THE
OXFORD ENCYCLOPEDIC
ENGLISH DICTIONARY

The
OXFORD
Encyclopedic
English Dictionary

EDITED BY

JOYCE M. HAWKINS

AND

ROBERT ALLEN

CLARENDON PRESS · OXFORD

Oxford University Press, Walton Street, Oxford OX2 6DP
Oxford New York Toronto
Delhi Bombay Calcutta Madras Karachi
Kuala Lumpur Singapore Hong Kong Tokyo
Nairobi Dar es Salaam Cape Town
Melbourne Auckland Madrid
and associated companies in
Berlin Ibadan

Oxford is a trade mark of Oxford University Press

Published in the United States by
Oxford University Press Inc., New York

British Library Cataloguing in Publication Data
Data available

Library of Congress Cataloging in Publication Data
Data available
ISBN 0-19-861248-6 Plain Edition
ISBN 0-19-861266-4 Thumb Index Edition

Printed in the United States of America

Contents

Preface

THIS dictionary is an innovative all-in-one reference book, providing within a single volume a comprehensive dictionary of current English and a concise world encyclopedia prepared from the authoritative lexical database assembled for the *Concise Oxford Dictionary* and other dictionaries of current English, supplemented by the encyclopedic resources held by the Oxford English Dictionaries Department.

Lexical coverage is generous and up to date, with special attention given to scientific and technical vocabulary. Definitions are presented in a straightforward readable style with the minimum of symbols and abbreviations. There are clear explanations of grammar, usage, and word origins, and pronunciation is indicated by means of the International Phonetic Alphabet.

The encyclopedic articles are the fullest to appear in an English dictionary of this size. They include accounts of famous people, organizations, and institutions, a history of every major langauge, about 3,000 entries for names of countries, cities, continents, oceans, lakes, rivers, and mountains, and articles (including historical information) on a wide range of subjects. Biographical entries are given for people who are world-famous, pioneers, statesmen who were in power at a time of significant change in their country's history, and people who have become legendary on their own spheres, together with a representative selection of lesser figures. A history of every independent country is included, and the numbers given for populations are based on the most recent statistics available.

The Appendices offer useful information that is more easily presented in a tabulated form than in an encyclopedic entry or dispersed through a number of such entries. The Chronology of World Events enables the reader to see at a glance what was taking place in different parts of the world at any date from the palaeolithic age onwards.

Throughout the work our aim has been to present as much information as possible in a clear and concise style so as to offer the maximum help and interest to the reader.

March 1991   JMH
                    REA

ACKNOWLEDGEMENTS. We are grateful to the following for their contributions: Dr David Munro, of Edinburgh University, selected about 3,000 names of countries, cities, rivers, mountains, etc. for inclusion and supplied information for these entries; Mr P. Teed compiled the first drafts of the Chronology of World Events and some of the Appendices, and Mr A. J. Augarde, Dr B. Blackburn, Dr A. F. D. Clayton, Dr R. Innskeep, Dr A. Sherratt, and Mr O. Stainer assisted with these; Mr A. Green, Mr K. R. Whettam, Mrs A. Willitts, and Mrs R. Winter undertook the proofreading. Illustrations are by Illustra Design and Information Design Unit. The table of the Beaufort Scale is reproduced by kind permission of the Meteorological Office (Crown Copyright).

Guide to Use of the Dictionary

1. USE OF CONVENTIONS

1.1 In this edition, a great deal of the information given in the dictionary entries is self-explanatory, and the use of special conventions has been kept to a minimum. The following pages are meant to explain the editorial approach and to assist the user by explaining the principles involved in assembling the information.

2. HEADWORD

2.1 The headword is printed in bold roman type, or in bold italic type if the word is not naturalized in English and is usually found in italics in printed matter:

saddle /ˈsæd(ə)l/ *n. & v.* —*n.* **1** a seat of leather etc., usu. raised at the front and rear, fastened on a horse etc. for riding. **2** a seat for the rider of a bicycle etc. **3** a joint of meat consisting

2.2.1 Variant spellings are given before the definition; in all such cases the form given as the headword is the preferred form. Variant forms are also given at their own places in the dictionary when these are three or more entries away from the main form:

saguaro /sæˈgwɑːrəʊ/ *n.* (also **sahuaro** /sæˈwɑːrəʊ/) (*pl.* **-os**) a giant cactus, *Carnegiea gigantea*, of the SW United States and Mexico. [Mex. Sp.]

2.2.2 Variant spellings given at the beginning of an entry normally apply to the whole entry, including any phrases and undefined derivatives (see below, 10–12).

2.2.3 When variants apply only to certain functions or senses of a word, these are given in brackets at the relevant point in the entry.

2.2.4 Words that are normally spelt with a capital initial are given in this form as the headword; when they are in some senses spelt with a small initial and in others with a capital initial this is indicated by repetition of the full word in the appropriate form within the entry.

2.2.5 Variant American spellings are indicated by the designation *US*. These variants are often found in American use in addition to the main forms given:

sabre /ˈseɪbə(r)/ *n. & v.* (*US* **saber**) —*n.* **1** a cavalry sword with a curved blade. **2** a cavalry soldier and horse. **3** a light fencing-sword with a tapering blade. —*v.tr.* cut down or wound with a sabre.

2.2.6 Pronunciation of variants is given when this differs significantly from the pronunciation of the headword.

2.3 Words that are different but spelt the same way (homographs) are distinguished by superior numerals:

bat[1] /bæt/ *n. & v.* —*n.* **1** an implement with a handle, usu. of wood and with a flat or curved surface, used for hitting balls in games. **2** a turn at using this. **3** a batsman, esp. in cricket, usu. described in some way (*an excellent bat*). **4** (usu. in *pl.*) an object like a table-tennis bat used to guide aircraft when taxiing. —*v.* (**batted, batting**) **1** *tr.* hit with or as with a bat. **2** *intr.* take a turn at batting. □ **bat around 1** *sl.* potter aimlessly. **2** *US* discuss (an idea or proposal). **off one's own bat** unprompted, unaided. **right off the bat** *US* immediately. [ME f. OE *batt* club, perh. partly f. OF *batte* club f. *battre* strike]

bat[2] /bæt/ *n.* any mouselike nocturnal mammal of the order Chiroptera, capable of flight by means of membranous wings extending from its forelimbs. □ **have bats in the belfry** be eccentric or crazy. **like a bat out of hell** very fast. [16th c., alt. of ME *bakke* f. Scand.]

bat[3] /bæt/ *v.tr.* (**batted, batting**) wink (one's eyelid) (now usu. in phr.). □ **not** (or **never**) **bat an eyelid** *colloq.* show no reaction or emotion. [var. of obs. *bate* flutter]

3. PRONUNCIATION

3.1.1 Guidance on pronunciation follows the system of the International Phonetic Alphabet (IPA), and is based on the pronunciation associated especially with southern England (sometimes called 'Received Pronunciation').

3.1.2 It is not possible in a dictionary of this size to show the many variations heard in educated speech in other parts of the English-speaking world.

3.2 The symbols used, with their values, are as follows:

3.2.1 *Consonants*:

b, d, f, h, k, l, m, n, p, r, s, t, v, w, and *z* have their usual English values. Other symbols are used as follows:

g	(get)	ŋ	(ring)	ʃ	(she)
tʃ	(chip)	θ	(thin)	ʒ	(decision)
dʒ	(jar)	ð	(this)	j	(yes)
x	(loch)				

3.2.2 *Vowels*:

short vowels		long vowels		diphthongs	
æ	(cat)	ɑː	(arm)	eɪ	(day)
e	(bed)	iː	(see)	aɪ	(my)
ə	(ago)	ɔː	(saw)	ɔɪ	(boy)
ɪ	(sit)	ɜː	(her)	əʊ	(no)
ɒ	(hot)	uː	(too)	aʊ	(how)
ʌ	(run)			ɪə	(near)
ʊ	(put)			eə	(hair)
				ʊə	(poor)
				aɪə	(fire)
				aʊə	(sour)

3.2.3.1 (ə) signifies the indeterminate sound as in gar*d*e*n*, car*n*a*l*, and rhyth*m*.

3.2.3.2 (r) at the end of a word indicates an r that is sounded when a word beginning with a vowel follows, as in *clutter up* and *an acre of land*.

3.2.4 The mark ˜ indicates a nasalized sound, as in the following sounds that are not natural in English:

æ̃	(timbre)
ɑ̃	(élan)
ɔ̃	(garçon)

3.2.5 The main or primary stress of a word is shown by ˈ preceding the relevant syllable; any secondary stress in words of three or more syllables is shown by ˌ preceding the relevant syllable.

3.3 With headwords consisting of two or more unhyphened words, the pronunciation is given only of the words that do not appear individually elsewhere in the dictionary.

3.4 Pronunciation of derivatives listed at the end of the entries is only given when there is a change of stress (as with many words in -*ation*) or some other significant change.

3.5 For the pronunciation of inflected forms, see below, 5.1.3.

3.6 For the pronunciation of prefixes, suffixes, and combining forms, see below, 14.3.

4. PART OF SPEECH

4.1 The grammatical identity of words as *noun*, *verb*, *adjective*, and so on, is given for all headwords and derivatives, and for compounds and phrases when necessary to aid clarity. The same part-of-speech label is used of groups of more than one word when the group has the function of that part of speech, e.g. **ad hoc, Parthian shot**.

4.2 When a headword has more than one part of speech, a list is given at the beginning of the entry, and the treatment of the successive parts of speech (in the same order as the list) is introduced by a bold dash in each case:

safe /seɪf/ *adj.* & *n.* —*adj.* **1 a** free of danger or injury. **b** (often foll. by *from*) out of or not exposed to danger (*safe from their enemies*). **2** affording security or not involving danger or risk (*put it in a safe place*). **3** reliable, certain; that can be reckoned on (*a safe catch; a safe method; is safe to win*). **4** prevented from escaping or doing harm (*have got him safe*). **5** (also **safe and sound**) uninjured; with no harm done. **6** cautious and unenterprising; consistently moderate. —*n.* **1** a strong lockable cabinet etc. for valuables. **2** = *meat safe*.

4.3 The standard part-of-speech names are used, and the following additional explanations should be noted:

4.3.1 Nouns used attributively are designated *attrib.* when their function is not fully adjectival (e.g. **model** in *a model student*; *the student is very model* is not acceptable usage).

4.3.2.1 Adjectives are labelled *attrib.* (= attributive) when they are placed before the word they modify (as in *a blue car*), and *predic.* (= predicative) when they occur (usually after a verb) in the predicate of a sentence (as in *the car is blue*).

4.3.2.2 Some adjectives are restricted in such use: for example **aware** is normally used predicatively and **undue** is normally used attributively.

4.3.3 The designation *absol.* (= absolute) refers to uses of transitive verbs with an object implied but not stated (as in *smoking kills* and *let me explain*).

4.3.4 The designation 'in *comb.*' (= in combination), or 'also in *comb.*', refers to uses of words (especially adjectives) as an element joined by a hyphen with another word, as with **crested**, which often appears in forms such as *red-crested, large-crested*, and so on.

5. INFLECTION

5.1.1 Inflection of words (i.e. plurals, past tenses, etc.) is given after the part of speech concerned:

safari /səˈfɑːrɪ/ *n.* (*pl.* **safaris**) **1** a hunting or scientific expedition, esp. in E. Africa (*go on safari*). **2** a sightseeing trip to see African animals in their natural habitat.

sag /sæg/ *v.* & *n.* —*v.intr.* (**sagged, sagging**) **1** sink or subside under weight or pressure, esp. unevenly. **2** have a downward bulge or curve in the middle. **3** fall in price. **4** (of a ship) drift from its course, esp. to leeward.

5.1.2 The forms given are normally those in use in British English. Variant American forms are identified by the label US; these variants are often found in American use in addition to the main forms given.

5.1.3 Pronunciation of inflected forms is given when this differs significantly from the pronunciation of the headword. The designation '*pronunc.* same' denotes that the pronunciation, despite a change of form, is the same as that of the headword.

5.2 In general, the inflection of nouns, verbs, adjectives, and adverbs is given when it is irregular (as described further below) or when, though regular, it causes difficulty (as with forms such as **budgeted, coos,** and **taxis**).

5.3 *Plurals of nouns*: nouns that form their plural regularly by adding -*s* (or -*es* when they end in -*s*, -*x*, -*z*, -*sh*, or soft -*ch*) receive no comment. Other plural forms are given, notably:

5.3.1 nouns ending in -*i* or -*o*.

5.3.2 nouns ending in -*y*.

5.3.3 nouns ending in Latinate forms such as -*a* and -*um*.

5.3.4 nouns with more than one plural form, e.g. **fish** and **aquarium**.

5.3.5 nouns with plurals involving a change in the stem, e.g. **foot, feet**.

5.3.6 nouns with a plural form identical to the singular form, e.g. **sheep**.

5.3.7 nouns in -*ful*, e.g. **handful**.

5.4 *Forms of verbs*:

The following forms are regarded as regular:

5.4.1 third person singular present forms adding -*s* to the stem (or -*es* to stems ending in -*s*, -*x*, -*z*, -*sh*, or soft -*ch*).

5.4.2 past tenses and past participles adding -*ed* to the stem, dropping a final silent *e* (e.g. **changed, danced**).

5.4.3 present participles adding -*ing* to the stem, dropping a final silent *e* (e.g. **changing, dancing**).

5.4.4 Other forms are given, notably:

5.4.4.1 doubling of a final consonant, e.g. **bat, batted, batting**.

5.4.4.2 strong and irregular forms involving a change in the stem, e.g. **come, came, come,** and **go, went, gone**.

5.5 *Comparative and Superlative of Adjectives and Adverbs*:

5.5.1 Words of one syllable adding -*er* or -*est*, those ending in silent *e* dropping the *e* (e.g. **braver, bravest**) are regarded as regular. Most one-syllable words have these forms, but participial adjectives (e.g. **pleased**) do not.

5.5.2 Those that double a final consonant (e.g. **hot, hotter, hottest**) are given, as are two-syllable words that have comparative and superlative forms in -*er* and -*est* (of which very many are forms ending in -*y*, e.g. **happy, happier, happiest**), and their negative forms (e.g. **unhappier, unhappiest**).

5.5.3 It should be noted that specification of these forms indicates only that they are available; it is usually also possible to form comparatives with *more* and superlatives with *most* (as in *more happy, most unhappy*), which is the standard way of proceeding with adjectives and adverbs that do not admit of inflection.

5.6 *Adjectives in -able formed from Transitive Verbs*:

These are given as derivatives when there is sufficient evidence of their currency; in general they are formed as follows:

5.6.1 Verbs drop silent final -*e* except after *c* and *g* (e.g. **movable** but **changeable**).

5.6.2 Verbs of more than one syllable ending in -*y* (preceded by a consonant or *qu*) change *y* to *i* (e.g. **enviable, undeniable**).

5.6.3 A final consonant is often doubled as in normal inflection (e.g. **conferrable, regrettable**).

6. DEFINITION

6.1 Definitions are listed in a numbered sequence in order of comparative familiarity and importance, with the most current and important senses first:

sail /seɪl/ n. & v. —n. **1** a piece of material (orig. canvas, now usu. nylon etc.) extended on rigging to catch the wind and propel a boat or ship. **2** a ship's sails collectively. **3 a** a voyage or excursion in a sailing-ship. **b** a voyage of specified duration. **4** a ship, esp. as discerned from its sails. **5** (collect.) ships in a squadron or company (a fleet of twenty sail). **6** (in pl.) Naut. **a** sl. a maker or repairer of sails. **b** hist. a chief petty officer in charge of rigging. **7** a wind-catching apparatus, usu. a set of boards, attached to the arm of a windmill. **8 a** the dorsal fin of a sailfish. **b** the tentacle of a nautilus. **c** the float of a Portuguese man-of-war. —v. **1** intr. travel on water by the use of sails or engine-power. **2** tr. **a** navigate (a ship etc.). **b** travel on (a sea). **3** tr. set (a toy boat) afloat. **4** intr. glide or move smoothly or in a stately manner. **5** intr. (often foll. by through) colloq. succeed easily (sailed through the exams).

6.2 They are subdivided into lettered senses (**a**, **b**, etc.) when these are closely related or call for collective treatment.

7. ILLUSTRATIVE EXAMPLES

Many examples of words in use are given to support, and in some cases supplement, the definitions. These appear in italics in brackets. They are meant to amplify meaning and (especially when following a grammatical point) illustrate how the word is used in context, as in the following sense of **saint**:

a very virtuous person; a person of great real or affected holiness (would try the patience of a saint).

8. GRAMMATICAL INFORMATION

8.1 Definitions are often accompanied by explanations in brackets of how the word or phrase in question is used in context. Often, the comment refers to words that usually follow (foll. by) or precede (prec. by) the word being explained. For example, at **sack**[1]:

sack[1] /sæk/ n. & v. —n. **1 a** a large strong bag, usu. made of hessian, paper, or plastic, for storing or conveying goods. **b** (usu. foll. by of) this with its contents (a sack of potatoes). **c** a quantity contained in a sack. **2** (prec. by the) colloq. dismissal from employment. **3** (prec. by the) US sl. bed. **4 a** a woman's short loose dress with a sacklike appearance. **b** archaic or hist. a woman's loose gown, or a silk train attached to the shoulders of this. **5** a man's or woman's loose-hanging coat not shaped to the back. —v.tr. **1** put into a sack or sacks. **2** colloq. dismiss from employment. □ **sack race** a race between competitors in sacks up to the waist or neck. □□ **sackful** n. (pl. -fuls). **sacklike** adj. [OE sacc f. L saccus f. Gk sakkos, of Semitic orig.]

sense 1b usually appears as a sack of (something), as the example further shows; and senses 2 and 3 always appear as the sack.

8.2 With verbs, the fact that a sense is transitive or intransitive can affect the construction. In the examples given below, **prevail** is intransitive (and the construction is prevail on a person) and **urge** is transitive (and the construction is urge a person on).

prevail /prɪˈveɪl/ v.intr. **1** (often foll. by against, over) be victorious or gain mastery. **2** be the more usual or predominant. **3** exist or occur in general use or experience; be current. **4** (foll. by on, upon) persuade.

urge /ɜːdʒ/ v. & n. —v.tr. **1** (often foll. by on) drive forcibly; impel; hasten (urged them on; urged the horses forward). **2** (often foll. by to + infin. or that + clause) encourage or entreat earnestly or persistently (urged them to go; urged them to action; urged that they should go).

8.3 The formula (foll. by to + infin.) means that the word is followed by a normal infinitive with to, as in want to leave and eager to learn.

8.4 The formula (foll. by that + clause) indicates the routine addition of a clause with that, as in said that it was late. (For the omission of that, as in said it was late, see the usage note in the entry for **that**.)

8.5 'pres. part.' and 'verbal noun' denote verbal forms in -ing that function as adjectives and nouns respectively, as in set him laughing and tired of asking.

9. USAGE

9.1 If the use of a word is restricted in any way, this is indicated by any of various labels printed in italics, as follows:

9.2 *Geographical*

9.2.1 *Brit.* indicates that the use is found chiefly in British English (and often also in Australian and New Zealand English, and in other parts of the Commonwealth) but not in American English.

9.2.2 *US* indicates that the use is found chiefly in American English (often including Canada and also in Australian and New Zealand English) but not in British English except as a conscious Americanism.

9.2.3 Other geographical designations (e.g. *Austral., NZ, S.Afr.*) restrict uses to the areas named.

9.2.4 These usage labels should be distinguished from comments of the type '(in the UK)' or '(in the US)' preceding definitions, which denote that the thing defined is associated with the country named. For example, **Pentagon** is a US institution, but the term is not restricted to American English.

9.3 *Register*

9.3.1 Levels of usage, or *registers*, are indicated as follows:

9.3.2 *formal* indicates uses that are normally restricted to formal (esp. written) English, e.g. **commence**.

9.3.3 *colloq.* (= colloquial) indicates a use that is normally restricted to informal (esp. spoken) English.

9.3.4 *sl.* (= slang) indicates a use of the most informal kind, unsuited to written English and often restricted to a particular social group.

9.3.5 *archaic* indicates a word that is restricted to special contexts such as legal or religious use, or is used for special effect.

9.3.6 *literary* indicates a word or use that is found chiefly in literature.

9.3.7 *poet.* (= poetic) indicates uses confined to poetry or other contexts with romantic connotations.

9.3.8 *joc.* (= jocular) indicates uses that are intended to be humorous or playful.

9.3.9 *derog.* (= derogatory) denotes uses that are intentionally disparaging.

9.3.10 *offens.* (= offensive) denotes uses that cause offence, whether intentionally or not.

9.3.11 *disp.* (= disputed) indicates a use that is disputed or controversial. Often this is enough to alert the user to a danger or difficulty; when further explanation is needed a usage note (see below) is used as well or instead.

9.3.12 *hist.* (= historical) denotes a word or use that is confined to historical reference, normally because the thing referred to no longer exists.

9.3.13 *propr.* (= proprietary) denotes a term that has the status of a trade mark (see the Note on Proprietary Status, p. xvii).

9.4 Subject

The many subject labels, e.g. *Law, Math., Naut.,* show that a word or sense is current only in a particular field of activity, and is not in general use.

9.5 Usage Notes

These are added to give extra information not central to the definition, and to explain points of grammar and usage. They are introduced by the symbol ¶. The purpose of these notes is not to prescribe usage but to alert the user to a difficulty or controversy attached to particular uses.

10. PHRASES AND IDIOMS

10.1 These are listed (together with compounds) in alphabetical order after the treatment of the main senses, introduced by the symbol □. The words *a, the, one,* and *person* do not count for purposes of alphabetical order:

□ **on the safe side** with a margin of security against risks. **safe bet** a bet that is certain to succeed. **safe-breaker** (or **-blower** or **-cracker**) a person who breaks open and robs safes. **safe conduct** **1** a privilege of immunity from arrest or harm, esp. on a particular occasion. **2** a document securing this. **safe deposit** a building containing strongrooms and safes let separately. **safe house** a place of refuge or rendezvous for spies etc. **safe keeping** preservation in a safe place. **safe light** *Photog.* a filtered light for use in a darkroom. **safe period** the time during and near the menstrual period when conception is least likely. **safe seat** a seat in Parliament etc. that is usually won with a large margin by a particular party.

10.2 They are normally defined under the earliest important word in the phrase, except when a later word is more clearly the key word or is the common word in a phrase with variants (in which case a cross-reference often appears at the entry for the earliest word):

make do 1 manage with the limited or inadequate means available. **2** (foll. *by with*) manage with (something) as an inferior substitute. **make an example of** punish as a warning to others. **make a fool of** see FOOL[1]. **make for 1** tend to result in (happiness etc.). **2** proceed towards (a place). **3** assault; attack. **4** confirm (an opinion). **make friends** (often foll. by *with*) become friendly. **make fun of** see FUN. **make good** see GOOD. **make a habit of** see HABIT. **make a hash of** see HASH[1]. **make hay** see HAY. **make head or tail of** see HEAD. **make a House** *Polit.* secure the presence of enough members for a quorum or support in the House of Commons. **make it** *colloq.* **1** succeed in reaching, esp. in time. **2** be successful. **3** (usu. foll. by *with*) *sl.* have sexual intercourse (with). **make it up 1** be reconciled, esp. after a quarrel. **2** fill in a deficit. **make it up to** remedy negligence, an injury, etc. to (a person). **make light of** see LIGHT[2]. **make love** see LOVE. **make a meal of** see MEAL[1]. **make merry** see MERRY.

11. COMPOUNDS

11.1 Compound terms forming one word (e.g. **bathroom, newspaper**) are listed as main entries; those consisting of two or more words (e.g. **chain reaction**) or joined by a hyphen (e.g. **chain-gang**) are given under the first element or occasionally as main entries.

12. DERIVATIVES

12.1 Words formed by adding a suffix to another word are in many cases listed at the end of the entry for the main word, introduced by the symbol □□. In this position they are not defined since they can be understood from the sense of the main word and that given at the suffix concerned:

□□ **saintdom** *n.* **sainthood** *n.* **saintlike** *adj.* **saintling** *n.* **saintship** *n.*

When further definition is called for they are given main entries in their own right (e.g. **changeable**).

12.2 For derivative words used in combination (e.g. **-crested** in *red-crested*), see 4.3.4 above.

13. ETYMOLOGY

13.1 A brief account of the etymology, or origin, of words is given in square brackets at the end of entries. It is not given for compound words of obvious formation (such as **bathroom** and **jellyfish**), for routinely formed derivatives (such as **changeable, muddy,** and **seller**), or for words consisting of clearly identified elements already explained (such as **Anglo-Saxon, overrun,** and many words in *in-, re-, un-,* etc.). It is also not always given for every word of a set sharing the same basic origin (such as the group from **proprietary** to **propriety**). Noteworthy features, such as an origin in Old English, are however always given.

13.2 More detailed information can be found in the *Oxford Dictionary of English Etymology* (ed. C. T. Onions *et al.,* 1966) and the *Concise Oxford Dictionary of English Etymology* (ed. T. F. Hoad, 1986).

13.3 The immediate source language is given first. Forms in other languages are not given if they are exactly or nearly the same as the English form given in the headword.

13.4 Words of Germanic origin are described as 'f. Gmc' or 'f. WG' (West Germanic) as appropriate; unrecorded or postulated forms are not normally given.

13.5 OE (Old English) is used for words that are known to have been used before AD 1150, and ME (Middle English) for words traceable to the period 1150–1500 (no distinction being made between early and late Middle English).

13.6 Words of Romance origin are referred to their immediate source, usually F (French) or OF (Old French) before 1400, and then to earlier sources when known.

13.6.1 AF (Anglo-French) denotes the variety of French current in England in the Middle Ages after the Norman Conquest.

13.6.2 Rmc (Romanic) denotes the vernacular descendants of Latin that are the source of French, Spanish, Italian, etc. Romanic forms are almost always of the 'unrecorded' or 'postulated' kind, and are not specified except to clarify a significant change of form. Often the formula 'ult. f. L' etc. (ultimately from Latin, etc.) is used to indicate that the route from Latin is via Romanic forms.

13.6.3 L (Latin) denotes classical Latin up to about AD 200; OL (Old Latin) Latin before about 75 BC; LL (Late Latin) Latin of about 200–600; med.L (medieval Latin) Latin of about 600–1500; mod.L (modern Latin) Latin in use (mainly for technical purposes) since about 1500.

13.6.4 Similar divisions for 'late', 'medieval', and 'modern' are made for Greek.

13.7 Many English words have corresponding forms in both French and Latin, and it cannot always be established which was the immediate source. In such cases the formula 'F or L' is used (e.g. **section** . . . F *section* or L *sectio*); in these cases the Latin form is the source of the French word and (either directly or indirectly) of the English word.

13.8 When the origin of a word cannot be reliably established, the forms 'orig. unkn.' (= origin unknown) and 'orig. uncert.' (= origin uncertain) are used, even if frequently canvassed speculative derivations exist (as with **gremlin** and **pommy**). In these cases the century of the first recorded occurrence of the word in English is given.

13.9 An equals sign (=) precedes words in other languages that are parallel formations from a common source (cognates) rather than sources of the English word.

14. PREFIXES, SUFFIXES, AND COMBINING FORMS

14.1 A large selection of these is given in the main body of the text; prefixes are given in the form **ex-**, **re-**, etc., and suffixes in the form **-ion**, **-ness**, etc. These entries should be consulted to explain the many routinely formed derivatives given at the end of entries (see above, 12).

14.2 Combining forms (e.g. **bio-**, **-graphy**) are semantically significant elements that can be attached to words or elements as explained in the usage note at the entry for **combine**.

14.3 The pronunciation given for a prefix, suffix, or combining form is an approximate one for purposes of articulating and (in some cases) identifying the headword;

pronunciation and stress may change considerably when they form part of a word.

15. CROSS-REFERENCES

15.1 These are introduced by any of a number of reference types, as follows:

15.1.1 '=' denotes that the meaning of the item at which the cross-reference occurs is the same as that of the item referred to.

15.1.2 'see' indicates that information will be found at the point referred to, and is widely used for encyclopedic matter and in the idiom sections of entries to deal with items that can be located at any of a number of words included in the idiom (see also above, 10.2).

15.1.3 'see also' indicates that further information can be found at the point referred to.

15.1.4 'cf.' denotes an item related or relevant to the one being consulted, and the reference often completes or clarifies the exact meaning of the item being treated.

15.1.5 'opp.' refers to a word or sense that is opposite to the one being treated, and again often completes or clarifies the sense.

15.1.6 References of the kind '*pl.* of' (= plural of), '*past* of' (= past tense of), etc., are given at entries for inflections and other related forms.

15.2 Cross-references preceded by any of these reference types appear in small capitals if the reference is to a main headword, and in italics if the reference is to a compound or idiom within an entry.

15.3 References in italics to compounds and defined phrases are to the entry for the first word unless another is specified.

Abbreviations and Symbols

Some abbreviations (especially of language-names) occur only in etymologies. Others may appear in italics. Abbreviations in general use (such as etc., i.e., and those for books of the Bible) are explained in the dictionary itself.

abbr.	abbreviation	Cat.	Catalan	emphat.	emphatic(ally)
ablat.	ablative	Celt.	Celtic	Engin.	Engineering
absol.	absolute(ly)	Ch.	Church	Engl.	England; English
acc.	according	Chem.	Chemistry	Entomol.	Entomology
accus.	accusative	Chin.	Chinese	erron.	erroneous(ly)
adj.	adjective	Cinematog.	Cinematography	esp.	especial(ly)
adv.	adverb	class.	classical	est.	estimated
Aeron.	Aeronautics	coarse sl.	coarse slang	etym.	etymology
AF	Anglo-French	cogn.	cognate	euphem.	euphemism
Afr.	Africa, African	collect.	collective(ly)	Eur.	Europe, European
Afrik.	Afrikaans	colloq.	colloquial(ly)	ex.	example
Akkad.	Akkadian	comb.	combination;	exc.	except
AL	Anglo-Latin		combining	exclam.	exclamation
alt.	alteration	compar.	comparative		
Amer.	America, American	compl.	complement	F	French
Anat.	Anatomy	Conchol.	Conchology	f.	from
anc.	ancient	conj.	conjunction	fam.	familiar
Anglo-Ind.	Anglo-Indian	conn.	connected	fem.	feminine
Anthropol.	Anthropology	constr.	construction	fig.	figurative(ly)
Antiq.	Antiquities, Antiquity	contr.	contraction	Finn.	Finnish
app.	apparently	Corn.	Cornish	fl.	floruit
Arab.	Arabic	corresp.	corresponding	Flem.	Flemish
Aram.	Aramaic	corrupt.	corruption	foll.	followed, following
arbitr.	arbitrary, arbitrarily	Criminol.	Criminology	form.	formation
Archaeol.	Archaeology	Crystallog.	Crystallography	Fr.	French
Archit.	Architecture			Frank.	Frankish
Arith.	Arithmetic	Da.	Danish	frequent.	frequentative(ly)
assim.	assimilated	decl.	declension		
assoc.	associated, association	def.	definite	G	German
Assyr.	Assyrian	Demog.	Demography	Gael.	Gaelic
Astrol.	Astrology	demons.	demonstrative	Gallo-Rom.	Gallo-Roman
Astron.	Astronomy	demons.adj.	demonstrative	gen.	general
Astronaut.	Astronautics		adjective	genit.	genitive
attrib.	attributive(ly)	demons.pron.	demonstrative	Geog.	Geography
attrib.adj.	attributive		pronoun	Geol.	Geology
	adjective	deriv.	derivative	Geom.	Geometry
augment.	augmentative	derog.	derogatory	Ger.	German
Austral.	Australia, Australian	dial.	dialect	Gk	Greek
aux.	auxiliary	different.	differentiated	Gk Hist.	Greek History
		dimin.	diminutive	Gmc	Germanic
back-form.	back-formation	disp.	disputed (use)	Goth.	Gothic
Bibl.	Biblical	dissim.	dissimilated	Gram.	Grammar
Bibliog.	Bibliography	distrib.	distributive		
Biochem.	Biochemistry	Du.	Dutch	Heb.	Hebrew
Biol.	Biology			Hind.	Hindustani
Bot.	Botany	E	English	Hist.	History
Braz.	Brazil, Brazilian	Eccl.	Ecclesiastical	hist.	with historical
Bret.	Breton	Ecol.	Ecology		reference
Brit.	British, in British use	Econ.	Economics	Horol.	Horology
Bulg.	Bulgarian	EFris.	East Frisian	Hort.	Horticulture
Burm.	Burmese	Egypt.	Egyptian	Hung.	Hungarian
Byz.	Byzantine	E.Ind.	East Indian, of the East		
			Indies	Icel.	Icelandic
c.	century	Electr.	Electricity	IE	Indo-European
c.	*circa*	elem.	elementary	illit.	illiterate
Can.	Canada, Canadian	ellipt.	elliptical(ly)	imit.	imitative

immed.	immediate(ly)	N.Amer.	North America, North	Pharm.	Pharmacy;
imper.	imperative		American		Pharmacology
impers.	impersonal	Nat.	National	Philol.	Philology
incept.	inceptive	Naut.	Nautical	Philos.	Philosophy
incl.	including; inclusive	neg.	negative(ly)	Phoen.	Phoenician
Ind.	of the subcontinent	N.Engl.	North of England	Phonet.	Phonetics
	comprising India,	neut.	neuter	Photog.	Photography
	Pakistan, and	Norm.	Norman	phr.	phrase
	Bangladesh	north.	northern	Phrenol.	Phrenology
ind.	indirect	Norw.	Norwegian	Physiol.	Physiology
indecl.	indeclinable	n.pl.	noun plural	pl.	plural
indef.	indefinite	num.	numeral	poet.	poetical
infin.	infinitive	NZ	New Zealand	Pol.	Polish
infl.	influence(d)			Polit.	Politics
instr.	instrumental (case)	O	Old (with languages)	pop.	popular, not technical;
int.	interjection	obj.	object; objective		population
interrog.	interrogative(ly)	OBret.	Old Breton	pop.L	popular Latin, informal
interrog.adj.	interrogative	OBrit.	Old British		spoken Latin
	adjective	obs.	obsolete	Port.	Portuguese
interrog.pron.	interrogative	Obstet.	Obstetrics	poss.	possessive
	pronoun	OBulg.	Old Bulgarian	poss.pron.	possessive
intr.	intransitive	occas.	occasional(ly)		pronoun
Ir.	Irish (language or	OCelt.	Old Celtic	prec.	preceded, preceding
	usage)	ODa.	Old Danish	predic.	predicate;
iron.	ironical(ly)	ODu.	Old Dutch		predicative(ly)
irreg.	irregular(ly)	OE	Old English	predic.adj.	predicative
It.	Italian	OF	Old French		adjective
		offens.	offensive	prep.	preposition
Jap.	Japan, Japanese	OFrank.	Old Frankish	pres.part.	present participle
Jav.	Javanese	OFris.	Old Frisian	prob.	probable, probably
joc.	jocular(ly)	OGael.	Old Gaelic	pron.	pronoun
		OHG	Old High German	pronunc.	pronunciation
L	Latin	OIcel.	Old Icelandic	propr.	proprietary term
lang.	language	OIr.	Old Irish	Prov.	Provençal
LG	Low German	OIt.	Old Italian	Psychol.	Psychology
LHeb.	Late Hebrew	OL	Old Latin		
lit.	literal(ly)	OLG	Old Low German	RC Ch.	Roman Catholic
LL	Late Latin	ON	Old Norse		Church
M	Middle (with	ONF	Old Northern French	redupl.	reduplicated
	languages)	ONorw.	Old Norwegian	ref.	reference
masc.	masculine	OPers.	Old Persian	refl.	reflexive(ly)
Math.	Mathematics	OPort.	Old Portuguese	rel.	related; relative
MDa.	Middle Danish	opp.	(as) opposed (to);	rel.adj.	relative adjective
MDu.	Middle Dutch		opposite (of)	Relig.	Religion
ME	Middle English	OProv.	Old Provençal	rel.pron.	relative pronoun
Mech.	Mechanics	orig.	origin; original(ly)	repr.	representing
Med.	Medicine	Ornithol.	Ornithology	Rhet.	Rhetoric
med.	medieval	OS	Old Saxon	rhet.	rhetorical(ly)
med.L	medieval Latin	OScand.	Old Scandinavian	Rmc	Romanic
metaph.	metaphorical	OSlav.	Old Slavonic	Rom.	Roman
metath.	metathesis	OSp.	Old Spanish	Rom.Hist.	Roman History
Meteorol.	Meteorology	OSw.	Old Swedish	Russ.	Russian
Mex.	Mexican				
MFlem.	Middle Flemish			S.Afr.	South Africa, South
MHG	Middle High German	Palaeog.	Palaeography		African
Mil.	Military	Parl.	Parliament;	S.Amer.	South America, South
Mineral.	Mineralogy		Parliamentary		American
mistransl.	mistranslation	part.	participle	Sc.	Scottish
MLG	Middle Low German	past part.	past participle	Scand.	Scandinavia,
mod.	modern	Pathol.	Pathology		Scandinavian
mod.L	modern Latin	pejor.	pejorative	Sci.	Science
MSw.	Middle Swedish	perf.	perfect (tense)	Shakesp.	Shakespeare
Mus.	Music	perh.	perhaps	sing.	singular
Mythol.	Mythology	Pers.	Persian	Sinh.	Sinhalese
		pers.	person(al)	Skr.	Sanskrit
n.	noun	Peruv.	Peruvian	sl.	slang

Slav.	Slavonic	tr.	transitive	v.aux.	auxiliary verb
Sociol.	Sociology	transf.	in transferred sense	Vet.	Veterinary
Sp.	Spanish	transl.	translation	v.intr.	intransitive verb
spec.	special(ly)	Turk.	Turkish	voc.	vocative
Stock Exch.	Stock Exchange	Typog.	Typography	v.refl.	reflexive verb
subj.	subject; subjunctive			v.tr.	transitive verb
superl.	superlative	ult.	ultimate(ly)		
Sw.	Swedish	uncert.	uncertain	WFris.	West Frisian
syll.	syllable	unexpl.	unexplained	WG	West Germanic
symb.	symbol	univ.	university	W.Ind.	West Indian, of the
syn.	synonym	unkn.	unknown		West Indies
		US	American, in American	WS	West Saxon
techn.	technical(ly)		use	WSlav.	West Slavonic
Telev.	Television	usu.	usual(ly)		
Teut.	Teutonic			Zool.	Zoology
Theatr.	Theatre, Theatrical	v.	verb		
Theol.	Theology	var.	variant(s)		

Symbols used in the Dictionary

¶ introduces notes on usage (see *Guide to the Use of the Dictionary* 9.5).

▢ introduces defined compounds, phrases, and idioms.

▢▢ introduces undefined derivatives formed by adding a suffix to the main word.

Note on Proprietary Status

This dictionary includes some words which are, or are asserted to be, proprietary names or trade marks. Their inclusion does not imply that they have acquired for legal purposes a non-proprietary or general significance, nor is any other judgement implied concerning their legal status. In cases where the editor has some evidence that a word is used as a proprietary name or trade mark this is indicated by the designation *propr.*, but no judgement concerning the legal status of such words is made or implied thereby.

The

OXFORD
Encyclopedic
English Dictionary

A

A¹ /eɪ/ n. (also **a**) (pl. **As** or **A's**) **1** the first letter of the alphabet. **2** Mus. the sixth note of the diatonic scale of C major. **3** the first hypothetical person or example. **4** the highest class or category (of roads, academic marks, etc.). **5** (usu. **a**) Algebra the first known quantity. **6** a human blood type of the ABO system. □ **A1** /eɪ ˈwʌn/ **1** Naut. **a** a first-class vessel in Lloyd's Register of Shipping. **b** first-class. **2** colloq. excellent, first-rate. **A1, A2,** etc. the standard paper sizes, each half the previous one, e.g. A4 = 297 × 210 mm, A5 = 210 × 148 mm. **from A to B** from one place to another (a means of getting from A to B). **from A to Z** over the entire range, completely.

A² /eɪ/ abbr. (also **A.**) **1** Brit. (of films) classified as suitable for an adult audience but not necessarily for children. ¶ Now replaced by PG. **2** = A LEVEL. **3** ampere(s). **4** answer. **5** Associate of. **6** atomic (energy etc.).

a¹ /ə, eɪ/ adj. (also **an** before a vowel) (called the indefinite article) **1** (as an unemphatic substitute) one, some, any. **2** one like (a Judas). **3** one single (not a thing in sight). **4** the same (all of a size). **5** in, to, or for each (twice a year; £20 a man; seven a side). [weakening of OE ān one; sense 5 orig. = A²]

a² /ə/ prep. (usu. as prefix) **1** to, towards (ashore; aside). **2** (with verb in pres. part. or infin.) in the process of; in a specified state (a-hunting; a-wandering; abuzz; aflutter). **3** on (afire; afoot). **4** in (nowadays). [weakening of OE prep. an, on (see ON)]

a³ abbr. atto-.

Å abbr. ångström(s).

a-¹ /eɪ, æ/ prefix not, without (amoral; agnostic; apetalous). [Gk a-, or L f. Gk, or F f. L f. Gk]

a-² /ə/ prefix implying motion onward or away, adding intensity to verbs of motion (arise; awake). [OE a-, orig. ar-]

a-³ /ə/ prefix to, at, or into a state (adroit; agree; amass; avenge). [ME a- (= OF prefix a-), (f. F) f. L ad- to, at]

a-⁴ /ə/ prefix **1** from, away (abridge). **2** (akin, anew). **3** out, utterly (abash; affray). **4** in, on, engaged in, etc. (see A²). [sense 1 f. ME a-, OF a-, f. L ab; sense 2 f. ME a- f. OE of prep.; sense 3 f. ME, AF a- = OF e-, es- f. L ex]

a-⁵ /ə, æ/ prefix assim. form of AD- before sc, sp, st.

-a¹ /ə/ suffix forming nouns from Greek, Latin, and Romanic feminine singular, esp.: **1** ancient or Latinized modern names of animals and plants (amoeba; campanula). **2** oxides (alumina). **3** geographical names (Africa). **4** ancient or Latinized modern feminine names (Lydia; Hilda).

-a² /ə/ suffix forming plural nouns from Greek and Latin neuter plural, esp. names (often from modern Latin) of zoological groups (phenomena; Carnivora).

-a³ /ə/ suffix colloq. sl. **1** of (kinda; coupla). **2** have (mighta; coulda). **3** to (oughta).

AA abbr. **1** Automobile Association. **2** Alcoholics Anonymous. **3** Mil. anti-aircraft. **4** Brit. (of films) classified as suitable for persons of over 14 years. ¶ Now replaced by PG.

AAA abbr. **1** (in the UK) Amateur Athletic Association. **2** American Automobile Association. **3** Australian Automobile Association.

Aachen /ˈɑːxən, ˈɑːk(ə)n/ (French **Aix-la-Chapelle** /ˌeɪkslæʃæˈpel/) an industrial city and spa in North Rhine-Westphalia in the west of Germany, near the Belgian and Dutch borders; pop. (1987) 239,200. German emperors were crowned in Aachen from the time of Charlemagne (who was born and buried there) until 1531.

Aalborg /ˈɔːlbɔːg/ (also **Ålborg**) an industrial city and port in north Jutland, Denmark, one of the country's oldest towns; pop. (1988) 154,700.

Aalst /ɑːlst/ (French **Alost** /æˈlɒst/) industrial city in East Flanders, Belgium, 22 km (14 miles) north-west of Brussels; pop. (1988) 76,700.

Aalto /ˈɑːltəʊ/, Hugo Henrik Alvar (1898–1976), Finnish architect, one of the most inventive of his generation, who worked extensively in Europe and America as well as in Finland, where he was responsible for the design of a number of public buildings. He is notable for his expressive and inventive use of timber (Finland's basic building material) for structure and decoration, and for the use of mixed materials in designs that were beautiful as a result of purely functional concerns.

A. & M. abbr. (Hymns) Ancient and Modern.

A. & R. abbr. **1** artists and recording. **2** artists and repertoire.

aardvark /ˈɑːdvɑːk/ n. a nocturnal mammal of southern Africa, Orycteropus afer, with a tubular snout and a long extendible tongue, that feeds on termites. Also called ant-bear, earth-hog. [Afrik. f. aarde earth + vark pig]

aardwolf /ˈɑːdwʊlf/ n. (pl. **aardwolves** /-wʊlvz/) an African mammal, Proteles cristatus, of the hyena family, with grey fur and black stripes, that feeds on insects. [Afrik. f. aarde earth + wolf wolf]

Aarhus /ˈɔːrhuːs/ (also **Århus**) the second-largest city of Denmark, on the coast in east Jutland; pop. (1988) 258,000.

Aaron /ˈeər(ə)n/ brother of Moses and traditional founder of the Jewish priesthood. □ **Aaron's beard** (see Ps. 133: 2) a popular name for several plants, especially a St John's wort Hypericum calycinum. **Aaron's rod** a popular name for several tall plants with flowering stems, especially a mullein, Verbascum thapsus. (Aaron's rod sprouted and blossomed as a sign that he was designated by God as high priest of the Hebrews; see Numbers 17: 8.)

A'asia abbr. Australasia.

aasvogel /ˈɑːsˌfəʊg(ə)l/ n. a vulture. [Afrik. f. aas carrion + vogel bird]

AAU abbr. US Amateur Athletic Union.

AB¹ /eɪˈbiː/ n. a human blood type of the ABO system.

AB² abbr. **1** able rating or seaman. **2** US Bachelor of Arts. [sense 1 f. able-bodied; sense 2 f. L Artium Baccalaureus]

ab- /əb, æb/ prefix off, away, from (abduct; abnormal; abuse). [F or L]

aba /ˈæbə/ n. (also **abba, abaya** /əˈbeɪjə/) a sleeveless outer garment worn by Arabs. [Arab. 'abā']

abaca /ˈæbəkə/ n. **1** Manila hemp. **2** the plant, Musa textilis, yielding this. [Sp. abacá]

aback /əˈbæk/ adv. **1** archaic backwards, behind. **2** Naut. (of a sail) pressed against the mast by a head wind. □ **take aback 1** surprise, disconcert (your request took me aback; I was greatly taken aback by the news). **2** (as **taken aback**) (of a ship) with the sails pressed against the mast by a head wind. [OE on bæc (as A², BACK)]

abacus /ˈæbəkəs/ n. (pl. **abacuses**) **1** an oblong frame with rows of wires or grooves along which beads are slid, used for calculating. Its provenance and date of origin are uncertain. The ancient Egyptians, Greeks, and Romans used a counting-board with vertical columns as an aid to reckoning; the frame may be a development of this, or may have been devised independently. It was in general use during the Middle Ages until the adoption of the nine figures and zero, and is still used in the Far East. **2** Archit. the flat slab on top of a capital, supporting the architrave. [L f. Gk abax abakos slab, drawing-board, f. Heb. 'ābāk dust (from use of board sprinkled with sand or dust for drawing geometrical diagrams)]

Abadan /ˌæbəˈdɑːn/ a city on an island of the same name on the Shatt al-Arab waterway in western Iran; pop. (1986) 294,000. It is a port and an oil-refining centre.

Abaddon /əˈbæd(ə)n/ n. **1** hell. **2** the Devil (Rev. 9:11). [Heb., = destruction]

abaft /əˈbɑːft/ adv. & prep. Naut. —adv. in the stern half of a ship. —*prep.* nearer the stern than; aft of. [A² + -*baft* f. OE *beæftan* f. *be* BY + *æftan* behind]

abalone /ˌæbəˈləʊnɪ/ *n.* any mollusc of the genus *Haliotis*, with a shallow ear-shaped shell having respiratory holes, and lined with mother-of-pearl, e.g. the ormer. [Amer. Sp. *abulón*]

abandon /əˈbænd(ə)n/ *v.* & *n.* —*v.tr.* **1** give up completely or before completion (*abandoned hope; abandoned the game*). **2 a** forsake or desert (a person or a post of responsibility). **b** leave or desert (a motor vehicle or ship). **3 a** give up to another's control or mercy. **b** *refl.* yield oneself completely to a passion or impulse. —*n.* lack of inhibition or restraint; reckless freedom of manner. □□ **abandoner** *n.* **abandonment** *n.* [ME f. OF *abandoner* f. *à bandon* under control ult. f. LL *bannus, -um* BAN]

abandoned /əˈbænd(ə)nd/ *adj.* **1 a** (of a person) deserted, forsaken (*an abandoned child*). **b** (of a building, vehicle, etc.) left empty or unused (*an abandoned cottage; an abandoned ship*). **2** (of a person or behaviour) unrestrained, profligate.

abase /əˈbeɪs/ *v.tr.* & *refl.* humiliate or degrade (another person or oneself). □□ **abasement** *n.* [ME f. OF *abaissier* (as A-³, *baissier* to lower ult. f. LL *bassus* short of stature): infl. by BASE²]

abash /əˈbæʃ/ *v.tr.* (usu. as **abashed** *adj.*) embarrass, disconcert. □□ **abashment** *n.* [ME f. OF *esbaïr* (es- = A-⁴ 3, *baïr* astound or *baer* yawn)]

abate /əˈbeɪt/ *v.* **1** *tr.* & *intr.* make or become less strong, severe, intense, etc. **2** *tr. Law* **a** quash (a writ or action). **b** put an end to (a nuisance). □□ **abatement** *n.* [ME f. OF *abatre* f. Rmc (as A-³, L *batt(u)ere* beat)]

abatis /ˈæbətɪs/ *n.* (also **abattis** /əˈbætɪs/) (*pl.* same /-tiːz/; **abatises, abattises**) *hist.* a defence made of felled trees with the boughs pointing outwards. □□ **abatised** *adj.* [F f. *abatre* fell: see ABATE]

abattoir /ˈæbəˌtwɑː(r)/ *n.* a slaughterhouse. [F (as ABATIS, -ORY¹)]

abaxial /æbˈæksɪəl/ *adj. Bot.* facing away from the stem of a plant, esp. of the lower surface of a leaf (cf. ADAXIAL). [AB- + AXIAL]

abaya (also **abba**) var. of ABA.

abbacy /ˈæbəsɪ/ *n.* (*pl.* **-ies**) the office, jurisdiction, or period of office of an abbot or abbess. [ME f. eccl.L *abbacia* f. *abbat-* ABBOT]

Abbasid /əˈbæsɪd/ *n.* & *adj.* —*n.* a member of a dynasty of caliphs ruling in Baghdad 750–1258, claiming descent from Abbas (566–652), uncle of Muhammad. —*adj.* of this dynasty.

abbatial /əˈbeɪʃ(ə)l/ *adj.* of an abbey, abbot, or abbess. [F *abbatial* or med.L *abbatialis* (as ABBOT)]

abbé /ˈæbeɪ/ *n.* (in France) an abbot; a male entitled to wear ecclesiastical dress. [F f. eccl.L *abbas abbatis* ABBOT]

abbess /ˈæbɪs/ *n.* a woman who is the head of certain communities of nuns. [ME f. OF *abbesse* f. eccl.L *abbatissa* (as ABBOT)]

Abbevillian /æbˈvɪlɪən/ *adj.* & *n.* —*adj.* of the earliest lower palaeolithic hand-axe industries in Europe, named after the type-site at Abbeville on the River Somme in northern France and dated to *c*.500,000 BC. The hand-axes were made by hammering flakes off a flint with a hard stone, giving them a rough appearance. (See also ACHEULIAN.) —*n.* the Abbevillian industry. [F *Abbevillien* f. *Abbeville*]

abbey /ˈæbɪ/ *n.* (*pl.* **-eys**) **1** the building(s) occupied by a community of monks or nuns. **2** the community itself. **3** a church or house that was once an abbey. □ **the Abbey** Westminster Abbey, in London. [ME f. OF *abbeie* etc. f. med.L *abbatia* ABBACY]

Abbey Theatre a theatre in Abbey Street, Dublin, first opened in 1904, staging chiefly Irish plays. W. B. Yeats was associated with its foundation. In 1925 it became the first State-subsidized theatre in the English-speaking world.

abbot /ˈæbət/ *n.* a man who is the head of an abbey of monks. □□ **abbotship** *n.* [OE *abbod* f. eccl.L *abbas -atis* f. Gk *abbas* father f. Aram. *'abbā*]

abbreviate /əˈbriːvɪˌeɪt/ *v.tr.* shorten, esp. represent (a word etc.) by a part of it. [ME f. LL *abbreviare* shorten f. *brevis* short: cf. ABRIDGE]

abbreviation /əˌbriːvɪˈeɪʃ(ə)n/ *n.* **1** an abbreviated form, esp. a shortened form of a word or phrase. **2** the process of abbreviating.

ABC¹ /ˌeɪbiːˈsiː/ *n.* **1** the alphabet. **2** the rudiments of any subject. **3** an alphabetical guide.

ABC² *abbr.* **1** Australian Broadcasting Corporation. **2** American Broadcasting Company.

ABC Islands the Dutch islands of Aruba, Bonaire, and Curaçao which lie in the Caribbean Sea near the coast of Venezuela. [acronym]

abdicate /ˈæbdɪˌkeɪt/ *v.tr.* **1** (usu. *absol.*) give up or renounce (the throne). **2** renounce (a responsibility, duty, etc.). □□ **abdication** /ˌæbdɪˈkeɪʃ(ə)n/ *n.* **abdicator** *n.* [L *abdicare abdicat-* (as AB-, *dicare* declare)]

abdomen /ˈæbdəmən/ *n.* **1** the part of the body containing the stomach, bowels, reproductive organs, etc. **2** *Zool.* the hinder part of an insect, crustacean, spider, etc. □□ **abdominal** /æbˈdɒmɪn(ə)l/ *adj.* **abdominally** /æbˈdɒmɪnəlɪ/ *adv.* [L]

abduct /əbˈdʌkt/ *v.tr.* **1** carry off or kidnap (a person) illegally by force or deception. **2** (of a muscle etc.) draw (a limb etc.) away from the middle line of the body. □□ **abduction** *n.* **abductor** *n.* [L *abducere abduct-* (as AB-, *ducere* draw)]

Abduh /ˈæbduː/, Muhammad (1849–1905), Egyptian Islamic scholar and jurist, leader of a movement in Egypt and other countries to modernize and revitalize Islam. As Grand Mufti of Egypt from 1899 he introduced reforms in Islamic law and education, seeking to break through the rigid acceptance of traditional doctrines and customs and presenting the faith as rational and progressive.

Abdul Hamid II /ˌæbdʊl ˈhæmɪd/ (1842–1918), the last sultan of Turkey, 1876–1909. An autocratic ruler, he suspended parliament and the constitution and was noted for ruthless suppression of his non-Muslim subjects, notably the Armenians. In 1909 he was deposed after the revolt of the Young Turks.

Abdullah¹ /æbˈdʊlə/ (1882–1951), Emir of Transjordan (1921–46) and its first king when the country (later called Jordan) became independent in 1946. He was assassinated in 1951.

Abdullah² /æbˈdʊlə/, Sheikh Muhammad (1905–82), Kashmiri Muslim leader, known as the Lion of Kashmir. In the 1930s he was an activist agitating against the arbitrary rule of the Hindu Maharajah of Kashmir. After accepting Indian sovereignty (1947) he eventually won for Kashmir a form of autonomy within India, although he was imprisoned for much of the time between 1953 and 1968 on suspicion of seeking its full independence.

Abdul Rahman /ˌæbdʊl ˈrɑːmən/, Tunku (= Prince) (1903–90), Malayan statesman. He negotiated Malayan independence from Britain (1957) and the formation of the Federation of Malaysia (1963), becoming Malaya's first Prime Minister and continuing in office as the first prime minister of Malaysia (1963–70).

abeam /əˈbiːm/ *adv.* **1** on a line at right angles to a ship's or an aircraft's length. **2** (foll. by *of*) opposite the middle of (a ship etc.). [A² + BEAM]

abed /əˈbed/ *adv. archaic* in bed. [OE (as A², BED)]

Abel /ˈɑːbel/, Niels Henrik (1802–29), Norwegian mathematician who, in his six productive years, published the first acceptable proof that equations of the fifth degree or above cannot be solved by methods analogous to those that had been known since the 16th c. for solving equations of degree 1, 2, 3, or 4, introduced rigorous argument into the theory of power series, and discovered startling new results on elliptic functions, as a result of which the theory of these and of their generalizations became one of the liveliest areas for 19th-c. mathematical research. After two years of travel, meeting mathematicians in Germany and France, he returned to Norway where he lived in poverty and died of consumption aged 26, at the height of his powers. □□ **Abelian** /əˈbiːlɪən/ *adj.*

Abelard /ˈæbɪˌlɑːd/, Peter (1079–1142), French scholar, theologian, and philosopher, whose lively, restless, independent mind impressed his contemporaries but brought him into frequent conflict with his masters and led to his being twice condemned for heresy. He lectured in Paris until his academic career was cut short in 1118 by the tragic issue of his love affair with his pupil Héloïse, niece of Fulbert, a canon of Notre-Dame.

æ *cat* ɑː *arm* e *bed* ɜː *her* ɪ *sit* iː *see* ɒ *hot* ɔː *saw* ʌ *run* ʊ *put* uː *too* ə *ago* aɪ *my*

Abelard was castrated at Fulbert's instigation; he entered a monastery, and made Héloïse become a nun. Abelard continued his highly controversial teaching, applying reason to the deepest mysteries of the faith, notably the doctrine of the Trinity. His doctrine of the Atonement, emphasizing the love of Christ, manifest in his life and passion, which calls forth a human response of love, has had a continuing influence. The lovers are now buried in one grave in Paris.

abele /əˈbiːl, ˈeɪb(ə)l/ n. the white poplar, *Populus alba.* [Du. *abeel* f. OF *abel, aubel* ult. f. L *albus* white]

Aberdeen[1] /ˌæbəˈdiːn/ a city and former county in Scotland, humorously credited with an extremely parsimonious population. □ **Aberdeen Angus 1** an animal of a Scottish breed of hornless black beef cattle. **2** this breed. [*Angus* former Scottish county]

Aberdeen[2] /ˌæbəˈdiːn/, George Hamilton Gordon, 4th Earl of (1784–1860), British Conservative statesman, Prime Minister of a coalition government 1852–5. He reluctantly involved his country in the Crimean War and was subsequently blamed for its mismanagement and obliged to resign.

Aberdonian /ˌæbəˈdəʊnɪən/ adj. & n. —adj. of Aberdeen. —n. a native or citizen of Aberdeen. [med.L *Aberdonia*]

Aberfan /ˌæbəˈvæn/ a village in South Wales where, in 1966, a slag-heap collapsed and mining waste overwhelmed nearby houses and a school, killing 28 adults and 116 children.

aberrant /əˈberənt/ adj. **1** esp. *Biol.* diverging from the normal type. **2** departing from an accepted standard. □□ **aberrance** n. **aberrancy** n. [L *aberrare aberrant-* (as AB-, *errare* stray)]

aberration /ˌæbəˈreɪʃ(ə)n/ n. **1** a departure from what is normal or accepted or regarded as right. **2** a moral or mental lapse. **3** *Biol.* deviation from a normal type. **4** *Optics* the failure of rays to converge at one focus because of a defect in a lens or mirror. **5** *Astron.* the apparent displacement of a celestial body, meteor, etc., caused by the observer's velocity and the finite speed of light. As the earth has two motions, there is a *diurnal* as well as an *annual* aberration; *planetary* aberration is effected by the additional element of the motion of the planet itself, during the time occupied by the passage of its light to the earth. □ **chromatic aberration** see CHROMATIC. [L *aberratio* (as ABERRANT)]

abet /əˈbet/ v.tr. (**abetted, abetting**) (usu. in **aid and abet**) encourage or assist (an offender or offence). □□ **abetment** n. [ME f. OF *abeter* f. *à* to + *beter* BAIT[1]]

abetter /əˈbetə(r)/ n. (also **abettor**) one who abets.

abeyance /əˈbeɪəns/ n. (usu. prec. by *in, into*) a state of temporary disuse or suspension. □□ **abeyant** adj. [AF *abeiance* f. OF *abeer* f. *à* to + *beer* f. med.L *batare* gape]

abhor /əbˈhɔː(r)/ v.tr. (**abhorred, abhorring**) regard with disgust and hatred. [ME f. F *abhorrer* or f. L *abhorrēre* (as AB-, *horrēre* shudder)]

abhorrence /əbˈhɒrəns/ n. **1** disgust; detestation. **2** a detested thing.

abhorrent /əbˈhɒrənt/ adj. **1** (often foll. by *to*) (of conduct etc.) inspiring disgust, repugnant; hateful, detestable. **2** (foll. by *to*) not in accordance with; strongly conflicting with (*abhorrent to the spirit of the law*). **3** (foll. by *from*) inconsistent with. □□ **abhorrer** n.

abide /əˈbaɪd/ v. (*past* **abided** or rarely **abode** /əˈbəʊd/) **1** tr. (usu. in *neg.* or *interrog.*) tolerate, endure (*can't abide him*). **2** intr. (foll. by *by*) **a** act in accordance with (*abide by the rules*). **b** remain faithful to (a promise). **3** intr. *archaic* **a** remain, continue. **b** dwell. **4** tr. *archaic* sustain, endure. □□ **abidance** n. [OE *ābīdan* (as A-[2], *bidan* BIDE)]

abiding /əˈbaɪdɪŋ/ adj. enduring, permanent (*an abiding sense of loss*). □□ **abidingly** adv.

Abidjan /ˌæbɪˈdʒɑːn/ the capital and chief port of the Ivory Coast; pop. (est. 1982) 1,850,000.

abigail /ˈæbɪɡeɪl/ n. a lady's maid. [character in Beaumont and Fletcher's *Scornful Lady*; cf. 1 Sam. 25]

ability /əˈbɪlɪtɪ/ n. (pl. **-ies**) **1** (often foll. by *to* + infin.) capacity or power (*has the ability to write songs*). **2** cleverness, talent; mental power (*a person of great ability; has many abilities*). [ME f. OF *ablete* f. L *habilitas -tatis* f. *habilis* able]

-ability /əˈbɪlɪtɪ/ suffix forming nouns of quality from, or corresponding to, adjectives in *-able* (*capability; vulnerability*). [F *-abilité* or L *-abilitas*: cf. *-ITY*]

ab initio /ˌæb ɪˈnɪʃɪəʊ/ adv. from the beginning. [L]

abiogenesis /ˌeɪbaɪəʊˈdʒenɪsɪs/ n. **1** the formation of living organisms from non-living substances. **2** the supposed spontaneous generation of living organisms. □□ **abiogenic** adj. [A-[1] + Gk *bios* life + GENESIS]

abject /ˈæbdʒekt/ adj. **1** miserable, wretched. **2** degraded, self-abasing, humble. **3** despicable. □□ **abjectly** adv. **abjectness** n. [ME f. L *abjectus* past part. of *abicere* (as AB-, *jacere* throw)]

abjection /æbˈdʒekʃ(ə)n/ n. a state of misery or degradation. [ME f. OF *abjection* or L *abjectio* (as ABJECT)]

abjure /əbˈdʒʊə(r)/ v.tr. **1** renounce on oath (an opinion, cause, claim, etc.). **2** swear perpetual absence from (one's country etc.). □□ **abjuration** /ˌæbdʒʊˈreɪʃ(ə)n/ n. [L *abjurare* (as AB-, *jurare* swear)]

ablation /æbˈleɪʃ(ə)n/ n. **1** the surgical removal of body tissue. **2** *Geol.* the wasting or erosion of a glacier, iceberg, or rock by melting or the action of water. **3** *Astronaut.* the evaporation or melting of part of the outer surface of a spacecraft through heating by friction with the atmosphere. □□ **ablate** v.tr. [F *ablation* or LL *ablatio* f. L *ablat-* (as AB-, *lat-* past part. stem of *ferre* carry)]

ablative /ˈæblətɪv/ n. & adj. *Gram.* —n. the case (esp. in Latin) of nouns and pronouns (and words in grammatical agreement with them) indicating an agent, instrument, or location. —adj. of or in the ablative. □ **ablative absolute** an absolute construction in Latin with a noun and participle or adjective in the ablative case (see ABSOLUTE). [ME f. OF *ablatif -ive* or L *ablativus* (as ABLATION)]

ablaut /ˈæblaʊt/ n. a change of vowel in related words or forms, esp. in Indo-European languages, arising from differences of accent and stress in the parent language, e.g. in *sing, sang, sung.* [G]

ablaze /əˈbleɪz/ predic.adj. & adv. **1** on fire (*set it ablaze; the house was ablaze*). **2** (often foll. by *with*) glittering, glowing. **3** (often foll. by *with*) greatly excited.

able /ˈeɪb(ə)l/ adj. (**abler, ablest**) **1** (often foll. by *to* + infin.; used esp. in *is able, will be able, was able,* etc., replacing tenses of *can*) having the capacity or power (*was not able to come*). **2** having great ability; clever, skilful. □ **able-bodied** fit, healthy. **able-bodied rating** (or **seaman**) *Naut.* one able to perform all duties. [ME f. OF *hable, able* f. L *habilis* handy f. *habēre* to hold]

-able /əb(ə)l/ suffix forming adjectives meaning: **1** that may or must be (*eatable; forgiveable; payable*). **2** that can be made the subject of (*dutiable; objectionable*). **3** that is relevant to or in accordance with (*fashionable; seasonable*). **4** (with active sense, in earlier word-formations) that may (*comfortable; suitable*). [F *-able* or L *-abilis* forming verbal adjectives f. verbs of first conjugation]

abloom /əˈbluːm/ predic.adj. blooming; in flower.

ablush /əˈblʌʃ/ predic.adj. blushing.

ablution /əˈbluːʃ(ə)n/ n. (usu. in pl.) **1** the ceremonial washing of parts of the body or sacred vessels etc. **2** *colloq.* the ordinary washing of the body. **3** a building containing washing-places etc. in a camp, ship, etc. □□ **ablutionary** adj. [ME f. OF *ablution* or L *ablutio* (as AB-, *lutio* f. *luere lut-* wash)]

ably /ˈeɪblɪ/ adv. capably, cleverly, competently.

-ably /əblɪ/ suffix forming adverbs corresponding to adjectives in *-able.*

ABM abbr. anti-ballistic missile.

abnegate /ˈæbnɪɡeɪt/ v.tr. **1** give up or deny oneself (a pleasure etc.). **2** renounce or reject (a right or belief). □□ **abnegator** n. [L *abnegare abnegat-* (as AB-, *negare* deny)]

abnegation /ˌæbnɪˈɡeɪʃ(ə)n/ n. **1** denial; the rejection or renunciation of a doctrine. **2** = SELF-ABNEGATION. [OF *abnegation* or LL *abnegatio* (as ABNEGATE)]

abnormal /æbˈnɔːm(ə)l/ adj. **1** deviating from what is normal or usual; exceptional. **2** relating to or dealing with what is

abnormal (*abnormal psychology*). □□ **abnormally** *adv.* [earlier and F *anormal, anomal* f. Gk *anōmalos* ANOMALOUS, assoc. with L *abnormis*: see ABNORMITY]

abnormality /ˌæbnɔːˈmælɪtɪ/ *n.* (*pl.* **-ies**) **1 a** an abnormal quality, occurrence, etc. **b** the state of being abnormal. **2** a physical irregularity.

abnormity /æbˈnɔːmɪtɪ/ *n.* (*pl.* **-ies**) **1** an abnormality or irregularity. **2** a monstrosity. [L *abnormis* (as AB-, *normis* f. *norma* rule)]

Abo /ˈæbəʊ/ *n.* & *adj.* (also **abo**) *Austral. sl.* usu. *offens.* —*n.* (*pl.* **Abos**) an Aboriginal. —*adj.* Aboriginal. [abbr.]

aboard /əˈbɔːd/ *adv.* & *prep.* **1** on or into (a ship, aircraft, train, etc.). **2** alongside. □ **all aboard!** a call that warns of the imminent departure of a ship, train, etc. [ME f. A² + BOARD & F *à bord*]

abode¹ /əˈbəʊd/ *n.* **1** a dwelling-place; one's home. **2** *archaic* a stay or sojourn. [verbal noun of ABIDE: cf. *ride, rode, road*]

abode² *past of* ABIDE.

abolish /əˈbɒlɪʃ/ *v.tr.* put an end to the existence or practice of (esp. a custom or institution). □□ **abolishable** *adj.* **abolisher** *n.* **abolishment** *n.* [ME f. F *abolir* f. L *abolēre* destroy]

abolition /ˌæbəˈlɪʃ(ə)n/ *n.* **1** the act or process of abolishing or being abolished. **2** an instance of this. [F *abolition* or L *abolitio* (as ABOLISH)]

abolitionist /ˌæbəˈlɪʃənɪst/ *n.* one who favours the abolition of a practice or institution, esp. of capital punishment or (formerly) of Negro slavery. □□ **abolitionism** *n.*

abomasum /ˌæbəˈmeɪs(ə)m/ *n.* (*pl.* **abomasa** /-sə/) the fourth stomach of a ruminant. [mod.L f. AB- + OMASUM]

A-bomb /ˈeɪbɒm/ *n.* = *atomic bomb.* [A (for ATOMIC) + BOMB]

Abomey /əˈbəʊmeɪ, ˌæbəˈmeɪ/ a town in southern Benin, formerly capital of the kingdom of Dahomey; pop. (1982) 54,400.

abominable /əˈbɒmɪnəb(ə)l/ *adj.* **1** detestable; loathsome; morally reprehensible. **2** *colloq.* very bad or unpleasant (*abominable weather*). □ **Abominable Snowman** an unidentified manlike or bearlike animal said to exist in the Himalayas; a yeti. □□ **abominably** *adv.* [ME f. OF f. L *abominabilis* f. *abominari* deprecate (as AB-, *ominari* f. OMEN)]

abominate /əˈbɒmɪneɪt/ *v.tr.* detest, loathe. □□ **abominator** *n.* [L *abominari* (as ABOMINABLE)]

abomination /əˌbɒmɪˈneɪʃ(ə)n/ *n.* **1** loathing. **2** an odious or degrading habit or act. **3** (often foll. by *to*) an object of disgust. [ME f. OF (as ABOMINATE)]

aboral /æbˈɔːr(ə)l/ *adj.* away from or opposite the mouth. [AB- + ORAL]

aboriginal /ˌæbəˈrɪdʒɪn(ə)l/ *adj.* & *n.* —*adj.* **1** (of races and natural phenomena) inhabiting or existing in a land from the earliest times or from before the arrival of colonists. **2** (usu. **Aboriginal**) of the Australian Aborigines. —*n.* **1** an aboriginal inhabitant. **2** (usu. **Aboriginal**) an aboriginal inhabitant of Australia. □□ **aboriginally** *adv.* [as ABORIGINE + -AL]

aborigine /ˌæbəˈrɪdʒɪnɪ/ *n.* (usu. in *pl.*) **1** an aboriginal inhabitant. **2** (usu. **Aborigine**) an aboriginal inhabitant of Australia. ¶ *Aboriginal* is the preferred singular form, *Aborigines* now the preferred plural, although *Aboriginals* is also acceptable. **3** an aboriginal plant or animal. [back-form. f. pl. *aborigines* f. L, prob. f. phr. *ab origine* from the beginning]

The Australian Aborigines, dark-skinned hunter-gatherers comprising several physically distinct groups, arrived in Australia in prehistoric times and brought with them the dingo. Before the arrival of Europeans they were scattered through the whole continent, including Tasmania. Their languages (except of Tasmania) are related to each other but not, apparently, to any other language family and have no literature of their own; estimated at several hundred in number they are almost or completely extinct, and of those that survive some have only a few hundred speakers in Australia. There are now roughly 160,000 Aborigines in Australia. Having become mostly urbanized many have recently moved to their traditional homeland areas in an attempt to preserve their culture.

abort /əˈbɔːt/ *v.* & *n.* —*v.* **1** *intr.* **a** (of a woman) undergo abortion; miscarry. **b** (of a foetus) suffer abortion. **2** *tr.* **a** effect the abortion of (a foetus). **b** effect abortion in (a mother). **3 a** *tr.* cause to end

fruitlessly or prematurely; stop in the early stages. **b** *intr.* end unsuccessfully or prematurely. **4 a** *tr.* abandon or terminate (a space flight or other technical project) before its completion, usu. because of a fault. **b** *intr.* terminate or fail to complete such an undertaking. **5** *Biol.* **a** *intr.* (of an organism) remain undeveloped; shrink away. **b** *tr.* cause to do this. —*n.* **1** a prematurely terminated space flight or other undertaking. **2** the termination of such an undertaking. [L *aboriri* miscarry (as AB-, *oriri ort-* be born)]

abortifacient /əˌbɔːtɪˈfeɪʃ(ə)nt/ *adj.* & *n.* —*adj.* effecting abortion. —*n.* a drug or other agent that effects abortion.

abortion /əˈbɔːʃ(ə)n/ *n.* **1** the expulsion of a foetus (naturally or esp. by medical induction) from the womb before it is able to survive independently, esp. in the first 28 weeks of a human pregnancy. **2** a stunted or deformed creature or thing. **3** the failure of a project or an action. **4** *Biol.* the arrest of the development of an organ. [L *abortio* (as ABORT)]

abortionist /əˈbɔːʃənɪst/ *n.* **1** a person who carries out abortions, esp. illegally. **2** a person who favours the legalization of abortion.

abortive /əˈbɔːtɪv/ *adj.* **1** fruitless, unsuccessful, unfinished. **2** resulting in abortion. **3** *Biol.* (of an organ etc.) rudimentary; arrested in development. □□ **abortively** *adv.* [ME f. OF *abortif -ive* f. L *abortivus* (as ABORT)]

ABO system /ˌeɪbiːˈəʊ/ *n.* a system of four types (A, AB, B, and O) by which human blood may be classified, based on the presence or absence of certain inherited antigens.

aboulia /əˈbuːlɪə/ *n.* (also **abulia**) the loss of will-power as a mental disorder. □□ **aboulic** *adj.* [Gk *a-* not + *boulē* will]

abound /əˈbaʊnd/ *v.intr.* **1** be plentiful. **2** (foll. by *in, with*) be rich; teem or be infested. [ME f. OF *abunder* etc. f. L *abundare* overflow (as AB-, *undare* f. *unda* wave)]

about /əˈbaʊt/ *prep.* & *adv.* —*prep.* **1 a** on the subject of; in connection with (*a book about birds; what are you talking about?*; *argued about money*). **b** relating to (*something funny about this*). **c** in relation to (*symmetry about a plane*). **d** so as to affect (*can do nothing about it; what are you going to do about it?*). **2** at a time near to (*come about four*). **3 a** in, round, surrounding (*wandered about the town; a scarf about her neck*). **b** all round from a centre (*look about you*). **4** here and there in; at points throughout (*toys lying about the house*). **5** at a point or points near to (*fighting going on about us*). **6** carried with (*have no money about me*). **7** occupied with (*what are you about?*). —*adv.* **1 a** approximately (*costs about a pound; is about right*). **b** *colloq.* used to indicate understatement (*just about had enough; it's about time they came*). **2** here and there; at points nearby (*a lot of flu about; I've seen him about recently*). **3** all round; in every direction (*look about*). **4** on the move; in action (*out and about*). **5** in partial rotation or alteration from a given position (*the wrong way about*). **6** in rotation or succession (*turn and turn about*). **7** *Naut.* on or to the opposite tack (*go about; put about*). □ **be about to** to be on the point of (doing something) (*was about to laugh*). [OE *onbūtan* (*on* = A², *būtan* BUT¹)]

about-face /əbaʊtˈfeɪs/ *n.*, *v.*, & *int.* —*n.* & *v.intr.* = ABOUT-TURN *n.* & *v.* —*int.* = ABOUT TURN *int.*

about-turn /əbaʊtˈtɜːn/ *n.*, *v.*, & *int.* —*n.* **1** a turn made so as to face the opposite direction. **2** a change of opinion or policy etc. —*v.intr.* make an about-turn. —*int.* (**about turn**) *Mil.* a command to make an about-turn. [orig. as int.]

above /əˈbʌv/ *prep.*, *adv.*, *adj.*, & *n.* —*prep.* **1** over; on the top of; higher (vertically, up a slope or stream etc.) than; over the surface of (*head above water; above the din*). **2** more than (*above twenty people; above average*). **3** higher in rank, position, importance, etc., than (*above all*). **4 a** too great or good for (*above one's station; is not above cheating at cards*). **b** beyond the reach of; not affected by (*above my understanding; above suspicion*). **5** *archaic* to an earlier time than (*not traced above the third century*). —*adv.* **1** at or to a higher point; overhead (*the floor above; the clouds above*). **2 a** upstairs (*lives above*). **b** upstream. **3** (of a text reference) further back on a page or in a book (*as noted above*). **4** on the upper side (*looks similar above and below*). **5** in addition (*over and above*). **6** *rhet.* in heaven (*Lord above!*). —*adj.* mentioned earlier; preceding (*the above argument*). —*n.* (prec. by *the*) what is mentioned above (*the above shows*). □ **above-board** *adj.* & *adv.* without concealment; fair or fairly;

b *but* d *dog* f *few* g *get* h *he* j *yes* k *cat* l *leg* m *man* n *no* p *pen* r *red* s *sit* t *top* v *voice*

open or openly. **above ground** alive. **above one's head** see HEAD. **above oneself** conceited, arrogant. [A² + OE *bufan* f. *be* = BY + *ufan* above]

ab ovo /æb ˈəʊvəʊ/ *adv.* from the very beginning. [L, = from the egg]

Abp. *abbr.* Archbishop.

abracadabra /ˌæbrəkəˈdæbrə/ *int. & n.* —*int.* a supposedly magic word used by conjurors in performing a trick. —*n.* **1** a spell or charm. **2** jargon or gibberish. [a mystical word engraved and used as a charm: L f. Gk]

abrade /əˈbreɪd/ *v.tr.* scrape or wear away (skin, rock, etc.) by rubbing. □□ **abrader** *n.* [L f. *radere ras-* scrape]

Abraham /ˈeɪbrəˌhæm/ the Hebrew patriarch from whom all Jews trace their descent (Gen. 11: 27–25: 10). In Gen. 14 he is made a contemporary of 'Amraphel king of Shinar', who may be Hammurabi (Shinar = Babylon). □ **Plains of Abraham** see separate entry.

Abrahams /ˈeɪbrəˌhæmz/, Harold Maurice (1899–1978), British sprinter, the only Englishman to have won the 100-metre dash in the Olympic Games. He achieved this at Paris in 1924, after a distinguished athletics career at Cambridge University. His exploits were the subject of the film *Chariots of Fire* (1981).

abrasion /əˈbreɪʒ(ə)n/ *n.* **1** the scraping or wearing away (of skin, rock, etc.). **2** a damaged area resulting from this. [L *abrasio* (as ABRADE)]

abrasive /əˈbreɪsɪv/ *adj. & n.* —*adj.* **1 a** tending to rub or graze. **b** capable of polishing by rubbing or grinding. **2** harsh or hurtful in manner. —*n.* an abrasive substance. [as ABRADE + -IVE]

abreact /ˌæbrɪˈækt/ *v.tr. Psychol.* release (an emotion) by abreaction. [back-form. f. ABREACTION]

abreaction /ˌæbrɪˈækʃ(ə)n/ *n. Psychol.* the free expression and consequent release of a previously repressed emotion. □□ **abreactive** *adj.* [AB- + REACTION after G *Abreagierung*]

abreast /əˈbrest/ *adv.* **1** side by side and facing the same way. **2 a** (often foll. by *with*) up to date. **b** (foll. by *of*) well-informed (*abreast of all the changes*). [ME f. A² + BREAST]

abridge /əˈbrɪdʒ/ *v.tr.* **1** shorten (a book, film, etc.) by using fewer words or making deletions. **2** curtail (liberty). □□ **abridgable** *adj.* **abridger** *n.* [ME f. OF *abreg(i)er* f. LL *abbreviare* ABBREVIATE]

abridgement /əˈbrɪdʒmənt/ *n.* (also **abridgment**) **1 a** a shortened version, esp. of a book; an abstract. **b** the process of producing this. **2** a curtailment (of rights). [F *abrégement* (as ABRIDGE)]

abroad /əˈbrɔːd/ *adv.* **1** in or to a foreign country or countries. **2** over a wide area; in different directions; everywhere (*scatter abroad*). **3** at large; freely moving about; in circulation (*there is a rumour abroad*). **4** *archaic* in or into the open; out of doors. **5** *archaic* wide of the mark; erring. □ **from abroad** from another country. [ME f. A² + BROAD]

abrogate /ˈæbrəˌgeɪt/ *v.tr.* repeal, annul, abolish (a law or custom). □□ **abrogation** /ˌæbrəˈgeɪʃ(ə)n/ *n.* **abrogator** *n.* [L *abrogare* (as AB-, *rogare* propose a law)]

abrupt /əˈbrʌpt/ *adj.* **1** sudden and unexpected; hasty (*his abrupt departure*). **2** (of speech, manner, etc.) uneven; lacking continuity; curt. **3** steep, precipitous. **4** *Bot.* truncated. **5** *Geol.* (of strata) suddenly appearing at the surface. □□ **abruptly** *adv.* **abruptness** *n.* [L *abruptus* past part. of *abrumpere* (as AB-, *rumpere* break)]

Abruzzi /əˈbrʊtsɪ/ a mountainous region on the Adriatic coast of east central Italy; pop. (1981) 1,217,800; capital, L'Aquila.

abs- /əbs, æbs/ *prefix* = AB-. [var. of L *ab-* used before *c, q, t*]

abscess /ˈæbsɪs/ *n.* a swollen area accumulating pus within a body tissue. □□ **abscessed** *adj.* [L *abscessus* a going away (as AB-, *cedere cess-* go)]

abscisic acid /æbˈsaɪzɪk/ *n.* a plant hormone which promotes leaf detachment and bud dormancy and inhibits germination. [L *abscis-* past part. stem of *abscindere* (as AB-, *scindere* to cut)]

abscissa /əbˈsɪsə/ *n.* (*pl.* **abscissae** /-siː/ or **abscissas**) *Math.* **1** (in a system of coordinates) the shortest distance from a point to the vertical or *y*-axis, measured parallel to the horizontal or *x*-axis; the Cartesian *x*-coordinate of a point (cf. ORDINATE). **2** the part of a line between a fixed point on it and an ordinate drawn

to it from any other point. [mod.L *abscissa* (*linea*) fem. past part. of *abscindere* *absciss-* (as AB-, *scindere* cut)]

abscission /əbˈsɪʒ(ə)n/ *n.* **1** the act or an instance of cutting off. **2** *Bot.* the natural detachment of leaves, branches, flowers, etc. [L *abscissio* (as ABSCISSA)]

abscond /əbˈskɒnd/ *v.intr.* depart hurriedly and furtively, esp. unlawfully or to avoid arrest. □□ **absconder** *n.* [L *abscondere* (as AB-, *condere* stow)]

abseil /ˈæbseɪl, -ziːl/ *v. & n. Mountaineering* —*v.intr.* descend a steep rock-face by using a doubled rope coiled round the body and fixed at a higher point. —*n.* a descent made by abseiling. [G *abseilen* f. *ab* down + *Seil* rope]

absence /ˈæbs(ə)ns/ *n.* **1** the state of being away from a place or person. **2** the time or duration of being away. **3** (foll. by *of*) the non-existence or lack of. □ **absence of mind** inattentiveness. [ME f. OF f. L *absentia* (as ABSENT)]

absent *adj. & v.* —*adj.* /ˈæbs(ə)nt/ **1 a** not present. **b** (foll. by *from*) not present at or in. **2** not existing. **3** inattentive to the matter in hand. —*v.refl.* /əbˈsent/ **1** stay away. **2** withdraw. □□ **absently** *adv.* (in sense 3 of *adj.*). [ME ult. f. L *absent-* pres. part. of *abesse* be absent]

absentee /ˌæbsənˈtiː/ *n.* a person not present, esp. one who is absent from work or school. □ **absentee landlord** a landlord who lets a property while living elsewhere.

absenteeism /ˌæbsənˈtiːɪz(ə)m/ *n.* the practice of absenting oneself from work or school etc., esp. frequently or illicitly.

absent-minded /ˌæbs(ə)ntˈmaɪndɪd/ *adj.* habitually forgetful or inattentive; with one's mind on other things. □□ **absent-mindedly** *adv.* **absent-mindedness** *n.*

absinth /ˈæbsɪnθ/ *n.* **1** a shrubby plant, *Atemisia absinthium*, or its essence. Also called WORMWOOD. **2** (usu. **absinthe**) a green aniseed-flavoured potent liqueur based on wormwood and turning milky when water is added. [F *absinthe* f. L *absinthium* f. Gk *apsinthion*]

absit omen /ˌæbsɪt ˈəʊmen/ *int.* may what is threatened not become fact. [L, = may this (evil) omen be absent]

absolute /ˈæbsəˌluːt, -ˌljuːt/ *adj. & n.* —*adj.* **1** complete, utter, perfect (*an absolute fool; absolute bliss*). **2** unconditional, unlimited (*absolute authority*). **3** despotic; ruling arbitrarily or with unrestricted power (*an absolute monarch*). **4** (of a standard or other concept) universally valid; not admitting exceptions; not relative or comparative. **5** *Gram.* **a** (of a construction) syntactically independent of the rest of the sentence, as in *dinner being over, we left the table; let us toss for it, loser to pay*. **b** (of an adjective or transitive verb) used or usable without an expressed noun or object (e.g. *the deaf, guns kill*). **6** (of a legal decree etc.) final. —*n. Philos.* **1** a value, standard, etc., which is objective and universally valid, not subjective or relative. **2** (prec. by *the*) **a** *Philos.* that which can exist without being related to anything else. **b** *Theol.* ultimate reality; God. □ **absolute alcohol** *Chem.* ethanol free from water or other impurities. **absolute magnitude** see MAGNITUDE. **absolute majority 1** a majority over all others combined. **2** more than half. **absolute pitch** *Mus.* **1** the ability to recognize the pitch of a note or produce any given note. **2** a fixed standard of pitch defined by the rate of vibration. **absolute temperature** one measured from absolute zero. **absolute zero** a theoretical lowest possible temperature, at which the particles whose motion constitutes heat would be minimal, calculated as −273.15 °C (or 0 °K). □□ **absoluteness** *n.* [ME f. L *absolutus* past part.: see ABSOLVE]

absolutely /ˈæbsəˌluːtlɪ, -ˌljuːtlɪ/ *adv.* **1** completely, utterly, perfectly (*absolutely marvellous; he absolutely denies it*). **2** independently; in an absolute sense (*God exists absolutely*). **3** (foll. by *neg.*) (no or none) at all (*absolutely no chance of winning; absolutely nowhere*). **4** *colloq.* in actual fact; positively (*it absolutely exploded*). **5** *Gram.* in an absolute way, esp. (of a verb) without a stated object. **6** /-ˈluːtlɪ, -ˈljuːtlɪ/ *colloq.* (used in reply) quite so; yes.

absolution /ˌæbsəˈluːʃ(ə)n, -ˈljuːʃ(ə)n/ *n.* **1** a formal release from guilt, obligation, or punishment. **2** an ecclesiastical declaration of forgiveness of sins. **3** a remission of penance. **4** forgiveness. [ME f. OF f. L *absolutio -onis* (as ABSOLVE)]

absolutism /ˈæbsəluːˌtɪz(ə)m, -ljuːˌtɪz(ə)m/ *n.* the acceptance of or belief in absolute principles in political, philosophical, ethical, or theological matters. □□ **absolutist** n. & adj.

absolve /əb'zɒlv/ v.tr. **1** (often foll. by *from*, *of*) **a** set or pronounce free from blame or obligation etc. **b** acquit; pronounce not guilty. **2** pardon or give absolution for (a sin etc.). □□ **absolver** n. [L *absolvere* (as AB-, *solvere solut-* loosen)]

absorb /əb'sɔːb, -'zɔːb/ v.tr. **1** include or incorporate as part of itself or oneself (*the country successfully absorbed its immigrants*). **2** take in; suck up (liquid, heat, knowledge, etc.) (*she quickly absorbed all she was taught*). **3** reduce the effect or intensity of; deal easily with (an impact, sound, difficulty, etc.). **4** consume (income, time, resources, etc.) (*his debts absorbed half his income*). **5** engross the attention of (*television absorbs them completely*). □□ **absorbable** adj. **absorbability** /-'bɪlɪtɪ/ n. **absorber** n. [ME f. F *absorber* or L *absorbēre absorpt-* (as AB-, *sorbēre* suck in)]

absorbed /əb'sɔːbd, -'zɔːbd/ adj. intensely engaged or interested (*he was absorbed in his work*). □□ **absorbedly** /-bɪdlɪ/ adv.

absorbent /əb'sɔːbənt, -'zɔːbənt/ adj. & n. —adj. having a tendency to absorb (esp. liquids). —n. **1** an absorbent substance. **2** any of the vessels in plants and animals (e.g. root tips) that absorb nutriment. □□ **absorbency** n. [L *absorbent-* f. *absorbēre* ABSORB]

absorbing /əb'sɔːbɪŋ, -'zɔːbɪŋ/ adj. engrossing; intensely interesting. □□ **absorbingly** adv.

absorption /əb'sɔːpʃ(ə)n, -'zɔːpʃ(ə)n/ n. **1** the process or action of absorbing or being absorbed. **2** disappearance through incorporation into something else. **3** mental engrossment. □□ **absorptive** adj. [L *absorptio* (as ABSORB)]

abstain /əb'steɪn/ v.intr. **1 a** (usu. foll. by *from*) restrain oneself; refrain from indulging in (*abstained from cakes and sweets; abstained from mentioning it*). **b** refrain from drinking alcohol. **2** formally decline to use one's vote. □□ **abstainer** n. [ME f. AF *astener* f. OF *abstenir* f. L *abstinēre abstent-* (as AB-, *tenēre* hold)]

abstemious /æb'stiːmɪəs/ adj. (of a person, habit, etc.) moderate, not self-indulgent, esp. in eating and drinking. □□ **abstemiously** adv. **abstemiousness** n. [L *abstemius* (as AB-, *temetum* strong drink)]

abstention /əb'stenʃ(ə)n/ n. the act or an instance of abstaining, esp. from voting. [F *abstention* or LL *abstentio -onis* (as ABSTAIN)]

abstinence /'æbstɪnəns/ n. **1** the act of abstaining, esp. from food or alcohol. **2** the habit of abstaining from pleasure, food, etc. [ME f. OF f. L *abstinentia* (as ABSTINENT)]

abstinent /'æbstɪnənt/ adj. practising abstinence. □□ **abstinently** adv. [ME f. OF f. L (as ABSTAIN)]

abstract adj., v., & n. —adj. /'æbstrækt/ **1 a** to do with or existing in thought rather than matter, or in theory rather than practice; not tangible or concrete (*abstract questions rarely concerned him*). **b** (of a word, esp. a noun) denoting a quality or condition or intangible thing rather than a concrete object. **2** (of painting or sculpture) see ABSTRACT ART. —v. /əb'strækt/ **1** tr. (often foll. by *from*) take out of; extract; remove. **2 a** tr. summarize (an article, book, etc.). **b** intr. do this as an occupation. **3** tr. & refl. (often foll. by *from*) disengage (a person's attention etc.); distract. **4** tr. (foll. by *from*) consider abstractly or separately from something else. **5** tr. euphem. steal. —n. /'æbstrækt/ **1** a summary or statement of the contents of a book etc. **2** an abstract work of art. **3** an abstraction or abstract term. □ **in the abstract** in theory rather than in practice. □□ **abstractly** /'æbstræktlɪ/ adv. **abstractor** /əb'stræktə(r)/ n. (in sense 2 of v.). [ME f. OF *abstract* or L *abstractus* past part. of *abstrahere* (as AB-, *trahere* draw)]

abstract art n. painting or sculpture that achieves its effect by grouping shapes and colours in satisfying patterns rather than by the recognizable representation of physical reality. Although such patterns are the structural basis of all artistic design, their elevation into a self-sufficient aesthetic is essentially a 20th-c. phenomenon. The first abstract works of art are generally considered to date from *c*.1910–14, and since then abstract art has polarized into two main divisions: hard-edged and geometric (akin to the linear and classical) or flowing and organic (akin to the painterly and romantic).

abstracted /əb'stræktɪd/ adj. inattentive to the matter in hand; preoccupied. □□ **abstractedly** adv.

abstract expressionism n. a development of abstract art of the kind produced in New York in the 1940s and early 1950s in which large canvases were covered by means of spontaneous painterly gestures whose disposition primarily expressed an intangible emotive feeling as opposed to having any descriptive function. Of its participants de Kooning retained some figurative elements, but many others avoided all such reference. Although initially inspired by European surrealism in its use of unconscious inspiration for pictorial creation, it is widely considered to be the first major American contribution to art and had enormous impact in Europe in the 1950s.

abstraction /əb'strækʃ(ə)n/ n. **1** the act or an instance of abstracting or taking away. **2 a** an abstract or visionary idea. **b** the formation of abstract ideas. **3 a** abstract qualities (esp. in art). **b** an abstract work of art. **4** absent-mindedness. [F *abstraction* or L *abstractio* (as ABSTRACT)]

abstractionism /əb'strækʃ(ə)nɪz(ə)m/ n. **1** the principles and practice of abstract art. **2** the pursuit or cult of abstract ideas. □□ **abstractionist** n.

abstruse /əb'struːs/ adj. hard to understand; obscure; profound. □□ **abstrusely** adv. **abstruseness** n. [F *abstruse* or L *abstrusus* (as AB-, *trusus* past part. of *trudere* push)]

absurd /əb'sɜːd/ adj. **1** (of an idea, suggestion, etc.) wildly unreasonable, illogical, or inappropriate. **2** (of a person) unreasonable or ridiculous in manner. **3** (of a thing) ludicrous, incongruous (*an absurd hat; the situation was becoming absurd*). □ **Theatre of the Absurd** see THEATRE. □□ **absurdly** adv. **absurdness** n. [F *absurde* or L *absurdus* (as AB-, *surdus* deaf, dull)]

absurdity /əb'sɜːdɪtɪ/ n. (pl. **-ies**) **1** wild inappropriateness or incongruity. **2** extreme unreasonableness. **3** an absurd statement or act. [F *absurdité* or LL *absurditas* (as ABSURD)]

ABTA /'æbtə/ abbr. Association of British Travel Agents.

Abu Dhabi /ˌæbuː 'dɑːbɪ/ **1** the largest of the member States of the United Arab Emirates; pop. (1980) 670,100. **2** its capital city (pop. 242,975), which is also the federal capital of the United Arab Emirates.

Abuja /ə'buːdʒə/ a newly built city designated since 1982 to replace Lagos and the capital of Nigeria. It is located in the Federal Capital Territory, at the geographical centre of the country.

abulia var. of ABOULIA.

Abu Musa /ˌæbuː 'muːsə/ a small island in the Persian Gulf administered by the emirate of Sharjah until occupied by Iran in 1971.

abundance /ə'bʌnd(ə)ns/ n. **1** a very great quantity, usu. considered to be more than enough. **2** wealth, affluence. **3** wealth of emotion (*abundance of heart*). **4** a call in solo whist undertaking to make nine tricks. [ME f. OF *abundance* f. L *abundantia* (as ABUNDANT)]

abundant /ə'bʌnd(ə)nt/ adj. **1** existing or available in large quantities; plentiful. **2** (foll. by *in*) having an abundance of (*a country abundant in fruit*). □□ **abundantly** adv. [ME f. L (as ABOUND)]

abuse v. & n. —v.tr. /ə'bjuːz/ **1** use to bad effect or for a bad purpose; misuse (*abused his position of power*). **2** insult verbally; maltreat. —n. /ə'bjuːs/ **1 a** an incorrect or improper use (*the abuse of power*). **b** an instance of this. **2** insulting language (*a torrent of abuse*). **3** unjust or corrupt practice. **4** maltreatment of a person (*child abuse*). □□ **abuser** /ə'bjuːzə(r)/ n. [ME f. OF *abus* (n.), *abuser* (v.) f. L *abusus*, *abuti* (as AB-, *uti us-* USE)]

Abu Simbel /ˌæbuː 'sɪmb(ə)l/ a former village in southern Egypt, site of two rock-cut temples built by Rameses II (13th c. BC), a monument to the greatest of the pharaohs and a constant reminder to possibly restive Nubian tribes of Egypt's might. The great temple, with its façade (31 m, 102 ft., high) bearing four colossal seated statues of Rameses, faces due east, and is dedicated to Amun-Ra and other principal State gods of the period; the small temple is dedicated to Hathor and Nefertari, first wife of Rameses. In 1963 an archaeological salvage operation was begun, comparable in scale to the original construction of the temples, in which engineers sawed up the monument and carried it up the hillside to be rebuilt, with its original orientation, well above the rising waters of Lake Nasser, whose level was affected by the building of the High Dam at Aswan.

abusive /ə'bju:sɪv/ adj. **1** using or containing insulting language. **2** (of language) insulting. □□ **abusively** adv. **abusiveness** n.

abut /ə'bʌt/ v. (**abutted**, **abutting**) **1** intr. (foll. by on) (of estates, countries, etc.) adjoin (another). **2** intr. (foll. by on, against) (of part of a building) touch or lean upon (another) with a projecting end or point (the shed abutted on the side of the house). **3** tr. abut on. [OF abouter (BUTT¹) and AL abuttare f. OF but end]

abutment /ə'bʌtmənt/ n. **1** the lateral supporting structure of a bridge, arch, etc. **2** the point of junction between such a support and the thing supported.

abutter /ə'bʌtə(r)/ n. Law the owner of an adjoining property.

abuzz /ə'bʌz/ adv. & adj. in a 'buzz' (see BUZZ n. 3); in a state of excitement or activity.

abysmal /ə'bɪzm(ə)l/ adj. **1** colloq. extremely bad (abysmal weather; the standard is abysmal). **2** profound, utter (abysmal ignorance). □□ **abysmally** adv. [archaic or poet. abysm = ABYSS, f. OF abi(s)me f. med.L abysmus]

abyss /ə'bɪs/ n. **1** a deep or seemingly bottomless chasm. **2 a** an immeasurable depth (abyss of despair). **b** a catastrophic situation as contemplated or feared (his loss brought him a step nearer the abyss). **3** (prec. by the) primal chaos, hell. [ME f. LL abyssus f. Gk abussos bottomless (as A-¹, bussos depth)]

abyssal /ə'bɪs(ə)l/ adj. **1** at or of the ocean depths or floor. **2** Geol. plutonic.

Abyssinia /ˌæbɪ'sɪnɪə/ a former name of Ethiopia. □□ **Abyssinian** adj. & n.

AC abbr. **1** (also **ac**) alternating current. **2** Brit. aircraftman. **3** before Christ. **4** Companion of the Order of Australia. [sense 3 f. L ante Christum]

Ac symb. Chem. the element actinium.

ac- /ək/ prefix assim. form of AD- before c, k, q.

äc abbr. account. [account current: see ACCOUNT n. 2, 3]

-ac /æk/ suffix forming adjectives which are often also (or only) used as nouns (cardiac; maniac) (see also -ACAL). [F -aque or L -acus or Gk -akos adj. suffix]

acacia /ə'keɪʃə/ n. **1** any tree of the genus Acacia, with yellow or white flowers, esp. A. senegal yielding gum arabic. **2** (also **false acacia**) the locust tree, Robinia pseudoacacia, grown for ornament. [L f. Gk akakia]

academe /'ækədi:m/ n. **1 a** the world of learning. **b** universities collectively. **2** literary a college or university. □ **grove** (or **groves**) **of Academe** a university environment. [Gk Akadēmos (see ACADEMY): used by Shakesp. (Love's Labour's Lost I. i. 13) and Milton (Paradise Regained iv. 244)]

academia /ˌækə'di:mɪə/ n. the academic world; scholastic life. [mod.L: see ACADEMY]

academic /ˌækə'demɪk/ adj. & n. —adj. **1 a** scholarly; to do with learning. **b** of or relating to a scholarly institution (academic dress). **2** abstract; theoretical; not of practical relevance. **3** Art conventional, over-formal. **4 a** of or concerning Plato's philosophy. **b** sceptical. —n. a teacher or scholar in a university or institute of higher education. □ **academic year** a period of nearly a year reckoned from the time of the main student intake, usu. from the beginning of the autumn term to the end of the summer term. □□ **academically** adv. [F académique or L academicus (as ACADEMY)]

academical /ˌækə'demɪk(ə)l/ adj. & n. —adj. belonging to a college or university. —n. (in pl.) university costume.

academician /ə,kædə'mɪʃ(ə)n/ n. a member of an Academy, esp. of the Royal Academy of Arts, the Académie française, or the USSR Academy of Sciences. [F académicien (as ACADEMIC)]

academicism /ˌækə'demɪˌsɪz(ə)m/ n. (also **academism** /ə'kædə,mɪz(ə)m/) academic principles or their application in art.

Académie française /æ,kæde'mi: frɑː'sez/ a French literary academy with a constant membership of 40, founded by Richelieu in 1635. Its functions include the compilation and periodic revision of a definitive dictionary of the French language, the first edition of which appeared in 1694. Its tendency is to defend traditional literary and linguistic rules and to discourage innovation. Nevertheless, membership is accounted a high literary honour and is coveted even by unorthodox writers who continue to experiment with the language (see FRENCH). [F, = French Academy]

academy /ə'kædəmɪ/ n. (pl. **-ies**) **1 a** a place of study or training in a special field (military academy; academy of dance). **b** hist. a place of study. **2** (usu. **Academy**) a society or institution of distinguished scholars, artists, scientists, etc. (Royal Academy). **3** Sc. a secondary school. **4** (**Academy**) the park and gymnasium in the outskirts of ancient Athens, sacred to the hero Academus, where Plato founded a school which survived until its dissolution by Justinian in AD 529. The name is applied by extension to the philosophical system of Plato, and also to the philosophical scepticism of the school in the 3rd and 2nd c. BC. □ **Academy award** (nicknamed 'Oscar') any of the awards of the Academy of Motion Picture Arts and Sciences (Hollywood, US) given annually for success in the film industry. [F académie or L academia f. Gk akadēmeia f. Akadēmos the hero after whom Plato's garden was named]

Acadia /ə'keɪdɪə/ a former French colony (Acadie; now Nova Scotia) on the eastern seaboard of North America. Founded in 1603, the colony was subject to considerable encroachment from British colonists and much of it was ceded to Britain by the Treaty of Utrecht in 1713. Some of its French inhabitants withdrew to French territory in the following year, and during the French and Indian War (1754–63) the remainder, who were considered to be a threat to the British position, were forcibly resettled in other British colonies to the south.

Acadian /ə'keɪdɪən/ n. & adj. —n. **1** a native or inhabitant of Acadia in Nova Scotia, esp. a French-speaking descendant of the early French settlers in Canada. **2** a descendant of French-speaking Nova Scotian immigrants in Louisiana. —adj. of or relating to Acadians. [F Acadie (see ACADIA)]

-acal /ək(ə)l/ suffix forming adjectives, often used to distinguish them from nouns in -ac (heliacal; maniacal).

acanthus /ə'kænθəs/ n. **1** any herbaceous plant or shrub of the genus Acanthus, with spiny leaves. **2** Archit. a conventionalized representation of an acanthus leaf, used esp. as a decoration for Corinthian column capitals. [L f. Gk akanthos f. akantha thorn perh. f. akē sharp point]

a cappella /ˌɑː kə'pelə, ˌæ kə'pelə/ adj. & adv. (also **alla cappella** /ˌælə/) Mus. (of choral music) unaccompanied. [It., = in church style]

Acapulco /ˌækə'pʊlkəʊ/ a port and holiday resort in the south of Mexico, on the Pacific coast; pop. (1980) 409,300.

acaricide /ə'kærɪˌsaɪd/ n. a preparation for destroying mites.

acarid /'ækərɪd/ n. any small arachnid of the order Acarina, including mites and ticks. [mod.L acarida f. acarus f. Gk akari mite]

acarpous /ə'kɑːpəs/ adj. Bot. (of a plant etc.) without fruit or that does not produce fruit. [A-¹ + Gk karpos fruit]

ACAS /'eɪkæs/ abbr. (in the UK) Advisory, Conciliation, and Arbitration Service. The service was set up in 1975 to provide such facilities as a means of avoiding or resolving industrial disputes, and to promote the improvement of collective bargaining. ACAS does not carry out arbitrations itself but may recommend arbitration (to be conducted by another body) for solving a dispute.

Accadian var. of AKKADIAN.

accede /æk'si:d/ v.intr. (often foll. by to) **1** take office, esp. become monarch. **2** assent or agree (acceded to the proposal). **3** (foll. by to) formally subscribe to a treaty or other agreement. [ME f. L accedere (as AC-, cedere cess- go)]

accelerando /ək,selə'rændəʊ, ə,tʃel-/ adv., adj., & n. Mus. —adj. & adv. with a gradual increase of speed. —n. (pl. **accelerandos** or **accelerandi** /-dɪ/) a passage performed accelerando. [It.]

accelerate /ək'seləˌreɪt/ v. **1** intr. **a** (of a moving body, esp. a vehicle) move or begin to move more quickly; increase speed. **b** (of a process) happen or reach completion more quickly. **2** tr. **a** cause to increase speed. **b** cause (a process) to happen more quickly. [L accelerare (as AC-, celerare f. celer swift)]

acceleration /ək,selə'reɪʃ(ə)n/ n. **1** the process or act of accelerating or being accelerated. **2** an instance of this. **3** (of a vehicle etc.) the capacity to gain speed (*the car has good acceleration*). **4** *Physics* the rate of change of velocity measured in terms of a unit of time. [F *accélération* or L *acceleratio* (as ACCELERATE)]

accelerative /ək'selərətɪv/ adj. tending to increase speed; quickening.

accelerator /ək'selə,reɪtə(r)/ n. **1** a device for increasing speed, esp. the pedal that controls the speed of a vehicle's engine. **2** *Physics* an apparatus for imparting high speeds to charged particles. **3** *Chem.* a substance that speeds up a chemical reaction.

accelerometer /ək,selə'rɒmɪtə(r)/ n. an instrument for measuring acceleration esp. of rockets. [ACCELERATE + -METER]

accent n. & v. —n. /'æks(ə)nt, -sent/ **1** a particular mode of pronunciation, esp. one associated with a particular region or group (*Liverpool accent; German accent; upper-class accent*). **2** prominence given to a syllable by stress or pitch. **3** a mark on a letter or word to indicate pitch, stress, or the quality of a vowel. **4** a distinctive feature or emphasis (*an accent on comfort*). **5** *Mus.* emphasis on a particular note or chord. —v.tr. /æk'sent/ **1** pronounce with an accent; emphasize (a word or syllable). **2** write or print accents on (words etc.). **3** accentuate. **4** *Mus.* play (a note etc.) with an accent. □□ **accentual** /ək'sentjʊəl/ adj. [L *accentus* (as AC-, *cantus* song) repr. Gk *prosōidia* (PROSODY), or through F *accent, accenter*]

accentor /ək'sentə(r)/ n. any bird of the genus *Prunella*, e.g. the hedge sparrow. [med.L *accentor* f. L *ad* to + *cantor* singer]

accentuate /æk'sentjʊ,eɪt/ v.tr. emphasize; make prominent. □□ **accentuation** /æk,sentjʊ'eɪʃ(ə)n/ n. [med.L *accentuare accentuat-* (as ACCENT)]

accept /ək'sept/ v.tr. **1** (also *absol.*) consent to receive (a thing offered). **2** (also *absol.*) give an affirmative answer to (an offer or proposal). **3** regard favourably; treat as welcome (*her mother-in-law never accepted her*). **4 a** believe, receive (an opinion, explanation, etc.) as adequate or valid. **b** be prepared to subscribe to (a belief, philosophy, etc.). **5** receive as suitable (*the hotel accepts traveller's cheques; the machine only accepts tokens*). **6 a** tolerate; submit to (*accepted the umpire's decision*). **b** (often foll. by *that* + clause) be willing to believe (*we accept that you meant well*). **7** undertake (an office or responsibility). **8** agree to meet (a draft or bill of exchange). □□ **accepted opinion** one generally held to be correct. □□ **accepter** n. [ME f. OF *accepter* or L *acceptare* f. *accipere* (as AC-, *capere* take)]

acceptable /ək'septəb(ə)l/ adj. **1 a** worthy of being accepted. **b** pleasing, welcome. **2** adequate, satisfactory. **3** tolerable (*an acceptable risk*). □□ **acceptability** /ək,septə'bɪlɪtɪ/ n. **acceptableness** n. **acceptably** adv. [ME f. OF f. LL *acceptabilis* (as ACCEPT)]

acceptance /ək'sept(ə)ns/ n. **1** willingness to receive (a gift, payment, duty, etc.). **2** an affirmative answer to an invitation or proposal. **3** (often foll. by *of*) a willingness to accept (conditions, a circumstance, etc.). **4 a** approval, belief (*found wide acceptance*). **b** willingness or ability to tolerate. **5 a** agreement to meet a bill of exchange. **b** a bill so accepted. [F f. *accepter* (as ACCEPT)]

acceptant /ək'sept(ə)nt/ adj. (foll. by *of*) willingly accepting. [F (as ACCEPTANCE)]

acceptation /,æksep'teɪʃ(ə)n/ n. a particular sense, or the generally recognized meaning, of a word or phrase. [ME f. OF f. med.L *acceptatio* (as ACCEPT)]

acceptor /ək'septə(r)/ n. **1** *Commerce* a person who accepts a bill. **2** *Physics* an atom or molecule able to receive an extra electron, esp. an impurity in a semiconductor. **3** *Chem.* a molecule or ion etc. to which electrons are donated in the formation of a bond. **4** *Electr.* a circuit able to accept a given frequency.

access /'ækses/ n. & v. —n. **1** a way of approaching or reaching or entering (*a building with rear access*). **2 a** (often foll. by *to*) the right or opportunity to reach or use or visit; admittance (*has access to secret files; was granted access to the prisoner*). **b** the condition of being readily approached; accessibility. **3** (often foll. by *of*) an attack or outburst (*an access of anger*). **4** (*attrib.*) *Brit.* (of broadcasting) allowed to minority or special-interest groups to undertake (*access television*). —v.tr. **1** *Computing* gain access to (data, a file, etc.). **2** accession. □ **access road** a road giving access only

to the properties along it. **access time** *Computing* the time taken to retrieve data from storage. [ME f. OF *acces* or L *accessus* f. *accedere* (as AC-, *cedere cess-* go)]

accessary var. of ACCESSORY.

accessible /ək'sesɪb(ə)l/ adj. (often foll. by *to*) **1** that can be readily be reached, entered, or used. **2** (of a person) readily available (esp. to subordinates). **3** (in a form) easy to understand. □□ **accessibility** /ək,sesɪ'bɪlɪtɪ/ n. **accessibly** adv. [F *accessible* or LL *accessibilis* (as ACCEDE)]

accession /ək'seʃ(ə)n/ n. & v. —n. **1** entering upon an office (esp. the throne) or a condition (as manhood). **2** (often foll. by *to*) a thing added (e.g. a book to a library); increase, addition. **3** *Law* the incorporation of one item of property in another. **4** assent; the formal acceptance of a treaty etc. —v.tr. record the addition of (a new item) to a library or museum. [F *accession* or L *accessio -onis* (as ACCEDE)]

accessorize /ək'sesə,raɪz/ v.tr. provide (a costume etc.) with accessories.

accessory /ək'sesərɪ/ n. & adj. (also **accessary**) —n. (pl. **-ies**) **1** an additional or extra thing. **2** (usu. in *pl.*) **a** a small attachment or fitting. **b** a small item of (esp. a woman's) dress (e.g. shoes, gloves, handbag). **3** (often foll. by *to*) a person who helps in or knows the details of an (esp. illegal) act, without taking part in it. —adj. additional; contributing or aiding in a minor way; dispensable. □ **accessory before** (or **after**) **the fact** a person who incites (or assists) another to commit a crime. □□ **accessorial** /,ækse'sɔːrɪəl/ adj. [med.L *accessorius* (as ACCEDE)]

acciaccatura /ə,tʃækə'tʊərə/ n. *Mus.* a grace-note performed as quickly as possible before an essential note of a melody. [It.]

accidence /'æksɪd(ə)ns/ n. the part of grammar that deals with the variable parts or inflections of words. [med.L sense of L *accidentia* (transl. Gk *parepomena*) neut. pl. of *accidens* (as ACCIDENT)]

accident /'æksɪd(ə)nt/ n. **1** an event that is without apparent cause, or is unexpected (*their early arrival was just an accident*). **2** an unfortunate event, esp. one causing physical harm or damage, brought about unintentionally. **3** occurrence of things by chance; the working of fortune (*accident accounts for much in life*). **4** *colloq.* an occurrence of involuntary urination or defecation. **5** an irregularity in structure. □ **accident-prone** (of a person) subject to frequent accidents. **by accident** unintentionally. [ME f. OF f. LL *accidens* f. L *accidere* (as AC-, *cadere* fall)]

accidental /,æksɪ'dent(ə)l/ adj. & n. —adj. **1** happening by chance, unintentionally, or unexpectedly. **2** not essential to a conception; subsidiary. —n. **1** *Mus.* a sign indicating a momentary departure from the key signature by raising or lowering a note. **2** something not essential to a conception. □□ **accidentally** adv. [ME f. LL *accidentalis* (as ACCIDENT)]

accidie /'æksɪdiː/ n. laziness, sloth, apathy. [ME f. AF *accidie* f. OF *accide* f. med.L *accidia*]

acclaim /ə'kleɪm/ v. & n. —v.tr. **1** welcome or applaud enthusiastically; praise publicly. **2** (foll. by compl.) hail as (*acclaimed him king; was acclaimed the winner*). —n. **1** applause; welcome; public praise. **2** a shout of acclaim. □□ **acclaimer** n. [ME f. L *acclamare* (as AC-, *clamare* shout: spelling assim. to *claim*)]

acclamation /,æklə'meɪʃ(ə)n/ n. **1** loud and eager assent to a proposal. **2** (usu. in *pl.*) shouting in a person's honour. **3** the act or process of acclaiming. □ **by acclamation** *US Polit.* (elected) unanimously and without ballot. [L *acclamatio* (as ACCLAIM)]

acclimate /'æklɪ,meɪt, ə'klaɪ-/ v.tr. *US* acclimatize. [F *acclimater* f. *à* to + *climat* CLIMATE]

acclimation /,æklaɪ'meɪʃ(ə)n/ n. acclimatization. [irreg. f. ACCLIMATE]

acclimatize /ə'klaɪmə,taɪz/ v. (also **-ise**) **1** tr. accustom to a new climate or to new conditions. **2** intr. become acclimatized. □□ **acclimatization** /-'zeɪʃ(ə)n/ n. [F *acclimater*: see ACCLIMATE]

acclivity /ə'klɪvɪtɪ/ n. (pl. **-ies**) an upward slope. □□ **acclivitous** adj. [L *acclivitas* f. *acclivis* (as AC-, *clivis* f. *clivus* slope)]

accolade /'ækə,leɪd, -'leɪd/ n. **1** the awarding of praise; an acknowledgement of merit. **2** a touch made with a sword as the bestowing of a knighthood. [F f. Prov. *acolada* (as AC-, L *collum* neck)]

b but d dog f few g get h he j yes k cat l leg m man n no p pen r red s sit t top v voice

accommodate /əˈkɒməˌdeɪt/ v.tr. **1** provide lodging or room for (*the flat accommodates three people*). **2** adapt, harmonize, reconcile (*must accommodate ourselves to new surroundings; cannot accommodate your needs to mine*). **3 a** do service or favour to; oblige (a person). **b** (foll. by *with*) supply (a person) with. [L *accommodare* (as AC-, *commodus* fitting)]

accommodating /əˈkɒməˌdeɪtɪŋ/ adj. obliging, compliant. □□ **accommodatingly** adv.

accommodation /əˌkɒməˈdeɪʃ(ə)n/ n. **1** (in *sing.* or US in *pl.*) lodgings; a place to live. **2** an adjustment or adaptation to suit a special or different purpose. **3** a convenient arrangement; a settlement or compromise. **4** (in *pl.*) US a seat in a vehicle etc. □ **accommodation address** an address used on letters to a person who is unable or unwilling to give a permanent address. **accommodation bill** a bill to raise money on credit. **accommodation ladder** a ladder up the side of a ship from a small boat. **accommodation road** a road for access to a place not on a public road. [F *accommodation* or L *accommodatio -onis* (as ACCOMMODATE)]

accompaniment /əˈkʌmpənɪmənt/ n. **1** *Mus.* an instrumental or orchestral part supporting or partnering a solo instrument, voice, or group. **2** an accompanying thing; an appendage. [F *accompagnement* (as ACCOMPANY)]

accompanist /əˈkʌmpənɪst/ n. (also **accompanyist** /-nɪɪst/) a person who provides a musical accompaniment.

accompany /əˈkʌmpənɪ/ v.tr. (**-ies, -ied**) **1** go with; escort, attend. **2** (usu. in *passive*; foll. by *with, by*) **a** be done or found with; supplement (*speech accompanied with gestures*). **b** have as a result (*pills accompanied by side effects*). **3** *Mus.* support or partner with accompaniment. [ME f. F *accompagner* f. *à* to + OF *compaing* COMPANION¹: assim. to COMPANY]

accomplice /əˈkʌmplɪs, -ˈkɒm-/ n. a partner in a crime or wrongdoing. [ME and F *complice* (prob. by assoc. with ACCOMPANY), f. LL *complex complicis* confederate: cf. COMPLICATE]

accomplish /əˈkʌmplɪʃ, əˈkɒm-/ v.tr. perform; complete; succeed in doing. [ME f. OF *acomplir* f. L *complēre* COMPLETE]

accomplished /əˈkʌmplɪʃd, əˈkɒm-/ adj. clever, skilled; well trained or educated.

accomplishment /əˈkʌmplɪʃmənt, əˈkɒm-/ n. **1** the fulfilment or completion (of a task etc.). **2** an acquired skill, esp. a social one. **3** a thing done or achieved.

accord /əˈkɔːd/ v. & n. —v. **1** *intr.* (often foll. by *with*) (esp. of a thing) be in harmony; be consistent. **2** *tr.* **a** grant (permission, a request, etc.). **b** give (a welcome etc.). —n. **1** agreement, consent. **2** harmony or harmonious correspondence in pitch, tone, colour, etc. □ **of one's own accord** on one's own initiative; voluntarily. **with one accord** unanimously; in a united way. [ME f. OF *acord, acorder* f. L *cor cordis* heart]

accordance /əˈkɔːd(ə)ns/ n. harmony, agreement. □ **in accordance with** in a manner corresponding to (*we acted in accordance with your wishes*). [ME f. OF *acordance* (as ACCORD)]

accordant /əˈkɔːd(ə)nt/ adj. (often foll. by *with*) in tune; agreeing. □□ **accordantly** adv. [ME f. OF *acordant* (as ACCORD)]

according /əˈkɔːdɪŋ/ adv. **1** (foll. by *to*) **a** as stated by or in (*according to my sister; according to their statement*). **b** in a manner corresponding to; in proportion to (*he lives according to his principles*). **2** (foll. by *as* + clause) in a manner or to a degree that varies as (*he pays according as he is able*).

accordingly /əˈkɔːdɪŋlɪ/ adv. **1** as suggested or required by the (stated) circumstances (*silence is vital so please act accordingly*). **2** consequently, therefore (*accordingly, he left the room*).

accordion /əˈkɔːdɪən/ n. a portable musical instrument with reeds blown by bellows and played by means of keys and buttons. □ **accordion pleat, wall**, etc. one folding like the bellows of an accordion. □□ **accordionist** n. [G *Akkordion* f. It. *accordare* to tune]

accost /əˈkɒst/ v.tr. **1** approach and address (a person), esp. boldly. **2** (of a prostitute) solicit. [F *accoster* f. It. *accostare* ult. f. L *costa* rib: see COAST]

accouchement /ˌæːkuːʃˈmɑ̃/ n. **1** childbirth. **2** the period of childbirth. [F f. *accoucher* act as midwife]

accoucheur /ˌækuːˈʃɜː(r)/ n. a male midwife. [F (as ACCOUCHEMENT)]

account /əˈkaʊnt/ n. & v. —n. **1** a narration or description (*gave a long account of the ordeal*). **2 a** an arrangement or facility at a bank or building society etc. for commercial or financial transactions, esp. for depositing and withdrawing money (*opened an account*). **b** the assets credited by such an arrangement (*has a large account; paid the money into her account*). **c** an arrangement at a shop for buying goods on credit (*has an account at the news-agent's*). **3 a** (often in *pl.*) a record or statement of money, goods, or services received or expended, with the balance (*firms must keep detailed accounts*). **b** (in *pl.*) the practice of accounting or reckoning (*is good at accounts*). **4** a statement of the administration of money in trust (*demand an account*). **5** the period during which transactions take place on a stock exchange; the period from one account day to the next. **6** counting, reckoning. —v.tr. (foll. by *to be* or compl.) consider, regard as (*account it a misfortune; account him wise; account him to be guilty*). ¶ Use with *as* (*we accounted him as wise*) is considered incorrect. □ **account day** a day of periodic settlement of stock exchange accounts. **account for 1** serve as or provide an explanation or reason for (*that accounts for their misbehaviour*). **2 a** give a reckoning of or answer for (money etc. entrusted). **b** answer for (one's conduct). **3** succeed in killing, destroying, disposing of, or defeating. **4** supply or make up a specified amount or proportion of (*rent accounts for 50% of expenditure*). **account rendered** a bill which has been sent but is not yet paid. **by all accounts** in everyone's opinion. **call to account** require an explanation from (a person). **give a good** (or **bad**) **account of oneself** make a favourable (or unfavourable) impression; be successful (or unsuccessful). **keep account of** keep a record of; follow closely. **leave out of account** fail or decline to consider. **money of account** denominations of money used in reckoning, but not current as coins. **of no account** unimportant. **of some account** important. **on account 1** (of goods) to be paid for later. **2** (of money) in part payment. **on account of** because of. **on no account** under no circumstances; certainly not. **on one's own account** for one's own purposes; at one's own risk. **settle** (or **square**) **accounts with 1** receive or pay money etc. owed to. **2** have revenge on. **take account of** (or **take into account**) consider along with other factors (*took their age into account*). **turn to account** (or **good account**) turn to one's advantage. [ME f. OF *acont, aconter* (as AC-, *conter* COUNT¹)]

accountable /əˈkaʊntəb(ə)l/ adj. **1** responsible; required to account for one's conduct (*accountable for one's actions*). **2** explicable, understandable. □□ **accountability** /-ˈbɪlɪtɪ/ n. **accountably** adv.

accountancy /əˈkaʊntənsɪ/ n. the profession or duties of an accountant.

accountant /əˈkaʊnt(ə)nt/ n. a professional keeper or inspector of accounts. [legal F f. pres. part. of OF *aconter* ACCOUNT]

accounting /əˈkaʊntɪŋ/ n. **1** the process of or skill in keeping and verifying accounts. **2** in senses of ACCOUNT v.

accoutre /əˈkuːtə(r)/ v.tr. (US **accouter**) (usu. as **accoutred** adj.) attire, equip, esp. with a special costume. [F *accoutrer* f. OF *acoustrer* (as A-³, *couture* sewing: cf. SUTURE)]

accoutrement /əˈkuːtrəmənt, -təmənt/ n. (US **accouterment** /-təmənt/) (usu. in *pl.*) **1** equipment, trappings. **2** *Mil.* a soldier's outfit other than weapons and garments. [F (as ACCOUTRE)]

Accra /əˈkrɑː/ the capital of Ghana, a port on the Gulf of Guinea; pop. (1984) 867,450; Greater Accra pop. 1,431,100.

accredit /əˈkredɪt/ v.tr. (**accredited, accrediting**) **1** (foll. by *to*) attribute (a saying etc.) to (a person). **2** (foll. by *with*) credit (a person) with (a saying etc.). **3** (usu. foll. by *to* or *at*) send (an ambassador etc.) with credentials; recommend by documents as an envoy (*was accredited to the sovereign*). **4** gain belief or influence for or make credible (an adviser, a statement, etc.). □□ **accreditation** /-ˈteɪʃ(ə)n/ n. [F *accréditer* (as AC-, *crédit* CREDIT)]

accredited /əˈkredɪtɪd/ adj. **1** (of a person or organization) officially recognized. **2** (of a belief) generally accepted; orthodox. **3** (of cattle, milk, etc.) having guaranteed quality.

accrete /əˈkriːt/ v. **1** *intr.* grow together or into one. **2** *intr.* (often foll. by *to*) form round or on, as round a nucleus. **3** *tr.* attract (such additions). [L *accrescere* (as AC-, *crescere cret-* grow)]

accretion /əˈkriːʃ(ə)n/ *n.* **1** growth by organic enlargement. **2 a** the growing of separate things into one. **b** the product of such growing. **3 a** extraneous matter added to anything. **b** the adhesion of this. **4** *Law* **a** = ACCESSION. **b** the increase of a legacy etc. by the share of a failing co-legatee. □□ **accretive** *adj.* [L *accretio* (as ACCRETE)]

accrue /əˈkruː/ *v.intr.* (**accrues, accrued, accruing**) (often foll. by *to*) come as a natural increase or advantage, esp. financial. □□ **accrual** *n.* **accrued** *adj.* [ME f. AF *acru(e)*, past part. of *acreistre* increase f. L *accrescere* ACCRETE]

acculturate /əˈkʌltʃəˌreɪt/ *v.* **1** *intr.* adapt to or adopt a different culture. **2** *tr.* cause to do this. □□ **acculturation** /-ˈreɪʃ(ə)n/ *n.* **acculturative** /-rətɪv/ *adj.*

accumulate /əˈkjuːmjʊˌleɪt/ *v.* **1** *tr.* **a** acquire an increasing number or quantity of; heap up. **b** produce or acquire (a resulting whole) in this way. **2** *intr.* grow numerous or considerable; form an increasing mass or quantity. [L *accumulare* (as AC-, *cumulus* heap)]

accumulation /əˌkjuːmjʊˈleɪʃ(ə)n/ *n.* **1** the act or process of accumulating or being accumulated. **2** an accumulated mass. **3** the growth of capital by continued interest. [L *accumulatio* (as ACCUMULATE)]

accumulative /əˈkjuːmjʊlətɪv/ *adj.* **1** arising from accumulation; cumulative (*accumulative evidence*). **2** arranged so as to accumulate. **3** acquisitive; given to hoarding. □□ **accumulatively** *adv.*

accumulator /əˈkjuːmjʊˌleɪtə(r)/ *n.* **1** *Brit.* a rechargeable electric cell. **2** a bet placed on a sequence of events, the winnings and stake from each being placed on the next. **3** a register in a computer used to contain the results of an operation. **4** a person who accumulates things.

accuracy /ˈækjʊrəsɪ/ *n.* exactness or precision, esp. arising from careful effort.

accurate /ˈækjʊrət/ *adj.* **1** careful, precise; lacking errors. **2** conforming exactly with the truth or with a given standard. □□ **accurately** *adv.* [L *accuratus* done carefully, past part. of *accurare* (as AC-, *cura* care)]

accursed /əˈkɜːsɪd, əˈkɜːst/ *adj.* (*archaic* **accurst** /əˈkɜːst/) **1** lying under a curse; ill-fated. **2** *colloq.* detestable, annoying. [past part. of *accurse*, f. A-² + CURSE]

accusal /əˈkjuːz(ə)l/ *n.* accusation.

accusation /ˌækjuːˈzeɪʃ(ə)n/ *n.* **1** the act or process of accusing or being accused. **2** a statement charging a person with an offence or crime. [ME f. OF f. L *accusatio -onis* (as ACCUSE)]

accusative /əˈkjuːzətɪv/ *n. & adj. Gram.* —*n.* the case of nouns, pronouns, and adjectives, expressing the object of an action or the goal of motion. —*adj.* of or in this case. □□ **accusatival** /-ˈtaɪv(ə)l/ *adj.* **accusatively** *adv.* [ME f. OF *accusatif -ive* or L (*casus*) *accusativus*, transl. Gk (*ptōsis*) *aitiatikē*]

accusatorial /əˌkjuːzəˈtɔːrɪəl/ *adj. Law* (of proceedings) involving accusation by a prosecutor and a verdict reached by an impartial judge or jury (opp. INQUISITORIAL). [L *accusatorius* (as ACCUSE)]

accusatory /əˈkjuːzətərɪ/ *adj.* (of language, manner, etc.) of or implying accusation.

accuse /əˈkjuːz/ *v.tr.* **1** (foll. by *of*) charge (a person etc.) with a fault or crime; indict (*accused them of murder; was accused of stealing a car*). **2** lay the blame on. □ **the accused** the person charged with a crime. □□ **accuser** *n.* **accusingly** *adv.* [ME *acuse* f. OF *ac(c)user* f. L *accusare* (as AC-, CAUSE)]

accustom /əˈkʌstəm/ *v.tr. & refl.* (foll. by *to*) make (a person or thing or oneself) used to (*the army accustomed him to discipline; was accustomed to their strange ways*). [ME f. OF *acostumer* (as AD-, *costume* CUSTOM)]

accustomed /əˈkʌstəmd/ *adj.* **1** (usu. foll. by *to*) used to (*accustomed to hard work*). **2** customary, usual.

ace /eɪs/ *n. & adj.* —*n.* **1 a** a playing-card, domino, etc., with a single spot and generally having the value 'one' or in card-games the highest value in each suit. **b** a single spot on a playing-card etc. **2 a** a person who excels in some activity. **b** *Aeron.* a pilot

who has shot down many enemy aircraft. **3 a** (in lawn tennis) a stroke (esp. a service) too good for the opponent to return. **b** a point scored in this way. —*adj. sl.* excellent. □ **ace up one's sleeve** (*US* **in the hole**) something effective kept in reserve. **play one's ace** use one's best resource. **within an ace of** on the verge of. [ME f. OF f. L *as* unity, AS²]

-acea /ˈeɪʃə/ *suffix* forming the plural names of orders and classes of animals (*Crustacea*) (cf. -ACEAN). [neut. pl. of L adj. suffix *-aceus* of the nature of]

-aceae /ˈeɪsiiː/ *suffix* forming the plural names of families of plants (*Rosaceae*). [fem. pl. of L adj. suffix *-aceus* of the nature of]

-acean /ˈeɪʃ(ə)n/ *suffix* **1** forming adjectives, = -ACEOUS. **2** forming nouns as the sing. of names in *-acea* (*crustacean*). [L *-aceus*: see -ACEA]

acedia /əˈsiːdɪə/ *n.* = ACCIDIE. [LL *acedia* f. Gk *akēdia* listlessness]

Aceldama /əˈkeldəˌmə/ a field near ancient Jerusalem purchased for a cemetery with the blood-money received by Judas Iscariot (Matt. 27: 8, Acts 1: 19). [Aram., = field of blood]

acellular /eɪˈseljʊlə(r)/ *adj. Biol.* **1** having no cells; not consisting of cells. **2** (esp. of protozoa) consisting of one cell only; unicellular.

-aceous /ˈeɪʃəs/ *suffix* forming adjectives, esp. from nouns in *-acea, -aceae* (*herbaceous; rosaceous*). [L *-aceus*: see -ACEA]

acephalous /əˈsefələs, əˈke-/ *adj.* **1** headless. **2** having no chief. **3** *Zool.* having no part of the body specially organized as a head. **4** *Bot.* with a head aborted or cut off. **5** *Prosody* lacking a syllable or syllables in the first foot. [med.L *acephalus* f. Gk *akephalos* headless (as A-¹, *kephalē* head)]

acerbic /əˈsɜːbɪk/ *adj.* **1** astringently sour; harsh-tasting. **2** bitter in speech, manner, or temper. □□ **acerbically** *adv.* **acerbity** *n.* (*pl.* **-ies**). [L *acerbus* sour-tasting]

acetabulum /ˌæsɪˈtæbjʊləm/ *n.* (*pl.* **acetabula** /-lə/) *Zool.* **1** the socket for the head of the thigh-bone, or of the leg in insects. **2** a cup-shaped sucker of various organisms, including tapeworms and cuttlefish. [ME f. L, = vinegar cup f. *acetum* vinegar + *-abulum* dimin. of *-abrum* holder]

acetal /ˈæsɪˌtæl/ *n. Chem.* any of a class of organic compounds formed by the condensation of two alcohol molecules with an aldehyde molecule. [as ACETIC + -AL]

acetaldehyde /ˌæsɪˈtældɪˌhaɪd/ *n.* a colourless volatile liquid aldehyde. Also called ETHANAL. ¶ *Chem.* formula: CH_3CHO. [ACETIC + ALDEHYDE]

acetate /ˈæsɪˌteɪt/ *n.* **1** a salt or ester of acetic acid, esp. the cellulose ester used to make textiles, gramophone records, etc. Also called ETHANOATE. **2** a fabric made from cellulose acetate. □ **acetate fibre** (or **silk**) fibre (or silk) made artificially from cellulose acetate. [ACETIC + -ATE¹ 2]

acetic /əˈsiːtɪk/ *adj.* of or like vinegar. □ **acetic acid** the clear liquid acid that gives vinegar its characteristic taste: also called ETHANOATE. ¶ *Chem.* formula: CH_3COOH. [F *acétique* f. L *acetum* vinegar]

aceto- /ˈæsɪtəʊ/ *comb. form Chem.* acetic, acetyl.

acetone /ˈæsɪˌtəʊn/ *n.* a colourless volatile liquid ketone valuable as a solvent of organic compounds esp. paints, varnishes, etc. Also called PROPANONE. ¶ *Chem.* formula: CH_3COCH_3. [ACETO- + -ONE]

acetous /ˈæsɪtəs/ *adj.* **1** having the qualities of vinegar. **2** producing vinegar. **3** sour. [LL *acetosus* sour (as ACETIC)]

acetyl /ˈæsɪtɪl, -ˌtaɪl/ *n. Chem.* the univalent radical of acetic acid. ¶ *Chem.* formula: CH_3CO-. □ **acetyl silk** = acetate silk. [ACETIC + -YL]

acetylcholine /ˌæsɪtɪlˈkəʊliːn, ˌæsɪtaɪl-/ *n.* a compound serving to transmit impulses from nerve fibres. [ACETYL + CHOLINE]

acetylene /əˈsetɪˌliːn/ *n.* a colourless hydrocarbon gas, burning with a bright flame, used esp. in welding and formerly in lighting. Also called ETHYNE. ¶ *Chem.* formula: C_2H_2. [ACETIC + -YL + -ENE]

acetylide /əˈsetɪˌlaɪd/ *n.* any of a class of salts formed from acetylene and a metal.

acetylsalicylic acid /ˌæsɪtaɪlˌsælɪˈsɪlɪk/ *n.* = ASPIRIN. [ACETYL + SALICYLIC ACID]

Achaea /əˈkiːə/ **1** a district of ancient Greece comprising SE

æ cat ɑː arm e bed ɜː her ɪ sit iː see ɒ hot ɔː saw ʌ run ʊ put uː too ə ago aɪ my

Thessaly and the north coast of the Peloponnese. **2** a Roman province comprising all the southern part of Greece.

Achaean /əˈkiːən/ *adj.* & *n.* —*adj.* **1** of or relating to Achaea in ancient Greece. **2** *literary* (esp. in Homeric contexts) Greek. —*n.* **1** an inhabitant of Achaea. **2** *literary* (usu. in *pl.*) a Greek. [L *Achaeus* f. Gk *Akhaios*]

Achaemenid /əˈkiːmənɪd/ *adj.* & *n.* (also **Achaemenian** /ˌækɪˈmiːnɪən/) —*adj.* of or relating to the dynasty ruling in Persia 553–330 BC, from Cyrus I to Darius III, that ended with the defeat of Darius by Alexander the Great. —*n.* a member of this dynasty. [L *Achaemenius* f. Gk *Akhaimenēs*, ancestor of the dynasty]

acharnement /ˌæʃɑːnˈmɑ̃/ *n.* **1** bloodthirsty fury; ferocity. **2** gusto. [F]

Achates /əˈkɑːtiːz/ *Gk* & *Rom. legend* a companion of Aeneas. His fidelity to his friend was so exemplary as to become proverbial (*fidus* (= faithful) *Achates*).

ache /eɪk/ *n.* & *v.* —*n.* **1** a continuous or prolonged dull pain. **2** mental distress. —*v.intr.* **1** suffer from or be the source of an ache (*I ached all over; my left leg ached*). **2** (foll. by *to* + infin.) desire greatly (*we ached to be at home again*). □□ **achingly** *adv.* [ME f. OE *æce, acan.* Dr Johnson is mainly responsible for the modern spelling, as he erroneously derived *ache* and the earlier form *ake* from Gk *akhos* (= pain, distress) and declared that the latter was 'more grammatically written *ache*']

Achebe /əˈtʃeɪbɪ/, Chinua (born Albert Chinualumgu, 1930–), Nigerian novelist, poet, and writer of short stories and essays. His novels, which include *Things Fall Apart* (1958), show traditional African society in its confrontation with European customs and values. In *A Man of the People* (1966) he gives a satirical account of corrupt government in newly independent Africa.

achene /əˈkiːn/ *n. Bot.* a small dry one-seeded fruit that does not open to liberate the seed (e.g. a strawberry pip). [mod.L *achaenium* (as A-¹, Gk *khainō* gape)]

Acheson /ˈeɪtʃɪs(ə)n/, Dean Gooderham (1893–1971), American politician, who worked with and later succeeded George C. Marshall (see entry) as Secretary of State. He urged international control of nuclear power, formulated plans for NATO, and implemented the Marshall Plan and the Truman Doctrine of US support for nations threatened by Communism.

Acheulian /əˈʃuːlɪən/ *adj.* & *n.* (also **Acheulean**) —*adj.* of the later stages of the lower palaeolithic hand-axe industries in Europe, named after the type-site at St-Acheul near Amiens in northern France. The hand-axes of this period are differentiated from those of the preceding Abbevillian by the use of an implement made of wood, antler, or bone to hammer flakes off a flint, giving these a less rough appearance than that produced by a hard stone. In Africa, where the industry seems to have originated, and where it survived much longer than elsewhere, the entire lower palaeolithic hand-axe sequence is referred to as Acheulian, with the African lower Acheulian representing the Abbevillian of Europe; remains occur at Olduvai Gorge in northern Tanzania and at Kalambo Falls near the SE end of Lake Tanganyika. The industries as a whole are dated to 1.500,000–200,000 BC. —*n.* the Acheulian industry. [F *acheuléen* f. St-*Acheul*]

achieve /əˈtʃiːv/ *v.tr.* **1 a** reach or attain by effort (*achieved victory*). **b** acquire, gain, earn (*achieved notoriety*). **2** accomplish or carry out (a feat or task). **3** *absol.* be successful; attain a desired level of performance. □□ **achievable** *adj.* **achiever** *n.* [ME f. OF *achever* f. *a chief* to a head]

achievement /əˈtʃiːvmənt/ *n.* **1** something achieved. **2 a** the act of achieving. **b** an instance of this. **3** *Psychol.* performance in a standardized test. **4** *Heraldry* **a** an escutcheon with adjuncts, or bearing, esp. in memory of a distinguished feat. **b** = HATCHMENT.

achillea /ˌækɪˈliːə/ *n.* any plant of the genus *Achillea*, comprising hardy perennial, usu. aromatic plants with flower-heads (often white or yellow) usu. in corymbs. [L f. Gk *Akhilleios* a plant supposed to have been used medicinally by Achilles]

Achilles /əˈkɪliːz/ *Gk legend* a hero of the Trojan War, son of Peleus and Thetis. During his infancy his mother plunged him in the Styx, thus making his body invulnerable except for the heel by which she held him. He was wounded in the heel during the Trojan War by an arrow shot by Paris, and died of this wound. □ **Achilles' heel,** a weak or vulnerable point. **Achilles' tendon,** a tendon attaching the calf muscles to the heel.

achiral /eɪˈkaɪər(ə)l/ *adj. Chem.* (of a crystal or molecule) not chiral.

achromat /ˈækrəʊˌmæt/ *n.* a lens made achromatic by correction.

achromatic /ˌækrəʊˈmætɪk/ *adj. Optics* **1** that transmits light without separating it into constituent colours (*achromatic lens*). **2** without colour (*achromatic fringe*). □□ **achromatically** *adv.* **achromaticity** /əˌkrəʊməˈtɪsɪtɪ/ *n.* **achromatism** /əˈkrəʊməˌtɪz(ə)m/ *n.* [F *achromatique* f. Gk *akhromatos* (as A-¹, CHROMATIC)]

achy /ˈeɪkɪ/ *adj.* (**achier, achiest**) full of or suffering from aches.

acid /ˈæsɪd/ *n.* & *adj.* —*n.* **1** *Chem.* **a** any of a class of substances that liberate hydrogen ions in water, are usu. sour and corrosive, turn litmus red, and have a pH of less than 7. **b** any compound or atom donating protons. (See below.) **2** (in general use) any sour substance. **3** *sl.* the drug LSD. —*adj.* **1** sharp-tasting, sour. **2** biting, sharp (*an acid wit*). **3** *Chem.* having the essential properties of an acid. **4** *Geol.* containing much silica. **5** (of a colour) intense, bright. □ **acid drop** *Brit.* a kind of sweet with a sharp taste. **acid-head** *sl.* a user of the drug LSD. **acid house** see separate entry. **acid radical** one formed by the removal of hydrogen ions from an acid. **acid rain** acid formed in the atmosphere esp. from industrial waste gases and falling with rain. **acid test** a severe or conclusive test. **2** a test in which acid is used to test for gold etc. **put the acid on** *Austral. sl.* seek to extract a loan or favour etc. from. □□ **acidic** /əˈsɪdɪk/ *adj.* **acidimeter** /ˌæsɪˈdɪmɪtə(r)/ *n.* **acidimetry** /ˌæsɪˈdɪmɪtrɪ/ *n.* **acidly** *adv.* **acidness** *n.* [F *acide* or L *acidus* f. *acēre* be sour]

The term was originally applied to the stony 'mineral acids', such as sulphuric acid, whose properties were attributed in the 17th c. to their consisting of particles with sharp points. Many organic compounds, however, also show acidic properties. The commonest modern definition of an acid is a substance which releases hydrogen ions when dissolved in water (or, by extension, in other alkaline substances), producing salts. Acids are now recognized as substances which are donors of hydrogen ions or protons or acceptors of electron pairs, but an unequivocal definition of the term has yet to be found. Acids play a highly important role in industry. Among the most useful mineral acids are sulphuric acid, which is the electrolyte commonly used in car batteries; hydrochloric acid, which is used in ore reduction, metal cleaning, and food processing; and nitric acid, which is used in the manufacture of explosives and fertilizers.

acid house *n.* a style of pop music with a simple repetitive very fast beat, synthesized sound, and a distinctive gurgling bass. The word 'acid' here is probably taken from the record *Acid Trax* by the American rock group Phuture (in Chicago slang 'acid burning' means 'stealing', and this type of music relies heavily on 'sampling' or stealing from other tracks); the popular theory that it refers to the drug LSD is denied by its followers. The word 'house' is short for 'Warehouse' (see HOUSE 19). Such music originated in Chicago as an offshoot of 'house' music in 1986; imported to Britain in 1988, it started a youth cult with its own set of behaviour and its own language, with parties held at venues kept secret until the very last moment.

acidify /əˈsɪdɪˌfaɪ/ *v.tr.* & *intr.* (**-ies, -ied**) make or become acid. □□ **acidification** /-fɪˈkeɪʃ(ə)n/ *n.*

acidity /əˈsɪdɪtɪ/ *n.* (*pl.* **-ies**) an acid quality or state, esp. an excessively acid condition of the stomach.

acidosis /ˌæsɪˈdəʊsɪs/ *n.* an over-acid condition of the body fluids or tissues. □□ **acidotic** /-ˈdɒtɪk/ *adj.*

acidulate /əˈsɪdjʊˌleɪt/ *v.tr.* make somewhat acid. □□ **acidulation** /-ˈleɪʃ(ə)n/ *n.* [L *acidulus* dimin. of *acidus* sour]

acidulous /əˈsɪdjʊləs/ *adj.* somewhat acid.

acinus /ˈæsɪnəs/ *n.* (*pl.* **acini** /-ˌnaɪ/) **1** any of the small elements that make up a compound fruit of the blackberry, raspberry, etc. **2** the seed of a grape or berry. **3** *Anat.* **a** any multicellular gland with saclike secreting ducts. **b** the terminus of a duct in such a gland. [L, = berry, kernel]

-acious /ˈeɪʃəs/ *suffix* forming adjectives meaning 'inclined to, full of' (*vivacious; pugnacious; voracious; capacious*). [L *-ax -acis*, added chiefly to verbal stems to form adjectives + -OUS]

-acity /ˈæsɪtɪ/ *suffix* forming nouns of quality or state corresponding to adjectives in *-acious*. [F *-acité* or L *-acitas -tatis*]

ack-ack /ˈækˈæk/ *adj. & n. colloq.* —*adj.* anti-aircraft. —*n.* an anti-aircraft gun etc. [formerly signallers' name for the letters *AA*]

ackee /ˈækiː/ *n.* (also **akee**) **1** a tropical tree, *Blighia sapida.* **2** its fruit, edible when cooked. [Kru *ákee*]

ack emma /æk ˈemə/ *adv. & n. Brit. colloq.* = A.M. [formerly signallers' name for the letters *AM*]

acknowledge /əkˈnɒlɪdʒ/ *v.tr.* **1 a** recognize; accept; admit the truth of (*acknowledged the failure of the plan*). **b** (often foll. by *to be* + compl.) recognize as (*acknowledged it to be a great success*). **c** (often foll. by *that* + clause or *to* + infin.) admit that something is so (*acknowledged that he was wrong; acknowledged him to be wrong*). **2** confirm the receipt of (*acknowledged her letter*). **3 a** show that one has noticed (*acknowledged my arrival with a grunt*). **b** express appreciation of (a service etc.). **4** own; recognize the validity of (*the acknowledged king*). □□ **acknowledgeable** *adj.* [obs. KNOWLEDGE *v.* after obs. *acknow* (as A-⁴, KNOW), or f. obs. noun *acknowledge*]

acknowledgement /əkˈnɒlɪdʒmənt/ *n.* (also **acknowledgment**) **1** the act or an instance of acknowledging. **2 a** a thing given or done in return for a service etc. **b** a letter confirming receipt of something. **3** (usu. in *pl.*) an author's statement of indebtedness to others.

aclinic line /əˈklɪnɪk/ *n.* = *magnetic equator.* [Gk *aklinēs* (as A-¹, *klinō* bend)]

acme /ˈækmɪ/ *n.* the highest point or period (of achievement, success, etc.); the peak of perfection (*displayed the acme of good taste*). [Gk, = highest point]

acne /ˈæknɪ/ *n.* a skin condition, usu. of the face, characterized by red pimples. □□ **acned** *adj.* [mod.L f. erron. Gk *aknas* for *akmas* accus. pl. of *akmē* facial eruption: cf. ACME]

acolyte /ˈækəˌlaɪt/ *n.* **1** a person assisting a priest in a service or procession. **2** an assistant; a beginner. [ME f. OF *acolyt* or eccl.L *acolytus* f. Gk *akolouthos* follower]

Aconcagua /ˌækɒnˈkɑːɡwə/ the highest mountain in South America (6,960 m, 22,834 ft.) in the Andes of Argentina. It is an extinct volcano.

aconite /ˈækəˌnaɪt/ *n.* **1 a** any poisonous plant of the genus *Aconitum*, esp. monkshood or wolfsbane. **b** the drug obtained from this. Also called ACONITINE. **2** (in full **winter aconite**) any ranunculaceous plant of the genus *Eranthis*, with yellow flowers. □□ **aconitic** /ˌækəˈnɪtɪk/ *adj. Chem.* [F *aconit* or L *aconitum* f. Gk *akoniton*]

aconitine /əˈkɒnɪˌtiːn/ *n. Pharm.* a poisonous alkaloid obtained from the aconite plant.

acorn /ˈeɪkɔːn/ *n.* the fruit of the oak, with a smooth nut in a rough cuplike base. □ **acorn barnacle** a multivalve marine cirriped, *Balanus balanoides*, living on rocks. **acorn worm** any marine wormlike animal of the phylum Hemichordata, having a proboscis and gill slits, and inhabiting seashores. [OE *æcern*, rel. to *æcer* ACRE, later assoc. with OAK and CORN¹]

acotyledon /əˌkɒtɪˈliːdən/ *n.* a plant with no distinct seed-leaves. □□ **acotyledonous** *adj.* [mod.L *acotyledones* pl. (as A-¹, COTYLEDON)]

acoustic /əˈkuːstɪk/ *adj. & n.* —*adj.* **1** relating to sound or the sense of hearing. **2** (of a musical instrument, gramophone, or recording) not having electrical amplification (*acoustic guitar*). **3** (of building materials) used for soundproofing or modifying sound. **4** *Mil.* (of a mine) that can be exploded by sound waves transmitted under water. —*n.* **1** (usu. in *pl.*) the properties or qualities (esp. of a room or hall etc.) in transmitting sound (*good acoustics; a poor acoustic*). **2** (in *pl.*; usu. treated as *sing.*) the science of sound (*acoustics is not widely taught*). □ **acoustic coupler** *Computing* a modem which converts digital signals into audible signals and vice versa, so that the former can be transmitted and received over telephone lines. □□ **acoustical** *adj.* **acoustically** *adv.* [Gk *akoustikos* f. *akouō* hear]

acoustician /ˌækuːˈstɪʃ(ə)n/ *n.* an expert in acoustics.

acquaint /əˈkweɪnt/ *v.tr. & refl.* (usu. foll. by *with*) make (a person or oneself) aware of or familiar with (*acquaint me with the facts*). □ **be acquainted with** have personal knowledge of (a person or thing). [ME f. OF *acointier* f. LL *accognitare* (as AC-, *cognoscere cognitum* come to know)]

acquaintance /əˈkweɪnt(ə)ns/ *n.* **1** (usu. foll. by *with*) slight knowledge (of a person or thing). **2** the fact or process of being acquainted (*our acquaintance lasted a year*). **3** a person one knows slightly. □ **make one's acquaintance** first meet or introduce oneself to another person. **make the acquaintance of** come to know. □□ **acquaintanceship** *n.* [ME f. OF *acointance* (as ACQUAINT)]

acquiesce /ˌækwɪˈes/ *v.intr.* **1** agree, esp. tacitly. **2** raise no objection. **3** (foll. by *in*) accept (an arrangement etc.). □□ **acquiescence** *n.* **acquiescent** *adj.* [L *acquiescere* (as AC-, *quiescere* rest)]

acquire /əˈkwaɪə(r)/ *v.tr.* **1** gain by and for oneself; obtain. **2** come into possession of (*acquired fame; acquired much property*). □ **acquired characteristic** *Biol.* a characteristic caused by the environment, not inherited. **acquired immune deficiency syndrome** *Med.* see AIDS. **acquired taste 1** a liking gained by experience. **2** the object of such a liking. □□ **acquirable** *adj.* [ME f. OF *aquerre* ult. f. L *acquirere* (as AC-, *quaerere* seek)]

acquirement /əˈkwaɪəmənt/ *n.* **1** something acquired, esp. a mental attainment. **2** the act or an instance of acquiring.

acquisition /ˌækwɪˈzɪʃ(ə)n/ *n.* **1** something acquired, esp. if regarded as useful. **2** the act or an instance of acquiring. [L *acquisitio* (as ACQUIRE)]

acquisitive /əˈkwɪzɪtɪv/ *adj.* keen to acquire things; avaricious; materialistic. □□ **acquisitively** *adv.* **acquisitiveness** *n.* [F *acquisitive* or LL *acquisitivus* (as ACQUIRE)]

acquit /əˈkwɪt/ *v.* (**acquitted, acquitting**) **1** *tr.* (often foll. by *of*) declare (a person) not guilty (*were acquitted of the offence*). **2** *refl.* **a** conduct oneself or perform in a specified way (*we acquitted ourselves well*). **b** (foll. by *of*) discharge (a duty or responsibility). [ME f. OF *aquiter* f. med.L *acquitare* pay a debt (as AC-, QUIT)]

acquittal /əˈkwɪt(ə)l/ *n.* **1** the process of freeing or being freed from a charge, esp. by a judgement of not guilty. **2** performance of a duty.

acquittance /əˈkwɪt(ə)ns/ *n.* **1** payment of or release from a debt. **2** a written receipt attesting settlement of a debt. [ME f. OF *aquitance* (as ACQUIT)]

Acre /ˈeɪkə(r)/ (also **Akko** /ˈækəʊ/) a seaport of Israel; pop. (est. 1982) 39,100. It was captured by the Christians in the Third Crusade in 1191, and recaptured, the last Christian stronghold in the Holy Land, in 1291.

acre /ˈeɪkə(r)/ *n.* **1** a measure of land, 4,840 sq. yds., 0.405 ha. **2** a piece of land; a field. **3** (in *pl.*) a large area. □□ **acred** *adj.* (also in *comb.*). [OE *æcer* f. Gmc]

acreage /ˈeɪkərɪdʒ/ *n.* **1** a number of acres. **2** an extent of land.

acrid /ˈækrɪd/ *adj.* (**acrider, acridest**) **1** bitterly pungent; irritating; corrosive. **2** bitter in temper or manner. □□ **acridity** /əˈkrɪdɪtɪ/ *n.* **acridly** *adv.* [irreg. f. L *acer acris* keen + -ID¹, prob. after *acid*]

acridine /ˈækrɪˌdiːn/ *n.* a colourless crystalline compound used in the manufacture of dyes and drugs. [ACRID + -INE⁴]

acriflavine /ˌækrɪˈfleɪvɪn, -viːn/ *n.* a reddish powder used as an antiseptic. [irreg. f. ACRIDINE + FLAVINE]

acrimonious /ˌækrɪˈməʊnɪəs/ *adj.* bitter in manner or temper. □□ **acrimoniously** *adv.* [F *acrimonieux, -euse* f. med.L *acrimoniosus* f. L *acrimonia* ACRIMONY]

acrimony /ˈækrɪmənɪ/ *n.* (*pl.* **-ies**) bitterness of temper or manner; ill feeling. [F *acrimonie* or L *acrimonia* pungency (as ACRID)]

acrobat /ˈækrəˌbæt/ *n.* **1** a performer of spectacular gymnastic feats. **2** a person noted for constant change of mind, allegiance, etc. □□ **acrobatic** /ˌækrəˈbætɪk/ *adj.* **acrobatically** /ˌækrəˈbætɪkəlɪ/ *adv.* [F *acrobate* f. Gk *akrobatēs* f. *akron* summit + *bainō* walk]

acrobatics /ˌækrəˈbætɪks/ *n.pl.* **1** acrobatic feats. **2** (as *sing.*) the art of performing these. **3** a skill requiring ingenuity (*mental acrobatics*).

acrogen /ˈækrədʒ(ə)n/ n. Bot. any non-flowering plant having a perennial stem with the growing point at its apex, e.g. a fern or moss. □□ **acrogenous** /əˈkrɒdʒɪnəs/ adj. [Gk akron tip + -GEN]

acromegaly /ˌækrəˈmegəlɪ/ n. Med. the abnormal growth of the hands, feet, and face, caused by excessive activity of the pituitary gland. □□ **acromegalic** /-mɪˈgælɪk/ adj. [F acromégalie f. Gk akron extremity + megas megal- great]

acronym /ˈækrənɪm/ n. a word, usu. pronounced as such, formed from the initial letters of other words (e.g. Ernie, laser, Nato). [Gk akron end + -onum- = onoma name]

acropetal /əˈkrɒpɪt(ə)l/ adj. Bot. developing from below upwards. □□ **acropetally** adv. [Gk akron tip + L petere seek]

acrophobia /ˌækrəˈfəʊbɪə/ n. Psychol. an abnormal dread of heights. □□ **acrophobic** adj. [Gk akron peak + -PHOBIA]

acropolis /əˈkrɒpəlɪs/ n. **1** a citadel or upper fortified part of an ancient Greek city. **2** (**Acropolis**) the ancient citadel at Athens, containing the Parthenon, Erechtheum, and other notable buildings, mostly dating from the 5th c. BC. [Gk akropolis f. akron summit + polis city]

across /əˈkrɒs/ prep. & adv. —prep. **1** to or on the other side of (walked across the road; lives across the river). **2** from one side to another side of (the cover stretched across the opening; a bridge across the river). **3** at or forming an angle (esp. a right angle) with (deep cuts across his legs). —adv. **1** to or on the other side (ran across; shall soon be across). **2** from one side to another (a blanket stretched across). **3** forming a cross (with cuts across). **4** (of a crossword clue or answer) read horizontally (cannot do nine across). □ **across the board** general; generally; applying to all. [ME f. OF a croix, en croix, later regarded as f. A² + CROSS]

acrostic /əˈkrɒstɪk/ n. **1** a poem or other composition in which certain letters in each line form a word or words. **2** a word-puzzle constructed in this way. □ **double acrostic** one using the first and last letters of each line. **single acrostic** one using the first letter only. **triple acrostic** one using the first, middle, and last letters. [F acrostiche or Gk akrostikhis f. akron end + stikhos row, line of verse, assim. to -IC]

acrylic /əˈkrɪlɪk/ adj. & n. —adj. **1** of material made with a synthetic polymer derived from acrylic acid. **2** Chem. of or derived from acrylic acid. —n. an acrylic fibre. □ **acrylic acid** a pungent liquid organic acid. ¶ Chem. formula: C₃H₄O₂. **acrylic resin** any of various transparent colourless polymers of acrylic acid. [acrolein f. L acer acris pungent + olēre to smell + -IN + -YL + -IC]

ACT abbr. Australian Capital Territory.

act /ækt/ n. & v. —n. **1** something done; a deed; an action. **2** the process of doing something (caught in the act). **3 a** a piece of entertainment, usu. one of a series in a programme. **b** the performer(s) of this. **4** a pretence; behaviour intended to deceive or impress (it was all an act). **5** a main division of a play or opera. **6 a** a written ordinance of a parliament or other legislative body. **b** a document attesting a legal transaction. **7** (often in pl.) the recorded decisions or proceedings of a committee, an academic body, etc. **8** (**Acts**) (in full **Acts of the Apostles**) a book of the New Testament immediately following the Gospels, relating the early history of the Church and dealing largely with the lives and work of St Peter and St Paul. It is traditionally ascribed to St Luke. —v. **1** intr. behave (see how they act under stress). **2** intr. perform actions or functions; operate effectively; take action (act as referee; the brakes failed to act; we must act quickly). **3** intr. (also foll. by on) exert energy or influence (the medicine soon began to act; alcohol acts on the brain). **4** intr. **a** perform a part in a play, film, etc. **b** pretend. **5** tr. **a** perform the part of (acted Othello; acts the fool). **b** perform (a play etc.). **c** portray (an incident) by actions. **d** feign (we acted indifference). □ **act for** be the (esp. legal) representative of. **act of God** the operation of uncontrollable natural forces. **act of grace** a privilege or concession that cannot be claimed as a right. **act on** (or **upon**) perform or carry out; put into operation (acted on my advice). **act out 1** translate (ideas etc.) into action. **2** Psychol. represent (one's subconscious desires etc.) in action. **act up** colloq. misbehave; give trouble (my car is acting up again). **get one's act together** sl. become properly organized; make preparations for an undertaking etc. **get into the act** sl. become a participant (esp. for profit). **put on an act** colloq. carry

out a pretence. □□ **actable** adj. (in sense 5 of v.). **actability** /-ˈbɪlɪtɪ/ n. (in sense 5 of v.). [ME ult. f. L agere act- do]

Actaeon /ækˈtiːən, ˈæk-/ Gk Mythol. a hunter who, because he accidentally saw Artemis bathing, was changed into a stag and killed by his own hounds.

ACTH abbr. adrenocorticotrophic hormone.

acting /ˈæktɪŋ/ n. & attrib. adj. —n. **1** the art or occupation of performing parts in plays, films, etc. **2** in senses of ACT v. —attrib.adj. serving temporarily or on behalf of another or others (acting manager; Acting Captain).

actinia /ækˈtɪnɪə/ n. (pl. **actiniae** /-nɪˌiː/) any sea anemone, esp. of the genus Actinia. [mod.L f. Gk aktis -inos ray]

actinide /ˈæktɪˌnaɪd/ n. (also **actinoid** /ˈæktɪˌnɔɪd/) Chem. any of the series of 15 radioactive elements having increasing atomic numbers from actinium (89) to lawrencium (102). □ **actinide series** this series of elements. [ACTINIUM + -IDE as in lanthanide]

actinism /ˈæktɪˌnɪz(ə)m/ n. the property of short-wave radiation that produces chemical changes, as in photography. □□ **actinic** /ækˈtɪnɪk/ adj. [Gk aktis -inos ray]

actinium /ækˈtɪnɪəm/ n. Chem. a radioactive metallic element of the actinide series, occurring naturally in pitchblende. It was first discovered in 1899. ¶ Symb.: **Ac**; atomic number 89.

actinoid var. of ACTINIDE.

actinometer /ˌæktɪˈnɒmɪtə(r)/ n. an instrument for measuring the intensity of radiation, esp. ultraviolet radiation. [Gk aktis -tinos ray + -METER]

actinomorphic /ˌæktɪnəˈmɔːfɪk/ adj. Biol. radially symmetrical. [as ACTINOMETER + Gk morphē form]

actinomycete /ˌæktɪnəʊmaɪˈsiːt/ n. any of the usu. non-motile filamentous anaerobic bacteria of the order Actinomycetales. [as ACTINOMORPHIC + -mycetes f. Gk mukēs -ētos mushroom]

action /ˈækʃ(ə)n/ n. & v. —n. **1** the fact or process of doing or acting (demanded action; put ideas into action). **2** forcefulness or energy as a characteristic (a woman of action). **3** the exertion of energy or influence (the action of acid on metal). **4** something done; a deed or act (not aware of his own actions). **5 a** a series of events represented in a story, play, etc. **b** sl. exciting activity (arrived late and missed the action; want some action). **6 a** armed conflict; fighting (killed in action). **b** an occurrence of this, esp. a minor military engagement. **7 a** the way in which a machine, instrument, etc. works (explain the action of an air pump). **b** the mechanism that makes a machine, instrument, etc. (e.g. a musical instrument, a gun, etc.) work. **c** the mode or style of movement of an animal or human (usu. described in some way) (a runner with good action). **8** a legal process; a lawsuit (bring an action). **9** (in imper.) a word of command to begin, esp. used by a film director etc. —v.tr. bring a legal action against. □ **action committee** (or **group** etc.) a body formed to take active steps, esp. in politics. **action-packed** colloq. full of action or excitement. **action painting** see separate entry. **action point** a proposal for action, esp. arising from a discussion etc. **action replay** a playback of part of a television broadcast, esp. a sporting event, often in slow motion. **action stations** positions taken up by troops etc. ready for battle. **go into action** start work. **out of action** not working. **take action** begin to act (esp. energetically in protest). [ME f. OF f. L actio -onis (as ACT)]

actionable /ˈækʃənəb(ə)l/ adj. giving cause for legal action. □□ **actionably** adv.

Action Directe /ˈæksjɔ̃ dɪˈrekt/ a group of extreme left-wing French terrorists. [F, = direct action]

action painting n. abstract painting in which the artist applies paint by random actions. The term was first used in 1952 to describe the approach to art of certain New York painters, including Jackson Pollock. Although it is often used as a synonym for abstract expressionism, not all the artists associated with the latter can be considered as action painters.

activate /ˈæktɪˌveɪt/ v.tr. **1** make active; bring into action. **2** Chem. cause reaction in; excite (a substance, molecules, etc.). **3** Physics make radioactive. □ **activated carbon** carbon, esp. charcoal, treated to increase its adsorptive power. **activated sludge** aerated sewage containing aerobic bacteria. □□ **activation** /-ˈveɪʃ(ə)n/ n. **activator** n.

active /ˈæktɪv/ adj. & n. —adj. **1 a** consisting in or marked by action; energetic; diligent (leads an active life; an active helper). **b** able to move about or accomplish practical tasks (infirmity made him less active). **2** working, operative (an active volcano). **3** originating action; not merely passive or inert (active support; active ingredients). **4** radioactive. **5** Gram. designating the voice that attributes the action of a verb to the person or thing from which it logically proceeds (e.g. of the verbs in guns kill; we saw him). —n. Gram. the active form or voice of a verb. □ **active carbon** = activated carbon (see ACTIVATE). **active list** Mil. a list of officers available for service. **active service** service in the armed forces during a war. □□ **actively** adv. **activeness** n. [ME f. OF actif -ive or L activus (as ACT v.)]

activism /ˈæktɪˌvɪz(ə)m/ n. a policy of vigorous action in a cause, esp. in politics. □□ **activist** n.

activity /ækˈtɪvɪtɪ/ n. (pl. **-ies**) **1 a** the condition of being active or moving about. **b** the exertion of energy; vigorous action. **2** (often in pl.) a particular occupation or pursuit (outdoor activities). **3** = RADIOACTIVITY. [F activité or LL activitas (as ACTIVE)]

actor /ˈæktə(r)/ n. **1** the performer of a part in a play, film, etc. **2** a person whose profession is performing such parts. [L, = doer, actor (as ACT, -OR¹)]

actress /ˈæktrɪs/ n. a female actor.

actual /ˈæktʃʊəl, ˈæktjʊəl/ adj. (usu. attrib.) **1** existing in fact; real (often as distinct from ideal). **2** existing now; current. ¶ Redundant use, as in tell me the actual facts, is disp., but common. □□ **actualize** v.tr. (also **-ise**). **actualization** /-ˈzeɪʃ(ə)n/ n. [ME f. OF actuel f. LL actualis f. agere ACT]

actuality /ˌæktʃʊˈælɪtɪ, ˌæktjʊ-/ n. (pl. **-ies**) **1** reality; what is the case. **2** (in pl.) existing conditions. [ME f. OF actualité entity or med.L actualitas (as ACTUAL)]

actually /ˈæktʃʊəlɪ/ adv. **1** as a fact, really (I asked for ten, but actually got nine). **2** as a matter of fact, even (strange as it may seem) (he actually refused!). **3** at present; for the time being.

actuary /ˈæktʃʊərɪ/ n. (pl. **-ies**) an expert in statistics, esp. one who calculates insurance risks and premiums. □□ **actuarial** /-ˈeərɪəl/ adj. **actuarially** /-ˈeərɪəlɪ/ adv. [L actuarius bookkeeper f. actus past part. of agere ACT]

actuate /ˈæktʃʊˌeɪt/ v.tr. **1** communicate motion to (a machine etc.). **2** cause the operation of (an electrical device etc.). **3** cause (a person) to act. □□ **actuation** /-ˈeɪʃ(ə)n/ n. **actuator** n. [med.L actuare f. L actus: see ACTUAL]

acuity /əˈkjuːɪtɪ/ n. sharpness, acuteness (of a needle, senses, understanding). [F acuité or med.L acuitas f. acuere sharpen: see ACUTE]

aculeate /əˈkjuːlɪət/ n. **1** Zool. having a sting. **2** Bot. prickly. **3** pointed, incisive. [L aculeatus f. aculeus sting, dimin. of acus needle]

acumen /ˈækjʊmən, əˈkjuːmən/ n. keen insight or discernment, penetration. [L acumen -minis anything sharp f. acuere sharpen: see ACUTE]

acuminate /əˈkjuːmɪnət/ adj. Biol. tapering to a point. [L acuminatus pointed (as ACUMEN)]

acupuncture /ˈækjuːˌpʌŋktʃə(r)/ n. a method (orig. Chinese) of treating various conditions by pricking the skin or tissues with needles. □□ **acupuncturist** n. [L acu with a needle + PUNCTURE]

acushla /əˈkʊʃlə/ n. Ir. darling. [Ir. a cuisle O pulse (of my heart)!]

acute /əˈkjuːt/ adj. & n. —adj. (**acuter, acutest**) **1** (of sensation or senses) keen, penetrating. **2** shrewd, perceptive (an acute critic). **3** (of a disease) coming sharply to a crisis; severe, not chronic. **4** (of a difficulty or controversy) critical, serious. **5 a** (of an angle) less than 90°. **b** sharp, pointed. **6** (of a sound) high, shrill. —n. = acute accent. □ **acute accent** a mark (ˊ) placed over letters in some languages to show quality, vowel length, pronunciation (e.g. maté), etc. **acute rheumatism** Med. = rheumatic fever. □□ **acutely** adv. **acuteness** n. [L acutus past part. of acuere sharpen f. acus needle]

ACW abbr. Brit. (preceding a name) Aircraftwoman.

-acy /əsɪ/ suffix forming nouns of state or quality (accuracy; piracy; supremacy), or an instance of it (conspiracy; fallacy) (see also -CRACY). [a branch of the suffix -CY from or after F -acie or L -acia or -atia or Gk -ateia]

acyl /ˈæsɪl, -aɪl/ n. Chem. the univalent radical of an organic acid. [G (as ACID, -YL)]

AD abbr. (of a date) of the Christian era. (See DIONYSIUS EXIGUUS.) ¶ Strictly, AD should precede a date (e.g. AD 410), but uses such as the tenth century AD are well established. [Anno Domini 'in the year of the Lord']

ad /æd/ n. colloq. an advertisement. [abbr.]

ad- /əd, æd/ prefix (also **a-** before sc, sp, st, **ac-** before c, k, q, **af-** before f, **ag-** before g, **al-** before l, **an-** before n, **ap-** before p, **ar-** before r, **as-** before s, **at-** before t) **1** with the sense of motion or direction to, reduction or change into, addition, adherence, increase, or intensification. **2** formed by assimilation of other prefixes (accurse; admiral; advance; affray). [(sense 1) (through OF a-) f. L ad to: (sense 2) a- repr. various prefixes other than ad-]

-ad¹ /əd, æd/ suffix forming nouns: **1** in collective numerals (myriad; triad). **2** in fem. patronymics (Dryad). **3** in names of poems and similar compositions (Iliad; Dunciad; jeremiad). [Gk -as -ada]

-ad² /əd/ suffix forming nouns (ballad; salad) (cf. -ADE¹). [F -ade]

adage /ˈædɪdʒ/ n. a traditional maxim, a proverb. [F f. L adagium (as AD-, root of aio say)]

adagio /əˈdɑːʒɪəʊ/ adv., adj., & n. Mus. —adv. & adj. in slow time. —n. (pl. **-os**) an adagio movement or passage. [It.]

Adam¹ /ˈædəm/ n. (in the Biblical and Koranic traditions) the first man. □ **Adam's ale** water. **Adam's apple** a projection of the thyroid cartilage of the larynx, esp. as prominent in men. **not know a person from Adam** be unable to recognize the person in question. [Heb. 'ādām man]

Adam² /ˈædəm/ Robert (1728–92), the principal architect of the 'Adam Revolution', son of William Adam, a leading Scottish architect. Robert's brothers also assisted him in the family practice. He began a Grand Tour in 1754, mainly in France and Italy, which gave him knowledge of ancient buildings and modern neoclassical theory. The brothers set up in London in 1758 and introduced a lighter, more decorative, style than the Palladianism of the previous half-century. Their Works in Architecture (1773, 1779, and posthumously 1822), published as advertisement, claim to have revolutionized architecture in Britain. Robert's actual buildings are almost exclusively domestic, and he was particularly successful as an interior designer.

adamant /ˈædəmənt/ adj. & n. —adj. stubbornly resolute; resistant to persuasion. —n. archaic diamond or other hard substance. □□ **adamance** n. **adamantine** /-ˈmæntaɪn/ adj. **adamantly** adv. [OF adamaunt f. L adamas adamant- untameable f. Gk (as A-¹, damaō to tame)]

Adams¹ /ˈædəmz/, John (1735–1826), 2nd President of the US, 1797–1801, after being Vice-President from 1789.

Adams² /ˈædəmz/, John Quincy (1767–1848), 6th President of the US 1825–9. He was the eldest son of President John Adams. As Secretary of State under Monroe, he had helped to shape the Monroe Doctrine.

Adam's Bridge a chain of small islands stretching across the Palk Strait between NW Sri Lanka and SE India.

Adam's Peak a holy mountain in Sri Lanka rising to a height of 2,243 m (7,282 ft.).

Adana /ˈædənə/ a city in southern Turkey, situated on the Seyhan River to the south of the Cilician Gates; pop. (1985) 776,000.

adapt /əˈdæpt/ v. **1** tr. **a** (foll. by to) fit, adjust (one thing to another). **b** (foll. by to, for) make suitable for a purpose. **c** alter or modify (esp. a text). **d** arrange for broadcasting etc. **2** intr. & refl. (usu. foll. by to) become adjusted to new conditions. □□ **adaptive** adj. **adaptively** adv. [F adapter f. L adaptare (as AD-, aptare f. aptus fit)]

adaptable /əˈdæptəb(ə)l/ adj. **1** able to adapt oneself to new conditions. **2** that can be adapted. □□ **adaptability** /-ˈbɪlɪtɪ/ n. **adaptably** adv.

adaptation /ˌædæpˈteɪʃ(ə)n/ n. **1** the act or process of adapting or being adapted. **2** a thing that has been adapted. **3** Biol. the process by which an organism or species becomes suited to its environment. [F f. LL adaptatio -onis (as ADAPT)]

adaptor /əˈdæptə(r)/ n. (also **adapter**) **1** a device for making equipment compatible. **2** a device for connecting several electrical plugs to one socket. **3** a person who adapts.

adaxial /æd'æksɪəl/ adj. Bot. facing toward the stem of a plant, esp. of the upper side of a leaf (cf. ABAXIAL). [AD- + AXIAL]

ADC abbr. **1** aide-de-camp. **2** analogue–digital converter.

add /æd/ v.tr. **1** join (one thing to another) as an increase or supplement (add your efforts to mine; add insult to injury). **2** put together (two or more numbers) to find a number denoting their combined value. **3** say in addition (added a remark; added that I was wrong). □ **add in** include. **add-on** something added to an existing object or quantity. **add to** increase; be a further item among (this adds to our difficulties). **add up 1** find the total of. **2** (foll. by to) amount to; constitute (adds up to a disaster). **3** colloq. make sense; be understandable. □□ **added** adj. [ME f. L addere (as AD-, dare put)]

addax /'ædæks/ n. a large antelope, Addax nasomaculatus, of North Africa, with twisted horns. [L f. an African word]

addendum /ə'dendəm/ n. (pl. **addenda** /-də/) **1** a thing (usu. something omitted) to be added, esp. (in pl.) as additional matter at the end of a book. **2** an appendix; an addition. [L, gerundive of addere ADD]

adder /'ædə(r)/ n. any of various small venomous snakes, esp. the common viper, Vipera berus, the only poisonous snake in Great Britain. □ **adder's tongue** any fern of the genus Ophioglossum. [OE nædre: n lost in ME by wrong division of a naddre: cf. APRON, AUGER, UMPIRE]

addict v. & n. —v.tr. & refl. /ə'dɪkt/ (usu. foll. by to) devote or apply habitually or compulsively; make addicted. —n. /'ædɪkt/ **1** a person addicted to a habit, esp. one dependent on a (specified) drug (drug addict; heroin addict). **2** colloq. an enthusiastic devotee of a sport or pastime (film addict). [L addicere assign (as AD-, dicere dict- say)]

addicted /ə'dɪktɪd/ adj. (foll. by to) **1** dependent on as a habit; unable to do without (addicted to heroin; addicted to smoking). **2** devoted (addicted to football).

addiction /ə'dɪkʃ(ə)n/ n. the fact or process of being addicted, esp. the condition of taking a drug habitually and being unable to give it up without incurring adverse effects. [L addictio: see ADDICT]

addictive /ə'dɪktɪv/ adj. (of a drug, habit, etc.) causing addiction or dependence.

Addington /'ædɪŋt(ə)n/, Henry, 1st Viscount Sidmouth (1757–1844), British Tory statesman, who succeeded William Pitt the Younger as Prime Minister 1801–4. As Home Secretary (1812–1821) he introduced repressive legislation in an attempt to suppress the Luddites and other protest groups.

Addis Ababa /ˌædɪs 'æbəbə/ the capital of Ethiopia, situated at 2,440 m (about 8,000 ft.); pop. (est. 1984) 1,412,000.

Addison[1] /'ædɪs(ə)n/, Joseph (1672–1719), English poet, dramatist, and essayist, whose name is inseparably linked with that of Sir Richard Steele for their cooperation in the daily journal The Spectator, and who was a close friend of Swift and other writers. A staunch Whig, he was an MP from 1708 until his death, holding various (chiefly minor) political offices. His tragedy Cato was produced with great success in 1713. In the history of English literature he is remarkable for his simple unornamented prose style which marked the end of the mannerisms and eccentricities of the 17th c. (See STEELE.)

Addison[2] /'ædɪs(ə)n/, Thomas (1793–1860), English physician, the first to describe what is now called Addison's disease, a condition characterized by great weakness and frequently a bronze pigmentation of the skin, and to ascribe it correctly to defective functioning of the adrenal glands which were not previously known to be the seat of any definite malady. Distinguished for his remarkable zeal in the investigation of disease, Addison had a great reputation as a clinical teacher, and Guy's Hospital in London attained fame as a school of medicine during his connection with it as physician and lecturer.

addition /ə'dɪʃ(ə)n/ n. **1** the act or process of adding or being added. **2** a person or thing added (a useful addition to the team). □ **in addition** (often foll. by to) as something added. [ME f. OF addition or f. L additio (as ADD)]

additional /ə'dɪʃən(ə)l/ adj. added, extra, supplementary. □□ **additionally** adv.

additive /'ædɪtɪv/ n. & adj. —n. a thing added, esp. a substance added to another so as to give it specific qualities (food additive). —adj. **1** characterized by addition (additive process). **2** to be added. [LL additivus (as ADD)]

addle /'æd(ə)l/ v. & adj. —v. **1** tr. muddle, confuse. **2** intr. (of an egg) become addled. —adj. **1** muddled, unsound (addle-brained; addle-head). **2** empty, vain. **3** (of an egg) addled. [OE adela filth, used as adj., then as verb]

addled /'æd(ə)ld/ adj. **1** (of an egg) rotten, producing no chick. **2** muddled. □ **Addled Parliament**, the parliament of James I, summoned in 1614, so known because it refused to accede to the king's financial requests, did not succeed in its attempts to curb his existing powers of taxation, and was dissolved without having passed any legislation. [ADDLE adj., assim. to past part. form]

Addo /æ'dəʊ/ a national park in Cape Province, South Africa, established in 1931 to protect the last of the Eastern Cape elephants.

address /ə'dres/ n. & v. —n. **1 a** the place where a person lives or an organization is situated. **b** particulars of this, esp. for postal purposes. **c** Computing the location of an item of stored information. **2** a discourse delivered to an audience. **3** skill, dexterity, readiness. **4** (in pl.) a courteous approach, courtship (pay one's addresses to). **5** archaic manner in conversation. —v.tr. **1** write directions for delivery (esp. the name and address of the intended recipient) on (an envelope, packet, etc.). **2** direct in speech or writing (remarks, a protest, etc.). **3** speak or write to, esp. formally (addressed the audience; asked me how to address a duke). **4** direct one's attention to. **5** Golf take aim at or prepare to hit (the ball). □ **address oneself to 1** speak or write to. **2** attend to. □□ **addresser** n. [ME f. OF adresser ult. f. L (as AD-, directus DIRECT): (n.) perh. f. F adresse]

addressee /ˌædre'siː/ n. the person to whom something (esp. a letter) is addressed.

Addressograph /ə'dresəʊˌɡrɑːf/ n. propr. a machine for printing addresses on envelopes.

adduce /ə'djuːs/ v.tr. cite as an instance or as proof or evidence. □□ **adducible** adj. [L adducere adduct- (as AD-, ducere lead)]

adduct /ə'dʌkt/ v.tr. draw towards a middle line, esp. draw (a limb) towards the middle line of the body. □□ **adduction** n.

adductor /ə'dʌktə(r)/ n. (in full **adductor muscle**) any muscle that moves one part of the body towards another or towards the middle line of the body.

-ade[1] /eɪd/ suffix forming nouns: **1** an action done (blockade; tirade). **2** the body concerned in an action or process (cavalcade). **3** the product or result of a material or action (arcade; lemonade; masquerade). [from or after F -ade f. Prov., Sp., or Port. -ada f. It. -ata f. L -ata fem. sing. past part. of verbs in -are]

-ade[2] /eɪd/ suffix forming nouns (decade) (cf. -AD[1]). [F -ade f. Gk -as -ada]

-ade[3] /eɪd/ suffix forming nouns: **1** = -ADE[1] (brocade). **2** a person concerned (renegade). [Sp. or Port. -ado, masc. form of -ada: see -ADE[1]]

Adelaide /'ædəˌleɪd/ the capital and chief port of South Australia, on the River Torrens; pop. (1986) 993,100.

Adélie Coast /æ'deɪlɪ/ (also **Adélie Land**, French Terre Adélie) that part of Antarctica first sighted in 1840 by Captain Dumont d'Urville of the French navy (he named it after his wife) and later claimed by France.

Aden /'eɪd(ə)n/ a port commanding the entrance to the Red Sea, capital of South Yemen 1967–90; pop. (1984) 318,000. A trading centre since Roman times, it was formerly under British rule, first as part of British India (from 1839), then from 1935 as a Crown Colony.

Adenauer /'ædəˌnaʊə(r)/, Konrad (1876–1967), German statesman, first Chancellor of the Federal Republic of Germany (1949–63). During his period in office a sound democratic system of government was established, friendship with the US and France was secured, and the West German people enjoyed the 'economic miracle' of a great growth in prosperity.

adenine /ˈædəˌniːn/ n. a purine derivative found in all living tissue as a component base of DNA or RNA. [G Adenin formed as ADENOIDS: see -INE⁴]

adenoids /ˈædɪˌnɔɪdz/ n.pl. Med. a mass of enlarged lymphatic tissue between the back of the nose and the throat, often hindering speaking and breathing in the young. □□ **adenoidal** /-ˈnɔɪd(ə)l/ adj. **adenoidally** /-ˈnɔɪdəlɪ/ adv. [Gk adēn -enos gland + -OID]

adenoma /ˌædɪˈnəʊmə/ n. (pl. **adenomas** or **adenomata** /-mətə/) a glandlike benign tumour. [mod.L f. Gk adēn gland + -OMA]

adenosine /əˈdenəˌsiːn/ n. a nucleoside of adenine and ribose present in all living tissue in a combined form (see AMP, ADP, ATP). [ADENINE + RIBOSE]

adept /ˈædept, əˈdept/ adj. & n. —adj. (foll. by at, in) thoroughly proficient. —n. a skilled performer; an expert. □□ **adeptly** adv. **adeptness** n. [L adeptus past part. of adipisci attain]

adequate /ˈædɪkwət/ adj. **1** sufficient, satisfactory (often with the implication of being barely so). **2** (foll. by to) proportionate. **3** barely sufficient. □□ **adequacy** n. **adequately** adv. [L adaequatus past part. of adaequare make equal (as AD-, aequus equal)]

à deux /ɑː ˈdɜː/ adv. & adj. **1** for two. **2** between two. [F]

ad fin. /æd ˈfɪn/ abbr. at or near the end. [L ad finem]

adhere /ədˈhɪə(r)/ v.intr. **1** (usu. foll. by to) (of a substance) stick fast to a surface, another substance, etc. **2** (foll. by to) behave according to; follow in detail (adhered to our plan). **3** (foll. by to) give support or allegiance. [F adhérer or L adhaerēre (as AD-, haerēre haes- stick)]

adherent /ədˈhɪərənt/ n. & adj. —n. **1** a supporter of a party, person, etc. **2** a devotee of an activity. —adj. **1** (foll. by to) faithfully observing a rule etc. **2** (often foll. by to) (of a substance) sticking fast. □□ **adherence** n. [F adhérent (as ADHERE)]

adhesion /ədˈhiːʒ(ə)n/ n. **1** the act or process of adhering. **2** the capacity of a substance to stick fast. **3** Med. an unnatural union of surfaces due to inflammation. **4** the maintenance of contact between the wheels of a vehicle and the road. **5** the giving of support or allegiance. ¶ More common in physical senses (e.g. the glue has good adhesion), with adherence used in abstract senses (e.g. adherence to principles). [F adhésion or L adhaesio (as ADHERE)]

adhesive /ədˈhiːsɪv/ adj. & n. —adj. sticky, enabling surfaces or substances to adhere to one another. —n. an adhesive substance, esp. one used to stick other substances together. □□ **adhesively** adv. **adhesiveness** n. [F adhésif -ive (as ADHERE)]

adhibit /ədˈhɪbɪt/ v.tr. (**adhibited, adhibiting**) **1** affix. **2** apply or administer (a remedy). □□ **adhibition** /ˌædhɪˈbɪʃ(ə)n/ n. [L adhibēre adhibit- (as AD-, habēre have)]

ad hoc /æd ˈhɒk/ adv. & adj. for a particular (usu. exclusive) purpose (an ad hoc appointment). [L, = to this]

ad hominem /æd ˈhɒmɪˌnem/ adv. & adj. **1** relating to or associated with a particular person. **2** (of an argument) appealing to the emotions and not to reason. [L, = to the person]

adiabatic /ˌeɪdaɪəˈbætɪk/ adj. & n. Physics —adj. **1** impassable to heat. **2** occurring without heat entering or leaving the system. —n. a curve or formula for adiabatic phenomena. □□ **adiabatically** adv. [Gk adiabatos impassable (as A-¹, diabainō pass)]

adiantum /ˌædɪˈæntəm/ n. **1** any fern of the genus Adiantum, e.g. maidenhair. **2** (in general use) a spleenwort. [L f. Gk adianton maidenhair (as A-¹, diantos wettable)]

adieu /əˈdjuː/ int. & n. —int. goodbye. —n. (pl. **adieus** or **adieux** /əˈdjuːz/) a goodbye. [ME f. OF f. à to + Dieu God]

Adi Granth /ˌɑːdɪ ˈɡrʌnt/ the single sacred scripture of Sikhism, compiled by religious teachers, containing religious poetry in several languages. After the death of the tenth and last guru (early 18th c.) the Adi Granth took the place of subsequent teachers. It is the main object of worship in the Sikh gurdwara. [Hindi (= first book), f. Skr.]

ad infinitum /æd ˌɪnfɪˈnaɪtəm/ adv. without limit; for ever. [L]

ad interim /æd ˈɪntərɪm/ adv. & adj. for the meantime. [L]

adios /ˌædɪˈɒs/ int. goodbye. [Sp. adiós f. a to + Dios God]

adipocere /ˈædɪpəˌsɪə(r)/ n. a greyish fatty or soapy substance generated in dead bodies subjected to moisture. [F adipocire f. L adeps adipis fat + F cire wax f. L cera]

adipose /ˈædɪˌpəʊz/ adj. of or characterized by fat; fatty. □ **adipose tissue** fatty connective tissue in animals. □□ **adiposity** /-ˈpɒsɪtɪ/ n. [mod.L adiposus f. adeps adipis fat]

Adirondack Mountains /ˌædɪˈrɒndæk/ (also **Adirondacks**) a range of mountains in New York State, source of the Hudson and Mohawk Rivers. Ancient glaciers have left rugged gorges, lakes, and waterfalls, and the region, with its forests, is now one of great scenic beauty.

adit /ˈædɪt/ n. **1** a horizontal entrance or passage in a mine. **2** a means of approach. [L aditus (as AD-, itus f. ire it- go)]

Adivasi /ˌædɪˈvɑːsɪ/ n. (pl. **Adivasis**) a member of the aboriginal tribal peoples of India. [Hindi adinivāsī original inhabitant]

Adj. abbr. (preceding a name) Adjutant.

adjacent /əˈdʒeɪs(ə)nt/ adj. (often foll. by to) lying near or adjoining. □□ **adjacency** n. [ME f. L adjacēre (as AD-, jacēre lie)]

adjective /ˈædʒɪktɪv/ n. & adj. —n. a word or phrase naming an attribute, added to or grammatically related to a noun or pronoun to modify it or describe it. —adj. additional; not standing by itself; dependent. □□ **adjectival** /ˌædʒɪkˈtaɪv(ə)l/ adj. **adjectivally** /ˌædʒɪkˈtaɪvəlɪ/ adv. [ME f. OF adjectif -ive ult. f. L adjicere adject- (as AD-, jacere throw)]

adjoin /əˈdʒɔɪn/ v.tr. **1** be next to and joined with. **2** archaic = ADD 1. [ME f. OF ajoindre, ajoign- f. L adjungere adjunct- (as AD-, jungere join)]

adjourn /əˈdʒɜːn/ v. **1** tr. **a** put off; postpone. **b** break off (a meeting, discussion, etc.) with the intention of resuming later. **2** intr. of persons at a meeting: **a** break off proceedings and disperse. **b** (foll. by to) transfer the meeting to another place. [ME f. OF ajorner (as AD-, jorn day ult. f. L diurnus DIURNAL): cf. JOURNAL, JOURNEY]

adjournment /əˈdʒɜːnmənt/ n. adjourning or being adjourned. □ **adjournment debate** a debate in the House of Commons on the motion that the House be adjourned, used as an opportunity for raising various matters.

adjudge /əˈdʒʌdʒ/ v.tr. **1** adjudicate (a matter). **2** (often foll. by that + clause, or to + infin.) pronounce judicially. **3** (foll. by to) award judicially. **4** archaic condemn. □□ **adjudgement** n. (also **adjudgment**). [ME f. OF ajuger f. L adjudicare: see ADJUDICATE]

adjudicate /əˈdʒuːdɪˌkeɪt/ v. **1** intr. act as judge in a competition, court, tribunal, etc. **2** tr. **a** decide judicially regarding (a claim etc.). **b** (foll. by to be + compl.) pronounce (was adjudicated to be bankrupt). □□ **adjudication** /-ˈkeɪʃ(ə)n/ n. **adjudicative** adj. **adjudicator** n. [L adjudicare (as AD-, judicare f. judex -icis judge)]

adjunct /ˈædʒʌŋkt/ n. **1** (foll. by to, of) a subordinate or incidental thing. **2** an assistant; a subordinate person, esp. one with temporary appointment only. **3** Gram. a word or phrase used to explain or amplify the predicate, subject, etc. □□ **adjunctive** /əˈdʒʌŋktɪv/ adj. **adjunctively** /əˈdʒʌŋktɪvlɪ/ adv. [L adjunctus: see ADJOIN]

adjure /əˈdʒʊə(r)/ v.tr. (usu. foll. by to + infin.) charge or request (a person) solemnly or earnestly, esp. under oath. □□ **adjuration** /ˌædʒʊəˈreɪʃ(ə)n/ n. **adjuratory** /-rətərɪ/ adj. [ME f. L adjurare (as AD-, jurare swear) in LL sense 'put a person to an oath']

adjust /əˈdʒʌst/ v. **1** tr. **a** arrange; put in the correct order or position. **b** regulate, esp. by a small amount. **2** tr. (usu. foll. by to) make suitable. **3** tr. harmonize (discrepancies). **4** tr. assess (loss or damages). **5** intr. (usu. foll. by to) make oneself suited to; become familiar with (adjust to one's surroundings). □□ **adjustable** adj. **adjustability** /-ˈbɪlɪtɪ/ n. **adjuster** n. **adjustment** n. [F adjuster f. OF ajoster ult. f. L juxta near]

adjutant /ˈædʒʊt(ə)nt/ n. **1 a** Mil. an officer who assists superior officers by communicating orders, conducting correspondence, etc. **b** an assistant. **2** (in full **adjutant bird**) a giant Indian stork. □ **Adjutant-General** a high-ranking Army administrative officer. □□ **adjutancy** n. [L adjutare frequent. of adjuvare: see ADJUVANT]

adjuvant /ˈædʒʊv(ə)nt/ adj. & n. —adj. helpful, auxiliary. —n. an adjuvant person or thing. [F adjuvant or L adjuvare (as AD-, juvare jut- help)]

Adler /ˈædlə(r)/, Alfred (1870–1937), Austrian psychologist and psychiatrist. At first a disciple of Freud, he eventually rejected Freud's basic tenets, particularly the emphasis on biological instincts as determinants of personality. Holding that those of society and culture were at least as significant, he saw human action as motivated by future expectations rather than by past events, striving to express dominance and seeking perfection both in the self and in the individual's contribution to his group. He introduced the concept of the 'inferiority complex', asserting that the most important key to the understanding of both personal and mass problems was the sense of inferiority and the individual's striving to compensate for this. □□ **Adlerian** /ædˈlɪərɪən/ adj.

ad lib /æd ˈlɪb/ v., adj., adv., & n. —v.intr. (**ad libbed, ad libbing**) speak or perform without formal preparation; improvise. —adj. improvised. —adv. as one pleases, to any desired extent. —n. something spoken or played extempore. [abbr. of AD LIBITUM]

ad libitum /æd ˈlɪbɪtəm/ adv. = AD LIB adv. [L, = according to pleasure]

ad litem /æd ˈlaɪtem/ adj. (of a guardian etc.) appointed for a lawsuit. [L]

Adm. abbr. (preceding a name) Admiral.

adman /ˈædmæn/ n. (pl. **admen**) colloq. a person who produces advertisements commercially.

admass /ˈædmæs/ n. esp. Brit. the section of the community that is regarded as readily influenced by advertising and mass communication.

admeasure /ədˈmeʒə(r)/ v.tr. apportion; assign in due shares. □□ **admeasurement** n. [ME f. OF amesurer f. med.L admensurare (as AD-, MEASURE)]

admin /ˈædmɪn/ n. colloq. administration. [abbr.]

adminicle /ədˈmɪnɪk(ə)l/ n. **1** a thing that helps. **2** (in Scottish law) collateral evidence of the contents of a missing document. □□ **adminicular** /ˌædmɪˈnɪkjʊlə(r)/ adj. [L adminiculum prop]

administer /ədˈmɪnɪstə(r)/ v. **1** tr. attend to the running of (business affairs etc.); manage. **2** tr. a be responsible for the implementation of (the law, justice, punishment, etc.). **b** Eccl. give out, or perform the rites of (a sacrament). **c** (usu. foll. by to) direct the taking of (an oath). **3** tr. a provide, apply (a remedy). **b** give, deliver (a rebuke). **4** intr. act as administrator. □□ **administrable** adj. [ME f. OF aministrer f. L administrare (as AD-, MINISTER)]

administrate /ədˈmɪnɪˌstreɪt/ v.tr. & intr. administer (esp. business affairs); act as an administrator. [L administrare (as ADMINISTER)]

administration /ədˌmɪnɪˈstreɪʃ(ə)n/ n. **1** management of a business. **2** the management of public affairs; government. **3** the government in power; the ministry. **4** US a President's period of office. **5** Law the management of another person's estate. **6** (foll. by of) **a** the administering of justice, an oath, etc. **b** application of remedies. [ME f. OF administration or L administratio (as ADMINISTRATE)]

administrative /ədˈmɪnɪstrətɪv/ adj. concerning or relating to the management of affairs. □□ **administratively** adv. [F administratif -ive or L administrativus (as ADMINISTRATION)]

administrator /ədˈmɪnɪˌstreɪtə(r)/ n. **1** a person who administers a business or public affairs. **2** a person capable of organizing (is no administrator). **3** Law a person appointed to manage the estate of a person who has died intestate. **4** a person who performs official duties in some sphere, e.g. in religion or justice. □□ **administratorship** n. **administratrix** n. [L (as ADMINISTER)]

admirable /ˈædmərəb(ə)l/ adj. **1** deserving admiration. **2** excellent. □□ **admirably** adv. [F f. L admirabilis (as ADMIRE)]

admiral /ˈædmər(ə)l/ n. **1 a** the commander-in-chief of a country's navy. **b** a naval officer of high rank, the commander of a fleet or squadron. **c** (**Admiral**) an admiral of the second grade. There are four grades: Admiral of the Fleet, Admiral, Vice Admiral, Rear Admiral. **2** any of various butterflies (red admiral; white admiral). □ **Admiral of the Fleet** an admiral of the first grade. **Fleet Admiral** US = Admiral of the Fleet. □□ **admiralship** n. [ME f. OF a(d)mira(i)l etc. f. med.L a(d)miralis etc., f. Arab. 'amīr

commander (cf. AMIR), assoc. with ADMIRABLE. The modern maritime use is due to the office of 'Amir of the Sea' created by the Arabs in Spain and Sicily and adopted successively by the Genoese, French, and English under Edward III.]

Admiralty /ˈædmərəltɪ/ n. (pl. **-ies**) **1** (hist. except in titles) (in the UK) the department administering the Royal Navy. **2** (**admiralty**) Law trial and decision of maritime questions and offences. □ **Admiralty Board** hist. a committee of the Ministry of Defence superintending the Royal Navy. [ME f. OF admiral(i)té (as ADMIRAL)]

Admiralty Islands an island group of Papua New Guinea in the western Pacific Ocean. In 1884 the islands became a German protectorate, but after 1920 they were administered as an Australian mandate.

admiration /ˌædmɪˈreɪʃ(ə)n/ n. **1** pleased contemplation. **2** respect, warm approval. **3** an object of this (was the admiration of the whole town). [F admiration or L admiratio (as ADMIRE)]

admire /ədˈmaɪə(r)/ v.tr. **1** regard with approval, respect, or satisfaction. **2** express one's admiration of. [F admirer or L admirari (as AD-, mirari wonder at)]

admirer /ədˈmaɪərə(r)/ n. **1** a woman's suitor. **2** a person who admires, esp. a devotee of an able or famous person.

admiring /ədˈmaɪərɪŋ/ adj. showing or feeling admiration (an admiring follower; admiring glances). □□ **admiringly** adv.

admissible /ədˈmɪsɪb(ə)l/ adj. **1** (of an idea or plan) worth accepting or considering. **2** Law allowable as evidence. **3** (foll. by to) capable of being admitted. □□ **admissibility** /-ˈbɪlɪtɪ/ n. [F admissible or med.L admissibilis (as ADMIT)]

admission /ədˈmɪʃ(ə)n/ n. **1** an acknowledgement (admission of error; admission that he was wrong). **2 a** the process or right of entering. **b** a charge for this (admission is £5). **3** a person admitted to a hospital. ¶ Has more general application in senses of ADMIT than admittance. [ME f. L admissio (as ADMIT)]

admit /ədˈmɪt/ v. (**admitted, admitting**) **1** tr. **a** (often foll. by to be, or that + clause) acknowledge; recognize as true. **b** accept as valid or true. **2** intr. (foll. by to) acknowledge responsibility for a deed, fault, etc. **3** tr. **a** allow (a person) entrance or access. **b** allow (a person) to be a member of (a class, group, etc.) or to share in (a privilege etc.). **c** (of a hospital etc.) bring in (a person) for residential treatment. **4** tr. (of an enclosed space) have room for; accommodate. **5** intr. (foll. by of) allow as possible. [ME f. L admittere admiss- (as AD-, mittere send)]

admittance /ədˈmɪt(ə)ns/ n. **1** the right or process of admitting or being admitted, usu. to a place (no admittance except on business). **2** Electr. the reciprocal of impedance. ¶ A more formal and technical word than admission.

admittedly /ədˈmɪtɪdlɪ/ adv. as an acknowledged fact (admittedly there are problems).

admix /ædˈmɪks/ v. **1** tr. & intr. (foll. by with) mingle. **2** tr. add as an ingredient.

admixture /ædˈmɪkstʃə(r)/ n. **1** a thing added, esp. a minor ingredient. **2** the act of adding this. [L admixtus past part. of admiscēre (as AD-, miscēre mix)]

admonish /ədˈmɒnɪʃ/ v.tr. **1** reprove. **2** (foll. by to + infin., or that + clause) urge. **3** give advice to. **4** (foll. by of) warn. □□ **admonishment** n. **admonition** /ˌædməˈnɪʃ(ə)n/ n. **admonitory** adj. [ME f. OF amonester ult. f. L admonēre (as AD-, monēre monit- warn)]

ad nauseam /æd ˈnɔːzɪˌæm, ˈnɔːsɪˌæm/ adv. to an excessive or disgusting degree. [L, = to sickness]

adnominal /ædˈnɒmɪn(ə)l/ adj. Gram. attached to a noun. [L adnomen -minis (added name)]

ado /əˈduː/ n. (pl. **ados**) fuss, busy activity; trouble, difficulty. □ **without more ado** immediately. [orig. in much ado = much to do, f. north. ME at do (= to do) f. ON at as sign of infin. + DO[1]]

-ado /ˈɑːdəʊ/ suffix forming nouns (desperado) (cf. -ADE[3]). [Sp. or Port. -ado f. L -atus past part. of verbs in -are]

adobe /əˈdəʊbɪ, əˈdəʊb/ n. **1** an unburnt sun-dried brick. **2** the clay used for making such bricks. [Sp. f. Arab.]

adolescent /ˌædəˈles(ə)nt/ adj. & n. —adj. between childhood and adulthood. —*n.* an adolescent person. □□ **adolescence** *n.* [ME f. OF f. L *adolescere* grow up]

Adonis /ə'dəʊnɪs/ *Gk Mythol.* a beautiful youth loved by both Aphrodite and Persephone. He was killed by a boar (the flower anemone was said to have sprung from his blood), but Zeus decreed that he should spend part of each year in the Underworld with Persephone and the summer months with Aphrodite. The traditional interpretation of the myth as symbolizing the cycle of the life of plants is by no means certain. —*n.* a handsome young man. □ **Adonis blue** a kind of butterfly, *Lysandra bellargus*. [L f. Gk f. Phoen. *adōn* lord]

adopt /ə'dɒpt/ *v.tr.* **1** take (a person) into a relationship, esp. another's child as one's own. **2** choose to follow (a course of action etc.). **3** take over (an idea etc.) from another person. **4** choose as a candidate for office. **5** *Brit.* (of a local authority) accept responsibility for the maintenance of (a road etc.). **6** accept; formally approve (a report, accounts, etc.). □□ **adoption** *n.*[F *adopter* or L *adoptare* (as AD-, *optare* choose)]

adoptive /ə'dɒptɪv/ *adj.* due to adoption (*adoptive son; adoptive father*). □□ **adoptively** *adv.* [ME f. OF *adoptif -ive* f. L *adoptivus* (as ADOPT)]

adorable /ə'dɔːrəb(ə)l/ *adj.* **1** deserving adoration. **2** *colloq.* delightful, charming. □□ **adorably** *adv.* [F f. L *adorabilis* (as ADORE)]

adore /ə'dɔː(r)/ *v.tr.* **1** regard with honour and deep affection. **2 a** worship as divine. **b** *RC Ch.* offer reverence to (the Host etc.). **3** *colloq.* like very much. □□ **adoration** /ˌædə'reɪʃ(ə)n/ *n.* **adoring** *adj.* **adoringly** *adv.* [ME f. OF *aourer* f. L *adorare* worship (as AD-, *orare* speak, pray)]

adorer /ə'dɔːrə(r)/ *n.* **1** a worshipper. **2** an ardent admirer.

adorn /ə'dɔːn/ *v.tr.* **1** add beauty or lustre to; be an ornament to. **2** furnish with ornaments; decorate. □□ **adornment** *n.* [ME f. OF a(u)rner f. L *adornare* (as AD-, *ornare* furnish, deck)]

ADP *abbr.* **1** adenosine diphosphate. **2** automatic data processing.

ad personam /ˌæd pə'səʊnæm/ *adv. & adj.* —*adv.* to the person. —*adj.* personal. [L]

Adrar des Iforas /æ'drɑː(r) deɪz ɪ'fɔːrɑː/ a mountainous region in the Sahara Desert in NW Africa.

ad rem /æd 'rem/ *adv. & adj.* to the point; to the purpose. [L, = to the matter]

adrenal /ə'driːn(ə)l/ *adj. & n.* —*adj.* **1** at or near the kidneys. **2** of the adrenal glands. —*n.* (in full **adrenal gland**) either of two ductless glands above the kidneys, secreting adrenalin. [AD- + RENAL]

adrenalin /ə'drenəlɪn/ *n.* (also **adrenaline**) **1** a hormone secreted by the adrenal glands, affecting circulation and muscular action, and causing excitement and stimulation. **2** the same substance obtained from animals or by synthesis, used as a stimulant.

adrenocorticotrophic hormone /əˌdriːnəˌkɔːtɪkə'trɒfɪk/ *n.* (also **adrenocorticotropic** /-'trɒpɪk/) a hormone secreted by the pituitary gland and stimulating the adrenal glands. ¶ Abbr.: **ACTH**. [ADRENAL + CORTEX + -TROPHIC, -TROPIC]

adrenocorticotrophin /əˌdriːnəˌkɔːtɪkə'trɒfɪn/ *n.* = ADRENO-CORTICOTROPHIC HORMONE. [ADRENOCORTICOTROPHIC (HORMONE) + -IN]

Adrian IV /'eɪdrɪən/ Nicholas Breakspear (*c.*1100–59), pope 1154–9, the only Englishman to have held that office. He reorganized the Church in Norway, assisted Henry II of England to gain control of Ireland, and opposed Frederick Barbarossa's claims to power, a dispute that was still in progress when he died.

Adriatic /ˌeɪdrɪ'ætɪk/ *adj. & n.* —*adj.* of the Adriatic Sea. —*n.* the Adriatic Sea. □ **Adriatic Sea** an arm of the Mediterranean Sea lying between Italy and the Balkan Peninsula. **Marriage of the Adriatic** a former Ascension-Day ceremony symbolizing the sea-power of Venice, during which the Doge dropped a ring into the water from his official barge.

adrift /ə'drɪft/ *adv. & predic.adj.* **1** drifting. **2** at the mercy of circumstances. **3** *colloq.* **a** unfastened. **b** out of touch. **c** absent

without leave. **d** (often foll. by *of*) failing to reach a target. **e** out of order. **f** ill-informed. [A² + DRIFT]

adroit /ə'drɔɪt/ *adj.* dextrous, skilful. □□ **adroitly** *adv.* **adroitness** *n.* [F f. *à droit* according to right]

adsorb /əd'sɔːb/ *v.tr.* (usu. of a solid) hold (molecules of a gas or liquid or solute) to its surface, causing a thin film to form. □□ **adsorbable** *adj.* **adsorbent** *adj. & n.* **adsorption** *n.* (also **adsorbtion**). [AD-, after ABSORB]

adsorbate /æd'sɔːbeɪt/ *n.* a substance adsorbed.

adsuki var. of ADZUKI.

adulate /'ædjʊˌleɪt/ *v.tr.* flatter obsequiously. □□ **adulation** /-'leɪʃ(ə)n/ *n.* **adulator** *n.* **adulatory** *adj.* [L *adulari adulat-* fawn on]

Adullamite /ə'dʌləˌmaɪt/ *n.* a member of a dissident political group. The term was originally applied to a group of Liberal MPs who seceded from their party (which was then in power) from dissatisfaction with its attempt at Parliamentary reform and brought about defeat of the Reform Bill of 1866. [f. cave of *Adullam* (1 Sam. 22: 1–2) where all who were distressed, in debt, or discontented came to join David when he fled from Saul]

adult /'ædʌlt, ə'dʌlt/ *adj. & n.* —*adj.* **1** mature, grown-up. **2 a** of or for adults (*adult education*). **b** *euphem.* sexually explicit; indecent (*adult films*). —*n.* **1** an adult person. **2** *Law* a person who has reached the age of majority. □□ **adulthood** *n.* **adultly** *adv.* [L *adultus* past part. of *adolescere* grow up: cf. ADOLESCENT]

adulterant /ə'dʌltərənt/ *adj. & n.* —*adj.* used in adulterating. —*n.* an adulterant substance.

adulterate *v. & adj.* —*v.tr.* /ə'dʌltəˌreɪt/ debase (esp. foods) by adding other or inferior substances. —*adj.* /ə'dʌltərət/ spurious, debased, counterfeit. □□ **adulteration** /-'reɪʃ(ə)n/ *n.* **adulterator** *n.* [L *adulterare adulterat-* corrupt]

adulterer /ə'dʌltərə(r)/ *n.* (*fem.* **adulteress** /-rɪs/) a person who commits adultery. [obs. *adulter* (v.) f. OF *avoutrer* f. L *adulterare*: see ADULTERATE]

adulterine /ə'dʌltəˌraɪn/ *adj.* **1** illegal, unlicensed. **2** spurious. **3** born of adultery. [L *adulterinus* f. *adulter*: see ADULTERY]

adulterous /ə'dʌltərəs/ *adj.* of or involved in adultery. □□ **adulterously** *adv.* [ME f. *adulter*: see ADULTERER]

adultery /ə'dʌltərɪ/ *n.* voluntary sexual intercourse between a married person and a person (married or not) other than his or her spouse. [ME f. OF *avoutrie* etc. f. *avoutre* adulterer f. L *adulter*, assim. to L *adulterium*]

adumbrate /'ædʌmˌbreɪt/ *v.tr.* **1** indicate faintly. **2** represent in outline. **3** foreshadow, typify. **4** overshadow. □□ **adumbration** /-'breɪʃ(ə)n/ *n.* **adumbrative** /ə'dʌmbrətɪv/ *adj.* [L *adumbrare* (as AD-, *umbrare* f. *umbra* shade)]

ad valorem /ˌæd və'lɔːrem/ *adv. & adj.* (of taxes) in proportion to the estimated value of the goods concerned. [L, = according to the value]

advance /əd'vɑːns/ *v., n., & adj.* —*v.* **1** *tr. & intr.* move or put forward. **2** *intr.* make progress. **3** *tr.* **a** pay (money) before it is due. **b** lend (money). **4** *tr.* give active support to; promote (a person, cause, or plan). **5** *tr.* put forward (a claim or suggestion). **6** *tr.* cause (an event) to occur at an earlier date (*advanced the meeting three hours*). **7** *tr.* raise (a price). **8** *intr.* rise (in price). **9** *tr.* (as **advanced** *adj.*) **a** far on in progress (*the work is well advanced*). **b** ahead of the times (*advanced ideas*). —*n.* **1** an act of going forward. **2** progress. **3** a payment made before the due time. **4** a loan. **5** (esp. in *pl.*; often foll. by *to*) an amorous or friendly approach. **6** a rise in price. —*attrib.adj.* done or supplied beforehand (*advance warning; advance copy*). □ **advanced** (or **advanced supplementary**) **level** (in the UK) a GCE examination of a standard higher than ordinary level and GCSE. **advance guard** a body of soldiers preceding the main body of an army. **advance on** approach threateningly. **in advance** ahead in place or time. □□ **advancer** *n.* [ME f. OF *avancer* f. LL *abante* in front f. L *ab* away + *ante* before: (n.) partly through F *avance*]

Advance Australia Fair an Australian patriotic song composed *c.*1878 by P. D. McCormick, a Scot, under the pen-name 'Amicus'.

advancement /əd'vɑːnsmənt/ *n.* the promotion of a person, cause, or plan. [ME f. F *avancement* f. *avancer* (as ADVANCE)]

advantage /əd'vɑːntɪdʒ/ n. & v. —n. **1** a beneficial feature; a favourable circumstance. **2** benefit, profit (is not to your advantage). **3** (often foll. by over) a better position; superiority in a particular respect. **4** (in lawn tennis) the next point won after deuce. —v.tr. **1** be beneficial or favourable to. **2** further, promote. □ **have the advantage of** be in a better position in some respect than. **take advantage of 1** make good use of (a favourable circumstance). **2** exploit or outwit (a person), esp. unfairly. **3** euphem. seduce. **to advantage** in a way which exhibits the merits (was seen to advantage). **turn to advantage** benefit from. □□ **advantageous** /ˌædvən'teɪdʒəs/ adj. **advantageously** /ˌædvən'teɪdʒəslɪ/ adv. [ME f. OF avantage, avantager f. avant in front f. LL abante: see ADVANCE]

advection /əd'vekʃ(ə)n/ n. Meteorol. transfer of heat by the horizontal flow of air. □□ **advective** adj. [L advectio f. advehere (as AD-, vehere vect- carry)]

Advent /'ædvent/ n. **1** the season before Christmas, including the four preceding Sundays. **2** the coming or second coming of Christ. **3** (advent) the arrival of esp. an important person or thing. □ **Advent calendar** Brit. a calendar for Advent, usu. of card with flaps to open each day revealing a picture or scene. **Advent Sunday** the first Sunday in Advent. [OE f. OF advent, auvent f. L adventus arrival f. advenire (as AD-, venire vent- come)]

Adventist /'ædventɪst/ n. a member of a Christian sect that believes in the imminent second coming of Christ. As a denomination they originated in the US, followers of William Miller (1782–1849), a millenarian preacher, who originally prophesied that Christ would return in 1843/4. The chief bodies now are the Second Advent Christians and the Seventh-day Adventists. □□ **Adventism** n.

adventitious /ˌædven'tɪʃəs/ adj. **1** accidental, casual. **2** added from outside. **3** Biol. formed accidentally or under unusual conditions. **4** Law (of property) coming from a stranger or by collateral succession rather than directly. □□ **adventitiously** adv. [L adventicius (as ADVENT)]

adventure /əd'ventʃə(r)/ n. & v. —n. **1** an unusual and exciting experience. **2** a daring enterprise; a hazardous activity. **3** enterprise (the spirit of adventure). **4** a commercial speculation. —v.intr. **1** (often foll. by into, upon) dare to go or come. **2** (foll. by on, upon) dare to undertake. **3** incur risk; engage in adventure. □ **adventure playground** a playground where children are provided with functional materials for climbing on, building with, etc. □□ **adventuresome** adj. [ME f. OF aventure, aventurer f. L adventurus about to happen (as ADVENT)]

adventurer /əd'ventʃərə(r)/ n. (fem. **adventuress** /-ɔrɪs/) **1** a person who seeks adventure, esp. for personal gain or enjoyment. **2** a financial speculator. [F aventurier (as ADVENTURE)]

adventurism /əd'ventʃəˌrɪz(ə)m/ n. a tendency to take risks, esp. in foreign policy. □□ **adventurist** n.

adventurous /əd'ventʃərəs/ adj. **1** rash, venturesome; enterprising. **2** characterized by adventures. □□ **adventurously** adv. **adventurousness** n. [ME f. OF aventuros (as ADVENTURE)]

adverb /'ædvɜːb/ n. a word or phrase that modifies or qualifies another word (esp. an adjective, verb, or other adverb) or a word-group, expressing a relation of place, time, circumstance, manner, cause, degree, etc. (e.g. gently, quite, then, there). □□ **adverbial** /əd'vɜːbɪəl/ adj. [F adverbe or L adverbium (as AD-, VERB)]

adversarial /ˌædvə'seərɪəl/ adj. **1** involving conflict or opposition. **2** opposed, hostile. [ADVERSARY + -IAL]

adversary /'ædvəsərɪ/ n. (pl. **-ies**) **1** an enemy. **2** an opponent in a sport or game; an antagonist. [ME f. OF adversarie f. L adversarius f. adversus: see ADVERSE]

adversative /əd'vɜːsətɪv/ adj. (of words etc.) expressing opposition or antithesis. □□ **adversatively** adv. [F adversatif -ive or LL adversativus f. adversari oppose f. adversus: see ADVERSE]

adverse /'ædvɜːs/ adj. (often foll. by to) **1** contrary, hostile. **2** hurtful, injurious. □□ **adversely** adv. **adverseness** n. [ME f. OF advers f. L adversus past part. of advertere (as AD-, vertere vers- turn)]

adversity /əd'vɜːsɪtɪ/ n. (pl. **-ies**) **1** the condition of adverse fortune. **2** a misfortune. [ME f. OF adversité f. L adversitas -tatis (as ADVERSE)]

advert[1] /'ædvɜːt/ n. Brit. colloq. an advertisement. [abbr.]

advert[2] /əd'vɜːt/ v.intr. (foll. by to) literary refer in speaking or writing. [ME f. OF avertir f. L advertere: see ADVERSE]

advertise /'ædvəˌtaɪz/ v. **1** tr. draw attention to or describe favourably (goods or services) in a public medium to promote sales. **2** tr. make generally or publicly known. **3** intr. (foll. by for) seek by public notice, esp. in a newspaper. **4** tr. (usu. foll. by of, or that + clause) notify. □□ **advertiser** n. [ME f. OF avertir (stem advertiss-): see ADVERT[2]]

In ancient times public criers walked through the streets announcing that a sale (e.g. of slaves or cattle) would take place. When public newspapers began to be printed regularly in the mid-17th c. they were able to carry announcements and advertisements, though the London Gazette in 1666 relegated advertisements 'of Books, Medicines, and other things, not properly the business of a Paper of Intelligence' to a supplement, but this form of advertising prospered. The growth of popular newspapers in the 19th c. enabled advertisements to reach a wider market; they became an essential tool of salesmanship, and advertising became an industry. Other media have become vehicles of advertising, each with its own technique and approach: posters, painted signs, and electric displays in public places deliver a message that has to be brief, simple, and direct; commercials are broadcast on radio and television; direct mail, which involves the sending of advertising matter through the post to a specific address, enables special groups of potential customers to be selectively targeted and to study material at their leisure; small gifts and handy items suitably emblazoned keep a company's name before the public.

advertisement /əd'vɜːtɪsmənt, -tɪzmənt/ n. **1** a public notice or announcement, esp. one advertising goods or services in newspapers, on posters, or in broadcasts. **2** the act or process of advertising. **3** archaic a notice to readers in a book etc. [earlier avert- f. F avertissement (as ADVERTISE)]

advice /əd'vaɪs/ n. **1** words given or offered as an opinion or recommendation about future action or behaviour. **2** (in pl.) communications from a distance. □ **take advice 1** obtain advice, esp. from an expert. **2** act according to advice given. [ME f. OF avis f. L ad to + visum past part. of vidēre see]

advisable /əd'vaɪzəb(ə)l/ adj. **1** (of a course of action etc.) to be recommended. **2** expedient. □□ **advisability** /-'bɪlɪtɪ/ n. **advisably** adv.

advise /əd'vaɪz/ v. **1** tr. (also absol.) give advice to. **2** tr. recommend; offer as advice (they advise caution; advised me to rest). **3** tr. (usu. foll. by of, or that + clause) inform, notify. **4** intr. (foll. by with) US consult. [ME f. OF aviser f. L ad to + visare frequent. of vidēre see]

advised /əd'vaɪzd/ adj. **1** judicious (well-advised). **2** deliberate, considered. □□ **advisedly** /-zɪdlɪ/ adv.

adviser /əd'vaɪzə(r)/ n. (also disp. **advisor**) **1** a person who advises, esp. one appointed to do so and regularly consulted. **2** US a person who advises students on education, careers, etc. ¶ The disputed form advisor is prob. influenced by the adj. advisory.

advisory /əd'vaɪzərɪ/ adj. & n. —adj. **1** giving advice; constituted to give advice (an advisory body). **2** consisting in giving advice. —n. (pl. **-ies**) US an advisory statement, esp. a bulletin about bad weather.

advocaat /ˌædvə'kɑːt/ n. a liqueur of eggs, sugar, and brandy. [Du., = ADVOCATE (being orig. an advocate's drink)]

advocacy /'ædvəkəsɪ/ n. **1** (usu. foll. by of) verbal support or argument for a cause, policy, etc. **2** the function of an advocate. [ME f. OF a(d)vocacie f. med.L advocatia (as ADVOCATE)]

advocate n. & v. —n. /'ædvəkət/ **1** (foll. by of) a person who supports or speaks in favour. **2** a person who pleads for another. **3 a** a professional pleader in a court of justice. **b** Sc. a barrister. —v.tr. /'ædvəˌkeɪt/ **1** recommend or support by argument (a cause, policy, etc.). **2** plead for, defend. □□ **advocateship** n. **advocatory** /'ædvəkeɪtərɪ/ adj. [ME f. OF avocat f. L advocatus past part. of advocare (as AD-, vocare call)]

advowson /əd'vaʊz(ə)n/ n. Brit. Eccl. (in ecclesiastical law) the right of recommending a member of the clergy for a vacant benefice, or of making the appointment. [ME f. AF a(d)voweson f. OF avoeson f. L advocatio -onis (as ADVOCATE)]

advt. abbr. advertisement.

adytum /ˈædɪtəm/ n. (pl. **adyta** /-tə/) the innermost part of an ancient temple. [L f. Gk aduton neut. of adutos impenetrable (as A-¹, duō enter)]

adze /ædz/ n. & v. (US **adz**) —n. a tool for cutting away the surface of wood, like an axe with an arched blade at right angles to the handle. —v.tr. dress or cut with an adze. [OE adesa]

adzuki /ədˈzuːkɪ/ n. (also **adsuki, azuki**) 1 an annual leguminous plant, Vigna angularis, native to China and Japan. 2 the small round red edible bean of this plant. [Jap. azuki]

-ae /iː/ suffix forming plural nouns, used in names of animal and plant families, tribes, etc. (Felidae; Rosaceae) and instead of -as in the plural of many non-naturalized or unfamiliar nouns in -a derived from Latin or Greek (larvae; actiniae). [pl. -ae of L nouns in -a or pl. -ai of some Gk nouns]

aedile /ˈiːdaɪl/ n. either of a pair of Roman magistrates who administered public works, maintenance of roads, public games, the corn-supply, etc. □□ **aedileship** n. [L aedilis concerned with buildings f. aedes building]

Aegean /ɪˈdʒiːən/ adj. & n. —adj. of the Aegean Sea. —n. the Aegean Sea. □ **Aegean Islands** a group of islands in the Aegean Sea forming a region of Greece. The principal islands of the group are Chios (Khios), Samos, Lesbos, the Cyclades, and the Dodecanese; pop. (1981) 428,500. **Aegean Sea** the part of the Mediterranean lying between Greece and Turkey.

aegis /ˈiːdʒɪs/ n. a protection; an impregnable defence. □ **under the aegis of** under the auspices of. [L f. Gk aigis mythical shield of Zeus or Athene]

aegrotat /ˈiːgrəʊˌtæt/ n. Brit. 1 a certificate that a university student is too ill to attend an examination. 2 an examination pass awarded in such circumstances. [L, = is sick f. aeger sick]

Ælfric /ˈælfrɪk/ (c.955–c.1020) Anglo-Saxon monk, a prose-writer and grammarian, whose chief works are the Catholic Homilies (990–2; collections of sermons) and the Lives of the Saints (993–6). Other surviving works include his popular Grammar which earned him the name of 'Grammaticus'. He is celebrated for his stylistic excellence and his educational principles.

-aemia /ˈiːmɪə/ comb. form (also **-haemia** /ˈhiːmɪə/, US **-emia**, **-hemia** /ˈhiːmɪə/) forming nouns denoting that a substance is (esp. excessively) present in the blood (bacteriaemia; pyaemia). [mod.L f. Gk -aimia f. haima blood]

Aeneas /ɪˈniːəs/ Gk & Rom. legend a Trojan leader, son of Anchises and Aphrodite. When Troy fell to the Greeks he escaped and after long wandering reached the Tiber. He was regarded by the Romans as the founder of their State, and is known as 'pious Aeneas' for his filial dutifulness and fidelity to his mission.

Aeneid /ˈiːnɪɪd/ a Latin hexameter epic poem in twelve books by Virgil, which relates the wanderings of the Trojan hero Aeneas (legendary founder of the Roman State) after the fall of Troy, his love affair with the Carthaginian queen Dido, his visit to his dead father Anchises in the Underworld, his arrival in Italy, and his eventual victory over the hostile Italian peoples led by Turnus. Closely modelled on the epics of Homer, it also contains a not totally optimistic celebration of the ideals and achievements of Augustus. Virgil's wish that the poem (unfinished at his death) be burned was not respected by his literary executors.

aeolian /iːˈəʊlɪən/ adj. (US **eolian**) wind-borne. □ **aeolian harp** a stringed instrument or toy that produces musical sounds when the wind passes through it. [L Aeolius f. AEOLUS f. Gk Aiolos]

Aeolian Islands /iːˈəʊlɪən/ the ancient name of the Lipari Islands. [as AEOLIAN]

Aeolian mode /iːˈəʊlɪən/ n. Mus. the mode represented by the natural diatonic scale A–A. [L Aeolius f. Aeolis in Asia Minor f. Gk Aiolis]

Aeolus /ˈiːələs/ Gk Mythol. the guardian (later thought of as a god) of the winds. [Gk Aiolos f. aiolos swift, changeable]

aeon /ˈiːɒn/ n. (also **eon**) 1 a very long or indefinite period. 2 an age of the universe. 3 Astron. a thousand million years. 4 an eternity. 5 Philos. (in Neoplatonism, Platonism, and Gnosticism)

a power existing from eternity, an emanation or phase of the supreme deity. [eccl.L f. Gk aiōn age]

aepyornis /ˌiːpɪˈɔːnɪs/ n. a gigantic flightless extinct bird of the genus Aepyornis, resembling a moa, known from remains found in Madagascar. [L f. Gk aipus high, ornis bird]

aerate /ˈeəreɪt/ v.tr. 1 charge (a liquid) with a gas, esp. carbon dioxide, e.g. to produce effervescence. 2 expose to the mechanical or chemical action of the air. □□ **aeration** /-ˈreɪʃ(ə)n/ n. **aerator** n. [L aer AIR + -ATE³, after F aérer]

aerenchyma /ˌeərənˈkaɪmə/ n. Bot. a soft plant tissue containing air spaces found esp. in many aquatic plants. [Gk aēr air + egkhuma infusion]

aerial /ˈeərɪəl/ n. & adj. —n. a metal rod, wire, or other structure by which signals are transmitted or received as part of a radio or television transmission or receiving system. —adj. 1 by or from or involving aircraft (aerial navigation; aerial photography). 2 **a** existing, moving, or happening in the air. **b** of or in the atmosphere, atmospheric. 3 **a** thin as air, ethereal. **b** immaterial, imaginary. **c** of air, gaseous. □□ **aeriality** /-ˈælɪtɪ/ n. **aerially** adv. [L aerius f. Gk aerios f. aēr air]

aerialist /ˈeərɪəlɪst/ n. a high-wire or trapeze artist.

aerie var. of EYRIE.

aeriform /ˈeərɪˌfɔːm/ adj. 1 of the form of air; gaseous. 2 unsubstantial, unreal. [L aer AIR + -FORM]

aero- /ˈeərəʊ/ comb. form 1 air. 2 aircraft. [Gk aero- f. aēr air]

aerobatics /ˌeərəˈbætɪks/ n.pl. 1 feats of expert and usu. spectacular flying and manoeuvring of aircraft. 2 (as sing.) a performance of these. [AERO- + ACROBATICS]

aerobe /ˈeərəʊb/ n. a micro-organism usu. growing in the presence of air, or needing air for growth. [F aérobie (as AERO-, Gk bios life)]

aerobic /eəˈrəʊbɪk, eəˈrɒb-/ adj. 1 of or relating to aerobics. 2 of or relating to aerobes.

aerobics /eəˈrəʊbɪks/ n.pl. vigorous exercises designed to increase the body's oxygen intake.

aerobiology /ˌeərəbaɪˈɒlədʒɪ/ n. the study of airborne micro-organisms, pollen, spores, etc., esp. as agents of infection.

aerodrome /ˈeərəˌdrəʊm/ n. Brit. a small airport or airfield. ¶ Now largely replaced by airfield and airport.

aerodynamics /ˌeərəʊdaɪˈnæmɪks/ n.pl. (usu. treated as sing.) the study of the interaction between the air and solid bodies moving through it. □□ **aerodynamic** adj. **aerodynamically** adv. **aerodynamicist** n.

aero-engine /ˈeərəʊˌendʒɪn/ n. an engine used to power an aircraft.

aerofoil /ˈeərəˌfɔɪl/ n. Brit. a structure with curved surfaces (e.g. a wing, fin, or tailplane) designed to give lift in flight.

aerogramme /ˈeərəˌgræm/ n. (also **aerogram**) an air letter in the form of a single sheet that is folded and sealed.

aerolite /ˈeərəˌlaɪt/ n. a stony meteorite.

aerology /eəˈrɒlədʒɪ/ n. the study of the upper levels of the atmosphere. □□ **aerological** /-əˈlɒdʒɪk(ə)l/ adj.

aeronautics /ˌeərəʊˈnɔːtɪks/ n.pl. (usu. treated as sing.) the science or practice of motion or travel in the air. □□ **aeronautic** adj. **aeronautical** adj. [mod.L aeronautica (as AERO-, NAUTICAL)]

aeronomy /eəˈrɒnəmɪ/ n. the science of the upper atmosphere.

aeroplane /ˈeərəˌpleɪn/ n. esp. Brit. a powered heavier-than-air flying vehicle with fixed wings. The first true aeroplane to achieve controlled sustained flight was that designed, built, and flown by the Wright brothers in 1903. [F aéroplane (as AERO-, PLANE¹)]

aerosol /ˈeərəˌsɒl/ n. 1 **a** a container used to hold a substance packed under pressure with a device for releasing it as a fine spray. **b** the releasing device. **c** the substance contained in an aerosol. The propellent gas must be non-toxic and non-inflammable; for this reason one of the chlorinated fluorocarbon refrigerants is often used, but fears have been expressed about the effects of accumulation of these gases in the upper atmosphere, where a photochemical reaction may reduce the amount of ozone. This in turn could lead to an increased amount of ultraviolet radiation reaching the earth, with consequent risks to health. Aerosols were first developed commercially in the US in the early 1940s. **2** a system of colloidal particles dispersed in a gas (e.g. fog or smoke). [AERO- + SOL²]

aerospace /ˈeərəʊˌspeɪs/ n. **1** the earth's atmosphere and outer space. **2** the technology of aviation in this region.

aerotrain /ˈeərəʊˌtreɪn/ n. a train that is supported on an air-cushion and guided by a track. [F *aérotrain* (as AERO-, TRAIN)]

aeruginous /ɪəˈruːdʒɪnəs/ adj. of the nature or colour of verdigris. [L *aeruginosus* f. *aerugo -inis* verdigris f. *aes aeris* bronze]

Aeschines /ˈiːskɪˌniːz/ (*c*.397–*c*.322 BC) Athenian orator and statesman, whose exchanges with his implacable opponent Demosthenes provide much of the evidence of the relations between Athens and Macedon 343–330 BC.

Aeschylus /ˈiːskɪləs/ (525/4–456 BC) Greek dramatist, who saw the collapse of tyranny and the rapid rise of democratic government at Athens, fought in the Persian Wars, and is regarded as the founder of Greek tragic drama. His seven extant plays are distinguished by magnificence of staging and spectacle (as in the oriental ceremony of the *Persians*), and by grandeur of language; his characters (e.g. Prometheus in *Prometheus Bound*) are strongly drawn, and behind them can be felt the presence and power of fate and of the gods; the chorus acts as a vehicle for profound reflections on events. His examination of the workings of providence is best seen in the *Oresteia*, a trilogy which traces the working-out, on the human and divine levels, of the blood-feud in the house of Agamemnon.

Aesculapian /ˌiːskjʊˈleɪpɪən/ adj. of or relating to medicine or physicians. [L *Aesculapius* f. Gk *Asklēpios* ASCLEPIUS]

Aesir /ˈiːsə(r)/ *Scand. Mythol.* the collective name of the gods.

Aesop /ˈiːsɒp/ (early 6th c. BC) Greek teller of moral animal fables who lived as a slave on the island of Samos.

aesthete /ˈiːsθiːt/ n. (*US* **esthete**) a person who has or professes to have a special appreciation of beauty. [Gk *aisthētēs* one who perceives, or f. AESTHETIC]

aesthetic /iːsˈθetɪk/ adj. & n. (*US* **esthetic**) **1** concerned with beauty or the appreciation of beauty. **2** having such appreciation; sensitive to beauty. **3** in accordance with the principles of good taste. —n. **1** (in *pl.*) the philosophy of the beautiful, esp. in art. **2** a set of principles of good taste and the appreciation of beauty. □□ **aesthetically** adv. **aestheticism** /-ˌsɪz(ə)m/ n. [Gk *aisthētikos* f. *aisthanomai* perceive]

Aesthetic movement n. a literary and artistic movement devoted to 'art for art's sake' which blossomed in the 1880s, heavily influenced by the Pre-Raphaelites, Ruskin, and Walter Pater, in which the adoption of sentimental archaism as the ideal of beauty was carried to extravagant lengths and often accompanied by affectation of speech and manner and eccentricity of dress. Its chief followers, who included Oscar Wilde, Aubrey Beardsley, and others associated with the *Yellow Book*, were greatly ridiculed in *Punch* and in Gilbert and Sullivan's opera *Patience* (1881).

aestival /ˈiːstɪv(ə)l, eˈstɑːv(ə)l, iːˈstɑːv(ə)l/ adj. (*US* **estival**) *formal* belonging to or appearing in summer. [ME f. OF *estival* f. L *aestivalis* f. *aestivus* f. *aestus* heat]

aestivate /ˈiːstɪˌveɪt, ˈiːs-/ v.intr. (*US* **estivate**) **1** *Zool.* spend the summer or dry season in a state of torpor. **2** *formal* pass the summer. [L *aestivare aestivat-*]

aestivation /ˌiːstɪˈveɪʃ(ə)n, ˌiːs-/ n. (*US* **estivation**) **1** *Bot.* the arrangement of petals in a flower-bud before it opens (cf. VERNATION). **2** *Zool.* spending the summer or dry season in a state of torpor.

aet. abbr. (also *aetat.*) *aetatis.*

aetatis /iːˈtɑːtɪs, aɪ-/ adj. of or at the age of.

aether var. of ETHER 2, 3.

aetiology /ˌiːtɪˈɒlədʒɪ/ n. (*US* **etiology**) **1** the assignment of a cause or reason. **2** the philosophy of causation. **3** *Med.* the science of the causes of disease. □□ **aetiologic** /-əˈlɒdʒɪk/ adj. **aetiological** /-əˈlɒdʒɪk(ə)l/ adj. **aetiologically** /-əˈlɒdʒɪkəlɪ/ adv. [LL *aetiologia* f. Gk *aitiologia* f. *aitia* cause]

AEU abbr. (in the UK) Amalgamated Engineering Union.

AEU(TASS) abbr. Technical, Administrative, and Supervisory Section of the AEU.

AF abbr. audio frequency.

af- /əf/ prefix assim. form of AD- before *f.*

afar /əˈfɑː(r)/ adv. at or to a distance. □ **from afar** from a distance. [ME f. A-², A-⁴ + FAR]

AFC abbr. **1** (in the UK) Air Force Cross. **2** Association Football Club.

AFDCS abbr. (in the UK) Association of First Division Civil Servants (cf. FDA).

affable /ˈæfəb(ə)l/ adj. **1** (of a person) approachable and friendly. **2** kind and courteous, esp. to inferiors. □□ **affability** /-ˈbɪlɪtɪ/ n. **affably** adv. [F f. L *affabilis* f. *affari* (as AD-, *fari* speak)]

affair /əˈfeə(r)/ n. **1** a concern; a business; a matter to be attended to (*that is my affair*). **2 a** a celebrated or notorious happening or sequence of events. **b** *colloq.* a noteworthy thing or event (*was a puzzling affair*). **3** = *love affair.* **4** (in *pl.*) **a** ordinary pursuits of life. **b** business dealings. **c** public matters (*current affairs*). [ME f. AF *afere* f. OF *afaire f. à faire* to do: cf. ADO]

affaire /æˈfeə(r)/ n. (also *affaire de cœur* /ˌæ ˌfeə də ˈkɜː(r)/) a love affair. [F]

affairé /æˈfeəreɪ/ adj. busy; involved. [F]

affect¹ /əˈfekt/ v.tr. **1** a produce an effect on. **b** (of a disease etc.) attack (*his liver is affected*). **2** move; touch the feelings of (*affected me deeply*). ¶ Often confused with *effect*, which as a verb means 'bring about; accomplish'. □□ **affecting** adj. **affectingly** adv. [F *affecter* or L *afficere affect-* influence (as AD-, *facere* do)]

affect² /əˈfekt/ v.tr. **1** pretend to have or feel (*affected indifference*). **2** (foll. by *to* + infin.) pretend. **3** assume the character or manner of; pose as (*affect the freethinker*). **4** make a show of liking or using (*she affects fancy hats*). [F *affecter* or L *affectare* aim at, frequent. of *afficere* (as AFFECT¹)]

affect³ /ˈæfekt/ n. *Psychol.* a feeling, emotion, or desire, esp. as leading to action. [G *Affekt* f. L *affectus* disposition f. *afficere* (as AFFECT¹)]

affectation /ˌæfekˈteɪʃ(ə)n/ n. **1** an assumed or contrived manner of behaviour, esp. in order to impress. **2** (foll. by *of*) a studied display. **3** pretence. [F *affectation* or L *affectatio* (as AFFECT²)]

affected /əˈfektɪd/ adj. **1** in senses of AFFECT¹, AFFECT². **2** artificially assumed or displayed; pretended (*an affected air of innocence*). **3** (of a person) full of affectation; artificial. **4** (prec. by adv.; often foll. by *towards*) disposed, inclined. □□ **affectedly** adv.

affection /əˈfekʃ(ə)n/ n. **1** (often foll. by *for, towards*) goodwill; fond or kindly feeling. **2** a disease; a diseased condition. **3** a mental state; an emotion. **4** a mental disposition. **5** the act or process of affecting or being affected. □□ **affectional** adj. (in sense 3). **affectionally** adv. [ME f. OF f. L *affectio -onis* (as AFFECT¹)]

affectionate /əˈfekʃ(ə)nət/ adj. loving, fond; showing love or tenderness. □□ **affectionately** adv. [F *affectionné* or med.L *affectionatus* (as AFFECTION)]

affective /əˈfektɪv/ adj. **1** concerning the affections; emotional. **2** *Psychol.* relating to affects. □□ **affectivity** /ˌæfekˈtɪvɪtɪ/ n. [F *affectif -ive* f. LL *affectivus* (as AFFECT¹)]

affenpinscher /ˈæfənˌpɪnʃə(r)/ n. **1** a dog of a small breed resembling the griffon. **2** this breed. [G f. *Affe* monkey + *Pinscher* terrier]

afferent /ˈæfərənt/ adj. *Physiol.* conducting inwards or towards (*afferent nerves; afferent vessels*) (opp. EFFERENT). [L *afferre* (as AD-, *ferre* bring)]

affiance /əˈfaɪəns/ v.tr. (usu. in *passive*) *literary* promise solemnly to give (a person) in marriage. [ME f. OF *afiancer* f. med.L *affidare* (as AD-, *fidus* trusty)]

affidavit /ˌæfɪˈdeɪvɪt/ n. a written statement confirmed by oath, for use as evidence in court. [med.L, = has stated on oath, f. *affidare*: see AFFIANCE]

affiliate v. & n. —v. /əˈfɪlɪˌeɪt/ **1** tr. (usu. in *passive*; foll. by *to, with*) attach or connect (a person or society) with a larger organization. **2** tr. (of an institution) adopt (persons as members, societies as branches). **3** intr. **a** (foll. by *to*) associate oneself with a society. **b** (foll. by *with*) associate oneself with a political party. —n. /əˈfɪlɪˌeɪt, -lɪɪt/ an affiliated person or organization. [med.L *affiliare* adopt (as AD-, *filius* son)]

affiliation /əˌfɪlɪˈeɪʃ(ə)n/ n. the act or process of affiliating or being affiliated. □ **affiliation order** *Brit.* a legal order that the man judged to be the father of an illegitimate child must help to support it. [F f. med.L *affiliatio* f. *affiliare*: see AFFILIATE]

affined /ə'faɪnd/ *adj.* related, connected. [*affine* (adj.) f. L *affinis* related: see AFFINITY]

affinity /ə'fɪnɪtɪ/ *n.* (*pl.* **-ies**) **1** (often foll. by *between*, or *disp.* to, *for*) a spontaneous or natural liking for or attraction to a person or thing. **2** relationship, esp. by marriage. **3** resemblance in structure between animals, plants, or languages. **4** a similarity of characters suggesting a relationship. **5** *Chem.* the tendency of certain substances to combine with others. [ME f. OF *afinité* f. L *affinitas -tatis* f. *affinis* related, lit. bordering on (as AD- + *finis* border)]

affirm /ə'fɜːm/ *v.* **1** *tr.* assert strongly; state as a fact. **2** *intr.* a *Law* make an affirmation. **b** make a formal declaration. **3** *tr. Law* confirm, ratify (a judgement). □□ **affirmatory** *adj.* **affirmer** *n.* [ME f. OF *afermer* f. L *affirmare* (as AD-, *firmus* strong)]

affirmation /ˌæfə'meɪʃ(ə)n/ *n.* **1** the act or process of affirming or being affirmed. **2** *Law* a solemn declaration by a person who conscientiously declines to take an oath. [F *affirmation* or L *affirmatio* (as AFFIRM)]

affirmative /ə'fɜːmətɪv/ *adj.* & *n.* —*adj.* **1** affirming; asserting that a thing is so. **2** (of a vote) expressing approval. —*n.* **1** an affirmative statement, reply, or word. **2** (prec. by *the*) a positive or affirming position. □ **affirmative action** esp. *US* action favouring those who often suffer from discrimination. **in the affirmative** with affirmative effect; so as to accept or agree to a proposal; yes (*the answer was in the affirmative*). □□ **affirmatively** *adv.* [ME f. OF *affirmatif -ive* f. LL *affirmativus* (as AFFIRM)]

affix *v.* & *n.* —*v.tr.* /ə'fɪks/ **1** (usu. foll. by *to*, *on*) attach, fasten. **2** add in writing (a signature or postscript). **3** impress (a seal or stamp). —*n.* /'æfɪks/ **1** an appendage; an addition. **2** *Gram.* an addition or element placed at the beginning (*prefix*) or end (*suffix*) of a root, stem, or word, or in the body of a word (*infix*), to modify its meaning. □□ **affixture** /ə'fɪkstʃə(r)/ *n.* [F *affixer*, *affixe* or med.L *affixare* frequent. of L *affigere* (as AD-, *figere fix-* fix)]

afflatus /ə'fleɪtəs/ *n.* a divine creative impulse; inspiration. [L f. *afflare* (as AD-, *flare flat-* to blow)]

afflict /ə'flɪkt/ *v.tr.* inflict bodily or mental suffering on. □ **afflicted with** suffering from. □□ **afflictive** *adj.* [ME f. L *afflictare*, or *afflict-* past part. stem of *affligere* (as AD-, *fligere flict-* dash)]

affliction /ə'flɪkʃ(ə)n/ *n.* **1** physical or mental distress, esp. pain or illness. **2** a cause of this. [ME f. OF f. L *afflictio -onis* (as AFFLICT)]

affluence /'æfluəns/ *n.* an abundant supply of money, commodities, etc.; wealth. [ME f. F. f. L *affluentia* f. *affluere*: see AFFLUENT]

affluent /'æfluənt/ *adj.* & *n.* —*adj.* **1** wealthy, rich. **2** abundant. **3** flowing freely or copiously. —*n.* a tributary stream. □ **affluent society** a society in which material wealth is widely distributed. □□ **affluently** *adv.* [ME f. OF f. L *affluere* (as AD-, *fluere flux-* flow)]

afflux /'æflʌks/ *n.* a flow towards a point; an influx. [med.L *affluxus* f. L *affluere*: see AFFLUENT]

afford /ə'fɔːd/ *v.tr.* **1** (prec. by *can* or *be able to*; often foll. by *to* + infin.) **a** have enough money, means, time, etc., for; be able to spare (*can afford £50*; *could not afford a holiday*; *can we afford to buy a new television?*). **b** be in a position to do something (esp. without risk of adverse consequences) (*can't afford to let him think so*). **2** yield a supply of. **3** provide (*affords a view of the sea*). □□ **affordable** *adj.* **affordability** /-'bɪlɪtɪ/ *n.* [ME f. OE *geforthian* promote (as Y-, FORTH), assim. to words in AF-]

afforest /ə'fɒrɪst, æ-/ *v.tr.* **1** convert into forest. **2** plant with trees. □□ **afforestation** /-'steɪʃ(ə)n/ *n.* [med.L *afforestare* (as AD-, *foresta* FOREST)]

affranchise /ə'fræntʃaɪz/ *v.tr.* release from servitude or an obligation. [OF *afranchir* (as ENFRANCHISE, with prefix A-³)]

affray /ə'freɪ/ *n.* a breach of the peace by fighting or rioting in public. [ME f. AF *afrayer* (v.) f. OF *esfreer* f. Rmc]

affricate /'æfrɪkət/ *n.* *Phonet.* a combination of a plosive with an immediately following fricative or spirant, e.g. *ch*. [L *affricare* (as AD-, *fricare* rub)]

affront /ə'frʌnt/ *n.* & *v.* —*n.* an open insult (*feel it an affront*; *offer an affront to*). —*v.tr.* **1** insult openly. **2** offend the modesty or

self-respect of. **3** face, confront. [ME f. OF *afronter* slap in the face, insult, ult. f. L *frons frontis* face]

Afghan /'æfgæn/ *n.* & *adj.* —*n.* **1 a** a native or national of Afghanistan. **b** a person of Afghan descent. **2** the official language of Afghanistan (also called PASHTO). **3** (**afghan**) a knitted and sewn woollen blanket or shawl. **4** (in full **Afghan coat**) a kind of sheepskin coat with the skin outside and usu. with a shaggy border. —*adj.* of or relating to Afghanistan or its people or language. □ **Afghan hound** a tall hunting dog with long silky hair. [Pashto *afghānī*]

Afghani /æf'gɑːnɪ/ *n.* (*pl.* **Afghanis**) the chief monetary unit of Afghanistan. [Pashto]

Afghanistan /æf'gænɪˌstæn/ a mountainous country in central Asia, dominated by the Hindu Kush, bordered by Iran to the west, Pakistan to the south and east, and the USSR to the north; pop. (est. 1988) 14,480,900; official languages, Pashto and a form of Persian (Dari); capital, Kabul. The principal industries are agriculture and sheep-raising. Conquered in the 4th c. BC by Alexander the Great, Afghanistan fell under Arab domination in the 7th c. AD, before being conquered by the Mongols. Part of the Indian Mughal empire, Afghanistan became independent in the mid-18th c. under Ahmen Khan, and in the 19th and early 20th c. became the focal point for conflicting Russian and British interests on the Northwest Frontier, the British fighting three wars against the Afghans between 1839 and 1919. A constitutional monarchy since 1930, Afghanistan became progressively politically unstable in the 1970s and was invaded by the Soviets in December 1979. A puppet regime was set up in Kabul but large parts of the country remained disaffected; the occupying forces were subjected to continuing attacks by Afghan guerrillas, while about 2–3 million people left as refugees. After the Soviet withdrawal in 1988–9 the regime remained strongly pro-Soviet, and the conflict persisted.

aficionado /əˌfɪsjə'nɑːdəʊ/ *n.* (*pl.* **-os**) a devotee of a sport or pastime (orig. of bullfighting). [Sp.]

afield /ə'fiːld/ *adv.* **1** away from home; to or at a distance (esp. *far afield*). **2** in the field. [OE (as A², FIELD)]

afire /ə'faɪə(r)/ *adv.* & *predic.adj.* **1** on fire. **2** intensely roused or excited.

aflame /ə'fleɪm/ *adv.* & *predic.adj.* **1** in flames. **2** = AFIRE 2.

aflatoxin /'æfləˌtɒksɪn/ *n.* *Chem.* any of several related toxic compounds produced by the fungus *Aspergillus flavus*, which cause tissue damage and cancer. [*Aspergillus* + *flavus* + TOXIN]

afloat /ə'fləʊt/ *adv.* & *predic.adj.* **1** floating in water or air. **2** at sea; on board ship. **3** out of debt or difficulty. **4** in general circulation; current. **5** full of or covered with a liquid. **6** in full swing. [OE (as A², FLOAT)]

AFM *abbr.* (in the UK) Air Force Medal.

afoot /ə'fʊt/ *adv.* & *predic.adj.* **1** in operation; progressing. **2** astir; on the move.

afore /ə'fɔː(r)/ *prep.* & *adv.* *archaic* before; previously; in front (of). [OE *onforan* (as A², FORE)]

afore- /ə'fɔː(r)/ *comb. form* before, previously (*aforementioned*; *aforesaid*).

aforethought /ə'fɔːθɔːt/ *adj.* premeditated (following a noun: *malice aforethought*).

a fortiori /ˌeɪ fɔːtɪ'ɔːraɪ/ *adv.* & *adj.* with a yet stronger reason (than a conclusion already accepted); more conclusively. [L]

afraid /ə'freɪd/ *predic.adj.* **1** (often foll. by *of*, or *that* or *lest* + clause) alarmed, frightened. **2** (foll. by *to* + infin.) unwilling or reluctant for fear of the consequences (*was afraid to go in*). □ **be afraid** (foll. by *that* + clause) *colloq.* admit or declare with (real or politely simulated) regret (*I'm afraid there's none left*). [ME, past part. of obs. *affray* (v.) f. AF *afrayer* f. OF *esfreer*]

afreet /'æfriːt/ *n.* (also **afrit**) a demon in Muslim mythology. [Arab. *'ifrīt*]

afresh /ə'freʃ/ *adv.* anew; with a fresh beginning. [A-² + FRESH]

Africa /'æfrɪkə/ the second-largest of the world's continents, a southward projection of the land mass which constitutes the Old World, surrounded by sea except where the isthmus of Suez joins it to Asia and divided almost exactly in two by the Equator, the northern half being dominated by the Sahara Desert. Its indigenous inhabitants are dark-skinned peoples varying in colour from light copper in the north to black in equatorial and southern parts. Egypt in the north-east was one of the world's earliest centres of civilization, and the Mediterranean coast has been subject to European influence since classical times, but much of the continent remained unknown to the outside world until voyages of discovery along the coast between the 15th and 17th centuries. The interior was explored and partitioned by European nations in the second half of the 19th c., Liberia and Ethiopia alone remaining under African rule. Since the Second World War most of the former colonies have secured their independence, but decolonization has left a legacy of instability which in many areas has yet to be satisfactorily resolved.

African /ˈæfrɪkən/ n. & adj. —n. **1** a native of Africa (esp. a dark-skinned person). **2** a person of African descent. —adj. of or relating to Africa. □ **African American** an American citizen of African origin or descent. **African elephant** the elephant, *Loxodonta africana*, of Africa, which is larger than the Indian elephant. **African violet** a saintpaulia, *Saintpaulia ionantha*, with heart-shaped velvety leaves and blue, purple, pink, or white flowers which resemble (but are unrelated to) English violets. They are native to tropical central and East Africa. [L *Africanus*]

Africana /ˌæfrɪˈkɑːnə/ n.pl. things connected with Africa.

Africander /ˌæfrɪˈkændə(r)/ n. (also **Afrikander**) one of a S. African breed of sheep or longhorn cattle. [Afrik. *Afrikaander* alt. of Du. *Afrikaner* after *Hollander* etc.]

African National Congress a South African political party and Black nationalist organization, founded in 1912, whose aim is to secure racial equality and Black representation in parliament. For many years it sponsored non-violent protests, strikes, marches, etc. In 1960, after police opened fire on a crowd of demonstrators at Sharpeville (see entry), the ANC and its more militant breakaway movement, the Pan-African Congress, were declared illegal by the South African government. Confronted by Afrikaner intransigence on racial issues, the ANC turned to sabotage and guerrilla warfare, operating both in and outside the Republic of South Africa, with its headquarters in Zambia. Prominent leaders include Oliver Tambo and Nelson Mandela. The ban on the ANC was lifted in February 1990, and discussions with the South African government began three months later; in August of that year the ANC leaders renounced violence directed against White rule.

Afrikaans /ˌæfrɪˈkɑːns/ n. a language that since 1925 has been one of the two official languages of the Republic of South Africa (the other being English). It is a development of 17th-c. Dutch brought to South Africa by settlers from Holland, and its subsequent isolation gave rise to various differences so that it is now considered to be a separate language. It is spoken by 4 million people—2 million White Afrikaners and about 2 million people of mixed race. [Du., = African]

Afrikaner /ˌæfrɪˈkɑːnə(r)/ n. **1** an Afrikaans-speaking White person in S. Africa, esp. one of Dutch descent. **2** Bot. a S. African species of *Gladiolus* or *Homoglossum*. [Afrik., formed as AFRICANDER]

afrit var. of AFREET.

Afro /ˈæfrəʊ/ adj. & n. —adj. (of a hairstyle) long and bushy, as naturally grown by some Blacks. —n. (pl. -os) an Afro hairstyle. [AFRO-, or abbr. of AFRICAN]

Afro- /ˈæfrəʊ/ comb. form African (*Afro-Asian*). [L *Afer Afr-* African]

Afro-American /ˌæfrəʊəˈmerɪkən/ adj. & n. —adj. of or relating to American Blacks or their culture. —n. an American Black.

Afro-Caribbean /ˌæfrəʊˌkærɪˈbiːən, -kəˈrɪbɪən/ n. & adj. —n. a person of African descent in or from the Caribbean. —adj. of or relating to the Afro-Caribbeans or their culture.

afrormosia /ˌæfrɔːˈməʊzɪə/ n. **1** an African tree, *Pericopsis* (formerly *Afrormosia*) *elata*, yielding a hard wood resembling teak and used for furniture. **2** this wood. [mod.L f. AFRO- + *Ormosia* genus of trees]

aft /ɑːft/ adv. Naut. & Aeron. at or towards the stern or tail. [prob. f. ME *baft*: see ABAFT]

after /ˈɑːftə(r)/ prep., conj., adv., & adj. —prep. **1 a** following in

time; later than (*after six months; after midnight; day after day*). **b** US in specifying time (*a quarter after eight*). **2** (with causal force) in view of (something that happened shortly before) (*after your behaviour tonight what do you expect?*). **3** (with concessive force) in spite of (*after all my efforts I'm no better off*). **4** behind (*shut the door you*). **5** in pursuit or quest of (*run after them; inquire after him; hanker after it; is after a job*). **6** about, concerning (*asked after her; asked after her health*). **7** in allusion to (*named him William after the prince*). **8** in imitation of (a person, word, etc.) (*a painting after Rubens; 'aesthete' is formed after 'athlete'*). **9** next in importance to (*the best book on the subject after mine*). **10** according to (*after a fashion*). —conj. in or at a time later than that when (*left after they arrived*). —adv. **1** later in time (*soon after; a week after*). **2** behind in place (*followed on after; look before and after*). —adj. **1** later, following (*in after years*). **2** Naut. nearer the stern (*after cabins; after mast; after-peak*). □ **after all 1** in spite of all that has happened or has been said etc. (*after all, what does it matter?*). **2** in spite of one's exertions, expectations, etc. (*they tried for an hour and failed after all; so you have come after all!*). **after-care** care of a patient after a stay in hospital or of a person on release from prison. **after-damp** choking gas left after an explosion of firedamp in a mine. **after-effect** an effect that follows after an interval or after the primary action of something. **after-image** an image retained by a sense-organ, esp. the eye, and producing a sensation after the cessation of the stimulus. **after one's own heart** see HEART. **after-taste** a taste remaining or recurring after eating or drinking. **after you** a formula used in offering precedence. [OE *æfter* f. Gmc]

afterbirth /ˈɑːftəˌbɜːθ/ n. Med. the placenta and foetal membranes discharged from the womb after childbirth.

afterburner /ˈɑːftəˌbɜːnə(r)/ n. an auxiliary burner in a jet engine to increase thrust.

afterglow /ˈɑːftəˌgləʊ/ n. a light or radiance remaining after its source has disappeared or been removed.

afterlife /ˈɑːftəˌlaɪf/ n. **1** Relig. life after death. **2** life at a later time.

aftermarket /ˈɑːftəˌmɑːkɪt/ n. **1** a market in spare parts and components. **2** US Stock Exch. a market in shares after their original issue.

aftermath /ˈɑːftəˌmæθ, -ˌmɑːθ/ n. **1** consequences; after-effects (*the aftermath of war*). **2** new grass growing after mowing or after a harvest. [AFTER adj. + *math* mowing f. OE *mæth* f. Gmc]

aftermost /ˈɑːftəˌməʊst/ adj. **1** last. **2** Naut. furthest aft. [AFTER adj. + -MOST]

afternoon /ˌɑːftəˈnuːn, attrib. ˈɑːft-/ n. & int. —n. **1** the time from noon or lunch-time to evening (*this afternoon; during the afternoon; afternoon tea*). **2** this time spent in a particular way (*had a lazy afternoon*). **3** a time compared with this, esp. the later part of something (*the afternoon of life*). —int. = good afternoon (see GOOD adj. 14).

afterpains /ˈɑːftəˌpeɪnz/ n.pl. pains caused by contraction of the womb after childbirth.

afters /ˈɑːftəz/ n.pl. Brit. colloq. the course following the main course of a meal.

aftershave /ˈɑːftəˌʃeɪv/ n. an astringent lotion for use after shaving.

afterthought /ˈɑːftəˌθɔːt/ n. an item or thing that is thought of or added later.

afterwards /ˈɑːftəwədz/ adv. (US **afterward**) later, subsequently. [OE *æftanwearde* adj. f. *æftan* AFTER + -WARD]

afterword /ˈɑːftəˌwɜːd/ n. concluding remarks in a book, esp. by a person other than its author.

Ag symb. Chem. the element silver. [L *argentum*]

ag- /əg/ prefix assim. form of AD- before g.

Aga /ˈɑːgə/ n. propr. a type of large cooking stove or range burning solid fuel or powered by gas, oil, or electricity. [Sw. f. Svenska Aktienbolaget Gasackumulator (Swedish Gas Accumulator Company), the original manufacturer]

aga /ˈɑːgə/ n. (in Muslim countries, esp. under the Ottoman Empire) a commander, a chief. [Turk. *ağa* master]

Agadir /ˌægəˈdɪə(r)/ a seaport and holiday resort on the Atlantic coast of Morocco; pop. (1982) 110,500.

Aga Khan /ˌɑːgə ˈkɑːn/ the leader of most of the Ismaili Muslims. Following the reign of the eighth Fatimid caliph a split in the Ismaili sect took place in 1094 over disagreement about the succession to the caliphate. The 'eastern' group, known as Nizaris after the candidate whom they supported, were based in Persia and known to those whom they opposed with violent methods as *Hashshīshīn* (hashish-takers) or, in its better-known form, 'Assassins'. The original *modus operandi* of the group did not survive; the Nizari community was reorganized in the 19th c. under the leadership of its imam (leader), known as the Aga Khan, who is traditionally based in the Indian subcontinent, although a much smaller remnant of the original Nizaris remains independent in Syria. The Aga Khan heads an enormous complex of services and welfare provisions for members of the community. [f. Turk. *aġa* master, *khān* ruler]

again /əˈgeɪn, əˈgen/ *adv.* **1** another time; once more. **2** as in a previous position or condition (*back again; home again; quite well again*). **3** in addition (*as much again; half as many again*). **4** further, besides (*again, what about the children?*). **5** on the other hand (*I might, and again I might not*). □ **again and again** repeatedly. [orig. a northern form of ME *ayen* etc., f. OE *ongēan, ongægn*, etc., f. Gmc]

against /əˈgeɪnst, əˈgenst/ *prep.* **1** in opposition to (*fight against the invaders; am against hanging; arson is against the law*). **2** into collision or in contact with (*ran against a rock; lean against the wall; up against a problem*). **3** to the disadvantage of (*his age is against him*). **4** in contrast to (*against a dark background; 99 as against 102 yesterday*). **5** in anticipation of or preparation for (*against his coming; against a rainy day; protected against the cold; warned against pickpockets*). **6** as a compensating factor to (*income against expenditure*). **7** in return for (*issued against payment of the fee*). □ **against the clock** see CLOCK[1] 3. **against the grain** see GRAIN. **against time** see TIME. [ME *ayenes* etc. f. *ayen* AGAIN + -t as in *amongst*: see AMONG]

agama /ˈægəmə/ *n.* any Old World lizard of the genus *Agama*. [Carib]

Agamemnon /ˌægəˈmemnən/ *Gk legend* king of Mycenae, or Argos, brother of Menelaus, and probably a historical person of the Mycenaean era. In the Homeric poems he is the commander-in-chief of the Greek expedition against Troy. On his return from Troy he was murdered by his wife Clytemnestra and her lover Aegisthus.

agamic /əˈgæmɪk/ *adj.* characterized by the absence of sexual reproduction. [as AGAMOUS + -IC]

agamogenesis /ˌægəməˈdʒenɪsɪs/ *n. Biol.* asexual reproduction. □□ **agamogenetic** /-dʒɪˈnetɪk/ *adj.* [as AGAMOUS + Gk *genesis* birth]

agamous /ˈægəməs/ *adj. Biol.* without (distinguishable) sexual organs. [LL *agamus* f. Gk *agamos* (as A-[1], *gamos* marriage)]

agapanthus /ˌægəˈpænθəs/ *n.* any African plant of the genus *Agapanthus*, esp. the ornamental African lily, with blue or white flowers. [mod.L f. Gk *agapē* love + *anthos* flower]

agape[1] /əˈgeɪp/ *adv. & predic.adj.* gaping, open-mouthed, esp. with wonder or expectation.

agape[2] /ˈægəˌpeɪ/ *n.* **1** a Christian feast in token of fellowship, esp. one held by early Christians in commemoration of the Last Supper. **2** *Theol.* Christian fellowship, esp. as distinct from erotic love. [Gk, = brotherly love]

agar /ˈeɪgɑː(r)/ *n.* (also **agar-agar** /ˌeɪgɑːˈeɪgɑː(r)/) a gelatinous substance obtained from any of various kinds of red seaweed and used in food, microbiological media, etc. [Malay]

agaric /ˈægərɪk/ *n.* any fungus of the family Agaricaceae, with cap and stalk, including the common edible mushroom. [L *agaricum* f. Gk *agarikon*]

Agassiz /ˈægəˌsiːz/, Jean Louis Rodolphe (1807–73), Swiss-born zoologist, geologist, and palaeontologist, who in 1837 was the first to propose that much of Europe had once been in the grip of an ice age. Agassiz lived in America from 1846 onwards and became an influential teacher and writer on many aspects of natural history. He was an opponent of Darwin's theory of evolution, holding that organisms were immutable and independent of each other.

agate /ˈægət/ *n.* **1** any of several varieties of hard usu. streaked chalcedony. **2** a coloured toy marble resembling this. [F *agate, -the*, f. L *achates* f. Gk *akhatēs*]

agave /əˈgeɪvɪ/ *n.* any plant of the genus *Agave*, with rosettes of narrow spiny leaves, and tall inflorescences, e.g. the American aloe, a tropical American plant with spiny leaves and a tall stem often 12 m (40 ft.) high, flowering only once, when the plant is mature, in 10–70 years. Some species are an important source of fibre (especially sisal) or of alcoholic beverages (the Mexican pulque) and spirit (mescal); a few are ornamental. [L f. Gk *Agauē*, proper name in myth f. *agauos* illustrious]

agaze /əˈgeɪz/ *adv.* gazing.

age /eɪdʒ/ *n. & v.* —*n.* **1 a** the length of time that a person or thing has existed or is likely to exist. **b** a particular point in or part of one's life, often as a qualification (*old age; voting age*). **2 a** *colloq.* (often in *pl.*) a long time (*took an age to answer; have been waiting for ages*). **b** a distinct period of the past (*golden age; Bronze age; Middle Ages*). **c** *Geol.* a period of time. **d** a generation. **3** the latter part of life; old age (*the peevishness of age*). —*v. (pres. part.* **ageing, aging**) **1** *intr.* show signs of advancing age (*has aged a lot recently*). **2** *intr.* grow old. **3** *intr.* mature. **4** *tr.* cause or allow to age. □ **age-long** lasting for a very long time. **age of consent** see CONSENT. **age of discretion** see DISCRETION. **age-old** having existed for a very long time. **come of age** reach adult status (esp. in Law at 18, formerly 21). **over age 1** old enough. **2** too old. **under age** not old enough, esp. not yet of adult status. [ME f. OF ult. f. L *aetas -atis* age]

-age /ɪdʒ/ *suffix* forming nouns denoting: **1** an action (*breakage; spillage*). **2** a condition or function (*bondage; a peerage*). **3** an aggregate or number of (*coverage; the peerage; acreage*). **4** fees payable for; the cost of using (*postage*). **5** the product of an action (*dosage; wreckage*). **6** a place; an abode (*anchorage; orphanage; parsonage*). [OF ult. f. L *-aticum* neut. of adj. suffix -ATIC]

aged *adj.* **1** /eɪdʒd/ **a** of the age of (*aged ten*). **b** that has been subjected to ageing. **c** (of a horse) over six years old. **2** /ˈeɪdʒɪd/ having lived long; old.

ageing /ˈeɪdʒɪŋ/ *n.* (also **aging**) **1** growing old. **2** giving the appearance of advancing age. **3** a change of properties occurring in some metals after heat treatment or cold working.

ageism /ˈeɪdʒɪz(ə)m/ *n.* (also **agism**) prejudice or discrimination on the grounds of age. □□ **ageist** *adj. & n.* (also **agist**).

ageless /ˈeɪdʒlɪs/ *adj.* **1** never growing or appearing old or outmoded. **2** eternal, timeless.

agency /ˈeɪdʒənsɪ/ *n. (pl.* **-ies**) **1 a** the business or establishment of an agent (*employment agency*). **b** the function of an agent. **2 a** active operation; action (*free agency*). **b** intervening action (*fertilized by the agency of insects*). **c** action personified (*an invisible agency*). **3** a specialized department of the United Nations. [med.L *agentia* f. L *agere* do]

agenda /əˈdʒendə/ *n.* **1** (*pl.* **agendas**) **a** a list of items of business to be considered at a meeting. **b** a series of things to be done. **2** (as *pl.*) **a** items to be considered. **b** things to be done. ¶ Now very common as a countable noun in sense 1 (cf. DATA, MEDIA). [L, neut. pl. of gerundive of *agere* do]

agent /ˈeɪdʒ(ə)nt/ *n.* **1 a** a person who acts for another in business, politics, etc. (*estate agent; insurance agent*). **b** a spy. **2 a** a person or thing that exerts power or produces an effect. **b** the cause of a natural force or effect on matter (*oxidizing agent*). **c** such a force or effect. □ **agent-general** a representative of an Australian State or Canadian province, usu. in London. □□ **agential** /əˈdʒenʃ(ə)l/ *adj.* [L *agent-* part. stem of *agere* do]

agent provocateur /ˌɑːʒã prəˌvɒkəˈtɜː(r)/ *n.* (*pl.* **agents provocateurs** pronunc. same) a person employed to detect suspected offenders by tempting them to overt self-incriminating action. [F, = provocative agent]

agglomerate *v., n., & adj.* —*v.tr. & intr.* /əˈglɒməˌreɪt/ **1** collect into a mass. **2** accumulate in a disorderly way. —*n.* /əˈglɒmərət/ **1** a mass or collection of things. **2** *Geol.* a mass of large volcanic fragments bonded under heat (cf. CONGLOMERATE). —*adj.* /əˈglɒmərət/ collected into a mass. □□ **agglomeration** /-ˈreɪʃ(ə)n/ *n.* **agglomerative** /əˈglɒmərətɪv/ *adj.* [L *agglomerare* (as AD-, *glomerare* f. *glomus -meris* ball)]

agglutinate /əˈgluːtɪˌneɪt/ *v.* **1** *tr.* unite as with glue. **2** *tr. & intr.*

Biol. cause or undergo adhesion (of bacteria, erythrocytes, etc.). **3** *tr.* (of language) combine (simple words) without change of form to express compound ideas. □□ **agglutination** /-ˈneɪʃ(ə)n/ *n.* **agglutinative** /əˈgluːtɪnətɪv/ *adj.* [L *agglutinare* (as AD-, *glutinare* f. *gluten -tinis* glue)]

agglutinin /əˈgluːtɪnɪn/ *n. Biol.* a substance or antibody causing agglutination. [AGGLUTINATE + -IN]

aggrandize /əˈgrændaɪz/ *v.tr.* (also **-ise**) **1** increase the power, rank, or wealth of (a person or State). **2** cause to appear greater than is the case. □□ **aggrandizement** /-dɪzmənt/ *n.* **aggrandizer** *n.* [F *agrandir* (stem *agrandiss-*), prob. f. It. *aggrandire* f. L *grandis* large: assim. to verbs in -IZE]

aggravate /ˈægrəveɪt/ *v.tr.* **1** increase the gravity of (an illness, offence, etc.). **2** *disp.* annoy, exasperate (a person). □□ **aggravation** /-ˈveɪʃ(ə)n/ *n.* [L *aggravare aggravat-* make heavy f. *gravis* heavy]

aggregate *n., adj., & v.* —*n.* /ˈægrɪgət/ **1** a collection of, or the total of, disparate elements. **2** pieces of crushed stone, gravel, etc. used in making concrete. **3 a** *Geol.* a mass of minerals formed into solid rock. **b** a mass of particles. —*adj.* /ˈægrɪgət/ **1** (of disparate elements) collected into one mass. **2** constituted by the collection of many units into one body. **3** *Bot.* **a** (of fruit) formed from several carpels derived from the same flower (e.g. raspberry). **b** (of a species) closely related. —*v.* /ˈægrɪˌgeɪt/ **1** *tr.* & *intr.* collect together; combine into one mass. **2** *tr. colloq.* amount to (a specified total). **3** *tr.* unite (*was aggregated to the group*). □ **in the aggregate** as a whole. □□ **aggregation** /-ˈgeɪʃ(ə)n/ *n.* **aggregative** /ˈægrɪˌgeɪtɪv/ *adj.* [L *aggregare aggregat-* herd together (as AD-, *grex gregis* flock)]

aggression /əˈgreʃ(ə)n/ *n.* **1** the act or practice of attacking without provocation, esp. beginning a quarrel or war. **2** an unprovoked attack. **3** self-assertiveness; forcefulness. **4** *Psychol.* hostile or destructive tendency or behaviour. [F *agression* or L *aggressio* attack f. *aggredi aggress-* (as AD-, *gradi* walk)]

aggressive /əˈgresɪv/ *adj.* **1** of a person: **a** given to aggression; openly hostile. **b** forceful; self-assertive. **2** (of an act) offensive, hostile. **3** of aggression. □□ **aggressively** *adv.* **aggressiveness** *n.*

aggressor /əˈgresə(r)/ *n.* a person or State that attacks without provocation. [L (as AGGRESSION)]

aggrieved /əˈgriːvd/ *adj.* having a grievance. □□ **aggrievedly** /-vɪdlɪ/ *adv.* [ME, past part. of *aggrieve* f. OF *agrever* make heavier (as AD-, GRIEVE¹)]

aggro /ˈægrəʊ/ *n. sl.* **1** aggressive troublemaking. **2** trouble, difficulty. [abbr. of AGGRAVATION (see AGGRAVATE) or AGGRESSION]

aghast /əˈgɑːst/ *adj.* (usu. *predic.*; often foll. by *at*) filled with dismay or consternation. [ME, past part. of obs. *agast, gast* frighten: see GHASTLY]

Aghios Nikolaos /ˈaɪɒs ˌnɪkɒˈlaɪɒs/ (Greek **Ayios Nikólaos**) a holiday resort on the north coast of Crete, east of Heraklion; pop. (1981) 8,100.

agile /ˈædʒaɪl/ *adj.* quick-moving, nimble, active. □□ **agilely** *adv.* **agility** /əˈdʒɪlɪtɪ/ *n.* [F f. L *agilis* f. *agere* do]

agin /əˈgɪn/ *prep. colloq.* or *dial.* against. [corrupt. of AGAINST or synonymous *again* obs. prep.]

Agincourt /ˈædʒɪnˌkɔː(r), -ˌkɔːt/ a village of NW France, scene of a great English victory (1415) in the Hundred Years War, when a small invading army under Henry V defeated a much larger French force. Indiscipline, muddy ground, and Henry's sound defensive tactics led to heavy losses among the heavily armoured French knights. Following his victory, Henry was able to occupy Normandy and consolidate his claim to the French throne by marrying Catherine, daughter of the mad king Charles VI.

aging var. of AGEING.

agio /ˈædʒɪəʊ/ *n.* (pl. **agios**) **1** the percentage charged on the exchange of one currency, or one form of money, into another more valuable. **2** the excess value of one currency over another. **3** money-exchange business. [It. *aggio*]

agism var. of AGEISM.

agitate /ˈædʒɪˌteɪt/ *v.* **1** *tr.* disturb or excite (a person or feelings). **2** *intr.* (often foll. by *for, against*) stir up interest or concern, esp.

publicly (*agitated for tax reform*). **3** *tr.* shake or move, esp. briskly. □□ **agitatedly** *adv.* [L *agitare agitat-* frequent. of *agere* drive]

agitation /ˌædʒɪˈteɪʃ(ə)n/ *n.* **1** the act or process of agitating or being agitated. **2** mental anxiety or concern. [F *agitation* or L *agitatio* (as AGITATE)]

agitato /ˌædʒɪˈtɑːtəʊ/ *adv. & adj. Mus.* in an agitated manner. [It.]

agitator /ˈædʒɪˌteɪtə(r)/ *n.* **1** a person who agitates, esp. publicly for a cause etc. **2** an apparatus for shaking or mixing liquid etc. [L (as AGITATE)]

agitprop /ˈædʒɪtˌprɒp, ˈæg-/ *n.* the dissemination of Communist political propaganda, esp. in plays, films, books, etc. [Russ. (as AGITATION, PROPAGANDA)]

aglet /ˈæglɪt/ *n.* **1** a metal tag attached to each end of a shoelace etc. **2** = AIGUILLETTE. [ME f. F *aiguillette* small needle, ult. f. L *acus* needle]

agley /əˈglɪ, -ˈliː/ *adv. Sc.* askew, awry. [A² + Sc. *gley* squint]

aglow /əˈgləʊ/ *adv. & adj.* —*adv.* glowingly. —*predic.adj.* glowing.

AGM *abbr.* annual general meeting.

agma /ˈægmə/ *n.* **1** the sound represented by the symbol /ŋ/. **2** this symbol. [Gk, lit. 'fragment']

agnail /ˈægneɪl/ *n.* **1** a piece of torn skin at the root of a fingernail. **2** the soreness resulting from this. [OE *angnægl* f. *nægl* NAIL *n.* 1: cf. HANGNAIL]

agnate /ˈægneɪt/ *adj. & n.* —*adj.* **1** descended esp. by male line from the same male ancestor (cf. COGNATE). **2** descended from the same forefather; of the same clan or nation. **3** of the same nature; akin. —*n.* one who is descended esp. by male line from the same male ancestor. □□ **agnatic** /-ˈnætɪk/ *adj.* **agnation** /-ˈneɪʃ(ə)n/ *n.* [L *agnatus* f. *ad* to + *gnasci* be born f. stem *gen-* beget]

Agnes /ˈægnɪs/, St (venerated as a virgin in Rome since the 4th c.) The legends of her martyrdom vary. Her emblem is a lamb (L *agnus*), and on her feast day (21 Jan.) two lambs providing wool for the pallium are blessed in her basilica in Rome.

Agni /ˈægni/ *Hinduism* the Vedic god of fire, the priest of the gods and the god of the priests. As mediator between gods and men, he takes offerings to the gods in the smoke of sacrifice and returns to the earth as lightning. [Skr., = fire, cogn. with L *ignis*]

agnosia /ægˈnəʊsɪə/ *n. Med.* the loss of the ability to interpret sensations. [mod.L f. Gk *agnōsia* ignorance]

agnostic /ægˈnɒstɪk/ *n. & adj.* —*n.* a person who believes that nothing is known, or can be known, of the existence or nature of God or of anything beyond material phenomena. —*adj.* of or relating to agnostics. □□ **agnosticism** /-ˌsɪz(ə)m/ *n.* [A-¹ + GNOSTIC]

Agnus Dei /ˌægnʊs ˈdeɪiː/ *n.* **1** a figure of a lamb bearing a cross or flag, as an emblem of Christ. **2** the part of the Roman Catholic mass beginning with the words 'Lamb of God'. [L, = lamb of God]

ago /əˈgəʊ/ *adv.* earlier, before the present (*ten years ago; long ago*). ¶ Note the construction *it is 10 years ago that* (not *since*) *I saw them*. [ME (*ago, agone*), past part. of obs. *ago* (v.) (as A-², GO¹)]

agog /əˈgɒg/ *adv. & adj.* —*adv.* eagerly, expectantly. —*predic.adj.* eager, expectant. [F *en gogues* f. *en* in + pl. of *gogue* fun]

à gogo /əˈgəʊgəʊ/ *adv.* in abundance (*whisky à gogo*). [F]

agonic /əˈgɒnɪk/ *adj.* having or forming no angle. □ **agonic line** a line passing through the two poles, along which a magnetic needle points directly north or south. [Gk *agōnios* without angle (as A-¹, *gōnia* angle)]

agonistic /ˌægəˈnɪstɪk/ *adj.* polemical, combative. □□ **agonistically** *adv.* [LL *agonisticus* f. Gk *agōnistikos* f. *agōnistēs* contestant f. *agōn* contest]

agonize /ˈægəˌnaɪz/ *v.* (also **-ise**) **1** *intr.* (often foll. by *over*) undergo (esp. mental) anguish; suffer agony. **2** *tr.* cause agony to. **3** *tr.* (as **agonized** *adj.*) expressing agony (*an agonized look*). **4** *intr.* struggle, contend. □□ **agonizingly** *adv.* [F *agoniser* or LL *agonizare* f. Gk *agōnizomai* contend f. *agōn* contest]

agony /ˈægənɪ/ *n.* (pl. **-ies**) **1** extreme mental or physical suffering. **2** a severe struggle. □ **agony aunt** *colloq.* a person (esp. a woman) who answers letters in an agony column. **agony column** *colloq.* **1** a column in a newspaper or magazine offering personal advice to readers who write in. **2** = *personal column.* [ME f. OF *agonie* or LL f. Gk *agōnia* f. *agōn* contest]

agoraphobe /ˈægərəˌfəʊb/ *n.* a person who suffers from agoraphobia.

agoraphobia /ˌægərəˈfəʊbɪə/ *n. Psychol.* an abnormal fear of open spaces or public places. □□ **agoraphobic** *adj. & n.* [mod.L f. Gk *agora* place of assembly, market-place + -PHOBIA]

agouti /əˈguːtɪ/ *n.* (also **aguti**) (*pl.* **agoutis**) any burrowing rodent of the genus *Dasyprocta* or *Myoprocta* of Central and S. America, related to the guinea-pig. [F *agouti* or Sp. *aguti* f. Tupi *aguti*]

AGR *abbr.* advanced gas-cooled (nuclear) reactor.

Agra /ˈɑːgrə/ a city (pop. (1981) 770,000) on the River Jumna in Uttar Pradesh, capital of the Mogul emperors from the early 16th c. to the mid-17th c. It is the site of the Taj Mahal.

agrarian /əˈgreərɪən/ *adj. & n.* —*adj.* **1** of or relating to the land or its cultivation. **2** relating to landed property. —*n.* a person who advocates a redistribution of landed property. [L *agrarius* f. *ager agri* field]

Agrarian Revolution *n.* the transformation of British agriculture during the 18th c., characterized by the acceleration of enclosures (see entry) and the consequent decline of the open-field system, as well as by the introduction of technological innovations such as the seed drill and the scientific rotation of crops.

agree /əˈgriː/ *v.* (**agrees, agreed, agreeing**) **1** *intr.* hold a similar opinion (*I agree with you about that; they agreed that it would rain*). **2** *intr.* (often foll. by *to*, or *to* + *infin.*) consent (*agreed to the arrangement; agreed to go*). **3** *intr.* (often foll. by *with*) **a** become or be in harmony. **b** suit; be good for (*caviar didn't agree with him*). **c** *Gram.* have the same number, gender, case, or person as. **4** *tr.* reach agreement about (*agreed a price*). **5** *tr.* consent to or approve of (terms, a proposal, etc.). **6** *tr.* bring (things, esp. accounts) into harmony. **7** *intr.* (foll. by *on*) decide by mutual consent (*agreed on a compromise*). □ **agree to differ** leave a difference of opinion etc. unresolved. **be agreed** have reached the same opinion. [ME f. OF *agreer* ult. f. L *gratus* pleasing]

agreeable /əˈgriːəb(ə)l/ *adj.* **1** (often foll. by *to*) pleasing. **2** (often foll. by *to*) (of a person) willing to agree (*was agreeable to going*). **3** (foll. by *to*) conformable. □□ **agreeableness** *n.* **agreeably** *adv.* [ME f. OF *agreable* f. *agreer* AGREE]

agreement /əˈgriːmənt/ *n.* **1** the act of agreeing; the holding of the same opinion (*reached agreement*). **2** mutual understanding. **3** an arrangement between parties as to a course of action etc. **4** *Gram.* having the same number, gender, case, or person. **5** a state of being harmonious. [ME f. OF (as AGREE)]

agribusiness /ˈægrɪˌbɪznɪs/ *n.* **1** agriculture conducted on strictly commercial principles, esp. using advanced technology. **2** an organization engaged in this. **3** the group of industries dealing with the produce of, and services to, farming. □□ **agribusinessman** /-ˈbɪznɪsmən/ *n.* (*pl.* **-men**). [AGRICULTURE + BUSINESS]

Agricola /əˈgrɪkələ/, Gnaeus Julius (40–93), Roman senator and general, whose career is known chiefly from his *Life* by his son-in-law Tacitus. Governor of Britain from 78, he completed the subjugation of Wales, advanced into Scotland (where he built a number of forts), and defeated the Caledonian Highland tribes at the battle of Mons Graupius. His fleet circumnavigated Britain.

agriculture /ˈægrɪˌkʌltʃə(r)/ *n.* the science or practice of cultivating the soil and rearing animals. (See below.) □□ **agricultural** /-ˈkʌltʃər(ə)l/ *adj.* **agriculturalist** /-ˈkʌltʃərəlɪst/ *n.* **agriculturally** /-ˈkʌltʃərəlɪ/ *adv.* **agriculturist** /-ˈkʌltʃərɪst/ *n.* [F *agriculture* or L *agricultura* f. *ager agri* field + *cultura* CULTURE]

The beginnings of agriculture date from the neolithic period, perhaps 9,000 years ago, and the gradual change from a life-style in which people obtained their food by hunting wild animals and gathering such berries, roots, etc., as nature provided to one in which they tended the animals they had caught, and planted crops in order to reap a harvest, is associated with the establishment of settled communities, as in the Tigris–Euphrates valley and beside the Nile. The type and development of farming have varied in different parts of the world, and methods used in one place have been (and still are) sometimes centuries ahead of

those of another. In Britain, the system of land-holding whereby each man held scattered strips in large unfenced areas was replaced in the 18th c. (see AGRARIAN REVOLUTION) by enclosed fields, enabling individual farmers to make use of new implements and improve the quality of cattle and sheep by careful stock-breeding. Labour-saving machinery and improved methods of transport made increased production possible, important inventions being the reaping-machine, reaper-and-binder, combine harvester, and tractor, use of pesticides and fertilizers increased the yield from crops while advances in the understanding of animal health did the same for livestock. In the 20th c. experiments in farm organization have aimed at greater efficiency in the use of both labour and land (e.g. in systems of collective farming, as in the USSR). Over-use of intensive methods of farming, however, has brought its own problems of soil erosion and environmental pollution.

agrimony /ˈægrɪmənɪ/ *n.* (*pl.* **-ies**) any perennial plant of the genus *Agrimonia*, esp. *A. eupatoria* with small yellow flowers. [ME f. OF *aigremoine* f. L *agrimonia* alt. of *argemonia* f. Gk *argemōnē* poppy]

Agrippa[1] /əˈgrɪpə/, Marcus Vipsanius (64/3–12 BC), the right-hand man of Augustus (whose daughter Julia was his third wife) during the latter's rise to power and principate, and thrice consul. Indispensable in military and civilian affairs, he played an important part in the naval victories over Sextus Pompeius and Mark Antony, and held commands in western and eastern provinces. His many buildings in Rome (paid for out of his own pocket) included baths, aqueducts, and sewers.

Agrippa[2] /əˈgrɪpə/ = HEROD AGRIPPA.

agro- /ˈægrəʊ/ *comb. form* agricultural (*agro-climatic; agro-ecological*). [Gk *agros* field]

agrochemical /ˌægrəʊˈkemɪk(ə)l/ *n.* a chemical used in agriculture.

agronomy /əˈgrɒnəmɪ/ *n.* the science of soil management and crop production. □□ **agronomic** /ˌægrəˈnɒmɪk/ *adj.* **agronomical** /ˌægrəˈnɒmɪk(ə)l/ *adj.* **agronomically** /ˌægrəˈnɒmɪkəlɪ/ *adv.* **agronomist** *n.* [F *agronomie* f. *agronome* agriculturist f. Gk *agros* field + -*nomos f. nemō* arrange]

aground /əˈgraʊnd/ *predic.adj. & adv.* (of a ship) on or on to the bottom of shallow water (*be aground; run aground*). [ME f. A[2] + GROUND[1]]

Aguascalientes /ˌɑːgwɒskælˈjenteɪz/ **1** a State of central Mexico; pop. (est. 1988) 684,250. **2** its capital city, a health resort noted for its mineral waters.

ague /ˈeɪgjuː/ *n.* **1** *hist.* a malarial fever, with cold, hot, and sweating stages. **2** a shivering fit. □□ **agued** *adj.* **aguish** *adj.* [ME f. OF f. med.L *acuta* (*febris*) acute (fever)]

aguti var. of AGOUTI.

AH *abbr.* in the year of the Hegira (AD 622); of the Muslim era. [L *anno Hegirae*]

ah /ɑː/ *int.* expressing surprise, pleasure, sudden realization, resignation, etc. ¶ The sense depends much on intonation. [ME f. OF *a*]

aha /ɑːˈhɑː, əˈhɑː/ *int.* expressing surprise, triumph, mockery, irony, etc. ¶ The sense depends much on intonation. [ME f. AH + HA]

Ahaggar Mountains see HOGGAR MOUNTAINS.

ahead /əˈhed/ *adv.* **1** further forward in space or time. **2** in the lead; further advanced (*ahead on points*). **3** in the line of one's forward motion (*roadworks ahead*). **4** straight forwards. □ **ahead of 1** further forward or advanced than. **2** in the line of the forward motion of. [orig. *Naut.*, f. A[2] + HEAD]

ahem /əˈhəm, əˈhem/ (not usu. clearly articulated) *int.* used to attract attention, gain time, or express disapproval. [lengthened form of HEM[2]]

ahimsa /əˈhɪmsɑː/ *n.* (in the Hindu, Buddhist, and Jainist tradition) respect for all living things and avoidance of violence towards others both in thought and deed. [Skr. f. *a* without + *himsa* injury]

Ahmadabad /ˈɑːmædəˌbæd/ an industrial city in the State of Gujarat in western India; pop. (1981) 2,515,000.

æ cat ɑː arm e bed ɜː her ɪ sit iː see ɒ hot ɔː saw ʌ run ʊ put uː too ə ago aɪ my

ahoy /ə'hɔɪ/ int. Naut. a call used in hailing. [AH + HOY[1]]

Ahriman /'ɑːrɪmən/ the evil spirit in the dualistic doctrine of Zoroastrianism. [Pers., f. Avestan angramainya dark or destructive spirit]

à huis clos /ˌɑː wiː 'kləʊ/ adv. in private. [F, = with closed doors]

Ahura Mazda /əˌhʊərə 'mæzdə/ (later called Ormazd) the creator god of ancient Iran (and, in particular, of Zoroastrianism), the force for good and the opponent of Ahriman. [Avestan, = the living wise one]

Ahvaz /ɑː'vɑːz/ (Arabic **Ahwāz**) the capital of the oil-producing province of Khuzestan in western Iran; pop. (1986) 580,000.

AI abbr. artificial insemination.

ai /'ɑːiː/ n. (pl. **ais**) the three-toed sloth of S. America, of the genus Bradypus. [Tupi ai, repr. its cry]

AID abbr. artificial insemination by donor.

aid /eɪd/ n. & v. —n. 1 help. 2 financial or material help, esp. given by one country to another. 3 a material source of help (teaching aid). 4 a person or thing that helps. 5 hist. a grant of subsidy or tax to a king. —v.tr. 1 (often foll. by to + infin.) help. 2 promote or encourage (sleep will aid recovery). □ **in aid of** in support of. **what's this** (or **all this**) **in aid of?** colloq. what is the purpose of this? [ME f. OF aide, aidier, ult. f. L adjuvare (as AD-, juvare jut- help)]

-aid /eɪd/ comb. form denoting an organization or event that raises money for charity (school aid). [20th c.: orig. in Band Aid, rock musicians campaigning for famine relief]

aide /eɪd/ n. 1 an aide-de-camp. 2 esp. US an assistant. 3 an unqualified assistant to a social worker. [abbr.]

aide-de-camp /ˌeɪddə'kɑ̃/ n. (pl. **aides-de-camp** pronunc. same) an officer acting as a confidential assistant to a senior officer. [F]

aide-mémoire /ˌeɪdme'mwɑː(r)/ n. (pl. **aides-mémoire** pronunc. same) **1 a** an aid to the memory. **b** a book or document meant to aid the memory. **2** Diplomacy a memorandum. [F f. aider to help + mémoire memory]

Aids /eɪdz/ n. (also **AIDS**) acquired immune deficiency syndrome, an often fatal syndrome caused by a virus transmitted in the blood, marked by severe loss of resistance to infection. The condition was first identified and named in the early 1980s but is thought to have existed considerably earlier. □ **Aids-related complex** the symptoms of a person affected with the Aids virus without necessarily developing the disease. [abbr.]

aigrette /'eɪgret, eɪ'gret/ n. 1 an egret. 2 its white plume. 3 a tuft of feathers or hair. 4 a spray of gems or similar ornament. [F]

Aigues-Mortes /eɪg'mɔːt/ a town in SE France, in the Rhone delta; pop. (1982) 4,106. Its name is derived from the Latin aquae mortuae (= dead waters), referring to the saline marshland which surrounds it. The site was chosen by St Louis (Louis IX) to serve as the military base and embarkation port for his two Crusades (1248 and 1270). He began to construct fortifications and his son Philip the Bold (1245–85) completed the vast rectangle of battlemented walls strengthened by 15 towers. The harbour has long been silted up.

aiguille /eɪ'gwiːl/ n. a sharp peak of rock, esp. in the Alps. [F: see AGLET]

aiguillette /ˌeɪgwɪ'let/ n. a tagged point hanging from the shoulder on the breast of some uniforms. [F: see AGLET]

AIH abbr. artificial insemination by husband.

aikido /'aɪkɪˌdəʊ/ n. a Japanese form of self-defence making use of the attacker's own movements without causing injury. [Jap. f. ai mutual + ki mind + dō way]

ail /eɪl/ v. 1 tr. archaic (only in 3rd person interrog. or indefinite constructions) trouble or afflict in mind or body (what ails him?). 2 intr. (usu. **be ailing**) be ill. [OE egl(i)an f. egle troublesome]

ailanthus /eɪ'lænθəs/ n. a tall deciduous tree of the genus Ailanthus, esp. A. altissima, native to China and Australasia. [mod.L ailantus f. Ambonese aylanto]

aileron /'eɪləˌrɒn/ n. a hinged surface in the trailing edge of an aeroplane wing, used to control lateral balance. [F, dimin. of aile wing f. L ala]

ailing /'eɪlɪŋ/ adj. 1 ill, esp. chronically. 2 in poor condition.

ailment /'eɪlmənt/ n. an illness, esp. a minor one.

aim /eɪm/ v. & n. —v. 1 intr. (foll. by at + verbal noun, or to + infin.) intend or try (aim at winning; aim to win). 2 tr. (usu. foll. by at) direct or point (a weapon, remark, etc.). 3 intr. take aim. 4 intr. (foll. by at, for) seek to attain or achieve. —n. 1 a purpose, a design, an object aimed at. 2 the directing of a weapon, missile, etc., at an object. □ **take aim** direct a weapon etc. at an object. [ME f. OF ult. f. L aestimare reckon]

aimless /'eɪmlɪs/ adj. without aim or purpose. □□ **aimlessly** adv. **aimlessness** n.

ain't /eɪnt/ contr. colloq. **1** am not; are not; is not (you ain't doing it right; she ain't nice). **2** has not; have not (we ain't seen him). ¶ Usually regarded as an uneducated use, and unacceptable in spoken and written English, except to represent dialect speech. [contr. of are not]

Aintree /'eɪntriː/ a suburb of Liverpool, in Merseyside, site of a racecourse over which the Grand National (see entry) has been run since 1839.

Ainu /'aɪnʊ/ n. (pl. same or **Ainus**) a member of the non-Mongoloid aboriginal inhabitants of the Japanese archipelago whose physical characteristics (light skin colour, round eyes, and exceptionally thick, wavy hair) set them apart dramatically from the majority population of the islands and have stimulated much speculation as to their possible Caucasoid origin. Archaeological evidence suggests that the Ainu were resident in the area as early as 5000 BC, thereby predating the great Mongoloid expansion. Forced by Japanese expansion to retreat to the northernmost islands (i.e. Hokkaido and Sakhalin) the Ainu are on the verge of cultural extinction and now number only a few hundred pure-blooded individuals. Assimilation has resulted in a shift from hunting and gathering to sedentary agriculture, and the Japanese language has all but replaced the unique Ainu language which is unrelated to any known form of speech. Traditional practices such as female tattooing and the iomande (bear sacrifice) have also declined as a result of Japanese cultural influence. [Ainu, = man]

air /eə(r)/ n. & v. —n. 1 an invisible gaseous substance surrounding the earth, a mixture mainly of oxygen and nitrogen. **2 a** the earth's atmosphere. **b** the free or unconfined space in the atmosphere (birds of the air; in the open air). **c** the atmosphere as a place where aircraft operate. **3 a** a distinctive impression or characteristic (an air of absurdity). **b** one's manner or bearing, esp. a confident one (with a triumphant air; does things with an air). **c** (esp. in pl.) an affected manner; pretentiousness (gave himself airs; airs and graces). **4** Mus. a melody; a melodious composition. **5** a breeze or light wind. —v.tr. **1** warm (washed laundry) to remove damp, esp. at a fire or in a heated cupboard. **2** expose (a room etc.) to the open air; ventilate. **3** express publicly (an opinion, grievance, etc.). **4** parade; show ostentatiously (esp. qualities). **5** refl. go out in the fresh air. □ **air bag** a safety device that fills with air on impact to protect the occupants of a vehicle in a collision. **air-bed** an inflatable mattress. **air bladder** a bladder or sac filled with air in fish or some plants (cf. swim-bladder). **air brake** a brake worked by air pressure. **2** a movable flap or other device on an aircraft to reduce its speed. **air-brick** a brick perforated with small holes for ventilation. **air-bridge** a portable bridge or walkway put against an aircraft door. **Air Chief Marshal** an RAF officer of high rank, below Marshal of the RAF and above Air Marshal. **Air Commodore** an RAF officer next above Group Captain. **air-conditioned** (of a room, building, etc.) equipped with air-conditioning. **air-conditioner** an air-conditioning apparatus. **air-conditioning 1** a system for regulating the humidity, ventilation, and temperature in a building. **2** the apparatus for this. **air-cooled** cooled by means of a current of air. **air corridor** = CORRIDOR 4. **air-cushion 1** an inflatable cushion. **2** the layer of air supporting a hovercraft or similar vehicle. **air force** a branch of the armed forces concerned with fighting or defence in the air. **air hostess** a stewardess in a passenger aircraft. **air lane** a path or course regularly used by aircraft (cf. LANE 4). **air letter** a sheet of light paper forming a letter for sending by airmail. **air line** a pipe supplying air, esp. to a diver. **Air Marshal** an RAF officer of high rank, below Air Chief Marshal and above Air Vice-Marshal. **Air Officer** any RAF officer above the rank of Group Captain. **air plant** a plant growing naturally without soil. **air pocket** an apparent vacuum in the air causing an aircraft to drop suddenly. **air power** the ability to defend and attack by means of aircraft, missiles, etc. **air pump** a device for pumping air into or out of a vessel. **air raid** see separate entry. **air rifle** a rifle using compressed air to propel pellets. **air sac** an extension of the lungs in birds or the tracheae in insects. **air-sea rescue** rescue from the sea by aircraft. **air speed** the speed of an aircraft relative to the air through which it is moving. **air terminal** a building in a city or town to which passengers report and which serves as a base for transport to and from an airport. **air time** time allotted for a broadcast. **air-to-air** from one aircraft to another in flight **air traffic controller** an airport official who controls air traffic by giving radio instructions to pilots concerning route, altitude, take-off, and landing. **Air Vice-Marshal** an RAF officer of high rank, just below Air Marshal. **air waves** *colloq.* radio waves used in broadcasting. **by air** by aircraft; in an aircraft. **in the air 1** (of opinions or feelings) prevalent; gaining currency. **2** (of projects etc.) uncertain, not decided. **on** (or **off**) **the air** in (or not in) the process of broadcasting. **take the air** go out of doors **tread** (or **walk**) **on air** feel elated. [ME f. F and L f. Gk *aēr*]

airbase /ˈeəbeɪs/ *n.* a base for the operation of military aircraft.

airborne /ˈeəbɔːn/ *adj.* **1** transported by air. **2** (of aircraft) in the air after taking off.

airbrush /ˈeəbrʌʃ/ *n. & v.* —*n.* an artist's device for spraying paint by means of compressed air. —*v.tr.* paint with an airbrush.

Airbus /ˈeəbʌs/ *n. propr.* a type of passenger aircraft.

aircraft /ˈeəkrɑːft/ *n.* (*pl.* **aircraft**) a machine capable of flight, esp. an aeroplane or helicopter. □ **aircraft-carrier** a warship that carries and serves as a base for aeroplanes.

aircraftman /ˈeəˌkrɑːftmən/ *n.* (*pl.* **-men**) the lowest rank in the RAF.

aircraftwoman /ˈeəkrɑːftˌwʊmən/ *n.* (*pl.* **-women**) the lowest rank in the WRAF.

aircrew /ˈeəkruː/ *n.* **1** the crew manning an aircraft. **2** (*pl.* **aircrew**) a member of such a crew.

Airedale /ˈeədeɪl/ *n.* **1** a large terrier of a rough-coated breed. **2** this breed. [*Airedale* in W. Yorkshire]

airer /ˈeərə(r)/ *n.* a frame or stand for airing or drying clothes etc.

airfield /ˈeəfiːld/ *n.* an area of land where aircraft take off and land, are maintained, etc.

airfoil /ˈeəfɔɪl/ *n. US* = AEROFOIL. [AIR + FOIL²]

airframe /ˈeəfreɪm/ *n.* the body of an aircraft as distinct from its engine(s).

airglow /ˈeəɡləʊ/ *n.* radiation from the upper atmosphere, detectable at night.

airgun /ˈeəɡʌn/ *n.* a gun using compressed air to propel pellets.

airhead /ˈeəhed/ *n.* **1** *Mil.* a forward base for aircraft in enemy territory. **2** esp. *US sl.* a silly or foolish person.

airing /ˈeərɪŋ/ *n.* **1** exposure to fresh air, esp. for exercise or an excursion. **2** exposure (of laundry etc.) to warm air. **3** public expression of an opinion etc. (*the idea will get an airing at tomorrow's meeting*).

airless /ˈeəlɪs/ *adj.* **1** stuffy; not ventilated. **2** without wind or breeze; still. □□ **airlessness** *n.*

airlift /ˈeəlɪft/ *n. & v.* —*n.* the transport of troops and supplies by air, esp. in a blockade or other emergency. —*v.tr.* transport in this way.

airline /ˈeəlaɪn/ *n.* an organization providing a regular public service of air transport on one or more routes.

airliner /ˈeəˌlaɪnə(r)/ *n.* a large passenger aircraft.

airlock /ˈeəlɒk/ *n.* **1** a stoppage of the flow in a pump or pipe, caused by an air bubble. **2** a compartment with controlled pressure and parallel sets of doors, to permit movement between areas at different pressures.

airmail /ˈeəmeɪl/ *n. & v.* —*n.* **1** a system of transporting mail by air. **2** mail carried by air. —*v.tr.* send by airmail.

airman /ˈeəmən/ *n.* (*pl.* **-men**) **1** a pilot or member of the crew of an aircraft, esp. in an air force. **2** a member of the RAF below commissioned rank.

airmiss /ˈeəmɪs/ *n.* a circumstance in which two or more aircraft in flight on different routes are less than a prescribed distance apart.

airmobile /eəˈməʊbaɪl/ *adj.* (of troops) that can be moved about by air.

airplane /ˈeəpleɪn/ *n. US* = AEROPLANE.

airplay /ˈeəpleɪ/ *n.* broadcasting (of recorded music).

airport /ˈeəpɔːt/ *n.* a complex of runways and buildings for the take-off, landing, and maintenance of civil aircraft, with facilities for passengers.

air raid *n.* an attack by aircraft with bombs etc. The first air raid in history took place when the Austrian army sent up hot-air balloons, with bombs but no pilots, to drift over Venice in the campaign of 1849. The first successful manned bombing flights were by Zeppelin raiders over London in the First World War.

airscrew /ˈeəskruː/ *n. Brit.* an aircraft propeller.

airship /ˈeəʃɪp/ *n.* a power-driven aircraft that is lighter than air. An airship may be *rigid*, having a rigid framework for maintaining the shape of its hull, *non-rigid* (also called a *blimp*), in which internal pressure maintains the shape of the envelope, *semi-rigid*, with a rigid longitudinal member to distribute the load and assist in maintaining the shape of its hull, or *hybrid*, with its design incorporating parts of an aeroplane or helicopter to supplement its lift. The airship developed from the balloon, elongated in shape and steered instead of having to drift with the wind; the problem was to build light enough engines. In 1852 a Frenchman, Henri Giffard, built an airship with a steam engine slung (for reasons of safety) well below the gas-bag, but its speed was so slow that it could be steered only on a windless day. In 1884 the French government financed the building of one that was really controllable and able to return to its base; it was powered by a 6.75 kW electric motor. By the turn of the century Germany had taken the lead with the designs of Count von Zeppelin, whose machines were used in successful passenger services, in the First World War for bombing raids on England, and subsequently for transatlantic flights. In the 1930s, however, a series of disasters with hydrogen-filled airships, including the British *R101* at Beauvais, France (1930), and the German *Hindenburg* in 1937, cost many lives and gave such aircraft the tragic reputation which terminated interest in their use for about 40 years, while developments in heavier-than-air aircraft made them commercially obsolete. In the 1970s and 1980s, however, interest revived, with non-flammable helium used instead of the potentially dangerous hydrogen as a lifting gas (see HELIUM).

airsick /ˈeəsɪk/ *adj.* affected with nausea due to travel in an aircraft. □□ **airsickness** *n.*

airspace /ˈeəspeɪs/ *n.* the air available to aircraft to fly in, esp. the part subject to the jurisdiction of a particular country.

airstrip /ˈeəstrɪp/ *n.* a strip of ground suitable for the take-off and landing of aircraft.

airtight /ˈeətaɪt/ *adj.* not allowing air to pass through.

airway /ˈeəweɪ/ *n.* **1 a** a recognized route followed by aircraft. **b** (often in *pl.*) = AIRLINE. **2** a ventilating passage in a mine.

airwoman /ˈeəˌwʊmən/ *n.* (*pl.* **-women**) **1** a woman pilot or member of the crew of an aircraft, esp. in an air force. **2** a member of the WRAF below commissioned rank.

airworthy /ˈeəwɜːðɪ/ *adj.* (of an aircraft) fit to fly.

airy /ˈeərɪ/ *adj.* (**airier**, **airiest**) **1** well-ventilated, breezy. **2** flippant, superficial. **3 a** light as air. **b** graceful, delicate. **4** insubstantial, ethereal, immaterial. □ **airy-fairy** *colloq.* unrealistic, impractical, foolishly idealistic. □□ **airily** *adv.* **airiness** *n.*

aisle /aɪl/ *n.* **1** part of a church, esp. one parallel to and divided by pillars from the nave, choir, or transept. **2** a passage between rows of pews, seats, etc. □□ **aisled** *adj.* [ME *ele*, *ile* f. OF *ele* f. L *ala* wing: confused with *island* and F *aile* wing]

ait /eɪt/ *n.* (also **eyot**) *Brit.* a small island, esp. in a river. [OE *iggath* etc. f. *īeg* ISLAND + dimin. suffix]

aitch /eɪtʃ/ n. the name of the letter H. □ **drop one's aitches** fail to pronounce the initial h in words. [ME f. OF ache]

aitchbone /ˈeɪtʃbəʊn/ n. **1** the buttock or rump bone. **2** a cut of beef lying over this. [ME nage-, nache-bone buttock, ult. f. L natis, -es buttock(s): for loss of n cf. ADDER, APRON]

Aix-en-Provence /ˌeɪksãprɒˈvãs/ a city of Provence in southern France; pop. (1982) 124,550. It was the home of the painter Paul Cézanne.

Aix-la-Chapelle see AACHEN.

Ajaccio /æˈjætʃɪˌəʊ/ a seaport on the west coast of Corsica; pop. (1982) 55,300. It was the birthplace of Napoleon I.

Ajanta /əˈdʒʌntə/ a village in south central India with caves containing Buddhist frescoes and sculptures of the 1st c. BC–7th c. AD, with the finest examples belonging to the Gupta period (5th–6th c. AD).

ajar[1] /əˈdʒɑː(r)/ adv. & predic.adj. (of a door) slightly open. [A² + obs. char f. OE cerr a turn]

ajar[2] /əˈdʒɑː(r)/ adv. out of harmony. [A² + JAR²]

Ajax /ˈeɪdʒæks/ Gk legend **1** a Greek hero of the Trojan war, son of Telamon king of Salamis. **2** another Greek, son of Oileus king of Locris, who was killed after a shipwreck on his homeward journey after the fall of Troy.

Ajman /ædʒˈmɑːn/ **1** the smallest of the seven emirates of the United Arab Emirates; pop. (1980) 64,300. **2** its capital city.

ajutage var. of ADJUTAGE.

AK abbr. US Alaska (in official postal use).

a.k.a. abbr. also known as.

Akbar /ˈækbɑː(r)/, Jalaludin Muhammad (1542–1605), Mogul emperor of India. Coming to the throne in 1556, Akbar spread the Mogul empire over most of India and established administrative efficiency, a coherent commercial system, and religious toleration. He was the first ruler of India who sought to unite the many different peoples and religions rather than to be the leading representative of one dominant race or creed.

akee var. of ACKEE.

akela /ɑːˈkeɪlə/ n. the adult leader of a group of Cub Scouts. [name of the leader of a wolf-pack in Kipling's Jungle Book]

Akhenaten /ˌæk(ə)ˈnɑːt(ə)n/ ('Glory of the Sun') the name taken by the pharaoh Amenophis IV (1353–1335 BC) when he founded his new capital, Akhetaten (see AMARNA) in celebration of his religious ideology. Unique in the history of ancient Egyptian religion, it advocated the recognition of the Aten (sun disc) as the sole deity, with the king as his only intermediary. The instigation of this belief became Akhenaten's main objective: temples to other gods were closed throughout the land, the name 'Amun' and the plural form 'gods' were systematically removed from inscriptions. His chief wife Nefertiti bore him six daughters but no sons, and he was succeeded by Tutankhamun, early in whose reign the new religion was abandoned.

akimbo /əˈkɪmbəʊ/ adv. (of the arms) with hands on the hips and elbows turned outwards. [ME in kenebowe, prob. f. ON]

akin /əˈkɪn/ predic.adj. **1** related by blood. **2** of similar or kindred character. [A-⁴ + KIN]

Akkad /ˈækæd/ the capital city (as yet undiscovered) which gave its name to an ancient kingdom, traditionally founded by Sargon (2334–2279 BC) in north central Mesopotamia (modern Iraq). Its power extended over Babylonia, Assyria, and Syria, and even penetrated into Asia Minor, until it was overwhelmed by invading tribes from the east c.2150 BC.

Akkadian /əˈkeɪdɪən/ (also **Accadian**) adj. & n. —adj. of Akkad or its people or language. —n. **1** the Akkadian language, known from cuneiform inscriptions, the oldest Hamito-Semitic language for which we have any evidence, used in Mesopotamia from about 3000 BC. Two dialects of Akkadian, Assyrian and Babylonian, were widely spoken in the Middle East for the next 2,000 years before they gave way to Aramaic. **2** an inhabitant of Akkad.

Aksai Chin /ˌæksaɪ ˈtʃɪn/ a region of the Himalayas occupied by China but claimed by India as part of Kashmir.

Aksum /ˈɑːksəm/ (also **Axum**) a town in the province of Tigre in northern Ethiopia. It was a religious centre and the capital of a powerful kingdom during the 1st–6th centuries AD. According to ancient Aksumite religious tradition their kings were descended from Menelik (legendary son of Solomon and Sheba) who brought to the country the Ark of the Covenant containing the original Tablets of the Law given to Moses. □□ **Aksumite** adj. & n.

Akureyri /ˌæːkuˈreɪrɪ/ the chief settlement of northern Iceland; pop. (1987) 13,856.

akvavit var. of AQUAVIT.

AL abbr. US Alabama (in official postal use).

Al symb. Chem. the element aluminium.

al- /æl, əl/ prefix assim. form of AD- before l.

-al /əl/ suffix **1** forming adjectives meaning 'relating to, of the kind of': **a** from Latin or Greek words (central; regimental; colossal; tropical) (cf. -IAL, -ICAL). **b** from English nouns (tidal). **2** forming nouns, esp. of verbal action (animal; rival; arrival; proposal; trial). [sense 1 f. F -el or L -alis adj. suffix rel. to -aris (-AR¹); sense 2 f. F -aille or f. (or after) L -alis etc. used as noun]

Ala. abbr. Alabama.

à la /ˈaː laː/ prep. after the manner of (à la russe). [F, f. À LA MODE]

Alabama /ˌæləˈbæmə/ a State in the south-eastern US bordering on the Gulf of Mexico; pop. (est. 1985) 3,894,000. Visited by Spanish explorers in the mid-16th c., and later settled by the French, it passed to Britain in 1763 and to the US in 1783, becoming the 22nd State of the US in 1819; capital, Montgomery.

alabaster /ˈæləˌbɑːstə(r), -ˌbæstə(r), æləˈb-/ n. & adj. —n. a translucent usu. white form of gypsum, often carved into ornaments. —adj. **1** of alabaster. **2** like alabaster in whiteness or smoothness. □□ **alabastrine** /-ˈbɑːstrɪn, -ˈbæstrɪn, -aɪn/ adj. [ME f. OF alabastre f. L alabaster, -trum, f. Gk alabast(r)os]

à la carte /ˌaː laː ˈkaːt/ adv. & adj. ordered as separately priced item(s) from a menu, not as part of a set meal. [F]

alack /əˈlæk/ int. (also **alack-a-day** /əˈlækəˌdeɪ/) archaic an expression of regret or surprise. [prob. f. AH + LACK]

alacrity /əˈlækrɪtɪ/ n. briskness or cheerful readiness. [L alacritas f. alacer brisk]

Aladdin /əˈlædɪn/ hero of a story in the Arabian Nights, who acquired a lamp the rubbing of which brought a genie to do the will of the owner. □ **Aladdin's cave** a treasure-house of jewels or other valuables. **Aladdin's lamp** a talisman enabling its holder to gratify any wish.

Alamein see EL ALAMEIN.

Alamo /ˈæləˌməʊ/ a mission in San Antonio, Texas, site of a siege in 1836 by Mexican forces during the Texan struggle for independence from Mexico. It was defended by a handful of volunteers (including Davy Crockett), all of whom were killed.

à la mode /ˌaː laː ˈməʊd/ adv. & adj. **1** in fashion; fashionable. **2 a** (of beef) braised in wine. **b** US served with ice-cream. [F, = in the fashion]

Åland Islands /ˈɔːlənd/ (Finnish **Ahvenanmaa**) a group of islands in the Gulf of Bothnia forming an autonomous region of Finland; pop. (1987) 23,761; capital, Mariehamn (Maarianhamina).

alar /ˈeɪlə(r)/ adj. **1** relating to wings. **2** winglike or wing-shaped. **3** axillary. [L alaris f. ala wing]

Alarcón /ˌæläˈkɒn/, Pedro Antonio de (1833–91), Spanish writer of novels and short stories, whose best-known work, the humorous short story El sombrero de tres picos (The Three-cornered Hat, 1874), used as the basis for a ballet by Manuel de Falla and into an opera by Hugo Wolf.

Alarcón (y Mendoza) see RUIZ DE ALARCÓN Y MENDOZA.

Alaric /ˈælərɪk/ (c.370–410), king of the Visigoths. Becoming king in 395, Alaric invaded first Greece (395–6) and then Italy (400–3), but was checked on each occasion by the Roman general Stilicho. He invaded Italy again in 408 and in 410 captured and sacked Rome.

alarm /əˈlɑːm/ n. & v. —n. **1** a warning of danger etc. (gave the alarm). **2 a** a warning sound or device (the burglar alarm was set off accidentally). **b** = alarm clock. **3** frightened expectation of danger or difficulty (were filled with alarm). —v.tr. **1** frighten or disturb. **2** arouse to a sense of danger. □ **alarm clock** a clock with a device that can be made to sound at the time set in advance. [ME f. OF *alarme* f. It. *allarme* f. *all'arme!* to arms]

alarming /ə'lɑːmɪŋ/ adj. disturbing, frightening. □□ **alarmingly** adv.

alarmist /ə'lɑːmɪst/ n. & adj. —n. a person given to spreading needless alarm. —adj. creating needless alarm. □□ **alarmism** n.

alarum /ə'lɑːrəm/ n. archaic = ALARM. □ **alarums and excursions** joc. confused noise and bustle.

Alas. abbr. Alaska.

alas /ə'læs, ə'lɑːs/ int. an expression of grief, pity, or concern. [ME f. OF *a las(se)* f. *a ah* + *las(se)* f. L *lassus* weary]

Alaska /ə'læskə/ the largest State of the US, in the extreme north-west of North America, with coasts in the Arctic Ocean, Bering Sea, and North Pacific; pop. (est. 1985) 401,850. About one-third of it lies within the Arctic Circle. It was discovered by Russian explorers (under Vitus Bering) in 1741, and further explored by Cook, Vancouver, and others during the last quarter of the 18th c. The territory was purchased from Russia in 1867 and became the 49th State of the US in 1959; capital, Juneau. □ **baked Alaska** sponge cake and ice-cream in a meringue covering. □□ **Alaskan** adj. & n.

alate /'eɪleɪt/ adj. having wings or winglike appendages. [L *alatus* f. *ala* wing]

alb /ælb/ n. a white vestment reaching to the feet, worn by some Christian priests at church ceremonies. [OE *albe* f. eccl.L *alba* fem. of L *albus* white]

albacore /'ælbə,kɔː(r)/ n. **1** a long-finned tunny, *Thunnus alalunga*. Also called GERMON. **2** any of various other related fish. [Port. *albacor, -cora*, f. Arab. *al* the + *bakr* young camel or *bakūr* premature, precocious]

Alba Iulia /ˌælbə 'juːlɪə/ a city in western Romania; pop. (1985) 64,400. Founded by the Romans in the 2nd c. AD, it was the capital of Transylvania and for a short time (1599–1601) capital of the united principalities of Transylvania, Moldavia, and Walachia.

Alban /'ɔːlbən/, St (3rd c.), the first British martyr. He was a pagan of Verulamium (now St Albans, Herts.) who was converted and baptized by a fugitive priest whom he sheltered. When soldiers searched his house he put on the priest's cloak and was arrested and condemned to death. Feast day, 20 June.

Albania /æl'beɪnɪə/ a small country in SE Europe, bordering on the Adriatic Sea; pop. (est. 1988) 3,147,350; official language, Albanian; capital, Tirana. Much of the land is mountainous and there are extensive forests, but the coastal areas are fertile. The economy is mainly agricultural but chemical and engineering industries are being developed and the rich mineral resources (which include copper and iron) exploited; all industry is nationalized. Although Albania was part of the Byzantine empire from the 6th c. and part of the Turkish from the 15th c., its mountain tribes always remained fiercely independent and central rule was never completely effective. It became an independent State as a result of the Balkan Wars in 1912, and after a brief period as a republic became a rather unstable monarchy under King Zog in 1928. Invaded by Italy in 1939, it became a Communist State under Enver Hoxha after the Second World War, and although under the influence first of the USSR and later that of China, has generally remained isolationist in policy and outlook. There were anti-Communist demonstrations in 1990–1.

Albanian /æl'beɪnɪən/ n. & adj. —n. **1 a** a native or national of Albania. **b** a person of Albanian descent. **2** the official language of Albania, constituting a separate branch of the Indo-European language group, spoken by some 3 million speakers of whom 2 million live in Albania and 1 million in Yugoslavia. There are two distinct dialects, Tosk in the north and Gheg in the south. —adj. of or relating to Albania or its people or language.

Albany /'ɔːlbənɪ/ the capital of New York State, on the Hudson River; pop. (1980) 101,730.

albata /æl'bɑːtə/ n. German silver; an alloy of nickel, copper, and zinc. [L *albata* whitened f. *albus* white]

albatross /'ælbə,trɒs/ n. **1 a** any long-winged stout-bodied bird of the family Diomedeidae related to petrels, inhabiting the Pacific and Southern Oceans. **b** a source of frustration or guilt; an encumbrance. **2** Brit. Golf a score of three strokes under par at any hole. [alt. (after L *albus* white) of 17th-c. *alcatras*, applied to various sea-birds, f. Sp. and Port. *alcatraz*, var. of Port. *alcatruz* f. Arab. *alḳādūs* the pitcher]

albedo /æl'biːdəʊ/ n. (pl. **-os**) the proportion of light or radiation reflected by a surface, esp. of a planet or moon. [eccl.L, = whiteness, f. L *albus* white]

Albee /'ɔːlbiː, 'æ-/ Edward Franklin (1928–), American playwright, associated with the Theatre of the Absurd, whose best works explore sexual fantasy, frustration, and domestic anguish. His works include the one-act satiric comedy *The American Dream* (1961), the more naturalistic marital tragicomedy of academe *Who's Afraid of Virginia Woolf?* (1962), and *A Delicate Balance* (1966), set in a hard-drinking domestic environment.

albeit /ɔːl'biːɪt/ conj. literary though (he tried, albeit without success).

Albena /æl'beɪnə/ a resort town in Bulgaria, on the coast of the Black Sea.

Albert[1] /'ælbət/, Prince (1819–61), prince of Saxe-Coburg-Gotha, husband to Queen Victoria. An intelligent and energetic consort, Albert breathed considerable life into the British court in the first twenty years of his wife's reign. He was one of the driving forces behind the Great Exhibition of 1851, and a decade later, just before his premature death from typhoid fever, his moderating influence was crucial in keeping Britain out of the American Civil War.

Albert[2] /'ælbət/, Lake a lake on the Zaïre–Uganda frontier in the rift valley of east central Africa, named after the Prince Consort by the English explorer Samuel Baker, who was the first European to sight it. It was renamed Lake Mobutu Sese Seko in 1973.

albert /'ælbət/ n. a watch-chain with a bar at one end for attaching to a buttonhole. [Prince ALBERT]

Alberta /æl'bɜːtə/ a prairie province in western Canada (from 1905), bounded on the south by the US and on the west by the Rocky Mountains; pop. (1986) 2,375,300; capital, Edmonton.

Alberti /æl'beərtɪ/, Leon Battista (1404–72), Italian architect, humanist, painter, writer on art, poet, and musician, justly described as 'the universal man of the early Renaissance'. Born in Genoa, he worked in Florence, and later in Rome (as a member of the papal court) and Mantua. In his works he emphasized the rational basis of all creative endeavour. He was the most representative figure in the change which took place at the Renaissance from the medieval attitude to art as a symbolic expression of theological truths to the humanistic outlook, and the new ideas of scientific naturalism found their fullest expression in his writings.

Albertus Magnus /æl'bɜːtəs/, St (c.1206–80), Dominican theologian, philosopher, and scientist, who taught Aquinas. Nicknamed the 'universal doctor', he was a pioneer in the study of Aristotle and other pagan Greek and Arabic authors. He was particularly interested in the physical sciences (which led to a reputation for magical powers) and in the problem of reconciling Christianity with pagan philosophy.

albescent /æl'bes(ə)nt/ adj. growing or shading into white. [L *albescere albescent-* f. *albus* white]

Albigenses /ˌælbɪ'dʒensiːz/ n.pl. the members of a heretical sect in southern France, 12th–13th c., named from the city of Albi. Their teaching was a form of Manichaean dualism, with a moral and social doctrine of extreme rigorism and an implacable hatred against the Church. The heresy spread rapidly, its advocates being admired for their austerity, until ruthlessly crushed in a crusade (1209–31) led by Simon de Montfort, and finally extirpated by the Dominican Inquisition. □□ **Albigensian** adj. [L f. *Albi* in S. France]

albino /æl'biːnəʊ/ n. (pl. **-os**) **1** a person or animal having a congenital absence of pigment in the skin and hair (which are white), and the eyes (which are usu. pink). **2** a plant lacking normal colouring. □□ **albinism** /'ælbɪ,nɪz(ə)m/ n. **albinotic**

/ˌælbɪˈnɒtɪk/ adj. [Sp. & Port. (orig. of White Negroes) f. albo L f. albus white + -ino = -INE¹]

Albion /ˈælbɪən/ (also **perfidious Albion**) Britain or England. [OE f. L f. Celt. Albio (unrecorded): F la perfide Albion with ref. to alleged treachery to other nations]

albite /ˈælbaɪt/ n. Mineral. a feldspar, usu. white, rich in sodium. [L albus white + -ITE¹]

Ålborg var. of AALBORG.

Albufeira /ˌælbuːˈfeɪrə/ a fishing village and holiday resort on the Algarve coast in southern Portugal; pop. (1981) 14,200.

album /ˈælbəm/ n. **1** a blank book for the insertion of photographs, stamps, etc. **2 a** a long-playing gramophone record. **b** a set of these. [L, = a blank tablet, neut. of albus white]

albumen /ˈælbjʊmɪn/ n. **1** egg-white. **2** Bot. the substance found between the skin and germ of many seeds, usu. the edible part; = ENDOSPERM. [L albumen -minis white of egg f. albus white]

albumin /ˈælbjʊmɪn/ n. any of a class of water-soluble proteins found in egg-white, milk, blood, etc. □□ **albuminous** /ælˈbjuːmɪnəs/ adj. [F albumine f. L albumin-: see ALBUMEN]

albuminoid /ælˈbjuːmɪˌnɔɪd/ n. = SCLEROPROTEIN.

albuminuria /ˌælbjuːmɪˈnjʊərɪə/ n. the presence of albumin in the urine, usu. as a symptom of kidney disease.

Albuquerque¹ /ˈælbəˌkɜːkɪ/ the largest city in the State of New Mexico, US; pop. (1982) 342,000.

Albuquerque² /ˈælbəˌkɜːkɪ/, Alfonso de (1453–1515), Portuguese colonial statesman. He first travelled east in 1503, and, after being appointed Viceroy of the Portuguese Indies three years later, conquered Goa and made it the capital of the Portuguese empire in the east. An active and enlightened administrator, Albuquerque made further conquests on Ceylon, Malacca, Ormuz, the Sunda Isles, and along the Malabar Coast, but was relieved of office as a result of a court intrigue at home and died on the passage back to Portugal.

alburnum /ælˈbɜːnəm/ n. = SAPWOOD. [L f. albus white]

Alcaeus /ælˈsiːəs/ (born c.620 BC) Greek lyric poet from the island of Lesbos, active in its troubled politics. The surviving fragments of his poetry include political poems, drinking-songs, and love-songs. His works were an important model for the Roman poet Horace.

alcahest var. of ALKAHEST.

alcaic /ælˈkeɪɪk/ adj. & n. —adj. of the verse metre invented by Alcaeus (see entry), occurring in four-line stanzas. —n. (in pl.) alcaic verses. [LL alcaicus f. Gk alkaikos f. Alkaios Alcaeus]

alcalde /ɑːlˈkɑːldeɪ/ n. a magistrate or mayor in a Spanish, Portuguese, or Latin American town. [Sp. f. Arab. al-ḳāḍī the judge: see CADI]

Alcatraz /ˌælkəˈtræz/ a rocky island in San Francisco Bay, California, named after its pelicans (Sp. álcatraces). It was the site in 1934–63 of a top-security Federal prison.

Alcestis /ælˈsestɪs/ Gk legend wife of Admetus king of Pherae in Thessaly, whose life she saved by consenting to die on his behalf. She was brought back from Hades by Hercules.

alchemy /ˈælkəmɪ/ n. (pl. **-ies**) **1** the medieval forerunner of chemistry, esp. seeking to turn base metals into gold or silver. (See below.) **2** a miraculous transformation or the means of achieving this. □□ **alchemic** /ælˈkemɪk/ adj. **alchemical** /ælˈkemɪk(ə)l/ adj. **alchemist** n. **alchemize** v.tr. (also **-ise**). [ME f. OF alkemie, alkamie f. med.L alchimia, -emia, f. Arab. alkīmiyā' f. al the + kīmiyā' f. Gk khēmia, -meia art of transmuting metals]

Alchemy was based on the possible transmutation of all matter, and was far wider in scope than the familiar attempts to turn base metals into gold. It attracted such medieval scholars as Roger Bacon and Albertus Magnus, and was patronized by princes including the 16th-c. Emperors Maximilian II and Rudolf II. The influential Swiss writer Paracelsus (16th c.) was primarily concerned with its medical application to his search for a chemical therapy for disease; his followers developed specialized chemical medicines and sought a universal elixir which they dreamed would prolong life and restore youth from old age. Alchemy made a considerable, if largely accidental, contribution to chemistry which separated only slowly from it; many leading

scientists, including Newton, retained a belief or interest in transmutation. The rise of the mechanical philosophy in the 17th c. gradually undermined alchemy and other forms of the occult, and later alchemists chose to emphasize its mystical aspects in esoteric movements such as that of the Rosicrucians.

alcheringa /ˌæltʃəˈrɪŋgə/ n. (in the mythology of some Australian Aboriginals) the 'golden age' when the first ancestors were created. [Aboriginal, = dream-time]

Alcibiades /ˌælsɪˈbaɪədiːz/ (c.450–404 BC) Athenian general and statesman. Educated in the household of Pericles, he became the pupil and friend of Socrates. In the Peloponnesian War he sponsored the unsuccessful expedition against Sicily, but fled to Sparta after being recalled for trial on a charge of sacrilege. He later held commands for Athens against Sparta and Persia, before his enemies finally forced him from Athens and had him murdered in Phrygia.

Alcock /ˈɔːlkɒk/, Sir John William (1892–1919), English aviator. He served as a pilot in the Royal Flying Corps during the First World War and was knighted after making the first direct non-stop transatlantic flight (16 hours 27 minutes) on 14–15 June 1919, from Newfoundland to Clifden, Ireland, with Sir Arthur Whitten Brown in a converted Vickers Vimy bomber.

alcohol /ˈælkəhɒl/ n. **1** (in full **ethyl alcohol**) a colourless volatile inflammable liquid forming the intoxicating element in wine, beer, spirits, etc., and also used as a solvent, as fuel, etc. Also called ETHANOL. ¶ Chem. formula: C_2H_5OH. **2** any liquor containing this. **3** Chem. any of a large class of organic compounds that contain one or more hydroxyl groups attached to carbon atoms. [F or med.L f. Arab. al-kuḥl f. al the + kuḥl KOHL]

alcoholic /ˌælkəˈhɒlɪk/ adj. & n. —adj. of, relating to, containing, or caused by alcohol. —n. a person suffering from alcoholism.

alcoholism /ˈælkəhɒˌlɪz(ə)m/ n. **1** an addiction to the consumption of alcoholic liquor. **2** the diseased condition resulting from this. [mod.L alcoholismus (as ALCOHOL)]

alcoholometer /ˌælkəhɒˈlɒmɪtə(r)/ n. an instrument for measuring alcoholic concentration. □□ **alcoholometry** n.

Alcott /ˈɔːlkɒt/, Louisa May (1832–88), American novelist. From an early age she published sketches and stories to support her impractical father and her family, including Hospital Sketches (1863), which recounted her experiences as a nurse in the Civil War. Her novel for girls Little Women (1868–9), a largely autobiographical work concerning a New England family in the 19th c., achieved wide and lasting popularity. She wrote many others in the same vein as well as adult novels, and was involved in various reform movements, including women's suffrage.

alcove /ˈælkəʊv/ n. a recess, esp. in the wall of a room or of a garden. [F f. Sp. alcoba f. Arab. al-ḳubba f. al the + ḳubba vault]

Alcuin /ˈælkwɪn/ (c.735–804), English scholar and theologian, inspirer of the 'Carolingian Renaissance'. Born and educated at York, he was invited to Charlemagne's court and became his adviser in religious and educational matters. He improved the palace library and, becoming Abbot of Tours in 796, established an important library and school there. He developed the type of minuscule handwriting which influenced the Roman type now used in printed books.

Aldabra /ælˈdæbrə/ a coral atoll in the Indian Ocean. From 1965 to 1976 it was part of the British Indian Ocean Territory; it has been administered as a nature reserve since 1976, when it became an outlying dependency of the Seychelles.

Aldebaran /ælˈdebərən/ a conspicuous red giant that is the brightest star in the constellation Taurus. [Arab., = the following (because it follows the Pleiades)]

aldehyde /ˈældɪˌhaɪd/ n. Chem. any of a class of compounds formed by the oxidation of alcohols (and containing the group —CHO). □□ **aldehydic** /ˌældɪˈhɪdɪk/ adj. [abbr. of mod.L alcohol dehydrogenatum alcohol deprived of hydrogen]

al dente /æl ˈdentɪ/ adj. (of pasta etc.) cooked so as to be still firm when bitten. [It., lit. 'to the tooth']

alder /ˈɔːldə(r)/ n. any tree of the genus Alnus, related to the birch, with catkins and toothed leaves. □ **alder buckthorn** a shrub, *Frangula alnus*, related to the buckthorn. [OE *alor, aler*, rel. to L *alnus*, with euphonic *d*]

alderman /ˈɔːldəmən/ *n.* (*pl.* **-men**) **1** esp. *hist.* a co-opted member of an English county or borough council, next in dignity to the Mayor. **2** *US* & *Austral.* the elected governor of a city. □□ **aldermanic** /-ˈmænɪk/ *adj.* **aldermanship** *n.* [OE *aldor* patriarch f. *ald* old + MAN]

Alderney /ˈɔːldənɪ/ one of the Channel Islands; pop. (1981) 2,100. —*n.* **1** an animal of a breed of small dairy cattle that came originally from Alderney. **2** this breed.

Aldine /ˈældaɪn/ *adj.* of the Italian printer Aldus Manutius (see entry), or the books printed by him or his family, or certain styles of display types. The device characteristic of Aldine books is a figure of a dolphin on an anchor. [L *Aldinus*, Latinized form of *Aldo*]

Aldis lamp /ˈɔːldɪs/ *n.* a hand lamp for signalling in Morse code. [A. C. W. *Aldis*, its inventor]

Aldiss /ˈɔːldɪs/, Brian Wilson (1925–   ), English novelist, short-story writer, and critic, best known for his works of science fiction and for his involvement with the cause of science fiction as a literary genre. He has edited many collections and anthologies and has written a history of the subject, *Billion Year Spree* (1973).

aldrin /ˈældrɪn/ *n.* a white crystalline chlorinated hydrocarbon used as an insecticide. [K. *Alder*, Ger. chemist d. 1958 + -IN]

Aldus Manutius /ˈɔːldəs məˈnjuːʃɪəs/ the Latinized name of Teobaldo Manucci, also known as Aldo Manuzio (1450–1515), Italian scholar, printer, and publisher, noted for the fine editions of Greek and Latin classics which were printed at his press in Venice. Among the scholars who worked with him was Erasmus. Aldus Manutius was responsible for the introduction of italic type (see ITALIC).

ale /eɪl/ *n.* beer, especially (**real ale**) that regarded as brewed and stored in the traditional way, with secondary fermentation in the container from which it is dispensed. *Ale* and *beer* seem originally to have been synonyms, but after the introduction into England of 'the wicked weed called hops' (*c.*1624) beer was commonly flavoured with hops. [OE *alu*, = ON *öl*]

aleatoric /ˌeɪlɪəˈtɒrɪk/ *adj.* **1** depending on the throw of a die or on chance. **2** *Mus.* & *Art* involving random choice by a performer or artist. [L *aleatorius* dice-player f. *alea* die]

aleatory /ˈeɪlɪətərɪ/ *adj.* = ALEATORIC. [as ALEATORIC]

alec /ˈælɪk/ *n.* (also **aleck**) *Austral.* *sl.* a stupid person. [shortening of SMART ALEC]

alee /əˈliː/ *adv.* & *predic.adj.* **1** on the lee or sheltered side of a ship. **2** to leeward. [ME, f. A² + LEE]

alehouse /ˈeɪlhaʊs/ *n. hist.* a tavern.

Alekhine /ˈælɪˌkiːn, ˈæljəkɪn/, Alexander (1892–1946), Russian-born chess player, who became a naturalized French citizen, world champion 1927–35 and from 1937 until his death.

Alembert /ˌæˈlãbeər/, Jean le Rond d' (1717–83), French philosopher and mathematician who collaborated with Diderot in the production of an encyclopedia (see DIDEROT).

alembic /əˈlembɪk/ *n.* **1** *hist.* an apparatus formerly used in distilling. **2** a means of refining or extracting. [ME f. OF f. med.L *alembicus* f. Arab. *al-'anbīḳ* f. al the + *'anbīḳ* still f. Gk *ambix, -ikos* cup, cap of a still]

Alentejo /ˌælənˈteɪʒəʊ/ a historic region of central Portugal. Its name is derived from an Arabic phrase meaning 'beyond the Tagus'.

aleph /ˈɑːlef/ *n.* the first letter of the Hebrew alphabet. [Heb. *'āleph*, lit. 'ox']

Aleppo /æˈlepəʊ/ (Arabic Ḥalab /haːˈlaːb/) the second-largest city of Syria, in the north of the country; pop. (1981) 976,700. The city is an ancient one, an important commercial centre between the Mediterranean and the countries of the East, especially after the destruction of Palmyra in 273; it was besieged, though not captured, during the Crusades.

alert /əˈlɜːt/ *adj., n.,* & *v.* —*adj.* **1** watchful or vigilant; ready to take action. **2** nimble (esp. of mental faculties); attentive. —*n.* **1** a warning call or alarm. **2 a** warning of an air raid. **b** the

duration of this. —*v.tr.* (often foll. by *to*) make alert; warn (*were alerted to the danger*). □ **on the alert** on the lookout against danger or attack. □□ **alertly** *adv.* **alertness** *n.* [F *alerte* f. It. *all'erta* to the watch-tower]

-ales /ˈeɪliːz/ *suffix* forming the plural names of orders of plants (*Rosales*). [pl. of L adj. suffix *-alis*: see -AL]

Aletschhorn /ˈɑːletʃˌhɔːn/ a mountain in Switzerland, in the Bernese Alps, rising to a height of 4,195 m (13,763 ft.). The Aletsch glaciers are amongst the largest in Europe.

aleuron /əˈljʊərɒn/ *n.* (also **aleurone** /-rəʊn/) *Biochem.* a protein found as granules in the seeds of plants etc. [Gk *aleuron* flour]

Aleut /əˈljuːt/ *n.* **1** a native of the Aleutian Islands. **2** the language of the Aleuts, distantly related to Eskimo. □□ **Aleutian** /əˈljuːʃ(ə)n/ *adj.* & *n.* [orig. unkn.]

Aleutian Islands /əˈljuːʃ(ə)n/ (also **Aleutians**) a group of islands in US possession, extending SW from Alaska.

A level /eɪ/ *n. Brit.* = *advanced level* (see ADVANCE).

alewife /ˈeɪlwaɪf/ *n.* (*pl.* **alewives**) *US* any of several species of fish allied to the herring. [corrupt. of 17th-c. *aloofe*: orig. uncert.]

Alexander[1] /ˌælɪɡˈzɑːndə(r)/ 'the Great' (356–323 BC), king of Macedon 336–323 BC, son of Philip II, tutored by the philosopher Aristotle. On his succession he immediately set about the invasion of the Persian empire; after liberating the Greek cities in Asia Minor, he defeated the Persians in Egypt, Syria, and Mesopotamia, and extended his conquests eastwards to Bactria and the Punjab. He died of a fever at Babylon, and his empire quickly fell apart after his death. Undoubtedly the greatest general of his country, and probably of antiquity, his remarkable achievements during his short life were due to his untiring energy, enquiring mind, and profound grasp of strategy both in war and in the foundation of new cities. His plans for the empire were grand and original but perhaps impossible of execution. Regarded as a god in his lifetime, he became a model for all later ancient imperialist conquerors and the subject of many fantastic legends.

Alexander[2] /ˌælɪɡˈzɑːndə(r)/ the name of three kings of Scotland:

Alexander I (*c.*1077–1124), son of Malcolm III, reigned 1107–24. During his reign the penetration of Anglo-Norman influences and the strengthening of feudal links between Scotland and England accelerated the drift of the hitherto remote northern kingdom into the mainstream of British social and political developments.

Alexander II (1198–1249), son of William I, reigned 1214–49. He generally restored friendly relations with England, while extending royal authority within his own realm.

Alexander III (1241–86), son of Alexander II, reigned 1249–86. He enjoyed a long and relatively peaceful reign, but his death in a riding accident left Scotland without a male heir to the throne, plunging the country into three decades of dynastic upheaval and struggle against English domination.

Alexander[3] /ˌælɪɡˈzɑːndə(r)/ the name of three emperors of Russia:

Alexander I (1777–1825), reigned 1801–25. Alexander came to the throne after the murder of his tyrannical father Paul, but, even though the new Tsar was a romantic liberal by temperament, he was unable to pursue reforming policies beyond limited administrative improvements. The first half of his reign was dominated by the military struggle with Napoleon, in which Russian arms, after many setbacks, finally emerged triumphant. In his later years Alexander became increasingly withdrawn and prone to religious conservatism and took less and less interest in improving the lot of his subjects.

Alexander II (1818–81), son of Nicholas I, reigned 1855–81. A conservative by nature, Alexander realized the need for at least a measure of reform to rescue Russia from the economic and political crisis into which it had sunk in the last years of his father's reign. Although a series of reforms were introduced, including the emancipation of the serfs in 1861, Alexander was unwilling to go too far. As his reign progressed, radical opposition hardened, throwing up a series of terrorist groups, one of which succeeded in assassinating the Tsar with a bomb in March 1881.

Alexander III (1845–94), son of Alexander II, reigned 1881–94. Coming to the throne after his father's murder, Alexander III stopped the policy of gradual liberal reform and fell back on repressive conservatism. Although his reign witnessed considerable economic development, his failure even to countenance social and political reform produced a dangerous situation to which his son and successor Nicholas II was to prove unequal.

Alexander[4] /ˌælɪɡˈzɑːndə(r)/, Harold Rupert Leofric George, 1st Earl (1891–1969), British field marshal. In the Second World War he supervised the evacuation from Dunkirk, the withdrawal from Burma, and the victorious campaigns in North Africa (1943) and in Sicily and Italy (1943–5). After the war he became Governor-General of Canada (1946–52).

Alexander Nevski /ˌælɪɡˈzɑːndə(r)ˈnefski/ (1220–63), Russian saint and national hero, called 'Nevski' from the River Neva, on the banks of which he defeated the Swedes.

alexanders /ˌælɪɡˈzɑːndəz/ n. an umbelliferous plant, *Smyrnium olusatrum*, formerly used in salads but superseded by celery. [OE f. med.L *alexandrum*]

Alexander technique /ˌælɪɡˈzɑːndə(r)/ n. a technique for controlling posture as an aid to improved well-being. [F. M. *Alexander*, physiotherapist d. 1955]

Alexandretta /ˌælɪɡzɑːnˈdretə/ the former name of Iskenderun (see entry).

Alexandria /ˌælɪɡˈzɑːndrɪə/ the chief port of Egypt; pop. (est. 1986) 2,893,000. Founded in 332 BC by Alexander the Great, after whom it is named, it became a major centre of Hellenistic and Jewish culture, with renowned libraries, and was the capital city until the Arab invasions c. AD 641. On an island off the coast was an early lighthouse, often considered one of the Seven Wonders of the World (see PHAROS).

Alexandrian /ˌælɪɡˈzɑːndrɪən/ adj. **1** of or characteristic of Alexandria in Egypt. **2 a** belonging to or akin to the schools of literature and philosophy of Alexandria. **b** (of a writer) derivative or imitative; fond of recondite learning.

alexandrine /ˌælɪɡˈzændraɪn/ adj. & n. —adj. (of a line of verse) having six iambic feet. —n. an alexandrine line. [F *alexandrin* f. *Alexandre* Alexander (the Great), the subject of an Old French poem in this metre]

alexandrite /ˌælɪɡˈzɑːndraɪt/ n. Mineral. a green variety of chrysoberyl. [Tsar *Alexander* I of Russia + -ITE[1]]

alexia /əˈleksɪə/ n. the inability to see words or to read, caused by a condition of the brain. [mod.L, A-[1] + Gk *lexis* speech f. *legein* to speak, confused with L *legere* to read]

alfalfa /ælˈfælfə/ n. a leguminous plant, *Medicago sativa*, with clover-like leaves and flowers used for fodder. Also called LUCERNE. [Sp. f. Arab. *al-faṣfaṣa*, a green fodder]

Alfonso /ælˈfɒnsəʊ/ the name of 13 kings of Spain:

Alfonso XIII (1886–1941), reigned 1886–1931. Alfonso ruled under the regency of his mother until 1902, during which time Spain lost her colonial possessions in the Philippines and Cuba to the US. He appointed Primo de Rivera dictator in 1923, but after the opening of the National Assembly in 1927 Spain was stricken with a worsening political crisis. Martial law was declared in 1930, but this failed to stop the striking and rioting and a year later Alfonso was forced to abdicate.

Alfred /ˈælfrɪd/ 'the Great' (849–99), king of Wessex 871–99. Alfred's military resistance to Danish invaders saved the south-west part of the country from Norse occupation and made him one of the great heroic figures of his age. Apart from his military victories, Alfred was also responsible for a considerable revival of learning and literature in the west of England, himself translating Latin works into English.

alfresco /ælˈfreskəʊ/ adv. & adj. in the open air (*we lunched alfresco; an alfresco lunch*). [It. *al fresco* in the fresh (air)]

alga /ˈælɡə/ n. (pl. **algae** /ˈælɡiː, ˈælɡiː/) (usu. in pl.) any of a large group of primitive mainly aquatic non-flowering photosynthetic plants, including seaweeds and many plankton. They may be single-celled or multicellular but, unlike higher plants, have no vascular (conducting) tissue and no absorbent root system. Algae constitute a form of life rather than a single related group and are now separated into a number of divisions or phyla, partly on the basis of their pigmentation. The primitive but widespread blue-green algae are related more to bacteria than to other algae; traces of them are reported in rocks several thousand million years old. The brown algae include the largest and most complex seaweeds, but another division, the green algae, are thought to be the ancestors of most land plants. Planktonic algae of various kinds provide the food which supports nearly all marine life. □□ **algal** adj. **algoid** adj. [L]

Algarve /ælˈɡɑːv/ the southernmost province of Portugal, on the Atlantic coast; pop. (est. 1986) 339,200; capital, Faro. [Arab. *al* the + *gharb* west]

algebra /ˈældʒɪbrə/ n. **1** the branch of mathematics that uses letters and other general symbols to represent numbers and quantities in formulae and equations. (See below.) **2** a system of this based on given axioms (*linear algebra; the algebra of logic*). □□ **algebraic** /ˌældʒɪˈbreɪɪk/ adj. **algebraical** /ˌældʒɪˈbreɪɪk(ə)l/ adj. **algebraically** /ˌældʒɪˈbreɪɪkəlɪ/ adv. **algebraist** /ˌældʒɪˈbreɪɪst/ n. [It. & Sp. & med.L, f. Arab. *al-jabr* f. *al* the + *jabr* reunion of broken parts (title of book written c.820 by Al-Khuwārizmī; see ALGORITHM) f. *jabara* reunite]

One of the earliest works on algebra was the *Arithmetica* by Diophantus of Alexandria (see entry). Abstract (or 'modern') algebra deals with systems (such as fields, rings, vector spaces, groups) that consist of elements (typically numbers, vectors, or geometrical transformations) and operations that may be performed with them (such as addition, multiplication, or composition of transformations). In abstract algebra attention is shifted from calculation that can be performed within particular systems to comparison between different systems.

Algeciras /ˌældʒɪˈsɪərəs/ a ferry port in southern Spain, opposite Gibraltar; pop. (1986) 97,200.

Algeria /ælˈdʒɪərɪə/ a North African country on the Mediterranean coast, consisting chiefly of desert, with fertile areas near the coast; pop. (est. 1988) 24,194,800; official language, Arabic; capital, Algiers. The people are mainly Arabs and Berbers and the economy is chiefly agricultural, though industrial development is proceeding; all major industries are under State control. The main exports are crude oil and (liquefied) natural gas, which are pumped from the Sahara to terminals on the coast. Algeria came under nominal Turkish rule in the 16th c., but the native peoples always retained a high degree of independence, dominating the Barbary coast until colonized by France in the mid-19th c. Heavily settled by French immigrants, Algeria was closely integrated with metropolitan France, but the refusal of the European settlers to grant equal rights to the native population led to increasing political instability and civil war in the 1950s, and in 1962 the country was granted independence as a result of a referendum and became a republic (one-party until November 1989). The departure of the French caused grave damage to the previously prosperous Algerian economy, with the result that the next two decades were characterized by slow attempts at economic recovery and limited external contacts. □□ **Algerian** adj. & n.

-algia /ˈældʒə/ comb. form Med. denoting pain in a part specified by the first element (*neuralgia*). □□ **-algic** comb. form forming adjectives. [Gk f. *algos* pain]

algicide /ˈælɡɪˌsaɪd/ n. a preparation for destroying algae.

algid /ˈældʒɪd/ adj. Med. cold, chilly. □□ **algidity** /ælˈdʒɪdɪtɪ/ n. [L *algidus* f. *algēre* be cold]

Algiers /ælˈdʒɪəz/ (French **Alger** /alˈʒeɪ/, Arabic **El Djezair** /dʒeˈzeə(r)/) the capital of Algeria and a leading Mediterranean seaport; pop. (1983) 1,721,600.

alginate /ˈældʒɪˌneɪt/ n. a salt or ester of alginic acid. [ALGA + -IN + -ATE[1]]

alginic acid /ælˈdʒɪnɪk/ n. an insoluble carbohydrate found (chiefly as salts) in many brown seaweeds. [ALGA + -IN + -IC]

algoid see ALGA.

Algol[1] /ˈælɡɒl/ an eclipsing binary star that is the second brightest in the constellation Perseus. [Arab., = the destruction]

Algol² /'ælgɒl/ n. a high-level computer programming language. [ALGORITHMIC (see ALGORITHM) + LANGUAGE]

algolagnia /ˌælgə'lægnɪə/ n. sexual pleasure got from inflicting pain on oneself or others; masochism or sadism. □□ **algolagnic** adj. & n. [mod.L f. G Algolagnie f. Gk algos pain + lagneia lust]

algology /æl'gɒlədʒɪ/ n. the study of algae. □□ **algological** /-'lɒdʒɪk(ə)l/ adj. **algologist** n.

Algonquian /æl'gɒŋkwɪən/ (also **Algonkian**) adj. & n. —n. 1 a member of a large group of North American Indian tribes speaking related languages, pushed northward and westward by colonial expansion in the 18th and 19th c. 2 any of their languages or dialects, forming one of the largest groups of American Indian languages and including Ojibwa, Cree, Blackfoot, Cheyenne, Fox, and Delaware, which are spoken mainly in the north Middle West of the US, Montana, and south central Canada. Many English and American words have been adopted from this group, e.g. moccasin, moose, pow-wow, squaw, toboggan. —adj. of or relating to the Algonquians or their languages. [f. ALGONQUIN + -IAN]

Algonquin /æl'gɒŋkwɪn/ adj. & n. —n. 1 an American Indian of a people encountered in the districts of Ottawa and Quebec; this people. 2 their language. —adj. of or relating to the Algonquins or their language. [F, perh. f. native word = 'at the place of spearing fish and eels']

algorithm /'ælgərɪð(ə)m/ n. (also **algorism** /'ælgərɪz(ə)m/) 1 Math. a process or set of rules used for calculation or problem-solving, esp. with a computer. 2 the Arabic or decimal notation of numbers. □□ **algorithmic** /ˌælgə'rɪðmɪk/ adj. [algorism ME ult. f. Pers. al-Kuwārizmī 9th-c. mathematician: algorithm infl. by Gk arithmos number (cf. f algorithme)]

alguacil /ˌælgwə'sɪl, ˌælgwəsɪl/ n. (also **alguazil** /ˌælgwə'zɪl, 'ælgwəzɪl/) 1 a mounted official at a bullfight. 2 a constable or an officer of justice in Spain or Spanish-speaking countries. [Sp. f. Arab. al-wazīr f. al the + wazir: see VIZIER]

Alhambra /æl'hæmbrə/ a fortified Moorish palace, the last stronghold of the Muslim kings of Granada, built between 1248 and 1354 near Granada in Spain. It is an outstanding piece of Moorish architecture with its marble courts and fountains, delicate columns and archways, and wall decorations of carved and painted stucco. [Arab., = red castle]

Ali /'ɑːlɪ/, Muhammad (1942–), American boxer who won the world heavyweight title first in 1964 and regained it twice subsequently (1974, 1978). On joining the Black Muslim movement he gave up his real name (Cassius Clay) and became known as Muhammad Ali. He is a vital figure in the history of the sport, both for his physical skill, with great speed allied to a formidable physique, and for his colourful flamboyant character.

alias /'eɪlɪəs/ adv. & n. —adv. also named or known as. —n. a false or assumed name. [L, = at another time, otherwise]

Ali Baba /'ælɪ 'bɑːbə/ the hero of a story supposed to be from the Arabian Nights, who discovered the magic formula ('Open Sesame!') which opened the cave in which forty robbers kept the treasure they had accumulated.

alibi /'ælɪˌbaɪ/ n. & v. —n. 1 a claim, or the evidence supporting it, that when an alleged act took place one was elsewhere. 2 disp. an excuse of any kind; a pretext or justification. —v. (alibis, alibied, alibiing) colloq. 1 tr. provide an alibi or offer an excuse for (a person). 2 intr. provide an alibi. [L, = elsewhere]

Alicante /ˌælɪ'kænteɪ/ a seaport on the Mediterranean coast of SE Spain; pop. (1986) 265,500.

Alice /'ælɪs/ the heroine of stories by Lewis Carroll.

Alice Springs /'ælɪs/ an administrative and supply centre, and railway terminus, serving the outback area of Northern Territory, Australia; pop. (1986) 22,900.

alicyclic /ˌælɪ'saɪklɪk/ adj. Chem. of, denoting, or relating to organic compounds combining a cyclic structure with aliphatic properties, e.g. cyclohexane. [G alicyclisch (as ALIPHATIC, CYCLIC)]

alidade /'ælɪˌdeɪd/ n. Surveying & Astron. an instrument for determining directions or measuring angles. [F f. med.L f. Arab. al-iḍāda the revolving radius f. ʿaḍud upper arm]

alien /'eɪlɪən/ adj. & n. —adj. 1 a (often foll. by to) unfamiliar;

not in accordance or harmony; unfriendly, hostile; unacceptable or repugnant (army discipline was alien to him; struck an alien note). b (often foll. by from) different or separated. 2 foreign; from a foreign country (help from alien powers). 3 of or relating to beings supposedly from other worlds. 4 Bot. (of a plant) introduced from elsewhere and naturalized in its new home. —n. 1 a foreigner, esp. one who is not a naturalized citizen of the country where he or she is living. 2 a being from another world. 3 Bot. an alien plant. □□ **alienness** n. [ME f. OF f. L alienus belonging to another (alius)]

alienable /'eɪlɪənəb(ə)l/ adj. Law able to be transferred to new ownership. □□ **alienability** /-'bɪlɪtɪ/ n.

alienage /'eɪlɪənɪdʒ/ n. the state or condition of being an alien.

alienate /'eɪlɪəˌneɪt/ v.tr. 1 a cause (a person) to become unfriendly or hostile. b (often foll. by from) cause (a person) to feel isolated or estranged from (friends, society, etc.). 2 transfer ownership of (property) to another person etc. □□ **alienator** n. [ME f. L alienare alienat- (as ALIEN)]

alienation /ˌeɪlɪə'neɪʃ(ə)n/ n. 1 the act or result of alienating. 2 (Theatr. **alienation effect**) a dramatic effect whereby an audience remains objective, not identifying with the characters or action of a play.

alienist /'eɪlɪənɪst/ n. US a psychiatrist, esp. a legal adviser on psychiatric problems. [F aliéniste (as ALIEN)]

aliform /'eɪlɪˌfɔːm/ adj. wing-shaped. [mod.L aliformis f. L ala wing: see -FORM]

alight¹ /ə'laɪt/ v.intr. 1 a (often foll. by from) descend from a vehicle. b dismount from a horse. 2 descend and settle; come to earth from the air. 3 (foll. by on) find by chance; notice. [OE ālīhtan (as A-², līhtan LIGHT² v.)]

alight² /ə'laɪt/ predic.adj. 1 on fire; burning (they set the old shed alight; is the fire still alight?). 2 lighted up; excited (eyes alight with expectation). [ME, prob. f. phr. on a light (= lighted) fire]

align /ə'laɪn/ v.tr. 1 put in a straight line or bring into line (three books were neatly aligned on the shelf). 2 esp. Polit. (usu. foll. by with) bring (oneself etc.) into agreement or alliance with (a cause, policy, political party, etc.). □□ **alignment** n. [F aligner f. phr. à ligne into line: see LINE¹]

alike /ə'laɪk/ adj. & adv. —adj. (usu. predic.) similar, like one another; indistinguishable. —adv. in a similar way or manner (all were treated alike). [ME f. OE gelīc and ON glíkr (LIKE¹)]

aliment /'ælɪmənt/ n. formal 1 food. 2 support or mental sustenance. □□ **alimental** /ˌælɪ'ment(ə)l/ adj. [ME f. F aliment or L alimentum f. alere nourish]

alimentary /ˌælɪ'mentərɪ/ adj. of, relating to, or providing nourishment or sustenance. □ **alimentary canal** Anat. the passage along which food is passed from the mouth to the anus during digestion. [L alimentarius (as ALIMENT)]

alimentation /ˌælɪmen'teɪʃ(ə)n/ n. 1 nourishment; feeding. 2 maintenance, support; supplying with the necessities of life. [F alimentation or med.L alimentatio f. alimentare (as ALIMENT)]

alimony /'ælɪmənɪ/ n. the money payable by a man to his wife or former wife or by a woman to her husband or former husband after they are separated or divorced. ¶ In UK use replaced by maintenance. [L alimonia nutriment f. alere nourish]

A-line /'eɪlaɪn/ adj. (of a garment) having a narrow waist or shoulders and somewhat flared skirt.

aliphatic /ˌælɪ'fætɪk/ adj. Chem. of, denoting, or relating to organic compounds in which carbon atoms form open chains, not aromatic rings. [Gk aleiphar -atos fat]

aliquot /'ælɪˌkwɒt/ adj. & n. —adj. (of a part or portion) contained by the whole an integral or whole number of times (4 is an aliquot part of 12). —n. 1 an aliquot part; an integral factor. 2 (in general use) any known fraction of a whole; a sample. [F aliquote f. L aliquot some, so many]

alive /ə'laɪv/ adj. (usu. predic.) 1 (of a person, animal, plant, etc.) living, not dead. 2 a (of a thing) existing; continuing; in operation or action (kept his interest alive). b under discussion; provoking interest (the topic is still very much alive today). 3 (of a person or animal) lively, active. 4 charged with an electric current; connected to a source of electricity. 5 (foll. by to) aware of;

alert or responsive to. **6** (foll. by *with*) **a** swarming or teeming with. **b** full of. □ **alive and kicking** *colloq.* very active; lively. **alive and well** still alive or active (esp. despite contrary assumptions or rumours). □□ **aliveness** *n.* [OE *on līfe* (as A[2], LIFE)]

alizarin /əˈlɪzərɪn/ *n.* **1** the red colouring matter of madder root, used in dyeing. **2** (*attrib.*) (of a dye) derived from or similar to this pigment. [F *alizarine* f. *alizari* madder f. Arab. *al-ˈiṣara* pressed juice f. ˈaṣara to press fruit]

alkahest /ˈælkəˌhest/ *n.* (also **alcahest**) the universal solvent sought by alchemists. [sham Arab., prob. invented by Paracelsus]

alkali /ˈælkəˌlaɪ/ *n.* (*pl.* **alkalis**). **1 a** any of a class of substances that liberate hydroxide ions in water, usu. form caustic or corrosive solutions, turn litmus blue, and have a pH of more than 7, e.g. caustic soda. (See below.) **b** any other substance with similar but weaker properties, e.g. sodium carbonate. **2** *Chem.* any substance that reacts with or neutralizes hydrogen ions. □ **alkali metal** any of the univalent group of metals, lithium, sodium, potassium, rubidium, and caesium, whose hydroxides are alkalis. Being very reactive, they are not found in the free state in nature. □□ **alkalimeter** /ˌælkəˈlɪmɪtə(r)/ *n.* **alkalimetry** /ˌælkəˈlɪmɪtrɪ/ *n.* [ME f. med.L, f. Arab. *al-ḳalī* calcined ashes f. ḳala fry]

Since the 17th c. alkalis or bases such as potash (potassium carbonate) and caustic soda (a mixture of sodium oxide and sodium hydroxide) have been thought of as substances which in some sense are opposed to acids. They neutralize acids, forming salts, have a caustic or acid taste, turn red litmus blue, and have a smooth soapy texture. It is now recognized that bases, at a molecular level, may be defined as any of the substances which accept a proton in solution or are capable of donating a pair of electrons to an acid. Whether a given substance functions as an acid or as a base depends upon its chemical environment. Well-known bases are sodium and potassium hydroxide, which are used to manufacture soaps and detergents; quicklime or calcium oxide, used in the manufacture of cement; and ammonia, which is used as a fertilizer and as a chemical intermediate.

alkaline /ˈælkəˌlaɪn/ *adj.* of, relating to, or having the nature of an alkali; rich in alkali. □ **alkaline earth 1** any of the bivalent group of metals, beryllium, magnesium, calcium, strontium, barium, and radium, which resemble the alkali metals in being very reactive and in forming basic hydroxides, although these are comparatively insoluble. **2** an oxide of the lime group. □□ **alkalinity** /ˌælkəˈlɪnɪtɪ/ *n.*

alkaloid /ˈælkəˌlɔɪd/ *n.* any of a series of nitrogenous organic compounds of plant origin, many of which are used as drugs, e.g. morphine, quinine. [G (as ALKALI)]

alkalosis /ˌælkəˈləʊsɪs/ *n.* *Med.* an excessive alkaline condition of the body fluids or tissues.

alkane /ˈælkeɪn/ *n.* *Chem.* any of a series of saturated aliphatic hydrocarbons having the general formula C_nH_{2n+2}, including methane, ethane, and propane. [ALKYL + -ANE[2]]

alkanet /ˈælkəˌnet/ *n.* **1 a** any plant of the genus *Alkanna*, esp. *A. tinctoria*, yielding a red dye from its roots. **b** the dye itself. **2** any of various similar plants. [ME f. Sp. *alcaneta* dimin. of *alcana* f. Arab. *al-ḥinnāʾ* the henna shrub]

alkene /ˈælkiːn/ *n.* *Chem.* any of a series of unsaturated aliphatic hydrocarbons containing a double bond and having the general formula C_nH_{2n}, including ethylene and propene. [ALKYL + -ENE]

alkyd /ˈælkɪd/ *n.* any of the group of synthetic resins derived from various alcohols and acids. [ALKYL + ACID]

alkyl /ˈælkaɪl, ˈælkɪl/ *n.* (in full **alkyl radical**) *Chem.* any radical derived from an alkane by the removal of a hydrogen atom. [G *Alkohol* ALCOHOL + -YL]

alkylate /ˈælkɪˌleɪt/ *v.tr.* *Chem.* introduce an alkyl radical into (a compound).

alkyne /ˈælkaɪn/ *n.* *Chem.* any of a series of unsaturated aliphatic hydrocarbons containing a triple bond and having the general formula C_nH_{2n-2}, including acetylene. [ALKYL + -YNE]

all /ɔːl/ *adj., n.,* & *adv.* —*adj.* **1 a** the whole amount, quantity, or extent of (*waited all day; all his life; we all know why; take it all*). **b**

(with *pl.*) the entire number of (*all the others left; all ten men; the children are all boys; film stars all*). **2** any whatever (*beyond all doubt*). **3** greatest possible (*with all speed*). —*n.* **1 a** all the persons or things concerned (*all were present; all were thrown away*). **b** everything (*all is lost; that is all*). **2** (foll. by *of*) **a** the whole of (*take all of it*). **b** every one (*all of us*). **c** *colloq.* as much as (*all of six feet tall*). **d** *colloq.* affected by; in a state of (*all of a dither*). **3** one's whole strength or resources (prec. by *my, your,* etc.). **4** (in games) on both sides (*two goals all*). ¶ Widely used with *of* in sense 2a, b, esp. when followed by a pronoun or by a noun implying a number of persons or things, as in *all of the children are here.* However, use with mass nouns (as in *all of the bread*) is often avoided. —*adv.* **1 a** entirely, quite (*dressed all in black; all round the room; the all-important thing*). **b** as an intensifier (*a book all about ships; stop all this grumbling*). **2** *colloq.* very (*went all shy*). **3** (foll. by *the* + compar.) **a** by so much; to that extent (*if they go, all the better*). **b** in the full degree to be expected (*that makes it all the worse*). □ **all along** all the time (*he was joking all along*). **all-American 1** representing the whole of (or only) America or the US. **2** truly American (*all-American boy*). **all and sundry** everyone. **all-around** *US* = *all-round.* **All Blacks** *colloq.* the New Zealand international Rugby Union football team, so called from the colour of their uniforms. **all but** very nearly (*it was all but impossible; he was all but drowned*). **all-clear** a signal that danger or difficulty is over. **All Fools' Day** 1 April. **all for** *colloq.* strongly in favour of. **All Hallows** see HALLOW. **all-important** crucial; vitally important. **all in** *colloq.* exhausted. **all-in** (*attrib.*) inclusive of all. **all in all** everything considered. **all-in wrestling** wrestling with few or no restrictions. **all manner of** see MANNER. **all of a sudden** see SUDDEN. **all one** (or **the same**) (usu. foll. by *to*) a matter of indifference (*it's all one to me*). **all out** involving all one's strength; at full speed (also (with hyphen) *attrib.: an all-out effort*). **all over 1** completely finished. **2** in or on all parts of (esp. the body) (*went hot and cold all over; mud all over the carpet*). **3** *colloq.* typically (*that is you all over*). **4** *sl.* effusively attentive to (a person). **all-purpose** suitable for many uses. **all right** (*predic.*) **1** satisfactory; safe and sound; in good condition. **2** satisfactorily, as desired (*it worked out all right*). **3 a** an interjection expressing consent or assent to a proposal or order. **b** as an intensifier (*that's the one all right*). **all-right** *attrib.adj. colloq.* fine, acceptable (*an all-right guy*). **all round 1** in all respects (*a good performance all round*). **2** for each person (*he bought drinks all round*). **all-round** (*attrib.*) (of a person) versatile. **all-rounder** *Brit.* a versatile person. **All Saints' Day** 1 Nov. **all the same** nevertheless, in spite of this (*he was innocent but was punished all the same*). **all set** *colloq.* ready to start. **All Souls' Day** 2 Nov. **all there** *colloq.* mentally alert. **all-time** (of a record etc.) hitherto unsurpassed. **all the time** see TIME. **all together** all at once; all in one place or in a group (*they came all together*) (cf. ALTOGETHER). **all told** in all. **all-up weight** the total weight of an aircraft with passengers, cargo, etc., when airborne. **all very well** *colloq.* an expression used to reject or to imply scepticism about a favourable or consoling remark. **all the way** the whole distance; completely. **at all** (with *neg.* or *interrog.*) in any way; to any extent (*did not swim at all; did you like it at all?*). **be all up with** see UP. **in all** in total number; altogether (*there were 10 people in all*). **on all fours** see FOUR. **one and all** everyone. [OE *all, eall*, prob. f. Gmc]

alla breve /ˌælə ˈbreɪveɪ/ *n.* *Mus.* a time signature indicating 2 or 4 minim beats in a bar. [It., = at the BREVE]

alla cappella var. of A CAPPELLA.

Allah /ˈælə/ *n.* the name of God among Arabs and Muslims. [Arab. ˈallāh contr. of al-ˈilāh f. al the + ilāh god]

Allahabad /ˈɑːləhəˌbɑːd/ a city in India at the confluence at the Jumna with the Ganges. It is a place of Hindu pilgrimage.

allantois /əˈlæntəʊɪs/ *n.* (*pl.* **allantoides** /-ˌdiːz/) *Zool.* one of several membranes that develop in embryonic reptiles, birds, or mammals. □□ **allantoic** /ˌælənˈtəʊɪk/ *adj.* [mod.L f. Gk *allantoeidēs* sausage-shaped]

allay /əˈleɪ/ *v.tr.* **1** diminish (fear, suspicion, etc.). **2** relieve or alleviate (pain, hunger, etc.). [OE *ālecgan* (as A[2], LAY[1])]

Allecto /əˈlektəʊ/ *Gk Mythol.* one of the Furies. [Gk, = the implacable one]

allegation /ˌælɪˈgeɪʃ(ə)n/ n. **1** an assertion, esp. an unproved one. **2** the act or an instance of alleging. [ME f. F allégation or L allegatio f. allegare allege]

allege /əˈledʒ/ v.tr. **1** (often foll. by that + clause, or to + infin.) declare to be the case, esp. without proof. **2** advance as an argument or excuse. □□ **alleged** adj. [ME f. AF alegier, OF esligier clear at law; confused in sense with L allegare: see ALLEGATION]

allegedly /əˈledʒɪdlɪ/ adv. as is alleged or said to be the case.

Allegheny Mountains /ˌælɪˈgeɪnɪ/ (also **Alleghenies**) a mountain range of the Appalachian system in the eastern US.

allegiance /əˈliːdʒ(ə)ns/ n. **1** loyalty (to a person or cause etc.). **2** the duty of a subject to his or her sovereign or government. [ME f. AF f. OF ligeance (as LIEGE): perh. assoc. with ALLIANCE]

allegorical /ˌælɪˈgɒrɪk(ə)l/ adj. (also **allegoric** /-rɪk/) consisting of or relating to allegory; by means of allegory. □□ **allegorically** adv.

allegorize /ˈælɪgəˌraɪz/ v.tr. (also **-ise**) treat as or by means of an allegory. □□ **allegorization** /-ˈzeɪʃ(ə)n/ n.

allegory /ˈælɪgərɪ/ n. (pl. **-ies**) **1** a story, play, poem, picture, etc., in which the meaning or message is represented symbolically. **2** the use of such symbols. **3** a symbol. □□ **allegorist** n. [ME f. OF allegorie f. L allegoria f. Gk allēgoria f. allos other + -agoria speaking]

allegretto /ˌælɪˈgretəʊ/ adv., adj., & n. Mus. —adv. & adj. in a fairly brisk tempo. —n. (pl. **-os**) an allegretto passage or movement. [It., dimin. of ALLEGRO]

allegro /əˈleɪgrəʊ, əˈleg-/ adv., adj., & n. Mus. —adv. & adj. in a brisk tempo. —n. (pl. **-os**) an allegro passage or movement. [It., = lively, gay]

allele /ˈæliːl/ n. (also **allel** /ˈælel/) one of the (usu. two) alternative forms of a gene. □□ **allelic** /əˈliːlɪk/ adj. [G Allel, abbr. of ALLELOMORPH]

allelomorph /əˈliːləˌmɔːf/ n. = ALLELE. □□ **allelomorphic** /-ˈmɔːfɪk/ adj. [Gk allēl- one another + morphē form]

alleluia /ˌælɪˈluːjə/ int. & n. (also **alleluya**, **hallelujah** /hæl-/) —int. God be praised. —n. **1** praise to God. **2** a song of praise to God. **3** RC Ch. the part of the mass including this. [ME f. eccl.L f. (Septuagint) Gk allēlouia f. Heb. hallˈlūyāh praise ye the Lord]

allemande /ˈælmɑ̃nd/ n. **1 a** the name of several German dances. **b** the music for any of these, esp. as a movement of a suite. **2 a** figure in a country dance. [F, = German (dance)]

Allen /ˈæl(ə)n/, Woody (real name Allen Stewart Konigsberg, 1935–), American film director, writer, and actor, best known for his comedy films such as Take the Money and Run (1969) and Annie Hall (1977). He also starred in the film version of his play Play it Again, Sam (1969).

Allenby /ˈælənbɪ/, Edmund Henry Hynman, 1st Viscount (1861–1936), British general of the First World War, a veteran of the Boer War, who commanded the cavalry division and later the Third Army on the Western Front. In 1917 he was sent to the Middle East to lead the Egyptian Expeditionary Force. Having captured Jerusalem in December 1917, he went on to inflict total defeat on the Turkish forces in Palestine in 1918.

Allende /æˈjendɪ/, Salvador (1908–73), Chilean statesman, President of Chile 1970–3, the first avowed Marxist to win a Latin American presidency in a free election. During his brief tenure in office he set the country on a socialist path and in the process incurred the antipathy of the Chilean military establishment. A military coup, led by General Pinochet and with some indirect support from the US, overthrew him in 1973, and he died in the fighting.

Allen key /ˈæl(ə)n/ n. propr. a spanner designed to fit into and turn an Allen screw. [Allen, name of the US manufacturer]

Allen screw /ˈæl(ə)n/ n. propr. a screw with a hexagonal socket in the head.

allergen /ˈælədʒ(ə)n/ n. any substance that causes an allergic reaction. □□ **allergenic** /ˌælədʒˈdʒenɪk/ adj. [ALLERGY + -GEN]

allergic /əˈlɜːdʒɪk/ adj. **1** (foll. by to) **a** having an allergy to. **b** colloq. having a strong dislike for (a person or thing). **2** caused by or relating to an allergy.

allergy /ˈælədʒɪ/ n. (pl. **-ies**) **1** Med. a condition of reacting

adversely to certain substances, esp. particular foods, pollen, fur, or dust. **2** colloq. an antipathy. □□ **allergist** n. [G Allergie, after Energie ENERGY, f. Gk allos other]

alleviate /əˈliːvɪˌeɪt/ v.tr. lessen or make less severe (pain, suffering, etc.). □□ **alleviation** /-ˈeɪʃ(ə)n/ n. **alleviative** /əˈliːvɪətɪv/ adj. **alleviator** n. **alleviatory** /əˈliːvɪətərɪ/ adj. [LL alleviare lighten f. L allevare (as AD-, levare raise)]

alley[1] /ˈælɪ/ n. (pl. **-eys**) **1** (also **alley-way**) **a** a narrow street. **b** a narrow passageway, esp. between or behind buildings. **2** a path or walk in a park or garden. **3** an enclosure for skittles, bowling, etc. **4** (in lawn tennis) either of the two side strips of a doubles court. □ **alley cat** a stray town cat often mangy or half wild. [ME f. OF alee walking, passage f. aler go f. L ambulare walk]

alley[2] var. of ALLY[2].

alliaceous /ˌælɪˈeɪʃəs/ adj. **1** of or relating to the genus Allium. **2** tasting or smelling like onion or garlic. [mod.L alliaceus f. L allium garlic]

alliance /əˈlaɪəns/ n. **1 a** union or agreement to cooperate, esp. of States by treaty or families by marriage. **b** the parties involved. **2** (**Alliance**) a political party formed by the allying of separate parties. **3** a relationship resulting from an affinity in nature or qualities etc. (the old alliance between logic and metaphysics). **4** Bot. a group of allied families. [ME f. OF aliance (as ALLY[1])]

allied /ˈælaɪd/ adj. **1 a** united or associated in an alliance. **b** (**Allied**) of or relating to Britain and her allies in the two world wars or to the Allies in the Gulf War of 1991. **2** connected or related (studied medicine and allied subjects).

Allier /ˈælɪˌeɪ/ a river of central France which rises in the Cévennes and flows north-west to meet the Loire near Nevers.

alligator /ˈælɪˌgeɪtə(r)/ n. **1** a large reptile of the crocodile family native to S. America and China, with upper teeth that lie outside the lower teeth and a head broader and shorter than that of the crocodile. **2** (in general use) any of several large members of the crocodile family. **3 a** the skin of such an animal or material resembling it. **b** (in pl.) shoes of this. □ **alligator clip** a clip with teeth for gripping. **alligator pear** an avocado. **alligator tortoise** a large freshwater snapping turtle. [Sp. el lagarto the lizard f. L lacerta]

alliterate /əˈlɪtəˌreɪt/ v. **1** intr. **a** contain alliteration. **b** use alliteration in speech or writing. **2** tr. **a** construct (a phrase etc.) with alliteration. **b** speak or pronounce with alliteration. □□ **alliterative** /əˈlɪtərətɪv/ adj. [back-form. f. ALLITERATION]

alliteration /əˌlɪtəˈreɪʃ(ə)n/ n. the occurrence of the same letter or sound at the beginning of adjacent or closely connected words (e.g. cool, calm, and collected). [mod.L alliteratio (as AD-, littera letter)]

allium /ˈælɪəm/ n. any plant of the genus Allium, usu. bulbous and strong smelling, e.g. onion and garlic. [L, = garlic]

allo- /ˈæləʊ, əˈlɒ/ comb. form other (allophone; allogamy). [Gk allos other]

allocate /ˈæləˌkeɪt/ v.tr. (usu. foll. by to) assign or devote to (a purpose, person, or place). □□ **allocable** /ˈæləkəb(ə)l/ adj. **allocation** /ˌæləˈkeɪʃ(ə)n/ n. **allocator** n. [med.L allocare f. locus place]

allocution /ˌæləˈkjuːʃ(ə)n/ n. formal or hortatory speech or manner of address. [L allocutio f. alloqui allocut- speak to]

allogamy /əˈlɒgəmɪ/ n. Bot. cross-fertilization in plants. [ALLO- + Gk -gamia f. gamos marriage]

allomorph /ˈæləˌmɔːf/ n. Linguistics any of two or more alternative forms of a morpheme. □□ **allomorphic** /ˌæləˈmɔːfɪk/ adj. [ALLO- + MORPHEME]

allopath /ˈæləˌpæθ/ n. one who practises allopathy. [F allopathe back-form. f. allopathie = ALLOPATHY]

allopathy /əˈlɒpəθɪ/ n. the treatment of disease by conventional means, i.e. with drugs having opposite effects to the symptoms (cf. HOMOEOPATHY). □□ **allopathic** /ˌæləˈpæθɪk/ adj. **allopathist** n. [G Allopathie (as ALLO-, -PATHY)]

allophone /ˈæləˌfəʊn/ n. Linguistics any of the variant sounds forming a single phoneme. □□ **allophonic** /ˌæləˈfɒnɪk/ adj. [ALLO- + PHONEME]

allot /ə'lɒt/ *v.tr.* (**allotted, allotting**) **1** give or apportion to (a person) as a share or task; distribute officially to (*they allotted us each a pair of boots; the men were allotted duties*). **2** (foll. by *to*) give or distribute officially to (*a sum was allotted to each charity*). [OF *aloter* f. *a* to + LOT]

allotment /ə'lɒtmənt/ *n.* **1** a small piece of land rented (usu. from a local authority) for cultivation. **2** a share allotted. **3** the action of allotting.

allotrope /'ælə₁trəυp/ *n.* any of two or more different physical forms in which an element can exist (*graphite, charcoal, and diamond are all allotropes of carbon*). [back-form. f. ALLOTROPY]

allotropy /ə'lɒtrəpɪ/ *n.* the existence of two or more different physical forms of a chemical element. □□ **allotropic** /₁ælə'trɒpɪk/ *adj.* **allotropical** /₁ælə'trɒpɪk(ə)l/ *adj.* [Gk *allotropos* of another form f. *allos* different + *tropos* manner f. *trepō* to turn]

allottee /əlɒ'tɪː/ *n.* a person to whom something is allotted.

allow /ə'laυ/ *v.* **1** *tr.* permit (a practice, a person to do something, a thing to happen, etc.) (*smoking is not allowed; we allowed them to speak*). **2** *tr.* give or provide; permit (a person) to have (a limited quantity or sum) (*we were allowed £500 a year*). **3** *tr.* provide or set aside for a purpose; add or deduct in consideration of something (*allow 10% for inflation*). **4** *tr.* **a** admit, agree, concede (*he allowed that it was so; 'You know best,' he allowed*). **b** US state; be of the opinion. **5** *refl.* permit oneself, indulge oneself in (conduct) (*allowed herself to be persuaded; allowed myself a few angry words*). **6** *intr.* (foll. by *of*) admit of. **7** *intr.* (foll. by *for*) take into consideration or account; make addition or deduction corresponding to (*allowing for wastage*). □□ **allowable** *adj.* **allowably** *adv.* [ME, orig. = 'praise', f. OF *alouer* f. L *allaudare* to praise, and med.L *allocare* to place]

allowance /ə'laυəns/ *n.* & *v.* —*n.* **1** an amount or sum allowed to a person, esp. regularly for a stated purpose. **2** an amount allowed in reckoning. **3** a deduction or discount (*an allowance on your old cooker*). **4** (foll. by *of*) tolerance of. —*v.tr.* **1** make an allowance to (a person). **2** supply in limited quantities. □ **make allowances** (often foll. by *for*) **1** take into consideration (mitigating circumstances) (*made allowances for his demented state*). **2** look with tolerance upon, make excuses for (a person, bad behaviour, etc.). [ME f. OF *alouance* (as ALLOW)]

allowedly /ə'laυɪdlɪ/ *adv.* as is generally allowed or acknowledged.

alloy /'ælɔɪ, ə'lɔɪ/ *n.* & *v.* —*n.* **1** a mixture of two or more metals, e.g. brass (a mixture of copper and zinc). **2** an inferior metal mixed esp. with gold or silver. —*v.tr.* **1** mix (metals). **2** debase (a pure substance) by admixture. **3** moderate. [F *aloi* (n.), *aloyer* (v.) f. OF *aloier, aleier* combine f. L *alligare* bind]

allseed /'ɔːlsiːd/ *n.* any of various plants producing much seed, esp. *Radiola linoides*.

allspice /'ɔːlspaɪs/ *n.* **1** the aromatic spice obtained from the ground berry of the pimento plant, *Pimenta dioica*. **2** the berry of this plant. **3** any of various other aromatic shrubs.

Allston /'ɔːlst(ə)n/, Washington (1779–1843), American landscape painter, the most important artistic personality of the first generation of romanticism in the US. His early works exhibit a taste for the monumental, apocalyptic, and melodramatic, in the same vein as J. M. W. Turner or John Martin (e.g. *The Deluge*, 1804, and his vast unfinished canvas, *Belshazzar's Feast*, 1817–43). More influential in America, however, were his later, visionary, and dreamlike paintings such as *The Moonlight Landscape* (1819).

allude /ə'luːd, ə'ljuːd/ *v.intr.* (foll. by *to*) **1** refer, esp. indirectly, covertly, or briefly to. **2** *disp.* mention. [L *alludere* (as AD-, *ludere lus-* play)]

allure /ə'ljυə(r)/ *v.* & *n.* —*v.tr.* attract, charm, or fascinate. —*n.* attractiveness, personal charm, fascination. □□ **allurement** *n.* [ME f. OF *alurer* attract (as AD-, *luere* LURE 1)]

allusion /ə'luːʒ(ə)n, ə'ljuː-/ *n.* (often foll. by *to*) a reference, esp. a covert, passing, or indirect one. ¶ Often confused with *illusion*. [F *allusion* or LL *allusio* (as ALLUDE)]

allusive /ə'luːsɪv, ə'ljuː-/ *adj.* **1** (often foll. by *to*) containing an allusion. **2** containing many allusions. □□ **allusively** *adv.* **allusiveness** *n.*

alluvial /ə'luːvɪəl/ *adj.* & *n.* —*adj.* of or relating to alluvium. —*n.* alluvium, esp. containing a precious metal.

alluvion /ə'luːvɪən/ *n.* **1** the wash of the sea against the shore, or of a river against its banks. **2 a** a large overflow of water. **b** matter deposited by this, esp. alluvium. **3** the formation of new land by the movement of the sea or of a river. [F f. L *alluvio -onis* f. *luere* wash]

alluvium /ə'luːvɪəm/ *n.* (pl. **alluvia** /-vɪə/ or **alluviums**) a deposit of usu. fine fertile soil left during a time of flood, esp. in a river valley or delta. [L neut. of *alluvius* adj. f. *luere* wash]

ally[1] /'ælaɪ/ *n.* & *v.* —*n.* (pl. **-ies**) **1** a State formally cooperating or united with another for a special purpose, esp. by a treaty. **2** a person or organization that cooperates with or helps another. —*v.tr.* /also ə'laɪ/ (**-ies, -ied**) (often foll. by *with*) combine or unite in alliance. □ **the Allies** the nations allied in opposition to the Central Powers in the First World War or to the Axis Powers in the Second World War, or to Iraq in the Gulf War of 1991. [ME f. OF *al(e)ier* f. L *alligare* bind: cf. ALLOY]

ally[2] /'ælɪ/ *n.* (also **alley**) (pl. **-ies** or **-eys**) a choice playing-marble made of marble, alabaster, or glass. [perh. dimin. of ALABASTER]

-ally /əlɪ/ *suffix* forming adverbs from adjectives in *-al* (cf. -AL, -LY[2], -ICALLY).

allyl /'ælɪl, -laɪl/ *n. Chem.* the unsaturated univalent radical $CH_2 = CH - CH_2$. [L *allium* garlic + -YL]

Alma-Ata /₁ælmə 'ɑːtə/ (formerly *Vernyi*) the capital of the Soviet republic of Kazakhstan; pop. (est. 1987) 1,108,000.

almacantar var. of ALMUCANTAR.

Almagest /'ælmə₁dʒest/ **1** the title of an Arabic version of Ptolemy's astronomical treatise. **2** (in the Middle Ages; also **almagest**) any of various other celebrated textbooks on astrology and alchemy. [f. Arab. *al* the, Gk *megistē* (*suntaxis*) the great (system)]

Alma Mater /₁ælmə 'mɑːtə(r), 'meɪtə(r)/ *n.* the university, school, or college one attends or attended. [L, = bounteous mother]

almanac /'ɔːlmə₁næk, 'ɒl-/ *n.* (also **almanack**) an annual calendar of months and days, usu. with astronomical data and other information. [ME f. med.L *almanac(h)* f. Gk *almenikhiaka*]

Almanach de Gotha /₁ɒlmə₁næk də 'gəυtə/ a formerly annual publication giving information about European royalty, nobility, and diplomats, published in French by Justus Perthes of Gotha since 1763.

almandine /'ælmən₁diːn, -₁daɪn/ *n.* a kind of garnet with a violet tint. [F, alt. of obs. *alabandine* f. med.L *alabandina* f. *Alabanda*, ancient city in Asia Minor]

Alma-Tadema /₁ælmə'tædɪmə/, Sir Lawrence (1836–1912), Dutch-born painter who settled in England in 1870 and was naturalized in 1873. With Leighton and Poynter he was typical of that meticulous painting style so popular in the late 19th c. that combined archaeological accuracy with contemporary concerns to produce idealized and often sentimental reconstructions of life in the classical world. His remarkable social and financial success has yet to be endorsed by posterity as an artistic one.

almighty /ɔːl'maɪtɪ/ *adj.* & *adv.* —*adj.* **1** having complete power; omnipotent. **2** (**the Almighty**) God. **3** *sl.* very great (*an almighty crash*). —*adv. sl.* extremely; very much. [OE *ælmihtig* (as ALL, MIGHTY)]

almond /'ɑːmənd/ *n.* **1** the oval nutlike seed (kernel) of the stone-fruit from the tree *Prunus dulcis*, of which there are sweet and bitter varieties. **2** the tree itself, of the rose family and allied to the peach and plum. □ **almond eyes** narrow almond-shaped eyes. **almond oil** the oil expressed from the seed (esp. the bitter variety), used for toilet preparations, flavouring, and medicinal purposes. **almond paste** = MARZIPAN. [ME f. OF *alemande* etc. f. med.L *amandula* f. L *amygdala* f. Gk *amugdalē*: assoc. with words in AL-]

almoner /'ɑːmənə(r)/ *n.* **1** *Brit.* a social worker attached to a hospital and seeing to the after-care of patients. ¶ Now usu. called *medical social worker*. **2** *hist.* an official distributor of alms. [ME f. AF *aumoner*, OF *aumonier*, ult. f. med.L *eleëmosynarius* (as ALMS)]

almost /'ɔːlməʊst/ adv. all but; very nearly. [OE ælmǣst for the most part (as ALL, MOST)]

alms /ɑːmz/ n.pl. hist. the charitable donation of money or food to the poor. [OE ælmysse, -messe, f. Gmc ult. f. Gk eleēmosunē compassionateness f. eleēmōn (adj.) f. eleos compassion]

almshouse /'ɑːmzhaʊs/ n. hist. a house founded by charity for the poor.

almucantar /ˌælmə'kæntə(r)/ n. (also **almacantar**) Astron. a line of constant altitude above the horizon. [ME f. med.L almucantarath or F almucantara etc., f. Arab. almuḳanṭarāt sundial f. ḳanṭara arch]

aloe /'æləʊ/ n. 1 any plant of the genus Aloe, usu. having toothed fleshy leaves. 2 (in pl.) (in full **bitter aloes**) a strong laxative obtained from the bitter juice of various species of aloe. 3 (also **American aloe**) an agave native to Central America. [OE al(e)we f. L aloē f. Gk]

aloetic /ˌæləʊ'etɪk/ adj. & n. —adj. of or relating to an aloe. —n. a medicine containing aloes. [Gk aloē aloe, on the false analogy of diuretic etc.]

aloft /ə'lɒft/ predic.adj. & adv. 1 high up; overhead. 2 upwards. [ME f. ON á lopt(i) f. á in, on, to + lopt air: cf. LIFT, LOFT]

alogical /eɪ'lɒdʒɪk(ə)l/ adj. 1 not logical. 2 opposed to logic.

alone /ə'ləʊn/ adj. & adv. —predic.adj. 1 a without others present (they wanted to be alone; the tree stood alone). b without others' help (succeeded alone). c lonely and wretched (felt alone). 2 (often foll. by in) standing by oneself in an opinion etc. (was alone in thinking this). —adv. only, exclusively (you alone can help me). □ **go it alone** act by oneself without assistance. □□ **aloneness** n. [ME f. ALL + ONE]

along /ə'lɒŋ/ prep. & adv. —prep. 1 from one end to the other end of (a handkerchief with lace along the edge). 2 on or through any part of the length of (was walking along the road). 3 beside or through the length of (shelves stood along the wall). —adv. 1 onward; into a more advanced state (come along; getting along nicely). 2 at or to a particular place; arriving (I'll be along soon). 3 in company with a person, esp. oneself (bring a book along). 4 beside or through part or the whole length of a thing. □ **along with** in addition to; together with. [OE andlang f. WG, rel. to LONG¹]

alongshore /əlɒŋ'ʃɔː(r)/ adv. along or by the shore.

alongside /əlɒŋ'saɪd/ adv. & prep. —adv. at or to the side (of a ship, pier, etc.). —prep. close to the side of; next to. □ **alongside of** side by side with; together or simultaneously with.

aloof /ə'luːf/ adj. & adv. —adj. distant, unsympathetic. —adv. away, apart (he kept aloof from his colleagues). □□ **aloofly** adv. **aloofness** n. [orig. Naut., f. A² + LUFF]

alopecia /ˌælə'piːʃə/ n. Med. the absence (complete or partial) of hair from areas of the body where it normally grows; baldness. [L f. Gk alōpekia fox-mange f. alōpēx fox]

Alost see AALST.

aloud /ə'laʊd/ adv. 1 audibly; not silently or in a whisper. 2 archaic loudly. [A² + LOUD]

alow /ə'ləʊ/ adv. & predic.adj. Naut. in or into the lower part of a ship. [A² + LOW¹]

alp /ælp/ n. 1 a a high mountain. b (**the Alps**) the high range of mountains extending from the Mediterranean coast of France and NW Italy through Switzerland to the western Hungarian plain, with many peaks over 3,700 m (12,000 ft.) 2 (in Switzerland) pasture-land on a mountainside. [orig. pl., f. F f. L Alpes f. Gk Alpeis]

alpaca /æl'pækə/ n. 1 a S. American mammal, Lama pacos, related to the llama, with long shaggy hair. 2 the wool from the animal. 3 fabric made from the wool, with or without other fibres. [Sp. f. Aymará or Quechua]

alpargata /ˌælpɑː'gɑːtə/ n. a light canvas shoe with a plaited fibre sole; an espadrille. [Sp.]

alpenhorn /'ælpənˌhɔːn/ n. a long wooden horn used by Alpine herdsmen to call their cattle. [G, = Alp-horn]

alpenstock /'ælpənˌstɒk/ n. a long iron-tipped staff used in hillwalking. [G, = Alp-stick]

alpha /'ælfə/ n. 1 the first letter of the Greek alphabet (A, α). 2 a first-class mark given for a piece of work or in an examination. 3 Astron. the chief star in a constellation. □ **alpha and omega** the beginning and the end; the most important features. **alpha particle** (or **ray**) a helium nucleus emitted by a radioactive substance, orig. regarded as a ray. [ME f. L f. Gk]

alphabet /'ælfəˌbet/ n. 1 the set of letters used in writing a language (the Russian alphabet). 2 a set of symbols or signs representing letters. [LL alphabetum f. Gk alpha, bēta, the first two letters of the alphabet]

Alphabetic script developed as a consonantal system in the Levant during the second millennium BC and had assumed a linear form composed of twenty-two signs, known as 'Phoenician', by the 11th c. BC, before it was transmitted to Greece. With the introduction of the first full vocalic system, the earliest Greek alphabet of c.750 BC achieved the final structural development of writing which passed back to the Semites and thence to the rest of the world, remaining principally unaltered to the present day. The alphabet is the most flexible method of writing ever invented, passing from one language to another with minimal difficulty; it is hard to overestimate its importance.

alphabetical /ˌælfə'betɪk(ə)l/ adj. (also **alphabetic** /-'betɪk/) 1 of or relating to an alphabet. 2 in the order of the letters of the alphabet. □□ **alphabetically** adv.

alphabetize /'ælfəbəˌtaɪz/ v.tr. (also **-ise**) arrange (words, names, etc.) in alphabetical order. □□ **alphabetization** /-'zeɪʃ(ə)n/ n.

alphanumeric /ˌælfənju:'merɪk/ adj. (also **alphameric** /ˌælfə'merɪk/, **alphanumerical**) containing both alphabetical and numerical symbols. [ALPHABETIC (see ALPHABETICAL) + NUMERICAL]

alpine /'ælpaɪn/ adj. & n. —adj. 1 a of or relating to high mountains. b growing or found on high mountains. 2 (**Alpine**) of or relating to the Alps. 3 (**Alpine**) of or belonging to an extremely artificial sub-racial grouping of people who, as a population, are short (c.163 cm (5 ft. 4 in.) tall on average) with intermediate colouring, and brachycephalic. —n. a plant native or suited to mountain districts. [L Alpinus: see ALP]

Alpinist /'ælpɪnɪst/ n. (also **alpinist**) a climber of high mountains, esp. the Alps. [F alpiniste (as ALPINE; see -IST)]

already /ɔːl'redɪ/ adv. 1 before the time in question (I knew that already). 2 as early or as soon as this (already at the age of six). [ALL adv. + READY]

alright /ɔːl'raɪt/ adv. disp. = all right.

Alsace /æl'sæs/ a French region west of the Rhine; pop. (1982) 1,566,000; capital, Strasbourg. It was annexed with part of Lorraine (the annexed territory was known as Alsace-Lorraine) after the Franco-Prussian war of 1870, and restored to France after the First World War.

Alsatian /æl'seɪʃ(ə)n/ n. 1 a a large dog of a breed of wolfhound. b this breed (also called German shepherd dog). 2 a native of Alsace. [Alsatia (= Alsace) + -AN]

alsike /'ælsɪk/ n. a species of clover, Trifolium hybridum. [Alsike in Sweden]

also /'ɔːlsəʊ/ adv. in addition; likewise; besides. □ **also-ran 1** a horse or dog etc. not among the winners in a race. 2 an undistinguished person. [OE alswā (as ALL adv., SO¹)]

Alta. abbr. Alberta.

Altai /'æltaɪ/ a territory of the Russian SFSR in SW Siberia; pop. (1985) 2,744,000; capital, Barnaul.

Altaic /æl'taɪk/ adj. & n. —adj. of the Altai Mountains in central Asia, or a family of languages comprising the Turkic, Mongolian, and Tungusic groups. —n. this family of languages, whose common features include vowel harmony, with all the vowels of a word belonging to the same class (i.e. either front or back).

Altai Mountains /'æltaɪ/ a mountain system of central Asia extending about 1,600 km (1,000 miles) in a south-easterly direction from Siberia in the USSR through Mongolia and NW China to the Gobi Desert.

Altamira¹ /ˌæltə'miːrə/ the site of a cave with palaeolithic rock paintings, south of Santander in NE Spain, discovered in 1879. The paintings are boldly executed polychrome figures of animals, including deer, wild boar, aurochs, and especially bison, depicted with a sure realism; they are dated to the upper Magdalenian period.

Altamira² /ˌæltəˈmɪərə/ a town in the State of Pará, NE Brazil, which attracted world attention in 1989 when it was the venue of a major rally of Amerindians and environmentalists who gathered to protest against the devastation of the Amazonian rain forest.

altar /ˈɔːltə(r), ˈɒl-/ n. **1** a table or flat-topped block, often of stone, for sacrifice or offering to a deity. **2** a Communion-table. □ **altar boy** a boy who serves as a priest's assistant in a service. **lead to the altar** marry (a woman). [OE *altar -er*, Gmc adoption of LL *altar*, *altarium* f. L *altaria* (pl.) burnt offerings, altar, prob. rel. to *adolēre* burn in sacrifice]

altarpiece /ˈɔːltəpiːs, ˈɒl-/ n. a piece of art, esp. a painting, set above or behind an altar.

altazimuth /ælˈtæzɪməθ/ n. an instrument for measuring the altitude and azimuth of celestial bodies. [ALTITUDE + AZIMUTH]

Altdorfer /ˈæltdɔːfə(r)/, Albrecht (*c.*1485–1538), German painter. In his early works he was preoccupied with the problem of setting figures in a landscape which reflected the mood of the human activity; in his late years he painted pure landscapes, miniatures on vellum, and is an important figure in the history of the appreciation of scenery for its own sake. Altdorfer was employed by the Emperor Maximilian, and together with Dürer and others illustrated the margins of the Emperor's prayer-book. From 1526 he was town architect of Regensburg in Bavaria.

alter /ˈɔːltə(r), ˈɒl-/ v. **1** tr. & intr. make or become different; change. **2** tr. US & Austral. castrate or spay. □□ **alterable** adj. **alteration** /-ˈreɪʃ(ə)n/ n. [ME f. OF *alterer* f. LL *alterare* f. L *alter* other]

alterative /ˈɔːltərətɪv, ˈɒl-/ adj. & n. —adj. **1** tending to alter. **2** (of a medicine) that alters bodily processes. —n. an alterative medicine or treatment. [ME f. med.L *alterativus* (as ALTER)]

altercate /ˈɔːltəˌkeɪt, ˈɒl-/ v.intr. (often foll. by *with*) dispute hotly; wrangle. □□ **altercation** /-ˈkeɪʃ(ə)n/ n. [L *altercari altercat-*]

alter ego /ˌæltər ˈiːɡəʊ, ˈeɡəʊ/ n. (pl. ***alter egos***) **1** an intimate and trusted friend. **2** a person's secondary or alternative personality. [L, = other self]

alternate v., adj., & n. —v. /ˈɔːltəˌneɪt, ˈɒl-/ **1** intr. (often foll. by *with*) (of two things) succeed each other by turns (*rain and sunshine alternated; elation alternated with depression*). **2** intr. (foll. by *between*) change repeatedly (between two conditions) (*the patient alternated between hot and cold fevers*). **3** tr. (often foll. by *with*) cause (two things) to succeed each other by turns (*the band alternated fast and slow tunes; we alternated criticism with reassurance*). —adj. /ɔːlˈtɜːnət, ɒl-/ **1** (with noun in pl.) every other (*comes on alternate days*). **2** (of things of two kinds) each following and succeeded by one of the other kind (*alternate joy and misery*). **3** (of a sequence etc.) consisting of alternate things. **4** Bot. (of leaves etc.) placed alternately on the two sides of the stem. **5** = ALTERNATIVE. —n. /ɔːlˈtɜːnət, ɒl-/ esp. US a deputy or substitute. □ **alternate angles** two angles, not adjoining one another, that are formed on opposite sides of a line that intersects two other lines. **alternating current** an electric current that reverses its direction at regular intervals. □□ **alternately** /ɔːlˈtɜːnətlɪ, ɒl-/ adv. [L *alternatus* past part. of *alternare* do things by turns f. *alternus* every other f. *alter* other]

alternation /ˌɔːltəˈneɪʃ(ə)n, ˌɒl-/ n. the action or result of alternating. □ **alternation of generations** a pattern of reproduction occurring in the life cycles of many lower plants (e.g. ferns) and some invertebrate animals (especially coelenterates), involving a regular alternation between two distinct forms, differently produced and often very different from each other. Generation is alternately sexual and asexual (as in ferns) or dioecious and parthenogenetic (as in some jellyfish).

alternative /ɔːlˈtɜːnətɪv, ɒl-/ adj. & n. —adj. **1** (of one or more things) available or usable instead of another (*an alternative route*). ¶ Use with reference to more than two options (e.g. *many alternative methods*) is common, and acceptable. **2** (of two things) mutually exclusive. **3** of or relating to practices that offer a

substitute for the conventional ones (*alternative medicine; alternative theatre*). —n. **1** any of two or more possibilities. **2** the freedom or opportunity to choose between two or more things (*I had no alternative but to go*). □ **Alternative Service Book,** a book containing the public liturgy of the Church of England published in 1980 for use as the alternative to the Book of Common Prayer. **the alternative society** a group of people dissociating themselves from conventional society and its values. □□ **alternatively** adv. [F *alternatif -ive* or med.L *alternativus* (as ALTERNATE)]

alternator /ˈɔːltəˌneɪtə(r), ˈɒl-/ n. a dynamo that generates an alternating current.

althorn /ˈælthɔːn/ n. Mus. an instrument of the saxhorn family, esp. the alto or tenor saxhorn in E flat. [G f. *alt* high f. L *altus* + HORN]

although /ɔːlˈðəʊ/ conj. = THOUGH conj. 1–3. [ME f. ALL adv. + THOUGH]

altimeter /ˈæltɪˌmiːtə(r)/ n. an instrument for showing height above sea or ground level, esp. one fitted to an aircraft. [L *altus* high + -METER]

altiplano /ˌæltɪˈplɑːnəʊ/ n. (pl. **-os**) a high-altitude plateau or plain, esp. that in the Andes in western Bolivia and southern Peru. [Amer. Sp., f. L *altus* high + *planum* plain]

altitude /ˈæltɪtjuːd/ n. **1** the height of an object in relation to a given point, esp. sea level or the horizon. **2** Geom. the length of the perpendicular from a vertex to the opposite side of a figure. **3** a high or exalted position (*a social altitude*). □ **altitude sickness** a sickness experienced at high altitudes. □□ **altitudinal** /ˌæltɪˈtjuːdɪn(ə)l/ adj. [ME f. L *altitudo* f. *altus* high]

alto /ˈæltəʊ/ n. (pl. **-os**) **1** = CONTRALTO. **2 a** the highest adult male singing-voice, above tenor. **b** a singer with this voice. **c** a part written for it. **3 a** (attrib.) denoting the member of a family of instruments pitched second- or third-highest. **b** an alto instrument, esp. an alto saxophone. □ **alto clef** a clef placing middle C on the middle line of the staff, used chiefly for viola music. [It. *alto* (*canto*) high (singing)]

altocumulus /ˌæltəʊˈkjuːmjʊləs/ n. (pl. **altocumuli** /-ˌlaɪ/) Meteorol. a cloud formation at medium altitude consisting of rounded masses with a level base. [mod.L f. L *altus* high + CUMULUS]

altogether /ˌɔːltəˈɡeðə(r)/ adv. **1** totally, completely (*you are altogether wrong*). **2** on the whole (*altogether it had been a good day*). **3** in total (*there are six bedrooms altogether*). ¶ Note that *all together* is used to mean 'all at once' or 'all in one place', as in *there are six bedrooms all together*. □ **in the altogether** colloq. naked. [ME f. ALL + TOGETHER]

alto-relievo /ˌæltəʊrɪˈliːvəʊ/ n. (pl. **-os**) Sculpture **1** a form of relief in which the sculptured shapes stand out from the background to at least half their actual depth. **2** a sculpture characterized by this. [ALTO + RELIEVO]

altostratus /ˌæltəʊˈstreɪtəs, -ˈstrɑːtəs/ n. (pl. **altostrati** /-tɪ/) a continuous and uniformly flat cloud formation at medium altitude. [mod.L f. L *altus* high + STRATUS]

altricial /ælˈtrɪʃ(ə)l/ adj. & n. —adj. (of a bird) whose young require care and feeding by the parents after hatching. —n. an altricial bird (cf. PRAECOCIAL). [L *altrix altricis* (fem.) nourisher f. *altor* f. *alere altus* nourish]

altruism /ˈæltruːˌɪz(ə)m/ n. **1** regard for others as a principle of action. **2** unselfishness; concern for other people. □□ **altruist** n. **altruistic** /ˌæltruːˈɪstɪk/ adj. **altruistically** /ˌæltruːˈɪstɪkəlɪ/ adv. [F *altruisme* f. It. *altrui* somebody else (infl. by L *alter* other)]

alum /ˈæləm/ n. **1** a double sulphate of aluminium and potassium. **2** any of a group of compounds of double sulphates of a monovalent metal (or group) and a trivalent metal. [ME f. OF f. L *alumen aluminis*]

alumina /əˈluːmɪnə/ n. the compound aluminium oxide occurring naturally as corundum and emery. [L *alumen* alum, after *soda* etc.]

aluminium /ˌæljʊˈmɪnɪəm/ n. (US **aluminum** /əˈluːmɪnəm/) a silvery light and malleable metallic element, having a valency of three. It is the most abundant metal in the earth's crust but it does not occur in uncombined form in nature and was obtained in the pure state only in 1825. Although very reactive, it forms a tough surface layer of oxide when exposed to air, protecting it against further corrosion. Its lightness, good thermal and electrical conductivity, and strength (when alloyed) have led to its widespread use in domestic utensils, engineering parts, and aircraft construction. The main commercial ore is bauxite, but aluminium is also a major constituent of clays and feldspars. ¶ Symb.: Al; atomic number 13. □ **aluminium bronze** an alloy of copper and aluminium. [*aluminium*, alt. (after *sodium* etc.) f. *aluminum*, earlier *alumium* f. ALUM + -IUM]

aluminize /ə'lu:mɪˌnaɪz/ *v.tr.* (also **-ise**) coat with aluminium. □□ **aluminization** /-'zeɪʃ(ə)n/ *n.*

alumnus /ə'lʌmnəs/ *n.* (*pl.* **alumni** /-nɪ/; *fem.* **alumna**, *pl.* **alumnae** /-nɪ/) a former pupil or student. [L, = nursling, pupil f. *alere* nourish]

alveolar /æl'vɪələ(r), ˌælvɪ'əʊlə(r)/ *adj.* **1** of an alveolus. **2** *Phonet.* (of a consonant) pronounced with the tip of the tongue in contact with the ridge of the upper teeth, e.g. *n*, *s*, *t*. [ALVEOLUS + -AR¹]

alveolus /æl'vɪələs, ˌælvɪ'əʊləs/ *n.* (*pl.* **alveoli** /-laɪ, -lɪ/) **1** a small cavity, pit, or hollow. **2** any of the many tiny air sacs of the lungs which allow for rapid gaseous exchange. **3** the bony socket for the root of a tooth. **4** the cell of a honeycomb. □□ **alveolate** *adj.* [L dimin. of *alveus* cavity]

always /'ɔ:lweɪz/ *adv.* **1** at all times; on all occasions (*they are always late*). **2** whatever the circumstances (*I can always sleep on the floor*). **3** repeatedly; often (*they are always complaining*). [ME, prob. distrib. genit. f. ALL + WAY + -'s¹]

alyssum /'ælɪsəm/ *n.* any plant of the genus *Alyssum*, widely cultivated and usu. having yellow or white flowers. [L f. Gk *alusson*]

Alzheimer's disease /'ælts,haɪməz/ *n.* a serious disorder of the brain manifesting itself in premature senility. [A. *Alzheimer*, Ger. neurologist d. 1915]

AM *abbr.* **1** amplitude modulation. **2** *US* Master of Arts. **3** Member of the Order of Australia. [(sense 2) L *artium Magister*]

Am *symb. Chem.* the element americium.

am *1st person sing. present of* BE.

a.m. *abbr.* before noon. [L *ante meridiem*]

amadavat /ˌæmədə'væt/ *n.* (also **avadavat** /ˌævə-/) either of two small brightly coloured S. Asian waxbills, the green *Amandava formosa* or esp. the red *A. amandava*. [*Ahmadabad* in India]

amadou /'æməˌdu:/ *n.* a spongy and combustible tinder prepared from dry fungi. [F f. mod.Prov., lit. = lover (because quickly kindled) f. L (as AMATEUR)]

amah /'ɑ:mə/ *n.* (in the Far East and India) a nursemaid or maid. [Port. *ama* nurse]

Amalfi /ə'mælfɪ/ a port and holiday resort about 40 km (25 miles) south-east of Naples, on the Gulf of Salerno; pop. (1981) 6,000.

amalgam /ə'mælgəm/ *n.* **1** a mixture or blend. **2** an alloy of mercury with one or more other metals, used esp. in dentistry. [ME f. F *amalgame* or med.L *amalgama* f. Gk *malagma* an emollient]

amalgamate /ə'mælgəˌmeɪt/ *v.* **1** *tr.* & *intr.* combine or unite to form one structure, organization, etc. **2** *intr.* (of metals) alloy with mercury. □□ **amalgamation** /-'meɪʃ(ə)n/ *n.* [med.L *amalgamare amalgamat-* (as AMALGAM)]

amanuensis /əˌmænju:'ensɪs/ *n.* (*pl.* **amanuenses** /-si:z/) **1** a person who writes from dictation or copies manuscripts. **2** a literary assistant. [L f. (*servus*) *a manu* secretary + -*ensis* belonging to]

amaranth /'æməˌrænθ/ *n.* **1** any plant of the genus *Amaranthus*, usu. having small green, red, or purple tinted flowers, e.g. prince's feather and pigweed. **2** an imaginary flower that never fades. **3** a purple colour. □□ **amaranthine** /ˌæmə'rænθaɪn/ *adj.* [F *amarante* or mod.L *amaranthus* f. L f. Gk *amarantos* everlasting f. *a-* not + *marainō* wither, alt. after *polyanthus* etc.]

Amarna /ə'mɑ:nə/, **Tell el-** the modern name of Akhetaten (= 'the horizon of the Aten'), the short-lived capital of ancient Egypt, founded by Akhenaten in the fifth year of his reign 450km (280 miles) north of Thebes and dismantled by his successors.

It is particularly famous for its lively and expressionistic art, which shows a conscious divergence from the old artistic conventions, and for the cuneiform tablets known as the Amarna Letters, discovered in 1887. These texts contain letters written by Assyrian and Mitannian kings, and by native chiefs and Egyptian governors in Syria and Palestine, providing valuable insight into Near Eastern diplomacy of the 14th c. BC.

amaryllis /ˌæmə'rɪlɪs/ *n.* **1** a plant genus with a single species, *Amaryllis belladonna*, a bulbous lily-like plant native to S. Africa with white or rose-pink flowers (also called *belladonna lily*). **2** any of various related plants formerly of this genus now transferred to other genera, notably *Hippeastrum*. [L f. Gk *Amarullis*, name of a country girl]

amass /ə'mæs/ *v.tr.* **1** gather or heap together. **2** accumulate (esp. riches). □□ **amasser** *n.* [F *amasser* or med.L *amassare* ult. f. L *massa* MASS¹]

amateur /'æmətə(r)/ *n.* **1** a person who engages in a pursuit (e.g. an art or sport) as a pastime rather than a profession. **2** (*attrib.*) for or done by amateurs (*amateur athletics*). **3** (foll. by *of*) a person who is fond of a thing. □□ **amateurism** *n.* [F f. It. *amatore* f. L *amator -oris* lover f. *amare* love]

amateurish /'æmətərɪʃ/ *adj.* characteristic of an amateur, esp. unskilful or inexperienced. □□ **amateurishly** *adv.* **amateurishness** *n.*

Amati /ə'mɑ:tɪ/ a family of Italian violin-makers, of whom three generations worked in Cremona: Andrea (*c.*1520–1611), his sons Antonio (1550–1638) and Girolamo (1551–1635), and, most famous of them all, Nicolò (1596–1684). From Nicolò's workshop came Antonio Stradivari and Andreas Guarneri, great-uncle of the celebrated Giuseppe Guarneri 'del Gesù'. The Amatis were responsible for the classic shape of the violin, flattening the body by deepening the middle curvature, sharpening the corners, and rounding the sound-holes in a more elegant shape.

amatory /'æmətərɪ/ *adj.* of or relating to sexual love or desire. [L *amatorius* f. *amare* love]

amaurosis /ˌæmə'rəʊsɪs/ *n.* the partial or total loss of sight, from disease of the optic nerve, retina, spinal cord, or brain. □□ **amaurotic** /-'rɒtɪk/ *adj.* [mod.L f. Gk f. *amauroō* darken f. *amauros* dim]

amaze /ə'meɪz/ *v.tr.* (often foll. by *at*, or *that* + clause, or *to* + infin.) surprise greatly; overwhelm with wonder (*am amazed at your indifference*; *was amazed to find them alive*). □□ **amazement** *n.* **amazing** *adj.* **amazingly** *adv.* **amazingness** *n.* [ME f. OE *āmasod* past part. of *āmasian*, of uncert. orig.]

Amazon¹ /'æməz(ə)n/ *n.* **1** a member of a mythical race of female warriors in Scythia and elsewhere. (See below.) **2** (**amazon**) a very tall, strong, or athletic woman. □□ **Amazonian** /ˌæmə'zəʊnɪən/ *adj.* [ME f. L f. Gk: expl. by the Greeks as 'breastless' (as if A-¹ + *mazos* breast), but prob. of foreign orig.]

   The Amazons were alleged to exist somewhere on the borders of the known world. Their name was explained by the Greeks as meaning 'without a breast', in connection with the fable that they destroyed the right breast so as not to interfere with the use of the bow, but this is probably the popular etymology of an unknown word. They caught the Greek imagination and appear in many legends. Amazons appear as allies of the Trojans in the Trojan war, and their queen, Penthesilea, was killed by Achilles. One of the labours of Hercules was to obtain the girdle of Hippolyta, queen of the Amazons. According to Athenian legend, Attica once suffered an invasion of Amazons, which Theseus repelled.

Amazon² /'æməz(ə)n/ a great river in South America, 6,570 km (4,080 miles) long, flowing into the Atlantic Ocean on the north coast of Brazil. It drains two-fifths of the continent and in terms of water-flow it is the largest river in the world. It bore various names after its discovery in 1500 and was finally named because of a legend that a tribe of female warriors lived somewhere on its banks. □□ **Amazonian** /ˌæmə'zəʊnɪən/ *adj.*

ambassador /æm'bæsədə(r)/ *n.* **1** an accredited diplomat sent by a State on a mission to, or as its permanent representative in, a foreign country. **2** a representative or promoter of a specified thing (*an ambassador of peace*). □ **ambassador-at-large** *US* an ambassador with special duties, not appointed to a particular country. □□ **ambassadorial** /ˌæmbæsəˈdɔːrɪəl/ *adj.* **ambassadorship** *n.* [ME f. F *ambassadeur* f. It. *ambasciator*, ult. f. L *ambactus* servant]

ambassadress /æmˈbæsədrɪs/ *n.* **1** a female ambassador. **2** an ambassador's wife.

ambatch /ˈæmbætʃ/ *n.* an African tree, *Aeschynomene elaphroxylon*, with very light spongy wood. [Ethiopic]

Ambato /æmˈbɑːtəʊ/ a picturesque market town and transportation centre in the Andes of central Ecuador; pop. (1982) 221,000. The town was almost totally destroyed by an earthquake in 1949.

amber /ˈæmbə(r)/ *n.* & *adj.* —*n.* **1 a** a yellowish translucent fossilized resin deriving from extinct (esp. coniferous) trees and used in jewellery. **b** the honey-yellow colour of this. **2** a yellow traffic-light meaning caution, showing between red for 'stop' and green for 'go'. —*adj.* made of or coloured like amber. [ME f. OF *ambre* f. Arab. *'anbar* ambergris, amber]

Amber is found chiefly along the southern shores of the Baltic Sea. It burns with an agreeable odour, often entombs the bodies of insects etc. which were trapped in the resin before it hardened, and when rubbed becomes charged with static electricity and has the property of attracting small particles (the word *electric* is derived from the Greek word for *amber*). It has been used for ornaments since the mesolithic period and seems to have been the basic commodity of regular prehistoric trade routes from the Baltic along the Elbe and Vistula rivers down to the Adriatic Sea.

ambergris /ˈæmbəɡrɪs, -ˌɡriːs/ *n.* a strong-smelling waxlike secretion of the intestine of the sperm whale, found floating in tropical seas and used in perfume manufacture. [ME f. OF *ambre gris* grey AMBER]

amberjack /ˈæmbəˌdʒæk/ *n.* US any large brightly-coloured marine fish of the genus *Seriola* found in tropical and subtropical Atlantic waters.

ambiance var. of AMBIENCE.

ambidextrous /ˌæmbɪˈdekstrəs/ *adj.* (also **ambidexterous**) **1** able to use the right and left hands equally well. **2** working skilfully in more than one medium. □□ **ambidexterity** /-ˈsterɪtɪ/ *n.* **ambidextrously** *adv.* **ambidextrousness** *n.* [LL *ambidexter* f. *ambi-* on both sides + *dexter* right-handed]

ambience /ˈæmbɪəns/ *n.* (also **ambiance**) the surroundings or atmosphere of a place. [AMBIENT + -ENCE or F *ambiance*]

ambient /ˈæmbɪənt/ *adj.* surrounding. [F *ambiant* or L *ambiens -entis* pres. part. of *ambire* go round]

ambiguity /ˌæmbɪˈɡjuːɪtɪ/ *n.* (pl. **-ies**) **1 a** a double meaning which is either deliberate or caused by inexactness of expression. **b** an example of this. **2** an expression able to be interpreted in more than one way (e.g. *dogs must be carried*). [ME f. OF *ambiguité* or L *ambiguitas* (as AMBIGUOUS)]

ambiguous /æmˈbɪɡjʊəs/ *adj.* **1** having an obscure or double meaning. **2** difficult to classify. □□ **ambiguously** *adv.* **ambiguousness** *n.* [L *ambiguus* doubtful f. *ambigere* f. *ambi-* both ways + *agere* drive]

ambisonics /ˌæmbɪˈsɒnɪks/ *n.pl.* a system of high-fidelity sound reproduction designed to reproduce the directional and acoustic properties of the sound source using two or more channels. [L *ambi-* on both sides + SONIC]

ambit /ˈæmbɪt/ *n.* **1** the scope, extent, or bounds of something. **2** precincts or environs. [ME f. L *ambitus* circuit f. *ambire*: see AMBIENT]

ambition /æmˈbɪʃ(ə)n/ *n.* **1** (often foll. by *to* + infin.) the determination to achieve success or distinction, usu. in a chosen field. **2** the object of this determination. [ME f. OF f. L *ambitio -onis* f. *ambire ambit-* canvass for votes: see AMBIENT]

ambitious /æmˈbɪʃəs/ *adj.* **1 a** full of ambition. **b** showing ambition (*an ambitious attempt*). **2** (foll. by *of*, or *to* + infin.) strongly determined. □□ **ambitiously** *adv.* **ambitiousness** *n.* [ME f. OF *ambitieux* f. L *ambitiosus* (as AMBITION)]

ambivalence /æmˈbɪvələns/ *n.* (also **ambivalency** /-ənsɪ/) the coexistence in one person's mind of opposing feelings, esp.

love and hate, in a single context. □□ **ambivalent** *adj.* **ambivalently** *adv.* [G *Ambivalenz* f. L *ambo* both, after *equivalence, -ency*]

ambivert /ˈæmbɪˌvɜːt/ *n.* Psychol. a person who fluctuates between being an introvert and an extrovert. □□ **ambiversion** /ˌæmbɪˈvɜːʃ(ə)n/ *n.* [L *ambi-* on both sides + *-vert* f. L *vertere* to turn, after EXTROVERT, INTROVERT]

amble /ˈæmb(ə)l/ *v.* & *n.* —*v.intr.* **1** move at an easy pace, in a way suggesting an ambling horse. **2** (of a horse etc.) move by lifting the two feet on one side together. **3** ride an ambling horse; ride at an easy pace. —*n.* an easy pace; the gait of an ambling horse. [ME f. OF *ambler* f. L *ambulare* walk]

amblyopia /ˌæmblɪˈəʊpɪə/ *n.* dimness of vision without obvious defect or change in the eye. □□ **amblyopic** /-ˈɒpɪk/ *adj.* [Gk f. *ambluōpos* (adj.) f. *amblus* dull + *ōps, ōpos* eye]

ambo /ˈæmbəʊ/ *n.* (pl. **-os** or **ambones** /-ˈbəʊniːz/) a stand for reading lessons in an early Christian church etc. [med.L f. Gk *ambōn* rim (in med.Gk = pulpit)]

amboyna /æmˈbɔɪnə/ *n.* the decorative wood of the SE Asian tree *Pterocarpus indicus*. [*Amboyna* Island in Indonesia]

Ambrose /ˈæmbrəʊz/, St (c.339–97), Doctor of the Church. He was a Roman governor at Milan when, a converted Christian though not yet baptized, he was elected bishop of Milan (374) by popular demand, and became a famous preacher and champion of orthodoxy. To him was partly due the conversion of St Augustine. His knowledge of Greek enabled him to introduce much Eastern theology into the West; he wrote on ascetical subjects, and encouraged monasticism. The so-called Athanasian Creed has been attributed to him. Feast day, 7 Dec.

ambrosia /æmˈbrəʊzɪə, -ʒə/ *n.* **1** Gk & Rom. Mythol.the food of the gods; the elixir of life. **2** anything very pleasing to taste or smell. **3** the food of certain bees and beetles. □□ **ambrosial** *adj.* **ambrosian** *adj.* [L f. Gk, = elixir of life f. *ambrotos* immortal]

ambry var. of AUMBRY.

ambulance /ˈæmbjʊləns/ *n.* **1** a vehicle specially equipped for conveying the sick or injured to and from hospital, esp. in emergencies. **2** a mobile hospital following an army. [F (as AMBULANT)]

ambulant /ˈæmbjʊlənt/ *adj.* Med. **1** (of a patient) able to walk about; not confined to bed. **2** (of treatment) not confining a patient to bed. [L *ambulare ambulant-* walk]

ambulatory /ˈæmbjʊlətərɪ/ *adj.* & *n.* —*adj.* **1** = AMBULANT. **2** of or adapted for walking. **3 a** movable. **b** not permanent. —*n.* (pl. **-ies**) a place for walking, esp. an aisle or cloister in a church or monastery. [L *ambulatorius* f. *ambulare* walk]

ambuscade /ˌæmbəˈskeɪd/ *n.* & *v.* —*n.* an ambush. —*v.* **1** *tr.* attack by means of an ambush. **2** *intr.* lie in ambush. **3** *tr.* conceal in an ambush. [F *embuscade* f. It. *imboscata* or Sp. *emboscada* f. L *imboscare*: see AMBUSH, -ADE¹]

ambush /ˈæmbʊʃ/ *n.* & *v.* —*n.* **1** a surprise attack by persons (e.g. troops) in a concealed position. **2 a** the concealment of troops etc. to make such an attack. **b** the place where they are concealed. **c** the troops etc. concealed. —*v.tr.* **1** attack by means of an ambush. **2** lie in wait for. [ME f. OF *embusche, embuschier*, f. a Rmc form = 'put in a wood': rel. to BUSH¹]

ameba US var. of AMOEBA.

ameer var. of AMIR.

ameliorate /əˈmiːlɪəˌreɪt/ *v.tr.* & *intr. formal* make or become better; improve. □□ **amelioration** /əˌmiːlɪəˈreɪʃ(ə)n/ *n.* **ameliorative** *adj.* **ameliorator** *n.* [alt. of MELIORATE after F *améliorer*]

amen /ɑːˈmen, eɪ-/ *int.* & *n.* —*int.* **1** uttered at the end of a prayer or hymn etc., meaning 'so be it'. **2** (foll. by *to*) expressing agreement or assent (*amen to that*). —*n.* an utterance of 'amen' (sense 1). [ME f. eccl.L f. Gk f. Heb. *'āmēn* certainly]

amenable /əˈmiːnəb(ə)l/ *adj.* **1** responsive, tractable. **2** (often foll. by *to*) (of a person) responsible to law. **3** (foll. by *to*) (of a thing) subject or liable. □□ **amenability** /-ˈbɪlɪtɪ/ *n.* **amenableness** *n.* **amenably** *adv.* [AF (Law) f. F *amener* bring to f. *a-* to + *mener* bring f. LL *minare* drive animals f. L *minari* threaten]

amend /əˈmend/ *v.tr.* **1** make minor improvements in (a text or a written proposal). **2** correct an error or errors in (a document). **3** make better; improve. ¶ Often confused with *emend*, a more technical word used in the context of textual correction. □□ **amendable** *adj.* **amender** *n.* [ME f. OF *amender* ult. f. L *emendare* EMEND]

amende honorable /ɔˌmãd ɒnɔːˈraːb(ə)l/ *n.* (*pl.* **amendes honorables** *pronunc.* same) a public or open apology, often with some form of reparation. (Originally a punishment known in France from the 12th c. to the Revolution, involving a public and humiliating acknowledgement of crime, imposed in cases of public scandal and frequently required before execution.) [F, = honourable reparation]

amendment /əˈmendmənt/ *n.* **1** a minor improvement in a document (esp. a legal or statutory one). **2** an article added to the US Constitution. [AMEND + -MENT]

amends /əˈmendz/ *n.* □ **make amends** (often foll. by *for*) compensate or make up (for). [ME f. OF *amendes* penalties, fine, pl. of *amende* reparation f. *amender* AMEND]

amenity /əˈmiːnɪtɪ, əˈmenɪtɪ/ *n.* (*pl.* **-ies**) **1** (usu. in *pl.*) a pleasant or useful feature. **2** pleasantness (of a place, person, etc.). □ **amenity-bed** *Brit.* a bed available in a hospital to give more privacy for a small payment. [ME f. OF *amenité* or L *amoenitas* f. *amoenus* pleasant]

Amenophis /ˌɑːmenˈəʊfɪs/ the name of four Egyptian pharaohs of the 18th Dynasty (1550–1307 BC). □□ **Amenophis IV** see AKHENATEN.

amenorrhoea /eɪˌmenəˈrɪə/ *n.* (*US* **amenorrhea**) *Med.* an abnormal absence of menstruation. [A-[1] + MENO- + Gk -*rrhoia* f. *rheō* flow]

ament /ˈament/ *n.* (also **amentum** /-təm/) (*pl.* **aments** or **amenta** /-tə/) a catkin. [L, = thong]

amentia /əˈmenʃə/ *n.* *Med.* severe congenital mental deficiency. [L f. *amens* *ament-* mad (as A-[1], *mens* mind)]

amerce /əˈmɜːs/ *v.tr.* **1** *Law* punish by fine. **2** punish arbitrarily. □□ **amercement** *n.* **amerciable** /-stəb(ə)l/ *adj.* [ME *amercy* f. AF *amercier* f. *a* at + *merci* MERCY]

America /əˈmerɪkə/ **1** a continent of the New World or western hemisphere, consisting of two great land-masses, North and South America, joined by the narrow isthmus of Central America. North America was probably visited by Norse seamen in the 8th or 9th c., but for the modern world the continent was discovered by Christopher Columbus, who reached the West Indies in 1492 and the South American mainland in 1498. **2** the United States of America.

The name of America dates from the early 16th c. The traditional explanation is that it derives from the Latin form (*Americus*) of the name of the explorer Amerigo Vespucci, who sailed along the west coast of South America in 1501 while seeking a sea route to the Orient; he concluded that the land mass was not a part of Asia. The name was later applied to the North and South continents. Another suggestion is that it was named after a Bristol merchant Richard Ameryk (or Amerik), who is said to have invested in Cabot's second voyage. As a customs collector he paid Cabot his pension of £20, but whether his name was used for the new land is a matter of speculation.

American /əˈmerɪkən/ *adj.* & *n.* —*adj.* **1** of, relating to, or characteristic of the United States or its inhabitants. **2** (usu. in *comb.*) of or relating to the continents of America (*Latin-American*). —*n.* **1** a native or citizen of the United States. **2** (usu. in *comb.*) a native or inhabitant of the continents of America (*North Americans*). **3** the English language as it is used in the United States. □ **American dream** the traditional ideals of the American people, such as equality, democracy, and material prosperity.

Americana /əˌmerɪˈkɑːnə/ *n.pl.* things connected with America, esp. with the United States.

American English *n.* the English language as spoken and written in the US. Serious and cultured speech and writing does not differ greatly from that used in Britain, but during the 300 years in which American English has been developing many new words or meanings have been added to make the languages distinct from each other. These include adoptions from languages with which the early settlers came in contact (e.g.

moccasin, pecan, racoon from Indian languages; *prairie, shanty* from French; *corral, lasso, ranch* from Spanish; *boss, sleigh* from Dutch), changes in meaning (e.g. *corn*, English = cereal plants, American = maize), survivals of 17th–18th-c. English (e.g. *guess* = suppose, *fall* = autumn, *gotten* = got), different words for the same thing (*elevator* = lift, *sidewalk* = pavement), and there are some notable differences in grammar and construction (e.g. the American *to teach school, I just ate, a quarter of ten*). There are also differences in spelling (e.g. *color* = colour) and pronunciation, but these are of slight importance in comparison with the use of words and phrases which give American English its distinctive character. Many American words have come into such general use outside the US (e.g. *blizzard, bogus, crank, deadline*) that few people realize their transatlantic origin.

American football *n.* a form of football played in the US between two teams of 11 players with an oval ball and an H-shaped goal, on a field marked out as a gridiron. Scoring is by points. Football in the US dates as far back as 1609, when colonists from England were kicking an air-filled bladder as they had done in Britain, but the modern game developed from 1876 onwards, when the sport had been taken up in the colleges, and the Rugby Union code was adopted as the basis of the rules. Emphasis is placed on strategy and tactics in both attack and defence, and the game itself is violent enough to require the wearing of helmets and other protective clothing.

American Independence, War of (also known as the **American Revolution**) the revolt of American colonists against British rule, 1775–83, triggered by colonial resentment at the commercial policies of Britain and by lack of American participation in political decisions which affected their interests. Disturbances such as the Boston Tea Party of 1773 developed into armed resistance in 1775 and full-scale war, with the Declaration of Independence a year later. The British were unable to provide sufficient manpower or coordinated leadership to crush the rebels, and following the American victory at Saratoga France and Spain lent their support, French sea-power eventually playing a crucial role in the decisive surrender of a British army at Yorktown in 1781. The war was ended by the Peace of Paris in 1783 and George Washington became the first President of the US in 1789.

American Indian *n.* a member of a group of indigenous peoples of North and South America and the Caribbean Islands, called Indians by the error of Columbus and other Europeans in the 15th-16th c., who thought they had reached part of India by a new route. They are characterized by medium skin pigmentation, coarse straight black hair, and certain blood features which are markedly different from those of the Mongoloid peoples whom they otherwise resemble and with whom they were formerly classified.

Americanism /əˈmerɪkəˌnɪz(ə)m/ *n.* **1 a** a word, sense, or phrase peculiar to or originating from the United States. **b** a thing or feature characteristic of or peculiar to the United States. **2** attachment to or sympathy for the United States.

Americanize /əˈmerɪkəˌnaɪz/ *v.* (also **-ise**) **1** *tr.* **a** make American in character. **b** naturalize as an American. **2** *intr.* become American in character. □□ **Americanization** /-ˈzeɪʃ(ə)n/ *n.*

American Legion see LEGION.

American organ *n.* a type of reed organ resembling the harmonium but in which air is sucked (not blown) through reeds.

American Revolution see AMERICAN INDEPENDENCE, WAR OF.

America's Cup a yachting trophy named after the yacht *America* which won it in 1851, originally presented by the Royal Yacht Squadron for a race round the Isle of Wight. The *America*'s owners gave the trophy to the New York Yacht Club as a perpetual international challenge trophy, and it remained in the club's possession for 132 years until the successful challenge by an Australian crew in September 1983. Since 1857 the race had been held in a course off Newport, Rhode Island; after the Australian victory was held in Perth, Western Australia, in 1957, where a US crew regained the trophy.

americium /ˌæməˈrɪsɪəm, -ˈʃɪəm/ *n.* *Chem.* an artificially made transuranic radioactive metallic element, first obtained in 1945 by bombarding plutonium with neutrons. It emits gamma radiation and this property has led to its use in industrial measuring equipment. ¶ Symb.: **Am**; atomic number 95. [*America* (where first made) + -IUM]

Amerind /ˈæmərɪnd/ *adj.* & *n.* (also **Amerindian** /ˌæməˈrɪndɪən/) = *American Indian.* □□ **Amerindic** /-ˈrɪndɪk/ *adj.* [portmanteau word]

amethyst /ˈæmɪθɪst/ *n.* a precious stone of a violet or purple variety of quartz. □□ **amethystine** /-ˈθɪstiːn/ *adj.* [ME f. OF *ametiste* f. L *amethystus* f. Gk *amethustos* not drunken, the stone being supposed to prevent intoxication]

Amharic /æmˈhærɪk/ *adj.* & *n.* —*n.* the official and commercial language of Ethiopia, spoken by some 9 million people (approximately one-third of the population) in the area of the capital, Addis Ababa, and the region to the north of it. It belongs to the Semitic language group but within the Ethiopic branch of this group is directly descended from Ge'ez. —*adj.* of this language. [*Amhara*, Ethiopian province + -IC]

amiable /ˈeɪmɪəb(ə)l/ *adj.* friendly and pleasant in temperament; likeable. □□ **amiability** /ˌeɪmɪəˈbɪlɪtɪ/ *n.* **amiableness** *n.* **amiably** *adv.* [ME f. OF f. LL *amicabilis* amicable: confused with F *aimable* lovable]

amianthus /ˌæmɪˈænθəs/ *n.* (also **amiantus** /-təs/) any fine silky-fibred variety of asbestos. [L f. Gk *amiantos* undefiled f. *a*- not + *miainō* defile, i.e. purified by fire, being incombustible: for -*h*- cf. AMARANTH]

amicable /ˈæmɪkəb(ə)l/ *adj.* showing or done in a friendly spirit (*an amicable meeting*). □□ **amicability** /ˌæmɪkəˈbɪlɪtɪ/ *n.* **amicableness** *n.* **amicably** *adv.* [LL *amicabilis* f. *amicus* friend]

amice[1] /ˈæmɪs/ *n.* a white linen cloth worn on the neck and shoulders by a priest celebrating the Eucharist. [ME f. med.L *amicia*, -*sia* (earlier *amit* f. OF), f. L *amictus* outer garment]

amice[2] /ˈæmɪs/ *n.* a cap, hood, or cape worn by members of certain religious orders. [ME f. OF *aumusse* f. med.L *almucia* etc., of unkn. orig.]

amicus curiae /æˌmiːkəs ˈkjʊərɪˌiː/ *n.* (pl. *amici curiae* /-sɪ/) *Law* an impartial adviser in a court of law. [mod.L, = friend of the court]

amid /əˈmɪd/ *prep.* (also **amidst** /əˈmɪdst/) **1** in the middle of. **2** in the course of. [ME *amidde(s)* f. OE *on* on + MID[1]]

amide /ˈeɪmaɪd, ˈæm-/ *n.* *Chem.* a compound formed from ammonia by replacement of one (or sometimes more than one) hydrogen atom by a metal or an acyl radical. [AMMONIA + -IDE]

amidships /əˈmɪdʃɪps/ *adv.* (US **amidship**) in or into the middle of a ship. [MIDSHIP after AMID]

amidst var. of AMID.

Amiens /ˈæmjæ̃/ the capital of Picardy in northern France; pop. (1982) 136,350. Its 13th-c. cathedral is the largest in France.

amigo /æˈmiːgəʊ/ *n.* (pl. -os) esp. US *colloq.* (often as a form of address) a friend or comrade, esp. in Spanish-speaking areas. [Sp.]

Amin /æˈmiːn/, Idi (1925–), Ugandan soldier, dictator, and head of State 1971–9. Having risen through the ranks of the army to become its commander, in 1971 he overthrew President Obote and seized power. His rule was characterized by the advancing of narrow tribal interests, expulsion of non-Africans (most notably the Ugandan Asians), and violence on a huge scale. With Tanzanian assistance he was overthrown in 1979.

amine /ˈeɪmiːn, ˈæm-/ *n.* *Chem.* a compound formed from ammonia by replacement of one or more hydrogen atoms by an organic radical or radicals. [AMMONIA + -INE[4]]

amino /əˈmiːnəʊ/ *n.* (attrib.) *Chem.* of, relating to, or containing the monovalent group –NH₂. [AMINE]

amino acid /əˈmiːnəʊ/ *n.* *Biochem.* any of a group of organic compounds containing both the carboxyl (COOH) and amino (NH₂) group, occurring naturally in plant and animal tissues and forming the basic constituents of proteins. [AMINE + ACID]

amir /əˈmɪə(r)/ *n.* (also **ameer**) the title of some Arab rulers. [Arab. *'amīr* commander f. *amara* command: cf. EMIR]

Amirante Islands /ˈæmɪˌrænt/ a group of coral islands in the Indian Ocean, forming part of the Seychelles.

Amis[1] /ˈeɪmɪs/, Sir Kingsley (1922–), English novelist and poet. He achieved popular success with his first novel *Lucky Jim* (1954) and its lower-middle-class anti-establishment hero; the provincial university setting marked a new development in fiction that Amis confirmed in *That Uncertain Feeling* (1955) and *Take a Girl Like You* (1960). In *I Like it Here* (1958) Amis displays a deliberate cultivation of a prejudiced and philistine pose which later hardened into an increasingly conservative and hostile view of contemporary life and manners. His subsequent work, of great versatility, includes satiric comedies and several volumes of poetry. He won the Booker Prize in 1986 for his novel *The Old Devils*.

Amis[2] /ˈeɪmɪs/, Martin Louis (1949–), English novelist, whose works include *The Rachel Papers* (1973), *Success* (1978), and *Money* (1984). He is the son of Sir Kingsley Amis (see entry).

Amish /ˈɑːmɪʃ, ˈeɪ-/ *adj.* belonging to a strict US Mennonite sect. [prob. f. G *Amisch* f. J. *Amen* 17th-c. Swiss preacher]

amiss /əˈmɪs/ *predic.adj.* & *adv.* —*predic.adj.* wrong; out of order; faulty (*knew something was amiss*). —*adv.* wrong; wrongly; inappropriately (*everything went amiss*). □ **take amiss** be offended by (*took my words amiss*). [ME prob. f. ON *à mis* so as to miss f. *à* on + *mis* rel. to MISS[1]]

amitosis /ˌæmɪˈtəʊsɪs/ *n.* *Biol.* a form of nuclear division that does not involve mitosis. [A-[1] + MITOSIS]

amitriptyline /ˌæmɪˈtrɪptɪˌliːn/ *n.* *Pharm.* an antidepressant drug that has a mild tranquillizing action. [AMINE + TRI- + *heptyl* (see HEPTANE) + -INE[4]]

amity /ˈæmɪtɪ/ *n.* friendship; friendly relations. [ME f. OF *amitié* ult. f. L *amicus* friend]

Amman /əˈmɑːn/ the capital of Jordan; pop. 777,500.

ammeter /ˈæmɪtə(r)/ *n.* an instrument for measuring electric current in amperes. [AMPERE + -METER]

ammo /ˈæməʊ/ *n.* *colloq.* ammunition. [abbr.]

Ammon /ˈæmən/ var. of AMUN.

ammonia /əˈməʊnɪə/ *n.* **1** a colourless strongly alkaline gas with a characteristic pungent smell. ¶ Chem. formula: NH₃. **2** (in full **ammonia water**) (in general use) a solution of ammonia gas in water. [mod.L f. SAL AMMONIAC]

ammoniacal /ˌæməˈnaɪək(ə)l/ *adj.* of, relating to, or containing ammonia or sal ammoniac. [ME *ammoniac* f. OF (*arm-*, *amm-*) f. L f. Gk *ammōniakos* of Ammon (cf. SAL AMMONIAC) + -AL]

ammoniated /əˈməʊnɪˌeɪtɪd/ *adj.* combined or treated with ammonia.

ammonite /ˈæməˌnaɪt/ *n.* any extinct cephalopod mollusc of the order Ammonoidea, with a flat coiled spiral shell found as a fossil. [mod.L *ammonites*, after med.L *cornu Ammonis*, = L *Ammonis cornu* (Pliny), horn of (Jupiter) Ammon]

ammonium /əˈməʊnɪəm/ *n.* the univalent ion NH₄₊, formed from ammonia. [mod.L (as AMMONIA)]

ammunition /ˌæmjʊˈnɪʃ(ə)n/ *n.* **1** a supply of projectiles (esp. bullets, shells, and grenades). **2** points used or usable to advantage in an argument. [obs. F *amunition*, corrupt. of (*la*) *munition* (the) MUNITION]

amnesia /æmˈniːzɪə/ *n.* a partial or total loss of memory. □□ **amnesiac** /-zɪˌæk/ *n.* **amnesic** *adj.* & *n.* [mod.L f. Gk, = forgetfulness]

amnesty /ˈæmnɪstɪ/ *n.* & *v.* —*n.* (pl. -**ies**) a general pardon, esp. for political offences. —*v.tr.* (-**ies**, -**ied**) grant an amnesty to. [F *amnestie* or L f. Gk *amnēstia* oblivion]

Amnesty International an international organization, founded in London in 1961, whose aim is to inform the public about violations of human rights and which actively seeks the release of political prisoners. It was awarded the Nobel Peace Prize in 1977.

amniocentesis /ˌæmnɪəʊsenˈtiːsɪs/ *n.* (pl. **amniocenteses** /-siːz/) *Med.* the sampling of amniotic fluid by insertion of a hollow needle to determine the condition of an embryo. [AMNION + Gk *kentēsis* pricking f. *kentō* to prick]

aʊ how eɪ day əʊ no eə hair ɪə near ɔɪ boy ʊə poor aɪə fire aʊə sour (*see over for consonants*)

amnion /'æmnɪən/ n. (pl. **amnia**) Zool. & Physiol. the innermost membrane that encloses the embryo of a reptile, bird, or mammal. □□ **amniotic** /ˌæmnɪ'ɒtɪk/ adj. [Gk, = caul (dimin. of amnos lamb)]

amoeba /ə'miːbə/ n. (US **ameba**) (pl. **amoebas** or **amoebae** /-biː/) any usu. aquatic protozoan of the genus Amoeba, esp. A. proteus, capable of changing shape. □□ **amoebic** adj. **amoeboid** adj. [mod.L f. Gk amoibē change]

amok /ə'mɒk/ adv. (also **amuck** /ə'mʌk/) □ **run amok** run about wildly in an uncontrollable violent rage. [Malay amok rushing in a frenzy]

among /ə'mʌŋ/ prep. (also **amongst** /ə'mʌŋst/) **1** surrounded by; in the company of (lived among the trees; be among friends). **2** in the number of (among us were those who disagreed). **3** an example of; in the class or category of (is among the richest men alive). **4 a** between; within the limits of (collectively or distributively); shared by (had £5 among us; divide it among you). **b** by the joint action or from the joint resources of (among us we can manage it). **5** with one another; by the reciprocal action of (was decided among the participants; talked among themselves). **6** as distinguished from; preeminent in the category of (she is one among many). [OE ongemang f. on ON + gemang assemblage (cf. MINGLE): -st = adverbial genitive -s + -t as in AGAINST]

amontillado /əˌmɒntɪ'lɑːdəʊ/ n. (pl. **-os**) a medium dry sherry. [Sp. f. Montilla in Spain + -ado = -ATE²]

amoral /eɪ'mɒr(ə)l/ adj. **1** not concerned with or outside the scope of morality (cf. IMMORAL). **2** having no moral principles. □□ **amoralism** n. **amoralist** n. **amorality** /-'rælɪtɪ/ n.

amoretto /ˌæmɒ'retəʊ/ n. (pl. **amoretti** /-tiː/) a Cupid. [It., dimin. of amore love f. L (as AMOUR)]

amorist /'æmərɪst/ n. a person who professes or writes of (esp. sexual) love. [L amor or F amour + -IST]

Amorite /'æməˌraɪt/ n. & adj. —n. a member of a group of semi-nomadic tribes, bearing Semitic personal names, from the east Syrian steppe and desert region. In the late 3rd and early 2nd millennium BC they founded a number of States and dynasties, including Mari on the Euphrates and the First Dynasty of Babylon, associated with Hammurabi I (d. 1750 BC). —adj. of the Amorites. [Heb. 'ĕmōrī f. Akkadian (Sumerian martu west)]

amoroso¹ /ˌæmə'rəʊsəʊ/ adv. & adj. Mus. in a loving or tender manner. [It.]

amoroso² /ˌæmə'rəʊsəʊ/ n. (pl. **-os**) a full rich type of sherry. [Sp., = amorous]

amorous /'æmərəs/ adj. **1** showing, feeling, or inclined to sexual love. **2** of or relating to sexual love. □□ **amorously** adv. **amorousness** n. [ME f. OF f. med.L amorosus f. L amor love]

amorphous /ə'mɔːfəs/ adj. **1** shapeless. **2** vague, ill-organized. **3** Mineral. & Chem. non-crystalline; having neither definite form nor structure. □□ **amorphously** adv. **amorphousness** n. [med.L amorphus f. Gk amorphos shapeless f. a- not + morphē form]

amortize /ə'mɔːtaɪz/ v.tr. (also **-ise**) Commerce **1** gradually extinguish (a debt) by money regularly put aside. **2** gradually write off the initial cost of (assets). **3** transfer (land) to a corporation in mortmain. □□ **amortization** /-'zeɪʃ(ə)n/ n. [ME f. OF amortir (stem amortiss-) ult. f. L ad to + mors mort- death]

Amos /'eɪmɒs/ **1** a Hebrew minor prophet (c.760 BC). **2** a book of the Old Testament containing his prophecies.

amount /ə'maʊnt/ n. & v. —n. **1** a quantity, esp. the total of a thing or things in number, size, value, extent, etc. (a large amount of money; came to a considerable amount). **2** the full effect or significance. —v.intr. (foll. by to) be equivalent to in number, size, significance, etc. (amounted to £100; amounted to a disaster). □ **any amount of** a great deal of. **no amount of** not even the greatest possible amount of. [ME f. OF amunter f. amont upward, lit. uphill, f. L ad montem]

amour /ə'mʊə(r)/ n. a love affair, esp. a secret one. [F, = love, f. L amor amoris]

amour propre /æˌmʊə 'prɒpr/ self-respect. [F]

AMP abbr. adenosine monophosphate.

amp¹ /æmp/ n. Electr. an ampere. [abbr.]

amp² /æmp/ n. colloq. an amplifier. [abbr.]

ampelopsis /ˌæmpɪ'lɒpsɪs/ n. any plant of the genus Ampelopsis or Parthenocissus, usu. a climber supporting itself by twining tendrils, e.g. Virginia creeper. [mod.L f. Gk ampelos vine + opsis appearance]

amperage /'æmpərɪdʒ/ n. Electr. the strength of an electric current in amperes.

Ampère /'æmpeə(r)/, André-Marie (1775–1836), French physicist, mathematician, and philosopher, a mathematical child prodigy who became one of the founders of electromagnetism and electrodynamics, and is best known for his analysis of the relationship between magnetic force and the electric current, begun shortly after he heard of Oersted's discovery in 1820. Ampère also developed a precursor of the galvanometer. The unit of electric current (see foll.) is named after him.

ampere /'æmpeə(r)/ n. Electr. the SI base unit of electric current (established in 1948 for international use), that constant current which, if maintained in two straight parallel conductors of infinite length, of negligible circular cross-section, and placed 1 metre apart in a vacuum, would produce between these conductors a force equal to 2×10^{-7} newton per metre of length. ¶ Symb.: **A**. [AMPÈRE]

ampersand /'æmpəˌsænd/ n. the sign & (= and). [corrupt. of and per se and ('&' by itself is 'and')]

amphetamine /æm'fetəmɪn, -ˌmiːn/ n. a synthetic drug used esp. as a stimulant. [abbr. of chemical name alpha-methyl phenethylamine]

amphi- /'æmfɪ/ comb. form **1** both. **2** of both kinds. **3** on both sides. **4** around. [Gk]

amphibian /æm'fɪbɪən/ adj. & n. —adj. **1** living both on land and in water. **2** Zool. of or relating to the class Amphibia. **3** (of a vehicle) able to operate on land and water. —n. **1** Zool. any vertebrate of the class Amphibia, typically having an aquatic larval stage with gills (e.g. a tadpole) and an air-breathing four-legged adult stage. There are about 2,400 living species, divided into two main groups: tailless forms (frogs and toads) and those with tails (e.g. newts and salamanders). Amphibians, which evolved from fish ancestors in the Devonian period, were the first vertebrates to live on land, preceding the reptiles. Unlike reptiles, however, their eggs lack shells and require water or damp conditions to survive, and so they cannot be completely independent of a moist environment. **2** (in general use) a creature living both on land and in water. **3** an amphibian vehicle.

amphibious /æm'fɪbɪəs/ adj. **1** living both on land and in water. **2** of or relating to or suited for both land and water. **3** Mil. **a** (of a military operation) involving forces landed from the sea. **b** (of forces) trained for such operations. **4** having a twofold nature; occupying two positions. □□ **amphibiously** adv.

amphibology /ˌæmfɪ'bɒlədʒɪ/ n. (pl. **-ies**) **1** a quibble. **2** an ambiguous wording. [ME f. OF amphibologie f. LL amphibologia for L f. Gk amphibolia ambiguity]

amphimixis /ˌæmfɪ'mɪksɪs/ n. Biol. true sexual reproduction with the fusion of gametes from two individuals (cf. APOMIXIS). □□ **amphimictic** adj. [mod.L, formed as AMPHI- + Gk mixis mingling]

amphioxus /ˌæmfɪ'ɒksəs/ n. any lancelet of the genus Branchiostoma (formerly Amphioxus). [mod.L, formed as AMPHI- + Gk oxus sharp]

amphipathic /ˌæmfɪ'pæθɪk/ adj. Chem. **1** of a substance or molecule that has both a hydrophilic and a hydrophobic part. **2** consisting of such parts. [AMPHI- + Gk pathikos (as PATHOS)]

amphipod /'æmfɪˌpɒd/ n. any crustacean of the largely marine order Amphipoda, having a laterally compressed abdomen with two kinds of limb, e.g. the freshwater shrimp (Gammarus pulex). [AMPHI- + Gk pous podos foot]

amphiprostyle /æm'fɪprəˌstaɪl/ n. & adj. —n. a classical building with a portico at each end. —adj. of or in this style. [L *amphiprostylus* f. Gk *amphiprostulos* (as AMPHI-, *prostulos* PROSTYLE)]

amphisbaena /ˌæmfɪsˈbiːnə/ n. **1** *Mythol.* & *poet.* a fabulous serpent with a head at each end. **2** *Zool.* any burrowing wormlike lizard of the family Amphisbaena, having no apparent division of head from body making both ends look similar. [ME f. L f. Gk *amphisbaina* f. *amphis* both ways + *bainō* go]

amphitheatre /ˈæmfɪˌθɪətə(r)/ n. (*US* **amphitheater**) **1** a round, usu. unroofed building with tiers of seats surrounding a central space. **2** a semicircular gallery in a theatre. **3** a large circular hollow. **4** the scene of a contest. [L *amphitheatrum* f. Gk *amphitheatron* (as AMPHI-, THEATRE)]

Amphitrite /ˌæmfɪˈtraɪtɪ/ Gk *Mythol.* a sea goddess, wife of Poseidon.

amphora /ˈæmfərə/ n. (pl. **amphorae** /-ˌriː/ or **amphoras**) a Greek or Roman vessel with two handles and a narrow neck. [L f. Gk *amphoreus*]

amphoteric /ˌæmfəˈterɪk/ adj. *Chem.* able to react as a base and an acid. [Gk *amphoteros* compar. of *amphō* both]

ampicillin /ˌæmpɪˈsɪlɪn/ n. *Pharm.* a semi-synthetic penicillin used esp. in treating infections of the urinary and respiratory tracts. [*amino* + *penicillin*]

ample /ˈæmp(ə)l/ adj. (**ampler, amplest**) **1 a** plentiful, abundant, extensive. **b** *euphem.* (esp. of a person) large, stout. **2** enough or more than enough. □□ **ampleness** n. **amply** adv. [F f. L *amplus*]

amplifier /ˈæmplɪˌfaɪə(r)/ n. an electronic device for increasing the strength of electrical signals, esp. for conversion into sound in radio etc. equipment.

amplify /ˈæmplɪˌfaɪ/ v. (**-ies, -ied**) **1** *tr.* increase the volume or strength of (sound, electrical signals, etc.). **2** *tr.* enlarge upon or add detail to (a story etc.). **3** *intr.* expand what is said or written. □□ **amplification** /-fɪˈkeɪʃ(ə)n/ n. [ME f. OF *amplifier* f. L *amplificare* (as AMPLE, -FY)]

amplitude /ˈæmplɪˌtjuːd/ n. **1 a** *Physics* the maximum extent of a vibration or oscillation from the position of equilibrium. **b** *Electr.* the maximum departure of the value of an alternating current or wave from the average value. **2 a** spaciousness, breadth; wide range. **b** abundance. □ **amplitude modulation** *Electr.* **1** the modulation of a wave by variation of its amplitude. **2** the system using such modulation. [F *amplitude* or L *amplitudo* (as AMPLE)]

ampoule /ˈæmpuːl/ n. a small capsule in which measured quantities of liquids or solids, esp. for injecting, are sealed ready for use. [F f. L AMPULLA]

ampulla /æmˈpʊlə/ n. (pl. **ampullae** /-liː/) **1 a** a Roman globular flask with two handles. **b** a vessel for sacred uses. **2** *Anat.* the dilated end of a vessel or duct. [L]

amputate /ˈæmpjʊˌteɪt/ v.tr. cut off by surgical operation (a part of the body, esp. a limb), usu. because of injury or disease. □□ **amputation** /-ˈteɪʃ(ə)n/ n. **amputator** n. [L *amputare* f. *amb*-about + *putare* prune]

amputee /ˌæmpjʊˈtiː/ n. a person who has lost a limb etc. by amputation.

Amritsar /æmˈrɪtsə(r)/ a city in Punjab in NW India; pop. (1981) 589,000. Founded in 1577 by Ram Das, fourth guru of the Sikhs, it became the centre of the Sikh faith and is the site of its holiest temple.

Amsterdam /ˌæmstəˈdæm/ the capital and largest city of The Netherlands, one of the major ports and commercial centres of Europe, built on about 100 islands separated by the canals for which it is noted; pop. (1987) 691,738. Its many industries include diamond-cutting.

amtrac /ˈæmtræk/ n. (also **amtrak**) *US* an amphibious tracked vehicle used for landing assault troops on a shore. [*amphibious* + *tractor*]

amu *abbr.* atomic mass unit.

amuck var. of AMOK.

Amu Darya /ˌɑːmuː ˈdɑːrɪə/ a great river of central Asia, 2,400 km (1,500 miles) long, rising in the Pamirs and flowing into the Aral Sea. In classical times it was known as the Oxus. For part of its length it forms the boundary between Afghanistan and the Soviet Union.

amulet /ˈæmjʊlɪt/ n. **1** an ornament or small piece of jewellery worn as a charm against evil. **2** something which is thought to give such protection. [L *amuletum*, of unkn. orig.]

Amun /ˈæmən/ (also **Ammon**) a god of the ancient Egyptians (originally the local god of Thebes) whose worship spread to Greece, where he was identified with Zeus, and to Rome, where he was known as Jupiter Ammon. As a national god of Egypt he was associated in a triad with Mut and Khonsu. He is represented in human form (rarely as ram-headed). His priesthood was important in State affairs except for a brief period when Akhenaten introduced the worship of Aten.

Amundsen /ˈɑːmʊns(ə)n/, Roald (1872–1928), Norwegian polar explorer. The most successful of the turn-of-the-century polar explorers, Amundsen made his name with a successful three-year navigation of the Northwest Passage in the small sailing vessel *Gjöa* (1903–6). In December 1911 he beat the British explorer Scott in the famous race to reach the South Pole which cost the latter his life. In the 1920s Amundsen devoted himself to aerial exploration of the polar regions, eventually disappearing on a search for the missing Italian airship expedition led by Umberto Nobile.

Amur /əˈmʊə(r)/ (Chinese *Heilung Jiang*) a river of NE Asia, forming for the greater part of its length the boundary between the Soviet Union and China.

amuse /əˈmjuːz/ v. **1** *tr.* cause (a person) to laugh or smile. **2** *tr.* & *refl.* (often foll. by *with, by*) interest or occupy; keep (a person) entertained. □□ **amusing** adj. **amusingly** adv. [ME f. OF *amuser* cause to muse (see MUSE²) f. causal *a* to + *muser* stare]

amusement /əˈmjuːzmənt/ n. **1** something that amuses, esp. a pleasant diversion, game, or pastime. **2 a** the state of being amused. **b** the act of amusing. **3** a mechanical device (e.g. a roundabout) for entertainment at a fairground etc. □ **amusement arcade** *Brit.* an indoor area for entertainment with automatic game-machines. [F f. *amuser*: see AMUSE, -MENT]

amygdaloid /əˈmɪgdəˌlɔɪd/ adj. shaped like an almond. □ **amygdaloid nucleus** a roughly almond-shaped mass of grey matter deep inside each cerebral hemisphere, associated with the sense of smell. [L *amygdala* f. Gk *amugdalē* almond]

amyl /ˈeɪmaɪl, ˈæmɪl/ n. (used *attrib.*) *Chem.* the monovalent group $C_5H_{11}-$, derived from pentane. Also called PENTYL. [L *amylum* starch, from which oil containing it was distilled]

amylase /ˈæmɪˌleɪz/ n. *Biochem.* any of several enzymes that convert starch and glycogen into simple sugars. [AMYL + -ASE]

amylopsin /ˌæmɪˈlɒpsɪn/ n. *Biochem.* an enzyme of the pancreas that converts starch into maltose. [AMYL after *pepsin*]

Amytal /ˈæmɪˌtæl/ n. *propr.* a name for amylobarbitone, a barbiturate drug used as a sedative and a hypnotic. [chem. name *amylethyl barbituric acid*]

an /æn, ən/ adj. the form of the indefinite article (see A¹) used before words beginning with a vowel sound (*an egg; an hour; an MP*). ¶ Now less often used before aspirated words beginning with *h* and stressed on a syllable other than the first (so *a hotel*, not *an hotel*).

an-¹ /ən, æn/ *prefix* not, without (*anarchy*) (cf. A-¹). [Gk *an-*]

an-² /ən, æn/ assim. form of AD- before *n*.

-an /ən/ *suffix* (also **-ean, -ian**) forming adjectives and nouns, esp. from names of places, systems, zoological classes or orders, and founders (*Mexican; Anglican; crustacean; European; Lutheran; Georgian; theologian*). [ult. f. L adj. endings -(*i*)*anus, -aeus*: cf. Gk -*aios, -eios*]

ana /ˈɑːnə/ n. **1** (as *pl.*) anecdotes or literary gossip about a person. **2** (as *sing.*) a collection of a person's memorable sayings. [= -ANA]

ana- /ˈænə/ *prefix* (usu. **an-** before a vowel) **1** up (*anadromous*). **2** back (*anamnesis*). **3** again (*anabaptism*). [Gk *ana* up]

-ana /ˈɑːnə/ *suffix* forming plural nouns meaning 'things associated with' (*Victoriana; Americana*). [neut. pl. of L adj. ending -*anus*]

Anabaptism /ˌænəˈbæptɪz(ə)m/ n. the doctrine that baptism should only be administered to believing adults. □□ **Anabaptist** n. [eccl.L anabaptismus f. Gk anabaptismos (as ANA-, BAPTISM)]

anabas /ˈænəbæs/ n. any of the freshwater fish of the climbing perch family native to Asia and Africa, esp. the genus Anabas, able to breathe air and move on land. [mod.L f. Gk past part. of anabainō walk up]

anabasis /əˈnæbəsɪs/ n. (pl. **anabases** /-ˌsiːz/) **1** the march of the younger Cyrus into Asia in 401 BC as narrated by Xenophon in his work Anabasis. **2** a military up-country march. [Gk, = ascent f. anabainō (as ANA-, bainō go)]

anabatic /ˌænəˈbætɪk/ adj. Meteorol. (of a wind) caused by air flowing upwards (cf. KATABATIC). [Gk anabatikos ascending (as ANABASIS)]

anabiosis /ˌænəbaɪˈəʊsɪs/ n. (pl. **anabioses** /-siːz/) revival after apparent death. □□ **anabiotic** /-ˈɒtɪk/ adj. [med.L f. Gk anabiōsis f. anabioō return to life]

anabolic /ˌænəˈbɒlɪk/ adj. Biochem. of or relating to anabolism. □ **anabolic steroid** any of a group of synthetic steroid hormones used to increase muscle size.

anabolism /əˈnæbəˌlɪz(ə)m/ n. Biochem. the synthesis of complex molecules in living organisms from simpler ones together with the storage of energy; constructive metabolism (opp. CATABOLISM). [Gk anabolē ascent (as ANA-, ballō throw)]

anabranch /ˈænəˌbrɑːntʃ/ n. esp. Austral. a stream that leaves a river and re-enters it lower down. [ANASTOMOSE + BRANCH]

anachronic /ˌænəˈkrɒnɪk/ adj. **1** out of date. **2** involving anachronism. [ANACHRONISM after synchronic etc.]

anachronism /əˈnækrəˌnɪz(ə)m/ n. **1 a** the attribution of a custom, event, etc., to a period to which it does not belong. **b** a thing attributed in this way. **2 a** anything out of harmony with its period. **b** an old-fashioned or out-of-date person or thing. □□ **anachronistic** /-ˈnɪstɪk/ adj. **anachronistically** /-ˈnɪstɪkəlɪ/ adv. [F anachronisme or Gk anakhronismos (as ANA-, khronos time)]

anacoluthon /ˌænəkəˈluːθɒn/ n. (pl. **anacolutha** /-ˈluːθə/) a sentence or construction which lacks grammatical sequence (e.g. while in the garden the door banged shut). □□ **anacoluthic** adj. [LL f. Gk anakolouthon (as AN-¹, akolouthos following)]

anaconda /ˌænəˈkɒndə/ n. a large non-poisonous snake living mainly in water or in trees that kills its prey by constriction. [alt. of anacondaia f. Sinh. henakandayā whip-snake f. hena lightning + kanda stem: orig. of a snake in Sri Lanka]

Anacreon /əˈnækrɪɒn/ (c.570–478 BC) Greek lyric poet who wrote for a number of courts in the Greek world. The surviving fragments of his work include love-songs and drinking-songs, iambic invectives, and elegiac epitaphs.

anacreontic /əˌnækrɪˈɒntɪk/ n. & adj. —n. a poem written after the manner of Anacreon. —adj. **1** after the manner of Anacreon. **2** convivial and amatory in tone. [LL anacreonticus f. Gk Anakreōn]

anacrusis /ˌænəˈkruːsɪs/ n. (pl. **anacruses** /-siːz/) **1** (in poetry) an unstressed syllable at the beginning of a verse. **2** Mus. an unstressed note or notes before the first bar-line. [Gk anakrousis (as ANA-, krousis f. krouō strike)]

anadromous /əˈnædrəməs/ adj. (of a fish, e.g. the salmon) that swims up a river from the sea to spawn (opp. CATADROMOUS). [Gk anadromos (as ANA-, dromos -running)]

anaemia /əˈniːmɪə/ n. (US anemia) a deficiency in the blood, usu. of red cells or their haemoglobin, resulting in pallor and weariness. □ **pernicious anaemia** a defective formation of red blood cells through a lack of vitamin B_{12} or folic acid. [mod.L f. Gk anaimia (as AN-¹, -AEMIA)]

anaemic /əˈniːmɪk/ adj. (US anemic) **1** relating to or suffering from anaemia. **2** pale; lacking in vitality.

anaerobe /ˈænəˌrəʊb, əˈneərəʊb/ n. an organism that grows without air, or requires oxygen-free conditions to live. □□ **anaerobic** /ˌæneəˈrəʊbɪk/ adj. [F anaérobie formed as AN-¹ + AEROBE]

anaesthesia /ˌænɪsˈθiːzɪə/ n. (US anesthesia) the absence of

sensation, esp. artificially induced insensitivity to pain usu. achieved by the administration of gases or the injection of drugs. □□ **anaesthesiology** /-ˈɒlədʒɪ/ n. [mod.L f. Gk anaisthēsia (as AN-¹, aisthēsis sensation)]

anaesthetic /ˌænɪsˈθetɪk/ adj. & n. (US anesthetic) —n. a substance that produces insensibility to pain etc. (See below.) —adj. producing partial or complete insensibility to pain etc. □ **general anaesthetic** an anaesthetic that affects the whole body, usu. with loss of consciousness. **local anaesthetic** an anaesthetic that affects a restricted area of the body. [Gk anaisthētos insensible (as ANAESTHESIA)]

Attempts at anaesthesia were made from ancient times by stupefying patients with wine or the juices of narcotic plants, but it was not until the 1840s that unconsciousness was produced by inhalation of anaesthetic gases (ether and nitrous oxide) in dentistry and surgery. The first such use of ether dates from 1842 when an American surgeon, C. W. Long, removed a tumour from the neck of a patient who had inhaled its vapour. Chloroform was introduced as an alternative to ether (which for a time it superseded) by the Scottish physician Sir James Young Simpson, but both substances had disadvantages and other anaesthetic agents were sought. Today new materials and methods are constantly being introduced. Anaesthetics may be given as gases, by inhalation; as drugs in solution, by injection or enema; or (for localized effect) sprayed on the skin. There are four main types of anaesthesia: general, in which the patient loses consciousness; spinal, in which anaesthetic is injected into the fluid surrounding the spinal cord, and the portion of the body below the site of the injection is anaesthetized; regional, injecting around nerve-roots and nerve tracts as they emerge from the spinal column, anaesthetizing only that area of the body supplied by those nerves; and local, in which the drug is injected or sprayed directly at the site of the operative incision. Anaesthesia may also be produced by other means, including acupuncture and hypnosis. The introduction of anaesthesia removed the necessity for the surgeon to concentrate on speed, in order to end the patient's ordeal as soon as possible, and widened the scope of surgery enormously.

anaesthetist /əˈniːsθətɪst/ n. a specialist in the administration of anaesthetics.

anaesthetize /əˈniːsθəˌtaɪz/ v.tr. (also **-ise**, US anesthetize) **1** administer an anaesthetic to. **2** deprive of physical or mental sensation. □□ **anaesthetization** /-ˈzeɪʃ(ə)n/ n.

anaglyph /ˈænəglɪf/ n. **1** Photog. a composite stereoscopic photograph printed in superimposed complementary colours. **2** an embossed object cut in low relief. □□ **anaglyphic** /-ˈglɪfɪk/ adj. [Gk anagluphē (as ANA-, gluphē f. gluphō carve)]

anaglypta /ˌænəˈglɪptə/ n. a type of thick embossed wallpaper, usu. for painting over. [L anaglypta work in bas-relief: cf. ANAGLYPH]

anagram /ˈænəˌgræm/ n. a word or phrase formed by transposing the letters of another word or phrase. □□ **anagrammatic** /-grəˈmætɪk/ adj. **anagrammatical** /-grəˈmætɪk(ə)l/ adj. **anagrammatize** /-ˈgræməˌtaɪz/ v.tr. (also **-ise**). [F anagramme or mod.L anagramma f. Gk ANA- + gramma -atos letter: cf. -GRAM]

anal /ˈeɪn(ə)l/ adj. relating to or situated near the anus. □ **anal retentive** (of a person) excessively orderly and fussy (supposedly owing to aspects of toilet-training in infancy). □□ **anally** adv. [mod.L analis (as ANUS)]

analects /ˈænəˌlekts/ n.pl. (also **analecta** /ˌænəˈlektə/) a collection of short literary extracts. [L f. Gk analekta things gathered f. analegō pick up]

analeptic /ˌænəˈleptɪk/ adj. & n. —adj. (of a drug etc.) restorative. —n. a restorative medicine or drug. [Gk analēptikos f. analambanō take back]

analgesia /ˌænælˈdʒiːzɪə, -sɪə/ n. the absence or relief of pain. [mod.L f. Gk, = painlessness]

analgesic /ˌænælˈdʒiːsɪk, -zɪk/ adj. & n. —adj. relieving pain. —n. an analgesic drug.

analog US var. of ANALOGUE.

analogize /əˈnæləˌdʒaɪz/ v. (also **-ise**) **1** tr. represent or explain by analogy. **2** intr. use analogy.

analogous /əˈnæləɡəs/ adj. (usu. foll. by to) partially similar or parallel; showing analogy. □□ **analogously** adv. [L analogus f. Gk analogos proportionate]

analogue /ˈænəˌlɒɡ/ n. (US **analog**) **1** an analogous or parallel thing. **2** (attrib.) (usu. **analog**) (of a computer or electronic process) using physical variables, e.g. voltage, weight, or length, to represent numbers (cf. DIGITAL). [F f. Gk analogon neut. adj.: see ANALOGOUS]

analogy /əˈnælədʒɪ/ n. (pl. **-ies**) **1** (usu. foll. by to, with, between) correspondence or partial similarity. **2** Logic a process of arguing from similarity in known respects to similarity in other respects. **3** Philol. the imitation of existing words in forming inflections or constructions of others, without the existence of corresponding intermediate stages. **4** Biol. the resemblance of function between organs essentially different. **5** an analogue. □□ **analogical** /ˌænəˈlɒdʒɪk(ə)l/ adj. **analogically** /ˌænəˈlɒdʒɪkəlɪ/ adv. [F analogie or L analogia proportion f. Gk (as ANALOGOUS)]

analysand /əˈnælɪˌsænd/ n. a person undergoing psychoanalysis.

analyse /ˈænəˌlaɪz/ v.tr. (US **analyze**) **1** examine in detail the constitution or structure of. **2** Chem. ascertain the constituents of (a sample of a mixture or compound). **3** find or show the essence or structure of (a book, music, etc.). **4** Gram. resolve (a sentence) into its grammatical elements. **5** psychoanalyse. □□ **analysable** adj. **analyser** n. [obs. analyse (n.) or F analyser f. analyse (n.) f. med.L ANALYSIS]

analysis /əˈnælɪsɪs/ n. (pl. **analyses** /-ˌsiːz/) **1 a** a detailed examination of the elements or structure of a substance etc. **b** a statement of the result of this. **2** Chem. the determination of the constituent parts of a mixture or compound. **3** psychoanalysis. **4** Math. the use of algebra and calculus in problem-solving. Analysis is the theory of functions and limiting operations on them, continuity, differentiation, and integration, treated by the strictest standards of logical reasoning. This huge subject emerged in the 19th c. from the work of Cauchy (see entry) and others. **5** Cricket a statement of the performance of a bowler, usu. giving the numbers of overs and maiden overs bowled, runs conceded, and wickets taken. □ **in the final** (or **last** or **ultimate**) **analysis** after all due consideration; in the end. [med.L f. Gk analusis (as ANA-, luō set free)]

analyst /ˈænəlɪst/ n. **1** a person skilled in (esp. chemical) analysis. **2** a psychoanalyst. [F analyste]

analytic /ˌænəˈlɪtɪk/ adj. **1** of or relating to analysis. **2** Philol. analytical. **3** Logic (of a statement etc.) such that its denial is self-contradictory; true by definition (see SYNTHETIC). [LL f. Gk analutikos (as ANALYSIS)]

analytical /ˌænəˈlɪtɪk(ə)l/ adj. **1** using analytic methods. **2** Philol. using separate words instead of inflections (cf. SYNTHETIC). □ **analytical geometry** geometry using coordinates. □□ **analytically** adv.

analyze US var. of ANALYSE.

anamnesis /ˌænəmˈniːsɪs/ n. (pl. **anamneses** /-siːz/) **1** recollection (esp. of a previous existence). **2** a patient's account of his or her medical history. **3** Eccl. the part of the anaphora recalling the Passion, Resurrection, and Ascension of Christ. [Gk, = remembrance]

anandrous /əˈnændrəs/ adj. Bot. having no stamens. [Gk anandros without males f. an- not + anēr andros male]

Ananias /ˌænəˈnaɪəs/ **1** the husband of Sapphira, struck dead because he lied (Acts 5). **2** the Jewish high priest before whom St Paul was brought (Acts 23).

anapaest /ˈænəˌpiːst/ n. (US **anapest**) Prosody a foot consisting of two short or unstressed syllables followed by one long or stressed syllable. □□ **anapaestic** /-ˈpiːstɪk/ adj. [L anapaestus f. Gk anapaistos reversed (because the reverse of a dactyl)]

anaphase /ˈænəˌfeɪz/ n. Biol. the stage of meiotic or mitotic cell division when the chromosomes move away from one another to opposite poles of the spindle. [ANA- + PHASE]

anaphora /əˈnæfərə/ n. **1** Rhet. the repetition of a word or phrase at the beginning of successive clauses. **2** Gram. the use of a word referring to or replacing a word used earlier in a sentence, to avoid repetition (e.g. do in I like it and so do they). **3** Eccl. the part of the Eucharist which contains the consecration, anamnesis, and communion. □□ **anaphoric** /ˌænəˈfɒrɪk/ adj. [L f. Gk, = repetition (as ANA-, pherō to bear)]

anaphrodisiac /ænˌæfrəˈdɪzɪˌæk/ adj. & n. —adj. tending to reduce sexual desire. —n. an anaphrodisiac drug.

anaphylaxis /ˌænəfɪˈlæksɪs/ n. (pl. **anaphylaxes** /-ksiːz/) Med. hypersensitivity of tissues to a dose of antigen, as a reaction against a previous dose. □□ **anaphylactic** adj. [mod.L f. F anaphylaxie (as ANA- + Gk phulaxis guarding)]

anaptyxis /ˌænəpˈtɪksɪs/ n. (pl. **anaptyxes** /-siːz/) Phonet. the insertion of a vowel between two consonants to aid pronunciation (as in went thataway). □□ **anaptyctic** adj. [mod.L f. Gk anaptuxis (as ANA-, ptussō fold)]

anarchism /ˈænəˌkɪz(ə)m/ n. the doctrine that all government should be abolished. [F anarchisme (as ANARCHY)]

anarchist /ˈænəkɪst/ n. an advocate of anarchism or of political disorder. □□ **anarchistic** /-ˈkɪstɪk/ adj. [F anarchiste (as ANARCHY)]

anarchy /ˈænəkɪ/ n. **1** disorder, esp. political or social. **2** lack of government in a society. □□ **anarchic** /əˈnɑːkɪk/ adj. **anarchical** /əˈnɑːkɪk(ə)l/ adj. **anarchically** /əˈnɑːkɪkəlɪ/ adv. [med.L f. Gk anarkhia (as AN-¹, arkhē rule)]

Anasazi /ænəˈsɑːzɪ/ adj. of an ancient culture of the southwestern US from which the Pueblo culture (which continues to the present) developed. Its earliest phases are known as the Basket Maker period. [Navaho, = ancient one (also = 'enemy ancestor')]

anastigmat /əˈnæstɪɡˌmæt/ n. a lens or lens-system made free from astigmatism by correction. [G f. anastigmatisch ANASTIGMATIC]

anastigmatic /ˌænəstɪɡˈmætɪk/ adj. free from astigmatism. [F ana-

anastomose /əˈnæstəˌməʊz/ v.intr. link by anastomosis. [F anastomoser (as ANASTOMOSIS)]

anastomosis /əˌnæstəˈməʊsɪs/ n. (pl. **anastomoses** /-siːz/) a cross-connection of arteries, branches, rivers, etc. [mod.L f. Gk f. anastomoō furnish with a mouth (as ANA-, stoma mouth)]

anastrophe /əˈnæstrəfɪ/ n. Rhet. the inversion of the usual order of words or clauses. [Gk anastrophē turning back (as ANA-, strephō to turn)]

anathema /əˈnæθəmə/ n. (pl. **anathemas**) **1** a detested thing or person (is anathema to me). **2 a** a curse of the Church, excommunicating a person or denouncing a doctrine. **b** a cursed thing or person. **c** a strong curse. [eccl.L, = excommunicated person, excommunication, f. Gk anathema thing devoted, (later) accursed thing, f. anatithēmi set up]

anathematize /əˈnæθəməˌtaɪz/ v.tr. & intr. (also **-ise**) curse. [F anathématiser f. L anathematizāre f. Gk anathematizo (as ANATHEMA)]

Anatolia /ˌænəˈtəʊlɪə/ (in history called Asia Minor; see entry) the western peninsula of Asia that now forms the greater part of Turkey, bounded by the Black Sea and the Aegean and Mediterranean Seas. Most of it consists of a high plateau; the mountain ranges in the east include Mount Ararat. □□ **Anatolian** adj. & n. [Gk anatolē east]

anatomical /ˌænəˈtɒmɪk(ə)l/ adj. **1** of or relating to anatomy. **2** structural. □□ **anatomically** adv. [F anatomique or LL anatomicus (as ANATOMY)]

anatomist /əˈnætəmɪst/ n. a person skilled in anatomy. [F anatomiste or med.L anatomista (as ANATOMIZE)]

anatomize /əˈnætəˌmaɪz/ v.tr. (also **-ise**) **1** examine in detail. **2** dissect. [F anatomiser or med.L anatomizare f. anatomia (as ANATOMY)]

anatomy /əˈnætəmɪ/ n. (pl. **-ies**) **1** the science of the bodily structure of animals and plants. **2** this structure. **3** colloq. a human body. **4** analysis. **5** the dissection of the human body, animals, or plants. [F anatomie or LL anatomia f. Gk (as ANA-, -TOMY)]

anatta (also **anatto**) var. of ANNATTO.

Anaxagoras /ˌænækˈsægərəs/ (*c*.500–*c*.428 BC) Greek philosopher, the last of the Ionian school, who lived in Athens and was a teacher and friend of Pericles. Few fragments of his writings have survived. He held that all matter was infinitely divisible and initially held together in a motionless uniform mixture until put into a system of circulation directed by Spirit or Intelligence, which created the sky and earth, from which the sun, moon, and stars were formed. His astronomy was not particularly fruitful, but his concept of an independent moving cause prepared the way for a fully teleological view of nature. There is now some dispute as to whether he was the first to give the true explanation of eclipses.

Anaximander /æˌnæksɪˈmændə(r)/ (*c*.610–*c*.545 BC) Greek philosopher and astronomer of the Ionian school, who lived in Miletus. Apart from one verbatim quotation, all that is known about him comes from indirect sources. He is reputed to have drawn the earliest map of the inhabited world, to have introduced the gnomon sundial into Greece, and to have taught a primitive form of evolutionary theory, in that he argued that life began in water and that man originated from fish. More significantly, he taught that all phenomena resulted from a single law which set the primordial substance into a vortex motion. This separated out contrasting qualities, such as hot/cold, wet/dry, and eventually formed the universe, with a flat cylindrically shaped cold damp earth at the centre, surrounded by fiery sun, moon, and stars.

Anaximenes /ˌænækˈsɪmɪˌniːz/ (*c*.546 BC) Greek philosopher of the Ionian school, who lived in Miletus. He maintained that the universe consists of 'air' or vapour which when rarefied becomes fire, when condensed becomes progressively wind, cloud, water, earth, stone. Anaximenes believed the earth to be flat and shallow, and his astronomy is retrograde from that of Anaximander, but his theory of condensation and rarefaction as a means of change from the basic form of matter to the diversity of natural substances was an important contribution to the thought of his time.

ANC *abbr.* African National Congress.

-ance /əns/ *suffix* forming nouns expressing: **1** a quality or state or an instance of one (*arrogance*; *protuberance*; *relevance*; *resemblance*). **2** an action (*assistance*; *furtherance*; *penance*). [from or after F -*ance* f. L -*antia*, -*entia* (cf. -ENCE) f. pres. part. stem -*ant-*, -*ent-*]

ancestor /ˈænsestə(r)/ *n.* (*fem.* **ancestress** /-strɪs/) **1** any (esp. remote) person from whom one is descended. **2** an early type of animal or plant from which others have evolved. **3** an early prototype or forerunner (*ancestor of the computer*). [ME f. OF *ancestre* f. L *antecessor* -*oris* f. *antecedere* (as ANTE-, *cedere cess-* go)]

ancestral /ænˈsestr(ə)l/ *adj.* belonging to or inherited from one's ancestors. [F *ancestrel* (as ANCESTOR)]

ancestry /ˈænsestrɪ/ *n.* (*pl.* -**ies**) **1** one's (esp. remote) family descent. **2** one's ancestors collectively. [ME alt. of OF *ancesserie* (as ANCESTOR)]

anchor /ˈæŋkə(r)/ *n.* & *v.* —*n.* **1** a heavy metal weight used to moor a ship to the sea-bottom or a balloon to the ground. **2** a thing affording stability. **3** a source of confidence. —*v.* **1** *tr.* secure (a ship or balloon) by means of an anchor. **2** *tr.* fix firmly. **3** *intr.* cast anchor. **4** *intr.* be moored by means of an anchor. □ **anchor escapement** a form of escapement in clocks and watches in which the teeth of the crown- or balance-wheel act on the pallets by recoil. **anchor-plate** a heavy piece of timber or metal, e.g. as support for suspension-bridge cables. **at anchor** moored by means of an anchor. **cast** (or **come to**) **anchor** let the anchor down. **weigh anchor** take the anchor up. [OE *ancor* f. L *anchora* f. Gk *agkura*]

Anchorage /ˈæŋkərɪdʒ/ the largest city in Alaska; pop. (1982) 194,700.

anchorage /ˈæŋkərɪdʒ/ *n.* **1** a place where a ship may be anchored. **2** the act of anchoring or lying at anchor. **3** anything dependable.

anchorite /ˈæŋkəˌraɪt/ *n.* (also **anchoret** /-rɪt/) (*fem.* **anchoress** /-rɪs/) **1** a hermit; a religious recluse. **2** a person of secluded habits. □□ **anchoretic** /-ˈretɪk/ *adj.* **anchoritic** /-ˈrɪtɪk/ *adj.* [ME

f. med.L *anc(h)orita*, eccl.L *anchoreta* f. eccl.Gk *anakhōrētēs* f. *anakhōreō* retire]

anchorman /ˈæŋkəmən/ *n.* (*pl.* -**men**) **1** a person who coordinates activities, esp. as compère in a broadcast. **2** a person who plays a crucial part, esp. at the back of a tug-of-war team or as the last runner in a relay race.

anchoveta /ˌæntʃəˈvetə/ *n.* a small Pacific anchovy caught for use as bait or to make fish-meal. [Sp., dimin. of *anchova*: cf. ANCHOVY]

anchovy /ˈæntʃəvɪ, ænˈtʃəʊvɪ/ *n.* (*pl.* -**ies**) any of various small silvery fish of the herring family usu. preserved in salt and oil and having a strong taste. □ **anchovy pear** a W. Indian fruit like a mango. **anchovy toast** toast spread with paste made from anchovies. [Sp. & Port. *ancho(v)a*, of uncert. orig.]

anchusa /ænˈkjuːzə, ænˈtʃuːzə/ *n.* any plant of the genus *Anchusa*, akin to borage. [L f. Gk *agkhousa*]

anchylose var. of ANKYLOSE.

anchylosis var. of ANKYLOSIS.

ancien régime /ˌɑ̃ːsjæ̃ reˈʒiːm/ *n.* (*pl. anciens régimes* pronunc. same) **1** the political and social system in France before the Revolution of 1789. **2** any superseded regime. [F, = old rule]

ancient¹ /ˈeɪnʃ(ə)nt/ *adj.* & *n.* —*adj.* **1** of long ago. **2** having lived or existed long. —*n.* archaic an old man. □ **ancient history 1** the history of the ancient civilizations of the Mediterranean area and the Near East before the fall of the Western Roman Empire in 476. **2** something already long familiar. **ancient lights** a window that a neighbour may not deprive of light by building. **ancient monument** *Brit.* an old building etc. preserved usu. under Government control. **the ancients** the people of ancient times, esp. the Greeks and Romans. □□ **ancientness** *n.* [ME f. AF *auncien* f. OF *ancien*, ult. f. L *ante* before]

ancient² /ˈeɪnʃ(ə)nt/ *n.* archaic = ENSIGN. [corrupt. of form *ensyne* etc. by assoc. with *ancien* = ANCIENT¹]

anciently /ˈeɪnʃəntlɪ/ *adv.* long ago.

ancillary /ænˈsɪlərɪ/ *adj.* & *n.* —*adj.* **1** (of a person, activity, or service) providing essential support to a central service or industry, esp. the medical service. **2** (often foll. by *to*) subordinate, subservient. —*n.* (*pl.* -**ies**) **1** an ancillary worker. **2** something which is ancillary; an auxiliary or accessory. [L *ancillaris* f. *ancilla* maidservant]

ancon /ˈæŋkən/ *n.* (*pl.* -**es** /æŋˈkəʊniːz/) *Archit.* **1** a console, usu. of two volutes, supporting or appearing to support a cornice. **2** each of a pair of projections on either side of a block of stone etc. for lifting or repositioning. [L f. Gk *agkōn* elbow]

-ancy /ənsɪ/ *suffix* forming nouns denoting a quality (*constancy*; *relevancy*) or state (*expectancy*; *infancy*) (cf. -ANCE). [from or after L -*antia*: cf. -ENCY]

and /ænd, ənd/ *conj.* **1 a** connecting words, clauses, or sentences, that are to be taken jointly (*cakes and buns*; *white and brown bread*; *buy and sell*; *two hundred and forty*). **b** implying progression (*better and better*). **c** implying causation (*do that and I'll hit you*; *she hit him and he cried*). **d** implying great duration (*he cried and cried*). **e** implying a great number (*miles and miles*). **f** implying addition (*two and two are four*). **g** implying variety (*there are books and books*). **h** implying succession (*walking two and two*). **2** *colloq.* to (*try and open it*). **3** in relation to (*Britain and the EEC*). □ **and/or** either or both of two stated possibilities (usually restricted to legal and commercial use). [OE *and*]

-and /ænd/ *suffix* forming nouns meaning 'a person or thing to be treated in a specified way' (*ordinand*). [L gerundive ending -*andus*]

Andalusia /ˌændəˈluːsɪə/ (also **Andalucia**) the southernmost region of Spain, bordering on the Atlantic Ocean and the Mediterranean Sea; pop. (1986) 6,875,600; capital, Seville. □□ **Andalusian** *adj.* & *n.* [VANDAL; named by Muslim conquerors after the Vandals who had settled there in the 5th c.]

Andaman and Nicobar Islands /ˈændəmən, ˈnɪkəˌbɑː(r)/ a Union Territory of India, consisting of two groups of islands in the Bay of Bengal; pop. (1981) 188,250; capital, Port Blair, in the Andaman Islands.

b *but* d *dog* f *few* g *get* h *he* j *yes* k *cat* l *leg* m *man* n *no* p *pen* r *red* s *sit* t *top* v *voice*

andante /ænˈdæntɪ/ *adv., adj., & n. Mus.* —*adv. & adj.* in a moderately slow tempo. —*n.* an andante passage or movement. [It., part. of *andare* go]

andantino /ˌændænˈtiːnəʊ/ *adv., adj., & n. Mus.* —*adv. & adj.* rather quicker (orig. slower) than andante. —*n.* (*pl.* -**os**) an andantino passage or movement. [It., dimin. of ANDANTE]

Andersen /ˈændəs(ə)n/, Hans Christian (1805–75), Danish author, son of a shoemaker and a washerwoman. He attempted to become an actor in Copenhagen but failed in this and nearly starved; then friends took pity on him and he eventually won the generous patronage of King Frederick VI, and received a university education. He was acknowledged in Scandinavia as a novelist and travel-writer before publishing the first of the fairy tales for which he is now celebrated. These appeared from 1835 and include such classics as 'The Snow Queen', 'The Ugly Duckling', and 'The Little Match Girl'. Andersen lived to see his native town of Odense illuminated in his honour, but he knew only too well how it felt to be humble and penniless, and some of his best-loved stories are those that tell of the plight of innocent helpless creatures in a harsh and dangerous world.

Anderson /ˈændəs(ə)n/, Elizabeth Garrett (1836–1917), pioneer of medical training for women. Debarred from entry to medical courses in Britain because of her sex, she studied privately and in 1865 obtained a licence to practise from the Society of Apothecaries. In the following year she opened a dispensary for women and children in Marylebone, which later became a hospital, the first to be staffed by medical women; its name was changed to the Elizabeth Garrett Anderson Hospital in 1918. Her influence was considerable in securing the admission of women to various qualifying bodies and to important medical societies.

Andes /ˈændiːz/ a major mountain range running the length of the Pacific coast of South America. It includes many volcanoes, and several peaks top 6,150 m (20,000 ft.). □□ **Andean** /ænˈdiːən, ˈæn-/ *adj.*

andesite /ˈændɪˌzaɪt/ *n.* a fine-grained brown or greyish intermediate volcanic rock. [ANDES + -ITE¹]

Andhra Pradesh /ˌɑːndrə prəˈdeʃ/ a State in SE India; pop. (1981) 53,403,600; capital, Hyderabad.

andiron /ˈændˌaɪən/ *n.* a metal stand (usu. one of a pair) for supporting burning wood in a fireplace; a firedog. [ME f. OF *andier*, of unkn. orig.: assim. to IRON]

Andorra /ænˈdɒrə/ a small autonomous principality in the southern Pyrenees, between France and Spain; pop. (est. 1988) 49,400; official language, Catalan; capital, Andorra la Vella. Its independence is said to arise from the granting of the lands by a son of Charlemagne to the counts of Urgel in Spain. Under a treaty of 1278 the sovereignty of Andorra is shared between France and the Spanish bishop of Urgel. □□ **Andorran** *adj. & n.*

Andre /ˈɑːndreɪ/, Carl (1935–), American minimal sculptor (see MINIMAL). He produces his works by stacking ready-made units such as bricks, cement blocks, or ceramic magnets according to a mathematically imposed modular system and without adhesives or joints. In Britain he is best known for the outcry about the alleged waste of public money on the purchase by the Tate Gallery of his *Equivalent VIII* (1966), which consists of 120 bricks arranged two deep in a rectangle.

Andrea del Sarto /ˈændrɪɔ del ˈsɑːtəʊ/ (1486–1531), Italian Renaissance painter who absorbed the style of poise and beauty developed by Bartolommeo and Raphael and influenced the mannerist experiments of his pupils Pontormo and Rosso (1494–1540). His reputation was largely made and marred by Vasari, who described his works as 'faultless' but represented him as a weakling under the thumb of a wicked wife—traits of character which Robert Browning (1855) and others have (unjustly) sought to link with the lack of vigour in his mellifluous style. He worked chiefly in Florence, where among his most important works are fresco cycles (*Nativity of the Virgin*, 1514; *Madonna del Sacco*, 1524) and grisailles which give the effect of relief sculpture. The appeal of his dreamy portraits and

dark-eyed Madonnas has never failed with the unsophisticated public.

Andrew /ˈændruː/, St (1st c.), one of the twelve Apostles, brother of St Peter. Since *c.*750 he has been regarded as the patron saint of Scotland. An apocryphal work dating probably from the 3rd c. describes his death by crucifixion but makes no mention of the X-shaped cross associated with his name. Feast day, 30 Nov.

Andrews /ˈændruːz/, Julie (1935–), English actress and singer, who created the role of Eliza Doolittle in *My Fair Lady* on Broadway in 1956. Her films *Mary Poppins* (1964) and *The Sound of Music* (1965) were well suited to her wholesome appeal and displayed her talents as a singer.

Androcles /ˈændrəˌkliːz/ a runaway slave in a story by Aulus Gellius (2nd c. AD) who extracted a thorn from the paw of a lion which later recognized and refrained from attacking him when he faced it in the arena.

androecium /ænˈdriːsɪəm/ *n.* (*pl.* **androecia** /-sɪə/) *Bot.* the stamens taken collectively. [mod.L f. Gk *andro-* male + *oikion* house]

androgen /ˈændrədʒ(ə)n/ *n.* a male sex hormone or other substance capable of developing and maintaining certain male sexual characteristics. □□ **androgenic** /-ˈdʒenɪk/ *adj.* [Gk *andro-* male + -GEN]

androgyne /ˈændrəˌdʒaɪn/ *adj. & n.* —*adj.* hermaphrodite. —*n.* a hermaphrodite person. [OF *androgyne* or L *androgynus* f. Gk *androgunos* (*anēr andros* male, *gunē* woman)]

androgynous /ænˈdrɒdʒɪnəs/ *adj.* **1** hermaphrodite. **2** *Bot.* with stamens and pistils in the same flower or inflorescence.

androgyny /ænˈdrɒdʒɪnɪ/ *n.* hermaphroditism.

android /ˈændrɔɪd/ *n.* a robot with a human appearance. [Gk *andro-* male, man + -OID]

Andromache /ænˈdrɒməkɪ/ *Gk legend* wife of Hector. After the fall of Troy she became the slave of Neoptolemus (son of Achilles), and after his death married Helenus, a brother of Hector.

Andromeda /ænˈdrɒmɪdə/ **1** *Gk legend* daughter of Cepheus, king of the Ethiopians. Her mother (Cassiopeia) boasted that she herself (or her daughter) was more beautiful than the Nereids, whereupon Poseidon in vengeance sent a sea-monster to ravage the country. To abate his wrath Andromeda was fastened to a rock and exposed to the monster, from which she was rescued by Perseus. The story is of a type that is widely distributed and may have had a share in forming the legend of St George and the Dragon. The traditional site in later time was Joppa (= Jaffa). **2** *Astron.* a constellation, conspicuous for its great spiral nebula (the **Andromeda Galaxy**) which is now known to be a spiral galaxy probably twice as massive as our own and located two million light-years away.

-androus /ˈændrəs/ *comb. form Bot.* forming adjectives meaning 'having specified male organs or stamens' (*monandrous*). [mod.L f. Gk *-andros* f. *anēr andros* male + -OUS]

-ane¹ /eɪn/ *suffix* var. of -AN; usu. with distinction of sense (*germane*; *humane*; *urbane*) but sometimes with no corresponding form in *-an* (*mundane*).

-ane² /eɪn/ *suffix Chem.* forming names of paraffins and other saturated hydrocarbons (*methane*; *propane*). [after *-ene*, *-ine*, etc.]

anecdotage /ˈænɪkˌdəʊtɪdʒ/ *n.* **1** *joc.* garrulous old age. **2** anecdotes. [ANECDOTE + -AGE: sense 1 after DOTAGE]

anecdote /ˈænɪkˌdəʊt/ *n.* a short account (or painting etc.) of an entertaining or interesting incident. □□ **anecdotal** /-ˈdəʊt(ə)l/ *adj.* **anecdotalist** /-ˈdəʊtəlɪst/ *n.* **anecdotic** /-ˈdɒtɪk/ *adj.* **anecdotist** *n.* [F *anecdote* or mod.L f. Gk *anekdota* things unpublished (as AN-¹, *ekdotos* f. *ekdidōmi* publish)]

anechoic /ˌænɪˈkəʊɪk/ *adj.* free from echo.

anele /əˈniːl/ *v.tr. archaic* anoint, esp. in extreme unction. [ME f. AN-¹ + *elien* f. OE *ele* f. L *oleum* oil]

anemia *US* var. of ANAEMIA.

anemic *US* var. of ANAEMIC.

anemograph /əˈneməˌɡrɑːf/ *n.* an instrument for recording on paper the direction and force of the wind. □□ **anemographic** /-ˈɡræfɪk/ *adj.* [Gk *anemos* wind + -GRAPH]

anemometer /ˌænɪˈmɒmɪtə(r)/ *n.* an instrument for measuring the force of the wind. [Gk *anemos* wind + -METER]

anemometry /ˌænɪ'mɒmɪtrɪ/ n. the measurement of the force of the wind. □□ **anemometric** /-mə'metrɪk/ adj. [Gk anemos wind + -METRY]

anemone /ə'nemənɪ/ n. **1** any plant of the genus *Anemone*, akin to the buttercup, with flowers of various vivid colours. **2** = PASQUE-FLOWER. [L f. Gk anemōnē wind-flower f. anemos wind]

anemophilous /ˌænɪ'mɒfɪləs/ adj. wind-pollinated. [Gk anemos wind + -philous (see -PHILIA)]

anent /ə'nent/ prep. archaic or Sc. concerning. [OE on efen on a level with]

-aneous /'eɪnɪəs/ suffix forming adjectives (cutaneous; miscellaneous). [L -aneus + -OUS]

aneroid /'ænəˌrɔɪd/ adj. & n. —adj. (of a barometer) that measures air-pressure by its action on the elastic lid of an evacuated box, not by the height of a column of fluid. —n. an aneroid barometer. [F anéroïde f. Gk a- not + nēros water]

anesthesia etc. US var. of ANAESTHESIA etc.

aneurin /ə'njʊərɪn, 'æn-/ n. = THIAMINE. [anti + polyneuritis + vitamin]

aneurysm /'ænjʊˌrɪz(ə)m/ n. (also **aneurism**) an excessive localized enlargement of an artery. □□ **aneurysmal** /-'rɪzm(ə)l/ adj. (also **aneurismal**). [Gk aneurusma f. aneurunō widen out f. eurus wide]

anew /ə'njuː/ adv. **1** again. **2** in a different way. [ME, f. A-⁴ + NEW]

anfractuosity /ˌænfræktjʊ'ɒsɪtɪ/ n. **1** circuitousness. **2** intricacy. [F anfractuosité f. LL anfractuosus f. L anfractus a bending]

angary /'æŋgərɪ/ n. Law the right of a belligerent (subject to compensation for loss) to seize or destroy neutral property under military necessity. [F angarie ult. f. Gk aggareia f. aggaros courier]

angel /'eɪndʒ(ə)l/ n. **1 a** an attendant or messenger of God. (See below.) **b** a conventional representation of this in human form with wings. **c** an attendant spirit (evil angel; guardian angel). **d** a member of the lowest order of the ninefold celestial hierarchy (see ORDER). **2 a** a very virtuous person. **b** an obliging person (be an angel and answer the door). **3** an old English coin bearing the figure of the archangel Michael piercing the dragon. **4** sl. a financial backer of an enterprise, esp. in the theatre. **5** an unexplained radar echo. □ **angel cake** a very light sponge cake. **angel-fish** any of various fish, esp. *Pterophyllum scalare*, with large dorsal and ventral fins. **angel-shark** = MONKFISH 2. **angels-on-horseback** a savoury of oysters wrapped in slices of bacon. [ME f. OF angele f. eccl.L angelus f. Gk aggelos messenger]

In the Bible angels are represented as an innumerable multitude of beings intermediate between God and man; they form the heavenly court. In the early Church interest in angels was peripheral; Dionysius the Pseudo-Areopagite speculatively arranged them in three hierarchies. In the Middle Ages there was speculation and controversy over their substance, form, and nature. Catholic Christianity in general teaches their existence, perfect spirituality, and creation before man, and enjoins a cult similar to that given to the saints; Protestants have shrunk from definition and speculation.

Angel Falls a waterfall in the Guiana Highlands of SE Venezuela with an uninterrupted fall of 978 m (3,210 ft.), making this the highest waterfall in the world. The falls were discovered in 1935 by the American aviator and prospector James Angel, after whom they are named.

angelic /æn'dʒelɪk/ adj. **1** like or relating to angels. **2** having characteristics attributed to angels, esp. sublime beauty or innocence. □ **Angelic Doctor** the nickname of St Thomas Aquinas. □□ **angelical** adj. **angelically** adv. [ME f. F angélique or LL angelicus f. Gk aggelikos (as ANGEL)]

angelica /æn'dʒelɪkə/ n. **1** an aromatic umbelliferous plant, *Angelica archangelica*, used in cooking and medicine. **2** its candied stalks. [med.L (herba) angelica angelic herb]

Angelico /æn'dʒelɪˌkəʊ/, Guido di Pietro, 'Fra Angelico' (c.1400–55), Italian painter who became a Dominican friar at Fiesole in 1408, regarded in the 19th c. as a saint but now recognized as a highly professional artist, well aware of progressive developments in contemporary Florentine painting. His art makes use of Masaccio's achievements in the representation of volume, and of the architectural forms of Michelozzo and Brunelleschi, yet is more conservative in its preference for intense local colour and graceful linear rhythms. His most celebrated works are the frescos in the convent of San Marco, Florence (c.1438–47) and the *Scenes from the Lives of SS Stephen and Lawrence* (1447–9) in the private chapel of Pope Nicholas V in the Vatican.

angelus /'ændʒɪləs/ n. **1** a Roman Catholic devotion commemorating the Incarnation, said at morning, noon, and sunset. **2** a bell rung to announce this. [opening words Angelus domini (L, = the angel of the Lord)]

anger /'æŋgə(r)/ n. & v. —n. extreme or passionate displeasure. —v.tr. make angry; enrage. [ME f. ON angr grief, angra vex]

Angers /'ɑ̃ʒeɪ/ the capital of the former province of Anjou in the Pays de la Loire region in western France; pop. (1982) 141,150.

Angevin /'ændʒɪvɪn/ n. & adj. —n. **1** a native or inhabitant of Anjou. **2** a Plantagenet, esp. any of the English kings from Henry II to John. —adj. **1** of Anjou. **2** of the Plantagenets. [F]

angina /æn'dʒaɪnə/ n. **1** an attack of intense constricting pain often causing suffocation. **2** (in full **angina pectoris** /'pektərɪs/) pain in the chest brought on by exertion, owing to an inadequate blood supply to the heart. [L, = spasm of the chest f. angina quinsy f. Gk agkhonē strangling]

angioma /ˌændʒɪ'əʊmə/ n. (pl. **angiomata** /-mətə/) a tumour produced by the dilatation or new formation of blood-vessels. [mod.L f. Gk aggeion vessel]

angiosperm /'ændʒɪəˌspɜːm/ n. any plant producing flowers and reproducing by seeds enclosed within a carpel, including herbaceous plants, herbs, shrubs, grasses and most trees (opp. GYMNOSPERM). □□ **angiospermous** /ˌændʒɪə'spɜːməs/ adj. [Gk aggeion vessel + sperma seed]

Angkor /'æŋkɔː(r)/ the capital of the ancient kingdom of Khmer, famous for its temples, especially the Angkor Wat (early 12th c.), decorated with relief sculptures. The site was overgrown with jungle when it was rediscovered in 1860.

Angle /'æŋg(ə)l/ n. (usu. in pl.) a member of a North German tribe, originally inhabitants of what is now Schleswig-Holstein, who came to England in the 5th c., founding kingdoms in Mercia, Northumbria, and East Anglia, and finally gave their name to England and the English. □□ **Anglian** adj. [L Anglus f. Gmc (OE Engle: cf. ENGLISH) f. Angul a district of Schleswig (now in N. Germany) (as ANGLE²)]

angle¹ /'æŋg(ə)l/ n. & v. —n. **1 a** the space between two meeting lines or surfaces. **b** the inclination of two lines or surfaces to each other. **2 a** a corner. **b** a sharp projection. **3 a** the direction from which a photograph etc. is taken. **b** the aspect from which a matter is considered. —v. **1** tr. & intr. move or place obliquely. **2** tr. present (information) from a particular point of view (was angled in favour of the victim). □ **angle brackets** brackets in the form ⟨ ⟩ (see BRACKET n. 3). **angle-iron** a piece of iron or steel with an L-shaped cross-section, used to strengthen a framework. **angle of repose** the angle beyond which an inclined body will not support another on its surface by friction. [ME f. OF angle or f. L angulus]

angle² /'æŋg(ə)l/ v. & n. —v.intr. **1** (often foll. by for) fish with hook and line. The first treatise on angling is that by Dame Juliana Barnes (1496); the most famous is Sir Izaac Walton's *Compleat Angler* (1653). **2** (foll. by for) seek an objective by devious or calculated means (angled for a pay rise). —n. archaic a fish-hook. [OE angul]

angled /'æŋg(ə)ld/ adj. **1** placed at an angle to something else. **2** presented to suit a particular point of view. **3** having an angle.

angler /'æŋglə(r)/ n. **1** a person who fishes with a hook and line. **2** = angler-fish. □ **angler-fish** any of various fishes that prey upon small fish, attracting them by filaments arising from the dorsal fin: also called frog-fish (see FROG¹).

Anglesey /'æŋgəlsɪ/ an island of NW Wales, separated from the mainland by the Menai Strait.

Anglican /ˈæŋglɪkən/ adj. & n. —adj. of or relating to the Church of England or any Church in communion with it. — n. a member of an Anglican Church. □□ **Anglicanism** n. [med.L Anglicanus (Magna Carta) f. Anglicus (Bede) f. Anglus ANGLE]

anglice /ˈæŋglɪsɪ/ adv. in English. [med.L]

Anglicism /ˈæŋglɪˌsɪz(ə)m/ n. 1 a peculiarly English word or custom. 2 Englishness. 3 preference for what is English. [L Anglicus (see ANGLICAN) + -ISM]

Anglicize /ˈæŋglɪˌsaɪz/ v.tr. (also -ise) make English in form or character.

Anglist /ˈæŋglɪst/ n. a student of or scholar in English language or literature. □□ **Anglistics** /-ˈglɪstɪks/ n. [G f. L Anglus English]

Anglo /ˈæŋgləʊ/ n. (pl. -os) US a person of British or northern-European origin. [abbr. of ANGLO-SAXON]

Anglo- /ˈæŋgləʊ/ comb. form 1 English (Anglo-Catholic). 2 of English origin (an Anglo-American). 3 English or British and (an Anglo-American agreement). [f. mod.L f. L Anglus English]

Anglo-Catholic /ˌæŋgləʊˈkæθəlɪk/ adj. & n. —adj. of a High Church Anglican group which emphasizes its unbroken connection with the early Church and seeks maximum accordance with the doctrine of the Catholic Church. —n. a member of this group.

Anglocentric /ˌæŋgləʊˈsentrɪk/ adj. centred on or considered in terms of England.

Anglo-French /ˌæŋgləʊˈfrentʃ/ adj. & n. —adj. 1 English (or British) and French. 2 of Anglo-French. —n. the French language as retained and separately developed in England after the Norman Conquest. It arose from the dialect of French carried to England by the Norman invaders in 1066, and remained the language of the English nobility for several centuries. It is still preserved in some archaic legal phraseology.

Anglo-Indian /ˌæŋgləʊˈɪndɪən/ adj. & n. —adj. 1 of or relating to England and India. 2 a of British descent or birth but living or having lived long in India. b of mixed British and Indian parentage. 3 (of a word) adopted into English from an Indian language. —n. an Anglo-Indian person.

Anglo-Latin /ˌæŋgləʊˈlætɪn/ adj. & n. —adj. of Latin as used in medieval England. —n. this form of Latin.

Anglomania /ˌæŋgləʊˈmeɪnɪə/ n. excessive admiration of English customs.

Anglo-Norman /ˌæŋgləʊˈnɔːmən/ adj. & n. —adj. 1 English and Norman. 2 of the Normans in England after the Norman Conquest. 3 of the dialect of French used by them. —n. the Anglo-Norman dialect.

Anglophile /ˈæŋgləʊˌfaɪl/ n. & adj. (also **Anglophil** /-fɪl/) — n. a person who is fond of or greatly admires England or the English. —adj. being or characteristic of an Anglophile.

Anglophobe /ˈæŋgləʊˌfəʊb/ n. & adj. —n. a person who greatly hates or fears England or the English. —adj. being or characteristic of an Anglophobe.

Anglophobia /ˌæŋgləʊˈfəʊbɪə/ n. intense hatred or fear of England or the English.

anglophone /ˈæŋgləʊˌfəʊn/ adj. & n. —adj. English-speaking. —n. an English-speaking person. [ANGLO-, after FRANCOPHONE]

Anglo-Saxon /ˌæŋgləʊˈsæks(ə)n/ adj. & n. —adj. 1 of the English Saxons (as distinct from the Old Saxons of the continent, and from the Angles) before the Norman Conquest. 2 of the Old English people as a whole before the Norman Conquest. 3 of English descent. —n. 1 an Anglo-Saxon person. 2 the Old English language (see ENGLISH). 3 a colloq. plain (esp. crude) English. b US the modern English language. [mod.L Anglo-Saxones, med.L Angli Saxones after OE Angulseaxe, -an]

Angola /æŋˈgəʊlə/ a country on the coast of Africa north of Namibia; pop. (est. 1988) 8,236,400; official language, Portuguese; capital, Luanda. The country is rich in mineral resources, including diamonds and oil. Discovered by the Portuguese at the end of the 15th c., the area was colonized by them a century later, and remained in Portuguese possession until it achieved independence in 1975 after a bitter anti-colonial war. □□ **Angolan** adj. & n.

angora /æŋˈgɔːrə/ n. 1 a fabric made from the hair of the angora goat or rabbit. 2 a long-haired variety of cat, goat, or rabbit. □ **angora wool** a mixture of sheep's wool and angora rabbit hair. [Angora former name of ANKARA]

angostura /ˌæŋgəˈstjʊərə/ n. (in full **angostura bark**) an aromatic bitter bark used as a flavouring, and formerly used as a tonic and to reduce fever. □ **Angostura Bitters** propr. a kind of tonic first made in Angostura. [Angostura, a town in Venezuela on the Orinoco, now Ciudad Bolívar]

angry /ˈæŋgrɪ/ adj. (**angrier**, **angriest**) 1 feeling or showing anger; extremely displeased or resentful. 2 (of a wound, sore, etc.) inflamed, painful. 3 suggesting or seeming to show anger (an angry sky). □□ **angrily** adv. [ME, f. ANGER + -Y¹]

angst /æŋst/ n. 1 anxiety. 2 a feeling of guilt or remorse. [G]

Ångström /ˈæŋstrəm, ˈɔːŋstrɔːm/, Anders Jonas (1814–1874), Swedish physicist. He wrote on terrestrial magnetism and on the conduction of heat, but his most important work was in the new field of spectroscopy. He proposed a relationship between the emission and absorption spectra of chemical elements, discovered in 1862 the presence of hydrogen in the sun's atmosphere, and six years later published his atlas of the solar spectrum. He measured his optical wavelengths in units of one ten-millionth of a millimetre (10^{-10} metre), later named the angstrom unit in his honour.

angstrom /ˈæŋstrəm/ n. (also **ångström** /ˈɒŋstrɔːm/) a unit of length equal to 10^{-10} metre. ¶ Symb.: Å. [A.J. ÅNGSTRÖM]

Anguilla /æŋˈgwɪlə/ the most northerly of the Leeward Islands in the West Indies; pop. (est. 1988) 6,700; official language, English; capital, Valley. The island is a British dependency with full self-government (see ST KITTS-NEVIS).

anguine /ˈæŋgwɪn/ adj. of or resembling a snake. [L anguinus f. anguis snake]

anguish /ˈæŋgwɪʃ/ n. severe misery or mental suffering. [ME f. OF anguisse choking f. L angustia tightness f. angustus narrow]

anguished /ˈæŋgwɪʃt/ adj. suffering or expressing anguish. [past part. of anguish (v.) f. OF anguissier f. eccl.L angustiare to distress, formed as ANGUISH]

angular /ˈæŋgjʊlə(r)/ adj. 1 a having angles or sharp corners. b (of a person) having sharp features; lean and bony. c awkward in manner. 2 forming an angle. 3 measured by angle (angular distance). □ **angular momentum** the quantity of rotation of a body, the product of its moment of inertia and angular velocity. **angular velocity** the rate of change of angular position of a rotating body. □□ **angularity** /-ˈlærɪtɪ/ n. **angularly** adv. [L angularis f. angulus ANGLE¹]

anhedral /ænˈhiːdr(ə)l/ n. & adj. Aeron. —n. the angle between wing and horizontal when the wing is inclined downwards. —adj. of or having an anhedral. [AN-¹ + -hedral (see -HEDRON)]

Anhui /ˈɑːnhweɪ/ (also **Anhwei**) a province in eastern China; pop. (est. 1986) 52,170,000; capital, Hefei (Hofei).

anhydride /ænˈhaɪdraɪd/ n. Chem. a substance obtained by removing the elements of water from a compound, esp. from an acid. [as ANHYDROUS + -IDE]

anhydrite /ænˈhaɪdraɪt/ n. a naturally occurring usu. rock-forming anhydrous mineral form of calcium sulphate. [as ANHYDROUS + -ITE¹ 2]

anhydrous /ænˈhaɪdrəs/ adj. Chem. without water, esp. water of crystallization. [Gk anudros (as AN-¹, hudōr water)]

aniline /ˈænɪˌliːn, -lɪn, -ˌlaɪn/ n. a colourless oily liquid, used in the manufacture of dyes, drugs, and plastics. □ **aniline dye** 1 any of numerous dyes made from aniline. 2 any synthetic dye. [G Anilin f. Anil indigo (from which it was orig. obtained), ult. f. Arab. an-nīl]

anima /ˈænɪmə/ n. Psychol. 1 the inner personality (opp. PERSONA). 2 Jung's term for the feminine part of a man's personality (opp. ANIMUS). [L, = mind, soul]

animadvert /ˌænɪmædˈvɜːt/ v.intr. (foll. by on) criticize, censure (conduct, a fault, etc.). □□ **animadversion** n. [L animadvertere f. animus mind + advertere (as AD-, vertere vers- turn)]

animal /ˈænɪm(ə)l/ n. & adj. —n. **1** a living organism which feeds on organic matter, usu. one with specialized sense-organs and nervous system, and able to respond rapidly to stimuli. **2** such an organism other than man. **3** a brutish or uncivilized person. **4** colloq. a person or thing of any kind (there is no such animal). —adj. **1** characteristic of animals. **2** of animals as distinct from vegetables (animal charcoal). **3** characteristic of the physical needs of animals; carnal, sensual. □ **animal husbandry** the science of breeding and caring for farm animals. **animal magnetism** hist. mesmerism. **animal spirits** natural exuberance. [L f. animale neut. of animalis having breath f. anima breath]

animalcule /ˌænɪˈmælkjuːl/ n. archaic a microscopic animal. □□ **animalcular** adj. [mod.L animalculum (as ANIMAL, -CULE)]

animalism /ˈænɪməˌlɪz(ə)m/ n. **1** the nature and activity of animals. **2** the belief that humans are not superior to other animals. **3** concern with physical matters; sensuality.

animality /ˌænɪˈmælɪtɪ/ n. **1** the animal world. **2** the nature or behaviour of animals. [F animalité f. animal (adj.)]

animalize /ˈænɪməˌlaɪz/ v.tr. (also **-ise**) **1** make (a person) bestial; sensualize. **2** convert to animal substance. □□ **animalization** /-ˈzeɪʃ(ə)n/ n.

animate adj. & v. —adj. /ˈænɪmət/ **1** having life. **2** lively. —v.tr. /ˈænɪˌmeɪt/ **1** enliven, make lively. **2** give life to. **3** inspire, actuate. **4** encourage. [L animatus past part. of animare give life to f. anima life, soul]

animated /ˈænɪˌmeɪtɪd/ adj. **1** lively, vigorous. **2** having life. **3** (of a film etc.) using techniques of animation. □□ **animatedly** adv. **animator** n. (in sense 3).

animation /ˌænɪˈmeɪʃ(ə)n/ n. **1** vivacity, ardour. **2** the state of being alive. **3** Cinematog. the technique of filming successive drawings or positions of puppets to create an illusion of movement when the film is shown as a sequence.

animé /ˈænɪˌmeɪ/ n. any of various resins, esp. a W. Indian resin used in making varnish. [F, of uncert. orig.]

animism /ˈænɪˌmɪz(ə)m/ n. **1** the attribution of a living soul to plants, inanimate objects, and natural phenomena. **2** the belief in a supernatural power that organizes and animates the material universe. □□ **animist** n. **animistic** /-ˈmɪstɪk/ adj. [L anima life, soul + -ISM]

animosity /ˌænɪˈmɒsɪtɪ/ n. (pl. **-ies**) a spirit or feeling of strong hostility. [ME f. OF animosité or LL animositas f. animosus spirited, formed as ANIMUS]

animus /ˈænɪməs/ n. **1** a display of animosity. **2** ill feeling. **3** a motivating spirit or feeling. **4** Psychol. Jung's term for the masculine part of a woman's personality (opp. ANIMA). [L, = spirit, mind]

anion /ˈænˌaɪən/ n. a negatively charged ion; an ion that is attracted to the anode in electrolysis (opp. CATION). [ANA- + ION]

anionic /ˌænaɪˈɒnɪk/ adj. **1** of an anion or anions. **2** having an active anion.

anise /ˈænɪs/ n. an umbelliferous plant, Pimpinella anisum, having aromatic seeds (see ANISEED). [ME f. OF anis f. L f. Gk anison anise, dill]

aniseed /ˈænɪˌsiːd/ n. the seed of the anise, used to flavour liqueurs and sweets etc. [ME f. ANISE + SEED]

anisette /ˌænɪˈzet/ n. a liqueur flavoured with aniseed. [F, dimin. of anis ANISE]

anisotropic /ˌænaɪsəˈtrɒpɪk/ adj. having physical properties that are different in different directions, e.g. the strength of wood along the grain differing from that across the grain (opp. ISOTROPIC). □□ **anisotropically** adv. **anisotropy** /-ˈsɒtrəpɪ/ n. [AN-¹ + ISOTROPIC]

Anjou /ɑ̃ˈʒuː/ a former province of western France, on the Loire. Henry II of England, as a Plantagenet, was Count of Anjou, but it was lost to the English Crown by King John in 1204.

Ankara /ˈæŋkərə / (formerly Angora) an inland city of Asia Minor, the capital of Turkey since 1923; pop. (1985) 2,251,500. Prominent in Roman times as the capital (Ancyra) of Galatia,

it later dwindled to insignificance until chosen by Kemal Atatürk in 1923 as his seat of government.

ankh /æŋk/ n. a device consisting of a looped bar with a shorter crossbar, used in ancient Egypt as a symbol of life. [Egypt., = life, soul]

ankle /ˈæŋk(ə)l/ n. & v. —n. **1** the joint connecting the foot with the leg. **2** the part of the leg between this and the calf. —v.intr. sl. walk. □ **ankle-bone** a bone forming the ankle. **ankle sock** a short sock just covering the ankle. [ME f. ON ankul- (unrecorded) f. Gmc: rel. to ANGLE¹]

anklet /ˈæŋklɪt/ n. an ornament or fetter worn round the ankle. [ANKLE + -LET, after BRACELET]

ankylose /ˈæŋkɪˌləʊz/ v.tr. & intr. (also **anchylose**) (of bones or a joint) stiffen or unite by ankylosis. [back-form. f. ANKYLOSIS after anastomose etc.]

ankylosis /ˌæŋkɪˈləʊsɪs/ n. (also **anchylosis**) **1** the abnormal stiffening and immobility of a joint by fusion of the bones. **2** such fusion. □□ **ankylotic** adj. [mod.L f. Gk agkulōsis f. agkuloō crook]

anna /ˈænə/ n. a former monetary unit of India and Pakistan, one-sixteenth of a rupee. [Hind. ānā]

Annaba /ˈænəbə/ (formerly Bône) a port on the Mediterranean coast of NE Algeria; pop. (1983) 348,322.

annal /ˈæn(ə)l/ n. **1** the annals of one year. **2** a record of one item in a chronicle. [back-form. f. ANNALS]

annalist /ˈænəlɪst/ n. a writer of annals. □□ **annalistic** /-ˈlɪstɪk/ adj. **annalistically** /-ˈlɪstɪkəlɪ/ adv.

annals /ˈæn(ə)lz/ n.pl. **1** a narrative of events year by year. **2** historical records. [F annales or L annales (libri) yearly (books) f. annus year]

Annapolis /əˈnæpəˌlɪs/ the capital of Maryland; pop. (1980) 31,700. It is the home of the US Naval Academy, which was founded in 1845.

Annapurna /ˌænəˈpɜːnə/ a ridge of the Himalayas, in north central Nepal. Its highest peak rises to 8,078 m (26,503 ft.).

annates /ˈæneɪts/ n.pl. RC Ch. the first year's revenue of a see or benefice, paid to the Pope. [F annate f. med.L annata year's proceeds f. annus year]

annatto /əˈnætəʊ/ n. (also **anatta** /-tə/, **anatto**) an orange-red dye from the pulp of a tropical fruit, used for colouring foods. [Carib name of the fruit-tree]

Anne¹ /æn/ (1665–1714) queen of England and Scotland (known as Great Britain from 1707) and Ireland, 1702–14. The last of the Stuart monarchs, daughter of the Catholic James II (but herself a staunch Protestant), she eventually succeeded her brother-in-law William III on the throne, there presiding over the Act of Union which completed the unification of Scotland and England. Although Anne was pregnant eighteen times none of the five children born alive survived childhood, and by the Act of Settlement the throne passed to the House of Hanover on her death. □ **Queen Anne's Bounty** duties called 'first fruits and tenths', payable originally to the pope but made payable to the Crown by Henry VIII, and directed by Queen Anne in 1704 to be used to provide for the augmentation of livings of the poorer clergy. The Bounty never increased by parliamentary and private grants, and in 1948 its administration became the responsibility of the Church Commissioners.

Anne² /æn/ St (1st c. BC), the mother of the Virgin Mary, first mentioned by name in the apocryphal gospel of James (2nd c.). The extreme veneration of St Anne in the late Middle Ages was attacked by Luther and other reformers. Her feast day (26 July) is observed with special devotion in Brittany (of which she is the patron saint) and Canada.

anneal /əˈniːl/ v. & n. —v.tr. **1** heat (metal or glass) and allow it to cool slowly, esp. to toughen it. **2** toughen. —n. treatment by annealing. □□ **annealer** n. [OE onǣlan f. on + ǣlan burn, bake f. āl fire]

Anne Boleyn /ˈbʊlɪn/ see BOLEYN.

annectent /əˈnekt(ə)nt/ adj. Biol. connecting (annectent link). [L annectere annectent- bind (as ANNEX)]

annelid /ˈænəlɪd/ n. any segmented worm of the phylum Annelida, e.g. earthworms, lugworms, etc. [F *annélide* or mod.L *annelida* (pl.) f. F *annelés* ringed animals f. OF *anel* ring f. L *anellus* dimin. of *anulus* ring]

annelidan /əˈnelɪd(ə)n/ adj. & n. —adj. of the annelids. —n. an annelid.

Anne of Cleves /kliːvz/ (1515–57) fourth wife of Henry VIII, whose marriage to her (1540) was the product of his minister Thomas Cromwell's attempt to forge a dynastic alliance with one of the Protestant German States. Henry, initially deceived by a flattering portrait of Anne painted by Holbein, took an instant dislike to his new wife and dissolved the marriage after six months. Cromwell paid for his blunder with his head.

annex /æˈneks, əˈn-/ v.tr. **1 a** add as a subordinate part. **b** (often foll. by *to*) append to a book etc. **2** incorporate (territory of another) into one's own. **3** add as a condition or consequence. **4** colloq. take without right. □□ **annexation** /-ˈseɪʃ(ə)n/ n. [ME f. OF *annexer* f. L *annectere* (as AN-², *nectere nex-* bind)]

annexe /ˈæneks/ n. (also **annex**) **1** a separate or added building, esp. for extra accommodation. **2** an addition to a document. [F *annexe* f. L *annexum* past part. of *annectere* bind: see ANNEX]

Annigoni /ˌæniˈɡəʊni/, Pietro (1910–), Italian artist, noted for his portraits of Queen Elizabeth II, President Kennedy, and others, painted in old-master style.

annihilate /əˈnaɪəˌleɪt, əˈnaɪɪl-/ v.tr. **1** completely destroy. **2** defeat utterly; make insignificant or powerless. □□ **annihilator** n. [LL *annihilare* (as AN-², *nihil* nothing)]

annihilation /əˌnaɪəˈleɪʃ(ə)n, əˌnaɪɪl-/ n. **1** the act or process of annihilating. **2** *Physics* the conversion of a particle and an antiparticle into radiation. [F *annihilation* or LL *annihilatio* (as ANNIHILATE)]

anniversary /ˌæniˈvɜːsəri/ n. (pl. **-ies**) **1** the date on which an event took place in a previous year. **2** the celebration of this. [ME f. L *anniversarius* f. *annus* year + *versus* turned]

Annobón /ˈænəˌbɒn/ (called *Pagalu* 1973–9) an island of Equatorial Guinea, in the Gulf of Guinea; pop. (1983) 2,000.

Anno Domini /ˌænəʊ ˈdɒmɪˌnaɪ/ adv. & n. —adv. in the year of our Lord, in the year of the Christian era. —n. colloq. advancing age (*suffering from Anno Domini*). [L, = in the year of the Lord]

annotate /ˈænəʊˌteɪt, ˈænəˌteɪt/ v.tr. add explanatory notes to (a book, document, etc.). □□ **annotatable** adj. **annotation** /-ˈteɪʃ(ə)n/ n. **annotative** adj. **annotator** n. [L *annotare* (as AD-, *nota* mark)]

announce /əˈnaʊns/ v.tr. **1** (often foll. by *that*) make publicly known. **2** make known the arrival or imminence of (a guest, dinner, etc.). **3** make known (without words) to the senses or the mind; be a sign of. □□ **announcement** n. [ME f. OF *annoncer* f. L *annuntiare* (as AD-, *nuntius* messenger)]

announcer /əˈnaʊnsə(r)/ n. a person who announces, esp. introducing programmes in broadcasting.

annoy /əˈnɔɪ/ v.tr. **1** cause slight anger or mental distress to. **2** (in *passive*) be somewhat angry (*am annoyed with you*; *was annoyed at my remarks*). **3** molest; harass repeatedly. □□ **annoyance** n. **annoyer** n. [ME f. OF *anuier*, *anui* etc., ult. f. L *in odio* hateful]

annual /ˈænjʊəl/ adj. & n. —adj. **1** reckoned by the year. **2** occurring every year. **3** living or lasting for one year. —n. **1** a book etc. published once a year; a yearbook. **2** a plant that lives only for a year or less. □ **annual general meeting** a yearly meeting of members or shareholders, esp. for holding elections and reporting on the year's events. **annual ring** a ring in the cross-section of a plant, esp. a tree, produced by one year's growth. □□ **annually** adv. [ME f. OF *annuel* f. LL *annualis* f. L *annalis* f. *annus* year]

annualized /ˈænjʊəˌlaɪzd/ adj. (of rates of interest, inflation, etc.) calculated on an annual basis, as a projection from figures obtained for a shorter period.

annuitant /əˈnjuːɪt(ə)nt/ n. a person who holds or receives an annuity. [ANNUITY + -ANT, by assim. to *accountant* etc.]

annuity /əˈnjuːɪti/ n. (pl. **-ies**) **1** a yearly grant or allowance.

2 an investment of money entitling the investor to a series of equal annual sums. **3** a sum payable in respect of a particular year. [ME f. F *annuité* f. med.L *annuitas -tatis* f. L *annuus* yearly (as ANNUAL)]

annul /əˈnʌl/ v.tr. (**annulled, annulling**) **1** declare (a marriage etc.) invalid. **2** cancel, abolish. □□ **annulment** n. [ME f. OF *anuller* f. LL *annullare* (as AD-, *nullus* none)]

annular /ˈænjʊlə(r)/ adj. ring-shaped; forming a ring. □ **annular eclipse** an eclipse of the sun in which the moon leaves a ring of sunlight visible round it. □□ **annularly** adv. [F *annulaire* or L *annularis* f. *an(n)ulus* ring]

annulate /ˈænjʊlət/ adj. having rings; marked with or formed of rings. □□ **annulation** /-ˈleɪʃ(ə)n/ n. [L *annulatus* (as ANNULUS)]

annulet /ˈænjʊlɪt/ n. **1** *Archit.* a small fillet or band encircling a column. **2** a small ring. [L *annulus* ring + -ET¹]

annulus /ˈænjʊləs/ n. (pl. **annuli** /-laɪ/) esp. *Math.* & *Biol.* a ring. [L *an(n)ulus*]

annunciate /əˈnʌnʃɪˌeɪt/ v.tr. **1** proclaim. **2** indicate as coming or ready. [LL *annunciare* f. L *annuntiare annuntiat-* announce]

annunciation /əˌnʌnsɪˈeɪʃ(ə)n/ n. **1** (**Annunciation**) **a** the announcing of the Incarnation, made by the angel Gabriel to Mary, related in Luke 1: 26–38. **b** the festival commemorating this (Lady Day) on 25 March. **2 a** the act or process of announcing. **b** an announcement. [ME f. OF *annonciation* f. LL *annuntiatio -onis* (as ANNUNCIATE)]

annunciator /əˈnʌnsɪˌeɪtə(r)/ n. **1** a device giving an audible or visible indication of which of several electrical circuits has been activated, of the position of a train, etc. **2** an announcer. [LL *annuntiator* (as ANNUNCIATE)]

annus mirabilis /ˌænəs mɪˈrɑːbɪlɪs/ n. a remarkable or auspicious year. [mod.L, = wonderful year]

anoa /əˈnəʊə/ n. any of several small deerlike water buffalo of the genus *Bubalus*, native to Sulawesi. [name in Sulawesi]

anode /ˈænəʊd/ n. *Electr.* **1** the positive electrode in an electrolytic cell or electronic valve or tube. **2** the negative terminal of a primary cell such as a battery (opp. CATHODE). □ **anode ray** a beam of particles emitted from the anode of a high-vacuum tube. □□ **anodal** adj. **anodic** /əˈnɒdɪk/ adj. [Gk *anodos* way up f. *ana* up + *hodos* way]

anodize /ˈænəˌdaɪz/ v.tr. (also **-ise**) coat (a metal, esp. aluminium) with a protective oxide layer by electrolysis. □□ **anodizer** n. [ANODE + -IZE]

anodyne /ˈænəˌdaɪn/ adj. & n. —adj. **1** able to relieve pain. **2** mentally soothing. —n. an anodyne drug or medicine. [L *anodynus* f. Gk *anōdunos* painless (as AN-¹, *odunē* pain)]

anoesis /ˌænəʊˈiːsɪs/ n. *Psychol.* consciousness with sensation but without thought. □□ **anoetic** /-ˈetɪk/ adj. [A-¹ + Gk *noēsis* understanding]

anoint /əˈnɔɪnt/ v.tr. **1** apply oil or ointment to, esp. as a religious ceremony (e.g. at baptism, or the consecration of a priest or king, or in ministering to the sick). **2** (usu. foll. by *with*) smear, rub. □□ **anointer** n. [ME f. AF *anoint* (adj.) f. OF *enoint* past part. of *enoindre* f. L *inungere* (as IN-², *ungere unct-* smear with oil)]

anomalistic /əˌnɒməˈlɪstɪk/ adj. *Astron.* of the anomaly or angular distance of a planet from its perihelion. □ **anomalistic month** a month measured between successive perigees of the moon. **anomalistic year** a year measured between successive perihelia of the earth.

anomalous /əˈnɒmələs/ adj. having an irregular or deviant feature; abnormal. □□ **anomalously** adv. **anomalousness** n. [LL *anomalus* f. Gk *anōmalos* (as AN-¹, *homalos* even)]

anomalure /əˈnɒməˌljʊə(r)/ n. any of the squirrel-like rodents of the family Anomaluridae, having tails with rough overlapping scales on the underside. [mod.L *anomalurus* f. Gk *anōmalos* ANOMALOUS + *oura* tail]

anomaly /əˈnɒməli/ n. (pl. **-ies**) **1** an anomalous circumstance or thing; an irregularity. **2** irregularity of motion, behaviour, etc. **3** *Astron.* the angular distance of a planet or satellite from its last perihelion or perigee. [L f. Gk *anōmalia* f. *anōmalos* ANOMALOUS]

w we z zoo ʃ she ʒ decision θ thin ð this ŋ ring x loch tʃ chip dʒ jar (*see over for vowels*)

anomy /ˈænəmɪ/ n. (also **anomie**) lack of the usual social or ethical standards in an individual or group. □□ **anomic** /əˈnɒmɪk/ adj. [Gk anomia f. anomos lawless: -ie f. F]

anon /əˈnɒn/ adv. archaic or literary soon, shortly (will say more of this anon). [OE on ān into one, on āne in one]

anon. /əˈnɒn/ abbr. anonymous; an anonymous author.

anonym /ˈænənɪm/ n. **1** an anonymous person or publication. **2** a pseudonym. [F anonyme f. Gk anōnumos: see ANONYMOUS]

anonymous /əˈnɒnɪməs/ adj. **1** of unknown name. **2** of unknown or undeclared source or authorship. **3** without character; featureless, impersonal. □□ **anonymity** /ˌænəˈnɪmɪtɪ/ n. **anonymously** adv. [LL anonymus f. Gk anōnumos nameless (as AN-¹, onoma name)]

anopheles /əˈnɒfɪˌliːz/ n. any of various mosquitoes of the genus Anopheles, many of which are carriers of the malarial parasite. [mod.L f. Gk anōphelēs unprofitable]

anorak /ˈænəˌræk/ n. a waterproof jacket of cloth or plastic, usu. with a hood, of a kind orig. used in polar regions. [Greenland Eskimo anoraq]

anorectic /ˌænəˈrektɪk/ adj. & n. (also **anorexic** /-ˈreksɪk/) —adj. involving, producing, or characterized by a lack of appetite, esp. in anorexia nervosa. —n. **1** an anorectic agent. **2** a person with anorexia. [Gk anorektos without appetite (as ANOREXIA): anorexic f. F anoréxique]

anorexia /ˌænəˈreksɪə/ n. **1** a lack or loss of appetite for food. **2** (in full **anorexia nervosa** /nɜːˈvəʊsə/) a psychological illness, esp. in young women, characterized by an obsessive desire to lose weight by refusing to eat. [LL f. Gk f. an- not + orexis appetite]

anosmia /æˈnɒzmɪə/ n. the loss of the sense of smell. □□ **anosmic** adj. [LL f. Gk f. an- not + osmē smell]

another /əˈnʌðə(r)/ adj. & pron. —adj. **1** an additional; one more (have another cake; after another six months). **2** a person like or comparable to (another Callas). **3** a different (quite another matter). **4** some or any other (will not do another man's work). — pron. **1** an additional one (have another). **2** a different one (take this book away and bring me another). **3** some or any other one (I love another). **4** Brit. an unnamed additional party to a legal action (X versus Y and another). **5** (also **A. N. Other** /ˌeɪ en ˈʌðə(r)/) a player unnamed or not yet selected. □ **another place** Brit. the other House of Parliament (used in the Commons to refer to the Lords, and vice versa). **such another** another of the same sort. [ME f. AN + OTHER]

Anouilh /ˈænuːˌiː/, Jean (1910–87), French dramatist, who first achieved success with Le Voyageur sans bagage (Traveller without Luggage, 1937), and has since been one of the most popular playwrights in France. Among his works are the romantic comedy L'Invitation au château (Ring Round the Moon, 1947), La Valse des toréadors (The Waltz of the Toreadors, 1952), L'Alouette (The Lark, 1953, on Joan of Arc), Becket (1959), and Antigone (1944), a concealed drama of the Resistance which played in Nazi-occupied Paris.

anovulant /æˈnɒvjʊlənt/ n. & adj. Pharm. —n. a drug preventing ovulation. —adj. preventing ovulation. [AN-¹ + ovulation (see OVULATE) + -ANT]

anoxia /əˈnɒksɪə/ n. Med. an absence or deficiency of oxygen reaching the tissues; severe hypoxia. □□ **anoxic** adj. [mod.L, formed as AN-¹ + OXYGEN + -IA¹]

anschluss /ˈænʃlʊs/ n. a unification, esp. the annexation of Austria by Germany in 1938. Any form of union of Austria with Germany was explicitly prohibited by the peace treaties signed after the First World War, though the majority of the German-speaking people of Austria would have welcomed it. Union came in 1938 when Hitler (himself an Austrian) forced the resignation of the Austrian Chancellor and his replacement by a pro-Nazi who invited German troops to enter the country on the pretext of restoring law and order. Anschluss was proclaimed, and later ratified by a plebiscite. The ban on such a union was reiterated when the Allied Powers recognized the second Austrian republic in 1946. [G f. anschliessen join]

Anselm /ˈænselm/, St (c.1033–1109), Italian-born philosopher and theologian, who became Archbishop of Canterbury in 1093. His uncompromising insistence on the spiritual independence of his office twice led to his being exiled, after conflicts with William II and Henry I. Of his theological writings the most famous is the study on the Atonement (Cur Deus Homo?). Like later Schoolmen (and unlike most of his predecessors) he preferred to defend the faith by intellectual reasoning rather than by basing arguments on scriptural and other written authorities. Feast day, 21 April.

anserine /ˈænsəˌraɪn/ adj. **1** of or like a goose. **2** silly. [L anserinus f. anser goose]

answer /ˈɑːnsə(r)/ n. & v. —n. **1** something said or done to deal with or in reaction to a question, statement, or circumstance. **2** the solution to a problem. —v. **1** tr. make an answer to (answer me; answer my question). **2** intr. (often foll. by to) make an answer. **3** tr. respond to the summons or signal of (answer the door; answer the telephone). **4** tr. be satisfactory for (a purpose or need). **5** intr. (foll. by for, to) be responsible (you will answer to me for your conduct). **6** intr. (foll. by to) correspond, esp. to a description. **7** intr. be satisfactory or successful. □ **answer back** answer a rebuke etc. impudently. **answering machine** a tape recorder which supplies a recorded answer to a telephone call. **answering service** a business that receives and answers telephone calls for its clients. **answer to the name of** be called. [OE andswaru, andswarian f. Gmc, = swear against (charge)]

answerable /ˈɑːnsərəb(ə)l/ adj. **1** (usu. foll. by to, for) responsible (answerable to them for any accident). **2** that can be answered.

answerphone /ˈɑːnsəˌfəʊn/ n. a telephone answering machine.

ant /ænt/ n. any small insect of a widely distributed hymenopterous family, living in complex social colonies, wingless (except for males in the mating season), and proverbial for industry. □ **ant-bear** = AARDVARK. **ant** (or **ant's**) **eggs** pupae of ants. **ant-lion** any of various dragonfly-like insects. **white ant** = TERMITE. [OE æmet(t)e, ēmete (see EMMET) f. WG]

ant- /ænt/ assim. form of ANTI- before a vowel or h (Antarctic).

-ant /ənt/ suffix **1** forming adjectives denoting attribution of an action (pendant; repentant) or state (arrogant; expectant). **2** forming nouns denoting an agent (assistant; celebrant; deodorant). [F -ant or L -ant-, -ent-, pres. part. stem of verbs: cf. -ENT]

antacid /æntˈæsɪd/ n. & adj. —n. a substance that prevents or corrects acidity esp. in the stomach. —adj. having these properties.

Antaeus /ænˈtiːəs/ Gk Mythol. a giant, son of Poseidon and Earth, living in Libya. He compelled all comers to wrestle with him and overcame and killed them until he was defeated by Hercules. That he was stronger when thrown, by contact with his mother the Earth, seems a later addition to the story.

antagonism /ænˈtægəˌnɪz(ə)m/ n. active opposition or hostility. [F antagonisme (as ANTAGONIST)]

antagonist /ænˈtægənɪst/ n. **1** an opponent or adversary. **2** Biol. a substance or organ that partially or completely opposes the action of another. □□ **antagonistic** /-ˈnɪstɪk/ adj. **antagonistically** /-ˈnɪstɪkəlɪ/ adv. [F antagoniste or LL antagonista f. Gk antagōnistēs (as ANTAGONIZE)]

antagonize /ænˈtægəˌnaɪz/ v.tr. (also **-ise**) **1** evoke hostility or opposition or enmity in. **2** (of one force etc.) counteract or tend to neutralize (another). □□ **antagonization** /-ˈzeɪʃ(ə)n/ n. [Gk antagōnizomai (as ANTI-, agōnizomai f. agōn contest)]

antalkali /æntˈælkəlaɪ/ n. (pl. **antalkalis**) any substance that counteracts an alkali.

Antalya /ænˈtæljə/ the chief seaport of the eastern Mediterranean coast of southern Turkey; pop. (1985) 258,100.

Antananarivo /ˌæntəˌnænəˈriːvəʊ/ the capital of Madagascar; pop. (1986) 703,000.

Antarctic /æntˈɑːktɪk/ adj. & n. —adj. of the south polar regions. —n. this region. □ **Antarctic Circle** the parallel of latitude 66° 32′ S., forming an imaginary line round this region. **Antarctic Ocean** the Southern Ocean. [ME f. OF antartique or L antarcticus f. Gk antarktikos (as ANTI-, arktikos ARCTIC)]

Antarctica /ænt'ɑːktɪkə/ a continent round the South Pole, situated mainly within the Antarctic Circle and almost entirely covered by ice-sheet. Only a few patches of moss and lichen grow—too few to support land animals, but there is abundant life in the sea, including whales, seals, and penguins. Exploration at first concentrated on reaching the South Pole. Scott pioneered the way in 1902, followed by Shackleton in 1908; in 1911 Amundsen was the first to reach the Pole, and Scott reached it a month later. The American aviator Richard Byrd flew over the South Pole in 1929. Although there is no permanent human habitation Norway, Australia, France, New Zealand, and the UK claim sectors of the continent (Argentina and Chile claim parts of the British sector); its exploitation is governed by international treaty of 1959.

ante /'æntɪ/ n. & v. —n. 1 a stake put up by a player in poker etc. before receiving cards. 2 an amount to be paid in advance. —v.tr. (**antes**, **anted**) 1 put up as an ante. 2 US **a** bet, stake. **b** (foll. by *up*) pay. [L, = before]

ante- /'æntɪ/ prefix forming nouns and adjectives meaning 'before, preceding' (*ante-room*; *antenatal*; *ante-post*). [L *ante* (prep. & adv.), = before]

anteater /'æntiːtə(r)/ n. any of various mammals feeding on ants and termites, e.g. a tamandua.

ante-bellum /ˌæntɪˈbeləm/ adj. occurring or existing before a particular war, esp. the US Civil War. [L f. *ante* before + *bellum* war]

antecedent /ˌæntɪˈsiːd(ə)nt/ n. & adj. —n. 1 a preceding thing or circumstance. 2 *Gram.* a word, phrase, clause, or sentence, to which another word (esp. a relative pronoun, usu. following) refers. 3 (in *pl.*) past history, esp. of a person. 4 *Logic* the statement contained in the 'if' clause of a conditional proposition. —adj. 1 (often foll. by *to*) previous. 2 presumptive, a priori. □□ **antecedence** n. **antecedently** adv. [ME f. F *antecedent* or L *antecedere* (as ANTE-, *cedere* go)]

antechamber /'æntɪˌtʃeɪmbə(r)/ n. a small room leading to a main one. [earlier *anti-*, f. F *antichambre* f. It. *anticamera* (as ANTE-, CHAMBER)]

antechapel /'æntɪˌtʃæp(ə)l/ n. the outer part at the west end of a college chapel.

antedate v. & n. —v.tr. /ˌæntɪˈdeɪt/ 1 exist or occur at a date earlier than. 2 assign an earlier date to (a document, event, etc.), esp. one earlier than its actual date. —n. /'æntɪˌdeɪt/ a date earlier than the actual one.

antediluvian /ˌæntɪdɪˈluːvɪən, -ˈljuːvɪən/ adj. 1 of or belonging to the time before the Biblical Flood. 2 *colloq.* very old or out of date. [ANTE- + L *diluvium* DELUGE + -AN]

antelope /'æntɪˌləʊp/ n. (pl. same or **antelopes**) 1 any of various deerlike ruminants of the family Bovidae, esp. abundant in Africa and typically tall, slender, graceful, and swift-moving with smooth hair and upward-pointing horns, e.g. gazelles, gnus, kudus, and impala. 2 leather made from the skin of any of these. [ME f. OF *antelop* or f. med.L *ant(h)alopus* f. late Gk *antholops*, of unkn. orig.]

antenatal /ˌæntɪˈneɪt(ə)l/ adj. 1 existing or occurring before birth. 2 relating to the period of pregnancy.

antenna /æn'tenə/ n. (pl. **antennae** /-niː/) 1 *Zool.* one of a pair of mobile appendages on the heads of insects, crustaceans, etc., sensitive to touch and taste; a feeler. 2 (pl. **antennas**) = AERIAL n. □□ **antennal** adj. (in sense 1). **antennary** adj. (in sense 1). [L, = sail-yard]

antenuptial /ˌæntɪˈnʌpʃ(ə)l/ adj. existing or occurring before marriage. □ **antenuptial contract** *S.Afr.* a contract between two persons intending to marry each other, setting out the terms and conditions of their marriage. [LL *antenuptialis* (as ANTE-, NUPTIAL)]

antependium /ˌæntɪˈpendɪəm/ n. (pl. **antependia** /-dɪə/) a veil or hanging for the front of an altar. [med.L (as ANTE-, *pendēre* hang)]

antepenult /ˌæntɪpɪˈnʌlt/ n. the last syllable but two in a word. [abbr. of LL *antepaenultimus* (as ANTE-, *paenultimus* PENULT)]

antepenultimate /ˌæntɪpɪˈnʌltɪmət/ adj. & n. —adj. last but two. —n. anything that is last but two.

ante-post /ˌæntɪˈpəʊst/ adj. *Brit.* (of betting) done at odds determined at the time of betting, in advance of the event concerned. [ANTE- + POST[1]]

anterior /æn'tɪərɪə(r)/ adj. 1 nearer the front. 2 (often foll. by *to*) earlier, prior. □□ **anteriority** /-rɪˈɒrɪtɪ/ n. **anteriorly** adv. [F *antérieur* or L *anterior* f. *ante* before]

ante-room /'æntɪˌruːm, -ˌrʊm/ n. 1 a small room leading to a main one. 2 *Mil.* a sitting-room in an officers' mess.

antheap /'ænθiːp/ n. = ANTHILL.

anthelion /æn'θiːlɪən/ n. (pl. **anthelia** /-lɪə/) a luminous halo projected on a cloud or fog-bank opposite to the sun. [Gk, neut. of *anthēlios* opposite to the sun (as ANTI-, *hēlios* sun)]

anthelmintic /ˌænθelˈmɪntɪk/ (also **anthelminthic** /-θɪk/) n. & adj. —n. any drug or agent used to destroy parasitic, esp. intestinal, worms, e.g. tapeworms, roundworms, and flukes. —adj. having the power to eliminate or destroy parasitic worms. [ANTI- + Gk *helmins helminthos* worm]

anthem /'ænθəm/ n. 1 an elaborate choral composition usu. based on a passage of scripture for (esp. Anglican) church use. 2 a solemn hymn of praise etc., esp. = *national anthem*. 3 a composition sung antiphonally. [OE *antefn*, *antifne* f. LL *antiphona* ANTIPHON]

anthemion /æn'θiːmɪən/ n. (pl. **anthemia** /-mɪə/) a flower-like ornament used in art. [Gk, = flower]

Anthemius /æn'θiːmɪəs/ of Tralles (6th c.), Greek mathematician, engineer, and artist chosen by Justinian in 532 to design Santa Sophia in Constantinople. His experiments included study of the effects of compressed steam, and he had an extensive reputation in the classical world for both these and artistic pursuits.

anther /'ænθə(r)/ n. *Bot.* the apical portion of a stamen containing pollen. □□ **antheral** adj. [F *anthère* or mod.L *anthera*, in L 'medicine extracted from flowers' f. Gk *anthēra* flowery, fem. adj. f. *anthos* flower]

antheridium /ˌænθəˈrɪdɪəm/ n. (pl. **antheridia** /-dɪə/) *Bot.* the male sex organ of algae, mosses, ferns, etc. [mod.L f. *anthera* (as ANTHER) + Gk *-idion* dimin. suffix]

anthill /'ænthɪl/ n. 1 a mound-like nest built by ants or termites. 2 a community teeming with people.

anthologize /æn'θɒləˌdʒaɪz/ v.tr. & intr. (also **-ise**) compile or include in an anthology.

anthology /æn'θɒlədʒɪ/ n. (pl. **-ies**) a published collection of passages from literature (esp. poems), songs, reproductions of paintings, etc. □□ **anthologist** n. [F *anthologie* or med.L f. Gk *anthologia* f. *anthos* flower + *-logia* collection f. *legō* gather]

Anthony[1] /'æntənɪ/, St (of Egypt; *c.*251–356), the founder of monasticism, a hermit who gave away his possessions and retired into the desert. The holiness and ordered discipline of his life attracted disciples, whom he organized into a community of hermits who lived under rule (this was an innovation). He used his influence in association with Athanasius against the Arians. In medieval times he was venerated as a healer. His emblems (pigs and bells) derive from the Hospitallers of St Antony (founded *c.*1100), who rang bells for alms and whose pigs were allowed to roam in the streets.

Anthony[2] /'æntənɪ/, St (of Padua; 1195–1231), Franciscan friar who converted many by his charismatic preaching. He is invoked as the finder of lost objects, possibly because of the story that a frightful apparition forced a novice to return a psalter borrowed without Anthony's permission. His devotion to the poor is commemorated by the alms known as St Anthony's bread.

anthozoan /ˌænθəˈzəʊən/ n. & adj. —n. any of the sessile marine coelenterates of the class Anthozoa, including sea anemones and corals. —adj. of or relating to this class. [mod.L *Anthozoa* f. Gk *anthos* flower + *zōia* animals]

anthracene /'ænθrəˌsiːn/ n. a colourless crystalline aromatic hydrocarbon obtained by the distillation of crude oils and used in the manufacture of chemicals. [Gk *anthrax -akos* coal + -ENE]

anthracite /'ænθrəˌsaɪt/ n. coal of a hard variety burning with little flame and smoke. □□ **anthracitic** /-'sɪtɪk/ adj. [Gk anthrakitis a kind of coal (as ANTHRACENE)]

anthrax /'ænθræks/ n. a disease of sheep and cattle transmissible to humans. [LL f. Gk, = carbuncle]

anthropo- /'ænθrəpəʊ/ comb. form human, mankind. [Gk anthrōpos human being]

anthropocentric /ˌænθrəpəʊ'sentrɪk/ adj. regarding mankind as the centre of existence. □□ **anthropocentrically** adv. **anthropocentrism** n.

anthropogenesis /ˌænθrəpəʊ'dʒenɪsɪs/ n. = ANTHROPOGENY.

anthropogeny /ˌænθrə'pɒdʒɪnɪ/ n. the study of the origin of man. □□ **anthropogenic** /ˌænθrəpəʊ'dʒenɪk/ adj.

anthropoid /'ænθrəˌpɔɪd/ adj. & n. —adj. **1** resembling a human being in form. **2** colloq. (of a person) apelike. —n. a being that is human in form only, esp. an anthropoid ape. [Gk anthrōpoeidēs (as ANTHROPO-, -OID)]

anthropology /ˌænθrə'pɒlədʒɪ/ n. **1** (also **social anthropology**) the study of mankind, esp. of its societies and customs. **2** (also **physical** or **biological anthropology**) the study of the structure and evolution of man as an animal. □□ **anthropological** /-pə'lɒdʒɪk(ə)l/ adj. **anthropologist** n.

Interest in the activities of other cultures is as old as written records, and anthropology traces its antecedents to the Greek travellers Xenophanes (6th c. BC) and Herodotus. Travellers' reports (e.g. those of Marco Polo) continued to be a popular form of proto-anthropology in the Middle Ages and Renaissance. The philosophical debates on the nature of man during the Enlightenment stimulated further interest in other cultures, but it was not until the advances of Saint-Simon and Comte that the foundation for a 'science of man' was laid. Modern academic anthropology traces its origin to the evolutionary theories of Darwin, which stimulated European interest in the 'primitive' peoples of the world who were seen to provide a living laboratory to test theories of cultural evolution and diffusion. The second half of the 19th c. saw an expansion of scholarly attention in and the quest for reliable information about the isolated and technologically less-developed peoples of the world. Initially ambitious comparative studies were undertaken on diverse topics including kinship systems, law, magic and religion, and culture, by a generation of library-bound scholars. At the turn of the present century advances by Durkheim saw a retreat from these evolutionary beginnings and a shift to the study of the ways in which societies maintain themselves. The functionalist revolution occasioned by Malinowski and Radcliffe-Brown in Britain and Boas in the US saw an increasing emphasis on ethnographic fieldwork studies utilizing the technique of participant-observation that has since become the single most important feature distinguishing anthropology from its sister discipline sociology, and recently structuralism has become an important theoretical mode.

anthropometry /ˌænθrə'pɒmɪtrɪ/ n. the scientific study of the measurements of the human body. □□ **anthropometric** /-pə'metrɪk/ adj.

anthropomorphic /ˌænθrəpə'mɔːfɪk/ adj. of or characterized by anthropomorphism. □□ **anthropomorphically** adv. [as ANTHROPOMORPHOUS + -IC]

anthropomorphism /ˌænθrəpə'mɔːfɪz(ə)m/ n. the attribution of a human form or personality to a god, animal, or thing. □□ **anthropomorphize** v.tr.

anthropomorphous /ˌænθrəpə'mɔːfəs/ adj. human in form. [Gk anthrōpomorphos (as ANTHROPO-, morphē form)]

anthroponymy /ˌænθrə'pɒnɪmɪ/ n. the study of personal names. [ANTHROPO- + Gk ŏnumia f. onoma name: cf. TOPONYMY]

anthropophagy /ˌænθrə'pɒfədʒɪ/ n. cannibalism. □□ **anthropophagous** adj. [Gk anthrōpophagia (as ANTHROPO-, phagŏ eat)]

anti /'æntɪ/ prep. & n. —prep. (also absol.) opposed to (is anti everything; seems to be rather anti). —n. (pl. **antis**) a person opposed to a particular policy etc. [ANTI-]

anti- /'æntɪ/ prefix (also **ant-** before a vowel or h) forming nouns and adjectives meaning: **1** opposed to; against (antivivisectionism). **2** preventing (antiscorbutic). **3** the opposite of

(anticlimax). **4** rival (antipope). **5** unlike the conventional form (anti-hero; anti-novel). **6** Physics the antiparticle of a specified particle (antineutrino; antiproton). [from or after Gk anti- against]

anti-aircraft /ˌæntɪ'eəkrɑːft/ adj. (of a gun, missile, etc.) used to attack enemy aircraft.

antiar /'æntɪˌɑː(r)/ n. = UPAS 1a, 2. [Jav. antjar]

Antibes /ɑ̃'tiːb/ a fishing-port and resort on the French Riviera; pop. (1982) 63,250.

antibiosis /ˌæntɪbaɪ'əʊsɪs/ n. an antagonistic association between two organisms (esp. micro-organisms), in which one is adversely affected (cf. SYMBIOSIS). [mod.L f. F antibiose (as ANTI-, SYMBIOSIS)]

antibiotic /ˌæntɪbaɪ'ɒtɪk/ n. & adj. Pharm. —n. any of various substances produced by micro-organisms or made synthetically, that can inhibit or destroy susceptible micro-organisms. The first antibiotic to be produced for therapeutic use was penicillin (see entry). —adj. functioning as an antibiotic. [F antibiotique (as ANTI-, Gk biōtikos fit for life f. bios life)]

antibody /'æntɪˌbɒdɪ/ n. (pl. **-ies**) any of various blood proteins produced in response to and then counteracting antigens. The capacity to develop immunity to infectious disease is essential for the survival of any animal. In vertebrates this is achieved by the formation of proteins which appear in the blood a few days after infection and which can combine specifically with the foreign substance. These proteins are known as antibodies and they are remarkably specific: immunity to diphtheria, for example, gives no protection against tetanus. All antibodies have the same basic structure of four polypeptide chains, small sections of which vary to determine their specific combining power. Combination with antibodies leads to the destruction of bacteria, viruses, or foreign substances and their elimination from the body. [transl. of G Antikörper (as ANTI-, Körper body)]

antic /'æntɪk/ n. & adj. —n. **1** (usu. in pl.) absurd or foolish behaviour. **2** an absurd or silly action. —adj. archaic grotesque, bizarre. [It. antico ANTIQUE, used as = grotesque]

anticathode /ˌæntɪ'kæθəʊd/ n. the target (or anode) of an X-ray tube on which the electrons from the cathode impinge and from which X-rays are emitted.

Antichrist /'æntɪˌkraɪst/ n. **1** an arch-enemy of Christ. **2** a postulated personal opponent of Christ expected by the early Church to appear before the end of the world. [ME f. OF antecrist f. eccl.L antichristus f. Gk antikhristos (as ANTI-, Khristos CHRIST)]

antichristian /ˌæntɪ'krɪstjən, -tɪən/ adj. **1** opposed to Christianity. **2** concerning the Antichrist.

anticipate /æn'tɪsɪˌpeɪt/ v.tr. **1** deal with or use before the proper time. **2** disp. expect, foresee; regard as probable (did not anticipate any difficulty). **3** forestall (a person or thing). **4** look forward to. □□ **anticipative** adj. **anticipator** n. **anticipatory** adj. [L anticipare f. anti- for ANTE- + -cipare f. capere take]

anticipation /ænˌtɪsɪ'peɪʃ(ə)n/ n. **1** the act or process of anticipating. **2** Mus. the introduction beforehand of part of a chord which is about to follow. [F anticipation or L anticipatio (as ANTICIPATE)]

anticlerical /ˌæntɪ'klerɪk(ə)l/ adj. & n. —adj. opposed to the influence of the clergy, esp. in politics. —n. an anticlerical person. □□ **anticlericalism** n.

anticlimax /ˌæntɪ'klaɪmæks/ n. a trivial conclusion to something significant or impressive, esp. where a climax was expected. □□ **anticlimactic** /-'mæktɪk/ adj. **anticlimactically** /-'mæktɪkəlɪ/ adv.

anticline /'æntɪˌklaɪn/ n. Geol. a ridge or fold of stratified rock in which the strata slope down from the crest (opp. SYNCLINE). □□ **anticlinal** /-'klaɪn(ə)l/ adj. [ANTI- + Gk klinō lean, after INCLINE]

anticlockwise /ˌæntɪ'klɒkwaɪz/ adv. & adj. —adv. in a curve opposite in direction to the movement of the hands of a clock. —adj. moving anticlockwise.

anticoagulant /ˌæntɪkəʊ'æɡjʊlənt/ n. & adj. —n. any drug or agent that retards or inhibits coagulation, esp. of the blood. —adj. retarding or inhibiting coagulation.

anticodon /ˌæntɪˈkəʊdɒn/ n. Biochem. a sequence of three nucleotides forming a unit of genetic code in a transfer RNA molecule that corresponds to a complementary codon in messenger RNA.

anticonvulsant /ˌæntɪkənˈvʌls(ə)nt/ n. & adj. —n. any drug or agent that prevents or reduces the severity of convulsions, esp. epileptic fits. —adj. preventing or reducing convulsions.

anticyclone /ˌæntɪˈsaɪkləʊn/ n. a system of winds rotating outwards from an area of high barometric pressure, producing fine weather. □□ **anticyclonic** /-ˈklɒnɪk/ adj.

antidepressant /ˌæntɪdɪˈpres(ə)nt/ n. & adj. —n. any drug or agent that alleviates depression. —adj. alleviating depression.

antidiuretic hormone /ˌæntɪˌdaɪjʊˈretɪk/ n. = VASOPRESSIN. [ANTI- + DIURETIC]

antidote /ˈæntɪˌdəʊt/ n. **1** a medicine etc. taken or given to counteract poison. **2** anything that counteracts something unpleasant or evil. □□ **antidotal** adj. [F antidote or L antidotum f. Gk antidoton neut. of antidotos given against (as ANTI- + stem of didonai give)]

antifreeze /ˈæntɪˌfriːz/ n. a substance (usu. ethylene glycol) added to water to lower its freezing-point, esp. in the radiator of a motor vehicle.

anti-g /ˌæntɪˈdʒiː/ adj. (of clothing for an astronaut etc.) designed to counteract the effects of high acceleration. [ANTI- + g symb. for acceleration due to gravity]

antigen /ˈæntɪdʒ(ə)n/ n. a foreign substance (e.g. toxin) which causes the body to produce antibodies. □□ **antigenic** /-ˈdʒenɪk/ adj. [G (as ANTIBODY, -GEN)]

Antigone /ænˈtɪɡəni/ Gk legend daughter of Oedipus and Jocasta. When the strife between her brothers Eteocles and Polynices resulted in the latter's death she buried his body by night, against the order of King Creon, and was ordered by him to be buried alive. She took her own life before the sentence was carried out, and Creon's son Haemon, who was betrothed to her, killed himself over her body.

anti-gravity /ˌæntɪˈɡrævɪti/ n. Physics a hypothetical force opposing gravity.

Antigua /ænˈtiːɡwə/ (also **Antigua Guatemala**) a Spanish colonial city in the Central Highlands of Guatemala. Founded in 1543, it was the capital of Guatemala until destroyed by an earthquake in 1773; pop. (1985) 27,000.

Antigua and Barbuda /ænˈtiːɡə, bɑːˈbuːdə/ a country comprising part of the Leeward Islands in the West Indies; pop. (1988) 70,925; official language, English; capital, St John's (on Antigua). Discovered in 1493 by Columbus and settled by the English in 1632, Antigua became a British colony with Barbuda as its dependency; the islands gained full independence as a member State of the Commonwealth in 1981. The economy, once dependent on sugar, is now much more diversified and contains a large element of tourism. □□ **Antiguan** adj. & n. **Barbudan** adj. & n.

anti-hero /ˈæntɪˌhɪərəʊ/ n. (pl. -oes) a central character in a story or drama who noticeably lacks conventional heroic attributes.

antihistamine /ˌæntɪˈhɪstəmɪn, -ˌmiːn/ n. a substance that counteracts the effects of histamine, used esp. in the treatment of allergies.

antiknock /ˈæntɪˌnɒk/ n. a substance added to motor fuel to prevent premature combustion.

Anti-Lebanon /ˌæntɪˈlebənən/ a range of mountains running north to south between Syria and Lebanon, east of the Lebanon range.

Antilles /ænˈtɪliːz/ a group of islands forming the greater part of the West Indies. The **Greater Antilles**, extending roughly east to west, comprise Cuba, Jamaica, Hispaniola (Haiti and the Dominican Republic), and Puerto Rico; the **Lesser Antilles**, to the south-east, include the Virgin Islands, Leeward Islands, Windward Islands, and various small islands to the north of Venezuela. **Netherlands Antilles** see separate entry.

antilog /ˈæntɪˌlɒɡ/ n. colloq. = ANTILOGARITHM. [abbr.]

antilogarithm /ˌæntɪˈlɒɡəˌrɪð(ə)m/ n. the number to which a logarithm belongs (100 is the common antilogarithm of 2).

antilogy /ænˈtɪlədʒɪ/ n. (pl. **-ies**) a contradiction in terms. [F antilogie f. Gk antilogia (as ANTI-, -LOGY)]

antimacassar /ˌæntɪməˈkæsə(r)/ n. a covering put over furniture, esp. over the back of a chair, as a protection from grease in the hair or as an ornament. [ANTI- + MACASSAR]

antimatter /ˈæntɪˌmætə(r)/ n. Physics matter composed solely of antiparticles (see entry).

antimetabolite /ˌæntɪmɪˈtæbəˌlaɪt/ n. Pharm. a drug that interferes with the normal metabolic processes within cells, usu. by combining with enzymes.

antimony /ˈæntɪmənɪ/ n. Chem. a semi-metallic element existing as a brittle silvery-white metal and in several non-metallic forms. The naturally-occurring sulphide was used as a cosmetic in ancient times, and was employed in alchemy. Antimony is widely used in alloys, especially with lead, where it increases hardness, and it was a component of the metal used for making printing-type where molten metal was used. ¶ Symb.: **Sb**; atomic number 51. □□ **antimonial** /-ˈməʊnɪəl/ adj. **antimonic** /-ˈməʊnɪk/ adj. **antimonious** /-ˈməʊnɪəs/ adj. [ME f. med.L antimonium (11th c.), of unkn. orig.]

antinode /ˈæntɪˌnəʊd/ n. Physics the position of maximum displacement in a standing wave system.

antinomian /ˌæntɪˈnəʊmɪən/ adj. & n. —adj. of or relating to the view that Christians are by grace released from the obligation of observing the moral law. It was attributed to St Paul by his opponents (Rom. 3: 8), and was held by many of the Gnostic sects, who held that as matter was so sharply opposed to spirit, bodily actions were indifferent. The teaching was revived at the Reformation as following from the Lutheran doctrine of justification by faith. —n. (**Antinomian**) hist. a person who holds this view. □□ **antinomianism** n. [med.L Antinomi, name of a sect in Germany (1535) alleged to hold this view (as ANTI-, Gk nomos law)]

antinomy /ænˈtɪnəmɪ/ n. (pl. **-ies**) **1** a contradiction between two beliefs or conclusions that are in themselves reasonable; a paradox. **2** a conflict between two laws or authorities. [L antinomia f. Gk (as ANTI-, nomos law)]

antinovel /ˈæntɪˌnɒv(ə)l/ n. a novel in which the conventions of the form are studiously avoided.

anti-nuclear /ˌæntɪˈnjuːklɪə(r)/ adj. opposed to the development of nuclear weapons or nuclear power.

Antioch /ˈæntɪˌɒk/ **1** the capital of Syria under the Seleucid kings, now Antakya (Hatay) in Turkey near the Syrian border; pop. (1985) 109,200. **2** a city in Phrygia near the Pisidian border, that became a Roman colony with the name Caesarea Antiochia.

Antiochus /ænˈtaɪəkəs/ the name of eight Seleucid kings:
Antiochus III 'the Great' (c.242–187 BC), reigned 223–187 BC, who restored and expanded the Seleucid empire. He regained the vassal kingdoms of Parthia and Bactria, and conquered Armenia, Syria, and Palestine; when he invaded Europe he came into conflict with the Romans, who defeated him by land and sea and severely limited his power.
Antiochus IV Epiphanes (c.215–163 BC), reigned 175–163 BC. His firm control of Judaea and his attempt to hellenize the Jews resulted in the revival of Jewish nationalism and the Maccabean revolt.

antioxidant /ˌæntɪˈɒksɪd(ə)nt/ n. an agent that inhibits oxidation, esp. used to reduce deterioration of products stored in air.

antiparticle /ˈæntɪˌpɑːtɪk(ə)l/ n. Physics an elementary particle having the same mass as a given particle but opposite electric or magnetic properties. Aristotle's physics was much concerned with pairs of Pythagorean contraries, such as hot and cold, wet and dry, gravity and lightness, and so forth. Physics from the 17th c. onwards tended to dispense with such dualities, replacing them by graduated properties. Hot and cold, for example, became different degrees of a single quality rather than contrary qualities. Modern elementary particle physics has vigorously reasserted the importance of opposed dualities in nature. For every elementary particle there is a corresponding 'antiparticle': the positron or anti-electron, discovered in 1932, has the same mass as the electron but possesses an equal and opposite charge; the anti-proton has the same mass as the proton, but again with an equal and opposite charge. When particle and antiparticle collide they annihilate each other, producing other particles and an enormous release of energy.

Antimatter is a hypothetical substance composed of anti-protons, anti-electrons, and anti-neutrons; it is theoretically as stable as ordinary matter. It is speculated that galaxies or even clusters of galaxies may exist which are composed entirely of antimatter.

antipasto /ˌæntɪˈpɑːstəʊ, -ˈpæstəʊ/ n. (pl. **-os** or **antipasti** /-tɪ/) an hors d'œuvre, esp. in an Italian meal. [It.]

antipathetic /ˌæntɪpəˈθetɪk/ adj. (usu. foll. by to) having a strong aversion or natural opposition. □□ **antipathetical** adj. **antipathetically** adv. [as ANTIPATHY after PATHETIC]

antipathic /ˌæntɪˈpæθɪk/ adj. of a contrary nature or character.

antipathy /ænˈtɪpəθɪ/ n. (pl. **-ies**) (often foll. by to, for, between) a strong or deep-seated aversion or dislike. [F antipathie or L antipathia f. Gk antipatheia f. antipathēs opposed in feeling (as ANTI-, pathos -eos feeling)]

anti-personnel /ˌæntɪˌpɜːsəˈnel/ adj. (of a bomb, mine, etc.) designed to kill or injure people rather than to damage buildings or equipment.

antiperspirant /ˌæntɪˈpɜːspɪrənt/ n. & adj. —n. a substance applied to the skin to prevent or reduce perspiration. —adj. that acts as an antiperspirant.

antiphlogistic /ˌæntɪfləˈdʒɪstɪk/ n. & adj. —n. any drug or agent that alleviates or reduces inflammation. —adj. alleviating or reducing inflammation.

antiphon /ˈæntɪf(ə)n/ n. 1 a hymn or psalm, the parts of which are sung or recited alternately by two groups. 2 a versicle or phrase from this. 3 a sentence sung or recited before or after a psalm or canticle. 4 a response. [eccl.L antiphona f. Gk (as ANTI-, phōnē sound)]

antiphonal /ænˈtɪfən(ə)l/ adj. & n. —adj. 1 sung or recited alternately by two groups. 2 responsive, answering. —n. a collection of antiphons. □□ **antiphonally** adv.

antiphonary /ænˈtɪfənərɪ/ n. (pl. **-ies**) a book of antiphons. [eccl.L antiphonarium (as ANTIPHON)]

antiphony /ænˈtɪfənɪ/ n. (pl. **-ies**) 1 antiphonal singing or chanting. 2 a response or echo.

antipode /ˈæntɪpəʊd/ n. (usu. foll. by of, to) the exact opposite. [see ANTIPODES]

antipodes /ænˈtɪpədiːz/ n.pl. 1 a (also **Antipodes**) a place diametrically opposite to another, esp. Australasia as the region on the opposite side of the earth to Europe. b places diametrically opposite to each other. 2 (usu. foll. by of, to) the exact opposite. □□ **antipodal** adj. **antipodean** /-ˈdiːən/ adj. & n. [F or LL f. Gk antipodes having the feet opposite (as ANTI-, pous podos foot)]

antipole /ˈæntɪpəʊl/ n. 1 the direct opposite. 2 the opposite pole.

antipope /ˈæntɪpəʊp/ n. a person set up as pope in opposition to one (held by others to be) canonically chosen. [F antipape f. med.L antipapa, assim. to POPE¹]

antiproton /ˌæntɪˈprəʊtɒn/ n. Physics the negatively charged antiparticle of a proton.

antipruritic /ˌæntɪprʊəˈrɪtɪk/ adj. & n. —adj. relieving itching. —n. an antipruritic drug or agent. [ANTI- + PRURITUS + -IC]

antipyretic /ˌæntɪpaɪˈretɪk/ adj. & n. —adj. preventing or reducing fever. —n. an antipyretic drug or agent.

antiquarian /ˌæntɪˈkweərɪən/ adj. & n. —adj. 1 of or dealing in antiques or rare books. 2 of the study of antiquities. —n. an antiquary. □□ **antiquarianism** n. [see ANTIQUARY]

antiquary /ˈæntɪkwərɪ/ n. (pl. **-ies**) a student or collector of antiques or antiquities. [L antiquarius f. antiquus ancient]

antiquated /ˈæntɪˌkweɪtɪd/ adj. old-fashioned; out of date. [eccl.L antiquare antiquat- make old]

antique /ænˈtiːk/ n., adj., & v. —n. an object of considerable age, esp. an item of furniture or the decorative arts having a high value. —adj. 1 of or existing from an early date. 2 old-fashioned, archaic. 3 of ancient times. —v.tr. (**antiques, antiqued, antiquing**) give an antique appearance to (furniture etc.) by artificial means. [F antique or L antiquus, anticus former, ancient f. ante before]

antiquity /ænˈtɪkwɪtɪ/ n. (pl. **-ies**) 1 ancient times, esp. the period before the Middle Ages. 2 great age (a city of great antiquity). 3 (usu. in pl.) physical remains or relics from ancient times, esp. buildings and works of art. 4 (in pl.) customs, events, etc., of ancient times. 5 the people of ancient times regarded collectively. [ME f. OF antiquité f. L antiquitas -tatis f. antiquus: see ANTIQUE]

antiracism /ˌæntɪˈreɪsɪz(ə)m/ n. the policy or practice of opposing racism and promoting racial tolerance. □□ **antiracist** n. & adj.

antirrhinum /ˌæntɪˈraɪnəm/ n. any plant of the genus Antirrhinum, esp. the snapdragon. [L f. Gk antirrhinon f. anti counterfeiting + rhis rhinos nose, from the resemblance of the flower to an animal's snout)]

antiscorbutic /ˌæntɪskɔːˈbjuːtɪk/ adj. & n. —adj. preventing or curing scurvy. —n. an antiscorbutic agent or drug.

anti-Semite /ˌæntɪˈsiːmaɪt, -ˈsemaɪt/ n. a person hostile to or prejudiced against Jews. □□ **anti-Semitic** /-sɪˈmɪtɪk/ adj. **anti-Semitism** /-ˈsemɪˌtɪz(ə)m/ n.

antisepsis /ˌæntɪˈsepsɪs/ n. the process of using antiseptics to eliminate undesirable micro-organisms such as bacteria, viruses, and fungi that cause disease. [mod.L (as ANTI-, SEPSIS)]

antiseptic /ˌæntɪˈseptɪk/ adj. & n. —adj. 1 counteracting sepsis esp. by preventing the growth of disease-causing micro-organisms. 2 sterile or free from contamination. 3 lacking character. —n. an antiseptic agent. In 1847 the Austrian physician Semmelweis ordered the use of a disinfectant solution by students attending women in childbirth, but without understanding why it prevented sepsis and without influencing his senior colleagues. Nearly twenty years later the antiseptic system was introduced into surgery by Lord Lister, who worked on the discoveries of Louis Pasteur. Until their time the mortality rate from surgical operations was very high because of infection of the tissues exposed at or after the operation, and septicaemia was a major hazard. Lister's introduction of antiseptics brought about a major revolution in the history of surgery. There were, however, a number of drawbacks: antiseptics strong enough to counter infection often also damaged body tissue. Hence arose the aseptic method, the keeping of wounds free from all contact with micro-organisms that may cause sepsis. □□ **antiseptically** adv.

antiserum /ˈæntɪˌsɪərəm/ n. (pl. **antisera** /-rə/) a blood serum containing antibodies against specific antigens, injected to treat or protect against specific diseases.

antisocial /ˌæntɪˈsəʊʃ(ə)l/ adj. 1 opposed or contrary to normal social instincts or practices. 2 not sociable. 3 opposed or harmful to the existing social order.

antistatic /ˌæntɪˈstætɪk/ adj. that counteracts the effects of static electricity.

antistrophe /ænˈtɪstrəfɪ/ n. the second section of an ancient Greek choral ode or of one division of it (see STROPHE). [LL f. Gk antistrophē f. antistrephō turn against]

antitetanus /ˌæntɪˈtetənəs/ adj. effective against tetanus.

antithesis /ænˈtɪθɪsɪs/ n. (pl. **antitheses** /-ˌsiːz/) 1 (foll. by of, to) the direct opposite. 2 (usu. foll. by of, between) contrast or opposition between two things. 3 a contrast of ideas expressed by parallelism of strongly contrasted words. [LL f. Gk antitithēmi set against (as ANTI-, tithēmi place)]

antithetical /ˌæntɪˈθetɪk(ə)l/ adj. (also **antithetic**) 1 contrasted, opposite. 2 connected with, containing, or using antithesis. □□ **antithetically** adv. [Gk antithetikos (as ANTITHESIS)]

antitoxin /ˌæntɪˈtɒksɪn/ n. an antibody that counteracts a toxin. □□ **antitoxic** adj.

antitrades /ˌæntɪˈtreɪdz, ˈæntɪ-/ n.pl. winds that blow in the opposite direction to (and usu. above) a trade wind.

antitrust /ˌæntɪˈtrʌst/ adj. US (of a law etc.) opposed to or controlling trusts or other monopolies (see TRUST n. 8c). Such laws were passed in the US from 1820 onwards, with the aim of making it illegal to do anything that interferes with free trade and competition.

antitype /ˈæntɪˌtaɪp/ n. **1** that which is represented by a type or symbol. **2** a person or thing of the opposite type. □□ **antitypical** /-ˈtɪpɪk(ə)l/ adj. [Gk antitupos corresponding as an impression to the die (as ANTI-, tupos stamp)]

antivenene /ˌæntɪvɪˈniːn/ n. (also **antivenin** /-ˈvenɪn/) an antiserum containing antibodies against specific poisons in the venom of esp. snakes, spiders, scorpions, etc. [ANTI- + L venenum poison + -ENE, -IN]

antiviral /ˌæntɪˈvaɪər(ə)l/ adj. effective against viruses.

antivivisectionism /ˌæntɪˌvɪvɪˈsekʃəˌnɪz(ə)m/ n. opposition to vivisection. □□ **antivivisectionist** n.

antler /ˈæntlə(r)/ n. **1** each of the branched horns of a stag or other (usu. male) deer. **2** a branch of this. □□ **antlered** adj. [ME f. AF, var. of OF antoillier, of unkn. orig.]

Antofagasta /ˌæntəʊfəˈɡæstə/ a port and the capital of the Antofagasta region on the Pacific coast of northern Chile; pop. (est. 1987) 204,600.

Antonine /ˈæntəˌnaɪn/ adj. of the Roman emperors Antoninus Pius and Marcus Aurelius Antoninus or their rule. □ **Antonines** n.pl. the Antonine emperors. [L Antoninus]

Antonine Wall a defensive fortification about 59 km (37 miles) long, built across the narrowest part of southern Scotland between the Firth of Forth and the Firth of Clyde c. AD 140, in the time of Antoninus Pius. It was intended to mark the frontier of the Roman province of Britain, and consisted of a turf wall with a broad ditch in front and a counterscarp bank on the outer edge, with 29 small forts linked by a military road. The Romans, however, were unable to consolidate their position and c.181 the wall was breached and the northern tribes forced a retreat from the Forth–Clyde frontier, eventually to that established earlier at Hadrian's Wall.

Antoninus Pius /ˌæntəˈnaɪnəs ˈpaɪəs/ (86–161), Roman emperor 137–161, the first of the Antonines (whose reigns Gibbon regarded as the summit of virtuous good government). Adopted as successor by Hadrian, he ruled in harmony with the Senate and pursued a policy of moderation and liberality. He was no great conqueror, but under his rule the frontier of Britain was temporarily advanced to the Antonine Wall.

antonomasia /ˌæntənəˈmeɪzɪə/ n. **1** the substitution of an epithet or title etc. for a proper name (e.g. the Maid of Orleans for Joan of Arc, his Grace for an archbishop). **2** the use of a proper name to express a general idea (e.g. a Scrooge for a miser). [L f. Gk f. antonomazō name instead (as ANTI-, + onoma name)]

Antony[1] /ˈæntənɪ/ var. of ANTHONY.

Antony[2] /ˈænt(ə)nɪ/, Mark (Marcus Antonius, c.83–30 BC), Roman general and triumvir, a supporter of Julius Caesar, after whose murder he was appointed one of the triumvirate of 43 BC, with Octavian and Lepidus. After the battle of Philippi he took charge of the eastern empire, where he established his association with Cleopatra. Quarrels with Octavian led finally to his defeat at the sea-battle of Actium in NW Greece in 31 BC and to his suicide the next year in Alexandria.

antonym /ˈæntənɪm/ n. a word opposite in meaning to another in the same language (e.g. bad and good) (opp. SYNONYM). □□ **antonymous** /ænˈtɒnɪməs/ adj. [F antonyme (as ANTI-, SYNONYM)]

Antrim /ˈæntrɪm/ a county of Northern Ireland; pop. (1981) 642,250; county town, Belfast.

antrum /ˈæntrəm/ n. (pl. **antra** /-trə/) Anat. a natural chamber or cavity in the body, esp. in a bone. □□ **antral** adj. [L f. Gk antron cave]

Antwerp /ˈæntwɜːp/ (French **Anvers** /ɑ̃ˈvɛə(r)/, Flemish **Antwerpen** /ˈɑːntveərpən/) a city and sea-port of Belgium; pop. (1988) 476,000.

Anubis /əˈnjuːbɪs/ Egyptian Mythol. the god of mummification, protector of tombs, represented with a dog's head, or as a dog

lying with head erect, or sometimes (in the Roman period) as a soldier in armour.

Anuradhapura /əˌnʊərədəˈpʊərə/ a town in Sri Lanka, the ancient capital of the island (4th c. BC–AD 760), site of the sacred bo tree (descended from Buddha's original tree at Buddh Gaya in India) and of numerous Buddhist foundations. There the Sinhalese ruler Mahinda was converted to Buddhism in the 3rd c. BC; pop. (1981) 36,000.

anuran /əˈnjʊərən, æ-/ n. & adj. any tailless amphibian of the order Anura, including frogs and toads. —adj. of or relating to this order. [mod.L Anura (AN-[1] + Gk oura tail)]

anus /ˈeɪnəs/ n. Anat. the excretory opening at the end of the alimentary canal. [L]

Anvers see ANTWERP.

anvil /ˈænvɪl/ n. **1** a block (usu. of iron) with a flat top, concave sides, and often a pointed end, on which metals are worked in forging. **2** Anat. a bone of the ear; the incus. [OE anfilte etc.]

anxiety /æŋˈzaɪətɪ/ n. (pl. **-ies**) **1** the state of being anxious. **2** concern about an imminent danger, difficulty, etc. **3** (foll. by for, or to + infin.) anxious desire. **4** a thing that causes anxiety (my greatest anxiety is that I shall fall ill). **5** Psychol. a nervous disorder characterized by a state of excessive uneasiness. [F anxieté or L anxietas -tatis (as ANXIOUS)]

anxious /ˈæŋkʃəs/ adj. **1** troubled; uneasy in the mind. **2** causing or marked by anxiety (an anxious moment). **3** (foll. by for, or to + infin.) earnestly or uneasily wanting or trying (anxious to please; anxious for you to succeed). □□ **anxiously** adv. **anxiousness** n. [L anxius f. angere choke]

any /ˈenɪ/ adj., pron., & adv. —adj. **1** (with interrog., neg., or conditional expressed or implied) **a** one, no matter which, of several (cannot find any answer). **b** some, no matter how much or many or of what sort (if any books arrive; have you any sugar?). **2** a minimal amount of (hardly any difference). **3** whichever is chosen (any fool knows that). **4 a** an appreciable or significant (did not stay for any length of time). **b** a very large (has any amount of money). —pron. **1** any one (did not know any of them). **2** any number (are any of them yours?). **3** any amount (is there any left?). —adv. (usu. with neg. or interrog.) at all, in some degree (is that any good?; do not make it any larger; without being any the wiser). □ **any more** to any further extent (don't like you any more). **any time** colloq. at any time. **any time** (or **day** or **minute** etc.) **now** colloq. at any time in the near future. **not having any** colloq. unwilling to participate. [OE ǽnig f. Gmc (as ONE, -Y[1])]

anybody /ˈenɪˌbɒdɪ/ n. & pron. **1 a** a person, no matter who. **b** a person of any kind. **c** whatever person is chosen. **2** a person of importance (are you anybody?). □ **anybody's** (of a contest) evenly balanced (it was anybody's game). **anybody's guess** see GUESS.

anyhow /ˈenɪˌhaʊ/ adv. **1** anyway. **2** in a disorderly manner or state (does his work anyhow; things are all anyhow).

anyone /ˈenɪˌwʌn/ pron. anybody. ¶ Written as two words to imply a numerical sense, as in any one of us can do it.

anyplace /ˈenɪˌpleɪs/ adv. US anywhere.

anything /ˈenɪˌθɪŋ/ pron. **1** a thing, no matter which. **2** a thing of any kind. **3** whatever thing is chosen. □ **anything but** not at all (was anything but honest). **like anything** colloq. with great vigour, intensity, etc.

anyway /ˈenɪˌweɪ/ adv. **1** in any way or manner. **2** at any rate. **3** in any case. **4** to resume (anyway, as I was saying).

anywhere /ˈenɪˌweə(r)/ adv. & pron. —adv. in or to any place. —pron. any place (anywhere will do).

anywise /ˈenɪˌwaɪz/ adv. archaic in any manner. [OE on ǽnige wīsan in any wise]

Anzac /ˈænzæk/ n. **1** a soldier in the Australian and New Zealand Army Corps (1914–18). **2** any person, esp. a member of the armed services, from Australia or New Zealand. □ **Anzac Day** 25 April, commemorating the Anzac landing at Gallipoli in 1915. [acronym]

Anzus /ˈænzəs/ n. (also **ANZUS**) Australia, New Zealand, and the US, as an alliance for the Pacific area. Signed in 1951 and known also as the Pacific Security Treaty, it recognized the common danger of an armed attack on any of these countries and declared its readiness to act to meet this. After New Zealand's declaration of an anti-nuclear policy (1985), which included the banning of nuclear-armed ships from its ports, the US suspended its security obligations to New Zealand (1986). [acronym]

AO *abbr.* Officer of the Order of Australia.

AOB *abbr.* any other business.

A-OK *abbr. US colloq.* excellent; in good order. [all systems OK]

Aorangi /aʊˈræŋi/ an administrative region in the Canterbury Plains of South Island, New Zealand; pop. (1986) 81,300; chief town, Timaru. Aorangi is the Maori name for Mount Cook.

aorist /ˈeərɪst/ *n. & adj. Gram.* —*n.* an unqualified past tense of a verb (esp. in Greek), without reference to duration or completion. —*adj.* of or designating this tense. □□ **aoristic** /eəˈrɪstɪk/ *adj.* [Gk *aoristos* indefinite f. *a-* not + *horizō* define, limit]

aorta /eɪˈɔːtə/ *n.* (pl. **aortas**) the main artery, giving rise to the arterial network through which oxygenated blood is supplied to the body from the heart. □□ **aortic** *adj.* [Gk *aortē* f. *a(e)irō* raise]

à outrance /ɑː ˈuːtrɑ̃s/ *adv.* **1** to the death. **2** to the bitter end. [F, = to the utmost]

Aouzou Strip /aʊˈzuː/ a narrow corridor of disputed desert land in north Chad, stretching the full length of the frontier separating Chad and Libya.

ap-[1] /æp/ *prefix* assim. form of AD- before *p*.

ap-[2] /æp/ *prefix* assim. form of APO- before a vowel or *h*.

apace /əˈpeɪs/ *adv. literary* swiftly, quickly. [OF *à pas* at (a considerable) pace]

Apache /əˈpætʃi/ *n.* (pl. same or **Apaches**) **1** a member of an Athapaskan-speaking American Indian tribe which migrated from Canada to what are now the southwestern US (primarily to Arizona and New Mexico with smaller numbers in Utah, Colorado, and Texas) over 1,000 years ago. The arid ecological conditions inhibited colonial expansion in the region with the result that the indigenous groups of the southwest (e.g. Apache, Navajo, and the various *pueblo* cultures) suffered less cultural disruption than most Amerindian groups. When contact finally came the Apache put up fierce resistance to colonial expansion and were, in the late 19th c., the last American Indian group to be conquered by the US cavalry—which has had a considerable effect on the popular imagination. Forcibly concentrated on reservations after 1887 and deprived of the freedom necessary to continue their traditional hunting and gathering by the policies of the US Bureau of Indian Affairs, Apache society has undergone profound restructuring in the 20th c. **2** (**apache**) (/əˈpæʃ/) a violent street ruffian, originally in Paris. [Mex. Sp.]

apanage var. of APPANAGE.

apart /əˈpɑːt/ *adv.* **1** separately; not together (*keep your feet apart*). **2** into pieces (*came apart in my hands*). **3 a** to or on one side. **b** out of consideration (placed after noun: *joking apart*). **4** to or at a distance. □ **apart from 1** excepting; not considering. **2** in addition to (*apart from roses we grow irises*). [ME f. OF *à* to + *part* side]

apartheid /əˈpɑːteɪt/ *n.* **1** a policy or system of segregation or discrimination on grounds of race, especially the South African policy in respect of Europeans and non-Europeans. Adopted by the successful Afrikaner National Party as a slogan in the 1948 election, apartheid intensified and institutionalized existing racial segregation, guaranteeing the dominance of the White minority. In the early 1960s domestic and international opposition to apartheid began to intensify, but despite rioting and terrorism at home and isolation abroad, the White regime maintained the apartheid system with only minor liberal alterations until Feb. 1991. **2** segregation in other contexts. [Afrik. (as APART, -HOOD)]

apartment /əˈpɑːtmənt/ *n.* **1** (in *pl.*) a suite of rooms, usu. furnished and rented. **2** a single room in a house. **3** *US* a flat.

□ **apartment house** *US* a block of flats. [F *appartement* f. It. *appartamento* f. *appartare* to separate f. *a parte* apart]

apathetic /æpəˈθetɪk/ *adj.* having or showing no emotion or interest. □□ **apathetically** *adv.* [APATHY, after PATHETIC]

apathy /ˈæpəθi/ *n.* (often foll. by *towards*) lack of interest or feeling; indifference. [F *apathie* f. L *apathia* f. Gk *apatheia* f. *apathēs* without feeling f. *a-* not + *pathos* suffering]

apatite /ˈæpətaɪt/ *n.* a naturally occurring crystalline mineral of calcium phosphate and fluoride, used in the manufacture of fertilizers. [G *Apatit* f. Gk *apatē* deceit (from its deceptive forms)]

ape /eɪp/ *n. & v.* —*n.* **1** any of the various primates of the family Pongidae characterized by the absence of a tail, e.g. the gorilla, chimpanzee, orang-utan, or gibbon. **2** (in general use) any monkey. **3 a** an imitator. **b** an apelike person. —*v.tr.* imitate, mimic. □ **ape-man** (pl. **-men**) any of various apelike primates held to be forerunners of present-day man. **go ape** *sl.* become crazy. **naked ape** present-day man. [OE *apa* f. Gmc]

Apeldoorn /ˈæpəldɔːn/ a town in the province of Gelderland, east central Netherlands, 27 km (17 miles) north of Arnhem; pop. (1987) 146,337. The Het Loo palace here has been a summer residence of the Dutch royal family since 1685.

Apelles /əˈpeliːz/ (4th c. BC) court portrait painter to Alexander the Great. From written sources he must be considered the greatest painter of antiquity, though none of his works has survived. Amongst his recorded works was a picture of Aphrodite rising from the sea, and a picture entitled *Calumny*, both of which were emulated by Botticelli in the 15th c.

Apennines /ˈæpɪnaɪnz/ a mountain range running the length of Italy from the north-west to the southern tip of the peninsula.

aperçu /æpɜːˈsjuː/ *n.* **1** a summary or survey. **2** an insight. [F, past part. of *apercevoir* perceive]

aperient /əˈpɪərɪənt/ *adj. & n.* —*adj.* laxative. —*n.* a laxative medicine. [L *aperire aperient-* to open]

aperiodic /ˌeɪpɪərɪˈɒdɪk/ *adj.* **1** not periodic; irregular. **2** *Physics* (of a potentially oscillating or vibrating system, e.g. an instrument with a pointer) that is adequately damped to prevent oscillation or vibration. **3** (of an oscillation or vibration) without a regular period. □□ **aperiodicity** /-rɪəˈdɪsɪti/ *n.*

aperitif /əˌperɪˈtiːf, əˈpe-/ *n.* an alcoholic drink taken before a meal to stimulate the appetite. [F *apéritif* f. med.L *aperitivus* f. L *aperire* to open]

aperture /ˈæpətjʊə(r)/ *n.* **1** an opening; a gap. **2** a space through which light passes in an optical or photographic instrument, esp. a variable space in a camera. [L *apertura* (as APERITIF)]

apery /ˈeɪpəri/ *n.* (pl. **-ies**) **1** mimicry. **2** an ape-house.

apetalous /eɪˈpetələs/ *adj. Bot.* (of flowers) having no petals. [mod.L *apetalus* f. Gk *apetalos* leafless f. *a-* not + *petalon* leaf]

APEX /ˈeɪpeks/ *abbr.* Association of Professional, Executive, Clerical, and Computer Staff.

Apex /ˈeɪpeks/ *n.* (also **APEX**) (often *attrib.*) a system of reduced fares for scheduled airline flights when paid for before a certain period in advance of departure. [Advance Purchase Excursion]

apex /ˈeɪpeks/ *n.* (pl. **apexes** or **apices** /ˈeɪpɪsiːz/) **1** the highest point. **2** a climax; a high point of achievement etc. **3** the vertex of a triangle or cone. **4** a tip or pointed end. [L, = peak, tip]

apfelstrudel /ˈæpfəlˌstruːd(ə)l/ *n.* a confection of flaky pastry filled with spiced apple. [G f. *Apfel* apple + STRUDEL]

aphaeresis /əˈfiərɪsɪs/ *n.* (pl. **aphaereses** /-ˌsiːz/) the omission of a letter or syllable at the beginning of a word as a morphological development (e.g. in the derivation of *adder*). [LL f. Gk *aphairesis* (as APO-, *haireō* take)]

aphasia /əˈfeɪzɪə/ *n. Med.* the loss of ability to understand or express speech, owing to brain damage. □□ **aphasic** *adj. & n.* [mod.L f. Gk f. *aphatos* speechless f. *a-* not + *pha-* speak]

aphelion /æpˈhiːlɪən, əˈfiːlɪən/ *n.* (pl. **aphelia** /-lɪə/) the point in a body's orbit where it is furthest from the sun (opp. PERIHELION).

¶ **Symb.: Q.** [Graecized f. mod.L *aphelium* f. Gk *aph' hēliou* from the sun]

aphesis /ˈæfɪsɪs/ *n.* (*pl.* **apheses** /-ˌsiːz/) the gradual loss of an unstressed vowel at the beginning of a word (e.g. of *e* from *esquire* to form *squire*). □□ **aphetic** /əˈfetɪk/ *adj.* **aphetically** /əˈfetɪkəlɪ/ *adv.* [Gk, = letting go (as APO-, *hiēmi* send)]

aphid /ˈeɪfɪd/ *n.* any small homopterous insect which feeds by sucking sap from leaves, stems, or roots of plants; a plant-louse. [back-form. f. *aphides*: see APHIS]

aphis /ˈeɪfɪs/ *n.* (*pl.* **aphides** /-ˌdiːz/) an aphid, esp. of the genus *Aphis* including the greenfly. [mod.L (Linnaeus) f. Gk (1523), perh. a misreading of *koris* bug]

aphonia /əˈfəʊnɪə/ *n.* (also **aphony** /ˈæfənɪ/) *Med.* the loss or absence of the voice through a disease of the larynx or mouth. [mod.L *aphonia* f. Gk f. *aphōnos* voiceless f. *a-* not + *phōnē* voice)]

aphorism /ˈæfəˌrɪz(ə)m/ *n.* **1** a short pithy maxim. **2** a brief statement of a principle. □□ **aphorist** *n.* **aphoristic** /-ˈrɪstɪk/ *adj.* **aphoristically** /-ˈrɪstɪkəlɪ/ *adv.* **aphorize** *v.intr.* (also **-ise**). [F *aphorisme* or LL f. Gk *aphorismos* definition f. *aphorizō* (as APO-, *horos* boundary)]

aphrodisiac /ˌæfrəˈdɪzɪˌæk/ *adj. & n.* —*adj.* that arouses sexual desire. —*n.* an aphrodisiac drug. [Gk *aphrodisiakos* f. *aphrodisios* f. *Aphroditē* APHRODITE]

Aphrodisias /ˌæfrəˈdɪsɪəs/ a ruined city in western Turkey, with a temple dedicated to Aphrodite.

Aphrodite /ˌæfrəˈdaɪtɪ/ *Gk Mythol.* the goddess of beauty, fertility, and sexual love, born of the sea-foam, identified by the Romans with Venus. Her cult was of eastern origin, and she was identified with Astarte, Ishtar, etc. The statue of Aphrodite (now lost) made by Praxiteles was the first important female nude. It was rejected by the people of the island of Cos, who found it too erotic, and acquired by Cnidos on the coast of Asia Minor, where it proved to be a great attraction to travellers, bringing fame to the town. [perh. f. Gk *aphros* foam]

aphyllous /əˈfɪləs/ *adj. Bot.* (of plants) having no leaves. [mod.L f. Gk *aphullos* f. *a-* not + *phullon* leaf]

Apia /ˈɑːpɪə/ the capital of Western Samoa in the central Pacific, situated on the north coast of the islands of Upolu; pop. (1981) 33,200. It was the home of Robert Louis Stevenson from 1890 until his death.

apian /ˈeɪpɪən/ *adj.* of or relating to bees. [L *apianus* f. *apis* bee]

apiary /ˈeɪpɪərɪ/ *n.* (*pl.* **-ies**) a place where bees are kept. □□ **apiarist** *n.* [L *apiarium* f. *apis* bee]

apical /ˈeɪpɪk(ə)l, ˈæp-/ *adj.* of, at, or forming an apex. □□ **apically** *adv.* [L *apex apicis*: see APEX]

apices *pl.* of APEX.

apiculture /ˈeɪpɪˌkʌltʃə(r)/ *n.* bee-keeping. □□ **apicultural** /-ˈkʌltʃər(ə)l/ *adj.* **apiculturist** /-ˈkʌltʃərɪst/ *n.* [L *apis* bee, after AGRICULTURE]

apiece /əˈpiːs/ *adv.* for each one; severally (*had five pounds apiece*). [A² + PIECE]

Apis /ˈɑːpɪs, ˈæ-/ *Egyptian Mythol.* a god always depicted as a bull (symbolizing strength in war and in fertility), worshipped especially at Memphis, where he was recognized as a manifestation of Ptah, the city's patron, then of Ra (and the solar disc was placed between his horns), and later of Osiris. A live bull, carefully chosen, was considered to be his incarnation and kept in an enclosure. When it died it was mummified and ceremonially interred, and a young black bull with suitable markings was installed in its place.

apish /ˈeɪpɪʃ/ *adj.* **1** of or like an ape. **2** silly, affected. □□ **apishly** *adv.* **apishness** *n.*

aplanat /ˈæpləˌnæt/ *n.* a reflecting or refracting surface made aplanatic by correction. [G]

aplanatic /ˌæpləˈnætɪk/ *adj.* (of a reflecting or refracting surface) free from spherical aberration. [Gk *aplanētos* free from error f. *a-* not + *planaō* wander]

aplasia /əˈpleɪzɪə/ *n. Med.* total or partial failure of development of an organ or tissue. □□ **aplastic** /əˈplæstɪk/ *adj.* [mod.L f. Gk f. *a-* not + *plasis* formation]

aplenty /əˈplentɪ/ *adv.* in plenty.

aplomb /əˈplɒm/ *n.* assurance; self-confidence. [F, = perpendicularity, f. *à plomb* according to a plummet]

apnoea /æpˈniːə/ *n.* (US **apnea**) *Med.* a temporary cessation of breathing. [mod.L f. Gk *apnoia* f. *apnous* breathless]

apo- /ˈæpə/ *prefix* **1** away from (*apogee*). **2** separate (*apocarpous*). [Gk *apo* from, away, un-, quite]

Apoc. *abbr.* **1** Apocalypse (New Testament). **2** Apocrypha.

apocalypse /əˈpɒkəlɪps/ *n.* **1** (**the Apocalypse**) Revelation (see REVELATION 3), the last book of the New Testament, recounting a divine revelation to St John. It describes visions of heaven and a prophetic account of the end of the world. **2** a revelation, esp. of the end of the world. **3** a grand or violent event resembling those described in the Apocalypse. [ME f. OF ult. f. Gk *apokalupsis* f. *apokaluptō* uncover, reveal]

apocalyptic /əˌpɒkəˈlɪptɪk/ *adj.* **1** of or resembling the Apocalypse. **2** revelatory, prophetic. □□ **apocalyptically** *adv.* [Gk *apokaluptikos* (as APOCALYPSE)]

apocarpous /ˌæpəˈkɑːpəs/ *adj. Bot.* (of ovaries) having distinct carpels not joined together (opp. SYNCARPOUS). [APO- + Gk *karpos* fruit]

apochromat /ˈæpəkrəˌmæt/ *n.* a lens or lens-system that reduces spherical and chromatic aberrations. □□ **apochromatic** /-krəˈmætɪk/ *adj.* [APO- + CHROMATIC]

apocope /əˈpɒkəpɪ/ *n.* the omission of a letter or letters at the end of a word as a morphological development (e.g. in the derivation of *curio*). [LL f. Gk *apokopē* (as APO-, *koptō* cut)]

Apocr. *abbr.* Apocrypha.

apocrine /ˈæpəˌkraɪn, -krɪn/ *adj. Biol.* (of a multicellular gland, e.g. the mammary gland) releasing some cytoplasm when secreting. [APO- + Gk *krinō* to separate]

Apocrypha /əˈpɒkrɪfə/ *n.pl.* **1** the Biblical books received by the early Church as part of the Greek version of the Old Testament (the Septuagint), but not included in the Hebrew Bible. They are included in the Vulgate (it was Jerome who introduced the term 'Apocrypha') and are regarded by the Roman Catholic Church as authoritative, but were refused the status of inspired Scripture at the Reformation. (Modern Bibles sometimes include them in the Old Testament or as an appendix, and sometimes omit them.) The books date from *c.*300 BC–*c.* AD 100, and are valuable as showing beliefs of the period when Christianity was not fully separated from Judaism. **2** (**apocrypha**) writings or reports not considered genuine. [ME f. eccl.L *apocrypha* (*scripta*) hidden writings f. Gk *apokruphos* f. *apokruptō* hide away]

apocryphal /əˈpɒkrɪf(ə)l/ *adj.* **1** of doubtful authenticity (orig. of some early Christian texts resembling those of the New Testament). **2** invented, mythical (*an apocryphal story*). **3** of or belonging to the Apocrypha.

apodal /ˈæpəd(ə)l/ *adj.* **1** without (or with undeveloped) feet. **2** (of fish) without ventral fins. [*apod* apodal creature f. Gk *apous* footless f. *a-* not + *pous podos* foot]

apodictic /ˌæpəˈdɪktɪk/ *adj.* (also **apodeictic** /-ˈdaɪktɪk/) **1** clearly established. **2** of clear demonstration. [L *apodicticus* f. Gk *apodeiktikos* (as APO-, *deiknumi* show)]

apodosis /əˈpɒdəsɪs/ *n.* (*pl.* **apodoses** /-ˌsiːz/) the main (consequent) clause of a conditional sentence (e.g. *I would agree* in *if you asked me I would agree*). [LL f. Gk f. *apodidōmi* give back (as APO-, *didōmi* give)]

apogee /ˈæpəˌdʒiː/ *n.* **1** the point in a celestial body's orbit where it is furthest from the earth (opp. PERIGEE). **2** the most distant or highest point. □□ **apogean** /ˌæpəˈdʒiːən/ *adj.* [F *apogée* or mod.L *apogaeum* f. Gk *apogeion* away from earth (as APO-, *gē* earth)]

apolitical /ˌeɪpəˈlɪtɪk(ə)l/ *adj.* not interested in or concerned with politics.

Apollinarius /əˌpɒlɪˈneərɪəs/ (*c.*310–*c.*390) bishop of Laodicea in Asia Minor, instigator of the first great Christological heresy, which asserted that Christ had a human body and soul but no human spirit, this being replaced by the divine Logos. The fundamental objection to this was that unless Christ's manhood was complete he could not redeem the whole of human nature. □□ **Apollinarian** *adj. & n.*

Apollo /ə'pɒləʊ/ **1** Gk Mythol. a god, in art the ideal type of manly beauty, son of Zeus and Leto and brother of Artemis. He is associated especially with music, archery, prophecy, medicine, and the care of flocks and herds. **2** the name given to the American space programme for landing men on the moon. Such a landing, to be achieved before 1970, was proposed by President J. F. Kennedy in 1961 following the first manned flights in space by the USSR, and achieved its declared object on 20 July 1969.

Apollonian /ˌæpə'ləʊnɪən/ adj. **1** of or relating to Apollo, the Greek and Roman sun-god, patron of music and poetry. **2** orderly, rational, self-disciplined. [L Apollonius f. Gk Apollōnios APOLLONIUS]

Apollonius /ˌæpə'ləʊnɪəs/ of Rhodes (3rd c. BC), Greek poet of Alexandria, where he was chief librarian, who spent part of his life in Rhodes and was a rival of the poet Callimachus. His Argonautica, a poem in Homeric style on the expedition of the Argonauts, was the first to place love—Medea's love for Jason, vividly portrayed—in the foreground of the action of an epic poem.

Apollyon /ə'pɒljən/ the Devil, the 'angel of the bottomless pit' in Rev. 9: 11. [L (Vulgate) f. Gk apolluōn pres. part. of apollumi (as APO-, ollumi destroy)]

apologetic /əˌpɒlə'dʒetɪk/ adj. & n. —adj. **1** regretfully acknowledging or excusing an offence or failure. **2** diffident. **3** of reasoned defence or vindication. —n. (usu. in pl.) a reasoned defence, esp. of Christianity. □□ **apologetically** adv. [F apologétique f. LL apologeticus f. Gk apologētikos f. apologeomai speak in defence]

apologia /ˌæpə'ləʊdʒɪə/ n. a formal defence of one's opinions or conduct. [L: see APOLOGY]

apologist /ə'pɒlədʒɪst/ n. a person who defends something by argument. [F apologiste f. Gk apologizomai render account f. apologos account]

apologize /ə'pɒləˌdʒaɪz/ v.intr. (also **-ise**) make an apology; express regret. [Gk apologizomai: see APOLOGIST]

apologue /'æpəˌlɒg/ n. a moral fable. [F apologue or L apologus f. Gk apologos story (as APO-, logos discourse)]

apology /ə'pɒlədʒɪ/ n. (pl. **-ies**) **1** a regretful acknowledgement of an offence or failure. **2** an assurance that no offence was intended. **3** an explanation or defence. **4** (foll. by for) a poor or scanty specimen of (this apology for a letter). [F apologie or LL apologia f. Gk (as APOLOGETIC)]

apolune /'æpəˌluːn, -ˌljuːn/ n. the point in a body's lunar orbit where it is furthest from the moon (opp. PERILUNE). [APO- + L luna moon, after apogee]

apomixis /ˌæpə'mɪksɪs/ n. (pl. **apomixes** /-siːz/) Biol. a form of asexual reproduction (cf. AMPHIMIXIS). □□ **apomictic** adj. [mod.L, formed as APO- + Gk mixis mingling]

apophthegm /'æpəˌθem, 'æpəfˌθem/ n. (US **apothegm**) a terse saying or maxim, an aphorism. □□ **apophthegmatic** /-θeg'mætɪk/ adj. [F apophthegme or mod.L apothegma f. Gk apophthegma -matos f. apophtheggomai speak out]

apoplectic /ˌæpə'plektɪk/ adj. **1** of, causing, suffering, or liable to apoplexy. **2** colloq. enraged. □□ **apoplectically** adv. [F apoplectique or LL apoplecticus f. Gk apoplēktikos f. apoplēssō strike completely (as APO-, plēssō strike)]

apoplexy /'æpəˌpleksɪ/ n. a sudden loss of consciousness, voluntary movement, and sensation caused by blockage or rupture of a brain artery; a stroke. [ME f. OF apoplexie f. LL apoplexia f. Gk apoplēxia (as APOPLECTIC)]

aposematic /ˌæpəsɪ'mætɪk/ adj. Zool. (of coloration, markings, etc.) serving to warn or repel. [APO- + Gk sēma sēmatos sign]

apostasy /ə'pɒstəsɪ/ n. (pl. **-ies**) **1** renunciation of a belief or faith, esp. religious. **2** abandonment of principles or of a party. **3** an instance of apostasy. [ME f. eccl.L f. NT Gk apostasia f. apostasis defection (as APO-, stat- stand)]

apostate /ə'pɒsteɪt/ n. & adj. —n. a person who renounces a former belief, adherence, etc. —adj. engaged in apostasy. □□ **apostatical** /ˌæpə'stætɪk(ə)l/ adj. [ME f. OF apostate or eccl.L apostata f. Gk apostatēs deserter (as APOSTASY)]

apostatize /ə'pɒstəˌtaɪz/ v.intr. (also **-ise**) renounce a former belief, adherence, etc. [med.L apostatizare f. apostata: see APOSTATE]

a posteriori /ˌeɪ pɒˌsterɪ'ɔːraɪ/ adj. & adv. —adj. (of reasoning) inductive, empirical; proceeding from effects to causes. —adv. inductively, empirically; from effects to causes (opp. A PRIORI). [L, = from what comes after]

apostle /ə'pɒs(ə)l/ n. **1** (**Apostle**) **a** the name given in the Gospels and later to the twelve chief disciples of Christ, Saints Peter, Andrew, James, John, Philip, Bartholomew, Thomas, Matthew, James (the Less), Thaddaeus, Simon, and Judas Iscariot. After the suicide of Judas his place was taken by Matthias; the term was applied also to Paul and Barnabas. **b** the first successful Christian missionary in a country or to a people. **2** a leader or outstanding figure, esp. of a reform movement (apostle of temperance). **3** a messenger or representative. □ **apostle-bird** any of various Australian birds, forming flocks of about a dozen. **Apostles' Creed** a statement of Christian belief used in the Western Church, dating (with minor variations in form) from the 4th c., by which time the legend that it was a joint composition by the twelve Apostles was current. **Apostle spoon** a spoon with a figure of an Apostle on the handle. □□ **apostleship** n. [OE apostol f. eccl.L apostolus f. Gk apostolos messenger (as APO-, stellō send forth)]

apostolate /ə'pɒstələt/ n. **1** the position or authority of an Apostle. **2** leadership in reform. [eccl.L apostolatus (as APOSTLE)]

apostolic /ˌæpə'stɒlɪk/ adj. **1** of or relating to the Apostles. **2** of the Pope regarded as the successor of St Peter. **3** of the character of an Apostle. □ **Apostolic Fathers** the Christian leaders immediately succeeding the Apostles. **apostolic succession** the uninterrupted transmission of spiritual authority from the Apostles through successive popes and other bishops from the Apostles. The continuity has been disputed; the necessity of it is taught by the Roman Catholic Church but denied by most Protestants. [F apostolique or eccl.L apostolicus f. Gk apostolikos (as APOSTLE)]

apostrophe[1] /ə'pɒstrəfɪ/ n. a punctuation mark used to indicate: **1** the omission of letters or numbers (e.g. can't; he's; 1 Jan. '92). **2** the possessive case (e.g. Harry's book; boys' coats). [F apostrophe or LL apostrophus f. Gk apostrophos accent of elision f. apostrephō turn away (as APO-, strephō turn)]

apostrophe[2] /ə'pɒstrəfɪ/ n. an exclamatory passage in a speech or poem, addressed to a person (often dead or absent) or thing (often personified). □□ **apostrophize** v.tr. & intr. (also **-ise**). [L f. Gk, lit. 'turning away' (as APOSTROPHE[1])]

apothecary /ə'pɒθəkərɪ/ n. (pl. **-ies**) archaic a chemist licensed to dispense medicines and drugs. □ **apothecaries' measure** (or **weight**) Brit. system of weight and liquid volume formerly used in pharmacy. ¶ 12 ounces = one pound; 20 fluid ounces = one pint. [ME f. OF apotecaire f. LL apothecarius f. L apotheca f. Gk apothēkē storehouse]

apothegm US var. of APOPHTHEGM.

apothem /'æpəˌθem/ n. Geom. a line from the centre of a regular polygon at right angles to any of its sides. [Gk apotithēmi put aside (as APO-, tithēmi place)]

apotheosis /əˌpɒθɪ'əʊsɪs/ n. (pl. **apotheoses** /-siːz/) **1** elevation to divine status; deification. **2** a glorification of a thing; a sublime example (apotheosis of the dance). **3** a deified ideal. [eccl.L f. Gk apotheoō make a god of (as APO-, theos god)]

apotheosize /ə'pɒθɪəˌsaɪz/ v.tr. (also **-ise**) **1** make divine; deify. **2** idealize, glorify.

apotropaic /ˌæpətrə'peɪɪk/ adj. supposedly having the power to avert an evil influence or bad luck. [Gk apotropaios (as APO-, trepō turn)]

appal /ə'pɔːl/ v.tr. (US **appall**) (**appalled, appalling**) **1** greatly dismay or horrify. **2** (as **appalling** adj.) colloq. shocking, unpleasant; bad. □□ **appallingly** adv. [ME f. OF apalir grow pale]

Appalachian Mountains /ˌæpə'leɪtʃ(ə)n/ (also **Appalachians**) a mountain system of eastern North America, which confined early European settlers to the eastern coastal belt.

□ **Appalachian Trail** a 2,000-mile (about 3,200-km) footpath through the Appalachians from Mount Katahdin in Maine to Springer Mountain in Georgia.

Appaloosa /ˌæpəˈluːsə/ *n.* **1** a horse of a North American breed having dark spots on a light background. **2** this breed. [*Opelousa* in Louisiana, or *Palouse*, a river in Idaho]

appanage /ˈæpənɪdʒ/ *n.* (also **apanage**) **1** provision for the maintenance of the younger children of kings etc. **2** a perquisite. **3** a natural accompaniment or attribute. [F ult. f. med.L *appanare* endow with the means of subsistence (as APO-, *panis* bread)]

apparat /ˌæpəˈrɑːt/ *n.* the administrative system of a Communist party, esp. in a Communist country. [Russ. f. G, = apparatus]

apparatchik /ˌæpəˈrɑːtʃɪk/ *n.* (*pl.* **apparatchiks** or **apparatchiki** /-ˌkiː/) **1 a** a member of a Communist *apparat*. **b** a Communist agent or spy. **2 a** a member of a political party in any country who executes policy; a jealous functionary. **b** an official of a public or private organization. [Russ.: see APPARAT]

apparatus /ˌæpəˈreɪtəs, ˈæp-/ *n.* **1** the equipment needed for a particular purpose or function, esp. scientific or technical. **2** a political or other complex organization. **3** *Anat.* the organs used to perform a particular process. **4** (in full **apparatus criticus**) a collection of variants and annotations accompanying a printed text and usu. appearing below it. [L f. *apparare apparat-* make ready for]

apparel /əˈpær(ə)l/ *n.* & *v.* —*n.* **1** *formal* clothing, dress. **2** embroidered ornamentation on some ecclesiastical vestments. —*v.tr.* (**apparelled, apparelling**; US **appareled, appareling**) *archaic* clothe. [ME *aparailen* (v.) f. OF *apareillier* f. Rmc *appariculare* (unrecorded) make equal or fit, ult. f. L *par* equal]

apparent /əˈpærənt/ *adj.* **1** readily visible or perceivable. **2** seeming. □ **apparent horizon** see HORIZON 1b. **apparent magnitude** see MAGNITUDE. **apparent time** solar time (see SOLAR *adj.*). □□ **apparently** *adv.* [ME f. OF *aparant* f. L (as APPEAR)]

apparition /ˌæpəˈrɪʃ(ə)n/ *n.* a sudden or dramatic appearance, esp. of a ghost or phantom; a visible ghost. [ME f. F *apparition* or f. L *apparitio* attendance (as APPEAR)]

appeal /əˈpiːl/ *v.* & *n.* —*v.* **1** *intr.* make an earnest or formal request; plead (*appealed for calm; appealed to us not to leave*). **2** *intr.* (usu. foll. by *to*) be attractive or of interest; be pleasing. **3** *intr.* (foll. by *to*) resort to or cite for support. **4** *Law* **a** *intr.* (often foll. by *to*) apply (to a higher court) for a reconsideration of the decision of a lower court. **b** *tr.* refer to a higher court to review (a case). **c** *intr.* (foll. by *against*) apply to a higher court to reconsider (a verdict or sentence). **5** *intr. Cricket* call on the umpire for a decision on whether a batsman is out. —*n.* **1** the act or an instance of appealing. **2** a formal or urgent request for public support, esp. financial, for a cause. **3** *Law* the referral of a case to a higher court. **4** attractiveness; appealing quality (*sex appeal*). □□ **appealer** *n.* [ME f. OF *apel, apeler* f. L *appellare* to address]

appealable /əˈpiːləb(ə)l/ *adj. Law* (of a case) that can be referred to a higher court for review.

appealing /əˈpiːlɪŋ/ *adj.* attractive, likeable. □□ **appealingly** *adv.*

appear /əˈpɪə(r)/ *v.intr.* **1** become or be visible. **2** be evident (*a new problem then appeared*). **3** seem; have the appearance of being (*appeared unwell; you appear to be right*). **4** present oneself publicly or formally, esp. on stage or as the accused or counsel in a lawcourt. **5** be published (*it appeared in the papers; a new edition will appear*). [ME f. OF *apareir* f. L *apparēre apparit-* come in sight]

appearance /əˈpɪərəns/ *n.* **1** the act or an instance of appearing. **2** an outward form as perceived (whether correctly or not), esp. visually (*has an appearance of prosperity; gives the appearance of trying hard*). **3** a semblance. □ **keep up appearances** maintain an impression or pretence of virtue, affluence, etc.

make (or **put in**) **an appearance** be present, esp. briefly. **to all appearances** as far as can be seen; apparently. [ME f. OF *aparance, -ence* f. LL *apparentia* (as APPEAR, -ENCE)]

appease /əˈpiːz/ *v.tr.* **1** make calm or quiet, esp. conciliate (a potential aggressor) by making concessions. **2** satisfy (an appetite, scruples). □□ **appeasement** *n.* (in a derog. sense, used especially of the British Prime Minister's efforts, 1937–9, to placate, and so stave off the threatened aggression of, the Axis powers). **appeaser** *n.* [ME f. AF *apeser*, OF *apaisier* f. *à* to + *pais* PEACE]

Appel /ˈɑːp(ə)l/, Karel (1921–), Dutch abstract expressionist painter, sculptor, and graphic artist, whose work is characterized by thick impasto and violent colours. His abstract images suggest human and animal forms or fantasy figures which have often been regarded as fraught with terror as well as a childlike naïvety.

appellant /əˈpelənt/ *n. Law* a person who appeals to a higher court. [ME f. F (as APPEAL, -ANT)]

appellate /əˈpelət/ *adj. Law* (esp. of a court) concerned with or dealing with appeals. [L *appellatus* (as APPEAL, -ATE²)]

appellation /ˌæpəˈleɪʃ(ə)n/ *n. formal* a name or title; nomenclature. [ME f. OF f. L *appellatio -onis* (as APPEAL, -ATION)]

appellative /əˈpelətɪv/ *adj.* **1** naming. **2** *Gram.* (of a noun) that designates a class; common. [LL *appellativus* (as APPEAL, -ATIVE)]

append /əˈpend/ *v.tr.* (usu. foll. by *to*) attach, affix, add, esp. to a written document etc. [L *appendere* hang]

appendage /əˈpendɪdʒ/ *n.* **1** something attached; an addition. **2** *Zool.* a leg or other projecting part of an arthropod.

appendant /əˈpend(ə)nt/ *adj.* & *n.* —*adj.* (usu. foll. by *to*) attached in a subordinate capacity. —*n.* an appendant person or thing. [OF *apendant* f. *apendre* formed as APPEND, -ANT]

appendectomy /ˌæpenˈdektəmɪ/ *n.* (also **appendicectomy** /-dɪˈsektəmɪ/) (*pl.* **-ies**) the surgical removal of the appendix. [APPENDIX + -ECTOMY]

appendicitis /əˌpendɪˈsaɪtɪs/ *n.* inflammation of the appendix. [APPENDIX + -ITIS]

appendix /əˈpendɪks/ *n.* (*pl.* **appendices** /-ˌsiːz/; **appendixes**) **1** (in full **vermiform appendix**) *Anat.* a small outgrowth of tissue forming a tube-shaped sac attached to the lower end of the large intestine. **2** subsidiary matter at the end of a book or document. [L *appendix -icis* f. *appendere* APPEND]

apperceive /ˌæpəˈsiːv/ *v.tr.* **1** be conscious of perceiving. **2** *Psychol.* compare (a perception) to previously held ideas so as to extract meaning from it. □□ **apperception** /-ˈsepʃ(ə)n/ *n.* **apperceptive** /-ˈseptɪv/ *adj.* [ME (in obs. sense 'observe') f. OF *aperceveir* ult. f. L *percipere* PERCEIVE]

appertain /ˌæpəˈteɪn/ *v.intr.* (foll. by *to*) **1** relate. **2** belong as a possession or right. **3** be appropriate. [ME f. OF *apertenir* f. LL *appertinēre* f. *pertinēre* PERTAIN]

appetence /ˈæpɪt(ə)ns/ *n.* (also **appetency** /-sɪ/) (foll. by *for*) longing or desire. [F *appétence* or L *appetentia* f. *appetere* seek after]

appetite /ˈæpɪˌtaɪt/ *n.* **1** a natural desire to satisfy bodily needs, esp. for food or sexual activity. **2** (usu. foll. by *for*) an inclination or desire. □□ **appetitive** /əˈpetɪtɪv/ *adj.* [ME f. OF *apetit* f. L *appetitus* f. *appetere* seek after]

appetizer /ˈæpɪˌtaɪzə(r)/ *n.* (also **-iser**) a small amount, esp. of food or drink, to stimulate an appetite. [*appetize* (back-form. f. APPETIZING)]

appetizing /ˈæpɪˌtaɪzɪŋ/ *adj.* (also **-ising**) stimulating an appetite, esp. for food. □□ **appetizingly** *adv.* [F *appétissant* irreg. f. *appétit*, ult. f. APPETITE]

Appian Way /ˈæpɪən/ (L *Via Appia*) the principal southward road from Rome in classical times, named after the censor Appius Claudius Caecus who in 312 BC built the section to Capua (c.210 km, 132 miles); it was later extended to Brindisi on the SE coast of Italy.

applaud /əˈplɔːd/ *v.* **1** *intr.* express strong approval or praise, esp. by clapping. **2** *tr.* express approval of (a person or action). [L *applaudere applaus-* clap hands]

applause /əˈplɔːz/ *n.* **1** an expression of approbation, esp. from an audience etc. by clapping. **2** emphatic approval. [med.L *applausus* (as APPLAUD)]

apple /ˈæp(ə)l/ *n.* **1** the fruit of a tree of the genus *Malus*, rounded in form and with a crisp flesh. **2** the tree bearing this. □ **apple of one's eye** a cherished person or thing. **apple-pie bed** a bed made (as a joke) with the sheets folded short, so that the legs cannot be accommodated. **apple-pie order** perfect order; extreme neatness. **she's apple** *Austral. sl.* everything is fine. **upset the apple-cart** spoil careful plans. [OE *æppel* f. Gmc]

applejack /ˈæp(ə)l̩dʒæk/ *n.* *US* a spirit distilled from fermented apple juice. [APPLE + JACK¹]

Appleton /ˈæpəlt(ə)n/, Sir Edward Victor (1892–1965), English physicist. His investigation of the Kennelly–Heaviside (or E) layer of the atmosphere led him to the discovery of a higher region of ionized gases (the Appleton layer, now resolved into two layers F1 and F2) from which short-wave radio waves were reflected back to earth. This work, for which he was awarded the Nobel Prize for physics in 1947, was important for long-range radio transmission and radar.

appliance /əˈplaɪəns/ *n.* a device or piece of equipment used for a specific task. [APPLY + -ANCE]

applicable /ˈæplɪkəb(ə)l, əˈplɪkəb(ə)l/ *adj.* (often foll. by *to*) **1** that may be applied. **2** having reference; appropriate. □□ **applicability** /-ˈbɪlɪtɪ/ *n.* **applicably** *adv.* [OF *applicable* or med.L *applicabilis* (as APPLY, -ABLE)]

applicant /ˈæplɪkənt/ *n.* a person who applies for something, esp. a post. [APPLICATION + -ANT]

application /ˌæplɪˈkeɪʃ(ə)n/ *n.* **1** the act of applying, esp. medicinal ointment to the skin. **2** a formal request, usu. in writing, for employment, membership, etc. **3 a** relevance. **b** the use to which something can or should be put. **4** sustained or concentrated effort; diligence. [ME f. F f. L *applicatio -onis* (as APPLY, -ATION)]

applicator /ˈæplɪˌkeɪtə(r)/ *n.* a device for applying a substance to a surface, esp. the skin. [APPLICATION + -OR¹]

applied /əˈplaɪd/ *adj.* (of a subject of study) put to practical use as opposed to being theoretical (cf. PURE *adj.* 9). □ **applied mathematics** see MATHEMATICS.

appliqué /æˈpliːkeɪ/ *n., adj., & v.* —*n.* ornamental work in which fabric is cut out and attached, usu. sewn, to the surface of another fabric to form pictures or patterns. —*adj.* executed in appliqué. —*v.tr.* (**appliqués, appliquéd, appliquéing**) decorate with appliqué; make using appliqué technique. [F, past part. of *appliquer* apply f. L *applicare*: see APPLY]

apply /əˈplaɪ/ *v.* (**-ies, -ied**) **1** *intr.* (often foll. by *for, to,* or *to* + infin.) make a formal request for something to be done, given, etc. (*apply for a job; apply for help to the governors; applied to be sent overseas*). **2** *intr.* have relevance (*does not apply in this case*). **3** *tr.* **a** make use of as relevant or suitable; employ (*apply the rules*). **b** operate (*apply the handbrake*). **4** *tr.* (often foll. by *to*) **a** put or spread on (*applied the ointment to the cut*). **b** administer (*applied the remedy; applied common sense to the problem*). **5** *refl.* (often foll. by *to*) devote oneself (*applied myself to the task*). □□ **applier** *n.* [ME f. OF *aplier* f. L *applicare* fold, fasten to]

appoggiatura /əˌpɒdʒəˈtʊərə/ *n. Mus.* a grace-note performed before an essential note of a melody and normally taking half its time-value. [It.]

appoint /əˈpɔɪnt/ *v.tr.* **1** assign a post or office to (*appoint him governor; appoint him to govern; appointed to the post*). **2** (often foll. by *for*) fix, decide on (a time, place, etc.) (*Wednesday was appointed for the meeting; 8.30 was the appointed time*). **3** prescribe; ordain (*Holy Writ appointed by the Church*). **4** *Law* **a** (also *absol.*) declare the destination of (property etc.). **b** declare (a person) as having an interest in property etc. (*Jones was appointed in the will*). **5** (as **appointed** *adj.*) equipped, furnished (*a badly appointed hotel*). □□ **appointee** /-ˈtiː/ *n.* **appointer** *n.* **appointive** *adj.* *US* [ME f. OF *apointer* f. *à point* to a point]

appointment /əˈpɔɪntmənt/ *n.* **1** an arrangement to meet at a specific time and place. **2 a** a post or office available for applicants, or recently filled (*took up the appointment on Monday*).

b a person appointed. **3** (usu. in *pl.*) **a** furniture, fittings. **b** equipment. [ME f. OF *apointement* (as APPOINT, -MENT)]

apport /əˈpɔːt/ *n.* **1** the production of material objects by supposedly occult means at a seance. **2** an object so produced. [ME (in obs. senses), f. OF *aport* f. *aporter* f. *à* to + *porter* bring]

apportion /əˈpɔːʃ(ə)n/ *v.tr.* (often foll. by *to*) share out; assign as a share. □□ **apportionable** *adj.* **apportionment** *n.* [F *apportionner* or f. med.L *apportionare* (as AD-, PORTION)]

apposite /ˈæpəzɪt/ *adj.* (often foll. by *to*) **1** apt; well chosen. **2** well expressed. □□ **appositely** *adv.* **appositeness** *n.* [L *appositus* past part. of *apponere* (as AD-, *ponere* put)]

apposition /ˌæpəˈzɪʃ(ə)n/ *n.* **1** placing side by side; juxtaposition. **2** *Gram.* the placing of a word next to another, esp. the addition of one noun to another, in order to qualify or explain the first (e.g. *William the Conqueror; my friend Sue*). □□ **appositional** *adj.* [ME f. F *apposition* or f. LL *appositio* (as APPOSITE, -ITION)]

appraisal /əˈpreɪz(ə)l/ *n.* the act or an instance of appraising.

appraise /əˈpreɪz/ *v.tr.* **1** estimate the value or quality of (*appraised her skills*). **2** (esp. of an official valuer) set a price on; value. □□ **appraisable** *adj.* **appraiser** *n.* **appraisive** *adj.* [APPRIZE by assim. to PRAISE]

appreciable /əˈpriːʃəb(ə)l/ *adj.* large enough to be noticed; significant; considerable (*appreciable progress has been made*). □□ **appreciably** *adv.* [F f. *apprécier* (as APPRECIATE)]

appreciate /əˈpriːʃɪˌeɪt, -sɪˌeɪt/ *v.* **1** *tr.* **a** esteem highly; value. **b** be grateful for (*we appreciate your sympathy*). **c** be sensitive to (*appreciate the nuances*). **2** *tr.* (often foll. by *that* + clause) understand; recognize (*I appreciate that I may be wrong*). **3 a** *intr.* (of property etc.) rise in value. **b** *tr.* raise in value. □□ **appreciative** /-ʃətɪv/ *adj.* **appreciatively** /-ʃətɪvlɪ/ *adv.* **appreciativeness** /-ʃətɪvnɪs/ *n.* **appreciator** *n.* **appreciatory** /-ʃjətərɪ/ *adj.* [LL *appretiare* appraise (as AD-, *pretium* price)]

appreciation /əˌpriːʃɪˈeɪʃ(ə)n, əˌpriːsɪ-/ *n.* **1** favourable or grateful recognition. **2** an estimation or judgement; a sensitive understanding or reaction (*a quick appreciation of the problem*). **3** an increase in value. **4** a (usu. favourable) review of a book, film, etc. [F f. LL *appretiatio -onis* (as APPRECIATE, -ATION)]

apprehend /ˌæprɪˈhend/ *v.tr.* **1** understand, perceive (*apprehend your meaning*). **2** seize, arrest (*apprehended the criminal*). **3** anticipate with uneasiness or fear (*apprehending the results*). [F *appréhender* or L *apprehendere* (as AD-, *prehendere prehens-* lay hold of)]

apprehensible /ˌæprɪˈhensɪb(ə)l/ *adj.* capable of being apprehended by the senses or the intellect (*an apprehensible theory; an apprehensible change in her expression*). □□ **apprehensibility** /-ˈbɪlɪtɪ/ *n.* [LL *apprehensibilis* (as APPREHEND, -IBLE)]

apprehension /ˌæprɪˈhenʃ(ə)n/ *n.* **1** uneasiness; dread. **2** understanding, grasp. **3** arrest, capture (*apprehension of the suspect*). **4** an idea; a conception. [F *appréhension* or LL *apprehensio* (as APPREHEND, -ION)]

apprehensive /ˌæprɪˈhensɪv/ *adj.* **1** (often foll. by *of, for*) uneasily fearful; dreading. **2** relating to perception by the senses or the intellect. **3** *archaic* perceptive; intelligent. □□ **apprehensively** *adv.* **apprehensiveness** *n.* [F *appréhensif* or med.L *apprehensivus* (as APPREHEND, -IVE)]

apprentice /əˈprentɪs/ *n. & v.* —*n.* **1** a person who is learning a trade by being employed in it for an agreed period at low wages. **2** a beginner; a novice. —*v.tr.* (usu. foll. by *to*) engage or bind as an apprentice (*was apprenticed to a builder*). □□ **apprenticeship** *n.* [ME f. OF *aprentis* f. *apprendre* learn (as APPREHEND), after words in -*tis*, -*tif*, f. L -*tivus*: see -IVE]

apprise /əˈpraɪz/ *v.tr.* inform. □ **be apprised of** be aware of. [F *appris -ise* past part. of *apprendre* learn, teach (as APPREHEND)]

apprize /əˈpraɪz/ *v.tr. archaic* **1** esteem highly. **2** appraise. [ME f. OF *apriser* f. *à* to + *pris* PRICE]

appro /ˈæprəʊ/ *n. Brit. colloq.* □ **on appro** = *on approval* (see APPROVAL). [abbr. of *approval* or *approbation*]

approach /əˈprəʊtʃ/ *v. & n.* —*v.* **1** *tr.* come near or nearer to (a place or time). **2** *intr.* come near or nearer in space or time (*the hour approaches*). **3** *tr.* make a tentative proposal or suggestion to (*approached me about a loan*). **4** *tr.* **a** be similar in character, quality, etc., to (*doesn't approach her for artistic skill*). **b** approximate to (*a population approaching 5 million*). **5** *tr.* attempt to influence or bribe. **6** *tr.* set about (a task etc.). **7** *intr.* *Golf* play an approach shot. **8** *intr.* *Aeron.* prepare to land. **9** *tr.* *archaic* bring near. —*n.* **1** an act or means of approaching (*made an approach; an approach lined with trees*). **2** an approximation (*an approach to an apology*). **3** a way of dealing with a person or thing (*needs a new approach*). **4** (usu. in *pl.*) a sexual advance. **5** *Golf* a stroke from the fairway to the green. **6** *Aeron.* the final part of a flight before landing. **7** *Bridge* a bidding method with a gradual advance to a final contract. □ **approach road** *Brit.* a road by which traffic enters a motorway. [ME f. OF *aproch(i)er* f. eccl.L *appropiare* draw near (as AD-, *propius* compar. of *prope* near)]

approachable /əˈprəʊtʃəb(ə)l/ *adj.* **1** friendly; easy to talk to. **2** able to be approached. □□ **approachability** /-ˈbɪlɪtɪ/ *n.*

approbate /ˈæprəˌbeɪt/ *v.tr.* US approve formally; sanction. [ME f. L *approbare* (as AD-, *probare* test f. *probus* good)]

approbation /ˌæprəˈbeɪʃ(ə)n/ *n.* approval, consent. □□ **approbative** /ˈæprəˌbeɪtɪv/ *adj.* **approbatory** *adj.* [ME f. OF f. L *approbatio -onis* (as APPROBATE, -ATION)]

appropriate *adj.* & *v.* —*adj.* /əˈprəʊprɪət/ (often foll. by *to*, *for*) **1** suitable or proper. **2** *formal* belonging or particular. —*v.tr.* /əˈprəʊprɪˌeɪt/ **1** take possession of, esp. without authority. **2** devote (money etc.) to special purposes. □□ **appropriately** *adv.* **appropriateness** *n.* **appropriation** /əˌprəʊprɪˈeɪʃ(ə)n/ *n.* **appropriator** /-ˌeɪtə(r)/ *n.* [LL *appropriatus* past part. of *appropriare* (as AD-, *proprius* own)]

approval /əˈpruːv(ə)l/ *n.* **1** the act of approving. **2** an instance of this; consent; a favourable opinion (*with your approval; looked at him with approval*). □ **on approval** (of goods supplied) to be returned if not satisfactory.

approve /əˈpruːv/ *v.* **1** *tr.* confirm; sanction (*approved his application*). **2** *intr.* give or have a favourable opinion. **3** *tr.* commend (*approved the new hat*). **4** *tr.* *archaic* (usu. *refl.*) demonstrate oneself to be (*approved himself a coward*). □ **approved school** *hist.* a residential place of training for young offenders. **approve of 1** pronounce or consider good or satisfactory; commend. **2** agree to. □□ **approvingly** *adv.* [ME f. OF *aprover* f. L (as APPROBATE)]

approx. *abbr.* **1** approximate. **2** approximately.

approximate *adj.* & *v.* —*adj.* /əˈprɒksɪmət/ **1** fairly correct or accurate; near to the actual (*the approximate time of arrival; an approximate guess*). **2** near or next (*your approximate neighbour*). —*v.tr.* & *intr.* /əˈprɒksɪˌmeɪt/ (often foll. by *to*) bring or come near (esp. in quality, number, etc.), but not exactly (*approximates to the truth; approximates the amount required*). □□ **approximately** /-mətlɪ/ *adv.* **approximation** /-ˈmeɪʃ(ə)n/ *n.* [LL *approximatus* past part. of *approximare* (as AD-, *proximus* very near)]

appurtenance /əˈpɜːtɪnəns/ *n.* (usu. in *pl.*) a belonging; an appendage; an accessory. [ME f. AF *apurtenaunce*, OF *apertenance* (as APPERTAIN, -ANCE)]

appurtenant /əˈpɜːtɪnənt/ *adj.* (often foll. by *to*) belonging or appertaining; pertinent. [ME f. OF *apartenant* pres. part. (as APPERTAIN)]

APR *abbr.* annual or annualized percentage rate (esp. of interest on loans or credit).

Apr. *abbr.* April.

après-ski /ˌæpreɪˈskiː/ *n.* & *adj.* —*n.* the evening, esp. its social activities, following a day's skiing. —*attrib.adj.* (of clothes, drinks, etc.) appropriate to social activities following skiing. [F]

apricot /ˈeɪprɪˌkɒt/ *n.* & *adj.* —*n.* **1 a** a juicy soft fruit, smaller than a peach, of an orange-yellow colour. **b** the tree, *Prunus armeniaca*, bearing it. **2** the ripe fruit's orange-yellow colour. —*adj.* orange-yellow (*apricot dress*). [Port. *albricoque* or Sp. *albaricoque* f. Arab. *al* the + *barḳuḳ* f. late Gk *praikokion* f. L *praecoquum* var. of *praecox* early-ripe: *apri-* after L *apricus* ripe, *-cot* by assim. to F *abricot*]

April /ˈeɪprɪl, -ˈeɪpr(ə)l/ *n.* the fourth month of the year. □ **April Fool** a person successfully tricked on 1 April. **April**

Fool's (or **Fools'**) **Day** 1 April. The custom of playing tricks on this day has been observed in many countries for hundreds of years, but its origin is unknown. [ME f. L *Aprilis*. The Romans considered this month to be sacred to Venus, goddess of love, and its name may be taken from that of her Greek equivalent APHRODITE]

a priori /ˌeɪ praɪˈɔːraɪ/ *adj.* & *adv.* —*adj.* **1** (of reasoning) deductive; proceeding from causes to effects (opp. A POSTERIORI). **2** (of concepts, knowledge, etc.) logically independent of experience; not derived from experience (opp. EMPIRICAL). **3** not submitted to critical investigation (*an a priori conjecture*). —*adv.* **1** in an a priori manner. **2** as far as one knows; presumptively. □□ **apriorism** /eɪˈpraɪəˌrɪz(ə)m/ *n.* [L, = from what is before]

apron /ˈeɪprən/ *n.* **1 a** a garment covering and protecting the front of a person's clothes, either from chest or waist level, and tied at the back. **b** official clothing of this kind (*bishop's apron*). **c** anything resembling an apron in shape or function. **2** *Theatr.* the part of a stage in front of the curtain. **3** the hard-surfaced area on an airfield used for manoeuvring or loading aircraft. **4** an endless conveyor belt. □ **tied to a person's apron-strings** dominated by or dependent on that person (usu. a woman). □□ **aproned** *adj.* **apronful** *n.* (*pl.* **-fuls**). [ME *naperon* etc. f. OF dimin. of *nape* table-cloth f. L *mappa*: for loss of *n* cf. ADDER]

apropos /ˈæprəˌpəʊ, -ˈpəʊ/ *adj.* & *adv.* —*adj.* **1** to the point or purpose; appropriate (*his comment was apropos*). **2** *colloq.* (often foll. by *of*) in respect of; concerning (*apropos the meeting; apropos of the talk*). —*adv.* **1** appropriately (*spoke apropos*). **2** (*absol.*) by the way; incidentally (*apropos, she's not going*). [F *à propos* f. *à* to + *propos* PURPOSE]

apse /æps/ *n.* **1** a large semicircular or polygonal recess, arched or with a domed roof, esp. at the eastern end of a church. **2** = APSIS. □□ **apsidal** /ˈæpsɪd(ə)l/ *adj.* [L APSIS]

apsis /ˈæpsɪs/ *n.* (*pl.* **apsides** /-ˌdiːz/) either of two points on the orbit of a planet or satellite that are nearest to or furthest from the body round which it moves. □□ **apsidal** *adj.* [L f. Gk (h)*apsis*, *-idos* arch, vault]

APT *abbr.* (in the UK) Advanced Passenger Train.

apt /æpt/ *adj.* **1** appropriate, suitable. **2** (foll. by *to* + infin.) having a tendency (*apt to lose his temper*). **3** clever; quick to learn (*an apt pupil; apt at the work*). □□ **aptly** *adv.* **aptness** *n.* [ME f. L *aptus* fitted, past part. of *apere* fasten]

apterous /ˈæptərəs/ *adj.* **1** *Zool.* (of insects) without wings. **2** *Bot.* (of seeds or fruits) having no winglike expansions. [Gk *apteros* f. *a-* not + *pteron* wing]

apteryx /ˈæptərɪks/ *n.* = KIWI. [mod.L f. Gk *a-* not + *pterux* wing]

aptitude /ˈæptɪˌtjuːd/ *n.* **1** a natural propensity or talent (*shows an aptitude for drawing*). **2** ability or fitness, esp. to acquire a particular skill. [F f. LL *aptitudo -inis* (as APT, -TUDE)]

Apuleius /ˌæpjʊˈliːəs/ (born *c.*123) Latin writer from Africa. Renowned as a declaimer, he wrote a variety of rhetorical and philosophical works. His most famous work is the *Metamorphoses* (better known as *The Golden Ass*), a picaresque novel which recounts the adventures of one Lucius who is transformed into an ass, and which includes the Cupid and Psyche tale. His writings are characterized by an exuberant and bizarre use of language.

Apulia /əˈpjuːlɪə/ (Italian **Puglia** /ˈpjuːlɪeɪ/) a region forming the south-east 'heel' of Italy; pop. (1981) 3,871,600; capital, Bari.

Aqaba /ˈækəbə/ Jordan's only port, at the head of the Gulf of Aqaba; pop. (est. 1983) 40,000.

aqua /ˈækwə/ *n.* the colour aquamarine. [abbr.]

aquaculture /ˈækwəˌkʌltʃə(r), -ˌkʌltʃə(r)/ *n.* the cultivation or rearing of aquatic plants or animals. [L *aqua* water + CULTURE, after *agriculture*]

aqua fortis /ˌækwə ˈfɔːtɪs/ *n.* *Chem.* nitric acid. [L, = strong water]

aqualung /ˈækwəˌlʌŋ/ *n.* & *v.* —*n.* a portable breathing-apparatus for divers, consisting of cylinders of compressed air strapped on the back, feeding air automatically through a mask or mouthpiece. It was first developed in 1943 by Jacques Cousteau and a French engineer Emile Gagnan. —*v.intr.* use an aqualung. [L *aqua* water + LUNG]

aquamarine /ˌækwəməˈriːn/ *n.* **1** a light bluish-green beryl. **2** its colour. [L *aqua marina* sea water]

aquanaut /ˈækwənɔːt/ *n.* an underwater swimmer or explorer. [L *aqua* water + Gk *nautēs* sailor]

aquaplane /ˈækwəˌpleɪn/ *n. & v.* —*n.* a board for riding on the water, pulled by a speedboat. —*v.intr.* **1** ride on an aquaplane. **2** (of a vehicle) glide uncontrollably on the wet surface of a road. [L *aqua* water + PLANE¹]

aqua regia /ˌækwə ˈriːdʒɪə/ *n.* *Chem.* a mixture of concentrated nitric and hydrochloric acids, a highly corrosive liquid attacking many substances unaffected by other reagents. [L, = royal water]

aquarelle /ˌækwəˈrel/ *n.* a painting in thin, usu. transparent water-colours. [F f. It. *acquarella* water-colour, dimin. of *acqua* f. L *aqua* water]

aquarium /əˈkweərɪəm/ *n.* (*pl.* **aquariums** or **aquaria** /-rɪə/) an artificial environment designed for keeping live aquatic plants and animals for study or exhibition, esp. a tank of water with transparent sides. [neut. of L *aquarius* of water (*aqua*) after *vivarium*]

Aquarius /əˈkweərɪəs/ **1** a constellation, traditionally regarded as contained in the figure of a water-carrier. **2** the eleventh sign of the zodiac (the Water-carrier) which the sun enters about 21 Jan. It contains no bright stars but possesses several good examples of planetary nebulae. —*n.* a person born when the sun is in this sign. □□ **Aquarian** *adj. & n.* [ME f. L (as AQUARIUM)]

aquatic /əˈkwætɪk/ *adj. & n.* —*adj.* **1** growing or living in or near water. **2** (of a sport) played in or on water. —*n.* **1** an aquatic plant or animal. **2** (in *pl.*) aquatic sports. [ME f. F *aquatique* or L *aquaticus* f. *aqua* water]

aquatint /ˈækwətɪnt/ *n.* **1** a print resembling a water-colour, produced from a copper plate etched with nitric acid. **2** the process of producing this. The effect is produced by coating a copper plate (or plates) with a porous resin ground, painting the design on it with varnish, immersing it in nitric acid, and inking it, when the protected parts, being less corroded by the acid, will take up less ink. Invented in the 18th c., its use as a landscape medium was pioneered by the topographical artist Paul Sandby in the 1770s, while its combination with line etching reached supreme heights in Goya's graphic work. Although it was somewhat eclipsed by new graphic techniques in the 19th c. there has been a revival of interest in this medium in recent years. [F *aquatinte* f. It. *acqua tinta* coloured water]

aquavit /ˈækwəvɪt, -ˌviːt/ (also **akvavit** /ˈækvə-/) *n.* an alcoholic spirit made from potatoes etc. [Scand.]

aqua vitae /ˌækwə ˈviːtaɪ/ *n.* a strong alcoholic spirit, esp. brandy. [L = water of life]

aqueduct /ˈækwɪˌdʌkt/ *n.* **1** an artificial channel for conveying water, esp. in the form of a bridge supported by tall columns across a valley. **2** *Physiol.* a small canal, esp. in the head of mammals. [L *aquae ductus* conduit f. *aqua* water + *ducere* duct- to lead]

aqueous /ˈeɪkwɪəs/ *adj.* **1** of, containing, or like water. **2** *Geol.* produced by water (*aqueous rocks*). □ **aqueous humour** see HUMOUR. [med.L *aqueus* f. L *aqua* water]

aquifer /ˈækwɪfə(r)/ *n.* *Geol.* a layer of rock or soil able to hold or transmit much water. [L *aqui-* f. *aqua* water + *-fer* bearing f. *ferre* bear]

Aquila /ˈækwɪlə/ a constellation, the Eagle, well seen during midsummer in the northern hemisphere. It contains the first-magnitude star Altair, twelfth brightest in the sky, and some rich star fields of the Milky Way.

aquilegia /ˌækwɪˈliːdʒə/ *n.* any (often blue-flowered) plant of the genus *Aquilegia*. Also called COLUMBINE. [mod. use of a med.L word: orig. unkn.]

aquiline /ˈækwɪˌlaɪn/ *adj.* **1** of or like an eagle. **2** (of a nose) curved like an eagle's beak. [L *aquilinus* f. *aquila* eagle]

Aquinas /əˈkwaɪnəs/, St Thomas (1225–74), a Doctor of the Church, 'the Angelic Doctor', philosopher and theologian, an Italian Dominican friar. His enormous works include many commentaries on Aristotle as well as the *Summa Contra Gentiles* (intended as a manual for those disputing with Spanish Muslims and Jews), and the *Summa Theologiae* (intended as an undergraduate textbook, left unfinished at his death). He probably also wrote hymns for the feast of Corpus Christi. His achievement was to make the work of Aristotle acceptable in Christian Western Europe; his own metaphysics, his account of the human mind, and his moral philosophy, were a development of Aristotle's, and his famous arguments for the existence of God (the 'Five Ways') were indebted to Aristotle and to Arabic philosophers. In theology he maintained a distinction between what could be discovered without special revelation and what could be known only by communication from God. Faith was the acceptance of propositions revealed by God out of trust in God who had revealed them. Feast day, 7 March.

Aquitaine /ˌækwɪˈteɪn/ **1** an ancient province of SW France, comprising at some periods the whole country from the Loire to the Pyrenees. By the marriage of Eleanor of Aquitaine to Henry II it became one of the English possessions in France. **2** a region of modern France; pop. (1982) 2,656,500; capital, Bordeaux.

AR *abbr.* US Arkansas (in official postal use).

Ar *symb.* *Chem.* the element argon.

ar- /ə(r)/ *prefix* assim. form of AD- before *r*.

-ar¹ /ə(r)/ *suffix* **1** forming adjectives (*angular; linear; nuclear; titular*). **2** forming nouns (*scholar*). [OF *-aire* or *-ier* or L *-aris*]

-ar² /ə(r)/ *suffix* forming nouns (*pillar*). [F *-er* or L *-ar, -are*, neut. of *-aris*]

-ar³ /ə(r)/ *suffix* forming nouns (*bursar; exemplar; mortar; vicar*). [OF *-aire* or *-ier* or L *-arius, -arium*]

-ar⁴ /ə(r)/ *suffix* assim. form of -ER¹, -OR¹ (*liar; pedlar*).

ARA *abbr.* Associate of the Royal Academy.

Arab /ˈærəb/ *n. & adj.* —*n.* **1** a member of a Semitic people inhabiting originally the Arabian peninsula and neighbouring countries, now also other parts of the Middle East and North Africa. **2** a horse of a breed orig. native to Arabia. —*adj.* of Arabia or the Arabs (esp. with ethnic reference). [F *Arabe* f. L *Arabs Arabis* f. Gk *Araps -abos* f. Arab. *'arab*]

arabesque /ˌærəˈbesk/ *n.* **1** *Ballet* a posture with one leg extended horizontally backwards, torso extended forwards, and arms outstretched. **2** a design of intertwined leaves, scrolls, etc. **3** *Mus.* a florid melodic section or composition. [F f. It. *arabesco* f. *arabo* Arab]

Arabia /əˈreɪbɪə/ a peninsula of SW Asia, largely desert, lying between the Red Sea and the Persian Gulf and bounded on the north by Jordan and Iraq.

Arabian /əˈreɪbɪən/ *adj. & n.* —*adj.* of or relating to Arabia (esp. with geographical reference) (*the Arabian desert*). —*n.* a native of Arabia. ¶ Now less common than *Arab* in this sense. □ **Arabian camel** a domesticated camel, *Camelus dromedarius*, native to the deserts of N. Africa and the Near East, with one hump: also called DROMEDARY. [ME f. OF *arabi* prob. f. Arab. *'arabī*, or f. L *Arabus, Arabius* f. Gk *Arabios*]

Arabian Desert see EASTERN DESERT.

Arabian Gulf see PERSIAN GULF.

Arabian Nights (in full *Arabian Nights' Entertainments*, also called the 'Thousand and One Nights') a collection of fairy stories and romances written in Arabic, linked together by a framework of Persian origin though the tales themselves are for the most part not Arabian but Persian in character, probably collected in Egypt at some time during the 14th–16th c.

Arabian Sea the north-western part of the Indian Ocean, between Arabia and India.

Arabic /ˈærəbɪk/ *n. & adj.* —*n.* the Semitic language of the Arabs, now spoken in much of N. Africa and the Middle East. (See below.) —*adj.* of or relating to Arabia (esp. with reference to language or literature). □ **arabic numeral** any of the numerals 0, 1, 2, 3, 4, 5, 6, 7, 8, and 9 which reached western Europe through Arabia by about AD 1200 but which probably originated in India. Different symbols are used in modern Arabic. (Cf. *roman numeral*.) [ME f. OF *arabic* f. L *arabicus* f. Gk *arabikos*]

Arabic is a Semitic language related to Hebrew and was originally confined to the Arabian peninsula, but during the Islamic conquests of the 7th c. it was carried eastwards to Iran and Syria and westwards to North Africa and Spain; it is now the official language of a number of countries in the Middle East and North Africa, being the native language of some 120 million people, and in addition is known to many millions of Muslims. There are many dialects of spoken Arabic but one common written language, which is based on 'classical' Arabic, the written form used in the Middle Ages when Arabic was the universal language of the Near and Middle East. It is the language of the Koran and of medieval Arabic literature, and was the chief medium of scientific and philosophical thought for some centuries, bequeathing to us words such as *alcohol*, *elixir*, *azimuth*, *zenith*. Arabic is written from right to left in a traditional script of uncertain origin which is used also for a number of other languages.

arabis /ˈærəbɪs/ *n.* any plant of the genus *Arabis*, low-growing or mat-forming with toothed leaves and usu. white flowers. Also called *rock cress* (see ROCK[1]), *wall cress*. [med.L f. Gk, = Arabian]

Arabist /ˈærəbɪst/ *n.* a student of Arabic civilization, language, etc.

Arabistan /ˌærəbɪˈstɑːn/ the Iraqi name for the Iranian province of Khuzestan.

arable /ˈærəb(ə)l/ *adj.* & *n.* —*adj.* **1** (of land) ploughed, or suitable for ploughing and crop production. **2** (of crops) that can be grown on arable land. —*n.* arable land or crops. [F *arable* or L *arabilis* f. *arare* to plough]

Arab League = LEAGUE OF ARAB STATES.

Araby /ˈærəbɪ/ *n. poet.* Arabia. [OF *Arabie* f. L *Arabia* f. Gk]

Arachne /əˈræknɪ/ *Gk legend* a woman of Colophon in Lydia, a skilful weaver who challenged Athene to a contest. Athene destroyed her work and Arachne hanged herself, but Athene changed her into a spider.

arachnid /əˈræknɪd/ *n.* any arthropod of the class Arachnida, having four pairs of walking legs and characterized by simple eyes, e.g. scorpions, spiders, mites, and ticks. □□ **arachnidan** *adj.* & *n.* [F *arachnide* or mod.L *arachnida* f. Gk *arakhnē* spider]

arachnoid /əˈræknɔɪd/ *n.* & *adj.* —*n.* Anat. (in full **arachnoid membrane**) one of the three membranes (see MENINX) that surround the brain and spinal cord of vertebrates. —*adj.* Bot. covered with long cobweb-like hairs. [mod.L *arachnoides* f. Gk *arakhnoeidēs* like a cobweb f. *arakhnē*: see ARACHNID]

arachnophobia /əˌræknəˈfəʊbɪə/ *n.* Psychol. an abnormal fear of spiders. [mod.L f. Gk *arakhne* spider + -PHOBIA]

Arafat /ˈærəfæt/, Yasser (1929–), Palestinian leader, who in 1969 became head of the Palestine Liberation Organization.

Arafura Sea /ˌærəˈfʊərə/ a sea lying between north Australia and the islands of east Indonesia.

Aragon /ˈærəgən/ a region of Spain, bounded on the north by the Pyrenees and on the east by Catalonia and Valencia; pop. (1986) 1,214,700; capital, Saragossa.

arak var. of ARRACK.

Arakan Coast /ˌɑːrəˈkɑːn/ the north-west coast of Burma, on the Bay of Bengal.

Araldite /ˈærəlˌdaɪt/ *n. propr.* an epoxy resin used as a strong heatproof cement to mend china, plastic, etc. [20th c.: orig. uncert.]

Aral Sea /ˈær(ə)l/ an inland sea of the USSR, east of the Caspian Sea. The diversion for irrigation of the water flowing into the Aral Sea has led to the area of the sea being reduced to two-thirds of its original size between 1960 and 1990.

Aramaic /ˌærəˈmeɪɪk/ *n.* & *adj.* —*n.* a Semitic language of ancient Syria which was used as the lingua franca in the Near East from the 6th c. BC and gradually replaced Hebrew as the language of the Jews in those parts. It was supplanted by Arabic

in the 7th c. AD. A modern form of Aramaic is still spoken in small communities in Syria and Turkey. One of its most important descendants is Syriac; Aramaic was written in the Hebrew alphabet from which the various Syriac scripts developed. —*adj.* of or in Aramaic. [L *Aramaeus* f. Gk *Aramaios* of Aram (bibl. name of Syria)]

Aran /ˈærən/ *adj.* of a type of patterned knitwear characteristic of the **Aran Islands**, a group of three islands off the west coast of Ireland.

Aranda /əˈrændə/ *n.* & *adj.* —*n.* (*pl.* same or **Arandas**) **1** a member of an Aboriginal people of central Australia, noted for their complex system of kinship reckoning. **2** the language of the Aranda. —*adj.* of the Aranda or their language. [native name]

Ararat /ˈærəˌræt/ either of two volcanic peaks of the Armenian plateau in eastern Turkey, near the frontiers of Russia and Iran, of which the higher (Great Ararat, 5,165 m, 16,946 ft.) last erupted in 1840. The mountains are the traditional site of the resting place of Noah's ark after the Flood (Gen. 8: 4).

arational /eɪˈræʃ(ə)n(ə)l/ *adj.* that does not purport to be rational.

Araucanian /ˌærɔːˈkeɪnɪən/ *n.* & *adj.* —*n.* **1** a member of an American Indian people of central Chile and adjacent regions of Argentina. **2** the group of languages spoken by the Araucanians. —*adj.* of the Araucanians or their language. [f. *Araucanía* region of Chile]

araucaria /ˌærɔːˈkeərɪə/ *n.* any evergreen conifer of the genus *Araucaria*, e.g. the monkey-puzzle tree. [mod.L f. *Arauco*, name of a province in Chile]

Arawak /ˈærəˌwæk/ *n.* & *adj.* —*n.* (*pl.* same or **Arawaks**) **1** a member of the American Indian peoples of the Greater Antilles and northern and western South America, speaking languages of the same linguistic family. They were forced out of the Antilles by the more warlike Carib Indians shortly before Spanish expansion in the Caribbean. **2** this family of languages. —*adj.* of the Arawaks or their language. □□ **Arawakan** *adj.* & *n.*

arbalest /ˈɑːbəˌlest/ *n.* (also **arblast** /ˈɑːblɑːst/) *hist.* a crossbow with a mechanism for drawing the string. [OE *arblast* f. OF *arbaleste* f. LL *arcubalista* f. *arcus* bow + BALLISTA]

arbiter /ˈɑːbɪtə(r)/ *n.* (*fem.* **arbitress** /-trɪs/) **1 a** an arbitrator in a dispute. **b** a judge; an authority (*arbiter of taste*). **2** (often foll. by *of*) a person who has entire control of something. □ **arbiter elegantiarum** (or **elegantiae**) /ˌeleˌgæntɪˈɑːrəm, ˌeleˈgænʃɪˌiː/ a judge of artistic taste and etiquette. [L]

arbitrage /ˈɑːbɪˌtrɑːʒ, -trɪdʒ/ *n.* the buying and selling of stocks or bills of exchange to take advantage of varying prices in different markets. [F f. *arbitrer* (as ARBITRATE)]

arbitrageur /ˌɑːbɪtrɑːˈʒɜː(r)/ *n.* (also **arbitrager** /ˈɑːbɪtrɪdʒə(r)/) a person who engages in arbitrage. [F]

arbitral /ˈɑːbɪtr(ə)l/ *adj.* concerning arbitration. [F *arbitral* or LL *arbitralis*: see ARBITER]

arbitrament /ɑːˈbɪtrəmənt/ *n.* **1** the deciding of a dispute by an arbiter. **2** an authoritative decision made by an arbiter. [ME f. OF *arbitrement* f. med.L *arbitramentum* (as ARBITRATE, -MENT)]

arbitrary /ˈɑːbɪtrərɪ/ *adj.* **1** based on or derived from uninformed opinion or random choice; capricious. **2** despotic. □□ **arbitrarily** *adv.* **arbitrariness** *n.* [L *arbitrarius* or F *arbitraire* (as ARBITER, -ARY[1])]

arbitrate /ˈɑːbɪˌtreɪt/ *v.tr.* & *intr.* decide by arbitration. [L *arbitrari* judge]

arbitration /ˌɑːbɪˈtreɪʃ(ə)n/ *n.* the settlement of a dispute by an arbitrator. [ME f. OF f. L *arbitratio -onis* (as ARBITER, -ATION)]

arbitrator /ˈɑːbɪˌtreɪtə(r)/ *n.* a person appointed to settle a dispute; an arbiter. □□ **arbitratorship** *n.* [ME f. LL (as ARBITRATION, -OR[1])]

arbitress see ARBITER.

arblast var. of ARBALEST.

arbor[1] /ˈɑːbə(r)/ *n.* **1** an axle or spindle on which something revolves. **2** US a device holding a tool in a lathe etc. [F *arbre* tree, axis, f. L *arbor*: refashioned on L]

arbor[2] US var. of ARBOUR.

arboraceous /ˌɑːbəˈreɪʃəs/ adj. **1** treelike. **2** wooded. [L arbor tree + -ACEOUS]

Arbor Day /ˈɑːbə/ n. a day set apart by law for the public planting of trees, originally in Nebraska in 1872. It is now observed throughout the US, usually in late April or early May, and has been adopted in Canada, Australia, and New Zealand. [L arbor tree]

arboreal /ɑːˈbɔːrɪəl/ adj. of, living in, or connected with trees. [L arboreus f. arbor tree]

arboreous /ɑːˈbɔːrɪəs/ adj. **1** wooded. **2** arboreal.

arborescent /ˌɑːbəˈres(ə)nt/ adj. treelike in growth or general appearance. □□ **arborescence** n. [L arborescere grow into a tree (arbor)]

arboretum /ˌɑːbəˈriːtəm/ n. (pl. **arboretums** or **arboreta** /-tə/) a botanical garden devoted to trees. [L f. arbor tree]

arboriculture /ˈɑːbərɪˌkʌltʃə(r)/ n. the cultivation of trees and shrubs. □□ **arboricultural** /-ˈkʌltʃər(ə)l/ adj. **arboriculturist** /-ˈkʌltʃərɪst/ n. [L arbor -oris tree, after agriculture]

arborization /ˌɑːbəraɪˈzeɪʃ(ə)n/ n. (also **-isation**) a treelike arrangement esp. in anatomy.

arbor vitae /ˌɑːbə ˈviːtaɪ, ˈvaɪtɪ/ n. any of the evergreen conifers of the genus Thuja, native to N. Asia and N. America, usu. of pyramidal habit with flattened shoots bearing scale leaves. [L, = tree of life]

arbour /ˈɑːbə(r)/ n. (US **arbor**) a shady garden alcove with the sides and roof formed by trees or climbing plants; a bower. □□ **arboured** adj. [ME f. AF erber f. OF erbier f. erbe herb f. L herba: phonetic change to ar- assisted by assoc. with L arbor tree]

Arbuthnot /ɑːˈbʌθnət/, John (1667–1735), Scottish physician, attendant on Queen Anne. He was friend of Swift and acquainted with Pope, Gray, and other literary men, and was the principal author of Memoirs of Martinus Scriblerus (c.1714), a satirical work directed against 'false tastes in learning'. His History of John Bull, a collection of pamphlets (1712) advocating the termination of the war with France, was the origin of 'John Bull', the typical Englishman.

arbutus /ɑːˈbjuːtəs/ n. any evergreen ericaceous tree or shrub of the genus Arbutus, having white or pink clusters of flowers and strawberry-like berries. Also called strawberry-tree. □ **trailing arbutus** US the mayflower, Epigaea repens. [L]

ARC abbr. **1** (in the UK) Agricultural Research Council. **2** Aids-related complex.

arc /ɑːk/ n. & v. —n. **1** part of the circumference of a circle or any other curve. **2** Electr. a luminous discharge between two electrodes. —v.intr. (**arced** /ɑːkt/; **arcing** /ˈɑːkɪŋ/) form an arc. □ **arc lamp** (or **light**) a light source using an electric arc. **arc welding** a method of using an electric arc to melt metals to be welded. [ME f. OF f. L arcus arc, curve]

arcade /ɑːˈkeɪd/ n. **1** a passage with an arched roof. **2** any covered walk, esp. with shops along one or both sides. **3** Archit. a series of arches supporting or set along a wall. □□ **arcaded** adj. [F f. Prov. arcada or It. arcata f. Rmc: rel. to ARCH¹]

Arcadia /ɑːˈkeɪdɪə/ a mountainous and, in antiquity, backward area in the central Peloponnese in Greece, in poetic fantasy the idyllic home of song-loving shepherds.

Arcadian /ɑːˈkeɪdɪən/ n. & adj. —n. an idealized peasant or country dweller, esp. in poetry. —adj. simple and poetically rural. □□ **Arcadianism** n. [L Arcadius f. Gk Arkadia ARCADIA]

Arcady /ˈɑːkədɪ/ n. poet. an ideal rustic paradise. [Gk Arkadia: see ARCADIAN]

arcane /ɑːˈkeɪn/ adj. mysterious, secret; understood by few. □□ **arcanely** adv. [F arcane or L arcanus f. arcēre shut up f. arca chest]

arcanum /ɑːˈkeɪnəm/ n. (pl. **arcana** /-nə/) (usu. in pl.) a mystery; a profound secret. [L neut. of arcanus: see ARCANE]

Arc de Triomphe /ˌɑːk də ˈtriːɒ̃f/ the ceremonial arch standing at the top of the Champs-Élysées in Paris, commissioned by Napoleon I to commemorate his victories in 1805–6. Inspired by the design of the Arch of Constantine in Rome, it was completed in 1836. The Unknown Soldier was buried under the centre of the arch on Armistice Day 1920.

arch¹ /ɑːtʃ/ n. & v. —n. **1 a** a curved structure as an opening or

a support for a bridge, roof, floor, etc. **b** an arch used in building as an ornament. **2** any arch-shaped curve, e.g. as on the inner side of the foot, the eyebrows, etc. —v. **1** tr. provide with or form into an arch. **2** tr. span like an arch. **3** intr. form an arch. [ME f. OF arche ult. f. L arcus arc]

arch² /ɑːtʃ/ adj. self-consciously or affectedly playful or teasing. □□ **archly** adv. **archness** n. [ARCH-, orig. in arch rogue etc.]

arch- /ɑːtʃ/ comb. form **1** chief, superior (archbishop; archdiocese; archduke). **2** pre-eminent of its kind (esp. in unfavourable senses) (arch-enemy). [OE arce- or OF arche-, ult. f. Gk arkhos chief]

Archaean /ɑːˈkiːən/ adj. & n. (US **Archean**) —adj. of or relating to the earlier part of the Precambrian era. —n. this time. [Gk arkhaios ancient f. arkhē beginning]

archaeology /ˌɑːkɪˈɒlədʒɪ/ n. (US **archeology**) the study of human history and prehistory through the excavation of sites and the analysis of physical remains. (See below.) □□ **archaeologic** /-ˈlɒdʒɪk/ adj. **archaeological** /-ˈlɒdʒɪk(ə)l/ adj. **archaeologist** n. **archaeologize** v.intr. (also **-ise**). [mod.L archaeologia f. Gk arkhaiologia ancient history (as ARCHAEAN, -LOGY)]

Archaeology, as a careful study rather than a romantic interest, is not much more than a hundred years old. The major methodological advances began in the second half of the 19th c., and the subject has developed at an increasing pace ever since. Excavation to recover new evidence is one approach, and whereas before the 19th c. the quest was for objects it is now for information of all kinds. Stratigraphy yields evidence of sequence: in a simple undisturbed series of layers the oldest must be at the bottom and the youngest at the top—but the sequence is rarely so simple, and is likely to show phases of rebuilding, periods of abandonment, etc. Typology (study in changes in forms of pottery, tools, etc.) can link finds from one site with those of another. Specialists in many fields have essential contributions to make: palaeontology, botany, and geology are but three of the disciplines that can contribute to the dating and interpretation of evidence, and the archaeologist can now call on scientific aids (e.g. aerial photography, radio-carbon dating) at most stages of the work. Specialized branches of archaeology include marine archaeology (exploration and recovery of ancient shipwrecks, and study of inundated sites), and industrial archaeology (concerned with the recording, while they still survive, of buildings, machines, and communications of the early industrial period—in Britain, notably those of the Industrial Revolution), but the purpose of the work remains the same—to unravel the long and complicated story of mankind's past.

archaeomagnetism /ˌɑːkɪəˈmægnɪtɪz(ə)m/ n. the remanent magnetism of magnetic materials in clay and rocks which have been heated above a certain temperature. On cooling, the orientation and intensity of their magnetism becomes fixed, determined by the direction and intensity of the earth's magnetic field at that time and (under certain conditions) enabling the date of the object or sample to be calculated. [Gk arkhaios ancient + MAGNETISM]

archaeopteryx /ˌɑːkɪˈɒptərɪks/ n. the oldest known fossil bird, Archaeopteryx lithographica, with teeth, feathers, and a reptilian tail. [Gk arkhaios ancient + pterux wing]

archaic /ɑːˈkeɪɪk/ adj. **1 a** antiquated. **b** (of a word etc.) no longer in ordinary use, though retained for special purposes. **2** primitive. **3** of an early period of art or culture, esp. the 7th–6th c. BC in Greece. □□ **archaically** adv. [F archaïque f. Gk arkhaïkos (as ARCHAEAN)]

archaism /ˈɑːkeɪɪz(ə)m/ n. **1** the retention or imitation of the old or obsolete, esp. in language or art. **2** an archaic word or expression. □□ **archaist** n. **archaistic** /-ˈɪstɪk/ adj. [mod.L f. Gk arkhaïsmos f. arkhaïzō (as ARCHAIZE, -ISM)]

archaize /ˈɑːkeɪaɪz/ v. (also **-ise**) **1** intr. imitate the archaic. **2** tr. make (a work of art, literature, etc.) imitate the archaic. [Gk arkhaïzō be old-fashioned f. arkhaios ancient]

Archangel /ˈɑːkˌeɪndʒ(ə)l/ (Russian **Arkhangelsk**) a port of the northern USSR, on the White Sea; pop. (est. 1987) 416,000.

archangel /ˈɑːkˌeɪndʒ(ə)l/ n. **1** an angel of the highest rank. **2** a member of the eighth order of the nine ranks of heavenly beings (see ORDER). □□ **archangelic** /-æn'dʒelɪk/ adj. [OE f. AF archangele f. eccl.L archangelus f. eccl.Gk arkhaggelos (as ARCH-, ANGEL)]

archbishop /ɑːtʃ'bɪʃəp/ n. the chief bishop of a province. [OE (as ARCH-, BISHOP)]

archbishopric /ɑːtʃ'bɪʃəprɪk/ n. the office or diocese of an archbishop. [OE (as ARCH-, BISHOPRIC)]

archdeacon /ɑːtʃ'diːkən/ n. **1** an Anglican cleric ranking below a bishop. **2** a member of the clergy of similar rank in other Churches. □□ **archdeaconry** n. (pl. **-ies**). **archdeaconship** n. [OE arce-, ercediacon, f. eccl.L archidiaconus f. eccl.Gk arkhidiakonos (as ARCH-, DEACON)]

archdiocese /ɑːtʃ'daɪəsɪs/ n. the diocese of an archbishop. □□ **archdiocesan** /ɑːtʃdaɪ'ɒsɪs(ə)n/ adj.

archduke /ɑːtʃ'djuːk/ n. (fem. **archduchess** /-'dʌtʃɪs/) hist. the chief duke (esp. as the title of a son of the Emperor of Austria). □□ **archducal** adj. **archduchy** /-'dʌtʃɪ/ n. (pl. **-ies**). [OF archeduc f. med.L archidux -ducis (as ARCH-, DUKE)]

Archean US var. of ARCHAEAN.

archegonium /ˌɑːkɪ'gəʊnɪəm/ n. (pl. **archegonia** /-nɪə/) Bot. the female sex organ in mosses, ferns, conifers, etc. [L, dimin. of Gk arkhegonos f. arkhe- chief + gonos race]

arch-enemy /ɑːtʃ'enəmɪ/ n. (pl. **-ies**) **1** a chief enemy. **2** the Devil.

archeology US var. of ARCHAEOLOGY.

archer /'ɑːtʃə(r)/ n. **1** a person who shoots with a bow and arrows. **2** (**the Archer**) the zodiacal sign or constellation Sagittarius. □ **archer-fish** a SE Asian fish that catches flying insects by shooting water at them from its mouth. [AF f. OF archier ult. f. L arcus bow]

archery /'ɑːtʃərɪ/ n. shooting with a bow and arrows, esp. as a sport. Bow and arrows were used in prehistoric times by hunters, and for recreation as well as in war by the ancient peoples of Egypt, India, and China. The sport of shooting developed as a pastime after the decline (16th c.) of the bow as a weapon. Modern archery is practised chiefly in the form of shooting at a target. [OF archerie f. archier (as ARCHER, -ERY)]

archetype /'ɑːkɪtaɪp/ n. **1 a** an original model; a prototype. **b** a typical specimen. **2** (in Jungian psychology) a primitive mental image inherited from man's earliest ancestors, and supposed to be present in the collective unconscious. **3** a recurrent symbol or motif in literature, art, etc. □□ **archetypal** /-'taɪp(ə)l/ adj. **archetypical** /-'tɪpɪk(ə)l/ adj. [L archetypum f. Gk arkhetupon (as ARCH-, tupos stamp)]

archidiaconal /ˌɑːkɪdaɪ'ækən(ə)l/ adj. of or relating to an archdeacon. □□ **archidiaconate** /-nət, -ˌneɪt/ n. [med.L archidiaconalis (as ARCH-, DIACONAL)]

archiepiscopal /ˌɑːkɪɪ'pɪskəp(ə)l/ adj. of or relating to an archbishop. □□ **archiepiscopate** /-pət, -ˌpeɪt/ n. [eccl.L archiepiscopus f. Gk arkhiepiskopos arch- bishop]

archil var. of ORCHIL.

Archilochus /ɑː'kɪləkəs/ (8th or 7th c. BC) Greek iambic and elegiac poet, author of satirical verse and fables.

archimandrite /ˌɑːkɪ'mændraɪt/ n. **1** the superior of a large monastery or group of monasteries in the Orthodox Church. **2** an honorary title given to a monastic priest. [F archimandrite or eccl.L archimandrita f. eccl. Gk arkhimandrites (as ARCH-, mandra monastery)]

Archimedean /ˌɑːkɪ'miːdɪən/ adj. of or associated with Archimedes (see entry). □ **Archimedean screw** a device of ancient origin for raising water by means of a spiral tube rotated by a handle. Its principle is also used in many other devices (e.g. a mincing machine).

Archimedes /ˌɑːkɪ'miːdiːz/ (c.287–212 BC) Greek mathematician and inventor, born at Syracuse and killed during the Roman invasion of that city. Popular history knew him as the inventor of marvellous machines used against the Romans in the siege of Syracuse, and of other devices such as the helical screw (still known by his name) for raising water, for his boast 'give me a place to stand on and I will move the earth', and for his discovery of the hydrostatic law (Archimedes' principle) that a

body totally or partially immersed in a fluid is subject to an upward force equal in magnitude to the weight of fluid it displaces. (Legend has it that he made this discovery while taking a bath, and ran through the streets shouting 'Eureka!'.) Among his mathematical discoveries are the ratio of the radius of a circle to its circumference, and formulas for the surface-area and volume of a sphere and of a cylinder.

archipelago /ˌɑːkɪ'peləˌgəʊ/ n. (pl. **-os** or **-oes**) **1** a group of islands. **2** a sea with many islands. [It. arcipelago f. Gk arkhi- chief + pelagos sea (orig. = the Aegean Sea)]

Archipenko /ˌɑːkɪ'peŋkəʊ/, Alexander Porfiryevich (1887–1964), Russian-born sculptor, who took American nationality in 1928. He introduced a new idiom into modern sculpture in works such as Walking Woman (1912), analysing the human figure into geometrical forms and opening parts of it with holes and concavities to create a contrast of solid and void. He combined sculpture and painting, producing works in which forms project from and develop a painted background, and from c.1946 experimented with 'light' sculpture, making structures of Plexiglas lit from within.

architect /'ɑːkɪˌtekt/ n. **1** a designer who prepares plans for buildings, ships, etc., and supervises their construction. **2** (foll. by of) a person who brings about a specified thing (the architect of his own fortune). [F architecte f. It. architetto, or L architectus f. Gk arkhitektōn (as ARCH-, tektōn builder)]

architectonic /ˌɑːkɪtek'tɒnɪk/ adj. & n. —adj. **1** of or relating to architecture or architects. **2** of or relating to the systematization of knowledge. —n. (in pl.; usu. treated as sing.) **1** the scientific study of architecture. **2** the study of the systematization of knowledge. [L architectonicus f. Gk arkhitektonikos (as ARCHITECT)]

architecture /'ɑːkɪˌtektʃə(r)/ n. **1** the art or science of designing and constructing buildings. **2** the style of a building as regards design and construction. **3** buildings or other structures collectively. □□ **architectural** /-'tektʃər(ə)l/ adj. **architecturally** /-'tektʃərəlɪ/ adv. [F architecture or L architectura f. architectus ARCHITECT)]

architrave /'ɑːkɪˌtreɪv/ n. **1** (in classical archi- tecture) a main beam resting across the tops of columns. **2** the moulded frame around a doorway or window. **3** a moulding round the exterior of an arch. [F f. It. (as ARCH-, trave f. L trabs trabis beam)]

archive /'ɑːkaɪv/ n. & v. —n. (usu. in pl.) **1** a collection of esp. public or corporate documents or records. **2** the place where these are kept. —v.tr. **1** place or store in an archive. **2** Computing transfer (data) to a less frequently used file, e.g. from disc to tape. □□ **archival** /ɑː'kaɪv(ə)l/ adj. [F archives (pl.) f. L archi(v)a f. Gk arkheia public records f. arkhē government]

archivist /'ɑːkɪvɪst/ n. a person who maintains and is in charge of archives.

archivolt /'ɑːkɪˌvəʊlt/ n. **1** a band of mouldings round the lower curve of an arch. **2** the lower curve itself from impost to impost of the columns. [F archivolte or It. archivolto (as ARC, VAULT)]

archlute /'ɑːtʃluːt, -ljuːt/ n. a bass lute with an extended neck and unstopped bass strings. [F archiluth (as ARCH-, LUTE¹)]

archon /'ɑːkən, 'ɑːkɒn/ n. each of the nine chief magistrates in ancient Athens. □□ **archonship** n. [Gk arkhōn ruler, = pres. part. of arkhō rule]

archway /'ɑːtʃweɪ/ n. **1** a vaulted passage. **2** an arched entrance.

Arctic /'ɑːktɪk/ adj. & n. —adj. **1** of the north polar regions. (See below.) **2** (**arctic**) colloq. (esp. of weather) very cold. —n. **1** the Arctic regions. **2** (**arctic**) US a thick waterproof overshoe. □ **Arctic Circle** the parallel of latitude 66° 33′ N, forming an imaginary line round this region. [ME f. OF artique f. L ar(c)ticus f. Gk arktikos f. arktos bear, Ursa Major].

With the important exception of Greenland, most of the land in the Arctic is free from snow in the summer. Plants are able to grow (and a number of animals can live on them) even though about a metre below the surface the soil is permanently frozen. Real exploration of Arctic regions began in the 16th c. when northern European nations tried to find a way to the rich trade of China and the East Indies by way of a North-east or North-west passage (see entries) across the Arctic Ocean at a time when the

w we   z zoo   ʃ she   ʒ decision   θ thin   ð this   ŋ ring   x loch   tʃ chip   dʒ jar   (see over for vowels)

longer but easier routes round Africa and South America were secured by Portugal and Spain. In the 19th c. attention turned to reaching the North Pole over the floating sea-ice (see NANSEN); in 1909 the American explorer R. E. Peary was the first man to reach the Pole; the American aviator Richard Byrd claimed to have flown over the North Pole in 1926. As air travel became more regular, flights were made over the polar ice. The last great advance in Arctic travel was the crossing of the polar ocean in 1958 by the atomic-powered submarine *Nautilus*, passing under the ice for 1,600 km (1,000 miles) from the Pacific to the Atlantic.

Arcturus /ɑːkˈtjʊərəs/ the brightest star in the northern sky, in the constellation Boötes. [Gk *arktos* bear + *ouros* guardian, because of its position in a line with the tail of Ursa Major]

arcuate /ˈɑːkjʊət/ *adj.* shaped like a bow; curved. [L *arcuatus* past part. of *arcuare* curve f. *arcus* bow, curve]

arcus senilis /ˌɑːkʊs seˈniːlɪs/ *n.* a narrow opaque band commonly encircling the cornea in old age. [L, lit. 'senile bow']

-ard /əd/ *suffix* **1** forming nouns in depreciatory senses (*drunkard*; *sluggard*). **2** forming nouns in other senses (*bollard*; *Spaniard*; *wizard*). [ME & OF f. G *-hard* hardy (in proper names)]

Ardennes /ɑːˈden/ a forested upland region including parts of Belgium, Luxembourg, and northern France, the scene of fierce fighting in both World Wars.

ardent /ˈɑːd(ə)nt/ *adj.* **1** eager, zealous; (of persons or feelings) fervent, passionate. **2** burning. □□ **ardency** *n.* **ardently** *adv.* [ME f. OF *ardant* f. L *ardens -entis* f. *ardēre* burn]

Ardnamurchan /ˌɑːdnəˈmɜːkən/ the most westerly point on the mainland of Scotland.

ardour /ˈɑːdə(r)/ *n.* (US **ardor**) zeal, burning enthusiasm, passion. [ME f. OF f. L *ardor -oris* f. *ardēre* burn]

arduous /ˈɑːdjuːəs/ *adj.* **1** hard to achieve or overcome; laborious, strenuous. **2** steep, difficult (*an arduous path*). □□ **arduously** *adv.* **arduousness** *n.* [L *arduus* steep, difficult]

are[1] *2nd sing. present* & *1st, 2nd, 3rd pl. present* of BE.

are[2] /ɑː(r)/ *n.* a metric unit of measure, equal to 100 square metres. [F f. L AREA]

area /ˈeərɪə/ *n.* **1** the extent or measure of a surface (*over a large area*; *3 acres in area*; *the area of a triangle*). **2** a region or tract (*the southern area*). **3** a space allocated for a specific purpose (*dining area*; *camping area*). **4** the scope or range of an activity or study. **5** *US* a space below ground level in front of the basement of a building. **6** (prec. by *the*) *Football* = *penalty area*. □□ **areal** *adj.* [L, = vacant piece of level ground]

areaway /ˈeərɪəˌweɪ/ *n. US* = AREA 5.

areca /ˈærɪkə, əˈriːkə/ *n.* any tropical palm of the genus *Areca*, native to Asia. □ **areca nut** the astringent seed of a species of areca, *A. catechu*: also called *betel-nut*. [Port. f. Malayalam *ádekka*]

areg *pl.* of ERG[2].

arena /əˈriːnə/ *n.* **1** the central part of an amphitheatre etc., where contests take place. **2** a scene of conflict; a sphere of action or discussion. □ **arena stage** a stage situated with the audience all round it. [L (*h*)*arena* sand, sand-strewn place of combat]

arenaceous /ˌærɪˈneɪʃəs/ *adj.* **1** (of rocks) containing sand; having a sandy texture. **2** sandlike. **3** (of plants) growing in sand. [L *arenaceus* (as ARENA, -ACEOUS)]

aren't /ɑːnt/ *contr.* **1** are not. **2** (in *interrog.*) am not (*aren't I coming too?*).

areola /æˈrɪələ/ *n.* (*pl.* **areolae** /-liː/) **1** *Anat.* a circular pigmented area, esp. that surrounding a nipple. **2** any of the spaces between lines on a surface, e.g. of a leaf or an insect's wing. □□ **areolar** *adj.* [L, dimin. of *area* AREA]

Areopagus /ˌærɪˈɒpəgəs/ **1** a hill at Athens, where (Acts 17) St Paul preached on the Unknown God. **2** the highest governmental council of ancient Athens, (later) a judicial court, meeting on this hill. [Gk *Areios pagos* hill of Ares]

Arequipa /ˌæreɪˈkiːpə/ the second-largest city in Peru, situated at the foot of the snow-capped El Misti volcano; pop. (est. 1988) 591,700.

Ares /ˈeəriːz/ *Gk Mythol.* the Greek war-god, son of Zeus and Hera. In Rome he was identified with Mars.

arête /æˈret/ *n.* a sharp mountain ridge. [F f. L *arista* ear of corn, fishbone, spine]

argali /ˈɑːgəlɪ/ *n.* (*pl.* same) a large Asiatic wild sheep, *Ovis ammon*, with massive horns. [Mongol]

argent /ˈɑːdʒ(ə)nt/ *n.* & *adj. Heraldry* silver; silvery white. [F f. L *argentum*]

argentiferous /ˌɑːdʒənˈtɪfərəs/ *adj.* containing natural deposits of silver. [L *argentum* + -FEROUS]

Argentina /ˌɑːdʒənˈtiːnə/ a country occupying much of the southern part of South America, characterized by heavily Europeanized cities and a large and often backward interior; pop. (est. 1988) 31,532,500; official language, Spanish; capital, Buenos Aires. The economy is chiefly agricultural, and meat-packing is one of the principal industries, but there has been recent growth in textile, plastic, and engineering industries and development of natural mineral resources, particularly copper. Substantial deposits of oil and natural gas occur in various parts of the country and are of major importance to Argentina's industries. Colonized by the Spanish in the 16th c., Argentina declared its independence in 1816 and played a crucial role in the overthrow of European rule in the rest of South America. After a period of semi-dictatorial rule, the country emerged as a democratic republic in the mid-19th c., but has since had recurrent problems with political instability, periodically falling under military rule, most notably at the time of Juan Peron. In 1982 the Argentinian claim to the Falkland Islands led to an unsuccessful war with Britain. [Sp., f. L *argentum* silver, because the Rio de la Plata (= silver river) district exported it.]

Argentine /ˈɑːdʒənˌtaɪn, -ˌtiːn/ *adj.* & *n.* (also **Argentinian** /-ˈtɪnɪən/) —*adj.* of or relating to Argentina. —*n.* **1** a native or national of Argentina. **2** a person of Argentine descent. □ **the Argentine** Argentina. [Sp. *Argentina* ARGENTINA]

argentine /ˈɑːdʒənˌtaɪn/ *adj.* of silver; silvery. [F *argentin* f. *argent* silver]

argil /ˈɑːdʒɪl/ *n.* clay, esp. that used in pottery. □□ **argillaceous** *adj.* [F *argille* f. L *argilla* f. Gk *argillos* f. *argos* white]

arginine /ˈɑːdʒɪˌniːn, -ˌnaɪn/ *n.* an amino acid present in many animal proteins and an essential nutrient in the vertebrate diet. [G *Arginin*, of uncert. orig.]

Argive /ˈɑːgaɪv/ *adj.* & *n.* —*adj.* **1** of Argos in ancient Greece. **2** *literary* (esp. in Homeric contexts) Greek. —*n.* **1** a citizen of Argos. **2** *literary* (usu. in *pl.*) a Greek. [L *Argivus* f. Gk *Argeios*]

argol /ˈɑːgɒl/ *n.* crude potassium hydrogen tartrate. [ME f. AF *argoile*, of unkn. orig.]

argon /ˈɑːgɒn/ *n. Chem.* an inert gaseous element, of the noble gas group. First isolated in 1894, argon is the earth's commonest noble gas, making up nearly one per cent of its atmosphere by volume. The gas is used in electric-light bulbs to prolong the life of the filament, and also in industry, e.g. in arc welding and the growing of semiconductor crystals, where an inert atmosphere is important. ¶ Symb.: **Ar**; atomic number 18. [Gk, neut. of *argos* idle f. *a-* not + *ergon* work]

Argonauts /ˈɑːgəˌnɔːts/ *n.pl. Gk legend* the heroes who accompanied Jason on board the ship *Argo* on the quest for the Golden Fleece. Their story is one of the oldest Greek sagas, known to Homer, and may reflect early explorations in the Black Sea, but it is diversified with typical fairy-tale elements. [Gk, = sailor in the *Argo*]

Argos /ˈɑːgɒs/ an ancient Greek town of the eastern Peloponnese, from which the peninsula of Argolis derived its name.

argosy /ˈɑːgəsɪ/ *n.* (*pl.* **-ies**) *poet.* a large merchant ship, orig. esp. from Ragusa (now Dubrovnik) or Venice. [prob. It. *Ragusea* (*nave*) Ragusan (vessel)]

argot /ˈɑːgəʊ/ *n.* the jargon of a group or class, formerly esp. of criminals. [F: orig. unkn.]

arguable /ˈɑːgjʊəb(ə)l/ *adj.* **1** that may be argued or reasonably proposed. **2** reasonable; supported by argument. □□ **arguably** *adv.*

argue /'ɑːgjuː/ v. (**argues, argued, arguing**) **1** intr. (often foll. by *with, about,* etc.) exchange views or opinions, especially heatedly or contentiously (with a person). **2** tr. & intr. (often foll. by *that* + clause) indicate; maintain by reasoning. **3** intr. (foll. by *for, against*) reason (*argued against joining*). **4** tr. treat by reasoning (*argue the point*). **5** tr. (foll. by *into, out of*) persuade (*argued me into going*). □ **argue the toss** colloq. dispute a decision or choice already made. □□ **arguer** n. [ME f. OF *arguer* f. L *argutari* prattle, frequent. of *arguere* make clear, prove, accuse]

argufy /'ɑːgjʊˌfaɪ/ v.intr. (**-ies, -ied**) colloq. argue excessively or tediously. [fanciful f. ARGUE: cf. SPEECHIFY]

argument /'ɑːgjʊmənt/ n. **1** an exchange of views, esp. a contentious or prolonged one. **2** (often foll. by *for, against*) a reason advanced; a reasoning process (*an argument for abolition*). **3** a summary of the subject-matter or line of reasoning of a book. **4** Math. an independent variable determining the value of a function. [ME f. OF f. L *argumentum* f. *arguere* (as ARGUE, -MENT)]

argumentation /ˌɑːgjʊmenˈteɪʃ(ə)n/ n. **1** methodical reasoning. **2** debate or argument. [F f. L *argumentatio* f. *argumentari* (as ARGUMENT, -ATION)]

argumentative /ˌɑːgjʊˈmentətɪv/ adj. **1** fond of arguing; quarrelsome. **2** using methodical reasoning. □□ **argumentatively** adv. **argumentativeness** n. [F *argumentatif* -ive or LL *argumentativus* (as ARGUMENT, -ATIVE)]

Argus /'ɑːgəs/ **1** Gk Mythol. a monster with many eyes, slain by Hermes. After his death he turned into a peacock, or Hera took his eyes to deck its tail. **2** Gk legend the dog of Ulysses, who recognized his master on his return from Troy after an absence of 20 years. — n. **1** a watchful guardian. **2** an Asiatic pheasant having markings on its tail resembling eyes. **3** a butterfly having markings resembling eyes. □ **Argus-eyed** vigilant. [ME f. L f. Gk *Argos*]

argute /ɑːˈgjuːt/ adj. literary **1** sharp or shrewd. **2** (of sounds) shrill. □□ **argutely** adv. [ME f. L *argutus* past part. of *arguere*: see ARGUE]

argy-bargy /ˌɑːdʒɪˈbɑːdʒɪ/ n. & v.joc. — n. (pl. **-ies**) a dispute or wrangle. — v.intr. (**-ies, -ied**) quarrel, esp. loudly. [orig. Sc.]

Århus see AARHUS.

aria /'ɑːrɪə/ n. Mus. a long accompanied song for solo voice in an opera, oratorio, etc. [It.]

Ariadne /ˌærɪˈædnɪ/ Gk Mythol. the daughter of Minos and Pasiphae. She helped Theseus to escape from the labyrinth of the Minotaur by providing him with a clue of thread. He then fled, taking her with him, but deserted her on the island of Naxos, where she was found and married by Dionysus. It is probable that she was originally a goddess, Minoan in origin.

Arian /'eərɪən/ n. & adj. — n. an adherent of the doctrine of Arius (see entry), who denied the divinity of Christ. — adj. of or concerning this doctrine. □□ **Arianism** n.

-arian /'eərɪən/ suffix forming adjectives and nouns meaning '(one) concerned with or believing in' (*agrarian; antiquarian; humanitarian; vegetarian*). [L *-arius* (see -ARY[1])]

Arianism /'eərɪənɪz(ə)m/ n. the principal heresy denying the divinity of Christ, named after its author Arius (see entry). Arianism maintained that the Son of God was not eternal but was created by the Father from nothing as an instrument for the creation of the world; the Son was therefore not coeternal with the Father, nor of the same substance. The heresy was condemned by the Council of Nicaea in 325 and again at Constantinople in 381, but though driven from the Empire it retained a foothold among Teutonic tribes until the conversion of the Franks to Catholicism (496).

arid /'ærɪd/ adj. **1 a** (of ground, climate, etc.) dry, parched. **b** too dry to support vegetation; barren. **2** un- interesting (*arid verse*). □□ **aridity** /əˈrɪdɪtɪ/ n. **aridly** adv. **aridness** n. [F *aride* or L *aridus* f. *arēre* be dry]

Aries /'eəriːz/ **1** a constellation, traditionally regarded as contained in the figure of a ram. **2** the first sign of the zodiac (the Ram), which the sun enters at the vernal equinox (see PRECESSION OF THE EQUINOXES). — n. (pl. same) a person born when the sun is in this sign. □□ **Arian** /-rɪən/ adj. & n. [ME f. L, = ram]

aright /əˈraɪt/ adv. rightly. [OE (as A[2], RIGHT)]

aril /'ærɪl/ n. Bot. an extra seed-covering, often coloured and hairy or fleshy, e.g. the red fleshy cup around a yew seed. □□ **arillate** adj. [mod.L *arillus*: cf. med.L *arilli* dried grape-stones]

Arion /əˈraɪən/ (7th c. BC) Greek poet and musician of Lesbos, said to have perfected the dithyramb. According to legend, sailors on a ship resolved to murder him but he leapt overboard and was carried safely ashore by one of the dolphins that had been attracted by his music.

Ariosto /ˌærɪˈɒstəʊ/, Ludovico (1474–1533), Italian poet. His *Orlando Furioso* (final version 1532), about the exploits of Roland (Orlando) and other knights of Charlemagne, was the greatest of the Italian romantic epics. It was a continuation of Boiardo's *Orlando Innamorato* (1487), and influenced Spenser's *Faerie Queene*.

-arious /'eərɪəs/ suffix forming adjectives (*gregarious; vicarious*). [L *-arius* (see -ARY[1]) + -OUS]

arise /əˈraɪz/ v.intr. (past **arose** /əˈrəʊz/; past part. **arisen** /əˈrɪz(ə)n/) **1** begin to exist; originate. **2** (usu. foll. by *from, out of*) result (*accidents can arise from carelessness*). **3** come to one's notice; emerge (*the question of payment arose*). **4** rise, esp. from the dead. [OE *ārīsan* (as A-[2], RISE)]

arisings /əˈraɪzɪŋz/ n.pl. materials forming the secondary or waste products of industrial operations.

Aristarchus[1] /ˌærɪˈstɑːkəs/ of Samos (3rd c. BC), Greek astronomer. Founder of an important school of Hellenic astronomy, he was aware of the rotation of the Earth and, by placing the sun at the centre of the universe, was able to account for the seasons. He knew that the sun must be larger than Earth and that the stars must be very distant. Many of his theories were more accurate than those of Ptolemy which replaced them.

Aristarchus[2] /ˌærɪˈstɑːkəs/ of Samothrace (c.217–145 BC), librarian at Alexandria who produced critical editions of the writings of Homer, Hesiod, Pindar, and other Greek authors, also commentaries and treatises upon their works, and is regarded as the originator of scientific scholarship.

Aristides /ˌærɪˈstaɪdiːz/ 'the Just' (5th c. BC), Athenian statesman and general. In the Persian Wars he commanded the Athenian army at the battle of Plataea in 479 BC, and was subsequently prominent in founding the Athenian empire. His renowned honesty was contrasted with the deceitfulness of his colleague and rival Themistocles.

Aristippus /æˈrɪstɪpəs/ the name of two Greek philosophers: the elder (late 5th c. BC), a native of Cyrene and friend of Socrates, is often called the founder of the Cyrenaic school, probably by confusion with the younger, his grandson, who taught that immediate pleasure is the only purpose of action.

aristocracy /ˌærɪˈstɒkrəsɪ/ n. (pl. **-ies**) **1 a** the highest class in society; the nobility. **b** the nobility as a ruling class. **2 a** government by the nobility or a privileged group. **b** a State governed in this way. **3** (often foll. by *of*) the best representatives or upper echelons (*aristocracy of intellect; aristocracy of labour*). [F *aristocratie* f. Gk *aristokratia* f. *aristos* best + *kratia* (as -CRACY)]

aristocrat /'ærɪstəˌkræt/ n. a member of the nobility. [F *aristocrate* (as ARISTOCRATIC)]

aristocratic /ˌærɪstəˈkrætɪk/ adj. **1** of or relating to the aristocracy. **2 a** distinguished in manners or bearing. **b** grand; stylish. □□ **aristocratically** adv. [F *aristocratique* f. Gk *aristokratikos* (as ARISTO- CRACY)]

Aristophanes /ˌærɪˈstɒfəniːz/ (c.450–c.385 BC) the greatest poet of Old Attic Comedy. His eleven surviving plays, characterized by fantasy of invention and exuberance of language, are largely occupied with topical themes; he satirizes politicians and intellectuals (e.g. Socrates), and parodies contemporary poets such as Aeschylus and Euripides. Political and social fantasy is a common theme, seen in the city of the birds ('Cloud-cuckoo-land') in the *Birds*, in the women's sex-strike for peace in the *Lysistrata*, and in the restoration of sight (and hence of proper discrimination) to the god of wealth in his last extant play, the *Plutus*.

Aristotelian /ˌærɪstəˈtiːlɪən/ n. & adj. — n. a disciple or student of the Greek philosopher Aristotle (see entry). — adj. of or concerning Aristotle or his ideas.

Aristotle /ˈærɪˌstɒt(ə)l/ (384–322 BC) Greek philosopher. A pupil of Plato, and tutor to Alexander the Great, in 335 BC he founded a school and library (the Lyceum) just outside Athens. His surviving written works, in the form of dry lecture notes, constitute a vast system of analysis, covering logic, physical science, zoology, psychology, metaphysics, ethics, politics, and rhetoric. In reasoning, he established the inductive method. In metaphysics, he reacted against the mystical speculation of Plato, whose Theory of Forms he rejected; for him form and matter were the inseparable constituents of all existing things. As an empirical scientific observer he had no rival in antiquity. The science in which he was most at home was biology, describing correctly the stomach of ruminants and the development of the chick embryo, and classifying animals by means of a scale ascending to man (without implying evolution). His work in this field was not fully appreciated until the 19th c.: Darwin acknowledges a debt to him. His influence in all fields has been immense: from the 9th c. it pervaded Islamic philosophy, theology, and science, and, after being lost to the West for some centuries, became the basis of scholasticism; in astronomy, his rejection of the idea of the plurality of planets was a serious handicap to later thinking. An ancient tradition describes him as bald, with thin legs, small eyes, and a lisp, and as being noticeably well-dressed. A number of extant statues (e.g. one in the Vienna Museum) probably represent him.

Arita /əˈriːtə/ n. (usu. attrib.) a type of Japanese porcelain characterized by asymmetric decoration. [Arita in Japan]

arithmetic n. & adj. —n. /əˈrɪθmətɪk/ 1 a the science of numbers. b one's knowledge of this (have improved my arithmetic). 2 the use of numbers; computation (a problem involving arithmetic). —adj. /ˌærɪθˈmetɪk/ (also **arithmetical** /-ˈmetɪk(ə)l/) of or concerning arithmetic. □ **arithmetic mean** the central number in an arithmetic progression. **arithmetic progression** 1 an increase or decrease by a constant quantity (e.g. 1, 2, 3, 4, etc., 9, 7, 5, 3, etc.). 2 a sequence of numbers showing this. □□ **arithmetician** /əˌrɪθməˈtɪʃ(ə)n/ n. [ME f. OF arismetique f. L arithmetica f. Gk arithmētikē (tekhnē) art of counting f. arithmos number]

-arium /ˈeərɪəm/ suffix forming nouns usu. denoting a place (aquarium; planetarium). [L, neut. of adjs. in -arius: see -ARY[1]]

Arius /ˈeərɪəs/ (c.250–c.336) a priest of Alexandria, who initiated the heresy named after him (see ARIANISM).

Ariz. abbr. Arizona.

Arizona /ˌærɪˈzəʊnə/ a State in the south-western US; pop. (est. 1985) 2,718,400; capital, Phoenix. It was acquired from Mexico in 1848 and 1854, and became the 48th State of the US in 1912.

Ark. abbr. Arkansas.

ark /ɑːk/ n. 1 = NOAH'S ARK 1. 2 archaic a chest or box. □ **Ark of the Covenant** (or **Testimony**) a chest or cupboard containing the scrolls or tables of Jewish Law. **out of the ark** colloq. very antiquated. [OE ærc f. L arca chest]

Arkansas /ˈɑːkənsɔː/ a State in the south central US, bordering on the Mississippi; pop. (est. 1985) 2,286,350; capital, Little Rock. It was acquired by the US in 1803 as part of the Louisiana Purchase and became the 25th State in 1836.

Arkwright /ˈɑːkraɪt/, Sir Richard (1732–92), English pioneer of mechanical cotton-spinning, using first animal- then water-power, so that his spinning machines became known as water frames. He also improved the preparatory processes, including carding, and established spinning mills in Lancashire, Derbyshire, and Scotland. He became rich and powerful, succeeding by fairly ruthless determination and by incorporating the work of others (which led to a number of patent actions); nevertheless he must be regarded as one who made a great contribution to the establishment of the cotton industry.

arm[1] /ɑːm/ n. 1 each of the two upper limbs of the human body from the shoulder to the hand. 2 a the forelimb of an animal. b the flexible limb of an invertebrate animal (e.g. an octopus). 3 a the sleeve of a garment. b the side part of a chair etc., used to support a sitter's arm. c a thing resembling an arm in branching from a main stem (an arm of the sea). d a large branch of a tree. 4 a control; a means of reaching (arm of the law). □ **an**

arm and a leg a large sum of money. **arm in arm** (of two or more persons) with arms linked. **arm-wrestling** a trial of strength in which each party tries to force the other's arm down on to a table on which their elbows rest. **as long as your** (or **my) arm** colloq. very long. **at arm's length 1** as far as an arm can reach. **2** far enough to avoid undue familiarity. **in arms** (of a baby) too young to walk. **in a person's arms** embraced. **on one's arm** supported by one's arm. **under one's arm** between the arm and the body. **within arm's reach** reachable without moving one's position. **with open arms** cordially. □□ **armful** n. (pl. **-fuls**). **armless** adj. [OE f. Gmc]

arm[2] /ɑːm/ n. & v. —n. 1 (usu. in pl.) a a weapon. b = FIREARM. 2 (in pl.) the military profession. 3 a branch of the military (e.g. infantry, cavalry, artillery, etc.). 4 (in pl.) heraldic devices (coat of arms). —v.tr. & refl. 1 (also absol.) supply with weapons. 2 supply with tools or other requisites or advantages (armed with the truth). 3 make (a bomb etc.) able to explode. □ **arms control** international disarmament or arms limitation, esp. by mutual agreement. **arms race** a contest for superiority in nuclear weapons, esp. between East and West. **in arms** armed. **lay down one's arms** cease fighting. **take up arms** begin fighting. **under arms** ready for war or battle. **up in arms** (usu. foll. by against, about) actively rebelling. □□ **armless** adj. [ME f. OF armes (pl.), armer, f. L arma arms, fittings]

armada /ɑːˈmɑːdə/ n. a fleet of warships, especially (**Armada**) a Spanish naval invasion force sent against England in 1588 by Philip II of Spain. The Armada, 129 ships strong and carrying almost 20,000 soldiers, was defeated in the Channel by a smaller English fleet before it could rendezvous with a Spanish army waiting in the Low Countries to be ferried across to England. The scattered survivors of the Armada tried to reach home by sailing north round Scotland, but many were lost to storms. [Sp. f. Rmc armata army]

armadillo /ˌɑːməˈdɪləʊ/ n. (pl. **-os**) any nocturnal insect-eating mammal of the family Dasypodidae, native to Central and S. America, with large claws for digging and a body covered in bony plates, often rolling itself into a ball when threatened. [Sp. dimin. of armado armed man f. L armatus past part. of armare ARM[2]]

Armageddon /ˌɑːməˈged(ə)n/ n. 1 a (in the New Testament) the last battle between good and evil before the Day of Judgement. b the place where this will be fought. 2 a bloody battle or struggle on a huge scale. [Gk f. Heb. har megiddōn hill of Megiddo: see Rev. 16: 16]

Armagh /ɑːˈmɑː/ 1 a county of Northern Ireland; pop. (1981) 118,820. 2 its county town; pop. (1981) 12,700.

Armagnac /ˈɑːmənjæk/ a district of Aquitaine in SW France, noted for its production of brandy.

armament /ˈɑːməmənt/ n. 1 (often in pl.) military weapons and equipment, esp. guns on a warship. 2 the process of equipping for war. 3 a force equipped for war. [L armamentum (as ARM[2], -MENT)]

armamentarium /ˌɑːməmenˈteərɪəm/ n. (pl. **armamentaria** /-rɪə/) 1 a set of medical equipment or drugs. 2 the resources available to a person engaged in a task. [L, = arsenal]

armature /ˈɑːmətjʊə(r)/ n. 1 a the rotating coil or coils of a dynamo or electric motor. b any moving part of an electrical machine in which a voltage is induced by a magnetic field. 2 a piece of soft iron placed in contact with the poles of a horseshoe magnet to preserve its power. Also called KEEPER. 3 Biol. the protective covering of an animal or plant. 4 a metal framework on which a sculpture is moulded with clay or similar material. 5 archaic arms; armour. [F f. L armatura armour (as ARM[2], -URE)]

armband /ˈɑːmbænd/ n. a band worn around the upper arm to hold up a shirtsleeve or as a form of identification etc.

armchair /ɑːmˈtʃeə(r), ˈɑːm-/ n. 1 a comfortable, usu. upholstered, chair with side supports for the arms. 2 (attrib.) theoretical rather than active or practical (an armchair critic).

Armenia /ɑːˈmiːnɪə/ 1 the country of the Armenians, a former kingdom in western Asia (Mount Ararat lies within it), most of which was under Turkish rule from the 16th c. and which is now divided between Turkey, Iran, and the USSR (see below). 2

---

b but d dog f few g get h he j yes k cat l leg m man n no p pen r red s sit t top v voice

the Armenian republic, a constituent republic of the USSR lying south of the Caucasus; pop. (est. 1987) 3,412,000; capital, Erivan.

In the early 19th c. the Russians advanced into the crumbling Ottoman empire, and in 1828 the Sultan was obliged to surrender part of the Armenian homeland. In 1915 the Turks, at war with Russia, suspected their Armenian subjects of sympathizing with kinsmen across the border and with the Western forces who had embarked on the Dardanelles campaign, and decided on mass deportation of 1,750,000 Armenians to the deserts of Syria and Mesopatamia. The long march involved massive loss of life and resulted in deep and lasting Armenian hatred towards the Turks.

Armenian /ɑːˈmiːnɪən/ n. & adj. —n. **1 a** a native of Armenia (see entry). **b** a person of Armenian descent. **2** the language of Armenia, which constitutes a separate branch of the Indo-European language group although its vocabulary has been substantially influenced by Iranian languages. There are some 4 million speakers of the modern language of whom about 3 million live in the Soviet Union. Its characteristic alphabet contains 38 letters and was invented in AD 400 by missionaries. **3** a member of the reputedly Monophysite Church established in Armenia c.300. —adj. of or relating to Armenia, its language, or the Christian Church established there.

armhole /ˈɑːmhəʊl/ n. each of two holes in a garment through which the arms are put, usu. into a sleeve.

armiger /ˈɑːmɪdʒə(r)/ n. a person entitled to heraldic arms. □□ **armigerous** /-ˈmɪdʒərəs/ adj. [L, = bearing arms, f. arma arms + gerere bear]

armillary /ɑːˈmɪlərɪ/ adj. relating to bracelets. □ **armillary sphere** hist. a representation of the celestial globe constructed from metal rings and showing the equator, the tropics, etc. [mod.L armillaris f. L armilla bracelet]

Arminian /ɑːˈmɪnɪən/ adj. & n. —adj. relating to the doctrine of Jacobus Arminius (Latinized name of Jakob Hermandszoon, 1560–1609), a Dutch Protestant theologian who rejected the Calvinist doctrines of predestination and election. —n. an adherent of this doctrine. □□ **Arminianism** n.

armistice /ˈɑːmɪstɪs/ n. a stopping of hostilities by common agreement of the opposing sides; a truce. □ **Armistice Day** 11 Nov., the anniversary of the armistice that ended the First World War, now replaced by Remembrance Sunday and (in the US) Veterans Day. [F armistice or mod.L armistitium, f. arma arms (ARM²) + -stitium stoppage]

armlet /ˈɑːmlɪt/ n. **1** a band worn round the arm. **2** a small inlet of the sea, or branch of a river.

armor US var. of ARMOUR.

armorer US var. of ARMOURER.

armory¹ /ˈɑːmərɪ/ n. (pl. **-ies**) heraldry. □□ **armorial** /ɑːˈmɔːrɪəl/ adj. [OF armoirie: see ARMOURY]

armory² US var. of ARMOURY.

armour /ˈɑːmə(r)/ n. & v. (US **armor**) —n. **1** a defensive covering, usu. of metal, formerly worn to protect the body in fighting. **2 a** (in full **armour-plate**) a protective metal covering for an armed vehicle, ship, etc. **b** armoured fighting vehicles collectively. **3** a protective covering or shell on certain animals and plants. **4** heraldic devices. —v.tr. (usu. as **armoured** adj.) provide with a protective covering, and often with guns (armoured car; armoured train). [ME f. OF armure f. L armatura: see ARMATURE]

armourer /ˈɑːmərə(r)/ n. (US **armorer**) **1** a maker or repairer of arms or armour. **2** an official in charge of a ship's or a regiment's arms. [AF armurer, OF -urier (as ARMOUR, -ER⁵)]

armoury /ˈɑːmərɪ/ n. (US **armory**) (pl. **-ies**) **1** a place where arms are kept; an arsenal. **2** an array of weapons, defensive resources, usable material, etc. **3** US a place where arms are manufactured. [ME f. OF armoirie, armoierie f. armoier to blazon f. arme ARM²: assim. to ARMOURY]

armpit /ˈɑːmpɪt/ n. **1** the hollow under the arm at the shoulder. **2** US colloq. a place or part considered disgusting or contemptible (the armpit of the world).

armrest /ˈɑːmrest/ n. = ARM¹ 3b.

Armstrong¹ /ˈɑːmstrɒŋ/, Edwin Howard (1890–1954), American electrical engineer, inventor of the superheterodyne radio receiver and the frequency modulation system in radio. The former involved him in bitter legal wrangles with Lee De Forest (see entry), inventor of the triode valve. The frequency modulation system, which is now dominant, removed the static that had ruined much early broadcasting; it created a carrier wave that natural static could not penetrate. Armstrong developed it during the 1930s, but since it required a basic change in existing transmitters and receivers the established radio industry was reluctant to accept it. The Second World War further delayed matters, and even after the war the system became accepted only slowly, while Armstrong was again involved in legal battles to protect his patent. Ill and depressed, he committed suicide in 1954.

Armstrong² /ˈɑːmstrɒŋ/, Louis (1900–71), known as 'Satchmo' (an abbreviation of 'Satchelmouth'), was born in New Orleans and grew up with the strains of ragtime about him, and became one of the great masters of Dixieland jazz. He learnt the trumpet in a waifs' home and played in jazz bands on the Mississippi river-boats, forming his own band in 1928. He was a distinctive singer as well as a trumpet player and had a brilliant talent for improvisation.

Armstrong³ /ˈɑːmstrɒŋ/, Neil Alden (1930–), American astronaut, the first man to set foot on the moon (30 July 1969).

army /ˈɑːmɪ/ n. (pl. **-ies**) **1** an organized force armed for fighting on land (see below). **2** (prec. by the) the military profession. **3** (often foll. by of) a very large number (an army of locusts; an army of helpers). **4** an organized body regarded as fighting for a particular cause (Salvation Army). □ **army ant** any ant of the subfamily Dorylinae, foraging in large groups. **Army List** Brit. an official list of commissioned officers. **army worm** any of various moth or fly larvae occurring in destructive swarms. [ME f. OF armee f. Rmc armata fem. past part. of armare arm]

In Britain, until the mid-17th c. the army consisted chiefly of soldiers engaged only for the duration of particular campaigns. In 1644 Oliver Cromwell raised his New Model Army, and from then onwards a regular standing army was maintained at all times. At the Restoration in 1660 the army became dependent on the Crown, but after the Revolution of 1688 Parliament took over from the king the control and payment of the army.

Arne /ɑːn/, Thomas (1710–78), English composer who made a distinctive contribution to 18th-c. theatrical music, especially with his operas Artaxerxes (1762), in the Italian style, and Thomas and Sally (1760) and Love in a Village (1762), which are purely English in flavour. His famous song 'Rule, Britannia' was composed for the masque Alfred (1740).

Arnhem /ˈɑːnəm/ the capital of the Dutch province of Gelderland, situated on the Rhine near its junction with the IJssel. Founded in the 13th c., it prospered in the Middle Ages as a river trading port. In September 1944 British airborne troops made a famous landing on the nearby Veluwe moorland but were overwhelmed by superior German forces.

Arnhem Land /ˈɑːnəm/ a peninsula in Northern Territory, Australia, situated to the west of the Gulf of Carpentaria. The chief town in Nhulunbuy.

arnica /ˈɑːnɪkə/ n. **1** any composite plant of the genus Arnica, having erect stems bearing yellow daisy-like flower heads, e.g. mountain tobacco. **2** a medicine prepared from this, used for bruises etc. [mod.L: orig. unkn.]

Arno /ˈɑːnəʊ/ a river of northern Italy, flowing through Florence and Pisa.

Arnold /ˈɑːnəld/, Matthew (1822–88), English poet and critic, eldest son of Thomas Arnold, headmaster of Rugby. He published his first volume of poetry (which contained 'The Forsaken Merman') in 1849. In 1851 he became an inspector of schools, and, while he continued to publish poetry (including 'The Scholar Gipsy' (1853), a pastoral lament, and 'Dover Beach' (1867), a characteristic expression of the religious doubts and personal affirmations of the 19th c.) he turned increasingly to prose, becoming, with such works as Culture and Anarchy, one of the most influential social critics of his time, whose views on religion, education, and the need for a more European culture, provided a challenge to the materialism and complacency of Victorian prosperity.

w we   z zoo   ʃ she   ʒ decision   θ thin   ð this   ŋ ring   x loch   tʃ chip   dʒ jar   (see over for vowels)

aroid /ˈeərɔɪd/ *adj.* of or relating to the family Araceae, including arums. [ARUM + -OID]

aroma /əˈrəʊmə/ *n.* **1** a fragrance; a distinctive and pleasing smell, often of food. **2** a subtle pervasive quality. [L f. Gk *arōma -atos* spice]

aromatherapy /əˌrəʊməˈθerəpɪ/ *n.* the use of plant extracts and essential oils in massage. □□ **aromatherapeutic** /-ˈpjuːtɪk/ *adj.* **aromatherapist** *n.*

aromatic /ˌærəˈmætɪk/ *adj. & n.* —*adj.* **1** fragrant, spicy; (of a smell) pleasantly pungent. **2** *Chem.* of organic compounds having an unsaturated ring, esp. containing a benzene ring. —*n.* an aromatic substance. □□ **aromatically** *adv.* **aromaticity** /ˌærəməˈtɪsɪtɪ/ *n.* [ME f. OF *aromatique* f. LL *aromaticus* f. Gk *arōmatikos* (as AROMA, -IC)]

aromatize /əˈrəʊməˌtaɪz/ *v.tr. Chem.* convert (a compound) into an aromatic structure. □□ **aromatization** /-ˈzeɪʃ(ə)n/ *n.*

arose *past of* ARISE.

around /əˈraʊnd/ *adv. & prep.* —*adv.* **1** on every side; all round; round about. **2** in various places; here and there; at random (*fool around; shop around*). **3** *colloq.* **a** in existence; available (*has been around for weeks*). **b** near at hand (*it's good to have you around*). —*prep.* **1** on or along the circuit of. **2** on every side of; enveloping. **3** here and there in or near (*chairs around the room*). **4** *US* (and increasingly *Brit.*) **a** round (*the church around the corner*). **b** approximately at; at a time near to (*come around four o'clock; happened around June*). □ **have been around** *colloq.* be widely experienced. [A² + ROUND]

arouse /əˈraʊz/ *v.tr.* **1** induce; call into existence (esp. a feeling, emotion, etc.). **2** awake from sleep. **3** stir into activity. **4** stimulate sexually. □□ **arousable** *adj.* **arousal** *n.* **arouser** *n.* [A-² + ROUSE]

Arp /ɑːp/, Jean (Hans Arp, 1887–1966), French painter, sculptor, and poet, born in Strasbourg which was then under German rule. He was associated with several of the most important movements in European art in the first half of the 20th c. —expressionism, constructivism, dada, surrealism—but is principally famous for the abstract sculptures, conveying a suggestion of organic forms and growth without reproducing actual plant and animal shapes, which he began to produce in the 1930s. His wife and occasional collaborator was the Swiss artist Sophie Taeuber (1889–1943).

arpeggio /ɑːˈpedʒɪəʊ/ *n.* (pl. **-os**) *Mus.* the notes of a chord played in succession, either ascending or descending. [It. f. *arpeggiare* play the harp f. *arpa* harp]

arquebus var. of HARQUEBUS.

arr. *abbr.* **1** *Mus.* arranged by. **2** arrives.

arrack /ˈærək/ *n.* (also **arak** /əˈræk/) an alcoholic spirit, esp. distilled from coco sap or rice. [Arab. *'araḳ* sweat, alcoholic spirit from grapes or dates]

arraign /əˈreɪn/ *v.tr.* **1** indict before a tribunal; accuse. **2** find fault with; call into question (an action or statement). □□ **arraignment** *n.* [ME f. AF *arainer* f. OF *araisnier* (ult. as AD-, L *ratio -onis* reason, discourse)]

Arran /ˈærən/ an island in the Firth of Clyde, Strathclyde region, in the west of Scotland.

arrange /əˈreɪndʒ/ *v.* **1** *tr.* put into the required order; classify. **2** *tr.* plan or provide for; cause to occur (*arranged a meeting*). **3** *tr.* settle beforehand the order or manner of. **4** *intr.* take measures; form plans; give instructions (*arrange to be there at eight; arranged for a taxi to come; will you arrange about the cake?*). **5** *intr.* come to an agreement (*arranged with her to meet later*). **6** *tr.* **a** *Mus.* adapt (a composition) for performance with instruments or voices other than those originally specified. **b** adapt (a play etc.) for broadcasting. **7** *tr.* settle (a dispute etc.). □□ **arrangeable** *adj.* **arranger** *n.* (esp. in sense 6). [ME f. OF *arangier* f. *à* to + *rangier* RANGE]

arrangement /əˈreɪndʒmənt/ *n.* **1** the act or process of arranging or being arranged. **2** the condition of being arranged; the manner in which a thing is arranged. **3** something arranged. **4** (in *pl.*) plans, measures (*make your own arrangements*). **5** *Mus.* a composition arranged for performance by different instruments

or voices (see ARRANGE 6a). **6** settlement of a dispute etc. [F (as ARRANGE, -MENT)]

arrant /ˈærənt/ *adj.* downright, utter, notorious (*arrant liar; arrant nonsense*). □□ **arrantly** *adv.* [ME, var. of ERRANT, orig. in phrases like *arrant* (= outlawed, roving) *thief*]

arras /ˈærəs/ *n. hist.* a rich tapestry, often hung on the walls of a room, or to conceal an alcove. [*Arras*, a town in NE France famous for the fabric]

Arrau /æˈraʊ/, Claudio (1903–), Chilean pianist, a renowned interpreter of the works of Chopin, Liszt, Beethoven, Mozart, Schumann, and Brahms.

array /əˈreɪ/ *n. & v.* —*n.* **1** an imposing or well-ordered series or display. **2** an ordered arrangement, esp. of troops (*battle array*). **3** *poet.* an outfit or dress (*in fine array*). **4 a** *Math.* an arrangement of quantities or symbols in rows and columns; a matrix. **b** *Computing* an ordered set of related elements. **5** *Law* a list of jurors empanelled. —*v.tr.* **1** deck, adorn. **2** set in order; marshal (forces). **3** *Law* empanel (a jury). [ME f. AF *araier*, OF *areer* ult. f. a Gmc root; = prepare]

arrears /əˈrɪəz/ *n.pl.* an amount still outstanding or uncompleted, esp. work undone or a debt unpaid. □ **in arrears** (or **arrear**) behindhand, esp. in payment. □□ **arrearage** *n.* [ME (orig. as adv.) f. OF *arere* f. med.L *adretro* (as AD-, *retro* backwards): first used in phr. *in arrear*]

arrest /əˈrest/ *v. & n.* —*v.tr.* **1 a** seize (a person) and take into custody, esp. by legal authority. **b** seize (a ship) by legal authority. **2** stop or check (esp. a process or moving thing). **3 a** attract (a person's attention). **b** attract the attention of (a person). —*n.* **1** the act of arresting or being arrested, esp. the legal seizure of a person. **2** a stoppage or check (*cardiac arrest*). □ **arrest of judgement** *Law* the staying of proceedings, notwithstanding a verdict, on the grounds of a material irregularity in the course of the trial. □□ **arrestingly** *adv.* [ME f. OF *arester* ult. f. L *restare* remain, stop]

arrestable /əˈrestəb(ə)l/ *adj.* **1** susceptible of arrest. **2** *Law* (of an offence) such that the offender may be arrested without a warrant.

arrester /əˈrestə(r)/ *n.* (also **arrestor**) a device, esp. on an aircraft carrier, for slowing an aircraft by means of a hook and cable after landing.

arrestment /əˈrestmənt/ *n. esp. Sc.* attachment of property for the satisfaction of a debt.

Arrhenius /əˈreɪnɪəs, əˈriː-/, Svante August (1859–1927), one of the founders of modern physical chemistry and the first Swede to win the Nobel Prize for chemistry, awarded in 1903 for his work on the physical chemistry of electrolytes.

arrière-pensée /ˌærjerpɑ̃ˈseɪ/ *n.* **1** an undisclosed motive. **2** a mental reservation. [F, = behind thought]

arris /ˈærɪs/ *n. Archit.* a sharp edge formed by the meeting of two flat or curved surfaces. [corrupt. f. F *areste*, mod. ARÊTE]

arrival /əˈraɪv(ə)l/ *n.* **1 a** the act of arriving. **b** an appearance on the scene. **2** a person or thing that has arrived. □ **new arrival** *colloq.* a newborn child. [ME f. AF *arrivaille* (as ARRIVE, -AL)]

arrive /əˈraɪv/ *v.intr.* (often foll. by *at, in*) **1** reach a destination; come to the end of a journey or a specified part of a journey (*arrived in Tibet; arrived at the station; arrived late*). **2** (foll. by *at*) reach (a conclusion, decision, etc.). **3** *colloq.* establish one's reputation or position. **4** *colloq.* (of a child) be born. **5** (of a thing) be brought (*the flowers have arrived*). **6** (of a time) come (*her birthday arrived at last*). [ME f. OF *ariver*, ult. as AD- + L *ripa* shore]

arriviste /ˌæriːˈviːst/ *n.* an ambitious or ruthlessly self-seeking person. [F f. *arriver* f. OF (as ARRIVE, -IST)]

arrogant /ˈærəgənt/ *adj.* (of a person, attitude, etc.) aggressively assertive or presumptuous; overbearing. □□ **arrogance** *n.* **arrogantly** *adv.* [ME f. OF (as ARROGATE, -ANT)]

arrogate /ˈærəˌgeɪt/ *v.tr.* **1** (often foll. by *to* oneself) claim (power, responsibility, etc.) without justification. **2** (often foll. by *to*) attribute unjustly (to a person). □□ **arrogation** /-ˈgeɪʃ(ə)n/ *n.* [L *arrogare arrogat-* (as AD-, *rogare* ask)]

arrondissement /æˌrɔ̃diːsˈmɑ̃/ *n.* **1** a subdivision of a French department, for local government administration purposes. **2** an administrative district of a large city, esp. Paris. [F]

Arrow /ˈærəʊ/, Kenneth Joseph (1921–), American economist, who in 1972 shared with Sir John Hicks the Nobel Prize for economics. Arrow's most startling theory, expounded in *Social Choice and Individual Values* (1951) showed the impossibility of aggregating the preferences of individuals into a single combined order of priorities for society as a whole. He is noted also for his work on general economic equilibrium and on risk-bearing and insurance.

arrow /ˈærəʊ/ n. 1 a sharp pointed wooden or metal stick shot from a bow as a weapon. 2 a drawn or printed etc. representation of an arrow indicating a direction; a pointer. □ **arrow-grass** a marsh plant of the genus *Triglochin*. **arrow worm** = CHAETOGNATH. **broad arrow** *Brit.* a mark formerly used on British prison clothing and other Government stores. □□ **arrowy** adj. [OE ar(e)we f. ON ör f. Gmc]

arrowhead /ˈærəʊˌhed/ n. 1 the pointed end of an arrow. 2 a water-plant, *Sagittaria sagittaria*, with arrow-shaped leaves. 3 a decorative device resembling an arrowhead.

arrowroot /ˈærəʊˌruːt/ n. a plant of the family Marantaceae from which a starch is prepared and used for nutritional and medicinal purposes.

arroyo /əˈrɔɪəʊ/ n. (pl. -os) *US* 1 a brook or stream. 2 a gully. [Sp.]

arse /ɑːs/ n. & v. (*US* **ass** /æs/) *coarse sl.* —n. the buttocks. —v.intr. (usu. foll. by *about*, *around*) play the fool. □ **arse-hole** 1 the anus. 2 *offens.* a term of contempt for a person. **arse-licking** obsequiousness for the purpose of gaining favour; toadying. ¶ Usually considered a taboo word. [OE ærs]

arsenal /ˈɑːsən(ə)l/ n. 1 a store of weapons. 2 a government establishment for the storage and manufacture of weapons and ammunition. 3 resources of anything compared with weapons (e.g. abuse), regarded collectively. [obs. F *arsenal* or It. *arzanale* f. Arab. *dārṣināʿa* f. *dār* house + *sināʿa* art, industry f. *ṣanaʿa* fabricate]

arsenic n. & adj. —n. /ˈɑːsənɪk/ 1 a non-scientific name for arsenic trioxide, a highly poisonous white powdery substance used in weed-killers, rat poison, etc. 2 *Chem.* a semi-metallic element existing as a brittle steel-grey solid and in several other allotropic forms. Arsenic occurs naturally as an element and in various minerals, including the sulphides orpiment and realgar, which were formerly used as dyes and pigments. In its elemental form it has a few specialized uses, but several of its compounds, which like the element are highly poisonous, are widely used as herbicides, pesticides, etc. ¶ Symb.: **As**; atomic number 33. —adj. /ɑːˈsenɪk/ 1 of or concerning arsenic. 2 *Chem.* containing arsenic with a valency of five. □ **red arsenic** = REALGAR. **white arsenic** = sense 1. □□ **arsenious** /ɑːˈsiːnɪəs/ adj. [ME f. OF f. L *arsenicum* f. Gk *arsenikon* yellow orpiment, identified with *arsenikos* male, but in fact f. Arab. *al-zarnīk* f. *al* the + *zarnīk* orpiment f. Pers. f. *zar* gold]

arsenical /ɑːˈsenɪk(ə)l/ adj. & n. —adj. of or containing arsenic. —n. a drug containing arsenic.

arsine /ˈɑːsiːn/ n. *Chem.* arsenic trihydride, a colourless poisonous gas smelling slightly of garlic. [ARSENIC after *amine*]

arsis /ˈɑːsɪs/ n. (pl. **arses** /-siːz/) a stressed syllable or part of a metrical foot in Greek or Latin verse (opp. THESIS). [ME f. LL f. Gk, = lifting f. *airō* raise]

arson /ˈɑːs(ə)n/ n. the act of maliciously setting fire to property. □□ **arsonist** n. [legal AF, OF, f. med.L *arsio -onis* f. L *ardēre ars-* burn]

arsphenamine /ɑːsˈfenəmiːn, -ˌmiːn/ n. a drug formerly used in the treatment of syphilis and parasitic diseases. [ARSENIC + PHENYL + AMINE]

art¹ /ɑːt/ n. 1 **a** human creative skill or its application. **b** work exhibiting this. 2 **a** (in pl.; prec. by *the*) the various branches of creative activity concerned with the production of imaginative designs, sounds, or ideas, e.g. painting, music, writing, considered collectively. **b** any one of these branches. 3 creative activity, esp. painting and drawing, resulting in visual representation (*interested in music but not art*). 4 human skill or workmanship as opposed to the work of nature (*art and nature had combined to make her a great beauty*). 5 (often foll. by *of*) a

skill, aptitude, or knack (*the art of writing clearly; keeping people happy is quite an art*). 6 (in pl.; usu. prec. by *the*) those branches of learning (esp. languages, literature, and history) associated with creative skill as opposed to scientific, technical, or vocational skills. □ **art and mystery** any of the special skills or techniques in a specified area. **art deco** see separate entry. **art form** 1 any medium of artistic expression. 2 an established form of composition (e.g. the novel, sonata, sonnet, etc.). **art nouveau** see separate entry. **art paper** smooth-coated high quality paper. **arts and crafts** decorative design and handicraft. [ME f. OF f. L *ars artis*]

art² /ɑːt/ *archaic* or *dial. 2nd sing. present* of BE.

art. /ɑːt/ abbr. article.

Artaud /ɑːˈtəʊ/, Antonin (1896–1948), French actor, director, and poet, one of the seminal influences on experimental theatre after the Second World War. An advocate of surrealism in the 1920s, he later developed the concept of a non-verbal Theatre of Cruelty, freeing the spectator's unconscious, which was embodied in his play *Les Cenci* (1935) and in a series of essays published as *Le Théâtre et son double* (1938).

Artaxerxes /ˌɑːtəˈzɜːksiːz/ the name of two kings of ancient Persia:

Artaxerxes I son of Xerxes, reigned 464–424 BC.

Artaxerxes II son of Darius II, reigned 404–358 BC.

art deco /ɑːt ˈdekəʊ/ n. a new style in the decorative arts which was defined by the Exposition Internationale des Arts Décoratifs et Industriels held in Paris in 1925. Although applied principally to the decorative arts and interior design of the 1920s and 1930s the term can be extended to analogous styles in architecture and painting. Concentrating on stylishness tuned to domestic use and popular consumption, it is characterized by geometric patterning, sharp edges, and flat bright colours, and often involved the use of enamel, chrome, bronze, and highly polished stone. The simplicity of the style can be seen as classicizing in spirit, attested by the Egyptian and Greek motifs which were often adopted (e.g. the schematized Egyptian scarab). Although it led to a re-confirmation, in both Europe and America, of the role of the craftsman-designer, popularization of the style often resulted in the mass production of less refined objects.

artefact /ˈɑːtɪˌfækt/ n. (also **artifact**) 1 a product of human art and workmanship. 2 *Archaeol.* a product of prehistoric or aboriginal workmanship as distinguished from a similar object naturally produced. 3 *Biol.* etc. a feature not naturally present, introduced during preparation or investigation (e.g. as in the preparation of a slide). □□ **artefactual** adj. (in senses 1 and 2). [L *arte* (ablat. of *ars* art) + *factum* (neut. past part. of *facere* make)]

artel /ɑːˈtel/ n. an association of craftsmen, peasants, etc., in the USSR. [Russ.]

Artemis /ˈɑːtɪmɪs/ *Gk Mythol.* a goddess who is probably pre-Hellenic. Daughter of Zeus, sister of Apollo, and a huntress, she is identified with Selene and Diana, and presided over birth, fertility, and fruitfulness. Her temple at Ephesus was one of the Seven Wonders of the World, but here her characteristics were those of an eastern nature-goddess, and her statue had rows of egg-shaped objects, either breasts or eggs (a symbol of fertility) across the chest. 'Great is Diana of the Ephesians' was the cry of the silversmiths at Ephesus when they found their trade in silver shrines of Diana threatened by St Paul's preaching (Acts 19: 24 ff.).

arterial /ɑːˈtɪərɪəl/ adj. 1 of or relating to an artery (*arterial blood*). 2 (esp. of a road) main, important, esp. linking large cities or towns. [F *artériel* f. *artère* artery]

arterialize /ɑːˈtɪərɪəˌlaɪz/ v.tr. (also **-ise**) 1 convert venous into arterial (blood) by reoxygenation esp. in the lungs. 2 provide with an arterial system. □□ **arterialization** /-ˈzeɪʃ(ə)n/ n.

arteriole /ɑːˈtɪərɪˌəʊl/ n. a small branch of an artery leading into capillaries. [F *artériole*, dimin. of *artère* ARTERY]

arteriosclerosis /ɑːˌtɪərɪəʊsklɪəˈrəʊsɪs/ n. the loss of elasticity and thickening of the walls of the arteries, esp. in old age;

hardening of the arteries. □□ **arteriosclerotic** /-ˈrɒtɪk/ *adj.* [ARTERY + SCLEROSIS]

artery /ˈɑːtərɪ/ *n.* (*pl.* **-ies**) **1** any of the muscular-walled tubes forming part of the blood circulation system of the body, carrying oxygen-enriched blood from the heart (cf. VEIN). **2** a main road or railway line. □□ **arteritis** /-ˈraɪtɪs/ *n.* [ME f. L *arteria* f. Gk *artēria* prob. f. *airō* raise]

artesian well /ɑːˈtiːzɪən, -ʒ(ə)n/ *n.* a well bored perpendicularly, esp. through rock, into water-bearing strata lying at an angle, so that natural pressure produces a constant supply of water with little or no pumping. [F. *artésien* f. *Artois*, see ARTOIS]

artful /ˈɑːtfʊl/ *adj.* (of a person or action) crafty, deceitful. □□ **artfully** *adv.* **artfulness** *n.*

arthritis /ɑːˈθraɪtɪs/ *n.* inflammation of a joint or joints. □□ **arthritic** /-ˈθrɪtɪk/ *adj.* & *n.* [L f. Gk f. *arthron* joint]

arthropod /ˈɑːθrəˌpɒd/ *n.* *Zool.* any invertebrate animal of the phylum Arthropoda, with a segmented body, jointed limbs, and an external skeleton. Insects, crustaceans, arachnids, centipedes, and millepedes are all arthropods, and, with well over a million species, the phylum is by far the largest in the animal kingdom. [Gk *arthron* joint + *pous podos* foot]

Arthur[1] /ˈɑːθə(r)/ a reputed king of Britain, historically perhaps a 5th- or 6th-c. chieftain or general, on whose life and court a mass of legends, in various tongues, have become centred, including the exploits of adventurous knights and the quest for the Holy Grail. The stories are recounted by Malory and others. Geoffrey of Monmouth (12th c.) places his court at Caerleon-on-Usk; the Norman writer Wace (12th c.) mentions the 'Round Table', a device to enable the knights to be seated in such a way that none had precedence.

Arthur[2] /ˈɑːθə(r)/, Chester Alan (1830–86), 21st President of the US, 1881–5. He became President after James Garfield was assassinated while in office.

Arthurian /ɑːˈθjʊərɪən/ *adj.* relating to or associated with King Arthur (see entry) or his court.

artichoke /ˈɑːtɪˌtʃəʊk/ *n.* **1** a European plant, *Cynara scolymus*, allied to the thistle. **2** (in full **globe artichoke**) the flower-head of the artichoke, the bracts of which have edible bases (see also JERUSALEM ARTICHOKE). [It. *articiocco* f. Arab. *al-karšūfa*]

article /ˈɑːtɪk(ə)l/ *n.* & *v.* —*n.* **1** (often in *pl.*) an item or commodity, usu. not further distinguished (*a collection of odd articles*). **2** a non-fictional essay, esp. one included with others in a newspaper, magazine, journal, etc. **3 a** a particular part (*an article of faith*). **b** a separate clause or portion of any document (*articles of apprenticeship*). **4** *Gram.* the definite or indefinite article. —*v.tr.* bind by articles of apprenticeship. □ **definite article** *Gram.* the word (*the* in English) preceding a noun and implying a specific or known instance (as in *the book on the table*; *the art of government*; *the famous public school in Berkshire*). **indefinite article** *Gram.* the word (e.g. *a*, *an*, *some* in English) preceding a noun and implying lack of specificity (as in *bought me a book*; *government is an art*; *went to a public school*). **the Thirty-nine Articles** see separate entry. [ME f. OF f. L *articulus* dimin. of *artus* joint]

articular /ɑːˈtɪkjʊlə(r)/ *adj.* of or relating to the joints. [ME f. L *articularis* (as ARTICLE, -AR¹)]

articulate *adj.* & *v.* —*adj.* /ɑːˈtɪkjʊlət/ **1** able to speak fluently and coherently. **2** (of sound or speech) having clearly distinguishable parts. **3** having joints. —*v.* /ɑːˈtɪkjʊˌleɪt/ **1** *tr.* **a** pronounce (words, syllables, etc.) clearly and distinctly. **b** express (an idea etc.) coherently. **2** *intr.* speak distinctly (*was quite unable to articulate*). **3** *tr.* (usu. in *passive*) connect by joints. **4** *tr.* mark with apparent joints. **5** *intr.* (often foll. by *with*) form a joint. □ **articulated lorry** *Brit.* a lorry consisting of two or more sections connected by a flexible joint. □□ **articulacy** *n.* **articulately** *adv.* **articulateness** *n.* **articulator** *n.* [L *articulatus* (as ARTICLE, -ATE²)]

articulation /ɑːˌtɪkjʊˈleɪʃ(ə)n/ *n.* **1 a** the act of speaking. **b** articulate utterance; speech. **2 a** the act or a mode of jointing. **b** a joint. [F *articulation* or L *articulatio* f. *articulare* joint (as ARTICLE, -ATION)]

artifact var. of ARTEFACT.

artifice /ˈɑːtɪfɪs/ *n.* **1** a clever device; a contrivance. **2 a** cunning. **b** an instance of this. **3** skill, dexterity. [F f. L *artificium* f. *ars artis* art, *-ficium* making f. *facere* make]

artificer /ɑːˈtɪfɪsə(r)/ *n.* **1** an inventor. **2** a craftsman. **3** a skilled mechanic in the armed forces. [ME f. AF, prob. alt. of OF *artificien*]

artificial /ˌɑːtɪˈfɪʃ(ə)l/ *adj.* **1** produced by human art or effort rather than originating naturally (*an artificial lake*). **2** formed in imitation of something natural (*artificial flowers*). **3** affected, insincere (*an artificial smile*). □ **artificial insemination** the injection of semen into the vagina or uterus other than by sexual intercourse. **artificial intelligence** see separate entry. **artificial kidney** an apparatus that performs the functions of the human kidney (outside the body), when one or both organs are damaged. The first 'artificial kidney' was demonstrated (on an animal) in 1913. **artificial respiration** the restoration or initiation of breathing by manual or mechanical or mouth-to-mouth methods. **artificial silk** rayon. □□ **artificiality** /-ʃɪˈælɪtɪ/ *n.* **artificially** *adv.* [ME f. OF *artificiel* or L *artificialis* (as ARTIFICE, -AL)]

artificial intelligence *n.* the theory and development of computer programs or systems to perform tasks that normally require human intelligence. Such tasks include decision-making and diagnosis, pattern and speech recognition, and natural language translation. Much effort has been devoted to investigating the basic processes of thought, learning, decision-making, and language use, and these aspects of artificial intelligence are closely related to work in other fields such as physiology, neurology, psychology, linguistics, and mathematics. At its most ambitious level the aim is to create computers and robots capable of mimicking a broad range of human behaviour. Doubts remain, however, about whether such systems are theoretically or practically possible, certainly as envisaged in much science fiction.

artillery /ɑːˈtɪlərɪ/ *n.* (*pl.* **-ies**) **1** large-calibre guns used in warfare on land. **2** a branch of the armed forces that uses these. □□ **artillerist** *n.* [ME f. OF *artillerie* f. *artiller* alt. of *atillier, atirier* equip, arm]

artilleryman /ɑːˈtɪlərɪˌmæn/ *n.* (*pl.* **-men**) a member of the artillery.

artisan /ˌɑːtɪˈzæn, ˈɑː-/ *n.* **1** a skilled (esp. manual) worker. **2** a mechanic. [F f. It. *artigiano*, ult. f. L *artitus* past part. of *artire* instruct in the arts]

artist /ˈɑːtɪst/ *n.* **1** a painter. **2** a person who practises any of the arts. **3** an artiste. **4** a person who works with the dedication and attributes associated with an artist (*an artist in crime*). **5** *colloq.* a devotee; a habitual practiser of a specified (usu. reprehensible) activity (*con artist*). □□ **artistry** *n.* [F *artiste* f. It. *artista* (as ART¹, -IST)]

artiste /ɑːˈtiːst/ *n.* a professional performer, esp. a singer or dancer. [F: see ARTIST]

artistic /ɑːˈtɪstɪk/ *adj.* **1** having natural skill in art. **2** made or done with art. **3** of art or artists. □□ **artistically** *adv.*

artless /ˈɑːtlɪs/ *adj.* **1** guileless, ingenuous. **2** not resulting from or displaying art. **3** clumsy. □□ **artlessly** *adv.*

art nouveau /ˌɑː nuːˈvəʊ/ *n.* a style of art, architecture, and design from the 1890s to the early 1900s in western Europe. As a decorative style it relied primarily on an organic and generative line that can be found equally in Beardsley's drawings, Mucha's posters, the architectural detail of van de Velde, and Guimard's designs for the Paris Métro. In its insistence on the introduction of good modern design into all aspects of life it became an international European style, but the movement nowhere survived the outbreak of the First World War to any significant extent. [F, = new art]

Artois /ˈɑːtwæ/ a former province of NW France. Known in Roman times as Artesium, the area gave its name to the artesian well which was first sunk here in the 12th c.

Arts and Crafts movement an English movement of the second half of the 19th c. which sought to revive, in an industrial age, the ideal of the handcrafted object. The notion of the craftsman employing traditional methods and style had both aesthetic and social implications. William Morris, influenced by J. J. Rousseau, and then by Pugin and Ruskin, translated the nostalgia for hand-crafted goods into an organized business venture. (see MORRIS[1]). In England the Arts and Crafts movement was closely associated with Pre-Raphaelitism and later with the Aesthetic movement. It influenced many artists and designers, including Walter Crane and C. R. Ashbee, who established the Guild and School of Arts and Crafts, London.

artwork /ˈɑːtwɜːk/ n. the illustrations in a printed work.

arty /ˈɑːtɪ/ adj. (**artier**, **artiest**) colloq. pretentiously or affectedly artistic. □ **arty-crafty** quaintly artistic; (of furniture etc.) seeking stylistic effect rather than usefulness or comfort. □□ **arti- ness** n.

Aruba /əˈruːbə/ a Dutch island in the Caribbean Sea, 24 km (15 miles) north of the Venezuelan coast. Formerly part of the Netherlands Antilles, it separated from that group in 1986 in advance of gaining full independence; pop. (est. 1988) 62,300; chief town, Oranjestad.

arum /ˈeərəm/ n. any plant of the genus Arum, usu. stemless with arrow-shaped leaves, e.g. lords and ladies. □ **arum lily** a tall lily-like plant, Zantedeschia aethiopica, with white spathe and spadix. [L f. Gk aron]

Arunachal Pradesh /ˌɑːrəˈnɑːtʃ(ə)l prəˈdeʃ/ a State of NE India, the North-east Frontier Agency of British India; pop. (1981) 628,050; capital, Itanagar.

Arunta /əˈrʌntə/ var. of ARANDA.

Arvand River /ˈɑːvənd/ the Iranian name for the Shatt al-Arab waterway between Iraq and Iran.

arvo /ˈɑːvəʊ/ n. Austral. sl. afternoon. [abbr.]

-ary[1] /ərɪ/ suffix **1** forming adjectives (budgetary; contrary; primary; unitary). **2** forming nouns (dictionary; fritillary; granary; January). [F -aire or L -arius 'connected with']

-ary[2] /ərɪ/ suffix forming adjectives (military). [F -aire or f. L -aris 'belonging to']

Aryan /ˈeərɪən/ n. & adj. —n. **1** a member of the peoples (not to be regarded as a race; see below) speaking any of the languages of the Indo-European (esp. Indo-Iranian) family. **2** the parent language of this family. **3** improperly (in Nazi ideology) a Caucasian not of Jewish descent. —adj. of or relating to Aryan or the Aryans. [Skr. āryas noble, earlier used as a national name]

The idea current in the 19th c. of an Aryan race corresponding to a definite Aryan language was taken up by nationalistic, historical, and romantic writers. It was given especial currency by M. A. de Gobineau, who linked it with the theory of the essential inferiority of certain races. The term 'Aryan race' was later revived and used for purposes of political propaganda in Nazi Germany.

aryl /ˈæraɪl, ˈærɪl/ n. Chem. any radical derived from or related to an aromatic hydrocarbon by removal of a hydrogen atom. [G Aryl (as AROMATIC, -YL)]

AS abbr. Anglo-Saxon.

As symb. Chem. the element arsenic.

as[1] /æz, unstressed əz/ adv., conj., & pron. —adv. & conj. (adv. as antecedent in main sentence; conj. in relative clause expressed or implied) . . . to the extent to which . . . is or does etc. (I am as tall as he; am as tall as he is; am not so tall as he; (colloq.) am as tall as him; as many as six; as recently as last week; it is not as easy as you think). —conj. (with relative clause expressed or implied) **1** (with antecedent so) expressing result or purpose (came early so as to meet us; we so arranged matters as to avoid a long wait; so good as to exceed all hopes). **2** (with antecedent adverb omitted) having concessive force (good as it is = although it is good; try as he might = although he might try). **3** (without antecedent adverb) **a** in the manner in which (do as you like; was regarded as a mistake; they rose as one man). **b** in the capacity or form of (I speak as your friend; Olivier as Hamlet; as a matter of fact). **c** during or at the time that (came up as I was speaking; fell just as I reached the door). **d** for the reason that; seeing that (as you are here, we can talk). **e** for instance (cathedral cities, as York). — rel.pron. (with verb of relative clause expressed or implied) **1**

that, who, which (I had the same trouble as you; he is a writer, as is his wife; such money as you have; such countries as France). **2** (with sentence as antecedent) a fact that (he lost, as you know). □ **as and when** to the extent and at the time that (I'll do it as and when I want to). **as for** with regard to (as for you, I think you are wrong). **as from** on and after (a specified date). **as if** (or **though**) as would be the case if (acts as if he were in charge; as if you didn't know!; looks as though we've won). **as it is** (or **as is**) in the existing circumstances or state. **as it were** in a way; to a certain extent (he is, as it were, infatuated). **as long as** see LONG[1]. **as much** see MUCH. **as of 1** = as from. **2** as at (a specified time). **as per** see PER. **as regards** see REGARD. **as soon as** see SOON. **as such** see SUCH. **as though** see as if. **as to** with respect to; concerning (said nothing as to money; as to you, I think you are wrong). **as was** in the previously existing circumstances or state. **as well** see WELL[1]. **as yet** until now or a particular time in the past (usu. with neg. and with implied reserve about the future: have received no news as yet). [reduced form of OE alswá ALSO]

as[2] /æs/ n. (pl. **asses**) a Roman copper coin. [L]

as- /əs/ prefix assim. form of AD- before s.

ASA abbr. **1** Amateur Swimming Association. **2** American Standards Association.

asafoetida /ˌæsəˈfiːtɪdə, -ˈfetɪdə/ n. (US **asafetida**) a resinous plant gum with a fetid ammoniac smell, formerly used in medi- cine, now as a herbal remedy and in Indian cooking. [ME f. med.L f. asa f. Pers. azā mastic + fetida (as FETID)]

a.s.a.p. abbr. as soon as possible.

asbestos /æzˈbestɒs, æs-/ n. **1** a fibrous silicate mineral that is incombustible. **2** this used as a heat-resistant or insulating material. □□ **asbestine** /-tɪn/ adj. [ME f. OF albeston, ult. f. Gk asbestos unquenchable f. a- not + sbestos f. sbennumi quench]

asbestosis /ˌæzbeˈstəʊsɪs, ˌæs-/ n. a lung disease resulting from the inhalation of asbestos particles.

ascarid /ˈæskərɪd/ n. (also **ascaris** /-rɪs/) a parasitic nematode worm of the genus Ascaris, e.g. the intestinal roundworm of mankind and other vertebrates. [mod.L ascaris f. Gk askaris]

ascend /əˈsend/ v. **1** intr. move upwards; rise. **2** intr. **a** slope upwards. **b** lie along an ascending slope. **3** tr. climb; go up. **4** intr. rise in rank or status. **5** tr. mount upon. **6** intr. (of sound) rise in pitch. **7** tr. go along (a river) to its source. **8** intr. Printing (of a letter) have part projecting upwards. □ **ascend the throne** become king or queen. [ME f. L ascendere (as AD-, scandere climb)]

ascendancy /əˈsend(ə)nsɪ/ n. (also **ascendency**) (often foll. by over) a superior or dominant condition or position.

ascendant /əˈsend(ə)nt/ adj. & n. —adj. **1** rising. **2** Astron. rising towards the zenith. **3** Astrol. just above the eastern horizon. **4** predominant. —n. Astrol. the point of the sun's apparent path that is ascendant at a given time (Aries in the ascendant), e.g. at the birth of a child. A planet close to this point is held to have special influence upon the life of a child then born. □ **in the ascendant 1** supreme or dominating. **2** rising; gaining power or authority. [ME f. OF f. L (as ASCEND, -ANT)]

ascender /əˈsendə(r)/ n. **1 a** a part of a letter that extends above the main part (as in b and d). **b** a letter having this. **2** a person or thing that ascends.

ascension /əˈsenʃ(ə)n/ n. **1** the act or an instance of ascending. **2** (**Ascension**) the ascent of Christ into heaven on the fortieth day after the Resurrection. □ **Ascension Day** the Thursday on which this is celebrated annually. **right ascension** Astron. longitude measured along the celestial equator. □□ **ascensional** adj. [ME f. OF f. L ascensio -onis (as ASCEND, -ION)]

Ascension Island a small island in the South Atlantic, incorporated with St Helena; pop. (1988) 1,007. It was discovered by the Portuguese, traditionally on Ascension Day in 1501, but remained uninhabited until a small British garrison was stationed there on the arrival of Napoleon for imprisonment on St Helena in 1815. It is now a British telecommunications centre and a US air base. The island has been strategically important during (and since) the military operations in the

Falkland Islands in 1982, serving as a base for British forces and a landing-point for aircraft travelling between Britain and the South Atlantic.

Ascensiontide /ə'senʃ(ə)n₁taɪd/ n. the period of ten days from Ascension Day to Whitsun Eve.

ascent /ə'sent/ n. **1** the act or an instance of ascending. **2 a** an upward movement or rise. **b** advancement or progress (*the ascent of man*). **3** a way by which one may ascend; an upward slope. [ASCEND, after *descent*]

ascertain /₁æsə'teɪn/ v.tr. **1** find out as a definite fact. **2** get to know. □□ **ascertainable** adj. **ascertainment** n. [ME f. OF *acertener*, stem *acertain-* f. *à* to + CERTAIN]

ascesis /ə'si:sɪs/ n. the practice of self-discipline. [Gk *askēsis* training f. *askeō* exercise]

ascetic /ə'setɪk/ n. & adj. —n. a person who practises severe self-discipline and abstains from all forms of pleasure, esp. for religious or spiritual reasons. —adj. relating to or characteristic of ascetics or asceticism; abstaining from pleasure. □□ **ascetically** adv. **asceticism** /-tɪ₁sɪz(ə)m/ n. [med.L *asceticus* or Gk *askētikos* f. *askētēs* monk f. *askeō* exercise]

Ascham /'æskəm/, Roger (1515/16–68), English humanist scholar and writer, tutor to the future Elizabeth I and Latin secretary to Queen Mary and later to Elizabeth. His works include *Toxophilus* (1545), a treatise on archery, and *The Scholemaster* (1570), a practical and influential treatise on education.

ascidian /ə'sɪdɪən/ n. Zool. any tunicate animal of the class Ascidiacea, often found in colonies, the adults sedentary on rocks or seaweeds, e.g. the sea squirt. [mod.L *Ascidia* f. Gk *askidion* dimin. of *askos* wineskin]

ASCII /'æskɪ/ abbr. Computing American Standard Code for Information Interchange.

ascites /ə'saɪti:z/ n. (pl. same) Med. the accumulation of fluid in the abdominal cavity causing swelling. [ME f. LL f. Gk f. *askitēs* f. *askos* wineskin]

Asclepius /ə'skli:pɪəs/ Gk Mythol. a hero and god of healing, often represented bearing a staff with a serpent coiled round it. The scroll or tablet which he sometimes bears probably represents medical learning.

ascorbic acid /ə'skɔ:bɪk/ n. a vitamin found in citrus fruits and green vegetables, essential in maintaining healthy connective tissue, a deficiency of which results in scurvy. Also called *vitamin C*.

Ascot /'æskət/ a racecourse near Windsor, Berks., and scene of an annual race-meeting in June, founded by Queen Anne in 1711. □ **Ascot week** this race-meeting.

ascribe /ə'skraɪb/ v.tr. (usu. foll. by *to*) **1** attribute or impute (*ascribes his well-being to a sound constitution*). **2** regard as belonging. □□ **ascribable** adj. [ME f. L *ascribere* (as AD-, *scribere* *script-* write)]

ascription /ə'skrɪpʃ(ə)n/ n. **1** the act or an instance of ascribing. **2** a preacher's words ascribing praise to God at the end of a sermon. [L *ascriptio -onis* (as ASCRIBE)]

asdic /'æzdɪk/ n. an early form of echo-sounder. [initials of Allied Submarine Detection Investigation Committee]

-ase /eɪz/ suffix Biochem. forming the name of an enzyme (*amylase*). [DIASTASE]

ASEAN /'æsɪən/ abbr. Association of South East Asian Nations, a regional organization formed by Indonesia, Malaysia, the Philippines, Singapore, and Thailand through the Bangkok Declaration of 1967. Brunei joined the organization in 1984. Although ASEAN has aimed to accelerate economic growth, its main success has been in the promotion of diplomatic collaboration, the exchange of cultural resources, and cooperation in transport and communication.

asepsis /eɪ'sepsɪs, ə-/ n. **1** the absence of harmful bacteria, viruses, or other micro-organisms. **2** a method of achieving asepsis in surgery.

aseptic /eɪ'septɪk/ adj. **1** free from contamination caused by harmful bacteria, viruses, or other micro-organisms. **2** (of a wound, instrument, or dressing) surgically sterile or sterilized. **3** (of a surgical method etc.) aiming at the elimination

of harmful micro-organisms, rather than counteraction (cf. ANTISEPTIC).

asexual /eɪ'seksjʊəl, æ-/ adj. Biol. **1** without sex or sexual organs. **2** (of reproduction) not involving the fusion of gametes. **3** without sexuality. □□ **asexuality** /-'ælɪtɪ/ n. **asexually** adv.

Asgard /'æzgɑ:d/ Scand. Mythol. a region in the centre of the universe, inhabited by the gods.

ASH /æʃ/ abbr. Action on Smoking and Health.

ash¹ /æʃ/ n. **1** (often in pl.) the powdery residue left after the burning of any substance. **2** (pl.) the remains of the human body after cremation or disintegration. **3** (**the Ashes**) Cricket see ASHES. **4** ashlike material thrown out by a volcano. □ **ash blonde 1** a very pale blonde colour. **2** a person with hair of this colour. **Ash Wednesday** the first day of Lent (from the custom of marking the foreheads of penitents with ashes on that day). [OE *æsce*]

ash² /æʃ/ n. **1** any forest-tree of the genus *Fraxinus*, with silver-grey bark, compound leaves, and hard, tough, pale wood. **2** its wood. **3** an Old English runic letter: = æ (named from a word of which it was the first letter). □ **ash-key** the winged seed of the ash-tree, growing in clusters resembling keys. **ash-plant** a sapling from an ash-tree, used as a walking-stick etc. [OE *æsc* f. Gmc]

ashamed /ə'ʃeɪmd/ adj. (usu. predic.) **1** (often foll. by *of* (= with regard to), *for* (= on account of), or *to* + infin.) embarrassed or disconcerted by shame (*ashamed of his aunt*; *ashamed of having lied*; *ashamed for you*; *ashamed to be seen with him*). **2** (foll. by *to* + infin.) hesitant, reluctant (but usu. not actually refusing or declining) (*am ashamed to admit that I was wrong*). □□ **ashamedly** /-mɪdlɪ/ adv. [OE *āscamod* past part. of *āscamian* feel shame (as A-², SHAME)]

Ashanti /ə'ʃæntɪ/ (also **Asante**) a region of central Ghana inhabited by the Ashanti, one of Ghana's principal ethnic groups. The regional capital, Kumasi, was the capital of the former Ashanti confederation, a tribal union (covering a wider area) that was forged in the 17th c. After a series of wars the area was formally annexed by Britain on 1 Jan. 1902 and became part of the British colony of the Gold Coast. —n. (pl. same) **1** a member of the people of this region. **2** their language, a dialect of Twi. [native name]

ashbin /'æʃbɪn/ n. a receptacle for the disposal of ashes.

ashcan /'æʃkæn/ n. US a dustbin.

Ash-can School a group of American painters active from c.1908 until the First World War. It was inspired largely by Robert Henri and its nucleus was formed by the group of The Eight, which he founded. The name of the school derives from its members' paintings of slum life and outcasts.

Ashcroft /'æʃkrɒft/, Dame Peggy (Edith Margaret Emily) (1907–), English stage and film actress, who played a number of Shakespearean roles including Desdemona to Paul Robeson's Othello (1930) and Juliet in John Gielgud's production of *Romeo and Juliet* (1935). Other outstanding performances include the role of Hedda Gabler (1954), for which she received a royal award. She also appeared in the television series *The Jewel in the Crown* (1984) and in the film *A Passage to India* (1985).

Ashdod /'æʃdɒd/ a seaport to the south of Tel Aviv on the Mediterranean coast of Israel; pop. (est. 1982) 62,000.

ashen¹ /'æʃ(ə)n/ adj. **1** of or resembling ashes. **2** ash-coloured; grey or pale.

ashen² /'æʃ(ə)n/ adj. **1** of or relating to the ash-tree. **2** archaic made of ash wood.

Asher /'æʃə(r)/ **1** a Hebrew patriarch, son of Jacob and Zilpah (Gen. 30: 12, 13). **2** the tribe of Israel traditionally descended from him.

Ashes, the a trophy for the winner of a series of test matches in cricket between England and Australia. The term originated in a mock obituary notice published in the *Sporting Times* 2 Sept. 1882, after the sensational victory of Australia: 'In Affectionate Remembrance of English Cricket Which died at the Oval on 29th August, 1882. Deeply lamented by a large circle of sorrowing friends and acquaintances. R.I.P. N.B.—The body will be cremated and the ashes taken to Australia.' Real ashes exist, kept in an urn at Lord's, and are said to be those of a bail (or a ball) burnt at Melbourne when England won the series of 1882–3.

ashet /ˈæʃɪt/ *n. Sc. & NZ* a large plate or dish. [F *assiette*]

Ashkenazi /ˌæʃkəˈnɑːzɪ/ *n.* (*pl.* **Ashkenazim** /-zɪm/) **1** an East European Jew. **2** a Jew of East European ancestry (cf. SEPHARDI). □□ **Ashkenazic** *adj.* [mod.Heb., f. *Ashkenaz* (Gen. 10: 3)]

Ashkhabad /ˌæʃkəˈbæd/ the capital of the Soviet republic of Turkmenistan; pop. (est. 1987) 382,000.

ashlar /ˈæʃlə(r)/ *n.* **1** a large square-cut stone used in building. **2** masonry made of ashlars. **3** such masonry used as a facing on a rough rubble or brick wall. [ME f. OF *aisselier* f. L *axilla* dimin. of *axis* board]

ashlaring /ˈæʃlərɪŋ/ *n.* **1** ashlar masonry. **2** the short upright boarding in a garret which cuts off the acute angle between the roof and the floor.

Ashley /ˈæʃlɪ/, Laura (1925–85), Welsh-born designer of textiles and clothes in traditional floral patterns and romantic neo-Victorian styles. The chain of shops under her name spread through Britain in the 1960s, and then to Europe, America, and Australia, selling home furnishings as well as fashions.

Ashmolean Museum /æʃˈməʊlɪən/ a museum of art and antiquities in Oxford, founded by the English antiquary Elias Ashmole (1617–92). In 1677 he deposited with Oxford University a number of items, some collected by himself, others forming the 'closett of Rarities' bequeathed to him by his friend John Tradescant (d. 1662), which formed the nucleus of the museum (opened in 1683), the first public institution of this kind in England, open to anyone who paid the entrance fee. From the first it was popular with the general public. The collection now includes archaeological material, European works of art, and Oriental works.

Ashmore and Cartier Islands /ˈæʃmɔː(r), ˈkɑːtɪeɪ/ an external territory of Australia, comprising the uninhabited Ashmore Reef and Cartier Island.

ashore /əˈʃɔː(r)/ *adv.* towards or on the shore or land (*sailed ashore; stayed ashore*).

ashpan /ˈæʃpæn/ *n.* a tray under a grate to catch the ash.

Ashquelon /ˈæʃkələn/ a resort on the Mediterranean coast of Israel, about 56 km (35 miles) south of Tel Aviv. It is the site of an ancient Philistine city (called *Ashkelon* in the Bible) which has given its name to a kind of onion (see SHALLOT and SCALLION).

ashram /ˈæʃrəm/ *n. Ind.* a place of religious retreat for Hindus; a hermitage. [Skr. *āshrama* hermitage]

Ashton /ˈæʃt(ə)n/, Sir Frederick (1904–88), British dancer, choreographer, and ballet director. He became chief choreographer of the Vic-Wells Ballet in 1935, remaining with the company when it became the Sadler's Wells and finally the Royal Ballet, and being appointed associate director in 1952 and director 1963–70. As brilliant in creating new works as in adapting historical ballets, he shows a soft, fluid, lyrical classicism. His important ballets include *Façade*, *Symphonic Variations* (1946), *Romeo and Juliet* (1955), *La Fille mal gardée* (1960), *The Dream* (1964), and *A Month in the Country* (1976).

ashtray /ˈæʃtreɪ/ *n.* a small receptacle for cigarette ash, stubs, etc.

Ashurbanipal /ˌæʃʊəˈbɑːnɪp(ə)l/ (668–627 BC) the last great king of Assyria. His principal campaigns were to Egypt (where he was ultimately unsuccessful), to Babylon (where he suppressed a revolt), and to Elam (where he sacked Susa). He is celebrated for his library of over 20,000 clay tablets at Nineveh, which included literary, religious, scientific, and administrative documents, many of them copies of ancient texts.

ashy /ˈæʃɪ/ *adj.* (**ashier, ashiest**) **1** = ASHEN[1]. **2** covered with ashes.

Asia /ˈeɪʃə/ the largest of the world's continents, constituting nearly one-third of the land mass, lying entirely north of the equator except for some SE Asian islands. It is connected to Africa by the isthmus of Suez, and generally divided from

Europe (which forms part of the same land mass) by a line running through the Ural Mountains and the Caspian Sea. The continent is currently dominated by the USSR, China, and India, the last two descended from long imperial traditions and civilizations stretching back into the ancient world, the first a product of progressive eastern expansion by European Russia. Many of the peripheral areas, particularly in the south, were colonized by European nations between the 17th and 19th centuries, emerging as indepedent States only after the Second World War.

Asia Minor the westernmost part of Asia (see ANATOLIA), now comprising Asiatic Turkey. The first major civilization established there was that of the Hittites in the 2nd millennium BC. The Greeks colonized the western coast (see IONIA), while the kingdoms of Lydia and Phrygia developed independently. The land was subjugated by various invaders, including Cyrus of Persia (546 BC) and Alexander the Great (333 BC). It was subsequently the Roman province of Asia and then part of the Byzantine empire. Conquered by the Turks, it became part of the Ottoman empire from the end of the 13th c. until the establishment of modern Turkey after the First World War. (See TURKEY.)

Asian /ˈeɪʃ(ə)n, -ʒ(ə)n/ *n. & adj.* —*n.* **1** a native of Asia. **2** a person of Asian descent. —*adj.* of or relating to Asia or its people, customs, or languages. □ **Asian Development Bank** a bank with 47 member countries (32 are from the Asia–Pacific region) that began operations in 1966, located in Manila in the Philippines. Its aim is to promote the economic and social progress of its developing member countries. [L *Asianus* f. Gk *Asianos* f. *Asia*]

Asiatic /ˌeɪʃɪˈætɪk, ˌeɪz-/ *n. & adj.* —*n. offens.* an Asian. —*adj.* Asian. [L *Asiaticus* f. Gk *Asiatikos*]

aside /əˈsaɪd/ *adv. & n.* —*adv.* **1** to or on one side; away. **2** out of consideration (placed after noun: *joking aside*). —*n.* **1** words spoken in a play for the audience to hear, but supposed not to be heard by the other characters. **2** an incidental remark. □ **aside from** *US* apart from. **set aside 1** put to one side. **2** keep for a special purpose or future use. **3** reject or disregard. **4** annul. **5** remove (land) from agricultural production to fallow, forestry, or other use. **take aside** engage (a person) esp. for a private conversation. [orig. *on side*: see A[2]]

A-side /ˈeɪsaɪd/ *n.* the side of a gramophone record regarded as the main one.

Asimov /ˈæsɪˌmɒf/, Isaac (1920–), Russian-born American author, whose prolific output includes science fiction, books on science for the layman, and essays on a wide variety of subjects. Among his best-known science fiction is *I, Robot* (1950) and the *Foundation* trilogy (1951–3 and 1982). He coined the term *robotic* (see entry).

asinine /ˈæsɪˌnaɪn/ *adj.* **1** stupid. **2** of or concerning asses; like an ass. □□ **asininity** /-ˈnɪnɪtɪ/ *n.* [L *asininus* f. *asinus* ass]

Asir Mountains /əˈsɪə(r)/ a range of mountains in the south-west of Saudi Arabia, running parallel to the coast of the Red Sea.

-asis /əsɪs/ *suffix* (usu. as **-iasis**) forming the names of diseases (*psoriasis; satyriasis*). [L f. Gk *-asis* in nouns of state f. verbs in *-aō*]

ask /ɑːsk/ *v.* **1** *tr.* call for an answer to or about (*ask her about it; ask him his name; ask a question of him*). **2** *tr.* seek to obtain from another person (*ask a favour of; ask to be allowed*). **3** *tr.* (usu. foll. by *out* or *over*, or *to* (a function etc.)) request the company of (*must ask them over; asked her to dinner*). **4** *intr.* (foll. by *for*) seek to obtain, meet, or be directed to (*ask for a donation; ask for the post office; asking for you*). **5** *tr. archaic* require (a thing). □ **ask after** inquire about (esp. a person). **ask for it** *sl.* invite trouble. **asking price** the price of an object set by the seller. **ask me another** *colloq.* I do not know. **for the asking** (obtainable) for nothing. **I ask you!** an exclamation of disgust, surprise, etc. **if you ask me** *colloq.* in my opinion. □□ **asker** *n.* [OE *āscian* etc. f. WG]

askance /əˈskæns, -ˈskɑːns/ *adv.* (also **askant** /-ˈskænt, -ˈskɑːnt/)

sideways or squinting. □ **look askance at** regard with suspicion or disapproval. [16th c.: orig. unkn.]

askari /æˈskɑːrɪ/ n. (pl. same or **askaris**) an East African soldier or policeman. [Arab. *'askarī* soldier]

askew /əˈskjuː/ adv. & predic.adj. —adv. obliquely; awry. —predic.adj. oblique; awry. [A² + SKEW]

aslant /əˈslɑːnt/ adv. & prep. —adv. obliquely or at a slant. —prep. obliquely across (*lay aslant the path*).

asleep /əˈsliːp/ predic.adj. & adv. **1 a** in or into a state of sleep (*he fell asleep*). **b** inactive, inattentive (*the nation is asleep*). **2** (of a limb etc.) numb. **3** *euphem.* dead.

ASLEF /ˈæzlef/ abbr. (in the UK) Associated Society of Locomotive Engineers and Firemen.

aslope /əˈsləʊp/ adv. & predic.adj. sloping; crosswise. [ME: orig. uncert.]

ASM abbr. air-to-surface missile.

Asmara /æsˈmɑːrə/ the capital of Eritrea, Ethiopia; pop. (est. 1984) 275,000.

asocial /eɪˈsəʊʃ(ə)l/ adj. **1** not social; antisocial. **2** colloq. inconsiderate of or hostile to others.

Asoka /əˈsəʊkə/ (died c.232 BC) Buddhist emperor of India from c.269 BC, ruling over the greater part of the peninsula. He embarked on a campaign of conquest, but after his conversion to Buddhism renounced war and sent out missionaries as far afield as Syria and Ceylon to spread his new faith.

asp /æsp/ n. **1** a small viper, *Vipera aspis*, native to Southern Europe, resembling the adder. **2** a small venomous snake, *Naja haje*, native to North Africa and Arabia. [ME f. OF *aspe* or L *aspis* f. Gk]

asparagus /əˈspærəgəs/ n. **1** any plant of the genus *Asparagus*. **2** one species of this, *A. officinalis*, with edible young shoots and leaves; this as food. □ **asparagus fern** a decorative plant, *Asparagus setaceus*. [L f. Gk *asparagos*]

aspartame /əˈspɑːteɪm/ n. a very sweet low-calorie substance used as a sweetener instead of sugar or saccharin. [contr. of the chem. name *1-methyl N-L-aspartyl-L-phenylalanine*, f. *aspartic acid* (invented name)]

aspect /ˈæspekt/ n. **1 a** a particular component or feature of a matter (*only one aspect of the problem*). **b** a particular way in which a matter may be considered. **2 a** a facial expression; a look (*a cheerful aspect*). **b** the appearance of a person or thing, esp. as presented to the mind of the viewer (*has a frightening aspect*). **3** the side of a building or location facing a particular direction (*southern aspect*). **4** *Gram.* a verbal category or form expressing inception, duration, or completion. **5** *Astrol.* the relative position of planets etc. measured by angular distance. □ **aspect ratio 1** *Aeron.* the ratio of the span to the mean chord of an aerofoil. **2** *Telev.* the ratio of picture width to height. □□ **aspectual** /æˈspektjʊəl/ adj. (in sense 4). [ME f. L *aspectus* f. *adspicere adspect-* look at (as AD-, *specere* look)]

Aspen /ˈæspən/ an old silver-mining town in Colorado, converted into a year-round resort.

aspen /ˈæspən/ n. a poplar tree, *Populus tremula*, with especially tremulous leaves. [earlier name *asp* f. OE *æspe* + -EN² forming adj. taken as noun]

asperity /əˈsperɪtɪ/ n. (pl. **-ies**) **1** harshness or sharpness of temper or tone. **2** roughness. **3** a rough excrescence. [ME f. OF *asperité* or L *asperitas* f. *asper* rough]

asperse /əˈspɜːs/ v.tr. (often foll. by *with*) attack the reputation of; calumniate. [ME, = besprinkle, f. L *aspergere aspers-* (as AD-, *spargere* sprinkle)]

aspersion /əˈspɜːʃ(ə)n/ n. □ **cast aspersions on** attack the reputation or integrity of. [L *aspersio* (as ASPERSE, -ION)]

asphalt /ˈæsfælt/ n. & v. —n. **1** a dark bituminous pitch occurring naturally or made from petroleum. Most asphalt is obtained from oil refineries, from the distillation of certain crude oils, but it can occur naturally in surface deposits. **2** a mixture of this with sand, gravel, etc., for surfacing roads etc. —v.tr. surface with asphalt. □□ **asphalter** n. **asphaltic** /-ˈfæltɪk/ adj. [ME, ult. f. LL *asphalton, -um*, f. Gk *asphalton*]

asphodel /ˈæsfədel/ n. **1** any plant of the genus *Asphodelus*, of the lily family. **2** *poet.* an immortal flower growing in Elysium. [L *asphodelus* f. Gk *asphodelos*: cf. DAFFODIL]

asphyxia /æsˈfɪksɪə/ n. a lack of oxygen in the blood, causing unconsciousness or death; suffocation. □□ **asphyxial** adj. **asphyxiant** adj. & n. [mod.L f. Gk *asphuxia* f. *a-* not + *sphuxis* pulse]

asphyxiate /æsˈfɪksɪeɪt/ v.tr. cause (a person) to have asphyxia; suffocate. □□ **asphyxiation** /-ˈeɪʃ(ə)n/ n. **asphyxiator** n.

aspic /ˈæspɪk/ n. a savoury meat jelly used as a garnish or to contain game, eggs, etc. [F, = ASP, from the colours of the jelly (compared to those of the asp)]

aspidistra /ˌæspɪˈdɪstrə/ n. a foliage plant of the genus *Aspidistra*, with broad tapering leaves, often grown as a house-plant. [mod.L f. Gk *aspis -idos* shield (from the shape of the leaves)]

aspirant /ˈæspɪrənt, əˈspaɪərənt/ adj. & n. (usu. foll. by *to, after, for*) —adj. aspiring. —n. a person who aspires. [F *aspirant* or f. L *aspirant-* (as ASPIRE, -ANT)]

aspirate /ˈæspərət/ adj., n., & v. *Phonet.* —adj. **1** pronounced with an exhalation of breath. **2** blended with the sound of *h*. —n. **1** a consonant pronounced in this way. **2** the sound of *h*. —v. /-ˌreɪt/ **1 a** tr. pronounce with a breath. **b** intr. make the sound of *h*. **2** tr. draw (fluid) by suction from a vessel or cavity. [L *aspiratus* past part. of *aspirare*: see ASPIRE]

aspiration /ˌæspɪˈreɪʃ(ə)n/ n. **1** a strong desire to achieve an end; an ambition. **2** the act or process of drawing breath. **3** the action of aspirating. [ME f. OF *aspiration* or L *aspiratio* (as ASPIRATE, -ATION)]

aspirator /ˈæspɪˌreɪtə(r)/ n. an apparatus for aspirating fluid. [L *aspirare* (as ASPIRATE, -OR¹)]

aspire /əˈspaɪə(r)/ v.intr. (usu. foll. by *to* or *after*, or *to* + infin.) **1** have ambition or strong desire. **2** *poet.* rise high. [ME f. F *aspirer* or L *aspirare* f. *ad* to + *spirare* breathe]

aspirin /ˈæsprɪn/ n. (pl. same or **aspirins**) **1** a white powder, acetylsalicylic acid, used to relieve pain and reduce fever. Aspirin was developed in Germany in the late 1890s, originally to reduce inflammation, and was discovered to have pain-relieving properties too. **2** a tablet of this. [G, formed as ACETYL + *spiraeic* (= *salicylic*) *acid* + -IN]

asquint /əˈskwɪnt/ predic.adj. & adv. (usu. **look asquint**). **1** to one side; from the corner of an eye. **2** with a squint. [ME perh. f. Du. *schuinte* slant]

Asquith /ˈæskwɪθ/, Herbert Henry, 1st Earl of Oxford and Asquith (1852–1928), British statesman, who succeeded Campbell-Bannerman as Liberal leader and Prime Minister in 1908. In the years before the First World War his administration had to face a host of problems, most notably the conflict with the House of Lords caused by the introduction of Lloyd George's People's Budget in 1909, Irish demands for Home Rule, industrial unrest, and the women's suffrage movement. After the beginning of the war Asquith proved increasingly unequal to the task of leadership and was eventually displaced by Lloyd George at the end of 1916. He remained leader of the Liberal Party until 1926, but the party's fortunes declined sharply after the wartime split with Lloyd George.

ass¹ /æs/ n. & v. —n. **1 a** either of two kinds of four-legged long-eared mammal of the horse genus *Equus*, *E. africana* of Africa and *E. hemionus* of Asia. **b** (in general use) a donkey. **2** a stupid person. —v.intr. sl. (foll. by *about, around*) act the fool. □ **asses' bridge** = PONS ASINORUM. **make an ass of** make (a person) look absurd or foolish. [OE *assa* through OCelt. f. L *asinus*]

ass² US var. of ARSE.

assagai var. of ASSEGAI.

assai /æˈsaɪ/ adv. *Mus.* very (*adagio assai*). [It.]

assail /əˈseɪl/ v.tr. **1** make a strong or concerted attack on. **2** make a resolute start on (a task). **3** make a strong or constant verbal attack on (*was assailed with angry questions*). □□ **assailable** adj. [ME f. OF *asail- stressed stem of *asalir* f. med.L *assalire* f. L *assilire* (as AD-, *salire* salt- leap)]

assailant /ə'seɪlənt/ n. a person who attacks another physically or verbally. [F (as ASSAIL)]

Assam /æ'sæm/ a State in NE India, formed in 1947; pop. (1981) 19,902,800; capital, Dispur. Parts have since been separated off as the States of Meghalaya and Nagaland and the Union Territories of Arunachal Pradesh and Mizoram. □□ **Assamese** /-'miːz/ adj. & n.

assassin /ə'sæsɪn/ n. 1 a killer, esp. of a political or religious leader. 2 hist. any of a group of Muslim fanatics in the time of the Crusades, sent on murder errands by Hasan-ben-Sabah (the 'Old Man of the Mountains') or later leaders and notorious for a series of killings of political and religious opponents (see AGA KHAN). [F assassin or f. med.L assassinus f. Arab. ḥaššāš hashish-eater]

assassinate /ə'sæsɪˌneɪt/ v.tr. kill (esp. a political or religious leader) for political or religious motives. □□ **assassination** /-ˈneɪʃ(ə)n/ n. **assassinator** n. [med.L assassinare f. assassinus: see ASSASSIN]

assault /ə'sɔːlt, ə'sɒlt/ n. & v. —n. 1 a violent physical or verbal attack. 2 a Law an act that threatens physical harm to a person (whether or not actual harm is done). b euphem. an act of rape. 3 (attrib.) relating to or used in an assault (assault craft; assault troops). 4 a vigorous start made to a lengthy or difficult task. 5 a final rush on a fortified place, esp. at the end of a prolonged attack. —v.tr. 1 make an assault on. 2 euphem. rape. □ **assault and battery** Law a threatening act that results in physical harm done to a person. **assault course** an obstacle course used in training soldiers etc. □□ **assaulter** n. **assaultive** adj. [ME f. OF asaut, assauter ult. f. L (salire salt-leap)]

assay /ə'seɪ, 'æseɪ/ n. & v. —n. 1 the testing of a metal or ore to determine its ingredients and quality. 2 Chem. etc. the determination of the content or strength of a substance. —v. 1 tr. make an assay of (a metal or ore). 2 tr. Chem. etc. perform a concentration on (a substance). 3 tr. show (content) on being assayed. 4 intr. make an assay. 5 tr. archaic attempt. □ **Assay Office** an establishment which awards hallmarks. □□ **assayer** n. [ME f. OF assaier, assai, var. of essayer, essai: see ESSAY]

assegai /'æsɪˌɡaɪ/ n. (also **assagai** /'æsəˌɡaɪ/) a slender iron-tipped spear of hard wood, esp. as used by S. African peoples. [obs. F azagaie or Port. azagaia f. Arab. az-zaġāyah f. al the + zaġāyah spear]

assemblage /ə'semblɪdʒ/ n. 1 the act or an instance of bringing or coming together. 2 a collection of things or gathering of people. 3 a the act or an instance of fitting together. b an object made of pieces fitted together. 4 a work of art made by grouping found or unrelated objects.

assemble /ə'semb(ə)l/ v. 1 tr. & intr. gather together; collect. 2 tr. arrange in order. 3 tr. esp. Mech. fit together the parts of. [ME f. OF asembler ult. f. L ad to + simul together]

assembler /ə'semblə(r)/ n. 1 a person who assembles a machine or its parts. 2 Computing a a program for converting instructions written in low-level symbolic code into machine code. b the low-level symbolic code itself; an assembly language.

assembly /ə'semblɪ/ n. (pl. **-ies**) 1 the act or an instance of assembling or gathering together. 2 a a group of persons gathered together, esp. as a deliberative body or a legislative council. b a gathering of the entire members of a school. 3 the assembling of a machine or structure or its parts. 4 Mil. a call to assemble, given by drum or bugle. □ **assembly language** Computing the low-level symbolic code converted by an assembler. **assembly line** machinery arranged in stages by which a product is progressively assembled. **assembly room** (or **shop**) a place where a machine or its components are assembled. **assembly rooms** public rooms in which meetings or social functions are held. [ME f. OF asemblee fem. past part. of asembler: see ASSEMBLE]

assent /ə'sent/ v. & n. —v.intr. (usu. foll. by to) 1 express agreement (assented to my view). 2 consent (assented to my request). —n. 1 mental or inward acceptance or agreement (a nod of assent). 2 consent or sanction, esp. official. □ **royal assent** assent of the sovereign to a bill passed by Parliament. □□

assenter n. (also **assentor**). [ME f. OF asenter, as(s)ente ult. f. L assentari (ad to, sentire think)]

assentient /ə'senʃ(ə)nt, -ʃɪənt/ adj. & n. —adj. assenting. —n. a person who assents. [L assentire (as ASSENT, -ENT)]

assert /ə'sɜːt/ v. 1 tr. declare; state clearly (assert one's beliefs; assert that it is so). 2 refl. insist on one's rights or opinions; demand recognition. 3 tr. vindicate a claim to (assert one's rights). □□ **assertor** n. [L asserere (as AD-, serere sert- join)]

assertion /ə'sɜːʃ(ə)n/ n. 1 a declaration; a forthright statement. 2 the act or an instance of asserting. 3 (also **self-assertion**) insistence on the recognition of one's rights or claims. [ME f. F assertion or L assertio (as ASSERT, -ION)]

assertive /ə'sɜːtɪv/ adj. 1 tending to assert oneself; forthright, positive. 2 dogmatic. □□ **assertively** adv. **assertiveness** n.

asses pl. of AS², ASS¹, ASS².

assess /ə'ses/ v.tr. 1 a estimate the size or quality of. b estimate the value of (a property) for taxation. 2 a (usu. foll. by on) fix the amount of (a tax etc.) and impose it on a person or community. b (usu. foll. by in, at) fine or tax (a person, community, etc.) in or at a specific amount (assessed them at £100). □□ **assessable** adj. **assessment** n. [ME f. F assesser f. L assidēre (as AD-, sedēre sit)]

assessor /ə'sesə(r)/ n. 1 a person who assesses taxes or estimates the value of property for taxation or insurance purposes. 2 a person called upon to advise a judge, committee of inquiry, etc., on technical questions. □□ **assessorial** /ˌæse'sɔːrɪəl/ adj. [ME f. OF assessour f. L assessor -oris assistant-judge (as ASSESS, -OR¹): sense 1 f. med.L]

asset /'æset/ n. 1 a a useful or valuable quality. b a person or thing possessing such a quality or qualities (is an asset to the firm). 2 (usu. in pl.) a property and possessions, esp. regarded as having value in meeting debts, commitments, etc. b any possession having value. □ **asset-stripping** Commerce the practice of taking over a company and selling off its assets to make a profit. [assets (taken as pl.), f. AF asetz f. OF asez enough, ult. f. L ad to + satis enough]

asseverate /ə'sevəˌreɪt/ v.tr. declare solemnly. □□ **asseveration** /-'reɪʃ(ə)n/ n. [L asseverare (as AD-, severus serious)]

assibilate /ə'sɪbɪˌleɪt/ v.tr. Phonet. 1 pronounce (a sound) as a sibilant or affricate ending in a sibilant. 2 alter (a syllable) to become this. □□ **assibilation** /-'leɪʃ(ə)n/ n. [L assibilare (as AD-, sibilare hiss)]

assiduity /ˌæsɪ'djuːɪtɪ/ n. (pl. **-ies**) 1 constant or close attention to what one is doing. 2 (usu. in pl.) constant attentions to another person. [L assiduitas (as ASSIDUOUS, -ITY)]

assiduous /ə'sɪdjʊəs/ adj. 1 persevering, hard-working. 2 attending closely. □□ **assiduously** adv. **assiduousness** n. [L assiduus (as ASSESS)]

assign /ə'saɪn/ v. & n. —v.tr. 1 (usu. foll. by to) a allot as a share or responsibility. b appoint to a position, task, etc. 2 fix (a time, place, etc.) for a specific purpose. 3 (foll. by to) ascribe or refer to (a reason, date, etc.) (assigned the manuscript to 1832). 4 (foll. by to) transfer formally (esp. personal property) to (another). —n. a person to whom property or rights are legally transferred. □□ **assignable** adj. **assigner** n. **assignor** n. (in sense 4 of v.). [ME f. OF asi(g)ner f. L assignare mark out to (as AD-, signum sign)]

assignation /ˌæsɪɡ'neɪʃ(ə)n/ n. 1 a an appointment to meet. b a secret appointment, esp. between illicit lovers. 2 the act or an instance of assigning or being assigned. [ME f. OF f. L assignatio -onis (as ASSIGN, -ATION)]

assignee /ˌæsaɪ'niː/ n. 1 a person appointed to act for another. 2 an assign. [ME f. OF assigné past part. of assigner ASSIGN]

assignment /ə'saɪnmənt/ n. 1 something assigned, esp. a task allotted to a person. 2 the act or an instance of assigning or being assigned. 3 a a legal transfer. b the document effecting this. [ME f. OF assignement f. med.L assignamentum (as ASSIGN, -MENT)]

assimilate /ə'sɪmɪˌleɪt/ v. 1 tr. a absorb and digest (food etc.) into the body. b absorb (information etc.) into the mind. c absorb (people) into a larger group. 2 tr. (usu. foll. by to, with) make like; cause to resemble. **3** *tr. Phonet.* make (a sound) more like another in the same or next word. **4** *intr.* be absorbed into the body, mind, or a larger group. □□ **assimilable** *adj.* **assimilation** /-ˈleɪʃ(ə)n/ *n.* **assimilative** *adj.* **assimilator** *n.* **assimilatory** /-lətərɪ/ *adj.* [ME f. L *assimilare* (as AD-, *similis* like)]

Assisi /əˈsiːsɪ/ a town in Umbria in central Italy, famous as the birthplace of St Francis; pop. (1981) 24,650.

assist /əˈsɪst/ *v. & n.* —*v.* **1** *tr.* (often foll. by *in* + verbal noun) help (a person, process, etc.) (*assisted them in running the playgroup*). **2** *intr.* (often foll. by *in, at*) take part or be present (*assisted in the ceremony*). —*n. US* **1** help; an act of helping. **2** *Baseball* etc. a player's action of helping to put out an opponent, score a goal, etc. □□ **assistance** *n.* **assister** *n.* [ME f. F *assister* f. L *assistere* take one's stand by (as AD-, *sistere* take one's stand)]

assistant /əˈsɪst(ə)nt/ *n.* **1** a helper. **2** (often *attrib.*) a person who assists, esp. as a subordinate in a particular job or role. **3** = *shop assistant*. [ME *assistent* f. med.L *assistens assistent-*present (as ASSIST, -ANT, -ENT)]

assize /əˈsaɪz/ *n.* (usu. in *pl.*) *hist.* a court sitting at intervals in each county of England and Wales to administer the civil and criminal law. ¶ In 1972 the civil jurisdiction of assizes was transferred to the High Court and the criminal jurisdiction to the Crown Court. [ME f. OF *as(s)ise*, fem. past part. of *aseeir* sit at, f. L *assidēre*: cf. ASSESS]

Assoc. *abbr.* (as part of a title) Association.

associable /əˈsəʊʃəb(ə)l/ *adj.* (usu. foll. by *with*) capable of being connected in thought. □□ **associability** /-ˈbɪlɪtɪ/ *n.* [F f. *associer* (as ASSOCIATE, -ABLE)]

associate *v., n., & adj.* —*v.* /əˈsəʊʃɪˌeɪt, -sɪˌeɪt/ **1** *tr.* connect in the mind (*associate holly with Christmas*). **2** *tr.* join or combine. **3** *refl.* make oneself a partner; declare oneself in agreement (*associate myself in your endeavour; did not want to associate ourselves with the plan*). **4** *intr.* combine for a common purpose. **5** *intr.* (usu. foll. by *with*) meet frequently or have dealings. —*n.* /əˈsəʊʃɪət, -sɪət/ **1** a business partner or colleague. **2** a friend or companion. **3** a subordinate member of a body, institute, etc. **4** a thing connected with another. —*adj.* /əˈsəʊʃɪət, -sɪət/ **1** joined in companionship, function, or dignity. **2** allied; in the same group or category. **3** of less than full status (*associate member*). □□ **associateship** /əˈsəʊʃɪətʃɪp, əˈsəʊs-/ *n.* **associator** /əˈsəʊʃɪˌeɪtə(r), əˈsəʊs-/ *n.* **associatory** /əˈsəʊʃɪətərɪ, əˈsəʊs-/ *adj.* [E f. L *associatus* past part. of *associare* (as AD-, *socius* sharing, allied)]

association /əˌsəʊsɪˈeɪʃ(ə)n/ *n.* **1** a group of people organized for a joint purpose; a society. **2** the act or an instance of associating. **3** fellowship or companionship. **4** a mental connection between ideas. **5** *Chem.* a loose aggregation of molecules. **6** *Ecol.* a group of associated plants. □ **Association Football** *Brit.* football played by sides of 11 with a round ball which may not be handled during play except by the goalkeepers. □□ **associational** *adj.* [F *association* or med.L *associatio* (as ASSOCIATE, -ATION)]

associative /əˈsəʊʃɪətɪv, əˈsəʊs-/ *adj.* **1** of or involving association. **2** *Math. & Computing* involving the condition that a group of quantities connected by operators (see OPERATOR 4) gives the same result whatever their grouping, as long as their order remains the same, e.g. $(a \times b) \times c = a \times (b \times c)$.

assonance /ˈæsənəns/ *n.* the resemblance of sound between two syllables in nearby words, arising from the rhyming of two or more accented vowels, but not consonants, or the use of identical consonants with different vowels, e.g. *sonnet*, *porridge*, and *killed*, *cold*, *culled*. □□ **assonant** *adj.* **assonate** /-ˌneɪt/ *v.intr.* [F f. L *assonare* respond to (as AD-, *sonus* sound)]

assort /əˈsɔːt/ *v.* **1** *tr.* (usu. foll. by *with*) classify or arrange in groups. **2** *intr.* suit; fit into; harmonize with (usu. *assort ill* or *well with*). [OF *assorter* f. *à* to + *sorte* SORT]

assortative /əˈsɔːtətɪv/ *adj.* assorting. □ **assortative mating** *Biol.* selective mating based on the similarity of the partners' characteristics etc.

assorted /əˈsɔːtɪd/ *adj.* **1** of various sorts put together; miscellaneous. **2** sorted into groups. **3** matched (*ill-assorted*; *poorly assorted*).

assortment /əˈsɔːtmənt/ *n.* a set of various sorts of things or people put together; a mixed collection.

ASSR *abbr.* Autonomous Soviet Socialist Republic.

Asst. *abbr.* Assistant.

assuage /əˈsweɪdʒ/ *v.tr.* **1** calm or soothe (a person, pain, etc.). **2** appease or relieve (an appetite or desire). □□ **assuagement** *n.* **assuager** *n.* [ME f. OF *as(s)ouagier* ult. f. L *suavis* sweet]

assume /əˈsjuːm/ *v.tr.* **1** (usu. foll. by *that* + clause) take or accept as being true, without proof, for the purpose of argument or action. **2** simulate or pretend (ignorance etc.). **3** undertake (an office or duty). **4** take or put on oneself or itself (an aspect, attribute, etc.) (*the problem assumed immense proportions*). **5** (usu. foll. by *to*) arrogate, usurp, or seize (credit, power, etc.) (*assumed to himself the right of veto*). □□ **assumable** *adj.* **assumedly** /-mɪdlɪ/ *adv.* [ME f. L *assumere* (as AD-, *sumere sumpt-* take)]

assuming /əˈsjuːmɪŋ/ *adj.* (of a person) taking too much for granted; arrogant, presumptuous.

assumption /əˈsʌmpʃ(ə)n/ *n.* **1** the act or an instance of assuming. **2 a** the act or an instance of accepting without proof. **b** a thing assumed in this way. **3** arrogance. **4** (**Assumption**) **a** the reception of the Virgin Mary bodily into heaven, according to Roman Catholic doctrine. **b** the feast in honour of this (15 August). The doctrine dates from the 4th c. and is held by the Roman Catholic and Orthodox Churches. In the Church of England the feast was removed from the Book of Common Prayer in 1549 and has not been officially restored. [ME f. OF *asompsion* or L *assumptio* (as ASSUME, -ION)]

assumptive /əˈsʌmptɪv/ *adj.* **1** taken for granted. **2** arrogant. [L *assumptivus* (as ASSUME, -IVE)]

assurance /əˈʃʊərəns/ *n.* **1** a positive declaration that a thing is true. **2** a solemn promise or guarantee. **3** insurance, esp. life insurance. Insurance companies tend to use the term *assurance* of policies where a sum is payable after a fixed number of years or on the death of the insured person, and *insurance* of policies relating to events such as fire, accident, or death within a limited period. In popular usage the word *insurance* is used in both cases. **4** certainty. **5 a** self-confidence. **b** impudence. [ME f. OF *aseürance* f. *aseürer* (as ASSURE, -ANCE)]

assure /əˈʃʊə(r)/ *v.tr.* **1** (often foll. by *of*) **a** make (a person) sure; convince (*assured him of my sincerity*). **b** tell (a person) confidently (*assured him the bus went to Westminster*). **2 a** make certain of; ensure the happening etc. of (*will assure her success*). **b** make safe (against overthrow etc.). **3** insure (esp. a life). **4** (as **assured** *adj.*) **a** guaranteed. **b** self-confident. □ **rest assured** remain confident. □□ **assurable** *adj.* **assurer** *n.* [ME f. OF *aseürer* ult. f. L *securus* safe, SECURE]

assuredly /əˈʃʊərɪdlɪ/ *adv.* certainly.

Assyria /əˈsɪrɪə/ an ancient country in what is now northern Iraq. It was originally centred on Ashur, a city-state on the west bank of the Tigris, which first became prominent and expanded its borders in the 14th c. BC. From the 8th to the late 7th c. BC Assyria was the dominant Near Eastern power and created an empire which stretched from the Persian Gulf to Egypt. The State fell in 612 BC, defeated by a coalition of Medes and Chaldeans. □□ **Assyrian** *adj. & n.*

Assyriology /əˌsɪrɪˈɒlədʒɪ/ *n.* the study of the language, history, and antiquities of Assyria. □□ **Assyriologist** *n.*

AST *abbr.* Atlantic Standard Time.

astable /eɪˈsteɪb(ə)l/ *adj.* **1** not stable. **2** *Electr.* of or relating to a circuit which oscillates spontaneously between unstable states.

Astaire /əˈsteə(r)/, Fred (real name Frederick Austerlitz, 1899–1987), American dancer, singer, and film actor. In the 1930s he starred in a number of musicals, including *Top Hat* (1935), *Follow the Fleet* (1936), and *Shall We Dance?* (1937), in a notable partnership with the actress Ginger Rogers (1911–), and is famed for his technical excellence and sophisticated style.

Astarte /əˈstɑːtɪ/ *Semitic Mythol.* a Phoenician goddess of fertility and sexual love, whose cult was widespread. She became identified with the Egyptian Isis, the Greek Aphrodite, and others. In the Bible she is referred to as Ashtaroth or Ashtoreth, and her worship is linked with that of Baal.

astatic /eɪˈstætɪk, ə-/ *adj.* **1** not static; unstable or unsteady. **2** *Physics* not tending to keep one position or direction. □ **astatic galvanometer** one in which the effect of the earth's magnetic field on the meter needle is greatly reduced. [Gk *astatos* unstable f. *a-* not + *sta-* stand]

astatine /ˈæstətiːn/ *n. Chem.* a radioactive element, the heaviest of the halogens, which occurs naturally in minute quantities but was first prepared artificially in 1940 by bombarding bismuth with alpha particles. ¶ Symb: **At**; atomic number 85. [formed as ASTATIC + -INE⁴]

aster /ˈæstə(r)/ *n.* any composite plant of the genus *Aster*, with bright daisy-like flowers, e.g. the Michaelmas daisy. □ **China aster** a related plant, *Callistephus chinensis*, cultivated for its bright and showy flowers. [L f. Gk *astēr* star]

-aster /ˈæstə(r)/ *suffix* **1** forming nouns denoting poor quality (*criticaster, poetaster*). **2** *Bot.* denoting incomplete resemblance (*oleaster; pinaster*). [L]

asterisk /ˈæstərɪsk/ *n. & v.* —*n.* a symbol (*) used in printing and writing to mark words etc. for reference, to stand for omitted matter, etc. —*v.tr.* mark with an asterisk. [ME f. LL *asteriscus* f. Gk *asteriskos* dimin. (as ASTER)]

asterism /ˈæstəˌrɪz(ə)m/ *n.* **1** a cluster of stars. **2** a group of three asterisks (⁂) calling attention to following text. [Gk *asterismos* (as ASTER, -ISM)]

astern /əˈstɜːn/ *adv. Naut. & Aeron.* (often foll. by *of*) **1** aft; away to the rear. **2** backwards. [A² + STERN²]

asteroid /ˈæstəˌrɔɪd/ *n.* **1** any of the minor planets revolving round the sun, mainly between the orbits of Mars and Jupiter. (See MINOR.) **2** *Zool.* a starfish. □□ **asteroidal** /ˌæstəˈrɔɪd(ə)l/ *adj.* [Gk *asteroeidēs* (as ASTER, -OID)]

asthenia /æsˈθiːnɪə/ *n. Med.* loss of strength; debility. [mod.L f. Gk *astheneia* f. *asthenēs* weak]

asthenic /æsˈθenɪk/ *adj. & n.* —*adj.* **1** of lean or long-limbed build. **2** *Med.* of or characterized by asthenia. —*n.* a lean long-limbed person.

asthma /ˈæsmə/ *n.* a usu. allergic respiratory disease, often with paroxysms of difficult breathing. [ME f. Gk *asthma -matos* f. *azō* breathe hard]

asthmatic /æsˈmætɪk/ *adj. & n.* —*adj.* relating to or suffering from asthma. —*n.* a person suffering from asthma. □□ **asthmatically** *adv.* [L *asthmaticus* f. Gk *asthmatikos* (as ASTHMA, -IC)]

Asti /ˈæstɪ/ *n.* (*pl.* **Astis**) an Italian white wine. □ **Asti spumante** /spuːˈmæntɪ/ a sparkling form of this. [*Asti* in Piedmont]

astigmatism /əˈstɪgməˌtɪz(ə)m/ *n.* a defect in the eye or in a lens resulting in distorted images, as light rays are prevented from meeting at a common focus. □□ **astigmatic** /ˌæstɪgˈmætɪk/ *adj.* [A-¹ + Gk *stigma -matos* point]

astilbe /əˈstɪlbɪ/ *n.* any plant of the genus *Astilbe*, with plumelike heads of tiny white or red flowers. [mod.L f. Gk *a-* not + *stilbē* fem. of *stilbos* glittering, from the inconspicuous (individual) flowers]

astir /əˈstɜː(r)/ *predic.adj. & adv.* **1** in motion. **2** awake and out of bed (*astir early; already astir*). **3** excited. [A² + STIR¹ *n.*]

Aston /ˈæst(ə)n/, Francis William (1877–1945), English physicist who worked in Cambridge with J. J. Thomson, and invented the mass spectrograph. With this apparatus he could separate electrically charged particles according to their atomic weights, and eventually discovered many of the 287 naturally occurring isotopes of non-radioactive elements, and in 1919 announced his whole-number rule governing their masses. He was awarded the Nobel Prize for chemistry in 1922.

astonish /əˈstɒnɪʃ/ *v.tr.* amaze; surprise greatly. □□ **astonishing** *adj.* **astonishingly** *adv.* **astonishment** *n.* [obs. *astone* f. OF *estoner* f. Gallo-Roman: see -ISH²]

Astor /ˈæstə(r)/, Nancy Witcher, Viscountess (1879–1964), English Conservative politician, who became the first woman to sit in the House of Commons when she succeeded her husband as MP for Plymouth in 1919.

astound /əˈstaʊnd/ *v.tr.* shock with alarm or surprise; amaze. □□ **astounding** *adj.* **astoundingly** *adv.* [obs. *astound* (adj.) = *astoned* past part. of obs. *astone*: see ASTONISH]

astraddle /əˈstræd(ə)l/ *adv. & predic.adj.* in a straddling position.

astragal /ˈæstrəg(ə)l/ *n. Archit.* a small semicircular moulding round the top or bottom of a column. [ASTRAGALUS]

astragalus /əˈstrægələs/ *n.* (*pl.* **-li** /-ˌlaɪ/) **1** *Anat.* = TALUS¹. **2** *Bot.* a leguminous plant of the genus *Astragalus*, e.g. the milk-vetch. [L f. Gk *astragalos* ankle-bone, moulding, a plant]

Astrakhan /ˌæstrəˈkɑːn/ a city in the Russian SFSR, on the delta of the River Volga; pop. (est. 1987) 509,000.

astrakhan /ˌæstrəˈkæn/ *n.* **1** the dark curly fleece of young lambs from Astrakhan. **2** a cloth imitating astrakhan. [ASTRAKHAN]

astral /ˈæstr(ə)l/ *adj.* **1** of or connected with the stars. **2** consisting of stars; starry. **3** *Theosophy* relating to or arising from a supposed ethereal existence, esp. of a counterpart of the body, associated with oneself in life and surviving after death. [LL *astralis* f. *astrum* star]

astray /əˈstreɪ/ *adv. & predic.adj.* **1** in or into error or sin (esp. *lead astray*). **2** out of the right way. □ **go astray** be lost or mislaid. [ME f. OF *estraié* past part. of *estraier* ult. f. L *extra* out of bounds + *vagari* wander]

astride /əˈstraɪd/ *adv. & prep.* —*adv.* **1** (often foll. by *of*) with a leg on each side. **2** with legs apart. —*prep.* with a leg on each side of; extending across.

astringent /əˈstrɪndʒ(ə)nt/ *adj. & n.* —*adj.* **1** causing the contraction of body tissues. **2** checking bleeding. **3** severe, austere. —*n.* an astringent substance or drug. □□ **astringency** *n.* **astringently** *adv.* [F f. L *astringere* (as AD-, *stringere* bind)]

astro- /ˈæstrəʊ/ *comb. form* **1** relating to the stars or celestial bodies. **2** relating to outer space. [Gk f. *astron* star]

astrochemistry /ˌæstrəʊˈkemɪstrɪ/ *n.* the study of molecules and radicals in interstellar space.

astrodome /ˈæstrəˌdəʊm/ *n.* a domed window in an aircraft for astronomical observations.

astrohatch /ˈæstrəˌhætʃ/ *n.* = ASTRODOME.

astrolabe /ˈæstrəˌleɪb/ *n.* an instrument, usu. consisting of a disc and pointer, formerly used to make astronomical measurements, esp. of the altitudes of celestial bodies, and as an aid in navigation. Its form and structure varied with the progress of astronomy and the purpose for which it was intended. In its earliest form (which dates from classical times) it consisted of a disc with the degrees of the circle marked round its edge, and a pivoted pointer along which a heavenly body could be sighted. From late medieval times it was used by mariners for calculating latitude, until replaced by the sextant. [ME f. OF *astrelabe* f. med.L *astrolabium* f. Gk *astrolabon*, neut. of *astrolabos* star-taking]

astrology /əˈstrɒlədʒɪ/ *n.* the study of the movements and relative positions of celestial bodies interpreted as an influence on human affairs. (See below.) □□ **astrologer** *n.* **astrological** /ˌæstrəˈlɒdʒɪk(ə)l/ *adj.* **astrologist** *n.* [ME f. OF *astrologie* f. L *astrologia* f. Gk (as ASTRO-, -LOGY)]

Astrology, long seen as applied astronomy, was developed by the Greeks and reached Christian Europe via the Arabs. It was a utilitarian science linked to medicine and agriculture, and also an ambitious philosophical system resting on the belief that the stars influenced the entire sublunar world. By studying eclipses, comets, and the movements of the planets in the zodiac, astrologers felt able to predict such effects as wars, plagues, and the weather. They found a key to a person's whole life in his horoscope, the disposition of the planets at his birth. In the Renaissance popes such as Paul III (1534–49) were enthusiastic patrons, and many rulers employed court astrologers for both political and medical assistance, Nostradamus (16th c.) being the best known. A papal bull of 1586 condemned judicial astrology, and the Protestant reformer Calvin was hostile, but its decline was slow and many leading scientists in the 17th c. thought it had at least a residual basis of truth.

Though it had lost its intellectual standing by 1700, popular writers such as Old Moore (see Francis MOORE) gave it a widespread appeal which has survived to the present day. It still retains a more reputable standing in many parts of the East.

astronaut /ˈæstrənɔːt/ n. a person who is trained to travel in a spacecraft. □□ **astronautical** /ˌæstrə'nɔːtɪk(ə)l/ adj. [ASTRO-, after aeronaut]

astronautics /ˌæstrə'nɔːtɪks/ n. the science of space travel.

astronomical /ˌæstrə'nɒmɪk(ə)l/ adj. (also **astronomic**) **1** of or relating to astronomy. **2** extremely large; too large to contemplate. □ **astronomical unit** a unit of measurement in astronomy equal to the mean distance from the centre of the earth to the centre of the sun, 1.495 × 10¹¹ metres or 92.9 million miles. **astronomical year** see YEAR n. 1. □□ **astronomically** adv. [L astronomicus f. Gk astronomikos]

astronomy /ə'strɒnəmɪ/ n. the scientific study of celestial bodies. (See below.) □□ **astronomer** n. [ME f. OF astronomie f. L f. Gk astronomia f. astronomos (adj.) star-arranging f. nemō arrange]

From time immemorial people have charted the positions and motions of the sun and moon, stars and planets, the original naked-eye results later refined by the use of the telescope and interpreted by the mathematics of celestial mechanics and positional astronomy. The classification and interpretation of celestial objects depend now on the use of the most sophisticated instruments to measure positions and brightness: radio telescopes, infrared detectors, ultraviolet and X-ray satellites are all used, while robot probes can visit the planets, nearest of our neighbours in space. Once the science of regular celestial phenomena, upon which timekeeping and navigation depended, astronomy has expanded to ask about the nature and content of the entire universe.

astrophysics /ˌæstrəʊ'fɪzɪks/ n. a branch of astronomy concerned with the physics and chemistry of celestial bodies. The science draws heavily on the applications of known physical laws to understand the observations of astronomers, and reveals in turn new laws operating in the extreme conditions of temperature and density not attainable on earth. □□ **astrophysical** adj. **astrophysicist** /-sɪst/ n.

Astroturf /ˈæstrəʊˌtɜːf/ n. propr. an artificial grass surface, esp. for sports fields. [Astrodome, name of a sports stadium in Texas where it was first used, + TURF]

Asturias /æs'tjʊərɪəs/ a region of NW Spain; pop. (1986) 1,114,100; capital, Oviedo. □ **Prince of the Asturias** the title of an eldest son of the king of Spain.

astute /ə'stjuːt/ adj. **1** shrewd; sagacious. **2** crafty. □□ **astutely** adv. **astuteness** n. [obs. F astut or L astutus f. astus craft]

Asunción /əˌsʊnsɪ'ɒn/ the capital and chief port of Paraguay; pop. (est. 1984) 729,300.

asunder /ə'sʌndə(r)/ adv. literary apart. [OE on sundran into pieces: cf. SUNDER]

asura /ə'sjʊərə/ n. a member of a class of divine beings in the Vedic period, which in Indian mythology are evil (opposed to the devas) and in Zoroastrianism are benevolent. (Cf. DEVA.)

Aswan /æs'wɑːn/ a city (pop. (est. 1986) 195,700) in southern Egypt near which are two dams across the Nile. The first was built in 1898–1902 to regulate the flooding of the Nile and control the supply of water for irrigation and other purposes. It is now superseded by the high dam, built in 1960–70 with Soviet aid, about 3.6 km (2¼ miles) long and 111 m (364 ft.) high, a feat of building comparable to that of the pyramids. Behind it is the enormous reservoir of Lake Nasser, and its controlled release not only ensures a steady supply of water for irrigation and domestic and industrial use but produces hydroelectric power sufficient to supply the greater part of Egypt's electricity.

asylum /ə'saɪləm/ n. **1** sanctuary; protection, esp. for those pursued by the law (seek asylum). **2** hist. any of various kinds of institution offering shelter and support to distressed or destitute individuals, esp. the mentally ill. □ **political asylum** protection given by a State to a political refugee from another country. [ME f. L f. Gk asulon refuge f. a- not + sulon right of seizure]

asymmetry /eɪ'sɪmɪtrɪ, æ'sɪmɪtrɪ/ n. lack of symmetry. □□ **asymmetric** /-'metrɪk/ adj. **asymmetrical** /-'metrɪk(ə)l/ adj. **asymmetrically** /-'metrɪkəlɪ/ adv. [Gk asummetria (as A-¹, SYMMETRY)]

asymptomatic /eɪˌsɪmptə'mætɪk/ adj. producing or showing no symptoms.

asymptote /ˈæsɪmpˌtəʊt, 'æsɪmˌtəʊt/ n. a line that continually approaches a given curve but does not meet it at a finite distance. □□ **asymptotic** /ˌæsɪmp'tɒtɪk/ adj. **asymptotically** /ˌæsɪmp'tɒtɪkəlɪ/ adv. [mod.L asymptota (linea line) f. Gk asumptōtos not falling together f. a- not + sun together + ptōtos falling f. piptō fall]

asynchronous /eɪ'sɪŋkrənəs/ adj. not synchronous. □□ **asynchronously** adv.

asyndeton /ə'sɪndɪt(ə)n/ n. (pl. **asyndeta** /-tə/) the omission of a conjunction. □□ **asyndetic** /ˌæsɪn'detɪk/ adj. [mod.L f. Gk asundeton (neut. adj.) f. a- not + sundetos bound together]

At symb. Chem. the element astatine.

at /æt, unstressed ət/ prep. **1** expressing position, exact or approximate (wait at the corner; at the top of the hill; met at Bath; is at school; at a distance). **2** expressing a point in time (see you at three; went at dawn). **3** expressing a point in a scale or range (at boiling-point; at his best). **4** expressing engagement or concern in a state or activity (at war; at work; at odds). **5** expressing a value or rate (sell at £10 each). **6 a** with or with reference to; in terms of (at a disadvantage; annoyed at losing; good at cricket; play at fighting; sick at heart; came at a run; at short notice; work at it). **b** by means of (starts at a touch; drank it at a gulp). **7** expressing: **a** motion towards (arrived at the station; went at them). **b** aim towards or pursuit of (physically or conceptually) (aim at the target; work at a solution; guess at the truth; laughed at us; has been at the milk again). □ **at all** see ALL. **at hand** see HAND. **at home** see HOME. **at it 1** engaged in an activity; working hard. **2** colloq. repeating a habitual (usu. disapproved of) activity (found them at it again). **at once** see ONCE. **at that** moreover (found one, and a good one at that). **at times** see TIME. **where it's at** sl. the fashionable scene or activity. [OE æt, rel. to L ad to]

at- /ət/ prefix assim. form of AD- before t.

Atabrine var. of ATEBRIN.

Atacama Desert /ˌætə'kɑːmə/ the most arid region of South America, extending for a distance of some 965 km (600 miles) southwards into Chile from the Peruvian border.

Atalanta /ˌætə'læntə/ Gk legend a huntress, averse to marriage, loved by Meleager. She would marry no one who could not beat her in a foot-race, but Melanion (or Hippomenes) won the race by throwing down three golden apples given to him by Aphrodite, which were so beautiful that Atalanta stopped to pick them up.

ataractic /ˌætə'ræktɪk/ adj. & n. (also **ataraxic** /-'ræksɪk/) —adj. calming or tranquillizing. —n. a tranquillizing drug. [Gk ataraktos calm: cf. ATARAXY]

ataraxy /ˈætəˌræksɪ/ n. (also **ataraxia** /ˌætə'ræksɪə/) calmness or tranquillity; imperturbability. [F ataraxie f. Gk ataraxia impassiveness]

Atatürk /ˈætəˌtɜːk/, Kemal (1881–1938), Turkish general and statesman. A successful general in the Gallipoli campaign in 1915, Atatürk organized the Turkish Nationalist Party after the war, and, elected President of a provisional government in 1920, launched a victorious campaign to drive Greek invaders from Turkish soil. With the official establishment of the Turkish republic in 1923, he was elected its first president and remained in power until his death, wielding almost dictatorial powers in his struggle to make Turkey a modern secular State. Known first as Mustapha Kemal, and then as Kemal Pasha, he took the name of Atatürk (= father-Turk) in 1934.

atavism /ˈætəˌvɪz(ə)m/ n. **1** a resemblance to remote ancestors rather than to parents in plants or animals. **2** reversion to an earlier type. □□ **atavistic** /-'vɪstɪk/ adj. **atavistically** /-'vɪstɪkəlɪ/ adv. [F atavisme f. L atavus great-grandfather's grandfather]

ataxy /ə'tæksɪ/ n. (also **ataxia** /-sɪə/) Med. the loss of full control of bodily movements. □□ **ataxic** adj. [mod.L ataxia f. Gk f. a- not + taxis order]

ATC abbr. Brit. **1** air traffic control. **2** Air Training Corps.

ate past of EAT.

-ate[1] /ət, eɪt/ suffix **1** forming nouns denoting: **a** status or office (doctorate; episcopate). **b** state or function (curate; magistrate; mandate). **2** Chem. forming nouns denoting the salt of an acid with a corresponding name ending in -ic (chlorate; nitrate). **3** forming nouns denoting a group (electorate). **4** Chem. forming nouns denoting a product (condensate; filtrate). [from or after OF -at or é(e) or f. L -atus noun or past part.: cf. -ATE[2]]

-ate[2] /ət, eɪt/ suffix **1** forming adjectives and nouns (associate; delegate; duplicate; separate). **2** forming adjectives from Latin or English nouns and adjectives (cordate; insensate; Italianate). [from or after (F -é f.) L -atus past part. of verbs in -are]

-ate[3] /eɪt/ suffix forming verbs (associate; duplicate; fascinate; hyphenate; separate). [from or after (F -er f.) L -are (past part. -atus): cf. -ATE[2]]

Atebrin /'ætəbrɪn/ n. (also **Atabrine** /-ˌbriːn/) propr. = QUIN-ACRINE. [-ATE[1] 2 + BRINE]

atelier /ə'telɪˌeɪ, 'ætəˌljeɪ/ n. a workshop or studio, esp. of an artist or designer. [F]

a tempo /ɑː 'tempoʊ/ adv. Mus. in the previous tempo. [It., lit. 'in time']

Aten /'ɑːt(ə)n/ Egyptian Mythol. the name by which the sun or solar disc was worshipped particularly during the reign of Akhenaten.

Athabasca /ˌæθə'bæskə/, **Lake** the fourth largest lake in Canada, situated in NE Alberta and NW Saskatchewan; area c.8,080 sq. km (3,120 sq. miles).

Athanasian Creed /ˌæθə'neɪʒ(ə)n/ n. an affirmation of Christian faith formerly much used in the Western Church, now less so. Its attribution to Athanasius (see entry) is now generally abandoned (see AMBROSE).

Athanasius /ˌæθə'neɪʃəs/, St (c.296–373), bishop of Alexandria, a great and consistent upholder of orthodoxy, especially against Arianism. He aided the ascetic movement in Egypt and introduced knowledge of monasticism to the West. Feast day, 2 May.

Atharva-Veda /əˌtɑːvə'veɪdə, -'viː-/ n. a collection of hymns and spells in old Sanskrit, traditionally called the fourth Veda but originating outside Vedic society, perhaps in the indigenous fourth varna. [Skr. atharvan priest, vēda knowledge]

atheism /'eɪθɪˌɪz(ə)m/ n. the theory or belief that God does not exist. □□ **atheist** n. **atheistic** /-'ɪstɪk/ adj. **atheistical** /-'ɪstɪk(ə)l/ adj. [F athéisme f. Gk atheos without God f. a- not + theos god]

atheling /'æθəlɪŋ/ n. hist. a prince or lord in Anglo-Saxon England. [OE ætheling = OHG ediling f. WG: see -ING[3]]

Athelstan /'æθəlstən/ (895–939), king of England 926–39. One of the most successful of England's Anglo-Saxon monarchs, Athelstan came to the thrones of Wessex and Mercia in 925 before becoming king of all England a year later. He successfully invaded both Scotland and Wales and inflicted a heavy defeat on an invading Danish army.

athematic /ˌæθɪ'mætɪk, ˌeɪ-/ adj. **1** Mus. not based on the use of themes. **2** Gram. (of a verb-form) having a suffix attached to the stem without a correcting (thematic) vowel.

athenaeum /ˌæθɪ'niːəm/ n. (US **atheneum**) **1** an institution for literary or scientific study. **2** a library. □ **the Athenaeum** a London club founded in 1824 for men of distinction in literature, art, and learning. [LL Athenaeum f. Gk Athēnaion temple of Athene (used as a place of teaching)]

Athene /ə'θiːnɪ/ Gk Mythol. the patron goddess of Athens, also extensively worshipped elsewhere in ancient Greece and its colonies, and almost certainly pre-Hellenic. Her cult-statues show her as female but fully armed, and in classical times the owl is regularly associated with her; she is identified with Minerva. A patroness of many arts and crafts, she became allegorized into a personification of wisdom. The principal

myth concerning her is that she sprang, fully armed and uttering her war-cry, from the head of Zeus.

Athenian /ə'θiːnɪən/ n. & adj. —n. a native or inhabitant of ancient or modern Athens. —adj. of or relating to Athens. [L Atheniensis f. Athenae f. Gk Athēnai Athens]

Athens /'æθɪnz/ (Greek **Athínai** /æ'θiːneɪ/) the capital of Greece, lying 6 km (nearly 4 miles) from its port Piraeus; pop. (1981) 3,027,331. It was a flourishing city-state from early times in ancient Greece, and by the mid-5th c. BC was established as leader of a league of Greek States from whom it exacted tribute. Under Pericles it became a cultural centre, and many of its best-known buildings (e.g. the Parthenon and Erechtheum) date from the extensive rebuilding that he commissioned. Athens recovered only slowly from defeat in the Peloponnesian War (404 BC). In 146 BC it became subject to Rome, but in the early Roman Empire enjoyed imperial favour and was still the cultural centre of the Greek world. Gothic invaders captured and sacked Athens in AD 267, and its importance declined as power and wealth were transferred to Constantinople. After its capture by the Turks in 1456 it declined to the status of a village until chosen as the capital of a newly independent Greece in 1834 after the successful revolt against Turkish rule.

atherosclerosis /ˌæθərəʊsklɪə'rəʊsɪs/ n. a form of arteri-osclerosis characterized by the degeneration of the arteries because of the build-up of fatty deposits. □□ **atherosclerotic** /-'rɒtɪk/ adj. [G Atherosklerose f. Gk athērē groats + SCLEROSIS]

Atherton Tableland /'æθət(ə)n/ a plateau in the Great Dividing Range in NE Queensland, Australia, the highest point is Mt Bartle Frere (1,612 m, 5,287 ft.)

Athinai see ATHENS.

athirst /ə'θɜːst/ predic.adj. poet. **1** (usu. foll. by for) eager (athirst for knowledge). **2** thirsty. [OE ofthyrst for ofthyrsted past part. of ofthyrstan be thirsty]

athlete /'æθliːt/ n. **1** a skilled performer in physical exercises, esp. in track and field events. **2** a healthy person with natural athletic ability. □ **athlete's foot** a fungal foot condition affecting esp. the skin between the toes. [L athleta f. Gk athlētēs f. athleō contend for a prize (athlon)]

athletic /æθ'letɪk/ adj. **1** of or relating to athletes or athletics (an athletic competition). **2** muscular or physically powerful. □□ **athletically** adv. **athleticism** /-'letɪˌsɪz(ə)m/ n. [F athlétique or L athleticus f. Gk athlētikos (as ATHLETE, -IC)]

athletics /æθ'letɪks/ n.pl. (usu. treated as sing.) **1 a** physical exercises, esp. track and field events. **b** the practice of these. (See below.) **2** US physical sports and games of any kind.

The sport of competing in athletics can be traced back at least to the Olympic Games in ancient Greece, but when they were abolished in AD 393 the sport became neglected. Evidence exists of athletic contests in England c.1154, but organized competitions were not held until the mid-19th c.

Athos /'æθɒs, 'eɪ-/, **Mount** a mountainous peninsula projecting into the Aegean Sea from the coast of Macedonia, an auto-nomous district of Greece since 1927. It is inhabited by monks of the Eastern Orthodox Church in twenty monasteries; the earliest monastic settlement dates from 962. A curious rule of the monks forbids women, or even female animals, to set foot on the peninsula. □□ **Athonite** /'æθənaɪt/ adj. & n.

athwart /ə'θwɔːt/ adv. & prep. —adv. **1** across from side to side (usu. obliquely). **2** perversely or in opposition. —prep. **1** from side to side of. **2** in opposition to. [A[2] + THWART]

-atic /'ætɪk/ suffix forming adjectives and nouns (aquatic; fanatic; idiomatic). [F -atique or L -aticus, often ult. f. Gk -atikos]

atilt /ə'tɪlt/ adv. tilted and nearly falling. [A[2] + TILT]

-ation /'eɪʃ(ə)n/ suffix **1** forming nouns denoting an action or an instance of it (alteration; flirtation; hesitation). **2** forming nouns denoting a result or product of action (plantation; starvation; vexation) (see also -FICATION). [from or after F -ation or L -atio -ationis f. verbs in -are: see -ION]

-ative /ətɪv, eɪtɪv/ *suffix* forming adjectives denoting a characteristic or propensity (*authoritative; imitative; pejorative; qualitative; talkative*). [from or after F *-atif -ative* or f. L *-ativus* f. past part. stem *-at-* of verbs in *-are* + *-ivus* (see *-IVE*): cf. *-ATIC*]

Atlanta /ətˈlæntə/ the capital and largest city of Georgia, US; pop. (1982) 428,150. Founded at the end of a railroad line in 1837, the city was originally called Terminus; in 1843 it was incorporated as Marthasville, and in 1845 its name was finally changed to Atlanta.

Atlantean /ətˈlæntɪən/ *adj. literary* of or like Atlas, esp. in physical strength. [L *Atlanteus* (as ATLAS)]

atlantes /ətˈlæntiːz/ *n.pl. Archit.* male figures carved in stone and used as columns to support the entablature of a Greek or Greek-style building. [Gk, pl. of *Atlas*: see ATLAS]

Atlantic /ətˈlæntɪk/ *n. & adj.* —*n.* (**the Atlantic**) the Atlantic Ocean. —*adj.* of or adjoining the Atlantic. □ **Atlantic Ocean** the ocean between Europe and Africa to the east, and North and South American to the west. **Atlantic Time** the standard time used in the most eastern parts of Canada and Central America. **Battle of the Atlantic** a succession of sea operations in the Atlantic, the Caribbean, and northern European waters during the Second World War, involving both submarine blockades and attacks on Allied shipping. German U-boats, sometimes assisted by Italian submarines, were the main weapon of attack, but surface vessels and aircraft also participated. About 2,800 Allied, mainly British, merchant ships were lost, placing the Allies in a critical situation, and the threat was not finally ended until the capture of the U-boats' bases by Allied land forces in 1944. [ME f. L *Atlanticus* f. Gk *Atlantikos* (as ATLAS, -IC): orig. of the Atlas Mountains, then of the sea near the W. African coast]

Atlantic Charter a declaration of eight common principles in international relations, intended to guide a postwar peace settlement, drawn up by the British Prime Minister Winston Churchill and the US President Franklin D. Roosevelt, on behalf of the British Empire and the US, at their meeting at sea in the western Atlantic in August 1941. It stipulated freely chosen governments, free trade, freedom of the seas, and disarmament of current aggressor States, and condemned territorial changes made against the wishes of local populations. In the following month other States, including the USSR, declared their support for these principles. The Atlantic Charter provided the ideological base for the United Nations organization.

Atlantis /ətˈlæntɪs/ *Gk legend* a fabled island in the ocean west of the Pillars of Hercules. It was beautiful and prosperous, and once ruled part of Europe and Africa, but its kings were defeated by the prehistoric Athenians when it attempted to conquer the rest (the story is told by Plato in the *Timaeus*), and it was overwhelmed by the sea. Memories of Atlantic islands, or of a great volcanic eruption, may lie behind the story.

Atlas /ˈætləs/ *Gk Mythol.* one of the Titans, who was punished for his part in their revolt against Zeus by being made to support the heavens (a popular explanation of why the sky does not fall). He became identified with the Atlas range in north-west Africa, or a peak of it (thought to be a sky-supporting mountain). According to a later story Perseus, with the aid of Medusa's head, turned him into a mountain.

atlas /ˈætləs/ *n.* **1** a book of maps or charts. **2** *Anat.* the cervical vertebra of the backbone articulating with the skull at the neck. [L f. Gk *Atlas -antos* ATLAS, whose picture appeared at the beginning of early atlases]

Atlas Mountains a range of mountains in North Africa extending from Morocco to Tunisia and rising to over 4,000 m (13,000 ft.). (See ATLAS.)

atm *abbr. Physics* atmosphere(s).

atman /ˈɑːtmæn/ *n. Hinduism & Buddhism* **1** the real self. **2** the supreme spiritual principle. [Skr. *ātmán* essence, breath]

atmosphere /ˈætməsˌfɪə(r)/ *n.* **1 a** the envelope of gases surrounding the earth, any other planet, or any substance. **b** the air in any particular place, esp. if unpleasant. **2 a** the pervading tone or mood of a place or situation, esp. with reference to the feelings or emotions evoked. **b** the feelings or emotions evoked by a work of art, a piece of music, etc. **3** *Physics* a unit of pressure equal to mean atmospheric pressure at sea level, 101,325 pascals. ¶ Abbr.: **atm.** □□ **atmospheric** /-ˈferɪk/ *adj.* **atmospherical** /-ˈferɪk(ə)l/ *adj.* **atmospherically** /-ˈferɪkəlɪ/ *adv.* [mod.L *atmosphaera* f. Gk *atmos* vapour: see SPHERE]

atmospherics /ˌætməsˈferɪks/ *n.pl.* **1** electrical disturbance in the atmosphere, esp. caused by lightning. **2** interference with telecommunications caused by this.

atoll /ˈætɒl/ *n.* a ring-shaped coral reef enclosing a lagoon. [Maldive *atolu*]

atom /ˈætəm/ *n.* **1 a** the smallest particle of a chemical element that can take part in a chemical reaction. (See below.) **b** this particle as a source of nuclear energy. **2** (usu. with *neg.*) the least portion of a thing or quality (*not an atom of pity*). □ **atom bomb** see separate entry. **atom-smasher** *colloq.* = ACCELERATOR 2. [ME f. OF *atome* f. L *atomus* f. Gk *atomos* indivisible]

Atomic theories have been known from antiquity, but did not receive their definitive verification until the present century. The atomic theory in ancient Greece was an attempt to explain the complexity of natural bodies and phenomena in terms of the arrangement and rearrangement of tiny indivisible particles, which differed from each other only in size, shape, and motion. The modern view of atoms is far more complex, in that atoms have an elaborate internal structure, they may under certain circumstances be transmuted into other atoms, they congregate together under electrical and gravitational forces, and there are about ninety naturally occurring species of atom and many others that can be created artificially. Atoms, which are roughly 10^{-8} cm in diameter, are each composed of a nucleus of about 10^{-12} cm diameter, containing neutrons and protons, which is surrounded by orbiting electrons. Each chemical element is composed of atoms of one kind only (see ELEMENT); the atoms of most elements can combine to form molecules.

atom bomb *n.* a bomb whose destructive power comes from the rapid release of nuclear energy by fission of heavy atomic nuclei, with damaging effects caused by heat, blast, and radioactivity. In it, a conventional explosive either pushes together two masses of fissile material or compresses a single mass. Small masses of such material are stable, but above a certain mass (critical mass) a chain reaction occurs with instantaneous release of energy. The first atom bomb to be used in war was exploded by the US 300 m above Hiroshima in Japan on 6 Aug. 1945, the second over Nagasaki three days later, resulting in the surrender of Japan and the end of the Second World War.

atomic /əˈtɒmɪk/ *adj.* **1** concerned with or using atomic energy or atomic bombs. **2** of or relating to an atom or atoms. □ **atomic bomb** see ATOM BOMB. **atomic clock** a clock in which the periodic process (time scale) is regulated by the vibrations of an atomic or molecular system, such as caesium or ammonia. **atomic energy** nuclear energy. **atomic mass** the mass of an atom measured in atomic mass units. **atomic mass unit** a unit of mass used to express atomic and molecular weights that is equal to one-twelfth of the mass of an atom of carbon-12. ¶ Abbr.: **amu. atomic number** the number of protons in the nucleus of an atom, which is characteristic of a chemical element and determines its place in the periodic table. ¶ Symb.: Z. **atomic particle** any one of the particles of which an atom is constituted. **atomic philosophy** atomism. **atomic physics** the branch of physics concerned with the structure of the atom and the characteristics of the elementary particles of which it is composed. **atomic pile** a nuclear reactor. **atomic power** nuclear power. **atomic spectrum** the emission or absorption spectrum arising from electron transitions inside an atom and characteristic of the element. **atomic structure** the structure of an atom as being a central positively charged nucleus surrounded by negatively charged orbiting electrons. **atomic theory 1** the concept of an atom as being composed of elementary particles. **2** the theory that all matter is made up of small indivisible particles called atoms, and that the atoms of any one element are identical in all respects but differ from those of other elements and only unite to form compounds in fixed proportions. **3** *Philos.* atomism. **atomic warfare** warfare involving the use of atom bombs. **atomic weight** = *relative atomic mass*. □□ **atomically** *adv.* [mod.L *atomicus* (as ATOM, -IC)]

atomicity /ˌætəˈmɪsɪtɪ/ *n.* **1** the number of atoms in the molecules of an element. **2** the state or fact of being composed of atoms.

atomism /ˈætəˌmɪz(ə)m/ *n.* *Philos.* **1** the theory that all matter consists of tiny individual particles. **2** *Psychol.* the theory that mental states are made up of elementary units. □□ **atomist** *n.* **atomistic** /-ˈmɪstɪk/ *adj.*

atomize /ˌætəˈmaɪz/ *v.tr.* (also **-ise**) reduce to atoms or fine particles. □□ **atomization** /-ˈzeɪʃ(ə)n/ *n.*

atomizer /ˈætəˌmaɪzə(r)/ *n.* (also **-iser**) an instrument for emitting liquids as a fine spray.

atomy /ˈætəmɪ/ *n.* (*pl.* **-ies**) *archaic* **1** a skeleton. **2** an emaciated body. [ANATOMY taken as *an atomy*]

atonal /eɪˈtəʊn(ə)l, ə-/ *adj.* *Mus.* not written in any key or mode. □□ **atonality** /-ˈnælɪtɪ/ *n.*

atone /əˈtəʊn/ *v.intr.* (usu. foll. by *for*) make amends; expiate (for a wrong). [back-form. f. ATONEMENT]

atonement /əˈtəʊnmənt/ *n.* **1** expiation; reparation for a wrong or injury. **2** the reconciliation of God and man. □ the **Atonement** the expiation by Christ of mankind's sin. **Day of Atonement** the most solemn religious fast of the Jewish year, eight days after the Jewish New Year. [*at one* + -MENT, after med.L *adunamentum* and earlier *onement* f. obs. *one* (v.) unite]

atonic /əˈtɒnɪk/ *adj.* **1** without accent or stress. **2** *Med.* lacking bodily tone. □□ **atony** /ˈætənɪ/ *n.*

atop /əˈtɒp/ *adv. & prep.* —*adv.* (often foll. by *of*) on the top. —*prep.* on the top of.

-ator /ˈeɪtə(r)/ *suffix* forming agent nouns, usu. from Latin words (sometimes via French) (*agitator*; *creator*; *equator*; *escalator*). See also -OR¹. [L *-ator*]

-atory /ətərɪ/ *suffix* forming adjectives meaning 'relating to or involving (a verbal action)' (*amatory*; *explanatory*; *predatory*). See also -ORY². [L *-atorius*]

ATP *abbr.* adenosine triphosphate.

atrabilious /ˌætrəˈbɪljəs/ *adj.* *literary* melancholy; ill-tempered. [L *atra bilis* black bile, transl. Gk *melagkholia* MELANCHOLY]

Atreus /ˈeɪtrɪəs/ *Gk legend* son of Pelops and brother of Thyestes, with whom he was at variance. He invited Thyestes to a banquet and served up to him the flesh of the latter's own children, at which the sun turned back on its course in horror.

atrium /ˈeɪtrɪəm/ *n.* (*pl.* **atriums** or **atria** /-trɪə/) **1 a** the central court of an ancient Roman house. **b** a usu. skylit central court rising through several storeys with galleries and rooms opening off at each level. **c** esp. *US* (in a modern house) a central hall or glazed court with rooms opening off it. **2** *Anat.* a cavity in the body, esp. one of the two upper cavities of the heart, receiving blood from the veins. □□ **atrial** *adj.* [L]

atrocious /əˈtrəʊʃəs/ *adj.* **1** very bad or unpleasant (*atrocious weather; their manners were atrocious*). **2** extremely savage or wicked (*atrocious cruelty*). □□ **atrociously** *adv.* **atrociousness** *n.* [L *atrox -ocis* cruel]

atrocity /əˈtrɒsɪtɪ/ *n.* (*pl.* **-ies**) **1** an extremely wicked or cruel act, esp. one involving physical violence or injury. **2** extreme wickedness. [F *atrocité* or L *atrocitas* (as ATROCIOUS, -ITY)]

atrophy /ˈætrəfɪ/ *v. & n.* —*v.* (**-ies, -ied**) **1** *intr.* waste away through undernourishment, ageing, or lack of use; become emaciated. **2** *tr.* cause to atrophy. —*n.* the process of atrophying; emaciation. [F *atrophie* or LL *atrophia* f. Gk f. *a-* not + *trophē* food)]

atropine /ˈætrəpiːn, -pɪn/ *n.* a poisonous alkaloid found in deadly nightshade, used in medicine to treat renal and biliary colic etc. [mod.L *Atropa belladonna* deadly nightshade f. Gk *Atropos* ATROPOS]

Atropos /ˈætrəpɒs/ *Gk Mythol.* one of the three Fates (see FATES). [Gk f. *atropos* inflexible]

attach /əˈtætʃ/ *v.* **1** *tr.* fasten, affix, join. **2** *tr.* (in *passive;* foll.

by *to*) be very fond of or devoted to (*am deeply attached to her*). **3** *tr.* attribute, assign (some function, quality, or characteristic) (*can you attach a name to it?; attaches great importance to it*). **4 a** *tr.* accompany; form part of (*no conditions are attached*). **b** *intr.* (foll. by *to*) be an attribute or characteristic (*great prestige attaches to the job*). **5** *refl.* (usu. foll. by *to*) take part in; join (*attached themselves to the expedition*). **6** *tr.* appoint for special or temporary duties. **7** *tr.* *Law* seize (a person or property) by legal authority. □□ **attachable** *adj.* **attacher** *n.* [ME f. OF *estachier* fasten f. Gmc: in Law sense through OF *atachier*]

attaché /əˈtæʃeɪ/ *n.* a person appointed to an ambassador's staff, usu. with a special sphere of activity (*military attaché; press attaché*). □ **attaché case** a small flat rectangular case for carrying documents etc. [F, past part. of *attacher*: see ATTACH]

attachment /əˈtætʃmənt/ *n.* **1** a thing attached or to be attached, esp. to a machine, device, etc., for a special function. **2** affection, devotion. **3** a means of attaching. **4** the act of attaching or the state of being attached. **5** legal seizure. **6** a temporary position in, or secondment to, an organization. [ME f. F *attachement* f. *attacher* (as ATTACH, -MENT)]

attack /əˈtæk/ *v. & n.* —*v.* **1** *tr.* act against with (esp. armed) force. **2** *tr.* seek to hurt or defeat. **3** *tr.* criticize adversely. **4** *tr.* act harmfully upon (*a virus attacking the nervous system*). **5** *tr.* vigorously apply oneself to; begin work on (*attacked his meal with gusto*). **6** *intr.* make an attack. **7** *intr.* be in a mode of attack. —*n.* **1** the act or process of attacking. **2** an offensive operation or mode of behaviour. **3** *Mus.* the action or manner of beginning a piece, passage, etc. **4** gusto, vigour. **5** a sudden occurrence of an illness. **6** a player or players seeking to score goals etc. □□ **attacker** *n.* [F *attaque, attaquer* f. It. *attacco* attack, *attaccare* ATTACH]

attain /əˈteɪn/ *v.* **1** *tr.* arrive at; reach (a goal etc.). **2** *tr.* gain, accomplish (an aim, distinction, etc.). **3** *intr.* (foll. by *to*) arrive at by conscious development or effort. □□ **attainable** *adj.* **attainability** /-ˈbɪlɪtɪ/ *n.* **attainableness** *n.* [ME f. AF *attain-*, *atein-*, OF *ataign-* stem of *ataindre* f. L *attingere* (as AD-, *tangere* touch)]

attainder /əˈteɪndə(r)/ *n.* *hist.* the forfeiture of land and civil rights suffered as a consequence of a sentence of death for treason or felony. □ **act** (or **bill**) **of attainder** an item of legislation inflicting attainder without judicial process. [ME f. AF, = OF *ateindre* ATTAIN used as noun: see -ER⁶]

attainment /əˈteɪnmənt/ *n.* **1** (often in *pl.*) something attained or achieved; an accomplishment. **2** the act or an instance of attaining.

attaint /əˈteɪnt/ *v.tr.* **1** *hist.* subject to attainder. **2 a** (of disease etc.) strike, affect. **b** taint. [ME f. obs. *attaint* (adj.) f. OF *ataint*, *ateint* past part. formed as ATTAIN: confused in meaning with TAINT]

Attalid /ˈætəlɪd/ *adj. & n.* —*adj.* of the Hellenistic dynasty which ruled from Pergamum in Asia Minor, founded by Philetaerus, the son of Attalus, in 282 BC. The Attalid kings established Pergamum as a leading cultural centre of the Greek world, and celebrated their military victories in splendid sculptural monuments. The kingdom was bequeathed to Rome by Attalus III on his death in 133 BC. —*n.* a member of this dynasty.

attar /ˈætɑː(r)/ *n.* (also **otto** /ˈɒtəʊ/) a fragrant essential oil, esp. from rose-petals. [Pers. ʿatar f. Arab. f. ʿiṭr perfume]

attempt /əˈtempt/ *v. & n.* —*v.tr.* **1** (often foll. by *to* + infin.) seek to achieve or complete (a task or action) (*attempted the exercise; attempted to explain*). **2** seek to climb or master (a mountain etc.). —*n.* (often foll. by *at, on,* or *to* + infin.) an act of attempting; an endeavour (*made an attempt at winning; an attempt to succeed; an attempt on his life*). □ **attempt the life of** *archaic* try to kill. □□ **attemptable** *adj.* [OF *attempter* f. L *attemptare* (as AD-, *temptare* TEMPT)]

Attenborough /ˈætənˌbərə/, Sir Richard (1923–), British film actor, producer, and director. From 1942 onwards he appeared in a number of war films and comedies, and extended his activity range into character roles such as Pinkie in *Brighton*

Rock (1947) and the murder suspect Christie in *10 Rillington Place* (1971). The films he directed include *Oh! What a Lovely War* (1969) and *Gandhi* (1982), both of which won a number of awards.

attend /əˈtend/ v. **1** tr. **a** be present at (*attended the meeting*). **b** go regularly to (*attends the local school*). **2** intr. **a** be present (*many members failed to attend*). **b** be present in a serving capacity; wait. **3** a tr. escort, accompany (*the king was attended by soldiers*). **b** intr. (foll. by *on*) wait on; serve. **4** intr. **a** (usu. foll. by *to*) turn or apply one's mind; focus one's attention (*attend to what I am saying; was not attending*). **b** (foll. by *to*) deal with (*shall attend to the matter myself*). **5** tr. (usu. in *passive*) follow as a result from (*the error was attended by serious consequences*). □□ **attender** n. [ME f. OF *atendre* f. L *attendere* (as AD-, *tendere tent-* stretch)]

attendance /əˈtend(ə)ns/ n. **1** the act of attending or being present. **2** the number of people present (*a high attendance*). □ **attendance allowance** (in the UK) a State benefit paid to disabled people in need of constant care at home. **attendance centre** Brit. a place where young offenders report by order of a court as a minor penalty. [ME f. OF *atendance* (as ATTEND, -ANCE)]

attendant /əˈtend(ə)nt/ n. & adj. —n. a person employed to wait on others or provide a service (*cloakroom attendant; museum attendant*). —adj. **1** accompanying (*attendant circumstances*). **2** waiting on; serving (*ladies attendant on the queen*). [ME f. OF (as ATTEND, -ANT)]

attendee /ˌætenˈdiː/ n. a person who attends (a meeting etc.).

attention /əˈtenʃ(ə)n/ n. & int. —n. **1** the act or faculty of applying one's mind (*give me your attention; attract his attention*). **2 a** consideration (*give attention to the problem*). **b** care (*give special attention to your handwriting*). **3** (in *pl.*) **a** ceremonious politeness (*he paid his attentions to her*). **b** wooing, courting (*she was the subject of his attentions*). **4** Mil. an erect attitude of readiness (*stand at attention*). —int. (in full **stand at attention!**) an order to assume an attitude of attention. [ME f. L *attentio* (as ATTEND, -ION)]

attentive /əˈtentɪv/ adj. **1** concentrating; paying attention. **2** assiduously polite. **3** heedful. □□ **attentively** adv. **attentiveness** n. [ME f. F *attentif -ive* f. *attente*, OF *atente*, fem. past part. of *atendre* ATTEND]

attenuate v. & adj. —v.tr. /əˈtenjʊˌeɪt/ **1** make thin. **2** reduce in force, value, or virulence. **3** Electr. reduce the amplitude of (a signal or current). —adj. /əˈtenjʊət/ **1** slender. **2** tapering gradually. **3** rarefied. □□ **attenuated** adj. **attenuation** /-ˈeɪʃ(ə)n/ n. **attenuator** n. [L *attenuare* (as AD-, *tenuis* thin)]

attest /əˈtest/ v. **1** tr. certify the validity of. **2** tr. enrol (a recruit) for military service. **3** intr. (foll. by *to*) bear witness to. **4** intr. enrol oneself for military service. □□ **attestable** adj. **attestor** n. [F *attester* f. L *attestari* (as AD-, *testis* witness)]

attestation /ˌæteˈsteɪʃ(ə)n/ n. **1** the act of attesting. **2** a testimony. [F *attestation* or LL *attestatio* (as ATTEST, -ATION)]

Attic /ˈætɪk/ adj. & n. —adj. of ancient Athens or Attica, or the form of Greek spoken there. —n. the form of Greek used by the ancient Athenians. □ **Attic salt** (or **wit**) refined wit. [L *Atticus* f. Gk *Attikos*]

attic /ˈætɪk/ n. **1** the uppermost storey in a house, usu. under the roof. **2** a room in the attic area. [F *attique*, as ATTIC: orig. (Archit.) a small order above a taller one]

Attica /ˈætɪkə/ a triangular promontory, constituting the easternmost part of central Greece. Its chief city is Athens, whose territory it was in ancient times.

atticism /ˈætɪˌsɪz(ə)m/ n. **1** extreme elegance of speech. **2** an instance of this. [Gk *Attikismos* (as ATTIC, -ISM)]

Attila /ˈætɪlə/ (406–53), king of the Huns 434–53. Having inflicted great devastation on the Eastern Roman Empire in 445–50, Attila invaded the Western Empire but was defeated at Châlons in 451. He and his army were the terror of Europe during his lifetime, earning Attila the nickname 'Scourge of God'. □ **Attila Line** (also called the *Sahin* (= *Falcon*) *Line*) the boundary separating Greek and Turkish-occupied Cyprus,

named after the Attila Plan, a secret Turkish plan of 1964 to partition the country.

attire /əˈtaɪə(r)/ v. & n. *formal* —v.tr. dress, esp. in fine clothes or formal wear. —n. clothes, esp. fine or formal. [ME f. OF *atir(i)er* equip f. *à tire* in order, of unkn. orig.]

Attis /ˈætɪs/ *Anatolian Mythol.* the youthful consort of Cybele. A subsidiary figure in the early cult, at Rome he attained official status under Claudius. His death and resurrection were celebrated in a spring festival, with a sacrifice for the crops; his symbol was the pine tree.

attitude /ˈætɪˌtjuːd/ n. **1 a** a settled opinion or way of thinking. **b** behaviour reflecting this (*I don't like his attitude*). **2 a** a bodily posture. **b** a pose adopted in a painting or a play, esp. for dramatic effect (*strike an attitude*). **3** the position of an aircraft, spacecraft, etc., in relation to specified directions. □ **attitude of mind** a settled way of thinking. □□ **attitudinal** /ˌætɪˈtjuːdɪn(ə)l/ adj. [F f. It. *attitudine* fitness, posture, f. LL *aptitudo -dinis* f. *aptus* fit]

attitudinize /ˌætɪˈtjuːdɪˌnaɪz/ v.intr. (also **-ise**) **1** practise or adopt attitudes, esp. for effect. **2** speak, write, or behave affectedly. [It. *attitudine* f. LL (as ATTITUDE) + -IZE]

Attlee /ˈætlɪ/, Clement Richard, 1st Earl Attlee (1883–1967), British statesman, leader of the Labour Party from 1935. As a result of the 1945 election Attlee became the first Labour Prime Minister to command an absolute majority in the House. His administration was notable at home for a series of measures setting up the modern Welfare State and abroad for progressive withdrawal from colonies.

attn. *abbr.* **1** attention. **2** for the attention of.

atto- /ˈætəʊ/ *comb. form Math.* denoting a factor of 10^{-18} (*attometre*). [Da. or Norw. *atten* eighteen + -O-]

attorney /əˈtɜːnɪ/ n. (*pl.* **-eys**) **1** a person, esp. a lawyer, appointed to act for another in business or legal matters. **2** US a qualified lawyer, esp. one representing a client in a lawcourt. □ **Attorney-General** the chief legal officer in England, the US, and other countries. **District Attorney** see DISTRICT. **power of attorney** the authority to act for another person in legal or financial matters. □□ **attorneyship** n. [ME f. OF *atorné* past part. of *atorner* assign f. *à* to + *torner* turn]

attract /əˈtrækt/ v.tr. **1** (also *absol.*) draw or bring to oneself or itself (*attracts many admirers; attracts attention*). **2** be attractive to; fascinate. **3** (of a magnet, gravity, etc.) exert a pull on (an object). □□ **attractable** adj. **attractor** n. [L *attrahere* (as AD-, *trahere tract-* draw)]

attractant /əˈtrækt(ə)nt/ n. & adj. —n. a substance which attracts (esp. insects). —adj. attracting.

attraction /əˈtrækʃ(ə)n/ n. **1 a** the act or power of attracting (*the attraction of foreign travel*). **b** a person or thing that attracts by arousing interest (*the fair is a big attraction*). **2** *Physics* the force by which bodies attract or approach each other (opp. REPULSION). **3** *Gram.* the influence exerted by one word on another which causes it to change to an incorrect form, e.g. *the wages of sin is death*. [F *attraction* or L *attractio* (as ATTRACT, -ION)]

attractive /əˈtræktɪv/ adj. **1** attracting or capable of attracting; interesting (*an attractive proposition*). **2** aesthetically pleasing or appealing. □□ **attractively** adv. **attractiveness** n. [F *attractif -ive* f. LL *attractivus* (as ATTRACT, -IVE)]

attribute v. & n. —v.tr. /əˈtrɪbjuːt/ (usu. foll. by *to*) **1** regard as belonging or appropriate to (*a poem attributed to Shakespeare*). **2** ascribe to; regard as the effect of a stated cause (*the delays were attributed to the heavy traffic*). —n. /ˈætrɪˌbjuːt/ **1 a** a quality ascribed to a person or thing. **b** a characteristic quality. **2** a material object recognized as appropriate to a person, office, or status (*a large car is an attribute of seniority*). **3** *Gram.* an attributive adjective or noun. □□ **attributable** /əˈtrɪbjʊtəb(ə)l/ adj. **attribution** /ˌætrɪˈbjuːʃ(ə)n/ n. [ME f. L *attribuere attribut-* (as AD-, *tribuere* assign): (n.) f. OF *attribut* or L *attributum*]

attributive /əˈtrɪbjʊtɪv/ adj. *Gram.* (of an adjective or noun) preceding the word described and expressing an attribute, as *old* in *the old dog* (but not in *the dog is old*) and *expiry* in *expiry* *date* (opp. PREDICATIVE). □□ **attributively** *adv.* [F *attributif -ive* (as ATTRIBUTE, -IVE)]

attrition /ə'trɪʃ(ə)n/ *n.* **1 a** the act or process of gradually wearing out, esp. by friction. **b** abrasion. **2** *Theol.* sorrow for sin, falling short of contrition. □ **war of attrition** a war in which one side wins by gradually wearing the other down with repeated attacks etc. □□ **attritional** *adj.* [ME f. LL *attritio* f. *atterere attrit-* rub]

attune /ə'tjuːn/ *v.tr.* **1** (usu. foll. by *to*) adjust (a person or thing) to a situation. **2** bring (an orchestra, instrument, etc.) into musical accord. [AT- + TUNE]

Atty. *abbr.* Attorney.

Atwood /'ætwʊd/, Margaret Eleanor (1939–   ), Canadian poet, novelist, and writer of short stories, children's books, and literary criticism. She is best known for her novels, often with themes of feminism and human rights; they include *The Edible Woman* (1969), *Surfacing* (1972), *Bodily Harm* (1981), and *The Handmaid's Tale* (1986).

atypical /eɪ'tɪpɪk(ə)l/ *adj.* not typical; not conforming to a type. □□ **atypically** *adv.*

AU *abbr.* **1** (also **au.**) astronomical unit. **2** ångström unit.

Au *symb. Chem.* the element gold. [L *aurum*]

aubade /əʊ'bɑːd/ *n.* a poem or piece of music appropriate to the dawn or early morning. [F f. Sp. *albada* f. *alba* dawn]

auberge /əʊ'bɛəʒ/ *n.* an inn. [F]

aubergine /'əʊbəˌʒiːn/ *n.* **1** a tropical plant, *Solanum melongena*, having erect or spreading branches bearing white or purple egg-shaped fruit. **2** this fruit eaten as a vegetable. Also called EGGPLANT. **3** the dark purple colour of this fruit. [F f. Cat. *alberginia* f. Arab. *al-bādinjān* f. Pers. *bādingān* f. Skr. *vātimgaṇa*]

Aubrey /'ɔːbrɪ/, John (1626–97), English antiquarian and polymath, author of a collection of 'Lives' of eminent persons. He was a pioneer of field archaeology, most of his researches being centred on the earthworks and monuments in Wiltshire (particularly Avebury and Stonehenge), and became one of the first Fellows of the Royal Society in 1663.

aubrietia /ɔː'briːʃə/ *n.* (also **aubretia**) any dwarf perennial rock-plant of the genus *Aubrieta*, having purple or pink flowers in spring. [mod.L f. Claude *Aubriet*, Fr. botanist d. 1743]

auburn /'ɔːbən/ *adj.* reddish brown (usu. of a person's hair). [ME, orig. yellowish white, f. OF *auborne*, *alborne*, f. L *alburnus* whitish f. *albus* white]

Aubusson /'əʊbuːˌsɔ̃/ *n.* **1** a kind of tapestry made at the town of Aubusson in central France, famous since the 16th c., and especially in the 18th c., for the manufacture of tapestries and carpets: **2** a carpet resembling this in design.

AUC *abbr.* (of a date) from the foundation of the city (of Rome). [L *ab urbe condita*]

Auckland /'ɔːklənd/ **1** the largest city and chief seaport of New Zealand; pop. (1988) 841,700. **2** the province of New Zealand comprising the northern part of North Island.

au courant /ˌəʊ kuː'rɑ̃/ *predic.adj.* (usu. foll. by *with*, *of*) knowing what is going on; well-informed. [F, = in the (regular) course]

auction /'ɔːkʃ(ə)n/ *n. & v.* —*n.* a sale of goods, usu. in public, in which articles are sold to the highest bidder. —*v.tr.* sell by auction. □ **auction bridge 1** see BRIDGE². **2** the sequence of bids made at bridge. **Dutch auction** a sale, usu. public, of goods in which the price is reduced by the auctioneer until a buyer is found. [L *auctio* increase, auction f. *augēre auct-* increase]

auctioneer /ˌɔːkʃə'nɪə(r)/ *n.* a person who conducts auctions professionally, by calling for bids and declaring goods sold. □□ **auctioneering** *n.*

audacious /ɔː'deɪʃəs/ *adj.* **1** daring, bold. **2** impudent. □□ **audaciously** *adv.* **audaciousness** *n.* **audacity** /ɔː'dæsɪtɪ/ *n.* [L *audax -acis* bold f. *audēre* dare]

Auden /'ɔːd(ə)n/, Wystan Hugh (1907–73), English poet. At Oxford he was the leading voice of a near-Marxist group (which included Day Lewis, MacNeice, and Spender) that responded to the public chaos of the 1930s. Auden collaborated with Isherwood in several Brechtian verse dramas (notably *The Ascent of F6*, 1936) and in *Journey to a War* (1939) recording a journey to

China, and with MacNeice in *Letters from Iceland* (1937). Britten set many of his poems to music and later used Auden's text for his opera *Paul Bunyan*. In 1939, with Isherwood, he settled in America (becoming a US citizen in 1946) where he met Chester Kallmann, who became his lifelong friend and with whom he collaborated in several opera libretti including Stravinsky's *The Rake's Progress*. His poetry now became increasingly Christian in tone, reflecting man's isolation. His absence from Europe during the war led to a poor reception of his work in England, but the high quality of his later works, such as *Nones* (1951) and *The Shield of Achilles* (1955) reinstated him as a major poet; he was elected Professor of Poetry at Oxford in 1956. Auden's progress from the didactic poems of his youth to the complexity of his later works offered a wide variety of models. He was a master of verse form, accommodating traditional patterns to a fresh contemporary language.

Audenarde see OUDENARDE.

audible /'ɔːdɪb(ə)l/ *adj.* capable of being heard. □□ **audibility** /-'bɪlɪtɪ/ *n.* **audibleness** *n.* **audibly** *adv.* [LL *audibilis* f. *audire* hear]

audience /'ɔːdɪəns/ *n.* **1 a** the assembled listeners or spectators at an event, esp. a stage performance, concert, etc. **b** the people addressed by a film, book, play, etc. **2** a formal interview with a person in authority. **3** *archaic* a hearing (*give audience to my plea*). [ME f. OF f. L *audientia* f. *audire* hear]

audile /'ɔːdaɪl/ *adj.* of or referring to the sense of hearing. [irreg. f. L *audire* hear, after *tactile*]

audio /'ɔːdɪəʊ/ *n.* (usu. *attrib.*) sound or the reproduction of sound. □ **audio frequency** a frequency capable of being perceived by the human ear. **audio typist** a person who types direct from a recording. [AUDIO-]

audio- /'ɔːdɪəʊ/ *comb. form* hearing or sound. [L *audire* hear + -o-]

audiology /ˌɔːdɪ'ɒlədʒɪ/ *n.* the science of hearing. □□ **audiologist** *n.*

audiometer /ˌɔːdɪ'ɒmɪtə(r)/ *n.* an instrument for testing hearing.

audiophile /'ɔːdɪəʊˌfaɪl/ *n.* a hi-fi enthusiast.

audiotape /'ɔːdɪəʊˌteɪp/ *n. & v.* —*n.* **1 a** magnetic tape on which sound can be recorded. **b** a length of this. **2** a sound recording on tape. —*v.tr.* record (sound, speech, etc.) on tape.

audiovisual /ˌɔːdɪəʊ'vɪʒʊəl/ *adj.* (esp. of teaching methods) using both sight and sound.

audit /'ɔːdɪt/ *n. & v.* —*n.* an official examination of accounts. —*v.tr.* (**audited, auditing**) **1** conduct an audit of. **2** *US* attend (a class) informally, without working for credits. [ME f. L *auditus* hearing f. *audire* audit- hear]

audition /ɔː'dɪʃ(ə)n/ *n. & v.* —*n.* **1** an interview for a role as a singer, actor, dancer, etc., consisting of a practical demonstration of suitability. **2** the power of hearing or listening. —*v.* **1** *tr.* interview (a candidate at an audition). **2** *intr.* be interviewed at an audition. [F *audition* or L *auditio* f. *audire* audit- hear]

auditive /'ɔːdɪtɪv/ *adj.* concerned with hearing. [F *auditif -ive* (as AUDITION, -IVE)]

auditor /'ɔːdɪtə(r)/ *n.* **1** a person who audits accounts. **2** a listener. □□ **auditorial** /-'tɔːrɪəl/ *adj.* [ME f. AF *auditour* f. L *auditor -oris* (as AUDITIVE, -OR)]

auditorium /ˌɔːdɪ'tɔːrɪəm/ *n.* (*pl.* **auditoriums** or **auditoria** /-rɪə/) the part of a theatre etc. in which the audience sits. [L neut. of *auditorius* (adj.): see AUDITORY, -ORIUM]

auditory /'ɔːdɪtərɪ/ *adj.* **1** concerned with hearing. **2** received by the ear. [L *auditorius* (as AUDITOR, -ORY²)]

Audubon /'ɔːdəbən/, John James (1785–1851), American naturalist and artist, remembered for his great illustrated work *The Birds of America* (1827–38). His elementary education in France made him barely literate and he contributed little else to ornithology, except an early attempt to trace the movements of birds by banding them. His book was compiled during his wanderings round America trying and failing to make a living in various small towns. He portrayed even the largest birds life-size, and painted them not in conventionally formal postures but in dramatic and sometimes violent action. Eventually he found a publisher in Britain and, published in parts, the book had lasting success, not only for the arresting quality of the engravings but also as a major contribution to the then rapidly growing knowledge of natural history.

AUEW abbr. (in the UK) Amalgamated Union of Engineering Workers.

au fait /əʊ ˈfeɪ/ predic.adj. (usu. foll. by *with*) having current knowledge; conversant (*fully au fait with the arrangements*). □ **put** (or **make**) *au fait* with instruct in. [F]

au fond /əʊ ˈfɔ̃/ adv. basically; at bottom. [F]

Aug. abbr. August.

Augean /ɔːˈdʒiːən/ adj. **1** Gk Mythol. of Augeas, legendary king whose vast stables had never been cleaned, and which Hercules cleaned in a day by diverting the river Alpheus to flow through them. **2** filthy; extremely dirty. [L Augeas f. Gk Augeias]

auger /ˈɔːgə(r)/ n. **1** a tool resembling a large corkscrew, for boring holes in wood. **2** a similar larger tool for boring holes in the ground. [OE nafogār f. nafu NAVE², + gār pierce: for loss of n cf. ADDER]

aught¹ /ɔːt/ n. (also **ought**) archaic (usu. implying neg.) anything at all. [OE āwiht f. Gmc]

aught² var. of OUGHT².

augite /ˈɔːdʒaɪt/ n. Mineral. a complex calcium magnesium aluminous silicate occurring in many igneous rocks. [L augites f. Gk augitēs f. augē lustre]

augment v. & n. —v.tr. & intr. /ɔːgˈment/ make or become greater; increase. —n. /ˈɔːgment/ Gram. a vowel prefixed to the past tenses in the older Indo-European languages. □ **augmented interval** Mus. a perfect or major interval that is increased by a semitone. □□ **augmenter** n. [ME f. OF augment (n.), F augmenter (v.), or LL augmentum, augmentare f. L augēre increase]

augmentation /ɔːgmenˈteɪʃ(ə)n/ n. **1** enlargement; growth; increase. **2** Mus. the lengthening of the time-values of notes in melodic parts. [ME f. F f. LL augmentatio -onis f. augmentare (as AUGMENT)]

augmentative /ɔːgˈmentətɪv/ adj. **1** having the property of increasing. **2** Gram. (of an affix or derived word) reinforcing the idea of the original word. [F augmentatif -ive or med.L augmentativus (as AUGMENT)]

Augrabies Falls /əˈgrɑːbiːz/ a waterfall on the Orange River in NW Cape Province, South Africa.

au gratin /əʊ græˈtæ̃/ adj. Cookery cooked with a crisp brown crust usu. of breadcrumbs or melted cheese. [F f. gratter, = by grating, f. GRATE¹]

Augsburg /ˈaʊgzbɜːg/ a city of Bavaria; pop. (1987) 246,000. □ **Augsburg Confession** a statement of the Lutheran position, mainly drawn up by Melanchthon and approved by Luther before being presented to the Emperor Charles V at Augsburg on 25 June 1530.

augur /ˈɔːgə(r)/ v. & n. —v. **1** intr. **a** (of an event, circumstance, etc.) suggest a specified outcome (usu. *augur well* or *ill*). **b** portend, bode (*all augured well for our success*). **2** tr. **a** foresee, predict. **b** portend. —n. a Roman religious official who observed natural signs, esp. the behaviour of birds, interpreting these as an indication of divine approval or disapproval of a proposed action. □□ **augural** adj. [L]

augury /ˈɔːgjərɪ/ n. (pl. **-ies**) **1** an omen; a portent. **2** the work of an augur; the interpretation of omens. [ME f. OF augurie or L augurium f. AUGUR]

August /ˈɔːgəst/ n. the eighth month of the year. [OE f. L Augustus AUGUSTUS]

august /ɔːˈgʌst/ adj. inspiring reverence and admiration; venerable, impressive. □□ **augustly** adv. **augustness** n. [F auguste or L augustus consecrated, venerable]

Augusta /ɔːˈgʌstə/ the capital of Maine; pop. (1980) 21,820.

Augustan /ɔːˈgʌst(ə)n/ adj. & n. —adj. **1** connected with, occurring during, or influenced by the reign of the Roman emperor Augustus, esp. as an outstanding period of Latin literature. **2** (of a nation's literature) refined and classical in style (in England of the literature of the 17th–18th c.). —n. a writer of the Augustan age of any literature. [L Augustanus f. Augustus]

Augustine¹ /ɔːˈgʌstɪn/, St (of Canterbury; died c.604), the first archbishop of Canterbury. Sent from Rome by Gregory the Great (then pope) to refound the Church in England, he and his party landed in Kent in 597 and were favourably received by King Ethelbert (whose wife was a Christian), who was afterwards converted. Augustine founded the first church and a monastery at Canterbury, and was consecrated as archbishop, but failed to reach agreement with representatives of the ancient Celtic Church which still survived in Britain and was at variance with Rome on questions of discipline and practice. Feast day, 26 May.

Augustine² /ɔːˈgʌstɪn/, St (of Hippo, 354–430), a Doctor of the Church. Born in North Africa of a pagan father and a Christian mother, he was early attracted to Manichaeism. He taught rhetoric in Rome and then in Milan, where he was influenced by the bishop, Ambrose, and embraced his Neoplatonic understanding of Christianity. Augustine henceforth lived a monastic life, first in retirement, then as priest and (after 395) as bishop of Hippo in North Africa. His episcopate was marked by continual controversy, with Manichees, Donatists, Pelagians, and pagan philosophy. Most of his vast literary output was pastoral or polemical. The *City of God*, a vindication of the Church against paganism, is perhaps his most famous work, apart from his *Confessions* which contains a striking account of his early life and conversion. Augustine died during the siege of Hippo by the Vandals. His theology has dominated all later Western theology, with its profound psychological insight and its sense of man's utter dependence on grace, expressed in his doctrine of predestination, and of the Church and the sacraments.

Augustine³ /ɔːˈgʌstɪn/ n. an Augustinian friar. [ME f. OF augustin f. L Augustinus: see AUGUSTINIAN]

Augustinian /ɔːgəˈstɪnɪən/ adj. & n. —adj. **1** of or relating to St Augustine of Hippo. **2** belonging to a religious order observing the 'rule of St Augustine' (based largely on his writings but not founded by him), especially the Augustinian Canons (founded in the 11th c.) and the Augustinian (or Austin) Friars, a mendicant order founded c.1250. —n. **1** an adherent of the doctrines of St Augustine. **2** a member of the order of Augustinian Friars. [L Augustinus Augustine]

Augustus /ɔːˈgʌstəs/ (63 BC–AD 14) the first Roman emperor. Born Gaius Octavius (subsequently known as Octavian), grand nephew of Julius Caesar, after whose murder he established his position in Italy as one of the triumvirate of 43 BC, he gained supreme power by his defeat of Antony at the battle of Actium in 31 BC. A constitutional settlement in 27 BC in theory restored the Republic but in practice regularized his sovereignty; in the same year he was given the title Augustus (L, = venerable). His rule was marked abroad by a series of expansionist military campaigns and at home by moral and religious reforms intended to restore old Roman values disrupted during the civil wars of previous decades. He energetically patronized the arts; the literature of his reign represents the high-point of Roman classicism.

auk /ɔːk/ n. any sea diving-bird of the family Alcidae, with heavy body, short wings, and black and white plumage, e.g. the guillemot, puffin, and razorbill. □ **great auk** an extinct flightless auk, *Alca impennis*. **little auk** a small arctic auk, *Plautus alle*. [ON álka]

auld /ɔːld/ adj. Sc. old. [OE ald, Anglian form of OLD]

auld lang syne /ɔːld læŋ ˈsaɪn/ n. times long past. [Sc., = old long since: also as the title and refrain of a song]

aumbry /ˈɔːmbrɪ/ n. (also **ambry** /ˈæmbrɪ/) (pl. **-ies**) **1** a small recess in the wall of a church. **2** hist. a small cupboard. [ME f. OF almarie, armarie f. L armarium closet, chest f. arma utensils]

au naturel /əʊ nætjəˈrel, -tjuˈrel/ predic.adj. & adv. Cookery uncooked; (cooked) in the most natural or simplest way. [F, = in the natural state]

Aung San /aʊŋ ˈsæn/ (1914–47), Burmese nationalist leader, who was instrumental in securing Burma's independence from British rule. A leader of the radicals from his student days, during the Second World War he accepted Japanese assistance and secret military training for his supporters. Returning to Burma in 1942 he became leader of the Japanese-sponsored Burma National Army which defected to the Allies in the closing weeks of the Pacific War. As head of the Anti-Fascist People's Freedom League he led the postwar Council of Ministers, and in January 1947 negotiated a promise of full self-government from the British, but on 19 July 1947 he and six of his colleagues were assassinated by political rivals during a meeting of the Council.

aunt /ɑːnt/ n. **1** the sister of one's father or mother. **2** an uncle's wife. **3** colloq. an unrelated woman friend of a child or children. □ **Aunt Sally 1** a game in which players throw sticks or balls at a wooden dummy. **2** the object of an unreasonable attack. **my** (or **my sainted** etc.) **aunt** sl. an exclamation of surprise, disbelief, etc. [ME f. AF aunte, OF ante, f. L amita]

auntie /ˈɑːntɪ/ n. (also **aunty**) (pl. **-ies**) colloq. **1** = AUNT. **2** (**Auntie**) an institution considered to be conservative or cautious, esp. the BBC.

au pair /əʊ ˈpeə(r)/ n. a young foreign person, esp. a woman, helping with housework etc. in exchange for room, board, and pocket money, esp. as a means of learning a language. [F]

aura /ˈɔːrə/ n. (pl. **aurae** /-riː/ or **auras**) **1** the distinctive atmosphere diffused by or attending a person, place, etc. **2** (in mystic or spiritualistic use) a supposed subtle emanation, visible as a sphere of white or coloured light, surrounding the body of a living creature. **3** a subtle emanation or aroma from flowers etc. **4** Med. premonitory symptom(s) in epilepsy etc. □□ **aural** adj. **auric** adj. [ME f. L f. Gk, = breeze, breath]

aural /ˈɔːr(ə)l/ adj. of or relating to or received by the ear. □□ **aurally** adv. [L auris ear]

Aurangzeb /ˈɔːrəŋˌzeb, ˈaʊ-/ (1618–1707), Mughal emperor of Hindustan 1658–1707, a period of great wealth and splendour for the empire. Having usurped the throne from his father, Aurangzeb assumed the title Alamgir—Conqueror of the World—and embarked on an expansionist policy. He increased the Mughal empire to its widest extent, but constant rebellions and wars greatly weakened it and it declined sharply after his death.

aureate /ˈɔːrɪət/ adj. **1** golden, gold-coloured. **2** resplendent. **3** (of a language) highly ornamented. [ME f. LL aureatus f. L aureus golden f. aurum gold]

Aurelian /ɔːˈriːlɪən/ (Lucius Domitius Aurelianus, c.215–75) Roman emperor, acclaimed by the army in 270, and murdered in a military plot in 275. By a series of campaigns he reunited the empire and repulsed barbarian invaders. He built new walls round Rome and established the State worship of the sun.

Aurelius /ɔːˈriːlɪəs/, Marcus (121–180), Roman emperor 161–180, the adopted successor of Antoninus Pius. Much of his reign was occupied with wars against Germanic tribes invading the empire from the north. He himself was by nature a philosophical contemplative; his Meditations (in Greek) are a collection of aphorisms and reflections based on a Stoic outlook and written down for his own guidance. His equestrian statue now stands on the Capitol in Rome.

aureole /ˈɔːrɪˌəʊl/ n. (also **aureola** /ɔːˈrɪələ/) **1** a halo or circle of light, esp. round the head or body of a portrayed religious figure. **2** a corona round the sun or moon. [ME f. L aureola (corona), = golden (crown), fem. of aureolus f. aureus f. aurum gold: aureole f. OF f. L aureola]

aureomycin /ˌɔːrɪəʊˈmaɪsɪn/ n. an antibiotic used esp. in lung diseases. [L aureus golden + Gk mukēs fungus + -IN]

au revoir /əʊ rəˈvwɑː(r)/ int. & n. goodbye (until we meet again). [F]

Auric /ɔːˈriːk/, Georges (1899–1983), French composer, the youngest member of Les Six (see SIX). His works include operas, ballets (notably Les Matelots, 1925), orchestral works, and songs, but he is probably best known for his film music such as the scores for The Lavender Hill Mob (1951) and Moulin Rouge (1952).

auric /ˈɔːrɪk/ adj. of or relating to trivalent gold. [L aurum gold]

auricle /ˈɔːrɪk(ə)l/ n. Anat. **1 a** a small muscular pouch on the surface of each atrium of the heart. **b** the atrium itself. **2** the external ear of animals. Also called PINNA. **3** an appendage shaped like the ear. [AURICULA]

auricula /ɔːˈrɪkjʊlə/ n. a primula, Primula auricula, with leaves shaped like bears' ears. [L, dimin. of auris ear]

auricular /ɔːˈrɪkjʊlə(r)/ adj. **1** of or relating to the ear or hearing. **2** of or relating to the auricle of the heart. **3** shaped like an auricle. □□ **auricularly** adv. [LL auricularis (as AURICULA)]

auriculate /ɔːˈrɪkjʊlət/ adj. having one or more auricles or ear-shaped appendages. [L]

auriferous /ɔːˈrɪfərəs/ adj. naturally bearing gold. [L aurifer f. aurum gold]

Auriga /ɔːˈraɪgə/ the Charioteer or Wagoner, a constellation in the northern hemisphere, near Orion, including the brilliant yellow star Capella, sixth brightest in the sky, several interesting variable stars, and three well-known galactic clusters. It is crossed by the luminous band of the Milky Way.

Aurignacian /ˌɔːrɪgˈneɪʃ(ə)n/ adj. & n. —adj. of an early upper palaeolithic industry occurring throughout Europe and the Near East, named after the type-site, a cave at Aurignac in southern France, and dated in most places to c.32,000–27,000 BC. This period (which follows the Mousterian and precedes the Solutrean) witnessed the first appearance of cave-paintings (e.g. those at Lascaux in the Dordogne region of France). —n. the Aurignacian industry. [F Aurignacien f. Aurignac]

aurochs /ˈɔːrɒks, ˈaʊrɒks/ n. (pl. same) an extinct wild ox, Bos primigenius, ancestor of domestic cattle and formerly native to many parts of the world. Also called URUS. [G f. OHG ūrohso f. ūr- urus + ohso ox]

Aurora /ɔːˈrɔːrə/ Rom. Mythol. goddess of the dawn, corresponding to the Greek Eos. Most of the stories about her consist of kidnappings of handsome men to live with her (see TITHONUS). [L, = dawn]

aurora /ɔːˈrɔːrə/ n. (pl. **auroras** or **aurorae** /-riː/) **1** a luminous electrical atmospheric phenomenon, usu. of streamers of light in the sky above the northern or southern magnetic pole. **2** poet. the dawn. □ **aurora australis** /ɔːˈstreɪlɪs/ a southern occurrence of aurora. **aurora borealis** /ˌbɒrɪˈeɪlɪs/ a northern occurrence of aurora. □□ **auroral** adj. [L, = dawn, goddess of dawn]

Auschwitz /ˈaʊʃvɪts/ a town in Poland (Polish Oświecim), site of a Nazi concentration camp in the Second World War.

auscultation /ˌɔːskəlˈteɪʃ(ə)n/ n. the act of listening, esp. to sounds from the heart, lungs, etc., as a part of medical diagnosis. □□ **auscultatory** /-ˈkʌltətərɪ/ adj. [L auscultatio f. auscultare listen to]

auspice /ˈɔːspɪs/ n. **1** (in pl.) patronage (esp. under the auspices of). **2** a forecast. [orig. 'observation of bird-flight in divination': F auspice or L auspicium f. auspex observer of birds f. avis bird]

auspicious /ɔːˈspɪʃəs/ adj. **1** of good omen; favourable. **2** prosperous. □□ **auspiciously** adv. **auspiciousness** n. [AUSPICE + -OUS]

Aussie /ˈɒzɪ, ˈɒsɪ/ n. & adj. (also **Ossie**, **Ozzie**) colloq. —n. **1** an Australian. **2** Australia. —adj. Australian. [abbr.]

Austen /ˈɒstɪn/, Jane (1775–1817), English novelist, born at Steventon, Hampshire, where her father was rector. She never married but led an uneventful life in the midst of a large and lively family, writing the witty, epigrammatic, and satiric novels which were to make her world-famous. Her major works, which portray the social life of the upper classes and praise the virtues of reason and intelligence rather than those of passion and impulse, all end with a happy marriage, achieved after the surmounting of obstacles: Sense and Sensibility (1811), Pride and Prejudice (1813), Northanger Abbey (1818), Mansfield Park (1814), Emma (1815), and Persuasion (1818).

austere /ɒˈstɪə(r), ɔːˈstɪə(r)/ adj. (**austerer**, **austerest**) **1** severely simple. **2** morally strict. **3** harsh, stern. □□ **austerely** adv. [ME f. OF f. L austerus f. Gk austēros severe]

austerity /ɒˈsteriti, ɔːˈsteriti/ n. (pl. **-ies**) **1** sternness; moral severity. **2** severe simplicity, e.g. of nationwide economies. **3** (esp. in pl.) an austere practice (*the austerities of a monk's life*).

Austerlitz /ˈaʊstəlɪts, ˈɔ-/ a town in central Czechoslovakia, scene in 1805 of Napoleon's defeat of the Austrians and Russians.

Austin[1] /ˈɒstɪn/ the capital of Texas, on the Colorado River; pop. (1982) 368,100.

Austin[2] /ˈɒstɪn, ˈɔ:stɪn/ n. = AUGUSTINIAN. [contr. of AUGUSTINE]

Austin[3] /ˈɔ:stɪn/, John (1790–1859), English jurist, a friend of Jeremy Bentham, by whom he was greatly influenced. Austin's importance lies in his strict delimitation of the sphere of law and its distinction from that of morality, and his examination of the connotations of such common legal terms and ideas as right, duty, liberty, injury, and punishment. He is regarded as the founder of analytical jurisprudence.

Austin[4] /ˈɔ:stɪn/, John Langshaw (1911–60), English philosopher, lecturer and later professor at Oxford University. He was a careful and witty exponent of the linguistic school of philosophy, seeking to elucidate philosophical problems by analysis of the words in which they are expressed. Two of his courses of lectures were published posthumously in 1962: *Sense and Sensibilia* discusses perception, *How to Do Things with Words* distinguishes 'performative' utterances (in which something is done, such as promising or making marriage vows) and utterances that convey information.

Austin Friars /ˈɔ:stɪn/ see AUGUSTINIAN.

austral /ˈɔ:str(ə)l, ˈɒstr(ə)l/ adj. **1** southern. **2** (**Austral**) of Australia or Australasia (*Austral English*). [ME f. L *australis* f. *Auster* south wind]

Australasia /ˌɒstrəˈleɪʒə, -ʃə/ a region consisting of Australia, New Zealand, and neighbouring islands of the SW Pacific. □□ **Australasian** adj. & n. f. F *Australasie*, formed as *Australia* + *Asia*]

Australia /ɒˈstreɪlɪə/ an island country and continent of the southern hemisphere in the SW Pacific, a member State of the British Commonwealth; pop. (1988) 16,260,400; official language, English; capital, Canberra. Much of the continent has a hot dry climate and a large part of the central area is desert or semi-desert; the most fertile areas are the eastern coastal plains and the SW corner of Western Australia. Agriculture has always been of vital importance to the economy, with cereal crops grown over wide areas and livestock producing wool, meat, and dairy products for export. There are significant mineral resources (including bauxite, coal, copper, iron, lead, uranium, and zinc), and fourteen oilfields produce nearly 70 per cent of the country's requirements. The people are mainly of European descent but there are about 160,000 Aborigines. [L (*terra*) *australis* (as AUSTRAL]

Human habitation in Australia dates from prehistoric times (see ABORIGINES). The existence of an unknown southern land (*terra australis*) was postulated in ancient Greek geographical writings and the idea was passed on in medieval writings and maps. Pre-17th c. European sightings of Australia are claimed but not firmly attested. From 1606 onwards its western coast was explored by the Dutch, and in 1642 Tasman proved that it was an island; it was visited by an Englishman, William Dampier, in 1688 and 1699. In 1770 Captain James Cook landed at Botany Bay on the eastern side of the continent and formally took possession of New South Wales. British colonization began in 1788 (also the settling of convicts at Port Jackson, discontinued in 1840). The interior was gradually explored and opened up in the 19th c. and political consolidation resulted in the declaration of a Commonwealth in 1901, when the six colonies (New South Wales, Victoria, Queensland, South Australia, Western Australia, and Tasmania) federated as sovereign States. Australia supported Great Britain heavily in each of the two World Wars, being threatened herself by Japanese invasion during the second, but although still maintaining ties with the former mother country has more and more pursued her own interests both domestically and internationally, the latter with particular reference to SE Asia and the South Pacific.

Australian /ɒˈstreɪlɪən/ n. & adj. —n. **1** a native or national of Australia. **2** a person of Australian descent. —adj. of or relating to Australia. □ **Australian bear** a koala bear. **Australian Rules** see separate entry. **Australian terrier** a wire-haired Australian breed of terrier. □□ **Australianism** n. [F *australien* f. L (as AUSTRAL)]

Australian Capital Territory federal territory (pop. (1986) 260,700) in New South Wales consisting of two enclaves ceded by New South Wales, one in 1911 to contain Canberra, the other in 1915 containing Jervis Bay.

Australian (National) Rules Football a form of football played by teams of 18 players with a ball shaped like that used in Rugby football. It is a fast-moving game with few rules apart from those aimed at protecting the player, forming the national code in the Australian Commonwealth and officially dating back to 1858.

Austral Islands see TUBUAI ISLANDS.

Australoid /ˈɒstrɔɪd/ adj. & n. —adj. of a race of people that diffused to Australia from Asia at a time of lower sea level. The Vedda of Sri Lanka and the Aborigines of Australia are the modern representatives. Their physical attributes are: dark skin, black wavy to curly hair, abundant facial and body hair, dolichocephalic head, splayed nose, wide mouth, and thick lips. Male height varies from 150–180 cm (4 ft. 10 in.– 6 ft.) with the women being c.10 cm (4 in.) shorter. —n. a person of Australoid ethnological type. [as AUSTRALIAN]

Australopithecus /ˌɒstrələʊˈpɪθɪkəs/ n. any extinct bipedal primate of the genus *Australopithecus* having apelike and human characteristics, or its fossilized remains. Such remains have been found in Southern and East Africa; they belong to the Upper Pliocene and Lower Pleistocene epochs, dating from c.5.5 million to 1 million years ago. □□ **australopithecine** /-ɪˌsiːn/ n. & adj. [mod.L f. L *australis* southern + Gk *pithēkos* ape]

Austria /ˈɒstrɪə/ (German **Österreich** /ˈɜːstəˌraɪk/) a country in central Europe, much of it mountainous, with the River Danube flowing through the north-east; pop. (est. 1988) 7,577,000; official language, German; capital, Vienna. Agriculture and forestry are important (timber is a valuable source of wealth) and there are considerable heavy industries; hydroelectric power has been developed and is exported. The Celtic tribes settled in the area were conquered by the Romans in 15–9 BC and it remained part of the Roman Empire, with the Danube as its frontier, until overrun by Germanic peoples in the 5th c. AD. Dominated from the early Middle Ages by the Hapsburg family, Austria became the centre of a massive Central European empire which held sway over the area until the First World War. The collapse of the Hapsburg empire in 1918 left Austria a weak and unstable country which was easily incorporated within the Nazi Reich in 1938. After the Second World War the country remained under Allied military occupation until 1955. Since regaining her sovereignty Austria has emerged as a prosperous and stable democratic republic with decidedly westward leanings. □□ **Austrian** adj. & n.

Austria-Hungary (also called the **Austro-Hungarian empire**) the 'Dual Monarchy', established by the Austrian emperor Francis Joseph after Austria's defeat by Prussia in 1866 in which Austria and Hungary became autonomous States under a common sovereign. The dualist system came under increasing pressure from the other subject nations, including Croatians, Serbs, Slovaks, Romanians, and Czechs, and failure to resolve these nationalist aspirations was one of the causes of the First World War. After their victory the Allies gave support to the emergent nations, and the Austro-Hungarian empire was dissolved by the Versailles peace settlement (1919).

Austrian Succession, War of the a complicated European conflict in which the key issue was the right of Maria Theresa of Austria to succeed to the lands of her father, the emperor Charles VI, and that of her husband Francis of Lorraine to the imperial title. (see PRAGMATIC SANCTION.)

Austro- /ˈɒstrəʊ/ comb. form Austrian; Austrian and (*Austro-Hungarian*).

AUT abbr. (in the UK) Association of University Teachers.

autarchy /ˈɔːtɑːkɪ/ n. (pl. **-ies**) **1** absolute sovereignty. **2** despotism. **3** an autarchic country or society. □□ **autarchic** /ɔːˈtɑːkɪk/ adj. **autarchical** /ɔːˈtɑːkɪk(ə)l/ adj. [mod.L *autarchia* (as AUTO-, Gk *-arkhia* f. *arkhō* rule)]

autarky /ˈɔːtɑːkɪ/ n. (pl. **-ies**) **1** self-sufficiency, esp. as an economic system. **2** a state etc. run according to such a system. □□ **autarkic** /ɔːˈtɑːkɪk/ adj. **autarkical** /ɔːˈtɑːkɪk(ə)l/ adj. **autarkist** n. [Gk *autarkeia* (as AUTO-, *arkeō* suffice)]

authentic /ɔːˈθentɪk/ adj. **1 a** of undisputed origin; genuine. **b** reliable or trustworthy. **2** Mus. (of a mode) containing notes between the final and an octave higher (cf. PLAGAL). □□ **authentically** adv. **authenticity** /ɔːθenˈtɪsɪtɪ/ n. [ME f. OF *autentique* f. LL *authenticus* f. Gk *authentikos* principal, genuine]

authenticate /ɔːˈθentɪkeɪt/ v.tr. **1** establish the truth or genuineness of. **2** validate. □□ **authentication** /-ˈkeɪʃ(ə)n/ n. **authenticator** n. [med.L *authenticare* f. LL *authenticus*: see AUTHENTIC]

author /ˈɔːθə(r)/ n. & v. —n. (fem. **authoress** /ˈɔːθrɪs, ˌɔːθəˈres/) **1** a writer, esp. of books. **2** the originator of an event, a condition, etc. (*the author of all my woes*). —v.tr. disp. be the author of (a book, the universe, a child, etc.). □□ **authorial** /ɔːˈθɔːrɪəl/ adj. [ME f. AF *autour*, OF *autor* f. L *auctor* f. *augēre auct-* increase, originate, promote]

authoritarian /ɔːˌθɒrɪˈteərɪən/ adj. & n. —adj. **1** favouring, encouraging, or enforcing strict obedience to authority, as opposed to individual freedom. **2** tyrannical or domineering. —n. a person favouring absolute obedience to a constituted authority. □□ **authoritarianism** n.

authoritative /ɔːˈθɒrɪtətɪv/ adj. **1** being recognized as true or dependable. **2** (of a person, behaviour, etc.) commanding or self-confident. **3** official; supported by authority (*an authoritative document*). □□ **authoritatively** adv. **authoritativeness** n.

authority /ɔːˈθɒrɪtɪ/ n. (pl. **-ies**) **1 a** the power or right to enforce obedience. **b** (often foll. by *for*, or to + infin.) delegated power. **2** (esp. in pl.) a person or body having authority, esp. political or administrative. **3 a** an influence exerted on opinion because of recognized knowledge or expertise. **b** such an influence expressed in a book, quotation, etc. (*an authority on vintage cars*). **c** a person whose opinion is accepted, esp. an expert in a subject. **4** the weight of evidence. [ME f. OF *autorité* f. L *auctoritas* f. *auctor*: see AUTHOR]

authorize /ˈɔːθəˌraɪz/ v.tr. (also **-ise**) **1** sanction. **2** (foll. by *to* + infin.) **a** give authority. **b** commission (a person or body) (*authorized to trade*). □□ **authorization** /ˌɔːθəraɪˈzeɪʃ(ə)n/ n. [ME f. OF *autoriser* f. med.L *auctorizare* f. *auctor*: see AUTHOR]

Authorized Version a popular appellation of the 1611 English translation of the Bible, ordered by James I (it is known in the US as the 'King James Version') and produced by about 50 scholars. On the title-page are the words 'appointed to be read in churches', but it has never otherwise been officially 'authorized'. It immediately won the hearts of the people, loved for its intrinsic merits rather than promoted by official recommendation, and remained for centuries the Bible of every English-speaking country.

authorship /ˈɔːθəʃɪp/ n. **1** the origin of a book or other written work (*of unknown authorship*). **2** the occupation of writing.

autism /ˈɔːtɪz(ə)m/ n. Psychol. a mental condition, usu. present from childhood, characterized by complete self-absorption and a reduced ability to respond to or communicate with the outside world. □□ **autistic** /ɔːˈtɪstɪk/ adj. [mod.L *autismus* (as AUTO-, -ISM)]

auto /ˈɔːtəʊ/ n. (pl. **-os**) US colloq. a motor car. [abbr. of AUTOMOBILE]

auto- /ˈɔːtəʊ/ comb. form (usu. **aut-** before a vowel) **1** self (*autism*). **2** one's own (*autobiography*). **3** by oneself or spontaneous (*auto-suggestion*). **4** by itself or automatic (*automobile*). [from or after Gk *auto-* f. *autos* self]

autobahn /ˈɔːtəʊˌbɑːn/ n. (pl. **autobahns** or **autobahnen** /-nən/) a German, Austrian, or Swiss motorway. [G f. *Auto* motor car + *Bahn* path, road]

autobiography /ˌɔːtəʊbaɪˈɒgrəfɪ/ n. (pl. **-ies**) **1** a personal account of one's own life, esp. for publication. **2** this as a process or literary form. □□ **autobiographer** n. **autobiographic** /ˌɔːtəʊˌbaɪəˈgræfɪk/ adj. **autobiographical** /-ˈgræfɪk(ə)l/ adj.

autocade /ˈɔːtəʊˌkeɪd/ n. US a motorcade. ¶ *Motorcade* is more usual. [AUTOMOBILE + CAVALCADE]

autocar /ˈɔːtəʊˌkɑː(r)/ n. archaic a motor vehicle.

autocephalous /ˌɔːtəʊˈsefələs/ adj. **1** (esp. of an Eastern Church) appointing its own head. **2** (of a bishop, Church, etc.) independent. [Gk *autokephalos* (as AUTO-, *kephalē* head)]

autochthon /ɔːˈtɒkθ(ə)n/ n. (pl. **autochthons** or **autochthones** /-θəˌniːz/) (usu. in pl.) the original or earliest known inhabitants of a country; aboriginals. □□ **autochthonal** adj. **autochthonic** /-ˈθɒnɪk/ adj. **autochthonous** adj. [Gk, = sprung from the earth (as AUTO-, *khthōn, -onos* earth)]

autoclave /ˈɔːtəʊˌkleɪv/ n. **1** a strong vessel used for chemical reactions at high pressures and temperatures. **2** a sterilizer using high-pressure steam. [AUTO- + L *clavus* nail or *clavis* key]

autocracy /ɔːˈtɒkrəsɪ/ n. (pl. **-ies**) **1** absolute government by one person. **2** the power exercised by such a person. **3** an autocratic country or society. [Gk *autokrateia* (as AUTOCRAT)]

autocrat /ˈɔːtəˌkræt/ n. **1** an absolute ruler. **2** a dictatorial person. □□ **autocratic** /-ˈkrætɪk/ adj. **autocratically** /-ˈkrætɪkəlɪ/ adv. [F *autocrate* f. Gk *autokratēs* (as AUTO-, *kratos* power)]

autocross /ˈɔːtəʊˌkrɒs/ n. motor-racing across country or on unmade roads. [AUTOMOBILE + CROSS-]

Autocue /ˈɔːtəʊˌkjuː/ n. propr. a device, unseen by the audience, displaying a television script to a speaker or performer as an aid to memory (cf. TELEPROMPTER).

auto-da-fé /ˌɔːtəʊdɑːˈfeɪ/ n. (pl. **autos-da-fé** /ˌɔːtəʊz-/) **1** a sentence of punishment by the Spanish Inquisition. **2** the execution of such a sentence, esp. the burning of a heretic. [Port., = act of the faith]

autodidact /ˈɔːtəʊˌdaɪdækt/ n. a self-taught person. □□ **autodidactic** /-ˈdæktɪk/ adj. [AUTO- + *didact* as DIDACTIC]

auto-erotism /ˌɔːtəʊˈerəˌtɪz(ə)m/ n. (also **auto-eroticism** /-ɪˈrɒtɪˌsɪz(ə)m/) Psychol. sexual excitement generated by stimulating one's own body; masturbation. □□ **auto-erotic** /-ɪˈrɒtɪk/ adj.

autofocus /ˈɔːtəʊˌfəʊkəs/ n. a device for focusing a camera etc. automatically.

autogamy /ɔːˈtɒgəmɪ/ n. Bot. self-fertilization in plants. □□ **autogamous** adj. [AUTO- + Gk *-gamia* f. *gamos* marriage]

autogenous /ɔːˈtɒdʒɪnəs/ adj. self-produced. □ **autogenous welding** a process of joining metal by melting the edges together, without adding material.

autogiro /ˌɔːtəʊˈdʒaɪərəʊ/ n. (also **autogyro**) (pl. **-os**) an early form of helicopter with freely rotating horizontal vanes and a propeller. It differs from the later helicopter in that its wings are not powered, but rotate in the slipstream. The aircraft itself is propelled forward by a conventional mounted engine and propeller. Originally the term 'autogiro' was the proprietary name used by its Spanish inventor, Juan de la Cierva, whose first autogiro flew in 1923. [Sp. (as AUTO-, *giro* gyration)]

autograft /ˈɔːtəˌgrɑːft/ n. Surgery a graft of tissue from one point to another of the same person's body.

autograph /ˈɔːtəˌgrɑːf/ n. & v. —n. **1 a** a signature, esp. that of a celebrity. **b** handwriting. **2** a manuscript in an author's own handwriting. **3** a document signed by its author. —v.tr. **1** sign (a photograph, autograph album, etc.). **2** write (a letter etc.) by hand. [F *autographe* or LL *autographum* f. Gk *autographon* neut. of *autographos* (as AUTO-, -GRAPH)]

autography /ɔːˈtɒgrəfɪ/ n. **1** writing done with one's own hand. **2** the facsimile reproduction of writing or illustration. □□ **autographic** /-ˈgræfɪk/ adj.

autogyro var. of AUTOGIRO.

autoharp /ˈɔːtəˌhɑːp/ n. a kind of zither with a mechanical device to allow the playing of chords.

autoimmune /ˌɔːtəʊɪˈmjuːn/ adj. Med. (of a disease) caused by antibodies produced against substances naturally present in the body. □□ **autoimmunity** n.

autointoxication /ˌɔːtəʊɪnˌtɒksɪˈkeɪʃ(ə)n/ n. Med. poisoning by a toxin formed within the body itself.

autolysis /ɔːˈtɒlɪsɪs/ n. the destruction of cells by their own enzymes. □□ **autolytic** /ˌɔːtəˈlɪtɪk/ adj. [G Autolyse (as AUTO-, -LYSIS)]

automat /ˈɔːtəˌmæt/ n. US **1** a slot-machine that dispenses goods. **2** a cafeteria containing slot-machines dispensing food and drink. [G f. F automate, formed as AUTOMATION]

automate /ˈɔːtəˌmeɪt/ v.tr. convert to or operate by automation (the ticket office has been automated). [back-form. f. AUTOMATION]

automatic /ˌɔːtəˈmætɪk/ adj. & n. —adj. **1** (of a machine, device, etc., or its function) working by itself, without direct human intervention. **2 a** done spontaneously, without conscious thought or intention (an automatic reaction). **b** necessary and inevitable (an automatic penalty). **3** Psychol. performed unconsciously or subconsciously. **4** (of a firearm) that continues firing until the ammunition is exhausted or the pressure on the trigger is released. **5** (of a motor vehicle or its transmission) using gears that change automatically according to speed and acceleration. —n. **1** an automatic device, esp. a gun or transmission. **2** colloq. a vehicle with automatic transmission. □ **automatic pilot** a device for keeping an aircraft on a set course. □□ **automatically** adv. **automaticity** /ˌɔːtəməˈtɪsɪtɪ/ n. [formed as AUTOMATON + -IC]

automation /ˌɔːtəˈmeɪʃ(ə)n/ n. **1** the use of automatic equipment to save mental and manual labour. **2** the automatic control of the manufacture of a product through its successive stages. [irreg. f. AUTOMATIC + -ATION]

automatism /ɔːˈtɒməˌtɪz(ə)m/ n. **1** Psychol. the performance of actions unconsciously or subconsciously; such action. **2** involuntary action. **3** unthinking routine. [F automatisme f. automate AUTOMATON]

automatize /ɔːˈtɒməˌtaɪz/ v.tr. (also **-ise**) **1** make (a process etc.) automatic. **2** subject (a business, enterprise, etc.) to automation. □□ **automatization** /-ˈzeɪʃ(ə)n/ n. [AUTOMATIC + -IZE]

automaton /ɔːˈtɒmət(ə)n/ n. (pl. **automata** /-tə/ or **automatons**) **1** a piece of mechanism with concealed motive power. **2** a person who behaves mechanically, like an automaton. [L f. Gk, neut. of automatos acting of itself: see AUTO-]

automobile /ˈɔːtəməˌbiːl/ n. US a motor car. [F (as AUTO-, MOBILE)]

automotive /ˌɔːtəˈməʊtɪv/ adj. concerned with motor vehicles.

autonomic /ˌɔːtəˈnɒmɪk/ adj. esp. Physiol. functioning involuntarily. □ **autonomic nervous system** see NERVOUS SYSTEM. [AUTONOMY + -IC]

autonomous /ɔːˈtɒnəməs/ adj. **1** having self-government. **2** acting independently or having the freedom to do so. □□ **autonomously** adv. [Gk autonomos (as AUTONOMY)]

autonomy /ɔːˈtɒnəmɪ/ n. (pl. **-ies**) **1** the right of self-government. **2** personal freedom. **3** freedom of the will. **4** a self-governing community. □□ **autonomist** n. [Gk autonomia f. autos self + nomos law]

autopilot /ˈɔːtəʊˌpaɪlət/ n. an automatic pilot. [abbr.]

autopista /ˈaʊtəʊˌpɪstə/ n. a Spanish motorway. [Sp. (as AUTOMOBILE, pista track)]

autopsy /ˈɔːtɒpsɪ, ɔːˈtɒpsɪ/ n. (pl. **-ies**) **1** a post-mortem examination. **2** any critical analysis. **3** a personal inspection. [F autopsie or mod.L autopsia f. Gk f. autoptēs eye-witness]

autoradiograph /ˌɔːtəˈreɪdɪəˌɡrɑːf/ n. a photograph of an object, produced by radiation from radioactive material in the object. □□ **autoradiographic** /ˌɔːtəˌreɪdɪəˈɡræfɪk/ adj. **autoradiography** /ˌɔːtəˌreɪdɪˈɒɡrəfɪ/ n.

autoroute /ˈɔːtəʊˌruːt/ n. a French motorway. [F (as AUTOMOBILE, ROUTE)]

autostrada /ˈɔːtəʊˌstrɑːdə/ n. (pl. **autostradas** or **autostrade** /-deɪ/) an Italian motorway. [It. (as AUTOMOBILE, strada road)]

auto-suggestion /ˌɔːtəʊsəˈdʒestʃ(ə)n/ n. a hypnotic or subconscious suggestion made by a person to himself or herself and affecting behaviour.

autotelic /ˌɔːtəˈtelɪk/ adj. having or being a purpose in itself. [AUTO- + Gk telos end]

autotomy /ɔːˈtɒtəmɪ/ n. Zool. the casting off of a part of the body when threatened, e.g. the tail of a lizard.

autotoxin /ˌɔːtəˈtɒksɪn/ n. a poisonous substance originating within an organism. □□ **autotoxic** adj.

autotrophic /ˌɔːtəˈtrɒfɪk/ adj. Biol. able to form complex nutritional organic substances from simple inorganic substances such as carbon dioxide (cf. HETEROTROPHIC). [AUTO- + Gk trophos feeder]

autotype /ˈɔːtəˌtaɪp/ n. **1** a facsimile. **2 a** a photographic printing process for monochrome reproduction. **b** a print made by this process.

autoxidation /ɔːˌtɒksɪˈdeɪʃ(ə)n/ n. Chem. oxidation by exposure to air at room temperature.

autumn /ˈɔːtəm/ n. **1** the third season of the year, when crops and fruits are gathered, and leaves fall, in the northern hemisphere from September to November and in the southern hemisphere from March to May. **2** Astron. the period from the autumnal equinox to the winter solstice. **3** a time of maturity or incipient decay. □ **autumn crocus** any plant of the genus Colchicum, esp. meadow saffron, of the lily family and unrelated to the true crocus. [ME f. OF autompne f. L autumnus]

autumnal /ɔːˈtʌmn(ə)l/ adj. **1** of, characteristic of, or appropriate to autumn (autumnal colours). **2** occurring in autumn (autumnal equinox). **3** maturing or blooming in autumn. **4** past the prime of life. [L autumnalis (as AUTUMN, -AL)]

Auvergne /əʊˈvɛən/ **1** an ancient province of south central France. It takes its name from the Arverni, a Celtic tribe living there in Roman times. **2** a region of modern France; pop. (1982) 1,332,700; capital, Clermont-Ferrand.

auxanometer /ˌɔːksəˈnɒmɪtə(r)/ n. an instrument for measuring the linear growth of plants. [Gk auxanō increase + -METER]

auxiliary /ɔːɡˈzɪljərɪ/ adj. & n. —adj. **1** (of a person or thing) that gives help. **2** (of services or equipment) subsidiary, additional. —n. (pl. **-ies**) **1** an auxiliary person or thing. **2** (in pl.) Mil. auxiliary troops. **3** Gram. an auxiliary verb. □ **auxiliary troops** Mil. foreign or allied troops in a belligerent nation's service. **auxiliary verb** Gram. one used in forming tenses, moods, and voices of other verbs. [L auxiliarius f. auxilium help]

auxin /ˈɔːksɪn/ n. a plant hormone that regulates growth. [G f. Gk auxō increase + -IN]

AV abbr. **1** audiovisual (teaching aids etc.). **2** Authorized Version (of the Bible).

avadavat var. of AMADAVAT.

avail /əˈveɪl/ v. & n. —v. **1** tr. help, benefit. **2** refl. (foll. by of) profit by; take advantage of. **3** intr. **a** provide help. **b** be of use, value, or profit. —n. (usu. in neg. or interrog. phrases) use, profit (of no avail; without avail; of what avail?). [ME f. obs. vail (v.) f. OF valoir be worth f. L valēre]

available /əˈveɪləb(ə)l/ adj. (often foll. by to, for) **1** capable of being used; at one's disposal. **2** within one's reach. □□ **availability** /-ˈbɪlɪtɪ/ n. **availableness** n. **availably** adv. [ME f. AVAIL + -ABLE]

avalanche /ˈævəlɑːnʃ/ n. & v. —n. **1** a mass of snow and ice, tumbling rapidly down a mountain. **2** a sudden appearance or arrival of anything in large quantities (faced with an avalanche of work). —v. **1** intr. descend like an avalanche. **2** tr. carry down like an avalanche. [F, alt. of dial. lavanche after avaler descend]

Avalon /ˈævələn/ **1** (in Arthurian legend) the place to which Arthur was conveyed after death. **2** Welsh Mythol. the kingdom of the dead.

avant-garde /ˌævɑ̃ˈɡɑːd/ n. & adj. —n. pioneers or innovators esp. in art and literature. —adj. (of ideas etc.) new, progressive. □□ **avant-gardism** n. **avant-gardist** n. [F, = vanguard]

Avar /ˈɑːvə(r)/ n. & adj. —n. **a** member of a Turkic people prominent in SE Europe in the 6th–9th c. In the 7th c. their kingdom extended from the Black Sea to the Adriatic. They were finally subdued by Charlemagne (791–9). —*adj.* of this people.

avarice /ˈævərɪs/ *n.* extreme greed for money or gain; cupidity. □□ **avaricious** /ˌævəˈrɪʃəs/ *adj.* **avariciously** /-ˈrɪʃəslɪ/ *adv.* **avariciousness** /-ˈrɪʃəsnɪs/ *n.* [ME f. OF f. L *avaritia* f. *avarus* greedy]

avast /əˈvɑːst/ *int. Naut.* stop, cease. [Du. *houd vast* hold fast]

avatar /ˈævəˌtɑː(r)/ *n.* **1** (in Hindu mythology) the descent of a deity or released soul to earth in bodily form. **2** incarnation; manifestation. **3** a manifestation or phase. [Skr. *avatāra* descent f. *áva* down + *tṛ-* pass over]

avaunt /əˈvɔːnt/ *int. archaic* begone. [ME f. AF f. OF *avant* ult. f. L *ab* from + *ante* before]

Ave. *abbr.* Avenue.

ave /ˈɑːveɪ, ˈɑːvɪ/ *int. & n.* —*int.* **1** welcome. **2** farewell. —*n.* **1** (**Ave**; in full **Ave Maria**) a prayer to the Virgin Mary, the opening line from Luke 1: 28. Also called *Hail Mary*. **2** a shout of welcome or farewell. [ME f. L, 2nd sing. imper. of *avēre* fare well]

Avebury /ˈeɪvbərɪ/ a village in Wiltshire on the site of one of Britain's most impressive henge monuments of the late neolithic period (3rd millennium BC).

avenge /əˈvendʒ/ *v.tr.* **1** inflict retribution on behalf of (a person, a violated right, etc.). **2** take vengeance for (an injury). □ **be avenged** avenge oneself. □□ **avenger** *n.* [ME f. OF *avengier* f. *à* to + *vengier* f. L *vindicare* vindicate]

avens /ˈæv(ə)nz/ *n.* any of various plants of the genus *Geum.* □ **mountain avens** a related plant (*Dryas octopetala*). [ME f. OF *avence* (med.L *avencia*), of unkn. orig.]

aventurine /əˈventjʊˌriːn/ *n. Mineral.* **1** brownish glass or mineral containing sparkling gold-coloured particles usu. of copper or gold. **2** a variety of spangled quartz resembling this. [F f. It. *avventurino* f. *avventura* chance (because of its accidental discovery)]

avenue /ˈævəˌnjuː/ *n.* **1 a** a broad road or street, often with trees at regular intervals along its sides. **b** a tree-lined approach to a country house. **2 a** way of approaching or dealing with something (*explored every avenue to find an answer*). [F, fem. past part. of *avenir* f. L *advenire* come to]

aver /əˈvɜː(r)/ *v.tr.* (**averred, averring**) assert, affirm. [ME f. OF *averer* (as AD-, L *verus* true)]

average /ˈævərɪdʒ/ *n., adj., & v.* —*n.* **1 a** the usual amount, extent, or rate. **b** the ordinary standard. **2** an amount obtained by dividing the total of given amounts by the number of amounts in the set. **3** *Law* the distribution of loss resulting from damage to a ship or cargo. —*adj.* **1** usual, ordinary. **2** estimated or calculated by average. —*v.tr.* **1** amount on average to (*the sale of the product averaged one hundred a day*). **2** do on average (*averages six hours' work a day*). **3 a** estimate the average of. **b** estimate the general standard of. □ **average adjustment** *Law* the apportionment of average. **average out** result in an average. **average out at** result in an average of. **batting average 1** *Cricket* a batsman's runs scored per completed innings. **2** *Baseball* a batter's safe hits per time at bat. **bowling average** *Cricket* a bowler's conceded runs per wicket taken. **law of averages** the principle that if one of two extremes occurs the other will also tend to so as to maintain the normal average. **on** (or **on an**) **average** as an average rate or estimate. □□ **averagely** *adv.* [F *avarie* damage to ship or cargo (see sense 3), f. It. *avaria* f. Arab. *ʿawārīya* damaged goods f. *ʿawār* damage at sea, loss: *-age* after *damage*]

averment /əˈvɜːmənt/ *n.* a positive statement; an affirmation, esp. *Law* one with an offer of proof. [ME f. AF, OF *aver(r)ement* (as AVER, -MENT)]

Avernus /əˈvɜːnəs/ a lake near Naples in Italy, filling the crater of an extinct volcano, regarded by the ancients as the entrance to the Underworld.

Averroës /əˈverəʊˌiːz/ (Arabic name ibn-Rushd, *c.*1126–98) Islamic philosopher, born at Cordoba in Spain, whose work crowned a 500-year tradition in Islamic thought. Of his scientific, philosophical, and religious writings the most influential were the commentaries on Aristotle which, through a

reliance upon Neoplatonism, interpreted Aristotle's writings in such a way as to make them consistent with Plato's. Reality, he held, consists of hierarchical levels of being which flow from the Ultimate One, who can be identified with Allah. Averroës' commentaries exercised a strong and controversial influence upon the succeeding centuries of Western philosophy and science.

averse /əˈvɜːs/ *predic.adj.* (often foll. by *to, from*) opposed, disinclined (*was not averse to helping me*). ¶ Construction with *to* is now more common. [L *aversus* (as AVERT)]

aversion /əˈvɜːʃ(ə)n/ *n.* **1** (usu. foll. by *to, from, for*) a dislike or unwillingness (*has an aversion to hard work*). **2** an object of dislike (*my pet aversion*). □ **aversion therapy** therapy designed to make a subject averse to an existing habit. [F *aversion* or L *aversio* (as AVERT, -ION)]

avert /əˈvɜːt/ *v.tr.* (often foll. by *from*) **1** turn away (one's eyes or thoughts). **2** prevent or ward off (an undesirable occurrence). □□ **avertable** *adj.* **avertible** *adj.* [ME f. L *avertere* (as AB-, *vertere* *vers-* turn): partly f. OF *avertir* f. Rmc]

Avesta /əˈvestə/ *n.* (usu. prec. by *the*) the sacred writings of Zoroastrianism, compiled by Zoroaster as a means of reforming an older tradition. (See ZEND-AVESTA.) [Pers. *avastāk* text]

Avestan /əˈvest(ə)n/ *adj. & n.* —*adj.* of or relating to the Avesta. —*n.* the ancient east-Iranian language in which the Avesta is written (often incorrectly called *Zend*), closely related to Vedic Sanskrit.

avian /ˈeɪvɪən/ *adj.* of or relating to birds. [L *avis* bird]

aviary /ˈeɪvɪərɪ/ *n.* (*pl.* **-ies**) a large enclosure or building for keeping birds. [L *aviarium* (as AVIAN, -ARY[1])]

aviate /ˈeɪvɪˌeɪt/ *v.* **1** *intr.* fly in an aeroplane. **2** *tr.* pilot (an aeroplane). [back-form. f. AVIATION]

aviation /ˌeɪvɪˈeɪʃ(ə)n/ *n.* **1** the skill or practice of operating aircraft. **2** aircraft manufacture. [F f. L *avis* bird]

aviator /ˈeɪvɪˌeɪtə(r)/ *n.* (*fem.* **aviatrix** /ˈeɪvɪətrɪks/) an airman or airwoman. [F *aviateur* f. L *avis* bird]

Avicenna /ˌævɪˈsenə/ (Arabic name ibn-Sina, 980–1037) Islamic philosopher who exercised a dominant influence upon medieval Islam. Born in Persia, he worked as physician at the courts of local princes, and his surviving works include treatises on philosophy, medicine, and religion. His philosophical system, while drawing heavily from Aristotle, is closer to Neoplatonism, and was the major influence on the development of 13th-c. scholasticism. He produced a philosophical encyclopaedia *Ash-Shifa* (*The Recovery*), and his *Canon of Medicine*, which combined his own medical knowledge with Roman and Arabic medicine, was a popular text in the medieval world.

aviculture /ˈeɪvɪˌkʌltʃə(r)/ *n.* the rearing and keeping of birds. □□ **aviculturist** /-ˈkʌltʃərɪst/ *n.* [L *avis* bird, after AGRICULTURE]

avid /ˈævɪd/ *adj.* (usu. foll. by *of, for*) eager, greedy. □□ **avidity** /əˈvɪdɪtɪ/ *n.* **avidly** *adv.* [F *avide* or L *avidus* f. *avēre* crave]

avifauna /ˈeɪvɪˌfɔːnə/ *n.* birds of a region or country collectively. [L *avis* bird + FAUNA]

Avignon /ˈæviːˌjɲɔ̃/ a city on the Rhône in southern France; pop. (1982) 174,250. From 1309 until 1377 it was the residence of the popes during their exile from Rome, and became papal property by purchase in 1348. After the papal court had returned to Rome two antipopes re-established a papal court in Avignon. The second of these was expelled in 1408, but the city remained in papal hands until the French Revolution.

avionics /ˌeɪvɪˈɒnɪks/ *n.* electronics as applied to aviation.

avitaminosis /eɪˌvɪtəmɪˈnəʊsɪs/ *n. Med.* a condition resulting from a deficiency of one or more vitamins.

avizandum /ˌævɪˈzændəm/ *n. Sc. Law* a period of time for further consideration of a judgement. [med.L, gerund of *avizare* consider (as ADVISE)]

avocado /ˌævəˈkɑːdəʊ/ *n.* (*pl.* **-os**) **1** (in full **avocado pear**) a pear-shaped fruit with rough leathery skin, a smooth oily edible flesh, and a large stone. **2** the tropical evergreen tree, *Persea americana*, native to Central America, bearing this fruit. Also called *alligator pear*. **3** the light green colour of the flesh of this fruit. [Sp., = advocate (substituted for Aztec *ahuacatl*)]

avocation /ˌævəˈkeɪʃ(ə)n/ n. **1** a minor occupation. **2** colloq. a vocation or calling. [L avocatio f. avocare call away]

avocet /ˈævəˌset/ n. any wading bird of the genus Recurvirostra with long legs and a long slender upward-curved bill and usu. black and white plumage. [F avocette f. It. avosetta]

Avogadro /ˌævəˈgɑːdrəʊ/, Amadeo (1776–1856), Italian physicist, best known for his hypothesis (or law), formulated in 1811 but ignored for the next fifty years, according to which equal volumes of gases at the same temperature and pressure contain equal numbers of molecules (the term which he coined for an aggregation of atoms), and from which it became relatively simple to derive both molecular weights and a system of atomic weights. A constant named in his honour is Avogadro's number, which is the number of molecules in 1 gram-molecular weight (mole) of a substance, and has a value of 6.02×10^{23}.

avoid /əˈvɔɪd/ v.tr. **1** keep away or refrain from (a thing, person, or action). **2** escape; evade. **3** Law **a** nullify (a decree or contract). **b** quash (a sentence). □□ **avoidable** adj. **avoidably** adv. **avoidance** n. **avoider** n. [AF avoider, OF evuider clear out, get quit of, f. vuide empty, VOID]

avoirdupois /ˌævədəˈpɔɪz/ n. (in full **avoirdupois weight**) a system of weights based on a pound of 16 ounces or 7,000 grains. [ME f. OF aveir de peis goods of weight f. aveir f. L habēre have + peis (see POISE¹)]

Avon /ˈeɪvən/ a county of SW England; pop. (1981) 915,200; county town, Bristol.

avouch /əˈvaʊtʃ/ v.tr. & intr. archaic or rhet. guarantee, affirm, confess. □□ **avouchment** n. [ME f. OF avochier f. L advocare (as AD-, vocare call)]

avow /əˈvaʊ/ v.tr. **1** admit, confess. **2 a** refl. admit that one is (avowed himself the author). **b** (as **avowed** adj.) admitted (the avowed author). □□ **avowal** n. **avowedly** /əˈvaʊɪdlɪ/ adv. [ME f. OF avouer acknowledge f. L advocare (as AD-, vocare call)]

avulsion /əˈvʌlʃ(ə)n/ n. **1** a tearing away. **2** Law a sudden removal of land by a flood etc. to another person's estate. [F avulsion or L avulsio f. avellere avuls- pluck away]

avuncular /əˈvʌŋkjʊlə(r)/ adj. like or of an uncle; kind and friendly, esp. towards a younger person. [L avunculus maternal uncle, dimin. of avus grandfather]

AWACS /ˈeɪwæks/ n. a long-range radar system for detecting enemy aircraft. [abbr. of airborne warning and control system]

await /əˈweɪt/ v.tr. **1** wait for. **2** (of an event or thing) be in store for (a surprise awaits you). [ME f. AF awaitier, OF aguaitier (as AD-, waitier WAIT)]

awake /əˈweɪk/ v. & adj. —v. (past **awoke** /əˈwəʊk/; past part. **awoken** /əˈwəʊkən/) **1** intr. **a** cease to sleep. **b** become active. **2** tr. (foll. by to) become aware of. **3** tr. rouse from sleep. —predic.adj. **1 a** not asleep. **b** vigilant. **2** (foll. by to) aware of. [OE āwæcnan, āwacian (as A-², WAKE¹)]

awaken /əˈweɪkən/ v.tr. & intr. **1** = AWAKE v. **2** tr. (often foll. by to) make aware. [OE onwæcnan etc. (as A-², WAKEN)]

award /əˈwɔːd/ v. & n. —v.tr. **1** give or order to be given as a payment, penalty, or prize (awarded him a knighthood; was awarded damages). **2** grant, assign. —n. **1** a payment, penalty, or prize awarded. **2** a judicial decision. □□ **awarder** n. [ME f. AF awarder, ult. f. Gmc: see WARD]

aware /əˈweə(r)/ predic.adj. **1** (often foll. by of, or that + clause) conscious; not ignorant; having knowledge. **2** well-informed. ¶ Also found in attrib. use in sense 2, as in a very aware person; this is disp. □□ **awareness** n. [OE gewær]

awash /əˈwɒʃ/ predic.adj. **1** level with the surface of water, so that it just washes over. **2** carried or washed by the waves; flooded.

away /əˈweɪ/ adv., adj., & n. —adv. **1** to or at a distance from the place, person, or thing in question (go away; give away; look away; they are away; 5 miles away). **2** towards or into non-existence (sounds die away; explain it away; idled their time away). **3** constantly, persistently, continuously (work away; laugh away). **4** without delay (ask away). —adj. Sport played on an opponent's ground etc. (away match; away win). —n. Sport an away match

or win. □ **away with** (as imper.) take away; let us be rid of. [OE onweg, aweg on one's way f. A² + WAY]

awe /ɔː/ n. & v. —n. reverential fear or wonder (stand in awe of). —v.tr. inspire with awe. □ **awe-inspiring** causing awe or wonder; amazing, magnificent. [ME age f. ON agi f. Gmc]

aweary /əˈwɪərɪ/ predic.adj. poet. (often foll. by of) weary. [aphetic a + WEARY]

aweigh /əˈweɪ/ predic.adj. Naut. (of an anchor) clear of the sea or river bed; hanging. [A² + WEIGH¹]

awesome /ˈɔːsəm/ adj. inspiring awe; dreaded. □□ **awesomely** adv. **awesomeness** n. [AWE + -SOME¹]

awestricken /ˈɔːˌstrɪkən/ adj. (also **awestruck** /-strʌk/) struck or afflicted with awe.

awful /ˈɔːfʊl/ adj. **1** colloq. **a** unpleasant or horrible (awful weather). **b** poor in quality; very bad (has awful writing). **c** (attrib.) excessive; large (an awful lot of money). **2** poet. inspiring awe. □□ **awfulness** n. [AWE + -FUL]

awfully /ˈɔːfəlɪ, -flɪ/ adv. **1** in an unpleasant, bad, or horrible way (he played awfully). **2** colloq. very (she's awfully pleased; thanks awfully). **3** poet. reverently.

awhile /əˈwaɪl/ adv. for a short time. [OE āne hwīle a while]

awkward /ˈɔːkwəd/ adj. **1** ill-adapted for use; causing difficulty in use. **2** clumsy or bungling. **3 a** embarrassed (felt awkward about it). **b** embarrassing (an awkward situation). **4** difficult to deal with (an awkward customer). □ **the awkward age** adolescence. □□ **awkwardly** adv. **awkwardness** n. [obs. awk backhanded, untoward (ME f. ON afugr turned the wrong way) + -WARD]

awl /ɔːl/ n. a small pointed tool used for piercing holes, esp. in leather. [OE æl]

awn /ɔːn/ n. a stiff bristle growing from the grain-sheath of grasses, or terminating a leaf etc. □□ **awned** adj. [ME f. ON ögn]

awning /ˈɔːnɪŋ/ n. a sheet of canvas or similar material stretched on a frame and used to shade a shop window, doorway, ship's deck, or other area from the sun or rain. [17th c. (Naut.): orig. uncert.]

awoke past of AWAKE.

awoken past part. of AWAKE.

AWOL /ˈeɪwɒl/ abbr. colloq. absent without leave.

awry /əˈraɪ/ adv. & adj. —adv. **1** crookedly or askew. **2** improperly or amiss. —predic.adj. crooked; deviant or unsound (his theory is awry). □ **go awry** go or do wrong. [ME f. A² + WRY]

axe /æks/ n. & v. (US **ax**) —n. **1** a chopping-tool, usu. of iron with a steel edge and wooden handle. **2** the drastic cutting or elimination of expenditure, staff, etc. —v.tr. (**axing**) **1** cut (esp. costs or services) drastically. **2** remove or dismiss. □ **axe-breaker** a hard-wooded Australian tree. **an axe to grind** private ends to serve. [OE æx f. Gmc]

axel /ˈæks(ə)l/ n. a jumping movement in skating, similar to a loop (see LOOP n. 7) but from one foot to the other. [Axel R. Paulsen, Norw. skater d. 1938]

axes pl. of AXIS¹.

axial /ˈæksɪəl/ adj. **1** forming or belonging to an axis. **2** round an axis (axial rotation; axial symmetry). □□ **axiality** /ˌæksɪˈælɪtɪ/ n. **axially** adv.

axil /ˈæksɪl/ n. the upper angle between a leaf and the stem it springs from, or between a branch and the trunk. [L axilla: see AXILLA]

axilla /ækˈsɪlə/ n. (pl. **axillae** /-liː/) **1** Anat. the armpit. **2** an axil. [L, = armpit, dimin. of ala wing]

axillary /ækˈsɪlərɪ/ adj. **1** Anat. of or relating to the armpit. **2** Bot. in or growing from the axil.

axiom /ˈæksɪəm/ n. **1** an established or widely accepted principle. **2** esp. Geom. a self-evident truth. [F axiome or L axioma f. Gk axiōma axiōmat- f. axios worthy]

axiomatic /ˌæksɪəˈmætɪk/ adj. **1** self-evident. **2** relating to or containing axioms. □□ **axiomatically** adv. [Gk axiōmatikos (as AXIOM)]

b but d dog f few g get h he j yes k cat l leg m man n no p pen r red s sit t top v voice

axis[1] /ˈæksɪs/ n. (pl. **axes** /-siːz/) **1 a** an imaginary line about which a body rotates or about which a plane figure is conceived as generating a solid. **b** a line which divides a regular figure symmetrically. **2** Math. a fixed reference line for the measurement of coordinates etc. **3** Bot. the central column of an inflorescence or other growth. **4** Anat. the second cervical vertebra. **5** Physiol. the central part of an organ or organism. **6 a** an agreement or alliance between two or more countries forming a centre for an eventual larger grouping of nations sharing an ideal or objective. **b** (**the Axis**) the alliance of Germany and Italy formed before and during the Second World War, later extended to include Japan and other countries; these countries as a group. The Rome–Berlin Axis began as a political association in 1936, becoming a military alliance in 1939. It collapsed with the fall of Mussolini and the surrender of Italy in 1943. [L, = axle, pivot]

axis[2] /ˈæksɪs/ n. a white spotted deer, Cervus axis, of S. Asia. Also called CHITAL. [L]

axle /ˈæks(ə)l/ n. a rod or spindle (either fixed or rotating) on which a wheel or group of wheels is fixed. [orig. axle-tree f. ME axel-tre f. ON ǫxull-tré]

Axminster /ˈæks‚mɪnstə(r)/ n. (in full **Axminster carpet**) a kind of machine-woven patterned carpet with a cut pile. [Axminster in S. England]

axolotl /ˈæksə‚lɒt(ə)l/ n. an aquatic newtlike salamander, Ambystoma mexicanum, from Mexico, which in natural conditions retains its larval form for life but is able to breed. [Nahuatl f. atl water + xolotl servant]

axon /ˈæksɒn/ n. Anat. & Zool. a long threadlike part of a nerve cell, conducting impulses from the cell body. [mod.L f. Gk axōn axis]

Axum var. of AKSUM.

ay var. of AYE[1].

Ayacucho /‚ɑːjɑːˈkuːtʃəʊ/ a commercial city in south central Peru; pop. (est. 1988) 94,200. In December 1824 the final defeat of Spanish forces at the battle of Ayacucho secured the independence of Peru. The Sendero Luminoso (Shining Path) guerrilla movement first emerged in the vicinity of Ayacucho during the 1980s.

ayah /ˈaɪə/ n. a native nurse or maidservant, esp. in India and other former British territories abroad. [Anglo-Ind. f. Port. aia nurse]

ayatollah /‚aɪəˈtɒlə/ n. a Shiite religious leader in Iran. [Pers. f. Arab., = token of God]

Ayckbourn /ˈeɪkbɔːn/, Alan (1939–), English playwright, whose first London success Relatively Speaking (1967) was followed by many others. The plays are comedies of surburban and middle-class life, showing a keen sense of social nuance and of domestic misery and insensitivity, and displaying the virtuosity of Ayckbourn's stagecraft.

aye[1] /aɪ/ adv. & n. (also **ay**) —adv. **1** archaic or dial. yes. **2** (in voting) I assent. **3** (as **aye aye**) Naut. a response accepting an order. —n. an affirmative answer or assent, esp. in voting. □ **the ayes have it** the affirmative votes are in the majority. [16th c.: prob. f. first pers. personal pron. expressing assent]

aye[2] /eɪ/ adv. archaic ever, always. □ **for aye** for ever. [ME f. ON ei, ey f. Gmc]

aye-aye /ˈaɪaɪ/ n. an arboreal nocturnal lemur, Daubentonia madagascariensis, native to Madagascar. [F f. Malagasy aiay]

Ayer /eə(r)/, Sir Alfred Jules (1910–89), English philosopher, a notable proponent of 'logical positivism' (see entry) and an opponent of the linguistic approach of J. L. Austin. In moral philosophy he was disinclined to defend any particular theory of moral judgement, holding that for all practical purposes a tolerant utilitarianism was the soundest basis for private conduct and public morality.

Ayers Rock /eəz/ a red rock-mass in Northern Territory, Australia, SW of Alice Springs. The largest monolith in the world, it is 348 m (1,143 ft.) high and about 9 km (6 miles) in circumference, rising in impressive isolation from the surrounding plain. It is named after Sir Henry Ayers, Premier of South Australia in 1872–3 when the rock was first recorded.

Ayios Nikólaos see AGHIOS NIKOLAOS.

Aylesbury /ˈeɪlzbəri/ n. (pl. **Aylesburys**) **1** a bird of a breed of large white domestic ducks. **2** this breed. [Aylesbury in S. England]

Aymara /ˈaɪmə‚rɑː/ n. (pl. same or **Aymaras**) **1** a member of an American Indian people mainly inhabiting the plateau lands of Bolivia and Peru near Lake Titicaca. **2** the language of the Aymara. [Bolivian Sp.]

Ayrshire /ˈeəʃə(r)/ n. **1** an animal of a mainly white breed of dairy cattle. **2** this breed. [name of a former Scottish county]

AZ abbr. US Arizona (in official postal use).

azalea /əˈzeɪlɪə/ n. any of various flowering deciduous shrubs of the genus Rhododendron, with large pink, purple, white, or yellow flowers. [mod.L f. Gk, fem. of azaleos dry (from the dry soil in which it was believed to flourish)]

Azania /əˈzeɪnɪə/ the alternative Black African name for South Africa.

azeotrope /əˈziːə‚trəʊp/ n. Chem. a mixture of liquids in which the boiling-point remains constant during distillation, at a given pressure, without change in composition. □□ **azeotropic** /ə‚ziːəˈtrɒpɪk/ adj. [A-1 + Gk zeō boil + tropos turning]

Azerbaijan /‚æzəbaɪˈdʒɑːn/ the Azerbaijan republic, a constituent republic of the USSR, lying between the Black and Caspian Seas and containing the Baku oilfields. Until the early 19th c. it formed part of Persia; pop. (est. 1987) 6,811,000; capital, Baku.

azide /ˈeɪzaɪd/ n. Chem. any compound containing the radical N_3–.

Azikiwe /‚ɑːzɪˈkiːweɪ/, (Benjamin) Nnamdi (1904–) Nigerian statesman. In the 1940s he exerted a strong influence on emerging Nigerian nationalism, and in 1944 founded the National Council of Nigeria and the Cameroons to oppose colonial rule. He was the first governor-general of an independent Nigeria (1960–3) and its first President (1963–6) when it became a republic. His civilian government was ousted by a military coup in 1966.

Azilian /əˈzɪlɪən/ adj. & n. —adj. of an early mesolithic industry in Europe, named after the type-site, a cave at Mas d'Azil in the French Pyrenees, succeeding the Magdalenian and dated to 10000–8000 BC. It is characterized by flat bore harpoons, painted pebbles, and microliths. —n. the Azilian industry. [Mas d'Azil]

azimuth /ˈæzɪməθ/ n. **1** the angular distance from a north or south point of the horizon to the intersection with the horizon of a vertical circle passing through a given celestial body. **2** the horizontal angle or direction of a compass bearing. □□ **azimuthal** /-ˈmjuː·θ(ə)l/ adj. [ME f. OF azimut f. Arab. as-sumūt f. al the + sumūt pl. of samt way, direction]

azine /ˈeɪziːn/ n. Chem. any organic compound with two or more nitrogen atoms in a six-atom ring. [AZO- +-INE[4]]

azo- /ˈæzəʊ, ˈeɪ-/ prefix Chem. containing two adjacent nitrogen atoms between carbon atoms. [F azote nitrogen f. Gk azōos without life]

azoic /əˈzəʊɪk/ adj. **1** having no trace of life. **2** Geol. (of an age etc.) having left no organic remains. [Gk azōos without life]

Azores /əˈzɔːz/ a group of volcanic islands in the North Atlantic, 1,287 km (800 miles) west of Portugal, in Portuguese possession but partially autonomous; pop. (est. 1986) 253,500; capital, Ponta Delgada.

Azov /ˈæzɒf/, **Sea of** an inland sea of the southern USSR, separated from the Black Sea by the Crimea and communicating with it by a narrow strait.

Azrael /ˈæzreɪ(ə)l/ Jewish & Islamic Mythol. the angel who severs the soul from the body at death. [Heb., = help of God]

AZT /‚eɪzed'tiː/ n. a drug intended for use against the Aids virus. [chem. name azidothymidine]

Aztec /ˈæztek/ n. & adj. —n. **1** a member of the native people dominant in Mexico before the Spanish conquest of the 16th century. (See below.) **2** the language of the Aztecs. —adj. of the Aztecs or their language (see also NAHUATL). [F Aztèque or Sp. Azteca f. Nahuatl aztecatl men of the north]

The people we call the Aztecs (who were also called *Mexica* or *Tenochca*) arrived in the central valley of Mexico after the collapse of the Toltec civilization in the 12th c., and at first were obliged to live in the less desirable, infertile regions, often on the brink of famine. By the early 15th c. they had risen to dominance of the area, and a century later commanded a territory that covered most of the central and southern part of present-day Mexico, exacting tribute from their subjects. They were a warring people who slew captives as human sacrifices to their chief god, but their life-style was comfortable or (for the rulers) luxurious, and the Spaniards under Cortés arrived to find a rich and elaborate civilization centred on the city of Tenochtitlán, which boasted vast pyramids, temples, and palaces with fountains, all so spectacular that they wondered if the sight was a dream.

azuki var. of ADZUKI.

azure /ˈæʒə(r), -zjə(r), ˈeɪ-/ *n. & adj.* —*n.* **1 a** a deep sky-blue colour. **b** *Heraldry* blue. **2** *poet.* the clear sky. —*adj.* **1 a** of the colour azure. **b** *Heraldry* blue. **2** serene, untroubled. [ME f. OF *asur, azur,* f. med.L *azzurum, azolum* f. Arab. *al* the + *lāzaward* f. Pers. *lāžward* lapis lazuli]

azygous /ˈæzɪɡəs/ *adj. & n. Anat.* —*adj.* (of any organic structure) single, not existing in pairs. —*n.* an organic structure occurring singly. [Gk *azugos* unyoked f. *a-* not + *zugon* yoke]

B

B¹ /biː/ *n.* (also **b**) (*pl.* **Bs** or **B's**) **1** the second letter of the alphabet. **2** *Mus.* the seventh note of the diatonic scale of C major. **3** the second hypothetical person or example. **4** the second highest class or category (of roads, academic marks, etc.). **5** *Algebra* (usu. **b**) the second known quantity. **6** a human blood type of the ABO system. □ **B film** a supporting film in a cinema programme.

B² *symb.* **1** *Chem.* the element boron. **2** *Physics* magnetic flux density.

B³ *abbr.* (also **B.**) **1** Bachelor. **2** bel(s). **3** bishop. **4** black (pencil-lead). **5** Blessed.

b *symb. Physics* barn.

b. *abbr.* **1** born. **2** *Cricket* **a** bowled by. **b** bye. **3** billion.

BA *abbr.* **1** Bachelor of Arts. **2** British Academy. **3** British Airways. **4** British Association.

Ba *symb. Chem.* the element barium.

BAA *abbr.* British Airports Authority.

baa /baː/ *v. & n.* —*v.intr.* (**baas, baaed** or **baa'd**) (esp. of a sheep) bleat. —*n.* (*pl.* **baas**) the cry of a sheep or lamb. [imit.]

Baader-Meinhof group /ˈbaːdə(r) ˈmaɪnhɒf/ see RED ARMY FACTION.

Baal /ˈbeɪ(ə)l/ (*pl.* **Baalim**) *Semitic Mythol.* any of the male deities of fertility whose cult was widespread in ancient Phoenician and Canaanite lands, strongly resisted by the Hebrew prophets. The name is found as a prefix to place-names (e.g. Baalbek) and as the last element in Phoenician names such as Hannibal and Jezebel. [Heb. *ba'al* lord]

Baalbek /ˈbaːlbek/ a town in eastern Lebanon, site of the ancient city of Heliopolis. Its principal monuments date from the Roman period, and include the Corinthian temples of Jupiter and Bacchus, and private houses with important mosaics.

baas /baːs/ *n. S.Afr.* boss, master (often as a form of address). [Du.: cf. BOSS¹]

baasskap /ˈbaːskaːp/ *n. S.Afr.* domination, esp. of non-Whites by Whites. [Afrik. f. *baas* master + *-skap* condition]

Baath /baːθ/ *n.* (also **Ba'ath**) *Polit.* (usu. *attrib.* or prec. by *the*) a pan-Arab socialist party founded in Syria in 1943. □□ **Baathist** *adj. & n.* [Arab. *ba'ṯ* resurrection, renaissance]

baba /ˈbaːbaː/ *n.* (in full **rum baba**) a small rich sponge cake, usu. soaked in rum-flavoured syrup. [F f. Pol.]

babacoote /ˈbaːbəˌkuːt/ *n.* = INDRI. [Malagasy *babakoto*]

Babbage /ˈbæbɪdʒ/, Charles (1791–1871), English mathematician and inventor, an outstanding example of a man ahead of his time, generally recognized as the pioneer of machine computing. His interest in the compilation of accurate tables of mathematical and astronomical functions through elimination of human error led to the construction (from 1823 onwards) of a mechanical computer or 'difference engine' which would not only perform calculations but also print the results. Because of the difficulties in constructing such a machine to a sufficient degree of accuracy, and of obtaining continuing financial support, neither this machine nor a subsequent analytical engine was ever finished, and Babbage became a frustrated and embittered man. Nevertheless he continued to innovate: in the field of operational research his analysis of the economies of the Post Office led to the introduction of the penny post, and he invented the heliograph and the ophthalmoscope. Tennyson's 'Every minute dies a man, Every minute one is born' drew from Babbage the remark that since the world's population was constantly increasing the second line should read 'And one and a sixteenth is born'. (Tennyson did in fact blur the assertion by changing 'minute' to 'moment'.)

Babbitt¹ /ˈbæbɪt/ *n.* **1** (in full **Babbitt metal**) any of a group of soft alloys of tin, antimony, copper, and usu. lead, used for lining bearings etc., to diminish friction. **2** (**babbitt**) a bearing-lining made of this. [I. *Babbitt*, Amer. inventor d. 1862]

Babbitt² /ˈbæbɪt/ *n.* a materialistic, complacent businessman. □□ **Babbittry** *n.* [George *Babbitt*, a character in the novel *Babbitt* (1922) by S. Lewis]

Babbitt³ /ˈbæbɪt/, Milton (1916–), American composer and mathematician, who became Professor of Music at Princeton University. His compositions (which include orchestral, piano, and choral music) developed from the twelve-note system of Schoenberg and Webern, and later employed electronic devices such as synthesizers and tape.

babble /ˈbæb(ə)l/ *v. & n.* —*v.* **1** *intr.* **a** talk in an inarticulate or incoherent manner. **b** chatter excessively or irrelevantly. **c** (of a stream etc.) murmur, trickle. **2** *tr.* repeat foolishly; divulge through chatter. —*n.* **1 a** incoherent speech. **b** foolish, idle, or childish talk. **2** the murmur of voices, water, etc. **3** *Telephony* background disturbance caused by interference from conversations on other lines. □□ **babblement** *n.* [ME f. MLG *babbelen*, or imit.]

babbler /ˈbæbl(ə)r/ *n.* **1** a chatterer. **2** a person who reveals secrets. **3** any of a large group of passerine birds with loud chattering voices.

babe /beɪb/ *n.* **1** *literary* a baby. **2** an innocent or helpless person (*babes and sucklings; babes in the wood*). **3** *US sl.* a young woman (often as a form of address). [ME: imit. of child's *ba, ba*]

babel /ˈbeɪb(ə)l/ *n.* **1** a confused noise, esp. of voices. **2** a noisy assembly. **3** a scene of confusion. □ **Tower of Babel** a visionary or unrealistic plan. The phrase refers to the biblical account (Gen. 11: 1–9) of the tower built in an attempt to reach heaven, which God frustrated by confusing the languages of its builders so that they could not understand one another. The story was probably inspired by the Babylonian ziggurat, and may be an attempt to explain the existence of different languages. [ME f. Heb. *Bābel* Babylon f. Akkad. *bab ili* gate of god.]

Babi /ˈbæbi/ *n.* a member of a Persian eclectic sect founded in 1844 by Mirza Ali Muhammad of Shiraz, emphasizing the coming of a new prophet or messenger of God (in Persian *Bab-ed-Din* gate (= intermediary) of the Faith, whence the founder's usual title of (the) *Bab*). The Baha'i faith is an offshoot of Babism. **2** the sect itself. □□ **Babism** *n.* [Pers. *Bab-ed-Din*, gate (= intermediary) of the Faith]

baboon /bəˈbuːn/ *n.* **1** any of various large Old World monkeys of the genus *Papio*, having a long doglike snout, large teeth, and naked callosities on the buttocks. **2** an ugly or uncouth person. [ME f. OF *babuin* or med.L *babewynus*, of unkn. orig.]

babu /ˈbaːbuː/ *n.* (also **baboo**) *Ind.* **1** a title of respect, esp. to Hindus. **2** *derog.* formerly, an English-writing Indian clerk. [Hindi *bābū*]

Babur /ˈbaːbʊ(r)/ (1483–1530), the first Mughal emperor, descended from Tamerlane. He invaded India *c.*1525 and conquered the territory from the Oxus to Patna.

babushka /bəˈbuːʃkə/ *n.* a headscarf tied under the chin. [Russ., = grandmother]

Babuyan Islands /ˌbaːbʊˈjaːn/ a group of twenty-four volcanic islands lying to the north of Luzon in the north Philippines.

baby /ˈbeɪbi/ *n. & v.* —*n.* (*pl.* **-ies**) **1** a very young child or infant, esp. one not yet able to walk. **2** an unduly childish person (*is a baby about injections*). **3** the youngest member of a family, team, etc. **4** (often *attrib.*) **a** a young or newly born animal. **b** a thing that is small of its kind (*baby car; baby rose*). **5** *sl.* a young woman; a sweetheart (often as a form of address). **6** *sl.* a person or thing regarded with affection or familiarity. **7** one's own responsibility, invention, concern, achievement, etc., regarded in a personal way. —*v.tr.* (**-ies, -ied**) **1** treat like a baby. **2** pamper. □ **baby boom** *colloq.* a temporary marked increase in the birthrate. **baby boomer** a person born during a baby boom, esp. after the Second World War. **baby-bouncer** *Brit.* a frame supported by elastic or springs, into which a child is harnessed to exercise its limbs. **Baby Buggy** (*pl.* **-ies**) *Brit. propr.* a kind of collapsible pushchair for a child. **baby carriage** *US* a pram. **baby grand** the smallest size of grand piano. **baby-snatcher** *colloq.* 1 a person who kidnaps babies. 2 = *cradle-snatcher*. **baby-talk** childish talk used by or to young children. **baby-walker** a wheeled frame in which a baby learns to walk. **carry** (or **hold**) **the baby** bear unwelcome responsibility. **throw away the baby with the bath-water** reject the essential with the inessential. □□ **babyhood** *n.* [ME, formed as BABE, -Y²]

Babygro /ˈbeɪbɪˌɡrəʊ/ *n.* (*pl.* **-os**) *propr.* a kind of all-in-one stretch garment for babies. [BABY + GROW]

babyish /ˈbeɪbɪʃ/ *adj.* 1 childish, simple. 2 immature. □□ **babyishly** *adv.* **babyishness** *n.*

Babylon /ˈbæbɪlən/ 1 the capital of Babylonia, first prominent under Hammurabi. The city (now in ruins) lay on the Euphrates and was noted for its luxury, its fortifications, and particularly for the 'Hanging Gardens' which were one of the Seven Wonders of the World. 2 *derog.* (among Blacks, esp. Rastafarians; used of anything which to the Black consciousness represents the degenerate or oppressive aspect of White culture): **a** White society. **b** the representatives of this, esp. the police. **c** London. [Gk f. Heb. *Bābel*]

Babylonia /ˌbæbɪˈləʊnɪə/ the ancient name for southern Mesopotamia (earlier called Sumer), which first became a political entity when an Amorite dynasty united Sumer and Akkad in the first half of the 2nd millennium BC. At this period its power ascended over Assyria and part of Syria. After *c.*1530 BC first the Hittites then other invaders, the Kassites, dominated the land, and it became part of the Assyrian empire. With the latter's decline Babylonia again became prominent under the Chaldeans 625–538 BC, only to fall to Cyrus the Great, whose entry into Babylon ended its power for ever. □□ **Babylonian** *adj.* & *n.*

babysit /ˈbeɪbɪsɪt/ *v.intr.* (**-sitting**; *past* and *past part.* **-sat**) look after a child or children while the parents are out. □□ **babysitter** *n.*

Bacardi /bəˈkɑːdɪ/ *n.* (*pl.* **Bacardis**) *propr.* a West Indian rum produced orig. in Cuba. [name of the company producing it]

baccalaureate /ˌbækəˈlɔːrɪət/ *n.* 1 the university degree of bachelor. 2 an examination intended to qualify successful candidates for higher education. [F *baccalauréat* or med.L *baccalaureatus* f. *baccalaureus* bachelor]

baccarat /ˈbækəˌrɑː/ *n.* a gambling card-game played by punters in turn against the banker. [F]

baccate /ˈbækeɪt/ *adj. Bot.* 1 bearing berries. 2 of or like a berry. [L *baccatus* berried f. *bacca* berry]

bacchanal /ˈbækən(ə)l/ *n.* & *adj.* —*n.* 1 a wild and drunken revelry. 2 a drunken reveller. 3 a priest, worshipper, or follower of Bacchus. —*adj.* 1 of or like Bacchus (see entry) or his rites. 2 riotous, roistering. [L *bacchanalis* f. *Bacchus* BACCHUS f. Gk *Bakkhos*]

Bacchanalia /ˌbækəˈneɪlɪə/ *n.pl.* 1 the Roman festival of Bacchus. 2 (**bacchanalia**) a drunken revelry. □□ **Bacchanalian** *adj.* & *n.* [L, neut. pl. of *bacchanalis*: see BACCHANAL]

bacchant /ˈbækənt/ *n.* & *adj.* —*n.* (*pl.* **bacchants** or **bacchantes** /bəˈkæntiːz/; *fem.* **bacchante** /bəˈkæntɪ/) 1 a priest, worshipper, or follower of Bacchus. 2 a drunken reveller. —*adj.* 1 of or like Bacchus or his rites. 2 riotous, roistering. □□ **bacchantic** /bəˈkæntɪk/ *adj.* [F *bacchante* f. L *bacchari* celebrate Bacchanal rites]

Bacchic /ˈbækɪk/ *adj.* = BACCHANAL *adj.* [L *bacchicus* f. Gk *bakkhikos* of Bacchus]

Bacchus /ˈbækəs/ Gk Mythol. the other name of DIONYSUS.

baccy /ˈbækɪ/ *n.* (*pl.* **-ies**) *Brit. colloq.* tobacco. [abbr.]

Bach /bɑːx/, Johann Sebastian (1685–1750), German composer, the greatest of a large family of musicians, who was described by Wagner as 'the most stupendous miracle in all music', though in his lifetime his reputation as a composer was restricted to a fairly narrow circle. His enormous output included violin concertos, suites, the six Brandenburg Concertos, many clavier works, and (while serving St Thomas's Church in Leipzig) over 250 sacred cantatas as well as the St Matthew and St John Passions, the Christmas Oratorio, and the collection of large-scale Mass movements known to us as the B minor Mass and regarded as one of the great Christian works of art, though Bach did not conceive of it as a unity. He composed nothing without purpose: he was a devout Protestant in the Lutheran tradition and his chorales faithfully and movingly represent the message of their words; he was renowned for his organ-playing and his organ pieces are a summation of the North German tradition which he knew and revered; his last (unfinished) work, *The Art of Fugue*, is an awe-inspiring attempt to exhaust the possibilities of canon and fugue upon a single melody. Bach symbolizes the musical Baroque in Germany except in one respect: he left the composing of opera to his erstwhile compatriot Handel.

Of his twenty children, his eldest son Wilhelm Friedmann Bach (1710–84) became an organist and composer, Carl Philipp Emanuel Bach (1714–88) wrote much church music, over 200 keyboard sonatas, and a celebrated treatise on clavier-playing, and Johann Christian Bach (1735–82) became music-master to the British royal family and composed 13 operas and many instrumental works.

bachelor /ˈbætʃələ(r)/ *n.* 1 an unmarried man. 2 a man or woman who has taken the degree of Bachelor of Arts or Science etc. 3 *hist.* a young knight serving under another's banner. □ **bachelor girl** an independent unmarried young woman. **bachelor's buttons** any of various button-like flowers, esp. the double buttercup. □□ **bachelorhood** *n.* **bachelorship** *n.* [ME & OF *bacheler* aspirant to knighthood, of uncert. orig.]

bacillary /bəˈsɪlərɪ/ *adj.* relating to or caused by bacilli.

bacilliform /bəˈsɪlɪˌfɔːm/ *adj.* rod-shaped.

bacillus /bəˈsɪləs/ *n.* (*pl.* **bacilli** /-laɪ/) 1 any rod-shaped bacterium. 2 (usu. in *pl.*) any pathogenic bacterium. [LL, dimin. of L *baculus* stick]

back /bæk/ *n., adv., v.,* & *adj.* —*n.* 1 **a** the rear surface of the human body from the shoulders to the hips. **b** the corresponding upper surface of an animal's body. **c** the spine (*fell and broke his back*). **d** the keel of a ship. 2 **a** any surface regarded as corresponding to the human back, e.g. of the head or hand, or of a chair. **b** the part of a garment that covers the back. 3 **a** the less active or visible or important part of something functional, e.g. of a knife or a piece of paper (*write it on the back*). **b** the side or part normally away from the spectator or the direction of motion or attention, e.g. of a car, house, or room (*stood at the back*). 4 **a** a defensive player in field games. **b** this position. 5 (**the Backs**) the grounds of Cambridge colleges which back on to the River Cam. —*adv.* 1 to the rear; away from what is considered to be the front (*go back a bit; ran off without looking back*). 2 **a** in or into an earlier or normal position or condition (*came back late; went back home; ran back to the car; put it back on the shelf*). **b** in return (*pay back*). 3 in or into the past (*back in June; three years back*). 4 at a distance (*stand back from the road*). 5 in check (*hold him back*). 6 (foll. by *of*) *US* behind (*was back of the house*). —*v.* 1 *tr.* **a** help with moral or financial support. **b** bet on the success of (a horse etc.). 2 *tr.* & *intr.* move, or cause (a vehicle etc.) to move, backwards. 3 *tr.* **a** put or serve as a back, background, or support to. **b** *Mus.* accompany. 4 *tr.* lie at the back of (*a beach backed by steep cliffs*). 5 *intr.* (of the wind) move round in an anticlockwise direction. —*adj.* 1 situated behind, esp. as remote or subsidiary (*backstreet; back teeth*). 2 of or relating to the past; not current (*back pay; back issue*). 3 reversed (*back flow*). □ **at a person's back** in pursuit or support. **at the back of one's mind** remembered but not consciously thought of. **back and forth** to and fro. **back bench** a back-bencher's seat in the House of Commons. **back-bencher** a member of Parliament not holding a senior office. **back-boiler** *Brit.* a boiler behind and integral with a domestic fire. **back-breaking** (esp. of manual work) extremely hard. **back country** esp. *Austral.* & *NZ* an area away from settled districts. **back-crawl** = BACKSTROKE. **back-cross** *Biol.* 1 cross a hybrid with one of its parents. 2 an instance or the product of this. **back door** a secret or ingenious means of gaining an objective. **back-door** adj. (of an activity) clandestine, underhand (a back-door deal). **back down** withdraw one's claim or point of view etc.; concede defeat in an argument etc. **back-down** n. an instance of backing down. **back-fill** refill an excavated hole with the material dug out of it. **back-formation 1** the formation of a word from its seeming derivative (e.g. laze from lazy). **2** a word formed in this way. **back number 1** an issue of a periodical earlier than the current one. **2** sl. an out-of-date person or thing. **the back of beyond** a very remote or inaccessible place. **back off 1** draw back, retreat. **2** abandon one's intention, stand, etc. **back on to** have its back adjacent to (the house backs on to a field). **back out** (often foll. by of) withdraw from a commitment. **back passage** colloq. the rectum. **back-pedal (-pedalled, -pedalling; US -pedaled, -pedaling) 1** pedal backwards on a bicycle etc. **2** reverse one's previous action or opinion. **back-projection** the projection of a picture from behind a translucent screen for viewing or filming. **back room** (often with hyphen) attrib.) a place where secret work is done. **back-scattering** the scattering of radiation in a reverse direction. **back seat** an inferior position or status. **back-seat driver** a person who is eager to advise without responsibility (orig. of a passenger in a car etc.). **back slang** slang using words spelt backwards (e.g. yob). **back-stop** = LONGSTOP. **back talk** US = BACKCHAT. **back to back** with backs adjacent and opposite each other (we stood back to back). **back-to-back** adj. esp. Brit. (of houses) with a party wall at the rear. **back to front 1** with the back at the front and the front at the back. **2** in disorder. **back-to-nature** (usu. attrib.) applied to a movement or enthusiast for the reversion to a simpler way of life. **back up 1** give (esp. moral) support to. **2** Computing make a spare copy of (data, a disk, etc.). **3** (of running water) accumulate behind an obstruction. **4** reverse (a vehicle) into a desired position. **5** US form a queue of vehicles etc., esp. in congested traffic. **back water** reverse a boat's forward motion using oars. **get** (or **put**) **a person's back up** annoy or anger a person. **get off a person's back** stop troubling a person. **go back on** fail to honour (a promise or commitment). **know like the back of one's hand** be entirely familiar with. **on one's back** injured or ill in bed. **on the back burner** see BURNER. **put one's back into** approach (a task etc.) with vigour. **see the back of** see SEE[1]. **turn one's back on 1** abandon. **2** ignore. **with one's back to** (or **up against**) **the wall** in a desperate situation; hard-pressed. □□ **backer** n. (in sense 1 of v.). **backless** adj. [OE bæc f. Gmc]

backache /ˈbækeɪk/ n. a (usu. prolonged) pain in one's back.

backbite /ˈbækbaɪt/ v.tr. slander; speak badly of. □□ **backbiter** n.

backblocks /ˈbækblɒks/ n.pl. Austral. & NZ land in the remote and sparsely inhabited interior.

backboard /ˈbækbɔːd/ n. **1** a board worn to support or straighten the back. **2** a board placed at or forming the back of anything.

backbone /ˈbækbəʊn/ n. **1** the spine. **2** the main support of a structure. **3** firmness of character. **4** US the spine of a book.

backchat /ˈbæktʃæt/ n. Brit. colloq. the practice of replying rudely or impudently.

backcloth /ˈbækklɒθ/ n. Brit. Theatr. a painted cloth at the back of the stage as a main part of the scenery.

backcomb /ˈbækkəʊm/ v.tr. comb (the hair) towards the scalp to make it look thicker.

backdate /bækˈdeɪt/ v.tr. **1** put an earlier date to (an agreement etc.) than the actual one. **2** make retrospectively valid.

backdrop /ˈbækdrɒp/ n. = BACKCLOTH.

backfire v. & n. —v.intr. /bækˈfaɪə(r)/ **1** undergo a mistimed explosion in the cylinder or exhaust of an internal-combustion engine. **2** (of a plan etc.) rebound adversely on the originator; have the opposite effect to what was intended. —n. /ˈbækfaɪə(r)/ an instance of backfiring.

backgammon /ˈbækˌgæmən, bækˈgæmən/ n. **1** a game for two played on a board with pieces moved according to throws of the dice. It is among the most ancient of all games, combining elements of chance and skill, and passed from one civilization

to another. **2** the most complete form of win in this. [BACK (because pieces go back and re-enter) + GAMMON[2]]

background /ˈbækgraʊnd/ n. **1** part of a scene, picture, or description, that serves as a setting to the chief figures or objects and foreground. **2** an inconspicuous or obscure position (kept in the background). **3** a person's education, knowledge, or social circumstances. **4** explanatory or contributory information or circumstances. **5** Physics low-intensity ambient radiation from radioisotopes present in the natural environment. **6** Electronics unwanted signals, such as noise in the reception or recording of sound. □ **background music** music intended as an unobtrusive accompaniment to some activity, or to provide atmosphere in a film etc.

backhand /ˈbækhænd/ n. Tennis etc. **1** a stroke played with the back of the hand turned towards the opponent. **2** (attrib.) of or made with a backhand (backhand volley).

backhanded /bækˈhændɪd/ adj. **1** (of a blow etc.) delivered with the back of the hand, or in a direction opposite to the usual one. **2** indirect; ambiguous (a backhanded compliment). **3** = BACKHAND adj.

backhander /ˈbækˌhændə(r)/ n. **1 a** a backhand stroke. **b** a backhanded blow. **2** colloq. an indirect attack. **3** Brit. sl. a bribe.

backing /ˈbækɪŋ/ n. **1 a** support. **b** a body of supporters. **c** material used to form a back or support. **2** musical accompaniment, esp. to a singer.

backlash /ˈbæklæʃ/ n. **1** an excessive or marked adverse reaction. **2 a** a sudden recoil or reaction between parts of a mechanism. **b** excessive play between such parts.

backlist /ˈbæklɪst/ n. a publisher's list of books published before the current season and still in print.

backlit /ˈbæklɪt/ adj. (esp. in photography) illuminated from behind.

backlog /ˈbæklɒg/ n. **1** arrears of uncompleted work etc. **2** a reserve; reserves (a backlog of goodwill). ¶ Orig. = a large log placed at the back of a fire to sustain it.

backmarker /ˈbækˌmɑːkə(r)/ n. Brit. a competitor who has the least favourable handicap in a race etc.

backmost /ˈbækməʊst/ adj. furthest back.

backpack /ˈbækpæk/ n. & v. —n. a rucksack. —v.intr. travel or hike with a backpack. □□ **backpacker** n.

backrest /ˈbækrest/ n. a support for the back.

backscratcher /ˈbækˌskrætʃə(r)/ n. **1** a rod terminating in a clawed hand for scratching one's own back. **2** a person who performs mutual services with another for gain.

backsheesh var. of BAKSHEESH.

backside /bækˈsaɪd, ˈbæk-/ n. colloq. the buttocks.

backsight /ˈbæksaɪt/ n. **1** the sight of a rifle etc. that is nearer the stock. **2** Surveying a sight or reading taken backwards or towards the point of starting.

backslapping /ˈbækˌslæpɪŋ/ adj. vigorously hearty.

backslash /ˈbækslæʃ/ n. a backward-sloping diagonal line; a reversesolidus(\).

backslide /ˈbækslaɪd/ v.intr. (past -slid; past part. -slid or -slidden) relapse into bad ways or error. □□ **backslider** n.

backspace /ˈbækspeɪs/ v.intr. move a typewriter carriage etc. back one or more spaces.

backspin /ˈbækspɪn/ n. a backward spin imparted to a ball causing it to fly off at an angle on hitting a surface.

backstage /bækˈsteɪdʒ/ adv. & adj. —adv. **1** Theatr. out of view of the audience, esp. in the wings or dressing-rooms. **2** not known to the public. —adj. /also ˈbæk-/ that is backstage; concealed.

backstairs /ˈbæksteəz/ n.pl. **1** stairs at the back or side of a building. **2** (also **backstair**) (attrib.) denoting underhand or clandestine activity.

backstay /ˈbæksteɪ/ n. a rope etc. leading downwards and aft from the top of a mast.

backstitch /ˈbækstɪtʃ/ n. & v. —n. sewing with overlapping stitches. —v.tr. & intr. sew using backstitch.

backstreet /ˈbækstriːt/ n. **1** a street in a quiet part of a town, away from the main streets. **2** (*attrib.*) denoting illicit or illegal activity (*a backstreet abortion*).

backstroke /ˈbækstrəʊk/ *n.* a swimming stroke performed on the back with the arms lifted alternately out of the water in a backward circular motion and the legs extended in a kicking action.

backtrack /ˈbæktræk/ *v.intr.* **1** retrace one's steps. **2** reverse one's previous action or opinion.

backup /ˈbækʌp/ *n.* **1** moral or technical support (*called for extra backup*). **2** a reserve. **3** *Computing* (often *attrib.*) **a** the procedure for making security copies of data (*backup facilities*). **b** the copy itself (*made a backup*). **4** *US* a queue of vehicles etc., esp. in congested traffic. □ **backup light** *US* a reversing light.

backveld /ˈbækvelt/ *n. S.Afr.* remote country districts, esp. those strongly conservative. □□ **backvelder** *n.*

backward /ˈbækwəd/ *adv. & adj.* —*adv.* = BACKWARDS. ¶ *Backwards* is now more common, esp. in literal senses. —*adj.* **1** directed to the rear or starting-point (*a backward look*). **2** reversed. **3** mentally retarded or slow. **4** reluctant, shy, unassertive. □□ **backwardness** *n.* [earlier *abackward*, assoc. with BACK]

backwardation /ˌbækwəˈdeɪʃ(ə)n/ *n.* esp. *Brit. Stock Exch.* the percentage paid by a person selling stock for the right of delaying the delivery of it (cf. CONTANGO).

backwards /ˈbækwədz/ *adv.* **1** away from one's front (*lean backwards; look backwards*). **2 a** with the back foremost (*walk backwards*). **b** in reverse of the usual way (*count backwards; spell backwards*). **3 a** into a worse state (*new policies are taking us backwards*). **b** into the past (*looked backwards over the years*). **c** (of a thing's motion) back towards the starting-point (*rolled backwards*). □ **backwards and forwards** in both directions alternately; to and fro. **bend** (or **fall** or **lean**) **over backwards** (often foll. by *to* + infin.) *colloq.* make every effort, esp. to be fair or helpful. **know backwards** be entirely familiar with.

backwash /ˈbækwɒʃ/ *n.* **1 a** receding waves created by the motion of a ship etc. **b** a backward current of air created by a moving aircraft. **2** repercussions.

backwater /ˈbækˌwɔːtə(r)/ *n.* **1** a place or condition remote from the centre of activity or thought. **2** stagnant water fed by a stream.

backwoods /ˈbækwʊdz/ *n.pl.* **1** remote uncleared forest land. **2** any remote or sparsely inhabited region.

backwoodsman /ˈbækˌwʊdzmən/ *n.* (*pl.* **-men**) **1** an inhabitant of backwoods. **2** an uncouth person.

backyard /bækˈjɑːd/ *n.* a yard at the back of a house etc. □ **in one's own backyard** *colloq.* near at hand.

baclava var. of BAKLAVA.

Bacolod /baˈkɒlɒd/ the chief city on the island of Negros in the central Philippines; pop. (1980) 262,400.

Bacon /ˈbeɪkən/, Francis, Baron Verulam and Viscount St Albans (1561–1626), English lawyer and philosopher, the pre-eminent legal figure of the late Elizabethan and early Stuart periods, eventually rising to become Lord Chancellor under James I before falling from favour after impeachment on charges of corruption. His radical philosophical beliefs, expounded in several books which have become literary classics, proved very influential, dominating the field for a century after his death. In science he advocated the inductive method and rejected the formulation of a priori hypotheses; application of this inspired the founding of the Royal Society in 1660. There are those who credit him with having written the plays of Shakespeare.

Bacon[2] /ˈbeɪkən/, Francis (1909–), British painter, born in Dublin of an English horse-trainer. Entirely self-taught, he began painting in the 1930s, working mainly from photographs or other paintings. His work displays human figures in repulsively distorted postures, their features blurred or erased, and is characterized by violent colours and a horrifying dramatic quality. In 1944 his *Three Studies* for the base of a *Crucifixion* made him overnight the most controversial painter in postwar England.

Bacon[3] /ˈbeɪkən/, Roger (*c.*1214–94), English medieval scholar. A Franciscan monk, Bacon taught at Oxford and Paris and was

best known for his scientific work, particularly in the field of optics. Although widely acclaimed in scholarly circles he fell foul of his own order, which eventually imprisoned him as a heretic. He is alleged to have prophesied flying machines, mechanical propulsion, and optical instruments such as the telescope and microscope, and to have described spectacles and the manufacture of gunpowder.

bacon /ˈbeɪkən/ *n.* cured meat from the back or sides of a pig. □ **bring home the bacon** *colloq.* **1** succeed in one's undertaking. **2** supply material provision or support. [ME f. OF f. Frank. *bako* = OHG *bahho* ham, flitch]

Baconian /beɪˈkəʊnɪən/ *adj. & n.* —*adj.* of or relating to the English philosopher Sir Francis Bacon (see BACON[1]), or to his inductive method of reasoning and philosophy. —*n.* **1** a supporter of the view that Bacon was the author of Shakespeare's plays. **2** a follower of Bacon.

bacteria *pl.* of BACTERIUM.

bactericide /bækˈtɪərɪˌsaɪd/ *n.* a substance capable of destroying bacteria. □□ **bactericidal** /-ˈsaɪd(ə)l/ *adj.*

bacteriology /bækˌtɪərɪˈɒlədʒɪ/ *n.* the study of bacteria. □□ **bacteriological** /-əˈlɒdʒɪk(ə)l/ *adj.* **bacteriologically** /-əˈlɒdʒɪkəlɪ/ *adv.* **bacteriologist** *n.*

bacteriolysis /bækˌtɪərɪˈɒlɪsɪs/ *n.* the rupture of bacterial cells.

bacteriolytic /bækˌtɪərɪəˈlɪtɪk/ *adj.* capable of lysing bacteria.

bacteriophage /bækˈtɪərɪəʊˌfeɪdʒ, -ˌfɑːʒ/ *n.* a virus parasitic on a bacterium, by infecting it and reproducing inside it. [BACTERIUM + Gk *phagein* eat]

bacteriostasis /bækˌtɪərɪəʊˈsteɪsɪs/ *n.* the inhibition of the growth of bacteria without destroying them. □□ **bacteriostatic** /-ˈstætɪk/ *adj.*

bacterium /bækˈtɪərɪəm/ *n.* (*pl.* **bacteria** /-rɪə/) a member of a large group of unicellular micro-organisms lacking organelles and an organized nucleus, some of which can cause disease. (See below.) □□ **bacterial** *adj.* [mod.L f. Gk *baktērion* dimin. of *baktron* stick]

Bacteria are very widely distributed in nature, not only in soil, water, and air, but also on or in many parts of the tissues of plants and animals. Traditionally included in the plant kingdom they are now usually grouped as members of the Protista. Bacteria form one of the main biologically interdependent groups of organisms in virtue of the chemical changes which many of them bring about (e.g. all forms of decay and the building up of nitrogen compounds in the soil; see CARBON CYCLE, NITROGEN CYCLE); the ability of some bacteria to incorporate atmospheric nitrogen into organic compounds is essential to life on earth. Bacterial classification is problematic because they are so uniform in shape, usually spherical (cocci) or rodlike (bacilli). Multiplication is usually by simple fission; some form spores, aerially dispersed; true sexual reproduction is rare. Because of the rapid growth rate and ease of culture of bacteria much modern biochemical knowledge has been derived from their study. The division between the apparently simple cells of bacteria and the larger nucleated cells of animals and plants is one of the most fundamental in biology, and bacterial cells are believed to be ancestral to nucleated cells. Bacteria were first observed by Leeuwenhoek in the 17th c. and first definitely implicated in a disease (anthrax) by Koch in 1876.

Bactria /ˈbæktrɪə/ the ancient name for a country that included the northern part of modern Afghanistan and parts of Soviet central Asia. Traditionally the home of Zoroaster and the Zend-Avesta, it was the seat of a powerful Indo-Greek kingdom in the 3rd and 2nd c. BC.

Bactrian /ˈbæktrɪən/ *adj.* of or relating to Bactria in central Asia. □ **Bactrian camel** a camel, *Camelus bactrianus*, native to central Asia, with two humps. [L *Bactrianus* f. Gk *Baktrianos*]

bad /bæd/ *adj., n., & adv.* —*adj.* (**worse** /wɜːs/; **worst** /wɜːst/) **1** inferior, inadequate, defective (*bad work; a bad driver; bad light*). **2 a** unpleasant, unwelcome (*bad weather; bad news*). **b** unsatisfactory, unfortunate (*a bad business*). **3** harmful (*is bad for you*). **4** (of food) decayed, putrid. **5** *colloq.* ill, injured (*am feeling bad today; a bad leg*). **6** *colloq.* regretful, guilty, ashamed (*feels bad about it*). **7** (of an unwelcome thing) serious, severe (*a bad headache; a* *bad mistake*). **8 a** morally wicked or offensive (*a bad man*; *bad language*). **b** naughty; badly behaved (*a bad child*). **9** worthless; not valid (*a bad cheque*). **10** (**badder, baddest**) *esp. US sl.* good, excellent. —*n.* **1 a** ill fortune (*take the bad with the good*). **b** ruin; a degenerate condition (*go to the bad*). **2** the debit side of an account (*£500 to the bad*). **3** (as *pl.*; *prec.* by *the*) bad or wicked people. —*adv. US colloq.* badly (*took it bad*). □ **bad blood** ill feeling. **bad books** see BOOK. **bad breath** unpleasant-smelling breath. **bad debt** a debt that is not recoverable. **bad egg** see EGG¹. **bad faith** see FAITH. **bad form** see FORM. **a bad job** *colloq.* an unfortunate state of affairs. **bad mouth** *US* malicious gossip or criticism. **bad-mouth** *v.tr. US* subject to malicious gossip or criticism. **bad news** *colloq.* an unpleasant or troublesome person or thing. **from bad to worse** into an even worse state. **in a bad way** ill; in trouble (*looked in a bad way*). **not** (or **not so**) **bad** *colloq.* fairly good. **too bad** *colloq.* (of circumstances etc.) regrettable but now beyond retrieval. □□ **baddish** *adj.* **badness** *n.* [ME, perh. f. OE *bæddel* hermaphrodite, womanish man: for loss of *l* cf. MUCH, WENCH]

baddy /ˈbædɪ/ *n.* (*pl.* **-ies**) *colloq.* a villain or criminal, esp. in a story, film, etc.

bade see BID.

Baden /ˈbɑːd(ə)n/ Austria's most famous spa town, situated 30 km (19 miles) south of Vienna in the province of Lower Austria; pop. (1981) 23,100. Known to the Romans as *Thermae Pannonicae*, it became a royal summer retreat and fashionable resort in the 19th c.

Baden-Powell /ˌbeɪdən'pəʊəl/, Robert Stephenson Smyth, 1st Baron Baden-Powell of Gilwell (1857–1941), English soldier, founder of the Boy Scouts (1908), Girl Guides (1910), and related organizations, which proved to be the most important British youth movements of the 20th c. He had become a national hero after his successful defence of Mafeking in the early part of the Second Boer War, but retired in 1910 to devote himself to the Boy Scout movement.

Baden-Württemberg /ˌbɑːdən'vʊətəmˌberk/ a 'Land' (State) of Germany; pop. (1987) 9,350,000; capital, Stuttgart.

Bader /ˈbɑːdə(r)/, Sir Douglas Robert Steuart (1910–82), British airman, a hero of the Second World War. Despite having lost both legs in a flying accident in 1931, he rejoined the RAF in 1939 and saw action during the evacuation from Dunkirk (1940) and the Battle of Britain. After the war he was noted for his work for disabled people.

badge /bædʒ/ *n.* **1** a distinctive emblem worn as a mark of office, membership, achievement, licensed employment, etc. **2** any feature or sign which reveals a characteristic condition or quality. [ME: orig. unkn.]

badger /ˈbædʒə(r)/ *n. & v.* —*n.* **1** an omnivorous grey-coated nocturnal mammal of the family Mustelidae with a white stripe flanked by black stripes on its head, which lives in sets. **2** a fishing-fly, brush, etc., made of its hair. —*v.tr.* pester, harass, tease. [16th c.: perh. f. BADGE, with ref. to its white forehead mark]

badinage /ˈbædɪnɑːʒ/ *n.* humorous or playful ridicule. [F f. *badiner* to joke]

badlands /ˈbædlændz/ *n.* extensive uncultivable eroded tracts in arid areas, especially the strikingly eroded areas of the US, characterized by sharp-crested ridges and pinnacles. Such topography is found where, owing to an arid climate or over-grazing, there is little vegetation to protect the land surface from erosion, so that streams and rivers have incised it with numerous gullies and ravines. The name was originally applied to parts of South Dakota and Nebraska, which the French trappers (applying the Indian name) found 'bad lands to cross'. Exposure of the rock layers has resulted in substantial finds of fossil vertebrates. [transl. F *mauvaises terres*]

badly /ˈbædlɪ/ *adv.* (**worse** /wɜːs/; **worst** /wɜːst/) **1** in a bad manner (*works badly*). **2** *colloq.* very much (*wants it badly*). **3** severely (*was badly defeated*).

badminton /ˈbædmɪnt(ə)n/ *n.* **1** a volleying game played by one or two players opposing an equivalent number across a net,

using rackets and a shuttlecock. It derives its name from Badminton (now in Avon), the seat of the Duke of Beaufort, where the game is supposed to have evolved about 1870 from the ancient game of battledore and shuttlecock. From the outset it gained popularity with army officers who took it to India and played it out of doors. The first laws were drawn up in Poona in the mid-1870s. **2** a summer drink of claret, soda, and sugar.

Badon Hill /ˈbeɪd(ə)n/ according to some sources, the site of a successful defensive fight by King Arthur's forces against the Saxons in AD 516. Another source implies that the battle was fought *c.*500 but does not connect it with Arthur. The location of the site is uncertain.

bad-tempered /bæd'tempəd/ *adj.* having a bad temper; irritable; easily annoyed. □□ **bad-temperedly** *adv.*

Baedeker /ˈbeɪdɪkə(r)/ *n.* any of various travel guidebooks published by the firm founded by the German Karl *Baedeker* (1801–59).

Baer /beə(r)/, Karl Ernest von (1792–1876), German biologist. His discovery that mammalian and human ova were not follicles of the ovary, but particles within these, was the chief of his many contributions to embryology. He also formulated a principle that in the developing embryo general characters appear before special ones, and his studies were used by Darwin in the theory of evolution.

Baffin /ˈbæfɪn/, William (*c.*1584–1622), English navigator and explorer who in 1616 discovered the largest island of the Canadian Arctic, which island (**Baffin Island**) and the strait (**Baffin Bay**) between it and Greenland are named after him. The record he established for attaining the most northerly latitude was not bested until the mid-19th c.

baffle /ˈbæf(ə)l/ *v. & n.* —*v.tr.* **1** confuse or perplex (a person, one's faculties, etc.). **2 a** frustrate or hinder (plans etc.). **b** restrain or regulate the progress of (fluids, sounds, etc.). —*n.* (also **baffle-plate**) a device used to restrain the flow of fluid, gas, etc., through an opening, often found in microphones etc. to regulate the emission of sound. □ **baffle-board** a device to prevent sound from spreading in different directions, esp. round a loudspeaker cone. □□ **bafflement** *n.* **baffling** *adj.* **bafflingly** *adv.* [perh. rel. to F *bafouer* ridicule, OF *beffer* mock]

baffler /ˈbæflə(r)/ *n.* = BAFFLE *n.*

BAFTA *abbr.* British Association of Film and Television Arts.

bag /bæg/ *n. & v.* —*n.* **1** a receptacle of flexible material with an opening at the top. **2 a** (usu. in *pl.*) a piece of luggage (*put the bags in the boot*). **b** a woman's handbag. **3** (in *pl.*; usu. foll. by *of*) *colloq.* a large amount; plenty (*bags of time*). **4** (in *pl.*) *Brit. colloq.* trousers. **5** *sl. derog.* a woman, esp. regarded as unattractive or unpleasant. **6** an animal's sac containing poison, honey, etc. **7** an amount of game shot by a sportsman. **8** (usu. in *pl.*) baggy folds of skin under the eyes. **9** *sl.* a person's particular interest or preoccupation, esp. in a distinctive style or category of music (*his bag is Indian music*). —*v.* (**bagged, bagging**) **1** *tr.* put in a bag. **2** *tr. colloq.* **a** secure; get hold of (*bagged the best seat*). **b** *colloq.* steal. **c** shoot (game). **d** (often in phr. **bags I**) *Brit. colloq.* claim on grounds of being the first to do so (*bagged first go*; *bags I go first*). **3 a** *intr.* hang loosely; bulge; swell. **b** *tr.* cause to do this. **4** *tr. Austral. sl.* criticize, disparage. □ **bag and baggage** with all one's belongings. **bag lady** *US* a homeless woman who carries her possessions around in shopping bags. **bag** (or **whole bag**) **of tricks** *colloq.* everything; the whole lot. **in the bag** *colloq.* achieved; as good as secured. □□ **bagful** *n.* (*pl.* **-fuls**). [ME, perh. f. ON *baggi*]

bagarre /bɑːˈgɑː(r)/ *n.* a scuffle or brawl. [F]

bagasse /bəˈgæs/ *n.* the dry pulpy residue left after the extraction of juice from sugar cane, usable as fuel or to make paper etc. [F f. Sp. *bagazo*]

bagatelle /ˌbægə'tel/ *n.* **1** a game in which small balls are struck into numbered holes on a board, with pins as obstructions. **2** a mere trifle; a negligible amount. **3** *Mus.* a short piece of music, esp. for the piano. [F f. It. *bagatella* dimin., perh. f. *baga* BAGGAGE]

Bagehot /ˈbædʒət/, Walter (1826–77), English economist and journalist, a banker and shipowner, editor of *The Economist* from 1860 until his death. His remarkable insight into economic and political questions is shown in his *The English Constitution* (1867), *Lombard Street* (1873), and *Economic Studies* (1880).

bagel /ˈbeɪg(ə)l/ *n.* (also **beigel**) *US* a hard bread roll in the shape of a ring. [Yiddish *beygel*]

baggage /ˈbægɪdʒ/ *n.* **1** everyday belongings packed up in suit-cases etc. for travelling; luggage. **2** the portable equipment of an army. **3** *joc.* or *derog.* a girl or woman. □ **baggage check** *US* a luggage ticket. [ME f. OF *bagage* f. *baguer* tie up or *bagues* bundles: perh. rel. to BAG]

baggy /ˈbægɪ/ *adj.* (**baggier**, **baggiest**) **1** hanging in loose folds. **2** puffed out. □□ **baggily** *adv.* **bagginess** *n.*

Baghdad /bægˈdæd/ the capital of Iraq, on the River Tigris. Under Caliph Harun-al-Rashid (d. 809) it became one of the greatest cities of Islam; pop. (est. 1985) 4,648,600.

bagman /ˈbægmən/ *n.* (pl. **-men**) **1** *Brit. sl.* a travelling salesman. **2** *Austral.* a tramp. **3** *US sl.* an agent who collects or distributes money for illicit purposes.

bagnio /ˈbɑːnjəʊ/ *n.* (pl. **-os**) **1** a brothel. **2** an Oriental prison. [It. *bagno* f. L *balneum* bath]

bagpipe /ˈbægpaɪp/ *n.* (usu. in *pl.*) a musical instrument with reeds that are sounded by the pressure of wind emitted from a bag squeezed by the player's arm and fed with air either by breath or by means of small bellows strapped to the waist. It generally has at least two pipes, one (the chanter) giving the melody and any others sounding a drone or drones. The bagpipe has been a popular instrument in the West from the Middle Ages and also appears, in widely varying forms, in Central and Eastern Europe and Asia; it is now associated especially with Scotland, Northumberland, and Ireland. □□ **bagpiper** *n.*

baguette /bæˈget/ *n.* **1** a long narrow French loaf. **2** a gem cut in a long rectangular shape. **3** *Archit.* a small moulding, semicircular in section. [F f. It. *bacchetto* dimin. of *bacchio* f. L *baculum* staff]

bah /bɑː/ *int.* an expression of contempt or disbelief. [prob. F]

Baha'i /bəˈhɑːɪ/ *n.* (pl. **Baha'is**) a member of a monotheistic religion founded in Persia in the 19th c. by Baha-ullah (1817–92) and his son Abdul Baha (1844–1921), that is a development of Babism. (See below.) □□ **Baha'ism** *n.* [Pers. *bahā* splendour]

The central tenet of the Baha'i faith is that the essence of all religions is one; thus all religious teachers are the messengers of one God. Its quest is for the general peace of mankind, whose unification it regards as necessary and inevitable; membership is open to all who accept its teachings, and members are now found in most countries of the world. Almost from its inception followers of this faith have been persecuted in Persia. The seat of its governing body, the Universal House of Justice, is in Haifa in Israel, adjacent to the golden-domed shrine of the Bab (see BABI) where his bones were buried in 1909 after freedom was given to religious minorities in the Ottoman empire.

Bahamas /bəˈhɑːməz/ a country consisting of an archipelago off the SE coast of Florida, part of the West Indies; pop. (est. 1988) 243,000; official language, English; capital, Nassau. It was here that Columbus made his first landfall in the New World (12 Oct. 1492). The islands were depopulated in the 16th c. as the Spaniards carried off most of the inhabitants to slavery and death. In 1648 a group of English Puritans settled there, and the islands were administered as a British colony from the 18th c. until they gained independence, as a member of the Commonwealth, in 1973. The subtropical climate and extensive beaches make tourism the main industry. □□ **Bahamian** /bəˈeɪmɪən/ *adj.* & *n.*

Bahasa Indonesia /bɑːˌhɑːsə ˌɪndəˈniːsɪə/ *n.* the official language of Indonesia (see INDONESIAN *n.* 3). [Indonesian *bahasa* language f. Skr. *bhāṣā* f. *bhāṣate* he speaks: see INDONESIAN]

Bahawalpur /bəˈhɑːwəlˌpʊə(r)/ a city of central Pakistan, in Punjab province; pop. (1981) 178,000.

Bahía see SALVADOR.

Bahía Blanca /bəˈhiːə ˈblæŋkə/ the principal port serving the southern Pampas of Argentina; pop. (1980) 220,800.

Bahrain /bɑːˈreɪn/ a sheikdom consisting of a group of islands in the Persian Gulf; pop. (est. 1988) 480,400; official language, Arabic; capital, Manama. The islands, famous in ancient times

for their pearls, were ruled by the Portuguese in the 16th c. and the Persians in the 17th c. They became a British protectorate in 1861 under a treaty by which the sheikh pledged himself to refrain from 'the prosecution of war, piracy, or slavery', and independent in 1971. Bahrain's economy is almost wholly dependent on the refining and export of oil, chiefly that coming by pipeline from Saudi Arabia. □□ **Bahraini** *adj.* & *n.*

Baikal /baɪˈkɑːl/, **Lake** a large lake in southern Siberia, the largest freshwater lake in Europe and Asia and the deepest lake in the world.

bail[1] /beɪl/ *n.* & *v.* —*n.* **1** money etc. required as security against the temporary release of a prisoner pending trial. **2** a person or persons giving such security. —*v.tr.* (usu. foll. by *out*) **1** release or secure the release of (a prisoner) on payment of bail. **2** (also **bale** by assoc. with *bale out* 1: see BALE[1]) release from a difficulty; come to the rescue of. □ **forfeit** (*colloq.* **jump**) **bail** fail to appear for trial after being released on bail. **go** (or **stand**) **bail** (often foll. by *for*) act as surety (for an accused person). □□ **bailable** *adj.* [ME f. OF *bail* custody, *bailler* take charge of, f. L *bajulare* bear a burden]

bail[2] /beɪl/ *n.* & *v.* —*n.* **1** *Cricket* either of the two crosspieces bridging the stumps. **2** the bar on a typewriter holding the paper against the platen. **3** a bar separating horses in an open stable. **4** *Austral.* & *NZ* a framework to secure the head of a cow during milking. —*v. Austral.* & *NZ* (usu. foll. by *up*) **1** *tr.* secure (a cow) during milking. **2 a** *tr.* make (a person) hold up his or her arms to be robbed. **b** *intr.* surrender by throwing up one's arms. **c** *tr.* buttonhole (a person). [ME f. OF *bail(e)*, perh. f. *bailler* enclose]

bail[3] /beɪl/ *v.tr.* (also **bale**) **1** (usu. foll. by *out*) scoop water out of (a boat etc.). **2** scoop (water etc.) out. □ **bail out** var. of *bale out* 1 (see BALE[1]). □□ **bailer** *n.* [obs. *bail* (n.) bucket f. F *baille* ult. f. L *bajulus* carrier]

bailee /beɪˈliː/ *n. Law* a person or party to whom goods are committed for a purpose, e.g. custody or repair, without transfer of ownership. [BAIL[1] + -EE]

bailey /ˈbeɪlɪ/ *n.* (pl. **-eys**) **1** the outer wall of a castle. **2** a court enclosed by it. [ME, var. of BAIL[2]]

Bailey bridge /ˈbeɪlɪ/ *n.* a temporary bridge of lattice steel designed for rapid assembly from prefabricated standard parts, designed by Sir Donald Bailey (1901–85) for military use in the Second World War. The bridge is built in its intended orientation beside the river and then 'launched' on rollers from one bank until it reaches the far side. Highway authorities still use such bridges for emergency work.

bailie /ˈbeɪlɪ/ *n. esp. hist.* a municipal officer and magistrate in Scotland. [ME, f. OF *bailli*s BAILIFF]

bailiff /ˈbeɪlɪf/ *n.* **1** a sheriff's officer who executes writs and processes and carries out distraints and arrests. **2** *Brit.* the agent or steward of a landlord. **3** *US* an official in a court of law who keeps order, looks after prisoners, etc. **4** *Brit.* (*hist.* except in formal titles) the sovereign's representative in a district, esp. the chief officer of a hundred. **5** the first civil officer in the Channel Islands. [ME f. OF *baillif* ult. f. L *bajulus* carrier, manager]

bailiwick /ˈbeɪlɪwɪk/ *n.* **1** *Law* the district or jurisdiction of a bailie or bailiff. **2** *joc.* a person's sphere of operations or particular area of interest. [BAILIE + WICK[2]]

bailment /ˈbeɪlmənt/ *n.* the act of delivering goods etc. for a (usu. specified) purpose.

bailor /ˈbeɪlə(r)/ *n. Law* a person or party that entrusts goods to a bailee. [BAIL[1] + -OR]

bailsman /ˈbeɪlzmən/ *n.* (pl. **-men**) a person who stands bail for another. [BAIL[1] + MAN]

bain-marie /ˌbæmæˈriː/ *n.* (pl. **bains-marie** *pronunc.* same) a cooking utensil consisting of a vessel of hot water in which a receptacle containing a sauce etc. can be slowly and gently heated; a double boiler. [F, transl. med.L *balneum Mariae* bath of Maria (an alleged Jewish alchemist)]

Bairam /baɪˈræm, ˈbaɪræm/ *n.* either of two annual Muslim festivals, **Greater Bairam**, celebrated concurrently with the annual pilgrimage (*hadj*) in the twelfth month of the Muslim lunar calendar and continuing for 3–4 days, and **Lesser**

Bairam, which follows the month of ritual fasting (Ramadan), the ninth month of the year, and lasts 2–3 days. [Turk. & Pers.]

Baird /beəd/, John Logie (1888–1946), Scottish pioneer of television. He started his work in the early 1920s, gave a demonstration in London in 1926, and made the first transatlantic transmission and demonstration of colour television in 1928.

bairn /beən/ n. Sc. & N.Engl. a child. [OE bearn]

Bairrada /baɪˈraːdə/ a wine-producing region of Portugal, in the coastal province of Beira Litoral.

bait[1] /beɪt/ n. & v. —n. 1 food used to entice a prey, esp. a fish or an animal. 2 an allurement; something intended to tempt or entice. 3 archaic a halt on a journey for refreshment or a rest. 4 = BATE. —v. 1 tr. a harass or annoy (a person). b torment (a chained animal). 2 tr. put bait on (a hook, trap, etc.) to entice a prey. 3 archaic a tr. give food to (horses on a journey). b intr. stop on a journey to take food or a rest. [ME f. ON beita hunt or chase]

bait[2] var. of BATE.

baize /beɪz/ n. a coarse usu. green woollen material resembling felt used as a covering or lining, esp. on the tops of billiard- and card-tables. [F baies (pl.) fem. of bai chestnut-coloured (BAY[4]), treated as sing.: cf. BODICE]

Baja California /ˈbæxə/ (also **North Baja**) a State of NW Mexico comprising that part of the Baja California (Lower California) peninsula lying to the north of the 28th parallel; pop. (est. 1988) 1,388,500; capital, Mexicali.

Baja California Sur /ˈbæxə, suə(r)/ (also **South Baja**) a State of NW Mexico comprising that part of the Baja California peninsula lying to the south of the 28th parallel; pop. (est. 1988) 395,100; capital, La Paz.

bajra /ˈbɑːdʒrə/ n. Ind. pearl millet or similar grain. [Hindi]

bake /beɪk/ v. & n. —v. 1 a tr. cook (food) by dry heat in an oven or on a hot surface, without direct exposure to a flame. b intr. undergo the process of being baked. 2 intr. colloq. a (usu. as be **baking**) (of weather etc.) be very hot. b (of a person) become hot. 3 a tr. harden (clay etc.) by heat. b intr. (of clay etc.) be hardened by heat. 4 a tr. (of the sun) affect by its heat, e.g. ripen (fruit). b intr. (e.g. of fruit) be affected by the sun's heat. —n. 1 the act or an instance of baking. 2 a batch of baking. 3 US a social gathering at which baked food is eaten. □ **baked Alaska** see ALASKA. **baked beans** baked haricot beans, usu. tinned in tomato sauce. **baking-powder** a mixture of sodium bicarbonate, cream of tartar, etc., used instead of yeast in baking. **baking-soda** sodium bicarbonate. [OE bacan]

bakehouse /ˈbeɪkhaʊs/ n. = BAKERY.

Bakelite /ˈbeɪkəlaɪt/ n. propr. any of various thermosetting resins or plastics made from formaldehyde and phenol and used for cables, buttons, plates, etc. [G Bakelit f. L.H. Baekeland its Belgian-born inventor d. 1944]

Baker /ˈbeɪkə(r)/, Dame Janet Abbott (1933–), English mezzo-soprano singer, whose voice is noted for its richness and intensity of feeling. In her many operatic roles she is as impressive as in the realm of Lieder, English and French songs, and oratorio.

baker /ˈbeɪkə(r)/ n. a person who bakes and sells bread, cakes, etc., esp. professionally. □ **baker's dozen** thirteen (so called from the former bakers' custom of adding an extra loaf to a dozen sold; the exact reason for this is unclear). [OE bæcere]

bakery /ˈbeɪkərɪ/ n. (pl. -ies) a place where bread and cakes are made or sold.

Bakewell /ˈbeɪkwel/, Robert (1725–95), English pioneer in scientific methods of livestock breeding and husbandry, who from his Leicestershire farm produced pedigree herds of sheep and cattle. Proper irrigation of his grassland gave him four cuts a year, while feeding and rigorously selective breeding greatly improved the meat-production from his animals. The first expenses of his experiments appear to have exceeded the profits, for he became bankrupt in 1776.

Bakewell tart /ˈbeɪkwel/ n. a baked open pie consisting of a pastry case lined with jam and filled with a rich almond paste. [Bakewell in Derbyshire]

baklava /ˈbækləvə, ˌbæklɑːˈvɑː/ n. (also **baclava**) a rich sweetmeat of flaky pastry, honey, and nuts. [Turk.]

baksheesh /ˈbækʃiːʃ/ n. (also **backsheesh**) (in some oriental countries) a small sum of money given as a gratuity or as alms. [ult. f. Pers. bak̲h̲šīš f. bak̲h̲šīdan give]

Bakst /bækst/, Léon (1866–1924), real name Lev Semuilovich Rosenberg, Russian painter and designer. Associated with Diaghilev's magazine The World of Art from 1899, he became one of the most influential members of the Diaghilev circle and the Ballets Russes. He designed the décor for such Diaghilev productions as Carnaval, Sheherazade (both 1910), Spectre de la rose (1911), L'après-midi d'un faune, Daphnis and Chloë (both 1912), and The Sleeping Princess (1921).

Baku /bæˈkuː/ the capital of the Soviet republic of Azerbaijan, on the Caspian Sea. It is an industrial port and a centre of the oil industry; pop. (est. 1987) 1,741,000.

Bakunin /bæˈkuːnɪn/, Mikhail Aleksandrovich (1814–76), Russian revolutionary, a leading exponent of anarchism. After taking part in the revolutions of 1848 he was exiled to Siberia, but escaped in 1861 and went to London. He participated in the First International, founded in 1864, but conflicted with Karl Marx by calling for violent means to destroy the existing political and social order, splitting the two factions for years to come.

Balaclava /ˌbæləˈklɑːvə/ a Crimean village, scene of a battle (1854) in the Crimean War. A Russian attempt to break the siege of Sebastopol was repulsed by the Franco-British army in a confused engagement most famous for the Charge of the Light Brigade. —n. (in full **Balaclava helmet**) a tight woollen garment covering the whole head and neck except for parts of the face, worn orig. by soldiers on active service in the Crimean War.

balalaika /ˌbæləˈlaɪkə/ n. a guitar-like musical instrument having a triangular body and 2–4 strings, popular in Russia and other Slav countries. [Russ.]

balance /ˈbæləns/ n. & v. —n. 1 an apparatus for weighing, esp. one with a central pivot, beam, and two scales. 2 a a counteracting weight or force. b (in full **balance-wheel**) the regulating device in a clock etc. 3 a an even distribution of weight or amount. b stability of body or mind (regained his balance). 4 a preponderating weight or amount (the balance of opinion). 5 a an agreement between or the difference between credits and debits in an account. b the difference between an amount due and an amount paid (will pay the balance next week). c an amount left over; the rest. 6 a Art harmony of design and proportion. b Mus. the relative volume of various sources of sound (bad balance between violins and trumpets). 7 (**the Balance**) the zodiacal sign or constellation Libra. —v. 1 tr. (foll. by with, against) offset or compare (one thing) with another (must balance the advantages with the disadvantages). 2 tr. counteract, equal, or neutralize the weight or importance of. 3 a tr. bring into or keep in equilibrium (balanced a book on her head). b intr. be in equilibrium (balanced on one leg). 4 tr. (usu. as **balanced** adj.) establish equal or appropriate proportions of elements in (a balanced diet; balanced opinion). 5 tr. weigh (arguments etc.) against each other. 6 a tr. compare and esp. equalize debits and credits of (an account). b intr. (of an account) have credits and debits equal. □ **balance of payments** the difference in value between payments into and out of a country. **balance of power** 1 a situation in which the chief States of the world have roughly equal power. 2 the power held by a small group when larger groups are of equal strength. **balance of trade** the difference in value between imports and exports. **balance sheet** a statement giving the balance of an account. **in the balance** uncertain; at a critical stage. **on balance** all things considered. **strike a balance** choose a moderate course or compromise. □□ **balanceable** adj. **balancer** n. [ME f. OF, ult. f. LL (libra) bilanx bilancis two-scaled (balance)]

Balanchine /ˌbælɑːˈʃiːn, ˈbælɒnˌtʃiːn/, George (1904–83), real name Georgi Melitonovich Balanchivadze, Russian-American dancer, choreographer, and ballet director. Diaghilev made him chief choreographer of his Ballets Russes in 1925; from this time dates his lifelong friendship with Stravinsky. In 1934 he went to the US, and started the company which later became the New York City Ballet. One of the greatest choreographers in ballet history, he became a dominant force of neoclassicism and a master of the plotless ballet. His numerous works include *Firebird* (1949), *Nutcracker* (1954), *A Midsummer Night's Dream* (1962), and *Slaughter on Tenth Avenue* (1968). He also choreographed opera, musicals, and films.

balata /ˈbælətə/ n. **1** any of several latex-yielding trees of Central America, esp. *Manilkara bidentata*. **2** the dried sap of this used as a substitute for gutta-percha. [ult. f. Carib]

Balaton /ˈbɒlə,tɒn/, **Lake** a lake in west central Hungary, situated in a leading resort and wine-producing region to the south of the Bakony Mountains. It is the largest and shallowest lake in central Europe.

Balboa /bælˈbəʊə/, Vasco Núñez de (1475–1517), Spanish explorer, especially of Central America. Settling in San Domingo in the new Spanish colony of Hispaniola in 1501, Balboa later (to escape his creditors) joined an expedition to Darien as a stowaway, but rose to command it after a mutiny (1510–11). In 1513 he reached the western coast of the isthmus after an epic 25-day march, thereby becoming the first European to see the Pacific Ocean. The arrival of a colonial governor in Panama marked a drastic downturn in Balboa's fortunes, however, and in 1517, after a series of disagreements with his superior, he was executed on a trumped-up charge of sedition.

Balbriggan /bælˈbrɪgən/ n. a knitted cotton fabric used for underwear etc. [*Balbriggan* in Ireland, where it was orig. made]

Balcon /ˈbælkən/, Michael (1896–1977), British film producer. He was responsible for several early Hitchcock films but is mainly remembered for his long association with Ealing Studios, during which he produced such famous comedies as *Kind Hearts and Coronets*, *Passport to Pimlico*, and *Whisky Galore* (all 1949), *The Man in the White Suit*, and *The Lavender Hill Mob* (both 1952).

balcony /ˈbælkənɪ/ n. (pl. **-ies**) **1** a usu. balustraded platform on the outside of a building, with access from an upper-floor window or door. **2 a** the tier of seats in a theatre above the dress circle. **b** the upstairs seats in a cinema etc. **c** *US* the dress circle in a theatre. □□ **balconied** adj. [It. *balcone*]

bald /bɔːld/ adj. **1** (of a person) with the scalp wholly or partly lacking hair. **2** (of an animal, plant, etc.) not covered with the usual hair, feathers, leaves, etc. **3** *colloq.* with the surface worn away (*a bald tyre*). **4 a** blunt, unelaborated (*a bald statement*). **b** undisguised (*the bald effrontery*). **5** meagre or dull (*a bald style*). **6** marked with white, esp. on the face (*a bald horse*). □ **bald eagle** a white-headed eagle (*Haliaeetus leucocephalus*), used as the emblem of the United States. □□ **balding** adj. (in senses 1–3). **baldish** adj. **baldly** adv. (in sense 4). **baldness** n. [ME *ballede*, orig. 'having a white blaze', prob. f. an OE root *ball-* 'white patch']

baldachin /ˈbɔːldəkɪn/ n. (also **baldaquin**) **1** a ceremonial canopy over an altar, throne, etc. **2** a rich brocade. [It. *baldacchino* f. *Baldacco* Baghdad, its place of origin]

Balder /ˈbɔːldə(r)/ *Scand. Mythol.* a son of Odin and god of the summer sun. He was invulnerable to all things except mistletoe, with which the evil spirit Loki by a trick induced the blind god Hödur to kill him.

balderdash /ˈbɔːldə,dæʃ/ n. senseless talk or writing; nonsense. [earlier = 'mixture of drinks': orig. unkn.]

baldhead /ˈbɔːldhed/ n. a person with a bald head.

baldmoney /ˈbɔːld,mʌnɪ/ n. (pl. **-eys**) an aromatic white-flowered umbelliferous mountain plant *Meum athamanticum*. [ME in sense 'gentian': orig. unkn.]

baldric /ˈbɔːldrɪk/ n. *hist.* a belt for a sword, bugle, etc., hung from the shoulder across the body to the opposite hip. [ME *baudry* f. OF *baudrei*: cf. MHG *balderich*, of unkn. orig.]

Baldwin /ˈbɔːldwɪn/, Stanley, 1st Earl (1867–1947), British Conservative statesman, Prime Minister 1923–4, 1924–9, and 1935–7. His second ministry was marked by the return to the gold standard, the General Strike of 1926, and the annexation of Ethopia by fascist Italy, his last by the abdication of King Edward VIII, which he handled skilfully. Although international relations continued to deteriorate with the German occupation of the Rhineland (1936) and the outbreak of the Spanish Civil War (1936), Baldwin opposed demands for rearmament, believing that the public would not support it.

bale¹ /beɪl/ n. & v. —n. **1** a bundle of merchandise or hay etc. tightly wrapped and bound with cords or hoops. **2** the quantity in a bale as a measure, esp. *US* 500 lb. of cotton. —v.tr. make up into bales. □ **bale** (or **bail**) **out 1** (of an airman) make an emergency parachute descent from an aircraft (cf. BAIL³). **2** = BAIL¹ v. 2. [ME prob. f. MDu., ult. identical with BALL¹]

bale² /beɪl/ n. *archaic* or *poet.* evil, destruction, woe, pain, misery. [OE *b(e)alu*]

bale³ var. of BAIL³.

Balearic Islands /ˌbælɪˈærɪk/ (also **Balearics**) a group of Mediterranean islands off the east coast of Spain, forming a province of that country, with four large islands (Majorca, Minorca, Ibiza, Formentera) and seven smaller ones; pop. (1986) 754,800; capital, Palma (on Majorca). Occupied by the Romans after the destruction of Carthage, the islands were subsequently conquered by Vandals and Moors, and then by Aragon in the 14th c.

baleen /bəˈliːn/ n. whalebone. □ **baleen whale** any of various whales of the suborder Mysticeti, having plates of baleen fringed with bristles for straining plankton from the water. [ME f. OF *baleine* f. L *balaena* whale]

baleful /ˈbeɪlfʊl/ adj. **1** (esp. of a manner, look, etc.) gloomy, menacing. **2** harmful, malignant, destructive. □□ **balefully** adv. **balefulness** n. [BALE² + -FUL]

Balenciaga /bæ,lenθɪˈɑːgə/, Cristóbal (1895–1972), Spanish-born couturier, who moved to Paris in 1937.

baler /ˈbeɪlə(r)/ n. a machine for making bales of hay, straw, metal, etc.

Balfour /ˈbælfʊə(r)/, Arthur James, 1st Earl of Balfour (1848–1930), British Conservative statesman and philosopher. An MP from 1874, Balfour entered the Cabinet of his uncle, the Earl of Salisbury, in 1886, and succeeded him as Prime Minister in 1902. His premiership saw the formation of the Committee of Imperial Defence and the creation of the Entente Cordiale with France, but the party split over the issue of tariff reform in 1905, forcing Balfour's resignation. During the First World War Balfour served as First Lord of the Admiralty (1915–16) and Foreign Secretary (1916–19), in which capacity he issued in 1917 the declaration, known by his name, in favour of a Jewish national home in Palestine.

Bali /ˈbɑːlɪ/ a mountainous island of Indonesia; pop. (1980) 2,469,900; capital, Singaradja.

Balinese /ˌbɑːlɪˈniːz/ n. & adj. —n. (pl. same) **1** a native of Bali. **2** the language of Bali. —adj. of or relating to Bali or its people or language.

balk var. of BAULK.

Balkan /ˈbɔːlkən, ˈbɒl-/ adj. of the Balkan Peninsula or States. □ **the Balkans** the Balkan States. **Balkan Mountains** a range of mountains stretching across central Bulgaria from the Yugoslav frontier to the Black Sea. **Balkan Peninsula** a peninsula of SE Europe, south of the Danube and Sava rivers, home of various peoples (Albanians, Vlachs, Greeks, Serbs, Bulgars, and Turks) with differing cultures. **Balkan States** the countries of this peninsula. **Balkan Wars** the wars of 1912–13 (see below). [Turk.]

From the 3rd to 7th c. the peninsula, nominally ruled by the Byzantine emperors, was invaded by successive migrations of Slavs; later, parts of it were conquered by Venice and other States. In 1356 the Ottoman invasion began: Constantinople fell to the Turks in 1453, and by 1478 most of the peninsula was in their power; the subject nations, though largely retaining their languages and religions, did not recover independence until the 19th c. In 1912–13 Turkey was attacked and defeated by other Balkan peoples in alliance, then the former allies fought over their gains. After the First World War the peninsula was divided between Greece, Bulgaria, Albania, and Yugoslavia, with Turkey retaining only Constantinople and the surrounding land.

Balkhash /bælˈkæʃ/, **Lake** a salt lake in the Soviet republic of Kazakhstan, with no outlet.

Balkis /ˈbɔːlkɪs, ˈbɒl-/ the name of the Queen of Sheba in Arabic literature.

balky var. of BAULKY.

ball¹ /bɔːl/ *n. & v.* —*n.* **1** a solid or hollow sphere, esp. for use in a game. **2 a** a ball-shaped object; material forming the shape of a ball (*ball of snow; ball of wool; rolled himself into a ball*). **b** a rounded part of the body (*ball of the foot*). **3** a solid non-explosive missile for a cannon etc. **4** a single delivery of a ball in cricket, baseball, etc., or passing of a ball in football. **5** (in *pl.*) *coarse sl.* **a** the testicles. **b** (usu. as an exclam. of contempt) nonsense, rubbish. **c** = balls-up. **d** courage, 'guts'. ¶ Sense 5 is usually considered a taboo use. —*v.* **1** *tr.* squeeze or wind into a ball. **2** *intr.* form or gather into a ball or balls. □ **ball-and-socket joint** *Anat.* a joint in which a rounded end lies in a concave cup or socket, allowing freedom of movement. **ball-bearing 1** a bearing in which the two halves are separated by a ring of small metal balls which reduce friction. **2** one of these balls. **ball game 1 a** any game played with a ball. **b** *US* a game of baseball. **2** esp. *US colloq.* a particular affair or concern (*a whole new ball game*). **the ball is in your** etc. **court** you etc. must be next to act. **ball lightning** a rare globular form of lightning. **ball-point (pen)** a pen with a tiny ball as its writing point. **balls** (or **ball**) **up** *coarse sl.* bungle; make a mess of. **balls-up** *n. coarse sl.* a mess; a confused or bungled situation. **have the ball at one's feet** have one's best opportunity. **keep the ball rolling** maintain the momentum of an activity. **on the ball** *colloq.* alert. **play ball** *colloq.* cooperate. **start** etc. **the ball rolling** set an activity in motion; make a start. [ME f. ON *böllr* f. Gmc]

ball² /bɔːl/ *n.* **1** a formal social gathering for dancing. **2** *sl.* an enjoyable time (esp. *have a ball*). [F *bal* f. LL *ballare* to dance]

ballad /ˈbæləd/ *n.* **1** a poem or song narrating a popular story. **2** a slow sentimental or romantic song. □ **ballad metre** = *common metre*. [ME f. OF *balade* f. Prov. *balada* dancing-song f. *balar* to dance]

ballade /bæˈlɑːd/ *n.* **1** a poem of one or more triplets of stanzas with a repeated refrain and an envoy. **2** *Mus.* a short lyrical piece, esp. for piano. [earlier spelling and pronunc. of BALLAD]

balladeer /ˌbæləˈdɪə(r)/ *n.* a singer or composer of ballads.

balladry /ˈbælədrɪ/ *n.* ballad poetry.

Ballarat /ˈbæləˌræt/ a mining and sheep-farming centre in the State of Victoria, Australia; pop. (1986) 78,300. The largest gold reserves in Australia were discovered here in 1851.

ballast /ˈbæləst/ *n. & v.* —*n.* **1** any heavy material placed in a ship or the car of a balloon etc. to secure stability. **2** coarse stone etc. used to form the bed of a railway track or road. **3** *Electr.* any device used to stabilize the current in a circuit. **4** anything that affords stability or permanence. —*v.tr.* **1** provide with ballast. **2** afford stability or weight to. [16th c.: f. LG or Scand., of uncert. orig.]

ballboy /ˈbɔːlbɔɪ/ *n.* (*fem.* **ballgirl** /-gɜːl/) (in lawn tennis) a boy or girl who retrieves balls that go out of play during a game.

ballcock /ˈbɔːlkɒk/ *n.* a floating ball on a hinged arm, whose movement up and down controls the water level in a cistern.

ballerina /ˌbæləˈriːnə/ *n.* a female ballet-dancer. [It., fem. of *ballerino* dancing-master f. *ballare* dance f. LL: see BALL²]

ballet /ˈbæleɪ/ *n.* **1 a** a dramatic or representational style of dancing and mime, using set steps and techniques and usu. (esp. in classical ballet) accompanied by music. (See below.) **b** a particular piece or performance of ballet. **c** the music for this. **2** a company performing ballet. □ **ballet-dancer** a dancer who specializes in ballet. □□ **balletic** /bəˈletɪk/ *adj.* [F f. It. *balletto* dimin. of *ballo* BALL²]

The art of ballet grew up in Renaissance Italy and reached its first great flowering in France at the court of Louis XIV who employed a young Italian, Lully, as his dancing master. The great schools of 'romantic' and 'classical' ballet developed in the 19th c., the former represented by such dancers as Marie Taglioni (1804–84) and Carlotta Grisi (1819–99) and the latter by the choreographer Marius Petipa (see entry), whose works include *The Sleeping Beauty* (1890) to music by Tchaikovsky. The early 20th c. was dominated by the productions of Diaghilev's Ballets Russes, involving the collaboration of outstanding dancers, choreographers, stage designers, and composers, but an equally important influence was that of the American dancer Isadora Duncan, who abandoned the traditional role of ballet as a narrative art for one of subjective response directly to the music. This forms the basis of the 'modern dance' movement, with which the names of Martha Graham (1894–) and Merce Cunningham (1919–) are associated.

balletomane /ˈbælɪtəʊˌmeɪn/ *n.* a devotee of ballet. □□ **balletomania** /-ˈmeɪnɪə/ *n.*

ballista /bəˈlɪstə/ *n.* (*pl.* **ballistae** /-stiː/) a catapult used in ancient warfare for hurling large stones etc. [L f. Gk *ballō* throw]

ballistic /bəˈlɪstɪk/ *adj.* **1** of or relating to projectiles. **2** moving under the force of gravity only. □ **ballistic missile** a missile which is initially powered and guided but falls under gravity on its target. □□ **ballistically** *adv.* [BALLISTA + -IC]

ballistics /bəˈlɪstɪks/ *n.pl.* (usu. treated as *sing.*) the science of projectiles and firearms.

ballocks var. of BOLLOCKS.

ballon d'essai /bæˌlɔ̃ deˈseɪ/ *n.* (*pl.* **ballons d'essai** pronunc. same) an experiment to see how a new policy etc. will be received. [F, = trial balloon]

balloon /bəˈluːn/ *n. & v.* —*n.* **1** a small inflatable rubber pouch with a neck, used as a child's toy or as decoration. **2** a large usu. round bag inflatable with hot air or gas to make it rise in the air, often carrying a basket for passengers. (See below.) **3** *colloq.* a balloon shape enclosing the words or thoughts of characters in a comic strip or cartoon. **4** a large globular drinking glass, usu. for brandy. —*v.* **1** *intr. & tr.* swell out or cause to swell out like a balloon. **2** *intr.* travel by balloon. **3** *tr. Brit.* hit or kick (a ball etc.) high in the air. □□ **balloonist** *n.* [F *ballon* or It. *ballone* large ball]

A small hot-air balloon was demonstrated in Lisbon in 1709, but attracted little attention. Napoleon, as a young general, used balloons for military observation in 1794, information about the enemy's movements being communicated by signalling. Barrage balloons, arranged in protective cordons round cities, were used in the First and Second World Wars to deter bombing attacks. Free balloons, both manned and unmanned, have had important functions in atmospheric research and weather prediction.

Man's efforts to fly succeeded on 21 Nov. 1783 when two Frenchmen, de Rozier and the Marquis d'Arlandes, were airborne under a hot-air balloon (built by the Montgolfier brothers) for 25 minutes and covered more than 8 km (5 miles). In 1804 two other intrepid Frenchmen, Biot and Gay-Lussac, undertook an ascent (the first ever made solely in the cause of science) to examine magnetic force and the constitution of the higher atmosphere and its electrical properties. Ballooning in the 19th c. was a story of steady and astonishing achievement, with flights across the English Channel and the Alps. By the end of the century the sport was so fashionable in London as to be rated a social grace, but lapsed at the end of the Edwardian era with the arrival of heavier-than-air flight. Interest in it has recently revived.

ballot /ˈbælət/ *n. & v.* —*n.* **1** a process of voting, in writing and usu. secret. **2** the total of votes recorded in a ballot. **3** the drawing of lots. **4** a paper or ticket etc. used in voting. —*v.* (**balloted, balloting**) **1** *intr.* (usu. foll. by *for*) **a** hold a ballot; give a vote. **b** draw lots for precedence etc. **2** *tr.* take a ballot of (*the union balloted its members*). □ **ballot-box** a sealed box into which voters put completed ballot-papers. **ballot-paper** a slip of paper used to register a vote. [It. *ballotta* dimin. of *balla* BALL¹]

ballpark /ˈbɔːlpɑːk/ *n. US* **1** a baseball ground. **2** (*attrib.*) *colloq.* approximate, rough (*a ballpark figure*). □ **in the right ballpark** *colloq.* close to one's objective; approximately correct.

ballroom /ˈbɔːlruːm, -rʊm/ *n.* a large room or hall for dancing. □ **ballroom dancing** formal social dancing as a recreation.

bally /ˈbælɪ/ *adj. & adv. Brit. sl.* a mild form of *bloody* (see BLOODY *adj.* 3) (*took the bally lot*). [alt. of BLOODY]

ballyhoo /ˌbælɪˈhuː/ *n.* **1** a loud noise or fuss; a confused state or commotion. **2** extravagant or sensational publicity. [19th or 20th c., orig. US (in sense 2): orig. unkn.]

Ballymena /ˌbælɪˈmiːnə/ a town in Co. Antrim, in the north-east of Northern Ireland; pop. (1981) 18,150.

ballyrag /ˈbælɪˌræg/ v.tr. (also **bullyrag** /ˈbʊl-/) (**-ragged, -ragging**) sl. play tricks on; scold, harass. [18th c.: orig. unkn.]

balm /bɑːm/ n. **1** an aromatic ointment for anointing, soothing, or healing. **2** a fragrant and medicinal exudation from certain trees and plants. **3** a healing or soothing influence or consolation. **4** an Asian and N. African tree yielding balm. **5** any aromatic herb, esp. one of the genus *Melissa*. **6** a pleasant perfume or fragrance. □ **balm of Gilead** (cf. Jer. 8: 22) **1 a** a fragrant resin formerly much used as an unguent. **b** a plant of the genus *Commiphora* yielding such resin. **2** the balsam fir or poplar. [ME f. OF ba(s)me f. L balsamum BALSAM]

balmoral /bælˈmɒr(ə)l/ n. **1** a type of brimless boat-shaped cocked hat with a cockade or ribbons attached, usu. worn by certain Scottish regiments. **2** a heavy leather walking-boot with laces up the front. [BALMORAL Castle]

Balmoral Castle /bælˈmɒr(ə)l/ a holiday residence of the British royal family near Braemar in Scotland. The estate was bought in 1847 by Prince Albert, who rebuilt the castle.

balmy /ˈbɑːmɪ/ adj. (**balmier, balmiest**) **1** mild and fragrant; soothing. **2** yielding balm. **3** sl. = BARMY. □□ **balmily** adv. **balminess** n.

balneology /ˌbælnɪˈɒlədʒɪ/ n. the scientific study of bathing and medicinal springs. □□ **balneological** /-nɪəˈlɒdʒɪk(ə)l/ adj. **balneologist** n. [L balneum bath + -LOGY]

baloney var. of BOLONEY.

BALPA abbr. British Air Line Pilots' Association.

balsa /ˈbɒlsə, ˈbɔːl-/ n. **1** (in full **balsa-wood**) a type of tough lightweight wood used for making models etc. **2** the tropical American tree, *Ochroma lagopus*, from which it comes. [Sp., = raft]

balsam /ˈbɒlsəm, ˈbɔːl-/ n. **1** any of several aromatic resinous exudations, such as balm, obtained from various trees and shrubs and used as a base for certain fragrances and medical preparations. **2** an ointment, esp. one composed of a substance dissolved in oil or turpentine. **3** any of various trees or shrubs which yield balsam. **4** any of several flowering plants of the genus *Impatiens*. **5** a healing or soothing agency. □ **balsam apple** any of various gourdlike plants of the genus *Momordica*, having warted orange-yellow fruits. **balsam fir** a N. American tree (*Abies balsamea*) which yields balsam. **balsam poplar** any of various N. American poplars, esp. *Populus balsamifera*, yielding balsam. □□ **balsamic** /-ˈsæmɪk/ adj. [OE f. L balsamum]

Balt /bɔːlt, bɒlt/ n. & adj. —n. **1** a native of one of the Baltic States of Lithuania, Latvia, and Estonia. **2** hist. a German inhabitant of any of these States. —adj. of or relating to the Balts. [L Balthae]

Baltic /ˈbɔːltɪk, ˈbɒl-/ n. & adj. —n. **1** (**the Baltic**) **a** the Baltic Sea. **b** the Baltic States, **2** —adj. of or relating to the Baltic or the group of languages called Baltic. [med.L Balticus f. LL Balthae dwellers near the Baltic Sea]

Baltic Exchange an association of companies, with headquarters in London, whose members are engaged in numerous international trading activities, especially the chartering of vessels to carry cargo. Other activities include the sale and purchase of ships, the chartering, sale, and purchase of aircraft, and commodity trading. The origins of the Exchange can be traced to the 18th c., when shipowners and merchants met in London coffee houses; foremost among these were the Jerusalem Coffee House and the Virginia and Maryland Coffee House, known from 1744 as the Virginia and Baltic since the cargoes dealt with came from the American colonies or from the countries on the Baltic seaboard. In 1900 it merged with the London Shipping Exchange.

Baltic Sea an almost land-locked sea in northern Europe, connected with the North Sea by a channel, and bordered by Sweden, Finland, the USSR, Poland, Germany, and Denmark.

Baltic States the former independent republics of Estonia, Latvia, and Lithuania.

Baltimore /ˈbɔːltɪˌmɔː(r), ˈbɒl-/ a seaport in north Maryland; pop. 774,113. [Lord Baltimore (d. 1632), English proprietor of territory which later became Maryland]

Baltistan /ˌbɔːltɪˈstɑːn, ˌbɒl-/ (also called **Little Tibet**) a region

of the Karakoram range of the Himalayas, to the south of K2, occupied by the Baltis, a Muslim tribe of Tibetan origin; chief town, Skardu.

Baluchistan /bəˌluːkɪˈstɑːin/ **1** a mountainous region of western Asia that includes part of SE Iran, SW Afghanistan, and west Pakistan. **2** a province of west Pakistan; pop. (1981) 4,332,000; capital, Quetta.

baluster /ˈbæləstə(r)/ n. each of a series of often ornamental short posts or pillars supporting a rail or coping etc. ¶ Often confused with *banister*. [F balustre f. It. balaustro f. L f. Gk balaustion wild-pomegranate flower]

balustrade /ˌbæləˈstreɪd/ n. a railing supported by balusters, esp. forming an ornamental parapet to a balcony, bridge, or terrace. [F (as BALUSTER)]

Balzac /ˈbælzæk/, Honoré de (1799–1850), French novelist, who studied law in Paris before turning to literature in 1819. His first successful novel was *Les Chouans* (1829). Thereafter his output became prodigious and his great series of coordinated interconnected novels and stories known collectively as *La Comédie humaine* appeared in 1842–8. The whole is a panorama of French society during the late 18th to early 19th c. and the underlying theme is the role of money in shaping personal and social relations. The breadth of Balzac's vision, and the vitality of his creations, have earned him a reputation as a writer of universal genius, and his work is an essential reference-point in the history of the European novel. Having struggled with insolvency most of his life he finally married the wealthy Polish lady, Mme Eveline Hanska, with whom he had corresponded since 1832 (*Lettres à l'Étrangère*, 1899–1906) shortly before his death.

Bamako /ˈbæməˌkəʊ/ the capital of Mali, pop. 600,000.

bambino /bæmˈbiːnəʊ/ n. (pl. ***bambini*** /-nɪ/) colloq. a young (esp. Italian) child. [It., dimin. of bambo silly]

bamboo /bæmˈbuː/ n. **1** a mainly tropical giant woody grass of the subfamily Bambusidae. **2** its hollow jointed stem, used as a stick or to make furniture etc. The pulp and fibre of some species are used in paper-making, or distilled to extract substances for use in medicines and chemical reactions. [Du. bamboes f. Port. mambu f. Malay]

bamboozle /bæmˈbuːz(ə)l/ v.tr. colloq. cheat, hoax, mystify. □□ **bamboozlement** n. **bamboozler** n. [c.1700: prob. of cant orig.]

Bamian /ˌbæmɪˈɑːn/ **1** a province of central Afghanistan. **2** its capital city; pop. (est. 1984) 8,000. Nearby are the remains of two colossal statues of Buddha and the ruins of the city of Ghulghuleh, which was destroyed by Genghis Khan c.1221.

ban /bæn/ v. & n. —v.tr. (**banned, banning**) forbid, prohibit, esp. formally. —n. **1** a formal or authoritative prohibition (*a ban on smoking*). **2** a tacit prohibition by public opinion. **3** a sentence of outlawry. **4** archaic a curse or execration. [OE bannan summon f. Gmc]

banal /bəˈnɑːl/ adj. trite, feeble, commonplace. □□ **banality** /-ˈnælɪtɪ/ n. (pl. **-ies**). **banally** adv. [orig. in sense 'compulsory', hence 'common to all', f. F f. ban (as BAN)]

banana /bəˈnɑːnə/ n. **1** a long curved fruit with soft pulpy flesh and yellow skin when ripe, growing in clusters. **2** (in full **banana-tree**) the tropical and subtropical treelike plant, *Musa sapientum*, bearing this. □ **banana republic** derog. a small State, esp. in Central America, dependent on the influx of foreign capital. **banana skin 1** the skin of a banana. **2** a cause of upset or humiliation; a blunder. **banana split** a sweet dish made with split bananas, ice-cream, sauce, etc. **go bananas** sl. become crazy or angry. [Port. or Sp., f. a name in Guinea]

banausic /bəˈnɔːsɪk/ adj. derog. **1 a** uncultivated. **b** materialistic. **2** suitable only for artisans. [Gk banausikos for artisans]

Banbury cake /ˈbænbərɪ/ n. a flat pastry with a spicy currant filling. [Banbury in S. England, where it was orig. made]

banc /bæŋk/ n. □ **in banc** Law sitting as a full court. [AF (= bench) f. med.L (as BANK²)]

band¹ /bænd/ n. & v. —n. **1** a flat thin strip or loop of material (e.g. paper, metal, rubber, or cloth) put round something esp. to hold it together or decorate it (*headband*). **2 a** a strip of material forming part of a garment (*hatband; waistband*). **b** a stripe of a different colour or material on an object. **3 a** a range of frequencies or wavelengths in a spectrum (esp. of radio frequencies). **b** a range of values within a series. **4** *Mech.* a belt connecting wheels or pulleys. **5** (in *pl.*) a collar having two hanging strips, worn by some lawyers, ministers, and academics in formal dress. **6** *archaic* a thing that restrains, binds, connects, or unites; a bond. —*v.tr.* **1** put a band on. **2 a** mark with stripes. **b** (as **banded** *adj.*) *Bot. & Zool.* marked with coloured bands or stripes. □ **band-saw** a mechanical saw with a blade formed by an endless toothed band. [ME f. OF *bande, bende* (sense 6 f. ON *band*) f. Gmc]

band² /bænd/ *n. & v.* —*n.* **1** an organized group of people having a common object, esp. of a criminal nature (*band of cutthroats*). **2 a** a group of musicians, esp. playing wind instruments (*brass band; military band*). **b** a group of musicians playing jazz, pop, or dance music. **c** *colloq.* an orchestra. **3** *US* a herd or flock. —*v.tr. & intr.* form into a group for a purpose (*band together for mutual protection*). □ **Band of Hope** an association promoting total abstinence from alcohol. [ME f. OF *bande, bander,* med.L *banda,* prob. of Gmc orig.]

Banda /ˈbændə/, Hastings Kamuzu (1906–), Malawi statesman, who studied medicine in the US and practised in Britain before returning to lead his country to independence. As its first President he created a highly autocratic regime, but his prestige overcame the tribal divisions which plagued many newly independent African countries so that Malawi, a poor country with few resources, became an oasis of calm in a troubled region.

bandage /ˈbændɪdʒ/ *n. & v.* —*n.* **1** a strip of material for binding up a wound etc. **2** a piece of material used as a blindfold. —*v.tr.* bind (a wound etc.) with a bandage. [F f. *bande* (as BAND¹)]

bandanna /bænˈdænə/ *n.* a large coloured handkerchief or neckerchief, usu. of silk or cotton, and often having white spots. [prob. Port. f. Hindi]

Bandaranaike /ˌbændərəˈnaɪkə/, Sirimavo Ratwatte Dias (1916–), Sinhalese stateswoman, Prime Minister of Sri Lanka 1960–5 and 1970–7, the world's first woman Prime Minister. After the assassination of her husband, S. W. R. D. Bandaranaike (1899–1959), Prime Minister 1956–9, she succeeded him in office.

Bandar Seri Begawan /ˈbændə ˌseri bəˈɡɑːwən/ the capital of Brunei; pop. (1981) 63,860. A deepwater port was opened in 1972 at nearby Muara.

Banda Sea /ˈbændə/ a sea in eastern Indonesia, between the central and south Molucca Islands.

b. & b. *abbr.* bed and breakfast.

bandbox /ˈbændbɒks/ *n.* a usu. circular cardboard box for carrying hats. □ **out of a bandbox** extremely neat. [BAND¹ + BOX¹]

bandeau /ˈbændəʊ, -ˈdəʊ/ *n.* (*pl.* **bandeaux** /-dəʊz/) a narrow band worn round the head. [F]

banderilla /ˌbændəˈriljə/ *n.* a decorated dart thrust into a bull's neck or shoulders during a bullfight. [Sp.]

banderole /ˌbændəˈrəʊl/ *n.* (also **banderol**) **1 a** a long narrow flag with a cleft end, flown at a masthead. **b** an ornamental streamer on a knight's lance. **2 a** a ribbon-like scroll. **b** a stone band resembling a banderole, bearing an inscription. [F *banderole* f. It. *banderuola* dimin. of *bandiera* BANNER]

bandicoot /ˈbændɪˌkuːt/ *n.* **1** any of the insect- and plant-eating marsupials of the family *Peramelidae.* **2** (in full **bandicoot rat**) *Ind.* a destructive rat, *Bandicota benegalensis.* [Telugu *pandikokku* pig-rat]

bandit /ˈbændɪt/ *n.* (*pl.* **bandits** or **banditti** /-ˈdɪti/) **1** a robber or murderer, esp. a member of a gang; a gangster. **2** an outlaw. □□ **banditry** *n.* [It. *bandito* (pl. *-iti*), past part. of *bandire* ban, = med.L *bannire* proclaim: see BANISH]

Bandjarmasin see BANJARMASIN.

bandmaster /ˈbændˌmɑːstə(r)/ *n.* the conductor of a (esp. military or brass) band. [BAND² + MASTER]

bandolier /ˌbændəˈlɪə(r)/ *n.* (also **bandoleer**) a shoulder belt with loops or pockets for cartridges. [Du. *bandelier* or F *bandoulière,* prob. formed as BANDEROLE]

bandsman /ˈbændzmən/ *n.* (*pl.* **-men**) a player in a (esp. military or brass) band.

bandstand /ˈbændstænd/ *n.* a covered outdoor platform for a band to play on, usu. in a park.

Bandung /ˈbænduŋ/ the capital of the province of West Java, Indonesia; pop. (1980) 1,462,600. Founded by the Dutch in 1810, it was the capital of the Dutch East Indies.

bandwagon /ˈbændˌwæɡən/ *n. US* a wagon used for carrying a band in a parade etc. □ **climb** (or **jump**) **on the bandwagon** join a party, cause, or group that seems likely to succeed.

bandwidth /ˈbændwɪtθ, -wɪdθ/ *n.* the range of frequencies within a given band (see BAND¹ n. 3a).

bandy¹ /ˈbændɪ/ *adj.* (**bandier, bandiest**) **1** (of the legs) curved so as to be wide apart at the knees. **2** (also **bandy-legged**) (of a person) having bandy legs. [perh. f. obs. *bandy* curved stick]

bandy² /ˈbændɪ/ *v.tr.* (**-ies, -ied**) **1** (often foll. by *about*) **a** pass (a story, rumour, etc.) to and fro. **b** throw or pass (a ball etc.) to and fro. **2** (often foll. by *about*) discuss disparagingly (*bandied her name about*). **3** (often foll. by *with*) exchange (blows, insults, etc.) (*don't bandy words with me*). [perh. f. F *bander* take sides f. *bande* BAND²]

bane /beɪn/ *n.* **1** the cause of ruin or trouble; the curse (esp. *the bane of one's life*). **2** *poet.* ruin; woe. **3** *archaic* (except in *comb.*) poison (*ratsbane*). □□ **baneful** *adj.* **banefully** *adv.* [OE *bana* f. Gmc]

baneberry /ˈbeɪnbəri/ *n.* (*pl.* **-ies**) **1** a plant of the genus *Actaea.* **2** the bitter poisonous berry of this plant.

bang /bæŋ/ *n., v., & adv.* —*n.* **1 a** a loud short sound. **b** an explosion. **c** the report of a gun. **2 a** a sharp blow. **b** the sound of this. **3** esp. *US* a fringe of hair cut straight across the forehead. **4** *coarse sl.* an act of sexual intercourse. **5** *sl.* a drug injection (cf. BHANG). —*v.* **1** *tr. & intr.* strike or shut noisily (*banged the door shut; banged on the table*). **2** *tr. & intr.* make or cause to make the sound of a blow or an explosion. **3** *tr.* esp. *US* cut (hair) in a bang. **4** *coarse sl.* **a** *intr.* have sexual intercourse. **b** *tr.* have sexual intercourse with. —*adv.* **1** with a bang or sudden impact. **2** *colloq.* exactly (*bang in the middle*). □ **bang off** *Brit. sl.* immediately. **bang on** *Brit. colloq.* exactly right. **bang-up** *US sl.* first-class, excellent (esp. *bang-up job*). **go bang 1** (of a door etc.) shut noisily. **2** explode. **3** *colloq.* be suddenly destroyed (*bang went their chances*). **go with a bang** go successfully. [16th c.: perh. f. Scand.]

Bangalore /ˌbæŋɡəˈlɔː(r)/ the capital of the State of Karnataka in central India; pop. (1981) 2,914,000.

banger /ˈbæŋə(r)/ *n. Brit.* **1** *sl.* a sausage. **2** *sl.* an old car, esp. a noisy one. **3** a loud firework.

Bangkok /bæŋˈkɒk/ the capital and chief port of Thailand; pop. (est. 1987) 5,609,350.

Bangladesh /ˌbæŋɡləˈdeʃ/ a Muslim country of the Indian subcontinent, in the Ganges delta; pop. (est. 1988) 109,963,550; official language, Bengali; capital, Dhaka. From 1857 the area formed part of India, under British rule, until 1947 when it became (as East Pakistan) one of the two geographical units of Pakistan. In response to serious internal political problems an independent republic was proclaimed in East Pakistan in 1971, taking the name of Bangladesh (Bengali, = land of Bengal), which became a member State of the Commonwealth in 1972. It is the world's chief producer of jute, which forms its main export, but the country remains one of the poorest in the world. The region is subject to frequent cyclones which cause immense damage and loss of life and crops. □□ **Bangladeshi** *adj. & n.*

bangle /ˈbæŋɡ(ə)l/ *n.* a rigid ornamental band worn round the arm or occas. the ankle. [Hindi *bangri* glass bracelet]

bangtail /ˈbæŋteɪl/ *n.* a horse, esp. with its tail cut straight across. **2 bangtail muster** *Austral.* the counting of cattle involving cutting across the tufts at the tail-ends as each is counted.

Bangui /ˈbæŋɡiː/ the capital of the Central African Republic; pop. (est. 1988) 596,800.

banian var. of BANYAN.

banish /ˈbænɪʃ/ *v.tr.* **1** formally expel (a person), esp. from a country. **2** dismiss from one's presence or mind. □□ **banishment** *n.* [ME f. OE *banir* ult. f. Gmc]

banister /ˈbænɪstə(r)/ *n.* (also **bannister**) **1** (in *pl.*) the uprights and handrail at the side of a staircase. **2** (usu. in *pl.*) an upright supporting a handrail. ¶ Often confused with *baluster*. [earlier *barrister*, corrupt. of BALUSTER]

Banjarmasin /ˌbændʒəˈmɑːsɪn, ˌbɑː-/ (also **Bandjarmasin**) a deepwater port and capital of the province of South Kalimantan, Indonesia; pop. (1980) 381,300.

banjo /ˈbændʒəʊ/ n. (pl. **-os** or **-oes**) a stringed musical instrument with a neck and head like a guitar and an open-backed body consisting of parchment stretched over a metal hoop. Its origin is supposed to be Africa, and it was in use among slaves of the southern US. It became the characteristic instrument of Negro minstrels, and in the 20th c. found a place in jazz bands. □□ **banjoist** n. [US southern corrupt. of earlier *bandore* ult. f. Gk *pandoura* three-stringed lute]

Banjul /bænˈdʒuːl/ (formerly *Bathurst*) the capital of The Gambia; pop. (1983) 44,536.

bank[1] /bæŋk/ n. & v. —n. **1 a** the sloping edge of land by a river. **b** the area of ground alongside a river (*had a picnic on the bank*). **2** a raised shelf of ground; a slope. **3** an elevation in the sea or a river bed. **4** the artificial slope of a road etc., enabling vehicles to maintain speed round a curve. **5** a mass of cloud, fog, snow, etc. **6** the edge of a hollow place (e.g. the top of a mine-shaft). —v. **1** tr. & intr. (often foll. by *up*) heap or rise into banks. **2** tr. heap up (a fire) tightly so that it burns slowly. **3 a** intr. (of a vehicle or aircraft or its occupant) travel with one side higher than the other in rounding a curve. **b** tr. cause (a vehicle or aircraft) to do this. **4** tr. contain or confine within a bank or banks. **5** tr. build (a road etc.) higher at the outer edge of a bend to enable fast cornering. [ME f. Gmc f. ON *banki* (unrecorded: cf. OIcel. *bakki*): rel. to BENCH]

bank[2] /bæŋk/ n. & v. —n. **1 a** a financial establishment which uses money deposited by customers for investment, pays it out when required, makes loans at interest, exchanges currency, etc. **b** a building in which this business takes place. **2** = *piggy bank*. **3 a** the money or tokens held by the banker in some gambling games. **b** the banker in such games. **4** a place for storing anything for future use (*blood bank; data bank*). —v. **1** tr. deposit (money or valuables) in a bank. **2** intr. engage in business as a banker. **3** intr. (often foll. by *at, with*) keep money (at a bank). **4** intr. act as banker in some gambling games. □ **bank balance** the amount of money held in a bank account at a given moment. **bank-bill 1** *Brit.* a bill drawn by one bank on another. **2** *US* = BANKNOTE. **bank-book** = PASSBOOK. **bank card** = *cheque card*. **bank holiday** see separate entry. **bank manager** a person in charge of a local branch of a bank. **bank on** rely on (*I'm banking on your help*). **bank statement** a printed statement of transactions and balance issued periodically to the holder of a bank account. [F *banque* or It. *banca* f. med.L *banca, bancus*, f. Gmc: rel. to BANK[1] f. F or It. (as foll.), referring to the fact that early bankers transacted their business at a bench (*banco*) in the market-place]

bank[3] /bæŋk/ n. **1** a row of similar objects, esp. of keys, lights, or switches. **2** a tier of oars. [ME f. OF *banc* f. Gmc: rel. to BANK[1], BENCH]

bankable /ˈbæŋkəb(ə)l/ adj. **1** acceptable at a bank. **2** reliable (*a bankable reputation*).

banker[1] /ˈbæŋkə(r)/ n. **1** a person who manages or owns a bank or group of banks. **2 a** a keeper of the bank or dealer in some gambling games. **b** a card-game involving gambling. **3** *Brit.* a result forecast identically (while other forecasts differ) in several football-pool entries on one coupon. □ **banker's card** = *cheque card*. **banker's order** an instruction to a bank to pay money or deliver property, signed by the owner or the owner's agent. [F *banquier* f. *banque* BANK[2]]

banker[2] /ˈbæŋkə(r)/ n. **1 a** a fishing boat off Newfoundland. **b** a Newfoundland fisherman. **2** *Austral. colloq.* a river flooded to the top of its banks. [BANK[1] + -ER[1]]

Bank for International Settlements a bank founded in 1930 to promote the cooperation of central banks and to provide facilities for international financial operations. Its main original function was to facilitate the mobilization and transfer of German reparation payments agreed after the First World War (and cancelled in 1932). It is located at Basle in Switzerland.

bank holiday a weekday kept as a public holiday, when banks are officially closed. In the 19th c. certain Saints' days (about 33 per annum) were kept as holidays at the Bank of England. In 1834 these were reduced to Good Friday, 1 May, 1 Nov., and Christmas Day. An Act of 1871 (originally intended as a social reform measure to guarantee workers more holiday) formally recognized certain days as bank holidays, and the number and date of these has been altered subsequently.

banking /ˈbæŋkɪŋ/ n. the business transactions of a bank.

banknote /ˈbæŋknəʊt/ n. a banker's promissory note, esp. from a central bank, payable to the bearer on demand, and serving as money.

Bank of England the central bank of England (see CENTRAL), originally incorporated in 1694 to raise and lend money to William III towards carrying on the war against France. It has the right of issuing legal-tender notes, manages the National Debt, and administers exchange-control regulations. The Government is its chief customer; it was nationalized in 1946.

bankroll /ˈbæŋkrəʊl/ n. & v. *US* —n. **1** a roll of banknotes. **2** funds. —v.tr. *colloq.* support financially.

bankrupt /ˈbæŋkrʌpt/ adj., n., & v. —adj. **1 a** insolvent; declared in law unable to pay debts. **b** undergoing the legal process resulting from this. **2** (often foll. by *of*) exhausted or drained (of some quality etc.); deficient, lacking. —n. **1 a** an insolvent person whose estate is administered and disposed of for the benefit of the creditors. **b** an insolvent debtor. **2** a person exhausted of or deficient in a certain attribute (*a moral bankrupt*). —v.tr. make bankrupt. □□ **bankruptcy** /-ˌrʌptsɪ/ n. (pl. **-ies**). [16th c.: f. It. *banca rotta* broken bench (as BANK[2], L *rumpere rupt-* break), assim. to L]

Banks /bæŋks/, Sir Joseph (1743–1820), English naturalist who accompanied Captain Cook on his first voyage round the world and collected and recorded many new species of plants. Banks became an influential figure in science: he was President of the Royal Society for over 40 years, and helped to establish the botanic gardens at Kew near London not only as a repository of thousands of living specimens from all over the world but as a centre for the introduction of plants to new regions, including breadfruit for the West Indies and tea from China to India. He also imported merino sheep from Spain and sent them on to Australia. His herbarium and library in London became a centre of taxonomic research, and after his death became part of the British Museum.

banksia /ˈbæŋksɪə/ n. any evergreen flowering shrub of the genus *Banksia*, native to Australia. □ **banksia rose** a Chinese climbing rose with small flowers. [Sir J. BANKS]

banner /ˈbænə(r)/ n. **1 a** a large rectangular sign bearing a slogan or design and usu. carried on two side-poles or a crossbar in a demonstration or procession. **b** a long strip of cloth etc. hung across a street or along the front of a building etc. and bearing a slogan. **2** a slogan or phrase used to represent a belief or principle. **3** a flag on a pole used as the standard of a king, knight, etc., esp. in battle. **4** (*attrib.*) *US* excellent, outstanding (*a banner year in sales*). □ **banner headline** a large newspaper headline, esp. one across the top of the front page. **join** (or **follow**) **the banner of** adhere to the cause of. □□ **bannered** adj. [ME f. AF *banere*, OF *baniere* f. Rmc ult. f. Gmc]

banneret /ˈbænərɪt/ n. *hist.* **1** a knight who commanded his own troops in battle under his own banner. **2** a knighthood given on the battlefield for courage. [ME & OF *baneret* f. *baniere* BANNER + -et as -ATE[1]]

bannister var. of BANISTER.

Bannister /ˈbænɪstə(r)/, Sir Roger Gilbert (1929–), British middle-distance runner, later a neurologist, who while a medical student became the first man to run a mile in under 4 minutes (6 May 1954) which, in its day, was the most coveted achievement in athletics.

bannock /ˈbænək/ n. *Sc.* & *N.Engl.* a round flat loaf, usu. unleavened. [OE *bannuc*, perh. f. Celt.]

Bannockburn /ˈbænəkˌbɜːn/ a village in central Scotland, scene of a decisive Scottish victory when the much larger English army of Edward II, advancing to break the siege of Stirling

Castle in 1314, was outmanoeuvred and defeated by Robert the Bruce on difficult ground a few miles from the castle. Bruce's victory virtually ended for several decades the Plantagenet attempt to reduce Scotland to the status of a vassal kingdom.

banns /bænz/ *n.pl.* a notice read out on three successive Sundays in a parish church, announcing an intended marriage and giving the opportunity for objections. The custom of announcing a forthcoming marriage during a church service was adopted early, but seems to have developed especially after Charlemagne's order for inquiry before marriage into possible consanguinity between the parties. It was ordered in England in 1200, and made compulsory throughout Christendom in 1215. The matter is regulated by statute, and the obtaining of a marriage licence is a civil and canonical equivalent. □ **forbid the banns** raise an objection to an intended marriage, esp. in church following the reading of the banns. [pl. of BAN]

banquet /'bæŋkwɪt/ *n. & v.* —*n.* **1** an elaborate usu. extensive feast. **2** a dinner for many people followed by speeches in favour of a cause or in celebration of an event. —*v.* (**banqueted, banqueting**) **1** *intr.* hold a banquet; feast. **2** *tr.* entertain with a banquet. □□ **banqueter** *n.* [F, dimin. of *banc* bench, BANK²]

banquette /bæŋ'ket/ *n.* **1** an upholstered bench along a wall, esp. in a restaurant or bar. **2** a raised step behind a rampart. [F f. It. *banchetta* dimin. of *banca* bench, BANK²]

banshee /'bænʃiː, -'ʃiː/ *n. Ir. & Sc.* a female spirit whose wailing warns of a death in a house. [Ir. *bean sídhe* f. OIr. *ben síde* woman of the fairies]

bantam /'bæntəm/ *n.* **1** any of several small breeds of domestic fowl, of which the cock is very aggressive. **2** a small but aggressive person. [app. f. *Bāntān* in Java, although the fowl is not native there]

bantamweight /'bæntəm,weɪt/ *n.* **1** a weight in certain sports intermediate between flyweight and featherweight, in the amateur boxing scale 51–4 kg but differing for professional boxers, wrestlers, and weightlifters. **2** a sportsman of this weight.

banter /'bæntə(r)/ *n. & v.* —*n.* good-humoured teasing. —*v.* **1** *tr.* ridicule in a good-humoured way. **2** *intr.* talk humorously or teasingly. □□ **banterer** *n.* [17th c.: orig. unkn.]

Banting[1] /'bæntɪŋ/, Sir Frederick Grant (1891–1941), Canadian surgeon who, in 1921, working with a science student, Charles Best, isolated the internal secretion of the pancreas, insulin. Banting had no significant experience in physiological research and the production of insulin originated from a wrongly conceived, badly conducted, and incorrectly interpreted series of experiments. None the less the discovery was a complex and dramatic event which revolutionized the treatment of diabetes, and he was awarded a Nobel Prize for medicine in 1923.

Banting[1] /'bæntɪŋ/, William (1797–1878), English undertaker who advocated a method of reducing weight by dieting.

Bantu /bæn'tuː/ *n. & adj.* —*n.* (*pl.* same or **Bantus**) **1** often *offens.* **a** a large group of Negroid peoples of central and southern Africa. **b** a member of any of these peoples. (See below.) **2** the group of languages spoken by them. —*adj.* of or relating to these peoples or languages. [Bantu, = people]
The Bantu people migrated to southern Africa, through the lake region of East Africa, by the 3rd c. AD. They are basically of Negro stock but vary considerably in physical appearance through admixture with other African peoples during and after their initial entry into southern Africa. It is believed that the Bantu introduced iron metallurgy to southern Africa at the time of their entry. Bantu languages belong to the Niger-Congo language group, and there are more than 300 of them (with 100 million speakers), of which Swahili is the most important. Their chief characteristics are that nearly all the words are tonal, and that all nouns belong to one of a set of classes, usually about eighteen. Most Bantu languages were not written down until the 19th c. Originally Arabs trading along the coast had brought their Arabic script, which was used for Swahili, but elsewhere the Roman alphabet has been used, sometimes with additional characters. Linguistic evidence suggests that the original home of these languages may have been in the Cameroon region.

Bantustan /,bæntuː'staːn/ *n. S.Afr.* often *offens.* any of several partially self-governing areas reserved for Black South Africans (see also HOMELAND). [BANTU + -*stan* as in *Hindustan*]

banyan /'bænɪən, -jən/ *n.* (also **banian**) **1** an Indian fig tree, *Ficus benghalensis*, the branches of which hang down and root themselves. **2** a Hindu trader. **3** a loose flannel jacket, shirt, or gown worn in India. [Port. *banian* f. Gujarati *vāṇiyo* man of trading caste, f. Skr.: applied orig. to one such tree under which banyans had built a pagoda]

banzai /baːnˈzaɪ/ *int.* **1** a Japanese battle cry. **2** a form of greeting used to the Japanese emperor. [Jap., = ten thousand years (of life to you)]

baobab /'beɪəʊˌbæb/ *n.* an African tree, *Adansonia digitata*, with an enormously thick trunk and large fruit containing edible pulp. [L (1592), prob. f. an Afr. lang.]

BAOR *abbr.* British Army of the Rhine.

bap /bæp/ *n. Brit.* a soft flattish bread roll. [16th c.: orig. unkn.]

baptism /'bæptɪz(ə)m/ *n.* **1 a** the religious rite, symbolizing admission to the Christian Church, of sprinkling the forehead with water, or (usu. only with adults) by immersion, generally accompanied by name-giving. **b** the act of baptizing or being baptized. **2** an initiation, e.g. into battle. **3** the naming of ships, church bells, etc. □ **baptism of fire 1** initiation into battle. **2** a painful new undertaking or experience. □□ **baptismal** /-'tɪzm(ə)l/ *adj.* [ME f. OF *ba(p)te(s)me* f. eccl.L *baptismus* f. eccl.Gk *baptismos* f. *baptizō* BAPTIZE]

baptist /'bæptɪst/ *n.* **1** a person who baptizes, esp. John the Baptist. **2** (**Baptist**) a Christian advocating baptism by total immersion, esp. of adults, as a symbol of membership of and initiation into the Church. (See below.) [ME f. OF *baptiste* f. eccl.L *baptista* f. eccl.Gk *baptistēs* f. *baptizō* BAPTIZE]
Baptists form one of the largest Protestant bodies, to be found in every continent and especially in the US. The exiled John Smyth founded the first group in Amsterdam in 1609, and in 1612 some of his followers returned to London and established a Baptist Church in England. Churches arising from this practice were known as General Baptists, and those founded by a group of Calvinists, who held that salvation was only for a particular few, as Strict or Particular Baptists. Rigid Calvinism was gradually modified and the merging of the two groups, begun in 1813, was largely completed by the end of the 19th c.

baptistery /'bæptɪstərɪ/ *n.* (also **baptistry** /-trɪ/) (*pl.* **-ies**) **1 a** the part of a church used for baptism. **b** *hist.* a building next to a church, used for baptism. **2** (in a Baptist chapel) a sunken receptacle used for total immersion. [ME f. OF *baptisterie* f. eccl.L *baptisterium* f. eccl.Gk *baptistērion* bathing-place f. *baptizō* BAPTIZE]

baptize /bæp'taɪz/ *v.tr.* (also **-ise**) **1** (also *absol.*) administer baptism to. **2** give a name or nickname to; christen. [ME f. OF *baptiser* f. eccl.L *baptizare* f. Gk *baptizō* immerse, baptize]

bar[1] /baː(r)/ *n., v., & prep.* —*n.* **1** a long rod or piece of rigid wood, metal, etc., esp. used as an obstruction, fastening, weapon, etc. **2 a** something resembling a bar in being (thought of as) straight, narrow, and rigid (*bar of soap; bar of chocolate*). **b** a band of colour or light, esp. on a flat surface. **c** the heating element of an electric fire. **d** = CROSSBAR. **e** Brit. a metal strip below the clasp of a medal, awarded as an extra distinction. **f** a sandbank or shoal at the mouth of a harbour or an estuary. **g** Brit. a rail marking the end of each chamber in the Houses of Parliament. **h** *Heraldry* a narrow horizontal stripe across a shield. **3 a** a barrier of any shape. **b** a restriction (*colour bar; a bar to promotion*). **4 a** a counter in a public house, restaurant, or café across which alcohol or refreshments are served. **b** a room in a public house in which customers may sit and drink. **c** *US* a public house. **d** a small shop or stall serving refreshments (*snack bar*). **e** a specialized department in a large store (*heel bar*). **5 a** an enclosure in which a prisoner stands in a lawcourt. **b** a public standard of acceptability, before which a person is said to be tried (*bar of conscience*). **c** a plea arresting an action or claim in a law case. **d** a particular court of law. **6** *Mus.* **a** any of the sections of usu. equal time-value into which a musical composition is divided by vertical lines across the staff. **b** = *bar-line*. **7** (**the Bar**) *Law* **a** barristers collectively. **b** the profession of barrister. —*v.tr.* (**barred, barring**) **1 a** fasten (a door, window, etc.) with a bar or bars. **b** (usu. foll. by *in, out*) shut or keep in or out (*barred him in*). **2** obstruct, prevent (*bar his progress*). **3 a** (usu. foll. by *from*) prohibit, exclude (*bar them from attending*). **b** exclude from consideration (cf. BARRING). **4** mark with stripes. **5** *Law* prevent or delay (an action) by objection. —*prep.* **1** except (*all were there bar a few*). **2** *Racing* except (the horses indicated: used in stating the odds, indicating the number of horses excluded) (*33–1 bar three*). □ **bar billiards** a form of billiards in which balls are knocked into holes in the table. **bar chart** a chart using bars to represent quantity. **bar-code** a machine-readable code in the form of a pattern of stripes printed on and identifying a commodity, used esp. for stock-control. **bar-line** *Mus.* a vertical line used to mark divisions between bars. **bar none** with no exceptions. **bar person** a barmaid or barman. **bar sinister** = *bend sinister* (see BEND[2]). **bar tracery** tracery with strips of stone across an aperture. **be called to the Bar** *Brit.* be admitted as a barrister. **be called within the Bar** *Brit.* be appointed a Queen's Counsel. **behind bars** in prison. **the outer Bar** barristers who are not Queen's Counsels. [ME f. OF *barre, barrer,* f. Rmc]

bar[2] /baː(r)/ *n. esp. Meteorol.* a unit of pressure, 10^5 newton per square metre, approx. one atmosphere. [Gk *baros* weight]

Barabbas /bəˈræbəs/ the robber whom Pontius Pilate released from prison to the Jews instead of Jesus Christ (Mark 15: 6–15).

barathea /ˌbærəˈθɪə/ *n.* a fine woollen cloth, sometimes mixed with silk or cotton, used esp. for coats, suits, etc. [19th c.: orig. unkn.]

barb /baːb/ *n. & v.* —*n.* **1** a secondary backward-facing projection from an arrow, fish-hook, etc., angled to make extraction difficult. **2** a deliberately hurtful remark. **3** a beardlike filament at the mouth of some fish, e.g. barbel and catfish. **4** any one of the fine hairlike filaments growing from the shaft of a feather, forming the vane. —*v.tr.* **1** provide (an arrow, a fish-hook, etc.) with a barb or barbs. **2** (as **barbed** *adj.*) (of a remark etc.) deliberately hurtful. □ **barbed wire** wire bearing sharp pointed spikes close together and used in fencing, or in warfare as an obstruction. [ME f. OF *barbe* f. L *barba* beard]

Barbados /baːˈbeɪdɒs/ the most easterly of the Caribbean islands; pop. (est. 1988) 256,800; official language, English; capital, Bridgetown. The geographical position of Barbados has influenced its history. Difficult of access in the days of sailing-ships, it became a British colony in 1652 and remained British without interruption until 1966 when it gained independence as a member State of the Commonwealth. The economy is based on tourism, sugar, and light manufacturing industries. □□ **Barbadian** *adj. & n.*

barbarian /baːˈbeərɪən/ *n. & adj.* —*n.* **1** an uncultured or brutish person; a lout. **2** a member of a primitive community or tribe. —*adj.* **1** rough and uncultured. **2** uncivilized. [orig. of any foreigner with a different language or customs: F *barbarien* f. *barbare* (as BARBAROUS)]

barbaric /baːˈbærɪk/ *adj.* **1** brutal; cruel (*flogging is a barbaric punishment*). **2** rough and uncultured; unrestrained. **3** of or like barbarians and their art or taste; primitive. □□ **barbarically** *adv.* [ME f. OF *barbarique* or L *barbaricus* f. Gk *barbarikos* f. *barbaros* foreign]

barbarism /ˈbaːbəˌrɪz(ə)m/ *n.* **1 a** the absence of culture and civilized standards; ignorance and rudeness. **b** an example of this. **2** a word or expression not considered correct; a solecism. **3** anything considered to be in bad taste. [F *barbarisme* f. L *barbarismus* f. Gk *barbarismos* f. *barbarizō* speak like a foreigner f. *barbaros* foreign]

barbarity /baːˈbærɪtɪ/ *n.* (pl. **-ies**) **1** savage cruelty. **2** an example of this.

barbarize /ˈbaːbəˌraɪz/ *v.tr. & intr.* (also **-ise**) make or become barbarous. □□ **barbarization** /-ˈzeɪʃ(ə)n/ *n.*

Barbarossa /ˌbaːbəˈrɒsə/ see FREDERICK I.

barbarous /ˈbaːbərəs/ *adj.* **1** uncivilized. **2** cruel. **3** coarse and unrefined. □□ **barbarously** *adv.* **barbarousness** *n.* [orig. of any foreign language or people: f. L f. Gk *barbaros* foreign]

Barbary /ˈbaːbərɪ/ (also **Barbary States**) *hist.* the name formerly applied to the Saracen countries of North and NW Africa,

and part of Spain, bordering on the Mediterranean Sea (see MAGHRIB), noted in the 16th–18th c. for its pirates. □ **Barbary ape** a macaque, *Macaca sylvana*, of North Africa and Gibraltar. [ult. f. Arab. *Barbar* BERBER, applied by ancient Arab geographers to the natives of N. Africa west and south of Egypt]

barbecue /ˈbaːbɪˌkjuː/ *n. & v.* —*n.* **1 a** a meal cooked on an open fire out of doors, esp. meat grilled on a metal appliance. **b** a party at which such a meal is cooked and eaten. **2 a** the metal appliance used for the preparation of a barbecue. **b** a fireplace, usu. of brick, containing such an appliance. —*v.tr.* (**barbecues, barbecued, barbecuing**) cook (esp. meat) on a barbecue. □ **barbecue sauce** a highly seasoned sauce, usu. containing chillies, in which meat etc. may be cooked. [Sp. *barbacòa* f. Haitian *barbacoa* wooden frame on posts]

barbel /ˈbaːb(ə)l/ *n.* **1** any large European freshwater fish of the genus *Barbus*, with fleshy filaments hanging from its mouth. **2** such a filament growing from the mouth of any fish. [ME f. OF f. LL *barbellus* dimin. of *barbus* barbel f. *barba* beard]

barbell /ˈbaːbel/ *n.* an iron bar with a series of graded discs at each end, used for weightlifting exercises. [BAR[1] + BELL[1]]

Barber /ˈbaːbə(r)/, Samuel (1910–81), American composer. His music is in the European traditional line; conservative in idiom, it is melodic and elegant, and includes operas, ballets, choral works, and orchestral and chamber music. His best-known works are the *Adagio for Strings* (1936) and the opera *Vanessa* (1958).

barber /ˈbaːbə(r)/ *n. & v.* —*n.* a person who cuts men's hair and shaves or trims beards as an occupation; a men's hairdresser. (See below.) —*v.tr.* **1** cut the hair, shave or trim the beard of. **2** cut or trim closely (*barbered the grass*). □ **barber's pole** a spirally painted striped red and white pole hung outside barbers' shops as a business sign. [ME & AF f. OF *barbeor* f. med.L *barbator -oris* f. *barba* beard]

Formerly the barber was also a regular practitioner in surgery and dentistry. The Company of Barber-surgeons was incorporated by Edward IV in 1461; under Henry VIII (1540) the title was altered to 'Company of Barbers and Surgeons' (to which women were admitted), and surgery passed out of the hands of the barbers. (See DENTISTRY, SURGERY.)

barberry /ˈbaːbərɪ/ *n.* (pl. **-ies**) **1** any shrub of the genus *Berberis*, with spiny shoots, yellow flowers, and ovoid red berries, often grown as hedges. **2** its berry. [ME f. OF *berberis*, of unkn. orig.: assim. to BERRY]

barber's (shop) music *n.* music like that formerly produced by customers waiting their turn in a barber's shop, where a simple musical instrument was provided for their amusement, especially in the 16th–17th c. The tradition ceased in England in the early part of the 18th c. but was maintained longer in America, where 'barber-shop harmony', a style of close-harmony singing for male voices, has enjoyed a 20th-c. revival.

barbet /ˈbaːbɪt/ *n.* any small brightly coloured tropical bird of the family Capitonidae, with bristles at the base of its beak. [F f. *barbe* beard]

barbette /baːˈbet/ *n.* a platform in a fort or ship from which guns can be fired over a parapet etc. without an embrasure. [F, dimin. of *barbe* beard]

barbican /ˈbaːbɪkən/ *n.* the outer defence of a city, castle, etc., esp. a double tower above a gate or drawbridge. [ME f. OF *barbacane*, of unkn. orig.]

Barbirolli /ˌbaːbɪˈrɒlɪ/, Sir John (Giovanni Battista) (1899–1970), English conductor, of Franco-Italian parentage. Originally a cellist, in 1924 he formed his own string orchestra to conduct and subsequently became conductor of major opera companies and orchestras in Britain and the US. In 1943 he returned to England as conductor of the Hallé Orchestra, Manchester, where he remained until his death.

barbitone /ˈbaːbɪˌtəʊn/ *n.* (*US* **barbital** /ˈbaːbɪt(ə)l/) a sedative drug. [as BARBITURIC ACID + -ONE, -al as in *veronal*]

barbiturate /baːˈbɪtjʊrət, -ˌreɪt/ *n.* any derivative of barbituric acid used in the preparation of sedative and sleep-inducing drugs. [BARBITURIC + -ATE[1]]

barbituric acid /ˌbaːbɪˈtjʊərɪk/ *n. Chem.* an organic acid from which various sedatives and sleep-inducing drugs are derived. [F *barbiturique* f. G *Barbitursäure* (*Säure* acid) f. the name *Barbara*]

Barbizon school /'bɑːbɪz(ə)n/ a group of French landscape painters, who came together in the 1840s, opposed to academic painting conventions and concerned with landscape painting for its own sake. They took the name of the small village, near Paris, where they worked. Théodore Rousseau was the leader of the group which included Daubigny, Diaz, Millet, and Dupré. Influenced by Constable and Dutch 17th-c. traditions they painted direct from nature, in the form of studies which were completed later in the studio. They were unlike the impressionists in this respect, but shared the same desire to return to nature for aesthetic inspiration. Their fresh naturalistic approach was closely linked to the spirit of the realist movement, though with a much more limited subject-range.

barbola /bɑːˈbəʊlə/ n. (in full **barbola work**) **1** the craft of making small models of fruit, flowers, etc. from a plastic paste. **2** articles, e.g. mirrors, decorated with such models. [arbitr. f. *barbotine* clay slip for ornamenting pottery]

Barbour /'bɑːbə(r)/, John (c.1320–95), Scottish poet, Archdeacon of Aberdeen (1357), who probably taught at Oxford and Paris. The only poem ascribed to him with certainty is *The Bruce*, a verse chronicle relating the deeds of Robert Bruce, king of Scotland, and his follower James Douglas, which contains a celebrated account of Bannockburn.

Barbuda see ANTIGUA AND BARBUDA.

barbule /'bɑːbjuːl/ n. a minute filament projecting from the barb of a feather. [L *barbula*, dimin. of *barba* beard]

barbwire /'bɑːbˌwaɪə(r)/ n. US = barbed wire (see BARB).

barcarole /'bɑːkəˌrəʊl/ n. (also **barcarolle** /-ˌrɒl/) **1** a song sung by Venetian gondoliers. **2** music in imitation of this. [F *barcarolle* f. Venetian It. *barcarola* boatman's song f. *barca* boat]

Barcelona /bɑːsɪˈləʊnə/ a city and province of Catalonia in NE Spain; pop. (city, 1986) 1,694,000.

Bar-Cochba /bɑːˈkɒkbə/ the name found in Christian sources (Jewish sources call him Simeon) for the leader of a Jewish rebellion in AD 132 against Hadrian's project to rebuild Jerusalem as a non-Jewish city, replacing the Jewish Temple with a temple of Jupiter. He claimed to be, and was accepted as, the Messiah. A number of letters in his handwriting have been found in archaeological excavations in Israel. [Aram., = son of a star]

bard[1] /bɑːd/ n. **1 a** *hist.* a Celtic minstrel. **b** the winner of a prize for Welsh verse at an Eisteddfod. **2** *poet.* a poet, esp. one treating heroic themes. □ **the Bard** (or **the Bard of Avon**) Shakespeare. □□ **bardic** *adj.* [Gael. & Ir. *bárd*, Welsh *bardd*, f. OCelt.]

bard[2] /bɑːd/ n. & v. —n. a rasher of fat bacon placed on meat or game before roasting. —v.tr. cover (meat etc.) with bards. [F *barde*, orig. = horse's breastplate, ult. f. Arab.]

Bardo /'bɑːdəʊ/ (also **Le Bardo**) a town in northern Tunisia, situated just north-west of Tunis; pop. (1984) 65,700.

Bardot /bɑːˈdəʊ/, Brigitte (1934–), French film actress with a coquettish appeal which won her the appellation of 'sex kitten'. Her films include *And God Created Woman* (1956). After retiring from acting she became an active supporter of animal welfare.

bardy /'bɑːdɪ/ n. (pl. **-ies**) *Austral.* an edible wood-boring grub. [Aboriginal]

bare /beə(r)/ adj. & v. —adj. **1** (esp. of part of the body) unclothed or uncovered (*with bare head*). **2** without appropriate covering or contents: **a** (of a tree) leafless. **b** unfurnished; empty (*bare rooms; the cupboard was bare*). **c** (of a floor) uncarpeted. **3 a** undisguised (*the bare truth*). **b** unadorned (*bare facts*). **4** (*attrib.*) **a** scanty (*a bare majority*). **b** mere (*bare necessities*). —v.tr. **1** uncover, unsheathe (*bared his teeth*). **2** reveal (*bared his soul*). □ **bare contract** *Law* a contract lacking a consideration and therefore void unless under seal. **bare of** without. **with one's bare hands** without using tools or weapons. □□ **bareness** n. [OE *bær*, *barian* f. Gmc]

bareback /'beəbæk/ adj. & adv. on an unsaddled horse, donkey, etc.

Barebones Parliament /'beəbəʊnz/ the nickname of Cromwell's Parliament of 1653, from one of its members, Praise-God Barbon, an Anabaptist leather-seller in Fleet Street.

barefaced /'beəfeɪst/ adj. undisguised; impudent (*barefaced cheek*). □□ **barefacedly** /-ˈfeɪsɪdlɪ/ adv. **barefacedness** n.

barefoot /'beəfʊt/ adj. & adv. (also **barefooted** /-ˈfʊtɪd/) with nothing on the feet. □ **barefoot doctor** a paramedical worker with basic medical training, esp. in China.

barège /bəˈreɪʒ/ n. a silky gauze made from wool or other material. [F f. *Barèges* in SW France, where it was orig. made]

bareheaded /beəˈhedɪd/ adj. & adv. without a covering for the head.

barely /'beəlɪ/ adv. **1** only just; scarcely (*barely escaped*). **2** scantily (*barely furnished*). **3** *archaic* openly, explicitly.

Barents /'bærənts/, Willem (d. 1597), Dutch explorer. The leader of several expeditions in search of the North-east passage to Asia, Barents discovered Spitsbergen and reached Novaya Zemlya, off the coast of which he died. Traces of his winter quarters were discovered undisturbed in the 1870s. The Barents Sea, a part of the Arctic Ocean north of the USSR, is named after him.

barf /bɑːf/ v. & n. *sl.* —v.intr. vomit or retch. —n. an attack of vomiting. [20th c.: orig. unkn.]

barfly /'bɑːflaɪ/ n. (pl. **-flies**) *colloq.* a person who frequents bars.

bargain /'bɑːgɪn/ n. & v. **1 a** an agreement on the terms of a transaction or sale. **b** this seen from the buyer's viewpoint (*a bad bargain*). **2** something acquired or offered cheaply. —v.intr. (often foll. by *with, for*) discuss the terms of a transaction (*expected him to bargain, but he paid up; bargained with her; bargained for the table*). □ **bargain away** part with for something worthless (*had bargained away the estate*). **bargain basement** the basement of a shop where bargains are displayed. **bargain for** (or *colloq.* **on**) (usu. with *neg.* actual or implied) be prepared for; expect (*didn't bargain for bad weather; more than I bargained for*). **bargain on** rely on. **drive a hard bargain** pursue one's own profit in a transaction keenly. **into** (*US* **in**) **the bargain** moreover; in addition to what was expected. **make** (or **strike**) **a bargain** agree a transaction. □□ **bargainer** n. [ME f. OF *bargaine, bargaignier*, prob. f. Gmc]

barge /bɑːdʒ/ n. & v. —n. **1** a long flat-bottomed boat for carrying freight on canals, rivers, etc. **2** a long ornamental boat used for pleasure or ceremony. **3** a boat used by the chief officers of a man-of-war. —v.intr. **1** (often foll. by *around*) lurch or rush clumsily about. **2** (foll. by *in, into*) **a** intrude or interrupt rudely or awkwardly (*barged in while we were kissing*). **b** collide with (*barged into her*). [ME f. OF perh. f. med.L *barica* f. Gk *baris* Egyptian boat]

bargeboard /'bɑːdʒbɔːd/ n. a board (often ornamental) fixed to the gable-end of a roof to hide the ends of the roof timbers. [perh. f. med.L *bargus* gallows]

bargee /bɑːˈdʒiː/ n. *Brit.* a person in charge of or working on a barge.

bargepole /'bɑːdʒpəʊl/ n. a long pole used for punting barges etc. and for fending off obstacles. □ **would not touch with a bargepole** refuse to be associated or concerned with (a person or thing).

Bari /'bɑːrɪ/ a seaport and capital of Apulia region in SE Italy, on the Adriatic; pop. (1981) 371,000.

barilla /bəˈrɪlə/ n. **1** any plant of the genus *Salsola* found chiefly in Spain and Sicily. **2** an impure alkali made by burning either this or kelp. [Sp.]

Bariloche see SAN CARLOS DE BARILOCHE.

Barisal /'bʌrɪsæl/ a port in southern Bangladesh, on the Ganges delta; pop. (1981) 172,900. It gives its name to the natural phenomenon known as 'Barisal guns', a sound like cannon-fire or thunder, possibly of seismic origin.

barite /'beəraɪt/ n. *US* = BARYTES.

baritone /'bærɪˌtəʊn/ n. & adj. —n. **1 a** the second-lowest adult male singing voice. **b** a singer with this voice. **c** a part written for it. **2 a** an instrument that is second-lowest in pitch in its family. **b** its player. —adj. of the second-lowest range. [It. *baritono* f. Gk *barutonos* f. *barus* heavy + *tonos* TONE]

barium /'beərɪəm/ n. *Chem.* a white reactive soft metallic element of the alkaline earth group, first isolated by Sir Humphrey

Davy in 1808. Barium and its compounds have a number of specialized uses, e.g. in water purification, the glass industry, pigments, and insecticides. It is used as an ingredient of signal flares and fireworks, where it imparts a bright yellowish-green colour to the flame. Its soluble compounds are poisonous, and the carbonate is used in rat poisons. ¶ Symb.: **Ba**; atomic number 56. □ **barium meal** a mixture of barium sulphate and water, which is opaque to X-rays, and is given to patients requiring radiological examination of the stomach and intestines. [BARYTA + -IUM]

bark[1] /baːk/ n. & v. —n. 1 the sharp explosive cry of a dog, fox, etc. 2 a sound resembling this cry. —v. 1 intr. (of a dog, fox, etc.) give a bark. 2 tr. & intr. speak or utter sharply or brusquely. 3 intr. cough fiercely. 4 tr. US sell or advertise publicly by calling out. □ **one's bark is worse than one's bite** one is not as ferocious as one appears. **bark up the wrong tree** be on the wrong track; make an effort in the wrong direction. [OE beorcan]

bark[2] /baːk/ n. & v. —n. 1 the tough protective outer sheath of the trunks, branches, and twigs of trees or woody shrubs. 2 this material used for tanning leather or dyeing material. —v.tr. 1 graze or scrape (one's shin etc.). 2 strip bark from (a tree etc.). 3 tan or dye (leather etc.) using the tannins found in bark. [ME f. OIcel. börkr bark-: perh. rel. to BIRCH]

bark[3] /baːk/ n. poet. a ship or boat. [= BARQUE]

barkeeper /'baːˌkiːpə(r)/ n. (also **barkeep**) US a person serving drinks in a bar.

barkentine esp. US var. of BARQUENTINE.

Barker /'baːkə(r)/, George Granville (1913–), English poet, a self-styled 'Augustinian anarchist', with a penchant for puns, distortion, and abrupt changes of tone. His Tone Confession of George Barker (1950, 1965) presents himself as irreverent, defiant, offhand, Rabelaisian, and guilt-ridden; some of his other works have a more sombre questioning tone.

barker /'baːkə(r)/ n. a tout at an auction, sideshow, etc., who calls out for custom to passers-by. [BARK[1] + -ER[1]]

Barkly Tableland /'baːklɪ/ a plateau region lying to the north-east of Tennant Creek in Northern Territory, Australia.

barley /'baːlɪ/ n. 1 any of various hardy awned cereals of the genus Hordeum widely used as food and in malt liquors and spirits such as whisky. 2 the grain produced from this (cf. pearl barley). □ **barley sugar** an amber-coloured sweet made of boiled sugar, traditionally shaped as a twisted stick. **barley water** a drink made from water and a boiled barley mixture. [OE bærlic (adj.) f. bære, bere barley]

barleycorn /'baːlɪˌkɔːn/ n. 1 the grain of barley. 2 a former unit of measure (about a third of an inch) based on the length of a grain of barley.

barleymow /'baːlɪˌməʊ/ n. Brit. a stack of barley.

barm /baːm/ n. 1 the froth on fermenting malt liquor. 2 archaic or dial. yeast or leaven. [OE beorma]

barmaid /'baːmeɪd/ n. a woman serving behind the bar of a public house, hotel, etc.

barman /'baːmən/ n. (pl. **-men**) a man serving behind the bar of a public house, hotel, etc.

barmbrack /'baːmbræk/ n. (also **barnbrack** /'baːn/) Ir. soft spicy bread with currants etc. [Ir. bairigen breac speckled cake]

Barmecide /'baːmɪˌsaɪd/ adj. & n. —adj. illusory, imaginary; such as to disappoint. —n. a giver of benefits that are illusory or disappointing. [the name of a wealthy man in the Arabian Nights' Entertainments who gave a beggar a feast consisting of ornate but empty dishes]

bar mitzvah /baː ˈmɪtzvə/ n. 1 the religious initiation ceremony of a Jewish boy who has reached the age of 13, when he is called upon to read from the Scriptures in a synagogue service. 2 the boy undergoing this ceremony, who thereby takes on the responsibilities of an adult under Jewish law. [Heb., = 'son of the commandment']

barmy /'baːmɪ/ adj. (**barmier**, **barmiest**) esp. Brit. sl. crazy, stupid. □□ **barmily** adv. **barminess** n. [earlier = frothy, f. BARM]

barn[1] /baːn/ n. 1 a large farm building for storing grain etc. 2

derog. a large plain or unattractive building. 3 US a large shed for storing road or railway vehicles. □ **barn dance 1** an informal social gathering for country dancing, orig. in a barn. 2 a dance for a number of couples forming a line or circle, with couples moving along it in turn. **barn-owl** a kind of owl, Tyto alba, frequenting barns. [OE bern, beren f. bere barley + ern, ærn house]

barn[2] /baːn/ n. Physics a unit of area, 10⁻²⁸ square metres, used esp. in particle physics. ¶ Symb.: **b**. [perh. f. phrase 'as big as a barn']

Barnabas /'baːnəbəs/, St (1st c.), a Levite, born in Cyprus, who became one of the earliest disciples of Christ at Jerusalem. He introduced St Paul to the Apostles and accompanied him in the first missionary journey to Cyprus and Asia Minor, returning to Cyprus after they disagreed and separated. He is the traditional founder of the Cypriot Church, and legend asserts that he was martyred at Salamis in Cyprus in AD 61. Feast day, 11 June.

barnacle /'baːnək(ə)l/ n. 1 any of various species of small marine crustaceans of the class Cirripedia which in adult form cling to rocks, ships' bottoms, etc. 2 a tenacious attendant or follower who cannot easily be shaken off. □ **barnacle goose** an Arctic goose, Branta leucopsis, which visits Britain in winter. □□ **barnacled** adj. [ME bernak (= med.L bernaca), of unkn. orig.]

Barnard /'baːnaːd/, Christiaan Neethling (1922–), South African surgeon, pioneer of human heart transplantation. He performed the first operation of this kind in Dec. 1967.

Barnardo /bə'naːdəʊ/, Thomas John (1845–1905), British philanthropist, founder of a chain of homes (formerly called 'Dr Barnardo's Homes') for destitute children, the first of which was opened in London in 1870.

Barnaul /ˌbaːnaˈuːl/ the capital of the Soviet territory of Altai in SW Siberia; pop. (est. 1987) 596,000.

barnbrack var. of BARMBRACK.

barney /'baːnɪ/ n. (pl. **-eys**) Brit. colloq. a noisy quarrel. [perh. dial.]

barnstorm /'baːnstɔːm/ v.intr. 1 tour rural districts giving theatrical performances (formerly often in barns). 2 US make a rapid tour holding political meetings. 3 US Aeron. give informal flying exhibitions; do stunt flying. □□ **barnstormer** n.

Barnum /'baːnəm/, Phineas Taylor (1810–91), American showman, famous for his extravagant advertising and exhibition of freaks at his American Museum in New York, and for his circus, opened in 1871, billed as 'The Greatest Show on Earth'.

barnyard /'baːnjaːd/ n. the area around a barn; a farmyard.

Baroda see VADODARA.

barograph /'bærəˌgraːf/ n. a barometer equipped to record its readings. [Gk baros weight + -GRAPH]

barometer /bə'rɒmɪtə(r)/ n. 1 an instrument measuring atmospheric pressure, esp. in forecasting the weather and determining altitude. The principle of the mercury barometer was established by the Italian physicist Torricelli (see entry) in 1644. A successful aneroid barometer (less sensitive than the mercury type but portable and more convenient) was devised in France in the 1840s. 2 anything which reflects changes in circumstances, opinions, etc. □□ **barometric** /ˌbærəʊ'metrɪk/ adj. **barometrical** /ˌbærəʊ'metrɪk(ə)l/ adj. **barometry** n.

baron /'bærən/ n. 1 a a member of the lowest order of the British nobility, styled Lord—. The use of the word as a title, as distinct from a description of a feudal relationship (see sense 3) or membership of a royal council, may be said to date from the creation of barons by patent, which began in the reign of Richard II. b a similar member of a foreign nobility, styled Baron—. 2 an important businessman or other powerful or influential person (sugar baron; newspaper baron). 3 hist. a person who held lands or property from the sovereign or a powerful overlord. □ **baron of beef** an undivided double sirloin. [ME f. AF barun, OF baron f. med.L baro, -onis man, of unkn. orig.]

baronage /'bærənɪdʒ/ n. 1 barons or nobles collectively. 2 an annotated list of barons or peers. [ME f. OF barnage (as BARON)]

baroness /'bærənɪs/ n. 1 a woman holding the rank of baron either as a life peerage or as a hereditary rank. 2 the wife or widow of a baron. [ME f. OF baronesse (as BARON)]

æ cat ɑː arm e bed ɜː her ɪ sit iː see ɒ hot ɔː saw ʌ run ʊ put uː too ə ago aɪ my

baronet /ˈbærənɪt/ n. a member of a British titled order, the lowest that is hereditary, ranking next below a baron and above all orders of knighthood except that of the Garter. *Baronets of England* were instituted by James I in 1611, to raise money for the settlement of Ulster by fees paid for the 'new dignity'; *Baronets of Scotland* (or *of Nova Scotia*) were instituted by Charles I similarly in 1625, for encouragement of the settling of Nova Scotia; *Baronets of Ireland* were instituted in 1619. Creation of the Scottish and Irish titles ceased in 1707 and 1801 respectively, after the Acts of Union relating to each country, and new baronetcies were *of Great Britain* until 1800 and *of the United Kingdom* from 1801. [ME f. AL *baronettus* (as BARON)]

baronetage /ˈbærənɪtɪdʒ/ n. **1** baronets collectively. **2** an annotated list of baronets.

baronetcy /ˈbærənɪtsɪ/ n. (pl. **-ies**) the domain, rank, or tenure of a baronet.

baronial /bəˈrəʊnɪəl/ adj. of, relating to, or befitting barons.

barony /ˈbærənɪ/ n. (pl. **-ies**) **1** the domain, rank, or tenure of a baron. **2** (in Ireland) a division of a county. **3** (in Scotland) a large manor or estate. [ME f. OF *baronie* (as BARON)]

baroque /bəˈrɒk/ adj. & n. —adj. **1** highly ornate and extravagant in style, esp. of European art, architecture, and music of the 17th and 18th c. **2** of or relating to this period. —n. **1** the baroque style. **2** baroque art collectively. [F (orig. = 'irregular pearl') f. Port. *barroco*, of unkn. orig.]

barouche /bəˈruːʃ/ n. a horse-drawn carriage with four wheels and a collapsible hood over the rear half, used esp. in the 19th c. [G (dial.) *Barutsche* f. It. *baroccio* ult. f. L *birotus* two-wheeled]

barque /bɑːk/ n. **1** a sailing-ship with the rear mast fore-and-aft-rigged and the remaining (usu. two) masts square-rigged. Until the mid-19th c. barques were relatively small sailing-ships, but later were built up to about 3,000 tons or more, sometimes with four or five masts. They are now virtually obsolete as trading vessels but some are used as sail training ships. **2** *poet.* any boat. [ME f. F prob. f. Prov. *barca* f. L *barca* ship's boat]

barquentine /ˈbɑːkəntiːn/ n. (also **barkentine**, **barquantine**) a sailing ship with the foremast square-rigged and the remaining (usu. two) masts fore-and-aft-rigged. [BARQUE after *brigantine*]

barrack[1] /ˈbærək/ n. & v. —n. (usu. in pl., often treated as sing.) **1** a building or building complex used to house soldiers. **2** any building used to accommodate large numbers of people. **3** a large building of a bleak or plain appearance. —v.tr. place (soldiers etc.) in barracks. □ **barrack-room lawyer** Brit. a pompously argumentative person. **barrack-square** a drill-ground near a barracks. [F *baraque* f. It. *baracca* or Sp. *barraca* soldier's tent, of unkn. orig.]

barrack[2] /ˈbærək/ v. Brit. **1** tr. shout or jeer at (players in a game, a performer, speaker, etc.). **2** intr. (of spectators at games etc.) shout or jeer. [app. f. BORAK]

barracouta /ˌbærəˈkuːtə/ n. (pl. same or **barracoutas**) **1** a long slender fish, *Thyrsites atun*, usu. found in southern oceans. **2** NZ a small narrow loaf of bread. [var. of BARRACUDA]

barracuda /ˌbærəˈkuːdə/ n. (pl. same or **barracudas**) a large and voracious tropical marine fish of the family Sphyraenidae. [Amer. Sp. *barracuda*]

barrage /ˈbærɑːʒ/ n. **1** a concentrated artillery bombardment over a wide area. **2** a rapid succession of questions or criticisms. **3** an artificial barrier, esp. in a river. **4** a heat or deciding event in fencing, show jumping, etc. □ **barrage balloon** a large anchored balloon, often with netting suspended from it, used (usu. as one of a series) as a defence against low-flying aircraft. [F f. *barrer* (as BAR[1])]

barramundi /ˌbærəˈmʌndɪ/ n. (pl. same or **barramundis**) any of various Australian freshwater fishes, esp. *Lates calcarifer*, used as food. [Aboriginal]

Barranquilla /ˌbærənˈkiːjə/ the chief port of Colombia. Founded in 1629, the city lies at the mouth of the Magdalena River near the Caribbean Sea; pop. (1985) 899,800.

barrator /ˈbærətə(r)/ n. **1** a malicious person causing discord.

2 *hist.* a vexatious litigant. [ME f. AF *baratour*, OF *barateor* trickster, f. *barat* deceit]

barratry /ˈbærətrɪ/ n. **1** fraud or gross negligence of a ship's master or crew at the expense of its owners or users. **2** *hist.* vexatious litigation or incitement to it. **3** *hist.* trade in the sale of Church or State appointments. □□ **barratrous** adj. [ME f. OF *baraterie* (as BARRATOR)]

barre /bɑː(r)/ n. a horizontal bar at waist level used in dance exercises. [F]

barré /ˈbæreɪ/ n. *Mus.* a method of playing a chord on the guitar etc. with a finger laid across the strings at a particular fret, raising their pitch. [F, past part. of *barrer* bar]

barrel /ˈbær(ə)l/ n. & v. —n. **1** a cylindrical container usu. bulging out in the middle, traditionally made of wooden staves with metal hoops round them. **2** the contents of this. **3** a measure of capacity, usu. varying from 30 to 40 gallons (in brewing = 36 imperial gallons; in the oil industry = 35 imperial or 42 US gallons).. **4** a cylindrical tube forming part of an object such as a gun or a pen. **5** the belly and loins of a four-legged animal, e.g. a horse. —v. (**barrelled**, **barrelling**; US **barreled**, **barreling**) **1** tr. put into a barrel or barrels. **2** intr. US sl. drive fast. □ **barrel-chested** having a large rounded chest. **barrel roll** an aerobatic manoeuvre in which an aircraft follows a single turn of a spiral while rolling once about its longitudinal axis. **barrel vault** Archit. a vault forming a half cylinder. **over a barrel** colloq. in a helpless position; at a person's mercy. [ME f. OF *baril* perh. f. Rmc.: rel to BAR[1]]

barrel-organ n. **1** an automatic pipe-organ much used in churches in the 19th c. Projections on a cylinder (barrel) that was turned by a handle (which also worked the bellows) opened pipes to produce the required notes for a predetermined tune. **2** a 19th-c. street-instrument (not of the organ type) producing notes by means of metal tongues struck by pins fixed in the barrel. The tone resembles that of a piano.

barren /ˈbærən/ adj. & n. —adj. (**barrener**, **barrenest**) **1 a** unable to bear young. **b** unable to produce fruit or vegetation. **2** meagre, unprofitable. **3** dull, unstimulating. **4** (foll. by *of*) lacking in (*barren of wit*). —n. a barren tract or tracts of land esp. (in pl.) in N. America. □□ **barrenly** adv. **barrenness** n. [ME f. AF *barai(g)ne*, OF *barhaine* etc., of unkn. orig.]

Barrett /ˈbærət/, Elizabeth, see BROWNING.[1]

barricade /ˌbærɪˈkeɪd/ n. & v. —n. a barrier, esp. one improvised across a street etc. —v.tr. block or defend with a barricade. [F f. *barrique* cask f. Sp. *barrica*, rel. to BARREL]

Barrie /ˈbærɪ/, Sir James Matthew (1860–1937), Scottish dramatist and novelist, son of a weaver, who wrote several sentimental stories before turning to drama. He achieved success with *Quality Street* (1901), the ever-popular comedy *The Admirable Crichton* (1902), and *Dear Brutus* (1917), and is above all remembered for his internationally celebrated children's play *Peter Pan* (1904) about the boy who would not grow up, the copyright of which he bequeathed to the Great Ormond Street Children's Hospital.

barrier /ˈbærɪə(r)/ n. **1** a fence or other obstacle that bars advance or access. **2** an obstacle or circumstance that keeps people or things apart, or prevents communication (*class barriers; a language barrier*). **3** anything that prevents progress or success. **4** a gate at a car park, railway station, etc., that controls access. **5** colloq. = sound barrier. □ **barrier cream** a cream used to protect the skin from damage or infection. **barrier reef** a coral reef separated from the shore by a broad deep channel. [ME f. AF *barrere*, OF *barriere*]

barring /ˈbɑːrɪŋ/ prep. except, not including. [BAR[1] + -ING[2]]

barrio /ˈbɑːrɪəʊ/ n. (pl. **-os**) (in the US) the Spanish-speaking quarter of a town or city. [Sp., = district of a town]

barrister /ˈbærɪstə(r)/ n. (in full **barrister-at-law**) **1** Brit. a person called to the bar and entitled to practise as an advocate in the higher courts. **2** US a lawyer. [16th c.: f. BAR[1], perh. after *minister*]

barrow[1] /ˈbærəʊ/ n. **1** Brit. a two-wheeled handcart used esp. by street vendors. **2** = WHEELBARROW. **3** a metal frame with two wheels used for transporting luggage etc. □ **barrow boy** *Brit.* a boy who sells wares from a barrow. [OE *bearwe* f. Gmc]

barrow[2] /ˈbærəʊ/ *n. Archaeol.* a mound of earth constructed in ancient times to cover one or more burials (often marked on maps as *tumulus*). The earliest barrows occurred in NW Europe in the late 5th and 4th millenniums BC and were elongated in shape (*long barrows*). In the late 4th millennium BC round barrows came into use, and continued to be constructed intermittently up to the 10th c. AD. The somewhat uniform appearance that these monuments tend to display today belies a wide range of burial practices and construction techniques. [OE *beorg* hill, hillock f. Gmc]

Barry /ˈbærɪ/, Sir Charles (1795–1860), English architect who made his reputation with his Italianate design of the Travellers' Club in Pall Mall, London (1830–2), and in 1836 won a competition to design the new Houses of Parliament after the old buildings had been destroyed by fire. These he formed in Gothic style, with details contributed by A. W. N. Pugin.

Barrymore /ˈbærɪˌmɔːr/ the name of an American family of actors. Lionel (1878–1954) withdrew from the theatre in 1925 and spent the rest of his life in films, where he had a long and distinguished career. Ethel (1879–1959), a beautiful woman with a warm and distinguished presence, gave some of her finest performances in later life. In 1928 a New York theatre was named after her. John (1882–1942), who was noted for his romantic good looks and perfect diction, was an excellent light comedian as well as a serious actor. His most spectacular success was as Hamlet, both in New York (1922) and in London (1925).

Barsac /bɑːˈsæk/ *n.* a sweet white wine from the district of Barsac, department of Gironde, in western France.

Bart. /bɑːt/ *abbr.* Baronet.

bartender /ˈbɑːˌtendə(r)/ *n.* a person serving behind the bar of a public house.

barter /ˈbɑːtə(r)/ *v. & n.* —*v.* **1** *tr.* exchange (goods or services) without using money. **2** *intr.* make such an exchange. —*n.* trade by exchange of goods. □□ **barterer** *n.* [prob. OF *barater*: see BARRATOR]

Barth[1] /bɑːθ/, John Simmons (1930–), American novelist, whose complex, elaborate, experimental novels include *The Sot-Weed Factor* (1960), and *Letters* (1979). His works have been more admired in American academic circles than in Britain.

Barth[2] /bɑːt, bɑːθ/, Karl (1886–1968), Swiss Protestant theologian. Under the shadow of the First World War he was led to a radical questioning of contemporary religious philosophy, with its positive attitude to science and the arts, its sympathy with mysticism, and its stress on feeling. Regarding this outlook as fundamentally erroneous, he sought a return to the principles of the Reformation and the teachings of the Bible. He emphasized the supremacy and transcendence of God and the worthlessness of human reason, asserting that our understanding of God is centred exclusively upon his revelation in Christ, and that man is utterly dependent upon divine grace. Though in English-speaking countries the greatest impact of his theology was in the 1930s, his potent astringent influence continued, and his personal prestige, based largely on his distinctive and forthright standpoint, has given him the position of the outstanding Protestant theologian of the 20th c.

Bartholomew /bɑːˈθɒləˌmjuː/, St (1st c.), one of the twelve Apostles. He is said to have been flayed alive in Armenia, and is hence regarded as the patron saint of tanners. Feast day, 12 Aug. □ **Massacre of St Bartholomew,** the massacre of Huguenots throughout France ordered by Charles IX at the instigation of his mother, Catherine de Médicis, and begun without warning on the feast of St Bartholomew, 1572.

bartizan /ˈbɑːtɪz(ə)n, ˌbɑːtɪˈzæn/ *n. Archit.* a battle-mented parapet or an overhanging corner turret at the top of a castle or church tower. □□ **bartizaned** *adj.* [var. of *bertisene*, erron. spelling of *bratticing*: see BRATTICE]

Bartók /ˈbɑːtɒk/, Béla (1881–1945), Hungarian composer, better known in his native country as a collector, with Kodály, of Magyar folk-songs, and as a pianist. He emigrated to the US in 1940, and there produced one of the works for which he is most famous, the *Concerto for Orchestra* (1943), dying in poverty two years later. His music is not obviously influenced by Hungarian idioms, and in his only opera, *Duke Bluebeard's Castle* (1911), he reveals an interest in Debussy and Schoenberg and also in recent developments in the study of psychology which led him to depict Bluebeard not as the standard bloodthirsty monster but as a personification of the loneliness and disillusionment of man. Bartók's string quartets, composed before he left for America, are regarded as his crowning achievement, combining perfectly balanced form and thematic integrity with the presentation of deeply personal emotions.

Bartolommeo /bɑːˌtɒlɒˈmeɪəʊ/, Fra Baccio della Porta (c.1472–1517), Florentine painter, who belonged to the period of transition from the early to the High Rennaissance. Deeply influenced by Savonarola, he entered the Dominican Order in 1499. His large-scale works are restrained and austere, and his ideals were balance and simplicity. He was one of the first to replace modern costume with generalized drapery in his religious figures.

Baruch /ˈbɑːrʊk/ a book of the Apocrypha, attributed in the text to Baruch, the scribe of Jeremiah (Jer. 36).

baryon /ˈbærɪˌɒn/ *n. Physics* an elementary particle that is of equal mass to or greater mass than a proton (i.e. is a nucleon or a hyperon). □□ **baryonic** /-ˈɒnɪk/ *adj.* [Gk *barus* heavy + -ON]

barysphere /ˈbærɪˌsfɪə(r)/ *n.* the dense interior of the earth, including the mantle and core, enclosed by the lithosphere. [Gk *barus* heavy + *sphaira* sphere]

baryta /bəˈraɪtə/ *n.* barium oxide or hydroxide. □□ **barytic** /-ˈrɪtɪk/ *adj.* [BARYTES, after *soda* etc.]

barytes /bəˈraɪtiːz/ *n.* a mineral form of barium sulphate. [Gk *barus* heavy, partly assim. to mineral names in -*ites*]

basal /ˈbeɪs(ə)l/ *adj.* **1** of, at, or forming a base. **2** fundamental. □ **basal metabolism** the chemical processes occurring in an organism at complete rest. [BASE¹ + -AL]

basalt /ˈbæsɔːlt/ *n.* **1** a dark basic volcanic rock whose strata sometimes form columns. **2** a kind of black stoneware resembling basalt. □□ **basaltic** /bəˈsɔːltɪk/ *adj.* [L *basaltes* var. of *basanites* f. Gk f. *basanos* touchstone]

bascule bridge /ˈbæskjuːl/ *n.* a type of drawbridge (see BRIDGE¹) which is raised and lowered using counterweights. [F, earlier *bacule* see-saw f. *battre* bump + *cul* buttocks]

base[1] /beɪs/ *n. & v.* —*n.* **1 a** a part that supports from beneath or serves as a foundation for an object or structure. **b** a notional structure or entity on which something draws or depends (*power base*). **2** a principle or starting-point; a basis. **3** esp. *Mil.* a place from which an operation or activity is directed. **4 a** a main or important ingredient of a mixture. **b** a substance, e.g. water, in combination with which pigment forms paint etc. **5** a substance used as a foundation for make-up. **6** *Chem.* a substance capable of combining with an acid to form a salt and water and usu. producing hydroxide ions when dissolved in water. The term includes alkalis but has wider application (see ALKALI). **7** *Math.* a number in terms of which other numbers or logarithms are expressed (see RADIX). **8** *Archit.* the part of a column between the shaft and pedestal or pavement. **9** *Geom.* a line or surface on which a figure is regarded as standing. **10** *Surveying* a known line used as a geometrical base for trigonometry. **11** *Electronics* the middle part of a transistor separating the emitter from the collector. **12** *Linguistics* a root or stem as the origin of a word or a derivative. **13** *Baseball* etc. one of the four stations that must be reached in turn when scoring a run. **14** *Bot. & Zool.* the end at which an organ is attached to the trunk. **15** *Heraldry* the lowest part of a shield. —*v.tr.* **1** (usu. foll. by *on*, *upon*) found or establish (*a theory based on speculation*; *his opinion was soundly based*). **2** (foll. by *at*, *in*, etc.) station (*troops were based in Malta*). □ **base hospital** esp. *Austral.* a hospital in a rural area, or (in warfare) removed from the field of action. **base pairing** *Biochem.* complementary binding by means of hydrogen bonds of a purine to a pyrimidine base in opposite strands of nucleic acids. **base rate** *Brit.* the interest rate set by the Bank of England, used as the basis for other banks' rates. **base unit** a unit that is defined arbitrarily and not by combinations of other units. [F *base* or L *basis* stepping f. Gk]

b *but* d *dog* f *few* g *get* h *he* j *yes* k *cat* l *leg* m *man* n *no* p *pen* r *red* s *sit* t *top* v *voice*

base² /beɪs/ *adj.* **1** lacking moral worth; cowardly, despicable. **2** menial. **3** not pure; alloyed (*base coin*). **4** (of a metal) low in value (opp. NOBLE, PRECIOUS). □□ **basely** *adv.* **baseness** *n.* [ME in sense 'of small height', f. F *bas* f. med.L *bassus* short (in L as a cognomen)]

baseball /ˈbeɪsbɔːl/ *n.* **1** a game evolved from rounders, with teams of nine players who in turn seek to strike the ball thrown by an opponent (the *pitcher*) and traverse a circuit of four points (*bases*). Long regarded as the American national game, it was played in simple form in both England and America (under the name 'base ball') from the mid-18th c., and is mentioned in Jane Austen's novel *Northanger Abbey*. The basic modern rules date from *c.*1845. **2** the ball used in this game.

baseboard /ˈbeɪsbɔːd/ *n. US* a skirting-board.

Basel see BASLE.

baseless /ˈbeɪslɪs/ *adj.* unfounded, groundless. □□ **baselessly** *adv.* **baselessness** *n.*

baseline /ˈbeɪslaɪn/ *n.* **1** a line used as a base or starting-point. **2** (in lawn tennis) the line marking each end of a court.

baseload /ˈbeɪsləʊd/ *n. Electr.* the permanent load on power supplies etc.

baseman /ˈbeɪsmən/ *n.* (*pl.* **-men**) *Baseball* a fielder stationed near a base.

basement /ˈbeɪsmənt/ *n.* the lowest floor of a building, usu. at least partly below ground level. [prob. Du., perh. f. It. *basamento* column-base]

bases *pl.* of BASE¹, BASIS.

bash /bæʃ/ *v.* & *n.* —*v.* **1** *tr.* **a** strike bluntly or heavily. **b** (often foll. by *up*) *colloq.* attack violently. **c** (often foll. by *down*, *in*, etc.) damage or break by striking forcibly. **2** *intr.* (foll. by *into*) collide with. —*n.* **1** a heavy blow. **2** *sl.* an attempt (*had a bash at painting*). **3** *sl.* a party or social event. [imit., perh. f. *bang*, *smash*, *dash*, etc.]

bashful /ˈbæʃfʊl/ *adj.* **1** shy, diffident, self-conscious. **2** sheepish. □□ **bashfully** *adv.* **bashfulness** *n.* [obs. *bash* (v.), = ABASH]

BASIC /ˈbeɪsɪk/ *n.* a computer programming language using familiar English words, designed for beginners and widely used on microcomputers. [*Beginner's All-purpose Symbolic Instruction Code*]

basic /ˈbeɪsɪk/ *adj.* & *n.* —*adj.* **1** forming or serving as a base. **2** fundamental. **3 a** simplest or lowest in level (*basic pay*; *basic requirements*). **b** vulgar (*basic humour*). **4** *Chem.* having the properties of or containing a base. **5** *Geol.* (of volcanic rocks etc.) having less than 50 per cent silica. **6** *Metallurgy* of or produced in a furnace etc. which is made of a basic material. —*n.* (usu. in *pl.*) the fundamental facts or principles. □ **basic dye** a dye consisting of salts of organic bases. **Basic English** a simplified form of English limited to 850 selected words intended for international communication. **basic industry** an industry of fundamental economic importance. **basic slag** fertilizer containing phosphates formed as a by-product during steel manufacture. **basic wage** *Austral.* & *NZ* the minimum living wage, fixed by industrial tribunal. □□ **basically** *adv.* [BASE¹ + -IC]

basicity /beɪˈsɪsɪtɪ/ *n. Chem.* the number of protons with which a base will combine.

basidium /bəˈsɪdɪəm/ *n.* (*pl.* **basidia** /-dɪə/) a microscopic spore-bearing structure produced by certain fungi. [mod.L f. Gk *basidion* dimin. of BASIS]

Basie /ˈbeɪsɪ/, 'Count' (1904–84), American jazz band-leader. He took up the piano at an early age, looking to figures such as 'Fats' Waller and Willie 'the Lion' Smith for his models, and became famous as leader of his own 'big band' from 1935.

Basil /ˈbæz(ə)l/, St, 'the Great' (*c.*330–79), a Doctor of the Church, brother of St Gregory of Nyssa and St Macrina. He was called from the hermit life to defend orthodoxy against the Arian emperor Valens, and in 370 was appointed bishop of Caesarea in Cappadocia. Eloquent, learned, and statesmanlike, he was endowed with a talent for organization, and the monastic rule which he put forward is still the basis of that followed in the Eastern Church. Feast day, 14 June.

basil /ˈbæz(ə)l/ *n.* an aromatic herb of the genus *Ocimum*, esp. *O.*

basilicum (in full **sweet basil**), whose leaves are used as a flavouring in savoury dishes. [ME f. OF *basile* f. med.L *basilicus* f. Gk *basilikos* royal]

basilar /ˈbæzɪlə(r)/ *adj.* of or at the base (esp. of the skull). [mod.L *basilaris* (as BASIS)]

basilica /bəˈzɪlɪkə/ *n.* **1** an ancient Roman public hall with an apse and colonnades, used as a lawcourt and place of assembly. **2** a similar building used as a Christian church. **3** a church having special privileges from the Pope. □□ **basilican** *adj.* [L f. Gk *basilikē* (*oikia*, *stoa*) royal (house, portico) f. *basileus* king]

Basilicata /bəˌsɪlɪˈkɑːtə/ a region of southern Italy, lying between the 'heel' of Apulia and the 'toe' of Calabria; pop. (1981) 610,200; capital, Potenza.

basilisk /ˈbæzɪlɪsk/ *n.* **1** a mythical reptile with a lethal breath and look. **2** any small American lizard of the genus *Basiliscus*, with a crest from its back to its tail. **3** *Heraldry* a cockatrice. [ME f. L *basiliscus* f. Gk *basiliskos* kinglet, serpent (so called, acc. to Pliny, from a spot resembling a crown on its head)]

basin /ˈbeɪs(ə)n/ *n.* **1** a wide shallow open container, esp. a fixed one for holding water. **2** a hollow rounded depression. **3** any sheltered area of water where boats can moor safely. **4** a round valley. **5** an area drained by rivers and tributaries. **6** *Geol.* **a** a rock formation where the strata dip towards the centre. **b** an accumulation of rock strata formed in this dip as a result of subsidence and sedimentation. □□ **basinful** *n.* (*pl.* **-fuls**). [ME f. OF *bacin* f. med.L *ba(s)cinus*, perh. f. Gaulish]

basipetal /beɪˈsɪpɪt(ə)l/ *adj. Bot.* (of each new part produced) developing nearer the base than the previous one did. □□ **basipetally** *adv.* [BASIS + L *petere* seek]

basis /ˈbeɪsɪs/ *n.* (*pl.* **bases** /-siːz/) **1** the foundation or support of something, esp. an idea or argument. **2** the main or determining principle or ingredient (*on a purely friendly basis*). **3** the starting-point for a discussion etc. [L f. Gk, = BASE¹]

bask /bɑːsk/ *v.intr.* **1** sit or lie back lazily in warmth and light (*basking in the sun*). **2** (foll. by *in*) derive great pleasure (from) (*basking in glory*). □ **basking shark** a very large shark, *Cetorhinus maximus*, which often lies near the surface. [ME, app. f. ON: rel. to BATHE]

Baskerville /ˈbæskəvɪl/, John (1706–75), English printer, who designed the typeface that bears his name.

basket /ˈbɑːskɪt/ *n.* **1** a container made of interwoven cane etc. **2** a container resembling this. **3** the amount held by a basket. **4** the goal in basketball, or a goal scored. **5** *euphem. colloq.* bastard. □ **basket of currencies** *Econ.* a group or range of selected currencies used to establish a value for some other unit of currency. **basket weave** a weave resembling that of a basket. □□ **basketful** *n.* (*pl.* **-fuls**). [AF & OF *basket*, AL *baskettum*, of unkn. orig.]

basketball /ˈbɑːskɪtbɔːl/ *n.* **1** a game played between teams of 5 or 6 players in which a goal is scored when the ball is thrown into a net fixed on a ring about 3 m (10 ft.) above the ground. It originated in the US in 1891, the invention of Dr J. A. Naismith (1861–1939), at Springfield, Mass. **2** the ball used in this game.

Basket Maker *n.* a member of a culture of the south-western US, forming the early stages of the Anasazi culture from the 1st c. BC until *c.*700 AD, so called from the basketry and other woven fragments found in early cave sites.

basketry /ˈbɑːskɪtrɪ/ *n.* **1** the art of making baskets. **2** baskets collectively.

basketwork /ˈbɑːskɪtˌwɜːk/ *n.* **1** material woven in the style of a basket. **2** the art of making this.

Basle /bɑːl/ (German **Basel** /ˈbɑːz(ə)l/) a commercial and industrial city on the Rhine in NE Switzerland; pop. (1986) 363,000. It is the focal point of the three-nation Regio Basiliensis which was set up in 1963 to coordinate the cultural and economic development of the French, German, and Swiss districts in the Upper Rhine Valley.

basmati /bæzˈmɑːtɪ/ *n.* (in full **basmati rice**) a superior kind of Indian rice. [Hindi, = fragrant]

Basque /bæsk, bɑːsk/ *n.* & *adj.* —*n.* **1** a member of a people living in the Western Pyrenees on both sides of the

French–Spanish border. **2** the language of this people. (See below.) —*adj.* of or relating to the Basques or their language. [F f. L *Vasco -onis*]

Culturally the Basques are one of the most distinct groups in Europe. While they do not differ physically from other European groups, their language, Basque, is not of the Indo-European language family and is unrelated to any other known tongue, though some similarities with Caucasian languages have been noted. This complex language, inherited from the ancient Vascones and predating the Roman conquest of the Iberian peninsula, is the only remnant of the languages spoken in SW Europe before the region was Romanized. It is spoken by some 700,000 people in the Pyrenees, but evidence of place-names suggests that it was originally current in a much wider area.

basque /bæsk/ *n.* a close-fitting bodice extending from the shoulders to the waist and often with a short continuation below waist level. [BASQUE]

Basra /ˈbæzrə/ an oil-port of Iraq, on the Shatt al-Arab waterway; pop. (est. 1985) 616,700.

bas-relief /ˈbæsrɪˌliːf/ *n.* sculpture or carving in which the figures project slightly from the background. [earlier *basse relieve* f. It. *basso rilievo* low relief: later altered to F form]

bass[1] /beɪs/ *n.* & *adj.* —*n.* **1 a** the lowest adult male singing voice. **b** a singer with this voice. **c** a part written for it. **2** the lowest part in harmonized music. **3 a** an instrument that is the lowest in pitch in its family. **b** its player. **4** *colloq.* **a** a bass guitar or double-bass. **b** its player. **5** the low-frequency output of a radio, record-player, etc., corresponding to the bass in music. —*adj.* **1** lowest in musical pitch. **2** deep-sounding. □ **bass clef** a clef placing F below middle C on the second highest line of the staff. **bass viol 1 a** a viola da gamba. **b** its player. **2** *US* a double-bass. □□ **bassist** *n.* (in sense 4). [alt. of BASE[2] after It. *basso*]

bass[2] /bæs/ *n.* (pl. same or **basses**) **1** the common perch. **2 a** a marine fish of the family Serranidae, with spiny fins. **b** a similar N. American marine fish, *Morone saxatilis*. **3** any of various American freshwater fish, esp. *Micropterus salmoides*. [earlier *barse* f. OE *bærs*]

bass[3] /bæs/ *n.* = BAST. [alt. f. BAST]

Bassein /bæˈseɪn/ a port on the Irrawaddy delta in SW Burma; pop. (1983) 144,100.

basset /ˈbæsɪt/ *n.* (in full **basset-hound**) **1** a sturdy hunting-dog of a breed with a long body, short legs, and big ears. **2** this breed. [F, dimin. of *bas basse* low: see BASE[2]]

Basseterre /bæsˈteə(r)/ the capital (on the island of St Kitts) of St Kitts and Nevis; pop. (1980) 14,300.

Basse-Terre /bæsˈteə(r)/ **1** the main island of Guadeloupe in the West Indies. **2** its capital city, situated on the SW corner of the island; pop. (1982) 13,650.

basset-horn /ˈbæsɪtˌhɔːn/ *n.* an alto clarinet in F, with a dark tone. [G, transl. of F *cor de bassette* f. It. *corno di bassetto* f. *corno* horn + *bassetto* dimin. of *basso* BASE[2]]

bassinet /ˌbæsɪˈnet/ *n.* a child's wicker cradle, usu. with a hood. [F, dimin. of *bassin* BASIN]

basso /ˈbæsəʊ/ *n.* (pl. **-os** or **bassi** /-sɪ/) a singer with a bass voice. □ **basso profondo** a bass singer with an exceptionally low range. [It., = BASS[1]; *profondo* deep]

bassoon /bəˈsuːn/ *n.* **1 a** a bass instrument of the oboe family, with a double reed. (See below.) **b** its player. **2** an organ stop with the quality of a bassoon. □□ **bassoonist** *n.* (in sense 1). [F *basson* f. *bas* BASS[1]]

The bassoon dates from about the 1660s. It has a range of about three-and-a-half octaves, and is a standard orchestral instrument. It is often used for comic effect but also has a capacity for melancholy which has not been overlooked by composers. The contrabassoon, or double bassoon, has a range an octave deeper than the bassoon's.

basso-rilievo /ˌbæsəʊrɪˈljeɪvəʊ/ *n.* (pl. **-os**) = BAS-RELIEF. [It.]

Bass Strait /bæs/ a channel separating the island of Tasmania from the mainland of Australia.

basswood /ˈbæswʊd/ *n.* **1** the American lime, *Tilia americana*. **2** the wood of this tree. [BASS[3] + WOOD]

bast /bæst/ *n.* the inner bark of lime, or other flexible fibrous bark, used as fibre in matting etc. [OE *bæst* f. Gmc]

bastard /ˈbɑːstəd, ˈbæ-/ *n.* & *adj.* —*n.* **1** a person born of parents not married to each other. **2** *sl.* **a** an unpleasant or despicable person. **b** a person of a specified kind (*poor bastard*; *rotten bastard*; *lucky bastard*). **3** *sl.* a difficult or awkward thing, undertaking, etc. —*adj.* **1** born of parents not married to each other; illegitimate. **2** (of things): **a** unauthorized, counterfeit. **b** hybrid. □□ **bastardy** *n.* (in sense 1 of *n.*). [ME f. OF f. med.L *bastardus*, perh. f. *bastum* pack-saddle]

bastardize /ˈbɑːstəˌdaɪz/ *v.tr.* (also **-ise**) **1** declare (a person) illegitimate. **2** corrupt, debase. □□ **bastardization** /-ˈzeɪʃ(ə)n/ *n.*

baste[1] /beɪst/ *v.tr.* moisten (meat) with gravy or melted fat during cooking. [16th c.: orig. unkn.]

baste[2] /beɪst/ *v.tr.* stitch loosely together in preparation for sewing; tack. [ME f. OF *bastir* sew lightly, ult. f. Gmc]

baste[3] /beɪst/ *v.tr.* beat soundly; thrash. [perh. figurative use of BASTE[1]]

Bastet /ˈbæstet/ *Egyptian Mythol.* a goddess usually shown as a woman with the head of a cat, wearing one gold earring.

Bastia /bæˈstiːə/ the chief port of Corsica; pop. (1982) 45,000.

Bastille /bæˈstiːl/ a fortress in Paris built in the 14th c. and used in the 17th–18th c. as a State prison. It became a symbol of despotism and its storming by the mob on 14 July 1789 marked the start of the French Revolution; the anniversary of this event is kept as a national holiday. [ME f. OF *bastille* f. Prov. *bastir* build: orig. of the fortress and prison in Paris, destroyed in 1789]

bastinado /ˌbæstɪˈneɪdəʊ/ *n.* & *v.* —*n.* punishment by beating with a stick on the soles of the feet. —*v.tr.* (**-oes, -oed**) punish (a person) in this way. [Sp. *bastonada* f. *baston* BATON]

bastion /ˈbæstɪən/ *n.* **1** a projecting part of a fortification built at an angle of, or against the line of, a wall. **2** a thing regarded as protecting (*bastion of freedom*). **3** a natural rock formation resembling a bastion. [F f. It. *bastione* f. *bastire* build]

Basutoland /bəˈsuːtəʊˌlænd/ the former name (until 1966) of Lesotho.

bat[1] /bæt/ *n.* & *v.* —*n.* **1** an implement with a handle, usu. of wood and with a flat or curved surface, used for hitting balls in games. **2** a turn at using this. **3** a batsman, esp. in cricket, usu. described in some way (*an excellent bat*). **4** (usu. in *pl.*) an object like a table-tennis bat used to guide aircraft when taxiing. —*v.* (**batted, batting**) **1** *tr.* hit with or as with a bat. **2** *intr.* take a turn at batting. □ **bat around 1** *sl.* potter aimlessly. **2** *US* discuss (an idea or proposal). **off one's own bat** unprompted, unaided. **right off the bat** *US* immediately. [ME f. OE *batt* club, perh. partly f. OF *batte* club f. *battre* strike]

bat[2] /bæt/ *n.* any mouselike nocturnal mammal of the order Chiroptera, capable of flight by means of membranous wings extending from its forelimbs. □ **have bats in the belfry** be eccentric or crazy. **like a bat out of hell** very fast. [16th c., alt. of ME *bakke* f. Scand.]

bat[3] /bæt/ *v.tr.* (**batted, batting**) wink (one's eyelid) (now usu. in phr.). □ **not** (or **never**) **bat an eyelid** *colloq.* show no reaction or emotion. [var. of obs. *bate* flutter]

Bata /ˈbɑːtə/ a seaport and the largest town of Equatorial Guinea; pop. (est. 1986) 17,000.

Batan Islands /bəˈtɑːn/ a group of islands in the northern Philippines, lying between the Babuyan Islands and Taiwan.

Batavia /bəˈteɪvɪə/ the former name (until 1949) of Djakarta.

batch /bætʃ/ *n.* & *v.* —*n.* **1** a number of things or persons forming a group or dealt with together. **2** an instalment (*have sent off the latest batch*). **3** the loaves produced at one baking. **4** (*attrib.*) using or dealt with in batches, not as a continuous flow (*batch production*). **5** *Computing* a group of records processed as a single unit. —*v.tr.* arrange or deal with in batches. [ME f. OE *bæcce* f. *bacan* BAKE]

Batdambang see BATTAMBANG.

bate /beɪt/ *n.* (also **bait**) *Brit. sl.* a rage; a cross mood (*is in an awful bate*). [BAIT[1] = state of baited person]

bateau /ˈbætəʊ/ n. (pl. **bateaux** /-əʊz/) a light river-boat, esp. of the flat-bottomed kind used in Canada. [F, = boat]

bated /ˈbeɪtɪd/ adj. □ **with bated breath** very anxiously. [past part. of obs. *bate* (v.) restrain, f. ABATE]

bateleur /ˌbætəˈlɜː(r)/ n. a short-tailed African eagle, *Terathopius ecaudatus*. [F, = juggler]

Bates[1] /beɪts/, Henry Walter (1825–92), English naturalist, a friend and colleague of A. R. Wallace with whom he travelled in Brazil, and author of *The Naturalist on the River Amazons* (1863). The phenomenon known as 'Batesian mimicry' is named after him: noting the resemblance of certain animals, especially insects, to their natural backgrounds, and the fact that certain edible species of butterfly resemble those avoided by predators, Bates suggested that, by natural selection, those who 'mimic' in this way are more likely to survive.

Bates[2] /beɪts/, Herbert Ernest (1905–74), English novelist and writer of short stories. His novels include *Love for Lydia* (1952) and *The Darling Buds of May* (1958); many of them were successfully dramatized for television.

bath /bɑːθ/ n. & v. —n. (pl. **baths** /bɑːðz/) **1 a** (in full **bath-tub**) a container for liquid, usu. water, used for immersing and washing the body. **b** this with its contents (*your bath is ready*). **2** the act or process of immersing the body for washing or therapy (*have a bath; take a bath*). **3 a** a vessel containing liquid in which something is immersed, e.g. a film for developing, for controlling temperature, etc. **b** this with its contents. **4** (usu. in pl.) a building with baths or a swimming pool, usu. open to the public. —v. *Brit.* **1** *tr.* wash (esp. a person) in a bath. **2** *intr.* take a bath. □ **bath cube** a cube of compacted bath salts. **bath salts** soluble salts used for softening or scenting bath-water. **Order of the Bath** an order of knighthood, so called from the ceremonial bath which originally preceded installation. [OE *bæth* f. Gmc]

Bath bun /bɑːθ/ n. *Brit.* a round spiced kind of bun with currants, often iced. [*Bath* in S. England, named from its hot springs]

Bath chair /bɑːθ/ n. a wheelchair for invalids.

Bath chap see CHAP[3].

bathe /beɪð/ v. & n. —v. **1** *intr.* immerse oneself in water, esp. to swim or esp. *US* wash oneself. **2** *tr.* immerse in or wash or treat with liquid esp. for cleansing or medicinal purposes. **3** *tr.* (of sunlight etc.) envelop. —n. *Brit.* immersion in liquid, esp. to swim. □ **bathing-costume** (or **-suit**) a garment worn for swimming. [OE *bathian* f. Gmc]

bather /ˈbeɪðə(r)/ n. **1** a person who bathes. **2** (in pl.) *Austral.* a bathing-suit.

bathhouse /ˈbɑːθhaʊs/ n. a building with baths for public use.

batholith /ˈbæθəlɪθ/ n. a dome of igneous rock extending inwards to an unknown depth. [G f. Gk *bathos* depth + -LITH]

Bath Oliver /ˌbɑːθ ˈɒlɪvə(r)/ n. *Brit. propr.* a kind of savoury biscuit. [Dr W. *Oliver* of *Bath* d. 1764, who invented it]

bathometer /bəˈθɒmɪtə(r)/ n. an instrument used to measure the depth of water. [Gk *bathos* depth + -METER]

bathos /ˈbeɪθɒs/ n. an unintentional lapse in mood from the sublime to the absurd or trivial; a commonplace or ridiculous feature offsetting an otherwise sublime situation; an anticlimax. □□ **bathetic** /bəˈθetɪk/ adj. **bathotic** /bəˈθɒtɪk/ adj. [Gk, = depth]

bathrobe /ˈbɑːθrəʊb/ n. *US* a loose coat usu. of towelling worn before and after taking a bath.

bathroom /ˈbɑːθruːm, -rʊm/ n. **1** a room containing a bath and usu. other washing facilities. **2** esp. *US* a room containing a lavatory.

Bathsheba /bæθˈʃiːbə, ˈbæθʃɪbə/ the wife of Uriah the Hittite (2 Sam. 11). She became one of the wives of David, who had caused her husband to be killed in battle, and was the mother of Solomon.

Bathurst /ˈbæθɜːst/ the former name (until 1973) of Banjul.

bathyscaphe /ˈbæθɪˌskæf/ n. a manned vessel for deep-sea diving. [Gk *bathus* deep + *skaphos* ship]

bathysphere /ˈbæθɪˌsfɪə(r)/ n. a spherical vessel for deep-sea observation. [Gk *bathus* deep + SPHERE]

batik /bəˈtiːk, ˈbætɪk/ n. a method (orig. used in Java) of producing coloured designs on textiles by applying wax to the parts to be left uncoloured; a piece of cloth treated in this way. [Jav., = painted]

Batista /bəˈtiːstə/, Fulgencio (full name Batista y Zalvídar, 1901–73), Cuban soldier and dictator, President of Cuba 1940–4 and 1954–9 after military coups in 1933 and 1952. Although supported by the US his second government was notoriously corrupt and ruthless, and was overthrown by an uprising under the leadership of Fidel Castro.

batiste /bæˈtiːst/ n. & adj. —n. a fine linen or cotton cloth. —adj. made of batiste. [F (earlier *batiche*), perh. rel. to *battre* BATTER[1]]

batman /ˈbætmən/ n. (pl. **-men**) *Mil.* an attendant serving an officer. [OF *bat*, *bast* f. med.L *bastum* pack-saddle + MAN]

baton /ˈbæt(ə)n/ n. **1** a thin stick used by a conductor to direct an orchestra, choir, etc. **2** *Athletics* a short stick or tube carried and passed on by the runners in a relay race. **3** a long stick carried and twirled by a drum major. **4** a staff of office or authority, esp. a Field Marshal's. **5** a policeman's truncheon. **6** *Heraldry* a narrow truncated bend. **7** *Horol.* a short bar replacing some figures on dials. □ **baton round** a rubber or plastic bullet. [F *bâton*, *baston* ult. f. LL *bastum* stick]

Baton Rouge /ˌbæt(ə) ˈruːʒ/ the capital of the State of Louisiana, situated on the east bank of the Mississippi; pop. (1982) 361,600.

batrachian /bəˈtreɪkɪən/ n. & adj. —n. any of the amphibians that discard gills and tails, esp. the frog and toad. —adj. of or relating to the batrachians. [Gk *batrakhos* frog]

bats /bæts/ *predic.adj. sl.* crazy. [f. phr. (*have*) *bats in the belfry*: see BAT[2]]

batsman /ˈbætsmən/ n. (pl. **-men**) **1** a person who bats or is batting, esp. in cricket. **2** a signaller using bats to guide aircraft on the ground. □□ **batsmanship** n. (in sense 1).

battalion /bəˈtælɪən/ n. **1** a large body of men ready for battle, esp. an infantry unit forming part of a brigade. **2** a large group of people pursuing a common aim or sharing a major undertaking. [F *battaillon* f. It. *battaglione* f. *battaglia* BATTLE]

Battambang /ˈbætəmˌbæŋ/ (also **Batdambang**) **1** the principal agricultural region of Cambodia, lying to the west of Phnom Penh. **2** its capital city, the second largest city in the country; pop. (1981) 551,860.

battels /ˈbæt(ə)lz/ n.pl. *Brit.* an Oxford college account for expenses, esp. for board and the supply of provisions. [perh. f. obs. *battle* (v.) fatten f. obs. *battle* (adj.) nutritious: cf. BATTEN[2]]

batten[1] /ˈbæt(ə)n/ n. & v. —n. **1** a long flat strip of squared timber or metal, esp. used to hold something in place or as a fastening against a wall etc. **2** a strip of wood used for clamping the boards of a door etc. **3** *Naut.* a strip of wood or metal for securing a tarpaulin over a ship's hatchway. —v.tr. strengthen or fasten with battens. □ **batten down the hatches 1** *Naut.* secure a ship's tarpaulins. **2** prepare for a difficulty or crisis. [OF *batant* part. of *batre* beat f. L *battuere*]

batten[2] /ˈbæt(ə)n/ v.intr. (foll. by on) thrive or prosper at another's expense. [ON *batna* get better f. *bati* advantage]

Battenberg /ˈbæt(ə)nˌbɜːg/ n. a kind of oblong cake, usu. of two colours of sponge and covered with marzipan. [*Battenberg* in Germany]

batter[1] /ˈbætə(r)/ v. **1 a** *tr.* strike repeatedly with hard blows, esp. so as to cause visible damage. **b** *intr.* (often foll. by *against*, *at*, etc.) strike repeated blows; pound heavily and insistently (*batter at the door*). **2** *tr.* (often in *passive*) a handle roughly, esp. over a long period. **b** censure or criticize severely. □ **battered baby** an infant that has suffered repeated violence from adults, esp. its parents. **battered wife** a wife subjected to repeated violence by her husband. **battering-ram** *hist.* a heavy beam, orig. with an end in the form of a carved ram's head, used in breaching fortifications. □□ **batterer** n. [ME f. AF *baterer* f. OF *batre* beat f. L *battuere*]

batter[2] /ˈbætə(r)/ n. **1** a fluid mixture of flour, egg, and milk or water, used in cooking, esp. for pancakes and for coating food before frying. **2** *Printing* an area of damaged type. [ME f. AF *batour* f. OF *bateüre* f. *batre*: see BATTER¹]

batter³ /'bætə(r)/ *n. Sport* a player batting, esp. in baseball.

batter⁴ /'bætə(r)/ *n. & v.* —*n.* **1** a wall etc. with a sloping face. **2** a receding slope. —*v.intr.* have a receding slope. [ME: orig. unkn.]

battered /'bætəd/ *adj.* (esp. of fish) coated in batter and deep-fried.

battery /'bætəri/ *n.* (*pl.* **-ies**) **1** a usu. portable container of a cell or cells carrying an electric charge, as a source of current. (See below.) **2** (often *attrib.*) esp. *Brit.* a series of cages for the intensive breeding and rearing of poultry or cattle. **3** a set of similar units of equipment, esp. connected. **4** a series of tests, esp. psychological. **5 a** a fortified emplacement for heavy guns. **b** an artillery unit of guns, men, and vehicles. **6** *Law* an act inflicting unlawful personal violence on another (see ASSAULT). **7** *Baseball* the pitcher and the catcher. [F *batterie* f. *batre*, *battre* strike f. L *battuere*]
The first electric battery was made in 1800 by Alessandro Volta, who caused a current to pass through a wire by attaching it to two different metals (zinc and copper) in a salt solution. Dry batteries derive from a Leclanché cell, with the electrolyte in the form of a paste or jelly instead of a liquid.

Batticaloa /ˌbætɪkəˈləʊə/ a city in the east of Sri Lanka, on an inlet of the Bay of Bengal; pop. (1981) 42,900.

batting /'bætɪŋ/ *n.* **1** the action of hitting with a bat. **2** cotton wadding prepared in sheets for use in quilts etc. □ **batting order** the order in which people act or take their turn, esp. of batsmen in cricket.

battle /'bæt(ə)l/ *n. & v.* —*n.* **1** a prolonged fight between large organized armed forces. **2** a contest; a prolonged or difficult struggle (*life is a constant battle*; *a battle of wits*). —*v.* **1** *intr.* struggle; fight persistently (*battled against the elements*; *battled for women's rights*). **2** *tr.* fight (one's way etc.). **3** *tr. US* engage in battle with. □ **battle-cruiser** *hist.* a heavy-gunned ship faster and more lightly armoured than a battleship. **battle-cry** a cry or slogan of participants in a battle or contest. **battle fatigue** = *combat fatigue*. **Battle of the Atlantic** see ATLANTIC. **Battle of Britain** see BRITAIN. **battle royal 1** a battle in which several combatants or all available forces engage; a free fight. **2** a heated argument. **half the battle** the key to the success of an undertaking. □□ **battler** *n.* [ME f. OF *bataille* ult. f. LL *battualia* gladiatorial exercises f. L *battuere* beat]

battleaxe /'bæt(ə)lˌæks/ *n.* **1** a large axe used in ancient warfare. **2** *colloq.* a formidable or domineering older woman.

battledore /'bæt(ə)lˌdɔː(r)/ *n. hist.* **1 a** (in full **battledore and shuttlecock**) a volleying game played with a shuttlecock and rackets, which dates at least from the 18th c. The game of badminton may have developed from it. **b** the racket used in this. **2** a kind of wooden utensil like a paddle, formerly used in washing, baking, etc. [15th c., perh. f. Prov. *batedor* beater f. *batre* beat]

battledress /'bæt(ə)lˌdres/ *n.* the everyday uniform of a soldier.

battlefield /'bæt(ə)lˌfiːld/ *n.* (also **battleground** /-ˌgraʊnd/) the piece of ground on which a battle is or was fought.

battlement /'bæt(ə)lmənt/ *n.* (usu. in *pl.*) **1** a parapet with recesses along the top of a wall, as part of a fortification. **2** a section of roof enclosed by this (*walking on the battlements*). □□ **battlemented** *adj.* [OF *bataillier* furnish with ramparts + -MENT]

battleship /'bæt(ə)lˌʃɪp/ *n.* a warship with the heaviest armour and the largest guns.

battue /bæ'tjuː, bæ'tuː/ *n.* **1 a** the driving of game towards hunters by beaters. **b** a shooting-party arranged in this way. **2** wholesale slaughter. [F, fem. past part. of *battre* beat f. L *battuere*]

batty /'bætɪ/ *adj.* (**battier, battiest**) *sl.* crazy. □□ **battily** *adv.* **battiness** *n.* [BAT² + -Y¹]

batwing /'bætwɪŋ/ *adj.* (esp. of a sleeve or a flame) shaped like the wing of a bat.

batwoman /'bætˌwʊmən/ *n.* (*pl.* **-women**) a female attendant serving an officer in the women's services. [as BATMAN + WOMAN]

bauble /'bɔːb(ə)l/ *n.* **1** a showy trinket or toy of little value. **2** a baton formerly used as an emblem by jesters. [ME f. OF *ba(u)bel* child's toy, of unkn. orig.]

Baucis /'bɔːkɪs/ *Gk Mythol.* the wife of Philemon (see PHILEMON¹).

baud /baʊd, bɔːd/ *n.* (*pl.* same or **bauds**) *Computing* etc. **1** a unit used to express the speed of electronic code signals, corresponding to one information unit per second. **2** (loosely) a unit of data-transmission speed of one bit per second. [J. M. E. *Baudot*, Fr. engineer d. 1903]

Baudelaire /ˈbəʊdəˌleə(r)/, Charles (1821–67), French poet and critic. In 1842 he inherited a large fortune and lived extravagantly until his family intervened and put his inheritance in trust, allowing him only a limited income, which he supplemented by following a literary career. He began writing reviews, and made translations of Edgar Allen Poe. His *Les Fleurs du mal* (1857), one of the great collections of French verse, is a series of 101 exquisitely composed lyrics in a variety of metres, exploring his own sense of isolation, exile and sin, boredom and melancholy, the attraction of evil and vice, and the fascination and degradation of Paris life. On publication he was fined and six of the poems were banned as offensive to public morals. By 1864 his resources were exhausted and he lived a dissipated life in Brussels while trying to earn a living by lecturing; he returned to Paris (1866) with general paralysis and died in obscurity, though by the end of the 19th c. leaders of the symbolist movement were acknowledging a debt to him. Like his poetic genius, his critical writing was little appreciated in his time but his stature is now universally recognized. His essays on Paris salons, on Delacroix, Gautier, Flaubert, and Wagner, were collected posthumously in *Curiosités esthétiques* and *L'Art romantique* (1868).

Bauhaus /'baʊhaʊs/ the school of design established by Gropius in Weimar in Germany in 1919, whence it moved to Dessau in 1925. Its style is characterized by emphasis on architectonic form and smooth linearity, employing the resources of modern technology while continuing to take account of the tradition of the Arts and Crafts movement. Gropius fostered the idea of the artist as craftsman and saw the school as exemplifying the need for cooperation amongst artists working in different disciplines, from architecture to painting, sculpture, weaving, and the design of objects for utilitarian use; Breuer's tubular steel chair is perhaps the best-known consumer design to have emerged. The socialist principles on which Bauhaus ideas rested incurred the inevitable hostility of the Nazis and the school was closed in 1933. The resultant movement abroad of teachers and pupils has ensured the international dissemination of its style and ideas. [G f. *Bau* building + *Haus* house]

baulk /bɔːlk, bɔːk/ *v. & n.* (also **balk**) —*v.* **1** *intr.* **a** refuse to go on. **b** (often foll. by *at*) hesitate. **2** *tr.* **a** thwart, hinder. **b** disappoint. **3** *tr.* **a** miss, let slip (a chance etc.). **b** ignore, shirk. —*n.* **1** a hindrance; a stumbling-block. **2 a** a roughly-squared timber beam. **b** a tie-beam of a house. **3** *Billiards* etc. the area on a billiard-table from which a player begins a game. **4** *Baseball* an illegal action made by a pitcher. **5** a ridge left unploughed between furrows. □□ **baulker** *n.* [OE *balc* f. ON *bálkr* f. Gmc]

baulky /'bɔːlkɪ/ *adj.* (also **balky**) (**-ier, -iest**) reluctant, perverse. □□ **baulkiness** *n.* [BAULK + -Y¹]

bauxite /'bɔːksaɪt/ *n.* a claylike mineral containing varying proportions of alumina, the chief source of aluminium. □□ **bauxitic** /-'sɪtɪk/ *adj.* [F f. *Les Baux* near Arles in S. France + -ITE¹]

Bavaria /bə'veərɪə/ (German **Bayern** /'baɪəːn/) a 'Land' (State) of Germany; pop. (1987) 11,043,000; capital, Munich. □□ **Bavarian** *adj. & n.*

bawd /bɔːd/ *n.* a woman who runs a brothel. [ME *bawdstrot* f. OF *baudetrot, baudestroyt* procuress]

bawdy /'bɔːdɪ/ *adj. & n.* —*adj.* (**bawdier, bawdiest**) humorously indecent. —*n.* bawdy talk or writing. □ **bawdy-house** a brothel. □□ **bawdily** *adv.* **bawdiness** *n.* [BAWD + -Y¹]

bawl /bɔːl/ *v.* **1** *tr.* speak or call out noisily. **2** *intr.* weep loudly. □ **bawl out** *colloq.* reprimand angrily. □□ **bawler** *n.* [imit.: cf. med.L *baulare* bark, Icel. *baula* (Sw. *böla*) to low]

b *but*   d *dog*   f *few*   g *get*   h *he*   j *yes*   k *cat*   l *leg*   m *man*   n *no*   p *pen*   r *red*   s *sit*   t *top*   v *voice*

Bax /bæks/, Sir Arnold (1883–1953), English composer, who was greatly influenced by the poetry of Yeats and by Irish folk music. He was born in London and had no Irish blood, but travelled in Ireland and wrote short stories under the pseudonym Dermot O'Byrne. His tone poems are the best known of his works today, but he also composed seven symphonies, chamber works, choral music, and some attractive piano pieces.

Baxter /'bækstə(r)/, James Keir (1926–72), New Zealand poet, noted especially for his lyric verse, which includes *Cressida* (1951), a sequence on an unhappy love affair, and for his published lectures on New Zealand poetry.

bay[1] /beɪ/ n. **1** a broad inlet of the sea where the land curves inwards. **2** a recess in a mountain range. □ **Bay State** US Massachusetts. [ME f. OF *baie* f. OSp. *bahia*]

bay[2] /beɪ/ n. **1** (in full **bay laurel**) a laurel, *Laurus nobilis*, having deep green leaves and purple berries. Also called SWEET BAY. **2** (in *pl.*) a wreath made of bay-leaves, for a victor or poet. □ **bay-leaf** the aromatic (usu. dried) leaf of the bay-tree, used in cooking. **bay rum** a perfume, esp. for the hair, distilled orig. from bayberry leaves in rum. [OF *baie* f. L *baca* berry]

bay[3] /beɪ/ n. **1** a space created by a window-line projecting outwards from a wall. **2** a recess; a section of wall between buttresses or columns, esp. in the nave of a church etc. **3** a compartment (*bomb bay*). **4** an area specially allocated or marked off (*sick bay; loading bay*). **5** *Brit.* the terminus of a branch line at a railway station also having through lines, usu. at the side of an outer platform. □ **bay window** a window built into a bay. [ME f. OF *baie* f. *ba(y)er* gape f. med.L *batare*]

bay[4] /beɪ/ adj. & n. —adj. (esp. of a horse) dark reddish-brown. —n. a bay horse with a black mane and tail. [OF *bai* f. L *badius*]

bay[5] /beɪ/ v. & n. —v. **1** intr. (esp. of a large dog) bark or howl loudly and plaintively. **2** tr. bay at. —n. the sound of baying, esp. in chorus from hounds in close pursuit. □ **at bay 1** cornered, apparently unable to escape. **2** in a desperate situation. **bring to bay** gain on in pursuit; trap. **hold** (or **keep**) **at bay** hold off (a pursuer). **stand at bay** turn to face one's pursuers. [ME f. OF *bai, baïer* bark f. It. *baiare*, of imit. orig.]

Bayard /'beɪɑːd/, Pierre du Terrail, Seigneur de (1473–1524), French soldier of great valour and chivalry, known as the knight 'sans peur et sans reproche' (fearless and above reproach).

bayberry /'beɪbərɪ/ n. (*pl.* -**ies**) any of various N. American plants of the genus *Myrica*, having aromatic leaves and bearing berries covered in a wax coating. [BAY[2] + BERRY]

Bayer /'baɪə(r)/, Johann Friedrich Wilhelm Adolf von (1835–1917), German organic chemist, best known for the discovery of synthetic indigo. He was taught by both Bunsen and Kekulé. A very fine chemical experimenter, he had a profound influence on organic chemistry and subsequently on the emerging field of biochemistry. He was awarded the 1905 Nobel Prize for chemistry for his work on dyes and hydro-aromatic compounds.

Bayern see BAVARIA.

Bayeux Tapestry /baɪ'jɜː/ a superb example of Anglo-Saxon embroidery (it is not really a tapestry) executed between 1066 and 1077, probably at Canterbury, for Odo, bishop of Bayeux and half-brother of William the Conqueror, and now exhibited at Bayeux in Normandy. It is 48 cm (19 in.) wide and, although incomplete, 70 m (230 ft.) long. In 79 racy and colourful scenes, accompanied by a Latin text and arranged like a strip cartoon, it tells the story of the Norman Conquest and the events that led up to it. It is an important historical record, relating incidents not recorded elsewhere, and is a source of information on such things as armour, clothes, and boats. The colours, of which there are eight, are used for decorative rather than descriptive purposes.

Baylis /'beɪlɪs/, Lilian Mary (1874–1937), English theatre manageress. An intensely religious and single-minded woman, she devoted herself to the founding and running of popular homes for drama and opera in London. Under her management the Old Vic acquired a reputation as the world's leading house of Shakespearean productions, and her initiative in reopening the old Sadler's Wells Theatre in 1931 led to the development of the Royal Ballet and the English National Opera.

Bay of Pigs Cochinos Bay, a bay on the SW coast of Cuba, where on 17 Apr. 1961 about 1,500 Cuban exiles, with the support of the American CIA, made an unsuccessful attempt to invade the country and overthrow the regime of Fidel Castro. The newly inaugurated President Kennedy refused the expected US air support, and the operation was a fiasco. Castro's prestige and popularity rose as a result of this, and Kennedy emphasized the need for strict presidential control of the CIA and its overseas activities.

Bay of Plenty an administrative region of North Island, New Zealand, situated between the Thames Valley and East Cape; pop. (1986) 187,500; chief town, Tauranga.

bayonet /'beɪə,net/ n. & v. —n. **1** a stabbing blade attachable to the muzzle of a rifle. **2** an electrical or other fitting engaged by being pushed into a socket and twisted. —v.tr. (**bayoneted**, **bayoneting**) stab with a bayonet. [F *baïonnette*, perh. f. *Bayonne* in SW France, where they were first made]

bayou /'baɪuː/ n. a marshy offshoot of a river etc. in the southern US. [Amer. F: cf. Choctau *bayuk*]

Bayreuth /baɪˈrɔɪt, -'rɔɪt/ a town in Bavaria, Germany, where Wagner made his home from 1874 and where he is buried. Festivals of his operas are held regularly in a theatre specially built (1872–6) to house performances of *Der Ring des Nibelungen*.

bazaar /bə'zɑː(r)/ n. **1** a market in an oriental country. **2** a fund-raising sale of goods, esp. for charity. **3** a large shop selling fancy goods etc. [Pers. *bāzār*, prob. through Turk. and It.]

bazooka /bə'zuːkə/ n. **1** a tubular short-range rocket-launcher used against tanks. **2** a crude trombone-like musical instrument. [app. f. *bazoo* mouth, of unkn. orig.]

BB abbr. double-black (pencil-lead).

BBC abbr. British Broadcasting Corporation, a public corporation originally having the monopoly of broadcasting in Britain, financed by a grant-in-aid from Parliament. It was established in 1927 by royal charter to carry on work previously performed by the British Broadcasting Company. □ **BBC English** English as supposedly pronounced by BBC announcers.

bbl. abbr. barrels (esp. of oil).

BC abbr. British Columbia.

BC abbr. (of a date) before Christ.

BCD /ˌbiːsiːˈdiː/ n. Computing a code representing decimal numbers as a string of binary digits. [abbr. for binary coded decimal]

BCE abbr. before the Common Era.

BCG abbr. Bacillus Calmette-Guérin, an anti-tuberculosis vaccine.

BD abbr. Bachelor of Divinity.

Bde abbr. Brigade.

bdellium /'delɪəm/ n. **1** any of various trees, esp. of the genus *Commiphora*, yielding resin. **2** this fragrant resin used in perfumes. [L f. Gk *bdellion* f. Heb. *bedhōlaḥ*]

Bdr. abbr. (before a name) Bombardier.

BDS abbr. Bachelor of Dental Surgery.

BE abbr. **1** Bachelor of Education. **2** Bachelor of Engineering. **3** bill of exchange.

Be symb. Chem. the element beryllium.

be /biː, bɪ/ v. & v.aux. (*sing. present* **am** /æm, əm/; **are** /ɑː(r), ə(r)/; **is** /ɪz/; *pl. present* **are**; *1st and 3rd sing. past* **was** /wɒz, wəz/; *2nd sing. past and pl. past* **were** /wɜː(r), wə(r)/; *present subj.* **be**; *past subj.* **were**; *pres. part.* **being**; *past part.* **been** /biːn, bɪn/) —v.intr. **1** (often prec. by *there*) exist, live (*I think, therefore I am; there is a house on the corner; there is no God*). **2 a** occur; take place (*dinner is at eight*). **b** occupy a position in space (*he is in the garden; she is from abroad; have you been to Paris?*). **3** remain, continue (*let it be*). **4** linking subject and predicate, expressing: **a** identity (*she is the person; today is Thursday*). **b** condition (*he is ill today*). **c** state or quality (*he is very kind; they are my friends*). **d** opinion (*I am against hanging*). **e** total (*two and two are four*). **f** cost or significance (*it is £5 to enter; it is nothing to me*). —v.aux. **1** with a past participle to form the passive mood (*it was done; it is said; we shall be helped*). **2** with a present participle to form continuous tenses (*we are coming; it is being cleaned*). **3** with an infinitive to express duty or commitment, intention, possibility, destiny, or hypothesis (*I am* *to tell you; we are to wait here; he is to come at four; it was not to be found; they were never to meet again; if I were to die).* **4** *archaic* with the past participle of intransitive verbs to form perfect tenses (*the sun is set; Babylon is fallen*). □ **be about** occupy oneself with (*is about his business*). **be-all and end-all** *colloq.* (often foll. by *of*) the whole being or essence. **be at** occupy oneself with (*what is he at?; mice have been at the food*). **been** (or **been and gone) and** *sl.* an expression of protest or surprise (*he's been and taken my car!*). **be off** *colloq.* go away; leave. **be that as it may** see MAY. **-to-be** of the future (in *comb.*: *bride-to-be*). [OE *beo(m), (e)am, is, (e)aron*; past f. OE *wæs* f. *wesan* to be; there are numerous Gmc cognates]

be- /bɪ/ *prefix* forming verbs: **1** (from transitive verbs) **a** all over; all round (*beset; besmear*). **b** thoroughly, excessively (*begrudge; belabour*). **2** (from intransitive verbs) expressing transitive action (*bemoan; bestride*). **3** (from adjectives and nouns) expressing transitive action (*befool; befoul*). **4** (from nouns) **a** affect with (*befog*). **b** treat as (*befriend*). **c** (forming adjectives in -ed) having; covered with (*bejewelled; bespectacled*). [OE *be-*, weak form of *bī* BY as in *bygone, byword*, etc.]

BEA *abbr.* British Epilepsy Association.

beach /biːtʃ/ *n. & v.* —*n.* a pebbly or sandy shore esp. of the sea between high- and low-water marks. —*v.tr.* run or haul up (a boat etc.) on to a beach. □ **beach-ball** a large inflated ball for games on the beach. **beach buggy** a low wide-wheeled motor vehicle for recreational driving on sand. **beach plum 1** a maritime N. American shrub, *Prunus maritima*. **2** its edible fruit. [16th c.: orig. unkn.]

beachcomber /ˈbiːtʃˌkəʊmə(r)/ *n.* **1** a vagrant who lives by searching beaches for articles of value. **2** a long wave rolling in from the sea.

beachhead /ˈbiːtʃhed/ *n. Mil.* a fortified position established on a beach by landing forces. [after *bridgehead*]

Beach-la-mar /ˌbiːtʃləˈmɑː(r)/ *n. Brit.* an English-based Creole language spoken in the W. Pacific. [corrupt. f. Port. *bicho do mar* BÊCHE-DE-MER]

beacon /ˈbiːkən/ *n.* **1 a** a fire or light set up in a high or prominent position as a warning etc. **b** *Brit.* (now often in placenames) a hill suitable for this. **2** a visible warning or guiding point or device (e.g. a lighthouse, navigation buoy, etc.). **3** a radio transmitter whose signal helps fix the position of a ship or air- craft. **4** *Brit.* = BELISHA BEACON. [OE *beacn* f. WG]

bead /biːd/ *n. & v.* —*n.* **1 a** a small usu. rounded and perforated piece of glass, stone, etc., for threading with others to make jewellery, or sewing on to fabric, etc. **b** (in *pl.*) a string of beads; a rosary. **2** a drop of liquid; a bubble. **3** a small knob in the foresight of a gun. **4** the inner edge of a pneumatic tyre that grips the rim of the wheel. **5** *Archit.* **a** a moulding like a series of beads. **b** a narrow moulding with a semicircular cross-section. —*v.* **1** *tr.* furnish or decorate with beads. **2** *tr.* string together. **3** *intr.* form or grow into beads. □ **draw a bead on** take aim at. **tell one's beads** use the beads of a rosary etc. in counting prayers. □□ **beaded** *adj.* [orig. = 'prayer' (for which the earliest use of beads arose): OE *gebed* f. Gmc, rel. to BID]

beading /ˈbiːdɪŋ/ *n.* **1** decoration in the form of or resembling a row of beads, esp. lacelike looped edging. **2** *Archit.* a bead moulding. **3** the bead of a tyre.

beadle /ˈbiːd(ə)l/ *n.* **1** *Brit.* a ceremonial officer of a church, college, etc. **2** *Sc.* a church officer attending on the minister. **3** *Brit. hist.* a minor parish officer dealing with petty offenders etc. □□ **beadleship** *n.* [ME f. OF *bedel* ult. f. Gmc]

beadsman /ˈbiːdzmən/ *n.* (*pl.* **-men**) *hist.* **1** a pensioner provided for by a benefactor in return for prayers. **2** an inmate of an almshouse.

beady /ˈbiːdɪ/ *adj.* (**beadier, beadiest**) **1** (of the eyes) small, round, and bright. **2** covered with beads or drops. □ **beady-eyed** with beady eyes. □□ **beadily** *adv.* **beadiness** *n.*

beagle /ˈbiːg(ə)l/ *n. & v.* —*n.* **1 a** a small hound of a breed with a short coat, used for hunting hares. **b** this breed. **2** *hist.* an informer or spy; a constable. —*v.intr.* (often as **beagling** *n.*) hunt with beagles. □□ **beagler** *n.* [ME f. OF *beegueule* noisy person, prob. f. *beer* open wide + *gueule* throat]

Beagle Channel /ˈbiːg(ə)l/ a channel in the islands of Tierra del Fuego at the southern tip of South America. It is named after the ship of Darwin's voyage (see DARWIN).

beak[1] /biːk/ *n.* **1 a** a bird's horny projecting jaws; a bill. **b** the similar projecting jaw of other animals, e.g. a turtle. **2** *sl.* a hooked nose. **3** *Naut. hist.* the projection at the prow of a warship. **4** a spout. □□ **beaked** *adj.* **beaky** *adj.* [ME f. OF *bec* f. L *beccus*, of Celt. orig.]

beak[2] /biːk/ *n. Brit. sl.* **1** a magistrate. **2** a schoolmaster. [19th c.: prob. f. thieves' cant]

beaker /ˈbiːk(ə)r/ *n.* **1** a tall drinking-vessel, usu. of plastic and tumbler-shaped. **2** a lipped cylindrical glass vessel for scientific experiments. **3** *archaic* or *literary* a large drinking-vessel with a wide mouth. **4** *Archaeol.* a wide-mouthed pottery vessel found in graves of the late neolithic period (3rd millennium BC) in western Europe. □ **Beaker Folk,** users of such prehistoric vessels. For a long time they were thought of as a mobile population directly responsible for the rapid spread of beaker pottery, but more recent theory holds that the distribution of these vessels can be accounted for by trade and exchange. [ME f. ON *bikarr*, perh. f. Gk *bikos* drinking-bowl]

Beale /biːl/, Dorothea (1831–1906), a pioneer, together with her friend Frances Buss, in higher education for women in Britain, and an enthusiastic advocate of women's suffrage. From 1858 until her death she was principal of Cheltenham Ladies' College, where she introduced a curriculum similar to that used in public schools for boys.

beam /biːm/ *n. & v.* —*n.* **1** a long sturdy piece of squared timber or metal spanning an opening or room, usu. to support the structure above. **2 a** a ray or shaft of light. **b** a directional flow of particles or radiation. **3** a bright look or smile. **4 a** a series of radio or radar signals as a guide to a ship or aircraft. **b** the course indicated by this (*off beam*). **5** the crossbar of a balance. **6 a** a ship's breadth at its widest point. **b** the width of a person's hips (esp. *broad in the beam*). **7** (in *pl.*) the horizontal cross-timbers of a ship supporting the deck and joining the sides. **8** the side of a ship (*land on the port beam*). **9** the chief timber of a plough. **10** the cylinder in a loom on which the warp or cloth is wound. **11** the main stem of a stag's antlers. **12** the lever in an engine connecting the piston-rod and crank. **13** the shank of an anchor. —*v.* **1** *tr.* emit or direct (light, radio waves, etc.). **2** *intr.* **a** shine. **b** look or smile radiantly. □ **beam-compass** (or **-compasses**) compasses with a beam connecting sliding sockets, used for large circles. **a beam in one's eye** a fault that is greater in oneself than in the person one is finding fault with (see Matt. 7: 3). **off beam** *colloq.* mistaken. **on the beam** *colloq.* on the right track. **on the beam-ends** (of a ship) on its side; almost capsizing. **on one's beam-ends** near the end of one's resources. [OE *beam* tree f. WG]

beamer /ˈbiːmə(r)/ *n. Cricket colloq.* a ball bowled at a batsman's head.

Beamon /ˈbiːmən/, Robert ('Bob'), (1946–   ), American athlete, who set a world record of 8.90 metres (29 ft. 2½ in.) in the long jump in 1968 at the Olympic Games in Mexico City.

beamy /ˈbiːmɪ/ *adj.* (of a ship) broad-beamed.

bean /biːn/ *n. & v.* —*n.* **1 a** any kind of leguminous plant with edible usu. kidney-shaped seeds in long pods. **b** one of these seeds. **2** a similar seed of coffee and other plants. **3** *US sl.* the head. **4** (in *pl.*; with *neg.*) *US sl.* anything at all (*doesn't know beans about it*). —*v.tr. US sl.* hit on the head. □ **bean curd** jelly or paste made from beans, used esp. in Asian cookery. **bean sprout** a sprout of a bean seed, esp. of the mung bean, used as food. **full of beans** *colloq.* lively; in high spirits. **not a bean** *Brit. sl.* no money. **old bean** *Brit. sl.* a friendly form of address, usu. to a man. [OE *bean* f. Gmc]

beanbag /ˈbiːnbæg/ *n.* **1** a small bag filled with dried beans and used esp. in children's games. **2** a large cushion filled usu. with polystyrene beads and used as a seat.

beanery /ˈbiːnərɪ/ *n.* (*pl.* **-ies**) *US sl.* a cheap restaurant.

beanfeast /ˈbiːnfiːst/ *n.* **1** *Brit. colloq.* a celebration; a merry time. **2** an employer's annual dinner given to employees. [BEAN + FEAST, beans and bacon being regarded as an indispensable dish]

beanie /'biːnɪ/ n. a small close-fitting hat worn on the back of the head. [perh. f. BEAN 'head' + -IE]

beano /'biːnəʊ/ n. (pl. -os) Brit. sl. a celebration; a party. [abbr. of BEANFEAST]

beanpole /'biːnpəʊl/ n. 1 a stick for supporting bean plants. 2 colloq. a tall thin person.

beanstalk /'biːnstɔːk/ n. the stem of a bean plant.

bear[1] /beə(r)/ v. (past **bore** /bɔː(r)/; past part. **borne**, **born** /bɔːn/) ¶ In the passive born is used with reference to birth (e.g. was born in July), except for borne by foll. by the name of the mother (e.g. was borne by Sarah). 1 tr. carry, bring, or take (esp. visibly) (bear gifts). 2 tr. show; be marked by; have as an attribute or characteristic (bear marks of violence; bears no relation to the case; bore no name). 3 tr. a produce, yield (fruit etc.). b give birth to (has borne a son; was born last week). 4 tr. a sustain (a weight, responsibility, cost, etc.). b stand, endure (an ordeal, difficulty, etc.). 5 tr. (usu. with neg. or interrog.) a tolerate; put up with (can't bear him; how can you bear it?). b admit of; be fit for (does not bear thinking about). 6 tr. carry in thought or memory (bear a grudge). 7 intr. veer in a given direction (bear left). 8 tr. bring or provide (something needed) (bear him company). 9 refl. behave (in a certain way). □ **bear arms 1** carry weapons; serve as a soldier. **2** wear or display heraldic devices. **bear away** (or **off**) win (a prize etc.). **bear down** exert downward pressure. **bear down on** approach rapidly or purposefully. **bear fruit** have results. **bear a hand** help. **bear hard on** oppress. **bear in mind** take into account having remembered. **bear on** (or **upon**) be relevant to. **bear out** support or confirm (an account or the person giving it). **bear repeating** be worth repetition. **bear up** raise one's spirits; not despair. **bear with** treat forbearingly; tolerate patiently. **bear witness** testify. [OE beran f. Gmc]

bear[2] /beə(r)/ n. & v. —n. 1 any large heavy mammal of the family Ursidae, having thick fur and walking on its soles. 2 a rough, unmannerly, or uncouth person. 3 Stock Exch. a person who sells shares for future delivery, hoping that prices will fall and that he or she will be able to buy them at a lower price before having to deliver them. The term (which dates from the 18th c.) is probably derived from the proverb 'to sell the bear's skin before one has caught the bear'. The associated term bull appears later, and was perhaps suggested by bear. 4 = TEDDY. 5 (the Bear) colloq. Russia. —v. Stock Exch. 1 intr. speculate for a fall in price. 2 tr. produce a fall in the price of (stocks etc.). □ **bear-baiting** hist. an entertainment involving setting dogs to attack a captive bear. **bear-hug** a tight embrace. **bear market** Stock Exch. a market with falling prices. **bear's breech** a kind of acanthus, Acanthus mollis. **bear's ear** auricula. **bear's foot** a hellebore, Helleborus fetidus. **the Great Bear** the constellation Ursa Major. **the Little Bear** the constellation Ursa Minor. **like a bear with a sore head** Brit. colloq. very irritable. [OE bera f. WG]

bearable /'beərəb(ə)l/ adj. that may be endured or tolerated. □□ **bearability** /-'bɪlɪtɪ/ n. **bearableness** n. **bearably** adv.

beard /'bɪəd/ n. & v. —n. 1 hair growing on the chin and lower cheeks of the face. 2 a similar tuft or part on an animal (esp. a goat). 3 the awn of a grass, sheath of barley, etc. —v.tr. oppose openly; defy. □□ **bearded** adj. **beardless** adj. [OE f. WG]

beardie /'bɪədɪ/ n. Brit. colloq. a bearded man.

Beardsley /'bɪədzlɪ/, Aubrey Vincent (1872–98), English artist and illustrator. Encouraged by Burne-Jones, his early work was influenced by the Pre-Raphaelites and his discovery of Japanese prints. His illustrations for Malory's Morte d'Arthur (1893) brought him to public notice, and in 1894 he became editor of the quarterly periodical The Yellow Book. In that year he illustrated Oscar Wilde's Salome and thereby gained much notoriety. The chief English representative of aestheticism in art, his genius for linear arabesque and acute sense of visual design give his prints and drawings a unique place in the corpus of English art: the quality of his designs for The Rape of the Lock bears witness to the tragedy of his early death.

bearer /'beərə(r)/ n. 1 a person or thing that bears, carries, or brings. 2 a carrier of equipment on an expedition etc. 3 a person who presents a cheque or other order to pay money. 4 (attrib.)

payable to the possessor (bearer stock). 5 hist. (in India etc.) a personal servant.

beargarden /'beəˌɡɑːd(ə)n/ n. a rowdy or noisy scene.

bearing /'beərɪŋ/ n. 1 a person's bodily attitude or outward behaviour. 2 (foll. by on, upon) relation or relevance to (his comments have no bearing on the subject). 3 endurability (beyond bearing). 4 a part of a machine that supports a rotating or other moving part. 5 direction or position relative to a fixed point, measured esp. in degrees. 6 (in pl.) a one's position relative to one's surroundings. b awareness of this; a sense of one's orientation (get one's bearings; lose one's bearings). 7 Heraldry a device or charge. 8 = ball-bearing (see BALL[1]). □ **bearing-rein** a fixed rein from bit to saddle that forces a horse to arch its neck.

bearish /'beərɪʃ/ adj. 1 like a bear, esp. in temper. 2 Stock Exch. causing or associated with a fall in prices.

Béarnaise sauce /ˌbeɪəˈneɪz/ n. a rich sauce thickened with egg yolks and flavoured with tarragon. [F, fem. of béarnais of Béarn in SW France]

bearskin /'beəskɪn/ n. 1 a the skin of a bear. b a wrap etc. made of this. 2 a tall furry hat worn ceremonially by some regiments.

Beas /biˈɑːs/ a river of northern India that rises in the Himalayas and flows through Himachal Pradesh to join the Sutlej River in the State of Punjab. It is one of the 'five rivers' that gave Punjab its name. In ancient times called the Hyphasis, it marked the eastern limit of Alexander the Great's conquests.

beast /biːst/ n. 1 an animal other than a human being, esp. a wild quadruped. 2 a a brutal person. b colloq. an objectionable or unpleasant person or thing (he's a beast for not inviting her; a beast of a problem). 3 (prec. by the) a human being's brutish or uncivilized characteristics (saw the beast in him). □ **beast of burden** an animal, e.g. an ox, used for carrying loads. **beast of prey** see PREY. [ME f. OF beste f. Rmc besta f. L bestia]

beastie /'biːstɪ/ n. Sc. or joc. a small animal.

beastly /'biːstlɪ/ adj. & adv. —adj. (**beastlier**, **beastliest**) 1 colloq. objectionable, unpleasant. 2 like a beast; brutal. —adv. colloq. very, extremely. □□ **beastliness** n.

beat /biːt/ v., n., & adj. —v. (past **beat**; past part. **beaten** /'biːt(ə)n/) 1 tr. a strike (a person or animal) persistently or repeatedly, esp. to harm or punish. b strike (a thing) repeatedly, e.g. to remove dust from (a carpet etc.), to sound (a drum etc.). 2 intr. (foll. by against, at, on, etc.) a pound or knock repeatedly (waves beat against the shore; beat at the door). b = beat down 3. 3 tr. a overcome; surpass; win a victory over. b complete an activity before (another person etc.). c be too hard for; perplex. 4 tr. (often foll. by up) stir (eggs etc.) vigorously into a frothy mixture. 5 tr. (often foll. by out) fashion or shape (metal etc.) by blows. 6 intr. (of the heart, a drum, etc.) pulsate rhythmically. 7 tr. (often foll. by out) a indicate (a tempo or rhythm) by gestures, tapping, etc. b sound (a signal etc.) by striking a drum or other means (beat a tattoo). 8 a intr. (of a bird's wings) move up and down. b tr. cause (wings) to move in this way. 9 tr. make (a path etc.) by trampling. 10 tr. strike (bushes etc.) to rouse game. 11 intr. Naut. sail in the direction from which the wind is blowing. —n. 1 a a main accent or rhythmic unit in music or verse (three beats to the bar; missed a beat and came in early). b the indication of rhythm by a conductor's movements (watch the beat). c (in popular music) a strong rhythm. d (attrib.) characterized by a strong rhythm (beat music). 2 a a stroke or blow (e.g. on a drum). b a measured sequence of strokes (the beat of the waves on the rocks). c a throbbing movement or sound (the beat of his heart). 3 a a route or area allocated to a police officer etc. b a person's habitual round. 4 Physics a pulsation due to the combination of two sounds or electric currents of similar but not equivalent frequencies. 5 colloq. = BEATNIK. —adj. 1 (predic.) sl. exhausted, tired out. 2 (attrib.) of the beat generation or its philosophy. □ **beat about** (often foll. by for) search (for an excuse etc.). **beat about the bush** discuss a matter without coming to the point. **beat the bounds** Brit. mark parish boundaries by striking certain points with rods. **beat one's breast** strike one's chest in anguish or sorrow. **beat the clock** complete a task within a stated time. **beat down 1 a** bargain with (a seller) to lower the price. **b** cause a seller to lower (the price). **2** strike (a resisting object) until it falls (*beat the door down*). **3** (of the sun, rain, etc.) radiate heat or fall continuously and vigorously. **beat the drum for** publicize, promote. **beaten at the post** defeated at the last moment. **beat generation** the members of a movement of young people esp. in the 1950s who rejected conventional society in their dress, habits, and beliefs. **beat in** crush. **beat it** *sl.* go away. **beat off** drive back (an attack etc.). **beat a retreat** withdraw; abandon an undertaking. **beat time** indicate or follow a musical tempo with a baton or other means. **beat a person to it** arrive or achieve something before another person. **beat up** give a beating to, esp. with punches and kicks. **beat-up** *adj. colloq.* dilapidated; in a state of disrepair. **it beats me** I do not understand (it). □□ **beatable** *adj.* [OE *bēatan* f. Gmc]

beaten /'biːt(ə)n/ *adj.* **1** outwitted; defeated. **2** exhausted; dejected. **3** (of gold or any other metal) shaped by a hammer. **4** (of a path etc.) well-trodden, much-used. □ **off the beaten track 1** in or into an isolated place. **2** unusual. [past part. of BEAT]

beater /'biːtə(r)/ *n.* **1** a person employed to rouse game for shooting. **2** an implement used for beating (esp. a carpet or eggs). **3** a person who beats metal.

beatific /ˌbiːə'tɪfɪk/ *adj.* **1** *colloq.* blissful (*a beatific smile*). **2 a** of or relating to blessedness. **b** making blessed. □□ **beatifically** *adv.* [F *béatifique* or L *beatificus* f. *beatus* blessed]

beatification /biːˌætɪfɪ'keɪʃ(ə)n/ *n.* **1** RC *Ch.* the act of formally declaring a dead person 'blessed', often a step towards canonization. **2** making or being blessed. [F *béatification* or eccl.L *beatificatio* (as BEATIFY)]

beatify /biː'ætɪfaɪ/ *v.tr.* (**-ies, -ied**) **1** RC *Ch.* announce the beatification of. **2** make happy. [F *béatifier* or eccl.L *beatificare* f. L *beatus* blessed]

beating /'biːtɪŋ/ *n.* **1** a physical punishment or assault. **2** a defeat. □ **take some** (or **a lot of**) **beating** be difficult to surpass.

beatitude /biː'ætɪtjuːd/ *n.* **1** blessedness. **2** (in *pl.*) the declarations of blessedness in Matt. 5: 3–11. **3** a title given to patriarchs in the Orthodox Church. [F *béatitude* or L *beatitudo* f. *beatus* blessed]

Beatles /'biːt(ə)lz/, **the** English rock group consisting of George Harrison (1943–), John Lennon (1940–80), Paul McCartney (1942–), and Ringo Starr (real name Richard Starkey, 1940–). In the 1960s both their music and their ideas caught the imagination of their generation throughout the world and focused attention on the fact that young people could make their own music.

beatnik /'biːtnɪk/ *n.* a member of the beat generation (see BEAT). [BEAT + -*nik* after *sputnik*, perh. infl. by US use of Yiddish -*nik* agent-suffix]

Beaton /'biːt(ə)n/, Sir Cecil Walter Hardy (1904–80), English photographer, noted for his fashion features and portraits of celebrities.

Beatty /'biːtɪ/, David, 1st Earl (1871–1936), British admiral. As commander of battle-cruiser squadrons he gained minor victories over German cruisers off Heligoland (1914) and the Dogger Bank (1915), and played a major role in the battle of Jutland. He was commander-in-chief of the Grand Fleet 1916–19 and received the German naval surrender in 1918. From 1919 to 1927 he was First Sea Lord.

beau /bəʊ/ *n.* (*pl.* **beaux** or **beaus** /bəʊz, bəʊ/) **1** esp. *US* an admirer; a boyfriend. **2** a fop; a dandy. [F, = handsome, f. L *bellus*]

Beaufort scale /'bəʊfət/ *n.* a scale of wind speed ranging from 0 (calm) to 12 (hurricane). It is named after the English admiral Sir Francis Beaufort (1774–1857) who devised it.

Beaufort Sea a part of the Arctic Ocean lying to the north of Alaska and Canada. It is named after Sir Francis Beaufort (see BEAUFORT SCALE).

beau geste /bəʊ 'ʒest/ *n.* (*pl.* **beaux gestes** pronunc. same) a generous or gracious act. [F, = splendid gesture]

beau ideal /ˌbəʊ iːdeɪ'æl/ *n.* (*pl.* **beaux ideals** /ˌbəʊz iːdeɪ'æl/) the highest type of excellence or beauty. [F *beau idéal* = ideal beauty: see BEAU, IDEAL]

Beaujolais /'bəʊʒəˌleɪ/ *n.* a red or white burgundy wine from the Beaujolais district of SE France.

Beaumarchais /ˌbəʊmɑːr'ʃeɪ/, Pierre Augustin Caron de (1732–99), French dramatist, best known for his comedies *Le Barbier de Séville* (1775) and *Le Mariage de Figaro* (1784) which inspired operas by Rossini and Mozart.

Beaumont /'bəʊmɒnt/, Francis (1584–1616), English dramatist, who entered the Inner Temple in 1600 and collaborated with John Fletcher in *Philaster* (1609), *The Maid's Tragedy* (1610–11), and many other plays. *The Knight of the Burning Pestle* (?1607) is attributed to Beaumont alone. He retired *c.*1613 when he married profitably; he is buried in Westminster Abbey.

beau monde /bəʊ 'mɒnd/ *n.* fashionable society. [F]

Beaune /bəʊn/ *n.* a red burgundy wine from the region round the town of Beaune in east central France.

beaut /bjuːt/ *n.* & *adj. Austral.* & *NZ sl.* —*n.* an excellent or beautiful person or thing. —*adj.* excellent; beautiful. [abbr. of BEAUTY]

beauteous /'bjuːtɪəs/ *adj. poet.* beautiful. [ME f. BEAUTY + -OUS, after *bounteous, plenteous*]

beautician /bjuː'tɪʃ(ə)n/ *n.* **1** a person who gives beauty treatment. **2** a person who runs or owns a beauty salon.

beautiful /'bjuːtɪfʊl/ *adj.* **1** delighting the aesthetic senses (*a beautiful voice*). **2** pleasant, enjoyable (*had a beautiful time*). **3** excellent (*a beautiful specimen*). □□ **beautifully** *adv.*

beautify /'bjuːtɪfaɪ/ *v.tr.* (**-ies, -ied**) make beautiful; adorn. □□ **beautification** /-fɪ'keɪʃ(ə)n/ *n.* **beautifier** /-ˌfaɪə(r)/ *n.*

beauty /'bjuːtɪ/ *n.* (*pl.* **-ies**) **1 a** a combination of qualities such as shape, colour, etc., that pleases the aesthetic senses, esp. the sight. **b** a combination of qualities that pleases the intellect or moral sense (*the beauty of the argument*). **2** *colloq.* **a** an excellent specimen (*what a beauty!*). **b** an attractive feature; an advantage (*that's the beauty of it!*). **3** a beautiful woman. □ **beauty is only skin-deep** a pleasing appearance is not a guide to character. **beauty parlour** (or **salon**) an establishment in which massage, manicure, hairdressing, make-up, etc., are offered to women. **beauty queen** the woman judged most beautiful in a competition. **beauty sleep** sleep before midnight, supposed to be health-giving. **beauty spot 1** a place known for its beauty. **2** a small natural or artificial mark such as a mole on the face, considered to enhance another feature. **beauty treatment** cosmetic treatment received in a beauty parlour. [ME f. AF *beuté*, OF *bealté, beauté*, ult. f. L (as BEAU)]

Beauvoir /'bəʊvwɑː(r)/, Simone de (1908–86), French existentialist novelist and feminist whose best-known work is the treatise *Le Deuxième Sexe* (*The Second Sex*, 1949). She formed a lifelong association with Sartre, whom she met in 1929.

beaux *pl.* of BEAU.

beaux arts /bəʊ'zɑː/ *n.pl.* **1** fine arts. **2** (*attrib.*) relating to the rules and conventions of the École des Beaux-Arts in Paris (later called Académie des Beaux Arts). [F *beaux-arts*]

beaver¹ /'biːvə(r)/ *n.* & *v.* —*n.* (*pl.* same or **beavers**) **1 a** any large amphibious broad-tailed rodent of the genus *Castor*, native to N. America, Europe, and Asia, and able to cut down trees and build dams. **b** its soft light-brown fur. **c** a hat of this. **2** (in full **beaver cloth**) a heavy woollen cloth like beaver fur. **3** (**Beaver**) a boy (or, from 1991, girl) aged six or seven who is an affiliate member of the Scout Association. —*v.intr. colloq.* (usu. foll. by *away*) work hard. □ **beaver lamb** lamb's wool made to look like beaver fur. **eager beaver** *colloq.* an over-zealous person. [OE *be(o)for* f. Gmc]

beaver² /'biːvə(r)/ *n. hist.* the lower portion of the face-guard of a helmet, when worn with a visor. In the 14th c. the term was applied to the movable face-guard; in the early part of the 15th c. the beaver was formed of overlapping plates, which could be raised or depressed to any degree desired by the wearer. In the 16th c. it again became confounded with the visor, and could be pushed up entirely over the top of the helmet, or drawn down. [OF *baviere* bib f. *baver* slaver f. *beve* saliva f. Rmc]

beaver³ /'biːvə(r)/ *n. sl.* a bearded man. [20th c.: orig. uncert.]

Beaverboard /'biːvəˌbɔːd/ *n. propr.* a kind of fibreboard. [BEAVER¹ + BOARD]

Beaverbrook /'biːvəbrʊk/, William Maxwell Aitken, 1st Baron

(1879–1964), British Conservative politician and newspaper proprietor, who made his fortune in Canadian business before coming to Britain and winning election to Parliament in 1910. A wartime Cabinet Minister, he built up a substantial newspaper empire, centred on the *Daily Express*, in the 1920s, and during the early years of the Second World War served again in the Cabinet, being Minister of Aircraft Production during the crucial years of 1940–2.

bebop /ˈbiːbɒp/ *n.* a type of jazz originating in the 1940s and characterized by complex harmony and rhythms. □□ **bebopper** *n.* [imit. of the typical rhythm]

becalm /bɪˈkɑːm/ *v.tr.* (usu. in *passive*) deprive (a ship) of wind.

became *past of* BECOME.

because /bɪˈkɒz/ *conj.* for the reason that; since. □ **because of** on account of; by reason of. [ME f. BY *prep.* + CAUSE, after OF *par cause de* by reason of]

béchamel /ˈbeɪʃəˌmel/ *n.* a kind of thick white sauce. [invented by the Marquis de *Béchamel*, Fr. courtier d. 1703]

bêche-de-mer /ˌbeʃ də ˈmeə(r)/ *n.* (*pl.* same or **bêches-de-mer** *pronunc.* same) **1** a kind of sea cucumber eaten in China usu. in long dried strips. **2** = BEACH-LA-MAR. [F, alt. of *biche de mer* f. Port. *bicho do mar* sea-worm]

Bechstein /ˈbekstaɪn/, Friedrich Wilhelm Carl (1826–1900), German piano-builder. His name is used to designate a piano manufactured by him or by the firm which he founded in 1856.

Bechuanaland /ˌbetʃʊˈɑːnəˌlænd/ the former name (until 1966) of Botswana.

beck[1] /bek/ *n.* N.Engl. a brook; a mountain stream. [ME f. ON *bekkr* f. Gmc]

beck[2] /bek/ *n. poet.* a gesture requesting attention, e.g. a nod, wave, etc. □ **at a person's beck and call** having constantly to obey a person's orders. [*beck* (v.) f. BECKON]

Bekenbauer /ˈbekənˌbaʊə(r)/, Franz (1945–), German Association Football player, under whose captaincy Bayern Munich won a number of championships and West Germany won the World Cup in 1974. After a spell in the US (1976–80) he returned to West Germany where he was manager of the national team that won the World Cup again in 1990.

Becker /ˈbekə(r)/, Boris (1967–), West German tennis-player, the youngest man to win the men's singles championship at Wimbledon, 1985.

Becket /ˈbekɪt/, St Thomas (c.1118–70), close and influential friend of Henry II who made him his chancellor and later (1162) Archbishop of Canterbury, a position Becket accepted with reluctance, foreseeing the inevitable clash between the interests of the King and those of the Church to which his service and loyalty were now transferred. He soon found himself in open opposition to Henry, on a matter of taxation and later over the coronation of Henry's son, and the King in anger uttered words which sent four knights to Canterbury in revenge. Becket was assassinated in his cathedral in the late afternoon of 29 Dec. He proved to be more potent in death than he had ever been in life: the murder aroused indignation throughout Europe, miracles were soon reported at his tomb, and Henry was obliged to do public penance there. The shrine became a major centre of pilgrimage until its destruction under Henry VIII (1538). Feast day, 29 Dec.

becket /ˈbekɪt/ *n. Naut.* a contrivance such as a hook, bracket, or rope-loop, for securing loose ropes, tackle, or spars. [18th c.: orig. unkn.]

Beckett /ˈbekɪt/, Samuel Barclay (1906–89), Irish dramatist, novelist, and poet, who spent five solitary years in Germany, France, and London, reviewing, translating, writing poems and a study of Proust (1931), before settling permanently in France. His trilogy comprising *Molloy* (1951), *Malone Dies* (1951), and *The Unnameable* (1953) was originally published in French; all three are desolate terminal interior monologues irradiated with flashes of black humour. His highly distinctive despairing yet exhilarating voice made its greatest impact with *Waiting for Godot* (1952), one of the most influential plays of the post-war period, and from this time Beckett established his association with the Theatre of the Absurd. His use of the stage and of

dramatic narrative and symbolism revolutionized drama in England. Subsequent plays include *Endgame* (1957), a one-act drama of frustration, irascibility, and senility, *Krapp's Last Tape* (1959), *Breath* (1966), a thirty-second play consisting of a pile of rubbish, a breath, and a cry, and *Not I* (1973), a disembodied monologue delivered by an actor of indeterminate sex of whom only the 'Mouth' is illuminated. Beckett was awarded the Nobel Prize for literature in 1969.

Beckford /ˈbekfəd/, William (1759–1844), English writer, the son of a Lord Mayor of London from whom he inherited an enormous fortune which he spent lavishly. He travelled in Europe, collected works of art and curios, and commissioned the building of Fonthill in Wiltshire, a Gothic extravaganza where he lived in almost complete and somewhat mysterious seclusion from 1796. He is remembered as the author of the fantastic oriental romance, *Vathek* (1786, originally written in French), and also wrote two notable travel-books.

beckon /ˈbekən/ *v.* **1** *tr.* attract the attention of; summon by gesture. **2** *intr.* (usu. foll. by *to*) make a signal to attract a person's attention; summon a person by doing this. [OE *bīecnan, bēcnan* ult. f. WG *baukna* BEACON]

becloud /bɪˈklaʊd/ *v.tr.* **1** obscure (*becloud the argument*). **2** cover with clouds.

become /bɪˈkʌm/ *v.* (*past* **became** /bɪˈkeɪm/; *past part.* **become**) **1** *intr.* (foll. by *compl.*) begin to be (*became president; will become famous*). **2** *tr.* **a** look well on; suit (*blue becomes him*). **b** befit (*it ill becomes you to complain*). **3** *intr.* (as **becoming** *adj.*) a flattering the appearance. **b** suitable; decorous. □ **become of** happen to (*what will become of me?*). □□ **becomingly** *adj.* **becomingness** *n.* [OE *becuman* f. Gmc: cf. BE-, COME]

Becquerel /ˈbekər(e)l/, Antoine-Henri (1852–1908), French physicist, who shared the 1903 Nobel Prize for physics with the Curies for his discovery of natural radioactivity in uranium salts (1896), and made a systematic study of the properties of this form of radiation. Initially, the rays emitted by radioactive substances were named after him.

becquerel /ˈbekəˌrel/ *n. Physics* the SI unit of radioactivity, corresponding to one disintegration per second. [A.-H. BECQUEREL]

bed /bed/ *n. & v.* —*n.* **1 a** a piece of furniture used for sleeping on, usu. a framework with a mattress and coverings. **b** such a mattress, with or without coverings. **2** any place used by a person or animal for sleep or rest; a litter. **3 a** a garden plot, esp. one used for planting flowers. **b** a place where other things may be grown (*osier bed*). **4** the use of a bed: **a** *colloq.* for sexual intercourse (*only thinks of bed*). **b** for rest (*needs his bed*). **5** something flat, forming a support or base as in: **a** the bottom of the sea or a river. **b** the foundations of a road or railway. **c** the slates etc. on a billiard-table. **6** a stratum, such as a layer of oysters etc. —*v.* (**bedded, bedding**) **1** *tr. & intr.* (usu. foll. by *down*) put or go to bed. **2** *tr. colloq.* have sexual intercourse with. **3** *tr.* (usu. foll. by *out*) plant in a garden bed. **4** *tr.* cover up or fix firmly in something. **5 a** *tr.* arrange as a layer. **b** *intr.* be or form a layer. □ **bed and board 1** lodging and food. **2** marital relations. **bed and breakfast 1** one night's lodging and breakfast in a hotel etc. **2** an establishment that provides this. **3** *Stock Exch.* an operation in which a shareholder sells a holding one evening while agreeing to buy it back again next morning, realizing either a gain or a loss in order to suit a tax requirement. **bed of roses** a life of ease. **brought to bed** (often foll. by *of*) delivered of a child. **get out of bed on the wrong side** be bad-tempered all day long. **go to bed 1** retire for the night. **2** have sexual intercourse. **3** (of a newspaper) go to press. **keep one's bed** stay in bed because of illness. **make the bed** tidy and arrange the bed for use. **make one's bed and lie in it** accept the consequences of one's acts. **put to bed 1** cause to go to bed. **2** make (a newspaper) ready for press. **take to one's bed** stay in bed because of illness. [OE *bed(d), beddian* f. Gmc]

B.Ed. *abbr.* Bachelor of Education.

bedabble /bɪˈdæb(ə)l/ *v.tr.* stain or splash with dirty liquid, blood, etc.

bedad /bɪˈdæd/ *int. Ir.* by God! [corrupt.: cf. GAD[2]]

bedaub /bɪˈdɔːb/ v.tr. smear or daub with paint etc.; decorate gaudily.

bedazzle /bɪˈdæz(ə)l/ v.tr. 1 dazzle. 2 confuse (a person). □□ **bedazzlement** n.

bedbug /ˈbedbʌg/ n. either of two flat, wingless, evil-smelling insects of the genus *Cimex* infesting beds and unclean houses and sucking blood.

bedchamber /ˈbedˌtʃeɪmbə(r)/ n. 1 *archaic* a bedroom. 2 (**Bed-chamber**) part of the title of some of the sovereign's attendants (*Lady of the Bedchamber*).

bedclothes /ˈbedkləʊðz/ n.pl. coverings for a bed, such as sheets, blankets, etc.

beddable /ˈbedəb(ə)l/ adj. colloq. sexually attractive. [BED + -ABLE]

bedder /ˈbedə(r)/ n. 1 a plant suitable for a garden bed. 2 *Brit.* colloq. a college bedmaker.

bedding /ˈbedɪŋ/ n. 1 a mattress and bedclothes. 2 a litter for cattle, horses, etc. 3 a bottom layer. 4 *Geol.* the stratification of rocks, esp. when clearly visible. □ **bedding plant** a plant suitable for a garden bed.

Beddoes /ˈbedəʊz/, Thomas Lovell (1803–49), English dramatic poet, much influenced by Jacobean tragedy. His finest play *Death's Jest-book*, posthumously published in 1850, shows his characteristic preoccupation with death and penchant for the macabre.

Bede /biːd/, the Venerable (*c*.673–735), monk of Jarrow, the 'Father of English History'. He is best known for his historical works including the *Ecclesiastical History of the English People* (completed in 731), a primary source for early English history, with vivid descriptions and based on careful research, separating fact from hearsay and tradition. This and specific works on the calculation of Easter did much to establish the practice of dating events from the Incarnation. He was honoured after his death with the title Venerable in recognition of the holiness of his life. Feast day, 27 May.

bedeck /bɪˈdek/ v.tr. adorn.

bedeguar /ˈbedɪˌgɑː(r)/ n. a mosslike growth on rose-bushes produced by a gall wasp. [F *bédegar* f. Pers. *bād-āwar* wind-brought]

bedel /ˈbiːd(ə)l, bɪˈdel/ n. (also **bedell**) *Brit.* a university official with chiefly processional duties. [= BEADLE]

bedevil /bɪˈdev(ə)l/ v.tr. (**bedevilled, bedevilling**; US **bedeviled, bedeviling**) 1 plague; afflict. 2 confound; confuse. 3 possess as if with a devil; bewitch. 4 treat with diabolical violence or abuse. □□ **bedevilment** n.

bedew /bɪˈdjuː/ v.tr. 1 cover or sprinkle with dew or drops of water. 2 *poet.* sprinkle with tears.

bedfellow /ˈbedˌfeləʊ/ n. 1 a person who shares a bed. 2 an associate.

Bedford cord /ˈbedfəd/ n. a tough woven fabric having prominent ridges, similar to corduroy. [*Bedford* in S. England]

Bedfordshire /ˈbedfədˌʃɪə(r)/ an east midland county of England; county town, Bedford.

bedight /bɪˈdaɪt/ adj. *archaic* arrayed; adorned. [ME past part. of *bedight* (v.) (as BE-, DIGHT)]

bedim /bɪˈdɪm/ v.tr. (**bedimmed, bedimming**) *poet.* make (the eyes, mind, etc.) dim.

bedizen /bɪˈdaɪz(ə)n, -ˈdɪz(ə)n/ v.tr. *poet.* deck out gaudily. [BE- + obs. *dizen* deck out]

bedjacket /ˈbedˌdʒækɪt/ n. a jacket worn when sitting up in bed.

bedlam /ˈbedləm/ n. 1 a scene of uproar and confusion (*the traffic was bedlam*). 2 *archaic* a madhouse; an asylum. 'Bedlam' was originally the popular name of the hospital of St Mary of Bethlehem, founded as a priory in 1247 at Bishopsgate, London, and by the 14th c. a mental hospital. In 1675 a new hospital was built in Moorfields, and this in turn was replaced by a building in the Lambeth Road in 1815 (now the Imperial War Museum), and transferred to Beckenham in Kent in 1931.

bedlinen /ˈbedˌlɪnɪn/ n. sheets and pillowcases.

Bedlington terrier /ˈbedlɪŋt(ə)n/ n. 1 a terrier of a breed with narrow head, long legs, and curly grey hair. 2 this breed. [*Bedlington* in Northumberland]

bedmaker /ˈbedˌmeɪkə(r)/ n. *Brit.* a person employed to clean and tidy students' rooms in a college.

Bedouin /ˈbeduɪn/ n. & adj. (also **Beduin**) (*pl.* same) —n. 1 a nomadic Arab of the desert. 2 a wanderer; a nomad. —adj. 1 of or relating to the Bedouin. 2 wandering; nomadic. [ME f. OF *beduin* ult. f. Arab. *badwiyyīn* (oblique case) dwellers in the desert f. *badw* desert]

bedpan /ˈbedpæn/ n. a receptacle used by a bedridden patient for urine and faeces.

bedplate /ˈbedpleɪt/ n. a metal plate forming the base of a machine.

bedpost /ˈbedpəʊst/ n. any of the four upright supports of a bedstead. □ **between you and me and the bedpost** colloq. in strict confidence.

bedraggle /bɪˈdræg(ə)l/ v.tr. 1 wet (a dress etc.) by trailing it, or so that it hangs limp. 2 (as **bedraggled** adj.) untidy; dishevelled. [BE- + DRAGGLE]

bedrest /ˈbedrest/ n. confinement of an invalid to bed.

bedridden /ˈbedˌrɪd(ə)n/ adj. 1 confined to bed by infirmity. 2 decrepit. [OE *bedreda* f. *ridan* ride]

bedrock /ˈbedrɒk/ n. 1 solid rock underlying alluvial deposits etc. 2 the underlying principles or facts of a theory, character, etc.

bedroll /ˈbedrəʊl/ n. esp. *US* portable bedding rolled into a bundle, esp. a sleeping-bag.

bedroom /ˈbedruːm, -rʊm/ n. 1 a room for sleeping in. 2 (*attrib.*) of or referring to sexual relations (*bedroom comedy*).

Beds. abbr. Bedfordshire.

bedside /ˈbedsaɪd/ n. 1 the space beside esp. a patient's bed. 2 (*attrib.*) of or relating to the side of a bed (*bedside lamp*). □ **bedside manner** (of a doctor) an approach or attitude to a patient.

bedsitter /bedˈsɪtə(r)/ n. (also **bedsit**) colloq. = BEDSITTING ROOM. [contr.]

bedsitting room /bedˈsɪtɪŋ/ n. *Brit.* a one-roomed unit of accommodation usu. consisting of combined bedroom and sitting-room with cooking facilities.

bedsock /ˈbedsɒk/ n. each of a pair of thick socks worn in bed.

bedsore /ˈbedsɔː(r)/ n. a sore developed by an invalid because of pressure caused by lying in bed.

bedspread /ˈbedspred/ n. an often decorative cloth used to cover a bed when not in use.

bedstead /ˈbedsted/ n. the framework of a bed.

bedstraw /ˈbedstrɔː/ n. 1 any herbaceous plant of the genus *Galium*, once used as straw for bedding. 2 (in full **Our Lady's bedstraw**) a bedstraw, *G. verum*, with yellow flowers.

bedtable /ˈbedˌteɪb(ə)l/ n. a portable table or tray with legs used by a person sitting up in bed.

bedtime /ˈbedtaɪm/ n. 1 the usual time for going to bed. 2 (*attrib.*) of or relating to bedtime (*bedtime drink*).

Beduin var. of BEDOUIN.

bedwetting /ˈbedˌwetɪŋ/ n. involuntary urination during the night.

bee /biː/ n. 1 any four-winged insect of the superfamily Apoidea which collects nectar and pollen, produces wax and honey, and lives in large communities. 2 any insect of a similar type. 3 (usu. **busy bee**) a busy person. 4 esp. *US* a meeting for communal work or amusement. □ **bee-bread** honey or pollen used as food by bees. **bee dance** a dance performed by worker bees to inform the colony of the location of food. **bee-eater** any bright-plumaged insect-eating bird of the family Meropidae with a long slender curved bill. **a bee in one's bonnet** an obsession. **bee-keeper** a keeper of bees. **bee-keeping** the occupation of keeping bees. **bee-master** a bee-keeper. **bee orchid** a kind of European orchid, *Ophrys apifera*, with bee-shaped flowers. **the bee's knees** sl. something outstandingly good (*thinks he's the bee's knees*). [OE *bēo* f. Gmc]

Beeb /biːb/ n. (prec. by *the*) *Brit.* colloq. the BBC. [abbr.]

beech /biːtʃ/ n. 1 any large forest tree of the genus *Fagus*, having smooth grey bark and glossy leaves. **2** (also **beechwood**) its wood. **3** *Austral.* any of various similar trees in Australia. □ **beech-fern** a fern, *Thelypteris phagopteris*, found in damp woods. **beech-marten** a white-breasted marten, *Martes foina*, of S. Europe and Asia. □□ **beechy** *adj.* [OE *bēce* f. Gmc]

Beecham /'bi:tʃəm/, Sir Thomas (1879–1961), English conductor and impresario, possessor of a keen wit, who was associated in one way or another with most of the leading British orchestras, founding the London Philharmonic in 1932 and the Royal Philharmonic in 1947. In the decade preceding the Second World War he was artistic director of the Royal Opera House. An ardent champion of Delius (whose friend and biographer he became) Beecham was a notable interpreter of Mozart, Haydn, Sibelius, Richard Strauss, and French composers.

beechmast /'bi:tʃmɑ:st/ *n.* (*pl.* same) the small rough-skinned fruit of the beech tree. [BEECH + MAST²]

beef /bi:f/ *n.* & *v.* —*n.* **1** the flesh of the ox, bull, or esp. the cow, for eating. **2** *colloq.* well-developed male muscle. **3** (*pl.* **beeves** /bi:vz/ or US **beefs**) a cow, bull, or ox fattened for beef; its carcass. **4** (*pl.* **beefs**) *sl.* a complaint; a protest. —*v.intr. sl.* complain. □ **beef tea** stewed extract of beef, given to invalids. **beef up** *sl.* strengthen, reinforce, augment. **beef-wood 1** any of various Australian and W. Indian hardwood trees. **2** the close-grained red timber of these. [ME f. AF, OF *boef* f. L *bos bovis* ox]

beefburger /'bi:f₁bɜ:gə(r)/ *n.* = HAMBURGER.

beefcake /'bi:fkeɪk/ *n.* esp. US *sl.* well-developed male muscles, esp. when displayed for admiration.

beefeater /'bi:f₁i:tə(r)/ *n.* **1** a warder in the Tower of London. **2** a Yeoman of the Guard. [f. obs. sense 'well-fed menial']

beefsteak /bi:f'steɪk, 'bi:f-/ *n.* a thick slice of lean beef, esp. from the rump, usu. for grilling or frying. □ **beefsteak fungus** a red edible fungus, *Fistulina hepatica*, resembling beef.

beefy /'bi:fɪ/ *adj.* (**beefier, beefiest**) **1** like beef. **2** solid; muscular. □□ **beefily** *adv.* **beefiness** *n.*

beehive /'bi:haɪv/ *n.* **1** an artificial habitation for bees. **2** a busy place. **3** anything resembling a wicker beehive in being domed.

beeline /'bi:laɪn/ *n.* a straight line between two places. □ **make a beeline for** hurry directly to.

Beelzebub /bi:'elzɪ₁bʌb/ (in the Gospels) the Devil, (in 2 Kings 1) the god of the Philistine city Ekron. The name is not found elsewhere in contemporary sources. [L, rendering (i) Gk *Beelzeboul* (Matt. 12: 24), (ii) Heb. *ba'al z*ᵉ*bûb* lord of flies]

been *past part.* of BE.

beep /bi:p/ *n.* & *v.* —*n.* **1** the sound of a motor-car horn. **2** any similar high-pitched noise. —*v.intr.* emit a beep. □□ **beeper** *n.* [imit.]

beer /bɪə(r)/ *n.* **1 a** an alcoholic drink made from yeast-fermented malt etc., flavoured with hops. **b** a glass of this, esp. a pint or half-pint. **2** any of several other fermented drinks, e.g. ginger beer. □ **beer and skittles** amusement (*life is not all beer and skittles*). **beer-cellar 1** an underground room for storing beer. **2** a basement or cellar for selling or drinking beer. **beer-engine** *Brit.* a machine that draws up beer from a barrel in a cellar. **beer garden** a garden where beer is sold and drunk. **beer hall** a large room where beer is sold and drunk. **beer-mat** a small table-mat for a beer-glass. **beer pump** US = *beer-engine*. [OE *bēor* f. LL *biber* drink f. L *bibere*]

Beerbohm /'bɪəbəʊm/, Sir Henry Maximilian ('Max') (1872–1956), English caricaturist, essayist, and critic. A central figure of the Aesthetic movement, he was well placed to comment on the avant-garde tendencies of the period, which he did with elegance and wit in collections of essays and of caricatures. His one completed novel *Zuleika Dobson* (1911) is a fantasized distillation of the atmosphere of *fin-de-siècle* Oxford.

beerhouse /'bɪəhaʊs/ *n. Brit.* a public house licensed to sell beer but not spirits.

Beersheba /bɪə'ʃi:bə/ a town in southern Israel on the northern edge of the Negev; pop. (1987) 114,600. In Old Testament times it marked the southern limit of Israelite territory (Judges 20; see also DAN 3).

beery /'bɪərɪ/ *adj.* (**beerier, beeriest**) **1** showing the influence

of drink in one's appearance or behaviour. **2** smelling or tasting of beer. □□ **beerily** *adv.* **beeriness** *n.*

beestings /'bi:stɪnz/ *n.pl.* (also treated as *sing.*) the first milk (esp. of a cow) after giving birth. [OE *bēsting* (implied by *bēost*), of unkn. orig.]

beeswax /'bi:zwæks/ *n.* & *v.* —*n.* **1** the wax secreted by bees to make honeycombs. **2** this wax refined and used to polish wood. —*v.tr.* polish (furniture etc.) with beeswax.

beeswing /'bi:zwɪŋ/ *n.* a filmy second crust on old port.

beet /bi:t/ *n.* any plant of the genus *Beta* with an edible root (see BEETROOT, *sugar beet*). [OE *bēte* f. L *beta*, perh. of Celt. orig.]

Beethoven /'beɪthəʊ(ə)n/, Ludwig van (1770–1827), German composer, born at Bonn in the Rhineland, who settled in Vienna in 1792 and remained there for the rest of his life. Always a man of brusque manner, his eccentricities grew after his discovery in 1798 that he was growing deaf, an affliction which worsened steadily in the next twenty years. Like Haydn, his teacher in Vienna, he was pre-eminently an instrumental composer, and he poured powerful new life into the forms of sonata, symphony, and concerto that had matured during the latter part of the 18th c., reshaping them as masterfully as his hero Napoleon (with whom he became disillusioned after the latter proclaimed himself emperor) was reshaping the map of Europe. Such works as the 'Eroica' and Fifth Symphonies, the so-called 'Emperor' Concerto, and the 'Appassionata' Sonata ripened in the climate of the Napoleonic Wars, but when the wars were over Beethoven turned in upon himself. In the piano sonatas of 1816–22 and the string quartets of 1824–6 the old structural forms are only latent; in his Ninth (and last) Symphony he broke with them altogether in the finale by introducing voices to sing Schiller's *Ode to Joy*. With his titanic expansion of 18th c. forms and techniques and the penetration of his later works with personal emotion he crowns the classic age of music and heralds the Romantic.

beetle¹ /'bi:t(ə)l/ *n.* & *v.* —*n.* **1** any insect of the order Coleoptera, with modified front wings forming hard protective cases closing over the back wings. **2** *colloq.* any similar, usu. black, insect. **3** *sl.* a type of compact rounded Volkswagen saloon car. **4** a dice game in which a beetle is drawn or assembled. —*v.intr. colloq.* (foll. by *about, away*, etc.) *Brit.* hurry, scurry. □ **beetle-crusher** *Brit. colloq.* a large boot or foot. [OE *bitula* biter f. *bītan* BITE]

beetle² /'bi:t(ə)l/ *n.* & *v.* —*n.* **1** a tool with a heavy head and a handle, used for ramming, crushing, driving wedges, etc. **2** a machine used for heightening the lustre of cloth by pressure from rollers. —*v.tr.* **1** ram, crush, drive, etc., with a beetle. **2** finish (cloth) with a beetle. [OE *bētel* f. Gmc]

beetle³ /'bi:t(ə)l/ *adj.* & *v.* —*adj.* (esp. of the eyebrows) projecting, shaggy, scowling. —*v.intr.* (usu. as **beetling** *adj.*) (of brows, cliffs, etc.) projecting; overhanging threateningly. □ **beetle-browed** with shaggy, projecting, or scowling eyebrows. [ME: orig. unkn.]

Beeton /'bi:t(ə)n/, Mrs Isabella Mary (1836–65), English author of a book of cookery and household management first published serially (1859–61).

beetroot /'bi:tru:t/ *n.* esp. *Brit.* **1** a beet, *Beta vulgaris*, with an edible spherical dark red root. **2** this root used as a vegetable.

beeves *pl.* of BEEF.

BEF *abbr. hist.* British Expeditionary Force.

befall /bɪ'fɔ:l/ *v.* (*past* **befell** /bɪ'fel/; *past part.* **befallen** /bɪ'fɔ:lən/) *poet.* **1** *intr.* happen (*so it befell*). **2** *tr.* happen to (a person etc.) (*what has befallen her?*). [OE *befeallan* (as BE-, *feallan* FALL)]

befit /bɪ'fɪt/ *v.tr.* (**befitted, befitting**) **1** be fitted or appropriate for; suit. **2** be incumbent on. □□ **befitting** *adj.* **befittingly** *adv.*

befog /bɪ'fɒg/ *v.tr.* (**befogged, befogging**) **1** confuse; obscure. **2** envelop in fog.

befool /bɪ'fu:l/ *v.tr.* make a fool of; delude.

before /bɪ'fɔ:(r)/ *conj., prep., & adv.* —*conj.* **1** earlier than the time when (*crawled before he walked*). **2** rather than that (*would starve before he stole*). —*prep.* **1 a** in front of (*before her in the queue*). **b** ahead of (*crossed the line before him*). **c** under the impulse of (*recoil before the attack*). **d** awaiting (*the future before them*). **2** earlier than; preceding (*Lent comes before Easter*). **3** rather than (*death* *before dishonour).* **4 a** in the presence of *(appear before the judge).* **b** for the attention of *(a plan put before the committee). —adv.* **1 a** earlier than the time in question; already *(heard it before).* **b** in the past *(happened long before).* **2** ahead *(go before).* **3** on the front *(hit before and behind).* □ **Before Christ** (of a date) reckoned backwards from the birth of Christ. **before God** a solemn oath meaning 'as God sees me'. **before time** see TIME. [OE *beforan* f. Gmc]

beforehand /bɪˈfɔːhænd/ *adv.* in anticipation; in advance; in readiness *(had prepared the meal beforehand).* □ **be beforehand with** anticipate; forestall. [ME f. BEFORE + HAND: cf. AF *avant main*]

befoul /bɪˈfaʊl/ *v.tr. poet.* **1** make foul or dirty. **2** degrade; defile *(befouled her name).*

befriend /bɪˈfrend/ *v.tr.* act as a friend to; help.

befuddle /bɪˈfʌd(ə)l/ *v.tr.* **1** make drunk. **2** confuse. □□ **befuddlement** *n.*

beg /beg/ *v.* (**begged, begging**) **1 a** *intr.* (usu. foll. by *for*) ask for (esp. food, money, etc.) *(begged for alms).* **b** *tr.* ask for (food, money, etc.) as a gift. **c** *intr.* live by begging. **2** *tr. & intr.* (usu. foll. by *for,* or *to* + *infin.*) ask earnestly or humbly *(begged for forgiveness; begged to be allowed out; please, I beg of you; beg your indulgence for a time).* **3** *tr.* ask formally for *(beg leave).* **4** *intr.* (of a dog etc.) sit up with the front paws raised expectantly. **5** *tr.* take or ask leave (to do something) *(I beg to differ; beg to enclose).* □ **beg one's bread** live by begging. **begging bowl** **1** a bowl etc. held out for food or alms. **2** an earnest appeal for help. **beg off 1** decline to take part in or attend. **2** get (a person) excused a penalty etc. **beg pardon** see PARDON. **beg the question 1** assume the truth of an argument or proposition to be proved, without arguing it. **2** *disp.* pose the question. **3** *colloq.* evade a difficulty. **go begging** (or **a-begging**) (of a chance or a thing) not be taken; be unwanted. [ME prob. f. OE *bedecian* f. Gmc: rel. to BID]

begad /bɪˈgæd/ *int. archaic colloq.* by God! [corrupt.: cf. GAD²]

began *past* of BEGIN.

begat *archaic past* of BEGET.

beget /bɪˈget/ *v.tr.* (**begetting;** *past* **begot** /bɪˈgɒt/; *archaic* **begat** /bɪˈgæt/; *past part.* **begotten** /bɪˈgɒt(ə)n/) *literary* **1** (usu. of a father, sometimes of a father and mother) procreate. **2** give rise to; cause *(beget strife).* □□ **begetter** *n.* [OE *begietan,* formed as BE- + GET = procreate]

beggar /ˈbegə(r)/ *n. & v.* —*n.* **1** a person who begs, esp. one who lives by begging. **2** a poor person. **3** *colloq.* a fellow *(poor beggar).* —*v.tr.* **1** reduce to poverty. **2** outshine. **3** exhaust the resources of *(beggar description).* □ **beggar-my-neighbour 1** a card-game in which a player seeks to capture an opponent's cards. **2** *(attrib.)* (esp. of national policy) self-aggrandizing at the expense of competitors. **beggars cannot** (or **must not**) **be choosers** those without other resources must take what is offered. [ME f. BEG + -AR³]

beggarly /ˈbegəlɪ/ *adj.* **1** poverty-stricken; needy. **2** intellectually poor. **3** mean; sordid. **4** ungenerous. □□ **beggarliness** *n.*

beggary /ˈbegərɪ/ *n.* extreme poverty.

begin /bɪˈgɪn/ *v.* (**beginning;** *past* **began** /bɪˈgæn/; *past part.* **begun** /bɪˈgʌn/) **1** *tr.* perform the first part of; start *(begin work; begin crying; begin to understand).* **2** *intr.* come into being; arise: **a** in time *(war began in 1939).* **b** in space *(Wales begins beyond the river).* **3** *tr.* (usu. foll. by *to* + *infin.*) start at a certain time *(then began to feel ill).* **4** *intr.* be begun *(the meeting will begin at 7).* **5** *intr.* **a** start speaking *('No,' he began).* **b** take the first step; be the first to do something *(who wants to begin?).* **6** *intr. colloq.* (usu. with neg.) show any attempt or likelihood *(can't begin to compete).* □ **begin at** start from. **begin on** (or **upon**) set to work at. **begin school** attend school for the first time. **begin with** take (a subject, task, etc.) first or as a starting-point. **to begin with** in the first place; as the first thing. [OE *beginnan* f. Gmc]

beginner /bɪˈgɪnə(r)/ *n.* a person just beginning to learn a skill etc. □ **beginner's luck** good luck supposed to attend a beginner at games etc.

beginning /bɪˈgɪnɪŋ/ *n.* **1** the time or place at which anything begins. **2** a source or origin. **3** the first part. □ **the beginning of the end** the first clear sign of a final result.

begone /bɪˈgɒn/ *int. poet.* go away at once!

begonia /bɪˈgəʊnjə/ *n.* any plant of the genus *Begonia* with brightly coloured sepals and no petals, and often having brilliant glossy foliage. [M. *Bégon,* Fr. patron of science d. 1710]

begorra /bɪˈgɒrə/ *int. Ir.* by God! [corrupt.]

begot *past* of BEGET.

begotten *past part.* of BEGET.

begrime /bɪˈgraɪm/ *v.tr.* make grimy.

begrudge /bɪˈgrʌdʒ/ *v.tr.* **1** resent; be dissatisfied at. **2** envy (a person) the possession of. □□ **begrudgingly** *adv.*

beguile /bɪˈgaɪl/ *v.tr.* **1** charm; amuse. **2** divert attention pleasantly from toil etc. **3** (usu. foll. by *of, out of,* or *into* + verbal noun) delude; cheat *(beguiled him into paying).* □□ **beguilement** *n.* **beguiler** *n.* **beguiling** *adj.* **beguilingly** *adv.* [BE- + obs. *guile* to deceive]

beguine /bɪˈgiːn/ *n.* **1** a popular dance of W. Indian origin. **2** its rhythm. [Amer. F f. F *béguin* infatuation]

begum /ˈbeɪgəm/ *n.* in the Indian subcontinent: **1** a Muslim lady of high rank. **2** (**Begum**) the title of a married Muslim woman, equivalent to Mrs. [Urdu *begam* f. E.Turk. *bīgam* princess, fem. of *big* prince: cf. BEY]

begun *past part.* of BEGIN.

behalf /bɪˈhɑːf/ *n.* □ **on** (US **in**) **behalf of** (or **on a person's behalf**) **1** in the interests of (a person, principle, etc.). **2** as representative of *(acting on behalf of my client).* [mixture of earlier phrases *on his halve* and *bihalfe him,* both = on his side: see BY, HALF]

Behan /ˈbiːən/, Brendan (1923–64), Irish playwright. He was arrested in 1939 for his involvement with the IRA, and his subsequent period of Borstal training is described in his autobiographical *Borstal Boy* (1958). His best-known plays are *The Hostage* (1958), a tragicomedy about an English soldier held hostage in a Dublin brothel, and *The Quare Fellow* (1956) set in an Irish prison on the eve of a hanging.

behave /bɪˈheɪv/ *v.* **1** *intr.* **a** act or react (in a specified way) *(behaved well).* **b** (esp. to or of a child) conduct oneself properly. **c** (of a machine etc.) work well (or in a specified way) *(the computer is not behaving today).* **2** *refl.* (esp. of or to a child) show good manners *(behaved herself).* □ **behave towards** treat (in a specified way). **ill-behaved** having bad manners or conduct. **well-behaved** having good manners or conduct. [BE- + HAVE]

behaviour /bɪˈheɪvjə(r)/ *n.* (US **behavior**) **1 a** the way one conducts oneself; manners. **b** the treatment of others; moral conduct. **2** the way in which a ship, machine, chemical substance, etc., acts or works. **3** *Psychol.* the response (of a person, animal, etc.) to a stimulus. □ **behaviour therapy** the treatment of neurotic symptoms by training the patient's reactions (see BEHAVIOURISM). **be on one's good** (or **best**) **behaviour** behave well when being observed. [BEHAVE after *demeanour* and obs. *haviour* f. *have*]

behavioural /bɪˈheɪvjər(ə)l/ *adj.* (US **behavioral**) of or relating to behaviour. □ **behavioural science** the scientific study of human behaviour (see BEHAVIOURISM). □□ **behaviouralist** *n.*

behaviourism /bɪˈheɪvjəˌrɪz(ə)m/ *n.* (US **behaviorism**) *Psychol.* **1** the theory that human behaviour is determined by conditioning rather than by thoughts or feelings, and that psychological disorders are best treated by altering behaviour patterns. (See J. B. WATSON.) **2** such study and treatment in practice. □□ **behaviourist** *n.* **behaviouristic** /-ˈrɪstɪk/ *adj.*

behead /bɪˈhed/ *v.tr.* **1** cut off the head of (a person), esp. as a form of execution. **2** kill by beheading. [OE *behēafdian* (as BE-, *hēafod* HEAD)]

beheld *past* and *past part.* of BEHOLD.

behemoth /bɪˈhiːmɒθ/ *n.* an enormous creature or thing. [ME f. Heb. *behēmōt* intensive pl. of *behēmāh* beast, perh. f. Egyptian *p-ehe-mau* water-ox]

behest /bɪˈhest/ *n. literary* a command; an entreaty *(went at his behest).* [OE *behǣs* f. Gmc]

behind /bɪˈhaɪnd/ *prep., adv., & n.* —*prep.* **1 a** in, towards, or to the rear of. **b** on the further side of *(behind the bush).* **c** hidden by *(something behind that remark).* **2 a** in the past in relation to (*trouble is behind me now*). **b** late in relation to (*behind schedule*). **3** inferior to; weaker than (*rather behind the others in his maths*). **4 a** in support of (*she's right behind us*). **b** responsible for; giving rise to (*the man behind the project; the reasons behind his resignation*). **5** in the tracks of; following. —*adv.* **1 a** in or to or towards the rear; further back (*the street behind; glance behind*). **b** on the further side (*a high wall with a field behind*). **2** remaining after departure (*leave behind; stay behind*). **3** (usu. foll. by *with*) **a** in arrears (*behind with the rent*). **b** late in accomplishing a task etc. (*working too slowly and getting behind*). **4** in a weak position; backward (*behind in Latin*). **5** following (*his dog running behind*). —*n.* **1** *colloq.* the buttocks. **2** (in Australian Rules) a kick etc. scoring one point. □ **behind a person's back** without a person's knowledge. **behind the scenes** see SCENE. **behind time** late. **behind the times** antiquated. **come from behind** win after lagging. **fall** (or **lag**) **behind** not keep up. **put behind one 1** refuse to consider. **2** get over (an unhappy experience etc.). [OE *behindan, bihindan* f. *bi* BY + *hindan* from behind, *hinder* below]

behindhand /bɪˈhaɪndhænd/ *adv. & predic.adj.* **1** (usu. foll. by *with, in*) late (in discharging a duty, paying a debt, etc.). **2** out of date; behind time. [BEHIND + HAND: cf. BEFOREHAND]

behold /bɪˈhəʊld/ *v.tr.* (*past & past part.* **beheld** /bɪˈheld/) *literary* (esp. in *imper.*) see, observe. □□ **beholder** *n.* [OE *bihaldan* (as BE-, *haldan* hold)]

beholden /bɪˈhəʊld(ə)n/ *predic.adj.* (usu. foll. by *to*) under obligation. [past part. (obs. except in this use) of BEHOLD, = bound]

behoof /bɪˈhuːf/ *n. archaic* (prec. by *to, for, on*; foll. by *of*) benefit; advantage. [OE *behōf*]

behove /bɪˈhəʊv/ *v.tr.* (*US* **behoove** /-ˈhuːv/) *formal* (prec. by *it* as subject; foll. by *to* + infin.) **1** be incumbent on. **2** (usu. with *neg.*) befit (*ill behoves him to protest*). [OE *behōfian* f. *behōf*: see BEHOOF]

Behrens /ˈbeərənz/, Peter (1868–1940), German architect, a leading influence in the growth of modern architecture and industrial design in Germany between 1900 and 1914. His most important building was the turbine factory built in 1909 for the electrical combine AEG; it was the first German building in steel and glass and was notable for its functional employment of modern materials for monumental effect.

Behring /ˈberiŋ/, Emil Adolf von (1854–1917), German bacteriologist and immunologist, one of the founders of immunology, who discovered in 1890 that animals can produce substances in the blood which counteract the effects of toxins released by invading bacteria. Behring and his colleagues quickly applied this knowledge of 'antitoxins' (now known to be types of antibody) to curing diphtheria and tetanus by injecting patients with blood serum taken from animals previously exposed to the disease. He was awarded a Nobel Prize in 1901.

beige /beɪʒ/ *n. & adj.* —*n.* a pale sandy fawn colour. —*adj.* of this colour. [F: orig. unkn.]

beigel var. of BAGEL.

Beijing /ˈbiːˈdʒɪŋ/ the Pinyin form of PEKING.

being /ˈbiːɪŋ/ *n.* **1** existence. **2** the nature or essence (of a person etc.) (*his whole being revolted*). **3** a human being. **4** anything that exists or is imagined. □ **in being** existing.

Beira[1] /ˈbeɪrə/ a historic region of north central Portugal, stretching from the Serra da Estrela mountains to the Atlantic coast and comprising the three provinces of Beira Alta, Beira Baixa, and Beira Litoral.

Beira[2] /ˈbeɪrə/ a seaport on the east coast of Mozambique; pop. (est. 1986) 269,700. A railway, road, and oil pipeline along the so-called Beira Corridor link landlocked Zimbabwe with the port of Beira.

Beirut /beɪˈruːt/ the capital and a port of Lebanon; pop. 702,000.

bejabers /bɪˈdʒeɪbəz/ *int.* (also **bejabbers** /-ˈdʒæbəz/) *Ir.* by Jesus! [corrupt.]

bejewelled /bɪˈdʒuːəld/ *adj.* (*US* **bejeweled**) adorned with jewels.

Bekaa /bɪˈkɑː/ a fertile valley in central Lebanon through which the Litani River flows NE–SW between the Lebanon and Anti-Lebanon mountains. The chief towns are Zahlé, Baalbek (see entry), and Hermel.

Bel *Babylonian & Assyrian Mythol.* = BAAL. □ **Bel and the Dragon** a book of the Apocrypha containing stories of Daniel, including his miraculous liberation from the lions' den.

bel /bel/ *n.* a unit used in the comparison of power levels in electrical communication or intensities of sound, corresponding to an intensity ratio of 10 to 1 (cf. DECIBEL). [A. G. BELL]

belabour /bɪˈleɪbə(r)/ *v.tr.* (*US* **belabor**) **1 a** thrash; beat. **b** attack verbally. **2** argue or elaborate (a subject) in excessive detail. [BE- + LABOUR = exert one's strength]

belated /bɪˈleɪtɪd/ *adj.* **1** coming late or too late. **2** overtaken by darkness. □□ **belatedly** *adv.* **belatedness** *n.* [past part. of obs. *belate* delay (as BE-, LATE)]

Belau see PALAU.

belay /bɪˈleɪ/ *v. & n.* —*v.* **1** *tr.* fix (a running rope) round a cleat, pin, rock, etc., to secure it. **2** *tr. & intr.* (usu. in *imper.*) *Naut. sl.* stop; enough! (esp. *belay there!*). —*n.* **1** an act of belaying. **2** a spike of rock etc. used for belaying. □ **belaying-pin** a fixed wooden or iron pin used for fastening a rope round. [Du. *beleggen*]

bel canto /bel ˈkæntəʊ/ *n.* **1** a lyrical style of operatic singing using a full rich broad tone and smooth phrasing. **2** (*attrib.*) (of a type of aria or voice) characterized by this type of singing. [It., = fine song]

belch /beltʃ/ *v. & n.* —*v.* **1** *intr.* emit wind noisily from the stomach through the mouth. **2** *tr.* **a** (of a chimney, volcano, gun, etc.) send (smoke etc.) out or up. **b** utter forcibly. —*n.* an act of belching. [OE *belcettan*]

beldam /ˈbeldəm/ *n.* (also **beldame**) *archaic* **1** an old woman; a hag. **2** a virago. [ME & OF *bel* beautiful + DAM[2], DAME]

beleaguer /bɪˈliːgə(r)/ *v.tr.* **1** besiege. **2** vex; harass. [Du. *belegeren* camp round (as BE-, *leger* a camp)]

Belém /beˈlem/ (also called **Pará** /pəˈrɑː/) a city and port that is the chief commercial centre of northern Brazil, at the mouth of the Amazon; pop. (1980) 756,000.

belemnite /ˈbeləmˌnaɪt/ *n.* any extinct cephalopod of the order Belemnoidea, having a bullet-shaped internal shell often found in fossilized form. [mod.L *belemnites* f. Gk *belemnon* dart + -ITE[1]]

bel esprit /ˌbel eˈspriː/ *n.* (pl. *beaux esprits* /ˌbəʊz eˈspriː/) a witty person. [F, lit. fine mind]

Belfast /belˈfɑːst/ the capital of Northern Ireland, a port at the mouth of the River Lagan; pop. (1987) 303,800.

belfry /ˈbelfrɪ/ *n.* (pl. **-ies**) **1** a bell tower or steeple housing bells, esp. forming part of a church. **2** a space for hanging bells in a church tower. □ **bats in the belfry** see BAT[2]. [ME f. OF *berfrei* f. Frank.: altered by assoc. with *bell*]

Belgian /ˈbeldʒ(ə)n/ *n. & adj.* —*n.* **1** a native or national of Belgium. **2** a person of Belgian descent. —*adj.* of or relating to Belgium. □ **Belgian hare** a dark-red long-eared breed of domestic rabbit.

Belgian Congo the former name (1908–60) of Zaïre.

Belgic /ˈbeldʒɪk/ *adj.* **1** of the ancient Belgae of N. Gaul (see BELGIUM). **2** of the Low Countries. [L *Belgicus* f. *Belgae*]

Belgium /ˈbeldʒəm/ a country in western Europe on the south shore of the North Sea and English Channel, now highly industrialized; pop. (est. 1988) 9,880,500; official languages, Flemish and French; capital, Brussels. The country takes its name from the Belgae, a Celtic people conquered by the Romans in the 1st c. BC. A low-lying area, prosperous in medieval times as a result of textile production and commerce, Belgium was on the border of French, Dutch, and Hapsburg spheres of influence in the 16th–18th c. and, as a result, frequently the site of military operations. After falling at various times under the rule of Burgundy, Spain, Austria, France, and The Netherlands it gained formal independence in 1839 as a consequence of a nationalist revolt that began in 1830, and Prince Leopold of Saxe-Coburg was elected as king. Occupied and devastated during both world wars, Belgium made a quick recovery after 1945, taking the first step towards European economic integration with the formation of the Benelux customs union with The Netherlands and Luxembourg in 1947.

Belgrade /bel'greɪd/ (Serbian **Beograd**) the capital of Yugoslavia, at the junction of the river Sava with the Danube; pop. (1981) 1,455,000.

Belial /'biːlɪəl/ n. the Devil. [Heb. b'liyya'al worthless]

belie /bɪ'laɪ/ v.tr. (**belying**) 1 give a false notion of; fail to corroborate (its appearance belies its age). 2 a fail to fulfil (a promise etc.). b fail to justify (a hope etc.). [OE belēogan (as BE-, lēogan LIE²)]

belief /bɪ'liːf/ n. 1 a a person's religion; religious conviction (has no belief). b a firm opinion (my belief is that he did it). c an acceptance (of a thing, fact, statement, etc.) (belief in the afterlife). 2 (usu. foll. by in) trust or confidence. □ **beyond belief** incredible. **to the best of my belief** in my genuine opinion. [ME f. OE gelēafa (as BELIEVE)]

believe /bɪ'liːv/ v. 1 tr. accept as true or as conveying the truth (I believe it; don't believe him; believes what he is told). 2 tr. think, suppose (I believe it's raining; Mr Smith, I believe?). 3 intr. (foll. by in) a have faith in the existence of (believes in God). b have confidence in (a remedy, a person, etc.) (believes in alternative medicine). c have trust in the advisability of (believes in telling the truth). 4 intr. have (esp. religious) faith. □ **believe one's ears** (or **eyes**) accept that what one apparently hears or sees etc. is true. **believe it or not** colloq. it is true though surprising. **make believe** (often foll. by that + clause, or to + infin.) pretend (let's make believe that we're young again). **would you believe it?** colloq. = believe it or not. □□ **believable** adj. **believability** /-,liːvə'bɪlɪti/ n. [OE belfan, belēfan, with change of prefix f. gelēfan f. Gmc: rel. to LIEF]

believer /bɪ'liːvə(r)/ n. 1 an adherent of a specified religion. 2 a person who believes, esp. in the efficacy of something (a great believer in exercise).

Belisarius /,belɪ'seərɪəs/ (?505–65) a general under Justinian.

Belisha beacon /bə'liːʃə/ n. Brit. a flashing orange ball surmounted on a striped post, marking some pedestrian crossings. [L. Hore-Belisha d. 1957, Minister of Transport 1934]

belittle /bɪ'lɪt(ə)l/ v.tr. 1 depreciate. 2 make small; dwarf. □□ **belittlement** n. **belittler** n. **belittlingly** adv.

Belitung /bɪ'liːtʊŋ/ an Indonesian island in the Java Sea between Borneo and Sumatra.

Belize /be'liːz/ a country on the Caribbean coast of Central America; pop. (est. 1988) 171,700; official language, English; capital, Belmopan. Remains of the Maya civilization have been found in this area. The British settled there in the 17th c., proclaiming the area (as British Honduras) a Crown colony in 1862. It adopted the name Belize (from a Mayan word, = muddy water) in 1973, and in 1981 became an independent State within the Commonwealth. Guatemala, which bounds it on the west and south, has always claimed the territory on the basis of old Spanish treaties. □ **Belize City** the principal seaport and former capital (until 1970) of the country; pop. (1980) 40,000. □□ **Belizian** adj. & n.

Bell¹ /bel/ Alexander Graham (1847–1922), Scottish scientist and inventor, who became interested in sound waves, speech, and helping the deaf. Emigrating to the US, he worked on transmission of messages by telegraphy and then by telephony, using electromagnetic principles. The three patents he took out between 1875 and 1877 were disputed by Edison, but upheld. Bell also invented the gramophone as a successful rival to Edison's phonograph, founded the huge Bell Telephone Company, and investigated the stability of flying machines.

Bell² /bel/ Currer, Ellis, and Acton, see BRONTË.

Bell³ /bel/, Gertrude Margaret Lowthian (1868–1926), English traveller and scholar. After a dozen years of world travel and mountaineering she began her solitary travels as a field archaeologist in the Middle East, acquiring a knowledge of the desert Arabs and local politics. Her writings include The Desert and the Sown (1907) and letters and diaries, all vividly conveying the landscapes and personalities of the desert.

bell¹ /bel/ n. & v. —n. 1 a hollow usu. metal object in the shape of a deep upturned cup usu. widening at the lip, made to sound a clear musical note when struck (either externally or by means of a clapper inside). (See below.) 2 a a sound or stroke of a bell,

esp. as a signal. b (prec. by a numeral) Naut. the time as indicated every half-hour of a watch by the striking of the ship's bell one to eight times. 3 anything that sounds like or functions as a bell, esp. an electronic device that rings etc. as a signal. 4 a any bell-shaped object or part, e.g. of a musical instrument. b the corolla of a flower when bell-shaped. 5 (in pl.) Mus. a set of cylindrical metal tubes of different lengths, suspended in a frame and played by being struck with a hammer. —v.tr. 1 provide with a bell or bells; attach a bell to. 2 (foll. by out) form into the shape of the lip of a bell. □ **bell-bottom** 1 a marked flare below the knee (of a trouser-leg). 2 (in pl.) trousers with bell-bottoms. **bell-bottomed** having bell-bottoms. **bell-buoy** a buoy equipped with a warning bell rung by the motion of the sea. **bell-founder** a person who casts large bells in a foundry. **bell-glass** a bell-shaped glass cover for plants. **bell-jar** a bell-shaped glass cover or container for use in a laboratory. **bell-metal** an alloy of copper and tin for making bells (the tin content being greater than in bronze). **bell-pull** a cord or handle which rings a bell when pulled. **bell-push** a button that operates an electric bell when pushed. **bell-ringer** a person who rings church bells or handbells. **bell-ringing** this as an activity. **bell-tent** a cone-shaped tent supported by a central pole. **bell-wether** 1 the leading sheep of a flock, with a bell on its neck. 2 a ringleader. **clear** (or **sound**) **as a bell** perfectly clear or sound. **ring a bell** colloq. revive a distant recollection; sound familiar. [OE belle: perh. rel. to BELL²]

Bells vary enormously in weight and size, from the huge broken bell at the Kremlin, dating from 1733 and weighing over 170 tons, to small handbells ranged in pitch order on a table. The oldest bell in England is thought to be that at Claughton, Lancs., cast in 1296. Bells occur all over the world, have various powers assigned to them, and possess their own special mystique, whether sinister and awesome or joyous.

bell² /bel/ n. & v. —n. the cry of a stag or buck at rutting-time. —v.intr. make this cry. [OE bellan bark, bellow]

belladonna /,belə'dɒnə/ n. 1 Bot. a poisonous plant, Atropa belladonna, with purple flowers and purple-black berries. Also called deadly nightshade. 2 Med. a drug prepared from this. □ **belladonna lily** a S. African amaryllis with white or pink flowers, Amaryllis belladonna. [mod.L f. It., = fair lady, perh. from its use as a cosmetic]

bellbird /'belbɜːd/ n. any of various birds with a bell-like song, esp. any Central or S. American bird of the genus Procnias, a New Zealand honey-eater, Anthornis melanura, and an Australian bird, Oreoica gutturalis.

bellboy /'belbɔɪ/ n. esp. US a page in a hotel or club.

belle /bel/ n. 1 a beautiful woman. 2 a woman recognized as the most beautiful (the belle of the ball). [F f. L bella fem. of bellus beautiful]

belle époque /,bel eɪ'pɒk/ n. the period of settled and comfortable life preceding the First World War. [F, = fine period]

belle laide /bel 'leɪd/ n. (pl. **belles laides** pronunc. same) a fascinatingly ugly woman. [F f. belle beautiful + laide ugly]

Bellerophon /bɪ'lerəfɒn/ Gk legend a hero who slew the monster Chimaera with the help of the winged horse Pegasus.

belles-lettres /bel 'letr/ n.pl. (also treated as sing.) writings or studies of a literary nature, esp. essays and criticisms. □□ **belletrism** /be'letrɪz(ə)m/ n. **belletrist** /be'letrɪst/ n. **belletristic** /,belə'trɪstɪk/ adj. [F, = fine letters]

bellflower /'bel,flaʊə(r)/ n. = CAMPANULA.

bellicose /'belɪkəʊz/ adj. eager to fight; warlike. □□ **bellicosity** /-'kɒsɪti/ n. [ME f. L bellicosus f. bellum war]

belligerence /bɪ'lɪdʒərəns/ n. (also **belligerency** /-rənsi/) 1 aggressive or warlike behaviour. 2 the status of a belligerent.

belligerent /bɪ'lɪdʒərənt/ adj. & n. —adj. 1 engaged in war or conflict. 2 given to constant fighting; pugnacious. —n. a nation or person engaged in war or conflict. □□ **belligerently** adv. [L belligerare wage war f. bellum war + gerere wage]

Bellini¹ /be'liːni/ the name of a family of Venetian painters. Jacopo (c.1400–70) was trained by Gentile da Fabriano: few of his paintings survive, but over 230 drawings are preserved in two sketchbooks (Louvre and British Museum). His elder son,

æ cat ɑː arm e bed ɜː her ɪ sit iː see ɒ hot ɔː saw ʌ run ʊ put uː too ə ago aɪ my

Gentile (c.1429–1507) was prominent as a portraitist and narrative painter. Giovanni, the younger son (c.1430–1516) transformed Venice into a major centre of Renaissance painting. He was deeply influenced by his brother-in-law Mantegna, but Giovanni's painting is always more fluent and poetic, and its serene contemplative qualities have hardly been equalled. In the 15th c. his work is dominated by Madonnas and other sacred subjects, but he showed astonishing adaptability as an old man, painting the newly fashionable pagan themes and mysterious allegories. Stylistically, he brought a sense of volume to a predominantly linear art, and, around 1500, moved to a more atmospheric method of painting which paralleled that of his young pupils Giorgione and Titian.

Bellini[2] /beˈliːniː/, Vincenzo (1801–35), Italian composer of 11 operas before his untimely death in France. He is most famous for *La sonnambula*, *Norma* (both 1831), and *I Puritani* (1835); the soprano aria 'Casta diva' ('Chaste goddess'), in which Norma prays for peace between the Romans and the Druids, is the supreme example of his gift for long-breathed melody, while in the last act of that opera, where Norma chooses to sacrifice her life, Bellini achieves his finest expression of tragic doomed grandeur.

bellman /ˈbelmən/ n. (pl. **-men**) hist. a town crier.

Belloc /ˈbelɒk/, Hilaire (1870–1953), versatile British writer (poet, essayist, historian, novelist), and Liberal MP (1906–10). A devout Roman Catholic, he collaborated with G. K. Chesterton in works often directly opposing the socialism of G. B. Shaw and H. G. Wells, notably in *The Servile State* (1912). He wrote biographies of Danton, Robespierre, Napoleon, and Cromwell, and numerous travel works including *The Path to Rome* (1902), but is today best known for his popular light verse, such as *The Bad Child's Book of Beasts* (1896) and *Cautionary Tales* (1907).

Bellow /ˈbeləʊ/, Saul (1915–   ), American novelist, born in Canada of Russian-Jewish parentage. His works range from the richly comic *The Adventures of Augie March* (1953), a picaresque account of a young Chicago Jew, to the semi-autobiographic *Herzog* (1964). He was awarded the Nobel Prize for literature in 1976.

bellow /ˈbeləʊ/ v. & n. —v. 1 intr. **a** emit a deep loud roar. **b** cry or shout with pain. 2 tr. utter loudly and usu. angrily. —n. a bellowing sound. [ME: perh. rel. to BELL[2]]

bellows /ˈbeləʊz/ n.pl. (also treated as sing.) 1 a device with an air bag that emits a stream of air when squeezed, esp.: **a** (in full **pair of bellows**) a kind with two handles used for blowing air on to a fire. **b** a kind used in a harmonium or small organ. 2 an expandable component, e.g. joining the lens to the body of a camera. [ME prob. f. OE *belga* pl. of *belig* belly]

belly /ˈbeli/ n. & v. —n. (pl. **-ies**) 1 the part of the human body below the chest, containing the stomach and bowels. 2 the stomach, esp. representing the body's need for food. 3 the front of the body from the waist to the groin. 4 the underside of a four-legged animal. 5 **a** a cavity or bulging part of anything. **b** the surface of an instrument of the violin family, across which the strings are placed. —v.tr. & intr. (**-ies**, **-ied**) (often foll. by *out*) swell or cause to swell; bulge. □ **belly button** colloq. the navel. **belly-dance** an oriental dance performed by a woman, involving voluptuous movements of the belly. **belly-dancer** a woman who performs belly-dances, esp. professionally. **belly-dancing** the performance of belly-dances. **belly-landing** a crash-landing of an aircraft on the underside of the fuselage, without lowering the undercarriage. **belly-laugh** a loud unrestrained laugh. [OE *belig* (orig. = bag) f. Gmc]

bellyache /ˈbeliˌeɪk/ n. & v. —n. colloq. a stomach pain. —v.intr. sl. complain noisily or persistently. □□ **bellyacher** n.

bellyband /ˈbeliˌbænd/ n. a band placed round a horse's belly, holding the shafts of a cart etc.

bellyflop /ˈbeliˌflɒp/ n. & v. colloq. —n. a dive into water in which the body lands with the belly flat on the water. —v.intr. (**-flopped, -flopping**) perform this dive.

bellyful /ˈbeliˌfʊl/ n. (pl. **-fuls**) 1 enough to eat. 2 colloq. enough or more than enough of anything (esp. unwelcome).

Belmopan /ˌbelməʊˈpæn/ the capital of Belize. Founded in

1970, it is one of the smallest capital cities in the world; pop. (est. 1986) 3,500.

Belo Horizonte /ˈbeləʊ ˌhɒrɪˈzɒnteɪ/ a city in eastern Brazil, capital of the State of Minas Gerais, situated at the centre of a rich mining and agricultural region; pop. (1980) 1,441,600. Built in 1895–7, it was Brazil's first planned modern city.

belong /bɪˈlɒŋ/ v.intr. 1 (foll. by *to*) **a** be the property of. **b** be rightly assigned to as a duty, right, part, member, characteristic, etc. **c** be a member of (a club, family, group, etc.). 2 have the right personal or social qualities to be a member of a particular group (*he's nice but just doesn't belong*). 3 (foll. by *in, under*): **a** be rightly placed or classified. **b** fit a particular environment. □□ **belongingness** n. [ME f. intensive BE- + *longen* belong f. OE *langian* (*gelang* at hand)]

belongings /bɪˈlɒŋɪŋz/ n.pl. one's movable possessions or luggage.

Belorussia /ˌbeləʊˈrʌʃə/ (also known as **White Russia**) the Belorussian SSR, a constituent republic of the USSR in the west of the country; pop. (est. 1987) 10,078,000; capital, Minsk. [Russ. *Belorussiya* f. *belyi* white + *Russiya* Russia]

Belorussian /ˌbeləʊˈrʌʃ(ə)n/ n. & adj. (also **Byelorussian** /ˌbjeləʊ-/) —n. 1 a native of Belorussia. 2 the language of Belorussia. —adj. of or relating to Belorussia or its people or language.

beloved /bɪˈlʌvɪd, predic. also -lʌvd/ adj. & n. —adj. much loved. —n. a much loved person. [obs. *belove* (v.)]

below /bɪˈləʊ/ prep. & adv. —prep. 1 lower in position (vertically, down a slope or stream, etc.) than. 2 beneath the surface of; at or to a greater depth than (*head below water*; *below 500 feet*). 3 lower or less than in amount or degree (*below freezing-point*; *temperature is 20 below*). 4 lower in rank, position, or importance than. 5 unworthy of. —adv. 1 at or to a lower point or level. 2 **a** downstairs (*lives below*). **b** downstream. 3 (of a text reference) further forward on a page or in a book (*as noted below*). 4 on the lower side (*looks similar above and below*). 5 rhet. on earth; in hell. □ **below stairs** in the basement of a house esp. as the part occupied by servants. [BE- + LOW[1]]

Bel Paese /ˌbel pɑːˈeɪzeɪ/ n. propr. a rich white mild creamy cheese of a kind orig. made in Italy. [It., = fair country]

Belsen /ˈbels(ə)n/ a village in NW Germany, site of a Nazi concentration camp in the Second World War.

Belshazzar /belˈʃæzə(r)/ (in Dan. 5) son of Nebuchadnezzar and last king of Babylon, who was killed in the sack of the city by Cyrus (538 BC) and whose doom was foretold by writing which appeared on the walls of his palace at a great banquet. In inscriptions and documents from Ur, however, he was the son of Nabonidos, last king of Babylon, and did not himself reign.

belt /belt/ n. & v. —n. 1 a strip of leather or other material worn round the waist or across the chest, esp. to retain or support clothes or to carry weapons or as a safety-belt. 2 a belt worn as a sign of rank or achievement. 3 **a** a circular band of material used as a driving medium in machinery. **b** a conveyor belt. **c** a flexible strip carrying machine-gun cartridges. 4 a strip of colour or texture etc. differing from that on each side. 5 a distinct region or extent (*cotton belt*; *commuter belt*; *a belt of rain*). 6 sl. a heavy blow. —v. 1 tr. put a belt round. 2 tr. (often foll. by *on*) fasten with a belt. 3 tr. **a** beat with a belt. **b** sl. hit hard. 4 intr. sl. rush, hurry (usu. with compl.: *belted along*; *belted home*). □ **below the belt** unfair or unfairly; disregarding the rules. **belt and braces** (of a policy etc.) of twofold security. **belt out** sl. sing or utter loudly and forcibly. **belt up** Brit. 1 sl. be quiet. 2 colloq. put on a seat belt. **tighten one's belt** live more frugally. **under one's belt** 1 (of food) eaten. 2 securely acquired (*has a degree under her belt*). □□ **belter** n. (esp. in sense of *belt out*). [OE f. Gmc f. L *balteus*]

Beltane /ˈbelteɪn/ n. an ancient Celtic festival celebrated on May Day. [Gael. *bealltainn*]

beltman /ˈbeltmæn/ n. (pl. **-men**) Austral. a member of a life-saving team of surfers.

beluga /bəˈluːgə/ n. 1 **a** a large kind of sturgeon, *Huso huso*. **b** caviare obtained from it. 2 a white whale. [Russ. *beluga* f. *belyi* white]

belvedere /ˈbelvɪˌdɪə(r)/ n. a summer-house or open-sided gallery usu. at rooftop level. [It. f. *bel* beautiful + *vedere* see]

belying *pres. part.* of BELIE.

BEM *abbr.* British Empire Medal.

bemire /bɪˈmaɪə(r)/ v.tr. **1** cover or stain with mud. **2** (in *passive*) be stuck in mud. [BE- + MIRE]

bemoan /bɪˈməʊn/ v.tr. **1** express regret or sorrow over; lament. **2** complain about. [BE- + MOAN]

bemuse /bɪˈmjuːz/ v.tr. stupefy or bewilder (a person). □□ **bemusedly** /-zɪdlɪ/ adv. **bemusement** n. [BE- + MUSE²]

ben¹ /ben/ n. Sc. a high mountain or mountain peak, esp. in names (*Ben Nevis*). [Gael. *beann*]

ben² /ben/ n. Sc. an inner room, esp. of a two-roomed cottage. [ellipt. use of *ben* (adv.), = within (OE *binnan*)]

Benares see VARANASI.

Ben Bella /ben ˈbelə/, Ahmed (1916–), Algerian leader, who worked for the independence of his country and became its first Prime Minister (1962–5) and President (1963–5).

bench /bentʃ/ n. & v. —n. **1** a long seat of wood or stone for seating several people. **2** a working-table, e.g. for a carpenter, mechanic, or scientist. **3** (prec. by *the*) **a** the office of judge or magistrate. **b** a judge's seat in a lawcourt. **c** a lawcourt. **d** judges and magistrates collectively. **4** (often in *pl.*) *Sport* an area to the side of a pitch, with seating where coaches and players not taking part can watch the game. **5** *Brit. Parl.* a seat appropriated as specified (*front bench*). **6** a level ledge in masonry or an earthwork, on a hill-slope, etc. —v.tr. **1** exhibit (a dog) at a show. **2** *Sport US* withdraw (a player) from the pitch to the benches. □ **bench test** esp. *Computing* n. a test made by benchmarking. —v.tr. run a series of tests on (a computer etc.) before its use. **King's** (or **Queen's**) **Bench** (in the UK) a division of the High Court of Justice. **on the bench** appointed a judge or magistrate. [OE *benc* f. Gmc]

bencher /ˈbentʃə(r)/ n. Brit. **1** Law a senior member of any of the Inns of Court. **2** (in *comb.*) Parl. an occupant of a specified bench (*backbencher*).

benchmark /ˈbentʃmɑːk/ n. & v. —n. **1** a surveyor's mark cut in a wall, pillar, building, etc., used as a reference point in measuring altitudes. **2** a standard or point of reference. **3** a means of testing a computer, usu. by a set of programs run on a series of different machines. —v.tr. evaluate (a computer) by a benchmark. □ **benchmark test** a test using a benchmark.

bend¹ /bend/ v. & n. —v. (*past* **bent**; *past part.* **bent** exc. in *bended knee*) **1 a** tr. force or adapt (something straight) into a curve or angle. **b** intr. (of an object) be altered in this way. **2** intr. move or stretch in a curved course (*the road bends to the left*). **3** intr. & tr. (often foll. by *down, over*, etc.) incline or cause to incline from the vertical (*bent down to pick it up*). **4** tr. interpret or modify (a rule) to suit oneself. **5** tr. & refl. (foll. by *to, on*) direct or devote (oneself or one's attention, energies, etc.). **6** tr. turn (one's steps or eyes) in a new direction. **7** tr. (in *passive*; foll. by *on*) have firmly decided; be determined (*was bent on selling; on pleasure bent*). **8 a** intr. stoop or submit (*bent before his master*). **b** tr. force to submit. **9** tr. Naut. attach (a sail or cable) with a knot. —n. **1** a curve in a road or other course. **2** a departure from a straight course. **3** a bent part of anything. **4** (in *pl.*; prec. by *the*) colloq. sickness due to too rapid decompression underwater. □ **bend over backwards** see BACKWARDS. **round the bend** colloq. crazy, insane. □□ **bendable** adj. [OE *bendan* f. Gmc]

bend² /bend/ n. **1** Naut. any of various knots for tying ropes (*fisherman's bend*). **2** Heraldry **a** a diagonal stripe from top right to bottom left of a shield. **b** (**bend sinister**) a diagonal stripe from top left to bottom right, as a sign of bastardy. [OE *bend* band, bond f. Gmc]

bender /ˈbendə(r)/ n. sl. a wild drinking-spree. [BEND¹ + -ER¹]

Bendigo /ˈbendɪˌgəʊ/ a former gold-mining town in the State of Victoria, Australia; pop. (1986) 64,800. It is said to have been named after a local prizefighter who adopted the nickname of an English pugilist (William Thompson, 1811–80) whom he admired.

bendy /ˈbendɪ/ adj. (**bendier**, **bendiest**) colloq. capable of bending; soft and flexible. □□ **bendiness** n.

beneath /bɪˈniːθ/ prep. & adv. —prep. **1** not worthy of; too demeaning for (*it was beneath him to reply*). **2** below, under. —adv. below, under, underneath. □ **beneath contempt** see CONTEMPT. [OE *binithan, bineothan* f. *bi* BY + *nithan* etc. below f. Gmc]

benedicite /ˌbenɪˈdaɪsɪtɪ/ n. a blessing, esp. a grace said at table in religious communities. [ME f. L, = bless ye: see BENEDICTION]

Benedict /ˈbenɪdɪkt/, St (*c*.480–*c*.550), a hermit, the 'Patriarch of Western monasticism', compiler of a monastic rule (chiefly at Monte Cassino in Italy) though he does not seem to have been ordained or to have contemplated founding an order. He was buried at Monte Cassino in the same grave as his sister, St Scholastica. Feast day, 21 March.

The rule of St Benedict was gradually adopted by most western monastic houses, sometimes with their own modifications. Relaxations of discipline were followed by attempts at reform, and resulted in the formation of separate orders, which remained largely independent of any wider organization. The Benedictines have rendered invaluable services to civilization, preparing the social organization of the Middle Ages during the chaos after the fall of the Roman Empire, preserving ideals of scholarship, and maintaining or restoring the use of good art in liturgical worship.

Benedictine /ˌbenɪˈdɪktɪn, (in sense 2) -ˌtiːn/ n. & adj. —n. **1** a monk or nun of an order following the rule of St Benedict. The monks are also called Black Monks from the colour of their habits. **2** propr. a liqueur based on brandy, orig. made by Benedictines in France. —adj. of St Benedict or the Benedictines. [F *bénédictine* or mod.L *benedictinus* f. *Benedictus* Benedict]

benediction /ˌbenɪˈdɪkʃ(ə)n/ n. **1** the utterance of a blessing, esp. at the end of a religious service or as a special Roman Catholic service. **2** the state of being blessed. [ME f. OF f. L *benedictio -onis* f. *benedicere -dict-* bless]

benedictory /ˌbenɪˈdɪktərɪ/ adj. of or expressing benediction. [L *benedictorius* (as BENEDICTION)]

Benedictus /ˌbenɪˈdɪktəs/ n. **1** the section of the Roman Catholic Mass beginning *Benedictus qui venit in nomine Domini* (Blessed is he who comes in the name of the Lord). **2** a canticle beginning *Benedictus Dominus Deus* (Blessed be the Lord God) from Luke 1: 68–79. [L, = blessed: see BENEDICTION]

benefaction /ˌbenɪˈfækʃ(ə)n/ n. **1** a donation or gift. **2** an act of giving or doing good. [LL *benefactio* (as BENEFIT)]

benefactor /ˈbenɪˌfæktə(r)/ n. (*fem.* **benefactress** /-trɪs/) a person who gives support (esp. financial) to a person or cause. [ME f. LL (as BENEFIT)]

benefice /ˈbenɪfɪs/ n. **1** a living from a church office. **2** the property attached to a church office, esp. that bestowed on a rector or vicar. □□ **beneficed** adj. [ME f. OF f. L *beneficium* favour f. *bene* well + *facere* do]

beneficent /bɪˈnefɪs(ə)nt/ adj. doing good; generous, actively kind. □□ **beneficence** n. **beneficently** adv. [L *beneficent-* (as BENEFICE)]

beneficial /ˌbenɪˈfɪʃ(ə)l/ adj. **1** advantageous; having benefits. **2** Law relating to the use or benefit of property; having rights to this use or benefit. □□ **beneficially** adv. [ME f. F *bénéficial* or LL *beneficialis* (as BENEFICE)]

beneficiary /ˌbenɪˈfɪʃərɪ/ n. (*pl.* **-ies**) **1** a person who receives benefits, esp. under a person's will. **2** a holder of a church living. [L *beneficiarius* (as BENEFICE)]

benefit /ˈbenɪfɪt/ n. & v. —n. **1** a favourable or helpful factor or circumstance; advantage, profit. **2** (often in *pl.*) payment made under insurance or social security (*sickness benefit*). **3** a public performance or game of which the proceeds go to a particular player or company or charitable cause. —v. (**benefited**, **benefiting**; US **benefitted**, **benefitting**) **1** tr. do good to; bring advantage to. **2** intr. (often foll. by *from, by*) receive an advantage or gain. □ **benefit of clergy 1** hist. exemption of the English tonsured clergy and nuns from the jurisdiction of the ordinary civil courts. **2** ecclesiastical sanction or approval (*marriage without benefit of clergy*). **the benefit of the doubt** a concession that a person is innocent, correct, etc., although doubt exists. **benefit society** a society for mutual insurance against illness or the effects of old age. [ME f. AF *benfet*, OF *bienfet*, f. L *benefactum* f. *bene facere* do well]

Benelux /ˈbenɪˌlʌks/ a collective name for Belgium, The Netherlands, and Luxembourg, especially with reference to their economic cooperation established in 1948. [*Belgium* + *Netherlands* + *Luxembourg*]

Beneš /ˈbeneʃ/, Edvard (1884–1948), Czechoslovak statesman, a founder (with Tomáš Masaryk) of modern Czechoslovakia, President of his country 1935–8 and 1946–8 and of its government in exile during the Second World War. He resigned in 1948 after the Communist coup.

benevolent /bɪˈnevələnt/ *adj.* **1** wishing to do good; actively friendly and helpful. **2** charitable (*benevolent fund*; *benevolent society*). □□ **benevolence** *n.* **benevolently** *adv.* [ME f. OF *benivolent* f. L *bene volens -entis* well wishing f. *velle* wish]

B.Eng. *abbr.* Bachelor of Engineering.

Bengali /beŋˈɡɔːlɪ/ *n.* & *adj.* —*n.* (*pl.* **Bengalis**) **1** a native of Bengal. **2** the language of Bengal, spoken by some 125 million people. It is a descendant of Sanskrit, written in a version of the Sanskrit Devanagari script, and is the official language of Bangladesh. —*adj.* of or relating to Bengal or its people or language.

Bengal light /beŋˈɡɔːl/ *n.* a kind of firework giving off a blue flame, used for signals.

Benghazi /benˈɡɑːzɪ/ a Mediterranean port in NE Libya; pop. (1984) 485,400. It was the co-capital of Libya from 1951 to 1972.

Benguela /beŋˈɡwelə/ a port and railway terminal of Angola, on the Atlantic coast; pop. 41,000. The railway provides an outlet for copper exports from the African interior.

Ben-Gurion /ˌbenˈɡʊrɪən/, David (1886–1973), Israeli statesman, born in Russian Poland. As Israel's first Prime Minister (1948–53, 1955–63) and Minister of Defence, he played the largest part in shaping the State of Israel during its formative years.

benighted /bɪˈnaɪtɪd/ *adj.* **1** intellectually or morally ignorant. **2** overtaken by darkness. □□ **benightedness** *n.* [obs. *benight* (v.)]

benign /bɪˈnaɪn/ *adj.* **1** gentle, mild, kindly. **2** fortunate, salutary. **3** (of the climate, soil, etc.) mild, favourable. **4** *Med.* (of a disease, tumour, etc.) not malignant. □□ **benignly** *adv.* [ME f. OF *benigne* f. L *benignus* f. *bene* well + -*genus* born]

benignant /bɪˈnɪɡnənt/ *adj.* **1** kindly, esp. to in- feriors. **2** salutary, beneficial. **3** *Med.* = BENIGN. □□ **benignancy** *n.* **benignantly** *adv.* [f. BENIGN or L *benignus*, after *malignant*]

benignity /bɪˈnɪɡnɪtɪ/ *n.* (*pl.* -**ies**) **1** kindliness. **2** an act of kindness. [ME f. OF *benignité* or L *benignitas* (as BENIGN)]

Benin /beˈnɪn/ a country of western Africa, immediately west of Nigeria; pop. (est. 1988) 4,497,100; official language, French; capital, Porto Novo. Known as Dahomey, and a centre of the slave trade, the country was conquered by the French in 1893 and became part of French West Africa. In 1960 it became fully independent and in 1975 adopted the name of Benin, a former African kingdom (in what is now southern Nigeria) that was powerful in the 14th–17th c. and was famous for its bronze and ivory sculptures. □ **Bight of Benin** a wide bay on the coast of Africa north of the Gulf of Guinea, bordered by Togo, Benin, and SW Nigeria. Lagos is its chief port. □□ **Beninese** /ˌbenɪˈniːz/ *adj.* & *n.*

benison /ˈbenɪz(ə)n/ *n. archaic* a blessing. [ME f. OF *beneiçun* f. L *benedictio -onis*]

Benjamin /ˈbendʒəmɪn/ **1** a Hebrew patriarch, the youngest and favourite son of Jacob (Gen. 35: 8, 42, etc.). **2** the smallest tribe of Israel, traditionally descended from him.

Bennett /ˈbenɪt/, (Enoch) Arnold (1867–1931), English novelist who began a versatile literary career in London writing stories for periodicals and editing the journal *Woman*. He lived in Paris (1902–12) where he was greatly influenced by the French realists, and wrote several successful plays, but his fame rests on his novels and stories set in the Potteries (the 'Five Towns') of his youth, notably *Anna of the Five Towns* (1902), *The Old Wives' Tale* (1908), and the *Clayhanger* series (1902–8), in which he portrays provincial life and culture in documentary detail.

Ben Nevis /ben ˈnevɪs/ the highest mountain in the British Isles (1,343 m, 4,406 ft.), in western Scotland.

bent[1] /bent/ *past* and *past part.* of BEND[1] *v.* —*adj.* **1** curved or having an angle. **2** *sl.* dishonest, illicit. **3** *sl.* sexually deviant. **4** (foll. by *on*) determined to do or have. —*n.* **1** an inclination or bias. **2** (foll. by *for*) a talent for something specified (*a bent for mimicry*).

bent[2] /bent/ *n.* **1 a** any stiff grass of the genus *Agrostis*. **b** any of various grasslike reeds, rushes, or sedges. **2** a stiff stalk of a grass usu. with a flexible base. **3** *archaic* or *dial.* a heath or unenclosed pasture. [ME repr. OE *beonet-* (in place-names), f. Gmc]

Bentham /ˈbentəm, -θəm/, Jeremy (1748–1832), English philosopher, the first major proponent of utilitarianism, advocating the organization of society to secure 'the greatest happiness of the greatest number' and concerned to reform the law by giving it a clear theoretical justification. He went beyond general theoretical foundations and produced intricate classifications of kinds of pleasures and pains, motives, dispositions, and offences, and attacked the concept of natural rights, which he called 'nonsense on stilts'. He also made plans for a model prison, which were taken seriously but never put into practice. Bentham exercised a decisive influence over 19th-c. British thought, particularly with reference to political reform. □□ **Benthamism** /ˈbenθəˌmɪz(ə)m/ *n.* **Benthamite** *n.* & *adj.*

benthos /ˈbenθɒs/ *n.* the flora and fauna found at the bottom of a sea or lake. □□ **benthic** *adj.* [Gk, = depth of the sea]

bentonite /ˈbentəˌnaɪt/ *n.* a kind of absorbent clay used esp. as a filler. [Fort *Benton* in Montana, US]

ben trovato /ˌben trəʊˈvɑːtəʊ/ *adj.* **1** well invented. **2** characteristic if not true. [It., = well found]

bentwood /ˈbentwʊd/ *n.* wood that is artificially shaped for use in making furniture.

benumb /bɪˈnʌm/ *v.tr.* **1** make numb; deaden. **2** paralyse (the mind or feelings). [orig. = deprived, as past part. of ME *benimen* f. OE *beniman* (as BE-, *niman* take)]

Benz /bents/, Karl Friedrich (1844–1929), German engineer, one of the great pioneers of the motor car, building the first car (a three-wheeled vehicle) to be driven by an internal-combustion engine, at Mannheim in Germany in 1885.

Benzedrine /ˈbenzɪˌdriːn/ *n. propr.* amphetamine. [BENZOIC + EPHEDRINE]

benzene /ˈbenziːn/ *n.* a colourless carcinogenic volatile liquid found in coal tar, petroleum, etc., and used as a solvent and in the manufacture of plastics etc. ¶ *Chem.* formula: C_6H_6. □ **benzene ring** the hexagonal unsaturated ring of six carbon atoms in the benzene molecule. □□ **benzenoid** *adj.* [BENZOIC + -ENE]

benzine /ˈbenziːn/ *n.* (also **benzin** /-zɪn/) a mixture of liquid hydrocarbons obtained from petroleum. [BENZOIN + -INE[4]]

benzoic /benˈzəʊɪk/ *adj.* containing or derived from benzoin or benzoic acid. □ **benzoic acid** a white crystalline substance used as a food preservative. ¶ *Chem.* formula: $C_7H_6O_2$. [BENZOIN + -IC]

benzoin /ˈbenzəʊɪn/ *n.* **1** a fragrant gum resin obtained from various E. Asian trees of the genus *Styrax*, and used in the manufacture of perfumes and incense. **2** the white crystalline constituent of this. Also called *gum benjamin*. [earlier *benjoin* ult. f. Arab. *lubān jāwī* incense of Java]

benzol /ˈbenzɒl/ *n.* (also **benzole** /-zəʊl/) benzene, esp. unrefined and used as a fuel.

benzoyl /ˈbenzəʊɪl/ *n.* (usu. *attrib.*) *Chem.* the radical C_6H_5CO.

benzyl /ˈbenzaɪl, -zɪl/ *n.* (usu. *attrib.*) *Chem.* the radical $C_6H_5CH_2$.

Beograd see BELGRADE.

Beowulf /ˈbeɪəˌwʊlf/ a legendary Swedish hero celebrated in the Old English epic poem 'Beowulf'. The historical events referred to in the poem belong to the first part of the 6th c., but the date of the poem itself is less certain since it includes both heathen and Christian religious elements.

bequeath /bɪˈkwiːð/ *v.tr.* **1** leave (a personal estate) to a person by a will. **2** hand down to posterity. □□ **bequeathal** *n.* **bequeather** *n.* [OE *becwethan* (as BE-, *cwethan* say: cf. QUOTH)]

bequest /bɪˈkwest/ n. **1** the act or an instance of bequeathing. **2** a thing bequeathed. [ME f. BE- + obs. *quiste* f. OE -*cwiss*, *cwide* saying]

berate /bɪˈreɪt/ v.tr. scold, rebuke. [BE- + RATE²]

Berber /ˈbɜːbə(r)/ n. & adj. —n. **1** a member of the indigenous mainly Muslim Caucasian peoples of N. Africa (now mainly in Morocco and Algeria) speaking related languages. **2** the Hamito-Semitic language or group of languages of these peoples. —adj. of the Berbers or their language. [Arab. *barbar*]

Berbera /ˈbɜːbərə/ a port on the north coast of Somalia, until 1941 the winter capital of British Somaliland; pop. 65,000.

berberis /ˈbɜːbərɪs/ n. = BARBERRY. [med.L & OF, of unkn. orig.]

berceuse /beəˈsɜːz/ n. (pl. **berceuses** pronunc. same) **1** a lullaby. **2** an instrumental piece in the style of a lullaby. [F]

bereave /bɪˈriːv/ v.tr. (esp. as **bereaved** adj.) (foll. by *of*) deprive of a relation, friend, etc., esp. by death. □□ **bereavement** n. [OE *berēafian* (as BE-, REAVE)]

bereft /bɪˈreft/ adj. (foll. by *of*) deprived (esp. of a non-material asset) (*bereft of hope*). [past part. of BEREAVE]

Berenice /ˌberɪˈnaɪsɪ/ (3rd c. BC) Egyptian queen, wife of Ptolemy III. During his absence on an expedition in Syria she dedicated her hair as a votive offering for his safe return. The hair was stolen, and legend said that it was carried to the heavens where it became the constellation *Coma Berenices*.

beret /ˈbereɪ/ n. a round flattish cap of felt or cloth. [F *béret* Basque cap f. Prov. *berret*]

Berg /beəg/, Alban (1885–1935), Austrian composer who studied with Schoenberg in Vienna, and together with Anton Webern became his greatest pupil. The emotional content of his music has done much to ease public acceptance of his use of 12-note music and serial techniques, and one of his best-loved works is the Violin Concerto (1935), composed as a memorial after the death of the 18-year-old daughter of Alma and Walter Gropius. His two operas, *Wozzeck* (1914–21) and *Lulu* (1928–35), the former based on a play by Georg Büchner and the latter on two plays by Wedekind, combine an expressionist violence with a deep compassion for his unfortunate hero and heroine. His music, together with that of Schoenberg and Webern, was condemned by Hitler as 'degenerate art'.

berg¹ /bɜːg/ n. = ICEBERG. [abbr.]

berg² /bɜːg/ n. S.Afr. a mountain or hill. □ **berg wind** a hot dry northerly wind blowing from the interior to coastal districts. [Afrik. f. Du.]

bergamot¹ /ˈbɜːgəˌmɒt/ n. **1** an aromatic herb, esp. *Mentha citrata*. **2** an oily perfume extracted from the rind of the fruit of the citrus tree *Citrus bergamia*, a dwarf variety of the Seville orange tree. **3** the tree itself. [*Bergamo* in N. Italy]

bergamot² /ˈbɜːgəˌmɒt/ n. a variety of fine pear. [F *bergamotte* f. It. *bergamotta* f. Turk. *begarmūdi* prince's pear f. *beg* prince + *armudi* pear]

Bergen¹ /ˈbɜːgən, ˈbeəgən/ a seaport in SW Norway, birthplace of the composer Edvard Grieg; pop. (1988) 209,830.

Bergen² see MONS.

Bergerac¹ /ˈbeəʒəˌræk/ a wine-producing region in the Dordogne in SW France.

Bergerac² see CYRANO DE BERGERAC.

Bergman¹ /ˈbeəgmən/, Ingmar (1918–), Swedish film and theatre director. After several films about the problems of the young he turned to studies of feminine psychology, one of which, *Smiles of a Summer Night* (1955), made him internationally famous. He achieved further worldwide success with *The Seventh Seal* and *Wild Strawberries* (both 1957), each of them, together with several subsequent films, concerned with man's isolation from God. In *Persona* (1966), *Cries and Whispers* (1972), and *Autumn Sonata* (1978) Bergman turned from metaphysics to study the relationships between women. *Fanny and Alexander* (1982) was announced as being his last film. Bergman is also important as a theatre director, notably at Stockholm's Royal Dramatic Theatre, and many of his players worked frequently with him in both media.

Bergman² /ˈbeəgmən/, Ingrid (1915–82), Swedish film and

stage actress, whose films include *Casablanca* (1943), *For Whom the Bell Tolls* (1943), and *Anastasia* (1956).

bergschrund /ˈbeəkʃrʊnt/ n. a crevasse or gap at the head of a glacier or névé. [G]

Bergson /ˈbɜːgs(ə)n, ˈbeək-/, Henri (1859–1941), French philosopher, whose ideas influenced the novelist Proust (whose cousin he married in 1891), impressed William James (who became a close friend), and reached a wide public throughout Europe. His philosophy is dualistic, dividing the world into life (or consciousness) and matter. In his most famous work *Creative Evolution* (1907) he interprets evolution as the continuous operation of a vital impulse (*élan vital*), which is a manifestation of a single original impulse seeking to impose itself upon matter, which resists it; latterly Bergson identified this force with a God whose being and purpose are love. We perceive matter through intellect, but it is through intuition (which is superior to intellect) that we perceive this life force and the reality of time, which is an indivisible flow of experience and not as measured in units. After the First World War Bergson spent much time attempting to promote international peace and cooperation. He was awarded the Nobel Prize for literature for 1927.

Beria /ˈberɪə/, Lavrenti Pavlovich (1899–1953), Soviet politician and head of the secret police (MVD). After Stalin's death (1953) he became a victim of the ensuing struggle for power in which Malenkov and Khrushchev were successful; he was executed after a secret trial.

beriberi /ˌberɪˈberɪ/ n. a disease causing inflammation of the nerves due to a deficiency of vitamin B₁. [Sinh., f. *beri* weakness]

Bering /ˈbeərɪŋ/, Vitus Jonassen (1681–1741), Danish navigator and explorer of Arctic Asia, who led several Russian expeditions aimed at discovering whether Asia and North America were connected by land. He sailed along the coast of Siberia, and in 1741 reached Alaska from the east. On the return journey his ship was wrecked and he died on an island which now bears his name. Also named after him are the Bering Sea (the northernmost part of the Pacific) and Bering Strait (between Asia and America, connecting the Bering Sea with the Arctic Ocean).

berk /bɜːk/ n. (also **burk**) Brit. sl. a fool; a stupid person. ¶ Usu. not considered *offens*. despite the etymology. [abbr. of *Berkeley* or *Berkshire Hunt*, rhyming sl. for *cunt*]

Berkeley /ˈbɑːklɪ/, George (1685–1753), Irish-born philosopher and bishop. His philosophical system originated in criticisms of Locke's. Berkeley denied the existence of matter, holding that only minds and mental events exist, and supported his view by a number of ingenious arguments. He maintained that material objects exist only by being perceived. To the objection that a tree, for example, would cease to exist if no one was looking at it he replied that God perceives everything, and that this gives trees, rocks, and stones an existence as continuous as common sense supposes: they are ideas in the mind of God. If there were no God material objects would leap in and out of existence; this was, in his view, a weighty argument for the existence of God.

berkelium /bɜːˈkiːlɪəm, ˈbɜːklɪəm/ n. Chem. an artificially made transuranic radioactive metallic element, first obtained in 1949 by bombarding americium wih helium ions. ¶ Symb.: **Bk**; atomic number 97. [mod.L f. *Berkeley* in California (where first made) + -IUM]

Berks. /bɑːks/ abbr. Berkshire.

Berkshire /ˈbɑːkʃɪə(r)/ a southern inland county of England; pop. (1981) 681,200; county town, Reading.

Berlin¹ /bɜːˈlɪn/ the capital of Germany (formerly of Prussia); pop. (1987) 3,102,500. From the Second World War until the reunification of Germany in 1990 it was divided into two parts: West Berlin (a State of the Federal Republic of Germany, forming an enclave within the German Democratic Republic) and East Berlin (the zone of the city that was Soviet-occupied at the end of the war, and later became capital of the German Democratic Republic). A fortified wall separating the two sectors was erected in 1961 by the Communist authorities to curb the flow of refugees to the West, and many people were killed or wounded while attempting to cross. Long regarded as a symbol of the ideological East–West division of Europe, it was opened in

November 1989 after the collapse of the Communist regime in East Germany, and subsequently dismantled.

Berlin[2] /bəˈlɪn/, Irving (1888–1989), Russian-born American song-writer, born Israel Baline, who emigrated with his family to the US when he was four. He began writing songs when he was 16 and in 1911 had a best-selling hit with *Alexander's Ragtime Band*. He formed his own publishing business in 1919 and in 1921 built, with Sam H. Harris, the Music Box Theater. Some of his best songs were written for films; his greatest commercial success was the song 'White Christmas' from *Holiday Inn* (1942).

Berliner /bɜːˈlɪnə(r)/ n. **1** a native or citizen of Berlin. **2** a lightly fried yeast bun with jam filling and vanilla icing. [G]

Berlioz /ˈbeəlɪəʊz/, Hector (1803–69), French composer, one of the most original of his time. He took as his inspiration such giants as Shakespeare and Beethoven, and his private life was as dramatic as his music. His *Symphonie fantastique* (1830) reflects his unhappy passion for Harriet Smithson, an Irish actress he had seen playing Ophelia, with a programme describing happy times with his beloved (represented by an *idée fixe*, or recurring melody) followed by fearful scenes where she is transformed into a very active participant in a Witches' Sabbath. A subsequent affair with a young pianist drove him to plan, in full detail, her murder and that of her lover, and in turn inspired the monodrama *Lélio* (1831–2) as a sequel to the *Symphonie*. Berlioz was an innovative orchestrator, and his *Grand traité d'instrumentation et d'orchestration moderne* (1843) affords a fascinating glimpse of his approach to the instruments of his day.

berm /bɜːm/ n. **1** a narrow path or grass strip beside a road, canal, etc. **2** a narrow ledge, esp. in a fortification between a ditch and the base of a parapet. [F *berme* f. Du. *berm*]

Bermuda /bɜːˈmjuːdə/ (also **Bermuda Islands, Bermudas**) a country comprising a group of about 150 small islands off the coast of North Carolina; pop. (est. 1988) 58,100; official language, English; capital, Hamilton. The climate is subtropical and tourism is the principal industry. The islands (now a British dependency with full internal self-government) were sighted early in the 16th c. by the Spaniard, Juan Bermúdez, from whom they take their name, but remained uninhabited until 1609 when an English expedition, on its way to Virginia, was shipwrecked there; its leader, Sir George Somers, later returned from Virginia to claim the islands for Britain. □ **Bermuda ketch, sloop**, etc. one that has a high tapering sail (**Bermuda rig**).**Bermuda shorts** (also **Bermudas**) close-fitting shorts reaching the knees. **Bermuda Triangle** the name given to an area of the western Atlantic between Bermuda and Florida, credited since the mid-19th c. with a number of unexplained disappearances of ships and aircraft. □□ **Bermudian** /bɜːˈmjuːdɪən/ *adj. & n.*

Bernadette /ˌbɜːnəˈdet/, St (1844–79), Marie Bernarde Soubirous (see LOURDES).

Bernadotte[1] /ˌbeənəˈdɒt/, Folke, Count (1895–1948), Swedish statesman. A member of the Swedish royal family, Bernadotte gained a deserved reputation as a neutral arbiter in international disputes. Charged with the position of UN mediator in Palestine after the Second World War, he was assassinated by Jewish extremists.

Bernadotte[2] /ˌbeənəˈdɒt/, Jean Baptiste (1763–1844), French soldier, one of Napoleon's marshals. He was adopted by Charles XIII of Sweden in 1810 and became king (as Charles XIV) in 1818, thus founding the present royal house.

Bernard[1] /berˈnɑːrd/, Claude (1813–78), French physiologist, pioneer of modern knowledge of the functioning of the body. Bernard used animal experiments to show the role of the pancreas in digestion, the method of regulation of body temperature, and the function of the nerves to the body's internal organs. He realized that the constant composition of the body fluids, the '*milieu interieur*', was essential for the optimal functioning of the body. He also discovered the biological importance of glycogen and investigated the action of curare, the paralysing drug still used in anaesthesia.

Bernard[2] /ˈbɜːnəd/, St (1090–1153), a saintly monk of strong personality, abbot of Clairvaux in France, where he founded a monastery which became one of the chief centres of the Cistercian order. Enjoying papal favour, he was an important religious force in Europe, and the Cistercian order grew rapidly under his influence; he preached the Second Crusade, and had Abelard (see entry) condemned for heresy. His writings reveal above all a faith inspired by sublime mysticism. Feast day, 20 Aug.

Bernard[3] /ˈbɜːnəd/, St (*c*.996–*c*.1081), a priest who founded two hospices to aid travellers in the Alps. The St Bernard passes, where the hospices were situated, and St Bernard dogs, once kept by the monks and trained to aid travellers, are named after him. Feast day, 28 May.

Berne /bɜːn/ (also **Bern**) a city on the River Aar, founded in 1191 and the capital of Switzerland since 1848; pop. (1986) 300,300. □ **Berne Convention** an international copyright agreement of 1885, later revised. The US has never been party to it.

Bernhardt /ˈbeənˌhɑːt/, Sarah (1844–1923), real name Rosine Bernard, French romantic and tragic actress. The 'divine Sarah' made her début in 1862, and her earliest successes (due largely to her beautiful voice and magnetic personality) were in Victor Hugo's *Ruy Blas* and *Hernani*, and as Phaedra in Racine's tragedy. The loss of a leg late in life, as the result of an accident, did not diminish her activity; numerous legends about her eccentricities were in circulation, some provoked by her undoubted unconventionality, others apocryphal.

Bernini /beəˈniːnɪ/, Gianlorenzo (1598–1680), Italian sculptor, painter, and architect, the outstanding figure of the Italian baroque, son of a sculptor (Pietro Bernini, 1562–1629). His works are original in their vigour, movement, and dramatic and emotional power, and he used a variety of materials (bronze, stucco, stone, and marble) to fuse sculpture, architecture, and painting into a magnificent decorative whole. Working chiefly in Rome, he became architect to St Peter's in 1629, for which he made the great baldacchino over the high altar, decorated the apse with the group of the Church Fathers supporting the chair of St Peter, and designed the colonnade round the piazza in front of the church. Although to the neoclassical taste of the 18th c. Bernini's approach to sculpture was anathema, changes of fashion and taste in the 20th c. have brought a more sympathetic recognition of his achievement.

Bernoulli /bɜːˈnuːiː/ the name of a Swiss family that produced many eminent mathematicians and scientists within three generations. Jakob (Jacques or James) Bernoulli (1654–1705) made substantial discoveries in the calculus, which he used to solve minimization problems, and he contributed to geometry and the theory of probabilities. His brother Johann (Jean or John, 1667–1748) also contributed to differential and integral calculus. Both were professors of mathematics at Basle. Daniel Bernoulli (1700–82), son of Johann, was professor of mathematics at St Petersburg and then held successively the chairs of botany, physiology, and physics at Basle. Although his original studies were in medicine, his greatest contributions were to hydrodynamics and various branches of mathematical physics. Other members of the family were also well-known mathematicians, astronomers, and scientists in their day.

Bernstein[1] /ˈbɜːnstaɪn/, Basil Bernard (1924–), English sociologist and educationist, who drew attention to the part played by forms of language in the perpetuation of different social groups. He is the author of *Class, Codes and Control* (1971–5).

Bernstein[2] /ˈbɜːnstaɪn/, Leonard (1918–90), American composer, conductor, and pianist, whose works include the symphony *The Age of Anxiety* (1947–9), musicals such as *West Side Story* (1957), his *Mass* (1970–1), and film music such as that for *On the Waterfront* (1954).

Berra /ˈbeərə/, Yogi (Lawrence Peter Berra, 1925–), American professional baseball player, famous especially as a catcher in the 1950s and early 1960s. The cartoon character Yogi Bear (1958) is popularly believed to have been named after him, though the animators (W. D. Hanna and J. R. Barbera) deny that this was their intention.

Berry[1] /ˈberɪ/ a former province of central France, now part of Centre region. Its capital was the city of Bourges.

au *how* eɪ *day* əʊ *no* eə *hair* ɪə *near* ɔɪ *boy* ʊə *poor* aɪə *fire* aʊə *sour*   (*see over for consonants*)

Berry[2] /ˈberɪ/, Charles Edward ('Chuck') (1931–), American rhythm-and-blues singer and prolific songwriter, whose style was much imitated.

berry /ˈberɪ/ n. & v. —n. (pl. **-ies**) **1** any small roundish juicy fruit without a stone. **2** Bot. a fruit with its seeds enclosed in a pulp (e.g. a banana, tomato, etc.). **3** any of various kernels or seeds (e.g. coffee bean etc.). **4** a fish egg or roe of a lobster etc. —v.intr. (**-ies, -ied**) **1** (usu. as **berrying** n.) go gathering berries. **2** form a berry; bear berries. □□ **berried** adj. (also in comb.). [OE berie f. Gmc]

berserk /bəˈsɜːk, -ˈzɜːk/ adj. & n. —adj. (esp. in **go berserk**) wild, frenzied; in a violent rage. —n. (also **berserker** /-kə(r)/) an ancient Norse warrior who fought with a wild frenzy. [Icel. berserkr (n.) prob. f. bern- BEAR[2] + serkr coat]

berth /bɜːθ/ n. & v. —n. **1** a fixed bunk on a ship, train, etc., for sleeping in. **2** a ship's place at a wharf. **3** room for a ship to swing at anchor. **4** adequate sea room. **5** colloq. a situation or appointment. **6** the proper place for anything. —v. **1** tr. moor (a ship) in its berth. **2** tr. provide a sleeping place for. **3** intr. (of a ship) come to its mooring-place. □ **give a wide berth to** stay away from. [prob. f. naut. use of BEAR[1] + -TH[2]]

bertha /ˈbɜːθə/ n. **1** a deep falling collar often of lace. **2** a small cape on a dress. [F berthe f. Berthe Bertha (the name)]

Bertillon /beərtɪˈjɔ̃/, Alphonse (1853–1914), French criminologist who devised a system of body-measurements for the identification of criminals. It was widely used in France and other countries until superseded by the technique of fingerprinting at the beginning of the 20th c.

Bertolucci /ˌbeətoˈluːtʃɪ/, Bernardo (1940–), Italian film director, whose films include The Spider's Stratagem (1970) and Last Tango in Paris (1972).

Berwick-upon-Tweed /ˈberɪk/ a town at the mouth of the River Tweed in NE England; pop. (1981) 13,000.

beryl /ˈberɪl/ n. **1** a kind of transparent precious stone, esp. pale green, blue, or yellow, and consisting of beryllium aluminium silicate in a hexagonal form. **2** a mineral species which includes this, emerald, and aquamarine. [ME f. OF f. L beryllus f. Gk bērullos]

beryllium /bəˈrɪlɪəm/ n. Chem. a very light hard greyish-white metallic element of the alkaline-earth metal series. First isolated in 1828, its chief use is in alloys, especially where lightness and a high melting-point are important, as in aircraft or space vehicles. The main commercial ore is beryl. ¶ Symb.: **Be**; atomic number 4. [BERYL + -IUM]

Berzelius /bɜːˈziːlɪəs/, Jöns Jakob (1779–1848), Swedish chemist, who was created a baron on his wedding day in 1835. Regarded by his contemporaries as a remarkably gifted analytical chemist he studied about 2,000 compounds, and by 1818 had determined the atomic weights of most of the then known elements, using oxygen as the standard. He discovered three new elements: cerium (1803), selenium (1817), and thorium (1829), suggested the basic principles of the modern notation of chemical formulae, and introduced the terms isomerism, polymer, protein, and catalysis.

Bes /bes/ Egyptian Mythol. a grotesque god depicted as having short legs, an obese body, and an almost bestial face, whose comic but frightening aspect had the effect of dispelling evil spirits.

Besançon /bezɑ̃ˈsɔ̃/ the regional capital of Franche-Comté in NE France; pop. (1982) 119,700. It was the birthplace of the writer Victor Hugo.

beseech /bɪˈsiːtʃ/ v.tr. (past and past part. **besought** /-ˈsɔːt/ or **beseeched**) **1** (foll. by for, or to + infin.) entreat. **2** ask earnestly for. □□ **beseeching** adj. [ME f. BE- + secan SEEK]

beset /bɪˈset/ v.tr. (**besetting**; past and past part. **beset**) **1** attack or harass persistently (beset by worries). **2** surround or hem in (a person etc.). **3** archaic cover round with (beset with pearls). □ **besetting sin** the sin that especially or most frequently tempts one. □□ **besetment** n. [OE besettan f. Gmc]

beside /bɪˈsaɪd/ prep. **1** at the side of; near. **2** compared with. **3** irrelevant to (beside the point). □ **beside oneself** overcome with worry, anger, etc. [OE be sīdan (as BY, SIDE)]

besides /bɪˈsaɪdz/ prep. & adv. —prep. in addition to; apart from. —adv. also; as well; moreover.

besiege /bɪˈsiːdʒ/ v.tr. **1** lay siege to. **2** crowd round oppressively. **3** harass with requests. □□ **besieger** n. [ME f. assiege by substitution of BE-, f. OF asegier f. Rmc]

besmear /bɪˈsmɪə(r)/ v.tr. **1** smear with greasy or sticky stuff. **2** sully (a reputation etc.). [OE bismierwan (as BE-, SMEAR)]

besmirch /bɪˈsmɜːtʃ/ v.tr. **1** soil, discolour. **2** dishonour; sully the reputation or name of. [BE- + SMIRCH]

besom /ˈbiːz(ə)m/ n. **1** a broom made of twigs tied round a stick. **2** esp. N.Engl. derog. or joc. a woman. [OE besema]

besotted /bɪˈsɒtɪd/ adj. **1** infatuated. **2** foolish, confused. **3** intoxicated, stupefied. [besot (v.) (as BE-, SOT)]

besought past and past part. of BESEECH.

bespangle /bɪˈspæŋg(ə)l/ v.tr. adorn with spangles.

bespatter /bɪˈspætə(r)/ v.tr. **1** spatter (an object) all over. **2** spatter (liquid etc.) about. **3** overwhelm with abuse etc.

bespeak /bɪˈspiːk/ v.tr. (past **bespoke** /-ˈspəʊk/; past part. **bespoken** /-ˈspəʊkən/ or as adj. **bespoke**) **1** engage in advance. **2** order (goods). **3** suggest; be evidence of (his gift bespeaks a kind heart). **4** literary speak to. [OE bisprecan (as BE-, SPEAK)]

bespectacled /bɪˈspektək(ə)ld/ adj. wearing spectacles.

bespoke past and past part. of BESPEAK. —adj. **1** (of goods, esp. clothing) made to order. **2** (of a tradesman) making goods to order.

bespoken past part. of BESPEAK.

besprinkle /bɪˈsprɪŋk(ə)l/ v.tr. **1** sprinkle or strew all over with liquid etc. **2** sprinkle (liquid etc.) over. [ME f. BE- + sprengen in the same sense]

Bessarabia /ˌbesəˈreɪbɪə/ a region in the south-west of the USSR. In 1918 it chose to become part of Romania, which was forced to cede it to the USSR in 1940. Most of it now forms part of the Moldavian SSR, the remainder part of the Ukranian SSR. □□ **Bessarabian** adj. & n.

Bessemer /ˈbesɪmə(r)/, Sir Henry (1813–98), English engineer and inventor, of French Huguenot extraction, remembered for the steel-making process which bears his name. The most important part of his career dates from the Crimean War, when the obvious imperfections in the artillery of the British army brought forward a large number of more or less able inventors. His proposals for the redesign of guns received little encouragement from the British War Office but a great deal from the Emperor Napoleon; experiments proved, however, that the material available for gun construction was inadequate for its purpose. Bessemer's efforts were then directed to the production of a stronger material, and led to a series of experiments and patents.

Bessemer process n. a process formerly much used for removing carbon, silicon, etc., from molten pig-iron by the passage of air, thus converting it into a material suitable for steelmaking. The process was invented by Henry Bessemer, but followed earlier work by William Kelly in the US. By 1860 Bessemer had evolved his converter, a large steel vessel lined with a refractory material and pivoted in such a way that it could be tilted to three positions. When the axis was horizontal it could be loaded with steel scrap on to which molten iron was poured. With the axis vertical a blast of air was blown through the mixture; the oxygen in the air combined with the carbon and some other elements to provide the heat needed to melt the steel scrap and reduce the amount of carbon and other impurities to a low level. After removal of molten slag from the surface and the addition of a small quantity of manganese the converter was tilted far enough to allow the finished steel to be poured out. It was the first successful method of making steel in quantity at low cost, so enabling it to be used on a large scale, but has been replaced by more modern techniques (see STEEL).

best /best/ adj., adv., n., & v. —adj. (superl. of GOOD) of the most excellent or outstanding or desirable kind (my best work; the best solution; the best thing to do would be to confess). —adv. (superl. of WELL[1]). **1** in the best manner (does it best). **2** to the greatest degree (like it best). **3** most usefully (is best ignored). —n. **1** that which is best (*the best is yet to come*). **2** the chief merit or advantage (*brings out the best in him*). **3** (foll. by *of*) a winning majority of (a certain number of games etc. played) (*the best of five*). **4** = *Sunday best.* —*v.tr. colloq.* defeat, outwit, outbid, etc. □ **all the best** an expression used to wish a person good fortune. **as best one can** (or **may**) as effectively as possible under the circumstances. **at best** on the most optimistic view. **at one's best** in peak condition etc. **at the best of times** even in the most favourable circumstances. **be for** (or **all for**) **the best** be desirable in the end. **best end of neck** the rib end of a neck of lamb etc. for cooking. **best man** the bridegroom's chief attendant at a wedding. **the best part of** most of. **best seller 1** a book or other item that has sold in large numbers. **2** the author of such a book. **do one's best** do all one can. **get the best of** defeat, outwit. **give a person the best** admit the superiority of that person. **had best** would find it wisest to. **make the best of** derive what limited advantage one can from (something unsatisfactory or unwelcome); put up with. **to the best of one's ability, knowledge**, etc. as far as one can do, know, etc. **with the best of them** as well as anyone. [OE *betest* (adj.), *bet(o)st* (adv.), f. Gmc]

bestial /ˈbestɪəl/ *adj.* **1** brutish, cruel, savage. **2** sexually depraved; lustful. **3** of or like a beast. □□ **bestialize** *v.tr.* (also **-ise**). **bestially** *adv.* [ME f. OF f. LL *bestialis* f. *bestia* beast]

bestiality /ˌbestɪˈælɪtɪ/ *n.* (*pl.* **-ies**) **1** bestial behaviour or an instance of this. **2** sexual intercourse between a person and an animal. [F *bestialité* (as BESTIAL)]

bestiary /ˈbestɪərɪ/ *n.* (*pl.* **-ies**) a moralizing medieval treatise on real and imaginary beasts. [med.L *bestiarium* f. L *bestia* beast]

bestir /bɪˈstɜː(r)/ *v.refl.* (**bestirred, bestirring**) exert or rouse (oneself).

bestow /bɪˈstəʊ/ *v.tr.* **1** (foll. by *on, upon*) confer (a gift, right, etc.). **2** deposit. □□ **bestowal** *n.* [ME f. BE- + OE *stow* a place]

bestrew /bɪˈstruː/ *v.tr.* (*past part.* **bestrewed** or **bestrewn** /-ˈstruːn/) **1** (foll. by *with*) cover or partly cover (a surface). **2** scatter (things) about. **3** lie scattered over. [OE *bestrēowian* (as BE-, STREW)]

bestride /bɪˈstraɪd/ *v.tr.* (*past* **bestrode** /-ˈstrəʊd/; *past part.* **bestridden** /-ˈstrɪd(ə)n/) **1** sit astride on. **2** stand astride over. [OE *bestrīdan*]

bet /bet/ *v. & n.* —*v.* (**betting**; *past and past part.* **bet** or **betted**) **1** *intr.* (foll. by *on* or *against* with ref. to the outcome) risk a sum of money etc. against another's on the basis of the outcome of an unpredictable event (esp. the result of a race, game, etc., or the outcome in a game of chance). **2** *tr.* risk (an amount) on such an outcome or result (*bet £10 on a horse*). **3** *tr.* risk a sum of money against (a person). **4** *tr. colloq.* feel sure (*bet they've forgotten it*). —*n.* **1** the act of betting (*make a bet*). **2** the money etc. staked (*put a bet on*). **3** *colloq.* an opinion, esp. a quickly formed or spontaneous one (*my bet is that he won't come*). **4** *colloq.* a choice or course of action (*she's our best bet*). □ **you bet** *colloq.* you may be sure. [16th c.: perh. a shortened form of ABET]

beta /ˈbiːtə/ *n.* **1** the second letter of the Greek alphabet (Β, β). **2** a second-class mark given for a piece of work or in an examination. **3** *Astron.* the second brightest star in a constellation. **4** the second member of a series. □ **beta-blocker** *Pharm.* a drug that prevents the stimulation of increased cardiac action, used to treat angina and reduce high blood pressure. **beta particle** a fast-moving electron emitted by radioactive decay of substances (such particles were orig. regarded as rays). [ME f. L f. Gk]

betake /bɪˈteɪk/ *v.refl.* (*past* **betook** /bɪˈtʊk/; *past part.* **betaken** /bɪˈteɪkən/) (foll. by *to*) go to (a place or person).

betatron /ˈbiːtətrɒn/ *n. Physics* an apparatus for accelerating electrons in a circular path by magnetic induction. [BETA + -TRON]

betel /ˈbiːt(ə)l/ *n.* the leaf of the Asian evergreen climbing plant *Piper betle*, chewed in the East with parings of the areca nut. □ **betel-nut** the areca nut. [Port. f. Malayalam *veṭṭila*]

Betelgeuse /ˈbiːt(ə)l,dʒɜːz/ a first-magnitude variable star in the constellation of Orion. Its Arabic name apparently means 'armpit of the Great One'. Variations in brightness by a factor of two

can occur over periods of a few years, and are associated with pulsations in the outer envelope of this red giant.

bête noire /beɪt ˈnwɑː(r)/ *n.* (*pl.* **bêtes noires** *pronunc.* same) a person or thing one particularly dislikes or fears. [F, = black beast]

bethink /bɪˈθɪŋk/ *v.refl.* (*past and past part.* **bethought** /-ˈθɔːt/) (foll. by *of, how*, or *that* + clause) *formal* **1** reflect; stop to think. **2** be reminded by reflection. [OE *bithencan* f. Gmc (as BE-, THINK)]

Bethlehem /ˈbeθlɪˌhem/ a small town 8 km (5 miles) south of Jerusalem, first mentioned in Egyptian records of the 14th c. BC; pop. (est. 1980) 14,000. The native city of King David and reputed birthplace of Jesus Christ, it contains a church built by Constantine in 330 over the supposed site of Christ's birth. St Jerome lived and worked in Bethlehem from 384, and it became a monastic centre.

betide /bɪˈtaɪd/ *v.* (only in infin. and 3rd sing. subj.) **1** *tr.* happen to (*woe betide him*). **2** *intr.* happen (*whate'er may betide*). [ME f. obs. *tide* befall f. OE *tīdan*]

betimes /bɪˈtaɪmz/ *adv. literary* early; in good time. [ME f. obs. *betime* (as BY, TIME)]

bêtise /beɪˈtiːz/ *n.* **1** a foolish or ill-timed remark or action. **2** a piece of folly. [F]

Betjeman /ˈbetʃəmən/, Sir John (1906–84), English poet, whose first collection (*Mount Zion*) was published in 1931. Others followed, including *New Bats in Old Belfries* (1945), *Collected Poems* (1958), and his blank-verse autobiography *Summoned by Bells* (1960), a nostalgic description of his boyhood and his life at Oxford University. His poems are witty and gently satiric, a comedy of manners, place-names, and contemporary allusions, capturing the spirit of his age and making him the most popular poet since Kipling. His 'topographical predilection' is displayed in many of his works, including those on architecture, such as *Ghastly Good Taste* (1933), and he fostered interest in Victorian and Edwardian buildings, campaigning enthusiastically for their preservation. He was appointed Poet Laureate in 1972.

betoken /bɪˈtəʊkən/ *v.tr.* **1** be a sign of; indicate. **2** augur. [OE (as BE-, *tācnian* signify: see TOKEN)]

betony /ˈbetənɪ/ *n.* **1** a purple-flowered plant, *Stachys officinalis.* **2** any of various similar plants. [ME f. OF *betoine* f. L *betonica*]

betook *past of* BETAKE.

betray /bɪˈtreɪ/ *v.tr.* **1** place (a person, one's country, etc.) in the hands or power of an enemy. **2** be disloyal to (another person, a person's trust, etc.). **3** reveal involuntarily or treacherously; be evidence of (*his shaking hand betrayed his fear*). **4** lead astray or into error. □□ **betrayal** *n.* **betrayer** *n.* [ME f. obs. *tray*, ult. f. L *tradere* hand over]

betroth /bɪˈtrəʊð/ *v.tr.* (usu. as **betrothed** adj.) bind with a promise to marry. □□ **betrothal** *n.* [ME f. BE- + *trouthe, treuthe* TRUTH, later assim. to TROTH]

better¹ /ˈbetə(r)/ *adj., adv., n., & v.* —*adj.* (*compar.* of GOOD). **1** of a more excellent or outstanding or desirable kind (*a better product; it would be better to go home*). **2** partly or fully recovered from illness (*feeling better*). —*adv.* (*compar.* of WELL¹). **1** in a better manner (*she sings better*). **2** to a greater degree (*like it better*). **3** more usefully or advantageously (*is better forgotten*). —*n.* **1** that which is better (*the better of the two*). **2** (usu. in pl.; prec. by *my* etc.) one's superior in ability or rank (*take notice of your betters*). —*v.* **1** *tr.* improve on; surpass (*I can better his offer*). **2** *tr.* make better; improve. **3** *refl.* improve one's position etc. **4** *intr.* become better; improve. □ **better feelings** one's conscience. **better half** *colloq.* one's wife or husband. **better off** in a better (esp. financial) position. **the better part of** most of. **for better or for worse** on terms accepting all results; whatever the outcome. **get the better of** defeat, outwit; win an advantage over. **go one better 1** outbid etc. by one. **2** outdo another person. **had better** would find it wiser to. [OE *betera* f. Gmc]

better² /ˈbetə(r)/ *n.* (also **bettor**) a person who bets.

betterment /ˈbetəmənt/ *n.* **1** making better; improvement. **2** *Econ.* enhanced value (of real property) arising from local improvements.

Betterton /ˈbetət(ə)n/, Thomas (1635–1710), the greatest English actor during the Restoration period.

Betti /'betɪ/, Ugo (1892–1953), Italian dramatist, who also wrote poetry, short stories, and a novel. His plays include *Delitto all'Isola della Capre* (*Crime on Goat Island* 1950, 1960) and *Corruzione al palazzo di giustizia* (*Corruption in the Palace of Justice*, 1949, 1962).

betting /'betɪŋ/ n. **1** gambling by risking money on an unpredictable outcome. **2** the odds offered in this. □ **betting-shop** *Brit.* a bookmaker's shop or office. **what's the betting?** *colloq.* it is likely or to be expected (*what's the betting he'll be late?*).

bettor var. of BETTER[2].

between /bɪ'twiːn/ prep. & adv. —prep. **1 a** at or to a point in the area or interval bounded by two or more other points in space, time, etc. (*broke down between London and Dover; we must meet between now and Friday*). **b** along the extent of such an area or interval (*there are five shops between here and the main road; works best between five and six; the numbers between 10 and 20*). **2** separating, physically or conceptually (*the distance between here and Leeds; the difference between right and wrong*). **3 a** by combining the resources of (*great potential between them; between us we could afford it*). **b** shared by; as the joint resources of (*£5 between them*). **c** by joint or reciprocal action (*an agreement between us; sorted it out between themselves*). ¶ Use in sense 3 with reference to more than two people or things is established and acceptable (e.g. *relations between Britain, France, and Germany*). **4** to and from (*runs between London and Sheffield*). **5** taking one and rejecting the other of (*decide between eating here and going out*). —adv. (also **in between**) at a point or in the area bounded by two or more other points in space, time, sequence, etc. (*not fat or thin but in between*). □ **between ourselves** (or **you and me**) in confidence. **between times** (or **whiles**) in the intervals between other actions; occasionally. [OE *betwēonum* f. Gmc (as BY, TWO)]

betwixt /bɪ'twɪkst/ prep. & adv. *archaic* between. □ **betwixt and between** *colloq.* neither one thing nor the other. [ME f. OE *betwēox* f. Gmc: cf. AGAINST]

BeV abbr. a billion (= 10[9]) electron-volts. Also called GeV.

Bevan /'bev(ə)n/, Aneurin (1897–1960), British Labour politician. In a Parliamentary career stretching from 1929 to 1960, Bevan's most notable contribution was the creation of the National Health Service during his time as Minister of Health 1945–51. The leader of the left wing of the Labour Party, he was defeated by Hugh Gaitskell in the contest for the party leadership in 1955.

bevatron /'bevə,trɒn/ n. a synchrotron used to accelerate protons to energies in the billion electronvolt range. [BeV + -TRON]

bevel /'bev(ə)l/ n. & v. —n. **1** a slope from the horizontal or vertical in carpentry and stonework; a sloping surface or edge. **2** (in full **bevel square**) a tool for marking angles in carpentry and stonework. —v. (**bevelled, bevelling**; *US* **beveled, beveling**) **1** tr. reduce (a square edge) to a sloping edge. **2** intr. slope at an angle; slant. □ **bevel gear** a gear working another gear at an angle to it by means of bevel wheels. **bevel wheel** a toothed wheel whose working face is oblique to the axis. [OF *bevel* (unrecorded) f. *baif* f. *baer* gape]

beverage /'bevərɪdʒ/ n. *formal* a drink (*hot beverage; alcoholic beverage*). [ME f. OF *be(u)vrage*, ult. f. L *bibere* drink]

Beveridge /'bevərɪdʒ/, William Henry, 1st Baron (1879–1963), British economist. Long-time Director of the London School of Economics, Beveridge was the chairman of the wartime committee appointed to investigate social insurance problems. His report, completed in 1942, was the blueprint for postwar legislation leading to the drawing up of a national insurance scheme.

Beverly Hills /'bevəlɪ/ an affluent and largely residential city in California, to the west of Los Angeles; pop. (1980) 32,400.

bevy /'bevɪ/ n. (pl. **-ies**) **1** a flock of quails or larks. **2** a company or group (orig. of women). [15th c.: orig. unkn.]

bewail /bɪ'weɪl/ v.tr. **1** greatly regret or lament. **2** wail over; mourn for. □□ **bewailer** n.

beware /bɪ'weə(r)/ v. (only in *imper.* or *infin.*) **1** intr. (often foll. by *of*, or *that*, *lest*, etc. + clause) be cautious, take heed (*beware of the dog; told us to beware; beware that you don't fall*). **2** tr. be cautious of (*beware the Ides of March*). [BE + WARE[3]]

Bewick /'bjuːɪk/, Thomas (1755–1828), English animal artist and wood engraver whose best works are the shrewdly observed and expressive animal studies which illustrate such books as *The History of British Birds* (1797, 1804).

bewilder /bɪ'wɪldə(r)/ v.tr. utterly perplex or confuse. □□ **bewilderedly** adv. **bewildering** adj. **bewilderingly** adv. **bewilderment** n. [BE- + obs. *wilder* lose one's way]

bewitch /bɪ'wɪtʃ/ v.tr. **1** enchant; greatly delight. **2** cast a spell on. □□ **bewitching** adj. **bewitchingly** adv. [ME f. BE- + OE *wiccian* enchant f. *wicca* WITCH]

bey /beɪ/ n. *hist.* (in the Ottoman Empire) the title of a governor of a province. [Turk.]

beyond /bɪ'jɒnd/ prep., adv., & n. —prep. **1** at or to the further side of (*beyond the river*). **2** outside the scope, range, or understanding of (*beyond repair; beyond a joke; it is beyond me*). **3** more than. —adv. **1** at or to the further side. **2** further on. —n. (prec. by *the*) the unknown after death. □ **the back of beyond** see BACK. [OE *beg(e)ondan* (as BY, YON, YONDER)]

bezant /'bez(ə)nt, bɪ'zænt/ n. **1** *hist.* a gold or silver coin orig. minted at Byzantium. **2** *Heraldry* a gold roundel. [ME f. OF *besanz -ant* f. L *Byzantius* Byzantine]

bezel /'bez(ə)l/ n. **1** the sloped edge of a chisel. **2** the oblique faces of a cut gem. **3 a** a groove holding a watch-glass or gem. **b** a rim holding a glass etc. cover. [OF *besel* (unrecorded: cf. F *béseau, bizeau*) of unkn. orig.]

bezique /bɪ'ziːk/ n. **1** a card-game for two with a double pack of 64 cards, including the ace to seven only in each suit. **2** a combination of the queen of spades and the jack of diamonds in this game. [F *bésigue*, perh. f. Pers. *bāzīgar* juggler]

bezoar /'biːzɔː(r), 'bezəʊˌɑː(r)/ n. a small stone which may form in the stomachs of certain animals, esp. ruminants, and which was once used as an antidote for various ills. [ult. f. Pers. *pādzahr* antidote, Arab. *bāzahr*]

b.f. abbr. **1** *Brit. colloq.* bloody fool. **2** brought forward. **3** *Printing* bold face.

Bhagavadgita /ˌbɑːgəvəd'giːtə/ n. the 'Song of the Lord' (i.e. Krishna), the most famous religious text of Hinduism, an independent work incorporated into the Mahabharata. Composed between the 2nd c. BC and 2nd c. AD, it is the earliest exposition of devotional religion (*bhakti*). Presented as a dialogue between the Kshatriya prince Arjuna and his divine charioteer Krishna, the poem stresses the importance of doing one's duty and of faith in god. [Skr.]

bhakti /'bɑːktɪ/ n. *Hinduism* devotional worship directed to one supreme deity, usually Vishnu (especially in his incarnations as Rama and Krishna) or Siva, by whose grace salvation may be attained by all regardless of sex, caste, or class. This is the religion of the majority of Hindus today. [Skr.]

bhang /bæŋ/ n. the leaves and flower-tops of Indian hemp used as a narcotic. [Port. *bangue*, Pers. *bang*, & Urdu etc. *bhāng* f. Skr. *bhaṅgā*]

bharal /'bʌr(ə)l/ n. (also **burhel**) a Himalayan wild sheep, *Pseudois nayaur*, with blue-black coat and horns curved rearward. [Hindi]

Bharat /'bərət/ the Hindi name for India.

Bharatpur /'bərət,pʊər/ a sanctuary for migratory birds, near an 18th-c. fort, in Rajasthan in eastern India.

Bhopal /bəʊ'pɑːl/ a city in central India, the capital of Madhya Pradesh; pop. (1981) 672,000. In December 1984 leakage of poisonous gas from an American-owned pesticide factory caused the death of about 2,500 people and thousands suffered injury.

b.h.p. abbr. brake horsepower.

Bhutan /buː'tɑːn/ a small independent kingdom, a protectorate of the Republic of India, lying on the south-east of the Himalayas; pop. (est. 1988) 1,503,180; official language, Dzongkha; capital, Thimphu. □□ **Bhutanese** /ˌbuːtə'niːz/ adj. & n.

Bhutto[1] /'buːtəʊ/, Benazir (1953–), Pakistani stateswoman, Prime Minister of Pakistan 1988–90, the first woman to be head of a Muslim State. She became leader of the Pakistan People's Party formed in 1967 by her father, Zulfikar Ali Bhutto (see entry).

Bhutto[2] /'buːtəʊ/, Zulfikar Ali (1928–79), Pakistani statesman, the first civilian President (1971–3) and later Prime Minister

(1973–7) of his country. He was ousted by a military coup and executed for conspiring to murder a political rival.

Bi *symb. Chem.* the element bismuth.

bi- /baɪ/ *comb. form* (often **bin-** before a vowel) forming nouns and adjectives meaning: **1** having two; a thing having two (*bilateral*; *binaural*; *biplane*). **2 a** occurring twice in every one or once in every two (*bi-weekly*). **b** lasting for two (*biennial*). **3** doubly; in two ways (*biconcave*). **4** *Chem.* a substance having a double proportion of the acid etc. indicated by the simple word (*bicarbonate*). **5** *Bot.* & *Zool.* (of division and subdivision) twice over (*bipinnate*). [L]

Biafra /bɪæˈfrə/ a State proclaimed in 1967 when part of eastern Nigeria, inhabited chiefly by the Ibo people, sought independence from the rest of the country. In the ensuing civil war the new State's troops were overwhelmed by numerically superior forces, and by 1970 it had ceased to exist. □□ **Biafran** *adj.* & *n.*

biannual /baɪˈænjʊəl/ *adj.* occurring, appearing, etc., twice a year (cf. BIENNIAL). □□ **biannually** *adv.*

Biarritz /bɪəˈrɪts/ a seaside resort in SW France, on the Bay of Biscay; pop. (1982) 28,000.

bias /ˈbaɪəs/ *n.* & *v.* —*n.* **1** (often foll. by *towards*, *against*) a predisposition or prejudice. **2** *Statistics* a systematic distortion of a statistical result due to a factor not allowed for in its derivation. **3** an edge cut obliquely across the weave of a fabric. **4** *Sport* **a** the irregular shape given to a bowl. **b** the oblique course this causes it to run. **5** *Electr.* a steady voltage, magnetic field, etc., applied to an electronic system or device. —*v.tr.* (**biased**, **biasing** or **biassed**, **biassing**) **1** (esp. as **biased** *adj.*) influence (usu. unfairly); prejudice. **2** give a bias to. □ **bias binding** a strip of fabric cut obliquely and used to bind edges. **on the bias** obliquely, diagonally. [F *biais*, of unkn. orig.]

biathlon /baɪˈæθlən/ *n.* *Sport* an athletic contest in skiing and shooting. □□ **biathlete** *n.* [BI-, after PENTATHLON]

biaxial /baɪˈæksɪəl/ *adj.* (esp. of crystals) having two axes along which polarized light travels with equal velocity.

bib¹ /bɪb/ *n.* **1** a piece of cloth or plastic fastened round a child's neck to keep the clothes clean while eating. **2** the top front part of an apron, dungarees, etc. **3** the edible marine fish *Trisopterus luscus* of the cod family. Also called POUT². □ **best bib and tucker** best clothes. **stick** (or **poke** etc.) **one's bib in** *Austral. sl.* interfere. [perh. f. BIB²]

bib² /bɪb/ *v.intr.* (**bibbed**, **bibbing**) *archaic* drink much or often. □□ **bibber** *n.* [ME, perh. f. L *bibere* drink]

bib-cock /ˈbɪbkɒk/ *n.* a tap with a bent nozzle fixed at the end of a pipe. [perh. f. BIB¹ + COCK¹]

bibelot /ˈbiːbləʊ/ *n.* a small curio or artistic trinket. [F]

Bible /ˈbaɪb(ə)l/ *n.* **1 a** the Christian scriptures consisting of the Old and New Testaments. (See below.) **b** the Jewish scriptures. **c** (**bible**) any copy of these (*three bibles on the table*). **d** a particular edition of the Bible (*New English Bible*). **2** *colloq.* any authoritative book (*Wisden is his Bible*). **3** the scriptures of any non-Christian religion. □ **Bible-basher** (or **-thumper** etc.) *sl.* a person given to Bible-bashing. **Bible-bashing** (or **-thumping** etc.) *sl.* aggressive fundamentalist preaching. **Bible belt** a region of the southern and central US, including Arkansas, Oklahoma, Texas, Tennessee, and parts of Kentucky, noted for its religious fundamentalism and its Bible salesmen. **Bible oath** a solemn oath taken on the Bible. [ME f. OF f. eccl.L *biblia* f. Gk *biblia* books (pl. of *biblion*), orig. dimin. of *biblos*, *bublos* papyrus]

The respect shown by Christ and the early Church to the scriptures of Judaism formed the basis of the Christian attitude to the Old Testament, the message therein being complemented by that of the New Testament, with the two together forming a single record of God's revelation. Although there was some allegorical interpretation, in the earlier phases of the modern scientific movement (16th and 17th c.) both Protestants and Catholics held to belief in the truth of the Bible's assertions on matters not only of history, doctrine, and ethics but also of cosmology and natural science, and it was not until the 19th c. that critical study began to interpret the Bible in its historical perspective and the circumstances and purpose of its compilation. Protestant reformers sought to make the Bible available to the laity in the vernacular (Luther's German translation of the New Testament appeared in 1522), and there are now translations of all or part of it in 1,763 languages.

biblical /ˈbɪblɪk(ə)l/ *adj.* **1** of, concerning, or contained in the Bible. **2** resembling the language of the Authorized Version of the Bible. □□ **biblically** *adv.*

biblio- /ˈbɪblɪəʊ/ *comb. form* denoting a book or books. [Gk f. *biblion* book]

bibliography /ˌbɪblɪˈɒgrəfɪ/ *n.* (*pl.* **-ies**) **1 a** a list of the books referred to in a scholarly work, usu. printed as an appendix. **b** a list of the books of a specific author or publisher, or on a specific subject, etc. **2 a** the history or description of books, including authors, editions, etc. **b** any book containing such information. □□ **bibliographer** *n.* **bibliographic** /-əˈgræfɪk/ *adj.* **bibliographical** /-əˈgræfɪk(ə)l/ *adj.* **bibliographically** /-əˈgræfɪkəlɪ/ *adv.* **bibliographize** *v.tr.* (also **-ise**). [F *bibliographie* f. mod.L *bibliographia* f. Gk (as BIBLE, -GRAPHY)]

bibliomancy /ˈbɪblɪəʊˌmænsɪ/ *n.* foretelling the future by the analysis of a randomly chosen passage from a book, esp. the Bible.

bibliomania /ˌbɪblɪəʊˈmeɪnɪə/ *n.* an extreme enthusiasm for collecting and possessing books. □□ **bibliomaniac** /-nɪˌæk/ *n.* & *adj.*

bibliophile /ˈbɪblɪəʊˌfaɪl/ *n.* (also **bibliophil** /-fɪl/) a person who collects or is fond of books. □□ **bibliophilic** /-ˈfɪlɪk/ *adj.* **bibliophily** /-ˈɒfɪlɪ/ *n.* [F *bibliophile* (as BIBLIO-, -PHILE)]

bibliopole /ˈbɪblɪəʊˌpəʊl/ *n.* a seller of (esp. rare) books. □□ **bibliopoly** /-ˈɒpəlɪ/ *n.* [L *bibliopola* f. Gk *bibliopōlēs* f. *biblion* book + *pōlēs* seller]

Bibliothèque nationale /ˌbɪblɪəˈtek ˌnæsjɒˈnɑːl/ the national library of France, in Paris. It had its origins in the libraries of medieval French kings who amassed their collections in the way that was then usual—by plunder and gifts. In the long reign of Louis XIV, when France was very prosperous, it grew to more than 70,000 volumes and part of the present building was erected. Its present name first came to be used during the French Revolution.

bibulous /ˈbɪbjʊləs/ *adj.* given to drinking alcoholic liquor. □□ **bibulously** *adv.* **bibulousness** *n.* [L *bibulus* freely drinking f. *bibere* drink]

bicameral /baɪˈkæmər(ə)l/ *adj.* (of a parliament or legislative body) having two chambers. □□ **bicameralism** *n.* [BI- + L *camera* chamber]

bicarb /ˈbaɪkɑːb/ *n. colloq.* = BICARBONATE 2. [abbr.]

bicarbonate /baɪˈkɑːbənɪt/ *n.* **1** *Chem.* any acid salt of carbonic acid. **2** (in full **bicarbonate of soda**) sodium bicarbonate used as an antacid or in baking powder.

bice /baɪs/ *n.* **1** any of various pigments made from blue or green basic copper carbonate. **2** any similar pigment made from smalt. **3** a shade of blue or green given by these. □ **blue bice** a shade of blue between ultramarine and azure derived from smalt. **green bice** a yellowish green colour derived by adding yellow orpiment to smalt. [orig. = brownish grey, f. OF *bis* dark grey, of unkn. orig.]

bicentenary /ˌbaɪsenˈtiːnərɪ/ *n.* & *adj.* —*n.* (*pl.* **-ies**) **1** a two-hundredth anniversary. **2** a celebration of this. —*adj.* of or concerning a bicentenary.

bicentennial /ˌbaɪsenˈtenɪəl/ *n.* & *adj.* esp. *US* —*n.* a bicentenary. —*adj.* **1** lasting two hundred years or occurring every two hundred years. **2** of or concerning a bicentenary.

bicephalous /baɪˈsefələs/ *adj.* having two heads.

biceps /ˈbaɪseps/ *n.* a muscle having two heads or attachments, esp. the one which bends the elbow. [L = two-headed, formed as BI- + -*ceps* f. *caput* head]

bicker /ˈbɪkə(r)/ *v.intr.* **1** quarrel pettily; wrangle. **2** *poet.* **a** (of a stream, rain, etc.) patter (over stones etc.). **b** (of a flame, light, etc.) flash, flicker. □□ **bickerer** *n.* [ME *biker*, *beker*, of unkn. orig.]

bicolour /ˈbaɪˌkʌlə(r)/ *adj.* & *n.* —*adj.* having two colours. —*n.* a bicolour blossom or animal.

biconcave /baɪˈkɒnkeɪv/ adj. (esp. of a lens) concave on both sides.

biconvex /baɪˈkɒnveks/ adj. (esp. of a lens) convex on both sides.

bicultural /baɪˈkʌltʃər(ə)l/ adj. having or combining two cultures.

bicuspid /baɪˈkʌspɪd/ adj. & n. —adj. having two cusps or points. —n. **1** the premolar tooth in humans. **2** a tooth with two cusps. □□ **bicuspidate** adj. [BI- + L cuspis -idis sharp point]

bicycle /ˈbaɪsɪk(ə)l/ n. & v. —n. a vehicle of two wheels held in a frame one behind the other, propelled by pedals and steered with handlebars attached to the front wheel. (See below.) —v.intr. ride a bicycle. □ **bicycle-chain** a chain transmitting power from the bicycle pedals to the wheels. **bicycle-clip** either of two metal clips used to confine a cyclist's trousers at the ankle. **bicycle-pump** a portable pump for inflating bicycle tyres. □□ **bicycler** n. **bicyclist** /-klɪst/ n. [F f. BI- + Gk kuklos wheel]

A two-wheeled conveyance (called a velocipede) was patented by Karl von Drais in Germany in 1817: a rider sat on a bar between the wheels and propelled himself by pushing the ground with each foot alternately. It was introduced into France and into England, where it was called a 'pedestrian curricle' or 'hobby-horse' or 'dandy-horse'), and achieved a certain popularity. A lever-drive arrangement worked by treadles was fitted to the back wheel c.1840, and in 1861 in France Pierre Michaux and his son added cranks and pedals to the front wheel; this machine became copied elsewhere. The early bicycle was a cumbersome and uncomfortable machine, with a heavy frame and iron tyres, putting considerable strain on the rider's limbs and hence known as the 'boneshaker'. Springs and wire-spoke wheels were introduced in the 1860s, also solid rubber tyres (c.1867), and the front wheel was made much larger so that the distance covered for each push of the pedals was longer. This machine became known as the 'ordinary' bicycle (and later by the derisory name 'penny farthing') after the introduction in the late 1870s of 'safety' bicycles with two medium-sized wheels and with the rider's seat set further back, reducing the chances of pitching head-first over the handlebars from a high position. The successful Rover safety bicycle of 1884/5, with smaller wheels and with a toothed gearwheel connected by an endless chain with the hub of the rear wheel, was essentially the modern machine. The diamond-shaped frame was common by the 1890s, and the next really new development did not take place until 1962 when the cross-frame was introduced, with one large tube as the main horizontal member from which two parallel tubes project (one for the seat and one for the handlebars), and with small wheels.

Many key modern technologies were developed for the bicycle, including wire-spoked wheels, ball-bearings, and pneumatic tyres. The machine had a great social effect and remains of major importance in both rich and poor countries.

bid /bɪd/ v. & n. —v. (**bidding**; past **bid**, archaic **bade** /beɪd, bæd/; past part. **bid**, archaic **bidden** /ˈbɪd(ə)n/) **1** tr. & intr. (past and past part. **bid**) (often foll. by for, against) **a** (esp. at an auction) offer (a certain price) (did not bid for the vase; bid against the dealer; bid £20). **b** offer to do work etc. for a stated price. **2** tr. archaic or literary **a** command; order (bid the soldiers shoot). **b** invite (bade her start). **3** tr. archaic or literary **a** utter (greeting or farewell) to (I bade him welcome). **b** proclaim (defiance etc.). **4** (past and past part. **bid**) Cards **a** intr. state before play how many tricks one intends to make. **b** tr. state (one's intended number of tricks). —n. **1 a** (esp. at an auction) an offer (of a price) (a bid of £5). **b** an offer (to do work, supply goods, etc.) at a stated price; a tender. **2** Cards a statement of the number of tricks a player proposes to make. **3** colloq. an attempt; an effort (a bid for power). □ **bid fair to** seem likely to. **make a bid for** try to gain (made a bid for freedom). □□ **bidder** n. [OE biddan ask f. Gmc, & OE bēodan offer, command]

biddable /ˈbɪdəb(ə)l/ adj. **1** obedient. **2** Cards (of a hand or suit) suitable for being bid. □□ **biddability** /-ˈbɪlɪtɪ/ n.

bidden archaic past part. of BID.

bidding /ˈbɪdɪŋ/ n. **1** the offers at an auction. **2** Cards the act of

making a bid or bids. **3** a command, request, or invitation. □ **bidding-prayer** one inviting the congregation to join in.

biddy /ˈbɪdɪ/ n. (pl. **-ies**) sl. derog. a woman (esp. old biddy). [pet-form of the name Bridget]

bide /baɪd/ v.intr. archaic or dial. remain; stay. □ **bide one's time** await one's best opportunity. [OE bīdan f. Gmc]

bidet /ˈbiːdeɪ/ n. a low oval basin used esp. for washing the genital area. [F, = pony]

Biedermeier /ˈbiːdəˌmaɪə(r)/ attrib.adj. **1** (of styles, furnishings, etc.) characteristic of the period 1815–48 in Germany. **2** derog. conventional; bourgeois. [Biedermaier a fictitious German poet (1854)]

Bielefeld /ˈbiːləˌfelt/ an industrial city in North Rhine-Westphalia in Germany; pop. (1987) 299,400.

biennial /baɪˈenɪəl/ adj. & n. —adj. **1** lasting two years. **2** recurring every two years (cf. BIANNUAL). —n. **1** Bot. a plant that takes two years to grow from seed to fruition and die (cf. ANNUAL, PERENNIAL). **2** an event celebrated or taking place every two years. □□ **biennially** adv. [L biennis (as BI-, annus year)]

biennium /baɪˈenɪəm/ n. (pl. **bienniums** or **biennia** /-nɪə/) a period of two years. [L (as BIENNIAL)]

bier /bɪə(r)/ n. a movable frame on which a coffin or a corpse is placed, or taken to a grave. [OE bēr f. Gmc]

Bierce /ˈbɪəs/, Ambrose Gwinnett (1842–?1914), American writer, who served in the American Civil War (1861–5) and later became a prominent journalist in California, London, and Washington. He is best known for his short stories—realistic, sardonic, and strongly influenced by Edgar Allan Poe. In 1913 he travelled to Mexico and mysteriously disappeared.

biff /bɪf/ n. & v. sl. —n. a sharp blow. —v.tr. strike (a person). [imit.]

biffin /ˈbɪfɪn/ n. Brit. a deep-red cooking-apple. [= beefing f. BEEF + -ING[1], with ref. to the colour]

bifid /ˈbaɪfɪd/ adj. divided by a deep cleft into two parts. [L bifidus (as BI-, fidus f. stem of findere cleave)]

bifocal /baɪˈfəʊk(ə)l/ adj. & n. —adj. having two focuses, esp. of a lens with a part for distant vision and a part for near vision. —n. (in pl.) bifocal spectacles.

bifurcate /ˈbaɪfəˌkeɪt/ v. & adj. —v.tr. & intr. divide into two branches; fork. —adj. forked; branched. [med.L bifurcare f. L bifurcus two-forked (as BI-, furca fork)]

bifurcation /ˌbaɪfəˈkeɪʃ(ə)n/ n. **1 a** a division into two branches. **b** either or both of such branches. **2** the point of such a division.

big /bɪg/ adj. & adv. —adj. (**bigger, biggest**) **1 a** of considerable size, amount, intensity, etc. (a big mistake; a big helping). **b** of a large or the largest size (big toe; big drum). **2** important; significant; outstanding (the big race; my big chance). **3 a** grown up (a big boy now). **b** elder (big sister). **4** colloq. **a** boastful (big words; big mouth). **b** often iron. generous (big of him). **c** ambitious (big ideas). **5** (usu. foll. by with) advanced in pregnancy; fecund (big with child; big with consequences). —adv. colloq. in a big manner, esp.: **1** effectively (went over big). **2** boastfully (talk big). **3** ambitiously (think big). □ **Big Apple** US sl. New York City. **big band** a large jazz or pop orchestra. **big bang** see separate entry. **Big Board** US colloq. the New York Stock Exchange. **Big Brother** an all-powerful supposedly benevolent dictator (as in Orwell's 1984). **big bud** a plant disease caused by the gall-mite. **big bug** sl. = BIGWIG. **big business** large-scale financial dealings, esp. when sinister or exploitative. **Big Chief** (or **Daddy**) sl. = BIGWIG. **big deal!** sl. iron. I am not impressed. **big dipper 1** a fairground switchback. **2** US = the Great Bear (see BEAR[2]). **big end** (in a motor vehicle) the end of the connecting-rod that encircles the crankpin. **big game** large animals hunted for sport. **big gun** sl. = BIGWIG. **big-head** colloq. a conceited person. **big-headed** colloq. conceited. **big-headedness** colloq. conceitedness. **big-hearted** generous. **big house 1** the principal house in a village etc. **2** sl. a prison. **big idea** often iron. the important intention or scheme. **big money** large amounts; high profit; high pay. **big name** a famous person. **big noise** (or **pot** or **shot**) colloq. sl. = BIGWIG. **big smoke** Brit. sl. **1** London. **2** any large town. **big stick** a display of force. **Big Three** (or **Four** etc.) the predominant few. **the big time** sl. success in a profession, esp. show business. **big-timer** *sl.* a person who achieves success. **big top** the main tent in a circus. **big tree** *US* a giant evergreen conifer, *Sequoiadendron giganteum*, usu. with a trunk of large girth. **big wheel 1** a Ferris wheel. **2** *US sl.* = BIGWIG. **come** (or **go**) **over big** make a great effect. **in a big way 1** on a large scale. **2** *colloq.* with great enthusiasm, display, etc. **look** (or **talk**) **big** boast. **think big** be ambitious. **too big for one's boots** (or **breeches**) *sl.* conceited. □□ **biggish** *adj.* **bigness** *n.* [ME: orig. unkn.]

bigamy /ˈbɪgəmɪ/ *n.* (*pl.* **-ies**) the crime of marrying when one is lawfully married to another person. □□ **bigamist** *n.* **bigamous** *adj.* [ME f. OF *bigamie* f. *bigame* bigamous f. LL *bigamus* (as BI-, Gk *gamos* marriage)]

big bang *n.* **1** the explosion of dense matter which, according to a current cosmological theory, marks the origin of the universe. In the beginning, a fireball of radiation at unbelievably high temperatures but occupying a tiny volume is believed to have formed. The density at this time was also extremely high, and the fireball expanded and cooled, infinitely fast at first, but more slowly as elementary particles condensed out from the radiation to form the matter which later accumulated into galaxies and stars. Currently, the galaxies are still retreating from one another in the wake of this initial explosion, and it is not known whether they contain sufficient mass to halt the expansion through their mutual gravitational attraction. What was left of the original radiation continued to cool, and may now be observed with microwave detectors at a temperature of three degrees above absolute zero. **2** *Stock Exch.* (in the UK) the introduction in 1986 of important changes in the regulations and procedures for trading, especially the widening of membership, the relaxation of rules for brokers, and the introduction of computerized communications.

bighorn /ˈbɪghɔːn/ *n.* an American sheep, *Ovis canadensis*, esp. native to the Rocky Mountains.

bight /baɪt/ *n.* **1** a curve or recess in a coastline, river, etc. **2** a loop of rope. [OE *byht*, MLG *bucht* f. Gmc: see BOW²]

bigot /ˈbɪgət/ *n.* an obstinate and intolerant believer in a religion, political theory, etc. □□ **bigotry** *n.* [16th c. f. F: orig. unkn.]

bigoted /ˈbɪgətɪd/ *adj.* unreasonably prejudiced and intolerant.

bigwig /ˈbɪgwɪg/ *n. colloq.* an important person.

Bihar /bɪˈhɑː(r)/ a State in NE India; pop. (1981) 69,823,150; capital, Patna.

Bihari /bɪˈhɑːrɪ/ *n.* **1** a native of Bihar. **2** a group of three closely related languages, descended from Sanskrit, spoken principally in Bihar. The three languages are Bhojpuri with 20 million speakers in western Bihar and eastern Uttar Pradesh, Maithili with 15 million speakers in northern Bihar and Nepal, and Magahi with 5 million speakers in central Bihar.

Bijagos, Ilhas dos see BISSAGOS.

bijou /ˈbiːʒuː/ *n. & adj.* —*n.* (*pl.* **bijoux** *pronunc.* same) a jewel; a trinket. —*attrib.adj.* (**bijou**) small and elegant. [F]

bijouterie /biːˈʒuːtərɪ/ *n.* jewellery; trinkets. [F (as BIJOU, -ERY)]

bike /baɪk/ *n. & v. colloq.* —*n.* a bicycle or motor cycle. —*v.intr.* ride a bicycle or motor cycle. [abbr.]

biker /ˈbaɪkə(r)/ *n.* a cyclist, esp. a motor cyclist.

bikini /bɪˈkiːnɪ/ *n.* (*pl.* **bikinis**) a two-piece swimsuit for women. □ **bikini briefs** women's scanty briefs. [*Bikini*, an atoll in the Marshall Islands in the Pacific where an atom bomb was exploded in 1946, perh. from the supposed 'explosive' effect]

Biko /ˈbiːkəʊ/, Stephen ('Steve') (1946–77), Black radical student leader in South Africa, an active opponent of apartheid, whose death after a few days in police custody made him a symbol of heroism in Black townships and beyond. Disclosures about the extensive injuries he had sustained while in prison provoked international concern.

bilabial /baɪˈleɪbɪəl/ *adj. Phonet.* (of a sound etc.) made with closed or nearly closed lips.

bilateral /baɪˈlætər(ə)l/ *adj.* **1** of, on, or with two sides. **2** affecting or between two parties, countries, etc. (*bilateral negotiations*). □ **bilateral symmetry** symmetry about a plane. □□ **bilaterally** *adv.*

Bilbao /bɪlˈbaːəʊ/ a seaport in the Basque Provinces, a region of northern Spain; pop. (1986) 378,200.

bilberry /ˈbɪlbərɪ/ *n.* (*pl.* **-ies**) **1** a hardy dwarf shrub, *Vaccinium myrtillus*, of N. Europe, growing on heaths and mountains, and having red drooping flowers and dark blue berries. **2** the small blue edible berry of this species. **3** any of various shrubs of the genus *Vaccinium* having dark blue berries. [orig. uncert.: cf. Da. *böllebær*]

bilbo /ˈbɪlbəʊ/ *n.* (*pl.* **-os** or **-oes**) *hist.* a sword noted for the temper and elasticity of its blade. [*Bilboa* = Bilbao in Spain]

bilboes /ˈbɪlbəʊz/ *n.pl. hist.* an iron bar with sliding shackles for a prisoner's ankles. [16th c.: orig. unkn.]

Bildungsroman /ˈbɪldʊnzrəʊˌmaːn/ *n.* a novel dealing with one person's early life and development. [G]

bile /baɪl/ *n.* **1** a bitter greenish-brown alkaline fluid which aids digestion and is secreted by the liver and stored in the gall-bladder. **2** bad temper; peevish anger. □ **bile-duct** the duct which conveys bile from the liver and the gall-bladder to the duodenum. [F f. L *bilis*]

bilge /bɪldʒ/ *n. & v.* —*n.* **1 a** the almost flat part of a ship's bottom, inside or out. **b** (in full **bilge-water**) filthy water that collects inside the bilge. **2** *sl.* nonsense; rot (*don't talk bilge*). —*v.* **1** *tr.* stave in the bilge of (a ship). **2** *intr.* spring a leak in the bilge. **3** *intr.* swell out; bulge. □ **bilge-keel** a plate or timber fastened under the bilge to prevent rolling. [prob. var. of BULGE]

bilharzia /bɪlˈhɑːtsɪə/ *n.* **1** a tropical flatworm of the genus *Schistosoma* (formerly *Bilharzia*) which is parasitic in blood vessels in the human pelvic region. Also called SCHISTOSOME. **2** the chronic tropical disease produced by its presence. Also called BILHARZIASIS, SCHISTOSOMIASIS. [mod.L f. T. *Bilharz*, Ger. physician d. 1862]

bilharziasis /ˌbɪlhɑːˈtsaɪəsɪs/ *n.* the disease of bilharzia. Also called SCHISTOSOMIASIS.

biliary /ˈbɪlɪərɪ/ *adj.* of the bile. [F *bilaire*: see BILE, -ARY²]

bilingual /baɪˈlɪŋgw(ə)l/ *adj. & n.* —*adj.* **1** able to speak two languages, esp. fluently. **2** spoken or written in two languages. —*n.* a bilingual person. □□ **bilingualism** *n.* [L *bilinguis* (as BI-, *lingua* tongue)]

bilious /ˈbɪlɪəs/ *adj.* **1** affected by a disorder of the bile. **2** bad-tempered. □□ **biliously** *adv.* **biliousness** *n.* [L *biliosus* f. *bilis* bile]

bilirubin /ˌbɪlɪˈruːbɪn/ *n.* the orange-yellow pigment occurring in bile. [G f. L *bilis* BILE + *ruber* red]

bilk /bɪlk/ *v.tr. sl.* **1** cheat. **2** give the slip to. **3** avoid paying (a creditor or debt). □□ **bilker** *n.* [orig. uncert., perh. = BALK: earliest use (17th c.) in cribbage, = spoil one's opponent's score]

bill¹ /bɪl/ *n. & v.* —*n.* **1 a** a printed or written statement of charges for goods supplied or services rendered. **b** the amount owed (*ran up a bill of £300*). **2** a draft of a proposed law. **3 a** a poster; a placard. **b** = HANDBILL. **4 a** a printed list, esp. a theatre programme. **b** the entertainment itself (*top of the bill*). **5** *US* a banknote (*ten dollar bill*). —*v.tr.* **1** put in the programme; announce. **2** (foll. by *as*) advertise. **3** send a note of charges to (*billed him for the books*). □ **bill of exchange** *Econ.* a written order to pay a sum of money on a given date to the drawer or to a named payee. **bill of fare** a menu. **2** a programme (for a theatrical event). **bill of health 1** *Naut.* a certificate regarding infectious disease on a ship or in a port at the time of sailing. **2 (clean bill of health) a** such a certificate stating that there is no disease. **b** a declaration that a person or thing examined has been found to be free of illness or in good condition. **bill of indictment** *hist.* or *US* a written accusation as presented to a grand jury. **bill of lading** *Naut.* **1** a shipmaster's detailed list of the ship's cargo. **2** *US* = WAYBILL. **Bill of Rights** see separate entry. **bill of sale** *Econ.* a certificate of transfer of personal property, esp. as a security against debt. □□ **billable** *adj.* [ME f. AF *bille*, AL *billa*, prob. alt. of med.L *bulla* seal, sealed documents, BULL²]

bill² /bɪl/ *n. & v.* —*n.* **1** the beak of a bird, esp. when it is slender, flattened, or weak, or belongs to a web-footed bird or a bird of the pigeon family. **2** the muzzle of a platypus. **3** a narrow promontory. **4** the point of an anchor-fluke. —*v.intr.* (of doves etc.) stroke a bill with a bill. □ **bill and coo** exchange caresses. □□ **billed** adj. (usu. in comb.). [OE bile, of unkn. orig.]

bill[3] /bɪl/ n. **1** hist. a weapon like a halberd with a hook instead of a blade. **2** = BILLHOOK. [OE bil, ult. f. Gmc]

billabong /ˈbɪləˌbɒŋ/ n. Austral. a branch of a river forming a backwater or a stagnant pool. [Aboriginal Billibang Bell River f. billa water]

billboard /ˈbɪlbɔːd/ n. esp. US a large outdoor board for advertisements etc.

billet[1] /ˈbɪlɪt/ n. & v. —n. **1 a** a place where troops etc. are lodged, usu. with civilians. **b** a written order requiring a householder to lodge the bearer, usu. a soldier. **2** colloq. a situation; a job. —v.tr. (**billeted, billeting**) **1** (usu. foll. by on, in, at) quarter (soldiers etc.). **2** (of a householder) provide (a soldier etc.) with board and lodging. □□ **billetee** /-ˈtiː/ n. **billeter** n. [ME f. AF billette, AL billetta, dimin. of billa BILL[1]]

billet[2] /ˈbɪlɪt/ n. **1** a thick piece of firewood. **2** a small metal bar. **3** Archit. each of a series of short rolls inserted at intervals in Norman decorative mouldings. [ME f. F billette small log, ult. prob. of Celtic orig.]

billet-doux /ˌbɪliˈduː/ n. (pl. **billets-doux** /-ˈduːz/) often joc. a love-letter. [F, = sweet note]

billfold /ˈbɪlfəʊld/ n. US a wallet for keeping banknotes.

billhead /ˈbɪlhed/ n. a printed account form.

billhook /ˈbɪlhʊk/ n. a sickle-shaped tool with a sharp inner edge, used for pruning, lopping, etc.

billiards /ˈbɪljədz/ n. **1** a game played on an oblong cloth-covered table, with three balls struck with cues into pockets round the edge of the table. (See below.) **2** (**billiard**) (in comb.) used in billiards (billiard-ball; billiard-table). [orig. pl., f. F billard billiards, cue, dimin. of bille log: see BILLET[2]]

There are many forms of the game, and its origin and age are uncertain; the reference to billiards in Shakespear's Antony and Cleopatra is an anachronism. In the 16th–17th c. it is well attested, and is known to have been a sport of royalty both in France and in Britain. By the mid-17th c. there were public as well as private tables. The game became associated with gambling and a dissipated life, and for a few years in the mid-18th c. it was classed as an unlawful game and tables were banned in public houses. Early tables were made entirely of wood, later with an iron top, until the slate top was introduced c.1826 to avoid problems of warping or rusting. Green was the colour of the fitted fabric covering until variants were introduced in the mid-20th c. Balls were propelled with a mace (a stick with a flat square head) until the straight cue was introduced in the early 19th c.; the two-piece cue became popular in the mid-1970s. The balls were made of ivory until towards the end of the 19th c., when the invention of celluloid made possible the use of synthetics, although at first these were not universally accepted. The phenomenal skill of the Australian player Walter Lindrum (1898–1960), which defied competition (especially in the early 1930s), helped to kill the game in favour of pool, where there is a greater element of chance; the most popular form of this is snooker (see entry).

Billingsgate /ˈbɪlɪŋzˌɡeɪt/ a London fish-market dating from the 16th c., known for the invective traditionally ascribed to the fish-porters.

billion /ˈbɪljən/ n. & adj. —n. (pl. same or (in sense 3) **billions**) (in sing. prec. by a or one) **1** a thousand million (1,000,000,000 or 10[9]). **2** (now less often, esp. Brit.) a million million (1,000,000,000,000 or 10[12]). **3** (in pl.) colloq. a very large number (billions of years). —adj. that amount to a billion. □□ **billionth** adj. & n. [F (as BI-, MILLION)]

billionaire /ˌbɪljəˈneə(r)/ n. a person possessing over a billion pounds, dollars, etc. [after MILLIONAIRE]

Bill of Rights 1 a bill passed in October 1689 confirming the deposition of James II and the accession of William and Mary, guaranteeing the Protestant succession, and laying down principles of parliamentary supremacy. **2** the first 10 amendments to the Constitution of the US, proposed by Congress in 1789 and ratified in 1791, spelling out individual rights that are regarded as inalienable. The First Amendment gives citizens freedom of religion, assembly, speech, and the press, and the right of petition. The next seven secure the rights of property and guarantee the rights of persons accused of crime. The Ninth protects rights held concurrently by the people and the federal government, and the Tenth assures the reserved rights of the States. **3** a statement of the rights of a class of people.

billon /ˈbɪlən/ n. an alloy of gold or silver with a predominating admixture of a base metal. [F f. bille BILLET[2]]

billow /ˈbɪləʊ/ n. & v. —n. **1** a wave. **2** a soft upward-curving flow. **3** any large soft mass. —v.intr. move or build up in billows. □□ **billowy** adj. [ON bylgja f. Gmc]

billposter /ˈbɪlˌpəʊstə(r)/ n. (also **billsticker** /-ˌstɪkə(r)/) a person who pastes up advertisements on hoardings. □□ **billposting** n.

billy[1] /ˈbɪli/ n. (pl. **-ies**) (in full **billycan**) (orig. Austral.) a tin or enamel cooking-pot with a lid and wire handle, for use out of doors. [perh. f. Aboriginal billa water]

billy[2] /ˈbɪli/ n. (pl. **-ies**) = BILLY-GOAT.

billycan /ˈbɪliˌkæn/ n. = BILLY[1].

billy-goat /ˈbɪliˌɡəʊt/ n. a male goat. [Billy, pet-form of the name William]

billy-oh /ˈbɪliəʊ/ n. □ **like billy-oh** sl. very much, hard, strongly, etc. (raining like billy-oh). [19th c.: orig. unkn.]

bilobate /baɪˈləʊbət/ adj. (also **bilobed** /-ˈləʊbd/) having or consisting of two lobes.

biltong /ˈbɪltɒŋ/ n. S.Afr. boneless meat salted and dried in strips. [Afrik., of uncert. orig.]

BIM abbr. British Institute of Management.

bimanal /ˈbɪmən(ə)l/ adj. (also **bimanous** /-nəs/) having two hands. [BI- + L manus hand]

bimbo /ˈbɪmbəʊ/ n. (pl. **-os** or **-oes**) sl. usu. derog. **1** a person. **2** a woman, esp. a young empty-headed one. [It., = little child]

bimetallic /ˌbaɪmɪˈtælɪk/ adj. **1** made of two metals. **2** of or relating to bimetallism. □ **bimetallic strip** a sensitive element in some thermostats made of two bands of different metals that expand at different rates when heated, causing the strip to bend. [F bimétallique (as BI-, METALLIC)]

bimetallism /baɪˈmetəˌlɪz(ə)m/ n. a system of allowing the unrestricted currency of two metals (e.g. gold and silver) at a fixed ratio to each other, as coined money. □□ **bimetallist** n.

bimillenary /ˌbaɪmɪˈlenəri/ adj. & n. —adj. of or relating to a two-thousandth anniversary. —n. (pl. **-ies**) a bimillenary year or festival.

bimonthly /baɪˈmʌnθli/ adj., adv., & n. —adj. occurring twice a month or every two months. —adv. twice a month or every two months. —n. (pl. **-ies**) a periodical produced bimonthly. ¶ Often avoided, because of the ambiguity of meaning, in favour of two-monthly and twice-monthly.

bin /bɪn/ n. & v. —n. a large receptacle for storage or for depositing rubbish. —v.tr. colloq. (**binned, binning**) store or put in a bin. □ **bin end** one of the last bottles from a bin of wine, usu. sold at a reduced price. **bin-liner** a bag (usu. of plastic) for lining a rubbish bin. [OE bin(n), binne]

bin- /bɪn, baɪn/ prefix var. of BI- before a vowel.

binary /ˈbaɪnəri/ adj. & n. —adj. **1 a** dual. **b** of or involving pairs. **2** of the arithmetical system using 2 as a base. —n. (pl. **-ies**) **1** something having two parts. **2** a binary number. **3** a binary star. □ **binary code** Computing a coding system using the binary digits 0 and 1 to represent a letter, digit, or other character in a computer (see BCD). **binary compound** Chem. a compound having two elements or radicals. **binary fission** the division of a cell or organism into two parts. **binary number** (or **digit**) one of two digits (usu. 0 or 1) in a binary system of notation. **binary star** a gravitationally-bound pair of stars revolving round a common centre. By no means uncommon, such pairs may be widely separated, or they may interact tidally if close together, one stripping material from the other. Close binary pairs may eclipse one another if their orbital plane lies in the line of sight. **binary system** a system in which information can be expressed by combinations of the digits 0 and 1 (corresponding to 'off' and 'on' in computing). **binary tree** a data structure in which a record is branched to the left when greater and to the right when less than the previous record. [LL *binarius* f. *bini* two together]

binate /'baɪneɪt/ *adj. Bot.* **1** growing in pairs. **2** composed of two equal parts. [mod.L *binatus* f. L *bini* two together]

binaural /baɪ'nɔːr(ə)l/ *adj.* **1** of or used with both ears. **2** (of sound) recorded using two microphones and usu. transmitted separately to the two ears.

bind /baɪnd/ *v. & n.* —*v.* (*past* and *past part.* **bound** /baʊnd/) (see also BOUNDEN). **1** *tr.* (often foll. by *to*, *on*, *together*) tie or fasten tightly. **2** *tr.* **a** restrain; put in bonds. **b** (as **-bound** *adj.*) constricted, obstructed (*snowbound*). **3** *tr. esp. Cookery* cause (ingredients) to cohere using another ingredient. **4** *tr.* fasten or hold together as a single mass. **5** *tr.* compel; impose an obligation or duty on. **6** *tr.* **a** edge (fabric etc.) with braid etc. **b** fix together and fasten (the pages of a book) in a cover. **7** *tr.* constipate. **8** *tr.* ratify (a bargain, agreement, etc.). **9** *tr.* (in *passive*) be required by an obligation or duty (*am bound to answer*). **10** *tr.* (often foll. by *up*) **a** put a bandage or other covering round. **b** fix together with something put round (*bound her hair*). **11** *tr.* indenture as an apprentice. **12** *intr.* (of snow etc.) cohere, stick. **13** *intr.* be prevented from moving freely. **14** *intr. sl.* complain. —*n.* **1** *colloq.* a nuisance; a restriction. **2** = BINE. □ **be bound up with** be closely associated with. **bind over** *Law* order (a person) to do something, esp. keep the peace. **bind up** bandage. **I'll be bound** a statement of assurance, or guaranteeing the truth of something. [OE *bindan*]

binder /'baɪndə(r)/ *n.* **1** a cover for sheets of paper, for a book, etc. **2** a substance that acts cohesively. **3** a reaping-machine that binds grain into sheaves. **4** a bookbinder.

bindery /'baɪndərɪ/ *n.* (*pl.* **-ies**) a workshop or factory for binding books.

bindi-eye /'bɪndɪˌaɪ/ *n. Austral.* a small perennial Australian herb, *Calotis cuneifolia*, which has a burlike fruit. [20th c.: orig. unkn.]

binding /'baɪndɪŋ/ *n. & adj.* —*n.* something that binds, esp. the covers, glue, etc., of a book. —*adj.* (often foll. by *on*) obligatory.

bindweed /'baɪndwiːd/ *n.* **1** convolvulus. **2** any of various species of climbing plants such as honeysuckle.

bine /baɪn/ *n.* **1** the twisting stem of a climbing plant, esp. the hop. **2** a flexible shoot. [orig. a dial. form of BIND]

Binet /'biːneɪ/, Alfred (1857–1911), French psychologist, father of intelligence testing as it is known today. He was requested by the French government to devise a test which would detect intellectually slow schoolchildren who might not benefit from the normal school curriculum at a time when school attendance became mandatory in France, and from 1905, together with another French psychologist, Theodore Simon, he produced tests (now known as *Binet*(-*Simon*) *tests*) thought to task general reasoning capacities rather than the perceptual-motor skills which had previously been used as an indicator of intellectual ability. Believing that bright and dull schoolchildren were simply advanced or retarded in their mental growth, Binet devised a 'mental-age' scale which described a student's performance in relation to the average performance of students of the same physical age.

binge /bɪndʒ/ *n. & v. sl.* —*n.* a spree; a period of uncontrolled eating, drinking, etc. —*v.intr.* go on a spree; indulge in uncontrolled eating, drinking, etc. [prob. orig. dial., = soak]

bingo /'bɪŋgəʊ/ *n. & int.* —*n.* a game for any number of players, each having a card of squares with numbers, which are marked off as numbers are randomly drawn by a caller. The player first covering all or a set of these wins a prize. —*int.* expressing sudden surprise, satisfaction, etc., as in winning at bingo. [prob. imit.: cf. dial. *bing* 'with a bang']

binman /'bɪnmæn/ *n.* (*pl.* **-men**) *colloq.* a dustman.

binnacle /'bɪnək(ə)l/ *n.* a built-in housing for a ship's compass. [earlier *bittacle*, ult. f. L *habitaculum* habitation f. *habitare* inhabit]

binocular /baɪ'nɒkjʊlə(r)/ *adj.* adapted for or using both eyes. [BIN- + L *oculus* eye]

binoculars /bɪ'nɒkjʊləz/ *n.pl.* an optical instrument with a lens for each eye, for viewing distant objects.

binomial /baɪ'nəʊmɪəl/ *n. & adj.* —*n.* **1** an algebraic expression of the sum or the difference of two terms. **2** a two-part name, esp. in taxonomy. —*adj.* consisting of two terms. □ **binomial classification** a system of classification using two terms, the first one indicating the genus and the second the species. **binomial distribution** a frequency distribution of the possible number of successful outcomes in a given number of trials in each of which there is the same probability of success. **binomial theorem** a formula for finding any power of a binomial without multiplying at length. □□ **binomially** *adv.* [F *binôme* or mod.L *binomium* (as BI-, Gk *nomos* part, portion)]

binominal /baɪ'nɒmɪn(ə)l/ *adj.* = BINOMIAL. [L *binominis* (as BI-, *nomen -inis* name)]

bint /bɪnt/ *n. sl.* usu. *offens.* a girl or woman. [Arab., = daughter, girl]

binturong /'bɪntjʊˌrɒŋ/ *n.* a civet, *Arctictis binturong*, of S. Asia, with a shaggy black coat and a prehensile tail. [Malay]

bio- /'baɪəʊ/ *comb. form* **1** life (*biography*). **2** biological (*biomathematics*). **3** of living beings (*biophysics*). [Gk *bios* (course of) human life]

biochemistry /ˌbaɪəʊ'kemɪstrɪ/ *n.* the study of the chemical and physico-chemical processes of living organisms. □□ **biochemical** *adj.* **biochemist** *n.*

biocoenosis /ˌbaɪəʊsiː'nəʊsɪs/ *n.* (*US* **biocenosis**) (*pl.* **-noses** /-siːz/) **1** an association of different organisms forming a community. **2** the relationship existing between such organisms. □□ **biocoenology** /-'nɒlədʒɪ/ *n.* **biocoenotic** /-'nɒtɪk/ *adj.* [mod.L f. BIO- + Gk *koinōsis* sharing f. *koinos* common]

biodegradable /ˌbaɪəʊdɪ'greɪdəb(ə)l/ *adj.* capable of being decomposed by bacteria or other living organisms. □□ **biodegradability** /-'bɪlɪtɪ/ *n.* **biodegradation** /ˌbaɪəʊˌdegrə'deɪʃ(ə)n/ *n.*

bioengineering /ˌbaɪəʊˌendʒɪ'nɪərɪŋ/ *n.* **1** the application of engineering techniques to biological processes. **2** the use of artificial tissues, organs, or organ components to replace damaged or absent parts of the body, e.g. artificial limbs, heart pacemakers, etc. □□ **bioengineer** *n. & v.*

bioethics /ˌbaɪəʊ'eθɪks/ *n.pl.* (treated as *sing.*) the ethics of medical and biological research. □□ **bioethicist** *n.*

biofeedback /ˌbaɪəʊ'fiːdbæk/ *n.* the technique of using the feedback of a normally automatic bodily response to a stimulus, in order to acquire voluntary control of that response.

bioflavonoid /ˌbaɪəʊ'fleɪvəˌnɔɪd/ *n.* = CITRIN. [BIO- + *flavonoid* f. FLAVINE + -OID]

biogenesis /ˌbaɪəʊ'dʒenɪsɪs/ *n.* **1** the synthesis of substances by living organisms. **2** the hypothesis that a living organism arises only from another similar living organism. □□ **biogenetic** /-dʒɪ'netɪk/ *adj.*

biogenic /ˌbaɪəʊ'dʒenɪk/ *adj.* produced by living organisms.

biogeography /ˌbaɪəʊdʒɪ'ɒgrəfɪ/ *n.* the scientific study of the geographical distribution of plants and animals. □□ **biogeographical** /-dʒɪə'græfɪk(ə)l/ *adj.*

biography /baɪ'ɒgrəfɪ/ *n.* (*pl.* **-ies**) **1 a** a written account of a person's life, usu. by another. **b** such writing as a branch of literature. **2** the course of a living (usu. human) being's life. □□ **biographer** *n.* **biographic** /ˌbaɪə'græfɪk/ *adj.* **biographical** /ˌbaɪə'græfɪk(ə)l/ *adj.* [F *biographie* or mod.L *biographia* f. med.Gk]

Bioko /bɪ'əʊkəʊ/ an island of Equatorial Guinea, in the eastern part of the Gulf of Guinea, known as Fernando Póo until 1973 and as Macias Nguema 1973–9; pop. (1983) 57,200.

biological /ˌbaɪə'lɒdʒɪk(ə)l/ *adj.* of or relating to biology or living organisms. □ **biological clock** an innate mechanism controlling the rhythmic physiological activities of an organism. **biological control** the control of a pest by the introduction of a natural enemy. **biological warfare** warfare involving the use of toxins or micro-organisms. □□ **biologically** *adv.*

biology /baɪ'ɒlədʒɪ/ *n.* **1** the study of living organisms. **2** the plants and animals of a particular area. The word was coined in the 19th c. as it began to be realized that all living things share fundamental similarities. □□ **biologist** *n.* [F *biologie* f. G *Biologie* (as BIO-, -LOGY)]

bioluminescence /ˌbaɪəʊˌluːmɪˈnes(ə)ns/ n. the emission of light by living organisms such as the firefly and glow-worm. □□ **bioluminescent** adj.

biomass /ˈbaɪəʊˌmæs/ n. the total quantity or weight of organisms in a given area or volume. [BIO- + MASS¹]

biomathematics /ˌbaɪəʊˌmæθɪˈmætɪks/ n. the science of the application of mathematics to biology.

biome /ˈbaɪəʊm/ n. **1** a large naturally occurring community of flora and fauna adapted to the particular conditions in which they occur, e.g. tundra. **2** the geographical region containing such a community. [BIO- + -OME]

biomechanics /ˌbaɪəʊmɪˈkæniks/ n. the study of the mechanical laws relating to the movement or structure of living organisms.

biometry /baɪˈɒmɪtrɪ/ n. (also **biometrics** /ˌbaɪəʊˈmetrɪks/) the application of statistical analysis to biological data. □□ **biometric** /ˌbaɪəʊˈmetrɪk/ adj. **biometrical** /ˌbaɪəʊˈmetrɪk(ə)l/ adj. **biometrician** /ˌbaɪəʊmɪˈtrɪʃ(ə)n/ n.

biomorph /ˈbaɪəʊˌmɔːf/ n. a decorative form based on a living organism. □□ **biomorphic** /-ˈmɔːfɪk/ adj. [BIO- + Gk morphē form]

bionic /baɪˈɒnɪk/ adj. **1** having artificial body parts or the superhuman powers resulting from these. **2** relating to bionics. □□ **bionically** adv. [BIO- after ELECTRONIC]

bionics /baɪˈɒnɪks/ n.pl. (treated as sing.) the study of mechanical systems that function like living organisms or parts of living organisms.

bionomics /ˌbaɪəˈnɒmɪks/ n.pl. (treated as sing.) the study of the mode of life of organisms in their natural habitat and their adaptations to their surroundings. □□ **bionomic** adj. [BIO- after ECONOMICS]

biophysics /ˌbaɪəʊˈfɪzɪks/ n.pl. (treated as sing.) the science of the physical properties of living organisms and their constituents, and the investigation of biological phenomena in general by means of the techniques of modern physics. □□ **biophysical** adj. **biophysicist** n.

biopsy /ˈbaɪɒpsɪ/ n. (pl. **-ies**) the examination of tissue removed from a living body to discover the presence, cause, or extent of a disease. [F biopsie f. Gk bios life + opsis sight, after necropsy]

biorhythm /ˈbaɪəʊˌrɪð(ə)m/ n. **1** any of the recurring cycles of biological processes thought to affect a person's emotional, intellectual, and physical activity. **2** any periodic change in the behaviour or physiology of an organism. □□ **biorhythmic** /-ˈrɪðmɪk/ adj. **biorhythmically** /-ˈrɪðmɪkəlɪ/ adv.

bioscope /ˈbaɪəˌskəʊp/ n. S.Afr. sl. a cinema.

biosphere /ˈbaɪəʊˌsfɪə(r)/ n. the regions of the earth's crust and atmosphere occupied by living organisms. [G Biosphäre (as BIO-, SPHERE)]

biosynthesis /ˌbaɪəʊˈsɪnθɪsɪs/ n. the production of organic molecules by living organisms. □□ **biosynthetic** /-ˈθetɪk/ adj.

biota /baɪˈəʊtə/ n. the animal and plant life of a region. [mod.L: cf. Gk biotē life]

biotechnology /ˌbaɪəʊtekˈnɒlədʒɪ/ n. the exploitation of biological processes for industrial and other purposes, esp. genetic manipulation of micro-organisms (for the production of antibiotics, hormones, etc.).

biotic /baɪˈɒtɪk/ adj. **1** relating to life or to living things. **2** of biological origin. [F biotique or LL bioticus f. Gk biōtikos f. bios life]

biotin /ˈbaɪətɪn/ n. a vitamin of the B complex, found in egg yolk, liver, and yeast, and involved in the metabolism of carbohydrates, fats, and proteins. [G f. Gk bios life + -IN]

biotite /ˈbaɪəˌtaɪt/ n. Mineral. a black, dark brown, or green micaceous mineral occurring as a constituent of metamorphic and igneous rocks. [J. B. Biot, Fr. physicist d. 1862]

bipartisan /ˌbaɪpɑːtɪˈzæn, baɪˈpɑːtɪz(ə)n/ adj. of or involving two (esp. political) parties. □□ **bipartisanship** n.

bipartite /baɪˈpɑːtaɪt/ adj. **1** consisting of two parts. **2** shared by or involving two parties. **3** Law (of a contract, treaty, etc.) drawn up in two corresponding parts or between two parties. [L bipartitus f. bipartire (as BI-, partire PART)]

biped /ˈbaɪped/ n. & adj. —n. a two-footed animal. —adj. two-footed. □□ **bipedal** adj. [L bipes -edis (as BI-, pes pedis foot)]

bipinnate /baɪˈpɪneɪt/ adj. (of a pinnate leaf) having leaflets that are further subdivided in a pinnate arrangement.

biplane /ˈbaɪpleɪn/ n. an early type of aeroplane having two sets of wings, one above the other.

bipolar /baɪˈpəʊlə(r)/ adj. having two poles or extremities. □□ **bipolarity** /-ˈlærɪtɪ/ n.

birch /bɜːtʃ/ n. & v. —n. **1** any tree of the genus Betula, having thin peeling bark, bearing catkins, and found predominantly in northern temperate regions. **2** (in full **birchwood**) the hard fine-grained pale wood of these trees. **3** NZ any of various similar trees. **4** (in full **birch-rod**) a bundle of birch twigs used for flogging. —v.tr. beat with a birch (in sense 4). □ **birch-bark 1** the bark of Betula papyrifera used to make canoes. **2** US such a canoe. □□ **birchen** adj. [OE bi(e)rce f. Gmc]

bird /bɜːd/ n. **1** a feathered vertebrate with a beak, with two wings and two feet, egg-laying and usu. able to fly. (See below.) **2** a game-bird. **3** Brit. sl. a young woman. **4** colloq. a person (a wily old bird). **5** sl. **a** a prison. **b** rhyming sl. a prison sentence (short for birdlime = time). □ **bird-bath** a basin in a garden etc. with water for birds to bathe in. **bird-call 1** a bird's natural call. **2** an instrument imitating this. **bird cherry** a wild cherry Prunus padus. **bird-fancier** a person who knows about, collects, breeds, or deals in, birds. **a bird in the hand** something secured or certain. **the bird is** (or **has**) **flown** the prisoner, quarry, etc., has escaped. **bird-** (or **birds'-**) **nesting** hunting for birds' nests, usu. to get eggs. **bird of paradise** any bird of the family Paradiseidae found chiefly in New Guinea, the males having very beautiful brilliantly coloured plumage. **bird of passage 1** a migrant. **2** any transient visitor. **bird of prey** see PREY. **bird sanctuary** an area where birds are protected and encouraged to breed. **the birds and the bees** euphem. sexual activity and reproduction. **bird's-eye** —n. **1** any of several plants having small bright round flowers, such as the germander speedwell. **2** a pattern with many small spots. —adj. of or having small bright round flowers (bird's-eye primrose). **bird's-eye view** a general view from above. **bird's-foot** (pl. **bird's-foots**) any plant like the foot of a bird, esp. of the genus Lotus, having claw-shaped pods. **bird's nest soup** soup made (esp. in Chinese cookery) from the dried gelatinous coating of the nests of swifts and other birds. **birds of a feather** people of like character. **bird-strike** a collision between a bird and an aircraft. **bird table** a raised platform on which food for birds is placed. **bird-watcher** a person who observes birds in their natural surroundings. **bird-watching** this occupation. **for** (or **strictly for**) **the birds** colloq. trivial, uninteresting. **get the bird** sl. **1** be dismissed. **2** be hissed at or booed. **like a bird** without difficulty or hesitation. **a little bird** an unnamed informant. [OE brid, of unkn. orig.]

The earliest known fossil bird, Archaeopteryx, comes from the Jurassic period, about 140 million years ago, and clearly shows the close relationship of birds to the dinosaur-like reptiles from which they are descended: it had feathers, and forelimbs modified as wings, but retained teeth, a long tail containing vertebrae, and other reptilian features. Modern birds, of which there are about 8,600 living species, are anatomically a comparatively uniform group, probably because of the structural demands that flight imposes. Their bones are often hollow for the sake of lightness. They are warm-blooded, and their feathers, besides making flight possible, function as an insulating layer to help conserve their body heat. Birds are primarily diurnal animals, with good colour vision, good hearing, and a poor sense of smell. They exhibit complex social and migratory behaviour, but are considered to behave more instinctively and with less ability to adapt than mammals.

birdbrain /ˈbɜːdbreɪn/ n. colloq. a stupid or flighty person. □□ **birdbrained** adj.

birdcage /ˈbɜːdkeɪdʒ/ n. **1** a cage for birds usu. made of wire or cane. **2** an object of a similar design.

birder /ˈbɜːdə(r)/ n. US a bird-watcher. □□ **birding** n.

birdie /ˈbɜːdɪ/ n. & v. —n. **1** colloq. a little bird. **2** Golf a score of one stroke less than par at any hole. —*v.tr.* (**birdies, birdied, birdying**) *Golf* play (a hole) in a birdie.

birdlime /ˈbɜːdlaɪm/ *n.* sticky material painted on to twigs to trap small birds.

birdseed /ˈbɜːdsiːd/ *n.* a blend of seed for feeding birds, esp. ones which are caged.

Birdseye /ˈbɜːdzaɪ/, Clarence (1886–1956), American businessman and inventor, famous for developing a process of rapid freezing of foods in small packages suitable for retail selling.

birdsong /ˈbɜːdsɒŋ/ *n.* the musical cry of a bird or birds.

birefringent /ˌbaɪrɪˈfrɪndʒ(ə)nt/ *adj. Physics* having two different refractive indices. □□ **birefringence** *n.*

bireme /ˈbaɪriːm/ *n. hist.* an ancient Greek warship, with two files of oarsmen on each side. [L *biremis* (as BI-, *remus* oar)]

biretta /bɪˈretə/ *n.* a square usu. black cap with three flat projections on top, worn by (esp. Roman Catholic) clergymen. [It. *berretta* or Sp. *birreta* f. LL *birrus* cape]

biriani /ˌbɪriˈɑːni/ *n.* (also **biryani**) an orig. Indian dish made with highly seasoned rice, and meat or fish etc. [Urdu]

Birmingham /ˈbɜːmɪŋəm/ an industrial city and the county town of West Midlands; pop. (1981) 920,000.

Biro /ˈbaɪərəʊ/ *n.* (*pl.* **-os**) *Brit. propr.* a kind of ball-point pen. [L. *Biró*, Hung. inventor d. 1985]

birth /bɜːθ/ *n. & v.* —*n.* 1 the emergence of a (usu. fully developed) infant or other young from the body of its mother. 2 *rhet.* the beginning or coming into existence of something (*the birth of civilization; the birth of socialism*). 3 **a** origin, descent, ancestry (*of noble birth*). **b** high or noble birth; inherited position. —*v.tr. US colloq.* 1 to give birth to. 2 to assist (a woman) to give birth. □ **birth certificate** an official document identifying a person by name, place, date of birth, and parentage. **birth control** the control of the number of children one conceives, esp. by contraception. **birth pill** the contraceptive pill. **birth rate** the number of live births per thousand of population per year. **give birth** bear a child etc. **give birth to 1** produce (young) from the womb. 2 cause to begin, found. [ME f. ON *byrth* f. Gmc: see BEAR¹, -TH²]

birthday /ˈbɜːθdeɪ/ *n.* 1 the day on which a person etc. was born. 2 the anniversary of this. □ **birthday honours** *Brit.* titles etc. given on a sovereign's official birthday. **in one's birthday suit** *joc.* naked.

birthmark /ˈbɜːθmɑːk/ *n.* an unusual brown or red mark on one's body at or from birth.

birthplace /ˈbɜːθpleɪs/ *n.* the place where a person was born.

birthright /ˈbɜːθraɪt/ *n.* a right of possession or privilege one has from birth, esp. as the eldest son.

birthstone /ˈbɜːθstəʊn/ *n.* a gemstone popularly associated with the month of one's birth.

Birtwhistle /ˈbɜːt,wɪs(ə)l/, Harrison Paul (1934–), English composer, whose works include the opera *Punch and Judy* (1966–7), the instrumental ensemble *Medusa* (1969–70), dramatic cantatas, and orchestral works.

biryani var. of BIRIANI.

Biscay /ˈbɪskeɪ/, **Bay of** part of the North Atlantic between the north coast of Spain and the west coast of France, notorious for storms.

biscuit /ˈbɪskɪt/ *n. & adj.* —*n.* 1 *Brit.* a small unleavened cake, usu. flat and crisp and often sweet. 2 fired unglazed pottery. 3 a light brown colour. —*adj.* biscuit-coloured. [ME f. OF *bescoit* etc. ult. f. L *bis* twice + *coctus* past part. of *coquere* cook]

bise /biːz/ *n.* a keen dry northerly wind in Switzerland, S. France, etc. [ME f. OF]

bisect /baɪˈsekt/ *v.tr.* divide into two (strictly, equal) parts. □□ **bisection** *n.* **bisector** *n.* [BI- + L *secare sect-* cut]

bisexual /baɪˈseksjʊəl/ *adj. & n.* —*adj.* 1 sexually attracted by persons of both sexes. 2 *Biol.* having characteristics of both sexes. 3 of or concerning both sexes. —*n.* a bisexual person. □□ **bisexuality** /-ˈælɪti/ *n.*

bish /bɪʃ/ *n. sl.* a mistake. [20th c.: orig. uncert.]

bishop /ˈbɪʃəp/ *n.* 1 a senior member of the Christian clergy usu. in charge of a diocese, and empowered to confer holy orders. 2 a chess piece with the top sometimes shaped like a mitre. 3 mulled and spiced wine. [OE *biscop*, ult. f. Gk *episkopos* overseer (as EPI-, *-skopos* -looking)]

bishopric /ˈbɪʃəprɪk/ *n.* 1 the office of a bishop. 2 a diocese. [OE *bisceoprīce* (as BISHOP, *rīce* realm)]

Bismarck¹ /ˈbɪzmɑːk/ the capital of North Dakota; capital, 44,490.

Bismarck² /ˈbɪzmɑːk/, Otto Eduard Leopold, Prince von (1815–98), German statesman. As minister-president and foreign minister of Prussia from 1862, Bismarck was the driving force behind the unification of Germany, orchestrating wars with Denmark (1864), Austria (1866), and France (1870–1) in order to achieve his end. As Chancellor of the new German empire from 1871 to 1890, he continued to dominate the political scene, attempting to crush opposition to the central government at home (see KULTURKAMPF) while consolidating Germany's position as a European power by creating a system of alliances. Although Bismarck was able to work very well with the ageing Wilhelm I, he quarrelled with Wilhelm II and was forced to resign in 1890.

Bismarck Sea an arm of the Pacific Ocean north-east of New Guinea and north of New Britain. In March 1943 the United States destroyed a large Japanese naval force in these waters.

bismuth /ˈbɪzməθ/ *n. Chem.* 1 a brittle reddish-white metallic element. Bismuth occurs in the free state in nature but was not identified as a separate element until the 18th c. It is a relatively poor conductor of heat and electricity. Its main use is as a component of alloys required to have a low melting-point. ¶ Symb.: **Bi**; atomic number 83. 2 any compound of this element used medicinally. [mod.L *bisemutum*, Latinization of G *Wismut*, of unkn. orig.]

bison /ˈbaɪs(ə)n/ *n.* (*pl.* same) either of two wild hump-backed shaggy-haired oxen of the genus *Bison*, native to N. America (*B. bison*) and Europe (*B. bonasus*). [ME f. L f. Gmc]

bisque¹ /bɪsk/ *n.* a rich shellfish soup, made esp. from lobster. [F]

bisque² /bɪsk/ *n. Tennis, Croquet, & Golf* an advantage of scoring one free point, or taking an extra turn or stroke. [F]

bisque³ /bɪsk/ *n.* = BISCUIT 2.

Bissagos Islands /bɪˈsɑːgəs/ (Portuguese **Ilhas dos Bijagós** /ˌviːˈʒɑːˈɡɒʃ/) a group of islands off the coast of Guinea-Bissau, West Africa.

Bissau /bɪˈsaʊ/ the capital of Guinea-Bissau; pop. (est. 1988) 125,000.

bistable /baɪˈsteɪb(ə)l/ *adj.* (of an electrical circuit etc.) having two stable states.

bister US var. of BISTRE.

bistort /ˈbɪstɔːt/ *n.* a herb, *Polygonum bistorta*, with a twisted root and a cylindrical spike of flesh-coloured flowers. [F *bistorte* or med.L *bistorta* f. *bis* twice + *torta* fem. past part. of *torquēre* twist]

bistoury /ˈbɪstərɪ/ *n.* (*pl.* **-ies**) a surgical scalpel. [F *bistouri*, *bistorie*, orig. = dagger, of unkn. orig.]

bistre /ˈbɪstə(r)/ *n. & adj.* (US **bister**) —*n.* 1 a brownish pigment made from the soot of burnt wood. 2 the brownish colour of this. —*adj.* of this colour. [F, of unkn. orig.]

bistro /ˈbiːstrəʊ/ *n.* (*pl.* **-os**) a small restaurant. [F]

bisulphate /baɪˈsʌlfeɪt/ *n.* (US **bisulfate**) *Chem.* a salt or ester of sulphuric acid.

bit¹ /bɪt/ *n.* 1 a small piece or quantity (*a bit of cheese; give me another bit; that bit is too small*). 2 (prec. by *a*) **a** a fair amount (*sold quite a bit; needed a bit of persuading*). **b** *colloq.* somewhat (*am a bit tired*). **c** (foll. by *of*) *colloq.* rather (*a bit of an idiot*). **d** (foll. by *of*) *colloq.* only a little; a mere (*a bit of a boy*). 3 a short time or distance (*wait a bit; move up a bit*). 4 *US sl.* a unit of 12½ cents (used only in even multiples). □ **bit by bit** gradually. **bit of all right** *sl.* a pleasing person or thing, esp. a woman. **bit of fluff** (or **skirt** or **stuff**) see FLUFF, SKIRT, STUFF. **bit on the side** *sl.* an extramarital sexual relationship. **bit part** a minor part in a play or a film. **bits and pieces** (or **bobs**) an assortment of small items. **do one's bit** *colloq.* make a useful contribution to an effort or cause. **every bit as** see EVERY. **not a bit** (or **not a bit of it**) not at all. **to bits** into pieces. [OE *bita* f. Gmc, rel. to BITE]

bit² *past of* BITE.

bit³ /bɪt/ n. & v. —n. **1** a metal mouthpiece on a bridle, used to control a horse. **2** a (usu. metal) tool or piece for boring or drilling. **3** the cutting or gripping part of a plane, pincers, etc. **4** the part of a key that engages with the lock-lever. **5** the copper head of a soldering-iron. —v.tr. **1** put a bit into the mouth of (a horse). **2** restrain. □ **take the bit between one's teeth 1** take decisive personal action. **2** escape from control. [OE *bite* f. Gmc, rel. to BITE]

bit⁴ /bɪt/ n. *Computing* a unit of information expressed as a choice between two possibilities; a 0 or 1 in binary notation. The term was coined in 1948 by the American engineer C. E. Shannon (see INFORMATION THEORY). [BINARY + DIGIT]

bitch /bɪtʃ/ n. & v. —n. **1** a female dog or other canine animal. **2** *sl. offens.* a malicious or spiteful woman. **3** *sl.* a very unpleasant or difficult thing or situation. —v. **1** *intr.* (often foll. by *about*) **a** speak scathingly. **b** complain. **2** *tr.* be spiteful or unfair to. [OE *bicce*]

bitchy /ˈbɪtʃɪ/ adj. (**bitchier**, **bitchiest**) *sl.* spiteful; bad-tempered. □□ **bitchily** adv. **bitchiness** n.

bite /baɪt/ v. & n. —v. (*past* **bit** /bɪt/; *past part.* **bitten** /ˈbɪt(ə)n/) **1** *tr.* cut or puncture using the teeth. **2** *tr.* (foll. by *off*, *away*, etc.) detach with the teeth. **3** *tr.* (of an insect, snake, etc.) wound with a sting, fangs, etc. **4** *intr.* (of a wheel, screw, etc.) grip, penetrate. **5** *intr.* accept bait or an inducement. **6** *intr.* have a (desired) adverse effect. **7** *tr.* (in *passive*) **a** take in; swindle. **b** (foll. by *by*, *with*, etc.) be infected by (enthusiasm etc.). **8** *tr.* (as **bitten** adj.) cause a glowing or smarting pain to (*frostbitten*). **9** *intr.* (foll. by *at*) snap at. —n. **1** an act of biting. **2** a wound or sore made by biting. **3 a** a mouthful of food. **b** a snack or light meal. **4** the taking of bait by a fish. **5** pungency (esp. of flavour). **6** incisiveness, sharpness. **7** = OCCLUSION 3. □ **bite back** restrain (one's speech etc.) by or as if by biting the lips. **bite** (or **bite on**) **the bullet** *sl.* behave bravely or stoically. **bite the dust** *sl.* **1** die. **2** fail; break down. **bite the hand that feeds one** hurt or offend a benefactor. **bite a person's head off** *colloq.* respond fiercely or angrily. **bite one's lip** see LIP. **bite off more than one can chew** take on a commitment one cannot fulfil. **once bitten twice shy** an unpleasant experience induces caution. **put the bite on** *US sl.* borrow or extort money from. **what's biting you?** *sl.* what is worrying you? □□ **biter** n. [OE *bītan* f. Gmc]

Bithynia /bɪˈθɪnɪə/ the ancient name for the region of NW Asia Minor west of Paphlagonia and bordering the Black Sea and the Sea of Marmara.

biting /ˈbaɪtɪŋ/ adj. **1** stinging; intensely cold (*a biting wind*). **2** sharp; effective (*biting wit*; *biting sarcasm*). □□ **bitingly** adv.

bitten *past part.* of BITE.

bitter /ˈbɪtə(r)/ adj. & n. —adj. **1** having a sharp pungent taste; not sweet. **2 a** causing or showing mental pain or resentment (*bitter memories*; *bitter rejoinder*). **b** painful or difficult to accept (*bitter disappointment*). **3 a** harsh; virulent (*bitter animosity*). **b** piercingly cold. —n. **1** *Brit.* beer strongly flavoured with hops and having a bitter taste. **2** (in *pl.*) liquor with a bitter flavour (esp. of wormwood) used as an additive in cocktails. □ **bitter-apple** = COLOCYNTH. **bitter orange** = SEVILLE ORANGE. **bitter pill** something unpleasant that has to be accepted. **bitter-sweet** adj. **1** sweet with a bitter after-taste. **2** arousing pleasure tinged with pain or sorrow. —n. **1 a** sweetness with a bitter after-taste. **b** pleasure tinged with pain or sorrow. **2** = *woody nightshade* (see NIGHTSHADE). **to the bitter end** to the very end in spite of difficulties. □□ **bitterly** adv. **bitterness** n. [OE *biter* prob. f. Gmc: *to the bitter end* may be assoc. with a Naut. word *bitter* = 'last part of a cable': see BITTS]

bitterling /ˈbɪtəlɪŋ/ n. a small brightly coloured freshwater fish, *Rhodeus amarus*, from Central Europe. [BITTER + -LING¹]

bittern /ˈbɪt(ə)n/ n. **1** any of a group of wading birds of the heron family, esp. of the genus *Botaurus* with a distinctive booming call. **2** *Chem.* the liquid remaining after the crystallization of common salt from sea water. [ME f. OF *butor* ult. f. L *butio* bittern + *taurus* bull; *-n* perh. f. assoc. with HERON]

bitts /bɪts/ n.pl. *Naut.* a pair of posts on the deck of a ship, for fastening cables etc. [ME prob. f. LG: cf. LG & Du. *beting*]

bitty /ˈbɪtɪ/ adj. (**bittier**, **bittiest**) made up of unrelated bits; scrappy. □□ **bittily** adv. **bittiness** n.

bitumen /ˈbɪtjʊmɪn/ n. **1** any of various tarlike mixtures of hydrocarbons derived from petroleum naturally or by distillation and used for road surfacing and roofing. **2** *Austral. colloq.* a tarred road. [L *bitumen -minis*]

bituminize /bɪˈtjuːmɪˌnaɪz/ v.tr. (also **-ise**) convert into, impregnate with, or cover with bitumen. □□ **bituminization** /-ˈzeɪʃ(ə)n/ n.

bituminous /bɪˈtjuːmɪnəs/ adj. of, relating to, or containing bitumen. □ **bituminous coal** a form of coal burning with a smoky flame.

bivalent /baɪˈveɪlənt/ adj. & n. —adj. **1** *Chem.* having a valency of two. **2** *Biol.* (of homologous chromosomes) associated in pairs. —n. *Biol.* any pair of homologous chromosomes. □□ **bivalency** n. [BI- + *valent-* pres. part. stem formed as VALENCE¹]

bivalve /ˈbaɪvælv/ n. & adj. —n. any of a group of aquatic molluscs of the class Bivalvia, with laterally compressed bodies enclosed within two hinged shells, e.g. oysters, mussels, etc. —adj. **1** with a hinged double shell. **2** *Biol.* having two valves, e.g. of a pea-pod.

bivouac /ˈbɪvʊˌæk/ n. & v. —n. a temporary open encampment without tents, esp. of soldiers. —v.intr. (**bivouacked**, **bivouacking**) camp in a bivouac, esp. overnight. [F, prob. f. Swiss G *Beiwacht* additional guard at night]

biweekly /baɪˈwiːklɪ/ adv., adj., & n. —adv. **1** every two weeks. **2** twice a week. —adj. produced or occurring biweekly. —n. (pl. **-ies**) a biweekly periodical. ¶ See the note at *bimonthly*.

biyearly /baɪˈjɪəlɪ/ adv. & adj. —adv. **1** every two years. **2** twice a year. —adj. produced or occurring biyearly. ¶ See the note at *bimonthly*.

biz /bɪz/ n. *colloq.* business. [abbr.]

bizarre /bɪˈzɑː(r)/ adj. strange in appearance or effect; eccentric; grotesque. □□ **bizarrely** adv. **bizarreness** n. [F, = handsome, brave, f. Sp. & Port. *bizarro* f. Basque *bizarra* beard]

bizarrerie /bɪˈzɑːrərɪ/ n. a bizarre quality; bizarreness. [F]

Bizerta /bɪˈzɜːtə/ (also **Bizerte**) a seaport on the northern coast of Tunisia; pop. (1984) 94,500.

Bizet /ˈbiːzeɪ/, Alexandre Césare Léopold, known as Georges (1838–75), French composer. His first major work was the symphony in C major (1855). Among his best-known works are the suites from his incidental music to Daudet's play *L'Arlésienne* (1872), and above all the opera *Carmen* which after a lukewarm reception in 1875 has become one of the best-loved works in the repertory.

Bk *symb. Chem.* the element berkelium.

bk. *abbr.* book.

BL *abbr.* **1** *Sc. & Ir.* Bachelor of Law. **2** British Library. **3** *hist.* British Leyland. **4** bill of lading.

bl. *abbr.* **1** barrel. **2** black.

blab /blæb/ v. & n. —v. (**blabbed**, **blabbing**) **1** *intr.* **a** talk foolishly or indiscreetly. **b** reveal secrets. **2** *tr.* reveal (a secret etc.) by indiscreet talk. —n. a person who blabs. [ME prob. f. Gmc]

blabber /ˈblæbə(r)/ n. & v. —n. (also **blabbermouth** /ˈblæbəˌmaʊθ/) a person who blabs. —v.intr. (often foll. by *on*) talk foolishly or inconsequentially, esp. at length.

Black, Joseph (1728–99), Scottish chemist, renowned for his study of the chemistry of gases and for formulating the concepts of latent heat and thermal capacity. He developed accurate techniques for following chemical reactions by weighing reactants and products. In studying the chemistry of alkalis he isolated a gas which he termed 'fixed air' (now known to be carbon dioxide), and investigated its chemistry, including its characteristic reaction with lime water.

black /blæk/ adj., n., & v. —adj. **1** very dark, having no colour from the absorption of all or nearly all incident light (like coal or soot). **2** completely dark from the absence of a source of light (*black night*). **3** (**Black**) **a** of the human group having dark-coloured skin, esp. of African or Aboriginal descent. **b** of or relating to Black people (*Black rights*). **4** (of the sky, a cloud, etc.) dusky; heavily overcast. **5** angry, threatening (*a black look*). **6** implying disgrace or condemnation (*in his black books*). **7** wicked, sinister, deadly (*black-hearted*). **8** gloomy, depressed, sullen (*a black mood*). **9** portending trouble or difficulty (*things looked black*). **10** (of hands, clothes, etc.) dirty, soiled. **11** (of humour or its representation) with sinister or macabre, as well as comic, import (*black comedy*). **12** (of tea or coffee) without milk. **13** *Brit.* **a** (of industrial labour or its products) boycotted, esp. by a trade union, in an industrial dispute. **b** (of a person) doing work or handling goods that have been boycotted. **14** dark in colour as distinguished from a lighter variety (*black bear, black pine*). —*n.* **1** a black colour or pigment. **2** black clothes or material (*dressed in black*). **3 a** (in a game or sport) a black piece, ball, etc. **b** the player using such pieces. **4** the credit side of an account (*in the black*). **5 (Black)** a member of a dark-skinned race, esp. a Negro or Aboriginal. —*v.tr.* **1** make black (*blacked his face*). **2** polish with blacking. **3** *Brit.* declare (goods etc.) 'black'. □ **Black Africa** the area of Africa, generally south of the Sahara, where Blacks predominate. **black and blue** discoloured by bruises. **Black and Tans** an armed force recruited to fight Sinn Fein in Ireland in 1921, wearing a mixture of military and constabulary uniforms. **black and white 1** recorded in writing or print (*down in black and white*). **2** (of film etc.) not in colour. **3** consisting of extremes only, oversimplified (*interpreted the problem in black and white terms*). **the black art** = *black magic*. **black beetle** the common cockroach, *Blatta orientalis*. **black belt 1** a black belt worn by an expert in judo, karate, etc. **2** a person qualified to wear this. **black body** *Physics* a hypothetical perfect absorber and radiator of energy, with no reflecting power. **black box 1** a flight-recorder in an aircraft. **2** any complex piece of equipment, usu. a unit in an electronic system, with contents which are mysterious to the user. **black bread** a coarse dark-coloured type of rye bread. **black bryony** a rooted climber, *Tamus communis*, with clusters of red berries. **Black Country** (usu. prec. by *the*) a district of the Midlands west of Birmingham, so called from the smoke and dust of the coal and iron trades in the 19th c. **black damp** = *choke-damp*. **Black Death** see separate entry. **black diamond** (in *pl.*) coal. **black disc** a long-playing gramophone record, as distinct from a compact disc. **black earth** = CHERNOZEM. **black economy** unofficial economic activity. **Black English** the form of English spoken by many Blacks, esp. as an urban dialect of the US. **black eye** bruised skin around the eye resulting from a blow. **black-eyed** (or **black-eye**) **bean** a variety of bean, *Vigna sinensis*, with seeds often dried and stored prior to eating (so called from its black hilum). **black-eyed Susan** any of several flowers, esp. of the genus *Rudbeckia*, with yellow-coloured petals and a dark centre. **black-face 1** a variety of sheep with a black face. **2** the make-up used by a non-Black performer playing a Negro role. **black flag** see FLAG¹. **Black Forest** see separate entry. **Black Friar** a Dominican friar (so called from the black cloak worn). **black frost** see FROST. **black game** (or **grouse**) a European grouse, *Lyrurus tetrix*. **black hole** see separate entry. **black ice** thin hard transparent ice, esp. on a road surface. **black in the face** livid with strangulation, exertion, or passion. **black lead** graphite. **black leopard** = PANTHER. **black letter** an old heavy style of type. **black light** *Physics* the invisible ultraviolet or infrared radiations of the electromagnetic spectrum. **black magic** magic involving supposed invocation of evil spirits. **Black Maria** *sl.* a police vehicle for transporting prisoners. **black mark** a mark of discredit. **black market** an illicit traffic in officially controlled or scarce commodities. **black marketeer** a person who engages in a black market. **Black Mass** a travesty of the Roman Catholic Mass in worship of Satan. **Black Monk** a Benedictine monk (so called from the colour of the habit). **Black Muslim** a member of an exclusively Black Islamic sect proposing a separate Black community, founded *c.*1930 in the US. **Black Nationalism** advocacy of the national civil rights of US (and occas. other) Blacks. **black nightshade** see NIGHTSHADE. **black out 1** **a** effect a blackout on. **b** undergo a blackout. **2** obscure windows etc. or extinguish all lights for protection esp. against an air attack. **Black Panther** *US* any of a group of

extremist fighters for Blacks' rights. **black pepper** pepper made by grinding the whole dried berry, including the husk, of the pepper plant. **Black Power** a movement in support of rights and political power for Blacks. It began in the US during the 1960s. **black pudding** a black sausage containing pork, dried pig's blood, suet, etc. **Black Rod** see separate entry. **black sheep** *colloq.* an unsatisfactory member of a family, group, etc.; a scoundrel. **black spot** a place of danger or difficulty, esp. on a road (*an accident black spot*). **black swan 1** something extremely rare. **2** an Australian swan, *Cygnus atratus*, with black plumage. **black tea** tea that is fully fermented before drying. **black tie 1** a black bow-tie worn with a dinner jacket. **2** *colloq.* formal evening dress. **black tracker** *Austral.* an Aboriginal employed to help find persons lost or hiding in the bush. **black velvet** a drink of stout and champagne. **Black Watch** (usu. prec. by *the*) the Royal Highland Regiment (so called from its dark tartan uniform). **black-water fever** a complication of malaria, in which blood cells are rapidly destroyed, resulting in dark urine. **black widow** a venomous spider of the genus *Latrodectus*, found in tropical and subtropical regions. The female of the North American species *L. mactans* devours its mate. □□ **blackish** *adj.* **blackly** *adv.* **blackness** *n.* [OE *blæc*]

blackamoor /ˈblækəˌmʊə(r), -ˌmɔː(r)/ *n. archaic* a dark-skinned person, esp. a Negro. [BLACK + MOOR²]

blackball /ˈblækbɔːl/ *v.tr.* reject (a candidate) in a ballot (orig. by voting with a black ball).

blackberry /ˈblækbəri/ *n. & v.* —*n.* (*pl.* -**ies**) **1** a climbing thorny rosaceous shrub, *Rubus fruticosus*, bearing white or pink flowers. Also called BRAMBLE. **2** a black fleshy edible fruit of this plant. —*v.intr.* (-**ies**, -**ied**) gather blackberries.

blackbird /ˈblækbɜːd/ *n.* **1** a common thrush, *Turdus merula*, of which the male is black with an orange beak. **2** *US* any of various birds, esp. a grackle, with black plumage. **3** *hist.* a kidnapped Negro or Polynesian on a slave-ship.

blackboard /ˈblækbɔːd/ *n.* a board with a smooth usu. dark surface for writing on with chalk.

blackboy /ˈblækbɔɪ/ *n.* any tree of the genus *Xanthorrhea*, native to Australia, with a thick dark trunk and a head of grasslike leaves. Also called *grass tree*.

blackbuck /ˈblækbʌk/ *n.* a small Indian gazelle, *Antilope cervicapra*, with a black back and white underbelly. Also called SASIN.

blackcap /ˈblækkæp/ *n.* a small warbler, *Sylvia atricapilla*, the male of which has a black-topped head.

blackcock /ˈblækkɒk/ *n.* the male of the black grouse (cf. *grey-hen*).

blackcurrant /blækˈkʌrənt/ *n.* **1** a widely cultivated shrub, *Ribes nigrum*, bearing flowers in racemes. **2** the small dark edible berry of this plant.

Black Death *n.* an epidemic of plague (chiefly bubonic) that decimated the population of Europe in the mid-14th c. It originated in central Asia and spread rapidly through Europe, carried by the fleas of black rats, reaching England in 1349 and killing between one third and one half of the population in a matter of months. Less severe outbreaks of plague occurred at irregular intervals throughout the next few centuries. The name dates from 1833 and is a translation from the German; the significance of 'black' is uncertain.

blacken /ˈblækən/ *v.* **1** *tr. & intr.* make or become black or dark. **2** *tr.* speak evil of, defame (*blacken someone's character*).

Blackett /ˈblækɪt/, Patrick Maynard Stuart, Baron (1897–1974), English physicist. During the Second World War he was involved in operational research, of great importance in the U-boat war, and was a member of the Maud Committee which dealt with the development of the atomic bomb. He modified Wilson's cloud chamber (a device for detecting ionized particles) for the study of cosmic rays, and in 1948 was awarded the Nobel Prize for physics for his discoveries in nuclear physics and cosmic radiation.

blackfellow /ˈblækˌfeləʊ/ *n. hist.* an Australian Aboriginal.

blackfish /ˈblækfɪʃ/ *n.* **1** any of several species of dark-coloured fish. **2** a salmon at spawning.

blackfly /'blækflaɪ/ n. (pl. **-flies**) any of various thrips or aphids, esp. *Aphis fabae*, infesting plants.

Black Forest (German **Schwarzwald**) /'ʃvɑːtsvɑːlt/) a hilly wooded region of SW Germany lying to the east of the Rhine valley. □ **black forest gateau** a chocolate sponge cake with layers of morello cherries or cherry jam and whipped cream, topped with icing, originally from southern Germany.

blackguard /'blægɑːd, -gəd/ n. & v. —n. a villain; a scoundrel; an unscrupulous, unprincipled person. —v.tr. abuse scurrilously. □□ **blackguardly** adj. [BLACK + GUARD: orig. applied collectively to menials etc.]

blackhead /'blækhed/ n. a black-topped pimple on the skin.

Black Hills a range of mountains in east Wyoming and west South Dakota, so called because the densely forested slopes appear dark from a distance.

black hole n. **1** (also called COLLAPSAR) a region in outer space with a gravitational field so intense that no matter or radiation can escape from it, formed most likely when a massive star exhausts its nuclear fuel and begins to collapse under the force of its own gravity. If the star is massive enough, no known force can counteract the increasing gravity, and it will collapse to a point of infinite density. Before this stage is reached, light itself will be trapped and the later stages of collapse lost from sight. A traveller unfortunate enough to pass near to a black hole would be torn apart by strong tidal forces as he crossed the boundary of the region within which light is trapped; in any case, he could never hope to return once that point had been passed. It is speculated that black holes of millions of solar masses may lurk at the centre of some galaxies, swallowing passing stars and increasing in mass. Such cannibalistic objects may provide the enormous energies seen in quasars. **2** a place of confinement for punishment, esp. in the armed services.

blacking /'blækɪŋ/ n. any black paste or polish, esp. for shoes.

blackjack[1] /'blækdʒæk/ n. **1** the card-game pontoon. **2** US a flexible leaded bludgeon. [BLACK + JACK[1]]

blackjack[2] /'blækdʒæk/ n. a pirates' black flag. [BLACK + JACK[1]]

blackjack[3] /'blækdʒæk/ n. a tarred-leather vessel for alcoholic liquor. [BLACK + JACK[2]]

blacklead /'blækled/ n. & v. —n. graphite. —v.tr. polish with graphite.

blackleg /'blækleg/ n. & v. —n. (often attrib.) Brit. derog. a person who fails or declines to take part in industrial action or who participates in strike-breaking by working for an employer whose regular workmen are on strike. —v.intr. (**-legged**, **-legging**) act as a blackleg.

blacklist /'blæklɪst/ n. & v. —n. a list of persons under suspicion, in disfavour, etc. —v.tr. put the name of (a person) on a blacklist.

blackmail /'blækmeɪl/ n. & v. —n. **1 a** an extortion of payment in return for not disclosing discreditable information, a secret, etc. **b** any payment extorted in this way. **2** the use of threats or moral pressure. —v.tr. **1** extort or try to extort money etc. from (a person) by blackmail. **2** threaten, coerce. □□ **blackmailer** n. [BLACK + obs. *mail* rent, OE *māl* f. ON *mál* agreement]

Black Monday Monday 19 Oct. 1987, when massive falls in the value of stocks on Wall Street triggered similar falls in markets around the world.

The term was originally applied to Easter Monday. Various historical explanations are offered for this, but all are untrustworthy; Mondays in general were held to be unlucky, and the common notion that rejoicing is naturally followed by calamity may have caused the day after Easter Day to be regarded as even more perilous than other Mondays.

Blackmore /'blækmɔː(r)/, Richard Doddridge (1825–1900), English writer who became a fruit-farmer and published novels, poems, and translations. His fame rests almost entirely on his enduringly popular romantic novel *Lorna Doone* (1869), set in 17th-c. Exmoor.

blackout /'blækaʊt/ n. **1** a temporary or complete loss of vision, consciousness, or memory. **2** a loss of power, radio reception, etc. **3** a compulsory period of darkness as a precaution against air raids. **4** a temporary suppression of the release of information, esp. from police or government sources. **5** a sudden darkening of a theatre stage.

Blackpool /'blækpuːl/ a seaside resort on the coast of Lancashire; pop. (1981) 148,500.

Black Prince the 16th-c. name given, for unknown reasons, to Edward Plantagenet (1330–76), eldest son of Edward III of England. A soldier of considerable ability, the Black Prince was responsible for some of the greatest English triumphs of the early years of the Hundred Years War, most notably that at Poitiers in 1356. His health failed at a relatively early age and he predeceased his father, although his own son eventually came to the throne as Richard II.

Black Rod (in full *Gentleman Usher of the Black Rod*) the chief gentleman usher of the Lord Chamberlain's department of the royal household, who is also usher to the House of Lords, so called from the ebony staff, surmounted by a golden lion, which he carries as his symbol of office. When the monarch is to deliver a speech in the House of Lords he summons the Commons to attend by knocking on their door (which has been shut against him) with his staff.

Black Sea a tideless virtually land-locked sea between the USSR, Turkey, Bulgaria, and Romania, connected to the Mediterranean Sea through the Bosporus and Sea of Marmara.

Blackshirts n. pl. any of various Fascist organizations. 'Blackshirts' was the colloquial name (in Italian *camicia nera*) given to the Squadre d'Azione (Italian, = Action Squad), the national combat groups, founded in Italy in 1919. Organized along paramilitary lines, they wore black shirts and patrolled cities to fight socialism and communism by violent means. In 1921 they were incorporated into the Fascist Party as a national militia. The term was also applied to the SS in Nazi Germany.

blacksmith /'blæksmɪθ/ n. a smith who works in iron.

Blackstone /'blækstəʊn/, Sir William (1723–80), English jurist. His major work was the *Commentaries on the Laws of England* (1765–9), based on the lectures that he had given at Oxford University.

blackthorn /'blækθɔːn/ n. **1** a thorny rosaceous shrub, *Prunus spinosa*, bearing white-petalled flowers before small blue-black fruits. Also called SLOE. **2** a cudgel or walking-stick made from its wood. □ **blackthorn winter** the time when the plant flowers, usu. marked by cold NE winds.

blacktop /'blæktɒp/ n. US a type of road-surfacing material.

bladder /'blædə(r)/ n. **1 a** any of various membranous sacs in some animals, containing urine (**urinary bladder**), bile (**gall-bladder**), or air (**swim-bladder**). **b** this or part of it or a similar object prepared for various uses. **2** an inflated pericarp or vesicle in various plants. **3** anything inflated and hollow. [OE *blǣdre* f. Gmc]

bladderwort /'blædəwɜːt/ n. any insect-consuming aquatic plant of the genus *Utricularia*, with leaves having small bladders for trapping insects.

bladderwrack /'blædəræk/ n. a common brown seaweed, *Fucus vesiculosus*, with fronds containing air bladders which give buoyancy to the plant.

blade /bleɪd/ n. **1 a** the flat part of a knife, chisel, etc., that forms the cutting edge. **b** = *razor-blade*. **2** the flattened functional part of an oar, spade, propeller, bat, skate, etc. **3 a** the flat, narrow, usu. pointed leaf of grass and cereals. **b** the whole of such plants before the ear is formed (*in the blade*). **c** Bot. the broad thin part of a leaf apart from the petiole. **4** (in full **blade-bone**) a flat bone, e.g. in the shoulder. **5** Archaeol. a long narrow flake (see FLAKE[1]3). **6** poet. a sword. **7** colloq. (usu. *archaic*) a carefree young fellow. □□ **bladed** adj. (also in comb.). [OE *blæd* f. Gmc]

blaeberry /'bleɪbərɪ/ n. (pl. **-ies**) Brit. = BILBERRY. [ME f. *blae* (Sc. and N.Engl. dial. f. ME *blo* f. ON *blár* f. Gmc: see BLUE[1]) + BERRY]

blag /blæg/ n. & v. sl. —n. robbery, esp. with violence; theft. —v.tr. & intr. (**blagged**, **blagging**) rob (esp. with violence); steal. □□ **blagger** n. [19th c.: orig. unkn.]

blague /blɑːg/ n. humbug, claptrap. [F]

blagueur /blaˈgɜː(r)/ n. a pretentious talker. [F]

blah /blɑː/ n. (also **blah-blah**) *colloq.* pretentious nonsense. [imit.]

blain /bleɪn/ n. an inflamed swelling or sore on the skin. [OE *blegen* f. WG]

Blake /bleɪk/, William (1757–1827), English artist and poet. He trained as an engraver but, despite the encouragement of patrons, never achieved prosperity or the recognition that his highly original works were posthumously accorded. His volumes of poetry, which, through a personal mythology, express a mystic sense of the energy of the universe and a protest against hypocrisy and constraint in conventional religion and art, mark a rejection of the Age of Enlightenment and the dawn of Romanticism; they include *Songs of Innocence* (1789), *Songs of Experience* (1794), and various long symbolic and prophetic works (*Milton* (1804–8) includes the short poem known as 'Jerusalem'). His major prose work, *The Marriage of Heaven and Hell* (engraved c.1790–3) is a collection of paradoxical and revolutionary aphorisms. His watercolours and engravings (illustrating, notably, the Book of Job and the works of Dante) are equally striking and unconventional, and are now very highly regarded.

blakey /ˈbleɪkɪ/ n. (also **Blakey**) (pl. **-eys**) a metal cap on the heel or toe of a shoe or boot. [*Blakey*, name of the manufacturer]

blame /bleɪm/ v. & n. —v.tr. **1** assign fault or responsibility to. **2** (foll. by *on*) assign the responsibility for (an error or wrong) to a person etc. (*blamed his death on a poor diet*). —n. **1** responsibility for a bad result; culpability (*shared the blame equally; put the blame on the bad weather*). **2** the act of blaming or attributing responsibility; censure (*she got all the blame*). □ **be to blame** (often foll. by *for*) be responsible; deserve censure (*she is not to blame for the accident*). **have only oneself to blame** be solely responsible (for something one suffers). **I don't blame you** etc. I think your etc. action was justifiable. □□ **blameable** adj. [ME f. OF *bla(s)mer* (v.), *blame* (n.) f. pop.L *blastemare* f. eccl.L *blasphemare* reproach f. Gk *blasphēmeō* blaspheme]

blameful /ˈbleɪmfʊl/ adj. deserving blame; guilty. □□ **blamefully** adv.

blameless /ˈbleɪmlɪs/ adj. innocent; free from blame. □□ **blamelessly** adv. **blamelessness** n.

blameworthy /ˈbleɪmˌwɜːðɪ/ adj. deserving blame. □□ **blameworthiness** n.

blanch /blɑːntʃ/ v. **1** tr. make white or pale by extracting colour. **2** intr. & tr. grow or make pale from shock, fear, etc. **3** tr. *Cookery* **a** peel (almonds etc.) by scalding. **b** immerse (vegetables or meat) briefly in boiling water. **4** tr. whiten (a plant) by depriving it of light. □ **blanch over** give a deceptively good impression of (a fault etc.) by misrepresentation. [ME f. OF *blanchir* f. *blanc* white, BLANK]

Blanchard /ˈblænʃɑːd/, Jean Pierre François (1753–1809), French balloonist. Before the invention of the balloon he designed a flapping-wing machine with four wings and a rudder, which he later tried (unsuccessfully) on a hydrogen balloon. Together with American Dr John Jeffries he made the first crossing of the English Channel by air, flying by balloon from Dover to Calais on 7 Jan. 1785, and was the first to fly a balloon in the US. Essentially a showman, by his many flights he stimulated others to awareness of the possibility of flight, but was killed in Paris making practice jumps by parachute from a balloon.

blancmange /bləˈmɒndʒ/ n. a sweet opaque gelatinous dessert made with flavoured cornflour and milk. [ME f. OF *blancmanger* f. *blanc* white, BLANK + *manger* eat f. L *manducare* MANDUCATE]

blanco /ˈblæŋkəʊ/ n. & v. *Mil.* —n. **1** a white substance for whitening belts etc. **2** a similar coloured substance. —v.tr. (**-oes, -oed**) treat with blanco. [F *blanc* white, BLANK]

bland /blænd/ adj. **1 a** mild, not irritating. **b** tasteless, unstimulating, insipid. **2** gentle in manner; suave. □□ **blandly** adv. **blandness** n. [L *blandus* soft, smooth]

blandish /ˈblændɪʃ/ v.tr. flatter; coax, cajole. [ME f. OF *blandir* (-ISH²) f. L *blandiri* f. *blandus* soft, smooth]

blandishment /ˈblændɪʃmənt/ n. (usu. in pl.) flattery; cajolery.

blank /blæŋk/ adj., n., & v. —adj. **1 a** (of paper) not written or printed on. **b** (of a document) with spaces left for a signature or details. **2 a** not filled; empty (*a blank space*). **b** unrelieved; sheer

(*a blank wall*). **3 a** having or showing no interest or expression (*a blank face*). **b** void of incident or result. **c** puzzled, nonplussed. **d** having (temporarily) no knowledge or understanding (*my mind went blank*). **4** (with neg. import) complete, downright (*a blank refusal; blank despair*). **5** *euphem.* used in place of an adjective regarded as coarse or abusive. —n. **1 a** a space left to be filled in a document. **b** a document having blank spaces to be filled. **2** (in full **blank cartridge**) a cartridge containing gunpowder but no bullet, used for training, etc. **3** an empty space or period of time. **4 a** a coin-disc before stamping. **b** a metal or wooden block before final shaping. **5 a** a dash written instead of a word or letter, esp. instead of an obscenity. **b** *euphem.* used in place of a noun regarded as coarse. **6** a domino with one or both halves blank. **7** a lottery ticket that gains no prize. **8** the white centre of the target in archery etc. —v.tr. **1** (usu. foll. by *off, out*) screen, obscure (*clouds blanked out the sun*). **2** (usu. foll. by *out*) cut (a metal blank). **3** *US* defeat without allowing to score. □ **blank cheque 1** a cheque with the amount left for the payee to fill in. **2** *colloq.* unlimited freedom of action (cf. CARTE BLANCHE). **blank test** *Chem.* a scientific test done without a specimen, to verify the absence of an effect of reagents etc. **blank verse** unrhymed verse, esp. iambic pentameters. **draw a blank** elicit no response; fail. □□ **blankly** adv. **blankness** n. [ME f. OF *blanc* white, ult. f. Gmc]

blanket /ˈblæŋkɪt/ n., adj., & v. —n. **1** a large piece of woollen or other material used esp. as a bed-covering or to wrap up a person or an animal for warmth. **2** (usu. foll. by *of*) a thick mass or layer that covers something (*blanket of fog; blanket of silence*). **3** *Printing* a rubber surface transferring an impression from a plate to paper etc. in offset printing. —*attrib.adj.* covering all cases or classes; inclusive (*blanket condemnation; blanket agreement*). —v.tr. (**blanketed, blanketing**) **1** cover with or as if with a blanket (*snow blanketed the land*). **2** stifle; keep quiet (*blanketed all discussion*). **3** *Naut.* take wind from the sails of (another craft) by passing to windward. □ **blanket bath** a body wash given to a bedridden patient. **blanket stitch** a stitch used to neaten the edges of a blanket or other material. **born on the wrong side of the blanket** illegitimate. **electric blanket** an electrically-wired blanket used for heating a bed. **wet blanket** *colloq.* a gloomy person preventing the enjoyment of others. [ME f. OF *blancquet, blanchet* f. *blanc* white, BLANK]

blankety /ˈblæŋkətɪ/ adj. & n. (also **blanky** /ˈblæŋkɪ/) *Brit. colloq.* = BLANK adj. 5.

blanky var. of BLANKETY.

blanquette /blɑˈket/ n. *Cookery* a dish consisting of white meat, e.g. veal, in a white sauce. [F (as BLANKET)]

Blantyre /blænˈtaɪə(r)/ the chief commercial and industrial city of Malawi; pop. (est. 1985) 355,200. The city was founded in 1876 as a Church of Scotland mission, and is named after the explorer David Livingstone's birthplace in Scotland.

blare /bleə(r)/ v. & n. —v. **1** tr. & intr. sound or utter loudly. **2** intr. make the sound of a trumpet. —n. a loud sound resembling that of a trumpet. [ME f. MDu. *blaren, bleren*, imit.]

blarney /ˈblɑːnɪ/ n. & v. —n. **1** cajoling talk; flattery. **2** nonsense. —v. (**-eys, -eyed**) **1** tr. flatter (a person) with blarney. **2** intr. talk flatteringly. [*Blarney*, an Irish castle near Cork with a stone said to confer a cajoling tongue on whoever kisses it]

blasé /ˈblɑːzeɪ/ adj. **1** unimpressed or indifferent because of over-familiarity. **2** tired of pleasure; surfeited. [F]

blaspheme /blæsˈfiːm/ v. **1** intr. talk profanely, making use of religious names, etc. **2** tr. talk profanely about; revile. □□ **blasphemer** n. [ME f. OF *blasfemer* f. eccl.L *blasphemare* f. Gk *blasphēmeō*: cf. BLAME]

blasphemy /ˈblæsfəmɪ/ n. (pl. **-ies**) **1** profane talk. **2** an instance of this. □□ **blasphemous** adj. **blasphemously** adv. [ME f. OF *blasfemie* f. eccl.L f. Gk *blasphēmia* slander, blasphemy]

blast /blɑːst/ n., v., & int. —n. **1** a strong gust of wind. **2 a** a destructive wave of highly compressed air spreading outwards from an explosion. **b** such an explosion. **3** the single loud note of a wind instrument, car horn, whistle, etc. **4** *colloq.* a severe reprimand. **5** a strong current of air used in smelting etc. —v. **1** tr. blow up (rocks etc.) with explosives. **2** tr. **a** wither, shrivel, or blight (a plant, animal, limb, etc.) (*blasted oak*). **b** destroy, ruin (*blasted her hopes*). **c** strike with divine anger; curse. **3** *intr.* & *tr.* make or cause to make a loud or explosive noise (*blasted away on his trumpet*). **4** *tr. colloq.* reprimand severely. **5** *colloq.* **a** *tr.* shoot; shoot at. **b** *intr.* shoot. —*int.* expressing annoyance. □ **at full blast** *colloq.* working at maximum speed etc. **blast-hole** a hole containing an explosive charge for blasting. **blast off** (of a rocket etc.) take off from a launching site. **blast-off** n. **1** the launching of a rocket etc. **2** the initial thrust for this. [OE *blæst* f. Gmc]

-blast /blɑːst/ *comb. form* Biol. **1** an embryonic cell (*erythroblast*) (cf. -CYTE). **2** a germ layer of an embryo (*epiblast*). [Gk *blastos* sprout]

blasted /ˈblɑːstɪd/ *adj.* & *adv.* —*attrib.adj.* damned; annoying (*that blasted dog!*). —*adv. colloq.* damned; extremely (*it's blasted cold*).

blaster /ˈblɑːstə(r)/ n. **1** in senses of BLAST v. **2** *Golf* a heavy lofted club for playing from a bunker.

blast-furnace n. a smelting-furnace into which compressed hot air is driven. This is the major means of smelting iron ore to produce molten iron. It consists of a tall steel tower, roughly cylindrical in shape and lined with a refractory material, charged from the top with a mixture of iron ore, coke, and limestone. Hot air is blown into the base of the tower through nozzles. The oxygen in the air reacts with the carbon in the coke to produce carbon monoxide which in turn combines with oxygen from the iron ore to produce carbon dioxide and pure iron. As the carbon dioxide passes up the tower it again reacts with carbon to produce carbon monoxide, and the cycle is repeated. The limestone combines with ash from the coke to form a liquid slag which absorbs sulphur in the iron and is collected at the bottom of the tower, floating above a pool of molten iron. The iron and the slag are tapped off separately from time to time and the gas exhausted from the top of the tower, after cleaning, is used to preheat the incoming blast of air and then is used as fuel for raising steam to drive the blowing-engines (air compressors) or to heat the coke-ovens. The whole process is therefore a well-integrated method of producing iron continuously on a large scale.

blastula /ˈblæstjʊlə/ n. (*pl.* **blastulae** /-ˌliː/ or *US* **blastulas**) Biol. an animal embryo at an early stage of development when it is a hollow ball of cells. [mod.L f. Gk *blastos* sprout]

blatant /ˈbleɪt(ə)nt/ *adj.* **1** flagrant, unashamed (*blatant attempt to steal*). **2** offensively noisy or obtrusive. □□ **blatancy** n. **blatantly** *adv.* [a word used by Spenser (1596), perh. after Sc. *blatand* = bleating]

blather /ˈblæðə(r)/ n. & v. (also **blether** /ˈbleðə(r)/) —n. foolish chatter. —*v.intr.* chatter foolishly. [ME *blather*, Sc. *blether*, f. ON *blathra* talk nonsense f. *blathr* nonsense]

blatherskite /ˈblæðəˌskaɪt/ (also **bletherskate** /ˈbleðəˌskeɪt/) n. **1** a person who blathers. **2** = BLATHER n. [BLATHER + *skite*, corrupt. of derog. use of SKATE²]

Blavatsky /blæˈvætskɪ/, Helen Petrovna (1831–91), Russian spiritualist, founder of the Theosophical Society.

blaze¹ /bleɪz/ n. & v. —n. **1** a bright flame or fire. **2 a** a bright glaring light (*the sun set in a blaze of orange*). **b** a full light (*a blaze of publicity*). **3** a violent outburst (of passion etc.) (*a blaze of patriotic fervour*). **4 a** a glow of colour (*roses were a blaze of scarlet*). **b** a bright display (*a blaze of glory*). —*v.intr.* **1** burn with a bright flame. **2** be brilliantly lighted. **3** be consumed with anger, excitement, etc. **4** show bright colours (*blazing with jewels*). **b** emit light (*stars blazing*). □ **blaze away** (often foll. by *at*) **1** fire continuously with rifles etc. **2** work enthusiastically. **blaze up 1** burst into flame. **2** burst out in anger. **like blazes** *sl.* **1** with great energy. **2** very fast. **what the blazes!** *sl.* what the hell! □□ **blazingly** *adv.* [OE *blæse* torch, f. Gmc: ult. rel. to BLAZE²]

blaze² /bleɪz/ n. & v. —n. **1** a white mark on an animal's face. **2** a mark made on a tree by slashing the bark esp. to mark a route. —*v.tr.* **1** mark (a tree or a path) by chipping bark. □ **blaze a trail 1** mark out a path or route. **2** be the first to do, invent, or study something; pioneer. [17th c.: ult. rel. to BLAZE¹]

blaze³ /bleɪz/ *v.tr.* proclaim as with a trumpet. □ **blaze abroad**

spread (news) about. [ME f. LG or Du. *blāzen* blow, f. Gmc *blæsan*]

blazer /ˈbleɪzə(r)/ n. **1** a coloured, often striped, summer jacket worn by schoolchildren, sportsmen, etc., esp. as part of a uniform. **2** a man's plain jacket, often dark blue, not worn with matching trousers. [BLAZE¹ + -ER¹]

blazon /ˈbleɪz(ə)n/ v. & n. —v.tr. **1** proclaim (esp. *blazon abroad*). **2** *Heraldry* **a** describe or paint (arms). **b** inscribe or paint (an object) with arms, names, etc. —n. **1** *Heraldry* **a** a shield, coat of arms, bearings, or a banner. **b** a correct description of these. **2** a record or description, esp. of virtues, etc. □□ **blazoner** n. **blazonment** n. [ME f. OF *blason* shield, of unkn. orig.; verb also f. BLAZE³]

blazonry /ˈbleɪzənrɪ/ n. *Heraldry* **1 a** the art of describing or painting heraldic devices or armorial bearings. **b** such devices or bearings. **2** brightly coloured display.

bleach /bliːtʃ/ v. & n. —v.tr. & intr. whiten by exposure to sunlight or by a chemical process. —n. **1** a bleaching substance. **2** the process of bleaching. □ **bleaching-powder** calcium hypochlorite used esp. to remove colour from materials. [OE *blǣcan* f. Gmc]

bleacher /ˈbliːtʃə(r)/ n. **1 a** a person who bleaches (esp. textiles). **b** a vessel or chemical used in bleaching. **2** (usu. in *pl.*) esp. *US* an outdoor uncovered bench-seat at a sports ground, arranged in tiers and very cheap.

bleak¹ /bliːk/ *adj.* **1** bare, exposed; windswept. **2** unpromising; dreary (*bleak prospects*). □□ **bleakly** *adv.* **bleakness** n. [16th c.: rel. to obs. adjs. *bleach*, *blake* (f. ON *bleikr*) pale, ult. f. Gmc: cf. BLEACH]

bleak² /bliːk/ n. any of various species of small river-fish, esp. *Alburnus alburnus*. [ME prob. f. ON *bleikja*, OHG *bleicha* f. Gmc]

blear /blɪə(r)/ *adj.* & v. *archaic* —*adj.* **1** (of the eyes or the mind) dim, dull, filmy. **2** indistinct. —*v.tr.* make dim or obscure; blur. [ME, of uncert. orig.]

bleary /ˈblɪərɪ/ *adj.* (**blearier**, **bleariest**) **1** (of the eyes or mind) dim; blurred. **2** indistinct. □ **bleary- eyed** having dim sight or wits. □□ **blearily** *adv.* **bleariness** n.

bleat /bliːt/ v. & n. —v. **1** intr. (of a sheep, goat, or calf) make a weak, wavering cry. **2** intr. & tr. (often foll. by *out*) speak or say feebly, foolishly, or plaintively. —n. **1** the sound made by a sheep, goat, etc. **2** a weak, plaintive, or foolish cry. □□ **bleater** n. **bleatingly** *adv.* [OE *blǣtan* (imit.)]

bleb /bleb/ n. **1** esp. *Med.* a small blister on the skin. **2** a small bubble in glass or on water. [var. of BLOB]

bleed /bliːd/ v. & n. —v. (*past* and *past part.* **bled** /bled/) **1** intr. emit blood. **2** tr. draw blood from surgically. **3 a** tr. extort money from. **b** intr. part with money lavishly; suffer extortion. **4** tr. (often foll. by *for*) suffer wounds or violent death (*bled for the Revolution*). **5** intr. **a** (of a plant) emit sap. **b** (of dye) come out in water. **6** tr. **a** allow (fluid or gas) to escape from a closed system through a valve etc. **b** treat (such a system) in this way. **7** *Printing* **a** intr. (of a printed area) be cut into when pages are trimmed. **b** tr. cut into the printed area of when trimming. **c** tr. extend (an illustration) to the cut edge of a page. —n. an act of bleeding (cf. NOSEBLEED). □ **one's heart bleeds** usu. *iron.* one is very sorrowful. [OE *blēdan* f. Gmc]

bleeder /ˈbliːdə(r)/ n. **1** *coarse sl.* a person (esp. as a term of contempt or disrespect) (*you bleeder, lucky bleeder*). **2** *colloq.* a haemophiliac.

bleeding /ˈbliːdɪŋ/ *adj.* & *adv. Brit. coarse sl.* expressing annoyance or antipathy (*a bleeding nuisance*). □ **bleeding heart 1** *colloq.* a dangerously soft-hearted person. **2** any of various plants, esp. *Dicentra spectabilis* having heart-shaped crimson flowers hanging from an arched stem.

bleep /bliːp/ n. & v. —n. an intermittent high-pitched sound made electronically. —*v.intr.* & tr. **1** make or cause to make such a sound, esp. as a signal. **2** tr. call (a person) by means of a bleeper. [imit.]

bleeper /ˈbliːpə(r)/ n. a small portable electronic device which emits a bleep when the wearer is contacted.

blemish /ˈblemɪʃ/ n. & v. —n. a physical or moral defect; a stain; a flaw (*not a blemish on his character*). —*v.tr.* spoil the beauty or perfection of; stain (*spots blemished her complexion*). [ME f. OF ble(s)*mir* (-ISH²) make pale, prob. of Gmc orig.]

blench /blentʃ/ *v.intr.* flinch; quail. [ME f. OE *blencan*, ult. f. Gmc]

blend /blend/ *v. & n.* —*v.* **1** *tr.* **a** mix (esp. sorts of tea, tobacco, etc.) together to produce a desired flavour etc. **b** produce by this method (*blended whisky*). **2** *intr.* form a harmonious compound; become one. **3 a** *tr. & intr.* (often foll. by *with*) mingle or be mingled (*truth blended with lies; blends well with the locals*). **b** *tr.* (often foll. by *in, with*) mix thoroughly. **4** *intr.* (esp. of colours): **a** pass imperceptibly into each other. **b** go well together; harmonize. —*n.* **1 a** a mixture, esp. of various sorts of tea, spirits, tobacco, fibre, etc. **b** a combination (of different abstract or personal qualities). **2** a portmanteau word. [ME prob. f. ON *blanda* mix]

blende /blend/ *n.* any naturally occurring metal sulphide, esp. zinc blende. [G f. *blenden* deceive, so called because while often resembling galena it yielded no lead]

blender /ˈblendə(r)/ *n.* **1** a mixing machine used in food preparation for liquidizing, chopping, or puréeing. **2 a** a thing that blends. **b** a person who blends.

Blenheim /ˈblenɪm/ a village in Bavaria, scene of a battle in 1704 (see MARLBOROUGH). —*n.* **1** a small spaniel of a red and white breed. **2** this breed. [the Duke of Marlborough's seat at Woodstock in S. England, named after his victory at Blenheim in Bavaria]

Blenheim Orange /ˈblenɪm/ *n.* a golden-coloured apple which ripens late in the season.

blenny /ˈblenɪ/ *n.* (*pl.* **-ies**) any of a family of small spiny-finned marine fish, esp. of the genus *Blennius*, having scaleless skins. [L *blennius* f. Gk *blennos* mucus, with reference to its mucous coating]

blent /blent/ *poet.* past and past part. of BLEND.

blepharitis /ˌblefəˈraɪtɪs/ *n.* inflammation of the eyelids. [Gk *blepharon* eyelid + -ITIS]

Blériot /ˈbleriˌəʊ/, Louis (1872–1936), French pioneer in aviation. Trained as an engineer, he built a successful flapping-wing model aircraft in 1901 and one of the first successful monoplanes in 1907. On 25 July 1909 he made aviation history by being the first to fly the English Channel, from Calais to Dover, in a monoplane (a balloon crossing had been made by Blanchard in 1785). Later he became an aircraft manufacturer, and between 1909 and 1914 his factory built over 800 aeroplanes of 40 different types; by the end of the First World War it was producing 18 aircraft a day.

blesbok /ˈblesbɒk/ *n.* (also **blesbuck** /-bʌk/) a subspecies of bontebok, native to southern Africa, having small lyre-shaped horns. [Afrik. f. *bles* BLAZE² (from the white mark on its forehead) + *bok* goat]

bless /bles/ *v.tr.* (*past* and *past part.* **blessed**, *poet.* **blest** /blest/) **1** (of a priest etc.) pronounce words, esp. in a religious rite, asking for divine favour; ask God to look favourably on (*bless this house*). **2 a** consecrate (esp. bread and wine). **b** sanctify by the sign of the cross. **3** call (God) holy; adore. **4** attribute one's good fortune to (an auspicious time, one's fate, etc.); thank (*bless the day I met her; bless my stars*). **5** (usu. in *passive*; often foll. by *with*) make happy or successful (*blessed with children; they were truly blessed*). **6** *euphem.* curse; damn (*bless the boy!*). □ (**God**) **bless me** (or **my soul**) an exclamation of surprise, pleasure, indignation, etc. (**God**) **bless you!** **1** an exclamation of endearment, gratitude, etc. **2** an exclamation made to a person who has just sneezed. **I'm** (or **well, I'm**) **blessed** (or **blest**) an exclamation of surprise etc. **not have a penny to bless oneself with** be impoverished. [OE *blǣdsian, blēdsian, blētsian,* f. *blōd* blood (hence mark with blood, consecrate): meaning infl. by its use at the conversion of the English to translate L *benedicare* praise]

blessed /ˈblesɪd, blest/ *adj.* (also *poet.* **blest**) **1 a** consecrated (*Blessed Sacrament*). **b** revered. **2** /blest/ (usu. foll. by *with*) often *iron.* fortunate (in the possession of) (*blessed with good health; blessed with children*). **3** *euphem.* cursed; damned (*blessed nuisance!*). **4 a** in paradise. **b** RC Ch. a title given to a dead person as an acknowledgement of his or her holy life; beatified. **5** bringing happiness; blissful (*blessed ignorance*). □□ **blessedly** *adv.*

blessedness /ˈblesɪdnɪs/ *n.* **1** happiness. **2** the enjoyment of divine favour. □ **single blessedness** *joc.* the state of being unmarried (perversion of Shakesp. *Midsummer Night's Dream* I. i. 78).

blessing /ˈblesɪŋ/ *n.* **1** the act of declaring, seeking, or bestowing (esp. divine) favour (*sought God's blessing; mother gave them her blessing*). **2** grace said before or after a meal. **3** a gift of God, nature, etc.; a thing one is glad of (*what a blessing he brought it!*). □ **blessing in disguise** an apparent misfortune that eventually has good results.

blest /blest/ *poet.* var. of BLESSED.

blether var. of BLATHER.

bletherskate var. of BLATHERSKITE.

blew *past* of BLOW¹, BLOW³.

blewits /ˈbluːɪts/ *n.* any fungus of the genus *Tricholoma*, with edible lilac-stemmed mushrooms. [prob. f BLUE¹]

Bligh /blaɪ/, William (1754–1817), British naval officer who, as captain, commanded HMS *Bounty*. He eventually rose to become a Vice Admiral, although his harsh temperament got him into trouble on at least one occasion other than the mutiny, when he was deposed by disaffected officers while acting as governor of New South Wales (1805–8).

blight /blaɪt/ *n. & v.* —*n.* **1** any plant disease caused by mildews, rusts, smuts, fungi, or insects. **2** any insect or parasite causing such a disease. **3** any obscure force which is harmful or destructive. **4** an unsightly or neglected urban area. —*v.tr.* **1** affect with blight. **2** harm, destroy. **3** spoil. [17th c.: orig. unkn.]

blighter /ˈblaɪtə(r)/ *n.* *Brit. colloq.* a person (esp. as a term of contempt or disparagement). [BLIGHT + -ER¹]

Blighty /ˈblaɪtɪ/ *n.* (*pl.* **-ies**) *sl.* (used by soldiers, esp. during the First World War) England; home. [Anglo-Ind. corrupt. of Hind. *bilāyatī, wilāyatī* foreign, European]

blimey /ˈblaɪmɪ/ *int.* (also **cor blimey** /kɔː/) *Brit. coarse sl.* an expression of surprise, contempt, etc. [corrupt. of (*God*) *blind me!*]

blimp /blɪmp/ *n.* **1** (also (**Colonel**) **Blimp**) a proponent of reactionary establishment opinions. **2 a** a small non-rigid airship. **b** a barrage balloon. **3** a soundproof cover for a cine-camera. □□ **blimpery** *n.* **blimpish** *adj.* [20th. c., of uncert. orig.: in sense 1, a pompous, obese, elderly character invented by cartoonist David Low (d. 1963), and used in anti-German or anti-Government drawings before and during the Second World War]

blind /blaɪnd/ *adj., v., n., & adv.* —*adj.* **1** lacking the power of sight. **2 a** without foresight, discernment, intellectual perception, or adequate information (*blind effort*). **b** (often foll. by *to*) unwilling or unable to appreciate (a factor, circumstance, etc.) (*blind to argument*). **3** not governed by purpose or reason (*blind forces*). **4** reckless (*blind hitting*). **5 a** concealed (*blind ditch*). **b** (of a door, window, etc.) walled up. **c** closed at one end. **6** *Aeron.* (of flying) without direct observation, using instruments only. **7** *Cookery* (of a flan case, pie base, etc.) baked without a filling. **8** *sl.* drunk. —*v.* **1** *tr.* deprive of sight, permanently or temporarily (*blinded by tears*). **2** *tr.* (often foll. by *to*) rob of judgement; deceive (*blinded them to the danger*). **3** *intr.* *sl.* go very fast and dangerously, esp. in a motor vehicle. —*n.* **1 a** a screen for a window, esp. on a roller, or with slats (*roller blind; Venetian blind*). **b** an awning over a shop window. **2 a** something designed or used to hide the truth; a pretext. **b** a legitimate business concealing a criminal enterprise (*he's a spy, and his job is just a blind*). **3** any obstruction to sight or light. **4** *Brit. sl.* a heavy drinking-bout. **5** *Cards* a stake put up by a poker player before the cards dealt are seen. **6** *US* = HIDE¹ *n.* —*adv.* blindly (*fly blind; bake it blind*). □ **blind alley 1** a cul-de-sac. **2** a course of action leading nowhere. **blind as a bat** completely blind. **blind coal** coal burning without a flame. **blind corner** a corner round which a motorist etc. cannot see. **blind date 1** a social engagement between a man and a woman who have not previously met. **2** either of the couple on a blind date. **blind drunk** extremely drunk. **blind gut** the caecum. **blind man's buff** see separate entry. **blind side** a direction in which one cannot see the approach of danger etc. **blind spot 1**

Anat. the point of entry of the optic nerve on the retina, insensitive to light. **2** an area in which a person lacks understanding or impartiality. **3** a point of unusually weak radio reception. **blind stamping** (or **tooling**) embossing a book cover without the use of colour or gold leaf. **blind-stitch** *n.* sewing visible on one side only. —*v.tr. & intr.* sew with this stitch. **blind to** incapable of appreciating. **blind with science** overawe with a display of (often spurious) knowledge. **go it blind** act recklessly or without proper consideration. **not a blind bit of** (or **not a blind**) *sl.* not the slightest; not a single (*took not a blind bit of notice; not a blind word out of him*). **turn a** (or **one's**) **blind eye to** pretend not to notice. □□ **blindly** *adv.* **blindness** *n.* [OE f. Gmc]

blinder /ˈblaɪndə(r)/ *n. colloq.* **1** an excellent piece of play in a game. **2** (in *pl.*) US blinkers.

blindfold /ˈblaɪndfəʊld/ *v., n., adj., & adv.* —*v.tr.* **1** deprive (a person) of sight by covering the eyes, esp. with a tied cloth. **2** deprive of understanding; hoodwink. —*n.* **1** a bandage or cloth used to blindfold. **2** any obstruction to understanding. —*adj. & adv.* **1** with eyes bandaged. **2** without care or circumspection (*went into it blindfold*). **3** *Chess* without sight of board and men. [replacing (by assoc. with FOLD¹) ME *blindfellen*, past part. *blindfelled* (FELL¹) strike blind]

blinding /ˈblaɪndɪŋ/ *n.* **1** the process of covering a newly made road etc. with grit to fill cracks. **2** such grit.

blind man's buff *n.* a game in which a blindfold player tries to catch others, who push him or her about. A sport with universal appeal, it is played under different names in many countries, and goes back to remote antiquity. In the Middle Ages it was played by adults in the street, with greater emphasis on the 'buffs' than is usual in its later version as a children's (indoor) party game. [obs. *buff* = buffet]

blindworm /ˈblaɪndwɜːm/ *n.* = SLOW-WORM.

blink /blɪŋk/ *v. & n.* —*v.* **1** shut and open the eyes quickly and usu. involuntarily. **2** *intr.* (often foll. by *at*) look with eyes opening and shutting. **3** *tr.* **a** (often foll. by *back*) prevent (tears) by blinking. **b** (often foll. by *away, from*) clear (dust etc.) from the eyes by blinking. **4** *tr.* **a** (foll. by *at*) *intr.* shirk consideration of; ignore; condone. **5** *intr.* **a** shine with an unsteady or intermittent light. **b** cast a momentary gleam. **6** *tr.* blink with (eyes). —*n.* **1** an act of blinking. **2** a momentary gleam or glimpse. **3** = ICEBLINK. □ **on the blink** *sl.* out of order, esp. intermittently. [partly var. of *blenk* = BLENCH, partly f. MDu. *blinken* shine]

blinker /ˈblɪŋkə(r)/ *n. & v.* —*n.* **1** (usu. in *pl.*) either of a pair of screens attached to a horse's bridle to prevent it from seeing sideways. **2** a device that blinks, esp. a vehicle's indicator. —*v.tr.* **1** obscure with blinkers. **2** (as **blinkered** *adj.*) having narrow and prejudiced views.

blinking /ˈblɪŋkɪŋ/ *adj. & adv. Brit. sl.* an intensive, esp. expressing disapproval (*a blinking idiot; a blinking awful time*). [BLINK + -ING² (euphem. for BLOODY)]

blip /blɪp/ *n. & v.* —*n.* **1** a quick popping sound, as of dripping water or an electronic device. **2** a small image of an object on a radar screen. **3** a minor deviation or error in a process or system. —*v.* (**blipped, blipping**) **1** *intr.* make a blip. **2** *tr.* strike briskly. [imit.]

Bliss /blɪs/, Sir Arthur (1891–1975), English composer, director of music at the BBC from 1942 to 1944 and Master of the Queen's Music from 1953 to 1975. He showed an interest in avant-garde music, particularly that of Schoenberg and Stravinsky, when he was in his twenties, composing in 1922, at Elgar's behest, *A Colour Symphony* for the Three Choirs Festival. In later years, however, he tended more to traditional forms, as in his symphony for orator, chorus, and orchestra *Morning Heroes* (1930), composed as a memorial to the victims of the First World War (who included his brother).

bliss /blɪs/ *n.* **1 a** perfect joy or happiness. **b** enjoyment; gladness. **2 a** being in heaven. **b** a state of blessedness. [OE *blīths, bliss* f. Gmc *blīthsjō* f. *blīthiz* BLITHE: sense infl. by BLESS]

blissful /ˈblɪsfʊl/ *adj.* perfectly happy; joyful. □ **blissful ignorance** fortunate unawareness of something unpleasant. □□ **blissfully** *adv.* **blissfulness** *n.*

blister /ˈblɪstə(r)/ *n. & v.* —*n.* **1** a small bubble on the skin filled

with serum and caused by friction, burning, etc. **2** a similar swelling on any other surface. **3** *Med.* anything applied to raise a blister. **4** *sl.* an annoying person. —*v.* **1** *tr.* raise a blister on. **2** *intr.* come up in a blister or blisters. **3** *tr.* attack sharply (*blistered them with his criticisms*). □ **blister copper** copper which is almost pure. **blister gas** a poison gas causing blisters on the skin. **blister pack** a bubble pack. □□ **blistery** *adj.* [ME perh. f. OF *blestre, blo(u)stre* swelling, pimple]

blithe /blaɪð/ *adj.* **1** *poet.* gay, joyous. **2** careless, casual (*with blithe indifference*). □□ **blithely** *adv.* **blitheness** *n.* **blithesome** /-səm/ *adj.* [OE *blīthe* f. Gmc]

blithering /ˈblɪðərɪŋ/ *adj. colloq.* **1** senselessly talkative. **2 a** (*attrib.*) utter; hopeless (*blithering idiot*). **b** contemptible. [*blither*, var. of BLATHER + -ING²]

B.Litt. *abbr.* Bachelor of Letters. [L *Baccalaureus Litterarum*]

blitz /blɪts/ *n. & v. colloq.* —*n.* **1 a** an intensive or sudden (esp. aerial) attack. **b** an energetic intensive attack, usu. on a specific task (*must have a blitz on this room*). **2** (**the Blitz**) the German air raids on London in 1940. —*v.tr.* attack, damage, or destroy by a blitz. [abbr. of BLITZKRIEG]

blitzkrieg /ˈblɪtskriːɡ/ *n.* an intense military campaign intended to bring about a swift victory, especially as used by Germany against various countries of Europe in the Second World War. [G, = lightning war]

blizzard /ˈblɪzəd/ *n.* a severe snowstorm with high winds. [US 'violent blow' (1829), 'snowstorm' (1859), perh. imit.]

bloat /bləʊt/ *v.* **1** *tr. & intr.* inflate, swell (*wind bloated the sheets; bloated with gas*). **2** *tr.* (as **bloated** *adj.*) **a** swollen, puffed. **b** puffed up with pride or excessive wealth (*bloated plutocrat*). **3** *tr.* cure (a herring) by salting and smoking lightly. [obs. *bloat* swollen, soft and wet, perh. f. ON *blautr* soaked, flabby]

bloater /ˈbləʊtə(r)/ *n.* a herring cured by bloating.

blob /blɒb/ *n.* **1** a small roundish mass; a drop of matter. **2** a drop of liquid. **3** a spot of colour. **4** *Cricket sl.* a score of 0. [imit.: cf. BLEB]

bloc /blɒk/ *n.* a combination of parties, governments, groups, etc. sharing a common purpose. □ **bloc vote** = *block vote*. [F, = block]

Bloch /blɒx/, Ernest (1880–1959), Swiss-born composer of Jewish descent, who lived in the US from 1916. His opera *Macbeth* was produced in 1909. Many of his works (which include the *Israel Symphony* (1912–16), *Schelomo*, a rhapsody for cello and orchestra (1916), and numerous orchestral compositions are inspired by Jewish folk-music and liturgy.

block /blɒk/ *n., v., & adj.* —*n.* **1 a** a solid hewn or unhewn piece of hard material, esp. of rock, stone, or wood (*block of ice*). **2 a** flat-topped block used as a base for chopping, beheading, standing something on, hammering on, or for mounting a horse from. **3 a** a large building, esp. when subdivided (*block of flats*). **b** a compact mass of buildings bounded by (usu. four) streets. **4** an obstruction; anything preventing progress or normal working (*a block in the pipe*). **5** a chock for stopping the motion of a wheel etc. **6** a pulley or system of pulleys mounted in a case. **7** (in *pl.*) any of a set of solid cubes etc., used as a child's toy. **8** *Printing* a piece of wood or metal engraved for printing on paper or fabric. **9** a head-shaped mould used for shaping hats or wigs. **10** *sl.* the head (*knock his block off*). **11** US **a** the area between streets in a town or suburb. **b** the length of such an area, esp. as a measure of distance (*lives three blocks away*). **12** a stolid, unimaginative, or hard-hearted person. **13** a large quantity or allocation of things treated as a unit, esp. shares, seats in a theatre, etc. **14** a set of sheets of paper used for writing, or esp. drawing, glued along one edge. **15** *Cricket* a spot on which a batsman blocks the ball before the wicket, and rests the bat before playing. **16** *Athletics* = *starting-block*. **17** *Amer. Football* a blocking action. **18** *Austral.* **a** a tract of land offered to an individual settler by a government. **b** a large area of land. —*v.tr.* **1 a** (often foll. by *up*) obstruct (a passage etc.) (*the road was blocked; you are blocking my view*). **b** put obstacles in the way of (progress etc.). **2** restrict the use or conversion of (currency or any other asset). **3** use a block for making (a hat, wig, etc.). **4** emboss or impress a design on (a book cover). **5** *Cricket* stop (a ball) with a bat defensively. **6** *Amer. Football* intercept (an opponent) with one's body. —*attrib.adj.* treating (many similar things) as one unit (*block booking*). □ **block and tackle** a system of pulleys and ropes, esp. for lifting. **block capitals** (or **letters**) letters printed without serifs, or written with each letter separate and in capitals. **block diagram** a diagram showing the general arrangement of parts of an apparatus. **block in 1** sketch roughly; plan. **2** confine. **block mountain** *Geol.* a mountain formed by natural faults. **block out 1 a** shut out (light, noise, etc.). **b** exclude from memory, as being too painful. **2** sketch roughly; plan. **block-ship** *Naut.* a ship used to block a channel. **block system** a system by which no railway train may enter a section that is not clear. **block tin** refined tin cast in ingots. **block up 1** confine; shut (a person etc.) in. **2** infill (a window, doorway, etc.) with bricks etc. **block vote** a vote proportional in power to the number of people a delegate represents. **mental** (or **psychological**) **block** a particular mental inability due to subconscious emotional factors. **on the block** *US* being auctioned. **put the blocks on** prevent from proceeding. □□ **blocker** *n.* [ME f. OF *bloc, bloquer* f. MDu. *blok*, of unkn. orig.]

blockade /blɒˈkeɪd/ *n. & v.* —*n.* **1** the surrounding or blocking of a place, esp. a port, by an enemy to prevent entry and exit of supplies etc. **2** anything that prevents access or progress. **3** *US* an obstruction by snow etc. —*v.tr.* **1** subject to a blockade. **2** obstruct (a passage, a view, etc.). □ **blockade-runner 1** a vessel which runs or attempts to run into a blockaded port. **2** the owner, master, or one of the crew of such a vessel. **run a blockade** enter or leave a blockaded port by evading the blockading force. □□ **blockader** *n.* [BLOCK + -ADE¹, prob. after *ambuscade*]

blockage /ˈblɒkɪdʒ/ *n.* **1** an obstruction. **2** a blocked state.

blockboard /ˈblɒkbɔːd/ *n.* a plywood board with a core of wooden strips.

blockbuster /ˈblɒkˌbʌstə(r)/ *n. sl.* **1** something of great power or size, esp. an epic film or a book. **2** a huge bomb capable of destroying a whole block of buildings.

blockhead /ˈblɒkhed/ *n.* a stupid person. □□ **blockheaded** *adj.*

blockhouse /ˈblɒkhaʊs/ *n.* **1** a reinforced concrete shelter used as an observation point etc. **2** *hist.* a one-storeyed timber building with loopholes, used as a fort. **3** a house made of squared logs.

blockish /ˈblɒkɪʃ/ *adj.* **1** resembling a block. **2** excessively dull; stupid, obtuse. **3** clumsy, rude, roughly hewn. □□ **blockishly** *adv.* **blockishness** *n.*

Bloemfontein /ˈbluːmfɒnˌteɪn/ the capital of Orange Free State and judicial capital of the Republic of South Africa; pop. (1985) 233,000.

bloke /bləʊk/ *n. Brit. sl.* a man, a fellow. [Shelta]

blond /blɒnd/ *adj. & n.* —*adj.* **1** (of hair) light-coloured; fair. **2** (of the complexion, as an indication of race) light-coloured. —*n.* a person, esp. a man, with fair hair and skin. □□ **blondish** *adj.* **blondness** *n.* [ME f. F f. med.L *blondus, blundus* yellow, perh. of Gmc orig.]

blonde /blɒnd/ *adj. & n.* —*adj.* (of a woman or a woman's hair) blond. —*n.* a blond-haired woman. [F fem. of *blond*; see BLOND]

Blondin /ˈblɒndɪn, ˈblɔ̃dæ̃/, Charles (Jean-François Gravelet, 1824–97), French acrobat, who walked across a tightrope suspended over Niagara Falls in 1859 and on subsequent occasions with acrobatics.

blood /blʌd/ *n. & v.* —*n.* **1** a liquid, usually red and circulating in the arteries and veins of vertebrates, that carries oxygen to and carbon dioxide from the tissues of the body. (See below.) **2** a corresponding fluid in invertebrates. **3** bloodshed, esp. killing. **4** passion, temperament. **5** race, descent, parentage (*of the same blood*). **6** a relationship; relations (*own flesh and blood; blood is thicker than water*). **7** a dandy; a man of fashion. —*v.tr.* **1** give (a hound) a first taste of blood. **2** initiate (a person) by experience. □ **bad blood** ill feeling. **blood-and-thunder** (*attrib.*) *colloq.* sensational, melodramatic. **blood bank** a place where supplies of blood or plasma for transfusion are stored. **blood bath** a massacre. **blood-brother** a brother by birth or by the

ceremonial mingling of blood. **blood count 1** the counting of the number of corpuscles in a specific amount of blood. **2** the number itself. **blood-curdling** horrifying. **blood donor** one who gives blood for transfusion. **blood feud** a feud between families involving killing or injury. **blood group** any one of the various types of human blood determining compatibility in transfusion. (See LANDSTEINER.) **blood-heat** the normal body temperature of a healthy human being, about 37 °C or 98.4 °F. **blood horse** a thoroughbred. **one's blood is up** one is in a fighting mood. **blood-letting 1** the surgical removal of some of a patient's blood. **2** *joc.* bloodshed. **blood-lust** the desire for shedding blood. **blood-money 1** money paid to the next of kin of a person who has been killed. **2** money paid to a hired murderer. **3** money paid for information about a murder or murderer. **blood orange** an orange with red or red-streaked pulp. **blood-poisoning** a diseased state caused by the presence of micro-organisms in the blood. **blood pressure** the pressure of the blood in the circulatory system, often measured for diagnosis since it is closely related to the force and rate of the heartbeat and the diameter and elasticity of the arterial walls. **blood-red** red as blood. **blood relation** (or **relative**) a relative by blood, not by marriage. **blood royal** the royal family. **blood serum** see SERUM. **blood sport** sport involving the wounding or killing of animals, esp. hunting. **blood sugar** the amount of glucose in the blood. **blood test** a scientific examination of blood, esp. for diagnosis. **blood transfusion** the injection of a volume of blood, previously taken from a healthy person, into a patient. **blood-vessel** a vein, artery, or capillary carrying blood. **blood-wort** any of various plants having red roots or leaves, esp. the red-veined dock. **first blood 1** the first shedding of blood, esp. in boxing. **2** the first point gained in a contest etc. **in one's blood** inherent in one's character. **make one's blood boil** infuriate one. **make one's blood run cold** horrify one. **new** (or **fresh**) **blood** new members admitted to a group, esp. as an invigorating force. **of the blood** royal. **out for a person's blood** set on getting revenge. **taste blood** be stimulated by an early success. **young blood 1** a younger member or members of a group. **2** a rake or fashionable young man. [OE *blōd* f. Gmc]

Most animal bodies depend upon a circulating fluid for transporting substances from one part to another. In vertebrates this fluid is blood, circulating in veins and arteries and pumped by the heart, carrying food, salts, oxygen, hormones, and cells and molecules of the immune system to tissues, and removing waste products; by virtue of its large volume and rapid circulation it evens out the temperature of the bodily parts. Blood consists of a mildly alkaline fluid (plasma) in which are suspended a number of different types of cell: red cells (erythrocytes), white cells (leucocytes), and platelets. Plasma consists chiefly of water and is driven easily along even the smallest blood-vessels. Red blood-cells (which give blood its colour) carry the protein haemoglobin, which can combine with oxygen and also with carbon dioxide, thus enabling the blood to carry oxygen from the lungs to the tissues and carbon dioxide in the reverse direction. The main function of white blood-cells (of which there are several types) is to protect the body against the invasion of foreign agents (e.g. bacteria) into its tissues. Platelets and other factors present in plasma are concerned in the clotting of blood, preventing haemorrhage.

Blood was formerly thought to be the medium of heredity, whence such phrases as *the blood royal, we are of the same blood, gambling is in his blood*, and *blood will tell*.

blooded /ˈblʌdɪd/ *adj.* **1** (of horses etc.) of good pedigree. **2** (in *comb.*) having blood or a disposition of a specified kind (*cold-blooded; red-blooded*).

bloodhound /ˈblʌdhaʊnd/ *n.* **1** a large hound of a breed used in tracking and having a very keen sense of smell. **2** this breed.

bloodless /ˈblʌdlɪs/ *adj.* **1** without blood. **2** unemotional; cold. **3** pale. **4** without bloodshed (*a bloodless coup*). **5** feeble; lifeless. □□ **bloodlessly** *adv.* **bloodlessness** *n.*

bloodshed /ˈblʌdʃed/ *n.* **1** the spilling of blood. **2** slaughter.

bloodshot /ˈblʌdʃɒt/ *adj.* (of an eyeball) inflamed, tinged with blood.

bloodstain /ˈblʌdsteɪn/ *n.* a discoloration caused by blood.

bloodstained /'blʌdsteɪnd/ adj. 1 stained with blood. 2 guilty of bloodshed.

bloodstock /'blʌdstɒk/ n. thoroughbred horses.

bloodstone /'blʌdstəʊn/ n. a type of green chalcedony spotted or streaked with red, often used as a gemstone.

bloodstream /'blʌdstri:m/ n. blood in circulation.

bloodsucker /'blʌd,sʌkə(r)/ n. 1 an animal or insect that sucks blood, esp. a leech. 2 an extortioner. □□ **bloodsucking** adj.

bloodthirsty /'blʌd,θɜ:stɪ/ adj. (**bloodthirstier, bloodthirstiest**) eager for bloodshed. □□ **bloodthirstily** adv. **bloodthirstiness** n.

bloodworm /'blʌdwɜ:m/ n. 1 any of a variety of bright-red midge-larvae. 2 a small tubifex worm used as food for aquarium fish.

bloody /'blʌdɪ/ adj., adv., & v. —adj. (**bloodier, bloodiest**) 1 a of or like blood. b running or smeared with blood (bloody bandage). 2 a involving, loving, or resulting from bloodshed (bloody battle). b sanguinary; cruel (bloody butcher). 3 coarse sl. expressing annoyance or antipathy, or as an intensive (a bloody shame; a bloody sight better; not a bloody chocolate left). 4 red. —adv. coarse sl. as an intensive (a bloody good job; I'll bloody thump him). —v.tr. (**-ies, -ied**) make bloody; stain with blood. □ **bloody hand** Heraldry the armorial device of a baronet. **Bloody Mary** a drink composed of vodka and tomato juice. **bloody-minded** colloq. deliberately uncooperative. **bloody-mindedly** colloq. in a perverse or uncooperative manner. **bloody-mindedness** colloq. perversity, contrariness. □□ **bloodily** adv. **bloodiness** n. [OE blōdig (as BLOOD, -Y¹)]

Bloody Assizes the trials held in SW England in 1685 of the supporters of the Duke of Monmouth after their defeat at Sedgemoor. The Government's representative, Judge Jeffreys, sentenced several hundred rebels to death and about 1,000 others to transportation to America as plantation slaves.

Bloody Sunday colloq. 1 Sunday 13 November 1887, when police violently broke up a socialist demonstration in Trafalgar Square, London, against the British Government's Irish policy. 2 any of various other Sundays when blood was shed, including 9 January 1905 (22 January in the New Style calendar) when troops attacked and killed hundreds of unarmed workers who had gathered in St Petersburg to present a petition to the Czar, and 30 January 1972 when British troops violently dispersed marchers in Londonderry who were protesting against the Government's policy of internment.

bloom¹ /blu:m/ n. & v. —n. 1 a a flower, esp. one cultivated for its beauty. b the state of flowering (in bloom). 2 a state of perfection or loveliness; the prime (in full bloom). 3 a (of the complexion) a flush; a glow. b a delicate powdery surface deposit on plums, grapes, leaves, etc., indicating freshness. c a cloudiness on a shiny surface. —v. 1 intr. bear flowers; be in flower. 2 intr. a come into, or remain in, full beauty. b flourish; be in a healthy, vigorous state. 3 tr. Photog. coat (a lens) so as to reduce reflection from its surface. □ **take the bloom off** make stale. **water-bloom** scum formed by algae on the surface of standing water. [ME f. ON blóm, blómi etc. f. Gmc: cf. BLOSSOM]

bloom² /blu:m/ n. & v. —n. a mass of puddled iron hammered or squeezed into a thick bar. —v.tr. make into bloom. [OE blōma]

bloomer¹ /'blu:mə(r)/ n. sl. a blunder. [= BLOOMING error]

bloomer² /'blu:mə(r)/ n. Brit. an oblong loaf with a rounded diagonally slashed top. [20th c.: orig. uncert.]

bloomer³ /'blu:mə(r)/ n. a plant that blooms (in a specified way) (early autumn bloomer).

bloomers /'blu:məz/ n.pl. 1 women's loose-fitting almost knee-length knickers. 2 colloq. any women's knickers. 3 hist. women's loose-fitting trousers, gathered at the knee or (orig.) the ankle. [Mrs A. Bloomer, Amer. social reformer d. 1894, who advocated a costume called 'rational dress' for women, invented by Mrs E. S. Miller and consisting of a short jacket, full skirt reaching to just below the knee, and trousers down to the ankle]

bloomery /'blu:mərɪ/ n. (pl. **-ies**) a factory that makes puddled iron into blooms.

Bloomfield /'blu:mfiəld/, Leonard (1887–1949), American linguistics scholar who counts as one of the founders of American linguistic structuralism. He wrote about Indo-European philology, Malayo-Polynesian languages, American-Indian languages, and theoretical linguistics but the work which reached the widest public was Language (1933), a textbook which contained important sections on historical and comparative linguistics but was largely dedicated to an account of the techniques and aims of the new descriptive linguistics (see DESCRIPTIVE).

blooming /'blu:mɪŋ/ adj. & adv. —adj. 1 flourishing; healthy. 2 Brit. sl. an intensive (a blooming miracle). —adv. Brit. sl. an intensive (was blooming difficult). [BLOOM¹ + -ING²: euphem. for BLOODY]

Bloomsbury /'blu:mzbərɪ, -brɪ/ n. & adj. —n. (in full **Bloomsbury Group**) a group of writers, artists, and philosophers living in or associated with Bloomsbury in London in the early 20th c. —adj. 1 associated with or similar to the Bloomsbury Group. 2 intellectual; highbrow.

blooper /'blu:pə(r)/ n. esp. US colloq. an embarrassing error. [imit. bloop + -ER¹]

blossom /'blɒsəm/ n. & v. —n. 1 a flower or a mass of flowers, esp. of a fruit-tree. 2 the stage or time of flowering (the cherry tree in blossom). 3 a promising stage (the blossom of youth). —v.intr. 1 open into flower. 2 reach a promising stage; mature, thrive. □□ **blossomy** adj. [OE blōstm(a) prob. formed as BLOOM¹]

blot /blɒt/ n. & v. —n. 1 a spot or stain of ink etc. 2 a moral defect in an otherwise good character; a disgraceful act or quality. 3 any disfigurement or blemish. —v. (**blotted, blotting**) 1 a tr. spot or stain with ink; smudge. b intr. (of a pen, ink, etc.) make blots. 2 tr. a use blotting-paper or other absorbent material to absorb excess ink. b (of blotting-paper etc.) soak up (esp. ink). 3 tr. disgrace (blotted his reputation). □ **blot one's copybook** damage one's reputation. **blot on the escutcheon** a disgrace to the family name. **blot out 1 a** obliterate (writing). b obscure (a view, sound, etc.). 2 obliterate (from the memory) as too painful. 3 destroy. **blotting-paper** unglazed absorbent paper used for soaking up excess ink. [ME prob. f. Scand.: cf. Icel. blettr spot, stain]

blotch /blɒtʃ/ n. & v. —n. 1 a discoloured or inflamed patch on the skin. 2 an irregular patch of ink or colour. —v.tr. cover with blotches. □□ **blotchy** adj. (**blotchier, blotchiest**). [17th c.: f. obs. plotch and BLOT]

blotter /'blɒtə(r)/ n. 1 a sheet or sheets of blotting-paper, usu. inserted into a frame. 2 US a temporary recording-book, esp. a police charge-sheet.

blotto /'blɒtəʊ/ adj. sl. very drunk, esp. unconscious from drinking. [20th c.: perh. f. BLOT]

blouse /blaʊz/ n. & v. —n. 1 a a woman's loose, usu. lightweight, upper garment, usu. buttoned and collared. b the upper part of a soldier's or airman's battledress. 2 a workman's or peasant's loose linen or cotton garment, usu. belted at the waist. —v.tr. make (a bodice etc.) loose like a blouse. [F, of unkn. orig.]

blouson /'blu:zɒn/ n. a short blouse-shaped jacket. [F]

blow¹ /bləʊ/ v. & n. —v. (past **blew** /blu:/; past part. **blown** /bləʊn/) 1 a intr. (of the wind or air, or impersonally) move along; act as an air-current (it was blowing hard). b intr. be driven by an air-current (waste paper blew along the gutter). c tr. drive with an air-current (blew the door open). 2 a tr. send out (esp. air) by breathing (blew cigarette smoke; blew a bubble). b intr. send a dir-ected air-current from the mouth. 3 tr. & intr. sound or be sounded by blowing (the whistle blew; they blew the trumpets). 4 tr. a direct an air-current at (blew the embers). b (foll. by off, away, etc.) clear of by means of an air-current (blew the dust off). 5 tr. (past part. **blowed**) sl. (esp. in imper.) curse, confound (blow it!; I'll be blowed!; let's take a taxi and blow the expense). 6 tr. a clear (the nose) of mucus by blowing. b remove contents from (an egg) by blowing through it. 7 a intr. puff, pant. b tr. (esp. in passive) exhaust of breath. 8 sl. a tr. depart suddenly from (blew the town yesterday). b intr. depart suddenly. 9 tr. shatter or send flying by an explosion (the bomb blew the tiles off the roof; blew them to smithereens). 10 tr. make or shape (glass or a bubble) by blowing air in. 11 tr. & intr. melt or cause to melt from overloading (the *fuse has blown*). **12** *intr*. (of a whale) eject air and water through a blow-hole. **13** *tr*. break into (a safe etc.) with explosives. **14** *tr. sl*. **a** squander, spend recklessly (*blew £20 on a meal*). **b** spoil, bungle (an opportunity etc.) (*he's blown his chances of winning*). **c** reveal (a secret etc.). **15** *intr*. (of a food-tin etc.) swell and eventually burst from internal gas pressure. **16** *tr*. work the bellows of (an organ). **17** *tr*. (of flies) deposit eggs in. **18** *intr. US & Austral. colloq.* boast. —*n*. **1 a** an act of blowing (e.g. one's nose, a wind instrument). **b** *colloq*. a turn or spell of playing jazz (on any instrument); a musical session. **2 a** a gust of wind or air. **b** exposure to fresh air. **3** = *fly-blow* (see FLY²). **4** *US* a boaster. □ **be blowed if one will** *colloq*. be unwilling to. **blow-ball** the globular seed-head of a dandelion etc. **blow-drier** (or **-dryer**) a dryer used for blow-drying. **blow-dry** arrange (the hair) while drying it with a hand-held drier. **blow the gaff** reveal a secret inadvertently. **blow-hole 1** the nostril of a whale, on the top of its head. **2** a hole (esp. in ice) for breathing or fishing through. **3** a vent for air, smoke, etc., in a tunnel etc. **blow hot and cold** *colloq*. vacillate. **blow in 1** break inwards by an explosion. **2** *colloq*. arrive unexpectedly. **blow-job** *coarse sl*. fellatio; cunnilingus. **blow a kiss** kiss one's hand and wave it to a distant person. **blow a person's mind** *sl*. cause a person to have drug-induced hallucinations or a similar experience. **blow off 1** escape or allow (steam etc.) to escape forcibly. **2** *sl*. break wind noisily. **blow on** (or **upon**) make stale; discredit. **blow out 1 a** extinguish by blowing. **b** send outwards by an explosion. **2** (of a tyre) burst. **3** (of a fuse etc.) melt. **blow-out** *n. colloq*. **1** a burst tyre. **2** a melted fuse. **3** a huge meal. **blow over** (of trouble etc.) fade away without serious consequences. **blow one's own trumpet** praise oneself. **blow one's top** (*US* **stack**) *colloq*. explode in rage. **blow up 1 a** shatter or destroy by an explosion. **b** explode, erupt. **2** *colloq*. rebuke strongly. **3** inflate (a tyre etc.). **4** *colloq*. **a** enlarge (a photograph). **b** exaggerate. **5** *colloq*. come to notice; arise. **6** *colloq*. lose one's temper. **blow-up** *n*. **1** *colloq*. an enlargement (of a photograph etc.). **2** an explosion. **blow the whistle on** see WHISTLE. [OE *blāwan* f. Gmc]

blow² /bləʊ/ *n*. **1 a** a hard stroke with a hand or weapon. **2** a sudden shock or misfortune. □ **at one blow** by a single stroke; in one operation. **blow-by-blow** (of a description etc.) giving all the details in sequence. **come to blows** end up fighting. **strike a blow for** (or **against**) help (or oppose). [15th c.: orig. unkn.]

blow³ /bləʊ/ *v. & n. archaic* —*v.intr*. (*past* **blew** /bluː/; *past part*. **blown** /bləʊn/) burst into or be in flower. —*n*. blossoming, bloom (*in full blow*). [OE *blōwan* f. Gmc]

blower /ˈbləʊə(r)/ *n*. **1** in senses of BLOW¹ *v*. **2** a device for creating a current of air. **3** *colloq*. a telephone.

blowfish /ˈbləʊfɪʃ/ *n*. any of several kinds of fish able to inflate their bodies when frightened etc.

blowfly /ˈbləʊflaɪ/ *n*. (*pl*. **-flies**) a meat-fly, a bluebottle.

blowgun /ˈbləʊɡʌn/ *n. US* = BLOWPIPE.

blowhard /ˈbləʊhɑːd/ *n. & adj. colloq*. —*n*. a boastful person. —*adj*. boastful; blustering.

blowlamp /ˈbləʊlæmp/ *n*. a portable device with a very hot flame used for burning off paint, soldering, etc.

blown *past part*. of BLOW¹, BLOW³.

blowpipe /ˈbləʊpaɪp/ *n*. **1** a tube used esp. by primitive peoples for propelling arrows or darts by blowing. **2** a tube used to intensify the heat of a flame by blowing air or other gas through it at high pressure. **3** a tube used in glass-blowing.

blowtorch /ˈbləʊtɔːtʃ/ *n. US* = BLOWLAMP.

blowy /ˈbləʊɪ/ *adj*. (**blowier, blowiest**) windy, windswept. □□ **blowiness** *n*.

blowzy /ˈblaʊzɪ/ *adj*. (**blowzier, blowziest**) **1** coarse-looking; red-faced. **2** dishevelled, slovenly. □□ **blowzily** *adv*. **blowziness** *n*. [obs. *blowze* beggar's wench, of unkn. orig.]

blub /blʌb/ *v.intr*. (**blubbed, blubbing**) *sl*. sob. [abbr. of BLUBBER¹]

blubber¹ /ˈblʌbə(r)/ *n. & v*. —*n*. **1** whale fat. **2** a spell of weeping. —*v*. **1** *intr*. sob loudly. **2** *tr*. sob out (words). □□ **blubberer** *n*. **blubberingly** *adv*. **blubbery** *adj*. [ME perh. imit. (obs. meanings 'foaming, bubble')]

blubber² /ˈblʌbə(r)/ *adj*. (of the lips) swollen, protruding. [earlier *blabber, blobber*, imit.]

bluchers /ˈbluːkəz/ *n.pl. hist*. strong leather half-boots or high shoes. [G. L. von *Blücher*, Prussian general d. 1819]

bludge /blʌdʒ/ *v. & n. Austral. & NZ sl*. —*v.intr*. avoid work. —*n*. an easy job or assignment. □ **bludge on** impose on. [back-form. f. BLUDGER]

bludgeon /ˈblʌdʒ(ə)n/ *n. & v*. —*n*. a club with a heavy end. —*v.tr*. **1** beat with a bludgeon. **2** coerce. [18th c.: orig. unkn.]

bludger /ˈblʌdʒə(r)/ *n. Austral. & NZ sl*. **1** a hanger-on. **2** a loafer. [orig. E sl., = pimp, f. obs. *bludgeoner* f. BLUDGEON]

blue¹ /bluː/ *adj., n., & v*. —*adj*. **1** having a colour like that of a clear sky. **2** sad, depressed; (of a state of affairs) gloomy, dismal (*feel blue; blue times*). **3** indecent, pornographic (*a blue film*). **4** with bluish skin through cold, fear, anger, etc. **5** *Brit*. politically conservative. **6** having blue as a distinguishing colour (*blue jay*). —*n*. **1** a blue colour or pigment. **2** blue clothes or material (*dressed in blue*). **3** *Brit*. **a** a person who has represented a university in a sport, esp. Oxford or Cambridge. **b** this distinction. **4** *Brit*. a supporter of the Conservative party. **5** any of various small blue-coloured butterflies of the family Lycaenidae. **6** blue powder used to whiten laundry. **7** *Austral. sl*. **a** an argument or row. **b** (as a nickname) a red-headed person. **8** a blue ball, piece, etc. in a game or sport. **9** (prec. by *the*) the clear sky. —*v.tr*. (**blues, blued, bluing** or **blueing**) **1** make blue. **2** treat with laundering blue. □ **blue baby** a baby with a blue complexion from lack of oxygen in the blood due to a congenital defect of the heart or great vessels. **blue bag** a lawyer's brief-bag. **blue blood** noble birth. **blue-blooded** of noble birth. **Blue Book** a report issued by Parliament or the Privy Council. **blue cheese** cheese produced with veins of blue mould, e.g. Stilton and Danish Blue. **blue-chip** (*attrib*.) of shares of reliable investment, though less secure than gilt-edged stock. **blue-collar** (*attrib*.) of manual or unskilled work. **blue dahlia** something rare or impossible. **blue ensign** see ENSIGN. **blue-eyed boy** esp. *Brit. colloq*. usu. *derog*. a favoured person; a favourite. **blue funk** esp. *Brit. colloq*. a state of great terror or panic. **blue-green alga** = CYANOBACTERIUM. **blue ground** = KIMBERLITE. **blue in the face** in a state of extreme anger or exasperation. **blue metal** broken blue stone used for road-making. **blue mould** a bluish fungus growing on food and other organic matter. **blue-pencil** (**-pencilled**, **-pencilling**; *US* **-penciled**, **-penciling**) censor or make cuts in (a manuscript, film, etc.). **Blue Peter** a blue flag with a white square raised on board a ship leaving port. **blue ribbon 1** a high honour. **2** *Brit*. the ribbon of the Order of the Garter. **blue rinse** a preparation for tinting grey hair. **blue roan** see ROAN¹. **blue rock** = *rock-dove* (see ROCK¹). **blue stone** (or **vitriol**) copper sulphate crystals. **blue tit** a common tit, *Parus caeruleus*, with a distinct blue crest on a black and white head. **blue water** open sea. **blue whale** a rorqual, *Balaenoptera musculus*, the largest known living mammal. **once in a blue moon** very rarely. **out of the blue** unexpectedly. □□ **blueness** *n*. [ME f. OF *bleu* f. Gmc]

blue² /bluː/ *v.tr*. (**blues, blued, bluing** or **blueing**) *sl*. squander (money). [perh. var. of BLOW¹]

Bluebeard /ˈbluːbɪəd/ the hero of a tale by Perrault. Bluebeard killed several wives in turn because they showed undue curiosity about a locked room (which contained the bodies of his previous wives). Local tradition in Brittany identifies him with Gilles de Retz (c.1400–40), a perpetrator of atrocities, though he had only one wife (who left him). *n*. **1** a man who murders his wives. **2** a person with a horrible secret.

bluebell /ˈbluːbel/ *n*. **1** a liliaceous plant, *Hyacinthoides nonscripta*, with clusters of bell-shaped blue flowers on a stem arising from a rhizome. Also called *wild hyacinth*, *wood hyacinth* (see HYACINTH). **2** *Sc*. a plant, *Campanula rotundifolia*, with solitary bell-shaped blue flowers on long stalks. Also called HAREBELL. **3** any of several plants with blue bell-shaped flowers.

blueberry /ˈbluːbərɪ/ *n*. (*pl*. **-ies**) **1** any of several plants of the genus *Vaccinium*, cultivated for their edible fruit. **2** the small blue-black fruit of these plants.

bluebird /ˈbluːbɜːd/ *n*. any of various N. American songbirds of the thrush family, esp. of the genus *Sialia*, with distinctive blue plumage usu. on the back or head.

bluebottle /'blu:ˌbɒt(ə)l/ *n.* **1** a large buzzing fly, *Calliphora vomitoria*, with a metallic-blue body. Also called BLOWFLY. **2** *Austral.* a Portuguese man-of-war. **3** a dark blue cornflower. **4** *Brit. colloq.* a policeman.

Bluefields /'blu:fiəldz/ a port on the Mosquito Coast of Nicaragua, situated on an inlet of the Caribbean Sea; pop. (1985) 18,000.

bluefish /'blu:fiʃ/ *n.* a voracious marine fish, *Pomatomus saltatrix*, inhabiting tropical waters and popular as a game-fish.

bluegrass /'blu:grɑːs/ *n.* *US* **1** any of several bluish-green grasses, esp. of Kentucky. **2** a kind of instrumental country-and-western music characterized by virtuosic playing of banjos, guitars, etc.

bluegum /'blu:gʌm/ *n.* any tree of the genus *Eucalyptus*, esp. *E. regnans* with blue-green aromatic leaves.

bluejacket /'blu:ˌdʒækɪt/ *n.* a seaman in the Navy.

Bluemantle /'blu:ˌmænt(ə)l/ *n.* one of four pursuivants of the English College of Arms.

Blue Mountains 1 a section of the Great Dividing Range in New South Wales, Australia. Part of it is a national park and nature reserve. **2** a range of mountains in eastern Jamaica. **3** a range of mountains running from central Oregon to SE Washington in the US.

blueprint /'blu:prɪnt/ *n.* & *v.* —*n.* **1** a photographic print of the final stage of engineering or other plans in white on a blue background. **2** a detailed plan, esp. in the early stages of a project or idea. —*v.tr.* *US* work out (a programme, plan, etc.).

Blue Riband (or **Ribbon**) **of the Atlantic** a trophy for the ship making the fastest eastward sea-crossing of the Atlantic Ocean. It was originally a notional trophy for which liners unofficially but enthusiastically competed. The early 'awards' are retrospective, but the *Acadia* (completed in 1840), the fastest of the original Cunard liners, is regarded as the first holder. Ships of all the great transatlantic lines have held it since, including the German *Kaiser Wilhelm der Grosse*, the Cunard *Mauretania*, the Italian *Rex*, the French *Normandie*, the British *Queen Mary*, and finally the American-owned *United States* (1952), with speeds rising progressively. An actual trophy, instituted in 1935, was accepted by the latest of these. Faster speeds were achieved later but award of the trophy was refused on the grounds that the challenge was intended for passenger-carrying craft operating a regular service.
The term 'blue ribbon' (see BLUE) is used to denote the highest honour attainable in any sphere.

Blue Ridge Mountains a range of the Appalachian Mountains stretching from south Pennsylvania to north Georgia. Mt Mitchell is the highest peak, rising to a height of 2,039 metres (6,684 ft.).

blues /blu:z/ *n.pl.* **1** (prec. by *the*) a bout of depression (*had a fit of the blues*). **2 a** (prec. by *the*; often treated as *sing.*) melancholic music of Black American folk origin, often in a twelve-bar sequence (*always singing the blues*). **b** (*pl.* same) (as *sing.*) a piece of such music (*the band played a blues*). □□ **bluesy** *adj.* (in sense 2).

bluestocking /'blu:ˌstɒkɪŋ/ *n.* usu. *derog.* an intellectual or literary woman. [from the '*Blue Stocking* Club', 18th-c. literary coterie, led by three ladies, formed to substitute for the card-playing, which then formed the chief recreation at evening parties, more intellectual modes of spending the time, including conversation on literary subjects, in which eminent men of letters often took part. Many of these eschewed formal dress and one habitually wore grey or 'blue' worsted stockings instead of black silk.]

bluet /'blu:ɪt/ *n.* *US* a blue-flowered plant of the genus *Houstonia*.

bluey /'blu:ɪ/ *n.* (*pl.* **-eys**) *Austral. colloq.* **1** a bundle carried by a bushman. **2** = BLUE *n.* 7b.

bluff¹ /blʌf/ *v.* & *n.* —*v.* **1** *intr.* make a pretence of strength or confidence to gain an advantage. **2** *tr.* mislead by bluffing. —*n.* an act of bluffing; a show of confidence or assertiveness

intended to deceive. □ **call a person's bluff** challenge a person thought to be bluffing. □□ **bluffer** *n.* [19th c. (orig. in poker) f. Du. *bluffen* brag]

bluff² /blʌf/ *adj.* & *n.* —*adj.* **1** (of a cliff, or a ship's bows) having a vertical or steep broad front. **2** (of a person or manner) blunt, frank, hearty. —*n.* a steep cliff or headland. □□ **bluffly** *adv.* (in sense 2 of *adj.*). **bluffness** *n.* (in sense 2 of *adj.*). [17th-c. Naut. word: orig. unkn.]

bluish /'blu:ɪʃ/ *adj.* somewhat blue.

Blumenbach /'blu:mənˌbɑːx/, Johann Friedrich (1752–1840), German physiologist and comparative anatomist who, out of respect for his formulation of one of the earliest racial classifications, is called the founder of Physical Anthropology. His research led to the division of modern man into five broad categories: Caucasian (white), Mongolian (yellow), Malayan (brown), Ethiopian (black), and American (red).

Blunden /'blʌnd(ə)n/, Edmund Charles (1869–1974), English poet and critic, whose *Undertones of War* (1928) is a sensitive account of his experiences in the First World War. His writings show his deep love of the English countryside.

blunder /'blʌndə(r)/ *n.* & *v.* —*n.* a clumsy or foolish mistake, esp. an important one. —*v.* **1** *intr.* make a blunder; act clumsily or ineptly. **2** *tr.* deal incompetently with; mismanage. **3** *intr.* move about blindly or clumsily; stumble. □□ **blunderer** *n.* **blunderingly** *adv.* [ME prob. f. Scand.: cf. MSw. *blundra* shut the eyes]

blunderbuss /'blʌndəˌbʌs/ *n.* *hist.* a short large-bored muzzle-loading usually flintlock gun for close-range use, common in the 18th c., with a flared muzzle, firing many balls or slugs at one shot. [alt. of Du. *donderbus* thunder gun, assoc. with BLUNDER]

blunge /blʌndʒ/ *v.tr.* (in ceramics etc.) mix (clay etc.) with water. □□ **blunger** *n.* [after *plunge*, *blend*]

Blunt /blʌnt/, Anthony Frederick (1907–83), English art historian. He was Director of the Courtauld Institute of Art from 1947 to 1974, Surveyor of the King's (later Queen's) Pictures from 1945 to 1972, and one of the leading figures in establishing art history as an academic discipline in Britain. In 1965 he confessed that he had been a Soviet agent since the 1930s, spied for the Soviet Union during his service at the War Office in the Second World War, and been instrumental in the escape of the spies Guy Burgess and Donald Maclean in 1951. These revelations became public in 1979, and he was subsequently stripped of the knighthood that he had been awarded in 1956.

blunt /blʌnt/ *adj.* & *v.* —*adj.* **1** (of a knife, pencil, etc.) lacking in sharpness; having a worn-down point or edge. **2** (of a person or manner) direct, uncompromising, outspoken. —*v.tr.* make blunt or less sharp. □□ **bluntly** *adv.* (in sense 2 of *adj.*). **bluntness** *n.* [ME perh. f. Scand.: cf. ON *blunda* shut the eyes]

blur /blɜː(r)/ *v.* & *n.* —*v.* (**blurred**, **blurring**) **1** *tr.* & *intr.* make or become unclear or less distinct. **2** *tr.* smear; partially efface. **3** *tr.* make (one's memory, perception, etc.) dim or less clear. —*n.* something that appears or sounds indistinct or unclear. □□ **blurry** *adj.* (**blurrier**, **blurriest**). [16th c.: perh. rel. to BLEAR]

blurb /blɜːb/ *n.* a (usu. eulogistic) description of a book, esp. printed on its jacket, as promotion by its publishers. [said to have been originated in 1907 by G. Burgess, Amer. humorist, in a comic book jacket embellished with a drawing of a pulchritudinous young lady whom he facetiously dubbed Miss Blinda Blurb]

blurt /blɜːt/ *v.tr.* (usu. foll. by *out*) utter abruptly, thoughtlessly, or tactlessly. [prob. imit.]

blush /blʌʃ/ *v.* & *n.* —*v.intr.* **1 a** develop a pink tinge in the face from embarrassment or shame. **b** (of the face) redden in this way. **2** feel embarrassed or ashamed. **3** be or become red or pink. —*n.* **1** the act of blushing. **2** a pink tinge. □ **at first blush** on the first glimpse or impression. **spare a person's blushes** refrain from causing embarrassment esp. by praise. [ME f. OE *blyscan*]

blusher /'blʌʃə(r)/ *n.* a cosmetic used to give a warmth of colour to the face.

b *but* d *dog* f *few* g *get* h *he* j *yes* k *cat* l *leg* m *man* n *no* p *pen* r *red* s *sit* t *top* v *voice*

bluster /ˈblʌstə(r)/ v. & n. —v.intr. **1** behave pompously and boisterously; utter empty threats. **2** (of the wind etc.) blow fiercely. —n. **1** noisily self-assertive talk. **2** empty threats. □□ **blusterer** n. **blustery** adj. [16th c.: ult. imit.]

Blyton /ˈblaɪt(ə)n/, Enid (1897–1968), English writer of over 600 books for children. Her writings attracted considerable criticism from educationists and others because of their mediocrity and limited vocabulary, and for some years libraries refused to stock them, but they were commercially successful. Her most celebrated character was Noddy (created in 1949).

BM abbr. **1** British Museum. **2** Bachelor of Medicine.

BMA abbr. British Medical Association.

B.Mus. abbr. Bachelor of Music.

BMX /ˌbiːemˈeks/ n. **1** organized bicycle-racing on a dirt-track, esp. for youngsters. **2** a kind of bicycle used for this. **3** (attrib.) of or related to such racing or the equipment used (BMX gloves). [abbr. of bicycle moto-cross]

Bn. abbr. Battalion.

bn. abbr. billion.

BO abbr. colloq. body odour.

bo¹ /bəʊ/ int. = BOO. [imit.]

bo² /bəʊ/ n. US colloq. (as a form of address) pal; old chap. [19th c.: perh. f. BOY]

boa /ˈbəʊə/ n. **1** any large non-poisonous snake from tropical America esp. of the genus Boa, which kills its prey by crushing and suffocating it in its coils. **2** any snake which is similar in appearance, such as Old World pythons. **3** a long thin stole made of feathers or fur. □ **boa constrictor** a large snake, Boa constrictor, native to tropical America and the West Indies, which crushes its prey. [L]

Boadicea /ˌbəʊədɪˈsiːə/ = BOUDICCA.

boar /bɔː(r)/ n. **1** (in full **wild boar**) the tusked wild pig, Sus scrofa, from which domestic pigs are descended. **2** an uncastrated male pig. **3** its flesh. **4** a male guinea-pig etc. [OE bār f. WG]

board /bɔːd/ n. & v. —n. **1 a** a flat thin piece of sawn timber, usu. long and narrow. **b** a piece of material resembling this, made from compressed fibres. **c** a thin slab of wood or a similar substance, often with a covering, used for any of various purposes (chessboard; ironing-board; notice-board). **d** thick stiff card used in bookbinding. **2** the provision of regular meals, usu. with accommodation, for payment. **3** archaic a table spread for a meal. **4** the directors of a company; any other specially constituted administrative body, e.g. a committee or group of councillors, examiners, etc. **5** (in pl.) the stage of a theatre (cf. tread the boards). **6** Naut. the side of a ship. —v. **1** tr. **a** go on board (a ship, train, aircraft, etc.). **b** force one's way on board (a ship etc.) in attack. **2 a** intr. receive regular meals, or (esp. of a schoolchild) meals and lodging, for payment. **b** tr. (often foll. by out) arrange accommodation away from home for (esp. a child). **c** tr. provide (a lodger etc.) with regular meals. **3** tr. (usu. foll. by up) cover with boards; seal or close. □ **board-game** a game played on a board. **board of trade** US a chamber of commerce. **go by the board** be neglected, omitted, or discarded. **on board** on or on to a ship, aircraft, oil rig, etc. **take on board** consider (a new idea etc.). [OE bord f. Gmc]

boarder /ˈbɔːdə(r)/ n. **1** a person who boards (see BOARD v. 2a), esp. a pupil at a boarding-school. **2** a person who boards a ship, esp. an enemy.

boarding-house /ˈbɔːdɪŋˌhaʊs/ n. an unlicensed establishment providing board and lodging, esp. to holiday-makers.

boarding-school /ˈbɔːdɪŋˌskuːl/ n. a school where pupils are resident in term-time.

boardroom /ˈbɔːdruːm, -rʊm/ n. a room in which a board of directors etc. meets regularly.

boardsailing /ˈbɔːdˌseɪlɪŋ/ n. = WINDSURFING. □□ **boardsailor** n. (also **boardsailer**).

boardwalk /ˈbɔːdwɔːk/ n. US **1** a wooden walkway across sand, marsh, etc. **2** a promenade along a beach.

boart var. of BORT.

Boas /ˈbəʊs/, Franz (1858–1942), American anthropologist.

Against the general trend of contemporary theory he founded the approach to anthropology that became dominant in the 20th c., insisting that cultural development must be explored by means of field studies reconstructing histories of particular cultures rather than by assuming there to be single, hier-archical, and racially correlated culture. He did much to destroy the theory of 'Nordic' superiority over 'inferior peoples'; his writings were burnt by the Nazis.

boast /bəʊst/ v. & n. —v. **1** intr. declare one's achievements, possessions, or abilities with indulgent pride and satisfaction. **2** tr. own or have as something praiseworthy etc. (the hotel boasts magnificent views). —n. **1** an act of boasting. **2** something one is proud of. □□ **boaster** n. **boastingly** adv. [ME f. AF bost, of unkn. orig.]

boastful /ˈbəʊstfʊl/ adj. **1** given to boasting. **2** characterized by boasting (boastful talk). □□ **boastfully** adv. **boastfulness** n.

boat /bəʊt/ n. & v. —n. **1** a small vessel propelled on water by an engine, oars, or sails. **2** (in general use) a ship of any size. (See below.) **3** an elongated boat-shaped jug used for holding sauce etc. —v.intr. travel or go in a boat, esp. for pleasure. □ **boat-hook** a long pole with a hook and a spike at one end, for moving boats. **boat-house** a shed at the edge of a river, lake, etc., for housing boats. **boat people** refugees who have left a country by sea. **boat race** a race between rowing crews, esp. (**Boat Race**) the one between Oxford and Cambridge (see separate entry). **boat-train** a train scheduled to meet or go on a boat. **in the same boat** sharing the same adverse circumstances. **push the boat out** colloq. celebrate lavishly. □□ **boatful** n. (pl. **-fuls**). [OE bāt f. Gmc]

Boat is the generic name for small open craft used (for practical purposes or for pleasure) on inland waterways and near coasts, as distinct from ships, which are sea-going. Some exceptions to this general definition are fishing boats, gunboats, patrol boats, mail boats, etc., some yachts, and submarines, possibly because they were originally called 'submarine boats'. Usage (especially by people ashore) is not always precise or consistent: railway authorities run 'boat trains' to take passengers to what everyone would call a 'ship'.

boatel var. of BOTEL.

boater /ˈbəʊtə(r)/ n. a flat-topped hardened straw hat with a brim.

boating /ˈbəʊtɪŋ/ n. rowing or sailing in boats as a sport or form of recreation.

boatload /ˈbəʊtləʊd/ n. **1** enough to fill a boat. **2** colloq. a large number of people.

boatman /ˈbəʊtmən/ n. (pl. **-men**) a person who hires out boats or provides transport by boat.

Boat Race an annual rowing competition on the Thames in London between eights of Oxford and Cambridge Universities. First rowed at Henley in 1829 (when Oxford won), then from Westminster to Putney in 1836 (when Cambridge were successful) it became an annual event in 1839. In 1845 the course was moved to its present location from Putney to Mortlake (6.8 km, 4¼ miles). The idea of such a race was originated largely by Charles Wordsworth (nephew of the poet), who had inaugurated the University cricket match a few years earlier.

boatswain /ˈbəʊs(ə)n/ n. (also **bo'sun**, **bosun**, **bo's'n**) a ship's officer in charge of equipment and the crew. □ **boatswain's chair** a seat suspended from ropes for work on the side of a ship or building. [OE bātswegen (as BOAT, SWAIN)]

bob¹ /bɒb/ v. & n. —v.intr. (**bobbed**, **bobbing**) **1** move quickly up and down; dance. **2** (usu. foll. by back, up) **a** bounce buoyantly. **b** emerge suddenly; become active or conspicuous again after a defeat etc. **3** curtsy. **4** (foll. by for) try to catch with the mouth alone (fruit etc. floating or hanging). —n. **1** a jerking or bouncing movement, esp. upward. **2** a curtsy. **3** one of several kinds of change in long peals in bell-ringing. [14th c.: prob. imit.]

bob² /bɒb/ n. & v. —n. **1** a short hairstyle for women and children. **2** a weight on a pendulum, plumb-line, or kite-tail. **3** = BOB-SLEIGH. **4** a horse's docked tail. **5** a short line at or towards the end of a stanza. **6** a knot of hair; a tassel-shaped curl. —*v.* (**bobbed, bobbing**) **1** *tr.* cut (a woman's or child's hair) so that it hangs clear of the shoulders. **2** *intr.* ride on a bob-sleigh. [ME: orig. unkn.]

bob[3] /bɒb/ *n.* (*pl.* same) *Brit. sl.* a former shilling (now = 5 decimal pence). [19th c.: orig. unkn.]

bob[4] /bɒb/ *n.* □ **bob's your uncle** *Brit. sl.* an expression of completion or satisfaction. [pet-form of the name *Robert*]

bobbin /ˈbɒbɪn/ *n.* **1 a** a cylinder or cone holding thread, yarn, wire, etc., used esp. in weaving and machine sewing. **b** a spool or reel. **2** a small bar and string for raising a door-latch. □ **bobbin-lace** lace made by hand with thread wound on bobbins. [F *bobine*]

bobbinet /ˈbɒbɪˌnet/ *n.* machine-made cotton net (imitating lace made with bobbins on a pillow). [BOBBIN + NET[1]]

bobble /ˈbɒb(ə)l/ *n.* a small woolly or tufted ball as a decoration or trimming. [dimin. of BOB[2]]

bobby[1] /ˈbɒbɪ/ *n.* (*pl.* -**ies**) *Brit. colloq.* a policeman. [Sir Robert Peel (see entry), Home Secretary at the passing of the Metropolitan Police Act, 1828]

bobby[2] /ˈbɒbɪ/ *n.* (*pl.* -**ies**) (in full **bobby calf**) *Austral. & NZ* an unweaned calf slaughtered for veal. [Eng. dial.]

bobby-dazzler /ˈbɒbɪˌdæzlə(r)/ *n. colloq.* a remarkable or excellent person or thing. [dial., rel. to DAZZLE]

bobby-pin /ˈbɒbɪpɪn/ *n. US, Austral., & NZ* a flat hairpin. [BOB[2] + -Y[2]]

bobby socks /ˈbɒbɪ ˌsɒks/ *n.pl.* esp. *US* short socks reaching just above the ankle.

bobcat /ˈbɒbkæt/ *n.* a small N. American lynx, *Felix rufus*, with a spotted reddish-brown coat and a short tail. [BOB[2] + CAT]

bobolink /ˈbɒbəlɪŋk/ *n.* a N. American oriole, *Dolichonyx oryzivorus*. [orig. *Bob (o') Lincoln*: imit. of its call]

bob-sled /ˈbɒbsled/ *n. US* = BOB-SLEIGH.

bob-sleigh /ˈbɒbsleɪ/ *n. & v.* —*n.* a sleigh with two axles, each of which has two runners, steered either by ropes or by a wheel; the winter sport in which such sleighs, normally manned by crews of four or two, are guided down a specially prepared descending track of solid ice with banked bends. —*v.intr.* race in a bob-sleigh. [BOB[2] + SLEIGH]

bobstay /ˈbɒbsteɪ/ *n.* the chain or rope holding down a ship's bowsprit. [prob. BOB[1] + STAY[2]]

bobtail /ˈbɒbteɪl/ *n.* a docked tail; a horse or a dog with a bobtail. [BOB[2] + TAIL[1]]

bocage /bəˈkɑːʒ/ *n.* the representation of silvan scenery in ceramics. [F f. OF *boscage*: see BOSCAGE]

Boccaccio /bɒˈkɑːtʃɪˌəʊ/, Giovanni (1313–75), Italian novelist, poet, and humanist, son of a Florentine merchant. He was a friend and admirer of Dante and endeavoured, apparently with little success, to interest Petrarch in his fellow poet. In 1348 he witnessed the Black Death in Florence. His most famous work, the *Decameron* (1348–58) is a collection of tales supposedly told by a group of ten young people fleeing from the pestilence. Boccaccio is an important figure in the history of narrative fiction and has provided inspiration to major writers in most periods of literature, including Chaucer, Shakespeare, Dryden, Keats, Longfellow, and Tennyson.

Boccherini /ˌbɒkəˈriːnɪ/, Luigi (1743–1805), Italian composer, famous in his teens as a virtuoso cellist, important chiefly for his works for the cello.

Boche /bɒʃ/ *n. & adj. sl. derog.* —*n.* **1** a German, esp. a soldier. **2** (prec. by *the*) Germans, esp. German soldiers, collectively. —*adj.* German. [F sl., orig. = rascal: applied to Germans in the First World War]

Bochum /ˈbɒʊxʊm/ an industrial city in the Ruhr Valley, North Rhine-Westphalia, Germany; pop. (1987) 381, 200.

bock /bɒk/ *n.* a strong dark German beer. [F f. G abbr. of *Eimbockbier* f. *Einbeck* in Hanover]

BOD *abbr.* biochemical oxygen demand.

bod /bɒd/ *n. Brit. colloq.* a person. [abbr. of BODY]

bode /bəʊd/ *v.* **1** *tr.* portend, foreshow. **2** *tr.* foresee, foretell

(evil). □ **bode well** (or **ill**) show good (or bad) signs for the future. □□ **boding** *n.* [OE *bodian* f. *boda* messenger]

bodega /bɒʊˈdiːgə/ *n.* a cellar or shop selling wine and food, esp. in a Spanish-speaking country. [Sp. f. L *apotheca* f. Gk *apothēkē* storehouse]

Bodensee see Lake CONSTANCE.

bodge var. of BOTCH.

Bodhgaya /ˌbɒdgəˈjɑː/ (also **Buddh Gaya** /ˌbʊd/) a village in the State of Bihar in India, where Siddhartha Gautama attained enlightment (see BUDDHA). A bo-tree here is said to be a descendant of the tree under which he meditated.

Bodhisattva /ˌbɒʊdɪˈsætvə/ *n.* one who is destined to become enlightened (the term is applied to the Buddha before his enlightenment). While the goal of the ancient schools of Buddhism (Hinayana, Theravada) is to attain nirvana oneself, that of Mahayana Buddhism is to become a bodhisattva, postponing one's own salvation in order to help others on the spiritual path. [Skr., = one whose essence is perfect knowledge]

bodice /ˈbɒdɪs/ *n.* **1** the part of a woman's dress (excluding sleeves) which is above the waist. **2** a woman's undergarment, like a vest, for the same part of the body. [orig. *pair of bodies* = stays, corsets]

bodiless /ˈbɒdɪlɪs/ *adj.* **1** lacking a body. **2** incorporeal, insubstantial.

bodily /ˈbɒdɪlɪ/ *adj. & adv.* —*adj.* of or concerning the body. —*adv.* **1** with the whole bulk; as a whole (*threw them bodily*). **2** in the body; as a person.

bodkin /ˈbɒdkɪn/ *n.* **1** a blunt thick needle with a large eye used esp. for drawing tape etc. through a hem. **2** a long pin for fastening hair. **3** a small pointed instrument for piercing cloth, removing a piece of type for correction, etc. [ME perh. f. Celt.]

Bodleian Library /ˈbɒdlɪən/ (*colloq.* **Bodley** /ˈbɒdlɪ/) the library of Oxford University. The first library was founded in the 14th c. and benefited from the manuscript collections donated by Humphrey, duke of Gloucester (1391–1447). It was refounded by Sir Thomas Bodley (1545–1613), diplomat and scholar, for the use both of the University of Oxford and the 'republic of the learned', and opened in 1602. In 1610 the Stationers' Company agreed to give to the library a copy of every book printed in England, and by various Copyright Acts it is now one of the six libraries entitled to receive on demand a copy of every book published in the UK. It also houses one of the world's most extensive collections of Western and Oriental manuscripts.

Bodoni /bəˈdəʊnɪ/, Giambattista (1740–1813), Italian painter. The typeface which he designed, and others based on it, are named after him.

Bodrum /ˈbɒdrəm/ a resort town on the Aegean coast of western Turkey, site of the ancient city of Halicarnassus (see entry).

body /ˈbɒdɪ/ *n. & v.* —*n.* (*pl.* -**ies**) **1** the physical structure, including the bones, flesh, and organs, of a person or an animal, whether dead or alive. **2** the trunk apart from the head and the limbs. **3 a** the main or central part of a thing (*body of the car*; *body of the attack*). **b** the bulk or majority; the aggregate (*body of opinion*). **4 a** a group of persons regarded collectively, esp. as having a corporate function (*governing body*). **b** (usu. foll. by *of*) a collection (*body of facts*). **5** a quantity (*body of water*). **6** a piece of matter (*heavenly body*). **7** *colloq.* a person. **8** a full or substantial quality of flavour, tone, etc., e.g. in wine, musical sounds, etc. —*v.tr.* (-**ies**, -**ied**) (usu. foll. by *forth*) give body or substance to. □ **body-blow** a severe setback. **body-building** the practice of strengthening the body, esp. shaping and enlarging the muscles, by exercise. **body-colour** an opaque pigment. **body language** the process of communicating through conscious or unconscious gestures and poses. **body-line bowling** *Cricket* persistent fast bowling on the leg side threatening the batsman's body. **body odour** the smell of the human body, esp. when unpleasant. **body politic** the nation or State as a corporate body. **body scanner** a scanning X-ray machine for taking tomograms of the whole body. **body shop** a workshop where repairs to the bodywork of vehicles are carried out. **body stocking** a woman's undergarment, usually made of knitted nylon, which covers the torso. **body warmer** a sleeveless quilted or padded jacket worn as an outdoor garment. **in a body** all together. **keep body and soul together** keep alive, esp. barely. **over my dead body** *colloq.* entirely without my assent. □□ **-bodied** *adj.* (in *comb.*) (*able-bodied*). [OE *bodig*, of unkn. orig.]

body-check /ˈbɒdɪˌtʃek/ *n. & v. Sport* —*n.* a deliberate obstruction of one player by another. —*v.tr.* obstruct in this way.

bodyguard /ˈbɒdɪˌɡɑːd/ *n.* a person or group of persons escorting and protecting another person (esp. a dignitary).

body-snatcher *n. hist.* a person who illicitly disinterred corpses for dissection. Prior to the Anatomy Act, 1832, there was no provision for supplying bodies to medical students for anatomical study, and disinterment was profitable though illegal. □□ **body-snatching** *n.*

bodywork /ˈbɒdɪˌwɜːk/ *n.* the outer shell of a vehicle.

Boeotia /bɪˈəʊʃə/ a region of central Greece, north of Attica. Its chief city is Thebes (see entry). In ancient times the people of Boeotia had a reputation for being dull, boorish, and thick-witted, but its contribution to literature was considerable; Hesiod, Pindar, and Plutarch were all Boeotians. □□ **Boeotian** *adj. & n.*

Boer /ˈbəʊə(r), bʊə(r)/ *n. & adj.* —*n.* **1** a South African of Dutch descent. **2** *hist.* an early Dutch inhabitant of the Cape. —*adj.* of or relating to the Boers. [Du.: see BOOR]

Boer Wars two wars fought by Great Britain in South Africa. The first (1880–1) began with the revolt of the Boer settlers in the Transvaal against British rule and ended after the British defeat at Majuba Hill with the establishment of an independent Boer Republic under British suzerainty. The second (1899–1902) was caused by the Boer refusal to grant equal rights to recent British immigrants and by the imperialist ambitions of Cecil Rhodes and some Conservative policitians. In the early stages of the war the Boers gained a series of remarkable victories, but after the arrival of Roberts and Kitchener the British succeeded in capturing the Boer capital Pretoria and driving the Boer leader Kruger into exile. The second half of the war was dominated by guerrilla warfare, victory eventually being obtained through the use of almost half a million British and imperial troops and the employment of blockhouses, barbed wire, and concentration camps to control the countryside.

Boethius /bəʊˈiːθɪəs/ (Anicius Manlius Severinus, *c.*480–524) Roman statesman and philosopher. After rising to high office under Theodoric, king of Italy, he was arrested, imprisoned, and finally executed on a charge of treason. A man of wide-ranging abilities, he wrote Latin commentaries and translations of Aristotle in addition to works on education, science, philosophy, and logic. His greatest work, *The Consolation of Philosophy*, written in a mixture of prose and verse while in prison, argued that the soul can attain happiness in affliction by realizing the value of goodness and meditating on the reality of God. While drawing upon Stoicism and Neoplatonism its thought echoed Christian sentiments and exercised considerable influence throughout the Middle Ages, especially among the scholastic theologians. It was frequently translated into European languages; renderings into English include those by King Alfred, Chaucer, and Queen Elizabeth I.

boffin /ˈbɒfɪn/ *n. esp. Brit. colloq.* a person engaged in scientific (esp. military) research. [20th c.: orig. unkn.]

Bofors gun /ˈbəʊfəz/ *n.* a type of light anti-aircraft gun. [*Bofors* in Sweden]

bog /bɒɡ/ *n. & v.* —*n.* **1 a** wet spongy ground. **b** a stretch of such ground. **2** *Brit. sl.* a lavatory. —*v.tr.* (**bogged, bogging**) (foll. by *down*; usu. in *passive*) impede (*was bogged down by difficulties*). □ **bog-bean** = BUCKBEAN. **bog myrtle** a deciduous shrub, *Myrica gale*, which grows in damp open places and has short upright catkins and aromatic grey-green leaves: also called *sweet-gale* (see GALE²). **bog oak** an ancient oak which has

been preserved in a black state in peat. **bog spavin** see SPAVIN. **bog-trotter** *sl. derog.* an Irishman. □□ **boggy** *adj.* (**boggier, boggiest**). **bogginess** *n.* [Ir. or Gael. *bogach* f. *bog* soft]

Bogarde /ˈbəʊɡɑːd/, Dirk (real name Derek Niven van den Bogaerde, 1921–), British actor, born in The Netherlands, whose films include *The Servant* (1963), *Death in Venice* (1971), *A Bridge too Far* (1977), and a number of light productions in which he played a romantic lead.

Bogart /ˈbəʊɡɑːt/, Humphrey (1899–1957), nicknamed 'Bogey', American film actor, who appeared in films from 1930 onwards in roles ranging from ruthless gangster to more sympathetic criminal and tough reckless characters, just outside conventional society but endowed with a romantic appeal. His films include *The Maltese Falcon* (1941), *Casablanca* (1942), and *The African Queen* (1951).

bogey¹ /ˈbəʊɡɪ/ *n. & v. Golf* —*n.* (*pl.* **-eys**) **1** a score of one stroke more than par at any hole. **2** (formerly) a score that a good player should do a hole or course in; par. —*v.tr.* (**-eys, -eyed**) play (a hole) in one stroke more than par. [perh. f. *Bogey* as an imaginary player]

bogey² /ˈbəʊɡɪ/ *n.* (also **bogy**) (*pl.* **-eys** or **-ies**) **1** an evil or mischievous spirit; a devil. **2** an awkward thing or circumstance. **3** *sl.* a piece of dried nasal mucus. [19th c., orig. as a proper name: cf. BOGLE]

bogeyman /ˈbəʊɡɪˌmæn/ *n.* (also **bogyman**) (*pl.* **-men**) a person (real or imaginary) causing fear or difficulty.

boggle /ˈbɒɡ(ə)l/ *v.intr. colloq.* **1** be startled or baffled (esp. *the mind boggles*). **2** (usu. foll. by *about, at*) hesitate, demur. [prob. f. dial. *boggle* BOGEY²]

bogie /ˈbəʊɡɪ/ *n. esp. Brit.* **1** a wheeled undercarriage pivoted below the end of a rail vehicle. **2** a small truck used for carrying coal, rubble, etc. [19th-c. north. dial. word: orig. unkn.]

bogle /ˈbəʊɡ(ə)l/ *n.* **1** = BOGEY². **2** a phantom. **3** a scarecrow. [orig. Sc. (16th c.), prob. rel. to BOGEY]

Bogotá /ˌbɒɡəˈtɑː/ the capital of Colombia, situated in the eastern Andes at 2,610 m (*c.*8,560 ft.); pop. (1985) 3,982,900.

bogus /ˈbəʊɡəs/ *adj.* sham, fictitious, spurious. □□ **bogusly** *adv.* **bogusness** *n.* [19th-c. US word: orig. unkn.]

bogy var. of BOGEY².

bogyman var. of BOGEYMAN.

bohea /bəʊˈhiː/ *n.* a black China tea, the last crop of the season and usu. regarded as of low quality. [*Bu-i* (Wuyi) Hills in China]

Bohemia /bəʊˈhiːmɪə/ an area of Czechoslovakia. A former Slavonic kingdom, it fell under Austrian rule in 1526, and by the Treaty of Versailles (1919) became a province of Czechoslovakia.

Bohemian /bəʊˈhiːmɪən/ *n. & adj.* —*n.* **1** a native of Bohemia, a Czech. **2** (also **bohemian**) a socially unconventional person, esp. an artist or writer. —*adj.* **1** of, relating to, or characteristic of Bohemia or its people. **2** (also **bohemian**) socially unconventional. □□ **bohemianism** *n.* (in sense 2). [BOHEMIA + -AN: sense 2 f. F *bohémien* gypsy]

Bohol /bəʊˈhɒl/ an island lying to the north of Mindanao in the central Philippines; pop. (1980) 806,000; chief town, Tagbilaran.

Bohr /bɔː(r)/, Niels Hendrik David (1885–1962), Danish physicist, one of the major early figures in the development of quantum physics. He worked with J. J. Thomson at Cambridge and with Rutherford at Manchester. Bohr's theory of the structure of the atom was a radical departure since it incorporated quantum theory for the first time, and is the basis for the present-day quantum mechanical models. He postulated that electrons orbited the nucleus at fixed distances, each orbit having a quantum (fixed amount) of energy, released (or absorbed) when electrons jumped from one quantum orbit to another. Taking the simplest case, the hydrogen atom, he could now account for the lines in its spectrum. In 1927 he proposed the principle of 'complementarity', that natural phenomena could be looked at in mutually exclusive ways, which accounted for the paradox of regarding subatomic particles both as waves and as particles. Bohr had returned to Copenhagen in 1916, and in the 1930s he was joined by Jewish and other physicists fleeing from Nazi persecution. In 1943, at risk of imprisonment as a patriot, he escaped from German-occupied Denmark and helped to develop the atom bomb, working first in Britain and then in the US. He became increasingly concerned about the human implications of atomic weapons and stressed the need for international cooperation in the study of the peaceful applications of atomic energy. Niels Bohr was awarded the 1922 Nobel Prize for physics for his contribution to atomic energy, and his son, Aage Niels Bohr (1922–) shared the 1975 Prize for his studies in the physics of the atomic nucleus.

boil[1] /bɔɪl/ v. & n. —v. **1** intr. **a** (of a liquid) start to bubble up and turn into vapour; reach a temperature at which this happens. **b** (of a vessel) contain boiling liquid (the kettle is boiling). **2 a** tr. bring (a liquid or vessel) to a temperature at which it boils. **b** tr. cook (food) by boiling. **c** intr. (of food) be cooked by boiling. **d** tr. subject to the heat of boiling water, e.g. to clean. **3** intr. **a** (of the sea etc.) undulate or seethe like boiling water. **b** (of a person or feelings) be greatly agitated, esp. by anger. —n. the act or process of boiling; boiling-point (on the boil; bring to the boil). □ **boil down 1** reduce volume by boiling. **2** reduce to essentials. **3** (foll. by to) amount to; signify basically. **boiled shirt** a dress shirt with a starched front. **boiled sweet** Brit. a sweet made of boiled sugar. **boil over 1** spill over in boiling. **2** lose one's temper; become over-excited. **make one's blood boil** see BLOOD. [ME f. AF boiller, OF boillir, f. L bullire to bubble f. bulla bubble]

boil[2] /bɔɪl/ n. an inflamed pus-filled swelling caused by infection of a hair follicle etc. [OE bȳl(e) f. WG]

Boileau(-Despréaux) /ˈbwɑːləʊ ˌdespreɪˈəʊ/, Nicholas (1636–1711), French critic and poet, friend of Racine, Molière, and La Fontaine. His Satires appeared in 1666–1711, and his didactic poem, Art Poétique (1674, based on Horace's Ars Poetica) defining principles of composition and criticism, earned him international recognition as the legislator and model for French neoclassicism at its apogee. Boileau was less important as a poet than as a founder of French literary criticism, where his influence has been profound.

boiler /ˈbɔɪlə(r)/ n. **1** a fuel-burning apparatus for heating a hot-water supply. **2** a tank for heating water, esp. for turning it to steam under pressure. **3** a metal tub for boiling laundry etc. **4** a fowl, vegetable, etc., suitable for cooking only by boiling. □ **boiler-room** a room with a boiler and other heating equipment, esp. in the basement of a large building. **boiler suit** a one-piece suit worn as overalls for heavy manual work.

boiling /ˈbɔɪlɪŋ/ adj. (also **boiling hot**) colloq. very hot.

boiling-point /ˈbɔɪlɪŋ/ n. **1** the temperature at which a liquid starts to boil. **2** high excitement (feelings reached boiling-point).

Boise /ˈbɔɪsɪ/ the capital of Idaho, situated on the River Boise; pop. (1980) 102,451.

Bois-le-Duc see 's-HERTOGENBOSCH.

boisterous /ˈbɔɪstərəs/ adj. **1** (of a person) rough; noisily exuberant. **2** (of the sea, weather, etc.) stormy, rough. □□ **boisterously** adv. **boisterousness** n. [var. of ME boist(u)ous, of unkn. orig.]

Bokassa /bəˈkæsə/, Jean Bédel (1921–), African military leader, who led a successful coup in 1966 and became President and later self-styled Emperor of the Central African Republic (see entry). In 1987 was tried and sentenced to death for his crimes.

Bokhara see BUKHARA.

bolas /ˈbəʊləs/ n. (as sing. or pl.) (esp. in S. America) a missile consisting of a number of balls connected by strong cord, which when thrown entangles the limbs of the quarry. [Sp. & Port., pl. of bola ball]

bold /bəʊld/ adj. **1** confidently assertive; adventurous, courageous. **2** forthright, impudent. **3** vivid, distinct, well-marked (bold colours; a bold imagination). **4** Printing (in full **bold-face** or **-faced**) printed in a thick black typeface. □ **as bold as brass** excessively bold or self-assured. **make** (or **be**) **so bold as to**

presume to; venture to. □□ **boldly** adv. **boldness** n. [OE bald dangerous f. Gmc]

Boldrewood /ˈbəʊldəˌwʊd/, Rolf (pseudonym of Thomas Alexander Browne, 1826–1915), Australian novelist, whose most enduring work was Robbery Under Arms, first published as a serial in 1882–3, a narration of the life and crimes of a bushranger under sentence of death.

bole[1] /bəʊl/ n. the stem or trunk of a tree. [ME f. ON bolr, perh. rel. to BALK[1]]

bole[2] /bəʊl/ n. fine compact earthy clay. [LL BOLUS]

bolero /bəˈleərəʊ/ n. (pl. -os) **1 a** a Spanish dance in simple triple time. **b** music for or in the time of a bolero. **2** /also ˈbɒlərəʊ/ a woman's short open jacket. [Sp.]

Boleyn /bʊˈlɪn, ˈbʊ-/, Anne (1507–36), second wife of Henry VIII and mother of Elizabeth I. Although the King had fallen deeply in love with Anne, and had divorced Catherine of Aragon in order to marry her, she fell from favour when she failed to provide him with the male heir he so desperately wanted. She was eventually executed because of suspected infidelities which were probably more the product of Henry's own suspicion, and of his desire for a new queen, than of any act of Anne's.

Bolívar /ˌbɒlɪˈvɑː(r)/, Simón (1783–1830), Venezuelan patriot and statesman, called 'the Liberator'. More than any other man Bolívar was responsible for the liberation of South America from Spanish rule. Although his military career was not without its failures, and although his dream of a South American federation was never realized, he liberated one area of the country after another and eventually had one country, Bolivia, named after him.

Bolivia /bəˈlɪvɪə/ a land-locked country in South America; pop. (1988) 6,448,300; official language, Spanish; capital, La Paz; legal capital and seat of the judiciary, Sucre. Bolivia's chief topographical feature is the Altiplano, the great central plateau between the two chains of the Andes. The main exports include tin and other minerals and natural gas; the coca plant, from the leaves of which cocaine is produced, grows freely. Oil is produced in quantities that are sufficient for home consumption. Part of the Inca empire, Bolivia became one of the most important parts of Spain's American empire following the discovery of major silver deposits soon after Pizarro's destruction of the Incas. It was freed from the Spanish in 1825 and named after the great liberator Bolívar, but since then it has been crippled by endemic poverty and political instability, losing land (including its Pacific coast) to surrounding countries in 19th- and early 20th-c. wars and suffering from almost continual coups and changes of government. □□ **Bolivian** adj. & n.

boll /bəʊl/ n. a rounded capsule containing seeds, esp. flax or cotton. □ **boll-weevil** a small American or Mexican weevil, Anthonomus grandis, whose larvae destroy cotton bolls. [ME f. MDu. bolle: see BOWL[1]]

Böll /bɜːl/, Heinrich (1917–), German author of novels and short stories, mostly on the subject of wartime and post war Germany, e.g. in Und sagte kein einziges Wort (And Never Said a Word, 1953). His more recent works, which include Guppenbild mit Dame (Group Portrait with Lady, 1971) and Fürsorgliche Belagerung (The Safety Net, 1979) show a concern for topical problems. He was awarded the Nobel Prize for literature in 1972.

Bollandists /ˈbɒləndɪsts/ n.pl. the Jesuit editors of the Acta Sanctorum, a critical edition of the lives of the saints, based on authentic sources and first edited by John Bolland (1596–1665).

bollard /ˈbɒlɑːd/ n. **1** Brit. a short metal, concrete, or plastic post in the road, esp. as part of a traffic island. **2** a short post on a quay or ship for securing a rope. [ME perh. f. ON bolr BOLE[1] + -ARD]

bollocking /ˈbɒləkɪŋ/ n. coarse sl. a severe reprimand.

bollocks /ˈbɒləks/ n. (also **ballocks**) coarse sl. ¶ Usually considered a taboo word. **1** the testicles. **2** (usu. as an exclam. of contempt) nonsense, rubbish. [OE bealluc, rel. to BALL[1]]

Bologna /bəˈləʊnjə/ a city in north Italy, capital of the region of Emilia-Romagna; pop. (1981) 459,000. Its university, which dates from the 11th c., is the oldest in Europe. □ **Bologna sausage** US a large smoked sausage made of bacon, veal, pork-suet, and other meats, and sold ready for eating.

bologna /bə'ləʊnjə/ n. US = BOLOGNA SAUSAGE.

bolometer /bə'lɒmɪtə(r)/ n. a sensitive electrical instrument for measuring radiant energy. □□ **bolometry** n. **bolometric** /ˌbəʊlə'metrɪk/ adj. [Gk *bolē* ray + -METER]

boloney /bə'ləʊnɪ/ n. (also **baloney**) (pl. **-eys**) sl. 1 humbug, nonsense. 2 = BOLOGNA SAUSAGE. [20th c.: orig. uncert.]

Bolshevik /'bɒlʃəvɪk/ n. & adj. —n. 1 hist. a member of the radical faction of the socialist party in Russia which, from 1903, favoured revolutionary tactics. (See below.) 2 a Russian communist. 3 (in general use) any revolutionary socialist. —adj. 1 of, relating to, or characteristic of the Bolsheviks. 2 communist. □□ **Bolshevism** n. **Bolshevist** n. [Russ., = a member of the majority, f. *bol'she* greater]

The Bolsheviks formed the majority faction of the Russian socialist party, led by Lenin, advocating no cooperation with moderate reformers and fomentation of revolution by a small political élite prepared to shape the ideas of the working class. After the successful overthrow of the Russian government in 1917 they eventually succeeded in seizing complete control of the country from the various other revolutionary groups. In March 1918 they were renamed the (Russian) Communist Party.

Bolshie /'bɒlʃɪ/ adj. & n. (also **Bolshy**) sl. —adj. (usu. **bolshie**) 1 uncooperative, rebellious, awkward; bad-tempered. 2 left-wing, socialist. —n. (pl. **-ies**) a Bolshevik. □□ **bolshiness** n. (in sense 1 of adj.). [abbr.]

Bolshoi Ballet /'bɒlʃɔɪ/ a Moscow ballet company, the most prestigious in the world, dating from 1776. The New Bolshoi Petrovsky Theatre (the present Bolshoi Theatre) opened in 1825 and by 1850 the company numbered 155 dancers. The first production of *Swan Lake*, with music by Tchaikovsky, was given in 1877. After the October Revolution the company was reorganized and new Soviet ballets such as the *The Red Poppy* (1927) were introduced. The company first appeared in London in 1956 and in New York in 1959, and performs regularly at the Kremlin Palace Theatre. [Russ., = great]

bolster[1] /'bəʊlstə(r)/ n. & v. —n. 1 a long thick pillow. 2 a pad or support, esp. in a machine. 3 *Building* a short timber cap over a post to increase the bearing of the beams it supports. —v.tr. (usu. foll. by *up*) 1 encourage, reinforce (*bolstered our morale*). 2 support with a bolster; prop up. □□ **bolsterer** n. [OE f. Gmc]

bolster[2] /'bəʊlstə(r)/ n. a chisel for cutting bricks. [20th c.: orig. uncert.]

bolt[1] /bəʊlt/ n., v., & adv. —n. 1 a sliding bar and socket used to fasten or lock a door, gate, etc. 2 a large usu. metal pin with a head, usu. riveted or used with a nut, to hold things together. 3 a discharge of lightning. 4 an act of bolting (cf. sense 4 of v.); a sudden escape or dash for freedom. 5 hist. an arrow for shooting from a crossbow. 6 a roll of fabric (orig. as a measure). —v. 1 tr. fasten or lock with a bolt. 2 tr. (foll. by *in*, *out*) keep (a person etc.) from leaving or entering by bolting a door. 3 tr. fasten together with bolts. 4 intr. **a** dash suddenly away, esp. to escape. **b** (of a horse) suddenly gallop out of control. 5 tr. gulp down (food) unchewed; eat hurriedly. 6 intr. (of a plant) run to seed. —adv. (usu. in **bolt upright**) rigidly, stiffly. □ **a bolt from the blue** a complete surprise. **bolt-hole** 1 a means of escape. 2 a secret refuge. **shoot one's bolt** do all that is in one's power. □□ **bolter** n. (in sense 4 of v.). [OE *bolt* arrow]

bolt[2] /bəʊlt/ v.tr. (also **boult**) sift (flour etc.). □□ **bolter** n. [ME f. OF *bulter, buleter*, of unkn. orig.]

Boltzmann /'bɒltsmən/, Ludwig (1844–1906), Austrian physicist who made fundamental contributions to the kinetic theory of gases, classical statistical mechanics, and thermodynamics. He was one of the first European scientists to recognize the importance of the electromagnetic theory of James Clerk Maxwell, but had difficulty in getting his own work on statistical mechanics accepted until the new discoveries in atomic physics at the turn of the century. Boltzmann introduced the so-called Maxwell-Boltzmann equation for the change in distribution of atoms due to collisions, and he correlated entropy with probability when he brought thermodynamics and molecular physics together.

bolus /'bəʊləs/ n. (pl. **boluses**) 1 a soft ball, esp. of chewed food. 2 a large pill. [LL f. Gk *bōlos* clod]

Bolzano /bɒl'tsɑːnəʊ/ 1 an autonomous province in the Trentino-Adige region of north Italy. 2 its capital city; pop. (1981) 104,606.

bomb /bɒm/ n. & v. —n. 1 **a** a container with explosive, incendiary material, smoke, or gas etc., designed to explode on impact or by means of a time-mechanism or remote-control device. **b** an ordinary object fitted with an explosive device (*letter-bomb*). 2 (prec. by *the*) the atomic or hydrogen bomb considered as a weapon with supreme destructive power. 3 *Brit. sl.* a large sum of money (*cost a bomb*). 4 a mass of solidified lava thrown from a volcano. 5 *US colloq.* a bad failure (esp. a theatrical one). 6 *sl.* a drugged cigarette. 7 *Med.* = **radium bomb**. —v. 1 tr. attack with bombs; drop bombs on. 2 tr. (foll. by *out*) drive (a person etc.) out of a building or refuge by using bombs. 3 intr. throw or drop bombs. 4 intr. esp. *US sl.* fail badly. 5 intr. *colloq.* (usu. foll. by *along*, *off*) move or go very quickly. 6 tr. *US sl.* criticize fiercely. □ **bomb-bay** compartment in an aircraft used to hold bombs. **bomb-disposal** the defusing or removal and detonation of an unexploded bomb. **bomb-sight** a device in an aircraft for aiming bombs. **bomb-site** an area where buildings have been destroyed by bombs. **go down a bomb** *colloq.*, often *iron.* be very well received. **like a bomb** *Brit. colloq.* 1 often *iron.* very successfully. 2 very fast. [F *bombe* f. It. *bomba* f. L *bombus* f. Gk *bombos* hum]

bombard /bɒm'bɑːd/ v.tr. 1 attack with a number of heavy guns or bombs. 2 (often foll. by *with*) subject to persistent questioning, abuse, etc. 3 *Physics* direct a stream of high-speed particles at (a substance). □□ **bombardment** n. [F *bombarder* f. *bombarde* f. med.L *bombarda* a stone-throwing engine: see BOMB]

bombardier /ˌbɒmbə'dɪə(r)/ n. 1 *Brit.* a non-commissioned officer in the artillery. 2 *US* a member of a bomber crew responsible for sighting and releasing bombs. [F (as BOMBARD)]

bombardon /bɒm'bɑːd(ə)n, 'bɒmbəd(ə)n/ n. *Mus.* 1 a type of valved bass tuba. 2 an organ stop imitating this. [It. *bombardone* f. *bombardo* bassoon]

bombasine var. of BOMBAZINE.

bombast /'bɒmbæst/ n. pompous or extravagant language. □□ **bombastic** /-'bæstɪk/ adj. **bombastically** /-'bæstɪkəlɪ/ adv. [earlier *bombace* cotton wool f. F f. med.L *bombax -acis* alt. f. *bombyx*; see BOMBAZINE]

Bombay /bɒm'beɪ/ a city and port on the west coast of India, that country's largest city and a commercial centre, long noted for its textile industry; pop. (1981) 8,227,000.

Bombay duck /bɒm'beɪ dʌk/ n. a dried fish, esp. bummalo, usu. eaten with curried dishes. [corrupt. of *bombil*: see BUMMALO]

bombazine /'bɒmbəˌziːn, -'ziːn/ n. (also **bombasine**) n. a twilled dress-material of worsted with or without an admixture of silk or cotton, esp., when black, formerly used for mourning. [F *bombasin* f. med.L *bombacinum* f. LL *bombycinus* silken f. *bombyx -ycis* silk or silkworm f. L *bombyx* f. Gk *bombux*]

bombe /bɒmb/ n. *Cookery* a dome-shaped dish or confection, freq. frozen. [F, = BOMB]

bomber /'bɒmə(r)/ n. 1 an aircraft equipped to carry and drop bombs. 2 a person using bombs, esp. illegally. □ **bomber jacket** a short leather or cloth jacket tightly gathered at the waist and cuffs.

bombora /bɒm'bɔːrə/ n. *Austral.* a dangerous sea area where waves break over a submerged reef. [Aboriginal]

bombproof /'bɒmpruːf/ adj. strong enough to resist the effects of blast from a bomb.

bombshell /'bɒmʃel/ n. **1** an overwhelming surprise or disappointment. **2** an artillery bomb. **3** *sl.* a very attractive woman (*blonde bombshell*).

bona fide /ˌbəʊnə ˈfaɪdɪ/ *adj. & adv.* —*adj.* genuine; sincere. —*adv.* genuinely; sincerely. [L, ablat. sing. of BONA FIDES]

bona fides /ˌbəʊnə ˈfaɪdiːz/ *n.* **1** esp. *Law* an honest intention; sincerity. **2** (as *pl.*) *colloq.* documentary evidence of acceptability (*his bona fides are in order*). [L, = good faith]

Bonaire /bɒˈneə(r)/ one of the two principal islands of the Netherlands Antilles, situated in the Caribbean Sea 60 km (37 miles) north of the Venezuelan coast; pop. (1981) 9,065; chief town, Kralendijk.

bonanza /bəˈnænzə/ *n. & adj.* —*n.* **1** a source of wealth or prosperity. **2** a large output (esp. of a mine). **3 a** prosperity; good luck. **b** a run of good luck. —*adj.* greatly prospering or productive. [orig. US f. Sp., = fair weather, f. L *bonus* good]

Bonaparte /ˈbəʊnəˌpɑːt/ the name of a Corsican family including the three French rulers named Napoleon.

bona vacantia /ˌbəʊnə vəˈkæntɪə/ *n. Law* goods without an apparent owner. [L, = ownerless goods]

Bonaventura /bɒnəvenˈtjʊərə/, St (1221–74) Giovanni di Fidanza, a Franciscan theologian, the 'Seraphic Doctor', from 1257 Minister General of his order, who wrote the official biography of St Francis and had a lasting influence as a spiritual writer. Feast day, 15 (formerly 14) July.

bon-bon /ˈbɒnbɒn/ *n.* a piece of confectionery; a sweet. [F f. *bon* good f. L *bonus*]

bonce /bɒns/ *n. Brit.* **1** *sl.* the head. **2** a large playing-marble. [19th c.: orig. unkn.]

Bond /bɒnd/, James. A secret agent in the spy novels of Ian Fleming.

bond /bɒnd/ *n. & v.* —*n.* **1 a** a thing that ties another down or together. **b** (usu. in *pl.*) a thing restraining bodily freedom (*broke his bonds*). **2** (often in *pl.*) **a** a uniting force (*sisterly bond*). **b** a restraint; a responsibility (*bonds of duty*). **3** a binding engagement; an agreement (*his word is his bond*). **4** *Commerce* a certificate issued by a government or a public company promising to repay borrowed money at a fixed rate of interest at a specified time; a debenture. **5** adhesiveness. **6** *Law* a deed by which a person is bound to make payment to another. **7** *Chem.* linkage between atoms in a molecule or a crystal. **8** *Building* the laying of bricks in one of various patterns in a wall in order to ensure strength (*English bond; Flemish bond*). —*v.* **1** *tr.* **a** lay (bricks) overlapping. **b** bind together (resin with fibres etc.). **2** *intr.* adhere; hold together. **3** *tr.* connect with a bond. **4** *tr.* place (goods) in bond. **5** *intr.* become emotionally attached. □ **bond paper** high-quality writing-paper. **bond-washing** dividend-stripping. **in bond** (of goods) stored in a bonded warehouse until the importer pays the duty owing (see BONDED). [ME var. of BAND[1]]

bondage /ˈbɒndɪdʒ/ *n.* **1** serfdom; slavery. **2** subjection to constraint, influence, obligation, etc. **3** sado-masochistic practices, including the use of physical restraints or mental enslavement. [ME f. AL *bondagium*: infl. by BOND]

bonded /ˈbɒndɪd/ *adj.* **1** (of goods) placed in bond. **2** (of material) reinforced by or cemented to another. **3** (of a debt) secured by bonds. □ **bonded warehouse** a Customs-controlled warehouse for the retention of imported goods until the duty owed is paid.

Bondi /ˈbɒndɪ/ a coastal resort in a suburb of Sydney, NSW, with a popular beach.

bondsman /ˈbɒndzmən/ *n.* (*pl.* **-men**) **1** a slave. **2** a person in thrall to another. [var. of *bondman* (f. archaic *bond* in serfdom or slavery) as though f. *bond's* genitive of BOND[1]]

bone /bəʊn/ *n. & v.* —*n.* **1** any of the pieces of hard tissue making up the skeleton in vertebrates. (See below.) **2** (in *pl.*) **a** the skeleton, esp. as remains after death. **b** the body, esp. as a seat of intuitive feeling (*felt it in my bones*). **3 a** the material of which bones consist. **b** a similar substance such as ivory, dentine, or whalebone. **4** a thing made of bone. **5** (in *pl.*) the essential part of a thing (*the bare bones*). **6** (in *pl.*) **a** dice. **b** castanets. **7** a strip of stiffening in a corset etc. —*v.* **1** *tr.* take out the bones from (meat or fish). **2** *tr.* stiffen (a garment)

with bone etc. **3** *tr. Brit. sl.* steal. □ **bone china** fine china made of clay mixed with the ash from bones. **bone-dry** quite dry. **bone idle** (or **lazy**) utterly idle or lazy. **bone-meal** crushed or ground bones used esp. as a fertilizer. **bone of contention** a source or ground of dispute. **bone-setter** a person who sets broken or dislocated bones, esp. without being a qualified surgeon. **bone spavin** see SPAVIN. **bone up** (often foll. by *on*) *colloq.* study (a subject) intensively. **close to** (or **near**) **the bone 1** tactless to the point of offensiveness. **2** destitute; hard up. **have a bone to pick** (usu. foll. by *with*) have a cause for dispute (with another person). **make no bones about 1** admit or allow without fuss. **2** not hesitate or scruple. **point the bone** (usu. foll. by *at*) *Austral.* **1** wish bad luck on. **2** cast a spell on in order to kill. **to the bone 1** to the bare minimum. **2** penetratingly. **work one's fingers to the bone** work very hard, esp. thanklessly. □□ **boneless** *adj.* [OE *bān* f. Gmc]

The human skeleton is conventionally regarded as consisting of two main parts: the skull, spine, and ribs, which support and protect body tissues and organs, and the limb bones and their attachments which function in conjunction with muscles as levers to provide movement. Bone itself is a living tissue, composed of special cells which secrete around them a material consisting of calcium salts (which provide hardness and strength in compression) and collagen fibres (which provide tensile strength); its formation is a complex process, beginning in the embryo. The material of bone varies considerably in density and compactness, that near the surface of a bone generally being more compact. Many bones have a central cavity containing marrow, a tissue which is the source of most of the cells of the blood and is also a site for the storage of fats. The calcium salts in bone are crucial in the regulation of the level of calcium throughout the body.

bonefish /ˈbəʊnfɪʃ/ *n. US* any of several species of large game-fish, esp. *Albula vulpes*, having many small bones.

bonehead /ˈbəʊnhed/ *n. sl.* a stupid person. □□ **boneheaded** *adj.*

boner /ˈbəʊnə(r)/ *n. sl.* a stupid mistake. [BONE + -ER[1]]

boneshaker /ˈbəʊnˌʃeɪkə(r)/ *n.* **1** a decrepit or uncomfortable old vehicle. **2** an old type of bicycle with solid tyres.

bonfire /ˈbɒnˌfaɪə(r)/ *n.* a large open-air fire for burning rubbish, as part of a celebration, or as a signal. □ **Bonfire Night** *Brit.* 5 Nov., on which fireworks are displayed and an effigy of Guy Fawkes burnt in memory of the Gunpowder Plot (see entry). **make a bonfire of** destroy by burning. [earlier *bonefire* f. BONE (bones being the chief material formerly used) + FIRE]

bongo[1] /ˈbɒŋgəʊ/ *n.* (*pl.* **-os** or **-oes**) either of a pair of small long-bodied drums usu. held between the knees and played with the fingers. [Amer. Sp. *bongó*]

bongo[2] /ˈbɒŋgəʊ/ *n.* (*pl.* same or **-os**) a rare antelope, *Tragelaphus euryceros*, native to the forests of central Africa, having spiralled horns and a chestnut-red coat with narrow white vertical stripes. [cf. Bangi *mbangani*, Lingala *mongu*]

Bonhoeffer /ˈbɒnˌhɜːfə(r)/, Dietrich (1906–45), German Lutheran theologian, an active opponent of Nazism both before and during the Second World War. Arrested in 1943, he was sent to Buchenwald concentration camp and executed in 1945.

bonhomie /ˌbɒnɒˈmiː/ *n.* geniality; good-natured friendliness. [F f. *bonhomme* good fellow]

bonhomous /ˈbɒnəməs/ *adj.* full of *bonhomie*.

Boniface /ˈbɒnɪfeɪs/, St (680–754), apostle of Germany, who laid the foundations of a settled ecclesiastical organization there. Originally named Wynfrith, he was born in Devon and went as a missionary to Frisia and Germany. His courage in felling the sacred oak of Thor won him instant success and many converts. In 741 he was given authority to reform the whole Frankish Church. The first papal legate north of the Alps, Boniface greatly assisted the spread of papal influence. He was martyred in Frisia. Feast day, 5 June.

Bonington /ˈbɒnɪŋt(ə)n/, Christian John Storey ('Chris') (1934–), English mountaineer. He made the first British ascent of the north face of the Eiger in 1962, and led expeditions to

Mount Everest, one by a hitherto unclimbed route in 1975 and another in 1985, when he reached the summit.

bonito /bəˈniːtəʊ/ n. (pl. **-os**) any of several tunny-like fish which are striped like mackerel and are common in tropical seas. [Sp.]

bonk /bɒŋk/ v. & n. —v. **1** tr. hit resoundingly. **2** intr. bang; bump. **3** coarse sl. **a** intr. have sexual intercourse. **b** tr. have sexual intercourse with. —n. an instance of bonking (a bonk on the head). □□ **bonker** n. [imit.: cf. BANG, BUMP¹, CONK²]

bonkers /ˈbɒŋkəz/ adj. sl. crazy. [20th c.: orig. unkn.]

bon mot /bɔ̃ ˈməʊ, bɒn-/ n. (pl. **bons mots** pronunc. same or /-məʊz/) a witty saying. [F]

Bonn /bɒn/ the seat of government of Germany, situated on the Rhine; pop. (1987) 291,400. From 1949 until the reunification of Germany in 1990 Bonn was the capital of the Federal Republic of Germany (West Germany).

Bonnard /bɒˈnɑː(r)/, Pierre (1867–1947), French painter and graphic artist, a distinguished upholder of the impressionist tradition and a member of the Nabi group. His works include domestic interior scenes, stage decor, and landscapes. His finest works radiate a sense of well-being that won him great popularity both with collectors and with the general public.

bonne bouche /bɒn ˈbuːʃ/ n. (pl. **bonne bouches** or **bonnes bouches** pronunc. same) a titbit, esp. to end a meal with. [F f. bonne fem. good + bouche mouth]

bonnet /ˈbɒnɪt/ n. **1 a** a woman's or child's hat tied under the chin and usu. with a brim framing the face. **b** a soft round brimless hat like a beret worn by men and boys in Scotland (cf. TAM-O'-SHANTER). **c** colloq. any hat. **2** Brit. a hinged cover over the engine of a motor vehicle. **3** the ceremonial feathered head-dress of an American Indian. **4** the cowl of a chimney etc. **5** a protective cap in various machines. **6** Naut. additional canvas laced to the foot of a sail. □ **bonnet monkey** an Indian macaque, Macaca radiata, with a bonnet-like tuft of hair. □□ **bonneted** adj. [ME f. OF bonet short for chapel de bonet cap of some kind of material (med.L bonetus)]

bonnethead /ˈbɒnɪtˌhed/ n. = SHOVELHEAD.

bonny /ˈbɒnɪ/ adj. (**bonnier**, **bonniest**) esp. Sc. & N.Engl. **1 a** physically attractive. **b** healthy looking. **2** good, fine, pleasant. □ **Bonny Prince Charlie** a romantic Jacobite name given to Charles Edward Stuart, elder son of the Stuart claimant to the British throne and leader of the 1745–6 Jacobite uprising. □□ **bonnily** adv. **bonniness** n. [16th c.: perh. f. F bon good]

bonsai /ˈbɒnsaɪ/ n. (pl. same) **1** the art of cultivating ornamental artificially dwarfed varieties of trees and shrubs. **2** a tree or shrub grown by this method. [Jap.]

bonspiel /ˈbɒnspiːl/ n. esp. Sc. a curling-match (usu. between two clubs). [16th c.: perh. f. LG]

bontebok /ˈbɒntɪˌbʌk/ n. (also **bontbok** /ˈbɒntbʌk/) (pl. same or **-boks**) a large chestnut antelope, Damaliscus dorcas, native to southern Africa, having a white tail and a white patch on its head and rump. [Afrik. f. bont spotted + bok BUCK¹]

bonus /ˈbəʊnəs/ n. **1** an unsought or unexpected extra benefit. **2 a** a usu. seasonal gratuity to employees beyond their normal pay. **b** an extra dividend or issue paid to the shareholders of a company. **c** a distribution of profits to holders of an insurance policy. [L bonus, bonum good (thing)]

bon vivant /ˌbɔ̃ viːˈvɑ̃/ n. (pl. **bon vivants** or **bons vivants** pronunc. same) a person indulging in good living; a gourmand. [F, lit. good liver f. vivre to live]

bon viveur /ˌbɔ̃ viːˈvɜː(r)/ n. (pl. **bon viveurs** or **bons viveurs** pronunc. same) = BON VIVANT. [pseudo-F]

bon voyage /ˌbɔ̃ vwaˈjaːʒ, vɔɪˈjaːʒ/ int. & n. an expression of good wishes to a departing traveller. [F]

bony /ˈbəʊnɪ/ adj. (**bonier**, **boniest**) **1** (of a person) thin with prominent bones. **2** having many bones. **3** of or like bone. **4** (of a fish) having bones rather than cartilage. □□ **boniness** n.

bonze /bɒnz/ n. a Japanese or Chinese Buddhist priest. [F bonze or Port. bonzo perh. f. Jap. bonzō f. Chin. fanseng religious person, or f. Jap. bō-zi f. Chin. fasi teacher of the law]

bonzer /ˈbɒnzə(r)/ adj. Austral. sl. excellent, first-rate. [perh. f. BONANZA]

boo /buː/ int., n., & v. —int. **1** an expression of disapproval or contempt. **2** a sound, made esp. to a child, intended to surprise. —n. an utterance of boo, esp. as an expression of disapproval or contempt made to a performer etc. —v. (**boos**, **booed**) **1** intr. utter a boo or boos. **2** tr. jeer at (a performer etc.) by booing. □ **can't** (or **wouldn't**) **say boo to a goose** is very shy or timid. [imit.]

boob¹ /buːb/ n. & v. sl. —n. **1** Brit. an embarrassing mistake. **2** a simpleton. —v.intr. Brit. make an embarrassing mistake. [abbr. of BOOBY]

boob² /buːb/ n. sl. a woman's breast. □ **boob tube** sl. **1** a woman's low-cut close-fitting usu. strapless top. **2** (usu. prec. by the) US television; one's television set. [earlier bubby, booby, of uncert. orig.]

booboo /ˈbuːbuː/ n. sl. a mistake. [BOOB¹]

boobook /ˈbuːbʊk, ˈbʊəbʊək/ n. Austral. a brown spotted owl, Ninox novae-seelandiae, native to Australia and New Zealand. [imit. of its call]

booby /ˈbuːbɪ/ n. (pl. **-ies**) **1** a stupid or childish person. **2** a small gannet of the genus Sula. □ **booby-hatch** esp. US sl. a mental hospital. **booby prize** a prize given to the least successful competitor in any contest. **booby trap 1** a trap intended as a practical joke, e.g. an object placed on top of a door ajar ready to fall on the next person to pass through. **2** Mil. an apparently harmless explosive device intended to kill or injure anyone touching it. **booby-trap** v.tr. place a booby trap or traps in or on. [prob. f. Sp. bobo (in both senses) f. L balbus stammering]

boodle /ˈbuːd(ə)l/ n. sl. money, esp. when gained or used dishonestly, e.g. as a bribe. [Du. boedel possessions]

boogie /ˈbuːɡɪ/ v. & n. —v.intr. (**boogies**, **boogied**, **boogying**) sl. dance enthusiastically to pop music. —n. **1** = BOOGIE-WOOGIE. **2** sl. a dance to pop music. [BOOGIE-WOOGIE]

boogie-woogie /ˌbuːɡɪˈwuːɡɪ/ n. a style of playing blues or jazz on the piano, marked by a persistent bass rhythm. [20th c.: orig. unkn.]

book /bʊk/ n. & v. —n. **1 a** a written or printed work consisting of pages glued or sewn together along one side and bound in covers. **b** a literary composition intended for publication (is working on her book). **2** a bound set of blank sheets for writing or keeping records in. **3** a set of tickets, stamps, matches, cheques, samples of cloth, etc., bound up together. **4** (in pl.) a set of records or accounts. **5** a main division of a literary work, or of the Bible (the Book of Deuteronomy). **6** (in full **book of words**) a libretto, script of a play, etc. **7** colloq. a magazine. **8** a telephone directory (his number's in the book). **9** a record of bets made and money paid out at a race meeting by a bookmaker. **10** a set of six tricks collected together in a card-game. **11** an imaginary record or list (the book of life). —v. **1** tr. **a** engage (a seat etc.) in advance; make a reservation of. **b** engage (a guest, supporter, etc.) for some occasion. **2** tr. **a** take the personal details of (an offender or rule-breaker). **b** enter in a book or list. **3** tr. issue a railway etc. ticket to. **4** intr. make a reservation (no need to book). □ **book club** a society which sells its members selected books on special terms. **book-end** a usu. ornamental prop used to keep a row of books upright. **book in** esp. Brit. register one's arrival at a hotel etc. **book learning** mere theory. **book-plate** a decorative label stuck in the front of a book bearing the owner's name. **book-rest** an adjustable support for an open book on a table. **book token** Brit. a voucher which can be exchanged for books to a specified value. **book up 1** buy tickets in advance for a theatre, concert, holiday, etc. **2** (as **booked up**) with all places reserved. **book value** the value of a commodity as entered in a firm's books (opp. market value). **bring to book** call to account. **closed** (or **sealed**) **book** a subject of which one is ignorant. **go by the book** proceed according to the rules. **the good Book** the Bible. **in a person's bad** (or **good**) **books** in disfavour (or favour) with a person. **in my book** in my opinion. **make a book** take bets and pay out winnings at a race meeting. **not in the book** disallowed. **on the books** contained in a list of members etc. **suits my book** is convenient to me. **take a leaf out of a person's book** imitate a person. **throw the book at** *colloq.* charge or punish to the utmost. [OE *bōc*, *bōcian*, f. Gmc. usu. taken to be rel. to BEECH (the bark of which was used for writing on)]

bookbinder /ˈbʊkˌbaɪndə(r)/ *n.* a person who binds books professionally. □□ **bookbinding** *n.*

bookcase /ˈbʊkkeɪs/ *n.* a set of shelves for books in the form of a cabinet.

bookie /ˈbʊkɪ/ *n. colloq.* = BOOKMAKER.

booking /ˈbʊkɪŋ/ *n.* the act or an instance of booking or reserving a seat, a room in a hotel, etc.; a reservation (see BOOK *v.* 1). □ **booking-clerk** an official selling tickets at a railway station. **booking-hall** (or **-office**) *Brit.* a room or area at a railway station in which tickets are sold.

bookish /ˈbʊkɪʃ/ *adj.* 1 studious; fond of reading. 2 acquiring knowledge from books rather than practical experience. 3 (of a word, language, etc.) literary; not colloquial. □□ **bookishly** *adv.* **bookishness** *n.*

bookkeeper /ˈbʊkˌkiːpə(r)/ *n.* a person who keeps accounts for a trader, a public office, etc. □□ **bookkeeping** *n.*

bookland /ˈbʊklænd/ *n. hist.* an area of common land granted by charter to a private owner.

booklet /ˈbʊklɪt/ *n.* a small book consisting of a few sheets usu. with paper covers.

bookmaker /ˈbʊkˌmeɪkə(r)/ *n.* a person who takes bets, esp. on horse-races, calculates odds, and pays out winnings. □□ **bookmaking** *n.*

bookman /ˈbʊkmən/ *n.* (*pl.* **-men**) a literary man, esp. a reviewer.

bookmark /ˈbʊkmɑːk/ *n.* (also **bookmarker**) a strip of leather, card, etc., used to mark one's place in a book.

bookmobile /ˈbʊkməˌbiːl/ *n. US* a mobile library. [after AUTOMOBILE]

Book of Common Prayer the official service book of the Church of England. It was compiled through the desire of Cranmer and others to simplify and condense the Latin service books of the medieval Church and produce in English a simple, convenient, and comprehensive guide for priest and people. It was first issued in 1549 under Edward VI, and its use ordered by Act of Parliament; after revision in the light of Protestant criticism it was reissued in 1552; abolished by the Catholic Queen Mary, reinstated under Elizabeth I (1559), it was again abolished (through Puritan objections), but revised and reissued in 1662, a version which remained almost unchanged until the 20th c.; a revised version was proposed in 1928. Measures of 1965 and 1974 authorized the use also of alternative services that follow forms sanctioned by the Church authorities, in an attempt to meet people's diverse spiritual needs, and the Alternative Service Book (issued in 1980) presents these services (in modern English) in their final form.

bookseller /ˈbʊkˌselə(r)/ *n.* a dealer in books.

bookshop /ˈbʊkʃɒp/ *n.* a shop where books are sold.

bookstall /ˈbʊkstɔːl/ *n.* a stand for selling books, newspapers, etc., esp. out of doors or at a station.

bookstore /ˈbʊkstɔː(r)/ *n. US* = BOOKSHOP.

booksy /ˈbʊksɪ/ *adj. colloq.* having literary or bookish pretensions.

bookwork /ˈbʊkwɜːk/ *n.* the study of books (as opposed to practical work).

bookworm /ˈbʊkwɜːm/ *n.* 1 *colloq.* a person devoted to reading. 2 the larva of a moth or beetle which feeds on the paper and glue used in books.

Boole /buːl/, George (1815–64), English mathematician, entirely self-taught, professor at Cork in Ireland from 1849 until his death. He wrote important works on differential equations and various other branches of mathematics, but is remembered chiefly for his development of an algebraic description of reasoning, now known as Boolean algebra (see below). The branch of mathematics known as mathematical (or symbolic)

logic developed mainly from his ideas. □ **Boolean algebra** a system of algebraic notation to represent logical propositions. **Boolean logic** the use of the logical operators 'and', 'or', and 'not' in retrieving information from a computer database.

boom[1] /buːm/ *n.* & *v.* —*n.* a deep resonant sound. —*v.intr.* make or speak with a boom. [imit.]

boom[2] /buːm/ *n.* & *v.* —*n.* a period of prosperity or sudden activity in commerce. —*v.intr.* (esp. of commercial ventures) be suddenly prosperous or successful. □ **boom town** a town undergoing sudden growth due to a boom. □□ **boomlet** *n.* [19th-c. US word, perhaps f. BOOM[1] (cf. *make things hum*)]

boom[3] /buːm/ *n.* 1 *Naut.* a pivoted spar to which the foot of a sail is attached, allowing the angle of the sail to be changed. 2 a long pole over a film or television set, carrying microphones and other equipment. 3 a floating barrier across the mouth of a harbour or river. [Du., = BEAM *n.*]

boomer /ˈbuːmə(r)/ *n.* 1 a large male kangaroo. 2 a N. American mountain beaver, *Aplodontia rufa.* 3 a large wave.

boomerang /ˈbuːməˌræŋ/ *n.* & *v.* —*n.* 1 a curved flat hardwood missile used by Australian Aborigines to kill prey, and often of a kind able to return in flight to the thrower. 2 a plan or scheme that recoils on its originator. —*v.intr.* 1 act as a boomerang. 2 (of a plan or action) backfire. [Aboriginal name, perh. modified]

boomslang /ˈbuːmslæŋ/ *n.* a large venomous tree-snake, *Dispholidus typus,* native to southern Africa. [Afrik. f. *boom* tree + *slang* snake]

boon[1] /buːn/ *n.* 1 an advantage; a blessing. 2 *archaic* **a** a thing asked for; a request. **b** a gift; a favour. [ME, orig. = prayer, f. ON *bón* f. Gmc]

boon[2] /buːn/ *adj.* close, intimate, favourite (usu. *boon companion*). [ME (orig. = jolly, congenial) f. OF *bon* f. L *bonus* good]

boondock /ˈbuːndɒk/ *n.* (usu. in *pl.*) *US sl.* rough or isolated country. [Tagalog *bundok* mountain]

Boone /buːn/, Daniel (*c.*1735–1820), American pioneer. Moving west from his native Pennsylvania, Boone made trips into the unexplored area of Kentucky from 1767 onwards, organizing settlements and successfully defending them against hostile Indians. He later moved further west to Missouri, being granted land there in 1799. As a hunter, trail-blazer, and fighter against the Indians he became a legend even during his own long life.

boor /bʊə(r)/ *n.* 1 a rude, ill-mannered person. 2 a clumsy person. □□ **boorish** *adj.* **boorishly** *adv.* **boorishness** *n.* [LG *būr* or Du. *boer* farmer: cf. BOWER[3]]

boost /buːst/ *v.* & *n. colloq.* —*v.tr.* 1 **a** promote or increase the reputation of (a person, scheme, commodity, etc.) by praise or advertising; push; increase or assist (*boosted his spirits; boost sales*). **b** push from below; assist (*boosted me up the tree*). 2 **a** raise the voltage in (an electric circuit etc.). **b** amplify (a radio signal). —*n.* 1 an act, process, or result of boosting; a push (*asked for a boost up the hill*). 2 **a** an advertisement campaign. **b** the resulting advance in value, reputation, etc. [19th-c. US word: orig. unkn.]

booster /ˈbuːstə(r)/ *n.* 1 a device for increasing electrical power or voltage. 2 an auxiliary engine or rocket used to give initial acceleration. 3 *Med.* a dose of an immunizing agent increasing or renewing the effect of an earlier one. 4 a person who boosts by helping or encouraging.

boot[1] /buːt/ *n.* & *v.* —*n.* 1 an outer covering for the foot, esp. of leather, reaching above the ankle, often to the knee. 2 *Brit.* the luggage compartment of a motor car, usu. at the rear. 3 *colloq.* a firm kick. 4 (prec. by *the*) *colloq.* dismissal, esp. from employment (*gave them the boot*). 5 a covering to protect the lower part of a horse's leg. 6 *hist.* an instrument of torture encasing and crushing the foot. —*v.tr.* 1 kick, esp. hard. 2 (often foll. by *out*) dismiss (a person) forcefully. 3 (usu. foll. by *up*) put (a computer) in a state of readiness (cf. BOOTSTRAP 2). □ **the boot is on the other foot** (or **leg**) the truth or responsibility is the other way round. **die with one's boots on** (of a soldier etc.) die fighting. **put the boot in 1** kick brutally. **2** act decisively against a person. **you bet your boots**

b *but*   d *dog*   f *few*   g *get*   h *he*   j *yes*   k *cat*   l *leg*   m *man*   n *no*   p *pen*   r *red*   s *sit*   t *top*   v *voice*

sl. it is quite certain. □□ **booted** *adj.* [ME f. ON *bóti* or f. OF *bote*, of unkn. orig.]

boot² /buːt/ *n.* □ **to boot** as well; to the good; in addition. [orig. = 'advantage': OE *bōt* f. Gmc]

bootblack /ˈbuːtblæk/ *n.* US a person who polishes boots and shoes.

bootee /buːˈtiː/ *n.* **1** a soft shoe, esp. a woollen one, worn by a baby. **2** a woman's short boot.

Boötes /bəʊˈəʊtiːz/ the Herdsman, a northern constellation containing Arcturus. [Gk, = ox-driver]

Booth /buːð/, William (1829–1912), founder (assisted by his wife, Catherine Booth, 1829–90) of the Salvation Army. He was for some time a Methodist revivalist preacher, and had a great love for the poor, whose souls he sought to save by his preaching while at the same time ministering to their bodily needs. Though he was ignorant of theology, the strength of his emotions and sympathies, combined with shrewd commercial sense, made the movement one of the most successful religious revivals of modern times.

booth /buːð, buːθ/ *n.* **1** a small temporary roofed structure of canvas, wood, etc., used esp. as a market stall, for puppet shows, etc. **2** an enclosure or compartment for various purposes, e.g. telephoning or voting. **3** a set of a table and benches in a restaurant or bar. [ME f. Scand.]

bootjack /ˈbuːtdʒæk/ *n.* a device for holding a boot by the heel to ease withdrawal of the leg.

bootlace /ˈbuːtleɪs/ *n.* a cord or leather thong for lacing boots.

bootleg /ˈbuːtleg/ *adj.* & *v.* —*adj.* (esp. of liquor) smuggled; illicitly sold. —*v.tr.* (**-legged, -legging**) make, distribute, or smuggle (illicit goods, esp. alcohol). □□ **bootlegger** *n.* [f. the smugglers' practice of concealing bottles in their boots]

bootless /ˈbuːtlɪs/ *adj. archaic* unavailing, useless. [OE *bōtlēas* (as BOOT², LESS)]

bootlicker /ˈbuːtˌlɪkə(r)/ *n. colloq.* a person who behaves obsequiously or servilely; a toady.

boots /buːts/ *n. Brit.* a hotel servant who cleans boots and shoes, carries luggage, etc.

bootstrap /ˈbuːtstræp/ *n.* **1** a loop at the back of a boot used to pull it on. **2** *Computing* a technique of loading a program into a computer by means of a few initial instructions which enable the introduction of the rest of the program from an input device. □ **pull oneself up by one's bootstraps** better oneself by one's own efforts.

booty /ˈbuːtɪ/ *n.* **1** plunder gained esp. in war or by piracy. **2** *colloq.* something gained or won. [ME f. MLG *būte, buite* exchange, of uncert. orig.]

booze /buːz/ *n.* & *v. colloq.* —*n.* **1** alcoholic drink. **2** the drinking of this (*on the booze*). —*v.intr.* drink alcoholic liquor, esp. excessively or habitually. □ **booze-up** *sl.* a drinking bout. [earlier *bouse, bowse,* f. MDu. *būsen* drink to excess]

boozer /ˈbuːzə(r)/ *n. colloq.* **1** a person who drinks alcohol, esp. to excess. **2** *Brit.* a public house.

boozy /ˈbuːzɪ/ *adj.* (**boozier, booziest**) *colloq.* intoxicated; addicted to drink. □□ **boozily** *adv.* **booziness** *n.*

bop¹ /bɒp/ *n.* & *v. colloq.* —*n.* **1** = BEBOP. **2 a** a spell of dancing, esp. to pop music. **b** an organized social occasion for this. —*v.intr.* (**bopped, bopping**) dance, esp. to pop music. □□ **bopper** *n.* [abbr. of BEBOP]

bop² /bɒp/ *v.* & *n. colloq.* —*v.tr.* (**bopped, bopping**) hit, punch lightly. —*n.* a light blow or hit. [imit.]

bo-peep /bəʊˈpiːp/ *n.* a game of hiding and suddenly reappearing, played with a young child. [BO¹ + PEEP¹]

Bophuthatswana /bəʊˌpuːtəˈtswɑːnə/ the tribal homeland of the Tswana people of South Africa, designated an independent republic in 1977 and comprising six separate territories; pop. (1985) 1,600,000; capital, Mmabatho.

bora¹ /ˈbɔːrə/ *n.* a strong cold dry NE wind blowing in the upper Adriatic. [It. dial. f. L *boreas* north wind: see BOREAL]

bora² /ˈbɔːrə/ *n. Austral.* an Aboriginal rite in which boys are initiated into manhood. [Aboriginal]

Bora-Bora /ˌbɔːrəˈbɔːrə/ an island in the Leeward group of the Society Islands in French Polynesia.

boracic /bəˈræsɪk/ *adj.* of borax; containing boron. □ **boracic acid** = boric acid. [med.L *borax -acis*]

borage /ˈbɒrɪdʒ/ *n.* any plant of the genus *Borago*, esp. *Borago officinalis* with bright blue flowers and leaves used as flavouring. [OF *bourrache* f. med.L *borrago* f. Arab. *'abu 'āraḳ* father of sweat (from its use as a diaphoretic)]

borak /ˈbɒræk/ *n. Austral.* & *NZ sl.* banter, ridicule. [Aboriginal Austral.]

borane /ˈbɔːreɪn/ *n. Chem.* any hydride of boron.

Borås /bʊˈrɔːs/ an industrial city in SW Sweden, founded in 1632 by Gustavus Adolphus; pop. (1987) 101,000.

borate /ˈbɔːreɪt/ *n.* a salt or ester of boric acid.

borax /ˈbɔːræks/ *n.* **1** the mineral salt sodium borate, occurring in alkaline deposits as an efflorescence or as crystals. **2** the purified form of this salt, used in making glass and china, and as an antiseptic. [ME f. OF *boras* f. med.L *borax* f. Arab. *būraḳ* f. Pers. *būrah*]

borazon /ˈbɔːrəˌzɒn/ *n.* a hard form of boron nitride, resistant to oxidation. [BORON + AZO- nitrogen + *-on*]

borborygmus /ˌbɔːbəˈrɪgməs/ *n.* (*pl.* **borborygmi** /-maɪ/) a rumbling of gas in the intestines. □□ **borborygmic** *adj.* [mod.L f. Gk]

Bordeaux /bɔːˈdəʊ/ an inland port on the River Garonne in SW France; pop. (1982) 211,200. —*n.* (*pl.* same /-ˈdəʊz/) any of various red, white, or rosé wines from the district of Bordeaux. □ **Bordeaux mixture** a fungicide for vines, fruit-trees, etc., composed of equal quantities of copper sulphate and calcium oxide in water.

bordello /bɔːˈdeləʊ/ *n.* (*pl.* **-os**) esp. US a brothel. [ME (f. It. *bordello*) f. OF *bordel* small farm, dimin. of *borde* ult. f. Frank.: see BOARD]

border /ˈbɔːdə(r)/ *n.* & *v.* —*n.* **1** the edge or boundary of anything, or the part near it. **2 a** the line separating two political or geographical areas, esp. countries. **b** the district on each side of this. **c** (**the Border**) a particular boundary and its adjoining districts, esp. between Scotland and England (usu. **the Borders**), or N. Ireland and the Irish Republic. **3** a distinct edging round anything, esp. for strength or decoration. **4** a long narrow bed of flowers or shrubs in a garden (*herbaceous border*). —*v.* **1** *tr.* be a border to. **2** *tr.* provide with a border. **3** *intr.* (usu. foll. by *on, upon*) **a** adjoin; come close to being. **b** approximate, resemble. □ **Border collie** a common working sheepdog of the North Country. **Border terrier 1** a small terrier of a breed with rough hair. **2** this breed. [ME f. OF *bordure*: cf. BOARD]

borderer /ˈbɔːdərə(r)/ *n.* a person who lives near a border, esp. that between Scotland and England.

borderland /ˈbɔːdəˌlænd/ *n.* **1** the district near a border. **2** an intermediate condition between two extremes. **3** an area for debate.

borderline /ˈbɔːdəˌlaɪn/ *n.* & *adj.* —*n.* **1** the line dividing two (often extreme) conditions. **2** a line marking a boundary. —*adj.* **1** on the borderline. **2** verging on an extreme condition; only just acceptable.

Borders /ˈbɔːdəz/ a local government region in southern Scotland; pop. (1981) 102,100; capital, Newtown St Boswells.

Bordone /bɔːˈdəʊnɪ/, Paris (1500–71), Venetian painter whose reputation in his own day rivalled that of Titian, under whom he may have studied. His chiaroscuro and rich colouring were highly praised and his popularity brought him commissions from all over Europe, but his works were too conventional and unoriginal for lasting fame.

bordure /ˈbɔːdjʊə(r)/ *n. Heraldry* a border round the edge of a shield. [ME form of BORDER]

bore¹ /bɔː(r)/ *v.* & *n.* —*v.* **1** *tr.* make a hole in, esp. with a revolving tool. **2** *tr.* hollow out (a tube etc.). **3** *tr.* **a** make (a hole) by boring or excavation. **b** make (one's way) through a crowd etc. **4** *intr.* (of an athlete, racehorse, etc.) push another competitor out of the way. **5** *intr.* drill a well (for oil etc.).

—*n.* **1** the hollow of a firearm barrel or of a cylinder in an internal-combustion engine. **2** the diameter of this; the calibre. **3** = BOREHOLE. [OE *borian* f. Gmc]

bore[2] /bɔː(r)/ *n.* & *v.* —*n.* a tiresome or dull person or thing. —*v.tr.* weary by tedious talk or dullness. □ **bore a person to tears** weary (a person) in the extreme. [18th c.: orig. unkn.]

bore[3] /bɔː(r)/ *n.* a high tidal wave rushing up a narrow estuary. Also called EAGRE. [ME, perh. f. ON *bára* wave]

bore[4] *past of* BEAR[1].

boreal /ˈbɔːrɪəl/ *adj.* **1** of the North or northern regions. **2** of the north wind. [ME f. F *boréal* or LL *borealis* f. L *Boreas* f. Gk *Boreas* god of the north wind]

boredom /ˈbɔːdəm/ *n.* the state of being bored; ennui.

borehole /ˈbɔːhəʊl/ *n.* **1** a deep narrow hole, esp. one made in the earth to find water, oil, etc. **2** *Austral.* a water-hole for cattle.

borer /ˈbɔːrə(r)/ *n.* **1** any of several worms, molluscs, insects, or insect larvae which bore into wood, other plant material, and rock. **2** a tool for boring.

Borg /bɔg/, Bjorn (1956–), Swedish tennis-player, who in 1980 won the men's singles championship at Wimbledon for the fifth year in succession, beating the record of three consecutive wins held by Fred Perry.

Borges /ˈbɔːxes/, Jorge Luis (1899–1986), Argentinian writer, whose international reputation was established by the publication of *Labyrinths*, a collection of stories, in Paris in 1953. His stories tend to be labyrinthine in form, metaphysical in speculation, and dreamlike.

boric /ˈbɔːrɪk/ *adj.* of or containing boron. □ **boric acid** an acid derived from borax, used as a mild antiseptic and in the manufacture of heat-resistant glass and enamels.

boring /ˈbɔːrɪŋ/ *adj.* that makes one bored; uninteresting, tedious, dull. □□ **boringly** *adv.* **boringness** *n.*

Born /bɔːn/, Max (1882–1970), German theoretical physicist, one of the founders of quantum mechanics. In 1921 he was appointed professor of theoretical physics at Göttingen, where he established a powerful group of theoreticians, but in 1933, being a Jew, he had to flee the Nazi regime and settled in Britain. After retirement from the chair of natural philosophy at Edinburgh University he returned to Göttingen to write mainly on the philosophy of physics and the social responsibility of scientists. He provided a link between wave mechanics and quantum theory by postulating a probabilistic interpretation of Schrödinger's wave equation, for which he was awarded the Nobel Prize for physics in 1954. He wrote extremely popular textbooks on optics and atomic physics.

born /bɔːn/ *adj.* **1** existing as a result of birth. **2 a** being such or likely to become such by natural ability or quality (*a born leader*). **b** (usu. foll. by *to* + infin.) having a specified destiny or prospect (*born lucky*; *born to be king*; *born to lead men*). **3** (in *comb.*) of a certain status by birth (*French-born*; *well-born*). □ **born-again** (*attrib.*) converted (esp. to fundamentalist Christianity). **born and bred** by birth and upbringing. **in all one's born days** *colloq.* in one's life so far. **not born yesterday** *colloq.* not stupid; shrewd. [past part. of BEAR[1]]

borne /bɔːn/ **1** *past part. of* BEAR[1]. **2** (in *comb.*) carried or transported by (*airborne*).

borné /ˈbɔːneɪ/ *adj.* **1** narrow-minded; of limited ideas. **2** having limitations. [F]

Borneo /ˈbɔːnɪˌəʊ/ a large island of the Malay Archipelago, comprising Kalimantan (a region of Indonesia), Sabah and Sarawak (now parts of Malaysia), and Brunei. □□ **Bornean** *adj.*

Bornholm /ˈbɔːnhəʊm/ a Danish island in the Baltic Sea; pop. (1988) 46,600. □ **Bornholm's disease** a viral infection with fever and pain in the muscles of the ribs. [*Bornholm* in Denmark]

boro- /ˈbɔːrəʊ/ *comb. form* indicating salts containing boron.

Borobudur /ˌbɔːrəʊbʊˈdʊ(r)/ a Buddhist monument in central Java, built *c.*800, abandoned *c.*1000, restored in 1907–11 and again in the 1980s. Designed for the purpose of worship,

veneration, and meditation, it consists of five square successively smaller terraces, one above the other, surmounted by three concentric galleries with open stupas culminating in a supreme closed stupa. Each of the square terraces is enclosed by a high wall; bas-reliefs on its vertical surfaces depict, in a continuous series, the life of the Buddha and successive stages towards perfection.

Borodin /ˈbɒrədɪn/, Alexander (1833–87), Russian composer (illegitimate son of a Russian prince), one of the group known as 'The Five' or 'The Mighty Handful' (the others were Balakirev, Musorgsky, Rimsky-Korsakov, and Cui). He earned his living as a scientist, but showed early musical talent. He composed symphonies, string quartets, songs, and piano music, but is best known for the epic opera *Prince Igor* (completed after his death by Rimsky-Korsakov and Glazunov).

boron /ˈbɔːrɒn/ *n. Chem.* a non-metallic yellow crystalline or brown amorphous element extracted from borax and boracic acid. The element, which is not found in the free state in nature, was first isolated by Sir Humphrey Davy in 1807. Boron and its compounds have a wide variety of specialized industrial uses, and trace amounts of it are essential to the growth of plants. ¶ Symb.: B; atomic number 5. [BORAX + -*on* f. *carbon* (which it resembles in some respects)]

boronia /bəˈrəʊnɪə/ *n. Austral.* any sweet-scented shrub of the genus *Boronia*. [F. *Borone*, It. botanist d. 1794]

borosilicate /ˌbɔːrəʊˈsɪlɪˌkeɪt/ *n.* any of many substances containing boron, silicon, and oxygen generally used in glazes and enamels and in the production of glass.

borough /ˈbʌrə/ *n.* **1** **a** a town represented in the House of Commons. **b** a town or district granted the status of a borough. **2** *Brit. hist.* a town with a municipal corporation and privileges conferred by a royal charter. **3** *US* a municipal corporation in certain States. **4** *US* each of five divisions of New York City. **5** *US* (in Alaska) a division corresponding to a county. [OE *burg, burh* f. Gmc: cf. BURGH] □ **pocket borough** *Brit. hist.* a borough where elections were controlled by a wealthy private person or family. **rotten borough** (in the 19th c.) a borough that was still represented by an MP although the population had become severely reduced in numbers. The choice of MP was often in the hands of one person or family. Such boroughs were abolished by the Reform Act of 1832.

Borovets /ˈbɒrəvets/ a ski resort in the Rila Mountains of western Bulgaria.

Borromini /ˌbɒrəˈmiːnɪ/, Francesco (1599–1667), Italian architect, one of the leading figures of Roman baroque. His style, at once passionate and mathematical, using subtle architectural forms but austere methods of decoration, was of tremendous importance in the development of the baroque in Italy, and even more in Austria and South Germany; it was repeatedly denounced in the 18th–19th c. Arriving at Rome in 1614, he worked as a mason at St Peter's, and on the Palazzo Barberini with Maderna and Bernini. Always neurotic, he committed suicide in a fit of melancholia.

Borrow /ˈbɒrəʊ/, George (1803–81), English writer whose travels in England, Europe, Russia, and the East provided material, inextricably combined with fiction, for his picaresque narrative *Lavengro* (1851) in which he meets gypsies, tinkers, and murderers and describes much of his comparative study of the languages of the countries he visits. He continues his adventures in *The Romany Rye* (1857), and *The Bible in Spain* (1843) gives a vivid account of a country racked by civil war during the author's travels as a distributor of Bibles.

borrow /ˈbɒrəʊ/ *v.* **1 a** *tr.* acquire temporarily with the promise or intention of returning. **b** *intr.* obtain money in this way. **2** *tr.* use (an idea, invention, etc.) originated by another; plagiarize. **3** *intr. Golf* **a** play the ball uphill so that it rolls back towards the hole. **b** allow for the wind or a slope. □ **borrowed time** an unexpected extension esp. of life. □□ **borrower** *n.* **borrowing** *n.* [OE *borgian* give a pledge]

borsch *var. of* BORTSCH.

Borstal /ˈbɔːst(ə)l/ *n. Brit. hist.* an institution for reforming and training young offenders. ¶ Now replaced by *detention centre* and *youth custody centre*. [*Borstal* in S. England, where the first of these was established in 1901]

bort /bɔːt/ *n.* (also **boart**) **1** an inferior or malformed diamond, used for cutting. **2** fragments of diamonds produced in cutting. [Du. *boort*]

bortsch /bɔːtʃ/ *n.* (also **borsch** /bɔːʃ/) a highly seasoned Russian or Polish soup with various ingredients including beetroot and cabbage and served with sour cream. [Russ. *borshch*]

borzoi /ˈbɔːzɔɪ/ *n.* **1** a large Russian wolfhound of a breed with a narrow head and silky, usu. white, coat. **2** this breed. [Russ. f. *borzyi* swift]

Bosanquet /ˈbəʊsənˌket/, Bernard James Tindall (1877–1936), English all-round cricketer, who played for Middlesex and for England and devised the style of bowling which became generally known as a 'googly' but in Australia was named after the inventor and called a 'bosie'.

boscage /ˈbɒskɪdʒ/ *n.* (also **boskage**) **1** masses of trees or shrubs. **2** wooded scenery. [ME f. OF *boscage* f. Gmc: cf. BUSH¹]

Bosch /bɒʃ/, Hieronymus (c.1450–1516), Dutch painter who took his name from his birthplace ('s Hertogenbosch), a strangely individual figure whose style has little in common with the mainstream of painting in the Low Countries. His works are characterized by creatures of fantasy, half-human half-animal, and demons, interspersed with human figures in a setting of imaginary architecture and landscape; his basic themes show an innocent central figure (Christ or a saint) besieged by horrific representations of evil and temptation, or stress in morbid vein the fearful consequences of human sin and folly. His turbulent and grotesque fantasy has appealed to modern taste and caused the surrealists to claim him as the forerunner of their school.

bosh /bɒʃ/ *n. & int. sl.* nonsense; foolish talk. [Turk. *boş* empty]

Boskop /ˈbɒskɒp/ a town in the Transvaal, South Africa, where a skull dome was found in 1913. The fossil itself is undated and morphologically shows no primitive features. At the time of discovery, this find became the type-fossil of a distinct 'Boskop race' but is now thought to be related to the Bushman-Hottentot types.

bosky /ˈbɒskɪ/ *adj.* (**boskier, boskiest**) *literary* wooded, bushy. [ME *bosk* thicket]

bo's'n var. of BOATSWAIN.

Bosnia and Hercegovina /ˈbɒznɪə, ˌhɜːtsɪɡəˈviːnə/ a constituent republic of Yugoslavia; pop. (1981) 4,124,250; capital, Sarajevo. □ **Bosnian** *adj & n.*

bosom /ˈbʊz(ə)m/ *n.* **1 a** a person's breast or chest, esp. a woman's. **b** *colloq.* each of a woman's breasts. **c** the enclosure formed by a person's breast and arms. **2** an emotional centre, esp. as the source of an enfolding relationship (*in the bosom of one's family*). **3** the part of a woman's dress covering the breast. □ **bosom friend** a very close or intimate friend. [OE *bōsm* f. Gmc]

bosomy /ˈbʊzəmɪ/ *adj.* (of a woman) having large breasts.

boson /ˈbəʊzɒn/ *n. Physics* any of several elementary particles obeying the relations stated by Bose and Einstein, with a zero or integral spin, e.g. photons (cf. FERMION). [S. N. Bose, Ind. physicist d. 1974]

Bosporus /ˈbɒspərəs/ (also **Bosphorus** /-fərəs/) a strait connecting the Black Sea and the Sea of Marmara, with Istanbul at its south end. It separates Europe from Asia Minor, and is spanned by two long suspension bridges. [Gk *bos* ox + *poros* passage, crossing; the name is linked with the story of Io (see entry) crossing it in escaping from Zeus]

BOSS /bɒs/ *n.* the Bureau of State Security, the former South African intelligence and security organization. It was replaced by the National Intelligence Service after evidence of corruption was revealed in 1978. Its activities against opponents of apartheid had caused much resentment in the countries where it operated. [abbr.]

boss¹ /bɒs/ *n. & v. colloq.* —*n.* **1** a person in charge; an employer, manager, or overseer. **2** *US* a person who controls or dominates a political organization. —*v.tr.* **1** (usu. foll. by *about, around*) treat domineeringly; give constant peremptory orders to. **2** be the master or manager of. [orig. US: f. Du. *baas* master]

boss² /bɒs/ *n.* **1** a round knob, stud, or other protuberance, esp. on the centre of a shield or in ornamental work. **2** *Archit.* a piece of ornamental carving etc. covering the point where the ribs in a vault or ceiling cross. **3** *Geol.* a large mass of igneous rock. **4** *Mech.* an enlarged part of a shaft. [ME f. OF *boce* f. Rmc]

bossa nova /ˌbɒsə ˈnəʊvə/ *n.* **1** a dance like the samba, originating in Brazil. **2** a piece of music for this or in its rhythm. [Port., = new flair]

boss-eyed /ˈbɒsaɪd/ *adj. Brit. colloq.* **1** having only one good eye; cross-eyed. **2** crooked; out of true. [dial. *boss* miss, bungle]

boss-shot /ˈbɒsʃɒt/ *n. Brit. dial. & sl.* **1** a bad shot or aim. **2** an unsuccessful attempt. [as BOSS-EYED]

bossy /ˈbɒsɪ/ *adj.* (**bossier, bossiest**) *colloq.* domineering; tending to boss. □ **bossy-boots** *colloq.* a domineering person. □□ **bossily** *adv.* **bossiness** *n.*

Boston /ˈbɒst(ə)n/ the capital city and a seaport of Massachusetts; pop. (1982) 560,847. It was founded c.1630 and named after Boston in Lincolnshire ('St Botulph's town'), which has associations with the Pilgrim Fathers. □ **Boston tea-party** a violent demonstration by American colonists who in 1773 boarded vessels moored in the harbour of Boston, Massachusetts, dressed as Red Indians, and threw the cargoes of tea into the water in protest at the imposition of a tax on tea by the British Parliament, in which the colonists had no representation. It occasioned the general revolt of the American colonies and the War of American Independence.

bosun (also **bo'sun**) var. of BOATSWAIN.

Boswell /ˈbɒzwəl/, James (1740–95), Scottish author and biographer. After travelling through Europe, where he met Rousseau and Voltaire, he practised law in England and Scotland, though his ambitions were directed towards literature and politics. A visit to Corsica in 1765 inspired him with zeal for the cause of Corsican liberty and resulted in his first substantial work, *An Account of Corsica* (1768). He first met Samuel Johnson in London (1762–3) and Boswell's *Journal of a Tour to the Hebrides* (1785) describes their travels together in 1773. The rest of his life was devoted to an unsuccessful pursuit of a political career and to assembling material for the most celebrated biography in the English language, *The Life of Samuel Johnson* (1791), which gives a vivid and intimate portrait of Johnson and an invaluable panorama of the age and its personalities, presented with the curious mix of naïve enthusiasm and sad worldliness that is the essential Boswell.

Bosworth Field /ˈbɒzwəθ/ the scene, near Market Bosworth in Leicestershire, of a battle (1485) in the Wars of the Roses, at which Henry Tudor defeated the Yorkist king Richard III, who died there. The battle is generally considered to mark the end of the Wars of the Roses, but Henry, crowned soon afterwards as Henry VII, was not really secure until a last Yorkist challenge was crushed at the battle of Stoke two years later.

bot /bɒt/ *n.* (also **bott**) any of various parasitic larvae of flies of the family Oestridae, infesting horses, sheep, etc. □ **bot-fly** (*pl.* **-flies**) any dipterous fly of the genus *Oestrus*, with stout hairy bodies. [prob. of LG orig.]

bot. *abbr.* **1** bottle. **2** botanic; botanical; botany. **3** bought.

botanize /ˈbɒtəˌnaɪz/ *v.intr.* (also **-ise**) study plants, esp. in their habitat.

Botany /ˈbɒtənɪ/ *n.* (in full **Botany wool**) merino wool, esp. from Australia. [BOTANY BAY]

botany /ˈbɒtənɪ/ *n.* **1** the study of the physiology, structure, genetics, ecology, distribution, classification, and economic importance of plants. (See below.) **2** the plant life of a particular area or time. □□ **botanic** /bəˈtænɪk/ *adj.* **botanical** /bəˈtænɪk(ə)l/ *adj.* **botanically** /bəˈtænɪkəlɪ/ *adv.* **botanist** *n.* [*botanic* f. F *botanique* or LL *botanicus* f. Gk *botanikos* f. *botanē* plant]

The study of plants has a long history: Theophrastus (c.300 BC) wrote about their form and function, and they remained of interest thereafter, especially because of their medicinal properties. John Ray (1627–1705) produced the first systematic account of English flora, and by the mid-18th c. Linnaeus had devised a systematic method of naming and classifying plants which is still used (though modified) today. Study of plant anatomy developed in the 17th c., and of plant physiology a century later, with important advances such as the discovery of photosynthesis. In the 20th c. botanical studies have contributed much to the development of agriculture and horticulture with discoveries such as plant hormones (widely used to accelerate or delay growth and the fruiting of crop plants), systematic breeding techniques, and advances in the understanding of plant biology and pathology.

Botany Bay a bay near Sydney, New South Wales, Australia, which was the site of Captain Cook's landing in 1770 and of an early penal settlement. Its name refers to the variety of its flora.

botch /bɒtʃ/ v. & n. (also **bodge**) —v.tr. **1** bungle; do badly. **2** patch or repair clumsily. —n. **1** bungled or spoilt work (made a botch of it). □□ **botcher** n. [ME: orig. unkn.]

botel /bəʊˈtel/ n. (also **boatel**) a waterside hotel with facilities for mooring boats. [blend of BOAT and HOTEL]

both /bəʊθ/ adj., pron., & adv. —adj. & pron. the two, not only one (both boys; both the boys; both of the boys; the boys are both here). ¶ Widely used with of, esp. when followed by a pronoun (e.g. both of us) or a noun implying separate rather than collective consideration, e.g. both of the boys suggests each boy rather than the two together. —adv. with equal truth in two cases (both the boy and his sister are here; are both here and hungry). □ **both ways** = each way. **have it both ways** alternate between two incompatible points of view to suit the needs of the moment. [ME f. ON báthir]

Botha /ˈbəʊtə/, Louis (1862–1919), South African soldier and statesman. One of the most successful Boer leaders in the Boer War, Botha became commander-in-chief in 1900 and waged guerrilla warfare against the more numerous British forces until the war ended. In 1910 he became the first President of the Union of South Africa, holding the post until his death.

Botham /ˈbəʊθəm/, Ian Terence (1955–   ), English all-round cricketer, who played in county and international matches from 1974 onwards in a highly successful but often controversial career and holds the record for the best all-round career in test-match cricket. He also played Football League soccer for Scunthorpe United.

bother /ˈbɒðə(r)/ v., n., & int. —v. **1** tr. **a** give trouble to; worry, disturb. **b** refl. (often foll. by about) be anxious or concerned. **2** intr. **a** (often foll. by about, or to + infin.) worry or trouble oneself (don't bother about that; didn't bother to tell me). **b** (foll. by with) be concerned. —n. **1 a** a person or thing that bothers or causes worry. **b** a minor nuisance. **2** trouble, worry, fuss. —int. esp. Brit. expressing annoyance or impatience. □ **cannot be bothered** will not make the effort needed. [Ir. bodhraim deafen]

botheration /ˌbɒðəˈreɪʃ(ə)n/ n. & int. colloq. = BOTHER n., int.

bothersome /ˈbɒðəsəm/ adj. causing bother; troublesome.

Bothnia /ˈbɒθnɪə/, **Gulf of** a northern arm of the Baltic Sea, between Sweden and Finland.

Bothwell /ˈbɒθwel/, James Hepburn, 4th Earl of (c.1536–78), third husband of Mary Queen of Scots. He was implicated in the murder of Darnley.

bothy /ˈbɒθɪ/ n. (also **bothie**) (pl. **-ies**) Sc. a small hut or cottage, esp. one for housing labourers. [18th c.: orig. unkn.: perh. rel. to BOOTH]

bo-tree /ˈbəʊtriː/ n. the Indian fig-tree, Ficus religiosa, regarded as sacred by Buddhists. Also called PIPAL or PEEPUL. [repr. Sinh. bogaha tree of knowledge (Buddha's enlightenment having occurred beneath such a tree)]

Botswana /bɒtˈswɑːnə/ an inland country of southern Africa, a member State of the Commonwealth; pop. (est. 1988) 1,211,800; official language, English; capital, Gaborone. The area was made the British Protectorate of Bechuanaland in 1885. In 1966 it became a republic within the Commonwealth

under the presidency of Sir Seretse Khama. Cattle-raising is the chief industry, though minerals (including diamonds, copper, nickel, and coal) were discovered in the 1960s and are becoming increasingly important as exports.

bott var. of BOT.

Botticelli /ˌbɒtɪˈtʃelɪ/, Alessandro di Mariano Filipepi (1445–1510), called Sandro, Florentine painter. A pupil of Filippo Lippi, he had his own studio by 1470 and enjoyed the patronage of the Medici from 1475. His mythological paintings such as Primavera (c.1478) and The Birth of Venus (c.1480) show the influence of Neoplatonic philosophy derived from Lorenzo de' Medici's circle. The preaching of Savonarola in the 1490s is said by Vasari to have altered the course of his art, which became increasingly ecstatic, intense, and mannered (e.g. in Mystic Nativity, 1500). During his lifetime his reputation was apparently restricted to a small circle and he died in obscurity. His fame was resurrected in the second half of the 19th c., when the Pre-Raphaelites imitated his wan elongated figures, Ruskin sang his praises, and Walter Pater wrote eloquently of him.

bottle /ˈbɒt(ə)l/ n. & v. —n. **1** a container, usu. of glass or plastic and with a narrow neck, for storing liquid. **2** the amount that will fill a bottle. **3** a baby's feeding-bottle. **4** = hot-water bottle. **5** a metal cylinder for liquefied gas. **6** Brit. sl. courage, confidence. —v.tr. **1** put into bottles or jars. **2** preserve (fruit etc.) in jars. **3** (foll. by up) **a** conceal or restrain for a time (esp. a feeling). **b** keep (an enemy force etc.) contained or entrapped. **4** (as **bottled** adj.) sl. drunk. □ **bottle bank** a place where used bottles may be deposited for recycling. **bottle-brush 1** a cylindrical brush for cleaning inside bottles. **2** any of various plants with a flower of this shape. **bottle-green** a dark shade of green. **bottle party** a party to which guests bring bottles of drink. **bottle tree** any of various Australian trees of the genus Brachychiton with a swollen bottle-shaped trunk. **hit the bottle** sl. drink heavily. **on the bottle** sl. drinking (alcoholic drink) heavily. □□ **bottleful** n. (pl. **-fuls**). [ME f. OF botele, botaille f. med.L butticula dimin. of LL buttis BUTT⁴]

bottle-feed /ˈbɒt(ə)lˌfiːd/ v.tr. (past and past part. **-fed**) feed (a baby) with milk by means of a bottle.

bottleneck /ˈbɒt(ə)lˌnek/ n. **1** a point at which the flow of traffic, production, etc., is constricted. **2** a narrow place causing constriction.

bottlenose /ˈbɒt(ə)lˌnəʊz/ n. (also **bottlenosed**) a swollen nose. □ **bottlenose dolphin** a dolphin, Tursiops truncatus, with a bottle-shaped snout.

bottler /ˈbɒtlə(r)/ n. **1** a person who bottles drinks etc. **2** Austral. & NZ sl. an excellent person or thing.

bottom /ˈbɒtəm/ n., adj., & v. —n. **1 a** the lowest point or part (bottom of the stairs). **b** the part on which a thing rests (bottom of a saucepan). **c** the underneath part (scraped the bottom of the car). **d** the furthest or inmost part (bottom of the garden). **2** colloq. **a** the buttocks. **b** the seat of a chair etc. **3 a** the less honourable, important, or successful end of a table, a class, etc. (at the bottom of the list of requirements). **b** a person occupying this place (he's always bottom of the class). **4** the ground under the water of a lake, a river, etc. (swam until he touched the bottom). **5** the basis; the origin (he's at the bottom of it). **6** the essential character; reality. **7** Naut. **a** the keel or hull of a ship. **b** a ship, esp. as a cargo-carrier. **8** staying power; endurance. —adj. **1** lowest (bottom button). **2** last (got the bottom score). —v. **1** tr. put a bottom to (a chair, saucepan, etc.). **2** intr. (of a ship) reach or touch the bottom. **3** tr. find the extent or real nature of; work out. **4** tr. (usu. foll. by on) base (an argument etc.) (reasoning bottomed on logic). **5** tr. touch the bottom or lowest point of. □ **at bottom** basically, essentially. **be at the bottom of** have caused. **bet one's bottom dollar** sl. stake all. **bottom dog** = UNDERDOG. **bottom drawer** Brit. linen etc. stored by a woman in preparation for her marriage. **bottom falls out** collapse occurs. **bottom gear** see GEAR. **bottom line** colloq. the underlying or ultimate truth; the ultimate, esp. financial, criterion. **bottom out** reach the lowest level. **bottoms up!** a call to drain one's glass. **bottom up** upside-down. **get to the**

bottom of fully investigate and explain. **knock the bottom out of** prove (a thing) worthless. □□ **bottommost** /ˈbɒtəmˌməʊst/ adj. [OE botm f. Gmc]

bottomless /ˈbɒtəmlɪs/ adj. **1** without a bottom. **2** (of a supply etc.) inexhaustible.

bottomry /ˈbɒtəmrɪ/ n. & v. Naut. —n. a system of using a ship as security against a loan to finance a voyage, the lender losing his or her money if the ship sinks. —v.tr. (**-ies, -ied**) pledge (a ship) in this way. [BOTTOM = ship + -RY, after Du. bodemerij]

botulism /ˈbɒtjʊˌlɪz(ə)m/ n. poisoning caused by a toxin produced by the bacillus Clostridium botulinum growing in poorly preserved food. [G Botulismus f. L botulus sausage]

Boucher /ˈbuːʃeɪ/, François (1703–70), French painter and decorative artist whose elegant, often frivolous, works sum up the spirit of the rococo style in France. As protégé of Mme de Pompadour and her brother the Marquis de Marigny, Boucher enjoyed both royal and aristocratic patronage; in 1755 he was appointed director of the Gobelins tapestry factory and, in 1765, King's Painter. In the spirit of Watteau, Boucher displayed little interest in the grand manner, preferring to paint light-hearted mythological subjects and scènes galantes. His art reflected the elegant social life of the period, his output ranging from large decorative paintings, popular engravings, tapestry design, and décors for the opera, to minor commissions such as the painting of fans and slippers. Boucher's artificial, rather frivolous subject-matter was by no means universally admired, incurring for example the disapproval of Diderot, who found his work lacking in la vérité.

Boucher de Perthes /ˈbuːʃeɪ də ˈpɛrt/, Jacques (1788–1868), French antiquarian who produced some of the first evidence of man-made stone tools in association with the bones of extinct (Pleistocene) animals from the valley of the River Somme in northern France. In the decade following 1837 he argued that these tools (and their makers) belonged to a remote pre-Celtic 'antediluvian' age, but it was not until the 1850s, when geologists supported his claims, that his findings were accepted.

bouclé /ˈbuːkleɪ/ n. **1** a looped or curled yarn (esp. wool). **2** a fabric, esp. knitted, made of this. [F, = buckled, curled]

Boudicca /ˈbuːdɪkə/ (pop. **Boadicea**, d. AD 62) a queen of the ancient Britons, ruler of the Iceni tribe in eastern England. When imperial agents maltreated her family after the death of her husband in AD 60, Boudicca led her forces in revolt against the Romans and sacked Colchester, St Albans, and London before being completely defeated by the Roman governor Paulinus. Boudicca committed suicide soon after her defeat, but her name became a symbol of native resistance to the Roman occupation.

boudoir /ˈbuːdwɑː(r)/ n. a woman's small private room or bedroom. [F, lit. sulking-place f. bouder sulk]

bouffant /ˈbuːfɑ̃/ adj. (of a dress, hair, etc.) puffed out. [F]

bougainvillaea /ˌbuːɡənˈvɪlɪə/ n. any tropical widely cultivated plant of the genus Bougainvillaea, with large coloured bracts (usu. purple, red, or white) almost concealing the inconspicuous flowers. [L. A. de BOUGAINVILLE[2]]

Bougainville[1] /ˈbuːɡənˌvɪl/ a volcanic island, the largest of the Solomon Islands. It is named after a French explorer (see BOUGAINVILLE[2]).

Bougainville[2] /ˈbuːɡənvɪl/, Louis Antoine de (1729–1811), French explorer. After a distinguished early military career, most notably as aide-de-camp to Montcalm during the unsuccessful defence of French Canada in 1759, Bougainville joined the French Navy and between 1766 and 1769 led the first successful French circumnavigation of the globe, visiting many of the islands of the South Pacific and compiling an invaluable scientific record of his findings. Afterwards he served in the War of American Independence before retiring to devote himself to science. The largest of the Solomon Islands is named after him.

bough /baʊ/ n. a branch of a tree, esp. a main one. [OE bōg, bōh f. Gmc]

bought past and past part. of BUY.

boughten /ˈbɔːt(ə)n/ adj. US or dial. bought at a shop, not home-made. [var. of past part. of BUY]

bougie /ˈbuːʒiː/ n. **1** Med. a thin flexible surgical instrument for exploring, dilating, etc. the passages of the body. **2** a wax candle. [F f. Arab. Bujiya Algerian town with a wax trade]

bouillabaisse /ˌbuːjəˈbes/ n. Cookery a rich, spicy fish-stew, orig. from Provence. [F]

bouilli /buːˈjiː/ n. Cookery stewed or boiled meat. [F, = boiled]

bouillon /ˈbuːjɔ̃, ˈbuːjɒn/ n. thin soup; broth. [F f. bouillir to boil]

boulder /ˈbəʊldə(r)/ n. a large stone worn smooth by erosion. □ **boulder-clay** Geol. a mixture of boulders etc. formed by deposition from massive bodies of melting ice, to give distinctive glacial formations. [short for boulderstone, ME f. Scand.]

boule[1] /buːl/ n. (also **boules** pronunc. same) a French form of bowls, played on rough ground with usu. metal balls. [F, = BOWL[2]]

boule[2] /ˈbuːlɪ/ n. a legislative body of an ancient Greek city or of modern Greece. [Gk boulē senate]

boule[3] var. of BUHL.

boules var. of BOULE[1].

boulevard /ˈbuːləˌvɑːd, ˈbuːlvɑː(r)/ n. **1** a broad tree-lined avenue. **2** esp. US a broad main road. [F f. G Bollwerk BULWARK, orig. of a promenade on a demolished fortification]

Boulez /ˈbuːlez/, Pierre (1925–), French composer and conductor who introduced to French audiences not only modern composers but also music of the Renaissance and baroque periods. In 1976 he became director of the French government's research institute into techniques of modern composition, and in his own works explored thoroughly and imaginatively the possibilities of serial music and of aleatory procedures. His use of instruments, both traditional and electronic, is brilliantly effective.

Boulle /buːl/, André-Charles (1642-1732), French cabinet-maker living in the reign of Louis XIV. (See BUHL.)

boulle var. of BUHL.

Boulogne /bʊˈlɔɪn/ (also **Boulogne-sur-Mer** /sjʊə ˈmer/) a fishing and ferry port on the NW coast of France; pop. (1982) 50,000.

Boult /bəʊlt/, Sir Adrian Cedric (1889–1983), English conductor, noted especially for his championship of English composers. He was music director of the BBC from 1930 to 1949 and chief conductor of its Symphony Orchestra 1930–50, then principal conductor of the London Philharmonic Orchestra 1950–7.

boult var. of BOLT[2].

Boulting /ˈbəʊltɪŋ/, John (1913–85) and Roy (1913–), twin brothers who worked together, interchanging responsibilities as film producer and director. They made a number of memorable films, including Brighton Rock (1947) and Seven Days to Noon (1950). From the late 1950s their main output was comedy and farce, including Private's Progress (1956) and I'm All Right Jack (1959).

Boulton /ˈbəʊlt(ə)n/, Matthew (1728–1809), pioneer, with his partner James Watt, in the manufacture of steam engines, providing the commercial expertise, optimism, and capacity for achievement necessary for such engines to succeed on a large scale.

bounce /baʊns/ v. & n. —v. **1 a** intr. (of a ball etc.) rebound. **b** tr. cause to rebound. **c** tr. & intr. bounce repeatedly. **2** intr. sl. (of a cheque) be returned by a bank when there are insufficient funds to meet it. **3** intr. **a** (foll. by about, up) (of a person, dog, etc.) jump or spring energetically. **b** (foll. by in, out, etc.) rush noisily, angrily, enthusiastically, etc. (bounced into the room; bounced out in a temper). **4** tr. colloq. (usu. foll. by into + verbal noun) hustle, persuade (bounced him into signing). **5** intr. colloq. talk boastfully. **6** tr. sl. eject forcibly (from a dancehall, club, etc.). —n. **1 a** a rebound. **b** the power of rebounding (this ball has a good bounce). **2** colloq. **a** a swagger, self-confidence (has a lot of bounce). **b** liveliness. **3** sl. an ejection. □ **bounce back** regain one's good health, spirits, prosperity, etc. [ME *bunsen* beat, thump, (perh. imit.), or f. LG *bunsen*, Du. *bons* thump]

bouncer /ˈbaʊnsə(r)/ *n.* **1** *sl.* a person employed to eject troublemakers from a dancehall, club, etc. **2** *Cricket* = BUMPER.

bouncing /ˈbaʊnsɪŋ/ *adj.* **1** (esp. of a baby) big and healthy. **2** boisterous.

bouncy /ˈbaʊnsɪ/ *adj.* (**bouncier**, **bounciest**) **1** (of a ball etc.) that bounces well. **2** cheerful and lively. **3** resilient, springy (*a bouncy sofa*). □□ **bouncily** *adv.* **bounciness** *n.*

bound[1] /baʊnd/ *v. & n.* —*v.intr.* **1 a** spring, leap (*bounded out of bed*). **b** walk or run with leaping strides. **2** (of a ball etc.) recoil from a wall or the ground; bounce. —*n.* **1** a springy movement upwards or outwards; a leap. **2** a bounce. □ **by leaps and bounds** see LEAP. [F *bond*, *bondir* (orig. of sound) f. LL *bombitare* f. L *bombus* hum]

bound[2] /baʊnd/ *n. & v.* —*n.* (usu. in *pl.*) **1** a limitation; a restriction (*beyond the bounds of possibility*). **2** a border of a territory; a boundary. —*v.tr.* **1** (esp. in *passive*; foll. by *by*) set bounds to; limit (*views bounded by prejudice*). **2** be the boundary of. □ **out of bounds 1** outside the part of a school etc. in which one is allowed to be. **2** beyond what is acceptable; forbidden. [ME f. AF *bounde*, OF *bonde* etc., f. med.L *bodina*, earlier *butina*, of unkn. orig.]

bound[3] /baʊnd/ *adj.* **1** (usu. foll. by *for*) ready to start or having started (*bound for stardom*). **2** (in *comb.*) moving in a specified direction (*northbound*; *outward bound*). [ME f. ON *búinn* past part. of *búa* get ready: -*d* euphonic, or partly after BIND[1]]

bound[4] /baʊnd/ *past* and *past part.* of BIND. □ **bound to** certain to (*he's bound to come*).

boundary /ˈbaʊndərɪ, -drɪ/ *n.* (*pl.* -**ies**) **1** a line marking the limits of an area, territory, etc. (*the fence is the boundary*; *boundary between liberty and licence*). **2** *Cricket* a hit crossing the limits of the field, scoring 4 or 6 runs. □ **boundary layer** the fluid immediately surrounding an object that is immersed and moving. **boundary rider** *Austral. & NZ* a person employed to ride round the fences etc. of a cattle or sheep station and keep them in good order. **boundary umpire** (in Australian Rules) an umpire on the sidelines who signals when the ball is out. [dial. *bounder* f. BOUND[2] + -ER[1] perh. after *limitary*]

bounden /ˈbaʊnd(ə)n/ *adj. archaic* obligatory. □ **bounden duty** solemn responsibility. [archaic past part. of BIND]

bounder /ˈbaʊndə(r)/ *n. colloq.* or *joc.* a cad; an ill-bred person.

boundless /ˈbaʊndlɪs/ *adj.* unlimited; immense (*boundless enthusiasm*). □□ **boundlessly** *adv.* **boundlessness** *n.*

bounteous /ˈbaʊntɪəs/ *adj. poet.* **1** generous, liberal. **2** freely given (*bounteous affection*). □□ **bounteously** *adv.* **bounteousness** *n.* [ME f. OF *bontif* f. *bonté* BOUNTY after *plenteous*]

bountiful /ˈbaʊntɪˌfʊl/ *adj.* **1** = BOUNTEOUS. **2** ample. □ **Lady Bountiful** a charitable but patronizing lady of a neighbourhood (after a character in Farquhar's *Beaux' Stratagem*, 1707). □□ **bountifully** *adv.* [BOUNTY + -FUL]

Bounty /ˈbaʊntɪ/ a ship, HMS *Bounty* which was bound from Tahiti to the Cape of Good Hope and the West Indies when on 28 April 1789 part of the crew mutinied against their commander, Lieutenant Bligh, either because he was an unduly stern disciplinarian or (more probably) because of the attractions of the women and way of life of the South Sea Islands. Bligh and 18 companions, set adrift in an open boat, succeeded in reaching Timor in the East Indies, nearly 6,400 km (4,000 miles) away. The mutineers returned to Tahiti whence some of them went on to Pitcairn Island, founding a settlement there which was not discovered until 1808; this was eventually adopted by the British Government as a colony.

bounty /ˈbaʊntɪ/ *n.* (*pl.* -**ies**) **1** liberality; generosity. **2** a gift or reward, made usu. by the State, esp.: **a** a sum paid for a valiant act. **b** a sum paid to encourage a trading enterprise etc. **c** a sum paid to army or navy recruits on enlistment. □ **bounty-hunter** a person who pursues a criminal or seeks an achievement for the sake of the reward. **King's** (or **Queen's**) **bounty** *hist.* a grant made to a mother of triplets. [ME f. OF *bonté* f. L *bonitas* -*tatis* f. *bonus* good]

bouquet /buːˈkeɪ, bəʊ-/ *n.* **1** a bunch of flowers, esp. for carrying at a wedding or other ceremony. **2** the scent of wine etc. **3** a favourable comment; a compliment. □ **bouquet garni** /ˈɡɑːnɪ/ *Cookery* a bunch of herbs used for flavouring stews etc. [F f. dial. var. of OF *bos*, *bois* wood]

Bourbaki /bʊəˈbɑːkɪ/, Nicolas. The pseudonym under which a group of mathematicians, mainly French, have been attempting to publish a complete account of the foundations of all known pure mathematics. Their approach is highly abstract and strictly axiomatic in style and spirit, intending to lay bare the structure of the entire field. Volumes in different areas of mathematics have been appearing since 1939 and, in spite of their idiosyncrasies, have been highly influential among mathematicians.

Bourbon /ˈbʊəbən, ˈbʊəbɔ̃/ the surname of a branch of the royal family of France, who became the ruling monarchs when Henry IV succeeded to the throne in 1589 and reached the peak of their power under Louis XIV in the late 17th c. The last Bourbon king was Louis Philippe, and the French monarchy came to an end when he was overthrown in 1848. Members of this family became kings of Spain (1700–1931 and from 1975) and of Naples. —*n.* **1** a chocolate-flavoured biscuit with chocolate-cream filling. **2** *US* a reactionary.

bourbon /ˈbɜːbən, ˈbʊə-/ *n. US* whisky distilled from maize and rye. [*Bourbon* County, Kentucky, where it was first made]

Bourbonnais /ˌbʊəbɒˈneɪ/ a former duchy and province of central France, now part of Burgundy and Centre regions. Its capital was the city of Moulins.

bourdon /ˈbʊəd(ə)n/ *n. Mus.* **1** a low-pitched stop in an organ or harmonium. **2** the lowest bell in a peal of bells. **3** the drone pipe of a bagpipe. [F, = bagpipe-drone, f. Rmc, imit.]

bourgeois /ˈbʊəʒwɑː/ *adj. & n.* often *derog.* —*adj.* **1 a** conventionally middle-class. **b** humdrum, unimaginative. **c** selfishly materialistic. **2** upholding the interests of the capitalist class; non-communist. —*n.* a bourgeois person. [F: see BURGESS]

bourgeoisie /ˌbʊəʒwɑːˈziː/ *n.* **1** the capitalist class. **2** the middle class. [F]

Bourgogne see BURGUNDY.

Bourguiba /bʊəˈɡiːbə/, Habib ben Ali (1903–), Tunisian nationalist and statesman, a moderate and democratic leader. Having negotiated the settlement that led to his country's autonomy he was its first Prime Minister after independence (1956) and was chosen as President when the country became a republic. He was deposed in 1987.

bourn[1] /bɔːn, bʊən/ *n.* a small stream. [ME: S. Engl. var. of BURN[2]]

bourn[2] /bɔːn, bʊən/ *n.* (also **bourne**) *archaic* **1** a goal; a destination. **2** a limit. [F *borne* f. OF *bodne* BOUND[2]]

bourrée /ˈbʊəreɪ/ *n.* **1** a lively French dance like a gavotte. **2** the music for this dance. [F]

bourse /bʊəs/ *n.* **1** (**Bourse**) the Paris equivalent of the Stock Exchange. **2** a money-market. [F, = purse, f. med.L *bursa*: cf. PURSE[1]]

boustrophedon /ˌbaʊstrəˈfiːd(ə)n, ˌbuː-/ *adj. & adv.* (of written words) from right to left and from left to right in alternate lines. [Gk (adv.) = as an ox turns in ploughing f. *bous* ox + -*strophos* turning]

bout /baʊt/ *n.* (often foll. by *of*) **1 a** a limited period (of intensive work or exercise). **b** a drinking session. **c** a period (of illness) (*a bout of flu*). **2 a** a wrestling- or boxing-match. **b** a trial of strength. [16th c.: app. the same as obs. *bought* bending]

boutique /buːˈtiːk/ *n.* a small shop or department of a store, selling (esp. fashionable) clothes or accessories. [F, = small shop, f. L (as BODEGA)]

boutonnière /ˌbuːtɒnɪˈeə(r)/ *n.* a spray of flowers worn in a buttonhole. [F]

Bouvet Island /ˈbuːveɪ/ an uninhabited Norwegian island in the South Atlantic, named after the French navigator François Lozier-Bouvet in 1739.

bouzouki /buːˈzuːkɪ/ *n.* (*pl.* **bouzoukis**) a Greek form of mandolin. [mod. Gk]

bovate /ˈbəʊveɪt/ *n. hist.* a measure of land, as much as one ox could plough in a year, varying from 10 to 18 acres. [med.L *bovata* f. L *bos bovis* ox]

bovine /'bəʊvaɪn/ *adj.* **1** of or relating to cattle. **2** stupid, dull. □□ **bovinely** *adv.* [LL *bovinus* f. L *bos bovis* ox]

Bovril /'bɒvrɪl/ *n. propr.* a concentrated essence of beef diluted with hot water to make a drink. [L *bos bovis* ox, cow]

bovver /'bɒvə(r)/ *n. Brit. sl.* deliberate troublemaking. □ **bovver boot** a heavy laced boot worn typically by skinheads. **bovver boy** a violent hooligan. [cockney pronunc. of BOTHER]

Bow /bəʊ/, Clara (1905–65), American actress, known as the 'It Girl' for her sexual magnetism, one of the most popular stars of the 1920s. She is remembered as portraying a flapper with expressive eyes and cupid's-bow mouth.

bow[1] /bəʊ/ *n. & v.* —*n.* **1 a** a slip-knot with a double loop. **b** a ribbon, shoelace, etc., tied with this. **c** a decoration (on clothing, or painted etc.) in the form of a bow. **2** a device for shooting arrows with a taut string joining the ends of a curved piece of wood etc. **3 a** a rod with horsehair stretched along its length, used for playing the violin, cello, etc. **b** a single stroke of a bow over strings. **4 a** a shallow curve or bend. **b** a rainbow. **5** = *saddle-bow.* **6** a metal ring forming the handle of scissors, a key, etc. **7** *US* the side-piece of a spectacle-frame. **8** *Archery* = BOWMAN[1]. —*v.tr.* (also *absol.*) use a bow on (a violin etc.) (*he bowed vigorously*). □ **bow-compass** (or **-compasses**) compasses with jointed legs. **bow-legged** having bandy legs. **bow-legs** bandy legs. **bow-saw** *Carpentry* a narrow saw stretched like a bowstring on a light frame. **bow-tie** a necktie in the form of a bow (sense 1). **bow-window** a curved bay window. **two strings to one's bow** a twofold resource. [OE *boga* f. Gmc: cf. BOW[2]]

bow[2] /baʊ/ *v. & n.* —*v.* **1** *intr.* incline the head or trunk, esp. in greeting or assent or acknowledgement of applause. **2** *intr.* submit (*bowed to the inevitable*). **3** *tr.* cause to incline (*bowed his head; bowed his will to hers*). **4** *tr.* express (thanks, assent, etc.) by bowing (*bowed agreement to the plan*). **5** *tr.* (foll. by *in, out*) usher or escort obsequiously (*bowed us out of the restaurant*). —*n.* an inclining of the head or body in greeting, assent, or in the acknowledgement of applause, etc. □ **bow and scrape** be obsequious; fawn. **bow down 1** bend or kneel in submission or reverence (*bowed down before the king*). **2** (usu. in *passive*) make stoop; crush (*was bowed down by care*). **bowing acquaintance** a person one acknowledges but does not know well enough to speak to. **bow out 1** make one's exit (esp. formally). **2** retreat, withdraw; retire gracefully. **make one's bow** make a formal exit or entrance. **take a bow** acknowledge applause. [OE *būgan*, f. Gmc: cf. BOW[1]]

bow[3] /baʊ/ *n. Naut.* **1** (often in *pl.*) the fore-end of a boat or a ship. **2** = BOWMAN[2]. □ **bow wave** a wave set up at the bows of a moving ship or in front of a body moving in air. **on the bow** within 45° of the point directly ahead. **shot across the bows** a warning. [LG *boog,* Du. *boeg,* ship's bow, orig. shoulder: see BOUGH]

bowdlerize /'baʊdlə,raɪz/ *v.tr.* (also **-ise**) expurgate (a book etc.). □□ **bowdlerism** *n.* **bowdlerization** /-'zeɪʃ(ə)n/ *n.* [T. Bowdler (d. 1825), who in 1818 published an expurgated edition of Shakespeare]

bowel /'baʊəl/ *n.* **1 a** the part of the alimentary canal below the stomach. **b** the intestine. **2** (in *pl.*) the depths; the innermost parts (*the bowels of the earth*). □ **bowel movement 1** discharge from the bowels; defecation. **2** the faeces discharged from the body. [ME f. OF *buel* f. L *botellus* little sausage]

Bowen /'bəʊɪn/, Elizabeth Dorothea Cole (1899–1973), Anglo-Irish novelist and writer of short stories. Her skill in describing landscape (urban and rural) and her sensibility to changes of light and atmosphere are distinguishing features of her prose; she wrote most confidently within a middle- and upper-middle-class social range. Among her best-known novels are *The Death of the Heart* (1938), and *The Heat of the Day* (1949) which centres on a tragic wartime love affair.

bower[1] /'baʊə(r)/ *n. & v.* —*n.* **1 a** a secluded place, esp. in a garden, enclosed by foliage; an arbour. **b** a summer-house. **2**

poet. an inner room; a boudoir. —*v. tr. poet.* embower. □□ **bowery** *adj.* [OE *būr* f. Gmc]

bower[2] /'baʊə(r)/ *n.* (in full **bower-anchor**) either of two anchors carried at a ship's bow. □ **best bower** the starboard bower. **bower-cable** the cable attached to a bower-anchor. **small bower** the port bower. [BOW[3] + -ER[1]]

bower[3] /'baʊə(r)/ *n.* either of two cards at euchre and similar games. □ **left bower** the jack of the same colour as the right bower. **right bower** the jack of trumps. [G *Bauer* peasant, jack at cards, rel. to Du. *boer*: see BOOR]

bowerbird /'baʊəbɜːd/ *n.* **1** any of various birds of the Ptilonorhynchidae family, native to Australia and New Guinea, the males of which construct elaborate bowers of feathers, grasses, shells, etc. during courtship. **2** a person who collects bric-à-brac.

bowery /'baʊərɪ/ *n.* (also **Bowery**) (*pl.* **-ies**) *US* a district known as a resort of drunks and down-and-outs. [orig. the Bowery, a street in New York City, f. Du. *bouwerij* farm]

bowfin /'bəʊfɪn/ *n.* a voracious American freshwater fish, *Amia calva*. [BOW[1] + FIN]

bowhead /'bəʊhed/ *n.* an Arctic whale, *Balaena mysticetus*.

Bowie /'bəʊɪ/, David (real name David Robert Jones, 1947–   ), English rock singer and composer, with an inventive theatrical style. His albums include *Space Oddity* (1969) and *Ziggy Stardust* (1972). Bowie also had a separate career as a film and stage actor; his films include *The Man Who Fell to Earth* (1976) and *Absolute Beginners* (1986), to which he contributed the theme.

bowie /'bəʊɪ/ *n.* (in full **bowie knife**) a long knife with a blade double-edged at the point, used as a weapon by American pioneers. It is named after James ('Jim') Bowie (1796–1836), American folk hero, a colonel in the Texan forces during the war with Mexico, who is said to have had a knife as his hunting-dagger.

bowl[1] /bəʊl/ *n.* **1 a** a usu. round deep basin used for food or liquid. **b** the quantity (of soup etc.) a bowl holds. **c** the contents of a bowl. **2 a** any deep-sided container shaped like a bowl (*lavatory bowl*). **b** the bowl-shaped part of a tobacco-pipe, spoon, balance, etc. **3** esp. *US* a bowl-shaped region or building, esp. an amphitheatre (*Hollywood Bowl*). □□ **bowlful** *n.* (*pl.* **-fuls**). [OE *bolle, bolla,* f. Gmc]

bowl[2] /bəʊl/ *n. & v.* —*n.* **1 a** a wooden or hard rubber ball, slightly asymmetrical so that it runs on a curved course, used in the game of bowls. **b** a wooden ball or disc used in playing skittles. **c** a large ball with indents for gripping, used in tenpin bowling. **2** (in *pl.*; usu. treated as *sing.*) **a** a game played with bowls (sense 1a) on grass. (See BOWLS.) **b** tenpin bowling. (See BOWLING.) **c** skittles. **3** a spell or turn of bowling in cricket. —*v.* **1 a** *tr.* roll (a ball, a hoop, etc.) along the ground. **b** *intr.* play bowls or skittles. **2** *tr.* (also *absol.*) *Cricket* etc. **a** deliver (a ball, an over, etc.) (*bowled six overs; bowled well*). **b** (often foll. by *out*) dismiss (a batsman) by knocking down the wicket with a ball (*soon bowled him out*). **c** (often foll. by *down*) knock (a wicket) over. **3** *intr.* (often foll. by *along*) go along rapidly by revolving, esp. on wheels (*the cart bowled along the road*). □ **bowl out** *Cricket* dismiss (a batsman or a side). **bowl over 1** knock down. **2** *colloq.* **a** impress greatly. **b** overwhelm (*bowled over by her energy*). [ME & F *boule* f. L *bulla* bubble]

bowler[1] /'bəʊlə(r)/ *n.* **1** *Cricket* etc. a member of the fielding side who bowls or is bowling. **2** a player at bowls.

bowler[2] /'bəʊlə(r)/ *n.* (in full **bowler hat**) a man's hard felt hat with a round dome-shaped crown. □ **bowler-hat (-hatted, -hatting)** *sl.* retire (a person) from the army etc. (*he's been bowler-hatted*). [J. Bowler, a hatter, who designed it in 1850]

bowline /'bəʊlɪn/ *n. Naut.* **1** a rope attaching the weather side of a square sail to the bow. **2** a simple knot for forming a non-slipping loop at the end of a rope. [ME f. MLG *bōline* (as BOW[3], LINE[1])]

bowling /'bəʊlɪŋ/ *n.* the game of bowls as a sport or recreation. (See below, and BOWLS.) □ **bowling-alley 1** a long enclosure for skittles or tenpin bowling. **2** a building containing these. **bowling-crease** *Cricket* the line from behind which a bowler delivers the ball. **bowling-green** a lawn used for playing bowls.

Bowling (as an indoor game) is of great antiquity. Related games were played in ancient Egypt; in Germany, congregations played at bowling in church cloisters (c.1400), with the target representing the Devil and the player who hit it adjudged free of sin (Luther approved of the game). In England, Edward III banned the game in 1361 (like football and golf it interfered with the practice of archery, which was of military use). Henry VIII built alleys at Whitehall but condemned the game in 1511 for its association with gambling. In 1895 the American Bowling Congress gave the game rules and standardized its equipment.

bowls /bəʊlz/ n. a game played with bowls (see BOWL²) on grass. One of the oldest games known in Britain, it is now played chiefly out of doors. An intentional imbalance (bias) of balls was introduced in the 16th c., greatly increasing the tactical scope of the game by allowing balls to run in curved paths round obstructions. It is fashionable to discount the legend, first published in a political pamphlet in 1624, that on 19 July 1588 Sir Francis Drake (who was known to like the game) was playing bowls on Plymouth Hoe when news came that the Spanish Armada had been sighted, and refused to leave until he had finished the game, but it could be true.

bowman¹ /ˈbəʊmən/ n. (pl. **-men**) an archer.

bowman² /ˈbaʊmən/ n. (pl. **-men**) the rower nearest the bow of esp. a racing boat.

bowser /ˈbaʊzə(r)/ n. **1** a tanker used for fuelling aircraft etc. **2** Austral. & NZ a petrol pump. [trade name, orig. propr.]

bowshot /ˈbəʊʃɒt/ n. the distance to which a bow can send an arrow.

bowsprit /ˈbəʊsprɪt/ n. Naut. a spar running out from a ship's bow to which the forestays are fastened. [ME f. Gmc (as BOW³, SPRIT)]

Bow Street Runners /bəʊ/ (also **Bow Street officers**) the common name for London's police force during the first half of the 19th c., coined because the main police court was situated in Bow Street. They had been formed c.1745 by Henry Fielding (see entry).

bowstring /ˈbəʊstrɪŋ/ n. & v. —n. the string of an archer's bow. —v.tr. strangle with a bowstring (a former Turkish method of execution).

bow-wow /ˈbaʊwaʊ, -ˈwaʊ/ int. & n. —int. an imitation of a dog's bark. —n. **1** colloq. a dog. **2** a dog's bark. [imit.]

bowyang /ˈbəʊjæŋ/ n. Austral. & NZ either of a pair of bands or straps worn round the trouser-legs below the knee. [dial. bowy-yangs etc.]

bowyer /ˈbəʊjə(r)/ n. a maker or seller of archers' bows.

box¹ /bɒks/ n. & v. —n. **1** a container, usu. with flat sides and of firm material such as wood or card, esp. for holding solids. **2 a** the amount that will fill a box. **b** Brit. a gift of a kind formerly given to tradesmen etc. at Christmas (Christmas-box). **3** a separate compartment for any of various purposes, e.g. for a small group in a theatre, for witnesses in a lawcourt, for horses in a stable or vehicle. **4** an enclosure or receptacle for a special purpose (often in comb.: money box; telephone box). **5** a facility at a newspaper office for receiving replies to an advertisement. **6** (prec. by the) colloq. television; one's television set (what's on the box?). **7** an enclosed area or space. **8** a space or area of print on a page, enclosed by a border. **9** Brit. a small country house for use when shooting, fishing, or for other sporting activity. **10** a protective casing for a piece of mechanism. **11** a light shield for protecting the genitals in sport, esp. in cricket. **12** (prec. by the) Football colloq. the penalty area. **13** Baseball the area occupied by the batter or the pitcher. **14** a coachman's seat. —v.tr. **1** put in or provide with a box. **2** (foll. by in, up) confine; restrain from movement. **3** (foll. by up) Austral. & NZ mix up (different flocks of sheep). □ **box camera** a simple box-shaped hand camera. **box the compass** Naut. recite the points of the compass in the correct order. **box girder** a hollow girder square in cross-section. **box junction** Brit. a road area at a junction marked with a yellow

grid, which a vehicle should enter only if its exit from it is clear. **box kite** a kite in the form of a long box open at each end. **box number** a number by which replies are made to a private advertisement in a newspaper. **box office 1** an office for booking seats and buying tickets at a theatre, cinema, etc. **2** the commercial aspect of the arts and entertainment (often attrib.: a box-office failure). **box pleat** a pleat consisting of two parallel creases forming a raised band. **box spanner** a spanner with a box-shaped end fitting over the head of a nut. **box spring** each of a set of vertical springs housed in a frame, e.g. in a mattress. □□ **boxful** n. (pl. **-fuls**). **boxlike** adj. [OE f. LL buxis f. L PYXIS]

box² /bɒks/ v. & n. —v. **1** tr. fight (an opponent) at boxing. **b** intr. practise boxing. **2** tr. slap (esp. a person's ears). —n. a slap with the hand, esp. on the ears. □ **box clever** colloq. act in a clever or effective way. [ME: orig. unkn.]

box³ /bɒks/ n. **1** any small evergreen tree or shrub of the genus Buxus, esp. B. sempervirens, a slow-growing tree with glossy dark green leaves which is often used in hedging. **2** its wood, used for carving, turning, engraving, etc. **3** any of various trees in Australasia which have similar wood or foliage, esp. those of several species of Eucalyptus. **4** = BOXWOOD. □ **box elder** the American ash-leaved maple, Acer negundo. [OE f. L buxus, Gk puxos]

Box and Cox /ˌbɒks ənd ˈkɒks/ n. & v. —n. (often attrib.) two persons sharing accommodation etc., and using it at different times. —v.intr. share accommodation, duties, etc. by a strictly timed arrangement. [the names of characters in a farce (1847) by J. M. Morton—a printer and a hatter to whom a landlady let the same room without their knowing it, the one being out at work all night and the other all day]

boxcar /ˈbɒkskɑː(r)/ n. US an enclosed railway goods wagon, usu. with sliding doors on the sides.

Boxer /ˈbɒksə(r)/ n. hist. a member of a fiercely nationalistic Chinese secret society that flourished in the late 19th c. Abetted by the Dowager Empress, in 1899 it led a Chinese uprising against Western domination and besieged the foreign legations in Peking. The uprising was eventually crushed by a combined European force, aided by Japan and the US, and the foreign powers took their opportunity to strengthen their hold over the Chinese. [transl. of Chin. i ho chuan, lit. 'righteous harmony fists']

boxer /ˈbɒksə(r)/ n. **1** a person who practises boxing, esp. for sport. **2 a** a medium-size dog of a breed with a smooth brown coat and puglike face. **b** this breed. □ **boxer shorts** men's underpants similar to shorts worn in boxing, with a shallow curved slit at each side.

boxing /ˈbɒksɪŋ/ n. the practice of fighting with the fists, esp. in padded gloves in a roped square, as a sport. It was organized in its modern form under the Queensberry Rules, compiled in the 1860s. It is both an amateur and a professional sport, with contestants divided into categories according to their weight, and fights are divided into 3-minute rounds. □ **boxing glove** each of a pair of heavily padded gloves used in boxing. **boxing weight** each of a series of fixed weight-ranges at which boxers are matched. The British professional scale is as follows: flyweight, bantamweight, featherweight, lightweight, light welterweight, welterweight, light middleweight, middleweight, light heavyweight, heavyweight. (See separate entries.) The weights and divisions are modified in the amateur scale.

Boxing Day /ˈbɒksɪŋ/ n. the first weekday after Christmas. [from the custom of giving tradesmen gifts or money: see BOX¹ n. 2b]

boxroom /ˈbɒksruːm, -rʊm/ n. Brit. a room or large cupboard for storing boxes, cases, etc.

boxwood /ˈbɒkswʊd/ n. **1** the wood of the box used esp. by engravers for the fineness of its grain and for its hardness. **2** = BOX³ 1.

boxy /ˈbɒksɪ/ adj. (**boxier, boxiest**) reminiscent of a box; (of a room or space) very cramped.

boy /bɔɪ/ n. & int. —n. **1** a male child or youth. **2** a young man, esp. regarded as not yet mature. **3** a male servant, attendant, etc. **4 (the boys)** *colloq.* a group of men mixing socially. —*int.* expressing pleasure, surprise, etc. □ **boy scout** = SCOUT[1] 4. (See SCOUT ASSOCIATION.) **boys in blue** *Brit.* policemen. □□ **boyhood** *n.* **boyish** *adj.* **boyishly** *adv.* **boyishness** *n.* [ME = servant, perh. ult. f. L *boia* fetter]

boyar /bɔʊˈjɑː(r)/ *n. hist.* a member of the old aristocracy in Russia. [Russ. *boyarin* grandee]

Boyce /bɔɪs/, William (1711–79), English composer and organist, who became Master of the King's Music in 1757. His compositions include songs, overtures, church anthems and services, and eight symphonies. He is noted also for his *Cathedral Music* (1760–73) an important anthology of English sacred music of the past 200 years which provided much of the repertory of English cathedrals for many more. He is buried beneath the dome of St Paul's Cathedral.

boycott /ˈbɔɪkɒt/ *v. & n.* —*v.tr.* **1** combine in refusing social or commercial relations with (a person, group, country, etc.) usu. as punishment or coercion. **2** refuse to handle (goods) to this end. —*n.* such a refusal. [Capt. C. C. *Boycott*, land-agent in Ireland, so treated in 1880. The Irish Land League ordered him to reduce rents after a bad harvest, and when he refused the tenants avoided any communication with him]

Boyd /bɔɪd/, Arthur Merric Bloomfield (1920–), Australian painter, potter, etcher, lithographer, and ceramic artist. He became well known in Australia for his large ceramic totem pole (weighing about 10 tons and built entirely by hand) at the entrance to the Olympic Pool, Melbourne, and for his series (20 pictures) *Love, Marriage and Death of a Half-Caste*. The latter was made the subject of the film *The Black Man and His Bride*, which won a Silver Medallion in the experimental section of the 1960 Australian Film Festival.

Boyer /ˈbwɑːjeɪ/, Charles (1897–1977), French film actor, known as 'the great lover' and famous for his suave charm and poise. His films include *Mayerling* (1936) and (with Greta Garbo) *Tovarich* (1937).

boyfriend /ˈbɔɪfrend/ *n.* a person's regular male companion or lover.

Boyle /bɔɪl/, Robert (1627–91), Irish-born natural philosopher, of aristocratic birth, a founder member of the Royal Society. He rejected the chemical views of the alchemists and Aristotelians and advanced a corpuscular view of matter, a precursor of the modern theory of chemical elements and a cornerstone of his mechanical philosophy which became very influential. He is best known for his experiments with the air pump, assisted initially by Robert Hooke, which led to the famous law named after him that the pressure of a fixed quantity of gas is inversely proportional to its volume at a constant temperature; this was published by Boyle in 1662 with information supplied by R. Towneley, and subsequently but independently by Edmé Mariotte in France in 1676.

Boyne /bɔɪn/ a river in the Republic of Ireland, scene of the victory of a Protestant (largely English) army under William III over the Catholic (Irish and French) forces of the recently deposed James II in 1690. Although the campaign dragged on for some months afterwards, the Battle of the Boyne effectively destroyed for some time James's chances of regaining his throne.

boyo /ˈbɔɪəʊ/ *n. (pl.* **-os**) *Welsh & Ir. colloq.* boy, fellow (esp. as a form of address).

Boys' Brigade the oldest of the national organizations for boys in Britain, founded by Sir William Smith in 1883 (and now with worldwide membership) with the aim of promoting 'Christian manliness', discipline, and self-respect. Each company is connected with a church.

boysenberry /ˈbɔɪzənbəri/ *n. (pl.* **-ies**) **1** a hybrid of several species of bramble. **2** the large red edible fruit of this plant. [R. *Boysen*, 20th-c. Amer. horticulturalist]

Boz /bɒz/ the pseudonym used by Charles Dickens in his *Pickwick Papers* and contributions to the *Morning Chronicle*.

BP *abbr.* **1** boiling-point. **2** blood pressure. **3** before the present (era). **4** British Petroleum. **5** British Pharmacopoeia.

Bp. *abbr.* Bishop.

BPC *abbr.* British Pharmaceutical Codex.

B.Phil. *abbr.* Bachelor of Philosophy.

Bq *abbr.* becquerel.

BR *abbr.* British Rail.

Br *symb. Chem.* the element bromine.

Br. *abbr.* **1** British. **2** Brother.

bra /brɑː/ *n. (pl.* **bras)** *colloq.* = BRASSIÈRE. [abbr.]

Brabant /brəˈbænt/ a former duchy in western Europe, now divided between Belgium and The Netherlands.

Brabham /ˈbræbəm/, Sir John Arthur ('Jack') (1926–), Australian motor-racing driver, three times world champion— 1959, 1960, and finally in 1966 when he became the first driver to win the championship in a car of his own construction.

brace /breɪs/ *n. & v.* —*n.* **1 a** a device that clamps or fastens tightly. **b** a strengthening piece of iron or timber in building. **2** (in *pl.*) *Brit.* straps supporting trousers from the shoulders. **3** a wire device for straightening the teeth. **4** (*pl.* same) a pair (esp. of game). **5** a rope attached to the yard of a ship for trimming the sail. **6 a** a connecting mark { or } used in printing. **b** *Mus.* a similar mark connecting staves to be performed at the same time. —*v.tr.* **1** fasten tightly, give firmness to. **2** make steady by supporting. **3** (esp. as **bracing** *adj.*) invigorate, refresh. **4** (often *refl.*) prepare for a difficulty, shock, etc. □ **brace and bit** a revolving tool with a D-shaped central handle for boring. □□ **bracingly** *adv.* **bracingness** *n.* [ME f. OF *brace* two arms, *bracier* embrace, f. L bra(c)*chia* arms]

bracelet /ˈbreɪslɪt/ *n.* **1** an ornamental band, hoop, or chain worn on the wrist or arm. **2** *sl.* a hand- cuff. [ME f. OF, dimin. of *bracel* f. L *bracchiale* f. bra(c)*chium* arm]

bracer /ˈbreɪsə(r)/ *n. colloq.* a tonic.

brachial /ˈbreɪkɪəl/ *adj.* **1** of or relating to the arm (*brachial artery*). **2** like an arm. [L *brachialis* f. bra(c)*chium* arm]

brachiate /ˈbreɪkɪˌeɪt/ *v. & adj.* —*v.intr.* (of certain apes and monkeys) move by using the arms to swing from branch to branch. —*adj. Biol.* **1** having arms. **2** having paired branches on alternate sides. □□ **brachiation** /-ˈeɪʃ(ə)n/ *n.* **brachiator** *n.* [L bra(c)- *chium* arm]

brachiopod /ˈbreɪkɪəˌpɒd, ˈbræk-/ *n.* any marine invertebrate of the phylum Brachiopoda (esp. a fossil one) having a two-valved chalky shell and a ciliated feeding arm. [mod.L f. Gk *brakhiōn* arm + *pous podos* foot]

brachiosaurus /ˌbreɪkɪəˈsɔːrəs, ˌbræk-/ *n.* any huge planteating dinosaur of the genus *Brachiosaurus* with forelegs longer than its hind legs. [mod.L f. Gk *brakhiōn* arm + *sauros* lizard]

brachistochrone /brəˈkɪstəˌkrəʊn/ *n.* a curve between two points along which a body can move in a shorter time than for any other curve. [Gk *brakhistos* shortest + *khronos* time]

brachy- /ˈbrækɪ/ *comb. form* short. [Gk *brakhus* short]

brachycephalic /ˌbrækɪsɪˈfælɪk/ *adj.* having a short rounded skull whose width is at least 80% of its length, i.e. with a cephalic index of equal to or greater than 80. Examples of brachycephalic populations occur in Central Europe from central France to central Russia, and from north Italy to Prussia. □□ **brachycephalous** /ˌbrækɪˈsefələs/ *adj.* **brachycephaly** *n.* [BRACHY- + Gk *kephalē* head]

brachylogy /brəˈkɪlədʒɪ/ *n. (pl.* **-ies**) **1** over-conciseness of expression. **2** an instance of this.

brack /bræk/ *n. Ir.* cake or bread containing dried fruit etc. [abbr. of BARMBRACK]

bracken /ˈbrækən/ *n.* **1** any large coarse fern, esp. *Pteridium aquilinum*, abundant on heaths and moorlands, and in woods. **2** a mass of such ferns. Also called BRAKE[5]. [north. ME f. ON]

bracket /ˈbrækɪt/ *n. & v.* —*n.* **1** a right-angled or other support attached to and projecting from a vertical surface. **2** a shelf fixed with such a support to a wall. **3** each of a pair of marks ( ) [ ] { } < > used to enclose words or figures. **4** a group classified as containing similar elements or falling between given limits (*income bracket*). **5** *Mil.* the distance between two artillery shots fired either side of the target to establish range. —*v.tr.* (**bracketed, bracketing**) **1** a couple (names etc.) with a brace. **b** imply a connection or equality between. **2 a** enclose in brackets as parenthetic or spurious. **b** *Math.* enclose in brackets as having specific relations to what precedes or follows. **3** *Mil.* establish the range of (a target) by firing two preliminary shots one short of and the other beyond it. [F *braguette* or Sp. *bragueta* codpiece, dimin. of F *brague* f. Prov. *braga* f. L *braca*, pl. *bracae* breeches]

brackish /'brækɪʃ/ *adj.* (of water etc.) slightly salty. □□ **brackishness** *n.* [obs. *brack* (adj.) f. MLG, MDu. *brac*]

bract /brækt/ *n.* a modified and often brightly coloured leaf, with a flower or an inflorescence in its axil. □□ **bracteal** *adj.* **bracteate** /-tɪɪt/ *adj.* [L *bractea* thin plate, gold-leaf]

brad /bræd/ *n.* a thin flat nail with a head in the form of slight enlargement at the top. [var. of ME *brod* goad, pointed instrument, f. ON *broddr* spike]

bradawl /'brædɔːl/ *n.* a small tool with a pointed end for boring holes by hand. [BRAD + AWL]

Bradbury[1] /'brædbərɪ/, Malcolm Stanley (1932–) English novelist and critic. His first three novels (*Eating People is Wrong*, 1959; *Stepping Westward*, 1965; and *The History Man*, 1975) are satirical campus novels with widely differing backgrounds, and *Rates of Exchange* (1983) is a witty satiric commentary on cultural exchange. His critical works, which include studies of Waugh (1962) and Bellow (1982), show a respect for pluralism with an admiration for the experimental and fictive devices of the American novel.

Bradbury[2] /'brædbərɪ/, Ray Douglas (1920–), American writer of science fiction, whose works include *Martian Chronicles* (1950) and *Fahrenheit 451* (1951). He is a richly imaginative writer with a distinctive blend of sentiment and cynicism.

Bradford /'brædfəd/ an industrial town in West Yorkshire; pop. (1981) 295,000.

Bradley /'brædlɪ/, James (1693–1762), English astronomer, appointed Savilian professor of astronomy at Oxford in 1721 and Astronomer Royal in 1742. His attempt to measure the distance of the stars by means of stellar parallax resulted in his discovery of the aberration of light announced in 1729, which he ascribed correctly to the combined effect of the velocity of light and the earth's annual orbital motion. He also observed the oscillation of the earth's axis, which he termed 'nutation'. His catalogue of star positions was published posthumously in two volumes in 1798 and 1805.

Bradman /'brædmən/, Sir Donald George (1908–), Australian cricketer whose career extended from 1927 to 1949. He scored 117 centuries in 338 innings in first-class cricket.

Bradshaw /'brædʃɔ/ *n.* a timetable of (esp. British) passenger trains. [f. G. *Bradshaw* (d. 1853), British printer and engraver, first publisher of *Bradshaw's Railway Guide*, a timetable of all passenger trains in Britain, issued until 1961]

bradycardia /ˌbrædɪ'kɑːdɪə/ *n. Med.* abnormally slow heart-action. [Gk *bradus* slow + *kardia* heart]

brae /breɪ/ *n. Sc.* a steep bank or hillside. [ME f. ON *brá* eyelash]

brag /bræg/ *v.* & *n.* —*v.* (**bragged**, **bragging**) **1** *intr.* talk boastfully. **2** *tr.* boast about. —*n.* **1** a card-game like poker. **2** a boastful statement; boastful talk. □□ **bragger** *n.* **braggingly** *adv.* [ME, orig. adj., = spirited, boastful; orig. unkn.]

Braga /'brɑːgə/ a city in the north of Portugal; pop. (est. 1984) 63,000. It is the seat of the Primate of Portugal.

Braganza /brə'gænzə/ (Portuguese **Bragança**) **1** a mountainous district of NE Portugal; pop. (est. 1986) 185,600. **2** its capital city. **3** the name of the dynasty that ruled Portugal from 1640 until the end of the monarchy in 1910, and Brazil (upon its independence from Portugal) from 1822 until the formation of a republic in 1889.

Bragg /bræg/, Sir William Henry (1862–1942), English physicist and a founder of solid state physics. His early work was on the ionization of X-rays and radioactivity, but in 1912 he began to collaborate with his son, William (later Sir Lawrence) Bragg (1890–1971) in developing the technique of X-ray diffraction for determining the atomic structure of crystals; for this they shared the 1915 Nobel Prize for physics. During the First World War he worked on submarine detection for the Admiralty; afterwards he returned to University College, London, where he established a research school for crystallography, and moved to

the Royal Institution of which he became the director in 1923. His son was appointed head of the same establishment in 1953. Their diffraction analysis of organic crystals was of fundamental importance in the emerging field of molecular biology.

braggadocio /ˌbrægə'dəʊtʃɪəʊ, -'dəʊʃɪəʊ/ *n.* empty boasting; a boastful manner of speech and behaviour. [*Braggadochio*, a braggart in Spenser's *Faerie Queene*, f. BRAG or BRAGGART + It. augment. suffix *-occio*]

braggart /'brægət/ *n.* & *adj.* —*n.* a person given to bragging. —*adj.* boastful. [F *bragard* f. *braguer* BRAG]

Brahe /'brɑːə/, Tycho (1546–1601), the greatest naked-eye astronomer, a Danish nobleman of great wealth but uncertain temper. He boasted a fine metal nose, substituted for his own which he lost in a duel. He built the great observatory of Uraniborg at Hveen in Åresund, which he equipped with many new and accurate instruments, using these to observe the planetary motions and star positions with great precision. His detailed tables of the position of Mars, in particular, were to be used later by his protégé Kepler to work out the laws of planetary dynamics. He was aware of the effects of atmospheric refraction on his observations, and made appropriate corrections. His observations of cometary orbits, published in the book *De Nova Stella* (1577), demonstrated that they followed regular sun-centred paths, but despite this he adhered to a geocentric picture of the orbits of the planets. The 'new star' which he observed in 1572, since named after him, is now known to have been a supernova.

Brahma /'brɑːmə/ *Hinduism* the creator god of late Vedic religion (see BRAHMAN), who later formed a triad with Vishnu and Siva. Little worshipped after the 5th c. AD, he has one known temple dedicated to him in India today. [masc. form of neut. BRAHMAN]

brahma /'brɑːmə/ *n.* = BRAHMAPUTRA. [abbr.]

Brahman /'brɑːmən/ *n.* **1** the supreme being of the Upanishads, often identified with the inner core of the individual (*atman*). It is the eternal and conscious ground of the universe, the source of dharma, and the special sphere of the priestly brahmin class. A neuter term, Brahman was personified in Hindu mythology as the male creator god (Brahma). **2** (also **brahman**; pl. **-mans**) a member of the highest Hindu class, whose members are traditionally eligible for the priesthood, versed in sacred knowledge (i.e. the Veda) □□ **Brahmanic** /-'mænɪk/ *adj.* **Brahmanical** /-'mænɪk(ə)l/ *adj.* [Skr., = sacred knowledge]

Brahmana /'brɑːmənə/ *n.* any of the lengthy commentaries on the Vedas, composed in Sanskrit *c.*900–700 BC, containing exegetical material relating to Vedic sacrificial ritual. [as BRAHMAN]

Brahmanism /'brɑːmənɪz(ə)m/ *n.* the complex sacrificial religion that emerged in post-Vedic India (*c.*900 BC) under the influence of the dominant priesthood (Brahmans). It was as a reaction to Brahman orthodoxy that heterodox sects such as Buddhism and Jainism were formed.

Brahmaputra /ˌbrɑːmə'puːtrə/ a river of southern Asia, rising in Tibet and flowing 2,900 km (1,800 miles) through the Himalayas and NE India to join the Ganges at its delta (in Bangladesh) on the Bay of Bengal.

brahmaputra /ˌbrɑːmə'puːtrə/ *n.* (also **brahma**) **1** any bird of a large Asian breed of domestic fowl. **2** this breed. [river BRAHMAPUTRA, from where it was brought]

Brahmin /'brɑːmɪn/ *n.* **1** = BRAHMAN. **2** *US* a socially or intellectually superior person. [var. of BRAHMAN]

Brahms /brɑːmz/, Johannes (1833–97), German composer and pianist. Welcomed as a genius in Leipzig by Schumann in 1853, he lived for most of the last 35 years of his life in Vienna. Firmly opposed to the 'New German' school of Liszt and the young Wagner, he eschewed programme music and opera and concentrated his energies on 'pure' and traditional forms. He wrote four symphonies, two piano concertos, the Violin Concerto and the Double Concerto, chamber and piano music, choral works including the highly successful *German Requiem* (1857–68), and nearly 200 songs, all of which, if classical in conception, are undeniably romantic and frequently lyrical in expression.

æ cat ɑː arm e bed ɜː her ɪ sit iː see ɒ hot ɔː saw ʌ run ʊ put uː too ə ago aɪ my

braid /breɪd/ n. & v. —n. **1** a woven band of silk or thread used for edging or trimming. **2** a length of entwined hair. —v.tr. **1** plait or intertwine (hair or thread). **2** trim or decorate with braid. □□ **braider** n. [OE *bregdan* f. Gmc]

braiding /'breɪdɪŋ/ n. **1** various types of braid collectively. **2** braided work.

Brăila /brəˈiːlə/ an industrial city and port on the Danube in east Romania; pop. (1985) 234,600.

Braille /breɪl/ n. & v. —n. a system of writing and printing for the blind, in which characters are represented by patterns of raised dots. —v.tr. print or transcribe in Braille. [L. *Braille*, its inventor (d. 1852). a blind French teacher who perfected his system in 1834]

Brain /breɪn/, Dennis (1921–57), English player of the French horn, regarded as the finest virtuoso of his day. Britten, Hindemith, and others composed works for him.

brain /breɪn/ n. & v. —n. **1** an organ of soft nervous tissue contained in the skull of vertebrates, functioning as the coordinating centre of sensation, and of intellectual and nervous activity. (See below.) **2** (in *pl.*) the substance of the brain, esp. as food. **3 a** a person's intellectual capacity (*has a poor brain*). **b** (often in *pl.*) intelligence; high intellectual capacity (*has a brain*; *has brains*). **4** (in *pl.*; prec. by *the*) *colloq.* **a** the cleverest person in a group. **b** a person who originates a complex plan or idea (*the brains behind the robbery*). **5** an electronic device with functions comparable to those of a brain. —v.tr. **1** dash out the brains of. **2** strike hard on the head. □ **brain-dead** suffering from brain death. **brain death** irreversible brain damage causing the end of independent respiration, regarded as indicative of death. **brain drain** *colloq.* the loss of skilled personnel by emigration. **brain fever** inflammation of the brain. **brain-pan** *colloq.* the skull. **brain stem** the central trunk of the brain, upon which the cerebrum and cerebellum are set, and which continues downwards to form the spinal cord. **brains** (*US* **brain**) **trust** a group of experts who give impromptu answers to questions, usu. publicly. **brain-teaser** (or **-twister**) *colloq.* a puzzle or problem. **brain trust** *US* a group of expert advisers. **on the brain** *colloq.* obsessively in one's thoughts. [OE *brægen* f. WG]

The human brain comprises that part of the nervous system contained in the skull. Like that of other vertebrates it arises, during development of the embryo, from the anterior end of a tube of nervous tissue which becomes the spinal cord. The brain directs an animal's activity and exerts control over internal physiological processes; in humans and perhaps some other animals it is the seat of consciousness. It consists of three main parts. (i) The forebrain, greatly developed into the cerebrum in man, consists of two 'hemispheres', joined by a bridge of nerve fibres and is responsible for the exercise of thought and control of the faculty of speech. Its wrinkled surface or cortex is coated with nerve-cells, which appear grey in contrast to the white of the deeper nerve-fibres. Deep in its substance are the thalamus and the hypothalamus, which have a number of functions, being concerned with the regulation of temperature and water balance, with hunger, thirst, and the sex drive, and with the experience of emotions such as anger. The left half of the cerebrum is associated with the right side of the body, regulating its posture and movements and appreciation of bodily sensations, and the right half with the left side. The functions of most of the cerebral cortex, the nature of the physical embodiment of memory and of consciousness itself, remain unknown. (ii) The midbrain, the upper part of the tapering brain-stem, contains cells concerned in eye-movements. (iii) The hindbrain, the lower part of the brain stem, contains the cells responsible for breathing and others which regulate the action of the heart, the flow of digestive juices, etc. The cerebellum, which lies behind the brain stem, plays an important role in the execution of highly skilled movements. In invertebrate animals the brain is similar but less developed; in the lower animals a collection of ganglia has an analogous function.

brainchild /'breɪntʃaɪld/ n. (pl. **-children**) *colloq.* an idea, plan, or invention regarded as the result of a person's mental effort.

Braine /breɪn/, John Gerard (1922–86), English novelist. His first novel *Room at the Top* (1957) was an instant success, with its hero

portraying an 'angry young man' of the 1950s. Braine's later novels express his increasing hostility to the radical views with which he was once identified.

brainless /'breɪnlɪs/ adj. stupid, foolish.

brainpower /'breɪnˌpaʊə(r)/ n. mental ability or intelligence.

brainstorm /'breɪnstɔːm/ n. **1** a violent or excited outburst often as a result of a sudden mental disturbance. **2** *colloq.* mental confusion. **3** *US* a brainwave. **4** a concerted intellectual treatment of a problem by discussing spontaneous ideas about it. □□ **brainstorming** n. (in sense 4).

brainwash /'breɪnwɒʃ/ v.tr. subject (a person) to a prolonged process by which ideas other than and at variance with those already held are implanted in the mind. □□ **brainwashing** n.

brainwave /'breɪnweɪv/ n. **1** (usu. in *pl.*) an electrical impulse in the brain. **2** *colloq.* a sudden bright idea.

brainy /'breɪnɪ/ adj. (**brainier**, **brainiest**) intellectually clever or active. □□ **brainily** adv. **braininess** n.

braise /breɪz/ v.tr. fry lightly and then stew slowly with a little liquid in a closed container. [F *braiser* f. *braise* live coals]

brake[1] /breɪk/ n. & v. —n. **1** (often in *pl.*) a device for checking the motion of a mechanism, esp. a wheel or vehicle, or for keeping it at rest. **2** anything that has the effect of hindering or impeding (*shortage of money was a brake on their enthusiasm*). —v. **1** *intr.* apply a brake. **2** *tr.* retard or stop with a brake. □ **brake block** a block used to hold a brake shoe. **brake drum** a cylinder attached to a wheel on which the brake shoe presses to brake. **brake fluid** fluid used in a hydraulic brake system. **brake horsepower** the power of an engine reckoned in terms of the force needed to brake it. **brake lining** a strip of fabric which increases the friction of the brake shoe. **brake shoe** a long curved block which presses on the brake drum to brake. **brake van** *Brit.* a railway coach or vehicle from which the train's brakes can be controlled. □□ **brakeless** adj. [prob. obs. *brake* in sense 'machine-handle, bridle']

brake[2] /breɪk/ n. a large estate car. [var. of BREAK[2]]

brake[3] /breɪk/ n. & v. —n. **1** a toothed instrument used for crushing flax and hemp. **2** (in full **brake harrow**) a heavy kind of harrow for breaking up large lumps of earth. —v.tr. crush (flax or hemp) by beating it. [ME, rel. to BREAK[1]]

brake[4] /breɪk/ n. **1** a thicket. **2** brushwood. [ME f. OF *bracu*, MLG *brake* branch, stump]

brake[5] /breɪk/ n. bracken. [ME, perh. shortened f. BRACKEN, *-en* being taken as a pl. ending]

brake[6] *archaic past* of BREAK[1].

brakeman /'breɪkmən/ n. (pl. **-men**) **1** *US* an official on a train, responsible for maintenance on a journey. **2** a person in charge of brakes. [BRAKE[1] + MAN]

brakesman /'breɪksmən/ n. (pl. **-men**) *Brit.* = BRAKEMAN 2.

Bramah /'bræmə/, Joseph (1749–1814), English inventor, one of the most versatile and influential engineers of the Industrial Revolution. Best known for his hydraulic press, used for heavy forging, he was responsible also for other important machine tools. In 1784 he patented a very successful lock, unpicked until 1851. To develop the precision machines needed for its manufacture he engaged Henry Maudslay who became a major innovator of machine tools and in turn encouraged other innovators. Bramah's own inventions included milling and planing machines, a beer-engine, a machine for numbering banknotes, and a water-closet.

Bramante /brəˈmæntɪ/, Donato di Angelo (1444–1514), the outstanding Italian architect of the High Renaissance. Strongly influenced by the remains of antiquity he adapted the circular temple to Christian usage, his work expressing the Renaissance striving for the ideal of classical perfection. Employed by Pope Julius II, his most important tasks were the works at the Vatican and the designing of the new St Peter's (begun in 1506), where his Greek-cross plan, crowned with a central dome, was the starting-point for all subsequent work on the basilica. Bramante's character seems to have been forceful and unscrupulous, and he was probably responsible for setting up his kinsman Raphael in Rome in opposition to Michelangelo.

bramble /ˈbræmb(ə)l/ n. **1** any of various thorny shrubs bearing fleshy red or black berries, esp. the blackberry bush, *Rubus fructicosus*. **2** the edible berry of these shrubs. **3** any of various other rosaceous shrubs with similar foliage, esp. the dog rose (*Rosa canina*). □□ **brambly** adj. [OE *bræmbel* (earlier *bræmel*): see BROOM]

brambling /ˈbræmblɪŋ/ n. the speckled finch, *Fringilla montifringilla*, native to northern Eurasia, the male having a distinctive red breast. [G *Brämling* f. WG (cf. BRAMBLE)]

Bramley /ˈbræmlɪ/ n. (pl. **-eys**) (in full **Bramley's seedling**) a large green variety of cooking apple. [M. *Bramley*, Engl. butcher in whose garden it may have first grown c.1850]

bran /bræn/ n. grain husks separated from the flour. □ **bran-tub** Brit. a lucky dip with prizes concealed in bran. [ME f. OF, of unkn. orig.]

Branagh /ˈbrænə/, Kenneth Charles (1960–), English actor, producer, and director, who has played in a wide variety of stage and film dramas. His acclaimed performances include several major Shakespearian roles with the Royal Shakespeare Company.

branch /brɑːntʃ/ n. & v. —n. **1** a limb extending from a tree or bough. **2** a lateral extension or subdivision, esp. of a river, road, or railway. **3** a conceptual extension or subdivision, as of a family, knowledge, etc. **4** a local division or office etc. of a large business, as of a bank, library, etc. —v.intr. (often foll. by *off*) **1** diverge from the main part. **2** divide into branches. **3** (of a tree etc) bear or send out branches. □ **branch out** extend one's field of interest. □□ **branched** adj. **branchlet** n. **branchlike** adj. **branchy** adj. [ME f. OF *branche* f. LL *branca* paw]

branchia /ˈbræŋkɪə/ n.pl. (also **branchiae** /-kɪˌiː/) gills. □□ **branchial** adj. **branchiate** /-kɪˌeɪt/ adj. [L *branchia*, pl. *-ae*, f. Gk *bragkhia* pl.]

Brancusi /bræŋˈkuːzɪ/, Constantin (1876–1957), Romanian sculptor, who worked mainly in Paris. He is noted for his originality in reducing forms to their ultimate—almost abstract—simplicity. His work influenced Epstein, and was admired by Henry Moore.

brand /brænd/ n. & v. —n. **1 a** a particular make of goods. **b** an identifying trade mark, label, etc. **2** (usu. foll. by *of*) a special or characteristic kind (*brand of humour*). **3** an identifying mark burned on livestock or (formerly) prisoners etc. with a hot iron. **4** an iron used for this. **5** a piece of burning, smouldering, or charred wood. **6** a stigma; a mark of disgrace. **7** *poet.* **a** a torch. **b** a sword. **8** a kind of blight, leaving leaves with a burnt appearance. —v.tr. **1** mark with a hot iron. **2** stigmatize; mark with disgrace (*they branded him a liar; was branded for life*). **3** impress unforgettably on one's mind. **4** assign a trademark or label to. □ **brand-new** completely or obviously new. □□ **brander** n. [OE f. Gmc]

Brandenburg /ˈbrændənˌbɜːg/ **1** a former region of Prussia. Its eastern part was ceded to Poland after the Second World War. **2** a 'Land' (State) of Germany, part of East Germany 1952–90; pop. (est. 1990) 2,700,000; capital, Potsdam.

Brandenburg Gate /ˈbrændənˌbɜːg/ one of the city gates of Berlin, the only one that survives. It was built in 1788–91 by Carl Langhans (1732–1808), chief architect to Frederick William II of Prussia, in neoclassical style, and surmounted by the Quadriga of Victory, a chariot drawn by four horses. After the construction of the Berlin Wall (1961) it stood in East Berlin, a conspicuous symbol of a divided city; it was reopened on 21 Dec. 1989.

brandish /ˈbrændɪʃ/ v.tr. wave or flourish as a threat or in display. □□ **brandisher** n. [OF *brandir* ult. f. Gmc, rel. to BRAND]

brandling /ˈbrændlɪŋ/ n. a red earthworm, *Eisenia foetida*, with rings of a brighter colour, which is often found in manure and used as bait. [BRAND + -LING[1]]

Brando /ˈbrændəʊ/, Marlon (1924–), American film actor, an exponent of Stanislavsky's 'method' style (see METHOD 5). His films include *A Streetcar Named Desire* (1951), *On the Waterfront* (1954), *The Godfather* (1972), and *Last Tango in Paris* (1972). Many of his portrayals include explosions of violence and scenes of physical suffering.

Brands Hatch /brændz hætʃ/ a motor circuit near Farningham in Kent, opened for Formula Three racing in 1949 and now used both for motor racing and for test-driving.

Brandt /brɑːnt/, Willy (Herbert Ernst Karl Frahm) (1913–), German statesman, Chancellor of West Germany 1969–74. His main achievement lay in his policy of détente and opening of relations with the USSR and countries of eastern Europe (*Ostpolitik*). He was awarded the Nobel Peace Prize in 1971.

brandy /ˈbrændɪ/ n. (pl. **-ies**) a strong alcoholic spirit distilled from wine or fermented fruit juice. □ **brandy-ball** Brit. a ball of brandy-flavoured sweet. **brandy butter** a rich sweet hard sauce made with brandy, butter, and sugar. **brandy-snap** a crisp rolled gingerbread wafer usu. filled with cream. [earlier *brand(e)wine* f. Du. *brandewijn* burnt (distilled) wine]

brank-ursine /ˌbræŋkˈɜːsaɪn/ n. the plant *Acanthus mollis* or *A. spinosus*, with three-lobed flowers and spiny leaves, used as a motif for the Corinthian capital. Also called *bear's breech* (see BEAR[2]). [F *branche ursine*, med.L *branca ursina* bear's claw: see BRANCH, URSINE]

brant US var. of BRENT.

Braque /brɑːk/, Georges (1882–1963), French painter who, with Picasso, inaugurated cubism. Painting at first in the manner of the fauves, with pure pigments and bright colours, he was impressed with the structural composition of the Cézanne exhibition of 1907 so that when he met Picasso in the following year he was ripe to join him in the researches which led to cubism, and the two worked in close association until Braque's mobilization in 1914 for the First World War. Braque was the first to make the collages which developed into synthetic cubism, introducing real elements and commercial lettering into pictures to contrast the real with the 'illusory' painted image. In 1915 he suffered a severe head wound, but contrived to paint in cubist style from 1917, and by the 1930s was recognized as an international master of still life.

brash[1] /bræʃ/ adj. **1** vulgarly or ostentatiously self-assertive. **2** hasty, rash. **3** impudent. □□ **brashly** adv. **brashness** n. [orig. dial., perh. f. RASH[1]]

brash[2] /bræʃ/ n. **1** loose broken rock or ice. **2** clippings from hedges, shrubs, etc. [18th c.: orig. unkn.]

brash[3] /bræʃ/ n. an eruption of fluid from the stomach. [16th c., perh. imit.]

Brasilia /brəˈzɪlɪə/ the capital (since 1960) of Brazil, built on a site that was chosen (in 1956) in an attempt to draw people away from the crowded coastal areas; pop. (1980) 1,176,748.

Brașov /bræˈʃɒv/ the second-largest city in Romania; pop. (1985) 346,600. It belonged to Hungary (its Hungarian name is *Brassó*) until after the First World War, when it was ceded to Germany (German name *Kronstadt*); in 1950–60 it was known as Orașul Stalin (Romanian, = Stalin City).

brass /brɑːs/ n. & adj. —n. **1** a yellow alloy of copper and zinc. **2 a** an ornament or other decorated piece of brass. **b** brass objects collectively. **3** *Mus.* brass wind instruments (including trumpet, horn, trombone) forming a band or a section of an orchestra. **4** Brit. sl. money. **5** (in full **horse-brass**) a round flat brass ornament for the harness of a draught-horse. **6** (in full **top brass**) colloq. persons in authority or of high (esp. military) rank. **7** an inscribed or engraved memorial tablet of brass. **8** colloq. effrontery (*then had the brass to demand money*). **9** a brass block or die used for making a design on a book binding. —adj. made of brass. □ **brass band** a group of musicians playing brass instruments, sometimes also with percussion. **brassed off** sl. fed up. **brass hat** Brit. colloq. an officer of high rank, usu. one with gold braid on the cap. **brass monkey** coarse sl. used in various phrases to indicate extreme cold. **brass-rubbing 1** the rubbing of heelball etc. over paper laid on an engraved brass to take an impression of its design. **2** the impression obtained by this. **brass tacks** sl. actual details; real business (*get down to brass tacks*). **not a brass farthing** colloq. no money or assets at all. [OE *bræs*, of unkn. orig.]

brassard /ˈbræsɑːd/ n. a band worn on the sleeve, esp. with a uniform. [F *bras* arm + -ARD]

b but d dog f few g get h he j yes k cat l leg m man n no p pen r red s sit t top v voice

brasserie /ˈbræsərɪ/ n. a restaurant, orig. one serving beer with food. [F. = brewery]

Brassey /ˈbræsɪ/, Thomas (1805–70), English engineer, the greatest railway contractor of the 19th c., who built over 10,000 km (6,500 miles) of railways in Europe, North and South America, Australia, and India. Brassey had a genius for recruiting and organizing men, both labourers and managers, who gave of their best. After building the railway from London to Southampton he was responsible for building that from Paris to Rouen and later to Le Havre, for which purposes he sent thousands of British navvies over to France to show his large labour force how to work. Despite this, one large viaduct (550 m long) collapsed but was rebuilt in record time so that the line was opened on time, as were all his subsequent lines. He never went to law over disputes and the reputation he gained for British civil engineering was of lasting value. His one failure was the Grand Trunk Railway of Canada, where lack of experience of local conditions caused costs to exceed estimates considerably, though Brassey bore much of the loss himself. It was said of him that he altered the world more effectively than did the conquests of Alexander the Great.

brassica /ˈbræsɪkə/ n. any cruciferous plant of the genus *Brassica*, having tap roots and erect branched stems, including cabbage, swede, Brussels sprout, mustard, rape, cauliflower, kohlrabi, calabrese, kale, and turnip. [L, = cabbage]

brassie /ˈbræsɪ/ n. (also **brassy**) (pl. **-ies**) a wooden-headed golf club with a brass sole.

brassière /ˈbræzɪə(r), -sɪˌeə(r)/ n. an undergarment worn by women to support the breasts. [F, = child's vest]

brassy¹ /ˈbrɑːsɪ/ adj. (**brassier**, **brassiest**) 1 impudent. 2 pretentious, showy. 3 loud and blaring. 4 of or like brass. □□ **brassily** adv. **brassiness** n.

brassy² var. of BRASSIE.

brat /bræt/ n. usu. derog. a child, esp. an ill-behaved one. □□ **bratty** adj. [perh. abbr. of Sc. *bratchart* hound, or f. *brat* rough garment]

Bratislava /ˌbrætɪˈslɑːvə/ a port on the Danube, the second-largest city of Czechoslovakia; pop. (1986) 417,000. It was the Hungarian capital from 1526 to 1784.

brattice /ˈbrætɪs/ n. a wooden partition or shaft-lining in a coalmine. [ME ult. f. OE *brittisc* BRITISH]

bratwurst /ˈbrætvʊəst, -vɜːst/ n. a type of small German pork sausage. [G f. *braten* fry, roast + *Wurst* sausage]

Braun¹ /brɔːn/, Karl Ferdinand (1850–1918), German physicist who made notable contributions to wireless telegraphy and to the development of the cathode ray tube, the essential precursor of television. He discovered the rectification properties of certain crystals and invented the coupled system of radio transmission. His demonstration that a beam of electrons could be deflected by a voltage difference between deflector plates in an evacuated tube, or by a magnetic field, led to the Braun tube, the forerunner of the cathode ray tube. He was awarded the Nobel Prize for physics, jointly with Guglielmo Marconi, in 1909.

Braun² /brɔːn/, Werner Magnus Maximilian von (1912–77), German designer of rocket engines in the 1930s and during the Second World War. After the war he joined the US team in New Mexico, leading the efforts which resulted in successful launches of satellites, interplanetary missions, and the landing of men on the moon in 1969.

Braunschweig see BRUNSWICK.

bravado /brəˈvɑːdəʊ/ n. a bold manner or a show of boldness intended to impress. [Sp. *bravata* f. *bravo*: cf. BRAVE, -ADO]

brave /breɪv/ adj., n., & v. —adj. 1 able or ready to face and endure danger or pain. 2 formal splendid, spectacular (*make a brave show*). —n. an American Indian warrior. —v.tr. defy; encounter bravely. □ **brave it out** behave defiantly under suspicion or blame. □□ **bravely** adv. **braveness** n. [ME f. F, ult. f. L *barbarus* BARBAROUS]

bravery /ˈbreɪvərɪ/ n. 1 brave conduct. 2 a brave nature. [F *braverie* or It. *braveria* (as BRAVE)]

bravo¹ /brɑːˈvəʊ/ int. & n. —int. expressing approval of a performer etc. —n. (pl. **-os**) a cry of bravo. [F f. It.]

bravo² /ˈbrɑːvəʊ/ n. (pl. **-oes** or **-os**) a hired ruffian or killer. [It.: see BRAVE]

bravura /brəˈvʊərə, -ˈvjʊərə/ n. (often attrib.) 1 a brilliant or ambitious action or display. 2 a a style of (esp. vocal) music requiring exceptional ability. b a passage of this kind. 3 bravado. [It.]

braw /brɔː/ adj. Sc. fine, good. [var. of *brawf* BRAVE]

brawl /brɔːl/ n. & v. —n. a noisy quarrel or fight. —v.intr. 1 quarrel noisily or roughly. 2 (of a stream) run noisily. □□ **brawler** n. [ME f. OProv., rel. to BRAY¹]

brawn /brɔːn/ n. 1 muscular strength. 2 muscle; lean flesh. 3 Brit. a jellied preparation of the chopped meat from a boiled pig's head. [ME f. AF *braun*, OF *braon* f. Gmc]

brawny /ˈbrɔːnɪ/ adj. (**brawnier**, **brawniest**) muscular, strong. □□ **brawniness** n.

Bray, **Vicar of** the hero of an 18th-c. song who kept his benefice from Charles II's reign to George I's by changing his beliefs to suit the times. The song is apparently based on an anecdote of an unidentified vicar of Bray, Berks., in T. Fuller *Worthies of England* (1662).

bray¹ /breɪ/ n. & v. —n. 1 the cry of a donkey. 2 a sound like this cry, e.g. that of a harshly-played brass instrument, a laugh, etc. —v. 1 intr. make a braying sound. 2 tr. utter harshly. [ME f. OF *braire*, perh. ult. f. Celt.]

bray² /breɪ/ v.tr. archaic pound or crush to small pieces, esp. with a pestle and mortar. [ME f. AF *braier*, OF *breier* f. Gmc]

braze¹ /breɪz/ v. & n. —v.tr. solder with an alloy of brass and zinc at a high temperature. —n. 1 a brazed joint. 2 the alloy used for brazing. [F *braser* solder f. *braise* live coals]

braze² /breɪz/ v.tr. 1 a make of brass. b cover or ornament with brass. 2 make hard like brass. [OE *bræsen* f. *bræs* BRASS]

brazen /ˈbreɪz(ə)n/ adj. & v. —adj. 1 (also **brazen-faced**) flagrant and shameless; insolent. 2 made of brass. 3 of or like brass, esp. in colour or sound. —v.tr. (foll. by *out*) face or undergo defiantly. □ **brazen it out** be defiantly unrepentant under censure. □□ **brazenly** adv. **brazenness** /ˈbreɪznnɪs/ n. [OE *bræsen* f. *bræs* brass]

brazier¹ /ˈbreɪzɪə(r), -ʒə(r)/ n. a portable heater consisting of a pan or stand for holding lighted coals. [F *brasier* f. *braise* hot coals]

brazier² /ˈbreɪzɪə(r), -ʒə(r)/ n. a worker in brass. □□ **braziery** n. [ME prob. f. BRASS + -IER, after *glass*, *glazier*]

Brazil¹ /brəˈzɪl/ a country in NE South America, the largest of that continent, comprising almost half its total area, and the fourth-largest in the world; pop. (1988) 150,685,100; official language, Portuguese; capital, Brasilia. In the north lies the Amazon basin with its tropical rain forests. Economically, Brazil is still mainly an agricultural country, but is rich in mineral resources (not yet fully exploited), including iron, gold, phosphates, and uranium. The land is split into an industrialized coastal belt, which makes it the most industrially advanced country in South America, and a vast underdeveloped interior. Colonized by the Portuguese in the 16th c., Brazil became an independent kingdom in 1826, remaining a liberal monarchy until the institution of a republic in 1889. It fell under dictatorial rule between the World Wars, and although not as troubled by instability as some of its neighbours, is still prone to socio-political unrest. The country is named after Brazil-wood; it was originally *Brasil*, short for Spanish and Portuguese *terra de brasil* red-dye-wood land (see BRAZIL²). □□ **Brazilian** adj. & n.

Brazil² /brəˈzɪl/ n. 1 a a lofty tree, *Bertholletia excelsa*, forming large forests in S. America. b (in full **Brazil nut**) a large three-sided nut with an edible kernel from this tree. 2 (in full **Brazil-wood**) a hard red wood from any tropical tree of the genus *Caesalpina*, that yields dyes. [Sp. & Port. *brasil*, med. L *brasilium* (orig. unkn.; perh. a corruption of an Oriental name for the dye-wood orig. so called)]

Brazzaville /ˈbræzəvɪl/ the capital and a major port of the People's Republic of the Congo, on the Congo River; pop. (est. 1984) 585,800.

BRCS abbr. British Red Cross Society.

breach /briːtʃ/ n. & v. —n. **1** (often foll. by of) the breaking of or failure to observe a law, contract, etc. **2 a** a breaking of relations; an estrangement. **b** a quarrel. **3 a** a broken state. **b** a gap, esp. one made by artillery in fortifications. —v.tr. **1** break through; make a gap in. **2** break (a law, contract, etc.). □ **breach of the peace** an infringement or violation of the public peace by any disturbance or riot etc. **breach of promise** the breaking of a promise, esp. a promise to marry. **stand in the breach** bear the brunt of an attack. **step into the breach** give help in a crisis, esp. by replacing someone who has dropped out. [ME f. OF breche, ult. f. Gmc]

bread /bred/ n. & v. —n. **1** baked dough made of flour usu. leavened with yeast and moistened, eaten as a staple food. **2 a** necessary food. **b** (also **daily bread**) one's livelihood. **3** sl. money. —v.tr. coat with breadcrumbs for cooking. □ **bread and butter 1** bread spread with butter. **2 a** one's livelihood. **b** routine work to ensure an income. **bread-and-butter letter** a letter of thanks for hospitality. **bread and circuses** the public provision of subsistence and entertainment. **bread and wine** the Eucharist. **bread basket 1** a basket for bread or rolls. **2** sl. the stomach. **bread bin** a container for keeping bread in. **bread sauce** a white sauce thickened with breadcrumbs. **cast one's bread upon the waters** do good without expecting gratitude or reward. **know which side one's bread is buttered** know where one's advantage lies. **take the bread out of a person's mouth** take away a person's living, esp. by competition etc. [OE brēad f. Gmc]

breadboard /ˈbredbɔːd/ n. **1** a board for cutting bread on. **2** a board for making an experimental model of an electric circuit.

breadcrumb /ˈbredkrʌm/ n. **1** a small fragment of bread. **2** (in pl.) bread crumbled for use in cooking.

breadfruit /ˈbredfruːt/ n. **1** a tropical evergreen tree, Artocarpus altilis, bearing edible usu. seedless fruit. **2** the fruit of this tree which when roasted becomes soft like new bread.

breadline /ˈbredlaɪn/ n. **1** subsistence level (esp. on the breadline). **2** US a queue of people waiting to receive free food.

breadth /bredθ/ n. **1** the distance or measurement from side to side of a thing; broadness. **2** a piece (of cloth etc.) of standard or full breadth. **3** extent, distance, room. **4** (usu. foll. by of) capacity to respect other opinions; freedom from prejudice or intolerance (esp. breadth of mind or view). **5** Art unity of the whole, achieved by the disregard of unnecessary details. □□ **breadthways** adv. **breadthwise** adv. [obs. brede, OE brǣdu, f. Gmc, rel. to BROAD]

breadwinner /ˈbredˌwɪnə(r)/ n. a person who earns the money to support a family.

break¹ /breɪk/ v. & n. —v. (past **broke** /brəʊk/ or archaic **brake** /breɪk/; past part. **broken** /ˈbrəʊkən/ or archaic **broke**) **1** tr. & intr. **a** separate into pieces under a blow or strain; shatter. **b** make or become inoperative, e.g. from damage (the toaster has broken). **c** break a bone in or dislocate (part of the body). **d** break the skin of (the head or crown). **2 a** tr. cause or effect an interruption in (broke our journey; the spell was broken; broke the silence). **b** intr. have an interval between spells of work (let's break now; we broke for tea). **3** tr. fail to observe or keep (a law, promise, etc.). **4 a** tr. & intr. make or become subdued or weakened; yield or cause to yield (broke his spirit; he broke under the strain). **b** tr. weaken the effect of (a fall, blow, etc.). **c** tr. = break in 3c. **d** tr. defeat, destroy (broke the enemy's power). **e** tr. defeat the object of (a strike, e.g. by engaging other personnel). **5** tr. surpass (a record). **6** intr. (foll. by with) quarrel or cease association with (another person etc.). **7** tr. **a** be no longer subject to (a habit). **b** (foll. by of) cause (a person) to be free of a habit (broke them of their addiction). **8** tr. & intr. reveal or be revealed; (cause to) become known (broke the news; the story broke on Friday). **9** intr. **a** (of the weather) change suddenly, esp. after a fine spell. **b** (of waves) curl over and dissolve into foam. **c** (of the day) dawn. **d** (of clouds) move apart; show a gap. **e** (of a storm) begin violently. **10** tr. Electr. disconnect (a circuit). **11** intr. **a** (of the voice) change with emotion. **b** (of a boy's voice) change in register etc. at puberty. **12** tr. **a** (often foll. by up) divide (a set etc.) into parts, e.g. by selling to different buyers. **b** change (a banknote etc.) for coins. **13** tr. ruin (an individual or institution) financially (see also BROKE adj.). **14** tr.

penetrate (e.g. a safe) by force. **15** tr. decipher (a code). **16** tr. make (a way, path, etc.) by separating obstacles. **17** intr. burst forth (the sun broke through the clouds). **18** Mil. **a** intr. (of troops) disperse in confusion. **b** tr. make a rupture in (ranks). **19 a** intr. (usu. foll. by free, loose, out, etc.) escape from constraint by a sudden effort. **b** tr. escape or emerge from (prison, bounds, cover, etc.). **20** tr. Tennis etc. win a game against (an opponent's service). **21** intr. Boxing etc. (of two fighters, usu. at the referee's command) come out of a clinch. **22** Mil. tr. demote (an officer). **23** intr. esp. Stock Exch. (of prices) fall sharply. **24** intr. Cricket (of a bowled ball) change direction on bouncing. **25** intr. Billiards etc. disperse the balls at the beginning of a game. **26** tr. unfurl (a flag etc.). **27** tr. Phonet. subject (a vowel) to fracture. **28** tr. fail to rejoin (one's ship) after absence on leave. **29** tr. disprove (an alibi). —n. **1 a** an act or instance of breaking. **b** a point where something is broken; a gap. **2** an interval, an interruption; a pause in work. **3** a sudden dash (esp. to escape). **4** colloq. **a** a piece of good luck; a fair chance. **b** (also **bad break**) an unfortunate remark or action, a blunder. **5** Cricket a change in direction of a bowled ball on bouncing. **6** Billiards etc. **a** a series of points scored during one turn. **b** the opening shot that disperses the balls. **7** Mus. (in jazz) a short unaccompanied passage for a soloist, usu. improvised. **8** Electr. a discontinuity in a circuit. □ **bad break** colloq. **1** a piece of bad luck. **2** a mistake or blunder. **break away** make or become free or separate (see also BREAKAWAY). **break the back of 1** do the hardest or greatest part of. **2** overburden (a person). **break bulk** see BULK. **break crop** a crop grown to avoid the continual growing of cereals. **break-dancing** an energetic style of street-dancing, developed by US Blacks. **break down 1 a** fail in mechanical action; cease to function. **b** (of human relationships etc.) fail, collapse. **c** fail in (esp. mental) health. **d** be overcome by emotion; collapse in tears. **2 a** demolish, destroy. **b** suppress (resistance). **c** force (a person) to yield under pressure. **3** analyse into components (see also BREAKDOWN). **break even** emerge from a transaction etc. with neither profit nor loss. **break a person's heart** see HEART. **break the ice 1** begin to overcome formality or shyness, esp. between strangers. **2** make a start. **break in 1** enter premises by force, esp. with criminal intent. **2** interrupt. **3 a** accustom to a habit etc. **b** wear etc. until comfortable. **c** tame or discipline (an animal); accustom (a horse) to saddle and bridle etc. **4** Austral. & NZ bring (virgin land) into cultivation. **break-in** n. an illegal forced entry into premises, esp. with criminal intent. **breaking and entering** (formerly) the illegal entering of a building with intent to commit a felony. **breaking-point** the point of greatest strain, at which a thing breaks or a person gives way. **break in on** disturb; interrupt. **break into 1** enter forcibly or violently. **2 a** suddenly begin, burst forth with (a song, laughter, etc.). **b** suddenly change one's pace for (a faster one) (broke into a gallop). **3** interrupt. **break-line** Printing the last line of a paragraph (usu. not of full length). **break of day** dawn. **break off 1** detach by breaking. **2** bring to an end. **3** cease talking etc. **break open** open forcibly. **break out 1** escape by force, esp. from prison. **2** begin suddenly; burst forth (then violence broke out). **3** (foll. by in) become covered in (a rash etc.). **4** exclaim. **5** release (a run-up flag). **6** US **a** open up (a receptacle) and remove its contents. **b** remove (articles) from a place of storage. **break-out** n. a forcible escape. **break point 1** a place or time at which an interruption or change is made. **2** Computing (usu. **breakpoint**) a place in a computer program where the sequence of instructions is interrupted, esp. by another program. **3 a** (in lawn tennis) a point which would win the game for the player(s) receiving service. **b** the situation at which the receiver(s) may break service by winning such a point. **4** = breaking-point. **break step** get out of step. **break up 1** break into small pieces. **2** disperse; disband. **3** end the school term. **4 a** terminate a relationship; disband. **b** cause to do this. **5** (of the weather) change suddenly (esp. after a fine spell). **6** esp. US **a** upset or be upset. **b** excite or be excited. **c** convulse or be convulsed (see also BREAKUP). **break wind** release gas from the anus. **break one's word** see WORD. [OE brecan f. Gmc]

break² /breɪk/ n. **1** a carriage-frame without a body, for breaking in young horses. **2** = BRAKE². [perh. = *brake* framework: 17th c., of unkn. orig.]

breakable /'breɪkəb(ə)l/ *adj. & n.* —*adj.* that may or is apt to be broken easily. —*n.* (esp. in *pl.*) a breakable thing.

breakage /'breɪkɪdʒ/ *n.* **1 a** a broken thing. **b** damage caused by breaking. **2** an act or instance of breaking.

breakaway /'breɪkəˌweɪ/ *n.* **1** the act or an instance of breaking away or seceding. **2** (*attrib.*) that breaks away or has broken away; separate. **3** *Austral.* a stampede, esp. at the sight or smell of water. **4** a false start in a race. **5** *Rugby Football* an outside second-row forward.

breakdown /'breɪkdaʊn/ *n.* **1 a** a mechanical failure. **b** a loss of (esp. mental) health and strength. **2** a collapse or disintegration (*breakdown of communication*). **3** a detailed analysis (of statistics etc.).

breaker /'breɪkə(r)/ *n.* **1** a person or thing that breaks something, esp. disused machinery. **2** a person who breaks in a horse. **3** a heavy wave that breaks.

breakfast /'brekfəst/ *n. & v.* —*n.* the first meal of the day. —*v.intr.* have breakfast. □□ **breakfaster** *n.* [BREAK¹ interrupt + FAST²]

breakneck /'breɪknek/ *adj.* (of speed) dangerously fast.

Breakspear /'breɪkspɪə(r)/, Nicholas, see ADRIAN IV.

breakthrough /'breɪkθruː/ *n.* **1** a major advance or discovery. **2** an act of breaking through an obstacle etc.

breakup /'breɪkʌp/ *n.* **1** disintegration, collapse. **2** dispersal.

breakwater /'breɪkˌwɔːtə(r)/ *n.* a barrier built out into the sea to break the force of waves.

Bream /briːm/, Julian Alexander (1933–), English guitarist and lutenist, whose outstanding talent attracted the attention of Segovia. Britten, Walton, and others have composed works for him.

bream¹ /briːm/ *n.* (*pl.* same) **1** a yellowish arch-backed fresh-water fish, *Abramis brama*. **2** (in full **sea bream**) a similarly shaped marine fish of the family Sparidae. [ME f. OF *bre(s)me* f. WG]

bream² /briːm/ *v.tr. Naut. hist.* clean (a ship's bottom) by burning and scraping. [prob. f. LG: rel. to BROOM]

breast /brest/ *n. & v.* —*n.* **1 a** either of two milk-secreting organs on the upper front of a woman's body. **b** the corresponding usu. rudimentary part of a man's body. **2 a** the upper front part of a human body; the chest. **b** the corresponding part of an animal. **3** the part of a garment that covers the breast. **4** the breast as a source of nourishment or emotion. —*v.tr.* **1** face, meet in full opposition (*breast the wind*). **2** contend with (*breast it out against difficulties*). **3** reach the top of (a hill). □ **breast-feed** (*past* and *past part.* **-fed**) feed (a baby) from the breast. **breast-high** as high as the breast; submerged to the breast. **breast-pin** a brooch etc. worn on the breast. **breast-stroke** a stroke made while swimming on the breast by extending arms forward and sweeping them back in unison. **breast the tape** see TAPE. **make a clean breast of** confess fully. □□ **breasted** *adj.* (also in *comb.*). **breastless** *adj.* [OE *brēost* f. Gmc]

breastbone /'brestbəʊn/ *n.* a thin flat vertical bone and cartilage in the chest connecting the ribs.

breastplate /'brestpleɪt/ *n.* a piece of armour covering the breast.

breastsummer /'bresəmə(r)/ *n. Archit.* a beam across a broad opening, sustaining a superstructure. [BREAST + SUMMER²]

breastwork /'brestwɜːk/ *n.* a low temporary defence or parapet.

breath /breθ/ *n.* **1 a** the air taken into or expelled from the lungs. **b** one respiration of air. **c** an exhalation of air that can be seen, smelt, or heard (*breath steamed in the cold air; bad breath*). **2 a** a slight movement of air; a breeze. **b** a whiff of perfume etc. **3** a whisper, a murmur (esp. of a scandalous nature). **4** the power of breathing; life (*is there breath in him?*). □ **below** (or **under**) **one's breath** in a whisper. **breath of fresh air 1** a small amount of or a brief time in the fresh air. **2** a refreshing change. **breath of life** a necessity. **breath test** *Brit.* a test of a person's alcohol consumption, using a breathalyser. **catch**

one's breath **1** cease breathing momentarily in surprise, suspense, etc. **2** rest after exercise to restore normal breathing. **draw breath** breathe; live. **hold one's breath** cease breathing temporarily. **in the same breath** (esp. of saying two contradictory things) within a short time. **out of breath** gasping for air, esp. after exercise. **take breath** pause for rest. **take one's breath away** astound; surprise; awe; delight. **waste one's breath** talk or give advice without effect. [OE *brǣth* f. Gmc]

Breathalyser /'breθəˌlaɪzə(r)/ *n.* (also **Breathalyzer**) *Brit. propr.* an instrument for measuring the amount of alcohol in the breath (and hence in the blood) of a driver. □□ **breathalyse** *v.tr.* (also **-lyze**). [BREATH + ANALYSE + -ER¹]

breathe /briːð/ *v.* **1** *intr.* take air into and expel it from the lungs. **2** *intr.* be or seem alive (*is she breathing?*). **3** *tr.* **a** utter; say (esp. quietly) (*breathed her forgiveness*). **b** express; display (*breathed defiance*). **4** *intr.* take breath, pause. **5** *tr.* send out or take in (as if) with breathed air (*breathed new life into them; breathed whisky*). **6** *intr.* (of wine, fabric, etc.) be exposed to fresh air. **7** *intr.* **a** sound, speak (esp. quietly). **b** (of wind) blow softly. **8** *tr.* allow (a horse etc.) to breathe; give rest after exertion. □ **breathe again** (or **freely**) recover from a shock, fear, etc., and be at ease. **breathe down a person's neck** follow or check up on a person, esp. menacingly. **breathe one's last** die. **breathe upon** tarnish, taint. **not breathe a word** keep quite secret. [ME f. BREATH]

breather /'briːðə(r)/ *n.* **1** *colloq.* **a** a brief pause for rest. **b** a short spell of exercise. **2** a safety-vent in the crankcase of a motor vehicle etc.

breathing /'briːðɪŋ/ *n.* **1** the process of taking air into and expelling it from the lungs. **2** *Phonet.* a sign in Greek indicating that an initial vowel or rho is aspirated (**rough breathing**) or not aspirated (**smooth breathing**). □ **breathing-space** time to breathe; a pause.

breathless /'breθlɪs/ *adj.* **1** panting, out of breath. **2** holding the breath because of excitement, suspense, etc. (*a state of breathless expectancy*). **3** unstirred by wind; still. □□ **breathlessly** *adv.* **breathlessness** *n.*

breathtaking /'breθˌteɪkɪŋ/ *adj.* astounding; awe-inspiring. □□ **breathtakingly** *adv.*

breathy /'breθɪ/ *adj.* (**breathier, breathiest**) (of a singing-voice etc.) containing the sound of breathing. □□ **breathily** *adv.* **breathiness** *n.*

breccia /'bretʃɪə/ *n. & v.* —*n.* a rock of angular stones etc. cemented by finer material. —*v.tr.* form into breccia. □□ **brecciate** *v.tr.* **brecciation** /-'eɪʃ(ə)n/ *n.* [It., = gravel, f. Gmc, rel. to BREAK¹]

Brecht /brext/, Bertolt (1898–1956), German dramatist, producer, and poet. His early plays showed kinship with expressionism and in 1928 he achieved outstanding success with *The Threepenny Opera* (an adaptation of John Gay's *The Beggar's Opera*) with music by Kurt Weill. From 1933 he lived in the US and Scandinavia, returning in 1949 to East Berlin where he founded the Berlin Ensemble. His enormous impact on 20th-c. drama derives from his attempts to develop a Marxist 'epic theatre', exploiting his famous 'alienation effect' which rejected Aristotelian principles, disposed of dramatic climaxes, and used songs to comment on the action as in *The Life of Galileo* (1937–9), *Mother Courage* (1941), and *The Caucasian Chalk Circle* (1948).

bred *past* and *past part.* of BREED.

Breda /'breɪdə/ a manufacturing town in SW Netherlands; pop. (1987) 120,212. It is remembered for the Compromise of Breda (1566), a protest against Spanish rule; the manifesto of Charles II (who live there in exile), stating his terms for accepting the throne of Britain (1660); and the Treaty of Breda, which ended the Anglo-Dutch war of 1665–7.

breech /briːtʃ/ *n. & v.* —*n.* **1 a** the part of a cannon behind the bore. **b** the back part of a rifle or gun barrel. **2** *archaic* the buttocks. —*v.tr. archaic* put (a boy) into breeches after being in petticoats since birth. □ **breech birth** (or **delivery**) the delivery of a baby with the buttocks or feet foremost. **breech-block** a metal block which closes the breech aperture in a gun. **breech-loader** a gun loaded at the breech, not through the muzzle. **breech-loading** (of a gun) loaded at the breech, not through the muzzle. [OE brōc, pl. brēc (treated as sing. in ME), f. Gmc]

breeches /ˈbrɪtʃɪz/ n.pl. (also **pair of breeches** sing.) **1** short trousers, esp. fastened below the knee, now used esp. for riding or in court costume. **2** colloq. any trousers, knickerbockers, or underpants. □ **Breeches Bible** the Geneva Bible of 1560 with breeches for aprons in Gen. 3: 7. **breeches buoy** a lifebuoy suspended from a rope which has canvas breeches for the user's legs. [pl. of BREECH]

breed /briːd/ v. & n. —v. (past and past part. **bred** /bred/) **1** tr. & intr. bear, generate (offspring). **2** tr. & intr. propagate or cause to propagate; raise (livestock). **3** tr. **a** yield, produce; result in (war breeds famine). **b** spread (discontent bred by rumour). **4** intr. arise; spread (disease breeds in the Tropics). **5** tr. bring up; train (bred to the law; Hollywood breeds stars). **6** tr. Physics create (fissile material) by nuclear reaction. —n. **1** a stock of animals or plants within a species, having a similar appearance, and usu. developed by deliberate selection. **2** a race; a lineage. **3** a sort, a kind. □ **bred and born** = born and bred. **bred in the bone** hereditary. **breeder reactor** a nuclear reactor that can create more fissile material than it consumes. **breed in** mate with or marry near relations. □□ **breeder** n. [OE brēdan: rel. to BROOD]

breeding /ˈbriːdɪŋ/ n. **1** the process of developing or propagating (animals, plants, etc.). **2** generation; childbearing. **3** the result of training or education; behaviour. **4** good manners (as produced by an aristocratic heredity) (has no breeding).

breeks /briːks/ n.pl. Sc. var. of BREECHES.

breeze[1] /briːz/ n. & v. —n. **1** a gentle wind. **2** Meteorol. a wind of 4–31 m.p.h. and between force 2 and force 6 on the Beaufort scale. **3** a wind blowing from land at night or sea during the day. **4** esp. Brit. colloq. a quarrel or display of temper. **5** esp. US colloq. an easy task. —v.intr. (foll. by in, out, along, etc.) colloq. come or go in a casual or lighthearted manner. [prob. f. OSp. & Port. briza NE wind]

breeze[2] /briːz/ n. small cinders. □ **breeze-block** any lightweight building block, esp. one made from breeze mixed with sand and cement. [F braise live coals]

breeze[3] /briːz/ n. a gadfly or cleg. [OE briosa, of unkn. orig.]

breezy /ˈbriːzɪ/ adj. (**breezier**, **breeziest**) **1 a** windswept. **b** pleasantly windy. **2** colloq. lively; jovial. **3** colloq. careless (with breezy indifference). □□ **breezily** adv. **breeziness** n.

Bremen /ˈbreɪmən/ **1** a 'Land' (State) of Germany; pop. (1987) 654,000. **2** its capital city, an industrial city and port on the River Weser; pop. (1987) 522,000.

bremsstrahlung /ˈbremzˌʃtraːlʊŋ/ n. Physics the electromagnetic radiation produced by the acceleration or esp. the deceleration of a charged particle after passing through the electric and magnetic fields of a nucleus. [G, = braking radiation]

Bren /bren/ n. (in full **Bren gun**) a lightweight quick-firing machine-gun. [Brno in Czechoslovakia (where orig. made) + Enfield in Greater London, England (where later made)]

Brendan /ˈbrend(ə)n/, St (c.486–c.575), abbot of Clonfert. The legend of the 'Navigation of St Brendan' (c.1050), describing his voyage with a band of monks to a promised land (possibly the Orkneys and Hebrides) was widely popular in the Middle Ages.

Brenner Pass /ˈbrenə(r)/ an Alpine pass on the Austro–Italian frontier, at an altitude of 1,371 m (4,450 ft.) on the route between Innsbruck and Bolzano.

brent /brent/ n. (US **brant**) (in full **brent-goose**) a small migratory goose, Branta bernicla. [16th c.: orig. unkn.]

Brescia /ˈbreʃə/ an industrial city in Lombardy in north Italy; pop. (1981) 206,650.

Breslau see WROCŁAW.

Bresson /ˈbresɔ̃/, Robert (1907–), French film director whose spare individual style depicts with meticulous detail the subject he wishes to explore, but omits everything extraneous to it. He preferred not to use professional actors. His films, which appear infrequently and are given thematic coherence by his Catholic beliefs, include Diary of a Country Priest (1951), The Trial of Joan of Arc (1962), The Devil, Probably (1977), and L'Argent (1983).

Brest /brest/ a port and naval base on the Atlantic coast of Brittany in NW France; pop. (1982) 160,350.

Brest-Litovsk /ˌbrestlɪˈtɒfsk/ a Polish town on the Russian frontier (now in the USSR), in which was signed the treaty of peace between Germany and Russia in March 1918.

Bretagne see BRITTANY.

brethren see BROTHER.

Breton[1] /ˈbret(ə)n, brəˈtɔ̃/ n. & adj. —n. **1** a native of Brittany. **2** the Celtic language of Brittany. (See below.) —adj. of or relating to Brittany or its people or language. [OF, = BRITON]

The language of the Bretons, belongs to the Brythonic branch of the Celtic language group. It is the only Celtic language now spoken on the European mainland, representing the modern development of the language brought from Cornwall and South Wales in the 5th and 6th c. by Britons fleeing from the Saxon invaders. Until the 20th c. it was widely spoken in Brittany, but official encouragement of the use of French contributed to its decline. Recently attempts have been made to revive its use in Brittany, but although it is taught in some schools its use is rare in the younger generation. [OF, = Briton]

Breton[2] /ˈbret(ə)n, brəˈtɔ̃/, André (1896–1966), French poet, essayist, and critic, founder and chief theorist of surrealism (see entry).

bretzel var. of PRETZEL.

Breughel var. of BRUEGEL and BRUEGHEL.

Breuil /ˈbrɜːɪ/, Henri (1877–1961), French archaeologist, noted for his work on palaeolithic cave-paintings.

breve /briːv/ n. **1** Mus. a note, now rarely used, having the time value of two semibreves. **2** a written or printed mark (˘) indicating a short or unstressed vowel. **3** hist. an authoritative letter from a sovereign or pope. [ME var. of BRIEF]

brevet /ˈbrevɪt/ n. & v. —n. (often attrib.) a document conferring a privilege from a sovereign or government, esp. a rank in the army, without the appropriate pay (was promoted by brevet; brevet major). —v.tr. (**breveted**, **breveting** or **brevetted**, **brevetting**) confer brevet rank on. [ME f. OF dimin. of bref BRIEF]

breviary /ˈbriːvɪərɪ/ n. (pl. **-ies**) RC Ch. a book containing the service for each day, to be recited by those in orders. [L breviarium summary f. breviare abridge: see ABBREVIATE]

brevity /ˈbrevɪtɪ/ n. **1** economy of expression; conciseness. **2** shortness (of time etc.) (the brevity of happiness). [AF breveté, OF brieveté f. bref BRIEF]

brew /bruː/ v. & n. —v. **1** tr. **a** make (beer etc.) by infusion, boiling, and fermentation. **b** make (tea etc.) by infusion or (punch etc.) by mixture. **2** intr. undergo either of these processes (the tea is brewing). **3** intr. (of trouble, a storm, etc.) gather force; threaten (mischief was brewing). **4** tr. bring about; set in train; concoct (brewed their fiendish scheme). —n. **1** an amount (of beer etc.) brewed at one time (this year's brew). **2** what is brewed (esp. with regard to its quality) (a good strong brew). **3** the action or process of brewing. □ **brew up** make tea. **brew-up** n. an instance of making tea. □□ **brewer** n. [OE brēowan f. Gmc]

brewery /ˈbruːərɪ/ n. (pl. **-ies**) a place where beer etc. is brewed commercially.

Brezhnev /ˈbreʒnef/, Leonid Ilyich (1906–83), Soviet statesman, effectively leader of the USSR from 1964, when he succeeded Khrushchev as First Secretary of the Communist Party, until his death. His period in power was marked by intensified persecution of dissidents at home and by attempted détente followed by renewed 'cold war' in 1968. He was largely responsible for the decision to invade Czechoslovakia in 1968, maintaining the doctrine that one socialist State may interfere in the affairs of another if the continuance of socialism is at risk.

Brian Boru /ˌbraɪən bəˈruː/ (926–1014) king of Munster in SW Ireland. Having defeated the Danes he became high king of Ireland, but was killed after a victory over the Danes at Clontarf.

briar[1] var. of BRIER[1].

briar[2] var. of BRIER[2].

bribe /braɪb/ v. & n. —v.tr. (often foll. by to + infin.) persuade (a person etc.) to act improperly in one's favour by a gift of money, services, etc. (bribed the guard to release the suspect). —n.

b but   d dog   f few   g get   h he   j yes   k cat   l leg   m man   n no   p pen   r red   s sit   t top   v voice

money or services offered in the process of bribing. □□ **bribable** *adj.* **briber** *n.* **bribery** *n.* [ME f. OF *briber, brimber* beg, of unkn. orig.]

bric-à-brac /ˈbrɪkəˌbræk/ *n.* (also **bric-a-brac, bricabrac**) miscellaneous, often old, ornaments, trinkets, furniture, etc., of no great value. [F f. obs. *à bric et à brac* at random]

brick /brɪk/ *n., v.,* & *adj.* —*n.* **1 a** a small, usu. rectangular, block of fired or sun-dried clay, used in building. **b** the material used to make these. **c** a similar block of concrete etc. **2** *Brit.* a child's toy building-block. **3** a brick-shaped solid object (*a brick of ice-cream*). **4** *sl.* a generous or loyal person. —*v.tr.* (foll. by *in, up*) close or block with brickwork. —*adj.* **1** built of brick (*brick wall*). **2** of a dull red colour. □ **bang** (or **knock** or **run**) **one's head against a brick wall** attempt the impossible. **brick-field** a place at which bricks are made. **brick-red** the colour of bricks. **like a load** (or **ton**) **of bricks** *colloq.* with crushing weight, force, or authority. **see through a brick wall** have miraculous insight. □□ **bricky** *adj.* [ME f. MLG, MDu. *bri(c)ke,* of unkn. orig.]

brickbat /ˈbrɪkbæt/ *n.* **1** a piece of brick, esp. when used as a missile. **2** an uncomplimentary remark.

brickfielder /ˈbrɪkˌfiːldə(r)/ *n. Austral.* a hot, dry north wind.

brickie /ˈbrɪkɪ/ *n. sl.* a bricklayer.

bricklayer /ˈbrɪkˌleɪə(r)/ *n.* a worker who builds with bricks. □□ **bricklaying** *n.*

brickwork /ˈbrɪkwɜːk/ *n.* **1** building in brick. **2** a wall, building, etc. made of brick.

brickyard /ˈbrɪkjɑːd/ *n.* a place where bricks are made.

bridal /ˈbraɪd(ə)l/ *adj.* of or concerning a bride or a wedding. □□ **bridally** *adv.* [orig. as noun, = wedding-feast, f. OE *brȳd-ealu* f. *brȳd* BRIDE + *ealu* ale-drinking]

Bride /braɪd/, St, see BRIDGET[1].

bride /braɪd/ *n.* a woman on her wedding day and for some time before and after it. □ **bride-cake** a wedding cake. **bride-price** money or goods given to a bride's family esp. in primitive societies. [OE *brȳd* f. Gmc]

bridegroom /ˈbraɪdgruːm, -grʊm/ *n.* a man on his wedding day and for some time before and after it. [OE *brȳdguma* (as BRIDE, *guma* man, assim. to GROOM)]

bridesmaid /ˈbraɪdzmeɪd/ *n.* a girl or unmarried woman attending a bride on her wedding day. [earlier *bridemaid,* f. BRIDE + MAID]

bridewell /ˈbraɪdwel, -wel/ *n. archaic* a prison; a reformatory. [St *Bride's* (or *Bridget's*) *Well* in London, between Fleet Street and the Thames, where such a building (formerly a royal palace) stood]

Bridge /brɪdʒ/, Frank (1879–1941), English composer, conductor, violinist, and violist. His compositions include chamber music, songs, and orchestral works, among them *The Sea* (1910–11). His later works, such as the string trio *Rhapsody* (1928) and *Oration* (for cello and orchestra, 1930) show stylistic elements akin to those of Schoenberg. Benjamin Britten, at the age of 14, was among his pupils.

bridge[1] /brɪdʒ/ *n.* & *v.* —*n.* **1 a** a structure carrying a road, path, railway, etc., across a stream, ravine, road, railway, etc. (See below.) **b** anything providing a connection between different things (*English is a bridge between nations*). **2** the superstructure on a ship from which the captain and officers direct operations. **3** the upper bony part of the nose. **4** *Mus.* an upright piece of wood on a violin etc. over which the strings are stretched. **5** = BRIDGEWORK. **6** *Billiards* etc. **a** a long stick with a structure at the end which is used to support a cue for a difficult shot. **b** a support for a cue formed by a raised hand. **7** = *land-bridge.* —*v.tr.* **1 a** be a bridge over (*a fallen tree bridges the stream*). **b** make a bridge over; span. **2** span as if with a bridge (*bridged their differences with understanding*). □ **bridge of asses** = *pons asinorum.* **bridge of boats** a bridge formed by mooring boats together abreast across a river etc. **Bridge of Sighs** a 16th-c. covered bridge in Venice between the doges' palace and the State prison, crossed by prisoners on their way to torture or execution. **bridge passage** *Mus.* a transitional piece between main themes. **bridging loan** a loan from a bank etc. to cover the short interval between buying a house etc. and selling another.

cross a (or **that**) **bridge when one comes to it** deal with a problem when and if it arises. □□ **bridgeable** *adj.* [OE *brycg* f. Gmc]

The main types of bridge are the girder, arch, suspension, cantilever, and drawbridge or bascule. (See also BAILEY BRIDGE.)

The simplest and oldest type consists of a straight beam or girder placed across a span, as a log may be set over a stream as a means of crossing. A variant of this is seen in the Dartmoor 'clapper' bridges, large stone slabs supported on dry stone piers; this type survives elsewhere, e.g. in Fukien province in China, where 200-tonne granite slabs 21 m (70 ft.) long were used.

Although the masonry arch was developed in China in the 4th millennium BC, it was the Romans who first used the semicircular arch extensively. The Pont du Gard (see entry) dates from *c.* AD 14, the Alcantara road-bridge over the River Tagus in Spain, with six granite arches, from *c.* AD 100. With increasing confidence, medieval and Renaissance engineers built arches with lower rise than the semicircle and coped with the resulting increased thrust on the abutment; these can be seen, for example, in the remaining elliptical arches of the bridge at Avignon (1171) and the segmented arches of the Ponte Vecchio in Florence (1345). As late as 1903 the Plauen bridge in Germany was built as a segmental arch in a hard slate. In 1779 the Coalbrookdale bridge in Shropshire heralded a new era of iron and steel arch bridges, including several with spans of over 500 m (1640 ft.), as in the Sydney Harbour Bridge (1932). A distorted arch is seen in the modern portal frame bridge, a solid rectangular framed structure with the corners braced.

The suspension bridge in its primitive form, widespread geographically, consists of three ropes hanging in a catenary from anchorages on each side, forming walkway and handrailing. The Lan Chin bridge in Tunnan Province, China (AD 65), has iron chains supporting a wooden deck, but in the West iron chains were not used until the early years of the Industrial Revolution, typically as in Telford's Menai bridge (1819–26). The American engineer J. A. Roebling (1806–69) invented today's method of using parallel stranded wire ropes for the suspension cables; famous examples include the Golden Gate bridge at San Francisco (1937).

The cantilever bridge, a refinement of the beam, has a central span supported on the ends of side-spans which are cantilevered out over piers, as in the Forth railway bridge in Scotland (1882–9) and the Quebec bridge (finally completed in (1917).

The drawbridge, lowered and raised by ropes or chains to allow or prevent passage, finds its modern development in designs that make use of counterweights and gears and that can be used over waterways, being raised to allow the passage of tall ships. London's Tower Bridge uses two bascules to span 61 m (200 ft.).

bridge[2] /brɪdʒ/ *n.* a card-game derived from whist, in which one player's cards are exposed and are played by his or her partner. Its two main forms are **auction bridge** (with competitive bidding for the right to name the trump suit), which was popular with the British in India in the 19th c., and **contract bridge,** where only the tricks bid and won count towards the game and which has now largely superseded other forms, under the influence of the American player Ely Culbertson (1891–1955). □ **bridge roll** a small soft bread roll. [19th c., orig. unkn., but prob. of Levantine origin since some form of the game seems to have been long known in the Near East]

bridgehead /ˈbrɪdʒhed/ *n. Mil.* a fortified position held on the enemy's side of a river or other obstacle.

Bridges /ˈbrɪdʒɪz/, Robert Seymour (1844–1930), English poet, who studied and for a time practised medicine. Author of many beautiful lyrics, Bridges was perhaps too subtle and severe a poet to appeal to a very wide public, though his long philosophical poem in the Victorian tradition, *The Testament of Beauty* (1929) was instantly popular. He wrote two influential essays, *Milton's Prosody* (1893) and *John Keats* (1895). His greatest contribution to literature was the publication of his friend Gerard Manley Hopkins's poems in 1918. From 1913 to 1930 he was Poet Laureate. Bridges was intimately associated with Oxford University Press, taking an active interest in questions of type,

w we z zoo ʃ she ʒ decision θ thin ð this ŋ ring x loch tʃ chip dʒ jar (*see over for vowels*)

spelling, and phonetics, and did much to encourage taste and accuracy in printing.

Bridget[1] /'brɪdʒɪt/, St (of Ireland), traditionally abbess of Kildare in the early 6th c. She was venerated in Ireland as a virgin saint, noted in miracle stories for her compassion, and her cult soon spread over most of western Europe. Details such as her sacred fire described by Gerald of Wales suggest that she may represent the Irish goddess Brig.

Bridget[2] /'brɪdʒɪt/, St (of Sweden; c.1303–73). After her husband's death she devoted herself to religion and founded the Order of Brigettines (c.1346) at Vadstena in Sweden. The revelations which she was held to have received in visions were highly regarded in the Middle Ages.

Bridgetown /'brɪdʒtaʊn/ a port and the capital of Barbados; pop. (1980) 7,466.

bridgework /'brɪdʒwɜːk/ n. Dentistry a dental structure used to cover a gap, joined to and supported by the teeth on either side.

bridle /'braɪd(ə)l/ n. & v. —n. **1 a** the headgear used to control a horse, consisting of buckled leather straps, a metal bit, and reins. **b** a restraining thing or influence (put a bridle on your tongue). **2** Naut. a mooring-cable. **3** Physiol. a ligament checking the motion of a part. —v. **1** tr. put a bridle on (a horse etc.). **2** tr. bring under control; curb. **3** intr. (often foll. by up) express offence, resentment, etc., esp. by throwing up the head and drawing in the chin. □ **bridle-path** (or **-road** or **-way**) a rough path or road fit only for riders or walkers, not vehicles. [OE brīdel]

bridoon /brɪ'duːn/ n. the snaffle and rein of a military bridle. [F bridon f. bride bridle]

Brie /briː/ n. a kind of soft cheese. [Brie in N. France]

brief /briːf/ adj., n., & v. —adj. **1** of short duration. **2** concise in expression. **3** abrupt, brusque (was rather brief with me). **4** scanty; lacking in substance (wearing a brief skirt). —n. **1** (in pl.) **a** women's brief pants. **b** men's brief underpants. **2** Law **a** a summary of the facts and legal points of a case drawn up for counsel. **b** a piece of work for a barrister. **3** instructions given for a task, operation, etc. (orig. a bombing plan given to an aircrew). **4** RC Ch. a letter from the Pope to a person or community on a matter of discipline. —v.tr. **1** Brit. Law instruct (a barrister) by brief. **2** instruct (an employee, a participant, etc.) in preparation for a task; inform or instruct thoroughly in advance (briefed him for the interview) (cf. DEBRIEF). □ **be brief** use few words. **hold a brief for 1** argue in favour of. **2** be retained as counsel for. **in brief** in short. **watching brief 1** a brief held by a barrister following a case for a client not directly involved. **2** a state of interest maintained in a proceeding not directly or immediately concerning one. □□ **briefly** adv. **briefness** n. [ME f. AF bref, OF brief, f. L brevis short]

briefcase /'briːfkeɪs/ n. a flat rectangular case for carrying documents etc.

briefing /'briːfɪŋ/ n. **1** a meeting for giving information or instructions. **2** the information or instructions given; a brief. **3** the action of informing or instructing.

briefless /'briːflɪs/ adj. Law (of a barrister) having no clients.

brier[1] /'braɪə(r)/ n. (also **briar**) any prickly bush esp. of a wild rose. □ **brier-rose** dog-rose. **sweet-brier** a wild rose, Rosa eglanteria, with small fragrant leaves and flowers. □□ **briery** adj. [OE brǣr, brēr, of unkn. orig.]

brier[2] /'braɪə(r)/ n. (also **briar**) **1** a white heath, Erica arborea, native to S. Europe. **2** a tobacco pipe made from its root. [19th-c. bruyer f. F bruyère heath]

Brig. abbr. Brigadier.

brig[1] /brɪg/ n. **1** a two-masted square-rigged ship, with an additional lower fore-and-aft sail on the gaff and a boom to the mainmast. **2** US a prison, esp. on a warship. [abbr. of BRIGANTINE]

brig[2] /brɪg/ n. Sc. & N.Engl. var. of BRIDGE[1].

brigade /brɪ'geɪd/ n. & v. —n. **1** Mil. **a** a subdivision of an army. **b** a British infantry unit consisting usu. of three battalions and forming part of a division. **c** a corresponding armoured unit. **2** an organized or uniformed band of workers (fire brigade). **3** colloq. any group of people with a characteristic in common (the couldn't-care-less brigade). —v.tr. form into a brigade. [F f. It. brigata company f. brigare be busy with f. briga strife]

brigadier /ˌbrɪgə'dɪə(r)/ n. Mil. **1** an officer commanding a brigade. **2 a** a staff officer of similar standing, above a colonel and below a major-general. **b** the titular rank granted to such an officer. □ **brigadier general** US an officer ranking next above colonel. [F (as BRIGADE, -IER)]

brigalow /'brɪgəˌləʊ/ n. Austral. any of various acacia trees, esp. Acacia harpophylla. [Aboriginal]

brigand /'brɪgənd/ n. a member of a robber band living by pillage and ransom, usu. in wild terrain. □□ **brigandage** n. **brigandish** adj. **brigandism** n. **brigandry** n. [ME f. OF f. It. brigante f. brigare: see BRIGADE]

brigantine /'brɪgənˌtiːn/ n. a sailing-ship with two masts, the foremast square-rigged, used in the 18th and 19th c. for short coastal and trading voyages. The name comes from the fact that they were favourite vessels of sea brigands. [OF brigandine or It. brigantino f. brigante BRIGAND]

Bright /braɪt/, John (1811–89), English Liberal politician and reformer. A noted orator, Bright was the leader, along with Richard Cobden, of the campaign to repeal the Corn Laws.

bright /braɪt/ adj. & adv. —adj. **1** emitting or reflecting much light; shining. **2** (of colour) intense, vivid. **3** clever, talented, quick-witted (a bright idea; a bright child). **4** cheerful, vivacious. —adv. esp. poet. brightly (the moon shone bright). □ **bright and early** very early in the morning. **bright-eyed and bushy-tailed** colloq. alert and sprightly. **the bright lights** the glamour and excitement of the city. **look on the bright side** be optimistic. □□ **brightish** adj. **brightly** adv. **brightness** n. [OE beorht, (adv.) beorhte, f. Gmc]

brighten /'braɪt(ə)n/ v.tr. & intr. **1** make or become brighter. **2** make or become more cheerful.

Brighton /'braɪt(ə)n/ a resort on the south coast of England, in East Sussex; pop. (1981) 146,000. It was patronized by the Prince of Wales (later George IV) from c.1780 to 1827, and has much Regency architecture and a Royal Pavilion rebuilt for him by John Nash in Oriental style.

Bright's disease /braɪts/ n. inflammation of the kidney from any of various causes; nephritis. It is named after the English physician Dr Richard Bright (1759–1858) whose researches, published in 1827, established its nature.

brill[1] /brɪl/ n. a European flat-fish, Scophthalmus rhombus, resembling a turbot. [15th c.: orig. unkn.]

brill[2] /brɪl/ adj. colloq. = BRILLIANT adj. 4. [abbr.]

brilliance /'brɪlɪəns/ n. (also **brilliancy** /-ənsɪ/) **1** great brightness; sparkling or radiant quality. **2** outstanding talent or intelligence.

brilliancy var. of BRILLIANCE.

brilliant /'brɪlɪənt/ adj. & n. —adj. **1** very bright; sparkling. **2** outstandingly talented or intelligent. **3** showy; outwardly impressive. **4** colloq. excellent, superb. —n. a diamond of the finest cut with many facets. □□ **brilliantly** adv. [F brillant part. of briller shine f. It. brillare, of unkn. orig.]

brilliantine /'brɪljənˌtiːn/ n. **1** an oily liquid dressing for making the hair glossy. **2** US a lustrous dress fabric. [F brillantine (as BRILLIANT)]

brim /brɪm/ n. & v. —n. **1** the edge or lip of a cup or other vessel, or of a hollow. **2** the projecting edge of a hat. —v.tr. & intr. (**brimmed**, **brimming**) fill or be full to the brim. □ **brim over** overflow. □□ **brimless** adj. **brimmed** adj. (usu. in comb.). [ME brimme, of unkn. orig.]

brim-full /brɪm'fʊl/ adj. (also **brimful**) (often foll. by of) filled to the brim.

brimstone /'brɪmstəʊn/ n. **1** archaic the element sulphur. **2** a butterfly, Gonepteryx rhamni, or moth, Opisthograptis luteolata, having yellow wings. [ME prob. f. OE bryne burning + STONE]

brindled /'brɪnd(ə)ld/ adj. (also **brindle**) brownish or tawny with streaks of other colour (esp. of domestic animals). [earlier brinded, brended f. brend, perh. of Scand. orig.]

Brindley /'brɪndlɪ/, James (1716–72), pioneer British canal builder, starting in 1760 with the Bridgewater canal to bring coal from the Duke of Bridgewater's mines at Worsley to Manchester. This included an aqueduct over the River Irwell at Barton, a wonder of the age. Altogether he designed some 600 km (375 miles) of waterway, completing the main canal system connecting all the major rivers of England. Brindley believed in building contour canals with the minimum of locks, embankments, cuttings, or tunnels, at the expense of greater lengths. His philosophy has proved correct in that canals built with many locks were the first to be abandoned.

brine /braɪn/ n. & v. —n. 1 water saturated or strongly impregnated with salt. 2 sea water. —v.tr. soak in or saturate with brine. [OE *brīne*, of unkn. orig.]

bring /brɪŋ/ v.tr. (past and past part. **brought** /brɔːt/) 1 a come conveying esp. by carrying or leading. b come with. 2 cause to come or be present (*what brings you here?*). 3 cause or result in (*war brings misery*). 4 be sold for; produce as income. 5 a prefer (a charge). b initiate (legal action). 6 cause to become or to reach a particular state (*brings me alive*; *brought them to their senses*; *cannot bring myself to agree*). 7 adduce (evidence, an argument, etc.). □ **bring about 1** cause to happen. **2** turn (a ship) around. **bring-and-buy sale** Brit. a kind of charity sale at which participants bring items for sale and buy what is brought by others. **bring back** call to mind. **bring down 1** cause to fall. **2** lower (a price). **3** sl. make unhappy or less happy. **4** colloq. damage the reputation of; demean. **bring forth 1** give birth to. **2** produce, emit, cause. **bring forward 1** move to an earlier date or time. **2** transfer from the previous page or account. **3** draw attention to; adduce. **bring home to** cause to realize fully (*brought home to me that I was wrong*). **bring the house down** receive rapturous applause. **bring in 1** introduce (legislation, a custom, fashion, topic, etc.). **2** yield as income or profit. **bring into play** cause to operate; activate. **bring low** overcome. **bring off** achieve successfully. **bring on 1** cause to happen or appear. **2** accelerate the progress of. **bring out 1** emphasize; make evident. **2** publish. **bring over** convert to one's own side. **bring round 1** restore to consciousness. **2** persuade. **bring through** aid (a person) through adversity, esp. illness. **bring to 1** restore to consciousness (*brought him to*). **2** check the motion of. **bring to bear** (usu. foll. by *on*) direct and concentrate (forces). **bring to mind** recall; cause one to remember. **bring to pass** cause to happen. **bring under** subdue. **bring up 1** rear (a child). **2** vomit, regurgitate. **3** call attention to. **4** (*absol.*) stop suddenly. **bring upon oneself** be responsible for (something one suffers). □□ **bringer** n. [OE *bringan* f. Gmc]

brinjal /ˈbrɪndʒ(ə)l/ n. (in India and Africa) an aubergine. [ult. Port. *berinjela* formed as AUBERGINE]

brink /brɪŋk/ n. 1 the extreme edge of land before a precipice, river, etc., esp. when a sudden drop follows. 2 the furthest point before something dangerous or exciting is discovered. □ **on the brink of** about to experience or suffer; in imminent danger of. [ME f. ON: orig. unkn.]

brinkmanship /ˈbrɪŋkmənʃɪp/ n. the art or policy of pursuing a dangerous course to the brink of catastrophe before desisting.

briny /ˈbraɪnɪ/ adj. & n. —adj. (**brinier, briniest**) of brine or the sea; salty. —n. (prec. by *the*) Brit. sl. the sea. □□ **brininess** n.

brio /ˈbriːəʊ/ n. dash, vigour, vivacity. [It.]

brioche /ˈbriːɒʃ/ n. a small rounded sweet roll made with a light yeast dough. [F]

briquette /brɪˈket/ n. (also **briquet**) a block of compressed coal dust used as fuel. [F *briquette*, dimin. of *brique* brick]

Brisbane /ˈbrɪzbən/ an Australian seaport, the capital of Queensland; pop. (1986) 1,171,300. It is named after the Scottish soldier and patron of astronomy (Sir) Thomas Brisbane, governor of New South Wales 1821–5.

brisk /brɪsk/ adj. & v. —adj. 1 quick, lively, keen (*a brisk pace*; *brisk trade*). 2 enlivening (*a brisk wind*). —v.tr. & intr. (often foll. by *up*) make or grow brisk. □□ **brisken** v.tr. & intr. **briskly** adv. **briskness** n. [prob. F *brusque* BRUSQUE]

brisket /ˈbrɪskɪt/ n. an animal's breast, esp. as a joint of meat. [AF f. OF *bruschet*, perh. f. ON]

brisling /ˈbrɪzlɪŋ, ˈbrɪs-/ n. a small herring or sprat. [Norw. & Da., = sprat]

bristle /ˈbrɪs(ə)l/ n. & v. —n. 1 a short stiff hair, esp. one of those on an animal's back. 2 this, or a man-made substitute, used in clumps to make a brush. —v. 1 a intr. (of the hair) stand upright, esp. in anger or pride. b tr. make (the hair) do this. 2 intr. show irritation or defensiveness. 3 intr. (usu. foll. by *with*) be covered or abundant (in). [ME *bristel, brestel* f. OE *byrst*]

bristletail /ˈbrɪs(ə)lˌteɪl/ n. = SILVERFISH.

bristly /ˈbrɪslɪ/ adj. (**bristlier, bristliest**) full of bristles; rough, prickly.

Bristol /ˈbrɪst(ə)l/ the county town of Avon in SW England; pop. (1981) 388,000. □ **Bristol board** a kind of fine smooth pasteboard for drawing on. **Bristol fashion** (functioning as *predic.adj.*) (in full **shipshape and Bristol fashion**) orig. Naut. with all in good order.

bristols /ˈbrɪst(ə)lz/ n.pl. Brit. sl. a woman's breasts. [rhyming sl. f. *Bristol cities* = *titties*]

Brit /brɪt/ n. colloq. a British person. [abbr.]

Brit. abbr. 1 British. 2 Britain.

Britain /ˈbrɪt(ə)n/ (in full **Great Britain**) the island containing England, Wales, and Scotland, and including the small adjacent islands. After the OE period *Britain* was used only as a historical term until about the time of Henry VIII and Edward VI, when it came into practical politics in connection with the efforts made to unite England and Scotland. In 1604 James I was proclaimed 'King of Great Britain', and this name was adopted for the United Kingdom at the Union of 1707, after which *South Britain* and *North Britain* were frequent in Acts of Parliament for England and Scotland respectively. (See GREAT BRITAIN.) □ **Battle of Britain** the series of air raids directed against Britain by the German air force (June 1940–April 1941), successfully resisted by the RAF, thereby frustrating this preliminary to a planned invasion of Britain. [13th c. *Bretayne* f. OF *Bretaigne* f. L *Britannia* (OE *Breoton* and variants)]

Britannia /brɪˈtænjə/ the personification of Britain, esp. as a helmeted woman with shield, helmet, and trident. It is said that one of Charles II's ladies, the Duchess of Richmond, sat as a model for Britannia to replace the figure which appears on Roman coins from the time of Hadrian or earlier and that King Charles was so pleased with the result that he ordered one of his new naval ships to be given this name. The first warship to be called *Britannia* was in service in 1682, and the name has been associated with the Royal Navy ever since. □ **Britannia metal** a silvery alloy of tin, antimony, and copper. **Britannia silver** silver that is about 96% pure. [L f. Gk *Brettania* f. *Brettanoi* Britons]

Britannic /brɪˈtænɪk/ adj. (esp. in **His** or **Her Britannic Majesty**) of Britain. [L *Britannicus* (as BRITANNIA)]

Briticism /ˈbrɪtɪˌsɪz(ə)m/ n. (also **Britishism** /-ˌʃɪz(ə)m/) an idiom used in Britain but not in other English-speaking countries. [BRITISH, after GALLICISM]

British /ˈbrɪtɪʃ/ adj. & n. —adj. 1 of or relating to Great Britain or the United Kingdom, or to its people or language. 2 of the British Commonwealth or (formerly) the British Empire (*British subject*). —n. 1 (prec. by *the*; treated as pl.) the British people. 2 US = British English. □ **British English** English as used in Great Britain, as distinct from that used elsewhere. **British Legion** = ROYAL BRITISH LEGION. **British summer time** = *summer time* (see SUMMER[1]). **British thermal unit** see THERMAL. □□ **Britishness** n. [OE *Brettisc* etc. f. Bret f. L *Britto* or OCelt.]

British Academy an institution founded in 1901 for the promotion of historical, philosophical, and philological studies.

British Antarctic Territory that part of Antarctica claimed by Britain. Designated in 1962, includes some 388,500 sq. km (150,058 sq. miles) of the continent of Antarctica as well as the adjacent South Orkney Islands and South Shetland Islands.

British Columbia /kəˈlʌmbɪə/ a province of Canada (from 1871), on the west coast, formed in 1866 by the union of Vancouver Island (a British colony from 1849) and the mainland area which was called New Caledonia; pop. (1986) 2,889,200; capital, Victoria.

British Council an organization established in 1934. Its royal charter (1930) defines its aims as the promotion of a wider knowledge of Britain and English abroad, and the development of closer cultural relations with other countries. Most of its funds are provided by Parliament.

British Empire British overseas possessions, acquired for commercial, strategic, or territorial reasons. The colonization of North America started in the early 17th c., although the colonies south of Canada were lost in the American Revolution in the late 18th c. British domination of India began under the auspices of the East India Company, also in the 17th c., while a series of small colonies, mostly in the West Indies, were gained in the colonial wars with France during the late 17th–early 19th c. Australia, New Zealand, and various possessions in the Far East were added in the 19th c. (notably Hong Kong), while extensive possessions in Africa came Britain's way in the last few decades of the 19th c. at the height of the imperialist age. The movement of the British colonies towards independence began in the mid-19th c. with the granting of self-government to Canada, Australia, New Zealand, and South Africa. This trend was accelerated by the two World Wars, with most of the remaining colonies gaining independence in the decade and a half following the end of the Second World War.

Britisher /ˈbrɪtɪʃə(r)/ n. a British subject, esp. of British descent. ¶ Not used in British English.

British Expeditionary Force hist. any of the British forces made available by the army reform of 1908 for service overseas against foreign countries. Such a force was sent to France in 1914 at the outbreak of the First World War; the force sent to France early in the Second World War (1939) was evacuated from Dunkirk (see entry) in 1940.

British Honduras /hɒnˈdjʊərəs/ the former name (until 1973) of Belize.

British Indian Ocean Territory a British dependency in the Indian Ocean, comprising the islands of the Chagos Archipelago. Ceded to Britain by France in 1814, the islands were administered from Mauritius until the designation of a separate dependency in 1965. There are no permanent inhabitants, but British and US naval personnel occupy the island of Diego Garcia.

Britishism var. of BRITICISM.

British Library the national library of Britain containing the former library departments of the British Museum (in which it is housed), to which George II presented the royal library in 1757. As one of the six copyright libraries it receives a copy of every book published in the UK. It was established separately from the British Museum in 1972, and new premises are being prepared.

British Museum a national museum of antiquities etc. in Bloomsbury, London, occupying the site of Montagu House, which was acquired in 1753 to house the library and collections of Sir Hans Sloane and the Harleian manuscripts purchased with funds granted by Parliament. The present buildings were erected from 1823 onwards. The original holdings have been greatly increased by gifts and purchases and by acquisitions from excavations, and now comprise one of the world's finest collections, particularly of Egyptian, Assyrian, Greek, Roman, and Oriental antiquities, including the Elgin Marbles and the Rosetta Stone. During the 19th c. the natural history collections grew so extensively that it became necessary to find new quarters for them, and in 1881 they were moved to South Kensington; in 1963 the Natural History Museum was made completely independent. The library departments of the British Museum were transferred in 1972 to the British Library.

British Somaliland a former British protectorate established on the Somali coast of East Africa in 1884. In 1960 it united with Italian Somaliland to form the independent State of Somalia.

Briton /ˈbrɪt(ə)n/ n. 1 one of the people of S. Britain before the Roman conquest. 2 a native or inhabitant of Great Britain or

(formerly) of the British Empire. [ME & OF Breton f. L Britto -onis f. OCelt.]

Brittany /ˈbrɪtənɪ/ (French **Bretagne** /breˈtæɲ/) a region of NW France forming a peninsula between the Bay of Biscay and the English Channel; pop. (1982) 2,707,900; capital, Rennes. Brittany was a duchy from 1196 until 1532, when it was incorporated into France.

Britten /ˈbrɪt(ə)n/, Edward Benjamin, Lord Britten of Aldeburgh, (1913–76), English musician, whose talents as a composer were matched by his outstanding abilities as conductor and pianist. His compositions dazzle in their unrelenting sharpness of vision, and his operas and other vocal works, the best known of his music, are doubly moving for their commemoration of his long friendship with the tenor Peter Pears. *Peter Grimes* (1945), after Crabbe's poem *The Borough* (1810), heralded a new beginning for English music following the privations of the Second World War, and in *Curlew River* (1964), *The Burning Fiery Furnace* (1966), and *The Prodigal Son* (1968) he invented a new musical genre, the church parable. He made settings of a wise and varied range of writers, including Rimbaud (*Les Illuminations*, 1939), Michelangelo (*Seven Sonnets*, 1940), John Donne (nine *Holy Sonnetts*, 1945), Henry James (*The Turn of the Screw*, 1954), Shakespeare (*A Midsummer Night's Dream*, 1960) and at the and of his life Thomas Mann (*Death in Venice*, 1973); his pacifism found public expression in the *War Requiem* (1961), which combines the Latin Mass with war poems by Wilfred Owen. Few composers have caught the public's imagination in their lifetime as vividly as did Britten; each new work was eagerly awaited and absorbed.

brittle /ˈbrɪt(ə)l/ adj. & n. —adj. hard and fragile; apt to break. —n. a brittle sweet made from nuts and set melted sugar. □ **brittle-bone disease** = OSTEOPOROSIS. **brittle-star** an echinoderm of the class Ophiuroidea, with long brittle arms radiating from a small central body. □□ **brittlely** adv. **brittleness** n. **brittly** adv. [ME ult. f. a Gmc root rel. to OE brēotan break up]

Brno /ˈbɜːnəʊ/ an industrial city in central Czechoslovakia; pop. (1986) 385,000. The Bren gun, which was developed here, is named after the city.

bro. abbr. brother.

broach /brəʊtʃ/ v. & n. —v.tr. 1 raise (a subject) for discussion. 2 pierce (a cask) to draw liquor. 3 open and start using contents of (a box, bale, bottle, etc.). 4 begin drawing (liquor). —n. 1 a bit for boring. 2 a roasting-spit. □ **broach spire** an octagonal church spire rising from a square tower without a parapet. [ME f. OF broche (n.), brocher (v.) ult. f. L brocc(h)us projecting]

broad /brɔːd/ adj. & n. —adj. 1 large in extent from one side to the other; wide. 2 (following a measurement) in breadth (2 *metres broad*). 3 spacious or extensive (*broad acres*; *a broad plain*). 4 full and clear (*broad daylight*). 5 explicit, unmistakable (*broad hint*). 6 general; not taking account of detail (*broad intentions*; *a broad inquiry*; *in the broadest sense of the word*). 7 chief or principal (*the broad facts*). 8 tolerant, liberal (*take a broad view*). 9 somewhat coarse (*broad humour*). 10 (of speech) markedly regional (*broad Scots*). —n. 1 the broad part of something (*broad of the back*). 2 *US sl.* a young woman. 3 (**the Broads**) large areas of fresh water in East Anglia, formed by the widening of rivers. The removal of peat in medieval times (with subsequent flooding) was probably an important factor in their formation. □ **broad arrow** see ARROW. **broad bean 1** a kind of bean, *Vicia faba*, with pods containing large edible flat seeds. **2** one of these seeds. **Broad Church** a group within the Anglican Church favouring a liberal interpretation of doctrine. **broad gauge** a railway track with a gauge wider than the standard one. **broad-leaved** (of a tree) deciduous and hard-timbered. **broad pennant** a short swallow-tailed pennant distinguishing the commodore's ship in a squadron. **broad spectrum** (of a medicinal substance) effective against a large variety of micro-organisms. □□ **broadness** n. **broadways** adv. **broadwise** adv. [OE brād f. Gmc]

broadcast /ˈbrɔːdkɑːst/ v., n., adj., & adv. —v. (past **broadcast** or **broadcasted**; past part. **broadcast**) 1 tr. **a** transmit (programmes or information) by radio or television. **b** disseminate (information) widely. 2 intr. undertake or take part in a radio or television transmission. 3 tr. scatter (seed etc.) over a large area, esp. by hand. —n. a radio or television programme or transmission. —*adj.* **1** transmitted by radio or television. **2 a** scattered widely. **b** (of information etc.) widely disseminated. —*adv.* over a large area. □□ **broadcaster** *n.* **broadcasting** *n.* [BROAD + CAST *past part.*]

broadcloth /ˈbrɔːdklɒθ/ *n.* a fine cloth of wool, cotton, or silk. [orig. with ref. to width and quality]

broaden /ˈbrɔːd(ə)n/ *v.tr.* & *intr.* make or become broader.

broadloom /ˈbrɔːdluːm/ *adj.* (esp. of carpet) woven in broad widths.

broadly /ˈbrɔːdlɪ/ *adv.* in a broad manner; widely (grinned broadly). □ **broadly speaking** disregarding minor exceptions.

broad-minded /brɔːdˈmaɪndɪd/ *adj.* tolerant or liberal in one's views. □□ **broad-mindedly** *adv.* **broad-mindedness** *n.*

broadsheet /ˈbrɔːdʃiːt/ *n.* a large sheet of paper printed on one side only, esp. with information.

broadside /ˈbrɔːdsaɪd/ *n.* **1** the firing of all guns from one side of a ship. **2** a vigorous verbal onslaught. **3** the side of a ship above the water between the bow and quarter. □ **broadside on** sideways on.

broadsword /ˈbrɔːdsɔːd/ *n.* a sword with a broad blade, for cutting rather than thrusting.

broadtail /ˈbrɔːdteɪl/ *n.* **1** the karacul sheep. **2** the fleece or wool from its lamb.

Broadway a street traversing the length of Manhattan Island, New York. One of the longest streets in the world, it extends for about 21 km (13 miles), and is famous for its theatres which formerly made its name synonymous with show business.

broadway /ˈbrɔːdweɪ/ *n.* a large open or main road.

brocade /brəˈkeɪd, brəʊ-/ *n.* & *v.* —*n.* a rich fabric with a silky finish woven with a raised pattern, and often with gold or silver thread. —*v.tr.* weave with this design. [Sp. & Port. brocado f. It. broccato f. brocco twisted thread]

broccoli /ˈbrɒkəlɪ/ *n.* **1** a variety of cabbage, similar to the cauliflower, with a loose cluster of greenish flower buds. **2** the flower-stalk and head used as a vegetable. [It., pl. of broccolo dimin. of brocco sprout]

broch /brɒk, brɒx/ *n.* (in Scotland) a prehistoric circular stone tower. [ON borg castle]

brochette /brɒˈʃet, brəˈʃet/ *n.* a skewer on which chunks of meat are cooked, esp. over an open fire. [F, dimin. of broche BROACH]

brochure /ˈbrəʊʃə(r), brəʊˈʃʊə(r)/ *n.* a pamphlet or leaflet, esp. one giving descriptive information. [F, lit. 'stitching', f. brocher stitch]

brock /brɒk/ *n.* (esp. in rural use) a badger. [OE broc(c) f. OBrit. brokkos]

Brocken /ˈbrɒkən/ the name of the highest of the Harz Mountains in northern Germany, reputed to be the scene of witches' Walpurgis-night revels. □ **Brocken spectre** a magnified shadow of the spectator thrown on a bank of cloud in high mountains when the sun is low, and often encircled by rainbow-like bands. This phenomenon was first observed on the Brocken.

brocket /ˈbrɒkɪt/ *n.* any small deer of the genus Mazama, native to Central and S. America, having short straight antlers. [ME f. AF broque (= broche BROACH)]

broderie anglaise /ˌbrəʊdərɪ ɑ̃ˈgleɪz/ *n.* open embroidery on white linen or cambric, esp. in floral patterns. [F, = English embroidery]

Brodsky /ˈbrɒtskɪ/, Joseph (1940–), Russian poet, who emigrated to the US in 1972 and has written both in Russian and in English. His poetry often has themes of loss and exile. He was awarded a Nobel Prize for literature in 1987.

brogue[1] /brəʊg/ *n.* **1** a strong outdoor shoe with ornamental perforated bands. **2** a rough shoe of untanned leather. [Gael. & Ir. brög f. ON brók]

brogue[2] /brəʊg/ *n.* a marked accent, esp. Irish. [18th c.: orig. unkn.: perh. allusively f. BROGUE[1]]

broil[1] /brɔɪl/ *v.* esp. US **1** *tr.* cook (meat) on a rack or a gridiron. **2** *tr.* & *intr.* make or become very hot, esp. from the sun. [ME f. OF bruler burn f. Rmc]

broil[2] /brɔɪl/ *n.* a row; a tumult. [obs. broil to muddle: cf. EMBROIL]

broiler /ˈbrɔɪlə(r)/ *n.* **1** a young chicken raised for broiling or roasting. **2** a gridiron etc. for broiling. **3** *colloq.* a very hot day. □ **broiler house** a building for rearing broiler chickens in close confinement.

broke /brəʊk/ *past* of BREAK[1]. —*predic.adj.* *colloq.* having no money; financially ruined. □ **go for broke** *sl.* risk everything in a strenuous effort. [(adj.) archaic past part. of BREAK[1]]

broken /ˈbrəʊkən/ *past part.* of BREAK[1]. —*adj.* **1** that has been broken; out of order. **2** (of a person) reduced to despair; beaten. **3** (of a language or of speech) spoken falteringly and with many mistakes, as by a foreigner (broken English). **4** disturbed, interrupted (broken time). **5** uneven (broken ground). □ **broken chord** *Mus.* a chord in which the notes are played successively. **broken-down 1** worn out by age, use, or ill-treatment. **2** out of order. **broken-hearted** overwhelmed with sorrow or grief. **broken-heartedness** grief. **broken home** a family in which the parents are divorced or separated. **broken reed** a person who has become unreliable or ineffective. **broken wind** heaves (see HEAVE *n.* 3). **broken-winded** (of a horse) disabled by ruptured air-cells in the lungs. □□ **brokenly** *adv.* **brokenness** *n.*

Broken Hill 1 a mining town in New South Wales, Australia; pop. (est. 1987) 24,170. In 1938 the Royal Flying Doctor Service established its heaquarters here. **2** the former name of Kabwe, a town in Zambia, site of a cave that has yielded human fossils in association with tools belonging to the early middle Stone Age of the Upper Pleistocene in Southern Africa, c.125,000 years old. The fossils are of the type Homo sapiens rhodesiensis (African Neanderthaloid) that apparently belong to the most recent threshold of human evolution from which fully modern man developed.

broker /ˈbrəʊkə(r)/ *n.* **1** an agent who buys and sells for others; a middleman. **2** a member of the Stock Exchange dealing in stocks and shares. ¶ In the UK from Oct. 1986 officially called **broker-dealer** and entitled to act as agent and principal in share dealings. **3** *Brit.* an official appointed to sell or appraise distrained goods. [ME f. AF brocour, of unkn. orig.]

brokerage /ˈbrəʊkərɪdʒ/ *n.* a broker's fee or commission.

broking /ˈbrəʊkɪŋ/ *n.* the trade or business of a broker.

brolga /ˈbrɒlgə/ *n.* Austral. a large Australian crane, Grus rubicunda, with a booming call. [Aboriginal]

brolly /ˈbrɒlɪ/ *n.* (pl. **-ies**) Brit. **1** *colloq.* an umbrella. **2** *sl.* a parachute. [abbr.]

bromate /ˈbrəʊmeɪt/ *n.* Chem. a salt or ester of bromic acid.

Bromberg see BYDGOSZCZ.

brome /brəʊm/ *n.* any oatlike grass of the genus Bromus, having slender stems with flowering spikes. [mod.L Bromus f. Gk bromos oat]

bromelia /brəʊˈmiːlɪə/ *n.* (also **bromeliad** /-lɪad/) any plant of the family Bromeliaceae (esp. of the genus Bromelia), native to the New World, having short stems with rosettes of stiff usu. spiny leaves, e.g. pineapple. [O. Bromel, Sw. botanist d. 1705]

bromic /ˈbrəʊmɪk/ *adj.* Chem. of or containing bromine. □ **bromic acid** a strong acid used as an oxidizing agent.

bromide /ˈbrəʊmaɪd/ *n.* **1** Chem. any binary compound of bromine. **2** Pharm. a preparation of usu. potassium bromide, used as a sedative. **3** a trite remark. □ **bromide paper** a photographic printing paper coated with silver bromide emulsion.

bromine /ˈbrəʊmiːn/ *n.* Chem. a non-metallic dark-red liquid element of the halogen group with a poisonous rank-smelling vapour, first discovered in 1826. The uncombined element has few uses but bromine compounds are used as petrol additives, insecticides, sedatives, laboratory reagents, etc. The main commercial source for bromine is sea water. ¶ Symb.: **Br**; atomic number 35. □□ **bromism** *n.* [F brome f. Gk brōmos stink]

bromo- /ˈbrəʊməʊ/ comb. form Chem. bromine.

bronc /brɒŋk/ *n.* US colloq. = BRONCO. [abbr.]

bronchi pl. of BRONCHUS.

bronchial /ˈbrɒŋkɪəl/ *adj.* of or relating to the bronchi or bronchioles. □ **bronchial tree** the branching system of bronchi and bronchioles conducting air from the windpipe to the lungs.

bronchiole /ˈbrɒŋkɪˌəʊl/ n. any of the minute divisions of a bronchus. □□ **bronchiolar** /-ˈəʊlə(r)/ adj.

bronchitis /brɒŋˈkaɪtɪs/ n. inflammation of the mucous membrane in the bronchial tubes. □□ **bronchitic** /-ˈkɪtɪk/ adj. & n.

broncho- /ˈbrɒŋkəʊ/ comb. form bronchi.

bronchocele /ˈbrɒŋkəˌsiːl/ n. a goitre.

bronchopneumonia /ˌbrɒŋkəʊnjuːˈməʊnɪə/ n. inflammation of the lungs, arising in the bronchi or bronchioles.

bronchoscope /ˈbrɒŋkəˌskəʊp/ n. a usu. fibre-optic instrument for inspecting the bronchi. □□ **bronchoscopy** /-ˈkɒskəpɪ/ n.

bronchus /ˈbrɒŋkəs/ n. (pl. **bronchi** /-kaɪ/) any of the major air passages of the lungs, esp. either of the two main divisions of the windpipe. [LL f. Gk brogkhos windpipe]

bronco /ˈbrɒŋkəʊ/ n. (pl. **-os**) a wild or half-tamed horse of the western US. □ **bronco-buster** US sl. a person who breaks in horses. [Sp., = rough]

Brontë /ˈbrɒnteɪ/, Charlotte (1816–55), Emily (1818–48), and Anne (1820–49), English novelists, the three surviving daughters of Patrick Prunty or Brontë, perpetual curate of Haworth in Yorkshire. Having lost their mother in 1821 they were educated (with their black-sheep brother, Branwell) largely at home. A lonely childhood in a remote neighbourhood intensified the imaginative powers that were to produce their remarkable novels; apart from work as governesses and, for Emily and Charlotte, a visit to Brussels, their experience of the outside world was unusually limited. All died young, Emily of consumption after publication but before the success of her masterpiece, Wuthering Heights (1847), Anne, also of consumption, after publishing two novels, and Charlotte shortly after her marriage to the Revd A. B. Nicholls, when she was already famous for her romantic tour-de-force, Jane Eyre (1847), and for her restrained Shirley (1849) and Villette (1853). Their works were published under the pseudonyms Currer, Ellis, and Acton Bell, including their unsuccessful first efforts, a joint book of poems, of which Emily's are now highly regarded.

brontosaurus /ˌbrɒntəˈsɔːrəs/ n. (also **brontosaur** /ˈbrɒntəˌsɔː(r)/) a large plant-eating dinosaur of the genus Brontosaurus, with a long whiplike tail and trunk-like legs. [Gk brontē thunder + sauros lizard]

Bronx /brɒŋks/, **the** a borough of New York City, north-east of the Harlem river. It is named after a Dutch settler, Jonas Bronck, who purchased land here in 1641.

bronze /brɒnz/ n., adj., & v. —n. 1 any of a group of alloys of copper and tin. (See below.) 2 its brownish colour. 3 a thing made of bronze, esp. as a work of art. —adj. made of or coloured like bronze. —v. 1 tr. give a bronzelike surface to. 2 tr. & intr. make or become brown; tan. □ **bronze medal** a medal usu. awarded to a competitor who comes third (esp. in sport). □□ **bronzy** adj. [F f. It. bronzo, prob. f. Pers. birinj copper]
    Bronze was first smelted in the Near East, the Aegean, and the Balkans in the late 4th and early 3rd millennium BC. It is harder than pure copper and therefore superior for making weapons and tools. Until the introduction of iron, bronze remained the sole metal for utilitarian purposes, and afterwards it continued in general use to the end of antiquity for sculpture, many domestic objects, and (after the 5th c. BC) for small-denomination coins. The bronze coin was introduced into Britain in 1860, but continued to be called a 'copper' (its original material; see PENNY).

Bronze Age the second stage in the classification of pre-historic periods (see PREHISTORY) when certain weapons and tools were usually made of bronze rather than stone. It began in the Near East and SE Europe in the late 4th and early 3rd millennium BC and is associated with the first European civilizations, the spread of the wheel, and the establishment of far-reaching trade networks. It is equated with the beginnings of urban life in China (beginning c.2000 BC), but develops only in the final stages of some of the Meso-American civilizations (c. AD 1000). In NW Europe the Bronze Age is unaccompanied by developments in civilized life but merely follows on from the Stone Age; in Africa and Australasia it does not appear at all. It ends in most areas with the general use of iron technology, in

the 8th c. BC in northern Europe and in the 5th c. AD in China; in Greece and other Aegean countries it ends c.1200 BC with the start of a Dark Age.

brooch /brəʊtʃ/ n. an ornament fastened to clothing with a hinged pin. [ME broche = BROACH n.]

brood /bruːd/ n. & v. —n. 1 the young of an animal (esp. a bird) produced at one hatching or birth. 2 colloq. the children in a family. 3 a group of related things. 4 bee or wasp larvae. 5 (attrib.) kept for breeding (brood-mare). —v. 1 intr. (often foll. by on, over, etc.) worry or ponder (esp. resentfully). 2 a intr. sit as a hen on eggs to hatch them. b tr. sit on (eggs) to hatch them. 3 intr. (usu. foll. by over) (of silence, a storm, etc.) hang or hover closely. □□ **broodingly** adv. [OE brōd f. Gmc]

brooder /ˈbruːdə(r)/ n. 1 a heated house for chicks, piglets, etc. 2 a person who broods.

broody /ˈbruːdɪ/ adj. (**broodier**, **broodiest**) 1 (of a hen) wanting to brood. 2 sullenly thoughtful or depressed. 3 colloq. (of a woman) wanting to have a baby. □□ **broodily** adv. **broodiness** n.

brook¹ /brʊk/ n. a small stream. □□ **brooklet** /-lɪt/ n. [OE brōc, of unkn. orig.]

brook² /brʊk/ v.tr. (usu. with neg.) literary tolerate, allow. [OE brūcan f. Gmc]

Brooke /brʊk/, Rupert Chawner (1887–1915), English poet and Cambridge scholar. His works include 'Tiara Tahiti' and other poems, but he is most famous for his wartime poetry 1914 and Other Poems (1915) and for his lighter verse, such as 'The Old Vicarage, Granchester'.

Brooklands /ˈbrʊkləndz/ a motor-racing track opened in 1907 near Weybridge in Surrey. Oval in shape, it was laid out like a horse-racing track because it was the world's first special motor course and there was no previous experience on which to rely. The course proved invaluable to British motor manufacturers and inventors who were hampered in testing their products by the prevailing speed limit of 20 m.p.h. on roads. During the Second World War the course was converted (and subsequently sold) for aeroplane manufacture.

brooklime /ˈbrʊklaɪm/ n. a kind of speedwell, Veronica becca-bunga, growing in wet areas.

Brooklyn /ˈbrʊklɪn/ a borough of New York City, at the south-west corner of Long Island; pop. (1980) 2,230,900. The Brooklyn Bridge links Long Island with lower Manhattan.

brookweed /ˈbrʊkwiːd/ n. a small herb, Samolus valerandi, having slender stems with tiny white flowers and growing in wet places.

broom /bruːm/ n. 1 a long-handled brush of bristles, twigs, etc. for sweeping (orig. one made of twigs of broom). 2 any of various shrubs, esp. Cytisus scoparius bearing bright yellow flowers. □ **new broom** a newly appointed person eager to make changes. [OE brōm]

broomrape /ˈbruːmreɪp/ n. any parasitic plant of the genus Orobanche, with tubular flowers on a leafless brown stem, and living on the roots of broom and similar plants. [BROOM + L rapum tuber]

broomstick /ˈbruːmstɪk/ n. the handle of a broom, esp. as allegedly ridden on through the air by witches.

Bros. abbr. Brothers (esp. in the name of a firm).

brose /brəʊz/ n. esp. Sc. Cookery a dish of oatmeal with boiling water or milk poured on it. [Sc. form of brewis broth: ME f. OF bro(u)ez, ult. f. Gmc]

broth /brɒθ/ n. 1 Cookery a a thin soup of meat or fish stock. b unclarified meat or fish stock. 2 Biol. meat stock as a nutrient medium for bacteria. [OE f. Gmc: rel. to BREW]

brothel /ˈbrɒθ(ə)l/ n. a house etc. where prostitution takes place. [orig. brothel-house f. ME brothel worthless man, prostitute, f. OE brēothan go to ruin]

brother /ˈbrʌðə(r)/ n. 1 a man or boy in relation to other sons and daughters of his parents. 2 a (often as a form of address) a close male friend or associate. b a male fellow member of a trade union etc. 3 (pl. also **brethren** /ˈbreðrɪn/) a a member of a male religious order, esp. a monk. b a fellow member of the

æ cat ɑː arm e bed ɜː her ɪ sit iː see ɒ hot ɔː saw ʌ run ʊ put uː too ə ago aɪ my

Christian Church, a religion, or (formerly) a guild etc. **4** a fellow human being. □ **brother german** see GERMAN. **brother-in-law** (*pl.* **brothers-in-law**) **1** the brother of one's wife or husband. **2** the husband of one's sister. **3** the husband of one's sister-in-law. **brother uterine** see UTERINE 2. □□ **brotherless** *adj.* **brotherly** *adj.* & *adv.* **brotherliness** *n.* [OE *brōthor* f. Gmc]

brotherhood /ˈbrʌðəˌhʊd/ *n.* **1 a** the relationship between brothers. **b** brotherly friendliness; companionship. **2 a** an association, society, or community of people linked by a common interest, religion, trade, etc. **b** its members collectively. **3** *US* a trade union. **4** community of feeling between all human beings. [ME alt. f. *brotherrede* f. OE *brōthor-rǽden* (cf. KINDRED) after words in -HOOD, -HEAD]

brougham /ˈbruːəm, bruːm/ *n. hist.* **1** a horse-drawn closed carriage with a driver perched outside in front. **2** a motor car with an open driver's seat. [Lord *Brougham*, d. 1868]

brought *past* and *past part.* of BRING.

brouhaha /ˈbruːhɑːˌhɑː/ *n.* commotion, sensation; hubbub, uproar. [F]

Brouwer /ˈbraʊə(r)/, Adriaen (1605/6–38), Flemish painter, who spent much of his short working life at Haarlem in Holland, where he was probably a pupil of Frans Hals. His most typical works represent peasants brawling and drinking, but although the subject-matter is humorously coarse his technique was delicate and sparkling.

brow /braʊ/ *n.* **1** the forehead. **2** (usu. in *pl.*) an eyebrow. **3** the summit of a hill or pass. **4** the edge of a cliff etc. **5** *colloq.* intellectual level. □□ **browed** *adj.* [OE *brū* f. Gmc]

browbeat /ˈbraʊbiːt/ *v.tr.* (*past* **-beat**; *past part.* **-beaten**) intimidate with stern looks and words. □□ **browbeater** *n.*

Brown[1] /braʊn/, Sir Arthur Whitten (1886–1948), aviator, born in Glasgow of American parents, knighted in 1919 for his pioneer transatlantic flight with J. W. Alcock.

Brown[2] /braʊn/, John (1800–59), American abolitionist, commemorated in the popular marching-song 'John Brown's Body'. The leader of an unsuccessful uprising in Virginia in 1859, he was captured and executed after he had seized the arsenal at Harper's Ferry, intending to arm the Black slaves and start a revolt. Although the revolt never materialized, Brown became a hero of the American abolitionists who played a crucial part in the outbreak of the American Civil War soon afterwards.

Brown[3] /braʊn/, Lancelot (1716–83), English landscape gardener, known as 'Capability' because he would tell his patrons that their estates had 'great capabilities'. He created natural-looking landscape parks, broken by serpentine waters and clumps of trees. Famous examples of his work are at Blenheim Palace in Oxfordshire and Chatsworth in Derbyshire.

brown /braʊn/ *adj., n.,* & *v.* —*adj.* **1** having the colour produced by mixing red, yellow, and black, as of dark wood or rich soil. **2** dark-skinned or suntanned. **3** (of bread) made from a dark flour as wholemeal or wheatmeal. **4** (of species or varieties) distinguished by brown coloration. —*n.* **1** a brown colour or pigment. **2** brown clothes or material (*dressed in brown*). **3** (in a game or sport) a brown ball, piece, etc. **4** (prec. by the) *Brit.* a brown mass of flying game-birds. —*v.tr.* & *intr.* make or become brown by cooking, sunburn, etc. □ **brown ale** a dark, mild, bottled beer. **brown bear** a large N. American bear, *Ursus arctos*, with shaggy usually brownish fur. **brown coal** = LIGNITE. **browned off** *Brit. sl.* fed up, disheartened. **brown fat** a dark-coloured adipose tissue with a rich supply of blood vessels. **brown holland** see HOLLAND. **brown owl 1** any of various owls, esp. the tawny owl. **2** (**Brown Owl**) an adult leader of a Brownie Guides pack. **brown rice** unpolished rice with only the husk of the grain removed. **brown sugar** unrefined or partially refined sugar. **in a brown study** see STUDY. □□ **brownish** *adj.* **brownness** *n.* **browny** *adj.* [OE *brūn* f. Gmc]

Browne /braʊn/, Sir Thomas (1605–82), English physician, author of *Religio Medici* (1642), a confession of Christian faith (qualified by an eclectic and generally sceptical attitude), and a collection of opinions on a vast number of subjects more or less connected with religion, expressed with a wealth of fancy and wide erudition.

Brownian movement /ˈbraʊnɪən/ *n.* (also **Brownian motion**) *Physics* the erratic random movement of microscopic particles in a liquid, gas, etc., as a result of continuous bombardment from molecules of the surrounding medium. [R. Brown, Sc. botanist (d. 1858) who discovered the phenomenon]

Brownie /ˈbraʊnɪ/ *n.* **1** (in full **Brownie Guide**) a member of the junior branch of the Girl Guides Association (see entry). **2** (**brownie**) *Cookery* **a** a small square of rich, usu. chocolate, cake with nuts. **b** *Austral.* & *NZ* a sweet currant-bread. **3** (**brownie**) a benevolent elf said to haunt houses and do household work secretly. □ **Brownie point** *colloq.* a notional credit for something done to please or win favour.

Browning[1] /ˈbraʊnɪŋ/, Elizabeth Barrett (1806–61), English poet, a semi-invalid from the age of 15. She is chiefly remembered today for her sensational romance with Robert Browning who rescued her from her domineering father and eloped with her to Italy in 1846. During her life her poetic reputation stood higher than Browning's; she was seriously considered a possible successor to Wordsworth as Poet Laureate. Her best-known works are her love poems *Sonnets from the Portuguese* (1850) and her verse novel *Aurora Leigh* (1857).

Browning[2] /ˈbraʊnɪŋ/, Robert (1812–89), English poet, son of a clerk in the Bank of England, who received most of his education from his father's library. The success of his long poem *Paracelsus* (1835) resulted in friendships with the writer John Forster and theatrical manager W. C. Macready who encouraged him to write for the stage; *Strafford* (1837) was successfully produced at Covent Garden but the poor reception of *Sordello* (1840) eclipsed his reputation for many years. In 1846 he married and eloped to Italy with Elizabeth Barrett; Elizabeth and Renaissance Italy inspired his greatest work and his reputation revived with *Men and Women* (1855) and *Dramatis Personae* (1864). His greatest triumph was *The Ring and the Book* (1868–9), a series of dramatic monologues, a form which Browning developed to perfection. Browning's experiments in form and content and his technical virtuosity have considerably influenced modern poets, notably Eliot and Pound.

browning /ˈbraʊnɪŋ/ *n. Brit. Cookery* browned flour or any other additive to colour gravy.

Brownshirts *n.pl.* the members of an early Nazi militia, the Storm Troops (German *Sturmabteilung* (abbr. SA) assault division), founded by Adolf Hitler in Munich in 1921, who wore brown uniforms reminiscent of Mussolini's Blackshirts. Their methods of violent intimidation of political opponents and of Jews played a key role in Hitler's rise to power. By 1933 they numbered some two million, double the size of the army, which was hostile to them. In 1934 Hitler had more than 70 members of the SA, and their leader Ernst Röhm, summarily executed by the SS on the 'night of the long knives' (see LONG[1]), and greatly reduced the Brownshirts' power.

brownstone /ˈbraʊnstəʊn/ *n. US* **1** a kind of reddish-brown sandstone used for building. **2** a building faced with this.

browse /braʊz/ *v.* & *n.* —*v.* **1** *intr.* & *tr.* read or survey desultorily. **2** *intr.* (often foll. by *on*) feed (on leaves, twigs, or scanty vegetation). **3** *tr.* crop and eat. —*n.* **1** twigs, young shoots, etc., as fodder for cattle. **2** an act of browsing. □□ **browser** *n.* [(n.) f. earlier *brouse* f. OF *brost* young shoot, prob. f. Gmc; (v.) f. F *broster*]

BRS *abbr.* British Road Services.

Bruce[1] /bruːs/ see ROBERT I 'the Bruce'.

Bruce[2] /bruːs/, James (1730–94), Scottish explorer. Consul-General at Algiers from 1763 to 1765, Bruce set off from Cairo in 1768 on an expedition to Abyssinia, discovering the source of the Blue Nile, after many hardships, in late 1770. Many of his accounts were dismissed by contemporaries as fabrications, but have since been vindicated by other observers.

brucellosis /ˌbruːsəˈləʊsɪs/ *n.* a disease caused by bacteria of the genus *Brucella*, affecting esp. cattle and causing undulant fever in humans. [*Brucella* f. Sir D. *Bruce*, Sc. physician d. 1931 + -OSIS]

brucite /'bru:saɪt/ n. a mineral form of magnesium hydroxide. [A. *Bruce*, US mineralogist d. 1818]

Bruckner /'brʊknə(r)/, Anton (1824–96), Austrian composer and virtuoso organist. He went to Vienna as professor of harmony, counterpoint, and organ at the Conservatory when he was 44. His friendship with Wagner began in 1865 but, although he dedicated his Third Symphony (1873–8) to him, he derived little from Wagner's music beyond a sense of the large-scale and a massive slow-moving harmonic thought. His music moved to maturity equally slowly, and Bruckner allowed himself to be persuaded by critical friends to alter the orchestration of his symphonies; for the most part editors have traced his original intentions, and the symphonies, together with the Masses, form the cornerstone upon which his fame rests.

Bruegel /'brɜ:g(ə)l/, Pieter (c.1525–69), Flemish artist, also known as 'Peasant Bruegel' and 'Pieter Bruegel the elder'. He joined the Antwerp guild in 1551 and after travelling to Italy settled there for eight years, producing graphic work in the main. In 1563 he moved to Brussels and worked in a variety of different genres, establishing his reputation as an artist of wide range and ability, with such pictures as *Hunters in the Snow* (1565), *The Procession to Calvary* (1564), and *The Blind Leading the Blind*. Both of his two sons (who spelt their name *Brueghel*) worked chiefly in Antwerp. Pieter Brueghel the younger (1564–1638) is known primarily as a very able copyist of his father's work, while Jon ('Velvet') Brueghel (1568–1623) was a celebrated still-life and mythological painter.

Bruges /bru:ʒ/ (Flemish **Brugge** /'brʊxə/) a city in NW Belgium, capital of the province of West Flanders; pop. (1988) 117,857.

Bruin /'bru:ɪn/ n. a personal name used for a bear. [ME f. Du., = BROWN: used as a name in *Reynard the Fox*]

bruise /bru:z/ n. & v. —n. 1 an injury appearing as an area of discoloured skin on a human or animal body, caused by a blow or impact. 2 a similar area of damage on a fruit etc. —v. 1 tr. **a** inflict a bruise on. **b** hurt mentally. 2 intr. be susceptible to bruising. 3 tr. crush or pound. [ME f. OE *brȳsan* crush, reinforced by AF *bruser*, OF *bruisier* break]

bruiser /'bru:zə(r)/ n. colloq. 1 a large tough-looking person. 2 a professional boxer.

bruit /bru:t/ v. & n. —v.tr. (often foll. by abroad, about) spread (a report or rumour). —n. archaic a report or rumour. [F, = noise f. *bruire* roar]

Brum /brʌm/ n. colloq. Birmingham (in England). [abbr. of BRUMMAGEM]

brumby /'brʌmbɪ/ n. (pl. **-ies**) Austral. a wild or unbroken horse. [19th c.: orig. unkn.]

brume /bru:m/ n. literary mist, fog. [F f. L *bruma* winter]

Brummagem /'brʌmədʒəm/ adj. 1 cheap and showy (*Brummagem goods*). 2 counterfeit. [dial. form of *Birmingham*, England, with ref. to counterfeit coins and plated goods once made there]

Brummell /'brʌm(ə)l/, George Bryan, 'Beau' (1778–1840), Regency dandy, arbiter of British fashion for the first decade and a half of the 19th c., owing his social position to his close friendship with the Prince of Wales (later George IV). Brummell quarrelled with his patron and fled to France to avoid his creditors in 1816, eventually dying penniless in a mental asylum in Caen.

Brummie /'brʌmɪ/ n. & adj. (also **Brummy**) colloq. —n. (pl. **-ies**) a native of Birmingham. —adj. of or characteristic of a Brummie (*a Brummie accent*). [BRUM]

brunch /brʌntʃ/ n. & v. —n. a late-morning meal eaten as the first meal of the day. —v.intr. eat brunch. [BR(EAKFAST) + (L)UNCH]

Brunei /'bru:naɪ/ a small oil-rich sultanate on the NW coast of Borneo, pop. (est. 1988) 316,565; official language, Malay; capital, Bandar Seri Begawan. By the early 16th c. Brunei's power extended over the whole of the island of Borneo and parts of the Philippines, but declined as Portuguese and Dutch influence grew, and in 1888 it was placed under British protection; it became fully independent in 1984. Its main industries are crude oil production and gas liquefying and distilling. □□ **Bruneian** adj.

Brunel /brʊ'nel/, Sir Marc Isambard (1769–1849), engineer who was born in France but fled to the US during the French Revolution, where he invented a mechanical method of producing ships' blocks. He came to England in 1799 and persuaded the government to finance first models then full-sized machines at Portsmouth dockyard; these must be regarded as the first examples of automation. He also designed other machines for woodworking, boot-making, knitting, and printing; he was a versatile civil engineer and built bridges, landing stages, and the first tunnelling shield, with which he built the first tunnel under the Thames, between 1825 and 1843.

His son Isambard Kingdom Brunel (1806–59) was equally versatile, designing the famous Clifton suspension bridge at Bristol, then in 1833 becoming chief engineer of the Great Western Railway before turning to steamship construction with the *Great Western* (1837), the first successful transatlantic steamship. A little-known but remarkable achievement was Brunel's design in 1855 of a prefabricated hospital for the Crimean War. Both father and son have a brilliant record of achievement.

Brunelleschi /ˌbru:ne'leskɪ/, properly Filippo di Ser Brunellesco (1377–1446), the most famous Florentine architect of the 15th c. He trained as a goldsmith, but began to study architecture soon after 1401 and went to Rome. He is often credited with the 'discovery' of perspective—i.e. he studied the mathematical laws underlying appearances, by use of which artists could give an appearance of reality and depth. He revived Roman architectural forms, and above all studied Roman construction; he was an engineer rather than a designer. His greatest feat was the construction of the dome of Florence cathedral, evolving a method, based on his Roman studies, of raising the dome without the use of temporary supports.

brunette /bru:'net/ n. & adj. —n. a woman with dark brown hair. —adj. (of a woman) having dark brown hair. [F, fem. of *brunet*, dimin. of *brun* BROWN]

Brunhild /'bru:nhɪlt/ (in the Nibelungenlied) wife of Gunther, who instituted the murder of Siegfried. In the Norse Versions she is a Valkyrie whom Sigurd (the Norse counterpart of Siegfried) wins by penetrating the wall of fire behind which she lies in an enchanted sleep.

Bruno /'bru:nəʊ/, (c.1032–1101), German founder of the Carthusian order (1084). He was never formally canonized but in 1514 his order obtained papal leave to keep his feast day (6 Oct.).

Brunswick /'brʌnzwɪk/ 1 a district and former duchy of northern Germany. 2 an industrial city in Lower Saxony, Germany; pop. (1987) 247,800.

brunt /brʌnt/ n. the chief or initial impact of an attack, task, etc. (esp. *bear the brunt of*). [ME: orig. unkn.]

brush /brʌʃ/ n. & v. —n. 1 an implement with bristles, hair, wire, etc. varying in firmness set into a block or projecting from the end of a handle, for any of various purposes, esp. cleaning or scrubbing, painting, arranging the hair, etc. 2 the application of a brush; brushing. 3 a (usu. foll. by with) a short esp. unpleasant encounter (*a brush with the law*). **b** a skirmish. 4 a the bushy tail of a fox. **b** a brushlike tuft. 5 Electr. **a** a piece of carbon or metal serving as an electrical contact esp. with a moving part. **b** (in full **brush discharge**) a brushlike discharge of sparks. 6 esp. US & Austral. **a** undergrowth, thicket; small trees and shrubs. **b** US such wood cut in faggots. **c** land covered with brush. **d** Austral. dense forest. 7 Austral. & NZ sl. a girl or young woman. —v. 1 tr. **a** sweep or scrub or put in order with a brush. **b** treat (a surface) with a brush so as to change its nature or appearance. 2 tr. **a** remove (dust etc.) with a brush. **b** apply (a liquid preparation) to a surface with a brush. 3 tr. & intr. graze or touch in passing. 4 intr. perform a brushing action or motion. □ **brush aside** dismiss or dispose of (a person, idea, etc.) curtly or lightly. **brushed aluminium** aluminium with a lustreless surface. **brushed fabric** fabric brushed so as to raise the nap. **brush off** rebuff; dismiss abruptly. **brush-off** n. a rebuff; an abrupt dismissal. **brush over** paint lightly. **brush turkey** Austral. a large mound-building bird, *Alectura lathami*. **brush up** 1 clean up or smarten. 2 revive one's former knowledge of (a subject). **brush-up** n. the process of cleaning up. □□ **brushlike** adj. **brushy** adj. [ME f. OF *brosse*]

brushless /ˈbrʌʃlɪs/ adj. not requiring the use of a brush.

brushwood /ˈbrʌʃwʊd/ n. **1** cut or broken twigs etc. **2** undergrowth; a thicket.

brushwork /ˈbrʌʃwɜːk/ n. **1** manipulation of the brush in painting. **2** a painter's style in this.

brusque /brʊsk, bruːsk, brʌsk/ adj. abrupt or offhand in manner or speech. □□ **brusquely** adv. **brusqueness** n. **brusquerie** /ˈbrʊskəˌriː/ n. [F f. It. *brusco* sour]

Brussels /ˈbrʌs(ə)lz/ (French **Bruxelles** /bruːˈsel/, Flemish **Brüssel**) a city on the River Senne, the capital of Brabant since the 14th c. and of Belgium since it achieved independence in 1830; pop. (1988) 970,346. The Commission of the European Communities has its headquarters here. □ **Brussels carpet** a carpet with a wool pile and a stout linen back. **Brussels lace** an elaborate needlepoint or pillow lace. **Brussels sprout** **1** a variety of cabbage with small compact cabbage-like buds borne close together along a tall single stem. **2** any of these buds used as a vegetable.

brut /bruːt/ adj. (of wine) unsweetened. [F]

brutal /ˈbruːt(ə)l/ adj. **1** savagely or coarsely cruel. **2** harsh, merciless. □□ **brutality** /-ˈtælɪtɪ/ n. (pl. **-ies**). **brutally** adv. [F *brutal* or med.L *brutalis* f. *brutus* BRUTE]

brutalism /ˈbruːtəˌlɪz(ə)m/ n. **1** brutality. **2** a heavy plain style of architecture etc.

brutalize /ˈbruːtəˌlaɪz/ v.tr. (also **-ise**) **1** make brutal. **2** treat brutally. □□ **brutalization** /-ˈzeɪʃ(ə)n/ n.

brute /bruːt/ n. & adj. —n. **1 a** a brutal or violent person or animal. **b** colloq. an unpleasant person. **2** an animal as opposed to a human being. —adj. **1** not possessing the capacity to reason. **2 a** animal-like, cruel. **3** stupid, sensual. **3** unthinking, merely material (*brute force*; *brute matter*). □□ **brutehood** n. **brutish** adj. **brutishly** adv. **brutishness** n. [F f. L *brutus* stupid]

Brutus[1] /ˈbruːtəs/ great-grandson of Aeneas and legendary founder of the British people, said to have brought a group of Trojans to England and founded Troynovant or New Troy (later called London), becoming the progenitor of a line of kings. His story is told (or more probably invented) by the historian Geoffrey of Monmouth (12th c.).

Brutus[2] /ˈbruːtəs/, Lucius Junius, traditional founder of the Roman republic. According to the legend (probably with a historical core), in 510 BC after the rape of his wife Lucretia by the son of King Tarquin the Proud, and her subsequent suicide, he led a popular uprising against the king (his uncle) and drove him from Rome; he and the father of Lucretia were elected as the first consuls of the Republic (509 BC).

Brutus[3] /ˈbruːtəs/, Marcus Junius (85–42 BC), Roman senator who claimed descent from Lucius Junius Brutus. With Cassius he was a leader of the conspirators who assassinated Julius Caesar in the name of the Republic in 44 BC. He and Cassius were defeated by Caesar's supporters, Antony and Octavian, at the battle of Philippi in 42 BC, after which he committed suicide.

bruxism /ˈbrʌksɪz(ə)m/ n. the involuntary or habitual grinding or clenching of the teeth. [Gk *brukhein* gnash the teeth]

bryology /braɪˈɒlədʒɪ/ n. the study of bryophytes. □□ **bryological** /-əˈlɒdʒɪk(ə)l/ adj. **bryologist** n. [Gk *bruon* moss]

bryony /ˈbraɪənɪ/ n. (pl. **-ies**) any climbing plant of the genus *Bryonia*, esp. *B. dioica* bearing greenish-white flowers and red berries. □ **black bryony** a similar unrelated plant, *Tamus communis*, bearing poisonous berries. [L *bryonia* f. Gk *bruōnia*]

bryophyte /ˈbraɪəˌfaɪt/ n. any plant of the division Bryophyta, including mosses and liverworts. □□ **bryophytic** /-ˈfɪtɪk/ adj. [mod.L *Bryophyta* f. Gk *bruon* moss + *phuton* plant]

bryozoan /ˌbraɪəˈzəʊən/ n. & adj. —n. any aquatic invertebrate animal of the phylum Bryozoa, forming colonies attached to rocks, seaweeds, etc. Also called POLYZOAN. —adj. of or relating to the phylum Bryozoa. □□ **bryozoology** /-ˈzəʊɒlədʒɪ/ n. [Gk *bruon* moss + *zōia* animals]

Brythonic /brɪˈθɒnɪk/ n. & adj. —n. the southern group of the Celtic languages, including Welsh, Cornish, and Breton. It grew from the language spoken by the Britons at the time of the Roman invasion, and borrowed a number of Latin words during the Roman occupation. When in the 5th c. Britain was invaded by Germanic-speaking peoples the language of the Britons died out in most parts but survived in the mountainous and more remote west—Wales, Cumberland, parts of the Scottish lowlands, and Cornwall—and was carried by British emigrants across the Channel, where it survives as the Breton language in Brittany. —adj. of or relating to this people or their languages. [W *Brython* Britons f. OCelt.]

BS abbr. **1** US Bachelor of Science. **2** Bachelor of Surgery. **3** Blessed Sacrament. **4** British Standard(s).

B.Sc. abbr. Bachelor of Science.

BSE abbr. bovine spongiform encephalopathy, a usu. fatal disease of cattle involving the central nervous system and causing extreme agitation. It is popularly known as 'mad cow disease'.

BSI abbr. British Standards Institution.

B-side /ˈbiːsaɪd/ n. the side of a gramophone record regarded as less important.

BST abbr. **1** British Summer Time. **2** British Standard Time (in use 1968–71). **3** bovine somatotrophin, a growth hormone found naturally in cows and introduced into cattle-feed to boost milk production.

BT abbr. British Telecom.

Bt. abbr. Baronet.

B.th.u. abbr. (also **B.t.u.**, **BTU**, **B.Th.U.**) British thermal unit(s).

bu. abbr. bushel(s).

bub /bʌb/ n. US colloq. a boy or a man, often used as a form of address. [earlier *bubby*, perh. a childish form of BROTHER or f. G *Bube* boy]

bubal /ˈbjuːb(ə)l/ n. = HARTEBEEST. [L *bubalus* f. Gk *boubalos* oxlike antelope]

bubble /ˈbʌb(ə)l/ n. & v. —n. **1 a** a thin sphere of liquid enclosing air etc. **b** an air-filled cavity in a liquid or a solidified liquid such as glass or amber. **2** the sound or appearance of boiling. **3** a transparent domed cavity. **4** a visionary or unrealistic project or enterprise (*the South Sea Bubble*). —v.intr. **1** rise in or send up bubbles. **2** make the sound of boiling. □ **bubble and squeak** Brit. cooked cabbage fried with cooked potatoes or meat. **bubble bath** **1** a preparation for adding to bath water to make it foam. **2** a bath with this added. **bubble car** Brit. a small motor car with a transparent dome. **bubble chamber** Physics an apparatus designed to make the tracks of ionizing particles visible as a row of bubbles in a liquid. **bubble gum** chewing-gum that can be blown into bubbles. **bubble memory** Computing a type of memory which stores data as a pattern of magnetized regions in a thin layer of magnetic material. **bubble over** (often foll. by *with*) be exuberant with laughter, excitement, anger, etc. **bubble pack** a small package enclosing goods in a transparent material on a backing. [ME: prob. imit.]

bubbly /ˈbʌblɪ/ adj. & n. —adj. (**bubblier**, **bubbliest**) **1** having or resembling bubbles. **2** exuberant. —n. colloq. champagne. □ **bubbly-jock** Sc. a turkeycock.

Buber /ˈbuːbə(r)/, Martin (1878–1965), Jewish religious philosopher, born in Vienna. He was sympathetic to chasidism (see entry) and was a committed Zionist (he settled in Palestine in 1938), in which he sought cultural as opposed to a purely political ideal. His most famous work *I and Thou* (1923) sums up much of his religious philosophy, taking the form of a dialogue between man and God in which man, addressed by God, tries to respond.

bubo /ˈbjuːbəʊ/ n. (pl. **-oes**) a swollen inflamed lymph node in the armpit or groin. [med.L *bubo -onis* swelling f. Gk *boubōn* groin]

bubonic /bjuːˈbɒnɪk/ adj. relating to or characterized by buboes. □ **bubonic plague** a contagious bacterial disease characterized by fever, delirium, and the formation of buboes.

buccal /ˈbʌk(ə)l/ adj. **1** of or relating to the cheek. **2** of or in the mouth. [L *bucca* cheek]

buccaneer /ˌbʌkəˈnɪə(r)/ n. & v. —n. **1** a pirate, orig. off the Spanish-American coasts. **2** an unscrupulous adventurer. —v.intr. be a buccaneer. □□ **buccaneering** n. & adj.

buccaneerish *adj.* [F *boucanier* f. *boucaner* cure meat on a barbecue f. *boucan* f. Tupi *mukem*]

buccinator /ˈbʌksɪˌneɪtə(r)/ *n.* a flat thin cheek muscle. [L f. *buccinare* blow a trumpet (*buccina*)]

Bucelas /buːˈseləs/ a small wine-producing region in central Portugal, north of Lisbon.

Bucephalus /bjuːˈsefələs/ the favourite horse of Alexander the Great, which was tamed by him as a boy and accompanied him on his campaigns until its death, after a battle, in 326 BC.

Buchan[1] /ˈbʌx(ə)n/, Alexander (1829–1907), Scottish meteorologist who wrote a standard textbook on the subject. After scrutinizing temperature records over a nine-year period, he proposed that at certain times the temperature deviated from the normal for that season; it is now thought that these 'Buchan's cold spells' are probably distributed at random. He also produced maps and tables of atmospheric circulation, and of ocean currents and temperatures, based largely on information gathered by the HMS *Challenger* expedition during 1872–6.

Buchan[2] /ˈbʌxən/, John, 1st Baron Tweedsmuir (1875–1940), Scottish novelist, who combined a literary career with public life (he was Governor-General of Canada 1935–40). He wrote non-fictional works but is remembered for his action-packed adventure stories, often featuring recurring heroes (such as Richard Hannay). Popular among these are *The Thirty-Nine Steps* (1915), *Greenmantle* (1916), and *The Three Hostages* (1924).

Buchanan /bjuːˈkænən/, James (1791–1868), 15th President of the US, 1857–61, who consistently leaned towards the proslavery side in the developing dispute over slavery in the territories.

Bucharest /ˌbuːkəˈrest/ the capital of Romania; pop. (1985) 1,975,800.

Buchenwald /ˈbʊkənˌvɑːlt, ˈbʊx-/ a village in eastern Germany, near Weimar, site of a Nazi concentration camp in the Second World War.

buck[1] /bʌk/ *n.* & *v.* —*n.* **1** the male of various animals, esp. the deer, hare, or rabbit. **2** *archaic* a fashionable young man. **3** (*attrib.*) **a** *sl.* male (*buck antelope*). **b** *US Mil.* of the lowest rank (*buck private*). —*v.* **1** *intr.* (of a horse) jump upwards with back arched and feet drawn together. **2** *tr.* **a** (usu. foll. by *off*) throw (a rider or burden) in this way. **b** *US* oppose, resist. **3** *tr.* & *intr.* (usu. foll. by *up*) *colloq.* **a** make or become more cheerful. **b** hurry. **4** *tr.* (as **bucked** *adj.*) *colloq.* encouraged, elated. □ **buck fever** *US* nervousness when called on to act. **buck-horn** horn of buck as a material for knife-handles etc. **buck-hound** a small kind of staghound. **buck rarebit** Welsh rarebit with a poached egg on top. **buck-tooth** an upper tooth that projects. □□ **bucker** *n.* [OE *buc* male deer, *bucca* male goat, f. ON]

buck[2] /bʌk/ *n.* *US* etc. *sl.* a dollar. □ **a fast buck** easy money. [19th c.: orig. unkn.]

buck[3] /bʌk/ *n.* *sl.* an article placed as a reminder before a player whose turn it is to deal at poker. □ **pass the buck** *colloq.* shift responsibility (to another). [19th c.: orig. unkn.]

buck[4] /bʌk/ *n.* **1** *US* a saw-horse. **2** a vaulting-horse. [Du. (*zaag*)*boc*]

buck[5] /bʌk/ *n.* the body of a cart. [perh. f. obs. *bouk* belly, f. OE *būc* f. Gmc]

buck[6] /bʌk/ *n.* conversation; boastful talk. [Hindi *buk buk*]

buckbean /ˈbʌkbiːn/ *n.* a bog plant, *Menyanthes trifoliata*, with white or pinkish hairy flowers. Also called *bog-bean*.

buckboard /ˈbʌkbɔːd/ *n.* *US* a horse-drawn vehicle with the body formed by a plank fixed to the axles. [BUCK[5] + BOARD]

bucket /ˈbʌkɪt/ *n.* & *v.* —*n.* **1 a** a roughly cylindrical open container, esp. of metal, with a handle, used for carrying, drawing, or holding water etc. **b** the amount contained in this (*need three buckets to fill the bath*). **2** (in *pl.*) large quantities of liquid, esp. rain or tears (*wept buckets*). **3** a compartment on the outer edge of a water wheel. **4** the scoop of a dredger or a grain-elevator. —*v.* (**bucketed**, **bucketing**) **1** *intr.* & *tr.* (often foll. by *along*) *Brit.* move or drive jerkily or bumpily. **2** *tr.* (often foll. by *down*) (of liquid, esp. rain) pour heavily. □ **bucket seat** a seat with a rounded back to fit one person, esp. in a car. **bucket-shop**

1 an office for gambling in stocks, speculating on markets, etc. **2** *colloq.* a travel agency specializing in cheap air tickets. □□ **bucketful** *n.* (*pl.* **-fuls**). [ME & AF *buket*, *buquet*, perh. f. OE *būc* pitcher]

buckeye /ˈbʌkaɪ/ *n.* **a** any shrub of the genus *Aesculus*, with large sticky buds and showy red or white flowers. **b** the shiny brown fruit of this plant.

Buckingham Palace /ˈbʌkɪŋəm/ the London residence of the British sovereign since 1837, adjoining St James's Park, Westminster. It was built for the Duke of Buckingham in the early 18th c., bought by George III in 1761, and redesigned by John Nash for George IV in 1825; the façade facing the Mall was redesigned in 1913.

Buckinghamshire /ˈbʌkɪŋəmˌʃɪə(r)/ a southern county of England; pop. (1981) 571,500; county town, Aylesbury.

buckle /ˈbʌk(ə)l/ *n.* & *v.* —*n.* **1** a flat often rectangular frame with a hinged pin, used for joining the ends of a belt, strap, etc. **2** a similarly shaped ornament, esp. on a shoe. —*v.* **1** *tr.* (often foll. by *up*, *on*, etc.) fasten with a buckle. **2** *tr.* & *intr.* (often foll. by *up*) give way or cause to give way under longitudinal pressure; crumple up. □ **buckle down** make a determined effort. **buckle to** (or **down to**) prepare for, set about (work etc.). **buckle to** get to work, make a vigorous start. [ME f. OF *boucle* f. L *buccula* cheek-strap of a helmet f. *bucca* cheek: sense 2 of *v.* f. F *boucler* bulge]

buckler /ˈbʌklə(r)/ *n.* **1** *hist.* a small round shield held by a handle. **2** *Bot.* any of several ferns of the genus *Dryopteris*, having buckler-shaped indusia. Also called *shield-fern*. [ME f. OF *bocler* lit. 'having a boss' f. *boucle* BOSS[2]]

Buckley's /ˈbʌklɪz/ *n.* (in full **Buckley's chance**) *Austral.* & *NZ colloq.* little or no chance. [19th c.: orig. uncert.; perh. f. the name of William Buckley (d. 1856), an escaped convict who lived for 32 years with Aborigines in south Victoria (but there are other explanations)]

buckling /ˈbʌklɪŋ/ *n.* a smoked herring. [G *Bückling* bloater]

bucko /ˈbʌkəʊ/ *n.* & *adj.* *Naut. sl.* —*n.* (*pl.* **-oes**) a swaggering or domineering fellow. —*adj.* blustering, swaggering, bullying. [BUCK[1] + -o]

buckram /ˈbʌkrəm/ *n.* & *adj.* —*n.* **1** a coarse linen or other cloth stiffened with gum or paste, and used as interfacing or in bookbinding. **2** *archaic* stiffness in manner. —*adj.* *archaic* starchy; formal. □ **men in buckram** a figment (Shakesp. *1 Henry IV* II. iv. 210–50). [ME f. AF *bukeram*, OF *boquerant*, perh. f. *Bokhara* in central Asia]

Bucks. /bʌks/ *abbr.* Buckinghamshire.

Buck's Fizz /bʌks/ *n.* a cocktail of champagne or sparkling white wine and orange juice. [*Buck's* Club in London + FIZZ]

buckshee /bʌkˈʃiː/ *adj.* & *adv.* *Brit. sl.* free of charge. [corrupt. of BAKSHEESH]

buckshot /ˈbʌkʃɒt/ *n.* coarse lead shot.

buckskin /ˈbʌkskɪn/ *n.* **1 a** the skin of a buck. **b** leather made from a buck's skin. **2** a thick smooth cotton or woollen cloth.

buckthorn /ˈbʌkθɔːn/ *n.* any thorny shrub of the genus *Rhamnus*, esp. *R. cathartica* with berries formerly used as a cathartic.

buckwheat /ˈbʌkwiːt/ *n.* a plant of the genus *Fagopyrum*, esp. *F. esculentum* with seeds used for fodder and for flour to make bread and pancakes. [MDu. *boecweite* beech wheat, its grains being shaped like beechmast]

bucolic /bjuːˈkɒlɪk/ *adj.* & *n.* —*adj.* of or concerning shepherds, the pastoral life, etc.; rural. —*n.* **1** (usu. in *pl.*) a pastoral poem or poetry. **2** a peasant. □□ **bucolically** *adv.* [L *bucolicus* f. Gk *boukolikos* f. *boukolos* herdsman f. *bous* ox]

bud[1] /bʌd/ *n.* & *v.* —*n.* **1 a** an immature knoblike shoot from which a stem, leaf, or flower develops. **b** a flower or leaf that is not fully open. **2** *Biol.* an asexual outgrowth from a parent organism that separates to form a new individual. **3** anything still undeveloped. —*v.* (**budded**, **budding**) **1** *intr.* *Bot.* & *Zool.* form a bud. **2** *intr.* begin to grow or develop (*a budding cricketer*). **3** *tr.* *Hort.* graft a bud (of a plant) on to another plant. □ **in bud** having newly formed buds. [ME: orig. unkn.]

bud[2] /bʌd/ n. US colloq. (as a form of address) = BUDDY. [abbr.]

Budapest /ˌbuːdəˈpest/ the capital of Hungary, formed in 1873 by the union of the hilly Buda on the right bank of the Danube with the low-lying Pest on the left bank; pop. (1988) 2,104,000.

Buddha /ˈbʊdə/ n. **1** a title given to successive teachers (past and future) of Buddhism, an honorific applied to an enlightened man. It usually denotes the founder of Buddhism, Siddhartha Gautama of the Sakyas (see SAKYAMUNI). Born a Kshatriya prince in the Nepalese Terai c.563 BC, he renounced kingdom, wife, and child to become an ascetic. After taking religious instruction from various teachers, he attained enlightenment (nirvana) c.525 BC through meditation beneath a bo-tree in the village of Bodhgaya in NE India. He then taught all who wanted to learn, regardless of sex, class, or caste, until his death in c.480 BC. **2** a statue or picture of the Buddha. [Skr., = enlightened, past part. of *budh* know]

Buddh Gaya see BODHGAYA.

Buddhism /ˈbʊdɪz(ə)m/ n. a widespread Asian religion or philosophy, founded by Siddhartha Gautama, entitled the Buddha, in NE India in the 5th c. BC. as a reaction against the sacrificial religion of orthodox brahminism. It is a religion without a god, in which human mistakes and human doom are linked in a relentless chain of cause and effect. There are two major traditions or 'vehicles': Theravada (often called Hinayana), and Mahayana; and, emerging from the latter, Vajrayana. The basic teachings of Buddhism are contained in the 'four noble truths': all existence is suffering; the cause of suffering is desire; freedom from suffering is nirvana; and the means of attaining nirvana is prescribed in the 'eightfold path' that combines ethical conduct, mental discipline, and wisdom. Central to this religious path are the doctrine of 'no-self' (*anatta*; Skr. *an-atman*) and the practice of meditation. The three 'jewels' of Buddhism are the Buddha, the doctrine (*dharma*), and the sangha. □□ **Buddhist** n. & adj. **Buddhistic** /-ˈdɪstɪk/ adj. **Buddhistical** /-ˈdɪstɪk(ə)l/ adj.

buddleia /ˈbʌdlɪə/ n. any shrub of the genus *Buddleia*, with fragrant lilac, yellow, or white flowers attractive to butterflies. [A. *Buddle*, Engl. botanist d. 1715]

buddy /ˈbʌdɪ/ n. & v. esp. US colloq. —n. (pl. **-ies**) (often as a form of address) a close friend or mate. —v.intr. (**-ies, -ied**) (often foll. by *up*) become friendly. [perh. corrupt. of *brother*, or var. of BUTTY[1]]

Budge /bʌdʒ/, John Donald ('Don') (1915–), Australian tennis player, the first to win the four major singles championships— Australia, France, Britain (Wimbledon), and the US—in one year (1938).

budge /bʌdʒ/ v. (usu. with *neg.*) **1** intr. **a** make the slightest movement. **b** change one's opinion (*he's stubborn, he won't budge*). **2** tr. cause or compel to budge (*nothing will budge him*). □ **budge up** (or **over**) make room for another person by moving. [F *bouger* stir ult. f. L *bullire* boil]

budgerigar /ˈbʌdʒərɪˌgɑː(r)/ n. a small green parrot, *Melopsittacus undulatus*, native to Australia, and bred in coloured varieties which are often kept as cage-birds. [Aboriginal, = good cockatoo]

budget /ˈbʌdʒɪt/ n. & v. —n. **1** the amount of money needed or available (for a specific item etc.) (*a budget of £200; mustn't exceed the budget*). **2 a** (**the Budget**) *Brit.* the usu. annual estimate of national revenue and expenditure. **b** an estimate or plan of expenditure in relation to income. **c** a private person's or family's similar estimate. **3** (*attrib.*) inexpensive. **4** *archaic* a quantity of material etc., esp. written or printed. —v.tr. & intr. (**budgeted, budgeting**) (often foll. by *for*) allow or arrange for in a budget (*have budgeted for a new car; can budget £60*). □ **budget account** (or **plan**) a bank account, or account with a store, into which one makes regular, usu. monthly, payments to cover bills. **on a budget** avoiding expense; cheap. □□ **budgetary** adj. [ME = pouch, f. OF *bougette* dimin. of *bouge* leather bag f. L *bulga* (f. Gaulish) knapsack: cf. BULGE]

budgie /ˈbʌdʒɪ/ n. colloq. = BUDGERIGAR. [abbr.]

Buenaventura /ˌbweɪnəvenˈtʊərə/ the chief Pacific port of Colombia, trading in tobacco, sugar, and coffee from the Cauca valley; pop. (1985) 122,500.

Buenos Aires /ˈbweɪnəs ˈaɪriːz/ the capital city and a port of Argentina; pop. (1980) 2,908,000.

buff /bʌf/ adj., n., & v. —adj. of a yellowish beige colour (*buff envelope*). —n. **1** a yellowish beige colour. **2** colloq. an enthusiast, esp. for a particular hobby (*railway buff*). **3** colloq. the human skin unclothed. **4 a** a velvety dull-yellow ox-leather. **b** (*attrib.*) (of a garment etc.) made of this (*buff gloves*). **5** (**the Buffs**) the former East Kent Regiment (from the colour of its uniform facings). —v.tr. **1** polish (metal, fingernails, etc.). **2** make (leather) velvety like buff, by removing the surface. □ **buff-stick** a stick covered with buff and used for polishing. **in the buff** colloq. naked. [orig. sense 'buffalo', prob. f. F *buffle*; sense 2 of *n.* orig. f. buff uniforms formerly worn by New York volunteer firemen, applied to enthusiastic fire-watchers]

Buffalo /ˈbʌfəˌləʊ/ an industrial city and major port of the St Lawrence Seaway, situated at the eastern end of Lake Erie, in New York State; pop. (1982) 348,000.

buffalo /ˈbʌfəˌləʊ/ n. & v. —n. (pl. same or **-oes**) **1** either of two species of ox, *Syncerus caffer*, native to Africa, or *Bubalus arnee*, native to Asia with heavy backswept horns. **2** a N. American bison, *Bison bison*. —v.tr. (**-oes, -oed**) US sl. overawe, outwit. □ **buffalo grass 1** a grass, *Buchloe dactyloides*, of the N. American plains. **2** a grass, *Stenotaphrum secundatum*, of Australia and New Zealand. [prob. f. Port. *bufalo* f. LL *bufalus* f. L *bubalus* f. Gk *boubalos* antelope, wild ox]

Buffalo Bill William Frederick Cody (1846–1917), American plainsman. Cody gained his nickname for killing a record number of buffalo in a single day, and, after working as an army scout and in a host of other itinerant jobs, devoted his life to show business, particularly a 'Wild West' show, which travelled all over the country giving performances purporting to portray life in the American West. As a result more of these dramatics than of any real frontier exploits, Cody became a national figure, and his death in 1917 was widely seen as symbolizing the end of an era.

buffer[1] /ˈbʌfə(r)/ n. & v. —n. **1 a** a device that protects against or reduces the effect of an impact. **b** *Brit.* such a device (usu. one of a pair) on the front and rear of a railway vehicle or at the end of a track. **2** *Biochem.* a substance that maintains the hydrogen ion concentration of a solution when an acid or alkali is added. **3** *Computing* a temporary memory area or queue for data to aid its transfer between devices or programs operating at different speeds etc. —v.tr. **1** act as a buffer to. **2** *Biochem.* treat with a buffer. □ **buffer State** a small State situated between two larger ones potentially hostile to one another and regarded as reducing the likelihood of open hostilities. **buffer stock** a reserve of commodity to offset price fluctuations. [prob. f. obs. *buff* (v.), imit. of the sound of a soft body struck]

buffer[2] /ˈbʌfə(r)/ n. *Brit. sl.* a silly or incompetent old man (esp. *old buffer*). [18th c.: prob. formed as BUFFER[1] or with the sense 'stutterer']

buffet[1] /ˈbʊfeɪ, ˈbʌfeɪ/ n. **1** a room or counter where light meals or snacks may be bought (*station buffet*). **2** a meal consisting of several dishes set out from which guests serve themselves (*buffet lunch*). **3** /also ˈbʌfɪt/ a sideboard or recessed cupboard for china etc. □ **buffet car** *Brit.* a railway coach serving light meals or snacks. [F f. OF *bufet* stool, of unkn. orig.]

buffet[2] /ˈbʌfɪt/ v. & n. —v. (**buffeted, buffeting**) **1** tr. **a** strike or knock repeatedly (*wind buffeted the trees*). **b** strike, esp. repeatedly, with the hand or fist. **2** tr. (of fate etc.) treat badly; plague (*cheerful though buffeted by misfortune*). **3 a** intr. struggle; fight one's way (through difficulties etc.). **b** tr. contend with (waves etc.). —n. **1** a blow, esp. of the hand or fist. **2** a shock. [ME f. OF dimin. of *bufe* blow]

buffeting /ˈbʌfɪtɪŋ/ n. **1** a beating; repeated blows. **2** *Aeron.* an irregular oscillation, caused by air eddies, of any part of an aircraft.

bufflehead /ˈbʌf(ə)lˌhed/ n. a duck, *Bucephala albeola*, native to N. America, with a head that appears over-large. [obs. *buffle* buffalo + HEAD]

buffo /'bʊfəʊ/ n. & adj. —n. (pl. *-os*) a comic actor, esp. in Italian opera. —adj. comic, burlesque. [It.]

Buffon /bu:'fɔ̃/, Georges-Louis Leclerc, Comte de (1707–88), French naturalist, appointed Keeper of the Jardin du Roi (Royal Botanical Garden) in 1739, which began his lifelong interest in natural history. He suggested that on scientific evidence the earth was much older than was generally accepted and he saw all life as the physical property of matter, thereby stressing the unity of all living species and minimizing the apparent differences between animals and plants. His work gives the impression that he is groping towards a concept of evolution, formulated in the next century by Darwin. These thoughts were expressed in a remarkable compilation of the animal kingdom, the *Histoire naturelle*, begun in 1749. At his death 36 volumes had been published, to which another 8 volumes were added posthumously.

buffoon /bə'fu:n/ n. **1** a jester; a mocker. **2** a stupid person. □□ **buffoonery** n. **buffoonish** adj. [F *bouffon* f. It. *buffone* f. med.L *buffo* clown f. Rmc]

bug /bʌg/ n. & v. —n. **1 a** any of various hemipterous insects with oval flattened bodies and mouthparts modified for piercing and sucking. **b** *US* any small insect. **2** *sl.* a micro-organism, esp. a bacterium, or a disease caused by it. **3** a concealed microphone. **4** *sl.* an error in a computer program or system etc. **5** *sl.* an obsession, enthusiasm, etc. —v. (**bugged**, **bugging**) **1** *tr. sl.* conceal a microphone in (esp. a building or room). **2** *tr. sl.* annoy, bother. **3** *intr.* (often foll. by *out*) *US sl.* leave quickly. □ **bug-eyed** with bulging eyes. [17th c.: orig. unkn.]

bugaboo /'bʌgəˌbu:/ n. a bogey (see BOGEY²) or bugbear. [prob. of dial. orig.: cf. Welsh *bwcïbo* the Devil, *bwci* hobgoblin]

Buganda /bu:'gændə, bju:-/ a former powerful kingdom of East Africa, on the north shore of Lake Victoria, now part of Uganda.

bugbear /'bʌgbeə(r)/ n. **1** a cause of annoyance or anger; a *bête noire*. **2** an object of baseless fear. **3** *archaic* a sort of hobgoblin or any being invoked to intimidate children. [obs. *bug* + BEAR²]

bugger /'bʌgə(r)/ n., v., & int. *coarse sl.* (except in sense 2 of n. and 3 of v.) ¶ Usually considered a taboo word. —n. **1 a** an unpleasant or awkward person or thing (*the bugger won't fit*). **b** a person of a specified kind (*he's a miserable bugger; you clever bugger!*). **2** a person who commits buggery. —v.tr. **1** as an exclamation of annoyance (*bugger the thing!*). **2** (often foll. by *up*) *Brit.* **a** ruin; spoil (*really buggered it up; no good, it's buggered*). **b** exhaust, tire out. **3** commit buggery with. —int. expressing annoyance. □ **bugger about** (or **around**) (often foll. by *with*) **1** mess about. **2** mislead; persecute. **bugger-all** nothing. **bugger off** (often in *imper.*) go away. [ME f. MDu. f. OF *bougre*, orig. 'heretic' f. med.L *Bulgarus* Bulgarian (member of the Greek Church)]

buggery /'bʌgərɪ/ n. **1** anal intercourse. **2** = BESTIALITY 2. [ME f. MDu. *buggerie* f. OF *bougerie*: see BUGGER]

buggy¹ /'bʌgɪ/ n. (pl. *-ies*) **1** a light, horse-drawn, esp. two-wheeled, vehicle for one or two people. **2** a small, sturdy, esp. open, motor vehicle (*beach buggy; dune buggy*). **3** *US* a pram. [18th c.: orig. unkn.]

buggy² /'bʌgɪ/ adj. (**buggier**, **buggiest**) infested with bugs.

bugle¹ /'bju:g(ə)l/ n. & v. —n. (also **bugle-horn**) a brass instrument like a small trumpet, used esp. by huntsmen and for military signals. —v. **1** *intr.* sound a bugle. **2** *tr.* sound (a note, a call, etc.) on a bugle. □□ **bugler** /'bju:glə(r)/ n. **buglet** /'bju:glɪt/ n. [ME, orig. = 'buffalo', f. OF f. L *buculus* dimin. of *bos* ox]

bugle² /'bju:g(ə)l/ n. a blue-flowered mat-forming plant, *Ajuga reptans*. [ME f. LL *bugula*]

bugle³ /'bju:g(ə)l/ n. a tube-shaped bead sewn on a dress etc. for ornament. [16th c.: orig. unkn.]

bugloss /'bju:glɒs/ n. **1** any of various bristly plants related to borage, esp. of the genus *Anchusa* with bright blue tubular flowers. **2** = *viper's bugloss* (see VIPER). [F *buglosse* or L *buglossus* f. Gk *bouglōssos* ox-tongued]

buhl /bu:l/ n. (also **boule**, **boulle**) **1** pieces of brass, tortoiseshell, etc., cut to make a pattern and used as decorative inlays esp. on furniture. **2** work inlaid with buhl. **3** (*attrib.*) inlaid with buhl. [(*buhl* Germanized) f. A. C. BOULLE]

build /bɪld/ v. & n. —v.tr. (*past* and *past. part.* **built** /bɪlt/) **1 a** construct (a house, vehicle, fire, road, model, etc.) by putting parts or material together. **b** commission, finance, and oversee the building of (*the council has built two new schools*). **2 a** (often foll. by *up*) establish, develop, make, or accumulate gradually (*built the business up from nothing*). **b** (often foll. by *on*) base (hopes, theories, etc.) (*ideas built on a false foundation*). **3** (as **built** adj.) having a specified build (*sturdily built; brick-built*). —n. **1** the proportions of esp. the human body (*a slim build*). **2** a style of construction; a make (*build of his suit was pre-war*). □ **build in** incorporate as part of a structure. **build in** (or **round** or **up**) surround with houses etc.; block up. **build on** add (an extension etc.). **build up 1** increase in size or strength. **2** praise; boost. **3** gradually become established. **build-up** n. **1** a favourable description in advance; publicity. **2** a gradual approach to a climax or maximum (*the build-up was slow but sure*). **built-in 1** forming an integral part of a structure. **2** forming an integral part of a person's character (*built-in integrity*). **built on sand** unstable. **built-up 1** (of a locality) densely covered by houses etc. **2** increased in height etc. by the addition of parts. **3** composed of separately prepared parts. [OE *byldan* f. *bold* dwelling f. Gmc: cf. BOWER¹, BOOTH]

builder /'bɪldə(r)/ n. **1** a contractor for building houses etc.; a master builder. **2** a person engaged as a bricklayer etc. on a building site.

building /'bɪldɪŋ/ n. **1** a permanent fixed structure forming an enclosure and providing protection from the elements etc. (e.g. a house, school, factory, or stable). **2** the constructing of such structures. □ **building line** a limit or boundary between a house and a street beyond which the owner may not build. **building site** an area before or during the construction of a house etc.

building society n. *Brit.* a society of investors that lends money to people buying houses etc. The earliest building societies date from the first part of the 19th c. They consisted of a group of people contributing to a fund which was used to purchase a house for each of its members, and were dissolved when this had been achieved. Later in the 19th c. societies were established on a permanent basis, and some still retain the word 'Permanent' in their titles. Since 1986 building societies have been able to widen the range of services they provide, competing with those of the high-street banks and offering further advantages (such as interest on credit balances in current accounts) which the banks have been forced to match. Some building societies have obtained the agreement of their members to become public companies.

built *past* and *past part.* of BUILD.

Bujumbura /ˌbu:dʒəm'bʊərə/ the capital of Burundi, on Lake Tanganyika; pop. (1986) 272,600.

Bukhara /bʊ'kɑ:rə/ a city in the Soviet republic of Uzbekistan; pop. (1987) 220,000. Situated in a large cotton-growing district, it is one of the oldest trade centres in central Asia.

Bukharin /bʊ'kɑ:rɪn/, Nikolai Ivanovich (1888–1938), Russian revolutionary leader. Editor of *Pravda* 1917–29, a member of the Central Committee of the Bolshevik party, and later editor of *Izvestia* (1934–7), he was a prominent member of the rightist opposition to Stalin's policies and became one of the victims of his purges—arrested, convicted, and shot. Bukharin was a model for Rubashov, hero of Koestler's novel *Darkness at Noon* (1940).

Bukovina /ˌbʊkə'vi:nə/ a region of SE Europe, divided between Romania and the USSR. Ceded to Austria by the Turks in 1775, after the First World War it was made part of Romania and so remained until the Second World War, when the northern part was occupied by the Soviets, who incorporated this section into the Ukranian SSR.

Bulawayo /ˌbu:lə'weɪəʊ/ an industrial city in western Zimbabwe; pop. (1982) 414,000. It was formerly the capital of Matabeleland.

bulb /bʌlb/ n. **1 a** an underground fleshy-leaved storage organ of some plants (e.g. lily, onion) sending roots downwards and leaves upwards. **b** a plant grown from this, e.g. a daffodil. **2** = light-bulb (see LIGHT¹). **3** any object or part shaped like a bulb. [L bulbus f. Gk bolbos onion]

bulbous /ˈbʌlbəs/ adj. **1** shaped like a bulb; fat or bulging. **2** having a bulb or bulbs. **3** (of a plant) growing from a bulb.

bulbul /ˈbʊlbʊl/ n. **1** any songbird of the family Pycnonotidae, of dull plumage with contrasting bright patches. **2** a singer or poet. [Pers. f. Arab., of imit. orig.]

Bulganin /bʌlˈɡɑːnɪn/, Nikolai Aleksandrovich (1895–1975), Soviet military leader and statesman. He was Chairman of the Council of Ministers 1955–8, during which time he shared power with Khrushchev, who replaced him.

Bulgar /ˈbʌlɡɑː(r)/ n. **1** a member of an ancient Finnish tribe that conquered the Slavs of the lower Danube area in the 7th c. AD and settled in what is now Bulgaria, becoming Slavonic in language. **2** a Bulgarian. [med.L Bulgarus f. OBulg. Blŭgarinŭ]

bulgar var. of BULGUR.

Bulgaria /bʌlˈɡeərɪə/ a country in SE Europe on the western shores of the Black Sea; pop. (est. 1988) 8,966,900; official language, Bulgarian; capital, Sofia. Until the Second World War Bulgaria was predominantly an agricultural country, but since then the industrial sector has been effectively built up and there is a substantial engineering industry. Conquered during the Dark Ages by Bulgar tribes from the east, the country became part of the Ottoman empire in the 14th c., remaining under Turkish rule until the Russo-Turkish wars of the late 19th c. Bulgaria fought on the German side in both World Wars, generally not enjoying good relations with her Balkan neighbours. Occupied by the Soviets after the Second World War, the State was one of the most consistently pro-Soviet members of the Warsaw Pact until the general collapse of Communism in eastern Europe at the end of 1989.

Bulgarian /bʌlˈɡeərɪən/ n. & adj. —n. **1 a** a native or national of Bulgaria. **b** a person of Bulgarian descent. **2** the official language of Bulgaria, belonging to the Slavonic group of languages within which it is most closely related to Serbo-Croat. —adj. of or relating to Bulgaria or its people or language. [med.L Bulgaria f. Bulgarus: see BULGAR]

bulge /bʌldʒ/ n. & v. —n. **1 a** a convex part of an otherwise flat or flatter surface. **b** an irregular swelling; a lump. **2** colloq. a temporary increase in quantity or number (baby bulge). **3** Naut. the bilge of a ship. **4** Mil. a salient. —v. **1** intr. swell outwards. **2** intr. be full or replete. **3** tr. swell (a bag, cheeks, etc.) by stuffing. □ **have** (or **get**) **the bulge on** sl. have or get an advantage over. □□ **bulgingly** adv. **bulgy** adj. [ME f. OF boulge, bouge f. L bulga: see BUDGET]

bulgur /ˈbʌlɡə(r)/ n. (also **bulgar**, **bulghur**) a cereal food of whole wheat partially boiled then dried, eaten esp. in Turkey. [Turk.]

bulimarexia /bjuːˌlɪməˈreksɪə/ n. esp. US = BULIMIA 2. □□ **bulimarexic** adj. & n. [BULIMIA + ANOREXIA]

bulimia /bjuːˈlɪmɪə/ n. Med. **1** insatiable overeating. **2** (in full **bulimia nervosa**) an emotional disorder in which bouts of extreme overeating are followed by depression and self-induced vomiting, purging, or fasting. □□ **bulimic** adj. & n. [mod.L f. Gk boulimia f. bous ox + limos hunger]

bulk /bʌlk/ n. & v. —n. **1 a** size; magnitude (esp. large). **b** a large mass, body, or person. **c** a large quantity. **2** a large shape, body, or person (jacket barely covered his bulk). **3** (usu. prec. by the; treated as pl.) the greater part or number (the bulk of the applicants are women). **4** roughage. **5** Naut. cargo, esp. unpackaged. —v. **1** intr. seem in respect of size or importance (bulks large in his reckoning). **2** tr. make (a book, a textile yarn, etc.) seem thicker by suitable treatment (bulked it with irrelevant stories). **3** tr. combine (consignments etc.). □ **break bulk** begin unloading (cargo). **bulk-buying 1** buying in large amounts at a discount. **2** the purchase by one buyer of all or most of a producer's output. **in bulk 1** in large quantities. **2** (of a cargo) loose, not packaged. [sense 'cargo' f. OIcel. búlki; sense 'mass' etc. perh. alt. f. obs. bouk (cf. BUCK³)]

bulkhead /ˈbʌlkhed/ n. an upright partition separating the

compartments in a ship, aircraft, vehicle, etc. [bulk stall f. ON bálkr + HEAD]

bulky /ˈbʌlkɪ/ adj. (**bulkier**, **bulkiest**) **1** taking up much space, large. **2** awkwardly large, unwieldy. □□ **bulkily** adv. **bulkiness** n.

bull¹ /bʊl/ n., adj., & v. —n. **1 a** an uncastrated male bovine animal. **b** a male of the whale, elephant, and other large animals. **2** (**the Bull**) the zodiacal sign or constellation Taurus. **3** Brit. the bull's-eye of a target. **4** Stock Exch. a person who buys shares in the hope that prices will rise and that he or she will be able to sell them at a higher price before being required to pay for them (cf. BEAR²). —adj. like that of a bull (bull neck). —v. **1** tr. & intr. act or treat violently. **2** Stock Exch. **a** intr. speculate for a rise. **b** tr. raise price of (stocks, etc.). □ **bull ant** Austral. = bulldog ant. **bull at a gate** a hasty or rash person. **bull-fiddle** US colloq. a double-bass. **bull-horn** a megaphone. **bull in a china shop** a reckless or clumsy person. **bull market** a market with shares rising in price. **bull-nose** (or **-nosed**) with rounded end. **bull session** US an informal group discussion. **bull's-eye 1** the centre of a target. **2** a large hard peppermint-flavoured sweet. **3** a hemisphere or thick disc of glass in a ship's deck or side to admit light. **4** a small circular window. **5 a** a hemispherical lens. **b** a lantern fitted with this. **6** a boss of glass at the centre of a blown glass sheet. **bull-terrier 1** a short-haired dog of a breed that is a cross between a bulldog and a terrier. **2** this breed. **take the bull by the horns** face danger or challenge boldly. □□ **bullish** adj. [ME f. ON boli = MLG, MDu bulle]

bull² /bʊl/ n. a papal edict. [ME f. OF bulle f. L bulla rounded object, in med.L 'seal']

bull³ /bʊl/ n. **1** (also **Irish bull**) an expression containing a contradiction in terms or implying ludicrous inconsistency. **2** sl. (cf. BULLSHIT) **a** unnecessary routine tasks or discipline. **b** nonsense. **c** trivial or insincere talk or writing. **d** US a bad blunder. [17th c.: orig. unkn.]

bullace /ˈbʊlɪs/ n. a thorny shrub, Prunus insititia, bearing globular yellow or purple-black fruits, of which the damson is the cultivated form. [ME f. OF buloce, beloce]

bulldog /ˈbʊldɒɡ/ n. **1 a** a dog of a sturdy powerful breed with a large head and smooth hair. **b** this breed. **2** a tenacious and courageous person. □ **bulldog ant** Austral. a large ant with a powerful sting. **bulldog clip** a strong sprung clip for papers.

bulldoze /ˈbʊldəʊz/ v.tr. **1** clear with a bulldozer. **2** colloq. **a** intimidate. **b** make (one's way) forcibly.

bulldozer /ˈbʊldəʊzə(r)/ n. **1** a powerful tractor with a broad curved vertical blade at the front for clearing ground. **2** a forceful and domineering person. [bulldose (or -doze) US = intimidate, f. BULL¹: second element uncert.]

bullet /ˈbʊlɪt/ n. a small round or cylindrical missile with a pointed end, fired from a rifle, revolver, etc. □ **bullet-headed** having a round head. [F boulet, boulette dimin. of boule ball f. L bulla bubble]

bulletin /ˈbʊlɪtɪn/ n. **1** a short official statement of news. **2** a regular list of information etc. issued by an organization or society. □ **bulletin-board** US a notice-board. [F f. It. bullettino dimin. of bulletta passport, dimin. of bulla seal, BULL²]

bulletproof /ˈbʊlɪtpruːf/ adj. & v. —adj. (of a material) designed to resist the penetration of bullets. —v.tr. make bulletproof.

bullfight /ˈbʊlfaɪt/ n. a sport of baiting and (usu.) killing a bull as a public spectacle. Bullfighting is the national spectator sport of Spain, found also in some parts of Latin America and southern France, taking place in an outdoor arena. An early type of bullfighting was practised by Minoans, Greeks, and Romans, and the sport seems to have been introduced into Spain in about the 11th c. □□ **bullfighter** n. **bullfighting** n.

bullfinch /ˈbʊlfɪntʃ/ n. a finch, Pyrrhula pyrrhula, with a short stout beak and bright plumage.

bullfrog /ˈbʊlfrɒɡ/ n. a large frog, Rana catesbiana, native to N. America, with a deep croak.

bullhead /ˈbʊlhed/ n. any of various marine fishes with large flattened heads.

bull-headed /bʊlˈhedɪd/ adj. obstinate; impetuous; blundering. □□ **bull-headedly** adv. **bull-headedness** n.

bullion /ˈbʊlɪən/ n. a metal (esp. gold or silver) in bulk before coining, or valued by weight. [AF = mint, var. of OF bouillon ult. f. L bullire boil]

bullish /ˈbʊlɪʃ/ adj. 1 like a bull, esp. in temper. 2 Stock Exch. causing or associated with a rise in prices.

bullock /ˈbʊlək/ n. & v. —n. a castrated bull. —v.intr. (often foll. by at) Austral. colloq. work very hard. [OE bulluc, dimin. of BULL¹]

bullocky /ˈbʊləkɪ/ n. Austral. & NZ colloq. a bullock-driver.

bullring /ˈbʊlrɪŋ/ n. an arena for bullfights.

Bull Run /bʊl/ a small river in East Virginia, scene of two important battles (1861 and 1862) in which the Federal side was defeated in the American Civil War.

bullshit /ˈbʊlʃɪt/ n. & v. coarse sl. —n. 1 (often as int.) nonsense, rubbish. 2 trivial or insincere talk or writing. —v.intr. (-**shitted**, -**shitting**) talk nonsense; bluff. □□ **bullshitter** n. [BULL³ + SHIT]

bulltrout /ˈbʊltraʊt/ n. Brit. a salmon trout.

bully¹ /ˈbʊlɪ/ n. & v. —n. (pl. -**ies**) a person who uses strength or power to coerce others by fear. —v.tr. (-**ies**, -**ied**) 1 persecute or oppress by force or threats. 2 (foll. by into + verbal noun) pressure or coerce (a person) to do something (bullied him into agreeing). □ **bully-boy** a hired ruffian. [orig. as a term of endearment, prob. f. MDu. boele lover]

bully² /ˈbʊlɪ/ adj. & int. colloq. —adj. very good; first-rate. —int. (foll. by for) expressing admiration or approval, or iron. (bully for them!). [perh. f BULLY¹]

bully³ /ˈbʊlɪ/ n. & v. (in full **bully off**) —n. (pl. -**ies**) the start of play in hockey in which two opponents strike each other's sticks three times and then go for the ball. —v.intr. (-**ies**, -**ied**) start play in this way. [19th c.: perh. f. bully scrum in Eton football, of unkn. orig.]

bully⁴ /ˈbʊlɪ/ n. (in full **bully beef**) corned beef. [F bouilli boiled beef f. bouillir BOIL¹]

bullyrag var. of BALLYRAG.

bully tree /ˈbʊlɪ/ n. = BALATA. [corrupt.]

bulrush /ˈbʊlrʌʃ/ n. 1 = reed-mace (see REED¹). 2 a rushlike water-plant, Scirpus lacustris, used for weaving. 3 Bibl. a papyrus plant. [perh. f. BULL¹ = large, coarse, as in bullfrog, bulltrout, etc.]

Bultmann /ˈbʊltmən/, Rudolf Karl (1884–1976), German Lutheran theologian, who held that the Gospels were a patchwork of traditional elements and insisted on the need for 'demythologizing' the whole Gospel story, extracting and reinterpreting the 'myths' (e.g. belief in a three-storied universe of heaven, earth, and hell) in order to disclose its real meaning. He emphasized what he saw as its 'existential' significance; his influence waned with the general decline of existentialism.

bulwark /ˈbʊlwək/ n. 1 a defensive wall, esp. of earth; a rampart; a mole or breakwater. 2 a person, principle, etc., that acts as a defence. 3 (usu. in pl.) a ship's side above deck. [ME f. MLG, MDu. bolwerk: see BOLE¹, WORK]

Bulwer-Lytton see LYTTON.

bum¹ /bʌm/ n. Brit. sl. the buttocks. □ **bum-bailiff** hist. a bailiff empowered to collect debts or arrest debtors for non-payment. **bum-boat** any small boat plying with provisions etc. for ships. **bum-sucker** sl. a toady. **bum-sucking** toadying. [ME bom, of unkn. orig.]

bum² /bʌm/ n., v., & adj. US sl. —n. a habitual loafer or tramp; a lazy dissolute person. —v. (**bummed**, **bumming**) 1 intr. (often foll. by about, around) loaf or wander around; be a bum. 2 tr. get by begging; cadge. —attrib.adj. of poor quality. □ **bum rap** imprisonment on a false charge. **bum's rush** forcible ejection. **bum steer** false information. **on the bum** vagrant, begging. [prob. abbr. or back-form. f. BUMMER]

bumble /ˈbʌmb(ə)l/ v.intr. 1 (foll. by on) speak in a rambling incoherent way. 2 (often as **bumbling** adj.) move or act ineptly; blunder. 3 make a buzz or hum. □□ **bumbler** n. [BOOM¹ + -LE⁴: partly f. bumble = blunderer]

bumble-bee /ˈbʌmb(ə)l,biː/ n. any large loud humming bee of the genus Bombus. [as BUMBLE]

bumf /bʌmf/ n. (also **bumph**) Brit. colloq. 1 usu. derog. papers, documents. 2 lavatory paper. [abbr. of bum-fodder]

bummalo /ˈbʌmə,ləʊ/ n. (pl. same) a small fish, Harpodon nehereus, of S. Asian coasts, dried and used as food (see BOMBAY DUCK). [perh. f. Marathi bombīl(a)]

bummer /ˈbʌmə(r)/ n. US sl. 1 an idler; a loafer. 2 an unpleasant occurrence. [19th c.: perh. f. G Bummler]

bump /bʌmp/ n., v., & adv. —n. 1 a dull-sounding blow or collision. 2 a swelling or dent caused by this. 3 an uneven patch on a road, field, etc. 4 Phrenol. any of various prominences on the skull thought to indicate different mental faculties. 5 (in narrow-river races where boats make a spaced start one behind another) the point at which a boat begins to overtake (and usu. touches) the boat ahead, thereby defeating it. 6 Aeron. **a** a rising air current causing this. —v. 1 **a** tr. hit or come against with a bump. **b** intr. (of two objects) collide. 2 intr. (foll. by against, into) hit with a bump; collide with. 3 tr. (often foll. by against, on) hurt or damage by striking (bumped my head on the ceiling; bumped the car while parking). 4 intr. (usu. foll. by along) move or travel with much jolting (we bumped along the road). 5 tr. (in a boat-race) gain a bump against. 6 tr. US displace, esp. by seniority. —adv. with a bump; suddenly; violently. □ **bump into** colloq. meet by chance. **bump off** sl. murder. **bump up** colloq. increase (prices etc.). [16th c., imit.: perh. f. Scand.]

bumper /ˈbʌmpə(r)/ n. 1 a horizontal bar or strip fixed across the front or back of a motor vehicle to reduce damage in a collision or as a trim. 2 (usu. attrib.) an unusually large or fine example (a bumper crop). 3 Cricket a ball rising high after pitching. 4 a brim-full glass of wine etc. □ **bumper car** = DODGEM.

bumph var. of BUMF.

bumpkin /ˈbʌmpkɪn/ n. a rustic or socially inept person. [perh. Du. boomken little tree or MDu. bommekijn little barrel]

bumptious /ˈbʌmpʃəs/ adj. offensively self-assertive or conceited. □□ **bumptiously** adv. **bumptiousness** n. [BUMP, after FRACTIOUS]

bumpy /ˈbʌmpɪ/ adj. (**bumpier**, **bumpiest**) 1 having many bumps (a bumpy road). 2 affected by bumps (a bumpy ride). □□ **bumpily** adv. **bumpiness** n.

bun /bʌn/ n. 1 a small usu. sweetened bread roll or cake, often with dried fruit. 2 Sc. a rich fruit cake or currant bread. 3 hair worn in the shape of a bun. □ **bun fight** Brit. sl. a tea party. **have a bun in the oven** sl. be pregnant. **hot cross bun** a bun marked with a cross, traditionally eaten on Good Friday. [ME: orig. unkn.]

buna /ˈbjuːnə, ˈbuːnɑ/ n. a synthetic rubber made by polymerization of butadiene. [G (as BUTADIENE, natrium sodium)]

Bunbury /ˈbʌnbərɪ/ n. a seaport and resort to the south of Perth in Western Australia; pop. (est. 1987) 25,250.

bunch /bʌntʃ/ n. & v. —n. 1 a cluster of things growing or fastened together (bunch of grapes; bunch of keys). 2 a collection; a set or lot (best of the bunch). 3 colloq. a group; a gang. —v. 1 tr. make into a bunch or bunches; gather into close folds. 2 intr. form into a group or crowd. □ **bunch grass** a N. American grass that grows in clumps. **bunch of fives** sl. a fist. □□ **bunchy** adj. [ME: orig. unkn.]

bunco /ˈbʌŋkəʊ/ n. & v. US sl. —n. (pl. -**os**) a swindle, esp. by card-sharping or a confidence trick. —v.tr. (-**oes**, -**oed**) swindle, cheat. [perh. f. Sp. banca a card-game]

buncombe var. of BUNKUM.

Bundesbank /ˈbʊndəs,bɑːŋk/ the central bank of Germany, established in 1875. Its headquarters are in Frankfurt. [G f. Bund federation + BANK²]

Bundesrat /ˈbʊndəs,rɑːt/ n. the Upper House of Parliament in Germany or in Austria. [G f. Bund federation + Rat council]

Bundestag /ˈbʊndəs,tɑːg/ n. the Lower House of Parliament in Germany. [G f. Bund federation + tagen confer]

bundle /ˈbʌnd(ə)l/ n. & v. —n. 1 a collection of things tied or fastened together. 2 a set of nerve fibres etc. banded together. 3 sl. a large amount of money. —v. 1 tr. (usu. foll. by up) tie in or make into a bundle (bundled up my squash kit). 2 tr. (usu. foll.

by *into*) throw or push, esp. quickly or confusedly (*bundled the papers into the drawer*). **3** *tr.* (usu. foll. by *out, off, away*, etc.) send (esp. a person) away hurriedly or unceremoniously (*bundled them off the premises*). **4** *intr.* sleep clothed with another person, esp. a fiancé(e), as a local custom. □ **be a bundle of nerves** (or **prejudices** etc.) be extremely nervous (or prejudiced etc.). **bundle up** dress warmly or cumbersomely. **go a bundle on** *sl.* be very fond of. □□ **bundler** *n.* [ME, perh. f. OE *byndelle* a binding, but also f. LG, Du *bundel*]

bung[1] /bʌŋ/ *n. & v.* —*n.* a stopper for closing a hole in a container, esp. a cask. —*v.tr.* **1** stop with a bung. **2** *Brit. sl.* throw, toss. □ **bunged up** closed, blocked. **bung-hole** a hole for filling or emptying a cask etc. [MDu. *bonghe*]

bung[2] /bʌŋ/ *adj. Austral. & NZ sl.* dead; ruined, useless. □ **go bung 1** die. **2** fail; go bankrupt. [Aboriginal]

bungalow /ˈbʌŋgəˌləʊ/ *n.* a one-storeyed house. [Gujarati *bangalo* f. Hind. *baṅglā* belonging to Bengal]

bungle /ˈbʌŋg(ə)l/ *v. & n.* —*v.* **1** *tr.* blunder over, mismanage, or fail at (a task). **2** *intr.* work badly or clumsily. —*n.* a bungled attempt; bungled work. □□ **bungler** *n.* [imit.: cf. BUMBLE]

Bunin /ˈbuːniːn/, Ivan Alekseyevich (1870–1953), Russian poet and novelist, who attained great popularity in the early 20th c. His first book of poems was published in 1891, and he translated works by Tennyson, Byron, and Longfellow. An opponent of modernism, he made love and rural life the most prominent themes in his prose works, which include *The Village* (a novel, 1910), *The Gentleman from San Francisco* (short stories, 1916), and *The Well of Days* (autobiography, 1910). He opposed the October Revolution and left Russia in 1918, eventually reaching France and permanent exile. In 1933 he became the first Russian to be awarded the Nobel Prize for literature.

bunion /ˈbʌnjən/ *n.* a swelling on the foot, esp. at the first joint of the big toe. [OF *buignon* f. *buigne* bump on the head]

bunk[1] /bʌŋk/ *n.* a sleeping-berth, esp. a shelflike bed against a wall, e.g. in a ship. □ **bunk-bed** each of two or more beds one above the other, forming a unit. **bunk-house** a house where workmen etc. are lodged. [18th c.: orig. unkn.]

bunk[2] /bʌŋk/ *n.* □ **do a bunk** *Brit. sl.* leave or abscond hurriedly. [19th c.: orig. unkn.]

bunk[3] /bʌŋk/ *n. sl.* nonsense, humbug. [abbr. of BUNKUM]

bunker /ˈbʌŋkə(r)/ *n. & v.* —*n.* **1** a large container or compartment for storing fuel. **2** a reinforced underground shelter, esp. for use in wartime. **3** a hollow filled with sand, used as an obstacle in a golf-course. —*v.tr.* **1** fill the fuel bunkers of (a ship etc.). **2** (usu. in *passive*) **a** trap in a bunker (in sense 3). **b** bring into difficulties. [19th c.: orig. unkn.]

Bunker Hill the first pitched battle (1775) of the War of American Independence (actually fought on Breed's Hill near Boston, Massachusetts). Although the British were able to drive the American rebels from their positions, the good performance of the untrained American irregulars gave considerable impetus to the revolution.

bunkum /ˈbʌŋkəm/ *n.* (also **buncombe**) nonsense; humbug. [orig. *buncombe* f. *Buncombe* County in N. Carolina, mentioned in a nonsense speech by its Congressman, c.1820]

bunny /ˈbʌnɪ/ *n.* (*pl.* **-ies**) **1** a child's name for a rabbit. **2** *Austral. sl.* a victim or dupe. **3** (in full **bunny girl**) a club hostess, waitress, etc., wearing a skimpy costume with ears and a tail suggestive of a rabbit. [dial. *bun* rabbit]

Bunsen /ˈbʌns(ə)n/, Robert Wilhelm Eberhard (1811–99), German chemist, a pioneer of chemical spectroscopy and photochemistry. His first important research was on organo-arsenic compounds, and he lost the use of his right eye in an explosion. In the 1860s he collaborated with Gustav Kirchhoff to develop the field of spectroscopy, when it was discovered that each element produced light of a characteristic wavelength. They realized that spectral analysis could be used for detecting new elements and for determining the composition of terrestrial and celestial matter (the sun and stars), and discovered the element caesium in 1860 and rubidium in the following year. Bunsen enjoyed designing chemical apparatus, including the

Bunsen battery (1841), grease-spot photometer (1844), absorptiometer (1855), actinometer (with Sir Henry Roscoe, 1856), effusion apparatus (1857), filter pump (1868), ice calorimeter (1870), and the vapour calorimeter (1887). His best-known device, the Bunsen (gas) burner (see entry) was developed in 1855, after a design by Peter Desdega or Michael Faraday.

Bunsen burner /ˈbʌns(ə)n/ *n.* a small adjustable gas burner used in scientific work as a source of great heat. [R. W. BUNSEN]

bunt[1] /bʌnt/ *n.* the baggy centre of a fishing-net, sail, etc. [16th c.: orig. unkn.]

bunt[2] /bʌnt/ *n.* a disease of wheat caused by the fungus *Tilletia caries*. [18th c.: orig. unkn.]

bunt[3] /bʌnt/ *v. & n.* —*v.* **1** *tr. & intr.* push with the head or horns; butt. **2** *tr. US Baseball* stop (a ball) with the bat without swinging. —*n.* an act of bunting. [19th c.: cf. BUTT[1]]

buntal /ˈbʌnt(ə)l/ *n.* the straw from a talipot palm. [Tagalog]

Bunter /ˈbʌntə(r)/, Billy. A schoolboy, noted for fatness and gluttony, in stories by Frank Richards (pseudonym of Charles Hamilton, 1875–1961).

bunting[1] /ˈbʌntɪŋ/ *n.* any of numerous seed-eating birds of the family Emberizidae, related to the finches and sparrows. [ME: orig. unkn.]

bunting[2] /ˈbʌntɪŋ/ *n.* **1** flags and other decorations. **2** a loosely-woven fabric used for these. [18th c.: orig. unkn.]

buntline /ˈbʌntlaɪn/ *n.* a line for confining the bunt (see BUNT[1]) when furling a sail.

Buñuel /buːˈnwel/, Luis (1900–83), Spanish film director, of whom it is said that he distinguished the cinema as much as the cinema did its best to extinguish him. In jokes, fierce independence, and original ideas he strayed far from the chic and fashionable. His early work was banned, and he had to leave Spain and go into exile in Mexico. His fiercest scorn was directed at the great institutions of civilization—the State and the Church—particularly at the idea that they conferred distinction or protection or allowed licence for dictatorship. He was profoundly influenced by surrealism (all his films propose a 'reality' composed as much of dreams and illusions as of verifiable events), and his first film *Un Chien andalou* (1928) was written and directed jointly with Salvador Dali, with whom he parted company when Dali supported Franco. Outstanding among his later works were the powerful and disturbing *Nazarin* (1958) and *Viridiana* (1961), and *The Discreet Charm of the Bourgeoisie* (1972).

bunya /ˈbʌnjə/ *n.* (also **bunya bunya** /ˈbʌnjəˌbʌnjə/) *Austral.* a tall coniferous tree, *Araucaria bidwillii*, bearing large nutritious cones. [Aboriginal]

Bunyan /ˈbʌnjən/, John (1628–88), English writer, son of a brazier. He served with the Parliamentary army during the Civil War, an experience perhaps reflected in his allegory *The Holy War* (1682). After a period of religious torment, he joined, in 1653, the Nonconformist Church at Bedford where he preached and came into conflict with the Quakers. He was arrested in 1660 for preaching without a licence and spent most of the next 12 years in prison, where he wrote his spiritual autobiography *Grace Abounding* (1666) and began his major work *The Pilgrim's Progress* (1678–84), an allegory in the form of a dream by the author. The work is remarkable for the beauty and simplicity of its language, the reality of its impersonations, and its humour; it has been translated into more than 100 languages.

bunyip /ˈbʌnjɪp/ *n. Austral.* **1** a fabulous monster inhabiting swamps and lagoons. **2** an imposter. [Aboriginal]

Buonaparte /ˈbɔːnəˌpɑːt/ var. of BONAPARTE.

buoy /bɔɪ/ *n. & v.* —*n.* **1** an anchored float serving as a navigation mark or to show reefs etc. **2** a lifebuoy. —*v.tr.* **1** (usu. foll. by *up*) **a** keep afloat. **b** sustain the courage or spirits of (a person etc.); uplift, encourage. **2** (often foll. by *out*) mark with a buoy or buoys. [ME prob. f. MDu. *bo(e)ye*, ult. f. L *boia* collar f. Gk *boeiai* ox-hides]

buoyancy /ˈbɔɪənsɪ/ *n.* **1** the capacity to be or remain buoyant. **2** resilience; recuperative power. **3** cheerfulness.

buoyant /ˈbɔɪənt/ *adj.* **1 a** able or apt to keep afloat or rise to the top of a liquid or gas. **b** (of a liquid or gas) able to keep something afloat. **2** light-hearted. □□ **buoyantly** adv. [F buoyant or Sp. boyante part. of boyar float f. boya BUOY]

bur /bɜ:(r)/ n. (also **burr**) **1 a** a prickly clinging seed-case or flower-head. **b** any plant producing these. **2** a person hard to shake off. **3** = BURR n. 2. □ **bur oak** a N. American oak, Quercus macrocarpa with large fringed acorn-cups. [ME: cf. Da. burre bur, burdock, Sw. kard-borre burdock]

Burbage /ˈbɜ:bɪdʒ/, Richard (c.1567–1619), the first outstanding English actor, creator of most of Shakespeare's great tragic roles—Hamlet, Othello, Lear, and Richard III. He was also associated in the building of the Globe Theatre, scene of his greatest triumphs. His father James (c.1530–97) built the first permanent playhouse in London, The Theatre, in 1576.

Burbank /ˈbɜ:bæŋk/ a city in California, to the north of Los Angeles, pop. (1980) 84,600. It is a centre of the film and television industries.

burble /ˈbɜ:b(ə)l/ v. & n. —v.intr. **1** speak ramblingly; make a murmuring noise. **2** Aeron. (of an air-flow) break up into turbulence. —n. **1** a murmuring noise. **2** rambling speech. □□ **burbler** n. [19th c.: imit.]

burbot /ˈbɜ:bət/ n. an eel-like flat-headed bearded freshwater fish, Lota lota. [ME: cf. OF barbote]

burden /ˈbɜ:d(ə)n/ n. & v. —n. **1** a load, esp. a heavy one. **2** an oppressive duty, obligation, expense, emotion, etc. **3** the bearing of loads (beast of burden). **4** (also archaic **burthen** /ˈbɜ:ð(ə)n/) a ship's carrying-capacity, tonnage. **5 a** the refrain or chorus of a song. **b** the chief theme or gist of a speech, book, poem, etc. —v.tr. load with a burden; encumber, oppress. □ **burden of proof** the obligation to prove one's case. □□ **burdensome** adj. [OE byrthen: rel. to BIRTH]

burdock /ˈbɜ:dɒk/ n. any plant of the genus Arctium, with prickly flowers and docklike leaves. [BUR + DOCK³]

bureau /ˈbjʊərəʊ, -ˈrəʊ/ n. (pl. **bureaux** or **bureaus** /-rəʊz/) **1 a** Brit. a writing-desk with drawers and usu. an angled top opening downwards to form a writing surface. **b** US a chest of drawers. **2 a** an office or department for transacting specific business. **b** a government department. [F, = desk, orig. its baize covering, f. OF burel f. bure, buire dark brown ult. f. Gk purros red]

bureaucracy /bjʊəˈrɒkrəsɪ/ n. (pl. **-ies**) **1 a** government by central administration. **b** a State or organization so governed. **2** the officials of such a government, esp. regarded as oppressive and inflexible. **3** conduct typical of such officials. [F bureaucratie: see BUREAU]

bureaucrat /ˈbjʊərəˌkræt, -rəʊˌkræt/ n. **1** an official in a bureaucracy. **2** an inflexible or insensitive administrator. □□ **bureaucratic** /-ˈkrætɪk/ adj. **bureaucratically** /-ˈkrætɪkəlɪ/ adv. [F bureaucrate (as BUREAUCRACY)]

bureaucratize /bjʊəˈrɒkrəˌtaɪz/ v.tr. (also **-ise**) govern by or transform into a bureaucratic system. □□ **bureaucratization** /-ˈzeɪʃ(ə)n/ n.

burette /bjʊəˈret/ n. (US **buret**) a graduated glass tube with an end-tap for measuring small volumes of liquid in chemical analysis. [F]

burg /bɜ:g/ n. US colloq. a town or city. [see BOROUGH]

burgage /ˈbɜ:gɪdʒ/ n. hist. (in England and Scotland) tenure of land in a town on a yearly rent. [ME f. med.L burgagium f. burgus BOROUGH]

Burgas /bʊəˈgæs/ an industrial port and health resort in Bulgaria, on the coast of the Black Sea; pop. (1987) 197,550.

burgee /bɜ:ˈdʒi:/ n. a triangular or swallow-tailed flag bearing the colours or emblem of a sailing-club. [18th c.: perh. = (ship-)owner, ult. F bourgeois: see BURGESS]

Burgenland /ˈbʊərgənˌlænt/ an agricultural province of eastern Austria; pop. (1981) 272,300; capital, Eisenstadt.

burgeon /ˈbɜ:dʒ(ə)n/ v. & n. literary —v.intr. **1** begin to grow rapidly; flourish. **2** put forth young shoots; bud. —n. a bud or young shoot. [ME f. OF bor-, burjon ult. f. LL burra wool]

burger /ˈbɜ:gə(r)/ n. **1** colloq. a hamburger. **2** (in comb.) a certain kind of hamburger or variation of it (beefburger; nutburger). [abbr.]

Burgess¹ /ˈbɜ:dʒɪs/, Anthony John Burgess Wilson (1917–),

English novelist and critic whose varied career has included a period as an education officer in Malaya and Borneo (1954–60) which inspired his first three novels, set in the Far East (Time for a Tiger, 1956; The Enemy in the Blanket, 1958; and Beds in the East, 1959). A Clockwork Orange (1962), an alarming vision of violence, high technology, and authoritarianism, appeared in a film version by Stanley Kubrick in 1971. His many other works include his comic trilogy which traces the literary, amorous, and digestive triumphs and misfortunes of the fitfully-inspired poet Enderby, the ambitious novel Earthly Powers (1980) in which real and fictitious characters mingle to produce an international panorama of the 20th c., critical works (notably on Joyce), screenplays, and a biography of Shakespeare.

Burgess² /ˈbɜ:dʒɪs/, Guy Francis de Moncy (1911–63), British Foreign Office official and Soviet spy, who fled to the USSR with Donald Maclean (see entry) in 1951.

burgess /ˈbɜ:dʒɪs/ n. **1** Brit. an inhabitant of a town or borough, esp. of one with full municipal rights. **2** Brit. hist. a Member of Parliament for a borough, corporate town, or university. **3** US a borough magistrate or governor. [ME f. OF burgeis ult. f. LL burgus BOROUGH]

burgh /ˈbʌrə/ n. hist. a Scottish borough or chartered town. ¶ This status was abolished in 1975. □□ **burghal** /ˈbɜ:g(ə)l/ adj. [Sc. form of BOROUGH]

burgher /ˈbɜ:gə(r)/ n. **1** a citizen or freeman, esp. of a Continental town. **2** S.Afr. hist. a citizen of a Boer republic. **3** a descendant of a Dutch or Portuguese colonist in Sri Lanka. [G Burger or Du. burger f. Burg, burg BOROUGH]

Burghley /ˈbɜ:lɪ/, William Cecil, 1st Baron (1521–98), English statesman and Lord Treasurer, and Queen Elizabeth I's most trusted councillor and minister.

burglar /ˈbɜ:glə(r)/ n. a person who commits burglary. □□ **burglarious** /-ˈgleərɪəs/ adj. [legal AF burgler, rel. to OF burgier pillage]

burglarize /ˈbɜ:gləˌraɪz/ v.tr. & intr. (also **-ise**) US = BURGLE.

burglary /ˈbɜ:glərɪ/ n. (pl. **-ies**) **1** entry into a building illegally with intent to commit theft, do bodily harm, or do damage. **2** an instance of this. ¶ Before 1968 in English law a crime under statute and in common law; after 1968 a statutory crime only (cf. HOUSEBREAKING). [legal AF burglarie: see BURGLAR]

burgle /ˈbɜ:g(ə)l/ v. **1** tr. commit burglary on (a building or person). **2** intr. commit burglary. [back-form. f BURGLAR]

burgomaster /ˈbɜ:gəˌmɑːstə(r)/ n. the mayor of a Dutch or Flemish town. [Du. burgemeester f. burg BOROUGH: assim. to MASTER]

Burgoyne /ˈbɜ:gɔɪn/, John (1722–92), English general and playwright, known as 'Gentleman Johnny', who capitulated to the Americans at Saratoga (1777) in the War of American Independence.

burgrave /ˈbɜ:greɪv/ n. hist. the ruler of a town or castle. [G Burggraf f. Burg BOROUGH + Graf COUNT²]

Burgundy /ˈbɜ:gəndɪ/ (French **Bourgogne** /bʊəˈgɒnj/) a former kingdom, now a region of east central France; pop. (1982) 1,596,000; capital, Dijon.

burgundy /ˈbɜ:gəndɪ/ n. (pl. **-ies**) **1 a** the wine (usu. red) of Burgundy in E. France. **b** a similar wine from another place. **2** the red colour of Burgundy wine.

burhel var. of BHARAL.

burial /ˈberɪəl/ n. **1 a** the burying of a dead body. **b** a funeral. **2** Archaeol. a grave or its remains. □ **burial-ground** a cemetery. [ME, erron. formed as sing. of OE byrgels f. Gmc: rel. to BURY]

burin /ˈbjʊərɪn/ n. **1** a steel tool for engraving on copper or wood. **2** Archaeol. a flint tool with a chisel point. [F]

burk var. of BERK.

burka /ˈbɜ:kə/ n. a long enveloping garment worn in public by Muslim women. [Hind. f. Arab. burka']

Burke¹ /bɜ:k/, Edmund (1729–97), British man of letters and politician. The son of Dublin lawyer, Burke produced a large corpus of political writings, much of it dealing with the issue of political emancipation in Britain and her colonies. His speeches were magnificently eloquent but lengthy and not well delivered;

his contemporaries called him the 'the dinner-gong'. In the last years of his life he devoted himself to attacking the radical excesses of the French Revolution, opposing the idea of peace with a regime that he saw as pernicious.

Burke[2] /bɜːk/, John (1787–1848), Irish-born genealogical and heraldic writer, first compiler of a 'Peerage and Baronetage' (1826), issued periodically since 1847.

Burke[3] /bɜːk/, Robert O'Hara (1820–61), Irish explorer and adventurer. After service in the Austrian army and the Irish constabulary, Burke emigrated to Australia in 1853 and became Inspector of Police in Victoria. In 1860–1 he successfully crossed Australia from south to north in the company of W. J. Wills (the first White men to do so). On the return journey, however, both he and his companion died of starvation.

Burke[4] /bɜːk/, William (1792–1829), Irish navvy, living in Edinburgh, who was hanged for having dug up corpses from cemeteries and smothered at least 15 persons in order to sell the bodies for dissection (see BODY-SNATCHER). William Hare, his landlord and fellow Irishman, was his accomplice.

Burkina /bɜːˈkiːnə/ an inland country of western Africa, bounded on its south by the Ivory Coast, Ghana, and Togo; pop. (est. 1988) 8,485,700; official language, French; capital, Ouagadougou. The country was a French protectorate from 1898, originally attached to Soudan (now Mali) and later partitioned between the Ivory Coast, Soudan, and Niger. In 1958 it became an autonomous republic within the French Community and a fully independent republic in 1960. □□ **Burkinan** *adj.* & *n.*

Burkitt's lymphoma /ˈbɜːkɪts/ *n. Med.* a malignant tumour of the lymphatic system, esp. affecting children of Central Africa. [D. P. *Burkitt*, Brit. surgeon b. 1911]

burl /bɜːl/ *n.* **1** a knot or lump in wool or cloth. **2** *US* a flattened knotty growth on a tree. [ME f. OF *bourle* tuft of wool, dimin. of *bourre* coarse wool f. LL *burra* wool]

burlap /ˈbɜːlæp/ *n.* **1** coarse canvas esp. of jute used for sacking etc. **2** a similar lighter material for use in dressmaking or furnishing. [17th c.: orig. unkn.]

burlesque /bɜːˈlesk/ *n., adj.,* & *v.* —*n.* **1 a** comic imitation, esp. in parody of a dramatic or literary work. **b** a performance or work of this kind. **c** bombast, mock-seriousness. **2** *US* a variety show, often including striptease. —*adj.* of or in the nature of burlesque. —*v.tr.* (**burlesques, burlesqued, burlesquing**) make or give a burlesque of. □□ **burlesquer** *n.* [F f. It. *burlesco* f. *burla* mockery]

burly /ˈbɜːlɪ/ *adj.* (**burlier, burliest**) of stout sturdy build; big and strong. □□ **burliness** *n.* [ME *borli* prob. f. an OE form = 'fit for the bower' (BOWER[1])]

Burma /ˈbɜːmə/ a country in SE Asia on the Bay of Bengal, centred on the Irrawaddy River; pop. (est. 1988) 39,632,200; official language, Burmese; capital, Yangon (formerly called Rangoon). Rice has traditionally been the mainstay of the country's economy, and teak is a valuable export. Burma is rich in minerals, including lead and zinc; petroleum products are the most important. An independent empire under the Pagan dynasty in the 11th–13th c., Burma fell to the Mongols and was generally split into small rival States until unified once again in 1757. As a result of the Burmese Wars of 1823–86 Burma was gradually annexed by the British, remaining under British administration until the Second World War. Occupied by the Japanese in 1942, the country became an independent republic in 1948, taking the formal name of the Union of Burma, changed in 1989 to Union of Myanmar. Since that time it has suffered periodic political disturbances, partially as a result of the general instability of SE Asia and partially as a result of religious and political differences within Burma itself. In 1962 an army coup led by Ne Win (see entry) overthrew the government and established an authoritarian State, continuing to maintain a policy of neutrality and limited foreign contact. A new constitution was adopted in 1974. In the late 1980s the pro-democracy movement gathered momentum and won the election held in May 1990.

Burman /ˈbɜːmən/ *adj.* & *n.* (*pl.* **Burmans**) = BURMESE.

Burmese /bɜːˈmiːz/ *n.* & *adj.* —*n.* (*pl.* same) **1 a** a native or national of Burma (now Myanmar) in SE Asia. **b** a person of

Burmese descent. **2** a member of the largest ethnic group of Burma. **3** the official language of Burma, spoken by three-quarters of its population (some 30 million people), a tonal language belonging to a branch of the Sino-Tibetan language group. It has a distinctive alphabet consisting almost entirely of circles or parts of circles in various combinations, which arose as a consequence of writing on palm leaves where straight lines were impossible. —*adj.* of or relating to Burma or its people or language.

burn[1] /bɜːn/ *v.* & *n.* —*v.* (*past* and *past part.* **burnt** or **burned**) **1** *tr.* & *intr.* be or cause to be consumed or destroyed by fire. **2** *intr.* **a** blaze or glow with fire. **b** be in the state characteristic of fire. **3** *tr.* & *intr.* be or cause to be injured or damaged by fire or great heat or by radiation. **4** *tr.* & *intr.* use or be used as a source of heat, light, or other energy. **5** *tr.* & *intr.* char or scorch in cooking (*burned the vegetables; the vegetables are burning*). **6** *tr.* produce (a hole, a mark, etc.) by fire or heat. **7** *tr.* **a** subject (clay, chalk, etc.) to heat for a purpose. **b** harden (bricks) by fire. **c** make (lime or charcoal) by heat. **8** *tr.* colour, tan, or parch with heat or light (*we were burnt brown by the sun*). **9** *tr.* & *intr.* put or be put to death by fire. **10** *tr.* **a** cauterize, brand. **b** (foll. by *in*) imprint by burning. **11** *tr.* & *intr.* make or be hot, give or feel a sensation or pain of or like heat. **12** *tr.* & *intr.* (often foll. by *with*) make or be passionate; feel or cause to feel great emotion (*burn with shame*). **13** *intr. sl.* drive fast. **14** *tr. US sl.* anger, infuriate. **15** *intr.* (foll. by *into*) (of acid etc.) gradually penetrate (into) causing disintegration. —*n.* **1** a mark or injury caused by burning. **2** the ignition of a rocket engine in flight, giving extra thrust. **3** *US, Austral.,* & *NZ* a forest area cleared by burning. **4** *sl.* a cigarette. **5** *sl.* a car race. □ **burn one's boats** (or **bridges**) commit oneself irrevocably. **burn the candle at both ends** exhaust one's strength or resources by undertaking too much. **burn down 1 a** destroy (a building) by burning. **b** (of a building) be destroyed by fire. **2** burn less vigorously as fuel fails. **burn one's fingers** suffer for meddling or rashness. **burn a hole in one's pocket** (of money) be quickly spent. **burning-glass** a lens for concentrating the sun's rays on an object to burn it. **burn low** (of fire) be nearly out. **burn the midnight oil** read or work late into the night. **burn out 1** be reduced to nothing by burning. **2** fail or cause to fail by burning. **3** (usu. *refl.*) esp. *US* suffer physical or emotional exhaustion. **4** consume the contents of by burning. **5** make (a person) homeless by burning his or her house. **burn-out** *n.* **1** physical or emotional exhaustion, esp. caused by stress. **2** depression, disillusionment. **burnt ochre** (or **sienna** or **umber**) a pigment darkened by burning. **burnt offering 1** an offering burnt on an altar as a sacrifice. **2** *joc.* overcooked food. **burnt-out** physically or emotionally exhausted. **burn up 1** get rid of by fire. **2** begin to blaze. **3** *US sl.* be or make furious. **have money to burn** have more money than one needs. [OE *birnan, bærnan* f. Gmc]

burn[2] /bɜːn/ *n. Sc.* a small stream. [OE *burna* etc. f. Gmc]

Burne-Jones /bɜːnˈdʒəʊnz/, Sir Edward Coley (1833–98), English painter of medieval and literary themes, friend of William Morris and Dante Gabriel Rossetti. He created an escapist dreamlike world in his paintings, which are much influenced by 15th-c. Italian artists, especially Botticelli; he also made many designs for tapestry and stained glass.

burner /ˈbɜːnə(r)/ *n.* the part of a gas cooker, lamp, etc. that emits and shapes the flame. □ **on the back** (or **front**) **burner** *colloq.* receiving little (or much) attention.

burnet /ˈbɜːnɪt/ *n.* **1** any rosaceous plant of the genus *Sanguisorba*, with pink or red flowers. **2** any of several diurnal moths of the family Zygaenidae, with crimson spots on greenish-black wings. [obs. *burnet* (adj.) dark brown f. OF *burnete*]

Burnett /bəˈnet/, Francis (Eliza) Hodgson (1849–1924), English author of novels and other works, remembered chiefly for her novels for children, including *Little Lord Fauntleroy* (1886) and *The Secret Garden* (1911).

Burney /ˈbɜːnɪ/, Francis ('Fanny') (1752–1840), English novelist who won fame and the praise of Samuel Johnson with her first novel *Evelina* (1778). She served Queen Charlotte at court (1786–91) and in 1793 married General d'Arblay with whom she was interned in France by Napoleon. Her diaries and letters provide

w *we*   z *zoo*   ʃ *she*   ʒ *decision*   θ *thin*   ð *this*   ŋ *ring*   x *loch*   tʃ *chip*   dʒ *jar*   (*see over for vowels*)

a vivid record of her time and the distinguished circles in which she moved.

burning /'bɜːnɪŋ/ *adj.* **1** ardent, intense (*burning desire*). **2** hotly discussed, exciting (*burning question*). **3** flagrant (*burning shame*). □ **burning bush 1** any of various shrubs with red fruits or red autumn leaves (with ref. to Exod. 3: 2). **2** fraxinella. □□ **burningly** *adv.*

burnish /'bɜːnɪʃ/ *v.tr.* polish by rubbing. □□ **burnisher** *n.* [ME f. OF *burnir* = *brunir* f. *brun* BROWN]

burnous /bɜːˈnuːs/ *n.* an Arab or Moorish hooded cloak. [F f. Arab. *burnus* f. Gk *birros* cloak]

Burns /bɜːnz/, Robert (1759–96), Scottish poet, son of a poor farmer in Ayrshire. He early developed an inclination for literature and also a tendency to dissipation. His *Poems, chiefly in the Scottish Dialect* (1786) was an immediate success and he was lionized by Edinburgh society. His best poems include his satires, 'Holy Willie's Prayer' (1785), 'The Twa Dogs' (1786), and 'The Jolly Beggars' (1786), and the broad humour of his narrative poem 'Tam o' Shanter' (1791); his songs, many of which were published in *The Scots Musical Museum* (1787–1803), have always been popular—'Auld Lang Syne', 'Ye Banks and Braes', and 'Scots wha hae'—as are his sentimental lyrics and rhetorical poems. His attractive appearance and gregarious temperament led him into many amorous entanglements. After returning unsuccessfully to farming he became an excise officer (1791) in Dumfries. Burns wrote, with equal facility in English and Scots, vividly and passionately on themes of country life, love, and animals, and with a deep sympathy for the oppressed. He was above all a patriot and his popularity with his fellow-countrymen is celebrated annually on his birthday on 25 Jan., with feasting and drinking.

burnt see BURN[1].

burp /bɜːp/ *v. & n. colloq.* —*v.* **1** *intr.* belch. **2** *tr.* make (a baby) belch, usu. by patting its back. —*n.* a belch. □ **burp gun** *US sl.* an automatic pistol. [imit.]

burr /bɜː(r)/ *n. & v.* —*n.* **1 a** a whirring sound. **b** a rough sounding of the letter *r*. **2** (also **bur**) **a** a rough edge left on cut or punched metal or paper. **b** a surgeon's or dentist's small drill. **3 a** a siliceous rock used for millstones. **b** a whetstone. **4** = BUR 1, 2. **5** the coronet of a deer's antler. —*v.* **1** *tr.* pronounce with a burr. **2** *intr.* speak indistinctly. **3** *intr.* make a whirring sound. [var. of BUR]

Burra /'bʌrə/, Edward (1905–76), English painter, draughtsman, and stage designer. An eccentric figure, he was fascinated by low-life and seedy subjects, which he experienced in places such as the streets of Harlem in New York and the dockside cafés of Marseilles, and which he depicted with warmth and humour. Usually he worked in water-colour, but on a large scale and using layers of pigment. In the mid-1930s he became fascinated with the bizarre and fantastic (*Dancing Skeletons*, 1934); later he painted occasional religious pictures, and in the 1950s and 1960s turned to landscape.

burrawang /'bʌrəˌwæŋ/ *n. Austral.* **1** any palmlike tree of the genus *Macrozamia*. **2** the nut produced by this tree. [Mount *Budawang* in New South Wales]

burrito /bəˈriːtəʊ/ *n.* (*pl.* **-os**) *US* a tortilla rolled round a savoury filling. [Amer. Sp., dimin. of *burro* BURRO]

burro /'bʌrəʊ/ *n.* (*pl.* **-os**) *US* a small donkey used as a pack-animal. [Sp.]

Burroughs[1] /'bʌrəz/, Edgar Rice (1875–1950), American novelist and writer of science fiction, remembered principally for his adventure stories about Tarzan (see entry).

Burroughs[2] /ˌbʌrəz/, William Seward (1914–), American novelist, best known for his frank accounts of life as a drug addict (*Junkie*, 1953; *The Naked Lunch*, 1959) and for his obsession with the underworld and homosexual fantasy (*Nova Express*, 1964; *The Wild Boys*, 1971).

burrow /'bʌrəʊ/ *n. & v.* —*n.* a hole or tunnel dug by a small animal, esp. a rabbit, as a dwelling. —*v.* **1** *intr.* make or live in a burrow. **2** *tr.* make (a hole etc.) by digging. **3** *intr.* hide oneself. **4** *intr.* (foll. by *into*) investigate, search. □□ **burrower** *n.* [ME, app. var. of BOROUGH]

Bursa /'bɜːsə/ a city in NW Turkey; pop. (1985) 614,100. Originally named Prusa, after its capture by the Turks in 1326 it was called Brusa or Bursa, and became the capital of the Ottoman Empire until 1413.

bursa /'bɜːsə/ *n.* (*pl.* **bursae** /-siː/ or **bursas**) *Anat.* a fluid-filled sac or saclike cavity to lessen friction. □□ **bursal** *adj.* [med.L = bag: cf. PURSE]

bursar /'bɜːsə(r)/ *n.* **1** a treasurer, esp. the person in charge of the funds and other property of a college. **2** the holder of a bursary. □□ **bursarship** *n.* [F *boursier* or (in sense 1) med.L *bursarius* f. *bursa* bag]

bursary /'bɜːsərɪ/ *n.* (*pl.* **-ies**) **1** a grant, esp. a scholarship. **2** the post or room of a bursar. □□ **bursarial** /-ˈseərɪəl/ *adj.* [med.L *bursaria* (as BURSAR)]

bursitis /bɜːˈsaɪtɪs/ *n.* inflammation of a bursa.

burst /bɜːst/ *v. & n.* —*v.* (*past* and *past part.* **burst**) **1 a** *intr.* break suddenly and violently apart by expansion of contents or internal pressure. **b** *tr.* cause to do this. **c** *tr.* send (a container etc.) violently apart. **2 a** *tr.* open forcibly. **b** *intr.* come open or be opened forcibly. **3 a** *intr.* (usu. foll. by *in, out*) make one's way suddenly, dramatically, or by force. **b** *tr.* break away from or through (*the river burst its banks*). **4** *tr. & intr.* fill or be full to overflowing. **5** *intr.* appear or come suddenly (*burst into flame*; *burst upon the view*; *sun burst out*). **6** *intr.* (foll. by *into*) suddenly begin to shed or utter (esp. *burst into tears* or *laughter* or *song*). **7** *intr.* be as if about to burst because of effort, excitement, etc. **8** *tr.* suffer bursting of (*burst a blood-vessel*). **9** *tr.* separate (continuous stationery) into single sheets. —*n.* **1** the act of or an instance of bursting; a split. **2** a sudden issuing forth (*burst of flame*). **3** a sudden outbreak (*burst of applause*). **4 a** a short sudden effort; a spurt. **b** a gallop. **5** an explosion. □ **burst out 1** suddenly begin (*burst out laughing*). **2** exclaim. [OE *berstan* f. Gmc]

burstproof /'bɜːstpruːf/ *adj.* (of a door lock) able to withstand a violent impact.

burthen *archaic* var. of BURDEN *n.* 4.

Burton[1] /'bɜːt(ə)n/, Richard (real name Richard Jenkins, 1925–84) Welsh actor, who played a number of Shakespearian roles and performed in the radio adaptation of Dylan Thomas's *Under Milk Wood* (1954) before becoming well known in films, including *The Robe* (1953), *The Spy Who Came in from the Cold* (1966), and *Anne of the Thousand Days* (1969). He often co-starred with Elizabeth Taylor (to whom he was twice married), most notably in *Cleopatra* (1962).

Burton[2] /'bɜːt(ə)n/, Sir Richard Francis (1821–90), explorer, anthropologist, and translator, one of the most flamboyant characters of his day. He joined the Indian Army in 1842 and subsequent travels took him to the forbidden City of Mecca, to expeditions in Africa (where, with Speke, he discovered Lake Tanganyika), to the Crimea, to Salt Lake City, and as consul to Brazil, Damascus, and Trieste. He published over 40 volumes of travel, several of folklore, and two of poetry and translations. He is best remembered for his unexpurgated version of the *Arabian Nights* (1885–8), *The Kama Sutra* (1883), *The Perfumed Garden* (1886), and other works of Arabian erotica. His interest in sexual behaviour and deviance and his detailed ethnographical notes led him to risk prosecution many times under the Obscene Publications Act of 1857.

burton[1] /'bɜːt(ə)n/ *n.* □ **go for a burton** *Brit. sl.* be lost or destroyed or killed. [20th c.: perh. *Burton* ale f. *Burton-on-Trent* in England]

burton[2] /'bɜːt(ə)n/ *n.* a light two-block tackle for hoisting. [ME *Breton tackles*: see BRETON]

Burundi /bʊˈrʌndɪ/ a country on the east side of Lake Tanganyika; pop. (est. 1988) 5,155,700; official languages, French and Kirundi; capital, Bujumbura. The area formed part of German East Africa before the First World War, after which it was administered by Belgium. It became an independent monarchy in 1962, and a republic in 1966. □□ **Burundian** *adj. & n.*

bury /'berɪ/ *v.tr.* (**-ies**, **-ied**) **1** place (a dead body) in the earth, in a tomb, or in the sea. **2** lose by death (*has buried three husbands*). **3 a** put under ground (*bury alive*). **b** hide (treasure, a bone, etc.) in the earth. **c** cover up; submerge. **4 a** put out of sight (*buried* *his face in his hands).* **b** consign to obscurity (*the idea was buried after brief discussion).* **c** put away; forget. **5** involve deeply (*buried himself in his work; was buried in a book).* □ **bury the hatchet** cease to quarrel. **burying-beetle** a sexton beetle. **burying-ground** (or **-place**) a cemetery. [OE *byrgan* f. WG: cf. BURIAL]

bus /bʌs/ *n. & v. —n. (pl.* **buses** or *US* **busses**) **1** a long-bodied passenger vehicle, esp. one serving the public on a fixed route. (See below.) **2** *colloq.* a motor car, aeroplane, etc. **3** *Computing* a defined set of conductors carrying data and control signals within a computer. *—v.* (**buses** or **busses, bussed, bussing**) **1** *intr.* go by bus. **2** *tr. US* transport by bus, esp. to promote racial integration. □ **bus lane** a part of a road's length marked off mainly for use by buses. **bus shelter** a shelter from rain etc. beside a bus stop. **bus station** a centre, esp. in a town, where (esp. long-distance) buses depart and arrive. **bus-stop 1** a regular stopping-place of a bus. **2** a sign marking this. [abbr. of OMNIBUS]

The bus originated in Paris in 1827. It was originally a horse-drawn vehicle, known as an omnibus (= 'a vehicle for all'), with the entrance at the rear. Later versions were motor-driven, first by petrol engines and then from c.1930 onwards by diesel engines. From early days passengers were carried on the roof as well as inside the vehicle, and from this practice there developed the form of the double-decker bus with upper and lower sections.

busbar /ˈbʌsbɑː(r)/ *n. Electr.* a system of conductors in a generating or receiving station on which power is concentrated for distribution.

busby /ˈbʌzbɪ/ *n. (pl.* **-ies**) (not in official use) a tall fur hat worn by hussars etc. [18th c.: orig. unkn.]

Bush /bʊʃ/, George Herbert Walter (1924–), 41st President of the US, from 1989.

bush[1] /bʊʃ/ *n.* **1** a shrub or clump of shrubs with stems of moderate length. **2** a thing resembling this, esp. a clump of hair or fur. **3** (esp. in Australia and Africa) a wild uncultivated district; woodland or forest. **4** *hist.* a bunch of ivy as a vintner's sign. □ **bush-baby** (*pl.* **-ies**) a small African tree-climbing lemur; a galago. **bush basil** a culinary herb, *Ocimum minimum.* **bush jacket** a light cotton jacket with a belt. **bush lawyer 1** *Austral. & NZ* a person claiming legal knowledge without qualifications for it. **2** *NZ* a bramble. **bush-ranger** *hist.* an Australian outlaw living in the bush. **bush sickness** a disease of animals due to a lack of cobalt in the soil. **bush telegraph** rapid spreading of information, a rumour, etc. **go bush** *Austral.* leave one's usual surroundings; run wild. [ME f. OE & ON, ult. f. Gmc]

bush[2] /bʊʃ/ *n. & v. —n.* **1** a metal lining for a round hole enclosing a revolving shaft etc. **2** a sleeve providing electrical insulation. *—v.tr.* provide with a bush. [MDu. *busse* BOX[1]]

bushbuck /ˈbʊʃbʌk/ *n.* a small antelope, *Tragelaphus scriptus,* of southern Africa, having a chestnut coat with white stripes. [BUSH[1] + BUCK[1], after Du. *boschbok* f. *bosch* bush]

bushed /bʊʃt/ *adj. colloq.* **1** *Austral. & NZ* a lost in the bush. **b** bewildered. **2** *US* tired out.

bushel /ˈbʊʃ(ə)l/ *n.* a measure of capacity for corn, fruit, liquids, etc. (*Brit.* 8 gallons, or 36.4 litres; *US* 64 US pints). The bushel formerly had a great variety of other values, varying not only from place to place but in the same place according to the commodity in question. Frequently it was a weight (not a measure) of so many pounds. □□ **bushelful** *n. (pl.* **-fuls**). [ME f. OF *buissiel* etc., perh. of Gaulish orig.]

bushfire /ˈbʊʃˌfaɪə(r)/ *n.* a fire in a forest or in scrub often spreading widely.

bushido /buːˈʃiːdəʊ/ *n.* the code of honour and morals evolved by the Japanese samurai. [Jap., = military knight's way]

bushing /ˈbʊʃɪŋ/ *n.* = BUSH[2] *n.*

bushman /ˈbʊʃmən/ *n. (pl.* **-men**) **1** a person who lives or travels in the Australian bush. **2** (**Bushman**) **a** a member of an aboriginal people in S. Africa. **b** the language of this people. [BUSH[1] + MAN: sense 2 after Du. *boschjesman* f. *bosch* bush]

bushmaster /ˈbʊʃˌmɑːstə(r)/ *n.* a venomous viper, *Lachesis muta,* of Central and S. America. [perh. f. Du. *boschmeester*]

bushveld /ˈbʊʃfelt/ *n.* open country consisting largely of bush. [BUSH[1] + VELD, after Afrik. *bosveld*]

bushwhack /ˈbʊʃwæk/ *v.* **1** *intr. US, Austral., & NZ* **a** clear woods and bush country. **b** live or travel in bush country. **2** *tr. US* ambush.

bushwhacker /ˈbʊʃˌwækə(r)/ *n.* **1** *US, Austral., & NZ* **a** a person who clears woods and bush country. **b** a person who lives or travels in bush country. **2** *US* a guerrilla fighter (orig. in the American Civil war).

bushy[1] /ˈbʊʃɪ/ *adj.* (**bushier, bushiest**) **1** growing thickly like a bush. **2** having many bushes. **3** covered with bush. □□ **bushily** *adv.* **bushiness** *n.*

bushy[2] /ˈbʊʃɪ/ *n. (pl.* **-ies**) *Austral. & NZ colloq.* a person who lives in the bush (as distinct from in a town).

busily /ˈbɪzɪlɪ/ *adv.* in a busy manner.

business /ˈbɪznɪs/ *n.* **1** one's regular occupation, profession, or trade. **2** a thing that is one's concern. **3 a** a task or duty. **b** a reason for coming (*what is your business?*). **4** serious work or activity (*get down to business*). **5** *derog.* **a** an affair, a matter (*sick of the whole business*). **b** a structure (*a lath-and-plaster business*). **6** a thing or series of things needing to be dealt with (*the business of the day*). **7** buying and selling; trade (*good stroke of business*). **8** a commercial house or firm. **9** *Theatr.* action on stage. **10** a difficult matter (*what a business it is!; made a great business of it*). □ **business card** a card printed with one's name and professional details. **the business end** *colloq.* the functional part of a tool or device. **business park** an area designed to accommodate businesses and light industry. **business person** a businessman or businesswoman. **business studies** training in economics, management, etc. **has no business to** has no right to. **in business 1** trading or dealing. **2** able to begin operations. **in the business of 1** engaged in. **2** intending to (*we are not in the business of surrendering*). **like nobody's business** *colloq.* extraordinarily. **make it one's business** to undertake to. **mind one's own business** not meddle. **on business** with a definite purpose, esp. one relating to one's regular occupation. **send a person about his** or **her business** dismiss a person; send a person away. [OE *bisignis* (as BUSY, -NESS)]

businesslike /ˈbɪznɪsˌlaɪk/ *adj.* efficient, systematic, practical.

businessman /ˈbɪznɪsmən/ *n. (pl.* **-men**; *fem.* **businesswoman**, *pl.* **-women**) a man or woman engaged in trade or commerce, esp. at a senior level (see also *business person*).

busk /bʌsk/ *v.intr.* perform (esp. music) for voluntary donations, usu. in the street or in subways. □□ **busker** *n.* **busking** *n.* [*busk* peddle etc. (perh. f. obs. F *busquer* seek)]

buskin /ˈbʌskɪn/ *n.* **1** either of a pair of thick-soled laced boots worn by an ancient Athenian tragic actor to gain height. **2** (usu. prec. by *the*) tragic drama; its style or spirit. **3** *hist.* either of a pair of calf- or knee-high boots of cloth or leather worn in the Middle Ages. □□ **buskined** *adj.* [prob. f. OF *bouzequin,* var. of *bro(u)sequin,* of unkn. orig.]

busman /ˈbʌsmən/ *n. (pl.* **-men**) the driver of a bus. □ **busman's holiday** leisure time spent in an activity similar to one's regular work.

Busoni /buːˈsəʊnɪ/, Ferruccio Benvenuto (1866–1924), Italian composer and conductor, a brilliant pianist (his best-known works are for that instrument), who from 1894 made his home in Berlin. His music found mixed favour in his lifetime but has become increasingly admired for its visionary nature. Deriving from the impressionistic late works of Liszt, it ventured into harmonic and rhythmic territory that became the preserve of Webern, Bartók, and Messiaen.

Buss /bʌs/, Frances Mary (1827–94), English educationist, who with her friend Dorothea Beale campaigned for higher education for women.

buss /bʌs/ *n. & v. archaic or US colloq. —n.* a kiss. *—v.tr.* kiss. [earlier *bass* (n. & v.): cf. F *baiser* f. L *basiare*]

bust[1] /bʌst/ *n.* **1 a** the human chest, esp. that of a woman; the bosom. **b** the circumference of the body at bust level (*a 36-inch bust*). **2** a sculpture of a person's head, shoulders, and chest. [F *buste* f. It. *busto,* of unkn. orig.]

bust[2] /bʌst/ *v., n., & adj. colloq. —v. (past and past part.* **busted**

or **bust**) **1** *tr.* & *intr.* burst, break. **2** *tr.* esp. *US* reduce (a soldier etc.) to a lower rank; dismiss. **3** *tr.* esp. *US* **a** raid, search. **b** arrest. —*n.* **1** a sudden failure; a bankruptcy. **2** a police raid. **3** a drinking-bout. **4** esp. *US* a punch; a hit. **5** a worthless thing. **6** a bad hand at cards. —*adj.* (also **busted**) **1** broken, burst, collapsed. **2** bankrupt. □ **bust up 1** bring or come to collapse; explode. **2** (of esp. a married couple) separate. **bust-up** *n.* **1** a quarrel. **2** a collapse; an explosion. **go bust** become bankrupt; fail. [orig. a (dial.) pronunc. of BURST]

bustard /ˈbʌstəd/ *n.* any large terrestrial bird of the family Otididae, with long neck, long legs, and stout tapering body. These birds, the heaviest flying-birds in the world, are chiefly centred in Africa but some species are found in southern Europe and in Asia, and one (*Choriotis australis*) in Australia. [ME f. OF *bistarde* f. L *avis tarda* slow bird (? = slow on the ground; but possibly a perversion of a foreign word)]

bustee /ˈbʌstiː/ *n. Ind.* a shanty town; a slum. [Hind. *bastī* dwelling]

buster /ˈbʌstə(r)/ *n.* **1** esp. *US sl.* mate; fellow (used esp. as a disrespectful form of address). **2** a violent gale.

bustier /ˈbʌstɪˌeɪ/ *n.* a strapless close-fitting bodice, usu. boned. [F]

bustle[1] /ˈbʌs(ə)l/ *v.* & *n.* —*v.* **1** *intr.* (often foll. by *about*) **a** work etc. showily, energetically, and officiously. **b** hasten (*bustled about the kitchen banging saucepans*). **2** *tr.* make (a person) hurry or work hard (*bustled him into his overcoat*). **3** *intr.* (as **bustling** *adj.*) *colloq.* full of activity. —*n.* excited activity; a fuss. □□ **bustler** *n.* [perh. f. *buskle* frequent. of *busk* prepare]

bustle[2] /ˈbʌs(ə)l/ *n. hist.* a pad or frame worn under a skirt and puffing it out behind. [18th c.: orig. unkn.]

busty /ˈbʌstɪ/ *adj.* (**bustier**, **bustiest**) (of a woman) having a prominent bust. □□ **bustiness** *n.*

busy /ˈbɪzɪ/ *adj., v.,* & *n.* —*adj.* (**busier**, **busiest**) **1** (often foll. by *in, with, at,* or pres. part.) occupied or engaged in work etc. with the attention concentrated (*busy at their needlework; he was busy packing*). **2** full of activity or detail; fussy (*a busy evening; a picture busy with detail*). **3** employed continuously; unresting (*busy as a bee*). **4** meddlesome; prying. **5** esp. *US* (of a telephone line) engaged. —*v.tr.* (**-ies, -ied**) (often *refl.*) keep busy; occupy (*the work busied him for many hours; busied herself with the accounts*). —*n.* (*pl.* **-ies**) *sl.* a detective; a policeman. □ **busy Lizzie** a house-plant, *Impatiens Walleriana*, with usu. toothed leaves and pendulous flowers. □□ **busily** /ˈbɪzɪlɪ/ *adv.* **busyness** /ˈbɪzɪnɪs/ *n.* (cf. BUSINESS). [OE *bisig*]

busybody /ˈbɪzɪˌbɒdɪ/ *n.* (*pl.* **-ies**) **1** a meddlesome person. **2** a mischief-maker.

but[1] /bʌt, bət/ *conj., prep., adv., pron., n.,* & *v.* —*conj.* **1 a** nevertheless, however (*tried hard but did not succeed; I am old, but I am not weak*). **b** on the other hand; on the contrary (*I am old but you are young*). **2** (prec. by *can* etc.; in *neg.* or *interrog.*) except, other than, otherwise than (*cannot choose but do it; what could we do but run?*). **3** without the result that (*it never rains but it pours*). **4** prefixing an interruption to the speaker's train of thought (*the weather is ideal—but is that a cloud on the horizon?*). —*prep.* except; apart from; other than (*everyone went but me; nothing but trouble*). —*adv.* **1** only; no more than; only just (*we can but try; is but a child; had but arrived; did it but once*). **2** introducing emphatic repetition; definitely (*wanted to see nobody, but nobody*). **3** *Austral.* & *NZ* though, however (*didn't like it, but*). —*rel.pron.* who not; that not (*there is not a man but feels pity*). —*n.* an objection (*ifs and buts*). —*v.tr.* (in *phr.* **but me no buts**) do not raise objections. □ **but for** without the help or hindrance etc. of (*but for you I'd be rich by now*). **but one** (or **two** etc.) excluding one (or two etc.) from the number (*next door but one; last but one*). **but that** (prec. by *neg.*) that (*I don't deny but that it's true*). **but that** (or *colloq.* **what**) other than that; except that (*who knows but that it is true?*). **but then** (or **yet**) however, on the other hand (*I won, but then the others were beginners*). [OE *be-ūtan, būtan, būta* outside, without]

but[2] /bʌt/ *n. Sc.* □ **but and ben** the outer and inner rooms of a two-roomed house (see BEN[2]). [BUT[1] = outside]

butadiene /ˌbjuːtəˈdaɪiːn/ *n. Chem.* a colourless gaseous hydrocarbon used in the manufacture of synthetic rubbers. ¶ Chem. formula: C_4H_6. [BUTANE + DI-[2] + -ENE: cf. BUNA]

butane /ˈbjuːteɪn, bjuːˈteɪn/ *n. Chem.* a gaseous hydrocarbon of the alkane series used in liquefied form as fuel. ¶ Chem. formula: C_4H_8. [BUTYL + -ANE]

butch /bʊtʃ/ *adj.* & *n. sl.* —*adj.* masculine; tough-looking. —*n.* **1** (often *attrib.*) **a** a mannish woman. **b** a mannish lesbian. **2** a tough, usu. muscular, youth or man. [perh. abbr. of BUTCHER]

butcher /ˈbʊtʃə(r)/ *n.* & *v.* —*n.* **1 a** a person whose trade is dealing in meat. **b** a person who slaughters animals for food. **2** a person who kills or has people killed indiscriminately or brutally. —*v.tr.* **1** slaughter or cut up (an animal) for food. **2** kill (people) wantonly or cruelly. **3** ruin (esp. a job or a musical composition) through incompetence. □ **the butcher, the baker, the candlestick-maker** people of all kinds or trades. **butcher-bird** a shrike of the genus *Lanius*, native to Australia and New Guinea, with a long hook-tipped bill for catching prey. **butcher's** *rhyming sl.* a look (short for *butcher's hook*). **butcher's-broom** a low spiny-leaved evergreen shrub, *Ruscus aculeatus*. **butcher's meat** slaughtered fresh meat excluding game, poultry, and bacon. □□ **butcherly** *adj.* [ME f. OF *bo(u)chier* f. *boc* BUCK[1]]

butchery /ˈbʊtʃərɪ/ *n.* (*pl.* **-ies**) **1** needless or cruel slaughter (of people). **2** the butcher's trade. **3** a slaughterhouse. [ME f. OF *boucherie* (as BUTCHER)]

Bute /bjuːt/, John Stuart, 3rd Earl of (1713–92), Scottish courtier and statesman, who through his influence with King George III became Prime Minister 1762–3. Bute was widely disliked and his influence with the King soon waned.

Buthelezi /ˌbuːtəˈleɪzɪ/, Mangosuthu Gatsha (1928–), Zulu leader and politician, head of a Black homeland in the Republic of South Africa and founder-president of the Inkatha movement (see INKATHA).

butle var. of BUTTLE.

Butler[1] /ˈbʌtlə(r)/, Reg(inald) Cotterell (1913–81), English sculptor, who was trained as an architect. During the Second World War he worked as a blacksmith (he was a conscientious objector), and after taking up sculpture as an assistant to Henry Moore (1947) he worked mainly in forged or cast metal. Butler shot to prominence in 1953 when he won the competition for a monument to the Unknown Political Prisoner, defeating Calder, Gabo, Hepworth, and other established artists.

Butler[2] /ˈbʌtlə(r)/, Samuel (1612–80), English poet. His reputation rests on his satirical poem *Hudibras* (1663–80, 3 parts), a mock romance derived from *Don Quixote*, with a loose narrative framework which give the author ample opportunity for digressions which included attacks on academic pedantry, the theological differences within the Puritan sects, the politics of the Civil War, and other contemporary concerns, in a distinctive style (8-syllable couplets with comic rhymes). It was highly approved by Charles II, who granted the author a pension, but Butler is said to have died in penury.

Butler[3] /ˈbʌtlə(r)/, Samuel (1835–1902), English novelist. The son of a clergyman, he emigrated in 1859 and became a successful sheep farmer in New Zealand. Returning to England in 1864 he studied painting for 10 years and turned to literature, publishing his satirical anti-utopian novel *Erewhon* (1872) and its sequel *Erewhon Revisited* (1901), several works of scientific controversy challenging aspects of Darwinism, and his semi-autobiographical *The Way of All Flesh* (published posthumously, 1903), a witty ironic study of the relations of parents to children and the stultifying effects of inherited family traits.

butler /ˈbʌtlə(r)/ *n.* the principal manservant of a household, usu. in charge of the wine cellar, pantry, etc. [ME f. AF *buteler*, OF *bouteillier*: see BOTTLE]

butt[1] /bʌt/ *v.* & *n.* —*v.* **1** *tr.* & *intr.* push with the head or horns. **2 a** *intr.* (usu. foll. by *against, upon*) come with one end flat against, meet end to end with, abut. **b** *tr.* (usu. foll. by *against*) place (timber etc.) with the end flat against a wall etc. —*n.* **1** a push with the head. **2** a join of two edges. □ **butt in** interrupt, meddle. [ME f. AF *buter*, OF *boter* f. Gmc: infl. by BUTT[2] and ABUT]

butt² /bʌt/ n. **1** (often foll. by of) an object (of ridicule etc.) (the butt of his jokes; made him their butt). **2 a** a mound behind a target. **b** (in pl.) a shooting-range. **c** a target. **3** a grouse-shooter's stand screened by low turf or a stone wall. [ME f. OF but goal, of unkn. orig.]

butt³ /bʌt/ n. **1** (also **butt-end**) the thicker end, esp. of a tool or a weapon (gun butt). **2 a** the stub of a cigar or a cigarette. **b** (also **butt-end**) a remnant (the butt of the evening). **3** esp. US sl. the buttocks. **4** (also **butt-end**) the square end of a plank meeting a similar end. **5** the trunk of a tree, esp. the part just above the ground. □ **butt weld** a weld in which the pieces are joined end to end. [Du. bot stumpy]

butt⁴ /bʌt/ n. a cask, esp. as a measure of wine or ale. [AL butta, bota, AF but, f. OF bo(u)t f. LL buttis]

butt⁵ /bʌt/ n. a flat-fish (e.g. a sole, plaice, or turbot). [MLG, MDu. but flat-fish]

butte /bjuːt/ n. US a high isolated steep-sided hill. [F, = mound]

butter /ˈbʌtə(r)/ n. & v. —n. **1 a** a pale yellow edible fatty substance made by churning cream and used as a spread or in cooking. **b** a substance of a similar consistency or appearance (peanut butter). **2** excessive flattery. —v.tr. spread, cook, or serve with butter (butter the bread; buttered carrots). □ **butter-and-eggs** any of several plants having two shades of yellow in the flower, e.g. toadflax. **butter-bean 1** the flat, dried, white lima bean. **2** a yellow-podded bean. **butter-cream** (or **-icing**) a mixture of butter, icing sugar, etc. used as a filling or a topping for a cake. **butter-fingers** colloq. a clumsy person prone to drop things. **butter-knife** a blunt knife used for cutting butter at table. **butter muslin** a thin, loosely-woven cloth with a fine mesh, orig. for wrapping butter. **butter-nut 1** a N. American tree, Juglans cinerea. **2** the oily nut of this tree. **butter up** colloq. flatter excessively. **look as if butter wouldn't melt in one's mouth** seem demure or innocent, probably deceptively. [OE butere f. L butyrum f. Gk bouturon]

butterball /ˈbʌtəˌbɔːl/ n. **1** a piece of butter shaped into a ball. **2** US = BUFFLEHEAD (because it is very fat in autumn). **3** US sl. a fat person.

butterbur /ˈbʌtəbɜː(r)/ n. any of several plants of the genus Petasites with large soft leaves, formerly used to wrap butter.

buttercup /ˈbʌtəˌkʌp/ n. any common yellow-flowered plant of the genus Ranunculus.

butterfat /ˈbʌtəˌfæt/ n. the essential fats of pure butter.

butterfish /ˈbʌtəˌfɪʃ/ n. = GUNNEL¹.

butterfly /ˈbʌtəˌflaɪ/ n. (pl. **-flies**) **1** any of a large group of insects of the order Lepidoptera, distinguished from moths in most instances by diurnal behaviour, clubbed or dilated antennae, thin bodies, and the usually erect position of the wings when at rest. **2** a showy or frivolous person. **3** (in pl.) colloq. a nervous sensation felt in the stomach. □ **butterfly net** a fine net on a ring attached to a pole, used for catching butterflies. **butterfly nut** a kind of wing-nut. **butterfly stroke** a stroke in swimming, with both arms raised and lifted forwards together. **butterfly valve** a valve with hinged semicircular plates. [OE buttor-flēoge (as BUTTER, FLY²)]

buttermilk /ˈbʌtəmɪlk/ n. a slightly acid liquid left after churning butter.

butterscotch /ˈbʌtəˌskɒtʃ/ n. a brittle sweet made from butter, brown sugar, etc. [SCOTCH]

butterwort /ˈbʌtəˌwɜːt/ n. any bog plant of the genus Pinguicula, esp. P. vulgaris with violet-like flowers and fleshy leaves that secrete a fluid to trap small insects for nutrient.

buttery¹ /ˈbʌtərɪ/ n. (pl. **-ies**) a room, esp. in a college, where provisions are kept and supplied to students etc. [ME f. AF boterie butt-store (as BUTT⁴)]

buttery² /ˈbʌtərɪ/ adj. like, containing, or spread with butter. □□ **butteriness** n.

buttle /ˈbʌt(ə)l/ v.intr. (also **butle**) joc. work as a butler. [back-form. f. BUTLER]

buttock /ˈbʌtək/ n. (usu. in pl.) **1** each of two fleshy protuberances on the lower rear part of the human body. **2** the corresponding part of an animal. [butt ridge + -OCK]

button /ˈbʌt(ə)n/ n. & v. —n. **1** a small disc or knob sewn on to a garment, either to fasten it by being pushed through a buttonhole, or as an ornament or badge. **2** a knob on a piece of esp. electronic equipment which is pressed to operate it. **3 a** a small round object (chocolate buttons). **b** (attrib.) anything resembling a button (button nose). **4 a** a bud. **b** a button mushroom. **5** Fencing a terminal knob on a foil making it harmless. —v. **1** tr. & intr. = button up 1. **2** tr. supply with buttons. □ **buttonball tree** (or **button wood**) US a plane-tree, Platanus occidentalis. **button chrysanthemum** a variety of chrysanthemum with small spherical flowers. **buttoned up** colloq. **1** formal and inhibited in manner. **2** silent. **button one's lip** esp. US sl. remain silent. **button mushroom** a young unopened mushroom. **button-through** (of a dress) fastened with buttons from neck to hem like a coat. **button up 1** fasten with buttons. **2** colloq. complete (a task etc.) satisfactorily. **3** colloq. become silent. **not worth a button** worthless. **on the button** esp. US sl. precisely. □□ **buttoned** adj. **buttonless** adj. **buttony** adj. [ME f. OF bouton, ult. f. Gmc]

buttonhole /ˈbʌt(ə)nˌhəʊl/ n. & v. —n. **1** a slit made in a garment to receive a button for fastening. **2** a flower or spray worn in a lapel buttonhole. —v.tr. **1** colloq. accost and detain (a reluctant listener). **2** make buttonholes in. □ **buttonhole stitch** a looped stitch used for making buttonholes.

buttonhook /ˈbʌt(ə)nˌhʊk/ n. a hook formerly used esp. for pulling the buttons on tight boots into place for fastening.

buttons /ˈbʌt(ə)nz/ n. colloq. a liveried page-boy. [from the rows of buttons on his jacket]

buttress /ˈbʌtrɪs/ n. & v. —n. **1 a** a projecting support of stone or brick etc. built against a wall. **b** a source of help or encouragement (she was a buttress to him in his trouble). **2** a projecting portion of a hill or mountain. —v.tr. (often foll. by up) **1** support with a buttress. **2** support by argument etc. (claim buttressed by facts). [ME f. OF (ars) bouterez thrusting (arch) f. bouteret f. bouter BUTT¹]

butty¹ /ˈbʌtɪ/ n. (pl. **-ies**) **1** colloq. or dial. a mate; a companion. **2** hist. a middleman negotiating between a mine-owner and the miners. **3** a barge or other craft towed by another. □ **butty-gang** a gang of men contracted to work on a large job and sharing the profits equally. [19th c.: perh. f. BOOTY in phr. play booty join in sharing plunder]

butty² /ˈbʌtɪ/ n. (pl. **-ies**) N.Engl. **1** a sandwich (bacon butty). **2** a slice of bread and butter. [BUTTER + -Y²]

butyl /ˈbjuːtaɪl/ n. Chem. the univalent alkyl radical C₄H₉. □ **butyl rubber** a synthetic rubber used in the manufacture of tyre inner tubes. [BUTYRIC (ACID) + -YL]

butyric acid /bjuːˈtɪrɪk/ n. Chem. either of two colourless syrupy liquid organic acids found in rancid butter or arnica oil. □□ **butyrate** /ˈbjuːtɪˌreɪt/ n. [L butyrum BUTTER + -IC]

buxom /ˈbʌksəm/ adj. (esp. of a woman) plump and healthy-looking; large and shapely; busty. □□ **buxomly** adv. **buxomness** n. [earlier sense pliant: ME f. stem of OE būgan BOW² + -SOME¹]

Buxtehude /ˈbʊkstəˌhuːdə/, Dietrich (c.1637–1707), Danish organist and composer. He worked as an organist in Lübeck from 1668 until his death, expanding the series of Sunday evening concerts traditionally given there to include a wide range of sacred vocal, organ, and chamber music. His skill as an organist inspired Bach to walk over 200 miles from Anstadt to hear him play, and his own organ works (preludes, fugues, chorale variations, etc.) give some idea of his mastery of the instrument as well as of his great contrapuntal gifts as a composer.

buy /baɪ/ v. & n. —v. (**buys, buying**; past and past part. **bought** /bɔːt/) **1** tr. **a** obtain in exchange for money etc. **b** (usu. in neg.) serve to obtain (money can't buy happiness). **2** tr. **a** procure (the loyalty etc.) of a person by bribery, promises, etc. **b** win over (a person) in this way. **3** tr. get by sacrifice, great effort, etc. (dearly bought; bought with our sweat). **4** tr. sl. accept, believe in, approve of (it's a good scheme, I'll buy it; he bought it, he's so gullible). **5** absol. be a buyer for a store etc. (buys for Selfridges; are you buying or selling?). —n. colloq. a purchase (that sofa was a good buy). □ **best buy** the purchase giving the best value in proportion to its price; a bargain. **buy in 1** buy a stock of. **2** withdraw (an item) at auction because of failure to reach the reserve price. **buy into** obtain a share in (an enterprise) by payment. **buy it** (usu. in *past*) *sl.* be killed. **buy off** get rid of (a claim, a claimant, a blackmailer) by payment. **buy oneself out** obtain one's release (esp. from the armed services) by payment. **buy out** pay (a person) to give up an ownership, interest, etc. **buy-out** *n.* the purchase of a controlling share in a company etc. **buy over** bribe. **buy time** delay an event, conclusion, etc., temporarily. **buy up 1** buy as much as possible of. **2** absorb (another firm etc.) by purchase. [OE *bycgan* f. Gmc]

buyer /ˈbaɪə(r)/ *n.* **1** a person employed to select and purchase stock for a large store etc. **2** a purchaser, a customer. □ **buyer's** (or **buyers'**) **market** an economic position in which goods are plentiful and cheap and buyers have the advantage.

buzz /bʌz/ *n.* & *v.* —*n.* **1** the hum of a bee etc. **2** the sound of a buzzer. **3 a** a confused low sound as of people talking; a murmur. **b** a stir; hurried activity (*a buzz of excitement*). **c** *colloq.* a rumour. **4** *sl.* a telephone call. **5** *sl.* a thrill; a euphoric sensation. —*v.* **1** *intr.* make a humming sound. **2 a** *tr.* & *intr.* signal or signal to with a buzzer. **b** *tr.* telephone. **3** *intr.* **a** (often foll. by *about*) move or hover busily. **b** (of a place) have an air of excitement or purposeful activity. **4** *tr. colloq.* throw hard. **5** *tr. Aeron. colloq.* fly fast and very close to (another aircraft). □ **buzz off** *sl.* go or hurry away. **buzz-saw** *US* a circular saw. **buzz-word** *sl.* **1** a fashionable piece of esp. technical or computer jargon. **2** a catchword; a slogan. [imit.]

buzzard /ˈbʌzəd/ *n.* **1** any of a group of predatory birds of the hawk family, esp. of the genus *Butea*, with broad wings well adapted for soaring flight. **2** *US* a turkey buzzard. [ME f. OF *busard, buson* f. L *buteo -onis* falcon]

buzzer /ˈbʌzə(r)/ *n.* **1** an electrical device, similar to a bell, that makes a buzzing noise. **2** a whistle or hooter.

BVM *abbr.* Blessed Virgin Mary.

bwana /ˈbwɑːnə/ *n. Afr.* master, sir. [Swahili]

BWI *abbr. hist.* British West Indies.

BWR *abbr.* boiling-water (nuclear) reactor.

by /baɪ/ *prep., adv., & n.* —*prep.* **1** near, beside, in the region of (*stand by the door; sit by me; path by the river*). **2** through the agency, means, instrumentality, or causation of (*by proxy; bought by a millionaire; a poem by Donne; went by bus; succeeded by persisting; divide four by two*). **3** not later than; as soon as (*by next week; by now; by the time he arrives*). **4 a** past, beyond (*drove by the church; came by us*). **b** passing through; via (*went by Paris*). **5** in the circumstances of (*by day; by daylight*). **6** to the extent of (*missed by a foot; better by far*). **7** according to; using as a standard or unit (*judge by appearances; paid by the hour*). **8** with the succession of (*worse by the minute; day by day; one by one*). **9** concerning; in respect of (*did our duty by them; Smith by name; all right by me*). **10** used in mild oaths (orig. = as surely as one believes in) (*by God; by gum; swear by all that is sacred*). **11** placed between specified lengths in two directions (*three feet by two*). **12** avoiding, ignoring (*pass by him; passed us by*). **13** inclining to (*north by north-west*). —*adv.* **1** near (*sat by, watching; lives close by*). **2** aside; in reserve (*put £5 by*). **3** past (*they marched by*). —*n.* = BYE. □ **by and by** before long; eventually. **by and large** on the whole, everything considered. **by the by** (or **bye**) incidentally, parenthetically. **by oneself 1 a** unaided. **b** without prompting. **2** alone; without company. [OE *bī, bi, be* f. Gmc]

by- /baɪ/ *prefix* (also **bye-**) subordinate, incidental, secondary (*by-effect; by-road*).

by-blow /ˈbaɪbləʊ/ *n.* **1** a side-blow not at the main target. **2** an illegitimate child.

Bydgoszcz /bɪdˈɡɒʃtʃ/ (German **Gromberg** /ˈbrɒmbeək/) an industrial port on the Brda River in north central Poland; pop. (1985) 361,000.

bye¹ /baɪ/ *n.* **1** *Cricket* a run scored from a ball that passes the batsman without being hit. **2** the status of an unpaired competitor in a sport, who proceeds to the next round as if having won. **3** *Golf* one or more holes remaining unplayed after the match has been decided. □ **by the bye** = *by the by*. **leg-bye**

Cricket a run scored from a ball that touches the batsman. [BY as noun]

bye² /baɪ/ *int. colloq.* = GOODBYE. [abbr.]

bye- *prefix* var. of BY-.

bye-bye¹ /ˈbaɪbaɪ, bəˈbaɪ/ *int. colloq.* = GOODBYE. [childish corrupt.]

bye-bye² /ˈbaɪbaɪ/ *n.* (also **bye-byes** /-baɪz/) (a child's word for) sleep. [ME, f. the sound used in lullabies]

by-election /ˈbaɪɪlekʃ(ə)n/ *n.* the election of an MP in a single constituency to fill a vacancy arising during a government's term of office.

Byelorussian var. of BELORUSSIAN.

by-form /ˈbaɪfɔːm/ *n.* a collateral form of a word etc.

bygone /ˈbaɪɡɒn/ *adj.* & *n.* —*adj.* past, antiquated (*bygone years*). —*n.* (in *pl.*) past offences (*let bygones be bygones*).

by-law /ˈbaɪlɔː/ *n.* (also **bye-law**) **1** *Brit.* a regulation made by a local authority or corporation. **2** a rule made by a company or society for its members. [ME prob. f. obs. *byrlaw* local custom (ON *býjar* genitive sing. of *býr* town, but assoc. with BY)]

byline /ˈbaɪlaɪn/ *n.* **1** a line in a newspaper etc. naming the writer of an article. **2** a secondary line of work. **3** a goal-line or touch-line.

byname /ˈbaɪneɪm/ *n.* a sobriquet; a nickname.

bypass /ˈbaɪpɑːs/ *n.* & *v.* —*n.* **1** a road passing round a town or its centre to provide an alternative route for through traffic. **2 a** a secondary channel or pipe etc. to allow a flow when the main one is closed or blocked. **b** an alternative passage for the circulation of blood during a surgical operation on the heart. —*v.tr.* **1** avoid; go round. **2** provide with a bypass.

bypath /ˈbaɪpɑːθ/ *n.* **1** a secluded path. **2** a minor or obscure branch of a subject.

byplay /ˈbaɪpleɪ/ *n.* a secondary action or sequence of events, esp. in a play.

by-product /ˈbaɪprɒdʌkt/ *n.* **1** an incidental or secondary product made in the manufacture of something else. **2** a secondary result.

Byrd¹ /bɜːd/, Richard Evelyn (1888–1957), American polar explorer, a career naval officer and aviator, leader of four scientific expeditions to the Antarctic. He claimed to have made the first aeroplane flight over the North Pole in 1926, made that over the South Pole in 1929, and led further expeditions to the Antarctic in 1933–4 and 1939–41.

Byrd² /bɜːd/, William (1543–1623), Roman Catholic composer under the Anglican Elizabeth I. He wrote for both Churches, and two of his finest works are the Anglican Great Service and the Latin Four-part Mass. As well as his expressive and beautifully crafted sacred music he left a huge quantity of music for virginals, of which the variations on popular tunes of the day remain widely known and loved, over 40 consort songs, a genre brought by him to a rich perfection, and consort music.

byre /ˈbaɪə(r)/ *n.* a cowshed. [OE *býre*: perh. rel. to BOWER]

byroad /ˈbaɪrəʊd/ *n.* a minor road.

Byron /ˈbaɪrən/, George Gordon, 6th Baron (1788–1824), English poet, born with a club foot which profoundly affected his temperament. Angered by contemptuous criticism of his first volume of verse (*Hours of Idleness*, 1807) Byron retaliated with his satire *English Bards and Scotch Reviewers* (1809). Soon afterwards he left England for extensive travels in Europe described in *Childe Harold's Pilgrimage* (1812–18), a work presenting, in the pilgrim, a truly 'Byronic' hero, aloof, cynical, melancholy, and rebellious. He became famous overnight and was lionized by literary and aristocractic circles. His marriage to Anne Isabella Milbanke in 1815 ended after the birth of their daughter Ada, while rumours of his incestuous relationship with his half-sister (Augusta Leigh) mounted and debts associated with his ancestral home, Newstead Abbey, increased. Ostracized and embittered Byron left England permanently, stayed with Shelley in Geneva, finally to settle in Italy. In *Beppo* (1818) he found a new ironic colloquial voice which he fully developed in his epic satire *Don Juan* (1819–24), a work which attacked hypocrisy and social conventions with subtle irony and wit. Though criticized

æ cat ɑː arm e bed ɜː her ɪ sit iː see ɒ hot ɔː saw ʌ run ʊ put uː too ə ago aɪ my

on moral grounds, Byron's poetry exerted enormous influence on the Romantic movement, as his name became a symbol of deep romantic melancholy. At the end of his life he was training troops for the Greeks against the Turks, a cause for which he had great enthusiasm.

Byronic /baɪˈrɒnɪk/ *adj.* **1** characteristic of Lord Byron or his romantic poetry. **2** (of a man) handsomely dark, mysterious, or moody.

byssinosis /ˌbɪsɪˈnəʊsɪs/ *n. Med.* a lung disease caused by prolonged inhalation of textile fibre dust. [mod.L f. Gk *bussinos* made of byssus + -osis]

byssus /ˈbɪsəs/ *n. hist.* (*pl.* **byssuses** or **byssi** /-saɪ/) **1** *hist.* a fine textile fibre and fabric of flax. **2** a tuft of tough silky filaments by which some molluscs adhere to rocks etc. [ME f. L f. Gk *bussos*]

bystander /ˈbaɪˌstændə(r)/ *n.* a person who stands by but does not take part; a mere spectator.

byte /baɪt/ *n. Computing* a group of eight binary digits, often used to represent one character. [20th c.: perh. based on BIT[4] and BITE]

byway /ˈbaɪweɪ/ *n.* **1** a byroad or bypath. **2** a minor activity.

byword /ˈbaɪwɜːd/ *n.* **1** a person or thing cited as a notable example (*is a byword for luxury*). **2** a familiar saying; a proverb.

Byzantine /bɪˈzæntaɪn, baɪ-, ˈbɪzənˌtiːn, ˈbɪzənˌtaɪn/ *adj.* & *n.* —*adj.* **1** of Byzantium or the Eastern Roman Empire. **2** (of a political situation etc.): **a** extremely complicated. **b** inflexible. **c** carried on by underhand methods. **3** *Archit.* & *Painting* of a highly decorated style developed in the Eastern Empire. —*n.* a citizen of Byzantium or the E. Roman Empire. □□ **Byzantinism** *n.* **Byzantinist** *n.* [F *byzantin* or L *Byzantinus* f. BYZANTIUM]

Byzantium /bɪˈzæntɪəm, baɪ-/ an ancient Greek city on the European side of the south end of the Bosporus, founded in the 7th c. BC and refounded as Constantinople by Constantine.

C

C¹ /siː/ *n.* (also **c**) (*pl.* **Cs** or **C's**) **1** the third letter of the alphabet. **2** *Mus.* the first note of the diatonic scale of C major (the major scale having no sharps or flats). **3** the third hypothetical person or example. **4** the third highest class or category (of academic marks etc.). **5** *Algebra* (usu. **c**) the third known quantity. **6** (as a Roman numeral) 100. **7** (**c**) the speed of light in a vacuum. **8** (also ©) copyright.

C² *symb. Chem.* the element carbon.

C³ *abbr.* (also **C.**) **1** Cape. **2** Conservative. **3** Command Paper (second series, 1870–99). **4** Celsius, Centigrade. **5** coulomb(s), capacitance.

c. *abbr.* **1** century; centuries. **2** chapter. **3** cent(s). **4** cold. **5** cubic. **6** colt. **7** *Cricket* caught by. **8** centi-.

c. *abbr. circa*, about.

c/- *abbr. Austral. & NZ* care of.

CA *abbr.* **1** *US* California (in official postal use). **2** *Sc. & Can.* chartered accountant.

Ca *symb. Chem.* the element calcium.

ca. *abbr. circa*, about.

CAA *abbr.* (in the UK) Civil Aviation Authority.

Caaba var. of KAABA.

CAB *abbr.* **1** Citizens' Advice Bureau. **2** *US* Civil Aeronautics Board. **3** Common Agricultural Bureaux (now **CAB International**) an institution founded in 1929 and consisting of four Institutes and eleven Bureaux whose purpose is to provide a scientific information service and mutual assistance in agricultural science to the countries contributing to its funds.

cab /kæb/ *n.* **1** a taxi. **2** the driver's compartment in a lorry, train, or crane. **3** *hist.* **a** a cabriolet or its improved successor the hansom. **b** any of various types of horse-drawn public carriage with two or four wheels. [abbr. of CABRIOLET]

cabal /kəˈbæl/ *n.* **1** a secret intrigue. **2** a political clique or faction. **3** *hist.* a committee of five ministers under Charles II, whose surnames happened to begin with C, A, B, A, and L. [F *cabale* f. med.L *cabala*, CABBALA]

cabala var. of CABBALA.

caballero /ˌkæbəˈljeərəʊ/ *n.* (*pl.* **-os**) a Spanish gentleman. [Sp.: see CAVALIER]

cabana /kəˈbɑːnə/ *n. US* a hut or shelter at a beach or swimming-pool. [Sp. *cabaña* f. LL (as CABIN)]

cabaret /ˈkæbəˌreɪ/ *n.* **1** an entertainment in a nightclub or restaurant while guests eat or drink at tables. **2** such a nightclub etc. [F, = wooden structure, tavern]

cabbage /ˈkæbɪdʒ/ *n.* **1 a** any of several cultivated varieties of *Brassica oleracea*, with thick green or purple leaves forming a round heart or head. **b** this head usu. eaten as vegetable. **2** *colloq. derog.* a person who is inactive or lacks interest. □ **cabbage palm** a palm tree, *Cordyline australis*, with edible cabbage-like terminal buds. **cabbage rose** a double rose with a large round compact flower. **cabbage tree** = *cabbage palm*. **cabbage white** a butterfly, *Pieris brassicae*, whose caterpillars feed on cabbage leaves. □□ **cabbagy** *adj.* [earlier *cabache*, *-oche* f. OF (Picard) *caboche* head, OF *caboce*, of unkn. orig.]

cabbala /kəˈbɑːlə, ˈkæbələ/ *n.* (also **cabala**, **kabbala**) **1** a pretended tradition of mystical interpretation of the Old Testament, using esoteric methods (including ciphers), that reached the height of its influence in the later Middle Ages. **2** mystic interpretation; any esoteric doctrine or occult lore. □□ **cabbalism** *n.* **cabbalist** *n.* **cabbalistic** /-ˈlɪstɪk/ *adj.* [med.L f. Rabbinical Heb. *ḳabbālā* tradition]

cabby /ˈkæbɪ/ *n.* (also **cabbie**) (*pl.* **-ies**) *colloq.* a taxi-driver. [CAB + -Y²]

caber /ˈkeɪbə(r)/ *n.* a roughly trimmed tree-trunk used in the Scottish Highland sport of tossing the caber. There is no universal standard size for the caber, but once tossed it must never be shortened; the Braemar caber is 19 ft. (5.79 m) long and weighs 120 lb (54.5 kg). [Gael. *cabar* pole]

cabin /ˈkæbɪn/ *n. & v.* —*n.* **1** a small shelter or house, esp. of wood. **2** a room or compartment in an aircraft or ship for passengers or crew. **3** a driver's cab. —*v.tr.* (**cabined**, **cabining**) confine in a small place, cramp. □ **cabin-boy** a boy who waits on a ship's officers or passengers. **cabin class** the intermediate class of accommodation in a ship. **cabin crew** the crew members on an aeroplane attending to passengers and cargo. **cabin cruiser** a large motor boat with living accommodation. [ME f. OF *cabane* f. Prov. *cabana* f. LL *capanna*, *cavanna*]

Cabinda /kəˈbɪndə/ **1** an enclave of Angola at the mouth of the Congo, separated from the rest of Angola by a wedge of Zaïre; pop. (1960) 58,550. **2** its capital city; pop. (1970) 21,120.

cabinet /ˈkæbɪnɪt/ *n.* **1 a** a cupboard or case with drawers, shelves, etc., for storing or displaying articles. **b** a piece of furniture housing a radio or television set etc. **2** (**Cabinet**) the committee of senior ministers responsible for controlling government policy. (See below.) **3** *archaic* a small private room. □ **cabinet-maker** a skilled joiner. **Cabinet Minister** *Brit.* a member of the Cabinet. **cabinet photograph** one of about 6 by 4 inches. **cabinet pudding** a steamed pudding with dried fruit. [CABIN + -ET¹, infl. by F *cabinet*]

The kings of England always had advisers. After the Restoration in 1660 a Cabinet (or Cabinet Council) developed, consisting of the major office-bearers and the king's most trusted members of the Privy Council, meeting as a committee in a private room (the *cabinet*, whence its name) and taking decisions without consulting the full Privy Council. In the time of Queen Anne it became the main machinery of executive government and the Privy Council became formal. From about 1717 the monarch (George I) ceased to attend, and from that time the Cabinet met independently. George III became obliged, through insanity and age, to leave more and more to his ministers, but it was not until after the Reform Act of 1832 that the royal power was dissolved and Cabinets came to depend, for their existence and policies, upon the support of a majority in the House of Commons.

cable /ˈkeɪb(ə)l/ *n. & v.* —*n.* **1** a thick rope of wire or hemp. **2** an encased group of insulated wires for transmitting electricity or electrical signals. **3** a cablegram. **4 a** *Naut.* the chain of an anchor. **b** a measure of 200 yards. **5** (in full **cable stitch**) a knitted stitch resembling twisted rope. **6** *Archit.* a rope-shaped ornament. —*v.* **1 a** *tr.* transmit (a message) by cablegram. **b** inform (a person) by cablegram. **c** *intr.* send a cablegram. **2** *tr.* furnish or fasten with a cable or cables. **3** *Archit. tr.* furnish with cables. □ **cable-car 1** a small cabin (often one of a series) suspended on an endless cable and drawn up and down a mountainside etc. by an engine at one end. **2** a carriage drawn along a cable railway. **cable-laid** (of rope) having three triple strands. **cable railway** a railway along which carriages are drawn by an endless cable. **cable television** a broadcasting system with signals transmitted by cable to subscribers' sets. [ME f. OF *chable*, ult. f. LL *capulum* halter f. Arab. *ḥabl*]

cablegram /ˈkeɪb(ə)lˌgræm/ *n.* a telegraph message sent by undersea cable etc.

cableway /ˈkeɪb(ə)lˌweɪ/ *n.* a transporting system with a usu. elevated cable.

cabman /ˈkæbmən/ *n.* (*pl.* **-men**) the driver of a cab.

cabochon /ˈkæbəˌʃɒn/ *n.* a gem polished but not faceted. □ **en cabochon** (of a gem) treated in this way. [F dimin. of *caboche*: see CABBAGE]

caboodle /kəˈbuːd(ə)l/ *n.* □ **the whole caboodle** *sl.* the whole lot (of persons or things). [19th c. *US*: perh. f. phr. *kit and boodle*]

---

b *but* d *dog* f *few* g *get* h *he* j *yes* k *cat* l *leg* m *man* n *no* p *pen* r *red* s *sit* t *top* v *voice*

caboose /kəˈbuːs/ n. **1** a kitchen on a ship's deck. **2** US a guard's van; a car on a freight train for workmen etc. [Du. *cabūse*, of unkn. orig.]

Cabora Bassa /kəˌbɔːrə ˈbæsə/ a lake on the Zambezi River in western Mozambique. Its waters are impounded by a dam and massive hydroelectric complex supplying power mainly to South Africa and to Maputo.

Cabot /ˈkæbət/, John (d. *c*.1498), Venetian explorer and navigator. He and his son Sebastian (d. 1557) sailed from Bristol in 1491 with a patent from Henry VII and discovered the mainland of North America a year before Columbus. The site of their landfall is uncertain (it may have been Cape Breton Island, or Labrador, or Newfoundland), but they believed themselves to be on the NE coast of Asia; Cabot returned to Bristol and reported his success. He undertook a second expedition in 1498 and appears to have returned to Bristol afterwards. Sebastian made further voyages of exploration after his father's death.

cabotage /ˈkæbəˌtɑːʒ, -tɪdʒ/ n. **1** *Naut.* coastal navigation and trade. **2** esp. *Aeron.* the reservation to a country of (esp. air) traffic operation within its territory. [F f. *caboter* to coast, perh. f. Sp. *cabo* CAPE²]

cabotin /ˌkɑːbɔˈtæ̃/ n. (*fem.* **cabotine** /-ˈtiːn/) a second-rate actor; a strolling player. [F, = strolling player, perh. formed as CABOTAGE, from the resemblance to vessels travelling from port to port]

cabriole /ˈkæbrɪˌəʊl/ n. a kind of curved leg characteristic of Queen Anne and Chippendale furniture. [F f. *cabrioler*, *caprioler* f. It. *capriolare* to leap in the air; from the resemblance to a leaping animal's foreleg: see CAPRIOLE]

cabriolet /ˌkæbrɪəʊˈleɪ/ n. **1** a light two-wheeled carriage with a hood, drawn by one horse, introduced into London from Paris in the early 19th c. **2** a motor car with a folding top. [F f. *cabriole* goat's leap (cf. CAPRIOLE), applied to its motion]

ca'canny /kɑːˈkænɪ/ n. **1** the practice of 'going slow' at work; a trade union policy of limiting output. **2** extreme caution. [Sc., = proceed warily: see CALL v. 16, CANNY]

cacao /kəˈkɑːəʊ, -ˈkeɪəʊ/ n. (*pl.* **-os**) **1** a seed pod from which cocoa and chocolate are made. **2** a small widely cultivated evergreen tree, *Theobroma cacao*, bearing these. [Sp. f. Nahuatl *cacauatl* (*uatl* tree)]

cachalot /ˈkæʃəˌlɒt, -ˌləʊt/ n. a sperm whale. [F f. Sp. & Port. *cachalote*, of unkn. orig.]

cache /kæʃ/ n. & v. —n. **1** a hiding-place for treasure, provisions, ammunition, etc. **2** what is hidden in a cache. —v.tr. put in a cache. [F f. *cacher* to hide]

cachectic /kəˈkektɪk/ adj. relating to or having the symptoms of cachexia.

cachet /ˈkæʃeɪ/ n. **1** a distinguishing mark or seal. **2** prestige. **3** *Med.* a flat capsule enclosing a dose of unpleasant-tasting medicine. [F f. *cacher* press ult. f. L *coactare* constrain]

cachexia /kəˈkeksɪə/ n. (also **cachexy** /-ksɪ/) a condition of weakness of body or mind associated with chronic disease. [F *cachexie* or LL *cachexia* f. Gk *kakhexia* f. *kakos* bad + *hexis* habit]

cachinnate /ˈkækɪˌneɪt/ v.intr. *literary* laugh loudly. □□ **cachinnation** /-ˈneɪʃ(ə)n/ n. **cachinnatory** /-ˈneɪtərɪ/ adj. [L *cachinnare cachinnat-*]

cacholong /ˈkæʃəˌlɒŋ/ n. a kind of opal. [F f. Mongolian *kashchilon* beautiful stone]

cachou /ˈkæʃuː/ n. **1** a lozenge to sweeten the breath. **2** var. of CATECHU. [F f. Port. *cachu* f. Malay *kāchu*: cf. CATECHU]

cachucha /kəˈtʃuːtʃə/ n. a Spanish solo dance. [Sp.]

cacique /kəˈsiːk/ n. **1** a W. Indian or American Indian native chief. **2** a political boss in Spain or Latin America. [Sp., of Carib orig.]

cack-handed /kækˈhændɪd/ adj. colloq. **1** awkward, clumsy. **2** left-handed. □□ **cack-handedly** adv. **cack-handedness** n. [dial. *cack* excrement]

cackle /ˈkæk(ə)l/ n. & v. —n. **1** a clucking sound as of a hen or a goose. **2** a loud silly laugh. **3** noisy inconsequential talk. —v. **1** intr. emit a cackle. **2** intr. talk noisily and inconsequentially. **3** tr. utter or express with a cackle. □ **cut the cackle** colloq. stop

talking aimlessly and come to the point. [ME prob. f. MLG, MDu. *kākelen* (imit.)]

cacodemon /ˌkækəˈdiːmən/ n. (also **cacodaemon**) **1** an evil spirit. **2** a malignant person. [Gk *kakodaimōn* f. *kakos* bad + *daimōn* spirit]

cacodyl /ˈkækəˌdaɪl/ n. a malodorous, toxic, spontaneously flammable liquid, tetramethyldiarsine. □□ **cacodylic** /-ˈdaɪlɪk/ adj. [Gk *kakōdēs* stinking f. *kakos* bad]

cacoethes /ˌkækəʊˈiːθiːz/ n. an urge to do something inadvisable. [L f. Gk *kakoēthes* neut. adj. f. *kakos* bad + *ēthos* disposition]

cacography /kəˈkɒgrəfɪ/ n. **1** bad handwriting. **2** bad spelling. □□ **cacographer** n. **cacographic** /ˌkækəˈgræfɪk/ adj. **cacographical** /ˌkækəˈgræfɪk(ə)l/ adj. [Gk *kakos* bad, after *orthography*]

cacology /kəˈkɒlədʒɪ/ n. **1** bad choice of words. **2** bad pronunciation. [LL *cacologia* f. Gk *kakologia* vituperation f. *kakos* bad]

cacomistle /ˈkækəˌmɪs(ə)l/ n. any racoon-like animal of several species of the genus *Bassariscus*, native to Central America, having a dark-ringed tail. [Amer. Sp. *cacomixtle* f. Nahuatl *tlacomiztli*]

cacophony /kəˈkɒfənɪ/ n. (*pl.* **-ies**) **1** a harsh discordant mixture of sound. **2** dissonance; discord. □□ **cacophonous** adj. [F *cacophonie* f. Gk *kakophōnia* f. *kakophōnos* f. *kakos* bad + *phōnē* sound]

cactus /ˈkæktəs/ n. (*pl.* **cacti** /-taɪ/ or **cactuses**) any succulent plant of the family Cactaceae, with a thick fleshy stem, usu. spines but no leaves, and brilliantly coloured flowers. □ **cactus dahlia** any kind of dahlia with quilled petals resembling a cactus flower. □□ **cactaceous** /-ˈteɪʃəs/ adj. [L f. Gk *kaktos* cardoon]

cacuminal /kæˈkjuːmɪn(ə)l/ adj. *Phonet.* pronounced with the tongue-tip curled up towards the hard palate. [L *cacuminare* make pointed f. *cacumen -minis* tree-top]

CAD abbr. computer-aided design.

cad /kæd/ n. a person (esp. a man) who behaves dishonourably. □□ **caddish** adj. **caddishly** adv. **caddishness** n. [abbr. of CADDIE in sense 'odd-job man']

cadastral /kəˈdæstr(ə)l/ adj. of or showing the extent, value, and ownership, of land for taxation. [F f. *cadastre* register of property f. Prov. *cadastro* f. It. *catast(r)o*, earlier *catastico* f. late Gk *katastikhon* list, register f. *kata stikhon* line by line]

cadaver /kəˈdeɪvə(r), -ˈdɑːvə(r)/ n. esp. *Med.* a corpse. □□ **cadaveric** /-ˈdævərɪk/ adj. [ME f. L f. *cadere* fall]

cadaverous /kəˈdævərəs/ adj. **1** corpselike. **2** deathly pale. [L *cadaverosus* (as CADAVER)]

Cadbury /ˈkædbərɪ/, George (1839–1922), English cocoa and chocolate manufacturer, a committed Quaker and enlightened social reformer. He and his brother Richard (1835–99) took over their father's business in 1861 and established Cadbury Brothers. They greatly improved working conditions, and in 1879 George Cadbury moved the works to a new factory on a rural site (which he called Bournville) outside Birmingham, where he subsequently built a housing estate intended primarily for his workers.

caddie /ˈkædɪ/ n. & v. (also **caddy**) —n. (*pl.* **-ies**) a person who assists a golfer during a match, by carrying clubs etc. —v.intr. (**caddies, caddied, caddying**) act as caddie. □ **caddie car** (or **cart**) a light two-wheeled trolley for transporting golf clubs during a game. [orig. Sc. f. F CADET]

caddis-fly /ˈkædɪs/ n. (*pl.* **-flies**) any small hairy-winged nocturnal insect of the order Trichoptera, living near water. [17th c.: orig. unkn.]

caddish see CAD.

caddis-worm /ˈkædɪs/ n. (also **caddis**) a larva of the caddis-fly, living in water and making protective cylindrical cases of sticks, leaves, etc., and used as fishing-bait. [as CADDIS-FLY]

caddy¹ /ˈkædɪ/ n. (*pl.* **-ies**) a small container, esp. a box for holding tea. [earlier *catty* weight of 1⅓ lb., f. Malay *kātī*]

caddy² var. of CADDIE.

cadence /ˈkeɪd(ə)ns/ n. **1** a fall in pitch of the voice, esp. at the end of a phrase or sentence. **2** intonation, tonal inflection. **3** *Mus.* a melodic or harmonic progression or device conventionally associated with the end of a musical composition, section, or phrase. **4** rhythm; the measure or beat of sound or movement. □□ **cadenced** adj. [ME f. OF f. It. cadenza, ult. f. L cadere fall]

cadential /kəˈdenʃ(ə)l/ adj. of a cadence or cadenza.

cadenza /kəˈdenzə/ n. Mus. a flourish inserted into the final cadence of any section of a vocal aria or a movement in a concerto, sonata, or other solo instrumental work. From the late 17th–18th c. such insertions were improvised by the performer, but in the 19th c. composers frequently wrote out their cadenzas. [It.: see CADENCE]

cadet /kəˈdet/ n. **1** a young trainee in the armed services or police force. **2** NZ an apprentice in sheep-farming. **3** a younger son. □□ **cadetship** n. [F f. Gascon dial. capdet, ult. f. L caput head]

cadge /kædʒ/ v. **1** tr. get or seek by begging. **2** intr. beg. □□ **cadger** n. [19th c., earlier = ? bind, carry: orig. unkn.]

cadi /ˈkɑːdɪ, ˈkeɪdɪ/ n. (also **kadi**) (pl. **-is**) a judge in a Muslim country. [Arab. ḳāḍī f. ḳaḍā to judge]

Cadiz /kəˈdɪz/ a city and port on the Andalusian coast of SW Spain; pop. (1986) 154,000. Originally a Phoenician settlement, it reached its highest importance in the 16th–18th c. as the headquarters of the Spanish fleets. In 1587 Sir Francis Drake burnt the ships of Philip II at anchor here.

Cadmean victory /kædˈmiːən/ n. = pyrrhic victory (see PYRRHIC[1]). [L Cadmeus f. Gk Kadmeios f. Kadmos CADMUS]

cadmium /ˈkædmɪəm/ n. a soft bluish-white metallic element, physically resembling tin but chemically related to zinc. Discovered in 1817, cadmium is obtained as a by-product of the extraction of zinc from its ores; the metal does not occur in the free state in nature. It is used as a component in low-melting-point alloys, as a coating on other metals to protect them against corrosion, and in the manufacture of pigments. Both the metal and its components are highly toxic. ¶ Symb.: **Cd**; atomic number 48. □ **cadmium cell** Electr. a standard primary cell. **cadmium yellow** an intense yellow pigment containing cadmium sulphide and used in paints etc. [obs. cadmia calamine f. L cadmia f. Gk kadm(e)ia (gē) Cadmean (earth), f. CADMUS: see -IUM]

Cadmus /ˈkædməs/ Gk legend the brother of Europa, whom he was sent to seek when she disappeared, and traditional founder of Thebes in Boeotia. To get water he killed a dragon which guarded a spring, and when (by Athene's advice) he sowed the dragon's teeth there came up a harvest of armed men, whom Cadmus disposed of by setting them to fight one another. He is also reputed to have introduced the alphabet into Greece.

cadre /ˈkɑːdə(r), ˈkɑːdrə/ n. **1** a basic unit, esp. of servicemen, forming a nucleus for expansion when necessary. **2** /also ˈkeɪdə(r)/ **a** a group of activists in a communist or any revolutionary party. **b** a member of such a group. [F f. It. quadro f. L quadrus square]

caduceus /kəˈdjuːsɪəs/ n. (pl. **caducei** /-sɪˌaɪ/) an Ancient Greek or Roman herald's wand, esp. as carried by the messenger-god Hermes or Mercury. [L f. Doric Gk karuk(e)ion f. kērux herald]

caducous /kəˈdjuːkəs/ adj. Biol. (of organs and parts) easily detached or shed at an early stage. □□ **caducity** /-sɪtɪ/ n. [L caducus falling f. cadere fall]

caecilian /siːˈsɪlɪən/ n. (also **coecilian**) any burrowing wormlike amphibian of the order Gymnophiona, having poorly developed eyes and no limbs. [L caecilia kind of lizard]

caecitis /sɪˈkaɪtɪs/ n. (US **cecitis**) inflammation of the caecum.

caecum /ˈsiːkəm/ n. (US **cecum**) (pl. **-ca** /-kə/) a blind-ended pouch at the junction of the small and large intestines. □□ **caecal** adj. [L for intestinum caecum f. caecus blind, transl. of Gk tuphlon enteron]

Cædmon /ˈkædmən/ (7th c.) English poet, said by Bede to have been an illiterate herdsman who received in a vision the power of song and put into English verse passages from the Scriptures. The only authentic fragment of his work is the hymn quoted by Bede.

Caen /kɑ̃/ a port on the coast of Normandy in NW France, capital of Basse-Normandie region; pop. (1982) 117,100. William the Conqueror is buried here.

Caenozoic var. of CENOZOIC.

Caernarfon /kəˈnɑːvən/ the county town of Gwynedd in NW Wales, on the shore of the Menai Strait; pop. (1981) 9,400. Its 13th-c. castle was the birthplace of Edward II.

Caerns. abbr. Caernarvonshire (a former county in Wales).

Caerphilly /keəˈfɪlɪ, kə-/ n. a kind of mild white cheese orig. made in the area near Caerphilly in Wales.

Caesar /ˈsiːzə(r)/ n. **1** Julius Caesar. **2** the title of the Roman emperors, esp. from Augustus to Hadrian. **3** an autocrat. **4** Med. sl. a Caesarean section; a case of this. □ **Caesar's wife** a person required to be above suspicion. [L, family name of Julius Caesar (see entry)]

Caesarea /ˌsiːzəˈriːə/ an ancient seaport on the Mediterranean coast of Israel, between Tel-Aviv and Haifa, named in honour of the Roman emperor Augustus Caesar.

Caesarean /sɪˈzeərɪən/ adj. & n. (also **Caesarian**, US **Ces-**) —adj. **1** of Caesar or the Caesars. **2** (of a birth) effected by Caesarean section. —n. a Caesarean section. □ **Caesarean section** an operation for delivering a child by cutting through the wall of the abdomen (Julius Caesar supposedly having been born this way). [L Caesarianus]

caesious /ˈsiːzɪəs/ adj. Bot. bluish or lavender. [L caesius]

caesium /ˈsiːzɪəm/ n. (US **cesium**) a soft silver-white metallic element of the alkali metal group. Discovered by spectroscopic means in 1860 by Bunsen and Kirchhoff, caesium is the most reactive of all metals apart from francium. It melts at 28.5 °C and so is liquid in a warm room. It is not used commercially in large quantities, although it has a few specialized applications. A specified transition of the caesium-133 atom is used in defining the second as a unit of time (see SECOND[2]). ¶ Symb.: **Cs**; atomic number 55. □ **caesium clock** an atomic clock that uses caesium. [as CAESIOUS (from its spectrum lines)]

caesura /sɪˈzjʊərə/ n. (pl. **caesuras**) Prosody **1** (in Greek and Latin verse) a break between words within a metrical foot. **2** (in modern verse) a pause near the middle of a line. □□ **caesural** adj. [L f. caedere caes- cut]

CAF abbr. US cost and freight.

cafard /kɑːˈfɑː(r)/ n. melancholia. [F, = cockroach, hypocrite]

café /ˈkæfeɪ, ˈkæfɪ/ n. (also **cafe** /also joc. kæf, keɪf/) **1** a small coffee-house or teashop; a simple restaurant. **2** US a bar. □ **café au lait** /əʊ ˈleɪ/ **1** coffee with milk. **2** the colour of this. **café noir** /ˈnwɑː(r)/ black coffee. **café society** the regular patrons of fashionable restaurants and nightclubs. [F, = coffee, coffee-house]

cafeteria /ˌkæfɪˈtɪərɪə/ n. a restaurant in which customers collect their meals on trays at a counter and usu. pay before sitting down to eat. [Amer. Sp. cafetería coffee-shop]

caff /kæf/ n. Brit. sl. = CAFÉ. [abbr.]

caffeine /ˈkæfiːn/ n. an alkaloid drug with stimulant action found in tea leaves and coffee beans. [F caféine f. café coffee]

caftan /ˈkæftæn/ n. (also **kaftan**) **1** a long usu. belted tunic worn by men in countries of the Near East. **2 a** a woman's long loose dress. **b** a loose shirt or top. [Turk. ḳaftān, partly through F cafetan]

Cagayan Islands /ˌkɑːɡəˈjɑːn/ a group of seven small islands in the Sulu Sea in the western Philippines.

Cage /keɪdʒ/, John (1912–), American composer, pianist, and writer, born in Los Angeles where he studied music with Schoenberg after a period in New York. He returned to New York in 1942 and there developed his ideas on the role of chance in music: his Music of Changes (for piano, 1951) was composed according to decisions made by tossing a coin. In 1938 he invented the 'prepared piano' (with pieces of metal, rubber, etc., inserted between the strings to alter the tone), and he occasionally uses electronic instruments. Perhaps his most notorious work is 4′ 33″ (1952), in which the 'performance' consists of four minutes thirty-three seconds of silence.

cage /keɪdʒ/ n. & v. —n. **1** a structure of bars or wires, esp. for confining animals or birds. **2** any similar open framework, esp. an enclosed platform or lift in a mine or the compartment for passengers in a lift. **3** colloq. a camp for prisoners of war. —v.tr. place or keep in a cage. □ **cage-bird** a bird of the kind customarily kept in a cage. [ME f. OF f. L cavea]

æ cat ɑː arm e bed ɜː her ɪ sit iː see ɒ hot ɔː saw ʌ run ʊ put uː too ə ago aɪ my

cagey /ˈkeɪdʒɪ/ adj. (also **cagy**) (**cagier**, **cagiest**) colloq. cautious and uncommunicative; wary. □□ **cagily** adv. **caginess** n. (also **cageyness**). [20th-c. US: orig. unkn.]

Cagliari /kælˈjɑːrɪ/ a seaport and the capital of Sardinia; pop. (1981) 233,850.

Cagney /ˈkægnɪ/, James (1904–86), American film actor, who played the part of a small-time crook, cocksure and aggressive, in films such as G-Men (1935) and Angels with Dirty Faces (1938).

cagoule /kəˈguːl/ n. a hooded thin windproof garment worn in mountaineering etc. [F]

cahoots /kəˈhuːts/ n.pl. □ **in cahoots** (often foll. by with) sl. in collusion. [19th c.: orig. uncert.]

CAI abbr. computer-assisted (or -aided) instruction.

caiman var. of CAYMAN.

Cain /keɪn/ the eldest son of Adam and murderer of his brother Abel. □ **raise Cain** colloq. make a disturbance; create trouble.

Caine /keɪn/, Michael (real name Maurice Micklewhite, 1933–), English film actor, born in London, noted for his dry laconic cockney manner. His films include The Ipcress File, Funeral in Berlin, and Billion Dollar Brain (1965–7), and Hannah and her Sisters (1986).

Cainozoic var. of CENOZOIC.

caique /kɑɪˈiːk/ n. **1** a light rowing-boat on the Bosporus. **2** a Levantine sailing-ship. [F f. It. caicco f. Turk. kayık]

cairn /keən/ n. **1** a mound of rough stones as a monument or landmark. **2** (in full **cairn terrier**) **a** a small terrier of a breed with short legs, a longish body, and a shaggy coat (perhaps so called from its being used to hunt among cairns). **b** this breed. [Gael. carn]

cairngorm /ˈkeəŋɡɔːm/ n. a yellow or wine-coloured semi-precious form of quartz. [found on Cairngorm, a mountain in Scotland f. Gael. carn gorm blue cairn]

Cairo /ˈkaɪrəʊ/ the capital of Egypt, a port on the Nile near the head of the delta, and the largest city in Africa; pop. (est. 1983) 11,000,000. Founded by the Fatimid Dynasty in 969 it was later fortified against the Crusaders by Saladin, whose citadel (built c.1179) still survives. Cairo's many mosques include that of Al Azhar (972), housing an Islamic university.

caisson /ˈkeɪs(ə)n, kəˈsuːn/ n. **1** a watertight chamber in which underwater construction work can be done. **2** a floating vessel used as a floodgate in docks. **3** an ammunition chest or wagon. □ **caisson disease** = decompression sickness. [F (f. It. cassone) assim. to caisse CASE²]

caitiff /ˈkeɪtɪf/ n. & adj. poet. or archaic —n. a base or despicable person; a coward. —adj. base, despicable, cowardly. [ME f. OF caitif, chaitif ult. f. L captivus CAPTIVE]

cajole /kəˈdʒəʊl/ v.tr. (often foll. by into, out of) persuade by flattery, deceit, etc. □□ **cajolement** n. **cajoler** n. **cajolery** n. [F cajoler]

cake /keɪk/ n. & v. —n. **1 a** a mixture of flour, butter, eggs, sugar, etc., baked in the oven. **b** a quantity of this baked in a flat round or ornamental shape and often iced and decorated. **2 a** other food in a flat round shape (fish cake). **b** = cattle-cake. **3** a flattish compact mass (a cake of soap). **4** Sc. & N.Engl. thin oaten bread. —v. **1** tr. & intr. form into a compact mass. **2** tr. (usu. foll. by with) cover (with a hard or sticky mass) (boots caked with mud). □ **cakes and ale** merrymaking. **have one's cake and eat it** colloq. enjoy both of two mutually exclusive alternatives. **like hot cakes** rapidly or successfully. **a piece of cake** colloq. something easily achieved. **a slice of the cake** participation in benefits. [ME f. ON kaka]

cakewalk /ˈkeɪkwɔːk/ n. **1** a dance developed from an American Black contest in graceful walking with a cake as a prize. **2** colloq. an easy task. **3** a form of fairground entertainment consisting of a promenade moved by machinery.

CAL abbr. computer-assisted learning.

Cal abbr. large calorie(s).

Cal. abbr. California.

cal abbr. small calorie(s).

Calabar /ˈkæləbɑː(r)/ a port and the capital of Cross River State in south Nigeria, situated at the mouth of the Calabar River

where it flows into the Gulf of Guinea; pop. (1983) 126,000. □ **Calabar bean** a poisonous seed of the tropical African climbing plant Physostigma venosum, yielding a medicinal extract.

calabash /ˈkæləbæʃ/ n. **1 a** an evergreen tree, Crescentia cujete, native to tropical America, bearing fruit in the form of large gourds. **b** a gourd from this tree. **2** the shell of this or a similar gourd used as a vessel for water, to make a tobacco pipe, etc. [F calebasse f. Sp. calabaza perh. f. Pers. karbuz melon]

calaboose /ˌkæləˈbuːs/ n. US a prison. [Black F calabouse f. Sp. calabozo dungeon]

calabrese /ˌkæləˈbriːz, ˌkæləˈbreɪseɪ/ n. a large succulent variety of sprouting broccoli. [It., = Calabrian]

Calabria /kəˈlæbrɪə/ the SW (formerly the SE) promontory of Italy. In antiquity the name was applied to the flat and arid but fertile SE promontory or 'heel' of Italy. The Lombards seized Calabria c. AD 700, whereupon the Byzantines transferred its name to the SW promontory or 'toe' of Italy, the Calabria of today. □□ **Calabrian** adj. & n.

Calais /ˈkæleɪ/ a ferry-port in NW France, on the coast of the English Channel; pop. (1982) 76,900. Captured by Edward III in 1347 after a long siege, it was saved from destruction by the surrender of six burghers (commemorated in Rodin's sculpture), and remained an English possession until retaken by the French in 1558, in the reign of Mary. The French terminal of the Channel Tunnel is at Fréthun, near Calais.

calamanco /ˌkæləˈmæŋkəʊ/ n. (pl. **-oes**) hist. a glossy woollen cloth chequered on one side. [16th c.: orig. unkn.]

calamander /ˈkæləˌmændə(r)/ n. a fine-grained red-brown ebony streaked with black, from the Asian tree Diospyros qualsita, used in furniture. [19th c.: orig. unkn.: perh. conn. with Sinh. word for the tree kalu-madīriya]

calamary /ˈkæləmərɪ/ n. (pl. **-ies**) any cephalopod mollusc with a long tapering penlike horny internal shell, esp. a squid of the genus Loligo. [med.L calamarium pen-case f. L calamus pen]

calamine /ˈkæləˌmaɪn/ n. **1** a pink powder consisting of zinc carbonate and ferric oxide used as a lotion or ointment. **2** a zinc mineral usu. zinc carbonate. [ME f. F f. med.L calamina alt. f. L cadmia: see CADMIUM]

calamint /ˈkæləmɪnt/ n. any aromatic herb or shrub of the genus Calamintha, esp. C. officinalis with purple or lilac flowers. [ME f. OF calament f. med.L calamentum f. LL calaminthe f. Gk kalaminthē]

calamity /kəˈlæmɪtɪ/ n. (pl. **-ies**) **1** a disaster, a great misfortune. **2 a** adversity. **b** deep distress. □ **Calamity Jane 1** the nickname of Martha Jane Burke (née Canary; d. 1903), a famous American horse-rider and markswoman. A colourful character (but not the beautiful heroine into which popular fiction transformed her) she was a prostitute, wore male clothing, carried a gun, and engaged in drinking bouts. **2** a prophet of disaster. □□ **calamitous** adj. **calamitously** adv. [ME f. F calamité f. L calamitas -tatis]

calando /kæˈlændəʊ/ adv. Mus. gradually decreasing in speed and volume. [It., = slackening]

calash /kəˈlæʃ/ n. hist. **1 a** a light low-wheeled carriage with a removable folding hood. **b** the folding hood itself. **2** Can. a two-wheeled horse-drawn vehicle. **3** a woman's hooped silk hood. [F calèche f. G Kalesche f. Pol. kolaska or Czech kolesa]

calc- /kælk/ comb. form lime or calcium. [G Kalk f. L CALX]

calcaneus /kælˈkeɪnɪəs/ n. (also **calcaneum** /-nɪəm/) (pl. **calcanei** /-nɪˌaɪ/ or **calcanea** /-nɪə/) the bone forming the heel. [L]

calcareous /kælˈkeərɪəs/ adj. (also **calcarious**) of or containing calcium carbonate; chalky. [L calcarius (as CALX)]

calceolaria /ˌkælsɪəˈleərɪə/ n. Bot. any plant of the genus Calceolaria, native to S. America, with slipper-shaped flowers. [mod.L f. L calceolus dimin. of calceus shoe + -aria fem. = -ARY¹]

calceolate /ˈkælsɪəˌleɪt/ adj. Bot. slipper-shaped.

calces pl. of CALX.

calciferol /kælˈsɪfəˌrɒl/ n. one of the D vitamins, routinely added to dairy products, essential for the deposition of calcium in bones. Also called ERGOCALCIFEROL, *vitamin* D_2. [CALCIFEROUS + -OL[1]]

calciferous /kæl'sɪfərəs/ adj. yielding calcium salts, esp. calcium carbonate. [L CALX lime + -FEROUS]

calcify /'kælsɪˌfaɪ/ v.tr. & intr. (-ies, -ied) 1 harden or become hardened by deposition of calcium salts; petrify. 2 convert or be converted to calcium carbonate. □□ **calcific** /-'sɪfɪk/ adj. **calcification** /-fɪ'keɪʃ(ə)n/ n.

calcine /'kælsɪn, -saɪn/ v. 1 tr. a reduce, oxidize, or desiccate by strong heat. b burn to ashes; consume by fire; roast. c reduce to calcium oxide by roasting or burning. 2 tr. consume or purify as if by fire. 3 intr. undergo any of these. □□ **calcination** /-'neɪʃ(ə)n/ n. [ME f. OF calciner or med.L calcinare f. LL calcina lime f. L CALX]

calcite /'kælsaɪt/ n. natural crystalline calcium carbonate. [G Calcit f. L CALX lime]

calcium /'kælsɪəm/ n. a soft grey metallic element of the alkaline earth group, first isolated by Sir Humphry Davy in 1808. A common element in the earth's crust, it occurs naturally in limestone, fluorite, and gypsum, but never uncombined. The metal now has a number of specialized uses. Calcium is also essential to life: many physiological processes depend on the movement of calcium ions, and calcium salts are an essential constituent of bone, teeth, and shells. ¶ Symb.: **Ca**; atomic number 20. □ **calcium carbide** a greyish solid used in the production of acetylene. **calcium carbonate** a white insoluble solid occurring naturally as chalk, limestone, marble, and calcite, and used in the manufacture of lime and cement. **calcium hydroxide** a white crystalline powder used in the manufacture of plaster and cement; slaked lime. **calcium oxide** a white crystalline solid from which many calcium compounds are manufactured: also called QUICKLIME, CALX. **calcium phosphate** the main constituent of animal bones, used as bone ash fertilizer. **calcium sulphate** a white crystalline solid occurring as anhydrite and gypsum. [L CALX lime + -IUM]

calcrete /'kælkriːt/ n. Geol. a conglomerate formed by the cementation of sand and gravel with calcium carbonate. [L calc lime + concrete]

calcspar /'kælkspɑː(r)/ n. = CALCITE. [CALC- + SPAR[3]]

calculable /'kælkjʊləb(ə)l/ adj. able to be calculated or estimated. □□ **calculability** /-'bɪlɪtɪ/ n. **calculably** adv.

calculate /'kælkjʊˌleɪt/ v. 1 tr. ascertain or determine beforehand, esp. by mathematics or by reckoning. 2 tr. plan deliberately. 3 intr. (foll. by on, upon) rely on; make an essential part of one's reckoning (calculated on a quick response). 4 tr. US colloq. suppose, believe. □□ **calculative** /-lətɪv/ adj. [LL calculare (as CALCULUS)]

calculated /'kælkjʊˌleɪtɪd/ adj. 1 (of an action) done with awareness of the likely consequences. 2 (foll. by to + infin.) designed or suitable; intended. □□ **calculatedly** adv.

calculating /'kælkjʊˌleɪtɪŋ/ adj. (of a person) shrewd, scheming. □□ **calculatingly** adv.

calculation /ˌkælkjʊ'leɪʃ(ə)n/ n. 1 the act or process of calculating. 2 a result got by calculating. 3 a reckoning or forecast. [ME f. OF f. LL calculatio (as CALCULATE)]

calculator /'kælkjʊˌleɪtə(r)/ n. 1 a device (esp. a small electronic one) used for making mathematical calculations. 2 a person or thing that calculates. 3 a set of tables used in calculation. [ME f. L (as CALCULATE)]

calculus /'kælkjʊləs/ n. (pl. **calculuses** or **calculi** /-ˌlaɪ/) 1 Math. a a particular method of calculation or reasoning (calculus of probabilities). b the infinitesimal calculuses of integration or differentiation (see integral calculus, differential calculus). Calculus emerged in the 17th c. from the work of Leibnitz, Newton, and their predecessors as the method of finding rates of change of varying quantities. It was developed for its main applications in mechanics and in geometry, where it provides techniques for finding tangents of curves and areas of curvilinear figures. 2 Med. a stone or concretion of minerals formed within the body. □□ **calculous** adj. (in sense 2). [L, = small stone used in reckoning on an abacus]

Calcutta /kæl'kʌtə/ the capital of the State of West Bengal, an important port and industrial centre and the second-largest city of India; pop. (1981) 9,166,000. Founded c.1690 by the East India Company, it was the capital of India from 1833 to 1912. □ **Black Hole of Calcutta** a dungeon in Fort William, Calcutta, where, following the capture of Calcutta by the Nawab of Bengal in 1756, 156 English prisoners were confined in a narrow cell 6 m (20 ft.) square for the night of 20 June, only 23 of them still being alive the next morning.

Caldecott /'kɒldɪˌkɒt/, Randolph (1846–86), English graphic artist and water-colour painter, best known for his illustrations to children's books.

Calder /'kɔːldə(r)/, Alexander (1898–1976), American sculptor and painter, famous as the inventor of the mobile. He held his first exhibition of mobiles in 1932; his non-moving sculptures he called by contrast 'stabiles'. Calder concentrated on free and uncontrolled movement in sculptural art rather than the carefully planned and controlled movements used by later kinetic artists.

caldera /kɑː'deərə/ n. a large volcanic depression. [Sp. f. LL caldaria boiling-pot]

Calderón de la Barca /'kɔːldəˌrɒn də lɑː 'bɑːkə, 'kɒl-/, Pedro (1600–81), Spanish dramatist and poet, author of some 120 plays.

caldron var. of CAULDRON.

Caledonian /ˌkælɪ'dəʊnɪən/ adj. & n. —adj. 1 of or relating to Scotland or (in Roman times) Caledonia (= northern Britain). 2 Geol. of a mountain-forming period in Europe in the Palaeozoic era. —n. a Scotsman. □ **Caledonian Canal** a system of lochs and canals in Scotland from Inverness on the east coast to Fort William in the west, linking the North Sea with the Atlantic Ocean. The work of Thomas Telford, it was opened in 1822.

calefacient /ˌkælɪ'feɪʃ(ə)nt/ n. & adj. Med. —n. a substance producing or causing a sensation of warmth. —adj. of this substance. [L calefacere f. calēre be warm + facere make]

calendar /'kælɪndə(r)/ n. & v. —n. 1 a system by which the beginning, length, and subdivisions of the year are fixed. (See Gregorian, Julian calendar.) 2 a chart or series of pages showing the days, weeks, and months of a particular year, or giving special seasonal information. 3 a timetable or programme of appointments, special events, etc. —v.tr. register or enter in a calendar or timetable etc. □ **calendar month** (or **year**) see MONTH, YEAR. □□ **calendric** /-'lendrɪk/ adj. **calendrical** /-'lendrɪk(ə)l/ adj. [ME f. AF calender, OF calendier f. L calendarium account-book (as CALENDS)]

calender /'kælɪndə(r)/ n. & v. —n. a machine in which cloth, paper, etc., is pressed by rollers to glaze or smooth it. —v.tr. press in a calender. [F calendre(r), of unkn. orig.]

calends /'kælɪndz/ n.pl. (also **kalends**) the first of the month in the ancient Roman calendar. [ME f. OF calendes f. L kalendae]

calendula /kə'lendjʊlə/ n. any plant of the genus Calendula, with large yellow or orange flowers, e.g. marigold. [mod.L dimin. of calendae (as CALENDS), perh. = little clock]

calenture /'kælentʃə(r)/ n. hist. a tropical delirium of sailors, who think the sea is green fields. [F f. Sp. calentura fever f. calentar be hot ult. f. L calēre be warm]

calf[1] /kɑːf/ n. (pl. **calves** /kɑːvz/) 1 a young bovine animal, used esp. of domestic cattle. 2 the young of other animals, e.g. elephant, deer, and whale. 3 Naut. a floating piece of ice detached from an iceberg. □ **calf-love** romantic attachment or affection between adolescents. **in** (or **with**) **calf** (of a cow) pregnant. □□ **calfhood** n. **calfish** adj. **calflike** adj. [OE cælf f. WG]

calf[2] /kɑːf/ n. (pl. **calves** /kɑːvz/) the fleshy hind part of the human leg below the knee. □□ **-calved** /kɑːvd/ adj. (in comb.). [ME f. ON kálfi, of unkn. orig.]

calfskin /'kɑːfskɪn/ n. calf-leather, esp. in bookbinding and shoemaking.

Calgary /'kælgərɪ/ a city in southern Alberta in SW Canada, situated to the east of the Rocky Mountains, on the edge of a rich agricultural and stock-raising area; pop. (1986) 636,100; metropolitan area pop. 671,300. Originally known as Fort Brisebois, Calgary was established in 1875 as a fort of the

Northwest Mounted Police. The Calgary Stampede, inaugurated in 1912, is an annual rodeo.

Cali /'kɑːliː/ an industrial city and transportation centre in western Colombia, capital of the Valle del Cauca department; pop. (1985) 1,350,550.

calibrate /'kælɪˌbreɪt/ v.tr. 1 mark (a gauge) with a standard scale of readings. 2 correlate the readings of (an instrument) with a standard. 3 determine the calibre of (a gun). 4 determine the correct capacity or value of. □□ **calibration** /-'breɪʃ(ə)n/ n. **calibrator** n. [CALIBRE + -ATE³]

calibre /'kælɪbə(r)/ n. (US **caliber**) 1 a the internal diameter of a gun or tube. b the diameter of a bullet or shell. 2 strength or quality of character; ability, importance (we need someone of your calibre). □□ **calibred** adj. (also in comb.). [F calibre or It. calibro, f. Arab. ḳālib mould]

caliche /kə'liːtʃɪ/ n. 1 a mineral deposit of gravel, sand, and nitrates, esp. Chile saltpetre, found in dry areas of America. 2 = CALCRETE. [Amer. Sp.]

calico /'kælɪˌkoʊ/ n. & adj. —n. (pl. **-oes** or US **-os**) 1 a cotton cloth, esp. plain white or unbleached. 2 US a printed cotton fabric. —adj. 1 made of calico. 2 US multicoloured, piebald. [earlier calicut f. Calicut in India]

Calicut /'kælɪˌkʌt/ a seaport in Kerala in SW India, on the Malabar coast; pop. (1981) 546,000.

Calif. abbr. California.

California /ˌkælɪ'fɔːnɪə/ a State on the Pacific coast of the US, ceded by Mexico in 1848; pop. (est. 1985) 23,667,950. The discovery of gold there in the same year led to a rapid influx of settlers. California became the 31st State of the US in 1850; capital, Sacramento. □ **Lower California** see BAJA CALIFORNIA. □□ **Californian** adj. & n.

californium /ˌkælɪ'fɔːnɪəm/ n. Chem. an artificially made transuranic radioactive metallic element, first obtained in 1950 by bombarding curium with helium ions. It is now used in industry and medicine as a source of neutrons. ¶ Symb.: **Cf**; atomic number 98. [CALIFORNIA (where it was first made) + -IUM]

Caligula /kə'lɪgjʊlə/ the nickname (lit. 'baby boot') of the Roman emperor Gaius, given to him as an infant by the soldiers on account of the military boots which he wore while in camp on the Rhine with his parents Germanicus and Agrippina. (See GAIUS.)

caliper var. of CALLIPER.

caliph /'keɪlɪf, 'kæl-/ n. esp. hist. the chief Muslim civil and religious ruler, regarded as the successor of Muhammad. (See below.) □□ **caliphate** n. [ME f. OF caliphe f. Arab. ḳalīfa successor]
The first caliph (Abu Bakr), who had been one of the Prophet Muhammad's earliest converts and most devoted disciples, was instituted by acclamation of the small Muslim community following the death of Muhammad in AD 632. He and the following three caliphs had had personal links with the Prophet and were dedicated to developing the community along the path he had marked out, being responsible for implementation of the precepts of Islamic rule and legislation; this also entailed military leadership as the community expanded across and beyond the Arabian Sea. Subsequently the caliphate became a hereditary position with the establishment of the Ummayyad and Abbasid dynasties (respectively 661–750 and 750–945), with the latter ruling in Baghdad until 1258 and then in Egypt until the Ottoman conquest (1517), though by the 11th c. most of the caliph's authority had been passed to a hierarchy of officials. The title was then held by the Ottoman sultans until the nationalist revolution of 1922, and the caliphate was abolished by Atatürk in 1924.

calisthenics var. of CALLISTHENICS.

calk US var. of CAULK.

call /kɔːl/ v. & n. —v. 1 intr. **a** (often foll. by out) cry, shout; speak loudly. **b** (of a bird or animal) emit its characteristic note or cry. **2** tr. communicate or converse with by telephone or radio. **3** tr. **a** bring to one's presence by calling; summon (will you call the children?). **b** arrange for (a person or thing) to come or be present (called a taxi). **4** intr. (often foll. by at, in, on) pay a brief visit (called at the house; called in to see you; come and call on me). **5** tr. **a** order

to take place; fix a time for (called a meeting). **b** direct to happen; announce (call a halt). **6 a** intr. require one's attention or consideration (duty calls). **b** tr. urge, invite, nominate (call to the bar). **7** tr. name; describe as (call her Della). **8** tr. consider; regard or estimate as (I call that silly). **9** tr. rouse from sleep (call me at 8). **10** intr. guess the outcome of tossing a coin etc. **11** intr. (foll. by for) order, require, demand (called for silence). **12** tr. (foll. by over) read out (a list of names to determine those present). **13** intr. (foll. by on, upon) invoke; appeal to; request or require (called on us to be quiet). **14** tr. Cricket (of an umpire) disallow a ball from (a bowler). **15** tr. Cards specify (a suit or contract) in bidding. **16** tr. Sc. drive (an animal, vehicle, etc.). —n. **1** a shout or cry; an act of calling. **2 a** the characteristic cry of a bird or animal. **b** an imitation of this. **c** an instrument for imitating it. **3** a brief visit (paid them a call). **4 a** an act of telephoning. **b** a telephone conversation. **5 a** an invitation or summons to appear or be present. **b** an appeal or invitation (from a specific source or discerned by a person's conscience etc.) to follow a certain profession, set of principles, etc. **6** (foll. by for, or to + infin.) a duty, need, or occasion (no call to be rude; no call for violence). **7** (foll. by for, on) a demand (not much call for it these days; a call on one's time). **8** a signal on a bugle etc.; a signalling-whistle. **9** Stock Exch. an option of buying stock at a fixed price at a given date. **10** Cards **a** a player's right or turn to make a bid. **b** a bid made. □ **at call** = on call. **call away** divert, distract. **call-box** a public telephone box or kiosk. **call-boy** a theatre attendant who summons actors when needed on stage. **call down 1** invoke. **2** reprimand. **call forth** elicit. **call-girl** a prostitute who accepts appointments by telephone. **call in** tr. **1** withdraw from circulation. **2** seek the advice or services of. **calling-card** US = visiting-card. **call in** (or **into**) **question** dispute; doubt the validity of. **call into play** give scope for; make use of. **call a person names** abuse a person verbally. **call off 1** cancel (an arrangement etc.). **2** order (an attacker or pursuer) to desist. **call of nature** a need to urinate or defecate. **call out 1** summon (troops etc.) to action. **2** order (workers) to strike. **call-over 1** a roll-call. **2** reading aloud of a list of betting prices. **call the shots** (or **tune**) be in control; take the initiative. **call-sign** (or **-signal**) a broadcast signal identifying the radio transmitter used. **call to account** see ACCOUNT. **call to mind** recollect; cause one to remember. **call to order 1** request to be orderly. **2** declare (a meeting) open. **call up 1** reach by telephone. **2** imagine, recollect. **3** summon, esp. to serve in the army. **call-up** n. the act or process of calling up (sense 3). **on call 1** (of a doctor etc.) available if required but not formally on duty. **2** (of money lent) repayable on demand. **within call** near enough to be summoned by calling. [OE ceallian f. ON kalla]

calla /'kælə/ n. 1 (in full **calla lily**) = arum lily. 2 an aquatic plant, Calla palustris. [mod.L]

Callaghan /'kæləhən/, (Leonard) James (1912–), British Labour politician, who became Prime Minister (1976–9) on Harold Wilson's resignation. The government did not command a majority in the House of Commons and therefore entered into an agreement with the Liberal Party (the Lib-Lab Pact) in 1977–8. Its position was weakened by widespread strikes in the so-called 'winter of discontent' (1978–9) called in protest at attempts to restrain increases in wages, and in 1979 the Conservatives, under Margaret Thatcher, won the election with a large majority.

Callao /kəl'jaːəʊ/ the principal seaport of Peru; pop. (est. 1988) 318,300.

Callas /'kæləs/, Maria (real name Calageropoulos, 1923–77), operatic coloratura soprano, born in America of Greek parents. Her highly individual voice and great dramatic talent were responsible for the revival of works by Rossini, Bellini, and Donizetti, and her range included Wagnerian roles as well as the Italian repertory.

caller /'kɔːlə(r)/ n. 1 a person who calls, esp. one who pays a visit or makes a telephone call. 2 Austral. a racing commentator.

calligraphy /kə'lɪgrəfɪ/ n. 1 handwriting, esp. when fine or pleasing. 2 the art of handwriting. □□ **calligrapher** n. **calligraphic** /-'græfɪk/ adj. **calligraphist** n. [Gk kalligraphia f. kallos beauty]

Callimachus /kəˈlɪməkəs/ (c. 305–c. 240 BC) Hellenistic poet and scholar, originally from Cyrene, who worked in the great library at Alexandria. His scholarly works included a vast critical catalogue of previous Greek literature. As a poet he exemplified a new ideal of short or episodic poetry, self-conscious, highly-polished, and learnedly allusive.

calling /ˈkɔːlɪŋ/ n. **1** a profession or occupation. **2** an inwardly felt call or summons; a vocation.

Calliope /kəˈlaɪəpɪ/ Gk & Rom. Mythol. the Muse of epic poetry. [Gk, = beautiful-voiced]

calliope /kəˈlaɪəpɪ/ n. US a keyboard instrument resembling an organ, with a set of steam whistles producing musical notes. [CALLIOPE]

calliper /ˈkælɪpə(r)/ n. & v. (also **caliper**) —n. **1** (in pl.) (also **calliper compasses**) compasses with bowed legs for measuring the diameter of convex bodies, or with out-turned points for measuring internal dimensions. **2** (in full **calliper splint**) a metal splint to support the leg. —v.tr. measure with callipers. [app. var. of CALIBRE]

callisthenics /ˌkælɪsˈθenɪks/ n.pl. (also **calisthenics**) gymnastic exercises to achieve bodily fitness and grace of movement. □□ **callisthenic** adj. [Gk kallos beauty + sthenos strength]

callop /ˈkæləp/ n. Austral. a gold-coloured freshwater fish, Plectroplites ambiguus, used as food. Also called golden perch. [Aboriginal]

callosity /kəˈlɒsɪtɪ/ n. (pl. **-ies**) a hard thick area of skin usu. occurring in parts of the body subject to pressure or friction. [F callosité or L callositas (as CALLOUS)]

callous /ˈkæləs/ adj. & n. —adj. **1** unfeeling, insensitive. **2** (of skin) hardened or hard. —n. = CALLUS 1. □□ **callously** adv. (in sense 1 of adj.). **callousness** n. [ME f. L callosus (as CALLUS) or F calleux]

callow /ˈkæləʊ/ adj. inexperienced, immature. □□ **callowly** adv. **callowness** n. [OE calu]

calluna /kəˈluːnə/ n. any common heather of the genus Calluna, native to Europe and N. Africa. [mod.L f. Gk kallunō beautify f. kallos beauty]

callus /ˈkæləs/ n. **1** a hard thick area of skin or tissue. **2** a hard tissue formed round bone ends after a fracture. **3** Bot. a new protective tissue formed over a wound. [L]

calm /kɑːm/ adj., n., & v. —adj. **1** tranquil, quiet, windless (a calm sea; a calm night). **2** (of a person or disposition) settled; not agitated (remained calm throughout the ordeal). **3** self-assured, confident (his calm assumption that we would wait). —n. **1** a state of being calm; stillness, serenity. **2** a period without wind or storm. —v.tr. & intr. (often foll. by down) make or become calm. □ **Calms of Cancer** a belt of high pressure surrounding the earth around latitudes 30°–35°N. **calms of Capricorn** a similar belt 30°–35°S. □□ **calmly** adv. **calmness** n. [ME ult. f. LL cauma f. Gk kauma heat]

calmative /ˈkælmətɪv, ˈkɑːm-/ adj. & n. Med. —adj. tending to calm or sedate. —n. a calmative drug etc.

calomel /ˈkæləˌmel/ n. a compound of mercury, esp. when used medicinally as a cathartic. [mod.L perh. f. Gk kalos beautiful + melas black]

Calor gas /ˈkælə/ n. propr. liquefied butane gas stored under pressure in containers for domestic use and used as a substitute for mains gas. [L calor heat]

caloric /ˈkælərɪk/ adj. & n. —adj. of heat or calories. —n. hist. a supposed material form or cause of heat. [F calorique f. L calor heat]

calorie /ˈkælərɪ/ n. (also **calory**) (pl. **-ies**) a unit of quantity of heat: **1** (in full **small calorie**) the amount needed to raise the temperature of 1 gram of water through 1 °C. ¶ Abbr.: **cal**. **2** (in full **large calorie**) the amount needed to raise the temperature of 1 kilogram of water through 1 °C, often used to measure the energy value of foods. ¶ Abbr.: **Cal**. [F, arbitr. f. L calor heat + -ie]

calorific /ˌkæləˈrɪfɪk/ adj. producing heat. □ **calorific value** the amount of heat produced by a specified quantity of fuel, food, etc. □□ **calorifically** adv. [L calorificus f. calor heat]

calorimeter /ˌkæləˈrɪmɪtə(r)/ n. any of various instruments for measuring quantity of heat, esp. to find calorific values. □□ **calorimetric** /-ˈmetrɪk/ adj. **calorimetry** n. [L calor heat + -METER]

calory var. of CALORIE.

calque /kælk/ n. Philol. = loan-translation. [F, = copy, tracing f. calquer trace ult. f. L calcare tread]

caltrop /ˈkæltrəp/ n. (also **caltrap**) **1** hist. a four-spiked iron ball thrown on the ground to impede cavalry horses. **2** Heraldry a representation of this. **3** any creeping plant of the genus Tribulus, with woody carpels usu. having hard spines. [(sense 3) OE calcatrippe f. med.L calcatrippa: (senses 1–2) ME f. OF chauchetrape f. chauchier tread, trappe trap: ult. the same word]

calumet /ˈkæljʊˌmet/ n. a N. American Indian peace-pipe. [F, ult. f. L calamus reed]

calumniate /kəˈlʌmnɪˌeɪt/ v.tr. slander. □□ **calumniation** /-ˈeɪʃ(ə)n/ n. **calumniator** n. **calumniatory** adj. [L calumniari]

calumny /ˈkæləmnɪ/ n. & v. —n. (pl. **-ies**) **1** slander; malicious representation. **2** an instance of this. —v.tr. (**-ies**, **-ied**) slander. □□ **calumnious** adj. [L calumnia]

calvados /ˈkælvəˌdɒs/ n. an apple brandy. [Calvados in France]

Calvary /ˈkælvərɪ/ n. **1** the place (just outside ancient Jerusalem) where Christ was crucified. **2** a representation of the Crucifixion. [ME f. LL calvaria skull, transl. Gk golgotha, Aram. gûlgûltâ (Matt. 27: 33)]

calve /kɑːv/ v. **1 a** intr. give birth to a calf. **b** tr. (esp. in passive) give birth to (a calf). **2** tr. (also absol.) (of an iceberg) break off or shed (a mass of ice). [OE calfian]

calves pl. of CALF¹, CALF².

Calvin /ˈkælvɪn/, John (1509–64), French Protestant theologian, the most important of the second generation of Reformers. Embracing Protestantism, he fled France, going first to Basle, where in 1536 he published the first edition of the Institutes of the Christian Religion, his systematic presentation of reformed Christianity, which was revised and extended throughout his life. This he tried to put into practice, first in Geneva, then in Strasbourg, then again in Geneva from 1541 until his death. Unlike Luther, Calvin envisaged a complete restructuring of society in accordance with Christian principles, an ideal which in practice proved inhumanly austere. The private morality of citizens was monitored, the power of excommunication readily used, and Calvin did not shrink from torture and persecution, most notoriously in the case of Servetus, Spanish theologian and physician, executed for Trinitarian and Christological heresy. His influence on Protestantism, through the Institutes and his vast work of scholarly and theological commentary on the Scriptures, has been enormous. (See CALVINISM.)

Calvinism /ˈkælvɪˌnɪz(ə)m/ n. the theological system of John Calvin and his successors, which finds concise expression in the Institutes of the Christian Religion (final edition, 1559). It is presented as derived from the Scriptures, Old and New Testaments being of equal authority, the true interpretation of which is assured by the inner witness of the Holy Spirit. Luther's characteristic doctrine of justification by faith alone becomes an overriding emphasis on the grace of God, which culminates in the central place given to the doctrine of predestination. Later Calvinism (beginning with Calvin's successor in Geneva, Theodore Beza) is much occupied by this doctrine and the question of signs by which the elect can be known, and in the 17th c. there was division between strict Calvinists and so-called Arminians who played down the doctrine. For Calvin himself it is not all-important, being rather the final assurance of the Christian life, and he finds room for a powerful doctrine of the Eucharist which stresses the role of the Spirit in a way that recalls the Greek Fathers. □□ **Calvinist** n. **Calvinistic** /-ˈnɪstɪk/ adj. **Calvinistical** /-ˈnɪstɪk(ə)l/ adj. [F calvinisme or mod.L calvinismus]

calx /kælks/ n. (pl. **calces** /ˈkælsiːz/) **1** a powdery metallic oxide formed when an ore or mineral has been heated. **2** calcium oxide. [L calx calcis lime prob. f. Gk khalix pebble, limestone]

Calypso /kəˈlɪpsəʊ/ Gk legend a nymph who kept Odysseus on her island, Ogygia, for seven years. [Gk, = she who conceals]

æ cat ɑ: arm e bed ɜ: her ɪ sit iː see ɒ hot ɔ: saw ʌ run ʊ put uː too ə ago aɪ my

calypso /kə'lɪpsəʊ/ n. (pl. **-os**) a W. Indian song in African rhythm, usu. improvised on a topical theme. [20th c.: orig. unkn.]

calyx /'keɪlɪks, 'kæl-/ n. (also **calix**) (pl. **calyces** /-lɪˌsiːz/ or **calyxes**) 1 Bot. the sepals collectively, forming the protective layer of a flower in bud. 2 Biol. any cuplike cavity or structure. [L f. Gk kalux case of bud, husk: cf. kaluptō hide]

cam /kæm/ n. a projection on a rotating part in machinery, shaped to impart reciprocal or variable motion to the part in contact with it. [Du. kam comb: cf. Du. kamrad cog-wheel]

camaraderie /ˌkæmə'rɑːdərɪ/ n. mutual trust and sociability among friends. [F]

Camargue /kæ'mɑːg/, **the** a region of the Rhône delta in SE France, characterized by numerous shallow salt lagoons. The region is known for its white horses and as a nature reserve.

camarilla /ˌkæmə'rɪlə/ n. a cabal or clique. [Sp., dimin. of camara chamber]

Camb. abbr. Cambridge.

Cambay /kæm'beɪ/, **Gulf of** (also **Gulf of Khambat**) an inlet of the Arabian Sea on the Gujarat coast of western India, north of Bombay.

camber /'kæmbə(r)/ n. & v. —n. 1 the slightly convex or arched shape of the surface of a road, ship's deck, aircraft wing, etc. 2 the slight sideways inclination of the front wheel of a motor vehicle. —v. 1 intr. (of a surface) have a camber. 2 tr. give a camber to; build with a camber. [F cambre arched f. L camurus curved inwards]

Camberwell Beauty /'kæmbəˌwel/ n. a deep purple butterfly, Nymphalis antiopa, with yellow-bordered wings. [Camberwell in London]

cambium /'kæmbɪəm/ n. (pl. **cambia** /-bɪə/ or **cambiums**) Bot. a cellular plant tissue responsible for the increase in girth of stems and roots. □□ **cambial** adj. [med.L, = change, exchange]

Cambodia /kæm'bəʊdɪə/ a country in SE Asia between Thailand and the south of Vietnam; pop. (est. 1988) 6,685,600; official language, Khmer; capital, Phnomh Penh. The economy is chiefly agricultural, with rice as the staple crop; there is little industry. Formerly part of the Khmer empire (see KHMER), the country, known as Kampuchea 1976–89, was made a French protectorate in 1863 and remained under French influence until it became fully independent in 1953. Civil war in 1970–5 undermined and finally overthrew the government, but the victorious Communist Khmer Rouge regime was itself toppled by a Vietnamese invasion in 1979; the country continued to be plagued by intermittent guerrilla activity. Vietnam withdrew its forces in 1989 after international pressure to do so. A UN peace plan was accepted in 1990. □□ **Cambodian** adj. & n.

Cambrian /'kæmbrɪən/ adj. & n. —adj. 1 Welsh. 2 Geol. of or relating to the first period in the Palaeozoic era, following the Precambrian era and preceding the Ordovician period, lasting from about 590 to 505 million years ago. It was a time of widespread seas, and is the first period in which fossils (notably trilobites) can be used in geological dating. Rocks of this period were first recognized in Wales (whence its name). —n. this period or system. [L Cambria var. of Cumbria f. Welsh Cymry Welshman or Cymru Wales]

cambric /'kæmbrɪk/ n. a fine white linen or cotton fabric. [Kamerijk, Flem. form of Cambrai in N. France, where it was orig. made]

Cambridge /'keɪmbrɪdʒ/ a city in Cambridgeshire on the River Cam, the seat of a major English university organized as a federation of colleges; pop. (1981) 91,150. The first historical trace of Cambridge as a University (studium generale) is in 1209; a number of scholars migrated from Oxford to Cambridge in 1209–14 after a conflict with townsmen during which two or three students were hanged. Its first recognition came in a royal writ to the Chancellor of Cambridge in 1230. The first college, Peterhouse, was founded in 1284 and another nine followed in the 14th and 15th centuries, but the University did not achieve real eminence until the 16th-c. Reformation when it produced Tyndale, Coverdale, Cranmer, and Latimer. After a prolonged period of stagnation, Cambridge was revived by its growth as a

centre of scientific research in the late 19th and early 20th c. Women's colleges were founded in the mid-19th c., but women did not receive full academic status until 1948. In 1990–1 there were 10,382 undergraduates in residence (6,121 men, 4,261 women) and 3,171 postgraduates (2,123 men, 1,048 women). □ **Cambridge blue** pale blue.

Cambridgeshire /'keɪmbrɪdʒʃə(r)/ an east midland county of England; pop. (1981) 591,300; county town, Cambridge. —n. a handicap horse-race run annually at Newmarket in Suffolk, England, in early October, inaugurated in 1839.

Cambs. abbr. Cambridgeshire.

Cambyses /kæm'baɪsiːz/ (d. 522 BC) son of Cyrus, king of Persia 530–522 BC. His main achievement was the conquest of Egypt in 525 BC.

camcorder /'kæmˌkɔːdə(r)/ n. a combined video camera and sound recorder. [camera + recorder]

came past of COME.

camel /'kæm(ə)l/ n. 1 either of two kinds of large cud-chewing mammals having slender cushion-footed legs and one hump (**Arabian camel**, Camelus dromedarius) or two humps (**Bactrian camel**, Camelus bactrianus). 2 a fawn colour. 3 an apparatus for providing additional buoyancy to ships etc. □ **camel** (or **camel's**) **-hair 1** the hair of a camel. 2 a a fine soft hair used in artists' brushes. b a fabric made of this. [OE f. L camelus f. Gk kamēlos, of Semitic orig.]

cameleer /ˌkæmə'lɪə(r)/ n. a camel-driver.

camellia /kə'miːlɪə/ n. any evergreen shrub of the genus Camellia, native to E. Asia, with shiny leaves and showy flowers. [J. Camellus or Kamel, 17th-c. Jesuit botanist]

camelopard /'kæmələˌpɑːd, kə'mel-/ n. archaic a giraffe. [L camelopardus f. Gk kamēlopardalis (as CAMEL, PARD)]

Camelot /'kæmɪˌlɒt/ (in Arthurian legend) the place where King Arthur held his court, stated by Malory to be Winchester.

camelry /'kæməlrɪ/ n. (pl. **-ies**) troops mounted on camels.

Camembert /'kæməmˌbeə(r)/ n. a kind of soft creamy cheese, usu. with a strong flavour. [Camembert in N. France, where it was orig. made]

cameo /'kæmɪˌəʊ/ n. (pl. **-os**) 1 a a small piece of onyx or other hard stone carved in relief with a background of a different colour. b a similar relief design using other materials. 2 a a short descriptive literary sketch or acted scene. b a small character part in a play or film, usu. brief and played by a distinguished actor. [ME f. OF camahieu and med.L cammaeus]

camera /'kæmrə, -ərə/ n. 1 an apparatus for taking photographs, consisting of a lightproof box to hold light-sensitive film, a lens, and a shutter mechanism, either for still photographs or for motion-picture film. (See below and PHOTOGRAPHY.) 2 Telev. a piece of equipment which forms an optical image and converts it into electrical impulses for transmission or storage. □ **camera obscura** see separate entry. **camera-ready** Printing (of copy) in a form suitable for immediate photographic reproduction. **in camera 1** Law in a judge's private room. 2 privately; not in public. **on camera** (esp. of an actor or actress) being filmed or televised at a particular moment. [orig. = chamber f. L camera f. Gk kamara vault etc.]

The photographic camera consists essentially of a light-tight chamber fitted in front with a lens to focus an image of the object being photographed on to the light-sensitive film or plate at the rear; an aperture, closed by a shutter, admits light for the brief period needed for the image to register. Cameras were developed during the 19th c. and originally used metal and then glass plates with a sensitized coating. Later, flexible roll-film of coated celluloid was used, enabling cameras to be made much smaller and more portable, and the tendency towards miniaturization has continued. Reflex cameras originally used two lenses, one to give an image for viewing on a ground-glass screen, the other to focus the image on the film; single-lens reflex cameras achieve a similar result by a complex arrangement of reflecting mirrors. Developments in photoelectric devices have enabled highly automated systems of focusing and exposure to be introduced. The television camera contains an 'electron gun' that converts an image into an electrical signal which is amplified for transmission (see TELEVISION).

cameraman /ˈkæmrəmən/ n. (pl. **-men**) a person who operates a camera professionally, esp. in film-making or television.

camera obscura /əbˈskjʊərə/ n. an apparatus that uses a darkened box or room with an aperture for projecting an image of a distant object on a screen within. Aristotle was aware of the principle on which this depends, and early astronomers used a form of it to watch the solar eclipse. In the early 17th c. Johann Kepler used it to record astronomical phenomena, and artists to trace an accurate outline of a subject. By the 18th c. it had become a craze and both amateurs and professionals (such as Canaletto) were using it for topographical painting. The *camera lucida* (L, = light chamber) was a similar device using a prism, and was employed mainly in copying drawings. [L, = dark chamber]

Cameron Highlands /ˈkæmərən/ a hill resort in Malaysia, named after the surveyor, William Cameron, who mapped the area in 1885.

Cameroon /ˌkæməˈruːn/ a country on the west coast of Africa between Nigeria and Gabon; pop. (est. 1988) 10,532,000; official languages, French and English; capital, Yaoundé. From 1884 to 1916 the territory was a German protectorate; it was then administered under League of Nations, later UN, trusteeship, part by France and part by Britain. In 1960 French Cameroons became an independent republic, to be joined in 1961 by part of the British Cameroons; the remainder became part of Nigeria. The French and British halves of the territory at first had separate governments but in 1972 merged as a United Republic. □□ **Cameroonian** adj. & n.

camiknickers /ˈkæmɪˌnɪkəz/ n.pl. Brit. a one-piece close-fitting undergarment worn by women. [CAMISOLE + KNICKERS]

camisole /ˈkæmɪˌsəʊl/ n. an under-bodice, usu. embroidered. [F f. It. *camiciola* or Sp. *camisola*: see CHEMISE]

camomile /ˈkæməˌmaɪl/ n. (also **chamomile**) any aromatic plant of the genus *Anthemis* or *Matricaria*, with daisy-like flowers. □ **camomile tea** an infusion of its dried flowers used as a tonic. [ME f. OF *camomille* f. LL *camomilla* or *chamomilla* f. Gk *khamaimēlon* earth-apple (from the apple-smell of its flowers)]

Camorra /kəˈmɒrə/ n. a secret society of lawless malcontents that evolved and became powerful in Naples and Neapolitan cities in the 19th c. Its members were involved in criminal activities of various kinds. [It. *camorra* smock-frock]

camouflage /ˈkæməˌflɑːʒ/ n. & v. —n. **1 a** the disguising of military vehicles, aircraft, ships, artillery, and installations by painting them or covering them to make them blend with their surroundings. **b** such a disguise. **2** the natural colouring of an animal which enables it to blend in with its surroundings. **3** a misleading or evasive precaution or expedient. —v.tr. hide or disguise by means of camouflage. [F f. *camoufler* disguise f. It. *camuffare* disguise, deceive]

camp¹ /kæmp/ n. & v. —n. **1 a** a place where troops are lodged or trained. **b** the military life (*court and camp*). **2** temporary overnight lodging in tents etc. in the open. **3 a** temporary accommodation of various kinds, usu. consisting of huts or tents, for detainees, homeless persons, and other emergency use. **b** a complex of buildings for holiday accommodation, usu. with extensive recreational facilities. **4** an ancient fortified site or its remains. **5** the adherents of a particular party or doctrine regarded collectively (*the Labour camp was jubilant*). **6** *S.Afr.* a portion of veld fenced off for pasture on farms. **7** *Austral.* & *NZ* an assembly place of sheep or cattle. —v.intr. **1** set up or spend time in a camp (in senses 1 and 2 of n.). **2** (often foll. by *out*) lodge in temporary quarters or in the open. **3** *Austral.* & *NZ* (of sheep or cattle) flock together esp. for rest. □ **camp-bed** a folding portable bed of a kind used in camping. **camp-fire** an open-air fire in a camp etc. **camp-follower 1** a civilian worker in a military camp. **2** a disciple or adherent. **camp-site** a place for camping. □□ **camping** n. [F f. It. *campo* f. L *campus* level ground]

camp² /kæmp/ adj., n., & v. colloq. —adj. **1** affected, effeminate. **2** homosexual. **3** done in an exaggerated way for effect. —n. a

camp manner or style. —v.intr. & tr. behave or do in a camp way. □ **camp it up** overact; behave affectedly. □□ **campy** adj. (**campier**, **campiest**). **campily** adv. **campiness** n. [20th c.: orig. uncert.]

campaign /kæmˈpeɪn/ n. & v. —n. **1** an organized course of action for a particular purpose, esp. to arouse public interest (e.g. before a political election). **2 a** a series of military operations in a definite area or to achieve a particular objective. **b** military service in the field (*on campaign*). —v.intr. conduct or take part in a campaign. □□ **campaigner** n. [F *campagne* open country f. It. *campagna* f. LL *campania*]

Campania /kæmˈpeɪnɪə/ a region of west central Italy; capital, Naples.

campanile /ˌkæmpəˈniːlɪ/ n. a bell-tower (usu. free-standing), esp. in Italy. [It. f. *campana* bell]

campanology /ˌkæmpəˈnɒlədʒɪ/ n. **1** the study of bells. **2** the art or practice of bell-ringing. □□ **campanologer** n. **campanological** /-nəˈlɒdʒɪk(ə)l/ adj. **campanologist** n. [mod.L *campanologia* f. LL *campana* bell]

campanula /kæmˈpænjʊlə/ n. any plant of the genus *Campanula*, with bell-shaped usu. blue, purple, or white flowers. Also called BELLFLOWER. [mod.L dimin. of L *campana* bell]

campanulate /kæmˈpænjʊlət/ adj. Bot. & Zool. bell-shaped.

Campbell¹ /ˈkæmb(ə)l/, Donald Malcolm (1921–67), son of Sir Malcolm Campbell and holder of the world water-speed record (1964), who also established a land-speed record of 403 m.p.h. (649 k.p.h.) at Lake Eyre, Australia, in 1964. His boats and cars were (like his father's) named *Bluebird*. He was killed in an attempt to achieve a water speed of 300 m.p.h. (482 k.p.h) on Coniston Water in England.

Campbell² /ˈkæmb(ə)l/, Sir Malcolm (1885–1948), English racing-driver, holder of the world land-speed record until 1950. In 1935 he became the first man to exceed 300 m.p.h. (483 k.p.h.), driving his car *Bluebird* on Bonneville Flats in Utah in the US. He also achieved the water-speed record in his boat of the same name in 1939.

Campbell³ /ˈkæmbəl/, (Ignatius) Roy(ston Dunnachie) (1901–57), South African poet, whose works include *The Flaming Terrapin* (1924), an exuberant allegorical narrative of the Flood, and *The Wayzgoose* (1928), a satire on South African life. His first autobiography *Broken Record* (1934) and the long poem *Flowering Rifle* (1939) show strong Fascist sympathies. During the Second World War he fought in Africa, and in 1941 published *Sons of the Mistral*, a selection of his best poems.

Campbell⁴ /ˈkæmb(ə)l/, Mrs Patrick (1865–1940), née Beatrice Stella Tanner, English actress, renowned for her eccentricity. She created the parts of Paula in *The Second Mrs Tanqueray* (1893), Agnes in *The Notorious Mrs Ebbsmith* (1895), both by Pinero, and the title role in *Magda* (1896), the English version of Sudermann's *Heimat*. George Bernard Shaw wrote the part of Eliza Doolittle in *Pygmalion* (1914) for her and exchanged letters with her over a long period.

Campbell⁵ /ˈkæmb(ə)l/, Thomas (1777–1844), Scottish poet, the son of a Glasgow merchant. He published *The Pleasures of Hope* (1799) and *Gertrude of Wyoming* (1809) among other volumes of verse, and is now chiefly remembered for his patriotic lyrics such as 'The Battle of Hohenlinden' and 'Ye Mariners of England', and for his ballads.

Campbell-Bannerman /ˌkæmbəlˈbænəmən/, Sir Henry (1836–1908), British Liberal statesman, Prime Minister 1905–8. His brief ministry, which ended with his resignation and death, saw the grant of self-government to the defeated Boer republics of the Transvaal (1906) and the Orange River Colony (1907), the passing of the important 1906 Trade Disputes Act which exempted Trade Unions from certain liabilities in connection with strikes, and the entente with Russia (1907).

Camp David the retreat in the Appalachian Mountains, Maryland, of the President of the US.

Campeachy wood /kæmˈpiːtʃɪ/ n. = LOGWOOD. [*Campeche* in Mexico, from where it was first exported]

Campeche /kæmˈpeɪtʃeɪ/ **1** a state in SE Mexico, on the Yucatán peninsula; pop. (est. 1988) 593,999. **2** its capital city, a seaport

b but   d dog   f few   g get   h he   j yes   k cat   l leg   m man   n no   p pen   r red   s sit   t top   v voice

on the Bay of Campeche in the Gulf of Mexico; pop. (est. 1979) 108,680.

camper /ˈkæmpə(r)/ n. **1** a person who camps out or lives temporarily in a tent, hut, etc., esp. on holiday. **2** a large motor vehicle with accommodation for camping out.

camphor /ˈkæmfə(r)/ n. a white translucent crystalline volatile substance with aromatic smell and bitter taste, used to make celluloid and in medicine. □□ **camphoric** /-ˈfɒrɪk/ adj. [ME f. OF camphore or med.L camphora f. Arab. kāfūr f. Skr. karpūram]

camphorate /ˈkæmfəˌreɪt/ v.tr. impregnate or treat with camphor.

Campion /ˈkæmpɪən/, St Edmund (1540–81), Jesuit priest and martyr. Ordained deacon of the Church of England but with Roman Catholic sympathies, he went abroad, becoming a Catholic and a Jesuit priest (1578). He was a member of the first Jesuit mission to England (1580). In 1581 he was arrested, charged with conspiracy against the Crown, tortured, and executed at Tyburn.

campion /ˈkæmpɪən/ n. **1** any plant of the genus *Silene*, with usu. pink or white notched flowers. **2** any of several similar cultivated plants of the genus *Lychnis*. [perh. f. obs. *campion* f. OF, = CHAMPION: transl. of Gk *lukhnis stephanōmatikē* a plant used for (champions') garlands]

campus /ˈkæmpəs/ n. (pl. **campuses**) **1** the grounds of a university or college. **2** esp. US a university, esp. as a teaching institution. [L, = field]

CAMRA /ˈkæmrə/ abbr. Campaign for Real Ale.

camshaft /ˈkæmʃɑːft/ n. a shaft with one or more cams attached to it.

Camus /kæˈmuː/, Albert (1913–60), French novelist, dramatist, and essayist, born in Algeria, the son of a farm labourer. He made his name as a journalist during the Second World War and became editor of the left-wing daily *Combat* (1944–7). Through his novels he illustrated the philosophy of the absurd, notably in *L'Étranger* (*The Outsider*, 1942) and *La Peste* (*The Plague*, 1947) and in his essays, *Le Mythe de Sisyphe* (*The Myth of Sisyphus*, 1942) and *L'Homme révolté* (*The Rebel*, 1951). He wrote several plays including *Caligula* (1945) and adaptations for the stage. In 1957 he was awarded the Nobel Prize for literature, and by the time of his death at the age of 46 he had achieved international recognition.

camwood /ˈkæmwʊd/ n. a hard red wood from a tree *Pterocarpus soyauxii*, native to W. Africa. [perh. f. Temne]

can¹ /kæn, kən/ v.aux. (3rd sing. present **can**; past **could** /kʊd/) (foll. by infin. without *to*, or absol.; present and past only in use) **1 a** be able to; know how to (*I can run fast; can he?; can you speak German?*). **b** be potentially capable of (*you can do it if you try*). **2** be permitted to (*can we go to the party?*). [OE *cunnan* know]

can² /kæn/ n. & v. —n. **1** a metal vessel for liquid. **2** a tin container in which food or drink is hermetically sealed to enable storage over long periods. **3** (prec. by *the*) sl. **a** prison (*sent to the can*). **b** US lavatory. —v.tr. (**canned, canning**) **1** put or preserve in a can. (See below.) **2** record on film or tape for future use. □ **can of worms** colloq. a complicated problem. **can-opener** n. a device for opening cans (in sense 2 of n.). **in the can** colloq. completed, ready (orig. of filmed or recorded material). □□ **canner** n. [OE *canne*]

Canning was introduced in the 19th c. The principle on which it is based was devised by a French confectioner, Nicolas Appert (1810), as a means of supplying preserved food for French troops. Food was heated to a high temperature in glass jars which were then sealed until use. The reason for its success was not known until the work of Louis Pasteur: heat destroyed the micro-organisms present in food, and sealing prevented others from entering. In the same year the technique was applied in England, using glass or metal containers, and tin-coated steel containers became widely used. Lids were soldered until the early 20th c., when a method was devised of sealing the cover to the can. The invention of tinned food considerably preceded the equally important invention of the tin-opener: opening was by means of a hammer and chisel until a domestic implement was devised in the mid-19th c.

Can. abbr. Canada; Canadian.

Cana /ˈkeɪnə/ a small town in Galilee in northern Israel, north-east of Nazareth, where Christ is said to have performed his first miracle by changing water into wine during a marriage feast (John 2: 1–11).

Canaan /ˈkeɪnən/ **1** the land, later known as Palestine, which the Israelites gradually conquered and occupied during the latter part of the 2nd millennium BC. The earliest known mention of the country by this name occurs in the Mari documents of the 18th c. BC. **2** a promised land. **3** heaven. □□ **Canaanite** /-naɪt/ adj. & n. [eccl.L f. eccl.Gk *Khanaan* f. Heb. *kʰnaʿan*]

Canada /ˈkænədə/ the second-largest country in the world, a member State of the Commonwealth, covering the entire northern half of North America with the exception of Alaska; pop. (1986) 25,354,000; official languages, English and French; capital, Ottawa. Both agriculture and industry are highly developed, and there are vast mineral resources. The Vikings established a settlement on the NE tip of Newfoundland c. AD 1000. John Cabot reached the east coast in 1497, Jacques Cartier explored the St Lawrence in 1535, and Samuel de Champlain founded Quebec in 1608 and penetrated the interior (1609–16). Eastern Canada was colonized by the French mainly in the 17th c., with the British emerging as the ruling colonial power after the Seven Years War (Treaty of Paris, 1763). Canada became a federation of provinces in 1867, and the last step in the attainment of its legal independence from the UK was taken with the signing of the Constitution Act of 1982. Through the late 19th and early 20th centuries the vast Canadian West was gradually opened up, but the country remains sparsely populated for its size. Although periodically affected by the dissatisfactions of part of the French-speaking minority, Canada has generally remained both stable and prosperous. □ **Canada balsam** *Biol.* a yellow resin obtained from the balsam fir and used for mounting preparations on microscope slides (its refractive index being similar to that of glass). **Canada goose** a wild goose, *Branta canadensis*, of N. America, with a brownish-grey body and white cheeks and breast.

Canadian /kəˈneɪdɪən/ n. & adj. —n. **1** a native or national of Canada. **2** a person of Canadian descent. —adj. of or relating to Canada. □ **Canadian Pacific Railway** the first transcontinental railway in Canada, completed in 1885. **Canadian shield** see SHIELD.

canaille /kəˈnɑːɪ/ n. the rabble; the populace. [F f. It. *canaglia* pack of dogs f. *cane* dog]

canal /kəˈnæl/ n. **1** an artificial waterway for inland navigation or irrigation. (See below.) **2** any of various tubular ducts in a plant or animal, for carrying food, liquid, or air. **3** *Astron.* any of a network of apparent linear markings on the planet Mars, which are observed from earth but not at close range. □ **canal boat** a long narrow boat for use on canals. **canal ray** a beam of positive ions moving through a bored hole in the cathode of a high-vacuum tube. [ME f. OF (earlier *chanel*) f. L *canalis* or It. *canale*]

Examples of irrigation canals date from the 5th millennium BC in Iraq. Early canals are also to be found in Egypt and China, where the Grand Canal, 1,700 km (1,060 miles) in length, begun in 109 BC, was completed in 1327. Many notable canals are designed to shorten sea passages: in France the Canal du Midi joined the Atlantic and Mediterranean in 1681, the Suez Canal joined the latter to the Red Sea in 1869, and in 1914 the Panama Canal joined the Atlantic and Pacific Oceans. The great advantage of inland water transport is its economy, due to the low resistance to movement of vessels and the level nature of the route. (Where changes in level are needed some form of lock is generally used.) In England canals were the arteries of the Industrial Revolution, greatly reducing the cost of transport to below that of land transport over inadequate roads. Brindley and Telford were the great canal builders between 1760 and 1840, by which time a network of some 6,800 km (4,250 miles) of canal was in being. Thereafter canal use declined in Britain, through the rise in railways and the restricted size of the early canals, but in Europe and North America canal use has grown in route length and in size of vessels, while in the late 20th c. canals in Britain have become increasingly popular recreational waterways. The Rhine, Rhône, and Danube will shortly be linked, while the Great

---

w we z zoo ʃ she ʒ decision θ thin ð this ŋ ring x loch tʃ chip dʒ jar (see over for vowels)

Lakes are accessible to ocean-going vessels by means of the St Lawrence Seaway.

Canaletto /ˌkænəˈletəʊ/ Giovanni Antonio Canale (1697–1768), Venetian view painter, especially popular with the English aristocracy, who commissioned his paintings of the Grand Canal and the festivals of Venice as mementoes of their Grand Tour. His early work is dramatic and freely handled, reflecting his training as a theatrical scene painter, but c.1730 he changed to a smoother more precise style, almost photographic in its topographical accuracy. From 1746 to 1755 Canaletto was in England, in a search for patronage which was of limited success, partly owing to the mannered mechanical style of his later work. His most important patron, Joseph Smith (British consul in Venice), sold a large collection of Canaletto's paintings and drawings to George III, and they remain in the British Royal Collection.

canalize /ˈkænəlaɪz/ v.tr. (also **-ise**) **1** make a canal through. **2** convert (a river) into a canal. **3** provide with canals. **4** give the desired direction or purpose to. □□ **canalization** /-ˈzeɪʃ(ə)n/ n. [F canaliser: see CANAL]

canapé /ˈkænəpɪ/ n. **1** a small piece of bread or pastry with a savoury on top, often served as an hors-d'œuvre. **2** a sofa. [F]

canard /kəˈnɑːd, ˈkænɑːd/ n. **1** an unfounded rumour or story. **2** an extra surface attached to an aeroplane forward of the main lifting surface, for extra stability or control. [F, = duck]

Canarese var. of KANARESE.

canary /kəˈneərɪ/ n. (pl. **-ies**) **1** any of various small finches of the genus *Serinus*, esp. *S. canaria*, a songbird native to the Canary Islands, with mainly yellow plumage. **2** hist. a sweet wine from the Canary Islands. □ **canary-coloured** coloured canary yellow. **canary creeper** a climbing plant, *Tropaeolum peregrinum*, with flowers of bright yellow deeply toothed petals which give the appearance of a small bird in flight. **canary grass** a Mediterranean plant *Phalaris canariensis*, grown as a crop plant for bird seed. **canary yellow** bright yellow. [Canary Islands f. F *Canarie* f. Sp. & L *Canaria* f. *canis* dog, one of the islands being noted in Roman times for large dogs]

Canary Islands /kəˈneərɪ/ (also **Canaries**) a group of islands, in Spanish possession since the 15th c., situated off the NW coast of Africa; pop. (1986) 1,614,900.

canasta /kəˈnæstə/ n. **1** a card-game using two packs and resembling rummy, the aim being to collect sets (or melds) of cards. **2** a set of seven cards in this game. [Sp., = basket]

canaster /kəˈnæstə(r)/ n. tobacco made from coarsely broken dried leaves. [orig. the container: Sp. *canastro* ult. f. Gk *kanastron*]

Canberra /ˈkænbərə/ the capital and seat of the federal government of Australia; pop. (1986) 285,800.

cancan /ˈkænkæn/ n. a lively stage-dance with high kicking, performed by women in long skirts and petticoats. Originally a decent and measured social dance invented by M. Masarié in 1830 as a variant of the quadrille, it appeared after 1844 in the French music-halls, developing there an increasingly uninhibited emphasis on the throwing up of the legs of the dancers and the display of their underwear, so that it was forbidden by the authorities. The best-known examples, however, are in Offenbach's operettas, notably *Orpheus in the Underworld*. [F]

cancel /ˈkæns(ə)l/ v. & n. —v. (**cancelled, cancelling**; US **canceled, canceling**) **1** tr. **a** withdraw or revoke (a previous arrangement). **b** discontinue (an arrangement in progress). **2** tr. obliterate or delete (writing etc.). **3** tr. mark or pierce (a ticket, stamp, etc.) to invalidate it. **4** tr. annul; make void; abolish. **5** (often foll. by *out*) **a** tr. (of one factor or circumstance) neutralize or counterbalance (another). **b** intr. (of two factors or circumstances) neutralize each other. **6** tr. Math. strike out (an equal factor) on each side of an equation or from the numerator and denominator of a fraction. —n. **1** a countermand. **2** the cancellation of a postage stamp. **3** Printing a new page or section inserted in a book to replace the original text, usu. to correct an error. **4** Mus. US a natural-sign. □□ **canceller** n. [ME f. F *canceller* f. L *cancellare* f. *cancelli* crossbars, lattice]

cancellate /ˈkænsɪlət/ adj. (also **cancellated** /-ˌleɪtɪd/) Biol. marked with crossing lines. [L *cancelli* lattice]

cancellation /ˌkænsəˈleɪʃ(ə)n/ n. **1** the act or an instance of cancelling or being cancelled. **2** something that has been cancelled, esp. a booking or reservation. [L *cancellatio* (as CANCEL)]

cancellous /ˈkænsɪləs/ adj. (of a bone) with pores. [L *cancelli* lattice]

Cancer /ˈkænsə(r)/ **1** a constellation, traditionally regarded as contained in the figure of a crab. It is most noted for its beautiful cluster of stars known as Praesepe or the Beehive, which appears as a misty patch of light to the naked eye, but was first resolved into individual stars by the telescope observations of Galileo. **b** the fourth sign of the zodiac (the Crab), which the sun enters at the summer solstice. —n. a person born when the sun is in this sign. □ **Calms of Cancer** see CALM. **Tropic of Cancer** see TROPIC. □□ **Cancerian** /-ˈsɪərɪən/ n. & adj. [ME f. L, = crab, cancer, after Gk *karkinos*]

cancer /ˈkænsə(r)/ n. **1 a** any malignant growth or tumour from an abnormal and uncontrolled division of body cells. **b** a disease caused by this. (See below.) **2** an evil influence or corruption spreading uncontrollably. □ **cancer stick** sl. a cigarette. □□ **cancerous** adj. [as CANCER]

Cancer is a disorder of the processes of growth, development, and repair during which cells undergo morphological and metabolic deviations from those inherent properties of the cells of the tissue of origin. Cancers result from the disruption in the control mechanisms normally exerted over cell reproduction and differentiation. A new growth of tissue arises spontaneously, is atypical in structure, loses or alters its normal biochemical characteristics, and follows an inexorable and purposeless growth pattern in which there is a failure of the normal control mechanisms to operate. As a consequence of these intrinsic cellular defects cancer cells do not conform to the restraints imposed on the proliferation of normal body cells. They do not form discrete isolated tumours but tend both to infiltrate neighbouring tissues and to spread to distant parts of the body, forming secondary growths or metastases. It is this disturbance of the fundamental cellular control processes, leading to the consequent disorder of cell behaviour, which characterizes cancer. As its aetiology is so imperfectly understood cancer defies definition and the above description does no more than detail in basic and general terms the abnormal changes underlying the cancerous process.

cancroid /ˈkæŋkrɔɪd/ adj. & n. —adj. **1** crablike. **2** resembling cancer. —n. a disease resembling cancer.

Cancún /kænˈkuːn/ a Caribbean resort in SE Mexico, on the NE coast of the Yucatán peninsula; pop. (1980) 27,500.

candela /kænˈdiːlə, -ˈdeɪlə/ n. the SI unit of luminous intensity (established in 1948 for international use; amended in 1967), the luminous intensity, in the perpendicular direction, of a surface of 1/600,000 square metre of a black body at the temperature of freezing platinum under a pressure of 101,325 newtons per square metre. ¶ Abbr.: **cd**. [L, = candle]

candelabrum /ˌkændɪˈlɑːbrəm/ n. (also **candelabra** /-brə/) (pl. **candelabra**, US **candelabrums, candelabras**) a large branched candlestick or lamp-holder. □ **candelabrum tree** a tropical E. African tree, *Euphorbia candelabrum*, with foliage shaped like a candelabrum. [L f. *candela* CANDLE]

candescent /kænˈdes(ə)nt/ adj. glowing with or as with white heat. □□ **candescence** n. [L *candēre* be white]

candid /ˈkændɪd/ adj. **1** frank; not hiding one's thoughts. **2** (of a photograph) taken informally, usu. without the subject's knowledge. □ **candid camera** a small camera for taking candid photographs. □□ **candidly** adv. **candidness** n. [F *candide* or L *candidus* white]

candida /ˈkændɪdə/ n. any yeastlike parasitic fungus of the genus *Candida*, esp. *C. albicans* causing thrush. [mod.L fem. of L *candidus*: see CANDID]

candidate /ˈkændɪdət, -ˌdeɪt/ n. **1** a person who seeks or is nominated for an office, award, etc. **2** a person or thing likely to gain some distinction or position. **3** a person entered for an examination. □□ **candidacy** n. **candidature** n. Brit. [F *candidat* or L *candidatus* white-robed (Roman candidates wearing white)]

candle /ˈkænd(ə)l/ n. & v. —n. **1** a cylinder or block of wax or tallow with a central wick, for giving light when burning. **2** = CANDLEPOWER. —*v.tr.* test (an egg) for freshness by holding it to the light. □ **cannot hold a candle to** cannot be compared with; is much inferior to. **not worth the candle** not justifying the cost or trouble. □□ **candler** *n*. [OE *candel* f. L *candela* f. *candēre* shine]

candlelight /ˈkænd(ə)lˌlaɪt/ *n*. **1** light provided by candles. **2** dusk.

Candlemas /ˈkænd(ə)lməs, -ˌmæs/ *n*. a feast with blessing of candles (2 Feb.), commemorating the Purification of the Virgin Mary and the presentation of Christ in the Temple. [OE *Candelmæsse* (as CANDLE, MASS²)]

candlepower /ˈkænd(ə)lˌpaʊə(r)/ *n*. a unit of luminous intensity.

candlestick /ˈkænd(ə)lstɪk/ *n*. a holder for one or more candles.

candlewick /ˈkænd(ə)lwɪk/ *n*. **1** a thick soft cotton yarn. **2** material made from this, usu. with a tufted pattern.

candour /ˈkændə(r)/ *n*. (*US* **candor**) candid behaviour or action; frankness. [F *candeur* or L *candor* whiteness]

C. & W. *abbr.* country-and-western.

candy /ˈkændɪ/ *n*. & *v*. —*n*. (*pl*. **-ies**) **1** (in full **sugar-candy**) sugar crystallized by repeated boiling and slow evaporation. **2** *US* sweets; a sweet. —*v.tr.* (**-ies, -ied**) (usu. as **candied** *adj*.) preserve by coating and impregnating with a sugar syrup (*candied fruit*). [F *sucre candi* candied sugar f. Arab. *ḳand* sugar]

candyfloss /ˈkændɪˌflɒs/ *n*. *Brit.* a fluffy mass of spun sugar wrapped round a stick.

candystripe /ˈkændɪˌstraɪp/ *n*. a pattern consisting of alternate stripes of white and a colour (usu. pink). □□ **candystriped** *adj*.

candytuft /ˈkændɪˌtʌft/ *n*. any of various plants of the genus *Iberis*, native to W. Europe, with white, pink, or purple flowers in tufts. [obs. *Candy* (*Candia* Crete) + TUFT]

cane /keɪn/ *n*. & *v*. —*n*. **1 a** the hollow jointed stem of giant reeds or grasses (*bamboo cane*). **b** the solid stem of slender palms (*malacca cane*). **2** = *sugar cane*. **3** a raspberry-cane. **4** material of cane used for wickerwork etc. **5 a** a cane used as a walking-stick or a support for a plant or an instrument of punishment. **b** any slender walking-stick. —*v.tr.* **1** beat with a cane. **2** weave cane into (a chair etc.). □ **cane-brake** *US* a tract of land overgrown with canes. **cane chair** a chair with a seat made of woven cane strips. **cane-sugar** sugar obtained from sugar-cane. **cane-trash** see TRASH. □□ **caner** *n*. (in sense 2 of *v*.). **caning** *n*. [ME f. OF f. L *canna* f. Gk *kanna*]

Canea /kəˈniːə/ (Greek **Khaniá** /xɑːˈnjɑː/) a port on the north coast of Crete, capital of the island from 1841 to 1971; pop. (1981) 47,340.

canine /ˈkeɪnaɪn, ˈkæn-/ *adj*. & *n*. —*adj*. **1** of a dog or dogs. **2** of or belonging to the family Canidae, including dogs, wolves, foxes, etc. —*n*. **1** a dog. **2** (in full **canine tooth**) a pointed tooth between the incisors and premolars. [ME f. *canin -ine* or f. L *caninus* f. *canis* dog]

canister /ˈkænɪstə(r)/ *n*. **1** a small container, usu. of metal and cylindrical, for storing tea etc. **2 a** a cylinder shot, tear-gas, etc., that explodes on impact. **b** such cylinders collectively. [L *canistrum* f. Gk f. *kanna* CANE]

canker /ˈkæŋkə(r)/ *n*. & *v*. —*n*. **1 a** a destructive fungus disease of trees and plants. **b** an open wound in the stem of a tree or plant. **2** *Zool*. an ulcerous ear disease of animals esp. cats and dogs. **3** *Med*. an ulceration esp. of the lips. **4** a corrupting influence. —*v.tr.* **1** consume with canker. **2** corrupt. **3** (as **cankered** *adj*.) soured, malignant, crabbed. □ **canker-worm** any caterpillar of various wingless moths which consume the buds and leaves of shade and fruit trees in N. America. □□ **cankerous** *adj*. [OE *cancer* & ONF *cancre*, OF *chancre* f. L *cancer* crab]

canna /ˈkænə/ *n*. any tropical plant of the genus *Canna* with bright flowers and ornamental leaves. [L: see CANE]

cannabis /ˈkænəbɪs/ *n*. **1** any hemp plant of the genus *Cannabis*, esp. Indian hemp. **2** a preparation of parts of this used as an intoxicant or hallucinogen. □ **cannabis resin** a sticky product, esp. from the flowering tops of the female cannabis plant. [L f. Gk]

canned /kænd/ *adj*. **1** pre-recorded (*canned laughter; canned music*). **2** supplied in a can (*canned beer*). **3** *sl*. drunk.

cannel /ˈkæn(ə)l/ *n*. (in full **cannel coal**) a bituminous coal burning with a bright flame. [16th c.: orig. N.Engl.]

cannelloni /ˌkænəˈləʊnɪ/ *n.pl*. tubes or rolls of pasta stuffed with meat or a vegetable mixture. [It. f. *cannello* stalk]

cannelure /ˈkænəljʊə(r)/ *n*. the groove round a bullet etc. [F f. *canneler* f. *canne* reed, CANE]

cannery /ˈkænərɪ/ *n*. (*pl*. **-ies**) a factory where food is canned.

Cannes /kæn/ a coastal resort on the Riviera in southern France, made fashionable in the 19th c. by visiting royalty and aristocracy; pop. (1982) 72,800. An important international film festival is held here annually.

cannibal /ˈkænɪb(ə)l/ *n*. & *adj*. —*n*. **1** a person who eats human flesh. (See below.) **2** an animal that feeds on flesh of its own species. —*adj*. of or like a cannibal. □□ **cannibalism** *n*. **cannibalistic** /-bəˈlɪstɪk/ *adj*. **cannibalistically** /-bəˈlɪstɪkəlɪ/ *adv*. [orig. pl. *Canibales* f. Sp.: var. of *Caribes* name of a W. Ind. nation]

Archaeological evidence suggests that cannibalism has occurred since palaeolithic times in many places throughout the world, although now, if it exists at all, it is limited to isolated parts of Melanesia and South America. Cannibalism is rarely associated with starvation, which is probably the least common motive for its occurrence; more often it is associated with ritual, religious, or magical beliefs. Anthropologists distinguish two categories of cannibalism: endocannibalism, in which the remains of relatives or other members of one's own group are consumed, and exocannibalism, in which the remains of one's enemies are consumed. The motivation underlying these two forms differs: in endocannibalism respect and reverence are shown toward one's deceased kinsmen; in exocannibalism the act is often associated with ritualized vengeance or with the means of absorbing the vitality or other qualities of vanquished foes. The parts of the body eaten and the methods of their preparation for consumption varied widely between societies and the particular organs or portions consumed frequently had ritual significance.

cannibalize /ˈkænɪbəˌlaɪz/ *v.tr.* (also **-ise**) use (a machine etc.) as a source of spare parts for others. □□ **cannibalization** /-ˈzeɪʃ(ə)n/ *n*.

cannikin /ˈkænɪkɪn/ *n*. a small can. [Du. *kanneken* (as CAN², -KIN)]

Canning /ˈkænɪŋ/, George (1770–1827), Foreign Secretary of Great Britain 1807–9 and 1822–7. Canning resigned his post in 1809 after a disagreement with his rival Castlereagh over a disastrous expedition in the Napoleonic Wars, but returned to office following the latter's suicide in 1822, whereupon he presided over a reversal of Britain's hitherto conservative foreign policy, being particularly responsible for the support of nationalist movements in various parts of Europe. He succeeded Lord Liverpool as Prime Minister on the latter's death in 1827, but died himself six months later.

Cannizzaro /ˌkænɪˈzɑːrəʊ/, Stanislao (1826–1910), Italian chemist, remembered for his revival of Avogadro's hypothesis, which had been neglected for fifty years. He also discovered a reaction (named after him) in which an aldehyde is converted into an acid and an alcohol in the presence of a strong alkali.

cannon /ˈkænən/ *n*. & *v*. —*n*. **1** *hist*. (*pl*. same) a large heavy gun installed on a carriage or mounting. It dates (in Europe) from the early 14th c. **2** an automatic aircraft gun firing shells. **3** *Billiards* the hitting of two balls successively by the cue-ball. **4** *Mech*. a hollow cylinder moving independently on a shaft. **5** (in full **cannon-bit**) a smooth round bit for a horse. —*v.intr.* **1** (usu. foll. by *against, into*) collide heavily or obliquely. **2** *Billiards* make a cannon shot. □ **cannon-ball** *hist*. a large usu. metal ball fired by a cannon. **cannon-bone** the tube-shaped bone between the hock and fetlock of a horse. **cannon-fodder** soldiers regarded merely as material to be expended in war. [F *canon* f. It. *cannone* large tube f. *canna* CANE: in Billiards sense f. older CAROM]

cannonade /ˌkænəˈneɪd/ *n*. & *v*. —*n*. a period of continuous heavy gunfire. —*v.tr.* bombard with a cannonade. [F f. It. *cannonata*]

cannot /ˈkænɒt, kæˈnɒt/ *v.aux.* can not.

cannula /ˈkænjʊlə/ n. (pl. **cannulae** /-liː/ or **cannulas**) Surgery a small tube for inserting into the body to allow fluid to enter or escape. [L, dimin. of canna cane]

cannulate /ˈkænjʊˌleɪt/ v.tr. Surgery introduce a cannula into.

canny /ˈkænɪ/ adj. (**cannier**, **canniest**) **1 a** shrewd, worldly-wise. **b** thrifty. **c** circumspect. **2** sly, drily humorous. **3** Sc. & N.Engl. pleasant, agreeable. □□ **cannily** adv. **canniness** n. [CAN¹ (in sense 'know') + -Y¹]

canoe /kəˈnuː/ n. & v. —n. a small narrow boat with pointed ends usu. propelled by paddling. (See below.) —v.intr. (**canoes**, **canoed**, **canoeing**) travel in a canoe. □□ **canoeist** n. [Sp. and Haitian canoa]

The term was applied to a small open boat used by primitive peoples, originally to those of West Indies aborigines (canoa is the native name found in use by Columbus) which were hollowed out of a single tree-trunk. It was extended to embrace similar craft, in which paddles were the motive force, all over the world, some of which (particularly among the Pacific islands) were remarkably large vessels in which two banks of paddlers, up to 20 or 30 a side, were used.

canon /ˈkænən/ n. **1 a** a general law, rule, principle, or criterion. **b** a church decree or law. **2** (fem. **canoness**) **a** a member of a cathedral chapter. **b** a member of certain RC orders. **3 a** a collection or list of sacred books etc. accepted as genuine. **b** the recognized genuine works of a particular author; a list of these. **4** the part of the Roman Catholic Mass containing the words of consecration. **5** Mus. a piece with different parts taking up the same theme successively, either at the same or at a different pitch. □ **canon law** ecclesiastical law, based on the New Testament, tradition, pronouncements by popes and councils of the Church, and decisions in particular cases. **canon regular** (or **regular canon**) see REGULAR adj. 9b. [OE f. L f. Gk kanōn, in ME also f. AF & OF canun, -on; in sense 2 ME f. OF canonie f. eccl.L canonicus: cf. CANONICAL]

cañon var. of CANYON.

canonic /kəˈnɒnɪk/ adj. = CANONICAL adj. [OE f. OF canonique or L canonicus f. Gk kanonikos (as CANON)]

canonical /kəˈnɒnɪk(ə)l/ adj. & n. —adj. **1 a** according to or ordered by canon law. **b** included in the canon of Scripture. **2** authoritative, standard, accepted. **3** of a cathedral chapter or a member of it. **4** Mus. in canon form. —n. (in pl.) the canonical dress of the clergy. □ **canonical hours** Eccl. the times fixed for a formal set of prayers or for the celebration of marriage. □□ **canonically** adv. [med.L canonicalis (as CANONIC)]

canonicate /kəˈnɒnɪkət/ n. = CANONRY.

canonicity /ˌkænəˈnɪsɪtɪ/ n. the status of being canonical. [L canonicus canonical]

canonist /ˈkænənɪst/ n. an expert in canon law. [ME f. F canoniste or f. med.L canonista: see CANON]

canonize /ˈkænəˌnaɪz/ v.tr. (also **-ise**) **1 a** declare officially to be a saint, usu. with a ceremony. **b** regard as a saint. **2** admit to the canon of Scripture. **3** sanction by Church authority. □□ **canonization** /-ˈzeɪʃ(ə)n/ n. [ME f. med.L canonizare: see CANON]

canonry /ˈkænənrɪ/ n. (pl. **-ies**) the office or benefice of a canon.

canoodle /kəˈnuːd(ə)l/ v.intr. colloq. kiss and cuddle amorously. [19th-c. US: orig. unkn.]

Canopic /kəˈnəʊpɪk/ adj. □ **Canopic jar** (or **vase**) each of a set of (usually four) urns for containing the different organs (liver, lungs, etc.) of an embalmed body in an ancient Egyptian burial. The lids, originally plain, were later modelled as the human, falcon, dog, and jackal heads of the four sons of Horus, protectors of the jars. [L Canopicus f. Canopus town in ancient Egypt]

canopy /ˈkænəpɪ/ n. & v. —n. (pl. **-ies**) **1 a** a covering hung or held up over a throne, bed, person, etc. **b** the sky. **c** an overhanging shelter. **2** Archit. a rooflike projection over a niche etc. **3** the uppermost layers of foliage etc. in a forest. **4** the expanding part of a parachute. **b** the cover of an aircraft's cockpit. —v.tr. (**-ies**, **-ied**) supply or be a canopy to. [ME f. med.L canopeum f. L conopeum f. Gk kōnōpeion couch with mosquito-curtains f. kōnōps gnat]

canorous /kəˈnɔːrəs/ adj. melodious, resonant. [L canorus f. canere sing]

Canova /kəˈnəʊvə/, Antonio (1757–1822), Italian sculptor who by the early 19th c. had developed an international reputation as the pre-eminent exponent of neoclassicism. Canova's sculpture readily reflected that 'noble simplicity' and 'calm grandeur' defined by Winckelmann as the essence of true classicism. His works range from heroic groups of classical subjects to funeral monuments and life-size busts: while on the one hand his fine carving reflects the ideality of his antique sources, his sense of invention and sophisticated treatment of problems such as multiple viewpoints were, in every sense, modern. His commissions included papal and royal monuments and figures executed for Napoleon and his family; Canova even attracted the commission for the statue of George Washington for North Carolina.

canst /kænst/ archaic 2nd person sing. of CAN¹.

cant¹ /kænt/ n. & v. —n. **1** insincere pious or moral talk. **2** ephemeral or fashionable catchwords. **3** language peculiar to a class, profession, sect, etc.; jargon. —v.intr. use cant. □ **canting arms** Heraldry arms containing an allusion to the name of the bearer. [earlier of musical sound, of intonation, and of beggars' whining; perh. from the singing of religious mendicants: prob. f. L canere sing]

cant² /kænt/ n. & v. —n. **1 a** a slanting surface, e.g. of a bank. **b** a bevel of a crystal etc. **2** an oblique push or movement that upsets or partly upsets something. **3** a tilted or sloping position. —v. **1** tr. push or pitch out of level; tilt. **2** intr. take or lie in a slanting position. **3** tr. impart a bevel to. **4** intr. Naut. swing round. □ **cant-dog** (or **-hook**) an iron hook at the end of a long handle, used for rolling logs. [ME f. MLG kant, kante, MDu. cant, point, side, edge, ult. f. L cant(h)us iron tire]

can't /kɑːnt/ contr. can not.

Cant. abbr. Canticles (Old Testament).

Cantab. /ˈkæntæb/ abbr. of Cambridge University. [L Cantabrigiensis]

cantabile /kænˈtɑːbɪlɪ/ adv., adj., & n. Mus. —adv. & adj. in a smooth singing style. —n. a cantabile passage or movement. [It., = singable]

Cantabria /kænˈtæbrɪə/ an autonomous region of northern Spain; pop. (1986) 524,670; capital, Santander. □□ **Cantabrian** adj. & n.

Cantabrigian /ˌkæntəˈbrɪdʒɪən/ adj. & n. —adj. of Cambridge or Cambridge University. —n. **1** a member of Cambridge University. **2** a native of Cambridge. [L Cantabrigia Cambridge]

cantal /ˈkænt(ə)l/ n. a type of hard strong French cheese. [name of a department of Auvergne, France]

cantaloup /ˈkæntəˌluːp/ n. (also **cantaloupe**) a small round ribbed variety of melon with orange flesh. [F cantaloup f. Cantaluppi near Rome, where it was first grown in Europe]

cantankerous /kænˈtæŋkərəs/ adj. bad-tempered, quarrelsome. □□ **cantankerously** adv. **cantankerousness** n. [perh. f. Ir. cant outbidding + rancorous]

cantata /kænˈtɑːtə/ n. Mus. a short narrative or descriptive composition with vocal solos and usu. chorus and orchestral accompaniment. Cantatas in the early 17th c. were of the nature of extended songs, but towards the end of the century the form began to expand until it comprised several sections, combining recitative, aria, and instrumental music. The great sacred cantatas of Bach and his contemporaries frequently incorporated melodies from the Lutheran chorales, sometimes harmonized simply so that the congregation could join in the singing at that point. The cantata declined after 1750, but isolated examples appear in the 20th c., e.g. by Britten (Cantata academica, 1959) and Stravinsky (Cantata, 1951–2). [It. cantata (aria) sung (air) f. cantare sing]

canteen /kænˈtiːn/ n. **1 a** a restaurant for employees in an office or factory etc. **b** a shop selling provisions or liquor in a barracks or camp. **2** a case or box of cutlery. **3** a soldier's or camper's water-flask or set of eating or drinking utensils. [F cantine f. It. cantina cellar]

canter /ˈkæntə(r)/ n. & v. —n. a gentle gallop. —v. **1** intr. (of a horse or its rider) go at a canter. **2** tr. make (a horse) canter. □

in a canter easily (*win in a canter*). [short for *Canterbury pace*, from the supposed easy pace of medieval pilgrims to Canterbury]

canterbury /ˈkæntəbərɪ/ n. (pl. **-ies**) a piece of furniture with partitions for holding music etc. [*Canterbury* in Kent]

Canterbury /ˈkæntəbərɪ/ a city in Kent, St Augustine's centre for the conversion of England to Christianity, now the seat of the archbishop, Primate of All England; pop. (1981) 39,700. St Augustine had been ordered to organize England into two ecclesiastical provinces, with archbishops at London and York. From the first, however, the place of London was taken by Canterbury. □ **Canterbury bell** a cultivated campanula with large flowers [after the bells of Canterbury pilgrims' horses: see CANTER].

Canterbury Plains a region on the central east coast of South Island, New Zealand, stretching southwards from the Banks Peninsula.

cantharides /kænˈθærɪˌdiːz/ n.pl. a preparation made from dried bodies of a beetle *Lytta vesicatoria*, causing blistering of the skin and formerly used in medicine and as an aphrodisiac. Also called *Spanish fly*. [L f. Gk *kantharis* Spanish fly]

canthus /ˈkænθəs/ n. (pl. **canthi** /-θaɪ/) the outer or inner corner of the eye, where the upper and lower lids meet. [L f. Gk *kanthos*]

canticle /ˈkæntɪk(ə)l/ n. 1 a song or chant with a Biblical text. 2 (also **Canticle of Canticles**) the Song of Solomon (see entry). [ME f. OF *canticle* (var. of *cantique*) or L *canticulum* dimin. of *canticum* f. *canere* sing]

cantilena /ˌkæntɪˈliːnə/ n. Mus. a simple or sustained melody. [It.]

cantilever /ˈkæntɪˌliːvə(r)/ n. & v. —n. 1 a long bracket or beam etc. projecting from a wall to support a balcony etc. 2 a beam or girder fixed at only one end. —v.intr. 1 project as a cantilever. 2 be supported by cantilevers. □ **cantilever bridge** a bridge made of cantilevers projecting from the piers and connected by girders. [17th c.: orig. unkn.]

cantillate /ˈkæntɪˌleɪt/ v.tr. & intr. chant or recite with musical tones. □□ **cantillation** /-ˈleɪʃ(ə)n/ n. [L *cantillare* sing low: see CHANT]

cantina /kænˈtiːnə/ n. a bar-room or wine-shop. [Sp. & It.]

canto /ˈkæntəʊ/ n. (pl. **-os**) a division of a long poem. [It., = song, f. L *cantus*]

Canton /kænˈtɒn/ (also **Guangzhou** /kwænˈdʒəʊ/) a city in south China, the capital of Guangdong province, situated on the Pearl River; pop. (est. 1986) 3,290,000. It is the leading industrial and commercial centre of southern China.

canton n. & v. —n. 1 /ˈkæntɒn/ **a** a subdivision of a country. **b** a State of the Swiss confederation. 2 /ˈkænt(ə)n/ *Heraldry* a square division, less than a quarter, in the upper (usu. dexter) corner of a shield. —v.tr. 1 /kænˈtuːn/ put (troops) into quarters. 2 /kænˈtɒn/ divide into cantons. □□ **cantonal** /ˈkæntən(ə)l, kænˈtɒn(ə)l/ adj. [OF, = corner (see CANT²): (v.) also partly f. F *cantonner*]

Cantonese /ˌkæntəˈniːz/ adj. & n. —adj. of Canton or the Cantonese dialect of Chinese. —n. (pl. same) 1 a native of Canton. 2 the dialect of Chinese spoken in SE China and Hong Kong.

cantonment /kænˈtuːnmənt/ n. 1 a lodging assigned to troops. 2 a permanent military station in India. [F *cantonnement*: see CANTON]

Cantor /ˈkæntɔː(r)/, Georg (1845–1918), Russian-born mathematician who spent most of his life in Germany, professor at Halle from 1869 until his death. He introduced the theory of sets which was later to be adopted as a satisfactory medium in which to express most concepts of mathematics. His analysis of the notion of real number and his study of infinite sets have led to a proper understanding of transfinite cardinal and ordinal numbers and of the logical foundations of most of mathematics.

cantor /ˈkæntɔː(r)/ n. 1 the leader of the singing in church; a precentor. 2 the precentor in a synagogue. [L, = singer f. *canere* sing]

cantorial /kænˈtɔːrɪəl/ adj. 1 of or relating to the cantor. 2 of the north side of the choir in a church (cf. DECANAL).

cantoris /kænˈtɔːrɪs/ adj. Mus. to be sung by the cantorial side of the choir in antiphonal singing (cf. DECANI). [L, genit. of CANTOR precentor]

cantrail /ˈkæntreɪl/ n. Brit. a timber etc. support for the roof of a railway carriage. [CANT² + RAIL]

cantrip /ˈkæntrɪp/ n. Sc. 1 a witch's trick. 2 a piece of mischief; a playful act. [18th c.: orig. unkn.]

Canuck /kəˈnʌk/ n. & adj. US sl. usu. derog. —n. 1 a Canadian, esp. a French Canadian. 2 a Canadian horse or pony. —adj. Canadian, esp. French Canadian. [app. f. *Canada*]

Canute var. of CNUT.

canvas /ˈkænvəs/ n. & v. —n. 1 **a** a strong coarse kind of cloth made from hemp or flax or other coarse yarn and used for sails and tents etc. and as a surface for oil-painting. **b** a piece of this. 2 a painting on canvas, esp. in oils. 3 an open kind of canvas used as a basis for tapestry and embroidery. 4 *sl.* the floor of a boxing or wrestling ring. 5 a racing-boat's covered end. —v.tr. (**canvassed, canvassing**; US **canvased, canvasing**) cover with canvas. □ **by a canvas** (in boat-racing) by a small margin (*win by a canvas*). **canvas-back** a wild duck *Aythya valisineria*, of N. America, with back feathers the colour of unbleached canvas. **under canvas 1** in a tent or tents. **2** with sails spread. [ME & ONF *canevas*, ult. f. L *cannabis* hemp]

canvass /ˈkænvəs/ v. & n. —v. 1 intr. solicit votes. **b** tr. solicit votes from (electors in a constituency). 2 tr. **a** ascertain opinions of. **b** seek custom from. **c** discuss thoroughly. 3 tr. Brit. propose (an idea or plan etc.). 4 intr. US check the validity of votes. —n. the process of or an instance of canvassing, esp. of electors. □□ **canvasser** n. [orig. = toss in a sheet, agitate, f. CANVAS]

canyon /ˈkænjən/ n. (also **cañon**) a deep gorge, often with a stream or river. [Sp. *cañón* tube, ult. f. L *canna* CANE]

canzonetta /ˌkænzəˈnetə/ n. (also **canzonet** /-ˈnet/) 1 a short light song. 2 a kind of madrigal. [It., dimin. of *canzone* song f. L *cantio -onis* f. *canere* sing]

caoutchouc /ˈkaʊtʃʊk/ n. raw rubber. [F f. Carib *cahuchu*]

CAP abbr. Common Agricultural Policy (of the EEC).

cap /kæp/ n. & v. —n. 1 **a** a soft brimless head-covering, usu. with a peak. **b** a head-covering worn in a particular profession (*nurse's cap*). **c** esp. Brit. a cap awarded as a sign of membership of a sports team. **d** an academic mortarboard or soft hat. **e** a special hat as part of Highland costume. 2 **a** a cover like a cap in shape or position (*kneecap; toecap*). **b** a device to seal a bottle or protect the point of a pen, lens of a camera, etc. 3 **a** = Dutch *cap*. **b** = percussion *cap*. 4 = CROWN n. 9b. —v.tr. (**capped, capping**) 1 **a** put a cap on. **b** cover the top or end of. **c** set a limit to (*rate-capping*). 2 **a** esp. Brit. award a sports cap to. **b** Sc. & NZ confer a university degree on. 3 **a** lie on top of; form the cap of. **b** surpass, excel. **c** improve on (a story, quotation, etc.) esp. by producing a better or more apposite one. □ **cap in hand** humbly. **cap of maintenance** a cap or hat worn as a symbol of official dignity or carried before the sovereign etc. **cap rock** a hard rock or stratum overlying a deposit of oil, gas, coal, etc. **cap sleeve** a sleeve extending only a short distance from the shoulder. **if the cap fits** (said of a generalized comment) it seems to be true (of a particular person). **set one's cap at** try to attract as a suitor. □□ **capful** n. (pl. **-fuls**). **capping** n. [OE *cæppe* f. LL *cappa*, perh. f. L *caput* head]

cap. abbr. 1 capital. 2 capital letter. 3 chapter. [L *capitulum* or *caput*]

capability /ˌkeɪpəˈbɪlɪtɪ/ n. (pl. **-ies**) 1 (often foll. by *of*, *for*, *to*) ability, power; the condition of being capable. 2 an undeveloped or unused faculty.

Capablanca /ˌkæpəˈblæŋkə/, José Raúl (1888–1942), Cuban chess-player, who was world champion from 1921 to 1927.

capable /ˈkeɪpəb(ə)l/ adj. 1 competent, able, gifted. 2 (foll. by *of*) **a** having the ability or fitness or necessary quality for. **b** susceptible of admitting of (explanation or improvement etc.). □□ **capably** adv. [F f. LL *capabilis* f. L *capere* hold]

capacious /kəˈpeɪʃəs/ adj. roomy; able to hold much. □□ **capaciously** adv. **capaciousness** n. [L *capax -acis* f. *capere* hold]

capacitance /kəˈpæsɪt(ə)ns/ n. Electr. 1 the ability of a system to store an electric charge. 2 the ratio of the change in an electric charge in a system to the corresponding change in its electric potential. ¶ Symb.: **C**. [CAPACITY + -ANCE]

capacitate /kə'pæsɪˌteɪt/ v.tr. **1** (usu. foll. by *for*, or *to* + infin.) render capable. **2** make legally competent.

capacitor /kə'pæsɪtə(r)/ n. *Electr.* a device of one or more pairs of conductors separated by insulators used to store an electric charge.

capacity /kə'pæsɪtɪ/ n. (pl. **-ies**) **1 a** the power of containing, receiving, experiencing, or producing (*capacity for heat, pain*, etc.). **b** the maximum amount that can be contained or produced etc. **c** the volume, e.g. of the cylinders in an internal-combustion engine. **d** (*attrib.*) fully occupying the available space, resources, etc. (*a capacity audience*). **2 a** mental power. **b** a faculty or talent. **3** a position or function (*in a civil capacity; in my capacity as a critic*). **4** legal competence. **5** *Electr.* capacitance. □ **measure of capacity** a measure used for vessels and liquids or grains etc. **to capacity** fully; using all resources (*working to capacity*). □□ **capacitative** /-tətɪv/ adj. (also **capacitive**) (in sense 5). [ME f. F f. L *capacitas* *-tatis* (as CAPACIOUS)]

caparison /kə'pærɪs(ə)n/ n. & v. —n. **1** (usu. in *pl.*) a horse's trappings. **2** equipment, finery. —v.tr. put caparisons on; adorn richly. [obs. F *caparasson* f. Sp. *caparazón* saddle-cloth f. *capa* CAPE¹]

cape¹ /keɪp/ n. **1** a sleeveless cloak. **2** a short sleeveless cloak as a fixed or detachable part of a longer cloak or coat. [F f. Prov. *capa* f. LL *cappa* CAP]

cape² /keɪp/ n. **1** a headland or promontory. **2** (**the Cape**) **a** the Cape of Good Hope. **b** the S. African province containing it (Cape Province). □ **Cape Coloured** adj. *S.Afr.* of the Coloured (see COLOURED 2) population of Cape Province. —n. a member of this population. **Cape doctor** *S.Afr. colloq.* a strong SE wind. **Cape Dutch** *archaic* Afrikaans. **Cape gooseberry 1** an edible soft roundish yellow berry enclosed in a lantern-like husk. **2** the plant, *Physalis peruviana*, bearing these. [ME f. OF *cap* f. Prov. *cap* ult. f. L *caput* head]

Cape Agulhas /ə'gʌlʌs/ the most southerly point of the continent of Africa, in Cape Province.

Cape Bon /bɒn/ a peninsula of NE Tunisia, extending into the Mediterranean Sea, noted for its resorts and its wine.

Cape Breton Island /'bret(ə)n/ an island that forms the north-eastern part of the Canadian province of Nova Scotia. Discovered by John Cabot in 1497, it was a French possession until 1763 and a separate colony from 1784 to 1820. Sydney is the chief town.

Cape Canaveral /kə'nævər(ə)l/ a cape on the east coast of Florida, known as Cape Kennedy from 1963 until 1973. It is the location of the John F. Kennedy Space Center which has been the principal US launching site for manned space flights since 1961.

Cape Cod a sandy peninsula in SE Massachusetts, which forms a wide curve enclosing Cape Cod Bay. The Cape Cod Canal, completed in 1914, links the bay with Buzzards Bay on the south-west. The Pilgrim Fathers (see entry) landed on the northern tip of Cape Cod in November 1620.

Cape Horn the southernmost point of South America, on an island south of Tierra del Fuego, belonging to Chile. It was discovered by the Dutch navigator Schouten in 1616 and named after Hoorn, his birthplace. The ocean region is notorious for storms, and until the opening of the Panama Canal in 1914 lay on a sea route between the Atlantic and Pacific Oceans.

Cape Johnson Depth /'dʒɒns(ə)n/ the deepest point of the Philippine Trench which drops to 10,497 m (34,440 ft.) below sea level off the east coast of the Philippines. It is named after the USS *Cape Johnson* which took soundings there in 1945.

Čapek /'tʃɑːpek/, Karel (1890–1938), Czech novelist and dramatist, born in Bohemia. He wrote several plays with his brother, Josef Čapek (1887–1945) (a painter and stage- designer) including *The Insect Play* (1921), a satire on human society and totalitarianism. Čapek's best-known independent work was *R.U.R.* (1920), set 'on a remote island in 1950–60' the title 'Rossum's Universal Robots' and the concept of the mechanical robot introduced a new word to the English language and opened up a whole new vein of science fiction. His other works include the play *The Makropoulos Affair* (1923), utopian romances, novels, travel works, and essays.

capelin /'kæplɪn/ n. (also **caplin**) a small smeltlike fish, *Mallotus*

villosus, of the N. Atlantic, used as food and as bait for catching cod etc. [F f. Prov. *capelan*: see CHAPLAIN]

Cape of Good Hope a mountainous promontory near the southern extremity of Africa, south of Cape Town. It was sighted towards the end of the 15th c. by the Portuguese explorer Dias and named Cape of Storms, and was rounded for the first time by Vasco da Gama in 1497.

Cape Province the southern province of the Republic of South Africa; pop. (1986) 4,901,200; capital, Cape Town.

caper¹ /'keɪpə(r)/ v. & n. —v.intr. jump or run about playfully. —n. **1** a playful jump or leap. **2 a** a fantastic proceeding; a prank. **b** *sl.* any activity or occupation. □ **cut a caper** (or **capers**) act friskily. □□ **caperer** n. [abbr. of CAPRIOLE]

caper² /'keɪpə(r)/ n. **1** a bramble-like S. European shrub, *Capparis spinosa*. **2** (in *pl.*) its flower buds cooked and pickled for use as flavouring esp. for a savoury sauce. [ME *capres* & F *câpres* f. L *capparis* f. Gk *kapparis*, treated as pl.: cf. CHERRY, PEA]

capercaillie /ˌkæpə'keɪlɪ/ n. (also **capercailzie** /-lzɪ/) a large European grouse, *Tetrao urogallus*. [Gael. *capull coille* horse of the wood]

capeskin /'keɪpskɪn/ n. a soft leather made from S. African sheepskin.

Capetian /kə'piːʃ(ə)n/ n. a member of a dynasty of kings of France, founded by Hugo Capet in 987 in succession to the Carolingian dynasty. It survived until 1328, giving way to the House of Valois. The extinction of the direct line of Capetians gave rise to Edward III's claim to the French throne and the start of the Hundred Years War.

Cape Town the legislative capital of the Republic of South Africa, at the foot of Table Mountain; pop. (est. 1985) 776,600.

Cape Verde Islands /vɜːd/ a country consisting of a group of islands in the Atlantic off the coast of Senegal, named after the most westerly cape of Africa; pop. (1988) 353,885; official language, Portuguese; capital, Praia. Settled by the Portuguese in the 15th c., the islands formed a Portuguese colony until they became independent in 1975. They have links with Guinea-Bissau, with which they were formerly administered, but the plan for federation with Guinea-Bissau was dropped in 1980. □□ **Cape Verdean** /vɜː'dɪən/ adj. & n.

Cape Wrath /rɒθ/ a promontory at the NW extremity of mainland Scotland.

Cape York a peninsula forming the most northerly point of the Australian mainland, on the Torres Strait.

capias /'kæpɪˌæs, 'keɪp-/ n. *Law* a writ ordering the arrest of the person named. [L, = you are to seize, f. *capere* take]

capillarity /ˌkæpɪ'lærɪtɪ/ n. a phenomenon at liquid boundaries resulting in the rise or depression of liquids in narrow tubes. Also called *capillary action*. [F *capillarité* (as CAPILLARY)]

capillary /kə'pɪlərɪ/ adj. & n. —adj. **1** of or like a hair. **2** (of a tube) of hairlike internal diameter. **3** of one of the delicate ramified blood vessels intervening between arteries and veins. —n. (pl. **-ies**) **1** a capillary tube. **2** a capillary blood vessel. □ **capillary action** = CAPILLARITY. [L *capillaris* f. *capillus* hair]

capital¹ /'kæpɪt(ə)l/ n., adj., & int. —n. **1** the most important town or city of a country or region, usu. its seat of government and administrative centre. **2 a** the money or other assets with which a company starts in business. **b** accumulated wealth, esp. as used in further production. **c** money invested or lent at interest. **3** capitalists generally. **4** a capital letter. —adj. **1 a** principal; most important; leading. **b** *colloq.* excellent, first-rate. **2 a** involving or punishable by death (*capital punishment; a capital offence*). **b** (of an error etc.) vitally harmful; fatal. **3** (of letters of the alphabet) large in size and of the form used to begin sentences and names etc. —int. expressing approval or satisfaction. □ **capital gain** a profit from the sale of investments or property. **capital goods** goods, esp. machinery, plant, etc., used or to be used in producing commodities (opp. *consumer goods*). **capital levy 1** the appropriation by the State of a fixed proportion of the wealth in the country. **2** a wealth tax. **capital punishment** see separate entry. **capital sum** a lump sum of money, esp. payable to an insured person. **capital territory** a territory containing the capital city of a country. **capital transfer tax**

hist. (in the UK) a tax levied on the transfer of capital by gift or bequest etc. ¶ Replaced in 1986 by *inheritance tax.* **make capital out of** use to one's advantage. **with a capital —** emphatically such (*art with a capital A*). □□ **capitally** *adv.* [ME f. OF f. L *capitalis* f. *caput -itis* head]

capital² /ˈkæpɪt(ə)l/ *n. Archit.* the head or cornice of a pillar or column. [ME f. OF *capitel* f. LL *capitellum* dimin. of L *caput* head]

capitalism /ˈkæpɪtəˌlɪz(ə)m/ *n.* **1 a** an economic system in which the production and distribution of goods depend on invested private capital and profit-making. **b** the possession of capital or wealth. **2** *Polit.* the dominance of private owners of capital and production for profit.

capitalist /ˈkæpɪtəlɪst/ *n. & adj.* —*n.* **1** a person using or possessing capital; a rich person. **2** an advocate of capitalism. —*adj.* of or favouring capitalism. □□ **capitalistic** /-ˈlɪstɪk/ *adj.* **capitalistically** /-ˈlɪstɪkəlɪ/ *adv.*

capitalize /ˈkæpɪtəˌlaɪz/ *v.* (also **-ise**) **1** *tr.* **a** convert into or provide with capital. **b** calculate or realize the present value of an income. **c** reckon (the value of an asset) by setting future benefits against the cost of maintenance. **2** *tr.* **a** write (a letter of the alphabet) as a capital. **b** begin (a word) with a capital letter. **3** *intr.* (foll. by *on*) use to one's advantage; profit from. □□ **capitalization** /-ˈzeɪʃ(ə)n/ *n.* [F *capitaliser* (as CAPITAL¹)]

capital punishment *n.* infliction of death by an authorized public authority as punishment for a crime. It was recognized by ancient legal systems, and methods of execution varied: the Babylonians used drowning, the Hebrews stoning, the Greeks allowed a free man to take poison (but slaves were beaten to death); Roman methods included hurling from the Tarpeian rock, strangulation, exposure to wild beasts, and crucifixion. In medieval Europe hanging and beheading were the usual methods; religious heretics were burnt at the stake. In more recent times, only hanging was used in Britain, the guillotine was introduced into France in the 18th c., the garrotte was used by Spain, and in the US the chief methods of execution were the electric chair and the gas chamber. In the 19th c. in Britain the death penalty, previously available for a wide range of offences (some quite trivial) was restricted to cases of treason and murder, and in 1965 was abolished for murder. Many western countries have abolished it.

capitation /ˌkæpɪˈteɪʃ(ə)n/ *n.* **1** a tax or fee at a set rate per person. **2** the levying of such a tax or fee. □ **capitation grant** a grant of a sum calculated from the number of people to be catered for, esp. in education. [F *capitation* or LL *capitatio* poll-tax f. *caput* head]

Capitol /ˈkæpɪt(ə)l/ **1** the temple of Jupiter in ancient Rome. **2** the seat of the US Congress in Washington DC. Its site was chosen by George Washington, who laid the first stone in 1793. [OF f. L (*caput* head)]

capitular /kəˈpɪtjʊlə(r)/ *adj.* **1** of or relating to a cathedral chapter. **2** *Anat.* of or relating to a terminal protuberance of a bone. [LL *capitularis* f. L *capitulum* CHAPTER]

capitulary /kəˈpɪtjʊlərɪ/ *n.* (pl. **-ies**) a collection of ordinances, esp. of the Frankish kings. [LL *capitularius* (as CAPITULAR)]

capitulate /kəˈpɪtjʊˌleɪt/ *v.intr.* surrender, esp. on stated conditions. □□ **capitulator** *n.* **capitulatory** /-lətərɪ/ *adj.* [med.L *capitulare* draw up under headings f. L *caput* head]

capitulation /kəˌpɪtjʊˈleɪʃ(ə)n/ *n.* **1** the act of capitulating; surrender. **2** a statement of the main divisions of a subject. **3** an agreement or set of conditions.

capitulum /kəˈpɪtjʊləm/ *n.* (pl. **capitula** /-lə/) *Bot.* an inflorescence with flowers clustered together like a head, as in the daisy family. [L, dimin. of *caput* head]

caplin var. of CAPELIN.

cap'n /kæpn/ *n. sl.* captain. [contr.]

capo /ˈkæpəʊ/ *n.* (in full **capo tasto** /ˈtæstəʊ/) (pl. **capos** or **capo tastos**) *Mus.* a device secured across the neck of a fretted instrument to raise equally the tuning of all strings by the required amount. [It. *capo tasto* head stop]

Capo di Monte /ˌkæpəʊ dɪ ˈmɒnteɪ/ the name of a palace near Naples, applied to a type of porcelain first produced there in the mid-18th c.

capon /ˈkeɪpən/ *n.* a domestic cock castrated and fattened for eating. □□ **caponize** *v.tr.* (also **-ise**). [OE f. AF *capun*, OF *capon*, ult. f. L *capo -onis*]

Capone /kəˈpəʊn/, Alphonso ('Al') (1899–1947), American gangster, born in Italy, notorious for his domination of organized crime in Chicago in the 1920s. He was eventually indicted for federal income tax evasion in 1931, and imprisoned.

caponier /ˌkæpəˈnɪə(r)/ *n.* a covered passage across a ditch round a fort. [Sp. *caponera*, lit. 'capon-pen']

capot /kəˈpɒt/ *n. & v.* —*n.* (in piquet) the winning of all the tricks by one player. —*v.tr.* (**capotted, capotting**) score a capot against (an opponent). [F]

Capote /kəˈpəʊt/, Truman (1924–84), American author, whose work ranges from the light-hearted story *Breakfast at Tiffany's* (1958) to the grim re-creation of a brutal multiple murder in *In Cold Blood* (1966).

capote /kəˈpəʊt/ *n. hist.* a long cloak with a hood, formerly worn by soldiers and travellers etc. [F, dimin. of *cape* CAPE¹]

Cappadocia /ˌkæpəˈdəʊʃə/ the ancient name for the region in the centre of Asia Minor (modern Turkey) between Lake Tuz and the Euphrates, north of Cilicia. It was an important centre of early Christianity. □□ **Cappadocian** *adj. & n.*

cappuccino /ˌkæpʊˈtʃiːnəʊ/ *n.* (pl. **-os**) coffee with milk made frothy with pressurized steam. [It., = CAPUCHIN]

Capri /ˈkæpriː, kəˈpriː/ an island off the west coast of Italy, in the Bay of Naples.

capriccio /kəˈprɪtʃɪəʊ/ *n.* (pl. **-os**) **1** a lively and usu. short musical composition. **2** a painting etc. representing a fantasy or a mixture of real and imaginary features. [It., = sudden start, orig. 'horror']

capriccioso /kəˌprɪtʃɪˈəʊsəʊ/ *adv., adj., & n. Mus.* —*adv. & adj.* in a free and impulsive style. —*n.* (pl. **-os**) a capriccioso passage or movement. [It., = capricious]

caprice /kəˈpriːs/ *n.* **1 a** an unaccountable or whimsical change of mind or conduct. **b** a tendency to this. **2** a work of lively fancy in painting, drawing, or music; a capriccio. [F f. It. CAPRICCIO]

capricious /kəˈprɪʃəs/ *adj.* **1** guided by or given to caprice. **2** irregular, unpredictable. □□ **capriciously** *adv.* **capriciousness** *n.* [F *capricieux* f. It. CAPRICCIOSO]

Capricorn /ˈkæprɪˌkɔːn/ (also **Capricornus** /-ˈkɔːnəs/) **1** a constellation, traditionally regarded as contained in the figure of a goat's horns. In the northern hemisphere it is visible in late summer. **2** the tenth sign of the zodiac (the Goat), which the sun enters at the winter solstice. —*n.* a person born when the sun is in this sign. □ **Calms of Capricorn** see CALM. **Tropic of Capricorn** see TROPIC. □□ **Capricornian** *n. & adj.* [ME f. OF *capricorne* f. L *capricornus* f. *caper -pri* goat + *cornu* horn]

caprine /ˈkæpraɪn/ *adj.* of or like a goat. [ME f. L *caprinus* f. *caper -pri* goat]

capriole /ˈkæprɪˌəʊl/ *n. & v.* —*n.* **1** a leap or caper. **2** a trained horse's high leap and kick without advancing. —*v.* **1** *intr.* (of a horse or its rider) perform a capriole. **2** *tr.* make (a horse) capriole. [F f. It. *capriola* leap, ult. f. *caper -pri* goat]

Capris /kəˈpriːz/ *n.pl.* (also **Capri pants**) women's close-fitting tapered trousers. [*Capri*, an island in the bay of Naples]

Caprivi Strip /kəˈpriːvɪ/ a narrow strip of Namibia that extends towards Zambia from the NE corner of Namibia and reaches the Zambezi River. It was part of German South West Africa until after the First World War, having been ceded by Britain in 1893 in order to give the German colony access to the Zambezi, and is named after Leo, Graf von Caprivi, German imperial chancellor 1890–4.

caps. *abbr.* capital letters.

Capsian /ˈkæpsɪən/ *adj. & n.* —*adj.* of or relating to a palaeolithic industry of North Africa and southern Europe (c.8000–4500 BC) noted for its microliths. —*n.* this culture. [L *Capsa* = Gafsa in Tunisia]

capsicum /ˈkæpsɪkəm/ *n.* **1** any plant of the genus *Capsicum*, having edible capsular fruits containing many seeds, esp. *C. annuum* yielding several varieties of pepper. **2** the fruit of any of these plants, which vary in size, colour, and pungency. [mod.L, perh. f. L *capsa* box]

capsid[1] /ˈkæpsɪd/ *n.* any bug of the family Capsidae, esp. one that feeds on plants. [mod.L *Capsus* a genus of them]

capsid[2] /ˈkæpsɪd/ *n.* the protein coat or shell of a virus. [F *capside* f. L *capsa* box]

capsize /kæpˈsaɪz/ *v.* **1** *tr.* upset or overturn (a boat). **2** *intr.* be capsized. □□ **capsizal** *n.* [*cap-* as in Prov. *capvirar*, F *chavirer*: *-size* unexpl.]

capstan /ˈkæpst(ə)n/ *n.* **1** a thick revolving cylinder with a vertical axis, for winding an anchor cable or a halyard etc. **2** a revolving spindle on a tape recorder, that guides the tape past the head. □ **capstan lathe** a lathe with a revolving tool-holder. [Prov. *cabestan*, ult. f. L *capistrum* halter f. *capere* seize]

capstone /ˈkæpstəʊn/ *n.* coping; a coping-stone.

capsule /ˈkæpsjuːl/ *n.* **1** a small soluble case of gelatine enclosing a dose of medicine and swallowed with it. **2** a detachable compartment of a spacecraft or nose-cone of a rocket. **3** an enclosing membrane in the body. **4 a** a dry fruit that releases its seeds when ripe. **b** the spore-producing part of mosses and liverworts. **5** *Biol.* an enveloping layer surrounding certain bacteria. **6** (*attrib.*) concise; highly condensed (*a capsule history of jazz*). □□ **capsular** *adj.* **capsulate** *adj.* [F f. L *capsula* f. *capsa* CASE[2]]

capsulize /ˈkæpsjʊˌlaɪz/ *v.tr.* (also **-ise**) put (information etc.) in compact form.

Capt. *abbr.* Captain.

captain /ˈkæptɪn/ *n.* & *v.* —*n.* **1 a** a chief or leader. **b** the leader of a team, esp. in sports. **c** a powerful or influential person (*captain of industry*). **2 a** the person in command of a merchant or passenger ship. **b** the pilot of a civil aircraft. **3** (as a title **Captain**) **a** an army or *US* Air Force officer next above lieutenant. **b** a Navy officer in command of a warship; one ranking below commodore or rear admiral and above commander. **c** *US* a police officer in charge of a precinct, ranking below Chief Officer. **4 a** a foreman. **b** a head boy or girl in a school. **c** *US* a supervisor of waiters or bellboys. **5 a** a great soldier or strategist. **b** an experienced commander. —*v.tr.* be captain of; lead. □ **captain-general** an honorary officer, esp. of artillery. **Captain of the Fleet** *Brit.* a Navy staff officer in charge of maintenance. □□ **captaincy** *n.* (*pl.* **-ies**). **captainship** *n.* [ME & OF *capitain* f. LL *capitaneus* chief f. L *caput capit-* head]

caption /ˈkæpʃ(ə)n/ *n.* & *v.* —*n.* **1** a title or brief explanation appended to an illustration, cartoon, etc. **2** wording appearing on a cinema or television screen as part of a film or broadcast. **3** the heading of a chapter or article etc. **4** *Law* a certificate attached to or written on a document. —*v.tr.* provide with a caption. [ME f. L *captio* f. *capere capt-* take]

captious /ˈkæpʃəs/ *adj.* given to finding fault or raising petty objections. □□ **captiously** *adv.* **captiousness** *n.* [ME f. F *captieux* or L *captiosus* (as CAPTION)]

captivate /ˈkæptɪˌveɪt/ *v.tr.* **1** overwhelm with charm or affection. **2** fascinate. □□ **captivatingly** *adv.* **captivation** /-ˈveɪʃ(ə)n/ *n.* [LL *captivare* take captive (as CAPTIVE)]

captive /ˈkæptɪv/ *n.* & *adj.* —*n.* a person or animal that has been taken prisoner or confined. —*adj.* **1 a** taken prisoner. **b** kept in confinement or under restraint. **2 a** unable to escape. **b** in a position of having to comply (*captive audience; captive market*). **3** of or like a prisoner (*captive state*). □ **captive balloon** a balloon held by a rope from the ground. [ME f. L *captivus* f. *capere capt-* take]

captivity /kæpˈtɪvɪtɪ/ *n.* (*pl.* **-ies**) **1 a** the condition or circumstances of being a captive. **b** a period of captivity. **2** (**the Captivity**) the captivity of the Jews in Babylon, to which they were deported by Nebuchadnezzar in 586 BC and from which they were released by Cyrus in 538 BC.

captor /ˈkæptə(r), -tɔː(r)/ *n.* a person who captures (a person, place, etc.). [L (as CAPTIVE)]

capture /ˈkæptʃə(r)/ *v.* & *n.* —*v.tr.* **1 a** take prisoner; seize as a prize. **b** obtain by force or trickery. **2** portray in permanent form (*could not capture the likeness*). **3** *Physics* absorb (a subatomic particle). **4** (in board games) make a move that secures the removal of (an opposing piece) from the board. **5** (of a stream)

divert the upper course of (another stream) by encroaching on its basin. **6** cause (data) to be stored in a computer. **7** *Astron.* (of a star or planet) bring (an object) to within its gravitational field. —*n.* **1** the act of capturing. **2** a thing or person captured. □□ **capturer** *n.* [F f. L *captura* f. *capere capt-* take]

Capuchin /ˈkæpjuːtʃɪn/ *n.* **1** a Franciscan friar of the new rule of 1529. **2** a cloak and hood formerly worn by women. **3** (**capuchin**) **a** any monkey of the genus *Cebus* of S. America, with cowl-like head hair. **b** a variety of pigeon with head and neck feathers resembling a cowl. [F f. It. *cappuccino* f. *cappuccio* cowl f. *cappa* CAPE[1]]

capybara /ˌkæpɪˈbɑːrə/ *n.* a very large semi-aquatic rodent, *Hydrochoerus hydrochaeris*, native to S. America. [Tupi]

car /kɑː(r)/ *n.* **1** (now the usual term for) a motor car (see entry). **2** (in *comb.*) **a** a wheeled vehicle, esp. of a specified kind (*tramcar*). **b** a railway carriage of a specified type (*dining-car*). **3** *US* any railway carriage or van. **4** the passenger compartment of a lift, cableway, balloon, etc. **5** *poet.* a wheeled vehicle; a chariot. □ **car bomb** a terrorist bomb concealed in or under a parked car. **car-boot sale** an outdoor sale at which participants sell unwanted possessions from the boots of their cars. **car coat** a short coat designed esp. for car drivers. **car park** an area for parking cars. **car phone** a radio-telephone for use in a motor vehicle. □□ **carful** *n.* (*pl.* **-fuls**). [ME f. AF & ONF *carre* ult. f. L *carrum*, *carrus*, of OCelt. orig.]

carabineer /ˌkærəbɪˈnɪə(r)/ *n.* (also **carabinier**) *hist.* **1** a soldier whose principal weapon is a carbine. **2** (**the Carabineers**) the Royal Scots Dragoon Guards. [F *carabinier* f. *carabine* CARBINE]

carabiniere /ˌkærəbɪˈnjɛərɪ/ *n.* (*pl.* **carabinieri** *pronunc.* same) an Italian gendarme. [It.]

caracal /ˈkærəˌkæl/ *n.* a lynx, *Felis caracal*, native to N. Africa and SW Asia. [F or Sp. f. Turk. *karakulak* f. *kara* black + *kulak* ear]

Caracalla /ˌkærəˈkælə/ the nickname (lit. 'a hooded Gallic cloak') of Marcus Aurelius Antoninus (188–217), Roman emperor 211–17, son of the emperor Septimius Severus. Sole ruler after the murder of his brother Geta in 212, he campaigned first in Germany and then in the east, where he hoped to repeat the conquests of Alexander the Great, but was assassinated in Mesopotamia. By an edict of 212 he granted Roman citizenship to all free inhabitants of the Roman Empire.

Caracas /kəˈrækəs/ the capital of Venezuela, famous as the birthplace of the revolutionary leader Simón Bolívar; pop. (1981) 1,163,000.

caracole /ˈkærəˌkəʊl/ *n.* & *v.* —*n.* a horse's half-turn to the right or left. —*v.* **1** *intr.* (of a horse or its rider) perform a caracole. **2** *tr.* make (a horse) caracole. [F]

caracul var. of KARAKUL.

carafe /kəˈræf, -rɑːf/ *n.* a glass container for water or wine, esp. at a table or bedside. [F f. It. *caraffa*, ult. f. Arab. *ġarrāfa* drinking vessel]

Carajás /ˌkærəˈʒɑːs/ a mining region in the State of Pará in north Brazil, the site of one of the richest deposits of iron ore in the world.

carambola /ˌkærəmˈbəʊlə/ *n.* **1** a small tree, *Averrhoa carambola*, native to SE Asia, bearing golden-yellow ribbed fruit. **2** this fruit. Also called *star fruit*. [Port., prob. of Indian or E. Indian orig.]

caramel /ˈkærəˌmel/ *n.* **1 a** sugar or syrup heated until it turns brown, then used as a flavouring or to colour spirits etc. **b** a kind of soft toffee made with sugar, butter, etc., melted and further heated. **2** the light-brown colour of caramel. [F f. Sp. *caramelo*]

caramelize /ˈkærəməˌlaɪz/ *v.* (also **-ise**) **1 a** *tr.* convert (sugar or syrup) into caramel. **b** *intr.* (of sugar or syrup) be converted into caramel. **2** *tr.* coat or cook (food) with caramelized sugar or syrup. □□ **caramelization** /-ˈzeɪʃ(ə)n/ *n.*

carapace /ˈkærəˌpeɪs/ *n.* the hard upper shell of a tortoise or a crustacean. [F f. Sp. *carapacho*]

carat /ˈkærət/ *n.* **1** a unit of weight for precious stones, now equivalent to 200 milligrams. **2** (*US* **karat**) a measure of purity of gold, pure gold being 24 carats. [F f. It. *carato* f. Arab. *qīrāṭ* weight of four grains, f. Gk *keration* fruit of the carob (dimin. of *keras* horn)]

Caratacus /kəˈrætəkəs/ (1st c. AD), son of Cunobelinus (see CYMBELINE). He took part in the resistance to the Roman invasion of AD 43, and when defeated fled first to the Welsh border and then to Yorkshire, where Cartimandua, queen of the Brigantes, surrendered him to the Romans in AD 51.

Caravaggio /ˌkærəˈvædʒɪˌəʊ/, properly Michelangelo Merisi da Caravaggio (1571–1610), Italian painter who was an important figure in the transition from late mannerism to the baroque, and had a far-reaching European influence, affecting Ribera, Rubens, Georges de la Tour, and, indirectly, Rembrandt. Born near Bergamo, he trained under a pupil of Titian, and was in Rome by 1592. Here he developed his characteristic style: using dramatic lighting, foreshortening, and unexpected poses, often making the figures seem unnervingly close to the spectator, he adopted a literal, realistic approach to traditional subjects, which revitalized religious art and rescued it from the nebulous unreality of late 16th-c. painting. In *The Death of the Virgin* the model was, reputedly, a drowned prostitute. Several of his altarpieces were rejected by the clergy on the grounds of indecorum, but he had powerful defenders, including cardinals and noblemen. Caravaggio's life was short and violent: forced to flee from Rome in 1606 after killing a man in a brawl, he spent his remaining years in Naples, Malta, and Sicily, dying of fever in 1610.

caravan /ˈkærəˌvæn/ *n. & v.* —*n.* **1 a** *Brit.* a vehicle equipped for living in and usu. towed by a motor vehicle or a horse. **b** *US* a covered motor vehicle equipped for living in. **2** a company of merchants or pilgrims etc. travelling together, esp. across a desert in Asia or N. Africa. **3** a covered cart or carriage. —*v.intr.* (**caravanned**, **caravanning**) travel or live in a caravan. □ **caravan site** (or **park**) a place where caravans are parked as dwellings, often with special amenities. □□ **caravanner** *n.* [F *caravane* f. Pers. *kārwān*]

caravanette /ˌkærəvæˈnet/ *n.* a motor vehicle with a caravan-like rear compartment for eating, sleeping, etc.

caravanserai /ˌkærəˈvænsɒrɪ, -ˌraɪ/ *n.* an Eastern inn with a central court where caravans (see CARAVAN 2) may rest. [Pers. *kārwānsarāy* f. *sarāy* palace]

caravel /ˈkærəˌvel/ *n.* (also **carvel** /ˈkɑːv(ə)l/) *hist.* a small light fast ship, chiefly Spanish and Portuguese of the 15th–17th c. [F *caravelle* f. Port. *caravela* f. Gk *karabos* horned beetle, light ship]

caraway /ˈkærəˌweɪ/ *n.* an umbelliferous plant, *Carum carvi*, bearing clusters of tiny white flowers. □ **caraway seed** its fruit used as flavouring and as a source of oil. [prob. OSp. *alcarahueya* f. Arab. *alkarāwiyā*, perh. f. Gk *karon*, *kareon* cumin]

carb /kɑːb/ *n. colloq.* a carburettor. [abbr.]

carbamate /ˈkɑːbəˌmeɪt/ *n. Chem.* a salt or ester of an amide of carbonic acid. [CARBONIC + AMIDE]

carbide /ˈkɑːbaɪd/ *n. Chem.* **1** a binary compound of carbon. **2** = *calcium carbide*.

carbine /ˈkɑːbaɪn/ *n.* a short firearm, usu. a rifle, orig. for cavalry use. [F *carabine* (this form also earlier in Engl.), weapon of the *carabin* mounted musketeer]

carbo- /ˈkɑːbəʊ/ *comb. form* carbon (*carbohydrate*; *carbolic*; *carboxyl*).

carbohydrate /ˌkɑːbəˈhaɪdreɪt/ *n. Biochem.* any of a large group of energy-producing organic compounds containing carbon, hydrogen, and oxygen, e.g. starch, glucose, and other sugars.

carbolic /kɑːˈbɒlɪk/ *n.* (in full **carbolic acid**) phenol, esp. when used as a disinfectant. □ **carbolic soap** soap containing this. [CARBO- + -OL¹ + -IC]

carbon /ˈkɑːbən/ *n.* **1** a non-metallic element occurring naturally as diamond, graphite, and charcoal, and in all organic compounds. (See below.) ¶ Symb.: **C**; atomic number 6. **2 a** = *carbon copy*. **b** = *carbon paper*. **3** a rod of carbon in an arc lamp. □ **carbon black** a fine carbon powder made by burning hydrocarbons in insufficient air. **carbon copy 1** a copy made with carbon paper. **2** a person or thing identical or similar to another (*is a carbon copy of his father*). **carbon cycle** see separate entry. **carbon dating** the determination of the age of an organic object from the ratio of isotopes which changes as carbon-14 decays. (See RADIOCARBON.) **carbon dioxide** a colourless odourless gas occurring naturally in the atmosphere and formed by respiration. ¶ Chem. formula: CO_2. **carbon disulphide** a

colourless liquid used as a solvent. ¶ Chem. formula: CS_2. **carbon fibre** a thin strong crystalline filament of carbon used as strengthening material in resins, ceramics, etc. **carbon-14** a long-lived radioactive carbon isotope of mass 14, used in radiocarbon dating, and as a tracer in biochemistry. **carbon monoxide** a colourless odourless toxic gas formed by the incomplete burning of carbon. ¶ Chem. formula: CO. **carbon paper** a thin carbon-coated paper used for making (esp. typed) copies. **carbon steel** a steel with properties dependent on the percentage of carbon present. **carbon tetrachloride** a colourless volatile liquid used as a solvent. ¶ Chem. formula: CCl_4. **carbon-12** a carbon isotope of mass 12, used in calculations of atomic mass units. [F *carbone* f. L *carbo -onis* charcoal]

The element occurs naturally as diamond and graphite; charcoal and coke are also composed of carbon. It has many economic uses, but its unique significance is that carbon compounds form the physical basis of all living organisms. Carbon has the property of combining with itself and other elements to form molecules consisting of rings or long chains of atoms, and an immense variety of compounds can therefore exist. The chemistry of such compounds found in living things or their remains was once thought to obey laws different from those governing other substances, whence the original separation of 'organic chemistry' as a distinct branch of the subject.

carbonaceous /ˌkɑːbəˈneɪʃəs/ *adj.* **1** consisting of or containing carbon. **2** of or like coal or charcoal.

carbonade /ˌkɑːbəˈneɪd/ *n.* a rich beef stew made with onions and beer. [F]

carbonado /ˌkɑːbəˈneɪdəʊ/ *n.* (*pl.* **-os**) a dark opaque or impure kind of diamond used as an abrasive, for drills etc. [Port.]

carbonate /ˈkɑːbəˌneɪt/ *n. & v.* —*n. Chem.* a salt of carbonic acid. —*v.tr.* **1** impregnate with carbon dioxide; aerate. **2** convert into a carbonate. □□ **carbonation** /-ˈneɪʃ(ə)n/ *n.* [F *carbonat* f. mod.L *carbonatum* (as CARBON)]

carbon cycle *n.* **1** *Biol.* the cycle in which carbon is absorbed from and replaced in the atmosphere. Carbon dioxide from the air is converted into more complex substances by plants, which are eaten by animals, and is finally released again into the air by the respiration of plants and animals or when organic substances decay. **2** *Physics* a cycle of thermonuclear reactions in stellar regions, in which carbon acts as a catalyst in the conversion of hydrogen into helium. The consequent energy released is held to be the source of the energy radiated by the sun and stars.

carbonic /kɑːˈbɒnɪk/ *adj. Chem.* containing carbon. □ **carbonic acid** a very weak acid formed from carbon dioxide dissolved in water. **carbonic acid gas** *archaic* carbon dioxide.

carboniferous /ˌkɑːbəˈnɪfərəs/ *adj. & n.* —*adj.* **1** producing coal. **2** (**Carboniferous**) *Geol.* of or relating to the fifth period in the Palaeozoic era, following the Devonian and preceding the Permian, lasting from about 360 to 286 million years ago. During this period seed-bearing plants first appeared, corals were widespread, and extensive limestone deposits were formed, rivers formed deltas, and luxuriant vegetation developed on coastal swamps. This vegetation was later drowned and buried under mud and sand, and subsequently became coal. In the US the Pennsylvanian and Mississippian periods correspond to the Carboniferous of other areas. —*n.* (**Carboniferous**) *Geol.* this period or system.

carbonize /ˈkɑːbəˌnaɪz/ *v.tr.* (also **-ise**) **1** convert into carbon by heating. **2** reduce to charcoal or coke. **3** coat with carbon. □□ **carbonization** /-ˈzeɪʃ(ə)n/ *n.*

carbonyl /ˈkɑːbəˌnaɪl/ *n.* (used *attrib.*) *Chem.* the divalent radical CO.

carborundum /ˌkɑːbəˈrʌndəm/ *n.* a compound of carbon and silicon used esp. as an abrasive. [CARBON + CORUNDUM]

carboxyl /kɑːˈbɒksɪl/ *n. Chem.* the univalent acid radical (—COOH), present in most organic acids. □□ **carboxylic** *adj.* [CARBON + OXYGEN + -YL]

carboy /ˈkɑːbɔɪ/ *n.* a large globular glass bottle usu. protected by a frame, for containing liquids. [Pers. *karāba* large glass flagon]

carbuncle /ˈkɑːbʌŋk(ə)l/ *n.* **1** a severe abscess in the skin. **2** a bright red gem. □□ **carbuncular** /-'bʌŋkjʊlə(r)/ adj. [ME f. OF charbucle etc. f. L carbunculus small coal f. carbo coal]

carburation /ˌkɑːbjʊ'reɪʃ(ə)n/ n. the process of charging air with a spray of liquid hydrocarbon fuel, esp. in an internal-combustion engine. [as CARBURET]

carburet /ˌkɑːbjʊ'ret/ v.tr. (**carburetted**, **carburetting**; US **carbureted**, **carbureting**) combine (a gas etc.) with carbon. [earlier carbure f. F f. L carbo (as CARBON)]

carburettor /ˌkɑːbjʊ'retə(r), ˌkɑːbə-/ n. (also **carburetter**, US **carburetor**) an apparatus for carburation of petrol and air in an internal-combustion engine. [as CARBURET + -OR¹]

carcajou /'kɑːkə,dʒuː, -kə,ʒuː/ n. US = WOLVERINE. [F, app. of Amer. Ind. orig.]

carcass /'kɑːkəs/ n. (also **carcase**) 1 the dead body of an animal, esp. a trunk for cutting up as meat. 2 the bones of a cooked bird. 3 derog. the human body, living or dead. 4 the skeleton, framework of a building, ship, etc. 5 worthless remains. □ **carcass meat** raw meat, not preserved. [ME f. AF carcois (OF charcois) & f. F carcasse: ult. orig. unkn.]

Carcassonne /ˌkɑːkə'sɒn/ a city in SW France, noted for its (much-restored) medieval fortifications; pop. (1975) 338,890. The fortress was besieged, but not captured, by the Black Prince in 1355.

Carchemish /'kɑːkɪmɪʃ/ an ancient city situated in a strategic position on the upper Euphrates, Hittite stronghold, annexed by Sargon II of Assyria in 717 BC.

carcinogen /kɑː'sɪnədʒ(ə)n/ n. any substance that produces cancer. [as CARCINOMA + -GEN]

carcinogenesis /ˌkɑːsɪnə'dʒenɪsɪs/ n. the production of cancer.

carcinogenic /ˌkɑːsɪnə'dʒenɪk/ adj. producing cancer. □□ **carcinogenicity** /-'nɪsɪtɪ/ n.

carcinoma /ˌkɑːsɪ'nəʊmə/ n. (pl. **carcinomata** /-tə/ or **carcinomas**) a cancer, esp. one arising in epithelial tissue. □□ **carcinomatous** adj. [L f. Gk karkinōma f. karkinos crab]

card¹ /kɑːd/ n. & v. —n. 1 thick stiff paper or thin pasteboard. 2 **a** a flat piece of this, esp. for writing or printing on. **b** = POSTCARD. **c** a card used to send greetings, issue an invitation, etc. (birthday card). **d** = visiting-card. **e** = business card. **f** a ticket of admission or membership. 3 **a** = PLAYING-CARD. **b** a similar card in a set designed for particular games, e.g. happy families. **c** (in pl.) card-playing; a card-game. 4 (in pl.) an employee's documents, esp. for tax and national insurance, held by the employer. 5 **a** a programme of events at a race-meeting etc. **b** Cricket a score-card. **c** a list of holes on a golf course, on which a player's scores are entered. 6 colloq. a person, esp. an odd or amusing one (what a card!; a knowing card). 7 a plan or expedient (sure card). 8 a printed or written notice, set of rules, etc., for display. 9 a small rectangular piece of plastic issued by a bank, building society, etc., with personal (often machine-readable) data on it, chiefly to obtain cash or credit (cheque card; credit card; do you have a card?). —v.tr. 1 fix to a card. 2 write on a card, esp. for indexing. □ **ask for** (or **get**) **one's cards** ask (or be told) to leave one's employment. **card-carrying** being a registered member of an organization, esp. a political party or trade union. **card-game** a game in which playing-cards are used. **card index** an index in which each item is entered on a separate card. **card-index** v.tr. make a card index of. **card-playing** the playing of card-games. **card-sharp** (or **-sharper**) a swindler at card-games. **card-table** a table for card-playing, esp. a folding one. **card up one's sleeve** a plan in reserve. **card vote** a block vote, esp. in trade-union meetings. **on** (US **in**) **the cards** possible or likely. **put** (or **lay**) **one's cards on the table** reveal one's resources, intentions, etc. [ME f. OF carte f. L charta f. Gk khartēs papyrus-leaf]

card² /kɑːd/ n. & v. —n. a toothed instrument, wire brush, etc., for raising a nap on cloth or for disentangling fibres before spinning. —v.tr. brush, comb, cleanse, or scratch with a card. □ **carding-wool** short-stapled wool. □□ **carder** n. [ME f. OF carde f. Prov. carda f. cardar tease, comb, ult. f. L carere card]

Card. abbr. Cardinal.

cardamom /'kɑːdəməm/ n. (also **cardamum**) 1 an aromatic SE Asian plant, Elettaria cardamomum. 2 the seed-capsules of this

used as a spice. [L cardamomum or F cardamome f. Gk kardamōmon f. kardamon cress + amōmon a spice plant]

Cardamom Mountains /'kɑːdəməm/ a range of mountains in western Cambodia, rising to a height of 1,813 m (5,886 ft.) at Phnomh Aural.

cardan joint /'kɑːd(ə)n/ n. Engin. a universal joint. [G. Cardano, It. mathematician d. 1576]

cardan shaft /'kɑːd(ə)n/ n. Engin. a shaft with a universal joint at one or both ends.

cardboard /'kɑːdbɔːd/ n. & adj. —n. pasteboard or stiff paper, esp. for making cards or boxes. —adj. 1 made of cardboard. 2 flimsy, insubstantial.

cardiac /'kɑːdɪˌæk/ adj. & n. —adj. 1 of or relating to the heart. 2 of or relating to the part of the stomach nearest the oesophagus. —n. a person with heart disease. [F cardiaque or L cardiacus f. Gk kardiakos f. kardia heart]

cardie var. of CARDY.

Cardiff /'kɑːdɪf/ the capital of Wales, at the mouth of the River Taff; pop. (1981) 278,900.

cardigan /'kɑːdɪgən/ n. a knitted jacket fastening down the front, usu. with long sleeves. [named after the 7th Earl of Cardigan (d. 1868), who led the disastrous Charge of the Light Brigade in the Crimean War]

Cardin /'kɑːdæ̃/, Pierre (1922–), French couturier, noted for his ready-to-wear clothes as well as for his haute couture. He was the first designer to show a collection of clothes for men (1960).

cardinal /'kɑːdɪn(ə)l/ n. & adj. —n. 1 (as a title **Cardinal**) a member of the Sacred College of the Roman Catholic Church. Cardinals hold the highest rank next to the pope, who is chosen from their number. 2 any small American songbird of the genus Richmondena, the males of which have scarlet plumage. 3 hist. a woman's cloak, orig. of scarlet cloth with a hood. —adj. 1 chief, fundamental; on which something hinges. 2 of deep scarlet (like a cardinal's cassock). □ **cardinal-flower** the scarlet lobelia. **cardinal humour** see HUMOUR. **cardinal numbers** those denoting quantity (one, two, three, etc.), as opposed to ordinal numbers (first, second, third, etc.). **cardinal points** the four main points of the compass (N., S., E., W.). **cardinal virtues** the chief moral attributes: justice, prudence, temperance, and fortitude. □□ **cardinalate** /-leɪt/ n. (in sense 1 of n.), as opposed to ordinal **cardinalship** n. (in sense 1 of n.). [ME f. OF f. L cardinalis f. cardo -inis hinge: in Eng. first applied to the four virtues on which conduct 'hinges']

cardio- /'kɑːdɪəʊ/ comb. form heart (cardiogram; cardiology). [Gk kardia heart]

cardiogram /'kɑːdɪəʊˌgræm/ n. a record of muscle activity within the heart, made by a cardiograph.

cardiograph /'kɑːdɪəʊˌgrɑːf/ n. an instrument for recording heart muscle activity. □□ **cardiographer** /-'ɒgrəfə(r)/ n. **cardiography** /-'ɒgrəfɪ/ n.

cardiology /ˌkɑːdɪ'ɒlədʒɪ/ n. the branch of medicine concerned with diseases and abnormalities of the heart. □□ **cardiologist** n.

cardiovascular /ˌkɑːdɪəʊ'væskjʊlə(r)/ adj. of or relating to the heart and blood vessels.

cardoon /kɑː'duːn/ n. a thistle-like plant, Cynara cardunculus, allied to the globe artichoke, with leaves used as a vegetable. [F cardon ult. f. L cardu(u)s thistle]

cardphone /'kɑːdfəʊn/ n. a public telephone operated by the insertion of a prepaid plastic machine-readable card instead of money.

cardy /'kɑːdɪ/ n. (also **cardie**) (pl. **-ies**) colloq. a cardigan. [abbr.]

care /keə(r)/ n. & v. —n. 1 worry, anxiety. 2 an occasion for this. 3 serious attention; heed, caution, pains (assembled with care; handle with care). 4 **a** protection, charge. **b** Brit. = child care. 5 a thing to be done or seen to. —v.intr. 1 (usu. foll. by about, for, whether) feel concern or interest. 2 (usu. foll. by for, about, and with neg. expressed or implied) feel liking, affection, regard, or deference (don't care for jazz). 3 (foll. by to + infin.) wish or be willing (should not care to be seen with him; would you care to try *them?*). □ **care for** provide for; look after. **care-label** a label attached to clothing, with instructions for washing etc. **care of** at the address of (*sent it care of his sister*). **have a care** take care; be careful. **I** (etc.) **couldn't** (*US* **could**) **care less** *colloq.* an expression of complete indifference. **in care** *Brit.* (of a child) taken into the care of a local authority. **take care 1** be careful. **2** (foll. by *to* + infin.) not fail or neglect. **take care of 1** look after; keep safe. **2** deal with. **3** dispose of. [OE *caru, carian,* f. Gmc]

careen /kəˈriːn/ v. **1** *tr.* turn (a ship) on one side for cleaning, caulking, or repair. **2 a** *intr.* tilt; lean over. **b** *tr.* cause to do this. **3** *intr. US* swerve about; career. ¶ Sense 3 is infl. by *career* (v.). □□ **careenage** *n.* [earlier as noun, = careened position of ship, f. F *carène* f. It. *carena* f. L *carina* keel]

career /kəˈrɪə(r)/ *n. & v.* —*n.* **1 a** one's advancement through life, esp. in a profession. **b** the progress through history of a group or institution. **2** a profession or occupation, esp. as offering advancement. **3** (*attrib.*) **a** pursuing or wishing to pursue a career (*career woman*). **b** working permanently in a specified profession (*career diplomat*). **4** swift course; impetus (*in full career*). —*v.intr.* **1** move or swerve about wildly. **2** go swiftly. [F *carrière* f. It. *carriera* ult. f. L *carrus* CAR]

careerist /kəˈrɪərɪst/ *n.* a person predominantly concerned with personal advancement.

carefree /ˈkeəfriː/ *adj.* free from anxiety or responsibility; light-hearted. □□ **carefreeness** *n.*

careful /ˈkeəfʊl/ *adj.* **1** painstaking, thorough. **2** cautious. **3** done with care and attention. **4** (usu. foll. by *that* + clause, or *to* + infin.) taking care; not neglecting. **5** (foll. by *for, of*) concerned for; taking care of. □□ **carefully** *adv.* **carefulness** *n.* [OE *carful* (as CARE, -FUL)]

careless /ˈkeəlɪs/ *adj.* **1** not taking care or paying attention. **2** unthinking, insensitive. **3** done without care; inaccurate. **4** light-hearted. **5** (foll. by *of*) not concerned about; taking no heed of. **6** effortless. □□ **carelessly** *adv.* **carelessness** *n.* [OE *carlēas* (as CARE, -LESS)]

carer /ˈkeərə(r)/ *n.* a person who cares for a sick or elderly person.

caress /kəˈres/ *v. & n.* —*v.tr.* **1** touch or stroke gently or lovingly; kiss. **2** treat fondly or kindly. —*n.* a loving or gentle touch or kiss. [F *caresse* (n.), *caresser* (v.), f. It. *carezza* ult. f. L *carus* dear]

caret /ˈkærət/ *n.* a mark (∧ , ⋏) indicating a proposed insertion in printing or writing. [L, = is lacking]

caretaker /ˈkeəˌteɪkə(r)/ *n.* **1** a person employed to look after something, esp. a house in the owner's absence, or *Brit.* a public building. **2** (*attrib.*) exercising temporary authority (*caretaker government*).

careworn /ˈkeəwɔːn/ *adj.* showing the effects of prolonged worry.

Carey /ˈkeərɪ/, George Leonard (1935–), English Anglican churchman, Archbishop of Canterbury from April 1991.

carfare /ˈkɑːfeə(r)/ *n. US* a passenger's fare to travel by bus.

cargo /ˈkɑːgəʊ/ *n.* (pl. **-oes** or **-os**) **1** goods carried on a ship or aircraft. **2** *US* goods carried in a motor vehicle. □ **cargo cult** (orig. in the Pacific Islands) a belief in the forthcoming arrival of ancestral spirits bringing cargoes of food and other goods. [Sp. (as CHARGE)]

carhop /ˈkɑːhɒp/ *n. US colloq.* a waiter at a drive-in restaurant.

Caria /ˈkeərɪə/ the ancient name for the region of SW Asia Minor south of the river Maeander and NW of Lycia. □□ **Carian** *adj. & n.*

cariama var. of SERIEMA.

Carib /ˈkærɪb/ *n. & adj.* —*n.* **1** a member of the pre-Columbian American Indian inhabitants of the Lesser Antilles and parts of the neighbouring South American coast, or of their descendants. (See below.) **2** the language of this people. —*adj.* of or relating to this people or their language. [Sp. *Caribe* f. Haitian]

A fearsome maritime people, the Caribs forced the peaceful Arawak-speaking peoples of the Antilles to migrate to South America to escape their depredations. Still expanding at the time of Spanish conquest the Caribs were supplanted, in turn, by European colonialism and have all but disappeared in the West Indies (where only a few hundred still remain on the island of

Dominica). On mainland South America Carib-speaking groups occupy territory in the NE and Amazon regions, living in small autonomous communities. Peculiarly, the Carib language was spoken only by men; their women, who were captured in raids on other tribes, spoke only Arawak. Male captives were tortured and eaten—hence giving the Carib name not only to the Caribbean Sea but also to the root of the English word 'cannibal'.

Caribbean /ˌkærɪˈbiːən, kəˈrɪbɪən/ *n. & adj.* —*n.* the Caribbean Sea. —*adj.* **1** of or relating to this sea or region. **2** of the Caribs or their language or culture. □ **Caribbean Community and Common Market** an organization established in 1973 to promote cooperation in economic affairs and social services etc. and to coordinate foreign policy among its members, all of which are independent States of this region. Its headquarters are at Georgetown, Guyana. **Caribbean Sea** the part of the Atlantic lying between the Antilles and the mainland of Central and South America.

caribou /ˈkærɪbuː/ *n.* (pl. same) a N. American reindeer. [Can. F, prob. f. Amer. Ind.]

caricature /ˈkærɪkətjʊə(r)/ *n. & v.* —*n.* **1** a grotesque usu. comic representation of a person by exaggeration of characteristic traits, in a picture, writing, or mime. **2** a ridiculously poor or absurd imitation or version. —*v.tr.* make or give a caricature of. □□ **caricatural** *adj.* **caricaturist** *n.* [F f. It. *caricatura* f. *caricare* load, exaggerate: see CHARGE]

CARICOM *abbr.* Caribbean Community and Common Market (see CARIBBEAN).

caries /ˈkeəriːz, -rɪˌiːz/ *n.* (pl. same) decay and crumbling of a tooth or bone. [L]

carillon /kəˈrɪljən, ˈkærɪljən/ *n.* **1** a set of bells sounded either from a keyboard or mechanically. **2** a tune played on bells. **3** an organ-stop imitating a peal of bells. [F f. OF *quarregnon* peal of four bells, alt. of Rmc *quaternio* f. L *quattuor* four]

carina /kəˈriːnə/ *n. Biol.* a keel-shaped structure, esp. the ridge of a bird's breastbone. □□ **carinal** *adj.* [L, = keel]

carinate /ˈkærɪˌneɪt/ *adj.* (of a bird) having a keeled breastbone (opp. RATITE). [L *carinatus* keeled f. *carina* keel]

caring /ˈkeərɪŋ/ *adj.* compassionate, esp. with reference to the professional care of the sick or elderly.

Carinthia /kəˈrɪnθɪə/ (German **Kärnten** /ˈkeənt(ə)n/) an Alpine province of southern Austria; pop. (1981) 536,700; capital, Klagenfurt.

carioca /ˌkærɪˈəʊkə/ *n.* **1 a** a Brazilian dance like the samba. **b** the music for this. **2** a native of Rio de Janeiro. [Port.]

cariogenic /ˌkeərɪəʊˈdʒenɪk/ *adj.* causing caries.

carious /ˈkeərɪəs/ *adj.* (of bones or teeth) decayed. [L *cariosus*]

carking /ˈkɑːkɪŋ/ *adj. archaic* burdensome (*carking care*). [part. of obs. *cark* (v.) f. ONF *carkier* f. Rmc, rel. to CHARGE]

carl /kɑːl/ *n. Sc.* a man; a fellow. [OE f. ON *karl,* rel. to CHURL]

carline /ˈkɑːlɪn/ *n.* any plant of the genus *Carlina,* esp. the thistle-like *C. vulgaris.* [F f. med.L *carlina* perh. for *cardina* (L *carduus* thistle), assoc. with *Carolus Magnus* Charlemagne]

carload /ˈkɑːləʊd/ *n.* **1** a quantity that can be carried in a car. **2** *US* the minimum quantity of goods for which a lower rate is charged for transport.

Carlovingian var. of CAROLINGIAN.

Carlow /ˈkɑːləʊ/ **1** a county in the province of Leinster in the Republic of Ireland. **2** its capital city; pop. (1981) 11,720.

Carlsbad see KARLOVY VARY.

Carlyle /kɑːˈlaɪl/, Thomas (1795–1881), Scottish historian and political philosopher. He had already embarked on a literary career when he married Jane Welsh in 1826, later celebrated for her brilliant letters. The Carlyles moved to London in 1834, shortly after the publication of the idiosyncratic *Sartor Resartus* (1833–4), where he established himself as 'the sage of Chelsea', revered almost as a prophet, and renowned for his history of the French Revolution (1837), his popular public lectures (*On Heroes and Hero-Worship,* 1840), and his attacks on the dehumanizing effects of utilitarian economics. He exalted the medieval past as a time of harmony and violently attacked the consequences of the Industrial Revolution, abhorred materialism, and showed genuine compassion for the poor; his views became increasingly anti-democratic. His important works include an edition of Cromwell's letters and speeches (1845) and a lengthy life of Frederick the Great (1858–65); a more human perspective is seen in his letters and in J. A. Froude's notoriously frank biography (1882–4).

carman /ˈkɑːmæn/ n. US **1** the driver of a van. **2** a carrier.

Carmel /ˈkɑːm(ə)l/, **Mount** a group of mountains in NW Israel ner the Mediterranean coast, rising to a height of 552 m (1,812 ft.) and sheltering the port of Haifa. On its SW slopes are caves that provided evidence of human occupation dating from the palaeolithic down to the mesolithic periods. The Carmelite order (see entry) was founded on Mount Carmel during the Crusades.

Carmelite /ˈkɑːmɪˌlaɪt/ n. & adj. —n. **1** a friar of the Order of Our Lady of Mount Carmel. (See below.) **2** a nun of a similar order. —adj. of or relating to the Carmelites. [F Carmelite or med.L carmelita f. Mt. Carmel in Palestine, where the order was founded]

   The 'Order of Our Lady of Mount Carmel' (also called 'White Friars' from the colour of their cloaks) was founded in Palestine by St Berthold c.1154; a corresponding order of nuns was established in 1452. In the 16th c., after discipline in the order had become relaxed, the 'discalced' reform movement, begun by St Teresa of Avila and St John of the Cross towards the end of the century, gradually spread, restoring the stricter rule. The order is contemplative and has produced great mystics.

Carmichael /kɑːˈmaɪk(ə)l/, Hoagy (real name Howard Hoagland, 1899–1981), American jazz musician, composer, and singer, and film actor. His best-known songs include 'Stardust' (1929), 'Two Sleepy People' (1938), and 'In the Cool, Cool, Cool of the Evening' (1951).

carminative /ˈkɑːmɪnətɪv/ adj. & n. —adj. relieving flatulence. —n. a carminative drug. [F carminatif -ive or med.L carminare heal (by incantation): see CHARM]

carmine /ˈkɑːmaɪn/ adj. & n. —adj. of a vivid crimson colour. —n. **1** this colour. **2** a vivid crimson pigment made from cochineal. [F carmin or med.L carminium perh. f. carmesinum crimson + minium cinnabar]

Carnac /ˈkɑːnæk/ a village in NW France, near the Atlantic coast of Brittany, site of a group of stone monuments dating from prehistoric times, chiefly the neolithic period. There are nearly 3,000 stones, which include single standing stones (menhirs), dolmens, and the long avenues of grey monoliths that march across the countryside, arranged in order of height so that they decrease steadily from about 3–3.7 metres (10–12 ft.) to 1–1.2 metres (3–4 ft.); some of these avenues end in semicircular or rectangular enclosures of standing stones.

carnage /ˈkɑːnɪdʒ/ n. great slaughter, esp. of human beings in battle. [F f. It. carnaggio f. med.L carnaticum f. L caro carnis flesh]

carnal /ˈkɑːn(ə)l/ adj. **1** of the body or flesh; worldly. **2** sensual, sexual. □ **carnal knowledge** Law sexual intercourse. □□ **carnality** /-ˈnælɪti/ n. **carnalize** v.tr. (also **-ise**). **carnally** adv. [ME f. LL carnalis f. caro carnis flesh]

Carnap /ˈkɑːnæp/, Rudolf (1891–1970), German-American philosopher, one of the originators of logical positivism, a founder and most influential member of the Vienna Circle, noted for his contributions to logic, the analysis of language, the theory of probability, and the philosophy of science. He thought the philosopher's task was to construct logically rigorous languages capable of expressing the truths of science, and attempted to fix meaning by stipulation and to define necessity in terms of it. At the heart of his view was the belief (modified over the years) that a statement is meaningful only if it can be verified by sensory observation; this led to a robust dismissal of the problems of traditional metaphysics.

carnassial /kɑːˈnæsɪəl/ adj. & n. —adj. (of a carnivore's upper premolar and lower molar teeth) adapted for shearing flesh. —n. such a tooth. Also called SECTORIAL. [F carnassier carnivorous]

carnation[1] /kɑːˈneɪʃ(ə)n/ n. **1** any of several cultivated varieties of clove-scented pink, with variously coloured showy flowers

(see also CLOVE[1] 2). **2** this flower. [orig. uncert.: in early use varying with coronation]

carnation[2] /kɑːˈneɪʃ(ə)n/ n. & adj. —n. a rosy pink colour. —adj. of this colour. [F f. It. carnagione ult. f. L caro carnis flesh]

carnauba /kɑːˈnaʊbə, -ˈnɔːbə, -ˈnaʊbə/ n. **1** a fan palm, Copernicia cerifera, native to NE Brazil. **2** (in full **carnauba wax**) the yellowish leaf-wax of this tree used as a polish etc. [Port.]

Carné /ˈkɑːneɪ/, Marcel (1909–   ), French film director, whose partnership with the scriptwriter Pierre Prévert produced some memorable films, including Le Jour se lève (1939), Les Enfants du Paradis (1945), and Les Portes de la Nuit (1946). His films are characterized by a fatalistic outlook and masterly evocation of atmosphere. Carné held a dominant position among film-makers of the 1930s and 1940s, but more recent evaluation, with modern taste for flexibility and freedom, has disliked the cold visual perfection of the studio-bound and rehearsed artistry of his films.

Carnegie /kɑːˈneɪɡɪ/, Andrew (1835–1919), son of a Scottish immigrant weaver, who built up a huge fortune in the steel industry in the US through his own shrewdness and energy. He retired from business in 1901 and devoted his wealth to charitable purposes on both sides of the Atlantic. One of his most notable achievements was the creation of the Carnegie Peace Fund to promote international peace.

carnelian var. of CORNELIAN.

carnet /ˈkɑːneɪ/ n. **1** a customs permit to take a motor vehicle across a frontier for a limited period. **2** a permit allowing use of a camp-site. [F, = notebook]

carnival /ˈkɑːnɪv(ə)l/ n. **1 a** the festivities usual during the period before Lent in Roman Catholic countries. **b** any festivities, esp. those occurring at a regular date. **2** merrymaking, revelry. **3** US a travelling funfair or circus. [It. carne-, carnovale f. med.L carnelevarium etc. Shrovetide f. L caro carnis flesh + levare put away]

carnivore /ˈkɑːnɪvɔː(r)/ n. **1 a** any mammal of the order Carnivora, with powerful jaws and teeth adapted for stabbing, tearing, and eating flesh, including cats, dogs, and bears. **b** any other flesh-eating mammal. **2** any flesh-eating plant.

carnivorous /kɑːˈnɪvərəs/ adj. **1** (of an animal) feeding on flesh. **2** (of a plant) digesting trapped insects or other animal substances. **3** of or relating to the order Carnivora. □□ **carnivorously** adv. **carnivorousness** n. [L carnivorus f. caro carnis flesh + -VOROUS]

Carnot /ˈkɑːnəʊ/, Nicolas Léonard Sadi (1796–1832), French scientist, noted for his contributions to thermodynamics. An army officer for most of his short life, Carnot became interested in the principles of operation of steam-engines and, in a book published in 1824, analysed the efficiency of such engines, using the notion of a cycle of reversible temperature and pressure changes of the gases within. Although Carnot's work had no influence on contemporary engine design, it was recognized after his death as being of crucial importance to the theory of thermodynamics.

carob /ˈkærəb/ n. **1** (in full **carob-tree**) an evergreen tree, Ceratonia siliqua, native to the Mediterranean, bearing edible pods. **2** its bean-shaped edible seed pod sometimes used as a substitute for chocolate. [obs. F carobe f. med.L carrubia, -um f. Arab. ḳarrūba]

carol /ˈkær(ə)l/ n. & v. —n. a joyous song, esp. a Christmas hymn. —v. (**carolled, carolling**; US **caroled, caroling**) **1** intr. sing carols, esp. outdoors at Christmas. **2** tr. & intr. sing joyfully. □□ **caroler** n. (also **caroller**). [ME f. OF carole, caroler, of unkn. orig.]

Caroline /ˈkærəˌlaɪn/ adj. **1** (also **Carolean** /-ˈliːən/) of the time of Charles I or II of England. **2** = CAROLINGIAN adj. 2. [L Carolus Charles]

Caroline Islands /ˈkærəˌlaɪn/ (also **Carolines**) a group of islands in the western Pacific Ocean, north of the equator, forming (with the exception of Palau and some smaller islands) the Federated States of Micronesia.

Carolingian /ˌkærəˈlɪndʒɪən/ adj. & n. (also **Carlovingian** /ˌkɑːləˈvɪndʒɪən/) —adj. **1** of or relating to a Frankish dynasty that ruled in western Europe from 750 to 987, many of whose members were called Charles, including Charlemagne (see entry). **2** of a style of script developed in France at the time of Charlemagne. —*n.* **1** a member of the Carolingian dynasty. **2** the Carolingian style of script. [F *carlovingien* f. *Karl* Charles after *mérovingien* (see MEROVINGIAN): reformed after L *Carolus*]

carom /ˈkærəm/ *n.* & *v.* *US Billiards* —*n.* a cannon. —*v.intr.* **1** make a carom. **2** (usu. foll. by *off*) strike and rebound. [abbr. of *carambole* f. Sp. *carambola*]

carotene /ˈkærəˌtiːn/ *n.* any of several orange-coloured plant pigments found in carrots, tomatoes, etc., acting as a source of vitamin A. [G *Carotin* f. L *carota* CARROT]

carotenoid /kəˈrɒtɪˌnɔɪd/ *n.* any of a group of yellow, orange, or brown pigments giving characteristic colour to plant organs, e.g. ripe tomatoes, carrots, autumn leaves, etc.

Carothers /kəˈrʌðəz/, Wallace Hume (1896–1937), American industrial chemist who in 1928 was appointed director of research in organic chemistry by the firm of E. I. du Pont de Nemours. He took up the study of long-chain molecules, now called polymers, developed (with J. A. Nieuwland) the synthetic rubber 'neoprene', and in the early 1930s the first melt-spun synthetic fibre, 'Nylon 66'. He committed suicide at the age of 41 before nylon had been commercially exploited, and it was left to others to follow his lead and discover the polyester fibres.

carotid /kəˈrɒtɪd/ *n.* & *adj.* —*n.* each of the two main arteries carrying blood to the head and neck. —*adj.* of or relating to either of these arteries. [F *carotide* or mod.L *carotides* f. Gk *karoōtides* (pl.) f. *karoō* stupefy (compression of these arteries bein thought to cause stupor)]

carouse /kəˈraʊz/ *v.* & *n.* —*v.intr.* **1** have a noisy or lively drinking-party. **2** drink heavily. —*n.* a noisy or lively drinking-party. □□ **carousal** *n.* **carouser** *n.* [orig. as adv. = right out, in phr. *drink carouse* f. G *gar aus trinken*]

carousel /ˌkærəˈsel, -ˈzel/ *n.* (*US* **carrousel**) **1** *US* a merry-go-round or roundabout. **2** a rotating delivery or conveyor system, esp. for passengers' luggage at an airport. **3** *hist.* a kind of equestrian tournament. [F *carrousel* f. It. *carosello*]

carp[1] /kɑːp/ *n.* (pl. same) any freshwater fish of the family Cyprinidae, esp. *Cyprinus carpio*, often bred for use as food. [ME f. OF *carpe* f. Prov. or f. LL *carpa*]

carp[2] /kɑːp/ *v.intr.* (usu. foll. by *at*) find fault; complain pettily. □□ **carper** *n.* [obs. ME senses 'talk, say, sing' f. ON *karpa* to brag: mod. sense (16th c.) from or infl. by L *carpere* pluck at, slander]

Carpaccio /kɑːˈpætʃɪˌəʊ/, Vittore (*c.*1450/60–1525/6), Venetian painter, noted especially for his paintings of Venice and for his lively narrative cycle of paintings *Scenes from the Life of St Ursula*.

carpal /ˈkɑːp(ə)l/ *adj.* & *n.* —*adj.* of or relating to the bones in the wrist. —*n.* any of the bones forming the wrist. [CARPUS + -AL]

Carpathian Mountains /kɑːˈpeɪθɪən/ (also **Carpathians**) a mountain system extending SE from southern Poland and Czechoslovakia into Romania.

carpel /ˈkɑːp(ə)l/ *n.* *Bot.* the female reproductive organ of a flower, consisting of a stigma, style, and ovary. □□ **carpellary** *adj.* [F *carpelle* or mod.L *carpellum* f. Gk *karpos* fruit]

Carpentaria /ˌkɑːpənˈteərɪə/, **Gulf of** a large bay indenting the eastern part of the north coast of Australia, between the Arnhem Land and Cape York peninsulas.

carpenter /ˈkɑːpɪntə(r)/ *n.* & *v.* —*n.* a person skilled in woodwork, esp. of a structural kind (cf. JOINER). —*v.* **1** *intr.* do carpentry. **2** *tr.* make by means of carpentry. **3** *tr.* (often foll. by *together*) construct; fit together. □ **carpenter ant** any large ant of the genus *Camponotus*, boring into wood to nest. **carpenter bee** any of various solitary bees, which bore into wood. [ME & AF; OF *carpentier* f. LL *carpentarius* f. *carpentum* wagon f. Gaulish]

carpentry /ˈkɑːpɪntrɪ/ *n.* **1** the work or occupation of a carpenter. **2** timber-work constructed by a carpenter. [ME f. OF *carpenterie* f. L *carpentaria*: see CARPENTER]

carpet /ˈkɑːpɪt/ *n.* & *v.* —*n.* **1 a** thick fabric for covering a floor or stairs. **b** a piece of this fabric. **2** an expanse or layer resembling a carpet in being smooth, soft, bright, or thick (*carpet of snow*).

—*v.tr.* (**carpeted, carpeting**) **1** cover with or as with a carpet. **2** *colloq.* reprimand, reprove. □ **carpet-bag** a travelling-bag of a kind orig. made of carpet-like material. **carpet-bagger 1** esp. *US* a political candidate in an area where the candidate has no local connections (orig. any of the adventurers from the northern States who went into the southern States after the American Civil War, in order to profit from the postwar reorganization, so called from the carpet-bag which held all their possessions). **2** an unscrupulous opportunist. **carpet bombing** intensive bombing. **carpet slipper** a kind of slipper with the upper made orig. of carpet-like material. **carpet-sweeper** a household implement with a revolving brush or brushes for sweeping carpets. **on the carpet 1** *colloq.* being reprimanded. **2** under consideration. **sweep under the carpet** conceal (a problem or difficulty) in the hope that it will be forgotten. [ME f. OF *carpite* or med.L *carpita*, f. obs. It. *carpita* woollen counterpane, ult. f. L *carpere* pluck, pull to pieces]

carpeting /ˈkɑːpɪtɪŋ/ *n.* **1** material for carpets. **2** carpets collectively.

carpology /kɑːˈpɒlədʒɪ/ *n.* the study of the structure of fruit and seeds. [Gk *karpos* fruit]

carport /ˈkɑːpɔːt/ *n.* a shelter with a roof and open sides for a car, usu. beside a house.

carpus /ˈkɑːpəs/ *n.* (pl. **carpi** /-paɪ/) the small bones between the forelimb and metacarpus in terrestrial vertebrates, forming the wrist in humans. [mod.L f. Gk *karpos* wrist]

Carracci /kɑːˈrɑːtʃɪ/ the name of a family of Italian painters from Bologna. Agostino (1557–1602) is remembered more for his teaching than his painting and probably dictated the training of the students in the so-called Carracci Academy at Bologna. His brother Annibale (1560–1609) was the most famous member of the family. His early work of the 1580s and 1590s revealed his ability in religious and landscape painting, but it was his move to Rome in 1595 that established his genius in the creation of paintings and decoration in the Grand Manner, in particular the Farnese Gallery in Rome. His combination of strong composition, tonal control, and use of gesture were to prove of immense and lasting influence in the 17th c., while his landscapes initiated the classical landscape with ruins developed by Claude and Poussin. His cousin Lodovico (1555–1619) established the Carracci studio in Bologna and helped pass on that style.

carrack /ˈkærək/ *n.* *hist.* a large merchant ship of northern and southern Europe in the 14th–17th c., the forerunner and first example of the larger three-masted ship which dominated naval architecture until the general introduction of steam propulsion in the mid-19th c. (See GALLEON.) [ME f. F *caraque* f. Sp. *carraca* f. Arab. *karākir*]

carrageen /ˈkærəˌgiːn/ *n.* (also **carragheen**) an edible red seaweed, *Chondrus crispus*, of the N. hemisphere. Also called *Irish moss*. [orig. uncert.: perh. f. Ir. *cosáinín carraige* carrageen, lit. 'little stem of the rock']

Carrara /kəˈrɑːrə/ a town in Tuscany in NW Italy, famous for its white marble; pop. (1981) 68,460.

carrel /ˈkær(ə)l/ *n.* **1** a small cubicle for a reader in a library. **2** *hist.* a small enclosure or study in a cloister. [OF *carole*, med.L *carola*, of unkn. orig.]

carriage /ˈkærɪdʒ/ *n.* **1** *Brit.* a railway passenger vehicle. **2** a wheeled passenger vehicle, esp. one with four wheels and pulled by horses. **3 a** the conveying of goods. **b** the cost of this (*carriage paid*). **4** the part of a machine (e.g. a typewriter) that carries other parts into the required position. **5** a gun-carriage. **6 a** manner of carrying oneself; one's bearing or deportment. □ **carriage and pair** a carriage with two horses pulling it. **carriage clock** a portable clock in a rectangular case with a handle on top. **carriage-dog** a dalmatian. [ME f. ONF *cariage* f. *carier* CARRY]

carriageway /ˈkærɪdʒˌweɪ/ *n.* *Brit.* the part of a road intended for vehicles.

carrick bend /ˈkærɪk/ *n.* *Naut.* a kind of knot used to join ropes. [BEND[2]: *carrick* perh. f. CARRACK]

carrier /ˈkærɪə(r)/ *n.* **1** a person or thing that carries. **2** a person or company undertaking to convey goods or passengers for payment. **3** = *carrier bag*. **4** a part of a bicycle etc. for carrying luggage or a passenger. **5** a person or animal that may transmit a disease or a hereditary characteristic without suffering from or displaying it. **6** = *aircraft-carrier*. **7** a substance used to support or convey a pigment, a catalyst, radioactive material, etc. **8** *Physics* a mobile electron or hole that carries a charge in a semiconductor. □ **carrier bag** *Brit*. a disposable plastic or paper bag with handles. **carrier pigeon** a pigeon trained to carry messages tied to its neck or leg. **carrier wave** a high-frequency electromagnetic wave modulated in amplitude or frequency to convey a signal.

carriole /ˈkærɪˌəʊl/ n. **1** a small open carriage for one. **2** a covered light cart. **3** a Canadian sledge. [F f. It. *carriuola*, dimin. of *carro* CAR]

carrion /ˈkærɪən/ n. & adj. —n. **1** dead putrefying flesh. **2** something vile or filthy. —adj. rotten, loathsome. □ **carrion crow** a black crow, *Corvus corone*, native to Europe, feeding mainly on carrion. **carrion flower** = STAPELIA. [ME f. AF & ONF *caroine, -oigne*, OF *charoigne* ult. f. L *caro* flesh]

Carroll /ˈkær(ə)l/, Lewis (pseudonym of Charles Lutwidge Dodgson, 1832–98), English writer and lecturer in mathematics at Oxford (1855–81), celebrated as author of the sophisticated children's classics (written for the daughter of the dean of his college, H. G. Liddell) *Alice's Adventures in Wonderland* (1865) and *Through the Looking Glass* (1871), both illustrated by Tenniel, describing a child's dream adventure. He also wrote nonsense verse, notably *The Hunting of the Snark* (1876), and experimented in portrait photography.

carrot /ˈkærət/ n. **1 a** an umbelliferous plant, *Daucus carota*, with a tapering orange-coloured root. **b** this root as a vegetable. **2** a means of enticement or persuasion. **3** (in *pl.*) *sl.* a red-haired person. □□ **carroty** adj. [F *carotte* f. L *carota* f. Gk *karōton*]

carrousel US var. of CAROUSEL.

carry /ˈkærɪ/ v. & n. —v. (-ies, -ied) **1** tr. support or hold up, esp. while moving. **2** tr. convey with one from one place to another. **3** tr. have on one's person (*carry a watch*). **4** tr. conduct or transmit (*pipe carries water; wire carries electric current*). **5** tr. take (a process etc.) to a specified point (*carry into effect; carry a joke too far*). **6** tr. (foll. by *to*) continue or prolong (*carry modesty to excess*). **7** tr. involve, imply; have as a feature or consequence (*carries a two-year guarantee; principles carry consequences*). **8** tr. (in reckoning) transfer (a figure) to a column of higher value. **9** tr. hold in a specified way (*carry oneself erect*). **10** tr. **a** (of a newspaper or magazine) publish; include in its contents, esp. regularly. **b** (of a radio or television station) broadcast, esp. regularly. **11** tr. (of a retailing outlet) keep a regular stock of (particular goods for sale) (*have stopped carrying that brand*). **12** intr. **a** (of sound, esp. a voice) be audible at a distance. **b** (of a missile) travel, penetrate. **13** tr. (of a gun etc.) propel to a specified distance. **14** tr. **a** win victory or acceptance for (a proposal etc.). **b** win acceptance from (*carried the audience with them*). **c** win, capture (a prize, a fortress, etc.). **d** US gain (a State or district) in an election. **e** *Golf* cause the ball to pass beyond (a bunker etc.). **15** tr. **a** endure the weight of; support (*columns carry the dome*). **b** be the chief cause of the effectiveness of; be the driving force in (*you carry the sales department*). **16** tr. be pregnant with (*is carrying twins*). **17** tr. **a** (of a motive, money, etc.) cause or enable (a person) to go to a specified place. **b** (of a journey) bring (a person) to a specified point. —n. (*pl.* -ies) **1** *Golf* the distance a ball travels before reaching the ground. **2** a portage between rivers etc. **3** the range of a gun etc. □ **carry-all 1** a light carriage (cf. CARRIOLE). **2** US a car with seats placed sideways. **3** US a large bag or case. **carry all before one** succeed; overcome all opposition. **carry away 1** remove. **2** inspire; affect emotionally or spiritually. **3** deprive of self-control (*got carried away*). **4** *Naut.* **a** lose (a mast etc.) by breakage. **b** break off or away. **carry back** take (a person) back in thought to a past time. **carry one's bat** *Cricket* be not out at the end of a side's completed innings. **carry the can** *colloq.* bear the responsibility or blame. **carry conviction** be convincing. **carry-cot** a portable cot for a baby. **carry the day** be victorious or successful. **carry forward** transfer to a new page or account. **carrying-on** (or

carryings-on) = *carry-on*. **carrying-trade** the conveying of goods from one country to another by water or air as a business. **carry it off** (or **carry it off well**) do well under difficulties. **carry off 1** take away, esp. by force. **2** win (a prize). **3** (esp. of a disease) kill. **4** render acceptable or passable. **carry on 1** continue (*carry on eating; carry on, don't mind me*). **2** engage in (a conversation or a business). **3** *colloq.* behave strangely or excitedly. **4** (often foll. by *with*) *colloq.* flirt or have a love affair. **5** advance (a process) by a stage. **carry-on** n. *Brit. sl.* **1** a state of excitement or fuss. **2** a questionable piece of behaviour. **3** a flirtation or love affair. **carry out** put (ideas, instructions, etc.) into practice. **carry-out** *attrib.adj.* & n. esp. *Sc.* & US = take-away. **carry over 1** = *carry forward*. **2** postpone (work etc.). **3** *Stock Exch.* keep over to the next settling-day. **carry-over** n. **1** something carried over. **2** *Stock Exch.* postponement to the next settling-day. **carry through 1** complete successfully. **2** bring safely out of difficulties. **carry weight** be influential or important. **carry with one** bear in mind. [ME f. AF & ONF *carier* (as CAR)]

carse /kɑːs/ n. *Sc.* fertile lowland beside a river. [ME, perh. f. *carrs* swamps]

carsick /ˈkɑːsɪk/ adj. affected with nausea caused by the motion of a car. □□ **carsickness** n.

Carson /ˈkɑːs(ə)n/ Rachel (1907–64), American zoologist, remembered as a pioneer ecologist and popularizer of scientific information. Her works include *The Sea Around Us* (1951) and *Silent Spring* (1963), a powerful attack on the indiscriminate use of pesticides and weedkillers.

Carson City /ˈkɑːs(ə)n/ the capital of Nevada; pop. (1980) 32,000.

cart /kɑːt/ n. & v. —n. **1** a strong vehicle with two or four wheels for carrying loads, usu. drawn by a horse. **2** a light vehicle for pulling by hand. **3** a light vehicle with two wheels for driving in, drawn by a single horse. —v.tr. **1** convey in or as in a cart. **2** *sl.* carry (esp. a cumbersome thing) with difficulty or over a long distance (*carted it all the way home*). □ **cart-horse** a thickset horse suitable for heavy work. **cart-load 1** an amount filling a cart. **2** a large quantity of anything. **cart off** remove, esp. by force. **cart-track** (or **-road**) a track or road too rough for ordinary vehicles. **cart-wright** a maker of carts. **in the cart** *sl.* in trouble or difficulty. **put the cart before the horse 1** reverse the proper order or procedure. **2** take an effect for a cause. □□ **carter** n. **cartful** n. (*pl.* -fuls). [ME f. ON *kartr* cart & OE *cræt*, prob. infl. by AF & ONF *carete* dimin. of *carre* CAR]

cartage /ˈkɑːtɪdʒ/ n. the price paid for carting.

Cartagena /ˌkɑːtəˈdʒiːnə, -ˈxenə/ **1** a port in SW Spain, on the Mediterranean Sea; pop. (1986) 168,800. Originally named Mastia, it was refounded as New Carthage (*Carthago Nova*) by Hasdrubal in 228 BC as a base for the Carthaginian conquest of Spain. It had a fine natural harbour and has been a naval port since the 16th c. **2** a port, resort, and oil-refining centre in NW Colombia, on the Caribbean Sea; pop. (1985) 531,400. Founded in 1533, it was an important city of the Spanish Main.

carte var. of QUART 4.

carte blanche /kɑːt ˈblɑ̃ʃ/ n. full discretionary power given to a person. [F, = blank paper]

cartel /kɑːˈtel/ n. **1** an informal association of manufacturers or suppliers to maintain prices at a high level, and control production, marketing arrangements, etc. **2** a political combination between parties. □□ **cartelize** /ˈkɑːtəˌlaɪz/ v.tr. & intr. (also **-ise**). [G *Kartell* f. F *cartel* f. It. *cartello* dimin. of *carta* CARD[1]]

Carter[1] /ˈkɑːtə(r)/ Elliott Cook (1908–), American composer, whose works incude the *Double Concerto* (1961) for harpsichord, piano, and two chamber orchestras, and *Symphony of Three Orchestras* (1976–7). In his *Cello Sonata* (1948) he developed 'metric modulation' whereby a new tempo is established from development of a cross-rhythm, giving an impression of the simultaneous existence of two tempos. His three string quartets (1951–72) have been described as the most significant compositions in the medium since those of Bartók.

Carter[2] /ˈkɑːtə(r)/, James Earl ('Jimmy') (1924–), 39th President of the US, 1977–81.

Cartesian /kɑːˈtiːzjən, -ʒ(ə)n/ adj. & n. —adj. of or relating to

Descartes, or his philosophy. —*n.* a follower of Descartes. □ **Cartesian coordinates** a system for locating a point by reference to its distance from two or three axes intersecting at right angles. **Cartesian diver** a toy device that rises and falls in liquid when the cover of a vessel is subjected to varying pressure. □□ **Cartesianism** *n.* [mod.L *Cartesianus* f. *Cartesius*, name of *Descartes*]

Carthage /ˈkɑːθɪdʒ/ a city on the north coast of Africa near Tunis, traditionally founded by Phoenicians from Tyre (in modern Lebanon) in 814 BC. It became a major force in the Mediterranean, with interests in North Africa, Spain, and Sicily, which brought it into conflict with Greece until the 3rd c. BC and then with Rome in the Punic Wars, until the Romans finally destroyed it in AD 146. □□ **Carthaginian** /kɑːθəˈdʒɪnɪən/ *adj.* & *n.* [Semitic, = new town]

Carthusian /kɑːˈθjuːzjən/ *n.* & *adj.* —*n.* a monk of a contemplative order founded by St Bruno in 1084. (See below.) —*adj.* of or relating to this order. [med.L *Carthusianus* f. L *Cart(h)usia* Chartreuse, near Grenoble]
  The Carthusian order is a strictly contemplative order of monks founded at the Grande Chartreuse (whence the name) in SE France by St Bruno in 1084. Their eremitical way of life, largely inspired by early eastern monasticism, is remarkable for its austerity and self-denial. The order includes a few houses of nuns.

Cartier /ˈkɑːtɪeɪ/, Jacques (1491–1557), French explorer of Canada, who made three exploring voyages to Canada between 1534 and 1541, sailing up the St Lawrence River and attempting to establish a settlement on the site of what is now Montreal.

Cartier-Bresson /kɑːtɪˌeɪbreˈsɔ̃/, Henri (1908–), French photographer, who did much to establish photographic journalism as an art form. The central idea of his work was the capturing of the 'decisive moment' of a scene or event, when the subject reveals the significance of the event of which it is a part. He built up a reputation as a humane and perceptive observer, features which he carried over into the making of films. From 1936 to 1939 he worked as assistant to the film director Jean Renoir, and in the late 1960s returned to filmmaking. During the Second World War he was taken prisoner in France, but escaped to join the Resistance and made a photographic record of the German occupation and retreat.

cartilage /ˈkɑːtɪlɪdʒ/ *n.* gristle, a firm flexible connective tissue forming the infant skeleton, which is mainly replaced by bone in adulthood. □□ **cartilaginoid** /-ˈlædʒɪˌnɔɪd/ *adj.* **cartilaginous** /-ˈlædʒɪnəs/ *adj.* [F f. L *cartilago -ginis*]

Cartland /ˈkɑːtlənd/, Dame Barbara Hamilton (1901–), English prolific writer of light romantic fiction.

cartogram /ˈkɑːtəˌɡræm/ *n.* a map with diagrammatic statistical information. [F *cartogramme* f. *carte* map, card]

cartography /kɑːˈtɒɡrəfɪ/ *n.* the science or practice of map-drawing. □□ **cartographer** *n.* **cartographic** /-təˈɡræfɪk/ *adj.* **cartographical** /-təˈɡræfɪk(ə)l/ *adj.* [F *cartographie* f. *carte* map, card]

cartomancy /ˈkɑːtəˌmænsɪ/ *n.* fortune-telling by interpreting a random selection of playing-cards. [F *cartomancie* f. *carte* CARD¹]

carton /ˈkɑːt(ə)n/ *n.* a light box or container, esp. one made of cardboard. [F (as CARTOON)]

cartoon /kɑːˈtuːn/ *n.* & *v.* —*n.* 1 a humorous drawing in a newspaper, magazine, etc., esp. as a topical comment. 2 a sequence of drawings, often with speech indicated, telling a story (*strip cartoon*). 3 a filmed sequence of drawings using the technique of animation. 4 a full-size drawing on stout paper as an artist's preliminary design for a painting, tapestry, mosaic, etc. —*v.* 1 *tr.* draw a cartoon of. 2 *intr.* draw cartoons. □□ **cartoonist** *n.* [It. *cartone* f. *carta* CARD¹]

cartouche /kɑːˈtuːʃ/ *n.* 1 a *Archit.* a scroll-like ornament, e.g. the volute of an Ionic capital. b a tablet imitating, or a drawing of, a scroll with rolled-up ends, used ornamentally or bearing an inscription. c an ornate frame. 2 *Archaeol.* an oval ring enclosing Egyptian hieroglyphs, usu. representing the name and title of a king. [F, = cartridge, f. It. *cartoccio* f. *carta* CARD¹]

cartridge /ˈkɑːtrɪdʒ/ *n.* 1 a case containing a charge of propelling explosive for firearms or blasting, with a bullet or shot if for small arms. 2 a spool of film, magnetic tape, etc., in a sealed container ready for insertion. 3 a component carrying the stylus on the pick-up head of a record-player. 4 an ink-container for insertion in a pen. □ **cartridge-belt** a belt with pockets or loops for cartridges (in sense 1). **cartridge paper** thick rough paper used for cartridges, for drawing, and for strong envelopes. [corrupt. of CARTOUCHE (but recorded earlier)]

cartwheel /ˈkɑːtwiːl/ *n.* 1 the (usu. spoked) wheel of a cart. 2 a circular sideways handspring with the arms and legs extended.

Cartwright /ˈkɑːtraɪt/, Edmund (1743–1823), English engineer, remembered chiefly as the inventor in 1785 of the power loom, but his record of achievements is a remarkable one. Starting as a clergyman he became interested in textile machinery and despite financial failures continued to innovate, with a wool-combing machine (1789), a rope-making machine (1792), and in 1797 an engine which used alcohol rather than steam, a thermodynamic development far ahead of its time. His achievements were recognized eventually by the government in 1809, who voted him £10,000, a just reward for innovations which had a profound effect on textile manufacture.

caruncle /ˈkærəŋk(ə)l, kəˈrʌŋk(ə)l/ *n.* 1 *Zool.* a fleshy excrescence, e.g. a turkeycock's wattles or the red prominence at the inner angle of the eye. 2 *Bot.* an outgrowth from a seed near the micropyle. □□ **caruncular** /-kjʊlə(r)/ *adj.* [obs. F f. L *caruncula* f. *caro carnis* flesh]

Caruso /kəˈruːsəʊ/, Enrico (1873–1921), Italian operatic tenor of the highest popularity. He appeared in both French and Italian opera, winning immense financial awards for appearances in person and for the recordings which made him a household name even among those who never attended operatic performances.

carve /kɑːv/ *v.* 1 *tr.* produce or shape (a statue, representation in relief, etc.) by cutting into a hard material (*carved a figure out of rock*; *carved it in wood*). 2 *tr.* a cut patterns, designs, letters, etc. in (hard material). b (foll. by *into*) form a pattern, design, etc., from (*carved it into a bust*). c (foll. by *with*) cover or decorate (material) with figures or designs cut in it. 3 *tr.* (*absol.*) cut (meat etc.) into slices for eating. □ **carve out 1** take from a larger whole. **2** establish (a career etc.) purposefully (*carved out a name for themselves*). **carve up** divide into several pieces; subdivide (territory etc.). **carve-up** *n. sl.* a sharing-out, esp. of spoils. **carving knife** a knife with a long blade, for carving meat. [OE *ceorfan* cut f. WG]

carvel /ˈkɑːv(ə)l/ *n.* var. of CARAVEL. □ **carvel-built** (of a boat) made with planks flush, not overlapping (cf. CLINKER-BUILT). [as CARAVEL]

carven /ˈkɑːv(ə)n/ *archaic past part.* of CARVE.

Carver /ˈkɑːvə(r)/ *n.* US a chair with arms, a rush seat, and a back having horizontal and vertical spindles. [J. *Carver*, first governor of Plymouth Colony, d. 1621, for whom a prototype was allegedly made]

carver /ˈkɑːvə(r)/ *n.* 1 a person who carves. 2 a a carving knife. b (in *pl.*) a knife and fork for carving. 3 *Brit.* the principal chair, with arms, in a set of dining-chairs, intended for the person who carves. ¶ To be distinguished (in sense 3) from *Carver*.

carvery /ˈkɑːvərɪ/ *n.* (*pl.* **-ies**) a buffet or restaurant with joints displayed, and carved as required, in front of customers.

carving /ˈkɑːvɪŋ/ *n.* a carved object, esp. as a work of art.

Cary /ˈkeərɪ/, (Arthur) Joyce (Lunel) (1888–1957), English novelist. His colourful exuberant novels include some set in Africa, where he had served briefly in the colonial service. In *The Horse's Mouth* (1944), one of a trilogy, he achieved a memorable portrait of an outrageous artist.

caryatid /ˌkærɪˈætɪd/ *n.* (*pl.* **caryatides** /-ˌdiːz/ or **caryatids**) *Archit.* a pillar in the form of a draped female figure, supporting an entablature. [F *caryatide* f. It. *cariatide* or L f. Gk *karuatis -idos* priestess at Caryae (*Karuai*) in Laconia]

caryopsis /ˌkærɪˈɒpsɪs/ *n.* (*pl.* **caryopses** /-siːz/) *Bot.* a dry one-seeded indehiscent fruit, as in wheat and maize. [mod.L f. Gk *karuon* nut + *opsis* appearance]

Casablanca /ˌkæsəˈblæŋkə/ a seaport and the largest city of Morocco, on the Atlantic coast; pop. (1982) 2,139,200.

Casals /kæˈsæls/, Pablo (or Pau) (1876–1973), Spanish cellist, conductor, and composer, the foremost cellist of his time, noted especially for his performances of Bach suites and the Dvořák concerto. He refused to perform in Hitler's Germany and went into voluntary exile from Spain in 1939 during the Franco regime, living first in Prades in the French Pyrenees, where he organized annual Bach festivals from 1950 to 1960, and then in Puerto Rico. His compositions include the oratorio *El Pessebre* (*The Manger*, 1943–60).

Casanova /ˌkæsəˈnəʊvə/ n. a man notorious for seducing women. [G. J. *Casanova* de Seingalt, Italian adventurer (d. 1798), famous for his memoirs, in French, describing his adventurous life, and particularly his pursuit of women, in a large number of European countries]

casbah var. of KASBAH.

cascade /kæsˈkeɪd/ n. & v. —n. **1** a small waterfall, esp. forming one in a series or part of a large broken waterfall. **2** a succession of electrical devices or stages in a process. **3** a quantity of material etc. draped in descending folds. **4** a process of disseminating information from senior to junior levels in an organization. —v.intr. fall in or like a cascade. [F f. It. *cascata* f. *cascare* to fall ult. f. L *casus*: see CASE¹]

Cascais /kæʃˈkaɪʃ/ a resort on the Atlantic coast of central Portugal, west of Lisbon; pop. (1981) 12,500.

cascara /kæsˈkɑːrə/ n. (in full **cascara sagrada** /səɡˈrɑːdə/) the bark of a Californian buckthorn, *Rhamnus purshiana*, used as a purgative. [Sp., = sacred bark]

case¹ /keɪs/ n. **1** an instance of something occurring. **2** a state of affairs, hypothetical or actual. **3 a** an instance of a person receiving professional guidance, e.g. from a doctor or social worker. **b** this person or the circumstances involved. **4** a matter under official investigation, esp. by the police. **5** *Law* **a** a cause or suit for trial. **b** a statement of the facts in a cause *sub judice*, drawn up for a higher court's consideration (*judge states a case*). **c** a cause that has been decided and may be cited (*leading case*). **6 a** the sum of the arguments on one side, esp. in a lawsuit (*that is our case*). **b** a set of arguments, esp. in relation to persuasiveness (*have a good case; have a weak case*). **c** a valid set of arguments (*have no case*). **7** *Gram.* **a** the relation of a word to other words in a sentence. **b** a form of a noun, adjective, or pronoun expressing this. **8** *colloq.* a comical person. **9** the position or circumstances in which one is. □ **as the case may be** according to the situation. **case history** information about a person for use in professional treatment, e.g. by a doctor. **case-law** the law as established by the outcome of former cases (cf. *common law, statute law*). **case-load** the cases with which a doctor etc. is concerned at one time. **case-study 1** an attempt to understand a person, institution, etc., from collected information. **2** a record of such an attempt. **3** the use of a particular instance as an exemplar of general principles. **in any case** whatever the truth is; whatever may happen. **in case 1** in the event that; if. **2** lest; in provision against a stated or implied possibility (*take an umbrella in case it rains; took it in case*). **in case of** in the event of. **in the case of** as regards. **in no case** under no circumstances. **in that case** if that is true; should that happen. **is** (or **is not**) **the case** is (or is not) so. [ME f. OF *cas* f. L *casus* fall f. *cadere cas-* to fall]

case² /keɪs/ n. & v. —n. **1** a container or covering serving to enclose or contain. **2** a container with its contents. **3** the outer protective covering of a watch, book, seed-vessel, sausage, etc. **4** an item of luggage, esp. a suitcase. **5** *Printing* a partitioned receptacle for type. **6** a glass box for showing specimens, curiosities, etc. —v.tr. **1** enclose in a case. **2** (foll. by *with*) surround. **3** *sl.* reconnoitre (a house etc.) esp. with a view to robbery. □ **case-bound** (of a book) in a hard cover. **case-harden 1** harden the surface of, esp. give a steel surface to (iron) by carbonizing. **2** make callous. **case-knife** a knife carried in a sheath. **case-shot 1** bullets in an iron case fired from a cannon. **2** shrapnel. **lower case** small letters. **upper case** capitals. [ME f. OF *casse, chasse*, f. L *capsa* f. *capere* hold]

casebook /ˈkeɪsbʊk/ n. a book containing a record of legal or medical cases.

casein /ˈkeɪsiːn, ˈkeɪsiːn/ n. the main protein in milk, esp. in coagulated form as in cheese. [L *caseus* cheese]

caseinogen /keɪˈsɪnədʒ(ə)n/ n. the soluble form of casein as it occurs in milk.

casemate /ˈkeɪsmeɪt/ n. **1** a chamber in the thickness of the wall of a fortress, with embrasures. **2** an armoured enclosure for guns on a warship. [F *casemate* & It. *casamatta* or Sp. *-mata*, f. *camata*, perh. f. Gk *khasma -atos* gap]

Casement /ˈkeɪsmənt/, Sir Roger David (1864–1916), Irish nationalist. He was a member of the British consular service in Africa and after retiring from this in 1912 went to Germany soon after the outbreak of the First World War to try to organize support for an Irish uprising. He was captured on his return to Ireland before the Easter rebellion of 1916, and subsequently hanged by the British for treason. Diaries reputedly written by him, containing descriptions of homosexual practices (suspicion of which had biased opinion against him) were not made available to the public until 1959.

casement /ˈkeɪsmənt/ n. **1** a window or part of a window hinged vertically to open like a door. **2** *poet.* a window. [ME f. AL *cassimentum* f. *cassa* CASE²]

casework /ˈkeɪswɜːk/ n. social work concerned with individuals, esp. involving understanding of the client's family and background. □□ **caseworker** n.

cash¹ /kæʃ/ n. & v. —n. **1** money in coins or notes, as distinct from cheques or orders. **2** (also **cash down**) money paid as full payment at the time of purchase, as distinct from credit. **3** *colloq.* wealth. —v.tr. give or obtain cash for (a note, cheque, etc.). □ **cash and carry 1** a system of wholesaling in which goods are paid for in cash and taken away by the purchaser. **2** a store where this system operates. **cash-book** a book in which receipts and payments of cash are recorded. **cash crop** a crop produced for sale, not for use as food etc. **cash desk** a counter or compartment in a shop where goods are paid for. **cash dispenser** an automatic machine from which customers of a bank etc. may withdraw cash, esp. by using a cashcard. **cash flow** the movement of money into and out of a business, as a measure of profitability, or as affecting liquidity. **cash in 1** obtain cash for. **2** *colloq.* (usu. foll. by *on*) profit (from); take advantage (of). **3** pay into a bank etc. **4** (in full **cash in one's checks**) *colloq.* die. **cash on delivery** a system of paying the carrier for goods when they are delivered. **cash register** a machine in a shop etc. with a drawer for money, recording the amount of each sale, totalling receipts, etc. **cash up** *Brit.* count and check cash takings at the end of a day's trading. □□ **cashable** adj. **cashless** adj. [obs. F *casse* box or It. *cassa* f. L *capsa* CASE²]

cash² /kæʃ/ n. (pl. same) *hist.* any of various small coins of China or the E. Indies. [ult. f. Port. *ca(i)xa* f. Tamil *kāsu* f. Skr. *karsha*]

cashcard /ˈkæʃkɑːd/ n. a plastic card (see CARD¹ n. 9) which enables the holder to draw money from a cash dispenser.

cashew /ˈkæʃuː, kæˈʃuː/ n. **1** a bushy evergreen tree, *Anacardium occidentale*, native to Central and S. America, bearing kidney-shaped nuts attached to fleshy fruits. **2** (in full **cashew nut**) the edible nut of this tree. □ **cashew apple** the edible fleshy fruit of this tree. [Port. f. Tupi (*a*)*caju*]

cashier¹ /kæˈʃɪə(r)/ n. a person dealing with cash transactions in a shop, bank, etc. [Du. *cassier* or F *caissier* (as CASH¹)]

cashier² /kæˈʃɪə(r)/ v.tr. dismiss from service, esp. from the armed forces with disgrace. [Flem. *kasseren* disband, revoke, f. F *casser* f. L *quassare* QUASH]

cashmere /ˈkæʃmɪə(r)/ n. **1** a fine soft wool, esp. that of a Kashmir goat. **2** a material made from this. [*Kashmir* in Asia]

cashpoint /ˈkæʃpɔɪnt/ n. = *cash dispenser*.

casing /ˈkeɪsɪŋ/ n. **1** a protective or enclosing cover or shell. **2** the material for this.

casino /kəˈsiːnəʊ/ n. (pl. **-os**) a public room or building for gambling. [It., dimin. of *casa* house f. L *casa* cottage]

cask /kɑːsk/ n. **1** a large barrel-like container made of wood, metal, or plastic, esp. one for alcoholic liquor. **2** its contents. **3** its capacity. [F *casque* or Sp. *casco* helmet]

casket /ˈkɑːskɪt/ n. **1** a small often ornamental box or chest for jewels, letters, etc. **2 a** a small wooden box for cremated ashes. **b** US a coffin, esp. a rectangular one. [perh. f. AF form of OF *cassette* f. It. *cassetta* dimin. of *cassa* f. L *capsa* CASE²]

Caslon /ˈkæzlən/, William (1692–1766), English typographer, who established a type foundry (continued by his son William, 1720–78), supplying printers on the Continent as well as in England. His name is applied to the type cut there, or an imitation of this.

Caspian Sea /ˈkæspɪən/ a land-locked salt lake enclosed by the USSR and Iran. It is the world's largest body of inland water and its surface lies 28 m (92 ft.) below sea level.

casque /kæsk/ n. **1** *hist.* or *poet.* a helmet. **2** *Zool.* a helmet-like structure, e.g. the process on the bill of the cassowary. [F f. Sp. *casco*]

Cassandra /kəˈsændrə/ *Gk legend* a daughter of Priam of Troy. She was loved by Apollo, who gave her the gift of prophecy, but when she cheated him he turned this into a curse by causing her prophecies, though true, to be disbelieved. —n. a person who prophesies disaster.

cassata /kəˈsɑːtə/ n. a type of ice-cream containing candied or dried fruit and nuts. [It.]

cassation /kəˈseɪʃ(ə)n/ n. *Mus.* an informal instrumental composition of the 18th c., similar to a divertimento and orig. often for outdoor performance. [It. *cassazione*]

cassava /kəˈsɑːvə/ n. **1 a** any plant of the genus *Manihot*, esp. the cultivated varieties M. *esculenta* (**bitter cassava**) and M. *dulcis* (**sweet cassava**), having starchy tuberous roots. **b** the roots themselves. **2** a starch or flour obtained from these roots. Also called TAPIOCA, MANIOC. [earlier *cas(s)avi* etc., f. Taino *casavi*, infl. by F *cassave*]

casserole /ˈkæsərəʊl/ n. & v. —n. **1** a covered dish, usu. of earthenware or glass, in which food is cooked, esp. slowly in the oven. **2** food cooked in a casserole. —v.tr. cook in a casserole. [F f. *cassole* dimin. of *casse* f. Prov. *casa* f. LL *cattia* ladle, pan f. Gk *kuathion* dimin. of *kuathos* cup]

cassette /kæˈset, kə-/ n. a sealed case containing a length of tape, ribbon, etc., ready for insertion in a machine, esp.: **1** a length of magnetic tape wound on to spools, ready for insertion in a tape recorder. **2** a length of photographic film, ready for insertion in a camera. [F, dimin. of *casse* CASE²]

cassia /ˈkæsɪə, ˈkæʃə/ n. **1** any tree of the genus *Cassia*, bearing leaves from which senna is extracted. **2** the cinnamon-like bark of this tree used as a spice. [L f. Gk *kasia* f. Heb. *qĕṣīʿāh* bark like cinnamon]

Cassiopeia /ˌkæsɪəˈpeɪə/ **1** *Gk Mythol.* the wife of Cepheus king of Ethiopia, and mother of Andromeda. She boasted herself more beautiful than the Nereids, thus incurring the wrath of Poseidon. **2** *Astron.* a northern constellation, recognizable by the 'W' pattern of its five brightest stars.

cassis /kæˈsiːs/ n. a syrupy usu. alcoholic blackcurrant flavouring for drinks etc. [F, = blackcurrant]

cassiterite /kəˈsɪtəˌraɪt/ n. a naturally occurring ore of tin dioxide, from which tin is extracted. Also called TINSTONE. [Gk *kassiteros* tin]

Cassius /ˈkæsjəs/ (Gaius Cassius Longinus, d. 42 BC) Roman general, with Marcus Junius Brutus one of the leaders of the conspiracy in 44 BC to assassinate Julius Caesar. He and Brutus were defeated by Caesar's supporters, Antony and Octavian, at the battle of Philippi in 42 BC; in the course of the battle he committed suicide.

cassock /ˈkæsək/ n. a long close-fitting usu. black or red garment worn by clergy, members of choirs, etc. □□ **cassocked** adj. [F *casaque* long coat f. It. *casacca* horseman's coat, prob. f. Turkic: cf. COSSACK]

cassoulet /ˈkæsuːleɪ/ n. a ragout of meat and beans. [F, dimin. of dial. *cassolo* stew-pan]

cassowary /ˈkæsəˌweərɪ/ n. (pl. **-ies**) any large flightless Australasian bird of the genus *Casuarius*, with heavy body, stout legs, a wattled neck, and a bony crest on its forehead. [Malay *kasuārī*, *kasavārī*]

cast /kɑːst/ v. & n. —v. (*past* and *past part.* **cast**) **1** tr. throw, esp. deliberately or forcefully. **2** tr. (often foll. by *on*, *over*) **a** direct or cause to fall (one's eyes, a glance, light, a shadow, a spell, etc.). **b** express (doubts, aspersions, etc.). **3** tr. throw out (a fishing-line) into the water. **4** tr. let down (an anchor or sounding-lead). **5** tr. **a** throw off, get rid of. **b** shed (skin etc.) esp. in the process of growth. **c** (of a horse) lose (a shoe). **6** tr. record, register, or give (a vote). **7** tr. **a** shape (molten metal or plastic material) in a mould. **b** make (a product) in this way. **8** tr. *Printing* make (type). **9** tr. **a** (usu. foll. by *as*) assign (an actor) to play a particular character. **b** allocate roles in (a play, film, etc.). **10** tr. (foll. by *in*, *into*) arrange or formulate (facts etc.) in a specified form. **11** tr. & *intr.* reckon, add up, calculate (accounts or figures). **12** tr. calculate and record details of (a horoscope). —n. **1 a** the throwing of a missile etc. **b** the distance reached by this. **2** a throw or a number thrown at dice. **3** a throw of a net, sounding-lead, or fishing-line. **4** *Fishing* **a** that which is cast, esp. the gut with hook and fly. **b** a place for casting (*a good cast*). **5 a** an object of metal, clay, etc., made in a mould. **b** a moulded mass of solidified material, esp. plaster protecting a broken limb. **6** the actors taking part in a play, film, etc. **7** form, type, or quality (*cast of features*; *cast of mind*). **8** a tinge or shade of colour. **9 a** (in full **cast in the eye**) a slight squint. **b** a twist or inclination. **10 a** a mass of earth excreted by a worm. **b** a mass of indigestible food thrown up by a hawk, owl, etc. **11** the form into which any work is thrown or arranged. **12 a** a wide area covered by a dog or pack to find a trail. **b** *Austral.* & *NZ* a wide sweep made by a sheepdog in mustering sheep. □ **cast about** (or **around** or **round**) make an extensive search (actually or mentally) (*cast about for a solution*). **cast adrift** leave to drift. **cast ashore** (of waves etc.) throw to the shore. **cast aside** give up using; abandon. **cast away 1** reject. **2** (in *passive*) be shipwrecked (cf. CASTAWAY). **cast one's bread upon the waters** see BREAD. **cast down** depress, deject (cf. DOWNCAST). **casting vote** a deciding vote usu. given by the chairperson when the votes on two sides are equal. ¶ From an obsolete sense of *cast* = turn the scale. **cast iron** see IRON. **cast-iron** adj. **1** made of cast iron. **2** hard, unchallengeable, unchangeable. **cast loose** detach; detach oneself. **cast lots** see LOT. **cast-net** a net thrown out and immediately drawn in. **cast off 1** abandon. **2** *Knitting* take the stitches off the needle by looping each over the next to finish the edge. **3** *Naut.* **a** set a ship free from a quay etc. **b** loosen and throw off (rope etc.). **4** *Printing* estimate the space that will be taken in print by manuscript copy. **cast-off** adj. abandoned, discarded. —n. a cast-off thing, esp. a garment. **cast on** *Knitting* make the first row of loops on the needle. **cast out** expel. **cast up 1** (of the sea) deposit on the shore. **2** add up (figures etc.). [ME f. ON *kasta*]

Castalia /kæˈsteɪlɪə/ a spring on Mount Parnassus, sacred to Apollo and the Muses. □□ **Castalian** adj.

castanet /ˌkæstəˈnet/ n. (usu. in *pl.*) a small concave piece of hardwood, ivory, etc., in pairs held in the hands and clicked together by the fingers as a rhythmic accompaniment, esp. by Spanish dancers. [Sp. *castañeta* dimin. of *castaña* f. L *castanea* chestnut]

castaway /ˈkɑːstəˌweɪ/ n. & adj. —n. a shipwrecked person. —adj. **1** shipwrecked. **2** cast aside; rejected.

caste /kɑːst/ n. **1** any of the Hindu hereditary classes (see below). **2** a more or less exclusive social class. **3** a system of such classes. **4** the position it confers. **5** *Zool.* a form of social insect having a particular function. □ **caste mark** a symbol on the forehead denoting a person's caste. **lose caste** descend in the social order. [Sp. and Port. *casta* lineage, race, breed, fem. of *casto* pure, CHASTE]

The term occurs first in Spanish, but was applied by the Portuguese in the 16th c. to denote the rigid social divisions found in India. The caste system, which ranks groups of individuals according to birth and occupation and is governed by rules of marriage and social intercourse within the group, extends even to the non-Hindu segments of South Asian society such as Indian Christians and Muslims. The term is frequently confused with the ancient and traditional division of society into four classes (varna) from which the caste system is erroneously said to have evolved. The true origin of caste may be the early trade and professional guilds listed in later Vedic literature.

casteism /ˈkɑːstɪz(ə)m/ n. often *derog.* the caste system.

Castel Gandolfo /ˌkæstel gænˈdɒlfəʊ/ the summer residence of the pope, situated on the western edge of Lake Albano, 16 km (10 miles) south-east of Rome.

castellan /ˈkæstələn/ n. *hist.* the governor of a castle. [ME f. ONF *castelain* f. med.L *castellanus*: see CASTLE]

castellated /ˈkæstəˌleɪtɪd/ adj. **1** having battlements. **2** castle-like. □□ **castellation** /-ˈleɪʃ(ə)n/ n. [med.L *castellatus*: see CASTLE]

caster /ˈkɑːstə(r)/ n. **1** var. of CASTOR¹. **2** a person who casts. **3** a machine for casting type.

castigate /ˈkæstɪˌɡeɪt/ v.tr. rebuke or punish severely. □□ **castigation** /-ˈɡeɪʃ(ə)n/ n. **castigator** n. **castigatory** adj. [L *castigare* reprove f. *castus* pure]

Castile /kæˈstiːl/ the central plateau of the Iberian peninsula, a former Spanish kingdom. Castile became an independent kingdom in the 10th c. and, with Aragon to the east, dominated the Spanish scene during the Middle Ages. The marriage of Isabella of Castile to Ferdinand of Aragon in 1469 effectively unified Spain into a single country. □ **Castile soap** a fine hard white or mottled soap made with olive oil and soda.

Castilian /kæˈstɪlɪən/ n. & adj. —n. **1** a native of Castile in Spain. **2** the language of Castile, standard spoken and literary Spanish. —adj. of or relating to Castile.

Castilla-La Mancha /kæˌstiːljɑ lɑː ˈmæntʃə/ an autonomous province in central Spain; pop. (1986) 1,665,000; administrative centre, Toledo.

Castilla-León /kæˈstiːləleɪˈɒn/ an autonomous region of northern Spain; pop. (1986) 2,600,300; capital, Valladolid.

casting /ˈkɑːstɪŋ/ n. an object made by casting, esp. of molten metal.

castle /ˈkɑːs(ə)l/ n. & v. —n. **1 a** a large fortified building or group of buildings; a stronghold. The term is also applied in proper names to ancient British or Roman earthworks. **b** a formerly fortified mansion. **2** *Chess* = ROOK². —v. *Chess* **1** intr. make a special move (once only in a game on each side) in which the king is moved two squares along the back rank and the nearer rook is moved to the square passed over by the king. **2** *tr.* move (the king) by castling. □ **castles in the air** (or **in Spain**) a visionary unattainable scheme; a day-dream. □□ **castled** adj. [AF & ONF *castel*, *chastel* f. L *castellum* dimin. of *castrum* fort]

Castlereagh /ˈkɑːsəlˌreɪ/ Robert Stewart, Viscount Castlereagh (1769–1822), British statesman. Having already held office as Secretary of Ireland and War Secretary, Castlereagh became Foreign Secretary in 1812, and as such represented his country at the Congress of Vienna, playing a central part in the establishment of a conservative system of relations between the great European powers, based on the maintenance of the balance of power. He committed suicide in 1822, his mind having apparently given way under the strain of work.

Castor /ˈkɑːstə(r)/ **1** *Gk Mythol.* one of the Dioscuri. **2** *Astron.* the more northerly of the two bright stars in the constellation Gemini. It is of special interest as a multiple star system, the three components visible in a moderate telescope being close binaries.

castor¹ /ˈkɑːstə(r)/ n. (also **caster**) **1** a small swivelled wheel (often one of a set) fixed to a leg (or the underside) of a piece of furniture. **2** a small container with holes in the top for sprinkling the contents. □ **castor action** swivelling of vehicle wheels to ensure stability. **castor sugar** finely granulated white sugar. [orig. a var. of CASTER (in the general sense)]

castor² /ˈkɑːstə(r)/ n. an oily substance secreted by beavers and used in medicine and perfumes. [F or L f. Gk *kastōr* beaver]

castor oil /ˈkɑːstə(r)/ n. **1** an oil from the seeds of a plant, *Ricinus communis*, used as a purgative and lubricant. **2** (in full **castor oil plant**) this plant. □ **castor oil bean** (or **castor bean**) a seed of the castor oil plant. [18th c.: orig. uncert.: perh. so called as having succeeded CASTOR² in the medical sense]

castrate /kæˈstreɪt/ v.tr. **1** remove the testicles of; geld. **2** deprive of vigour. □□ **castration** n. **castrator** n. [L *castrare*]

castrato /kæˈstrɑːtəʊ/ n. (pl. **castrati** /-tɪ/) *hist.* a male singer castrated in boyhood so as to retain a soprano or alto voice. [It., past part. of *castrare*: see CASTRATE]

Castries /ˈkæstriːs/ the capital and a port of the island of St Lucia; pop. (1988) 52,900.

Castro /ˈkæstrəʊ/ Fidel (1927–), Cuban statesman. Castro led a successful uprising against the regime of President Batista in 1959, setting up a Communist regime in Cuba which he has led ever since. The abortive US and Cuban invasion of the 'Bay of Pigs' (April 1961) boosted his popularity, as did his successful survival of the missile crisis in October 1962 and of several assassination plots. A keen promoter of revolution in other Latin-American countries, he has achieved considerable status in the Third World through his leadership of the Non-Aligned Movement.

casual /ˈkæʒʊəl, -zjʊəl/ adj. & n. —adj. **1** accidental; due to chance. **2** not regular or permanent; temporary, occasional (*casual work*; *a casual affair*). **3 a** unconcerned, uninterested (*was very casual about it*). **b** made or done without great care or thought (*a casual remark*). **c** acting carelessly or unmethodically. **4** (of clothes) informal. —n. **1** a casual worker. **2** (usu. in *pl.*) casual clothes or shoes. □□ **casually** adv. **casualness** n. [ME f. OF *casuel* & L *casualis* f. *casus* CASE¹]

casualty /ˈkæʒʊəltɪ, ˈkæzjʊ-/ n. (pl. **-ies**) **1** a person killed or injured in a war or accident. **2** a thing lost or destroyed. **3** = *casualty department*. **4** an accident, mishap, or disaster. □ **casualty department** (or **ward**) the part of a hospital where casualties are treated. [ME f. med.L *casualitas* (as CASUAL), after ROYALTY etc.]

casuarina /ˌkæsjʊˈriːnə/ n. any tree of the genus *Casuarina*, native to Australia and SE Asia, having tiny scale leaves on slender jointed branches, resembling gigantic horsetails. [mod.L *casuarius* cassowary (from the resemblance between branches and feathers)]

casuist /ˈkæʒjuːɪst, ˈkæʒʊɪst/ n. **1** a person, esp. a theologian, who resolves problems of conscience, duty, etc., often with clever but false reasoning. **2** a sophist or quibbler. □□ **casuistic** /-ˈɪstɪk/ adj. **casuistical** /-ˈɪstɪk(ə)l/ adj. **casuistically** /-ˈɪstɪkəlɪ/ adv. **casuistry** n. [F *casuiste* f. Sp. *casuista* f. L *casus* CASE¹]

casus belli /ˌkɑːzəs ˈbelɪ, ˌkeɪsəs/ n. an act or situation provoking or justifying war. [L]

CAT abbr. **1** computer-assisted (or -aided) testing. **2** *Med.* computerized axial tomography.

cat /kæt/ n. & v. —n. **1** a small soft-furred four-legged domesticated animal, *Felis catus*. **2 a** any wild animal of the genus *Felis*, e.g. a lion, tiger, or leopard. **b** = *wild cat*. **3** a catlike animal of any other species (*civet cat*). **4** *colloq.* a malicious or spiteful woman. **5** *sl.* a jazz enthusiast. **6** *Naut.* = CATHEAD. **7** = *cat-o'-nine-tails*. **8** a short tapered stick in the game of tipcat. —v.tr. (also *absol.*) (**catted**, **catting**) *Naut.* raise (an anchor) from the surface of the water to the cathead. □ **cat-and-dog** (of a relationship etc.) full of quarrels. **cat burglar** a burglar who enters by climbing to an upper storey. **cat flap** (or **door**) a small swinging flap in an outer door, for a cat to pass in and out. **cat-ice** thin ice unsupported by water. **cat-o'-nine-tails** *hist.* a rope whip with nine knotted lashes for flogging sailors, soldiers, or criminals. **cat's cradle** a child's game in which a loop of string is held between the fingers and patterns are formed. **Cat's-eye** *Brit. propr.* one of a series of reflector studs set into a road. **cat's-eye** a precious stone of Sri Lanka and Malabar. **cat's-foot** any small plant of the genus *Antennaria*, having soft woolly leaves and growing on the surface of the ground. **cat's-paw** **1** a person used as a tool by another (from the fable of the monkey who used the paw of his friend the cat to rake roasted chestnuts out of the fire). **2** a slight breeze rippling the surface of the water. **cat's-tail** = *reed-mace* (see REED¹). **cat's whiskers** (or **pyjamas**) *sl.* an excellent person or thing. **let the cat out of the bag** reveal a secret, esp. involuntarily. **like a cat on hot bricks** (or **on a hot tin roof**) very agitated or agitatedly. **put** (or **set**) **the cat among the pigeons** cause trouble. **rain cats and dogs** rain very hard. [OE *catt(e)* f. LL *cattus*]

cata- /ˈkætə/ prefix (usu. **cat-** before a vowel or *h*) **1** down, downwards (*catadromous*). **2** wrongly, badly (*catachresis*). [Gk *kata* down]

catabolism /kə'tæbə,lɪz(ə)m/ *n.* (also **katabolism**) *Biochem.* the breakdown of complex molecules in living organisms to form simpler ones with the release of energy; destructive metabolism (opp. ANABOLISM). □□ **catabolic** /,kætə'bɒlɪk/ *adj.* [Gk *katabolē* descent f. *kata* down + *bolē* f. *ballō* throw]

catachresis /,kætə'kriːsɪs/ *n.* (*pl.* **catachreses** /-siːz/) an incorrect use of words. □□ **catachrestic** /-'kriːstɪk, -'krestɪk/ *adj.* [L f. Gk *katakhrēsis* f. *khraomai* use]

cataclasis /,kætə'kleɪsɪs/ *n.* (*pl.* **cataclases** /-siːz/) *Geol.* the natural process of fracture, shearing, or breaking up of rocks. □□ **cataclastic** /-'klæstɪk/ *adj.* [mod.L f. Gk *kataklasis* breaking down]

cataclasm /'kætə,klæz(ə)m/ *n.* a violent break; a disruption. [Gk *kataklasma* (as CATA-, *klaō* to break)]

cataclysm /'kætə,klɪz(ə)m/ *n.* **1 a** a violent, esp. social or political, upheaval or disaster. **b** a great change. **2** a great flood or deluge. □□ **cataclysmal** /-'klɪzm(ə)l/ *adj.* **cataclysmic** /-'klɪzmɪk/ *adj.* **cataclysmically** /-'klɪzmɪkəlɪ/ *adv.* [F *cataclysme* f. L *cataclysmus* f. Gk *kataklusmos* f. *klusmos* flood f. *kluzō* wash]

catacomb /'kætə,kuːm, -,kəʊm/ *n.* (often in *pl.*) **1** an underground cemetery, esp. a Roman subterranean gallery with recesses for tombs. (See below.) **2** a similar underground construction; a cellar. [F *catacombes* f. LL *catacumbas* (see below), of unkn. orig.]

The term *catacumbas* was used as early as the 5th c. in connection with the subterranean cemetery under the Basilica of St Sebastian, on the Appian Way, near Rome, in which the bodies of the Apostles Peter and Paul were said to have been deposited. In later times it was applied (in the plural) to all the subterranean cemeteries lying around Rome (which, after having been long covered up and forgotten, were fortuitously discovered in 1578), and extended to similar works elsewhere. Since Roman legislation regarded every burial-place as sacrosanct, Christians could use the catacombs in the era of the persecutions, and their violation was extremely rare. The stucco paintings which often covered the walls are the first examples of Christian art.

catadromous /kə'tædrəməs/ *adj.* (of a fish, e.g. the eel) that swims down rivers to the sea to spawn (cf. ANADROMOUS). [Gk *katadromos* f. *kata* down + *dromos* running]

catafalque /'kætə,fælk/ *n.* a decorated wooden framework for supporting the coffin of a distinguished person during a funeral or while lying in state. [F f. It. *catafalco*, of unkn. orig.: cf. SCAFFOLD]

Catalan /'kætəlæn/ *n.* & *adj.* —*n.* **1** a native of Catalonia in Spain. **2** a Romance language most closely related to Provençal. Traditionally it is the language of Catalonia, but it is also spoken in Andorra (where it has official status), the Balearic Islands, and some parts of southern France. —*adj.* of or relating to Catalonia or its people or language. [F f. Sp.]

catalase /'kætə,leɪz/ *n. Biochem.* an enzyme that catalyses the reduction of hydrogen peroxide. [CATALYSIS]

catalepsy /'kætə,lepsɪ/ *n.* a state of trance or seizure with loss of sensation and consciousness accompanied by rigidity of the body. □□ **cataleptic** /-'leptɪk/ *adj.* & *n.* [F *catalepsie* or LL *catalepsia* f. Gk *katalēpsis* (as CATA-, *lēpsis* seizure)]

catalogue /'kætə,lɒg/ *n.* & *v.* (*US* **catalog**) —*n.* **1** a complete list of items (e.g. articles for sale, books held by a library), usu. in alphabetical or other systematic order and often with a description of each. **2** an extensive list (*a catalogue of crimes*). **3** *US* a university course-list etc. —*v.tr.* (**catalogues, catalogued, cataloguing**; *US* **catalogs, cataloged, cataloging**) **1** make a catalogue of. **2** enter in a catalogue. □□ **cataloguer** *n.* (*US* **cataloger**). [F f. LL *catalogus* f. Gk. *katalogos* f. *katalegō* enrol (as CATA-, *legō* choose)]

catalogue raisonné /'kætə,lɒg 'reɪzɒ'neɪ/ *n.* a descriptive catalogue with explanations or comments. [F, = explained catalogue]

Catalonia /,kætə'ləʊnɪə/ an autonomous region of NE Spain; pop. (1986) 5,977,000; capital, Barcelona.

catalpa /kə'tælpə/ *n.* any tree of the genus *Catalpa*, with heart-shaped leaves, trumpet-shaped flowers, and long pods. [Amer. Ind. (Creek)]

catalyse /'kætə,laɪz/ *v.tr.* (*US* **catalyze**) *Chem.* produce (a reaction) by catalysis. [as CATALYSIS after *analyse*]

catalysis /kə'tælɪsɪs/ *n.* (*pl.* **catalyses** /-siːz/) *Chem.* & *Biochem.* the acceleration of a chemical or biochemical reaction by a catalyst. [Gk *katalusis* dissolution (as CATA-, *luō* set free)]

catalyst /'kætəlɪst/ *n.* **1** *Chem.* a substance that, without itself undergoing any permanent chemical change, increases the rate of a reaction. **2** a person or thing that precipitates a change. [as CATALYSIS after *analyst*]

catalytic /,kætə'lɪtɪk/ *adj.* *Chem.* relating to or involving catalysis. □ **catalytic converter** a device incorporated in the exhaust system of a motor vehicle, with a catalyst for converting pollutant gases into harmless products. **catalytic cracker** a device for cracking (see CRACK *v.* 9) petroleum oils by catalysis.

catalyze *US* var. of CATALYSE.

catamaran /,kætəmə'ræn/ *n.* **1** a boat with twin hulls in parallel. **2** a raft of yoked logs or boats. **3** *colloq.* a quarrelsome woman. [Tamil *kaṭṭumaram* tied wood]

catamite /'kætə,maɪt/ *n.* **1** a boy kept for homosexual practices. **2** the passive partner in sodomy. [L *catamitus* through Etruscan f. Gk *Ganumēdēs* Ganymede, cupbearer of Zeus]

catamountain /'kætə,maʊntɪn/ *n.* **1** a lynx, leopard, puma, or other tiger-cat. **2** a wild quarrelsome person. [ME f. *cat of the mountain*]

catananche /,kætə'næŋkɪ/ *n.* any composite plant of the genus *Catananche*, with blue or yellow flowers. [mod.L f. L *catanancē* plant used in love-potions f. Gk *katanagkē* (as CATA-, *anagkē* compulsion)]

Catania /kə'tɑːnɪə/ a seaport situated at the foot of Mt. Etna, on the east coast of Sicily; pop. (1981) 380,300.

cataplexy /'kætə,pleksɪ/ *n.* sudden temporary paralysis due to fright etc. □□ **cataplectic** /-'plektɪk/ *adj.* [Gk *kataplēxis* stupefaction]

catapult /'kætə,pʌlt/ *n.* & *v.* —*n.* **1** a forked stick etc. with elastic for shooting stones. **2** *hist.* a military machine worked by a lever and ropes for hurling large stones etc. **3** a mechanical device for launching a glider, an aircraft from the deck of a ship, etc. —*v.* **1** *tr.* **a** hurl from or launch with a catapult. **b** fling forcibly. **2** *intr.* leap or be hurled forcibly. [F *catapulte* or L *catapulta* f. Gk *katapeltēs* (as CATA-, *pallō* hurl)]

cataract /'kætə,rækt/ *n.* **1 a** a large waterfall or cascade. **b** a downpour; a rush of water. **2** *Med.* a condition in which the eye-lens becomes progressively opaque resulting in blurred vision. [L *cataracta* f. Gk *katarrhaktēs* down-rushing; in med. sense prob. f. obs. sense 'portcullis']

catarrh /kə'tɑː(r)/ *n.* **1** inflammation of the mucous membrane of the nose, air passages, etc. **2** a watery discharge in the nose or throat due to this. □□ **catarrhal** *adj.* [F *catarrhe* f. LL *catarrhus* f. Gk *katarrhous* f. *katarrheō* flow down]

catarrhine /'kætə,raɪn/ *adj.* & *n.* *Zool.* —*adj.* (of primates) having nostrils close together, and directed downwards, e.g. a baboon, chimpanzee, or human. —*n.* such an animal (cf. PLATYRRHINE). [CATA- + *rhis rhinos* nose]

catastrophe /kə'tæstrəfɪ/ *n.* **1** a great and usu. sudden disaster. **2** the denouement of a drama. **3** a disastrous end; ruin. **4** an event producing a subversion of the order of things. □□ **catastrophic** /-'strɒfɪk/ *adj.* **catastrophically** /-'strɒfɪkəlɪ/ *adv.* [L *catastropha* f. Gk *katastrophē* (as CATA-, *strophē* turning f. *strephō* turn)]

catastrophism /kə'tæstrə,fɪz(ə)m/ *n.* *Geol.* the theory that changes in the earth's crust have occurred in sudden violent and unusual events. □□ **catastrophist** *n.*

catatonia /,kætə'təʊnɪə/ *n.* **1** schizophrenia with intervals of catalepsy and sometimes violence. **2** catalepsy. □□ **catatonic** /-'tɒnɪk/ *adj.* & *n.* [G *Katatonie* (as CATA-, TONE)]

catawba /kə'tɔːbə/ *n.* **1** a US variety of grape. **2** a white wine made from it. [River *Catawba* in S. Carolina]

catboat /'kætbəʊt/ *n.* a sailing-boat with a single mast placed well forward and carrying only one sail. [perh. f. *cat* a former type of coaler in NE England, + BOAT]

catcall /ˈkætkɔːl/ *n. & v.* —*n.* a shrill whistle of disapproval made at meetings etc. —*v.* **1** *intr.* make a catcall. **2** *tr.* make a catcall at.

catch /kætʃ/ *v. & n.* —*v.* (*past* and *past part.* **caught** /kɔːt/) **1** *tr.* **a** lay hold of so as to restrain or prevent from escaping; capture in a trap, in one's hands, etc. **b** (also **catch hold of**) get into one's hands so as to retain, operate, etc. (*caught hold of the handle*). **2** *tr.* detect or surprise (a person, esp. in a wrongful or embarrassing act) (*caught me in the act; caught him smoking*). **3** *tr.* **a** intercept and hold (a moving thing) in the hands etc. (*failed to catch the ball; a bowl to catch the drips*). **b** *Cricket* dismiss (a batsman) by catching the ball before it reaches the ground. **4** *tr.* **a** contract (a disease) by infection or contagion. **b** acquire (a quality or feeling) from another's example (*caught her enthusiasm*). **5** *tr.* **a** reach in time and board (a train, bus, etc.). **b** be in time to see etc. (a person or thing about to leave or finish) (*if you hurry you'll catch them; caught the end of the performance*). **6** *tr.* **a** apprehend with the senses or the mind (esp. a thing occurring quickly or briefly) (*didn't catch what he said*). **b** (of an artist etc.) reproduce faithfully. **7 a** *intr.* become fixed or entangled; be checked (*the bolt began to catch*). **b** *tr.* cause to do this (*caught her tights on a nail*). **c** *tr.* (often foll. by *on*) hit, deal a blow to (*caught him on the nose; caught his elbow on the table*). **8** *tr.* draw the attention of; captivate (*caught his eye; caught her fancy*). **9** *intr.* begin to burn. **10** *tr.* (often foll. by *up*) reach or overtake (a person etc. ahead). **11** *tr.* check suddenly (*caught his breath*). **12** *tr.* (foll. by *at*) grasp or try to grasp. —*n.* **1 a** an act of catching. **b** *Cricket* a chance or act of catching the ball. **2 a** an amount of a thing caught, esp. of fish. **b** a thing or person caught or worth catching, esp. in marriage. **3 a** a question, trick, etc., intended to deceive, incriminate, etc. **b** an unexpected or hidden difficulty or disadvantage. **4** a device for fastening a door or window etc. **5** *Mus.* a round, esp. with words arranged to produce a humorous effect. □ **catch-all** (often *attrib.*) a thing designed to be all-inclusive. **catch-as-catch-can** a style of wrestling with few holds barred. **catch at a straw** see STRAW. **catch crop** a crop grown between two staple crops (in position or time). **catch one's death** see DEATH. **catch fire** see FIRE. **catch it** *sl.* be punished or in trouble. **catch me!** etc. (often foll. by *pres. part.*) *colloq.* you may be sure I etc. shall not. **catch on** *colloq.* **1** (of a practice, fashion, etc.) become popular. **2** (of a person) understand what is meant. **catch out 1** detect in a mistake etc. **2** take unawares; cause to be bewildered or confused. **3** = sense 3b of *v.* **catch-phrase** a phrase in frequent use. **catch the sun 1** be in a sunny position. **2** become sunburnt. **catch up 1 a** (often foll. by *with*) reach a person etc. ahead (*he caught up in the end; he caught us up; he caught up with us*). **b** (often foll. by *with*, *on*) make up arrears (of work etc.) (*must catch up with my correspondence*). **2** snatch or pick up hurriedly. **3** (often in *passive*) **a** involve; entangle (*caught up in suspicious dealings*). **b** fasten up (*hair caught up in a ribbon*). □□ **catchable** *adj.* [ME f. AF & ONF *cachier*, OF *chacier*, ult. f. L *captare* try to catch]

catcher /ˈkætʃə(r)/ *n.* **1** a person or thing that catches. **2** *Baseball* a fielder who stands behind the batter.

catchfly /ˈkætʃflaɪ/ *n.* (*pl.* **-ies**) any plant of the genus *Silene* or *Lychnis* with a sticky stem.

catching /ˈkætʃɪŋ/ *adj.* **1 a** (of a disease) infectious. **b** (of a practice, habit, etc.) likely to be imitated. **2** attractive; captivating.

catchline /ˈkætʃlaɪn/ *n.* *Printing* a short line of type esp. at the head of copy or as a running headline.

catchment /ˈkætʃmənt/ *n.* the collection of rainfall. □ **catchment area 1** the area from which rainfall flows into a river etc. **2** the area served by a school, hospital, etc.

catchpenny /ˈkætʃˌpeni/ *adj.* intended merely to sell quickly; superficially attractive.

catch-22 /ˌkætʃˌtwentiˈtuː/ *n.* (often *attrib.*) *colloq.* a dilemma or circumstance from which there is no escape because of mutually conflicting or dependent conditions. [title of a novel by J. Heller (1961), set in the Second World War, in which the hero wishes not to fly any more missions and decides to go crazy, only to be told that anyone who wants to get out of combat duty is not really crazy]

catchup var. of KETCHUP.

catchweight /ˈkætʃweɪt/ *adj. & n.* —*adj.* unrestricted as regards weight. —*n.* unrestricted weight, as a weight category in sports.

catchword /ˈkætʃwɜːd/ *n.* **1** a word or phrase in common (often temporary) use; a topical slogan. **2** a word so placed as to draw attention. **3** *Theatr.* an actor's cue. **4** *Printing* the first word of a page given at the foot of the previous one.

catchy /ˈkætʃi/ *adj.* (**catchier, catchiest**) **1** (of a tune) easy to remember; attractive. **2** that snares or entraps; deceptive. **3** (of the wind etc.) fitful, spasmodic. □□ **catchily** *adv.* **catchiness** *n.* [CATCH + -Y¹]

cate /keɪt/ *n. archaic* (usu. in *pl.*) choice food, delicacies. [obs. *acate* purchase f. AF *acat*, OF *achat* f. *acater*, *achater* buy: see CATER]

catechetical /ˌkætɪˈketɪk(ə)l/ *adj.* (also **catechetic**) **1** of or by oral teaching. **2** according to the catechism of a Church. **3** consisting of or proceeding by question and answer. □□ **catechetically** *adv.* **catechetics** *n.* [eccl.Gk *katēkhētikos* f. *katēkhētēs* oral teacher: see CATECHIZE]

catechism /ˈkætɪkɪz(ə)m/ *n.* **1 a** a summary of the principles of a religion in the form of questions and answers. **b** a book containing this. **2** a series of questions put to anyone. □□ **catechismal** /-ˈkɪzm(ə)l/ *adj.* [eccl.L *catechismus* (as CATECHIZE)]

catechist /ˈkætɪkɪst/ *n.* a religious teacher, esp. one using a catechism.

catechize /ˈkætɪkaɪz/ *v.tr.* (also **-ise**) **1** instruct by means of question and answer, esp. from a catechism. **2** put questions to; examine. □□ **catechizer** *n.* [LL *catechizare* f. eccl.Gk *katēkhizō* f. *katēkheō* make hear (as CATA-, *ēkheō* sound)]

catechu /ˈkætɪˌtʃuː/ *n.* (also **cachou** /ˈkæʃuː/) gambier or similar vegetable extract, containing tannin. [mod.L f. Malay *kachu*]

catechumen /ˌkætɪˈkjuːmən/ *n.* a Christian convert under instruction before baptism. [ME f. OF *catechumene* or eccl.L *catechumenus* f. Gk *katēkheō*: see CATECHIZE]

categorical /ˌkætɪˈɡɒrɪk(ə)l/ *adj.* unconditional, absolute; explicit, direct (*a categorical refusal*). □ **categorical imperative** *Ethics* an unconditional moral obligation derived from pure reason; the bidding of conscience as ultimate moral law. □□ **categorically** *adv.* [F *catégorique* or LL *categoricus* f. Gk *katēgorikos*: see CATEGORY]

categorize /ˈkætɪɡəˌraɪz/ *v.tr.* (also **-ise**) place in a category or categories. □□ **categorization** /-ˈzeɪʃ(ə)n/ *n.*

category /ˈkætɪɡəri/ *n.* (*pl.* **-ies**) **1** a class or division. **2** *Philos.* **a** one of a possibly exhaustive set of classes among which all things might be distributed. **b** one of the a priori conceptions applied by the mind to sense-impressions. **c** any relatively fundamental philosophical concept. □□ **categorial** /-ˈɡɔːrɪəl/ *adj.* [F *catégorie* or LL *categoria* f. Gk *katēgoria* statement f. *katēgoros* accuser]

catena /kæˈtiːnə/ *n.* (*pl.* **catenae** /-niː/ or **catenas**) **1** a connected series of patristic comments on Scripture. **2** a series or chain. [L, = chain: orig. *catena patrum* chain of the Fathers (of the Church)]

catenary /kəˈtiːnəri/ *n. & adj.* —*n.* (*pl.* **-ies**) a curve formed by a uniform chain hanging freely from two points not in the same vertical line. —*adj.* of or resembling such a curve. □ **catenary bridge** a suspension bridge hung from such chains. [L *catenarius* f. *catena* chain]

catenate /ˈkætɪˌneɪt/ *v.tr.* connect like links of a chain. □□ **catenation** /-ˈneɪʃ(ə)n/ *n.* [L *catenare catenat-* (as CATENARY)]

cater /ˈkeɪtə(r)/ *v.intr.* **1** supply food. **2** (foll. by *for*) **a** provide meals for. **b** provide entertainment for. **3** (foll. by *to*) pander to (evil inclinations). [obs. noun *cater* (now *caterer*), f. *acater* f. AF *acatour* buyer f. *acater* buy f. Rmc]

cateran /ˈkætərən/ *n. Sc.* a Highland irregular fighting man; a marauder. [ME f. med.L *cateranus* & Gael. *ceathairne* peasantry]

cater-cornered /ˈkætəˌkɔːnəd/ *adj. & adv.* (also **cater-corner**, **catty-cornered** /ˈkætɪ-/) *US* —*adj.* placed or situated diagonally. —*adv.* diagonally. [dial. adv. *cater* diagonally (cf. obs. *cater* the four on dice f. F *quatre* f. L *quattuor* four)]

caterer /ˈkeɪtərə(r)/ n. a person who supplies food for social events, esp. professionally.

catering /ˈkeɪtərɪŋ/ n. the profession or work of a caterer.

caterpillar /ˈkætəˌpɪlə(r)/ n. **1 a** the larva of a butterfly or moth. **b** (in general use) any similar larva of various insects. **2** (**Caterpillar**) **a** (in full **Caterpillar track** or **tread**) propr. a steel band passing round the wheels of a tractor etc. for travel on rough ground. **b** a vehicle with these tracks, e.g. a tractor or tank. [perh. AF var. of OF chatepelose lit. hairy cat, infl. by obs. piller ravager]

caterwaul /ˈkætəˌwɔːl/ v. & n. —v.intr. make the shrill howl of a cat. —n. a caterwauling noise. [ME f. CAT + -waul etc. imit.]

catfish /ˈkætfɪʃ/ n. any of various esp. freshwater fish, usu. having whisker-like barbels round the mouth.

catgut /ˈkætgʌt/ n. a material used for the strings of musical instruments and surgical sutures, made of the twisted intestines of the sheep, horse, or ass (but not the cat).

Cath. abbr. **1** Cathedral. **2** Catholic.

Cathar /ˈkæθə(r)/ n. (pl. **Cathars** or **Cathari** /-rɪ/) a member of a medieval sect which sought to achieve great spiritual purity. □□ **Catharism** n. **Catharist** n. [med.L Cathari (pl.) f. Gk katharoi pure]

catharsis /kəˈθɑːsɪs/ n. (pl. **catharses** /-ˌsiːz/) **1** an emotional release in drama or art. **2** Psychol. the process of freeing repressed emotion by association with the cause, and elimination by abre-action. **3** Med. purgation. [mod.L f. Gk katharsis f. kathairō cleanse: sense 1 f. Aristotle's Poetics]

cathartic /kəˈθɑːtɪk/ adj. & n. —adj. **1** effecting catharsis. **2** purgative. —n. a cathartic drug. □□ **cathartically** adv. [LL catharticus f. Gk kathartikos (as CATHARSIS)]

Cathay /kæˈθeɪ/ n. (also **Khitai**) hist. or poet. the name by which China was known to medieval Europe, the Khitans being a people of Manchu race, to the NE of China, who established an empire over northern China during the two centuries ending in 1123. [med.L Cataya]

cathead /ˈkæthed/ n. Naut. a horizontal beam from each side of a ship's bow for raising and carrying the anchor.

cathectic see CATHEXIS.

cathedral /kəˈθiːdr(ə)l/ n. the principal church of a diocese, containing the bishop's throne. □ **cathedral city** a city in which there is a cathedral. [ME (as adj.) f. OF cathedral or f. LL cathedralis f. L f. Gk kathedra seat]

Cather /ˈkæθə(r)/, Willa Sibert (1876–1974), American novelist, brought up in Nebraska, which provides the setting for some of her best works. Her major novels include One of Ours (1922), the historical novel Death Comes for the Archbishop (1927) which is based on the work of the French Catholic missionary Father Latour in New Mexico, and Shadows on the Rock (1933) which tells of the French Canadians at Quebec.

Catherine II /ˈkæθrɪn/, 'the Great' (1729–96), Russian empress, reigned 1762–96. A German princess, Catherine deposed her husband Peter III in 1762 and ruled in his place. She attempted a wide-reaching series of social and political reforms, but entrenched aristocratic interests prevented these from developing very far, and in later years her reign became increasingly conservative. Abroad, Russia played an important part in European affairs, participating in the three partitions of Poland and forming close links with Prussia and Austria, while to the south and east further territorial advances were made at the expense of the Turks and Tartars.

Catherine de Medici[1] /ˈkæθərɪn də ˈmedɪtʃɪ, -ˈdiːtʃɪ/ (1519–89), queen of France. The wife of Henry II of France, Catherine ruled as regent during the minorities of their three sons, Francis II, Charles IX, and Henry III. She proved unable or unwilling to control the confused situation during the French religious wars, contributing substantially to the disorder and bloodshed through her own plotting and her instigation of the massacre of the Huguenots on St Bartholomew's Eve 1572.

Catherine of Aragon /ˈkæθrɪn, ˈærəgən/ (1485–1536), first wife of Henry VIII, youngest daughter of Ferdinand and Isabella of Spain, mother of Mary I. Originally married to Henry's elder brother Arthur, Catherine was eventually married to Henry several years after Arthur had died at the age of fifteen. The marriage was a reasonably happy one until about 1525 when the king, concerned by Catherine's failure to produce a male heir, fell in love with Anne Boleyn. His attempts to divorce his wife on the debatable grounds that Catherine's involvement with his brother made the marriage illegal did not gain the approval of the Vatican and led to a break with Rome.

Catherine wheel /ˈkæθrɪn/ n. **1** a firework in the form of a flat coil which spins when fixed and lit. **2** a circular window with radial divisions. [mod.L Catharina f. Gk Aikaterina name of a saint said to have been tortured on a spiked wheel (and then beheaded) at Alexandria in the 4th c.]

catheter /ˈkæθɪtə(r)/ n. Med. a tube for insertion into a body cavity for introducing or removing fluid. [LL f. Gk kathetēr f. kathiēmi send down]

catheterize /ˈkæθɪtəˌraɪz/ v.tr. (also **-ise**) Med. insert a catheter into.

cathetometer /ˌkæθɪˈtɒmɪtə(r)/ n. a telescope mounted on a graduated scale along which it can slide, used for accurate measurement of small vertical distances. [L cathetus f. Gk kathetos perpendicular line (as CATHETER + -METER)]

cathexis /kəˈθeksɪs/ n. (pl. **cathexes** /-siːz/) Psychol. concentration of mental energy in one channel. □□ **cathectic** adj. [Gk kathexis retention]

cathode /ˈkæθəʊd/ n. (also **kathode**) Electr. **1** the negative electrode in an electrolytic cell or electronic valve or tube. **2** the positive terminal of a primary cell such as a battery (opp. ANODE). □ **cathode ray** a beam of electrons emitted from the cathode of a high-vacuum tube. **cathode-ray tube** a high-vacuum tube in which cathode rays produce a luminous image on a fluorescent screen (as in a television set and an oscilloscope). ¶ Abbr.: **CRT**. (See below.) □□ **cathodal** adj. **cathodic** /kəˈθɒdɪk/ adj. [Gk kathodos descent f. kata down + hodos way]

The study of the discharge of high-voltage electricity through glass tubes containing gases at low pressure late last century revealed that a highly energetic radiation was being emitted from the region of the cathode or negative terminal of the tube. J. J. Thomson in 1897 established that cathode rays consisted of streams of high-velocity electrons. Cathode rays now have many applications in science and industry. The modern television tube, for example, is an advanced form of cathode-ray tube. It is highly evacuated and produces cathode rays through the evaporation of electrons from a heated cathode. The electrons are accelerated and focused by a specially designed and positively charged anode, and fall on a luminous screen where they produce a pinpoint of light. A metal grid or mesh inserted between cathode and anode may be charged positively or negatively, thereby increasing or reducing the brightness of the spot. When an external signal is not being received by the tube, special electrical circuits cause the electron beam to set up a scanning pattern which covers the whole screen with uniform illumination. When a signal is received at the grid from a television transmitter it controls the intensity of the electron beam, and, therefore, the brightness of the spot on the screen, in such a manner that the electrical signals received are translated into the pictures seen on the screen.

catholic /ˈkæθəlɪk, ˈkæθlɪk/ adj. & n. —adj. **1** of interest or use to all; universal. **2** all-embracing; of wide sympathies or interests (has catholic tastes). **3** (**Catholic**) **a** of the Roman Catholic religion. **b** including all Christians. **c** including all of the Western Church. —n. (**Catholic**) a Roman Catholic. □□ **catholically** adv. **Catholicism** /kəˈθɒlɪˌsɪz(ə)m/ n. **catholicity** /ˌkæθəˈlɪsɪtɪ/ n. **catholicly** adv. [ME f. OF catholique or LL catholicus f. Gk katholikos universal f. kata in respect of + holos whole]

catholicize /kəˈθɒlɪˌsaɪz/ v.tr. & intr. (also **-ise**) **1** make or become catholic. **2** (**Catholicize**) make or become a Roman Catholic.

Catiline /ˈkætɪˌlaɪn/ (Lucus Sergius Catilina, d. 62 BC), Roman nobleman and conspirator. Repeatedly thwarted in his ambition to be elected consul, in 63 BC he planned an uprising in Italy; his fellow-conspirators in Rome were successfully suppressed and executed on the initiative of the consul Cicero, and Catiline died fighting in Etruria in early 62 BC.

cation /ˈkætˌaɪən/ n. a positively charged ion; an ion that is attracted to the cathode in electrolysis (opp. ANION). [CATA- + ION]

cationic /ˌkætaɪˈɒnɪk/ adj. **1** of a cation or cations. **2** having an active cation.

catkin /ˈkætkɪn/ n. a spike of usu. downy or silky male or female flowers hanging from a willow, hazel, etc. [obs. Du. katteken kitten]

catlick /ˈkætlɪk/ n. colloq. a perfunctory wash.

catlike /ˈkætlaɪk/ adj. **1** like a cat. **2** stealthy.

catmint /ˈkætmɪnt/ n. a white-flowered plant, Nepeta cataria, having a pungent smell attractive to cats. Also called CATNIP.

catnap /ˈkætnæp/ n. & v. —n. a short sleep. —v.intr. (-napped, -napping) have a catnap.

catnip /ˈkætnɪp/ n. = CATMINT. [CAT + dial. nip catmint, var. of dial. nep]

Cato /ˈkeɪtəʊ/, Marcus Porcius 'the Censor' (234–149 BC), Roman statesman, orator, and writer, for later ages the embodiment of traditional Roman values. Of peasant stock, as a young man he fought in the Second Punic War, and thereafter remained an implacable enemy of Carthage. As censor in 184 BC he engaged in a vigorous programme of moral and social reform, and attempted to stem the growing influence of Greek culture on Roman life. His many writings included a lost history of Rome and an extant work on agriculture. His grandson, Cato the Younger (95–46 BC), was an opponent of the dictatorial ambitions of Julius Caesar.

catoptric /kəˈtɒptrɪk/ adj. of or relating to a mirror, a reflector, or reflection. □□ **catoptrics** n. [Gk katoptrikos f. katoptron mirror]

catsuit /ˈkætsuːt, -sjuːt/ n. a close-fitting garment with trouser legs, covering the body from neck to feet.

catsup /ˈkætsəp/ esp. US var. of KETCHUP.

cattery /ˈkætərɪ/ n. (pl. **-ies**) a place where cats are boarded or bred.

cattish /ˈkætɪʃ/ adj. = CATTY. □□ **cattishly** adv. **cattishness** n.

cattle /ˈkæt(ə)l/ n.pl. **1** any bison, buffalo, yak, or domesticated bovine animal, esp. of the genus Bos. **2** archaic livestock. □ **cattle-cake** Brit. a concentrated food for cattle, in cake form. **cattle-grid** Brit. a grid covering a ditch, allowing vehicles to pass over but not cattle, sheep, etc. **cattle-guard** US = cattle-grid. **cattle-plague** rinderpest. **cattle-stop** NZ = cattle-grid. [ME & AF catel f. OF chatel CHATTEL]

cattleman /ˈkæt(ə)lmən/ n. (pl. **-men**) US a person who tends or rears cattle.

cattleya /ˈkætlɪə/ n. any epiphytic orchid of the genus Cattleya, with handsome violet, pink, or yellow flowers. [mod.L f. W. Cattley, Engl. patron of botany d. 1832]

catty /ˈkætɪ/ adj. (**cattier, cattiest**) **1** sly, spiteful; deliberately hurtful in speech. **2** catlike. □□ **cattily** adv. **cattiness** n.

catty-cornered var. of CATER-CORNERED.

Catullus /kəˈtʌləs/, Gaius Valerius (c.84–c.54 BC), Roman poet, originally from Verona. His one book of verse contains poems in a variety of metres on a variety of subjects; he is best known for his intensely expressed poems to Lesbia, the nickname of one Clodia, probably the fast-living wife of the prominent Q. Metellus Celer. He also wrote personal poems to other friends and enemies, and a number of longer mythological pieces. His importance for later Latin poetry lies both in the impetus he gave to the development of love-elegy, and in his cultivation of an Alexandrian refinement and learning.

catwalk /ˈkætwɔːk/ n. **1** a narrow footway along a bridge, above a theatre stage, etc. **2** a narrow platform or gangway used in fashion shows etc.

Caucasian /kɔːˈkeɪʒ(ə)n, -ˈkeɪzɪən/ adj. & n. —adj. **1** of or relating to the White or light-skinned division of mankind. (See below.) **2** of or relating to the Caucasus. —n. a Caucasian person. □ **Caucasian languages** a group of languages spoken in the region of the Caucasus. Of the 40 known only a few are committed to writing. The main language of the group

is Georgian, which belongs to the southern group. [Caucasus, mountains in the USSR, its supposed place of origin]

This is one of the major racial divisions of man defined by Blumenbach. The physical attributes of Caucasians are highly variable: a wide range in body build, variable in nose-form and in the quantity and type of body and facial hair; a wide range in head-shape and in the form of the lips and mouth; and skin-colour ranging from extremely light to dark. The original distribution of this race extended from the Arctic to Africa north of the Sahara, and from the Azores in the North Atlantic to Samarkand in Soviet Central Asia.

Caucasoid /ˈkɔːkəˌsɔɪd/ adj. of or relating to the Caucasian division of mankind.

Caucasus /ˈkɔːkəsəs/ a mountain range in Georgia, USSR, between the Black and Caspian Seas, rising to over 5,500 m (18,000 ft.).

Cauchy /ˈkəʊʃɪ/, Augustin Louis, Baron (1789–1857), prolific and enormously influential French mathematician. It is said that more concepts and theorems have been named after Cauchy than after any other mathematician. His textbooks and many of his original writings introduced new standards of criticism and rigorous argument in the calculus from which grew the field of mathematics known as analysis. He transformed the theory of complex functions by discovering his integral theorems and introducing the calculus of residues. He founded the modern theory of elasticity, produced fundamental new ideas about the solution of differential equations, and contributed substantially in 1845 to the founding of the theory of groups.

caucus /ˈkɔːkəs/ n. **1** US **a** a meeting of the members of a political party, esp. in the Senate etc., to decide policy. **b** a bloc of such members. **c** this system as a political force. **2** often derog. (esp. in the UK) **a** a usu. secret meeting of a group within a larger organization or party. **b** such a group. [18th-c. US, perh. f. Algonquin cau'-cau-as'u adviser]

caudal /ˈkɔːd(ə)l/ adj. **1** of or like a tail. **2** of the posterior part of the body. □□ **caudally** adv. [mod.L caudalis f. L cauda tail]

caudate /ˈkɔːdeɪt/ adj. having a tail. [see CAUDAL]

caudillo /kaʊˈdiːljəʊ/ n. (pl. **-os**) (in Spanish-speaking countries) a military or political leader. [Sp. f. LL capitellum dimin. of caput head]

caught past and past part. of CATCH.

caul /kɔːl/ n. **1 a** the inner membrane enclosing a foetus. **b** part of this occasionally found on a child's head at birth, thought to bring good luck. The superstition existed among many sailors at least until the early 20th c. that possession of the caul of a new-born child was a sure protection against death by drowning. **2** hist. **a** a woman's close-fitting indoor head-dress. **b** the plain back part of a woman's indoor head-dress. **3** the omentum. [ME perh. f. OF cale small cap]

cauldron /ˈkɔːldrən/ n. (also **caldron**) a large deep bowl-shaped vessel for boiling over an open fire; an ornamental vessel resembling this. [ME f. AF & ONF caudron, ult. f. L caldarium hot bath f. calidus hot]

cauliflower /ˈkɒlɪˌflaʊə(r)/ n. **1** a variety of cabbage with a large immature flower-head of small usu. creamy-white flower-buds. **2** the flower-head eaten as a vegetable. □ **cauliflower cheese** a savoury dish of cauliflower in a cheese sauce. **cauliflower ear** an ear thickened by repeated blows, esp. in boxing. [earlier cole-florie etc. f. obs. F chou fleuri flowered cabbage, assim. to COLE and FLOWER]

caulk /kɔːk/ v.tr. (US **calk**) **1** stop up (the seams of a boat etc.) with oakum etc. and waterproofing material, or by driving plate-junctions together. **2** make (esp. a boat) watertight by this method. □□ **caulker** n. [OF dial. cauquer tread, press with force, f. L calcare tread f. calx heel]

causal /ˈkɔːz(ə)l/ adj. **1** of, forming, or expressing a cause or causes. **2** relating to, or of the nature of, cause and effect. □□ **causally** adv. [LL causalis: see CAUSE]

causality /kɔːˈzælɪtɪ/ n. **1** the relation of cause and effect. **2** the principle that everything has a cause.

causation /kɔːˈzeɪʃ(ə)n/ n. **1** the act of causing or producing an effect. **2** = CAUSALITY. [F *causation* or L *causatio* pretext etc., in med.L the action of causing, f. *causare* CAUSE]

causative /ˈkɔːzətɪv/ *adj.* **1** acting as cause. **2** (foll. by *of*) producing; having as effect. **3** *Gram.* expressing cause. ▫▫ **causatively** *adv.* [ME f. OF *causatif* or f. LL *causativus*: see CAUSATION]

cause /kɔːz/ *n. & v.* —*n.* **1 a** that which produces an effect, or gives rise to an action, phenomenon, or condition. **b** a person or thing that occasions something. **c** a reason or motive; a ground that may be held to justify something (*no cause for complaint*). **2** a reason adjudged adequate (*show cause*). **3** a principle, belief, or purpose which is advocated or supported (*faithful to the cause*). **4 a** a matter to be settled at law. **b** an individual's case offered at law (*plead a cause*). **5** the side taken by any party in a dispute. —*v.tr.* **1** be the cause of, produce, make happen (*caused a commotion*). **2** (foll. by *to* + infin.) induce (*caused me to smile*; *caused it to be done*). ▫ **in the cause of** to maintain, defend, or support (*in the cause of justice*). **make common cause with** join the side of. ▫▫ **causable** *adj.* **causeless** *adj.* **causer** *n.* [ME f. OF f. L *causa*]

'cause /kɒz/ *conj. & adv. colloq.* = BECAUSE. [abbr.]

cause célèbre /ˌkɔːz seˈlebr/ *n.* (*pl.* **causes célèbres** *pronunc.* same) a lawsuit that attracts much attention. [F]

causerie /ˈkəʊzərɪ/ *n.* (*pl.* **causeries** *pronunc.* same) an informal article or talk, esp. on a literary subject. [F f. *causer* talk]

causeway /ˈkɔːzweɪ/ *n.* **1** a raised road or track across low or wet ground or a stretch of water. **2** a raised path by a road. [earlier *cauce, causeway* f. ONF *caucié* ult. f. L CALX lime, limestone]

causey /ˈkɔːzɪ/ *n. archaic or dial.* = CAUSEWAY.

caustic /ˈkɔːstɪk/ *adj. & n.* —*adj.* **1** that burns or corrodes organic tissue. **2** sarcastic, biting. **3** *Chem.* strongly alkaline. **4** *Physics* formed by the intersection of reflected or refracted parallel rays from a curved surface. —*n.* **1** a caustic substance. **2** *Physics* a caustic surface or curve. ▫ **caustic potash** potassium hydroxide. **caustic soda** sodium hydroxide. ▫▫ **caustically** *adv.* **causticity** /-ˈtɪsɪtɪ/ *n.* [L *causticus* f. Gk *kaustikos* f. *kaustos* burnt f. *kaiō* burn]

cauterize /ˈkɔːtəˌraɪz/ *v.tr.* (also **-ise**) *Med.* burn or coagulate (tissue) with a heated instrument or caustic substance, esp. to stop bleeding. ▫▫ **cauterization** /-ˈzeɪʃ(ə)n/ *n.* [F *cautériser* f. LL *cauterizare* f. Gk *kautēriazō* f. *kautērion* branding-iron f. *kaiō* burn]

cautery /ˈkɔːtərɪ/ *n.* (*pl.* **-ies**) *Med.* **1** an instrument or caustic for cauterizing. **2** the operation of cauterizing. [L *cauterium* f. Gk *kautērion*: see CAUTERIZE]

caution /ˈkɔːʃ(ə)n/ *n. & v.* —*n.* **1** attention to safety; prudence, carefulness. **2 a** esp. *Brit.* a warning, esp. a formal one in law. **b** a formal warning and reprimand. **3** *colloq.* an amusing or surprising person or thing. —*v.tr.* **1** (often foll. by *against*, or *to* + infin.) warn or admonish. **2** esp. *Brit.* issue a caution to. ▫ **caution money** *Brit.* a sum deposited as security for good conduct. [ME f. OF f. L *cautio -onis* f. *cavēre caut-* take heed]

cautionary /ˈkɔːʃənərɪ/ *adj.* that gives or serves as a warning (*a cautionary tale*).

cautious /ˈkɔːʃəs/ *adj.* careful, prudent; attentive to safety. ▫▫ **cautiously** *adv.* **cautiousness** *n.* [ME f. OF f. L: see CAUTION]

Cauvery /ˈkɑːvərɪ/ (also **Kaveri**) a sacred river in south India that rises in north Kerala and flows east and south-east to the Bay of Bengal south of Pondicherry.

cavalcade /ˌkævəlˈkeɪd/ *n.* a procession or formal company of riders, motor vehicles, etc. [F f. It. *cavalcata* f. *cavalcare* ride ult. f. L *caballus* pack-horse]

cavalier /ˌkævəˈlɪə(r)/ *n. & adj.* —*n.* **1** *hist.* (**Cavalier**) a supporter of Charles I in the English Civil War. The term originally had pejorative connotations, referring to the supposedly over-enthusiastic attitude of the king's supporters towards the prospect of war. **2** a courtly gentleman, esp. as a lady's escort. **3** *archaic* a horseman. —*adj.* offhand, supercilious, blasé. ▫▫ **cavalierly** *adv.* [F f. It. *cavaliere*: see CHEVALIER]

cavalry /ˈkævəlrɪ/ *n.* (*pl.* **-ies**) (usu. treated as *pl.*) soldiers on horseback or in armoured vehicles. ▫ **cavalry twill** a strong fabric in a double twill. [F *cavallerie* f. It. *cavalleria* f. *cavallo* horse f. L *caballus*]

cavalryman /ˈkævəlrɪmən/ *n.* (*pl.* **-men**) a soldier of a cavalry regiment.

Cavan /ˈkævən/ **1** an inland county of the Republic of Ireland, though in the province of Ulster. **2** its capital city; pop. (1981) 3,240.

cavatina /ˌkævəˈtiːnə/ *n.* **1** a short simple song. **2** a similar piece of instrumental music, usu. slow and emotional. [It.]

cave[1] /keɪv/ *n. & v.* —*n.* **1** a large hollow in the side of a cliff, hill, etc., or underground. **2** *Brit. hist.* a dissident political group. —*v.intr.* explore caves, esp. interconnecting or underground. ▫ **cave-bear** an extinct kind of large bear, whose bones have been found in caves. **cave-dweller** = CAVEMAN. **cave in 1 a** (of a wall, earth over a hollow, etc.) subside, collapse. **b** cause (a wall, earth, etc.) to do this. **2** yield or submit under pressure; give up. **cave-in** *n.* a collapse, submission, etc. **cave-painting** picture(s) of animals etc. on the interior of a cave, especially by prehistoric peoples. ▫▫ **cavelike** *adj.* **caver** *n.* [ME f. OF f. L *cava* f. *cavus* hollow: *cave* in prob. f. E. Anglian dial. *calve in*]

cave[2] /ˈkeɪvɪ/ *int. Brit. school sl.* look out! (as a warning cry). ▫ **keep cave** act as lookout. [L, = beware]

caveat /ˈkævɪˌæt/ *n.* **1** a warning or proviso. **2** *Law* a process in court to suspend proceedings. [L, = let a person beware]

caveat emptor /ˈkævɪˌæt ˈemptɔː(r)/ *n.* the principle that the buyer alone is responsible if dissatisfied. [L, = let the buyer beware]

Cavell /ˈkæv(ə)l/, Edith (1865–1915), English nurse, executed by the Germans in 1915. Arrested by the German military authorities for helping British soldiers to escape from occupied Belgium, she was shot as a spy, a serious blunder on the part of the Germans who thereby gave British propaganda considerable fuel for allegations of German atrocities.

caveman /ˈkeɪvmæn/ *n.* (*pl.* **-men**) **1** a prehistoric man living in a cave. **2** a primitive or crude person.

Cavendish /ˈkævəndɪʃ/, Henry (1731–1810), English natural philosopher, nephew of the 3rd Duke of Devonshire. He was of independent means so that he did not have to study for a profession. Indeed, he was described as the 'richest of the learned, and the most learned of the rich'. A shy and eccentric man, he pursued his research for its own sake in his private laboratory, and troubled little about publishing his results. He identified hydrogen ('inflammable air') as a separate gas, studied carbon dioxide ('fixed air'), and determined their densities relative to common air in 1766, established that water was a compound in 1784, and determined the density of the earth by means of John Mitchel's torsion balance in 1798. The full extent of his discoveries in electrostatics was not known until his manuscripts were published by James Clerk Maxwell in 1879: he had anticipated Coulomb, Ohm, and Faraday, deduced the inverse square law of electrical attraction and repulsion, and discovered specific inductive capacity (not his term). The Cavendish Laboratory at Cambridge was named in his honour in 1874.

cavern /ˈkæv(ə)n/ *n.* **1** a cave, esp. a large or dark one. **2** a dark cavelike place, e.g. a room. ▫▫ **cavernous** *adj.* **cavernously** *adv.* [ME f. OF *caverne* or f. L *caverna* f. *cavus* hollow]

caviare /ˈkævɪˌɑː(r), ˌkævɪˈɑː(r)/ *n.* (*US* **caviar**) the pickled roe of sturgeon or other large fish, eaten as a delicacy. [early forms repr. It. *caviale*, Fr. *caviar*, prob. f. med.Gk *khaviari*]

cavil /ˈkævɪl/ *v. & n.* —*v.intr.* (**cavilled, cavilling;** *US* **caviled, caviling**) (usu. foll. by *at, about*) make petty objections; carp. —*n.* a trivial objection. ▫▫ **caviller** *n.* [F *caviller* f. L *cavillari* f. *cavilla* mockery]

caving /ˈkeɪvɪŋ/ *n.* exploring caves as a sport or pastime.

cavitation /ˌkævɪˈteɪʃ(ə)n/ *n.* **1** the formation of a cavity in a structure. **2** the formation of bubbles, or of a vacuum, in a liquid.

cavity /ˈkævɪtɪ/ *n.* (*pl.* **-ies**) **1** a hollow within a solid body. **2** a decayed part of a tooth. ▫ **cavity wall** a wall formed from two skins of brick or blockwork with a space between. [F *cavité* or LL *cavitas* f. L *cavus* hollow]

cavort /kəˈvɔːt/ *v.intr.* caper excitedly; gambol, prance. [US, perh. f. CURVET]

Cavour /kə'vuə(r)/, Camillo Benso, Count di (1810–61), Italian statesman. Premier of Sardinia from 1852, Cavour was the driving force behind the unification of Italy, organizing the movement behind his monarch Victor Emmanuel II and actively participating in international affairs, notably the Crimean War and the Franco-Austrian War, in order to win wide support for the project, which finally came to fruition with unification in 1860–1.

cavy /'keɪvɪ/ n. (pl. **-ies**) any small rodent of the family Caviidae, native to S. America and having a sturdy body and vestigial tail, including guinea pigs. [mod.L *cavia* f. Galibi *cabiai*]

caw /kɔː/ n. & v. —n. the harsh cry of a rook, crow, etc. —v.intr. utter this cry. [imit.]

Cawnpore see KANPUR.

Caxton /'kækstən/, William (c.1422–91), the first English printer. Having learned the art of printing on the Continent, Caxton printed his first English text in 1474 and went on to produce about 80 other texts (many of them his own translations of French romances) before his death, doing more than any other person to popularize printed books in Britain.

cay /keɪ/ n. a low insular bank or reef of coral, sand, etc. (cf. KEY²). [Sp. *cayo* shoal, reef f. F *quai*: see QUAY]

Cayenne /keɪ'en/ the capital and chief port of French Guiana; pop. (est. 1988) 38,100.

cayenne /keɪ'en/ n. (in full **cayenne pepper**) a pungent red powder obtained from various plants of the genus *Capsicum* and used for seasoning. [Tupi *kyynha* assim. to CAYENNE]

Cayley¹ /'keɪlɪ/, Arthur (1821–95), English mathematician and barrister, who wrote almost 1,000 mathematical papers on topics in algebra and geometry. These include articles on determinants, the newly developing group theory, and the algebra of matrices. He also studied dynamics and physical astronomy. The Cayley numbers, a generalization of complex numbers, are named after him.

Cayley² /'keɪlɪ/, Sir George (1773–1857), the father of British aeronautics, a mechanical genius best known for his understanding of the principles of flight, his model gliders, and his 'man-carrier', a glider which carried his coachman across Brompton Dale, Yorkshire, in 1853. At one time MP for Scarborough, his research, inventions, and designs covered schemes and devices for land reclamation, artificial limbs, theatre architecture, railways, lifeboats, finned projectiles, optics, electricity, hot-air engines, and what was later called the caterpillar tractor (1825). He was a founder of the original Regent Street Polytechnic Institution (1838).

cayman /'keɪmən/ n. (also **caiman**) any of various S. American alligator-like reptilians, esp. of the genus *Caiman*. [Sp. & Port. *caiman*, f. Carib *acayuman*]

Cayman Islands /'keɪmən/ (also **Caymans**) three islands in the Caribbean Sea, a British dependency, south of Cuba; pop. (est. 1988) 23,700; official language, English; capital, George Town. Columbus, discovering the islands in 1503, named them *Las Tortugas* (Sp., = the turtles) because of their abundance of turtles. A British colony was established towards the end of the 17th c., and in the 19th c. the Caymans became noted for the building of schooners.

CB abbr. **1** citizens' band. **2** (in the UK) Companion of the Order of the Bath.

Cb symb. US Chem. the element columbium.

CBC abbr. Canadian Broadcasting Corporation.

CBE abbr. Commander of the Order of the British Empire.

CBI abbr. (in the UK) Confederation of British Industry.

CBS abbr. US Columbia Broadcasting System.

CC abbr. **1** Brit. **a** City Council. **b** County Council. **c** County Councillor. **2** Cricket Club. **3** Companion of the Order of Canada.

cc abbr. (also **c.c.**) **1** cubic centimetre(s). **2** carbon copy.

CD abbr. **1** compact disc. **2** Civil Defence. **3** Corps Diplomatique. **4** Conference on Disarmament.

Cd symb. Chem. the element cadmium.

Cd. abbr. Command Paper (1900–18).

cd abbr. candela.

Cdr. abbr. Mil. Commander.

Cdre. abbr. Commodore.

CD-ROM /ˌsiːdiː'rɒm/ abbr. compact disc read-only memory (for retrieval of text or data on a VDU screen).

CDT abbr. US Central Daylight Time.

CD-video /ˌsiːdiː 'vɪdɪəʊ/ n. a systm of simultaneously reproducing high-quality sound and video pictures from a compact disc.

CE abbr. **1** Church of England. **2** civil engineer. **3** Common Era.

Ce symb. Chem. the element cerium.

ceanothus /ˌsiːə'nəʊθəs/ n. any shrub of the genus *Ceanothus*, with small blue or white flowers. [mod.L f. Gk *keanōthos* kind of thistle]

cease /siːs/ v. & n. —v.tr. & intr. stop; bring or come to an end (*ceased breathing*). —n. (in **without cease**) unending. □ **cease fire** Mil. stop firing. **cease-fire** n. **1** the order to do this. **2** a period of truce; a suspension of hostilities. [ME f. OF *cesser*, L *cessare* frequent. of *cedere* *cess-* yield]

ceaseless /'siːslɪs/ adj. without end; not ceasing. □ **ceaselessly** adv.

Ceauçescu /ˌtʃaʊ'ʃesku:/, Nicolae (1918–89), Romanian Communist statesman, first President of the republic of Romania 1974–89. Noted for his independence of the USSR, for many years he held absolute power, making his wife Elena his deputy and appointing many other members of his family to high office. His regime became increasingly tyrannical, oppressive, and corrupt, with officials living in comfort or luxury while the mass of the people existed in poverty. Its downfall was sudden: an uprising on 21 Dec. 1989 resulted in the arrest and summary trial of Ceauçescu and his wife, and their execution on Christmas Day.

Cebu /seɪ'buː/ **1** an island of the south central Philippines; pop. (1980) 2,091,600. **2** its chief city and port; pop. (1980) 490,280.

Cecilia /sɪ'siːljə/, St (2nd or 3rd c.), one of the most venerated martyrs in the early Roman Church. Her body is said to have been found entire and uncorrupted in 1599 in the church in Rome which bears her name. She is frequently represented as playing on the organ, and is the patron saint of church music. Feast day, 22 Nov.

cecitis US var. of CAECITIS.

cecum US var. of CAECUM.

cedar /'siːdə(r)/ n. **1** any spreading evergreen conifer of the genus *Cedrus*, bearing tufts of small needles and cones of papery scales. **2** any of various similar conifers yielding timber. **3** (in full **cedar wood**) the fragrant durable wood of any cedar tree. □□ **cedarn** adj. poet. [ME f. OF *cedre* f. L *cedrus* f. Gk *kedros*]

cede /siːd/ v.tr. give up one's rights to or possession of. [F *céder* or L *cedere* yield]

cedilla /sɪ'dɪlə/ n. **1** a mark written under the letter *c*, esp. in French, to show that it is sibilant (as in façade) **2** a similar mark under *s* in Turkish and other oriental languages. [Sp. *cedilla* dimin. of *zeda* f. Gk *zēta* letter Z]

Ceefax /'siːfæks/ n. Brit. propr. a teletext service provided by the BBC. (Cf. ORACLE 4.) [repr. pronunc. of *seeing* + *facsimile*]

CEGB abbr. (in the UK) Central Electricity Generating Board.

ceilidh /'keɪlɪ/ n. orig. Ir. & Sc. an informal gathering for conversation, music, dancing, songs, and stories. [Gael.]

ceiling /'siːlɪŋ/ n. **1 a** the upper interior surface of a room or other similar compartment. **b** the material forming this. **2** an upper limit on prices, wages, performance, etc. **3** Aeron. the maximum altitude a given aircraft can reach. **4** Naut. the inside planking of a ship's bottom and sides. [ME *celynge*, *siling*, perh. ult. f. L *caelum* heaven or *celare* hide]

celadon /'selə₁dɒn/ n. & adj. —n. **1** a willow-green colour. **2** a grey-green glaze used on some pottery. **3** Chinese pottery glazed in this way. —adj. of a grey-green colour. [F, f. the name of a character in d'Urfé's *L'Astrée* (1607–27)]

celandine /'selən₁daɪn/ n. either of two yellow-flowered plants, the greater celandine, *Chelidonium majus*, and the lesser celandine, *Ranunculus ficaria*. [ME and OF *celidoine* ult. f. Gk *khelidōn* swallow: the flowering of the plant was associated with the arrival of swallows]

-cele /siːl/ *comb. form* (also **-coele**) *Med.* swelling, hernia (*gastrocele*). [Gk *kēlē* tumour]

Celebes see SULAWESI.

celebrant /ˈselɪbrənt/ *n.* a person who performs a rite, esp. a priest at the Eucharist. [F. *célébrant* or L *celebrare celebrant-*: see CELEBRATE]

celebrate /ˈselɪˌbreɪt/ *v.* **1** *tr.* mark (a festival or special event) with festivities etc. **2** *tr.* perform publicly and duly (a religious ceremony etc.). **3 a** *tr.* officiate at (the Eucharist). **b** *intr.* officiate, esp. at the Eucharist. **4** *intr.* engage in festivities, usu. after a special event etc. **5** *tr.* (as **celebrated** *adj.*) publicly honoured, widely known. □□ **celebration** /-ˈbreɪʃ(ə)n/ *n.* **celebrator** *n.* **celebratory** *adj.* [L *celebrare* f. *celeber -bris* frequented, honoured]

celebrity /sɪˈlebrɪtɪ/ *n.* (*pl.* **-ies**) **1** a well-known person. **2** fame. [F *célébrité* or L *celebritas* f. *celeber*: see CELEBRATE]

celeriac /sɪˈlerɪˌæk/ *n.* a variety of celery with a swollen turnip-like stem-base used as a vegetable. [CELERY: *-ac* is unexplained]

celerity /sɪˈlerɪtɪ/ *n. archaic* or *literary* swiftness (esp. of a living creature). [ME f. F *célérité* f. L *celeritas -tatis* f. *celer* swift]

celery /ˈselərɪ/ *n.* an umbelliferous plant, *Apium graveolens*, with closely packed succulent leaf-stalks used as a vegetable. □ **celery pine** an Australasian tree, *Phyllocladus trichomanoides*, with branchlets like celery leaves. [F *céleri* f. It. dial. *selleri* f. L *selinum* f. Gk *selinon* parsley]

celesta /sɪˈlestə/ *n. Mus.* a small keyboard instrument resembling a glockenspiel, with hammers striking steel plates suspended over wooden resonators, giving an ethereal bell-like sound. [pseudo-L f. F *céleste*: see CELESTE]

celeste /sɪˈlest/ *n. Mus.* **1** an organ and harmonium stop with a soft tremulous tone. **2** = CELESTA. [F *céleste* heavenly f. L *caelestis* f. *caelum* heaven]

celestial /sɪˈlestɪəl/ *adj.* **1** heavenly; divinely good or beautiful; sublime. **2 a** of the sky; of the part of the sky commonly observed in astronomy etc. **b** of heavenly bodies. □ **celestial equator** the great circle of the sky in the plane perpendicular to the earth's axis. **celestial horizon** see HORIZON 1c. **celestial mechanics** the mathematical description of the positions and motions of astronomical objects on the celestial sphere. **celestial navigation** navigation by the stars etc. **celestial pole** the point on the celestial sphere directly above the earth's geographic pole (north or south). This is the point in the sky around which the stars and planets rotate during the course of the night, currently (in the northern hemisphere) within one degree of the bright star Polaris, but because of the precession of the equinoxes it appears to trace out a circle on the celestial sphere over a period of some 26,000 years. **celestial sphere** the abstract sphere of unit radius on which the positions of celestial objects are projected to form a map of the heavens whose poles and equator are projections of the corresponding terrestrial features. □□ **celestially** *adv.* [ME f. OF f. med.L *caelestialis* f. L *caelestis*: see CELESTE]

celiac *US* var. of COELIAC.

celibate /ˈselɪbət/ *adj. & n.* —*adj.* **1** committed to abstention from sexual relations and from marriage, esp. for religious reasons. **2** abstaining from sexual relations. —*n.* a celibate person. □□ **celibacy** *n.* [F *célibat* or L *caelibatus* unmarried state f. *caelebs -ibis* unmarried]

cell /sel/ *n.* **1** a small room, esp. in a prison or monastery. **2** a small compartment, e.g. in a honeycomb. **3** a small group as a nucleus of political activity, esp. of a subversive kind. **4** *hist.* a small monastery or nunnery dependent on a larger one. **5** *Biol.* **a** the structural and functional usu. microscopic unit of an organism, consisting of cytoplasm and a nucleus enclosed in a membrane. (See below.) **b** an enclosed cavity in an organism etc. **6** *Electr.* a vessel for containing electrodes within an electrolyte for current-generation or electrolysis. □□ **celled** *adj.* (also in comb.). [ME f. OF *celle* or f. L *cella* storeroom etc.]

Nearly all organisms are composed of cells (the simplest consist of a single cell), which are microscopic structures bounded by a membrane and capable of metabolism, self-repair, and reproduction. The word was first applied to dead cork cells by Robert Hooke in 1665, but the universal importance of living cells was not appreciated until the 19th c. Cells arise most commonly by the division of other cells, but sometimes by fusion (as of gametes in sexual reproduction). There are two basic types of cell: those of bacteria, lacking nuclei and other complex structures, and animal and plant cells, which are larger and more complex and possess a nucleus. This nucleus contains the genetic information (see DNA), the surrounding cytoplasm contains various structures and carries out most of the cell's metabolism, and the cell membrane regulates the exchange of materials with its environment. The activities of the cell are to a large extent controlled by the information in its DNA. In large organisms such as humans there are many specialized types of cell lacking some of the features described above; for example, red blood cells have no nuclei, and nerve cells in adults, although nucleated, are unable to reproduce. Most plant cells differ from those of animals in having a thick wall of cellulose outside the cell membrane, a large fluid-filled cavity within the cytoplasm, and (in green plants) structures that contain chlorophyll.

cellar /ˈselə(r)/ *n. & v.* —*n.* **1** a room below ground level in a house, used for storage, esp. of wine or coal. **2** a stock of wine in a cellar (*has a good cellar*). —*v.tr.* store or put in a cellar. [ME f. AF *celer*, OF *celier* f. LL *cellarium* storehouse]

cellarage /ˈselərɪdʒ/ *n.* **1** cellar accommodation. **2** the charge for the use of a cellar or storehouse.

cellarer /ˈselərə(r)/ *n.* a monastic officer in charge of wine.

cellaret /ˌseləˈret/ *n.* a case or sideboard for holding wine bottles in a dining-room.

Cellini /tʃeˈliːnɪ/, Benvenuto (1500–71), Florentine goldsmith and metal-worker, one of the most important mannerist sculptors. While in the service of Francis I of France, 1540–5, he created the salt-cellar of gold and enamel (now in Vienna), which is the greatest example of goldsmith's work that has survived from the Italian Renaissance. The rest of his life was spent in Florence; here he cast the bronze *Perseus* (1545–54) which is regarded as his materpiece. His autobiography, translated by Goethe in the 18th c., is famous for its racy style and its vivid picture of a proud, quarrelsome, Renaissance craftsman.

cello /ˈtʃeləʊ/ *n.* (*pl.* **-os**) violoncello, an instrument like a large violin with four strings and a range of over three octaves, played supported on the floor in an upright or slanting position between the seated player's knees □□ **cellist** *n.* [abbr. of VIOLONCELLO]

Cellophane /ˈseləˌfeɪn/ *n. propr.* a thin transparent wrapping material made from viscose, first produced in Switzerland in 1908. [CELLULOSE + *-phane* (cf. DIAPHANOUS)]

cellphone /ˈselfəʊn/ *n.* a small portable radio-telephone having access to a cellular radio system.

cellular /ˈseljʊlə(r)/ *adj.* **1** of or having small compartments or cavities. **2** of open texture; porous. **3** *Physiol.* of or consisting of cells. □ **cellular blanket** a blanket of open texture. **cellular plant** a plant with no distinct stem, leaves, etc. **cellular radio** a system of mobile radio-telephone transmission with an area divided into 'cells' each served by its own small transmitter. □□ **cellularity** /-ˈlærɪtɪ/ *n.* **cellulate** *adj.* **cellulation** /-ˈleɪʃ(ə)n/ *n.* **cellulous** *adj.* [F *cellulaire* f. mod.L *cellularis*: see CELLULE]

cellule /ˈseljuːl/ *n. Biol.* a small cell or cavity. [F *cellule* or L *cellula* dimin. of *cella* CELL]

cellulite /ˈseljʊˌlaɪt/ *n.* a lumpy form of fat, esp. on the hips and thighs of women, causing puckering of the skin. [F (as CELLULE)]

cellulitis /ˌseljʊˈlaɪtɪs/ *n.* inflammation of cellular tissue.

celluloid /ˈseljʊˌlɔɪd/ *n.* **1** a transparent flammable plastic made from camphor and cellulose nitrate. **2** cinema film. [irreg. f. CELLULOSE]

cellulose /ˈseljʊˌləʊz, -ˌləʊs/ *n.* **1** *Biochem.* a carbohydrate forming the main constituent of plant-cell walls, used in the production of textile fibres. (See below.) **2** (in general use) a paint or lacquer consisting of esp. cellulose acetate or nitrate in solution. □□ **cellulosic** /-ˈləʊsɪk/ *adj.* [F (as CELLULE)]

Cellulose, the main structural material of plants, is a carbohydrate consisting of long unbranched chains of glucose molecules and is the most abundant organic compound on earth. It is a major constituent of wood, from which it is produced industrially. Paper and plant-based textile fibres such as cotton consist largely of cellulose, and in chemically modified forms it is used in the manufacture of rayon, certain plastics, and many other products. It is important in the human diet since it is a constituent of dietary fibre.

celom US var. of COELOM.

Celsius[1] /'selsɪəs/, Anders (1701–44), Swedish astronomer, best known for his thermometer scale. He was appointed professor of astronomy at Uppsala in 1730, and six years later joined an expedition to measure a meridian in the north, which successfully verified Newton's theory that the earth is flattened at the poles. In 1742 he advocated a metric thermometer scale with 100° as the freezing-point of water and 0° as the boiling-point, but the thermometer which was introduced at the Uppsala Observatory in 1747 had its scale reversed. It was long known as the 'Swedish thermometer' and only in the early 19th c. did Celsius' name become associated with it.

Celsius[2] /'selsɪəs/ adj. of or denoting a temperature on the Celsius scale. □ **Celsius scale** a scale of temperature on which water freezes at 0° and boils at 100° under standard conditions. (See CELSIUS[1].)

Celt /kelt, selt/ n. (also **Kelt**) a member of a group of west European peoples, including the pre-Roman inhabitants of Britain and Gaul and their descendants, especially in Ireland, Wales, Scotland, Cornwall, Brittany, and the Isle of Man. (See below.) [L *Celtae* (pl.) f. Gk *Keltoi*]

The Celts occupied a large part of Europe in the Iron Age. Their unity is recognizable by common speech (see CELTIC) and common artistic tradition, but they did not constitute one race or group of tribes ethnologically. The origins of their culture can be traced back to the Bronze Age of the upper Danube in the 13th c. BC, with successive stages represented by the urnfield and Hallstatt cultures. Spreading over western and central Europe from perhaps as early as 900 BC, they reached the height of their power in the La Tène period of the 5th–1st c. BC. The ancients knew them as fierce fighters and superb horsemen, with savage religious rites conducted by the Druid priesthood. They were farmers, who cultivated fields on a regular basis with ox-drawn ploughs in place of manual implements, revolutionary changes which permanently affected people's way of life. But Celtic political sense was weak, and the numerous tribes, continually warring against each other, were crushed between the migratory Germans and the power of Rome, to be ejected or assimilated by the former or conquered outright by the latter.

celt /kelt/ n. Archaeol. a stone or metal prehistoric implement with a chisel edge. [med.L *celtes* chisel]

Celtic /'keltɪk, 'seltɪk/ adj. & n. —adj. of or relating to the Celts or their languages. —n. a sub-group of the Indo-European language group, today spoken in the British Isles and in Brittany, divided into two groups, Goidelic (consisting of Irish, Scots Gaelic, and Manx) and Brythonic (consisting of Welsh, Cornish, and Breton). There is widespread evidence that a Celtic language was spoken in mainland Europe before and during the Roman period. □ **Celtic cross** a Latin cross with a circle round the centre. □□ **Celticism** /-ˌsɪz(ə)m/ n. [L *celticus* (as CELT) or F *celtique*]

Celtic Sea the part of the Atlantic Ocean between Ireland and SW England.

cembalo /'tʃembəˌləʊ/ n. (pl. **-os**) a harpsichord. [abbr. of CLAVICEMBALO]

cement /sɪ'ment/ n. & v. —n. **1** a powdery substance made by calcining lime and clay, mixed with water to form mortar or used in concrete (see also *Portland cement*). **2** any similar substance that hardens and fastens on setting. **3** a uniting factor or principle. **4** a substance for filling cavities in teeth. **5** (also **cementum**) Anat. a thin layer of bony material that fixes teeth to the jaw. —v.tr. **1 a** unite with or as with cement. **b** establish or strengthen (a friendship etc.). **2** apply cement to. **3** line or cover with cement. □ **cement-mixer** a machine (usu. with a

revolving drum) for mixing cement with water. □□ **cementer** n. [ME f. OF *ciment* f. L *caementum* quarry stone f. *caedere* hew]

cementation /ˌsiːmen'teɪʃ(ə)n/ n. **1** the act or process of cementing or being cemented. **2** the heating of iron with charcoal powder to form steel.

cemetery /'semɪt(ə)rɪ/ n. (pl. **-ies**) a burial ground, esp. one not in a churchyard. [LL *coemeterium* f. Gk *koimētērion* dormitory f. *koimaō* put to sleep]

C.Eng. abbr. Brit. chartered engineer.

cenobite US var. of COENOBITE.

cenotaph /'senəˌtɑːf/ n. a tomblike monument, esp. a war memorial, to a person whose body is elsewhere. □ **the Cenotaph** a monument, designed by Sir Edward Lutyens, erected in 1919–20 in Whitehall, London, as a memorial to the British servicemen who died in the First World War. An inscription now commemorates also those who died in the Second World War. [F *cénotaphe* f. LL *cenotaphium* f. Gk *kenos* empty + *taphos* tomb]

Cenozoic /ˌsiːnə'zəʊɪk/ adj. & n. (also **Cainozoic** /ˌkaɪnə-/, **Caenozoic** /ˌsiːn-/) Geol. —adj. of or relating to the most recent geological era, following the Mesozoic and lasting from about 65 million years ago to the present day. It includes the Tertiary and Quaternary periods, and is characterized by the rapid evolution of mammals (whence its name). —n. this era. (cf. MESOZOIC, PALAEOZOIC.) [Gk *kainos* new + *zōion* animal]

censer /'sensə(r)/ n. a vessel in which incense is burnt, esp. during a religious procession or ceremony. [ME f. AF *censer*, OF *censier* aphetic of *encensier* f. *encens* INCENSE[1]]

censor /'sensə(r)/ n. & v. —n. **1** an official authorized to examine printed matter, films, news, etc., before public release, and to suppress any parts on the grounds of obscenity, a threat to security, etc. **2** Rom.Hist. either of two annual magistrates responsible for holding censuses and empowered to supervise public morals. **3** Psychol. an impulse which is said to prevent certain ideas and memories from emerging into consciousness. —v.tr. **1** act as a censor of. **2** make deletions or changes in. ¶ As a verb, often confused with *censure*. □□ **censorial** /-'sɔːrɪəl/ adj. **censorship** n. [L f. *censēre* assess: in sense 3 mistransl. of G *Zensur* censorship]

censorious /sen'sɔːrɪəs/ adj. severely critical; fault-finding; quick or eager to criticize. □□ **censoriously** adv. **censoriousness** n. [L *censorius*: see CENSOR]

censure /'sensjə(r)/ v. & n. —v.tr. criticize harshly; reprove. ¶ Often confused with *censor*. —n. harsh criticism; expression of disapproval. □□ **censurable** adj. [ME f. OF f. L *censura* f. *censēre* assess]

census /'sensəs/ n. (pl. **censuses**) the official count of a population or of a class of things, often with various statistics noted. [L f. *censēre* assess]

cent /sent/ n. **1 a** a monetary unit valued at one-hundredth of a dollar or other metric unit. **b** a coin of this value. **2** colloq. a very small sum of money. **3** see PER CENT. [F *cent* or It. *cento* or L *centum* hundred]

cent. abbr. century.

centaur /'sentɔː(r)/ n. **1** a member of a tribe of wild creatures in Greek mythology with the head, arms, and torso of a man and the body and legs of a horse. The legend of their existence may have arisen from the ancient inhabitants of Thessaly having tamed horses and appearing to their neighbours mounted on horseback. **2** (**the Centaur**) Astron. the southern constellation Centaurus. [ME f. L *centaurus* f. Gk *kentauros*, of unkn. orig.]

Centaurus /sen'tɔːrəs/ a southern constellation, the Centaur, famous for its brightest member, alpha Centauri, third-brightest in the sky and actually a triple star system of which the least bright component is the nearest star beyond our solar system, at a distance of 4.34 light-years.

centaury /'sentɔːrɪ/ n. (pl. **-ies**) any plant of the genus *Centaurium*, esp. *C. erythraea*, formerly used in medicine. [LL *centaurea* ult. f. Gk *kentauros* CENTAUR: from the legend that it was discovered by the centaur Chiron]

centavo /sen'tɑːvəʊ/ n. a small coin of Spain, Portugal, and some

æ cat ɑː arm e bed ɜː her ɪ sit iː see ɒ hot ɔː saw ʌ run ʊ put uː too ə ago aɪ my

Latin American countries, worth one-hundredth of the standard unit. [Sp. f. L *centum* hundred]

centenarian /ˌsentɪˈneərɪən/ n. & adj. —n. a person a hundred or more years old. —adj. a hundred or more years old.

centenary /senˈtiːnərɪ/ n. & adj. —n. (pl. **-ies**) **1** a hundredth anniversary. **2** a celebration of this. —adj. **1** of or relating to a centenary. **2** occurring every hundred years. [L *centenarius* f. *centeni* a hundred each f. *centum* a hundred]

centennial /senˈtenɪəl/ adj. & n. —adj. **1** lasting for a hundred years. **2** occurring every hundred years. —n. US = CENTENARY n. [L *centum* a hundred, after BIENNIAL]

center US var. of CENTRE.

centerboard US var. of CENTREBOARD.

centerfold US var. of CENTREFOLD.

centering US var. of CENTRING.

centesimal /senˈtesɪm(ə)l/ adj. reckoning or reckoned by hundredths. □□ **centesimally** adv. [L *centesimus* hundredth f. *centum* hundred]

centi- /ˈsentɪ/ comb. form **1** one-hundredth, esp. of a unit in the metric system (*centigram*; *centilitre*). **2** hundred. ¶ Abbr.: **c**. [L *centum* hundred]

centigrade /ˈsentɪˌɡreɪd/ adj. **1** = CELSIUS. **2** having a scale of a hundred degrees. ¶ In sense 1 *Celsius* is usually preferred in technical use. [F f. L *centum* hundred + *gradus* step]

centigram /ˈsentɪˌɡræm/ n. (also **centigramme**) a metric unit of mass, equal to one-hundredth of a gram.

centilitre /ˈsentɪˌliːtə(r)/ n. (US **centiliter**) a metric unit of capacity, equal to one-hundredth of a litre.

centime /ˈsɑ̃tiːm/ n. **1** a monetary unit valued at one-hundredth of a franc. **2** a coin of this value. [F f. L *centum* a hundred]

centimetre /ˈsentɪˌmiːtə(r)/ n. (US **centimeter**) a metric unit of length, equal to one-hundredth of a metre. □ **centimetre-gram-second system** the system using these as basic units of length, mass, and time. ¶ Abbr.: **cgs system**.

centipede /ˈsentɪˌpiːd/ n. any arthropod of the class Chilopoda, with a wormlike body of many segments each with a pair of legs. [F *centipède* or L *centipeda* f. *centum* hundred + *pes pedis* foot]

cento /ˈsentəʊ/ n. (pl. **-os**) a composition made up of quotations from other authors. [L, = patchwork garment]

Central /ˈsentr(ə)l/ a local government region in central Scotland; pop. (1981) 272,100.

central /ˈsentr(ə)l/ adj. **1** of, at, or forming the centre. **2** from the centre. **3** chief, essential, most important. □ **central heating** a method of warming a building by pipes, radiators, etc., fed from a central source of heat. **central nervous system** see NERVOUS SYSTEM. **central processor** (or **processing unit**) the principal operating part of a computer. □□ **centrality** /-ˈtrælɪtɪ/ n. **centrally** adv. [F *central* or L *centralis* f. *centrum* CENTRE]

Central African Republic a country of central Africa, bounded by Chad, Sudan, Zaïre, and the Cameroon Republic; pop. (est. 1988) 2,736,500; official language, French; capital, Bangui. Formerly the French colony of Ubanghi Shari, it became a republic within the French Community in 1958 and a fully independent State in 1960. In 1976 its President, Jean Bédel Bokassa, who had come to power after a military coup in 1966, declared himself Emperor and changed the country's name to Central African Empire, but it reverted to the name of Republic after he had been ousted in 1979 following widespread unrest and allegations of atrocities.

Central America the narrow southern part of North America, south of Mexico.

Central American Common Market an economic organization comprising Guatemala, Honduras, El Salvador, Nicaragua, and Costa Rica, set up in 1960 and with headquarters in Guatemala City, that sought to reduce trade barriers, stimulate exports, and encourage industrialization by means of regional cooperation. It lost impetus in the 1970s because of war, internal recession, and ideological differences among member States, and by the mid-1980s it was in a state of suspension.

central bank n. a national bank that provides financial and

banking services for its country's government and commercial banking system, as well as implementing the government's monetary policy, and issues currency. Major central banks include the Bank of England in the UK, the Federal Reserve Bank of the US, the Deutsche Bundesbank in Germany, and France's Banque de France.

Central Criminal Court the Old Bailey.

Central Intelligence Agency a federal agency in the US, established in 1947, responsible for coordinating government intelligence activities.

centralism /ˈsentrəˌlɪz(ə)m/ n. a system that centralizes (esp. an administration) (see also *democratic centralism*). □□ **centralist** n.

centralize /ˈsentrəˌlaɪz/ v. (also **-ise**) **1** tr. & intr. bring or come to a centre. **2** tr. **a** concentrate (administration) at a single centre. **b** subject (a State) to this system. □□ **centralization** /-ˈzeɪʃ(ə)n/ n.

Central Powers Germany and Austria-Hungary before 1914.

centre /ˈsentə(r)/ n. & v. (US **center**) —n. **1** the middle point, esp. of a line, circle, or sphere, equidistant from the ends or from any point on the circumference or surface. **2** a pivot or axis of rotation. **3 a** a place or group of buildings forming a central point in a district, city, etc., or a main area for an activity (*shopping centre*; *town centre*). **b** (with preceding word) a piece or set of equipment for a number of connected functions (*music centre*). **4** a point of concentration or dispersion; a nucleus or source. **5** a political party or group holding moderate opinions. **6** the filling in a chocolate etc. **7** *Sport* **a** the middle player in a line or group in some field games. **b** a kick or hit from the side to the centre of the pitch. **8** (in a lathe etc.) a conical adjustable support for the workpiece. **9** (attrib.) of or at the centre. —v. **1** intr. (foll. by *in*, *on*; disp. foll. by *round*) have as its main centre. **2** tr. place in the centre. **3** tr. mark with a centre. **4** tr. (foll. by *in* etc.) concentrate. **5** tr. *Sport* kick or hit (the ball) from the side to the centre of the pitch. □ **centre-bit** a boring tool with a centre point and side cutters. **centre forward** *Sport* the middle player or position in a forward line. **centre half** *Sport* the middle player or position in a half-back line. **centre of attention 1** a person or thing that draws general attention. **2** *Physics* the point to which bodies tend by gravity. **centre of gravity** (or **mass**) the point at which the weight of a body may be considered to act. **centre-piece 1** an ornament for the middle of a table. **2** a principal item. **centre spread** the two facing middle pages of a newspaper etc. □□ **centred** adj. (often in comb.). **centremost** adj. **centric** adj. **centrical** adj. **centricity** /-ˈtrɪsɪtɪ/ n. [ME f. OF *centre* or L *centrum* f. Gk *kentron* sharp point]

centreboard /ˈsentəˌbɔːd/ n. (US **centerboard**) a board for lowering through a boat's keel to prevent leeway.

centrefold /ˈsentəˌfəʊld/ n. (US **centerfold**) a printed and usu. illustrated sheet folded to form the centre spread of a magazine etc.

centreing var. of CENTRING.

-centric /ˈsentrɪk/ comb. form forming adjectives with the sense 'having a (specified) centre' (*anthropocentric*; *eccentric*). [after concentric etc. f. Gk *kentrikos*: see CENTRE]

centrifugal /ˌsentrɪˈfjuːɡ(ə)l, senˈtrɪfjʊɡ(ə)l/ adj. moving or tending to move from a centre (cf. CENTRIPETAL). □ **centrifugal force** an apparent force that acts outwards on a body moving about a centre. □□ **centrifugally** adv. [mod.L *centrifugus* f. L *centrum* centre + *fugere* flee]

centrifuge /ˈsentrɪˌfjuːdʒ/ n. & v. —n. a machine with a rapidly rotating device designed to separate liquids from solids or other liquids (e.g. cream from milk). (See below.) —v.tr. **1** subject to the action of a centrifuge. **2** separate by centrifuge. □□ **centrifugation** /-fjʊˈɡeɪʃ(ə)n/ n.

Centrifugal force is generated in a mechanically-driven bowl or cylinder, usually of metal, which turns inside a stationary casing. Higher forces are generated using smaller machines, since these contain less material and can be rotated faster without damaging the apparatus. There are two main types of centrifuge. In one type (used, for example, for separating cream from milk, or particles from a liquid in which they are suspended) constituents of greater density are impelled to the periphery and those of lesser density collect near the middle, so that a heterogeneous liquid eventually separates into distinct layers. In the other type, a filtering centrifuge, liquid in which particles are suspended is placed inside a revolving cylinder that has a perforated wall lined with a filter (e.g. a cloth or fine screen): liquid passes through the wall, impelled by centrifugal force, leaving behind a cake of solids on the filter medium.

centring /ˈsentrɪŋ/ (also **centreing** /ˈsentərɪŋ/, US **centering** /ˈsentərɪŋ/) n. a temporary frame used to support an arch, dome, etc., while under construction.

centriole /ˈsentrɪˌəʊl/ n. Biol. a minute organelle usu. within a centrosome involved esp. in the development of spindles in cell division. [med.L centriolum dimin. of centrum centre]

centripetal /senˈtrɪpɪt(ə)l/ adj. moving or tending to move towards a centre (cf. CENTRIFUGAL). □ **centripetal force** the force acting on a body causing it to move about a centre. □□ **centripetally** adv. [mod.L centripetus f. L centrum centre + petere seek]

centrist /ˈsentrɪst/ n. Polit. often derog. a person who holds moderate views. □□ **centrism** n.

centromere /ˈsentrəmɪə(r)/ n. Biol. the point on a chromosome to which the spindle is attached during cell division. [L centrum centre + Gk meros part]

centrosome /ˈsentrəˌsəʊm/ n. Biol. a distinct part of the cytoplasm in a cell, usu. near the nucleus, that contains the centriole. [G Centrosoma f. L centrum centre + Gk sōma body]

centuple /ˈsentjʊp(ə)l/ n., adj., & v. —n. a hundredfold amount. —adj. increased a hundredfold. —v.tr. multiply by a hundred; increase a hundredfold. [F centuple or eccl.L centuplus, centuplex f. L centum hundred]

centurion /senˈtjʊərɪən/ n. the commander of a century in the ancient Roman army. [ME f. L centurio -onis (as CENTURY)]

century /ˈsentʃərɪ, -tjʊrɪ/ n. (pl. **-ies**) **1 a** a period of one hundred years. **b** any of the centuries reckoned from the birth of Christ (twentieth century = 1901–2000; fifth century BC = 500–401 BC). ¶ In modern use often reckoned as (e.g.) 1900–1999. **2 a** a score etc. of a hundred in a sporting event, esp. a hundred runs by one batsman in cricket. **b** a group of a hundred things. **3 a** a company in the ancient Roman army, orig. of 100 men. **b** an ancient Roman political division for voting. □ **century plant** a plant, Agave americana, flowering once in many years and yielding sap from which tequila is distilled: also called American aloe (see ALOE). [L centuria f. centum hundred]

cep /sep/ n. an edible mushroom, Boletus edulis, with a stout stalk and brown smooth cap. [F cèpe f. Gascon cep f. L cippus stake]

cephalic /sɪˈfælɪk, ke-/ adj. of or in the head. □ **cephalic index** Anthropol. a number expressing the ratio of a head's greatest breadth and length. [F céphalique f. L cephalicus f. Gk kephalikos f. kephalē head]

-cephalic /sɪˈfælɪk/ comb. form = -CEPHALOUS.

Cephalonia /ˌsefəˈləʊnɪə/ (Greek **Kefallinia** /ˌkefəlɪˈniːə/) a Greek island in the Ionian Sea; pop. (1981) 31,300; capital, Argostolion.

cephalopod /ˈsefələˌpɒd/ n. any mollusc of the class Cephalopoda, having a distinct head with a ring of tentacles round the mouth. The group, which is entirely marine, contains about 700 living species, including octopuses, squid, cuttlefish, and nautiluses, but fossil species are much more numerous, and include the ammonites and belemnites. Cephalopods have large brains and are the most intelligent of all invertebrates, octopuses in particular having been shown to exhibit considerable learning ability. They are also notable for their well-developed eyes, which are quite similar to the vertebrate eye, and their ability to swim by a form of jet propulsion. Giant squid, which are rarely found but can grow to at least 18 m (60 ft.) long including tentacles, are the world's largest invertebrates. [Gk kephalē head + pous podos foot]

cephalothorax /ˌsefələʊˈθɔːræks/ n. (pl. **-thoraces** /-rəˌsiːz/ or **-thoraxes**) Anat. the fused head and thorax of a spider, crab, or other arthropod.

-cephalous /ˈsefələs/ comb. form -headed (brachycephalous; dolichocephalic). [Gk kephalē head]

cepheid /ˈsiːfiɪd, ˈsefiɪd/ n. (in full **cepheid variable**) Astron. any of a class of variable stars with a regular cycle of brightness, caused by pulsations of the surface layers. A precise relationship exists between the total luminosity of the star and the period of pulsation, allowing its distance to be inferred. [f. delta Cephei, the original example, in the constellation Cepheus named after a mythical king (Gk Kēpheus)]

ceramic /sɪˈræmɪk, kɪ-/ adj. & n. —adj. **1** made of (esp.) clay and permanently hardened by heat (a ceramic bowl). **2** of or relating to ceramics (the ceramic arts). —n. **1** a ceramic article or product. **2** a substance, esp. clay, used to make ceramic articles. [Gk keramikos f. keramos pottery]

ceramics /sɪˈræmɪks, kɪ-/ n.pl. **1** ceramic products collectively (exhibition of ceramics). **2** (usu. treated as sing.) the art of making ceramic articles.

ceramist /ˈserəmɪst/ n. a person who makes ceramics.

Ceram Sea /ˈseɪrəm/ (also **Seram Sea**) a section of the western Pacific Ocean in the central Molucca Islands.

cerastes /sɪˈræstiːz/ n. any viper of the genus Cerastes, esp. C. cerastes having a sharp upright spike over each eye and moving forward in a lateral motion. [L f. Gk kerastēs f. keras horn]

cerastium /sɪˈræstɪəm/ n. any plant of the genus Cerastium, with white flowers and often horn-shaped capsules. [mod.L f. Gk kerastes horned f. keras horn]

Cerberus /ˈsɜːbərəs/ Gk Mythol. the monstrous watchdog with three heads (or fifty heads, according to Hesiod) guarding the entrance to Hades. The heroes who visited Hades during their lifetime (e.g. Aeneas) appeased him with a cake (whence the phrase 'a sop to Cerberus'); Orpheus lulled him to sleep with his lyre; one of the twelve labours of Hercules was to bring him up from the Underworld.

cere /sɪə(r)/ n. a waxy fleshy covering at the base of the upper beak in some birds. [L cera wax]

cereal /ˈsɪərɪəl/ n. & adj. —n. **1** (usu. in pl.) **a** any kind of grain used for food. **b** any grass producing this, e.g. wheat, maize, rye, etc. **2** a breakfast food made from a cereal and requiring no cooking. —adj. of edible grain or products of it. [L cerealis f. CERES]

cerebellum /ˌserɪˈbeləm/ n. (pl. **cerebellums** or **cerebella** /-lə/) the part of the brain at the back of the skull in vertebrates, which coordinates and regulates muscular activity. □□ **cerebellar** adj. [L dimin. of CEREBRUM]

cerebral /ˈserɪbr(ə)l/ adj. **1** of the brain. **2** intellectual rather than emotional. **3** = CACUMINAL. □ **cerebral hemisphere** each of the two halves of the vertebrate cerebrum. **cerebral palsy** Med. spastic paralysis from brain damage before or at birth, with jerky or uncontrolled movements. □□ **cerebrally** adv. [L cerebrum brain]

cerebration /ˌserɪˈbreɪʃ(ə)n/ n. working of the brain. □ **unconscious cerebration** action of the brain with results reached without conscious thought. □□ **cerebrate** /ˈserɪˌbreɪt/ v.intr.

cerebro- /ˈserɪbrəʊ/ comb. form brain (cerebrospinal).

cerebrospinal /ˌserɪbrəʊˈspaɪn(ə)l/ adj. of the brain and spine.

cerebrovascular /ˌserɪbrəʊˈvæskjʊlə(r)/ adj. of the brain and its blood vessels.

cerebrum /ˈserɪbrəm/ n. (pl. **cerebra** /-brə/) the principal part of the brain in vertebrates, located in the front area of the skull, which integrates complex sensory and neural functions. [L, = brain]

cerecloth /ˈsɪəklɒθ/ n. hist. waxed cloth used as a waterproof covering or (esp.) as a shroud. [earlier cered cloth f. cere to wax f. L cerare f. cera wax]

cerement /ˈsɪəmənt/ n. (usu. in pl.) literary grave-clothes; cerecloth. [first used by Shakesp. in Hamlet (1602): app. f. CERECLOTH]

ceremonial /ˌserɪˈməʊnɪəl/ adj. & n. —adj. **1** with or concerning ritual or ceremony. **2** formal (a ceremonial bow). —n. **1** a system of rites etc. to be used esp. at a formal or religious occasion. **2** the formalities or behaviour proper to any occasion (*with all due ceremonial*). **3** *RC Ch.* a book containing an order of ritual. □□ **ceremonialism** *n.* **ceremonialist** *n.* **ceremonially** *adv.* [LL *caerimonialis* (as CEREMONY)]

ceremonious /ˌserɪˈməʊnɪəs/ *adj.* **1** excessively polite; punctilious. **2** having or showing a fondness for ritualistic observance or formality. □□ **ceremoniously** *adv.* **ceremoniousness** *n.* [F *cérémonieux* or LL *caerimoniosus* (as CEREMONY)]

ceremony /ˈserɪmənɪ/ *n.* (*pl.* **-ies**) **1** a formal religious or public occasion, esp. celebrating a particular event or anniversary. **2** formalities, esp. of an empty or ritualistic kind (*ceremony of exchanging compliments*). **3** excessively polite behaviour (*bowed low with great ceremony*). □ **Master of Ceremonies 1** (also **MC**) a person introducing speakers at a banquet, or entertainers in a variety show. **2** a person in charge of ceremonies at a state or public occasion. **stand on ceremony** insist on the observance of formalities. **without ceremony** informally. [ME f. OF *ceremonie* or L *caerimonia* religious worship]

Cerenkov radiation /tʃeˈrenkɒf/ *n.* (also **Cherenkov**) the electromagnetic radiation emitted by particles moving in a medium at speeds faster than that of light in the same medium. [P. A. *Cherenkov*, Russian physicist b. 1904]

Ceres /ˈsɪəriːz/ **1** *Rom. Mythol.* an ancient Italian corn-goddess, commonly identified in antiquity with Demeter. **2** *Astron.* the largest of the asteroids, and the first to be discovered (1 Jan. 1801).

ceresin /ˈserɪsɪn/ *n.* a hard whitish wax used with or instead of beeswax. [mod.L *ceres* f. L *cera* wax + -IN]

cerise /səˈriːz, -ˈriːs/ *adj.* & *n.* —*adj.* of a light clear red. —*n.* this colour. [F, = CHERRY]

cerium /ˈsɪərɪəm/ *n. Chem.* a silvery metallic element of the lanthanide series. The most abundant of the rare-earth elements, cerium was first isolated in pure form in 1875, although as a mixture with other rare earths it had been identified by Berzelius and others at the beginning of the 19th c. The pure metal is alloyed to make cigarette-lighter flints, and cerium dioxide is widely used for polishing glass. ¶ Symb.: **Ce**; atomic number 58. [named after the asteroid *Ceres*, discovered (1801) about the same time as this]

cermet /ˈsɜːmet/ *n.* a heat-resistant material made of ceramic and sintered metal. [*ceramic* + *metal*]

CERN /sɜːn/ *abbr.* European Council (or Organization) for Nuclear Research (tr. F *Conseil Européen* (later *Organisation Européene) pour la Recherche Nucléaire*), an organization of European countries, established in 1954, with headquarters at Meyrin near Geneva, for research into the fundamental structure of matter by teams of scientists from its member countries. It is not concerned with nuclear research of a military nature.

cero- /ˈsɪərəʊ/ *comb. form* wax (cf. CEROGRAPHY, CEROPLASTIC). [L *cera* or Gk *kēros* wax]

cerography /sɪəˈrɒgrəfɪ/ *n.* the technique of engraving or designing on or with wax.

ceroplastic /ˌsɪərəʊˈplæstɪk/ *adj.* **1** modelled in wax. **2** of or concerning wax-modelling.

cert /sɜːt/ *n. sl.* (esp. **dead cert**) **1** an event or result regarded as certain to happen. **2** a horse strongly tipped to win. [abbr. of CERTAIN, CERTAINTY]

cert. /sɜːt/ *abbr.* **1** a certificate. **2** certified.

certain /ˈsɜːt(ə)n, -tɪn/ *adj.* & *pron.* —*adj.* **1 a** (often foll. by *of*, or *that* + clause) confident, convinced (*certain that I put it here*). **b** (often foll. by *that* + clause) indisputable; known for sure (*it is certain that he is guilty*). **2** (often foll. by *to* + infin.) **a** that may be relied on to happen (*it is certain to rain*). **b** destined (*certain to become a star*). **3** definite, unfailing, reliable (*a certain indication of the coming storm; his touch is certain*). **4** (of a person, place, etc.) that might be specified, but is not (*a certain lady; of a certain age*). **5** some though not much (*a certain reluctance*). **6** (of a person, place, etc.) existing, though probably unknown to the reader or hearer (*a certain John Smith*). —*pron.* (as *pl.*) some but not all (*certain of them were wounded*). □ **for certain** without doubt. **make certain** = *make sure* (see SURE). [ME f. OF ult. f. L *certus* settled]

certainly /ˈsɜːtənlɪ, -tɪnlɪ/ *adv.* **1** undoubtedly, definitely. **2** confidently. **3** (in affirmative answer to a question or command) yes; by all means.

certainty /ˈsɜːtəntɪ, -tɪntɪ/ *n.* (*pl.* **-ies**) **1 a** an undoubted fact. **b** a certain prospect (*his return is a certainty*). **2** (often foll. by *of*, or *that* + clause) an absolute conviction (*has a certainty of his own worth*). **3** (often foll. by *to* + infin.) a thing or person that may be relied on (*a certainty to win the Derby*). □ **for a certainty** beyond the possibility of doubt. [ME f. AF *certainté*, OF *-eté* (as CERTAIN)]

Cert. Ed. *abbr.* (in the UK) Certificate in Education.

certifiable /ˌsɜːtɪˈfaɪəb(ə)l, ˈsɜːt-/ *adj.* **1** able or needing to be certified. **2** *colloq.* insane.

certificate /səˈtɪfɪkət/ *n.* & *v.* —*n.* a formal document attesting a fact, esp. birth, marriage, or death, a medical condition, a level of achievement, a fulfilment of requirements, ownership of shares, etc. —*v.tr.* /-ˌkeɪt/ (esp. as **certificated** *adj.*) provide with or license or attest by a certificate. □ **Certificate of Secondary Education** *hist.* **1** an examination set for secondary-school pupils in England and Wales. **2** the certificate gained by passing it. ¶ Replaced in 1988 by the *General Certificate of Secondary Education*. □□ **certification** /ˌsɜːtɪfɪˈkeɪʃ(ə)n/ *n.* [F *certificat* or med.L *certificatum* f. *certificare*: see CERTIFY]

certify /ˈsɜːtɪˌfaɪ/ *v.tr.* (**-ies, -ied**) **1** make a formal statement of; attest; attest to (*certified that he had witnessed the crime*). **2** declare by certificate (that a person is qualified or competent) (*certified as a trained bookkeeper*). **3** officially declare insane (*he should be certified*). □ **certified cheque** a cheque the validity of which is guaranteed by a bank. **certified mail** *US* = *recorded delivery* (see RECORD). **certified milk** milk guaranteed free from the tuberculosis bacillus. [ME f. OF *certifier* f. med.L *certificare* f. L *certus* certain]

certiorari /ˌsɜːtɪɔːˈreəraɪ/ *n. Law* a writ from a higher court requesting the records of a case tried in a lower court. [LL passive of *certiorare* inform f. *certior* compar. of *certus* certain]

certitude /ˈsɜːtɪˌtjuːd/ *n.* a feeling of absolute certainty or conviction. [ME f. LL *certitudo* f. *certus* certain]

cerulean /səˈruːlɪən/ *adj.* & *n. literary* —*adj.* deep blue like a clear sky. —*n.* this colour. [L *caeruleus* sky-blue f. *caelum* sky]

cerumen /səˈruːmen/ *n.* the yellow waxy substance in the outer ear. □□ **ceruminous** *adj.* [mod.L f. L *cera* wax]

ceruse /ˈsɪəruːs, sɪˈruːs/ *n.* white lead. [ME f. OF f. L *cerussa*, perh. f. Gk *kēros* wax]

Cervantes /sɜːˈvæntiːz/, Miguel de (1547–1616) (full surname Cervantes Saavedra), Spanish novelist and dramatist, born of an ancient and impoverished family. He lost the use of his left hand at the battle of Lepanto (1571), was captured by pirates (1575), and spent the next five years as a prisoner in Algiers. The rest of his life was spent trying to earn a living from literature and humble government employment. His first novel *La Galatea* (1585) was followed by his masterpiece *Don Quixote* (1605, 1615), a satirical romance about an amiable knight who imagines himself called upon to roam the world in search of adventure on his horse Rosinante, accompanied by the shrewd squire Sancho Panza. Don Quixote and Quixotism have been described as the genius of the Spanish nation but he has been adopted by many other countries, is the source of plots of several 17th-c. English plays, and continues to inspire innumerable imitations. Among Cervantes' other surviving works are sixteen plays and *Novelas Ejemplares* (1613; short stories).

cervelat /ˈsɜːvəˌlɑː, -ˌlæt/ *n.* a kind of smoked pork sausage. [obs. F f. It. *cervellata*]

cervical /sɜːˈvaɪk(ə)l, ˈsɜːvɪk(ə)l/ *adj. Anat.* **1** of or relating to the neck (*cervical vertebrae*). **2** of or relating to the cervix. □ **cervical screening** examination of a large number of apparently healthy women for cervical cancer. **cervical smear** a specimen of cellular material from the neck of the womb for detection of cancer. [F *cervical* or mod.L *cervicalis* f. L *cervix -icis* neck]

cervine /ˈsɜːvaɪn/ *adj.* of or like a deer. [L *cervinus* f. *cervus* deer]

cervix /ˈsɜːvɪks/ *n.* (*pl.* **cervices** /-ˌsiːz/) *Anat.* **1** the neck. **2** any necklike structure, esp. the neck of the womb. [L]

Cesarean (also **Cesarian**) *US* var. of CAESAREAN.

cesarevitch /sɪˈzærɪvɪtʃ/ *n.* (also **cesarewitch** /-wɪtʃ/) **1** *hist.* the eldest son of the emperor of Russia (cf. TSAREVICH). **2** (**Cesarewitch**) a handicap horse-race run annually at Newmarket in Suffolk, England, in late October, inaugurated in 1839 and named in honour of the state visit of the Russian prince who became Alexander II. [Russ. *tsesarevich*]

cesium *US* var. of CAESIUM.

cess[1] /ses/ *n.* (also **sess**) *Sc., Ir.,* & *Ind.* etc. a tax, a levy. [properly *sess* for obs. *assess* n.: see ASSESS]

cess[2] /ses/ *n. Ir.* □ **bad cess to** may evil befall (*bad cess to their clan*). [perh. f. CESS[1]]

cessation /seˈseɪʃ(ə)n/ *n.* **1** a ceasing (*cessation of the truce*). **2** a pause (*resumed fighting after the cessation*). [ME f. L *cessatio* f. *cessare* CEASE]

cesser /ˈsesə(r)/ *n. Law* a coming to an end; a cessation (of a term, a liability, etc.). [AF & OF, = CEASE]

cession /ˈseʃ(ə)n/ *n.* **1** (often foll. by *of*) the ceding or giving up (of rights, property, and esp. of territory by a State). **2** the territory etc. so ceded. [ME f. OF *cession* or L *cessio* f. *cedere* cessgo away]

cessionary /ˈseʃənərɪ/ *n.* (*pl.* **-ies**) *Law* = ASSIGN *n.*

cesspit /ˈsespɪt/ *n.* **1** a pit for the disposal of refuse. **2** = CESSPOOL. [*cess* in CESSPOOL + PIT[1]]

cesspool /ˈsespuːl/ *n.* **1** an underground container for the temporary storage of liquid waste or sewage. **2** a centre of corruption, depravity, etc. [perh. alt., after POOL[1], f. earlier *cesperalle*, f. *suspiral* vent, water-pipe, f. OF *souspirail* air-hole f. L *suspirare* breathe up, sigh (as SUB-, *spirare* breathe)]

cestode /ˈsestəʊd/ *n.* (also **cestoid** /ˈsestɔɪd/) any flatworm of the class Cestoda, including tapeworms. [L *cestus* f. Gk *kestos* girdle]

CET *abbr.* Central European Time.

cetacean /sɪˈteɪʃ(ə)n/ *n.* & *adj.* —*n.* any marine mammal of the order Cetacea with streamlined hairless body and dorsal blowhole for breathing, including whales, dolphins, and porpoises. —*adj.* of cetaceans. □□ **cetaceous** *adj.* [mod.L *Cetacea* f. L *cetus* f. Gk *kētos* whale]

cetane /ˈsiːteɪn/ *n. Chem.* a colourless liquid hydrocarbon of the alkane series used in standardizing ratings of diesel fuel. □ **cetane number** a measure of the ignition properties of diesel fuel. [f. SPERMACETI after *methane* etc.]

ceteris paribus /ˌsetərɪs ˈpærɪˌbʊs/ *adv.* other things being equal. [L]

Ceuta /ˈseɪuːtə, ˈθe-/ a Spanish enclave in Morocco, held since 1580, on the coast of North Africa; pop. (1981, with Melilla) 53,600. It consists of a free port and a military post, and overlooks the Mediterranean approach to the Strait of Gibraltar.

Cévennes /seˈven/ a mountain range on the southern edge of the Massif Central in France.

Ceylon /sɪˈlɒn/ the former name (until 1972) of Sri Lanka. □ **Ceylon moss** a red seaweed, *Gracilaria lichenoides*, from E. India.

Cézanne /seɪˈzæn/, Paul (1839–1906), French painter, associated with the impressionists but concerned less with fleeting impressions than with the structural analysis of nature, which made him a forerunner of cubism. Born in Aix-en-Provence, he was a schoolfellow of Zola, who introduced him to Manet and Courbet. He exhibited with the impressionists in 1874 and 1877, and was closest to Pissarro, near whose home he settled in 1872. His work, consisting mainly of still life and landscape, is dominated by his search for the cube, the cone, and the cylinder in nature. An exhibition in 1895 strengthened his influence on the younger French artists, and his painting became known in England through the Post-Impressionist exhibitions of 1910 and 1912, where it was made the foundation of the new aesthetic attitude of Clive Bell and Roger Fry, emphasizing pure form, which dominated English criticism in the 1930s.

CF *abbr. Brit.* Chaplain to the Forces.

Cf *symb. Chem.* the element californium.

cf. *abbr.* compare. [L *confer* imper. of *conferre* compare]

c.f. *abbr.* carried forward.

CFC *abbr. Chem.* chloro-fluorocarbon, any of various usu. gaseous compounds of carbon, hydrogen, chlorine, and fluorine, used in refrigerants, aerosol propellants, etc., and thought to be harmful to the ozone layer in the earth's atmosphere.

CFE *abbr.* College of Further Education.

cg *abbr.* centigram(s).

CGS *abbr.* Chief of General Staff.

cgs *abbr.* centimetre-gram-second.

CH *abbr.* (in the UK) Companion of Honour.

ch. *abbr.* **1** church. **2** chapter. **3** chestnut.

cha var. of CHAR[3].

Chablis /ˈʃæblɪ/ *n.* (*pl.* same /-lɪz/) a dry white burgundy wine. [*Chablis* in E. France]

cha-cha /ˈtʃɑːtʃɑː/ (also **cha-cha-cha** /ˌtʃɑːtʃɑːˈtʃɑː/) *n.* & *v.* —*n.* **1** a ballroom dance with a Latin-American rhythm. **2** music for or in the rhythm of a cha-cha. —*v.intr.* (**cha-chas, cha-chaed** /-tʃɑːd/ or **cha-cha'd, cha-chaing** /-tʃɑːɪŋ/) dance the cha-cha. [Amer. Sp.]

Chaco see GRAN CHACO.

chaconne /ʃəˈkɒn/ *n. Mus.* **1 a** a musical form consisting of variations on a ground bass. **b** a musical composition in this style. **2** *hist.* a dance performed to this music. [F f. Sp. *chacona*]

Chad[1] /tʃæd/ an inland country in north central Africa, bordering in the north on Libya; pop. (est. 1988) 4,778,000; official language, French; capital, Ndjaména. Much of the northern area is desert, merging into the Sahara, but there are mineral deposits of uranium, tungsten, and perhaps oil. The population comprises a remarkable mixture of peoples, languages, and religions, living mainly by agriculture with cotton as the chief crop. French expeditions entered the region in 1890, and by 1913 the country was organized as a French colony. It became autonomous within the French Community in 1958, and fully independent as a republic in 1960. □□ **Chadian** *adj.* & *n.*

Chad[2] /tʃæd/, **Lake** a shallow lake on the frontiers of Chad, Niger, and Nigeria in north central Africa. Its size varies seasonally from *c.*10,360 sq. km (4,000 sq. miles) to *c.*25,900 sq. km (10,000 sq. miles).

Chadic /ˈtʃædɪk/ *adj.* of a group of languages spoken in the region of Lake Chad in north central Africa, of which the most important is Hausa.

chador /ˈtʃʌdə(r)/ *n.* (also **chadar, chuddar**) a large piece of cloth worn in some countries by Muslim women, wrapped around the body to leave only the face exposed. [Pers. *chador*, Hindi *chador*]

Chadwick /ˈtʃædwɪk/, Sir James (1891–1974), English physicist, appointed in 1923 as assistant director to Rutherford at the Cavendish Laboratory, Cambridge, where he researched the artificial disintegration (transmutation) of elements such as beryllium when bombarded by alpha particles, which led, in 1932, to the discovery of the neutron, for which he received the 1935 Nobel Prize for physics. In the Second World War he was involved with the atomic bomb project, and afterwards stressed the importance of university research into nuclear physics.

chaetognath /ˈkiːtəɡˌnæθ/ *n.* any dart-shaped worm of the phylum Chaetognatha, usu. living among marine plankton, and having a head with external thorny teeth. [mod.L *Chaetognatha* f. Gk *khaitē* long hair + *gnathos* jaw]

chafe /tʃeɪf/ *v.* & *n.* —*v.* **1** *tr.* & *intr.* make or become sore or damaged by rubbing. **2** *tr.* rub (esp. the skin to restore warmth or sensation). **3** *tr.* & *intr.* make or become annoyed; fret (*was chafed by the delay*). —*n.* **1 a** an act of chafing. **b** a sore resulting from this. **2** a state of annoyance. [ME f. OF *chaufer* ult. f. L *calefacere* f. *calēre* be hot + *facere* make]

chafer /ˈtʃeɪfə(r)/ *n.* any of various large slow-moving beetles of the family Scarabeidae, esp. the cockchafer. [OE *ceafor, cefer* f. Gmc]

chaff /tʃɑːf/ *n.* & *v.* —*n.* **1** the husks of corn or other seed separated by winnowing or threshing. **2** chopped hay and straw used as fodder. **3** light-hearted joking; banter. **4** worthless things; rubbish. **5** strips of metal foil released in the atmosphere to obstruct radar detection. —*v.* **1** *tr.* & *intr.* tease; banter. **2** *tr.*

chop (straw etc.). □ **chaff-cutter** a machine for chopping fodder. **separate the wheat from the chaff** distinguish good from bad. □□ **chaffy** adj. [OE ceaf, cæf prob. f. Gmc: sense 3 of n. & 1 of v. perh. f. CHAFE]

chaffer /ˈtʃæfə(r)/ v. & n. —v.intr. haggle; bargain. —n. bargaining; haggling. □□ **chafferer** n. [ME f. OE ceapfaru f. ceap bargain + faru journey]

chaffinch /ˈtʃæfɪntʃ/ n. Brit. a common European finch, Fringilla coelebs, the male of which has a blue-grey head with pinkish cheeks. [OE ceaffinc: see CHAFF, FINCH]

chafing-dish /ˈtʃeɪfɪŋ/ n. 1 a cooking pot with an outer pan of hot water, used for keeping food warm. 2 a dish with a spirit-lamp etc. for cooking at table. [obs. sense of CHAFE = warm]

Chagall /ʃəˈgɑːl/, Marc (1887–1985), Russian-born painter, of Jewish family, who from 1910 spent most of his working life in Paris, where he joined the avant-garde circle of Soutine, Delaunay, and Modigliani. He returned to Russia and set up an art school in 1917, but his style of painting—imaginative, inspired by folk art and by the more sophisticated naïveté of the fauves—was not acceptable to the authorities, and he returned to Paris in 1923; from 1941 to 1947 he lived in the US. His achievements include graphic work (illustrations to Gogol's Dead Souls and La Fontaine's Fables, 1923–30), theatre design (the costumes and décor for Stravinsky's Firebird, 1945, murals for the Metropolitan Opera House, New York, 1966) and a series of paintings inspired by the Bible, culminating in 17 large pictures (now in a museum at Nice). His autobiography, Ma vie, was published in 1931.

Chagas' disease /ˈtʃɑːgəs/ (also **Chagas's disease**) n. a kind of sleeping sickness caused by a protozoan transmitted by blood-sucking bugs. [C. Chagas, Braz. physician d. 1934]

Chagos Archipelago /ˈtʃeɪgəs/ an island group in the Indian Ocean, formerly a dependency of Mauritius and now part of the strategic British Indian Ocean Territory.

chagrin /ˈʃægrɪn, ʃəˈgriːn/ n. & v. —n. acute vexation or mortification. —v.tr. affect with chagrin. [F chagrin(er), of uncert. orig.]

Chain /tʃeɪn/, Sir Ernst Boris (1906–79), British biochemist, born in Germany. (See FLOREY.)

chain /tʃeɪn/ n. & v. —n. 1 a a connected flexible series of esp. metal links as decoration or for a practical purpose. b something resembling this (formed a human chain). 2 (in pl.) a fetters used to confine prisoners. b any restraining force. 3 a sequence, series, or set (chain of events; mountain chain). 4 a group of associated hotels, shops, newspapers, etc. 5 a badge of office in the form of a chain worn round the neck (mayoral chain). 6 a a jointed measuring-line consisting of linked metal rods. b its length (66 ft.). (See GUNTER.) 7 Chem. a group of (esp. carbon) atoms bonded in sequence in a molecule. 8 a figure in a quadrille or similar dance. 9 (in pl.) Naut. channels (see CHANNEL²). 10 (also **chain-shot**) hist. two cannon-balls or half balls joined by a chain and used in sea battles for bringing down a mast etc. —v.tr. 1 (often foll. by up) secure or confine with a chain. 2 confine or restrict (a person) (is chained to the office). □ **chain-armour** armour made of interlaced rings. **chain bridge** a suspension bridge on chains. **chain drive** a system of transmission by endless chains. **chain-gang** a team of convicts chained together and forced to work in the open air. **chain-gear** a gear transmitting motion by means of an endless chain. **chain-letter** one of a sequence of letters the recipient of which is requested to send copies to a specific number of other people. **chain-link** made of wire in a diamond-shaped mesh (chain-link fencing). **chain-mail** = chain-armour. **chain reaction** 1 Physics a self-sustaining nuclear reaction, esp. one in which a neutron from a fission reaction initiates a series of these reactions. 2 Chem. a self-sustaining molecular reaction in which intermediate products initiate further reactions. 3 a series of events, each caused by the previous one. **chain-saw** a motor-driven saw with teeth on an endless chain. **chain-smoker** a person who smokes continually, esp. one who lights a cigarette etc. from the stub of the last one smoked. **chain-stitch** 1 an ornamental embroidery or crochet stitch resembling chains. 2 a stitch made by a sewing machine using a single thread that is hooked through its own loop on the underside of the fabric sewn. **chain store** one of a

series of shops owned by one firm and selling the same sort of goods. **chain-wale** = CHANNEL². **chain-wheel** a wheel transmitting power by a chain fitted to its edges. [ME f. OF cha(e)ine f. L catena]

chair /tʃeə(r)/ n. & v. —n. 1 a separate seat for one person, of various forms, usu. having a back and four legs. 2 a a professorship (offered the chair in physics). b a seat of authority, esp. on a board of directors. c a mayoralty. 3 a a chairperson. b the seat or office of a chairperson (will you take the chair?; I'm in the chair). 4 US = electric chair. 5 an iron or steel socket holding a railway rail in place. 6 hist. = sedan chair. —v.tr. 1 act as chairperson of or preside over (a meeting). 2 Brit. carry (a person) aloft in a chair or in a sitting position, in triumph. 3 install in a chair, esp. as a position of authority. □ **chair-bed** a chair that unfolds into a bed. **chair-borne** colloq. (of an administrator) not active. **chair-car** a railway carriage with chairs instead of long seats; a parlour car. **chair-lift** a series of chairs on an endless cable for carrying passengers up and down a mountain etc. **take a chair** sit down. [ME f. AF chaere, OF chaiere f. L cathedra f. Gk kathedra: see CATHEDRAL]

chairlady /ˈtʃeəˌleɪdɪ/ n. (pl. -ies) = CHAIRWOMAN.

chairman /ˈtʃeəmən/ n. (pl. -men; fem. **chairwoman**, pl. -women) 1 a person chosen to preside over a meeting. 2 the permanent president of a committee, a board of directors, a firm, etc. 3 the master of ceremonies at an entertainment etc. 4 hist. either of two sedan-bearers. □□ **chairmanship** n.

chairperson /ˈtʃeəˌpɜːs(ə)n/ n. a chairman or chairwoman (used as a neutral alternative).

chaise /ʃeɪz/ n. 1 esp. hist. a horse-drawn carriage for one or two persons, esp. one with an open top and two wheels. 2 = post-chaise (see POST²). [F var. of chaire, formed as CHAIR]

chaise longue /ʃeɪz ˈlɒŋ/ n. a sofa with only one arm rest. [F, lit. long chair]

chalaza /kəˈleɪzə/ n. (pl. **chalazae** /-ziː/) each of two twisted membranous strips joining the yolk to the ends of an egg. [mod.L f. Gk, = hailstone]

Chalcedon /kælˈsiːd(ə)n/ a city in Asia Minor, where the fourth ecumenical council of the Church was held in 451, at which was drawn up the important statement of faith affirming the two natures, human and divine, united in the single person of Christ unconfusedly, unchangeably, indivisibly, and inseparably. □□ **Chalcedonian** /-sɪˈdəʊnɪən/ adj.

chalcedony /kælˈsedənɪ/ n. a type of quartz occurring in several different forms, e.g. onyx, agate, tiger's eye, etc. □□ **chalcedonic** /ˌkælsɪˈdɒnɪk/ adj. [ME f. L c(h)alcedonius f. Gk khalkēdōn; both the origin of the name (which is unlikely to be from CHALCEDON) and its early application are obscure]

Chalcis /ˈkælsɪs/ (Greek **Khalkis** /xælˈkiːs/) the chiejf town of the island of Euboea, on the coast opposite mainland Greece; pop. (1981) 44,800. Aristotle died here in 322 BC.

chalcolithic /ˌkælkəˈlɪθɪk/ adj. Archaeol. of a prehistoric period in which both stone and bronze implements were used. [Gk khalkos copper + lithos stone]

chalcopyrite /ˌkælkəˈpaɪraɪt/ n. a yellow mineral of copper-iron sulphide, which is the principal ore of copper. [Gk khalkos copper + PYRITE]

Chaldea /kælˈdiːə/ the country of the Chaldeans, the southern part of Babylonia (the names are virtually synonymous). [Assyr. Kaldu]

Chaldean /kælˈdiːən/ n. & adj. —n. 1 a a member of a Semitic people originating from Arabia, who settled in the neighbourhood of Ur c.800 BC and ruled Babylonia 625–538 BC. They were famous as astronomers. The biblical reference to 'Ur of the Chaldees' in the time of Abraham is an anachronism. b the Semitic language of the Chaldeans. 2 an astrologer. 3 a member of the Uniat (formerly Nestorian) sect in Iran etc. —adj. 1 of or relating to ancient Chaldea or its people or language. 2 of or relating to astrology. 3 of or relating to the Uniat sect. [L Chaldaeus f. Gk Khaldaios f. Assyr. Kaldu]

Chaldee /kælˈdiː/ n. 1 the language of the Chaldeans. 2 a native of ancient Chaldea. 3 the Aramaic language as used in Old Testament books. [ME, repr. L Chaldaei (pl.) (as CHALDEAN)]

chalet /ˈʃæleɪ/ n. **1** a small suburban house or bungalow, esp. with an overhanging roof. **2** a small, usu. wooden, hut or house on a beach or in a holiday camp. **3** a Swiss cowherd's hut, or wooden cottage, with overhanging eaves. [Swiss F]

Chaliapin /ʃælˈjɑːpɪn/, Fyodor Ivanovich (1873–1938), Russian bass singer, most famous for his role as Boris Godunov in Mussorgsky's opera.

chalice /ˈtʃælɪs/ n. **1** literary a goblet. **2** a wine-cup used in the Communion service. [ME f. OF f. L calix -icis cup]

chalk /tʃɔːk/ n. & v. —n. **1** a white soft earthy limestone (calcium carbonate) formed from the skeletal remains of sea creatures. **2** a a similar substance (calcium sulphate), sometimes coloured, used for writing or drawing. **b** a piece of this (a box of chalks). **3** a series of strata consisting mainly of chalk. **4** = French chalk. —v.tr. **1** rub, mark, draw, or write with chalk. **2** (foll. by up) **a** write or record with chalk. **b** register (a success etc.). **c** charge (to an account). □ **as different as chalk and** (or **from**) **cheese** fundamentally different. **by a long chalk** Brit. by far (from the use of chalk to mark the score in games). **chalk and talk** traditional teaching (employing blackboard, chalk, and interlocution). **chalk out** sketch or plan a thing to be accomplished. **chalk-pit** a quarry in which chalk is dug. **chalk-stone** a concretion of urates like chalk in tissues and joints esp. of hands and feet. **chalk-stripe** a pattern of thin white stripes on a dark background. **chalk-striped** having chalk-stripes. [OE cealc ult. f. WG f. L CALX]

chalkboard /ˈtʃɔːkbɔːd/ n. US = BLACKBOARD.

chalky /ˈtʃɔːkɪ/ adj. (**chalkier, chalkiest**) **1 a** abounding in chalk. **b** white as chalk. **2** like or containing chalk stones. □□ **chalkiness** n.

challenge /ˈtʃælɪndʒ/ n. & v. —n. **1 a** a summons to take part in a contest or a trial of strength etc., esp. to a duel. **b** a summons to prove or justify something. **2** a demanding or difficult task (rose to the challenge of the new job). **3** Law an objection made to a jury member. **4** a call to respond, esp. a sentry's call for a password etc. **5** an invitation to a sporting contest, esp. one issued to a reigning champion. **6** Med. a test of immunity after immunization treatment. —v.tr. **1** (often foll. by to + infin.) **a** invite to take part in a contest, game, debate, duel, etc. **b** invite to prove or justify something. **2** dispute, deny (I challenge that remark). **3 a** stretch, stimulate (challenges him to produce his best). **b** (as **challenging** adj.) demanding; stimulatingly difficult. **4** (of a sentry) call to respond. **5** claim (attention, etc.). **6** Law object to (a jury member, evidence, etc.). **7** Med. test by a challenge. □□ **challengeable** /-dʒəb(ə)l/ adj. **challenger** n. [ME f. OF c(h)alenge, c(h)alenger f. L calumnia calumniari calumny]

Challenger Deep /ˈtʃælɪndʒə(r)/ the deepest part of the Mariana Trench in the Pacific Ocean, discovered by HMS Challenger II in 1948.

challis /ˈʃælɪs, ˈʃælɪ/ n. a lightweight soft clothing fabric. [perh. f. a surname]

chalybeate /kəˈlɪbɪət/ adj. (of mineral water etc.) impregnated with iron salts. [mod.L chalybeatus f. L chalybs f. Gk khalups -ubos steel]

chamaephyte /ˈkæmɪfaɪt/ n. a plant whose buds are on or near the ground. [Gk khamai on the ground + -PHYTE]

chamber /ˈtʃeɪmbə(r)/ n. **1 a** a hall used by a legislative or judicial body. **b** the body that meets in it. **c** any of the houses of a parliament (Chamber of Deputies; second chamber). **2** (in pl.) Brit. Law **a** rooms used by a barrister or group of barristers, esp. in the Inns of Court. **b** a judge's room used for hearing cases not needing to be taken in court. **3** poet. or archaic a room, esp. a bedroom. **4** Mus. (attrib.) of or for a small group of instruments (chamber orchestra; chamber music). **5** an enclosed space in machinery etc. (esp. the part of a gun-bore that contains the charge). **6 a** a cavity in a plant or in the body of an animal. **b** a compartment in a structure. **7** = chamber-pot. □ **Chamber of Commerce** an association to promote local commercial interests. **chamber-pot** a receptacle for urine etc., used in a bedroom. **chamber tomb** a tomb (esp. a megalithic structure) containing a chamber or chambers for deposition of the dead. [ME f. OF chambre f. L CAMERA]

chambered /ˈtʃeɪmbəd/ adj. (of a tomb) containing a burial chamber.

Chamberlain[1] /ˈtʃeɪmbəlɪn/, Arthur Neville (1869–1940), son of Joseph Chamberlain. A Conservative MP from 1918, he succeeded Baldwin as Prime Minister in 1937 and proved a strong leader, but his policy of personal diplomacy and appeasement of Hitler caused increasing discontent in his own party. Although Chamberlain is unfairly blamed for failing to prevent a war which was almost certainly inevitable, his war leadership was certainly inadequate and in May 1940 he was replaced by Winston Churchill.

Chamberlain[2] /ˈtʃeɪmbəlɪn/, Joseph (1836–1914), a successful industrialist who became a Liberal MP (1876), leaving the party in 1886 because of Gladstone's support of Irish Home Rule and leading the Liberal Unionists into an alliance with the Conservatives. As Colonial Secretary he was the spokesman for imperialist interests, playing a leading role in the Second Boer War.

chamberlain /ˈtʃeɪmbəlɪn/ n. **1** an officer managing the household of a sovereign or a great noble. **2** the treasurer of a corporation etc. □ **Lord Chamberlain (of the Household)** the official in charge of the Royal Household, formerly the licenser of plays. **Lord Great Chamberlain of England** the hereditary holder of a ceremonial office. □□ **chamberlainship** n. [ME f. OF chamberlain etc. f. Frank. f. L camera CAMERA]

chambermaid /ˈtʃeɪmbəˌmeɪd/ n. **1** a housemaid at a hotel etc. **2** US a housemaid.

Chambers /ˈtʃeɪmbəz/, Sir William (1723–96), architect, born in Sweden of Scottish parents, founder-member of the British Royal Academy and designer of Somerset House in London (1776). Travels in the Far East and studies in France and Italy helped to mould his eclectic but conservative style.

Chambertin /ˈʃɑːbə,tæ̃/ n. a high-quality dry red burgundy wine. [Gevrey Chambertin region in E. France]

chambray /ˈʃæmbreɪ/ n. a linen-finished gingham cloth with a white weft and a coloured warp. [irreg. f. Cambrai: see CAMBRIC]

chambré /ˈʃɑːbreɪ/ adj. (of red wine) brought to room temperature. [F, past part. of chambrer f. chambre room: see CHAMBER]

chameleon /kəˈmiːlɪən/ n. **1** any of a family of small lizards having grasping tails, long tongues, protruding eyes, and the power of changing colour. **2** a variable or inconstant person. □□ **chameleonic** /-ˈɒnɪk/ adj. [ME f. L f. Gk khamaileōn f. khamai on the ground + leōn lion]

chamfer /ˈtʃæmfə(r)/ v. & n. —v.tr. bevel symmetrically (a right-angled edge or corner). —n. a bevelled surface at an edge or corner. [back-form. f. chamfering f. F chamfrain f. chant edge (CANT[2]) + fraint broken f. OF fraindre break f. L frangere]

chamois /ˈʃæmwɑː/ n. (pl. same /-wɑːz/) **1** an agile goat antelope, Rupicapra rupicapra, native to the mountains of Europe and Asia. **2** /ˈʃæmɪ, ˈʃæmwɑː/ (in full **chamois leather**) **a** soft pliable leather from sheep, goats, deer, etc. **b** a piece of this for polishing etc. [F: cf. Gallo-Roman camox]

chamomile var. of CAMOMILE.

champ[1] /tʃæmp/ v. & n. —v. **1** tr. & intr. munch or chew noisily. **2** tr. (of a horse etc.) work (the bit) noisily between the teeth. **3** intr. fret with impatience (is champing to be away). —n. a chewing noise or motion. □ **champ at the bit** be restlessly impatient. [prob. imit.]

champ[2] /tʃæmp/ n. sl. a champion. [abbr.]

champagne /ʃæmˈpeɪn/ n. **1 a** a white sparkling wine from Champagne. **b** (loosely) a similar wine from elsewhere. ¶ Use in sense b is strictly incorrect. **2** a pale cream or straw colour. [Champagne, former province in E. France, famous for its vineyards]

Champagne-Ardenne /ʃæm,peɪnaˈden/ a region of NE France comprising part of the Ardennes forest and the vine-growing Plain of Champagne; pop. (1982) 1,345,900; capital, Reims.

champaign /ʃæmˈpeɪn/ n. literary **1** open country. **2** an expanse of open country. [ME f. OF champagne f. LL campania: cf. CAMPAIGN]

champers /ˈʃæmpəz/ n. sl. champagne.

champerty /ˈtʃæmpəti/ n. (pl. **-ies**) Law an illegal agreement in which a person not naturally interested in a lawsuit finances it with a view to sharing the disputed property. □□ **champertous** adj. [ME f. AF *champartie* f. OF *champart* feudal lord's share of produce, f. L *campus* field + *pars* part]

champion /ˈtʃæmpiən/ n., v., adj., & adv. —n. **1** (often attrib.) a person (esp. in a sport or game), an animal, plant, etc., that has defeated or surpassed all rivals in a competition etc. **2 a** a person who fights or argues for a cause or on behalf of another person. **b** hist. a knight etc. who fought in single combat on behalf of a king etc. —v.tr. support the cause of, defend, argue in favour of. —adj. colloq. or dial. first-class, splendid. —adv. colloq. or dial. splendidly, well. □ **Champion of England** (or **King's** or **Queen's Champion**) a hereditary official at coronations. [ME f. OF f. med.L *campio -onis* fighter f. L *campus* field]

championship /ˈtʃæmpiənʃɪp/ n. **1** (often in pl.) a contest for the position of champion in a sport etc. **2** the position of champion over all rivals. **3** the advocacy or defence (of a cause etc.).

Champlain /ʃæmˈpleɪn/, Samuel de (1567–1635), French explorer and colonial statesman. Champlain began his seaborne career in the service of Spain, but later entered French service, making his first voyage to Canada in 1603. Between 1604 and 1607 he explored the eastern seaboard of North America and in 1608 established the colony of Quebec, of which he became Lieutenant Governor. Much of his subsequent career was spent exploring the Canadian interior and defending his settlements against hostile Indians. After his capture and imprisonment by the English (1629–32), he returned to Canada for a final spell as Governor (1633–5). Lake Champlain, in the north-east US, is named after him; he visited it in 1609.

champlevé /ˌʃɑ̃ləˈveɪ/ n. & adj. —n. a type of enamel-work in which hollows made in a metal surface are filled with coloured enamels. —adj. of or relating to champlevé (cf. CLOISONNÉ). [F, = raised field]

Champollion /ʃɑ̃pɒlˈjɔ̃/, Jean-François (1790–1832), French Egyptologist, who in 1822 succeeded in deciphering some of the hieroglyphic inscriptions on the Rosetta stone (see entry).

chance /tʃɑːns/ n., adj., & v. —n. **1 a** a possibility (*just a chance we will catch the train*). **b** (often in pl.) probability (*the chances are against it*). **2** a risk (*have to take a chance*). **3 a** an undesigned occurrence (*just a chance that they met*). **b** the absence of design or discoverable cause (*here merely because of chance*). **4** an opportunity (*didn't have a chance to speak to him*). **5** the way things happen; fortune; luck (*we'll just leave it to chance*). **6** (often **Chance**) the course of events regarded as a power; fate (*blind Chance rules the universe*). **7** Cricket an opportunity for dismissing a batsman. —adj. fortuitous, accidental (*a chance meeting*). —v. **1** tr. colloq. risk (*we'll chance it and go*). **2** intr. (often foll. by *that* + clause, or *to* + infin.) happen without intention (*it chanced that I found it; I chanced to find it*). □ **by any chance** as it happens; perhaps. **by chance** without design; unintentionally. **chance one's arm** make an attempt though unlikely to succeed. **chance on** (or **upon**) happen to find, meet, etc. **game of chance** a game decided by luck, not skill. **the off chance** the slight possibility. **on the chance** (often foll. by *of*, or *that* + clause) in view of the possibility. **stand a chance** have a prospect of success etc. **take a chance** (or **chances**) behave riskily; risk failure. **take a** (or **one's**) **chance on** (or **with**) consent to take the consequences of; trust to luck. [ME f. AF *ch(e)aunce*, OF *chéance chëoir* fall ult. f. L *cadere*]

chancel /ˈtʃɑːns(ə)l/ n. the part of a church near the altar, reserved for the clergy, the choir, etc., usu. enclosed by a screen or separated from the nave by steps. [ME f. OF f. L *cancelli* lattice]

chancellery /ˈtʃɑːnsələri/ n. (pl. **-ies**) **1 a** the position, office, staff, department, etc., of a chancellor. **b** the official residence of a chancellor. **2** US an office attached to an embassy or consulate. [ME f. OF *chancellerie* (as CHANCELLOR)]

chancellor /ˈtʃɑːnsələ(r)/ n. **1** a State or legal official of various kinds. **2** the head of the government in some European countries, e.g. Germany. **3** the non-resident honorary head of a university. **4** a bishop's law officer. **5** US the president of a chancery court. □ **Chancellor of the Duchy of Lancaster** a member of the government legally representing the Queen as Duke of Lancaster, often a Cabinet Minister employed on non-departmental work. **Chancellor of the Exchequer** the finance minister of the United Kingdom, who prepares the budget. His office dates from the reign of Henry III, and was originally that of assistant to the treasurer of the Exchequer; it has become of prime importance since that of Treasurer came to be held not by an individual but by the Lords Commissioners of the Treasury (see TREASURY). **Chancellor of the Garter** etc. a government officer who seals commissions etc. **Lord** (or **Lord High**) **Chancellor** an officer presiding in the House of Lords, the Chancery Division, or the Court of Appeal. □□ **chancellorship** n. [OE f. AF *c(h)anceler*, OF -*ier* f. LL *cancellarius* porter, secretary, f. *cancelli* lattice]

chance-medley /ˌtʃɑːnsˈmedlɪ/ n. (pl. **-eys**) **1** Law a fight, esp. homicidal, beginning unintentionally. **2** inadvertency. [AF *chance medlee* (see MEDDLE) mixed chance]

chancery /ˈtʃɑːnsəri/ n. (pl. **-ies**) **1** Law (**Chancery**) the Lord Chancellor's court, a division of the High Court of Justice. **2** hist. the records office of an order of knighthood. **3** hist. the court of a bishop's chancellor. **4** an office attached to an embassy or consulate. **5** a public record office. **6** US a court of equity. □ **in chancery** sl. (of a boxer or wrestler) with the head held under the opponent's arm and being pummelled. [ME, contracted f. CHANCELLERY]

Chan Chan /tʃæn tʃæn/ the capital of the pre-Inca kingdom of Chimu. Its extensive ruins are situated on the north coast of Peru, near Trujillo. The main building material used was adobe.

chancre /ˈʃæŋkə(r)/ n. a painless ulcer developing in venereal disease etc. [F f. L CANCER]

chancroid /ˈʃæŋkrɔɪd/ n. ulceration of lymph nodes in the groin, from venereal disease.

chancy /ˈtʃɑːnsɪ/ adj. (**chancier**, **chanciest**) subject to chance; uncertain; risky. □□ **chancily** adv. **chanciness** n.

chandelier /ˌʃændɪˈlɪə(r)/ n. an ornamental branched hanging support for several candles or electric light bulbs. [F (*chandelle* f. as CANDLE)]

Chandigarh /ˌtʃʌndɪˈɡɑː(r)/ **1** a Union Territory in India, created in 1966. **2** a city in this Territory, capital of both Punjab and (at present) Haryana States; pop. (1981) 450,050.

Chandler /ˈtʃɑːndlə(r)/, Raymond (1888–1959), American author of thrillers and detective stories, including *The Big Sleep* (1939), *Farewell, My Lovely* (1940), and *The Long Goodbye* (1954), all of which have been filmed.

chandler /ˈtʃɑːndlə(r)/ n. a dealer in candles, oil, soap, paint, groceries, etc. □ **corn chandler** a dealer in corn. **ship** (or **ship's**) **chandler** a dealer in cordage, canvas, etc. [ME f. AF *chaundeler*, OF *chandelier* (as CANDLE)]

chandlery /ˈtʃɑːndləri/ n. the goods sold by a chandler.

Chanel /ʃəˈnel/, Gabrielle Bonheur ('Coco') (1883–1971), French couturière and perfume manufacturer, noted for her simple but sophisticated designs, which were of great influence especially between the two World Wars.

Changchun /ˌtʃæŋˈtʃʊn/ an industrial city in NE China, capital of Jilin province; pop. (est. 1986) 1,860,000.

change /tʃeɪndʒ/ n. & v. —n. **1 a** the act or an instance of making or becoming different. **b** an alteration or modification (*the change in her expression*). **2 a** money given in exchange for money in larger units or a different currency. **b** money returned as the balance of that given in payment. **c** = *small change*. **3** a new experience; variety (*fancied a change; for a change*). **4 a** the substitution of one thing for another; an exchange (*change of scene*). **b** a set of clothes etc. put on in place of another. **5** (in full **change of life**) colloq. the menopause. **6** (usu. in pl.) the different orders in which a peal of bells can be rung. **7** (**Change**) (also **'Change**) hist. a place where merchants etc. met to do business. **8** (of the moon) arrival at a fresh phase, esp. at the new moon. —v. **1** tr. & intr. undergo, show, or subject to change; make or become different (*the wig changed his appearance; changed from an introvert into an extrovert*). **2** tr. **a** take or use another instead of; go from one to another (*change one's socks; changed his doctor; changed trains*). **b** (usu. foll. by *for*) give up or get rid of in exchange (*changed the car for a van*). **3** tr. **a** give or get change in smaller denominations for (*can you change a ten-pound note?*). **b** (foll. by *for*) exchange (a sum of money) for (*changed his dollars for pounds*). **4** *tr.* & *intr.* put fresh clothes or coverings on (*changed the baby as he was wet; changed into something loose*). **5** *tr.* (often foll. by *with*) give and receive, exchange (*changed places with him; we changed places*). **6** *intr.* change trains etc. (*changed at Crewe*). **7** *intr.* (of the moon) arrive at a fresh phase, esp. become new. □ **change colour** blanch or flush. **change down** engage a lower gear in a vehicle. **change gear** engage a different gear in a vehicle. **change hands 1** pass to a different owner. **2** substitute one hand for another. **change one's mind** adopt a different opinion or plan. **change of air** a different climate; variety. **change of heart** a conversion to a different view. **change over** change from one system or situation to another. **change-over** *n.* such a change. **change step** alter one's step so that the opposite leg marks time (e.g. to the beat of a drum). **change the subject** begin talking of something different, esp. to avoid embarrassment. **change one's tune 1** voice a different opinion from that expressed previously. **2** change one's style of language or manner, esp. from an insolent to a respectful tone. **change up** engage a higher gear in a vehicle. **get no change out of** *sl.* **1** fail to get information from. **2** fail to get the better of (in business etc.). **ring the changes (on)** vary the ways of expressing, arranging, or doing something. □□ **changeful** *adj.* **changer** *n.* [ME f. AF *chaunge*, OF *change, changer* f. LL *cambiare*, L *cambire* barter, prob. of Celt. orig.]

changeable /ˈtʃeɪndʒəb(ə)l/ *adj.* **1** irregular, inconstant. **2** that can change or be changed. □□ **changeability** /-ˈbɪlɪtɪ/ *n.* **changeableness** *n.* **changeably** *adv.* [ME f. OF, formed as CHANGE]

changeless /ˈtʃeɪndʒlɪs/ *adj.* unchanging. □□ **changelessly** *adv.* **changelessness** *n.*

changeling /ˈtʃeɪndʒlɪŋ/ *n.* a child believed to be substituted for another by stealth, esp. an elf-child left by fairies.

Changsha /tʃæŋˈʃɑː/ the capital of Hunan province in SE China, on the Xiang Jiang river; pop. (est. 1986) 1,160,000.

channel[1] /ˈtʃæn(ə)l/ *n.* & *v.* —*n.* **1 a** a length of water wider than a strait, joining two larger areas, esp. seas. **b** (**the Channel**) the English Channel between Britain and France. **2** a medium of communication; an agency for conveying information (*through the usual channels*). **3** *Broadcasting* **a** a band of frequencies used in radio and television transmission, esp. as used by a particular station. **b** a service or station using this. **4** the course in which anything moves; a direction. **5 a** a natural or artificial hollow bed of water. **b** the navigable part of a waterway. **6** a tubular passage for liquid. **7** *Electronics* a lengthwise strip on recording tape etc. **8** a groove or a flute, esp. in a column. —*v.tr.* (**channelled, channelling**; *US* **channeled, channeling**) **1** guide, direct (*channelled them through customs*). **2** form channels in; groove. [ME f. OF *chanel* f. L *canalis* CANAL]

channel[2] /ˈtʃæn(ə)l/ *n. Naut.* any of the broad thick planks projecting horizontally from a ship's side abreast of the masts, used to widen the basis for the shrouds. [for *chain-wale*: cf. *gunnel* for *gunwale*]

Channel Country an area of SW Queensland and NE South Australia watered intermittently by channels such as Cooper's Creek and Warburton Creek. The rich grasslands produced by the summer rains provide grazing for cattle. The region is traversed by 'beef roads' such as the Strzelecki Track and the Diamanta Devel Road, down which beasts for slaughter are conveyed in 'trains' of linked cattle-trucks.

Channel Islands a group of islands in the English Channel off the NW coast of France, of which the largest are Jersey, Guernsey, and Alderney. They are the only portions of the former dukedom of Normandy that still owe allegiance to England, to which they have been attached since the Norman Conquest in 1066.

channelize /ˈtʃænəlaɪz/ *v.tr.* (also **-ise**) convey in, or as if in, a channel; guide.

Channel Tunnel a tunnel under the English Channel, linking the coasts of England and France. Such a scheme was first put forward in 1802 by a French engineer, who perceived the possibility of tunnelling through the layer of soft chalk rock

that is continuous from one side of the Channel to the other. Napoleon showed interest, but Britain was again at war with France in 1803 and no move was made. The proposal was revived again at intervals and digging actually started in 1882, but fear of invasion from the Continent brought hostile reaction in Britain until the 1950s, when the development of air power and guided missiles had made the Channel no longer the natural defence that it had been hitherto; a railway tunnel is currently being constructed beneath it, with terminals near Folkestone in England and Calais in France.

chanson de geste /ʃɑ̃ˌsɔ̃ də ˈʒest/ *n.* (*pl.* **chansons** *pronunc.* same) any of a group of French historical verse romances, mostly connected with Charlemagne, composed in the 11th–13th c. [F, = song of heroic deeds]

chant /tʃɑːnt/ *n.* & *v.* —*n.* **1 a** a spoken singsong phrase, esp. one performed in unison by a crowd etc. **b** a repetitious singsong way of speaking. **2** *Mus.* **a** a short musical passage in two or more phrases used for singing unmetrical words, e.g. psalms, canticles. **b** the psalm or canticle so sung. **c** a song, esp. monotonous or repetitive. **3** a musical recitation, esp. of poetry. —*v.tr.* & *intr.* **1** talk or repeat monotonously (*a crowd chanting slogans*). **2** sing or intone (a psalm etc.). [ME (orig. as verb) f. OF *chanter* sing f. L *cantare* frequent. of *canere cant-* sing]

chanter /ˈtʃɑːntə(r)/ *n. Mus.* the melody-pipe, with finger-holes, of a bagpipe.

chanterelle /ˌtʃæntəˈrel/ *n.* an edible fungus, *Cantharellus cibarius*, with a yellow funnel-shaped cap and smelling of apricots. [F f. mod.L *cantharellus* dimin. of *cantharus* f. Gk *kantharos* a kind of drinking vessel]

chanteuse /ʃɑːnˈtɜːz/ *n.* a female singer of popular songs. [F]

chanticleer /ˌtʃæntɪˈklɪə(r), ˌtʃɑːn-, ˈʃæn-, ˈʃɑːn-/ *n. literary* a name given to a domestic cock, esp. in fairy tales etc. [ME f. OF *chantecler* (as CHANT, CLEAR), a name in *Reynard the Fox*]

Chantilly /ʃænˈtɪlɪ, ˌʃɑːtiːˈjiː/ *n.* **1** a delicate kind of bobbin-lace. **2** sweetened or flavoured whipped cream. [*Chantilly* near Paris]

chantry /ˈtʃɑːntrɪ/ *n.* (*pl.* **-ies**) **1** an endowment for a priest or priests to celebrate masses for the founder's soul. **2** the priests, chapel, altar, etc., endowed. [ME f. AF *chaunterie*, OF *chanterie* f. *chanter* CHANT]

chanty var. of SHANTY[2].

Chanukkah var. of HANUKKAH.

Chanute /ʃæˈnuːt/, Octave (1832–1910), Franco-American aviation pioneer, who went to America at the age of 6. Educated as a railway engineer, he built the first glider in 1896 and later produced others of which the most successful was the biplane type which made over 700 flights without accident and inspired the Wright brothers. His encouragement to them and to the serious study of aeronautics greatly assisted them in making the world's first controlled powered flight on 17 Dec. 1903.

Chao Phraya /tʃaʊ ˈpraɪə/ a major waterway of central Thailand, formed by the junction of the Ping and Nan rivers near the port of Nakhon Sawan.

Chaos /ˈkeɪɒs/ *Gk Mythol.* the first created being, scarcely personified, from which came the primeval deities Gaia (Earth), Tartarus, Erebus (Darkness), and Nyx (Night). [Gk, = gaping void]

chaos /ˈkeɪɒs/ *n.* **1** utter confusion. **2** the formless matter supposed to have existed before the creation of the universe. □□ **chaotic** /keɪˈɒtɪk/ *adj.* **chaotically** /-ˈɒtɪkəlɪ/ *adv.* [F or L f. Gk *khaos*: *-otic* after *erotic* etc.]

chaos theory *n.* the mathematical study of complex systems whose development is highly sensitive to slight changes in conditions, so that small events can give rise to strikingly great consequences. For example, a slight turn of a tap can change a steady flow of water to an irregularly splashing stream; a tiny disruption of the atmosphere in the Arctic Circle might lead to the development of a hurricane in the tropics. The study, which has applications in many fields (including physics, biology, ecology, and economics), has two main aspects. On the one hand, processes that seem random or irregular may actually be following certain laws, which could be discovered. On the other hand, processes thought to be regular may turn out to be 'chaotic'. This aspect has further diminished scientists' confidence in the predictability of natural phenomena. Because of their complexity and the large number of conditions that may affect them at any stage, many systems that used to be thought predictable from the laws of nature, e.g. the movements of the planets in the solar system, have been shown to be 'chaotic' in the technical sense: for sufficiently far in the future even their approximate positions may be beyond calculation.

chap¹ /tʃæp/ v. & n. —v. (**chapped, chapping**) **1** intr. (esp. of the skin; also of dry ground etc.) crack in fissures, esp. because of exposure and dryness. **2** tr. (of the wind, cold, etc.) cause to chap. —n. (usu. in pl.) **1** a crack in the skin. **2** an open seam. [ME, perh. rel. to MLG, MDu. kappen chop off]

chap² /tʃæp/ n. colloq. a man; a boy; a fellow. [abbr. of CHAPMAN]

chap³ /tʃæp/ n. the lower jaw or half of the cheek, esp. of a pig as food. ☐ **chap-fallen** dispirited, dejected (with the lower jaw hanging). [16th c.: var. of CHOP², of unkn. orig.]

chap. abbr. chapter.

chaparejos /ˌʃæpəˈreɪəʊs, ˌtʃæp-/ n.pl. US a cowboy's leather protection for the front of the legs. [Mex. Sp.]

chaparral /ˌtʃæpəˈræl, ˌʃæp-/ n. US dense tangled brushwood; undergrowth. ☐ **chaparral cock** = ROADRUNNER. [Sp. f. chaparra evergreen oak]

chapatti /tʃəˈpɑːtɪ, -ˈpætɪ/ n. (also **chapati, chupatty**) (pl. **-is** or **chupatties**) Ind. a flat thin cake of unleavened wholemeal bread. [Hindi capāti]

chap-book /ˈtʃæpbʊk/ n. hist. a small pamphlet containing tales, ballads, tracts, etc., hawked by chapmen. [19th c.: see CHAPMAN]

chape /tʃeɪp/ n. **1** the metal cap of a scabbard-point. **2** the back-piece of a buckle attaching it to a strap etc. **3** a sliding loop on a belt or strap. [ME f. OF, = cope, hood, formed as CAP]

chapeau-bras /ˌʃæpəʊˈbrɑː/ n. (pl. **chapeaux-bras** pronunc. same) a three-cornered flat silk hat often carried under the arm. [F f. chapeau hat + bras arm]

chapel /ˈtʃæp(ə)l/ n. **1 a** a place for private Christian worship in a large church or esp. a cathedral, with its own altar and dedication (Lady chapel). **b** a place of Christian worship attached to a private house or institution. **2** Brit. **a** a place of worship for nonconformist bodies. **b** (predic.) an attender at or believer in nonconformist worship (they are strictly chapel). **c** a chapel service. **d** attendance at a chapel. **3** an Anglican church subordinate to a parish church. **4** Printing **a** the members or branch of a printers' trade union at a specific place of work. The name reflects the early connection of printing with the production of religious texts. **b** a meeting of them. ☐ **chapel of ease** an Anglican chapel for the convenience of remote parishioners. **chapel of rest** an undertaker's mortuary. **chapel royal** a chapel in a royal palace. **father of the chapel** (or **the chapel**) the shop steward of a printers' chapel. [ME f. OF chapele f. med.L cappella dimin. of cappa cloak: the first chapel was a sanctuary in which St Martin's sacred cloak (cappella) was preserved]

chapelry /ˈtʃæpəlrɪ/ n. (pl. **-ies**) a district served by an Anglican chapel.

chaperon /ˈʃæpəˌrəʊn/ n. & v. (also **chaperone**) —n. **1** a person, esp. an older woman, who ensures propriety by accompanying a young unmarried woman on social occasions. **2** a person who takes charge of esp. young people in public. —v.tr. act as a chaperon to. ☐☐ **chaperonage** /ˈʃæpərənɪdʒ/ n. [F, = hood, chaperon, dimin. of chape cope, formed as CAP]

chaplain /ˈtʃæplɪn/ n. a member of the clergy attached to a private chapel, institution, ship, regiment, etc. ☐☐ **chaplaincy** n. (pl. **-ies**). [ME f. AF & OF c(h)apelain f. med.L cappellanus, orig. custodian of the cloak of St Martin: see CHAPEL]

chaplet /ˈtʃæplɪt/ n. **1** a garland or circlet for the head. **2** a string of 55 beads (one-third of the rosary number) for counting prayers, or as a necklace. **3** a bead-moulding. ☐☐ **chapleted** adj. [ME f. OF chapelet, ult. f. LL cappa CAP]

Chaplin /ˈtʃæplɪn/, Sir Charles Spencer ('Charlie') (1889–1977), English film actor and director, considered by many the greatest screen mimic and clown. In 1914 he made 35 short slapstick comedies, mostly playing the Tramp, which remained his usual characterization for more than 25 years. He soon achieved worldwide fame, making his first full-length film The Kid in 1921. The peak of his career was marked by The Gold Rush (1925), The Circus (1928), and City Lights (1931), all of which—like Modern Times (1936) and The Great Dictator (1940), his first sound film and his last appearance as a tramp—he also directed. His four later films were of less interest.

Chapman /ˈtʃæpmən/, George (c.1560–1634), English poet and dramatist. He is chiefly known for his translation of Homer, animated by 'a daring fiery spirit' (Pope) and commemorated in a sonnet by Keats, but Swinburne and others have drawn attention to the remarkable quality of his dramatic works. Chapman was renowned as a scholar and is perhaps the 'rival poet' of Shakespeare's 'Sonnets'.

chapman /ˈtʃæpmən/ n. (pl. **-men**) hist. a pedlar. [OE cēapman f. cēap barter]

chappal /ˈtʃæp(ə)l/ n. an Indian sandal, usu. of leather. [Hindi]

chappie /ˈtʃæpɪ/ n. colloq. = CHAP².

chappy /ˈtʃæpɪ/ adj. full of chaps; chapped (chappy knuckles).

chaps /tʃæps, ʃæps/ n. = CHAPAREJOS. [abbr.]

chapstick /ˈtʃæpstɪk/ n. US a cylinder of a cosmetic substance used to prevent chapping of the lips.

chapter /ˈtʃæptə(r)/ n. **1** a main division of a book. **2** a period of time (in a person's life, a nation's history, etc.). **3** a series or sequence (a chapter of misfortunes). **4** a the canons of a cathedral or other religious community or knightly order. **b** a meeting of these. **5** an Act of Parliament numbered as part of a session's proceedings. **6** US a local branch of a society. ☐ **chapter and verse** an exact reference or authority. **chapter house 1** a building used for the meetings of a chapter. **2** US the place where a college fraternity or sorority meets. [ME f. OF chapitre f. L capitulum dimin. of caput -itis head]

char¹ /tʃɑː(r)/ v.tr. & intr. (**charred, charring**) **1** make or become black by burning; scorch. **2** burn or be burnt to charcoal. [app. back-form. f. CHARCOAL]

char² /tʃɑː(r)/ n. & v. Brit. colloq. —n. = CHARWOMAN. —v.intr. (**charred, charring**) work as a charwoman. [earlier chare f. OE cerr a turn, cierran to turn]

char³ /tʃɑː(r)/ n. (also **cha** /tʃɑː/) Brit. sl. tea. [Chin. cha]

char⁴ /tʃɑː(r)/ n. (also **charr**) (pl. same) any small troutlike fish of the genus Salvelinus. [17th c.: orig. unkn.]

charabanc /ˈʃærəˌbæŋ/ n. Brit. hist. a long vehicle, originally horse-drawn and open, later an early form of motor coach, with seating on transverse benches facing forward. [F char à bancs seated carriage]

character /ˈkærɪktə(r)/ n. & v. —n. **1** the collective qualities or characteristics, esp. mental and moral, that distinguish a person or thing. **2** a moral strength (has a weak character). **b** esp. good reputation. **3 a** a person in a novel, play, etc. **b** a part played by an actor; a role. **4** colloq. a person, esp. an eccentric or outstanding individual (he's a real character). **5 a** a printed or written letter, symbol, or distinctive mark (Chinese characters). **b** Computing any of a group of symbols representing a letter etc. **6** a written description of a person's qualities; a testimonial. **7** a characteristic (esp. of a biological species). —v.tr. archaic inscribe; describe. ☐ **character actor** an actor who specializes in playing eccentric or unusual persons. **character assassination** a malicious attempt to harm or destroy a person's good reputation. **in** (or **out of**) **character** consistent (or inconsistent) with a person's character. ☐☐ **characterful** adj. **characterfully** adv. **characterless** adj. [ME f. OF caractere f. L character f. Gk kharaktēr stamp, impress]

characteristic /ˌkærɪktəˈrɪstɪk/ adj. & n. —adj. typical, distinctive (with characteristic expertise). —n. **1** a characteristic feature or quality. **2** Math. the whole number or integral part of a logarithm. ☐ **characteristic curve** a graph showing the relationship between two variable but interdependent quantities. **characteristic radiation** radiation the wavelengths of which are peculiar to the element which emits them. ☐☐ **characteristically** adv. [F caractéristique or med.L characterizare f. Gk kharaktērizō]

characterize /ˈkærɪktəˌraɪz/ v.tr. (also **-ise**) **1 a** describe the character of. **b** (foll. by *as*) describe as. **2** be characteristic of. **3** impart character to. □□ **characterization** /-'zeɪʃ(ə)n/ *n*. [F *caractériser* or med.L *characterizare* f. Gk *kharaktērizō*]

charade /ʃə'rɑːd/ *n*. **1 a** (usu. in *pl*., treated as *sing*.) a game of guessing a word from a written or acted clue given for each syllable and for the whole. **b** one such clue. **2** an absurd pretence. [F f. mod.Prov. *charrado* conversation f. *charra* chatter]

charas /'tʃɑːrəs/ *n*. a narcotic resin from the flower-heads of hemp; cannabis resin. [Hindi]

charcoal /'tʃɑːkəʊl/ *n*. **1 a** an amorphous form of carbon consisting of a porous black residue from partially burnt wood, bones, etc. **b** (usu. in *pl*.) a piece of this used for drawing. **2** a drawing in charcoal. **3** (in full **charcoal grey**) a dark grey colour. □ **charcoal biscuit** a biscuit containing wood-charcoal to aid digestion. [ME COAL = charcoal: first element perh. *chare* turn (cf. CHAR¹, CHAR²)]

chard /tʃɑːd/ *n*. a kind of beet, *Beta vulgaris*, with edible broad white leaf-stalks and green blades. Also called *seakale beet*. [F *carde*, and *chardon* thistle: cf. CARDOON]

Chardonnay /'ʃɑːdɒˌneɪ/ *n*. **1** a variety of white grape used for making champagne and other wines. **2** the vine on which this grape grows. **3** a wine made from Chardonnay grapes. [F]

Charente /ʃæ'rɑ̃t/ a river of western France, that rises in the Massif Central and flows 360 km (225 miles) westwards to the Bay of Biscay, near Rochefort.

charge /tʃɑːdʒ/ *v*. & *n*. —*v*. **1** *tr*. **a** ask (an amount) as a price (*charges £5 a ticket*). **b** ask (a person) for an amount as a price (*you forgot to charge me*). **2** *tr*. **a** (foll. by *to*, *up to*) debit the cost of to (a person or account) (*charge it to my account*; *charge it up to me*). **b** debit (a person or an account) (*bought a new car and charged the company*). **3** *tr*. **a** (often foll. by *with*) accuse (of an offence) (*charged him with theft*). **b** (foll. by *that* + clause) make an accusation that. **4** *tr*. (foll. by *to* + infin.) instruct or urge. **5** (foll. by *with*) **a** *tr*. entrust with. **b** *refl*. undertake. **6 a** *intr*. make a rushing attack; rush headlong. **b** *tr*. make a rushing attack on; throw oneself against. **7** *tr*. (often foll. by *up*) **a** give an electric charge to (a body). **b** store energy in (a battery). **8** *tr*. (often foll. by *with*) load or fill (a vessel, gun, etc.) to the full or proper extent. **9** *tr*. (usu. as **charged** *adj*.) **a** (foll. by *with*) saturated with (*air charged with vapour*). **b** (usu. foll. by *with*) pervaded (with strong feelings etc.) (*atmosphere charged with emotion*; *a charged atmosphere*). —*n*. **1 a** a price asked for goods or services. **b** a financial liability or commitment. **2** an accusation, esp. against a prisoner brought to trial. **3 a** a task, duty, or commission. **b** care, custody, responsible possession. **c** a person or thing entrusted; a minister's congregation. **4 a** an impetuous rush or attack, esp. in a battle. **b** the signal for this. **5** the appropriate amount of material to be put into a receptacle, mechanism, etc. at one time, esp. of explosive for a gun. **6 a** a property of matter that is a consequence of the interaction between its constituent particles and exists in a positive or negative form, causing electrical phenomena. **b** the quantity of this carried by a body. **c** energy stored chemically for conversion into electricity. **d** the process of charging a battery. **7** an exhortation; directions, orders. **8** a burden or load. **9** *Heraldry* a device; a bearing. □ **charge account** *US* a credit account at a shop etc. **charge card** a credit card for which the account must be paid in full when a statement is issued. **charge-hand** *Brit*. a worker, ranking below a foreman, in charge of others on a particular job. **charge-nurse** *Brit*. a nurse in charge of a ward etc. **charge-sheet** *Brit*. a record of cases and charges made at a police station. **free of charge** gratis. **give a person in charge** hand a person over to the police. **in charge** having command. **lay to a person's charge** accuse a person of. **put a person on a charge** charge a person with a specified offence. **return to the charge** begin again, esp. in argument. **take charge** (often foll. by *of*) assume control or direction. □□ **chargeable** *adj*. [ME f. OF *charger* f. LL *car(ri)care* load f. L *carrus* CAR]

chargé d'affaires /ˌʃɑːʒeɪ dæ'feə(r)/ *n*. (also **chargé**) (*pl*. **chargés** *pronunc*. same) **1** an ambassador's deputy. **2** an envoy to a minor country. [F, = in charge (of affairs)]

Charge of the Light Brigade a British cavalry charge during the battle of Balaclava in the Crimean War. A misunderstanding between the commander of the Light Brigade, Lord Cardigan, and his superiors, Lords Raglan and Lucan, led to the British cavalry being committed to an attack up a valley heavily held on three sides by the Russians. Immortalized in verse by Tennyson, the charge in fact destroyed some of the finest light cavalry in the world to very little military purpose.

charger¹ /'tʃɑːdʒə(r)/ *n*. **1 a** a cavalry horse. **b** *poet*. any horse. **2** an apparatus for charging a battery. **3** a person or thing that charges.

charger² /'tʃɑːdʒə(r)/ *n*. *archaic* a large flat dish. [ME f. AF *chargeour*]

chariot /'tʃærɪət/ *n*. & *v*. —*n*. **1** *hist*. **a** a two-wheeled vehicle drawn by horses, used in ancient warfare and racing. Chariots were known in Mesopotamia from the end of the 3rd millennium BC, and spread from there to Europe and Asia. **b** a four-wheeled carriage with back seats only. **2** *poet*. a stately or triumphal vehicle. —*v.tr*. *literary* convey in or as in a chariot. [ME f. OF, augment. of *char* CAR]

charioteer /ˌtʃærɪə'tɪə(r)/ *n*. a chariot-driver.

charisma /kə'rɪzmə/ *n*. (*pl*. **charismata** /kə'rɪzmətə/) **1 a** the ability to inspire followers with devotion and enthusiasm. **b** an attractive aura; great charm. **2** a divinely conferred power or talent. [eccl.L f. Gk *kharisma* f. *kharis* favour, grace]

charismatic /ˌkærɪz'mætɪk/ *adj*. **1** having charisma; inspiring enthusiasm. **2** (of Christian worship) characterized by spontaneity, ecstatic utterances, etc. □ **charismatic movement** a neo-pentecostal movement affecting Roman Catholic, Anglican, and other Christian Churches. □□ **charismatically** *adv*.

charitable /'tʃærɪtəb(ə)l/ *adj*. **1** generous in giving to those in need. **2** of, relating to, or connected with a charity or charities. **3** apt to judge favourably of persons, acts, and motives. □□ **charitableness** *n*. **charitably** *adv*. [ME f. OF f. *charité* CHARITY]

charity /'tʃærɪtɪ/ *n*. (*pl*. **-ies**) **1 a** a giving voluntarily to those in need; alms-giving. **b** the help, esp. money, so given. **2** an institution or organization for helping those in need. **3 a** kindness, benevolence. **b** tolerance in judging others. **c** love of one's fellow men. □ **Charity Commission** (in the UK) a board established to control charitable trusts. [OE f. OF *charité* f. L *caritas -tatis* f. *carus* dear]

charivari /ˌʃɑːrɪ'vɑːrɪ/ *n*. (also **shivaree** /ˌʃɪvə'riː/) **1** a serenade of banging saucepans etc. to a newly-married couple. **2** a medley of sounds; a hubbub. [F, = serenade with pans, trays, etc., to an unpopular person]

charlady /'tʃɑːˌleɪdɪ/ *n*. (*pl*. **-ies**) = CHARWOMAN.

charlatan /'ʃɑːlət(ə)n/ *n*. a person falsely claiming a special knowledge or skill. □□ **charlatanism** *n*. **charlatanry** *n*. [F f. It. *ciarlatano* f. *ciarlare* babble]

Charlemagne /'ʃɑːləˌmeɪn/ (Latin *Carolus magnus* Charles the Great, 742–814), military and political colossus of the Dark Ages, who ruled the Franks in northern Europe 768–814. Famed in legend for being defeated at Roncesvalles, his successful conquests were prodigious. Had he not conquered the Saxons, whom he severely Christianized, and the Bavarians, Germany could hardly have come into existence. He gave to government new moral drive and religious responsibility. The political cohesion of his empire could not last, but the influence of his court scholars persisted in the Carolingian Renaissance. His coronation by Pope Leo III in Rome on Christmas Day, 800, is taken to have inaugurated the Holy Roman Empire, though he himself despised 'Babylonian pride' in rulers and remained at heart a Frank.

Charleroi /'ʃɑːləˌrwɑː/ a city in the province of Hainaut in SW Belgium; pop. (1988) 208,900.

Charles¹ /tʃɑːlz/ the name of two kings of Britain:
    Charles I (1600–49), son of James I, reigned 1625–49. His reign was dominated by the deepening religious and constitutional crisis that eventually resulted in the English Civil War. The King's attempt to rule without Parliament (1629–40) eventually failed when he became involved in war with Scotland, and the Long Parliament proved so uncooperative that an open breach and war between the two sides followed in 1642. The King was

finally defeated and surrendered to the Scots in 1646. Handed over to Parliament in 1647, he escaped and negotiated with the Scots to fight on his behalf in return for religious concessions, but the Royalist forces were defeated at Preston (1648) and the English army demanded Charles's death. He was tried by a special parliamentary court and beheaded in London in January 1649.

Charles II (1630–85), son of Charles I, reigned 1660–85. After his father's death Charles II was crowned in Scotland, but was forced into exile after the defeat of his invading army at Worcester in 1651. He remained in exile on the Continent for nine years before he was restored after the collapse of Cromwell's regime in 1660. Charles displayed considerable adroitness in handling the difficult constitutional situation left by the preceding two decades of strife, but his failure to produce a Protestant heir left the future of the Stuart dynasty in doubt after his death.

Charles² /tʃɑːlz/ the name of ten kings of France:
Charles VII (1403–61), reigned 1422–61. His reign witnessed the final defeat of the English forces in France and the end of the Hundred Years War. At the time of his father's death, the English were in firm occupation of much of northern France, including Reims (thus denying Charles his coronation). After the intervention of Joan of Arc, however, the French experienced a dramatic military revival. Charles was crowned in 1429 and the English gradually driven out until in 1453 only Calais remained in their hands. Charles achieved a considerable modernization of the administration of the army and did a great deal to lay the foundations of French power in the following decades, being so well aided in these and other tasks as to earn the sobriquet 'the Well-Served'.

Charles³ /tʃɑːlz/ the name of four kings of Spain:
Charles I (1500–58), reigned 1516–56, Holy Roman Emperor (as Charles V) 1519–56. The son of Philip I of Spain and grandson of the Emperor Maximilian I, Charles came to the throne of Spain in 1516 and united it with that of the Empire when he inherited the latter in 1519. Tied down by such wide responsibilities, Charles was never able to give proper consideration or attention to national and international problems. In Germany his reign was characterized by the struggle against the newly formed Protestant religion, in Spain he had to confront a serious revolt in Castile, and for most of his reign he was engaged in a war with France (1521–44). Exhausted by these struggles, Charles handed Naples (1554), The Netherlands (1555), and Spain (1556) over to his son Philip II and the imperial crown (1556) to his brother Ferdinand, and retired to a monastery in Spain.

Charles II (1661–1700), reigned 1665–1700. The last Hapsburg to be king of Spain, Charles inherited a kingdom already in the throes of decline and proved unequal to the task of regenerating it. His choice of Philip of Anjou, grandson of Louis XIV of France, as his successor brought on the War of the Spanish Succession, which began after his death.

Charles IV (1748–1819), reigned 1788–1808. A weak ruler, Charles was dominated by his mother Maria Louisa and his favourite Manuel de Godoy (Prime Minister from 1792). He was unable to stand up to Napoleon, with the result that his fleet was destroyed along with that of France at Trafalgar in 1805. Following the French invasion of Spain in 1807, Charles was forced to abdicate. He died in exile in Rome.

Charles⁴ /tʃɑːlz/ (1682–1718), king of Sweden (as Charles XII) 1697–1718. One of the most accomplished soldier-kings of his time, Charles embarked on the Great Northern War, three years after his accession, against the encircling powers of Denmark, Poland-Saxony, and Russia. In the early years he won a series of brilliant victories, most notably against the Russians at Narva in 1700, but in 1709 he embarked on an ill-fated expedition deep into Russia which ended in disaster at Poltava. Following the destruction of his army, Charles was interned in Turkey until 1715, leaving his country to fight on leaderless against almost all the surrounding nations. He resumed his military career after his return but was killed while besieging the Norwegian fortress of Fredrikshald in 1718.

Charles' Law /tʃɑːlz/ (also **Charles's Law** /ˈtʃɑːlzɪz/) n. Chem. the law stating that the volume of an ideal gas at constant

pressure is directly proportional to the absolute temperature. [J. A. C. *Charles*, Fr. scientist d. 1823]

Charles Martel /tʃɑːlz mɑːˈtel/ (c.688–741), the virtual ruler of the eastern part of the Frankish kingdom from 715 and the whole kingdom from 731, after being in charge of the palace under the decadent Merovingian kings. His nickname *Martel*, which means 'the hammer', was gained by his victory at Poitiers in 732 which effectively checked the Muslim advance into Europe. His rule marked the beginning of Carolingian power; Charlemagne was his grandson.

Charles's Wain /ˌtʃɑːlzɪz ˈweɪn/ see WAIN.

Charleston /ˈtʃɑːlst(ə)n/ **1** the capital of West Virginia; pop. (1980) 63,970. **2** a city and the main port of South Carolina; pop. (1980) 69,510. The bombardment of Fort Sumter, in its harbour, by Confederate troops in April 1861 marked the beginning of the American Civil War.

charleston /ˈtʃɑːlst(ə)n/ n. & v. (also **Charleston**) —n. a lively American dance of the 1920s with side-kicks from the knee. —v.intr. dance the charleston. [*Charleston* in S. Carolina]

charley horse /ˈtʃɑːlɪ/ n. US sl. stiffness or cramp in an arm or leg. [19th c.: orig. uncert.]

charlie /ˈtʃɑːlɪ/ n. Brit. sl. **1** a fool. **2** (in pl.) a woman's breasts. [dimin. of the name *Charles*]

charlock /ˈtʃɑːlɒk/ n. a wild mustard, *Sinapis arvensis*, with yellow flowers. Also called *field mustard*. [OE *cerlic*, of unkn. orig.]

Charlotte /ˈʃɑːlət/ the largest city and principal commercial centre of North Carolina; pop. (1982) 324,000. The city is named after the wife of King George III.

charlotte /ˈʃɑːlət/ n. a pudding made of stewed fruit with a casing or layers or covering of bread, sponge cake, biscuits, or breadcrumbs (*apple charlotte*). □ **charlotte russe** /ˈruːs/ custard etc. enclosed in sponge cake or a casing of sponge fingers. [F]

Charlotte Amalie /ˌʃɑːlət əˈmɑːljə/ the capital of the US Virgin Islands, on the island of St Thomas; pop. (1980) 11,750.

Charlotte Dundas /ˌʃɑːlət dʌnˈdæs/ the first vessel to use steam propulsion commercially, built on the River Clyde. The engine drove a single paddle-wheel and the ship made her first voyage in 1802.

Charlottetown /ˈʃɑːlətˌtaʊn/ the capital and chief port of Prince Edward Island; pop. (1986) 15,800.

Charlton /ˈtʃɑːlt(ə)n/, Robert ('Bobby') (1937–), English footballer, who played for Manchester United (1954–73) and for England (1957–73).

charm /tʃɑːm/ n. & v. —n. **1 a** the power or quality of giving delight or arousing admiration. **b** fascination, attractiveness. **c** (usu. in pl.) an attractive or enticing quality. **2** a trinket on a bracelet etc. **3 a** an object, act, or word(s) supposedly having occult or magic power; a spell. **b** a thing worn to avert evil etc.; an amulet. **4** *Physics* a property of matter manifested by some elementary particles. —v.tr. **1** delight, captivate (*charmed by the performance*). **2** influence or protect as if by magic (*leads a charmed life*). **3 a** gain by charm (*charmed agreement out of him*). **b** influence by charm (*charmed her into consenting*). **4** cast a spell on, bewitch. □ **charm-bracelet** a bracelet hung with small trinkets. **like a charm** perfectly, wonderfully. □□ **charmer** n. [ME f. OF *charme*, *charmer* f. L *carmen* song]

charmeuse /ʃɑːˈmɜːz/ n. a soft smooth silky dress-fabric. [F, fem. of *charmeur* (as CHARM)]

charming /ˈtʃɑːmɪŋ/ adj. **1** delightful, attractive, pleasing. **2** (often as int.) iron. expressing displeasure or disapproval. □□ **charmingly** adv.

charmless /ˈtʃɑːmlɪs/ adj. lacking charm; unattractive. □□ **charmlessly** adv. **charmlessness** n.

charnel-house /ˈtʃɑːn(ə)lˌhaʊs/ n. a house or vault in which dead bodies or bones are piled. [ME & OF *charnel* burying-place f. med.L *carnale* f. LL *carnalis* CARNAL]

Charollais /ˈʃærəˌleɪ/ n. (also **Charolais**) (pl. same) **1** an animal of a breed of large white beef-cattle. **2** this breed. [Monts du *Charollais* in E. France]

Charon /ˈkɛərən/ *Gk Mythol.* the aged ferryman who, for a fee of one obol, ferried the souls of the dead across the rivers Styx and

Acheron to Hades. It was usual for the Greeks to place a coin in the mouth of the dead for this fee.

charpoy /'tʃɑːpɔɪ/ n. Ind. a light bedstead. [Hind. chārpāi]

charr var. of CHAR⁴.

chart /tʃɑːt/ n. & v. —n. **1** a geographical map or plan, esp. for navigation by sea or air. **2** a sheet of information in the form of a table, graph, or diagram. **3** (usu. in pl.) colloq. a listing of the currently most popular gramophone records. —v.tr. make a chart of, map. [F charte f. L charta CARD¹]

chartbuster /'tʃɑːtˌbʌstə(r)/ n. colloq. a best-selling popular song, record, etc.

charter /'tʃɑːtə(r)/ n. & v. —n. **1 a** a written grant of rights, by the sovereign or legislature, esp. the creation of a borough, company, university, etc. **b** a written constitution or description of an organization's functions etc. **2** a contract to hire an aircraft, ship, etc., for a special purpose. **3** = CHARTER-PARTY. —v.tr. **1** grant a charter to. **2** hire (an aircraft, ship, etc.). □ **chartered accountant**, **engineer**, **librarian**, **surveyor**, etc. Brit. a member of a professional body that has a royal charter. **chartered libertine** a person allowed to do as he or she pleases. **charter flight** a flight by a chartered aircraft. **charter-member** an original member of a society, corporation, etc. **Great Charter** = MAGNA CARTA. □□ **charterer** n. [ME f. OF chartre f. L chartula dimin. of charta CARD¹]

charter-party /'tʃɑːtəˌpɑːtɪ/ n. (pl. **-ies**) a deed between a ship-owner and a merchant for the hire of a ship and the delivery of cargo. [F charte partie f. med.L charta partita divided charter, indenture]

Chartism /'tʃɑːtɪz(ə)m/ n. hist. the principles of the popular movement in Britain for electoral and social reform, 1837–48, whose principles were set out in a manifesto called The People's Charter. □□ **Chartist** n. [L charta charter + -ISM]

Chartres /ʃɑːtr/ a city in NW France, noted for its fine Gothic cathedral (mid-13th c.); pop. (1982) 36,700.

chartreuse /ʃɑːˈtrɜːz/ n. **1** a pale green or yellow liqueur of brandy and aromatic herbs etc. **2** the pale yellow or pale green colour of this. **3** a dish of fruit enclosed in jelly etc. [La Grande Chartreuse (Carthusian monastery near Grenoble)]

charwoman /'tʃɑːˌwʊmən/ n. (pl. **-women**) a woman employed as a cleaner in houses or offices.

chary /'tʃeərɪ/ adj. (**charier**, **chariest**) **1** cautious, wary (chary of employing such people). **2** sparing; ungenerous (chary of giving praise). **3** shy. □□ **charily** adv. **chariness** n. [OE cearig]

Charybdis /kəˈrɪbdɪs/ Gk legend a dangerous whirlpool in a narrow channel of the sea (later identified with the Strait of Messina, where there is no whirlpool), opposite the cave of Scylla.

Chas. abbr. Charles.

chase¹ /tʃeɪs/ v. & n. —v. **1** tr. pursue in order to catch. **2** tr. (foll. by from, out of, to, etc.) drive. **3** intr. **a** (foll. by after) hurry in pursuit of (a person). **b** (foll. by round etc.) colloq. act or move about hurriedly. **4** tr. (usu. foll. by up) colloq. pursue (overdue work, payment, etc. or the person responsible for it). **5** tr. colloq. **a** try to attain. **b** court persistently and openly. —n. **1** pursuit. **2** unenclosed hunting-land. **3** (prec. by the) hunting, esp. as a sport. **4** an animal etc. that is pursued. **5** = STEEPLECHASE. □ **go and chase oneself** (usu. in imper.) colloq. depart. [ME f. OF chace chacier, ult. f. L capere take]

chase² /tʃeɪs/ v.tr. emboss or engrave (metal). [app. f. earlier enchase f. F enchâsser (as EN-¹, CASE²)]

chase³ /tʃeɪs/ n. Printing a metal frame holding composed type. [F châsse f. L capsa CASE²]

chase⁴ /tʃeɪs/ n. **1** the part of a gun enclosing the bore. **2** a trench or groove cut to receive a pipe etc. [F chas enclosed space f. Prov. ca(u)s f. med.L capsum thorax]

chaser /'tʃeɪsə(r)/ n. **1** a person or thing that chases. **2** a horse for steeplechasing. **3** colloq. a drink taken after another of a different kind, e.g. beer after spirits. **4** US colloq. an amorous pursuer of women.

Chasid, Chasidism varr. of HASID, HASIDISM.

chasm /'kæz(ə)m/ n. **1** a deep fissure or opening in the earth, rock, etc. **2** a wide difference of feeling, interests, etc.; a gulf. **3**

archaic a hiatus. □□ **chasmic** adj. [L chasma f. Gk khasma gaping hollow]

chasse /ʃɑːs/ n. a liqueur taken after coffee etc. [F f. chasser CHASE¹]

chassé /'ʃæseɪ/ n. & v. —n. a gliding step in dancing. —v.intr. (**chasséd**; **chasséing**) make this step. [F, = chasing]

chassis /'ʃæsɪ/ n. (pl. same /-sɪz/) **1** the base-frame of a motor vehicle, carriage, etc. **2** a frame to carry radio etc. components. [F châssis ult. f. L capsa CASE²]

chaste /tʃeɪst/ adj. **1** abstaining from extramarital, or from all, sexual intercourse. **2** (of behaviour, speech, etc.) pure, virtuous, decent. **3** (of artistic etc. style) simple, unadorned. □ **chaste-tree** an ornamental shrub, Vitex agnus-castus, with blue or white flowers. □□ **chastely** adv. **chasteness** n. [ME f. OF f. L castus]

chasten /'tʃeɪs(ə)n/ v.tr. **1** (esp. as **chastening**, **chastened** adjs.) subdue, restrain (a chastening experience; chastened by his failure). **2** discipline, punish. **3** moderate. □□ **chastener** n. [obs. chaste (v.) f. OF chastier f. L castigare CASTIGATE]

chastise /tʃæsˈtaɪz/ v.tr. **1** rebuke or reprimand severely. **2** punish, esp. by beating. □□ **chastisement** n. **chastiser** n. [ME, app. irreg. formed f. obs. verbs chaste, chasty: see CHASTEN]

chastity /'tʃæstɪtɪ/ n. **1** being chaste. **2** sexual abstinence; virginity. **3** simplicity of style or taste. □ **chastity belt** hist. a garment designed to prevent a woman from having sexual intercourse. [ME f. OF chasteté f. L castitas -tatis f. castus CHASTE]

chasuble /'tʃæzjʊb(ə)l/ n. a loose sleeveless usu. ornate outer vestment worn by a priest celebrating Mass or the Eucharist. [ME f. OF chesible, later -uble, ult. f. L casula hooded cloak, little cottage, dimin. of casa cottage]

chat¹ /tʃæt/ v. & n. —v.intr. (**chatted**, **chatting**) talk in a light familiar way. —n. **1** informal conversation or talk. **2** an instance of this. □ **chat show** Brit. a television or radio programme in which celebrities are interviewed informally. **chat up** Brit. colloq. chat to, esp. flirtatiously or with an ulterior motive. [ME: shortening of CHATTER]

chat² /tʃæt/ n. any of various small birds with harsh calls, esp. a stonechat or whinchat or any of certain American or Australian warblers. [prob. imit.]

château /'ʃætəʊ/ n. (pl. **châteaux** /-təʊz/) a large French country house or castle, often giving its name to wine made in its neighbourhood. [F f. OF chastel CASTLE]

Chateaubriand /ˌʃætəʊbriˈɑ̃/, François-René, Vicomte de (1768–1848), French writer and diplomat, a major figure of early French romanticism. The Revolution interrupted his career and in 1791 he travelled to America, returning in 1792 to fight with the Royalists. Between 1793 and 1800 he lived in exile in England where he published his Essai sur les révolutions (1797). His literary reputation was established with Atala (1801) but he won great celebrity with Le Génie du Christianisme (1802), a work of Christian apologetics which contributed to the post-revolution religious revival in France. His political career began with the restoration of Louis XVIII—as a minister at Ghent, then as ambassador in London (1822). Mémoires d'outre-tombe (1849–50), considered a masterpiece, gives an eloquent account of the author's life against the background of political upheaval.

chateaubriand /ˌʃætəʊˈbriːɑ̃/ n. a thick fillet of beef steak. CHATEAUBRIAND]

chatelaine /'ʃætəˌleɪn/ n. **1** the mistress of a large house. **2** hist. a set of short chains attached to a woman's belt, for carrying keys etc. [F châtelaine, fem. of -ain lord of a castle, f. med.L castellanus CASTELLAN]

Chatham /'tʃætəm/, 1st Earl of, see PITT¹.

Chatham Islands /'tʃætəm/ an island group comprising the islands of Pitt and Chatham, situated in the SW Pacific Ocean to the east of New Zealand.

chattel /'tʃæt(ə)l/ n. (usu. in pl.) a moveable possession; any possession or piece of property other than real estate or a freehold. □ **chattel mortgage** US the conveyance of chattels by mortgage as security for a debt. **goods and chattels** personal possessions. [ME f. OF chatel: see CATTLE]

chatter /'tʃætə(r)/ v. & n. —v.intr. **1** talk quickly, incessantly, trivially, or indiscreetly. **2** (of a bird) emit short quick notes. **3** (of the teeth) click repeatedly together (usu. from cold). **4** (of a tool) clatter from vibration. —*n.* **1** chattering talk or sounds. **2** the vibration of a tool. □□ **chatterer** *n.* **chattery** *adj.* [ME: imit.]

chatterbox /ˈtʃætəˌbɒks/ *n.* a talkative person.

Chatterton /ˈtʃætət(ə)n/, Thomas (1753–70), English poet with a precocious literary talent, chiefly remembered for his fabricated poems purported to be the work of Thomas Rowley, an imaginary 15th-c. monk. Poverty and lack of recognition drove him to suicide at the age of 17. The Rowley poems were first published in 1777 by Thomas Tyrwhitt and controversy about their authenticity continued until Skeat proved them to be spurious in his 1871 edition. Chatterton's tragic life had a powerful effect on the Romantic poets who followed.

chatty /ˈtʃætɪ/ *adj.* (**chattier, chattiest**) **1** fond of chatting; talkative. **2** resembling chat; informal and lively (*a chatty letter*). □□ **chattily** *adv.* **chattiness** *n.*

Chaucer /ˈtʃɔːsə(r)/, Geoffrey (c.1342–1400), English poet, son of a London vintner. He held various positions at court and in the Customs service, and travelled to Europe on numerous diplomatic missions during which he may have met Boccaccio and Petrarch. He enjoyed the patronage of John of Gaunt (to whom he was related by marriage) and received pensions from Richard II and Henry IV. Chaucer translated part of the French poem, *Le Roman de la Rose*; his *The Book of the Duchess* (c.1370) was perhaps influenced by Dante's *Divine Comedy*. These poems, and *The Parliament of Fowls* (c.1380) are in the European dream allegory tradition; *Troilus and Criseyde* (1385) was based on Boccaccio's *Il Filostrato*. His best-known work, *The Canterbury Tales* (begun 1387), is a cycle of linked tales told by a group of pilgrims (ranging from Knight to Plowman, all vividly introduced in *The Prologue*) who meet in Southwark in London before their pilgrimage to Canterbury. Chaucer helped to establish the East Midland dialect of Middle English as the fully developed English literary language; many regard his work as the starting-point of English literature. He is buried in Poets' Corner in Westminster Abbey.

Chaucerian /tʃɔːˈsɪərɪən/ *adj.* & *n.* —*adj.* of or relating to the English poet Chaucer or his style. —*n.* a student of Chaucer.

chaud-froid /ʃəʊˈfrwɑː/ *n.* a dish of cold cooked meat or fish in jelly or sauce. [F f. *chaud* hot + *froid* cold]

chauffeur /ˈʃəʊfə(r), -ˈfɜː(r)/ *n.* & *v.* —*n.* (*fem.* **chauffeuse** /-ˈfɜːz/) a person employed to drive a private or hired motor car. —*v.tr.* drive (a car or a person) as a chauffeur. [F, = stoker]

chaulmoogra /tʃɔːlˈmuːɡrə/ *n.* any tree of the genus *Hydnocarpus*, esp. *H. wightiana*, with seeds yielding an oil formerly used in the treatment of leprosy. [Bengali]

chautauqua /tʃɔːˈtɔːkwə, ʃɔː-/ *n.* US a summer school or similar educational course. [*Chautauqua* in New York State]

chauvinism /ˈʃəʊvɪ,nɪz(ə)m/ *n.* **1** exaggerated or aggressive patriotism. **2** excessive or prejudiced support or loyalty for one's cause or group or sex (*male chauvinism*). [*Chauvin*, a Napoleonic veteran in the Cogniards' *Cocarde Tricolore* (1831)]

chauvinist /ˈʃəʊvɪnɪst/ *n.* **1** a person exhibiting chauvinism. **2** (in full **male chauvinist**) a man showing excessive loyalty to men and prejudice against women. □□ **chauvinistic** /-ˈnɪstɪk/ *adj.* **chauvinistically** /-ˈnɪstɪkəlɪ/ *adv.*

Ch.B. *abbr.* Bachelor of Surgery. [L *Chirurgiae Baccalaureus*]

cheap /tʃiːp/ *adj.* & *adv.* —*adj.* **1** low in price; worth more than its cost (*a cheap holiday; cheap labour*). **2** charging low prices; offering good value (*a cheap restaurant*). **3** of poor quality; inferior (*cheap housing*). **4 a** costing little effort or acquired by discreditable means and hence of little worth (*cheap popularity; a cheap joke*). **b** contemptible; despicable (*a cheap criminal*). —*adv.* cheaply (*got it cheap*). □ **cheap and nasty** of low cost and bad quality. **dirt cheap** very cheap. **feel cheap** feel ashamed or contemptible. **on the cheap** cheaply. □□ **cheapish** *adj.* **cheaply** *adv.* **cheapness** *n.* [obs. phr. *good cheap* f. *cheap* a bargain f. OE *cēap* barter, ult. f. L *caupo* innkeeper]

cheapen /ˈtʃiːpən/ *v.tr.* & *intr.* make or become cheap or cheaper; depreciate, degrade.

cheapjack /ˈtʃiːpdʒæk/ *n.* & *adj.* —*n.* a seller of inferior goods at low prices. —*adj.* inferior, shoddy. [CHEAP + JACK¹]

cheapo /ˈtʃiːpəʊ/ *attrib.adj. sl.* cheap.

cheapskate /ˈtʃiːpskeɪt/ *n.* esp. US *colloq.* a mean or contemptible person.

cheat /tʃiːt/ *v.* & *n.* —*v.* **1** *tr.* **a** (often foll. by *into, out of*) deceive or trick (*cheated into parting with his savings*). **b** (foll. by *of*) deprive of (*cheated of a chance to reply*). **2** *intr.* gain unfair advantage by deception or breaking rules, esp. in a game or examination. **3** *tr.* avoid (something undesirable) by luck or skill (*cheated the bad weather*). **4** *tr. archaic* divert attention from, beguile (time, tedium, etc.). —*n.* **1** a person who cheats. **2** a trick, fraud, or deception. **3** an act of cheating. □ **cheat on** *colloq.* be sexually unfaithful to. □□ **cheatingly** *adv.* [ME *chete* f. *achete*, var. of ESCHEAT]

cheater /ˈtʃiːtə(r)/ *n.* **1** a person who cheats. **2** (in *pl.*) US *sl.* spectacles.

check¹ /tʃek/ *v., n.,* & *int.* —*v.* **1** *tr.* (also *absol.*) **a** examine the accuracy, quality, or condition of. **b** (often foll. by *that* + clause) make sure; verify; establish to one's satisfaction (*checked that the doors were locked; checked the train times*). **2** *tr.* **a** stop or slow the motion of; curb, restrain (*progress was checked by bad weather*). **b** *colloq.* find fault with; rebuke. **3** *tr. Chess* move a piece into a position that directly threatens (the opposing king). **4** *intr.* US agree or correspond when compared. **5** *tr.* US mark with a tick etc. **6** *tr.* US deposit (luggage etc.) for storage or dispatch. **7** *intr.* (of hounds) pause to ensure or regain scent. —*n.* **1** a means or act of testing or ensuring accuracy, quality, satisfactory condition, etc. **2 a** a stopping or slowing of motion; a restraint on action. **b** a rebuff or rebuke. **c** a person or thing that restrains. **3** *Chess* (also as *int.*) **a** the exposure of a king to direct attack from an opposing piece. **b** an announcement of this by the attacking player. **4** US a bill in a restaurant. **5** esp. US a token of identification for left luggage etc. **6** US *Cards* a counter used in various games. **7** a temporary loss of the scent in hunting. **8** a crack or flaw in timber. —*int.* US expressing assent or agreement. □ **check in 1** arrive or register at a hotel, airport, etc. **2** record the arrival of. **check-in** *n.* the act or place of checking in. **check into** register one's arrival at (a hotel etc.). **check-list** a list for reference and verification. **check-nut** = *lock-nut.* **check off** mark on a list etc. as having been examined or dealt with. **check on** examine carefully or in detail; ascertain the truth about; keep a watch on (a person, work done, etc.). **check out 1** (often foll. by *of*) leave a hotel etc. with due formalities. **2** US investigate; examine for authenticity or suitability. **check over** examine for errors; verify. **check-rein** a rein attaching one horse's rein to another's bit, or preventing a horse from lowering its head. **check through** inspect or examine exhaustively; verify successive items of. **check up** ascertain, verify, make sure. **check-up** *n.* a thorough (esp. medical) examination. **check up on** = *check on.* **check-valve** a valve allowing flow in one direction only. **in check** under control, restrained. □□ **checkable** *adj.* [ME f. OF *eschequier* play chess, give check to, and OF *eschec*, ult. f. Pers. šāh king]

check² /tʃek/ *n.* **1** a pattern of small squares. **2** fabric having this pattern. [ME, prob. f. CHEQUER]

check³ US var. of CHEQUE.

checked /tʃekt/ *adj.* having a check pattern.

checker¹ /ˈtʃekə(r)/ *n.* **1** a person or thing that verifies or examines, esp. in a factory etc. **2** US a cashier in a supermarket etc.

checker² /ˈtʃekə(r)/ *n.* **1** var. of CHEQUER. **2** US **a** (in *pl.*, usu. treated as *sing.*) the game of draughts. **b** = CHECKERMAN.

checkerberry /ˈtʃekəbərɪ/ *n.* (*pl.* **-ies**) **1** a wintergreen, *Gaultheria procumbens*. **2** the fruit of this plant. [*checkers* berries of service-tree]

checkerboard /ˈtʃekəˌbɔːd/ *n.* US = DRAUGHTBOARD.

checkerman /ˈtʃekəˌmæn/ *n.* (*pl.* **-men**) each of the 'men' in a game of draughts.

checking account /ˈtʃekɪŋ/ *n.* US a current account at a bank. [CHECK³]

checkmate /ˈtʃekmeɪt/ *n.* & *v.* —*n.* **1** (also as *int.*) Chess **a** check from which a king cannot escape. **b** an announcement of this. **2** a final defeat or deadlock. —*v.tr.* **1** Chess put into checkmate. **2** defeat; frustrate. [ME f. OF *eschec mat* f. Pers. šāh māt the king is dead]

checkout /'tʃekaʊt/ n. **1** an act of checking out. **2** a point at which goods are paid for in a supermarket etc.

checkpoint /'tʃekpɔɪnt/ n. a place, esp. a barrier or manned entrance, where documents, vehicles, etc., are inspected.

checkroom /'tʃekruːm, -rʊm/ n. US **1** a cloakroom in a hotel or theatre. **2** an office for left luggage etc.

Cheddar /'tʃedə(r)/ n. a kind of firm smooth cheese orig. made in Cheddar in Somerset.

cheek /tʃiːk/ n. & v. —n. **1 a** the side of the face below the eye. **b** the side-wall of the mouth. **2 a** impertinent speech. **b** impertinence; cool confidence (had the cheek to ask for more). **3** sl. either buttock. **4 a** either of the side-posts of a door etc. **b** either of the jaws of a vice. **c** either of the side-pieces of various parts of machines arranged in lateral pairs. —v.tr. speak impertinently to. □ **cheek-bone** the bone below the eye. **cheek by jowl** close together; intimate. **turn the other cheek** accept attack etc. meekly; refuse to retaliate. [OE cē(a)ce, cēoce]

cheeky /'tʃiːkɪ/ adj. (**cheekier, cheekiest**) impertinent, impudent. □□ **cheekily** adv. **cheekiness** n.

cheep /tʃiːp/ n. & v. —n. the weak shrill cry of a young bird. —v.intr. make such a cry. [imit.: cf. PEEP²]

cheer /'tʃɪə(r)/ n. & v. —n. **1** a shout of encouragement or applause. **2** mood, disposition (full of good cheer). **3** (in pl.; as int.) Brit. colloq. **a** expressing good wishes on parting or before drinking. **b** expressing gratitude. —v. **1** tr. **a** applaud with shouts. **b** (usu. foll. by on) urge or encourage with shouts. **2** intr. shout for joy. **3** tr. gladden; comfort. □ **cheer-leader** a person who leads cheers of applause etc. **cheer up** make or become less depressed. **three cheers** three successive hurrahs for a person or thing honoured. [ME f. AF chere face etc., OF chiere f. LL cara face f. Gk kara head]

cheerful /'tʃɪəfʊl/ adj. **1** in good spirits, noticeably happy (a cheerful disposition). **2** bright, pleasant (a cheerful room). **3** willing, not reluctant. □□ **cheerfully** adv. **cheerfulness** n.

cheerio /ˌtʃɪrɪ'əʊ/ int. Brit. colloq. expressing good wishes on parting or before drinking.

cheerless /'tʃɪəlɪs/ adj. gloomy, dreary, miserable. □□ **cheerlessly** adv. **cheerlessness** n.

cheerly /'tʃɪəlɪ/ adv. & adj. —adv. esp. Naut. heartily, with a will. —adj. archaic cheerful.

cheery /'tʃɪərɪ/ adj. (**cheerier, cheeriest**) lively; in good spirits; genial, cheering. □□ **cheerily** adv. **cheeriness** n.

cheese¹ /tʃiːz/ n. **1 a** a food made from the pressed curds of milk. **b** a complete cake of this with rind. **2** a conserve having the consistency of soft cheese (lemon cheese). **3** a round flat object, e.g. the heavy flat wooden disc used in skittles. □ **cheese-cutter 1** a knife with a broad curved blade. **2** a device for cutting cheese by pulling a wire through it. **cheese-fly** (pl. **-flies**) a small black fly, Piophila casei, breeding in cheese. **cheese-head** the squat cylindrical head of a screw etc. **cheese-mite** any mite of the genus Tyroglyphus feeding on cheese. **cheese-paring** adj. stingy. —n. stinginess. **cheese plant** = Swiss cheese plant. **cheese-skipper** = cheese-fly. **cheese straw** a thin cheese-flavoured strip of pastry. **hard cheese** sl. bad luck. [OE cēse etc. ult. f. L caseus]

cheese² /tʃiːz/ v.tr. Brit. sl. (as **cheesed** adj.) (often foll. by off) bored, fed up. □ **cheese it** stop it, leave off. [19th c.: orig. unkn.]

cheese³ /tʃiːz/ n. (also **big cheese**) sl. an important person. [perh. f. Hind. chīz thing]

cheeseboard /'tʃiːzbɔːd/ n. **1** a board from which cheese is served. **2** a selection of cheeses.

cheeseburger /'tʃiːzˌbɜːgə(r)/ n. a hamburger with cheese in or on it.

cheesecake /'tʃiːzkeɪk/ n. **1** a tart filled with sweetened curds etc. **2** sl. the portrayal of women in a sexually attractive manner.

cheesecloth /'tʃiːzklɒθ/ n. thin loosely woven cloth, used orig. for wrapping cheese.

cheesemonger /'tʃiːzˌmʌŋgə(r)/ n. a dealer in cheese, butter, etc.

cheesewood /'tʃiːzwʊd/ n. **1** an Australian tree of the genus Pittosporum. **2** its hard yellowish wood.

cheesy /'tʃiːzɪ/ adj. (**cheesier, cheesiest**) **1** like cheese in taste, smell, appearance, etc. **2** sl. inferior; cheap and nasty. □□ **cheesiness** n.

cheetah /'tʃiːtə/ n. a swift-running feline, Acinonyx jubatus, with a leopard-like spotted coat. [Hindi cītā, perh. f. Skr. citraka speckled]

chef /ʃef/ n. a (usu. male) cook, esp. the chief cook in a restaurant etc. [F, = head]

chef-d'œuvre /ʃeɪ'dɜːvr/ n. (pl. **chefs-d'œuvre** pronunc. same) a masterpiece. [F]

cheiro- comb. form var. of CHIRO-.

Cheka /'tʃekə/ n. an organization, set up in 1917 under the Soviet regime, for the investigation of counter-revolutionary activities. Lenin had always envisaged the need for terror to protect his revolution, and this was its purpose. Under its first head, Dzerzhinsky, it helped to stabilize Lenin's regime by removing real and alleged enemies of the Soviet State; its headquarters, the Lubyanka prison in Moscow, contained offices and places for torture and execution. In 1922 the Cheka was abolished and immediately replaced by the GPU, later retitled the Ogpu (see entry). [Russ. abbr., = Extraordinary Commission (for combating counter-revolution, sabotage, and speculation)]

Chekhov /'tʃekɒf/, Anton Pavlovich (1860–1904), Russian dramatist and short-story writer, who studied medicine in Moscow where he began writing short humorous stories for journals. His first successful play was Ivanov (1887) but his status rests on his four later plays, The Seagull (1895), Uncle Vanya (1900), The Three Sisters (1901), and The Cherry Orchard (1904). These productions established the reputation and style of the Moscow Arts Theatre, of which Stanislavsky was a co-founder; in 1901 Chekhov married Olga Knipper, an actress at the theatre. In his revolutionary form of drama, using innovative idiomatic dialogue where communication between characters can convey non-communication, and where the smallest surface details can adopt a symbolic significance, Chekhov had an immense influence on 20th-c. drama. Shaw paid tribute to him in Heartbreak House.

Chekiang see ZHEJIANG.

chela¹ /'kiːlə/ n. (pl. **chelae** /-liː/) a prehensile claw of crabs, lobsters, scorpions, etc. [mod.L f. L chele, or Gk khēlē claw]

chela² /'tʃeɪlə/ n. **1** (in esoteric Buddhism) a novice qualifying for initiation. **2** a disciple; a pupil. [Hindi, = servant]

chelate- /'kiːleɪt/ n., adj., & v. —n. Chem. a usu. organometallic compound containing a bonded ring of atoms including a metal atom. —adj. **1** Chem. of a chelate. **2** Zool. & Anat. of or having chelae. —v.intr. Chem. form a chelate. □□ **chelation** /-'leɪʃ(ə)n/ n.

Chellean /'ʃelɪən/ adj. Archaeol. = ABBEVILLIAN. [F chelléen f. Chelles near Paris]

chelonian /kɪ'ləʊnɪən/ n. & adj. —n. any reptile of the order Chelonia, including turtles, terrapins, and tortoises, having a shell of bony plates covered with horny scales. —adj. of or relating to this order. [mod.L Chelonia f. Gk khelōnē tortoise]

Chelsea bun /'tʃelsɪ/ n. a kind of currant bun in the form of a flat spiral. [Chelsea in London]

Chelsea pensioner /'tʃelsɪ/ n. an inmate of the Chelsea Royal Hospital for old or disabled soldiers.

Chelsea ware /'tʃelsɪ/ n. any of various soft-paste porcelains made at Chelsea in the 18th c.

Chelyabinsk /ˌtʃel'jæbɪnsk/ a Soviet industrial city on the eastern slopes of the Ural Mountains in western Siberia; pop. (est. 1987) 1,119,000.

chemi- comb. form var. of CHEMO-.

chemical /'kemɪk(ə)l/ adj. & n. —adj. of, made by, or employing chemistry or chemicals. —n. a substance obtained or used in chemistry. □ **chemical bond** the force holding atoms together in a molecule or crystal. **chemical engineer** one engaged in chemical engineering, esp. professionally. **chemical engineering** the design, manufacture, and operation of industrial chemical plants. **chemical reaction** a process that involves change in the structure of atoms, molecules, or ions. **chemical warfare** warfare using poison gas and other chemicals. **fine chemicals** chemicals of high purity usu. used in small amounts.

heavy chemicals bulk chemicals used in industry and agriculture. □□ **chemically** adv. [chemic alchemic f. F chimique or mod.L chimicus, chymicus, f. med.L alchymicus: see ALCHEMY]

chemico- /ˈkemɪkəʊ/ comb. form chemical; chemical and (chemico-physical).

chemiluminescence /ˌkemɪˌluːmɪˈnes(ə)ns, -ˌljuːmɪˈnes(ə)ns/ n. the emission of light during a chemical reaction. □□ **chemiluminescent** adj. [G Chemilumineszenz (as CHEMI-, LUMINESCENCE)]

chemin de fer /ʃəˌmæ̃ də ˈfeə(r)/ n. a form of baccarat. [F, = railway, lit. road of iron]

chemise /ʃəˈmiːz/ n. hist. a woman's loose-fitting under-garment or dress hanging straight from the shoulders. [ME f. OF f. LL camisia shirt]

chemisorption /ˌkemɪˈsɔːpʃ(ə)n/ n. adsorption by chemical bonding. [CHEMI- + ADSORPTION (see ADSORB)]

chemist /ˈkemɪst/ n. 1 Brit. **a** a dealer in medicinal drugs, usu. also selling other medical goods and toiletries. **b** an authorized dispenser of medicines. 2 a person practising or trained in chemistry. [earlier chymist f. F chimiste f. mod.L chimista f. alchimista ALCHEMIST (see ALCHEMY)]

chemistry /ˈkemɪstrɪ/ n. (pl. -ies) 1 the study of the elements and the compounds they form and the reactions they undergo. 2 any complex (esp. emotional) change or process (the chemistry of fear). 3 colloq. a person's personality or temperament.

Chemnitz /ˈkemnɪts/ an industrial city of SE Germany, on the Chemnitz River, called Karl-Marx-Stadt from 1953 until the reunification of Germany in 1990; pop. (est. 1990) 310,000.

chemo- /ˈkiːməʊ/ comb. form (also **chemi-** /ˈkemɪ/) chemical.

chemosynthesis /ˌkiːməˈsɪnθɪsɪs/ n. the synthesis of organic compounds by energy derived from chemical reactions.

chemotherapy /ˌkiːməˈθerəpɪ/ n. the treatment of disease, esp. cancer, by use of chemical substances. □□ **chemotherapist** n.

chemurgy /ˈkemɜːdʒɪ/ n. US the chemical and industrial use of organic raw materials. □□ **chemurgic** /-ˈmɜːdʒɪk/ adj. [CHEMO-, after metallurgy]

Chenab /tʃɪˈnæb/ a river of northern India that rises in the Himalayas and flows through Himachal Pradesh and Jammu and Kashmir to join the Sutlej River (in Punjab) to become the Panjnad. It is one of the 'five rivers' that gave Punjab its name.

Chengchow see ZHENGZHOU.

Chengdu /tʃeŋˈduː/ the capital of Sichuan province in central China; pop. (est. 1986) 2,580,000.

chenille /ʃəˈniːl/ n. 1 a tufty velvety cord or yarn, used in trimming furniture etc. 2 fabric made from this. [F, = hairy caterpillar f. L canicula dimin. of canis dog]

cheongsam /tʃɪɒŋˈsæm/ n. a Chinese woman's garment with a high neck and slit skirt. [Chin.]

Cheops /ˈkiːɒps/ = KHUFU.

cheque /tʃek/ n. (US **check**) 1 a written order to a bank to pay the stated sum from the drawer's account. 2 the printed form on which such an order is written. □ **cheque-book** a book of forms for writing cheques. **cheque-book journalism** the payment of large sums for exclusive rights to material for (esp. personal) newspaper stories. **cheque card** a card issued by a bank to guarantee the honouring of cheques up to a stated amount. [special use of CHECK¹ to mean 'device for checking the amount of an item']

chequer /ˈtʃekə(r)/ n. & v. (also **checker**) —n. 1 (often in pl.) a pattern of squares often alternately coloured. 2 (in pl.) (usu. as **checkers**) US the game of draughts. —v.tr. 1 mark with chequers. 2 variegate; break the uniformity of. 3 (as **chequered** adj.) with varied fortunes (a chequered career). □ **chequer-board** 1 a chessboard. 2 a pattern resembling it. [ME f. EXCHEQUER]

Chequers /ˈtʃekəz/ a Tudor mansion in the Chilterns near Princes Risborough, Bucks., presented to the British nation in 1917 by Lord and Lady Lee of Fareham to serve as a country seat of the Prime Minister in office.

Cher /ʃeə(r)/ a river of central France that rises in the Massif Central and flows 350 km (220 miles) northwards to meet the Loire near Tours.

Cherbourg /ˈʃɜːbʊəg, ˈfeə-/ a seaport and naval base on the Normandy coast of NW France; pop. (1982) 40,500.

Cherenkov radiation var. of CERENKOV RADIATION.

cherish /ˈtʃerɪʃ/ v.tr. 1 protect or tend (a child, plant, etc.) lovingly. 2 hold dear, cling to (hopes, feelings, etc.). [ME f. OF cherir f. cher f. L carus dear]

Chernobyl /tʃəˈnɒbɪl, -ˈnəʊbɪl/ a city near Kiev in Ukraine in the USSR, where in April 1986 explosions at a nuclear power station resulted in a serious escape of radioactivity which spread in the atmosphere to a number of countries of Europe.

chernozem /ˈtʃɜːnəʊˌzem/ n. a fertile black soil rich in humus, found in temperate regions, esp. S. Russia. Also called black earth. [Russ. f. chernyĭ black + zemlya earth]

Cherokee /ˈtʃerəkɪ/ n. & adj. —n. 1 **a** an American Indian tribe formerly inhabiting much of the southern US. **b** a member of this tribe. 2 the language of this tribe. —adj. of or relating to the Cherokees or their language. □ **Cherokee rose** a fragrant white rose, Rosa laevigata, of the southern US. [Cherokee Tsálāgî]

cheroot /ʃəˈruːt/ n. a cigar with both ends open. [F cheroute f. Tamil shuruṭṭu roll]

cherry /ˈtʃerɪ/ n. & adj. —n. (pl. -ies) 1 **a** a small soft round stone-fruit. **b** any of several trees of the genus Prunus bearing this or grown for its ornamental flowers. 2 (in full **cherry wood**) the wood of a cherry. 3 US sl. **a** virginity. **b** a virgin. —adj. of a light red colour. □ **cherry brandy** a dark-red liqueur of brandy in which cherries have been steeped. **cherry-laurel** Brit. a small evergreen tree, Prunus laurocerasus, with white flowers and cherry-like fruits. **cherry-picker** colloq. a crane for raising and lowering people. **cherry-pie 1** a pie made with cherries. 2 a garden heliotrope. **cherry plum 1** a tree, Prunus cerasifera, native to SW Asia, with solitary white flowers and red fruits. 2 the fruit of this tree. **cherry tomato** a miniature tomato with a strong flavour. [ME f. ONF cherise (taken as pl.: cf. PEA) f. med.L ceresia perh. f. L f. Gk kerasos]

chersonese /ˈkɜːsəˌniːs/ n. a peninsula, esp. (**Chersonese**) the ancient name for (i) the Thracian or Gallipoli peninsula on the north side of the Hellespont, (ii) the Crimea (the Tauric Chersonese). [L chersonesus f. Gk khersonēsos f. khersos dry + nēsos island]

chert /tʃɜːt/ n. a flintlike form of quartz composed of chalcedony. □□ **cherty** adj. [17th c.: orig. unkn.]

cherub /ˈtʃerəb/ n. 1 (pl. **cherubim** /-bɪm/) an angelic being of the second order of the celestial hierarchy. 2 **a** a representation of a winged child or the head of a winged child. **b** a beautiful or innocent child. □□ **cherubic** /tʃɪˈruːbɪk/ adj. **cherubically** /tʃɪˈruːbɪkəlɪ/ adv. [ME f. OE cherubin and f. Heb. kᵉrūḇ, pl. kᵉrūḇîm]

Cherubini /ˌkeruˈbiːnɪ/, Luigi (1760–1842), Italian composer. Born in Florence, he spent most of his composing career in Paris, where he discarded the Italian operatic style in his attempts to create a truer drama involving less artificial characters; in this he was following the lead of Gluck, and when he visited Vienna in 1805 he in his turn influenced Beethoven (especially in Fidelio). Cherubini's sacred music (including seven Masses and two Requiem Masses) is scrupulous in its attention to the demands of the words.

chervil /ˈtʃɜːvɪl/ n. an umbelliferous plant, Anthriscus cerefolium, with small white flowers, used as a herb for flavouring soup, salads, etc. [OE cerfille f. L chaerephylla f. Gk khairephullon]

Ches. abbr. Cheshire.

Chesapeake Bay /ˈtʃesəˌpiːk/ a large inlet of the Atlantic Ocean on the coast of the US, 320 km (200 miles) in length, bordering on Virginia and Maryland.

Cheshire¹ /ˈtʃeʃə(r)/ a north midlands county of England; pop. (1981) 932,400; county town, Chester. —n. a crumbly cheese originally made in Cheshire. □ **like a Cheshire cat,** with a broad fixed grin. The phrase was popularized through Lewis Carroll's Alice's Adventures in Wonderland (1865). Its origin is uncertain: suggested explanations include a reference to Cheshire cheeses made in the shape of a cat, or to the lion rampant on Cheshire inn-signs.

Cheshire² /ˈtʃeʃə(r)/, (Geoffrey) Leonard (1917–), British airman, who was awarded the VC in 1944 and later founded homes (named after him) for the disabled and incurably sick in 45 countries.

chess *n.* a game of skill played between two persons on a chequered board divided into 64 squares. Each player has 16 'men' (king, queen, 2 bishops, 2 knights, 2 castles or rooks, 8 pawns), which are moved according to strict rules in simulation of a battle where the object is to manœuvre the opponent's king into a position (*checkmate*) from which escape is impossible. Many moves are named after the great players who originated them. The game seems to be a descendant (5th c.) of an earlier Indian game and to have reached Persia and Arab countries and spread thence until by the 13th c. it was known all over western Europe. [ME f. OF *esches*, pl. of *eschec* (CHECK¹); in medieval Latin the game was called *scacci*, but Spanish and Portuguese preserved the Arabic name *chat-ranj* f. Skr. *chaturanga*, = the four *angas* or members of an army (elephants, horses, chariots, foot-soldiers)]

chessboard /ˈtʃesbɔːd/ *n.* a chequered board of 64 squares on which chess and draughts are played.

chessman /ˈtʃesmæn/ *n.* (*pl.* **-men**) any of the 32 pieces and pawns with which chess is played.

chest /tʃest/ *n.* 1 a large strong box, esp. for storage or transport e.g. of blankets, tea, etc. 2 a the part of a human or animal body enclosed by the ribs. b the front surface of the body from neck to waist. 3 a small cabinet for medicines etc. 4 a the treasury or financial resources of an institution. b the money available from it. □ **chest of drawers** a piece of furniture consisting of a set of drawers in a frame. **chest-voice** the lowest register of the voice in singing or speaking. **get a thing off one's chest** *colloq.* disclose a fact, secret, etc., to relieve one's anxiety about it. **play (one's cards, a thing,** etc.) **close to one's chest** *colloq.* be cautious or secretive about. □□ **-chested** *adj.* (in *comb.*). [OE *cest*, *cyst* f. Gmc f. L f. Gk *kistē*]

Chester /ˈtʃestə(r)/ the county town of Cheshire; pop. (1981) 82,350.

chesterfield /ˈtʃestəˌfiːld/ *n.* 1 a sofa with arms and back of the same height and curved outwards at the top. 2 a man's plain overcoat usu. with a velvet collar. [19th-c. Earl of *Chesterfield*]

Chesterton /ˈtʃestət(ə)n/, Gilbert Keith (1874–1936), English essayist, novelist, and poet, who made his name in journalism. With Belloc he opposed the agnostic socialism of Wells and Shaw, praising the virtues of the Merry England of 'Beef and Beer'. His best-known novel is *The Napoleon of Notting Hill* (1904), but he is also widely remembered for his creation of detective priest Father Brown, who first appears in *The Innocence of Father Brown* (1911). Chesterton became a Roman Catholic in 1922.

chestnut /ˈtʃesnʌt/ *n.* & *adj.* —*n.* 1 a a glossy hard brown edible nut. b the tree *Castanea sativa*, bearing flowers in catkins and nuts enclosed in a spiny fruit. Also called *Spanish chestnut* or *sweet chestnut*. 2 any other tree of the genus *Castanea*. 3 = *horse chestnut*. 4 (in full **chestnut-wood**) the heavy wood of any chestnut tree. 5 a horse of a reddish-brown or yellowish-brown colour. 6 *colloq.* a stale joke or anecdote. 7 a small hard patch on a horse's leg. 8 a reddish-brown colour. —*adj.* of the colour chestnut. □ **liver chestnut** a dark kind of chestnut horse. [obs. *chesten* f. OF *chastaine* f. L *castanea* f. Gk *kastanea*]

chesty /ˈtʃesti/ *adj.* (**chestier**, **chestiest**) 1 *Brit. colloq.* inclined to or symptomatic of chest disease. 2 *colloq.* having a large chest or prominent breasts. 3 *US sl.* arrogant. □□ **chestily** *adv.* **chestiness** *n.*

chetnik /ˈtʃetnɪk/ *n. hist.* a member of a guerrilla force in the Balkans, especially the group led by Mihailovich during the Second World War. [Serbian *četnik* f. *četa* band, troop]

cheval-glass /ʃəˈvæl/ *n.* a tall mirror swung on an upright frame. [F *cheval* horse, frame]

Chevalier /ʃəˈvælˌeɪ/, Maurice (1888–1972), French singer and actor. He gained an international reputation in the Paris music halls of the 1920s before starring in successful Hollywood musicals such as *Love Me Tonight* (1932) and later in *Love in the Afternoon* (1957) and *Gigi* (1958).

chevalier /ʃeˈvælɪə(r)/ *n.* 1 a a member of certain orders of knighthood, and of modern French orders, as the Legion of Honour. b *archaic* or *hist.* a knight. 2 *hist.* the title of the Old and

Young Pretenders. 3 a chivalrous man; a cavalier. [ME f. AF *chevaler*, OF *chevalier* f. med.L *caballarius* f. L *caballus* horse]

chevet /ʃəˈveɪ/ *n.* the apsidal end of a church, sometimes with an attached group of apses. [F, = pillow, f. L *capitium* f. *caput* head]

Cheviot /ˈtʃeviət, ˈtʃiːv-/ *n.* 1 a a large sheep of a breed with short thick wool. b this breed. 2 (**cheviot**) the wool or cloth obtained from this breed. [CHEVIOT HILLS]

Cheviot Hills /ˈtʃeviət, ˈtʃiːv-/ (also **Cheviots**) a range of hills on the border between England and Scotland.

chèvre /ʃevr/ *n.* a variety of goat's-milk cheese. [F, = goat, she-goat]

chevron /ˈʃevrən/ *n.* 1 a badge in a V shape on the sleeve of a uniform indicating rank or length of service. 2 *Heraldry & Archit.* a bent bar of an inverted V shape. 3 any V-shaped line or stripe. [ME f. OF ult. f. L *caper* goat: cf. L *capreoli* pair of rafters]

chevrotain /ˈʃevrəˌteɪn/ (also **chevrotin** /-tɪn/) *n.* any small deerlike animal of the family Tragulidae, native to Africa and SE Asia, having small tusks. Also called *mouse deer*. [F, dimin. of OF *chevrot* dimin. of *chèvre* goat]

chevy var. of CHIVVY.

chew /tʃuː/ *v.* & *n.* —*v.tr.* (also *absol.*) work (food etc.) between the teeth; crush or indent with the teeth. —*n.* 1 an act of chewing. 2 something for chewing, esp. a chewy sweet. □ **chew the cud** reflect, ruminate. **chew the fat** (or **rag**) *sl.* 1 chat. 2 grumble. **chewing-gum** flavoured gum, esp. chicle, for chewing. **chew on** 1 work continuously between the teeth (*chewed on a piece of string*). 2 think about; meditate on. **chew out** *US colloq.* reprimand. **chew over** 1 discuss, talk over. 2 think about; meditate on. □□ **chewable** *adj.* **chewer** *n.* [OE *cēowan*]

chewy /ˈtʃuːɪ/ *adj.* (**chewier**, **chewiest**) 1 needing much chewing. 2 suitable for chewing. □□ **chewiness** *n.*

Cheyenne¹ /ʃaɪˈæn/ the capital of Wyoming; pop. (1980) 47,280.

Cheyenne² /ʃaɪˈæn/ *n.* & *adj.* —*n.* 1 a an American Indian tribe formerly living between the Missouri and Arkansas rivers. b a member of this tribe. 2 the language of this tribe. —*adj.* of or relating to the Cheyennes or their language. [Canadian F f. Dakota *Sahiyena*]

Cheyne–Stokes respiration /tʃeɪnˈstəʊks/ *n. Med.* (a breathing cycle with a gradual decrease of movement to a complete stop, followed by a gradual increase. [J. *Cheyne*, Sc. physician d. 1836, and W. *Stokes*, Ir. physician d. 1878]

chez /ʃeɪ/ *prep.* at the house or home of. [F f. OF *chiese* f. L *casa* cottage]

chi /kaɪ/ *n.* the twenty-second letter of the Greek alphabet (*X, χ*). □ **chi-rho** a monogram of chi and rho as the first two letters of Greek *Khristos* Christ. **chi-square test** a method of comparing observed and theoretical values in statistics. [ME f. Gk *khi*]

Chiang Kai-shek /ˌtʃjæŋ kaɪˈʃek/ (also **Jiang Jie Shi**, 1887–1975), Chinese leader who achieved military prominence as a general in the army of Sun Yat-sen, and after the latter's death in 1925 launched a campaign to unite China. In the 1930s he concentrated more on defeating the Chinese Communists than on resisting the invading Japanese, but despite his efforts he proved unable to establish order and was defeated by the Communists after the end of the Second World War. Forced to abandon mainland China in 1949, he set up a separate Nationalist Chinese State on Taiwan.

Chiangmai /dʒɪæŋˈmaɪ/ a city on the Ping River in NW Thailand, principal city of the region since 1296 when it was capital of the kingdom of Lan Na, powerful until the 16th c.; pop. (1980) 1,313,850.

Chianti /kɪˈæntɪ/ *n.* (*pl.* **Chiantis**) a dry red Italian wine. [*Chianti*, an area in Tuscany, Italy]

Chiapas /tʃɪˈɑːpəs/ a State of southern Mexico; pop. (est. 1988) 2,518,700; capital, Tuxtla Gutiérrez.

chiaroscuro /kɪˌɑːrəˈskʊərəʊ/ *n.* 1 the treatment of light and shade in drawing and painting. 2 the use of contrast in literature etc. 3 (*attrib.*) half-revealed. [It. f. *chiaro* CLEAR + *oscuro* dark, OBSCURE]

chiasma /kaɪˈæzmə/ *n.* (*pl.* **chiasmata** /-tə/) *Biol.* the point at which paired chromosomes remain in contact after crossing over during meiosis. [mod.L f. Gk *chiasma* a cross-shaped mark]

chiasmus /kaɪˈæzməs/ *n.* inversion in the second of two parallel phrases of the order followed in the first (e.g. *to stop too fearful and too faint to go*). □□ **chiastic** *adj.* [mod.L f. Gk *khiasmos* crosswise arrangement f. *khiazō* mark with letter CHI]

Chibcha /ˈtʃɪbtʃə/ *n. & adj.* —*n.* (*pl.* same) **1** a member of an Indian people of Colombia with an ancient civilization that was flourishing at the time the Spaniards first encountered them in 1537. **2** the language of this people. —*adj.* of the Chibcha or their language. □□ **Chibchan** *adj. & n.* [Sp.]

chibouk /tʃɪˈbuːk/ *n.* (also **chibouque**) a long Turkish tobacco-pipe. [Turk. *çubuk* tube]

chic /ʃiːk/ *adj. & n.* —*adj.* (**chic-er, chic-est**) stylish, elegant (in dress or appearance). —*n.* stylishness, elegance. □□ **chicly** *adv.* [F]

Chicago /ʃɪˈkɑːɡəʊ/ a city in Illinois, on Lake Michigan, the third-largest city of the US and the original home of the sky-scraper; pop. (1982) 2,997,155.

chicane /ʃɪˈkeɪn/ *n. & v.* —*n.* **1** chicanery. **2** an artificial barrier or obstacle on a motor racecourse. **3** *Bridge* a hand without trumps, or without cards of one suit. —*v. archaic* **1** *intr.* use chicanery. **2** *tr.* (usu. foll. by *into, out of*, etc.) cheat (a person). [F *chicane*(r) quibble]

chicanery /ʃɪˈkeɪnəri/ *n.* (*pl.* -**ies**) **1** clever but misleading talk; a false argument. **2** trickery, deception. [F *chicanerie* (as CHICANE)]

chicano /tʃɪˈkɑːnəʊ/ *n.* (*pl.* -**os**) *US* an American of Mexican origin. [Sp. *mejicano* Mexican]

Chichén Itzá /tʃiˈtʃen ɪtˈsɑː/ a site in northern Yucatán, Mexico, which was the centre of the Maya empire after AD 918, with elaborate ceremonial buildings centred on a sacred well.

Chichester /ˈtʃɪtʃɪstə(r)/, Sir Francis Charles (1901–72), English yachtsman, who in 1960 won the first solo transatlantic race in his yacht *Gipsy Moth III*, and in 1966–7 sailed alone round the world in *Gipsy Moth IV*, for which exploit he was knighted by Queen Elizabeth II on his return. His yachts were named after the Gipsy Moth aircraft in which he had made a solo flight to Australia in 1929.

chichi /ˈʃiːʃiː/ *adj. & n.* —*adj.* **1** (of a thing) frilly, showy. **2** (of a person or behaviour) fussy, affected. —*n.* **1** over-refinement, pretentiousness, fussiness. **2** a frilly, showy, or pretentious object. [F]

Chichimec /tʃiːtʃɪˈmek/ *n.* (*pl.* same) a member of a horde of invaders who entered the central valley of Mexico from the north west *c.*950–1300, and came to be known as the Toltec after the founding of their capital, Tula, in 968. In 1300 Chichimec farmers left their drought-stricken land and converged on Tula, contributing to its destruction. [Sp. f. Nahuatl]

chick[1] /tʃɪk/ *n.* **1** a young bird, esp. one newly hatched. **2** *sl.* **a** a young woman. **b** a child. [ME: shortening of CHICKEN]

chick[2] /tʃɪk/ *n. Ind.* a screen for a doorway etc., made from split bamboo and twine. [Hindi *chik*]

chickadee /ˈtʃɪkədiː/ *n. US* any of various small birds of the tit family, esp. *Parus atricapillus* with a distinctive dark-crowned head. [imit.]

chicken /ˈtʃɪkɪn/ *n., adj., & v.* —*n.* (*pl.* same or **chickens**) **1** a young bird of a domestic fowl. **2 a** a domestic fowl prepared as food. **b** its flesh. **3** a youthful person (usu. with *neg.*: *is no chicken*). **4** *colloq.* a children's pastime testing courage, usu. recklessly. —*adj. colloq.* cowardly. —*v.intr.* (foll. by *out*) *colloq.* withdraw from or fail in some activity through fear or lack of nerve. □ **chicken-and-egg problem** (or **dilemma** etc.) the unresolved question as to which of two things caused the other. **chicken brick** an earthenware container in two halves for roasting a chicken in its own juices. **chicken cholera** see CHOLERA. **chicken-feed 1** food for poultry. **2** *colloq.* an unimportant amount, esp. of money. **chicken-hearted** (or -**livered**) easily frightened; lacking nerve or courage. **chicken-wire** a light wire netting with a hexagonal mesh. [OE *cīcen, cȳcen* f. Gmc]

chickenpox /ˈtʃɪkɪnˌpɒks/ *n.* an infectious disease, esp. of children, with a rash of small blisters. Also called VARICELLA.

chick-pea /ˈtʃɪkpiː/ *n.* **1** a leguminous plant, *Cicer arietinum*, with short swollen pods containing yellow beaked seeds. **2** this seed used as a vegetable. [orig. *ciche pease* f. L *cicer*: see PEASE]

chickweed /ˈtʃɪkwiːd/ *n.* any of numerous small plants, esp. *Stellaria media*, a garden weed with slender stems and tiny white flowers.

chicle /ˈtʃɪk(ə)l, ˈtʃiːkliː/ *n.* the milky juice of the sapodilla tree, used in the manufacture of chewing-gum. [Amer. Sp. f. Nahuatl *tzictli*]

chicory /ˈtʃɪkəri/ *n.* (*pl.* -**ies**) **1** a blue flowered plant, *Cichorium intybus*, cultivated for its salad leaves and its root. **2** its root, roasted and ground for use with or instead of coffee. **3** *US* = ENDIVE. [ME f. obs. F *cicorée* endive f. med.L *cic(h)orea* f. L *cichorium* f. Gk *kikhorion* SUCCORY]

chide /tʃaɪd/ *v.tr. & intr.* (*past* **chided** or **chid** /tʃɪd/; *past part.* **chided** or **chidden** /ˈtʃɪd(ə)n/) *archaic* or *literary* scold, rebuke. □□ **chider** *n.* **chidingly** *adv.* [OE *cīdan*, of unkn. orig.]

chief /tʃiːf/ *n. & adj.* —*n.* **1 a** a leader or ruler. **b** the head of a tribe, clan, etc. **2** the head of a department; the highest official. **3** *Heraldry* the upper third of a shield. —*adj.* (usu. *attrib.*) **1** first in position, importance, influence, etc. (*chief engineer*). **2** prominent, leading. □ **Chief of Staff** the senior staff officer of a service or command. -**in-Chief** supreme (*Commander-in-Chief*). □□ **chiefdom** *n.* [ME f. OF *ch(i)ef* ult. f. L *caput* head]

chiefly /ˈtʃiːfli/ *adv.* above all; mainly but not exclusively.

chieftain /ˈtʃiːft(ə)n/ *n.* (*fem.* **chieftainess** /-nɪs/) the leader of a tribe, clan, etc. □□ **chieftaincy** /-sɪ/ *n.* (*pl.* -**ies**). **chieftainship** *n.* [ME f. OF *chevetaine* f. LL *capitaneus* CAPTAIN: assim. to CHIEF]

chiffchaff /ˈtʃɪftʃæf/ *n.* a small European bird, *Phylloscopus collybita*, of the warbler family. [imit.]

chiffon /ˈʃɪfɒn/ *n. & adj.* —*n.* a light diaphanous fabric of silk, nylon, etc. —*adj.* **1** made of chiffon. **2** (of a pie-filling, dessert, etc.) light-textured. [F f. *chiffe* rag]

chiffonier /ˌʃɪfəˈnɪə(r)/ *n.* a movable low cupboard with a side-board top. [F *chiffonnier, -ière* rag-picker, chest of drawers for odds and ends]

chigger /ˈtʃɪɡə(r)/ *n.* **1** = CHIGOE. **2** any harvest mite of the genus *Leptotrombidium* with parasitic larvae. [var. of CHIGOE]

chignon /ˈʃiːnjɒ̃/ *n.* a coil or mass of hair at the back of a woman's head. [F, orig. = nape of the neck]

chigoe /ˈtʃɪɡəʊ/ *n.* a tropical flea, *Tunga penetrans*, the females of which burrow beneath the skin causing painful sores. Also called CHIGGER. [Carib]

Chihuahua /tʃɪˈwɑːwə/ **1** the largest State in Mexico; pop. (est. 1988) 2,238,500. **2** its capital city; pop. (1980) 406,830.

chihuahua /tʃɪˈwɑːwə/ *n.* **1** a very small dog of a smooth-haired large-eyed breed originating in Mexico. **2** this breed. [CHIHUAHUA]

chilblain /ˈtʃɪlbleɪn/ *n.* a painful itching swelling of the skin usu. on a hand, foot, etc., caused by exposure to cold and by poor circulation. □□ **chilblained** *adj.* [CHILL + BLAIN]

child /tʃaɪld/ *n.* (*pl.* **children** /ˈtʃɪldrən/) **1 a** a young human being below the age of puberty. **b** an unborn or newborn human being. **2** one's son or daughter (at any age). **3** (foll. by *of*) a descendant, follower, adherent, or product of (*children of Israel*; *child of God*; *child of nature*). **4** a childish person. □ **child abuse** maltreatment of a child, esp. by physical violence or sexual molestation. **child benefit** (in the UK) regular payment by the State to the parents of a child up to a certain age. **child care** the care of children, esp. by a local authority. **child-minder** a person who looks after children for payment. **child's play** an easy task. □□ **childless** *adj.* **childlessness** *n.* [OE *cild*]

childbed /ˈtʃaɪldbed/ *n. archaic* = CHILDBIRTH.

childbirth /ˈtʃaɪldbɜːθ/ *n.* the act of giving birth to a child.

Childe /tʃaɪld/ *n. archaic* a youth of noble birth (*Childe Harold*). [var. of CHILD]

Childermas /ˈtʃɪldəˌmæs/ *n. archaic* the feast of the Holy Innocents, 28 Dec. [OE *cildramæsse* f. *cildra* genit. pl. of *cild* CHILD + *mæsse* MASS[2]]

Childers /ˈtʃɪldəz/, (Robert) Erskine (1870–1922), English-born writer and political activist, a supporter of Irish Home Rule. He settled in Ireland in 1920 and became director of publicity for the Irish republicans; he was court-martialled and shot for his involvement in the civil war following the establishment of the Irish Free State. As a writer he is remembered for his novel *The Riddle of the Sands* (1903), in which two amateur yachtsman sailing in the Baltic discover German preparations for an invasion of England.

childhood /'tʃaɪldhʊd/ n. the state or period of being a child. □ **second childhood** a person's dotage. [OE *cildhād*]

childish /'tʃaɪldɪʃ/ adj. 1 of, like, or proper to a child. 2 immature, silly. □□ **childishly** adv. **childishness** n.

childlike /'tʃaɪldlaɪk/ adj. having the good qualities of a child as innocence, frankness, etc.

childproof /'tʃaɪldpruːf/ adj. that cannot be damaged or operated by a child.

children pl. of CHILD.

Chile /'tʃɪli/ a country occupying a long coastal strip down the southern half of the west of South America, between the Andes and the Pacific Ocean; pop. (est. 1988) 12,638,000; official language, Spanish; capital, Santiago. The country's mineral wealth is considerable and includes copper, iron, nitrates, coal, and oil; Chile is one of the world's chief exporters of copper. Most of Chile was incorporated in the Inca empire and became part of the Spanish Viceroyalty of Peru after Pizarro's conquest, although the tribes of the south generally held out successfully against both imperial powers. Chilean independence was proclaimed in 1810 by O'Higgins and finally achieved in 1818 with help from Argentina. Chilean territory was pushed northwards in 1879–83 at the expense of Bolivia, and although difficulties with Argentina were solved without war in 1902, relations with her eastern neighbour have since periodically deteriorated. Chile was ruled by a right-wing military dictatorship after the overthrow of the Marxist democrat Allende in 1973 (see PINOCHET), until a democratically elected President took office in March 1990. □ **Chile pine** a monkey-puzzle tree. **Chile saltpetre** (also **Chile nitre**) naturally occurring sodium nitrate. □□ **Chilean** adj. & n.

chili var. of CHILLI.

chiliad /'kɪliˌæd/ n. 1 a thousand. 2 a thousand years. [LL *chilias chiliad-* f. Gk *khilias -ados*]

chiliasm /'kɪliˌæz(ə)m/ n. the doctrine of or belief in Christ's prophesied reign of 1,000 years on earth (see MILLENNIUM). [Gk *khiliasmos*: see CHILIAD]

chiliast /'kɪliˌæst/ n. a believer in chiliasm. □□ **chiliastic** /-'æstɪk/ adj. [LL *chiliastes*: see CHILIAD, CHILIASM]

chill /tʃɪl/ n., v., & adj. —n. 1 a an unpleasant cold sensation; lowered body temperature. b a feverish cold (*catch a chill*). 2 unpleasant coldness (of air, water, etc.). 3 a a depressing influence (*cast a chill over*). b a feeling of fear or dread accompanied by coldness. 4 coldness of manner. —v. 1 tr. & intr. make or become cold. 2 tr. depress, dispirit. 3 tr. cool (food or drink); preserve by cooling. 4 tr. harden (molten metal) by contact with cold material. —adj. literary chilly. □ **take the chill off** warm slightly. □□ **chiller** n. **chillingly** adv. **chillness** n. **chillsome** adj. literary. [OE *cele, ciele*, etc.: in mod. use the verb is the oldest (ME), and is of obscure orig.]

chilli /'tʃɪli/ n. (pl. **-ies**) (also US **chili**) a small hot-tasting dried red pod of a capsicum, *Capsicum frutescens*, used as seasoning and in curry powder, cayenne pepper, etc. □ **chilli con carne** /kɒn 'kɑːni/ a stew of chilli-flavoured minced beef and beans. **chilli sauce** a hot sauce made with tomatoes, chillies, and spices. [Sp. *chile, chili*, f. Aztec *chilli*]

chilly /'tʃɪli/ adj. (**chillier, chilliest**) 1 (of the weather or an object) somewhat cold. 2 (of a person or animal) feeling somewhat cold; sensitive to the cold. 3 unfriendly; unemotional. □□ **chilliness** n.

Chiltern Hills /'tʃɪltən/ (also **Chilterns**) a range of hills in southern England, north of the Thames. □ **apply for the Chiltern Hundreds** (of an MP) to apply for the stewardship of a district (formerly called a *hundred*) which includes part of the Chiltern Hills and is Crown property, and hence to be allowed to resign his seat. Resignation is not normally permitted once

an MP has been elected, but the holding of an office of profit under the Crown disqualifies a person from being an MP, and by a legal fiction this stewardship is held to be such an office.

chimaera var. of CHIMERA.

Chimborazo /ˌtʃɪmbəˈrɑːzəʊ/ the highest peak of the Andes in Ecuador, rising to a height of 6,310 m (20,487 ft.).

chime[1] /tʃaɪm/ n. & v. —n. 1 a a set of attuned bells. b the series of sounds given by this. c (usu. in pl.) a set of attuned bells as a door bell. 2 agreement, correspondence, harmony. —v. 1 a intr. (of bells) ring. b tr. sound (a bell or chime) by striking. 2 tr. show (the hour) by chiming. 3 intr. (usu. foll. by *together, with*) be in agreement, harmonize. □ **chime in** 1 interject a remark. 2 join in harmoniously. 3 (foll. by *with*) agree with. □□ **chimer** n. [ME, prob. f. *chym(b)e* bell f. OE *cimbal* f. L *cymbalum* f. Gk *kumbalon* CYMBAL]

chime[2] /tʃaɪm/ n. (also **chimb**) the projecting rim at the end of a cask. [ME: cf. MDu., MLG *kimme*]

chimera /kaɪˈmɪərə, kɪ-/ (also **chimaera**) n. 1 (in Greek mythology) a fire-breathing female monster with a lion's head, a goat's body, and a serpent's tail, killed by Bellorophon. 2 a fantastic or grotesque product of the imagination; a bogey. 3 any fabulous beast with parts taken from various animals. 4 *Biol*. a an organism containing genetically different tissues, formed by grafting, mutation, etc. b a nucleic acid formed by laboratory manipulation. 5 any cartilaginous fish of the family Chimaeridae, usu. having a long tapering caudal fin. □□ **chimeric** /-'merɪk/ adj. **chimerical** /-'merɪk(ə)l/ adj. **chimerically** /-'merɪkəlɪ/ adv. [L f. Gk *khimaira* she-goat, chimera]

chimney /'tʃɪmnɪ/ n. (pl. **-eys**) 1 a vertical channel conducting smoke or combustion gases etc. up and away from a fire, furnace, engine, etc. 2 the part of this which projects above a roof. 3 a glass tube protecting the flame of a lamp. 4 a narrow vertical crack in a rock-face, often used by mountaineers to ascend. □ **chimney-breast** a projecting interior wall surrounding a chimney. **chimney-piece** an ornamental structure around an open fireplace; a mantelpiece. **chimney-pot** an earthenware or metal pipe at the top of a chimney, narrowing the aperture and increasing the up draught. **chimney-stack** 1 a number of chimneys grouped in one structure. 2 = sense 2. **chimney-sweep** a person whose job is removing soot from inside chimneys. [ME f. OF *cheminée* f. LL *caminata* having a fire-place, f. L *caminus* f. Gk *kaminos* oven]

chimp /tʃɪmp/ n. colloq. = CHIMPANZEE. [abbr.]

chimpanzee /ˌtʃɪmpənˈziː/ n. a Central and West African ape of the genus *Pan*, of which there are two species: *P. troglodytes*, which resembles man more closely than does any other ape, and the pygmy chimpanzee *P. paniscus*. [F *chimpanzé* f. Kongo]

Chimu /tʃiːˈmuː/ n. (pl. same) a member or the language of a South American Indian civilization of Peru, the largest and most important civilization before the Inca. The large-scale irrigation systems and increased urbanization which marked their great efflorescence in the 14th c. anticipated subsequent developments by their Inca conquerers, to whom they passed their culture and engineering skills. Chimu social organization, with its distinctive hierarchical structure, was imperfectly copied by the Inca who had not yet established a permanent ruling class at the time of the Spanish conquest. The Chimu language died out in the 19th c. [Sp., f. Amer. Indian]

chin /tʃɪn/ n. the front of the lower jaw. □ **chin-strap** a strap for fastening a hat etc. under the chin. **chin up** colloq. cheer up. **chin-wag** sl. n. a talk or chat. —v.intr. (**-wagged, -wagging**) have a gossip. **keep one's chin up** colloq. remain cheerful, esp. in adversity. **take on the chin** 1 suffer a severe blow from (a misfortune etc.). 2 endure courageously. □□ **-chinned** adj. (in comb.). [OE *cin(n)* f. Gmc]

China /'tʃaɪnə/ a country in eastern Asia, the third-largest and most populous in the world; pop. (est. 1988) 1,088,169,200; official language, Chinese; capital, Peking. It is essentially an agricultural country, cereals being produced in the northern provinces and rice and sugar in the south; cotton, tea, hemp, jute, and flax are the most important crops, while the culture of silkworms is one of the oldest industries. Mineral resources are

b *but* d *dog* f *few* g *get* h *he* j *yes* k *cat* l *leg* m *man* n *no* p *pen* r *red* s *sit* t *top* v *voice*

considerable and include coal, iron ore, and oil, in which the country has been self-sufficient since 1973. Chinese civilization stretches back until at least the 3rd millennium BC, the country being ruled by a series of dynasties, including a Mongol one in the 13th–14th c., until the Ch'ing (or Manchu) dynasty was overthrown by Sun Yat-sen in 1912. The country was stricken by civil war (1927–37 and 1946-9; see KUOMINTANG and MAO TSE-TUNG) and by Japanese invasion, and soon after the end of the Second World War the corrupt and ineffective Kuomintang government was overthrown by the Communists, the People's Republic of China being declared in 1949. Until quite recently, China remained generally closed to Western economic or political penetration, both under its old imperial rulers and its new Communist ones. In the ancient and medieval past, however, China was undoubtedly more civilized in many ways than Europe, and after the stagnation and chaos of the late 19th and early 20th centuries the country is now emerging as a world power. A pro-democracy movement in June 1989 was ruthlessly repressed.

china /ˈtʃaɪnə/ n. & adj. —n. **1** a kind of fine white or translucent ceramic ware, porcelain, etc. **2** things made from ceramic, esp. household tableware. **3** rhyming sl. one's 'mate', i.e. husband or wife (short for china plate). —adj. made of china. □ **china clay** kaolin. **China tea** smoke-cured tea from a small-leaved tea plant grown in China. [orig. China ware (from China in Asia): name f. Pers. chīnī]

Chinagraph /ˈtʃaɪnəˌɡrɑːf/ n. propr. a waxy coloured pencil used to write on china, glass, etc.

Chinaman /ˈtʃaɪnəmən/ n. (pl. -**men**) **1** archaic or derog. (now usu. offens.) a native of China. **2** Cricket a ball bowled by a left-handed bowler that spins from off to leg.

China Sea a part of the Pacific Ocean off the coast of China, divided by the island of Taiwan into the East China Sea in the north and the South China Sea in the south.

Chinatown /ˈtʃaɪnəˌtaʊn/ n. a district of any non-Chinese town, esp. a city or seaport, in which the population is predominantly Chinese.

chinch /tʃɪntʃ/ n. (in full **chinch-bug**) US **1** a small insect, Blissus leucopterus, that destroys the shoots of grasses and grains. **2** a bedbug. [Sp. chinche f. L cimex -icis]

chincherinchee /ˌtʃɪntʃərɪnˈtʃiː/ n. a white-flowered bulbous plant, Ornithogalum thyrsoides, native to S. Africa. [imit. of the squeaky rubbing of its stalks]

chinchilla /tʃɪnˈtʃɪlə/ n. **1 a** any small rodent of the genus Chinchilla, native to S. America, having soft silver-grey fur and a bushy tail. **b** its highly valued fur. **2** a breed of cat or rabbit. [Sp. prob. f. S. Amer. native name]

chin-chin /tʃɪnˈtʃɪn/ int. Brit. colloq. a toast; a greeting or farewell. [Chin. qingqing (pr. ch-)]

Chindit /ˈtʃɪndɪt/ n. hist. a member of the Allied forces behind the Japanese lines in Burma (now Myanmar) in 1943–5, during the Second World War. [Burm. chinthé, a mythical creature]

Chindwin /tʃɪnˈdwɪn/ a river in western Burma, the principal tributary of the Irrawaddy. It was the scene of much fighting in 1942–4, during the Second World War.

chine[1] /tʃaɪn/ n. & v. —n. **1 a** a backbone, esp. of an animal. **b** a joint of meat containing all or part of this. **2** a ridge or arête. —v.tr. cut (meat) across or along the backbone. [ME f. OF eschine f. L spina SPINE]

chine[2] /tʃaɪn/ n. a deep narrow ravine in the Isle of Wight or Dorset. [OE cinu chink etc. f. Gmc]

chine[3] /tʃaɪn/ n. the join between the side and the bottom of a ship etc. [var. of CHIME[2]]

Chinese /tʃaɪˈniːz/ adj. & n. —adj. **a** of or relating to China. **b** of Chinese descent. —n. **1** the Chinese language. (See below.) **2** (pl. same) **a** a native or national of China. **b** a person of Chinese descent. □ **Chinese cabbage** = Chinese leaf. **Chinese gooseberry** = kiwi fruit. **Chinese lantern 1** a collapsible paper lantern. **2** a solanaceous plant, Physalis alkekengi, bearing white flowers and globular orange fruits enclosed in an orange-red papery calyx. **Chinese leaf** a lettuce-like cabbage, Brassica chinensis. **Chinese puzzle** a very intricate puzzle or problem.

Chinese water chestnut see water chestnut 2. **Chinese white** zinc oxide as a white pigment.

Chinese is a member of the Sino-Tibetan language group, a tonal language with no inflexions, declension, or conjugations. It is estimated that there are some 800 million speakers in China and neighbouring countries. There are many dialects, including Mandarin (based on the pronunciation of Peking), and Cantonese (spoken in the south-east and in Hong Kong). Chinese script is ideographic; the characters were in origin pictographic, with each sign standing for an object, and they gradually gave way to non-pictorial ideographs representing not only tangible objects but also abstract concepts. Despite its complexity the script makes written communication possible between people speaking mutually incomprehensible dialects. Examples of Chinese writing date back well beyond 1000 BC. Traditionally Chinese books were arranged in vertical columns and read from right to left, but they are now usually composed horizontally. Until the beginning of the 20th c. the greater part of written Chinese was in a style which imitated that of the Chinese classics, most of which were written before 200 BC, and this written style became far removed from current speech. A reform movement was started to make the literature available to the masses, and many simplified characters were introduced. A system of spelling (Pinyin) using the Roman alphabet has been officially adopted, in stages, since 1958.

Ch'ing /tʃɪŋ/ the name of a Chinese dynasty established by the Manchus, 1644–1912. Its overthrow in 1912 ended imperial rule in China and plunged the country into prolonged civil war.

Chin Hills /tʃɪn/ a range of hills in NW Burma, close to the frontier with India.

chink[1] /tʃɪŋk/ n. **1** an unintended crack that admits light or allows an attack. **2** a narrow opening; a slit. [16th c.: rel. to CHINE[2]]

chink[2] /tʃɪŋk/ v. & n. —v. **1** intr. make a slight ringing sound, as of glasses or coins striking together. **2** tr. cause to make this sound. —n. this sound. [imit.]

Chink /tʃɪŋk/ n. sl. offens. a Chinese. □□ **Chinky** adj. [abbr.]

chinless /ˈtʃɪnlɪs/ adj. colloq. weak or feeble in character. □ **chinless wonder** Brit. an ineffectual esp. upper class person.

Chino- /ˈtʃaɪnəʊ/ comb. form = SINO-.

chino /ˈtʃiːnəʊ/ n. US (pl. -**os**) **1** a cotton twill fabric, usu. khaki-coloured. **2** (in pl.) a garment, esp. trousers, made from this. [Amer. Sp., = toasted]

chinoiserie /ʃiːnˈwɑːzərɪ/ n. **1** the imitation of Chinese motifs and techniques in painting and in decorating furniture. **2** an object or objects in this style. [F]

Chinook /ʃəˈʊk, tʃə-, -ˈnuːk/ n. (pl. same) a member of a North American Indian tribe originally inhabiting the region round Columbus River in Oregon.

chinook /ʃəˈnʊk, tʃə-, -ˈnuːk/ n. **1** a warm dry wind which blows east of the Rocky Mountains. **2** a warm wet southerly wind west of the Rocky Mountains. □ **chinook salmon** a large salmon, Oncorhynchus tshawytscha, of the N. Pacific. [CHINOOK]

chintz /tʃɪnts/ n. & adj. —n. a printed multicoloured cotton fabric with a glazed finish. —adj. made from or upholstered with this fabric. [earlier chints (pl.) f. Hindi chīnt f. Skr. citra variegated]

chintzy /ˈtʃɪntsɪ/ adj. (**chintzier, chintziest**) **1** like chintz. **2** gaudy, cheap. **3** characteristic of the décor associated with chintz soft furnishings. □□ **chintzily** adv. **chintziness** n.

chionodoxa /ˌkaɪənəˈdɒksə/ n. any liliaceous plant of the genus Chionodoxa, having early-blooming blue flowers. Also called glory-of-the-snow. [mod.L f. Gk khiōn snow + doxa glory]

Chios /ˈkaɪɒs/ (Greek **Khios** /ˈkiːɒs/) a Greek island in the Aegean Sea; pop. (1981) 48,700.

chip /tʃɪp/ n. & v. —n. **1** a small piece removed by or in the course of chopping, cutting, or breaking, esp. from hard material such as wood or stone. **2** the place where such a chip has been made. **3 a** (usu. in pl.) a strip of potato, deep fried. **b** (in pl.) US potato crisps. **4** a counter used in some gambling games to represent money. **5** Electronics = MICROCHIP. **6 a** a thin strip of wood, straw, etc., used for weaving hats, baskets, etc. **b** a basket made from these. **7** *Football* etc. & *Golf* a short shot, kick, or pass with the ball describing an arc. —*v.* (**chipped, chipping**) **1** *tr.* (often foll. by *off, away*) cut or break (a piece) from a hard material. **2** *intr.* (often foll. by *at, away at*) cut pieces off (a hard material) to alter its shape, break it up, etc. **3** *intr.* (of stone, china, etc.) be susceptible to being chipped; be apt to break at the edge (*will chip easily*). **4** *tr.* (also *absol.*) *Football* etc. & *Golf* strike or kick (the ball) with a chip (cf. sense 7 of *n.*). **5** *tr.* (usu. as **chipped** *adj.*) cut (potatoes) into chips. □ **chip heater** *Austral.* & *NZ* a domestic water-heater that burns wood chips. **chip in** *colloq.* **1** interrupt or contribute abruptly to a conversation (*chipped in with a reminiscence*). **2** contribute (money or resources). **a chip off the old block** a child who resembles a parent, esp. in character. **a chip on one's shoulder** *colloq.* a disposition or inclination to feel resentful or aggrieved. **chip shot** = sense 7 of *n.* **have had one's chips** *Brit. colloq.* be unable to avoid defeat, punishment, etc. **when the chips are down** *colloq.* when it comes to the point. [ME f. OF *cipp, cyp* beam]

chipboard /ˈtʃɪpbɔːd/ *n.* a rigid sheet or panel made from compressed wood chips and resin.

chipmunk /ˈtʃɪpmʌŋk/ *n.* any ground squirrel of the genus *Tamias* or *Eutamias*, having alternate light and dark stripes running down the body. [Algonquian]

chipolata /ˌtʃɪpəˈlɑːtə/ *n.* *Brit.* a small thin sausage. [F f. It. *cipollata* a dish of onions f. *cipolla* onion]

Chippendale /ˈtʃɪpənˌdeɪl/ *adj.* **1** (of furniture) designed or made by the English cabinet-maker Thomas Chippendale (d. 1779). **2** in the ornately elegant style of Chippendale's furniture.

chipper /ˈtʃɪpə(r)/ *adj.* esp. *US colloq.* **1** cheerful. **2** smartly dressed. [perh. f. N.Engl. dial. *kipper* lively]

chippie var. of CHIPPY.

chipping /ˈtʃɪpɪŋ/ *n.* **1** a small fragment of stone, wood, etc. **2** (in *pl.*) these used as a surface for roads, roofs, etc.

chippy /ˈtʃɪpɪ/ *n.* (also **chippie**) (*pl.* **-ies**) *Brit. colloq.* **1** a fish-and-chip shop. **2** a carpenter.

Chips /tʃɪps/ *n.* *Naut. sl.* a ship's carpenter.

chiral /ˈkaɪr(ə)l/ *adj.* *Chem.* (of a crystal etc.) not superposable on its mirror image. □□ **chirality** /-ˈrælɪtɪ/ *n.* [Gk *kheir* hand]

Chirico /ˈkɪrɪˌkəʊ/, Giorgio de (1888–1978), Italian painter, born in Greece, a precursor of surrealism. Holding that 'good sense and logic have no place in a work of art' he painted unrelated objects against unexpected backgrounds, and from this developed a style that became known as 'metaphysical painting' in which there was more symbolic content. During the 1920s he painted his most powerful and distinctive works, notably a series featuring horses on unreal seashores with broken classical columns; his later work became repetitive and obsessed with technical refinement.

chiro- /ˈkaɪrəʊ/ (also **cheiro-**) *comb. form* of the hand. [Gk *kheir* hand]

chirography /kaɪəˈrɒgrəfɪ/ *n.* handwriting, calligraphy.

chiromancy /ˈkaɪrəʊˌmænsɪ/ *n.* palmistry.

chiropody /kɪˈrɒpədɪ/ *n.* the treatment of the feet and their ailments. □□ **chiropodist** *n.* [CHIRO- + Gk *pous podos* foot]

chiropractic /ˌkaɪrəʊˈpræktɪk/ *n.* the diagnosis and manipulative treatment of mechanical disorders of the joints, esp. of the spinal column. □□ **chiropractor** /ˈkaɪrəʊ-/ *n.* [CHIRO- + Gk *praktikos*: see PRACTICAL]

chiropteran /ˌkaɪəˈrɒptərən/ *n.* any member of the order Chiroptera, with membraned limbs serving as wings, including bats and flying foxes. □□ **chiropterous** *adj.* [CHIRO- + Gk *pteron* wing]

chirp /tʃɜːp/ *v.* & *n.* —*v.* **1** *intr.* (usu. of small birds, grasshoppers, etc.) utter a short sharp high-pitched note. **2** *tr.* & *intr.* (esp. of a child) speak or utter in a lively or jolly way. —*n.* a chirping sound. □□ **chirper** *n.* [ME, earlier *chirk, chirt*: imit.]

chirpy /ˈtʃɜːpɪ/ *adj. colloq.* (**chirpier, chirpiest**) cheerful, lively. □□ **chirpily** *adv.* **chirpiness** *n.*

chirr /tʃɜː(r)/ *v.* & *n.* (also **churr**) —*v.intr.* (esp. of insects) make a prolonged low trilling sound. —*n.* this sound. [imit.]

chirrup /ˈtʃɪrəp/ *v.* & *n.* —*v.intr.* (**chirruped, chirruping**) (esp. of small birds) chirp, esp. repeatedly; twitter. —*n.* a chirruping sound. □□ **chirrupy** *adj.* [trilled form of CHIRP]

chisel /ˈtʃɪz(ə)l/ *n.* & *v.* —*n.* a hand tool with a squared bevelled blade for shaping wood, stone, or metal. —*v.* **1** *tr.* (**chiselled, chiselling**; *US* **chiseled, chiseling**) cut or shape with a chisel. **2** *tr.* (as **chiselled** *adj.*) (of facial features) clear-cut, fine. **3** *tr.* & *intr. sl.* cheat, swindle. □□ **chiseller** *n.* [ME f. ONF ult. f. LL *cisorium* f. L *caedere caes-* cut]

chit[1] /tʃɪt/ *n.* **1** *derog.* or *joc.* a young, small, or frail girl or woman (esp. *a chit of a girl*). **2** a young child. [ME, = whelp, cub, kitten, perh. = dial. *chit* sprout]

chit[2] /tʃɪt/ *n.* **1** a note of requisition; a note of a sum owed, esp. for food or drink. **2** esp. *Brit.* a note or memorandum. [earlier *chitty*: Anglo-Ind. f. Hindi *ciṭṭhī* pass f. Skr. *citra* mark]

chital /ˈtʃiːt(ə)l/ *n.* = AXIS[2]. [Hindi *cītal*]

chit-chat /ˈtʃɪtˌtʃæt/ *n.* & *v. colloq.* —*n.* light conversation; gossip. —*v.intr.* (**-chatted, -chatting**) talk informally; gossip. [redupl. of CHAT[1]]

chitin /ˈkaɪtɪn/ *n.* *Chem.* a polysaccharide forming the major constituent in the exoskeleton of arthropods and in the cell walls of fungi. □□ **chitinous** *adj.* [F *chitine* irreg. f. Gk *khitōn*: see CHITON]

chiton /ˈkaɪt(ə)n/ *n.* **1** a long woollen tunic worn by ancient Greeks. **2** any marine mollusc of the class Amphineura, having a shell of overlapping plates. [Gk *khitōn* tunic]

Chittagong /ˈtʃɪtəˌgɒŋ/ a seaport in SE Bangladesh, on the Bay of Bengal; pop. (1981) 1,391,900.

chitterling /ˈtʃɪtəlɪŋ/ *n.* (usu. in *pl.*) the smaller intestines of pigs etc., esp. as cooked for food. [ME: orig. uncert.]

chivalrous /ˈʃɪvəlrəs/ *adj.* **1** (usu. of a male) gallant, honourable, courteous. **2** involving or showing chivalry. □□ **chivalrously** *adv.* [ME f. OF *chevalerous*: see CHEVALIER]

chivalry /ˈʃɪvəlrɪ/ *n.* **1** the medieval knightly system with its religious, moral, and social code. **2** the combination of qualities expected of an ideal knight, esp. courage, honour, courtesy, justice, and readiness to help the weak. **3** a man's courteous behaviour, esp. towards women. **4** *archaic* knights, noblemen, and horsemen collectively. □□ **chivalric** *adj.* [ME f. OF *chevalerie* etc. f. med.L *caballerius* for LL *caballarius* horseman: see CAVALIER]

chive /tʃaɪv/ *n.* a small alliaceous plant, *Allium schoenoprasum*, having purple-pink flowers and dense tufts of long tubular leaves which are used as a herb. [ME f. OF *cive* f. L *cepa* onion]

chivvy /ˈtʃɪvɪ/ *v.tr.* (**-ies, -ied**) (also **chivy, chevy** /ˈtʃevɪ/) harass, nag; pursue. [*chevy* (n. & v.), prob. f. the ballad of *Chevy Chase*, a place on the Scottish border]

chlamydia /kləˈmɪdɪə/ *n.* (*pl.* **chlamydiae** /-dɪˌiː/) any parasitic bacterium of the genus *Chlamydia*, some of which cause diseases such as trachoma, psittacosis, and non-specific urethritis. [mod.L f. Gk *khlamus -udos* cloak]

chlamydomonas /ˌklæmɪdəˈməʊnəs/ *n.* any unicellular green freshwater alga of the genus *Chlamydomonas*. [mod.L (as CHLAMYDIA)]

chlor- var. of CHLORO-.

chloral /ˈklɔːr(ə)l/ *n.* **1** a colourless liquid aldehyde used in making DDT. **2** (in full **chloral hydrate**) *Pharm.* a colourless crystalline solid made from chloral and used as a sedative. [F f. *chlore* chlorine + *alcool* alcohol]

chloramphenicol /ˌklɔːræmˈfenɪˌkɒl/ *n.* *Pharm.* an antibiotic prepared from *Streptomyces venezuelae* or produced synthetically and used esp. against typhoid fever. [CHLORO- + AMIDE + PHENO- + NITRO- + GLYCOL]

chlorate /ˈklɔːreɪt/ *n.* *Chem.* any salt of chloric acid.

chlorella /klɔːˈrelə/ *n.* any non-motile unicellular green alga of the genus *Chlorella*. [mod.L, dimin. of Gk *khlōros* green]

chloric acid /ˈklɔːrɪk/ *n.* *Chem.* a colourless liquid acid with strong oxidizing properties. [CHLORO- + -IC]

chloride /ˈklɔːraɪd/ *n.* *Chem.* **1** any compound of chlorine with another element or group. **2** any bleaching agent containing chloride. [CHLORO- + -IDE]

chlorinate /ˈklɔːrɪˌneɪt/ *v.tr.* **1** impregnate or treat with chlorine

2 *Chem.* cause to react or combine with chlorine. □□ **chlorinator** *n.*

chlorination /ˌklɔːrɪˈneɪʃ(ə)n/ *n.* **1** the treatment of water with chlorine to disinfect it. **2** *Chem.* a reaction in which chlorine is introduced into a compound.

chlorine /ˈklɔːriːn/ *n. Chem.* a non-metallic gaseous element of the halogen group, first isolated in 1774 and named in 1810 by Sir Humphry Davy for its colour. It is obtained mainly from sea water and from salt deposits. The yellowish-green gas is toxic and has a powerful irritating smell; it was used as a poison gas in the First World War. Chlorine is added to water supplies as a disinfectant, and is a constituent of many commercial chemical compounds, including bleaches, antiseptics, insecticides, dyes, and synthetic rubbers. ¶ Symb.; **Cl**; atomic number 17. [Gk *khlōros* green + -INE⁴]

chlorite /ˈklɔːraɪt/ *n. Chem.* any salt of chlorous acid. □□ **chloritic** /-ˈrɪtɪk/ *adj.*

chloro- /ˈklɔːrəʊ/ *comb. form* (also **chlor-** esp. before a vowel) **1** *Bot.* & *Mineral.* green. **2** *Chem.* chlorine. [Gk *khlōros* green: in sense 2 f. CHLORINE]

chloro-fluorocarbon see CFC.

chloroform /ˈklɒrəˌfɔːm, ˈklɔːrə-/ *n.* & *v.* —*n.* a colourless volatile sweet-smelling liquid used as a solvent and formerly used as a general anaesthetic. ¶ Chem. formula: CHCl₃. —*v.tr.* render (a person) unconscious with this. [F *chloroforme* formed as CHLORO- + *formyle*: see FORMIC (ACID)]

Chloromycetin /ˌklɔːrəʊmaɪˈsiːtɪn/ *n. propr.* = CHLORAMPHENICOL. [CHLORO- + Gk *mukēs* -ētos fungus]

chlorophyll /ˈklɒrəfɪl/ *n.* the green pigment found in most plants, responsible for light absorption to provide energy for photosynthesis. □□ **chlorophyllous** /-ˈfɪləs/ *adj.* [F *chlorophylle* f. Gk *phullon* leaf: see CHLORO-]

chloroplast /ˈklɒrəʊˌplæst/ *n.* a plastid containing chlorophyll, found in plant cells undergoing photosynthesis. [G: (as CHLORO-, PLASTID)]

chlorosis /kləˈrəʊsɪs, klɔː-/ *n.* **1** *hist.* a severe form of anaemia from iron deficiency esp. in young women, causing a greenish complexion (cf. GREENSICK). **2** *Bot.* a reduction or loss of the normal green coloration of plants. □□ **chlorotic** *adj.* [CHLORO- + -OSIS]

chlorous acid /ˈklɔːrəs/ *n. Chem.* a pale yellow liquid acid with oxidizing properties. ¶ Chem. formula: HClO₂. [CHLORO- + -OUS]

chlorpromazine /klɔːˈprɒməˌziːn/ *n. Pharm.* a drug used as a sedative and to control nausea and vomiting. [F (as CHLORO-, PROMETHAZINE)]

Ch.M. *abbr.* Master of Surgery. [L *Chirurgiae Magister*]

choc /tʃɒk/ *n.* & *adj. colloq.* chocolate. □ **choc-ice** a bar of ice-cream covered with a thin coating of chocolate. [abbr.]

chocho /ˈtʃəʊtʃəʊ/ *n.* (pl. **-os**) *W.Ind.* = CHOKO.

chock /tʃɒk/ *n., v.,* & *adv.* —*n.* a block or wedge of wood to check motion, esp. of a cask or a wheel. —*v.tr.* **1** fit or make fast with chocks. **2** (usu. foll. by *up*) *Brit.* cram full. —*adv.* as closely or tightly as possible. [prob. f. OF *couche, coche,* of unkn. orig.]

chock-a-block /ˈtʃɒkəˌblɒk/ *adj.* & *adv.* crammed close together; crammed full (*a street chock-a-block with cars*). [orig. Naut., with ref. to tackle with the two blocks run close together]

chocker /ˈtʃɒkə(r)/ *adj. Brit. sl.* fed up, disgusted. [CHOCK-A-BLOCK]

chock-full /ˈtʃɒkfʊl, -ˈfʊl/ *adj.* & *adv.* = CHOCK-A-BLOCK (*chock-full of rubbish*). [CHOCK + FULL¹: ME *chokkefulle* (rel. to CHOKE¹) is doubtful]

chocolate /ˈtʃɒkələt, ˈtʃɒklət/ *n.* & *adj.* —*n.* **1 a** a food preparation in the form of a paste or solid block made from roasted and ground cacao seeds, usually sweetened. **b** a sweet made of or coated with this. **c** a drink made with chocolate. **2** a deep brown colour. —*adj.* **1** made from or of chocolate. **2** chocolate-coloured. □ **chocolate-box 1** a decorated box filled with chocolates. **2** (*attrib.*) stereotypically pretty or romantic. □□ **chocolatey** *adj.* (also **chocolaty**). [F *chocolat* or Sp. *chocolate* f. Aztec *chocolatl*]

Choctaw /ˈtʃɒktɔː/ *n.* (pl. same or **Choctaws**) **1 a** a member of a North American people originally inhabiting Mississippi and

Alabama. **b** the language of this people. **2** (in skating) a step from one edge of a skate to the other edge of the other skate in the opposite direction. [native name]

choice /tʃɔɪs/ *n.* & *adj.* —*n.* **1 a** the act or an instance of choosing. **b** a thing or person chosen (*not a good choice*). **2** a range from which to choose. **3** (usu. foll. by *of*) the élite, the best. **4** the power or opportunity to choose (*what choice have I?*). —*adj.* of superior quality; carefully chosen. □□ **choicely** *adv.* **choiceness** *n.* [ME f. OF *chois* f. *choisir* CHOOSE]

choir /ˈkwaɪə(r)/ *n.* **1** a regular group of singers, esp. taking part in church services. **2** the part of a cathedral or large church between the altar and the nave, used by the choir and clergy. **3** a company of singers, birds, angels etc. (*a heavenly choir*). **4** *Mus.* a group of instruments of one family playing together. □ **choir organ** the softest of three parts making up a large organ having its row of keys the lowest of the three. **choir-stall** = STALL¹ *n.* 3a. [ME f. OF *quer* f. L *chorus*: see CHORUS]

choirboy /ˈkwaɪəˌbɔɪ/ *n.* a boy who sings in a church or cathedral choir.

choke¹ /tʃəʊk/ *v.* & *n.* —*v.* **1** *tr.* hinder or impede the breathing of (a person or animal) esp. by constricting the windpipe or (of gas, smoke, etc.) by being unbreathable. **2** *intr.* suffer a hindrance or stoppage of breath. **3** *tr.* & *intr.* make or become speechless from emotion. **4** *tr.* retard the growth of or kill (esp. plants) by the deprivation of light, air, nourishment, etc. **5** *tr.* (often foll. by *back*) suppress (feelings) with difficulty. **6** *tr.* block or clog (a passage, tube, etc.). **7** *tr.* (as **choked** *adj.*) *colloq.* disgusted, disappointed. **8** *tr.* enrich the fuel mixture in (an internal-combustion engine) by reducing the intake of air. —*n.* **1** the valve in the carburettor of an internal-combustion engine that controls the intake of air, esp. to enrich the fuel mixture. **2** *Electr.* an inductance coil used to smooth the variations of an alternating current or to alter its phase. □ **choke-chain** a chain looped round a dog's neck to exert control by pressure on its windpipe when the dog pulls. **choke-cherry** (pl. **-cherries**) an astringent N. American cherry, *Prunus virginiana.* **choke-damp** carbon dioxide in mines, wells, etc. **choke down** swallow with difficulty. **choke up** block (a channel etc.). [ME f. OE *ācēocian* f. *cēoce, cēce* CHEEK]

choke² /tʃəʊk/ *n.* the centre part of an artichoke. [prob. confusion of the ending of *artichoke* with CHOKE¹]

chokeberry /ˈtʃəʊkbərɪ/ *n.* (pl. **-ies**) *Bot.* **1** any rosaceous shrub of the genus *Aronia.* **2** its scarlet berry-like fruit.

choker /ˈtʃəʊkə(r)/ *n.* **1** a close-fitting necklace or ornamental neckband. **2** a clerical or other high collar.

choko /ˈtʃəʊkəʊ/ *n.* (pl. **-os**) *Austral.* & *NZ* a succulent green pear-shaped vegetable like a cucumber in flavour. [Braz. Ind. *chocho*]

choky¹ /ˈtʃəʊkɪ/ *n.* (also **chokey**) (pl. **-ies** or **-eys**) *Brit. sl.* prison. [orig. Anglo-Ind., f. Hindi *caukī* shed]

choky² /ˈtʃəʊkɪ/ *adj.* (**chokier, chokiest**) tending to choke or to cause choking.

cholangiography /ˌkɒlændʒɪˈɒɡrəfɪ/ *n. Med.* X-ray examination of the bile ducts, used to find the site and nature of any obstruction. [CHOLE- + Gk *aggeion* vessel + -GRAPHY]

chole- /ˈkɒlɪ/ *comb. form* (also **chol-** esp. before a vowel) *Med.* & *Chem.* bile. [Gk *kholē* gall, bile]

cholecalciferol /ˌkɒlɪkælˈsɪfəˌrɒl/ *n.* one of the D vitamins, produced by the action of sunlight on a cholesterol derivative widely distributed in the skin, a deficiency of which results in rickets in children and osteomalacia in adults. Also called *vitamin D₃.* [CHOLE- + CALCIFEROL]

cholecystography /ˌkɒlɪsɪsˈtɒɡrəfɪ/ *n. Med.* X-ray examination of the gall-bladder, esp. used to detect the presence of any gallstones. [CHOLE- + CYSTO- + -GRAPHY]

choler /ˈkɒlə(r)/ *n.* **1** *hist.* one of the four humours, bile. **2** *poet.* or *archaic* anger, irascibility. [ME f. OF *colere* bile, anger f. L *cholera* f. Gk *kholera* diarrhoea, in LL = bile, anger, f. Gk *kholē* bile]

cholera /ˈkɒlərə/ *n. Med.* an infectious and often fatal disease of the small intestine caused by the bacterium *Vibrio cholerae,* resulting in severe vomiting and diarrhoea. Cholera came to Europe from the East, spreading along the ancient trade routes, through Asia and eastern Europe from its traditional home in the Ganges valley. With the great increase of international trade and commerce in the 19th c. the disease found its way to western Europe, the first large epidemic being in 1831–2, and the low standard of public and personal hygiene at that time gave it every chance of spreading. It is the classic example of a mainly water-borne disease, and where the domestic water supply has been purified cholera epidemics have nearly always ceased. A vaccine is now available. □ **chicken** (or **fowl**) **cholera** an infectious disease of fowls. □□ **choleraic** /-ˈreɪɪk/ adj. [ME f. L f. Gk *kholera*: see CHOLER]

choleric /ˈkɒlərɪk/ adj. irascible, angry. □□ **cholerically** adv. [ME f. OF *cholerique* f. L *cholericus* f. Gk *kholerikos*: see CHOLER]

cholesterol /kəˈlestəˌrɒl/ n. *Biochem.* a sterol found in most body tissues, including the blood, where high concentrations promote arteriosclerosis. [*cholesterin* f. Gk *kholē* bile + *stereos* stiff]

choli /ˈtʃəʊlɪ/ n. (pl. **cholis**) a type of short-sleeved bodice worn by Indian women. [Hindi *colī*]

choliamb /ˈkəʊlɪˌæmb/ n. *Prosody* = SCAZON. □□ **choliambic** /ˌkəʊlɪˈæmbɪk/ adj. [LL *choliambus* f. Gk *khōliambos* f. *khōlos* lame: see IAMBUS]

choline /ˈkəʊliːn, -lɪn/ n. *Biochem.* a basic nitrogenous organic compound occurring widely in living matter. [G *Cholin* f. Gk *kholē* bile]

chomp /tʃɒmp/ v.tr. = CHAMP[1]. [imit.]

Chomsky /ˈtʃɒmskɪ/, Avram Noam (1928–), American linguistics scholar associated since 1957 with the theory of generative-transformational grammar which reacted against the static and taxonomic forms of American linguistic structuralism. He views language as the result of innate capacity, common to all persons, arguing that linguistics is a part of psychology. Chomsky was also a leading critic of the American involvement in the Vietnam war of 1961–76.

chondrite /ˈkɒndraɪt/ n. a stony meteorite containing small mineral granules. [G *Chondrit* f. Gk *khondros* granule]

chondrocranium /ˌkɒndrəʊˈkreɪnɪəm/ n. *Anat.* the embryonic skull composed of cartilage and later replaced by bone. [Gk *khondros* grain, cartilage]

Chonqing /tʃʊŋˈkɪŋ/ (also **Chungking**) a city in Sichuan province in central China; pop. (est. 1986) 2,780,000. It was the capital of China from 1938 to 1946, while both Peking and Nanking were held by the Japanese.

choo-choo /ˈtʃuːtʃuː/ n. *colloq.* (esp. as a child's word) a railway train or locomotive, esp. a steam engine. [imit.]

chook /tʃʊk/ n. (also **chookie**) *Austral.* & *NZ colloq.* **1** a chicken or fowl. **2** *sl.* an older woman. [E dial. *chuck* chicken]

choose /tʃuːz/ v. (*past* **chose** /tʃəʊz/; *past part.* **chosen** /ˈtʃəʊz(ə)n/) **1** *tr.* select out of a greater number. **2** *intr.* (usu. foll. by *between*, *from*) take or select one or another. **3** *tr.* (usu. foll. by *to* + infin.) decide, be determined (*chose to stay behind*). **4** *tr.* (foll. by complement) select as (*was chosen king*). **5** *tr. Theol.* (esp. as **chosen** adj.) destine to be saved (*God's chosen people*). □ **cannot choose but** *archaic* must. **nothing** (or **little**) **to choose between them** they are equivalent. □□ **chooser** n. [OE *cēosan* f. Gmc]

choosy /ˈtʃuːzɪ/ adj. (**choosier**, **choosiest**) *colloq.* fastidious. □□ **choosily** adv. **choosiness** n.

chop[1] /tʃɒp/ v. & n. —v.tr. (**chopped**, **chopping**) **1** (usu. foll. by *off*, *down*, etc.) cut or fell by a blow, usu. with an axe. **2** (often foll. by *up*) cut (esp. meat or vegetables) into small pieces. **3** strike (esp. a ball) with a short heavy edgewise blow. **4** *Brit. colloq.* dispense with; shorten or curtail. —n. **1** a cutting blow, esp. with an axe. **2** a thick slice of meat (esp. pork or lamb) usu. including a rib. **3** a short heavy edgewise stroke or blow in tennis, cricket, boxing, etc. **4** the broken motion of water, usu. owing to the action of the wind against the tide. **5** (prec. by *the*) *Brit. sl.* **a** dismissal from employment. **b** the action of killing or being killed. □ **chop logic** argue pedantically. [ME, var. of CHAP[1]]

chop[2] /tʃɒp/ n. (usu. in pl.) the jaw of an animal etc. [16th-c. var. (occurring earlier) of CHAP[3], of unkn. orig.]

chop[3] /tʃɒp/ v.intr. (**chopped**, **chopping**) □ **chop and change** vacillate; change direction frequently. [ME, perh. rel. to *chap* f. OE *cēapian* (as CHEAP)]

chop[4] /tʃɒp/ n. *Brit. archaic* a trade mark; a brand of goods. □ **not much chop** esp. *Austral.* & *NZ* no good. [orig. in India & China, f. Hindi *chāp* stamp]

chop-chop /tʃɒpˈtʃɒp/ adv. & int. (pidgin English) quickly, quick. [f. Chin. dial. *k'wâi-k'wâi*]

Chopin /ˈʃəʊpæ̃/, Fryderyk (Frédéric) (1810–49), Polish composer and pianist. He left Poland in 1830 and in 1831, while in Stuttgart, heard that Warsaw had been captured by the Russians. He never returned to his native land, moving to Paris in 1831 and remaining there, apart from a tour of Britain as a concert pianist and a year in Majorca and Spain, for the rest of his short life. For some years he was the lover of the French writer George Sand, but their affair ended before his death from tuberculosis. He was famous as a pianist, and his piano music represents for many the perfect expression of poetry in music. His works range from the dreamy lyricism of the Nocturnes to the fire and spirit of the Polonaises, while some of the larger-scale works such as the four Ballades combine and contrast these qualities. The Victorian conception of him as a consumptive drawing-room balladeer of the keyboard has long been exposed as a false trail leading hearers away from the true, poetic, heroic Chopin.

chopper /ˈtʃɒpə(r)/ n. **1 a** *Brit.* a short axe with a large blade. **b** a butcher's cleaver. **2** *colloq.* a helicopter. **3** a device for regularly interrupting an electric current or light-beam. **4** *colloq.* a type of bicycle or motor cycle with high handlebars. **5** (in pl.) *Brit. sl.* teeth. **6** *US sl.* a machine-gun.

choppy /ˈtʃɒpɪ/ adj. (**choppier**, **choppiest**) (of the sea, the weather, etc.) fairly rough. □□ **choppily** adv. **choppiness** n. [CHOP[1] + -Y[1]]

chopstick /ˈtʃɒpstɪk/ n. each of a pair of small thin sticks of wood or ivory etc., held both in one hand as eating utensils by the Chinese, Japanese, etc. [pidgin Engl. f. *chop* = quick + STICK; equivalent of Cantonese *k'wâi-tsze* nimble ones]

chopsuey /tʃɒpˈsuːɪ/ n. (pl. **-eys**) a Chinese-style dish of meat stewed and fried with bean sprouts, bamboo shoots, onions, and served with rice. [Cantonese *shap sui* mixed bits]

choral /ˈkɔːr(ə)l/ adj. of, for, or sung by a choir or chorus. □ **choral society** a group which meets regularly to sing choral music. □□ **chorally** adv. [med.L *choralis* f. L *chorus*: see CHORUS]

chorale /kɔːˈrɑːl/ n. (also **choral**) **1** a stately and simple hymn tune; a harmonized version of this. **2** esp. *US* a choir or choral society. [G *Choral(gesang)* f. med.L *cantus choralis*]

chord[1] /kɔːd/ n. *Mus.* a group of (usu. three or more) notes sounded together, as a basis of harmony. □□ **chordal** adj. [orig. *cord* f. ACCORD: later confused with CHORD[2]]

chord[2] /kɔːd/ n. **1** *Math.* & *Aeron.* etc. a straight line joining the ends of an arc, the wings of an aeroplane, etc. **2** *Anat.* = CORD. **3** *poet.* the string of a harp etc. **4** *Engin.* one of the two principal members, usu. horizontal, of a truss. □ **strike a chord 1** recall something to a person's memory. **2** elicit sympathy. **touch the right chord** appeal skilfully to the emotions. □□ **chordal** adj. [16th-c. refashioning of CORD after L *chorda*]

chordate /ˈkɔːdeɪt/ n. & adj. —n. any animal of the phylum Chordata, possessing a notochord at some stage during its development. —adj. of or relating to the chordates. [mod.L *chordata* f. L *chorda* CHORD[2] after *Vertebrata* etc.]

chore /tʃɔː(r)/ n. a tedious or routine task, esp. domestic. [orig. dial. & US form of CHAR[2]]

chorea /kɒˈrɪə/ n. *Med.* a disorder characterized by jerky involuntary movements affecting esp. the shoulders, hips, and face. □ **Huntington's chorea** chorea accompanied by a progressive dementia. **Sydenham's chorea** chorea esp. in children as one of the manifestations of rheumatic fever: also called ST VITUS's DANCE. [L f. Gk *khoreia* (as CHORUS)]

choreograph /ˈkɒrɪəˌɡrɑːf/ v.tr. compose the choreography for (a ballet etc.). □□ **choreographer** /-ɪˈɒɡrəfə(r)/ n. [back-form. f. CHOREOGRAPHY]

choreography /ˌkɒrɪˈɒɡrəfɪ/ n. **1** the design or arrangement of a ballet or other staged dance. **2** the sequence of steps and movements in dance. **3** the written notation for this. □□ **choreographic** /ˌkɒrɪəˈɡræfɪk/ adj. **choreographically** /ˌkɒrɪəˈɡræfɪkəlɪ/ adv. [Gk *khoreia* dance + -GRAPHY]

choreology /ˌkɒrɪˈɒlədʒɪ/ n. the study and description of the movements of dancing. □□ **choreologist** n.

choriambus /ˌkɒrɪˈæmbəs/ n. (pl. **choriambi** /-baɪ/) Prosody a metrical foot consisting of two short (unstressed) syllables between two long (stressed) ones. □□ **choriambic** adj. [LL Gk khoriambos f. khoreios of the dance + IAMBUS]

choric /ˈkɔːrɪk/ adj. of, like, or for a chorus in drama or recitation. [LL choricus f. Gk khorikos (as CHORUS)]

chorine /ˈkɔːriːn/ adj. US a chorus girl. [CHORUS + -INE³]

chorion /ˈkɔːrɪən/ n. the outermost membrane surrounding an embryo of a reptile, bird, or mammal. □□ **chorionic** /-ˈɒnɪk/ adj. [Gk khorion]

chorister /ˈkɒrɪstə(r)/ n. 1 a member of a choir, esp. a choirboy. 2 US the leader of a church choir. [ME, ult. f. OF cueriste f. quer CHOIR]

chorography /kəˈrɒgrəfɪ/ n. the systematic description of regions or districts. □□ **chorographer** n. **chorographic** /ˌkɒrəˈgræfɪk/ adj. [F chorographie or L f. Gk khōrographia f. khōra region]

choroid /ˈkɔːrɔɪd/ adj. & n. —adj. like a chorion in shape or vascularity. —n. (in full **choroid coat** or **membrane**) a layer of the eyeball between the retina and the sclera. [Gk khoroeidēs for khorioeidēs: see CHORION]

chorology /kəˈrɒlədʒɪ/ n. the study of the geographical distribution of animals and plants. □□ **chorological** /ˌkɔːrəˈlɒdʒɪk(ə)l/ adj. **chorologist** n. [Gk khōra region + -LOGY]

chortle /ˈtʃɔːt(ə)l/ v. & n. —v.intr. colloq. chuckle gleefully. —n. a gleeful chuckle. [portmanteau word coined by Lewis Carroll, prob. f. CHUCKLE + SNORT]

chorus /ˈkɔːrəs/ n. & v. —n. (pl. **choruses**) 1 a group (esp. a large one) of singers; a choir. 2 a piece of music composed for a choir. 3 the refrain or the main part of a popular song, in which a chorus participates. 4 any simultaneous utterance by many persons etc. (a chorus of disapproval followed). 5 a group of singers and dancers performing in concert in a musical comedy, opera, etc. 6 Gk Antiq. a in Greek tragedy, a group of performers who comment together in voice and movement on the main action. b an utterance of the chorus. 7 esp. in Elizabethan drama, a character who speaks the prologue and other linking parts of the play. 8 the part spoken by this character. —v.tr. & intr. (of a group) speak or utter simultaneously. □ **chorus girl** a young woman who sings or dances in the chorus of a musical comedy etc. **in chorus** (uttered) together; in unison. [L f. Gk khoros]

chose past of CHOOSE.

chosen past part. of CHOOSE.

Chou En-lai /ˌtʃəʊ enˈlaɪ/ (also **Zhou Enlai,** 1898–1976), Chinese statesman. One of the founders of the Chinese Communist party, he joined Sun Yat-sen in 1924 and organized the revolt in Shanghai in 1927 before forming a partnership with Mao Tse-tung, whose lieutenant he became. On the formation of the Communist regime in 1949 Chou became Premier.

chough /tʃʌf/ n. any corvine bird of the genus Pyrrhocorax, with a glossy blue-black plumage and red legs. [ME, prob. orig. imit.]

choux pastry /ʃuː/ n. very light pastry enriched with eggs. [F, pl. of chou cabbage, rosette]

chow /tʃaʊ/ n. 1 sl. food. 2 offens. a Chinese. 3 a a dog of a Chinese breed with long hair and bluish-black tongue. b this breed. [shortened f. CHOW-CHOW]

chow-chow /ˈtʃaʊtʃaʊ/ n. 1 = CHOW. 2 a Chinese preserve of ginger, orange-peel, etc., in syrup. 3 a mixed vegetable pickle. [pidgin Engl.]

chowder /ˈtʃaʊdə(r)/ n. US a soup or stew usu. of fresh fish, clams, or corn with bacon, onions, etc. [perh. F chaudière pot: see CAULDRON]

chow mein /tʃaʊ ˈmeɪn/ n. a Chinese-style dish of fried noodles with shredded meat or shrimps etc. and vegetables. [Chin. chao mian fried flour]

Chr. abbr. Chronicles (Old Testament).

chrestomathy /krɛsˈtɒməθɪ/ n. (pl. **-ies**) a selection of passages used esp. to help in learning a language. [F chrestomathie or Gk khrēstomatheia f. khrēstos useful + -matheia learning]

Chrétien de Troyes /kretɪˌæ̃ də ˈtrwɑː/ (12th c.) French poet who lived and worked at the court of Marie de Champagne and is regarded as the greatest of the writers of courtly romances. He probably wrote a romance of Tristan; his four extant volumes of romances are: Erec (c.1170), Cligés (1176), Yvain (c.1177–81), and Lancelot (c.1177–81). His unfinished Perceval, part of which survives, introduced the Holy Grail to literature. His writings greatly influenced subsequent Arthurian literature.

chrism /ˈkrɪz(ə)m/ n. a consecrated oil or unguent used esp. for anointing in Catholic and Greek Orthodox rites. [OE crisma f. eccl.L f. Gk khrisma anointing]

chrisom /ˈkrɪz(ə)m/ n. 1 = CHRISM. 2 (in full **chrisom-cloth**) hist. a white robe put on a child at baptism, and used as its shroud if it died within the month. [ME, as pop. pronunc. of CHRISM]

Christ /kraɪst/ n. & int. —n. 1 the title, also now treated as a name, given to Jesus of Nazareth, believed by Christians to have fulfilled the Old Testament prophecies of a coming Messiah. 2 the Messiah as prophesied in the Old Testament. 3 an image or picture of Jesus. —int. sl. expressing surprise, anger, etc. □□ **Christhood** n. **Christlike** adj. **Christly** adj. [OE Crīst f. L Christus f. Gk khristos anointed one f. khriō anoint: transl. of Heb. māšīaḥ MESSIAH]

Christadelphian /ˌkrɪstəˈdelfɪən/ n. & adj. —n. a member of a Christian sect founded in America in 1848 by John Thomas, rejecting the beliefs and development associated with the term 'Christian', calling themselves 'Christadelphians' (= brothers of Christ) and claiming to return to the beliefs and practices of the earliest disciples. The core of their faith is that Christ will return in power to set up a worldwide theocracy beginning at Jerusalem, and that belief in this is necessary for salvation. —adj. of or adhering to this sect and its beliefs. [CHRIST + Gk adelphos brother]

Christchurch /ˈkraɪsttʃɜːtʃ/ a city on South Island, New Zealand, the capital of Canterbury region; pop. (1988) 300,700. The city was founded in 1850 by English Anglican colonists.

christen /ˈkrɪs(ə)n/ v.tr. 1 give a Christian name to at baptism as a sign of admission to a Christian Church. 2 give a name to anything, esp. formally or with a ceremony. 3 colloq. use for the first time. □□ **christener** n. **christening** n. [OE crīstnian make Christian]

Christendom /ˈkrɪsəndəm/ n. Christians worldwide, regarded as a collective body. [OE cristendōm f. cristen CHRISTIAN + -DOM]

Christian /ˈkrɪstɪən, ˈkrɪstʃ(ə)n/ adj. & n. —adj. 1 of Christ's teaching or religion. 2 believing in or following the religion of Jesus Christ. 3 showing the qualities associated with Christ's teaching. 4 colloq. (of a person) kind, fair, decent. —n. 1 a a person who has received Christian baptism. b an adherent of Christ's teaching. 2 a person exhibiting Christian qualities. □ **Christian era** the era reckoned from the traditional date of Christ's birth. **Christian name** a forename, esp. as given at baptism. **Christian Science** see separate entry. □□ **Christianize** v.tr. & intr. (also **-ise**). **Christianization** /ˌkrɪstɪənaɪˈzeɪʃ(ə)n/ n. **Christianly** adv. [Christianus f. Christus CHRIST]

Christianity /ˌkrɪstɪˈænɪtɪ/ n. 1 the Christian religion; its beliefs and practices. (See below.) 2 being a Christian; Christian quality or character. 3 = CHRISTENDOM. [ME cristianite f. OF crestienté f. crestien CHRISTIAN]

At first Christianity was simply a Jewish sect which believed that Jesus of Nazareth was the Messiah (or 'Christ', = anointed one). Largely owing to the former Pharisee, Paul of Tarsus, it quickly became an independent, mainly Gentile, organization. In the early centuries Christians experienced intermittent persecution by the State, though there was no clear legal basis for this until the reign of the Emperor Decius (AD 250). By the 3rd c. Christianity was widespread throughout the Roman Empire; in 313 Constantine ended persecution and in 380 Theodosius recognized it as the State religion. There were frequent disputes between Christians mainly over the status of Christ and the nature of the Trinity, and later over grace and Church organization. Division between East and West, in origin largely cultural and linguistic, intensified, culminating in the Schism of 1054, sealed by the Crusades. In the West the organization of the Church, focused on the Roman papacy, was fragmented by the Reformation of the 16th c. In the 20th c. the ecumenical movement has sought to heal these ancient wounds.

Christian Science *n.* the doctrine of the Church of Christ, Scientist, a Christian sect founded in Boston in 1879 by Mrs Mary Baker Eddy to 'reinstate primitive Christianity and its lost element of healing'. She taught that God and his perfect spiritual creation are the only ultimate reality, and that his law is always available to bring regeneration and healing to humanity. The movement flourished and spread to other English-speaking countries, to Germany, and to many other countries. Since her death (1910) the affairs of the organization have been administered by a board of directors. Worship includes readings from *Science and Health with Key to the Scriptures* by the foundress. □ **Christian Scientist** an adherent of Christian Science.

Christie[1] /'kristi/ *n.* (also **Christy**) (*pl.* **-ies**) *Skiing* a sudden turn in which the skis are kept parallel, used for changing direction fast or stopping short. [abbr. of *Christiania* (now Oslo) in Norway]

Christie[2] /'kristi/, Dame Agatha (1890–1976), English author of detective fiction. The first of her novels, *The Mysterious Affair at Styles* (1920; introducing the Belgian detective Hercule Poirot who reappeared in many further novels), was followed by 66 further works in the genre, including *The Murder of Roger Ackroyd* (1926), *Murder on the Orient Express* (1934), *Death on the Nile* (1937), and *Ten Little Niggers* (1939); the settings for some of these were provided by her experiences while accompanying her second husband, Sir Max Mallowan (1904–78), on his archaeological expeditions in the Middle East. Her other works include two self-portraits and several plays: *The Mousetrap* (1952) has had a record run of over 30 years on the London stage, and a number of her stories have been filmed. Her prodigious international success has been achieved by her brisk humorous dialogue and her ingenious plots which sustain suspense while misdirecting the reader.

Christingle /krɪ'stɪŋg(ə)l/ *n.* a lighted candle set in an orange received at a Christingle service. □ **Christingle service** a children's Advent service, originally in the Moravian Church and recently popularized outside it, at which each participant is given an orange (symbolizing the world) set with a candle (symbolizing Christ as the Light of the World) and other symbolical decorations. [f. CHRIST; origin of second element unknown]

Christmas /'krɪsməs/ *n.* & *int.* — *n.* (*pl.* **Christmases**) **1** (also **Christmas Day**) the annual festival of Christ's birth, celebrated on 25 Dec. (See below.) **2** the season in which this occurs; the time immediately before and after 25 Dec. — *int. sl.* expressing surprise, dismay, etc. □ **Christmas-box** a present or gratuity given at Christmas esp. to tradesmen and employees. **Christmas cake** *Brit.* a rich fruit cake usu. covered with marzipan and icing and eaten at Christmas. **Christmas card** a card sent with greetings at Christmas. The Christmas card, as we know it, dates from the mid-19th c. **Christmas Eve** the day or the evening before Christmas Day. **Christmas pudding** *Brit.* a rich boiled pudding eaten at Christmas, made with flour, suet, dried fruit, etc. **Christmas rose** a white-flowered winterblooming evergreen, *Helleborus niger.* **Christmas tree** an evergreen (usu. spruce) or artificial tree set up with decorations at Christmas. The Christmas tree originated in Germany, where it was known from the 16th c., and spread elsewhere from there. It became fashionable in England after Prince Albert introduced it into his family. □□ **Christmassy** *adj.* [OE *Crīstes mæsse* (MASS[2])]

The festival of Christ's birth has been celebrated in the Western Church on 25 Dec. from about the end of the 4th c., and in the East formerly on 6 Jan. in conjunction with the Epiphany. There is no biblical or other direct evidence of the season of Christ's nativity, and the date may have been chosen to oppose the pagan celebration of the rebirth of the sun after the winter solstice. It has always been marked by the merrymaking characteristic of the Roman Saturnalia and similar festivals, and many of the things now associated with Christmas (e.g. evergreens, lights, red colour) belong to the rituals of 'bringing back the year' which it replaced.

Christmas Island 1 an island in the Indian Ocean to the south of Java, administered as an external territory of Australia since 1958; pop. (1986) 2,000. **2** the former name of Kiritimati.

Christo- /'kristəʊ/ *comb. form* Christ.

Christology /kris'tolədʒi/ *n.* the branch of theology relating to Christ.

Christopher /'kristəfə(r)/, St, legendary martyr, adopted as the patron saint of travellers. According to tradition he was martyred in Asia Minor. He is represented as a giant who carried travellers across a river; once he carried a child whose weight bowed him down, as the child was Christ and his weight that of the world. His feast day (25 July) was dropped from the Roman calendar in 1969. [Gk, = one who bore Christ]

Christ's Hospital a boys' school founded in London in 1552 for poor children, which has since moved to Horsham, Sussex. Pupils wear a distinctive uniform of long dark-blue belted gowns and yellow stockings.

Christy var. of CHRISTIE. [abbr.]

chroma /'krəʊmə/ *n.* purity or intensity of colour. [Gk *khrōma* colour]

chromate /'krəʊmeit/ *n. Chem.* a salt or ester of chromic acid.

chromatic /krə'mætik/ *adj.* **1** of or produced by colour; in (esp. bright) colours. **2** *Mus.* **a** of or having notes not belonging to a diatonic scale. **b** (of a scale) ascending or descending by semitones. □ **chromatic aberration** *Optics* the failure of different wavelengths of electromagnetic radiation to come to the same focus after refraction. **chromatic semitone** *Mus.* an interval between a note and its flat or sharp. □□ **chromatically** *adv.* **chromaticism** /-tɪ,sɪz(ə)m/ *n.* [F *chromatique* or L *chromaticus* f. Gk *khrōmatikos* f. *khrōma -atos* colour]

chromaticity /ˌkrəʊmə'tɪsɪti/ *n.* the quality of colour regarded independently of brightness.

chromatid /'krəʊmətɪd/ *n.* either of two threadlike strands into which a chromosome divides longitudinally during cell division. [Gk *khrōma -atos* colour + -ID[2]]

chromatin /'krəʊmətɪn/ *n.* the material in a cell nucleus that stains with basic dyes and consists of protein, RNA, and DNA, of which eukaryotic chromosomes are composed. [G: see CHROMATID]

chromato- /'krəʊmətəʊ/ *comb. form* (also **chromo-** /'krəʊməʊ/) colour (*chromatopsia*). [Gk *khrōma -atos* colour]

chromatography /ˌkrəʊmə'tɒgrəfi/ *n. Chem.* the separation of the components of a mixture by slow passage through or over a material which adsorbs them differently so that they appear as layers, often of different colours. □□ **chromatograph** /-'mætə,grɑːf/ *n.* **chromatographic** /-mətəʊ'græfik/ *adj.* [G *Chromatographie* (as CHROMATO-, -GRAPHY)]

chromatopsia /ˌkrəʊmə'tɒpsiə/ *n. Med.* abnormally coloured vision. [CHROMATO- + Gk *-opsia* seeing]

chrome /krəʊm/ *n.* **1** chromium, esp. as plating. **2** (in full **chrome yellow**) a yellow pigment obtained from lead chromate. □ **chrome leather** leather tanned with chromium salts. **chrome-nickel** (of stainless steel) containing chromium and nickel. **chrome steel** a hard fine-grained steel containing much chromium and used for tools etc. [F, = chromium, f. Gk *khrōma* colour]

chromic /'krəʊmik/ *adj. Chem.* of or containing trivalent chromium. □ **chromic acid** an acid that exists only in solution or in the form of chromate salts.

chromite /'krəʊmait/ *n.* **1** *Mineral.* a black mineral of chromium and iron oxides, which is the principal ore of chromium. **2** *Chem.* a salt of bivalent chromium.

chromium /'krəʊmiəm/ *n. Chem.* a hard white metallic transition element, first isolated in 1798. It is often plated on to other metals for decorative purposes and to prevent corrosion, and it is an important component of many alloys, notably stainless steel. Chromium compounds, many of which are brightly coloured, are used as pigments, in dyeing, and in the tanning of leather. ¶ Symb.: **Cr**; atomic number 24. □ **chromium steel** = *chrome steel.* [mod.L f. F CHROME]

chromium-plate /ˌkrəʊmiəm'pleit/ *n.* & *v.* — *n.* an electrolytically deposited protective coating of chromium. — *v.tr.*

1 coat with this. **2** (as **chromium-plated** adj.) pretentiously decorative.

chromo-¹ /'krəʊməʊ/ comb. form Chem. chromium.

chromo-² comb. form var. of CHROMATO-.

chromolithograph /ˌkrəʊməʊ'lɪθəˌgrɑːf/ n. & v. —n. a coloured picture printed by lithography. —v.tr. print or produce by this process. □□ **chromolithographer** /-'θɒgrəfə(r)/ n. **chromolithographic** /-ˌlɪθə'græfɪk/ adj. **chromolithography** /-lɪ'θɒgrəfɪ/ n.

chromosome /'krəʊməˌsəʊm/ n. Biochem. any of a number of rod-like or threadlike structures found in the nuclei of the cells of living organisms and carrying the genetic information in the form of genes. They can normally be seen as separate structures only when the cell is dividing. A normal undivided chromosome contains a single DNA double helix (associated with protein) in which the genes are arranged in linear order. The number of chromosomes per cell varies between species. Man has 23 pairs (see DIPLOID) of which one pair determines the sex of the individual: a female carries two similar X-chromosomes in each cell while a male has one X- and one smaller Y-chromosome. The genetic material of a bacterium is now also referred to as a chromosome. □ **chromosome map** a plan showing the relative positions of genes along the length of a chromosome. □□ **chromosomal** adj. [G Chromosom (as CHROMO-², -SOME³)]

chromosphere /'krəʊməˌsfɪə(r)/ n. the region immediately above the photosphere of the sun which, together with the corona, constitutes its outer atmosphere. Material in this region is at temperatures of 10,000–20,000 °C, and is subject to magnetic forces originating within the sun that may occasionally lift and propel it outwards for thousands of kilometres as solar flares. □□ **chromospheric** /-'sferɪk/ adj. [CHROMO-² + SPHERE]

Chron. abbr. Chronicles (Old Testament).

chronic /'krɒnɪk/ adj. **1** persisting for a long time (usu. of an illness or a personal or social problem). **2** having a chronic complaint. **3** colloq. disp. habitual, inveterate (a chronic liar). **4** Brit. colloq. very bad; intense, severe. □□ **chronically** adv. **chronicity** /krɒ'nɪsɪtɪ/ n. [F chronique f. L chronicus (in LL of disease) f. Gk khronikos f. khronos time]

chronicle /'krɒnɪk(ə)l/ n. & v. —n. **1** a register of events in order of their occurrence. **2** a narrative, a full account. **3** (**Chronicles**) the name of two of the historical books of the Old Testament or Hebrew bible recording the history of Israel and Judah from the Creation until the return from Exile (536 BC), with interest concentrated on the religious aspects, especially the Temple and worship. —v.tr. record (events) in the order of their occurrence. □□ **chronicler** n. [ME f. AF cronicle ult. f. L chronica f. Gk khronika annals: see CHRONIC]

chrono- /'krɒnəʊ/ comb. form time. [Gk khronos time]

chronograph /'krɒnəˌgrɑːf, 'krəʊnə-, -ˌgræf/ n. **1** an instrument for recording time with extreme accuracy. **2** a stopwatch. □□ **chronographic** /-'græfɪk/ adj.

chronological /ˌkrɒnə'lɒdʒɪk(ə)l/ adj. **1** (of a number of events) arranged or regarded in the order of their occurrence. **2** of or relating to chronology. □□ **chronologically** adv.

chronology /krə'nɒlədʒɪ/ n. (pl. **-ies**) **1** the study of historical records to establish the dates of past events. **2 a** the arrangement of events, dates, etc. in the order of their occurrence. **b** a table or document displaying this. □□ **chronologist** n. **chronologize** v.tr. (also **-ise**). [mod.L chronologia (as CHRONO-, -LOGY)]

chronometer /krə'nɒmɪtə(r)/ n. a time-measuring instrument, esp. one keeping accurate time in spite of movement or of variations in temperature, humidity, and air pressure. The longitude of a ship at sea may be found by comparing local time with Greenwich Mean Time; the former can be computed by astronomical observation, but without an accurate marine timekeeper it was not easy to ascertain Greenwich time. By 1785 French and English clockmakers had evolved a chronometer with an accuracy of better than one second a day, employing special balance-wheels and springs. Modern chronometers use a quartz crystal kept in oscillation at a constant frequency by electronic means. Since the advent of radio time signals the need for expensive marine chronometers scarcely exists.

chronometry /krə'nɒmɪtrɪ/ n. the science of accurate time-measurement. □□ **chronometric** /ˌkrɒnə'metrɪk/ adj. **chronometrical** /ˌkrɒnə'metrɪk(ə)l/ adj. **chronometrically** /ˌkrɒnə'metrɪkəlɪ/ adv.

chrysalis /'krɪsəlɪs/ n. (pl. **chrysalises** or **chrysalides** /krɪ'sælɪˌdiːz/) **1 a** a quiescent pupa of a butterfly or moth. **b** the hard outer case enclosing it. **2** a preparatory or transitional state. [L f. Gk khrusallis -idos f. khrusos gold]

chrysanth /krɪ'sænθ/ n. colloq. any of the autumn-blooming cultivated varieties of chrysanthemum. [abbr.]

chrysanthemum /krɪ'sænθəməm/ n. any composite plant of the genus Chrysanthemum, having brightly coloured flowers. [L f. Gk khrusanthemon f. khrusos gold + anthemon flower]

chryselephantine /ˌkrɪselɪ'fæntaɪn/ adj. (of ancient Greek sculpture) overlaid with gold and ivory. [Gk khruselephantinos f. khrusos gold + elephas ivory]

chrysoberyl /'krɪsəˌberɪl/ n. a yellowish-green gem consisting of a beryllium salt. [L chrysoberyllus f. Gk khrusos gold + bērullos beryl]

chrysolite /'krɪsəˌlaɪt/ n. a precious stone, a yellowish-green or brownish variety of olivine. [ME f. OF crisolite f. med.L crisolitus f. L chrysolithus f. Gk khrusolithos f. khrusos gold + lithos stone]

chrysoprase /'krɪsəˌpreɪz/ n. **1** an apple-green variety of chalcedony containing nickel and used as a gem. **2** (in the New Testament) prob. a golden-green variety of beryl. [ME f. OF crisopace f. L chrysopassus var. of L chrysoprasus f. Gk khrusoprasos f. khrusos gold + prason leek]

Chrysostom /'krɪsəstəm/, St John (c.347–407), bishop of Constantinople, Doctor of the Church. His name (Gk, = goldenmouthed) is a tribute to the eloquence of his preaching, and his sermons on books of the Bible established his title as the greatest of Christian expositors. As Patriarch of Constantinople his combination of honesty, asceticism, and tactlessness in his attempts at reforming the corrupt state of the court, clergy, and people offended many, including the Empress Eudoxia, who with some reason took all attempts at moral reform as a censure on herself; he was banished and died in exile. Feast day, 27 Jan.

chthonic /'kθɒnɪk, 'θɒnɪk/ (also **chthonian** /'kθəʊnɪən, 'θəʊ-/) adj. of, relating to, or inhabiting the underworld. [Gk khthōn earth]

chub /tʃʌb/ n. a thick-bodied coarse-fleshed river fish, Leuciscus cephalus. [15th c.: orig. unkn.]

chubby /'tʃʌbɪ/ adj. (**chubbier, chubbiest**) plump and rounded (esp. of a person or a part of the body). □□ **chubbily** adv. **chubbiness** n. [CHUB]

Chubu /'tʃuːbuː/ a region of Japan on the island of Honshu; pop. (1986) 20,694,000; capital, Nagoya.

chuck¹ /tʃʌk/ v. & n. —v.tr. **1** colloq. fling or throw carelessly or with indifference. **2** colloq. (often foll. by in, up) give up; reject (chucked in my job). **3** touch playfully, esp. under the chin. —n. a playful touch under the chin. □ **the chuck** sl. dismissal (he got the chuck). **chucker-out** colloq. a person employed to expel troublesome people from a gathering etc. **chuck it** sl. stop, desist. **chuck out** colloq. **1** expel (a person) from a gathering etc. **2** get rid of, discard. [16th c., perh. f. F chuquer, choquer to knock]

chuck² /tʃʌk/ n. & v. —n. **1** a cut of beef between the neck and the ribs. **2** a device for holding a workpiece in a lathe or a tool in a drill. —v.tr. fix (wood, a tool, etc.) to a chuck. [var. of CHOCK]

chuck³ /tʃʌk/ n. US colloq. food. □ **chuck-wagon 1** a provision-cart on a ranch etc. **2** a roadside eating-place. [19th c.: perh. f. CHUCK²]

chuckle /'tʃʌk(ə)l/ v. & n. —v.intr. laugh quietly or inwardly. —n. a quiet or suppressed laugh. □□ **chuckler** n. [chuck cluck]

chucklehead /'tʃʌkəlˌhed/ n. colloq. a stupid person. □□ **chuckleheaded** adj. [chuckle clumsy, prob. rel. to CHUCK²]

chuddar var. of CHADOR.

chuff /tʃʌf/ v.intr. (of a steam engine etc.) work with a regular sharp puffing sound. [imit.]

chuffed /tʃʌft/ adj. Brit. sl. delighted. [dial. chuff pleased]

chug /tʃʌg/ v. & n. —v.intr. (**chugged, chugging**) **1** emit a regular muffled explosive sound, as of an engine running slowly. **2** move with this sound. —*n.* a chugging sound. [imit.]

Chugoku /tʃuː'gəʊkuː/ a region of Japan on the island of Honshu; pop. (1986) 7,764,000; capital, Hiroshima.

chukar /tʃʌˈkɑː(r)/ *n.* a red-legged partridge, *Alectoris chukar*, native to India. [Hindi *cakor*]

Chukchi Sea /ˈtʃuːktʃɪ/ an arm of the Arctic Ocean lying between North America and the Soviet Union and to the north of the Bering Strait.

chukker /ˈtʃʌkə(r)/ *n.* (also **chukka**) each of the periods of play into which a game of polo is divided. □ **chukka boot** an ankle-high leather boot as worn for polo. [Hindi *cakkar* f. Skr. *cakra* wheel]

chum¹ /tʃʌm/ *n.* & *v.* —*n. colloq.* (esp. among schoolchildren) a close friend. —*v.intr.* (often foll. by *with*) share rooms. □ **chum up** (often foll. by *with*) become a close friend (of). □□ **chummy** *adj.* (**chummier, chummiest**). **chummily** *adv.* **chumminess** *n.* [17th c.: prob. short for *chamber-fellow*]

chum² /tʃʌm/ *n.* & *v. US* —*n.* **1** refuse from fish. **2** chopped fish used as bait. —*v.* **1** *intr.* fish using chum. **2** *tr.* bait (a fishing place) using chum. [19th c.: orig. unkn.]

chump /tʃʌmp/ *n.* **1** *colloq.* a foolish person. **2** *Brit.* the thick end, esp. of a loin of lamb or mutton (*chump chop*). **3** a short thick block of wood. **4** *Brit. sl.* the head. □ **off one's chump** *Brit. sl.* crazy. [18th c.: blend of CHUNK and LUMP¹]

chunder /ˈtʃʌndə(r)/ *v.intr.* & *n. Austral. sl.* vomit. [20th c.: orig. unkn.]

Chungking see CHONGQING.

chunk /tʃʌŋk/ *n.* **1** a thick solid slice or piece of something firm or hard. **2** a substantial amount or piece. [prob. var. of CHUCK²]

chunky /ˈtʃʌŋkɪ/ *adj.* (**chunkier, chunkiest**) **1** containing or consisting of chunks. **2** short and thick; small and sturdy. **3** (of clothes) made of a thick material. □□ **chunkiness** *n.*

Chunnel /ˈtʃʌn(ə)l/ *n. colloq.* a tunnel under the English Channel linking England and France. (See CHANNEL TUNNEL.) [portmanteau word f. *Channel tunnel*]

chunter /ˈtʃʌntə(r)/ *v.intr. Brit. colloq.* mutter, grumble. [prob. imit.]

chupatty var. of CHAPATTI.

church /tʃɜːtʃ/ *n.* & *v.* —*n.* **1** a building for public (usu. Christian) worship. **2** a meeting for public worship in such a building (*go to church; met after church*). **3** (**Church**) the body of all Christians. **4** (**Church**) the clergy or clerical profession (*went into the Church*). **5** (**Church**) an organized Christian group or society of any time, country, or distinct principles of worship (*the primitive Church; Church of Scotland; High Church*). **6** (**Church**) institutionalized religion as a political or social force (*Church and State*). —*v.tr.* bring (esp. a woman after childbirth) to church for a service of thanksgiving. □ **Church Army** see separate entry. **Church Commissioners** a body managing the finances of the Church of England. **Church of England, Church of Scotland** see separate entries. **church school** a school founded by or associated with the Church of England. **Church Slavonic** see SLAVONIC. [OE *cirice, circe*, etc. f. med. Gk *kurikon* f. Gk *kuriakon* (*dōma*) Lord's (house) f. *kurios* Lord: cf. KIRK]

Church Army a voluntary Anglican organization of lay workers, founded in 1882 on the model of the Salvation Army, for evangelistic purposes. Its activities include welfare work.

churchgoer /ˈtʃɜːtʃˌɡəʊə(r)/ *n.* a person who goes to church, esp. regularly. □□ **churchgoing** *n.* & *adj.*

Churchill /ˈtʃɜːtʃɪl/, Sir Winston Leonard Spencer (1874– 1965), British statesman. After an early career as a soldier and war correspondent, Churchill was elected as a Conservative MP in 1901, but joined the Liberals after the Conservative Party split over free trade. Having served as President of the Board of Trade, Home Secretary, and First Lord of the Admiralty, he lost his position of prominence after the Dardanelles fiasco and left politics to return to the army. Out of Parliament between 1922 and 1924, he returned as Conservative Chancellor of the Exchequer under Baldwin, failing to cope adequately with the economic crisis, and after the government's fall in 1929 did not

hold office again for a decade. Something of a political outcast, Churchill persistently warned of the threat of German military expansion in the 1930s, and on the outbreak of war returned to public life as First Lord of the Admiralty. He replaced Chamberlain as Prime Minister in May 1940 and served as war leader until 1945, becoming a symbol of British resistance in the darkest days of the conflict. After the victory, defeated in the general election of 1945, he campaigned for Western unity against the Communist threat and was returned to office in 1951, finally resigning at the age of 80 in 1955. A powerful orator, he was the originator or popularizer of a number of slogans and phrases. His writings include *The Second World War* (1948–53) and *A History of the English-speaking Peoples* (1956–8); he was awarded the Nobel Prize for literature in 1953.

churchman /ˈtʃɜːtʃmən/ *n.* (*pl.* **-men**) **1** a member of the clergy or of a church. **2** a supporter of the church.

Church of England the English branch of the Western or Latin Church, rejecting the pope's authority since the Reformation and having the monarch as its titular head and nominator of its bishops and archbishops. A synod held at Whitby in 664 resolved the earlier conflict between the indigenous Celtic Church, dominated by missionaries from Ireland and Scotland, and the Roman customs, introduced by St Augustine's mission (597), in favour of the latter. The English Church remained part of the Western Catholic Church until the 16th c. when, against a background of religious dissatisfaction and growing national self-awareness, Henry VIII failed to obtain a divorce from Catherine of Aragon and subsequently repudiated papal supremacy, bringing the Church under the control of the Crown. Some of Henry's advisers, notably Thomas Cromwell and Archbishop Cranmer, were deeply influenced by the Protestant Reformation, and the influence of Continental Protestantism reached a peak in the reign of Edward VI. The Church achieved its definitive form under Elizabeth I, when the Book of Common Prayer became its service-book and the Thirty-nine Articles its statement of doctrine. The aim of the Church of England has been, while rejecting the claims of Rome, to maintain its continuity with earlier tradition.

Church of Scotland the national (Presbyterian) Church of Scotland. At the Reformation the Calvinist party in Scotland, under John Knox, reformed the established Church and organized it on Presbyterian lines (1560). During the next century there were repeated attempts by the Stuart monarchs to impose episcopalianism, and the Church of Scotland was not finally established as Presbyterian until 1690. Its statement of doctrine is the *Westminster Confession* (1643). Like many Protestant Churches it has had a complicated history of schism and reunification.

churchwarden /tʃɜːtʃˈwɔːd(ə)n/ *n.* **1** either of two elected lay representatives of a parish, assisting with routine administration. **2** a long-stemmed clay pipe.

churchwoman /ˈtʃɜːtʃˌwʊmən/ *n.* (*pl.* **-women**) **1** a woman member of the clergy or of a church. **2** a woman supporter of the Church.

churchy /ˈtʃɜːtʃɪ/ *adj.* **1** obtrusively or intolerantly devoted to the Church or opposed to religious dissent. **2** like a church. □□ **churchiness** *n.*

churchyard /ˈtʃɜːtʃjɑːd/ *n.* the enclosed ground around a church, esp. as used for burials.

churinga /tʃʌˈrɪŋɡə/ *n.* (*pl.* same or **churingas**) a sacred object, esp. an amulet, among the Australian Aboriginals. [Aboriginal]

churl /tʃɜːl/ *n.* **1** an ill-bred person. **2** *archaic* a peasant; a person of low birth. **3** *archaic* a surly or mean person. [OE *ceorl* f. a WG root, = man]

churlish /ˈtʃɜːlɪʃ/ *adj.* surly; mean. □□ **churlishly** *adv.* **churlishness** *n.* [OE *cierlisc, ceorlisc* f. *ceorl* CHURL]

churn /tʃɜːn/ *n.* & *v.* —*n.* **1** *Brit.* a large milk-can. **2** a machine for making butter by agitating milk or cream. —*v.* **1** *tr.* agitate (milk or cream) in a churn. **2** *tr.* produce (butter) in this way. **3** *tr.* (usu. foll. by *up*) cause distress to; upset, agitate. **4** *intr.* (of a liquid) seethe, foam violently (*the churning sea*). **5** *tr.* agitate or move (liquid) vigorously, causing it to foam. □ **churn out** produce routinely or mechanically, esp. in large quantities. [OE *cyrin* f. Gmc]

churr var. of CHIRR.

Churrigueresque /ˌtʃʊrɪgəˈresk/ *adj.* of the lavishly ornamented late Spanish baroque style. [J. de *Churriguera*, Spanish architect (d. 1725)]

chute[1] /ʃuːt/ *n.* **1** a sloping channel or slide, with or without water, for conveying things to a lower level. **2** a slide into a swimming-pool. [F *chute* fall (of water etc.), f. OF *cheoite* fem. past part. of *cheoir* fall f. L *cadere*; in some senses = SHOOT]

chute[2] /ʃuːt/ *n. colloq.* parachute. □□ **chutist** *n.* [abbr.]

chutney /ˈtʃʌtnɪ/ *n.* (*pl.* **-eys**) a pungent orig. Indian condiment made of fruits or vegetables, vinegar, spices, sugar, etc. [Hindi *caṭnī*]

chutzpah /ˈxuːtzpə/ *n. sl.* shameless audacity; cheek. [Yiddish]

chyle /kaɪl/ *n.* a milky fluid consisting of lymph and absorbed food materials from the intestine after digestion. □□ **chylous** *adj.* [LL *chylus* f. Gk *khulos* juice]

chyme /kaɪm/ *n.* the acidic semisolid and partly digested food produced by the action of gastric secretion. □□ **chymous** *adj.* [LL *chymus* f. Gk *khumos* juice]

chypre /ˈʃiːpr/ *n.* a heavy perfume made from sandalwood. [F, = Cyprus, perh. where it was first made]

CI *abbr.* **1** Channel Islands. **2** *hist.* Order of the Crown of India.

Ci *abbr.* curie.

CIA *abbr.* (in the US) Central Intelligence Agency.

ciao /tʃaʊ/ *int. colloq.* **1** goodbye. **2** hello. [It.]

ciborium /sɪˈbɔːrɪəm/ *n.* (*pl.* **ciboria** /-rɪə/) **1** a vessel with an arched cover used to hold the Eucharist. **2** *Archit.* **a** a canopy. **b** a shrine with a canopy. [med.L f. Gk *kibōrion* seed-vessel of the water-lily, a cup made from it]

cicada /sɪˈkɑːdə, -ˈkeɪdə/ *n.* (also **cicala** /sɪˈkɑːlə/) any transparent-winged large insect of the family Cicadidae, the males of which make a loud rhythmic chirping sound. [L *cicada*, It. f. L *cicala*, It. *cigala*]

cicatrice /ˈsɪkətrɪs/ *n.* (also **cicatrix** /ˈsɪkətrɪks/) (*pl.* **cicatrices** /ˌsɪkəˈtraɪsiːz/) **1** any mark left by a healed wound; a scar. **2** *Bot.* **a** a mark on a stem etc. left when a leaf or other part becomes detached. **b** a scar on the bark of a tree. □□ **cicatricial** /ˌsɪkəˈtrɪʃ(ə)l/ *adj.* [ME f. OF *cicatrice* or L *cicatrix -icis*]

cicatrize /ˈsɪkətraɪz/ *v.* (also **-ise**) **1** *tr.* heal (a wound) by scar formation. **2** *intr.* (of a wound) heal by scar formation. □□ **cicatrization** /-ˈzeɪʃ(ə)n/ *n.* [F *cicatriser*: see CICATRICE]

cicely /ˈsɪsəlɪ/ *n.* (*pl.* **-ies**) any of various umbelliferous plants, esp. sweet cicely (see SWEET). [app. f. L *seselis* f. Gk, assim. to the woman's Christian name]

Cicero /ˈsɪsəˌrəʊ/, Marcus Tullius (106–43 BC), Roman statesman, orator, and writer. The greatest forensic and political orator of his time, in politics he was a somewhat conservative upholder of Republican values and a supporter of Pompey against the ambitions of Julius Caesar; his proudest success was the suppression, during his consulship of 63 BC, of the conspiracy of Catiline. He died in the proscriptions of 43 BC, a victim of Antony, whom he had savagely attacked in the *Philippics* after the death of Julius Caesar. As an orator and writer he established a model for Latin prose; his surviving works include many speeches, treatises on rhetoric, philosophical works (chiefly adaptations into Latin of the teachings of the several Greek schools), and books of letters, which form a close record of his personal and political interests and activities.

cicerone /ˌtʃɪtʃəˈrəʊnɪ, ˌsɪsəˈrəʊnɪ/ *n.* (*pl.* **ciceroni** *pronunc.* same) a guide who gives information about antiquities, places of interest, etc. to sightseers. [It.: see CICERONIAN]

Ciceronian /ˌsɪsəˈrəʊnɪən/ *adj.* (of language) eloquent, classical, or rhythmical, in the style of Cicero.

cichlid /ˈsɪklɪd/ *n.* any tropical freshwater fish of the family Cichlidae, esp. the kinds kept in aquariums. [mod.L *Cichlidae* f. Gk *kikhlē* a kind of fish]

CID *abbr.* (in the UK) Criminal Investigation Department.

Cid /sɪd/, **The** the title in Spanish literature of Ruy Diaz, count of Bivar, 11th-c. champion of Christianity against the Moors.

-cide /saɪd/ *suffix* forming nouns meaning: **1** a person or substance that kills (*regicide*; *insecticide*). **2** the killing of (*infanticide*; *suicide*). [F f. L *-cida* (sense 1), *-cidium* (sense 2), *caedere* kill]

cider /ˈsaɪdə(r)/ *n.* (also **cyder**) **1** *Brit.* an alcoholic drink made from fermented apple-juice. **2** *US* an unfermented drink made from apple-juice. □ **cider-press** a press for crushing apples to make cider. [ME f. OF *sidre*, ult. f. Heb. *šēḵār* strong drink]

ci-devant /ˌsiːdəˈvɑ̃/ *adj.* & *adv.* that has been (with person's earlier name or status); former or formerly. [F, = heretofore]

CIE *abbr. hist.* Companion (of the Order) of the Indian Empire.

c.i.f. *abbr.* cost, insurance, freight (as being included in a price).

cig /sɪg/ *n. colloq.* cigarette, cigar. [abbr.]

cigala /sɪˈgɑːlə/ *n.* = CICADA. [F *cigale*, It. & Prov. *cigala* f. L *cicada*]

cigar /sɪˈgɑː(r)/ *n.* a cylinder of tobacco rolled in tobacco leaves for smoking. [F *cigare* or Sp. *cigarro*]

cigarette /ˌsɪgəˈret/ *n.* (*US* also **cigaret**) **1** a thin cylinder of finely-cut tobacco rolled in paper for smoking. **2** a similar cylinder containing a narcotic or medicated substance. □ **cigarette card** a small picture card of a kind formerly included in a packet of cigarettes. **cigarette-end** the unsmoked remainder of a cigarette. [F, dimin. of *cigare* CIGAR]

cigarillo /ˌsɪgəˈrɪləʊ/ *n.* (*pl.* **-os**) a small cigar. [Sp., dimin. of *cigarro* CIGAR]

ciggy /ˈsɪgɪ/ *n.* (*pl.* **-ies**) *colloq.* cigarette. [abbr.]

CIGS *abbr. hist.* Chief of the Imperial General Staff.

cilice /ˈsɪlɪs/ *n.* **1** haircloth. **2** a garment of this. [F f. L *cilicium* f. Gk *kilikion* f. *Kilikia* CILICIA]

Cilicia /sɪˈlɪʃə/ the ancient name for the eastern half of the south coast of Asia Minor. □□ **Cilician** *adj.*

Cilician Gates /sɪˈlɪʃ(ə)n, saɪ-/ a mountain pass in the Taurus Mountains in Cilicia (now southern Turkey).

cilium /ˈsɪlɪəm/ *n.* (*pl.* **cilia** /-lɪə/) **1** a short minute hairlike vibrating structure on the surface of some cells, causing currents in the surrounding fluid. **2** an eyelash. □□ **ciliary** *adj.* **ciliate** /-ˌeɪt, -ət/ *adj.* **ciliated** *adj.* **ciliation** /-ˈeɪʃ(ə)n/ *n.* [L, = eyelash]

cill var. of SILL.

cimbalom /ˈsɪmbələm/ *n.* a dulcimer. [Magyar f. It. *cembalo*]

Cimmerian /sɪˈmɪərɪən/ *n.* & *adj.* —*n.* **1** a member of an ancient nomadic people, the earliest known inhabitants of the Crimea, who overran Asia Minor in the 7th c. BC. They overthrew Phrygia *c.*676 BC, and terrorized Ionia, but were gradually destroyed by epidemics and in wars with Lydia and Assyria. **2** *Gk legend* a member of a people who live in perpetual mist and darkness, near the land of the dead. —*adj.* of the Cimmerians. [L *Cimmerius* f. Gk *Kimmerios*, Assyr. *Gimirri* (the 'Gomer' of Gen. 10: 2, Ezek. 38: 6)]

C.-in-C. *abbr.* Commander-in-Chief.

cinch /sɪntʃ/ *n.* & *v.* —*n.* **1** *colloq.* **a** a sure thing; a certainty. **b** an easy task. **2** a firm hold. **3** esp. *US* a girth for a saddle or pack. —*v.tr.* **1 a** tighten as with a cinch (*cinched at the waist with a belt*). **b** secure a grip on. **2** *sl.* make certain of. **3** esp. *US* put a cinch (sense 3) on. [Sp. *cincha*]

cinchona /sɪŋˈkəʊnə/ *n.* **1 a** any evergreen tree or shrub of the genus *Cinchona*, native to S. America, with fragrant flowers and yielding cinchona bark. **b** the bark of this tree, containing quinine. **2** any drug from this bark formerly used as a tonic and to stimulate the appetite. □□ **cinchonic** /-ˈkɒnɪk/ *adj.* **cinchonine** /ˈsɪŋkəˌniːn/ *n.* [mod.L f. Countess of Chinchón d. 1641, introducer of drug into Spain]

Cincinnati /ˌsɪnsɪˈnætɪ/ an industrial city in Ohio, on the Ohio River; pop. (1982) 380,100.

cincture /ˈsɪŋktʃə(r)/ *n.* **1** *literary* a girdle, belt, or border. **2** *Archit.* a ring at either end of a column-shaft. [L *cinctura* f. *cingere* *cinct-* gird]

cinder /ˈsɪndə(r)/ *n.* **a** the residue of coal or wood etc. that has stopped giving off flames but still has combustible matter in it. **b** slag. **c** (in *pl.*) ashes. □ **burnt to a cinder** made useless by burning. □□ **cindery** *adj.* [OE *sinder*, assim. to the unconnected F *cendre* and L *cinis* ashes]

Cinderella /ˌsɪndəˈrelə/ *n.* **1** a person or thing of unrecognized or disregarded merit or beauty. **2** a neglected or despised member of a group. [the name of a girl, uncared-for and disregarded by her family, in a fairy tale by Perrault; analogous stories exist in the folklore of various countries]

cine- /ˈsɪnɪ/ *comb. form* cinematographic (*cine-camera*; *cine-photography*). [abbr.]

cineaste /ˈsɪnɪˌæst/ *n.* (also **cineast**) a cinema enthusiast. [F *cinéaste* (as CINE-): cf. ENTHUSIAST]

cinema /ˈsɪnɪˌmɑː, -mə/ *n.* **1** *Brit.* a theatre where motion-picture films (see FILM *n.* 3) are shown. **2 a** films collectively. **b** the production of films as an art or industry; cinematography. (See below.) □ **cinema organ** *Mus.* a kind of organ with extra stops and special effects. [F *cinéma*: see CINEMATOGRAPH]

Photographic motion pictures projected on to a screen became available to the general public from about 1895. The earliest pictures, shown either as sideshows at fairgrounds or as items in music-hall programmes, were all short and silent; they included slapstick comedy, trick pictures, short romances, and five-minute dramas. More important were the films recording actual happenings, such as the Derby of 1896, the Boer War, the funeral of Queen Victoria, and travel all over the world. From 1900 to 1914 the film industry was international, led by France, Italy, Britain, and America; films made in any country could be sold in any other, and their length increased from a few minutes to two hours. During the First World War the demand for films grew at a time when European producers were least able to meet it, and America became the foremost film-making country, Hollywood in California, with its strong clear light, being the chief centre of production. America consolidated this position in the 1920s, developing the star-system and film publicity simultaneously. The cinema became the people's entertainment, lavish, luxurious, often lurid, available at the price of a few pence. Sound films evolved in the late 1920s, and (because of the language barrier) forced national film industries to develop independently. In 1932 a three-colour process known as Technicolor was developed, adding gaiety and brilliance to the spectacle but (unlike the introduction of sound) often no greater sense of realism. Since the Second World War the increasing popularity of television has seriously threatened the prosperity of the cinema industry, taking over the 'domestic' film and, with its immediacy of transmission, the newsreel. New techniques, such as wide screens, were hurried forward, and costly and elaborate productions, including a number of science fiction and horror films, had some success in attracting audiences back to the cinema.

CinemaScope /ˈsɪnəməˌskəʊp/ *n. propr.* a wide-screen process in which special lenses are used to compress a wide image into a standard frame and then expand it again during projection. The resulting image is almost two and a half times as wide as it is high. The process was copyrighted by Twentieth Century-Fox in 1952, and similar processes were later adopted by other studios.

cinematheque /ˈsɪnɪməˌtek/ *n.* **1** a film library or archive. **2** a small cinema. [F]

cinematic /ˌsɪnɪˈmætɪk/ *adj.* **1** having the qualities characteristic of the cinema. **2** of or relating to the cinema. □□ **cinematically** *adv.*

cinematograph /ˌsɪnɪˈmætəˌɡrɑːf/ (also **kinematograph** /ˌkɪn-/) *n.* an apparatus for showing motion-picture films. [F *cinématographe* (machine patented by the Lumière brothers in 1895) f. Gk *kinēma -atos* movement f. *kineō* move]

cinematography /ˌsɪnɪməˈtɒɡrəfɪ/ *n.* the art of making motion-picture films. □□ **cinematographer** *n.* **cinematographic** /-ˌmætəˈɡræfɪk/ *adj.* **cinematographically** /-ˌmætəˈɡræfɪkəlɪ/ *adv.*

cinéma-vérité /ˌsɪnɪˌmɑː verɪˈteɪ/ *n. Cinematog.* **1** the art or process of making realistic (esp. documentary) films which avoid artificiality and artistic effect. This style of film-making developed in the late 1950s and early 1960s, having been made possible by the production for television of hand-held 16 mm cameras and portable sound equipment. In order to achieve immediacy and truth there was no script and no director, and the film crew consisted only of a cameraman and a sound-man. The style developed concurrently in France and in the US, where it was known as direct cinema. **2** such films collectively. [F, = cinema truth]

cineraria /ˌsɪnəˈreərɪə/ *n.* any of several varieties of the composite plant, *Cineraria cruentus*, having bright flowers and ash-coloured down on its leaves. [mod.L, fem. of L *cinerarius* of ashes f. *cinis -eris* ashes, from the ash-coloured down on the leaves]

cinerarium /ˌsɪnəˈreərɪəm/ *n.* (*pl.* **cinerariums**) a place where a cinerary urn is deposited. [LL, neut. of *cinerarius*: see CINERARIA]

cinerary /ˈsɪnərərɪ/ *adj.* of ashes. □ **cinerary urn** an urn for holding the ashes after cremation. [L *cinerarius*: see CINERARIA]

cinereous /sɪˈnɪərɪəs/ *adj.* (esp. of a bird or plumage) ash-grey. [L *cinereus* f. *cinis -eris* ashes]

ciné-vérité /ˈsɪnɪˌverɪˌteɪ/ *n. Cinematog.* = CINÉMA-VÉRITÉ.

Cingalese /ˌsɪŋɡəˈliːz/ *adj. & n.* (*pl.* same) *archaic* Sinhalese. [F *cing(h)alais*: see SINHALESE]

cingulum /ˈsɪŋɡjʊləm/ *n.* (*pl.* **cingula** /-lə/) *Anat.* a girdle, belt, or analogous structure, esp. a ridge surrounding the base of the crown of a tooth. [L, = belt]

cinnabar /ˈsɪnəˌbɑː(r)/ *n.* **1** a bright red mineral form of mercuric sulphide from which mercury is obtained. **2** vermilion. **3** a moth (*Callimorpha jacobaeae*) with reddish marked wings. [ME f. L *cinnabaris* f. Gk *kinnabari*, of oriental orig.]

cinnamon /ˈsɪnəmən/ *n.* **1** an aromatic spice from the peeled, dried, and rolled bark of a SE Asian tree. **2** any tree of the genus *Cinnamomum*, esp. *C. zeylanicum* yielding the spice. **3** yellowish-brown. [ME f. OF *cinnamome* f. L *cinnamomum* f. Gk *kinnamōmon*, and L *cinnamon* f. Gk *kinnamon*, f. Semitic (cf. Heb. *ḳinnāmôn*)]

cinque /sɪŋk/ *n.* (also **cinq**) the five on dice. [ME f. OF *cinc*, *cink*, f. L *quinque* five]

cinquecento /ˌtʃɪŋkwɪˈtʃentəʊ/ *n.* the style of Italian art and literature of the 16th c., with a reversion to classical forms. □□ **cinquecentist** *n.* [It., = 500, used with ref. to the years 1500–99]

cinquefoil /ˈsɪŋkfɔɪl/ *n.* **1** any plant of the genus *Potentilla*, with compound leaves of five leaflets. **2** *Archit.* a five-cusped ornament in a circle or arch. [ME f. L *quinquefolium* f. *quinque* five + *folium* leaf]

Cinque Ports /sɪŋk ˈpɔːts/ a group of medieval ports in SE England (originally five: Dover, Hastings, Hythe, Romney, and Sandwich; Rye and Winchelsea were added later) formerly allowed various trading privileges in exchange for providing the bulk of England's navy. The origins of the association are unknown, but it existed long before its first real charter was granted by Edward I. Most of the old privileges were abolished in the 19th c. and the Wardenship of the Cinque Ports is now a purely honorary post. [ME f. OF *cink porz*, L *quinque portus* five ports]

Cintra see SINTRA.

cion *US* var. of SCION 1.

cipher /ˈsaɪfə(r)/ *n. & v.* (also **cypher**) —*n.* **1 a** a secret or disguised way of writing. **b** a thing written in this way. **c** the key to it. **2** the arithmetical symbol (0) denoting no amount but used to occupy a vacant place in decimal etc. numeration (as in 12.05). **3** a person or thing of no importance. **4** the interlaced initials of a person or company etc.; a monogram. **5** any Arabic numeral. **6** continuous sounding of an organ-pipe, caused by a mechanical defect. —*v.* **1** *tr.* put into secret writing, encipher. **2 a** *tr.* (usu. foll. by *out*) work out by arithmetic, calculate. **b** *intr.* *archaic* do arithmetic. [ME, f. OF *cif(f)re*, ult. f. Arab *ṣifr* ZERO]

cipolin /ˈsɪpəlɪn/ *n.* an Italian white-and-green marble. [F *cipolin* or It. *cipollino* f. *cipolla* onion]

circa /ˈsɜːkə/ *prep.* (preceding a date) about. [L]

circadian /sɜːˈkeɪdɪən/ *adj. Physiol.* occurring or recurring about once per day. [irreg. f. L *circa* about + *dies* day]

Circassian /sɜːˈkæsɪən/ *adj. & n.* —*adj.* of a group of tribes of the Caucasus, whose women were remarkable for their beauty.

—*n.* a member of these tribes. [*Circassia* district in N. Caucasus (Russ. *Cherkés* tribe calling themselves Adighe)]

Circe /'sɜːsɪ/ *Gk legend* an enchantress who lived with her wild animals on the fabled island of Aeaea. When Odysseus visited the island his companions were changed into pigs by her potions, but he protected himself by the herb called *moly* and forced her to restore his men into human form. The island was later identified with the promontory of Circeii on the coast of Italy near Naples, where the great bulk of Monte Circeo rises like an island floating in the marshes.

circinate /'sɜːsɪˌneɪt/ *adj. Bot. & Zool.* rolled up with the apex in the centre, e.g. of young fronds of ferns. [L *circinatus* past part. of *circinare* make round f. *circinus* pair of compasses]

circle /'sɜːk(ə)l/ *n. & v.* —*n.* **1 a** a round plane figure whose circumference is everywhere equidistant from its centre. **b** the line enclosing a circle. **2** a roundish enclosure or structure. **3** a ring. **4** a curved upper tier of seats in a theatre etc. (*dress circle*). **5** a circular route. **6** *Archaeol.* a group of (usu. large embedded) stones arranged in a circle. **7** *Hockey* = *striking-circle*. **8** persons grouped round a centre of interest. **9** a set or class or restricted group (*literary circles; not done in the best circles*). **10** a period or cycle (*the circle of the year*). **11** (in full **vicious circle**) **a** an unbroken sequence of reciprocal cause and effect. **b** an action and reaction that intensify each other (cf. *virtuous circle*). **c** the fallacy of proving a proposition from another which depends on the first for its own proof. —*v.* **1** *intr.* (often foll. by *round, about*) move in a circle. **2** *tr.* **a** revolve round. **b** form a circle round. □ **circle back** move in a wide loop towards the starting-point. **come full circle** return to the starting-point. **go round in circles** make no progress despite effort. **great** (or **small**) **circle** a circle on the surface of a sphere whose plane passes (or does not pass) through the sphere's centre. **run round in circles** *colloq.* be fussily busy with little result. □□ **circler** *n.* [ME f. OF *cercle* f. L *circulus* dimin. of *circus* ring]

circlet /'sɜːklɪt/ *n.* **1** a small circle. **2** a circular band, esp. of gold or jewelled etc., as an ornament.

circs /sɜːks/ *n.pl. colloq.* circumstances. [abbr.]

circuit /'sɜːkɪt/ *n.* **1 a** a line or course enclosing an area; the distance round. **b** the area enclosed. **2** *Electr.* **a** the path of a current. **b** the apparatus through which a current passes. **3 a** the journey of a judge in a particular district to hold courts. **b** this district. **c** the lawyers following a circuit. **4** a chain of theatres or cinemas etc. under a single management. **5** *Brit.* a motor-racing track. **6 a** a sequence of sporting events (*the US tennis circuit*). **b** a sequence of athletic exercises. **7** a roundabout journey. **8 a** a group of local Methodist churches forming a minor administrative unit. **b** the journey of an itinerant minister within this. □ **circuit-breaker** an automatic device for stopping the flow of current in an electrical circuit. [ME f. OF, f. L *circuitus* f. CIRCUM- + *ire it-* go]

circuitous /sɜːˈkjuːɪtəs/ *adj.* **1** indirect (and usu. long). **2** going a long way round. □□ **circuitously** *adv.* **circuitousness** *n.* [med.L *circuitosus* f. *circuitus* CIRCUIT]

circuitry /'sɜːkɪtrɪ/ *n.* (*pl.* **-ies**) **1** a system of electric circuits. **2** the equipment forming this.

circular /'sɜːkjʊlə(r)/ *adj. & n.* —*adj.* **1 a** having the form of a circle. **b** moving or taking place along a circle (*circular tour*). **2** *Logic* (of reasoning) depending on a vicious circle. **3** (of a letter or advertisement etc.) printed for distribution to a large number of people. —*n.* a circular letter, leaflet, etc. □ **circular saw** a power saw with a rapidly rotating toothed disc. □□ **circularity** /-'lærɪtɪ/ *n.* **circularly** *adv.* [ME f. AF *circuler*, OF *circulier*, *cerclier* f. LL *circularis* f. L *circulus* CIRCLE]

circularize /'sɜːkjʊləˌraɪz/ *v.tr.* (also **-ise**) **1** distribute circulars to. **2** *US* seek opinions of (people) by means of a questionnaire. □□ **circularization** /-'zeɪʃ(ə)n/ *n.*

circulate /'sɜːkjʊˌleɪt/ *v.* **1** *intr.* go round from one place or person etc. to the next and so on; be in circulation. **2** *tr.* **a** cause to go round; put into circulation. **b** give currency to (a report etc.). **c** circularize. **3** *intr.* be actively sociable at a party, gathering, etc. □ **circulating library** a small library with books lent to a group of subscribers in turn. **circulating medium** notes or

gold etc. used in exchange. □□ **circulative** *adj.* **circulator** *n.* [L *circulare circulat-* f. *circulus* CIRCLE]

circulation /ˌsɜːkjʊˈleɪʃ(ə)n/ *n.* **1 a** a movement to and fro, or from and back to a starting point, esp. of a fluid in a confined area or circuit. **b** the movement of blood from and to the heart. **c** a similar movement of sap etc. **2 a** the transmission or distribution (of news or information or books etc.). **b** the number of copies sold, esp. of journals and newspapers. **3 a** currency, coin, etc. **b** the movement or exchange of this in a country etc. □ **in** (or **out of**) **circulation** participating (or not participating) in activities etc. [F *circulation* or L *circulatio* f. *circulare* CIRCULATE]

circulatory /ˌsɜːkjʊˈleɪtərɪ, ˈsɜːkjʊlətərɪ/ *adj.* of or relating to the circulation of blood or sap.

circum- /'sɜːkəm/ *comb. form* round, about, around, used: **1** adverbially (*circumambient; circumfuse*). **2** prepositionally (*circumlunar; circumocular*). [from or after L *circum* prep. = round, about]

circumambient /ˌsɜːkəmˈæmbɪənt/ *adj.* (esp. of air or another fluid) surrounding. □□ **circumambience** *n.* **circumambiency** *n.*

circumambulate /ˌsɜːkəmˈæmbjʊˌleɪt/ *v.tr. & intr. formal* walk round or about. □□ **circumambulation** /-ˈleɪʃ(ə)n/ *n.* **circumambulatory** *adj.* [CIRCUM- + *ambulate* f. L *ambulare* walk]

circumcircle /'sɜːkəmˌsɜːk(ə)l/ *n. Geom.* a circle touching all the vertices of a triangle or polygon.

circumcise /'sɜːkəmˌsaɪz/ *v.tr.* **1** cut off the foreskin, as a Jewish or Muslim rite or a surgical operation. **2** cut off the clitoris (and sometimes the labia), usu. as a religious rite. **3** *Bibl.* purify (the heart etc.). [ME f. OF f. L *circumcidere circumcis-* (as CIRCUM-, *caedere* cut)]

circumcision /ˌsɜːkəmˈsɪʒ(ə)n/ *n.* **1** the act or rite of circumcising or being circumcised. **2** (**Circumcision**) *Eccl.* the feast of the Circumcision of Christ, 1 Jan. [ME f. OF *circoncision* f. LL *circumcisio -onis* (as CIRCUMCISE)]

circumference /sɜːˈkʌmfərəns/ *n.* **1** the enclosing boundary, esp. of a circle or other figure enclosed by a curve. **2** the distance round. □□ **circumferential** /ˌsɜːkʌmfəˈrenʃ(ə)l/ *adj.* **circumferentially** /ˌsɜːkʌmfəˈrenʃəlɪ/ *adv.* [ME f. OF *circonference* f. L *circumferentia* (as CIRCUM-, *ferre* bear)]

circumflex /'sɜːkəmˌfleks/ *n. & adj.* —*n.* (in full **circumflex accent**) a mark (ˆ or ⌢) placed over a vowel in some languages to indicate a contraction, length, or a special quality. —*adj. Anat.* curved, bending round something else (*circumflex nerve*). [L *circumflexus* (as CIRCUM-, *flectere flex-* bend), transl. of Gk *perispōmenos* drawn around]

circumfluent /sɜːˈkʌmflʊənt/ *adj.* flowing round, surrounding. □□ **circumfluence** *n.* [L *circumfluere* (as CIRCUM-, *fluere* flow)]

circumfuse /ˌsɜːkəmˈfjuːz/ *v.tr.* pour round or about. [CIRCUM- + L *fundere fus-* pour]

circumjacent /ˌsɜːkəmˈdʒeɪs(ə)nt/ *adj.* situated around. [L *circumjacēre* (as CIRCUM-, *jacēo* lie)]

circumlocution /ˌsɜːkəmləˈkjuːʃ(ə)n/ *n.* **1 a** a roundabout expression. **b** evasive talk. **2** the use of many words where fewer would do; verbosity. □□ **circumlocutional** *adj.* **circumlocutionary** *adj.* **circumlocutionist** *n.* **circumlocutory** /-ˈlɒkjʊtərɪ/ *adj.* [ME f. F *circumlocution* or L *circumlocutio* (as CIRCUM-, LOCUTION), transl. of Gk PERIPHRASIS]

circumlunar /ˌsɜːkəmˈluːnə(r), -ˈljuːnə(r)/ *adj.* moving or situated around the moon.

circumnavigate /ˌsɜːkəmˈnævɪˌgeɪt/ *v.tr.* sail round (esp. the world). □□ **circumnavigation** /-ˈgeɪʃ(ə)n/ *n.* **circumnavigator** *n.* [L *circumnavigare* (as CIRCUM-, NAVIGATE)]

circumpolar /ˌsɜːkəmˈpəʊlə(r)/ *adj.* **1** *Geog.* around or near one of the earth's poles. **2** *Astron.* (of a star or motion etc.) above the horizon at all times in a given latitude.

circumscribe /'sɜːkəmˌskraɪb/ *v.tr.* **1** (of a line etc.) enclose or outline. **2** lay down the limits of; confine, restrict. **3** *Geom.* draw (a figure) round another, touching it at points but not cutting it (cf. INSCRIBE). □□ **circumscribable** /-ˈskraɪbəb(ə)l/ *adj.* **circumscriber** *n.* **circumscription** /-ˈskrɪpʃ(ə)n/ *n.* [L *circumscribere* (as CIRCUM-, *scribere script-* write)]

aʊ *how* eɪ *day* əʊ *no* eə *hair* ɪə *near* ɔɪ *boy* ʊə *poor* aɪə *fire* aʊə *sour*   (*see over for consonants*)

circumsolar /ˌsɜːkəmˈsəʊlə(r)/ *adj.* moving or situated around or near the sun.

circumspect /ˈsɜːkəmˌspekt/ *adj.* wary, cautious; taking everything into account. □□ **circumspection** /-ˈspekʃ(ə)n/ *n.* **circumspectly** *adv.* [ME f. L *circumspicere circumspect-* (as CIRCUM-, *specere spect-* look)]

circumstance /ˈsɜːkəmst(ə)ns/ *n.* **1 a** a fact, occurrence, or condition, esp. (in *pl.*) the time, place, manner, cause, occasion etc., or surroundings of an act or event. **b** (in *pl.*) the external conditions that affect or might affect an action. **2** (often foll. by *that* + clause) an incident, occurrence, or fact, as needing consideration (*the circumstance that he left early*). **3** (in *pl.*) one's state of financial or material welfare (*in reduced circumstances*). **4** ceremony, fuss (*pomp and circumstance*). **5** full detail in a narrative (*told it with much circumstance*). □ **in** (or **under**) **the** (or **these**) **circumstances** the state of affairs being what it is. **in** (or **under**) **no circumstances** not at all; never. □□ **circumstanced** *adj.* [ME f. OF *circonstance* or L *circumstantia* (as CIRCUM-, *stantia* f. *sto* stand)]

circumstantial /ˌsɜːkəmˈstænʃ(ə)l/ *adj.* **1** given in full detail (*a circumstantial account*). **2** (of evidence, a legal case, etc.) tending to establish a conclusion by inference from known facts hard to explain otherwise. **3 a** depending on circumstances. **b** adventitious, incidental. □□ **circumstantiality** /-ʃɪˈælɪtɪ/ *n.* **circumstantially** *adv.* [L *circumstantia*: see CIRCUMSTANCE]

circumterrestrial /ˌsɜːkəmtəˈrestrɪəl/ *adj.* moving or situated around the earth.

circumvallate /ˌsɜːkəmˈvæleɪt/ *v.tr.* surround with or as with a rampart. [L *circumvallare circumvallat-* (as CIRCUM-, *vallare* f. *vallum* rampart)]

circumvent /ˌsɜːkəmˈvent/ *v.tr.* **1 a** evade (a difficulty); find a way round. **b** baffle, outwit. **2** entrap (an enemy) by surrounding. □□ **circumvention** *n.* [L *circumvenire circumvent-* (as CIRCUM-, *venire* come)]

circumvolution /ˌsɜːkəmvəˈljuːʃ(ə)n/ *n.* **1** rotation. **2** the winding of one thing round another. **3** a sinuous movement. [ME f. L *circumvolvere circumvolut-* (as CIRCUM-, *volvere* roll)]

circus /ˈsɜːkəs/ *n.* (*pl.* **circuses**) **1** a travelling show of performing animals, acrobats, clowns, etc. (see below.) **2** *colloq.* **a** a scene of lively action; a disturbance. **b** a group of people in a common activity, esp. sport. **3** *Brit.* an open space in a town, where several streets converge (*Piccadilly Circus*). **4** a circular hollow surrounded by hills. **5** *Rom. Antiq.* **a** a rounded or oval arena with tiers of seats, for equestrian and other sports and games. **b** a performance given there (*bread and circuses*). [L, = ring]

Roman circuses in no way resembled those of the present day: they were arenas used for chariot-racing and gladiatorial combats. The modern circus dates from the late 18th c., when ex-sergeant-major Philip Astley gave horse-riding displays in London, at first in a field and then in 'Astley's Royal Amphitheatre of Arts', an arena to which he had added a stage for singing, dancing, and pantomime. This form of entertainment proved so popular that similar shows were started elsewhere in England and in other countries of Europe, some permanent, others as 'tenting' circuses, with performers and equipment travelling in caravans and wagons (later by train). From the early 19th c. they were often combined with the travelling menageries and wild animals' performances that had become very popular, of which the most celebrated was the combined circus and menagerie owned by the Sangers. America was the home of the really big circus. Barnum and his partners opened their first show at Brooklyn in 1871, and combined in 1880 with his great rivals Cooper and Bailey. After losing its popularity in England in the early 20th c., the circus enjoyed a revival through the large and elaborate productions of C. B. Cochran (1912) and after the First World War by new circuses such as that of Bertram Mills, but circuses are now rare in Britain. In the USSR, however, the circus continued to flourish while State-subsidized.

ciré /ˈsɪəreɪ/ *n. & adj.* —*n.* a fabric with a smooth shiny surface obtained esp. by waxing and heating. —*adj.* having such a surface. [F, = waxed]

cire perdue /ˌsɪə pɜːˈdjuː/ *n.* a method of bronze-casting using a clay core and a wax coating placed in a mould: the wax is melted in the mould and bronze poured into the space left, producing a hollow bronze figure when the core is discarded. [F, = lost wax]

cirque /sɜːk/ *n.* **1** *Geol.* a deep bowl-shaped hollow at the head of a valley or on a mountainside. **2** *poet.* **a** a ring. **b** an amphitheatre or arena. [F f. L CIRCUS]

cirrhosis /sɪˈrəʊsɪs/ *n.* a chronic disease of the liver marked by the degeneration of cells and the thickening of surrounding tissues, as a result of alcoholism, hepatitis, etc. □□ **cirrhotic** /sɪˈrɒtɪk/ *adj.* [mod.L f. Gk *kirrhos* tawny]

cirriped /ˈsɪrɪˌped/ *n.* (also **cirripede** /ˈsɪrɪˌpiːd/) any marine crustacean of the class Cirripedia, having a valved shell and usu. sessile when adult, e.g. a barnacle. [mod.L *Cirripedia* f. L *cirrus* curl (from the form of the legs) + *pes pedis* foot]

cirro- /ˈsɪrəʊ/ *comb. form* cirrus (cloud).

cirrocumulus /ˌsɪrəʊˈkjuːmjʊləs/ *n.* (*pl.* **-li** /-laɪ/) a form of usually high cloud consisting of small roundish fleecy clouds in contact with one another, known as 'mackerel sky'. [CIRRUS + CUMULUS]

cirrostratus /ˌsɪrəʊˈstreɪtəs/ *n.* (*pl.* **-ti** /-taɪ/) thin usually high white cloud composed mainly of fine ice-crystals and producing halo phenomena. [CIRRUS + STRATUS]

cirrus /ˈsɪrəs/ *n.* (*pl.* **cirri** /-raɪ/) **1** *Meteorol.* a form of white wispy cloud, esp. at high altitude. **2** *Bot.* a tendril. **3** *Zool.* a long slender appendage or filament. □□ **cirrose** *adj.* **cirrous** *adj.* [L, = curl]

cis- /sɪs/ *prefix* (opp. TRANS- or ULTRA-). **1** on this side of; on the side nearer to the speaker or writer (*cisatlantic*). **2** *Rom. Antiq.* on the Roman side of (*cisalpine*). **3** (of time) closer to the present (*cis-Elizabethan*). **4** *Chem.* (of an isomer) having two atoms or groups on the same side of a given plane in the molecule. [L *cis* on this side of]

cisalpine /sɪsˈælpaɪn/ *adj.* on the southern side of the Alps.

cisatlantic /ˌsɪsətˈlæntɪk/ *adj.* on this side of the Atlantic.

cisco /ˈsɪskəʊ/ *n.* (*pl.* **-oes**) any of various freshwater whitefish of the genus *Coregonus*, native to N. America. [19th c.: orig. unkn.]

Ciskei /sɪsˈkaɪ/ a tribal homeland of the Xhosa people of South Africa, designated an independent republic in 1981; pop. (1985) 925,000; capital, Bisho.

cislunar /sɪsˈluːnə(r)/ *adj.* between the earth and the moon.

Cisneros /θiːsˈneɪrəʊs/, Francisco Jiménez de (1437–1517), Spanish statesman. One of the major contributors to the growth of Spanish power in the late 15th and early 16th c., Cisneros became primate of Spain in 1495 and later a Cardinal and Inquisitor General for Castile and Léon.

cispontine /sɪsˈpɒntaɪn/ *adj.* on the north side of the Thames in London. [CIS- (orig. the better-known side) + L *pons pont-* bridge]

cissy *var.* of SISSY.

cist[1] /sɪst, kɪst/ *n.* (also **kist** /kɪst/) *Archaeol.* a coffin or burial-chamber made from stone or a hollowed tree. [Welsh, = CHEST]

cist[2] /sɪst/ *n. Gk Antiq.* a box used for sacred utensils. [L *cista* f. Gk *kistē* box]

Cistercian /sɪˈstɜːʃ(ə)n/ *n. & adj.* —*n.* a monk or nun of an order founded in 1098. (See below.) —*adj.* of the Cistercians. [F *cistercien* f. L *Cistercium* Cîteaux near Dijon in France, where the order was founded]

The Cistercian order was founded in 1098 for strict observance of the Rule of St Benedict, and Cistercian houses spread throughout Europe in the 12th–13th c. The monks are now divided into two observances, the strict observance (following the original rule), known popularly as Trappists, and the common observance, which has certain relaxations.

cistern /ˈsɪst(ə)n/ *n.* **1** a tank for storing water, esp. one in a roof-space supplying taps or as part of a flushing lavatory. **2** an underground reservoir for rainwater. [ME f. OF *cisterne* f. L *cisterna* (as CIST[2])]

cistus /ˈsɪstəs/ *n.* any shrub of the genus *Cistus*, with large white or red flowers. Also called *rock rose*. [mod.L f. Gk *kistos*]

citadel /ˈsɪtəd(ə)l, -ˌdel/ *n.* **1** a fortress, usu. on high ground protecting or dominating a city. **2** a meeting-hall of the Salvation Army. [F *citadelle* or It. *citadella*, ult. f. L *civitas -tatis* city]

citation /saɪˈteɪʃ(ə)n/ n. 1 the citing of a book or other source; a passage cited. 2 a mention in an official dispatch. 3 a note accompanying an award, describing the reasons for it.

cite /saɪt/ v.tr. 1 adduce as an instance. 2 quote (a passage, book, or author) in support of an argument etc. 3 mention in an official dispatch. 4 summon to appear in a lawcourt. □□ **citable** adj. [ME f. F f. L citare f. ciēre set moving]

citified /ˈsɪtɪˌfaɪd/ adj. (also **cityfied**) usu. derog. city-like or urban in appearance or behaviour.

citizen /ˈsɪtɪz(ə)n/ n. 1 a member of a State or Commonwealth, either native or naturalized (British citizen). 2 (usu. foll. by of) a an inhabitant of a city. b a freeman of a city. 3 US a civilian. □ **citizen of the world** a person who is at home anywhere; a cosmopolitan. **Citizens' Advice Bureau** (in the UK) an office at which the public can receive free advice and information on civil matters. **citizen's arrest** an arrest by an ordinary person without a warrant, allowable in certain cases. **citizen's band** a system of local intercommunication by individuals on special radio frequencies. □□ **citizenhood** n. **citizenry** n. **citizenship** n. [ME f. AF citesein, OF citeain ult. f. L civitas -tatis city: cf. DENIZEN]

Citlaltepetl /ˌsiːtlælˈteɪpet(ə)l/ the highest peak in Mexico, in the east of the country, north of the city of Orizaba after which it is sometimes named (Pico de Orizaba). It rises to a height of 5,699 m (18,503 ft.) and is an extinct volcano, inactive since 1687. Its Aztec name means 'star mountain'.

citole /sɪˈtəʊl/ n. a small cittern. [ME f. OF: rel. to CITTERN with dimin. suffix]

citric /ˈsɪtrɪk/ adj. derived from citrus fruit. □ **citric acid** a sharp-tasting water-soluble organic acid found in the juice of lemons and other sour fruits. □□ **citrate** n. [F citrique f. L citrus citron]

citrin /ˈsɪtrɪn/ n. a group of substances occurring mainly in citrus fruits and blackcurrants, and formerly thought to be a vitamin. Also called BIOFLAVONOID.

citrine /ˈsɪtrɪn/ adj. & n. —adj. lemon-coloured. —n. a transparent yellow variety of quartz. Also called false topaz. [ME f. OF citrin (as CITRUS)]

citron /ˈsɪtrən/ n. 1 a shrubby tree, Citrus medica, bearing large lemon-like fruits with thick fragrant peel. 2 this fruit. [F f. L CITRUS, after limon lemon]

citronella /ˌsɪtrəˈnelə/ n. 1 any fragrant grass of the genus Cymbopogon, native to S. Asia. 2 the scented oil from these, used in insect repellent, and perfume and soap manufacture. [mod.L, formed as CITRON + dimin. suffix]

citrus /ˈsɪtrəs/ n. 1 any tree of the genus Citrus, including citron, lemon, lime, orange, and grapefruit. 2 (in full **citrus fruit**) a fruit from such a tree. □□ **citrous** adj. [L, = citron-tree or thuja]

cittern /ˈsɪt(ə)n/ n. hist. a wire-stringed lutelike instrument usu. played with a plectrum. [L cithara, Gk kithara a kind of harp, assim. to GITTERN]

city /ˈsɪtɪ/ n. (pl. **-ies**) 1 a a large town. b Brit. (strictly) a town created a city by charter and containing a cathedral. c US a municipal corporation occupying a definite area. 2 (the City) a the part of London governed by the Lord Mayor and the Corporation. b the business part of this. c commercial circles; high finance. 3 (attrib.) of a city or the City. □ **City Company** a corporation descended from an ancient trade-guild. **city desk** a department of a newspaper dealing with business news or US with local news. **City editor 1** the editor dealing with financial news in a newspaper or magazine. 2 (**city editor**) US the editor dealing with local news. **city father** (usu. in pl.) a person concerned with or experienced in the administration of a city. **city hall** US municipal offices or officers. **city manager** US an official directing the administration of a city. **city page** Brit. the part of a newspaper or magazine dealing with the financial and business news. **city slicker** usu. derog. 1 a smart and sophisticated city-dweller. 2 a plausible rogue as found in cities. **city-state** esp. hist. a city that with its surrounding territory forms an independent state. **City Technology College** (in the UK) any of a number of schools founded to teach (esp. technological subjects) in inner-city areas, taking pupils aged 11–18 and financed jointly by the government and industry, and operating independently of local

education authorities. The first such school opened in Birmingham in 1987. □□ **cityward** adj. & adv. **citywards** adv. [ME f. OF cité f. L civitas -tatis f. civis citizen]

cityfied var. of CITIFIED.

cityscape /ˈsɪtɪˌskeɪp/ n. 1 a view of a city (actual or depicted). 2 city scenery.

Ciudad Bolívar /θjuːˈðaːð bɒˈliːvɑː(r), sjuː-/ a city in SE Venezuela, capital of the State of Bolívar, on the Orinoco River; pop. (1981) 183,000. Its name was formerly Angostura (= 'narrows'), and was changed in 1846 to honour the country's liberator, Simón Bolívar.

civet /ˈsɪvɪt/ n. 1 (in full **civet-cat**) any catlike animal of the mongoose family, esp. Civettictis civetta of Central Africa, having well developed anal scent glands. 2 a strong musky perfume obtained from the secretions of these scent glands. [F civette f. It. zibetto f. med.L zibethum f. Arab. azzabād f. al the + zabād this perfume]

civic /ˈsɪvɪk/ adj. 1 of a city; municipal. 2 of or proper to citizens (civic virtues). 3 of citizenship, civil. □ **civic centre** Brit. the area where municipal offices and other public buildings are situated; the buildings themselves. □□ **civically** adv. [F civique or L civicus f. civis citizen]

civics /ˈsɪvɪks/ n.pl. (usu. treated as sing.) the study of the rights and duties of citizenship.

civil /ˈsɪv(ə)l, -ɪl/ adj. 1 of or belonging to citizens. 2 of ordinary citizens and their concerns, as distinct from military or naval or ecclesiastical matters. 3 polite, obliging, not rude. 4 Law relating to civil law (see below), not criminal or political matters (civil court; civil lawyer). 5 (of the length of a day, year, etc.) fixed by custom or law, not natural or astronomical. □ **civil aviation** non-military, esp. commercial aviation. **civil commotion** a riot or similar disturbance. **civil defence** the organization and training of civilians for the protection of lives and property during and after attacks in wartime. **civil disobedience** the refusal to comply with certain laws or to pay taxes etc. as a peaceful form of political protest. **civil engineer** an engineer who designs or maintains roads, bridges, dams, etc. **civil engineering** this work. **civil law 1** law concerning private rights (opp. criminal law). 2 hist. Roman or non-ecclesiastical law. **civil libertarian** an advocate of increased civil liberty. **civil liberty** (often in pl.) freedom of action and speech subject to the law. **civil list** (in the UK) an annual allowance voted by Parliament for the royal family's household expenses. **civil marriage** a marriage solemnized as a civil contract without religious ceremony. **civil rights** the rights of citizens to political and social freedom and equality. **civil service** see separate entry. **civil state** being single or married or divorced etc. **civil war** see separate entry. **civil year** see YEAR 2. □□ **civilly** adv. [ME f. OF f. L civilis f. civis citizen]

civilian /sɪˈvɪlɪən/ n. & adj. —n. a person not in the armed services or the police force. —adj. of or for civilians.

civilianize /sɪˈvɪlɪəˌnaɪz/ v.tr. (also **-ise**) make civilian in character or function. □□ **civilianization** /-ˈzeɪʃ(ə)n/ n.

civility /sɪˈvɪlɪtɪ/ n. (pl. **-ies**) 1 politeness. 2 an act of politeness. [ME f. OF civilité f. L civilitas -tatis (as CIVIL)]

civilization /ˌsɪvɪlaɪˈzeɪʃ(ə)n, ˌsɪvɪlɪ-/ n. (also **-isation**) 1 an advanced stage or system of social development. 2 those peoples of the world regarded as having this. 3 a people or nation (esp. of the past) regarded as an element of social evolution (ancient civilizations; the Inca civilization). 4 making or becoming civilized.

civilize /ˈsɪvɪˌlaɪz/ v.tr. (also **-ise**) 1 bring out of a barbarous or primitive stage of society. 2 enlighten; refine and educate. □□ **civilizable** adj. **civilizer** n. [F civiliser (as CIVIL)]

civil service n. the body of full-time officers employed by a State in the administration of civil (non-military) affairs. The Roman Empire had such a service, and there was one in China from the 7th c.; in the 19th c. many European countries copied Napoleon's system of an organized hierarchy. The term 'civil service' was originally applied to the part of the service of the East India Company carried on by covenanted servants who did not belong to the army or navy. □ **civil servant** a member of the civil service.

civil war *n.* war between citizens of the same country:

English Civil War the war between Charles I and his Parliamentary opponents, 1642–9. After several years of warfare, the better-organized Parliamentary forces gained the upper hand in 1644–5. Royalist resistance collapsed in 1646 and an attempt by Charles to regain power in alliance with the Scots was defeated at Preston in 1648, Charles himself being executed at the behest of the Parliamentary army in 1649. Fought against a background of confused political and religious issues, the English Civil War dramatically changed the nature of English society and government, even though the attempt to find an alternative to the monarchy eventually ended with the restoration of Charles II after the death of Oliver Cromwell, the dominant figure of the entire period.

American Civil War the war between the northern US States (usually known as the Union) and the Confederate States of the South, 1861–5. The southern States, having seceded from the Federal Union over the issues of slavery and States' rights, maintained a military resistance to the superior industrial strength of the north for four years. Although its armies won some impressive victories in the first two years of the war, the Confederacy failed to gain foreign recognition and was gradually overwhelmed by superior military might and naval blockade. By the time the main Confederate army surrendered in April 1865, most of the South, including its capital Richmond, had already fallen to Union soldiers.

Spanish Civil War the conflict between Nationalist and Republican forces in Spain, 1936–9. It began with a widespread military uprising against the leftist republican government in July 1936; the Nationalists were extensively aided by Germany and Italy, the Republicans by Russia and by an International Brigade of volunteers from Europe and America. In bitter fighting the Nationalists, led by Franco, gradually gained control of the countryside but failed to capture the capital, Madrid. Various attempts to bring the war to an end failed until after long periods of prolonged stalemate Franco finally succeeded in capturing Barcelona and Madrid in early 1939.

civvies /ˈsɪvɪz/ *n.pl. sl.* civilian clothes. [abbr.]

Civvy Street /ˈsɪvɪ/ *n. sl.* civilian life. [abbr.]

CJ *abbr.* Chief Justice.

CJD *abbr.* Creutzfeldt-Jakob disease.

Cl *symb. Chem.* the element chlorine.

cl *abbr.* **1** centilitre(s). **2** class.

clack /klæk/ *v. & n.* —*v.intr.* **1** make a sharp sound as of boards struck together. **2** chatter, esp. loudly. —*n.* **1** a clacking sound. **2** clacking talk. □□ **clacker** *n.* [ME, = to chatter, prob. f. ON *klaka*, of imit. orig.]

Clactonian /klækˈtəʊnɪən/ *adj. & n.* —*adj.* of the lower palaeolithic industries represented by the flint implements found at Clacton, Essex, dated to *c.*250,000–200,000 BC. —*n.* these industries.

clad¹ /klæd/ *adj.* **1** clothed. **2** provided with cladding. [past part. of CLOTHE]

clad² /klæd/ *v.tr.* (**cladding**; *past* and *past part.* **cladded** or **clad**) provide with cladding. [app. f. CLAD¹]

cladding /ˈklædɪŋ/ *n.* a covering or coating on a structure or material etc.

clade /kleɪd/ *n. Biol.* a group of organisms evolved from a common ancestor. [Gk *klados* branch]

cladistics /kləˈdɪstɪks/ *n.pl.* (usu. treated as *sing.*) *Biol.* a method of classification of animals and plants on the basis of shared characteristics, which are assumed to indicate common ancestry. □□ **cladism** /ˈklædɪz(ə)m/ *n.* [as CLADE + -IST + -ICS]

cladode /ˈkleɪdəʊd/ *n.* a flattened leaflike stem. [Gk *kladōdēs* many-shooted f. *klados* shoot]

claim /kleɪm/ *v. & n.* —*v.tr.* **1 a** (often foll. by *that* + clause) demand as one's due or property. **b** (usu. *absol.*) submit a request for payment under an insurance policy. **2 a** represent oneself as having or achieving (*claim victory; claim accuracy*). **b** (foll. by *to* + infin.) profess (*claimed to be the owner*). **c** assert, contend (*claim that one knows*). **3** have as an achievement or a consequence (*could then claim five wins; the fire claimed many victims*). **4** (of a thing) deserve

(one's attention etc.). —*n.* **1 a** a demand or request for something considered one's due (*lay claim to; put in a claim*). **b** an application for compensation under the terms of an insurance policy. **2** (foll. by *to, on*) a right or title to a thing (*his only claim to fame; have many claims on my time*). **3** a contention or assertion. **4** a thing claimed. **5** a statement of the novel features in a patent. **6** *Mining* a piece of land allotted or taken. □ **no claim** (or **claims**) **bonus** a reduction of an insurance premium after an agreed period without a claim under the terms of the policy. □□ **claimable** *adj.* **claimer** *n.* [ME f. OF *claime* f. *clamer* call out f. L *clamare*]

claimant /ˈkleɪmənt/ *n.* a person making a claim, esp. in a lawsuit or for a State benefit.

Clair /kleə(r)/, René (real name René Chomette 1898–1981), French film director, the fantastic nature of whose work contained elements of surrealism, though humour and satire were always at their core. He made a number of silent films, notably *An Italian Straw Hat* (1927), and his early sound films included the classics *Sous les Toits de Paris* (1930), *Le Million*, and *A Nous la Liberté* (both 1931). His British and American work was less successful, but he regained his touch on returning to France in films such as *Les Belles de Nuit* (1952). He was invariably involved in writing the scripts.

clairaudience /kleəˈrɔːdɪəns/ *n.* the supposed faculty of perceiving, as if by hearing, what is inaudible. □□ **clairaudient** *adj. & n.* [F *clair* CLEAR, + AUDIENCE, after CLAIRVOYANCE]

clairvoyance /kleəˈvɔɪəns/ *n.* **1** the supposed faculty of perceiving things or events in the future or beyond normal sensory contact. **2** exceptional insight. [F *clairvoyance* f. *clair* CLEAR + *voir voy-* see]

clairvoyant /kleəˈvɔɪənt/ *n. & adj.* —*n.* (*fem.* **clairvoyante**) a person having clairvoyance. —*adj.* having clairvoyance. □□ **clairvoyantly** *adv.*

clam /klæm/ *n. & v.* —*n.* **1** any bivalve mollusc, esp. the edible N. American hard or round clam (*Mercenaria mercenaria*) or the soft or long clam (*Mya arenaria*). **2** *colloq.* a shy or withdrawn person. —*v.intr.* (**clammed**, **clamming**) **1** dig for clams. **2** (foll. by *up*) *colloq.* refuse to talk. [16th c.: app. f. *clam* a clamp]

clamant /ˈkleɪmənt/ *adj. literary* noisy; insistent, urgent. □□ **clamantly** *adv.* [L *clamare clamant-* cry out]

clamber /ˈklæmbə(r)/ *v. & n.* —*v.intr.* climb with hands and feet, esp. with difficulty or laboriously. —*n.* a difficult climb. [ME, prob. f. *clamb*, obs. past tense of CLIMB]

clammy /ˈklæmɪ/ *adj.* (**clammier**, **clammiest**) **1** unpleasantly damp and sticky or slimy. **2** (of weather) cold and damp. □□ **clammily** *adv.* **clamminess** *n.* [ME f. *clam* to daub]

clamour /ˈklæmə(r)/ *n. & v.* (*US* **clamor**) —*n.* **1** loud or vehement shouting or noise. **2** a protest or complaint; an appeal or demand. —*v.* **1** *intr.* make a clamour. **2** *tr.* utter with a clamour. □□ **clamorous** *adj.* **clamorously** *adv.* **clamorousness** *n.* [ME f. OF f. L *clamor -oris* f. *clamare* cry out]

clamp¹ /klæmp/ *n. & v.* —*n.* **1** a device, esp. a brace or band of iron etc., for strengthening other materials or holding things together. **2** a device for immobilizing an illegally parked car. —*v.tr.* **1** strengthen or fasten with a clamp. **2** place or hold firmly. **3** immobilize (an illegally parked car) by fixing a clamp to one of its wheels. □ **clamp down 1** (often foll. by *on*) be rigid in enforcing a rule etc. **2** (foll. by *on*) try to suppress. **clamp-down** *n.* severe restriction or suppression. [ME prob. f. MDu., MLG *klamp(e)*]

clamp² /klæmp/ *n.* **1** a heap of potatoes or other root vegetables stored under straw or earth. **2** a pile of bricks for burning. **3** a pile of turf or peat or garden rubbish etc. [16th c.: prob. f. Du. *klamp* heap (in sense 2 related to CLUMP)]

clan /klæn/ *n.* **1** a group of people with a common ancestor, esp. in the Scottish Highlands. **2** a large family as a social group. **3** a group with a strong common interest. **4 a** a genus, species, or class. **b** a family or group of animals, e.g. elephants. [ME f. Gael. *clann* f. L *planta* sprout]

clandestine /klænˈdestɪn/ *adj.* surreptitious, secret. □□ **clandestinely** *adv.* **clandestinity** /-ˈtɪnɪtɪ/ *n.* [F *clandestin* or L *clandestinus* f. *clam* secretly]

clang /klæŋ/ *n. & v.* —*n.* a loud resonant metallic sound as of a bell or hammer etc. —v. 1 intr. make a clang. 2 tr. cause to clang. [imit.: infl. by L clangere resound]

clanger /ˈklæŋə(r)/ n. sl. a mistake or blunder. □ **drop a clanger** commit a conspicuous indiscretion.

clangour /ˈklæŋgə(r)/ n. (US **clangor**) 1 a prolonged or repeated clanging noise. 2 an uproar or commotion. □□ **clangorous** adj. **clangorously** adv. [L clangor noise of trumpets etc.]

clank /klæŋk/ n. & v. —n. a sound as of heavy pieces of metal meeting or a chain rattling. —v. 1 intr. make a clanking sound. 2 tr. cause to clank. □□ **clankingly** adv. [imit.: cf. CLANG, CLINK¹, Du. klank]

clannish /ˈklænɪʃ/ adj. usu. derog. 1 (of a family or group) tending to hold together. 2 of or like a clan. □□ **clannishly** adv. **clannishness** n.

clanship /ˈklænʃɪp/ n. 1 a patriarchal system of clans. 2 loyalty to one's clan.

clansman /ˈklænzmən/ n. (pl. **-men**; fem. **clanswoman**, pl. **-women**) a member or fellow-member of a clan.

clap¹ /klæp/ v. & n. —v. (**clapped, clapping**) 1 a intr. strike the palms of one's hands together as a signal or repeatedly as applause. b tr. strike (the hands) together in this way. 2 tr. applaud or show one's approval of (esp. a person) in this way. 3 tr. (of a bird) flap (its wings) audibly. 4 tr. put or place quickly or with determination (clapped him in prison; clap a tax on whisky). —n. 1 the act of clapping, esp. as applause. 2 an explosive sound, esp. of thunder. 3 a slap, a pat. □ **clap eyes on** colloq. see. **clap on the back** = slap on the back. **clapped out** Brit. sl. worn out (esp. of machinery etc.); exhausted. [OE clappian throb, beat, of imit. orig.]

clap² /klæp/ n. coarse sl. venereal disease, esp. gonorrhoea. [OF clapoir venereal bubo]

clapboard /ˈklæpbɔːd, ˈklæbəd/ n. US = WEATHERBOARD. [Anglicized f. LG klappholt cask-stave]

clapper /ˈklæpə(r)/ n. the tongue or striker of a bell. □ **like the clappers** Brit. sl. very fast or hard.

clapperboard /ˈklæpəˌbɔːd/ n. Cinematog. a device of hinged boards struck together to synchronize the starting of picture and sound machinery in filming.

clapper bridge n. a rough bridge consisting of a series of slabs or planks resting on piles of stones. (See BRIDGE¹.) [perh. f. L claperius heap of stones (orig. unkn.)]

claptrap /ˈklæptræp/ n. 1 insincere or pretentious talk, nonsense. 2 language used or feelings expressed only to gain applause. [CLAP¹ + TRAP¹]

claque /klæk, klɑːk/ n. a group of people hired to applaud in a theatre etc. [F f. claquer to clap]

claqueur /klæˈkɜː(r), klɑː-/ n. a member of a claque. [F (as CLAQUE)]

clarabella /ˌklærəˌbelə, ˈklɑː-/ n. an organ-stop of flute quality. [fem. forms of L clarus clear and bellus pretty]

Clare¹ /kleə(r)/ a county in the province of Munster in the Republic of Ireland; pop. (est. 1986) 91,300; capital, Ennis.

Clare² /kleə(r)/, John (1793–1864), English poet, son of a Northamptonshire labourer. In 1820 he published his successful Poems Descriptive of Rural Life and Scenery, followed by other collections of verse with the same theme. In 1837 he was certified insane and spent the rest of his life in an asylum, where he continued to write, always in his own dialect and idosyncratic grammar and never succumbing to the current taste for artificial poetic diction.

Clare³ /kleə(r)/, St (1194–1253), foundress of the 'Poor Clares', an order of Franciscan nuns named after her. Born at Assisi, she joined St Francis c.1212, and when a few years later he set up a separate community for women to live on Franciscan lines she became its abbess. The order spread through Italy and into Europe. She was canonized two years after her death and in 1958 Pope Pius XII declared her the patron saint of television, alluding to an incident during her last illness when from her sickbed she miraculously saw and heard the Christmas midnight mass being held in the Church of St Francis on the far side of Assisi. Feast day, 11 (formerly 12) Aug.

clarence /ˈklærəns/ n. hist. a four-wheeled closed carriage with seats for four inside and two on the box. [Duke of Clarence, afterwards William IV]

Clarenceux /ˈklærənˌsjuː/ n. Heraldry (in the UK) the title given to the second King of Arms, with jurisdiction south of the Trent (cf. NORROY, King of Arms). [ME f. AF f. Duke of Clarence f. Clare in Suffolk]

Clarendon /ˈklærəndən/, Edward Hyde, Earl of (1609–74), English statesman and historian, Lord Chancellor under Charles II and Chancellor of Oxford University from 1660 until his fall in 1667, and author of a successful and prestigious history of the English Civil War. The new printing house into which Oxford University Press moved in 1713, and the laboratory which houses the university physics department (founded in 1872), are named after him.

claret /ˈklærət/ n. & adj. —n. 1 red wine, esp. from Bordeaux. 2 a deep purplish-red. 3 archaic sl. blood. —adj. claret-coloured. [ME f. OF (vin) claret f. med.L claratum (vinum) f. L clarus clear]

clarify /ˈklærɪˌfaɪ/ v. (**-ies, -ied**) 1 tr. & intr. make or become clearer. 2 tr. a free (liquid, butter, etc.) from impurities. b make transparent. c purify. □□ **clarification** /-fɪˈkeɪʃ(ə)n/ n. **clarificatory** /-fɪˈkeɪtərɪ/ n. **clarifier** n. [ME f. OF clarifier f. L clarus clear]

clarinet /ˌklærɪˈnet/ n. 1 a a woodwind instrument with a single-reed mouthpiece, a cylindrical tube with a flared end, holes, and keys. It has a range of just over three octaves, but the highest notes are not generally scored for except by some modern composers seeking a squeaky harsh sound. The clarinet dates from the early 18th c., and has been a standard orchestral instrument since the end of that century. b its player. 2 an organ-stop with a quality resembling a clarinet. □□ **clarinettist** n. (US **clarinetist**). [F clarinette, dimin. of clarine a kind of bell]

clarion /ˈklærɪən/ n. & adj. —n. 1 a clear rousing sound. 2 hist. a shrill narrow-tubed war trumpet. 3 an organ-stop with the quality of a clarion. —adj. clear and loud. [ME f. med.L clario -onis f. L clarus clear]

clarity /ˈklærɪtɪ/ n. the state or quality of being clear, esp. of sound or expression. [ME f. L claritas f. clarus clear]

Clark /klɑːk/, William (1770–1838), US army officer who jointly commanded the Lewis and Clark expedition (1804–6) across the American continent.

Clarke¹ /klɑːk/, Arthur Charles (1917–), English writer of science fiction stories and novels, including The Nine Billion Names of God (1967) and A Space Odyssey (1968), and of many non-fiction works on space travel.

Clarke² /klɑːk/, Marcus Andrew Hislop (1846–81), English writer, who emigrated to Australia in 1863, where he worked on a sheep station before becoming a journalist. He is remembered for his celebrated novel For the Term of his Natural Life (1874), a powerful and sympathetic portrayal of an Austrlian penal settlement, and for his shorter stories of Australian life.

clarkia /ˈklɑːkɪə/ n. any plant of the genus Clarkia, with showy white, pink, or purple flowers. [mod.L f. W. CLARK]

clary /ˈkleərɪ/ n. (pl. **-ies**) any of various aromatic herbs of the genus Salvia. [ME f. obs. F clarie repr. med.L sclarea]

clash /klæʃ/ n. & v. —n. 1 a a loud jarring sound as of metal objects being struck together. b a collision, esp. with force. 2 a a conflict or disagreement. b a discord of colours etc. —v. 1 a intr. make a clashing sound. b tr. cause to clash. 2 intr. collide; coincide awkwardly. 3 intr. (often foll. by with) a come into conflict or be at variance. b (of colours) be discordant. □□ **clasher** n. [imit.: cf. clack, clang, crack, crash]

clasp /klɑːsp/ n. & v. —n. 1 a a device with interlocking parts for fastening. b a buckle or brooch. c a metal fastening on a book-cover. 2 a an embrace; a person's reach. b a grasp or handshake. 3 a bar of silver on a medal-ribbon with the name of the battle etc. at which the wearer was present. —v. 1 tr. fasten with or as with a clasp. 2 tr. a grasp, hold closely. b embrace, encircle. 3 intr. fasten a clasp. □ **clasp hands** shake hands with fervour or affection. **clasp one's hands** interlace one's fingers. **clasp-knife** a folding knife, usu. with a catch holding the blade when open. □□ **clasper** n. [ME: orig. unkn.]

clasper /ˈklɑːspə(r)/ n. (in pl.) the appendages of some male fish and insects used to hold the female in copulation.

class /klɑːs/ n. & v. —n. 1 any set of persons or things grouped together, or graded or differentiated from others esp. by quality (*first class; economy class*). 2 a a division or order of society (*upper class; professional classes*). b a caste system, a system of social classes. c (**the classes**) *archaic* the rich or educated. 3 *colloq.* distinction or high quality in appearance, behaviour, etc.; stylishness. 4 a a group of students or pupils taught together. b the occasion when they meet. c their course of instruction. 5 *US* all the college or school students of the same standing or graduating in a given year (*the class of 1990*). 6 (in conscripted armies) all the recruits of a given year (*the 1950 class*). 7 *Brit.* a division of candidates according to merit in an examination. 8 *Biol.* a grouping of organisms, the next major rank below a division or phylum. —v.tr. assign to a class or category. □ **class-conscious** aware of and reacting to social divisions or one's place in a system of social class. **class-consciousness** this awareness. **class-list** *Brit.* a list of candidates in an examination with the class achieved by each. **class war** conflict between social classes. **in a class of** (or **on**) **its** (or **one's**) **own** unequalled. **no class** *colloq.* lacking quality or distinction. [L *classis* assembly]

classic /ˈklæsɪk/ adj. & n. —adj. 1 a of the first class; of acknowledged excellence. b remarkably typical; outstandingly important (*a classic case*). 2 a of ancient Greek and Latin literature, art, or culture. b (of style in art, music, etc.) simple, harmonious, well-proportioned; in accordance with established forms (cf. ROMANTIC). 3 having literary or historic associations (*classic ground*). 4 (of clothes) made in a simple elegant style not much affected by changes in fashion. —n. 1 a classic writer, artist, work, or example. 2 a an ancient Greek or Latin writer. b (in pl.) the study of ancient Greek and Latin literature and history. c *archaic* a scholar of ancient Greek and Latin. 3 a follower of classic models (cf. ROMANTIC). 4 a garment in classic style. 5 (in pl.) *Brit.* the classic races. □ **classic races** *Brit.* the five main flat races, namely the Two Thousand and the One Thousand Guineas, the Derby, the Oaks, and the St Leger. [F *classique* or L *classicus* f. *classis* class]

classical /ˈklæsɪk(ə)l/ adj. 1 a of ancient Greek or Latin literature or art. (See below.) b (of language) having the form used by the ancient standard authors (*classical Latin; classical Hebrew*). c based on the study of ancient Greek and Latin (*a classical education*). d learned in classical studies. 2 a (of music) serious or conventional; following traditional principles and intended to be of permanent rather than ephemeral value (cf. POPULAR, LIGHT). b of the period from c.1750–1800 (cf. ROMANTIC). 3 a in or following the restrained style of classical antiquity (cf. ROMANTIC). b in or relating to a long-established style. 4 *Physics* relating to the concepts which preceded relativity and quantum theory. □□ **classicalism** n. **classicalist** n. **classicality** /-ˈkælɪtɪ/ n. **classically** adv. [L *classicus* (as CLASSIC)]

Classical art refers, in the first instance, to the art of the Greeks and Romans: the term was originally applied to literature and its present usage in the visual arts dates back to the 17th c., when it was assumed that antique art had set the standard for all future achievement. In the late 18th c. it took on a second meaning as the antithesis to Romantic. In the 20th c. classicism tends to denote clarity, logicality, and adherence to recognized canons of form and conscious craftsmanship, in contrast to an irrational display of personal emotion.

classicism /ˈklæsɪˌsɪz(ə)m/ n. 1 the following of a classic style. 2 a classical scholarship. b the advocacy of a classical education. 3 an ancient Greek or Latin idiom. □□ **classicist** n.

classicize /ˈklæsɪˌsaɪz/ v. (also **-ise**) 1 tr. make classic. 2 intr. imitate a classical style.

classified /ˈklæsɪˌfaɪd/ adj. 1 arranged in classes or categories. 2 (of information etc.) designated as officially secret. 3 *Brit.* (of a road) assigned to a category according to its importance. 4 *Brit.* (of newspaper advertisements) arranged in columns according to various categories.

classify /ˈklæsɪˌfaɪ/ v.tr. (**-ies, -ied**) 1 a arrange in classes or categories. b assign (a thing) to a class or category. 2 designate as officially secret or not for general disclosure. □□ **classifiable**

adj. **classification** /-fɪˈkeɪʃ(ə)n/ n. **classificatory** /-ˈkeɪtərɪ/ adj. **classifier** n. [back-form. f. *classification* f. F (as CLASS)]

classless /ˈklɑːslɪs/ adj. making or showing no distinction of classes (*classless society; classless accent*). □□ **classlessness** n.

classmate /ˈklɑːsmeɪt/ n. a fellow-member of a class, esp. at school.

classroom /ˈklɑːsruːm, -rʊm/ n. a room in which a class of students is taught, esp. in a school.

classy /ˈklɑːsɪ/ adj. (**classier, classiest**) *colloq.* superior, stylish. □□ **classily** adv. **classiness** n.

clastic /ˈklæstɪk/ adj. *Geol.* composed of broken pieces of older rocks. □ **clastic rocks** conglomerates, sandstones, etc. [F *clastique* f. Gk *klastos* broken in pieces]

clathrate /ˈklæθreɪt/ n. *Chem.* a solid in which one component is enclosed in the structure of another. [L *clathratus* f. *clathri* lattice-bars f. Gk *klēthra*]

clatter /ˈklætə(r)/ n. & v. —n. 1 a rattling sound as of many hard objects struck together. 2 noisy talk. —v. 1 intr. a make a clatter. b fall or move etc. with a clatter. 2 tr. cause (plates etc.) to clatter. [OE, of imit. orig.]

Claude /kləʊd/ French landscape painter, Claude Gellée, called Le Lorrain and in England known as Claude Lorraine (1600–82), living in Rome from 1627, whose paintings are harmonious evocations of the pastoral serenity of the Golden Age. Apprenticed as a pastry-cook to the Roman painter Agostino Tassi, he became his assistant and worked with him on villa decoration. The influence of the late mannerists is evident in the nuns and picturesque paraphernalia of his early paintings, but in his mature works he concentrates on the poetic power of light and atmosphere, letting the sun shine directly out of the picture, and raising the viewpoint so that the eye can roam over a spacious panorama to the distant horizon. His paintings were so much in demand that he recorded them in the form of sketches in his *Liber Veritatis* to guard against forgeries. Claude was particularly admired in England, where he inspired a revolution in landscape gardening in the mid-18th c. and was a profound influence on the painters Wilson and Turner.

claudication /ˌklɔːdɪˈkeɪʃ(ə)n/ n. *Med.* a cramping pain, esp. in the leg, caused by arterial obstruction; limping. [L *claudicare* limp f. *claudus* lame]

Claudius /ˈklɔːdɪəs/ Tiberius Claudius Nero Germanicus (10 BC–AD 54), Roman emperor 41–54. Neglected in early life because of his physical infirmities, and largely devoted to historical and antiquarian studies, he was proclaimed emperor by the Praetorian Guard after the murder of Caligula. He took part personally in the invasion of Britain in 43. The power of his wives and freedmen was notorious; his fourth wife, Agrippina, the mother of Nero, is said to have killed him with a dish of poisoned mushrooms.

clause /klɔːz/ n. 1 *Gram.* a distinct part of a sentence, including a subject and predicate. 2 a single statement in a treaty, law, bill, or contract. □□ **clausal** adj. [ME f. OF f. L *clausula* conclusion f. *claudere* claus- shut]

Clausewitz /ˈklaʊzəvɪts/, Karl von (1780–1831), Prussian soldier and military theorist, whose monumental study *On War* was perhaps the most influential strategical work of the 19th c. Unfortunately his efforts to place military operations in the context of national and international politics were misinterpreted by his disciples (including many of the 19th and early 20th centuries' most important soldiers and statesmen) as establishing war as the ultimate and most desirable means of political action.

claustral /ˈklɔːstr(ə)l/ adj. 1 of or associated with the cloister; monastic. 2 narrow-minded. [ME f. LL *claustralis* f. *claustrum* CLOISTER]

claustrophobia /ˌklɔːstrəˈfəʊbɪə/ n. an abnormal fear of confined places. □□ **claustrophobe** /ˈklɔːstrəfəʊb/ n. [mod.L f. L *claustrum*: see CLOISTER]

claustrophobic /ˌklɔːstrəˈfəʊbɪk/ adj. 1 suffering from claustrophobia. 2 inducing claustrophobia. □□ **claustrophobically** adv.

clavate /ˈkleɪveɪt/ adj. Bot. club-shaped. [mod.L clavatus f. L clava club]

clave[1] /kleɪv, klɑːv/ n. Mus. a hardwood stick used in pairs to make a hollow sound when struck together. [Amer. Sp. f. Sp., = keystone, f. L clavis key]

clave[2] past of CLEAVE[2].

clavicembalo /ˌklævɪˈtʃembəˌləʊ/ n. (pl. -os) a harpsichord. [It.]

clavichord /ˈklævɪˌkɔːd/ n. a small stringed keyboard instrument with a very soft tone developed in the 14th c. and in use from the early 15th. The strings are struck by brass blades, or 'tangents', to produce a clear and quiet tone for domestic music-making. It was a favourite instrument of both Johann Sebastian Bach and his son C. P. E. Bach. [ME f. med.L clavichordium f. L clavis key, chorda string: see CHORD[2]]

clavicle /ˈklævɪk(ə)l/ n. the collar-bone. □□ **clavicular** /kləˈvɪkjʊlə(r)/ adj. [L clavicula dimin. of clavis key (from its shape)]

clavier /kləˈvɪə(r), ˈklævɪə(r)/ n. Mus. 1 any keyboard instrument. 2 its keyboard. [F clavier or G Klavier f. med.L claviarius, orig. = key-bearer, f. L clavis key]

claviform /ˈklævɪˌfɔːm/ adj. club-shaped. [L clava club]

claw /klɔː/ n. & v. —n. 1 a a pointed horny nail on an animal's or bird's foot. b a foot armed with claws. 2 the pincers of a shellfish. 3 a device for grappling, holding, etc. —v. 1 tr. & intr. scratch, maul, or pull (a person or thing) with claws. 2 tr. & intr. Sc. scratch gently. 3 intr. Naut. beat to windward. □ **claw back** 1 regain laboriously or gradually. 2 recover (money paid out) from another source (e.g. taxation). **claw-back** n. 1 the act of clawing back. 2 money recovered in this way. **claw-hammer** a hammer with one side of the head forked for extracting nails. □□ **clawed** adj. (also in comb.). **clawer** n. **clawless** adj. [OE clawu, clawian]

Clay /kleɪ/, Cassius, see Muhammad ALI.

clay /kleɪ/ n. 1 a stiff sticky earth, used for making bricks, pottery, ceramics, etc. 2 poet. the substance of the human body. 3 (in full **clay pipe**) a tobacco-pipe made of clay. □ **clay-pan** Austral. a natural hollow in clay soil, retaining water after rain. **clay pigeon** a breakable disc thrown up from a trap as a target for shooting. □□ **clayey** adj. **clayish** adj. **claylike** adj. [OE clǣg f. WG]

claymore /ˈkleɪmɔː(r)/ n. 1 hist. a a Scottish two-edged broadsword. b a broadsword, often with a single edge, having a basketwork structure protecting the hilt. 2 US a type of anti-personnel mine. [Gael. claidheamh mór great sword]

-cle /k(ə)l/ suffix forming (orig. diminutive) nouns (article; particle). [as -CULE]

clean /kliːn/ adj., adv., v., & n. —adj. 1 (often foll. by of) free from dirt or contaminating matter, unsoiled. 2 clear; unused or unpolluted; preserving what is regarded as the original state (clean air; clean page). 3 free from obscenity or indecency. 4 a attentive to personal hygiene and cleanliness. b (of children and animals) toilet-trained or house-trained. 5 complete, clear-cut, unobstructed, even. 6 a (of a ship, aircraft, or car) streamlined, smooth. b well-formed, slender and shapely (clean-limbed; the car has clean lines). 7 adroit, skilful (clean fielding). 8 (of a nuclear weapon) producing relatively little fallout. 9 a free from ceremonial defilement or from disease. b (of food) not prohibited. 10 a free from any record of a crime, offence, etc. (a clean driving-licence). b sl. free from suspicion; not carrying incriminating material. 11 (of a taste, smell, etc.) sharp, fresh, distinctive. 12 (of timber) free from knots. —adv. 1 completely, outright, simply (clean bowled; cut clean through; clean forgot). 2 in a clean manner. —v. 1 tr. (also foll. by of) & intr. make or become clean. 2 tr. eat all the food on (one's plate). 3 tr. Cookery remove the innards of (fish or fowl). 4 intr. make oneself clean. —n. the act or process of cleaning or being cleaned (give it a clean). □ **clean bill of health** see BILL[1]. **clean break** a quick and final separation. **clean-cut** sharply outlined. **clean down** clean by brushing or wiping. **clean hands** freedom from guilt. **clean-living** of upright character. **clean out** 1 clean thoroughly. 2 sl. empty or deprive (esp. of money). **clean-shaven** without beard, whiskers, moustache. **clean sheet** (or **slate**) freedom from commitments or imputations; the removal of these from one's record. **clean up** 1 a clear (a mess) away. b (also absol.) put (things) tidy. c make (oneself) clean. 2 restore order or morality to. 3 sl. a acquire as gain or profit. b make a gain or profit. **clean-up** n. an act of cleaning up. **come clean** colloq. own up; confess everything. **make a clean breast of** see BREAST. **make a clean job of** colloq. do thoroughly. **make a clean sweep of** see SWEEP. □□ **cleanable** adj. **cleanish** adj. **cleanness** n. [OE clǣne (adj. & adv.), clǣne (adv.), f. WG]

cleaner /ˈkliːnə(r)/ n. 1 a person employed to clean the interior of a building. 2 (usu. in pl.) a commercial establishment for cleaning clothes. 3 a device or substance for cleaning. □ **take to the cleaners** sl. 1 defraud or rob (a person) of all his or her money. 2 criticize severely.

cleanly[1] /ˈkliːnlɪ/ adv. 1 in a clean way. 2 efficiently; without difficulty. [OE clǣnlīce: see CLEAN, -LY[2]]

cleanly[2] /ˈklenlɪ/ adj. (**cleanlier**, **cleanliest**) habitually clean; with clean habits. □□ **cleanlily** adv. **cleanliness** n. [OE clǣnlic: see CLEAN, -LY[1]]

cleanse /klenz/ v.tr. 1 usu. formal. make clean. 2 (often foll. by of) purify from sin or guilt. 3 archaic cure (a leper etc.). □ **cleansing cream** cream for removing unwanted matter from the face, hands, etc. **cleansing department** Brit. a local service of refuse collection etc. □□ **cleanser** n. [OE clǣnsian (see CLEAN)]

cleanskin /ˈkliːnskɪn/ n. Austral. 1 an unbranded animal. 2 sl. a person free from blame, without a police record, etc.

clear /klɪə(r)/ adj., adv., & v. —adj. 1 free from dirt or contamination. 2 (of weather, the sky, etc.) not dull or cloudy. 3 a transparent. b lustrous, shining; free from obscurity. 4 (of soup) not containing solid ingredients. 5 (of a fire) burning with little smoke. 6 a distinct, easily perceived by the senses. b unambiguous, easily understood (make a thing clear; make oneself clear). c manifest; not confused or doubtful (clear evidence). 7 that discerns or is able to discern readily and accurately (clear thinking; clear-sighted). 8 (usu. foll. by about, on, or that + clause) confident, convinced, certain. 9 (of a conscience) free from guilt. 10 (of a road etc.) unobstructed, open. 11 a net, without deduction (a clear £1000). b complete (three clear days). 12 (often foll. by of) free, unhampered; unencumbered by debt, commitments, etc. 13 (foll. by of) not obstructed by. —adv. 1 clearly (speak loud and clear). 2 completely (he got clear away). 3 apart, out of contact (keep clear; stand clear of the doors). 4 (foll. by to) US all the way. —v. 1 tr. & intr. make or become clear. 2 a tr. (often foll. by of) free from prohibition or obstruction. b tr. & intr. make or become empty or unobstructed. c tr. free (land) for cultivation or building by cutting down trees etc. d tr. cause people to leave (a room etc.). 3 tr. (often foll. by of) show or declare (a person) to be innocent (cleared them of complicity). 4 tr. approve (a person) for special duty, access to information, etc. 5 tr. pass over or by safely or without touching, esp. by jumping. 6 tr. make (an amount of money) as a net gain or to balance expenses. 7 tr. pass (a cheque) through a clearing-house. 8 tr. pass through (a customs office etc.). 9 tr. remove (an obstruction, an unwanted object, etc.) (clear them out of the way). 10 tr. (also absol.) Football send (the ball) out of one's defensive zone. 11 intr. (often foll. by away, up) (of physical phenomena) disappear, gradually diminish (mist cleared by lunch-time; my cold has cleared up). 12 tr. (often foll. by off) discharge (a debt). □ **clear the air** 1 make the air less sultry. 2 disperse an atmosphere of suspicion, tension, etc. **clear away** 1 remove completely. 2 remove the remains of a meal from the table. **clear-cut** sharply defined. **clear the decks** prepare for action, esp. fighting. **clear off** 1 get rid of. 2 colloq. go away. **clear out** 1 empty. 2 remove. 3 colloq. go away. **clear one's throat** cough slightly to make one's voice clear. **clear up** 1 tidy up. 2 solve (a mystery etc.). 3 (of weather) become fine. **clear the way** 1 remove obstacles. 2 stand aside. **clear a thing with** get approval or authorization for a thing from (a person). **in clear** not in cipher or code. **in the clear** free from suspicion or difficulty. **out of a clear sky** as a complete surprise. □□ **clearable** adj. **clearer** n. **clearly** adv. **clearness** n. [ME f. OF cler f. L clarus]

clearance /ˈklɪərəns/ n. 1 the removal of obstructions etc., esp. removal of buildings, persons, etc., so as to clear land. 2 clear space allowed for the passing of two objects or two parts in machinery etc. 3 special authorization or permission (esp. for an aircraft to take off or land, or for access to information etc.). **4 a** the clearing of a person, ship, etc., by customs. **b** a certificate showing this. **5** the clearing of cheques. **6** *Football* a kick sending the ball out of a defensive zone. **7** making clear. □ **clearance order** an order for the demolition of buildings. **clearance sale** *Brit.* a sale to get rid of superfluous stock.

clearcole /ˈklɪəkəʊl/ *n. & v.* —*n.* a mixture of size and whiting or white lead, used as a primer for distemper. —*v.tr.* paint with clearcole. [F *claire colle* clear glue]

clearing /ˈklɪərɪŋ/ *n.* **1** in senses of CLEAR *v.* **2** an area in a forest cleared for cultivation. □ **clearing bank** *Brit.* a bank which is a member of a clearing-house. **clearing-house 1** a bankers' establishment where cheques and bills from member banks are exchanged, so that only the balances need be paid in cash. **2** an agency for collecting and distributing information etc.

clearstory *US* var. of CLERESTORY.

clearway /ˈklɪəweɪ/ *n. Brit.* a main road (other than a motorway) on which vehicles are not normally permitted to stop.

cleat /kliːt/ *n.* **1** a piece of metal, wood, etc., bolted on for fastening ropes to, or to strengthen woodwork etc. **2** a projecting piece on a spar, gangway, boot, etc., to give footing or prevent a rope from slipping. **3** a wedge. [OE: cf. CLOT]

cleavage /ˈkliːvɪdʒ/ *n.* **1** the hollow between a woman's breasts, esp. as exposed by a low-cut garment. **2** a division or splitting. **3** the splitting of rocks, crystals, etc., in a preferred direction.

cleave[1] /kliːv/ *v.* (*past* **clove** /kləʊv/ or **cleft** /kleft/ or **cleaved**; *past part.* **cloven** /ˈkləʊv(ə)n/ or **cleft** or **cleaved**) *literary* **1 a** *tr.* chop or break apart, split, esp. along the grain or the line of cleavage. **b** *intr.* come apart in this way. **2** *tr.* make one's way through (air or water). □□ **cleavable** *adj.* [OE *clēofan* f. Gmc]

cleave[2] /kliːv/ *v.intr.* (*past* **cleaved** or **clave** /kleɪv/) (foll. by *to*) *literary* stick fast; adhere. [OE *cleofian, clifian* f. WG: cf. CLAY]

cleaver /ˈkliːvə(r)/ *n.* **1** a tool for cleaving, esp. a heavy chopping tool used by butchers. **2** a person who cleaves.

cleavers /ˈkliːvəz/ *n.* (also **clivers** /ˈklɪvəz/) (treated as *sing.* or *pl.*) a plant, *Galium aparine*, having hooked bristles on its stem that catch on clothes etc. Also called GOOSEGRASS. [OE *clife*, formed as CLEAVE[2]]

clef /klef/ *n. Mus.* any of several symbols placed at the beginning of a staff, indicating the pitch of the notes written on it. [F f. L *clavis* key]

cleft[1] /kleft/ *adj.* split, partly divided. □ **cleft palate** a congenital split in the roof of the mouth. **in a cleft stick** in a difficult position, esp. one allowing neither retreat nor advance. [past part. of CLEAVE[1]]

cleft[2] /kleft/ *n.* a split or fissure; a space or division made by cleaving. [OE (rel. to CLEAVE[1]): assim. to CLEFT[1]]

cleg /kleg/ *n. Brit.* a horsefly. [ON *kleggi*]

cleistogamic /ˌklaɪstəˈɡæmɪk/ *adj. Bot.* (of a flower) permanently closed and self-fertilizing. [Gk *kleistos* closed + *gamos* marriage]

clematis /ˈklemətɪs, kləˈmeɪtɪs/ *n.* any erect or climbing plant of the genus *Clematis*, bearing white, pink, or purple flowers and feathery seeds, e.g. old man's beard. [L f. Gk *klēmatis* f. *klēma* vine branch]

Clemenceau /ˌklemãˈsəʊ/, Georges (1841–1929), French statesman. A radical politician and journalist, Clemenceau made his name as a critic of government corruption and an exponent of the recapture of Alsace and Lorraine, lost to Germany in the Franco-Prussian War. A persistent opponent of the government during the early years of the First World War, he became Premier himself in November 1917 and saw France through to victory in 1918. At the Versailles peace talks he pushed hard for a punitive settlement with Germany but lost popularity when he failed to obtain all that he demanded (including the Rhine as a frontier) and retired from politics soon afterwards, having failed to be elected President in 1920.

Clemens /ˈklemənz/, Samuel Langhorne (1835–1910) see Mark TWAIN.

Clement[1] /ˈklemənt/ of Alexandria, St (*c.*150–*c.*215), Greek theologian, head of the theological school at Alexandria from 190 to 202, when he was forced to flee from persecution. He was succeeded by his pupil Origen. In his writings Clement explained and supplemented the Christian faith with the ideas of Greek philosophy.

Clement[2] /ˈklemənt/ of Rome, St (1st c. AD), probably the third bishop of Rome after St Peter, author of an epistle written *c.* AD 96 to the Church at Corinth, insisting that certain deposed presbyters must be reinstated. Many other writings were circulated in the early Church under his name, and in later tradition he became the subject of a variety of legends. Feast day, 23 Nov.

clement /ˈklemənt/ *adj.* **1** mild (*clement weather*). **2** merciful. □□ **clemency** *n.* [ME f. L *clemens -entis*]

clementine /ˈklemənˌtiːn, -ˌtaɪn/ *n.* a small citrus fruit, thought to be a hybrid between a tangerine and sweet orange. [F *clémentine*]

clench /klentʃ/ *v. & n.* —*v.tr.* **1** close (the teeth or fingers) tightly. **2** grasp firmly. **3** = CLINCH *v.* **4.** —*n.* **1** a clenching action. **2** a clenched state. [OE f. Gmc: cf. CLING]

Cleopatra /ˌkliːəˈpætrə/ (69–30 BC) the last Ptolemaic ruler of Egypt (as Cleopatra VII from 51 BC), famous for her brief liaison with Julius Caesar and for her longer political and romantic alliance with Mark Antony (the famous meeting described by Shakespeare took place at Tarsus in 41 BC), by whom she had three children. She and Antony were defeated by Octavian at the battle of Actium in 31 BC, after which she committed suicide by the bite of an asp.

Cleopatra's Needles a pair of granite obelisks erected at Heliopolis by Tuthmosis III *c.*1475 BC. They were moved to Alexandria in 12 BC and moved again in 1878, one being set up on the Thames Embankment in London and the other in Central Park, New York. They have no connection with Cleopatra.

clepsydra /ˈklepsɪdrə, -ˈsɪdrə/ *n.* an ancient time-measuring device worked by a flow of water. [L f. Gk *klepsudra* f. *kleptō* steal + *hudōr* water]

clerestory /ˈklɪəstərɪ, -ˌstɔːrɪ/ *n.* (*US* **clearstory**) (*pl.* **-ies**) **1** an upper row of windows in a cathedral or large church, above the level of the aisle roofs. **2** *US* a raised section of the roof of a railway carriage, with windows or ventilators. [ME f. CLEAR + STOREY]

clergy /ˈklɜːdʒɪ/ *n.* (*pl.* **-ies**) (usu. treated as *pl.*) **1** (usu. prec. by *the*) the body of all persons ordained for religious duties in the Christian churches. **2** a number of such persons (*ten clergy were present*). [ME, partly f. OF *clergé* f. eccl.L *clericatus*, partly f. OF *clergie* f. *clerc* CLERK]

clergyman /ˈklɜːdʒɪmən/ *n.* (*pl.* **-men**) a member of the clergy, esp. of the Church of England.

cleric /ˈklerɪk/ *n.* a member of the clergy. [(orig. adj.) f. eccl.L f. Gk *klērikos* f. *klēros* lot, heritage, as in Acts 1: 17]

clerical /ˈklerɪk(ə)l/ *adj.* **1** of the clergy or clergymen. **2** of or done by a clerk or clerks. □ **clerical collar** a stiff upright white collar fastening at the back, as worn by the clergy in some Churches. **clerical error** an error made in copying or writing out. □□ **clericalism** *n.* **clericalist** *n.* **clerically** *adv.* [eccl.L *clericalis* (as CLERIC)]

clerihew /ˈklerɪˌhjuː/ *n.* a short comic or nonsensical verse, usu. in two rhyming couplets with lines of unequal length and referring to a famous person. [E. *Clerihew* Bentley, Engl. writer d. 1956, its inventor]

clerk /klɑːk/ *n. & v.* —*n.* **1** a person employed in an office, bank, shop, etc., to keep records, accounts, etc. **2** a secretary, agent, or record-keeper of a local council (*town clerk*), court, etc. **3** a lay officer of a church (*parish clerk*), college chapel, etc. **4** a senior official in Parliament. **5** *US* an assistant in a shop or hotel. **6** *archaic* a clergyman. —*v.intr.* work as a clerk. □ **clerk in holy orders** *formal* a clergyman. **clerk of the course** the judges' secretary etc. in horse or motor racing. **clerk of the works** (or **of works**) an overseer of building works etc. □□ **clerkdom** *n.* **clerkess** *n. Sc.* **clerkish** *adj.* **clerkly** *adj.* **clerkship** *n.* [OE *cleric, clerc*, & OF *clerc*, f. eccl.L *clericus* CLERIC]

Clermont-Ferrand /ˌkleəmɔ̃feˈrɑ̃/ a city in France, capital of the Auvergne region, at the centre of the Massif Central; pop. (1982) 151,000. The philosopher Blaise Pascal was born here.

Cleveland[1] /ˈkliːvlənd/ a county of NE England; pop. (1981) 570,200; county town, Middlesbrough.

Cleveland[2] /ˈkliːvlənd/ a major port and industrial city of NE Ohio, situated on Lake Erie; pop. (1982) 558,900.

Cleveland[3] /ˈkliːvlənd/, (Stephen) Grover (1837–1908), 22nd (1885–9) and 24th (1893–7) President of the US.

clever /ˈklevə(r)/ adj. (**cleverer**, **cleverest**) 1 skilful, talented; quick to understand and learn. 2 adroit, dextrous. 3 (of the doer or the thing done) ingenious, cunning. □ **clever Dick** (or **clogs** etc.) colloq. a person who is or purports to be smart or knowing. **not too clever** Austral. colloq. unwell, indisposed. □□ **cleverly** adv. **cleverness** n. [ME, = adroit: perh. rel. to CLEAVE[2], with sense 'apt to seize']

clevis /ˈklevɪs/ n. 1 a U-shaped piece of metal at the end of a beam for attaching tackle etc. 2 a connection in which a bolt holds one part that fits between the forked ends of another. [16th c.: rel. to CLEAVE[1]]

clew /kluː/ n. & v. —n. 1 Naut. **a** a lower or after corner of a sail. **b** a set of small cords suspending a hammock. 2 archaic **a** a ball of thread or yarn, esp. with reference to the legend of Theseus and the labyrinth. **b** = CLUE. —v.tr. Naut. 1 (foll. by up) draw the lower ends of (a sail) to the upper yard or the mast ready for furling. 2 (foll. by down) let down (a sail) by the clews in unfurling. [OE cliwen, cleowen]

clianthus /klɪˈænθəs/ n. any leguminous plant of the genus Clianthus, native to Australia and New Zealand, bearing drooping clusters of red pealike flowers. [mod.L, app. f. Gk klei-, kleos glory + anthos flower]

cliché /ˈkliːʃeɪ/ n. 1 a hackneyed phrase or opinion. 2 Brit. a metal casting of a stereotype or electrotype. [F f. clicher to stereotype]

clichéd /ˈkliːʃeɪd/ adj. (also **cliché'd**) hackneyed; full of clichés.

click /klɪk/ n. & v. —n. 1 a slight sharp sound as of a switch being operated. 2 a sharp non-vocal suction, used as a speech-sound in some languages. 3 a catch in machinery acting with a slight sharp sound. 4 (of a horse) an action causing a hind foot to touch the shoe of a fore foot. —v. 1 **a** intr. make a click. **b** tr. cause (one's tongue, heels, etc.) to click. 2 intr. colloq. **a** become clear or understandable (often prec. by it as subject: when I saw them it all clicked). **b** be successful, secure one's object. **c** (foll. by with) become friendly, esp. with a person of the opposite sex. **d** come to an agreement. □ **click beetle** any of a family of beetles (Elateridae) that make a click in recovering from being overturned. □□ **clicker** n. [imit.: cf. Du. klikken, F cliquer]

client /ˈklaɪənt/ n. 1 a person using the services of a lawyer, architect, social worker, or other professional person. 2 a customer. 3 Rom.Hist. a plebeian under the protection of a patrician. 4 archaic a dependant or hanger-on. □□ **clientship** n. [ME f. L cliens -entis f. cluere hear, obey]

clientele /ˌkliːɒnˈtel/ n. 1 clients collectively. 2 customers, esp. of a shop. 3 the patrons of a theatre etc. [L clientela clientship & F clientèle]

cliff /klɪf/ n. a steep rock-face, esp. at the edge of the sea. □ **cliff-hanger** a story etc. with a strong element of suspense; a suspenseful ending to an episode of a serial. **cliff-hanging** full of suspense. □□ **clifflike** adj. **cliffy** adj. [OE clif f. Gmc]

climacteric /klaɪˈmæktərɪk, ˌklaɪmækˈterɪk/ n. & adj. —n. 1 Med. the period of life when fertility and sexual activity are in decline. 2 a supposed critical period in life (esp. occurring at intervals of seven years). —adj. 1 Med. occurring at the climacteric. 2 constituting a crisis; critical. [F climatérique or L climactericus f. Gk klimaktērikos f. klimaktēr critical period f. klimax -akos ladder]

climactic /klaɪˈmæktɪk/ adj. of or forming a climax. □□ **climactically** adv. [CLIMAX + -IC, perh. after SYNTACTIC or CLIMACTERIC]

climate /ˈklaɪmɪt/ n. 1 the prevailing weather conditions of an area. 2 a region with particular weather conditions. 3 the prevailing trend of opinion or public feeling. □□ **climatic** /-ˈmætɪk/ adj. **climatical** /-ˈmætɪk(ə)l/ adj. **climatically** /-ˈmætɪkəlɪ/ adv. [ME f. OF climat or LL clima climat- f. Gk klima f. klinō slope]

climatology /ˌklaɪməˈtɒlədʒɪ/ n. the scientific study of climate. □□ **climatological** /-təˈlɒdʒɪk(ə)l/ adj. **climatologist** n.

climax /ˈklaɪmæks/ n. & v. —n. 1 the event or point of greatest intensity or interest; a culmination or apex. 2 a sexual orgasm. 3 Rhet. **a** a series arranged in order of increasing importance etc. **b** the last term in such a series. 4 Ecol. a state of equilibrium reached by a plant community. —v.tr. & intr. colloq. bring or come to a climax. [LL f. Gk klimax -akos ladder, climax]

climb /klaɪm/ v. & n. —v. 1 tr. & intr. (often foll. by up) ascend, mount, go or come up, esp. by using one's hands. 2 intr. (of a plant) grow up a wall, tree, trellis, etc. by clinging with tendrils or by twining. 3 intr. make progress from one's own efforts, esp. in social rank, intellectual or moral strength, etc. 4 intr. (of an aircraft, the sun, etc.) go upwards. 5 intr. slope upwards. —n. 1 an ascent by climbing. 2 **a** a place, esp. a hill, climbed or to be climbed. **b** a recognized route up a mountain etc. □ **climb down** 1 descend with the help of one's hands. 2 withdraw from a stance taken up in argument, negotiation, etc. **climb-down** n. such a withdrawal. **climbing-frame** a structure of joined bars etc. for children to climb on. **climbing-iron** a set of spikes attachable to a boot for climbing trees or ice slopes. □□ **climbable** adj. [OE climban f. WG, rel. to CLEAVE[2]]

climber /ˈklaɪmə(r)/ n. 1 a mountaineer. 2 a climbing plant. 3 a person with strong social etc. aspirations.

clime /klaɪm/ n. literary 1 a region. 2 a climate. [LL clima: see CLIMATE]

clinch /klɪntʃ/ v. & n. —v. 1 tr. confirm or settle (an argument, bargain, etc.) conclusively. 2 intr. Boxing & Wrestling (of participants) become too closely engaged. 3 intr. colloq. embrace. 4 tr. secure (a nail or rivet) by driving the point sideways when through. 5 tr. Naut. fasten (a rope) with a particular half hitch. —n. 1 **a** a clinching action. **b** a clinched state. 2 colloq. an (esp. amorous) embrace. 3 Boxing & Wrestling an action or state in which participants become too closely engaged. [16th-c. var. of CLENCH]

clincher /ˈklɪntʃə(r)/ n. colloq. a remark or argument that settles a matter conclusively.

clincher-built var. of CLINKER-BUILT.

cline /klaɪn/ n. Biol. the graded sequence of differences within a species etc. □□ **clinal** adj. [Gk klinō to slope]

cling /klɪŋ/ v. & n. —v.intr. (past and past part. **clung** /klʌŋ/) 1 (foll. by to) adhere, stick, or hold on (by means of stickiness, suction, grasping, or embracing). 2 (foll. by to) remain persistently or stubbornly faithful (to a friend, habit, idea, etc.). 3 maintain one's grasp; keep hold; resist separation. —n. = CLINGSTONE. □ **cling film** a very thin clinging transparent plastic film, used as a covering esp. for food. **cling together** remain in one body or in contact. □□ **clinger** n. **clingingly** adv. [OE clingan f. Gmc: cf. CLENCH]

clingstone /ˈklɪŋstəʊn/ n. a variety of peach or nectarine in which the flesh adheres to the stone (cf. FREESTONE 2).

clingy /ˈklɪŋɪ/ adj. (**clingier**, **clingiest**) liable to cling. □□ **clinginess** n.

clinic /ˈklɪnɪk/ n. 1 Brit. a private or specialized hospital. 2 a place or occasion for giving specialist medical treatment or advice (eye clinic; fertility clinic). 3 a gathering at a hospital bedside for the teaching of medicine or surgery. 4 US a conference or short course on a particular subject (golf clinic). □□ **clinician** /klɪˈnɪʃ(ə)n/ n. [F clinique f. Gk klinikē (tekhnē) clinical, lit. bedside (art)]

clinical /ˈklɪnɪk(ə)l/ adj. 1 Med. **a** of or for the treatment of patients. **b** taught or learnt at the hospital bedside. 2 dispassionate, coldly detached. □ **clinical death** death judged by observation of a person's condition. **clinical medicine** medicine dealing with the observation and treatment of patients. **clinical thermometer** a thermometer with a small range, for taking a person's temperature. □□ **clinically** adv. [L clinicus f. Gk klinikos f. klinē bed]

clink[1] /klɪŋk/ n. & v. —n. a sharp ringing sound. —v. 1 intr. make a clink. 2 tr. cause (glasses etc.) to clink. [ME, prob. f. MDu. klinken; cf. CLANG, CLANK]

clink[2] /klɪŋk/ n. (often prec. by in) sl. prison. [16th c.: orig. unkn.]

clinker[1] /ˈklɪŋkə(r)/ n. 1 a mass of slag or lava. 2 a stony residue from burnt coal. [earlier *clincard* etc. f. obs. Du. *klinkaerd* f. *klinken* CLINK[1]]

clinker[2] /ˈklɪŋkə(r)/ n. 1 *Brit. sl.* something excellent or outstanding. 2 *US sl.* a mistake or blunder. [CLINK[1] + -ER[1]]

clinker-built /ˈklɪŋkəˌbɪlt/ adj. (also **clincher-built** /ˈklɪntʃəˌbɪlt/) (of a boat) having external planks overlapping downwards and secured with clinched copper nails. [*clink* N.Engl. var. of CLINCH + -ER[1]]

clinkstone /ˈklɪŋkstəʊn/ n. a kind of feldspar that rings like iron when struck.

clinometer /klaɪˈnɒmɪtə(r)/ n. *Surveying* an instrument for measuring slopes. [Gk *klinō* to slope + -METER]

Clio /ˈklaɪəʊ/ *Gk & Rom. Mythol.* the Muse of history. [Gk *kleiō* celebrate]

cliometrics /ˌklaɪəˈmetrɪks/ n.pl. (usu. treated as *sing.*) a method of historical research making much use of statistical information and methods. [CLIO + METRIC + -ICS]

clip[1] /klɪp/ n. & v. —n. 1 a device for holding things together or for attachment to an object as a marker, esp. a paper-clip or a device worked by a spring. 2 a piece of jewellery fastened by a clip. 3 a set of attached cartridges for a firearm. —v.tr. (**clipped**, **clipping**) 1 fix with a clip. 2 grip tightly. 3 surround closely. □ **clip-on** attached by a clip. [OE *clyppan* embrace f. WG]

clip[2] /klɪp/ v. & n. —v.tr. (**clipped**, **clipping**) 1 cut with shears or scissors, esp. cut short or trim (hair, wool, etc.). 2 trim or remove the hair or wool of (a person or animal). 3 *colloq.* hit smartly. 4 a omit (a letter etc.) from a word. b omit letters or syllables of (words pronounced). 5 *Brit.* remove a small piece of (a ticket) to show that it has been used. 6 cut (an extract) from a newspaper etc. 7 *sl.* swindle, rob. 8 pare the edge of (a coin). —n. 1 an act of clipping, esp. shearing or hair-cutting. 2 *colloq.* a smart blow, esp. with the hand. 3 a short sequence from a motion picture. 4 the quantity of wool clipped from a sheep, flock, etc. 5 *colloq.* speed, esp. rapid. □ **clip-joint** *sl.* a club etc. charging exorbitant prices. **clip a person's wings** prevent a person from pursuing ambitions or acting effectively. □□ **clippable** adj. [ME f. ON *klippa*, prob. imit.]

clipboard /ˈklɪpbɔːd/ n. a small board with a spring clip for holding papers etc. and providing support for writing.

clip-clop /ˈklɪpklɒp/ n. & v. —n. a sound such as the beat of a horse's hooves. —v.intr. (**-clopped**, **-clopping**) make such a sound. [imit.]

clipper /ˈklɪpə(r)/ n. 1 (usu. in *pl.*) any of various instruments for clipping hair, fingernails, hedges, etc. 2 a fast sailing-ship, esp. one with raking bows and masts. (See below.) 3 a fast horse.

The term 'clipper' is loosely used as a generic name for types of very fast sailing-ship; it is said to refer to the fact that such ships could 'clip' the passage-time of the regular packet ships, themselves very fast in their day, and was first applied to the speedy schooners built in Virginia and Maryland in the early 19th c. The hull design was long and low with a very sharply-raked stem, and was later combined with the three-masted square rig, making the beautiful clipper-ships of the mid-19th c. the finest productions of the age of sail. The first British clippers were built for the tea trade, a profitable cargo, with the first arrivals in London from China each year commanding the highest prices. The opening of the Suez Canal in 1869 struck at the *raison d'être* of the tea-clippers, making the long trip round the Cape of Good Hope unprofitable.

clippie /ˈklɪpɪ/ n. *Brit. colloq.* a bus conductress.

clipping /ˈklɪpɪŋ/ n. a piece clipped or cut from something, esp. from a newspaper.

clique /kliːk/ n. a small exclusive group of people. □□ **cliquey** adj. (**cliquier**, **cliquiest**). **cliquish** adj. **cliquishness** n. **cliquism** n. [F f. *cliquer* CLICK]

C.Lit. abbr. *Brit.* Companion of Literature.

clitic /ˈklɪtɪk/ n. (often *attrib.*) an enclitic or proclitic. □□ **cliticization** /-tɪkaɪˈzeɪʃ(ə)n/ n.

clitoris /ˈklɪtərɪs, ˈklaɪ-/ n. a small erectile part of the female genitals at the upper end of the vulva. □□ **clitoral** adj. [mod.L f. Gk *kleitoris*]

clivers var. of CLEAVERS.

Cllr. abbr. *Brit.* Councillor.

cloaca /kləʊˈeɪkə/ n. (*pl.* **cloacae** /-siː/) 1 the genital and excretory cavity at the end of the intestinal canal in birds, reptiles, etc. 2 a sewer. □□ **cloacal** adj. [L, = sewer]

cloak /kləʊk/ n. & v. —n. 1 an outdoor over-garment, usu. sleeveless, hanging loosely from the shoulders. 2 a covering (*cloak of snow*). 3 (in *pl.*) = CLOAKROOM. —v.tr. 1 cover with a cloak. 2 conceal, disguise. □ **cloak-and-dagger** involving intrigue and espionage. **under the cloak of** using as a pretext. [ME f. OF *cloke*, dial. var. of *cloche* bell, cloak (from its bell shape) f. med.L *clocca* bell: see CLOCK[1]]

cloakroom /ˈkləʊkruːm, -rʊm/ n. 1 a room where outdoor clothes or luggage may be left by visitors, clients, etc. 2 *Brit. euphem.* a lavatory.

clobber[1] /ˈklɒbə(r)/ n. *Brit. sl.* clothing or personal belongings. [19th c.: orig. unkn.]

clobber[2] /ˈklɒbə(r)/ v.tr. *sl.* 1 hit repeatedly; beat up. 2 defeat. 3 criticize severely. [20th c.: orig. unkn.]

cloche /klɒʃ, kləʊʃ/ n. 1 a small translucent cover for protecting or forcing outdoor plants. 2 (in full **cloche hat**) a woman's close-fitting bell-shaped hat. [F, = bell, f. med.L *clocca*: see CLOCK[1]]

clock[1] /klɒk/ n. & v. —n. 1 an instrument for measuring time, driven mechanically or electrically and indicating hours, minutes, etc., by hands on a dial or by displayed figures. (See below.) 2 a any measuring device resembling a clock. b *colloq.* a speedometer, taximeter, or stopwatch. 3 time taken as an element in competitive sports etc. (*ran against the clock*). 4 *Brit. sl.* a person's face. 5 a downy seed-head, esp. that of a dandelion. —v.tr. 1 *colloq.* a (often foll. by *up*) attain or register (a stated time, distance, or speed, esp. in a race). b time (a race) with a stopwatch. 2 *Brit. sl.* hit, esp. on the head. □ **clock golf** a game in which a golf ball is putted into a hole from successive points in a circle. **clock in** (or **on**) register one's arrival at work, esp. by means of an automatic recording clock. **clock off** (or **out**) register one's departure similarly. **clock radio** a combined radio and alarm clock. **round the clock** all day and (usu.) night. **watch the clock** = CLOCK-WATCH. [ME f. MDu., MLG *klocke* f. med.L *clocca* bell, perh. f. Celt.]

The first true mechanical clock dates from c.1280. Such clocks were large weight-driven structures fitted into towers, and known as turret clocks; they had no dial or clock-hands, but sounded a signal which alerted a keeper to toll a bell. In the 14th c. public striking-clocks made their appearance, using a foliot or weighted arm as an oscillating flywheel controlled by a toothed wheel and an escapement mechanism. The first spring-driven clocks appeared c.1500, and led to the development of watches (i.e. spring clocks small enough to be carried on the person). The 17th c. (c.1670 in England) saw the anchor escapement, and the use of the swinging pendulum by Huygens from 1657. This was a great advance because its period of swing is independent of the friction of gears to which the foliot was subject; grandfather clocks and bracket clocks using this reached a high pitch of excellence in the hands of great English clock-makers such as Tompion. By 1620 another important invention was in use, the balance-wheel, followed (in the last quarter of the 17th c.) by the balance-spring, whose frequency of oscillation was controlled by a spiral spring of the now familiar type. Electrically driven clocks were introduced by 1840, and the quartz clock in 1927–30, using a quartz crystal maintained in oscillation at a fixed high frequency. A more accurate type of pendulum clock was manufactured by the Shortt-Synchronome Corporation in 1921–4, with the master pendulum enclosed in an airtight nearly evacuated chamber. Most accurate of all is the caesium clock, depending on the vibration of atoms of caesium.

clock[2] /klɒk/ n. an ornamental pattern on the side of a stocking or sock near the ankle. [16th c.: orig. unkn.]

clock-watch /ˈklɒkwɒtʃ/ v.intr. work over-anxiously to time, esp. so as not to exceed minimum working hours. □□ **clock-watcher** n. **clock-watching** n.

clockwise /ˈklɒkwaɪz/ adj. & adv. in a curve corresponding in direction to the movement of the hands of a clock.

clockwork /ˈklɒkwɜːk/ n. **1** a mechanism like that of a mechanical clock, with a spring and gears. **2** (attrib.) **a** driven by clockwork. **b** regular, mechanical. □ **like clockwork** smoothly, regularly, automatically.

clod /klɒd/ n. **1** a lump of earth, clay, etc. **2** sl. a silly or foolish person. **3** meat cut from the neck of an ox. □□ **cloddy** adj. [ME: var. of CLOT]

cloddish /ˈklɒdɪʃ/ adj. loutish, foolish, clumsy. □□ **cloddishly** adv. **cloddishness** n.

clodhopper /ˈklɒdˌhɒpə(r)/ n. **1** (usu. in pl.) colloq. a large heavy shoe. **2** = CLOD 2.

clodhopping /ˈklɒdˌhɒpɪŋ/ adj. = CLODDISH.

clodpoll /ˈklɒdpɒl/ n. sl. = CLOD 2.

clog /klɒɡ/ n. & v. —n. **1** a shoe with a thick wooden sole. **2** archaic an encumbrance or impediment. **3** a block of wood to impede an animal's movement. —v. (**clogged, clogging**) **1** (often foll. by up) **a** tr. obstruct, esp. by accumulation of glutinous matter. **b** intr. become obstructed. **2** tr. impede, hamper. **3** tr. & intr. (often foll. by up) fill with glutinous or choking matter. □ **clog-dance** a dance performed in clogs. [ME: orig. unkn.]

cloggy /ˈklɒɡɪ/ adj. (**cloggier, cloggiest**) **1** lumpy, knotty. **2** sticky.

cloisonné /ˈklwɑːzɒˌneɪ/ n. & adj. —n. **1** an enamel finish produced by forming areas of different colours separated by strips of wire placed edgeways on a metal backing. **2** this process. —adj. (of enamel) made by this process. [F f. cloison compartment]

cloister /ˈklɔɪstə(r)/ n. & v. —n. **1** a covered walk, often with a wall on one side and a colonnade open to a quadrangle on the other, esp. in a convent, monastery, college, or cathedral. **2** monastic life or seclusion. **3** a convent or monastery. —v.tr. seclude or shut up usu. in a convent or monastery. □□ **cloistral** adj. [ME f. OF cloistre f. L claustrum, clostrum lock, enclosed place f. claudere claus- CLOSE²]

cloistered /ˈklɔɪstəd/ adj. **1** secluded, sheltered. **2** monastic.

clomp var. of CLUMP v. 2.

clone /kləʊn/ n. & v. —n. **1 a** a group of organisms produced asexually from one stock or ancestor. **b** one such organism. **2** a person or thing regarded as identical with another. —v.tr. propagate as a clone. □□ **clonal** adj. [Gk klōn twig, slip]

clonk /klɒŋk/ n. & v. —n. an abrupt heavy sound of impact. —v. **1** intr. make such a sound. **2** tr. colloq. hit. [imit.]

clonus /ˈkləʊnəs/ n. Physiol. a spasm with alternate muscular contractions and relaxations. □□ **clonic** adj. [Gk klonos turmoil]

clop /klɒp/ n. & v. —n. the sound made by a horse's hooves. —v.intr. (**clopped, clopping**) make this sound. [imit.]

cloqué /ˈklɒʊkeɪ/ n. a fabric with an irregularly raised surface. [F, = blistered]

close¹ /kləʊs/ adj., adv., & n. —adj. **1** (often foll. by to) situated at only a short distance or interval. **2 a** having a strong or immediate relation or connection (close friend; close relative). **b** in intimate friendship or association (were very close). **c** corresponding almost exactly (close resemblance). **d** fitting tightly (close cap). **e** (of hair etc.) short, near the surface. **3** in or almost in contact (close combat; close proximity). **4** dense, compact, with no or only slight intervals (close texture; close writing; close formation; close thicket). **5** in which competitors are almost equal (close contest; close election). **6** leaving no gaps or weaknesses, rigorous (close reasoning). **7** concentrated, searching (close examination; close attention). **8** (of air etc.) stuffy or humid. **9** closed, shut. **10** limited or restricted to certain persons etc. (close corporation; close scholarship). **11 a** hidden, secret, covered. **b** secretive. **12** (of a danger etc.) directly threatening, narrowly avoided (that was close). **13** niggardly. **14** (of a vowel) pronounced with a relatively narrow opening of the mouth. **15** narrow, confined, contracted. **16** under prohibition. —adv. **1** (often foll. by by, on, to, upon) at only a short distance or interval (they live close by; close to the church). **2** closely, in a close manner (shut close). —n. **1** an enclosed space. **2** Brit. a street closed at one end. **3** Brit. the precinct of a cathedral. **4** Brit. a school playing-field or playground. **5** Sc. an entry from the street to a common stairway or to a court at the back. □ **at close quarters** very close together. **close-fisted** niggardly.

close-fitting (of a garment) fitting close to the body. **close-grained** without gaps between fibres etc. **close harmony** harmony in which the notes of the chord are close together. **close-hauled** (of a ship) with the sails hauled aft to sail close to the wind. **close-knit** tightly bound or interlocked; closely united in friendship. **close-mouthed** reticent. **close score** Mus. a score with more than one part on the same staff. **close season** Brit. the season when something, esp. the killing of game etc., is illegal. **close-set** separated only by a small interval or intervals. **close shave** colloq. a narrow escape. **close to the wind** see WIND¹. **close-up 1** a photograph etc. taken at close range and showing the subject on a large scale. **2** an intimate description. **go close** (of a racehorse) win or almost win. □□ **closely** adv. **closeness** n. **closish** adj. [ME f. OF clos f. L clausum enclosure & clausus past part. of claudere shut]

close² /kləʊz/ v. & n. —v. **1 a** tr. shut (a lid, box, door, room, house, etc.). **b** intr. be shut (the door closed slowly). **c** tr. block up. **2 a** tr. & intr. bring or come to an end. **b** intr. finish speaking (closed with an expression of thanks). **c** tr. settle (a bargain etc.). **3 a** intr. end the day's business. **b** tr. end the day's business at (a shop, office, etc.). **4** tr. & intr. bring or come into contact (close ranks). **5** tr. make (an electric circuit etc.) continuous. **6** intr. (foll. by with) express agreement (with an offer, terms, or the person offering them). **7** intr. (often foll. by with) come within striking distance; grapple. **8** intr. (foll. by on) (of a hand, box, etc.) grasp or entrap. —n. **1** a conclusion, an end. **2** Mus. a cadence. □ **close down 1** (of a shop, factory, etc.) discontinue business, esp. permanently. **2** Brit. (of a broadcasting station) end transmission esp. until the next day. **close one's eyes 1** (foll. by to) pay no attention. **2** die. **close in 1** enclose. **2** come nearer. **3** (of days) get successively shorter with the approach of the winter solstice. **close out** US discontinue, terminate, dispose of (a business). **close up 1** (often foll. by to) move closer. **2** shut, esp. temporarily. **3** block up. **4** (of an aperture) grow smaller. **5** coalesce. **closing-time** the time at which a public house, shop, etc., ends business. □□ **closable** adj. **closer** n. [ME f. OF clos- stem of clore f. L claudere shut]

closed /kləʊzd/ adj. **1** not giving access; shut. **2** (of a shop etc.) having ceased business temporarily. **3** (of a society, system, etc.) self-contained; not communicating with others. **4** (of a sport etc.) restricted to specified competitors etc. □ **closed book** see BOOK. **closed-circuit** (of television) transmitted by wires to a restricted set of receivers. **closed-end** having a predetermined extent (cf. open-ended). **closed season** US = close season (see CLOSE¹). **closed shop 1** a place of work etc. where all employees must belong to an agreed trade union. **2** this system. **closed syllable** a syllable ending in a consonant. **closed universe** the condition that there is sufficient matter in the universe to halt the expansion driven by the big bang and cause eventual re-collapse. Current observations suggest that the amount of visible matter is only a tenth of that required for closure, but apparent uncertainties in the masses of galaxies leave open the possibility of there being large quantities of 'dark matter'.

closet /ˈklɒzɪt/ n. & v. —n. **1** a small or private room. **2** a cupboard or recess. **3** = water-closet. **4** (attrib.) secret, covert (closet homosexual). —v.tr. (**closeted, closeting**) shut away, esp. in private conference or study. □ **Clerk of the Closet** (in the UK) the sovereign's principal chaplain. **closet play** a play to be read rather than acted. [ME f. OF, dimin. of clos: see CLOSE¹]

closure /ˈkləʊʒə(r)/ n. & v. —n. **1** the act or process of closing. **2** a closed condition. **3** something that closes or seals, e.g. a cap or tie. **4** a procedure for ending a debate and taking a vote, esp. in Parliament. —v.tr. apply the closure to (a motion, speakers, etc.). [ME f. OF f. LL clausura f. claudere claus- CLOSE²]

clot /klɒt/ n. & v. —n. **1 a** a thick mass of coagulated liquid, esp. of blood exposed to air. **b** a mass of material stuck together. **2** Brit. colloq. a silly or foolish person. —v.tr. & intr. (**clotted, clotting**) form into clots. □ **clotted cream** esp. Brit. thick cream obtained by slow scalding. [OE clot(t) f. WG: cf. CLEAT]

cloth /klɒθ/ n. (pl. **cloths** /klɒθs, klɒðz/) **1** woven or felted material. **2** a piece of this. **3** a piece of cloth for a particular purpose; a tablecloth, dishcloth, etc. **4** woollen woven fabric as used for clothes. **5 a** profession or status, esp. of the clergy, as shown by

clothes (*respect due to his cloth*). **b** (prec. by *the*) the clergy. □ **cloth-cap** relating to or associated with the working class. **cloth-eared** *colloq.* somewhat deaf. **cloth of gold** (or **silver**) tissue of gold (or silver) threads interwoven with silk or wool. [OE *clāth*, of unkn. orig.]

clothe /kləʊð/ *v.tr.* (*past* and *past part.* **clothed** or *formal* **clad**) **1** put clothes on; provide with clothes. **2** cover as with clothes or a cloth. **3** (foll. by *with*) endue (with qualities etc.). [OE: rel. to CLOTH]

clothes /kləʊz/ *n.pl.* **1** garments worn to cover the body and limbs. **2** bedclothes. □ **clothes-horse 1** a frame for airing washed clothes. **2** *colloq.* an affectedly fashionable person. **clothes-line** a rope or wire etc. on which washed clothes are hung to dry. **clothes-moth** any moth of the family Tineidae, with a larva destructive to wool, fur, etc. **clothes-peg** *Brit.* a clip or forked device for securing clothes to a clothes-line. **clothes-pin** *US* a clothes-peg. [OE *clāthas* pl. of *clāth* CLOTH]

clothier /ˈkləʊðɪə(r)/ *n.* a seller of men's clothes. [ME *clother* f. CLOTH]

clothing /ˈkləʊðɪŋ/ *n.* clothes collectively.

Clotho /ˈkləʊθəʊ/ *Gk Mythol.* one of the three Fates (see FATES). [Gk, = she who spins]

cloture /ˈkləʊtʃə(r), -tjʊə(r)/ *n.* & *v.* *US* —*n.* the closure of a debate. —*v.tr.* closure. [F *clôture* f. OF CLOSURE]

clou /kluː/ *n.* **1** the point of greatest interest; the chief attraction. **2** the central idea. [F, = nail]

cloud /klaʊd/ *n.* & *v.* —*n.* **1** a visible mass of condensed watery vapour floating in the atmosphere high above the general level of the ground. **2** a mass of smoke or dust. **3** (foll. by *of*) a great number of insects, birds, etc., moving together. **4 a** a state of gloom, trouble, or suspicion. **b** a frowning or depressed look (*a cloud on his brow*). **5** a local dimness or a vague patch of colour in or on a liquid or a transparent body. **6** an unsubstantial or fleeting thing. **7** obscurity. —*v.* **1** *tr.* cover or darken with clouds or gloom or trouble. **2** *intr.* (often foll. by *over, up*) become overcast or gloomy. **3** *tr.* make unclear. **4** *tr.* variegate with vague patches of colour. □ **cloud-castle** a daydream. **cloud chamber** a device containing vapour for tracking the paths of charged particles, X-rays, and gamma rays. **clouded leopard** a mottled arboreal S. Asian feline, *Neofelis nebulosa*. **cloud-hopping** movement of an aircraft from cloud to cloud esp. for concealment. **cloud-land** a utopia or fairyland. **in the clouds 1** unreal, imaginary, mystical. **2** (of a person) abstracted, inattentive. **on cloud nine** (or **seven**) *colloq.* extremely happy. **under a cloud** out of favour, discredited, under suspicion. **with one's head in the clouds** day-dreaming, unrealistic. □□ **cloudless** *adj.* **cloudlessly** *adv.* **cloudlet** *n.* [OE *clūd* mass of rock or earth, prob. rel. to CLOD]

cloudberry /ˈklaʊdbərɪ/ *n.* (*pl.* **-ies**) a small mountain bramble, *Rubus chamaemorus*, with a white flower and an orange-coloured fruit.

cloudburst /ˈklaʊdbɜːst/ *n.* a sudden violent rainstorm.

cloud-cuckoo-land /klaʊdˈkʊkuːˌlænd/ *n.* a fanciful or ideal place. [transl. of Gk *Nephelokokkugia* f. *nephelē* cloud + *kokkux* cuckoo (in Aristophanes' *Birds*)]

cloudscape /ˈklaʊdskeɪp/ *n.* **1** a picturesque grouping of clouds. **2** a picture or view of clouds. [CLOUD *n.*, after *landscape*]

cloudy /ˈklaʊdɪ/ *adj.* (**cloudier, cloudiest**) **1 a** (of the sky) covered with clouds, overcast. **b** (of weather) characterized by clouds. **2** not transparent; unclear. □□ **cloudily** *adv.* **cloudiness** *n.*

Clouet /ˈkluːeɪ/ the name of a family of painters descended from Jean Clouet the elder (b. 1420), a Fleming, who was painter to the Duke of Burgundy in 1475. The more famous Jean Clouet (*c.*1485–1541), thought to be his son, was a portrait painter belonging to the school of Flemish naturalism; his drawings have been compared to those of Holbein. His son François (d. 1572) worked in the international mannerist style and painted portraits and genre scenes.

Clough /klʌf/, Arthur Hugh (1819–61), English poet. A fellow of Oriel College, Oxford, he resigned in 1848 because of religious doubts, and some of his best-known poems express his spiritual anguish.

clough /klʌf/ *n. dial.* a steep valley usu. with a torrent bed; a ravine. [OE *clōh* f. Gmc]

clout /klaʊt/ *n.* & *v.* —*n.* **1** a heavy blow. **2** *colloq.* influence, power of effective action esp. in politics or business. **3** *dial.* a piece of cloth or clothing (*cast not a clout*). **4** *Archery hist.* a piece of canvas on a frame, used as a mark. **5** a nail with a large flat head. **6** a patch. —*v.tr.* **1** hit hard. **2** mend with a patch. [OE *clūt*, rel. to CLEAT, CLOT]

clove[1] /kləʊv/ *n.* **1 a** a dried flower-bud of a tropical plant, *Eugenia aromatica*, used as a pungent aromatic spice. **b** this plant. **2** (in full **clove gillyflower** or **clove pink**) a clove-scented pink, *Dianthus caryophyllus*, the original of the carnation and other double pinks. [ME f. *clou* (*de girofle*) nail (of gillyflower), from its shape, GILLYFLOWER being orig. the name of the spice; later applied to the similarly scented pink]

clove[2] /kləʊv/ *n.* any of the small bulbs making up a compound bulb of garlic, shallot, etc. [OE *clufu*, rel. to CLEAVE[1]]

clove[3] *past* of CLEAVE[1].

clove hitch /kləʊv/ *n.* a knot by which a rope is secured by passing it twice round a spar or rope that it crosses at right angles. [old past part. of CLEAVE[1], as showing parallel separate lines]

cloven /ˈkləʊv(ə)n/ *adj.* split, partly divided. □ **cloven hoof** (or **foot**) the divided hoof of ruminant quadrupeds (e.g. oxen, sheep, goats); also ascribed to the god Pan, and so to the Devil. **show the cloven hoof** reveal one's evil nature. □□ **cloven-footed** /-ˈfʊtɪd/ *adj.* **cloven-hoofed** /-ˈhuːfd/ *adj.* [past part. of CLEAVE[1]]

clover /ˈkləʊvə(r)/ *n.* any leguminous fodder plant of the genus *Trifolium*, having dense flower heads and leaves each consisting of usu. three leaflets. □ **clover leaf** a junction of roads intersecting at different levels with connecting sections forming the pattern of a four-leaved clover. **in clover** in ease and luxury. [OE *clāfre* f. Gmc]

Clovis /ˈkləʊvɪs/ the name of a city in eastern New Mexico in the US, applied to the remains of a prehistoric industry first found at the Blackwater Draw site near by, and especially to a type of projectile point often found in association with bones of the mammoth. The points are heavy, leaf-shaped, with parallel or slightly convex sides, and some are fluted for part of their length. They precede the Folsom type, dating from the 10th millennium BC and earlier.

clown /klaʊn/ *n.* & *v.* —*n.* **1** a comic entertainer, esp. in a pantomime or circus, usu. with traditional costume and make-up. (See GRIMALDI.) **2** a silly, foolish, or playful person. **3** *archaic* a rustic. —*v.* **1** *intr.* (often foll. by *about, around*) behave like a clown; act foolishly or playfully. **2** *tr.* perform (a part, an action, etc.) like a clown. □□ **clownery** *n.* **clownish** *adj.* **clownishly** *adv.* **clownishness** *n.* [16th c.: perh. of LG orig.]

cloy /klɔɪ/ *v.tr.* (usu. foll. by *with*) satiate or sicken with an excess of sweetness, richness, etc. □□ **cloyingly** *adv.* [ME f. obs. *acloy* f. AF *acloyer*, OF *encloyer* f. Rmc: cf. ENCLAVE]

cloze /kləʊz/ *n.* the exercise of supplying a word that has been omitted from a passage as a test of readability or comprehension (usu. *attrib.*: *cloze test*). [CLOSURE]

club /klʌb/ *n.* & *v.* —*n.* **1** a heavy stick with a thick end, used as a weapon etc. **2** a stick used in a game, esp. a stick with a head used in golf. **3 a** a playing-card of a suit denoted by a black trefoil. **b** (in *pl.*) this suit. **4** an association of persons united by a common interest, usu. meeting periodically for a shared activity (*tennis club*; *yacht club*). **5** an organization or premises offering members social amenities, meals and temporary residence, etc. **6** an organization offering subscribers certain benefits (*book club*). **7** a group of persons, nations, etc., having something in common. **8** = CLUBHOUSE. **9** a structure or organ, esp. in a plant, with a knob at the end. —*v.* (**clubbed, clubbing**) **1** *tr.* beat with or as with a club. **2** *intr.* (foll. by *together, with*) combine for joint action, esp. making up a sum of money for a purpose. **3** *tr.* contribute (money etc.) to a common stock. □ **club-class** a class of fare on aircraft etc. designed for the business traveller. **club-foot** a congenitally deformed foot. **club-footed** having a club-foot. **club-man** (*pl.* **-men**) a member of one or more clubs (in sense 5 of *n.*). **club-root** a disease of cabbages etc. with swelling at the base of the stem. **club sandwich** US a sandwich with two layers of filling between three slices of toast or bread. **in the club** Brit. sl. pregnant. **on the club** colloq. receiving relief from the funds of a benefit society. □□ **clubber** n. [ME f. ON klubba assim. form of klumba club, rel. to CLUMP]

clubbable /ˈklʌbəb(ə)l/ adj. sociable; fit for membership of a club. □□ **clubbability** /-ˈbɪlɪtɪ/ n. **clubbableness** n.

clubby /ˈklʌbɪ/ adj. (**clubbier, clubbiest**) esp. US sociable; friendly.

clubhouse /ˈklʌbhaʊs/ n. the premises used by a club.

clubland /ˈklʌblænd/ n. Brit. an area where many clubs are, esp. St James's in London.

clubmoss /ˈklʌbmɒs/ n. any pteridophyte of the family Lycopodiaceae, bearing upright spikes of spore-cases.

cluck /klʌk/ n. & v. —n. 1 a guttural cry like that of a hen. 2 sl. a silly or foolish person (dumb cluck). —v.intr. emit a cluck or clucks. [imit.]

clucky /ˈklʌkɪ/ adj. (of a hen) sitting on eggs.

clue /kluː/ n. & v. —n. 1 a fact or idea that serves as a guide, or suggests a line of inquiry, in a problem or investigation. 2 a piece of evidence etc. in the detection of a crime. 3 a verbal formula serving as a hint as to what is to be inserted in a crossword. 4 a the thread of a story. b a train of thought. —v.tr. (**clues, clued, cluing** or **clueing**) provide a clue to. □ **clue in** (or **up**) sl. inform. **not have a clue** colloq. be ignorant or incompetent. [var. of CLEW]

clueless /ˈkluːlɪs/ adj. colloq. ignorant, stupid. □□ **cluelessly** adv. **cluelessness** n.

Cluj /kluːʒ/ a city in west central Romania; pop. (1985) 309,800. Founded by German colonists in the 12th c., Cluj became a noted centre of learning and cultural capital of Transylvania.

clump /klʌmp/ n. & v. —n. 1 (foll. by of) a cluster of plants, esp. trees or shrubs. 2 an agglutinated mass of blood-cells etc. 3 a thick extra sole on a boot or shoe. —v. 1 a intr. form a clump. b tr. heap or plant together. 2 intr. (also **clomp** /klɒmp/) walk with heavy tread. 3 tr. colloq. hit. □□ **clumpy** adj. (**clumpier, clumpiest**). [MLG klumpe, MDu. klompe: see CLUB]

clumsy /ˈklʌmzɪ/ adj. (**clumsier, clumsiest**) 1 awkward in movement or shape; ungainly. 2 difficult to handle or use. 3 tactless. □□ **clumsily** adv. **clumsiness** n. [obs. clumse be numb with cold (prob. f. Scand.)]

clung past and past part. of CLING.

clunk /klʌŋk/ n. & v. —n. a dull sound as of thick pieces of metal meeting. —v.intr. make such a sound. [imit.]

Cluny /ˈkluːnɪ/ a town in eastern France where a monastery was founded in 910 with the object of returning to the strict Benedictine rule, cultivation of the spiritual life, and stress on the choir office. Other houses followed suit, and the order became centralized and influential in the 11th–12th c. □□ **Cluniac** /-ˌɪæk/ adj. & n.

cluster /ˈklʌstə(r)/ n. & v. —n. 1 a close group or bunch of similar things growing together. 2 a close group or swarm of people, animals, faint stars, gems, etc. 3 a group of successive consonants or vowels. —v. 1 tr. bring into a cluster or clusters. 2 intr. be or come into a cluster or clusters. 3 intr. (foll. by round, around) gather, congregate. □ **cluster bomb** an anti-personnel bomb spraying pellets on impact. **cluster pine** a Mediterranean pine Pinus pinaster with clustered cones: also called PINASTER. [OE clyster: cf. CLOT]

clustered /ˈklʌstəd/ adj. 1 growing in or brought into a cluster. 2 Archit. (of pillars, columns, or shafts) several close together, or disposed round or half detached from a pier.

clutch¹ /klʌtʃ/ v. & n. —v. 1 tr. seize eagerly; grasp tightly. 2 intr. (foll. by at) snatch suddenly. —n. 1 a a tight grasp. b (foll. by at) grasping. 2 (in pl.) grasping hands, esp. as representing a cruel or relentless grasp or control. 3 a (in a motor vehicle) a device for connecting and disconnecting the engine to the transmission. b the pedal operating this. c an arrangement for connecting or disconnecting working parts of a machine. □ **clutch bag** a slim flat handbag without handles. [ME clucche, clicche f. OE clyccan crook, clench, f. Gmc]

clutch² /klʌtʃ/ n. 1 a set of eggs for hatching. 2 a brood of chickens. [18th c.: prob. S.Engl. var. of cletch f. cleck to hatch f. ON klekja, assoc. with CLUTCH¹]

Clutha /ˈkluːθə/ a river at the southern end of South Island, New Zealand.

clutter /ˈklʌtə(r)/ n. & v. —n. 1 a crowded and untidy collection of things. 2 an untidy state. —v.tr. (often foll. by up, with) crowd untidily, fill with clutter. [partly var. of clotter coagulate, partly assoc. with CLUSTER, CLATTER]

Clwyd /ˈkluːɪd/ a county in NE Wales: pop. (1981) 393,600; county town, Mold.

Clyde /klaɪd/ a river in SW Scotland, famous for the shipbuilding industries along its banks.

Clydesdale /ˈklaɪdzdeɪl/ n. 1 a a horse of a heavy powerful breed, used as draught-horses. b this breed. 2 a kind of small terrier. [orig. bred near the river Clyde in Scotland: see DALE]

clypeus /ˈklɪpɪəs/ n. (pl. **clypei** /-pɪaɪ/) the hard protective area of an insect's head. □□ **clypeal** adj. **clypeate** adj. [L, = round shield]

clyster /ˈklɪstə(r)/ n. & v. archaic —n. an enema. —v.tr. treat with an enema. [ME f. OF clystere or f. L f. Gk klustēr syringe f. kluzō wash out]

Clytemnestra /klaɪtɪmˈnestrə/ Gk legend sister of Helen and the Dioscuri, wife of Agamemnon (see AGAMEMNON).

CM abbr. Member of the Order of Canada.

Cm. Brit. Command Paper (1986–   ).

Cm symb. Chem. the element curium.

cm abbr. centimetre(s).

Cmd. abbr. Brit. Command Paper (1918–56).

Cmdr. abbr. Commander.

Cmdre. abbr. Commodore.

CMEA abbr. Council for Mutual Economic Assistance (see COMECON).

CMG abbr. (in the UK) Companion (of the Order) of St Michael and St George.

Cmnd. abbr. Brit. Command Paper (1956–86).

CNAA abbr. Council for National Academic Awards.

CND abbr. (in the UK) Campaign for Nuclear Disarmament. Its first president was Bertrand Russell (1958).

cnr. abbr. corner.

Cnut /kəˈnjuːt/ (c.994–1035), Danish king of England, reigned 1017–35. Having succeeded his father as king of Denmark in 1014, Cnut became king of England after the murder in 1016 of Edmund Ironside, king of Wessex, ending a prolonged struggle for the throne. As king, he presided over a period of relative peace, depending more and more on English rather than Danish advisers. He is most commonly remembered for the occasion on which he demonstrated his inability to stop the rising tide to fawning courtiers who had told him he was all-powerful.

CO abbr. 1 Commanding Officer. 2 conscientious objector. 3 US Colorado (in official postal use).

Co symb. Chem. the element cobalt.

Co. abbr. 1 company. 2 county. □ **and Co.** /kəʊ/ colloq. and the rest of them; and similar things.

co- /kəʊ/ prefix 1 added to: a nouns, with the sense 'joint, mutual, common' (co-author; coequality). b adjectives and adverbs, with the sense 'jointly, mutually' (co-belligerent; coequal; coequally). c verbs, with the sense 'together with another or others' (cooperate; co-author). 2 Math. a of the complement of an angle (cosine). b the complement of (co-latitude; coset). [orig. a form of COM-]

c/o abbr. care of.

coach /kəʊtʃ/ n. & v. —n. 1 a single-decker bus, usu. comfortably equipped for longer journeys. 2 a railway carriage. 3 a horse-drawn carriage, usu. closed, esp. a State carriage or a stagecoach. 4 a an instructor or trainer in sport. b a private tutor. 5 US economy-class seating in an aircraft. 6 Austral. a docile cow or bullock used as a decoy to attract wild cattle. —v. 1 tr. a train or teach (a pupil, sports team, etc.) as a coach. b give hints to; prime with facts. 2 intr. travel by stagecoach (in the old coaching days). □ **coach-built** (of motor-car bodies) individually built by craftsmen. **coach-house** an outhouse for carriages. **coach station** a stopping-place for a number of coaches, usu. with buildings and amenities. [F *coche* f. Magyar *kocsi* (adj.) f. *Kocs* in Hungary]

coachload /ˈkəʊtʃləʊd/ *n.* a number of people, esp. holidaymakers, taken by coach.

coachman /ˈkəʊtʃmən/ *n.* (*pl.* **-men**) the driver of a horse-drawn carriage.

coachwood /ˈkəʊtʃwʊd/ *n. Austral.* any tree esp. *Ceratopetalum apetalum* with close-grained wood suitable for cabinet-making.

coachwork /ˈkəʊtʃwɜːk/ *n.* the bodywork of a road or rail vehicle.

coadjutor /kəʊˈædʒʊtə(r)/ *n.* an assistant, esp. an assistant bishop. [ME f. OF *coadjuteur* f. LL *coadjutor* (as CO-, *adjutor* f. *adjuvare* -*jut*- help)]

coagulant /kəʊˈægjʊlənt/ *n.* a substance that produces coagulation.

coagulate /kəʊˈægjʊˌleɪt/ *v.tr.* & *intr.* **1** change from a fluid to a solid or semisolid state. **2** clot, curdle. **3** set, solidify. □□ **coagulable** *adj.* **coagulative** /-lətɪv/ *adj.* **coagulator** *n.* [ME f. L *coagulare* f. *coagulum* rennet]

coagulation /kəʊˌægjʊˈleɪʃ(ə)n/ *n.* the process by which a liquid changes to a semisolid mass. [as COAGULATE]

coagulum /kəʊˈægjʊləm/ *n.* (*pl.* **coagula** /-lə/) a mass of coagulated matter. [L: see COAGULATE]

Coahuila /ˌkəʊəˈwiːlə/ a State of northern Mexico; pop. (est. 1988) 1,906,100; capital, Saltillo.

coal /kəʊl/ *n.* & *v.* —*n.* **1 a** a hard black or blackish rock, mainly carbonized plant matter, found in underground seams and used as a fuel and in the manufacture of gas, tar, etc. (See below.) **b** *Brit.* a piece of this for burning. **2** a red-hot piece of coal, wood, etc. in a fire. —*v.* **1** *intr.* take in a supply of coal. **2** *tr.* put coal into (an engine, fire, etc.). □ **coal-bed** a stratum of coal. **coal-black** completely black. **coal-fired** heated or driven by coal. **coal gas** mixed gases extracted from coal and used for lighting and heating. **coal-hole** *Brit.* a compartment or small cellar for storing coal. **coal measures** a series of rocks formed by seams of coal with intervening strata. **coal oil** *US* petroleum or paraffin. **coal-sack** **1** a sack for carrying coal. **2** a black patch in the Milky Way, esp. the one near the Southern Cross. **coal-scuttle** a container for coal to supply a domestic fire. **coal-seam** a stratum of coal suitable for mining. **coals to Newcastle** something brought or sent to a place where it is already plentiful. **coal tar** a thick black oily liquid distilled from coal and used as a source of benzene. **coal-tit** (or **cole-tit**) a small greyish bird, *Parus ater*, with a black head: also called COALMOUSE. **haul** (or **call**) **over the coals** reprimand. □□ **coaly** *adj.* [OE *col* f. Gmc]

Coal is the most abundant form of solid fuel, formed from the remains of trees and other plant material, mostly during the Carboniferous period. It consists chiefly of carbon, formed by the plants from carbon dioxide in the air by the process of photosynthesis, and this stored energy is released when the coal is burnt with oxygen from the air to produce carbon dioxide again. There is a wide variety of coal types, from black anthracite (almost pure carbon) through bituminous coal which contains tarry substances (mostly hydrocarbon compounds which form gases when heated), to lignite, a soft brown coal of later formation and with lower calorific value. Coal is widely used as a fuel in industry for the production of heat and electric power, formerly also for producing gas. Although oil and natural gas are competitive fuels at present, both are limited in quantity, whereas coal deposits are sufficient for several hundred years. Layers of coal near the surface are mined by opencast methods, removing and later replacing the covering soil. Deeper layers are mined by sinking shafts and digging the coal layers by machine, leaving pillars to support the ground above. Both methods have severe social problems; surface mining can leave derelict areas, while underground mining is dirty and dangerous work which cannot at present be done entirely by machines.

coaler /ˈkəʊlə(r)/ *n.* a ship etc. transporting coal.

coalesce /ˌkəʊəˈles/ *v.intr.* **1** come together and form one whole. **2** combine in a coalition. □□ **coalescence** *n.* **coalescent** *adj.* [L *coalescere* (as CO-, *alescere alit*- grow f. *alere* nourish)]

coalface /ˈkəʊlfeɪs/ *n.* an exposed surface of coal in a mine.

coalfield /ˈkəʊlfiːld/ *n.* an extensive area with strata containing coal.

coalfish /ˈkəʊlfɪʃ/ *n.* = SAITHE.

coalition /ˌkəʊəˈlɪʃ(ə)n/ *n.* **1** *Polit.* a temporary alliance for combined action, esp. of distinct parties forming a government, or of States. **2** fusion into one whole. □□ **coalitionist** *n.* [med.L *coalitio* (as COALESCE)]

coalman /ˈkəʊlmən/ *n.* (*pl.* **-men**) a man who carries or delivers coal.

coalmine /ˈkəʊlmaɪn/ *n.* a mine in which coal is dug. □□ **coalminer** *n.*

coalmouse /ˈkəʊlmaʊs/ *n.* (also **colemouse**) (*pl.* **-mice**) = *coaltit*. [OE *colmāse* f. *col* COAL + *māse* as TITMOUSE]

Coalport /ˈkəʊlpɔːt/ *n.* a kind of china and porcelain produced at Coalport, a town in Shropshire.

coaming /ˈkəʊmɪŋ/ *n.* a raised border round the hatches etc. of a ship to keep out water. [17th c.: orig. unkn.]

coarse /kɔːs/ *adj.* **1 a** rough or loose in texture or grain; made of large particles. **b** (of a person's features) rough or large. **2** lacking refinement or delicacy; crude, obscene (*coarse humour*). **3** rude, uncivil. **4** inferior, common. □ **coarse fish** *Brit.* any freshwater fish other than salmon and trout. □□ **coarsely** *adv.* **coarseness** *n.* **coarsish** *adj.* [ME: orig. unkn.]

coarsen /ˈkɔːs(ə)n/ *v.tr.* & *intr.* make or become coarse.

coast /kəʊst/ *n.* & *v.* —*n.* **1 a** the border of the land near the sea; the seashore. **b** (**the Coast**) *US* the Pacific coast of the US. **2 a** a run, usu. downhill, on a bicycle without pedalling or in a motor vehicle without using the engine. **b** *US* a toboggan slide or slope. —*v.intr.* **1** ride or move, usu. downhill, without use of power, free-wheel. **2** make progress without much effort. **3** *US* slide down a hill on a toboggan. **4 a** sail along the coast. **b** trade between ports on the same coast. □ **the coast is clear** there is no danger of being observed or caught. **coast-to-coast** across an island or continent. □□ **coastal** *adj.* [ME f. OF *coste, costeier* f. L *costa* rib, flank, side]

coaster /ˈkəʊstə(r)/ *n.* **1** a ship that travels along the coast from port to port. **2** a small tray or mat for a bottle or glass. **3** *US* **a** a sledge for coasting. **b** a roller-coaster.

coastguard /ˈkəʊstɡɑːd/ *n.* **1** an organization keeping watch on the coasts and on local shipping to save life, prevent smuggling, etc. **2** a member of this.

coastline /ˈkəʊstlaɪn/ *n.* the line of the seashore, esp. with regard to its shape (*a rugged coastline*).

coastwise /ˈkəʊstwaɪz/ *adj.* & *adv.* along, following, or connected with the coast.

coat /kəʊt/ *n.* & *v.* —*n.* **1** an outer garment with sleeves and often extending below the hips; an overcoat or jacket. **2 a** an animal's fur, hair, etc. **b** *Physiol.* a structure, esp. a membrane, enclosing or lining an organ. **c** a skin, rind, or husk. **d** a layer of a bulb etc. **3 a** a layer or covering. **b** a covering of paint etc. laid on a surface at one time. —*v.tr.* **1** (usu. foll. by *with, in*) **a** apply a coat of paint etc. to; provide with a layer or covering. **b** (as **coated** *adj.*) covered with. **2** (of paint etc.) form a covering to. □ **coat armour** coats of arms. **coat dress** a woman's tailored dress resembling a coat. **coat-hanger** see HANGER[1]. **coat of arms** the heraldic bearings or shield of a person, family, or corporation. **coat of mail** a jacket of mail armour (see MAIL[2]). **on a person's coat-tails** undeservedly benefiting from another's success. □□ **coated** *adj.* (also in *comb.*). [ME f. OF *cote* f. Rmc f. Frank., of unkn. orig.]

coatee /kəʊˈtiː/ *n.* **1** a woman's or infant's short coat. **2** *archaic* a close-fitting short coat.

coati /kəʊˈɑːtɪ/ *n.* (*pl.* **coatis**) any racoon-like flesh-eating mammal of the genus *Nasua*, with a long flexible snout and a long usu. ringed tail. [Tupi f. *cua* belt + *tim* nose]

coatimundi /ˌkəʊəˈtiːmʌndɪ/ *n.* (*pl.* **coatimundis**) = COATI. [as COATI + Tupi *mondi* solitary]

coating /ˈkəʊtɪŋ/ n. **1** a thin layer or covering of paint etc. **2** material for making coats.

co-author /ˌkəʊˈɔːθə(r)/ n. & v. —n. a joint author. —v.tr. be a joint author of.

coax /kəʊks/ v.tr. **1** (usu. foll. by *into*, or *to* + infin.) persuade (a person) gradually or by flattery. **2** (foll. by *out of*) obtain (a thing from a person) by coaxing. **3** manipulate (a thing) carefully or slowly. □□ **coaxer** n. **coaxingly** adv. [16th c.: f. 'make a *cokes* of' f. obs. *cokes* simpleton, of unkn. orig.]

coaxial /kəʊˈæksɪəl/ adj. **1** having a common axis. **2** *Electr.* (of a cable or line) transmitting by means of two concentric conductors separated by an insulator. □□ **coaxially** adv.

cob[1] /kɒb/ n. **1** a roundish lump of coal etc. **2** *Brit.* a domed loaf of bread. **3** *Brit.* = *corn-cob* (see CORN[1]). **4** (in full **cob-nut**) a large hazelnut. **5** a sturdy riding- or driving-horse with short legs. **6** a male swan. [ME: orig. unkn.]

cob[2] /kɒb/ n. a material for walls, made from compressed earth, clay, or chalk reinforced with straw. [17th c.: orig. unkn.]

cobalt /ˈkəʊbɔːlt, -bɒlt/ n. *Chem.* a hard silvery-white metallic element similar in many respects to nickel. The metal was known to Paracelsus, though its discovery is usually credited to G. Brandt (d. 1768) in 1733. There are important deposits from which it is mined in Zaïre and in Canada. Its main use is as a component of magnetic alloys and those designed for use at high temperatures. Cobalt compounds have been used since ancient times to colour ceramics, and they are also widely used as catalysts. The element is essential in small quantities to living organisms. ¶ Symb.: **Co**; atomic number 27. □ **cobalt blue 1** a pigment containing a cobalt salt. **2** the deep-blue colour of this. □□ **cobaltic** /kəˈbɔːltɪk/ adj. **cobaltous** /kəˈbɔːltəs/ adj. [G *Kobalt* etc., prob. = KOBOLD goblin or demon of the mines, the ore having been so called by the miners on account of its worthlessness (as then supposed) and from its bad effects upon their health and upon the silver ores with which it occurred, effects due mainly to the arsenic and sulphur with which it was combined]

cobber /ˈkɒbə(r)/ n. *Austral.* & *NZ colloq.* a companion or friend. [19th c.: perh. rel. to E dial. *cob* take a liking to]

Cobbett /ˈkɒbɪt/, William (1762–1835), English political reformer. A brilliant radical journalist, Cobbett was one of the leaders of the post-1815 campaign for political and social reform in England. Despite brief periods in prison and exile, Cobbett did much to expose the shortcomings of early 19th-c. industrial society, although his own reforming ideas looked back rather than forward.

cobble[1] /ˈkɒb(ə)l/ n. & v. —n. **1** (in full **cobblestone**) a small rounded stone of a size used for paving. **2** (in *pl.*) *Brit.* coal in lumps of this size. —v.tr. pave with cobbles. [ME *cobel(-ston)*, f. COB[1]]

cobble[2] /ˈkɒb(ə)l/ v.tr. **1** mend or patch up (esp. shoes). **2** (often foll. by *together*) join or assemble roughly. [back-form. f. COBBLER]

cobbler /ˈkɒblə(r)/ n. **1** a person who mends shoes, esp. professionally. **2** an iced drink of wine etc., sugar, and lemon (*sherry cobbler*). **3 a** a pie topped with scones. **b** esp. *US* a fruit pie with a rich thick crust. **4** (in *pl.*) *Brit. sl.* nonsense. **5** *Austral.* & *NZ sl.* the last sheep to be shorn. □ **cobbler's wax** a resinous substance used for waxing thread. [ME, of unkn. orig.: sense 4 f. rhyming sl. *cobbler's awls* = *balls*: sense 5 with pun on LAST[3]]

Cobden /ˈkɒbd(ə)n/, Richard (1804–65), British political reformer. A Manchester industrialist, Cobden was one of the leading spokesmen of the free-trade movement in Britain, leading, with John Bright, the Anti-Corn Law League in its successful campaign for the repeal of the Corn Laws in the early 1840s.

co-belligerent /ˌkəʊbɪˈlɪdʒərənt/ n. & adj. —n. any of two or more nations engaged in war as allies. —adj. of or as a co-belligerent. □□ **co-belligerence** n. **co-belligerency** n.

coble /ˈkəʊb(ə)l/ n. a flat-bottomed fishing-boat in Scotland and NE England. [OE, perh. f. Celt.]

COBOL /ˈkəʊbɒl/ n. *Computing* a programming language designed for use in commerce. [*common business oriented language*]

cobra /ˈkəʊbrə, ˈkɒbrə/ n. any venomous snake of the genus *Naja*, native to Africa and Asia, with a neck dilated like a hood when excited. [Port. f. L *colubra* snake]

cobweb /ˈkɒbweb/ n. **1 a** a fine network of threads spun by a spider from a liquid secreted by it, used to trap insects etc. **b** the thread of this. **2** anything compared with a cobweb, esp. in flimsiness of texture. **3** a trap or insidious entanglement. **4** (in *pl.*) a state of languishing; fustiness. □□ **cobwebbed** adj. **cobwebby** adj. [ME *cop(pe)web* f. obs. *coppe* spider]

coca /ˈkəʊkə/ n. **1** a S. American shrub, *Erythroxylum coca*. **2** its dried leaves, chewed as a stimulant. [Sp. f. Quechua *cuca*]

Coca-Cola /ˌkəʊkəˈkəʊlə/ n. *propr.* an aerated non-alcoholic drink sometimes flavoured with cola seeds.

cocaine /kəˈkeɪn, kəʊ-/ n. a drug derived from coca or prepared synthetically, used as a local anaesthetic and as a stimulant. [COCA + -INE[4]]

coccidiosis /ˌkɒksɪdɪˈəʊsɪs/ n. a disease of birds and mammals caused by any of various parasitic protozoa, esp. of the genus *Eimeria*, affecting the intestine. [*coccidium* (mod.L f. Gk *kokkis* dimin. of *kokkos* berry) + -OSIS]

coccus /ˈkɒkəs/ n. (pl. **cocci** /-kɪ/) any spherical or roughly spherical bacterium. □□ **coccal** adj. **coccoid** adj. [mod.L f. Gk *kokkos* berry]

coccyx /ˈkɒksɪks/ n. (pl. **coccyges** /-ˌdʒiːz/ or **coccyxes**) the small triangular bone at the base of the spinal column in humans and some apes. □□ **coccygeal** /kɒkˈsɪdʒɪəl/ adj. [L f. Gk *kokkux -ugos* cuckoo (from being shaped like its bill)]

Cochabamba /ˌkɒtʃəˈbæmbə/ the third-largest city in Bolivia, situated at the centre of a rich agricultural region; pop. (1985) 317,250.

Cochin /ˈkəʊtʃɪn/ a seaport and naval base on the Malabar coast of SW India, in the State of Kerala; pop. (1981) 686,000.

cochin /ˈkəʊtʃɪn/ n. (in full **cochin-china**) **1** a fowl of an Asian breed with feathery legs. **2** this breed. [COCHIN-CHINA]

Cochin-China /ˈkɒtʃɪˈtʃaɪnə/ the former name for the southern region of what is now Vietnam. Part of French Indo-China from 1862, in 1946 it became a French overseas territory then merged officially with Vietnam in 1949.

cochineal /ˈkɒtʃɪˌniːl, -ˌniːl/ n. **1** a scarlet dye used esp. for colouring food. **2** the dried bodies of the female of the Mexican insect, *Dactylopius coccus*, yielding this. [F *cochenille* or Sp. *cochinilla* f. L *coccinus* scarlet f. Gk *kokkos* berry]

cochlea /ˈkɒklɪə/ n. (pl. **cochleae** /-klɪˌiː/) the spiral cavity of the internal ear. □□ **cochlear** adj. [L, = snail-shell, f. Gk *kokhlias*]

Cochran /ˈkɒkrən/, Sir Charles Blake (1872–1951), American theatrical producer, one of the master showmen of his day. He is famous especially for the musical revues which he produced from 1914 onwards, his most memorable productions being those at the London Pavilion between 1918 and 1931; three of these were by Noel Coward, several of whose plays he later promoted.

cock[1] /kɒk/ n. & v. —n. **1 a** a male bird, esp. of a domestic fowl. **b** a male lobster, crab, or salmon. **c** = WOODCOCK. **2** *Brit. sl.* (usu. **old cock** as a form of address) a friend; a fellow. **3** *coarse sl.* the penis. **4** *Brit. sl.* nonsense. ¶ In senses 3, 4 usually considered a taboo word. **5 a** a firing lever in a gun which can be raised to be released by the trigger. **b** the cocked position of this (*at full cock*). **6** a tap or valve controlling flow. —v.tr. **1** raise or make upright or erect. **2** turn or move (the eye or ear) attentively or knowingly. **3** set aslant, or turn up the brim of (a hat). **4** raise the cock of (a gun). □ **at half cock** only partly ready. **cock-a-doodle-doo** a cock's crow. **cock-and-bull story** an absurd or incredible account. **cock crow** dawn. **cocked hat** a brimless triangular hat pointed at the front, back, and top. **cock-fight** a fight between cocks as sport. **cock-fighting** this sport. **cock-of-the-rock** a S. American bird, *Rupicola rupicola*, having a crest and bright orange plumage. **cock-of-the-walk** a dominant or arrogant person. **cock-of-the-wood 1** a capercaillie. **2** *US* a red-crested woodpecker. **cock-shy 1 a** a target for throwing at with sticks, stones, etc. **b** a throw at this. **2** an object of ridicule or criticism. **cock a snook** see SNOOK[1]. **cock sparrow 1** a male sparrow. **2** a lively quarrelsome person. **cock up** *Brit. sl.* bungle; make a mess of. **cock-up** n. *Brit. sl.* a muddle or mistake. **knock into a cocked hat** defeat utterly. [OE *cocc* and OF *coq* prob. f. med.L *coccus*]

cock² /kɒk/ n. & v. —n. a small pile of hay, straw, etc. with vertical sides and a rounded top. —v.tr. pile into cocks. [ME, perh. of Scand. orig.]

cockade /kɒˈkeɪd/ n. a rosette etc. worn in a hat as a badge of office or party, or as part of a livery. □□ **cockaded** adj. [F *cocarde* orig. in *bonnet à la coquarde*, f. fem. of obs. *coquard* saucy f. *coq* COCK¹]

cock-a-hoop /ˌkɒkəˈhuːp/ adj. & adv. —adj. exultant; crowing boastfully. —adv. exultantly. [16th c.: orig. in phr. *set cock a hoop* denoting some action preliminary to hard drinking]

cock-a-leekie /ˌkɒkəˈliːkɪ/ n. (also **cocky-leeky** /ˌkɒkɪ-/) a soup traditionally made in Scotland with boiling fowl and leeks. [COCK¹ + LEEK]

cockalorum /ˌkɒkəˈlɔːrəm/ n. colloq. a self-important little man. [18th c.: arbitr. f. COCK¹]

cockatiel /ˌkɒkəˈtiːl/ n. (also **cockateel**) Austral. a small delicately coloured crested parrot, *Nymphicus hollandicus*. [Du. *kaketielje*]

cockatoo /ˌkɒkəˈtuː/ n. 1 any of several parrots of the family Cacatuinae, having powerful beaks and erectile crests. 2 Austral. & NZ colloq. a small farmer. [Du. *kaketoe* f. Malay *kakatua*, assim. to COCK¹]

cockatrice /ˈkɒkətrɪs, -ˌtraɪs/ n. 1 = BASILISK 1. 2 Heraldry a fabulous animal, a cock with a serpent's tail. [ME f. OF *cocatris* f. L *calcare* tread, track, rendering Gk *ikhneumōn* tracker: see ICHNEUMON]

cockboat /ˈkɒkbəʊt/ n. a small ship's-boat. [obs. *cock* small boat (f. OF *coque*) + BOAT]

cockchafer /ˈkɒkˌtʃeɪfə(r)/ n. a large nocturnal beetle, *Melolontha melolontha*, which feeds on leaves and whose larva feeds on roots of crops etc. Also called *May-bug*. [perh. f. COCK¹ as expressing size or vigour + CHAFER]

Cockcroft /ˈkɒkkrɒft/, Sir John Douglas (1897–1967), English physicist, who joined Rutherford's group at the Cavendish Laboratory, Cambridge, in 1922, and ten years later, working with E. T. S. Walton, succeeded in 'splitting the atom' by means of artificially accelerated protons. With their novel high-energy particle accelerator the researchers bombarded lithium atoms with protons (the nuclei of hydrogen atoms) and produced alpha particles (helium nuclei); this pioneering experiment demonstrated the transmutation of elements and Einstein's theory of the equivalence of mass and energy. It ushered in the whole field of nuclear and particle physics relying on particle accelerators, and for their work the two shared the 1951 Nobel Prize for physics. After the Second World War Cockcroft emerged as one of the leading scientific figures, and was the first director of the Atomic Energy Research Establishment at Harwell.

cocker /ˈkɒkə(r)/ n. (in full **cocker spaniel**) 1 a small spaniel of a breed with a silky coat. 2 this breed. [as COCK¹, from use in hunting woodcocks etc.]

cockerel /ˈkɒkər(ə)l/ n. a young cock. [ME: dimin. of COCK¹]

Cockerell /ˈkɒkər(ə)l/, Sir Christopher Sydney (1910–), English engineer, who in 1955 patented the vessel that was later called the hovercraft (see entry).

cock-eyed /ˈkɒkaɪd/ adj. colloq. 1 crooked, askew, not level. 2 (of a scheme etc.) absurd, not practical. 3 drunk. 4 squinting. [19th c.: app. f. COCK¹ + EYE]

cockle¹ /ˈkɒk(ə)l/ n. 1 a any edible mollusc of the genus *Cardium*, having a chubby ribbed bivalve shell. b its shell. 2 (in full **cockle-shell**) a small shallow boat. □ **warm the cockles of one's heart** make one contented; be satisfying. [ME f. OF *coquille* shell ult. f. Gk *kogkhulion* f. *kogkhē* CONCH]

cockle² /ˈkɒk(ə)l/ n. 1 any of various plants, esp. the pink-flowered corn-cockle, *Agrostemma githago*, growing among corn, esp. wheat. 2 a disease of wheat that turns the grains black. [OE *coccul*, perh. ult. f. LL *coccus*]

cockle³ /ˈkɒk(ə)l/ v. & n. —v. 1 intr. pucker, wrinkle. 2 tr. cause to cockle. —n. a pucker or wrinkle in paper, glass, etc. [F *coquiller* blister (bread in cooking) f. *coquille*: see COCKLE¹]

cockney /ˈkɒknɪ/ n. & adj. —n. (pl. -eys) 1 a a native of East London, esp. (according to Minsheu (early 17th c.) 'one born within the sound of Bow Bells'). A distinctive feature is its use of rhyming slang (see RHYME). b the dialect or accent typical of this area. 2 Austral. a young snapper fish, *Chrysophrys auratus*. —adj. of or characteristic of cockneys or their dialect or accent. □□ **cockneyism** n. [ME *cokeney* cock's egg, later derog. for 'cocksman']

cockpit /ˈkɒkpɪt/ n. 1 a a compartment for the pilot (or the pilot and crew) of an aircraft or spacecraft. b a similar compartment for the driver in a racing car. c a space for the helmsman in some small yachts. 2 an arena of war or other conflict. 3 a place where cock-fights are held. [orig. in sense 3, f. COCK¹ + PIT¹]

cockroach /ˈkɒkrəʊtʃ/ n. any of various flat brown insects, esp. *Blatta orientalis*, infesting kitchens, bathrooms, etc. [Sp. *cucaracha*, assim. to COCK¹, ROACH¹]

cockscomb /ˈkɒkskəʊm/ n. 1 the crest or comb of a cock. 2 a garden plant *Celosia cristata*, with a terminal plume of tiny white or red flowers.

cocksfoot /ˈkɒksfʊt/ n. any pasture grass of the genus *Dactylis*, with broad leaves and green or purplish spikes.

cocksure /ˌkɒkˈʃʊə(r), -ˈʃɔː(r)/ adj. 1 presumptuously or arrogantly confident. 2 (foll. by *of*, *about*) absolutely sure. □□ **cocksurely** adv. **cocksureness** n. [*cock* = God + SURE]

cocktail /ˈkɒkteɪl/ n. 1 a usu. alcoholic drink made by mixing various spirits, fruit juices, etc. 2 a dish of mixed ingredients (*fruit cocktail*; *shellfish cocktail*). 3 any hybrid mixture. □ **cocktail dress** a usu. short evening dress suitable for wearing at a drinks party. **cocktail stick** a small pointed stick for serving an olive, cherry, small sausage, etc. [orig. unkn.: cf. earlier sense 'docked horse' f. COCK¹: the connection is unclear]

cocky¹ /ˈkɒkɪ/ adj. (**cockier, cockiest**) 1 conceited, arrogant. 2 saucy, impudent. □□ **cockily** adv. **cockiness** n. [COCK¹ + -Y¹]

cocky² /ˈkɒkɪ/ n. (pl. -ies) Austral. & NZ colloq. = COCKATOO 2. [abbr.]

cocky-leeky var. of COCK-A-LEEKIE.

coco /ˈkəʊkəʊ/ n. (also **cocoa**) (pl. **cocos** or **cocoas**) a tall tropical palm tree, *Cocos nucifera*, bearing coconuts. [Port. & Sp. *coco* grimace: the base of the shell resembles a face]

cocoa /ˈkəʊkəʊ/ n. 1 a powder made from crushed cacao seeds, often with other ingredients. 2 a drink made from this. The Aztec Indians were the first to make such a drink, and in the 16th c. the Spaniards brought it to Europe, where it was enjoyed as an expensive luxury. □ **cocoa bean** a cacao seed. **cocoa butter** a fatty substance obtained from cocoa beans and used for confectionery, cosmetics, etc. [alt. of CACAO]

coco-de-mer /ˌkəʊkəʊ-de-ˈmeə(r)/ n. a tall palm-tree, *Lodoicea maldivica*, of the Seychelles. [F]

coconut /ˈkəʊkənʌt/ n. (also **cocoanut**) 1 a a large ovate brown seed of the coco, with a hard shell and edible white fleshy lining enclosing a milky juice. b = COCO. c the edible white fleshy lining of a coconut. 2 sl. the human head. □ **coconut butter** a solid oil obtained from the lining of the coconut, and used in soap, candles, ointment, etc. **coconut ice** a sweet of sugar and desiccated coconut. **coconut matting** a matting made of fibre from coconut husks. **coconut shy** a fairground sideshow where balls are thrown to dislodge coconuts. **double coconut** a very large nut of the coco-de-mer. [COCO + NUT]

cocoon /kəˈkuːn/ n. & v. —n. 1 a silky case spun by many insect larvae for protection as pupae. b a similar structure made by other animals. 2 a protective covering, esp. to prevent corrosion of metal equipment. —v. 1 tr. & intr. wrap in or form a cocoon. 2 tr. spray with a protective coating. [F *cocon* f. mod. Prov. *coucoun* dimin. of *coca* shell]

Cocos Islands /ˈkəʊkəs/ (also **Keeling Islands** /ˈkiːlɪŋ/) a group of 27 small coral islands in the Indian Ocean, administered as an external territory of Australia since 1955. The islands were discovered in 1609 by Captain William Keeling of the East India Company; pop. (1986) 616.

cocotte /kəˈkɒt/ n. 1 a a small fireproof dish for cooking and serving an individual portion of food. b a deep cooking pot with a tight-fitting lid and handles. **2** *archaic* a fashionable prostitute. [F]

Cocteau /kɒkˈtəʊ/, Jean Maurice (1889–1963), French dramatist and film director. His plays include *La Machine infernale* (1934), based on the Oedipus legend, *Les Parents terribles* (1938), and *L'Aigle à deux têtes* (1946). He is better known outside France, however, for his films, some of which were adaptations of his plays. His reputation as a film-maker rests mainly on *Le Sang d'un poète* (1930), *La Belle et la bête* (1946), *Orphée* (1950), and *Le Testament d'Orphée* (1960), all of which show how poetry derives from the ordinary rather than from the obscure; they mingle myth and reality, often by the use of trick photography. His dramatic writing, with its singular blend of poetry, irony, and fantasy, proved a constant source of inspiration and controversy.

COD *abbr.* **1 a** cash on delivery. **b** *US* collect on delivery. **2** Concise Oxford Dictionary.

cod[1] /kɒd/ *n.* (*pl.* same) any large marine fish of the family Gadidae, used as food, esp. *Gadus morhua*. □ **cod-liver oil** an oil pressed from the fresh liver of cod, which is rich in vitamins D and A. [ME: orig. unkn.]

cod[2] /kɒd/ *n. & v. Brit. sl.* —*n.* **1** a parody. **2** a hoax. **3** (*attrib.*) = MOCK *adj.* —*v.* (**codded, codding**) **1 a** *intr.* perform a hoax. **b** *tr.* play a trick on; fool. **2** *tr.* parody. [19th c.: orig. unkn.]

cod[3] /kɒd/ *n.* (*sl.*) nonsense. [abbr. of CODSWALLOP]

coda /ˈkəʊdə/ *n.* **1** *Mus.* the concluding passage of a basic structure. **2** *Ballet* the concluding section of a dance. **3** a concluding event or series of events. [It. f. L *cauda* tail]

coddle /ˈkɒd(ə)l/ *v.tr.* **1 a** treat as an invalid; protect attentively. **b** (foll. by *up*) strengthen by feeding. **2** cook (an egg) in water below boiling point. □□ **coddler** *n.* [prob. dial. var. of *caudle* invalids' gruel]

code /kəʊd/ *n. & v.* —*n.* **1** a system of words, letters, figures, or symbols, used to represent others for secrecy or brevity. **2** a system of prearranged signals, esp. used to ensure secrecy in transmitting messages. **3** *Computing* a piece of program text. **4 a** a systematic collection of statutes, a body of laws so arranged as to avoid inconsistency and overlapping. **b** a set of rules on any subject. **5 a** the prevailing morality of a society or class (*code of honour*). **b** a person's standard of moral behaviour. —*v.tr.* put (a message, program, etc.) into code. □ **code-book** a list of symbols etc. used in a code. **code-name** (or **-number**) a word or symbol (or number) used for secrecy or convenience instead of the usual name. □□ **coder** *n.* [ME f. OF f. L CODEX]

codeine /ˈkəʊdiːn/ *n.* an alkaloid derived from morphine and used to relieve pain. [Gk *kōdeia* poppy-head + -INE[4]]

co-determination /ˌkəʊdɪˌtɜːmɪˈneɪʃ(ə)n/ *n.* cooperation between management and workers in decision-taking. [CO- + DETERMINATION, after G *Mitbestimmung*]

codex /ˈkəʊdeks/ *n.* (*pl.* **codices** /ˈkəʊdɪˌsiːz, ˈkɒd-/) **1** an ancient manuscript text in book form which between 1st–4th c. AD gradually replaced the continuous roll previously used for written documents. **2** a collection of pharmaceutical descriptions of drugs etc. [L, = block of wood, tablet, book]

codfish /ˈkɒdfɪʃ/ *n.* = COD[1].

codger /ˈkɒdʒə(r)/ *n.* (usu. in **old codger**) *colloq.* a person, esp. an old or strange one. [perh. var. of *cadger*: see CADGE]

codices *pl.* of CODEX.

codicil /ˈkəʊdɪsɪl, ˈkɒd-/ *n.* an addition explaining, modifying, or revoking a will or part of one. □□ **codicillary** /ˌkɒdɪˈsɪlərɪ/ *adj.* [L *codicillus*, dimin. of CODEX]

codicology /ˌkəʊdɪˈkɒlədʒɪ/ *n.* the study of manuscripts. □□ **codicological** /-kəˈlɒdʒɪk(ə)l/ *adj.* **codicologically** /-kəˈlɒdʒɪkəlɪ/ *adv.* [F *codicologie* f. L *codex codicis*: see CODEX]

codify /ˈkəʊdɪˌfaɪ, ˈkɒd-/ *v.tr.* (**-ies, -ied**) arrange (laws etc.) systematically into a code. □□ **codification** /-fɪˈkeɪʃ(ə)n/ *n.* **codifier** *n.*

codling[1] /ˈkɒdlɪŋ/ *n.* (also **codlin**) **1** any of several varieties of cooking-apple, having a long tapering shape. **2** a small moth, *Carpocapsa pomonella*, the larva of which feeds on apples. □ **codlings-and-cream** the great willow-herb, *Epilobium angustifolium*. [ME f. AF *quer de lion* lion-heart]

codling[2] /ˈkɒdlɪŋ/ *n.* a small codfish.

codomain /ˈkəʊdəʊˌmeɪn/ *n. Math.* a set that includes all the possible expressions of a given function. [CO- 2 + DOMAIN]

codon /ˈkəʊdɒn/ *n. Biochem.* a sequence of three nucleotides, forming a unit of genetic code in a DNA or RNA molecule. [CODE + -ON]

codpiece /ˈkɒdpiːs/ *n. hist.* an appendage like a small bag or flap at the front of a man's breeches. [ME, f. *cod* scrotum + PIECE]

co-driver /kəʊˈdraɪvə(r)/ *n.* a person who shares the driving of a vehicle with another, esp. in a race, rally, etc.

codswallop /ˈkɒdzˌwɒləp/ *n. Brit. sl.* nonsense. [20th c.: orig. unkn.]

Cody /ˈkəʊdɪ/, William Frederick, see BUFFALO BILL.

Coe /kəʊ/, Sebastian (1956–), English middle-distance runner, who broke a number of world records at different distances and won a gold medal in the 1500 metres event at the Olympic Games in 1980 and 1984.

coecilian var. of CAECILIAN.

coed /ˈkəʊed, kəʊˈed/ *n. & adj. colloq.* —*n.* **1** a coeducational system or institution. **2** esp. *US* a female student at a coeducational institution. —*adj.* coeducational. [abbr.]

coeducation /ˌkəʊedjuːˈkeɪʃ(ə)n/ *n.* the education of pupils of both sexes together. □□ **coeducational** *adj.*

coefficient /ˌkəʊɪˈfɪʃ(ə)nt/ *n.* **1** *Math.* a quantity placed before and multiplying an algebraic expression (e.g. 4 in $4x^y$). **2** *Physics* a multiplier or factor that measures some property (*coefficient of expansion*). [mod.L *coefficiens* (as CO-, EFFICIENT)]

coelacanth /ˈsiːləˌkænθ/ *n.* a large bony marine fish, *Latimeria chalumnae*, formerly thought to be extinct, having a trilobed tail-fin and fleshy pectoral fins. [mod.L *Coelacanthus* f. Gk *koilos* hollow + *akantha* spine]

-coele *comb. form* var. of -CELE.

coelenterate /siːˈlentəˌreɪt/ *n.* any marine animal of the phylum Coelenterata with a simple tube-shaped or cup-shaped body and a digestive system with a single opening surrounded by a ring of tentacles, e.g. jellyfish, hydras, corals, and sea anemones. [mod.L *Coelenterata* f. Gk *koilos* hollow + *enteron* intestine]

coeliac /ˈsiːlɪˌæk/ *adj.* (*US* **celiac**) of or affecting the belly. □ **coeliac disease** a digestive disease of the small intestine brought on by contact with dietary gluten. [L *coeliacus* f. Gk *koiliakos* f. *koilia* belly]

coelom /ˈsiːləm, ˈsiːləʊm/ *n.* (*US* **celom**) (*pl.* **-oms** or **-omata** /-ˈləʊmətə/) *Zool.* the principal body cavity in animals, between the intestinal canal and the body wall. □□ **coelomate** *adj. & n.* [Gk *koilōma* cavity]

coelostat /ˈsiːləˌstæt/ *n. Astron.* an instrument with a rotating mirror that continuously reflects the light from the same area of sky allowing the path of a celestial body to be monitored. [L *caelum* sky + -STAT]

coenobite /ˈsiːnəˌbaɪt/ *n.* (*US* **cenobite**) a member of a monastic community. □□ **coenobitic** /-ˈbɪtɪk/ *adj.* **coenobitical** /-ˈbɪtɪk(ə)l/ *adj.* [OF *cenobite* or eccl.L *coenobita* f. LL *coenobium* f. Gk *koinobion* convent f. *koinos* common + *bios* life]

coenzyme /ˈkəʊˌenzaɪm/ *n. Biochem.* a non-proteinaceous compound that assists in the action of an enzyme.

coequal /kəʊˈiːkw(ə)l/ *adj. & n. archaic* or *literary* —*adj.* equal with one another. —*n.* an equal. □□ **coequality** /ˌkəʊiːˈkwɒlɪtɪ/ *n.* **coequally** *adv.* [ME f. L or eccl.L *coaequalis* (as CO-, EQUAL)]

coerce /kəʊˈɜːs/ *v.tr.* (often foll. by *into*) persuade or restrain (an unwilling person) by force (*coerced you into signing*). □□ **coercible** *adj.* [ME f. L *coercēre* restrain (as CO-, *arcēre* restrain)]

coercion /kəʊˈɜːʃ(ə)n/ *n.* **1** the act or process of coercing. **2** government by force. □□ **coercive** *adj.* **coercively** *adv.* **coerciveness** *n.* [OF *cohercion*, *-tion* f. L *coer(c)tio*, *coercitio -onis* (as COERCE)]

coeval /kəʊˈiːv(ə)l/ *adj. & n.* —*adj.* **1** having the same age or date of origin. **2** living or existing at the same epoch. **3** having the same duration. —*n.* a coeval person, a contemporary. □□ **coevality** /-ˈvælɪtɪ/ *n.* **coevally** *adv.* [LL *coaevus* (as CO-, L *aevum* age)]

coexist /ˌkəʊɪgˈzɪst/ v.intr. (often foll. by with) **1** exist together (in time or place). **2** (esp. of nations) exist in mutual tolerance though professing different ideologies etc. □□ **coexistence** n. **coexistent** adj. [LL coexistere (as CO-, EXIST)]

coextensive /ˌkəʊɪkˈstensɪv/ adj. extending over the same space or time.

C. of E. abbr. Church of England.

coffee /ˈkɒfi/ n. **1 a** a drink made from the roasted and ground beanlike seeds of a tropical shrub. **b** a cup of this. **2 a** any shrub of the genus Coffea, yielding berries containing one or more seeds. **b** these seeds raw, or roasted and ground. **3** a pale brown colour, of coffee mixed with milk. □ **coffee bar** a bar or café serving coffee and light refreshments from a counter. **coffee bean** the beanlike seeds of the coffee shrub. **coffee-cup** a small cup for serving coffee. **coffee-essence** a concentrated extract of coffee usu. containing chicory. **coffee-house** a place serving coffee and other refreshments. **coffee-mill** a small machine for grinding roasted coffee beans. **coffee-morning** a morning gathering at which coffee is served, often in aid of charity. **coffee nibs** coffee beans removed from their shells. **coffee-shop** a small informal restaurant, esp. in a hotel or department store. **coffee-table** a small low table. **coffee-table book** a large lavishly illustrated book. [ult. f. Turk. kahveh f. Arab. ḳahwa, the drink]

coffer /ˈkɒfə(r)/ n. **1** a box, esp. a large strongbox for valuables. **2** (in pl.) a treasury or store of funds. **3** a sunken panel in a ceiling etc. □ **coffer-dam** a watertight enclosure pumped dry to permit work below the waterline on building bridges etc., or for repairing a ship. □□ **coffered** adj. [ME f. OF coffre f. L cophinus f. Gk kophinos basket]

coffin /ˈkɒfɪn/ n. & v. —n. **1** a long narrow usu. wooden box in which a corpse is buried or cremated. **2** the part of a horse's hoof below the coronet. —v.tr. (**coffined, coffining**) put in a coffin. □ **coffin-bone** a bone in a horse's hoof. **coffin corner** US Football the corner between the goal-line and sideline. **coffin-joint** the joint at the top of a horse's hoof. **coffin-nail** sl. a cigarette. [ME f. OF cof(f)in little basket etc. f. L cophinus: see COFFER]

coffle /ˈkɒf(ə)l/ n. a line of animals, slaves, etc., fastened together. [Arab. ḳāfila caravan]

cog /kɒg/ n. **1** each of a series of projections on the edge of a wheel or bar transferring motion by engaging with another series. **2** an unimportant member of an organization etc. □ **cog-wheel** a wheel with cogs. □□ **cogged** adj. [ME: prob. of Scand. orig.]

cogent /ˈkəʊdʒ(ə)nt/ adj. (of arguments, reasons, etc.) convincing, compelling. □□ **cogency** n. **cogently** adv. [L cogere compel (as CO-, agere act- drive)]

cogitable /ˈkɒdʒɪtəb(ə)l/ adj. able to be grasped by the mind; conceivable. [L cogitabilis (as COGITATE)]

cogitate /ˈkɒdʒɪteɪt/ v.tr. & intr. ponder, meditate. □□ **cogitation** /-ˈteɪʃ(ə)n/ n. **cogitative** /-tətɪv/ adj. **cogitator** n. [L cogitare think (as CO-, AGITATE)]

cogito /ˈkɒgɪtəʊ/ n. Philos. the principle establishing the existence of a being from the fact of its thinking or awareness. [L, = I think, in Fr. philosopher Descartes's formula (1641) cogito, ergo sum I think, therefore I exist]

cognac /ˈkɒnjæk/ n. a high-quality brandy, properly that distilled in Cognac in W. France.

cognate /ˈkɒgneɪt/ adj. & n. —adj. **1** related to or descended from a common ancestor (cf. AGNATE). **2** Philol. (of a word) having the same linguistic family or derivation (as another); representing the same original word or root (e.g. English father, German Vater, Latin pater). —n. **1** a relative. **2** a cognate word. □ **cognate object** Gram. an object that is related in origin and sense to the verb governing it (as in live a good life). □□ **cognately** adv. **cognateness** n. [L cognatus (as CO-, natus born)]

cognition /kɒgˈnɪʃ(ə)n/ n. **1** Philos. knowing, perceiving, or conceiving as an act or faculty distinct from emotion and volition. **2** a result of this; a perception, sensation, notion, or intuition. □□ **cognitional** adj. **cognitive** /ˈkɒgnɪtɪv/ adj. [L cognitio (as CO-, gnoscere gnit- apprehend)]

cognizable /ˈkɒgnɪzəb(ə)l, ˈkɒn-/ adj. (also **-isable**) **1** perceptible, recognizable; clearly identifiable. **2** within the jurisdiction of a court. □□ **cognizably** adv. [COGNIZANCE + -ABLE]

cognizance /ˈkɒgnɪz(ə)ns, ˈkɒn-/ n. (also **cognisance** /-z(ə)ns/) **1** knowledge or awareness; perception, notice. **2** the sphere of one's observation or concern. **3** Law the right of a court to deal with a matter. **4** Heraldry a distinctive device or mark. □ **have cognizance of** know, esp. officially. **take cognizance of** attend to; take account of. [ME f. OF conoisance ult. f. L cognoscent- f. cognitio: see COGNITION]

cognizant /ˈkɒgnɪz(ə)nt, ˈkɒn-/ adj. (also **cognisant** /-z(ə)nt/) (foll. by of) having knowledge or being aware of.

cognomen /kɒgˈnəʊmen/ n. **1** a nickname. **2** an ancient Roman's personal name or epithet, as in Marcus Tullius Cicero, Publius Cornelius Scipio Africanus. [L]

cognoscente /ˌkɒnjəˈʃenti/ n. (pl. **cognoscenti** /-tɪ/) (usu. in pl.) a connoisseur. [It., lit. one who knows]

cohabit /kəʊˈhæbɪt/ v.intr. (**cohabited, cohabiting**) live together, esp. as husband and wife without being married to one another. □□ **cohabitant** n. **cohabitation** /-ˈteɪʃ(ə)n/ n. **cohabitee** /-ˈtiː/ n. **cohabiter** n. [L cohabitare (as CO-, habitare dwell)]

cohere /kəʊˈhɪə(r)/ v.intr. **1** (of parts or a whole) stick together, remain united. **2** (of reasoning etc.) be logical or consistent. [L cohaerēre cohaes- (as CO-, haerēre stick)]

coherent /kəʊˈhɪərənt/ adj. **1** (of a person) able to speak intelligibly and articulately. **2** (of speech, an argument, etc.) logical and consistent; easily followed. **3** cohering; sticking together. **4** Physics (of waves) having a constant phase relationship. □□ **coherence** n. **coherency** n. **coherently** adv. [L cohaerēre cohaerent- (as COHERE)]

cohesion /kəʊˈhiːʒ(ə)n/ n. **1 a** the act or condition of sticking together. **b** a tendency to cohere. **2** Chem. the force with which molecules cohere. □□ **cohesive** /-sɪv/ adj. **cohesively** /-sɪvli/ adv. **cohesiveness** /-sɪvnɪs/ n. [L cohaes- (see COHERE) after adhesion]

Cohn /kəʊn/, Ferdinand Julius (1828–98), German botanist, noted for his studies of the life histories of algae, bacteria, and other micro-organisms. He was the first to devise a systematic classification of bacteria into genera and species, and is regarded as a founder of bacteriology. It was Cohn who recognized the importance of the work of the then unknown Robert Koch (see entry) on anthrax.

coho /ˈkəʊhəʊ/ n. (also **cohoe**) (pl. **-os** or **-oes**) a silver salmon, Oncorhynchus kisutch, of the N. Pacific. [19th c.: orig. unkn.]

cohort /ˈkəʊhɔːt/ n. **1** an ancient Roman military unit, equal to one-tenth of a legion. **2** a band of warriors. **3 a** persons banded or grouped together, esp. in a common cause. **b** a group of persons with a common statistical characteristic. **4** US a companion or colleague. [ME f. F cohorte or L cohors cohort- enclosure, company]

COHSE /ˈkəʊzɪ/ abbr. (in the UK) Confederation of Health Service Employees.

COI abbr. (in the UK) Central Office of Information.

coif /kɔɪf/ n. hist. **1** a close-fitting cap, esp. as worn by nuns under a veil. **2** a protective metal skullcap worn under armour. [ME f. OF coife f. LL cofia helmet]

coiffeur /kwaˈfɜː(r)/ n. (fem. **coiffeuse** /-ˈfɜːz/) a hairdresser. [F]

coiffure /kwaˈfjʊə(r)/ n. the way hair is arranged; a hairstyle. [F]

coign /kɔɪn/ n. □ **coign of vantage** a favourable position for observation or action. [earlier spelling of COIN in the sense 'cornerstone']

coil¹ /kɔɪl/ n. & v. —n. **1** anything arranged in a joined sequence of concentric circles. **2** a length of rope, a spring, etc., arranged in this way. **3** a single turn of something coiled, e.g. a snake. **4** a lock of hair twisted and coiled. **5** an intra-uterine contraceptive device in the form of a coil. **6** Electr. a device consisting of a coiled wire for converting low voltage to high voltage, esp. for transmission to the sparking plugs of an internal-combustion engine. **7** a piece of wire, piping, etc., wound in circles or spirals. **8** a roll of postage stamps. —v. **1** tr. arrange in a series of concentric loops or rings. **2** *tr.* & *intr.* twist or be twisted into a circular or spiral shape. **3** *intr.* move sinuously. [OF *coillir* f. L *colligere* COLLECT¹]

coil² /kɔɪl/ *n.* □ **this mortal coil** the difficulties of earthly life (with ref. to Shakesp. *Hamlet* III. i. 67). [16th c.: orig. unkn.]

Coimbatore /ˌkɔʊɪmbəˈtɔː(r)/ a city in Tamil Nadu in southern India; pop. (1981) 917,000.

Coimbra /kɔʊˈɪmbrə/ a university city in central Portugal; pop. (est. 1984) 74,600.

coin /kɔɪn/ *n.* & *v.* —*n.* **1** a piece of flat usu. round metal stamped and issued by authority as money. **2** (*collect.*) metal money. —*v.tr.* **1** make (coins) by stamping. **2** make (metal) into coins. **3** invent or devise (esp. a new word or phrase). □ **coin-box 1** a telephone operated by inserting coins. **2** the receptacle for these. **coin money** make much money quickly. **coin-op** a launderette etc. with automatic machines operated by inserting coins. **to coin a phrase** *iron.* introducing a banal remark or cliché. [ME f. OF, = stamping-die, f. L *cuneus* wedge]

coinage /ˈkɔɪnɪdʒ/ *n.* **1** the act or process of coining. Coinage is reputed to be the invention of the Lydians of Asia Minor, probably in the mid-7th c. BC. **2 a** coins collectively. **b** a system or type of coins in use (*decimal coinage*; *bronze coinage*). **3** an invention, esp. of a new word or phrase. [ME f. OF *coigniage*]

coincide /ˌkɔʊɪnˈsaɪd/ *v.intr.* **1** occur at or during the same time. **2** occupy the same portion of space. **3** (often foll. by *with*) be in agreement; have the same view. [med.L *coincidere* (as CO-, INCIDENT)]

coincidence /kɔʊˈɪnsɪd(ə)ns/ *n.* **1 a** occurring or being together. **b** an instance of this. **2** a remarkable concurrence of events or circumstances without apparent causal connection. **3** *Physics* the presence of ionizing particles etc. in two or more detectors simultaneously, or of two or more signals simultaneously in a circuit. [med.L *coincidentia* (as COINCIDE)]

coincident /kɔʊˈɪnsɪd(ə)nt/ *adj.* **1** occurring together in space or time. **2** (foll. by *with*) in agreement; harmonious. □□ **coincidently** *adv.*

coincidental /kɔʊˌɪnsɪˈdent(ə)l/ *adj.* **1** in the nature of or resulting from a coincidence. **2** happening or existing at the same time. □□ **coincidentally** *adv.*

coiner /ˈkɔɪnə(r)/ *n.* **1** a person who coins money, esp. *Brit.* the maker of counterfeit coin. **2** a person who invents or devises something (esp. a new word or phrase).

Cointreau /ˈkwɑːntrəʊ/ *n. propr.* a colourless orange-flavoured liqueur. [F]

coir /ˈkɔɪə(r)/ *n.* fibre from the outer husk of the coconut, used for ropes, matting, etc. [Malayalam *kāyar* cord f. *kāyaru* be twisted]

coition /kɔʊˈɪʃ(ə)n/ *n. Med.* = COITUS. [L *coitio* f. *coire* coit- go together]

coitus /ˈkɔʊɪtəs/ *n. Med.* sexual intercourse. □ **coitus interruptus** /ˌɪntəˈrʌptəs/ sexual intercourse in which the penis is withdrawn before ejaculation. □□ **coital** *adj.* [L (as COITION)]

Coke /kɔʊk/ *n. propr.* Coca-Cola. [abbr.]

coke¹ /kɔʊk/ *n.* & *v.* —*n.* **1** a solid substance left after the gases have been extracted from coal. **2** a residue left after the incomplete combustion of petrol etc. —*v.tr.* convert (coal) into coke. [prob. f. N.Engl. dial. *colk* core, of unkn. orig.]

coke² /kɔʊk/ *n. sl.* cocaine. [abbr.]

Col. *abbr.* **1** Colonel. **2** Colossians (New Testament).

col /kɒl/ *n.* **1** a depression in the summit-line of a chain of mountains, generally affording a pass from one slope to another. **2** *Meteorol.* a low-pressure region between anticyclones. [F, = neck, f. L *collum*]

col. *abbr.* column.

col- /kɒl/ *prefix* assim. form of COM- before l.

cola /ˈkɔʊlə/ *n.* (also **kola**) **1** any small tree of the genus *Cola*, native to W. Africa, bearing seeds containing caffeine. **2** a carbonated drink usu. flavoured with these seeds. □ **cola nut** a seed of the tree. [W.Afr.]

colander /ˈkʌləndə(r)/ *n.* a perforated vessel used to strain off liquid in cookery. [ME, ult. f. L *colare* strain]

co-latitude /kɒʊˈlætɪˌtjuːd/ *n. Astron.* the complement of the latitude, the difference between it and 90°.

Colbert /ˈkɒlbeə(r)/, Jean Baptiste (1619–83), French statesman, one of Louis XIV's most competent ministers, who achieved an impressive series of reforms, particularly of the country's finances. He also improved industry and commerce and established the French navy as one of the most formidable in Europe. His reforms, however, could not keep pace with the demands of Louis' war policies and of the extensive royal building programme, and by the end of Louis' reign French finances were in a desperate situation.

colchicine /ˈkɒltʃɪˌsiːn, ˈkɒlk-/ *n.* a yellow alkaloid obtained from colchicum, used in the treatment of gout.

colchicum /ˈkɒltʃɪkəm, ˈkɒlkɪ-/ *n.* **1** any liliaceous plant of the genus *Colchicum*, esp. meadow saffron. **2** its dried corm or seed. Also called *autumn crocus*. [L f. Gk *kolkhikon* of Kolkhis (COLCHIS)]

Colchis /ˈkɒlkɪs/ the Greek name (*Kolkhis*) for the region south of the Caucasus mountains at the east end of the Black Sea, the goal of Jason's expedition for the Golden Fleece.

cold /kɒʊld/ *adj.*, *n.*, & *adv.* —*adj.* **1** of or at a low or relatively low temperature, esp. when compared with the human body. **2** not heated; cooled after being heated. **3** (of a person) feeling cold. **4** lacking ardour, friendliness, or affection; undemonstrative, apathetic. **5** depressing, dispiriting, uninteresting (*cold facts*). **6 a** dead. **b** *colloq.* unconscious. **7** *colloq.* at one's mercy (*had me cold*). **8** sexually frigid. **9** (of soil) slow to absorb heat. **10** (of a scent in hunting) having become weak. **11** (in children's games) far from finding or guessing what is sought. **12** without preparation or rehearsal. —*n.* **1 a** the prevalence of a low temperature, esp. in the atmosphere. **b** cold weather; a cold environment (*went out into the cold*). **2** an infection in which the mucous membrane of the nose and throat becomes inflamed, causing running at the nose, sneezing, sore throat, etc. —*adv.* esp. *US* completely, entirely (*was stopped cold mid-sentence*). □ **catch a cold 1** become infected with a cold. **2** encounter trouble or difficulties. **cold call** sell goods or services by making unsolicited calls on prospective customers by telephone or in person. **cold cathode** a cathode that emits electrons without being heated. **cold chisel** a chisel suitable for cutting metal, stone, etc. **cold comfort** poor or inadequate consolation. **cold cream** ointment for cleansing and softening the skin. **cold cuts** slices of cold cooked meats. **cold feet** *colloq.* loss of nerve or confidence. **cold frame** an unheated frame with a glass top for growing small plants. **cold front** the forward edge of an advancing mass of cold air. **cold fusion** nuclear fusion at room temperature esp. as a possible energy source. **cold shoulder** a show of intentional unfriendliness. **cold-shoulder** *v.tr.* be deliberately unfriendly to. **cold sore** inflammation and blisters in and around the mouth, caused by a virus infection. **cold storage 1** storage in a refrigerator or other cold place for preservation. **2** a state in which something (esp. an idea) is put aside temporarily. **cold sweat** a state of sweating induced by fear or illness. **cold table** a selection of dishes of cold food. **cold turkey** *US sl.* **1** a series of blunt statements or behaviour. **2** abrupt withdrawal from addictive drugs; the symptoms of this. **cold war** a state of hostility between nations without actual fighting, consisting in threats, violent propaganda, subversive political activities or the like, specifically those between the USSR and the Western powers after the Second World War. Having lasted into the 1980s the cold war was formally and officially ended in Nov. 1990 by a declaration of friendship and a treaty agreeing a great reduction of conventional armaments in Europe. **cold wave 1** a temporary spell of cold weather over a wide area. **2** a kind of permanent wave for the hair using chemicals and without heat. **in cold blood** without feeling or passion; deliberately, ruthlessly. **out in the cold** ignored, neglected. **throw** (or **pour**) **cold water on** be discouraging or depreciatory about. □□ **coldish** *adj.* **coldly** *adv.* **coldness** *n.* [OE *cald* f. Gmc, rel. to L *gelu* frost]

cold-blooded /kɒʊldˈblʌdɪd/ *adj.* **1** having a body temperature varying with that of the environment (e.g. of fish); poikilothermic. **2** callous; deliberately cruel. □□ **cold-bloodedly** *adv.* **cold-bloodedness** *n.*

cold-hearted /kəʊldˈhɑːtɪd/ adj. lacking affection or warmth; unfriendly. □□ **cold-heartedly** adv. **cold-heartedness** n.

Colditz /ˈkəʊldɪts/ a town in east Germany, near Leipzig, noted for its castle which was used as a top-security camp for Allied prisoners in the Second World War.

cold-short /ˈkəʊldʃɔːt/ adj. (of a metal) brittle in its cold state. [Sw. kallskör f. kall cold + skör brittle: assim. to SHORT]

cole /kəʊl/ n. (usu. in comb.) **1** cabbage. **2** = RAPE². [ME f. ON kál f. L caulis stem, cabbage]

colemouse var. of COALMOUSE.

coleopteron /ˌkɒlɪˈɒptəˌrɒn/ n. any insect of the order Coleoptera, with front wings modified into sheaths to protect the hinder wings, e.g. a beetle or weevil. □□ **coleopterist** n. **coleopterous** adj. [mod.L Coleoptera f. Gk koleopteros f. koleon sheath + pteron wing]

coleoptile /ˌkɒlɪˈɒptaɪl/ n. Bot. a sheath protecting a young shoot tip in grasses. [Gk koleon sheath + ptilon feather]

Coleraine /kəʊlˈreɪn/ a town in the north of Northern Ireland, on the River Brann in Co. Derry; pop. (1981) 16,000.

Coleridge /ˈkəʊləˌrɪdʒ/, Samuel Taylor (1772–1834), English poet, critic, and philosopher, whose intense friendship with William Wordsworth began in 1797. Their jointly produced Lyrical Ballads (1798) revolutionized literary taste and sensibility and effectively started the English Romantic movement; Coleridge's own great contribution to the movement is found in his supernatural poems, 'The Ancient Mariner', 'Christabel', and 'Kubla Khan'. The simplicity and lucidness of his poetical expression contrasts with the involved fashion of his prose. He was instrumental in introducing 18th-c. German thought into England, and his debt to Kant and German philosophy may be seen in his major critical work, Biographia Literaria (1817). His unhappy marriage, his continuing opium addiction, and his hopeless love for Sarah Hutchinson contributed to his decline, recorded in his pessimistic poem 'Dejection: an Ode' (1802), and his ardent support for the French Revolution also turned to disillusion. His final position was that of Romantic conservative and Christian radical.

coleseed /ˈkəʊlsiːd/ n. = COLE 2.

coleslaw /ˈkəʊlslɔː/ n. a dressed salad of sliced raw cabbage, carrot, onion, etc. [Du. koolsla: see COLE, SLAW]

cole-tit var. of coal-tit.

Colette /kɒˈlet/ the pen-name of Sidonie Gabrielle (1873–1954), French novelist, noted for her sensuous feeling for nature and for her vivid insight into the crises of womanhood, often in the older woman, as in Chéri (1920) and La Fin de Chéri (1921).

coleus /ˈkəʊlɪəs/ n. any plant of the genus Coleus, having variegated coloured leaves. [mod.L f. Gk koleon sheath]

coley /ˈkəʊlɪ/ n. (pl. **-eys**) Brit. any of various fish used as food, esp. the saithe or rock-salmon. [perh. f. coal-fish]

colic /ˈkɒlɪk/ n. a severe spasmodic abdominal pain. □□ **colicky** adj. [ME f. F colique f. LL colicus: see COLON²]

Colima /kɒˈliːmə/ **1** a State of SW Mexico, on the Pacific coast; pop. (est. 1988) 419,400. **2** its capital city; pop. (est. 1984) 58,000.

coliseum /ˌkɒlɪˈsiːəm/ n. US = COLOSSEUM.

colitis /kəˈlaɪtɪs/ n. inflammation of the lining of the colon.

Coll /kɒl/ an island in the Inner Hebrides, west of Scotland.

Coll. abbr. College.

collaborate /kəˈlæbəˌreɪt/ v.intr. (often foll. by with) **1** work jointly, esp. in a literary or artistic production. **2** cooperate traitorously with an enemy. □□ **collaboration** /-ˈreɪʃ(ə)n/ n. **collaborationist** /-ˈreɪʃənɪst/ n. & adj. **collaborative** /-rətɪv/ adj. **collaborator** n. [L collaborare collaborat- (as COM-, laborare work)]

collage /ˈkɒlɑːʒ, kəˈlɑːʒ/ n. **1** a form of art in which various materials (e.g. photographs, pieces of paper, matchsticks) are arranged and glued to a backing. **2** a work of art done in this way. **3** a collection of unrelated things. □□ **collagist** n. [F, = gluing]

collagen /ˈkɒlədʒ(ə)n/ n. a protein found in animal connective tissue, yielding gelatin on boiling. [F collagène f. Gk kolla glue + -gène = -GEN]

collapsar /kɒˈlæpsɑː(r)/ n. Astron. = black hole 1.

collapse /kəˈlæps/ n. & v. —n. **1** the tumbling down or falling in of a structure; folding up; giving way. **2** a sudden failure of a plan, undertaking, etc. **3** a physical or mental breakdown. —v. **1 a** intr. undergo or experience a collapse. **b** tr. cause to collapse. **2** intr. colloq. lie or sit down and relax, esp. after prolonged effort (collapsed into a chair). **3 a** intr. (of furniture etc.) be foldable into a small space. **b** tr. fold (furniture) in this way. □□ **collapsible** adj. **collapsibility** /-ˈbɪlɪtɪ/ n. [L collapsus past part. of collabi (as COM-, labi slip)]

collar /ˈkɒlə(r)/ n. & v. —n. **1** the part of a shirt, dress, coat, etc., that goes round the neck, either upright or turned over. **2** a band of linen, lace, etc., completing the upper part of a costume. **3** a band of leather or other material put round an animal's (esp. a dog's) neck. **4** a restraining or connecting band, ring, or pipe in machinery. **5** a coloured marking resembling a collar round the neck of a bird or animal. **6** Brit. a piece of meat rolled up and tied. —v.tr. **1** seize (a person) by the collar or neck. **2** capture, apprehend. **3** colloq. accost. **4** sl. take, esp. illicitly. □ **collar-beam** a horizontal beam connecting two rafters and forming with them an A-shaped roof-truss. **collar-bone** either of two bones joining the breastbone and the shoulder-blades. **collared dove** a dove, Streptopelia decaoto, having distinct neck-markings. □□ **collared** adj. (also in comb.). **collarless** adj. [ME f. AF coler, OF colier, f. L collare f. collum neck]

collate /kəˈleɪt/ v.tr. **1** analyse and compare (texts, statements, etc.) to identify points of agreement and difference. **2** Bibliog. verify the order of (sheets) by their signatures. **3** assemble (information) from different sources. **4** (often foll. by to) Eccl. appoint (a clergyman) to a benefice. □□ **collator** n. [L collat- past part. stem of conferre compare]

collateral /kɒˈlætər(ə)l/ n. & adj. —n. **1** security pledged as a guarantee for repayment of a loan. **2** a person having the same descent as another but by a different line. —adj. **1** descended from the same stock but by a different line. **2** side by side; parallel. **3 a** additional but subordinate. **b** contributory. **c** connected but aside from the main subject, course, etc. □□ **collaterality** /-ˈrælɪtɪ/ n. **collaterally** adv. [ME f. med.L collateralis (as COM-, LATERAL)]

collation /kɒˈleɪʃ(ə)n/ n. **1** the act or an instance of collating. **2** RC Ch. a light meal allowed during a fast. **3** a light informal meal. [ME f. OF f. L collatio -onis (see COLLATE): sense 2 f. Cassian's Collationes Patrum (= Lives of the Fathers) read by Benedictines and followed by a light meal]

colleague /ˈkɒliːg/ n. a fellow official or worker, esp. in a profession or business. [F collègue f. L collega (as COM-, legare depute)]

collect¹ /kəˈlekt/ v., adj., & adv. —v. **1** tr. & intr. bring or come together; assemble, accumulate. **2** tr. systematically seek and acquire (books, stamps, etc.), esp. as a continuing hobby. **3 a** tr. obtain (taxes, contributions, etc.) from a number of people. **b** intr. colloq. receive money. **4** tr. call for; fetch (went to collect the laundry). **5 a** refl. regain control of oneself esp. after a shock. **b** tr. concentrate (one's energies, thoughts, etc.). **c** tr. (as collected adj.) calm and cool; not perturbed or distracted. **6** tr. infer, gather, conclude. —adj. & adv. US to be paid for by the receiver (of a telephone call, parcel, etc.). □□ **collectable** adj. **collectedly** adv. [F collecter or med.L collectare f. L collectus past part. of colligere (as COM-, legere pick)]

collect² /ˈkɒlekt, -ɪkt/ n. a short prayer of the Anglican and Roman Catholic Church, esp. one assigned to a particular day or season. [ME f. OF collecte f. L collecta fem. past part. of colligere: see COLLECT¹]

collectible /kəˈlektɪb(ə)l/ adj. & n. —adj. worth collecting. —n. an item sought by collectors.

collection /kəˈlekʃ(ə)n/ n. **1** the act or process of collecting or being collected. **2** a group of things collected together, esp. systematically. **3** (foll. by of) an accumulation; a mass or pile (a collection of dust). **4 a** the collecting of money, esp. in church or for a charitable cause. **b** the amount collected. **5** the regular removal of mail, esp. from a postbox, for dispatch. **6** (in pl.) Brit. college examinations held at the end of a term, esp. at Oxford University. [ME f. OF f. L collectio -onis (as COLLECT¹)]

collective /kəˈlektɪv/ adj. & n. —adj. **1** formed by or constituting a collection. **2** taken as a whole; aggregate (our collective *opinion*). **3** of or from several or many individuals; common. —*n.* **1 a** = *collective farm.* **b** any cooperative enterprise. **c** its members. **2** = *collective noun.* □ **collective bargaining** negotiation of wages etc. by an organized body of employees. **collective farm** a jointly-operated esp. State-owned amalgamation of several smallholdings. **collective noun** *Gram.* a noun that is grammatically singular and denotes a collection or number of individuals (e.g. *assembly, family, troop*). **collective ownership** ownership of land, means of production, etc., by all for the benefit of all. **collective unconscious** *Psychol.* (in Jungian theory) the part of the unconscious mind derived from ancestral memory and experience common to all mankind, as distinct from the personal unconscious.   □□ **collectively** *adv.* **collectiveness** *n.* **collectivity** /-ˈtɪvɪtɪ/ *n.* [F *collectif* or L *collectivus* (as COLLECT¹)]

collectivism /kəˈlektɪˌvɪz(ə)m/ *n.* the theory and practice of the collective ownership of land and the means of production.   □□ **collectivist** *n.* **collectivistic** /-ˈvɪstɪk/ *adj.*

collectivize /kəˈlektɪˌvaɪz/ *v.tr.* (also **-ise**) organize on the basis of collective ownership.   □□ **collectivization** /-ˈzeɪʃ(ə)n/ *n.*

collector /kəˈlektə(r)/ *n.* **1** a person who collects, esp. things of interest as a hobby. **2** a person who collects money etc. due (*tax-collector; ticket-collector*). **3** *Electronics* the region in a transistor that absorbs carriers of a charge. □ **collector's item** (or **piece**) a valuable object, esp. one of interest to collectors. [ME f. AF *collectour* f. med.L *collector* (as COLLECT¹)]

colleen /kɒˈliːn/ *n. Ir.* a girl. [Ir. *cailín,* dimin. of *caile* country-woman]

college /ˈkɒlɪdʒ/ *n.* **1** an establishment for further or higher education, sometimes part of a university. **2** an establishment for specialized professional education (*business college; college of music; naval college*). **3** the buildings or premises of a college (*lived in college*). **4** the students and teachers in a college. **5** *Brit.* a public school. **6** an organized body of persons with shared functions and privileges (*College of Physicians*). □ **College of Arms** (in the UK) a corporation recording lineage and granting arms. **college of education** *Brit.* a training college for schoolteachers. **college pudding** a small baked or steamed suet pudding with dried fruit.   □□ **collegial** /kəˈliːdʒ(ə)l/ *adj.* [ME f. OF *college* or L *collegium* f. *collega* (as COLLEAGUE)]

collegian /kəˈliːdʒ(ə)n/ *n.* a member of a college. [med.L *collegianus* (as COLLEGE)]

collegiate /kəˈliːdʒət/ *adj.* constituted as or belonging to a college; corporate. □ **collegiate church 1** a church endowed for a chapter of canons but without a bishop's see. **2** *US & Sc.* a church or group of churches established under a joint pastorate.   □□ **collegiately** *adv.* [LL *collegiatus* (as COLLEGE)]

collenchyma /kɒˈleŋkɪmə/ *n. Bot.* a tissue of cells with thick cellulose cell walls, strengthening young stems etc. [Gk *kolla* glue + *egkhuma* infusion]

Colles' fracture /ˈkɒlɪs/ *n.* a fracture of the lower end of the radius with a backward displacement of the hand. [A. *Colles,* Ir. surgeon d. 1843]

collet /ˈkɒlɪt/ *n.* **1** a flange or socket for setting a gem in jewellery. **2** *Engin.* a segmented band or sleeve put round a shaft or spindle and tightened to grip it. **3** *Horol.* a small collar to which the inner end of a balance spring is attached. [F, dimin. of COL]

collide /kəˈlaɪd/ *v.intr.* (often foll. by *with*) **1** come into abrupt or violent impact. **2** be in conflict. [L *collidere collis-* (as COM-, *laedere* strike, damage)]

collie /ˈkɒlɪ/ *n.* **1** a sheepdog orig. of a Scottish breed, with a long pointed nose and usu. dense long hair. **2** this breed. [perh. f. *coll* COAL (as being orig. black)]

collier /ˈkɒlɪə(r)/ *n.* **1** a coalminer. **2 a** a coal-ship. **b** a member of its crew. [ME, f. COAL + -IER]

colliery /ˈkɒlɪərɪ/ *n.* (*pl.* **-ies**) a coalmine and its associated buildings.

colligate /ˈkɒlɪˌɡeɪt/ *v.tr.* bring into connection (esp. isolated facts by a generalization).   □□ **colligation** /-ˈɡeɪʃ(ə)n/ *n.* [L *colligare colligat-* (as COM-, *ligare* bind)]

collimate /ˈkɒlɪˌmeɪt/ *v.tr.* **1** adjust the line of sight of (a telescope etc.). **2** make (telescopes or rays) accurately parallel.   □□

collimation /-ˈmeɪʃ(ə)n/ *n.* [L *collimare,* erron. for *collineare* align (as COM-, *linea* line)]

collimator /ˈkɒlɪˌmeɪtə(r)/ *n.* **1** a device for producing a parallel beam of rays or radiation. **2** a small fixed telescope used for adjusting the line of sight of an astronomical telescope, etc.

collinear /kəˈlɪnɪə(r)/ *adj. Geom.* (of points) lying in the same straight line.   □□ **collinearity** /-ˈærɪtɪ/ *n.* **collinearly** *adv.*

Collins¹ /ˈkɒlɪnz/ *n.* an iced drink made of gin or whisky etc. with soda, lemon or lime juice, and sugar. [20th c.: orig. unkn.]

Collins² /ˈkɒlɪnz/, (William) Wilkie (1824–89), English novelist, a friend and collaborator of Charles Dickens. He is remembered as the writer of the first full-length detective stories in English; his finest works in this genre were *The Woman in White* (1860) and *The Moonstone* (1868). His ingenious and meticulously constructed plots influenced Dickens's later works.

collision /kəˈlɪʒ(ə)n/ *n.* **1** a violent impact of a moving body, esp. a vehicle or ship, with another or with a fixed object. **2** the clashing of opposed interests or considerations. **3** *Physics* the action of particles striking or coming together. □ **collision course** a course or action that is bound to cause a collision or conflict.   □□ **collisional** *adj.* [ME f. LL *collisio* (as COLLIDE)]

collocate /ˈkɒləˌkeɪt/ *v.tr.* **1** place together or side by side. **2** arrange; set in a particular place. **3** (often foll. by *with*) *Linguistics* juxtapose (a word etc.) with another.   □□ **collocation** /-ˈkeɪʃ(ə)n/ *n.* [L *collocare collocat-* (as COM-, *locare* to place)]

collocutor /ˈkɒləˌkjuːtə(r), kəˈlɒkjuːtə(r)/ *n.* a person who takes part in a conversation. [LL f. *colloqui* (as COM-, *loqui locut-* talk)]

collodion /kəˈləʊdɪən/ *n.* a syrupy solution of cellulose nitrate in a mixture of alcohol and ether, used in photography and surgery. [Gk *kollōdēs* gluelike f. *kolla* glue]

collogue /kəˈləʊɡ/ *v.intr.* (**collogues, collogued, colloguing**) (foll. by *with*) talk confidentially. [prob. alt. of obs. *colleague* conspire, by assoc. with L *colloqui* converse]

colloid /ˈkɒlɔɪd/ *n.* **1** *Chem.* **a** a substance consisting of ultramicroscopic particles. **b** a mixture of such a substance uniformly dispersed through a second substance esp. to form a viscous solution. **2** *Med.* a substance of a homogeneous gelatinous consistency.   □□ **colloidal** /-ˈlɔɪd(ə)l/ *adj.* [Gk *kolla* glue + -OID]

collop /ˈkɒləp/ *n.* a slice, esp. of meat or bacon; an escalope. [ME, = fried bacon and eggs, of Scand. orig.]

colloquial /kəˈləʊkwɪəl/ *adj.* belonging to or proper to ordinary or familiar conversation, not formal or literary.   □□ **colloquially** *adv.* [L *colloquium* COLLOQUY]

colloquialism /kəˈləʊkwɪəˌlɪz(ə)m/ *n.* **1** a colloquial word or phrase. **2** the use of colloquialisms.

colloquium /kəˈləʊkwɪəm/ *n.* (*pl.* **colloquiums** or **colloquia** /-kwɪə/) an academic conference or seminar. [L: see COLLOQUY]

colloquy /ˈkɒləkwɪ/ *n.* (*pl.* **-quies**) **1** the act of conversing. **2** a conversation. **3** *Eccl.* a gathering for discussion of theological questions. [L *colloquium* (as COM-, *loqui* speak)]

collotype /ˈkɒləˌtaɪp/ *n. Printing* **1** a thin sheet of gelatin exposed to light, treated with reagents, and used to make high quality prints by lithography. **2** a print made by this process. [Gk *kolla* glue + TYPE]

collude /kəˈluːd, -ˈljuːd/ *v.intr.* come to an understanding or conspire together, esp. for a fraudulent purpose.   □□ **colluder** *n.* [L *colludere collus-* (as COM-, *ludere lus-* play)]

collusion /kəˈluːʒ(ə)n, -ˈljuːʒ(ə)n/ *n.* **1** a secret understanding, esp. for a fraudulent purpose. **2** *Law* such an understanding between ostensible opponents in a lawsuit.   □□ **collusive** *adj.* **collusively** *adv.* [ME f. OF *collusion* or L *collusio* (as COLLUDE)]

collyrium /kəˈlɪrɪəm/ *n.* (*pl.* **collyria** /-rɪə/) a medicated eyelotion. [L f. Gk *kollurion* poultice f. *kollura* coarse bread-roll]

collywobbles /ˈkɒlɪˌwɒb(ə)lz/ *n.pl. colloq.* **1** a rumbling or pain in the stomach. **2** a feeling of strong apprehension. [fanciful, f. COLIC + WOBBLE]

Colo. *abbr.* Colorado.

colobus /ˈkɒləbəs/ *n.* any leaf-eating monkey of the genus *Colobus,* native to Africa, having shortened thumbs. [mod.L f. Gk *kolobos* docked]

colocynth /ˈkɒləsɪnθ/ n. (also **coloquintida** /ˌkɒləˈkwɪntɪdə/) **1 a** a plant of the gourd family, *Citrullus colocynthis*, bearing a pulpy fruit. **b** this fruit. **2** a bitter purgative drug obtained from the fruit. [L *colocynthis* f. Gk *kolokunthis*]

Cologne /kəˈləʊn/ (German **Köln** /kɜːln/) German city on the west bank of the Rhine; pop. (1987) 914,300. Founded by the Romans, Cologne rose to prominence through the see established there, the Archbishop of Cologne becoming one of the most powerful German secular princes in the Middle Ages. At that time it was famous for the shrine of the Wise Men of the East, the 'Three Kings of Cologne'.

cologne /kəˈləʊn/ n. (in full **cologne water**) eau-de-Cologne or a similar scented toilet water. [abbr.]

Colombia /kəˈlɒmbɪə/ a country in the extreme NW of South America, having a coastline on both the Atlantic and the Pacific Ocean; pop. (1985) 27,867,300; official language, Spanish; capital, Bogotá. The Pacific coastal plain is humid and swampy, and most of the population is concentrated in the temperate valleys of the Andes. The economy is mainly agricultural, coffee being the chief export. Mineral resources are rich and include gold, silver, platinum (one of the world's richest deposits), emeralds, and salt, as well as oil, coal, and natural gas. Inhabited by the Chibcha and other Indian peoples, Colombia was conquered by the Spanish in the early 16th c., and under Spanish rule the capital Bogotá developed such a reputation for intellectual and social life as to be called 'the Athens of South America'. Like the rest of Spain's South American empire, Colombia achieved independence in the early 19th c., although the resulting Republic of Great Colombia lasted only until 1830, when first Venezuela and then Ecuador broke away to become independent States in their own right. The remaining State was known as New Granada, changing its name to Colombia in 1863. The country was stricken by civil war between 1949 and 1953, and since then has struggled with endemic poverty and social problems. It is notorious for its drugs traffic. □□ **Colombian** adj. & n.

Colombo /kəˈlʌmbəʊ/ the capital and chief port of Sri Lanka; pop. (1981) 585,776.

Colón /kɒˈlɒn/ the chief port of Panama, at the Caribbean end of the Panama Canal; pop. (1980) 59,000. Its name is the Spanish form of 'Columbus'; that of the neighbouring port Cristóbal is Spanish for 'Christopher'.

colon[1] /ˈkəʊlən, -lɒn/ n. a punctuation mark (:), used esp. to introduce a quotation or a list of items or to separate clauses when the second expands or illustrates the first; also between numbers in a statement of proportion (as in 10:1) and in Biblical references (as in Exodus 3: 2). [L f. Gk *kōlon* limb, clause]

colon[2] /ˈkəʊlən, -lɒn/ n. Anat. the lower and greater part of the large intestine, from the caecum to the rectum. □□ **colonic** /kəˈlɒnɪk/ adj. [ME, ult. f. Gk *kolon*]

colonel /ˈkɜːn(ə)l/ n. **1** an army officer in command of a regiment, immediately below a brigadier in rank. **2** US an officer of corresponding rank in the Air Force. **3** = *lieutenant-colonel*. □ **Colonel Blimp** see BLIMP n. 1. □□ **colonelcy** n. (pl. **-ies**). [obs. F *coronel* f. It. *colonnello* f. *colonna* COLUMN]

colonial /kəˈləʊnɪəl/ adj. & n. —adj. **1** of, relating to, or characteristic of a colony or colonies, esp. of a British Crown Colony. **2** (esp. of architecture or furniture) built or designed in, or in a style characteristic of, the period of the British colonies in America before independence. —n. **1** a native or inhabitant of a colony. **2** a house built in colonial style. □ **colonial goose** Austral. & NZ a boned and stuffed roast leg of mutton. □□ **colonially** adv.

colonialism /kəˈləʊnɪəˌlɪz(ə)m/ n. **1** a policy of acquiring or maintaining colonies. **2** derog. this policy regarded as the esp. economic exploitation of weak or backward peoples by a larger power. □□ **colonialist** n.

colonist /ˈkɒlənɪst/ n. a settler in or inhabitant of a colony.

colonize /ˈkɒləˌnaɪz/ v. (also **-ise**) **1** tr. **a** establish a colony or colonies in (a country or area). **b** settle as colonists. **2** intr. establish or join a colony. **3** tr. US Polit. plant voters in (a district) for party purposes. **4** tr. Biol. (of plants and animals) become

established (in an area). □□ **colonization** /-ˈzeɪʃ(ə)n/ n. **colonizer** n.

colonnade /ˌkɒləˈneɪd/ n. a row of columns, esp. supporting an entablature or roof. □□ **colonnaded** adj. [F f. *colonne* COLUMN]

colony /ˈkɒlənɪ/ n. (pl. **-ies**) **1 a** a group of settlers in a new country (whether or not already inhabited) fully or partly subject to the mother country. **b** the settlement or its territory. **2 a** people of one nationality or race or occupation in a city, esp. if living more or less in isolation or in a special quarter. **b** a separate or segregated group (*nudist colony*). **3** Biol. a collection of animals, plants, etc., connected, in contact, or living close together. [ME f. L *colonia* f. *colonus* farmer f. *colere* cultivate]

colophon /ˈkɒləˌfɒn, -fən/ n. **1** a publisher's device or imprint, esp. on the title-page. **2** a tailpiece in a manuscript or book, often ornamental, giving the writer's or printer's name, the date, etc. [LL f. Gk *kolophōn* summit, finishing touch]

colophony /kəˈlɒfənɪ/ n. = ROSIN. [L *colophonia* (resin) from Colophon in Asia Minor]

coloquintida var. of COLOCYNTH.

color etc. US var. of COLOUR etc.

Colorado /ˌkɒləˈrɑːdəʊ/ a State in the central US, named from the great Colorado River which rises there and flows into the Gulf of California; pop. (est. 1985) 2,899,700; capital, Denver. Part of it was acquired by the Louisiana Purchase in 1803 and the rest ceded by Mexico in 1848. It became the 38th State in 1876. □ **Colorado beetle** a yellow and black striped beetle, *Leptinotarsa decemlineata*, the larva of which is highly destructive to the potato plant.

coloration /ˌkʌləˈreɪʃ(ə)n/ n. (also **colouration**) **1** colouring; a scheme or method of applying colour. **2** the natural (esp. variegated) colour of living things or animals. [F *coloration* or LL *coloratio* f. *colorare* COLOUR]

coloratura /ˌkɒlərəˈtʊərə/ n. **1** elaborate ornamentation of a vocal melody. **2** a singer (esp. a soprano) skilled in coloratura singing. [It. f. L *colorare* COLOUR]

colorific /ˌkɒləˈrɪfɪk, ˌkʌl-/ adj. **1** producing colour. **2** highly coloured. [F *colorifique* or mod.L *colorificus* (as COLOUR)]

colorimeter /ˌkɒləˈrɪmɪtə(r), ˌkʌl-/ n. an instrument for measuring the intensity of colour. □□ **colorimetric** /-ˈmetrɪk/ adj. **colorimetry** n. [L *color* COLOUR + -METER]

colossal /kəˈlɒs(ə)l/ adj. **1** of immense size; huge, gigantic. **2** colloq. remarkable, splendid. **3** Archit. (of an order) having more than one storey of columns. **4** Sculpture (of a statue) about twice life size. □□ **colossally** adv. [F f. *colosse* COLOSSUS]

Colosseum /ˌkɒləˈsiːəm/ the medieval name given to the *Amphitheatrum Flavium*, a vast amphitheatre in Rome begun by Vespasian c. AD 75 and continued and completed by Titus and Domitian. It was capable of holding 50,000 people, with seating in three tiers and standing-room above; an elaborate system of staircases served all parts. The arena, floored with timber and surrounded by a fence, was the scene of gladiatorial combats, fights between men and beasts, and large-scale mock battles. —**colosseum** n. a large stadium or amphitheatre. [med.L, neut. of *colosseus* gigantic (as COLOSSUS)]

Colossians /kəˈlɒʃ(ə)nz/ **Epistle to the Colossians** a book of the New Testament, an epistle of St Paul to the Church at Colossae in Phrygia, Asia Minor.

colossus /kəˈlɒsəs/ n. (pl. **colossi** /-saɪ/ or **colossuses**) **1** a statue much bigger than life size. **2** a gigantic person, animal, building, etc. **3** an imperial power personified. □ **Colossus of Rhodes** a huge bronze statue of the sun-god Helios, one of the Seven Wonders of the World, said by Pliny to have been over 30.5 m (100 ft.) high. Built c. 292–280 BC, it commemorated the raising of the siege of Rhodes in 305–304 BC, and stood beside (not astride) the harbour entrance at Rhodes for about 50 years but was destroyed in an earthquake in 224 BC. [L f. Gk *kolossos*]

colostomy /kəˈlɒstəmɪ/ n. (pl. **-ies**) Surgery an operation on the colon to make an opening in the abdominal wall to provide an artificial anus. [as COLON[2] + Gk *stoma* mouth]

colostrum /kəˈlɒstrəm/ n. the first secretion from the mammary glands occurring after giving birth. [L]

colotomy /kəˈlɒtəmɪ/ n. (pl. **-ies**) Surgery an incision in the colon. [as COLON² + -TOMY]

colour /ˈkʌlə(r)/ n. & v. (US **color**) —n. **1 a** the sensation produced on the eye by rays of light when resolved as by a prism, selective reflection, etc., into different wavelengths (black being the effect produced by no light or by a surface reflecting no rays, and white the effect produced by rays of unresolved light). (See below.). **b** perception of colour; a system of colours. **2** one, or any mixture, of the constituents into which light can be separated as in a spectrum or rainbow, sometimes including (loosely) black and white. **3** a colouring substance, esp. paint. **4** the use of all colours, not only black and white, as in photography and television. **5 a** pigmentation of the skin, esp. when dark. **b** this as a ground for prejudice or discrimination. **6** ruddiness of complexion (a healthy colour). **7** (in pl.) appearance or aspect (see things in their true colours). **8** (in pl.) **a** Brit. a coloured ribbon or uniform etc. worn to signify membership of a school, club, team, etc. **b** the flag of a regiment or ship. **c** a national flag. **9** quality, mood, or variety in music, literature, speech, etc.; distinctive character or timbre. **10** a show of reason; a pretext (lend colour to; under colour of). —v. **1** tr. apply colour to, esp. by painting or dyeing or with coloured pens or pencils. **2** tr. influence (an attitude coloured by experience). **3** tr. misrepresent, exaggerate, esp. with spurious detail (a highly coloured account). **4** intr. take on colour; blush. □ **colour bar** the denial of services and facilities to non-White people. **colour-blind** unable to distinguish certain colours. **colour-blindness** the condition of being colour-blind. **colour code** use of colours as a standard means of identification. **colour-code** v.tr. identify by means of a colour code. **colour-fast** dyed in colours that will not fade or be washed out. **colour-fastness** the condition of being colour-fast. **colour scheme** an arrangement or planned combination of colours esp. in interior design. **colour-sergeant** the senior sergeant of an infantry company. **colour supplement** Brit. a magazine with coloured illustrations, issued as a supplement to a newspaper. **colour wash** coloured distemper. **colour-wash** v.tr. paint with coloured distemper. **Queen's** (or **King's** or **regimental**) **colour** a flag carried by a regiment. **show one's true colours** reveal one's true character or intentions. **under false colours** falsely, deceitfully. **with flying colours** see FLYING. [ME f. OF color, colorer f. L color, colorare]

White light is composed of a mixture of colours, and (as Newton established) is separated by a prism into its constituent colours, ranging from violet light, which has the highest frequency (shortest wavelength), to red light, which has the lowest frequency (longest wavelength). Colour perceived depends chiefly on the relative intensities of the mixture of optical frequencies present in the light received. The human retina possesses three types of specialized receptors which are able to distinguish between these various frequencies, and the gradual increase in frequency from the red end to the violet end of the visible spectrum is perceived as six or seven distinct bands or hues, with progressive colour shading within each hue.

colourable /ˈkʌlərəb(ə)l/ adj. (US **colorable**) **1** specious, plausible. **2** counterfeit. □□ **colourably** adv.

colourant /ˈkʌlərənt/ n. (US **colorant**) a colouring substance.

colouration var. of COLORATION.

coloured /ˈkʌləd/ adj. & n. (US **colored**) —adj. **1** having colour(s). **2** (**Coloured**) **a** wholly or partly of non-White descent. **b** S.Afr. of mixed White and non-White descent. **c** of or relating to Coloured people (a Coloured audience). —n. (**Coloured**) **1** a Coloured person. **2** S.Afr. a person of mixed descent speaking Afrikaans or English as the mother tongue.

colourful /ˈkʌləfʊl/ adj. (US **colorful**) **1** having much or varied colour; bright. **2** full of interest; vivid, lively. □□ **colourfully** adv. **colourfulness** n.

colouring /ˈkʌlərɪŋ/ n. (US **coloring**) **1** the process of or skill in using colour(s). **2** the style in which a thing is coloured, or in which an artist uses colour. **3** facial complexion.

colourist /ˈkʌlərɪst/ n. (US **colorist**) a person who uses colour, esp. in art.

colourless /ˈkʌləlɪs/ adj. (US **colorless**) **1** without colour. **2** lacking character or interest. **3** dull or pale in hue. **4** neutral, impartial, indifferent. □□ **colourlessly** adv.

coloury /ˈkʌlərɪ/ adj. US (**colory**) having a distinctive colour, esp. as indicating good quality.

colposcopy /ˌkɒlˈpɒskəpɪ/ n. examination of the vagina and the neck of the womb. □□ **colposcope** n. [Gk kolpos womb + -SCOPY]

Colt /ˈkəʊlt/, Samuel (1814–62), American inventor, who is remembered chiefly for the automatic pistol named after him. He is said to have conceived his idea of a revolving-breech firearm while watching the turning of the ship's steering-wheel when he sailed as a deck hand to India. Colt patented his invention, but although popular with individuals his 'six-shooter' failed to interest the US army, and his first company went out of business in 1842. His luck turned when he received a large government order on the outbreak of the war with Mexico in 1846, and success and fortune followed. The revolver was the 19th century's most important development in small arms.

colt /kəʊlt/ n. **1** a young uncastrated male horse, usu. less than four years old. **2** Sport a young or inexperienced player; a member of a junior team. □□ **colthood** n. **coltish** adj. **coltishly** adv. **coltishness** n. [OE, = young ass or camel]

colter US var. of COULTER.

Coltrane /kɒlˈtreɪn/, John William (1926–67), American jazz musician. His instrument was the saxophone, and he formed his own band in 1960; he was a leading figure in avant-garde jazz.

coltsfoot /ˈkəʊltsfʊt/ n. (pl. **coltsfoots**) a wild composite plant, Tussilago farfara, with large leaves and yellow flowers. Its Latin name refers to the fact that a cough medicine (L tussis cough) was formerly made from it.

colubrine /ˈkɒljʊˌbraɪn/ adj. **1** snakelike. **2** of the subfamily Colubrinae of non-poisonous snakes. [L colubrinus f. coluber snake]

Columba /kəˈlʌmbə/, St (c.521–97), Irish-born abbot and missionary. After founding several churches and monasteries in his own country he established himself c.563 with twelve companions on the island of Iona off the west coast of Scotland, and lived there for 34 years evangelizing the mainland and establishing monasteries in the neighbouring islands. Feast day, 9 June.

Columbia¹ /kəˈlʌmbɪə/ the capital of South Carolina; pop. (1980) 101,200.

Columbia², District of see DISTRICT OF COLUMBIA.

Columbine /ˈkɒləmˌbaɪn/ a character in Italian comedy, the mistress of Harlequin. She appears in the harlequinade of English pantomime as a short-skirted dancer. [F Colombine f. It. Colombina f. colombino dovelike]

columbine /ˈkɒləmˌbaɪn/ n. any plant of the genus Aquilegia, esp. A. vulgaris, having purple-blue flowers. Also called AQUILEGIA. [ME f. OF colombine f. med.L colombina herba dovelike plant f. L columba dove (from the supposed resemblance of the flower to a cluster of 5 doves)]

columbite /kəˈlʌmbaɪt/ n. US Chem. an ore of iron and niobium found in America. [Columbia, a poetic name for America, + -ITE¹]

columbium /kəˈlʌmbɪəm/ n. US Chem. = NIOBIUM.

Columbus¹ /kəˈlʌmbəs/ the capital and largest city of Ohio; pop. (1982) 570,600.

Columbus² /kəˈlʌmbəs/, Christopher (1451–1506), Italian explorer. A Genoese by birth, Columbus persuaded Ferdinand and Isabella of Spain to sponsor an expedition to sail westwards across the Atlantic in search of Asia and prove that the world was round. Sailing with three small ships in 1492, he discovered the New World (actually various Caribbean islands; he himself remained convinced that he had in fact found the coast of Asia) and returned home to a hero's welcome. Columbus made three further voyages to the New World between 1493 and 1504, but failed to find the expected riches of semi-mythical Cathay. A romantic visionary, unsuited either to organization or to intrigue, Columbus was out of his depth in the faction-ridden politics both at the Spanish court and within the new colonies he established. Out of favour, he died in poverty and obscurity at Valladolid in NW Spain.

w we   z zoo   ʃ she   ʒ decision   θ thin   ð this   ŋ ring   x loch   tʃ chip   dʒ jar   (see over for vowels)

column /ˈkɒləm/ n. 1 Archit. an upright cylindrical pillar often slightly tapering and usu. supporting an entablature or arch, or standing alone as a monument. 2 a structure or part shaped like a column. 3 a vertical cylindrical mass of liquid or vapour. 4 a a vertical division of a page, chart, etc., containing a sequence of figures or words. b the figures or words themselves. 5 a part of a newspaper regularly devoted to a particular subject (gossip column). 6 a Mil. an arrangement of troops in successive lines, with a narrow front. b Naut. a similar arrangement of ships. □ **column-inch** a quantity of print (esp. newsprint) occupying a one-inch length of a column. **dodge the column** colloq. shirk one's duty; avoid work. □□ **columnar** /kəˈlʌmnə(r)/ adj. **columned** adj. [ME f. OF columpne & L columna pillar]

columnist /ˈkɒləmnɪst, -mɪst/ n. a journalist contributing regularly to a newspaper.

colure /kəˈlʊə(r)/ n. Astron. either of two great circles intersecting at right angles at the celestial poles and passing through the ecliptic at either the equinoxes or the solstices. [ME f. LL colurus f. Gk kolouros truncated]

colza /ˈkɒlzə/ n. = RAPE². [F kolza(t) f. LG kölsāt (as COLE, SEED)]

COM abbr. computer output on microfilm or microfiche.

com- /kɒm, kəm, kʌm/ prefix (also **co-, col-, con-, cor-**) with, together, jointly, altogether. ¶ com- is used before b, m, p, and occas. before vowels and f; co- esp. before vowels, h, and gn; col- before l, cor- before r, and con- before other consonants. [L com-, cum with]

coma¹ /ˈkəʊmə/ n. (pl. **comas**) a prolonged deep unconsciousness, caused esp. by severe injury or excessive use of drugs. [med.L f. Gk kōma deep sleep]

coma² /ˈkəʊmə/ n. (pl. **comae** /-miː/) 1 Astron. a cloud of gas and dust surrounding the nucleus of a comet. 2 Bot. a tuft of silky hairs at the end of some seeds. [L f. Gk komē hair of head]

Comanche /kəˈmæntʃɪ/ n. & adj. —n. 1a North American Indian people of Texas and Oklahoma. 2 their language. —adj. of the Comanches or their language. [Sp.]

Comaneci /ˌkh:ɒməˈnetʃ/, Nadia (1961–), Romanian gymnast, who became the first competitor in the history of the Olympic Games to be awarded the maximum score (10.00) when she won three gold medals for her performances at the Montreal Olympics in 1976.

comatose /ˈkəʊməˌtəʊz/ adj. 1 in a coma. 2 drowsy, sleepy, lethargic.

comb /kəʊm/ n. & v. —n. 1 a toothed strip of rigid material for tidying and arranging the hair, or for keeping it in place. 2 a part of a machine having a similar design or purpose. 3 a the red fleshy crest of a fowl, esp. a cock. b an analogous growth in other birds. 4 a honeycomb. —v.tr. 1 arrange or tidy (the hair) by drawing a comb through. 2 curry (a horse). 3 dress (wool or flax) with a comb. 4 search (a place) thoroughly. □ **comb out 1** tidy and arrange (hair) with a comb. 2 remove with a comb. 3 search or attack systematically. 4 search out and get rid of (anything unwanted). □□ **combed** adj. [OE camb f. Gmc]

combat /ˈkɒmbæt, ˈkʌm-/ n. & v. —n. a fight, struggle, or contest. —v. (**combated, combating**) 1 intr. engage in combat. 2 tr. engage in combat with. 3 tr. oppose; strive against. □ **combat fatigue** a mental disorder caused by stress in wartime combat. **single combat** a duel. [F combat f. combattre f. LL (as COM-, L batuere fight)]

combatant /ˈkɒmbət(ə)nt, ˈkʌm-/ n. & adj. —n. a person engaged in fighting. —adj. 1 fighting. 2 for fighting.

combative /ˈkɒmbətɪv, ˈkʌm-/ adj. ready or eager to fight; pugnacious. □□ **combatively** adv. **combativeness** n.

combe var. of COOMB.

comber¹ /ˈkəʊmə(r)/ n. 1 a person or thing that combs, esp. a machine for combing cotton or wool very fine. 2 a long curling wave; a breaker.

comber² /ˈkəʊmə(r)/ n. Brit. a fish of the perch family, Serranus cabrilla. [18th c.: orig. unkn.]

combination /ˌkɒmbɪˈneɪʃ(ə)n/ n. 1 the act or an instance of combining; the process of being combined. 2 a combined state (in combination with). 3 a combined set of things or people. 4 a sequence of numbers or letters used to open a combination lock. 5 Brit. a motor cycle with side-car attached. 6 (in pl.) Brit. a single undergarment for the body and legs. 7 a group of things chosen from a larger number without regard to their arrangement. 8 a united action. b Chess a coordinated and effective sequence of moves. 9 Chem. a union of substances in a compound with new properties. □ **combination lock** a lock that can be opened only by a specific sequence of movements. □□ **combinative** /ˈkɒmbɪnətɪv/ adj. **combinational** adj. **combinatory** /ˈkɒmbɪnətərɪ/ adj. [obs. F combination or LL combinatio (as COMBINE)]

Combination Acts British laws of 1799–1800 making illegal the confederacy of persons to further their own interests, affect the rate of wages, etc. Formulated in the wake of naval mutinies and the Irish rebellion, and to prevent seditious revolutionary ideas from spreading to England after the French Revolution, the laws were supposed to apply to masters and men alike, but in fact the masters were allowed to combine freely and restrictions were enforced against working-class unions; most of the legislation was repealed in 1824.

combinatorial /ˌkɒmbɪnəˈtɔːrɪəl/ adj. Math. relating to combinations of items.

combine v. & n. —v. /kəmˈbaɪn/ 1 tr. & intr. join together; unite for a common purpose. 2 tr. possess (qualities usually distinct) together (combines charm and authority). 3 a intr. coalesce in one substance. b tr. cause to do this. c intr. form a chemical compound. 4 intr. cooperate. 5 /ˈkɒmbaɪn/ tr. harvest (crops etc.) by means of a combine harvester. —n. /ˈkɒmbaɪn/ a combination of esp. commercial interests to control prices etc. □ **combine harvester** a mobile machine that reaps and threshes in one operation. **combining form** Gram. a linguistic element used in combination with another element to form a word (e.g. Anglo- = English, bio- = life, -graphy writing). ¶ In this dictionary, combining form is used of an element that contributes to the particular sense of words (as with both elements of biography), as distinct from a prefix or suffix that adjusts the sense of or determines the function of words (as with un-, -able, and -ation). □□ **combinable** adj. [ME f. OF combiner or LL combinare (as COM-, L bini two)]

combing /ˈkəʊmɪŋ/ n. (in pl.) hairs combed off. □ **combing wool** long-stapled wool, suitable for combing and making into worsted.

combo /ˈkɒmbəʊ/ n. (pl. **-os**) sl. a small jazz or dance band. [abbr. of COMBINATION + -o]

combs /kɒmz/ n.pl. colloq. combinations (see COMBINATION 6).

combust /kəmˈbʌst/ v.tr. subject to combustion. [obs. combust (adj.) f. L combustus past part. (as COMBUSTION)]

combustible /kəmˈbʌstɪb(ə)l/ adj. & n. —adj. 1 capable of or used for burning. 2 excitable; easily irritated. —n. a combustible substance. □□ **combustibility** /-ˈbɪlɪtɪ/ n. [F combustible or med.L combustibilis (as COMBUSTION)]

combustion /kəmˈbʌstʃ(ə)n/ n. 1 burning; consumption by fire. 2 Chem. the development of light and heat from the chemical combination of a substance with oxygen. □□ **combustive** adj. [ME f. F combustion or LL combustio f. L comburere combust- burn up]

come /kʌm/ v. & n. —v.intr. (past **came** /keɪm/; past part. **come**) 1 move, be brought towards, or reach a place thought of as near or familiar to the speaker or hearer (come and see me; shall we come to your house?; the books have come). 2 reach or be brought to a specified situation or result (you'll come to no harm; have come to believe it; has come to be used wrongly; came into prominence). 3 reach or extend to a specified point (the road comes within a mile of us). 4 traverse or accomplish (with compl.: have come a long way). 5 occur, happen; become present instead of future (how did you come to break your leg?). 6 take or occupy a specified position in space or time (it comes on the third page; Nero came after Claudius; it does not come within the scope of the inquiry). 7 become perceptible or known (the church came into sight; the news comes as a surprise; it will come to me). 8 be available (the dress comes in three sizes; this model comes with optional features). 9 become (with compl.: the handle has come loose). 10 (foll. by of) a be descended from (comes *of a rich family*). **b** be the result of (*that comes of complaining*). **11** *colloq.* play the part of; behave like (with compl.: *don't come the bully with me*). **12** *sl.* have a sexual orgasm. **13** (*in subj.*) *colloq.* when a specified time is reached (*come next month*). **14** (as *int.*) expressing caution or reserve (*come, it cannot be that bad*). —*n. sl.* semen ejaculated at a sexual orgasm. □ **as . . . as they come** typically or supremely so (*is as tough as they come*). **come about** happen; take place. **come across 1** be effective or understood. **2** (foll. by *with*) *sl.* hand over what is wanted. **3** meet or find by chance (*came across an old jacket*). **come again** *colloq.* **1** make a further effort. **2** (as *imper.*) what did you say? **come along 1** make progress; move forward. **2** (as *imper.*) hurry up. **come and go 1** pass to and fro; be transitory. **2** pay brief visits. **come apart** fall or break into pieces, disintegrate. **come at 1** reach, discover; get access to. **2** attack (*came at me with a knife*). **come-at-able** /-ˈætəb(ə)l/ *adj.* reachable, accessible. **come away 1** become detached or broken off (*came away in my hands*). **2** (foll. by *with*) be left with a feeling, impression, etc. (*came away with many misgivings*). **come back 1** return. **2** recur to one's memory. **3** become fashionable or popular again. **4** *US* reply, retort. **come before** be dealt with by (a judge etc.). **come between 1** interfere with the relationship of. **2** separate; prevent contact between. **come by 1** pass; go past. **2** call on a visit (*why not come by tomorrow?*). **3** acquire, obtain (*came by a new bicycle*). **come clean** see CLEAN. **come down 1** come to a place or position regarded as lower. **2** lose position or wealth (*has come down in the world*). **3** be handed down by tradition or inheritance. **4** be reduced; show a downward trend (*prices are coming down*). **5** (foll. by *against*, *in favour of*) reach a decision or recommendation (*the report came down against change*). **6** (foll. by *to*) signify or betoken basically; be dependent on (a factor) (*it comes down to who is willing to go*). **7** (foll. by *on*) criticize harshly; rebuke, punish. **8** (foll. by *with*) begin to suffer from (a disease). **come for 1** come to collect or receive. **2** attack (*came for me with a hammer*). **come forward 1** advance. **2** offer oneself for a task, post, etc. **come-hither** *attrib.adj. colloq.* (of a look or manner) enticing, flirtatious. **come in 1** enter a house or room. **2** take a specified position in a race etc. (*came in third*). **3** become fashionable or seasonable. **4 a** have a useful role or function. **b** (with compl.) prove to be (*came in very handy*). **c** have a part to play (*where do I come in?*). **5** be received (*more news has just come in*). **6** begin speaking, esp. in radio transmission. **7** be elected; come to power. **8** *Cricket* begin an innings. **9** (foll. by *for*) receive; be the object of (usu. something unwelcome) (*came in for much criticism*). **10** (foll. by *on*) join (an enterprise etc.). **11** (of a tide) turn to high tide. **12** (of a train, ship, or aircraft) approach its destination. **come into 1** see senses 2, 7 of *v*. **2** receive, esp. as heir. **come near** see NEAR. **come of age** see AGE. **come off 1** *colloq.* (of an action) succeed; be accomplished. **2** (with compl.) fare; turn out (*came off badly; came off the winner*). **3** *coarse sl.* have a sexual orgasm. **4** be detached or detachable (from). **5** fall (from). **6** be reduced or subtracted from (£5 *came off the price*). **come off it** (as *imper.*) *colloq.* an expression of disbelief or refusal to accept another's opinion, behaviour, etc. **come on 1** continue to come. **2** advance, esp. to attack. **3** make progress; thrive (*is really coming on*). **4** (foll. by *to* + infin.) begin (*it came on to rain*). **5** appear on the stage, field of play, etc. **6** be heard or seen on the telephone, etc. **7** arise to be discussed. **8** (as *imper.*) expressing encouragement. **9** = **come upon**. **come-on** *n. sl.* a lure or enticement. **come out 1** emerge; become known (*it came out that he had left*). **2** appear or be published (*comes out every Saturday*). **3 a** declare oneself; make a decision (*came out in favour of joining*). **b** openly declare that one is a homosexual. **4** *Brit.* go on strike. **5 a** be satisfactorily visible in a photograph etc., or present in a specified way (*the dog didn't come out; he came out badly*). **b** (of a photograph) be produced satisfactorily or in a specified way (*only three have come out; they all came out well*). **6** attain a specified result in an examination etc. **7** (of a stain etc.) be removed. **8** make one's début on stage or in society. **9** (foll. by *in*) be covered with (*came out in spots*). **10** (of a problem) be solved. **11** (foll. by *with*) declare openly; disclose. **come over 1** come from some distance or nearer to the speaker (*came over from Paris; come over here a moment*). **2** change sides or one's opinion. **3 a** (of a feeling etc.) overtake or affect (a person). **b** *colloq.* feel suddenly (*came

over faint*). **4** appear or sound in a specified way (*you came over very well; the ideas came over clearly*). **5** affect or influence (*I don't know what came over me*). **come round 1** pay an informal visit. **2** recover consciousness. **3** be converted to another person's opinion. **4** (of a date or regular occurrence) recur; be imminent again. **come through 1** be successful; survive. **2** be received by telephone. **3** survive or overcome (a difficulty) (*came through the ordeal*). **come to 1** recover consciousness. **2** *Naut.* bring a vessel to a stop. **3** reach in total; amount to. **4** *refl.* **a** recover consciousness. **b** stop being foolish. **5** have as a destiny; reach (*what is the world coming to?*). **come to hand** become available; be recovered. **come to light** see LIGHT[1]. **come to nothing** have no useful result in the end; fail. **come to pass** happen, occur. **come to rest** cease moving. **come to one's senses** see SENSE. **come to that** *colloq.* in fact; if that is the case. **come under 1** be classified as or among. **2** be subject to (influence or authority). **come up 1** come to a place or position regarded as higher. **2** attain wealth or position (*come up in the world*). **3** (of an issue, problem, etc.) arise; present itself; be mentioned or discussed. **4** (often foll. by *to*) **a** approach a person, esp. to talk. **b** approach or draw near to a specified time, event, etc. (*is coming up to eight o'clock*). **5** (foll. by *to*) match (a standard etc.). **6** (foll. by *with*) produce (an idea etc.), esp. in response to a challenge. **7** (of a plant etc.) spring out of the ground. **8** become brighter (e.g. with polishing); shine more brightly. **come up against** be faced with or opposed by. **come upon 1** meet or find by chance. **2** attack by surprise. **come what may** no matter what happens. **have it coming to one** *colloq.* be about to get one's deserts. **how come?** *colloq.* how did that happen? **if it comes to that** in that case. **to come** future; in the future (*the year to come; many problems were still to come*). [OE *cuman* f. Gmc]

comeback /ˈkʌmbæk/ *n.* **1** a return to a previous (esp. successful) state. **2** *sl.* a retaliation or retort. **3** *Austral.* a sheep bred from crossbred and purebred parents for both wool and meat.

Comecon /ˈkɒmɪˌkɒn/ *n.* the English name for an economic organization of Soviet-bloc countries, founded in 1949 and analogous to the European Economic Community. Its headquarters are in Moscow. [abbr. of Council for Mutual Economic Assistance, transl. Russ. title]

comedian /kəˈmiːdɪən/ *n.* **1** a humorous entertainer on stage, television, etc. **2** an actor in comedy. [F *comédien* f. *comédie* COMEDY]

Comédie Française /ˌkɒmeɪˈdiː frãˈseɪz/ the French national theatre (used for both comedy and tragedy), in Paris, founded in 1680 by Louis XIV and reconstituted by Napoleon in 1803. It is organized as a cooperative society in which each actor holds a share or part-share. [F, = French comedy]

comedienne /kəˌmiːdɪˈen/ *n.* a female comedian. [F fem. (as COMEDIAN)]

comedist /ˈkɒmɪdɪst/ *n.* a writer of comedies.

comedo /ˈkɒmɪˌdəʊ/ *n.* (pl. **comedones** /-ˈdəʊniːz/) *Med.* a blackhead. [L, = glutton f. *comedere* eat up]

comedown /ˈkʌmdaʊn/ *n.* **1** a loss of status; decline or degradation. **2** a disappointment.

comedy /ˈkɒmɪdɪ/ *n.* (pl. **-ies**) **1 a** a play, film, etc., of an amusing or satirical character, usu. with a happy ending. **b** the dramatic genre consisting of works of this kind (*she excels in comedy*) (cf. TRAGEDY). **2** an amusing or farcical incident or series of incidents in everyday life. **3** humour, esp. in a work of art etc. □ **comedy of manners** see MANNER. □□ **comedic** /kəˈmiːdɪk/ *adj.* [ME f. OF *comedie* f. L *comoedia* f. Gk *kōmōidia* f. *kōmōidos* comic poet f. *kōmos* revel]

comely /ˈkʌmlɪ/ *adj.* (**comelier**, **comeliest**) (usu. of a woman) pleasant to look at. □□ **comeliness** /ˈkʌmlɪnɪs/ *n.* [ME *cumelich*, *cumli* prob. f. *becumelich* f. BECOME]

comer /ˈkʌmə(r)/ *n.* **1** a person who comes, esp. as an applicant, participant, etc. (*offered the job to the first comer*). **2** *colloq.* a person likely to be a success. □ **all comers** any applicants (with reference to a position, or esp. a challenge to a champion, that is unrestricted in entry).

comestible /kəˈmestɪb(ə)l/ *n.* (usu. in *pl.*) *formal* or *joc.* food. [ME f. F f. med.L *comestibilis* f. L *comedere comest-* eat up]

comet /'kɒmɪt/ n. a luminous object seen in the night sky, originally considered a supernatural omen, but now recognized as an object orbiting the sun, consisting of an icy nucleus and a tail of evaporated gas and dust particles. Originating in a belt of material perhaps more than a light-year from the sun, comets are seen in the inner solar system only if perturbed from their orbits by the outer planets. Most escape back to interstellar space, but a few are trapped near the sun, and reappear regularly as periodic comets, of which the best-known is Halley's. □□ **cometary** adj. [ME f. OF *comete* f. L *cometa* f. Gk *komētes* long-haired (star)]

comeuppance /kʌm'ʌpəns/ n. colloq. one's deserved fate or punishment (got his comeuppance). [COME + UP + -ANCE]

comfit /'kʌmfɪt/ n. archaic a sweet consisting of a nut, seed, etc., coated in sugar. [ME f. OF *confit* f. L *confectum* past part. of *conficere* prepare: see CONFECTION]

comfort /'kʌmfət/ n. & v. —n. 1 consolation; relief in affliction. 2 a a state of physical well-being; being comfortable (live in comfort). b (usu. in pl.) things that make life easy or pleasant (has all the comforts). 3 a cause of satisfaction (a comfort to me that you are here). 4 a person who consoles or helps one (he's a comfort to her in her old age). 5 US a warm quilt. —v.tr. 1 soothe in grief; console. 2 make comfortable (comforted by the warmth of the fire). □ **comfort station** US euphem. a public lavatory. [ME f. OF *confort(er)* f. LL *confortare* strengthen (as COM-, L *fortis* strong)]

comfortable /'kʌmftəb(ə)l, -fətəb(ə)l/ adj. & n. —adj. 1 ministering to comfort; giving ease (a comfortable pair of shoes). 2 free from discomfort; at ease (I'm quite comfortable thank you). 3 colloq. having an adequate standard of living; free from financial worry. 4 having an easy conscience (did not feel comfortable about refusing him). 5 with a wide margin (a comfortable win). —n. US a warm quilt. □□ **comfortableness** n. **comfortably** adv. [ME f. AF *confortable* (as COMFORT)]

comforter /'kʌmfətə(r)/ n. 1 a person who comforts. 2 a baby's dummy. 3 archaic a woollen scarf. 4 US a warm quilt. [ME f. AF *confortour*, OF *-ēor* (as COMFORT)]

comfortless /'kʌmfətlɪs/ adj. 1 dreary, cheerless. 2 without comfort.

comfrey /'kʌmfrɪ/ n. (pl. -eys) any of various plants of the genus *Symphytum*, esp. *S. officinale* having large hairy leaves and clusters of usu. white or purple bell-shaped flowers. [ME f. AF *cumfrie*, ult. f. L *conferva* (as COM-, *fervēre* boil)]

comfy /'kʌmfɪ/ adj. (comfier, comfiest) colloq. comfortable. □□ **comfily** adv. **comfiness** n. [abbr.]

comic /'kɒmɪk/ adj. & n. —adj. 1 (often attrib.) of, or in the style of, comedy (a comic actor; comic opera). 2 causing or meant to cause laughter; funny (comic to see his struggles). —n. 1 a professional comedian. 2 a a children's periodical, mainly in the form of comic strips. b a similar publication intended for adults. □ **comic opera** 1 an opera with much spoken dialogue, usu. with humorous treatment. 2 this genre of opera. **comic strip** a horizontal series of drawings in a comic, newspaper, etc., telling a story. [L *comicus* f. Gk *kōmikos* f. *kōmos* revel]

comical /'kɒmɪk(ə)l/ adj. funny; causing laughter. □□ **comicality** /-'kælɪtɪ/ n. **comically** adv. [COMIC]

coming /'kʌmɪŋ/ adj. & n. —attrib.adj. 1 approaching, next (in the coming week; this coming Sunday). 2 of potential importance (a coming man). —n. arrival; approach.

Comino /kɒ'miːnəʊ/ the smallest of the three main islands of Malta.

Comintern /'kɒmɪn,tɜːn/ n. the Third International (see INTERNATIONAL n. 2), a communist organization founded in 1919 and dissolved in 1943. [Russ. *Komintern* f. Russ. forms of *communist*, *international*]

comitadji /,kɒmɪ'tædʒɪ/ n. (also **komitadji**, **komitaji**) a member of an irregular band of soldiers in the Balkans. [Turk. *komitacı*, lit. 'member of a (revolutionary) committee']

comity /'kɒmɪtɪ/ n. (pl. -ies) 1 courtesy, civility; considerate behaviour towards others. 2 a an association of nations etc. for mutual benefit. b (in full **comity of nations**) the mutual recognition by nations of the laws and customs of others. [L *comitas* f. *comis* courteous]

comma /'kɒmə/ n. 1 a punctuation mark (,) indicating a pause between parts of a sentence, or dividing items in a list, string of figures, etc. 2 Mus. a definite minute interval or difference of pitch. □ **comma bacillus** a comma-shaped bacillus causing cholera. [L f. Gk *komma* clause]

command /kə'mɑːnd/ v. & n. —v.tr. 1 (often foll. by to + infin., or that + clause) give formal order or instructions to (commands us to obey; commands that it be done). 2 (also absol.) have authority or control over. 3 a (often refl.) restrain, master. b gain the use of; have at one's disposal or within reach (skill, resources, etc.) (commands an extensive knowledge of history; commands a salary of £40,000). 4 deserve and get (sympathy, respect, etc.). 5 Mil. dominate (a strategic position) from a superior height; look down over. —n. 1 an authoritative order; an instruction. 2 mastery, control, possession (a good command of languages; has command of the resources). 3 the exercise or tenure of authority, esp. naval or military (has command of this ship). 4 Mil. a a body of troops etc. (Bomber Command). b a district under a commander (Western Command). 5 Computing a an instruction causing a computer to perform one of its basic functions. b a signal initiating such an operation. □ **at command** ready to be used at will. **at** (or **by**) **a person's command** in pursuance of a person's bidding. **command module** the control compartment in a spacecraft. **Command Paper** (in the UK) a paper laid before Parliament by command of the Crown. **command performance** (in the UK) a theatrical or film performance given by royal command. **command post** the headquarters of a military unit. **in command of** commanding; having under control. **under command of** commanded by. **word of command** 1 Mil. an order for a movement in a drill etc. 2 a prearranged spoken signal for the start of an operation. [ME f. AF *comaunder*, OF *comander* f. LL *commandare* COMMEND]

commandant /,kɒmən'dænt, -'dɑːnt, 'kɒm-/ n. a commanding officer, esp. of a particular force, military academy, etc. □ **Commandant-in-Chief** the supreme commandant. □□ **commandantship** n. [F *commandant*, or It. or Sp. *commandante* (as COMMAND)]

commandeer /,kɒmən'dɪə(r)/ v.tr. 1 seize (men or goods) for military purposes. 2 take possession of without authority. [S.Afr. Du. *kommanderen* f. F *commander* COMMAND]

commander /kə'mɑːndə(r)/ n. 1 a person who commands, esp.: a a naval officer next in rank below captain. b = *wing commander*. 2 an officer in charge of a London police district. 3 (in full **knight commander**) a member of a higher class in some orders of knighthood. 4 a large wooden mallet. □ **commander-in-chief** the supreme commander, esp. of a nation's forces. **Commander of the Faithful** a title of a Caliph. □□ **commandership** n. [ME f. OF *comandere*, *-ēor* f. Rmc (as COMMAND)]

commanding /kə'mɑːndɪŋ/ adj. 1 dignified, exalted, impressive. 2 (of a hill or other high point) giving a wide view. 3 (of an advantage, a position, etc.) controlling; superior (has a commanding lead). □□ **commandingly** adv.

commandment /kə'mɑːndmənt/ n. a divine command. □ **the Ten Commandments** the divine rules of conduct given by God to Moses on Mount Sinai, according to Exod. 20: 1–17. [ME f. OF *comandement* (as COMMAND)]

commando /kə'mɑːndəʊ/ n. (pl. -os) Mil. 1 a a unit of British amphibious shock troops. The Commandos were British troops of Combined Operations Command during the Second World War. They were trained originally (in 1940) as shock troops for the repelling of the threatened German invasion of England, later for the carrying out of raids on the Continent and elsewhere. b a member of such a unit. c a similar unit or member of such a unit elsewhere. 2 a a party of men called out for military service. b a body of troops. 3 (in the Boer War) a unit of the Boer army composed of the militia of an electoral district. 4 (attrib.) of or concerning a commando (a commando operation). [Port. f. *commandar* COMMAND]

comme ci, comme ça /kɒm,si: kɒm'sɑ:/ adv. & adj. so so; middling or middlingly. [F, = like this, like that]

commedia dell'arte /kɒ,meɪdɪə del'ɑːteɪ/ n. an improvised kind of popular comedy performed by professional actors developed in 16th-c. Italy, and extended throughout Europe until the end of the 18th c., in which stock character types (e.g. Harlequin, Columbine, Pantaloon) adapted their comic dialogue and action according to a few basic plots (commonly love intrigues) and to popular needs. It had an enormous influence on European drama as seen in the work of Jonson, Molière, and Goldoni. [It., = comedy of art]

comme il faut /ˌkɒm iːl ˈfəʊ/ adj. & adv. —predic.adj. (esp. of behaviour, etiquette, etc.) proper, correct. —adv. properly, correctly. [F, = as is necessary]

commemorate /kəˈmeməˌreɪt/ v.tr. 1 celebrate in speech or writing. 2 a preserve in memory by some celebration. b (of a stone, plaque, etc.) be a memorial of. □□ **commemorative** /kəˈmemərətɪv/ adj. **commemorator** n. [L commemorare (as COM-, memorare relate f. memor mindful)]

commemoration /kəˌmeməˈreɪʃ(ə)n/ n. 1 an act of commemorating. 2 a service or part of a service in memory of a person, an event, etc. [ME f. F commemoration or L commemoratio (as COMMEMORATE)]

commence /kəˈmens/ v.tr. & intr. formal begin. [ME f. OF com-(m)encier f. Rmc (as COM-, L initiare INITIATE)]

commencement /kəˈmensmənt/ n. formal 1 a beginning. 2 esp. US a ceremony of degree conferment. [ME f. OF (as COMMENCE)]

commend /kəˈmend/ v.tr. 1 (often foll. by to) entrust, commit (commends his soul to God). 2 praise (commends her singing voice). 3 recommend (method commends itself). □ **commend me to** archaic remember me kindly to. **highly commended** (of a competitor etc.) just missing the top places. [ME f. L commendare (as COM-, mendare = mandare entrust: see MANDATE)]

commendable /kəˈmendəb(ə)l/ adj. praiseworthy. □□ **commendably** adv. [ME f. OF f. L commendabilis (as COMMEND)]

commendation /ˌkɒmenˈdeɪʃ(ə)n/ n. 1 an act of commending or recommending (esp. a person to another's favour). 2 praise. [ME f. OF f. L commendatio (as COMMEND)]

commendatory /kəˈmendətərɪ/ adj. commending, recommending. [LL commendatorius (as COMMEND)]

commensal /kəˈmens(ə)l/ adj. & n. —adj. 1 Biol. of, relating to, or exhibiting commensalism. 2 (of a person) eating at the same table as another. —n. 1 Biol. a commensal organism. 2 one who eats at the same table as another. □□ **commensality** /ˌkɒmenˈsælɪtɪ/ n. [ME f. F commensal or med.L commensalis (in sense 2) (as COM-, mensa table)]

commensalism /kəˈmensəˌlɪz(ə)m/ n. Biol. an association between two organisms in which one benefits and the other derives no benefit or harm.

commensurable /kəˈmenʃərəb(ə)l, -sjərəb(ə)l/ adj. 1 (often foll. by with, to) measurable by the same standard. 2 (foll. by to) proportionate to. 3 Math. (of numbers) in a ratio equal to the ratio of integers. □□ **commensurability** /-ˈbɪlɪtɪ/ n. **commensurably** adv. [LL commensurabilis (as COM-, MEASURE)]

commensurate /kəˈmenʃərət, -sjərət/ adj. 1 (usu. foll. by with) having the same size, duration, etc.; coextensive. 2 (often foll. by to, with) proportionate. □□ **commensurately** adv. [LL commensuratus (as COM-, MEASURE)]

comment /ˈkɒment/ n. & v. —n. 1 a a remark, esp. critical; an opinion (passed a comment on her hat). b commenting; criticism (his behaviour aroused much comment; an hour of news and comment). 2 a an explanatory note (e.g. on a written text). b written criticism or explanation (e.g. of a text). 3 (of a play, book, etc.) a critical illustration; a parable (his art is a comment on society). —v.intr. 1 (often foll. by on, upon, or that + clause) make (esp. critical) remarks (commented on her choice of friends). 2 (often foll. by on, upon) write explanatory notes. □ **no comment** colloq. I decline to answer your question. □□ **commenter** n. [ME f. L commentum contrivance (in LL also = interpretation), neut. past part. of comminisci devise, or F commenter (v.)]

commentary /ˈkɒməntərɪ/ n. (pl. -ies) 1 a set of explanatory or critical notes on a text etc. 2 a descriptive spoken account (esp. on radio or television) of an event or a performance as it happens. [L commentarius, -ium adj. used as noun (as COMMENT)]

commentate /ˈkɒmənˌteɪt/ v.intr. disp. act as a commentator. [back-form. f. COMMENTATOR]

commentator /ˈkɒmənˌteɪtə(r)/ n. 1 a person who provides a commentary on an event etc. 2 the writer of a commentary. 3 a person who writes or speaks on current events. [L f. commentari frequent. of comminisci devise]

commerce /ˈkɒmɜːs/ n. 1 financial transactions, esp. the buying and selling of merchandise, on a large scale. 2 social intercourse (the daily commerce of gossip and opinion). 3 archaic sexual intercourse. [F commerce or L commercium (as COM-, mercium f. merx mercis merchandise)]

commercial /kəˈmɜːʃ(ə)l/ adj. & n. —adj. 1 of, engaged in, or concerned with, commerce. 2 having profit as a primary aim rather than artistic etc. value; philistine. 3 (of chemicals) supplied in bulk more or less unpurified. —n. 1 a television or radio advertisement. 2 archaic a commercial traveller. □ **commercial art** art used in advertising, selling, etc. **commercial broadcasting** television or radio broadcasting in which programmes are financed by advertisements. **commercial traveller** a firm's travelling salesman or saleswoman who visits shops to get orders. **commercial vehicle** a vehicle used for carrying goods or fare-paying passengers. □□ **commercialism** n. **commerciality** /-ʃɪˈælɪtɪ/ n. **commercially** adv.

commercialize /kəˈmɜːʃəˌlaɪz/ v.tr. (also -ise) 1 exploit or spoil for the purpose of gaining profit. 2 make commercial. □□ **commercialization** /-ˈzeɪʃ(ə)n/ n.

commère /ˈkɒmeə(r)/ n. Brit. a female compère. [F, fem. of COMPÈRE]

Commie /ˈkɒmɪ/ n. sl. derog. a Communist. [abbr.]

commination /ˌkɒmɪˈneɪʃ(ə)n/ n. 1 the threatening of divine vengeance. 2 a the recital of divine threats against sinners in the Anglican Liturgy for Ash Wednesday. b the service that includes this. [ME f. L comminatio f. comminari threaten]

comminatory /ˈkɒmɪnətərɪ/ adj. threatening, denunciatory. [med.L comminatorius (as COMMINATION)]

commingle /kəˈmɪŋg(ə)l/ v.tr. & intr. literary mingle together.

comminute /ˈkɒmɪˌnjuːt/ v.tr. 1 reduce to small fragments. 2 divide (property) into small portions. □ **comminuted fracture** a fracture producing multiple bone splinters. □□ **comminution** /-ˈnjuːʃ(ə)n/ n. [L comminuere comminut- (as COM-, minuere lessen)]

commis /ˈkɒmɪ, ˈkɒmɪs/ n. (pl. **commis** /ˈkɒmɪ, ˈkɒmɪz/) a junior waiter or chef. [orig. = deputy, clerk, f. F, past part. of commettre entrust (as COMMIT)]

commiserate /kəˈmɪzəˌreɪt/ v. 1 intr. (usu. foll. by with) express or feel pity. 2 tr. archaic express or feel pity for (commiserate you on your loss). □□ **commiseration** /-ˈreɪʃ(ə)n/ n. **commiserative** /-rətɪv/ adj. **commiserator** n. [L commiserari (as COM-, miserari pity f. miser wretched)]

commissar /ˈkɒmɪˌsɑː(r)/ n. 1 an official of the Soviet Communist Party responsible for political education and organization. 2 hist. the head of a government department in the USSR before 1946. [Russ. komissar f. F commissaire (as COMMISSARY)]

commissariat /ˌkɒmɪˈseərɪət, -ˈsærɪæt/ n. 1 esp. Mil. a a department for the supply of food etc. b the food supplied. 2 hist. a government department of the USSR before 1946. [F commissariat & med.L commissariatus (as COMMISSARY)]

commissary /ˈkɒmɪsərɪ, kəˈmɪs-/ n. (pl. **-ies**) 1 a deputy or delegate. 2 a representative or deputy of a bishop. 3 Mil. an officer responsible for the supply of food etc. to soldiers. 4 US a a restaurant in a film studio etc. b the food supplied. 5 US Mil. a store for the supply of food etc. to soldiers. □□ **commissarial** /-ˈseərɪəl/ adj. **commissaryship** n. [ME f. med.L commissarius person in charge (as COMMIT)]

commission /kəˈmɪʃ(ə)n/ n. & v. —n. 1 a the authority to perform a task or certain duties. b a person or group entrusted esp. by a government with such authority (set up a commission to look into it). c an instruction, command, or duty given to such a group or person (their commission was to simplify the procedure; my commission was to find him). 2 an order for something, esp. a work of art, to be produced specially. 3 Mil. a a warrant conferring the rank of officer in the army, navy, or air force. **b** the rank so conferred. **4 a** the authority to act as agent for a company etc. in trade. **b** a percentage paid to the agent from the profits of goods etc. sold, or business obtained (*his wages are low, but he gets 20 per cent commission*). **c** the pay of a commissioned agent. **5** the act of committing (*a crime, sin, etc.*). **6** the office or department of a commissioner. —*v.tr.* **1** authorize or empower by a commission. **2 a** give (an artist etc.) a commission for a piece of work. **b** order (a work) to be written (*commissioned a new concerto*). **3** *Naut.* **a** give (an officer) the command of a ship. **b** prepare (a ship) for active service. **4** bring (a machine, equipment, etc.) into operation. □ **commission-agent** a bookmaker. **commission of the peace 1** Justices of the Peace. **2** the authority given to them. **in commission** (of a warship etc.) manned, armed, and ready for service. **out of commission** (esp. of a ship) not in service, not in working order. **Royal Commission 1** a commission of inquiry appointed by the Crown at the instance of the Government. **2** a committee so appointed. [ME f. OF f. L *commissio -onis* (as COMMIT)]

commissionaire /kəˌmɪʃəˈneə(r)/ *n.* esp. *Brit.* a uniformed door-attendant at a theatre, cinema, hotel, etc. [F (as COMMISSIONER)]

commissioner /kəˈmɪʃənə(r)/ *n.* **1** a person appointed by a commission to perform a specific task, e.g. the head of the London police, a delegate to the General Assembly of the Church of Scotland, etc. **2** a person appointed as a member of a government commission (*Charity Commissioner; Civil Service Commissioner*). **3** a representative of the supreme authority in a district, department, etc. □ **Commissioner for Oaths** a solicitor authorized to administer an oath to a person making an affidavit. **Lord** (or **Lord High**) **Commissioner** the representative of the Crown at the General Assembly of the Church of Scotland. [ME f. med.L *commissionarius* (as COMMISSION)]

commissure /ˈkɒmɪˌsjʊə(r)/ *n.* **1** a junction, joint, or seam. **2** *Anat.* **a** the joint between two bones. **b** a band of nerve tissue connecting the hemispheres of the brain, the two sides of the spinal cord, etc. **c** the line where the upper and lower lips, or eyelids, meet. **3** *Bot.* any of several joints etc. between different parts of a plant. □□ **commissural** /kɒmɪˈsjʊərəl/ *adj.* [ME f. L *commissura* junction (as COMMIT)]

commit /kəˈmɪt/ *v.tr.* (**committed**, **committing**) **1** (usu. foll. by *to*) entrust or consign for: **a** safe keeping (*I commit him to your care*). **b** treatment, usu. destruction (*committed the book to the flames*). **2** perpetrate, do (esp. a crime, sin, or blunder). **3** pledge, involve, or bind (esp. oneself) to a certain course or policy (*does not like committing herself; committed by the vow he had made*). **4** (as **committed** *adj.*) (often foll. by *to*) **a** morally dedicated or politically aligned (*a committed Christian; committed to the cause; a committed socialist*). **b** obliged (to take certain action) (*felt committed to staying there*). **5** *Polit.* refer (a bill etc.) to a committee. □ **commit to memory** memorize. **commit to prison** consign officially to custody, esp. on remand. □□ **committable** *adj.* **committer** *n.* [ME f. L *committere* join, entrust (as COM-, *mittere miss-* send)]

commitment /kəˈmɪtmənt/ *n.* **1** an engagement or (esp. financial) obligation that restricts freedom of action. **2** the process or an instance of committing oneself; a pledge or undertaking.

committal /kəˈmɪt(ə)l/ *n.* **1** the act of committing a person to an institution, esp. prison or a mental hospital. **2** the burial of a dead body.

committee /kəˈmɪti/ *n.* **1 a** a body of persons appointed for a specific function by, and usu. out of, a larger body. **b** such a body appointed by Parliament etc. to consider the details of proposed legislation. **c** (**Committee**) *Brit.* the whole House of Commons when sitting as a committee. **2** /ˌkɒmɪˈtiː/ *Law* a person entrusted with the charge of another person or another person's property. □ **committee-man** (*pl.* **-men**) *fem.* **committee-woman**, *pl.* **-women**) a member of a committee, esp. a habitual member of committees. **committee stage** *Brit.* the third of five stages of a bill's progress through Parliament when it may be considered in detail and amendments made. **select committee** a small parliamentary committee appointed for a special purpose. **standing committee** a committee that

is permanent during the existence of the appointing body. [COM-MIT + -EE]

commix /kəˈmɪks/ *v.tr.* & *intr.* *archaic* or *poet.* mix. □□ **commixture** *n.* [ME: back-form. f. *commixt* past part. f. L *commixtus* (as COM-, MIXED)]

commode /kəˈməʊd/ *n.* **1** a chest of drawers. **2** (also **night-commode**) **a** a bedside table with a cupboard containing a chamber-pot. **b** a chamber-pot concealed in a chair with a hinged cover. **3** = CHIFFONIER. [F, adj. (as noun) f. L *commodus* convenient (as COM-, *modus* measure)]

commodious /kəˈməʊdɪəs/ *adj.* **1** roomy and comfortable. **2** *archaic* convenient. □□ **commodiously** *adv.* **commodiousness** *n.* [F *commodieux* or f. med.L *commodiosus* f. L *commodus* (as COMMODE)]

commodity /kəˈmɒdɪtɪ/ *n.* (*pl.* **-ies**) **1** *Commerce* an article or raw material that can be bought and sold, esp. a product as opposed to a service. **2** a useful thing. [ME f. OF *commodité* or f. L *commoditas* (as COMMODE)]

commodore /ˈkɒməˌdɔː(r)/ *n.* **1** a naval officer above a captain and below a rear-admiral. **2** the commander of a squadron or other division of a fleet. **3** the president of a yacht-club. **4** the senior captain of a shipping line. □ **Commodore-in-Chief** the supreme officer in the air force. [prob. f. Du. *komandeur* f. F *commandeur* COMMANDER]

common /ˈkɒmən/ *adj.* & *n.* —*adj.* (**commoner**, **commonest**) **1 a** occurring often (*a common mistake*). **b** ordinary; of ordinary qualities; without special rank or position (*no common mind; common soldier; the common people*). **2 a** shared by, coming from, or done by, more than one (*common knowledge; by common consent; our common benefit*). **b** belonging to, open to, or affecting, the whole community or the public (*common land*). **3** *derog.* low-class; vulgar; inferior (*a common little man*). **4** of the most familiar type (*common cold; common nightshade*). **5** *Math.* belonging to two or more quantities (*common denominator; common factor*). **6** *Gram.* (of gender) referring to individuals of either sex (e.g. *teacher*). **7** *Prosody* (of a syllable) that may be either short or long. **8** *Mus.* having two or four beats, esp. four crotchets, in a bar. **9** *Law* (of a crime) of lesser importance (cf. GRAND, PETTY). —*n.* **1** a piece of open public land, esp. in a village or town. **2** *sl.* = *common sense* (*use your common*). **3** *Eccl.* a service used for each of a group of occasions. **4** (in full **right of common**) *Law* a person's right over another's land, e.g. for pasturage. □ **Common Agricultural Bureaux** see CAB. **Common Agricultural Policy** see separate entry. **common carrier** a person or firm undertaking to transport any goods or person in a specified category. **common chord** *Mus.* any note with its major or minor third and perfect fifth. **common crier** see CRIER. **common denominator** see DENOMINATOR. **Common Era** the Christian era. **common ground** a point or argument accepted by both sides in a dispute. **common jury** a jury with members of no particular social standing (cf. *special jury*). **common law** law derived from custom and judicial precedent rather than statutes (cf. *case-law* (see CASE¹)). **common-law husband** (or **wife**) a partner in a marriage recognized by common law, esp. after a period of cohabitation. **Common Market** the European Economic Community. **common metre** a hymn stanza of four lines with 8, 6, 8, and 6 syllables. **common noun** (or **name**) *Gram.* a name denoting a class of objects or a concept as opposed to a particular individual (e.g. *boy, chocolate, beauty*). **common or garden** *colloq.* ordinary. **Common Prayer** the Church of England liturgy orig. set forth in the *Book of Common Prayer* (see entry). **common-room 1** a room in some colleges, schools, etc., which members may use for relaxation or work. **2** the members who use this. **common salt** see SALT. **common seal** the official seal of a corporate body. **common sense** sound practical sense, esp. in everyday matters. **Common Serjeant** see SERJEANT. **common soldier** see SOLDIER. **common stock** *US* = *ordinary shares*. **common weal** public welfare. **common year** see YEAR **2**. **in common 1** in joint use; shared. **2** of joint interest (*have little in common*). **in common with** in the same way as. **least** (or **lowest**) **common denominator**, **multiple** see DENOMINATOR, MULTIPLE. **out of the common** unusual. □□ **commonly** *adv.* **commonness** *n.* [ME f. OF *comun* f. L *communis*]

commonable /ˈkɒmənəb(ə)l/ *adj.* **1** (of an animal) that may be pastured on common land. **2** (of land) that may be held in common. [obs. *common* to exercise right of common + -ABLE]

commonage /ˈkɒmənɪdʒ/ *n.* **1** = *right of common* (see COMMON *n.* 4). **2 a** land held in common. **b** the state of being held in common. **3** the common people; commonalty.

Common Agricultural Policy the system in the EEC, set out in the Treaty of Rome (1957), for establishing common prices for most agricultural products within the Community, a single fund for price supports, and levies on imports. It also lays down a common policy for the export of agricultural products to countries outside the Community.

commonality /ˌkɒməˈnælɪtɪ/ *n.* (*pl.* **-ies**) **1** the sharing of an attribute. **2** a common occurrence. **3** = COMMONALTY. [var. of COMMONALTY]

commonalty /ˈkɒmənəltɪ/ *n.* (*pl.* **-ies**) **1** the common people. **2** the general body (esp. of mankind). **3** a corporate body. [ME f. OF *comunalté* f. med.L *communalitas -tatis* (as COMMON)]

commoner /ˈkɒmənə(r)/ *n.* **1** one of the common people, as opposed to the aristocracy. **2** a person who has the right of common. **3** a student at a British university who does not have a scholarship. [ME f. med.L *communarius* f. *communa* (as COMMUNE¹)]

commonplace /ˈkɒmənˌpleɪs/ *adj.* & *n.* —*adj.* lacking originality; trite. —*n.* **1 a** an everyday saying; a platitude (*uttered a commonplace about the weather*). **b** an ordinary topic of conversation. **2** anything usual or trite. **3** a notable passage in a book etc. copied into a commonplace-book. □ **commonplace-book** a book into which notable extracts from other works are copied for personal use. □□ **commonplaceness** *n.* [transl. of L *locus communis* = Gk *koinos topos* general theme]

commons /ˈkɒmənz/ *n.pl.* **1** (**the Commons**) = *House of Commons.* **2 a** the common people. **b** (prec. by *the*) the common people regarded as a part of a political, esp. British, system. **3** provisions shared in common; daily fare. □ **short commons** insufficient food. [ME pl. of COMMON]

commonsensical /ˌkɒmənˈsensɪk(ə)l/ *adj.* possessing or marked by common sense. [*common sense* (see COMMON)]

commonweal /ˈkɒmənˌwiːl/ *n.* archaic **1** = *common weal.* **2** = COMMONWEALTH.

commonwealth /ˈkɒmənˌwelθ/ *n.* **1 a** an independent State or community, esp. a democratic republic. **b** such a community or organization of shared interests in a non-political field (*the commonwealth of learning*). **2** (**the Commonwealth**) **a** (in full **the British Commonwealth of Nations**) an international association consisting of the UK together with States that were previously part of the British Empire, and dependencies. **b** the republican period of government in Britain between the execution of Charles I in 1649 and the Restoration in 1660. **c** *US* a part of the title of some of the States of the US. **d** the title of the federated Australian States. □ **Commonwealth Day** the name since 1959 of a day each year commemorating the British Commonwealth. It was formerly called *Empire Day*, celebrated until 1965 on 24 May (Queen Victoria's birthday) and now on the second Monday in March, originally commemorating assistance given to Britain by the colonies in the Boer War of 1899–1902. **New Commonwealth**, those countries which have achieved self-government within the Commonwealth since 1945. [COMMON + WEALTH]

Commonwealth Development Corporation an organization set up in 1948 to assist commercial and industrial development in British dependent territories and in certain cases any Commonwealth or other developing country.

commotion /kəˈməʊʃ(ə)n/ *n.* **1 a** a confused and noisy disturbance or outburst. **b** loud and confusing noise. **2** a civil insurrection. [ME f. OF *commotion* or L *commotio* (as COM-, MOTION)]

communal /ˈkɒmjʊn(ə)l/ *adj.* **1** relating to or benefiting a community; for common use (*communal baths*). **2** of a commune, esp. the Paris Commune. □□ **communality** /-ˈnælɪtɪ/ *n.* **communally** *adv.* [F f. LL *communalis* (as COMMUNE¹)]

communalism /ˈkɒmjʊnəˌlɪz(ə)m/ *n.* **1** a principle of political organization based on federated communes. **2** the principle of communal ownership etc. □□ **communalist** *n.* **communalistic** /-ˈlɪstɪk/ *adj.*

communalize /ˈkɒmjʊnəˌlaɪz/ *v.tr.* (also **-ise**) make communal. □□ **communalization** /-ˈzeɪʃ(ə)n/ *n.*

communard /ˈkɒmjʊˌnɑːd/ *n.* **1** a member of a commune. **2** (also **Communard**) *hist.* a supporter of the Paris Commune. [F (as COMMUNE¹)]

commune¹ /ˈkɒmjuːn/ *n.* **1 a** a group of people, not necessarily related, sharing living accommodation, goods, etc., esp. as a political act. **b** a communal settlement esp. for the pursuit of shared interests. **2 a** the smallest French territorial division for administrative purposes. **b** a similar division elsewhere. □ **the Commune (of Paris)** (i) a body which usurped the municipal government of Paris and in this capacity played a leading part in the Reign of Terror until suppressed in 1794; (ii) the government on communalistic principles established in Paris for a short time in 1871 after the Franco-Prussian war and the collapse of the Second Empire. [F f. med.L *communia* neut. pl. of L *communis* common]

commune² /kəˈmjuːn/ *v.intr.* **1** (usu. foll. by *with*) **a** speak confidentially and intimately (*communed together about their loss; communed with his heart*). **b** feel in close touch (with nature etc.) (*communed with the hills*). **2** *US* receive Holy Communion. [ME f. OF *comuner* share f. *comun* COMMON]

communicable /kəˈmjuːnɪkəb(ə)l/ *adj.* **1** (esp. of a disease) able to be passed on. **2** *archaic* communicative. □□ **communicability** /-ˈbɪlɪtɪ/ *n.* **communicably** *adv.* [ME f. OF *communicable* or LL *communicabilis* (as COMMUNICATE)]

communicant /kəˈmjuːnɪkənt/ *n.* **1** a person who receives Holy Communion, esp. regularly. **2** a person who imparts information. [L *communicare communicant-* (as COMMON)]

communicate /kəˈmjuːnɪˌkeɪt/ *v.* **1** *tr.* **a** transmit or pass on by speaking or writing (*communicated his ideas*). **b** transmit (heat, motion, etc.). **c** pass on (an infectious illness). **d** impart (feelings etc.) non-verbally (*communicated his affection*). **2** *intr.* succeed in conveying information, evoking understanding etc. (*he communicates well*). **3** *intr.* (often foll. by *with*) share a feeling or understanding; relate socially. **4** *intr.* (often foll. by *with*) (of a room etc.) have a common door (*my room communicates with yours*). **5 a** *tr.* administer Holy Communion to. **b** *intr.* receive Holy Communion. □□ **communicator** *n.* **communicatory** *adj.* [L *communicare communicat-* (as COMMON)]

communication /kəˌmjuːnɪˈkeɪʃ(ə)n/ *n.* **1 a** the act of imparting, esp. news. **b** an instance of this. **c** the information etc. communicated. **2 a** a means of connecting different places, such as a door, passage, road, or railway. **3** social intercourse (*it was difficult to maintain communication in the uproar*). **4** (in *pl.*) the science and practice of transmitting information esp. by electronic or mechanical means. **5** (in *pl.*) *Mil.* the means of transport between a base and the front. **6** a paper read to a learned society. □ **communication cord** *Brit.* a cord or chain in a railway carriage that may be pulled to stop the train in an emergency. **communication** (or **communications**) **satellite** an artificial satellite used to relay telephone circuits or broadcast programmes. **communication theory** the study of the principles and methods by which information is conveyed.

communicative /kəˈmjuːnɪkətɪv/ *adj.* **1** open, talkative, informative. **2** ready to communicate. □□ **communicatively** *adv.* [LL *communicativus* (as COMMUNICATE)]

communion /kəˈmjuːnɪən/ *n.* **1** a sharing, esp. of thoughts etc.; fellowship (*their minds were in communion*). **2** participation; a sharing in common (*communion of interests*). **3** (**Communion, Holy Communion**) **a** the Eucharist. **b** participation in the Communion service. **c** (*attrib.*) of or used in the Communion service (*Communion-table; Communion-cloth; Communion-rail*). **4** fellowship, esp. between branches of the Catholic Church. **5** a body or group within the Christian faith (*the Methodist communion*). □ **communion of saints** fellowship between Christians living and dead. [ME f. OF *communion* or L *communio* f. *communis* common]

communiqué /kəˈmjuːnɪˌkeɪ/ n. an official communication, esp. a news report. [F, = communicated]

communism /ˈkɒmjʊˌnɪz(ə)m/ n. **1** a political theory derived from Marx (see entry and MARXISM) advocating class war and leading to a society in which all property is publicly owned and each person is paid and works according to his or her needs and abilities. (See below.) **2** (usu. **Communism**) **a** the communistic form of society established in the USSR and elsewhere. **b** any movement or political doctrine advocating communism. **3** = COMMUNALISM. [F communisme f. commun COMMON]

Communism took practical form with the triumph of the Bolsheviks in the Russian Revolution in 1917, and although it has adopted many different forms in different countries, it has generally been defined in terms of the Soviet system. Perhaps the most important political force in the 20th c., Communism embraces a revolutionary ideology based on the overthrow of the capitalist system, and, in theory at least, on the notion of constant progress towards the perfect stateless society. The end of 1989 saw the collapse of bureaucratic Communism in the countries of eastern Europe against a background of its failure to meet people's economic expectations, a shift towards democracy in the USSR itself, and the known intention of the Soviet leader, Mikhail Gorbachev, not to give military assistance to other Communist regimes.

Communism Peak the highest peak in the Soviet Union, rising to 7,495 m (24,590 ft.) in the Pamir Mountains of Tadjikistan.

communist /ˈkɒmjʊnɪst/ n. & adj. —n. **1** a person advocating or practising communism. **2** (**Communist**) a member of a Communist Party. —adj. of or relating to communism (a communist play). □□ **communistic** /-ˈnɪstɪk/ adj. [COMMUNISM]

communitarian /kəˌmjuːnɪˈteərɪən/ n. & adj. —n. a member of a communistic community. —adj. of or relating to such a community. [COMMUNITY + -ARIAN after unitarian etc.]

community /kəˈmjuːnɪtɪ/ n. (pl. **-ies**) **1 a** all the people living in a specific locality. **b** a specific locality, including its inhabitants. **2** a body of people having a religion, a profession, etc., in common (the immigrant community). **3** fellowship of interests etc.; similarity (community of intellect). **4** a monastic, socialistic, etc. body practising common ownership. **5** joint ownership or liability (community of goods). **6** (prec. by the) the public. **7** a body of nations unified by common interests. **8** Ecol. a group of animals or plants living or growing together in the same area. □ **community centre** a place providing social etc. facilities for a neighbourhood. **community charge** (in the UK) a tax levied locally on every adult in a community. **community chest** US a fund for charity and welfare work in a community. **community home** Brit. a centre for housing young offenders and other juveniles in need of custodial care. **community service order** an order for a convicted offender to perform a period of unpaid work in the community. **community singing** singing by a large crowd or group, esp. of old popular songs or hymns. **community spirit** a feeling of belonging to a community, expressed in mutual support etc. [ME f. OF comuneté f. L communitas -tatis (as COMMON)]

communize /ˈkɒmjʊˌnaɪz/ v.tr. (also **-ise**) **1** make (land etc.) common property. **2** make (a person etc.) communistic. □□ **communization** /-ˈzeɪʃ(ə)n/ n. [L communis COMMON]

commutable /kəˈmjuːtəb(ə)l/ adj. **1** convertible into money; exchangeable. **2** Law (of a punishment) able to be commuted. **3** within commuting distance. □□ **commutability** /-ˈbɪlɪtɪ/ n. [L commutabilis (as COMMUTE)]

commutate /ˈkɒmjuːˌteɪt/ v.tr. Electr. **1** regulate the direction of (an alternating current), esp. to make it a direct current. **2** reverse the direction (of an electric current). [L commutare commutat- (as COMMUTE)]

commutation /ˌkɒmjuːˈteɪʃ(ə)n/ n. **1** the act or process of commuting or being commuted (in legal and exchange senses). **2** Electr. the act or process of commutating or being commutated. **3** Math. the reversal of the order of two quantities. □ **commutation ticket** US a season ticket. [F commutation or L commutatio (as COMMUTE)]

commutative /kəˈmjuːtətɪv/ adj. **1** relating to or involving substitution. **2** Math. unchanged in result by the interchange of the order of quantities. [F commutatif or med.L commutativus (as COMMUTE)]

commutator /ˈkɒmjuːˌteɪtə(r)/ n. **1** Electr. a device for reversing electric current. **2** an attachment connected with the armature of a dynamo which directs and makes continuous the current produced.

commute /kəˈmjuːt/ v. **1** intr. travel to and from one's daily work, usu. in a city, esp. by car or train. **2** tr. Law (usu. foll. by to) change (a judicial sentence etc.) to another less severe. **3** tr. (often foll. by into, for) **a** change (one kind of payment) for another. **b** make a payment etc. to change (an obligation etc.) for another. **4** tr. **a** exchange; interchange (two things). **b** change (to another thing). **5** tr. Electr. commutate. **6** intr. Math. have a commutative relation. **7** intr. US buy and use a season ticket. [L commutare commutat- (as COM-, mutare change)]

commuter /kəˈmjuːtə(r)/ n. a person who travels some distance to work, esp. in a city, usu. by car or train.

Como /ˈkəʊməʊ/, **Lake** a lake in the foothills of the Alps in north Italy, formed by a natural widening of the River Adda.

Comodoro Rivadavia /ˌkəʊməˈdɔːrəʊ ˌriːvəˈdɑːviə/ the largest seaport in Patagonia and chief centre of oil production in Argentina; pop. (1980) 99,000.

Comorin /ˈkɒmərɪn/, **Cape** a cape at the southern tip of India, in Tamil Nadu.

Comoros /kɒˈmɔːrəʊz/ a country consisting of a group of islands in the Indian Ocean north of Madagascar; pop. (est. 1988) 429,500; official languages, French and Arabic; capital, Moroni. The islands were first visited by the English at the end of the 16th c. At that time and for long afterwards Arab interest was dominant. In the mid-19th c. they came under French protection, until in 1974 all but one of the four major islands voted for independence. □□ **Comoran** adj. & n.

comose /ˈkəʊməʊs/ adj. Bot. (of seeds etc.) having hairs, downy. [L comosus (as COMA²)]

comp /kɒmp/ n. & v. colloq. —n. **1** a competition. **2** Printing a compositor. **3** Mus. an accompaniment. —v. **1** Mus. **a** tr. accompany. **b** intr. play an accompaniment. **2** Printing **a** intr. work as a compositor. **b** tr. work as a compositor on. [abbr.]

compact¹ adj., v., & n. —adj. /kəmˈpækt/ **1** closely or neatly packed together. **2** (of a piece of equipment, a room, etc.) well-fitted and practical though small. **3** (of style etc.) condensed; brief. **4** (esp. of the human body) small but well-proportioned. **5** (foll. by of) composed or made up of. —v.tr. /kəmˈpækt/ **1** join or press firmly together. **2** condense. **3** (usu. foll. by of) compose; make up. —n. /ˈkɒmpækt/ **1** a small flat usu. decorated case for face-powder and a mirror etc. **2** an object formed by compacting powder. **3** US a medium-sized motor car. □ **compact disc** /ˈkɒmpækt/ a disc on which information or sound is recorded digitally and reproduced by reflection of laser light. □□ **compaction** n. **compactly** adv. **compactness** n. **compactor** n. [ME f. L compingere compact- (as COM-, pangere fasten)]

compact² /ˈkɒmpækt/ n. an agreement or contract between two or more parties. [L compactum f. compacisci compact- (as COM-, pacisci covenant): cf. PACT]

compages /kəmˈpeɪdʒiːz/ n. (pl. same) **1** a framework; a complex structure. **2** something resembling a compages in complexity etc. [L compages (as COM-, pages f. pangere fasten)]

companion¹ /kəmˈpænjən/ n. & v. —n. **1 a** (often foll. by in, of) a person who accompanies, associates with, or shares with, another (a companion in adversity; they were close companions). **b** a person, esp. an unmarried or widowed woman, employed to live with and assist another. **2** a handbook or reference book on a particular subject (A Companion to North Wales). **3** a thing that matches another (the companion of this book-end is over there). **4** (**Companion**) a member of the lowest grade of some orders of knighthood (Companion of the Bath). **5** Astron. a star etc. that accompanies another. **6** equipment or a piece of equipment that combines several uses. —v. **1** tr. accompany. **2** intr. literary (often foll. by with) be a companion. □ **companion in arms** a fellow-soldier. **Companion of Honour** (in the UK) a member of an order founded in 1917. **Companion of Literature** (in the UK) a member of an order founded in 1961. **companion-set** a set of fireside implements on a stand. [ME f. OF *compaignon* ult. f. L *panis* bread]

companion² /kəmˈpænjən/ n. *Naut.* **1** a raised frame with windows let into the quarterdeck of a ship to allow light into the cabins etc. below. **2** = *companion-way*. □ **companion-hatch** a wooden covering over a companion-way. **companion hatchway** an opening in a deck leading to a cabin. **companion ladder** a ladder from a deck to a cabin. **companion-way** a staircase to a cabin. [obs. Du. *kompanje* quarterdeck f. OF *compagne* f. It. *(camera della) compagna* pantry, prob. ult. rel. to COMPANION¹]

companionable /kəmˈpænjənəb(ə)l/ adj. agreeable as a companion; sociable. □□ **companionableness** n. **companionably** adv.

companionate /kəmˈpænjənɪt/ adj. **1** well-suited; (of clothes) matching. **2** of or like a companion.

companionship /kəmˈpænjənʃɪp/ n. good fellowship; friendship.

company /ˈkʌmpənɪ/ n. & v. —n. (pl. **-ies**) **1 a** a number of people assembled; a crowd; an audience (*addressed the company*). **b** guests or a guest (*am expecting company*). **2** a state of being a companion or fellow; companionship, esp. of a specific kind (*enjoys low company*; *do not care for his company*). **3 a** a commercial business. **b** (usu. **Co.**) the partner or partners not named in the title of a firm (*Smith and Co.*). **4** a troupe of actors or entertainers. **5** *Mil.* a subdivision of an infantry battalion usu. commanded by a major or a captain. **6** a group of Guides. —v. (**-ies, -ied**) **1** tr. archaic accompany. **2** intr. literary (often foll. by *with*) be a companion. □ **company officer** a captain or a lower commissioned officer. **company Sergeant-major** see SERGEANT. **err** (or **be**) **in good company** discover that one's companions, or better people, have done the same as oneself. **good** (or **bad**) **company 1** a pleasant (or dull) companion. **2** a suitable (or unsuitable) associate or group of friends. **in company** not alone. **in company with** together with. **keep company** (often foll. by *with*) associate habitually. **keep** (archaic **bear**) **a person company** accompany a person; be sociable. **part company** (often foll. by *with*) cease to associate. **ship's company** the entire crew. [ME f. AF *compainie*, OF *compai(g)nie* f. Rmc (as COMPANION¹)]

comparable /ˈkɒmpərəb(ə)l/ adj. **1** (often foll. by *with*) able to be compared. **2** (often foll. by *to*) fit to be compared; worth comparing. ¶ Use with *to* and *with* corresponds to the senses at *compare*; *to* is more common. □□ **comparability** /-ˈbɪlɪtɪ/ n. **comparableness** n. **comparably** adv. [ME f. OF f. L *comparabilis* (as COMPARE)]

comparative /kəmˈpærətɪv/ adj. & n. —adj. **1** perceptible by comparison; relative (*in comparative comfort*). **2** estimated by comparison (*the comparative merits of the two ideas*). **3** of or involving comparison (esp. of sciences etc.). **4** *Gram.* (of an adjective or adverb) expressing a higher degree of a quality, but not the highest possible (e.g. *braver, more fiercely*) (cf. POSITIVE, SUPERLATIVE). —n. *Gram.* **1** the comparative expression or form of an adjective or adverb. **2** a word in the comparative. □□ **comparatively** adv. [ME f. L *comparativus* (as COMPARE)]

comparator /kəmˈpærətə(r)/ n. *Engin.* a device for comparing a product, an output, etc., with a standard, esp. an electronic circuit comparing two signals.

compare /kəmˈpeə(r)/ v. & n. —v. **1** tr. (usu. foll. by *to*) express similarities in; liken (*compared the landscape to a painting*). **2** tr. (often foll. by *to, with*) estimate the similarity or dissimilarity of; assess the relation between (*compared radio with television*; *that lacks quality compared to this*). ¶ In current use *to* and *with* are generally interchangeable, but *with* often implies a greater element of formal analysis, as in *compared my account with yours*. **3** intr. (often foll. by *with*) bear comparison (*compares favourably with the rest*). **4** intr. (often foll. by *with*) be equal or equivalent to. **5** tr. *Gram.* form the comparative and superlative degrees of (an adjective or an adverb). —n. literary comparison (*beyond compare*; *without compare*; *has no compare*). □ **compare notes** exchange ideas or opinions. [ME f. OF *comparer* f. L *comparare* (as COM-, *parare* f. *par* equal)]

comparison /kəmˈpærɪs(ə)n/ n. **1** the act or an instance of comparing. **2** a simile or semantic illustration. **3** capacity for being likened; similarity (*there's no comparison*). **4** (in full **degrees of comparison**) *Gram.* the positive, comparative, and superlative forms of adjectives and adverbs. □ **bear** (or **stand**) **comparison** (often foll. by *with*) be able to be compared favourably. **beyond comparison 1** totally different in quality. **2** greatly superior; excellent. **in comparison with** compared to. [ME f. OF *comparesoun* f. L *comparatio -onis* (as COMPARE)]

compartment /kəmˈpɑːtmənt/ n. & v. —n. **1** a space within a larger space, separated from the rest by partitions, e.g. in a railway carriage, wallet, desk, etc. **2** *Naut.* a watertight division of a ship. **3** an area of activity etc. kept apart from others in a person's mind. —v.tr. put into compartments. □□ **compartmentation** /-ˈteɪʃ(ə)n/ n. [F *compartiment* f. It. *compartimento* f. LL *compartiri* (as COM-, *partiri* share)]

compartmental /ˌkɒmpɑːtˈment(ə)l/ adj. consisting of or relating to compartments or a compartment. □□ **compartmentally** adv.

compartmentalize /ˌkɒmpɑːtˈmentəˌlaɪz/ v.tr. (also **-ise**) divide into compartments or categories. □□ **compartmentalization** /-ˈzeɪʃ(ə)n/ n.

compass /ˈkʌmpəs/ n. & v. —n. **1** (in full **magnetic compass**) an instrument showing the direction of magnetic north and bearings from it. (See below.) **2** (usu. in pl.) an instrument for taking measurements and describing circles, with two arms connected at one end by a movable joint. **3** a circumference or boundary. **4** area, extent; scope (e.g. of knowledge or experience) (*beyond my compass*). **5** the range of tones of a voice or a musical instrument. —v.tr. literary **1** hem in. **2** grasp mentally. **3** contrive, accomplish. **4** go round. □ **compass card** a circular rotating card showing the 32 principal bearings, forming the indicator of a magnetic compass. **compass rose** a circle of the principal directions marked on a chart. **compass-saw** a saw with a narrow blade, for cutting curves. **compass window** a bay window with a semicircular curve. □□ **compassable** adj. [ME f. OF *compas* ult. f. L *passus* PACE¹]

In early times navigation was by observation of landmarks or of the stars. The mariner's compass is reported in China *c*.1100, western Europe 1187, Arabia *c*.1220, and Scandinavia *c*.1300; its actual use may well be considerably earlier in each of these areas. In very small and simple compasses the compass card is fixed and the magnetic needle swings round above it; in all aircraft and ships' magnetic compasses, however, the card is laid on top of the needle and attached to it, so that the needle swings it round. In a ship the compass card not only rotates on a pivot but is arranged so that it nearly floats on a quantity of alcohol; this liquid lessens the weight on the pivot, making the compass more sensitive, and the casing of the whole is swung on gimbals so that it remains face upwards in spite of the rocking of the ship. This kind of compass, which points to the magnetic north (whose position varies over the years) is subject to a number of errors (deviations can be caused by adjacent metal fitments etc.) but is carried as an emergency instrument even when a gyrocompass is fitted.

compassion /kəmˈpæʃ(ə)n/ n. pity inclining one to help or be merciful. [ME f. OF f. eccl.L *compassio -onis* f. *compati* (as COM-, *pati* pass- suffer)]

compassionate /kəmˈpæʃənət/ adj. sympathetic, pitying. □ **compassionate leave** Brit. leave granted on grounds of bereavement etc. □□ **compassionately** adv. [obs. F *compassioné* f. *compassioner* feel pity (as COMPASSION)]

compatible /kəmˈpætəb(ə)l/ adj. **1** (often foll. by *with*) **a** able to coexist; well-suited; mutually tolerant (*a compatible couple*). **b** consistent (*their views are not compatible with their actions*). **2** (of equipment, machinery, etc.) capable of being used in combination. □□ **compatibility** /-ˈbɪlɪtɪ/ n. **compatibly** adv. [F f. med.L *compatibilis* (as COMPASSION)]

compatriot /kəmˈpætrɪət/ n. a fellow-countryman. □□ **compatriotic** /-ˈɒtɪk/ adj. [F *compatriote* f. LL *compatriota* (as COM-, *patriota* PATRIOT)]

compeer /ˈkɒmpɪə(r), -ˈpɪə(r)/ n. **1** an equal, a peer. **2** a comrade. [ME f. OF *comper* (as COM-, PEER²)]

compel /kəm'pel/ v.tr. (**compelled, compelling**) 1 (usu. foll. by to + infin.) force, constrain (compelled them to admit it). 2 bring about (an action) by force (compel submission). 3 (as **compelling** adj.) rousing strong interest, attention, conviction, or admiration. 4 archaic drive forcibly. □□ **compellable** adj. **compellingly** adv. [ME f. L compellere compuls- (as COM-, pellere drive)]

compendious /kəm'pendɪəs/ adj. (esp. of a book etc.) comprehensive but fairly brief. □□ **compendiously** adv. **compendiousness** n. [ME f. OF compendieux f. L compendiosus brief (as COMPENDIUM)]

compendium /kəm'pendɪəm/ n. (pl. **compendiums** or **compendia** /-dɪə/) 1 esp. Brit. a usu. one-volume handbook or encyclopedia. 2 a a summary or abstract of a larger work. b an abridgement. 3 a a collection of games in a box. b any collection or mixture. 4 a package of writing paper, envelopes, etc. [L, = what is weighed together, f. compendere (as COM-, pendere weigh)]

compensate /'kɒmpen,seɪt/ v. 1 tr. (often foll. by for) recompense (a person) (compensated him for his loss). 2 intr. (usu. foll. by for a thing, to a person) make amends (compensated for the insult; will compensate to her in full). 3 tr. counterbalance. 4 tr. Mech. provide (a pendulum etc.) with extra or less weight etc. to neutralize the effects of temperature etc. 5 intr. Psychol. offset a disability or frustration by development in another direction. □□ **compensative** /-sətɪv/ adj. **compensator** n. **compensatory** /-'pensətərɪ, -'seɪtərɪ/ adj. [L compensare (as COM-, pensare frequent. of pendere pens- weigh)]

compensation /,kɒmpen'seɪʃ(ə)n/ n. 1 a the act of compensating. b the process of being compensated. 2 something, esp. money, given as a recompense. 3 Psychol. a an act of compensating. b the result of compensating. 4 US a salary or wages. □ **compensation pendulum** Physics a pendulum designed to neutralize the effects of temperature variation. □□ **compensational** adj. [ME f. OF f. L compensatio (as COMPENSATE)]

compère /'kɒmpeə(r)/ n. & v. Brit. —n. a person who introduces and links the artistes in a variety show etc.; a master of ceremonies. —v. 1 tr. act as a compère to. 2 intr. act as compère. [F, = godfather f. Rmc (as COM-, L pater father)]

compete /kəm'pi:t/ v.intr. 1 (often foll. by with, against a person, for a thing) strive for superiority or supremacy (competed with his brother; compete against the Russians; compete for the victory). 2 (often foll. by in) take part (in a contest etc.) (competed in the hurdles). [L competere competit-, in late sense 'strive after or contend for (something)' (as COM-, petere seek)]

competence /'kɒmpɪt(ə)ns/ n. (also **competency** /'kɒmpɪtənsɪ/) 1 (often foll. by for, or to + infin.) ability; the state of being competent. 2 an income large enough to live on, usu. unearned. 3 Law the legal capacity (of a court, a magistrate, etc.) to deal with a matter.

competent /'kɒmpɪt(ə)nt/ adj. 1 a (usu. foll. by to + infin. or for) adequately qualified or capable (not competent to drive). b effective (a competent batsman). 2 Law (of a judge, court, or witness) legally qualified or qualifying. □□ **competently** adv. [ME f. OF competent or L competent- (as COMPETE)]

competition /,kɒmpə'tɪʃ(ə)n/ n. 1 (often foll. by for) competing, esp. in an examination, in trade, etc. 2 an event or contest in which people compete. 3 a the people competing against a person. b the opposition they represent. [LL competitio rivalry (as COMPETITIVE)]

competitive /kəm'petɪtɪv/ adj. 1 involving, offered for, or by competition (competitive contest). 2 (of prices etc.) low enough to compare well with those of rival traders. 3 (of a person) having a strong urge to win; keen to compete. □□ **competitively** adv. **competitiveness** n. [competit-, past part. stem of L competere COMPETE]

competitor /kəm'petɪtə(r)/ n. a person who competes; a rival, esp. in business or commerce. [F compétiteur or L competitor (as COMPETE)]

compilation /,kɒmpɪ'leɪʃ(ə)n/ n. 1 a the act of compiling. b the process of being compiled. 2 something compiled, esp. a book etc. composed of separate articles, stories, etc. [ME f. OF f. L compilatio -onis (as COMPILE)]

compile /kəm'paɪl/ v.tr. 1 a collect (material) into a list, volume, etc. b make up (a volume etc.) from such material. 2 accumulate (a large number of) (compiled a score of 160). 3 Computing produce (a machine-coded form of a high-level program). [ME f. OF compiler or its apparent source, L compilare plunder, plagiarize]

compiler /kəm'paɪlə(r)/ n. 1 Computing a program for translating a high-level programming language into machine code. 2 a person who compiles.

complacency /kəm'pleɪsənsɪ/ n. (also **complacence**) 1 smug self-satisfaction. 2 tranquil pleasure. [med.L complacentia f. L complacēre (as COM-, placēre please)]

complacent /kəm'pleɪs(ə)nt/ adj. 1 smugly self-satisfied. 2 calmly content. ¶ Often confused with complaisant. □□ **complacently** adv. [L complacēre: see COMPLACENCY]

complain /kəm'pleɪn/ v.intr. 1 (often foll. by about, at, or that + clause) express dissatisfaction (complained at the state of the room; is always complaining). 2 (foll. by of) a announce that one is suffering from (an ailment) (complained of a headache). b state a grievance concerning (complained of the delay). 3 make a mournful sound; groan, creak under a strain. □□ **complainer** n. **complainingly** adv. [ME f. OF complaindre (stem complaign-) f. med.L complangere bewail (as COM-, plangere planct- lament)]

complainant /kəm'pleɪnənt/ n. Law a plaintiff in certain lawsuits.

complaint /kəm'pleɪnt/ n. 1 an act of complaining. 2 a grievance. 3 an ailment or illness. 4 US Law the plaintiff's case in a civil action. [ME f. OF complainte f. complaint past part. of complaindre: see COMPLAIN]

complaisant /kəm'pleɪz(ə)nt/ adj. 1 politely deferential. 2 willing to please; acquiescent. ¶ Often confused with complacent. □□ **complaisance** n. [F f. complaire (stem complais-) acquiesce to please, f. L complacēre: see COMPLACENCY]

compleat archaic var. of COMPLETE.

complement n. & v. —n./'kɒmplɪmənt/ 1 a something that completes. b one of a pair, or one of two things that go together. 2 (often **full complement**) the full number needed to man a ship, fill a conveyance, etc. 3 Gram. a word or phrase added to a verb to complete the predicate of a sentence. 4 Biochem. a group of proteins in the blood capable of lysing bacteria etc. 5 Math. any element not belonging to a specified set or class. 6 Geom. the amount by which an angle is less than 90° (cf. SUPPLEMENT). —v.tr. /'kɒmplɪ,ment/ 1 complete. 2 form a complement to (the scarf complements her dress). □□ **complemental** /-'ment(ə)l/ adj. [ME f. L complementum (as COMPLETE)]

complementarity /,kɒmplɪ,men'tærɪtɪ/ n. (pl. **-ies**) 1 a complementary relationship or situation. 2 Physics the concept that a single model may not be adequate to explain atomic systems in different experimental conditions.

complementary /,kɒmplɪ'mentərɪ/ adj. 1 completing; forming a complement. 2 (of two or more things) complementing each other. □ **complementary angle** either of two angles making up 90°. **complementary colour** a colour that combined with a given colour makes white or black. □□ **complementarily** adv. **complementariness** n.

complete /kəm'pli:t/ adj. & v. —adj. 1 having all its parts; entire (the set is complete). 2 finished (my task is complete). 3 of the maximum extent or degree (a complete surprise; a complete stranger). 4 (also **compleat** after Walton's Compleat Angler) joc. accomplished (the complete horseman). —v.tr. 1 finish. 2 a make whole or perfect. b make up the amount of (completes the quota). 3 fill in the answers to (a questionnaire etc.). 4 (usu. absol.) Law conclude a sale of property. □ **complete with** having (as an important accessory) (comes complete with instructions). □□ **completely** adv. **completeness** n. **completion** /-'pli:ʃ(ə)n/ n. [ME f. OF complet or L completus past part. of complēre fill up]

complex /'kɒmpleks/ n. & adj. —n. 1 a building, a series of rooms, a network, etc. made up of related parts (the arts complex). 2 Psychol. a related group of usu. repressed feelings or thoughts which cause abnormal behaviour or mental states. 3 (in general use) a preoccupation or obsession (has a complex about punctuality). 4 Chem. a compound in which molecules or ions form coordinate bonds to a metal atom or ion. —adj. 1 consisting of related parts; composite. **2** complicated (*a complex problem*). **3** *Math.* containing real and imaginary parts (cf. IMAGINARY). □ **complex sentence** a sentence containing a subordinate clause or clauses. □□ **complexity** /kəmˈpleksɪtɪ/ *n.* (*pl.* **-ies**).

complexly *adv.* [F *complexe* or L *complexus* past part. of *complectere* embrace, assoc. with *complexus* plaited]

complexion /kəmˈplekʃ(ə)n/ *n.* **1** the natural colour, texture, and appearance, of the skin, esp. of the face. **2** an aspect; a character (*puts a different complexion on the matter*). □□ **complexioned** *adj.* (also in *comb.*) [ME f. OF f. L *complexio -onis* (as COMPLEX): orig. = combination of supposed qualities determining the nature of a body]

complexionless /kəmˈplekʃənlɪs/ *adj.* pale-skinned.

compliance /kəmˈplaɪəns/ *n.* **1** the act or an instance of complying; obedience to a request, command, etc. **2** *Mech.* **a** the capacity to yield under an applied force. **b** the degree of such yielding. **3** unworthy acquiescence. □ **in compliance with** according to (a wish, command, etc.).

compliant /kəmˈplaɪənt/ *adj.* disposed to comply; yielding, obedient. □□ **compliantly** *adv.*

complicate /ˈkɒmplɪˌkeɪt/ *v.tr.* & *intr.* **1** (often foll. by *with*) make or become difficult, confused, or complex. **2** (as **complicated** *adj.*) complex; intricate. □□ **complicatedly** *adv.* **complicatedness** *n.* [L *complicare complicat-* (as COM-, *plicare* fold)]

complication /ˌkɒmplɪˈkeɪʃ(ə)n/ *n.* **1 a** an involved or confused condition or state. **b** a complicating circumstance; a difficulty. **2** *Med.* a secondary disease or condition aggravating a previous one. [F *complication* or LL *complicatio* (as COMPLICATE)]

complicity /kəmˈplɪsɪtɪ/ *n.* partnership in a crime or wrongdoing. [*complice* (see ACCOMPLICE) + -ITY]

compliment *n.* & *v.* —*n.* /ˈkɒmplɪmənt/ **1 a** a spoken or written expression of praise. **b** an act or circumstance implying praise (*their success was a compliment to their efforts*). **2** (in *pl.*) **a** formal greetings, esp. as a written accompaniment to a gift etc. (*with the compliments of the management*). **b** praise (*my compliments to the cook*). —*v.tr.* /ˈkɒmplɪˌment/ **1** (often foll. by *on*) congratulate; praise (*complimented him on his roses*). **2** (often foll. by *with*) present as a mark of courtesy (*complimented her with his attention*). □ **compliments of the season** greetings appropriate to the time of year, esp. Christmas. **compliments slip** a printed slip of paper sent with a gift etc., esp. from a business firm. **pay a compliment to** praise. **return the compliment 1** give a compliment in return for another. **2** retaliate or recompense in kind. [F *complimenter* f. It. *complimento* ult. f. L (as COMPLEMENT)]

complimentary /ˌkɒmplɪˈmentərɪ/ *adj.* **1** expressing a compliment; praising. **2** (of a ticket for a play etc.) given free of charge, esp. as a mark of favour. □□ **complimentarily** *adv.*

compline /ˈkɒmplɪn, -plaɪn/ *n. Eccl.* **1** the last of the canonical hours of prayer. **2** the service taking place during this. [ME f. OF *complie*, fem. past part. of obs. *complir* complete, ult. f. L *complēre* fill up]

comply /kəmˈplaɪ/ *v.intr.* (**-ies**, **-ied**) (often foll. by *with*) act in accordance (with a wish, command, etc.) (*complied with her expectation; had no choice but to comply*). [It. *complire* f. Cat. *complir*, Sp. *cumplir* f. L *complēre* fill up]

compo /ˈkɒmpəʊ/ *n.* & *adj.* —*n.* (*pl.* **-os**) a composition of plaster etc., e.g. stucco. —*adj.* = COMPOSITE. □ **compo rations** a large pack of food designed to last for several days. [abbr.]

component /kəmˈpəʊnənt/ *n.* & *adj.* —*n.* **1** a part of a larger whole, esp. part of a motor vehicle. **2** *Math.* one of two or more vectors equivalent to a given vector. —*adj.* being part of a larger whole (*assembled the component parts*). □□ **componential** /ˌkɒmpəˈnenʃ(ə)l/ *adj.* [L *componere component-* (as COM-, *ponere* put)]

comport /kəmˈpɔːt/ *v.refl. literary* conduct oneself; behave. □ **comport with** suit, befit. □□ **comportment** *n.* [L *comportare* (as COM-, *portare* carry)]

compos var. of COMPOS MENTIS.

compose /kəmˈpəʊz/ *v.* **1 a** *tr.* construct or create (a work of art, esp. literature or music). **b** *intr.* compose music (*gave up composing in 1917*). **2** *tr.* constitute; make up (*six tribes which composed the German nation*). ¶ Preferred to *comprise* in this sense.

3 *tr.* put together to form a whole, esp. artistically; order; arrange (*composed the group for the photographer*). **4** *tr.* **a** (often *refl.*) calm; settle (*compose your expression; composed himself to wait*). **b** (as **composed** *adj.*) calm, settled. **5** *tr.* settle (a dispute etc.). **6** *tr. Printing* **a** set up (type) to form words and blocks of words. **b** set up (a manuscript etc.) in type. □ **composed of** made up of, consisting of (*a flock composed of sheep and goats*). □□ **composedly** /-zɪdlɪ/ *adv.* [F *composer*, f. L *componere* (as COM-, *ponere* put)]

composer /kəmˈpəʊzə(r)/ *n.* a person who composes (esp. music).

composite /ˈkɒmpəzɪt, -ˌzaɪt/ *adj., n.,* & *v.* —*adj.* **1** made up of various parts; blended. **2** (esp. of a synthetic building material) made up of recognizable constituents. **3** *Archit.* of the fifth classical order of architecture, consisting of elements of the Ionic and Corinthian orders. **4** *Bot.* of the plant family Compositae. —*n.* **1** a thing made up of several parts or elements. **2** a synthetic building material. **3** *Bot.* any plant of the family Compositae, having a head of many small flowers forming one bloom, e.g. the daisy or the dandelion. **4** *Polit.* a resolution composed of two or more related resolutions. —*v.tr. Polit.* amalgamate (two or more similar resolutions). □□ **compositely** *adv.* **compositeness** *n.* [F f. L *compositus* past part. of *componere* (as COM-, *ponere posit-* put)]

composition /ˌkɒmpəˈzɪʃ(ə)n/ *n.* **1 a** the act of putting together; formation or construction. **b** something so composed; a mixture. **c** the constitution of such a mixture; the nature of its ingredients (*the composition is two parts oil to one part vinegar*). **2 a** a literary or musical work. **b** the act or art of producing such a work. **c** an essay, esp. written by a schoolchild. **d** an artistic arrangement (of parts of a picture, subjects for a photograph, etc.). **3** mental constitution; character (*jealousy is not in his composition*). **4** (often *attrib.*) a compound artificial substance, esp. one serving the purpose of a natural one. **5** *Printing* the setting-up of type. **6** *Gram.* the formation of words into a compound word. **7** *Law* **a** a compromise, esp. a legal agreement to pay a sum in lieu of a larger sum, or other obligation (*made a composition with his creditors*). **b** a sum paid in this way. **8** *Math.* the combination of functions in a series. □□ **compositional** *adj.* **compositionally** *adv.* [ME f. OF, f. L *compositio -onis* (as COMPOSITE)]

compositor /kəmˈpɒzɪtə(r)/ *n. Printing* a person who sets up type for printing. [ME f. AF *compositour* f. L *compositor* (as COMPOSITE)]

compos mentis /ˌkɒmpɒs ˈmentɪs/ *adj.* (also **compos**) having control of one's mind; sane. [L]

compossible /kəmˈpɒsɪb(ə)l/ *adj. formal* (often foll. by *with*) able to coexist. [OF f. med.L *compossibilis* (as COM-, POSSIBLE)]

compost /ˈkɒmpɒst/ *n.* & *v.* —*n.* **1 a** a mixed manure, esp. of organic origin. **b** a loam soil or other medium with added compost, used for growing plants. **2** a mixture of ingredients (*a rich compost of lies and innuendo*). —*v.tr.* **1** treat (soil) with compost. **2** make (manure, vegetable matter, etc.) into compost. □ **compost heap** (or **pile**) a layered structure of garden refuse, soil, etc., which decays to become compost. [ME f. OF *composte* f. L *compos(i)tum* (as COMPOSITE)]

composure /kəmˈpəʊʒə(r)/ *n.* a tranquil manner; calmness. [COMPOSE + -URE]

compote /ˈkɒmpəʊt, -pɒt/ *n.* fruit preserved or cooked in syrup. [F f. OF *composte* (as COMPOSITE)]

compound[1] /ˈkɒmpaʊnd/ *n., adj.,* & *v.* —*n.* **1** a mixture of two or more things, qualities, etc. **2** (also **compound word**) a word made up of two or more existing words. **3** *Chem.* a substance formed from two or more elements chemically united in fixed proportions. —*adj.* **1 a** made up of several ingredients. **b** consisting of several parts. **2** combined; collective. **3** *Zool.* consisting of individual organisms. **4** *Biol.* consisting of several or many parts. —*v.* /kəmˈpaʊnd/ **1** *tr.* mix or combine (ingredients, ideas, motives, etc.) (*grief compounded with fear*). **2** *tr.* increase or complicate (difficulties etc.) (*anxiety compounded by discomfort*). **3** *tr.* make up (a composite whole). **4** *tr.* (also *absol.*) settle (a debt, dispute, etc.) by concession or special arrangement. **5** *tr. Law* **a** condone (a liability or offence) in exchange for money etc. **b**

forbear from prosecuting (a felony) from private motives. **6** *intr.* (usu. foll. by *with, for*) *Law* come to terms with a person, for forgoing a claim etc. for an offence. **7** *tr.* combine (words or elements) into a word. □ **compound eye** an eye consisting of numerous visual units, as found in insects and crustaceans. **compound fracture** a fracture complicated by a skin wound. **compound interest** interest payable on capital and its accumulated interest (cf. *simple interest*). **compound interval** *Mus.* an interval exceeding one octave. **compound leaf** a leaf consisting of several or many leaflets. **compound sentence** a sentence with more than one subject or predicate. **compound time** *Mus.* music having more than one group of simple-time units in each bar. □□ **compoundable** /kəmˈpaʊndəb(ə)l/ *adj.* [ME *compoun(e)* f. OF *compondre* f. L *componere* (as COM-, *ponere* put: -*d* as in *expound*)]

compound² /ˈkɒmpaʊnd/ *n.* **1** a large open enclosure for housing workers etc., esp. miners in S. Africa. **2** an enclosure, esp. in India, China, etc., in which a factory or a house stands (cf. KAMPONG). **3** a large enclosed space in a prison or prison camp. **4** = POUND³. [Port. *campon* or Du. *kampong* f. Malay]

comprador /ˌkɒmprəˈdɔː(r)/ *n.* (also **compradore**) **1** *hist.* a Chinese business agent of a foreign company. **2** an agent of a foreign power. [Port. *comprador* buyer f. LL *comparator* f. L *comparare* purchase]

comprehend /ˌkɒmprɪˈhend/ *v.tr.* **1** grasp mentally; understand (a person or a thing). **2** include; take in. [ME f. OF *comprehender* or L *comprehendere comprehens-* (as COM-, *prehendere* grasp)]

comprehensible /ˌkɒmprɪˈhensɪb(ə)l/ *adj.* **1** that can be understood; intelligible. **2** that can be included or contained. □□ **comprehensibility** /-ˈbɪlɪtɪ/ *n.* **comprehensibly** *adv.* [F *compréhensible* or L *comprehensibilis* (as COMPREHEND)]

comprehension /ˌkɒmprɪˈhenʃ(ə)n/ *n.* **1 a** the act or capability of understanding, esp. writing or speech. **b** an extract from a text set as an examination, with questions designed to test understanding of it. **2** inclusion. **3** *Eccl. hist.* the inclusion of Nonconformists in the Anglican Church. [F *compréhension* or L *comprehensio* (as COMPREHENSIBLE)]

comprehensive /ˌkɒmprɪˈhensɪv/ *adj. & n.* —*adj.* **1** complete; including all or nearly all elements, aspects, etc. (*a comprehensive grasp of the subject*). **2** of or relating to understanding (*the comprehensive faculty*). **3** (of motor-vehicle insurance) providing complete protection. —*n.* (in full **comprehensive school**) *Brit.* a secondary school catering for children of all abilities from a given area. □□ **comprehensively** *adv.* **comprehensiveness** *n.* [F *compréhensif -ive* or LL *comprehensivus* (as COMPREHENSIBLE)]

compress *v. & n.* —*v.tr.* /kəmˈpres/ **1** squeeze together. **2** bring into a smaller space or shorter extent. —*n.* /ˈkɒmpres/ a pad of lint etc. pressed on to part of the body to relieve inflammation, stop bleeding, etc. □ **compressed air** air at more than atmospheric pressure. □□ **compressible** /kəmˈpresɪb(ə)l/ *adj.* **compressibility** /-ˈbɪlɪtɪ/ *n.* **compressive** /kəmˈpresɪv/ *adj.* [ME f. OF *compresser* or LL *compressare* frequent. of L *comprimere compress-* (as COM-, *premere* press)]

compression /kəmˈpreʃ(ə)n/ *n.* **1** the act of compressing or being compressed. **2** the reduction in volume (causing an increase in pressure) of the fuel mixture in an internal-combustion engine before ignition. [F f. L *compressio* (as COMPRESS)]

compressor /kəmˈpresə(r)/ *n.* an instrument or device for compressing, esp. a machine used for increasing the pressure of air or other gases.

comprise /kəmˈpraɪz/ *v.tr.* **1** include; comprehend. **2** consist of, be composed of (*the book comprises 350 pages*). **3** *disp.* make up, compose (*the essays comprise his total work*). □□ **comprisable** *adj.* [ME f. F, fem. past part. of *comprendre* COMPREHEND]

compromise /ˈkɒmprəˌmaɪz/ *n. & v.* —*n.* **1** the settlement of a dispute by mutual concession (*reached a compromise by bargaining*). **2** (often foll. by *between*) an intermediate state between conflicting opinions, actions, etc., reached by mutual concession or modification (*a compromise between ideals and material necessity*). —*v.* **1 a** *intr.* settle a dispute by mutual concession (*compromised

over the terms*). **b** *tr. archaic* settle (a dispute) by mutual concession. **2** *tr.* bring into disrepute or danger esp. by indiscretion or folly. □□ **compromiser** *n.* **compromisingly** *adv.* [ME f. OF *compromis* f. LL *compromissum* neut. past part. of *compromittere* (as COM-, *promittere* PROMISE)]

compte rendu /ˌkɔ̃trɑːˈdjuː/ *n.* (*pl.* **comptes rendus** pronunc. same) a report; a review; a statement. [F]

Comptometer /kɒmpˈtɒmɪtə(r)/ *n. propr.* an early type of calculating-machine. [app. f. F *compte* COUNT¹ + -METER]

Compton /ˈkɒmpt(ə)n/, Arthur Holly (1892–1962), American physicist who, in 1923, observed that the wavelength of X-rays increased when scattered by electrons. This became known as the Compton effect and demonstrates the dual particle and wave properties of electromagnetic radiation and matter predicted by quantum theory. He shared the 1927 Nobel Prize for physics with C. T. R. Wilson, the inventor of the cloud chamber, a device that Compton had used in this research. During the Second World War he developed plutonium production at Chicago for the Manhattan Project (see entry).

Compton-Burnett /ˌkɒmptənbɜːˈnet/, Dame Ivy (1884–1969), English novelist. She embarked on her serious literary career with *Pastors and Masters* (1925) which, with other early works, notably *Brothers and Sisters* (1929), reflected her brittle deflationary wit and satirical exuberance. Her highly individual novels, composed almost entirely in dialogue, including *A House and Its Head* (1935), *A Family and a Fortune* (1939), and *Manservant and Maidservant* (1947), set in large gloomy houses, portray inward-looking self-contained high-Victorian households ruled by a tyrannical parent or grandparent. They deal with domestic crime ranging from adultery, incest, child abuse, to murder and fraud, providing the author with an ideal environment in which to examine the misuse of power.

comptroller /kənˈtrəʊlə(r)/ *n.* a controller (used in the title of some financial officers) (*Comptroller and Auditor General*). [var. of CONTROLLER, by erron. assoc. with COUNT¹, L *computus*]

compulsion /kəmˈpʌlʃ(ə)n/ *n.* **1** a constraint; an obligation. **2** *Psychol.* an irresistible urge to a form of behaviour, esp. against one's conscious wishes. □ **under compulsion** because one is compelled. [ME f. F f. LL *compulsio -onis* (as COMPEL)]

compulsive /kəmˈpʌlsɪv/ *adj.* **1** compelling. **2** resulting or acting from, or as if from, compulsion (*a compulsive gambler*). **3** *Psychol.* resulting or acting from compulsion against one's conscious wishes. **4** irresistible (*compulsive entertainment*). □□ **compulsively** *adv.* **compulsiveness** *n.* [med.L *compulsivus* (as COMPEL)]

compulsory /kəmˈpʌlsərɪ/ *adj.* **1** required by law or a rule (*is compulsory to keep dogs on leads*). **2** essential; necessary. □ **compulsory purchase** the enforced purchase of land or property by a local authority etc., for public use. □□ **compulsorily** *adv.* **compulsoriness** *n.* [med.L *compulsorius* (as COMPEL)]

compunction /kəmˈpʌŋkʃ(ə)n/ *n.* (usu. with *neg.*) **1** the pricking of the conscience. **2** a slight regret; a scruple (*without compunction; have no compunction in refusing him*). □□ **compunctious** /-ʃəs/ *adj.* **compunctiously** /-ʃəslɪ/ *adv.* [ME f. OF *componction* f. eccl.L *compunctio -onis* f. L *compungere compunct-* (as COM-, *pungere* prick)]

compurgation /ˌkɒmpɜːˈɡeɪʃ(ə)n/ *n. Law hist.* an acquittal from a charge or accusation obtained by the oaths of witnesses. □□ **compurgatory** /kəmˈpɜːɡətərɪ/ *adj.* [med.L *compurgatio* f. L *compurgare* (as COM-, *purgare* purify)]

compurgator /ˈkɒmpɜːˌɡeɪtə(r)/ *n. Law hist.* a witness who swore to the innocence or good character of an accused person.

computation /ˌkɒmpjuːˈteɪʃ(ə)n/ *n.* **1** the act or an instance of reckoning; calculation. **2** the use of a computer (see entry). **3** a result obtained by calculation.□□ **computational** *adj.*

compute /kəmˈpjuːt/ *v.* **1** *tr.* (often foll. by *that* + clause) reckon or calculate (a number, an amount, etc.). **2** *intr.* make a reckoning, esp. using a computer. □□ **computability** /-təˈbɪlɪtɪ/ *n.* **computable** /-ˈpjuːtəb(ə)l/, ˈkɒm-/ *adj.* [F *computer* or L *computare* (as COM-, *putare* reckon)]

computer /kəmˈpjuːtə(r)/ *n.* **1** a usu. electronic device for storing and processing data (usu. in binary form), according to instructions given to it in a variable program. (See below.) **2** a person who computes or makes calculations. ◻ **computer-literate** able to use computers; familiar with the operation of computers. **computer science** the study of the principles and use of computers. **computer virus** a hidden code within a computer program intended to corrupt a system or destroy data stored in it.

The characteristic feature of all digital computers is the ability to store, and hence change rapidly, the operating program; they can operate at their own speed (up to several million instructions per second) and can therefore perform tasks too large to be completed in a human time-scale. The two major components of a computing system are the hardware (its physical elements) and the software (programs controlling the system). The three main elements of the hardware are the central processing unit (which processes the data), the memory (which stores the data before and after processing), and the peripheral (input/output) devices, which link the computer with the outside world by enabling information to be fed into the machine and produced by it (as a printout, magnetic tape, or display on a VDU) after processing. Information is converted into binary form (see BINARY SCALE) for storage and manipulation, the digits 0 and 1 representing the 'off' and 'on' positions of electronic switches. Computers are unusual tools in that their function can be altered by the software, without physical change, and hence a single machine can be used for a variety of disparate purposes.

Computing history is usually considered to start with Charles Babbage (see entry) who, between 1822 and 1871, designed a series of uncompleted machines able to perform calculations on different formulae. In 1936 the English mathematician Alan Turing showed that a single machine (the future computer) could process any problem if given rules for the solution. The Second World War provided the stimulus for the construction of practical machines in Germany, the UK, and the US. Since 1945 there has been an accelerating reduction in size and cost coupled with increased power and reliability as valves (first generation) were replaced by transistors (second generation) and these by integrated circuits of diminishing size and increasing complexity (third generation), followed by large-scale integration of circuits (4th generation); microelectronic technologies are likely to produce further innovations, with 'parallel processing' an increasingly common feature. Advances have led to rapid improvements in the performance of all types of systems and to the development of minicomputers and the widely-used microcomputer or personal computers. The boundaries between systems are frequently blurred: many personal computers are now more powerful than mainframe computers of the 1960s, and minicomputers are frequently used for applications that required mainframe computers in the late 1970s and early 1980s. The availability of low-cost optical discs, such as CD-ROM, together with improvements in computer graphics, are likely to lead to multimedia applications which will use sound, images, and moving pictures as well as more traditional data. (See also ARTIFICIAL INTELLIGENCE.)

computerize /kəm'pjuːtəˌraɪz/ v.tr. (also **-ise**) **1** equip with a computer; install a computer in. **2** store, perform, or produce by computer. ◻◻ **computerization** /-'zeɪʃ(ə)n/ n.

comrade /'kɒmreɪd, -rɪd/ n. **1 a** (usu. of males) a workmate, friend, or companion. **b** (also **comrade-in-arms**) a fellow soldier etc. **2** Polit. a fellow socialist or communist (often as a form of address). ◻◻ **comradely** adj. **comradeship** n. [earlier cama-camerade f. F camerade, camarade (orig. fem.) f. Sp. camarada roommate (as CHAMBER)]

comsat /'kɒmsæt/ n. a communication satellite. [abbr.]

Comte /kɔ̃t/, Auguste (1798–1857), French positivist philosopher. A republican who rebelled against his Catholic upbringing, he sought to come to terms with the changing political and industrial world. In his historical study of the progress of the human mind he discerned three phases—the theological, the metaphysical, and the positive; with the discrediting of the former types of explanation only the last phase survives in mature sciences, where there is simply a study of relations of succession and resemblance which are subsumed under laws. Comte attempted to show that sciences each evolve from one another developing their own laws in due course, and held that the latest and last science was sociology which had not yet reached its positive stage.

con[1] /kɒn/ n. & v. sl. —n. a confidence trick. —v.tr. (**conned, conning**) swindle; deceive (conned him into thinking he had won). ◻ **con man** = confidence man. [abbr.]

con[2] /kɒn/ n., prep., & adv. —n. (usu. in pl.) a reason against. —prep. & adv. against (cf. PRO[2]). [L contra against]

con[3] /kɒn/ n. sl. a convict. [abbr.]

con[4] /kɒn/ v.tr. (US **conn**) (**conned, conning**) Naut. direct the steering of (a ship). [app. weakened form of obs. cond, condie, f. F conduire f. L conducere CONDUCT]

con[5] /kɒn/ v.tr. (**conned, conning**) archaic (often foll. by over) study, learn by heart (conned his part well). [ME cunn-, con; forms of CAN[1]]

con- /kɒn, kən/ prefix assim. form of COM- before c, d, f, g, j, n, q, s, t, v, and sometimes before vowels.

conacre /'kɒnˌeɪkə(r)/ n. Ir. the letting by a tenant of small portions of land prepared for crops or grazing. [CORN[1] + ACRE]

Conakry /'kɒnəˌkriː/ the capital and chief port of Guinea; pop. (est. 1983) 705,300.

con amore /ˌkɒn æ'mɔːrɪ/ adv. **1** with devotion or zeal. **2** (**con amore**) Mus. tenderly. [It., = with love]

conation /kə'neɪʃ(ə)n/ n. Philos. & Psychol. **1** the desire to perform an action. **2** voluntary action; volition. ◻◻ **conative** /'kɒnətɪv, 'kəʊ-/ adj. [L conatio f. conari try]

con brio /kɒn 'briːəʊ/ adv. Mus. with vigour. [It.]

concatenate /kən'kætɪˌneɪt/ v. & adj. —v.tr. link together (a chain of events, things, etc.). —adj. joined; linked. ◻◻ **concatenation** /-'neɪʃ(ə)n/ n. [LL concatenare (as COM-, catenare f. catena chain)]

concave /'kɒnkeɪv/ adj. having an outline or surface curved like the interior of a circle or sphere (cf. CONVEX). ◻◻ **concavely** adv. **concavity** /-'kævɪtɪ/ n. [L concavus (as COM-, cavus hollow), or through F concave]

conceal /kən'siːl/ v.tr. **1** (often foll. by from) keep secret (concealed her motive from him). **2** not allow to be seen; hide (concealed the letter in her pocket). ◻◻ **concealer** n. **concealment** n. [ME f. OF conceler f. L concelare (as COM-, celare hide)]

concede /kən'siːd/ v.tr. **1 a** (often foll. by that + clause) admit (a defeat etc.) to be true (conceded that his work was inadequate). **b** admit defeat in. **2** (often foll. by to) grant, yield, or surrender (a right, a privilege, points or a start in a game, etc.). **3** Sport allow an opponent to score (a goal) or to win (a match), etc. ◻◻ **conceder** n. [F concéder or L concedere concess- (as COM-, cedere yield)]

conceit /kən'siːt/ n. **1** personal vanity; pride. **2** literary **a** a far-fetched comparison, esp. as a stylistic affectation; a convoluted or unlikely metaphor. **b** a fanciful notion. [ME f. CONCEIVE after deceit, deceive, etc.]

conceited /kən'siːtɪd/ adj. vain, proud. ◻◻ **conceitedly** adv. **conceitedness** n.

conceivable /kən'siːvəb(ə)l/ adj. capable of being grasped or imagined; understandable. ◻◻ **conceivability** /-'bɪlɪtɪ/ n. **conceivably** adv.

conceive /kən'siːv/ v. **1** intr. become pregnant. **2** tr. become pregnant with (a child). **3** (often foll. by that + clause) **a** imagine, fancy, think (can't conceive that he could be guilty). **b** (usu. in passive) formulate, express (a belief, a plan, etc.). ◻ **conceive of** form in the mind; imagine. [ME f. OF conceiv- stressed stem of conceivre f. L concipere concept- (as COM-, capere take)]

concelebrate /kən'selɪˌbreɪt/ v.intr. RC Ch. **1** (of two or more priests) celebrate the mass together. **2** (esp. of a newly ordained priest) celebrate the mass with the ordaining bishop. ◻◻ **concelebrant** /-brənt/ n. **concelebration** /-'breɪʃ(ə)n/ n. [L concelebrare (as COM-, celebrare CELEBRATE)]

concentrate /'kɒnsənˌtreɪt/ v. & n. —v. **1** intr. (often foll. by on, upon) focus all one's attention or mental ability. **2** tr. bring together (troops, power, attention, etc.) to one point; focus. **3** tr.

increase the strength of (a liquid etc.) by removing water or any other diluting agent. **4** *tr.* (as **concentrated** *adj.*) (of hate etc.) intense, strong. —*n.* **1** a concentrated substance. **2** a concentrated form of esp. food. □□ **concentratedly** *adv.* **concentrative** *adj.* **concentrator** *n.* [after *concentre* f. F *concentrer* (as CON- + CENTRE)]

concentration /ˌkɒnsənˈtreɪʃ(ə)n/ *n.* **1 a** the act or power of concentrating (*needs to develop concentration*). **b** an instance of this (*interrupted my concentration*). **2** something concentrated (*a concentration of resources*). **3** something brought together; a gathering. **4** the weight of substance in a given weight or volume of material. □ **concentration camp 1** a camp for the detention of political prisoners, internees, etc., esp. in Nazi Germany. **2** any of the camps (instituted by Lord Kitchener) where noncombatants of a district were accommodated during the Second Boer War of 1899–1902. A similar type of camp had been introduced in Cuba in 1896–7 during the struggle for independence from Spanish rule. The Spanish general Valeriano Weyler y Nicolau, nicknamed 'the Butcher', instituted a system of 'reconcentration', in which many thousands of Cubans were forced into camps where they died of starvation and disease.

concentre /kɒnˈsentə(r)/ *v.tr.* & *intr.* (*US* **concenter**) bring or come to a common centre. [F *concentrer*: see CONCENTRATE]

concentric /kɒnˈsentrɪk/ *adj.* (often foll. by *with*) (esp. of circles) having a common centre (cf. ECCENTRIC). □□ **concentrically** *adv.* **concentricity** /ˌkɒnsenˈtrɪsɪti/ *n.* [ME f. OF *concentrique* or med.L *concentricus* (as COM-, *centricus* as CENTRE)]

Concepción /kɒnˌsepsɪˈəʊn/ an industrial city in south central Chile; pop. (est. 1987) 294,400. Its port, on the Pacific coast, is Talcahuano.

concept /ˈkɒnsept/ *n.* **1** a general notion; an abstract idea (*the concept of evolution*). **2** *colloq.* an idea or invention to help sell or publicize a commodity (*a new concept in swimwear*). **3** *Philos.* an idea or mental picture of a group or class of objects formed by combining all their aspects. [LL *conceptus* f. *concept-*: see CONCEIVE]

conception /kənˈsepʃ(ə)n/ *n.* **1** the act or an instance of conceiving; the process of being conceived. **2** an idea or plan, esp. as being new or daring (*the whole conception showed originality*). □ **no conception of** an inability to imagine. □□ **conceptional** *adj.* [ME f. OF f. L *conceptio -onis* (as CONCEPT)]

conceptive /kənˈseptɪv/ *adj.* **1** conceiving mentally. **2** of conception. [L *conceptivus* as CONCEPT]

conceptual /kənˈseptjʊəl/ *adj.* of mental conceptions or concepts. □□ **conceptually** *adv.* [med.L *conceptualis* (*conceptus* as CONCEPT)]

conceptualism /kənˈseptjʊəˌlɪz(ə)m/ *n.* *Philos.* the theory that universals exist, but only as concepts in the mind. □□ **conceptualist** *n.*

conceptualize /kənˈseptjʊəˌlaɪz/ *v.tr.* (also **-ise**) form a concept or idea of. □□ **conceptualization** /-ˈzeɪʃ(ə)n/ *n.*

concern /kənˈsɜːn/ *v.* & *n.* —*v.tr.* **1 a** be relevant or important to (*this concerns you*). **b** relate to; be about. **2** (usu. *refl.*; often foll. by *with*, *in*, *about*, or *to* + *infin.*) interest or involve oneself (*don't concern yourself with my problems*). **3** worry, affect (*it concerns me that he is always late*). —*n.* **1** anxiety, worry (*felt a deep concern*). **2 a** a matter of interest or importance to one (*no concern of mine*). **b** (usu. in *pl.*) affairs, private business (*meddling in my concerns*). **3** a business, a firm (*quite a prosperous concern*). **4** *colloq.* a complicated or awkward thing (*have lost the whole concern*). □ **have a concern in** have an interest or share in. **have no concern with** have nothing to do with. **to whom it may concern** to those who have a proper interest in the matter (as an address to the reader of a testimonial, reference, etc.). [F *concerner* or LL *concernere* (as COM-, *cernere* sift, discern)]

concerned /kənˈsɜːnd/ *adj.* **1** involved, interested (*the people concerned*; *concerned with proving his innocence*). **2** (often foll. by *that*, *about*, *at*, *for*, or *to* + *infin.*) troubled, anxious (*concerned about him*; *concerned to hear that*). □ **as** (or **so**) **far as I am concerned** as regards my interests. **be concerned** (often foll. by *in*) take part. **I am not concerned** it is not my business. □□ **concernedly** /-ˈsɜːnɪdlɪ/ *adv.* **concernedness** /-ˈsɜːnɪdnɪs/ *n.*

concerning /kənˈsɜːnɪŋ/ *prep.* about, regarding.

concernment /kənˈsɜːnmənt/ *n.* *formal* **1** an affair or business. **2** importance. **3** (often foll. by *with*) a state of being concerned; anxiety.

concert *n.* & *v.* —*n.* /ˈkɒnsət/ **1** a musical performance of usu. several separate compositions. **2** agreement, accordance, harmony. **3** a combination of voices or sounds. —*v.tr.* /kənˈsɜːt/ arrange (by mutual agreement or coordination). □ **concert-goer** a person who often goes to concerts. **concert grand** the largest size of grand piano, used for concerts. **concert-master** esp. *US* the leading first-violin player in some orchestras. **concert overture** *Mus.* a piece like an overture but intended for independent performance. **concert performance** *Mus.* a performance (of an opera etc.) without scenery, costumes, or action. **concert pitch 1** *Mus.* the pitch (slightly higher than the ordinary) internationally agreed in 1960 whereby the A above middle C = 440 Hz, the previous standard being slightly lower at between 435 (European) and 439 (British). This note is generally carried about through the medium of a tuning-fork and in an orchestra is given out by the oboe, one of the instruments least affected by temperature change. **2** a state of unusual readiness, efficiency, and keenness (for action etc.). **in concert 1** (often foll. by *with*) acting jointly and accordantly. **2** (*predic.*) (of a musician) in a performance. [F *concert* (n.), *concerter* (v.) f. It. *concertare* harmonize]

concerted /kənˈsɜːtɪd/ *adj.* **1** combined together; jointly arranged or planned (*a concerted effort*). **2** *Mus.* arranged in parts for voices or instruments.

concertina /ˌkɒnsəˈtiːnə/ *n.* & *v.* —*n.* a musical instrument held in the hands and stretched and squeezed like bellows, having reeds and a set of buttons at each end to control the valves. —*v.tr.* & *intr.* (**concertinas**, **concertinaed** /-nəd/ or **concertina'd**, **concertining**) compress or collapse in folds like those of a concertina (*the car concertinaed into the bridge*). [CONCERT + -INA]

concertino /ˌkɒntʃəˈtiːnəʊ/ *n.* (*pl.* **-os**) *Mus.* **1** a simple or short concerto. **2** a solo instrument or solo instruments playing in a concerto. [It., dimin. of CONCERTO]

concerto /kənˈtʃeətəʊ, -ˈtʃɜːtəʊ/ *n.* (*pl.* **-os** or **concerti** /-tɪ/) *Mus.* a composition for a solo instrument or instruments accompanied by an orchestra. (See below.) □ **concerto grosso** /ˈgrɒsəʊ, ˈgrəʊ-/ (*pl.* **concerti grossi** /-sɪ/ or **concerto grossos**) a composition for a group of solo instruments accompanied by an orchestra. [It. (see CONCERT): *grosso* big]

In the 16th and early 17th c. the term was used fairly broadly, as in its application to the motets for voices and organ by the Italian composer Viadana (1602). Later in the 17th c. came the *concerto grosso* of Corelli and his contemporaries, in which a small body of instruments was offset against a larger ensemble. The concerto for an individual player was developed by J. S. Bach in his harpsichord concertos, and Handel's organ concertos were also an important development, being among the first to provide a cadenza in which the soloist could display his skill by extemporization. By this time the concerto was usually a three-movement form, and the classical composers continued this principle. Mozart composed nearly fifty concertos for various instrumental combinations, and established the modern style, but since the 19th c. it has been usual for the composer to write out the cadenza.

concession /kənˈseʃ(ə)n/ *n.* **1 a** the act or an instance of conceding (*made the concession that we were right*). **b** a thing conceded. **2** a reduction in price for a certain category of person. **3 a** the right to use land or other property, granted esp. by a government or local authority, esp. for a specific use. **b** the right, given by a company, to sell goods, esp. in a particular territory. **c** the land or property used or given. □□ **concessionary** *adj.* (also **concessional**). [F *concession* f. L *concessio* (as CONCEDE)]

concessionaire /kənˌseʃəˈneə(r)/ *n.* (also **concessionnaire**) the holder of a concession or grant, esp. for the use of land or trading rights. [F *concessionnaire* (as CONCESSION)]

concessive /kənˈsesɪv/ *adj.* **1** of or tending to concession. **2** *Gram.* **a** (of a preposition or conjunction) introducing a phrase or clause which might be expected to preclude the action of the main clause, but does not (e.g. *in spite of*, *although*). **b** (of a phrase or clause) introduced by a concessive preposition or conjunction. [LL *concessivus* (as CONCEDE)]

conch /kɒŋk, kɒntʃ/ n. (pl. **conchs** /kɒŋks/ or **conches** /ˈkɒntʃɪz/) **1 a** a thick heavy spiral shell, occasionally bearing long projections, of various marine gastropod molluscs of the family Strombidae. **b** any of these gastropods. **2** *Archit.* the domed roof of a semicircular apse. **3** = CONCHA. [L *concha* shell f. Gk *kogkhē*]

concha /ˈkɒŋkə/ n. (pl. **conchae** /-kiː/) *Anat.* any part resembling a shell, esp. the depression in the external ear leading to its central cavity. [L: see CONCH]

conchie /ˈkɒntʃɪ/ n. (also **conchy**) (pl. **-ies**) *derog. sl.* a conscientious objector. [abbr.]

conchoidal /kɒŋˈkɔɪd(ə)l/ adj. *Mineral.* (of a solid fracture etc.) resembling the surface of a bivalve shell.

conchology /kɒŋˈkɒlədʒɪ/ n. *Zool.* the scientific study of shells. □□ **conchological** /-kəˈlɒdʒɪk(ə)l/ adj. **conchologist** n. [Gk *kogkhē* shell + -LOGY]

conchy var. of CONCHIE.

concierge /ˌkɒ̃sɪˈeəʒ, ˌkɒn-/ n. (esp. in France) a door-keeper or porter of a block of flats etc. [F, prob. ult. f. L *conservus* fellow slave]

conciliar /kənˈsɪlɪə(r)/ adj. of or concerning a council, esp. an ecclesiastical council. [med.L *consiliarius* counsellor]

conciliate /kənˈsɪlɪeɪt/ v.tr. **1** make calm and amenable; pacify. **2** gain (esteem or goodwill). **3** *archaic* reconcile, make compatible. □□ **conciliative** /-ˈsɪlɪətɪv/ adj. **conciliator** n. **conciliatory** /-ˈsɪlɪətərɪ/ adj. **conciliatoriness** /-ˈsɪlɪətərɪnɪs/ n. [L *conciliare* combine, gain (*concilium* COUNCIL)]

conciliation /kənˌsɪlɪˈeɪʃ(ə)n/ n. the use of conciliating measures; reconcilement. [L *conciliatio* (as CONCILIATE)]

concinnity /kənˈsɪnɪtɪ/ n. elegance or neatness of literary style. □□ **concinnous** adj. [L *concinnitas* f. *concinnus* well-adjusted]

concise /kənˈsaɪs/ adj. (of speech, writing, style, or a person) brief but comprehensive in expression. □□ **concisely** adv. **conciseness** n. [F *concis* or L *concisus* past part. of *concidere* (as COM-, *caedere* cut)]

concision /kənˈsɪʒ(ə)n/ n. (esp. of literary style) conciseness. [ME f. L *concisio* (as CONCISE)]

conclave /ˈkɒŋkleɪv/ n. **1** a private meeting. **2** *RC Ch.* **a** the assembly of cardinals for the election of a pope. **b** the meeting-place for a conclave. [ME f. OF f. L *conclave* lockable room (as COM-, *clavis* key)]

conclude /kənˈkluːd/ v. **1** tr. & intr. bring or come to an end. **2** tr. (often foll. by *from*, or *that* + clause) infer (from given premisses) (*what did you conclude?*; *concluded from the evidence that he had been mistaken*). **3** tr. settle, arrange (a treaty etc.). **4** intr. (usu. foll. by *to* + infin.) esp. *US* decide. [ME f. L *concludere* (as COM-, *claudere* shut)]

conclusion /kənˈkluːʒ(ə)n/ n. **1** a final result; a termination. **2** a judgement reached by reasoning. **3** the summing-up of an argument, article, book, etc. **4** a settling; an arrangement (*the conclusion of peace*). **5** *Logic* a proposition that is reached from given premisses; the third and last part of a syllogism. □ **in conclusion** lastly, to conclude. **try conclusions with** engage in a trial of skill etc. with. [ME f. OF *conclusion* or L *conclusio* (as CONCLUDE)]

conclusive /kənˈkluːsɪv/ adj. decisive, convincing. □□ **conclusively** adv. **conclusiveness** n. [LL *conclusivus* (as CONCLUSION)]

concoct /kənˈkɒkt/ v.tr. **1** make by mixing ingredients (*concocted a stew*). **2** invent (a story, a lie, etc.). □□ **concocter** n. **concoction** /-ˈkɒkʃ(ə)n/ n. **concoctor** n. [L *concoquere concoct-* (as COM-, *coquere* cook)]

concomitance /kənˈkɒmɪt(ə)ns/ n. (also **concomitancy**) **1** coexistence. **2** *Theol.* the doctrine of the coexistence of the body and blood of Christ both in the bread and in the wine of the Eucharist. [med.L *concomitantia* (as CONCOMITANT)]

concomitant /kənˈkɒmɪt(ə)nt/ adj. & n. —adj. going together; associated (*concomitant circumstances*). —n. an accompanying thing. □□ **concomitantly** adv. [LL *concomitari* (as COM-, *comitari* f. L *comes -mitis* companion)]

Concord /ˈkɒŋkɔːd/ **1** the capital of New Hampshire; pop. (1980) 30,400. **2** a town in NE Massachusetts; pop. (1980) 16,300. Battles here and at Lexington in April 1775 marked the start of the War of American Independence.

concord /ˈkɒŋkɔːd, ˈkɒŋ-/ n. **1** agreement or harmony between people or things. **2** a treaty. **3** *Mus.* a chord that is pleasing or satisfactory in itself. **4** *Gram.* agreement between words in gender, number, etc. [ME f. OF *concorde* f. L *concordia* f. *concors* of one mind (as COM-, *cors* f. *cor cordis* heart)]

concordance /kənˈkɔːd(ə)ns, kən-/ n. **1** agreement. **2** a book containing an alphabetical list of the important words used in a book or by an author, usu. with citations of the passages concerned. [ME f. OF f. med.L *concordantia* (as CONCORDANT)]

concordant /kənˈkɔːd(ə)nt/ adj. **1** (often foll. by *with*) agreeing, harmonious. **2** *Mus.* in harmony. □□ **concordantly** adv. [ME f. OF f. L *concordare* f. *concors* (as CONCORD)]

concordat /kənˈkɔːdæt/ n. an agreement, esp. between the Roman Catholic Church and a State. [F *concordat* or L *concordatum* neut. past part. of *concordare* (as CONCORDANCE)]

Concorde /ˈkɒŋkɔːd/ a supersonic airliner, the product of Anglo-French cooperation, which made its maiden flight in 1969 and has been in commercial service since 1976.

concourse /ˈkɒŋkɔːs, ˈkɒŋ-/ n. **1** a crowd. **2** a coming together; a gathering (*a concourse of ideas*). **3** an open central area in a large public building, a railway station, etc. [ME f. OF *concours* f. L *concursus* (as CONCUR)]

concrescence /kənˈkres(ə)ns/ n. *Biol.* coalescence; growing together. □□ **concrescent** adj. [CON-, after *excrescence* etc.]

concrete /ˈkɒŋkriːt, ˈkɒŋ-/ adj., n., & v. —adj. **1 a** existing in a material form; real. **b** specific, definite (*concrete evidence*; *a concrete proposal*). **2** *Gram.* (of a noun) denoting a material object as opposed to an abstract quality, state, or action. —n. (often attrib.) a composition of gravel, sand, cement, and water, used for building. (See below.) —v. **1** tr. **a** cover with concrete. **b** embed in concrete. **2 a** tr. & intr. form into a mass; solidify. **b** tr. make concrete instead of abstract. □ **concrete-mixer** a machine, usu. with a revolving drum, used for mixing concrete. **concrete music** music constructed by mixing recorded sounds. **concrete poetry** poetry using unusual typographical layout to enhance the effect on the page. **in the concrete** in reality or in practice. □□ **concretely** adv. **concreteness** n. [F *concret* or L *concretus* past part. of *concrescere* (as COM-, *crescere cret-* GROW)]

Concrete was used by the Romans as a building material. Its modern use dates from the 19th c. (see PORTLAND CEMENT). Reinforced concrete was developed in France and England in the mid-19th c.; metal rods, bars, or mesh embedded in the concrete provided the tensile strength which concrete itself lacks. Prestressed concrete was invented by a German builder *c.*1886 and further developed by the French engineer Eugène Freyssinet in the early 20th c.; in it the reinforcing metal bars are stretched while the concrete is wet and released when it has set round them, thereby compressing the concrete longitudinally and reducing its tendency to bend under a load. It has been used with notable success in the building of bridges.

concretion /kənˈkriːʃ(ə)n/ n. **1 a** a hard solid concreted mass. **b** the forming of this by coalescence. **2** *Med.* a stony mass formed within the body. **3** *Geol.* a small round mass of rock particles embedded in limestone or clay. □□ **concretionary** adj. [F f. L *concretio* (as CONCRETE)]

concretize /ˈkɒŋkrɪtaɪz, ˈkɒŋ-/ v.tr. (also **-ise**) make concrete instead of abstract. □□ **concretization** /-ˈzeɪʃ(ə)n/ n.

concubinage /kənˈkjuːbɪnɪdʒ/ n. **1** the cohabitation of a man and woman not married to each other. **2** the state of being or having a concubine. [ME f. F (as CONCUBINE)]

concubine /ˈkɒŋkjʊbaɪn/ n. **1** a woman who lives with a man as his wife. **2** (among polygamous peoples) a secondary wife. □□ **concubinary** /kənˈkjuːbɪnərɪ/ adj. [ME f. OF f. L *concubina* (as COM-, *cubina* f. *cubare* lie)]

concupiscence /kənˈkjuːpɪs(ə)ns/ n. *formal* sexual desire. □□ **concupiscent** adj. [ME f. OF f. LL *concupiscentia* f. L *concupiscere* begin to desire (as COM-, inceptive f. *cupere* desire)]

concur /kənˈkɜː(r)/ v.intr. (**concurred**, **concurring**) **1** happen together; coincide. **2** (often foll. by *with*) **a** agree in opinion. **b** express agreement. **3** combine together for a cause; act in combination. [L *concurrere* (as COM-, *currere* run)]

concurrent /kən'kʌrənt/ *adj.* **1** (often foll. by *with*) **a** existing or in operation at the same time (*served two concurrent sentences*). **b** existing or acting together. **2** *Geom.* (of three or more lines) meeting at or tending towards one point. **3** agreeing, harmonious. □□ **concurrence** *n.* **concurrently** *adv.*

concuss /kən'kʌs/ *v.tr.* **1** subject to concussion. **2** shake violently. **3** *archaic* intimidate. [L *concutere concuss-* (as COM-, *cutere = quatere* shake)]

concussion /kən'kʌʃ(ə)n/ *n.* **1** *Med.* temporary unconsciousness or incapacity due to injury to the head. **2** violent shaking; shock. [L *concussio* (as CONCUSS)]

condemn /kən'dem/ *v.tr.* **1** express utter disapproval of; censure (*was condemned for his irresponsible behaviour*). **2 a** find guilty; convict. **b** (usu. foll. by *to*) sentence to (a punishment, esp. death). **c** bring about the conviction of (*his looks condemn him*). **3** pronounce (a building etc.) unfit for use or habitation. **4** (usu. foll. by *to*) doom or assign (to something unwelcome or painful) (*condemned to spending hours at the kitchen sink*). **5 a** declare (smuggled goods, property, etc.) to be forfeited. **b** pronounce incurable. □ **condemned cell** a cell for a prisoner condemned to death. □□ **condemnable** /-'demnəb(ə)l/ *adj.* **condemnation** /ˌkɒndem'neɪʃ(ə)n/ *n.* **condemnatory** /-'demnətərɪ/ *adj.* [ME f. OF *condem(p)ner* f. L *condemnare* (as COM-, *damnare* DAMN)]

condensate /kən'denseɪt, 'kɒndən,seɪt/ *n.* a substance produced by condensation.

condensation /ˌkɒndɛn'seɪʃ(ə)n/ *n.* **1** the act of condensing. **2** any condensed material (esp. water on a cold surface). **3** an abridgement. **4** *Chem.* the combination of molecules with the elimination of water or other small molecules. □ **condensation trail** = *vapour trail*. [LL *condensatio* (as CONDENSE)]

condense /kən'dens/ *v.* **1** *tr.* make denser or more concentrated. **2** *tr.* express in fewer words; make concise. **3** *tr.* & *intr.* reduce or be reduced from a gas or solid to a liquid. □ **condensed milk** milk thickened by evaporation and sweetened. □□ **condensable** *adj.* [F *condenser* or L *condensare* (as COM-, *densus* thick)]

condenser /kən'densə(r)/ *n.* **1** an apparatus or vessel for condensing vapour. **2** *Electr.* = CAPACITOR. **3** a lens or system of lenses for concentrating light. **4** a person or thing that condenses.

condescend /ˌkɒndɪ'send/ *v.intr.* **1** (usu. foll. by *to* + infin.) be gracious enough (to do a thing) esp. while showing one's sense of dignity or superiority (*condescended to attend the meeting*). **2** (foll. by *to*) behave as if one is on equal terms with (an inferior), usu. while maintaining an attitude of superiority. **3** (as **condescending** *adj.*) patronizing; kind to inferiors. □□ **condescendingly** *adv.* [ME f. OF *condescendre* f. eccl.L *condescendere* (as COM-, DESCEND)]

condescension /ˌkɒndɪ'senʃ(ə)n/ *n.* **1** a patronizing manner. **2** affability towards inferiors. [obs. F f. eccl.L *condescensio* (as CONDESCEND)]

condign /kən'daɪn/ *adj.* (of a punishment etc.) severe and well-deserved. □□ **condignly** *adv.* [ME f. OF *condigne* f. L *condignus* (as COM-, *dignus* worthy)]

condiment /'kɒndɪmənt/ *n.* a seasoning or relish for food. [ME f. L *condimentum* f. *condire* pickle]

condition /kən'dɪʃ(ə)n/ *n.* & *v.* —*n.* **1** a stipulation; something upon the fulfilment of which something else depends. **2 a** the state of being or fitness of a person or thing (*arrived in bad condition; not in a condition to be used*). **b** an ailment or abnormality (*a heart condition*). **3** (in *pl.*) circumstances, esp. those affecting the functioning or existence of something (*working conditions are good*). **4** *archaic* social rank (*all sorts and conditions of men*). **5** *Gram.* a clause expressing a condition. **6** *US* a subject in which a student must pass an examination within a stated time to maintain a provisionally granted status. —*v.tr.* **1 a** bring into a good or desired state or condition. **b** make fit (esp. dogs or horses). **2** teach or accustom to adopt certain habits etc. (*conditioned by society*). **3** govern, determine (*his behaviour was conditioned by his drunkenness*). **4 a** impose conditions on. **b** be

essential to (*the two things condition each other*). **5** test the condition of (textiles etc.). **6** *US* subject (a student) to re-examination. □ **conditioned reflex** a reflex response to a non-natural stimulus, established by training. **in** (or **out of**) **condition** in good (or bad) condition. **in no condition to** certainly not fit to. **on condition that** with the stipulation that. [ME f. OF *condicion* (n.), *condicionner* (v.) or med.L *condicionare* f. L *condicio -onis* f. *condicere* (as COM-, *dicere* say)]

conditional /kən'dɪʃən(ə)l/ *adj.* & *n.* —*adj.* **1** (often foll. by *on*) dependent; not absolute; containing a condition or stipulation (*a conditional offer*). **2** *Gram.* (of a clause, mood, etc.) expressing a condition. —*n.* *Gram.* **1** a conditional clause etc. **2** the conditional mood. □ **conditional discharge** *Law* an order made by a criminal court whereby an offender will not be sentenced for an offence unless a further offence is committed within a stated period. □□ **conditionality** /-'nælɪtɪ/ *n.* **conditionally** *adv.* [ME f. OF *condicionel* or f. LL *conditionalis* (as CONDITION)]

conditioner /kən'dɪʃənə(r)/ *n.* an agent that brings something into good condition, esp. a substance applied to the hair.

condo /'kɒndəʊ/ *n.* (*pl.* **-os**) *US colloq.* a condominium. [abbr.]

condolatory /kən'dəʊlətərɪ/ *adj.* expressing condolence. [CONDOLE, after *consolatory* etc.]

condole /kən'dəʊl/ *v.intr.* (foll. by *with*) express sympathy with a person over a loss, grief, etc. ¶ Often confused with *console*. [LL *condolēre* (as COM-, *dolēre* suffer)]

condolence /kən'dəʊləns/ *n.* (often in *pl.*) an expression of sympathy (*sent my condolences*).

condom /'kɒndɒm/ *n.* a rubber sheath worn on the penis during sexual intercourse as a contraceptive or to prevent infection. [18th c.: orig. unkn.]

condominium /ˌkɒndə'mɪnɪəm/ *n.* **1** the joint control of a State's affairs by other States. **2** *US* a building containing flats which are individually owned. [mod.L (as COM-, *dominium* DOMINION)]

condone /kən'dəʊn/ *v.tr.* **1** forgive or overlook (an offence or wrongdoing). **2** approve or sanction, usu. reluctantly. **3** (of an action) atone for (an offence); make up for. □□ **condonation** /ˌkɒndə'neɪʃ(ə)n/ *n.* **condoner** *n.* [L *condonare* (as COM-, *donare* give)]

condor /'kɒndɔː(r)/ *n.* **1** (in full **Andean condor**) a large vulture, *Vultur gryphus*, of S. America, having black plumage with a white neck ruff and a fleshy wattle on the forehead. **2** (in full **California condor**) a small vulture, *Gymnogyps californianus*, of California. [Sp. f. Quechua *cuntur*]

condottiere /ˌkɒndɒtɪ'jeərɪ/ *n.* (*pl.* **condottieri** *pronunc.* same) *hist.* a leader or a member of a troop of mercenaries in Italy etc. [It. f. *condotto* troop under contract (*condotta*) (as CONDUCT)]

conduce /kən'djuːs/ *v.intr.* (foll. by *to*) (usu. of an event or attribute) lead or contribute to (a result). [L *conducere conduct-* (as COM-, *ducere duct-* lead)]

conducive /kən'djuːsɪv/ *adj.* often foll. by *to*) contributing or helping (towards something) (*not a conducive atmosphere for negotiation; good health is conducive to happiness*).

conduct *n.* & *v.* —*n.* /'kɒndʌkt/ **1** behaviour (esp. in its moral aspect). **2** the action or manner of directing or managing (business, war, etc.). **3** *Art* mode of treatment, execution. **4** leading, guidance. —*v.* /kən'dʌkt/ **1** *tr.* lead or guide (a person or persons). **2** *tr.* direct or manage (business etc.). **3** *tr.* (also *absol.*) be the conductor of (an orchestra, choir, etc.). **4** *tr.* *Physics* transmit (heat, electricity, etc.) by conduction. **5** *refl.* behave (*conducted himself appropriately*). □ **conducted tour** a tour led by a guide on a fixed itinerary. **conduct sheet** a record of a person's offences and punishments. □□ **conductible** /kən'dʌktɪb(ə)l/ *adj.* **conductibility** /kən,dʌktɪ'bɪlɪtɪ/ *n.* [ME f. L *conductus* (as COM-, *ducere duct-* lead): (v.) f. OF *conduite* past part. of *conduire*]

conductance /kən'dʌkt(ə)ns/ *n.* *Physics* the power of a specified material to conduct electricity.

conduction /kən'dʌkʃ(ə)n/ *n.* **1 a** the transmission of heat through a substance from a region of higher temperature to a region of lower temperature. **b** the transmission of electricity through a substance by the application of an electric field. **2** the transmission of impulses along nerves. **3** the conducting of liquid through a pipe etc. [F *conduction* or L *conductio* (as CONDUCT)]

conductive /kən'dʌktɪv/ *adj.* having the property of conducting (esp. heat, electricity, etc.). □ **conductive education** a system of education for children and adults with motor disorders. □□ **conductively** *adv.*

conductivity /ˌkɒndʌk'tɪvɪtɪ/ *n.* the conducting power of a specified material.

conductor /kən'dʌktə(r)/ *n.* **1** a person who directs the performance of an orchestra or choir etc. **2** (*fem.* **conductress** /-trɪs/) **a** a person who collects fares in a bus etc. **b** *US* an official in charge of a train. **3** *Physics* **a** a thing that conducts or transmits heat or electricity, esp. regarded in terms of its capacity to do this (*a poor conductor*). **b** = *lightning-conductor*. **4** a guide or leader. **5** a manager or director. □ **conductor rail** a rail transmitting current to an electric train etc. □□ **conductorship** *n.* [ME f. F *conducteur* f. L *conductor* (as CONDUCT)]

conductus /kən'dʌktəs/ *n.* (*pl.* **conducti** /-taɪ/) a musical composition of the 12th–13th c., with Latin text. [med.L: see CONDUIT]

conduit /'kɒndɪt, -djʊɪt/ *n.* **1** a channel or pipe for conveying liquids. **2 a** a tube or trough for protecting insulated electric wires. **b** a length or stretch of this. [ME f. OF *conduit* f. med.L *conductus* CONDUCT n.]

condyle /'kɒndɪl/ *n.* *Anat.* a rounded process at the end of some bones, forming an articulation with another bone. □□ **condylar** *adj.* **condyloid** *adj.* [F f. L *condylus* f. Gk *kondulos* knuckle]

cone /kəʊn/ *n.* & *v.* —*n.* **1** a solid figure with a circular (or other curved) plane base, tapering to a point. **2** a thing of a similar shape, solid or hollow, e.g. as used to mark off areas of roads. **3** the dry fruit of a conifer. **4** an ice-cream cornet. **5** any of the minute cone-shaped structures in the retina. **6** a conical mountain esp. of volcanic origin. **7** (in full **cone-shell**) any marine gastropod mollusc of the family Conidae. **8** *Pottery* a ceramic pyramid, melting at a known temperature, used to indicate the temperature of a kiln. —*v.tr.* **1** shape like a cone. **2** (foll. by *off*) *Brit.* mark off (a road etc.) with cones. [F *cône* f. L *conus* f. Gk *kōnos*]

coney var. of CONY.

Coney Island /'kəʊnɪ/ a resort on the Atlantic coast in Brooklyn, New York City, forming part of Long Island since the silting up of a creek. It has been developed as a pleasure ground since the 1840s.

confab /'kɒnfæb/ *n.* & *v. colloq.* —*n.* = CONFABULATION (see CONFABULATE). —*v.intr.* (**confabbed**, **confabbing**) = CONFABULATE. [abbr.]

confabulate /kən'fæbjʊˌleɪt/ *v.intr.* **1** converse, chat. **2** *Psychol.* fabricate imaginary experiences as compensation for the loss of memory. □□ **confabulation** /-'leɪʃ(ə)n/ *n.* **confabulatory** *adj.* [L *confabulari* (as COM-, *fabulari* f. *fabula* tale)]

confect /kən'fekt/ *v.tr. literary* make by putting together ingredients. [L *conficere confect-* put together (as COM-, *facere* make)]

confection /kən'fekʃ(ə)n/ *n.* **1** a dish or delicacy made with sweet ingredients. **2** mixing, compounding. **3** a fashionable or elaborate article of women's dress. □□ **confectionary** *adj.* (in sense 1). [ME f. OF f. L *confectio -onis* (as CONFECT)]

confectioner /kən'fekʃənə(r)/ *n.* a maker or retailer of confectionery.

confectionery /kən'fekʃənərɪ/ *n.* sweets and other confections.

confederacy /kən'fedərəsɪ/ *n.* (*pl.* **-ies**) **1** a league or alliance, esp. of confederate States; **the Confederacy** the Confederate States (see CONFEDERATE). **2** a league for an unlawful or evil purpose; a conspiracy. **3** the condition or fact of being confederate; alliance; conspiracy. [ME, AF, OF *confederacie* (as CONFEDERATE)]

confederate /kən'fedərət/ *adj.*, *n.*, & *v.* —*adj.* esp. *Polit.* allied; joined by an agreement or treaty. —*n.* **1** an ally, esp. (in a bad sense) an accomplice. **2** (**Confederate**) a supporter of the Confederate States. —*v.* /-ˌreɪt/ (often foll. by *with*) **1** *tr.* bring (a person, State, or oneself) into alliance. **2** *intr.* come into alliance. □ **Confederate States** the 11 southern States (Alabama,

Arkansas, Florida, Georgia, Louisiana, Mississippi, North Carolina, South Carolina, Tennessee, Texas, Virginia) which seceded from the United States in 1860–1 and formed a confederacy of their own (thus precipitating the American Civil War) which was finally overthrown in 1865, after which they were reunited to the US. [LL *confoederatus* (as COM-, FEDERATE)]

confederation /kənˌfedə'reɪʃ(ə)n/ *n.* **1** a union or alliance of States etc. **2** the act or an instance of confederating; the state of being confederated. [F *confédération* (as CONFEDERATE)]

Confederation of British Industry an organization founded in 1965 (combining earlier associations) to promote the prosperity of British business. Membership, which totals about 50,000 companies, is voluntary. The organization provides its members with a wide range of services and practical advice, and voices the views of the management side of industry in the UK.

confer /kən'fɜː(r)/ *v.* (**conferred, conferring**) **1** *tr.* (often foll. by *on, upon*) grant or bestow (a title, degree, favour, etc.). **2** *intr.* (often foll. by *with*) converse, consult. □□ **conferrable** *adj.* [L *conferre* (as COM-, *ferre* bring)]

conferee /ˌkɒnfə'riː/ *n.* **1** a person on whom something is conferred. **2** a participant in a conference.

conference /'kɒnfərəns/ *n.* **1** consultation, discussion. **2** a meeting for discussion, esp. a regular one held by an association or organization. **3** an annual assembly of the Methodist Church. **4** an association in commerce, sport, etc. **5** the linking of several telephones, computer terminals, etc., so that each user may communicate with the others simultaneously. □ **in conference** engaged in discussion. □□ **conferential** /ˌkɒnfə'renʃ(ə)l/ *adj.* [F *conférence* or med.L *conferentia* (as CONFER)]

Conference on Disarmament a committee of which 40 nations are members that seeks to negotiate multilateral disarmament. It was constituted in 1962 as the Committee on Disarmament (with 18 nations as members) and adopted its present title in 1984. It meets in Geneva.

conferment /kən'fɜːmənt/ *n.* **1** the conferring of a degree, honour, etc. **2** an instance of this.

conferral /kən'fɜːr(ə)l/ *n.* esp. *US* = CONFERMENT.

confess /kən'fes/ *v.* **1 a** *tr.* (also *absol.*) acknowledge or admit (a fault, wrongdoing, etc.). **b** *intr.* (foll. by *to*) admit to (*confessed to having lied*). **2** *tr.* admit reluctantly (*confessed it would be difficult*). **3 a** *tr.* (also *absol.*) declare (one's sins) to a priest. **b** *tr.* (of a priest) hear the confession of. **c** *refl.* declare one's sins to a priest. [ME f. OF *confesser* f. Rmc f. L *confessus* past part. of *confitēri* (as COM-, *fatēri* declare, avow)]

confessant /kən'fes(ə)nt/ *n.* a person who confesses to a priest.

confessedly /kən'fesɪdlɪ/ *adv.* by one's own or general admission.

confession /kən'feʃ(ə)n/ *n.* **1 a** confessing or acknowledgement of a fault, wrongdoing, a sin to a priest, etc. **b** an instance of this. **c** a thing confessed. **2** (in full **confession of faith**) **a** a declaration of one's religious beliefs. **b** a statement of one's principles. □□ **confessionary** *adj.* [ME f. OF f. L *confessio -onis* (as CONFESS)]

confessional /kən'feʃ(ə)n(ə)l/ *n.* & *adj.* —*n.* an enclosed stall in a church in which a priest hears confessions. —*adj.* **1** of or relating to confession. **2** denominational. [F f. It. *confessionale* f. med.L, neut. of *confessionalis* (as CONFESSION)]

confessor /kən'fesə(r)/ *n.* **1** a person who makes a confession. **2** /also 'kɒn-/ a priest who hears confessions and gives spiritual counsel. **3** a person who avows a religion in the face of its suppression, but does not suffer martyrdom. [ME f. AF *confessur*, OF *-our*, f. eccl.L *confessor* (as CONFESS)]

confetti /kən'fetɪ/ *n.* small pieces of coloured paper thrown by wedding guests at the bride and groom. [It., = sweetmeats f. L (as COMFIT)]

confidant /ˌkɒnfɪ'dænt, 'kɒn-/ *n.* (*fem.* **confidante** pronunc. same) a person trusted with knowledge of one's private affairs. [18th-c. for earlier CONFIDENT *n.*, prob. to represent the pronunc. of F *confidente* (as CONFIDE)]

confide /kən'faɪd/ *v.* **1** *tr.* (usu. foll. by *to*) tell (a secret etc.) in confidence. **2** *tr.* (foll. by *to*) entrust (an object of care, a task, etc.) to. **3** *intr.* (foll. by *in*) **a** have trust or confidence in. **b** talk confidentially to. □□ **confidingly** *adv.* [L *confidere* (as COM-, *fidere* trust)]

confidence /ˈkɒnfɪd(ə)ns/ *n.* **1** firm trust (*have confidence in his ability*). **2 a** a feeling of reliance or certainty. **b** a sense of self-reliance; boldness. **3 a** something told confidentially. **b** the telling of private matters with mutual trust. □ **confidence man** a man who robs by means of a confidence trick. **confidence trick** (*US* **game**) a swindle in which the victim is persuaded to trust the swindler in some way. **in confidence** as a secret. **in a person's confidence** trusted with a person's secrets. **take into one's confidence** confide in. [ME f. L *confidentia* (as CONFIDE)]

confident /ˈkɒnfɪd(ə)nt/ *adj.* & *n.* —*adj.* **1** feeling or showing confidence; self-assured, bold (*spoke with a confident air*). **2** (often foll. by *of*, or *that* + clause) assured, trusting (*confident of your support*; *confident that he will come*). —*n. archaic* = CONFIDANT. □□ **confidently** *adv.* [F f. It. *confidente* (as CONFIDE)]

confidential /ˌkɒnfɪˈdenʃ(ə)l/ *adj.* **1** spoken or written in confidence. **2** entrusted with secrets (*a confidential secretary*). **3** confiding. □□ **confidentiality** /-ʃɪˈælɪtɪ/ *n.* **confidentially** *adv.*

configuration /kənˌfɪɡjʊˈreɪʃ(ə)n, -ɡəˈreɪʃ(ə)n/ *n.* **1 a** an arrangement of parts or elements in a particular form or figure. **b** the form, shape, or figure resulting from such an arrangement. **2** *Astron.* & *Astrol.* the relative position of planets etc. **3** *Psychol.* = GESTALT. **4** *Physics* the distribution of electrons among the energy levels of an atom, or of nucleons among the energy levels of a nucleus, as specified by quantum numbers. **5** *Chem.* the fixed three-dimensional relationship of the atoms in a molecule. **6** *Computing* **a** the interrelating or interconnecting of a computer system or elements of it so that it will accommodate a particular specification. **b** an instance of this. □□ **configurational** *adj.* **configure** *v.tr.* (in senses 1, 2, 6). [LL *configuratio* f. L *configurare* (as COM-, *figurare* fashion)]

confine *v.* & *n.* —*v.tr.* /kənˈfaɪn/ (often foll. by *in*, *to*, *within*) **1** keep or restrict (within certain limits etc.). **2** hold captive; imprison. —*n.* /ˈkɒnfaɪn/ (usu. in *pl.*) a limit or boundary (*within the confines of the town*). □ **be confined** be in childbirth. [(v.) f. F *confiner*, (n.) ME f. F *confins* (pl.), f. L *confinia* (as COM-, *finia* neut. pl. f. *finis* end, limit)]

confinement /kənˈfaɪnmənt/ *n.* **1** the act or an instance of confining; the state of being confined. **2** the time of a woman's giving birth.

confirm /kənˈfɜːm/ *v.tr.* **1** provide support for the truth or correctness of; make definitely valid (*confirmed my suspicions*; *confirmed his arrival time*). **2** (foll. by *in*) encourage (a person) in (an opinion etc.). **3** establish more firmly (power, possession, etc.). **4** ratify (a treaty, possession, title, etc.); make formally valid. **5** administer the religious rite of confirmation to. □□ **confirmative** *adj.* **confirmatory** *adj.* [ME f. OF *confermer* f. L *confirmare* (as COM-, FIRM¹)]

confirmand /ˈkɒnfəˌmænd/ *n. Eccl.* a person who is to be or has just been confirmed.

confirmation /ˌkɒnfəˈmeɪʃ(ə)n/ *n.* **1 a** the act or an instance of confirming; the state of being confirmed. **b** an instance of this. **2 a** a religious rite confirming a baptized person, esp. at the age of discretion, as a member of the Christian Church. **b** a ceremony of confirming persons of about this age in the Jewish faith. [ME f. OF f. L *confirmatio -onis* (as CONFIRM)]

confirmed /kənˈfɜːmd/ *adj.* firmly settled in some habit or condition (*confirmed in his ways*; *a confirmed bachelor*).

confiscate /ˈkɒnfɪˌskeɪt/ *v.tr.* **1** take or seize by authority. **2** appropriate to the public treasury (by way of a penalty). □□ **confiscable** /kənˈfɪskəb(ə)l/ *adj.* **confiscation** /-ˈskeɪʃ(ə)n/ *n.* **confiscator** *n.* **confiscatory** /kənˈfɪskətərɪ/ *adj.* [L *confiscare* (as COM-, *fiscare* f. *fiscus* treasury)]

conflagration /ˌkɒnfləˈɡreɪʃ(ə)n/ *n.* a great and destructive fire. [L *conflagratio* f. *conflagrare* (as COM-, *flagrare* blaze)]

conflate /kənˈfleɪt/ *v.tr.* blend or fuse together (esp. two variant texts into one). □□ **conflation** /-ˈfleɪʃ(ə)n/ *n.* [L *conflare* (as COM-, *flare* blow)]

conflict *n.* & *v.* —*n.* /ˈkɒnflɪkt/ **1 a** a state of opposition or hostilities. **b** a fight or struggle. **2** (often foll. by *of*) **a** the clashing of opposed principles etc. **b** an instance of this. **3** *Psychol.* **a** the opposition of incompatible wishes or needs in a person. **b** an instance of this. **c** the distress resulting from this. —*v.intr.* /kənˈflɪkt/ **1** clash; be incompatible. **2** (often foll. by *with*) struggle or contend. **3** (as **conflicting** *adj.*) contradictory. □ **in conflict** conflicting. □□ **confliction** /kənˈflɪkʃ(ə)n/ *n.* **conflictual** /kənˈflɪktʃʊəl/ *adj.* [ME f. L *confligere conflict-* (as COM-, *fligere* strike)]

confluence /ˈkɒnflʊəns/ *n.* **1** a place where two rivers meet. **2 a** a coming together. **b** a crowd of people. [L *confluere* (as COM-, *fluere* flow)]

confluent /ˈkɒnflʊənt/ *adj.* & *n.* —*adj.* flowing together, uniting. —*n.* a stream joining another.

conflux /ˈkɒnflʌks/ *n.* = CONFLUENCE. [LL *confluxus* (as CONFLUENCE)]

conform /kənˈfɔːm/ *v.* **1** *intr.* comply with rules or general custom. **2** *intr.* & *tr.* (often foll. by *to*) be or make accordant or suitable. **3** *tr.* (often foll. by *to*) form according to a pattern; make similar. **4** *intr.* (foll. by *to*, *with*) comply with; be in accordance with. □□ **conformer** *n.* [ME f. OF *conformer* f. L *conformare* (as COM-, FORM)]

conformable /kənˈfɔːməb(ə)l/ *adj.* **1** (often foll. by *to*) similar. **2** (often foll. by *with*) consistent. **3** (often foll. by *to*) adapted. **4** tractable, submissive. **5** *Geol.* (of strata in contact) lying in the same direction. □□ **conformability** /-ˈbɪlɪtɪ/ *n.* **conformably** *adv.* [med.L *conformabilis* (as CONFORM)]

conformal /kənˈfɔːm(ə)l/ *adj.* (of a map) showing any small area in its correct shape. □□ **conformally** *adv.* [LL *conformalis* (as CONFORM)]

conformance /kənˈfɔːməns/ *n.* (often foll. by *to*, *with*) = CONFORMITY 1, 2.

conformation /ˌkɒnfɔːˈmeɪʃ(ə)n/ *n.* **1** the way in which a thing is formed; shape, structure. **2** (often foll. by *to*) adjustment in form or character; adaptation. **3** *Chem.* any spatial arrangement of atoms in a molecule from the rotation of part of the molecule about a single bond. [L *conformatio* (as CONFORM)]

conformist /kənˈfɔːmɪst/ *n.* & *adj.* —*n.* **1** a person who conforms to an established practice; a conventional person. **2** *Brit.* a person who conforms to the practices of the Church of England. —*adj.* (of a person) conforming to established practices; conventional. □□ **conformism** *n.*

conformity /kənˈfɔːmɪtɪ/ *n.* **1** (often foll. by *to*, *with*) action or behaviour in accordance with established practice; compliance. **2** (often foll. by *to*, *with*) correspondence in form or manner; likeness, agreement. **3** *Brit.* compliance with the practices of the Church of England. [ME f. OF *conformité* or LL *conformitas* (as CONFORM)]

confound /kənˈfaʊnd/ *v.* & *int.* —*v.tr.* **1** throw into perplexity or confusion. **2** mix up; confuse (in one's mind). **3** *archaic* defeat, overthrow. —*int.* expressing annoyance (*confound you!*). [ME f. AF *confo(u)ndre*, OF *confondre* f. L *confundere* mix up (as COM-, *fundere fus-* pour)]

confounded /kənˈfaʊndɪd/ *adj. colloq.* damned (*a confounded nuisance!*). □□ **confoundedly** *adv.*

confraternity /ˌkɒnfrəˈtɜːnɪtɪ/ *n.* (pl. **-ies**) a brotherhood, esp. religious or charitable. [ME f. OF *confraternité* f. med.L *confraternitas* (as COM-, FRATERNITY)]

confrère /ˈkɒnfreə(r)/ *n.* a fellow member of a profession, scientific body, etc. [ME f. OF f. med.L *confrater* (as COM-, *frater* brother)]

confront /kənˈfrʌnt/ *v.tr.* **1 a** face in hostility or defiance. **b** face up to and deal with (a problem, difficulty, etc.). **2** (of a difficulty etc.) present itself to (*countless obstacles confronted us*). **3** (foll. by *with*) **a** bring (a person) face to face with (a circumstance), esp. by way of accusation (*confronted them with the evidence*). **b** set (a thing) face to face with (another) for comparison. **4** meet or stand facing. □□ **confrontation** /ˌkɒnfrʌnˈteɪʃ(ə)n/ *n.* **confrontational** /ˌkɒnfrʌnˈteɪʃən(ə)l/ *adj.* [F *confronter* f. med.L *confrontare* (as COM-, *frontare* f. *frons frontis* face)]

Confucianism /kənˈfjuːʃənɪz(ə)m/ *n.* a system of philosophical and ethical teachings founded by Confucius in the 6th c. BC and developed by Mencius (Meng-tzu) in the 4th c. BC, one of the two major Chinese ideologies (see TAOISM). The basic concepts are ethical ones: love for one's fellows, filial piety, decorum, virtue; and the ideal of the superior man. The publication in AD 1190 of the four great Confucian texts revitalized Confucianism throughout China. A second series of texts, the 'five classics', includes the I Ching. □□ **Confucianist** n.

Confucius /kən'fju:ʃəs/ (Latinization of Chinese *Kongfuze* Kong the master) the most influential Chinese philosopher (551–479 BC), founder of Confucianism. The most reliable source of his teachings is the Lun yu (Chinese, = conversations), published in 1890. □□ **Confucian** adj. & n.

confusable /kən'fju:zəb(ə)l/ adj. that is able or liable to be confused. □□ **confusability** /-'bɪlɪtɪ/ n.

confuse /kən'fju:z/ v.tr. **1 a** disconcert, perplex, bewilder. **b** embarrass. **2** mix up in the mind; mistake (one for another). **3** make indistinct (*that point confuses the issue*). **4** (as **confused** adj.) mentally decrepit. **5** (often as **confused** adj.) throw into disorder (*a confused jumble of clothes*). □□ **confusedly** /kən'fju:zɪdlɪ/ adv. **confusing** adj. **confusingly** adv. [19th-c. back-form. f. *confused* (14th c.) f. OF *confus* f. L *confusus*: see CONFOUND]

confusion /kən'fju:ʒ(ə)n/ n. **1 a** the act of confusing (*the confusion of fact and fiction*). **b** an instance of this; a misunderstanding (*confusions arise from a lack of communication*). **2 a** the result of confusing; a confused state; disorder (*thrown into confusion by his words; trampled in the confusion of battle*). **b** (foll. by *of*) a disorderly jumble (*a confusion of ideas*). **3 a** civil commotion (*confusion broke out at the announcement*). **b** an instance of this. [ME f. OF *confusion* or L *confusio* (as CONFUSE)]

confute /kən'fju:t/ v.tr. **1** prove (a person) to be in error. **2** prove (an argument) to be false. □□ **confutation** /ˌkɒnfju:'teɪʃ(ə)n/ n. [L *confutare* restrain]

conga /'kɒŋgə/ n. & v. —n. **1** a Latin-American dance of African origin, usu. with several persons in a single line, one behind the other. **2** (also **conga drum**) a tall, narrow, low-toned drum beaten with the hands. —v.intr. (**congas, congaed** /-gəd/ or **conga'd, congaing** /-gəɪŋ/) perform the conga. [Amer. Sp. f. Sp. *conga* (fem.) of the Congo]

congé /'kɒ̃ʒeɪ/ n. an unceremonious dismissal; leave-taking. [F: earlier *congee*, ME f. OF *congié* f. L *commeatus* leave of absence f. *commeare* go and come (as COM-, *meare* go): now usu. treated as mod. F]

congeal /kən'dʒi:l/ v.tr. & intr. **1** make or become semi-solid by cooling. **2** (of blood etc.) coagulate. □□ **congealable** adj. **congealment** n. [ME f. OF *congeler* f. L *congelare* (as COM-, *gelare* f. *gelu* frost)]

congelation /ˌkɒndʒɪ'leɪʃ(ə)n/ n. **1** the process of congealing. **2** a congealed state. **3** a congealed substance. [ME f. OF *congelation* or L *congelatio* (as CONGEAL)]

congener /kən'dʒi:nə(r)/ n. a thing or person of the same kind or category as another, esp. animals or plants of a specified genus (*the goldfinch is a congener of the canary*). [L (as CON-, GENUS)]

congeneric /ˌkɒndʒɪ'nerɪk/ adj. **1** of the same genus, kind, or race. **2** allied in nature or origin; akin. □□ **congenerous** /kən'dʒenərəs/ adj.

congenial /kən'dʒi:nɪəl/ adj. **1** (often foll. by *with, to*) (of a person, character, etc.) pleasant because akin to oneself in temperament or interests. **2** (often foll. by *to*) suited or agreeable. □□ **congeniality** /-'ælɪtɪ/ n. **congenially** adv. [CON- + GENIAL¹]

congenital /kən'dʒenɪt(ə)l/ adj. **1** (esp. of a disease, defect, etc.) existing from birth. **2** that is (or as if) such from birth (*a congenital liar*). □□ **congenitally** adv. [L *congenitus* (as COM-, *genitus* past part. of *gigno* beget)]

conger /'kɒŋgə(r)/ n. (in full **conger eel**) any large marine eel of the family Congridae. [ME f. OF *congre* f. L *conger, congrus*, f. Gk *goggros*]

congeries /kən'dʒɪərɪːz, -'dʒerɪˌiːz/ n. (pl. same) a disorderly collection; a mass or heap. [L, formed as CONGEST]

congest /kən'dʒest/ v.tr. (esp. as **congested** adj.) affect with congestion; obstruct, block (*congested streets; congested lungs*). □□ **congestive** adj. [L *congerere congest-* (as COM-, *gerere* bring)]

congestion /kən'dʒestʃ(ə)n/ n. abnormal accumulation, crowding, or obstruction, esp. of traffic etc. or of blood or mucus in a part of the body. [F f. L *congestio -onis* (as CONGEST)]

conglomerate /kən'glɒmərət/ adj., n., & v. —adj. **1** gathered into a rounded mass. **2** Geol. (of rock) made up of small stones held together (cf. AGGLOMERATE). —n. **1** a number of things or parts forming a heterogeneous mass. **2** a group or corporation formed by the merging of separate and diverse firms. **3** Geol. conglomerate rock. —v.tr. & intr. /kən'glɒməˌreɪt/ collect into a coherent mass. □□ **conglomeration** /kənˌglɒmə'reɪʃ(ə)n/ n. [L *conglomeratus* past part. of *conglomerare* (as COM-, *glomerare* f. *glomus -eris* ball)]

Congo /'kɒŋgəʊ/ **1** the former name of the Zaïre River. **2** a country in Africa, with a short Atlantic coastline, lying on the Equator with Zaïre to the east, and the Zaïre River and its tributary the Ubanghi forming most of its eastern boundary; pop. (est. 1988) 2,153,700; official language, French; capital, Brazzaville. There are some oil deposits but production is low. Colonized in the 19th c. by France and Belgium, the area has suffered severely as a result of the decolonizing process, being the scene of continued fighting in the 1960s and 1970s. □□ **Congolese** /ˌkɒŋgə'liːz/ adj. & n.

congou /'kɒŋguː, -gəʊ/ n. a variety of black China tea. [Chin. dial. *kung hu tē* tea laboured for]

congrats /kən'græts/ n.pl. & int. colloq. congratulations. [abbr.]

congratulate /kən'grætjʊˌleɪt/ v.tr. & refl. (often foll. by *on, upon*) **1** tr. express pleasure at the happiness or good fortune or excellence of (a person) (*congratulated them on their success*). **2** refl. think oneself fortunate or clever. □□ **congratulant** adj. & n. **congratulator** n. **congratulatory** /-lətərɪ/ adj. [L *congratulari* (as COM-, *gratulari* show joy f. *gratus* pleasing)]

congratulation /kənˌgrætjʊ'leɪʃ(ə)n/ n. **1** congratulating. **2** (also as int.; usu. in pl.) an expression of this (*congratulations on winning!*). [L *congratulatio* (as CONGRATULATE)]

congregant /'kɒŋgrɪgənt/ n. a member of a congregation (esp. Jewish). [L *congregare* (as CONGREGATE)]

congregate /'kɒŋgrɪˌgeɪt/ v.intr. & tr. collect or gather into a crowd or mass. [ME f. L *congregare* (as COM-, *gregare* f. *grex gregis* flock)]

congregation /ˌkɒŋgrɪ'geɪʃ(ə)n/ n. **1** the process of congregating; collection into a crowd or mass. **2** a crowd or mass gathered together. **3 a** a body assembled for religious worship. **b** a body of persons regularly attending a particular church etc. **c** RC Ch. a body of persons obeying a common religious rule. **d** RC Ch. any of several permanent committees of the Roman Catholic College of Cardinals. **4** (**Congregation**) Brit. (in some universities) a general assembly of resident senior members. [ME f. OF *congregation* or L *congregatio* (as CONGREGATE)]

congregational /ˌkɒŋgrɪ'geɪʃən(ə)l/ adj. **1** of a congregation. **2** (**Congregational**) of or adhering to Congregationalism.

Congregationalism /ˌkɒŋgrɪ'geɪʃənəˌlɪz(ə)m/ n. a system of ecclesiastical organization whereby individual churches are largely self-governing. The system derives from the belief that Christ is the sole head of his Church and all members of the Church, as Christians, are 'priests unto God'. Originally known as Independents, Congregationalists formed the backbone of Cromwell's army, but were persecuted under the 1662 Act of Uniformity. The independence of Congregational churches did not prevent them from forming County Associations for mutual support; in 1832 these Associations combined, and in 1972 the Congregational Church in England and Wales combined with the Presbyterian Church of England to form the United Reformed Church. □□ **Congregationalist** n. **Congregationalize** v.tr. (also **-ise**).

congress /'kɒŋgres/ n. **1** a formal meeting of delegates for discussion. **2** (**Congress**) a national legislative body, esp. that of the US. The US Congress, established by the Constitution of 1787, is composed of two houses, the upper or Senate, made up of two members for each State, each sitting for six years (one-third of whom come up for re-election every two years), and the lower, or House of Representatives, composed of 435 members (re-elected every two years) divided between the States on the basis of population by the method of major fractions in which each State elects one member for each ratio quotient and major fraction thereof. **3** a society or organization. **4** coming together, meeting. □ **Library of Congress** the US national library, in Washington, DC. It was established in 1800, originally for the benefit of members of Congress, and was at first housed in the Capitol, moving to its present site in 1897. □□ **congressional** /kənˈgreʃən(ə)l/ adj. [L congressus f. congredi (as COM-, gradi walk)]

congressman /ˈkɒŋgresmən/ n. (pl. **-men**; fem. **congresswoman**, pl. **-women**) a member of the US Congress.

Congreve /ˈkɒŋgriːv/, William (1670–1729), English dramatist, who gave up law for literature and achieved fame with The Old Bachelor (1693). Of his other plays, the best known are The Double Dealer (1693) and The Way of the World (1700), both brilliant examples of the sparkling and at times coarse wit of Restoration comedy. He wrote little for the stage after 1700. He lived comfortably, holding several sinecures and enjoying the company of Swift, Pope, Steele, and the Duchess of Marlborough who bore him a daughter.

congruence /ˈkɒŋgrʊəns/ n. (also **congruency** /-ənsɪ/) **1** agreement, consistency. **2** Geom. the state of being congruent. [ME f. L congruentia (as CONGRUENT)]

congruent /ˈkɒŋgrʊənt/ adj. **1** (often foll. by with) suitable, agreeing. **2** Geom. (of figures) coinciding exactly when superimposed. □□ **congruently** adv. [ME f. L congruere agree]

congruous /ˈkɒŋgrʊəs/ adj. (often foll. by with) suitable, agreeing; fitting. □□ **congruity** /-ˈgruːɪtɪ/ n. **congruously** adv. [L congruus (as CONGRUENT)]

conic /ˈkɒnɪk/ adj. & n. —adj. of a cone. —n. **1** a conic section. **2** (in pl.) the study of conic sections. □ **conic section** a figure formed by the intersection of a cone and a plane. [mod.L conicus f. Gk kōnikos (as CONE)]

conical /ˈkɒnɪk(ə)l/ adj. cone-shaped. □□ **conically** adv.

conidium /kəˈnɪdɪəm/ n. (pl. **conidia** /-dɪə/) a spore produced asexually by various fungi. [mod.L dimin. f. Gk konis dust]

conifer /ˈkɒnɪfə(r), ˈkəʊn-/ n. any evergreen tree of a group usu. bearing cones, including pines, yews, cedars, and redwoods. □□ **coniferous** /kəˈnɪfərəs/ adj. [L (as CONE, -FEROUS)]

coniform /ˈkəʊnɪfɔːm/ adj. cone-shaped. [L conus cone + -FORM]

coniine /ˈkəʊnɪˌiːn/ n. a poisonous alkaloid found in hemlock, that paralyses the nerves. [L conium f. Gk kōneion hemlock]

conjectural /kənˈdʒektʃər(ə)l/ adj. based on, involving, or given to conjecture. □□ **conjecturally** adv. [F f. L conjecturalis (as CONJECTURE)]

conjecture /kənˈdʒektʃə(r)/ n. & v. —n. **1 a** the formation of an opinion on incomplete information; guessing. **b** an opinion or conclusion reached in this way. **2 a** (in textual criticism) the guessing of a reading not in the text. **b** a proposed reading. —v. **1** tr. & intr. guess. **2** tr. (in textual criticism) propose (a reading). □□ **conjecturable** adj. [ME f. OF conjecture or L conjectura f. conjicere (as COM-, jacere throw)]

conjoin /kənˈdʒɔɪn/ v.tr. & intr. join, combine. [ME f. OF conjoign- pres. stem of conjoindre f. L conjungere (as COM-, jungere junct- join)]

conjoint /kənˈdʒɔɪnt/ adj. associated, conjoined. □□ **conjointly** adv. [ME f. OF, past part. (as CONJOIN)]

conjugal /ˈkɒndʒʊg(ə)l/ adj. of marriage or the relation between husband and wife. □ **conjugal rights** those rights (esp. to sexual relations) regarded as exercisable in law by each partner in a marriage. □□ **conjugality** /-ˈgælɪtɪ/ n. **conjugally** adv. [L conjugalis f. conjux consort (as COM-, -jux -jugis f. root of jungere join)]

conjugate v., adj., & n. —v. /ˈkɒndʒʊˌgeɪt/ **1** tr. Gram. give the different forms of (a verb). **2** intr. **a** unite sexually. **b** (of gametes) become fused. **3** intr. Chem. (of protein) combine with non-protein. —adj. /ˈkɒndʒʊgət/ **1** joined together, esp. as a pair. **2** Gram. derived from the same root. **3** Biol. fused. **4** Chem. (of an acid or base) related by loss or gain of an electron. **5** Math. joined in a reciprocal relation, esp. having the same real parts, and equal magnitudes but opposite signs of imaginary parts. —n. /ˈkɒndʒʊgət/ a conjugate word or thing. □□ **conjugately** /ˈkɒndʒʊgətlɪ/ adv. [L conjugare yoke together (as COM-, jugare f. jugum yoke)]

conjugation /ˌkɒndʒʊˈgeɪʃ(ə)n/ n. **1** Gram. a system of verbal inflection. **2 a** the act or an instance of conjugating. **b** an instance of this. **3** Biol. the fusion of two gametes in reproduction. □□ **conjugational** adj. [L conjugatio (as CONJUGATE)]

conjunct /kənˈdʒʌŋkt/ adj. joined together; combined; associated. [ME f. L conjunctus (as CONJOIN)]

conjunction /kənˈdʒʌŋkʃ(ə)n/ n. **1 a** the action of joining; the condition of being joined. **b** an instance of this. **2** Gram. a word used to connect clauses or sentences or words in the same clause (e.g. and, but, if). **3 a** a combination (of events or circumstances). **b** a number of associated persons or things. **4** Astron. & Astrol. the alignment of two bodies in the solar system so that they have the same longitude as seen from the earth. □ **in conjunction with** together with. □□ **conjunctional** adj. [ME f. OF conjonction f. L conjunctio -onis (as CONJUNCT)]

conjunctiva /ˌkɒndʒʌŋkˈtaɪvə, kənˈdʒʌŋktɪvə/ n. (pl. **conjunctivas**) Anat. the mucous membrane that covers the front of the eye and lines the inside of the eyelids. □□ **conjunctival** adj. [med.L (membrana) conjunctiva (as CONJUNCTIVE)]

conjunctive /kənˈdʒʌŋktɪv/ adj. & n. —adj. **1** serving to join; connective. **2** Gram. of the nature of a conjunction. —n. Gram. a conjunctive word. □□ **conjunctively** adv. [LL conjunctivus (as CONJOIN)]

conjunctivitis /kənˌdʒʌŋktɪˈvaɪtɪs/ n. inflammation of the conjunctiva.

conjuncture /kənˈdʒʌŋktʃə(r)/ n. a combination of events; a state of affairs. [obs. F f. It. congiuntura (as CONJOIN)]

conjuration /ˌkɒndʒʊˈreɪʃ(ə)n/ n. an incantation; a magic spell. [ME f. OF f. L conjuratio -onis (as CONJURE)]

conjure /ˈkʌndʒə(r)/ v. **1** intr. perform tricks which are seemingly magical, esp. by rapid movements of the hands. **2** tr. (usu. foll. by out of, away, to, etc.) cause to appear or disappear as if by magic (conjured a rabbit out of a hat; conjured them to a desert island; his pain was conjured away). **3** tr. call upon (a spirit) to appear. **4** intr. perform marvels. **5** tr. /kənˈdʒʊə(r)/ (often foll. by to + infin.) appeal solemnly to (a person). □ **conjure up 1** bring into existence or cause to appear as if by magic. **2** cause to appear to the eye or mind; evoke. [ME f. OF conjurer plot, exorcise f. L conjurare band together by oath (as COM-, jurare swear)]

conjuror /ˈkʌndʒərə(r)/ n. (also **conjurer**) a performer of conjuring tricks. [CONJURE + -ER¹ & AF conjurour (OF -eor) f. med.L conjurator (as CONJURE)]

conk¹ /kɒŋk/ v.intr. (usu. foll. by out) colloq. **1** (of a machine etc.) break down. **2** (of a person) become exhausted and give up; faint; die. [20th c.: orig. unkn.]

conk² /kɒŋk/ n. & v. sl. —n. **1 a** the nose. **b** the head. **2 a** a punch on the nose or head. **b** a blow. —v.tr. punch on the nose; hit on the head etc. [19th c.: perh. = CONCH]

conker /ˈkɒŋkə(r)/ n. **1** the hard fruit of a horse chestnut. **2** (in pl.) Brit. a children's game played with conkers on strings, one hit against another to try to break it. [dial. conker snail-shell (orig. used in the game), assoc. with CONQUER]

con moto /kɒn ˈməʊtəʊ/ adv. Mus. with movement. [It., = with movement]

conn US var. of CON⁴.

Conn. abbr. Connecticut.

Connacht see CONNAUGHT.

connate /ˈkɒneɪt/ adj. **1** existing in a person or thing from birth; innate. **2** formed at the same time. **3** allied, congenial. **4** Bot. (of organs) congenitally united so as to form one part. **5** Geol. (of water) trapped in sedimentary rock during its deposition. [LL connatus past part. of connasci (as COM-, nasci be born)]

connatural /kəˈnætʃər(ə)l/ adj. **1** (often foll. by to) innate; belonging naturally. **2** of like nature. □□ **connaturally** adv. [LL connaturalis (as COM-, NATURAL)]

Connaught /kəˈnɔːt/ (also **Connacht**) a province of the Republic of Ireland; pop. (est. 1986) 430,700.

connect /kəˈnekt/ v. **1 a** tr. (often foll. by to, with) join (one thing with another) (connected the hose to the tap). **b** tr. join (two things)

b but d dog f few g get h he j yes k cat l leg m man n no p pen r red s sit t top v voice

(a track connected the two villages). **c** intr. be joined or joinable (the two parts do not connect). **2** tr. (often foll. by with) associate mentally or practically (did not connect the two ideas; never connected me with the theatre). **3** intr. (foll. by with) (of a train etc.) be synchronized at its destination with another train etc., so that passengers can transfer (the train connects with the boat). **4** tr. put into communication by telephone. **5 a** tr. (usu. in passive; foll. by with) unite or associate with others in relationships etc. (am connected with the royal family). **b** intr. form a logical sequence; be meaningful. **6** intr. colloq. hit or strike effectively. □ **connecting-rod** the rod between the piston and the crankpin etc. in an internal-combustion engine or between the wheels of a locomotive. □□ **connectable** adj. **connector** n. [L connectere connex- (as COM-, nectere bind)]

connected /kəˈnektɪd/ adj. **1** joined in sequence. **2** (of ideas etc.) coherent. **3** related or associated. □ **well-connected** associated, esp. by birth, with persons of good social position. □□ **connectedly** adv. **connectedness** n.

Connecticut /kəˈnetɪkət/ a State of the US, bordering on the Atlantic; pop. (est. 1985) 3,107,600; capital, Hartford. A Puritan settlement in the 17th c., it was one of the original 13 States of the US (1788).

connection /kəˈnekʃ(ə)n/ n. (also Brit. **connexion**) **1 a** the act of connecting; the state of being connected. **b** an instance of this. **2** the point at which two things are connected (broke at the connection). **3 a** a thing or person that connects; a link (a radio formed the only connection with the outside world; cannot see the connection between the two ideas). **b** a telephone link (got a bad connection). **4** arrangement or opportunity for catching a connecting train etc.; the train etc. itself (missed the connection). **5** Electr. **a** the linking up of an electric current by contact. **b** a device for effecting this. **6** (often in pl.) a relative or associate, esp. one with influence (has connections in the Home Office; heard it through a business connection). **7** a relation of ideas; a context (in this connection I have to disagree). **8** sl. a supplier of narcotics. **9** a religious body, esp. Methodist. □ **in connection with** with reference to. **in this** (or **that**) **connection** with reference to this (or that). □□ **connectional** adj. [L connexio (as CONNECT): spelling -ct- after CONNECT]

connective /kəˈnektɪv/ adj. & n. —adj. serving or tending to connect. —n. something that connects. □ **connective tissue** Anat. a fibrous tissue that supports, binds, or separates more specialized tissue.

Connery /ˈkɒnərɪ/, Sean (Thomas Connery, 1930–), Scottish-born actor, known for his portrayal of James Bond in films of Ian Fleming's spy thrillers.

conning tower /ˈkɒnɪŋ/ n. **1** the superstructure of a submarine from which steering, firing, etc., are directed on or near the surface, and which contains the periscope. **2** the armoured pilot-house of a warship. [CON⁴ + -ING¹]

connivance /kəˈnaɪv(ə)ns/ n. **1** (often foll. by at, in) conniving (connivance in the crime). **2** tacit permission (done with his connivance). [F connivence or L conniventia (as CONNIVE)]

connive /kəˈnaɪv/ v.intr. **1** (foll. by at) disregard or tacitly consent to (a wrongdoing). **2** (usu. foll. by with) conspire. □□ **conniver** n. [F conniver or L connivēre shut the eyes (to)]

connoisseur /ˌkɒnəˈsɜː(r)/ n. (often foll. by of, in) an expert judge in matters of taste (a connoisseur of fine wine). □□ **connoisseurship** n. [F, obs. spelling of connaisseur f. pres. stem of connaître know + -eur -OR¹: cf. reconnoitre]

connotation /ˌkɒnəˈteɪʃ(ə)n/ n. **1** that which is implied by a word etc. in addition to its literal or primary meaning (a letter with sinister connotations). **2** the act of connoting or implying.

connote /kəˈnəʊt/ v.tr. **1** (of a word etc.) imply in addition to the literal or primary meaning. **2** (of a fact) imply as a consequence or condition. **3** mean, signify. □□ **connotative** /ˈkɒnəˌteɪtɪv, kəˈnəʊtətɪv/ adj. [med.L connotare mark in addition (as COM-, notare f. nota mark)]

connubial /kəˈnjuːbɪəl/ adj. of or relating to marriage or the relationship of husband and wife. □□ **connubiality** /-bɪˈælɪtɪ/ n. **connubially** adv. [L connubialis f. connubium (nubium f. nubere marry)]

conoid /ˈkəʊnɔɪd/ adj. & n. —adj. (also **conoidal** /-ˈnɔɪd(ə)l/) cone-shaped. —n. a cone-shaped object.

conquer /ˈkɒŋkə(r)/ v.tr. **1** overcome and control (an enemy or territory) by military force. **b** absol. be victorious. **2** overcome (a habit, emotion, disability, etc.) by effort (conquered his fear). **3** climb (a mountain) successfully. □□ **conquerable** adj. [ME f. OF conquerre f. Rmc f. L conquirere (as COM-, quaerere seek, get)]

conqueror /ˈkɒŋkərə(r)/ n. **1** a person who conquers. **2** Brit. = CONKER. [ME f. AF conquerour (OF -eor) f. conquerre (as CONQUER)]

conquest /ˈkɒŋkwest/ n. **1** the act or an instance of conquering; the state of being conquered. **2 a** a conquered territory. **b** something won. **3** a person whose affection or favour has been won. **4** (**the Conquest** or **Norman Conquest**) the conquest of England by William of Normandy in 1066. □ **make a conquest of** win the affections of. [ME f. OF conquest(e) f. Rmc (as CONQUER)]

conquistador /kɒnˈkwɪstə،dɔː(r)/ n. (pl. **conquistadores** /-rez/ or **conquistadors**) a conqueror, esp. one of the Spanish soldiers and adventurers who conquered South and Central America in the 16th c. While the initial object of most of their expeditions was the search for the fabled riches of the area, they ended by overthrowing the Aztec, Mayan, and Inca civilizations and establishing Spanish colonies. [Sp.]

Conrad /ˈkɒnræd/, Joseph (Teodor Josef Konrad Korzeniowski, 1857–1924), British novelist (he became a British subject in 1886), born of Polish parents in the Russian-dominated Ukraine. He was orphaned at an early age, went to sea in 1874, became a Master Mariner in 1894, when he settled in England and produced his first novel Almayer's Folly (1895). He established his reputation with The Nigger of the Narcissus (1897) and Lord Jim (1900), and continued his success with Nostromo (1904) in which he explores man's vulnerability and corruptibility, a theme he carries to terrifying conclusions in his story 'Heart of Darkness' (1902) and The Secret Agent (1907). The sea supplies the setting for most of his works and his narrative technique is characterized by breaks in time sequence, sometimes using a narrator, Marlow, to provide a commentary similar to a Greek chorus. He was a leading modernist and is considered by some critics to be among the great novelists in the English language.

Conran /ˈkɒnræn/, Sir Terence Orby (1931–), English designer of household furniture and furnishings, who established the 'Habitat' chain of shops, seeking to supply well-designed practical goods.

con-rod /ˈkɒnrɒd/ n. colloq. connecting-rod. [abbr.]

Cons. abbr. Conservative.

consanguineous /ˌkɒnsæŋˈgwɪnɪəs/ adj. descended from the same ancestor; akin. □□ **consanguinity** n. [L consanguineus (as COM-, sanguis -inis blood)]

conscience /ˈkɒnʃ(ə)ns/ n. **1** a moral sense of right and wrong esp. as felt by a person and affecting behaviour (my conscience won't allow me to do that). **2** an inner feeling as to the goodness or otherwise of one's behaviour (my conscience is clear; has a guilty conscience). □ **case of conscience** a matter in which one's conscience has to decide a conflict of principles. **conscience clause** a clause in a law, ensuring respect for the consciences of those affected. **conscience money** a sum paid to relieve one's conscience, esp. about a payment previously evaded. **conscience-stricken** (or **-struck**) made uneasy by a bad conscience. **for conscience** (or **conscience'**) **sake** to satisfy one's conscience. **freedom of conscience** a system allowing all persons freedom of choice in matters of religion, moral issues, etc. **in all conscience** colloq. by any reasonable standard; by all that is fair. **on one's conscience** causing one feelings of guilt. **prisoner of conscience** a person imprisoned by a State for holding political or religious views it does not tolerate. □□ **conscienceless** adj. [ME f. OF f. L conscientia f. conscire be privy to (as COM-, scire know)]

conscientious /ˌkɒnʃɪˈenʃəs/ adj. (of a person or conduct) diligent and scrupulous. □ **conscientious objector** a person who for reasons of conscience objects to conforming to a requirement, esp. that of military service. □□ **conscientiously** adv. **conscientiousness** n. [F conscientieux f. med.L conscientiosus (as CONSCIENCE)]

conscious /ˈkɒnʃəs/ *adj. & n.* —*adj.* **1** awake and aware of one's surroundings and identity. **2** (usu. foll. by *of*, or *that* + clause) aware, knowing (*conscious of his inferiority*). **3** (of actions, emotions, etc.) realized or recognized by the doer; intentional (*made a conscious effort not to laugh*). **4** (in *comb.*) aware of; concerned with (*appearance-conscious*). —*n.* (prec. by *the*) the conscious mind. □□ **consciously** *adv.* [L *conscius* knowing with others or in oneself f. *conscire* (as COM-, *scire* know)]

consciousness /ˈkɒnʃəsnɪs/ *n.* **1** the state of being conscious (*lost consciousness during the fight*). **2 a** awareness, perception (*had no consciousness of being ridiculed*). **b** (in *comb.*) awareness of (*class-consciousness*). **3** the totality of a person's thoughts and feelings, or of a class of these (*moral consciousness*). □ **consciousness-raising** the activity of increasing esp. social or political sensitivity or awareness.

conscribe /kənˈskraɪb/ *v.tr.* = CONSCRIPT *v.* [L *conscribere* (as CONSCRIPTION)]

conscript *v. & n.* —*v.tr.* /kənˈskrɪpt/ enlist by conscription. —*n.* /ˈkɒnskrɪpt/ a person enlisted by conscription. [(v.) backform. f. CONSCRIPTION: (n.) f. F *conscrit* f. L *conscriptus* (as CONSCRIPTION)]

conscription /kənˈskrɪpʃ(ə)n/ *n.* compulsory enlistment for State service, esp. military service. [F f. LL *conscriptio* levying of troops f. L *conscribere conscript-* enrol (as COM-, *scribere* write)]

consecrate /ˈkɒnsɪˌkreɪt/ *v.tr.* **1** make or declare sacred; dedicate formally to a religious or divine purpose. **2** (in Christian belief) make (bread and wine) into the body and blood of Christ. **3** (foll. by *to*) devote (one's life etc.) to (a purpose). **4** ordain (esp. a bishop) to a sacred office. □□ **consecration** /-ˈkreɪʃ(ə)n/ *n.* **consecrator** *n.* **consecratory** *adj.* [ME f. L *consecrare* (as COM-, *secrare* = *sacrare* dedicate f. *sacer* sacred)]

consecution /ˌkɒnsɪˈkjuːʃ(ə)n/ *n.* **1** logical sequence (in argument or reasoning). **2** sequence, succession (of events etc.). [L *consecutio* f. *consequi consecut-* overtake (as COM-, *sequi* pursue)]

consecutive /kənˈsekjʊtɪv/ *adj.* **1 a** following continuously. **b** in unbroken or logical order. **2** *Gram.* expressing consequence. □ **consecutive intervals** *Mus.* intervals of the same kind (esp. fifths or octaves), occurring in succession between two voices or parts in harmony. □□ **consecutively** *adv.* **consecutiveness** *n.* [F *consécutif -ive* f. med.L *consecutivus* (as CONSECUTION)]

consensual /kənˈsensjʊəl, -ˈsenʃʊəl/ *adj.* of or by consent or consensus. □□ **consensually** *adv.* [L *consensus* (see CONSENSUS) + -AL]

consensus /kənˈsensəs/ *n.* (often foll. by *of*) **1 a** general agreement (of opinion, testimony, etc.). **b** an instance of this. **2** (*attrib.*) majority view, collective opinion (*consensus politics*). [L, = agreement (as CONSENT)]

consent /kənˈsent/ *v. & n.* —*v.intr.* (often foll. by *to*) express willingness, give permission, agree. —*n.* voluntary agreement, permission, compliance. □ **age of consent** the age at which consent to sexual intercourse is valid in law. **consenting adult** **1** an adult who consents to something, esp. a homosexual act. **2** a homosexual. [ME f. OF *consentir* f. L *consentire* (as COM-, *sentire* *sens-* feel)]

consentient /kənˈsenʃ(ə)nt/ *adj.* **1** agreeing, united in opinion. **2** concurrent. **3** (often foll. by *to*) consenting. [L *consentient-* (as CONSENT)]

consequence /ˈkɒnsɪkwəns/ *n.* **1** the result or effect of an action or condition. **2 a** importance (*it is of no consequence*). **b** social distinction (*persons of consequence*). **3** (in *pl.*) a game in which a narrative is made up by the players, each ignorant of what has already been contributed. □ **in consequence** as a result. **take the consequences** accept the results of one's choice or action. [ME f. OF f. L *consequentia* (as CONSEQUENT)]

consequent /ˈkɒnsɪkwənt/ *adj. & n.* —*adj.* **1** (often foll. by *on*, *upon*) following as a result or consequence. **2** logically consistent. —*n.* **1** a thing that follows another. **2** *Logic* the second part of a conditional proposition, dependent on the antecedent. [ME f. OF f. L *consequi* (as CONSECUTION)]

consequential /ˌkɒnsɪˈkwenʃ(ə)l/ *adj.* **1** following as a result or consequence. **2** resulting indirectly (*consequential damage*). **3** (of

a person) self-important. □□ **consequentiality** /-ʃɪˈælɪtɪ/ *n.* **consequentially** *adv.* [L *consequentia*]

consequently /ˈkɒnsɪˌkwentlɪ/ *adv. & conj.* as a result; therefore.

conservancy /kənˈsɜːvənsɪ/ *n.* (pl. **-ies**) **1** *Brit.* a commission etc. controlling a port, river, etc. (*Thames Conservancy*). **2** a body concerned with the preservation of natural resources (*Nature Conservancy*). **3** conservation; official preservation (of forests etc.). [18th-c. alt. of obs. *conservacy* f. AF *conservacie* f. AL *conservatia* f. L *conservatio* (as CONSERVE)]

conservation /ˌkɒnsəˈveɪʃ(ə)n/ *n.* preservation, esp. of the natural environment. □ **conservation area** an area containing a noteworthy environment and specially protected by law against undesirable changes. **conservation of energy** (or **mass** or **momentum** etc.) *Physics* the principle that the total quantity of energy etc. of any system not subject to external action remains constant. □□ **conservational** *adj.* [ME f. OF *conservation* or L *conservatio* (as CONSERVE)]

conservationist /ˌkɒnsəˈveɪʃənɪst/ *n.* a supporter or advocate of environmental conservation.

conservative /kənˈsɜːvətɪv/ *adj. & n.* —*adj.* **1 a** averse to rapid change. **b** (of views, taste, etc.) moderate, avoiding extremes (*conservative in his dress*). **2** (of an estimate etc.) purposely low; moderate, cautious. **3** (**Conservative**) of or characteristic of Conservatives or the Conservative Party. **4** tending to conserve. —*n.* **1** a conservative person. **2** (**Conservative**) a supporter or member of the Conservative Party. □ **Conservative Judaism** Judaism allowing only minor changes in traditional ritual etc. **Conservative Party** see separate entry. **conservative surgery** surgery that seeks to preserve tissues as far as possible. □□ **conservatism** *n.* **conservatively** *adv.* **conservativeness** *n.* [ME f. LL *conservativus* (as CONSERVE)]

Conservative Party a political party disposed to maintain existing institutions and promote private enterprise. The modern Conservative Party in Britain emerged from the old Tory Party under Peel in the 1830s and 1840s. Under Disraeli it was the party committed to traditional institutions, social reform, and the defence of the Empire. After the First World War the Conservatives benefited from the decline of their traditional opponents, the Liberals, and dominated the political scene until defeated in the general election of 1945 by the Labour Party. The two-party system continued, with the Conservatives in power 1951-64, 1970–4, and from 1979; the emphasis of policy was on privatization of nationalized industries etc., reduction in direct taxation, reliance on market forces, and less governmental control.

conservatoire /kənˈsɜːvəˌtwɑː(r)/ *n.* a (usu. European) school of music or other arts. [F f. It. *conservatorio* (as CONSERVATORY)]

conservator /ˈkɒnsəˌveɪtə(r), kənˈsɜːvətə(r)/ *n.* a person who preserves something; an official custodian (of a museum etc.). [ME f. AF *conservatour*, OF *-ateur* f. L *conservator -oris* (as CONSERVE)]

conservatorium /kənˌsɜːvəˈtɔːrɪəm/ *n.* *Austral.* = CONSERVATOIRE.

conservatory /kənˈsɜːvətərɪ/ *n.* (pl. **-ies**) **1** a greenhouse for tender plants, esp. one attached to and communicating with a house. **2** esp. *US* = CONSERVATOIRE. [LL *conservatorium* (as CONSERVE): sense 2 through It. *conservatorio*]

conserve /kənˈsɜːv/ *v. & n.* —*v.tr.* **1** store up; keep from harm or damage, esp. for later use. **2** *Physics* maintain a quantity of (heat etc.). **3** preserve (food, esp. fruit), usu. with sugar. —*n.* /also ˈkɒnsɜːv/ **1** fruit etc. preserved in sugar. **2** fresh fruit jam. [ME f. OF *conserver* f. L *conservare* (as COM-, *servare* keep)]

consider /kənˈsɪdə(r)/ *v.tr.* (often *absol.*) **1** contemplate mentally, esp. in order to reach a conclusion. **2** examine the merits of (a course of action, a candidate, claim, etc.). **3** give attention to. **4** reckon with; take into account. **5** (foll. by *that* + clause) have the opinion. **6** (foll. by compl.) believe; regard as (*consider it to be genuine; consider it settled*). **7** (as **considered** *adj.*) formed after careful thought (*a considered opinion*). □ **all things considered** taking everything into account. [ME f. OF *considerer* f. L *considerare* examine]

considerable /kənˈsɪdərəb(ə)l/ *adj.* **1** enough in amount or extent to need consideration. **2** much; a lot of (*considerable pain*). **3** notable, important. □□ **considerably** *adv.*

considerate /kən'sɪdərət/ *adj.* **1** thoughtful towards other people; careful not to cause hurt or inconvenience. **2** *archaic* careful. □□ **considerately** *adv.*

consideration /kən,sɪdə'reɪʃ(ə)n/ *n.* **1** the act of considering; careful thought. **2** thoughtfulness for others; being considerate. **3** a fact or a thing taken into account in deciding or judging something. **4** compensation; a payment or reward. **5** *Law* (in a contractual agreement) anything given or promised or forborne by one party in exchange for the promise or undertaking of another. **6** *archaic* importance or consequence. □ **in consideration of** in return for; on account of. **take into consideration** include as a factor, reason, etc.; make allowance for. **under consideration** being considered. [ME f. OF f. L *consideratio -onis* (as CONSIDER)]

considering /kən'sɪdərɪŋ/ *prep.* **1** in view of; taking into consideration (*considering their youth; considering that it was snowing*). **2** (without compl.) *colloq.* all in all; taking everything into account (*not so bad, considering*).

consign /kən'saɪn/ *v.tr.* (often foll. by *to*) **1** hand over; deliver to a person's possession or trust. **2** assign; commit decisively or permanently (*consigned it to the dustbin; consigned to years of misery*). **3** transmit or send (goods), usu. by a public carrier. □□ **consignee** /,kɒnsaɪ'niː/ *n.* **consignor** *n.* [ME f. F *consigner* or L *consignare* mark with a seal (as COM-, SIGN)]

consignment /kən'saɪnmənt/ *n.* **1** the act or an instance of consigning; the process of being consigned. **2** a batch of goods consigned.

consist /kən'sɪst/ *v.intr.* **1** (foll. by *of*) be composed; have specified ingredients or elements. **2** (foll. by *in, of*) have its essential features as specified (*its beauty consists in the use of colour*). **3** (usu. foll. by *with*) harmonize; be consistent. [L *consistere* exist (as COM-, *sistere* stop)]

consistency /kən'sɪstənsɪ/ *n.* (also **consistence**) (*pl.* **-ies** or **-es**) **1** the degree of density, firmness, or viscosity, esp. of thick liquids. **2** the state of being consistent; conformity with other or earlier attitudes, practice, etc. **3** the state or quality of holding or sticking together and retaining shape. [F *consistence* or LL *consistentia* (as CONSIST)]

consistent /kən'sɪst(ə)nt/ *adj.* (usu. foll. by *with*) **1** compatible or in harmony; not contradictory. **2** (of a person) constant to the same principles of thought or action. □□ **consistently** *adv.* [L *consistere* (as CONSIST)]

consistory /kən'sɪstərɪ/ *n.* (*pl.* **-ies**) **1** *RC Ch.* the council of cardinals (with or without the pope). **2** (in full **consistory court**) (in the Church of England) a court presided over by a bishop, for the administration of ecclesiastical law in a diocese. **3** (in other Churches) a local administrative body. □□ **consistorial** /,kɒnsɪ'stɔːrɪəl/ *adj.* [ME f. AF *consistorie*, OF *-oire* f. LL *consistorium* (as CONSIST)]

consociation /kən,səʊʃɪ'eɪʃ(ə)n, kən,səʊsɪ'eɪʃ(ə)n/ *n.* **1** close association, esp. of Churches or religious communities. **2** *Ecol.* a closely-related sub-group of plants having one dominant species. [L *consociatio, -onis* f. *consociare* (as COM-, *socius* fellow)]

consolation /,kɒnsə'leɪʃ(ə)n/ *n.* **1** the act or an instance of consoling; the state of being consoled. **2** a consoling thing, person, or circumstance. □ **consolation prize** a prize given to a competitor who just fails to win a main prize. □□ **consolatory** /kən'sɒlətərɪ/ *adj.* [ME f. OF f. L *consolatio -onis* (as CONSOLE¹)]

console¹ /kən'səʊl/ *v.tr.* comfort, esp. in grief or disappointment. ¶ Often confused with *condole*. □□ **consolable** *adj.* **consoler** *n.* **consolingly** *adv.* [F *consoler* f. L *consolari*]

console² /'kɒnsəʊl/ *n.* **1** a panel or unit accommodating a set of switches, controls, etc. **2** a cabinet for television or radio equipment etc. **3** *Mus.* a cabinet with the keyboards, stops, pedals, etc., of an organ. **4** an ornamented bracket supporting a shelf etc. □ **console table** a table supported by a bracket against a wall. [F, perh. f. *consolider* (as CONSOLIDATE)]

consolidate /kən'sɒlɪ,deɪt/ *v.* **1** *tr. & intr.* make or become strong or solid. **2** *tr.* reinforce or strengthen (one's position, power, etc.). **3** *tr.* combine (territories, companies, debts, etc.) into one

whole. □□ **consolidation** /kən,sɒlɪ'deɪʃ(ə)n/ *n.* **consolidator** *n.* **consolidatory** *adj.* [L *consolidare* (as COM-, *solidare* f. *solidus* solid)]

Consolidated Fund the Exchequer account at the Bank of England into which public monies (such as tax receipts) are paid and from which the main payments are made that are not dependent on annual votes in Parliament. These include interest on the National Debt, grants to the Royal Family, and payments on the Civil List. It was established by William Pitt the Younger in 1786 and so called because it 'consolidated various revenues into a single fund'.

consols /'kɒnsɒlz/ *n.pl.* British government securities without redemption date and with fixed annual interest. The present bonds, called *consolidated annuities* or *consolidated stock*, are the result of merging several loans at various times from the 18th c. onwards. [abbr. of *consolidated annuities*]

consommé /kən'sɒmeɪ/ *n.* a clear soup made with meat stock. [F, past part. of *consommer* f. L *consummare* (as CONSUMMATE)]

consonance /'kɒnsənəns/ *n.* **1** agreement, harmony. **2** *Prosody* a recurrence of similar-sounding consonants. **3** *Mus.* a harmonious combination of notes; a harmonious interval. [ME f. OF *consonance* or L *consonantia* (as CONSONANT)]

consonant /'kɒnsənənt/ *n. & adj.* —*n.* **1** a speech sound in which the breath is at least partly obstructed, and which to form a syllable must be combined with a vowel. **2** a letter or letters representing this. —*adj.* (foll. by *with, to*) **1** consistent; in agreement or harmony. **2** similar in sound. **3** *Mus.* making a concord. □□ **consonantal** /-'nænt(ə)l/ *adj.* **consonantly** *adv.* [ME f. F f. L *consonare* (as COM-, *sonare* sound f. *sonus*)]

con sordino /,kɒn sɔː'diːnəʊ/ *adv. Mus.* with the use of a mute. [It.]

consort¹ *n. & v.* —*n.* /'kɒnsɔːt/ **1** a wife or husband, esp. of royalty (*prince consort*). **2** a ship sailing with another. —*v.* /kən'sɔːt/ **1** *intr.* (usu. foll. by *with, together*) **a** keep company; associate. **b** harmonize. **2** *tr.* class or bring together. [ME f. F f. L *consors sharer, comrade (as COM-, *sors sortis* lot, destiny)]

consort² /'kɒnsɔːt/ *n. Mus.* a group of players or instruments, esp. playing English music in about 1570 to 1720. The term 'broken consort' refers to an ensemble of mixed instruments (e.g. viols, recorders, and lutes) and 'whole consort' to a complete set of a single type. □ **consort song** a song for solo voice and a consort usually of viols. [earlier form of CONCERT]

consortium /kən'sɔːtɪəm/ *n.* (*pl.* **consortia** /-tɪə/ or **consortiums**) **1** an association, esp. of several business companies. **2** *Law* the right of association with a husband or wife (*loss of consortium*). [L, = partnership (as CONSORT¹)]

conspecific /,kɒnspɪ'sɪfɪk/ *adj. Biol.* of the same species.

conspectus /kən'spektəs/ *n.* **1** a general or comprehensive survey. **2** a summary or synopsis. [L f. *conspicere conspect-* (as COM-, *spicere* look at)]

conspicuous /kən'spɪkjʊəs/ *adj.* **1** clearly visible; striking to the eye; attracting notice. **2** remarkable of its kind (*conspicuous extravagance*). □□ **conspicuously** *adv.* **conspicuousness** *n.* [L *conspicuus* (as CONSPECTUS)]

conspiracy /kən'spɪrəsɪ/ *n.* (*pl.* **-ies**) **1** a secret plan to commit a crime or do harm, often for political ends; a plot. **2** the act of conspiring. □ **conspiracy of silence** an agreement to say nothing. [ME f. AF *conspiracie*, alt. form of OF *conspiration* f. L *conspiratio -onis* (as CONSPIRE)]

conspirator /kən'spɪrətə(r)/ *n.* a person who takes part in a conspiracy. □□ **conspiratorial** /-'tɔːrɪəl/ *adj.* **conspiratorially** /-'tɔːrɪəlɪ/ *adv.* [ME f. AF *conspiratour*, OF *-teur* (as CONSPIRE)]

conspire /kən'spaɪə(r)/ *v.intr.* **1** combine secretly to plan and prepare an unlawful or harmful act. **2** (often foll. by *against*, or *to* + infin.) (of events or circumstances) seem to be working together, esp. disadvantageously. [ME f. OF *conspirer* f. L *conspirare* agree, plot (as COM-, *spirare* breathe)]

Constable /'kʌnstəb(ə)l/, John (1776–1837), English painter. Never a prodigy, his style developed slowly towards a radical naturalism that took prosaic landscape and subjected it to rigorous visual analysis (e.g. *The Hay Wain*, 1820). Increasingly, however, his interests in paint handling as such, and a more generalized view of nature, saw the development of a florid, almost mannered, late style that replaced observation with expressive, almost rhetorical, statements about growth, change, and decay (e.g. *The Valley Farm*, 1835). Although he had no immediate followers in England, the exhibition of his work at Paris in 1824 was a revelation to French artists such as Delacroix and contemporary landscape painters. His personal achievement ranks, with that of Turner, as the greatest splendour of English landscape painting.

constable /ˈkʌnstəb(ə)l/ *n.* **1** *Brit.* **a** a policeman or policewoman. **b** (also **police constable**) a police officer of the lowest rank. **2** the governor of a royal castle. **3** *hist.* the principal officer in a royal household. □ **Chief Constable** the head of the police force of a county or other region. [ME f. OF *conestable* f. LL *comes stabuli* count of the stable]

constabulary /kənˈstæbjʊləri/ *n. & adj.* —*n.* (pl. **-ies**) an organized body of police; a police force. —*attrib.adj.* of or concerning the police force. [med.L *constabularius* (as CONSTABLE)]

Constance /ˈkɒnstəns/, **Lake** (German **Bodensee** /ˈbəʊdənˌzeɪ/) a lake on the north side of the Swiss Alps, at the meeting-point of Germany, Switzerland, and Austria, forming part of the course of the River Rhine.

constancy /ˈkɒnstənsi/ *n.* **1** the quality of being unchanging and dependable; faithfulness. **2** firmness, endurance. [L *constantia* (as CONSTANT)]

constant /ˈkɒnst(ə)nt/ *adj. & n.* —*adj.* **1** continuous (*needs constant attention*). **2** occurring frequently (*receive constant complaints*). **3** (often foll. by *to*) unchanging, faithful, dependable. —*n.* **1** anything that does not vary. **2** *Math.* a component of a relationship between variables that does not change its value. **3** *Physics* **a** a number expressing a relation, property, etc., and remaining the same in all circumstances. **b** such a number that remains the same for a substance in the same conditions. □□ **constantly** *adv.* [ME f. OF f. L *constare* (as COM-, *stare* stand)]

constantan /ˈkɒnstənˌtæn/ *n.* an alloy of copper and nickel used in electrical equipment. [CONSTANT + -AN]

Constantine¹ /ˈkɒnstənˌtaɪn/ 'the Great' (d. 337), Roman emperor from 306, who in his youth spent time at the court of Diocletian where he learned the new Byzantine ideas of absolute sovereignty. In 312 he defeated his rival Maxentius at a battle near Rome, adopting the labarum (see entry) as a standard (reportedly after a vision of the Cross). Shortly afterwards toleration and imperial favour were given to the Christian faith. His policy was to unite the Church to the secular State by the closest possible ties, and he involved himself in its internal affairs. After 324 he fixed his capital at Byzantium (rebuilt and inaugurated as Constantinople in 330), a move which led to an increasing imperial control of the Eastern Church and incidentally left the bishop of Rome as the most prominent figure in the West; the secular importance of the papacy in the Middle Ages dates from this time. His reign, though not free from blemishes, was marked by humanizing reforms and by liberal endowment of church building, especially at the holy sites in Palestine; in the Eastern Church he is venerated as a saint (feast day, 21 May).

Constantine² /ˈkɒnstənˌtaɪn/ a city in NE Algeria; pop. (1983) 448,578. As Cirta (or Kirtha) it was the capital of the Roman province of Numidia. It was destroyed in 311 but rebuilt soon afterwards by Constantine the Great, and given his name. Its port is Skikda.

Constantinople /ˌkɒnstæntɪˈnəʊp(ə)l/ a city (modern Istanbul) on the European side of the south end of the Bosporus, founded in 324 and inaugurated (330) as the second capital of the Roman Empire by Constantine the Great on the site of Byzantium. Subsequently the seat of the Byzantine emperors, it was captured by the Ottoman Turks in 1453.

Constanza /kənˈstæntsə/ the chief port of Romania, on the Black Sea; pop. (1985) 323,200. The roman poet Ovid lived in exile here; it was at the extreme edge of the Roman Empire and subject to barbarian attacks.

constellate /ˈkɒnstəˌleɪt/ *v.tr.* **1** form into (or as if into) a constellation. **2** adorn as with stars.

constellation /ˌkɒnstəˈleɪʃ(ə)n/ *n.* **1** a group of fixed stars forming a recognizable pattern in the sky and identified by some imaginative name describing their form or identifying them with a mythological figure. Eighty-eight are officially recognized by modern astronomers, many identical with those of the ancient Egyptians. **2** a group of associated persons, ideas, etc. [ME f. OF f. LL *constellatio -onis* (as COM-, *stella* star)]

consternate /ˈkɒnstəˌneɪt/ *v.tr.* (usu. in *passive*) dismay; fill with anxiety. [L *consternare* (as COM-, *sternere* throw down)]

consternation /ˌkɒnstəˈneɪʃ(ə)n/ *n.* anxiety or dismay causing mental confusion. [F *consternation* or L *consternatio* (as CONSTERNATE)]

constipate /ˈkɒnstɪˌpeɪt/ *v.tr.* (esp. as **constipated** *adj.*) affect with constipation. [L *constipare* (as COM-, *stipare* press)]

constipation /ˌkɒnstɪˈpeɪʃ(ə)n/ *n.* **1** a condition with hardened faeces and difficulty in emptying the bowels. **2** a restricted state. [ME f. OF *constipation* or LL *constipatio* (as CONSTIPATE)]

constituency /kənˈstɪtjʊənsi/ *n.* (pl. **-ies**) **1** a body of voters in a specified area who elect a representative member to a legislative body. **2** the area represented in this way. **3** a body of customers, supporters, etc.

constituent /kənˈstɪtjʊənt/ *adj. & n.* —*adj.* **1** composing or helping to make up a whole. **2** able to make or change a (political etc.) constitution (*constituent assembly*). **3** appointing or electing. —*n.* **1** a member of a constituency (esp. political). **2** a component part. **3** *Law* a person who appoints another as agent. [L *constituent-* partly through F *-ant* (as CONSTITUTE)]

constitute /ˈkɒnstɪˌtjuːt/ *v.tr.* **1** be the components or essence of; make up, form. **2 a** be equivalent or tantamount to (*this constitutes an official warning*). **b** formally establish (*does not constitute a precedent*). **3** give legal or constitutional form to; establish by law. □□ **constitutor** *n.* [L *constituere* (as COM-, *statuere* set up)]

constitution /ˌkɒnstɪˈtjuːʃ(ə)n/ *n.* **1** the act or method of constituting; the composition (of something). **2 a** the body of fundamental principles or established precedents according to which a State or other organization is acknowledged to be governed. **b** a (usu. written) record of this. **3** a person's physical state as regards vitality, health, strength, etc. **4** a person's mental or psychological make-up. **5** *hist.* a decree or ordinance. [ME f. OF *constitution* or L *constitutio* (as CONSTITUTE)]

constitutional /ˌkɒnstɪˈtjuːʃən(ə)l/ *adj. & n.* —*adj.* **1** of, consistent with, authorized by, or limited by a political constitution (*a constitutional monarchy*). **2** inherent in, stemming from, or affecting the physical or mental constitution. —*n.* a walk taken regularly to maintain or restore good health. □□ **constitutionality** /-ˈnælɪti/ *n.* **constitutionalize** *v.tr.* (also **-ise**). **constitutionally** *adv.*

constitutionalism /ˌkɒnstɪˈtjuːʃənəˌlɪz(ə)m/ *n.* **1** a constitutional system of government. **2** the adherence to or advocacy of such a system. □□ **constitutionalist** *n.*

constitutive /ˈkɒnstɪˌtjuːtɪv/ *adj.* **1** able to form or appoint. **2** component. **3** essential. □□ **constitutively** *adv.* [LL *constitutivus* (as CONSTITUTE)]

constrain /kənˈstreɪn/ *v.tr.* **1** compel; urge irresistibly or by necessity. **2 a** confine forcibly; imprison. **b** restrict severely as regards action, behaviour, etc. **3** bring about by compulsion. **4** (as **constrained** *adj.*) forced, embarrassed (*a constrained voice*; *a constrained manner*). □□ **constrainedly** /kənˈstreɪnɪdli/ *adv.* [ME f. OF *constraindre* f. L *constringere* (as COM-, *stringere strict-* tie)]

constraint /kənˈstreɪnt/ *n.* **1** the act or result of constraining or being constrained; restriction of liberty. **2** something that constrains; a limitation on motion or action. **3** the restraint of natural feelings or their expression; a constrained manner. [ME f. OF *constreinte*, fem. past part. (as CONSTRAIN)]

constrict /kənˈstrɪkt/ *v.tr.* **1** make narrow or tight; compress. **2** *Biol.* cause (organic tissue) to contract. □□ **constriction** *n.* **constrictive** *adj.* [L (as CONSTRAIN)]

constrictor /kənˈstrɪktə(r)/ *n.* **1** any snake (esp. a boa) that kills by coiling round its prey and compressing it. **2** *Anat.* any muscle that compresses or contracts an organ or part of the body. [mod.L (as CONSTRICT)]

construct *v. & n.* —*v.tr.* /kənˈstrʌkt/ **1** make by fitting parts together; build, form (something physical or abstract). 2 *Geom.* draw or delineate, esp. accurately to given conditions (*construct a triangle*). —*n.* /'kɒnstrʌkt/ 1 a thing constructed, esp. by the mind. 2 *Linguistics* a group of words forming a phrase. □□ **constructor** *n.* [L *construere construct-* (as COM-, *struere* pile, build)]

construction /kən'strʌkʃ(ə)n/ *n.* 1 the act or a mode of constructing. 2 a thing constructed. 3 an interpretation or explanation (*they put a generous construction on his act*). 4 *Gram.* an arrangement of words according to syntactical rules. □□ **constructional** *adj.* **constructionally** *adv.* [ME f. OF f. L *constructio -onis* (as CONSTRUCT)]

constructionism /kən'strʌkʃəˌnɪz(ə)m/ *n.* = CONSTRUCTIVISM.

constructive /kən'strʌktɪv/ *adj.* 1 **a** of construction; tending to construct. **b** tending to form a basis for ideas (*constructive criticism*). 2 helpful, positive (*a constructive approach*). 3 derived by inference; not expressed (*constructive permission*). 4 belonging to the structure of a building. □□ **constructively** *adv.* **constructiveness** *n.* [LL *constructivus* (as CONSTRUCT)]

constructivism /kən'strʌktɪˌvɪz(ə)m/ *n.* an artistic movement which gained momentum in the 1920s as two distinct trends — that of Russian constructivism and a separate international movement. The Russian movement stemmed from the work of artists such as Tatlin (1885–1953), Antony Pevsner, and Naum Pevsner (Gabo), who sought to 'construct' sculptural forms using materials as various as sheet metal, tubing, wire, perspex, and glass, and were as concerned with negative space as positive form. Opinion varies as to the founder and to the specific moment of the movement's birth. Tatlin, influenced by Picasso's cubist collages, was experimenting with 'hanging reliefs' of wood and iron as early as 1913, and his theories were most spectacularly expressed in his projected monument of 1920 to the Third Communist International, a leaning spiral with vertical glass chambers continually revolving at varying speeds. The constructivist school outside Russia was more diverse and is consequently less capable of categorization. Related ideas can be detected in aspects of the de Stijl movement in The Netherlands and the Bauhaus in Germany, and the later presence in England of Gabo, Pevsner, and others exerted some influence there. □□ **constructivist** *n.* [Russ. *konstruktivizm* (as CONSTRUCT)]

construe /kən'stru:/ *v.tr.* (**construes, construed, construing**) 1 interpret (words or actions) (*their decision can be construed in many ways*). 2 (often foll. by *with*) combine (words) grammatically ('*rely*' *is construed with* '*on*'). 3 analyse the syntax of (a sentence). 4 translate word for word. □□ **construable** *adj.* **construal** *n.* [ME f. L *construere* CONSTRUCT]

consubstantial /ˌkɒnsəb'stænʃ(ə)l/ *adj.* *Theol.* of the same substance (esp. of the three persons of the Trinity). □□ **consubstantiality** /-ʃɪ'ælɪtɪ/ *n.* [ME f. eccl.L *consubstantialis*, transl. Gk *homoousios* (as COM-, SUBSTANTIAL)]

consubstantiation /ˌkɒnsəbˌstænʃɪ'eɪʃ(ə)n/ *n.* *Theol.* the presence in the Eucharist, after consecration of the elements, of the real substances of the body and blood of Christ coexisting with those of the bread and wine. The doctrine asserting this, associated especially with Luther, was formulated in opposiiton to the medieval doctrine of transubstantiation. [mod.L *consubstantiatio*, after *transubstantiatio* TRANSUBSTANTIATION]

consuetude /'kɒnswɪˌtju:d/ *n.* a custom, esp. one having legal force in Scotland. □□ **consuetudinary** /ˌkɒnswɪ'tju:dɪnərɪ/ *adj.* [ME f. OF *consuetude* or L *consuetudo -dinis* f. *consuetus* accustomed]

consul /'kɒns(ə)l/ *n.* 1 an official appointed by a State to live in a foreign city and protect the State's citizens and interests there. 2 *hist.* either of two annually elected chief magistrates in ancient Rome. 3 any of the three chief magistrates of the French republic (1799–1804). □□ **consular** /'kɒnsjʊlə(r)/ *adj.* **consulship** *n.* [ME f. L, rel. to *consulere* take counsel]

consulate /'kɒnsjʊlət/ *n.* 1 the building officially used by a consul. 2 the office, position, or period of office of consul. 3 *hist.* government by consuls. 4 *hist.* the period of office of a consul. 5 *hist.* (**Consulate**) the government of France by three consuls (1799–1804). [ME f. L *consulatus* (as CONSUL)]

consult /kən'sʌlt/ *v.* 1 *tr.* seek information or advice from (a

person, book, watch, etc.). 2 *intr.* (often foll. by *with*) refer to a person for advice, an opinion, etc. 3 *tr.* seek permission or approval from (a person) for a proposed action. 4 *tr.* take into account; consider (feelings, interests, etc.). □□ **consultative** /-tətɪv/ *adj.* [F *consulter* f. L *consultare* frequent. of *consulere* consult-take counsel]

consultancy /kən'sʌltənsɪ/ *n.* (*pl.* **-ies**) the professional practice or position of a consultant.

consultant /kən'sʌlt(ə)nt/ *n.* 1 a person providing professional advice etc., esp. for a fee. 2 a senior specialist in a branch of medicine responsible for patients in a hospital. [prob. F (as CONSULT)]

consultation /ˌkɒnsəl'teɪʃ(ə)n/ *n.* 1 a meeting arranged to consult (esp. with a consultant). 2 the act or an instance of consulting. 3 a conference. [ME f. OF *consultation* or L *consultatio* (as CONSULTANT)]

consulting /kən'sʌltɪŋ/ *attrib.adj.* giving professional advice to others working in the same field or subject (*consulting physician*).

consumable /kən'sju:məb(ə)l/ *adj.* & *n.* —*adj.* that can be consumed; intended for consumption. —*n.* (usu. in *pl.*) a commodity that is eventually used up, worn out, or eaten.

consume /kən'sju:m/ *v.tr.* 1 eat or drink. 2 completely destroy; reduce to nothing or to tiny particles (*fire consumed the building*). 3 (as **consumed** *adj.*) possessed by or entirely taken up (foll. by *with*: *consumed with rage*). 4 use up (time, energy, etc.). □□ **consumingly** *adv.* [ME f. L *consumere* (as COM-, *sumere* sumpt- take up): partly through F *consumer*]

consumer /kən'sju:mə(r)/ *n.* 1 a person who consumes, esp. one who uses a product. 2 a purchaser of goods or services. □ **consumer durable** a household product with a relatively long useful life (e.g. a radio or washing-machine). **consumer goods** goods put to use by consumers, not used in producing other goods (opp. *capital goods* (see CAPITAL¹)). **consumer research** investigation of purchasers' needs and opinions. **consumer society** a society in which the marketing of goods and services is an important social and economic activity.

consumerism /kən'sju:məˌrɪz(ə)m/ *n.* the protection or promotion of consumers' interests in relation to the producer. □□ **consumerist** *adj.* & *n.*

consummate *v.* & *adj.* —*v.tr.* /'kɒnsəˌmeɪt/ 1 complete; make perfect. 2 complete (a marriage) by sexual intercourse. —*adj.* /kən'sʌmɪt, 'kɒnsəmɪt/ complete, perfect; fully skilled (*a consummate general*). □□ **consummately** *adv.* **consummative** *adj.* **consummator** /'kɒnsəˌmeɪtə(r)/ *n.* [L *consummare* (as COM-, *summare* complete f. *summus* utmost)]

consummation /ˌkɒnsə'meɪʃ(ə)n/ *n.* 1 completion, esp. of a marriage by sexual intercourse. 2 a desired end or goal; perfection. [ME f. OF *consommation* or L *consummatio* (as CONSUMMATE)]

consumption /kən'sʌmpʃ(ə)n/ *n.* 1 the act or an instance of consuming; the process of being consumed. 2 any disease causing wasting of tissues, esp. pulmonary tuberculosis. 3 an amount consumed. 4 the purchase and use of goods etc. [ME f. OF *consomption* f. L *consumptio* (as CONSUME)]

consumptive /kən'sʌmptɪv/ *adj.* & *n.* —*adj.* 1 of or tending to consumption. 2 tending to or affected with pulmonary tuberculosis. —*n.* a consumptive patient. □□ **consumptively** *adv.* [med.L *consumptivus* (as CONSUMPTION)]

cont. *abbr.* 1 contents. 2 continued.

contact /'kɒntækt/ *n.* & *v.* —*n.* 1 the state or condition of touching, meeting, or communicating. 2 a person who is or may be communicated with for information, supplies, assistance, etc. 3 *Electr.* **a** a connection for the passage of a current. **b** a device for providing this. 4 a person likely to carry a contagious disease through being associated with an infected person. 5 (usu. in *pl.*) *colloq.* a contact lens. —*v.tr.* /'kɒntækt, kən'tækt/ 1 get into communication with (a person). 2 begin correspondence or personal dealings with. □ **contact lens** a small lens placed directly on the eyeball to correct the vision. **contact print** a photographic print made by placing a negative directly on sensitized paper etc. and illuminating it. **contact sport** a sport in which participants necessarily come into bodily contact with one another. □□ **contactable** adj. [L contactus f. contingere (as COM-, tangere touch)]

Contadora /ˌkɒntəˈdɔːrə/ one of the Pearl Islands, in the Gulf of Panama. □ **Contadora Group** a group of countries (Colombia, Panama, Venezuela, and Mexico) whose representatives met on the island in Jan. 1983 with the aim of finding a means of bringing peace to Central America.

contagion /kənˈteɪdʒ(ə)n/ n. **1 a** the communication of disease from one person to another by bodily contact. **b** a contagious disease. **2** a contagious or harmful influence. **3** moral corruption, esp. when tending to be widespread. [ME f. L contagio (as COM-, tangere touch)]

contagious /kənˈteɪdʒəs/ adj. **1 a** (of a person) likely to transmit disease by contact. **b** (of a disease) transmitted in this way. **2** (of emotions, reactions, etc.) likely to affect others (contagious enthusiasm). □ **contagious abortion** brucellosis of cattle. □□ **contagiously** adv. **contagiousness** n. [ME f. LL contagiosus (as CONTAGION)]

contain /kənˈteɪn/ v.tr. **1** hold or be capable of holding within itself; include, comprise. **2** (of measures) consist of or be equal to (a gallon contains eight pints). **3** prevent (an enemy, difficulty, etc.) from moving or extending. **4** control or restrain (oneself, one's feelings, etc.). **5** (of a number) be divisible by (a factor) without a remainder. □□ **containable** adj. [ME f. OF contenir f. L continēre content- (as COM-, tenēre hold)]

container /kənˈteɪnə(r)/ n. **1** a vessel, box, etc., for holding particular things. **2** a large boxlike receptacle of standard design for the transport of goods, esp. one readily transferable from one form of transport to another (also attrib.: container ship).

containerize /kənˈteɪnəraɪz/ v.tr. (also -**ise**) **1** pack in or transport by container. **2** adapt to transport by container. □□ **containerization** /-ˈzeɪʃ(ə)n/ n.

containment /kənˈteɪnmənt/ n. the action or policy of preventing the expansion of a hostile country or influence.

contaminate /kənˈtæmɪˌneɪt/ v.tr. **1** pollute, esp. with radioactivity. **2** infect. □□ **contaminant** n. **contamination** /-ˈneɪʃ(ə)n/ n. **contaminator** n. [L contaminare (as COM-, tamen- rel. to tangere touch)]

contango /kənˈtæŋgəʊ/ n. (pl. -**os**) Brit. Stock Exch. **1** the postponement of the transfer of stock from one account day to the next. **2** a percentage paid by the buyer for such a postponement. □ **contango day** the eighth day before settling day. [19th c.: prob. an arbitrary formation]

conte /kɒ̃t/ n. **1** a short story (as a form of literary composition). **2** a medieval narrative tale. [F]

contemn /kənˈtem/ v.tr. literary despise; treat with disregard. □□ **contemner** /-ˈtemə(r), -ˈtemnə(r)/ n. [ME f. OF contemner or L contemnere (as COM-, temnere tempt- despise)]

contemplate /ˈkɒntəmˌpleɪt/ v. **1** tr. survey with the eyes or in the mind. **2** tr. regard (an event) as possible. **3** tr. intend; have as one's purpose (we contemplate leaving tomorrow). **4** intr. meditate. □□ **contemplation** /-ˈpleɪʃ(ə)n/ n. **contemplator** n. [L contemplari (as COM-, templum place for observations)]

contemplative /kənˈtemplətɪv/ adj. & n. —adj. of or given to (esp. religious) contemplation; meditative. —n. a person whose life is devoted to religious contemplation. □□ **contemplatively** adv. [ME f. OF contemplatif -ive, or L contemplativus (as CONTEMPLATE)]

contemporaneous /kənˌtempəˈreɪnɪəs/ adj. (usu. foll. by with) **1** existing or occurring at the same time. **2** of the same period. □□ **contemporaneity** /-ˈniːɪtɪ/ n. **contemporaneously** adv. **contemporaneousness** n. [L contemporaneus (as COM-, temporaneus f. tempus -oris time)]

contemporary /kənˈtempərərɪ/ adj. & n. —adj. **1** living or occurring at the same time. **2** approximately equal in age. **3** following modern ideas or fashion in style or design. —n. (pl. -**ies**) **1** a person or thing living or existing at the same time as another. **2** a person of roughly the same age as another. □□ **contemporarily** adv. **contemporariness** n. **contemporarize** v.tr. (also -**ise**). [med.L contemporarius (as CONTEMPORANEOUS)]

contempt /kənˈtempt/ n. **1** a feeling that a person or a thing is beneath consideration or worthless, or deserving scorn or extreme reproach. **2** the condition of being held in contempt. **3** (in full **contempt of court**) disobedience to or disrespect for a court of law and its officers. □ **beneath contempt** utterly despicable. **hold in contempt** despise. [ME f. L contemptus (as CONTEMN)]

contemptible /kənˈtemptɪb(ə)l/ adj. deserving contempt; despicable. □□ **contemptibility** n. **contemptibly** adv. [ME f. OF or LL contemptibilis (as CONTEMN)]

contemptuous /kənˈtemptjʊəs/ adj. (often foll. by of) showing contempt, scornful; insolent. □□ **contemptuously** adv. [med.L contemptuosus f. L contemptus (as CONTEMPT)]

contend /kənˈtend/ v. **1** intr. (usu. foll. by with) strive, fight. **2** intr. compete (contending emotions). **3** tr. (usu. foll. by that + clause) assert, maintain. □□ **contender** n. [OF contendre or L contendere (as COM-, tendere tent- stretch, strive)]

content[1] /kənˈtent/ adj., v., & n. —predic.adj. **1** satisfied; adequately happy; in agreement. **2** (foll. by to + infin.) willing. —v.tr. make content; satisfy. —n. a contented state; satisfaction. □ **to one's heart's content** to the full extent of one's desires. [ME f. OF f. L contentus satisfied, past part. of continēre (as CONTAIN)]

content[2] /ˈkɒntent/ n. **1** (usu. in pl.) what is contained in something, esp. in a vessel, book, or house. **2** the amount of a constituent contained (low sodium content). **3** the substance or material dealt with (in a speech, work of art, etc.) as distinct from its form or style. **4** the capacity or volume of a thing. [ME f. med.L contentum (as CONTAIN)]

contented /kənˈtentɪd/ adj. (often foll. by with, or to + infin.) **1** happy, satisfied. **2** (foll. by with) willing to be content (was contented with the outcome). □□ **contentedly** adv. **contentedness** n.

contention /kənˈtenʃ(ə)n/ n. **1** a dispute or argument; rivalry. **2** a point contended for in an argument (it is my contention that you are wrong). □ **in contention** competing, esp. with a good chance of success. [ME f. OF contention or L contentio (as CONTEND)]

contentious /kənˈtenʃəs/ adj. **1** argumentative, quarrelsome. **2** likely to cause an argument; disputed, controversial. □□ **contentiously** adv. **contentiousness** n. [ME f. OF contentieux f. L contentiosus (as CONTENTION)]

contentment /kənˈtentmənt/ n. a satisfied state; tranquil happiness.

conterminous /kɒnˈtɜːmɪnəs/ adj. (often foll. by with) **1** having a common boundary. **2** coextensive, coterminous. □□ **conterminously** adv. [L conterminus (as COM-, terminus boundary)]

contessa /kɒnˈtesə/ n. an Italian countess. [It. f. LL comitissa: see COUNTESS]

contest n. & v. —n. /ˈkɒntest/ **1** a process of contending; a competition. **2** a dispute; a controversy. —v.tr. /kənˈtest/ **1** challenge or dispute (a decision etc.). **2** debate (a point, statement, etc.). **3** contend or compete for (a prize, parliamentary seat, etc.); compete in (an election). □□ **contestable** /kənˈtestəb(ə)l/ adj. **contester** /kənˈtestə(r)/ n. [L contestari (as COM-, testis witness)]

contestant /kənˈtest(ə)nt/ n. a person who takes part in a contest or competition.

contestation /ˌkɒntesˈteɪʃ(ə)n/ n. **1** a disputation. **2** an assertion contended for. [L contestatio partly through F (as CONTEST)]

context /ˈkɒntekst/ n. **1** the parts of something written or spoken that immediately precede and follow a word or passage and clarify its meaning. **2** the circumstances relevant to something under consideration (must be seen in context). □ **out of context** without the surrounding words or circumstances and so not fully understandable. □□ **contextual** /kənˈtekstjʊəl/ adj. **contextualize** /kənˈtekstjʊəˌlaɪz/ v.tr. (also -**ise**). **contextualization** /kənˈtekstjʊəlaɪˌzeɪʃ(ə)n/ n. **contextually** /kənˈtekstjʊəlɪ/ adv. [ME f. L contextus (as COM-, texere text- weave)]

contiguity /ˌkɒntɪˈgjuːɪtɪ/ n. **1** being contiguous; proximity; contact. **2** Psychol. the proximity of ideas or impressions in place or time, as a principle of association.

contiguous /kənˈtɪgjʊəs/ adj. (usu. foll. by with, to) touching, esp. along a line; in contact. □□ **contiguously** adv. [L contiguus (as COM-, tangere touch)]

æ cat ɑː arm e bed ɜː her ɪ sit iː see ɒ hot ɔː saw ʌ run ʊ put uː too ə ago aɪ my

continent¹ /ˈkɒntɪnənt/ n. **1** any of the main continuous expanses of land (Europe, Asia, Africa, N. and S. America, Australia, Antarctica). **2 (the Continent)** Brit. the mainland of Europe as distinct from the British Isles. **3** continuous land; a mainland. [L terra continens (see CONTAIN) continuous land]

continent² /ˈkɒntɪnənt/ adj. **1** able to control movements of the bowels and bladder. **2** exercising self-restraint, esp. sexually. □□ **continence** n. **continently** adv. [ME f. L (as CONTAIN)]

continental /ˌkɒntɪˈnent(ə)l/ adj. & n. —adj. **1** of or characteristic of a continent. **2 (Continental)** Brit. of, relating to, or characteristic of mainland Europe. —n. an inhabitant of mainland Europe. □ **continental breakfast** a light breakfast of coffee, rolls, etc. **continental climate** a climate having wide variations of temperature. **continental drift** see separate entry. **continental quilt** Brit. a duvet. **continental shelf** an area of relatively shallow seabed between the shore of a continent and the deeper ocean. **continental slope** the relatively steep slope between the outer edge of the continental shelf and the ocean bed. □□ **continentally** adv.

Continental Divide the main series of mountain ridges in North America, chiefly the crests of the Rocky Mountains, which forms a watershed separating the rivers flowing eastwards into the Atlantic Ocean or the Gulf of Mexico from those flowing westwards into the Pacific. It is also called the Great Divide.

continental drift n. the postulated movement of the existing continents to their present positions after having at one time formed a single land mass. The idea of such lateral displacement is generally ascribed to the German meteorologist Alfred Wegener, although similar but less detailed suggestions had been put forward by earlier writers. Wegener's theory was based on similarities in the types of rock and in the flora and fauna (both fossil and living) of the continents, and in the correspondence of the outline of the coasts of South America and Africa, but the concept that the masses of rock forming the continents could drift across the rocks that form the weaker suboceanic portion of the earth's crust gained little credence before the 1960s. Since then information from the floors of the oceans, from seismic studies, from palaeomagnetic surveys, and from radiometric dating of rocks have shown that the theory is valid. It is now evident that the present continental land masses of South America, Africa, Australia, Antarctica, and the Indian subcontinent once formed a single supercontinent, termed Gondwanaland, which began splitting up about 200–150 million years ago. The precise geophysical mechanisms involved in the drift of the continents and, indeed, plate tectonics—a theory which expands upon that of continental drift—are still hotly debated.

contingency /kənˈtɪndʒənsɪ/ n. (pl. **-ies**) **1** a future event or circumstance regarded as likely to occur, or as influencing present action. **2** something dependent on another uncertain event or occurrence. **3** uncertainty of occurrence. **4 a** one thing incident to another. **b** an incidental expense etc. □ **contingency fund** a fund to cover incidental or unforeseen expenses. [earlier contingence f. LL contingentia (as CONTINGENT)]

contingent /kənˈtɪndʒ(ə)nt/ adj. & n. —adj. **1** (usu. foll. by on, upon) conditional, dependent (on an uncertain event or circumstance). **2** associated. **3** (usu. foll. by to) incidental. **4 a** that may or may not occur. **b** fortuitous; occurring by chance. **5** true only under existing or specified conditions. —n. a body (esp. of troops, ships, etc.) forming part of a larger group. □□ **contingently** adv. [L contingere (as COM-, tangere touch)]

continual /kənˈtɪnjʊəl/ adj. constantly or frequently recurring; always happening. □□ **continually** adv. [ME f. OF continuel f. continuer (as CONTINUE)]

continuance /kənˈtɪnjʊəns/ n. **1** a state of continuing in existence or operation. **2** the duration of an event or action. **3** US Law an adjournment. [ME f. OF (as CONTINUE)]

continuant /kənˈtɪnjʊənt/ n. & adj. Phonet. —n. a speech sound in which the vocal tract is only partly closed, allowing the breath to pass through and the sound to be prolonged (as with f, r, s, v). —adj. of or relating to such a sound. [F continuant and L continuare (as CONTINUE)]

continuation /kənˌtɪnjʊˈeɪʃ(ə)n/ n. **1** the act or an instance of continuing; the process of being continued. **2** a part that continues something else. **3** Brit. Stock Exch. the carrying over of an account to the next settling day. □ **continuation day** Stock Exch. = contango day. [ME f. OF f. L continuatio -onis (as CONTINUE)]

continuative /kənˈtɪnjʊətɪv/ adj. tending or serving to continue. [LL continuativus (as CONTINUATION)]

continue /kənˈtɪnjuː/ v. (**continues, continued, continuing**) **1** tr. (often foll. by verbal noun, or to + infin.) persist in, maintain, not stop (an action etc.). **2 a** tr. (also absol.) resume or prolong (a narrative, journey, etc.). **b** intr. recommence after a pause (the concert will continue shortly). **3** tr. be a sequel to. **4** intr. **a** remain in existence or unchanged. **b** (with compl.) remain in a specified state (the weather continued fine). **5** tr. US Law adjourn (proceedings). □□ **continuable** adj. **continuer** n. [ME f. OF continuer f. L continuare make or be CONTINUOUS]

continuity /ˌkɒntɪˈnjuːɪtɪ/ n. (pl. **-ies**) **1 a** the state of being continuous. **b** an unbroken succession. **c** a logical sequence. **2** the detailed and self-consistent scenario of a film or broadcast. **3** the linking of broadcast items. □ **continuity girl** (or **man**) the person responsible for agreement of detail between different sessions of filming. [F continuité f. L continuitas -tatis (as CONTINUOUS)]

continuo /kənˈtɪnjʊəʊ/ n. (pl. **-os**) Mus. an accompaniment providing a bass line and harmonies which are indicated by figures, usu. played on a keyboard instrument. [basso continuo (It., = continuous bass)]

continuous /kənˈtɪnjʊəs/ adj. **1** unbroken, uninterrupted, connected throughout in space or time. **2** Gram. = PROGRESSIVE. □ **continuous assessment** the evaluation of a pupil's progress throughout a course of study, as well as or instead of by examination. **continuous creation** the creation of the universe or the matter in it regarded as a continuous process. **continuous stationery** a continuous ream of paper, usu. perforated to form single sheets. □□ **continuously** adv. **continuousness** n. [L continuus uninterrupted f. continēre (as COM-, tenēre hold)]

continuum /kənˈtɪnjʊəm/ n. (pl. **continua** /-jʊə/) anything seen as having a continuous, not discrete, structure (space-time continuum). [L, neut. of continuus: see CONTINUOUS]

contort /kənˈtɔːt/ v.tr. twist or force out of normal shape. [L contorquēre contort- (as COM-, torquēre twist)]

contortion /kənˈtɔːʃ(ə)n/ n. **1** the act or process of twisting. **2** a twisted state, esp. of the face or body. [L contortio (as CONTORT)]

contortionist /kənˈtɔːʃənɪst/ n. an entertainer who adopts contorted postures.

contour /ˈkɒntʊə(r)/ n. & v. —n. **1** an outline, esp. representing or bounding the shape or form of something. **2** the outline of a natural feature, e.g. a coast or mountain mass. **3** a line separating differently coloured parts of a design. —v.tr. **1** mark with contour lines. **2** carry (a road or railway) round the side of a hill. □ **contour line** a line on a map joining points of equal altitude. **contour map** a map marked with contour lines. **contour ploughing** ploughing along lines of constant altitude to minimize soil erosion. [F f. It. contorno f. contornare draw in outline (as COM-, tornare turn)]

Contra /ˈkɒntrə/ n. (pl. **Contras**) a member of a counter-revolutionary guerrilla force in Nicaragua, opposing the Sandinista government, supported by the US 1982–9. It was officially disbanded in 1990. [abbr. of Sp. contrarevolucionario counter-revolutionary]

contra- /ˈkɒntrə/ comb. form **1** against, opposite (contradict). **2** Mus. (of instruments, organ-stops, etc.) pitched an octave below (contra-bassoon). [L contra against]

contraband /ˈkɒntrəbænd/ n. & adj. —n. **1** goods that have been smuggled, or imported or exported illegally. **2** prohibited trade; smuggling. **3** (in full **contraband of war**) goods forbidden to be supplied by neutrals to belligerents. —adj. **1** forbidden to be imported or exported (at all or without payment of duty). **2** concerning traffic in contraband (contraband trade). □□ **contrabandist** n. [Sp. contrabanda f. It. (as CONTRA-, bando proclamation)]

contrabass /ˈkɒntrəˌbeɪs/ n. Mus. = double-bass. [It. (basso BASS¹)]

contraception /ˌkɒntrəˈsepʃ(ə)n/ n. the intentional prevention of pregnancy; the use of contraceptives. [CONTRA- + CONCEPTION]

contraceptive /ˌkɒntrəˈseptɪv/ adj. & n. —adj. preventing pregnancy. —n. a contraceptive device or drug.

contract n. & v. —n. /ˈkɒntrækt/ **1** a written or spoken agreement between two or more parties, intended to be enforceable by law. **2** a document recording this. **3** marriage regarded as a binding commitment. **4** Bridge etc. an undertaking to win the number of tricks bid. —v. /kənˈtrækt/ **1** tr. & intr. make or become smaller. **2 a** intr. (usu. foll. by with) make a contract. **b** intr. (usu. foll. by for, or to + infin.) enter formally into a business or legal arrangement. **c** tr. (often foll. by out) arrange (work) to be done by contract. **3** tr. catch or develop (a disease). **4** tr. form or develop (a friendship, habit, etc.). **5** tr. enter into (marriage). **6** tr. incur (a debt etc.). **7** tr. shorten (a word) by combination or elision. **8** tr. draw (one's muscles, brow, etc.) together. □ **contract bridge** see BRIDGE². **contract in** (or **out**) (also refl.) Brit. choose to be involved in (or withdraw or remain out of) a scheme or commitment. □□ **contractive** adj. [earlier as adj., = contracted: OF, f. L contractus (as COM-, trahere tract- draw)]

contractable /kənˈtræktəb(ə)l/ adj. (of a disease) that can be contracted.

contractible /kənˈtræktɪb(ə)l/ adj. that can be shrunk or drawn together.

contractile /kənˈtræktaɪl/ adj. capable of or producing contraction. □□ **contractility** /ˌkɒntrækˈtɪlɪtɪ/ n.

contraction /kənˈtrækʃ(ə)n/ n. **1** the act of contracting. **2** Med. (usu. in pl.) shortening of the uterine muscles during childbirth. **3** shrinking, diminution. **4 a** a shortening of a word by combination or elision. **b** a contracted word or group of words. [F f. L contractio -onis (as CONTRACT)]

contractor /kənˈtræktə(r)/ n. a person who undertakes a contract, esp. to provide materials, conduct building operations, etc. [LL (as CONTRACT)]

contractual /kənˈtræktjʊəl/ adj. of or in the nature of a contract. □□ **contractually** adv.

contradict /ˌkɒntrəˈdɪkt/ v.tr. **1** deny or express the opposite of (a statement). **2** deny or express the opposite of a statement made by (a person). **3** be in opposition to or in conflict with (new evidence contradicted our theory). □□ **contradictor** n. [L contradicere contradict- (as CONTRA-, dicere say)]

contradiction /ˌkɒntrəˈdɪkʃ(ə)n/ n. **1 a** statement of the opposite; denial. **b** an instance of this. **2** inconsistency. □ **contradiction in terms** a self-contradictory statement or group of words. [ME f. OF f. L contradictio -onis (as CONTRADICT)]

contradictory /ˌkɒntrəˈdɪktərɪ/ adj. **1** expressing a denial or opposite statement. **2** (of statements etc.) mutually opposed or inconsistent. **3** (of a person) inclined to contradict. **4** Logic (of two propositions) so related that one and only one must be true. □□ **contradictorily** adv. **contradictoriness** n. [ME f. LL contradictorius (as CONTRADICT)]

contradistinction /ˌkɒntrədɪˈstɪŋkʃ(ə)n/ n. a distinction made by contrasting.

contradistinguish /ˌkɒntrədɪˈstɪŋgwɪʃ/ v.tr. (usu. foll. by from) distinguish two things by contrasting them.

contraflow /ˈkɒntrəˌfləʊ/ n. Brit. a flow (esp. of road traffic) alongside, and in a direction opposite to, an established or usual flow, esp. as a temporary or emergency arrangement.

contrail /ˈkɒntreɪl/ n. a condensation trail, esp. from an aircraft. [abbr.]

contraindicate /ˌkɒntrəˈɪndɪˌkeɪt/ v.tr. Med. act as an indication against (the use of a particular substance or treatment). □□ **contraindication** /-ˈkeɪʃ(ə)n/ n.

contralto /kənˈtræltəʊ/ n. (pl. **-os**) **1 a** the lowest female singing-voice. **b** a singer with this voice. **2** a part written for contralto. [It. (as CONTRA-, ALTO)]

contraposition /ˌkɒntrəpəˈzɪʃ(ə)n/ n. **1** opposition or contrast. **2** Logic conversion of a proposition from all A is B to all not-B is not-A. □□ **contrapositive** /-ˈpɒzɪtɪv/ adj. & n. [LL contrapositio (as CONTRA-, ponere posit- place)]

contraption /kənˈtræpʃ(ə)n/ n. often derog. or joc. a machine or device, esp. a strange or cumbersome one. [19th c.: perh. f. CONTRIVE, INVENTION: assoc. with TRAP¹]

contrapuntal /ˌkɒntrəˈpʌnt(ə)l/ adj. Mus. of or in counterpoint. □□ **contrapuntally** adv. **contrapuntist** n. [It. contrappunto counterpoint]

contrariety /ˌkɒntrəˈraɪtɪ/ n. **1** opposition in nature, quality, or action. **2** disagreement, inconsistency. [ME f. OF contrarieté f. LL contrarietas -tatis (as CONTRARY)]

contrariwise /kənˈtreərɪˌwaɪz/ adv. **1** on the other hand. **2** in the opposite way. **3** perversely. [ME f. CONTRARY + -WISE]

contrary /ˈkɒntrərɪ/ adj., n., & adv. —adj. **1** (usu. foll. by to) opposed in nature or tendency. **2** /kənˈtreərɪ/ colloq. perverse, self-willed. **3** (of a wind) unfavourable, impeding. **4** mutually opposed. **5** opposite in position or direction. —n. (pl. **-ies**) (prec. by the) the opposite. —adv. (foll. by to) in opposition or contrast (contrary to expectations it rained). □ **on the contrary** intensifying a denial of what has just been implied or stated. **to the contrary** to the opposite effect (can find no indication to the contrary). □□ **contrarily** /ˈkɒntrərɪlɪ/ (/kənˈtreərɪlɪ/ in sense 2 of adj.) adv. **contrariness** /ˈkɒntrərɪnɪs/ (/kənˈtreərɪnɪs/ in sense 2 of adj.) n. [ME f. AF contrarie, OF contraire, f. L contrarius f. contra against]

contrast n. & v. —n. /ˈkɒntrɑːst/ **1 a** a juxtaposition or comparison showing striking differences. **b** a difference so revealed. **2** (often foll. by to) a thing or person having qualities noticeably different from another. **3 a** the degree of difference between tones in a television picture or a photograph. **b** the change of apparent brightness or colour of an object caused by the juxtaposition of other objects. —v. /kənˈtrɑːst/ (often foll. by with) **1** tr. distinguish or set together so as to reveal a contrast. **2** intr. have or show a contrast. □□ **contrastingly** /kənˈtrɑːstɪŋlɪ/ adv. **contrastive** /kənˈtrɑːstɪv/ adj. [F contraste, contraster, f. It. contrasto f. med.L contrastare (as CONTRA-, stare stand)]

contrasty /ˈkɒntrɑːstɪ/ adj. (of photographic negatives, transparencies, or prints or of a television picture) showing a high degree of contrast.

contra-suggestible /ˌkɒntrəsəˈdʒestɪb(ə)l/ adj. Psychol. tending to respond to a suggestion by believing or doing the contrary.

contrate wheel /ˈkɒntreɪt/ n. = crown wheel. [med.L & Rmc contrata: see COUNTRY]

contravene /ˌkɒntrəˈviːn/ v.tr. **1** infringe (a law or code of conduct). **2** (of things) conflict with. □□ **contravener** n. [LL contravenire (as CONTRA-, venire vent- come)]

contravention /ˌkɒntrəˈvenʃ(ə)n/ n. **1** infringement. **2** an instance of this. □ **in contravention of** infringing, violating (a law etc.). [F f. med.L contraventio (as CONTRAVENE)]

contretemps /ˈkɔ̃ːntrəˌtɑ̃ː/ n. **1** an awkward or unfortunate occurrence. **2** an unexpected mishap. [F]

contribute /kənˈtrɪbjuːt, disp. ˈkɒntrɪˌbjuːt/ v. (often foll. by to) **1** tr. give (money, an idea, help, etc.) towards a common purpose (contributed £5 to the fund). **2** intr. help to bring about a result etc. (contributed to their downfall). **3** tr. (also absol.) supply (an article etc.) for publication with others in a journal etc. □□ **contributive** /kənˈtrɪb-/ adj. [L contribuere contribut- (as COM-, tribuere bestow)]

contribution /ˌkɒntrɪˈbjuːʃ(ə)n/ n. **1** the act of contributing. **2** something contributed, esp. money. **3** an article etc. contributed to a publication. [ME f. OF contribution or LL contributio (as CONTRIBUTE)]

contributor /kənˈtrɪbjʊtə(r)/ n. a person who contributes (esp. an article or literary work).

contributory /kənˈtrɪbjʊtərɪ/ adj. & n. —adj. **1** that contributes. **2** operated by means of contributions (contributory pension scheme). —n. Brit. Law a person liable to contribute towards the payment of a wound-up company's debts. □ **contributory negligence** Law negligence on the part of the injured party through failure to take precautions against an accident. [med.L contributorius (as CONTRIBUTE)]

contrite /ˈkɒntraɪt, kənˈtraɪt/ adj. **1** completely penitent. **2** feeling remorse or penitence; affected by guilt. **3** (of an action) showing a contrite spirit. □□ **contritely** adv. **contriteness** n. [ME f. OF contrit f. L contritus bruised (as COM-, terere trit- rub)]

b but d dog f few g get h he j yes k cat l leg m man n no p pen r red s sit t top v voice

contrition /kən'trɪʃ(ə)n/ n. the state of being contrite; thorough penitence. [ME f. OF f. LL *contritio -onis* (as CONTRITE)]

contrivance /kən'traɪv(ə)ns/ n. **1** something contrived, esp. a mechanical device or a plan. **2** an act of contriving, esp. deceitfully. **3** inventive capacity.

contrive /kən'traɪv/ v.tr. **1** devise; plan or make resourcefully or with skill. **2** (often foll. by *to* + infin.) manage (*contrived to make matters worse*). □□ **contrivable** adj. **contriver** n. [ME f. OF *controver* find, imagine f. med.L *contropare* compare]

contrived /kən'traɪvd/ adj. planned so carefully as to seem unnatural; artificial, forced (*the plot seemed contrived*).

control /kən'trəʊl/ n. & v. —n. **1** the power of directing, command (*under the control of*). **2** the power of restraining, esp. self-restraint. **3** a means of restraint; a check. **4** (usu. in *pl.*) a means of regulating prices etc. **5** (usu. in *pl.*) switches and other devices by which a machine, esp. an aircraft or vehicle, is controlled (also *attrib.*: *control panel*; *control room*). **6 a** a place where something is controlled or verified. **b** a person or group that controls something. **7** a standard of comparison for checking the results of a survey or experiment. —v.tr. (**controlled**, **controlling**) **1** have control or command of; dominate. **2** exert control over; regulate. **3** hold in check; restrain (*told him to control himself*). **4** serve as control to. **5** check, verify. □ **controlling interest** a means of determining the policy of a business etc., esp. by ownership of a majority of the stock. **control rod** a rod of neutron-absorbing material used to vary the output power of a nuclear reactor. **control tower** a tall building at an airport etc. from which air traffic is controlled. **in control** (often foll. by *of*) directing an activity. **out of control** no longer subject to containment, restraint, or guidance. **under control** being controlled; in order. □□ **controllable** adj. **controllability** /-'bɪlɪtɪ/ n. **controllably** adv. [ME f. AF *contreroller* keep a copy of a roll of accounts, f. med.L *contrarotulare* (as CONTRA-, *rotulus* ROLL n.): (n.) perh. f. F *contrôle*]

controller /kən'trəʊlə(r)/ n. **1** a person or thing that controls. **2** a person in charge of expenditure, esp. a steward or comptroller. □□ **controllership** n. [ME *counterroller* f. AF *controllour* (as CONTROL)]

controversial /ˌkɒntrə'vɜːʃ(ə)l/ adj. **1** causing or subject to controversy. **2** of controversy. **3** given to controversy. □□ **controversialism** n. **controversialist** n. **controversially** adv. [LL *controversialis* (as CONTROVERSY)]

controversy /ˈkɒntrəˌvɜːsɪ, disp. kən'trɒvəsɪ/ n. (pl. **-ies**) a prolonged argument or dispute, esp. when conducted publicly. [ME f. L *controversia* (as CONTROVERT)]

controvert /ˈkɒntrəˌvɜːt, -ˈvɜːt/ v.tr. **1** dispute, deny. **2** argue about; discuss. □□ **controvertible** adj. [orig. past part.; f. F *controvers(e)* f. L *controversus* (as CONTRA-, *vertere vers-* turn)]

contumacious /ˌkɒntjʊ'meɪʃəs/ adj. insubordinate; stubbornly or wilfully disobedient, esp. to a court order. □□ **contumaciously** adv. [L *contumax*, perh. rel. to *tumēre* swell]

contumacy /ˈkɒntjʊməsɪ/ n. stubborn refusal to obey or comply. [L *contumacia* f. *contumax*: see CONTUMACIOUS]

contumelious /ˌkɒntjʊ'miːlɪəs/ adj. reproachful, insulting, or insolent. □□ **contumeliously** adv. [ME f. OF *contumelieus* f. L *contumeliosus* (as CONTUMELY)]

contumely /ˈkɒntjuːmlɪ/ n. **1** insolent or reproachful language or treatment. **2** disgrace. [ME f. OF *contumelie* f. L *contumelia* (as COM-, *tumēre* swell)]

contuse /kən'tjuːz/ v.tr. injure without breaking the skin; bruise. □□ **contusion** n. [L *contundere contus-* (as COM-, *tundere* thump)]

conundrum /kə'nʌndrəm/ n. **1** a riddle, esp. one with a pun in its answer. **2** a hard or puzzling question. [16th c.: orig. unkn.]

conurbation /ˌkɒnɜː'beɪʃ(ə)n/ n. an extended urban area, esp. one consisting of several towns and merging suburbs. [CON- + L *urbs urbis* city + -ATION]

conure /kɒ'njʊə(r)/ n. any medium-sized parrot of the genus *Pyrrhura*, with mainly green plumage and a long gradated tail. [mod.L *conurus* f. Gk *kōnos* cone + *oura* tail]

convalesce /ˌkɒnvə'les/ v.intr. recover one's health after illness or medical treatment. [ME f. L *convalescere* (as COM-, *valēre* be well)]

convalescent /ˌkɒnvə'les(ə)nt/ adj. & n. —adj. recovering from an illness. —n. a convalescent person. □□ **convalescence** n.

convection /kən'vekʃ(ə)n/ n. **1** transference of heat in a gas or liquid by upward movement of the heated and less dense medium. **2** *Meteorol.* the transfer of heat by the upward flow of hot air or downward flow of cold air. □ **convection current** circulation that results from convection. □□ **convectional** adj. **convective** adj. [LL *convectio* f. L *convehere convect-* (as COM-, *vehere vect-* carry)]

convector /kən'vektə(r)/ n. a heating appliance that circulates warm air by convection.

convenance /ˈkɒvəˌnɑːs/ n. (usu. in *pl.*) conventional propriety. [F f. *convenir* be fitting (as CONVENE)]

convene /kən'viːn/ v. **1** tr. summon or arrange (a meeting etc.). **2** intr. assemble. **3** tr. summon (a person) before a tribunal. □□ **convenable** adj. **convener** n. **convenor** n. [ME f. L *convenire convent-* assemble, agree, fit (as COM-, *venire* come)]

convenience /kən'viːnɪəns/ n. **1** the quality of being convenient; suitability. **2** freedom from difficulty or trouble; material advantage (*for convenience*). **3** an advantage (*a great convenience*). **4** a useful thing, esp. an installation or piece of equipment. **5** *Brit.* a lavatory, esp. a public one. □ **at one's convenience** at a time or place that suits one. **at one's earliest convenience** as soon as one can. **convenience food** food, esp. complete meals, sold in convenient form and requiring very little preparation. **convenience store** *US* a large shop with extended opening hours. **make a convenience of** take advantage of (a person) insensitively. [ME f. L *convenientia* (as CONVENE)]

convenient /kən'viːnɪənt/ adj. **1** (often foll. by *for, to*) **a** serving one's comfort or interests; easily accessible. **b** suitable. **c** free of trouble or difficulty. **2** available or occurring at a suitable time or place (*will try to find a convenient moment*). **3** well situated for some purpose (*convenient for the shops*). □□ **conveniently** adv. [ME (as CONVENE)]

convent /ˈkɒnv(ə)nt, -vent/ n. **1** a religious community, esp. of nuns, under vows. **2** the premises occupied by this. **3** (in full **convent school**) a school attached to and run by a convent. [ME f. AF *covent*, OF *convent* f. L *conventus* assembly (as CONVENE)]

conventicle /kən'ventɪk(ə)l/ n. esp. *hist.* **1** a secret or unlawful religious meeting, esp. of dissenters. **2** a building used for this. [ME f. L *conventiculum* (place) of assembly, dimin. of *conventus* (as CONVENE)]

convention /kən'venʃ(ə)n/ n. **1 a** general agreement, esp. agreement on social behaviour etc. by implicit consent of the majority. **b** a custom or customary practice, esp. an artificial or formal one. **2 a** a formal assembly or conference for a common purpose. **b** *US* an assembly of the delegates of a political party to select candidates for office. **c** *hist.* a meeting of Parliament without a summons from the sovereign. **3 a** a formal agreement. **b** an agreement between States, esp. one less formal than a treaty. **4** *Cards* an accepted method of play (in leading, bidding, etc.) used to convey information to a partner. **5** the act of convening. [ME f. OF f. L *conventio -onis* (as CONVENE)]

conventional /kən'venʃən(ə)l/ adj. **1** depending on or according with convention. **2** (of a person) attentive to social conventions. **3** usual; of agreed significance. **4** not spontaneous or sincere or original. **5** (of weapons or power) non-nuclear. **6** *Art* following tradition rather than nature. □□ **conventionalism** n. **conventionalist** n. **conventionality** /-'nælɪtɪ/ n. **conventionalize** v.tr. (also **-ise**). **conventionally** adv. [F *conventionnel* or LL *conventionalis* (as CONVENTION)]

conventioneer /kənˌvenʃə'nɪə(r)/ n. *US* a person attending a convention.

conventual /kən'ventjʊəl/ adj. & n. —adj. **1** of or belonging to a convent. **2** of the less strict branch of the Franciscans, living in large convents. —n. **1** a member or inmate of a convent. **2** a conventual Franciscan. [ME f. med.L *conventualis* (as CONVENT)]

converge /kən'vɜːdʒ/ v.intr. **1** come together as if to meet or join. **2** (of lines) tend to meet at a point. **3** (foll. by *on, upon*) approach from different directions. **4** *Math.* (of a series) approximate in the sum of its terms towards a definite limit. [LL *convergere* (as COM-, *vergere* incline)]

convergent /kən'vɜːdʒ(ə)nt/ adj. **1** converging. **2** Biol. (of unrelated organisms) having the tendency to become similar while adapting to the same environment. **3** Psychol. (of thought) tending to reach only the most rational result. □□ **convergence** n. **convergency** n.

conversant /kən'vɜːs(ə)nt, 'kɒnvəs(ə)nt/ adj. (foll. by with) well experienced or acquainted with a subject, person, etc. □□ **conversance** n. **conversancy** n. [ME f. OF, pres. part. of converser CONVERSE¹]

conversation /ˌkɒnvə'seɪʃ(ə)n/ n. **1** the informal exchange of ideas by spoken words. **2** an instance of this. □ **conversation piece 1** a small genre painting of a group of figures. **2** a thing that serves as a topic of conversation because of its unusualness etc. **conversation stopper** colloq. an unexpected remark, esp. one that cannot readily be answered. [ME f. OF f. L conversatio -onis (as CONVERSE¹)]

conversational /ˌkɒnvə'seɪʃən(ə)l/ adj. **1** of or in conversation. **2** fond of or good at conversation. **3** colloquial. □□ **conversationally** adv.

conversationalist /ˌkɒnvə'seɪʃənəlɪst/ n. one who is good at or fond of conversing.

conversazione /ˌkɒnvəˌsætsɪ'əʊnɪ/ n. (pl. **conversaziones** or **conversazioni** pronunc. same) a social gathering held by a learned or art society. [It. f. L (as CONVERSATION)]

converse¹ v. & n. —v.intr. /kən'vɜːs/ (often foll. by with) engage in conversation (conversed with him about various subjects). —n. /'kɒnvɜːs/ archaic conversation. □□ **converser** /kən'vɜːsə(r)/ n. [ME f. OF converser f. L conversari keep company (with), frequent. of convertere (CONVERT)]

converse² /'kɒnvɜːs/ adj. & n. —adj. opposite, contrary, reversed. —n. **1** something that is opposite or contrary. **2** a statement formed from another statement by the transposition of certain words, e.g. some philosophers are men from some men are philosophers. **3** Math. a theorem whose hypothesis and conclusion are the conclusion and hypothesis of another. □□ **conversely** /'kɒnvɜːslɪ, kən'vɜːslɪ/ adv. [L conversus, past part. of convertere (CONVERT)]

conversion /kən'vɜːʃ(ə)n/ n. **1 a** the act or an instance of converting or the process of being converted, esp. in belief or religion. **b** an instance of this. **2 a** an adaptation of a building for new purposes. **b** a converted building. **3** transposition, inversion. **4** Theol. the turning of sinners to God. **5** the transformation of fertile into fissile material in a nuclear reactor. **6** Rugby Football the scoring of points by a successful kick at goal after scoring a try. **7** Psychol. the change of an unconscious conflict into a physical disorder or disease. [ME f. OF f. L conversio -onis (as CONVERT)]

convert v. & n. —v. /kən'vɜːt/ **1** tr. (usu. foll. by into) change in form, character, or function. **2** tr. cause (a person) to change beliefs, opinion, party, etc. **3** tr. change (moneys, stocks, units in which a quantity is expressed, etc.) into others of a different kind. **4** tr. make structural alterations in (a building) to serve a new purpose. **5** tr. (also absol.) **a** Rugby Football score extra points from (a try) by a successful kick at goal. **b** Amer. Football complete (a touchdown) by kicking a goal or crossing the goal-line. **6** intr. be converted or convertible (the sofa converts into a bed). **7** tr. Logic interchange the terms of (a proposition). —n. /'kɒnvɜːt/ (often foll. by to) a person who has been converted to a different belief, opinion, etc. □ **convert to one's own use** wrongfully make use of (another's property). [ME f. OF convertir ult. f. L convertere convers- turn about (as COM-, vertere turn)]

converter /kən'vɜːtə(r)/ n. (also **convertor**) **1** a person or thing that converts. **2** Electr. **a** an electrical apparatus for the interconversion of alternating current and direct current. **b** Electronics an apparatus for converting a signal from one frequency to another. **3** a reaction vessel used in making steel. □ **converter reactor** a nuclear reactor that converts fertile material into fissile material.

convertible /kən'vɜːtɪb(ə)l/ adj. & n. —adj. **1** that may be converted. **2** (of currency etc.) that may be converted into other forms, esp. into gold or US dollars. **3** (of a car) having a folding or detachable roof. **4** (of terms) synonymous. —n. a car with a

folding or detachable roof. □□ **convertibility** /-'bɪlɪtɪ/ n. **convertibly** adv. [OF f. L convertibilis (as CONVERT)]

convex /'kɒnveks/ adj. having an outline or surface curved like the exterior of a circle or sphere (cf. CONCAVE). □□ **convexity** /-'veksɪtɪ/ n. **convexly** adv. [L convexus vaulted, arched]

convey /kən'veɪ/ v.tr. **1** transport or carry (goods, passengers, etc.). **2** communicate (an idea, meaning, etc.). **3** Law transfer the title to (property). **4** transmit (sound, smell, etc.). □□ **conveyable** adj. [ME f. OF conveier f. med.L conviare (as COM-, L via way)]

conveyance /kən'veɪəns/ n. **1 a** the act or process of carrying. **b** the communication (of ideas etc.). **c** transmission. **2 a** means of transport; a vehicle. **3** Law **a** the transfer of property from one owner to another. **b** a document effecting this. □□ **conveyancer** n. (in sense 3). **conveyancing** n. (in sense 3).

conveyor /kən'veɪə(r)/ n. (also **conveyer**) a person or thing that conveys. □ **conveyor belt** an endless moving belt for conveying articles or materials, esp. in a factory.

convict v. & n. —v.tr. /kən'vɪkt/ **1** (often foll. by of) prove to be guilty (of a crime etc.). **2** declare guilty by the verdict of a jury or the decision of a judge. —n. /'kɒnvɪkt/ **1** a person found guilty of a criminal offence. **2** chiefly hist. a person serving a prison sentence, esp. in a penal colony. [ME f. L convincere convict- (as COM-, vincere conquer): noun f. obs. convict convicted]

conviction /kən'vɪkʃ(ə)n/ n. **1 a** the act or process of proving or finding guilty. **b** an instance of this (has two previous convictions). **2 a** the action or resulting state of being convinced. **b** a firm belief or opinion. **c** an act of convincing. [L convictio (as CONVICT)]

convince /kən'vɪns/ v.tr. **1** (often foll. by of, or that + clause) persuade (a person) to believe or realize. **2** (as **convinced** adj.) firmly persuaded (a convinced pacifist). □□ **convincer** n. **convincible** adj. [L (as CONVICT)]

convincing /kən'vɪnsɪŋ/ adj. **1** able to or such as to convince. **2** leaving no margin of doubt, substantial (a convincing victory). □□ **convincingly** adv.

convivial /kən'vɪvɪəl/ adj. **1** fond of good company; sociable and lively. **2** festive (a convivial atmosphere). □□ **conviviality** /-'ælɪtɪ/ n. **convivially** adv. [L convivialis f. convivium feast (as COM-, vivere live)]

convocation /ˌkɒnvə'keɪʃ(ə)n/ n. **1** the act of calling together. **2** a large formal gathering of people, esp.: **a** Brit. a provincial synod of the Anglican clergy of Canterbury or York. **b** Brit. a legislative or deliberative assembly of a university. □□ **convocational** adj. [ME f. L convocatio (as CONVOKE)]

convoke /kən'vəʊk/ v.tr. formal call (people) together to a meeting etc.; summon to assemble. [L convocare convocat- (as COM-, vocare call)]

convoluted /'kɒnvəˌluːtɪd/ adj. **1** coiled, twisted. **2** complex, intricate. □□ **convolutedly** adv. [past part. of convolute f. L convolutus (as COM-, volvere volut- roll)]

convolution /ˌkɒnvə'luːʃ(ə)n/ n. **1** coiling, twisting. **2** a coil or twist. **3** complexity. **4** a sinuous fold in the surface of the brain. □□ **convolutional** adj. [med.L convolutio (as CONVOLUTED)]

convolve /kən'vɒlv/ v.tr. & intr. (esp. as **convolved** adj.) roll together; coil up. [L convolvere (as CONVOLUTED)]

convolvulus /kən'vɒlvjʊləs/ n. any twining plant of the genus Convolvulus, with trumpet-shaped flowers, e.g. bindweed. [L]

convoy /'kɒnvɔɪ/ n. & v. —n. **1** a group of ships travelling together or under escort. **2** a supply of provisions etc. under escort. **3** a group of vehicles travelling on land together or under escort. **4** the act of travelling or moving in a group or under escort. —v.tr. **1** (of a warship) escort (a merchant or passenger vessel). **2** escort, esp. with armed force. [OF convoyer var. of conveier CONVEY]

convulsant /kən'vʌls(ə)nt/ adj. & n. Pharm. —adj. producing convulsions. —n. a drug that may produce convulsions. [F f. convulser (as CONVULSE)]

convulse /kən'vʌls/ v.tr. **1** (usu. in passive) affect with convulsions. **2** cause to laugh uncontrollably. **3** shake violently; agitate, disturb. [L convellere convuls- (as COM-, vellere pull)]

convulsion /kən'vʌlʃ(ə)n/ n. **1** (usu. in pl.) violent irregular motion of a limb or limbs or the body caused by involuntary contraction of muscles, esp. as a disorder of infants. **2** a violent natural disturbance, esp. an earthquake. **3** violent social or political agitation. **4** (in *pl.*) uncontrollable laughter. □□ **convulsionary** *adj.* [F *convulsion* or L *convulsio* (as CONVULSE)]

convulsive /kən'vʌlsɪv/ *adj.* **1** characterized by or affected with convulsions. **2** producing convulsions. □□ **convulsively** *adv.*

cony /'kəʊnɪ/ *n.* (also **coney**) (*pl.* **-ies** or **-eys**) **1 a** a rabbit. **b** its fur. **2** *Bibl.* a hyrax. [ME *cuning(g)* f. AF *coning*, OF *conin*, f. L *cuniculus*]

coo /kuː/ *n.*, *v.*, & *int.* —*n.* a soft murmuring sound like that of a dove or pigeon. —*v.* (**coos, cooed**) **1** *intr.* make the sound of a coo. **2** *intr.* & *tr.* talk or say in a soft or amorous voice. —*int.* *Brit. sl.* expressing surprise or incredulity. □□ **cooingly** *adv.* [imit.]

cooee /'kuːiː/ *n.*, *int.*, & *v. colloq.* —*n.* & *int.* a sound used to attract attention, esp. at a distance. —*v.intr.* (**cooees, cooeed, cooeeing**) make this sound. □ **within cooee** (or **a cooee**) **of** *Austral.* & *NZ colloq.* very near to. [imit. of a signal used by Australian Aboriginals and copied by settlers]

Cook[1] /kʊk/, **Mark** James (1728–79), English explorer. Cook first went to sea as a common sailor, but rose to the rank of Master in the Royal Navy as a result of his navigational skills, charting the St Lawrence Channel and the coasts of Newfoundland and Labrador during his service in North America (1759–67). Between 1768 and 1771 he conducted an expedition to the Pacific to observe the transit of Venus, charting the coasts of Australia, New Zealand, and New Guinea before returning via the Cape of Good Hope. Promoted to Commander, he returned to the Pacific in 1772–5 to search for the fabled Antarctic continent, visiting Tahiti, the New Hebrides, and New Caledonia on a voyage notable for the success of Cook's health measures (only one member of his crew dying during the entire voyage). His final voyage (1776–9), to discover a passage round North America from the Pacific side, was marked by further pioneer charting work, but eventually ended in disaster when Cook was killed in a skirmish with native peoples in Hawaii. Cook's surveying work added immeasurably to contemporary knowledge of the Pacific; he died a European hero.

Cook[2] /kʊk/, Thomas (1808–92), English tourist agent. Zealous in the cause of temperance, in 1841 he organized the first publicly advertised excursion train in England, carrying 570 passengers from Leicester to Loughborough and back, to attend a temperance meeting, for the price of one shilling. The success of this induced him to make the organizing of excursions at home and abroad a regular occupation.

Cook[3] /kʊk/, **Mount** the highest peak in New Zealand, a mountain in the Southern Alps on South Island, rising to a height of 3,764 m (12,349 ft.). It is named after James Cook, the explorer.

cook /kʊk/ *v.* & *n.* —*v.* **1** *tr.* prepare (food) by heating it. **2** *intr.* (of food) undergo cooking. **3** *tr. colloq.* falsify (accounts etc.); alter to produce a desired result. **4** *tr. sl.* ruin, spoil. **5** *tr.* (esp. as **cooked** *adj.*) *Brit. sl.* fatigue, exhaust. **6** *tr.* & *intr.* *US colloq.* do or proceed successfully. **7** *intr.* (as **be cooking**) *colloq.* be happening or about to happen (*went to find out what was cooking*). —*n.* a person who cooks, esp. professionally or in a specified way (*a good cook*). □ **cook-chill 1** the process of cooking and refrigerating food ready for reheating at a later time. **2** (*attrib.*) (of food) prepared in this way. **cook a person's goose** ruin a person's chances. **cook up** *colloq.* invent or concoct (a story, excuse, etc.). □□ **cookable** *adj.* & *n.* [OE *cōc* f. pop.L *cocus* for L *coquus*]

cookbook /'kʊkbʊk/ *n. US* a cookery book.

cooker /'kʊkə(r)/ *n.* **1 a** a container or device for cooking food. **b** *Brit.* an appliance powered by gas, electricity, etc., for cooking food. **2** *Brit.* a fruit etc. (esp. an apple) that is more suitable for cooking than for eating raw.

cookery /'kʊkərɪ/ *n.* (*pl.* **-ies**) **1** the art or practice of cooking. **2** *US* a place or establishment for cooking. □ **cookery book** *Brit.* a book containing recipes and other information about cooking.

cookhouse /'kʊkhaʊs/ *n.* **1** a camp kitchen. **2** an outdoor kitchen in warm countries. **3** a ship's galley.

cookie /'kʊkɪ/ *n.* **1** *US* a small sweet biscuit. **2** *US sl.* a person. **3** *Sc.* a plain bun. □ **the way the cookie crumbles** *US colloq.* how things turn out; the unalterable state of affairs. [Du. *koekje* dimin. of *koek* cake]

cooking /'kʊkɪŋ/ *n.* **1** the art or process by which food is cooked. **2** (*attrib.*) suitable for or used in cooking (*cooking apple*; *cooking utensils*).

Cook Islands /kʊk/ a group of islands in the SW Pacific Ocean between Tonga and French Polynesia with the status of a self-governing territory in free association with New Zealand; pop. (1986) 17,185. The islands were visited by Captain Cook in 1773.

cookout /'kʊkaʊt/ *n. US* a gathering with an open-air cooked meal; a barbecue.

cookshop /'kʊkʃɒp/ *n. NZ* the kitchen of a sheep-station.

Cookson /'kʊks(ə)n/, Catherine Anne (1906–), English prolific writer of light romantic fiction.

Cook Strait /kʊk/ a passage separating the North and South Island of New Zealand. It was visited in 1642 by the Dutch explorer Abel Tasman, who believed it to be a bay; Captain Cook discovered in 1770 that it was in fact a strait.

cookware /'kʊkweə(r)/ *n.* utensils for cooking, esp. dishes, pans, etc.

cool /kuːl/ *adj.*, *n.*, & *v.* —*adj.* **1** of or at a fairly low temperature, fairly cold (*a cool day; a cool bath*). **2** suggesting or achieving coolness (*cool colours; cool clothes*). **3** calm, unexcited. **4** lacking zeal or enthusiasm. **5** unfriendly; lacking cordiality (*got a cool reception*). **6** (of jazz playing) restrained, relaxed. **7** calmly audacious (*a cool customer*). **8** (prec. by *a*) *colloq.* at least; not less than (*cost me a cool thousand*). **9** *sl.* esp. *US* excellent, marvellous. —*n.* **1** coolness. **2** cool air; a cool place. **3** *sl.* calmness, composure (*keep one's cool; lose one's cool*). —*v.tr.* & *intr.* (often foll. by *down*, *off*) make or become cool. □ **cool-bag** (or **-box**) an insulated container for keeping food cool. **cool-headed** not easily excited. **cool one's heels** see HEEL[1]. **cooling-off period** an interval to allow for a change of mind before commitment to action. **cooling tower** a tall structure for cooling hot water before reuse, esp. in industry. **cool it** *sl.* relax, calm down. □□ **coolish** *adj.* **coolly** /'kuːllɪ/ *adv.* **coolness** *n.* [OE *cōl, cōlian*, f. Gmc: cf. COLD]

coolabah /'kuːlə₁bɑː/ *n.* (also **coolibah** /-lɪ₁bɑː/) *Austral.* any of various gum-trees, esp. *Eucalyptus microtheca*. [Aboriginal]

coolant /'kuːlənt/ *n.* **1** a cooling agent, esp. fluid, to remove heat from an engine, nuclear reactor, etc. **2** a fluid used to lessen the friction of a cutting tool. [COOL + -ANT after *lubricant*]

cooler /'kuːlə(r)/ *n.* **1** a vessel in which a thing is cooled. **2** *US* a refrigerator. **3** a long drink, esp. a spritzer. **4** *sl.* prison or a prison cell.

coolibah var. of COOLABAH.

Coolidge /'kuːlɪdʒ/, (John) Calvin (1872–1933), 30th President of the US, 1923–9. Highly popular personally, he was seen as an embodiment of thrift, caution, and honesty in a decade when corruption in public life was common, even in his own administration.

coolie /'kuːlɪ/ *n.* (also **cooly**) (*pl.* **-ies**) an unskilled native labourer in Eastern countries. □ **coolie hat** a broad conical hat as worn by coolies. [perh. f. *Kulī*, an aboriginal tribe of Gujarat, India]

coomb /kuːm/ *n.* (also **combe**) *Brit.* **1** a valley or hollow on the side of a hill. **2** a short valley running up from the coast. [OE *cumb*: cf. CWM]

coon /kuːn/ *n.* **1** *US* a racoon. **2** *sl. offens.* a Black. [abbr.]

coon-can /kuːn'kæn/ *n.* a simple card-game like rummy (orig. Mexican). [Sp. *con quién* with whom?]

coonskin /'kuːnskɪn/ *n.* **1** the skin of a racoon. **2** a cap etc. made of this.

coop /kuːp/ *n.* & *v.* —*n.* **1** a cage placed over sitting or fattening fowls. **2** a fowl-run. **3** a small place of confinement, esp. a prison. **4** *Brit.* a basket used in catching fish. —*v.tr.* **1** put or keep (a fowl) in a coop. **2** (often foll. by *up*, *in*) confine (a person) in a small space. [ME *cupe* basket f. MDu., MLG *kūpe*, ult. f. L *cupa* cask]

co-op /ˈkəʊɒp/ *n. colloq.* **1** *Brit.* a cooperative society or shop. **2** a cooperative business or enterprise. [abbr.]

Cooper[1] /ˈkuːpə(r)/, Gary (Frank James Cooper, 1901–61), American film actor, whose part in *The Virginian* (1929) established the kind of character for which he is chiefly remembered—tough, reticent, brave, and laconic. Although he is associated mainly with westerns many of his best films were action dramas or comedy-romances.

Cooper[2] /ˈkuːpə(r)/, James Fenimore (1789–1851), American novelist. After being dismissed from Yale he spent a short time in the US Navy and then settled down as a country proprietor and novelist. *The Pioneers* (1823) was the first of *The Leather Stocking Tales*, called after the deerskin leggings of their hero Natty Bumppo; the sequels were *The Last of the Mohicans* (1826), *The Prairie* (1827), *The Pathfinder* (1840) and *The Deerslayer* (1841), giving a vivid picture of American Indian and frontier life. During the years 1826–33 he travelled in Europe and published highly critical accounts of European society, including *England, with Sketches of Society in the Metropolis* (1837), and later vigorously expressed the defects and dangers of democracy in America in *The American Democrat* (1838).

cooper /ˈkuːpə(r)/ *n. & v.* —*n.* a maker or repairer of casks, barrels, etc. —*v.tr.* make or repair (a cask). [ME f. MDu., MLG *kūper* f. *kūpe* COOP]

cooperage /ˈkuːpərɪdʒ/ *n.* **1** the work or establishment of a cooper. **2** money payable for a cooper's work.

cooperate /kəʊˈɒpəˌreɪt/ *v.intr.* (also **co-operate**) **1** (often foll. by *with*) work or act together. **2** (of things) concur in producing an effect. □□ **cooperant** *adj.* **cooperator** *n.* [eccl.L *cooperari* (as CO-, *operari* f. *opus operis* work)]

cooperation /kəʊˌɒpəˈreɪʃ(ə)n/ *n.* (also **co-operation**) **1** working together to the same end. **2** *Econ.* the formation and operation of cooperatives. [ME f. L *cooperatio* (as COOPERATE): partly through F *coopération*]

cooperative /kəʊˈɒpərətɪv/ *adj. & n.* (also **co-operative**) —*adj.* **1** of or affording cooperation. **2** willing to cooperate. **3** *Econ.* (of a farm, shop, or other business, or a society owning such businesses) owned and run jointly by its members, with profits shared among them. —*n.* a cooperative farm or society or business. □□ **cooperatively** *adv.* **cooperativeness** *n.* [LL *cooperativus* (as COOPERATE)]

co-opt /kəʊˈɒpt/ *v.tr.* appoint to membership of a body by invitation of the existing members. □□ **co-optation** /-ˈteɪʃ(ə)n/ *n.* **co-option** *n.* **co-optive** *adj.* [L *cooptare* (as CO-, *optare* choose)]

coordinate *v., adj., & n.* (also **co-ordinate**) —*v.* /kəʊˈɔːdɪˌneɪt/ **1** *tr.* bring (various parts, movements, etc.) into a proper or required relation to ensure harmony or effective operation etc. **2** *intr.* work or act together effectively. **3** *tr.* make coordinate. —*adj.* /kəʊˈɔːdɪnət/ **1** equal in rank or importance. **2** in which the parts are coordinated; involving coordination. **3** *Gram.* (of parts of a compound sentence) equal in status (cf. SUBORDINATE). **4** *Chem.* denoting a type of covalent bond in which one atom provides both the shared electrons. —*n.* /kəʊˈɔːdɪnət/ **1** *Math.* each of a system of magnitudes used to fix the position of a point, line, or plane. **2** a person or thing equal in rank or importance. **3** (in *pl.*) matching items of clothing. □□ **coordinately** /-nətlɪ/ *adv.* **coordination** /-ˈneɪʃ(ə)n/ *n.* **coordinative** /-ˌneɪtɪv/ *adj.* **coordinator** /-ˌneɪtə(r)/ *n.* [CO- + L *ordinare ordinat-* f. *ordo -inis* order]

coot /kuːt/ *n.* **1** any black aquatic bird of the genus *Fulica*, esp. *F. atra* with the upper mandible extended backwards to form a white plate on the forehead. **2** *colloq.* a stupid person. [ME, prob. f. LG]

cootie /ˈkuːtɪ/ *n. sl.* a body louse. [perh. f. Malay *kutu* a biting parasite]

cop[1] /kɒp/ *n. & v. sl.* —*n.* **1** a policeman. **2** *Brit.* a capture or arrest (*it's a fair cop*). —*v.tr.* (**copped, copping**) **1** catch or arrest (an offender). **2** receive, suffer. **3** take, seize. □ **cop it** get into trouble; be punished. **2** be killed. **cop out 1** withdraw; give up an attempt. **2** go back on a promise. **3** escape. **cop-out** *n.* **1** a cowardly or feeble evasion. **2** an escape; a way of escape. **cop-shop** a police station. **not much** (or **no**) **cop** *Brit.* of little

or no value or use. [perh. f. obs. *cap* arrest f. OF *caper* seize f. L *capere*: (n.) cf. COPPER[2]]

cop[2] /kɒp/ *n.* (in spinning) a conical ball of thread wound on a spindle. [OE *cop* summit]

Copacabana Beach /ˌkɒpəkəˈbænə/ a beach resort on the Atlantic coast of Brazil, near the entrance to Guanabara Bay, Rio de Janeiro.

copacetic /ˌkəʊpəˈsetɪk, -ˈsiːtɪk/ *adj. US sl.* excellent; in good order. [20th c.: orig. unkn.]

copaiba /kəˈpaɪbə/ *n.* an aromatic oil or resin from any plant of the genus *Copaifera*, used in medicine and perfumery. [Sp. & Port. f. Guarani *cupauba*]

copal /ˈkəʊp(ə)l/ *n.* a resin from any of various tropical trees, used for varnish. [Sp. f. Aztec *copalli* incense]

Copán /kəʊˈpæn/ an ancient Mayan city, flourishing *c.*300–900, that was the southernmost point of the Mayan empire, in western Honduras near the Guatemalan frontier.

copartner /kəʊˈpɑːtnə(r)/ *n.* a partner or associate, esp. when sharing equally. □□ **copartnership** *n.*

cope[1] /kəʊp/ *v.intr.* **1** (foll. by *with*) deal effectively or contend successfully with a person or task. **2** manage successfully; deal with a situation or problem (*found they could no longer cope*). [ME f. OF *coper, colper* f. *cop, colp* blow f. med.L *colpus* f. L *colaphus* f. Gk *kolaphos* blow with the fist]

cope[2] /kəʊp/ *n. & v.* —*n.* **1** *Eccl.* a long cloaklike vestment worn by a priest or bishop in ceremonies and processions. **2** esp. *poet.* a covering compared with a cope. —*v.tr.* cover with a cope or coping. [ME ult. f. LL *cappa* CAP, CAPE[1]]

copeck /ˈkəʊpek, ˈkɒpek/ *n.* (also **kopeck, kopek**) a Russian coin and monetary unit worth one-hundredth of a rouble. [Russ. *kopeĭka* dimin. of *kop'ē* lance (from the figure of Ivan IV bearing a lance instead of a sword in 1535)]

Copenhagen /ˌkəʊpənˈheɪgən/ (Danish **København** /ˈkopənˌhaʊn/) the capital and chief port of Denmark; pop. (1988) 468,700.

copepod /ˈkəʊpɪˌpɒd/ *n.* any small aquatic crustacean of the class *Copepoda*, many of which form the minute components of plankton. [Gk *kōpē* oar-handle + *pous podos* foot]

coper /ˈkəʊpə(r)/ *n.* a horse-dealer. [obs. *cope* buy, f. MDu., MLG *kōpen*, G *kaufen*: rel. to CHEAP]

Copernicus /kəˈpɜːnɪkəs/, Nicolaus (Latinized name Koppernigk, 1473–1543), Polish astronomer, canon of the cathedral at Frauenberg, the figure most closely associated with the overthrow of the ancient Greek Earth-centred cosmology. He developed his theories of a moving Earth, which he first published in outline in 1530, to a generally favourable reception. Not until 1543, however, was the full substance of his studies published in *De Revolutionibus Orbium Coelestium*, a copy of which, according to tradition, first reached Copernicus on his deathbed. Eschewing the complex system of epicyclic motions required to explain planetary motions in the Ptolemaic theory, he proposed the simpler model of a system of planets, including the Earth, all orbiting the sun. Still influenced by classical ideas of perfection, he supposed the orbits of the planets to be determined by combinations of perfect circles; but the most important break with tradition was in removing the Earth from the centre of the universe, a move which was to find much opposition in the Roman Catholic Church during the next century.

copestone /ˈkəʊpstəʊn/ *n.* **1** = *coping-stone*. **2** a finishing touch. [COPE[2] + STONE]

copiable /ˈkɒpɪəb(ə)l/ *adj.* that can or may be copied.

copier /ˈkɒpɪə(r)/ *n.* a machine or person that copies (esp. documents).

copilot /ˈkəʊˌpaɪlət/ *n.* a second pilot in an aircraft.

coping /ˈkəʊpɪŋ/ *n.* the top (usu. sloping) course of masonry in a wall or parapet. □ **coping-stone** a stone used in a coping.

coping saw /ˈkəʊpɪŋ/ *n.* a D-shaped saw for cutting curves in wood. [*cope* cut wood f. OF *coper*: see COPE[1]]

copious /ˈkəʊpɪəs/ *adj.* **1** abundant, plentiful. **2** producing much. **3** providing much information. **4** profuse in speech. □□

copiously adv. **copiousness** n. [ME f. OF copieux or f. L copiosus f. copia plenty]

copita /kə'pi:tə/ n. **1** a tulip-shaped sherry-glass. **2** a glass of sherry. [Sp., dimin. of copa cup]

coplanar /kəʊ'pleɪnə(r)/ adj. Geom. in the same plane. □□ **coplanarity** /-plə'nærɪtɪ/ n.

Copland /'kəʊplənd/, Aaron (1900–90), American composer, pianist, and conductor. The son of immigrant Jewish parents from Lithuania, he was concerned to establish a distinctive 'American' style in music, borrowing from jazz in his Piano Concerto (1926) and Music for the Theater (1925), from Shaker music in the evocative and popular Appalachian Spring (1944), and from other folk and traditional songs in the ballet scores Billy the Kid (1938) and Rodeo (1942). He furthered the cause of his country's music in his work as a conductor and in his establishment of the American Composers' Alliance (1937).

Copley /'kɒplɪ/, John Singleton (1738–1815), American painter. His shrewd and forceful realism marked him out as one of the most talented of colonial portraitists: his power of characterization enabled him to create the most convincing expressions of the aristocratic ideal in 18th-c. American painting, and he had a special gift for the portrayal of older people of the professional classes. Urged by Reynolds and Benjamin West, he sailed for Europe in 1774, and settled in England, remaining there until his death. He enjoyed a short period of success, especially with history pictures such as The Death of Chatham (1779–80), but his popularity waned and his last years were menaced by debt.

copolymer /kəʊ'pɒlɪmə(r)/ n. Chem. a polymer with units of more than one kind. □□ **copolymerize** v.tr. & intr. (also **-ise**).

copper¹ /'kɒpə(r)/ n., adj., & v. —n. **1** Chem. a malleable red-brown metallic element of the transition series occurring naturally esp. in cuprite and malachite. (See below.) ¶ Symb.: **Cu**; atomic number 29. **2** a bronze coin. **3** a large metal vessel for boiling esp. laundry. **4** any of various butterflies with copper-coloured wings. —adj. made of or coloured like copper. —v.tr. cover (a ship's bottom, a pan, etc.) with copper. □ **Copper Age** the prehistoric period when some weapons and tools were made of copper, either before or in place of bronze. **copper beech** a variety of beech with copper-coloured leaves. **copper belt** a copper-mining area of Central Africa. **copper-bit** a soldering tool pointed with copper. **copper-bottomed 1** having a bottom sheathed with copper (esp. of a ship or pan). **2** genuine or reliable (esp. financially). **copper pyrites** a double sulphide of copper and iron: also called CHALCOPYRITE. **copper sulphate** a blue crystalline solid used in electroplating, textile dyeing, etc. **copper vitriol** copper sulphate. [OE copor, coper, ult. f. L cyprium aes Cyprus metal (Cyprus was the principal source of copper in Roman times)]

Copper is found in the native state as well as in the form of ores. It was the earliest metal to be used by man, first by itself and then later alloyed with tin to form bronze. A ductile easily worked metal, it is a very good conductor of heat and electricity. Copper is a component of many alloys, but it is still used mainly in its pure state, especially for electrical wiring. Copper compounds are used in the production of green pigments, insecticides, and fungicides. In trace amounts the element is essential to living organisms.

copper² /'kɒpə(r)/ n. Brit. sl. a policeman. [COP¹ + ER¹]

copperas /'kɒpərəs/ n. green iron-sulphate crystals. [ME coperose f. OF couperose f. med.L cup(e)rosa: perh. orig. aqua cuprosa copper water]

Copperbelt /'kɒpə,belt/ a province of central Zambia; pop. (1980) 1,248,900; capital, Ndola. Copper, cobalt, and uranium are mined here.

copperhead /'kɒpə,hed/ n. **1** a venomous viper, Agkistrodon contortrix, native to N. America. **2** a venomous cobra, Denisonia superba, native to Australia.

copperplate /'kɒpə,pleɪt/ n. & adj. —n. **1 a** a polished copper plate for engraving or etching. **b** a print made from this. **2** an ornate style of handwriting resembling that orig. used in engravings. —adj. of or in copperplate writing.

coppersmith /'kɒpəsmɪθ/ n. a person who works in copper.

coppery /'kɒpərɪ/ adj. of or like copper, esp. in colour.

coppice /'kɒpɪs/ n. & v. —n. an area of undergrowth and small trees, grown for periodic cutting. —v.tr. cut back (young trees) periodically to stimulate growth of shoots. □□ **coppiced** adj. [OF copeïz ult. f. med.L colpus blow: see COPE¹]

copra /'kɒprə/ n. the dried kernels of the coconut. [Port. f. Malayalam koppara coconut]

co-precipitation /,kəʊprɪˌsɪpɪ'teɪʃ(ə)n/ n. Chem. the simultaneous precipitation of more than one compound from a solution.

copro- /'kɒprəʊ/ comb. form dung, faeces. [Gk kopros dung]

co-production /,kəʊprə'dʌkʃ(ə)n/ n. a production of a play, broadcast, etc., jointly by more than one company.

coprolite /'kɒprə,laɪt/ n. Archaeol. fossil dung or a piece of it.

coprophagous /kɒ'prɒfəgəs/ adj. Zool. dung-eating. [COPRO-]

coprophilia /,kɒprə'fɪlɪə/ n. an abnormal interest in faeces and defecation.

coprosma /kə'prɒzmə/ n. any small evergreen plant of the genus Coprosma, native to Australasia. [mod.L f. Gk kopros dung + osmē smell]

copse /kɒps/ n. **1** = COPPICE. **2** (in general use) a small wood. □□ **copsy** adj. [shortened f. COPPICE]

copsewood /'kɒpswʊd/ n. undergrowth.

Copt /kɒpt/ n. **1** a native Egyptian in the Hellenistic and Roman periods. **2** a native Christian of the independent Egyptian (Coptic) Church. [F Copte or mod.L Coptus f. Arab. al-kibt, al-kubt Copts f. Coptic Gyptios f. Gk Aiguptios Egyptian]

Coptic /'kɒptɪk/ n. & adj. —n. the language of the Copts, that represents the final stage of ancient Egyptian, with an alphabet largely based on the Greek but with some letters borrowed from Egyptian demotic, and now surviving only as the liturgical language of the Coptic Church. In the 3rd c. AD Coptic was the prevailing language of Christian Egypt. After the Arab conquest in 642 it began to give way to Arabic but did not die out as a spoken language until the 17th c. □ **Coptic Church** the native Christian Church in Egypt, traditionally founded by St Mark. It became isolated from the rest of Christendom in 451 when it adhered to the Monophysite doctrine condemned by the Council of Chalcedon, and its numbers declined when the conquest of Egypt by Muslim Arabs in the 7th c. was followed by centuries of persecution. There is a small Uniat Coptic Church dating from 1741. —adj. of or relating to the Copts.

copula /'kɒpjʊlə/ n. (pl. **copulas**) Logic & Gram. a connecting word, esp. a part of the verb be connecting a subject and predicate. □□ **copular** adj. [L (as CO-, apere fasten)]

copulate /'kɒpjʊˌleɪt/ v.intr. (often foll. by with) have sexual intercourse. □□ **copulatory** adj. [L copulare fasten together (as COPULA)]

copulation /,kɒpjʊ'leɪʃ(ə)n/ n. **1** sexual union. **2** a grammatical or logical connection. [ME f. OF f. L copulatio (as COPULATE)]

copulative /'kɒpjʊlətɪv/ adj. **1** serving to connect. **2** Gram. **a** (of a word) that connects words or clauses linked in sense (cf. DISJUNCTIVE). **b** connecting a subject and predicate. **3** relating to sexual union. □□ **copulatively** adv. [ME f. OF copulatif -ive or LL copulativus (as COPULATIVE)]

copy /'kɒpɪ/ n. & v. —n. (pl. **-ies**) **1** a thing made to imitate or be identical to another. **2** a single specimen of a publication or issue (ordered twenty copies). **3 a** matter to be printed. **b** material for a newspaper or magazine article (scandals make good copy). **c** the text of an advertisement. **4 a** a model to be copied. **b** a page written after a model (of penmanship). —v. (**-ies, -ied**) **1** tr. **a** make a copy of. **b** (often foll. by out) transcribe. **2** intr. make a copy, esp. clandestinely. **3** tr. (foll. by to) send a copy of (a letter) to a third party. **4** tr. do the same as; imitate. □ **copy-edit** edit (copy) for printing. **copy editor** a person who edits copy for printing. **copy-typist** a person who makes typewritten transcripts of documents. [ME f. OF copie, copier, ult. f. L copia abundance (in med.L = transcript)]

copybook /'kɒpɪˌbʊk/ n. **1** a book containing models of handwriting for learners to imitate. **2** (attrib.) **a** a tritely conventional. **b** accurate, exemplary.

copycat /ˈkɒpɪˌkæt/ n. colloq. (esp. as a child's word) a person who copies another, esp. slavishly.

copydesk /ˈkɒpɪˌdesk/ n. the desk at which copy is edited for printing.

copyhold /ˈkɒpɪˌhəʊld/ n. Brit. hist. 1 tenure of land based on manorial records. 2 land held in this way. □□ **copyholder** n.

copyist /ˈkɒpɪɪst/ n. 1 a person who makes (esp. written) copies. 2 an imitator. [earlier copist f. F copiste or med.L copista (as COPY)]

copyreader /ˈkɒpɪˌriːdə(r)/ n. a person who reads and edits copy for a newspaper or book. □□ **copyread** v.tr.

copyright /ˈkɒpɪˌraɪt/ n., adj., & v. —n. the exclusive legal right granted for a specified period to an author, designer, etc., or another appointed person, to print, publish, perform, film, or record original literary, artistic, or musical material. (See below.) —adj. (of such material) protected by copyright. —v.tr. secure copyright for (material). □ **copyright library** Brit. a library entitled to receive from the publisher a free copy of each book published in the UK. The libraries so entitled are the British Library, Bodleian, Cambridge University. National Library of Wales, Scottish National Library, and Trinity College, Dublin.
  Protection of rights was made necessary by the invention of printing (15th c.). Rulers issued monopoly rights to individuals or guilds, and at first the only protection available to the author was against unauthorized publication; once published it was out of the author's control. The first English statute recognizing the author's rights was passed in 1710, and gave protection for 28 years only; in 1790 a similar copyright law was passed in the US. In Britain, in general copyright subsists for the author's lifetime plus 50 years; in the US protection lasts for 28 years, renewable for a second 28-year term. Legislation has recently been introduced to protect rights in computer programs and computer-stored material.

copywriter /ˈkɒpɪˌraɪtə(r)/ n. a person who writes or prepares copy (esp. of advertising material) for publication. □□ **copywriting** n.

coq au vin /ˌkɒk əʊ ˈvæ̃/ n. a casserole of chicken pieces cooked in wine. [F]

coquetry /ˈkɒkɪtrɪ, ˈkəʊk-/ n. (pl. -ies) 1 coquettish behaviour. 2 a coquettish act. 3 trifling with serious matters. [F coquetterie f. coqueter (as COQUETTE)]

coquette /kɒˈket, kəˈket/ n. 1 a woman who flirts. 2 any crested humming-bird of the genus Lophornis. □□ **coquettish** adj. **coquettishly** adv. **coquettishness** n. [F, fem. of coquet wanton, dimin. of coq cock]

coquina /kəˈkiːnə/ n. US a soft limestone of broken shells, used in road-making. [Sp., = cockle]

coquito /kəˈkiːtəʊ/ n. (pl. -os) a palm-tree, Jubaea chilensis, native to Chile, yielding honey from its sap, and fibre. [Sp., dimin. of coco coconut]

Cor. abbr. 1 Corinthians (New Testament). 2 US corner.

cor /kɔː(r)/ int. Brit. sl. expressing surprise, alarm, exasperation, etc. □ **cor blimey** see BLIMEY. [corrupt. of God]

cor- /kər/ prefix assim. form of COM- before r.

coracle /ˈkɒrək(ə)l/ n. Brit. a small boat, occasionally circular but more often rectangular with rounded corners, constructed of wickerwork and made watertight originally with animal hides but more recently with pitch or some other watertight material, used for river and coastal transport by the ancient Britons and still used by fishermen on the rivers and lakes of Wales and Ireland. [Welsh corwgl (corwg = Ir. currach boat: cf. CURRACH)]

coracoid /ˈkɒrəˌkɔɪd/ n. (in full **coracoid process**) a short projection from the shoulder-blade in vertebrates. [mod.L coracoides f. Gk korakoeidēs raven-like f. korax -akos raven]

coral /ˈkɒr(ə)l/ n. & adj. —n. 1 **a** a hard usually red, pink, or white calcareous substance secreted by various marine coelenterates for support and habitation, esp. that forming the skeleton of the precious coral (Corallium rubrun) of the Mediterranean and Red Sea. **b** pop. a similar substance produced by marine algae etc. 2 a rock-like aggregation of these substances, sometimes forming reefs and islands. 3 any marine coelenterate of the class Anthozoa, esp. of the order Madreporaria (the stony

or true corals) which have a calcareous skeleton and are the main reef-forming types. 4 the yellowish- or reddish-pink colour of some corals. 5 the unimpregnated roe of a lobster or scallop. —adj. 1 like coral, esp. in colour. 2 made of coral. □ **coral island** (or **reef**) one formed by the growth of coral. **coral rag** limestone containing beds of petrified corals. **coral-snake** any of various brightly coloured poisonous snakes, esp. Micrurus nigrocinctus, native to Central America. [ME f. OF f. L corallum f. Gk korallion, prob. of Semitic orig.]

coralline /ˈkɒrəˌlaɪn/ n. & adj. —n. 1 any seaweed of the genus Corallina having a calcareous jointed stem. 2 (in general use) the name of various plantlike compound organisms. —adj. 1 coral-red. 2 of or like coral. [F corallin & It. corallina f. LL corallinus (as CORAL)]

corallite /ˈkɒrəˌlaɪt/ n. 1 the coral skeleton of a marine polyp. 2 fossil coral. [L corallum CORAL]

coralloid /ˈkɒrəˌlɔɪd/ adj. & n. —adj. like or akin to coral. —n. a coralloid organism.

Coral Sea a part of the Pacific lying between Australia, New Guinea, and Vanuatu.

coram populo /ˌkɔːrəm ˈpɒpjʊˌləʊ/ adv. in public. [L, = in the presence of the people]

cor anglais /kɔːr ˈɒŋgleɪ, ã̃ˈgleɪ/ n. (pl. **cors anglais** pronunc. same) Mus. 1 an alto woodwind instrument of the oboe family. 2 its player. 3 an organ stop with the quality of a cor anglais. [F, = English horn]

corbel /ˈkɔːb(ə)l/ n. & v. Archit. —n. 1 a projection of stone, timber, etc., jutting out from a wall to support a weight. 2 a short timber laid longitudinally under a beam to help support it. —v.tr. & intr. (**corbelled**, **corbelling**; US **corbeled**, **corbeling**) (foll. by out, off) support or project on corbels. □ **corbel-table** a projecting course resting on corbels. [ME f. OF, dimin. of corp: see CORBIE]

corbie /ˈkɔːbɪ/ n. Sc. 1 a raven. 2 a carrion crow. □ **corbie-steps** the steplike projections on the sloping sides of a gable. [ME f. OF corb, corp f. L corvus crow]

Corcovado /ˌkɔːkəˈvɑːdəʊ/ a peak rising to 711 m (2,310 ft.) on the south side of Rio de Janeiro. The gigantic concrete statue of 'Christ the Redeemer' stands on its summit.

Corcyra /kɔːˈsaɪərə/ the former name of Corfu.

cord /kɔːd/ n. & v. —n. 1 **a** long thin flexible material made from several twisted strands. **b** a piece of this. 2 Anat. a structure in the body resembling a cord (spinal cord). 3 **a** ribbed fabric, esp. corduroy. **b** (in pl.) corduroy trousers. **c** a cordlike rib on fabric. 4 an electric flex. 5 a measure of cut wood (usu. 128 cu.ft., 3.6 cubic metres). 6 a moral or emotional tie (cords of affection; fourfold cord of evidence). —v.tr. 1 fasten or bind with cord. 2 (as **corded** adj.) **a** (of cloth) ribbed. **b** provided with cords. **c** (of muscles) standing out like taut cords. □□ **cordlike** adj. [ME f. OF corde f. L chorda f. Gk khordē gut, string of musical instrument]

cordage /ˈkɔːdɪdʒ/ n. cords or ropes, esp. in the rigging of a ship. [ME f. F (as CORD)]

cordate /ˈkɔːdeɪt/ adj. heart-shaped. [mod.L cordatus f. L cor cordis heart]

Corday /kɔːˈdeɪ/, Charlotte (1768–93), French noblewoman, a supporter of the revolutionary Girondist party, who assassinated Marat in his bath and was guillotined for her crime.

cordelier /ˌkɔːdɪˈlɪə(r)/ n. a Franciscan friar of the strict rule (wearing a knotted cord round the waist). [ME f. OF f. cordele dimin. of corde CORD]

cordial /ˈkɔːdɪəl/ adj. & n. —adj. 1 heartfelt, sincere. 2 warm, friendly. —n. 1 a fruit-flavoured drink. 2 a comforting or pleasant-tasting medicine. □□ **cordiality** /-ˈælɪtɪ/ n. **cordially** adv. [ME f. med.L cordialis f. L cor cordis heart]

cordillera /ˌkɔːdɪˈljeərə/ n. a system or group of usu. parallel mountain ranges together with intervening plateaux etc., esp. of the Andes and in Central America and Mexico. [Sp. f. cordilla dimin. of cuerda CORD]

cordite /ˈkɔːdaɪt/ n. a smokeless explosive made from cellulose nitrate and nitroglycerine. [CORD (from its appearance) + -ITE[1]]

cordless /'kɔːdlɪs/ adj. (of an electrical appliance, telephone, etc.) working from an internal source of energy etc. (esp. a battery) and without a connection to a mains supply or central unit.

Cordoba /'kɔːdəbə/ a city in southern Spain, founded by the Carthaginians, held by the Moors from 711 to 1236; pop. (1986) 304,800. As capital of the most powerful of the Arab Spanish States it flourished as a centre of learning, earning the title of 'the Athens of the West'. It began to decline after the overthrow of the caliphate in 1031.

Córdoba /'kɔːdəbə/ a city in central Argentina, capital of Córdoba province; pop. (1980) 982,000. Its university has been one of the principal centres of learning in South America since it was founded in 1613.

cordon /'kɔːd(ə)n/ n. & v. —n. 1 a line or circle of police, soldiers, guards, etc., esp. preventing access to or from an area. 2 a an ornamental cord or braid. b the ribbon of a knightly order. 3 a fruit-tree trained to grow as a single stem. 4 Archit. a string-course. —v.tr. (often foll. by off) enclose or separate with a cordon of police etc. [It. cordone augmentative of corda CORD, & F cordon (as CORD)]

cordon bleu /ˌkɔːdɒn 'blɜː, ˌkɔːdɔ̃/ adj. & n. Cookery —adj. of the highest class. —n. a cook of this class. [F, = blue ribbon, orig. that worn by Knights-grand-cross of the French order of the Holy Ghost, the highest order of chivalry under the Bourbon kings; hence extended to other first-class distinctions]

cordon sanitaire /ˌkɔːdɒn ˌsænɪ'teə(r)/ n. 1 a guarded line between infected and uninfected districts. 2 any measure designed to prevent communication or the spread of undesirable influences.

cordovan /'kɔːdəv(ə)n/ n. a kind of soft leather. [Sp. cordovan of Cordova (Cordoba) where it was orig. made]

corduroy /'kɔːdərɔɪ, -djʊ,rɔɪ/ n. 1 a thick cotton fabric with velvety ribs. 2 (in pl.) corduroy trousers. □ **corduroy road** a road made of tree-trunks laid across a swamp. [18th c.: prob. f. CORD ribbed fabric + obs. duroy coarse woollen fabric]

cordwainer /'kɔːd,weɪnə(r)/ n. Brit. archaic a shoemaker (usu. in names of guilds etc.). [obs. cordwain CORDOVAN]

cordwood /'kɔːdwʊd/ n. wood that is or can easily be measured in cords.

CORE abbr. US Congress of Racial Equality.

core /kɔː(r)/ n. & v. —n. 1 the horny central part of various fruits, containing the seeds. 2 a the central or most important part of anything (also attrib.: core curriculum). b the central part, of different character from the surroundings. 3 the central region of the earth. 4 the central part of a nuclear reactor, containing the fissile material. 5 a magnetic structural unit in a computer, storing one bit of data (see BIT⁴). 6 the inner strand of an electric cable, rope, etc. 7 a piece of soft iron forming the centre of an electromagnet or an induction coil. 8 an internal mould filling a space to be left hollow in a casting. 9 an internal part cut out (esp. of rock etc. in boring). 10 Archaeol. a piece of flint from which flakes or blades have been removed. —v.tr. remove the core from. □ **core memory** Computing the memory of a computer consisting of many cores. **core time** (in a flexitime system) the central part of the working day, when all employees must be present. □□ **corer** n. [ME: orig. unkn.]

corelation var. of CORRELATION.

co-religionist /ˌkɔːrɪ'lɪdʒənɪst/ n. (US coreligionist) an adherent of the same religion.

corella /kə'relə/ n. Austral. either of two small white cockatoos, Cacatua tenuirostris or C. sanguinea. [app. Latinized f. Aboriginal ca-rall]

Corelli[1] /kə'relɪ/, Arcangelo (1653–1713), Italian violinist and composer. His best-known works are for the violin: four sets of trio sonatas, one of sonatas for solo violin, and one of concerti grossi (for a solo group of instruments and small orchestra). With their idiomatic writing and beautiful melodies they had an important influence abroad, on Purcell, Bach, Handel, and Couperin, among others.

Corelli[2] /kə'relɪ/, Marie (pseudonym of Mary Mackay, 1855–1924), English author of romantic melodramas, the first of

which was A Romance of Two Worlds (1886). She achieved outstanding success at the turn of the century, but her popularity turned to ridicule long before her death.

coreopsis /ˌkɒrɪ'ɒpsɪs/ n. any composite plant of the genus Coreopsis, having rayed usu. yellow flowers. [mod.L f. Gk koris bug + opsis appearance, with ref. to the shape of the seed]

co-respondent /ˌkəʊrɪ'spɒnd(ə)nt/ n. (US corespondent) a person cited in a divorce case as having committed adultery with the respondent.

corf /kɔːf/ n. (pl. **corves** /kɔːvz/) Brit. 1 a basket in which fish are kept alive in the water. 2 a small wagon, formerly a large basket, used in mining. [MDu., MLG korf, OHG chorp, korb f. L corbis basket]

Corfu /kɔː'fuː/ (Greek **Kérkira** /'keəkɪrə/) one of the largest of the Ionian islands, off the west coast of Greece; pop. (1981) 96,500.

corgi /'kɔːgɪ/ n. (pl. **corgis**) (in full **Welsh corgi**) 1 a dog of a short-legged breed with foxlike head. 2 this breed. [Welsh f. cor dwarf + ci dog]

coriaceous /ˌkɒrɪ'eɪʃəs/ adj. like leather; leathery. [LL coriaceus f. corium leather]

coriander /ˌkɒrɪ'ændə(r)/ n. 1 a plant, Coriandrum sativum, with leaves used for flavouring and small round aromatic fruits. 2 (also **coriander seed**) the dried fruit used for flavouring curries etc. [ME f. OF coriandre f. L coriandrum f. Gk koriannon]

Corinthian /kə'rɪnθɪən/ adj. & n. —adj. 1 of ancient Corinth in southern Greece. 2 Archit. of an order characterized by ornate decoration and flared capitals with rows of acanthus leaves, used esp. by the Romans. 3 archaic profligate. —n. a native of Corinth. □ **(Epistle to the) Corinthians** either of two books of the New Testament, epistles of St Paul to the Church at Corinth. [L Corinthius f. Gk Korinthios + -AN]

Coriolanus /ˌkɒrɪə'leɪnəs/, Gnaeus Marcius (5th c. BC), Roman general, said to have left Rome after opposing the distribution of corn to the starving people and being charged with tyrannical conduct. He led a Volscian army against Rome in 491 BC, and was turned back only by the pleas of his mother Veturia and his wife Volumnia; he was subsequently put to death by the Volscians.

Coriolis /ˌkɒrɪ'əʊlɪs/, Gaspard Gustave de (1792–1843), French engineer and mathematician whose name is applied to the effect (which he described) whereby a body moving relative to a rotating frame of reference is accelerated in that frame in a direction perpendicular both to its direction of motion and to the axis of rotation of the frame. It helps to explain, for example, the movement of an air mass or the rotation of a rocket over the surface of the earth (clockwise in the northern hemisphere, anticlockwise in the southern).

corium /'kɔːrɪəm/ n. Anat. the dermis. [L, = skin]

Cork /kɔːk/ a city in the Republic of Ireland, capital of Cork county in the province of Ulster; pop. (est. 1986) 173,700.

cork /kɔːk/ n. & v. —n. 1 the buoyant light-brown bark of the cork-oak. 2 a bottle-stopper of cork or other material. 3 a float of cork used in fishing etc. 4 Bot. a protective layer of dead cells immediately below the bark of woody plants. 5 (attrib.) made of cork. —v.tr. (often foll. by up) 1 stop or confine. 2 restrain (feelings etc.). 3 blacken with burnt cork. □ **cork-oak** a S. European oak, Quercus suber. **cork-tipped** Brit. (of a cigarette) having a filter of corklike material. □□ **corklike** adj. [ME f. Du. & LG kork f. Sp. alcorque cork sole, perh. f. Arab.]

corkage /'kɔːkɪdʒ/ n. a charge made by a restaurant or hotel for serving wine etc. when brought in by customers.

corked /kɔːkt/ adj. 1 stopped with a cork. 2 (of wine) spoilt by a decayed cork. 3 blackened with burnt cork.

corker /'kɔːkə(r)/ n. sl. an excellent or astonishing person or thing.

corking /'kɔːkɪŋ/ adj. sl. strikingly large or splendid.

corkscrew /'kɔːkskruː/ n. & v. —n. 1 a spirally twisted steel device for extracting corks from bottles. 2 (often attrib.) a thing with a spiral shape. —v.tr. & intr. move spirally; twist.

corkwood /'kɔːkwʊd/ n. 1 any shrub of the genus Duboisia, yielding a light porous wood. 2 this wood.

corky /ˈkɔːkɪ/ adj. (**corkier**, **corkiest**) 1 corklike. 2 (of wine) corked.

corm /kɔːm/ n. Bot. an underground swollen stem base of some plants, e.g. crocus. [mod.L cormus f. Gk kormos trunk with boughs lopped off]

cormorant /ˈkɔːmərənt/ n. any diving sea bird of the family Phalacrocoracidae, esp. Phalacrocorax carbo having lustrous black plumage. [ME f. OF cormaran f. med.L corvus marinus sea-raven: for ending -ant cf. peasant, tyrant]

corn¹ /kɔːn/ n. & v. —n. 1 a any cereal before or after harvesting, esp. the chief crop of a region: wheat, oats, or (in the US and Australia) maize. b a grain or seed of a cereal plant. 2 colloq. something corny or trite. —v.tr. (as **corned** adj.) sprinkled or preserved with salt or brine (corned beef). □ **corn-cob** the cylindrical centre of the maize ear to which rows of grains are attached. **corn-cob pipe** a tobacco-pipe made from a corn-cob. **corn-cockle** see COCKLE². **corn dolly** a symbolic or decorative figure made of plaited straw. **corn exchange** a place for trade in corn. **corn-factor** Brit. a dealer in corn. **Corn Laws** see separate entry. **corn marigold** a daisy-like yellow-flowered plant, Chrysanthemum segetum, growing amongst corn. **corn on the cob** maize cooked and eaten from the corn-cob. **corn-salad** = lamb's lettuce (see LAMB). **corn-spurry** see SPURRY. **corn-whiskey** US whisky distilled from maize. [OE f. Gmc: rel. to L granum grain]

corn² /kɔːn/ n. a small area of horny usu. tender skin esp. on the toes, extending into subcutaneous tissue. [ME f. AF f. L cornu horn]

cornbrash /ˈkɔːnbræʃ/ n. Geol. Brit. an earthy limestone layer of the Jurassic period. [CORN¹ + BRASH²]

corncrake /ˈkɔːnkreɪk/ n. a rail, Crex crex, inhabiting grassland and nesting on the ground.

cornea /ˈkɔːnɪə/ n. the transparent circular part of the front of the eyeball. □□ **corneal** adj. [med.L cornea tela horny tissue, f. L corneus horny f. cornu horn]

Corneille /kɔːˈneɪ/, Pierre (1606–84), French dramatic poet, leader of classical French tragedy until he was eclipsed by Racine. Médée (1635), Le Cid (1637), and Cinna (1640) are among his masterpieces. His characters, more sublime than those of Racine, are often torn between duty and passion but may rise to superhuman heights of self-sacrifice.

cornel /ˈkɔːn(ə)l/ n. any plant of the genus Cornus, esp. a dwarf kind, C. suecica. [ME f. L cornus]

cornelian /kɔːˈniːlɪən/ n. (also **carnelian** /kɑː-/) 1 a dull red or reddish-white variety of chalcedony. 2 this colour. [ME f. OF corneline; car- after L caro carnis flesh]

corneous /ˈkɔːnɪəs/ adj. hornlike, horny. [L corneus f. cornu horn]

corner /ˈkɔːnə(r)/ n. & v. —n. 1 a place where converging sides or edges meet. 2 a projecting angle, esp. where two streets meet. 3 the internal space or recess formed by the meeting of two sides, esp. of a room. 4 a difficult position, esp. one from which there is no escape (driven into a corner). 5 a secluded or remote place. 6 a region or quarter, esp. a remote one (from the four corners of the earth). 7 the action or result of buying or controlling the whole available stock of a commodity, thereby dominating the market. 8 Boxing & Wrestling a an angle of the ring, esp. one where a contestant rests between rounds. b a contestant's supporters offering assistance at the corner between rounds. 9 Football & Hockey a free kick or hit from a corner of the pitch after the ball has been kicked over the goal-line by a defending player. 10 a triangular cut of gammon or ham. —v. 1 tr. force (a person or animal) into a difficult or inescapable position. 2 tr. a establish a corner in (a commodity). b dominate (dealers or the market) in this way. 3 intr. (esp. of or in a vehicle) go round a corner. □ **corner shop** a small local shop, esp. at a street corner. **just round** (or **around**) **the corner** colloq. very near, imminent. [ME f. AF ult. f. L cornu horn]

cornerstone /ˈkɔːnəstəʊn/ n. 1 a a stone in a projecting angle of a wall. b a foundation-stone. 2 an indispensable part or basis of something.

cornerwise /ˈkɔːnəwaɪz/ adv. diagonally.

cornet¹ /ˈkɔːnɪt/ n. 1 Mus. a a brass instrument resembling a

trumpet but shorter and wider. b its player. c an organ stop with the quality of a cornet. d a cornetto. 2 Brit. a conical wafer for holding ice-cream. □□ **cornetist** /kɔːˈnetɪst, ˈkɔːnɪtɪst/ n. **cornettist** /kɔːˈnetɪst/ n. [ME f. OF ult. f. L cornu horn]

cornet² /ˈkɔːnɪt/ n. Brit. hist. the fifth commissioned officer in a cavalry troop, who carried the colours. □□ **cornetcy** n. (pl. **-ies**). [earlier sense 'pennon, standard' f. F cornette dimin. of corne ult. f. L cornua horns]

cornett /ˈkɔːnɪt/ n. Mus. = CORNETTO. [var. of CORNET¹]

cornetto /kɔːˈnetəʊ/ n. (pl. **cornetti** /-tɪ/) Mus. an old woodwind instrument like a flageolet. [It., dimin. of corno horn (as CORNET¹)]

cornfield /ˈkɔːnfiːld/ n. a field in which corn is being grown.

cornflake /ˈkɔːnfleɪk/ n. 1 (in pl.) a breakfast cereal of toasted flakes made from maize flour. 2 a flake of this cereal.

cornflour /ˈkɔːnˌflaʊə(r)/ n. 1 a fine-ground maize flour. Also called CORNSTARCH. 2 a flour of rice or other grain.

cornflower /ˈkɔːnˌflaʊə(r)/ n. any plant of the genus Centaurea growing among corn, esp. C. cyanus, with deep-blue flowers.

cornice /ˈkɔːnɪs/ n. 1 Archit. a an ornamental moulding round the wall of a room just below the ceiling. b a horizontal moulded projection crowning a building or structure, esp. the uppermost member of the entablature of an order, surmounting the frieze. 2 Mountaineering an overhanging mass of hardened snow at the edge of a precipice. □□ **corniced** adj. [F corniche etc. f. It. cornice, perh. f. L cornix -icis crow]

corniche /ˈkɔːnɪʃ, kɔːˈniːʃ/ n. (in full **corniche road**) 1 a road cut into the edge of a cliff etc. 2 a coastal road with wide views. [F: see CORNICE]

Cornish /ˈkɔːnɪʃ/ adj. & n. —adj. of or relating to Cornwall. —n. the ancient Celtic language of Cornwall, belonging to the Brythonic branch of the Celtic language group. It was formerly spoken in Cornwall but gradually died out in the 17th–18th c., though attempts are being made to revive it. □ **Cornish cream** clotted cream. **Cornish pasty** seasoned meat and vegetables baked in a pastry envelope.

Corn Laws legislation first introduced in 1815 in an attempt to maintain the prosperity enjoyed by British agriculture during the Napoleonic Wars. The original Corn Law allowed foreign grain to be imported only after the price of home-grown wheat had risen above 80 shillings a quarter, but this had the unintended effect of forcing bread prices so high that both consumer and producer suffered. A sliding scale of import duties was introduced in 1828, but opposition to the Corn Laws continued to mount and they were eventually repealed by Peel in 1846, an act which split the Conservative Party.

cornstarch /ˈkɔːnstɑːtʃ/ n. = CORNFLOUR.

cornstone /ˈkɔːnstəʊn/ n. Brit. Geol. a mottled red and green limestone usu. formed under arid conditions, esp. in the Devonian period.

cornucopia /ˌkɔːnjʊˈkəʊpɪə/ n. 1 a a symbol of plenty consisting of a goat's horn overflowing with flowers, fruit, and corn. b an ornamental vessel shaped like this. 2 an abundant supply. □□ **cornucopian** adj. [LL f. L cornu copiae horn of plenty]

Cornwall /ˈkɔːnw(ə)l/ a county occupying the extreme SW peninsula of England; pop. (1981) 426,500; county town, Truro. The Celtic language of the ancient Cornish kingdom was still spoken there until the 18th c.

corny /ˈkɔːnɪ/ adj. (**cornier**, **corniest**) 1 colloq. a trite. b feebly humorous. c sentimental. d old-fashioned; out of date. 2 of or abounding in corn. □□ **cornily** adv. **corniness** n. [CORN¹ + -Y¹: sense 1 f. sense 'rustic']

corolla /kəˈrɒlə/ n. Bot. a whorl or whorls of petals forming the inner envelope of a flower. [L, dimin. of corona crown]

corollary /kəˈrɒlərɪ/ n. & adj. —n. (pl. **-ies**) 1 a a proposition that follows from (and is often appended to) one already proved. b an immediate deduction. 2 (often foll. by of) a natural consequence or result. —adj. 1 supplementary, associated. 2 (often foll. by to) forming a corollary. [ME f. L corollarium money paid for a garland, gratuity: neut. adj. f. COROLLA]

Coromandel Coast /ˌkɒrəˈmænd(ə)l/ the east coast of Tamil

Nadu in SE India, from Point Calimere to the mouth of the Krishna River.

corona[1] /kəˈrəʊnə/ n. (pl. **coronae** /-niː/) **1 a** a small circle of light round the sun or moon. **b** the rarefied gaseous envelope of the sun, normally visible only during a total solar eclipse, when it is seen as a pearly glow round the disc of the obscuring moon, extending for several times the radius of the sun. It consists of an extremely rarified gas of electrically charged particles, heated to a temperature of millions of degrees by sound waves originating in the surface layers of the sun. There is evidence of such regions in other stars. **2** a circular chandelier hung from a roof. **3** Anat. a crown or crownlike structure. **4** Bot. a crownlike outgrowth from the inner side of a corolla. **5** Archit. a broad vertical face of a cornice, usu. of considerable projection. **6** Electr. the glow around a conductor at high potential. [L, = crown]

corona[2] /kəˈrəʊnə/ n. a long cigar with straight sides. [Sp. La Corona the crown]

coronach /ˈkɒrənək, -nəx/ n. Sc. & Ir. a funeral-song or dirge. [Ir. coranach, Gael. corranach f. comh- together + rànach outcry]

coronagraph /kəˈrəʊnəˌgrɑːf/ n. an instrument for observing the sun's corona, esp. other than during a solar eclipse.

coronal[1] /kəˈrəʊn(ə)l, ˈkɒrən(ə)l/ adj. **1** Astron. & Bot. of a corona. **2** Anat. of the crown of the head. □ **coronal bone** the frontal bone of the skull. **coronal plane** an imaginary plane dividing the body into dorsal and ventral parts. **coronal suture** a transverse suture of the skull separating the frontal bone from the parietal bones. [F coronal or L coronalis (as CORONA[1])]

coronal[2] /ˈkɒrən(ə)l/ n. **1** a circlet (esp. of gold or gems) for the head. **2** a wreath or garland. [ME, app. f. AF f. corone CROWN]

coronary /ˈkɒrənəri/ adj. & n. —adj. Anat. resembling or encircling like a crown. —n. (pl. **-ies**) = coronary thrombosis. □ **coronary artery** an artery supplying blood to the heart. **coronary thrombosis** Med. a blockage of the blood flow caused by a blood clot in a coronary artery. [L coronarius f. corona crown]

coronation /ˌkɒrəˈneɪʃ(ə)n/ n. the ceremony of crowning a sovereign or a sovereign's consort. □ **Coronation stone** the stone of Scone on which Scottish kings were crowned, brought to England by Edward I and now preserved in the coronation chair at Westminster Abbey. [ME f. OF f. med.L coronatio -onis f. coronare to crown f. CORONA[1]]

coroner /ˈkɒrənə(r)/ n. **1** an officer of a county, district, or municipality, holding inquests on deaths thought to be violent or accidental, and inquiries in cases of treasure trove. **2** hist. an officer charged with maintaining the rights of the private property of the Crown. □□ **coronership** n. [ME f. AF cor(o)uner f. coro(u)ne CROWN]

coronet /ˈkɒrənɪt, -net/ n. **1** a small crown (esp. as worn, or used as a heraldic device, by a peer or peeress). **2** a circlet of precious materials, esp. as a woman's head-dress or part of one. **3** a garland for the head. **4** the lowest part of a horse's pastern. **5** a ring of bone at the base of a deer's antler. □□ **coroneted** adj. [OF coronet(t)e dimin. of corone CROWN]

Corot /ˈkɒrəʊ/, Jean-Baptiste Camille (1796–1875), French landscape artist, trained in the neoclassical tradition, who was an important influence on the impressionist landscape painters, especially Pissarro. At 26 he abandoned a commercial career for art. He was in Italy, the subject of many of his landscapes, in 1825–8 and again in 1834 and 1843. Corot was friendly with the Barbizon group, but his works remained poetic and essentially classical in spirit, becoming more misty and ethereal in the 1850s and 1860s. Throughout his career he painted charmingly direct portraits and figure studies, and he retained his powers into old age, The Studio (1870) and Sens Cathedral (1874) being among his masterpieces.

corozo /kəˈrəʊzəʊ/ n. (pl. **-os**) Bot. any of various palm-trees native to S. America. □ **corozo-nut** a seed of one species of palm, Phytelephas macrocarpa, which when hardened forms vegetable ivory: also called ivory-nut. [Sp.]

Corp. abbr. **1** Corporal. **2** US Corporation.

corpora pl. of CORPUS.

corporal[1] /ˈkɔːp(ə)l/ n. **1** a non-commissioned army or air-force officer ranking next below sergeant. **2** (in full **ship's corporal**) Brit. an officer under the master-at-arms, attending to police matters. **3** US a freshwater fallfish, Semotilis corporalis. [obs. F, var. of caporal f. It. caporale prob. f. L corporalis (as CORPORAL[2]), confused with It. capo head]

corporal[2] /ˈkɔːp(ə)l/ adj. of or relating to the human body (cf. CORPOREAL). □ **corporal punishment** punishment inflicted on the body, esp. by beating. □□ **corporally** adv. [ME f. OF f. L corporalis f. corpus body]

corporal[3] /ˈkɔːp(ə)l/ n. a cloth on which the vessels containing the consecrated elements are placed during the celebration of the Eucharist. [OE f. OF corporal or med.L corporale pallium body cloth (as CORPORAL[2])]

corporality /ˌkɔːpəˈrælɪti/ n. (pl. **-ies**) **1** material existence. **2** a body. [ME f. LL corporalitas (as CORPORAL[2])]

corporate /ˈkɔːpərət/ adj. **1** forming a corporation (corporate body; body corporate). **2** forming one body of many individuals. **3** of or belonging to a corporation or group (corporate responsibility). **4** corporative. □□ **corporately** adv. **corporatism** n. [L corporare corporat- form into a body (corpus -oris)]

corporation /ˌkɔːpəˈreɪʃ(ə)n/ n. **1** a group of people authorized to act as an individual and recognized in law as a single entity, esp. in business. **2** the municipal authorities of a borough, town, or city. **3** joc. a protruding stomach. [LL corporatio (as CORPORATE)]

corporative /ˈkɔːpərətɪv/ adj. **1** of a corporation. **2** governed by or organized in corporations, esp. of employers and employed. □□ **corporativism** n.

corporeal /kɔːˈpɔːrɪəl/ adj. **1** bodily, physical, material, esp. as distinct from spiritual (cf. CORPORAL[2]). **2** Law consisting of material objects. □□ **corporeality** /-ˈælɪti/ n. **corporeally** adv. [LL corporealis f. L corporeus f. corpus -oris body]

corporeity /ˌkɔːpəˈriːɪti/ n. **1** the quality of being or having a material body. **2** bodily substance. [F corporéité or med.L corporeitas f. L corporeus (as CORPOREAL)]

corposant /ˈkɔːpəz(ə)nt/ n. a luminous electrical discharge sometimes seen on a ship or aircraft during a storm. [OSp., Port., It. corpo santo holy body]

corps /kɔː(r)/ n. (pl. **corps** /kɔːz/) **1** Mil. **a** a body of troops with special duties (intelligence corps; Royal Army Medical Corps). **b** a main subdivision of an army in the field, consisting of two or more divisions. **2** a body of people engaged in a special activity (diplomatic corps; press corps). [F (as CORPSE)]

corps de ballet /ˌkɔː də ˈbæleɪ/ n. the company of ensemble dancers in a ballet. [F]

corps d'élite /ˌkɔː deɪˈliːt/ n. a select group. [F]

corps diplomatique /ˌkɔː dɪpləmæˈtiːk/ n. a diplomatic corps. [F]

corpse /kɔːps/ n. a dead (usu. human) body. □ **corpse-candle 1** a lambent flame seen in a churchyard or over a grave, regarded as an omen of death. **2** a lighted candle placed beside a corpse before burial. [ME corps, var. spelling of cors (CORSE), f. OF cors f. L corpus body]

corpulent /ˈkɔːpjʊlənt/ adj. bulky in body, fat. □□ **corpulence** n. **corpulency** n. [ME f. L corpulentus f. corpus body]

corpus /ˈkɔːpəs/ n. (pl. **corpora** /ˈkɔːpərə/ or **corpuses**) **1** a body or collection of writings, texts, spoken material, etc. **2** Anat. a structure of a special character in the animal body. [ME f. L, = body]

Corpus Christi /ˌkɔːpəs ˈkrɪstɪ/ n. a feast commemorating the institution and gift of the Eucharist, celebrated on the Thursday after Trinity Sunday. In medieval times it was the occasion when the guilds of many towns performed religious plays. [ME f. L, = Body of Christ]

corpuscle /ˈkɔːpʌs(ə)l/ n. a minute body or cell in an organism, esp. (in pl.) the red or white cells in the blood of vertebrates. □□ **corpuscular** /kɔːˈpʌskjʊlə(r)/ adj. [L corpusculum (as CORPUS)]

corpus delicti /ˌkɔːpəs dɪˈlɪktaɪ/ n. Law the facts and circumstances constituting a breach of a law. [L, = body of offence]

corpus luteum /ˌkɔːpəs ˈluːtɪəm/ n. Anat. a body developed in the ovary after discharge of the ovum, remaining in existence only if pregnancy has begun. [mod.L f. CORPUS + *luteus*, *-um* yellow]

corral /kɒˈrɑːl/ n. & v. —n. **1** US a pen for cattle, horses, etc. **2** an enclosure for capturing wild animals. **3** esp. US hist. a defensive enclosure of wagons in an encampment. —v.tr. (**corralled**, **corralling**) **1** put or keep in a corral. **2** form (wagons) into a corral. **3** US colloq. acquire. [Sp. & OPort. (as KRAAL)]

corrasion /kəˈreɪʒ(ə)n/ n. Geol. erosion of the earth's surface by rock material being carried over it by water, ice, etc. [L *corradere corras-* scrape together (as COM-, *radere* scrape)]

correct /kəˈrekt/ adj. & v. —adj. **1** true, right, accurate. **2** (of conduct, manners, etc.) proper, right. **3** in accordance with good standards of taste etc. —v.tr. **1** set right; amend (an error, omission, etc., or the person responsible for it). **2** mark the errors in (written or printed work etc.). **3** substitute the right thing for (the wrong one). **4 a** admonish or rebuke (a person). **b** punish (a person or fault). **5** counteract (a harmful quality). **6** adjust (an instrument etc.) to function accurately or accord with a standard. □□ **correctly** adv. **correctness** n. [ME (adj. through F) f. L *corrigere correct-* (as COM-, *regere* guide)]

correction /kəˈrekʃ(ə)n/ n. **1 a** the act or process of correcting. **b** an instance of this. **2** a thing substituted for what is wrong. **3** archaic punishment (*house of correction*). □□ **correctional** adj. [ME f. OF f. L *correctio -onis* (as CORRECT)]

correctitude /kəˈrektɪˌtjuːd/ n. correctness, esp. conscious correctness of conduct. [19th c., f. CORRECT + RECTITUDE]

corrective /kəˈrektɪv/ adj. & n. —adj. serving or tending to correct or counteract something undesired or harmful. —n. a corrective measure or thing. □□ **correctively** adv. [F *correctif -ive* or LL *correctivus* (as CORRECT)]

corrector /kəˈrektə(r)/ n. a person who corrects or points out faults. [ME f. AF *correctour* f. L *corrector* (as CORRECT)]

Correggio /kɒˈredʒɪˌəʊ/, Antonio Allegri (*c.*1489–1534), Italian painter, influenced by Mantegna and Leonardo, from whom he derived the soft indistinct outlines of his style of sentimental elegance and conscious allure. He was probably in Parma, the scene of his greatest activity, by 1518. There he decorated two domes, those of S. Giovanni Evangelista (1520) and Parma cathedral (*The Assumption of the Virgin*, 1526), developing the illusionism of Mantegna, henceforth almost always used in ceiling decoration, whereby the figures are seen in sharp foreshortening as if the event really were taking place in the sky above. His mythologies, such as *The Loves of Jupiter*, have a lyrical sensuous air which anticipates the rococo of the 18th c.

correlate /ˈkɒrəˌleɪt, ˈkɒrɪ-/ v. & n. —v. **1** intr. (foll. by *with*, *to*) have a mutual relation. **2** tr. (usu. foll. by *with*) bring into a mutual relation. —n. each of two related or complementary things (esp. so related that one implies the other). [back-form. f. CORRELATION, CORRELATIVE]

correlation /ˌkɒrəˈleɪʃ(ə)n, ˌkɒrɪ-/ n. (also **corelation** /ˌkəʊrɪ-/) **1** a mutual relation between two or more things. **2 a** interdependence of variable quantities. **b** a quantity measuring the extent of this. **3** the act of correlating. □□ **correlational** adj. [med.L *correlatio* (as CORRELATIVE)]

correlative /kɒˈrelətɪv, kə-/ adj. & n. —adj. **1** (often foll. by *with*, *to*) having a mutual relation. **2** Gram. (of words) corresponding to each other and regularly used together (as *neither* and *nor*). —n. a correlative word or thing. □□ **correlatively** adv. **correlativity** /-ˈtɪvɪtɪ/ n. [med.L *correlativus* (as COM-, RELATIVE)]

correspond /ˌkɒrɪˈspɒnd/ v.intr. **1 a** (usu. foll. by *to*) be analogous or similar. **b** (usu. foll. by *to*) agree in amount, position, etc. **c** (usu. foll. by *with*, *to*) be in harmony or agreement. **2** (usu. foll. by *with*) communicate by interchange of letters. □ **corresponding member** an honorary member of a learned society etc. with no voice in the society's affairs. □□ **correspondingly** adv. [F *correspondre* f. med.L *correspondere* (as COM-, RESPOND)]

correspondence /ˌkɒrɪˈspɒnd(ə)ns/ n. **1** (usu. foll. by *with*, *to*, *between*) agreement, similarity, or harmony. **2 a** communication by letters. **b** letters sent or received. □ **correspondence college** (or **school**) a college conducting correspondence courses. **correspondence column** the part of a newspaper etc. that

contains letters from readers. **correspondence course** a course of study conducted by post. [ME f. OF f. med.L *correspondentia* (as CORRESPOND)]

correspondent /ˌkɒrɪˈspɒnd(ə)nt/ n. & adj. —n. **1** a person who writes letters to a person or a newspaper, esp. regularly. **2** a person employed to contribute material for publication in a periodical or for broadcasting (*our chess correspondent*; *the BBC's Moscow correspondent*). **3** a person or firm having regular business relations with another, esp. in another country. —adj. (often foll. by *to*, *with*) archaic corresponding. □□ **correspondently** adv. [ME f. OF *correspondent* or med.L (as CORRESPOND)]

corrida /kɒˈriːdə/ n. **1** a bullfight. **2** bullfighting. [Sp. *corrida de toros* running of bulls]

corridor /ˈkɒrɪˌdɔː(r)/ n. **1** a passage from which doors lead into rooms (orig. an outside passage connecting parts of a building, now usu. a main passage in a large building). **2** a passage in a railway carriage from which doors lead into compartments. **3** a strip of the territory of one State passing through that of another, esp. securing access to the sea. **4** a route to which aircraft are restricted, esp. over a foreign country. □ **corridors of power** places where covert influence is said to be exerted in government. [F f. It. *corridore* corridor for *corridojo* running-place f. *correre* run, by confusion with *corridore* runner]

corrie /ˈkɒrɪ/ n. Sc. a circular hollow on a mountainside; a cirque. [Gael. *coire* cauldron]

corrigendum /ˌkɒrɪˈɡendəm, -ˈdʒendəm/ n. (pl. **corrigenda** /-də/) a thing to be corrected, esp. an error in a printed book. [L, neut. gerundive of *corrigere*: see CORRECT]

corrigible /ˈkɒrɪdʒɪb(ə)l/ adj. **1** capable of being corrected. **2** (of a person) submissive; open to correction. □□ **corrigibly** adv. [ME f. F f. med.L *corrigibilis* (as CORRECT)]

corroborate /kəˈrɒbəˌreɪt/ v.tr. confirm or give support to (a statement or belief, or the person holding it), esp. in relation to witnesses in a lawcourt. □□ **corroboration** /-ˈreɪʃ(ə)n/ n. **corroborative** /-rətɪv/ adj. **corroborator** n. **corroboratory** /-rətərɪ/ adj. [L *corroborare* strengthen (as COM-, *roborare* f. *robur -oris* strength)]

corroboree /kəˈrɒbərɪ/ n. **1** a festive or warlike dance-drama with song of Australian Aboriginals. **2** a noisy party. [Aboriginal dial.]

corrode /kəˈrəʊd/ v. **1 a** tr. wear away, esp. by chemical action. **b** intr. be worn away; decay. **2** tr. destroy gradually (*optimism corroded by recent misfortunes*). □□ **corrodible** adj. [ME f. L *corrodere corros-* (as COM-, *rodere* gnaw)]

corrosion /kəˈrəʊʒ(ə)n/ n. **1** the process of corroding, esp. of a rusting metal. **2 a** damage caused by corroding. **b** a corroded area.

corrosive /kəˈrəʊsɪv/ adj. & n. —adj. tending to corrode or consume. —n. a corrosive substance. □ **corrosive sublimate** mercuric chloride, a strong acid poison, used as a fungicide, antiseptic, etc. □□ **corrosively** adv. **corrosiveness** n. [ME f. OF *corosif -ive* (as CORRODE)]

corrugate /ˈkɒrʊˌɡeɪt/ v. **1** tr. (esp. as **corrugated** adj.) form into alternate ridges and grooves, esp. to strengthen (*corrugated iron*; *corrugated paper*). **2** tr. & intr. contract into wrinkles or folds. □□ **corrugation** /-ˈɡeɪʃ(ə)n/ n. [L *corrugare* (as COM-, *rugare* f. *ruga* wrinkle)]

corrugator /ˈkɒrʊˌɡeɪtə(r)/ n. Anat. either of two muscles that contract the brow in frowning. [mod.L (as CORRUGATE)]

corrupt /kəˈrʌpt/ adj. & v. —adj. **1** morally depraved; wicked. **2** influenced by or using bribery or fraudulent activity. **3** (of a text, language, etc.) harmed (esp. made suspect or unreliable) by errors or alterations. **4** rotten. —v. **1** tr. & intr. make or become corrupt or depraved. **2** tr. affect or harm by errors or alterations. **3** tr. infect, taint. □ **corrupt practices** fraudulent activity, esp. at elections. □□ **corrupter** n. **corruptible** adj. **corruptibility** /-ˈbɪlɪtɪ/ n. **corruptive** adj. **corruptly** adv. **corruptness** n. [ME f. OF *corrupt* or L *corruptus* past part. of *corrumpere corrupt-* (as COM-, *rumpere* break)]

corruption /kəˈrʌpʃ(ə)n/ n. **1** moral deterioration, esp. widespread. **2** use of corrupt practices, esp. bribery or fraud. **3 a** irregular alteration (of a text, language, etc.) from its original state. **b** an irregularly altered form of a word. **4** decomposition, esp. of a corpse or other organic matter. [ME f. OF *corruption* or L *corruptio* (as CORRUPT)]

corsac /ˈkɔːsæk/ n. (also **corsak**) a fox, *Vulpes corsac*, of Central Asia. [Turki]

corsage /kɔːˈsɑːʒ/ n. **1** a small bouquet worn by a woman. **2** the bodice of a woman's dress. [ME f. OF f. *cors* body: see CORPSE]

corsair /ˈkɔːseə(r)/ n. **1** a pirate ship. **2** a pirate. **3** *hist.* a privateer, esp. of the Barbary Coast. [F *corsaire* f. med.L *cursarius* f. *cursus* inroad f. *currere* run]

corsak var. of CORSAC.

corse /kɔːs/ n. archaic a corpse. [var. of CORPSE]

corselet var. of CORSLET, CORSELETTE.

corselette /ˈkɔːslɪt, ˈkɔːsəˌlet/ n. (also **corselet**) a woman's foundation garment combining corset and brassière.

corset /ˈkɔːsɪt/ n. & v. —n. **1** a closely-fitting undergarment worn by women to support the abdomen. **2** a similar garment worn by men and women because of injury, weakness, or deformity. —v.tr. (**corseted, corseting**) **1** provide with a corset. **2** control closely. □□ **corseted** adj. **corsetry** n. [ME f. OF, dimin. of *cors* body: see CORPSE]

corsetière /ˈkɔːsɪˌtjeə(r)/ n. a woman who makes or fits corsets. [F, fem. of *corsetier* (as CORSET, -IER)]

Corsica /ˈkɔːsɪkə/ an island off the west coast of Italy, under French rule, birthplace of Napoleon I (who was known as 'the Corsican'); pop. (1982) 240,178; capital, Ajaccio. □□ **Corsican** adj. & n.

corslet /ˈkɔːslɪt/ n. (also **corselet**) **1** a garment (usu. tight-fitting) covering the trunk but not the limbs. **2** *hist.* a piece of armour covering the trunk. [OF *corselet*, dimin. formed as CORSET]

Cort /kɔːt/, Henry (1740–1800), English ironmaster. Initially a supplier of wrought iron for naval and ordnance use, Cort set up his own forge near Fareham in Hampshire. In 1783 he patented a process for producing iron bars by passing iron through grooved rollers to avoid the laborious business of hammering. A year later he patented the puddling process for refining molten pig-iron by constant stirring to accelerate decarbonization; this process gave Britain a worldwide lead in the industry and earned Cort the title 'the Great Finer'. In spite of his success he was ruined by a dishonest partner, who embezzled naval funds.

cortège /kɔːˈteɪʒ/ n. **1** a procession, esp. for a funeral. **2** a train of attendants. [F]

Cortes /ˈkɔːtes, -tez/ n. the legislative assembly of Spain and formerly of Portugal. [Sp. & Port., pl. of *corte* COURT]

Cortés /ˈkɔːtez/, Hernando (1485–1547), Spanish conqueror of Mexico. The first of the conquistadors, Cortés successfully overthrew the Aztec empire with a tiny army of adventurers, taking its capital city in 1519 and deposing the emperor Montezuma.

cortex /ˈkɔːteks/ n. (pl. **cortices** /-tɪˌsiːz/) **1** *Anat.* the outer part of an organ, esp. of the brain (**cerebral cortex**) or kidneys (**renal cortex**). **2** *Bot.* **a** an outer layer of tissue immediately below the epidermis. **b** bark. □□ **cortical** /ˈkɔːtɪk(ə)l/ adj. [L *cortex, -icis* bark]

Corti /ˈkɔːtɪ/ n. □ **organ of Corti** *Anat.* a structure in the inner ear of mammals, responsible for converting sound signals into nerve impulses. [A. Corti, It. anatomist d. 1876]

corticate /ˈkɔːtɪˌkeɪt/ adj. (also **corticated**) **1** having bark or rind. **2** barklike. [L *corticatus* (as CORTEX)]

corticotrophic hormone /ˌkɔːtɪkəʊˈtrɒfɪk/ adj. (also **corticotropic**) = ADRENOCORTICOTROPHIC HORMONE.

corticotrophin /ˌkɔːtɪkəʊˈtrəʊfɪn/ n. (also **corticotropin**) = ADRENOCORTICOTROPHIN.

cortisone /ˈkɔːtɪˌzəʊn/ n. *Biochem.* a steroid hormone produced by the adrenal cortex or synthetically, used medicinally esp. against inflammation and allergy. [Chem. name 17-hydroxy-11-dehydrocorticosterone]

corundum /kəˈrʌndəm/ n. *Mineral.* extremely hard crystallized alumina, used esp. as an abrasive, and varieties of which, e.g. ruby and sapphire, are used for gemstones. [Tamil *kurundam* f. Skr. *kuruvinda* ruby]

Corunna /kəˈrʌnə/ (Spanish **La Coruña**) /læ kɒˈruːnjə/ a seaport in NW Spain; pop. (1981) 232,360. The Armada sailed from here to attack England in 1588, and the town was sacked by Francis Drake in 1589. It was the site of a battle (1809) in the Peninsular War (see Sir John MOORE⁴).

coruscate /ˈkɒrəˌskeɪt/ v.intr. **1** give off flashing light; sparkle. **2** be showy or brilliant. □□ **coruscation** /-ˈskeɪʃ(ə)n/ n. [L *coruscare* glitter]

corvée /kɔːˈveɪ/ n. **1** *hist.* a day's work of unpaid labour due to a lord from a vassal. **2** labour exacted in lieu of paying taxes. **3** an onerous task. [ME f. OF ult. f. L *corrogare* ask for, collect (as COM-, *rogare* ask)]

corves pl. of CORF.

corvette /kɔːˈvet/ n. *Naut.* **1** a small naval escort-vessel. **2** *hist.* a flush-decked warship with one tier of guns. [F f. MDu. *korf* kind of ship + dimin. -ETTE]

corvine /ˈkɔːvaɪn/ adj. of or akin to the raven or crow. [L *corvinus* f. *corvus* raven]

corybantic /ˌkɒrɪˈbæntɪk/ adj. wild, frenzied. [*Corybantes* priests of Cybele performing wild dances (L f. Gk *Korubantes*)]

corymb /ˈkɒrɪmb/ n. *Bot.* a flat-topped cluster of flowers with the flower-stalks proportionally longer lower down the stem. □□ **corymbose** adj. [F *corymbe* or L *corymbus* f. Gk *korumbos* cluster]

coryphée /ˈkɒrɪˌfeɪ/ n. a leading dancer in a *corps de ballet*. [F f. Gk *koruphaios* leader of a chorus f. *koruphē* head]

coryza /kəˈraɪzə/ n. **1** a catarrhal inflammation of the mucous membrane in the nose; a cold in the head. **2** any disease with this as a symptom. [L f. Gk *koruza* running at the nose]

Cos /kɒs/ (Greek **Kós**) a Greek island in the SE Aegean Sea.

cos¹ /kɒs/ n. a variety of lettuce with crisp narrow leaves forming a long upright head. [L f. Gk *Kōs*, Cos, where it originated]

cos² /kɒs, kɒz/ abbr. cosine.

cos³ /kɒz/ conj. & adv. (also **'cos**) colloq. because. [abbr.]

Cosa Nostra /ˌkəʊzə ˈnɒstrə/ n. a US criminal organization resembling and related to the Mafia. [It., = our affair]

cosec /ˈkəʊsek/ abbr. cosecant.

cosecant /kəʊˈsiːkənt/ n. *Math.* the ratio of the hypotenuse (in a right-angled triangle) to the side opposite an acute angle; the reciprocal of sine. [mod.L *cosecans* and F *cosécant* (as CO-, SECANT)]

coseismal /kəʊˈsaɪzm(ə)l/ adj. & n. —adj. of or relating to points of simultaneous arrival of an earthquake wave. —n. a straight line or a curve connecting these points. [CO- + SEISMAL (see SEISMIC)]

coset /ˈkəʊset/ n. *Math.* a set composed of all the products obtained by multiplying on the right or on the left each element of a subgroup in turn by one particular element of the group containing the subgroup. [CO- + SET²]

cosh¹ /kɒʃ/ n. & v. *Brit. colloq.* —n. a heavy blunt weapon. —v.tr. hit with a cosh. [19th c.: orig. unkn.]

cosh² /kɒʃ, kɒsˈeɪtʃ/ abbr. *Math.* hyperbolic cosine.

co-signatory /kəʊˈsɪgnətərɪ/ n. & adj. (US **cosignatory**) —n. (pl. **-ies**) a person or State signing (a treaty etc.) jointly with others. —adj. signing jointly.

cosine /ˈkəʊsaɪn/ n. *Math.* the ratio of the side adjacent to an acute angle (in a right-angled triangle) to the hypotenuse. [mod.L *cosinus* (as CO-, SINE)]

cosmea /ˈkɒzmɪə/ n. = COSMOS². [mod.L, formed as COSMOS²]

cosmetic /kɒzˈmetɪk/ adj. & n. —adj. **1** intended to adorn or beautify the body, esp. the face. **2** intended to improve only appearances; superficially improving or beneficial (*a cosmetic change*). **3** (of surgery or a prosthetic device) imitating, restoring, or enhancing the normal appearance. —n. a cosmetic preparation, esp. for the face. □□ **cosmetically** adv. [F *cosmétique* f. Gk *kosmētikos* f. *kosmeō* adorn f. *kosmos* order, adornment]

cosmic /ˈkɒzmɪk/ adj. **1** of the universe or cosmos, esp. as distinct from the earth. **2** of or for space travel. □ **cosmic dust** small particles of matter distributed throughout space. **cosmic rays** (or **radiation**) radiations from space etc. that reach the earth from all directions, usu. with high energy and penetrative power. □□ **cosmical** adj. **cosmically** adv.

cosmogony /kɒz'mɒgɒnɪ/ n. (pl. **-ies**) **1** the origin of the universe. **2** a theory about this. □□ **cosmogonic** /-mɔ'gɒnɪk/ adj. **cosmogonical** /-mɔ'gɒnɪk(ə)l/ adj. **cosmogonist** n. [Gk kosmogonia f. kosmos world + -gonia -begetting]

cosmography /kɒz'mɒgrɒfɪ/ n. (pl. **-ies**) a description or mapping of general features of the universe. □□ **cosmographer** n. **cosmographic** /-mɔ'græfɪk/ adj. **cosmographical** /-mɔ'græfɪk(ə)l/ adj. [ME f. F cosmographie or f. LL f. Gk kosmographia (as COSMOS[1], -GRAPHY)]

cosmology /kɒz'mɒlɔdʒɪ/ n. the science or theory of the creation and development of the universe. While ancient cosmologies supposed the world to be supported on the backs of elephants standing upon tortoises, or placed Earth at the centre of a universe of concentric crystal spheres, modern science debates whether an infinite and unchanging universe is maintained by the continuous creation of matter from the void, or whether a big bang both created and dispersed matter in an expansion which continues today, and which may be reversed if the universe is dense enough. The last of these interpretations is favoured by the detection of a radiation field permeating the universe, believed to be the cool remnant of the initial fireball. □□ **cosmological** /-mɔ'lɒdʒɪk(ə)l/ adj. **cosmologist** n. [F cosmologie or mod.L cosmologia (as COSMOS[1], -LOGY)]

cosmonaut /'kɒzmɔˌnɔːt/ n. a Soviet astronaut. [Russ. kosmonavt, as COSMOS[1], after astronaut]

cosmopolis /kɒz'mɒpɒlɪs/ n. a cosmopolitan city. [Gk kosmos world + polis city]

cosmopolitan /ˌkɒzmɔ'pɒlɪt(ə)n/ adj. & n. —adj. **1 a** of or from or knowing many parts of the world. **b** consisting of people from many or all parts. **2** free from national limitations or prejudices. **3** Ecol. (of a plant, animal, etc.) widely distributed. —n. **1** a cosmopolitan person. **2** Ecol. a widely distributed animal or plant. □□ **cosmopolitanism** n. **cosmopolitanize** v.tr. & intr. (also **-ise**). [COSMOPOLITE + -AN]

cosmopolite /kɒz'mɒpɔˌlaɪt/ n. & adj. —n. **1** a cosmopolitan person. **2** Ecol. = COSMOPOLITAN n. 2. —adj. free from national attachments or prejudices. [F f. Gk kosmopolitēs f. kosmos world + politēs citizen]

cosmos[1] /'kɒzmɒs/ n. **1** the universe, esp. as a well-ordered whole. **2 a** an ordered system of ideas etc. **b** a sum total of experience. [Gk kosmos]

cosmos[2] /'kɒzmɒs/ n. any composite plant of the genus Cosmos, bearing single dahlia-like blossoms of various colours. [mod.L f. Gk kosmos in sense 'ornament']

COSPAR abbr. Committee on Space Research.

Cossack /'kɒsæk/ n. & adj. —n. **1 a** a member of those Russians who sought a free life in the steppes or on the frontiers of imperial Russia and were allowed privileges by the Tsars, including autonomy for their settlements in southern Russia (especially the Ukraine) and Siberia in return for service in protecting the frontiers. **b** a descendant of these, noted for warlike qualities and for horsemanship. **2** a member of a Cossack military unit. —adj. of, relating to, or characteristic of the Cossacks. [F cosaque f. Russ. kazak f. Turki quzzāq nomad, adventurer]

cosset /'kɒsɪt/ v.tr. (**cosseted, cosseting**) pamper. [dial. cosset = pet lamb, prob. f. AF coscet, cozet f. OE cotsǣta cottager (as COT[2], SIT)]

cost /kɒst/ v. & n. —v. (past and past part. cost) **1** tr. be obtainable for (a sum of money); have as a price (what does it cost?; it cost me £50). **2** tr. involve as a loss or sacrifice (it cost them much effort; it cost him his life). **3** tr. (past and past part. costed) fix or estimate the cost or price of. **4** colloq. **a** tr. be costly to (it'll cost you). **b** intr. be costly. —n. **1** what a thing costs; the price paid or to be paid. **2** a loss or sacrifice; an expenditure of time, effort, etc. **3** (in pl.) legal expenses, esp. those allowed in favour of the winning party or against the losing party in a suit. □ **at all costs** (or **at any cost**) no matter what the cost or risk may be. **at cost** at the initial cost; at cost price. **at the cost of** at the expense of losing or sacrificing. **cost accountant** an accountant who records costs and (esp. overhead) expenses in a business concern.

cost-benefit assessing the relation between the cost of an operation and the value of the resulting benefits (cost-benefit analysis). **cost** (or **costing**) **clerk** a clerk who records costs and expenses in a business concern. **cost a person dear** (or **dearly**) involve a person in a high cost or a heavy penalty. **cost-effective** effective or productive in relation to its cost. **cost of living** the level of prices esp. of the basic necessities of life. **cost-plus** calculated as the basic cost plus a profit factor. **cost price** the price paid for a thing by one who later sells it. **cost push** Econ. factors other than demand that cause inflation. **to a person's cost** at a person's expense; with loss or disadvantage to a person. [ME f. OF coster, couster, coust ult. f. L constare stand firm, stand at a price (as COM-, stare stand)]

Costa /'kɒstə/, Lúcio (1902–63), Brazilian architect, town planner, and art historian, who achieved a worldwide reputation with his plan for the new capital Brasilia, which was chosen by an international jury in 1956.

Costa Blanca /'kɒstə 'blæŋkə/ a resort region on the Mediterranean coast of SE Spain. [Sp., = white coast]

Costa Brava /'kɒstə 'brɑːvə/ a resort region to the north of Barcelona, on the Mediterranean coast of NE Spain. [Sp., = wild coast]

Costa del Sol /'kɒstə del 'sɒl/ a resort region on the Mediterranean coast of south Spain. Marbella and Torremolinos are the principal resort towns. [Sp., = coast of the sun]

costal /'kɒst(ə)l/ adj. of the ribs. [F f. mod.L costalis f. L costa rib]

co-star /'kɒustɑː(r)/ n. & v. —n. a cinema or stage star appearing with another or others of equal importance. —v. (**-starred, -starring**) **1** intr. take part as a co-star. **2** tr. (of a production) include as a co-star.

costard /'kɒstəd/ n. Brit. **1** a large ribbed variety of apple. **2** archaic joc. the head. [ME f. AF f. coste rib f. L costa]

Costa Rica /ˌkɒstə 'riːkə/ a country in Central America on the Isthmus of Panama, with Nicaragua to the north and Panama to the south-east. The population is chiefly of European stock; pop. (est. 1988) 2,888,200; official language, Spanish; capital, San José. Colonized by Spain in the early 16th c., Costa Rica achieved independence in 1823 and finally emerged as a separate country in 1838 after 14 years within the Federation of Central America. Since then it has been one of the most stable and prosperous States in the region, enjoying high literacy and standards of living. The economy is chiefly agricultural, and the forests which cover most of the land produce valuable timber. In 1948 the army was abolished, the President declaring it unnecessary as the country loved peace. □□ **Costa Rican** adj. & n.

costate /'kɒsteɪt/ adj. ribbed; having ribs or ridges. [L costatus f. costa rib]

coster /'kɒstə(r)/ n. Brit. = COSTERMONGER. [abbr.]

costermonger /'kɒstəˌmʌŋgə(r)/ n. Brit. a person who sells fruit, vegetables, etc., in the street from a barrow. [COSTARD + MONGER]

costive /'kɒstɪv/ adj. **1** constipated. **2** niggardly. □□ **costively** adv. **costiveness** n. [ME f. OF costivé f. L constipatus: see CONSTIPATE]

costly /'kɒstlɪ/ adj. (**costlier, costliest**) **1** costing much; expensive. **2** of great value. □□ **costliness** n.

costmary /'kɒstˌmeərɪ/ n. (pl. **-ies**) an aromatic composite plant, Balsamita major, formerly used in medicine and for flavouring ale. [OE cost f. L costum f. Gk kostos f. Arab. ḳust an aromatic plant + (St) Mary (with whom it was associated in medieval times)]

costume /'kɒstjuːm/ n. & v. —n. **1** a style or fashion of dress, esp. that of a particular place, time, or class. **2** a set of clothes. **3** clothing for a particular activity (swimming-costume). **4** an actor's clothes for a part. **5** a woman's matching jacket and skirt. —v.tr. provide with a costume. □ **costume jewellery** artificial jewellery worn to adorn clothes. **costume play** (or **piece**) a play in which the actors wear historical costume. [F f. It. f. L consuetudo CUSTOM]

costumier /kɒ'stjuːmɪə(r)/ n. (also **costumer** /-mə(r)/) a person who makes or deals in costumes, esp. for theatrical use. [F costumier (as COSTUME)]

cosy /ˈkəʊzɪ/ *adj.*, *n.*, & *v.* (US **cozy**) —*adj.* (**cosier**, **cosiest**) **1** comfortable and warm; snug. **2** *derog.* complacent. **3** warm and friendly. —*n.* (*pl.* **-ies**) **1** a cover to keep something hot, esp. a teapot or a boiled egg. **2** a canopied corner seat for two. —*v.tr.* (**-ies**, **-ied**) (often foll. by *along*) *colloq.* reassure, esp. deceptively. □ **cosy up to** US *colloq.* **1** ingratiate oneself with. **2** snuggle up to. □□ **cosily** *adv.* **cosiness** *n.* [18th c. f. Sc., of unkn. orig.]

cot[1] /kɒt/ *n.* **1** *Brit.* a small bed with high sides, esp. for a baby or very young child. **2** a hospital bed. **3** US a small folding bed. **4** *Ind.* a light bedstead. **5** *Naut.* a kind of swinging bed hung from deck beams, formerly used by officers. □ **cot-case** a person too ill to leave his or her bed. **cot-death** the unexplained death of a baby while sleeping. [Anglo-Ind., f. Hindi *khāṭ* bedstead, hammock]

cot[2] /kɒt/ *n.* & *v.* —*n.* **1** a small shelter; a cote (*bell-cot*; *sheep-cot*). **2** *poet.* a cottage. —*v.tr.* (**cotted**, **cotting**) put (sheep) in a cot. [OE f. Gmc, rel. to COTE]

cot[3] /kɒt/ *abbr. Math.* cotangent.

cotangent /kəʊˈtændʒ(ə)nt/ *n. Math.* the ratio of the side adjacent to an acute angle (in a right-angled triangle) to the opposite side.

cote /kəʊt/ *n.* a shelter, esp. for animals or birds; a shed or stall (*sheep-cote*). [OE f. Gmc, rel. to COT[2]]

coterie /ˈkəʊtərɪ/ *n.* **1** an exclusive group of people sharing interests. **2** a select circle in society. [F, orig. = association of tenants, ult. f. MLG *kote* COTE]

coterminous /kəʊˈtɜːmɪnəs/ *adj.* (often foll. by *with*) having the same boundaries or extent (in space, time, or meaning). [CO- + TERMINUS + -OUS]

coth /kɒθ/ *abbr. Math.* hyperbolic cotangent.

co-tidal line /kəʊˈtaɪd(ə)l/ *n.* a line on a map connecting points at which tidal levels (as high tide or low tide) occur simultaneously.

cotillion /kəˈtɪljən/ *n.* **1** any of various French dances with elaborate steps, figures, and ceremonial. **2** US **a** a ballroom dance resembling a quadrille. **b** a formal ball. [F *cotillon* petticoat, dimin. of *cotte* f. OF *cote* COAT]

Cotman /ˈkɒtmən/, John Sell (1782–1842), English artist, whose importance as a landscape painter transcends his position as drawing-master to the East Anglian gentry. His early watercolours (e.g. *Greta Bridge*, 1805) have been compared in their compositional daring to Chinese painting. In 1817–20 he visited Normandy and developed a more richly coloured style. From 1834 he lived and taught in London and there developed his considerable skills as an engraver to become one of the most distinctive British etchers of the 19th c.

cotoneaster /kəˌtəʊnɪˈæstə(r)/ *n.* any rosaceous shrub of the genus *Cotoneaster*, bearing usu. bright red berries. [mod.L f. L *cotoneum* QUINCE + -ASTER]

Cotonou /ˌkɒtəˈnuː/ the largest city, chief port, and de facto capital of Benin, on the Guinea coast of West Africa; pop. (1982) 487,000.

Cotopaxi /ˌkɒtəˈpæksɪ/ the highest active volcano in the world, rising to 5,896 m (19,142 ft.) in the Andes of central Ecuador. Its Quechua name means 'shining peak'.

Cotswold Hills /ˈkɒtswəʊld/ (also **Cotswolds**) a range of limestone hills, largely in Gloucestershire, noted for sheep pastures and formerly a centre of the woollen industry.

cotta /ˈkɒtə/ *n. Eccl.* a short surplice. [It., formed as COAT]

cottage /ˈkɒtɪdʒ/ *n.* **1** a small simple house, esp. in the country. **2** a dwelling forming part of a farm establishment, used by a worker. □ **cottage cheese** soft white cheese made from curds of skimmed milk without pressing. **cottage hospital** *Brit.* a small hospital not having resident medical staff. **cottage industry** a business activity partly or wholly carried on at home. **cottage loaf** a loaf formed of two round masses, the smaller on top of the larger. **cottage pie** *Brit.* a dish of minced meat topped with browned mashed potato. □□ **cottagey** *adj.* [ME f. AF, formed as COT[2], COTE]

cottager /ˈkɒtɪdʒə(r)/ *n.* a person who lives in a cottage.

cottar /ˈkɒtə(r)/ *n.* (also **cotter**) **1** *Sc.* & *hist.* a farm-labourer or

tenant occupying a cottage in return for labour as required. **2** *Ir. hist.* = COTTIER. [COT[2] + -ER[1] (Sc. *-ar*)]

Cottbus /ˈkɒtbʊs/ an industrial city in SE Germany, on the River Spree; pop. (1986) 125,800.

cotter /ˈkɒtə(r)/ *n.* **1** a bolt or wedge for securing parts of machinery etc. **2** (in full **cotter pin**) a split pin that opens after passing through a hole. [17th c. (rel. to earlier *cotterel*): orig. unkn.]

cottier /ˈkɒtɪə(r)/ *n. Brit.* **1** a cottager. **2** *hist.* an Irish peasant under cottier tenure. □ **cottier tenure** *hist.* the letting of land in small portions at a rent fixed by competition. [ME f. OF *cotier* f. med.L *cotarius*: see COTERIE]

cotton /ˈkɒt(ə)n/ *n.* & *v.* —*n.* **1** a soft white fibrous substance covering the seeds of certain plants. **2** (in full **cotton plant**) such a plant, esp. any of the genus *Gossypium*. **b** cotton-plants cultivated as a crop for the fibre or the seeds. **3** thread or cloth made from the fibre. **4** (*attrib.*) made of cotton. —*v.intr.* (foll. by *to*) be attracted by (a person). □ **cotton-cake** compressed cotton seed used as food for cattle. **cotton candy** US candyfloss. **cotton-gin** a machine for separating cotton from its seeds. **cotton-grass** any grasslike plant of the genus *Eriophorum*, with long white silky hairs. **cotton on** (often foll. by *to*) *colloq.* begin to understand. **cotton-picking** US *sl.* unpleasant, wretched. **cotton waste** refuse yarn used to clean machinery etc. **cotton wool 1** esp. *Brit.* fluffy wadding of a kind orig. made from raw cotton. **2** US raw cotton. □□ **cottony** *adj.* [ME f. OF *coton* f. Arab. *kuṭn*]

cottontail /ˈkɒt(ə)nˌteɪl/ *n.* any rabbit of the genus *Sylvilagus*, native to America, having a mainly white fluffy tail.

cottonwood /ˈkɒt(ə)nˌwʊd/ *n.* **1** any of several poplars, native to N. America, having seeds covered in white cottony hairs. **2** any of several trees native to Australia, esp. a downy-leaved tree, *Bedfordia arborescens*.

cotyledon /ˌkɒtɪˈliːd(ə)n/ *n.* **1** an embryonic leaf in seed-bearing plants. **2** any succulent plant of the genus *Umbilicus*, e.g. pennywort. □□ **cotyledonary** *adj.* **cotyledonous** *adj.* [L, = pennywort, f. Gk *kotulēdōn* cup-shaped cavity f. *kotulē* cup]

coucal /ˈkuːkæl/ *n.* any ground-nesting bird of the genus *Centropus*, related to the cuckoos. [F, perh. f. *coucou* cuckoo + *alouette* lark]

couch[1] /kaʊtʃ/ *n.* & *v.* —*n.* **1** an upholstered piece of furniture for several people; a sofa. **2** a long padded seat with a headrest at one end, esp. one on which a psychiatrist's or doctor's patient reclines during examination. —*v.* **1** *tr.* (foll. by *in*) express in words of a specified kind (*couched in simple language*). **2** *tr.* lay on or as on a couch. **3** *intr.* **a** (of an animal) lie, esp. in its lair. **b** lie in ambush. **4** *tr.* lower (a spear etc.) to the position for attack. **5** *tr. Med.* treat (a cataract) by displacing the lens of the eye. □ **couch potato** US *sl.* a young person who likes lazing at home. [ME f. OF *couche*, *coucher* f. L *collocare* (as COM-, *locare* place)]

couch[2] /kuːtʃ, kaʊtʃ/ *n.* (in full **couch grass**) any of several grasses of the genus *Agropyron*, esp. *A. repens*, having long creeping roots. [var. of QUITCH]

couchant /ˈkaʊtʃ(ə)nt/ *adj.* (placed after noun) *Heraldry* (of an animal) lying with the body resting on the legs and the head raised. [F, pres. part. of *coucher*: see COUCH[1]]

couchette /kuːˈʃet/ *n.* **1** a railway carriage with seats convertible into sleeping-berths. **2** a berth in this. [F, = little bed, dimin. of *couche* COUCH[1]]

coudé /kuːˈdeɪ/ *adj.* & *n.* —*adj.* of or relating to a telescope in which rays are bent to a focus off the axis. —*n.* such a telescope. [F, past part. of *couder* bend at right angles f. *coude* elbow formed as CUBIT]

Couéism /ˈkuːeɪˌɪz(ə)m/ *n.* a system of usu. optimistic auto-suggestion as psychotherapy. [E. Coué, Fr. psychologist d. 1926]

cougar /ˈkuːgə(r)/ *n.* US a puma. [F, repr. Guarani *guaçu ara*]

cough /kɒf/ *v.* & *n.* —*v.intr.* **1** expel air from the lungs with a sudden sharp sound produced by abrupt opening of the glottis, to remove an obstruction or congestion. **2** (of an engine, gun, etc.) make a similar sound. **3** *sl.* confess. —*n.* **1** an act of coughing. **2** a condition of the respiratory organs causing coughing. **3** a tendency to cough. □ **cough drop** (or **sweet**) a medicated lozenge to relieve a cough. **cough mixture** a liquid medicine to relieve a cough. **cough out 1** eject by coughing. **2** say with a cough. **cough up 1** = *cough out.* **2** *sl.* bring out or give (money or information) reluctantly. □□ **cougher** *n.* [ME *coghe, cowhe,* rel. to MDu. *kuchen,* MHG *kūchen,* of imit. orig.]

could *past of* CAN¹.

couldn't /ˈkʊd(ə)nt/ *contr.* could not.

coulée /ˈkuːleɪ, ˈkuːlɪ/ *n. Geol.* **1** a solidified lava-flow. **2** *US* a deep ravine. [F, fem. past part. of *couler* flow, f. L *colare* strain, filter]

coulisse /kuːˈliːs/ *n.* **1** (usu. in *pl.*) *Theatr.* a piece of side scenery or a space between two of these; the wings. **2** a place of informal discussion or negotiation. [F f. *coulis* sliding: see PORTCULLIS]

couloir /ˈkuːlwɑː(r)/ *n.* a steep narrow gully on a mountainside. [F f. *couler* glide: see COULÉE]

Coulomb /ˈkuːlɒm/, Charles-Augustin de (1736–1806), French military engineer. He had a good grasp of mathematics and was a skilful experimenter, conducting mental research on structural mechanics, elasticity, friction, electricity, and magnetism. He is best known for Coulomb's Law, established with a sensitive torsion balance in 1785, according to which the forces between two electrical charges are proportional to the product of the sizes of the charges and inversely proportional to the square of the distance between them. At last the inverse-square law of electrostatic force had been verified and the quantity of electric charge could be defined. A unit of electric charge, the coulomb, has been named in his honour.

coulomb /ˈkuːlɒm/ *n. Electr.* the SI unit of electric charge, equal to the quantity of electricity conveyed in one second by a current of one ampere. ¶ Symb.: **C**. [C.-A. de COULOMB]

coulometry /kuːˈlɒmɪtrɪ/ *n. Chem.* a method of chemical analysis by measurement of the number of coulombs used in electrolysis. □□ **coulometric** /ˌkuːləˈmetrɪk/ *adj.*

coulter /ˈkəʊltə(r)/ *n.* (*US* **colter**) a vertical cutting blade fixed in front of a ploughshare. [OE f. L *culter*]

coumarin /ˈkuːmərɪn/ *n.* an aromatic substance found in many plants and formerly used for flavouring food. [F *coumarine* f. Tupi *cumarú* tonka bean]

coumarone /ˈkuːmərəʊn/ *n.* an organic liquid obtained from coal tar by synthesis and used in paints and varnishes. □ **coumarone resin** a thermoplastic resin formed by polymerization of coumarone. [COUMARIN + -ONE]

council /ˈkaʊns(ə)l/ *n.* **1 a** an advisory, deliberative, or administrative body of people formally constituted and meeting regularly. **b** a meeting of such a body. **2 a** the elected local administrative body of a parish, district, town, city, or administrative county and its paid officers and workforce. **b** (*attrib.*) (esp. of housing) provided by a local council (*council flat; council estate*). **3** a body of persons chosen as advisers (*Privy Council*). **4** an ecclesiastical assembly (*ecumenical council*). □ **council-chamber** a room in which a council meets. **council-house** a building in which a council meets. **council of war 1** an assembly of officers called in a special emergency. **2** any meeting held to plan a response to an emergency. **the Queen** (or **King**) **in Council** the Privy Council as issuing Orders in Council or receiving petitions etc. [ME f. AF *cuncile* f. L *concilium* convocation, assembly f. *calare* summon: cf. COUNSEL]

councillor /ˈkaʊnsələ(r)/ *n.* an elected member of a council, esp. a local one. □□ **councillorship** *n.* [ME, alt. of COUNSELLOR: assim. to COUNCIL]

councilman /ˈkaʊns(ə)lmən/ *n.* (*pl.* **-men**; *fem.* **councilwoman**, *pl.* **-women**) *esp. US* a member of a council; a councillor.

Council of Europe an association of European States, independent of the European Community. It meets in Strasbourg. Founded in 1949, it is committed to the principles of freedom and the rule of law, and to safeguarding the political and cultural heritage of Europe. Its executive organ is the Committee of Ministers, and most of its conclusions take the form of international agreements (known as *European Conventions*) or recommendations to governments. One of the Council's principal achievements is the European Convention of Human Rights (1950) under which was established the European Commission and the European Court of Human Rights.

counsel /ˈkaʊns(ə)l/ *n. & v.* —*n.* **1** advice, esp. formally given. **2**

consultation, esp. to seek or give advice. **3** (*pl.* same) a barrister or other legal adviser; a body of these advising in a case. **4** a plan of action. —*v.tr.* (**counselled, counselling;** *US* **counseled, counseling**) **1** (often foll. by *to* + infin.) advise (a person). **2 a** give advice to (a person) on social or personal problems, esp. professionally. **b** assist or guide (a person) in resolving personal difficulties. **3** (often foll. by *that*) recommend (a course of action). □ **counsel of despair** action to be taken when all else fails. **counsel of perfection 1** advice that is ideal but not feasible. **2** advice guiding towards moral perfection. **keep one's own counsel** not confide in others. **Queen's** (or **King's**) **Counsel** *Brit.* a counsel to the Crown, taking precedence over other barristers. **take counsel** (usu. foll. by *with*) consult. [ME f. OF *c(o)unseil, conseiller* f. L *consilium* consultation, advice]

counselling /ˈkaʊnsəlɪŋ/ *n.* (*US* **counseling**) **1** the act or process of giving counsel. **2** the process of assisting and guiding clients, esp. by a trained person on a professional basis, to resolve esp. personal, social, or psychological problems and difficulties (cf. COUNSEL *v.* 2b).

counsellor /ˈkaʊnsələ(r)/ *n.* (*US* **counselor**) **1** a person who gives counsel; an adviser. **2** a person trained to give guidance on personal, social, or psychological problems (*marriage guidance counsellor*). **3** a senior officer in the diplomatic service. **4 a** (also **counselor-at-law**) *US* a barrister. **b** (also **counsellor-at-law**) *Ir.* an advising barrister. □ **Counsellor of State** *Brit.* a temporary regent during a sovereign's absence. [ME f. OF *conseiller* (f. L *consiliarius*), *conseillour, -eur* (f. L *consiliator*): see COUNSEL]

count¹ /kaʊnt/ *v. & n.* —*v.* **1** *tr.* determine the total number or amount of, esp. by assigning successive numbers (*count the stations*). **2** *intr.* repeat numbers in ascending order; conduct a reckoning. **3 a** *tr.* (often foll. by *in*) include in one's reckoning or plan (*you can count me in; fifteen people, counting the guide*). **b** *intr.* be included in a reckoning or plan. **4** *tr.* consider (a thing or a person) to be (lucky etc.) (*count no man happy until he is dead*). **5** *intr.* (often foll. by *for*) have value; matter (*his opinion counts for a great deal*). —*n.* **1 a** the act of counting; a reckoning (*after a count of fifty*). **b** the sum total of a reckoning (*blood count; pollen count*). **2** *Law* each charge in an indictment (*guilty on ten counts*). **3** a count of up to ten seconds by a referee when a boxer is knocked down. **4** *Polit.* the act of counting the votes after a general or local election. **5** one of several points under discussion. **6** the measure of the fineness of a yarn expressed as the weight of a given length or the length of a given weight. **7** *Physics* the number of ionizing particles detected by a counter. □ **count against** be reckoned to the disadvantage of. **count one's blessings** be grateful for what one has. **count one's chickens** be over-optimistic or hasty in anticipating good fortune. **count the cost** consider the risks before taking action. **count the days** (or **hours** etc.) be impatient. **count down** recite numbers backwards to zero, esp. as part of a rocket-launching procedure. **counting-house** a place where accounts are kept. **count noun** a countable noun (see COUNTABLE 2). **count on** (or **upon**) depend on, rely on; expect confidently. **count out 1** count while taking from a stock. **2** complete a count of ten seconds over (a fallen boxer etc.), indicating defeat. **3** (in children's games) select (a player) for dismissal or a special role by use of a counting rhyme etc. **4** *colloq.* exclude from a plan or reckoning (*I'm too tired, count me out*). **5** *Brit. Polit.* procure the adjournment of (the House of Commons) when fewer than 40 members are present. **count up** find the sum of. **keep count** take note of how many there are etc. **lose count** fail to take note of the number etc. **not counting** excluding from the reckoning. **out for the count 1** *Boxing* defeated by being unable to rise within ten seconds. **2 a** defeated or demoralized. **b** soundly asleep. **take the count** *Boxing* be defeated. [ME f. OF *co(u)nter, co(u)nte* f. LL *computus, computare* COMPUTE]

count² /kaʊnt/ *n.* a foreign noble corresponding to an earl. □ **Count Palatine** *hist.* a high official of the Holy Roman Empire with royal authority within his domain. □□ **countship** *n.* [OF *conte* f. L *comes comitis* companion]

countable /ˈkaʊntəb(ə)l/ *adj.* **1** that can be counted. **2** *Gram.* (of a noun) that can form a plural or be used with the indefinite article (e.g. *book, kindness*).

countdown /ˈkaʊntdaʊn/ *n.* **1 a** the act of counting down, esp. at the launching of a rocket etc. **b** the procedures carried out during this time. **2** the final moments before any significant event.

countenance /ˈkaʊntɪnəns/ n. & v. —n. **1 a** the face. **b** the facial expression. **2** composure. **3** moral support. —v.tr. give approval to (an act etc.) (*cannot countenance this breach of the rules*). **2** (often foll. by *in*) encourage (a person or a practice). □ **change countenance** alter one's expression as an effect of emotion. **keep one's countenance** maintain composure, esp. by refraining from laughter. **keep a person in countenance** support or encourage a person. **lose countenance** become embarrassed. **out of countenance** disconcerted. [ME f. AF c(o)untenance, OF contenance bearing f. contenir: see CONTAIN]

counter[1] /ˈkaʊntə(r)/ n. **1 a** a long flat-topped fitment in a shop, bank, etc., across which business is conducted with customers. **b** a similar structure used for serving food etc. in a cafeteria or bar. **2 a** a small disc used for keeping the score etc. esp. in table-games. **b** a token representing a coin. **c** something used in bargaining; a pawn (*a counter in the struggle for power*). **3** an apparatus used for counting. **4** *Physics* an apparatus used for counting individual ionizing particles etc. **5** a person or thing that counts. □ **over the counter** by ordinary retail purchase. **under the counter** (esp. of the sale of scarce goods) surreptitiously, esp. illegally. [AF count(e-)our, OF conteo(i)r, f. med.L computatorium (as COMPUTE)]

counter[2] /ˈkaʊntə(r)/ v., adv., adj., & n. —v. **1 tr. a** oppose, contradict (*countered our proposal with their own*). **b** meet by a countermove. **2** intr. **a** make a countermove. **b** make an opposing statement ('*I shall!' he countered*). **3** intr. *Boxing* give a return blow while parrying. —adv. **1** in the opposite direction (*ran counter to the fox*). **2** contrary (*his action was counter to my wishes*). —adj. **1** opposed; opposite. **2** duplicate; serving as a check. —n. **1 a** a parry; a countermove. **2** something opposite or opposed. □ **act** (or **go**) **counter to** disobey (instructions etc.). **go** (or **hunt** or **run**) **counter** run or ride against the direction taken by a quarry. **run counter to** act contrary to. [ME f. OF countre f. L contra against: see COUNTER-]

counter[3] /ˈkaʊntə(r)/ n. **1** the part of a horse's breast between the shoulders and under the neck. **2** the curved part of the stern of a ship. **3** *Printing* a part of a printing-type etc. that is completely enclosed by an outline (e.g. the loop of P). [17th c.: orig. unkn.]

counter[4] /ˈkaʊntə(r)/ n. the back part of a shoe or a boot round the heel. [abbr. of counterfort buttress]

counter- /ˈkaʊntə(r)/ comb. form denoting: **1** retaliation, opposition, or rivalry (*counter-threat; counter-cheers*). **2** opposite direction (*counter-current*). **3** correspondence, duplication, or substitution (*counterpart; countersign*). [from or after AF countre-, OF contre f. L contra against]

counteract /ˌkaʊntəˈrækt/ v.tr. **1** hinder or oppose by contrary action. **2** neutralize. □□ **counteraction** n. **counteractive** adj.

counter-attack /ˈkaʊntərəˌtæk/ n. & v. —n. an attack in reply to an attack by an enemy or opponent. —v.tr. & intr. attack in reply.

counter-attraction /ˈkaʊntərəˌtrækʃ(ə)n/ n. **1** a rival attraction. **2** the attraction of a contrary tendency.

counterbalance /ˈkaʊntəˌbæləns/ n. & v. —n. **1** a weight balancing another. **2** an argument, force, etc., balancing another. —v.tr. act as a counterbalance to.

counterblast /ˈkaʊntəˌblɑːst/ n. (often foll. by *to*) an energetic or violent verbal or written reply to an argument etc.

counterchange /ˈkaʊntəˌtʃeɪndʒ/ v. **1 tr.** change (places or parts); interchange. **2 tr.** *literary* chequer, esp. with contrasting colours etc. **3 intr.** change places or parts. [F contrechanger (as COUNTER-, CHANGE)]

countercharge /ˈkaʊntəˌtʃɑːdʒ/ n. & v. —n. a charge or accusation in return for one received. —v.tr. make a countercharge against.

countercheck /ˈkaʊntəˌtʃek/ n. & v. —n. **1 a** a restraint that opposes something. **b** a restraint that operates against another. **2** a second check, esp. for security or accuracy. **3** *archaic* a retort. —v.tr. make a countercheck on.

counter-claim /ˈkaʊntəˌkleɪm/ n. & v. —n. **1** a claim made against another claim. **2** *Law* a claim made by a defendant in a suit against the plaintiff. —v.tr. & intr. make a counter-claim (for).

counter-clockwise /ˌkaʊntəˈklɒkwaɪz/ adv. & adj. US = ANTICLOCKWISE.

counter-culture /ˈkaʊntəˌkʌltʃə(r)/ n. a way of life etc. opposed to that usually considered normal.

counter-espionage /ˌkaʊntərˈespɪəˌnɑːʒ, -ɪdʒ/ n. action taken to frustrate enemy spying.

counterfeit /ˈkaʊntəfɪt, -ˌfiːt/ adj., n., & v. —adj. **1** (of a coin, writing, etc.) made in imitation; not genuine; forged. **2** (of a claimant etc.) pretended. —n. a forgery; an imitation. —v.tr. **1 a** imitate fraudulently (a coin, handwriting, etc.); forge. **b** make an imitation of. **2** simulate (feelings etc.) (*counterfeited interest*). **3** resemble closely. □□ **counterfeiter** n. [ME f. OF countrefet, -fait, past part. of contrefaire f. Rmc]

counterfoil /ˈkaʊntəˌfɔɪl/ n. the part of a cheque, receipt, etc., retained by the payer and containing details of the transaction.

counter-intelligence /ˌkaʊntərɪnˈtelɪdʒ(ə)ns/ n. = COUNTER-ESPIONAGE.

counterirritant /ˌkaʊntərˈɪrɪt(ə)nt/ n. **1** *Med.* something used to produce surface irritation of the skin, thereby counteracting more painful symptoms. **2** anything resembling a counterirritant in its effects. □□ **counterirritation** /-ˈteɪʃ(ə)n/ n.

countermand /ˌkaʊntəˈmɑːnd/ v. & n. —v.tr. **1** *Mil.* **a** revoke (an order or command). **b** recall (forces etc.) by a contrary order. **2** cancel an order for (goods etc.). —n. an order revoking a previous one. [ME f. OF contremander f. med.L contramandare (as CONTRA-, mandare order)]

countermarch /ˈkaʊntəˌmɑːtʃ/ v. & n. —v.intr. & tr. esp. *Mil.* march or cause to march in the opposite direction, e.g. with the front marchers turning and marching back through the ranks. —n. an act of countermarching.

countermeasure /ˈkaʊntəˌmeʒə(r)/ n. an action taken to counteract a danger, threat, etc.

countermine /ˈkaʊntəˌmaɪn/ n. & v. —n. **1** *Mil.* **a** a mine dug to intercept another dug by an enemy. **b** a submarine mine sunk to explode an enemy's mines. **2** a counterplot. —v.tr. make a countermine against.

countermove /ˈkaʊntəˌmuːv/ n. & v. —n. a move or action in opposition to another. —v.intr. make a countermove. □□ **countermovement** n.

counter-offensive /ˈkaʊntərəˌfensɪv/ n. **1** *Mil.* an attack made from a defensive position in order to effect an escape. **2** any attack made from a defensive position.

counterpane /ˈkaʊntəˌpeɪn/ n. a bedspread. [alt. (with assim. to pane in obs. sense 'cloth') f. obs. counterpoint f. OF contrepointe alt. f. cou(l)tepointe f. med.L culcita puncta quilted mattress]

counterpart /ˈkaʊntəˌpɑːt/ n. **1 a** a person or thing extremely like another. **b** a person or thing forming a natural complement or equivalent to another. **2** *Law* one of two copies of a legal document. □ **counterpart funds** US funds etc. in a local currency equivalent to goods etc. received from abroad.

counterplot /ˈkaʊntəˌplɒt/ n. & v. —n. a plot intended to defeat another plot. —v. (**-plotted, -plotting**) **1** intr. make a counterplot. **2** tr. make a counterplot against.

counterpoint /ˈkaʊntəˌpɔɪnt/ n. & v. —n. **1** *Mus.* **a** the art or technique of setting, writing, or playing a melody or melodies in conjunction with another, according to fixed rules. (See below.) **b** a melody played in conjunction with another. **2** a contrasting argument, plot, idea, or literary theme, etc., used to set off the main element. —v.tr. **1** *Mus.* add counterpoint to. **2** set (an argument, plot, etc.) in contrast to (a main element). □ **strict counterpoint** an academic exercise in writing counterpoint, not necessarily intended as a composition. [OF contrepoint f. med.L contrapunctum pricked or marked opposite, i.e. to the original melody (as CONTRA-, pungere punct- prick)]

The practice of adding a part or parts to an existing melody according to more or less strict rules arose in sacred music of the 9th c., and from simple progressions in parallel octaves and fifths the intricate art of counterpoint developed until in the 16th and early 17th c. it embraced rhythmically and melodically distinct movement in as many parts as the composer felt he could control. Fugue and canon are familiar contrapuntal forms.

counterpoise /ˈkaʊntəˌpɔɪz/ n. & v. —n. **1** a force etc. equivalent to another on the opposite side. **2** a state of equilibrium. **3** a counterbalancing weight. —v.tr. **1** counterbalance. **2** compensate.

3 bring into or keep in equilibrium. [ME f. OF *contrepeis, -pois, contrepeser* (as COUNTER-, *peis, pois* f. L *pensum* weight: cf. POISE¹)]

counter-productive /ˌkaʊntəprəˈdʌktɪv/ *adj.* having the opposite of the desired effect.

counter-reformation /ˌkaʊntəˌrefəˈmeɪʃ(ə)n/ *n.* **1** (**Counter-Reformation**) *hist.* the reform of the Church of Rome in Europe from the mid-16th to the mid-17th c. Though stimulated by Protestant opposition, reform movements within the Roman Catholic Church had begun almost simultaneously with the Lutheran schism, aimed at countering the abuses of the Renaissance age. The Jesuit order became the spearhead of the movement both within Europe and as a missionary force in America and the East, while the power of the papacy triumphed over those Catholics who wished for conciliation with the Protestants and over those French and Spanish bishops who opposed papal claims. Spain, the strongest military power of the day, constituted itself the secular arm of the Counter-Reformation in Europe, and the Inquisition was extended to other countries. Although most of northern Europe remained Protestant, South Germany and Poland were brought back to the Roman obedience. **2** a reformation running counter to another.

counter-revolution /ˌkaʊntəˌrevəˈluːʃ(ə)n/ *n.* a revolution opposing a former one or reversing its results. □□ **counter-revolutionary** *adj.* & *n.* (*pl.* **-ies**).

counterscarp /ˈkaʊntəˌskɑːp/ *n. Mil.* the outer wall or slope of a ditch in a fortification. [F *contrescarpe* f. It. *contrascarpa* (as CONTRA-, SCARP)]

countershaft /ˈkaʊntəˌʃɑːft/ *n.* **1** an intermediate shaft driven by a main shaft and transmitting motion to a particular machine etc. **2** US = LAYSHAFT.

countersign /ˈkaʊntəˌsaɪn/ *v.* & *n.* —*v.tr.* **1** add a signature to (a document already signed by another). **2** ratify. —*n.* **1** a watchword or password spoken to a person on guard (cf. PAROLE). **2** a mark used for identification etc. □□ **counter-signature** /-ˈsɪɡnətʃə(r)/ *n.* [F *contresigner* (v.), *contresigne* (n.) f. It. *contrasegno* (as COUNTER-, SIGN)]

countersink /ˈkaʊntəˌsɪŋk/ *v.tr.* (*past* and *past part.* **-sunk**) **1** enlarge and bevel (the rim of a hole) so that a screw or bolt can be inserted flush with the surface. **2** sink (a screw etc.) in such a hole.

counterstroke /ˈkaʊntəˌstrəʊk/ *n.* a blow given in return for another.

counter-tenor /ˈkaʊntəˌtenə(r)/ *n. Mus.* **1** a male alto singing-voice. **b** a singer with this voice. **2** a part written for counter-tenor. [ME f. F *contre-teneur* f. obs. It. *contratenore* (as CONTRA-, TENOR)]

countervail /ˌkaʊntəˈveɪl, ˈkaʊntə-/ *v.* **1** *tr.* counterbalance. **2** *tr.* & *intr.* (often foll. by *against*) oppose forcefully and usu. successfully. □ **countervailing duty** a tax put on imports to offset a subsidy in the exporting country or a tax on similar goods not from abroad. [ME f. AF *contrevaloir* f. L *contra valēre* be of worth against]

countervalue /ˈkaʊntəˌvælju:/ *n.* an equivalent value, esp. in military strategy.

counterweight /ˈkaʊntəˌweɪt/ *n.* a counterbalancing weight.

countess /ˈkaʊntɪs/ *n.* **1** the wife or widow of a count or an earl. **2** a woman holding the rank of count or earl. [ME f. OF *contesse, cuntesse,* f. LL *comitissa* fem. of *comes* COUNT²]

countless /ˈkaʊntlɪs/ *adj.* too many to be counted.

countrified /ˈkʌntrɪˌfaɪd/ *adj.* (also **countryfied**) often *derog.* rural or rustic, esp. of manners, appearance, etc. [past part. of *countrify* f. COUNTRY]

country /ˈkʌntrɪ/ *n.* (*pl.* **-ies**) **1 a** the territory of a nation with its own government; a State. **b** a territory possessing its own language, people, culture, etc. **2** (often *attrib.*) rural districts as opposed to towns or the capital (*a cottage in the country; a country town*). **3** the land of a person's birth or citizenship; a fatherland or motherland. **4 a** a territory, esp. an area of interest or knowledge. **b** a region associated with a particular person, esp. a writer (*Hardy country*). **5** *Brit.* a national population, esp. as voters (*the country won't stand for it*). □ **across country** not keeping to roads. **country-and-western** rural or cowboy songs originating in the US, and usu. accompanied by a guitar etc. **country club** a sporting and social club in a rural setting. **country cousin** often *derog.* a person with a countrified appearance or manners. **country dance** a traditional sort of dance, esp. English, with couples facing each

other in long lines. **country gentleman** a gentleman with landed property. **country house** a usu. large house in the country, often the seat of a country gentleman. **country music** = *country-and-western.* **country party** a political party supporting agricultural interests. **country seat** a large country house belonging to an aristocratic family. **country-wide** extending throughout a nation. **go** (or **appeal**) **to the country** *Brit.* test public opinion after an adverse or doubtful vote in the House of Commons, or at the end of a government's term of office, by dissolving Parliament and holding a general election. **in the country** *Cricket sl.* far from the wickets; in the deep field. **line of country** a subject about which a person is knowledgeable. **unknown country** an unfamiliar place or topic. [ME f. OF *cuntree,* f. med.L *contrata* (*terra*) (land) lying opposite (CONTRA)]

countryfied var. of COUNTRIFIED.

countryman /ˈkʌntrɪmən/ *n.* (*pl.* **-men;** *fem.* **countrywoman,** *pl.* **-women**) **1** a person living in a rural area. **2 a** (also **fellow-countryman**) a person of one's own country or district. **b** (often in *comb.*) a person from a specified country or district (*north-countryman*).

countryside /ˈkʌntrɪˌsaɪd/ *n.* **1 a** a rural area. **b** rural areas in general. **2** the inhabitants of a rural area.

county /ˈkaʊntɪ/ *n.* & *adj.* —*n.* (*pl.* **-ies**) **1 a** any of the territorial divisions of some countries, forming the chief unit of local administration. **b** US a political and administrative division of a State. **2** the people of a county, esp. the leading families. —*adj.* having the social status or characteristics of county families. □ **county borough** *hist.* a large borough ranking as a county for administrative purposes. **county corporate** *hist.* a city or town ranking as an administrative county. **county council** the elected governing body of an administrative county. **county court** a judicial court for civil cases (in the US for civil and criminal cases). **county cricket** cricket matches between teams representing counties. **county family** an aristocratic family with an ancestral seat in a county. **County Palatine** the territory of a Count or Earl Palatine. **county town** (US **seat**) the administrative capital of a county. [ME f. AF *counté,* OF *conté, cunté,* f. L *comitatus* (as COUNT²)]

coup /ku:/ *n.* (*pl.* **coups** /ku:z/) **1** a notable or successful stroke or move. **2** = COUP D'ÉTAT. **3** *Billiards* a direct pocketing of the ball. [F f. med.L *colpus* blow: see COPE¹]

coup de grâce /ˌku: də ˈɡrɑːs/ *n.* a finishing stroke, esp. to kill a wounded animal or person. [F, lit. stroke of grace]

coup de main /ˌku: də ˈmæ̃/ *n.* a sudden vigorous attack. [F, lit. stroke of the hand]

coup d'état /ˌku: deɪˈtɑː/ *n.* a violent or illegal seizure of power. [F, lit. stroke of the State]

coup d'œil /ku: ˈdɔɪ/ *n.* **1** a comprehensive glance. **2** a general view. [F, lit. stroke of the eye]

coupe /ku:p/ *n.* **1** a shallow glass or dish used for serving fruit, ice-cream, etc. **2** fruit, ice-cream, etc. served in this. [F, = goblet]

coupé /ˈku:peɪ/ *n.* (US **coupe** /ku:p/) **1** a car with a hard roof, esp. one with two seats and a sloping rear. **2** *hist.* a four-wheeled enclosed carriage for two passengers and a driver. [F, past part. of *couper* cut (formed as COUP)]

Couperin /ˈku:pəˌræ̃/, François (1668–1733), French composer, organist, and harpsichordist. As a composer at the court of Louis XIV he participated in concerts at Versailles, Fontainebleau, and Sceaux, and many of his over 230 harpsichord pieces, nearly all with descriptive titles, were composed for such royal surroundings. He combined elements of the prevailing Italian style with the French tradition, and the resulting delicacy of idiom and strength of invention have been aptly compared with the painting of Watteau. His treatise on playing the harpsichord (1716) influenced Bach.

couple /ˈkʌp(ə)l/ *n.* & *v.* —*n.* **1** (usu. foll. by *of;* often as *sing.*) **a** two (*a couple of girls*). **b** about two (*a couple of hours*). **2** (often as *sing.*) **a** a married or engaged pair. **b** a pair of partners in a dance, a game, etc. **c** a pair of rafters. **3** (*pl.* **couple**) a pair of hunting dogs (*six couple of hounds*). **4** (in *pl.*) a pair of joined collars used for holding hounds together. **5** *Mech.* a pair of equal and parallel forces acting in opposite directions, and tending to cause rotation about an axis perpendicular to the plane containing them. —*v.* **1** *tr.* fasten or link together; connect (esp. railway carriages). **2** *tr.* (often foll. by *together, with*) associate in thought or speech (*papers coupled their names; couple our congratulations with our best wishes*). **3** *intr.* copulate. **4** *tr. Physics* connect (oscillators) with a coupling. [ME f. OF *cople, cuple, copler, cupler* f. L *copulare*, L COPULA]

coupler /ˈkʌplə(r)/ *n.* **1** *Mus.* **a** a device in an organ for connecting two manuals, or a manual with pedals, so that they both sound when only one is played. **b** (also **octave coupler**) a similar device for connecting notes with their octaves above or below. **2** anything that connects two things, esp. a transformer used for connecting electric circuits.

couplet /ˈkʌplɪt/ *n. Prosody* two successive lines of verse, usu. rhyming and of the same length. [F dimin. of *couple*, formed as COUPLE]

coupling /ˈkʌplɪŋ/ *n.* **1 a** a link connecting railway carriages etc. **b** a device for connecting parts of machinery. **2** *Physics* a connection between two systems, causing one to oscillate when the other does so. **3** *Mus.* **a** the arrangement of items on a gramophone record. **b** each such item.

coupon /ˈkuːpɒn/ *n.* **1** a form etc. in a newspaper, magazine, etc., which may be filled in and sent as an application for a purchase, information, etc. **2** *Brit.* an entry form for a football pool or other competition. **3** a voucher given with a retail purchase, a certain number of which entitle the holder to a discount etc. **4 a** a detachable ticket entitling the holder to a ration of food, clothes, etc., esp. in wartime. **b** a similar ticket entitling the holder to payment, goods, services, etc. [F, = piece cut off f. *couper* cut: see COUPÉ]

courage /ˈkʌrɪdʒ/ *n.* the ability to disregard fear; bravery. □ **courage of one's convictions** the courage to act on one's beliefs. **lose courage** become less brave. **pluck up** (or **take**) **courage** muster one's courage. **take one's courage in both hands** nerve oneself to a venture. [ME f. OF *corage*, f. L *cor* heart]

courageous /kəˈreɪdʒəs/ *adj.* brave, fearless. □□ **courageously** *adv.* **courageousness** *n.* [ME f. AF *corageous*, OF *corageus* (as COURAGE)]

courante /kʊˈrɑːnt/ *n.* **1** *hist.* a running or gliding dance. **2** *Mus.* the music used for this, esp. as a movement of a suite. [F, fem. pres. part. (as noun) of *courir* run f. L *currere*]

Courbet /kʊəˈbeɪ/, Gustave (1819–77), French painter, who set himself up as the leader of the realist school of painting, choosing his themes from contemporary life and not excluding what was ugly or vulgar. He was an innovator in his choice of subject-matter, which he used for its pictorial value rather than for emotional impact.

courgette /kʊəˈʒet/ *n.* a small green variety of vegetable marrow. Also called ZUCCHINI. [F, dimin. of *courge* gourd]

courier /ˈkʊrɪə(r)/ *n.* **1** a person employed, usu. by a travel company, to guide and assist a group of tourists. **2** a special messenger. [ME f. obs. F, f. It. *corriere*, & f. OF *coreor*, both f. L *currere* run]

Courrèges /kʊəˈreʒ/, André (1923–), French fashion designer, who opened a fashion house in Paris in 1961 and became known for his futuristic, youth-oriented, unisex styles.

course /kɔːs/ *n. & v.* —*n.* **1** a continuous onward movement or progression. **2 a** a line along which a person or thing moves; a direction taken (*has changed course; the course of the winding river*). **b** a correct or intended direction or line of movement. **c** the direction taken by a ship or aircraft. **3 a** the ground on which a race (or other sport involving extensive linear movement) takes place. **b** a series of fences, hurdles, or other obstacles to be crossed in a race etc. **4 a** a series of lectures, lessons, etc., in a particular subject. **b** a book for such a course (*A Modern French Course*). **5** any of the successive parts of a meal. **6** *Med.* a sequence of medical treatment etc. (*prescribed a course of antibiotics*). **7** a line of conduct (*disappointed by the course he took*). **8** *Archit.* a continuous horizontal layer of brick, stone, etc., in a building. **9** a channel in which water flows. **10** the pursuit of game (esp. hares) with hounds, esp. greyhounds, by sight rather than scent. **11** *Naut.* a sail on a square-rigged ship (*fore course; main course*). —*v.* **1** *intr.* (esp. of liquid) run, esp. fast (*blood coursed through his veins*). **2** *tr.* (also *absol.*) a use (hounds) to hunt. **b** pursue (hares etc.) in hunting. □ **the course of nature** ordinary events or procedure. **in course of** in the process of. **in the course of** during. **in the course of time** as time goes by; eventually. **a**

matter of course the natural or expected thing. **of course** naturally; as is or was to be expected; admittedly. **on** (or **off**) **course** following (or deviating from) the desired direction or goal. **run** (or **take**) **its course** (esp. of an illness) complete its natural development. □□ **courser** *n.* (in sense 2 of *v.*). [ME f. OF *cours* f. L *cursus* f. *currere curs-* run]

courser[1] /ˈkɔːsə(r)/ *n. poet.* a swift horse. [ME f. OF *corsier* f. Rmc]

courser[2] /ˈkɔːsə(r)/ *n.* any fast-running plover-like bird of the genus *Cursorius*, native to Africa and Asia, having long legs and a slender bill. [LL *cursorius* adapted for running]

court /kɔːt/ *n. & v.* —*n.* **1** (in full **court of law**) **a** an assembly of judges or other persons acting as a tribunal in civil and criminal cases. **b** = COURTROOM. **2 a** an enclosed quadrangular area for games, which may be open or covered (*tennis-court; squash-court*). **b** an area marked out for lawn tennis etc. (*hit the ball out of court*). **3 a** a small enclosed street in a town, having a yard surrounded by houses, and adjoining a larger street. **b** *Brit.* = COURTYARD. **c** (**Court**) the name of a large house, block of flats, street, etc. (*Grosvenor Court*). **d** (at Cambridge University) a college quadrangle. **e** a subdivision of a building, usu. a large hall extending to the ceiling with galleries and staircases. **4 a** the establishment, retinue, and courtiers of a sovereign. **b** a sovereign and his or her councillors, constituting a ruling power. **c** a sovereign's residence. **d** an assembly held by a sovereign; a State reception. **5** attention paid to a person whose favour, love, or interest is sought (*paid court to her*). **6 a** the qualified members of a company or a corporation. **b** (in some Friendly Societies) a local branch. **c** a meeting of a court. —*v.tr.* **1 a** try to win the affection or favour of (a person). **b** pay amorous attention to (*courting couples*). **2** seek to win (applause, fame, etc.). **3** invite (misfortune) by one's actions (*you are courting disaster*). □ **court-card** a playing-card that is a king, queen, or jack (orig. *coat-card*). **court circular** *Brit.* a daily report of royal court affairs, published in some newspapers. **court dress** formal dress worn at a royal court. **court-house 1** a building in which a judicial court is held. **2** *US* a building containing the administrative offices of a county. **Court leet** see LEET[1]. **Court of Appeal** a court of law hearing appeals against judgements in the Crown Court, High Court, County Court, etc. **Court of Arches** the ecclesiastical court of appeal for the province of Canterbury, so known because it was formerly held at the church of St Mary-le-Bow, famous for its arched crypt. **Court of St James's** the court of the British sovereign. **Court of Protection** *Brit.* the department of the Supreme Court attending to the affairs of the mentally unfit. **court of record** a court whose proceedings are recorded and available as evidence of fact. **Court of St James's** the British sovereign's court. **Court of Session** the supreme civil court in Scotland. **court of summary jurisdiction** a court having the authority to use summary proceedings and arrive at a judgement or conviction. **court order** a direction issued by a court or a judge, usu. requiring a person to do or not do something. **court plaster** *hist.* sticking-plaster for cuts etc. (formerly used by ladies at court for face-patches). **court roll** *hist.* a manorial-court register of holdings. **court shoe** a woman's light, usu. high-heeled, shoe with a low-cut upper. **court tennis** *US* real tennis. **go to court** take legal action. **in court** appearing as a party or an advocate in a court of law. **out of court 1** (of a plaintiff) not entitled to be heard. **2** (of a settlement) arranged before a hearing or judgement can take place. **3** not worthy of consideration (*that suggestion is out of court*). [ME f. AF *curt*, OF *cort*, ult. f. L *cohors*, *-hortis* yard, retinue: (v.) after OIt. *corteare*, OF *courtoyer*]

Courtauld /ˈkɔːtəʊld/, Samuel (1876–1947), English industrialist, a director of the family silk firm and one of the earliest British collectors of French impressionist and post-impressionist paintings. He presented his collection to the University of London, endowed the Courtauld Institute of Art, and made over to it the house in Portman Square, London, which had been his residence.

court bouillon /ˌkʊə(r) buˈjɔ̃/ *n.* stock usu. made from wine, vegetables, etc., often used in fish dishes. [F f. *court* short + BOUILLON]

courteous /ˈkɜːtɪəs/ *adj.* polite, kind, or considerate in manner; well-mannered. □□ **courteously** *adv.* **courteousness** *n.* [ME f. OF *corteis, curteis* f. Rmc (as COURT): assim. to words in -OUS]

courtesan /ˌkɔːtɪˈzæn, ˈkɔːt-/ *n. literary* **1** a prostitute, esp. one with wealthy or upper-class clients. **2** the mistress of a wealthy man. [F *courtisane* f. It. *cortigiana*, fem. of *cortigiano* courtier f. *corte* COURT]

courtesy /ˈkɜːtɪsɪ/ *n.* (*pl.* **-ies**) **1** courteous behaviour; good manners. **2** a courteous act. **3** *archaic* = CURTSY. □ **by courtesy** by favour, not by right. **by courtesy of** with the formal permission of (a person etc.). **courtesy light** a light in a car that is switched on by opening a door. **courtesy title** a title held by courtesy, usu. having no legal validity, e.g. a title given to the heir of a duke etc. [ME f. OF *curtesie*, *co(u)rtesie* f. *curteis* etc. COURTEOUS]

courtier /ˈkɔːtɪə(r)/ *n.* a person who attends or frequents a sovereign's court. [ME f. AF *courte(i)our*, f. OF f. *cortoyer* be present at court]

courtly /ˈkɔːtlɪ/ *adj.* (**courtlier, courtliest**) **1** polished or refined in manners. **2** obsequious. **3** punctilious. □ **courtly love** the conventional medieval tradition of knightly love for a lady, and the etiquette used in its (esp. literary) expression. □□ **courtliness** *n.* [COURT]

court martial /ˌkɔːt ˈmɑːʃ(ə)l/ *n.* & *v.* —*n.* (*pl.* **courts martial**) a judicial court for trying members of the armed services. —*v.tr.* (**court-martial**) (**-martialled, -martialling;** US **-martialed, -martialing**) try by a court martial.

Courtrai see KORTRIJK.

courtroom /ˈkɔːtruːm, -rʊm/ *n.* the place or room in which a court of law meets.

courtship /ˈkɔːtʃɪp/ *n.* **1 a** courting with a view to marriage. **b** the courting behaviour of male animals, birds, etc. **c** a period of courting. **2** an attempt, often protracted, to gain advantage by flattery, attention, etc.

courtyard /ˈkɔːtjɑːd/ *n.* an area enclosed by walls or buildings, often opening off a street.

couscous /ˈkuːskuːs/ *n.* a N. African dish of wheat grain or coarse flour steamed over broth, often with meat or fruit added. [F f. Arab. *kuskus* f. *kaskasa* to pound]

cousin /ˈkʌz(ə)n/ *n.* **1** (also **first cousin, cousin-german**) the child of one's uncle or aunt. **2** (usu. in *pl.*) applied to the people of kindred races or nations (*our American cousins*). **3** *hist.* a title formerly used by a sovereign in addressing another sovereign or a noble of his or her own country. □ **second cousin** a child of one's parent's first cousin. □□ **cousinhood** *n.* **cousinly** *adj.* **cousinship** *n.* [ME f. OF *cosin, cusin,* f. L *consobrinus* mother's sister's child]

Cousteau /ˈkuːstəʊ/, Jacques-Yves (1910–), French oceanographer and film director. A naval officer keenly interested in underwater exploration, he began using a camera under water in 1939 as an aid to research. He made a number of short films recording underwater expeditions and three feature films, *The Silent World* (1956), *World Without Sun* (1964), and *Voyage to the Edge of the World* (jointly with Philippe Cousteau, 1976). He has also made several series for television.

couth /kuːθ/ *adj.* joc. cultured; well-mannered. [back-form. as antonym of UNCOUTH]

couture /kuːˈtjʊə(r)/ *n.* the design and manufacture of fashionable clothes; = HAUTE COUTURE. [F, = sewing, dressmaking]

couturier /kuːˈtjʊərɪˌeɪ/ *n.* (*fem.* **couturière** /-ˈrɪeə(r)/) a fashion designer or dressmaker. [F]

couvade /kuːˈvɑːd/ *n.* a custom by which a father behaves as if undergoing labour and childbirth when his child is being born. [F f. *couver* hatch f. L *cubare* lie down]

couvert /kuːˈveə(r)/ *n.* = COVER *n.* 6. [F]

couverture /ˌkuːvəˈtjʊə(r)/ *n.* chocolate for covering sweets, cakes, etc. [F, = covering]

covalency /kəʊˈveɪlənsɪ/ *n.* Chem. **1** the linking of atoms by a covalent bond. **2** the number of pairs of electrons an atom can share with another.

covalent /kəʊˈveɪlənt/ *adj.* Chem. of, relating to, or characterized by covalency. □ **covalent bond** Chem. a bond formed by sharing of electrons usu. in pairs by two atoms in a molecule. □□ **covalence** *n.* **covalently** *adv.* [co- + valent, after trivalent etc.]

cove[1] /kəʊv/ *n.* & *v.* —*n.* **1** a small, esp. sheltered, bay or creek. **2** a sheltered recess. **3** *Archit.* a concave arch or arched moulding, esp. one formed at the junction of a wall with a ceiling. —*v.tr.*

Archit. **1** provide (a room, ceiling, etc.) with a cove. **2** slope (the sides of a fireplace) inwards. [OE *cofa* chamber f. Gmc]

cove[2] /kəʊv/ *n.* Brit. sl. archaic a fellow; a chap. [16th-c. cant: orig. unkn.]

coven /ˈkʌv(ə)n/ *n.* an assembly of witches. [var. of *covent*; see CONVENT]

covenant /ˈkʌvənənt/ *n.* & *v.* —*n.* **1** an agreement; a contract. **2** Law **a** a contract drawn up under a seal, esp. undertaking to make regular payments to a charity. **b** a clause of a covenant. **3** (**Covenant**) *Bibl.* the agreement between God and the Israelites (see *Ark of the Covenant*). —*v.tr. & intr.* agree, esp. by legal covenant. □ **land of the Covenant** Canaan. □□ **covenantal** /-ˈnænt(ə)l/ *adj.* **covenantor** *n.* [ME f. OF, pres. part. of *co(n)venir*, formed as CONVENE]

covenanted /ˈkʌvənəntɪd/ *adj.* bound by a covenant.

covenanter /ˈkʌvənəntə(r)/ *n.* **1** a person who covenants. **2** (**Covenanter**) *hist.* an adherent of the Scottish National Covenant of 1638 and the Solemn League and Covenant (1643; see separate entry), proclamations defending Presbyterianism and resisting the religious policies of Charles I. The name was later applied to those who opposed the reintroduction of episcopacy to Scotland in 1662. The Covenanters were ruthlessly persecuted in 1678–85.

Covent Garden /ˈkʌvənt/ a district in central London, originally the convent garden of the Abbey of Westminster. It was the site for 300 years of London's chief fruit and vegetable market, which in 1974 was moved to Nine Elms, Battersea. The first Covent Garden Theatre was opened in 1732 and such famous plays as Goldsmith's *She Stoops to Conquer* (1773) and Sheridan's *The Rivals* (1775) were first performed there. It was several times destroyed and reconstructed, and since 1946 has been the home of London's chief opera and ballet companies.

Coventry /ˈkɒvəntrɪ/ an industrial city in West Midlands, central England; pop. (1981) 313,900. □ **send a person to Coventry** refuse to associate with or speak to a person. The origin of the phrase is unknown. One suggestion is based on Clarendon's statement that during the English Civil War Royalists taken prisoner at Birmingham were sent to Coventry, which was a Parliamentary stronghold; soldiers of the rival faction who were sent there would be cut off from social intercourse—whence, perhaps, the phrase.

cover /ˈkʌvə(r)/ *v.* & *n.* —*v.tr.* **1** (often foll. by *with*) protect or conceal by means of a cloth, lid, etc. **2 a** extend over; occupy the whole surface of (*covered in dirt; covered with writing*). **b** (often foll. by *with*) strew thickly or thoroughly (*covered the floor with straw*). **c** lie over; be a covering to (*the blanket scarcely covered him*). **3 a** protect; clothe. **b** (as **covered** *adj.*) wearing a hat; having a roof. **4** include; comprise; deal with (*the talk covered recent discoveries*). **5** travel (a specified distance) (*covered sixty miles*). **6** *Journalism* **a** report (events, a meeting, etc.). **b** investigate as a reporter. **7** be enough to defray (expenses, a bill, etc.) (*£20 should cover it*). **8 a** *refl.* take precautionary measures so as to protect oneself (*had covered myself by saying I might be late*). **b** (*absol.;* foll. by *for*) deputize or stand in for (a colleague etc.) (*will you cover for me?*). **9** *Mil.* **a** aim a gun etc. at. **b** (of a fortress, guns, etc.) command (a territory). **c** stand behind (a person in the front rank). **d** protect (an exposed person etc.) by being able to return fire. **10 a** esp. *Cricket* stand behind (another player) to stop any missed balls. **b** (in team games) mark (a corresponding player of the other side). **11** (also *absol.*) (in some card-games) play a card higher than (one already played to the same trick). **12** (of a stallion, a bull, etc.) copulate with. —*n.* **1** something that covers or protects, esp.: **a** a lid. **b** the binding of a book. **c** either board of this. **d** an envelope or the wrapper of a parcel (*under separate cover*). **e** the outer case of a pneumatic tyre. **f** (in *pl.*) bedclothes. **2 a** hiding-place; a shelter. **3** woods or undergrowth sheltering game or covering the ground (see COVERT). **4 a** a pretence; a screen (*under cover of humility*). **b** a spy's pretended identity or activity, intended as concealment. **c** *Mil.* a supporting force protecting an advance party from attack. **5 a** funds, esp. obtained by insurance, to meet a liability or secure against a contingent loss. **b** the state of being protected (*third-party cover*). **6 a** place setting at table, esp. in a restaurant. **7** *Cricket* = *cover-point*. □ **break cover** (of an animal, esp. game, or a hunted person) leave a place of shelter, esp. vegetation. **cover charge** an extra charge levied per head in a restaurant, nightclub, etc. **cover crop** a crop grown for the protection and enrichment of the soil. **cover-drive** *Cricket* a drive past cover-point. **cover girl** a female model whose picture appears on magazine covers etc. **cover in** provide with a roof etc. **covering letter** (or **note**) an explanatory letter sent with an enclosure. **cover note** *Brit.* a temporary certificate of current insurance. **cover-point** *Cricket* **1** a fielding position on the off side and halfway to the boundary. **2** a fielder at this position. **cover story** a news story in a magazine, that is illustrated or advertised on the front cover. **cover one's tracks** conceal evidence of what one has done. **cover up 1** completely cover or conceal. **2** conceal (circumstances etc., esp. illicitly) (also *absol.: refused to cover up for them*). **cover-up** *n.* an act of concealing circumstances, esp. illicitly. **from cover to cover** from beginning to end of a book etc. **take cover** use a natural or prepared shelter against an attack. □□ **coverable** *adj.* **coverer** *n.* [ME f. OF *covrir, cuvrir* f. L *cooperire* (as CO-, *operire* opert- cover)]

coverage /ˈkʌvərɪdʒ/ *n.* **1** an area or an amount covered. **2** *Journalism* the amount of press etc. publicity received by a particular story, person, etc. **3** a risk covered by an insurance policy. **4** an area reached by a particular broadcasting station or advertising medium.

coverall /ˈkʌvərˌɔːl/ *n. & adj.* esp. *US* —*n.* **1** something that covers entirely. **2** (usu. in *pl.*) a full-length protective outer garment often zipped up the front. —*attrib.adj.* covering entirely (*a coverall term*).

Coverdale /ˈkʌvəˌdeɪl/, Miles (1488–1568), translator of the first complete printed English Bible (1535), produced while he was in exile on the Continent for preaching against confession and images. In 1539, with R. Grafton, he issued the Great Bible; under Elizabeth I he became a Puritan leader.

covering /ˈkʌvərɪŋ/ *n.* something that covers, esp. a bedspread, blanket, etc., or clothing.

coverlet /ˈkʌvəlɪt/ *n.* a bedspread. [ME f. AF *covrelet, -lit* f. OF *covrir* cover + *lit* bed]

covert /ˈkʌvət/ *adj. & n.* —*adj.* secret or disguised (*a covert glance; covert operations*). —*n.* **1** a shelter, esp. a thicket hiding game. **2** a feather covering the base of a bird's flight-feather. □ **covert coat** a short, light, overcoat worn for shooting, riding, etc. □□ **covertly** *adv.* **covertness** *n.* [ME f. OF *covert* past part. of *covrir* COVER]

coverture /ˈkʌvətjʊə(r), -tʃə(r)/ *n.* **1** covering; shelter. **2** *Law hist.* the position of a married woman, considered to be under her husband's protection. [ME f. OF (as COVERT)]

covet /ˈkʌvɪt/ *v.tr.* (**coveted, coveting**) desire greatly (esp. something belonging to another person) (*coveted her friend's earrings*). □□ **covetable** *adj.* [ME f. OF *cu-, coveitier* f. Rmc]

covetous /ˈkʌvɪtəs/ *adj.* (usu. foll. by *of*) **1** greatly desirous (esp. of another person's property). **2** grasping, avaricious. □□ **covetously** *adv.* **covetousness** *n.* [ME f. OF *coveitous* f. Gallo-Roman]

covey /ˈkʌvɪ/ *n.* (*pl.* **-eys**) **1** a brood of partridges. **2** a small party or group of people or things. [ME f. OF *covee* f. Rmc f. L *cubare* lie]

covin /ˈkʌvɪn/ *n.* **1** *Law* a conspiracy to commit a crime etc. against a third party. **2** *archaic* fraud, deception. [ME f. OF *covin(e)* f. med.L *convenium -ia* f. *convenire*: see CONVENE]

coving *n.* = COVE[1] *n.* 3.

cow[1] /kaʊ/ *n.* **1** a fully grown female of any bovine animal, esp. of the genus *Bos*, used as a source of milk and beef. **2** the female of other large animals, esp. the elephant, whale, and seal. **3** *derog. sl.* **a** a woman esp. a coarse or unpleasant one. **b** *Austral. & NZ* an unpleasant person, thing, situation, etc. □ **cow-fish 1** any of several small plant-eating mammals, e.g. the manatee. **2** a marine fish, *Lactoria diaphana*, covered in hard bony plates and having hornlike spines over the eyes and on other parts of the body. **cow-heel** the foot of a cow or an ox stewed to a jelly. **cow-lick** a projecting lock of hair. **cow-parsley** a hedgerow plant *Anthriscus sylvestris*, having lacelike umbels of flowers: also called *Queen Anne's lace*. **cow-pat** a flat round piece of cow-dung. **cow-tree** a tree, *Brosimum galactodendron*, native to S. America, yielding a milklike juice which is used as a substitute for cow's milk. **cow-wheat** any plant of the genus *Melampyrum*, esp. M.

pratense growing on heathland. **till the cows come home** *colloq.* an indefinitely long time. [OE *cū* f. Gmc, rel. to L *bos*, Gk *bous*]

cow[2] /kaʊ/ *v.tr.* (usu. in *passive*) intimidate or dispirit (*cowed by ill-treatment*). [prob. f. ON *kúga* oppress]

cowage /ˈkaʊɪdʒ/ *n.* (also **cowhage**) a climbing plant, *Mucuna pruritum*, having hairy pods which cause stinging and itching. [Hindi *kawāñch*]

Coward /ˈkaʊəd/, Sir Noël Pierce (1899–1973), English playwright, actor, and composer, whose life from an early age was dedicated to the theatre. His plays of the 1920s, which matched the contemporary mood of smart sophistication, established his popularity, and his continuing production of plays, revues, musical plays, operettas, and films, spiced with wit and sweetened with sentimentality, added to it. Among his best-known works are the plays *Private Lives* (1930), *Cavalcade* (1931), *Blithe Spirit* (1941), and the operetta *Bitter Sweet* (1929).

coward /ˈkaʊəd/ *n. & adj.* —*n.* a person who is easily frightened or intimidated by danger or pain. —*adj. poet.* easily frightened. [ME f. OF *cuard, couard* ult. f. L *cauda* tail]

cowardice /ˈkaʊədɪs/ *n.* a lack of bravery. [ME f. OF *couardise* (as COWARD)]

cowardly /ˈkaʊədlɪ/ *adj. & adv.* —*adj.* **1** of or like a coward; lacking courage. **2** (of an action) done against one who cannot retaliate. —*adv. archaic* like a coward; with cowardice. □□ **cowardliness** *n.*

cowbane /ˈkaʊbeɪn/ *n.* = water hemlock.

cowbell /ˈkaʊbel/ *n.* **1** a bell worn round a cow's neck for easy location of the animal. **2** a similar bell used as a percussion instrument.

cowberry /ˈkaʊbərɪ/ *n.* (*pl.* **-ies**) **1** an evergreen shrub, *Vaccinium vitis-idaea*, bearing dark-red berries. **2** the berry of this plant.

cowboy /ˈkaʊbɔɪ/ *n.* **1** (*fem.* **cowgirl**) a person who herds and tends cattle, esp. in the western US. **2** this as a conventional figure in American folklore, esp. in films. **3** *colloq.* an unscrupulous or reckless person in business, esp. an unqualified one.

cowcatcher /ˈkaʊˌkætʃə(r)/ *n.* *US* a peaked metal frame at the front of a locomotive for pushing aside obstacles on the line.

cower /ˈkaʊə(r)/ *v.intr.* **1** crouch or shrink back, esp. in fear; cringe. **2** stand or squat in a bent position. [ME f. MLG *kūren* lie in wait, of unkn. orig.]

Cowes /kaʊz/ a town on the Isle of Wight, famous internationally as a yachting centre.

cowhage var. of COWAGE.

cowherd /ˈkaʊhɜːd/ *n.* a person who tends cattle.

cowhide /ˈkaʊhaɪd/ *n.* **1 a** a cow's hide. **b** leather made from this. **2** a leather whip made from cowhide.

cowhouse /ˈkaʊhaʊs/ *n.* a shed or shelter for cows.

cowl /kaʊl/ *n.* **1 a** the hood of a monk's habit. **b** a loose hood. **c** a monk's hooded habit. **2** the hood-shaped covering of a chimney or ventilating shaft. **3** the removable cover of a vehicle or aircraft engine. □□ **cowled** *adj.* (in sense 1). [OE *cugele, cūle* f. eccl.L *cuculla* f. L *cucullus* hood of a cloak]

cowling /ˈkaʊlɪŋ/ *n.* = COWL 3.

cowman /ˈkaʊmən/ *n.* (*pl.* **-men**) **1** = COWHERD. **2** *US* a cattle-owner.

co-worker /kəʊˈwɜːkə(r)/ *n.* a person who works in collaboration with another.

Cowper /ˈkuːpə(r)/, William (1731–1800), English poet. He suffered from acute melancholia and turned to evangelical Christianity for consolation. With the curate John Newton he wrote *Olney Hymns* (1779) to which Cowper contributed 'Oh! for a closer walk with God' amongst other congregational favourites. His famous comic ballad, *John Gilpin* appeared in 1782; his long poem *The Task* (1785) is notable for its intimate sketches of rural scenes. After the death of his close friend Mary Unwin he wrote 'The Castaway' (1803) expressing man's isolation, a theme which recurs in many of his poems.

cowpoke /ˈkaʊpəʊk/ *n.* *US* = COWBOY 1.

cowpox /ˈkaʊpɒks/ *n.* a disease of cows, of which the virus was formerly used in vaccination against smallpox.

aʊ how eɪ day əʊ no eə hair ɪə near ɔɪ boy ʊə poor aɪə fire aʊə sour (*see over for consonants*)

cowpuncher /'kaʊˌpʌntʃə(r)/ n. US = COWBOY 1.

cowrie /'kaʊrɪ/ n. (also **cowry**) (pl. **-ies**) **1** any gastropod mollusc of the family Cypraeidae, having a smooth glossy and usu. brightly-coloured shell. **2** its shell, esp. used as money in parts of Africa and S. Asia. [Urdu & Hindi kauṛī]

cowshed /'kaʊʃed/ n. **1** a shed for cattle that are not at pasture. **2** a milking-shed.

cowslip /'kaʊslɪp/ n. **1** a primula, *Primula veris*, with fragrant yellow flowers and growing in pastures. **2** US a marsh marigold. [OE *cūslyppe* f. cū cow[1] + *slyppe* slimy substance, i.e. cow-dung]

Cox /kɒks/ n. (in full **Cox's orange pippin**) a variety of eating-apple with a red-tinged green skin. [R. Cox, amateur Eng. fruit grower d. 1825]

cox /kɒks/ n. & v. —n. a coxswain, esp. of a racing-boat. —v. **1** intr. act as a cox (*coxed for Cambridge*). **2** tr. act as cox for (*coxed the winning boat*). [abbr.]

coxa /'kɒksə/ n. (pl. **coxae** /-si:/) **1** Anat. the hip-bone or hip-joint. **2** Zool. the first segment of an insect's leg. □□ **coxal** adj. [L]

coxcomb /'kɒkskəʊm/ n. an ostentatiously conceited man; a dandy. □□ **coxcombry** /-kəmrɪ/ n. (pl. **-ies**). [= *cock's comb* (see COCK[1]), orig. (a cap worn by) a jester]

Cox's Bazaar /'kɒksɪz/ a seaport in the Chittagong region of SE Bangladesh; pop. (1981) 29,600.

coxswain /'kɒkswein, -s(ə)n/ n. & v. —n. **1** a person who steers, esp. in a rowing-boat. **2** the senior petty officer in a small ship. —v. **1** intr. act as a coxswain. **2** tr. act as a coxswain of. □□ **coxswainship** n. [ME f. cock (see COCKBOAT) + SWAIN: cf. BOATSWAIN]

Coy. abbr. esp. Mil. Company.

coy /kɔɪ/ adj. (**coyer, coyest**) **1** archly or affectedly shy. **2** irritatingly reticent (*always coy about her age*). **3** (esp. of a girl) modest or shy. □□ **coyly** adv. **coyness** n. [ME f. OF coi, quei f. L quietus QUIET]

coyote /kɔɪ'əʊtɪ, 'kɔɪəʊt/ n. (pl. same or **coyotes**) a wolflike wild dog, *Canis latrans*, native to N. America. [Mex. Sp. f. Aztec *coyotl*]

coypu /'kɔɪpu:/ n. (pl. **coypus**) an aquatic beaver-like rodent, *Myocastor coypus*, native to S. America and kept in captivity for its fur. [Araucan]

coz /kʌz/ n. archaic cousin. [abbr.]

cozen /'kʌz(ə)n/ v. literary **1** tr. (often foll. by of, out of) cheat, defraud. **2** tr. (often foll. by into) beguile; persuade. **3** intr. act deceitfully. □□ **cozenage** n. [16th-c. cant, perh. rel. to COUSIN]

Cozumel /ˌkəʊzə'mel/ a resort island in the Caribbean, off the NE Coast of the Yucatán peninsula of Mexico.

cozy US var. of COSY.

CP abbr. **1** Cape Province. **2** Communist Party. **3** Austral. Country Party.

cp. abbr. compare.

c.p. abbr. candlepower.

Cpl. abbr. Corporal.

CPO abbr. Chief Petty Officer.

CPR abbr. Canadian Pacific Railway.

CPRE abbr. Council for the Protection of Rural England.

cps abbr. (also **c.p.s.**) **1** Computing characters per second. **2** cycles per second.

CPS abbr. (in the UK) Crown Prosecution Service.

CPSA abbr. (in the UK) Civil and Public Services Association.

CPU abbr. Computing central processing unit.

CPVE abbr. Brit. Certificate of Pre-Vocational Education, a qualification introduced in 1986 for students aged 16 or over who complete a one-year course of preparation for work or for further vocational study or training.

CR abbr. Community of the Resurrection.

Cr symb. Chem. the element chromium.

Cr. abbr. **1** Councillor. **2** creditor.

crab[1] /kræb/ n. **1 a** any of numerous ten-footed crustaceans having the first pair of legs modified as pincers. **b** the flesh of a crab, esp. *Cancer pagurus*, as food. **2** (**the Crab**) the zodiacal sign or constellation Cancer. **3** (in full **crab-louse**) (often in pl.) a

parasitic louse, *Phthirus pubis*, infesting hairy parts of the body and causing extreme irritation. **4** a machine for hoisting heavy weights. □ **catch a crab** Rowing effect a faulty stroke in which the oar is jammed under water or misses the water altogether. **crab-grass** US a creeping grass infesting lawns. **crab-pot** a wicker trap for crabs. □□ **crablike** adj. [OE *crabba*, rel. to ON *krafla* scratch]

crab[2] /kræb/ n. **1** (in full **crab-apple**) a small sour apple-like fruit. **2** (in full **crab tree** or **crab-apple tree**) any of several trees bearing this fruit. **3** a sour person. [ME, perh. alt. (after CRAB[1] or CRABBED) of earlier *scrab*, prob. of Scand. orig.]

crab[3] /kræb/ v. (**crabbed, crabbing**) colloq. **1** tr. & intr. criticize adversely or captiously; grumble. **2** tr. act so as to spoil (*the mistake crabbed his chances*). [orig. of hawks fighting, f. MLG *krabben*]

Crabbe /kræb/, George (1754–1832), English poet. His early life was spent at Aldeburgh, Suffolk, where he experienced much hardship. Crabbe's grimly realistic narrative poems, written in heroic couplets, were once immensely popular; they include the story of Peter Grimes, made the subject of an opera by Benjamin Britten.

crabbed /'kræbɪd/ adj. **1** irritable or morose. **2** (of handwriting) ill-formed and hard to decipher. **3** perverse or cross-grained. **4** difficult to understand. □□ **crabbedly** adv. **crabbedness** n. [ME f. CRAB[1], assoc. with CRAB[2]]

crabby /'kræbɪ/ adj. (**crabbier, crabbiest**) = CRABBED 1,3. □□ **crabbily** adv. **crabbiness** n.

Crab Nebula an irregular patch of luminous gas in the constellation Taurus, believed to be the remnant of a supernova explosion seen by Chinese astronomers in 1054. At its centre is the first pulsar to be observed visually. The nebula is also a strong source of high-energy radiation.

crabwise /'kræbwaɪz/ adv. & attrib.adj. (of movement) sideways or backwards like a crab.

crack /kræk/ n., v., & adj. —n. **1 a** a sudden sharp or explosive noise (*the crack of a whip; a rifle crack*). **b** (in a voice) a sudden harshness or change in pitch. **2** a sharp blow (*a crack on the head*). **3 a** a narrow opening formed by a break (*entered through a crack in the wall*). **b** a partial fracture, with the parts still joined (*the teacup has a crack in it*). **c** a chink (*looked through the crack formed by the door; a crack of light*). **4** colloq. a mischievous or malicious remark or aside (*a nasty crack about my age*). **5** colloq. an attempt (*I'll have a crack at it*). **6** the exact moment (*at the crack of noon; the crack of dawn*). **7** colloq. a first-rate player, horse, etc. **8** dial. colloq. conversation; good company; fun (*only went there for the crack*). **9** sl. a potent hard crystalline form of cocaine broken into small pieces and inhaled or smoked for its stimulating effect. —v. **1** tr. & intr. break without a complete separation of the parts (*cracked the window; the cup cracked on hitting the floor*). **2** intr. & tr. make or cause to make a sudden sharp or explosive sound. **3** intr. & tr. break or cause to break with a sudden sharp sound. **4** intr. & tr. give way or cause to give way (under torture etc.); yield. **5** intr. (of the voice, esp. of an adolescent boy or a person under strain) become dissonant; break. **6** tr. colloq. find a solution to (a problem, code, etc.). **7** tr. say (a joke etc.) in a jocular way. **8** tr. colloq. hit sharply or hard (*cracked her head on the ceiling*). **9** tr. Chem. decompose (heavy oils) by heat and pressure with or without a catalyst to produce lighter hydrocarbons (such as petrol). **10** tr. break (wheat) into coarse pieces. —attrib.adj. colloq. excellent; first-rate (*a crack regiment; a crack shot*). □ **crack a bottle** open a bottle, esp. of wine, and drink it. **crack-brained** crazy. **crack a crib** sl. break into a house. **crack-down** colloq. severe measures (esp. against law-breakers etc.). **crack down on** colloq. take severe measures against. **crack-jaw** colloq. —adj. (of a word) difficult to pronounce. —n. such a word. **crack of doom** a thunder-peal announcing the Day of Judgement. **crack up** colloq. **1** collapse under strain. **2** praise. **crack-up** n. colloq. **1** a mental breakdown. **2** a car crash. **crack-willow** a species of willow, *Salix fragilis*, with brittle branches. **fair crack of the whip** colloq. a fair chance to participate etc. **get cracking** colloq. begin promptly and vigorously. **have a crack at** colloq. attempt. [OE *cracian* resound]

cracked /krækt/ adj. **1** having cracks. **2** (predic.) sl. crazy. □

cracked wheat wheat that has been crushed into small pieces.

cracker /ˈkrækə(r)/ n. **1** a paper cylinder both ends of which are pulled at Christmas etc. making a sharp noise and releasing a small toy etc. **2** a firework exploding with a sharp noise. **3** (usu. in pl.) an instrument for cracking (nutcrackers). **4** a thin dry biscuit often eaten with cheese. **5** sl. Brit. a notable or attractive person. **6** US a biscuit. **7** US offens. = poor White. □ **cracker-barrel** US (of philosophy etc.) homespun; unsophisticated.

crackerjack /ˈkrækəˌdʒæk/ adj. & n. US sl. —adj. exceptionally fine or expert. —n. an exceptionally fine thing or person.

crackers /ˈkrækəz/ predic.adj. Brit. sl. crazy.

cracking /ˈkrækɪŋ/ adj. & adv. sl. —adj. **1** outstanding; very good (a cracking performance). **2** (attrib.) fast and exciting (a cracking speed). —adv. outstandingly (a cracking good time).

crackle /ˈkræk(ə)l/ v. & n. —v.intr. make a repeated slight cracking sound (radio crackled; fire was crackling). —n. **1** such a sound. **2 a** paintwork, china, or glass decorated with a pattern of minute surface cracks. **b** the smooth surface of such paintwork etc. □□ **crackly** adj. [CRACK + -LE⁴]

crackling /ˈkræklɪŋ/ n. **1** the crisp skin of roast pork. **2** joc. or offens. attractive women regarded collectively as objects of sexual desire. □ **bit of crackling** colloq. an attractive woman.

cracknel /ˈkrækn(ə)l/ n. a light crisp biscuit. [ME f. F craquelin f. MDu. krākelinc f. krāken CRACK]

crackpot /ˈkrækpɒt/ n. & adj. sl. —n. an eccentric or impractical person. —adj. mad, unworkable (a crackpot scheme).

cracksman /ˈkræksmən/ n. (pl. **-men**) sl. a burglar, esp. a safe-breaker.

cracky /ˈkrækɪ/ adj. covered with cracks. □□ **crackiness** n.

Cracow /ˈkrækaʊ/ (Polish **Kraków** /ˈkrɑːkuːf/) an industrial city in southern Poland, on the River Vistula; pop. (1985) 716,000.

-cracy /krəsɪ/ comb. form denoting a particular form of government, rule, or influence (aristocracy; bureaucracy). [from or after F -cratie f. med.L -cratia f. Gk -kratia f. kratos strength, power]

cradle /ˈkreɪd(ə)l/ n. & v. —n. **1 a** a child's bed or cot, esp. one mounted on rockers. **b** a place in which a thing begins, esp. a civilization etc., or is nurtured in its infancy (cradle of choral singing; cradle of democracy). **2** a framework resembling a cradle, esp.: **a** that on which a ship, a boat, etc., rests during construction or repairs. **b** that on which a worker is suspended to work on a ceiling, a ship, the vertical side of a building, etc. **c** the part of a telephone on which the receiver rests when not in use. —v.tr. **1** contain or shelter as if in a cradle (cradled his head in her arms). **2** place in a cradle. □ **cradle-snatcher** sl. a person amorously attached to a much younger person. **cradle-song** a lullaby. **from the cradle** from infancy. **from the cradle to the grave** from infancy till death (esp. of State welfare). [OE cradol, perh. rel. to OHG kratto basket]

cradling /ˈkreɪdlɪŋ/ n. Archit. a wooden or iron framework, esp. one used as a structural support in a ceiling.

craft /krɑːft/ n. & v. —n. **1** skill, esp. in practical arts. **2 a** (esp. in comb.) a trade or an art (statecraft; handicraft; priestcraft; the craft of pottery). **b** the members of a craft. **3** (pl. **craft**) a boat or vessel. **b** an aircraft or spacecraft. **4** cunning or deceit. **5** (**the Craft**) the brotherhood of Freemasons. —v.tr. make in a skilful way (crafted a poem; a well-crafted piece of work). □ **craft-brother** a fellow worker in the same trade. **craft-guild** hist. a guild of workers of the same trade. [OE cræft]

craftsman /ˈkrɑːftsmən/ n. (pl. **-men**; fem. **craftswoman**, pl. **-women**) **1** a skilled and usu. time-served worker. **2** a person who practises a handicraft. **3** a private soldier in the Royal Electrical and Mechanical Engineers. □□ **craftsmanship** n. [ME, orig. craft's man]

crafty /ˈkrɑːftɪ/ adj. (**craftier**, **craftiest**) cunning, artful, wily. □□ **craftily** adv. **craftiness** n. [OE cræftig]

crag¹ /kræg/ n. Brit. a steep or rugged rock. [ME, of Celt. orig.]

crag² /kræg/ n. Geol. rock consisting of a shelly sand. [18th c.: perh. f. CRAG¹]

craggy /ˈkrægɪ/ adj. (**craggier**, **craggiest**) **1** (esp. of a person's face) rugged; rough-textured. **2** (of a landscape) having crags. □□ **craggily** adv. **cragginess** n.

cragsman /ˈkrægzmən/ n. (pl. **-men**) a skilled climber of crags.

Craiova /krəˈjəʊvə/ a city in the mineral-rich Oltenia region of SW Romania; pop. (1985) 275,100.

crake /kreɪk/ n. **1** any rail (see RAIL³), esp. a corncrake. **2** the cry of a corncrake. [ME f. ON krāka (imit.): cf. CROAK]

cram /kræm/ v. —v. (**crammed**, **cramming**) **1** tr. **a** fill to bursting; stuff (the room was crammed). **b** (foll. by in, into) force (a thing) into (cram the sandwiches into the bag). **2** tr. & intr. prepare for an examination by intensive study. **3** tr. (often foll. by with) feed (poultry etc.) to excess. **4** tr. & intr. colloq. eat greedily. □ **cram-full** as full as possible. **cram in** push in to bursting point (crammed in another five minutes' work). [OE crammian f. Gmc]

crambo /ˈkræmbəʊ/ n. a game in which a player gives a word or verse-line to which each of the others must find a rhyme. [earlier crambe, app. allusive f. L crambe repetita cabbage served up again]

crammer /ˈkræmə(r)/ n. a person or institution that crams pupils for examinations.

cramp /kræmp/ n. & v. —n. **1 a** a painful involuntary contraction of a muscle or muscles from the cold, exertion, etc. **b** = writer's cramp (see WRITER). **2** (also **cramp-iron**) a metal bar with bent ends for holding masonry etc. together. **3** a portable tool for holding two planks etc. together; a clamp. **4** a restraint. —v.tr. **1** affect with cramp. **2** confine narrowly. **3** restrict (energies etc.). **4** (as **cramped** adj.) (of handwriting) small and difficult to read. **5** fasten with a cramp. □ **cramp a person's style** prevent a person from acting freely or naturally. **cramp up** confine narrowly. [ME f. OF crampe f. MDu., MLG krampe, OHG krampfo f. adj. meaning 'bent': cf. CRIMP]

crampon /ˈkræmpɒn/ n. (US **crampoon** /-ˈpuːn/) (usu. in pl.) **1** an iron plate with spikes fixed to a boot for walking on ice, climbing, etc. **2** a metal hook for lifting timber, rock, etc.; a grappling-iron. [ME f. F (as CRAMP)]

cran /kræn/ n. Sc. a measure for fresh herrings (37½ gallons). [= Gael. crann, of uncert. orig.]

Cranach /ˈkrænɒk/, Lucas, the Elder (1472–1553), German painter, who takes his name from the small town of Kronach in South Germany where he was born. He is noted for his portraits, which include several of Martin Luther, and for his religious pictures such as Rest on the Flight into Egypt, which shows the holy family resting in the glade of a German pine forest. His son, also called Lucas (1515–86), continued working in the same tradition.

cranage /ˈkreɪnɪdʒ/ n. **1** the use of a crane or cranes. **2** the money paid for this.

cranberry /ˈkrænbərɪ/ n. (pl. **-ies**) **1** any evergreen shrub of the genus Vaccinium, esp. V. macrocarpon of America and V. oxycoccos of Europe, yielding small red acid berries. **2** a berry from this used for a sauce and in cooking. Also called fen-berry. [17th c.: named by Amer. colonists f. G Kranbeere, LG kranebere crane-berry]

Crane /kreɪn/, Stephen (1871–1900), American writer. His first novel, Maggie: A Girl of the Streets (1893), was too grim to find a readership, but his next work The Red Badge of Courage (1895), a study of an inexperienced soldier and his reactions to the ordeal of battle in the American Civil War, was hailed as a masterpiece of psychological realism, though Crane himself had no personal experience of war. He came to England, where he developed a close friendship with Conrad, to whose work his own has been compared. His other writings include verse, short stories, and sketches.

crane /kreɪn/ n. & v. —n. **1** a machine for moving heavy objects, usu. by suspending them from a projecting arm or beam. **2** any tall wading bird of the family Gruidae, with long legs, long neck, and straight bill. **3** a moving platform supporting a television camera or cine-camera. —v.tr. **1** (also absol.) stretch out (one's neck) in order to see something. **2** tr. move (an object) by a crane. □ **crane-fly** (pl. **-flies**) any fly of the family Tipulidae, having two wings and long legs: also called daddy-long-legs. [OE cran, rel. to L grus, Gk geranos]

cranesbill /ˈkreɪnzbɪl/ n. any of various plants of the genus Geranium, having beaked fruits.

cranial /ˈkreɪnɪəl/ *adj.* of or relating to the skull. □ **cranial index** the ratio of the width and length of a skull. [CRANIUM + -AL]

craniate /ˈkreɪnɪət/ *adj. & n.* —*adj.* having a skull. —*n.* a craniate animal. [mod.L *craniatus* f. CRANIUM]

cranio- /ˈkreɪnɪəʊ/ *comb. form* cranium.

craniology /ˌkreɪnɪˈɒlədʒɪ/ *n.* the scientific study of the shape and size of the human skull. □□ **craniological** /ˌkreɪnɪəˈlɒdʒɪk(ə)l/ *adj.* **craniologist** *n.*

craniometry /ˌkreɪnɪˈɒmɪtrɪ/ *n.* the scientific measurement of skulls. □□ **craniometric** /-nɪəˈmetrɪk/ *adj.*

craniotomy /ˌkreɪnɪˈɒtəmɪ/ *n.* (*pl.* **-ies**) **1** surgical removal of a portion of the skull. **2** surgical perforation of the skull of a dead foetus to ease delivery.

cranium /ˈkreɪnɪəm/ *n.* (*pl.* **craniums** or **crania** /-nɪə/) **1** the skull. **2** the part of the skeleton that encloses the brain. [ME f. med.L f. Gk *kranion* skull]

crank[1] /kræŋk/ *n. & v.* —*n.* **1** part of an axle or shaft bent at right angles for interconverting reciprocal and circular motion. **2** an elbow-shaped connection in bell-hanging. —*v.tr.* **1** cause to move by means of a crank. **2 a** bend into a crank-shape. **b** furnish or fasten with a crank. □ **crank up 1** start (a car engine) by turning a crank. **2** *sl.* increase (speed etc.) by intensive effort. [OE *cranc*, app. f. *crincan*, rel. to *cringan* fall in battle, orig. 'curl up']

crank[2] /kræŋk/ *n.* **1 a** an eccentric person, esp. one obsessed by a particular theory (*health-food crank*). **b** *US* a bad-tempered person. **2** *literary* a fanciful turn of speech (*quips and cranks*). [back-form. f. CRANKY]

crank[3] /kræŋk/ *adj. Naut.* liable to capsize. [perh. f. *crank* weak, shaky, or CRANK[1]]

crankcase /ˈkræŋkkeɪs/ *n.* a case enclosing a crankshaft.

crankpin /ˈkræŋkpɪn/ *n.* a pin by which a connecting-rod is attached to a crank.

crankshaft /ˈkræŋkʃɑːft/ *n.* a shaft driven by a crank (see CRANK[1] *n.* 1).

cranky /ˈkræŋkɪ/ *adj.* (**crankier, crankiest**) **1** *colloq.* eccentric, esp. obsessed with a particular theory (*cranky ideas about women*). **2** working badly; shaky. **3** esp. *US* ill-tempered or crotchety. □□ **crankily** *adv.* **crankiness** *n.* [perh. f. obs. *crank* rogue feigning sickness]

Cranmer /ˈkrænmə(r)/, Thomas (1489–1556), Anglican cleric and martyr. He was appointed Archbishop of Canterbury in 1532 after his support for Henry VIII in the annulment of the king's marriage with Catherine of Aragon. Protestant in outlook, he was largely responsible for English liturgical reform, particularly under Edward VI, and for the compilation of the Book of Common Prayer. After the accession of Mary Tudor, Cranmer was tried for high treason, then for heresy, and finally burnt at the stake in Oxford.

crannog /ˈkrænəɡ/ *n.* an ancient lake-dwelling in Scotland or Ireland. [Ir. f. *crann* tree, beam]

cranny /ˈkrænɪ/ *n.* (*pl.* **-ies**) a chink, a crevice, a crack. □□ **crannied** /-ɪd/ *adj.* [ME f. OF *crané* past part. of *craner* f. *cran* f. pop.L *crena* notch]

crap[1] /kræp/ *n. & v. coarse sl.* —*n.* **1** (often as *int.*) nonsense, rubbish (*he talks crap*). **2** faeces. —*v.intr.* (**crapped, crapping**) defecate. ¶ Usually considered a taboo word. □ **crap out** *US* **1** be unsuccessful. **2** withdraw from a game etc. [earlier senses 'chaff, refuse from fat-boiling': ME f. Du. *krappe*]

crap[2] /kræp/ *n. US* a losing throw of 2, 3, or 12 in craps. □ **crap game** a game of craps. [formed as CRAPS]

crape /kreɪp/ *n.* **1** crêpe, usu. of black silk or imitation silk, formerly used for mourning clothes. **2** a band of this formerly worn round a person's hat etc. as a sign of mourning. □ **crape fern** a NZ fern, *Leptopteris superba*, with tall dark-green fronds. **crape hair** artificial hair used in stage make-up. □□ **crapy** *adj.* [earlier *crispe, crespe* f. F *crespe* CRÊPE]

crappy /ˈkræpɪ/ *adj.* (**crappier, crappiest**) *coarse sl.* **1** rubbishy, cheap. **2** disgusting.

craps /kræps/ *n.pl. US* a gambling game played with dice. □

shoot craps play craps. [19th c.: perh. f. *crab* lowest throw at dice]

crapulent /ˈkræpjʊlənt/ *adj.* **1** given to indulging in alcohol. **2** resulting from drunkenness. **3 a** drunk. **b** suffering from the effects of drunkenness. □□ **crapulence** *n.* **crapulous** *adj.* [LL *crapulentus* very drunk f. L *crapula* inebriation f. Gk *kraipalē* drunken headache]

craquelure /ˈkrækəˌljʊə(r)/ *n.* a network of fine cracks in a painting or its varnish. [F]

crash[1] /kræʃ/ *v., n., & adv.* —*v.* **1** *intr. & tr.* make or cause to make a loud smashing noise (*the cymbals crashed; crashed the plates together*). **2** *tr. & intr.* throw, drive, move, or fall with a loud smashing noise. **3** *intr. & tr.* **a** collide or cause (a vehicle) to collide violently with another vehicle, obstacle, etc.; overturn at high speed. **b** fall or cause (an aircraft) to fall violently on to the land or the sea (*crashed the plane; the airman crashed into the sea*). **4** *intr.* (usu. foll. by *into*) collide violently (*crashed into the window*). **5** *intr.* undergo financial ruin. **6** *tr. colloq.* enter without permission (*crashed the cocktail party*). **7** *intr. colloq.* be heavily defeated (*crashed to a 4–0 defeat*). **8** *intr. Computing* (of a machine or system) fail suddenly. **9** *tr. colloq.* pass (a red traffic-light etc.). **10** *intr.* (often foll. by *out*) *sl.* sleep for a night, esp. in an improvised setting. —*n.* **1 a** a loud and sudden smashing noise (*a thunder crash; the crash of crockery*). **b** a breakage (esp. of crockery, glass, etc.). **2 a** a violent collision, esp. of one vehicle with another or with an object. **b** the violent fall of an aircraft on to the land or sea. **3** ruin, esp. financial. **4** *Computing* a sudden failure which puts a system out of action. **5** (*attrib.*) done rapidly or urgently (*a crash course in first aid*). —*adv.* with a crash (*the window went crash*). □ **crash barrier** a barrier intended to prevent a car from leaving the road etc. **crash-dive** —*v.* **1** *intr.* **a** (of a submarine or its pilot) dive hastily and steeply in an emergency. **b** (of an aircraft or airman) dive and crash. **2** *tr.* cause to crash-dive. —*n.* such a dive. **crash-halt** a sudden stop by a vehicle. **crash-helmet** a helmet worn esp. by a motorcyclist to protect the head in a crash. **crash-land 1** *intr.* (of an aircraft or airman) land hurriedly with a crash, usu. without lowering the undercarriage. **2** *tr.* cause (an aircraft) to crash-land. **crash landing** a hurried landing with a crash. **crash pad** *sl.* a place to sleep, esp. in an emergency. **crash-stop** = *crash-halt*. **crash-tackle** *Football* a vigorous tackle. [ME: imit.]

crash[2] /kræʃ/ *n.* a coarse plain linen, cotton, etc., fabric. [Russ. *krashenina* coloured linen]

crashing /ˈkræʃɪŋ/ *adj. colloq.* overwhelming (*a crashing bore*).

crasis /ˈkreɪsɪs/ *n.* (*pl.* **crases** /-siːz/) the contraction of two adjacent vowels in ancient Greek into one long vowel or diphthong. [Gk *krasis* mixture]

crass /kræs/ *adj.* **1** grossly stupid (*a crass idea*). **2** gross (*crass stupidity*). **3** *literary* thick or gross. □□ **crassitude** *n.* **crassly** *adv.* **crassness** *n.* [L *crassus* solid, thick]

Crassus /ˈkræsəs/, Marcus Licinius (d. 53 BC), Roman politician, nicknamed 'Dives' for his riches. He defeated Spartacus in 71 BC, though Pompey claimed the credit for the victory. Having failed to achieve the supreme position which he sought, Crassus joined Caesar and Pompey in the First Triumvirate (60 BC). In 55 BC he was made consul and given a special command in Syria, where he hoped to regain a millitary reputation equal to that of his allies by a victory over the Parthians, but after some successes he was defeated and killed.

-crat /kræt/ *comb. form* a member or supporter of a particular form of government or rule (*autocrat; democrat*). [from or after F *-crate*: see -CRACY]

cratch /krætʃ/ *n.* a rack used for holding food for farm animals out of doors. [ME f. OF *creche* f. Gmc: rel. to CRIB]

crate /kreɪt/ *n. & v.* —*n.* **1** a large wickerwork basket or slatted wooden case etc. for packing esp. fragile goods for transportation. **2** *sl.* an old aeroplane or other vehicle. —*v.tr.* pack in a crate. □□ **crateful** *n.* (*pl.* **-fuls**). [ME, perh. f. Du. *krat* basket etc.]

crater /ˈkreɪtə(r)/ *n. & v.* —*n.* **1** the mouth of a volcano. **2** a bowl-shaped cavity, esp. that made by the explosion of a shell or bomb. **3** *Astron.* a hollow with a raised rim on the surface of a planet or moon, caused by the impact of a meteorite. **4** *Antiq.* a large ancient Greek bowl, used for mixing wine. —*v.tr.* form a crater in. □□ **craterous** *adj.* [L f. Gk *kratēr* mixing-bowl: see CRASIS]

-cratic /ˈkrætɪk/ *comb. form* (also **-cratical**) denoting a particular kind of government or rule (*autocratic; democratic*). □□ **-cratically** *comb. form* (*adv.*) [from or after F *-cratique*: see -CRACY]

cravat /krəˈvæt/ *n.* **1** a scarf worn by men inside an open-necked shirt. **2** *hist.* a necktie. □□ **cravatted** *adj.* [F *cravate* f. G *Krawat, Kroat* f. Serbo-Croatian *Hrvat* Croat]

crave /kreɪv/ *v.* **1** *tr.* **a** long for (*craved affection*). **b** beg for (*craves a blessing*). **2** *intr.* (foll. by *for*) long for; beg for (*craved for comfort*). □□ **craver** *n.* [OE *crafian*, rel. to ON *krefja*]

craven /ˈkreɪv(ə)n/ *adj.* & *n.* —*adj.* (of a person, behaviour, etc.) cowardly; abject. —*n.* a cowardly person. □□ **cravenly** *adv.* **cravenness** *n.* [ME *cravand* etc. perh. f. OF *cravanté* defeated, past part. of *cravanter* ult. f. L *crepare* burst; assim. to -EN³]

craving /ˈkreɪvɪŋ/ *n.* (usu. foll. by *for*) a strong desire or longing.

craw /krɔː/ *n. Zool.* the crop of a bird or insect. □ **stick in one's craw** be unacceptable. [ME, rel. to MDu. *crāghe*, MLG *krage*, MHG *krage* neck, throat]

crawfish /ˈkrɔːfɪʃ/ *n.* & *v.* —*n.* (*pl.* same) a large marine spiny lobster. —*v.intr. US* retreat; back out. [var. of CRAYFISH]

Crawford /ˈkrɔːfəd/, Osbert Guy Stanhope (1886–1957), British archaeologist, a pioneer in the use of aerial photography for the detection of previously unlocated or buried archaeological sites and monuments.

crawl /krɔːl/ *v.* & *n.* —*v.intr.* **1** move slowly, esp. on hands and knees. **2** (of an insect, snake, etc.) move slowly with the body close to the ground etc. **3** walk or move slowly (*the train crawled into the station*). **4** (often foll. by *to*) *colloq.* behave obsequiously or ingratiatingly in the hope of advantage. **5** (often foll. by *with*) be covered or filled with crawling or moving things, or with people etc. compared to this. **6** (esp. of the skin) feel a creepy sensation. **7** swim with a crawl stroke. —*n.* **1** an act of crawling. **2** a slow rate of movement. **3** a high-speed swimming stroke with alternate overarm movements and rapid straight-legged kicks. **4** (usu. in *comb.*) *colloq.* a leisurely journey between places of interest (*church-crawl*). **b** = pub-crawl. □□ **crawlingly** *adv.* **crawly** *adj.* (in senses 5, 6 of *v.*). [ME: orig. unkn.: cf. Sw. *kravla*, Da. *kravle*]

crawler /ˈkrɔːlə(r)/ *n.* **1** *sl.* a person who behaves obsequiously in the hope of advantage. **2** anything that crawls, esp. an insect. **3** a tractor moving on an endless chain. **4** (usu. in *pl.*) esp. *US* a baby's overall for crawling in; rompers.

cray /kreɪ/ *n. Austral. & NZ* = CRAYFISH.

crayfish /ˈkreɪfɪʃ/ *n.* (*pl.* same) **1** a small lobster-like freshwater crustacean. **2** a crawfish. [ME f. OF *crevice, crevis*, ult. f. OHG *krebiz* CRAB¹: assim. to FISH¹]

crayon /ˈkreɪən, -ɒn/ *n.* & *v.* —*n.* **1** a stick or pencil of coloured chalk, wax, etc. used for drawing. **2** a drawing made with this. —*v.tr.* draw with crayons. [F f. *craie* f. L *creta* chalk]

craze /kreɪz/ *v.* & *n.* —*v.* **1** *tr.* (usu. as **crazed** *adj.*) make insane (*crazed with grief*). **2** **a** *tr.* produce fine surface cracks on (pottery glaze etc.). **b** *intr.* develop such cracks. —*n.* **1** **a** a usu. temporary enthusiasm (*a craze for hula hoops*). **b** the object of this. **2** an insane fancy or condition. [ME, orig. = break, shatter, perh. f. ON]

crazy /ˈkreɪzɪ/ *adj.* (**crazier, craziest**) **1** *colloq.* (of a person, an action, etc.) insane or mad; foolish. **2** *colloq.* (usu. foll. by *about*) extremely enthusiastic. **3** *sl.* **a** exciting, unrestrained. **b** excellent. **4** (*attrib.*) (of paving, a quilt, etc.) made of irregular pieces fitted together. **5** *archaic* (of a ship, building, etc.) unsound, shaky. □ **crazy bone** *US* the funny bone. **like crazy** *colloq.* = *like mad* (see MAD). □□ **crazily** *adv.* **craziness** *n.*

creak /kriːk/ *n.* & *v.* —*n.* a harsh scraping or squeaking sound. —*v.intr.* **1** make a creak. **2** **a** move with a creaking noise. **b** move stiffly and awkwardly. **c** show weakness or frailty under strain. □□ **creakingly** *adv.* [ME, imit.: cf. CRAKE, CROAK]

creaky /ˈkriːkɪ/ *adj.* (**creakier, creakiest**) **1** liable to creak. **2** **a** stiff or frail (*creaky joints*). **b** (of a practice, institution, etc.)

decrepit, dilapidated, outmoded. □□ **creakily** *adv.* **creakiness** *n.*

cream /kriːm/ *n., v., & adj.* —*n.* **1** **a** the fatty content of milk which gathers at the top and can be made into butter by churning. **b** this eaten (often whipped) with a dessert, as a cake-filling, etc. (*strawberries and cream; cream gateau*). **2** the part of a liquid that gathers at the top. **3** (usu. prec. by *the*) the best or choicest part of something, esp.: **a** the point of an anecdote. **b** an élite group of people (*the cream of the nation*). **4** a creamlike preparation, esp. a cosmetic (*hand cream*). **5** a very pale yellow or off-white colour. **6** **a** a dish or sweet like or made with cream. **b** a soup or sauce containing milk or cream. **c** a full-bodied mellow sweet sherry. **d** a biscuit with a creamy sandwich filling. **e** a chocolate-covered usu. fruit-flavoured fondant. —*v.* **1** *tr.* **a** take the cream from (milk). **b** take the best or a specified part from. **2** *tr.* work (butter etc.) to a creamy consistency. **3** *tr.* treat (the skin etc.) with cosmetic cream. **4** *tr.* add cream to (coffee etc.). **5** *intr.* (of milk or any other liquid) form a cream or scum. **6** *tr. US colloq.* defeat (esp. in a sporting contest). —*adj.* pale yellow; off-white. □ **cream bun** (or **cake**) a bun or cake filled or topped with cream. **cream cheese** a soft rich cheese made from unskimmed milk and cream. **cream-coloured** pale yellowish white. **cream cracker** *Brit.* a crisp dry unsweetened biscuit usu. eaten with cheese. **cream-laid** (or **-wove**) laid (or wove) cream-coloured paper. **cream off 1** take (the best or a specified part) from a whole (*creamed off the brightest pupils*). **2** = sense 1b of *v.* **cream of tartar** purified and crystallized potassium hydrogen tartrate, used in medicine, baking powder, etc. **cream puff 1** a cake made of puff pastry filled with cream. **2** an ineffectual or effeminate person. **cream soda** a carbonated vanilla-flavoured soft drink. **cream tea** afternoon tea with scones, jam, and cream. [ME f. OF *cre(s)me* f. LL *cramum* (perh. f. Gaulish) & eccl.L *chrisma* CHRISM]

creamer /ˈkriːmə(r)/ *n.* **1** a flat dish used for skimming the cream off milk. **2** a machine used for separating cream from milk. **3** *US* a jug for cream. **4** an additive serving as a substitute for milk or cream in tea or coffee.

creamery /ˈkriːmərɪ/ *n.* (*pl.* **-ies**) **1** a factory producing butter and cheese. **2** a shop where milk, cream, etc., are sold; a dairy. [CREAM, after F *crémerie*]

creamy /ˈkriːmɪ/ *adj.* (**creamier, creamiest**) **1** like cream in consistency or colour. **2** rich in cream. □□ **creamily** *adv.* **creaminess** *n.*

crease¹ /kriːs/ *n.* & *v.* —*n.* **1** **a** a line in paper etc. caused by folding. **b** a fold or wrinkle. **2** *Cricket* a line marking the position of the bowler or batsman (see POPPING-CREASE, *bowling-crease*). **3** an area near the goal in ice hockey or lacrosse into which the puck or the ball must precede the players. —*v.* **1** *tr.* make creases in (material). **2** *intr.* become creased (*linen creases badly*). **3** *tr. & intr. sl.* (often foll. by *up*) make or become incapable through laughter. **4** *tr.* esp. *US sl.* **a** tire out. **b** stun or kill. [earlier *creast* = CREST ridge in material]

crease² var. of KRIS.

create /kriːˈeɪt/ *v.* **1** *tr.* **a** (of natural or historical forces) bring into existence; cause (*poverty creates resentment*). **b** (of a person or persons) make or cause (*create a diversion; create a good impression*). **2** *tr.* originate (*an actor creates a part*). **3** *tr.* invest (a person) with a rank (*created him a lord*). **4** *intr. sl. Brit.* make a fuss; grumble. □□ **creatable** *adj.* [ME f. L *creare*]

creatine /ˈkriːətiːn/ *n.* a product of protein metabolism found in the muscles of vertebrates. [Gk *kreas* meat + -INE⁴]

creation /kriːˈeɪʃ(ə)n/ *n.* **1** **a** the act of creating. **b** an instance of this. **2** **a** (usu. **the Creation**) the creating of the universe regarded as an act of God. **b** (usu. **Creation**) everything so created; the universe. **3** a product of human intelligence, esp. of imaginative thought or artistic ability. **4** **a** the act of investing with a title or rank. **b** an instance of this. [ME f. OF f. L *creatio -onis* (as CREATE)]

creationism /kriːˈeɪʃənɪz(ə)m/ *n. Theol.* a theory attributing all matter, biological species, etc., to separate acts of creation, rather than to evolution. □□ **creationist** *n.*

creative /kriːˈeɪtɪv/ *adj.* **1** inventive and imaginative. **2** creating or able to create. □□ **creatively** adv. **creativeness** n. **creativity** /-ˈtɪvɪtɪ/ n.

creator /kriːˈeɪtə(r)/ n. **1** a person who creates. **2** (as **the Creator**) God. [ME f. OF creat(o)ur f. L creator -oris (as CREATE)]

creature /ˈkriːtʃə(r)/ n. **1 a** an animal, as distinct from a human being. **b** any living being (we are all God's creatures). **2** a person of a specified kind (poor creature). **3** a person owing status to and obsequiously subservient to another. **4** anything created; a creation. □ **creature comforts** material comforts such as good food, warmth, etc. **creature of habit** a person set in an unvarying routine. □□ **creaturely** adj. [ME f. OF f. LL creatura (as CREATE)]

crèche /kreʃ, kreɪʃ/ n. **1** a day nursery for babies and young children. **2** US a representation of a Nativity scene. [F (as CRATCH)]

Crécy /ˈkresɪ/ a village in Picardy in northern France, scene of the first great English victory (1346) of the Hundred Years War. The invading English army of Edward III was attacked in a strong defensive position by a much larger French force. English longbowmen, however, wrought havoc in the ranks of the attacking French knights, whose disorganized charges made little impact on the English position. After repeated assaults lasting almost until nightfall, the French army retreated in confusion, leaving thousands of dead on the field, including a large portion of the nobility.

credal see CREED.

credence /ˈkriːd(ə)ns/ n. **1** belief. **2** (in full **credence table**) a small side-table, shelf, or niche which holds the elements of the Eucharist before they are consecrated. □ **give credence to** believe. **letter of credence** a letter of introduction, esp. of an ambassador. [ME f. OF f. med.L credentia f. credere believe]

credential /krɪˈdenʃ(ə)l/ n. (usu. in pl.) **1** evidence of a person's achievements or trustworthiness, usu. in the form of certificates, references, etc. **2** a letter or letters of introduction. [med.L credentialis (as CREDENCE)]

credenza /krɪˈdenzə/ n. a sideboard or cupboard. [It. f. med.L (as CREDENCE)]

credibility /ˌkredɪˈbɪlɪtɪ/ n. **1** the condition of being credible or believable. **2** reputation, status. □ **credibility gap** an apparent difference between what is said and what is true.

credible /ˈkredɪb(ə)l/ adj. **1** (of a person or statement) believable or worthy of belief. **2** (of a threat etc.) convincing. □□ **credibly** adv. [ME f. L credibilis f. credere believe]

credit /ˈkredɪt/ n. & v. —n. **1** (usu. of a person) a source of honour, pride, etc. (is a credit to the school). **2** the acknowledgement of merit (must give him credit for consistency). **3** a good reputation (his credit stands high). **4 a** belief or trust (I place credit in that). **b** something believable or trustworthy (that statement has credit). **5 a** a person's financial standing; the sum of money at a person's disposal in a bank etc. **b** the power to obtain goods etc. before payment (based on the trust that payment will be made). **6** (usu. in pl.) an acknowledgement of a contributor's services to a film, television programme, etc. **7** a grade above a pass in an examination. **8** a reputation for solvency and honesty in business. **9 a** (in bookkeeping) the acknowledgement of being paid by an entry on the credit side of an account. **b** the sum entered. **c** the credit side of an account. **10** US a certificate indicating that a student has completed a course. —v.tr. (**credited, crediting**) **1** believe (cannot credit it). **2** (usu. foll. by to, with) enter on the credit side of an account (credited £20 to him; credited him with £20). □ **credit account** Brit. an account with a shop etc. for obtaining goods or services before payment. **credit card** a card from a bank etc. authorizing the obtaining of goods on credit. **credit note** a note given by a shop etc. in return for goods returned, stating the value of goods owed to the customer. **credit rating** an estimate of a person's suitability to receive commercial credit. **credit sale** the sale of goods on credit. **credit title** a person's name appearing at the beginning or end of a film or broadcast etc. as an acknowledgement. **credit transfer** a transfer from one person's bank account to another's. **credit a person with** ascribe (a good quality) to a person. **do credit to** (or **do a person credit**) enhance the reputation of. **get credit for** be given credit for. **give a person credit for 1** enter (a sum) to a person's credit. **2** ascribe (a good quality) to a person. **give credit to** believe. **letter of credit** a letter from a banker authorizing a person to draw money up to a specified amount, usu. from another bank. **on credit** with an arrangement to pay later. **to one's credit** in one's praise, commendation, or defence (to his credit, he refused the offer). [F crédit f. It. credito or L creditum f. credere credit- believe, trust]

creditable /ˈkredɪtəb(ə)l/ adj. (often foll. by to) bringing credit or honour. □□ **creditability** /-ˈbɪlɪtɪ/ n. **creditably** adv.

creditor /ˈkredɪtə(r)/ n. **1** a person to whom a debt is owing. **2** a person or company that gives credit for money or goods (cf. DEBTOR). [ME f. AF creditour (OF -eur) f. L creditor -oris (as CREDIT)]

creditworthy /ˈkredɪtˌwɜːðɪ/ adj. considered suitable to receive commercial credit. □□ **creditworthiness** n.

credo /ˈkreɪdəʊ, ˈkriː-/ n. (pl. **-os**) **1** (**Credo**) a statement of belief; a creed, esp. the Apostles' or Nicene creed beginning in Latin with credo. **2** a musical setting of the Nicene Creed. [ME f. L, = I believe]

credulous /ˈkredjʊləs/ adj. **1** too ready to believe; gullible. **2** (of behaviour) showing such gullibility. □□ **credulity** /krɪˈdjuːlɪtɪ/ n. **credulously** adv. **credulousness** n. [L credulus f. credere believe]

Cree /kriː/ n. & adj. —n. (pl. same or **Crees**) **1 a** an American Indian people of Central America. **b** a member of this people. **2** the Algonquian language of this people. —adj. of or relating to the Crees or their language. [Canadian F Cris (earlier Cristinaux) f. Algonquian]

creed /kriːd/ n. **1** a set of principles or opinions, esp. as a philosophy of life (his creed is moderation in everything). **2 a** (often **the Creed**) = Apostles' Creed (see APOSTLE). **b** a brief formal summary of Christian doctrine (cf. NICENE CREED, Athanasian Creed). **c** the Creed as part of the Mass. □□ **credal** /ˈkriːd(ə)l/ adj. **creedal** adj. [OE crēda f. L CREDO]

Creek /kriːk/ n. & adj. —n. **1 a** an American Indian tribe now settled in Oklahoma. **b** a member of this tribe. **2** their Muskogean language. **3** a confederacy of several tribes and languages of which the Creek proper were the most numerous. —adj. of this people or their language. [CREEK]

creek /kriːk/ n. **1** Brit. **a** a small bay or harbour on a sea-coast. **b** a narrow inlet on a sea-coast or in a river-bank. **2** esp. US a tributary of a river; a stream. **3** Austral. & NZ a stream or brook. □ **up the creek** sl. **1** in difficulties or trouble. **2** crazy. [ME crike f. ON kriki nook (or partly f. OF crique f. ON), & ME crēke f. MDu. krēke (or f. crike by lengthening): ult. orig. unkn.]

creel /kriːl/ n. **1** a large wicker basket for fish. **2** an angler's fishing-basket. [ME, orig. Sc.: ult. orig. unkn.]

creep /kriːp/ v. & n. —v.intr. (past and past part. **crept** /krept/) **1** move with the body prone and close to the ground; crawl. **2** (often foll. by in, out, up, etc.) come, go, or move slowly and stealthily or timidly (crept out without being seen). **3** enter slowly (into a person's affections, life, awareness, etc.) (a feeling crept over her; crept into her heart). **4** colloq. act abjectly or obsequiously in the hope of advancement. **5** (of a plant) grow along the ground or up a wall by means of tendrils etc. **6** (as **creeping** adj.) developing slowly and steadily (creeping inflation). **7** (of the flesh) feel as if insects etc. were creeping over it, as a result of fear, horror, etc. **8** (of metals etc.) undergo creep. —n. **1 a** the act of creeping. **b** an instance of this. **2** (in pl.; prec. by the) colloq. a nervous feeling of revulsion or fear (gives me the creeps). **3** sl. an unpleasant person. **4** the gradual downward movement of disintegrated rock due to gravitational forces etc. **5** (of metals etc.) a gradual change of shape under stress. **6** a low arch under a railway embankment, road, etc. □ **creeping barrage** a barrage moving ahead of advancing troops. **creeping Jenny** any of various creeping plants, esp. moneywort. **creeping Jesus** sl. an abject or hypocritical person. **creep up on** approach (a person) stealthily or unnoticed. [OE crēopan f. Gmc]

creeper /ˈkriːpə(r)/ n. **1** Bot. any climbing or creeping plant. **2** any bird that climbs, esp. a treecreeper. **3** sl. a soft-soled shoe.

creepy /ˈkriːpɪ/ adj. (**creepier, creepiest**) **1** colloq. having or producing a creeping of the flesh (*I feel creepy; a creepy film*). **2** given to creeping. □□ **creepily** *adv.* **creepiness** *n.* [CREEP]

creepy-crawly /ˌkriːpɪˈkrɔːlɪ/ *n.* & *adj. Brit. colloq.* —*n.* (*pl.* -**ies**) an insect, worm, etc. —*adj.* creeping and crawling.

creese var. OF KRIS.

cremate /krɪˈmeɪt/ *v.tr.* consume (a corpse etc.) by fire. (See below.) □□ **cremation** /-ˈmeɪʃ(ə)n/ *n.* **cremator** *n.* [L *cremare* burn]

The practice of cremation was not common in primitive times, but in the ancient civilized world it was the normal custom except in Egypt, Judaea, and China. Belief in the resurrection of the body made the practice repugnant to the early Christians, and by the 5th c. Christian influence had caused it to be abandoned throughout the Roman Empire. It was revived in the West in the 19th c.; in the East it has remained the most general method of disposal of the dead.

crematorium /ˌkreməˈtɔːrɪəm/ *n.* (*pl.* **crematoria** or **crematoriums**) a place for cremating corpses in a furnace. [mod.L (as CREMATE, -ORY)]

crematory /ˈkremətərɪ/ *adj.* & *n.* —*adj.* of or relating to cremation. —*n.* (*pl.* -**ies**) *US* = CREMATORIUM.

crème /krem/ *n.* **1** = CREAM *n.* 6a. **2 a** a name for various creamy liqueurs (*crème de cassis*). □ **crème brûlée** /bruːˈleɪ/ a pudding of cream or custard topped with caramelized sugar. **crème caramel** a custard coated with caramel. **crème de la crème** /ˌkrem də lɑː ˈkrem/ the best part; the élite. **crème de menthe** /də ˈmɑːt, ˈmɒnt/ a peppermint-flavoured liqueur. [F, = cream]

crenate /ˈkriːneɪt/ *adj. Bot.* & *Zool.* having a notched edge or rounded teeth. □□ **crenated** *adj.* **crenation** /-ˈneɪʃ(ə)n/ *n.* **crenature** /ˈkrenətjʊə(r), ˈkriː-/ *n.* [mod.L *crenatus* f. pop.L *crena* notch]

crenel /ˈkren(ə)l/ *n.* (also **crenelle** /krɪˈnel/) an indentation or gap in the parapet of a tower, castle, etc., orig. for shooting through etc. [ME f. OF *crenel*, ult. f. pop.L *crena* notch]

crenellate /ˈkrenəˌleɪt/ *v.tr.* provide (a tower etc.) with battlements or loopholes. □□ **crenellation** /-ˈleɪʃ(ə)n/ *n.* [F *créneler* (as CRENEL)]

Creole /ˈkriːəʊl/ *n.* & *adj.* —*n.* **1 a** a descendant of European (esp. Spanish) settlers in the W. Indies or Central or S. America. **b** a White descendant of French settlers in the southern US. **c** a person of mixed European and Black descent. **2** a language formed from the contact of a European language (esp. English, French, or Portuguese) with another (esp. African) language. —*adj.* **1** of or relating to a Creole or Creoles. **2** (usu. **creole**) of Creole origin or production (*creole cooking*). [F *créole*, *criole* f. Sp. *criollo*, prob. f. Port. *crioulo* home-born slave f. *criar* breed f. L *creare* CREATE]

creolize /ˈkriːəˌlaɪz/ *v.tr.* (also -**ise**) form a Creole from (another language). □□ **creolization** /-ˈzeɪʃ(ə)n/ *n.*

creosote /ˈkriːəˌsəʊt/ *n.* & *v.* —*n.* **1** (in full **creosote oil**) a dark-brown oil distilled from coal tar, used as a wood-preservative. **2** a colourless oily fluid distilled from wood tar, used as an antiseptic. —*v.tr.* treat with creosote. [G *Kreosote* f. Gk *kreas* flesh + *sōtēr* preserver, with ref. to its antiseptic properties]

crêpe /kreɪp/ *n.* **1** a fine often gauzelike fabric with a wrinkled surface. **2** a thin pancake, usu. with a savoury or sweet filling. **3** (also **crêpe rubber**) a very hard-wearing wrinkled sheet rubber used for the soles of shoes etc. □ **crêpe de Chine** /də ˈʃiːn/ a fine silk crêpe. **crêpe paper** thin crinkled paper. **crêpe Suzette** /suːˈzet/ a small dessert pancake flamed in alcohol at the table. □□ **crêpey** *adj.* **crêpy** *adj.* [F f. OF *crespe* curled f. L *crispus*]

crepitate /ˈkrepɪˌteɪt/ *v.intr.* **1** make a crackling sound. **2** *Zool.* (of a beetle) eject pungent fluid with a sharp report. □□ **crepitant** *adj.* [L *crepitare* frequent. of *crepare* creak]

crepitation /ˌkrepɪˈteɪʃ(ə)n/ *n.* **1** *Med.* = CREPITUS. **2** the action or sound of crackling or rattling.

crepitus /ˈkrepɪtəs/ *n.* *Med.* **1** a grating noise from the ends of a fractured bone rubbing together. **2** a similar sound heard from the chest in pneumonia etc. [L f. *crepare* rattle]

crept past and past part. OF CREEP.

crepuscular /krɪˈpʌskjʊlə(r)/ *adj.* **1 a** of twilight. **b** dim. **2** *Zool.* appearing or active in twilight. [L *crepusculum* twilight]

Cres. *abbr.* Crescent.

cresc. *abbr.* (also **cres.**) *Mus.* = CRESCENDO.

crescendo /krɪˈʃendəʊ/ *n.*, *adv.*, *adj.*, & *v.* —*n.* (*pl.* -**os**) **1** *Mus.* a passage gradually increasing in loudness. **2 a** progress towards a climax (*a crescendo of emotions*). **b** *disp.* a climax (*reached a crescendo then died away*). —*adv.* & *adj.* with a gradual increase in loudness. —*v.intr.* (-**oes**, -**oed**) increase gradually in loudness or intensity. [It., part. of *crescere* grow (as CRESCENT)]

crescent /ˈkrez(ə)nt, ˈkres-/ *n.* & *adj.* —*n.* **1** the curved sickle shape of the waxing or waning moon. **2** anything of this shape, esp. *Brit.* a street forming an arc. **3 a** the crescent-shaped emblem of Islam or Turkey. (See below.) **b** (**the Crescent**) the world or power of Islam. —*adj.* **1** *poet.* increasing. **2** crescent-shaped. □□ **crescentic** /-ˈsentɪk/ *adj.* [ME f. AF *cressaunt*, OF *creissant*, f. L *crescere* grow]

As an emblem of Turkey or Islam the crescent has an ambiguous history. In the non-Islamic Western world it was regarded as the quintessential emblem of 'the Muslim Orient' from the mid-15th c. Early uses of the symbol do not suggest a specific religious significance (although the new moon itself is of great importance in Islam, for its appearance defines the first and last days of Ramadan and the start of the annual pilgrimage). It was first adopted officially by Sultan Selim III for use on the flag of his newly organized army and navy, but was given up when he was deposed in 1807. It was re-instituted in 1827, and subsequently became the central motif of many national flags (e.g. Turkey, Tunisia, Egypt until 1958, Pakistan, Malaysia, Mauritania, Algeria).

cresol /ˈkriːsɒl/ *n.* any of three isomeric phenols present in creosote and used as disinfectants. □□ **cresyl** /ˈkriːsɪl/ *adj.* [CREOSOTE + -OL²]

cress /kres/ *n.* any of various cruciferous plants usu. with pungent edible leaves, e.g. watercress. [OE *cresse* f. WG]

cresset /ˈkresɪt/ *n.* *hist.* a metal container for oil, coal, etc., lighted and usu. mounted on a pole for illumination. [ME f. OF *cresset*, *craisset*, f. *craisse* = *graisse* GREASE]

Cressida /ˈkresɪdə/ (in medieval legends of the Trojan War) the daughter of Calchas, a priest. She was faithless to her lover Troilus, a son of Priam.

crest /krest/ *n.* & *v.* —*n.* **1 a** a comb or tuft of feathers, fur, etc. on a bird's or animal's head. **b** something resembling this, esp. a plume of feathers on a helmet. **c** a helmet; the top of a helmet. **2** the top of something, esp. of a mountain, wave, roof, etc. **3** *Heraldry* **a** a device above the shield and helmet of a coat of arms. **b** such a device reproduced on writing paper or on a seal, signifying a family. **4 a** a line along the top of the neck of some animals. **b** the hair growing from this; a mane. **5** *Anat.* a ridge along the surface of a bone. —*v.* **1** *tr.* reach the crest of (a hill, wave, etc.). **2** *tr.* **a** provide with a crest. **b** serve as a crest to. **3** *intr.* (of a wave) form into a crest. □ **on the crest of a wave** at the most favourable moment in one's progress. □□ **crested** *adj.* (also in *comb.*). **crestless** *adj.* [ME f. OF *creste* f. L *crista* tuft]

Cresta run /ˈkrestə/ a hazardously winding steeply banked channel of ice built each year as a tobogganing course at St Moritz, Switzerland, by the St Moritz Tobogganing Club, who draw up rules for racing on it. A run down the Cresta valley was first built in 1884.

crestfallen /ˈkrestˌfɔːlən/ *adj.* **1** dejected, dispirited. **2** with a fallen or drooping crest.

cretaceous /krɪˈteɪʃəs/ *adj.* & *n.* —*adj.* **1** of the nature of chalk. **2** (**Cretaceous**) *Geol.* of or relating to the last period of the Mesozoic era, following the Jurassic and preceding the Tertiary, lasting from about 144 to 65 million years ago, during which time the climate was warm and the sea level rose. It is characterized especially in NW Europe by the deposition of chalk (whence its name). This period saw the emergence of the first flowering plants and the continued dominance of dinosaurs, although they died out before the end of it. —*n.* *Geol.* this era or system. [L *cretaceus* f. *creta* chalk]

Crete /ˈkriːt/ (Greek **Kríti** /ˈkriːtɪ/) an island in the eastern Mediterranean, noted for remains of the Minoan civilization; pop. (1981) 502,100. It fell to Rome in 67 BC and was subsequently ruled by Byzantines, Venetians, and Turks; it has been under Greek rule since 1913. □□ **Cretan** adj. & n.

cretic /ˈkriːtɪk/ n. Prosody a foot containing one short or unstressed syllable between two long or stressed ones. [L Creticus f. Gk Krētikos (as CRETAN)]

cretin /ˈkretɪn/ n. **1** a person who is deformed and mentally retarded as the result of a thyroid deficiency. **2** colloq. a stupid person. □□ **cretinism** n. **cretinize** v.tr. (also -ise). **cretinous** adj. [F crétin f. Swiss F. creitin, crestin f. L Christianus CHRISTIAN]

cretonne /kreˈtɒn, ˈkre-/ n. (often attrib.) a heavy cotton fabric with a usu. floral pattern printed on one or both sides, used for upholstery. [F f. Creton in Normandy]

Creutzfeldt-Jakob disease /ˌkrɔɪtsfelt ˈjækob/ n. a type of spongiform encephalopathy affecting human beings, characterized by progressive dementia. [H. G. Creutzefldt (d. 1964) and A. Jakob (d. 1931), German physicians]

crevasse /krəˈvæs/ n. **1** a deep open crack, esp. in a glacier. **2** US a breach in a river levee. [F f. OF crevace: see CREVICE]

crevice /ˈkrevɪs/ n. a narrow opening or fissure, esp. in a rock or building etc. [ME f. OF crevace f. crever burst f. L crepare]

crew[1] /kruː/ n. & v. —n. (often treated as pl.) **1 a** a body of people manning a ship, aircraft, train, etc. **b** such a body as distinguished from the captain or officers. **c** a body of people working together; a team. **2** colloq. a company of people; a gang (a motley crew). —v. **1** tr. supply or act as a crew or member of a crew for. **2** intr. act as a crew or member of a crew. □ **crew cut** an oblong man's haircut which is short all over the head. **crew neck** a close-fitting round neckline, esp. on a sweater. [ME f. OF creüe increase, fem. past part. of croistre grow f. L crescere]

crew[2] past of CROW[2].

crewel /ˈkruːəl/ n. a thin worsted yarn used for tapestry and embroidery. □ **crewel-work** a design worked in crewel on linen or cloth. [ME crule etc., of unkn. orig.]

crewman /ˈkruːmən/ n. (pl. -men) a member of a crew.

crib /krɪb/ n. & v. —n. **1 a** a child's bed with barred or latticed sides; a cot. **b** a model of the Nativity of Christ, with a manger as a bed. **2** a barred container or rack for animal fodder. **3** colloq. **a** a translation of a text for the (esp. surreptitious) use of students. **b** plagiarized work etc. **4** a small house or cottage. **5** a framework lining the shaft of a mine. **6** colloq. **a** cribbage. **b** a set of cards given to the dealer at cribbage by all the players. **7** heavy crossed timbers used in foundations in loose soil etc. **8** sl. a brothel. **9** Austral. & NZ a light meal; food. —v.tr. (also absol.) (**cribbed, cribbing**) **1** colloq. copy (another person's work) unfairly or without acknowledgement. **2** confine in a small space. **3** colloq. pilfer, steal. **4** colloq. grumble. □ **crib-biting** a horse's habit of biting the manger while noisily breathing in and swallowing. □□ **cribber** n. [OE crib(b)]

cribbage /ˈkrɪbɪdʒ/ n. a card game for two, three, or four players, in which the dealer may score from the cards in the crib (see CRIB 6b). The game was invented by the English poet Sir John Suckling (1609–42) and seems to be developed from an older game called Noddy. □ **cribbage-board** a board with pegs and holes used for scoring at cribbage. [17th c.: orig. unkn.]

cribo /ˈkriːbəʊ, ˈkraɪbəʊ/ n. (pl. -os) a large harmless snake, Drymarchon corais, of tropical America. Also called gopher snake (see GOPHER[1]). [19th c.: orig. unkn.]

cribriform /ˈkrɪbrɪˌfɔːm/ adj. Anat. & Bot. having numerous small holes. [L cribrum sieve + -FORM]

cribwork /ˈkrɪbwɜːk/ n. = CRIB n. 7.

Crichton /ˈkraɪt(ə)n/, James (1560–85), Scottish adventurer, frequently known as 'the Admirable Crichton'. An accomplished swordsman, staunch Catholic, and intellectual prodigy, Crichton led a mercurial career abroad, supposedly disputing scientific questions in twelve languages in Paris at the age of 17, serving in the French army, and making a considerable impact on Italian universities before being killed in a brawl in Mantua.

Crick /ˈkrɪk/, Francis Harry Compton (1916–), British bio-

physicist who together with J. D. Watson proposed a model for the structure of the DNA molecule, for which he shared a Nobel Prize in 1962.

crick /krɪk/ n. & v. —n. a sudden painful stiffness in the neck or the back etc. —v.tr. produce a crick in (the neck etc.). [ME: orig. unkn.]

cricket[1] /ˈkrɪkɪt/ n. & v. —n. a game played on a grass pitch with ball, bats, and two wickets between teams of 11 players each. Scoring is by runs. Members of the batting side take it in turns to defend each wicket from attack by a ball bowled by a member of the fielding side and to strike the ball out of reach of the fieldsmen, so that the batsman can score one or more runs by running to (and from) the wicket at the opposite end before the ball is returned. The game was first played in England in Tudor times and has spread as a major sport throughout the Commonwealth. The laws (which are complicated) were first drawn up in 1744. —v.intr. (**cricketed, cricketing**) play cricket. □ **cricket-bag** a long bag used for carrying a cricketer's bat etc. **not cricket** Brit. colloq. underhand or unfair behaviour (from the game's tradition of fair play and generous applause for the achievements of players of both sides). □□ **cricketer** n. [16th c.: orig. uncert.]

cricket[2] /ˈkrɪkɪt/ n. any of various grasshopper-like insects of the order Orthoptera, the males of which produce a characteristic chirping sound. [ME f. OF criquet f. criquer creak etc. (imit.)]

cricoid /ˈkraɪkɔɪd/ adj. & n. —adj. ring-shaped. —n. (in full **cricoid cartilage**) Anat. the ring-shaped cartilage of the larynx. [mod.L cricoides f. Gk krikoeidēs f. krikos ring]

cri de cœur /ˌkriː də ˈkɜː(r)/ n. (pl. **cris de cœur** pronunc. same) a passionate appeal, complaint, or protest. [F, = cry from the heart]

cried past and past part. of CRY.

crier /ˈkraɪə(r)/ n. (also **cryer**) **1** a person who cries. **2** an officer who makes public announcements in a court of justice. □ **town** (or **common**) **crier** hist. an officer employed by a town council etc. to make public announcements in the streets or marketplace. [ME f. AF criour, OF criere f. crier CRY]

crikey /ˈkraɪkɪ/ int. sl. an expression of astonishment. [euphem. for CHRIST]

crim /krɪm/ n. & adj. Austral. sl. = CRIMINAL. [abbr.]

crime /kraɪm/ n. & v. —n. **1 a** an offence punishable by law. **b** illegal acts as a whole (resorted to crime). **2** an evil act (a crime against humanity). **3** colloq. a shameful act (a crime to tease them). **4** a soldier's offence against military regulations. —v.tr. Mil. etc. charge with or convict of an offence. □ **crime-sheet** Mil. a record of a defendant's offences. **crime wave** a sudden increase in crime. **crime-writer** a writer of detective fiction or thrillers. [ME f. OF f. L crimen -minis judgement, offence]

Crimea /kraɪˈmɪə/ a peninsula of the USSR lying between the Sea of Azov and the Black Sea. It was the scene of inconclusive but bloody fighting between Russia and Turkey, France, and Britain in 1854–6. □□ **Crimean** adj.

Crimean War /kraɪˈmiːən/ a mid-19th-c. war between Russia and an alliance of Great Britain, France, Sardinia, and Turkey. Russian aggression against Turkey led to war in 1853, with Turkey's European allies intervening to destroy Russian naval power in the Black Sea in 1854. The main theatre of the war was the Crimean peninsula where an Anglo-French army eventually captured the fortress city of Sebastopol in 1855 after a lengthy siege. A peace treaty was signed early in 1856, but although the allied armies had been successful the war was chiefly remembered for the deficiencies it exposed in the British army, particularly with regard to medical services; both sides sustained heavy losses.

crime passionnel /ˌkriːm pæsjɒˈnel/ n. (pl. **crimes passionnels** pronunc. same) a crime, esp. murder, committed in a fit of sexual jealousy. [F, = crime of passion]

criminal /ˈkrɪmɪn(ə)l/ n. & adj. —n. a person who has committed a crime or crimes. —adj. **1** of, involving, or concerning crime (criminal records). **2** having committed (and usu. been convicted of) a crime. **3** Law relating to or expert in criminal law rather than civil or political matters (criminal code; criminal lawyer). **4** *colloq.* scandalous, deplorable. □ **criminal law** law concerned with punishment of offenders (opp. *civil law*). **criminal libel** see LIBEL. □□ **criminality** /-ˈnælɪtɪ/ *n.* **criminally** *adv.* [ME f. LL *criminalis* (as CRIME)]

criminalistic /ˌkrɪmɪnəˈlɪstɪk/ *adj.* relating to criminals or their habits.

criminalistics /ˌkrɪmɪnəˈlɪstɪks/ *n.pl.* esp. *US* forensic science.

criminology /ˌkrɪmɪˈnɒlədʒɪ/ *n.* the scientific study of crime. □□ **criminological** /-nəˈlɒdʒɪk(ə)l/ *adj.* **criminologist** *n.* [L *crimen -minis* CRIME + -OLOGY]

crimp /krɪmp/ *v.* & *n.* —*v.tr.* **1** compress into small folds or ridges; frill. **2** make narrow wrinkles or flutings in; corrugate. **3** make waves in (the hair) with a hot iron. —*n.* a crimped thing or form. □ **put a crimp in** *US sl.* thwart; interfere with. □□ **crimper** *n.* **crimpy** *adj.* **crimpily** *adv.* **crimpiness** *n.* [ME, prob. ult. f. OHG *krimphan*]

Crimplene /ˈkrɪmpliːn/ *n. propr.* a synthetic crease-resistant fibre and fabric.

crimson /ˈkrɪmz(ə)n/ *adj., n.,* & *v.* —*adj.* of a rich deep red inclining to purple. —*n.* this colour. —*v.tr.* & *intr.* make or become crimson. [ME *cremesin, crimesin,* ult. f. Arab. *ḳirmizī* KERMES]

cringe /krɪndʒ/ *v.* & *n.* —*v.intr.* **1** shrink back in fear or apprehension; cower. **2** (often foll. by *to*) behave obsequiously. —*n.* the act or an instance of cringing. □□ **cringer** *n.* [ME *crenge, crenche,* OE *cringan, crincan:* see CRANK[1]]

cringle /ˈkrɪŋg(ə)l/ *n. Naut.* an eye of rope containing a thimble for another rope to pass through. [LG *kringel* dimin. of *kring* ring f. root of CRANK[1]]

crinkle /ˈkrɪŋk(ə)l/ *n.* & *v.* —*n.* a wrinkle or crease in paper, cloth, etc. —*v.* **1** *intr.* form crinkles. **2** *tr.* form crinkles in. □ **crinkle-cut** (of vegetables) cut with wavy edges. □□ **crinkly** *adj.* [ME f. OE *crincan:* see CRANK[1]]

crinoid /ˈkrɪnɔɪd/ *n.* & *adj.* —*n.* any echinoderm of the class Crinoidea, usu. sedentary with feathery arms, e.g. sea lilies and feather stars. —*adj.* lily-shaped. □□ **crinoidal** /-ˈnɔɪd(ə)l/ *adj.* [Gk *krinoeidēs* f. *krinon* lily]

crinoline /ˈkrɪnəlɪn/ *n.* **1** a stiffened or hooped petticoat formerly worn to make a long skirt stand out. **2** a stiff fabric of horsehair etc. used for linings, hats, etc. [F f. L *crinis* hair + *linum* thread]

cripple /ˈkrɪp(ə)l/ *n.* & *v.* —*n.* a person who is permanently lame. —*v.tr.* **1** make a cripple of; lame. **2** disable, impair. **3** weaken or damage (an institution, enterprise, etc.) seriously (*crippled by the loss of funding*). □□ **crippledom** *n.* **cripplehood** *n.* **crippler** *n.* [OE *crypel,* rel. to CREEP]

cris var. of KRIS.

crisis /ˈkraɪsɪs/ *n.* (*pl.* **crises** /-siːz/) **1 a** a decisive moment. **b** a time of danger or great difficulty. **2** the turning-point, esp. of a disease. [L f. Gk *krisis* decision f. *krinō* decide]

crisp /krɪsp/ *adj., n.,* & *v.* —*adj.* **1** hard but brittle. **2 a** (of air) bracing. **b** (of a style or manner) lively, brisk and decisive. **c** (of features etc.) neat and clear-cut. **d** (of paper) stiff and crackling. **e** (of hair) closely curling. —*n.* **1** (in full **potato crisp**) *Brit.* a thin fried slice of potato sold in packets etc. and eaten as a snack or appetizer. **2 a** thing overdone in roasting etc. (*burnt to a crisp*). —*v.tr.* & *intr.* **1** make or become crisp. **2** curl in short stiff folds or waves. □□ **crisply** *adv.* **crispness** *n.* [OE f. L *crispus* curled]

crispate /ˈkrɪspeɪt/ *adj.* **1** crisped. **2** *Bot.* & *Zool.* having a wavy margin. [L *crispare* curl]

crispbread /ˈkrɪspbred/ *n.* **1** a thin crisp biscuit of crushed rye etc. **2** these collectively (*a packet of crispbread*).

crisper /ˈkrɪspə(r)/ *n.* a compartment in a refrigerator for storing fruit and vegetables.

crispy /ˈkrɪspɪ/ *adj.* (**crispier, crispiest**) **1** crisp, brittle. **2** curly. **3** brisk. □□ **crispiness** *n.*

criss-cross /ˈkrɪskrɒs/ *n., adj., adv.,* & *v.* —*n.* **1** a pattern of crossing lines. **2** the crossing of lines or currents etc. —*adj.* crossing; in cross lines (*criss-cross marking*). —*adv.* crosswise; at cross purposes. —*v.* **1** *intr.* **a** intersect repeatedly. **b** move

crosswise. **2** *tr.* mark or make with a criss-cross pattern. [15th c., f. *Christ's cross:* later treated as redupl. of CROSS]

crista /ˈkrɪstə/ *n.* (*pl.* **cristae** /-tiː/) **1** *Anat.* & *Zool.* a ridge or crest. **2** *Anat.* an infold of the inner membrane of a mitochondrion. □□ **cristate** *adj.* [L]

cristobalite /krɪˈstəʊbəˌlaɪt/ *n. Mineral.* a principal form of silica, occurring as opal. [G *Cristobalit* f. Cerro San *Cristóbal* in Mexico]

crit /krɪt/ *n. colloq.* **1** = CRITICISM 2. **2** = CRITIQUE. **3** *Physics* critical mass. [abbr.]

criterion /kraɪˈtɪərɪən/ *n.* (*pl.* **criteria** /-rɪə/) a principle or standard that a thing is judged by. □□ **criterial** *adj.* [Gk *kritērion* means of judging (cf. CRITIC)]

critic /ˈkrɪtɪk/ *n.* **1** a person who censures. **2** a person who reviews or judges the merits of literary, artistic, or musical works etc., esp. regularly or professionally. **3** a person engaged in textual criticism. [L *criticus* f. Gk *kritikos* f. *kritēs* judge f. *krinō* judge, decide]

critical /ˈkrɪtɪk(ə)l/ *adj.* **1 a** making or involving adverse or censorious comments or judgements. **b** expressing or involving criticism. **2** skilful at or engaged in criticism. **3** providing textual criticism (*a critical edition of Milton*). **4 a** of or at a crisis; involving risk or suspense (*in a critical condition; a critical operation*). **b** decisive, crucial (*of critical importance; at the critical moment*). **5 a** *Math.* & *Physics* marking transition from one state etc. to another (*critical angle*). **b** *Physics* (of a nuclear reactor) maintaining a self-sustaining chain reaction. □ **critical apparatus** = APPARATUS 4. **critical mass** *Physics* the amount of fissile material needed to maintain a nuclear chain reaction. **critical path** the sequence of stages determining the minimum time needed for an operation. **critical temperature** *Chem.* the temperature above which a gas cannot be liquefied. □□ **criticality** /-ˈkælɪtɪ/ *n.* (in sense 5). **critically** *adv.* **criticalness** *n.* [L *criticus:* see CRITIC]

criticaster /ˌkrɪtɪˈkæstə(r), ˈkrɪt-/ *n.* a minor or inferior critic.

criticism /ˈkrɪtɪsɪz(ə)m/ *n.* **1 a** a finding fault; censure. **b** a statement or remark expressing this. **2 a** the work of a critic. **b** an article, essay, etc., expressing or containing an analytical evaluation of something. □ **the higher criticism** criticism dealing with the origin and character etc. of texts, esp. of Biblical writings. **the lower criticism** textual criticism of the Bible. [CRITIC or L *criticus* + -ISM]

criticize /ˈkrɪtɪsaɪz/ *v.tr.* (also **-ise**) (also *absol.*) **1** find fault with; censure. **2** discuss critically. □□ **criticizable** *adj.* **criticizer** *n.*

critique /krɪˈtiːk/ *n.* & *v.* —*n.* a critical essay or analysis; an instance or the process of formal criticism. —*v.tr.* (**critiques, critiqued, critiquing**) discuss critically. [F f. Gk *kritikē tekhnē* critical art]

critter /ˈkrɪtə(r)/ *n.* **1** *dial.* or *joc.* a creature. **2** *derog.* a person. [var. of CREATURE]

croak /krəʊk/ *n.* & *v.* —*n.* **1** a deep hoarse sound as of a frog or a raven. **2** a sound resembling this. —*v.* **1 a** *intr.* utter a croak. **b** *tr.* utter with a croak or in a dismal manner. **2** *sl.* **a** *intr.* die. **b** *tr.* kill. [ME: imit.]

croaker /ˈkrəʊkə(r)/ *n.* **1** an animal that croaks. **2** a prophet of evil.

croaky /ˈkrəʊkɪ/ *adj.* (**croakier, croakiest**) (of a voice) croaking; hoarse. □□ **croakily** *adv.* **croakiness** *n.*

Croat /ˈkrəʊæt/ *n.* & *adj.* —*n.* **1 a** a native of Croatia in Yugoslavia. **b** a person of Croatian descent. **2** the Slavonic dialect of the Croats (cf. SERBO-CROAT). —*adj.* of or relating to the Croats or their dialect. [mod.L *Croatae* f. Serbo-Croatian *Hrvat*]

Croatia /krəʊˈeɪʃə/ (Serbian **Hrvatska** /ˈhɜːvætskə/) a constituent republic of Yugoslavia; pop. (1981) 4,601,450; capital, Zagreb. □□ **Croatian** *adj.* & *n.*

croc /krɒk/ *n. colloq.* a crocodile. [abbr.]

Croce /ˈkrɒtʃeɪ/, Benedetto (1866–1952), Italian philosopher. Born into a family of wealthy landowners, Croce spent most of his life engaged in academic pursuits. His philosophy, which coincided with a revival of historical idealism in Italy, arose out of his aesthetic theory. Aesthetic experience is interpreted as

aʊ how eɪ day əʊ no eə hair ɪə near ɔɪ boy ʊə poor aɪə fire aʊə sour (*see over for consonants*)

an intuition of the universal spirit which manifests itself in the practical activities of human personality. While reflection upon these intuitions requires rational concepts the former are more primitive than the latter; consequently history and art are seen as more primitive than science. Practical action is grounded in economic activity yet this must be made subject to the regulation of an ethic which expresses universal spiritual values. Croce broke with the Fascist regime in 1925 and thereafter became a leading antagonist. Following the demise of Fascism he became leader of the Liberal party and served briefly as a Cabinet minister in 1944.

croceate /ˈkrəʊsɪˌeɪt/ adj. saffron-coloured. [L croceus f. CROCUS]

crochet /ˈkrəʊʃeɪ, -ʃɪ/ n. & v. —n. 1 a handicraft in which yarn is made up into a patterned fabric by means of a hooked needle. 2 work made in this way. —v. (**crocheted** /-ʃeɪd/; **crocheting** /-ʃeɪɪŋ/) 1 tr. make by crocheting. 2 intr. do crochet. □□ **crocheter** /ˈkrəʊʃeɪə(r)/ n. [F, dimin. of croc hook]

crocidolite /krəʊˈsɪdəˌlaɪt/ n. a fibrous blue or green silicate of iron and sodium; blue asbestos. [Gk krokis -idos nap of cloth]

crock¹ /krɒk/ n. & v. colloq. —n. 1 an inefficient, broken-down, or worn-out person. 2 a worn-out vehicle, ship, etc. —v. 1 intr. (foll. by up) break down, collapse. 2 tr. (often foll. by up) disable, cause to collapse. [orig. Sc., perh. f. Flem.]

crock² /krɒk/ n. 1 an earthenware pot or jar. 2 a broken piece of earthenware. [OE croc(ca)]

crockery /ˈkrɒkərɪ/ n. earthenware or china dishes, plates, etc. [obs. crocker potter: see CROCK²]

crocket /ˈkrɒkɪt/ n. Archit. a small carved ornament (usu. a bud or curled leaf) on the inclined side of a pinnacle etc. [ME f. var. of OF crochet: see CROCHET]

Crockett /ˈkrɒkɪt/, David ('Davy') (1786–1836), American politician, soldier, and frontier fighter. Between 1827 and 1835 he was a member of the House of Representatives and cultivated the image of a rough backwoods legislator. On leaving politics he returned to the frontier, where he took up the cause of Texan independence and was killed at the battle of Alamo.

Crockford /ˈkrɒkfəd/ short for Crockford's Clerical Directory, a reference book of Anglican clergy first issued in 1860. [J. Crockford (d. 1865), nominal first publisher]

crocodile /ˈkrɒkəˌdaɪl/ n. 1 a any large tropical amphibious reptile of the order Crocodilia (see CROCODILIAN), usually of the genus Crocodylus, found in tropical regions. Its long snout is narrower than that of the alligator, and when the jaws are closed the fourth tooth on each side of the lower jaw projects outside the snout, whereas in the alligator it fits into a socket in the upper jaw. b leather from its skin, used to make bags, shoes, etc. 2 Brit. colloq. a line of schoolchildren etc. walking in pairs. □ **crocodile clip** a clip with teeth for gripping. **crocodile tears** insincere grief (from the belief that crocodiles wept while devouring or alluring their prey). [ME f. OF cocodrille f. med.L cocodrillus f. L crocodilus f. Gk krokodilos f. krokē pebble + drilos worm]

crocodilian /ˌkrɒkəˈdɪlɪən/ n. & adj. —n. a large heavy amphibious reptile of the order Crocodilia, which includes crocodiles, alligators, and caymans. Crocodilians have a long snout, strong jaws, short legs with webbed toes and with claws, and a powerful tail. In evolutionary sequence they are the last living link with prehistoric reptiles resembling the dinosaurs, and are the closest living relatives of the birds. —adj. of the crocodilians.

crocus /ˈkrəʊkəs/ n. (pl. **crocuses**) any dwarf plant of the genus Crocus, growing from a corm and having brilliant usu. yellow or purple flowers. [ME, = saffron, f. L f. Gk krokos crocus, of Semitic orig.]

Croesus /ˈkriːsəs/ the last king of Lydia c.560–546 BC, friendly to Greeks despite his subjugation of the Greek cities on the coast of Asia Minor, and proverbial for his wealth. His empire, with its capital at Sardis, was overthrown by the Persian king Cyrus. At this point his fate becomes the theme of legend; Cyrus is said to have cast him on a pyre from which he was saved by the miraculous intervention of Apollo.

croft /krɒft/ n. & v. Brit. —n. 1 an enclosed piece of (usu. arable)

land. 2 a small rented farm in Scotland or N. England. —v.intr. farm a croft; live as a crofter. [OE: orig. unkn.]

crofter /ˈkrɒftə(r)/ n. Brit. a person who rents a smallholding, esp. a joint tenant of a divided farm in parts of Scotland.

croissant /ˈkrwʌsɑ̃/ n. a crescent-shaped roll made of rich yeast pastry. [F, formed as CRESCENT]

Cro-Magnon /krəʊˈmænjɒn, -ˈmægnən/ the name of a hill of Cretaceous limestone in the Dordogne department of France, in a cave at the base of which skeletons of five individuals were found in 1868 among deposits of upper palaeolithic age. It had previously been supposed that modern man did not exist in palaeolithic times. The name is now applied in a more general sense to describe a particular race of modern man (Homo sapiens sapiens) that is associated with the upper palaeolithic Aurignacian industry found throughout western Europe and particularly SW France from between c.34,000 and 29,000 years BP. The geographical origin of the fully modern Cro-Magnon 'race' is uncertain but its appearance in western Europe heralded the apparent decline and disappearance of the existing Neanderthal populations and their middle palaeolithic industries. The group persisted in mesolithic and neolithic times, and some authorities consider that it survived in the Guanches, the earliest inhabitants (now extinct) of the Canary Islands.

Crome /krəʊm/, John (1768–1821), English artist, born in Norwich. His fame as a landscape painter rests on his traditional position between the beginnings of naturalism in Richard Wilson (d. 1782) and its maturity in John Constable. He helped found the Norwich Society of Artists in 1803, and was its acknowledged principal. Although his landscapes are obviously indebted to Dutch artists such as Hobbema and Rembrandt, the unity of pictorial and emotional tone in such pictures as Slate Quarries shows a tendency towards the more personal interpretation of nature that would be developed between 1800 and 1850.

cromlech /ˈkrɒmlek/ n. 1 a dolmen; a megalithic tomb. 2 (in Brittany) a circle of upright prehistoric stones. [Welsh f. crom fem. of crwm bent + llech flat stone]

Crompton¹ /ˈkrɒmpt(ə)n/, Richmal (pseudonym of Richmal Crompton Lamburn, 1890–1969), English author of the 'William' books, about a mishievous schoolboy and his family, friends, and enemies. The first of these, Just—William, was published in book form in 1922.

Crompton² /ˈkrɒmptən/, Samuel (1753–1827), English inventor of the spinning mule (see MULE¹ 4).

Cromwell¹ /ˈkrɒmwel/, Oliver (1599–1658), English general and statesman. A Puritan squire from Huntingdon, Cromwell was among the Parliamentary opponents of Charles I, but only became a national figure as a soldier during the English Civil War, playing a decisive part in the victories of Marston Moor and Naseby and in the formation of the New Model Army. His rise to pre-eminence continued with his victories at Preston, Dunbar, and Worcester and his subjugation of Ireland, and with the collapse of parliamentary government after the King's execution he became Lord Protector, an office he held from 1653 until his death.

Cromwell² /ˈkrɒmwel/, Thomas (c.1485–1540), chief minister to Henry VIII. Rising from humble origins in the service of Cardinal Wolsey, Cromwell succeeded the latter as the King's chief adviser. During the 1530s he presided over the King's divorce from Catherine of Aragon and break with the Roman Catholic Church, as well as the dissolution of the monasteries and a series of administrative reforms strengthening the central government. He fell from favour over Henry's marriage to Anne of Cleves and was executed on a trumped-up charge of treason.

crone /krəʊn/ n. 1 a withered old woman. 2 an old ewe. [ME, ult. f. ONF carogne CARRION]

Cronin /ˈkrəʊnɪn/, Archibald Joseph (1896–1981), Scottish novelist who practised as a physician until the success of his first novel made him devote himself to writing. His novels include Hatter's Castle (1931), The Citadel (1937), telling of the struggles of an idealistic young doctor, and The Stars Look Down (1935), about a mining community, all written with rare sympathy and understanding and a rich panorama of characters.

b but   d dog   f few   g get   h he   j yes   k cat   l leg   m man   n no   p pen   r red   s sit   t top   v voice

cronk /krɒŋk/ adj. Austral. colloq. **1** unsound; liable to collapse. **2 a** fraudulent. **b** (of a horse) dishonestly run, unfit. [19th c.: cf. CRANK³]

Cronus /ˈkrɒnəs/ Gk Mythol. the youngest son of Heaven and Earth, and leader of his brothers the Titans. By the advice of his mother he castrated his father, who therefore no longer approached Earth but left room for the Titans between them. Cronus then married his sister Rhea and swallowed all his male children because he was fated to be overcome by one of them. Rhea wrapped a stone in swaddling-clothes when Zeus was born and hid the baby away in Crete. Cronus swallowed the stone, and Zeus eventually dethroned him as ruler of the universe. The story is largely derived from Asia Minor and is almost certainly pre-Hellenic.

crony /ˈkrəʊnɪ/ n. (pl. **-ies**) a close friend or companion. [17th-c. chrony, university sl. f. Gk khronios long-standing f. khronos time]

crook /krʊk/ n., v., & adj. —n. **1** the hooked staff of a shepherd or bishop. **2 a** a bend, curve, or hook. **b** anything hooked or curved. **3** colloq. **a** a rogue; a swindler. **b** a professional criminal. —v.tr. & intr. bend, curve. —adj. **1** crooked. **2** Austral. & NZ colloq. **a** unsatisfactory, out of order; (of a person) unwell, injured. **b** unpleasant. **c** dishonest, unscrupulous. **d** bad-tempered, irritable, angry. □ **crook-back** a hunchback. **crook-backed** hunchbacked. **go crook** (usu. foll. by at, on) Austral. & NZ colloq. lose one's temper; become angry. □□ **crookery** n. [ME f. ON krókr hook]

crooked /ˈkrʊkɪd/ adj. (**crookeder, crookedest**) **1 a** not straight or level; bent, curved, twisted. **b** deformed, bent with age. **2** colloq. not straightforward; dishonest. **3** /krʊkt/ Austral. & NZ sl. = CROOK adj. **2**. **4** (foll. by on) Austral. sl. hostile to. □□ **crookedly** adv. **crookedness** n. [ME f. CROOK, prob. after ON krókóttr]

Crookes /krʊks/, Sir William (1832–1919), English physicist and chemist who combined scientific research in his private laboratory with business, and edited several photographic and scientific journals. He lacked mathematical skills but was a brilliant experimenter in the mould of Faraday, his model, and employed several adept assistants. His interest in spiritualism and psychic research caused several controversies. In 1861, shortly after the spectroscopic discoveries of Bunsen and Kirchhoff, he discovered the element thallium. This led him indirectly to the invention of the radiometer in 1875, a device with mica vanes rotated by daylight radiation which confirmed the kinetic theory of gases. In 1876 he began investigating electrical discharges (cathode rays) in vacuum tubes, for which he developed the Crookes' tube (the precursor of the X-ray tube). He finally took up the study of radioactivity, and in 1903 invented the spinthariscope for detecting alpha particles.

croon /kruːn/ v. & n. —v.tr. & intr. hum or sing in a low subdued voice, esp. in a sentimental manner. —n. such singing. □□ **crooner** n. [ME (orig. Sc. & N.Engl.) f. MDu. & MLG krōnen groan, lament]

crop /krɒp/ n. & v. —n. **1 a** the produce of cultivated plants, esp. cereals. **b** the season's total yield of this (a good crop). **2 a** group or an amount produced or appearing at one time (this year's crop of students). **3** (in full **hunting crop**) the stock or handle of a whip. **4 a** a style of hair cut very short. **b** the cropping of hair. **5** Zool. **a** the pouch in a bird's gullet where food is prepared for digestion. **b** a similar organ in other animals. **6** the entire tanned hide of an animal. **7** a piece cut off or out of something. —v. (**cropped, cropping**) **1** tr. **a** cut off. **b** (of animals) bite off (the tops of plants). **2** tr. cut (hair, cloth, edges of a book, etc.) short. **3** tr. gather or reap (produce). **4** tr. (foll. by with) sow or plant (land) with a crop. **5** intr. (of land) bear a crop. □ **crop circle** a circular depression in a standing crop. Such circles, which often appear with associated depressions forming straight lines, are variously attributed to whirlwinds, fungi, visiting spaceships, and common hoaxers. **crop-dusting** the sprinkling of powdered insecticide or fertilizer on crops, esp. from the air. **crop-eared** having the ears (esp. of animals) or hair cut short. **crop-full** having a full crop or stomach. **crop out** Geol. appear at the surface. **crop-over** a W. Indian celebration marking the end of the sugar-cane harvest. **crop up 1**

(of a subject, circumstance, etc.) appear or come to one's notice unexpectedly. **2** Geol. appear at the surface. [OE crop(p)]

cropper /ˈkrɒpə(r)/ n. a crop-producing plant of specified quality (a good cropper; a heavy cropper). □ **come a cropper** sl. **1** fall heavily. **2** fail badly.

croquet /ˈkrəʊkeɪ, -kɪ/ n. & v. —n. **1** a game played on a lawn, with wooden balls which are driven through a series of square-topped hoops by mallets. It owes its origin to paille maille (or Pell-Mell; whence the name of the London street Pall Mall, where it was played), a game known in France from the 16th c. **2** the act of croqueting a ball. —v.tr. (**croqueted** /-keɪd/; **croqueting** /-keɪɪŋ/) drive away (one's opponent's ball in croquet) by placing one's own against it and striking one's own. [perh. dial. form of F CROCHET hook]

croquette /krəˈket/ n. a fried breaded roll or ball of mashed potato or minced meat etc. [F f. croquer crunch]

crore /krɔː(r)/ n. Ind. **1** ten million. **2** one hundred lakhs (of rupees, units of measurement, persons, etc.). [Hindi k(a)rōr, ult. f. Skr. koṭi apex]

Crosby /ˈkrɒzbɪ/, Bing (real name Harry Lillis Crosby, 1904–77), American singer and actor, the most famous of all crooners, whose songs include 'Pennies from Heaven', 'Blue Skies', 'White Christmas', and 'The Bells of St Mary's' (all featured in films with those titles) with Bob Hope and Dorothy Lamour.

crosier /ˈkrəʊzɪə(r), -ʒə(r)/ n. (also **crozier**) **1** a hooked staff carried by a bishop as a symbol of pastoral office. **2** a crook. [orig. = bearer of a crook, f. OF crocier & OF croisier f. crois CROSS]

cross /krɒs/ n., v., & adj. —n. **1** an upright post with a transverse bar, as used in antiquity for crucifixion. **2 a** (**the Cross**) in Christianity, the cross on which Christ was crucified. **b** a representation of this as an emblem of Christianity. **c** = sign of the cross. **3** a staff surmounted by a cross and borne before an archbishop or in a religious procession. **4 a** a thing or mark shaped like a cross, esp. a figure made by two short intersecting lines (+ or ×). **b** a monument in the form of a cross, esp. one in the centre of a town or on a tomb. **5** a cross-shaped decoration indicating rank in some orders of knighthood or awarded for personal valour. **6 a** an intermixture of animal breeds or plant varieties. **b** an animal or plant resulting from this. **7** (foll. by between) a mixture or compromise of two things. **8 a** a crosswise movement, e.g. of an actor on stage. **b** Football etc. a pass of the ball across the direction of play. **c** Boxing a blow with a crosswise movement of the fist. **9** a trial or affliction; something to be endured (bear one's crosses). —v. **1** tr. (often foll. by over; also absol.) go across or to the other side of (a road, river, sea, etc.). **2 a** intr. intersect or be across one another (the roads cross near the bridge). **b** tr. cause to do this; place crosswise (cross one's legs). **3** tr. **a** draw a line or lines across. **b** Brit. mark (a cheque) with two parallel lines, and often an annotation, to indicate that it must be paid into a named bank account. **4** tr. (foll. by off, out, through) cancel or obliterate or remove from a list with lines drawn across. **5** tr. (often refl.) make the sign of the cross on or over. **6** intr. **a** pass in opposite or different directions. **b** (of letters between two correspondents) each be dispatched before receipt of the other. **c** (of telephone lines) become wrongly interconnected so that intrusive calls can be heard. **7** tr. **a** cause to interbreed. **b** cross-fertilize (plants). **8** tr. thwart or frustrate (crossed in love). **9** tr. sl. cheat. —adj. **1** (often foll. by with) peevish, angry. **2** (usu. attrib.) transverse; reaching from side to side. **3** (usu. attrib.) intersecting. **4** (usu. attrib.) contrary, opposed, reciprocal. □ **as cross as two sticks** extremely angry or peevish. **at cross purposes** misunderstanding or conflicting with one another. **cross one's fingers** (or **keep one's fingers crossed**) **1** put one finger across another as a sign of hoping for good luck. **2** trust in good luck. **cross the floor** join the opposing side in a debating-assembly. **cross one's heart** make a solemn pledge, esp. by crossing one's front. **cross one's mind** (of a thought etc.) occur to one, esp. transiently. **cross a person's palm** (usu. foll. by with) pay a person for a favour. **cross the path of 1** meet with (a person). **2** thwart. **cross swords** (often foll. by with) encounter in opposition; have an argument or dispute. **cross wires** (or **get one's wires crossed**) **1** become wrongly connected by telephone. **2** have a misunderstanding. **on the cross 1** diagonally. **2** *sl.* fraudulently, dishonestly. □□ **crossly** *adv.* **crossness** *n.* [OE *cros* f. ON *kross* f. OIr. *cros* f. L *crux cruc-*]

cross- /krɒs/ *comb. form* **1** denoting movement or position across something (*cross-channel*; *cross-country*). **2** denoting interaction (*cross-breed*; *cross-cultural*; *cross-fertilize*). **3 a** passing from side to side; transverse (*crossbar*; *cross-current*). **b** having a transverse part (*crossbow*). **4** describing the form or figure of a cross (*cross-keys*; *crossroads*).

crossbar /ˈkrɒsbɑː(r)/ *n.* a horizontal bar, esp. held on a pivot or between two upright bars etc., e.g. of a bicycle or of a football goal.

cross-bedding /ˈkrɒsˌbedɪŋ/ *n. Geol.* lines of stratification crossing the main rock strata. Also called *false bedding*.

cross-bench /ˈkrɒsbentʃ/ *n. Brit.* a seat in Parliament (now only the House of Lords) occupied by a member not taking the whip from a political party. □□ **cross-bencher** *n.*

crossbill /ˈkrɒsbɪl/ *n.* any stout finch of the genus *Loxia*, having a bill with crossed mandibles for opening pine cones.

crossbones /ˈkrɒsbəʊnz/ *n.* a representation of two crossed thigh-bones (see SKULL).

crossbow /ˈkrɒsbəʊ/ *n.* chiefly *hist.* a bow fixed across a wooden stock, with a groove for an arrow and a mechanism for drawing and releasing the string. □□ **crossbowman** *n.* (*pl.* **-men**)

cross-breed /ˈkrɒsbriːd/ *n.* & *v.* —*n.* **1** a breed of animals or plants produced by crossing. **2** an individual animal or plant of a cross-breed. —*v.tr.* (*past* and *past part.* **-bred**) produce by crossing.

cross-check /ˈkrɒstʃek/ *v.* & *n.* —*v.tr.* check by a second or alternative method, or by several methods. —*n.* an instance of cross-checking.

cross-country /krɒsˈkʌntrɪ/ *adj.* & *adv.* **1** across fields or open country. **2** not keeping to main or direct roads.

cross-cut /ˈkrɒskʌt/ *adj.* & *n.* —*adj.* cut across the main grain or axis. —*n.* a diagonal cut, path, etc. □ **cross-cut saw** a saw for cutting across the grain of wood.

cross-dating /ˈkrɒsˌdeɪtɪŋ/ *n. Archaeol.* dating by correlation with another site or level.

crosse /krɒs/ *n.* a stick with a triangular net at the end for conveying the ball in lacrosse. [F f. OF *croce*, *croc* hook]

cross-examine /ˌkrɒsɪɡˈzæmɪn/ *v.tr.* examine (esp. a witness in a lawcourt) to check or extend testimony already given. □□ **cross-examination** /-ˈneɪʃ(ə)n/ *n.* **cross-examiner** *n.*

cross-eyed /ˈkrɒsaɪd/ *adj.* (as a disorder) having one or both eyes turned permanently inwards towards the nose.

cross-fade /ˈkrɒsfeɪd/ *v.intr. Radio* etc. fade in one sound as another is faded out.

cross-fertilize /krɒsˈfɜːtɪˌlaɪz/ *v.tr.* (also **-ise**) **1** fertilize (an animal or plant) from one of a different species. **2** help by the interchange of ideas etc. □□ **cross-fertilization** /-ˈzeɪʃ(ə)n/ *n.*

crossfire /ˈkrɒsˌfaɪə(r)/ *n.* **1** firing in two crossing directions simultaneously. **2 a** attack or criticism from several sources at once. **b** a lively or combative exchange of views etc.

cross-grain /ˈkrɒsɡreɪn/ *n.* a grain in timber, running across the regular grain.

cross-grained /ˈkrɒsɡreɪnd/ *adj.* **1** (of timber) having a cross-grain. **2** perverse, intractable.

cross-hair /ˈkrɒsheə(r)/ *n.* a fine wire at the focus of an optical instrument for use in measurement.

cross-hatch /ˈkrɒshætʃ/ *v.tr.* shade with intersecting sets of parallel lines.

cross-head /ˈkrɒshed/ *n.* **1** a bar between the piston-rod and connecting-rod in a steam engine. **2** = CROSS-HEADING.

cross-heading /ˈkrɒsˌhedɪŋ/ *n.* a heading to a paragraph printed across a column in the body of an article in a newspaper etc.

crossing /ˈkrɒsɪŋ/ *n.* **1** a place where things (esp. roads) cross. **2** a place at which one may cross a street etc. (*pedestrian crossing*). **3** a journey across water (*had a smooth crossing*). **4** the intersection

of a church nave and transepts. **5** *Biol.* mating. □ **crossing over** *Biol.* an exchange of genes between homologous chromosomes (cf. RECOMBINATION).

cross-legged /krɒsˈleɡd, -ˈleɡɪd, ˈkrɒs-/ *adj.* with one leg crossed over the other.

cross-link /ˈkrɒslɪŋk/ *n.* (also **cross-linkage**) *Chem.* a bond between chains of atoms in a polymer etc.

crossmatch /krɒsˈmætʃ/ *v.tr. Med.* test the compatibility of (a donor's and a recipient's blood). □□ **crossmatching** *n.*

crossover /ˈkrɒsˌəʊvə(r)/ *n.* & *adj.* —*n.* a point or place of crossing from one side to the other. —*adj.* having a crossover.

crosspatch /ˈkrɒspætʃ/ *n. colloq.* a bad-tempered person. [CROSS *adj.* 1 + obs. *patch* fool, clown]

crosspiece /ˈkrɒspiːs/ *n.* a transverse beam or other component of a structure etc.

cross-ply /ˈkrɒsplaɪ/ *adj.* (of a tyre) having fabric layers with cords lying crosswise.

cross-pollinate /krɒsˈpɒlɪˌneɪt/ *v.tr.* pollinate (a plant) from another. □□ **cross-pollination** /-ˈneɪʃ(ə)n/ *n.*

cross-question /krɒsˈkwestʃ(ə)n/ *v.tr.* = CROSS-EXAMINE.

cross-refer /ˌkrɒsrɪˈfɜː(r)/ *v.intr.* (**-referred**, **-referring**) refer from one part of a book, article, etc., to another.

cross-reference /ˈkrɒsˌrefərəns/ *n.* & *v.* —*n.* a reference from one part of a book, article, etc., to another. —*v.tr.* provide with cross-references.

crossroad /ˈkrɒsrəʊd/ *n.* **1** (usu. in *pl.*) an intersection of two or more roads. **2** *US* a road that crosses a main road or joins two main roads. □ **at the crossroads** at a critical point in one's life.

cross-ruff /ˈkrɒsrʌf/ *n.* & *v. Bridge* etc. —*n.* the alternate trumping of partners' leads. —*v.intr.* play in this way.

cross-section /krɒsˈsekʃ(ə)n/ *n.* **1 a** a cutting of a solid at right angles to an axis. **b** a plane surface produced in this way. **c** a representation of this. **2** a representative sample, esp. of people. **3** *Physics* a quantity expressing the probability of interaction between particles. □□ **cross-sectional** *adj.*

cross-stitch /ˈkrɒsstɪtʃ/ *n.* **1** a stitch formed of two stitches crossing each other. **2** needlework done using this stitch.

crosstalk /ˈkrɒstɔːk/ *n.* **1** unwanted transfer of signals between communication channels. **2** *Brit.* witty talk; repartee.

cross-trees /ˈkrɒstriːz/ *n.pl. Naut.* a pair of horizontal timbers at the top of a lower mast, supporting the topmast.

cross-voting /ˈkrɒsˌvəʊtɪŋ/ *n.* voting for a party not one's own, or for more than one party.

crosswalk /ˈkrɒswɔːk/ *n. US* a pedestrian crossing.

crossways /ˈkrɒsweɪz/ *adv.* = CROSSWISE.

crosswind /ˈkrɒswɪnd/ *n.* a wind blowing across one's direction of travel.

crosswise /ˈkrɒswaɪz/ *adj.* & *adv.* **1** in the form of a cross; intersecting. **2** transverse or transversely.

crossword /ˈkrɒswɜːd/ *n.* (also **crossword puzzle**) a puzzle of a grid of squares and blanks into which words crossing vertically and horizontally have to be filled from clues. Invention of the crossword is attributed to a journalist, Arthur Wynne, whose puzzle (called a 'word-cross') appeared in a Sunday newspaper, the *New York World*, on 21 Dec. 1913.

crotch /krɒtʃ/ *n.* a place where something forks, esp. the legs of the human body or a garment (cf. CRUTCH). [perh. = ME & OF *croc(he)* hook, formed as CROOK]

crotchet /ˈkrɒtʃɪt/ *n.* **1** *Mus.* a note having the time value of a quarter of a semibreve and usu. representing one beat, drawn as a large dot with a stem. Also called *quarter note*. **2** a whimsical fancy. **3** a hook. [ME f. OF *crochet* dimin. of *croc* hook (see CROTCH)]

crotchety /ˈkrɒtʃɪtɪ/ *adj.* peevish, irritable. □□ **crotchetiness** *n.* [CROTCHET + -Y¹]

croton /ˈkrəʊt(ə)n/ *n.* **1** any small tree or shrub of the genus *Croton*, producing a capsule-like fruit. **2** any small tree or shrub of the genus *Codiaeum*, esp. *C. variegatum*, with coloured ornamental leaves. □ **croton oil** a powerful purgative obtained from the fruit of *Croton tiglium*. [mod.L f. Gk *krotōn* sheep-tick, croton (from the shape of its seeds)]

crouch /kraʊtʃ/ *v. & n.* —*v.intr.* lower the body with the limbs close to the chest, esp. for concealment, or (of an animal) before pouncing; be in this position. —*n.* an act of crouching; a crouching position. [ME, perh. f. OF *crochir* be bent f. *croc* hook: cf. CROOK]

croup[1] /kruːp/ *n.* an inflammation of the larynx and trachea in children, with a hard cough and difficulty in breathing. □□ **croupy** *adj.* [*croup* to croak (imit.)]

croup[2] /kruːp/ *n.* the rump or hindquarters esp. of a horse. [ME f. OF *croupe*, rel. to CROP]

croupier /ˈkruːpɪə(r), -ˌeɪ/ *n.* **1** the person in charge of a gaming-table, raking in and paying out money etc. **2** the assistant chairperson at a public dinner, seated at the foot of the table. [F, orig. = rider on the croup: see CROUP[2]]

croûton /ˈkruːtɒn/ *n.* a small piece of fried or toasted bread served with soup or used as a garnish. [F f. *croûte* CRUST]

crow[1] /krəʊ/ *n.* **1** any large black bird of the genus *Corvus*, having a powerful black beak. **2** any similar bird of the family Corvidae, e.g. the raven, rook, and jackdaw. **3** *sl. derog.* a woman, esp. an old or ugly one. □ **as the crow flies** in a straight line. **crow-bill** forceps for extracting bullets etc. **crow's-foot** (*pl.* **-feet**) **1** (usu. in *pl.*) a wrinkle at the outer corner of a person's eye. **2** *Mil.* a caltrop. **crow's-nest** a barrel or platform fixed at the masthead of a sailing vessel as a shelter for a lookout man. **crow steps** corbie-steps. **crow-toe** *archaic* or *dial.* any of various flowers, esp. the bluebell or buttercup. **eat crow** *US* submit to humiliation. [OE *crāwe* ult. f. WG]

crow[2] /krəʊ/ *v. & n.* —*v.intr.* **1** (*past* **crowed** or **crew** /kruː/) (of a cock) utter its characteristic loud cry. **2** (of a baby) utter happy cries. **3** (usu. foll. by *over*) express unrestrained gleeful satisfaction. —*n.* **1** the cry of a cock. **2** a happy cry of a baby. [OE *crāwan*, of imit. orig.]

crowbar /ˈkrəʊbɑː(r)/ *n.* an iron bar with a flattened end, used as a lever.

crowberry /ˈkrəʊbərɪ/ *n.* (*pl.* **-ies**) **1 a** a heathlike evergreen shrub *Empetrum nigrum*, bearing black berries. **b** the flavourless edible berry of this plant. **2** *US* a cranberry.

crowd /kraʊd/ *n. & v.* —*n.* **1** a large number of people gathered together, usu. without orderly arrangement. **2** a mass of spectators; an audience. **3** *colloq.* a particular company or set of people (*met the crowd from the sales department*). **4** (prec. by *the*) the mass or multitude of people (*go along with the crowd*). **5** a large number (of things). **6** actors representing a crowd. —*v.* **1 a** *intr.* come together in a crowd. **b** *tr.* cause to do this. **c** *intr.* force one's way. **2** *tr.* a (foll. by *into*) force or compress into a confined space. **b** (often foll. by *with*; usu. in *passive*) fill or make abundant with (*was crowded with tourists*). **3** *tr.* **a** (of a number of people) come aggressively close to. **b** *colloq.* harass or pressure (a person). □ **crowd out** exclude by crowding. □□ **crowdedness** *n.* [OE *crūdan* press, drive]

crowfoot /ˈkrəʊfʊt/ *n.* any of various aquatic plants of the genus *Ranunculus*, with white buttercup-like flowers held above the water.

crown /kraʊn/ *n. & v.* —*n.* **1** a monarch's ornamental and usu. jewelled head-dress. **2** (**the Crown**) **a** the monarch, esp. as head of State. **b** the power or authority residing in the monarchy. **3 a** a wreath of leaves or flowers etc. worn on the head, esp. as an emblem of victory. **b** an award or distinction gained by a victory or achievement, esp. in sport. **4** a crown-shaped thing, esp. a device or ornament. **5** the top part of a thing, esp. of the head or a hat. **6 a** the highest or central part of an arched or curved thing (*crown of the road*). **b** a thing that completes or forms the summit. **7** the part of a plant just above and below the ground. **8** the upper part of a cut gem above the girdle. **9 a** the part of a tooth projecting from the gum. **b** an artificial replacement or covering for this. **10 a** a former British coin equal to five shillings (25p). **b** any of several foreign coins with a name meaning 'crown', esp. the krona or krone. **11** a former size of paper, 504 × 384 mm. —*v.tr.* **1** put a crown on (a person or a person's head). **2** invest (a person) with a royal crown or authority. **3** be

a crown to; encircle or rest on the top of. **4 a** (often as **crowning** *adj.*) be or cause to be the consummation, reward, or finishing touch to (*the crowning glory*). **b** bring (efforts) to a happy issue. **5** fit a crown to (a tooth). **6** *sl.* hit on the head. □ **crown cap** a cork-lined metal cap for a bottle. **Crown Colony** a British colony controlled by the Crown. **Crown Court** a court of criminal jurisdiction in England and Wales. **Crown Derby** a soft-paste porcelain made at Derby and often marked with a crown above the letter 'D'. **crown glass** see GLASS. **crown green** a kind of bowling-green rising towards the middle. **crown imperial** a tall fritillary, *Fritillaria imperialis*, with a flower-cluster at the top of the stalk. **crown jewels** the regalia and other jewellery worn by the sovereign on certain State occasions. **Crown Office** (in the UK) an office of the Supreme Court transacting common-law business of Chancery. **crown of thorns** any starfish of the genus *Acanthaster* feeding on coral. **Crown prince** a male heir to a sovereign throne. **Crown princess 1** the wife of a Crown prince. **2** a female heir to a sovereign throne. **crown roast** a roast of rib-pieces of pork or lamb arranged like a crown. **crown saw** a cylinder with a toothed edge for making a circular hole. **crown wheel** a wheel with teeth set at right angles to its plane, esp. in the gears of motor vehicles. [ME f. AF *corune*, OF *corone* f. L *corona*]

Crozet Islands /krəʊˈzeɪ/ a group of five small French islands in the southern Indian Ocean.

crozier var. of CROSIER.

CRT *abbr.* cathode-ray tube.

cru /kruː/ *n.* **1** a French vineyard or wine-producing region. **2** the grade of wine produced from it. [F f. *crû* grown]

cruces *pl.* of CRUX.

crucial /ˈkruːʃ(ə)l/ *adj.* **1** decisive, critical. **2** *disp.* very important. □□ **cruciality** /-ʃɪˈælɪtɪ/ *n.* (*pl.* **-ies**). **crucially** *adv.* [F f. L *crux crucis* cross]

crucian /ˈkruːʃ(ə)n/ *n.* a yellow cyprinoid fish, *Carassius carassius*, allied to the goldfish. [LG *karusse* etc.]

cruciate /ˈkruːʃɪeɪt/ *adj. Zool.* cross-shaped. [mod.L *cruciatus* f. L (as CRUCIBLE)]

crucible /ˈkruːsɪb(ə)l/ *n.* **1** a melting-pot for metals etc. **2** a severe test or trial. [ME f. med.L *crucibulum* night-lamp, crucible, f. L *crux crucis* cross]

crucifer /ˈkruːsɪfə(r)/ *n.* a cruciferous plant.

cruciferous /kruːˈsɪfərəs/ *adj. Bot.* of the family Cruciferae, having flowers with four petals arranged in a cross. [LL *crucifer* (as CRUCIAL, -FEROUS)]

crucifix /ˈkruːsɪfɪks/ *n.* a model or image of a cross with a figure of Christ on it. [ME f. OF f. eccl.L *crucifixus* f. L *cruci fixus* fixed to a cross]

crucifixion /ˌkruːsɪˈfɪkʃ(ə)n/ *n.* **1 a** a crucifying or being crucified. **b** an instance of this. (See below.) **2** (**Crucifixion**) **a** the crucifixion of Christ. **b** a representation of this. [eccl.L *crucifixio* (as CRUCIFIX)]

Crucifixion was a form of capital punishment used by various ancient peoples including the Persians, Carthaginians, and Romans; it was normally confined to slaves and other persons with no civil rights. The condemned man was first flogged and then made to carry a cross-beam to the place of execution, where a stake had been fixed in the ground. He was fastened to the beam by nails or cords, and it was drawn up and fixed to the stake so that his feet were clear of the ground; sometimes the feet were fastened to the upright. Some support for the body was provided by a projecting ledge, but a footrest is rarely attested. Death apparently resulted from exhaustion, perhaps caused by the difficulty of breathing when the body's weight is suspended by the arms in this way; it could be hastened by breaking the legs. The penalty was abolished by the emperor Constantine.

cruciform /ˈkruːsɪˌfɔːm/ *adj.* cross-shaped (esp. of a church with transepts). [L *crux crucis* cross + -FORM]

crucify /ˈkruːsɪˌfaɪ/ *v.tr.* (**-ies, -ied**) **1** put to death by fastening to a cross. **2 a** cause extreme pain to. **b** persecute, torment. **c** *sl.* defeat thoroughly in an argument, match, etc. □□ **crucifier** *n.* [ME f. OF *crucifier* f. LL *crucifigere* (as CRUCIFIX)]

cruck /krʌk/ n. *Brit. hist.* either of a pair of curved timbers extending to the ground in the framework of a type of medieval house-roof. [var. of CROOK]

crud /krʌd/ n. *sl.* **1 a** a deposit of unwanted impurities, grease, etc. **b** a corrosive deposit in a nuclear reactor. **2** an unpleasant person. **3** nonsense. □□ **cruddy** *adj.* (**cruddier, cruddiest**). [var. of CURD]

crude /kruːd/ *adj. & n.* —*adj.* **1 a** in the natural or raw state; not refined. **b** rough, unpolished; lacking finish. **2 a** (of an action or statement or manners) rude, blunt. **b** offensive, indecent (*a crude gesture*). **3 a** *Statistics* (of figures) not adjusted or corrected. **b** rough (*a crude estimate*). —*n.* natural mineral oil. □□ **crudely** *adv.* **crudeness** *n.* **crudity** *n.* [ME f. L *crudus* raw, rough]

crudités /ˌkruːdɪˈteɪ/ n.pl. an hors d'œuvre of mixed raw vegetables often served with a sauce into which they are dipped. [F]

cruel /ˈkruːəl/ *adj. & v.* —*adj.* (**crueller, cruellest** or **crueler, cruelest**) **1** indifferent to or gratified by another's suffering. **2** causing pain or suffering, esp. deliberately. —*v.tr.* (**cruelled, cruelling**) *Austral. sl.* thwart, spoil. □□ **cruelly** *adv.* **cruelness** *n.* [ME f. OF f. L *crudelis,* rel. to *crudus* (as CRUDE)]

cruelty /ˈkruːəltɪ/ n. (pl. **-ies**) **1** a cruel act or attitude; indifference to another's suffering. **2** a succession of cruel acts; a continued cruel attitude (*suffered much cruelty*). **3** *Law* physical or mental harm inflicted (whether or not intentional), esp. as a ground for divorce. [OF *crualté* ult. f. L *crudelitas*]

cruet /ˈkruːɪt/ n. **1** a small container for salt, pepper, oil, or vinegar for use at table. **2** (in full **cruet-stand**) a stand holding cruets. **3** *Eccl.* a small container for the wine and water in the celebration of the Eucharist. [ME through AF f. OF *crue* pot f. OS *krūka:* rel. to CROCK²]

Crufts /krʌfts/ an annual dog-show held in London, first organized in 1886 by Charles Cruft, British dog-breeder.

Cruikshank /ˈkrʊkʃæŋk/, George (1792–1878), English painter, illustrator, and caricaturist, the most eminent political cartoonist of his day (the private life of the Prince Regent was one of his targets). His other drawings include illustrations for Grimms's stories and later for the works of Charles Dickens.

cruise /kruːz/ *v. & n.* —*v.* **1** *intr.* make a journey by sea calling at a series of ports usu. according to a predetermined plan, esp. for pleasure. **2** *intr.* sail about without a precise destination. **3** *intr.* **a** (of a motor vehicle or aircraft) travel at a moderate or economical speed. **b** (of a vehicle or its driver) travel at random, esp. slowly. **4** *intr.* achieve an objective, win a race etc., with ease. **5** *intr. & tr. sl.* walk or drive about (the streets etc.) in search of a sexual (esp. homosexual) partner. —*n.* a cruising voyage, esp. as a holiday. □ **cruise missile** one able to fly at a low altitude and guide itself by reference to the features of the region it traverses. **cruising speed** a comfortable and economical speed for a motor vehicle, below its maximum speed. [prob. f. Du. *kruisen* f. *kruis* CROSS]

cruiser /ˈkruːzə(r)/ n. **1** a warship of high speed and medium armament. **2** = *cabin cruiser.* **3** *US* a police patrol car. [Du. *kruiser* (as CRUISE)]

cruiserweight /ˈkruːzəˌweɪt/ n. esp. *Brit.* = *light heavyweight* (see HEAVYWEIGHT).

cruller /ˈkrʌlə(r)/ n. *US* a small cake made of a rich dough twisted or curled and fried in fat. [prob. f. Du. *krullen* curl]

crumb /krʌm/ n. & v. —n. **1 a** a small fragment, esp. of bread. **b** a small particle (*a crumb of comfort*). **2** the soft inner part of a loaf of bread. **3** *sl.* an objectionable person. —*v.tr.* **1** cover with breadcrumbs. **2** break into crumbs. [OE *cruma*]

crumble /ˈkrʌmb(ə)l/ *v. & n.* —*v.* **1** *tr. & intr.* break or fall into crumbs or fragments. **2** *intr.* (of power, a reputation, etc.) gradually disintegrate. —*n.* **1** a mixture of flour and fat, rubbed to the texture of breadcrumbs and cooked as a topping for fruit etc. (*apple crumble; vegetable crumble*). **2** a crumbly or crumbled substance. [ME f. OE, formed as CRUMB]

crumbly /ˈkrʌmblɪ/ *adj.* (**crumblier, crumbliest**) consisting of, or apt to fall into, crumbs or fragments. □□ **crumbliness** *n.*

crumbs /krʌmz/ int. *Brit. sl.* expressing dismay or surprise. [euphem. for *Christ*]

crumby /ˈkrʌmɪ/ *adj.* (**crumbier, crumbiest**) **1** like or covered in crumbs. **2** = CRUMMY.

crumhorn var. of KRUMMHORN.

crummy /ˈkrʌmɪ/ *adj.* (**crummier, crummiest**) *colloq.* dirty, squalid; inferior, worthless. □□ **crummily** *adv.* **crumminess** *n.* [var. of CRUMBY]

crump /krʌmp/ n. & v. *Mil. sl.* —n. the sound of a bursting bomb or shell. —*v.intr.* make this sound. [imit.]

crumpet /ˈkrʌmpɪt/ n. **1** a soft flat cake of a yeast mixture cooked on a griddle and eaten toasted and buttered. **2** *Brit. joc.* or *offens.* **a** a sexually attractive person, esp. a woman. **b** women regarded collectively, esp. as objects of sexual desire. **3** *archaic sl.* the head. [17th c.: orig. uncert.]

crumple /ˈkrʌmp(ə)l/ *v. & n.* —*v.* **1** *tr. & intr.* (often foll. by *up*) **a** crush or become crushed into creases. **b** ruffle, wrinkle. **2** *intr.* (often foll. by *up*) collapse, give way. —*n.* a crease or wrinkle. □ **crumple zone** a part of a motor vehicle, esp. the extreme front and rear, designed to crumple easily in a crash and absorb impact. □□ **crumply** *adj.* [obs. *crump* (v. & adj.) (make or become) curved]

crunch /krʌntʃ/ *v. & n.* —*v.* **1** *tr.* **a** crush noisily with the teeth. **b** grind (gravel, dry snow, etc.) under foot, wheels, etc. **2** *intr.* (often foll. by *up, through*) make a crunching sound in walking, moving, etc. —*n.* **1** crunching; a crunching sound. **2** *colloq.* a decisive event or moment. [earlier *cra(u)nch,* assim. to *munch*]

crunchy /ˈkrʌntʃɪ/ *adj.* (**crunchier, crunchiest**) that can be or has been crunched or crushed into small pieces; hard and crispy. □□ **crunchily** *adv.* **crunchiness** *n.*

crupper /ˈkrʌpə(r)/ n. **1** a strap buckled to the back of a saddle and looped under the horse's tail to hold the harness back. **2** the hindquarters of a horse. [ME f. OF *cropiere* (cf. CROUP²)]

crural /ˈkrʊər(ə)l/ *adj. Anat.* of the leg. [F *crural* or L *cruralis* f. *crus cruris* leg]

crusade /kruːˈseɪd/ n. & v. —n. **1 a** (**Crusade**) any of several medieval military expeditions made by western European Christians in the 11th–13th c. to recover the Holy Land from the Saracen Muslims. (See below.) **b** a war instigated by the Church for alleged religious ends. **2** a vigorous campaign in favour of a cause. —*v.intr.* engage in a crusade. □□ **crusader** *n.* [earlier *croisade* (F f. *croix* cross) or *crusado* (Sp. f. *cruz* cross)]

The first Crusade (1096–9) resulted in the capture of Jerusalem and the establishment of Crusader States in the Holy Land, but the second (1147–9) failed to stop a Muslim resurgence, and Jerusalem fell to Saladin in 1187. The third (1189–92) recaptured some lost ground but not Jerusalem, while the fourth (1202–4) was diverted against the Byzantine Empire, which was fatally weakened by the resultant sack of Constantinople. The fifth (1217–21) was sidetracked to Egypt, where it accomplished nothing, and although the sixth (1228–9) resulted in the return of Jerusalem to Christian hands the city was lost to the Turks in 1244. The seventh (1248–54) ended in disaster in Egypt, while the eighth and last (1270–1) petered out when its leader Louis IX of France died on his way east, and the Holy Land was left in Muslim hands until the 20th c. Although undertaken in a religious cause, the Crusades were carried on like most other medieval wars and were generally badly organized and indecisive.

cruse /kruːz/ n. *archaic* an earthenware pot or jar. [OE *crūse,* of unkn. orig.]

crush /krʌʃ/ *v. & n.* —*v.tr.* **1** compress with force or violence, so as to break, bruise, etc. **2** reduce to powder by pressure. **3** crease or crumple by rough handling. **4** defeat or subdue completely (*crushed by my reply*). —*n.* **1** an act of crushing. **2** a crowded mass of people. **3** a drink made from the juice of crushed fruit. **4** *colloq.* **a** (usu. foll. by *on*) a (usu. passing) infatuation. **b** the object of an infatuation (*who's the latest crush?*). □ **crush bar** a place in a theatre for audiences to buy drinks in the intervals. **crush barrier** a barrier, esp. a temporary one, for restraining a crowd. □□ **crushable** *adj.* **crusher** *n.* **crushingly** *adv.* [ME f. AF *crussir, corussier,* OF *croissir, cruissir,* gnash (teeth), crack, f. Rmc]

crust /krʌst/ n. & v. —n. **1 a** the hard outer part of a loaf of bread. **b** a piece of this with some soft bread attached. **c** a hard dry scrap of bread. **d** esp. *Austral. sl.* a livelihood (*what do you do for a crust?*). **2** the pastry covering of a pie. **3** a hard casing of a softer thing, e.g. a harder layer over soft snow. **4** *Geol.* the outer portion of the earth. **5 a** a coating or deposit on the surface of anything. **b** a hard dry formation on the skin, a scab. **6** a deposit of tartar formed in bottles of old wine. **7 a** *sl.* impudence (*you have a crust!*). **b** a superficial hardness of manner. —*v.tr. & intr.* **1** cover or become covered with a crust. **2** form into a crust. □□ **crustal** *adj.* (in sense 4 of *n.*). [ME f. OF *crouste* f. L *crusta* rind, shell]

crustacean /krʌˈsteɪʃ(ə)n/ *n. & adj.* —*n.* any arthropod of the class Crustacea, having a hard shell and usu. aquatic, e.g. the crab, lobster, and shrimp. —*adj.* of or relating to crustaceans. □□ **crustaceology** /-ʃɪˈɒlədʒɪ/ *n.* **crustaceous** /-ʃəs/ *adj.* [mod.L *crustaceus* f. *crusta*: see CRUST]

crusted /ˈkrʌstɪd/ *adj.* **1 a** having a crust. **b** (of wine) having deposited a crust. **2** antiquated, venerable (*crusted prejudice*).

crusty /ˈkrʌstɪ/ *adj.* (**crustier, crustiest**) **1** having a crisp crust (*a crusty loaf*). **2** irritable, curt. **3** hard, crustlike. □□ **crustily** *adv.* **crustiness** *n.*

crutch /krʌtʃ/ *n.* **1** a support for a lame person, usu. with a crosspiece at the top fitting under the armpit (*pair of crutches*). **2** any support or prop. **3** the crotch of the human body or garment. [OE *cryc(c)* f. Gmc]

Crutched Friars /krʌtʃt/ an order of mendicant friars. Of uncertain origin, they were established in Italy by 1169; they came to England in 1244, and similar orders existed in France and the Low Countries from the 13th c. The word 'crutched' means 'cross-bearing'; in 1243 they bore a cross upon the top of their staves, but subsequently wore a cross of scarlet cloth on the breast of their habit, which Pope Pius II in 1460 appointed to be blue. The order was suppressed in 1656. [obs. *crouch* cross]

crux /krʌks/ *n.* (*pl.* **cruxes** or **cruces** /ˈkruːsiːz/) **1** the decisive point at issue. **2** a difficult matter; a puzzle. [L, = cross]

Crux Australis /krʌks ɔːˈstreɪlɪs/ the Southern Cross (see entry). [L]

cruzado /kruːˈzɑːdəʊ/ *n.* (*pl.* **-os**) the chief monetary unit of Brazil from 1986. [Port. *cruzado, crusado*, = marked with the cross]

cruzeiro /kruːˈzeərəʊ/ *n.* (*pl.* **-os**) the former monetary unit of Brazil; from 1986 one-thousandth of a cruzado. [Port., = large cross]

cry /kraɪ/ *v. & n.* —*v.* (**cries, cried**) **1** *intr.* (often foll. by *out*) make a loud or shrill sound, esp. to express pain, grief, etc., or to appeal for help. **2 a** *intr.* shed tears; weep. **b** *tr.* shed (tears). **3** *tr.* (often foll. by *out*) say or exclaim loudly or excitedly. **4** *intr.* (of an animal, esp. a bird) make a loud call. **5** *tr.* (of a hawker etc.) proclaim (wares etc.) in the street. —*n.* (*pl.* **cries**) **1** a loud inarticulate utterance of grief, pain, fear, joy, etc. **2** a loud excited utterance of words. **3** an urgent appeal or entreaty. **4** a spell of weeping. **5 a** public demand; a strong movement of opinion. **b** a watchword or rallying call. **6** the natural utterance of an animal, esp. of hounds on the scent. **7** the street-call of a hawker etc. □ **cry-baby** a person, esp. a child, who sheds tears frequently. **cry down** disparage, belittle. **cry one's eyes** (or **heart**) **out** weep bitterly. **cry for the moon** ask for what is unattainable. **cry from the heart** a passionate appeal or protest. **cry off** *colloq.* withdraw from a promise or undertaking. **cry out for** demand as a self-evident requirement or solution. **cry over spilt milk** see MILK. **cry stinking fish** disparage one's own efforts, products, etc. **cry up** praise, extol. **cry wolf** see WOLF. **a far cry 1** a long way. **2** a very different thing. **for crying out loud** *colloq.* an exclamation of surprise or annoyance. **in full cry** (of hounds) in keen pursuit. [ME f. OF *crier, cri* f. L *quiritare* wail]

cryer var. of CRIER.

crying /ˈkraɪɪŋ/ *attrib.adj.* (of an injustice or other evil) flagrant, demanding redress (*a crying need; a crying shame*).

cryo- /ˈkraɪəʊ/ *comb. form* (extreme) cold. [Gk *kruos* frost]

cryobiology /ˌkraɪəʊbaɪˈɒlədʒɪ/ *n.* the biology of organisms

below their normal temperatures. □□ **cryobiological** /-ˌbaɪəˈlɒdʒɪk(ə)l/ *adj.* **cryobiologist** *n.*

cryogen /ˈkraɪədʒ(ə)n/ *n.* a freezing-mixture; a substance used to produce very low temperatures.

cryogenics /ˌkraɪəʊˈdʒenɪks/ *n.* the branch of physics dealing with the production and effects of very low temperatures. Modern techniques have reduced temperatures to a tiny fraction of 1 kelvin; the laws of physics suggest, however, that the absolute zero of temperature is in principle unattainable. Low temperature environments are becoming increasingly important in science and in industry. At very low temperatures many elements and alloys entirely lose their electrical resistance and become superconductors; this has many applications, e.g. in the production of powerful electromagnets. At very low temperatures also the thermal 'noise' produced by vibrating atoms is greatly reduced and various types of electrical devices, including detectors of electromagnetic signals, become much more sensitive and discriminating. □□ **cryogenic** *adj.*

cryolite /ˈkraɪəʊˌlaɪt/ *n. Mineral.* a lustrous mineral of sodium-aluminium fluoride, used in the manufacture of aluminium.

cryopump /ˈkraɪəʊˌpʌmp/ *n.* a vacuum pump using liquefied gases.

cryostat /ˈkraɪəʊˌstæt/ *n.* an apparatus for maintaining a very low temperature.

cryosurgery /ˌkraɪəʊˈsɜːdʒərɪ/ *n.* surgery using the local application of intense cold for anaesthesia or therapy.

crypt /krɪpt/ *n.* an underground room or vault, esp. one beneath a church, used usu. as a burial-place. [ME f. L *crypta* f. Gk *kruptē* f. *kruptos* hidden]

cryptanalysis /ˌkrɪptəˈnælɪsɪs/ *n.* the art or process of deciphering cryptograms by analysis. □□ **cryptanalyst** /-ˈænəlɪst/ *n.* **cryptanalytic** /-ˌænəˈlɪtɪk/ *adj.* **cryptanalytical** /-ˌænəˈlɪtɪk(ə)l/ *adj.* [CRYPTO- + ANALYSIS]

cryptic /ˈkrɪptɪk/ *adj.* **1 a** obscure in meaning. **b** (of a crossword clue etc.) indirect; indicating the solution in a way that is not obvious. **c** secret, mysterious, enigmatic. **2** *Zool.* (of coloration etc.) serving for concealment. □□ **cryptically** *adv.* [LL *crypticus* f. Gk *kruptikos* (as CRYPTO-)]

crypto /ˈkrɪptəʊ/ *n.* (*pl.* **-os**) *colloq.* a person having a secret allegiance to a political creed etc., esp. communism. [as CRYPTO-]

crypto- /ˈkrɪptəʊ/ *comb. form* concealed, secret (*crypto-communist*). [Gk *kruptos* hidden]

cryptocrystalline /ˌkrɪptəʊˈkrɪstəˌlaɪn/ *adj.* having a crystalline structure visible only when magnified.

cryptogam /ˈkrɪptəˌgæm/ *n.* a plant that has no true flowers or seeds, e.g. ferns, mosses, algae, and fungi. □□ **cryptogamic** /-ˈgæmɪk/ *adj.* **cryptogamous** /-ˈtɒgəməs/ *adj.* [F *cryptogame* f. mod.L *cryptogamae* (*plantae*) formed as CRYPTO- + Gk *gamos* marriage]

cryptogram /ˈkrɪptəˌgræm/ *n.* a text written in cipher.

cryptography /krɪpˈtɒgrəfɪ/ *n.* the art of writing or solving ciphers. □□ **cryptographer** *n.* **cryptographic** /-təˈgræfɪk/ *adj.* **cryptographically** /-təˈgræfɪkəlɪ/ *adv.*

cryptomeria /ˌkrɪptəˈmɪərɪə/ *n.* a tall evergreen tree, *Cryptomeria japonica*, native to China and Japan, with long curved spirally arranged leaves and short cones. Also called *Japanese cedar*. [CRYPTO- + Gk *meros* part (because the seeds are enclosed by scales)]

crystal /ˈkrɪst(ə)l/ *n. & adj.* —*n.* **1 a** a clear transparent mineral, esp. rock crystal. **b** a piece of this. **2** (in full **crystal glass**) **a** highly transparent glass; flint glass. **b** articles made of this. **3** the glass over a watch-face. **4** *Electronics* a crystalline piece of semiconductor. **5** *Chem.* **a** an aggregation of molecules with a definite internal structure and the external form of a solid enclosed by symmetrically arranged plane faces. **b** a solid whose constituent particles are symmetrically arranged. —*adj.* (usu. *attrib.*) made of, like, or clear as crystal. □ **crystal ball** a glass globe used in crystal-gazing. **crystal class** *Crystallog.* any of 32 categories of crystals classified according to their symmetry. **crystal clear** unclouded, transparent. **crystal-gazing** the process of concentrating one's gaze on a crystal ball supposedly in order to obtain a picture of future events etc. **crystal lattice** Crystallog. the regular repeating pattern of atoms, ions, or molecules in a crystalline substance. **crystal set** a simple early form of radio receiving apparatus with a crystal touching a metal wire as the rectifier. **crystal system** Crystallog. any of seven possible unique combinations of unit cells, crystal lattices, and symmetry elements of a crystal class. [OE f. OF cristal f. L crystallum f. Gk krustallos ice, crystal]

crystalline /ˈkrɪstəˌlaɪn/ adj. **1** of, like, or clear as crystal. **2** Chem. & Mineral. having the structure and form of a crystal. □ **crystalline lens** a transparent lens enclosed in a membranous capsule behind the iris of the eye. □□ **crystallinity** /-ˈlɪnɪti/ n. [ME f. OF cristallin f. L crystallinus f. Gk krustallinos (as CRYSTAL)]

crystallite /ˈkrɪstəˌlaɪt/ n. **1** a small crystal. **2** an individual perfect crystal or grain in a metal etc. **3** Bot. a region of cellulose etc. with a crystal-like structure.

crystallize /ˈkrɪstəˌlaɪz/ v. (also **-ise**) **1** tr. & intr. form or cause to form crystals. **2** (often foll. by out) **a** intr. (of ideas or plans) become definite. **b** tr. make definite. **3** tr. & intr. coat or impregnate or become coated or impregnated with sugar (crystallized fruit). □□ **crystallizable** adj. **crystallization** /-ˈzeɪʃ(ə)n/ n.

crystallography /ˌkrɪstəˈlɒgrəfi/ n. the science of crystal form and structure. □□ **crystallographer** n. **crystallographic** /-ləˈgræfik/ adj.

crystalloid /ˈkrɪstəˌlɔɪd/ adj. & n. —adj. **1** crystal-like. **2** having a crystalline structure. —n. a substance that in solution is able to pass through a semipermeable membrane (cf. COLLOID).

Crystal Palace a large building of iron and glass, like a giant greenhouse, designed by (Sir) Joseph Paxton for the Great Exhibition of 1851 in Hyde Park, London, and re-erected at Sydenham near Croydon; it was accidentally burnt down in 1936.

CS abbr. **1** Civil Service. **2** chartered surveyor. **3** Court of Session.

Cs symb. Chem. the element caesium.

c/s abbr. cycles per second.

csardas /ˈtʃɑːdæʃ/ n. (also **czardas**) (pl. same) a Hungarian dance with a slow start and a quick wild finish. [Magyar csárdás f. csárda inn]

CSC abbr. **1** Civil Service Commission. **2** Conspicuous Service Cross.

CSE abbr. hist. (in the UK) Certificate of Secondary Education. ¶ Replaced in 1988 by GCSE.

CS gas /siːˈes/ n. a gas causing tears and choking, used to control riots etc. [B. B. Corson & R. W. Stoughton, Amer. chemists]

CSI abbr. Companion of the Order of the Star of India.

CSIRO abbr. Commonwealth Scientific and Industrial Research Organization.

CSM abbr. (in the UK) Company Sergeant-Major.

CST abbr. (in the US) Central Standard Time.

CSU abbr. (in the UK) Civil Service Union.

CT abbr. US Connecticut (in official postal use).

ct. abbr. **1** carat. **2** cent.

CTC abbr. **1** (in the UK) Cyclists' Touring Club. **2** (in the UK) City Technology College.

ctenoid /ˈtiːnɔɪd/ adj. Zool. (of fish scales) characterized by tiny toothlike processes (cf. PLACOID). [Gk kteis ktenos comb]

ctenophore /ˈtiːnəˌfɔː(r), ˈtɛn-/ n. any marine animal of the phylum Ctenophora, having a jellyfish-like body bearing rows of cilia, e.g. sea gooseberries. [mod.L ctenophorus (as CTENOID)]

Ctesiphon /ˈtɛsɪf(ə)n/ an ancient city on the Tigris near Baghdad, capital of the Parthian kingdom from c.224 and then of Persia under the Sassanian dynasty. It was taken by the Arabs in 636.

CU abbr. Cambridge University.

Cu symb. Chem. the element copper.

cu. abbr. cubic.

cub /kʌb/ n. & v. —n. **1** the young of a fox, bear, lion, etc. **2** an ill-mannered young man. **3** (**Cub**) (in full **Cub Scout**) a member of the junior branch of the Scout Association (see entry). **4** (in full **cub reporter**) colloq. a young or inexperienced newspaper reporter. **5** US an apprentice. —v.tr. (**cubbed, cubbing**) (also absol.) give birth to (cubs). □□ **cubhood** n. [16th c.: orig. unkn.]

Cuba /ˈkjuːbə/ a Caribbean country, the largest and furthest west of the islands of the West Indies, situated at the mouth of the Gulf of Mexico; pop. (est. 1988) 10,354,000; official language, Spanish; capital, Havana. Sugar is the mainstay of the economy and is the principal export; other main exports include nickel and tobacco. One of the first parts of the New World to be discovered and colonized by Spain, Cuba remained under Spanish rule until the Spanish-American War of 1898. Thereafter it was nominally independent but heavily under American influence, until granted full autonomy in 1934. The country was stricken by instability, however, and after several periods of dictatorship was taken over by a Communist rebellion in 1959, since which time it has leant heavily on Russian aid under the presidency of Fidel Castro. In 1962 Cuba became the focus of cold war manoeuvres when on 22 Oct. President Kennedy announced a US blockade of the island in order to compel the USSR to dismantle the missile bases which it had installed there. On 28 Oct. Khrushchev agreed to do so, and the crisis was over; the prospect of nuclear war had never seemed closer.

Cuban /ˈkjuːbən/ adj. & n. —adj. of or relating to Cuba or its people. —n. a native or national of Cuba. □ **Cuban heel** a moderately high straight heel of a man's or woman's shoe.

Cubango see OKAVANGO.

cubby /ˈkʌbi/ n. (pl. **-ies**) (in full **cubby-hole**) **1** a very small room. **2** a snug or confined space. [dial. cub stall, pen, of LG orig.]

cube /kjuːb/ n. & v. —n. **1** a solid contained by six equal squares. **2** a cube-shaped block. **3** Math. the product of a number multiplied by its square. —v.tr. **1** find the cube of (a number). **2** cut (food for cooking etc.) into small cubes. □ **cube root** the number which produces a given number when cubed. □□ **cuber** n. [F cube or L cubus f. Gk kubos]

cubeb /ˈkjuːbɛb/ n. **1** a climbing plant, Piper cubeba, bearing pungent berries. **2** this berry crushed for use in medicated cigarettes. [ME f. OF cubebe, quibibe ult. f. Arab. kobāba, kubāba]

cubic /ˈkjuːbɪk/ adj. **1** cube-shaped. **2** of three dimensions. **3** involving the cube (and no higher power) of a number (cubic equation). **4** Crystallog. having three equal axes at right angles. □ **cubic content** the volume of a solid expressed in cubic metres. **cubic metre** etc. the volume of a cube whose edge is one metre etc. [F cubique or L cubicus f. Gk kubikos (as CUBE)]

cubical /ˈkjuːbɪk(ə)l/ adj. cube-shaped. □□ **cubically** adv.

cubicle /ˈkjuːbɪk(ə)l/ n. **1** a small partitioned space, screened for privacy. **2** a small separate sleeping-compartment. [L cubiculum f. cubare lie down]

cubiform /ˈkjuːbɪˌfɔːm/ adj. cube-shaped.

cubism /ˈkjuːbɪz(ə)m/ n. a style and movement in art, esp. painting, in which objects are so presented as to give the effect of an assemblage of geometrical figures. This style, created by Picasso and Braque, was inaugurated by Picasso's Demoiselles d'Avignon (1906–7) and Braque's Nude (1907–8). It was a reaction against the optical realism of impressionism, and developed from Cézanne's structural analysis; its aim was to depict the permanent structure of things as perceived in their solid tangible reality. In the first phase, known as analytical cubism, the artists confined their colour range and subject-matter, made the picture-space artificially shallow, and depicted objects as a series of planes, as they would be seen from a variety of different viewpoints. In the later phase, synthetic cubism (1912 onwards), they experimented with collages, sticking pieces of newspaper, matchboxes, etc., on to the canvas and combining them with drawing or painting. The movement ended c.1920, but its influence was strong until the 1940s. □□ **cubist** n. & adj. [F cubisme (as CUBE)]

cubit /ˈkjuːbɪt/ n. an ancient measure of length, approximately equal to the length of a forearm. [ME f. L cubitum elbow, cubit]

cubital /ˈkjuːbɪt(ə)l/ adj. **1** Anat. of the forearm. **2** Zool. of the corresponding part in animals. [ME f. L cubitalis (as CUBIT)]

cuboid /ˈkjuːbɔɪd/ adj. & n. —adj. cube-shaped; like a cube. —n. **1** Geom. a rectangular parallelepiped. **2** (in full **cuboid bone**)

æ cat ɑ: arm e bed ɜ: her ɪ sit i: see ɒ hot ɔ: saw ʌ run ʊ put u: too ə ago aɪ my

Anat. the outer bone of the tarsus. □□ **cuboidal** /-'bɔɪd(ə)l/ *adj.* [mod.L *cuboides* f. Gk *kuboeidēs* (as CUBE)]

cucking-stool /ˈkʌkɪŋˌstuːl/ *n. hist.* a chair on which disorderly women were ducked as a punishment. [ME f. obs. *cuck* defecate]

cuckold /ˈkʌkəʊld/ *n. & v.* —*n.* the husband of an adulteress. —*v.tr.* make a cuckold of. □□ **cuckoldry** *n.* [ME *cukeweld*, *cokewold*, f. OF *cucu* cuckoo]

cuckoo /ˈkʊkuː/ *n. & adj.* —*n.* any bird of the family Cuculidae, having a characteristic cry, esp. the migratory European bird *Cuculus canorus* which deposits its eggs in the nests of small birds, who hatch and rear the chicks as their own. —*predic.adj. sl.* crazy, foolish. □ **cuckoo clock** a clock that strikes the hour with a sound like a cuckoo's call, usu. with the emergence on each note of a mechanical cuckoo. **cuckoo flower 1** a meadow plant, *Cardamine pratensis*, with pale lilac flowers. **2** = *ragged robin.* **cuckoo in the nest** an unwelcome intruder. **cuckoo-pint** a wild arum, *Arum maculatum*, with arrow-shaped leaves and scarlet berries: also called *lords and ladies* (see LORD). **cuckoo-spit** froth exuded by larvae of insects of the family Cercopidae on leaves, stems, etc. [ME f. OF *cucu*, imit.]

cucumber /ˈkjuːkʌmbə(r)/ *n.* **1** a long green fleshy fruit, used in salads. **2** the climbing plant, *Cucumis sativus*, yielding this fruit. [ME f. OF *co(u)combre* f. L *cucumer*]

cucurbit /kjuːˈkɜːbɪt/ *n.* = GOURD. □□ **cucurbitaceous** /-ˈteɪʃəs/ *adj.* [L *cucurbita*]

cud /kʌd/ *n.* half-digested food returned from the first stomach of ruminants to the mouth for further chewing. [OE *cwidu*, *cudu* what is chewed, corresp. to OHG *kuti*, *quiti* glue]

cuddle /ˈkʌd(ə)l/ *v. & n.* —*v.* **1** *tr.* hug, embrace, fondle. **2** *intr.* nestle together, lie close and snug. —*n.* a prolonged and fond hug. □□ **cuddlesome** *adj.* [16th c.: perh. f. dial. *couth* snug]

cuddly /ˈkʌdlɪ/ *adj.* (**cuddlier**, **cuddliest**) tempting to cuddle; given to cuddling.

cuddy /ˈkʌdɪ/ *n.* (pl. **-ies**) *Sc.* **1** a donkey. **2** a stupid person. [perh. a pet-form of the name *Cuthbert*]

cudgel /ˈkʌdʒ(ə)l/ *n. & v.* —*n.* a short thick stick used as a weapon. —*v.tr.* (**cudgelled**, **cudgelling**; *US* **cudgeled**, **cudgeling**) beat with a cudgel. □ **cudgel one's brains** think hard about a problem. **take up the cudgels** (often foll. by *for*) make a vigorous defence. [OE *cycgel*, of unkn. orig.]

Cudlipp /ˈkʌdlɪp/, Hugh (1913–), British journalist, noted for his flamboyant style on the *Daily Mirror*, where he was features editor from 1935 and later (after the Second World War) editorial director. His overall formula for success, based on the presentation of sex, crime, and rabble-rousing politics, dramatically increased the paper's circulation. He gave his own account of this in his book *Publish and Be Damned* (1953).

cudweed /ˈkʌdwiːd/ *n.* any wild composite plant of the genus *Gnaphalium*, with scales and round flower-heads, formerly given to cattle that had lost their cud.

cue[1] /kjuː/ *n. & v.* —*n.* **1 a** the last words of an actor's speech serving as a signal to another actor to enter or speak. **b** a similar signal to a singer or player etc. **2 a** a stimulus to perception etc. **b** a signal for action. **c** a hint on how to behave in particular circumstances. **3** a facility for or an instance of cueing audio equipment (see sense 2 of *v.*). —*v.tr.* (**cues**, **cued**, **cueing** or **cuing**) **1** give a cue to. **2** put (a piece of audio equipment, esp. a record-player or tape recorder) in readiness to play a particular part of the recorded material. □ **cue-bid** *Bridge* an artificial bid to show a particular card etc. in the bidder's hand. **cue in 1** insert a cue for. **2** give information to. **on cue** at the correct moment. **take one's cue from** follow the example or advice of. [16th c.: orig. unkn.]

cue[2] /kjuː/ *n. & v. Billiards* etc. —*n.* a long straight tapering rod for striking the ball. —*v.* (**cues**, **cued**, **cueing** or **cuing**) **1** *tr.* strike (a ball) with a cue. **2** *intr.* use a cue. □ **cue-ball** the ball that is to be struck with the cue. □□ **cueist** *n.* [var. of QUEUE]

Cuenca /ˈkwenkə/ the third-largest city in Ecuador, founded in 1557, known as the 'marble city' because of its many fine buildings; pop. (1982) 272,400.

cuesta /ˈkwestə/ *n. Geog.* a gentle slope, esp. one ending in a steep drop. [Sp., = slope, f. L *costa*: see COAST]

cuff[1] /kʌf/ *n.* **1 a** the end part of a sleeve. **b** a separate band of linen worn round the wrist so as to appear under the sleeve. **c** the part of a glove covering the wrist. **2** *US* a trouser turn-up. **3** (in *pl.*) *colloq.* handcuffs. □ **cuff-link** a device of two joined studs etc. to fasten the sides of a cuff together. **off the cuff** *colloq.* without preparation, extempore. □□ **cuffed** *adj.* (also in *comb.*). [ME: orig. unkn.]

cuff[2] /kʌf/ *v. & n.* —*v.tr.* strike with an open hand. —*n.* such a blow. [16th c.: perh. imit.]

Cufic var. of KUFIC.

cui bono? /kwiː ˈbɒnəʊ, ˈbəʊ-/ who stands, or stood, to gain? (with the implication that this person is responsible). [L, = to whom (is it) a benefit?]

cuirass /kwɪˈræs/ *n.* **1** *hist.* a piece of armour consisting of breastplate and back-plate fastened together. **2** a device for artificial respiration. [ME f. OF *cuirace*, ult. f. LL *coriaceus* f. *corium* leather]

cuirassier /ˌkwɪrəˈsɪə(r)/ *n. hist.* a cavalry soldier wearing a cuirass. [F (as CUIRASS)]

cuish var. of CUISSE.

cuisine /kwɪˈziːn/ *n.* a style or method of cooking, esp. of a particular country or establishment. [F f. L *coquina* f. *coquere* to cook]

cuisse /kwɪs/ *n.* (also **cuish** /kwɪʃ/) (usu. in *pl.*) *hist.* thigh armour. [ME, f. OF *cuisseaux* pl. of *cuissel* f. LL *coxale* f. *coxa* hip]

Culbertson /ˈkʌlbəts(ə)n/, Ely (1891–1955), American authority on contract bridge, whose activities in the early 1930s helped to establish this form of the game in preference to auction bridge.

Culdees /ˈkʌldiːz/ *n.pl.* the name given to certain Irish and Scottish monks in the 8th and following centuries. They appear to have been anchorites in origin, who banded together, usually in groups of 13 (on the analogy of Christ and his Apostles). They were gradually brought under canonical rule along with the secular clergy. [prob. f. Ir. *célé dé* companion]

cul-de-sac /ˈkʌldəˌsæk, ˈkʊl-/ *n.* (pl. **culs-de-sac** pronunc. same) **1** a street or passage closed at one end. **2** a route or course leading nowhere; a position from which one cannot escape. **3** *Anat.* = DIVERTICULUM. [F, = sack-bottom]

-cule /kjuːl/ *suffix* forming (orig. diminutive) nouns (*molecule*). [F *-cule* or L *-culus*]

culinary /ˈkʌlɪnərɪ/ *adj.* of or for cooking or the kitchen. □□ **culinarily** *adv.* [L *culinarius* f. *culina* kitchen]

cull /kʌl/ *v. & n.* —*v.tr.* **1** select, choose, or gather from a large quantity or amount (*knowledge culled from books*). **2** pick or gather (flowers, fruit, etc.). **3** select (animals) according to quality, esp. poor surplus specimens for killing. —*n.* **1** an act of culling. **2** an animal or animals culled. □□ **culler** *n.* [ME f. OF *coillier* etc. ult. f. L *colligere* COLLECT[1]]

cullet /ˈkʌlɪt/ *n.* recycled waste or broken glass used in glass-making. [var. of COLLET]

Culloden /kəˈlɒd(ə)n/ a moor near Inverness in NE Scotland, site of the final engagement of the Jacobite uprising of 1745–6, the last pitched battle fought on British soil. Having withdrawn into the Highlands before the Hanoverian army commanded by the Duke of Cumberland, the small and poorly supplied Jacobite army turned on its pursuers. Superior fire-power smashed the attacking Highland clan regiments, and a ruthless pursuit after the battle effectively prevented any chance of saving the Jacobite cause.

culm[1] /kʌlm/ *n.* **1** coal-dust, esp. of anthracite. **2** *Geol.* strata under coal measures, esp. in SW England. [ME, prob. rel. to COAL]

culm[2] /kʌlm/ *n. Bot.* the stem of a plant, esp. of grasses. □□ **culmiferous** /-ˈmɪfərəs/ *adj.* [L *culmus* stalk]

culminant /ˈkʌlmɪnənt/ *adj.* **1** at or forming the top. **2** *Astron.* on the meridian. [as CULMINATE + -ANT]

culminate /ˈkʌlmɪˌneɪt/ *v.* **1** *intr.* (usu. foll. by *in*) reach its highest or final point (*the antagonism culminated in war*). **2** *tr.* bring to its highest or final point. **3** *intr. Astron.* be on the meridian. □□ **culmination** /-'neɪʃ(ə)n/ n. [LL *culminare culminat-* f. *culmen* summit]

culottes /kjuː'lɒts/ n.pl. women's (usu. short) trousers cut to resemble a skirt. [F, = knee-breeches]

culpable /'kʌlpəb(ə)l/ adj. deserving blame. □□ **culpability** /-'bɪlɪti/ n. **culpably** adv. [ME f. OF *coupable* f. L *culpabilis* f. *culpare* f. *culpa* blame]

culprit /'kʌlprɪt/ n. a person accused of or guilty of an offence. [17th c.: orig. in the formula *Culprit, how will you be tried?*, said by the Clerk of the Crown to a prisoner pleading Not Guilty: perh. abbr. of AF *Culpable: prest d'averrer* etc. (You are) guilty: (I am) ready to prove etc.]

cult /kʌlt/ n. **1** a system of religious worship esp. as expressed in ritual. **2 a** devotion or homage to a person or thing (*the cult of aestheticism*). **b** a popular fashion esp. followed by a specific section of society. **3** (*attrib.*) denoting a person or thing popularized in this way (*cult film*; *cult figure*). □□ **cultic** adj. **cultism** n. **cultist** n. [F *culte* or L *cultus* worship f. *colere cult-* inhabit, till, worship]

cultivar /'kʌltɪˌvɑː(r)/ n. Bot. a plant variety produced by cultivation. [CULTIVATE + VARIETY]

cultivate /'kʌltɪˌveɪt/ v.tr. **1 a** prepare and use (soil etc.) for crops or gardening. **b** break up (the ground) with a cultivator. **2 a** raise or produce (crops). **b** culture (bacteria etc.). **3 a** (often as **cultivated** adj.) apply oneself to improving or developing (the mind, manners, etc.). **b** pay attention to or nurture (a person or a person's friendship). □□ **cultivable** adj. **cultivatable** adj. **cultivation** /-'veɪʃ(ə)n/ n. [med.L *cultivare* f. *cultiva (terra)* arable (land) (as CULT)]

cultivator /'kʌltɪˌveɪtə(r)/ n. **1** a mechanical implement for breaking up the ground and uprooting weeds. **2** a person or thing that cultivates.

cultural /'kʌltʃər(ə)l/ adj. of or relating to the cultivation of the mind or manners, esp. through artistic or intellectual activity. □□ **culturally** adv.

Cultural Revolution a political upheaval in China, 1966–8, initiated by Marshal Lin Piao's calls for a return to revolutionary Maoist beliefs and attacks on the liberal ideals which had become prevalent in the early 20th c. Largely carried forward by the Red Guard, the Cultural Revolution resulted in a large-scale bloodless purge in party posts and the appearance of a virtual cult around the Chinese leader Mao Tse-tung, who had been in semi-retirement since 1959. It led, however, to considerable economic dislocation and was gradually brought to a halt by Chou En-lai.

culture /'kʌltʃə(r)/ n. & v. —n. **1 a** the arts and other manifestations of human intellectual achievement regarded collectively (*a city lacking in culture*). **b** a refined understanding of this; intellectual development (*a person of culture*). **2** the customs, civilization, and achievements of a particular time or people (*studied Chinese culture*). **3** improvement by mental or physical training. **4 a** the cultivation of plants; the rearing of bees, silkworms, etc. **b** the cultivation of the soil. **5** a quantity of micro-organisms and the nutrient material supporting their growth. —v.tr. maintain (bacteria etc.) in conditions suitable for growth. □ **culture shock** the feeling of disorientation experienced by a person suddenly subjected to an unfamiliar culture or way of life. **culture vulture** colloq. a person eager to acquire culture. **the two cultures** the arts and science. [ME f. F *culture* or L *cultura* (as CULT): (v.) f. obs. F *culturer* or med.L *culturare*]

cultured /'kʌltʃəd/ adj. having refined taste and manners and a good education. □ **cultured pearl** a pearl formed by an oyster after the insertion of a foreign body into its shell.

cultus /'kʌltəs/ n. a system of religious worship; a cult. [L: see CULT]

culverin /'kʌlvərɪn/ n. hist. **1** a long cannon. **2** a small firearm. [ME f. OF *coulevrine* f. *couleuvre* snake ult. f. L *colubra*]

culvert /'kʌlvət/ n. **1** an underground channel carrying water across a road etc. **2** a channel for an electric cable. [18th c.: orig. unkn.]

cum /kʌm/ prep. (usu. in comb.) with, combined with, also used as (*a bedroom-cum-study*). [L]

cumber /'kʌmbə(r)/ v. & n. —v.tr. literary hamper, hinder, inconvenience. —n. a hindrance, obstruction, or burden. [ME, prob. f. ENCUMBER]

Cumberland /'kʌmbələnd/, William Augustus, Duke of Cumberland (1721–65), third son of George II. Hanoverian commander at the battle of Culloden, Cumberland gained great notoriety (and the nickname 'the Butcher') for the severity of his suppression of the Jacobite clans in the aftermath of his victory.

cumbersome /'kʌmbəsəm/ adj. inconvenient in size, weight, or shape; unwieldy. □□ **cumbersomely** adv. **cumbersomeness** n. [ME f. CUMBER + -SOME[1]]

Cumbria /'kʌmbrɪə/ **1** an ancient kingdom of northern Britain. **2** a county of NW England; pop. (1981) 481,200; county town, Carlisle. □□ **Cumbrian** adj. & n. [med. L f. Welsh *Cymry* Welshman]

cumbrous /'kʌmbrəs/ adj. = CUMBERSOME. □□ **cumbrously** adv. **cumbrousness** n. [CUMBER + -OUS]

cum grano salis /kʌm ˌgrɑːnəʊ 'sɑːlɪs/ adv. with a grain of salt (see *take with a pinch of salt* (see SALT)). [L]

cumin /'kʌmɪn/ n. (also **cummin**) **1** an umbelliferous plant, *Cuminum cyminum*, bearing aromatic seeds. **2** these seeds used as flavouring, esp. ground and used in curry powder. [ME f. OF *cumin, comin* f. L *cuminum* f. Gk *kuminon*, prob. of Semitic orig.]

cummerbund /'kʌmərˌbʌnd/ n. a waist sash. [Hind. & Pers. *kamar-band* loin-band]

cummin var. of CUMIN.

Cummings /'kʌmɪŋz/, E(dward) E(stlin) (1894–1962), American writer, whose early poems attracted attention for their experimental typography and technical skill, and created some scandal for the frankness of his vocabulary and the sharpness of his satire. His other works include essays, plays, and *Tom* (1935), a satirical ballet based on H. B. Stowe's *Uncle Tom's Cabin*. His experimental novel *The Enormous Room* (1922), an account of his three-month internment in a French detention camp in 1917, won him an international reputation for its brilliant prose and its iconoclastic views. His iconoclasm extended to having his name presented with lower-case initials.

cumquat var. of KUMQUAT.

cumulate v. & adj. —v.tr. & intr. /'kjuːmjʊˌleɪt/ accumulate, amass; combine. —adj. /'kjuːmjʊlət/ heaped up, massed. □□ **cumulation** /-'leɪʃ(ə)n/ n. [L *cumulare* f. *cumulus* heap]

cumulative /'kjuːmjʊlətɪv/ adj. **1 a** increasing or increased in amount, force, etc., by successive additions (*cumulative evidence*). **b** formed by successive additions (*learning is a cumulative process*). **2** Stock Exch. (of shares) entitling holders to arrears of interest before any other distribution is made. □ **cumulative error** an error that increases with the size of the sample revealing it. **cumulative voting** a system in which each voter has as many votes as there are candidates and may give all to one candidate. □□ **cumulatively** adv. **cumulativeness** n.

cumulo- /'kjuːmjʊləʊ/ comb. form cumulus (cloud).

cumulonimbus /ˌkjuːmjʊləʊ'nɪmbəs/ n. a form of cloud consisting of a tall dense mass, present during thunderstorms.

cumulus /'kjuːmjʊləs/ n. (pl. **cumuli** /-ˌlaɪ/) a cloud formation consisting of rounded heaps heaped on each other above a horizontal base. □□ **cumulous** adj. [L, = heap]

Cunard /kjuː'nɑːd/, Sir Samuel (1787–1865), British-Canadian shipowner. A native of Nova Scotia, Cunard was one of the pioneers of the regular transatlantic passenger service, founding the steamship company which still bears his name with the aid of a contract to carry the mails between Britain and Canada.

cuneate /'kjuːnɪət/ adj. wedge-shaped. [L *cuneus* wedge]

cuneiform /'kjuːnɪˌfɔːm/ adj. & n. —adj. **1** wedge-shaped. **2** of, relating to, or using an ancient system of writing with wedge-shaped marks impressed on soft clay with a straight length of reed, bone, wood, or metal, or incised into stone etc. —n. cuneiform writing. It was used (though perhaps not invented) by the Sumerians, whose originally pictographic script had by the 3rd millennium BC become simplified into stylized patterns of short straight strokes (some with phonetic values) that were more suitable for impressing on the clay which had become increasingly the material on which writing was done. The dissemination of their civilization led to its use in modified forms for a number of languages in the Near East until towards the end of the 1st millennium BC. Cuneiform scripts remained undeciphered until the 19th c. when H. C. Rawlinson, British consul in Baghdad, discovered at Behistun in Persia a rock bearing a trilingual inscription; one text was in Persian characters, already partially deciphered, which served as a key to the others. [F *cunéiforme* or mod.L *cuneiformis* f. L *cuneus* wedge]

Cunene /kjuːˈneɪnə/ a river of Angola that rises near the city of Huambo and flows 250 km (156 miles) south as far as the frontier with Namibia, which it then follows westwards to the Atlantic.

cunjevoi /ˈkʌndʒɪˌvɔɪ/ n. Austral. **1** the green arum or spoon lily *Alocasia macrorrhiza*. **2** a sea squirt. [Aboriginal]

cunnilingus /ˌkʌnɪˈlɪŋgəs/ n. (also **cunnilinctus** /-ˈlɪŋktəs/) oral stimulation of the female genitals. [L f. *cunnus* vulva + *lingere* lick]

cunning /ˈkʌnɪŋ/ adj. & n. —adj. (**cunninger**, **cunningest**) **1 a** skilled in ingenuity or deceit. **b** selfishly clever or crafty. **2** ingenious (*a cunning device*). **3** US attractive, quaint. —n. **1** craftiness; skill in deceit. **2** skill, ingenuity. □□ **cunningly** adv. **cunningness** n. [ME f. ON *kunnandi* knowing f. *kunna* know: cf. CAN¹]

cunt /kʌnt/ n. coarse sl. **1** the female genitals. **2** offens. an unpleasant or stupid person. ¶ A highly taboo word. [ME f. Gmc]

CUP abbr. Cambridge University Press.

cup /kʌp/ n. & v. —n. **1** a small bowl-shaped container, usu. with a handle for drinking from. **2 a** its contents (*a cup of tea*). **b** = CUPFUL. **3** a cup-shaped thing, esp. the calyx of a flower or the socket of a bone. **4** flavoured wine, cider, etc., usu. chilled. **5** an ornamental cup-shaped trophy as a prize for victory or prowess, esp. in a sports contest. **6** one's fate or fortune (*a bitter cup*). **7** either of the two cup-shaped parts of a brassière. **8** the chalice used or the wine taken at the Eucharist. **9** Golf the hole on a putting-green or the metal container in it. —v.tr. (**cupped**, **cupping**) **1** form (esp. one's hands) into the shape of a cup. **2** take or hold as in a cup. **3** hist. bleed (a person) by using a glass in which a partial vacuum is formed by heating. □ **cup-cake** a small cake baked in a cup-shaped foil or paper container and often iced. **Cup Final** a final match in a competition for a cup. **cup lichen** a lichen, *Cladonia pyxidata*, with cup-shaped processes arising from the thallus. **one's cup of tea** colloq. what interests or suits one. **cup-tie** a match in a competition for a cup. **in one's cups** while drunk; drunk. [OE *cuppe* f. med.L *cuppa* cup, prob. differentiated from L *cupa* tub]

cupbearer /ˈkʌpˌbeərə(r)/ n. a person who serves wine, esp. an officer of a royal or noble household.

cupboard /ˈkʌbəd/ n. a recess or piece of furniture with a door and (usu.) shelves, in which things are stored. □ **cupboard love** a display of affection meant to secure some gain. [ME f. CUP + BOARD]

cupel /ˈkjuːp(ə)l/ n. & v. —n. a small flat porous vessel used in assaying gold or silver in the presence of lead. —v.tr. (**cupelled**, **cupelling**; US **cupeled**, **cupeling**) assay or refine in a cupel. □□ **cupellation** /-ˈleɪʃ(ə)n/ n. [F *coupelle* f. LL *cupella* dimin. of *cupa*: see CUP]

cupful /ˈkʌpfʊl/ n. (pl. **-fuls**) **1** the amount held by a cup, esp. US a half-pint or 8-ounce measure in cookery. **2** a cup full of a substance (*drank a cupful of water*). ¶ A *cupful* is a measure, and so *three cupfuls* is a quantity regarded in terms of a cup; *three cups full* denotes the actual cups, as in *three cups full of water*. Sense 2 is an intermediate use.

Cupid /ˈkjuːpɪd/ Rom. Mythol. the god of love, identified by the Romans with Eros. He is often pictured as a beautiful naked boy with wings, carrying bow and arrows with which he wounds his victims. —n. (also **cupid**) a representation of Cupid. □ **Cupid's bow** the upper lip etc. shaped like the double-curved bow carried by Cupid. [ME f. L *Cupido* f. *cupere* desire]

cupidity /kjuːˈpɪdɪtɪ/ n. greed for gain; avarice. [ME f. OF *cupidité* or L *cupiditas* f. *cupidus* desirous]

cupola /ˈkjuːpələ/ n. **1 a** a rounded dome forming a roof or ceiling. **b** a small rounded dome adorning a roof. **2** a revolving dome protecting mounted guns on a warship or in a fort. **3** (in full **cupola-furnace**) a furnace for melting metals. □□ **cupolaed** /-ləd/ adj. [It. f. LL *cupula* dimin. of *cupa* cask]

cuppa /ˈkʌpə/ n. (also **cupper** /ˈkʌpə(r)/) Brit. colloq. **1** a cup of. **2** a cup of tea. [corruption]

cuprammonium /ˌkjuːprəˈməʊnɪəm/ n. a complex ion of divalent copper and ammonia, solutions of which dissolve cellulose. [LL *cuprum* + AMMONIUM]

cupreous /ˈkjuːprɪəs/ adj. of or like copper. [LL *cupreus* f. *cuprum* copper]

cupric /ˈkjuːprɪk/ adj. of copper, esp. divalent copper. □□ **cupriferous** /-ˈprɪfərəs/ adj. [LL *cuprum* copper]

cupro- /ˈkjuːprəʊ/ comb. form copper (*cupro-nickel*).

cupro-nickel /ˌkjuːprəʊˈnɪk(ə)l/ n. an alloy of copper and nickel, esp. in the proportions 3:1 as used in 'silver' coins.

cuprous /ˈkjuːprəs/ adj. of copper, esp. monovalent copper. [LL *cuprum* copper]

cupule /ˈkjuːpjuːl/ n. Bot. & Zool. a cup-shaped organ, receptacle, etc. [LL *cupula* CUPOLA]

cur /kɜː(r)/ n. **1** a worthless or snappy dog. **2** a contemptible person. [ME, prob. orig. in *cur-dog*, perh. f. ON *kurr* grumbling]

curable /ˈkjʊərəb(ə)l/ adj. that can be cured. □□ **curability** /-ˈbɪlɪtɪ/ n. [CURE]

Curaçao /ˌkjʊərəˈsaʊ/ the largest island of The Netherlands Antilles, situated in the Caribbean Sea 60 km (37 miles) north of the Venezuelan coast; pop. (1981) 147,388; chief town, Willemstad.

curaçao /ˌkjʊərəˈsaʊ/ n. (also **curaçoa** /-ˈsəʊə/) (pl. **-os** or **curaçoas**) a liqueur of spirits flavoured with the peel of bitter oranges, orig. produced in Curaçao.

curacy /ˈkjʊərəsɪ/ n. (pl. **-ies**) a curate's office or the tenure of it.

curare /kjʊəˈrɑːrɪ/ n. a resinous bitter substance prepared from S. American plants of the genera *Strychnos* and *Chondodendron*, paralysing the motor nerves, used by American Indians to poison arrows and blowpipe darts, and formerly used as a muscle relaxant in surgery. [Carib]

curassow /ˈkjʊərəsəʊ/ n. any game bird of the family Cracidae, found in Central and S. America. [Anglicized f. CURAÇAO]

curate /ˈkjʊərət/ n. **1** a member of the clergy engaged as assistant to a parish priest. **2** archaic an ecclesiastical pastor. □ **curate-in-charge** a curate appointed to take charge of a parish in place of a priest. **curate's egg** a thing that is partly good and partly bad. [ME f. med.L *curatus* f. *cura* CURE]

curative /ˈkjʊərətɪv/ adj. & n. —adj. tending or able to cure (esp. disease). —n. a curative medicine or agent. [F *curatif* -ive f. med.L *curativus* f. *curare* CURE]

curator /kjʊəˈreɪtə(r)/ n. a keeper or custodian of a museum or other collection. □□ **curatorial** /ˌkjʊərəˈtɔːrɪəl/ adj. **curatorship** n. [ME f. AF *curatour* (OF *-eur*) or L *curator* (as CURATIVE)]

curb /kɜːb/ n. & v. —n. **1** a check or restraint. **2** a strap etc. fastened to the bit and passing under a horse's lower jaw, used as a check. **3** an enclosing border or edging such as the frame round the top of a well or a fender round a hearth. **4** = KERB. —v.tr. **1** restrain. **2** put a curb on (a horse). □ **curb roof** a roof of which each face has two slopes, the lower one steeper. [ME f. OF *courber* f. L *curvare* bend, CURVE]

curcuma /ˈkɜːkjʊmə/ n. **1** the spice turmeric. **2** any tuberous plant of the genus *Curcuma*, yielding this and other commercial substances. [med.L or mod.L f. Arab. *kurkum* saffron f. Skr. *kuṅkumaᵐ*]

curd /kɜːd/ n. **1** (often in pl.) a coagulated substance formed by the action of acids on milk, which may be made into cheese or eaten as food. **2** a fatty substance found between flakes of boiled salmon flesh. **3** the edible head of a cauliflower. □ **curds and whey** the result of acidulating milk. **curd soap** a white soap made of tallow and soda. □□ **curdy** adj. [ME: orig. unkn.]

curdle /ˈkɜːd(ə)l/ v.tr. & intr. make into or become curds; congeal.

□ **make one's blood curdle** fill one with horror. □□ **curdler** *n.* [frequent. form of CURD (as verb)]

cure /ˈkjʊə(r)/ *v. & n.* —*v.* **1** *tr.* (often foll. by *of*) restore (a person or animal) to health (*was cured of pleurisy*). **2** *tr.* eliminate (a disease, evil, etc.). **3** *tr.* preserve (meat, fruit, tobacco, or skins) by salting, drying, etc. **4** *tr.* **a** vulcanize (rubber). **b** harden (concrete or plastic). **5** *intr.* effect a cure. **6** *intr.* undergo a process of curing. —*n.* **1** restoration to health. **2** a thing that effects a cure. **3** a course of medical or healing treatment. **4** **a** the office or function of a curate. **b** a parish or other sphere of spiritual ministration. **5** **a** the process of curing rubber or plastic. **b** (with qualifying adj.) the degree of this. □ **cure-all** a panacea; a universal remedy. □□ **curer** *n.* [ME f. OF *curer* f. L *curare* take care of f. *cura* care]

curé /ˈkjʊəreɪ/ *n.* a parish priest in France etc. [F f. med.L *curatus*: see CURATE]

curettage /kjʊəˈretɪdʒ, -rɪˈtɑːdʒ/ *n.* the use of or an operation involving the use of a curette. [F (as CURETTE)]

curette /kjʊəˈret/ *n. & v.* —*n.* a surgeon's small scraping-instrument. —*v.tr. & intr.* clean or scrape with a curette. [F, f. *curer* cleanse (as CURE)]

curfew /ˈkɜːfjuː/ *n.* **1** **a** a regulation restricting or forbidding the public circulation of people, esp. requiring people to remain indoors between specified hours, usu. at night. **b** the hour designated as the beginning of such a restriction. **c** a daily signal indicating this. **2** *hist.* **a** a medieval regulation requiring people to extinguish fires at a fixed hour in the evening. **b** the hour for this. **c** the bell announcing it. **3** the ringing of a bell at a fixed evening hour. [ME f. AF *coeverfu*, OF *cuevrefeu* f. the stem of *couvrir* COVER + *feu* fire]

Curia /ˈkjʊərɪə/ *n.* (also **curia**) the papal court; the government departments of the Vatican. □□ **Curial** *adj.* [L: orig. a division of an ancient Roman tribe, the senate house at Rome, a feudal court of justice]

Curie /ˈkjʊəri/, Marie (1867–1934) and Pierre (1859–1906), pioneers of radioactivity. Born Marja Sklodowska in Poland, Marie studied physics at the Sorbonne in Paris and married Pierre in 1895. They worked together on the mineral pitchblende, seeking to discover why it was so radioactive even after uranium had been extracted from it. Pierre earned their living by teaching, and working in a rough shed they discovered the elements polonium and radium in the mineral; for this they shared the 1903 Nobel Prize for physics with Becquerel. Marie succeeded to her husband's chair of physics at the Sorbonne after his accidental death, and continued her work on radioactivity, receiving a second Nobel Prize in 1911, this one for chemistry, for her isolation of radium; she was the first scientist to be awarded two Prizes. She also studied radioactive decay and the applications of radioactivity to medicine, pioneered mobile X-ray units, headed the French Radiological Service during the First World War, and afterwards worked in the newly-established Radium Institute. She died of leukaemia, undoubtedly caused by prolonged exposure to radioactive materials; neither the Curies nor anyone else had realized the dangers. Pierre's early researches were on piezoelectricity (which he discovered with his brother Jacques in 1880) and on the effects of temperature on magnetism. He discovered that at a certain temperature (the Curie point) ferromagnetic substances lose their magnetism and exhibit paramagnetism. Their elder daughter, Irène, married the physicist J.-F. Joliot. The curie, a unit of radioactivity, was named after Pierre and the element curium after Marie and Pierre Curie.

curie /ˈkjʊəri/ *n.* **1** a unit of radioactivity, corresponding to 3.7 × 10¹⁰ disintegrations per second. ¶ Abbr.: **Ci.** **2** a quantity of radioactive substance having this activity. [P. CURIE]

curio /ˈkjʊərɪəʊ/ *n.* (*pl.* **-os**) a rare or unusual object or person. [19th-c. abbr. of CURIOSITY]

curiosa /ˌkjʊərɪˈəʊsə/ *n.pl.* **1** curiosities. **2** erotic or pornographic books. [neut. pl. of L *curiosus*: see CURIOUS]

curiosity /ˌkjʊərɪˈɒsɪtɪ/ *n.* (*pl.* **-ies**) **1** an eager desire to know; inquisitiveness. **2** strangeness. **3** a strange, rare, or interesting object. [ME f. OF *curiouseté* f. L *curiositas -tatis* (as CURIOUS)]

curious /ˈkjʊərɪəs/ *adj.* **1** eager to learn; inquisitive. **2** strange, surprising, odd. **3** *euphem.* (of books etc.) erotic, pornographic. □□ **curiously** *adv.* **curiousness** *n.* [ME f. OF *curios* f. L *curiosus* careful f. *cura* care]

Curitiba /ˌkʊərɪˈtiːbə/ a city in SE Brazil, capital of Paraná State; pop. (1980) 842,800.

curium /ˈkjʊərɪəm/ *n.* an artificially made transuranic radioactive metallic element, first produced in 1944 by bombarding plutonium with helium ions. ¶ Symb.: **Cm**; atomic number 96. [M. and P. CURIE]

curl /kɜːl/ *v. & n.* —*v.* **1** *tr. & intr.* (often foll. by *up*) bend or coil into a spiral; form or cause to form curls. **2** *intr.* move in a spiral form (*smoke curling upwards*). **3 a** *intr.* (of the upper lip) be raised slightly on one side as an expression of contempt or disapproval. **b** *tr.* cause (the lip) to do this. **4** *intr.* play curling. —*n.* **1** a lock of curled hair. **2** anything spiral or curved inwards. **3 a** a curling movement or act. **b** the state of being curled. **4** a disease of plants in which the leaves are curled up. □ **curl up** **1** lie or sit with the knees drawn up. **2** *colloq.* writhe with embarrassment or horror. **make a person's hair curl** *colloq.* shock or horrify a person. **out of curl** lacking energy. [ME; earliest form *crolled, crulled* f. obs. adj. *crolle, crulle* curly f. MDu. *krul*]

curler /ˈkɜːlə(r)/ *n.* **1** a pin or roller etc. for curling the hair. **2** a player in the game of curling.

curlew /ˈkɜːljuː/ *n.* any wading bird of the genus *Numenius*, esp. *N. arquatus*, possessing a usu. long slender down-curved bill. [ME f. OF *courlieu, courlis* orig. imit., but assim. to *courliu* courier f. *courre* run + *lieu* place]

curlicue /ˈkɜːlɪkjuː/ *n.* a decorative curl or twist. [CURLY + CUE² (= pigtail) or Q¹]

curling /ˈkɜːlɪŋ/ *n.* **1** in senses of CURL *v.* **2** a game played on ice, esp. in Scotland, in which large flat rounded stones are hurled along a defined space (the *rink*) towards a mark (the *tee*). In its earlier form it seems to have been akin to quoits, but is now more like bowls. Scotland's 'ain game' may have originated in the Low Countries: two of Breughel's landscapes (16th c.) show a similar game being played on frozen ponds. There are references to the game from 1620 onwards, and it developed in Scotland whence it spread to other countries where the climatic conditions are suitable. □ **curling-tongs** (or **-iron** or **-pins**) a heated device for twisting the hair into curls.

curly /ˈkɜːlɪ/ *adj.* (**curlier, curliest**) **1** having or arranged in curls. **2** moving in curves. □ **curly kale** see KALE. □□ **curliness** *n.*

curmudgeon /kəˈmʌdʒ(ə)n/ *n.* a bad-tempered person. □□ **curmudgeonly** *adj.* [16th c.: orig. unkn.]

currach /ˈkʌrə/ *n.* (also **curragh**) *Ir.* a coracle. [Ir.: cf. CORACLE]

Curragh /ˈkʌrə/, **the** a plain in County Kildare in the Republic of Ireland, noted for the breeding of racehorses. The Irish Derby is run annually on its racecourse.

currajong var. of KURRAJONG.

currant /ˈkʌrənt/ *n.* **1** a dried fruit of a small seedless variety of grape grown in the Levant and much used in cookery. **2 a** any of various shrubs of the genus *Ribes* producing red, white, or black berries. **b** a berry of these shrubs. □ **flowering currant** an ornamental species of currant native to N. America. [ME *raysons of coraunce* f. AF, = grapes of Corinth (the orig. source)]

currawong /ˈkʌrəˌwɒŋ/ *n. Austral.* any crowlike songbird of the genus *Strepera*, possessing a resonant call. [Aboriginal]

currency /ˈkʌrənsɪ/ *n.* (*pl.* **-ies**) **1 a** the money in general use in a country. **b** any other commodity used as a medium of exchange. **2** the condition of being current; prevalence (e.g. of words or ideas). **3** the time during which something is current. **4** *Austral. Hist.* a native-born Australian, as distinguished from English-born (called *sterling*) (*currency lads and lasses*).

current /ˈkʌrənt/ *adj. & n.* —*adj.* **1** belonging to the present time; happening now (*current events; the current week*). **2** (of money, opinion, a rumour, a word, etc.) in general circulation or use. —*n.* **1** a body of water, air, etc., moving in a definite direction, esp. through a stiller surrounding body. **2 a** an ordered movement of electrically charged particles. **b** a quantity representing the intensity of such movement. **3** (usu. foll. by *of*) a general tendency or course (of events, opinions, etc.). □ **current account** a bank account from which money may be drawn without notice. **pass current** be generally accepted as true or genuine. □□ **currentness** n. [ME f. OF *corant* f. L *currere* run]

currently /ˈkʌrəntlɪ/ adv. at the present time; now.

curricle /ˈkʌrɪk(ə)l/ n. hist. a light open two-wheeled carriage drawn by two horses abreast. [L *curriculum*: see CURRICULUM]

curriculum /kəˈrɪkjʊləm/ n. (pl. **curricula** /-lə/) 1 the subjects that are studied or prescribed for study in a school (*not part of the school curriculum*). 2 any programme of activities. □□ **curricular** adj. [L, = course, race-chariot, f. *currere* run]

curriculum vitae /kəˈrɪkjʊləm ˈviːtaɪ/ n. a brief account of one's education, qualifications, and previous occupations. [L, = course of life]

currier /ˈkʌrɪə(r)/ n. a person who dresses and colours tanned leather. [ME f. OF *corier*, f. L *coriarius* f. *corium* leather]

currish /ˈkɜːrɪʃ/ adj. 1 like a cur; snappish. 2 ignoble. □□ **currishly** adv. **currishness** n.

curry[1] /ˈkʌrɪ/ n. & v. —n. (pl. **-ies**) a dish of meat, vegetables, etc., cooked in a sauce of hot-tasting spices, usu. served with rice. —v.tr. (**-ies, -ied**) prepare or flavour with a sauce of hot-tasting spices (*curried eggs*). □ **curry-powder** a preparation of turmeric and other spices for making curry. [Tamil]

curry[2] /ˈkʌrɪ/ v.tr. (**-ies, -ied**) 1 groom (a horse) with a curry-comb. 2 treat (tanned leather) to improve its properties. 3 thrash. □ **curry-comb** a hand-held metal serrated device for grooming horses. **curry favour** ingratiate oneself. [ME f. OF *correier* ult. f. Gmc]

curse /kɜːs/ n. & v. —n. 1 a solemn utterance intended to invoke a supernatural power to inflict destruction or punishment on a person or thing. 2 the evil supposedly resulting from a curse. 3 a violent exclamation of anger; a profane oath. 4 a thing that causes evil or harm. 5 (prec. by *the*) colloq. menstruation. 6 a sentence of excommunication. —v. 1 tr. a utter a curse against. b (in *imper.*) may God curse. 2 tr. (usu. in *passive*; foll. by *with*) afflict with (*cursed with blindness*). 3 intr. utter expletive curses; swear. 4 tr. excommunicate. □□ **curser** n. [OE *curs, cursian*, of unkn. orig.]

cursed /ˈkɜːsɪd, kɜːst/ adj. damnable, abominable. □□ **cursedly** adv. **cursedness** n.

cursillo /kʊəˈsɪləʊ/ n. (pl. **-os**) RC Ch. a short informal spiritual retreat by a group of devotees esp. in Latin America. [Sp., = little course]

cursive /ˈkɜːsɪv/ adj. & n. —adj. (of writing) done with joined characters. —n. cursive writing (cf. PRINT v. 4, UNCIAL). □□ **cursively** adv. [med.L (*scriptura*) *cursiva* f. L *currere* curs- run]

cursor /ˈkɜːsə(r)/ n. 1 Math. etc. a transparent slide engraved with a hairline and forming part of a slide-rule. 2 Computing a movable indicator on a VDU screen identifying a particular position in the display, esp. the position that the program will operate on with the next keystroke. [L, = runner (as CURSIVE)]

cursorial /kɜːˈsɔːrɪəl/ adj. Anat. having limbs adapted for running. [as CURSOR + -IAL]

cursory /ˈkɜːsərɪ/ adj. hasty, hurried (*a cursory glance*). □□ **cursorily** adv. **cursoriness** n. [L *cursorius* of a runner (as CURSOR)]

curst archaic var. of CURSED.

curt /kɜːt/ adj. noticeably or rudely brief. □□ **curtly** adv. **curtness** n. [L *curtus* cut short, abridged]

curtail /kɜːˈteɪl/ v.tr. 1 cut short; reduce; terminate esp. prematurely (*curtailed his visit to America*). 2 (foll. by *of*) archaic deprive of. □□ **curtailment** n. [obs. *curtal* horse with docked tail f. F *courtault* f. *court* short f. L *curtus*: assim. to *tail*]

curtain /ˈkɜːt(ə)n/ n. & v. —n. 1 a piece of cloth etc. hung up as a screen, usu. moveable sideways or upwards, esp. at a window or between the stage and auditorium of a theatre. 2 Theatr. **a** the rise or fall of the stage curtain at the beginning or end of an act or scene. **b** = curtain-call. 3 a partition or cover. 4 (in *pl.*) sl. the end. —v.tr. 1 furnish or cover with a curtain or curtains. 2 (foll. by *off*) shut off with a curtain or curtains. □ **curtain-call** Theatr. an audience's summons to actor(s) to take a bow after

the fall of the curtain. **curtain-fire** Mil. a concentration of rapid and continuous fire. **curtain lecture** a wife's private reproof to her husband, orig. behind bed-curtains. **curtain-raiser** 1 Theatr. a piece prefaced to the main performance. 2 a preliminary event. **curtain-wall** 1 Fortification the plain wall of a fortified place, connecting two towers etc. 2 Archit. a piece of plain wall not supporting a roof. [ME f. OF *cortine* f. LL *cortina* transl. Gk *aulaia* f. *aulē* court]

curtana /kɜːˈteɪnə, -ˈtɑːnə/ n. Brit. an unpointed sword borne before English sovereigns at their coronation, as an emblem of mercy. [ME f. AL *curtana* (*spatha* sword) f. AF *curtain*, OF *cortain* name of Roland's similar sword f. *cort* short (as CURT)]

curtilage /ˈkɜːtɪlɪdʒ/ n. an area attached to a dwelling-house and forming one enclosure with it. [ME f. AF *curtilage*, OF *co(u)rtillage* f. *co(u)rtil* small court f. *cort* COURT]

Curtiss /ˈkɜːtɪs/, Glenn Hammond (1878–1930), pioneer American pilot and designer of aircraft and engines. Like some motor manufacturers he began by building and selling bicycles; then he built motor cycles (1901), on one of which he achieved 136.3 mph in 1907, and his first aeroplane in 1909. He obtained America's first pilot's licence, and won the first international Gordon Bennett Cup in 1911. In 1912 he built the world's first successful flying boat.

curtsy /ˈkɜːtsɪ/ n. & v. (also **curtsey**) —n. (pl. **-ies** or **-eys**) a woman's or girl's formal greeting or salutation made by bending the knees and lowering the body. —v.intr. (**-ies, -ied** or **-eys, -eyed**) make a curtsy. [var. of COURTESY]

curule /ˈkjʊəruːl/ adj. Rom.Hist. designating or relating to the authority exercised by the senior Roman magistrates, chiefly the consul and praetor, who were entitled to use the *sella curulis* ('curule seat' or seat of office). [L *curulis* f. *currus* chariot (in which the chief magistrate was conveyed to the seat of office)]

curvaceous /kɜːˈveɪʃəs/ adj. colloq. (esp. of a woman) having a shapely curved figure.

curvature /ˈkɜːvətʃə(r)/ n. 1 the act or state of curving. 2 a curved form. 3 Geom. **a** the deviation of a curve from a straight line, or of a curved surface from a plane. **b** the quantity expressing this. [OF f. L *curvatura* (as CURVE)]

curve /kɜːv/ n. & v. —n. 1 a line or surface having along its length a regular deviation from being straight or flat, as exemplified by the surface of a sphere or lens. 2 a curved form or thing. 3 a curved line on a graph. 4 Baseball a ball caused to deviate by the pitcher's spin. —v.tr. & intr. bend or shape so as to form a curve. □□ **curved** adj. [orig. as adj. (in *curve line*) f. L *curvus* bent: (v.) f. L *curvare*]

curvet /kɜːˈvet/ n. & v. —n. a horse's leap with the forelegs raised together and the hind legs raised with a spring before the forelegs reach the ground. —v.intr. (**curvetted, curvetting** or **curveted, curveting**) (of a horse or rider) make a curvet. [It. *corvetta* dimin. of *corva* CURVE]

curvi- /ˈkɜːvɪ/ comb. form curved. [L *curvus* curved]

curvifoliate /ˌkɜːvɪˈfəʊlɪət/ adj. Bot. with the leaves bent back.

curviform /ˈkɜːvɪfɔːm/ adj. having a curved shape.

curvilinear /ˌkɜːvɪˈlɪnɪə(r)/ adj. contained by or consisting of curved lines. □□ **curvilinearly** adv. [CURVI- after *rectilinear*]

curvirostral /ˌkɜːvɪˈrɒstr(ə)l/ adj. with a curved beak.

curvy /ˈkɜːvɪ/ adj. (**curvier, curviest**) 1 having many curves. 2 (of a woman's figure) shapely. □□ **curviness** n.

cuscus[1] /ˈkʌskəs/ n. the aromatic fibrous root of an Indian grass, *Vetiveria zizanoides*, used for making fans etc. [Pers. *k̠as̠k̠as̠*]

cuscus[2] /ˈkʌskəs/ n. any of several nocturnal, usu. arboreal, marsupial mammals of the genus *Phalanger*, native to New Guinea and N. Australia. [native name]

cusec /ˈkjuːsek/ n. a unit of flow (esp. of water) equal to one cubic foot per second. [abbr.]

Cush /kʊʃ/ 1 the eldest son of Ham and grandson of Noah. 2 the southern part of ancient Nubia (see entry), first mentioned in Egyptian records of the Middle Kingdom (see EGYPT). In the Old Testament is the country of the descendants of Cush.

cush /kʊʃ/ n. esp. Billiards colloq. a cushion. [abbr.]

cushat /ˈkʌʃət/ n. Sc. a woodpigeon. [OE *cūscute*, of unkn. orig.]

cush-cush /ˈkʊʃkʊʃ/ n. a yam, *Dioscorea trifida*, native to S. America. [native name]

Cushing /ˈkʊʃɪŋ/, Harvey Williams (1869–1939), American surgeon who introduced techniques that greatly increased the likelihood of success in neurosurgical operations, and was the first to describe (in 1932) a hormonal disorder named after him.

cushion /ˈkʊʃ(ə)n/ n. & v. —n. **1** a bag of cloth etc. stuffed with a mass of soft material, used as a soft support for sitting or leaning on etc. **2** a means of protection against shock. **3** the elastic lining of the sides of a billiard-table, from which the ball rebounds. **4** a body of air supporting a hovercraft etc. **5** the frog of a horse's hoof. —v.tr. **1** provide or protect with a cushion or cushions. **2** provide with a defence; protect. **3** mitigate the adverse effects of (*cushioned the blow*). **4** quietly suppress. **5** place or bounce (the ball) against the cushion in billiards. □□ **cushiony** adj. [ME f. OF *co(i)ssin, cu(i)ssin* f. Gallo-Roman f. L *culcita* mattress, cushion]

Cushitic /kʊˈʃɪtɪk/ n. & adj. —n. a group of E. African languages of the Hamitic type, spoken mainly in Ethiopia and Somalia. —adj. of this group. [CUSH + -ITE¹ + -IC]

cushy /ˈkʊʃɪ/ adj. (**cushier, cushiest**) colloq. **1** (of a job etc.) easy and pleasant. **2** US (of a seat, surroundings, etc.) soft, comfortable. □□ **cushiness** n. [Anglo-Ind. f. Hind. *khūsh* pleasant]

cusp /kʌsp/ n. **1** an apex or peak. **2** the horn of a crescent moon etc. **3** Astrol. the initial point of a house. **4** Archit. a projecting point between small arcs in Gothic tracery. **5** Geom. the point at which two arcs meet from the same direction terminating with a common tangent. **6** Bot. a pointed end, esp. of a leaf. **7** a cone-shaped prominence on the surface of a tooth esp. a molar or premolar. **8** a pocket or fold in a valve of the heart. □□ **cuspate** /-speɪt/ adj. **cusped** adj. **cuspidal** adj. [L *cuspis, -idis* point, apex]

cuspidor /ˈkʌspɪdɔː(r)/ n. US a spittoon. [Port., = spitter f. *cuspir* spit f. L *conspuere*]

cuss /kʌs/ n. & v. colloq. —n. **1** a curse. **2** usu. derog. a person; a creature. —v.tr. & intr. curse. □ **cuss-word** US a swear-word. [var. of CURSE]

cussed /ˈkʌsɪd/ adj. colloq. awkward and stubborn. □□ **cussedly** adv. **cussedness** n. [var. of CURSED]

custard /ˈkʌstəd/ n. **1** a dish made with milk and eggs, usu. sweetened. **2** a sweet sauce made with milk and flavoured cornflour. □ **custard-apple** a W. Indian fruit, *Annona reticulata*, with a custard-like pulp. **custard-pie** **1** a pie containing custard, commonly thrown in slapstick comedy. **2** (*attrib.*) denoting slapstick comedy. **custard powder** a preparation of cornflour etc. for making custard. [ME, earlier *crusta(r)de* f. AF f. OF *crouste* CRUST]

Custer /ˈkʌstə(r)/, George Armstrong (1839–76), US cavalry general, who earned distinction in numerous battles in the American Civil War but led his men to their deaths in a clash with the Indians at Little Bighorn in Montana. Assessment of him varies, and controversy over his conduct in the final battle still continues.

custodian /kʌˈstəʊdɪən/ n. a guardian or keeper, esp. of a public building etc. □□ **custodianship** n. [CUSTODY + -AN, after *guardian*]

custody /ˈkʌstədɪ/ n. **1** guardianship; protective care. **2** imprisonment. □ **take into custody** arrest. □□ **custodial** /kʌˈstəʊdɪəl/ adj. [L *custodia* f. *custos -odis* guardian]

custom /ˈkʌstəm/ n. **1 a** the usual way of behaving or acting (*a slave to custom*). **b** a particular established way of behaving (*our customs seem strange to foreigners*). **2** Law established usage having the force of law. **3** business patronage; regular dealings or customers (*lost a lot of custom*). **4** (in pl.; also treated as sing.) **a** a duty levied on certain imported and exported goods. **b** the official department that administers this. **c** the area at a port, frontier, etc., where customs officials deal with incoming goods, baggage, etc. □ **custom-built** (or **-made** etc.) made to a customer's order. **custom-house** the office at a port or frontier etc. at which customs duties are levied. **customs union** a group of States with an agreed common tariff, and usu. free trade with

each other. [ME and OF *custume* ult. f. L *consuetudo -dinis*: see CONSUETUDE]

customary /ˈkʌstəmərɪ/ adj. & n. —adj. usual; in accordance with custom. **2** Law in accordance with custom. —n. (pl. **-ies**) Law a book etc. listing the customs and established practices of a community. □□ **customarily** adv. **customariness** n. [med.L *custumarius* f. *custuma* f. AF *custume* (as CUSTOM)]

customer /ˈkʌstəmə(r)/ n. **1** a person who buys goods or services from a shop or business. **2** a person one has to deal with (*an awkward customer*). [ME f. AF *custumer* (as CUSTOMARY), or f. CUSTOM + -ER¹]

customize /ˈkʌstəˌmaɪz/ v.tr. (also **-ise**) make to order or modify according to individual requirements.

cut /kʌt/ v. & n. —v. (**cutting**; past and past part. **cut**) **1** tr. (also absol.) penetrate or wound with a sharp-edged instrument (*cut his finger; the knife won't cut*). **2** tr. & intr. (often foll. by *into*) divide or be divided with a knife etc. (*cut the bread; cut the cloth into metre lengths*). **3** tr. **a** trim or reduce the length of (hair, a hedge, etc.) by cutting. **b** detach all or the significant part of (flowers, corn, etc.) by cutting. **4** tr. (foll. by *loose, open*, etc.) make loose, open, etc. by cutting. **5** tr. (esp. as **cutting** adj.) cause sharp physical or mental pain to (*a cutting remark; a cutting wind; was cut to the quick*). **6** tr. (often foll. by *down*) **a** reduce (wages, prices, time, etc.). **b** reduce or cease (services etc.). **7** tr. **a** shape or fashion (a coat, gem, key, record, etc.) by cutting. **b** make (a path, tunnel, etc.) by removing material. **8** tr. perform, execute, make (*cut a caper; cut a sorry figure*). **9** tr. (also absol.) cross, intersect (*the line cuts the circle at two points; the two lines cut*). **10** intr. (foll. by *across, through*, etc.) pass or traverse, esp. in a hurry or as a shorter way (*cut across the grass*). **11** tr. **a** ignore or refuse to recognize (a person). **b** renounce (a connection). **12** tr. esp. US deliberately fail to attend (a class etc.). **13** Cards **a** tr. divide (a pack) into two parts. **b** intr. select a dealer etc. by dividing the pack. **14** Cinematog. **a** tr. edit (a film or tape). **b** intr. (often in *imper.*) stop filming or recording. **c** intr. (foll. by *to*) go quickly to (another shot). **15** tr. switch off (an engine etc.). **16** tr. **a** hit (a ball) with a chopping motion. **b** Golf slice (the ball). **17** tr. US dilute, adulterate. **18** tr. (as **cut** adj.) Brit. sl. drunk. **19** intr. Cricket (of the ball) turn sharply on pitching. **20** intr. sl. run. **21** tr. castrate. —n. **1** an act of cutting. **2** a division or wound made by cutting. **3** a stroke with a knife, sword, whip, etc. **4 a** a reduction (in prices, wages, etc.). **b** a cessation (of a power supply etc.). **5** an excision of part of a play, film, book, etc. **6** a wounding remark or act. **7** the way or style in which a garment, the hair, etc., is cut. **8** a piece of meat etc. cut from a carcass. **9** colloq. commission; a share of profits. **10** Tennis & Cricket etc. a stroke made by cutting. **11** ignoring of or refusal to recognize a person. **12 a** an engraved block for printing. **b** = WOODCUT. **13** a railway cutting. **14** a new channel made for a river. □ **a cut above** colloq. noticeably superior to. **be cut out** (foll. by *for*, or *to* + infin.) be suited (*was not cut out to be a teacher*). **cut across 1** transcend or take no account of (normal limitations etc.) (*their concern cuts across normal rivalries*). **2** see sense 10 of v. **cut-and-come-again** abundance. **cut and dried 1** completely decided; prearranged; inflexible. **2** (of opinions etc.) ready-made, lacking freshness. **cut and run** sl. run away. **cut and thrust 1** a lively interchange of argument etc. **2** the use of both the edge and the point of a sword. **cut back 1** reduce (expenditure etc.). **2** prune (a tree etc.). **3** Cinematog. repeat part of a previous scene for dramatic effect. **cut-back** n. an instance or the act of cutting back, esp. a reduction in expenditure. **cut both ways 1** serve both sides of an argument etc. **2** (of an action) have both good and bad effects. **cut one's coat according to one's cloth 1** adapt expenditure to resources. **2** limit ambition to what is feasible. **cut a corner** go across and not round it. **cut corners** do a task etc. perfunctorily or incompletely, esp. to save time. **cut a dash** see DASH. **cut dead** completely refuse to recognize (a person). **cut down 1 a** bring or throw down by cutting. **b** kill by means of a sword or disease. **2** see sense 6 of v. **3** reduce the length of (*cut down the trousers to make shorts*). **4** (often foll. by *on*) reduce one's consumption (*tried to cut down on beer*). **cut a person down to size** colloq. ruthlessly expose the limitations of a person's importance, ability, etc. **cut one's eye-teeth** attain worldly wisdom. **cut glass** glass with patterns and designs cut on it. **cut in 1** interrupt. **2** pull in too closely in front of another vehicle (esp. having overtaken it). **3** give a share of profits etc. to (a person). **4** connect (a source of electricity). **5** join in a card-game by taking the place of a player who cuts out. **6** interrupt a dancing couple to take over from one partner. **cut into 1** make a cut in (*they cut into the cake*). **2** interfere with and reduce (*travelling cuts into my free time*). **cut it fine** see FINE[1]. **cut it out** (usu. in *imper.*) *sl.* stop doing that (esp. quarrelling). **cut the knot** solve a problem in an irregular but efficient way. **cut-line 1** a caption to an illustration. **2** the line in squash above which a served ball must strike the wall. **cut loose 1** begin to act freely. **2** see sense 4 of *v.* **cut one's losses** (or a **loss**) abandon an unprofitable enterprise before losses become too great. **cut the mustard** *US sl.* reach the required standard. **cut no ice** *sl.* **1** have no influence or importance. **2** achieve little or nothing. **cut off 1** remove (an appendage) by cutting. **2 a** (often in *passive*) bring to an abrupt end or (esp. early) death. **b** intercept, interrupt; prevent from continuing (*cut off supplies; cut off the gas*). **c** disconnect (a person engaged in a telephone conversation) (*was suddenly cut off*). **3 a** prevent from travelling or venturing out (*was cut off by the snow*). **b** (as **cut off** *adj.*) isolated, remote (*felt cut off in the country*). **4** disinherit (*was cut off without a penny*). **cut-off** *n.* **1** the point at which something is cut off. **2** a device for stopping a flow. **3** *US* a short cut. **cut out 1** remove from the inside by cutting. **2** make by cutting from a larger whole. **3** omit; leave out. **4** *colloq.* stop doing or using (something) (*managed to cut out chocolate; let's cut out the arguing*). **5** cease or cause to cease functioning (*the engine cut out*). **6** outdo or supplant (a rival). **7** *US* detach (an animal) from the herd. **8** *Cards* be excluded from a card-game as a result of cutting the pack. **cut-out 1** a figure cut out of paper etc. **2** a device for automatic disconnection, the release of exhaust gases, etc. **cut-out box** *US* = *fuse-box* (see FUSE[1]). **cut-price** (or **-rate**) selling or sold at a reduced price. **cut short 1** interrupt; terminate prematurely (*cut short his visit*). **2** make shorter or more concise. **cut one's teeth on** acquire initial practice or experience from (something). **cut a tooth** have it appear through the gum. **cut up 1** cut into pieces. **2** destroy utterly. **3** (usu. in *passive*) distress greatly (*was very cut up about it*). **4** criticize severely. **5** *US* behave in a comical or unruly manner. **cut up rough** *Brit. sl.* show anger or resentment. **cut up well** *sl.* bequeath a large fortune. **have one's work cut out** see WORK. [ME *cutte, kitte, kette*, perh. f. OE *cyttan* (unrecorded)]

cutaneous /kju:'teɪnɪəs/ *adj.* of the skin. [mod.L *cutaneus* f. L *cutis* skin]

cutaway /'kʌtəˌweɪ/ *adj.* **1** (of a diagram etc.) with some parts left out to reveal the interior. **2** (of a coat) with the front below the waist cut away.

cutch var. of COUCH[2].

cute /kju:t/ *adj. colloq.* **1** esp. *US* **a** attractive, quaint. **b** affectedly attractive. **2** clever, ingenious. □□ **cutely** *adv.* **cuteness** *n.* [shortening of ACUTE]

Cuthbert /'kʌθbət/, St (d. 687), English monk and missionary, who became bishop of Lindisfarne. Feast day, 20 Mar.

cuticle /'kju:tɪk(ə)l/ *n.* **1 a** the dead skin at the base of a fingernail or toenail. **b** the epidermis or other superficial skin. **2** *Bot.* a thin surface film on plants. □□ **cuticular** /-'tɪkjʊlə(r)/ *adj.* [L *cuticula*, dimin. of *cutis* skin]

cutie /'kju:tɪ/ *n. sl.* an attractive young woman.

cutis /'kju:tɪs/ *n. Anat.* the true skin or dermis, underlying the epidermis. [L, = skin]

cutlass /'kʌtləs/ *n.* a short sword with a slightly curved blade, esp. of the type formerly used by sailors. [F *coutelas* ult. f. L *cultellus*: see CUTLER]

cutler /'kʌtlə(r)/ *n.* a person who makes or deals in knives and similar utensils. [ME f. AF *cotillere*, OF *coutelier* f. *coutel* f. L *cultellus* dimin. of *culter* COULTER]

cutlery /'kʌtlərɪ/ *n.* knives, forks, and spoons for use at table. [OF & F *coutel()erie* (as CUTLER)]

cutlet /'kʌtlɪt/ *n.* **1** a neck-chop of mutton or lamb. **2** a small piece of veal etc. for frying. **3** a flat cake of minced meat or nuts

and breadcrumbs etc. [F *côtelette*, OF *costelet* dimin. of *coste* rib f. L *costa*]

cutpurse /'kʌtpɜːs/ *n. archaic* a pickpocket; a thief.

cutter /'kʌtə(r)/ *n.* **1** a tailor etc. who takes measurements and cuts cloth. **2** *Naut.* **a** a small fast sailing-ship. **b** a small boat carried by a large ship. **3** *Cricket* a ball turning sharply on pitching. **4** *US* a light horse-drawn sleigh.

cutthroat /'kʌtθrəʊt/ *n. & adj.* —*n.* **1** a murderer. **2** (in full **cutthroat razor**) a razor having a long blade set in a handle and usu. folding like a penknife. **3** a species of trout, *Salmo clarki*, with a red mark under the jaw. —*adj.* **1** (of competition) ruthless and intense. **2** (of a card-game) three-handed.

cutting /'kʌtɪŋ/ *n. & adj.* —*n.* **1** a piece cut from a newspaper etc. **2** a piece cut from a plant for propagation. **3** an excavated channel through high ground for a railway or road. —*adj.* see CUT *v.* 5. □□ **cuttingly** *adv.*

cuttle /'kʌt(ə)l/ *n.* = CUTTLEFISH. □ **cuttle-bone** the internal shell of the cuttlefish crushed and used for polishing teeth etc. or as a supplement to the diet of a cage-bird. [OE *cudele*, ME *codel*, rel. to *cod* bag, with ref. to its ink-bag]

cuttlefish /'kʌt(ə)lfɪʃ/ *n.* any marine cephalopod mollusc of the genera *Sepia* and *Sepiola*, having ten arms and ejecting a black fluid when threatened or pursued.

cutty /'kʌtɪ/ *adj.* in *Sc. & N.Engl.* —*adj.* cut short; abnormally short. —*n.* (*pl.* **-ies**) a short tobacco pipe. □ **cutty-stool** *hist.* a stool of repentance.

Cutty Sark /ˌkʌtɪ 'sɑːk/ the only survivor of the British tea-clippers (see CLIPPER), launched in 1869 and now preserved as a museum ship at Greenwich, London. The name comes from a poem by Robert Burns which tells of a Scottish farmer who was chased by the young witch Nannie who wore only her 'cutty sark' (= short shift); the ship's figurehead is a representation of the witch with her arm outstretched to catch the tail of the farmer's grey mare on which he was escaping.

cutwater /'kʌtˌwɔːtə(r)/ *n.* **1** the forward edge of a ship's prow. **2** a wedge-shaped projection from a pier or bridge.

cutworm /'kʌtwɜːm/ *n.* any of various caterpillars that eat through the stems of young plants level with the ground.

cuvée /kju:'veɪ/ *n.* a blend or batch of wine. [F, = vatful f. *cuve* cask f. L *cupa*]

cuvette /kju:'vet/ *n.* a shallow vessel for liquid. [F, dimin. of *cuve* cask f. L *cupa*]

Cuvier /'kuːvɪˌeɪ/, Georges Jean Léopold Nicolas Frédéric, Baron (1769–1832), French naturalist who founded the science of palaeontology with a study of fossil elephants. Pioneering also in comparative anatomy, he was the first to classify the lower invertebrate animals. Later he realized that each such species could be derived from another by small changes in their structure, an observation which proved crucial in the emergence of the theory of evolution. He himself believed resolutely in the conventional view that the world had been created by God and quarrelled publicly with the early proponents of evolutionary ideas, notably Lamarck. He sought favour with the new political regimes of early 19th-c. France, and was given responsibility for the reorganization of the French universities.

Cuzco /'kʌskəʊ/ a city in the Andes in southern Peru that was the capital of the Inca empire until the Spanish conquest (1533); pop. (est. 1988) 255,300.

c.v. *abbr.* curriculum vitae.

CVO *abbr.* Commander of the Royal Victorian Order.

CVS *abbr.* chorionic villus sample, a test on a pregnant woman to detect any chromosomal abnormalities in the foetus.

Cwlth. *abbr.* Commonwealth.

cwm /kuːm/ *n.* **1** (in Wales) = COOMB. **2** *Geog.* a cirque. [Welsh]

c.w.o. *abbr.* cash with order.

cwt. *abbr.* hundredweight.

-cy /sɪ/ *suffix* (see also -ACY, -ANCY, -CRACY, -ENCY, -MANCY). **1** denoting state or condition (*bankruptcy; idiocy*). **2** denoting rank or status (*captaincy*). [from or after L *-cia, -tia*, Gk *-k(e)ia, -t(e)ia*]

cyan /'saɪæn/ *adj. & n.* —*adj.* of a greenish-blue. —*n.* a greenish-blue colour. [Gk *kuan(e)os* dark blue]

cyanamide /saɪˈænəˌmaɪd/ n. Chem. a colourless crystalline amide of cyanogen; any salt of this, esp. the calcium one which is used as a fertilizer. ¶ Chem. formula: CH_2N_2. [CYANOGEN + AMIDE]

cyanic acid /saɪˈænɪk/ n. an unstable colourless pungent acid gas. ¶ Chem. formula: HCNO. [CYANOGEN]

cyanide /ˈsaɪəˌnaɪd/ n. any of the highly poisonous salts or esters of hydrocyanic acid, esp. the potassium salt used in the extraction of gold and silver. [CYANOGEN + -IDE]

cyanobacterium /ˌsaɪəˌnəʊbækˈtɪərɪəm/ n. any prokaryotic organism of the division Cyanobacteria, found in many environments and capable of photosynthesizing. Also called blue-green alga (see BLUE[1]). [CYANOGEN + BACTERIUM]

cyanocobalamin /ˌsaɪəˌnəʊkəˈbæləmɪn/ n. a vitamin of the B complex, found in foods of animal origin such as liver, fish, and eggs, a deficiency of which can cause pernicious anaemia. Also called vitamin B_{12}. [CYANOGEN + cobalamin f. COBALT + VITAMIN]

cyanogen /saɪˈænədʒ(ə)n/ n. Chem. a colourless highly poisonous gas intermediate in the preparation of many fertilizers. ¶ Chem. formula: C_2N_2. [F cyanogène f. Gk kuanos dark-blue mineral, as being a constituent of Prussian blue]

cyanosis /ˌsaɪəˈnəʊsɪs/ n. Med. a bluish discoloration of the skin due to the presence of oxygen-deficient blood. □□ **cyanotic** /-ˈnɒtɪk/ adj. [mod.L f. Gk kuanōsis blueness (as CYANOGEN)]

Cybele /sɪˈbiːlɪ/ Anatolian Mythol. a mother-goddess worshipped especially in Phrygia and later in Greece (where she was associated with Demeter), Rome, and the Roman provinces, with her consort Attis.

cybernation /ˌsaɪbəˈneɪʃ(ə)n/ n. control by machines. □□ **cybernate** /ˈsaɪ-/ v.tr. [f. CYBERNETICS + -ATION]

cybernetics /ˌsaɪbəˈnetɪks/ n.pl. (usu. treated as sing.) the science of communications and automatic control systems in both machines and living things. □□ **cybernetic** adj. **cybernetician** /-ˈtɪʃ(ə)n/ n. **cyberneticist** /-sɪst/ n. [Gk kubernētēs steersman]

cycad /ˈsaɪkæd/ n. Bot. any of the palmlike plants of the order Cycadales (including fossil forms) inhabiting tropical and subtropical regions and often growing to a great height. [mod.L cycas, cycad- f. supposed Gk kukas, scribal error for koikas, pl. of koix Egyptian palm]

Cyclades /ˈsɪklədiːz/ (Greek **Kikládhes** /kɪkˈlɑːðiːs/ a group of islands in the Aegean Sea, regarded in antiquity as circling around the sacred island of Delos. They are the site of a Bronze Age civilization noted for developments in metallurgy and for angular figurines in white marble. The Cyclades form a department of modern Greece; pop. (1981) 88,450; capital, Síros. □□ **Cycladic** /saɪˈklædɪk, sɪ-/ adj. [L f. Gk (kuklos circle) f. Gk Kuklades f. kuklos circle (of islands)]

cyclamate /ˈsaɪkləˌmeɪt, ˈsɪk-/ n. any of various salts or esters of sulphamic acid formerly used as artificial sweetening agents. [Chem. name cyclohexylsulphamate]

cyclamen /ˈsɪkləmən/ n. 1 any plant of the genus Cyclamen, originating in Europe, having pink, red, or white flowers with reflexed petals, often grown in pots. 2 the shade of colour of the red or pink cyclamen flower. [med.L f. Gk kuklaminos, perh. f. kuklos circle, with ref. to its bulbous roots]

cycle /ˈsaɪk(ə)l/ n. & v. —n. 1 a a recurrent round or period (of events, phenomena, etc.). b the time needed for one such round or period. 2 a Physics etc. a recurrent series of operations or states. b Electr. = HERTZ. 3 a series of songs, poems, etc., usu. on a single theme. 4 a bicycle, tricycle, or similar machine. —v.intr. 1 ride a bicycle etc. 2 move in cycles. □ **cycle-track** (or **-way**) a path or road for bicycles. [ME f. OF, or f. LL cyclus f. Gk kuklos circle]

cyclic /ˈsaɪklɪk/ adj. 1 a recurring in cycles. b belonging to a chronological cycle. 2 Chem. with constituent atoms forming a ring. 3 of a cycle of songs etc. 4 Bot. (of a flower) with its parts arranged in whorls. 5 Math. of a circle or cycle. [F cyclique or L cyclicus f. Gk kuklikos (as CYCLE)]

cyclical /ˈsaɪklɪk(ə)l, ˈsɪk-/ adj. = CYCLIC 1. □□ **cyclically** adv.

cyclist /ˈsaɪklɪst/ n. a rider of a bicycle.

cyclo- /ˈsaɪkləʊ/ comb. form circle, cycle, or cyclic (cyclometer; cyclorama). [Gk kuklos circle]

cycloalkane /ˌsaɪkləʊˈælkeɪn/ n. Chem. a saturated cyclic hydrocarbon.

cyclo-cross /ˈsaɪkləʊˌkrɒs/ n. cross-country racing on bicycles, a sport mainly confined to Europe (especially Luxembourg, the Low Countries, and Russia) but found also in the US, especially near Chicago.

cyclograph /ˈsaɪkləˌgrɑːf/ n. an instrument for tracing circular arcs.

cyclohexane /ˌsaɪkləʊˈhekseɪn/ n. Chem. a colourless liquid cycloalkane used as a solvent and paint remover. ¶ Chem. formula: C_6H_{12}.

cycloid /ˈsaɪklɔɪd/ n. Math. a curve traced by a point on a circle when the circle is rolled along a straight line. □□ **cycloidal** /-ˈklɔɪd(ə)l/ adj. [Gk kukloeidēs (as CYCLE, -OID)]

cyclometer /saɪˈklɒmɪtə(r)/ n. 1 an instrument for measuring circular arcs. 2 an instrument for measuring the distance traversed by a bicycle etc.

cyclone /ˈsaɪkləʊn/ n. 1 a system of winds rotating inwards to an area of low barometric pressure; a depression. 2 a violent hurricane of limited diameter. □□ **cyclonic** /-ˈklɒnɪk/ adj. **cyclonically** /-ˈklɒnɪkəlɪ/ adv. [prob. repr. Gk kuklōma wheel, coil of a snake]

cyclopedia /ˌsaɪkləˈpiːdɪə/ n. (also **cyclopaedia**) an encyclopedia. □□ **cyclopedic** adj. [shortening of ENCYCLOPEDIA]

cycloparaffin /ˌsaɪkləˈpærəfɪn/ n. Chem. = CYCLO-ALKANE.

Cyclopean /ˌsaɪkləˈpiːən, -ˈkləʊpɪən/ adj. (also **Cyclopian**) 1 (of ancient masonry) made with massive irregular blocks. 2 of or resembling a Cyclops.

cyclopropane /ˌsaɪkləʊˈprəʊpeɪn/ n. Chem. a colourless gaseous cycloalkane used as a general anaesthetic. ¶ Chem. formula: C_3H_6.

Cyclops /ˈsaɪklɒps/ n. 1 (pl. **Cyclops** or **Cyclopses** or **Cyclopes** /saɪˈkləʊpiːz/) Gk Mythol. (in Homer) a race of one-eyed giants who are savage and pastoral; (in Hesiod) three one-eyed giants who make thunderbolts and are craftsmen. 2 (**cyclops**) (pl. **cyclops** or **cyclopes**) Zool. a crustacean of the genus Cyclops, with a single central eye. [L f. Gk Kuklōps f. kuklos circle + ōps eye]

cyclorama /ˌsaɪkləʊˈrɑːmə/ n. a circular panorama, curved wall, or cloth at the rear of a stage, esp. one used to represent the sky. □□ **cycloramic** /-ˈræmɪk/ adj.

cyclostome /ˈsaɪkləˌstəʊm/ n. any fishlike jawless vertebrate of the subclass Cyclostomata, having a large sucking mouth, e.g. a lamprey. □□ **cyclostomate** /-ˈklɒstəmət/ adj. [CYCLO- + Gk stoma mouth]

cyclostyle /ˈsaɪkləˌstaɪl/ n. & v. —n. an apparatus for printing copies of writing from a stencil. —v.tr. print or reproduce with this.

cyclothymia /ˌsaɪkləʊˈθaɪmɪə/ n. Psychol. a disorder characterized by the occurrence of marked swings of mood from cheerfulness to misery. □□ **cyclothymic** adj. [CYCLO- + Gk thumos temper]

cyclotron /ˈsaɪkləˌtrɒn/ n. Physics an apparatus in which charged atomic and subatomic particles are accelerated by an alternating electric field while following an outward spiral or circular path in a constant magnetic field. It was invented in 1929 by the American physicist E. O. Lawrence, who was awarded a Nobel Prize in 1939.

cyder var. of CIDER.

cygnet /ˈsɪgnɪt/ n. a young swan. [ME f. AF cignet dimin. of OF cigne swan f. med.L cycnus f. Gk kuknos]

Cygnus /ˈsɪgnəs/ a summer constellation, the Swan (named after a disguise adopted by Zeus on one of his many earthly escapades) or Northern Cross. It contains a host of objects of great astronomical interest, including the yellow supergiant star Deneb, the brightest dwarf nova SS Cygni, and the X-ray source Cygnus X-1 which is believed to be a binary star system which includes a black hole. [L, = swan]

cylinder /ˈsɪlɪndə(r)/ n. 1 a a uniform solid or hollow body with straight sides and a circular section. b a thing of this shape, e.g. a container for liquefied gas. 2 a cylinder-shaped part of various machines, esp. a piston-chamber in an engine. 3 Printing a metal roller. □ **cylinder saw** = *crown saw*. **cylinder seal** *Antiq*. a small cylindrical object of precious or semi-precious stone, shell, clay, faience, glass, occasionally metal, and possibly wood, which is usually pierced through its long axis for suspension and is always engraved with a design. It is particularly characteristic of Mesopotamia from the late 4th to the 1st millennium BC, where it served first as a mark of property and later as a signature to authenticate clay documents. □□ **cylindrical** /-'lɪndrɪk(ə)l/ *adj*. **cylindrically** /-'lɪndrɪkəlɪ/ *adv*. [L *cylindrus* f. Gk *kulindros* f. *kulindō* roll]

cyma /'saɪmə/ *n*. **1** *Archit*. an ogee moulding of a cornice. **2** = CYME. [mod.L f. Gk *kuma* wave, wavy moulding]

cymbal /'sɪmb(ə)l/ *n*. a musical instrument consisting of a concave brass or bronze plate, struck with another or with a stick etc. to make a ringing sound. □□ **cymbalist** *n*. [ME f. L *cymbalum* f. Gk *kumbalon* f. *kumbē* cup]

Cymbeline /'sɪmbə,liːn/ Cunobelinus (d. *c*.42 AD), king of the Catuvellauni, the most powerful Belgic tribe in ancient Britain, who occupied a wide area from Northants to SE England. He made Camulodunum (Colchester) his capital, and established a mint there. He was prominent in medieval fable, whence Shakespeare derived the material for his drama 'Cymbeline'.

cymbidium /sɪm'bɪdɪəm/ *n*. any tropical orchid of the genus *Cymbidium*, with a recess in the flower-lip. [mod.L f. Gk *kumbē* cup]

cymbiform /'sɪmbɪ,fɔːm/ *adj*. *Anat*. & *Bot*. boat-shaped. [L *cymba* f. Gk *kumbē* boat + -FORM]

cyme /saɪm/ *n*. *Bot*. an inflorescence in which the primary axis bears a single terminal flower that develops first, the system being continued by the axes of secondary and higher orders each with a flower (cf. RACEME). □□ **cymose** *adj*. [F, var. of *cime* summit, ult. f. Gk *kuma* wave]

Cymric /'kɪmrɪk/ *adj*. Welsh. [Welsh *Cymru* Wales]

Cynewulf /'kɪnɪ,wʊlf/ (late 8th–9th c.), Anglo-Saxon poet, probably from Northumbria or Mercia. Of the many poems that have been attributed to him modern scholarship restricts attribution to four poems in the Exeter Book and the Vercelli Book which end with his name in runes: *Juliana*; *Elene*, the story of the Finding of the Cross by St Helena; *The Fates of the Apostles*; and *Christ II*, a poem on the Ascension.

Cynic /'sɪnɪk/ *n*. & *adj*. —*n*. a member of an ancient Greek sect of philosophers founded by Antisthenes, a pupil of Socrates, who were characterized by an ostentatious contempt for ease, wealth, and the enjoyments of life. The most famous was Diogenes, a pupil of Antisthenes, who carried these principles to an extreme of asceticism. The movement flourished in the 3rd c. BC and revived in the 1st c. AD, when the Cynic beggar philosophers became a common sight in the Roman Empire. —*adj*. of the Cynics. [L *Cynicus* f. Gk *kunikos* f. *kuōn kunos* dog, nickname of Diogenes]

cynic /'sɪnɪk/ *n*. & *adj*. —*n*. a person who has little faith in human sincerity and goodness. —*adj*. = CYNICAL. □□ **cynicism** /-,sɪz(ə)m/ *n*. [CYNIC]

cynical /'sɪnɪk(ə)l/ *adj*. **1** of or characteristic of a cynic; incredulous of human goodness. **2** (of behaviour etc.) disregarding normal standards. **3** sneering, mocking. □□ **cynically** *adv*.

cynocephalus /,saɪnəʊ'sefələs/ *n*. **1** a fabled dog-headed man. **2** any flying lemur of the genus *Cynocephalus*, native to SE Asia. [Gk *kunokephalos* f. *kuōn kunos* dog + *kephalē* head]

cynosure /'saɪnə,zjʊə(r), 'sɪn-/ *n*. **1** a centre of attraction or admiration. **2** a guiding star. [F *cynosure* or L *cynosura* f. Gk *kunosoura* dog's tail, Ursa Minor f. *kuōn kunos* dog + *oura* tail]

cypher var. of CIPHER.

cy pres /siː 'preɪ/ *adv*. & *adj*. *Law* as near as possible to the testator's or donor's intentions when these cannot be precisely followed. [AF, = *si près* so near]

cypress /'saɪprəs/ *n*. **1** any coniferous tree of the genus *Cupressus* or *Chamaecyparis*, with hard wood and dark foliage. **2** this, or branches from it, as a symbol of mourning. [ME f. OF *cipres* f. LL *cypressus* f. Gk *kuparissos*]

Cyprian[1] /'sɪprɪən/ *n*. & *adj*. = CYPRIOT. [L *Cyprius* of Cyprus]

Cyprian[2] /'sɪprɪən/, St (d. 258), bishop of Carthage, author of an esteemed work on the nature of true unity in the Church in its relation to the episcopate, martyred in the reign of the emperor Valerian. Feast day, (in the RC Missal) 16 Sept.; in the Book of Common Prayer (by confusion with Cyprian, a converted magician of Antioch, who lived *c*.300) 26 Sept.

cyprinoid /'sɪprɪ,nɔɪd/ *adj*. & *n*. —*adj*. of or like carp. —*n*. a carp or related fish. [L *cyprinus* f. Gk *kuprinos* carp]

Cypriot /'sɪprɪət/ *n*. & *adj*. (also **Cypriote** /-əʊt/) —*n*. **1** a native or national of Cyprus. **2** the dialect of Greek used in Cyprus. —*adj*. of Cyprus or its people or dialect. [Gk *Kupriōtēs* f. *Kupros* Cyprus in E. Mediterranean]

cypripedium /,sɪprɪ'piːdɪəm/ *n*. any orchid of the genus *Cypripedium*, esp. the lady's slipper. [mod.L f. Gk *Kupris* Aphrodite + *pedilon* slipper]

Cyprus /'saɪprəs/ a large island in the eastern Mediterranean about 80 km (50 miles) south of the Turkish coast; pop. (est. 1980) 662,000; official languages, Greek and Turkish; capital, Nicosia. The island was colonized from Greece in the first half of the 14th c. BC. In classical times it was noted for its copper (which is named after it) and its cult of Aphrodite. Placed at the crossroads of a number of ancient civilizations, its Greek population was successively subject to Assyrian, Egyptian, Persian, Ptolemaic, and Roman overlordship. In medieval times it was ruled by Byzantines, Arabs, Franks, and Venetians, until conquered in 1571 by the Turks, who held it until 1878 when it was placed under British administration. It was annexed by Britain in 1914 and made a Crown Colony in 1925. The island's recent history has been dominated by tension between the two major communities, the Greek Cypriots (some of whom favour *enosis* or union with Greece) and the Turkish Cypriots. After a period of virtual civil war from 1955 Cyprus became an independent republic within the Commonwealth in 1960, but its constitution proved unworkable. In 1974 Turkey invaded the island and established a 'Turkish Federated State' in northern Cyprus; this has not been recognized by the UN.

cypsela /'sɪpsɪlə/ *n*. (*pl*. **cypselae** /-,liː/) *Bot*. a dry single-seeded fruit formed from a double ovary of which only one develops into a seed, characteristic of the daisy family Compositae. [mod.L f. Gk *kupselē* hollow vessel]

Cyrano de Bergerac /'sɪrɑː,nəʊ də 'beəʒəræk/, Savinien (1619–55), soldier, libertine, and duellist, famous for his grotesque appearance and long nose. He became a dramatist and novelist and is the subject of a highly successful play by Edmond Rostand. Two of his novels are about flights to the moon, with propulsion by bottles of dew (which vanished sunward in the morning), lodestones, and finally an array of rockets.

Cyrenaic /,saɪrɪ'neɪɪk/ *adj*. & *n*. —*adj*. of the hedonistic school of philosophy founded *c*.400 BC by Aristippus of Cyrene, a pupil of Socrates. Its ethical doctrines anticipated those of the Epicureans. —*n*. a philosopher of this school.

Cyrenaica /,saɪrə'neɪkə/ a region of NE Libya, bordering on the Mediterranean Sea.

Cyrene /saɪ'riːnɪ/ an ancient Greek colony in North Africa, near the coast in what is now Libya. From the 4th c. BC it was one of the great intellectual centres, with a noted medical school.

Cyril[1] /'sɪrɪl/, St (d. 444), Patriarch of Alexandria, Doctor of the Church, best known for his vehement opposition to the views of Nestorius whose condemnation he secured at the Council of Ephesus in 431. His extensive writings show his precision, accuracy, and skill as a theologian but often reveal intransigence and misunderstanding of his opponents' thought. Feast day, 9 Feb.

Cyril[2] /'sɪrɪl/, St (826–69), Greek missionary, to whom is ascribed the invention of the Cyrillic alphabet (see entry). He and his brother Methodius (*c*.815–85) became known as the 'Apostles of the Slavs'. Dispatched to Moravia, they taught in the vernacular, which they adopted also for the liturgy, and circulated a Slavonic version of the Scriptures. They met with hostility from the German bishops there, but received papal support. Feast day in the Eastern Church 11 May, in the Western Church 14 Feb.

Cyrillic /sɪ'rɪlɪk/ *adj*. & *n*. —*adj*. of one of the two principal

Slavonic alphabets (the other is the Roman) in use today. It was based on Greek uncials, and was reputedly introduced by St Cyril and his brother St Methodius in their missionary work amongst southern Slavs. It has remained, with some changes, the method of writing the languages (which include Russian) of those Slavonic peoples whose Christianity and culture came, directly or indirectly, from the Greek civilization of medieval Constantinople. —n. this script.

Cyrus[1] /ˈsaɪrəs/ 'the Great', son of Cambyses, king of Persia 559–529 BC and founder of the Achaemenid dynasty. He subjected the Medes after the capture of their king Astyages in 549 BC, and went on to conquer Asia Minor, Babylonia, Syria, Palestine, and most of the Iranian plateau. He ruled his empire with wisdom and moderation.

Cyrus[2] /ˈsaɪrəs/ 'the Younger' (d. 401 BC), son of Darius II (who ruled over Persia 424–405 BC). As commander of Persian forces in Asia Minor he helped the Spartan naval commander Lysander to defeat the Athenians in the Peloponnesian War. On the death of his father Cyrus led an army of mercenaries (in which the historian Xenophon enlisted) against his elder brother, who had succeeded to the throne as Artaxerxes II, but was killed in battle at Cunaxa, about 72 km (45 miles) north of Babylon.

cyst /sɪst/ n. **1** Med. a sac containing morbid matter, a parasitic larva, etc. **2** Biol. **a** a hollow organ, bladder, etc., in an animal or plant, containing a liquid secretion. **b** a cell or cavity enclosing reproductive bodies, an embryo, parasite, micro-organism, etc. [LL cystis f. Gk kustis bladder]

cysteine /ˈsɪstɪˌiːn, -tɪɪn/ n. Biochem. a sulphur-containing amino acid, essential in the human diet and a constituent of many enzymes. [CYSTINE + -eine (var. of -INE⁴)]

cystic /ˈsɪstɪk/ adj. **1** of the urinary bladder. **2** of the gall-bladder. **3** of the nature of a cyst. □ **cystic fibrosis** Med. a hereditary disease affecting the exocrine glands and usu. resulting in respiratory infections. [F cystique or mod.L cysticus (as CYST)]

cystitis /sɪˈstaɪtɪs/ n. an inflammation of the urinary bladder, often caused by infection, and usu. accompanied by frequent painful urination.

cysto- /ˈsɪstəʊ/ comb. form the urinary bladder (cystoscope; cystotomy). [Gk kustē, kustis bladder]

cystoscope /ˈsɪstəˌskəʊp/ n. an instrument inserted in the urethra for examining the urinary bladder. □□ **cystoscopic** /-ˈskɒpɪk/ adj. **cystoscopy** /sɪˈstɒskəpɪ/ n.

cystotomy /sɪˈstɒtəmɪ/ n. (pl. **-ies**) a surgical incision into the urinary bladder.

-cyte /saɪt/ comb. form Biol. a mature cell (leucocyte) (cf. -BLAST). [Gk kutos vessel]

cytidine /ˈsaɪtɪˌdiːn/ n. a nucleoside obtained from RNA by hydrolysis. [G Cytidin (as -CYTE)]

cyto- /ˈsaɪtəʊ/ comb. form Biol. cells or a cell. [as -CYTE]

cytochrome /ˈsaɪtəˌkrəʊm/ n. Biochem. a compound consisting of a protein linked to a haem, which is involved in electron transfer reactions.

cytogenetics /ˌsaɪtəʊdʒɪˈnetɪks/ n. the study of inheritance in relation to the structure and function of cells. □□ **cytogenetic**

adj. **cytogenetical** adj. **cytogenetically** adv. **cytogeneticist** /-sɪst/ n.

cytology /saɪˈtɒlədʒɪ/ n. the study of cells. □□ **cytological** /ˌsaɪtəˈlɒdʒɪk(ə)l/ adj. **cytologically** /ˌsaɪtəˈlɒdʒɪkəlɪ/ adv. **cytologist** n.

cytoplasm /ˈsaɪtəʊˌplæz(ə)m/ n. the protoplasmic content of a cell apart from its nucleus. □□ **cytoplasmic** /-ˈplæzmɪk/ adj.

cytosine /ˈsaɪtəʊˌsiːn/ n. one of the principal component bases of the nucleotides and the nucleic acids DNA and RNA, derived from pyrimidine.

cytotoxic /ˌsaɪtəʊˈtɒksɪk/ adj. toxic to cells.

czar etc. var. of TSAR etc.

czardas var. of CSARDAS.

Czech /tʃek/ n. & adj. —n. **1** a native or national of Czechoslovakia. **2** a native of the western and central parts of Czechoslovakia, namely Bohemia and Moravia. **3** the Slavonic language spoken by some 10 million people in these parts. It is one of the two official languages of Czechoslovakia (cf. SLOVAK). —adj. of or relating to Czechoslovakia or its people or language. □ **Czech Republic** one of the two constituent republics of Czechoslovakia, comprising the former provinces of Bohemia, Moravia, and Silesia. [Pol. spelling of Bohemian Čech]

Czechoslovak /ˌtʃekəˈsləʊvæk/ n. & adj. —n. a native or national of Czechoslovakia. —adj. of or relating to Czechoslovakia. [CZECH + SLOVAK]

Czechoslovakia /ˌtʃekəsləˈvækɪə/ a country in central Europe, between Germany in the west and the USSR in the east; pop. (est. 1988) 15,620,700; official languages, Czech and Slovak; capital, Prague. The country has long been industrialized. Economic planning is in the hands of the government, industry is nationalized, and agriculture is mainly run by State or cooperative farms. Czechoslovakia was created out of the northern part of the old Austro-Hungarian empire after the latter's collapse at the end of the First World War. It incorporated the Czechs (who had enjoyed freedom within their own State of Bohemia until the rise of Hapsburg power in the 16th and 17th c.) of Bohemia and Moravia in the west with the Slovaks of Slovakia in the east. Czech history between the two World Wars represents a brave and enlightened attempt at integration, undermined by economic trouble and eventually crushed by the Nazi takeover of first the Sudetenland (1938) and then the rest of Bohemia-Moravia (1939). After the Second World War, power was seized by the Communists and Czechoslovakia remained under Soviet domination, an attempt at liberalization being crushed by Soviet military intervention in 1968, until Communist supremacy was overthrown in a peaceful revolution in Dec. 1989, followed by the introduction of democratic reforms. In August 1990 the official name of the country was changed to the Czech and Slovak Federal Republic. □□ **Czechoslovakian** adj. & n.

Czerny /ˈtʃeənɪ/, Karl (1791–1857), Austrian pianist, teacher, and composer. He was a pupil of Beethoven, the teacher of Liszt, and a pianist/composer at a time when the piano was undergoing important structural developments. The bulk of his output is made up of over 1,000 exercises and studies for this instrument, but he also composed operas, symphonies, and sacred works.

D

D¹ /diː/ n. (also **d**) (pl. **Ds** or **D's**) **1** the fourth letter of the alphabet. **2** *Mus.* the second note of the diatonic scale of C major. **3** (as a Roman numeral) 500. **4** = DEE. **5** the fourth highest class or category (of academic marks etc.).

D² *symb. Chem.* the element deuterium.

D³ *abbr.* (also **D.**) **1** *US* Democrat. **2** dimension (3-D).

d. *abbr.* **1** died. **2** departs. **3** delete. **4** daughter. **5** *Brit.* (predecimal) penny. **6** depth. **7** deci-. [sense 5 f. L *denarius* silver coin]

'd v. *colloq.* (usu. after pronouns) had, would (I'd; he'd). [abbr.]

DA *abbr.* **1** *US* District Attorney. **2** *sl.* = *duck's arse* (see DUCK¹).

D/A *abbr. Computing* digital to analogue.

da *abbr.* deca-.

dab¹ /dæb/ v. & n. —v. (**dabbed, dabbing**) **1** *tr.* press (a surface) briefly with a cloth, sponge, etc., without rubbing, esp. in cleaning or to apply a substance. **2** *tr.* press (a sponge etc.) lightly on a surface. **3** *tr.* (foll. by *on*) apply (a substance) by dabbing a surface. **4** *intr.* (usu. foll. by *at*) aim a feeble blow; tap. **5** *tr.* strike lightly; tap. —n. **1** a brief application of a cloth, sponge, etc., to a surface without rubbing. **2** a small amount of something applied in this way (*a dab of paint*). **3** a light blow or tap. **4** (in pl.) *Brit. sl.* fingerprints. □□ **dabber** n. [ME, imit.]

dab² /dæb/ n. any flat-fish of the genus *Limanda*. [15th c.: orig. unkn.]

dab³ /dæb/ adj. esp. *Brit. colloq.* □ **dab hand** (usu. foll. by *at*) a person especially skilled (in) (*a dab hand at cooking*). [17th c.: orig. unkn.]

dabble /'dæb(ə)l/ v. **1** *intr.* (usu. foll. by *in, at*) take a casual or superficial interest or part (in a subject or activity). **2** *intr.* move the feet, hands, etc. about in (usu. a small amount of) liquid. **3** *tr.* wet partly or intermittently; moisten, stain, splash. □□ **dabbler** n. [16th c.: f. Du. *dabbelen* or DAB¹]

dabchick /'dæbtʃɪk/ n. = *little grebe* (see GREBE). [16th c., in earlier forms *dap-, dop-*: perh. rel. to OE *dūfedoppa*, DEEP, DIP]

da capo /dɑː ˈkɑːpəʊ/ adv. *Mus.* repeat from the beginning. [It.]

Dacca see DHAKA.

dace /deɪs/ n. (pl. same) any small freshwater fish, esp. of the genus *Leuciscus*, related to the carp. [OF *dars*: see DART]

dacha /'dætʃə/ n. a country house or cottage in Russia. [Russ., = gift]

Dachau /'dæxaʊ, -kaʊ/ a city of Germany, in southern Bavaria, site of a Nazi concentration camp from 1933 and during the Second World War.

dachshund /'dækshʊnd/ n. **1** a dog of a short-legged long-bodied breed. **2** this breed. [G, = badger-dog]

Dacia /'deɪʃə/ an ancient country of SE Europe in what is now the northern and western part of Romania.

dacoit /dəˈkɔɪt/ n. (in India or Burma) a member of a band of armed robbers. [Hindi *ḍakait* f. *ḍākā* gang-robbery]

dactyl /'dæktɪl/ n. a metrical foot (‿‿) consisting of one long (or stressed) syllable followed by two short (or unstressed). [ME f. L *dactylus* f. Gk *daktulos* finger, the three bones corresponding to the three syllables]

dactylic /dæk'tɪlɪk/ adj. & n. —adj. of or using dactyls. —n. (usu. in pl.) dactylic verse. [L *dactylicus* f. Gk *daktulikos* (as DACTYL)]

dad /dæd/ n. *colloq.* father. [perh. imit. of a child's *da, da* (cf. DADDY)]

Dada /'dɑːdɑː/ n. an early 20th-c. international movement in art, literature, music, and film, repudiating and mocking artistic and social conventions. (See below.) □□ **Dadaism** /-də‚ɪz(ə)m/ n. **Dadaist** /-dəɪst/ n. & adj. **Dadaistic** /-ɪstɪk/ adj. [F (the title of an early 20th-c. review) f. *dada* hobby-horse]

Dada is a French word for a child's hobby-horse, said to have been chosen at random from a dictionary and used as a label by a group of artists and writers who were refugees from the First World War in Switzerland. The movement was born in Zurich in 1916 and spread to Paris, Cologne, and New York. It was essentially nihilistic and self-destructive and was absorbed by the surrealists during the 1920s, although, unlike surrealism, it was always against politics (and against everything else, including, logically, Dada). The leading figures were the poet Tzara, the sculptor Arp, and the painters Ernst and Duchamp.

daddy /'dædɪ/ n. (pl. **-ies**) *colloq.* **1** father. **2** (usu. foll. by *of*) the oldest or supreme example (*had a daddy of a headache*). □ **daddy-long-legs 1** a crane-fly. **2** *US* a harvestman. [DAD + -Y³]

dado /'deɪdəʊ/ n. (pl. **-os**) **1** the lower part of the wall of a room when visually distinct from the upper part. **2** the plinth of a column. **3** the cube of a pedestal between the base and the cornice. [It., = DIE²]

Dadra and Nagar Haveli /'dɑːdrə, ‚nɑːgə həˈveɪlɪ/ a Union Territory in western India; pop. (1981) 103,700; capital, Silvassa.

Daedalus /'diːdələs/ *Gk legend* a craftsman who is said to have built the labyrinth for Minos, king of Crete. Minos imprisoned him and his son Icarus, but they escaped on wings which Daedalus made. Icarus was killed when he flew so near the sun that the wax attaching his wings melted and he fell into the Aegean Sea, but Daedalus reached Sicily safely. Daedalus was considered the inventor of carpentry and of such things as the saw, axe, plumb-line, auger, and glue, as well as the mast and yards of boats, and is credited with making figures which had open eyes, walked, and moved their arms. It is uncertain whether a historical artist gave rise to the legends, or whether Daedalus is a mythological figure representing accomplished craftsmanship.

daemon var. of DEMON 5.

daemonic var. of DEMONIC.

daff /dæf/ n. *colloq.* = DAFFODIL. [abbr.]

daffodil /'dæfədɪl/ n. **1 a** a bulbous plant, *Narcissus pseudonarcissus*, with a yellow trumpet-shaped crown. **b** any of various other large-flowered plants of the genus *Narcissus*. **c** a flower of any of these plants. **2** a pale-yellow colour. [earlier *affodill*, as ASPHODEL]

daffy /'dæfɪ/ adj. (**daffier, daffiest**) *sl.* = DAFT. □□ **daffily** adv. **daffiness** n. [*daff* simpleton + -Y²]

daft /dɑːft/ adj. esp. *Brit. colloq.* **1** silly, foolish, crazy. **2** (foll. by *about*) fond of; infatuated with. [ME *daffte* = OE *gedæfte* mild, meek, f. Gmc]

dag¹ /dæg/ n. & v. *Austral.* & *NZ* —n. (usu. in pl.) a lock of wool clotted with dung on the hinder parts of a sheep. —v.tr. (**dagged, dagging**) remove dags from (a sheep). □ **rattle one's dags** *sl.* hurry up. □□ **dagger** n. [orig. Engl. dial.]

dag² /dæg/ n. *Austral.* & *NZ sl.* an eccentric or noteworthy person; a character (*he's a bit of a dag*). [orig. Engl. dial., = a dare, challenge]

da Gama see GAMA.

Dagestan /‚dægɪˈstɑːn/ an autonomous Soviet republic of the RSFSR on the western shore of the Caspian Sea; pop. (est. 1987) 1,800,000; capital, Makhachkala.

dagga /'dægə/ n. *S.Afr.* **1** hemp used as a narcotic. **2** any plant of the genus *Leontis* used similarly. [Afrik. f. Hottentot *dachab*]

dagger /'dægə(r)/ n. **1** a short stabbing-weapon with a pointed and edged blade. **2** *Printing* = OBELUS. □ **at daggers drawn** in bitter enmity. **look daggers at** glare angrily or venomously at. [ME, perh. f. obs. *dag* pierce, infl. by OF *dague* long dagger]

dago /'deɪgəʊ/ n. (pl. **-os**) *sl. offens.* a foreigner, esp. a Spaniard, Portuguese, or Italian. [Sp. *Diego* = James]

Dagon /'deɪgɒn/ a national deity of the ancient Philistines, represented as a fish-tailed man. [Heb. *Dāgōn*]

---

daguerreotype /dəˈgerəʊˌtaɪp/ n. **1** a photograph taken by an early photographic process employing an iodine-sensitized silvered plate and mercury vapour. **2** this process. [L. *Daguerre*, Fr. inventor d. 1851]

dah /dɑː/ n. esp. *US Telegraphy* (in the Morse system) = DASH (cf. DIT). [imit.]

Dahl /dɑːl/, Roald (1916–90), Welsh-born writer, whose works include idiosyncratic short stories published in such collections as *Kiss Kiss* (1960) and the screenplay for the film *Chitty-Chitty-Bang-Bang* (1967). He is noted especially for his stories for children, which include *Charlie and the Cholocate Factory* (1964) and *George's Marvellous Medicine* (1981), and for *Revolting Rhymes* (1982), gruesomely comic versions of traditional tales. Many adult readers dislike his works in which they find a mixture of the glutinous and the cruel, but they are enormously popular with children.

dahlia /ˈdeɪlɪə/ n. any composite garden plant of the genus *Dahlia*, of Mexican origin, cultivated for its many-coloured single or double flowers. [A. *Dahl*, Sw. botanist d. 1789]

Dahomey /dəˈhəʊmɪ/ the former name (until 1975) of Benin.

Dáil /dɔɪl/ n. (in full **Dáil Éireann** /ˈeɪrən/) the lower house of parliament in the Republic of Ireland, composed of 166 members elected on a basis of proportional representation. It was first established in 1919 when the Irish republicans elected to Westminster in the 1918 election proclaimed an Irish State. [Ir., = assembly (of Ireland)]

daily /ˈdeɪlɪ/ adj., adv., & n. —adj. **1** done, produced, or occurring every day or every weekday. **2** constant, regular. —adv. **1** every day; from day to day. **2** constantly. —n. (pl. **-ies**) *colloq.* **1** a daily newspaper. **2** *Brit.* a charwoman or domestic help working daily. □ **daily bread** necessary food; a livelihood. **daily dozen** *Brit. colloq.* regular exercises, esp. on rising. [ME f. DAY + -LY¹, -LY²]

Daimler /ˈdaɪmlə(r)/, Gottlieb (1834–90), German engineer who contributed to the development of the internal-combustion engine. An employee of Nikolaus Otto, he produced a small engine using the Otto cycle in 1884 and made it propel a bicycle in 1886, using petrol vapour. He was a pioneer in the manufacture of motor cars, and was the original designer of the type /pronunc. ˈdeɪmlə(r)/ named after him.

daimon /ˈdaɪməʊn/ n. = DEMON 5. □□ **daimonic** /-ˈmɒnɪk/ adj. [Gk, = deity]

dainty /ˈdeɪntɪ/ adj. & n. —adj. (**daintier, daintiest**) **1** delicately pretty. **2** delicate of build or in movement. **3** (of food) choice. **4** fastidious; having delicate taste and sensibility. —n. (pl. **-ies**) a choice morsel; a delicacy. □□ **daintily** adv. **daintiness** n. [AF *dainté*, OF *daintié, deintié* f. L *dignitas -tatis* f. *dignus* worthy]

daiquiri /ˈdækərɪ, ˈdaɪ-/ n. (pl. **daiquiris**) a cocktail of rum, lime-juice, etc. [*Daiquiri* in Cuba]

dairy /ˈdeərɪ/ n. (pl. **-ies**) **1** a building or room for the storage, processing, and distribution of milk and its products. **2** a shop where milk and milk products are sold. **3** (attrib.) **a** of, containing, or concerning milk and its products (and sometimes eggs). **b** used for dairy products (dairy cow). [ME *deierie* f. *deie* maidservant f. OE *dæge* kneader of dough]

dairying /ˈdeərɪɪŋ/ n. the business of producing, storing, and distributing milk and its products.

dairymaid /ˈdeərɪˌmeɪd/ n. a woman employed in a dairy.

dairyman /ˈdeərɪmən/ n. (pl. **-men**) **1** a man dealing in dairy products. **2** a man employed in a dairy.

dais /ˈdeɪɪs/ n. a low platform, usu. at the upper end of a hall and used to support a table, lectern, etc. [ME f. OF *deis* f. L *discus* disc, dish, in med.L = table]

daisy /ˈdeɪzɪ/ n. (pl. **-ies**) **1 a** a small composite plant, *Bellis perennis*, bearing flowers each with a yellow disc and white rays. **b** any other plant with daisy-like flowers, esp. the larger ox-eye daisy, the Michaelmas daisy, or the Shasta daisy. **2** *sl.* a first-rate specimen of anything. □ **daisy-chain** a string of daisies threaded together. **daisy-cutter** *Cricket* a ball bowled so as to roll along the ground. **daisy wheel** *Computing* a disc of spokes extending radially from a central hub, each terminating in a printing character, used as a printer in word processors and

typewriters. **pushing up the daisies** *sl.* dead and buried. [OE *dæges ēage* day's eye, the flower opening in the morning]

Dak. *abbr.* Dakota.

Dakar /ˈdækɑː(r)/ the capital of Senegal, a port on the Atlantic coast of West Africa; pop. approx. 1,000,000.

Dakota /dəˈkəʊtə/ a former territory of the US, organized in 1889 into the States of North Dakota and South Dakota.

dal var. of DHAL.

Dalai Lama /ˌdælaɪ ˈlɑːmə/ n. the spiritual head of Tibetan Buddhism, formerly also the chief ruler of Tibet (see LAMA). The title is applied to a series of reincarnate lamas. Believed to be the reincarnation of the bodhisattva Ávalokitesvara, the Dalai Lama is the head of the dominant Tibetan Buddhist order and was, until the establishment of Chinese Communist rule in 1959, the spiritual and temporal ruler of Tibet. He lived in the strictest seclusion and was worshipped with almost divine honours. When he died, the lamas professed to search for a child who gave evidence that the soul of the deceased had entered into him; when found, the child succeeded to the office. [Mongolian *dalai* ocean; see LAMA]

Dalcroze /dælˈkrəʊz/ see JAQUES-DALCROZE.

dale /deɪl/ n. a valley, esp. in N. England. [OE *dæl* f. Gmc]

Dalek /ˈdɑːlek/ n. a type of robot appearing in 'Dr Who', a BBC Television science-fiction serial from 1963. [invented word, named after an encyclopaedia volume covering DAL–LEK]

dalesman /ˈdeɪlzmən/ n. (pl. **-men**) an inhabitant of the dales in Northern England.

Dalhousie /dælˈhaʊzɪ/, James Ramsay, 1st Marquis (1812–60), British colonial administrator who, as Governor-General of India between 1847 and 1856, was responsible for a series of reforms and innovations, notably the introduction of railways and of telegraphic communications. His policies, however, took insufficient account of the conservatism of the native peoples of India and contributed to the mounting discontent with British rule which eventually led to the Indian Mutiny.

Dali /ˈdɑːlɪ/, Salvador (1904–89), Spanish Cubist painter, who went to Paris in 1928 and in 1929 was welcomed by André Breton into the surrealist movement. He was expelled from it—by Breton—in 1938, since he rejected its Marxist connections, while retaining the Freudian elements. His pictures are extremely detailed representations of improbable juxtapositions, partly abstract, claimed to be paranoiac in content and deriving from the subconscious. He was in the US 1940–55, after which he returned to Spain as an avowed supporter of Franco. He made two films with Buñuel (1928, 1930), contributed a dream sequence of Hitchcock's *Spellbound* (1945), and wrote two autobiographies.

Dalian /ˌdɑːlɪˈæn/ a port and shipbuilding centre in Liaoning province in NE China. (See LÜDA).

Dallapiccola /ˌdælæˈpɪkələ/, Luigi (1904–75), Italian composer and pianist. His concern for liberty and opposition to Fascism is expressed in two of his best-known works, *Canti di Prigionia* (1938–41) and the opera *Il Prigioniero* (1944–8). His musical style combines the serial technique of Schoenberg and Webern, a typically Italian love of grateful vocal writing, and a concern for colour and sonority.

Dallas /ˈdæləs/ a city in NE Texas; pop. (1982) 943,800. President John F. Kennedy was assassinated here in Nov. 1963.

dalliance /ˈdælɪəns/ n. a leisurely or frivolous passing of time. [DALLY + -ANCE]

dally /ˈdælɪ/ v.intr. (**-ies, -ied**) **1** delay; waste time, esp. frivolously. **2** (often foll. by *with*) play about; flirt, treat frivolously (*dallied with her affections*). □ **dally away** waste or fritter (one's time, life, etc.). [ME f. OF *dalier* chat]

Dalmatian /dælˈmeɪʃ(ə)n/ adj. & n. —adj. of Dalmatia, the central region of the coast of Yugoslavia. —n. **1** a dog of a large white short-haired breed with dark spots. **2** this breed. [*Dalmatia* in Yugoslavia]

dalmatic /dælˈmætɪk/ n. a wide-sleeved long loose vestment open at the sides, worn by deacons and bishops, and by a monarch at his or her coronation. [ME f. OF *dalmatique* or LL *dalmatica* (*vestis*) of Dalmatian wool]

Dalriada /dæl'riːədə/ an ancient Gaelic kingdom in northern Ireland whose people (known as *Scoti*) established a colony in SW Scotland from about the late 5th c. By the 9th c. Irish Dalriada had declined but the people of Scottish Dalriada gradually acquired dominion over the whole of Scotland, giving that country its present name.

dal segno /dæl 'seɪnjəʊ/ *adv. Mus.* repeat from the point marked by a sign. [It., = from the sign]

Dalton /'dɔːlt(ə)n/, John (1766–1844), English chemist, Quaker schoolmaster, son of a weaver, possessor of insatiable curiosity, the founding father of modern atomic theory. His interest in meteorology led to the study of gases, and in 1801 he formulated the celebrated law of partial pressures named after him, according to which the total pressure of a mixture of gases is equal to the sum of the pressures that each gas would exert separately. Because of criticism he decided to furnish experimental proof; he took up his friend William Henry's study on the solubility of gases, and this resulted in his most fundamental work: his atomic theory and concept of atomic weight. He defined an atom as the smallest part of a substance that could participate in a chemical reaction, argued that elements are composed of atoms, and that elements combine in definite proportions. This allowed him, in 1803, to produce the first table of comparative atomic weights. In 1794 he published the first detailed description of 'Daltonism' or colour-blindness, based on his own inability to distinguish green from red.

dam¹ /dæm/ *n. & v.* —*n.* **1** a barrier constructed to hold back water and raise its level, forming a reservoir or preventing flooding. (See below.) **2** a barrier constructed in a stream by a beaver. **3** anything functioning as a dam does. **4** a causeway. —*v.tr.* (**dammed**, **damming**) **1** furnish or confine with a dam. **2** (often foll. by *up*) block up; hold back; obstruct. [ME f. MLG, MDu.]

One of the earliest dams, dating from *c.*2500 BC, is to be found in Egypt, and there are others in Iran, Iraq, and China, made of earth or masonry. Earth dams are still used, with a waterproof core of clay to prevent seepage and with the earth compacted and protected from erosion. Where site conditions are suitable concrete is used. Gravity dams rely on the weight of the dam for stability; arch dams, with a curved structure having its convex face upstream, rely on lateral thrust from solid rock abutments to resist the horizontal pressure of water, just as an arch bridge supports a vertical load. The main uses for dams are to generate electricity by means of water turbines, to store water for irrigation, industrial, or domestic water supplies, and to supply canals with water. It is estimated that at present one-tenth of the stream-flow of the world's rivers is regulated by dams; by the year 2000 two-thirds could be regulated.

dam² /dæm/ *n.* the female parent of an animal, esp. a four-footed one. [ME: var. of DAME]

damage /'dæmɪdʒ/ *n. & v.* —*n.* **1** harm or injury impairing the value or usefulness of something, or the health or normal function of a person. **2** (in *pl.*) *Law* a sum of money claimed or awarded in compensation for a loss or an injury. **3** the loss of what is desirable. **4** (prec. by *the*) *sl.* cost (*what's the damage?*). —*v.tr.* **1** inflict damage on. **2** (esp. as **damaging** *adj.*) detract from the reputation of (*a most damaging admission*). □□ **damagingly** *adv.* [ME f. OF *damage* (n.), *damagier* (v.), f. *dam*(*me*) loss f. L *damnum* loss, damage]

Daman and Diu /dəˌmaːn, 'diːuː/ a Union Territory of India; pop. (1981) 79,000. Until 1987 the district of Daman (on the west coast of India north of Bombay) and the island of Diu were administered with Goa, which now forms a separate State.

Damaraland /də'maːrəˌlænd/ a plateau region of central Namibia inhabited chiefly by the Damara and Herero peoples.

damascene /'dæməˌsiːn, ˌdæmə'siːn/ *v., n., & adj.* —*v.tr.* decorate (metal, esp. iron or steel) by etching or inlaying esp. with gold or silver, or with a watered pattern produced in welding. —*n.* a design or article produced in this way. —*adj.* of, relating to, or produced by this process. [*Damascene* of Damascus, f. L *Damascenus* f. Gk *Damaskēnos*]

Damascus /də'maːskəs/ the capital of Syria since the country's independence in 1946; pop. (1981) 1,251,000. It has existed as a city for over 4,000 years and has always been a centre of trade and travel.

damask /'dæməsk/ *n., adj., & v.* —*n.* **1 a** a figured woven fabric (esp. silk or linen) with a pattern visible on both sides. **b** twilled table linen with woven designs shown by the reflection of light. **2** a tablecloth made of this material. **3** *hist.* steel with a watered pattern produced in welding. —*adj.* **1** made of or resembling damask. **2** coloured like a damask rose, velvety pink or vivid red. —*v.tr.* **1** weave with figured designs. **2** = DAMASCENE *v.* **3** ornament. □ **damask rose** an old sweet-scented variety of rose, with very soft velvety petals, used to make attar. [ME, ult. f. L *Damascus*]

dame /deɪm/ *n.* **1** (**Dame**) **a** (in the UK) the title given to a woman with the rank of Knight Commander or holder of the Grand Cross in the Orders of Chivalry. **b** a woman holding this title. **2** *Brit.* a comic middle-aged female character in modern pantomime, usu. played by a man. **3** *archaic* a mature woman. **4** *US sl.* a woman. □ **dame-school** *hist.* a small primary school of the 18th c., usually kept by one female teacher, for the children of poor families. [ME f. OF f. L *domina* mistress]

damfool /'dæmfuːl/ *adj. colloq.* foolish, stupid. [DAMN + FOOL¹]

Damietta /ˌdæmɪ'etə/ (Arabic **Dumyât** /dʊm'jaːt/) **1** the eastern branch of the Nile delta. **2** a port at the mouth of this; pop. (est. 1986) 121,200.

dammar /'dæmə(r)/ *n.* **1** any E. Asian tree, esp. one of the genus *Agathis* or *Shorea*, yielding a resin used in varnish-making. **2** this resin. [Malay *damar*]

dammit /'dæmɪt/ *int.* damn it.

damn /dæm/ *v., n., adj., & adv.* —*v.tr.* **1** (often *absol.* or as *int.* of anger or annoyance, = *may God damn*) curse (a person or thing). **2** doom to hell; cause the damnation of. **3** condemn, censure (*a review damning the performance*). **4 a** (often as **damning** *adj.*) (of a circumstance, piece of evidence, etc.) show or prove to be guilty; bring condemnation upon (*evidence against them was damning*). **b** be the ruin of. —*n.* **1** an uttered curse. **2** *sl.* a negligible amount (*not worth a damn*). —*int. & adv. colloq.* = DAMNED. □ **damn all** *sl.* nothing at all. **damn well** *colloq.* (as an emphatic) simply (*damn well do as I say*). **damn with faint praise** commend so unenthusiastically as to imply disapproval. **I'm** (or **I'll be**) **damned if** *colloq.* I certainly do not, will not, etc. **not give a damn** see GIVE. **well I'm** (or **I'll be**) **damned** *colloq.* exclamation of surprise, dismay, etc. □□ **damningly** *adv.* [ME f. OF *damner* f. L *damnare* inflict loss on f. *damnum* loss]

damnable /'dæmnəb(ə)l/ *adj.* hateful, annoying. □□ **damnably** *adv.* [ME f. OF *damnable* (as DAMN)]

damnation /dæm'neɪʃ(ə)n/ *n. & int.* —*n.* condemnation to eternal punishment, esp. in hell. —*int.* expressing anger or annoyance. [ME f. OF *damnation* (as DAMN)]

damnatory /'dæmnətərɪ/ *adj.* conveying or causing censure or damnation. [L *damnatorius* (as DAMN)]

damned /dæmd/ *adj. & adv. colloq.* —*adj.* damnable, infernal, unwelcome. —*adv.* extremely (*damned hot; damned lovely*). □ **damned well** (as an emphatic) simply (*you've damned well got to*). **do one's damnedest** do one's utmost.

damnify /'dæmnɪˌfaɪ/ *v.tr.* (**-ies**, **-ied**) *Law* cause injury to. □□ **damnification** /-fɪ'keɪʃ(ə)n/ *n.* [OF *damnifier* etc. f. LL *damnificare* injure (as DAMN)]

Damocles /'dæməˌkliːz/ a courtier who excessively praised the happiness of Dionysius, ruler of Syracuse (4th c. BC). To show him how precarious this happiness was, Dionysius seated him at a banquet with a sword hung by a single hair over his head. □ **sword of Damocles** an imminent danger at a time of apparent well-being.

Damon /'deɪmən/ a Syracusan whose friend Phintias was sentenced to death. Damon went bail for Phintias, who returned at the last moment and saved him, and was reprieved. □ **Damon and Pythias** (erron. for *Phintias*) faithful friends.

damp /dæmp/ *adj., n., & v.* —*adj.* slightly wet; moist. —*n.* **1** diffused moisture in the air, on a surface, or in a solid, esp. as a cause of inconvenience or danger. **2** dejection; discouragement. **3** = FIREDAMP. —*v.tr.* **1** make damp; moisten. **2** (often foll. by *down*) **a** take the force or vigour out of (*damp one's enthusiasm*).

b make flaccid or spiritless. **c** make (a fire) burn less strongly by reducing the flow of air to it. **3** reduce or stop the vibration of (esp. the strings of a musical instrument). **4** quieten. □ **damp (or damp-proof) course** a layer of waterproof material in the wall of a building near the ground, to prevent rising damp. **damp off** (of a plant) die from a fungus attack in damp conditions. **damp squib** an unsuccessful attempt to impress etc. □□ **damply** adv. **dampness** n. [ME f. MLG, = vapour etc., OHG dampf steam f. WG]

dampen /'dæmpən/ v. **1** v.tr. & intr. make or become damp. **2** tr. make less forceful or vigorous; stifle, choke. □□ **dampener** n.

damper /'dæmpə(r)/ n. **1** a person or thing that discourages, or tempers enthusiasm. **2** a device that reduces shock or noise. **3** a metal plate in a flue to control the draught, and so the rate of combustion. **4** Mus. a pad silencing a piano string except when removed by means of a pedal or by the note's being struck. **5** esp. Austral. & NZ unleavened bread or cake of flour and water baked in wood ashes. □ **put a damper on** take the vigour or enjoyment out of.

Dampier /'dæmpɪə(r)/, William (1652–1715), English explorer and adventurer. Having already established a reputation as a hydrographer, Dampier was involved in buccaneering activities in Panama before setting out on a privateering expedition along the west coast of America in 1683. He crossed the Pacific to the Philippines, China, and Australia, was marooned on the Nicobar Islands in 1688, and eventually got back to England in 1691. In 1699 he revisited Australia, commissioned by the British government to explore the coast, and circumnavigated the globe again, despite being wrecked on Ascension Island on the way home. His later privateering activities were marred by drunkenness and brutality which caused trouble both with his own crews and with the British authorities.

damsel /'dæmz(ə)l/ n. archaic or literary a young unmarried woman. [ME f. OF dam(e)isele ult. f. L domina mistress]

damselfish /'dæmz(ə)lfɪʃ/ n. a small brightly-coloured fish, Chromis chromis, found in or near coral reefs.

damselfly /'dæmz(ə)l,flaɪ/ n. (pl. **-flies**) any of various insects of the order Odonata, like a dragonfly but with its wings folded over the body when resting.

damson /'dæmz(ə)n/ n. & adj. —n. **1** (in full **damson plum**) **a** a small dark-purple plumlike fruit. **b** the small deciduous tree, Prunus institia, bearing this. **2** a dark-purple colour. —adj. damson-coloured. □ **damson cheese** a solid preserve of damsons and sugar. [ME damacene, -scene, -sene f. L damascenum (prunum plum) of Damascus: see DAMASCENE]

Dan /dæn/ **1** Hebrew patriarch, son of Jacob and Bilhah (Gen. 30: 6). **2** the tribe of Israel traditionally descended from him. **3** an ancient town in the north of Canaan, where the tribe of Dan settled. In Old Testament times it marked the northern limit of Israelite territory (Judges 20; see also BEERSHEBA).

Dan. abbr. Daniel (Old Testament).

dan[1] /dæn/ n. **1** any of twelve degrees of advanced proficiency in judo. **2** a person who has achieved any of these. [Jap.]

dan[2] /dæn/ n. (in full **dan buoy**) a small buoy used as a marker in deep-sea fishing, or to mark the limits of an area cleared by minesweepers. [17th c.: orig. unkn.]

Dana[1] /'deɪnə/, James Dwight (1813–95), American naturalist, geologist, and mineralogist, an influential teacher whose works became standard textbooks in their subjects. At the age of 24 he produced A System of Mineralogy, founding a classification of minerals based on chemistry and physics; in spite of the reorganization of material made necessary by the development of scientific techniques the book still appears under his name. His view of the earth as a unit, with its physical features changing and developing progressively, was an evolutionary one, but he did not accept the theory of the evolution of species, constructed by Charles Darwin (with whom he corresponded), until the last edition of his Manual of Geology, published shortly before his death.

Dana[2] /'deɪnə/, Richard Henry (1815–82), American author, who wrote a realistic and lively account of his voyage from Boston round Cape Horn to California, published anonymously in 1840 as Two years Before the Mast.

Danae /'dænɑːɪ/ Gk Mythol. the daughter of Acrisius, king of Argos. An oracle foretold that she would bear a son who would kill her father. In an attempt to evade this he imprisoned her in a tower, but Zeus visited her in the form of a shower of gold and she conceived Perseus, who after many adventures killed Acrisius by accident.

Danaids /'dænɑːɪdz/ n.pl. Gk legend the daughters of Danaus, king of Argos, who were compelled to marry the sons of his brother Aegyptus but murdered their husbands on the wedding night, except for Hypermnestra, who helped her husband to escape. They were punished in Hades by being set to fill a leaky jar with water.

Da Nang /dɑː 'næŋ/ a port and city (formerly called Tourane) in central Vietnam, on the South China Sea; pop. (est.) 500,000. During the Vietnam War it was used as a US military base.

dance /dɑːns/ v. & n. —v. **1** intr. move about rhythmically alone or with a partner or in a set, usu. in fixed steps or sequences to music, for pleasure or as entertainment. **2** intr. move in a lively way; skip or jump about. **3** tr. **a** perform (a specified dance or form of dancing). **b** perform (a specified role) in a ballet etc. **4** intr. move up and down (on water, in the field of vision, etc.). **5** tr. move (esp. a child) up and down; dandle. —n. **1 a** a piece of dancing; a sequence of steps in dancing. **b** a special form of this. **2** a single round or turn of a dance. **3** a social gathering for dancing, a ball. **4** a piece of music for dancing to or in a dance rhythm. **5** a dancing or lively motion. □ **dance attendance on** follow or wait on (a person) obsequiously. **dance of death** see separate entry. **dance to a person's tune** accede obsequiously to a person's demands and wishes. **lead a person a dance** (or **merry dance**) Brit. cause a person much trouble in following a course one has instigated. □□ **danceable** adj. [ME f. OF dance, danse (n.), dancer, danser (v.), f. Rmc, of unkn. orig.]

dancehall /'dɑːnshɔːl/ n. a public hall for dancing.

dance of death n. a medieval conceit in which skeletal figures seized popes, kings, merchants, beggars, emphasizing the equality of all men before Death. The earliest dated painting (c.1425) was a mural in a Parisian cemetery, but the most famous example is the series of 41 woodcuts after drawings by Holbein (c.1523–6), based on a mural in Basle, first printed in Lyons in 1538 and immediately popular.

dancer /'dɑːnsə(r)/ n. **1** a person who performs a dance. **2** a person whose profession is dancing.

d. and c. n. dilatation (of the cervix) and curettage (of the uterus), performed after a miscarriage or for the removal of cysts, tumours, etc.

dandelion /'dændɪ,laɪən/ n. a composite plant, Taraxacum officinale, with jagged leaves and a large bright-yellow flower on a hollow stalk, followed by a globular head of seeds with downy tufts. □ **dandelion clock** the downy seed-head of a dandelion. **dandelion coffee** dried and powdered dandelion roots; a drink made from this. [F dent-de-lion transl. med.L dens leonis lion's tooth]

dander /'dændə(r)/ n. colloq. temper, anger, indignation. □ **get one's dander up** lose one's temper; become angry. [19th c.: orig. uncert.]

dandify /'dændɪ,faɪ/ v.tr. (**-ies, -ied**) cause to resemble a dandy.

dandle /'dænd(ə)l/ v.tr. **1** dance (a child) on one's knees or in one's arms. **2** pamper, pet. [16th c.: orig. unkn.]

dandruff /'dændrʌf/ n. **1** dead skin in small scales among the hair. **2** the condition of having this. [16th c.: -ruff perh. rel. to ME rove scurfiness f. ON hrufa or MLG, MDu. rōve]

dandy /'dændɪ/ n. & adj. —n. (pl. **-ies**) **1** a man unduly devoted to style, smartness, and fashion in dress and appearance. **2** colloq. an excellent thing. —adj. (**dandier, dandiest**) esp. US colloq. very good of its kind; splendid, first-rate. □ **dandy-brush** a brush for grooming a horse. **dandy roll** (or **roller**) a device for solidifying, and impressing a watermark in, paper during manufacture. □□ **dandyish** adj. **dandyism** n. [18th c.: perh. orig. = Andrew, in Jack-a-dandy]

Dane /deɪn/ n. **1** a native or national of Denmark. **2** hist. a Viking

b but   d dog   f few   g get   h he   j yes   k cat   l leg   m man   n no   p pen   r red   s sit   t top   v voice

invader of England in the 9th–11th c. □ **Great Dane 1** a dog of a very large short-haired breed. **2** this breed. [ME f. ON *Danir* (pl.), LL *Dani*]

Danegeld /ˈdeɪngeld/ *n. hist.* **1** a land-tax levied in Anglo-Saxon England (especially 991–1016), originally to bribe the invading Danes to go away, turned into a permanent levy for national defence by the Norman kings. **2** appeasement by bribery. [OE (as DANE + ON *gjald* payment)]

Danelaw /ˈdeɪnlɔː/ *n. hist.* the part of N. & E. England occupied or administered by Danes from the late 9th c. and administered according to their laws until after the Norman Conquest. [OE *Dena lagu* Danes' law]

danger /ˈdeɪndʒə(r)/ *n.* **1** liability or exposure to harm. **2** a thing that causes or is likely to cause harm. **3** the status of a railway signal directing a halt or caution. □ **danger list** a list of those dangerously ill, esp. in a hospital. **danger money** extra payment for dangerous work. **in danger of** likely to incur or to suffer from. [earlier sense 'jurisdiction, power': ME f. OF *dangier* ult. f. L *dominus* lord]

dangerous /ˈdeɪndʒərəs/ *adj.* involving or causing danger. □□ **dangerously** *adv.* **dangerousness** *n.* [ME f. AF *dangerous*, *daungerous*, OF *dangereus* (as DANGER)]

dangle /ˈdæŋg(ə)l/ *v.* **1** *intr.* be loosely suspended, so as to be able to sway to and fro. **2** *tr.* hold or carry loosely suspended. **3** *tr.* hold out (a hope, temptation, etc.) enticingly. □□ **dangler** *n.* [16th c. (imit.): cf. Sw. *dangla*, Da. *dangle*]

Daniel /ˈdænj(ə)l/ **1** a Hebrew prophet (6th c. BC), captive at Babylon, who spent his life at the court there, interpreted the dreams of Nebuchadnezzar, and was delivered by God from the lions' den into which he had been thrown as the result of a trick. The stories are regarded as legendary. **2** the book of the Old Testament bearing his name but probably written at the outbreak of persecution of the Jews under Seleucid rule *c.*167 BC. —*n.* an upright judge, a person of infallible wisdom (alluding to Sus. 45–64, where Daniel showed the evidence against Susannah to be false).

Daniell cell /ˈdænj(ə)l/ *n. Physics & Chem.* a primary voltaic cell with a copper anode and a zinc-amalgam cathode giving a standard electromotive force when either copper sulphate or sulphuric acid is used as the electrolyte. [John *Daniell*, Brit. chemist d. 1845, its inventor]

Danish /ˈdeɪnɪʃ/ *adj. & n.* —*adj.* of or relating to Denmark or its people or language. —*n.* the official language of Denmark (where it is spoken by the 5 million inhabitants) and also of Greenland and the Faeroes. It belongs to the Scandinavian language group. **2** (prec. by *the*; treated as *pl.*) the Danish people. □ **Danish blue** a soft salty white cheese with blue veins. **Danish pastry** a cake of sweetened yeast pastry topped with icing, fruit, nuts, etc. [ME f. AF *danes*, OF *daneis* f. med.L *Danensis* (as DANE)]

dank /dæŋk/ *adj.* disagreeably damp and cold. □□ **dankly** *adv.* **dankness** *n.* [ME prob. f. Scand.: cf. Sw. *dank* marshy spot]

d'Annunzio /dɑːˈnʊntsɪˌəʊ/, Gabriele (1863–1938), Italian poet, novelist, and dramatist. A fervent patriot, in the First World War he effectively urged the entry of Italy on the side of the Allies and himself took part in some spectacular exploits. All his work exudes a sensuous enjoyment of life; the Nietzchian hedonists (untroubled by conscience) who are the heroes of his novels may be said to anticipate Fascism. His flamboyance, his grand passion for the actress Eleanora Duse, and the erotic and decadent aspects of some of his works, made him a controversial figure both as a man and as a writer.

danse macabre /ˌdɑ̃s məˈkɑːbr/ *n.* = DANCE OF DEATH. [F (as DANCE, MACABRE)]

danseur /dɑ̃ˈsɜː(r)/ *n.* (*fem.* **danseuse** /-ˈsɜːz/) a ballet-dancer. [F, = dancer]

Dante Alighieri /ˈdæntɪ ˌælɪɡˈjeərɪ/ (1265–1321), Italian poet and philosopher, born in Florence of a Guelph family. He became active in political life, and in 1301 went into exile in various Italian cities after his party lost power. Early in life he fell in love with the girl whom he celebrates under the name of 'Beatrice'. His first major work, as an innovative poet of courtly love, was the collection of his poems for her, after her death, into a

visionary narrative, the 'Vita Nuova' (*c.*1292–4). He promised more for her, and eventually achieved this in his masterpiece (finished just before his death), the 'Commedia' ('Divina' was added by Boccaccio), a classical and Christian autobiographical epic in the form of an imagined visit to Hell and Purgatory (the 'Inferno' and 'Purgatorio') with Virgil as guide, and finally to the spheres of Heaven (the 'Paradiso') with Beatrice, now a blessed spirit, as guide. His works are vividly pictorial with dramatic encounters, a gift to illustrators. His writings included a pioneering work (in Latin) on the value of vernacular Italian as a literary language, displacing Latin.

danthonia /dænˈθəʊnɪə/ *n. Austral. & NZ* any tufted pasture grass of the genus *Danthonia*. [mod.L f. E. *Danthoine* 19th-c. Fr. botanist]

Danton /dɑ̃ˈtɔ̃/, Georges Jacques (1759–94), French revolutionary, a noted orator, who won great popularity among the Paris mob in the early days of the French Revolution. Initially an ally of Robespierre and the Jacobins, he later revolted against their radicalism and attempted to form an opposition, only to be arrested and executed on Robespierre's orders.

Danube /ˈdænjuːb/ a river about 2,850 km (1,770 miles) long that rises in the Black Forest in SW Germany and flows into the Black Sea. The Danube, which is Europe's second longest river, is known as the *Donau* in Germany and Austria, *Dunaj* in Czechoslovakia, *Duna* in Hungary, and *Dunarea* in Romania. The capital cities of Vienna, Budapest, and Belgrade are situated on it.

Danubian /dæˈnjuːbɪən/ *adj.* of the River Danube. □ **Danubian principalities** the former principalities of Moldavia and Wallachia, united in 1861 to form the State of Romania.

Danzig see GDANSK.

Dão /daʊ/ a river and noted wine-producing region of north central Portugal.

dap /dæp/ *v.* (**dapped, dapping**) **1** *intr.* fish by letting the bait bob on the water. **2** *tr. & intr.* dip lightly. **3** *tr. & intr.* bounce on the ground. [cf. DAB[1]]

Daphne /ˈdæfnɪ/ *Gk Mythol.* a nymph who was turned into a laurel-bush to save her from the pursuit of Apollo.

daphne /ˈdæfnɪ/ *n.* any flowering shrub of the genus *Daphne*, e.g. the spurge laurel or mezereon. [ME, = laurel, f. Gk *daphnē*]

daphnia /ˈdæfnɪə/ *n.* any freshwater branchiopod crustacean of the genus *Daphnia*, enclosed in a transparent carapace and with long antennae and prominent eyes. Also called *freshwater flea*. [mod.L f. DAPHNE, f. DAPHNE]

Daphnis /ˈdæfnɪs/ *Gk legend* a Sicilian shepherd, son or favourite of Hermes. According to one version of the legend he was struck with blindness for his infidelity to the nymph Echenaïs who loved him; he consoled himself by making pastoral music, of which he was the inventor, or it was first invented by the other shepherds, who sang of his misfortunes.

Da Ponte /dɑː ˈpɒntɪ/, Lorenzo Emanuela Conegliano (1749–1838), Italian poet and librettist for many composers, most notably for Mozart's *Marriage of Figaro, Don Giovanni*, and *Così fan tutte*.

dapper /ˈdæpə(r)/ *adj.* **1** neat and precise, esp. in dress or movement. **2** sprightly. □□ **dapperly** *adv.* **dapperness** *n.* [ME f. MLG, MDu. *dapper* strong, stout]

dapple /ˈdæp(ə)l/ *v. & n.* —*v.* **1** *tr.* mark with spots or rounded patches of colour or shade. **2** *intr.* become marked in this way. —*n.* **1** a dappled effect. **2** a dappled animal, esp. a horse. □ **dapple grey 1** (of an animal's coat) grey or white with darker spots. **2** a horse of this colour. [ME *dappled, dappeld*, (adj.), of unkn. orig.]

DAR *abbr.* Daughters of the American Revolution (see DAUGHTER).

darbies /ˈdɑːbɪz/ *n.pl. Brit. sl.* handcuffs. [allusive use of *Father Darby's bands*, some rigid form of agreement for debtors (16th c.)]

Darby and Joan /ˌdɑːbɪ, ˈdʒəʊn/ *n.* a devoted old married couple. □ **Darby and Joan club** *Brit.* a club for people over 60. [18th c.: perh. f. a poem of 1735 in the *Gentleman's Magazine* containing the lines 'Old Darby, with Joan by his side, You've often regarded with wonder: He's dropsical, she is sore-eyed, Yet they're never happy asunder']

Dardanelles /ˌdɑːdəˈnelz/ a narrow strait between Europe and Asiatic Turkey, anciently called the Hellespont. It was the scene of an unsuccessful attack on Turkey by British and French troops in 1915, with Australian and New Zealand contingents playing a major part.

dare /deə(r)/ v. & n. —v.tr. (3rd sing. present usu. **dare** before an expressed or implied infinitive without to) **1** (foll. by infin. with or without to) venture (to); have the courage or impudence (to) (dare he do it?; if they dare to come; how dare you?; I dare not speak; I do not dare to jump). **2** (usu. foll. by to + infin.) defy or challenge (a person) (I dare you to own up). **3** literary attempt; take the risk of (dare all things; dared their anger). —n. **1** an act of daring. **2** a challenge, esp. to prove courage. □ **I dare say 1** (often foll. by that + clause) it is probable. **2** probably; I grant that much (I dare say, but you are still wrong). □□ **darer** n. [OE durran with Gmc cognates: cf. Skr. dhṛṣ, Gk tharseō be bold]

daredevil /ˈdeəˌdev(ə)l/ n. & adj. —n. a recklessly daring person. —adj. recklessly daring. □□ **daredevilry** n. **daredeviltry** n.

Dar es Salaam /dɑːr es səˈlɑːm/ the former capital and chief port of Tanzania, founded in 1866 by the sultan of Zanzibar, who built his summer palace there; pop. (1978) approx. 757,346. Its Arabic name means 'haven of peace'.

Darfur /dɑːˈfʊə(r)/ a region in the west of Sudan; pop. (1983) 3,093,700.

darg /dɑːg/ n. Sc., N.Engl., & Austral. **1** a day's work. **2** a definite amount of work; a task. [ME f. daywork or daywark day-work]

Darien /ˈdeərɪən, ˈdæ-/ a sparsely populated province of eastern Panama; pop. (est. 1988) 39,200. The name was formerly applied to the whole of the Isthmus of Panama. At the end of the 19th c. an unsuccessful attempt was made by Scottish settlers to establish a colony in the tropical wilderness of the eastern region with the aim of controlling trade between the Atlantic and Pacific Oceans. □ **Gulf of Darien** a part of the Caribbean Sea, between Panama and Colombia.

daring /ˈdeərɪŋ/ n. & adj. —n. adventurous courage. —adj. adventurous, bold; prepared to take risks. □□ **daringly** adv.

dariole /ˈdærɪˌəʊl/ n. a savoury or sweet dish cooked and served in a small mould usu. shaped like a flowerpot. [ME f. OF]

Darius /dəˈraɪəs/ 'the Great' (c.550–486 BC), king of Persia 521–486 BC. He divided the empire into provinces governed by satraps, and (a true successor of Cyrus) centralized authority while allowing each province its own form of government and institutions. He developed commerce, building a network of roads, exploring the Indus valley, and connecting the Nile with the Red Sea by canal. His campaigns were designed to consolidate the empire. After suppressing a revolt of the Greek cities in Ionia (499–494 BC) he prepared to punish the mainland Greeks for their interference, but his expeditions ended in a Greek victory at Marathon (490 BC), and he died soon afterwards.

Darjeeling /dɑːˈdʒiːlɪŋ/ n. a high-quality tea from Darjeeling, a town and district of West Bengal.

dark /dɑːk/ adj. & n. —adj. **1** with little or no light. **2** of a deep or sombre colour. **3** (of a person) with deep brown or black hair, complexion, or skin. **4** gloomy, depressing, dismal (dark thoughts). **5** evil, sinister (dark deeds). **6** sullen, angry (a dark mood). **7** remote, secret, mysterious, little-known (the dark and distant past; keep it dark). **8** ignorant, unenlightened. —n. **1** absence of light. **2** nightfall (don't go out after dark). **3** a lack of knowledge. **4** a dark area or colour, esp. in painting (the skilled use of lights and darks). □ **the Dark Ages** (or **Age**) **1** see separate entry. **2** any period of supposed unenlightenment. **the Dark Continent** a name for Africa, esp. when little known to Europeans. **dark glasses** spectacles with dark-tinted lenses. **dark horse** a little-known person who is unexpectedly successful or prominent. **dark star** an invisible star known to exist from reception of physical data other than light. **in the dark** lacking information. □□ **darkish** adj. **darkly** adv. **darkness** n. **darksome** poet. adj. [OE deorc prob. f. Gmc]

Dark Ages a term denoting the obscurity or barbarity of the period in the West between the fall of the Roman Empire and the high Middle Ages, c.500–1100. Obscurity can delight historians who piece together the evidence; barbarity may imply an underestimate of classical influences on the newly settled Germanic peoples. Broadly, however, there was political fragmentation, a hiatus in city life, a lack of major learned centres, and an emphasis on waterways rather than roads. The Devil was accorded great power, symptomatic of an age which made peculiarly little distinction between nature and the supernatural (good or evil), and inhibiting of human development. The Dark Ages may be said to have ended when St Anselm became the first medieval thinker to deny that the Devil had a rightful dominion over men.

The term Dark Age has been applied to a similar period in the history of Greece and other Aegean countries from the end of the Bronze Age until the beginning of the historical period, when the region seems to have been heavily depopulated, its material culture stagnant, there was no building of palaces and fortresses, and the art of writing (associated with the palace bureaucracies) was apparently lost. The period falls between two cultural phases that have been comparatively well explored, but some features such as ship-building and the extraction of silver, and strong oral tradition resulting in the emergence of the Homeric poems as we have them, are at variance with the generally humble picture of Dark Age Greece and suggest that it has been painted too black.

darken /ˈdɑːkən/ v. **1** tr. make dark or darker. **2** intr. become dark or darker. □ **never darken a person's door** keep away permanently. □□ **darkener** n.

Darkhan /dɑːˈkɑːn/ an industrial and mining city in northern Mongolia, established in 1961; pop. (est. 1988) 80,000.

darkie var. of DARKY.

darkling /ˈdɑːklɪŋ/ adj. & adv. poet. in the dark; in the night.

darkroom /ˈdɑːkruːm, -rʊm/ n. a room for photographic work, with normal light excluded.

darky /ˈdɑːkɪ/ n. (also **darkie**) (pl. **-ies**) sl. offens. a Black person.

darling /ˈdɑːlɪŋ/ n. & adj. —n. **1** a beloved or lovable person or thing. **2** a favourite. **3** colloq. a pretty or endearing person or thing. —adj. **1** beloved, lovable. **2** favourite. **3** colloq. charming or pretty. [OE dēorling (as DEAR, -LING¹)]

Darling River a river of SE Australia, flowing 2,757 km (1,712 miles) in a generally south-westward course to join the Murray River.

darn¹ /dɑːn/ v. & n. —v.tr. **1** mend (esp. knitted material, or a hole in it) by interweaving yarn across the hole with a needle. **2** embroider with a large running stitch. —n. a darned area in material. □ **darning needle 1** a long needle with a large eye, used in darning. **2** US a dragonfly. [16th c.: perh. f. obs. dern hide]

darn² /dɑːn/ v.tr., int., adj., & adv. (US **durn** /dɜːn/) colloq. = DAMN (in imprecatory senses). [corrupt. of DAMN]

darned /dɑːnd/ adj. & adv. (US **durned** /dɜːnd/) colloq. = DAMNED.

darnel /ˈdɑːn(ə)l/ n. any of several grasses of the genus Lolium, growing in some countries as weeds among cereal crops. It was known first as the English name for the weed called Lolium in the Vulgate. Now rare in Britain, it appears to have been more common when seed-corn was imported from Mediterranean regions, where it abounds. It is a health hazard when infested by ergot, to which it is particularly susceptible, dangerous to grazing animals and formerly liable to contaminate rye flour. [ME: cf. Walloon darnelle]

darner /ˈdɑːnə(r)/ n. a person or thing that darns, esp. a darning needle.

darning /ˈdɑːnɪŋ/ n. **1** the action of a person who darns. **2** things to be darned.

Darnley /ˈdɑːnlɪ/, Lord (1545–67), Henry Stewart (or Stuart), Scottish nobleman, second husband of his cousin Mary Queen of Scots and father of James I of England. He was implicated in the murder of Riccio, her secretary, and was killed in mysterious circumstances at Edinburgh.

dart /dɑːt/ n. & v. —n. **1** a small pointed missile used as a weapon or in a game. **2** (in pl.; usu. treated as sing.) an indoor game in which darts are thrown at a circular target to score points. (See below.) **3** a sudden rapid movement. **4** *Zool.* a dartlike structure, such as an insect's sting or the calcareous projections of a snail (used during copulation). **5** a tapering tuck stitched in a garment. —*v.* **1** *intr.* (often foll. by *out, in, past,* etc.) move or go suddenly or rapidly (*darted into the shop*). **2** *tr.* throw (a missile). **3** *tr.* direct suddenly (a glance etc.). [ME f. OF *darz, dars,* f. Frank.]

Darts is a predominantly British indoor game in which light usually feathered darts are thrown at a target (a dartboard) marked with concentric circles and a bull's-eye in the centre, and now divided by radiating lines into numbered sectors. The game is associated with inns, taverns, and public houses, and dates from the time of George III or earlier.

dartboard /ˈdɑːtbɔːd/ *n.* a circular board marked with numbered segments, used as a target in darts.

darter /ˈdɑːtə(r)/ *n.* **1** any large water-bird of the genus *Anhinga*, having a narrow head and long thin neck. **2** any of various small quick-moving freshwater fish of the family Percidae, native to N. America.

Dartmoor /ˈdɑːtmʊə(r)/ **1** a moorland district in Devon that was a royal forest in Saxon times, now a national park. **2** a prison near Princetown in this district, originally built to hold French prisoners of war from the Napoleonic Wars. □ **Dartmoor pony 1** a small pony of a shaggy-coated breed. **2** this breed.

Darwin[1] /ˈdɑːwɪn/ the capital of the Northern Territory, Australia; pop. (1986) 68,500. Darwin was almost completely destroyed by Hurricane Tracy in 1974.

Darwin[2] /ˈdɑːwɪn/, Charles Robert (1809–82), English natural historian, geologist, voyager/collector, revolutionary thinker, botanist and zoologist of remarkable powers, who propounded the theory of evolution by natural selection, to the consternation of certain theologians at this threat to the beliefs that they found comfortable. Grandson of the eminent physician Erasmus Darwin and son of a Shrewsbury doctor and the daughter of the potter Josiah Wedgwood, he failed to complete his medical training at Edinburgh and just scraped a degree at Cambridge in vague preparation for a life in the Church. At twenty-two, seizing his one great opportunity, a post as gentleman-naturalist to HMS *Beagle* on her circumnavigation of the globe, he set out as an untried amateur and returned five years later to take his place amongst the élite of the learned societies. Marrying his cousin Emma Wedgwood and retiring into a massively productive isolation in Kent, visited only by a chosen handful of scientists, he published an astonishing series of books, monographs, and papers. *On the Origin of Species* (1859) and *The Descent of Man* (1871) changed our concept of nature and of man's place within it. The Newton of biology, he is buried in Westminster Abbey.

Darwinian /dɑːˈwɪnɪən/ *adj.* & *n.* —*adj.* of or relating to Darwin's theory of the evolution of species by the action of natural selection. —*n.* an adherent of this theory. □□ **Darwinism** /ˈdɑː-/ *n.* **Darwinist** /ˈdɑː-/ *n.*

dash /dæʃ/ *v.* & *n.* —*v.* **1** *intr.* rush hastily or forcefully (*dashed up the stairs*). **2** *tr.* strike or fling with great force, esp. so as to shatter (*dashed it to the ground; the cup was dashed from my hand*). **3** *tr.* frustrate, daunt, dispirit (*dashed their hopes*). **4** *tr. colloq.* (esp. **dash it** or **dash it all**) = DAMN *v.* 1 —*n.* **1** a rush or onset; a sudden advance (*made a dash for shelter*). **2** a horizontal stroke in writing or printing to mark a pause or break in sense or to represent omitted letters or words. **3** impetuous vigour or the capacity for this. **4** showy appearance or behaviour. **5** *US* a sprinting-race. **6** the longer signal of the two used in Morse code (cf. DOT[1] *n.* 3). **7** a slight admixture, esp. of a liquid. **8** = DASHBOARD. □ **cut a dash** make a brilliant show. **dash down** (or **off**) write or finish hurriedly. [ME, prob. imit.]

dashboard /ˈdæʃbɔːd/ *n.* **1** the surface below the windscreen of a motor vehicle or aircraft, containing instruments and controls. **2** *hist.* a board of wood or leather in front of a carriage, to keep out mud.

dashiki /ˈdɑːʃɪkɪ/ *n.* a loose brightly-coloured shirt worn by American Blacks. [W. Afr.]

dashing /ˈdæʃɪŋ/ *adj.* **1** spirited, lively. **2** showy. □□ **dashingly** *adv.* **dashingness** *n.*

dashpot /ˈdæʃpɒt/ *n.* a device for damping shock or vibration.

dassie /ˈdæsɪ, ˈdɑːsɪ/ *n. S.Afr.* **1** the Cape hyrax *Procavia capensis.* Also called *rock-rabbit* (see ROCK[1]). **2** a small coastal fish *Diplodus sargus* with rows of black stripes. [Afrik. f. Du. *dasje* dimin. of *das* badger]

dastardly /ˈdæstədlɪ/ *adj.* cowardly, despicable. □□ **dastardliness** *n.* [*dastard* base coward, prob. f. *dazed* past part. + -ARD, or obs. *dasart* dullard, DOTARD]

dasyure /ˈdæsɪˌjʊə(r)/ *n.* any small flesh-eating marsupial of the genus *Dasyurus.* [F f. mod.L *dasyurus* f. Gk *dasus* rough + *oura* tail]

DAT *abbr.* digital audio tape.

data /ˈdeɪtə/ *n.pl.* (also treated as *sing.,* as in *that is all the data we have,* although the singular form is strictly *datum*) **1** known facts or things used as a basis for inference or reckoning. **2** quantities or characters operated on by a computer etc. □ **data bank 1** a store or source of data. **2** = DATABASE. **data capture** the action or process of entering data into a computer. **data processing** a series of operations on data, esp. by a computer, to retrieve or classify etc. information. **data processor** a machine, esp. a computer, that carries out data processing. **data protection** legal control over access to data stored in computers. [pl. of DATUM]

database /ˈdeɪtəˌbeɪs/ *n.* a structured set of data held in a computer, esp. one that is accessible in various ways.

datable /ˈdeɪtəb(ə)l/ *adj.* (often foll. by *to*) capable of being dated (to a particular time).

date[1] /deɪt/ *n.* & *v.* —*n.* **1** a day of the month, esp. specified by a number. **2** a particular day or year, esp. when a given event occurred. **3** a statement (usu. giving the day, month, and year) in a document or inscription etc., of the time of composition or publication. **4** the period to which a work of art etc. belongs. **5** the time when an event happens or is to happen. **6** *colloq.* **a** an engagement or appointment, esp. with a person of the opposite sex. **b** *US* a person with whom one has a social engagement. —*v.* **1** *tr.* mark with a date. **2** *tr.* **a** assign a date to (an object, event, etc.). **b** (foll. by *to*) assign to a particular time, period, etc. **3** *intr.* (often foll. by *from, back to,* etc.) have its origins at a particular time. **4** *intr.* be recognizable as from a past or particular period; become evidently out of date (*a design that does not date*). **5** *tr.* indicate or expose as being out of date (*that hat really dates you*). **6** *colloq.* **a** *tr.* make an arrangement with (a person) to meet socially. **b** *intr.* meet socially by agreement (*they are now dating regularly*). □ **date-line** see separate entry. **date-stamp** *n.* **1** an adjustable rubber stamp etc. used to record a date. **2** the impression made by this. —*v.tr.* mark with a date-stamp. **out of date** (*attrib.* **out-of-date**) old-fashioned, obsolete. **to date** until now. **up to date** (*attrib.* **up-to-date**) meeting or according to the latest requirements, knowledge, or fashion; modern. [ME f. OF f. med.L *data,* fem. past part. of *dare* give: from the L formula used in dating letters, *data* (*epistola*) (letter) given or delivered (at a particular time or place)]

date[2] /deɪt/ *n.* **1** a dark oval single-stoned fruit. **2** (in full **date-palm**) the tall tree *Phoenix dactylifera,* native to W. Asia and N. Africa, bearing this fruit. [ME f. OF f. L *dactylus* f. Gk *daktulos* finger, from the shape of its leaf]

dateless /ˈdeɪtlɪs/ *adj.* **1** having no date. **2** of immemorial age. **3** not likely to become out of date.

date-line *n.* **1** the imaginary north–south line through the Pacific Ocean, partly along the meridian farthest (i.e. 180°) from Greenwich, east and west of which the date differs (east being one day earlier). It was officially adopted world-wide in 1884 (see GREENWICH MEAN TIME). **2** a line at the head of a dispatch or special article in a newspaper showing the date and place of writing.

dative /ˈdeɪtɪv/ *n.* & *adj. Gram.* —*n.* the case of nouns and pronouns (and words in grammatical agreement with them) indicating an indirect object or recipient. —*adj.* of or in the dative. □□ **datival** /dəˈtaɪv(ə)l/ *adj.* **dativally** /dəˈtaɪvəlɪ/ *adv.* [ME f. L (*casus*) *dativus* f. *dare* dat- give]

---

aʊ *how* eɪ *day* əʊ *no* eə *hair* ɪə *near* ɔɪ *boy* ʊə *poor* aɪə *fire* aʊə *sour* (*see over for consonants*)

Datong /dɑːˈtʊŋ/ a city of northern China in Shanxi province; pop. (est. 1984) 981,000. Nearby are the Yungang Caves which contain the earliest examples of Buddhist stone carvings in China.

datum /ˈdeɪtəm, ˈdɑːtəm/ n. (pl. **data**: see DATA as main entry). **1** a piece of information. **2** a thing known or granted; an assumption or premiss from which inferences may be drawn (see *sense-datum*). **3** a fixed starting-point of a scale etc. (*datum-line*). [L, = thing given, neut. past part. of *dare* give]

datura /dəˈtjʊərə/ n. any poisonous plant of the genus *Datura*, e.g. the thorn apple. [mod.L f. Hindi *dhatura*]

daub /dɔːb/ v. & n. —v.tr. **1** spread (paint, plaster, or some other thick substance) crudely or roughly on a surface. **2** coat or smear (a surface) with paint etc. **3 a** (also *absol.*) paint crudely or unskilfully. **b** lay (colours) on crudely and clumsily. —n. **1** paint or other substance daubed on a surface. **2** plaster, clay, etc., for coating a surface, esp. mixed with straw and applied to laths or wattles to form a wall. **3** a crude painting. [ME f. OF *dauber* f. L *dealbare* whitewash f. *albus* white]

daube /dəʊb/ n. a stew of braised meat (usu. beef) with wine etc. [F]

dauber /ˈdɔːbə(r)/ n. a person or implement that daubs, esp. in painting. □ **get one's dauber down** US sl. become dispirited or depressed.

Daubigny /dəʊˈbiːnjiː/, Charles-François (1817–79), French landscape painter, of the Barbizon school. His landscapes, in which nature is observed purely for its own sake, reflect his love of rivers, beaches, and canals; he often painted from a boat.

Daudet /ˈdəʊdeɪ/, Alphonse (1840–97), French novelist, best known for his sketches of life in his native Provence (*Lettres de mon moulin*, 1868), for his semi-autobiographical *Le petit chose* (1868), and as the creator of Tartarin, a caricature of the Frenchman of the Midi, whose comic exploits are first related in *Tartarin de Tarascon* (1872). His other novels portray the social, political, and professional life of Paris.

daughter /ˈdɔːtə(r)/ n. **1** a girl or woman in relation to either or both of her parents. **2** a female descendant. **3** (foll. by *of*) a female member of a family, nation, etc. **4** (foll. by *of*) a woman who is regarded as the spiritual descendant of, or as spiritually attached to, a person or thing. **5** a product or attribute personified as a daughter in relation to its source (*Fortune and its daughter Confidence*). **6** *Physics* a nuclide formed by the radioactive decay of another. **7** *Biol.* a cell etc. formed by the division etc. of another. □ **Daughters of the American Revolution** a US patriotic society, first organized in 1890, whose aims include fostering the study of US history and supporting educational projects for the underprivileged. Membership is limited to descendants of soldiers or others of the Revolutionary period who aided the cause of independence. **daughter-in-law** (pl. **daughters-in-law**) the wife of one's son. □□ **daughterhood** n. **daughterly** adj. [OE *dohtor* f. Gmc]

daunt /dɔːnt/ v.tr. discourage, intimidate. □□ **daunting** adj. **dauntingly** adv. [ME f. AF *daunter*, OF *danter*, *donter* f. L *domitare* frequent. of *domare* tame]

dauntless /ˈdɔːntlɪs/ adj. intrepid, persevering. □□ **dauntlessly** adv. **dauntlessness** n.

dauphin /ˈdɔːfɪn, ˈdəʊfæ̃/ n. hist. the title borne by the eldest son of the king of France from 1349 to 1830. Originally a personal name, it became the title of the lords of an area of SE France which was thence called Dauphiné. In 1349 the French Crown acquired the lands and the title, and Charles V, ceding it to his eldest son in 1368, established the practice of passing both title and lands to the Crown prince. [ME f. F, ult. f. L *delphinus* DOLPHIN, as a family name]

Dauphiné /ˌdəʊfiˈneɪ/ a region and former province of SE France (see DAUPHIN). Its capital was Grenoble.

Davao /ˈdɑːvaʊ/ a seaport in the southern Philippines, on the island of Mindanao; pop. (1980) 610,300. Founded in 1849, it is the largest city on the island and the third-largest city in the Philippines.

Davenport /ˈdævənˌpɔːt/ n. **1** *Brit.* an ornamental writing-desk

with drawers and a sloping surface for writing. **2** *US* a large heavily upholstered sofa. [19th c.: from the name *Davenport*]

David[1] /dɑːˈviːd/ the principal city of western Panama; pop. (1980) 50,600.

David[2] /ˈdeɪvɪd/ (died *c*.970 BC) youngest son of Jesse of Bethlehem, and slayer of a Philistine (see GOLIATH). On the death of Saul (whose son Jonathan was his close friend) he became king of Judah and later of the whole of Israel, making Jerusalem his capital and reigning there for 33 years. He is traditionally regarded as the author of the Psalms, but it is unlikely that more than a fraction of the Psalter is his work.

David[3] /ˈdeɪvɪd/ the name of two kings of Scotland:

David I (1084–1153), son of Malcolm III, reigned 1124–53. He reasserted some measure of Scottish independence from English feudal domination at the time of the civil wars of Stephen and Matilda, but was decisively defeated at the Battle of the Standard in Yorkshire in 1138.

David II (1324–71), son of Robert the Bruce, reigned 1329–71. His long reign witnessed a renewal of the Wars of Independence, with Edward III taking advantage of the Scots king's minority to introduce the son of John de Baliol as an English puppet in his place. After coming of age David was defeated by the English at Neville's Cross (1346) and spent eleven years in captivity. His death without issue in 1371 left the throne to the Stuarts.

David[4] /ˈdeɪvɪd/, Elizabeth (1913–), British author of a number of books on Continental cookery, which include not only recipes for dishes but comments on their preparation and history.

David[5] /dɑːˈviːd/, Jacques-Louis (1748–1825), French neoclassical painter of scenes from Roman history, stoic and austere in their style and morality, and recorder of events in the Revolutionary and Napoleonic eras. He became actively involved in the Revolution, voted the death of Louis XVI, and supported Robespierre: in *The Tennis-Court Oath* (1789) and *The Death of Marat* (1793) he treated contemporary events with a grandeur hitherto reserved for history painting. Imprisoned after the fall of Robespierre, he returned to prominence under Napoleon, recording Napoleonic ceremonies in a less austere style. His last years were spent in exile in Brussels. David responded best to direct contact with nature, as in his portraits, and was an excellent teacher; his pupils included Ingres.

David[6] /ˈdeɪvɪd/, St (6th c.), patron saint of Wales. Little is known of his life; the claim that he was elected bishop of the Welsh Church because of his eloquence, and that he made a pilgrimage to Jerusalem, where he was consecrated, seem not to be historically valid. Feast day, 1 Mar.

Davies[1] /ˈdeɪvɪs/, Sir Peter Maxwell (1934–), English composer, conductor, and teacher. From 1971 he has made his home in Orkney, where the landscape and solitude have had an undoubted effect upon his music. He has composed in a variety of styles for the theatre, ranging from the opera *Taverner* (1970), in which a strong dramatic impulse is given full outlet, and *The Lighthouse* (1980), to the violent and pitiful depiction of madness in *Eight Songs for a Mad King* (1969).

Davies[2] /ˈdeɪvɪs/, William Henry (1871–1940), English poet, author of *The Autobiography of a Super-Tramp* (1908), which had a preface by G. B. Shaw. His best-known poems record his sharp and intense response to the natural world. In *Young Emma*, published posthumously in 1980, he tells the story of his courtship of a girl much younger than himself.

Davies[3] /ˈdeɪvɪs/, (William) Robertson (1913–), Canadian novelist, playwright, and journalist, who won international recognition with his Deptford trilogy of novels ('Deptford' being the fictional name for his native city of Thamesville, Ontario), *Fifth Business* (1970), *The Manticore* (1972), and *World of Wonders* (1975). Other novels include the satiric romances *Tempest-tost* (1951), *Leaven of Malice* (1954), and *A Mixture of Frailties* (1958), and the highly coloured satire *The Rebel Angels* (1981).

Davis[1] /ˈdeɪvɪs/, Bette (Ruth Elizabeth Davis, 1908–89), American film actress, noted for the dramatic intensity of her performances, usually in portrayals of neurotic women. Her films include *Dangerous* (1935), *Jezebel* (1938), and *All About Eve* (1950). Later she starred in a series of macabre films, including *Watcher in the Woods* (1980).

b *but* d *dog* f *few* g *get* h *he* j *yes* k *cat* l *leg* m *man* n *no* p *pen* r *red* s *sit* t *top* v *voice*

Davis[2] /'deɪvɪs/, Joe (1901–78) and Fred (1913–   ), English billiards and snooker players. Joe Davis was dominant in snooker for many years, adding a new dimension of skill to the game and holding the world championship from 1927 until his retirement in 1946. He was also world billiards champion 1928–32. His brother Fred Davis was world snooker champion eight times between 1948 and 1956 and world champion in billiards in 1980.

Davis[3] /'deɪvɪs/, Miles Dewey (1926–   ), American jazz trumpeter, composer, and bandleader, noted for the economy of his style and the purity of his tone. His albums include *Birth of the Cool* (1949), *Sketches of Spain* (1959–60), and *Bitches Brew* (1969).

Davis[4] /'deɪvɪs/, Steve (1957–   ), English snooker player, who won a number of national and international events in the 1980s, becoming UK Professional Champion six times between 1980 and 1987 and World Professional Champion four times during the same period.

Davis Strait /'deɪvɪs/ a sea passage 645 km (400 miles) long separating Greenland from Baffin Island and connecting Baffin Bay with the Atlantic Ocean. The strait is named after the English explorer John Davis (1550–1605) who sailed through it in 1587.

davit /'dævɪt, 'deɪvɪt/ n. a small crane on board a ship, esp. one of a pair for suspending or lowering a lifeboat. [AF & OF *daviot*dimin. of *Davi* David]

Davos /dɑː'vəʊs/ a resort and winter sports centre in eastern Switzerland; pop. (1980) 10,500.

Davy /'deɪvɪ/, Sir Humphry (1778–1829), English chemist, a pioneer of electrochemistry and the inventor of a miner's safety lamp. After indifferent schooling and an apprenticeship with an apothecary-surgeon he discovered nitrous oxide (laughing gas), and as a result was invited to join the Royal Institution in London. He applied Volta's electrochemical battery to chemistry and, by means of electrolytic decomposition, discovered the elements sodium, potassium, magnesium, calcium, strontium, and barium during 1807–8. Davy identified and named the element chlorine after he had demonstrated that, contrary to Lavoisier, oxygen was not a constituent of acids, determined the properties of iodine, and demonstrated that diamond was a form of carbon. He appointed Faraday his assistant in 1813, and it has been said that this was his greatest discovery.

Davy Jones /ˌdeɪvɪ 'dʒəʊnz/ *nautical sl.* the evil spirit of the sea, first mentioned in the 18th c. □ **Davy Jones's locker** the bottom of the sea, especially as the grave of those who are drowned or buried at sea. [orig. unkn.]

Davy lamp /'deɪvɪ/ n. an early type of safety lamp for miners, with wire gauze enclosing the flame, named after Sir Humphry Davy who invented it in 1816. The action of the gauze was to quench, by its sudden cooling effect, any flame which might tend to emerge from inside and ignite the methane found in underground collieries. A very similar lamp was devised almost simultaneously by George Stephenson.

daw /dɔː/ n. = JACKDAW. [ME: cf. OHG *tāha*]

dawdle /'dɔːd(ə)l/ v. & n. —v. **1** *intr.* **a** walk slowly and idly. **b** delay; waste time. **2** *tr.* (foll. by *away*) waste (time). —n. an act or instance of dawdling. □□ **dawdler** n. [perh. rel. to dial. *daddle*, *doddle* idle, dally]

Dawkins /'dɔːkɪnz/, Richard (1941–   ), English biologist, whose book *The Selfish Gene* (1976) did much to popularize the theory of sociobiology (see entry). His second book, *The Blind Watchmaker* (1986) discusses evolution by natural selection and suggests that the theory can answer the biggest question of all — why do we exist?

dawn /dɔːn/ n. & v. —n. **1** the first light of day; daybreak. **2** the beginning or incipient appearance of something. —v.*intr.* **1** (of a day) begin; grow light. **2** (often foll. by *on, upon*) begin to become evident or understood (by a person). □ **dawn chorus** the singing of many birds at the break of day. [orig. as verb: back-form. f. *dawning*, ME f. earlier *dawing* after Scand. (as DAY)]

dawning /'dɔːnɪŋ/ n. **1** daybreak. **2** the first beginning of something.

day /deɪ/ n. **1** the time between sunrise and sunset. **2 a** a period

of 24 hours as a unit of time, esp. from midnight to midnight, corresponding to a complete revolution of the earth on its axis. **b** a corresponding period on other planets (*Martian day*). **3** daylight (*clear as day*). **4** the time in a day during which work is normally done (*an eight-hour day*). **5 a** (also *pl.*) a period of the past or present (*the modern day; the old days*). **b** (prec. by *the*) the present time (*the issues of the day*). **6** the lifetime of a person or thing, esp. regarded as useful or productive (*have had my day; in my day things were different*). **7** a point of time (*will do it one day*). **8 a** the date of a specific festival. **b** a day associated with a particular event or purpose (*graduation day; payday; Christmas day*). **9** a particular date; a date agreed on. **10** a day's endeavour, or the period of an endeavour, esp. as bringing success (*win the day*). □ **all in a** (or **the**) **day's work** part of normal routine. **at the end of the day** in the final reckoning, when all is said and done. **call it a day** end a period of activity, esp. resting content that enough has been done. **day after day** without respite. **day and night** all the time. **day-boy** (or **-girl**) *Brit.* a boy or girl who goes daily from home to school, esp. a school that also has boarders. **day by day** gradually. **day care** the supervision of young children during the working day. **day centre** a place providing care for the elderly or handicapped during the day. **day-dream** n. a pleasant fantasy or reverie. —v.*intr.* indulge in this. **day-dreamer** a person who indulges in day-dreams. **day in, day out** routinely, constantly. **day labourer** an unskilled labourer hired by the day. **day lily** any plant of the genus *Hemerocallis*, whose flowers last only a day. **day nursery** a nursery where children are looked after during the working day. **day off** a day's holiday from work. **Day of Judgement** = *Judgement Day*. **day of reckoning** see RECKONING. **day of rest** the Sabbath. **day out** a trip or excursion for a day. **day-owl** any owl hunting by day esp. the short-eared owl. **day release** *Brit.* a system of allowing employees days off work for education. **day return** a fare or ticket at a reduced rate for a journey out and back in one day. **day-room** a room, esp. a communal room in an institution, used during the day. **day-school** a school for pupils living at home. **day-to-day** mundane, routine. **day-trip** a trip or excursion completed in one day. **day-tripper** a person who goes on a day-trip. **not one's day** a day of successive misfortunes for a person. **on one's day** at one's peak of capability. **one of these days** before very long. **one of those days** a day when things go badly. **some day** at some point in the future. **that will be the day** *colloq.* that will never happen. **this day and age** the present time or period. □□ **dayless** *adj.* [OE *dæg* f. Gmc]

Dayak var. of DYAK.

daybook /'deɪbʊk/ n. an account-book in which a day's transactions are entered, for later transfer to a ledger.

daybreak /'deɪbreɪk/ n. the first appearance of light in the morning.

Day-Glo /'deɪɡləʊ/ n. & adj. —n. *propr.* a make of fluorescent paint or other colouring. —adj. coloured with or like this. [DAY + GLOW]

Day-Lewis /deɪ'luːɪs/, Cecil (1904–72), poet and critic, born in Ireland. During the 1930s he was associated with a group of left-wing poets which included Auden and Spender, and his early volumes of verse (*Transitional Poems*, 1929; *The Magnetic Mountain*, 1933) have a distinct revolutionary flavour. At this time he also wrote detective fiction under the pseudonym of 'Nicholas Blake'. After 1940 he became an increasingly establishment figure, consolidating his literary reputation with translations of Valéry and Virgil, further collections of original verse and an autobiography, *The Buried Day* (1960). He was Professor of Poetry at Oxford 1951–6, and was appointed Poet Laureate in 1968.

daylight /'deɪlaɪt/ n. **1** the light of day. **2** dawn (*before daylight*). **3 a** openness, publicity. **b** open knowledge. **4** a visible gap or interval, e.g. between boats in a race. **5** (usu. in *pl.*) *sl.* one's life or consciousness (orig. the internal organs) esp. as representing vulnerability to fear, attack, etc. (*scared the daylights out of me; beat the living daylights out of them*). □ **daylight robbery** *colloq.* a blatantly excessive charge. **daylight saving** the achieving of longer evening daylight, esp. in summer, by setting the time an hour ahead of the standard time. **see daylight** begin to understand what was previously obscure.

daylong /ˈdeɪlɒŋ/ adj. lasting for a day.

dayside /ˈdeɪsaɪd/ n. **1** US staff, esp. of a newspaper, who work during the day. **2** Astron. the side of a planet that faces the sun.

daytime /ˈdeɪtaɪm/ n. the part of the day when there is natural light.

daywork /ˈdeɪwɜːk/ n. work paid for according to the time taken.

daze /deɪz/ v. & n. —v.tr. stupefy, bewilder. —n. a state of confusion or bewilderment (in a daze). □□ **dazedly** /-zɪdlɪ/ adv. [ME dased past part., f. ON dasathr weary]

dazzle /ˈdæz(ə)l/ v. & n. —v. **1** tr. blind temporarily or confuse the sight of by an excess of light. **2** tr. impress or overpower (a person) with knowledge, ability, or any brilliant display or prospect. **3** intr. archaic (of eyes) be dazzled. —n. bright confusing light. □□ **dazzlement** n. **dazzler** n. **dazzling** adj. **dazzlingly** adv. [ME, f. DAZE + -LE⁴]

dB abbr. decibel(s).

DBE abbr. (in the UK) Dame Commander of the Order of the British Empire.

DBS abbr. **1** direct-broadcast satellite. **2** direct broadcasting by satellite.

DC abbr. **1** (also **d.c.**) direct current. **2** District of Columbia. **3** da capo. **4** District Commissioner.

DCB abbr. (in the UK) Dame Commander of the Order of the Bath.

DCL abbr. Doctor of Civil Law.

DCM abbr. (in the UK) Distinguished Conduct Medal.

DCMG abbr. (in the UK) Dame Commander of the Order of St Michael and St George.

DCVO abbr. (in the UK) Dame Commander of the Royal Victorian Order.

DD abbr. Doctor of Divinity.

D-Day /ˈdiːdeɪ/ n. **1** the day (6 June 1944) on which British and American forces invaded northern France in the Second World War. **2** the day on which an important operation is to begin or a change to take effect. [D for day + DAY]

DDT abbr. dichlorodiphenyltrichloroethane, a colourless chlorinated hydrocarbon used as an insecticide.

DE abbr. US Delaware (in official postal use).

de- /dɪ, diː/ prefix **1** forming verbs and their derivatives: **a** down, away (descend; deduct). **b** completely (declare; denude; deride). **2** added to verbs and their derivatives to form verbs and nouns implying removal or reversal (decentralize; de-ice; demoralization). [from or after L de (adv. & prep.) = off, from: sense 2 through OF des- f. L dis-]

deacon /ˈdiːkən/ n. & v. —n. **1** (in Episcopal churches) a minister of the third order, below bishop and priest. **2** (in Nonconformist churches) a lay officer attending to a congregation's secular affairs. **3** (in the early Church) an appointed minister of charity. —v.tr. appoint or ordain as a deacon. □□ **deaconate** n. **deaconship** n. [OE diacon f. eccl.L diaconus f. Gk diakonos servant]

deaconess /ˌdiːkəˈnes, ˈdiːkənɪs/ n. a woman in the early Church and in some modern Churches with functions analogous to a deacon's. [DEACON, after LL diaconissa]

deactivate /diːˈæktɪˌveɪt/ v.tr. make inactive or less reactive. □□ **deactivation** /-ˈveɪʃ(ə)n/ n. **deactivator** n.

dead /ded/ adj., adv., & n. —adj. **1** no longer alive. **2** colloq. extremely tired or unwell. **3** benumbed; affected by loss of sensation (my fingers are dead). **4** (foll. by to) unappreciative or unconscious of; insensitive to. **5** no longer effective or in use; obsolete, extinct. **6** (of a match, of coal, etc.) no longer burning; extinguished. **7** inanimate. **8 a** lacking force or vigour; dull, lustreless, muffled. **b** (of sound) not resonant. **c** (of sparkling wine etc.) no longer effervescent. **9 a** quiet; lacking activity (the dead season). **b** motionless, idle. **10 a** (of a microphone, telephone, etc.) not transmitting any sound, esp. because of a fault. **b** (of a circuit, conductor, etc.) carrying or transmitting no current; not connected to a source of electricity (a dead battery). **11** (of the ball in a game) out of play. **12** abrupt, complete, exact, unqualified, unrelieved (come to a dead stop; a dead faint; a dead calm; in dead

silence; a dead certainty). **13** without spiritual life. —adv. **1** absolutely, exactly, completely (dead on target; dead level; dead tired). **2** colloq. very, extremely (dead good; dead easy). —n. (prec. by the) **1** (treated as pl.) those who have died. **2** a time of silence or inactivity (the dead of night). □ **dead-and-alive** Brit. (of a place, person, activity, etc.) dull, monotonous; lacking interest. **dead as the dodo** see DODO. **dead as a doornail** see DOORNAIL. **dead bat** Cricket a bat held loosely so that it imparts no motion to the ball when struck. **dead beat 1** colloq. exhausted. **2** Physics (of an instrument) without recoil. **dead-beat** n. **1** colloq. a penniless person. **2** US sl. a person constantly in debt. **dead centre 1** the exact centre. **2** the position of a crank etc. in line with the connecting-rod and not exerting torque. **dead cert** see CERT. **dead duck** sl. an unsuccessful or useless person or thing. **dead end 1** a closed end of a road, passage, etc. **2** (often with hyphen) attrib.) a situation offering no prospects of progress or advancement. **dead from the neck up** colloq. stupid. **dead hand** an oppressive persisting influence, esp. posthumous control. **dead heat 1** a race in which two or more competitors finish exactly level. **2** the result of such a race. **dead-heat** v.intr. run a dead heat. **dead language** a language no longer commonly spoken, e.g. Latin. **dead letter** a law or practice no longer observed or recognized. **dead lift** the exertion of one's utmost strength to lift something. **dead loss 1** colloq. a useless person or thing. **2** a complete loss. **dead man's fingers 1** a kind of orchis, Orchis mascula. **2** any soft coral of the genus Alcyonium, with spongy lobes. **3** the finger-like divisions of a lobster's or crab's gills. **dead man's handle** (or **pedal** etc.) a controlling-device on an electric train, allowing power to be connected only as long as the operator presses on it. **dead march** a funeral march. **dead men** colloq. bottles after the contents have been drunk. **dead-nettle** any plant of the genus Lamium, having nettle-like leaves but without stinging hairs. **dead-on** exactly right. **dead reckoning** Naut. calculation of a ship's position from the log, compass, etc., when observations are impossible. **dead ringer** see RINGER. **dead shot** one who is extremely accurate. **dead time** Physics the period after the recording of a pulse etc. when the detector is unable to record another. **dead to the world** colloq. fast asleep; unconscious. **dead weight** (or **dead-weight**) **1 a** an inert mass. **b** a heavy weight or burden. **2** a debt not covered by assets. **3** the total weight carried on a ship. **dead wood** colloq. one or more useless people or things. **make a dead set at** see SET². **wouldn't be seen dead in** (or **with** etc.) colloq. shall have nothing to do with; shall refuse to wear etc. □□ **deadness** n. [OE dēad f. Gmc, rel. to DIE¹]

deadbolt /ˈdedbəʊlt/ n. esp. US a bolt engaged by turning a knob or key, rather than by spring action.

deaden /ˈded(ə)n/ v. **1** tr. & intr. deprive of or lose vitality, force, brightness, sound, feeling, etc. **2** tr. (foll. by to) make insensitive. □□ **deadener** n.

deadeye /ˈdedaɪ/ n. **1** Naut. a circular wooden block with a groove round the circumference to take a lanyard, used singly or in pairs to tighten a shroud. **2** US colloq. an expert marksman.

deadfall /ˈdedfɔːl/ n. US a trap in which a raised weight is made to fall on and kill esp. large game.

deadhead /ˈdedhed/ n. & v. —n. **1** a faded flower-head. **2** a passenger or member of an audience who has made use of a free ticket. **3** a useless or unenterprising person. —v. **1** tr. remove deadheads from (a plant). **2** intr. US (of a driver etc.) complete a journey with an empty train, bus, etc.

deadlight /ˈdedlaɪt/ n. Naut. **1** a shutter inside a porthole. **2** US a skylight that cannot be opened.

deadline /ˈdedlaɪn/ n. **1** a time-limit for the completion of an activity etc. **2** hist. a line beyond which prisoners were not allowed to go. Such a line was marked round a military prison at Andersonville, Georgia, US, c.1864; a prisoner going beyond it was liable to be shot down.

deadlock /ˈdedlɒk/ n. & v. —n. **1** a situation, esp. one involving opposing parties, in which no progress can be made. **2** a type of lock requiring a key to open or close it. —v.tr. & intr. bring or come to a standstill.

deadly /ˈdedlɪ/ adj. & adv. —adj. (**deadlier**, **deadliest**) **1 a**

causing or able to cause fatal injury or serious damage. **b** poisonous (*deadly snake*). **2** intense, extreme (*deadly dullness*). **3** (of an aim etc.) extremely accurate or effective. **4** deathlike (*deadly pale*; *deadly faintness*; *deadly gloom*). **5** *colloq.* dreary, dull. **6** implacable. —*adv.* **1** like death; as if dead (*deadly faint*). **2** extremely, intensely (*deadly serious*). □ **deadly nightshade** = BELLADONNA. **deadly sin** a sin regarded as leading to damnation for a person's soul. **seven deadly sins** traditionally pride, covetousness, lust, envy, gluttony, anger, sloth. They are listed (with minor variation) by the monk John Cassian (d. 435), St Gregory the Great, and St Thomas Aquinas. □□ **deadliness** *n.* [OE *dēadlic*, *dēadlīce* (as DEAD, -LY¹)]

deadpan /ˈdedpæn/ *adj.* & *adv.* with a face or manner totally lacking expression or emotion.

Dead Sea a bitter salt lake or inland sea in the Jordan valley on the Israel–Jordan border. Its surface is 400 m (1,300 ft.) below sea level. □ **Dead Sea scrolls** a once considerable collection of Hebrew and Aramaic manuscripts discovered in caves near Qumran, at the NE end of the Dead Sea, between 1947 and 1956, chiefly in fragments. They belonged to the library of a splinter Jewish sect, generally equated with the Essenes, who settled in a large building (or monastery) at Qumran from the mid-1st c. BC until the Jewish revolt against Roman rule AD 66–70, and are presumed to have been hidden, stored in the jars in which they were found, for safe keeping when the destruction of the centre seemed imminent. They include texts of many books of the Old Testament, commentaries, psalms, an apocalyptic work, and documents containing the rules of the life of the religious community. They are important for the evidence they provide on the history of the Old Testament text, scripts of the period, and the life and doctrines of a Jewish sect at the time when Christianity was born.

deadstock /ˈdedstɒk/ *n.* slaughtered farm stock, esp. diseased animals.

de-aerate /diːˈeəˌreɪt/ *v.tr.* remove air from. □□ **de-aeration** /-ˈreɪʃ(ə)n/ *n.*

deaf /def/ *adj.* **1** wholly or partly without hearing (*deaf in one ear*). **2** (foll. by *to*) refusing to listen or comply. **3** insensitive to harmony, rhythm, etc. (*tone-deaf*). □ **deaf-aid** *Brit.* a hearing-aid. **deaf-and-dumb alphabet** (or **language** etc.) = sign language. ¶ *Sign language* is preferred in official use. **deaf as a post** completely deaf. **deaf mute** a deaf and dumb person. **fall on deaf ears** be ignored. **turn a deaf ear** (usu. foll. by *to*) be unresponsive. □□ **deafly** *adv.* **deafness** *n.* [OE *dēaf* f. Gmc]

deafen /ˈdef(ə)n/ *v.tr.* **1** (often as **deafening** *adj.*) overpower with sound. **2** deprive of hearing by noise, esp. temporarily. □□ **deafeningly** *adv.*

deal¹ /diːl/ *v.* & *n.* —*v.* (*past* and *past part.* **dealt** /delt/) **1** *intr.* (foll. by *with*) **a** take measures concerning (a problem, person, etc.), esp. in order to put something right. **b** do business with; associate with. **c** discuss or treat (a subject). **d** (often foll. by *by*) behave in a specified way towards a person (*dealt honourably by them*). **2** *intr.* (foll. by *in*) sell or be concerned with commercially (*deals in insurance*). **3** *tr.* (often foll. by *out*, *round*) distribute or apportion to several people etc. **4** *tr.* (also *absol.*) distribute (cards) to players for a game or round. **5** *tr.* cause to be received; administer (*deal a heavy blow*). **6** *tr.* assign as a share or deserts to a person (*Providence dealt them much happiness*). **7** *tr.* (foll. by *in*) *colloq.* include (a person) in an activity (*you can deal me in*). —*n.* **1** (usu. **a good** or **great deal**) *colloq.* **a** a large amount (*a good deal of trouble*). **b** to a considerable extent (*is a great deal better*). **2** *colloq.* a business arrangement; a transaction. **3** a specified form of treatment given or received (*gave them a rough deal*; *got a fair deal*). **4 a** the distribution of cards by dealing. **b** a player's turn to do this (*it's my deal*). **c** the round of play following this. **d** a set of hands dealt to players. □ **it's a deal** *colloq.* expressing assent to an agreement. [OE *dǣl*, *dǣlan*, f. Gmc]

deal² /diːl/ *n.* **1** fir or pine timber, esp. sawn into boards of a standard size. **2 a** a board of this timber. **b** such timber collectively. [ME f. MLG, MDu. *dele* plank f. Gmc]

dealer /ˈdiːlə(r)/ *n.* **1 a** a person or business dealing in (esp. retail) goods (*contact your dealer*; *car-dealer*; *a dealer in tobacco*). **2** the player dealing at cards. **3** a jobber on the Stock Exchange. ¶ In the UK from Oct. 1986 the name has been merged with **broker** (see BROKER 2, JOBBER 1). □□ **dealership** *n.* (in sense 1).

dealings /ˈdiːlɪŋz/ *n.pl.* contacts or transactions, esp. in business. □ **have dealings with** associate with.

dealt *past* and *past part.* of DEAL¹.

Dean¹ /diːn/, Christopher Colin (1958–), English skater, who in partnership with Jayne Torvill won many championships in ice-dancing in 1981–4.

Dean² /diːn/, James (real name James Byron, 1931–55), American actor, whose particular appeal was youth. In his three films *East of Eden* (1955), *Rebel Without a Cause* (released posthumously in 1955), and *Giant* (released in 1956) he embodied vulnerable adolescent uncertainty and social antagonism. He was killed when his sports car crashed while travelling at speed.

dean¹ /diːn/ *n.* **1 a** the head of the chapter of a cathedral or collegiate church. **b** (usu. **rural dean**) *Brit.* a member of the clergy exercising supervision over a group of parochial clergy within a division of an archdeaconry. **2 a** a college or university official, esp. one of several fellows of a college, with disciplinary and advisory functions. **b** the head of a university faculty or department or of a medical school. **3** = DOYEN. □ **Dean of Faculty** the president of the Faculty of Advocates in Scotland. [ME f. AF *deen*, OF *deien*, f. LL *decanus* f. *decem* ten; orig. = chief of a group of ten]

dean² var. of DENE¹.

deanery /ˈdiːnərɪ/ *n.* (pl. **-ies**) **1** a dean's house or office. **2** *Brit.* the group of parishes presided over by a rural dean.

dear /dɪə(r)/ *adj.*, *n.*, *adv.*, & *int.* —*adj.* **1 a** beloved or much esteemed. **b** as a merely polite or ironic form (*my dear man*). **2** used as a formula of address, esp. at the beginning of letters (*Dear Sir*). **3** (often foll. by *to*) precious; much cherished. **4** (usu. in *superl.*) earnest, deeply felt (*my dearest wish*). **5 a** high-priced relative to its value. **b** having high prices. **c** (of money) available as a loan only at a high rate of interest. —*n.* (esp. as a form of address) dear person. —*adv.* at a high price or great cost (*buy cheap and sell dear*; *will pay dear*). —*int.* expressing surprise, dismay, pity, etc. (*dear me!*; *oh dear!*; *dear, dear!*). □ **Dear John** *colloq.* a letter terminating a personal relationship. **for dear life** see LIFE. □□ **dearly** *adv.* (esp. in sense 3 of *adj.*). **dearness** *n.* [OE *dēore* f. Gmc]

dearie /ˈdɪərɪ/ *n.* (esp. as a form of address) usu. *joc.* or *iron.* my dear. □ **dearie me!** *int.* expressing surprise, dismay, etc.

dearth /dɜːθ/ *n.* scarcity or lack, esp. of food. [ME, formed as DEAR]

deasil /ˈdesɪl/ *adv.* *Sc.* in the direction of the sun's apparent course (considered as lucky); clockwise. [Gael. *deiseil*]

death /deθ/ *n.* **1** the final cessation of vital functions in an organism; the ending of life. **2** the event that terminates life. **3 a** the fact or process of being killed or killing (*stone to death*; *fight to the death*). **b** the fact or state of being dead (*eyes closed in death*; *their deaths caused rioting*). **4 a** the destruction or permanent cessation of something (*was the death of our hopes*). **b** *colloq.* something terrible or appalling. **5** (usu. **Death**) a personification of death, esp. as a destructive power, usu. represented by a skeleton. **6** a lack of religious faith or spiritual life. □ **as sure as death** quite certain. **at death's door** close to death. **be in at the death 1** be present when an animal is killed, esp. in hunting. **2** witness the (esp. sudden) ending of an enterprise etc. **be the death of 1** cause the death of. **2** be very harmful to. **catch one's death** *colloq.* catch a serious chill etc. **death adder** any of various venomous snakes of the genus *Acanthopis* esp. *A. antarcticus* of Australia. **death cap** a poisonous toadstool, *Amanita phalloides*. **death cell** a prison cell for a person condemned to death. **death certificate** an official statement of the cause and date and place of a person's death. **death duty** *Brit. hist.* a tax levied on property after the owner's death. ¶ Replaced in 1975 by *capital transfer tax* and in 1986 by *inheritance tax*. **death grant** *Brit.* a State grant towards funeral expenses. **death-knell 1** the tolling of a bell to mark a person's death. **2** an event that heralds the end or destruction of something. **death-mask** a cast taken of a dead person's face. **death penalty** punishment by being put to death. **death rate** the number of deaths per thousand of population per year. **death-rattle** a gurgling sound sometimes heard in a dying person's throat. **death-roll 1** those killed in an accident, battle, etc. **2** a list of these. **death row** US a prison block or section for prisoners sentenced to death. **death's head** a human skull as an emblem of mortality. **death's head moth** a large dark hawk moth, *Acherontia atropos*, with skull-like markings on the back of the thorax. **death squad** an armed paramilitary group formed to kill political enemies etc. **death tax** US a tax on property payable on the owner's death. **death-toll** the number of people killed in an accident, battle, etc. **death-trap** *colloq.* a dangerous or unhealthy building, vehicle, etc. **death-warrant 1** an order for the execution of a condemned person. **2** anything that causes the end of an established practice etc. **death-watch** (in full **death-watch beetle**) a small beetle (*Xestobium rufovillosum*) which makes a sound like a watch ticking, once supposed to portend death, and whose larva bores in old wood. **death-wish** *Psychol.* a desire (usu. unconscious) for the death of oneself or another. **do to death 1** kill. **2** overdo. **fate worse than death** *colloq.* a disastrous misfortune or experience. **like death warmed up** *sl.* very tired or ill. **put to death** kill or cause to be killed. **to death** to the utmost, extremely (*bored to death; worked to death*). □□ **deathless** *adj.* **deathlessness** *n.* **deathlike** *adj.* [OE *dēath* f. Gmc: rel. to DIE¹]

deathbed /ˈdeθbed/ *n.* a bed as the place where a person is dying or has died.

deathblow /ˈdeθbləʊ/ *n.* **1** a blow or other action that causes death. **2** an event or circumstance that abruptly ends an activity, enterprise, etc.

deathly /ˈdeθlɪ/ *adj.* & *adv.* —*adj.* (**deathlier, deathliest**) suggestive of death (*deathly silence*). —*adv.* in a deathly way (*deathly pale*).

Death Valley a deep arid desert basin in SE California and SW Nevada, the hottest and driest part of North America and one of the hottest places on earth. It formed an obstacle to the movements of pioneer settlers, whence it name.

deb /deb/ *n. colloq.* a débutante. [abbr.]

débâcle /deɪˈbɑːk(ə)l/ *n.* (US **debacle**) **1 a** an utter defeat or failure. **b** a sudden collapse or downfall. **2** a confused rush or rout; a stampede. **3 a** a break-up of ice in a river, with resultant flooding. **b** a sudden rush of water carrying along blocks of stone and other debris. [F f. *débâcler* unbar]

debag /diːˈbæg/ *v.tr.* (**debagged, debagging**) *Brit. sl.* remove the trousers of (a person), esp. as a joke.

debar /dɪˈbɑː(r)/ *v.tr.* (**debarred, debarring**) (foll. by *from*) exclude from admission or from a right; prohibit from an action (*was debarred from entering*). □□ **debarment** *n.* [ME f. F *débarrer*, OF *desbarrer* (as DE-, BAR¹)]

debark¹ /diːˈbɑːk, dɪ-/ *v.tr.* & *intr.* land from a ship. □□ **debarkation** /-ˈkeɪʃ(ə)n/ *n.* [F *débarquer* (as DE-, BARK³)]

debark² /diːˈbɑːk/ *v.tr.* remove the bark from (a tree).

debase /dɪˈbeɪs/ *v.tr.* **1** lower in quality, value, or character. **2** depreciate (coin) by alloying etc. □□ **debasement** *n.* **debaser** *n.* [DE- + obs. *base* for ABASE]

debatable /dɪˈbeɪtəb(ə)l/ *adj.* **1** questionable; subject to dispute. **2** capable of being debated. □□ **debatably** *adv.* [OF *debatable* or AL *debatabilis* (as DEBATE)]

debate /dɪˈbeɪt/ *v.* & *n.* —*v.* **1** *tr.* (also *absol.*) discuss or dispute about (an issue, proposal, etc.) esp. formally in a legislative assembly, public meeting, etc. **2 a** *tr.* consider, ponder (a matter). **b** *intr.* consider different sides of a question. —*n.* **1** a formal discussion on a particular matter, esp. in a legislative assembly etc. **2** debating, discussion (*open to debate*). □ **debating point** an inessential matter used to gain advantage in a debate. □□ **debater** *n.* [ME f. OF *debatre, debat* f. Rmc (as DE-, BATTLE)]

debauch /dɪˈbɔːtʃ/ *v.* & *n.* —*v.tr.* **1** corrupt morally. **2** make intemperate or sensually indulgent. **3** deprave or debase (taste or judgement). **4** (as **debauched** *adj.*) dissolute. **5** seduce (a woman). —*n.* **1** a bout of sensual indulgence. **2** debauchery. □□ **debaucher** *n.* [F *débauche(r)*, OF *desbauche*, of unkn. orig.]

debauchee /ˌdɪbɔːˈtʃiː, ˌdeb-/ *n.* a person addicted to excessive sensual indulgence. [F *débauché* past part.: see DEBAUCH]

debauchery /dɪˈbɔːtʃərɪ/ *n.* excessive sensual indulgence.

debenture /dɪˈbentʃə(r)/ *n.* **1** *Brit.* an acknowledgement of indebtedness, esp. a bond of a company or corporation acknowledging a debt and providing for payment of interest at fixed intervals. **2** US (in full **debenture bond**) a fixed-interest bond of a company or corporation, backed by general credit rather than specified assets. □ **debenture stock** *Brit.* stock comprising debentures, with only the interest secured. [ME f. L *debentur* are owing f. *debēre* owe: assim. to -URE]

debilitate /dɪˈbɪlɪteɪt/ *v.tr.* enfeeble, enervate. □□ **debilitatingly** *adv.* **debilitation** /-ˈteɪʃ(ə)n/ *n.* **debilitative** /-tətɪv/ *adj.* [L *debilitare* (as DEBILITY)]

debility /dɪˈbɪlɪtɪ/ *n.* feebleness, esp. of health. [ME f. OF *debilité* f. L *debilitas -tatis* f. *debilis* weak]

debit /ˈdebɪt/ *n.* & *v.* —*n.* **1** an entry in an account recording a sum owed. **2** the sum recorded. **3** the total of such sums. **4** the debit side of an account —*v.tr.* (**debited, debiting**) **1** (foll. by *against, to*) enter (an amount) on the debit side of an account (*debited £500 against me*). **2** (foll. by *with*) enter (a person) on the debit side of an account (*debited me with £500*). [F *débit* f. L *debitum* DEBT]

debonair /ˌdebəˈneə(r)/ *adj.* **1** carefree, cheerful, self-assured. **2** having pleasant manners. □□ **debonairly** *adv.* [ME f. OF *debonaire = de bon aire* of good disposition]

debouch /dɪˈbaʊtʃ, -ˈbuːʃ/ *v.intr.* **1** (of troops or a stream) issue from a ravine, wood, etc., into open ground. **2** (often foll. by *into*) (of a river, road, etc.) merge into a larger body or area. □□ **debouchment** *n.* [F *déboucher* (as DE-, *bouche* mouth)]

Debrecen /ˈdebrətˌsen/ an industrial and commercial city in eastern Hungary; pop. (1988) 217,000.

Debrett /dɪˈbret/, John (*c.*1750–1822), compiler of a 'Peerage of England, Scotland and Ireland' first issued in 1803 and until fairly recently issued annually.

debrief /diːˈbriːf/ *v.tr. colloq.* interrogate (a person, e.g. a diplomat or pilot) about a completed mission or undertaking. □□ **debriefing** *n.*

debris /ˈdebriː, ˈdeɪ-/ *n.* **1** scattered fragments, esp. of something wrecked or destroyed. **2** *Geol.* an accumulation of loose material, e.g. from rocks or plants. [F *débris* f. obs. *débriser* break down (as DE-, *briser* break)]

de Broglie /də ˈbrɒɡliː/, Louis (1892–1987) French physicist, whose name is applied to the wave which in wave mechanics is taken as accounting for or representing the wave-like properties of particles of matter, especially elementary particles. He was awarded a Nobel Prize in 1929.

debt /det/ *n.* **1** something that is owed, esp. money. **2** a state of obligation to pay something owed (*in debt; out of debt; get into debt*). □ **debt-collector** a person who is employed to collect debts for creditors. **debt of honour** a debt not legally recoverable, esp. a sum lost in gambling. **in a person's debt** under an obligation to a person. [ME *det(te)* f. OF *dette* (later *debte*) ult. f. L *debitum* past part. of *debēre* owe]

debtor /ˈdetə(r)/ *n.* a person who owes a debt, esp. money. [ME f. OF *det(t)or, -our* f. L *debitor* (as DEBT)]

debug /diːˈbʌɡ/ *v.tr.* (**debugged, debugging**) **1** *colloq.* trace and remove concealed listening devices from (a room etc.). **2** *colloq.* identify and remove defects from (a machine, computer program, etc.). **3** remove bugs from.

debunk /diːˈbʌŋk/ *v.tr. colloq.* **1** show the good reputation or aspirations of (a person, institution, etc.) to be spurious. **2** expose the falseness of (a claim etc.). □□ **debunker** *n.*

debus /diːˈbʌs/ *v.tr.* & *intr.* (**debussed, debussing**) *esp. Mil.* unload (personnel or stores) or alight from a motor vehicle.

Debussy /dəˈbjuːsɪ/, Achille-Claude (1862–1918), French composer and critic, whose music was stimulated and influenced by events in Paris that ranged from the impressionist and symbolist movements, and the current preoccupation with the old church modes and with plainchant, to the sonorities of a Javanese gamelan at the World Exhibition in Paris in 1889. Cultivating a distinctively French musical outlook (eventually styling himself 'musicien français'), he was an innovator of the first degree, using block chords, harmony based on the whole-tone scale, and a declamatory yet lyrical style of vocal composition. His opera *Pelléas et Mélisande* (1893–5) turns away from Wagner in its reticence and its focusing not on the motives and thoughts of the protagonists but on their position 'at the mercy of life or destiny'. Such works as the *Prélude à l'après-midi d'un faune* (1894, produced by Diaghilev as a ballet in 1912 with Nijinsky in the title role) and *La mer* (inspired by Hokusai's painting of a wave) led to criticisms that he allowed effect to take the place of structure, but it was his feeling for colour and texture (not only in his orchestral works but also in the impressionistic piano Préludes, Images, Estampies, etc.) that made him such an important influence on later composers, including Webern, Berg, Bartók, Varèse, and Boulez.

début /ˈdeɪbjuː, -buː/ *n.* (*US* **debut**) **1** the first public appearance of a performer on stage etc. **2** the first appearance of a débutante in society. [F f. *débuter* lead off]

débutante /ˈdebjuːˌtɑːnt, ˈdeɪb-/ *n.* (*US* **debutante**) a (usu. wealthy) young woman making her social début. [F, fem. part. of *débuter*: see DÉBUT]

Dec. *abbr.* December.

dec. *abbr.* **1** deceased. **2** declared.

deca- /ˈdekə/ *comb. form* (also **dec-** before a vowel) **1** having ten. **2** tenfold. **3** ten, esp. of a metric unit (*decagram*; *decalitre*). [Gk *deka* ten]

decade /ˈdekeɪd, *disp.* dɪˈkeɪd/ *n.* **1** a period of ten years. **2** a set, series, or group of ten. □□ **decadal** /ˈdekəd(ə)l/ *adj.* [ME f. F *décade* f. LL *decas -adis* f. Gk f. *deka* ten]

decadence /ˈdekəd(ə)ns/ *n.* **1** moral or cultural deterioration, esp. after a peak or culmination of achievement. **2** decadent behaviour; a state of decadence. [F *décadence* f. med.L *decadentia* f. *decadere* DECAY]

decadent /ˈdekəd(ə)nt/ *adj. & n.* —*adj.* **1 a** in a state of moral or cultural deterioration; showing or characterized by decadence. **b** of a period of decadence. **2** self-indulgent. —*n.* a decadent person. □□ **decadently** *adv.* [F *décadent* (as DECADENCE)]

decaffeinate /diːˈkæfɪˌneɪt/ *v.tr.* **1** remove the caffeine from. **2** reduce the quantity of caffeine in (usu. coffee).

decagon /ˈdekəgən/ *n.* a plane figure with ten sides and angles. □□ **decagonal** /dɪˈkægən(ə)l/ *adj.* [med.L *decagonum* f. Gk *dekagōnon* (as DECA-, -GON)]

decagynous /deˈkædʒɪnəs/ *adj. Bot.* having ten pistils. [mod.L *decagynus* (as DECA-, Gk *gūne* woman)]

decahedron /ˌdekəˈhiːdrən/ *n.* a solid figure with ten faces. □□ **decahedral** *adj.* [DECA- + -HEDRON after POLYHEDRON]

decal /ˈdiːkæl/ *n.* = DECALCOMANIA 2. [abbr.]

decalcify /diːˈkælsɪˌfaɪ/ *v.tr.* (**-ies**, **-ied**) remove lime or calcareous matter from (a bone, tooth, etc.). □□ **decalcification** /-fɪˈkeɪʃ(ə)n/ *n.* **decalcifier** *n.*

decalcomania /diːˌkælkəˈmeɪnɪə/ *n.* *US* **1** a process of transferring designs from specially prepared paper to the surface of glass, porcelain, etc. **2** a picture or design made by this process. [F *décalcomanie* f. *décalquer* transfer]

decalitre /ˈdekəˌliːtə(r)/ *n.* a metric unit of capacity, equal to 10 litres.

Decalogue /ˈdekəˌlɒg/ *n.* the Ten Commandments. [ME f. F *décalogue* or eccl.L *decalogus* f. Gk *dekalogos* (after *hoi deka logoi* the Ten Commandments)]

Decameron /dɪˈkæmərən/ a work by Boccaccio, written between 1348 and 1358, containing 100 tales supposedly told in 10 days by a party of 7 young ladies and 3 young men who had fled from the plague in Florence. [It. f. Gk f. *deka* ten + *hēmera* day]

decametre /ˈdekəˌmiːtə(r)/ *n.* a metric unit of length, equal to 10 metres.

decamp /dɪˈkæmp/ *v.intr.* **1** break up or leave a camp. **2** depart suddenly; abscond. □□ **decampment** *n.* [F *décamper* (as DE-, CAMP[1])]

decanal /dɪˈkeɪn(ə)l, ˈdekə-/ *adj.* **1** of a dean or deanery. **2** of

the south side of a choir, the side on which the dean sits (cf. CANTORIAL). [med.L *decanalis* f. LL *decanus* DEAN[1]]

decandrous /dɪˈkændrəs/ *adj. Bot.* having ten stamens. [DECA- + Gk *andr-* man (= male organ)]

decani /dɪˈkeɪnaɪ/ *adj. Mus.* to be sung by the decanal side in antiphonal singing (cf. CANTORIS). [L, genit. of *decanus* DEAN[1]]

decant /dɪˈkænt/ *v.tr.* gradually pour off (liquid, esp. wine or a solution) from one container to another, esp. without disturbing the sediment. [med.L *decanthare* (as DE-, L *canthus* f. Gk *kanthos* canthus, used of the lip of a beaker)]

decanter /dɪˈkæntə(r)/ *n.* a stoppered glass container into which wine or spirit is decanted.

decapitate /dɪˈkæpɪˌteɪt/ *v.tr.* **1** behead (esp. as a form of capital punishment). **2** cut the head or end from. □□ **decapitation** /-ˈteɪʃ(ə)n/ *n.* **decapitator** *n.* [LL *decapitare* (as DE-, *caput -itis* head)]

decapod /ˈdekəˌpɒd/ *n.* **1** any crustacean of the chiefly marine order Decapoda, characterized by five pairs of walking legs, e.g. shrimps, crabs, and lobsters. **2** any of various molluscs of the class Cephalopoda, having ten tentacles, e.g. squids and cuttlefish. □□ **decapodan** /dɪˈkæpəd(ə)n/ *adj.* [F *décapode* f. Gk *deka* ten + *pous podos* foot]

decarbonize /diːˈkɑːbəˌnaɪz/ *v.tr.* (also **-ise**) remove carbon or carbonaceous deposits from (an internal-combustion engine etc.). □□ **decarbonization** /-ˈzeɪʃ(ə)n/ *n.*

decastyle /ˈdekəˌstaɪl/ *n. & adj. Archit.* —*n.* a ten-columned portico. —*adj.* having ten columns. [Gk *dekastulos* f. *deka* ten + *stulos* column]

decasyllable /ˈdekəˌsɪləb(ə)l/ *n.* a metrical line of ten syllables. □□ **decasyllabic** /-sɪˈlæbɪk/ *adj. & n.*

decathlon /dɪˈkæθlən/ *n.* an athletic contest in which each competitor takes part in the ten different events which it comprises, which has featured in the Olympic Games since 1912. □□ **decathlete** /-liːt/ *n.* [DECA- + Gk *athlon* contest]

decay /dɪˈkeɪ/ *v. & n.* —*v.* **1 a** *intr.* rot, decompose. **b** *tr.* cause to rot or decompose. **2** *intr. & tr.* decline or cause to decline in quality, power, wealth, energy, beauty, etc. **3** *intr. Physics* a (usu. foll. by *to*) (of a substance etc.) undergo change by radioactivity. **b** undergo a gradual decrease in magnitude of a physical quantity. —*n.* **1** a rotten or ruinous state; a process of wasting away. **2** decline in health, quality, etc. **3** *Physics* **a** change into another substance etc. by radioactivity. **b** a decrease in the magnitude of a physical quantity, esp. the intensity of radiation or amplitude of oscillation. **4** decayed tissue. □□ **decayable** *adj.* [ME f. OF *decair* f. Rmc (as DE-, L *cadere* fall)]

Deccan /ˈdekən/ a triangular plateau of southern India, bounded by the Malabar and Coromandel coasts, and by the Vindhaya mountains in the north.

decease /dɪˈsiːs/ *n. & v. formal esp. Law* —*n.* death. —*v.intr.* die. [ME f. OF *deces* f. L *decessus* f. *decedere* (as DE-, *cedere cess-* go)]

deceased /dɪˈsiːst/ *adj. & n. formal* —*adj.* dead. —*n.* (usu. prec. by *the*) a person who has died, esp. recently.

decedent /dɪˈsiːd(ə)nt/ *n.* *US Law* a deceased person. [L *decedere* die: see DECEASE]

deceit /dɪˈsiːt/ *n.* **1** the act or process of deceiving or misleading, esp. by concealing the truth. **2** a dishonest trick or stratagem. **3** willingness to deceive. [ME f. OF f. past part. of *deceveir* f. L *decipere* deceive (as DE-, *capere* take)]

deceitful /dɪˈsiːtfʊl/ *adj.* **1** (of a person) using deceit, esp. habitually. **2** (of an act, practice, etc.) intended to deceive. □□ **deceitfully** *adv.* **deceitfulness** *n.*

deceive /dɪˈsiːv/ *v.* **1** *tr.* make (a person) believe what is false, mislead purposely. **2** *tr.* be unfaithful to, esp. sexually. **3** *intr.* use deceit. **4** *tr. archaic* disappoint (esp. hopes). □ **be deceived** be mistaken or deluded. **deceive oneself** persist in a mistaken belief. □□ **deceivable** *adj.* **deceiver** *n.* [ME f. OF *deceivre* or *deceiv-* stressed stem of *deceveir* (as DECEIT)]

decelerate /diːˈseləˌreɪt/ *v.* **1** *intr. & tr.* begin or cause to begin to reduce speed. **2** *tr.* make slower (*decelerated motion*). □□ **deceleration** /-ˈreɪʃ(ə)n/ *n.* **decelerator** *n.* **decelerometer** /-ˈrɒmɪtə(r)/ *n.* [DE- after ACCELERATE]

December /dɪˈsembə(r)/ *n.* the twelfth month of the year. [ME

f. OF *decembre* f. L *December* f. *decem* ten: orig. the tenth month of the Roman year]

Decembrist /dɪˈsembrɪst/ *n.* a member of a group of Russian revolutionaries who in December 1825 led an unsuccessful revolt among the soldiers of the emperor Nicholas I in an attempt to deprive him of his throne. [transl. Russ. *dekabrist*]

decency /ˈdiːsənsɪ/ *n.* (*pl.* **-ies**) **1** correct and tasteful standards of behaviour as generally accepted. **2** conformity with current standards of behaviour or propriety. **3** avoidance of obscenity. **4** (in *pl.*) the requirements of correct behaviour. [L *decentia* f. *decēre* be fitting]

decennial /dɪˈsenɪ(ə)l/ *adj.* **1** lasting ten years. **2** recurring every ten years. □□ **decennially** *adv.* [L *decennis* of ten years f. *decem* ten + *annus* year]

decent /ˈdiːs(ə)nt/ *adj.* **1 a** conforming with current standards of behaviour or propriety. **b** avoiding obscenity. **2** respectable. **3** acceptable, passable; good enough. **4** *Brit.* kind, obliging, generous (*was decent enough to apologize*). □□ **decently** *adv.* [F *décent* or L *decēre* be fitting]

decentralize /diːˈsentrəˌlaɪz/ *v.tr.* (also **-ise**) **1** transfer (powers etc.) from a central to a local authority. **2** reorganize (a centralized institution, organization, etc.) on the basis of greater local autonomy. □□ **decentralist** /-lɪst/ *n.* & *adj.* **decentralization** /-ˈzeɪʃ(ə)n/ *n.*

deception /dɪˈsepʃ(ə)n/ *n.* **1** the act or an instance of deceiving; the process of being deceived. **2** a thing that deceives; a trick or sham. [ME f. OF or LL *deceptio* f. *decipere* (as DECEIT)]

deceptive /dɪˈseptɪv/ *adj.* apt to deceive; easily mistaken for something else or as having a different quality. □□ **deceptively** *adv.* **deceptiveness** *n.* [OF *deceptif -ive* or LL *deceptivus* (as DECEPTION)]

decerebrate /diːˈserɪbrət/ *adj.* having had the cerebrum removed.

deci- /ˈdesɪ/ *comb. form* one-tenth, esp. of a unit in the metric system (*decilitre*; *decimetre*). [L *decimus* tenth]

decibel /ˈdesɪbel/ *n.* a unit (one-tenth of a bel) used in the comparison of two power levels relating to electrical signals or sound intensities, one of the pair usually being taken as a standard. ¶ Abbr.: **dB.**

decide /dɪˈsaɪd/ *v.* **1 a** *intr.* (often foll. by *on*, *about*) come to a resolution as a result of consideration. **b** *tr.* (usu. foll. by *to* + infin., or *that* + clause) have or reach as one's resolution about something (*decided to stay*; *decided that we should leave*). **2** *tr.* **a** cause (a person) to reach a resolution (*was unsure about going but the weather decided me*). **b** resolve or settle (a question, dispute, etc.). **3** *intr.* (usu. foll. by *between*, *for*, *against*, *in favour of*, or *that* + clause) give a judgement concerning a matter. □□ **decidable** *adj.* [ME f. F *décider* or f. L *decidere* (as DE-, *cædere* cut)]

decided /dɪˈsaɪdɪd/ *adj.* **1** (usu. *attrib.*) definite, unquestionable (*a decided difference*). **2** (of a person, esp. as a characteristic) having clear opinions, resolute, not vacillating. □□ **decidedness** *n.*

decidedly /dɪˈsaɪdɪdlɪ/ *adv.* undoubtedly, undeniably.

decider /dɪˈsaɪdə(r)/ *n.* **1** a game, race, etc., to decide between competitors finishing equal in a previous contest. **2** any person or thing that decides.

deciduous /dɪˈsɪdjʊəs/ *adj.* **1** (of a tree) shedding its leaves annually. **2** (of leaves, horns, teeth, etc.) shed periodically. **3** (of an ant etc.) shedding its wings after copulation. **4** fleeting, transitory. □□ **deciduousness** *n.* [L *deciduus* f. *decidere* f. *cadere* fall]

decigram /ˈdesɪˌɡræm/ *n.* (also **decigramme**) a metric unit of mass, equal to 0.1 gram.

decile /ˈdesɪl, -saɪl/ *n. Statistics* any of the nine values of a random variable which divide a frequency distribution into ten groups, each containing one-tenth of the total population. [F *décile*, ult. f. L *decem* ten]

decilitre /ˈdesɪˌliːtə(r)/ *n.* a metric unit of capacity, equal to 0.1 litre.

decimal /ˈdesɪm(ə)l/ *adj.* & *n.* —*adj.* **1** (of a system of numbers, weights, measures, etc.) based on the number ten, in which the smaller units are related to the principal units as powers of

ten (units, tens, hundreds, thousands, etc.). **2** of tenths or ten; reckoning or proceeding by tens. —*n.* a decimal fraction. □ **decimal fraction** a fraction whose denominator is a power of ten, esp. when expressed positionally by units to the right of a decimal point. **decimal point** a full point or dot placed before a numerator in a decimal fraction. **decimal scale** a scale with successive places denoting units, tens, hundreds, etc. □□ **decimally** *adv.* [mod.L *decimalis* f. L *decimus* tenth]

decimalize /ˈdesɪməˌlaɪz/ *v.tr.* (also **-ise**) **1** express as a decimal. **2** convert to a decimal system (esp. of coinage). □□ **decimalization** /-ˈzeɪʃ(ə)n/ *n.*

decimate /ˈdesɪˌmeɪt/ *v.tr.* **1** *disp.* destroy a large proportion of. ¶ Now the usual sense, although often deplored as an inappropriate use. **2** *orig. Mil.* kill or remove one in every ten of. □□ **decimation** /-ˈmeɪʃ(ə)n/ *n.* **decimator** *n.* [L *decimare* take the tenth man f. *decimus* tenth]

decimetre /ˈdesɪˌmiːtə(r)/ *n.* a metric unit of length, equal to 0.1 metre.

decipher /dɪˈsaɪfə(r)/ *v.tr.* **1** convert (a text written in cipher) into an intelligible script or language. **2** determine the meaning of (anything obscure or unclear). □□ **decipherable** *adj.* **decipherment** *n.*

decision /dɪˈsɪʒ(ə)n/ *n.* **1** the act or process of deciding. **2** a conclusion or resolution reached, esp. as to future action, after consideration (*have made my decision*). **3** (often foll. by *of*) **a** the settlement of a question. **b** a formal judgement. **4** a tendency to decide firmly; resoluteness. [ME f. OF *decision* or L *decisio* (as DECIDE)]

decisive /dɪˈsaɪsɪv/ *adj.* **1** that decides an issue; conclusive. **2** (of a person, esp. as a characteristic) able to decide quickly and effectively. □□ **decisively** *adv.* **decisiveness** *n.* [F *décisif -ive* f. med.L *decisivus* (as DECIDE)]

Decius /ˈdiːsɪəs/, Gaius Messius Quintus (d. 251), Roman emperor 249–251, noted for his persecution of the Christians which resulted from his belief that the restoration of State cults was essential to the preservation of the empire. □□ **Decian** *adj.*

deck /dek/ *n.* & *v.* —*n.* **1 a** a platform in a ship covering all or part of the hull's area at any level and serving as a floor. **b** the accommodation on a particular deck of a ship. **2** anything compared to a ship's deck, e.g. the floor or compartment of a bus. **3** a component, usu. a flat horizontal surface, that carries a particular recording medium (such as a disc or tape) in sound-reproduction equipment. **4** *US* **a** a pack of cards. **b** *sl.* a packet of narcotics. **5** *sl.* the ground. **6** any floor or platform, esp. the floor of a pier or a platform for sunbathing. —*v.tr.* **1** (often foll. by *out*) decorate, adorn. **2** furnish with or cover as a deck. □ **below deck** (or **decks**) in or into the space below the main deck. **deck-chair** a folding chair of wood and canvas, of a kind used on deck on passenger ships. **deck-hand** a person employed in cleaning and odd jobs on a ship's deck. **deck quoits** a game in which rope quoits are aimed at a peg. **deck tennis** a game in which a quoit of rope, rubber, etc., is tossed to and fro over a net. **on deck 1** in the open air on a ship's main deck. **2** esp. *US* ready for action, work, etc. [ME, = covering f. MDu. *dec* roof, cloak]

-decker /ˈdekə(r)/ *comb. form* having a specified number of decks or layers (*double-decker*).

deckle /ˈdek(ə)l/ *n.* a device in a paper-making machine for limiting the size of the sheet. □ **deckle-edge** the rough uncut edge formed by a deckle. □□ **deckle-edged** *adj.* [G *Deckel* dimin. of *Decke* cover]

declaim /dɪˈkleɪm/ *v.* **1** *intr.* & *tr.* speak or utter rhetorically or affectedly. **2** *intr.* practise oratory or recitation. **3** *intr.* (foll. by *against*) protest forcefully. **4** *intr.* deliver an impassioned (rather than reasoned) speech. □□ **declaimer** *n.* [ME f. F *déclamer* or f. L *declamare* (as DE-, CLAIM)]

declamation /ˌdeklərˈmeɪʃ(ə)n/ *n.* **1** the act or art of declaiming. **2** a rhetorical exercise or set speech. **3** an impassioned speech; a harangue. □□ **declamatory** /dɪˈklæmətərɪ/ *adj.* [F *déclamation* or L *declamatio* (as DECLAIM)]

declarant /dɪˈkleərənt/ *n.* a person who makes a legal declaration. [F *déclarant* part. of *déclarer* (as DECLARE)]

declaration /ˌdeklə'reɪʃ(ə)n/ n. **1** the act or process of declaring. **2 a** a formal, emphatic, or deliberate statement or announcement. **b** a statement asserting or protecting a legal right. **3 a** written public announcement of intentions, terms of an agreement, etc. **4** Cricket an act of declaring an innings closed. **5** Cards **a** the naming of trumps. **b** an announcement of a combination held. **6** Law **a** a plaintiff's statement of claim. **b** an affirmation made instead of taking an oath. **7** (in full **declaration of the poll**) a public official announcement of the votes cast for candidates in an election. [ME f. L declaratio (as DECLARE)]

Declaration of Independence a document drawn up by Thomas Jefferson, Benjamin Franklin, John Adams, Roger Sherman, and Robert Livingstone declaring the US to be independent of the British Crown, signed on 4 July 1776 by the Congressional representatives of eleven States.

Declaration of Indulgence any of the declarations made by the two Stuart kings Charles II and James II dispensing with repressive legislation against religious nonconformists. The first two declarations, issued by Charles II in 1662 and 1672, were rejected by Parliament. Two, issued by James II in 1687–8, represented attempts to stimulate a Roman Catholic revival, and led to the trial of seven Anglican bishops who refused to comply with the King's wishes.

declare /dɪ'kleə(r)/ v. **1** tr. announce openly or formally (declare war; declare a dividend). **2** tr. pronounce (a person or thing) to be something (declared him to be an impostor; declared it invalid). **3** tr. (usu. foll. by that + clause) assert emphatically; state explicitly. **4** tr. acknowledge possession of (dutiable goods, income, etc.). **5** tr. (as **declared** adj.) who admits to be such (a declared atheist). **6** tr. (also absol.) Cricket close (an innings) voluntarily before all the wickets have fallen. **7** tr. Cards **a** (also absol.) name (the trump suit). **b** announce that one holds (certain combinations of cards etc.). **8** tr. (of things) make evident, prove (your actions declare your honesty). **9** intr. (foll. by for, against) take the side of one party or another. □ **declare oneself** reveal one's intentions or identity. **well, I declare** (or **I do declare**) an exclamation of incredulity, surprise, or vexation. □□ **declarable** adj. **declarative** /-'klærətɪv/ adj. **declaratively** /-'klærətɪvlɪ/ adv. **declaratory** /-'klærətərɪ/ adj. **declaredly** /-rɪdlɪ/ adv. **declarer** n. [ME f. L declarare (as DE-, clarare f. clarus clear)]

déclassé /deɪ'klæseɪ/ adj. (fem. **déclassée**) that has fallen in social status. [F]

declassify /di:'klæsɪfaɪ/ v.tr. (**-ies, -ied**) declare (information etc.) to be no longer secret. □□ **declassification** /-fɪ'keɪʃ(ə)n/ n.

declension /dɪ'klenʃ(ə)n/ n. **1** Gram. **a** the variation of the form of a noun, pronoun, or adjective, by which its grammatical case, number, and gender are identified. **b** the class in which a noun etc. is put according to the exact form of this variation. **2** deterioration, declining. □□ **declensional** adj. [OF declinaison f. decliner DECLINE after L declinatio: assim. to ASCENSION etc.]

declination /ˌdeklɪ'neɪʃ(ə)n/ n. **1** a downward bend or turn. **2** Astron. the angular distance of a star etc. north or south of the celestial equator. **3** Physics the angular deviation of a compass needle from true north. **4** US a formal refusal. □□ **declinational** adj. [ME f. L declinatio (as DECLINE)]

decline /dɪ'klaɪn/ v. & n. —v. **1** intr. deteriorate; lose strength or vigour; decrease. **2** a tr. reply with formal courtesy that one will not accept (an invitation, honour, etc.). **b** tr. refuse, esp. formally and courteously (declined to be made use of; declined doing anything). **c** tr. turn away from (a challenge, battle, discussion, etc.). **d** intr. give or send a refusal. **3** intr. slope downwards. **4** intr. bend down, droop. **5** tr. Gram. state the forms of (a noun, pronoun, or adjective) corresponding to cases, number, and gender. **6** intr. (of a day, life, etc.) draw to a close. **7** intr. decrease in price etc. **8** tr. bend down. —n. **1** gradual loss of vigour or excellence (on the decline). **2** decay, deterioration. **3** setting; the last part of the course (of the sun, of life, etc.). **4** a fall in price. **5** archaic tuberculosis or a similar wasting disease. □ **declining years** old age. □□ **declinable** adj. **decliner** n. [ME f. OF decliner f. L declinare (as DE-, clinare bend)]

declivity /dɪ'klɪvɪtɪ/ n. (pl. **-ies**) a downward slope, esp. a piece of sloping ground. □□ **declivitous** adj. [L declivitas f. declivis f. DE-, clivus slope)]

declutch /di:'klʌtʃ/ v.intr. disengage the clutch of a motor vehicle. □ **double-declutch** release and re-engage the clutch twice when changing gear.

Deco /'dekəʊ/ n. (also **deco**) (usu. attrib.) = art deco. [F décoratif DECORATIVE]

decoct /dɪ'kɒkt/ v.tr. extract the essence from by decoction. [ME f. L decoquere boil down]

decoction /dɪ'kɒkʃ(ə)n/ n. **1** a process of boiling down so as to extract some essence. **2** the extracted liquor resulting from this. [ME f. OF decoction or LL decoctio (as DE-, L coquere coct- boil)]

decode /di:'kəʊd/ v.tr. convert (a coded message) into intelligible language. □□ **decodable** adj.

decoder /di:'kəʊdə(r)/ n. **1** a person or thing that decodes. **2** an electronic device for analysing signals and feeding separate amplifier-channels.

decoke v. & n. Brit. colloq. —v.tr. /di:'kəʊk/ remove carbon or carbonaceous material from (an internal-combustion engine). —n. /'di:kəʊk/ the process of decoking.

decollate /dɪ'kɒleɪt/ v.tr. formal **1** behead. **2** truncate. □□ **decollation** /ˌdi:kɒ'leɪʃ(ə)n/ n. [L decollare decollat- (as DE-, collum neck)]

décolletage /ˌdeɪkɒl'tɑːʒ/ n. a low neckline of a woman's dress etc. [F (as DE-, collet collar of a dress)]

décolleté /deɪ'kɒlteɪ/ adj. & n. —adj. (also **décolletée**) **1** (of a dress etc.) having a low neckline. **2** (of a woman) wearing a dress with a low neckline. —n. a low neckline. [F (as DÉCOLLETAGE)]

decolonize /di:'kɒlənaɪz/ v.tr. (also **-ise**) (of a State) withdraw from (a colony), leaving it independent. □□ **decolonization** /-'zeɪʃ(ə)n/ n.

decolorize /di:'kʌləraɪz/ v. (also **-ise**) **1** tr. remove the colour from. **2** intr. lose colour. □□ **decolorization** /-'zeɪʃ(ə)n/ n.

decommission /ˌdi:kə'mɪʃ(ə)n/ v.tr. **1** close down (a nuclear reactor etc.). **2** take (a ship) out of service.

decompose /ˌdi:kəm'pəʊz/ v. **1** intr. decay, rot. **2** tr. separate (a substance, light, etc.) into its elements or simpler constituents. **3** intr. disintegrate; break up. □□ **decomposition** /ˌdi:kɒmpə'zɪʃ(ə)n/ n. [F décomposer (as DE-, COMPOSE)]

decompress /ˌdi:kəm'pres/ v.tr. subject to decompression; relieve or reduce the compression on.

decompression /ˌdi:kəm'preʃ(ə)n/ n. **1** release from compression. **2** a gradual reduction of air pressure on a person who has been subjected to high pressure (esp. underwater). □ **decompression chamber** an enclosed space for subjecting a person to decompression. **decompression sickness** a condition caused by the sudden lowering of air pressure and formation of bubbles in the blood: also called caisson disease, the bends (see BEND 14).

decompressor /ˌdi:kəm'presə(r)/ n. a device for reducing pressure in the engine of a motor vehicle.

decongestant /ˌdi:kən'dʒest(ə)nt/ adj. & n. —adj. that relieves (esp. nasal) congestion. —n. a medicinal agent that relieves nasal congestion.

deconsecrate /di:'kɒnsɪˌkreɪt/ v.tr. transfer (esp. a building) from sacred to secular use. □□ **deconsecration** /-'kreɪʃ(ə)n/ n.

deconstruct /ˌdi:kən'strʌkt/ v.tr. subject to deconstruction. □□ **deconstructive** adj. [back-form. f. DECONSTRUCTION]

deconstruction /ˌdi:kən'strʌkʃ(ə)n/ n. a method of critical analysis of philosophical and literary language. □□ **deconstructionism** n. **deconstructionist** adj. & n. [F déconstruction (as DE-, CONSTRUCTION)]

decontaminate /ˌdi:kən'tæmɪˌneɪt/ v.tr. remove contamination from (an area, person, clothes, etc.). □□ **decontamination** /-'neɪʃ(ə)n/ n.

decontrol /ˌdi:kən'trəʊl/ v. & n. —v.tr. (**decontrolled, decontrolling**) release (a commodity etc.) from controls or restrictions, esp. those imposed by the State. —n. the act of decontrolling.

décor /'deɪkɔː(r), 'de-/ n. **1** the furnishing and decoration of a room etc. **2** the decoration and scenery of a stage. [F f. décorer (as DECORATE)]

decorate /'dekəˌreɪt/ v.tr. **1** provide with adornments. **2** provide (a room or building) with new paint, wallpaper, etc. **3** serve as an adornment to. **4** confer an award or distinction on. □ **Decorated style** *Archit.* the second stage of English Gothic (14th c.), with increasing use of decoration and geometrical tracery. [L *decorare decorat-* f. *decus -oris* beauty]

decoration /ˌdekəˈreɪʃ(ə)n/ *n.* **1** the process or art of decorating. **2** a thing that decorates or serves as an ornament. **3** a medal etc. conferred and worn as an honour. **4** (in *pl.*) flags etc. put up on an occasion of public celebration. □ **Decoration Day** *US* Memorial Day. [F *décoration* or LL *decoratio* (as DECORATE)]

decorative /ˈdekərətɪv/ *adj.* serving to decorate. □□ **decoratively** *adv.* **decorativeness** *n.* [F *décoratif* (as DECORATE)]

decorator /ˈdekəˌreɪtə(r)/ *n.* a person who decorates, esp. one who paints or papers houses professionally.

decorous /ˈdekərəs/ *adj.* **1** respecting good taste or propriety. **2** dignified and decent. □□ **decorously** *adv.* **decorousness** *n.* [L *decorus* seemly]

decorticate /diːˈkɔːtɪˌkeɪt/ *v.tr.* **1** remove the bark, rind, or husk from. **2** remove the outside layer from (the kidney, brain, etc.). [L *decorticare decorticat-* (as DE-, *cortex -icis* bark)]

decortication /diːˌkɔːtɪˈkeɪʃ(ə)n/ *n.* **1** the removal of the outside layer from an organ (e.g. the kidney) or structure. **2** an operation removing the blood clot and scar tissue formed after bleeding in the chest cavity.

decorum /dɪˈkɔːrəm/ *n.* **1 a** seemliness, propriety. **b** behaviour required by politeness or decency. **2** a particular requirement of this kind. **3** etiquette. [L, neut. of *decorus* seemly]

découpage /ˌdeɪkuːˈpɑːʒ/ *n.* the decoration of surfaces with paper cut-outs. [F, = the action of cutting out]

decouple /diːˈkʌp(ə)l/ *v.tr.* **1** *Electr.* make the interaction between (oscillators etc.) so weak that there is little transfer of energy between them. **2** separate, disengage, dissociate.

decoy *n. & v.* —*n.* /ˈdiːkɔɪ, dɪˈkɔɪ/ **1 a** a person or thing used to lure an animal or person into a trap or danger. **b** a bait or enticement. **2** a pond with narrow netted arms into which wild duck may be tempted in order to catch them. —*v.tr.* /dɪˈkɔɪ, ˈdiːkɔɪ/ (often foll. by *into, out of*) allure or entice, esp. by means of a decoy. [17th c.: perh. f. Du. *de kooi* the decoy f. *de* THE + *kooi* f. L *cavea* cage]

decrease *v. & n.* —*v.tr. & intr.* /dɪˈkriːs/ make or become smaller or fewer. —*n.* /ˈdiːkriːs/ **1** the act or an instance of decreasing. **2** the amount by which a thing decreases. □□ **decreasingly** *adv.* [ME f. OF *de(s)creiss-*, pres. stem of *de(s)creistre* ult. f. L *decrescere* (as DE-, *crescere cret-* grow)]

decree /dɪˈkriː/ *n. & v.* —*n.* **1** an official order issued by a legal authority. **2** a judgement or decision of certain lawcourts, esp. in matrimonial cases. —*v.tr.* (**decrees, decreed, decreeing**) ordain by decree. □ **decree absolute** a final order for divorce, enabling either party to remarry. **decree nisi** a provisional order for divorce, made absolute unless cause to the contrary is shown within a fixed period. [ME f. OF *decré* f. L *decretum* neut. past part. of *decernere* decide (as DE-, *cernere* sift)]

decrement /ˈdekrɪmənt/ *n.* **1** *Physics* the ratio of the amplitudes in successive cycles of a damped oscillation. **2** the amount lost by diminution or waste. **3** the act of decreasing. [L *decrementum* (as DECREASE)]

decrepit /dɪˈkrepɪt/ *adj.* **1** weakened or worn out by age and infirmity. **2** worn out by long use; dilapidated. □□ **decrepitude** *n.* [ME f. L *decrepitus* (as DE-, *crepitus* past part. of *crepare* creak)]

decrepitate /dɪˈkrepɪˌteɪt/ *v.* **1** *tr.* roast or calcine (a mineral or salt) until it stops crackling. **2** *intr.* crackle under heat. □□ **decrepitation** /-ˈteɪʃ(ə)n/ *n.* [prob. mod.L *decrepitare* f. DE- + L *crepitare* crackle]

decrescendo /ˌdiːkreˈʃendəʊ, ˌdeɪkrɪ-/ *adv., adj., & n.* (*pl.* **-os**) = DIMINUENDO. [It., part. of *decrescere* DECREASE]

decrescent /dɪˈkres(ə)nt/ *adj.* (usu. of the moon) waning, decreasing. [L *decrescere*: see DECREASE]

decretal /dɪˈkriːt(ə)l/ *n.* **1** a papal decree. **2** (in *pl.*) a collection of these, forming part of canon law. [ME f. med.L *decretale* f. LL (*epistola*) *decretalis* (letter) of decree f. L *decernere*: see DECREE]

decriminalize /diːˈkrɪmɪnəˌlaɪz/ *v.tr.* (also **-ise**) cease to treat

(an action etc.) as criminal. □□ **decriminalization** /-ˈzeɪʃ(ə)n/ *n.*

decry /dɪˈkraɪ/ *v.tr.* (**-ies, -ied**) disparage, belittle. □□ **decrier** *n.* [after F *décrier*: cf. *cry down*]

decrypt /diːˈkrɪpt/ *v.tr.* decipher (a cryptogram), with or without knowledge of its key. □□ **decryption** *n.* [DE- + CRYPTOGRAM]

decumbent /dɪˈkʌmbənt/ *adj.* *Bot. & Zool.* (of a plant, shoot, or bristles) lying along the ground or a surface. [L *decumbere decumbent-* lie down]

decurve /diːˈkɜːv/ *v.tr. & intr.* *Zool. & Bot.* (esp. as **decurved** *adj.*) curve or bend down (*a decurved bill*). □□ **decurvature** *n.*

decussate /diːˈkʌseɪt/ *adj. & v.* —*adj.* **1** X-shaped. **2** *Bot.* with pairs of opposite leaves etc. each at right angles to the pair below. —*v.tr. & intr.* **1** arrange or be arranged in a decussate form. **2** intersect. □□ **decussation** /-ˈseɪʃ(ə)n/ *n.* [L *decussatus* past part. of *decussare* divide in a cross shape f. *decussis* the numeral ten or the shape X f. *decem* ten]

dedans /dəˈdɑ̃/ *n.* **1** (in real tennis) the open gallery at the end of the service side of a court. **2** the spectators watching a match. [F, = inside]

Dedekind /ˈdeɪdɪkɪnd/, Richard (1831–1916), German mathematician, professor at Brunswick from 1862 until his death. His analysis of the properties that characterize real numbers and his description of real numbers as Dedekind sections of rational numbers solved the 2,000-year-old question of what numbers are and supplied a satisfactory foundation on which mathematical analysis could be rigorously based. He is remembered also for his theory of rings of algebraic integers which, simplifying and extending the work of Eduard Kummer, cast the theory of algebraic numbers into its very general modern form. Like Georg Cantor, he introduced collections of numbers, treating these collections as entities that are of interest in their own right, whose relationships to each other may be studied by means of set theory. Thus he was one of the principal founders of abstract algebra and 'modern maths'.

dedicate /ˈdedɪˌkeɪt/ *v.tr.* **1** (foll. by *to*) devote (esp. oneself) to a special task or purpose. **2** (foll. by *to*) address (a book, piece of music, etc.) as a compliment to a friend, patron, etc. **3** (often foll. by *to*) devote (a building etc.) to a deity or a sacred person or purpose. **4** (as **dedicated** *adj.*) **a** (of a person) devoted to an aim or vocation; having single-minded loyalty or integrity. **b** (of equipment, esp. a computer) designed for a specific purpose. □□ **dedicatee** /-kəˈtiː/ *n.* **dedicative** *adj.* **dedicator** *n.* **dedicatory** *adj.* [L *dedicare* (DE-, *dicare* declare, dedicate)]

dedication /ˌdedɪˈkeɪʃ(ə)n/ *n.* **1** the act or an instance of dedicating; the process of being dedicated. **2** the words with which a book etc. is dedicated. **3** a dedicatory inscription. [ME f. OF *dedicacion* or L *dedicatio* (as DEDICATE)]

deduce /dɪˈdjuːs/ *v.tr.* **1** (often foll. by *from*) infer; draw as a logical conclusion. **2** *archaic* trace the course or derivation of. □□ **deducible** *adj.* [L *deducere* (as DE-, *ducere duct-* lead)]

deduct /dɪˈdʌkt/ *v.tr.* (often foll. by *from*) subtract, take away, withhold (an amount, portion, etc.). [L (as DEDUCE)]

deductible /dɪˈdʌktɪb(ə)l/ *adj. & n.* —*adj.* that may be deducted, esp. from tax to be paid or taxable income. —*n. US* = EXCESS *n.* 6.

deduction /dɪˈdʌkʃ(ə)n/ *n.* **1 a** the act of deducting. **b** an amount deducted. **2 a** the inferring of particular instances from a general law (cf. INDUCTION). **b** a conclusion deduced. [ME f. OF *deduction* or L *deductio* (as DEDUCE)]

deductive /dɪˈdʌktɪv/ *adj.* of or reasoning by deduction. □□ **deductively** *adv.* [med.L *deductivus* (as DEDUCE)]

dee /diː/ *n.* **1** the letter D. **2 a** a thing shaped like this. **b** *Physics* either of two hollow semicircular electrodes in a cyclotron. [the name of the letter]

deed /diːd/ *n. & v.* —*n.* **1** a thing done intentionally or consciously. **2** a brave, skilful, or conspicuous act. **3** actual fact or performance (*kind in word and deed; in deed and not in name*). **4** *Law* a written or printed document often used for a legal transfer of ownership and bearing the disposer's signature. —*v.tr. US* convey or transfer by legal deed. □ **deed-box** a strong box for keeping deeds and other documents. **deed of covenant**

an agreement to pay a specified amount regularly to a charity etc., enabling the recipient to recover the tax paid by the donor on an equivalent amount of income. **deed poll** a deed made and executed by one party only, esp. to change one's name (the paper being polled or cut even, not indented). [OE *dēd* f. Gmc: cf. DO¹]

deejay /ˈdiːˈdʒeɪ/ *n. sl.* a disc jockey. [abbr. *DJ*]

deem /diːm/ *v.tr. formal* regard, consider, judge (*deem it my duty; was deemed sufficient*). [OE *dēman* f. Gmc, rel. to DOOM]

de-emphasize /diːˈemfəˌsaɪz/ *v.tr.* (also **-ise**) **1** remove emphasis from. **2** reduce emphasis on.

deemster /ˈdiːmstə(r)/ *n.* a judge in the Isle of Man. [DEEM + -STER]

deep /diːp/ *adj., n.,* & *adv.* —*adj.* **1 a** extending far down from the top (*deep hole; deep water*). **b** extending far in from the surface or edge (*deep wound; deep plunge; deep shelf; deep border*). **2** (*predic.*) **a** extending to or lying at a specified depth (*water 6 feet deep; ankle-deep in mud*). **b** in a specified number of ranks one behind another (*soldiers drawn up six deep*). **3** situated far down or back or in (*hands deep in his pockets*). **4** coming or brought from far down or in (*deep breath; deep sigh*). **5** low-pitched, full-toned, not shrill (*deep voice; deep note; deep bell*). **6** intense, vivid, extreme (*deep disgrace; deep sleep; deep colour; deep secret*). **7** heartfelt, absorbing (*deep affection; deep feelings; deep interest*). **8** (*predic.*) fully absorbed or overwhelmed (*deep in a book; deep in debt*). **9** profound, penetrating, not superficial; difficult to understand (*deep thinker; deep thought; deep insight; deep learning*). **10** *Cricket* distant from the batsman (*deep mid-off*). **11** *Football* distant from the front line of one's team. **12** *sl.* cunning or secretive (*a deep one*). —*n.* **1** (*prec. by the*) *poet.* the sea. **2** a deep part of the sea. **3** an abyss, pit, or cavity. **4** (*prec. by the*) *Cricket* the position of a fielder distant from the batsman. **5** a deep state (*deep of the night*). **6** *poet.* a mysterious region of thought or feeling. —*adv.* deeply; far down or in (*dig deep; read deep into the night*). □ **deep breathing** breathing with long breaths, esp. as a form of exercise. **deep-drawn** (of metal etc.) shaped by forcing through a die when cold. **deep-fry** (**-fries, -fried**) fry (food) in an amount of fat or oil sufficient to cover it. **deep kiss** a kiss with contact between tongues. **deep-laid** (of a scheme) secret and elaborate. **deep mourning** mourning expressed by wearing only black clothes. **deep-mouthed** (esp. of a dog) having a deep voice. **deep-rooted** (esp. of convictions) firmly established. **deep sea** the deeper parts of the ocean. **deep-seated** (of emotion, disease, etc.) firmly established, profound. **Deep South** the States of the US bordering the Gulf of Mexico. **deep space** the regions beyond the solar system or the earth's atmosphere. **deep therapy** curative treatment with short-wave X-rays of high penetrating power. **go off** (or **go in off**) **the deep end** *colloq.* give way to anger or emotion. **in deep water** (or **waters**) in trouble or difficulty. **jump** (or **be thrown**) **in at the deep end** face a difficult problem, undertaking, etc., with little experience of it. □□ **deeply** *adv.* **deepness** *n.* [OE *dēop* (adj.), *dīope, dēope* (adv.), f. Gmc: rel. to DIP]

deepen /ˈdiːpən/ *v.tr.* & *intr.* make or become deep or deeper.

deep-freeze /diːpˈfriːz/ *n.* & *v.* —*n.* **1** a refrigerator in which food can be quickly frozen and kept for long periods at a very low temperature. **2** a suspension of activity. —*v.tr.* (**-froze, -frozen**) freeze or store (food) in a deep-freeze.

deer /dɪə(r)/ *n.* (*pl.* same) any four-hoofed grazing animal of the family Cervidae, the males of which usu. have deciduous branching antlers. □ **deer fly** any bloodsucking fly of the genus *Chrysops*. **deer-forest** an extensive area of wild land reserved for the stalking of deer. **deer-hound** a large rough-haired greyhound. **deer-lick** a spring or damp spot impregnated with salt etc. where deer come to lick. [OE *dēor* animal, deer]

deerskin /ˈdɪəskɪn/ *n.* & *adj.* —*n.* leather from a deer's skin. —*adj.* made from a deer's skin.

deerstalker /ˈdɪəˌstɔːkə(r)/ *n.* **1** a soft cloth cap with peaks in front and behind and ear-flaps often joined at the top. **2** a person who stalks deer.

de-escalate /diːˈeskəˌleɪt/ *v.tr.* reduce the level or intensity of. □□ **de-escalation** /-ˈleɪʃ(ə)n/ *n.*

deface /dɪˈfeɪs/ *v.tr.* **1** spoil the appearance of; disfigure. **2** make illegible. □□ **defaceable** *adj.* **defacement** *n.* **defacer** *n.* [ME f. F *défacer* f. OF *desfacier* (as DE-, FACE)]

de facto /diː ˈfæktəʊ, deɪ/ *adv., adj.,* & *n.* —*adv.* in fact, whether by right or not. —*adj.* that exists or is such in fact (*a de facto ruler*). —*n.* (in full **de facto wife** or **husband**) a person living with another as if married. [L]

defalcate /ˈdiːfælˌkeɪt/ *v.intr. formal* misappropriate property in one's charge, esp. money. □□ **defalcator** *n.* [med.L *defalcare* lop (as DE-, L *falx -cis* sickle)]

defalcation /ˌdiːfælˈkeɪʃ(ə)n/ *n. formal* **1** *Law* **a** a misappropriation of money. **b** an amount misappropriated. **2** a shortcoming. **3** defection. [ME f. med.L *defalcatio* (as DEFALCATE)]

defame /dɪˈfeɪm/ *v.tr.* attack the good reputation of; speak ill of. □□ **defamation** /ˌdefəˈmeɪʃ(ə)n, ˌdiːf-/ *n.* **defamatory** /dɪˈfæmətərɪ/ *adj.* **defamer** *n.* [ME f. OF *diffamer* etc. f. L *diffamare* spread evil report (as DIS-, *fama* report)]

defat /diːˈfæt/ *v.tr.* (**defatted, defatting**) remove fat or fats from.

default /dɪˈfɔːlt, -ˈfɒlt/ *n.* & *v.* —*n.* **1** failure to fulfil an obligation, esp. to appear, pay, or act in some way. **2** lack, absence. **3** a preselected option adopted by a computer program when no alternative is specified by the user or programmer. —*v.* **1** *intr.* fail to fulfil an obligation, esp. to pay money or to appear in a lawcourt. **2** *tr.* declare (a party) in default and give judgement against that party. □ **go by default 1** be ignored because of absence. **2** be absent. **in default of** because of the absence of. **judgement by default** judgement given for the plaintiff on the defendant's failure to plead. **win by default** win because an opponent fails to be present. [ME f. OF *defaut(e)* f. *defaillir* fail f. Rmc (as DE-, L *fallere* deceive): cf. FAIL]

defaulter /dɪˈfɔːltə(r), -ˈfɒltə(r)/ *n.* a person who defaults, esp. *Brit.* a soldier guilty of a military offence.

defeasance /dɪˈfiːz(ə)ns/ *n.* the act or process of rendering null and void. [ME f. OF *defesance* f. *de(s)faire* undo (as DE-, *faire* make f. L *facere*)]

defeasible /dɪˈfiːzɪb(ə)l/ *adj.* **1** capable of annulment. **2** liable to forfeiture. □□ **defeasibility** /-ˈbɪlɪtɪ/ *n.* **defeasibly** *adv.* [AF (as DEFEASANCE)]

defeat /dɪˈfiːt/ *v.* & *n.* —*v.tr.* **1** overcome in a battle or other contest. **2** frustrate, baffle. **3** reject (a motion etc.) by voting. **4** *Law* annul. —*n.* the act or process of defeating or being defeated. [ME f. OF *deffait, desfait* past part. of *desfaire* f. med.L *disfacere* (as DIS-, L *facere* do)]

defeatism /dɪˈfiːtɪz(ə)m/ *n.* **1** an excessive readiness to accept defeat. **2** conduct conducive to this. □□ **defeatist** *n.* & *adj.* [F *défaitisme* f. *défaite* DEFEAT]

defecate /ˈdefɪˌkeɪt/ *v.intr.* discharge faeces from the body. □□ **defecation** /-ˈkeɪʃ(ə)n/ *n.* [earlier as adj., = purified, f. L *defaecare* (as DE-, *faex faecis* dregs)]

defect /ˈdiːfekt/ *n.* & *v.* —*n.* [also /dɪˈfekt/] **1** lack of something essential or required; imperfection. **2** a shortcoming or failing. **3** a blemish. **4** the amount by which a thing falls short. —*v.intr.* abandon one's country or cause in favour of another. □□ **defector** *n.* [L *defectus* f. *deficere* desert, fail (as DE-, *facere* do)]

defection /dɪˈfekʃ(ə)n/ *n.* **1** the abandonment of one's country or cause. **2** ceasing in allegiance to a leader, party, religion, or duty. [L *defectio* (as DEFECT)]

defective /dɪˈfektɪv/ *adj.* & *n.* —*adj.* **1** having a defect or defects; incomplete, imperfect, faulty. **2** mentally subnormal. **3** (usu. foll. by *in*) lacking, deficient. **4** *Gram.* not having all the usual inflections. —*n.* a mentally defective person. □□ **defectively** *adv.* **defectiveness** *n.* [ME f. OF *defectif -ive* or LL *defectivus* (as DEFECT)]

defence /dɪˈfens/ *n.* (*US* **defense**) **1** the act of defending from or resisting attack. **2 a** a means of resisting attack. **b** a thing that protects. **c** the military resources of a country. **3** (in *pl.*) fortifications. **4 a** a justification, vindication. **b** a speech or piece of writing used to this end. **5 a** the defendant's case in a lawsuit. **b** the counsel for the defendant. **6 a** the action or role of defending one's goal etc. against attack. **b** the players in a team who perform this role. □ **defence mechanism 1** the body's reaction against disease organisms. **2** a usu. unconscious mental process to avoid conscious conflict or anxiety. □□ **defenceless** adj. **defencelessly** adv. **defencelessness** n. [ME f. OF defens(e) f. LL defensum, -a, past part. of defendere: see DEFEND]

defend /dɪˈfend/ v.tr. (also absol.) **1** (often foll. by against, from) resist an attack made on; protect (a person or thing) from harm or danger. **2** support or uphold by argument; speak or write in favour of. **3** conduct the case for (a defendant in a lawsuit). □□ **defendable** adj. **defender** n. [ME f. OF defendre f. L defendere: cf. OFFEND]

defendant /dɪˈfend(ə)nt/ n. a person etc. sued or accused in a court of law. [ME f. OF, part. of defendre: see DEFEND]

Defender of the Faith a title (transl. L Fidei defensor) conferred on Henry VIII by Pope Leo X in 1521 in recognition of his treatise defending the seven sacraments against Luther. It was recognized by Parliament as an official style of the English monarch in 1544, and has been borne by all subsequent sovereigns.

defenestration /ˌdiːfenɪˈstreɪʃ(ə)n/ n. formal or joc. the action of throwing (esp. a person) out of a window. □□ **defenestrate** /diːˈfenɪstreɪt/ v.tr. [mod.L defenestratio (as DE-, L fenestra window)]

defense US var. of DEFENCE.

defensible /dɪˈfensɪb(ə)l/ adj. **1** justifiable; supportable by argument. **2** that can be easily defended militarily. □□ **defensibility** /-ˈbɪlɪti/ n. **defensibly** adv. [ME f. LL defensibilis (as DEFEND)]

defensive /dɪˈfensɪv/ adj. **1** done or intended for defence or to defend. **2** (of a person or attitude) concerned to challenge criticism. □ **on the defensive 1** expecting criticism. **2** in an attitude or position of defence. □□ **defensively** adv. **defensiveness** n. [ME f. F défensif -ive f. med.L defensivus (as DEFEND)]

defer[1] /dɪˈfɜː(r)/ v.tr. (**deferred**, **deferring**) **1** put off to a later time; postpone. **2** US postpone the conscription of (a person). □ **deferred payment** payment by instalments. □□ **deferment** n. **deferrable** adj. **deferral** n. [ME, orig. the same as DIFFER]

defer[2] /dɪˈfɜː(r)/ v.intr. (**deferred**, **deferring**) (foll. by to) yield or make concessions in opinion or action. □□ **deferrer** n. [ME f. F déferer f. L deferre (as DE-, ferre bring)]

deference /ˈdefərəns/ n. **1** courteous regard, respect. **2** compliance with the advice or wishes of another (pay deference to). □ **in deference to** out of respect for. [F déférence (as DEFER[2])]

deferential /ˌdefəˈrenʃ(ə)l/ adj. showing deference; respectful. □□ **deferentially** adv. [DEFERENCE, after PRUDENTIAL etc.]

defiance /dɪˈfaɪəns/ n. **1** open disobedience; bold resistance. **2** a challenge to fight or maintain a cause, assertion, etc. □ **in defiance of** disregarding; in conflict with. [ME f. OF (as DEFY)]

defiant /dɪˈfaɪənt/ adj. **1** showing defiance. **2** openly disobedient. □□ **defiantly** adv.

defibrillation /ˌdiːfɪbrɪˈleɪʃ(ə)n/ n. Med. the stopping of the fibrillation of the heart. □□ **defibrillator** /ˌdiːˈfɪbrɪleɪtə(r)/ n.

deficiency /dɪˈfɪʃənsi/ n. (pl. **-ies**) **1** the state or condition of being deficient. **2** (usu. foll. by of) a lack or shortage. **3** a thing lacking. **4** the amount by which a thing, esp. revenue, falls short. □ **deficiency disease** a disease caused by the lack of some essential or important element in the diet.

deficient /dɪˈfɪʃ(ə)nt/ adj. **1** (usu. foll. by in) incomplete; not having enough of a specified quality or ingredient. **2** insufficient in quantity, force, etc. **3** (in full **mentally deficient**) incapable of adequate social or intellectual behaviour through imperfect mental development. □□ **deficiently** adv. [L deficiens part. of deficere (as DEFECT)]

deficit /ˈdefɪsɪt/ n. **1** the amount by which a thing (esp. a sum of money) is too small. **2** an excess of liabilities over assets in a given period, esp. a financial year (opp. SURPLUS). □ **deficit financing** financing of (esp. State) spending by borrowing. **deficit spending** spending, esp. by the State, financed by borrowing. [F déficit f. L deficit 3rd sing. pres. of deficere (as DEFECT)]

defier /dɪˈfaɪə(r)/ n. a person who defies.

defilade /ˌdefɪˈleɪd/ v. & n. —v.tr. secure (a fortification) against enfilading fire. —n. this precaution or arrangement. [DEFILE[2] + -ADE]

defile[1] /dɪˈfaɪl/ v.tr. **1** make dirty; pollute, befoul. **2** corrupt. **3** desecrate, profane. **4** deprive (esp. a woman) of virginity. **5** make ceremonially unclean. □□ **defilement** n. **defiler** n. [ME defoul f. OF defouler trample down, outrage (as DE-, fouler tread, trample) altered after obs. befile f. OE befȳlan (BE-, fūl FOUL)]

defile[2] /dɪˈfaɪl/ n. & v. —n. /also ˈdiːfaɪl/ **1** a narrow way through which troops can only march in file. **2** a gorge. —v.intr. march in file. [F défiler and défilé past part. (as DE-, FILE[2])]

define /dɪˈfaɪn/ v.tr. **1** give the exact meaning of (a word etc.). **2** describe or explain the scope of (define one's position). **3** make clear, esp. in outline (well-defined image). **4** mark out the boundary or limits of. **5** (of properties) make up the total character of. □□ **definable** adj. **definer** n. [ME f. OF definer ult. f. L definire (as DE-, finire finish, f. finis end)]

definite /ˈdefɪnɪt/ adj. **1** having exact and discernible limits. **2** clear and distinct; not vague. ¶ See the note at definitive. □ **definite article** see ARTICLE. **definite integral** see INTEGRAL. □□ **definiteness** n. [L definitus past part. of definire (as DEFINE)]

definitely /ˈdefɪnɪtli/ adv. & int. —adv. **1** in a definite manner. **2** certainly; without doubt (they were definitely there). —int. colloq. yes, certainly.

definition /ˌdefɪˈnɪʃ(ə)n/ n. **1 a** the act or process of defining. **b** a statement of the meaning of a word or the nature of a thing. **2 a** the degree of distinctness in outline of an object or image (esp. of an image produced by a lens or shown in a photograph or on a cinema or television screen). **b** making or being distinct in outline. [ME f. OF f. L definitio (as DEFINE)]

definitive /dɪˈfɪnɪtɪv/ adj. **1** (of an answer, treaty, verdict, etc.) decisive, unconditional, final. ¶ Often confused in this sense with definite, which does not have connotations of authority and conclusiveness: a definite no is a firm refusal, whereas a definitive no is an authoritative judgement or decision that something is not the case. **2** (of an edition of a book etc.) most authoritative. **3** Philately (of a series of stamps) for permanent use, not commemorative etc. □□ **definitively** adv. [ME f. OF definitif -ive f. L definitivus (as DEFINE)]

deflagrate /ˈdefləɡreɪt/ v.tr. & intr. burn away with sudden flame. □□ **deflagration** /-ˈreɪʃ(ə)n/ n. **deflagrator** n. [L deflagrare (as DE-, flagrare blaze)]

deflate /dɪˈfleɪt/ v. **1 a** tr. let air or gas out of (a tyre, balloon, etc.). **b** intr. be emptied of air or gas. **2 a** tr. cause to lose confidence or conceit. **b** intr. lose confidence. **3** Econ. **a** tr. subject (a currency or economy) to deflation. **b** intr. pursue a policy of deflation. **4** tr. reduce the importance of, depreciate. □□ **deflator** n. [DE- + INFLATE]

deflation /dɪˈfleɪʃ(ə)n/ n. **1** the act or process of deflating or being deflated. **2** Econ. reduction of the amount of money in circulation to increase its value as a measure against inflation. **3** Geol. the removal of particles of rock etc. by the wind. □□ **deflationary** adj. **deflationist** n.

deflect /dɪˈflekt/ v. **1** tr. & intr. bend or turn aside from a straight course or intended purpose. **2** (often foll. by from) **a** tr. cause to deviate. **b** intr. deviate. [L deflectere (as DE-, flectere flex- bend)]

deflection /dɪˈflekʃ(ə)n/ n. (also **deflexion**) **1** the act or process of deflecting or being deflected. **2** a lateral bend or turn; a deviation. **3** Physics the displacement of a pointer on an instrument from its zero position. [LL deflexio (as DEFLECT)]

deflector /dɪˈflektə(r)/ n. a thing that deflects, esp. a device for deflecting a flow of air etc.

defloration /ˌdiːflɔːˈreɪʃ(ə)n/ n. deflowering. [ME f. OF or f. LL defloratio (as DEFLOWER)]

deflower /dɪˈflaʊə(r)/ v.tr. **1** deprive (esp. a woman) of virginity. **2** ravage, spoil. **3** strip of flowers. [ME f. OF deflourer, des-, ult. f. LL deflorare (as DE-, L flos floris flower)]

defocus /diːˈfəʊkəs/ v.tr. & intr. (**defocused**, **defocusing** or **defocussed**, **defocussing**) put or go out of focus.

Defoe /dɪˈfəʊ/, Daniel (1660–1731), English novelist and journalist, born in London, the son of a butcher. His very varied career included several unsuccessful business ventures and secret service work for both Whigs and Tories, but he was best known to his contemporaries as a political journalist. His verse satire The

True-Born Englishman (1701), in defence of William of Orange, won him fame and the King's friendship. However, he was pilloried and imprisoned for his pamphlet *The Shortest Way with the Dissenters* (1702) in which he (though himself a Dissenter) ironically demanded the suppression of dissent. Having produced more than 500 pamphlets, books, and a thrice-weekly political journal *The Review* (1704–13), he was nearly 60 when he turned to fiction, producing in 1719 his greatest and most enduring novel, *Robinson Crusoe*; other fictional and semi-fictional works followed, notably *Captain Singleton* (1720), *Moll Flanders* and *Colonel Jack* (1722), *A Journal of the Plague Year* (1722), and *Roxana* (1724). He was a master of vivid narrative with a journalist's eye for realistic detail, and is regarded by many as the first true English novelist, and the spokesman of the rising middle classes.

defoliate /diːˈfəʊlɪˌeɪt/ *v.tr.* remove leaves from, esp. as a military tactic. □□ **defoliant** *n.* & *adj.* **defoliation** /-ˈeɪʃ(ə)n/ *n.* **defoliator** *n.* [LL *defoliare* f. *folium* leaf]

De Forest /dəˈfɒrɪst/, Lee (1873–1961), American physicist and electrical engineer, whose triode valve (patented in 1907) became the basic amplifier until superseded by the transistor in 1947. This device, which made possible the large-scale amplification of signals, was crucial to the development of radio communication, television, and computers. De Forest was one of the pioneers of radio broadcasting, successfully transmitting a live broadcast of a performance by Enrico Caruso in 1910. In the early 1920s he developed a method of converting sound waves into light of varying intensity for recording and reproducing sound on cinema film.

deforest /diːˈfɒrɪst/ *v.tr.* clear of forests or trees. □□ **deforestation** /-ˈsteɪʃ(ə)n/ *n.*

deform /dɪˈfɔːm/ *v.* **1** *tr.* make ugly, deface. **2** *tr.* put out of shape, misshape. **3** *intr.* undergo deformation; be deformed. □□ **deformable** *adj.* [ME f. OF *deformer* etc. f. med.L *difformare* ult. f. L *deformare* (as DE-, *formare* f. *forma* shape)]

deformation /ˌdiːfɔːˈmeɪʃ(ə)n/ *n.* **1** disfigurement. **2** *Physics* **a** (often foll. by *of*) change in shape. **b** a quantity representing the amount of this change. **3** a perverted form of a word (e.g. *dang* for *damn*). □□ **deformational** *adj.* [ME f. OF *deformation* or L *deformatio* (as DEFORM)]

deformed /dɪˈfɔːmd/ *adj.* (of a person or limb) misshapen.

deformity /dɪˈfɔːmɪtɪ/ *n.* (pl. **-ies**) **1** the state of being deformed; ugliness, disfigurement. **2** a malformation, esp. of body or limb. **3** a moral defect; depravity. [ME f. OF *deformité* etc. f. L *deformitas -tatis* f. *deformis* (as DE-, *forma* shape)]

defraud /dɪˈfrɔːd/ *v.tr.* (often foll. by *of*) cheat by fraud. □□ **defrauder** *n.* [ME f. OF *defrauder* or L *defraudare* (as DE-, FRAUD)]

defray /dɪˈfreɪ/ *v.tr.* provide money to pay (a cost or expense). □□ **defrayable** *adj.* **defrayal** *n.* **defrayment** *n.* [F *défrayer* (as DE-, obs. *frai(t)* cost, f. med.L *fredum, -us* fine for breach of the peace)]

defrock /diːˈfrɒk/ *v.tr.* deprive (a person, esp. a priest) of ecclesiastical status. [F *défroquer* (as DE-, FROCK)]

defrost /diːˈfrɒst/ *v.* **1** *tr.* **a** free (the interior of a refrigerator) of excess frost, usu. by turning it off for a period. **b** remove frost or ice from (esp. the windscreen of a motor vehicle). **2** *tr.* unfreeze (frozen food). **3** *intr.* become unfrozen. □□ **defroster** *n.*

deft /deft/ *adj.* neatly skilful or dextrous; adroit. □□ **deftly** *adv.* **deftness** *n.* [ME, var. of DAFT in obs. sense 'meek']

defunct /dɪˈfʌŋkt/ *adj.* **1** no longer existing. **2** no longer used or in fashion. **3** dead or extinct. □□ **defunctness** *n.* [L *defunctus* dead, past part. of *defungi* (as DE-, *fungi* perform)]

defuse /diːˈfjuːz/ *v.tr.* **1** remove the fuse from (an explosive device). **2** reduce the tension or potential danger in (a crisis, difficulty, etc.).

defy /dɪˈfaɪ/ *v.tr.* (**-ies, -ied**) **1** resist openly; refuse to obey. **2** (of a thing) present insuperable obstacles to (*defies solution*). **3** (foll. by *to* + infin.) challenge (a person) to do or prove something. **4** *archaic* challenge to combat. [ME f. OF *defier* f. Rmc (as DIS-, L *fidus* faithful)]

deg. *abbr.* degree.

dégagé /deɪˈɡɑːʒeɪ/ *adj.* (*fem.* **dégagée**) easy, unconstrained. [F, past part. of *dégager* set free]

Degas /dəˈɡɑː/, Edgar (1834–1917), French artist, born in Paris of a wealthy family. His early work evinced his training at the École des Beaux-Arts, where he greatly admired Ingres. This academic influence was to survive in his lifelong concentration on the human form, characterized by a sure sense of draughtsmanship, even after his introduction to the impressionist circle. He exhibited with Manet, Monet, Renoir, Cézanne, Sisley, Pissarro, and Fantin-Latour, evidence of his firm position in the inner circle of impressionist painters in Paris. Degas has in common with the impressionists an imagery which concentrates on everyday events. He explored subjects as diverse as horse-racing, bathers, and ballet-dancers, often finely executed in pastel, and he also produced a series of bronze statuettes, unique in his group. There is evidence that his daring compositional experiments were influenced by photography.

degas /diːˈɡæs/ *v.tr.* (**degassed, degassing**) remove unwanted gas from.

de Gaulle see GAULLE.

degauss /diːˈɡaʊs/ *v.tr.* neutralize the magnetism in (a thing) by encircling it with a current-carrying conductor. □□ **degausser** *n.* [DE- + GAUSS]

degenerate *adj.*, *n.*, & *v.* —*adj.* /dɪˈdʒenərət/ **1** having lost the qualities that are normal and desirable or proper to its kind; fallen from former excellence. **2** *Biol.* having changed to a lower type. —*n.* /dɪˈdʒenərət/ a degenerate person or animal. —*v.intr.* /dɪˈdʒenəˌreɪt/ become degenerate. □□ **degeneracy** *n.* **degenerately** *adv.* [L *degeneratus* past part. of *degenerare* (as DE-, *genus -eris* race)]

degeneration /dɪˌdʒenəˈreɪʃ(ə)n/ *n.* **1 a** the process of becoming degenerate. **b** the state of being degenerate. **2** *Med.* morbid deterioration of tissue or change in its structure. [ME f. F *dégénération* or f. LL *degeneratio* (as DEGENERATE)]

degenerative /dɪˈdʒenərətɪv/ *adj.* **1** of or tending to degeneration. **2** (of disease) characterized by progressive often irreversible deterioration.

degrade /dɪˈɡreɪd/ *v.* **1** *tr.* reduce to a lower rank, esp. as a punishment. **2** *tr.* bring into dishonour or contempt. **3** *tr. Chem.* reduce to a simpler molecular structure. **4** *tr. Physics* reduce (energy) to a less convertible form. **5** *tr. Geol.* wear down (rocks etc.) by disintegration. **6** *intr.* degenerate. **7** *intr. Chem.* disintegrate. □□ **degradable** *adj.* **degradation** /ˌdeɡrəˈdeɪʃ(ə)n/ *n.* **degradative** /-ˈdeɪtɪv/ *adj.* **degrader** *n.* [ME f. OF *degrader* f. eccl.L *degradare* (as DE-, L *gradus* step)]

degrading /dɪˈɡreɪdɪŋ/ *adj.* humiliating; causing a loss of self-respect. □□ **degradingly** *adv.*

degrease /diːˈɡriːs/ *v.tr.* remove unwanted grease or fat from.

degree /dɪˈɡriː/ *n.* **1** a stage in an ascending or descending scale, series, or process. **2** a stage in intensity or amount (*to a high degree*; *in some degree*). **3** relative condition (*each is good in its degree*). **4** *Math.* a unit of measurement of angles, one-ninetieth of a right angle or the angle subtended by one-three-hundred-and-sixtieth of the circumference of a circle. ¶ Symb.: ° (as in 45°). **5** *Physics* a unit in a scale of temperature, hardness, etc. ¶ Abbr.: **deg.** (or omitted in the Kelvin scale of temperature). **6** *Med.* an extent of burns on a scale characterized by the destruction of the skin. **7** an academic rank conferred by a college or university after examination or after completion of a course, or conferred as an honour on a distinguished person. **8** a grade of crime or criminality (*murder in the first degree*). **9** a step in direct genealogical descent. **10** social or official rank. **11** *Math.* the highest power of unknowns or variables in an equation etc. (*equation of the third degree*). **12** a masonic rank. **13** a thing placed like a step in a series; a tier or row. **14** *Mus.* the classification of a note by its position in the scale. □ **by degrees** a little at a time; gradually. **degree of freedom 1** *Physics* the independent direction in which motion can occur. **2** *Chem.* the number of independent factors required to specify a system at equilibrium. **3** *Statistics* the number of independent values or quantities which can be assigned to a statistical distribution. **degrees of comparison** see COMPARISON. **forbidden** (or

prohibited) degrees a number of degrees of descent too few to allow of marriage between two related persons. **to a degree** *colloq.* considerably. □□ **degreeless** *adj.* [ME f. OF *degré* f. Rmc (as DE-, L *gradus* step)]

degressive /dɪˈgresɪv/ *adj.* **1** (of taxation) at successively lower rates on low amounts. **2** reducing in amount. [L *degredi* (as DE-, *gradi* walk)]

de haut en bas /də ˌəʊt ã ˈbɑː/ *adv.* in a condescending or superior manner. [F, = from above to below]

de Havilland /də ˈhævɪlənd/, Sir Geoffrey (1882–1965), English aircraft designer and manufacturer. Having built the BE series of fighters in the First World War he started the company named after him (1920), and designed and built many famous light aircraft including the Moth series and also the Gipsy series of aircraft engines, the Mosquito of the Second World War, and some of the first jet-propelled aircraft.

dehisce /dɪˈhɪs/ *v.intr.* gape or burst open (esp. of a pod or seed-vessel or of a cut or wound). □□ **dehiscence** *n.* **dehiscent** *adj.* [L *dehiscere* (as DE-, *hiscere* incept. of *hiare* gape)]

dehorn /diːˈhɔːn/ *v.tr.* remove the horns from (an animal).

dehumanize /diːˈhjuːmənaɪz/ *v.tr.* (also **-ise**) **1** deprive of human characteristics. **2** make impersonal or machine-like. □□ **dehumanization** /-ˈzeɪʃ(ə)n/ *n.*

dehumidify /ˌdiːhjuːˈmɪdɪˌfaɪ/ *v.tr.* (**-ies, -ied**) reduce the degree of humidity of; remove moisture from (a gas, esp. air). □□ **dehumidification** /-fɪˈkeɪʃ(ə)n/ *n.* **dehumidifier** *n.*

dehydrate /diːˈhaɪdreɪt, ˌdiːhaɪˈdreɪt/ *v.* **a** remove water from (esp. foods for preservation and storage in bulk). **b** make dry, esp. make (the body) deficient in water. **c** render lifeless or uninteresting. **2** *intr.* lose water. □□ **dehydration** /-ˈdreɪʃ(ə)n/ *n.* **dehydrator** *n.*

dehydrogenate /ˌdiːhaɪˈdrɒdʒɪˌneɪt/ *v.tr. Chem.* remove a hydrogen atom or atoms from (a compound). □□ **dehydrogenation** /-ˈneɪʃ(ə)n/ *n.*

Deianira /ˌdaɪəˈnaɪrə/ *Gk Mythol.* the wife of Hercules, who was tricked into smearing poison on a garment which caused his death.

de-ice /diːˈaɪs/ *v.tr.* **1** remove ice from. **2** prevent the formation of ice on.

de-icer /diːˈaɪsə(r)/ *n.* a device or substance for de-icing, esp. a windscreen or ice on an aircraft.

deicide /ˈdiːɪˌsaɪd, ˈdeɪɪs-/ *n.* **1** the killer of a god. **2** the killing of a god. [eccl.L *deicida* f. L *deus* god + -CIDE]

deictic /ˈdaɪktɪk/ *adj. & n. Philol. & Gram.* —*adj.* pointing, demonstrative. —*n.* a deictic word. [Gk *deiktikos* f. *deiktos* capable of proof f. *deiknumi* show]

deify /ˈdiːɪˌfaɪ, ˈdeɪɪ-/ *v.tr.* (**-ies, -ied**) **1** make a god of. **2** regard or worship as a god. □□ **deification** /-fɪˈkeɪʃ(ə)n/ *n.* [ME f. OF *deifier* f. eccl.L *deificare* f. *deus* god]

Deighton /ˈdeɪt(ə)n/, Len (1929–   ), English writer, noted especially for his spy thrillers, several of which were adapted as films and for television. The best known include his first novel *The Ipcress File* (1962), *Funeral in Berlin* (1964), and the trilogy *Berlin Game, Mexico Set, London Match* (1983–5).

deign /deɪn/ *v.* **1** *intr.* (foll. by *to* + infin.) think fit, condescend. **2** *tr.* (usu. with *neg.*) *archaic* condescend to give (an answer etc.). [ME f. OF *degnier, deigner, daigner* f. L *dignare, -ari* deem worthy f. *dignus* worthy]

Dei gratia /ˌdeɪɪ ˈgrɑːtɪə, -ʃɪə/ *adv.* by the grace of God. [L]

deinstitutionalize /diːˌɪnstɪˈtjuːʃənəˌlaɪz/ *v.tr.* (also **-ise**) (usu. as **deinstitutionalized** *adj.*) remove from an institution or from the effects of institutional life. □□ **deinstitutionalization** /-ˈzeɪʃ(ə)n/ *n.*

deionize /diːˈaɪəˌnaɪz/ *v.tr.* (also **-ise**) remove the ions or ionic constituents from (water, air, etc.). □□ **deionization** /-ˈzeɪʃ(ə)n/ *n.* **deionizer** *n.*

Deirdre /ˈdɪədrɪ/ *Irish legend* the tragic heroine of the tale of 'The Sons of Usnach', of whom it was prophesied that her beauty would bring banishment and death to heroes. King Conchubar of Ulster destined her for his wife, but she fell in love with Naoise, son of Usnach, who with his brothers carried her off to Scotland. They were lured back by Conchubar and treacherously slain, and Deirdre took her own life. The legend has been dramatized by G. W. Russell (Æ), Synge, and Yeats.

deism /ˈdiːɪz(ə)m, ˈdeɪ-/ *n.* belief in the existence of a supreme being (creator of the world) without accepting revelation (cf. THEISM), especially the system of natural religion developed in England in the 17th–18th c. by anti-Christian rationalists influenced by Locke's empiricism. Never widely accepted in England, it had a great influence in France (where Voltaire and J.-J. Rousseau were among its exponents) and in Germany. □□ **deist** *n.* **deistic** /-ˈɪstɪk/ *adj.* **deistical** /-ˈɪstɪk(ə)l/ *adj.* [L *deus* god + -ISM]

deity /ˈdiːɪtɪ, ˈdeɪɪ-/ *n.* (*pl.* **-ies**) **1** a god or goddess. **2** divine status, quality, or nature. **3** (**the Deity**) the Creator, God. [ME f. OF *deité* f. eccl.L *deitas -tatis* transl. Gk *theotēs* f. *theos* god]

déjà vu /ˌdeɪʒɑː ˈvuː/ *n.* **1** *Psychol.* an illusory feeling of having already experienced a present situation. **2** something tediously familiar. [F, = already seen]

deject /dɪˈdʒekt/ *v.tr.* (usu. as **dejected** *adj.*) make sad or dispirited; depress. □□ **dejectedly** *adv.* [ME f. L *dejicere* (DE-, *jacĕre* throw)]

dejection /dɪˈdʒekʃ(ə)n/ *n.* a dejected state; low spirits. [ME f. L *dejectio* (as DEJECT)]

de jure /diː ˈdʒʊərɪ, deɪ ˈjʊəreɪ/ *adj. & adv.* —*adj.* rightful. —*adv.* rightfully; by right. [L]

Dekabrist /ˈdekəbrɪst/ *n.* = DECEMBRIST. [Russ.]

Dekker /ˈdekə(r)/, Thomas (1570?–1632), English playwright, author of *The Shoemaker's Holiday* (1600), a cheerful comedy of London life. Middleton collaborated with him in the first part of *The Honest Whore* (1604), and John Ford and William Rowley in *The Witch of Edmonton* (1623). His writings are marked by a racy wit, sunny simplicity, and sympathy for the poor and oppressed.

dekko /ˈdekəʊ/ *n.* (*pl.* **-os**) *Brit. sl.* a look or glance (*took a quick dekko*). [Hindi *dekho*, imper. of *dekhnā* look]

de Kooning /də ˈkuːnɪŋ/, Willem (1904–   ), American painter, who shared with Jackson Pollock the unofficial leadership of the abstract expressionist group. Unlike Pollock, he usually retained figurative elements in his painting. He achieved notoriety with his *Women* series (1950–3), which shocked the public and dismayed critics who believed in a rigorously abstract art.

Del. *abbr.* Delaware.

Delacroix /ˌdeləˈkrwɑː/, Ferdinand-Victor-Eugène (1798–1863), French painter, the greatest of the French romantics, though he himself claimed to be 'un pur classique'. His main artistic education came from study of Old Masters, especially Rubens and Veronese. In 1832 he visited Morocco, which both provided exotic subject-matter and stimulated his lifelong interest in colour. From the 1830s he experimented with complementary colours, purifying his palette to exclude black and earth colours, in an anticipation of impressionist methods which led Cézanne to say 'we are all in Delacroix'. Delacroix never painted modern life, preferring literary, historical, and typically romantic subject-matter, but to his great admirer, Baudelaire, he was modern because he expressed the spirit of his age. His *Journal* (1822–4 and 1847–63) is a revealing record of his views on literature, music, and art, as well as of his personal struggles and philosophy.

de la Mare /də læ ˈmeə(r)/, Walter (1873–1956), English poet and novelist whose highly individual works, addressed to adults and children, have a dreamlike quality suggesting eeriness and mystery. These include the poem 'The Listeners' (1912) and for children the story of *The Three Mulla Mulgars* (1910) and the verse collection *Peacock Pie* (1913).

delate /dɪˈleɪt/ *v.tr. archaic* **1** inform against; impeach (a person). **2** report (an offence). □□ **delation** /-ˈleɪʃ(ə)n/ *n.* **delator** *n.* [L *delat-* (as DE-, *lat-* past part. stem of *ferre* carry)]

Delaunay /dəˈləʊneɪ/, Robert (1885–1941), French painter, who through most of his career experimented with the abstract qualities of colour, notably in his series of paintings of the Eiffel Tower. By 1912 his work had become completely abstract, as in the beautiful *Circular Forms* series. Apollinaire gave the name Orphism to his work.

Delaware /ˈdeləˌweə(r)/ a State of the US on the Atlantic coast, one of the original 13 States of the US (1787); pop. (est. 1985) 594,300; capital, Dover.

delay /dɪˈleɪ/ v. & n. —v. 1 tr. postpone; defer. 2 tr. make late (was delayed at the traffic lights). 3 intr. loiter; be late (don't delay!). —n. 1 the act or an instance of delaying; the process of being delayed. 2 time lost by inaction or the inability to proceed. 3 a hindrance. □ **delayed-action** (attrib.) (esp. of a bomb, camera, etc.) operating some time after being primed or set. **delay line** Electr. a device producing a desired delay in the transmission of a signal. □□ **delayer** n. [ME f. OF delayer (v.), delai (n.), prob. f. des- DIS- + laier leave: see RELAY]

dele /ˈdiːlɪ/ v. & n. Printing —v.tr. (**deled, deleing**) delete or mark for deletion (a letter, word, etc., struck out of a text). —n. a sign marking something to be deleted; a deletion. [L, imper. of delēre: see DELETE]

delectable /dɪˈlektəb(ə)l/ adj. esp. literary. delightful, pleasant. □□ **delectability** /-ˈbɪlɪtɪ/ n. **delectably** adv. [ME f. OF f. L delectabilis f. delectare DELIGHT]

delectation /ˌdiːlekˈteɪʃ(ə)n/ n. literary pleasure, enjoyment (sang for his delectation). [ME f. OF (as DELECTABLE)]

delegacy /ˈdelɪgəsɪ/ n. (pl. -ies) 1 a system of delegating. 2 a an appointment as a delegate. b a body of delegates; a delegation.

delegate n. & v. —n. /ˈdelɪgət/ 1 an elected representative sent to a conference. 2 a member of a committee. 3 a member of a deputation. —v.tr. /ˈdelɪgeɪt/ 1 (often foll. by to) a commit (authority, power, etc.) to an agent or deputy. b entrust (a task) to another person. 2 send or authorize (a person) as a representative; depute. □□ **delegable** /ˈdelɪgəb(ə)l/ adj. [ME f. L delegatus (as DE-, legare depute)]

delegation /ˌdelɪˈgeɪʃ(ə)n/ n. 1 a body of delegates; a deputation. 2 the act or process of delegating or being delegated. [L delegatio (as DELEGATE)]

delete /dɪˈliːt/ v.tr. remove or obliterate (written or printed matter), esp. by striking out. □□ **deletion** /-ˈliːʃ(ə)n/ n. [L delēre delet- efface]

deleterious /ˌdelɪˈtɪərɪəs/ adj. harmful (to the mind or body). □□ **deleteriously** adv. [med.L deleterius f. Gk dēlētērios noxious]

Delft /delft/ a town in the Dutch province of South Holland, 5 km (3 miles) south-east of the Hague; pop. (1987) 88,100. From the 17th c. onwards the town has been noted for its pottery (see DELFT). The painters Pieter de Hooch (1629–83) and Jan Vermeer lived here; William the Silent, who freed The Netherlands from Spanish rule, was assassinated in Delft in 1584.

delft /delft/ n. (also **delftware** /ˈdelftweə(r)/) glazed, usu. blue and white, earthenware, made in Delft.

Delhi /ˈdelɪ/ a Union Territory of India, containing Old and New Delhi. □ **Old Delhi** a city of India on the River Jumna. It was made the capital of the Mughal empire in 1638 by Shah Jahan, who there built the Red Fort containing the imperial Mughal palace. **New Delhi** the present capital of India, adjoining Old Delhi, originally built 1912–29 to replace Calcutta as the capital of British India; pop. (1981) 6,196,414.

deli /ˈdelɪ/ n. (pl. **delis**) esp. US colloq. a delicatessen shop. [abbr.]

Delian /ˈdiːlɪən/ adj. & n. —adj. of Delos. —n. a native or inhabitant of Delos. □ **Delian League** the modern name given to the alliance of Greek city-states formed in 478–447 BC against the Persians, with its headquarters on Delos. Command of the joint forces and control of the treasury were in Athenian hands, and Athens used the alliance increasingly in her own interest; after the end of the war with Persia the treasury was moved from Delos to Athens and disaffection among the allies was firmly suppressed. Pericles encouraged the conversion of the alliance into an empire, the contributions became a form of tribute, and the reserve brought from Delos was used for the rebuilding of Athenian temples. The league was disbanded on the defeat of Athens in the Peloponnesian War (404 BC), but again united under Athens' leadership against Spartan aggression in 377–338 BC.

deliberate adj. & v. —adj. /dɪˈlɪbərət/ 1 a intentional (a deliberate foul). b fully considered; not impulsive (made a deliberate choice). 2 slow in deciding; cautious (a ponderous and deliberate

mind). 3 (of movement etc.) leisurely and unhurried. —v. /dɪˈlɪbəˌreɪt/ 1 intr. think carefully; take counsel (the jury deliberated for an hour). 2 tr. consider, discuss carefully (deliberated the question). □□ **deliberately** /dɪˈlɪbərətlɪ/ adv. **deliberateness** /dɪˈlɪbərətnɪs/ n. **deliberator** /dɪˈlɪbəˌreɪtə(r)/ n. [L deliberatus past part. of deliberare (as DE-, librare weigh f. libra balance)]

deliberation /dɪˌlɪbəˈreɪʃ(ə)n/ n. 1 careful consideration. 2 a the discussion of reasons for and against. b a debate or discussion. 3 a caution and care. b (of movement) slowness or ponderousness. [ME f. OF f. L deliberatio -onis (as DELIBERATE)]

deliberative /dɪˈlɪbərətɪv/ adj. of, or appointed for the purpose of, deliberation or debate (a deliberative assembly). □□ **deliberatively** adv. **deliberativeness** n. [F délibératif -ive or L deliberativus (as DELIBERATE)]

Delibes /dəˈliːb/, (Clément Philibert) Léo (1836–91), French composer and organist. He wrote a number of operas and operettas, but his best-known works are the ballets Coppélia (1870) and Sylvia (1876).

delicacy /ˈdelɪkəsɪ/ n. (pl. -ies) 1 (esp. in craftsmanship or artistic or natural beauty) fineness or intricacy of structure or texture; gracefulness. 2 susceptibility to injury or disease; weakness. 3 the quality of requiring discretion or sensitivity (a situation of some delicacy). 4 a choice or expensive food. 5 a consideration for the feelings of others. b avoidance of immodesty or vulgarity. 6 (esp. in a person, a sense, or an instrument) accuracy of perception; sensitiveness. [ME f. DELICATE + -ACY]

delicate /ˈdelɪkət/ adj. 1 a fine in texture or structure; soft, slender, or slight. b of exquisite quality or workmanship. c (of colour) subtle or subdued; not bright. d subtle, hard to appreciate. 2 (of a person) easily injured; susceptible to illness. 3 a requiring careful handling; tricky (a delicate situation). b (of an instrument) highly sensitive. 4 deft (a delicate touch). 5 (of a person) avoiding the immodest or offensive. 6 (esp. of actions) considerate. 7 (of food) dainty; suitable for an invalid. □ **in a delicate condition** archaic pregnant. □□ **delicately** adv. **delicateness** n. [ME f. OF delicat or L delicatus, of unkn. orig.]

delicatessen /ˌdelɪkəˈtes(ə)n/ n. 1 a shop selling cooked meats, cheeses, and unusual or foreign prepared foods. 2 (often attrib.) such foods collectively (a delicatessen counter). [G Delikatessen or Du. delicatessen f. F délicatesse f. délicat (as DELICATE)]

delicious /dɪˈlɪʃəs/ adj. 1 highly delightful and enjoyable to the taste or sense of smell. 2 (of a joke etc.) very witty. □□ **deliciously** adv. **deliciousness** n. [ME f. OF f. LL deliciosus f. L deliciae delight]

delict /dɪˈlɪkt, ˈdiː-/ n. archaic a violation of the law; an offence. [L delictum neut. past part. of delinquere offend (as DE-, linquere leave)]

delight /dɪˈlaɪt/ v. & n. —v. 1 tr. (often foll. by with) please greatly (the gift delighted them; was delighted that you won; delighted with the result). 2 intr. (often foll. by in, or to + infin.) take great pleasure; be highly pleased (delighted in her success; was delighted to help). —n. 1 great pleasure. 2 something giving pleasure (her singing is a delight). □□ **delighted** adj. **delightedly** adv. [ME f. OF delitier, delit, f. L delectare frequent. of delicere: alt. after light etc.]

delightful /dɪˈlaɪtfʊl/ adj. causing great delight; pleasant, charming. □□ **delightfully** adv. **delightfulness** n.

Delilah /dɪˈlaɪlə/ n. a seductive and wily temptress. [Delilah, woman who betrayed Samson to the Philistines (Judges 16)]

delimit /dɪˈlɪmɪt/ v.tr. (**delimited, delimiting**) 1 determine the limits of. 2 fix the territorial boundary of. □□ **delimitation** /-ˈteɪʃ(ə)n/ n. [F délimiter f. L delimitare (as DE-, limitare f. limes -itis boundary)]

delimitate /dɪˈlɪmɪˌteɪt/ v.tr. = DELIMIT.

delineate /dɪˈlɪnɪˌeɪt/ v.tr. portray by drawing etc. or in words (delineated her character). □□ **delineation** /-ˈeɪʃ(ə)n/ n. **delineator** n. [L delineare delineat- (as DE-, lineare f. linea line)]

delinquency /dɪˈlɪŋkwənsɪ/ n. (pl. -ies) 1 a a crime, usu. not of a serious kind; a misdeed. b minor crime in general, esp. that of young people (juvenile delinquency). 2 wickedness (moral delinquency; an act of delinquency). 3 neglect of one's duty. [eccl. L delinquentia f. L delinquens part. of delinquere (as DELICT)]

delinquent /dɪ'lɪŋkwənt/ n. & adj. —n. an offender (*juvenile delinquent*). —adj. **1** guilty of a minor crime or a misdeed. **2** failing in one's duty. **3** US in arrears. □□ **delinquently** adv.

deliquesce /ˌdelɪ'kwes/ v.intr. **1** become liquid, melt. **2** Chem. dissolve in water absorbed from the air. □□ **deliquescence** n. **deliquescent** adj. [L *deliquescere* (as DE-, *liquescere* incept. of *liquēre* be liquid)]

delirious /dɪ'lɪrɪəs/ adj. **1** affected with delirium; temporarily or apparently mad; raving. **2** wildly excited, ecstatic. **3** (of behaviour) betraying delirium or ecstasy. □□ **deliriously** adv.

delirium /dɪ'lɪrɪəm/ n. **1** an acutely disordered state of mind involving incoherent speech, hallucinations, and frenzied excitement, occurring in metabolic disorders, intoxication, fever, etc. **2** great excitement, ecstasy. □ **delirium tremens** /'triːmenz/ a psychosis of chronic alcoholism involving tremors and hallucinations. [L f. *delirare* be deranged (as DE-, *lira* ridge between furrows)]

Delius /'diːlɪəs/, Frederick (1862–1934), English composer, born in Yorkshire of German parents, who spent his life abroad, settling in France in the 1890s. From 1928, left paralysed, blind, and helpless after what was thought to be an attack of syphilis, he transmitted his work through the medium of a Yorkshireman, Eric Fenby. Best known for such pastoral works as *Brigg Fair* (1907) and *On Hearing the First Cuckoo in Spring* (1912), Delius also wrote two operas which are still performed, *A Village Romeo and Juliet* (1900–1) and *Fennimore and Gerda* (1909–10), which, together with his songs, reveals his love of Scandinavian life and literature: he had visited Norway in 1887 and there became a close friend of Grieg.

deliver /dɪ'lɪvə(r)/ v.tr. **1 a** distribute (letters, parcels, ordered goods, etc.) to the addressee or the purchaser. **b** (often foll. by *to*) hand over (*delivered the boy safely to his teacher*). **2** (often foll. by *from*) save, rescue, or set free (*delivered him from his enemies*). **3 a** give birth to (*delivered a girl*). **b** (in passive; often foll. by *of*) give birth (*was delivered of a child*). **c** assist at the birth of (*delivered six babies that week*). **d** assist in giving birth (*delivered the patient successfully*). **4 a** (often *refl.*) utter or recite (an opinion, a speech, etc.) (*delivered himself of the observation; delivered the sermon well*). **b** (of a judge) pronounce (a judgement). **5** (often foll. by *up*, *over*) abandon; resign; hand over (*delivered his soul up to God*). **6** present or render (an account). **7** launch or aim (a blow, a ball, or an attack). **8** Law hand over formally (esp. a sealed deed to a grantee). **9** colloq. = *deliver the goods*. **10** US cause (voters etc.) to support a candidate. □ **deliver the goods** colloq. carry out one's part of an agreement. □□ **deliverable** adj. **deliverer** n. [ME f. OF *delivrer* f. Gallo-Roman (as DE-, LIBERATE)]

deliverance /dɪ'lɪvərəns/ n. **1 a** the act or an instance of rescuing; the process of being rescued. **b** a rescue. **2 a** formally expressed opinion. [ME f. OF *delivrance* (as DELIVER)]

delivery /dɪ'lɪvərɪ/ n. (pl. **-ies**) **1 a** the delivering of letters etc. **b** a regular distribution of letters etc. (*two deliveries a day*). **c** something delivered. **2 a** the process of childbirth. **b** an act of this. **3** deliverance. **4 a** an act of throwing, esp. of a cricket ball. **b** the style of such an act (*a good delivery*). **5** the act of giving or surrendering (*delivery of the town to the enemy*). **6 a** the uttering of a speech etc. **b** the manner or style of such a delivery (*a measured delivery*). **7** Law **a** the formal handing over of property. **b** the transfer of a deed to a grantee or a third party. □ **take delivery of** receive (something purchased). [ME f. AF *delivree* fem. past part. of *delivrer* (as DELIVER)]

dell /del/ n. a small *usu.* wooded hollow or valley. [OE f. Gmc]

Della Cruscan /ˌdelə 'krʌskən/ adj. & n. —adj. **1** of or relating to the Academy della Crusca in Florence, concerned with the purity of Italian. **2** of or concerning a late 18th-c. school of English poets with an artificial style. —n. a member of the Academy della Crusca or the late 18th-c. school of English poets. [It. (*Accademia*) *della Crusca* (Academy) of the bran (with ref. to sifting)]

Della Robbia /ˌdelə 'rɒbɪə/, Luca (1400–82), Florentine sculptor, trained in the workshop of Florence cathedral, for which he executed a marble *Singing Gallery* of child musicians (1431–8) in his characteristically sweet and charming style. He

invented vitreous glazes to colour sculpture modelled in terracotta, thus making it possible for polychromatic sculpture to be used in outdoor settings without suffering from damp. The workshop, and the secret of the technique, were passed on to his nephew, Andrea (1434–1525), but the later productions of the family declined in quality as a result of mass production.

delocalize /diː'ləʊkəˌlaɪz/ v.tr. (also **-ise**) **1 a** detach or remove (a thing) from its place. **b** not limit to a particular location. **2** (as **delocalized** adj.) Chem. (of electrons) shared among more than two atoms in a molecule. □□ **delocalization** /-'zeɪʃ(ə)n/ n.

Delos /'diːlɒs/ a small island regarded as the centre of the Cyclades. According to legend the birthplace of Apollo and Artemis, it was from earliest historical times sacred to Apollo.

delouse /diː'laʊs/ v.tr. rid (a person or animal) of lice.

Delphi /'delfɪ, -faɪ/ (Greek **Dhelfoi** /ðel'fiː/) one of the most important religious sanctuaries of the ancient Greek world, dedicated to Apollo and situated on the lower southern slopes of Mt. Parnassus above the Gulf of Corinth. Reputedly the navel of the earth, it was the seat of the Delphic Oracle, whose often riddling responses to a wide range of religious, political, and moral questions were delivered in a state of ecstasy by the Pythia, the priestess of Apollo; a male prophet put the question to her and interpreted her answer. Influential in the earlier periods of Greek history, its influence declined in Hellenistic times although it was still a centre of information for the Greek world. Under the Roman Empire there were other oracles and other methods of divination (e.g. astrology) which provided alternative sources of prophecy, and its decline was almost complete when Christianity became the official religion under Constantine.

Delphic /'delfɪk/ adj. (also **Delphian** /-fɪən/) **1** (of an utterance, prophecy, etc.) obscure, ambiguous, or enigmatic. **2** of or concerning the ancient Greek oracle at Delphi.

delphinium /del'fɪnɪəm/ n. any ranunculaceous garden plant of the genus *Delphinium*, with tall spikes of *usu.* blue flowers. [mod.L f. Gk *delphinion* larkspur f. *delphin* dolphin]

delphinoid /'delfɪˌnɔɪd/ adj. & n. —adj. **1** of the family that includes dolphins, porpoises, grampuses, etc. **2** dolphin-like. —n. **1** a member of the delphinoid family of aquatic mammals. **2** a dolphin-like animal. [Gk *delphinoeidēs* f. *delphin* dolphin]

delta /'deltə/ n. **1** a triangular tract of deposited earth, alluvium, etc., at the mouth of a river, formed by its diverging outlets. **2 a** the fourth letter of the Greek alphabet (Δ, δ). **b** a fourth-class mark given for a piece of work or in an examination. **3** Astron. the fourth star in a constellation. **4** Math. an increment of a variable. □ **delta connection** Electr. a triangular arrangement of three-phase windings with circuit wire from each angle. **delta rays** Physics rays of low penetrative power consisting of slow electrons ejected from an atom by the impact of ionizing radiation. **delta rhythm** (or **wave**) low-frequency electrical activity of the brain during sleep. **delta wing** the triangular swept-back wing of an aircraft. □□ **deltaic** /del'teɪɪk/ adj. [ME f. Gk f. Phoen. *daleth*]

deltiology /ˌdeltɪ'ɒlədʒɪ/ n. the collecting and study of postcards. □□ **deltiologist** n. [Gk *deltion* dimin. of *deltos* writing-tablet + -LOGY]

deltoid /'deltɔɪd/ adj. & n. —adj. triangular; like a river delta. —n. (in full **deltoid muscle**) a thick triangular muscle covering the shoulder joint and used for raising the arm away from the body. [F *deltoïde* or mod.L *deltoides* f. Gk *deltoeidēs* (as DELTA, -OID)]

delude /dɪ'luːd, -'ljuːd/ v.tr. deceive or mislead (*deluded by false optimism*). □□ **deluder** n. [ME f. L *deludere* mock (as DE-, *ludere lus-* play)]

deluge /'deljuːdʒ/ n. & v. —n. **1** a great flood. **2** (**the Deluge**) the biblical Flood (Gen. 6–8). **3** a great outpouring (of words, paper, etc.). **4** a heavy fall of rain. —v.tr. **1** flood. **2** inundate with a great number or amount (*deluged with complaints*). [ME f. OF f. L *diluvium*, rel. to *lavare* wash]

delusion /dɪ'luːʒ(ə)n, -'ljuːʒ(ə)n/ n. **1** a false belief or impression. **2** Psychol. this as a symptom or form of mental disorder. □

æ cat ɑ: arm e bed ɜ: her ɪ sit iː see ɒ hot ɔ: saw ʌ run ʊ put uː too ə ago aɪ my

delusions of grandeur a false idea of oneself as being important, noble, famous, etc. □□ **delusional** adj. [ME f. LL delusio (as DELUDE)]

delusive /dɪˈluːsɪv, -ˈljuːsɪv/ adj. **1** deceptive or unreal. **2** disappointing. □□ **delusively** adv. **delusiveness** n.

delusory /dɪˈluːsərɪ, dɪˈljuː-/ adj. = DELUSIVE. [LL delusorius (as DELUSION)]

delustre /diːˈlʌstə(r)/ v.tr. (US **deluster**) remove the lustre from (a textile).

de luxe /də ˈlʌks, ˈluks/ adj. **1** luxurious or sumptuous. **2** of a superior kind. [F, = of luxury]

delve /delv/ v. **1** intr. (often foll. by in, into) **a** search energetically (delved into his pocket). **b** make a laborious search in documents etc.; research (delved into his family history). **2** tr. & intr. poet. dig. □□ **delver** n. [OE delfan f. WG]

Dem. abbr. US Democrat.

demagnetize /diːˈmæɡnɪˌtaɪz/ v.tr. (also **-ise**) remove the magnetic properties of. □□ **demagnetization** /-ˈzeɪʃ(ə)n/ n. **demagnetizer** n.

demagogue /ˈdeməˌɡɒɡ/ n. (US **-gog**) **1** a political agitator appealing to the basest instincts of a mob. **2** hist. a leader of the people, esp. in ancient times. □□ **demagogic** /-ˈɡɒɡɪk/ adj. **demagoguery** /-ˈɡɒɡərɪ/ n. **demagogy** /-ˈɡɒɡɪ/ n. [Gk dēmagōgos f. dēmos the people + agōgos leading]

demand /dɪˈmɑːnd/ n. & v. —n. **1** an insistent and peremptory request, made as of right. **2** Econ. the desire of purchasers or consumers for a commodity (no demand for solid tyres these days). **3** an urgent claim (care of her mother makes demands on her). —v.tr. **1** (often foll. by of, from, or to + infin., or that + clause) ask for (something) insistently and urgently, as of right (demanded to know; demanded five pounds from him; demanded that his wife be present). **2** require or need (a task demanding skill). **3** insist on being told (demanded her business). **4** (as **demanding** adj.) making demands; requiring skill, effort, etc. (a demanding but worthwhile job). □ **demand feeding** the practice of feeding a baby when it cries for a feed rather than at set times. **demand note 1 a** written request for payment. **2** US a bill payable at sight. **demand pull** Econ. available money as a factor causing economic inflation. **in demand** sought after. **on demand** as soon as a demand is made (a cheque payable on demand). □□ **demandable** adj. **demander** n. **demandingly** adv. [ME f. OF demande (n.), demander (v.) f. L demandare entrust (as DE-, mandare order: see MANDATE)]

demantoid /dɪˈmæntɔɪd/ n. a lustrous green garnet. [G]

demarcation /ˌdiːmɑːˈkeɪʃ(ə)n/ n. **1** the act of marking a boundary or limits. **2** the trade-union practice of strictly assigning specific jobs to different unions. □ **demarcation dispute** an inter-union dispute about who does a particular job. □□ **demarcate** /ˈdiː-/ v.tr. **demarcator** /ˈdiː-/ n. [Sp. demarcación f. demarcar mark the bounds of (as DE-, MARK¹)]

démarche /deɪˈmɑːʃ/ n. a political step or initiative. [F f. démarcher take steps (as DE-, MARCH¹)]

dematerialize /ˌdiːməˈtɪərɪəˌlaɪz/ v.tr. & intr. (also **-ise**) make or become non-material or spiritual (esp. of psychic phenomena etc.). □□ **dematerialization** /-ˈzeɪʃ(ə)n/ n.

deme /diːm/ n. **1 a** a political division of Attica in ancient Greece. **b** an administrative division in modern Greece. **2** Biol. a local population of closely related plants or animals. [Gk dēmos the people]

demean¹ /dɪˈmiːn/ v.tr. (usu. refl.) lower the dignity of (would not demean myself to take it). [DE- + MEAN², after debase]

demean² /dɪˈmiːn/ v.refl. (with adv.) behave (demeaned himself well). [ME f. OF demener f. Rmc (as DE-, L minare drive animals f. minari threaten)]

demeanour /dɪˈmiːnə(r)/ n. (US **demeanor**) outward behaviour or bearing. [DEMEAN², prob. after obs. havour behaviour]

dement /dɪˈment/ n. archaic a demented person. [orig. adj. f. F dément or L demens (as DEMENTED)]

demented /dɪˈmentɪd/ adj. mad; crazy. □□ **dementedly** adv. **dementedness** n. [past part. of dement verb f. OF dementer or f.

LL dementare f. demens out of one's mind (as DE-, mens mentis mind)]

démenti /deɪˈmɑtɪ/ n. an official denial of a rumour etc. [F f. démentir accuse of lying]

dementia /dɪˈmenʃə/ n. Med. a chronic or persistent disorder of the mental processes marked by memory disorders, personality changes, impaired reasoning, etc., due to brain disease or injury. □ **dementia praecox** /ˈpriːkɒks/ schizophrenia. [L f. demens (as DEMENTED)]

demerara /ˌdeməˈreərə/ n. light-brown cane sugar coming orig. and chiefly from Demerara. [Demerara in Guyana]

demerit /diːˈmerɪt/ n. **1** a quality or action deserving blame; a fault. **2** US a mark given to an offender. □□ **demeritorious** /-ˈtɔːrɪəs/ adj. [ME f. OF de(s)merite or L demeritum neut. past part. of demereri deserve]

demersal /dɪˈmɜːs(ə)l/ adj. (of a fish etc.) being or living near the sea-bottom (cf. PELAGIC). [L demersus past part. of demergere (as DE-, mergere plunge)]

demesne /dɪˈmiːn, -ˈmeɪn/ n. **1 a** a sovereign's or State's territory; a domain. **b** land attached to a mansion etc. **c** landed property; an estate. **2** (usu. foll. by of) a region or sphere. **3** Law hist. possession (of real property) as one's own. □ **held in demesne** (of an estate) occupied by the owner, not by tenants. [ME f. AF, OF demeine (later AF demesne) belonging to a lord f. L dominicus (as DOMINICAL)]

Demeter /dɪˈmiːtə(r)/ Gk Mythol. the corn-goddess, identified in Italy with Ceres, daughter of Cronos and mother of Persephone. [Gk mētēr mother]

demi- /ˈdemɪ/ prefix **1** half; half-size. **2** partially or imperfectly such (demigod). [ME f. F f. med.L dimedius half, for L dimidius]

demigod /ˈdemɪˌɡɒd/ n. (fem. **-goddess** /-ˌɡɒdɪs/) **1 a** a partly divine being. **b** the offspring of a god or goddess and a mortal. **2** colloq. a person of compelling beauty, powers, or personality.

demijohn /ˈdemɪˌdʒɒn/ n. a bulbous narrow-necked bottle holding from 3 to 10 gallons and usu. in a wicker cover. [prob. corrupt. of F dame-jeanne Lady Jane, assim. to DEMI- + the name John]

demilitarize /diːˈmɪlɪtəˌraɪz/ v.tr. (also **-ise**) remove a military organization or forces from (a frontier, a zone, etc.). □□ **demilitarization** /-ˈzeɪʃ(ə)n/ n.

De Mille /də ˈmɪl/, Cecil Blount (1881–1959), American film producer-director. In 1915 he created in Carmen the first of the lavish spectacles that were to become synonymous with his name. The Ten Commandments (1923) was his best-known film; he remade it more than 30 years later. The Bible also provided the source material for The King of Kings (1927), The Sign of the Cross (1932), and Samson and Delilah (1949), history inspired Cleopatra (1934) and The Crusades (1935), while The Plainsman (1937) and Union Pacific (1939) were westerns. The quintessential Hollywood showman, he displayed unrivalled skill in creating spectacular effects and handling crowds.

demi-mondaine /ˈdemɪmɒnˌdeɪn, -mɔ̃ˌdeɪn/ n. a woman of a demi-monde.

demi-monde /ˈdemɪˌmɒnd, -ˈmɔ̃d/ n. **1 a** hist. a class of women in 19th-c. France considered to be of doubtful social standing and morality. **b** a similar class of women in any society. **2** any group considered to be on the fringes of respectable society. [F, = half-world]

demineralize /diːˈmɪnərəˌlaɪz/ v.tr. (also **-ise**) remove salts from (sea water etc.). □□ **demineralization** /-ˈzeɪʃ(ə)n/ n.

demi-pension /dəmɪˈpɑ̃sjɔ̃/ n. hotel accommodation with bed, breakfast, and one main meal per day. [F (as DEMI-, PENSION²)]

demirep /ˈdemɪˌrep/ n. archaic a woman of doubtful sexual reputation. [abbr. of demi-reputable]

demise /dɪˈmaɪz/ n. & v. —n. **1** death (left a will on her demise; the demise of the agreement). **2** Law conveyance or transfer (of property, a title, etc.) by demising. —v.tr. Law **1** convey or grant (an estate) by will or lease. **2** transmit (a title etc.) by death. [AF use of past part. of OF de(s)mettre DISMISS, in refl. abdicate]

demisemiquaver /ˌdemɪˈsemɪˌkweɪvə(r), ˈdemɪ-/ n. Mus. a note having the time value of half a semiquaver and represented by a large dot with a three-hooked stem. Also called *thirty-second note*.

demist /di:ˈmɪst/ v.tr. clear mist from (a windscreen etc.). □□ **demister** n.

demit /dɪˈmɪt/ v.tr. (**demitted, demitting**) (often *absol.*) resign or abdicate (an office etc.). □□ **demission** /-ˈmɪʃ(ə)n/ n. [F *démettre* f. L *demittere* (as DE-, *mittere miss-* send)]

demitasse /ˈdemɪˌtæs, dəmɪˈtæs/ n. **1** a small coffee-cup. **2** its contents. [F, = half-cup]

demiurge /ˈdemɪˌɜːdʒ/ n. **1** (in the philosophy of Plato) the creator of the universe. **2** (in Gnosticism etc.) a heavenly being subordinate to the Supreme Being. □□ **demiurgic** /-ˈɜːdʒɪk/ adj. [eccl.L f. Gk *dēmiourgos* craftsman f. *dēmios* public f. *dēmos* people + *-ergos* working]

demo /ˈdemoʊ/ n. (pl. **-os**) colloq. = DEMONSTRATION 2, 3. [abbr.]

demob /di:ˈmɒb/ v. & n. Brit. colloq. —v.tr. (**demobbed, demobbing**) demobilize. —n. demobilization. [abbr.]

demobilize /di:ˈmoʊbɪˌlaɪz/ v.tr. (also **-ise**) disband (troops, ships, etc.). □□ **demobilization** /-ˈzeɪʃ(ə)n/ n. [F *démobiliser* (as DE-, MOBILIZE)]

democracy /dɪˈmɒkrəsɪ/ n. (pl. **-ies**) **1 a** a system of government by the whole population, usu. through elected representatives. **b** a State so governed. **c** any organization governed on democratic principles. **2** a classless and tolerant form of society. **3** US **a** the principles of the Democratic Party. **b** its members. [F *démocratie* f. LL *democratia* f. Gk *dēmokratia* f. *dēmos* the people + -CRACY]

democrat /ˈdeməˌkræt/ n. **1** an advocate of democracy. **2** (**Democrat**) (in the US) a member of the Democratic Party. □□ **democratism** /dɪˈmɒkrəˌtɪz(ə)m/ n. [F *démocrate* (as DEMOCRACY), after *aristocrate*]

democratic /ˌdeməˈkrætɪk/ adj. **1** of, like, practising, advocating, or constituting democracy or a democracy. **2** favouring social equality. □ **democratic centralism** an organizational system in which policy is decided centrally and is binding on all members. **Democratic Party** one of the two main US political parties (the other being the Republican Party). The name dates from c.1828, but the party existed earlier under other names; it claims Thomas Jefferson as its founder. In modern times the party is broadly liberal, supporting social reform and international commitment. □□ **democratically** adv. [F *démocratique* f. med.L *democraticus* f. Gk *dēmokratikos* f. *dēmokratia* DEMOCRACY]

democratize /dɪˈmɒkrəˌtaɪz/ v.tr. (also **-ise**) make (a State, institution, etc.) democratic. □□ **democratization** /-ˈzeɪʃ(ə)n/ n.

Democritus /dɪˈmɒkrɪtəs/ (5th c. BC) Greek philosopher, one of the founders of the atomic theory, according to which all things in an infinite universe are composed of the random groupings of atoms moving in a void. The later sobriquet 'the laughing philosopher' alludes to his ethical ideal of cheerfulness.

démodé /ˌdeɪmɒˈdeɪ/ adj. out of fashion. [F, past part. of *démoder* (as DE-, *mode* fashion)]

demodulate /di:ˈmɒdjʊˌleɪt/ v.tr. Physics extract (a modulating signal) from its carrier. □□ **demodulation** /ˌdi:mɒdjʊˈleɪʃ(ə)n/ n. **demodulator** n.

demography /dɪˈmɒɡrəfɪ/ n. the study of the statistics of births, deaths, disease, etc., as illustrating the conditions of life in communities. □□ **demographer** n. **demographic** /ˌdeməˈɡræfɪk/ adj. **demographical** /ˌdeməˈɡræfɪk(ə)l/ adj. **demographically** /ˌdeməˈɡræfɪkəlɪ/ adv. [Gk *dēmos* the people + -GRAPHY]

demoiselle /ˌdemwæˈzel/ n. **1** Zool. a small crane, *Anthropoides virgo*, native to Asia and N. Africa. **2 a** a damselfly. **b** a damselfish. **3** archaic a young woman. [F, = DAMSEL]

demolish /dɪˈmɒlɪʃ/ v.tr. **1 a** pull down (a building). **b** completely destroy or break. **2** overthrow (an institution). **3** refute (an argument, theory, etc.). **4** joc. eat up completely and quickly. □□ **demolisher** n. **demolition** /ˌdeməˈlɪʃ(ə)n/ n. **demolitionist** /ˌdeməˈlɪʃənɪst/ n. [F *démolir* f. L *demoliri* (as DE-, *moliri* molit- construct f. *moles* mass)]

demon /ˈdi:mən/ n. **1 a** an evil spirit or devil, esp. one thought

to possess a person. **b** the personification of evil passion. **2** a malignant supernatural being; the Devil. **3** (often *attrib.*) a forceful, fierce, or skilful performer (*a demon on the tennis court; a demon player*). **4** a cruel or destructive person. **5** (also **daemon**) **a** an inner or attendant spirit; a genius (*the demon of creativity*). **b** a supernatural being in ancient Greece. □ **demon bowler** *Cricket* a very fast bowler. **a demon for work** colloq. a person who works strenuously. [ME f. med.L *demon* f. L *daemon* f. Gk *daimōn* deity]

demonetize /di:ˈmʌnɪˌtaɪz/ v.tr. (also **-ise**) withdraw (a coin etc.) from use as money. □□ **demonetization** /-ˈzeɪʃ(ə)n/ n. [F *démonétiser* (as DE-, L *moneta* MONEY)]

demoniac /dɪˈmoʊnɪˌæk/ adj. & n. —adj. **1** fiercely energetic or frenzied. **2 a** supposedly possessed by an evil spirit. **b** of or concerning such possession. **3** of or like demons. —n. a person possessed by an evil spirit. □□ **demoniacal** /ˌdi:məˈnaɪək(ə)l/ adj. **demoniacally** /ˌdi:məˈnaɪəkəlɪ/ adv. [ME f. OF *demoniaque* f. eccl.L *daemoniacus* f. *daemonium* f. Gk *daimonion* dimin. of *daimōn*: see DEMON)]

demonic /dɪˈmɒnɪk/ adj. (also **daemonic**) **1** = DEMONIAC. **2** having or seeming to have supernatural genius or power. [LL *daemonicus* f. Gk *daimonikos* (as DEMON)]

demonism /ˈdi:məˌnɪz(ə)m/ n. belief in the power of demons.

demonize /ˈdi:məˌnaɪz/ v.tr. (also **-ise**) **1** make into or like a demon. **2** represent as a demon.

demonolatry /ˌdi:məˈnɒlətrɪ/ n. the worship of demons.

demonology /ˌdi:məˈnɒlədʒɪ/ n. the study of demons etc. □□ **demonologist** n.

demonstrable /ˈdemɒnstrəb(ə)l, dɪˈmɒnstrəb(ə)l/ adj. capable of being shown or logically proved. □□ **demonstrability** /-ˈbɪlɪtɪ/ n. **demonstrably** adv. [ME f. L *demonstrabilis* (as DEMONSTRATE)]

demonstrate /ˈdemənˌstreɪt/ v. **1** tr. show evidence of (feelings etc.). **2** tr. describe and explain (a scientific proposition, machine, etc.) by experiment, practical use, etc. **3** tr. **a** logically prove the truth of. **b** be proof of the existence of. **4** intr. take part in or organize a public demonstration. **5** intr. act as a demonstrator. [L *demonstrare* (as DE-, *monstrare* show)]

demonstration /ˌdemənˈstreɪʃ(ə)n/ n. **1** (foll. by *of*) **a** the outward showing of feeling etc. **b** an instance of this. **2** a public meeting, march, etc., for a political or moral purpose. **3 a** the exhibiting or explaining of specimens or experiments as a method of esp. scientific teaching. **b** an instance of this. **4** proof provided by logic, argument, etc. **5** Mil. a show of military force. □□ **demonstrational** adj. [ME f. OF *demonstration* or L *demonstratio* (as DEMONSTRATE)]

demonstrative /dɪˈmɒnstrətɪv/ adj. & n. —adj. **1** given to or marked by an open expression of feeling, esp. of affection (*a very demonstrative person*). **2** (usu. foll. by *of*) logically conclusive; giving proof (*the work is demonstrative of their skill*). **3 a** serving to point out or exhibit. **b** involving esp. scientific demonstration (*demonstrative technique*). **4** Gram. (of an adjective or pronoun) indicating the person or thing referred to (e.g. *this, that, those*). —n. Gram. a demonstrative adjective or pronoun. □□ **demonstratively** adv. **demonstrativeness** n. [ME f. OF *demonstratif -ive* f. L *demonstrativus* (as DEMONSTRATION)]

demonstrator /ˈdemənˌstreɪtə(r)/ n. **1** a person who takes part in a political demonstration etc. **2** a person who demonstrates, esp. machines, equipment, etc., to prospective customers. **3** a person who teaches by demonstration, esp. in a laboratory etc. [L (as DEMONSTRATE)]

demoralize /dɪˈmɒrəˌlaɪz/ v.tr. (also **-ise**) **1** destroy (a person's) morale; make hopeless. **2** archaic corrupt (a person's) morals. □□ **demoralization** /-ˈzeɪʃ(ə)n/ n. **demoralizing** adj. **demoralizingly** adv. [F *démoraliser* (as DE-, MORAL)]

Demosthenes /dɪˈmɒsθəˌni:z/ (384–322 BC) the greatest Athenian orator. His political speeches are largely taken up with the cause of Greek liberty against the pretensions of Philip II of Macedon, whom he attacked in the *Philippics*. Unsurpassed in the force, directness, and flexibility of his oratory, his devotion to liberty was unquestionable, but his methods and policies

b but   d dog   f few   g get   h he   j yes   k cat   l leg   m man   n no   p pen   r red   s sit   t top   v voice

were not the best suited to attain this, and those of his opponents were no less directed to maintaining the power and independence of Athens. The real problem of his day was how the Greek city-states could be united to counter the military power of the new national State of Macedon, and failure to achieve this (except with Thebes) led to their defeat in 338 BC. Demosthenes was finally driven to suicide in exile.

demote /dɪˈməʊt, diː-/ v.tr. reduce to a lower rank or class. □□ **demotion** /-ˈməʊʃ(ə)n/ n. [DE- + PROMOTE]

demotic /dɪˈmɒtɪk/ n. & adj. —n. **1** the popular colloquial form of a language. **2** a popular simplified form of ancient Egyptian writing, a cursive script based partially on hieratic, which dates from c.650 BC and was gradually replaced by Greek in the Ptolemaic period. —adj. **1** (esp. of language) popular, colloquial, or vulgar. **2** of or concerning the ancient Egyptian or modern Greek demotic. [Gk dēmotikos f. dēmotēs one of the people (dēmos)]

demotivate /ˌdiːˈməʊtɪˌveɪt/ v.tr. (also absol.) cause to lose motivation; discourage. □□ **demotivation** /-ˈveɪʃ(ə)n/ n.

demount /diːˈmaʊnt/ v.tr. **1** take (apparatus, a gun, etc.) from its mounting. **2** dismantle for later reassembly. □□ **demountable** adj. & n. [F démonter: cf. DISMOUNT]

Dempsey /ˈdempsɪ/, William Harrison ('Jack') (1895–1983), American boxer, world heavyweight champion 1919–26.

demulcent /dɪˈmʌls(ə)nt/ adj. & n. —adj. soothing. —n. an agent that forms a protective film soothing irritation or inflammation in the mouth. [L demulcēre (as DE-, mulcēre soothe)]

demur /dɪˈmɜː(r)/ v. & n. —v.intr. (**demurred, demurring**) **1** (often foll. by to, at) raise scruples or objections. **2** Law put in a demurrer. —n. (also **demurral** /dɪˈmʌr(ə)l/) (usu. in neg.) **1** an objection (agreed without demur). **2** the act or process of objecting. □□ **demurrant** /dɪˈmʌrənt/ n. (in sense 2 of v.). [ME f. OF demeure (n.), demeurer (v.) f. Rmc (as DE-, L morari delay)]

demure /dɪˈmjʊə(r)/ adj. (**demurer, demurest**) **1** composed, quiet, and reserved; modest. **2** affectedly shy and quiet; coy. **3** decorous (a demure high collar). □□ **demurely** adv. **demureness** n. [ME, perh. f. AF demuré f. OF demoré past part. of demorer remain, stay (as DEMUR): infl. by OF meür f. L maturus ripe]

demurrable /dɪˈmʌrəb(ə)l/ adj. esp. Law open to objection.

demurrage /dɪˈmʌrɪdʒ/ n. **1 a** a rate or amount payable to a shipowner by a charterer for failure to load or discharge a ship within the time agreed. **b** a similar charge on railway trucks or goods. **2** such a detention or delay. [OF demo(u)rage f. demorer (as DEMUR)]

demurrer /dɪˈmʌrə(r)/ n. Law an objection raised or exception taken. [AF (infin. as noun), = DEMUR]

demy /dɪˈmaɪ/ n. Printing a size of paper, 564 × 444 mm. [ME, var. of DEMI-]

demystify /diːˈmɪstɪˌfaɪ/ v.tr. (**-ies, -ied**) **1** clarify (obscure beliefs or subjects etc.). **2** reduce or remove the irrationality in (a person). □□ **demystification** /-fɪˈkeɪʃ(ə)n/ n.

demythologize /ˌdiːmɪˈθɒləˌdʒaɪz/ v.tr. (also **-ise**) **1** remove mythical elements from (a legend, famous person's life, etc.). **2** reinterpret what some consider to be the mythological elements in (the Bible). (See BULTMANN.)

den /den/ n. **1** a wild animal's lair. **2** a place of crime or vice (den of iniquity; opium den). **3** a small private room for pursuing a hobby etc. [OE denn f. Gmc, rel. to DEAN²]

denarius /dɪˈneərɪəs/ n. (pl. **denarii** /-rɪˌaɪ/) an ancient Roman silver coin. [L, = (coin) of ten asses (as DENARY: see AS²)]

denary /ˈdiːnərɪ/ adj. of ten; decimal. □ **denary scale** = decimal scale. [L denarius containing ten (deni by tens)]

denationalize /diːˈnæʃənəˌlaɪz/ v.tr. (also **-ise**) **1** transfer (a nationalized industry or institution etc.) from public to private ownership. **2 a** deprive (a nation) of its status or characteristics as a nation. **b** deprive (a person) of nationality or national characteristics. □□ **denationalization** /-ˈzeɪʃ(ə)n/ n. [F dénationaliser (as DE-, NATIONAL)]

denaturalize /diːˈnætʃərəˌlaɪz/ v.tr. (also **-ise**) **1** change the nature or properties of; make unnatural. **2** deprive of the rights of citizenship. **3** = DENATURE v. **1**. □□ **denaturalization** /-ˈzeɪʃ(ə)n/ n.

denature /diːˈneɪtʃə(r)/ v.tr. **1** change the properties of (a protein etc.) by heat, acidity, etc. **2** make (alcohol) unfit for drinking esp. by the addition of another substance. □□ **denaturant** n. **denaturation** /diːˌnætʃəˈreɪʃ(ə)n/ n. [F dénaturer (as DE-, NATURE)]

dendrite /ˈdendraɪt/ n. **1 a** a stone or mineral with natural treelike or mosslike markings. **b** such marks on stones or minerals. **2** Chem. a crystal with branching treelike growth. **3** Zool. & Anat. a branching process of a nerve-cell conducting signals to a cell body. [F f. Gk dendritēs (adj.) f. dendron tree]

dendritic /denˈdrɪtɪk/ adj. **1** of or like a dendrite. **2** treelike in shape or markings. □□ **dendritically** adv.

dendrochronology /ˌdendrəʊkrəˈnɒlədʒɪ/ n. **1** a system of dating using the characteristic patterns of annual growth rings of trees to assign dates to timber. Trees add a ring of growth each year, and variations in climate affect the width of these rings, with a dry year producing limited growth and a wet year luxuriant growth and a broader ring. By matching sequences of these rings from a tree of known date (e.g. one still alive) with those from an earlier (dead) tree overlapping in age, a master plot of tree-ring patterns can be built up, and timber of unknown date from within the area of this plot can be dated exactly by matching its rings. **2** the study of these growth rings. □□ **dendrochronological** /-ˌkrɒnəˈlɒdʒɪk(ə)l/ adj. **dendrochronologist** n. [Gk dendron tree + CHRONOLOGY]

dendroid /ˈdendrɔɪd/ adj. tree-shaped. [Gk dendrōdēs treelike + -OID]

dendrology /denˈdrɒlədʒɪ/ n. the scientific study of trees. □□ **dendrological** /-drəˈlɒdʒɪk(ə)l/ adj. **dendrologist** n. [Gk dendron tree + -LOGY]

dene¹ /diːn/ n. (also **dean**) Brit. **1** a narrow wooded valley. **2** a vale (esp. as the ending of place-names). [OE denu, rel. to DEN]

dene² /diːn/ n. Brit. a bare sandy tract, or a low sand-hill, by the sea. [orig. unkn.: cf. DUNE]

dengue /ˈdeŋgɪ/ n. an infectious viral disease of the tropics causing a fever and acute pains in the joints. [W. Ind. Sp., f. Swahili denga, dinga, with assim. to Sp. dengue fastidiousness, with ref. to the stiffness of the patient's neck and shoulders]

Deng Xiaoping /deŋ ʃaʊˈpɪŋ/ (also **Teng Hsiao-p'ing**) (1904–) Chinese Communist statesman, who held various prominent posts until he was discredited during the Cultural Revolution. Reinstated in 1977, he became the most prominent exponent of economic modernization, and improved relations with the West. Since then he has been the effective leader of China, with senior government posts in the hands of his supporters.

Den Haag see the HAGUE.

deniable /dɪˈnaɪəb(ə)l/ adj. that may be denied.

denial /dɪˈnaɪəl/ n. **1** the act or an instance of denying. **2** a refusal of a request or wish. **3** a statement that a thing is not true; a rejection (denial of the accusation). **4** a disavowal of a person as one's leader etc. **5** = SELF-DENIAL.

denier /ˈdenjə(r)/ n. a unit of weight by which the fineness of silk, rayon, or nylon yarn is measured. [orig. the name of a small coin: ME f. OF f. L denarius]

denigrate /ˈdenɪˌgreɪt/ v.tr. defame or disparage the reputation of (a person); blacken. □□ **denigration** /-ˈgreɪʃ(ə)n/ n. **denigrator** n. **denigratory** /-ˈgreɪtərɪ/ adj. [L denigrare (as DE-, nigrare f. niger black)]

denim /ˈdenɪm/ n. **1** (often attrib.) a usu. blue hard-wearing cotton twill fabric used for jeans, overalls, etc. (a denim skirt). **2** (in pl.) colloq. jeans, overalls, etc. made of this. [for serge de Nim f. Nîmes in S. France]

Denis¹ /deˈniː/, Maurice (1870–1943), French painter, designer, and writer on art theory, a leading member of the Nabis. A devout Roman Catholic, he set himself to revive religious painting; he also designed stained glass.

Denis² /ˈdenɪs/, St (c.250), patron saint of France. According to a 6th-c. biography he was one of a group of seven sent to convert Gaul, became bishop of Paris, and was martyred. He was later identified with Dionysius the Areopagite. Feast day, 9 Oct.

denitrify /diːˈnaɪtrɪˌfaɪ/ v.tr. (**-ies, -ied**) remove the nitrates or nitrites from (soil etc.). □□ **denitrification** /-fɪˈkeɪʃ(ə)n/ n.

denizen /ˈdenɪz(ə)n/ n. **1** a foreigner admitted to certain rights in his or her adopted country. **2** a naturalized foreign word, animal, or plant. **3** (usu. foll. by of) poet. an inhabitant or occupant. □□ **denizenship** n. [ME f. AF deinzein f. OF deinz within f. L de from + intus within + -ein f. L -aneus: see -ANEOUS]

Denmark /ˈdenmɑːk/ a Scandinavian country consisting of the greater part of the Jutland peninsula and the neighbouring islands, between the North Sea and the Baltic; pop. (est. 1988) 5,125,700; official language, Danish; capital, Copenhagen. Denmark emerged as a separate country during the Viking period of the 10th and 11th c. In the 14th c. Denmark and Norway were united under a Danish king, the union being joined between 1389–97 and 1523 by Sweden. Territory was lost to Sweden as a result of wars in the mid-17th c. and Norway was ceded to Sweden after the Napoleonic Wars. More territory was lost to the south when Schleswig-Holstein was taken by Prussia in 1864 (although the northern part of Schleswig was returned to Denmark in 1920). Denmark remained neutral in the First World War, but was occupied by the Germans for much of the Second. Since the war, however, Denmark has been stable and prosperous, her economy built largely around agriculture, particularly dairy products.

denominate /dɪˈnɒmɪˌneɪt/ v.tr. **1** give a name to. **2** call or describe (a person or thing) as. [L denominare (as DE-, NOMINATE)]

denomination /dɪˌnɒmɪˈneɪʃ(ə)n/ n. **1** a Church or religious sect. **2** a class of units within a range or sequence of numbers, weights, money, etc. (money of small denominations). **3 a** a name or designation, esp. a characteristic or class name. **b** a class or kind having a specific name. **4** the rank of a playing-card within a suit, or of a suit relative to others. □ **denominational education** education according to the principles of a Church or sect. □□ **denominational** adj. [ME f. OF denomination or L denominatio (as DENOMINATE)]

denominative /dɪˈnɒmɪnətɪv/ adj. serving as or giving a name. [LL denominativus (as DENOMINATION)]

denominator /dɪˈnɒmɪˌneɪtə(r)/ n. Math. the number below the line in a vulgar fraction; a divisor. □ **common denominator 1** a common multiple of the denominators of several fractions. **2** a common feature of members of a group. **least** (or **lowest**) **common denominator** the lowest common multiple as above. [F dénominateur or med.L denominator (as DE-, NOMINATE)]

de jours /də nɔː ˈʒʊə(r)/ adj. (placed after noun) of the present time. [F, = of our days]

denote /dɪˈnəʊt/ v.tr. **1** be a sign of; indicate (the arrow denotes direction). **2** (usu. foll. by that + clause) mean, convey. **3** stand as a name for; signify. □□ **denotation** /ˌdiːnəˈteɪʃ(ə)n/ n. **denotative** /-tətɪv/ adj. [F dénoter or f. L denotare (as DE-, notare mark f. nota NOTE)]

denouement /deɪˈnuːmɑ̃/ n. (also **dénouement**) **1** the final unravelling of a plot or complicated situation. **2** the final scene in a play, novel, etc., in which the plot is resolved. [F dénouement f. dénouer unknot (as DE-, L nodare f. nodus knot)]

denounce /dɪˈnaʊns/ v.tr. **1** accuse publicly; condemn (denounced him as a traitor). **2** inform against (denounced her to the police). **3** give notice of the termination of (an armistice, treaty, etc.). □□ **denouncement** n. **denouncer** n. [ME f. OF denoncier f. L denuntiare (as DE-, nuntiare make known f. nuntius messenger)]

de nouveau /də nuːˈvəʊ/ adv. starting again; anew. [F]

de novo /diː ˈnəʊvəʊ, deɪ/ adv. starting again; anew. [L]

Denpasar /denˈpɑːsɑː(r)/ the chief city and seaport of the island of Bali; pop. (1980) 261,200.

dense /dens/ adj. **1** closely compacted in substance; thick (dense fog). **2** crowded together (the population is less dense on the outskirts). **3** colloq. stupid. □□ **densely** adv. **denseness** n. [F dense or L densus]

densitometer /ˌdensɪˈtɒmɪtə(r)/ n. an instrument for measuring the photographic density of an image on a film or photographic print.

density /ˈdensɪtɪ/ n. (pl. **-ies**) **1** the degree of compactness of a substance. **2** Physics degree of consistency measured by the quantity of mass per unit volume. **3** the opacity of a photo-

graphic image. **4** a crowded state. **5** stupidity. [F densité or L densitas (as DENSE)]

dent /dent/ n. & v. —n. **1** a slight mark or hollow in a surface made by, or as if by, a blow with a hammer etc. **2** a noticeable effect (lunch made a dent in our funds). —v.tr. **1** mark with a dent. **2** have (esp. an adverse) effect on (the news dented our hopes). [ME, prob. f INDENT¹]

dental /ˈdent(ə)l/ adj. **1** of the teeth; of or relating to dentistry. **2** Phonet. (of a consonant) produced with the tongue-tip against the upper front teeth (as th) or the ridge of the teeth (as n, s, t). □ **dental floss** a thread of floss silk etc. used to clean between the teeth. **dental mechanic** a person who makes and repairs artificial teeth. **dental surgeon** a dentist. □□ **dentalize** v.tr. (also **-ise**). [LL dentalis f. L dens dentis tooth]

dentalium /denˈteɪlɪəm/ n. (pl. **dentalia** /-lɪə/) **1** any marine mollusc of the genus Dentalium, having a conical foot protruding from a tusklike shell. **2** this shell used as an ornament or as a form of currency. [mod.L f. LL dentalis: see DENTAL]

dentate /ˈdenteɪt/ adj. Bot. & Zool. toothed; with toothlike notches; serrated. [L dentatus f. dens dentis tooth]

denticle /ˈdentɪk(ə)l/ n. Zool. a small tooth or toothlike projection, scale, etc. □□ **denticulate** /denˈtɪkjʊlət/ adj. [ME f. L denticulus dimin. of dens dentis tooth]

dentifrice /ˈdentɪfrɪs/ n. a paste or powder for cleaning the teeth. [F f. L dentifricium f. dens dentis tooth + fricare rub]

dentil /ˈdentɪl/ n. Archit. each of a series of small rectangular blocks as a decoration under the moulding of a cornice in classical architecture. [obs. F dentille dimin. of dent tooth f. L dens dentis]

dentilingual /ˌdentɪˈlɪŋgw(ə)l/ adj. Phonet. formed by the teeth and the tongue.

dentine /ˈdentiːn/ n. (US **dentin** /-tɪn/) a hard dense bony tissue forming the bulk of a tooth. □□ **dentinal** /ˈdentɪn(ə)l/ adj. [L dens dentis tooth + -INE⁴]

dentist /ˈdentɪst/ n. a person who is qualified to treat the diseases and conditions that affect the mouth, jaws, teeth, and their supporting tissues, esp. the repair and extraction of teeth and the insertion of artificial ones. (See below.) □□ **dentistry** n. [F dentiste f. dent tooth]

Dental disease was recognized in ancient times in Babylonia and in Egypt, from where a papyrus of c.1500 BC contains prescriptions for diseases of the teeth and gums, though preventive and restorative work seem to have been unknown. The Etruscans had reached a high level of dental surgery by the 9th c. BC, and dentistry was highly developed in ancient India: Hindu writings describe extraction, scaling, and filling, and the fitting of artificial teeth. In early medieval times barbers and barber-surgeons were the dentists (see BARBER). Dentistry was taught in some hospitals from the early 19th c., and the first separate school of dental surgery was started at Baltimore in the US in 1839. Some instruments, notably the forceps, are of great antiquity, but many date from the early 19th c.; the principle of the dental drill was invented in 1829 by James Nasmyth, the Scottish engineer who invented the steam hammer. The development of anaesthetics and X-rays greatly benefited dentistry. The modern tendency is for the preservation of the natural teeth for as long as possible.

dentition /denˈtɪʃ(ə)n/ n. **1** the type, number, and arrangement of teeth in a species etc. **2** the cutting of teeth; teething. [L dentitio f. dentire to teethe]

denture /ˈdentʃə(r)/ n. a removable artificial replacement for one or more teeth carried on a removable plate or frame. [F f. dent tooth]

denuclearize /diːˈnjuːklɪəˌraɪz/ v.tr. (also **-ise**) remove nuclear armaments from (a country etc.). □□ **denuclearization** /-ˈzeɪʃ(ə)n/ n.

denude /dɪˈnjuːd/ v.tr. **1** make naked or bare. **2** (foll. by of) **a** strip of clothing, a covering, etc. **b** deprive of a possession or attribute. **3** Geol. lay (rock or a formation etc.) bare by removing what lies above. □□ **denudation** /ˌdiːnjuːˈdeɪʃ(ə)n/ n. **denudative** /-dətɪv/ adj. [L denudare (as DE-, nudus naked)]

denumerable /dɪˈnjuːmərəb(ə)l/ adj. Math. countable by correspondence with the infinite set of integers. □□ **denumerability** /-ˈbɪlɪtɪ/ n. **denumerably** adv. [LL denumerare (as DE-, numerare NUMBER)]

denunciation /dɪˌnʌnsɪˈeɪʃ(ə)n/ n. **1** the act of denouncing (a person, policy, etc.); public condemnation. **2** an instance of this. □□ **denunciate** /-ˈnʌnsɪˌeɪt/ v.tr. **denunciative** /-ˈnʌnsɪətɪv/ adj. **denunciator** /-ˈnʌnsɪˌeɪtə(r)/, -ˈnʌnʃɪˌeɪtə(r)/ n. **denunciatory** /dɪˈnʌnsɪətərɪ, -ˈnʌnʃɪətərɪ/ adj. [F dénonciation or L denunciatio (as DENOUNCE)]

Denver /ˈdenvə(r)/ the capital and largest city of Colorado; pop. (1982) 505,600.

deny /dɪˈnaɪ/ v.tr. (-ies, -ied) **1** declare untrue or non-existent (denied the charge; denied that it is so; denied having lied). **2** repudiate or disclaim (denied his faith; denied his signature). **3** (often foll. by to) refuse (a person or thing, or something to a person) (this was denied to me; denied him the satisfaction). **4** refuse access to (a person sought) (denied him his son). □ **deny oneself** be abstinent. □□ **denier** n. [ME f. OF denier f. L denegare (as DE-, negare say no)]

deoch an doris /ˌdɒx ən ˈdɒrɪs, ˌdɒk/ n. (also **doch an dorris**) Sc. & Ir. a drink taken at parting; a stirrup-cup. [Gael. deoch an doruis drink at the door]

deodar /ˈdiːəˌdɑː(r)/ n. the Himalayan cedar Cedrus deodara, the tallest of the cedar family, with drooping branches bearing large barrel-shaped cones. [Hindi dě' odār f. Skr. deva-dāru divine tree]

deodorant /diːˈəʊdərənt/ n. (often attrib.) a substance sprayed or rubbed on to the body or sprayed into the air to remove or conceal unpleasant smells (a roll-on deodorant; has a deodorant effect). [as DEODORIZE + -ANT]

deodorize /diːˈəʊdəˌraɪz/ v.tr. (also **-ise**) remove or destroy the (usu. unpleasant) smell of. □□ **deodorization** /-ˈzeɪʃ(ə)n/ n. **deodorizer** n. [DE- + L odor smell]

Deo gratias /ˌdeɪəʊ ˈɡrɑːtɪəs, -ˈʃəs/ int. thanks be to God. [L, = (we give) thanks to God]

deontic /diːˈɒntɪk/ adj. Philos. of or relating to duty and obligation as ethical concepts. [Gk deont- part. stem of dei it is right]

deontology /ˌdiːɒnˈtɒlədʒɪ/ n. Philos. the study of duty. □□ **deontological** /-təˈlɒdʒɪk(ə)l/ adj. **deontologist** n.

Deo volente /ˌdeɪəʊ vəˈlenteɪ/ adv. God willing; if nothing prevents it. [L]

deoxygenate /diːˈɒksɪdʒəˌneɪt/ v.tr. remove oxygen, esp. free oxygen, from. □□ **deoxygenation** /-ˈneɪʃ(ə)n/ n.

deoxyribonucleic acid /ˌdiːɒksɪˌraɪbəʊnjuˈkleɪɪk/ n. see DNA. [DE- + OXYGEN + RIBONUCLEIC (ACID)]

dep. abbr. **1** departs. **2** deputy.

depart /dɪˈpɑːt/ v. **1** intr. **a** (usu. foll. by from) go away; leave (the train departs from this platform). **b** (usu. foll. by for) start; set out (trains depart for Crewe every hour). **2** intr. (usu. foll. by from) diverge; deviate (departs from standard practice). **3 a** intr. leave by death; die. **b** tr. formal or literary leave by death (departed this life). [ME f. OF departir ult. f. L dispertire divide]

departed /dɪˈpɑːtɪd/ adj. & n. —adj. bygone (departed greatness). —n. (prec. by the) euphem. a particular dead person or dead people (we are here to mourn the departed).

department /dɪˈpɑːtmənt/ n. **1** a separate part of a complex whole, esp.: **a** a branch of municipal or State administration (Housing Department; Department of Social Security). **b** a branch of study and its administration at a university, school, etc. (the physics department). **c** a specialized section of a large store (hardware department). **2** colloq. an area of special expertise. **3** an administrative district in France and other countries. □ **department store** a large shop stocking many varieties of goods in different departments. [F département (as DEPART)]

departmental /ˌdiːpɑːtˈment(ə)l/ adj. of or belonging to a department. □ **departmental store** = department store. □□ **departmentalism** n. **departmentalize** v.tr. (also **-ise**). **departmentalization** /-ˈzeɪʃ(ə)n/ n. **departmentally** adv.

departure /dɪˈpɑːtʃə(r)/ n. **1** the act or an instance of departing. **2** (often foll. by from) a deviation (from the truth, a standard, etc.). **3** (often attrib.) the starting of a train, an aircraft, etc. (the departure was late; departure lounge). **4** a new course of action or thought (driving a car is rather a departure for him). **5** Naut. the amount of a ship's change of longitude. [OF departeüre (as DEPART)]

depasture /diːˈpɑːstʃə(r)/ v. **1** tr. (of cattle) graze upon. **b** intr. graze. **c** tr. put (cattle) to graze. **2** tr. (of land) provide pasturage for (cattle). □□ **depasturage** /-ɪdʒ/ n.

dépaysé /deɪˈpeɪzeɪ/ adj. (fem. *dépaysée* pronunc. same) removed from one's habitual surroundings. [F, = removed from one's own country]

depend /dɪˈpend/ v.intr. **1** (often foll. by on, upon) be controlled or determined (success depends on hard work; it depends on whether they agree; it depends how you tackle the problem). **2** (foll. by on, upon) **a** be unable to do without (depends on her mother). **b** rely on (I'm depending on you to come). **3** (foll. by on, upon) be grammatically dependent on. **4** (often foll. by from) archaic poet. hang down. □ **depend upon it!** you may be sure! **it** (or **it all** or **that**) **depends** expressing uncertainty or qualification in answering a question (Will they come? It depends). [ME f. OF dependre ult. f. L dependēre (as DE-, pendēre hang)]

dependable /dɪˈpendəb(ə)l/ adj. reliable. □□ **dependability** /-ˈbɪlɪtɪ/ n. **dependableness** n. **dependably** adv.

dependant /dɪˈpend(ə)nt/ n. (US **dependent**) **1** a person who relies on another esp. for financial support. **2** a servant. [F dépendant pres. part. of dépendre (as DEPEND)]

dependence /dɪˈpend(ə)ns/ n. **1** the state of being dependent, esp. on financial or other support. **2** reliance; trust; confidence (shows great dependence on his judgement). [F dépendance (as DEPEND)]

dependency /dɪˈpendənsɪ/ n. (pl. **-ies**) **1** a country or province controlled by another. **2** anything subordinate or dependent.

dependent /dɪˈpend(ə)nt/ adj. & n. —adj. **1** (usu. foll. by on) depending, conditional, or subordinate. **2** unable to do without (esp. a drug). **3** maintained at another's cost. **4** Math. (of a variable) having a value determined by that of another variable. **5** Gram. (of a clause, phrase, or word) subordinate to a sentence or word. —n. US var. of DEPENDANT. □□ **dependently** adv. [ME, earlier -ant = DEPENDANT]

depersonalization /dɪˌpɜːsənəlaɪˈzeɪʃ(ə)n/ n. (also **-isation**) esp. Psychol. the loss of one's sense of identity.

depersonalize /diːˈpɜːsənəˌlaɪz/ v.tr. (also **-ise**) **1** make impersonal. **2** deprive of personality.

depict /dɪˈpɪkt/ v.tr. **1** represent in a drawing or painting etc. **2** portray in words; describe (the play depicts him as vain and petty). □□ **depicter** n. **depiction** /-ˈpɪkʃ(ə)n/ n. **depictive** adj. **depictor** n. [L depingere depict- (as DE-, pingere paint)]

depilate /ˈdepɪˌleɪt/ v.tr. remove the hair from. □□ **depilation** /-ˈleɪʃ(ə)n/ n. [L depilare (as DE-, pilare f. pilus hair)]

depilatory /dɪˈpɪlətərɪ/ adj. & n. —adj. that removes unwanted hair. —n. (pl. **-ies**) a depilatory substance.

deplane /diːˈpleɪn/ v. esp. US **1** intr. disembark from an aeroplane. **2** tr. remove from an aeroplane.

deplete /dɪˈpliːt/ v.tr. (esp. in passive) **1** reduce in numbers or quantity (depleted forces). **2** empty out; exhaust (their energies were depleted). □□ **depletion** /-ˈpliːʃ(ə)n/ n. [L deplēre (as DE-, plēre plet- fill)]

deplorable /dɪˈplɔːrəb(ə)l/ adj. **1** exceedingly bad (a deplorable meal). **2** that can be deplored. □□ **deplorably** adv.

deplore /dɪˈplɔː(r)/ v.tr. **1** grieve over; regret. **2** be scandalized by; find exceedingly bad. □□ **deploringly** adv. [F déplorer or It. deplorare f. L deplorare (as DE-, plorare bewail)]

deploy /dɪˈplɔɪ/ v. **1** Mil. **a** tr. cause (troops) to spread out from a column into a line. **b** intr. (of troops) spread out in this way. **2** tr. bring (arguments, forces, etc.) into effective action. □□ **deployment** n. [F déployer f. L displicare (as DIS-, plicare fold) & LL deplicare explain]

deplume /diːˈpluːm/ v.tr. **1** strip of feathers, pluck. **2** deprive of honours etc. [ME f. F déplumer or f. med.L deplumare (as DE-, L pluma feather)]

depolarize /diːˈpəʊləˌraɪz/ v.tr. (also **-ise**) Physics reduce or remove the polarization of. □□ **depolarization** /-ˈzeɪʃ(ə)n/ n.

depoliticize /ˌdiːpəˈlɪtɪˌsaɪz/ v.tr. (also **-ise**) **1** make (a person, an organization, etc.) non-political. **2** remove from political activity or influence. □□ **depoliticization** /-ˈzeɪʃ(ə)n/ n.

depolymerize /diːˈpɒlɪməˌraɪz/ v.tr. & intr. (also **-ise**) Chem. break down into monomers or other smaller units. □□ **depolymerization** /-ˈzeɪʃ(ə)n/ n.

deponent /dɪˈpəʊnənt/ adj. & n. —adj. Gram. (of a verb, esp. in Latin or Greek) passive or middle in form but active in meaning. —n. **1** Gram. a deponent verb. **2** Law **a** a person making a deposition under oath. **b** a witness giving written testimony for use in court etc. [L deponere (as DE-, ponere posit- place): adj. from the notion that the verb had laid aside the passive sense]

depopulate /diːˈpɒpjʊˌleɪt/ v. **1** tr. reduce the population of. **2** intr. decline in population. □□ **depopulation** /-ˈleɪʃ(ə)n/ n. [L depopulari (as DE-, populari lay waste f. populus people)]

deport /dɪˈpɔːt/ v.tr. **1 a** remove (an immigrant or foreigner) forcibly to another country; banish. **b** exile (a native) to another country. **2** refl. conduct (oneself) or behave (in a specified manner) (deported himself well). □□ **deportable** adj. **deportation** /ˌdiːpɔːˈteɪʃ(ə)n/ n. [OF deporter and (sense 1) F déporter (as DE-, L portare carry)]

deportee /ˌdiːpɔːˈtiː/ n. a person who has been or is being deported.

deportment /dɪˈpɔːtmənt/ n. bearing, demeanour, or manners, esp. of a cultivated kind. [F déportement (as DEPORT)]

depose /dɪˈpəʊz/ v. **1** tr. remove from office, esp. dethrone. **2** intr. Law (usu. foll. by to, or that + clause) bear witness, esp. on oath in court. [ME f. OF deposer after L deponere: see DEPONENT, POSE¹]

deposit /dɪˈpɒzɪt/ n. & v. —n. **1 a** Brit. a sum of money kept in an account in a bank. **b** anything stored or entrusted for safe keeping, usu. in a bank. **2 a** a sum payable as a first instalment on an item bought on hire purchase, or as a pledge for a contract. **b** a returnable sum payable on the short-term hire of a car, boat, etc. **3 a** a natural layer of sand, rock, coal, etc. **b** a layer of precipitated matter on a surface, e.g. fur on a kettle. —v.tr. (**deposited, depositing**) **1 a** put or lay down in a (usu. specified) place (deposited the book on the floor). **b** (of water, wind, etc.) leave (matter etc.) lying in a displaced position. **2 a** store or entrust for keeping. **b** pay (a sum of money) into a bank account, esp. a deposit account. **3** pay (a sum) as a first instalment or as a pledge for a contract. □ **deposit account** Brit. a bank account that pays interest but from which money cannot usu. be withdrawn without notice or loss of interest. **on deposit** (of money) placed in a deposit account. [L depositum (n.), med.L depositare f. L deponere deposit- (as DEPONENT)]

depositary /dɪˈpɒzɪtərɪ/ n. (pl. **-ies**) a person to whom something is entrusted; a trustee. [LL depositarius (as DEPOSIT)]

deposition /ˌdiːpəˈzɪʃ(ə)n, ˌdep-/ n. **1** the act or an instance of deposing, esp. a monarch; dethronement. **2** Law **a** the process of giving sworn evidence; allegation. **b** an instance of this. **c** evidence given under oath; a testimony. **3** the act or an instance of depositing. **4** (**the Deposition**) **a** the taking down of the body of Christ from the Cross. **b** a representation of this. [ME f. OF f. L depositio -onis f. deponere: see DEPOSIT]

depositor /dɪˈpɒzɪtə(r)/ n. a person who deposits money, property, etc.

depository /dɪˈpɒzɪtərɪ/ n. (pl. **-ies**) **1 a** a storehouse for furniture etc. **b** a store (of wisdom, knowledge, etc.) (the book is a depository of wit). **2** = DEPOSITARY. [LL depositorium (as DEPOSIT)]

depot /ˈdepəʊ/ n. **1** a storehouse. **2** Mil. **a** a storehouse for equipment etc. **b** the headquarters of a regiment. **3 a** a building for the servicing, parking, etc. of esp. buses, trains, or goods vehicles. **b** US a railway or bus station. [F dépôt, OF depost f. L (as DEPOSIT)]

deprave /dɪˈpreɪv/ v.tr. pervert or corrupt, esp. morally. □□ **depravation** /ˌdeprəˈveɪʃ(ə)n/ n. [ME f. OF depraver or L depravare (as DE-, pravare f. pravus crooked)]

depravity /dɪˈprævɪtɪ/ n. (pl. **-ies**) **1 a** moral corruption; wickedness. **b** an instance of this; a wicked act. **2** Theol. the innate corruptness of human nature. [DE- + obs. pravity f. L pravitas (as DEPRAVE)]

deprecate /ˈdeprɪˌkeɪt/ v.tr. **1** express disapproval of or a wish

against; deplore (deprecate hasty action). ¶ Often confused with depreciate. **2** plead earnestly against. **3** archaic pray against. □□ **deprecatingly** adv. **deprecation** /-ˈkeɪʃ(ə)n/ n. **deprecative** /ˈdeprɪkətɪv/ adj. **deprecator** n. **deprecatory** /-ˈkeɪtərɪ/ adj. [L deprecari (as DE-, precari pray)]

depreciate /dɪˈpriːʃɪˌeɪt, -sɪˌeɪt/ v. **1** tr. & intr. diminish in value (the car has depreciated). **2** tr. disparage; belittle (they are always depreciating his taste). **3** tr. reduce the purchasing power of (money). □□ **depreciatingly** adv. **depreciatory** /dɪˈpriːʃɪətərɪ/ adj. [LL depretiare (as DE-, pretiare f. pretium price)]

depreciation /dɪˌpriːʃɪˈeɪʃ(ə)n, -sɪˈeɪʃ(ə)n/ n. **1** the amount of wear and tear (of a property etc.) for which a reduction may be made in a valuation, an estimate, or a balance sheet. **2** Econ. a decrease in the value of a currency. **3** the act or an instance of depreciating; belittlement.

depredation /ˌdeprɪˈdeɪʃ(ə)n/ n. (usu. in pl.) **1** despoiling, ravaging, or plundering. **2** an instance or instances of this. [F déprédation f. LL depraedatio (as DE-, praedatio -onis f. L praedari plunder)]

depredator /ˈdeprɪˌdeɪtə(r)/ n. a despoiler or pillager. □□ **depredatory** /ˈdeprɪˌdeɪtərɪ, dɪˈpredɪtərɪ/ adj. [LL depraedator (as DEPREDATION)]

depress /dɪˈpres/ v.tr. **1** push or pull down; lower (depressed the lever). **2** make dispirited or dejected. **3** Econ. reduce the activity of (esp. trade). **4** (as **depressed** adj.) **a** dispirited or miserable. **b** Psychol. suffering from depression. □ **depressed area** an area suffering from economic depression. □□ **depressible** adj. **depressing** adj. **depressingly** adv. [ME f. OF depresser f. LL depressare (as DE-, pressare frequent. of premere press)]

depressant /dɪˈpres(ə)nt/ adj. & n. —adj. **1** that depresses. **2** Med. sedative. —n. **1** Med. an agent, esp. a drug, that sedates. **2** an influence that depresses.

depression /dɪˈpreʃ(ə)n/ n. **1 a** Psychol. a state of extreme dejection or morbidly excessive melancholy; a mood of hopelessness and feelings of inadequacy, often with physical symptoms. **b** a reduction in vitality, vigour, or spirits. **2 a** a long period of financial and industrial decline; a slump. **b** (**the Depression**) the depression of 1929–34. (See below.) **3** Meteorol. a lowering of atmospheric pressure, esp. the centre of a region of minimum pressure or the system of winds round it. **4** a sunken place or hollow on a surface. **5 a** a lowering or sinking (often foll. by of: depression of freezing-point). **b** pressing down. **6** Astron. & Geog. the angular distance of an object below the horizon or a horizontal plane. [ME f. OF or L depressio (as DE-, premere press- press)]

The Great Depression of 1929–34 began with an agricultural crisis caused by over-production and led to a financial collapse, with massive speculation, a sudden loss of confidence, and consequent withdrawal of funds, resulting in widespread business failures and massive unemployment (13.7 million in the US, 5.6 million in Germany, and 2.8 million in Britain). The most dramatic results of the Depression were the introduction of extensive State-controlled economic planning, such as the American New Deal, and the rise of right-wing movements such as the German Nazi Party.

depressive /dɪˈpresɪv/ adj. & n. —adj. **1** tending to depress. **2** Psychol. involving or characterized by depression. —n. Psychol. a person suffering or with a tendency to suffer from depression. [F dépressif -ive or med.L depressivus (as DEPRESSION)]

depressor /dɪˈpresə(r)/ n. **1** Anat. **a** (in full **depressor muscle**) a muscle that causes the lowering of some part of the body. **b** a nerve that lowers blood pressure. **2** Surgery an instrument for pressing down an organ etc. [L (as DEPRESSION)]

depressurize /diːˈpreʃəˌraɪz/ v.tr. (also **-ise**) cause an appreciable drop in the pressure of the gas inside (a container), esp. to the ambient level. □□ **depressurization** /-ˈzeɪʃ(ə)n/ n.

deprivation /ˌdeprɪˈveɪʃ(ə)n, ˌdiːpraɪ-/ n. **1** (usu. foll. by of) the act or an instance of depriving; the state of being deprived (deprivation of liberty; suffered many deprivations). **2 a** a deposition from esp. an ecclesiastical office. **b** an instance of this. [med.L deprivatio (as DEPRIVE)]

deprive /dɪˈpraɪv/ v.tr. **1** (usu. foll. by of) strip, dispossess; debar from enjoying (illness deprived him of success). **2** (as **deprived** adj.) **a** (of a child etc.) suffering from the effects of a poor or loveless home. **b** (of an area) with inadequate housing, facilities, employment, etc. **3** *archaic* depose (esp. a clergyman) from office. □□ **deprivable** *adj.* **deprival** *n.* [ME f. OF *depriver* f. med.L *deprivare* (as DE-, L *privare* deprive)]

de profundis /ˌdeɪ prəˈfʊndɪs/ *adv. & n.* —*adv.* from the depths (of sorrow etc.). —*n.* a cry from the depths. [opening L words of Ps. 130]

Dept. *abbr.* Department.

depth /depθ/ *n.* **1 a** deepness (*the depth is not great at the edge*). **b** the measurement from the top down, from the surface inwards, or from the front to the back (*depth of the drawer is 12 inches*). **2** difficulty; abstruseness. **3 a** sagacity; wisdom. **b** intensity of emotion etc. (*the poem has little depth*). **4** an intensity of colour, darkness, etc. **5** (in *pl.*) **a** deep water, a deep place; an abyss. **b** a low, depressed state. **c** the lowest or inmost part (*the depths of the country*). **6** the middle (*in the depth of winter*). □ **depth-bomb** (or **-charge**) a bomb capable of exploding under water, esp. for dropping on a submerged submarine etc., devised in Britain and used during the First World War. **depth psychology** psychoanalysis to reveal hidden motives etc. **in depth** comprehensively, thoroughly, or profoundly. **in-depth** *adj.* thorough; done in depth. **out of one's depth 1** in water over one's head. **2** engaged in a task or on a subject too difficult for one. [ME (as DEEP, -TH²)]

depthless /ˈdepθlɪs/ *adj.* **1** extremely deep; fathomless. **2** shallow, superficial.

depurate /ˈdepjʊəˌreɪt/ *v.tr. & intr.* make or become free from impurities. □□ **depuration** /-ˈreɪʃ(ə)n/ *n.* **depurative** /dɪˈpjʊərətɪv/ *adj. & n.* **depurator** *n.* [med.L *depurare* (as DE-, *purus* pure)]

deputation /ˌdepjʊˈteɪʃ(ə)n/ *n.* a group of people appointed to represent others, usu. for a specific purpose; a delegation. [ME f. LL *deputatio* (as DEPUTE)]

depute *v. & n.* —*v.tr.* /dɪˈpjuːt/ (often foll. by *to*) **1** appoint as a deputy. **2** delegate (a task, authority, etc.) (*deputed the leadership to her*). —*n.* /ˈdepjuːt/ *Sc.* a deputy. [ME f. OF *député* past part. of *deputer* f. L *deputare* regard as, allot (as DE-, *putare* think)]

deputize /ˈdepjʊˌtaɪz/ *v.intr.* (also **-ise**) (usu. foll. by *for*) act as a deputy or understudy.

deputy /ˈdepjʊtɪ/ *n.* (pl. **-ies**) **1** a person appointed or delegated to act for another or others (also *attrib.: deputy manager*). **2** *Polit.* a parliamentary representative in certain countries, e.g. France. **3** a coalmine official responsible for safety. □ **by deputy** by proxy. **Chamber of Deputies** the lower legislative assembly in some parliaments. **deputy lieutenant** *Brit.* the deputy of the Lord Lieutenant of a county. □□ **deputyship** *n.* [ME var. of DEPUTE *n.*]

De Quincey /də ˈkwɪnsɪ/, Thomas (1785–1859), English essayist and critic, who ran away from school to homeless wanderings in Wales and London where he was befriended by a young prostitute, Ann. He then went to Oxford where he first took opium for toothache and became a lifelong addict. His acquaintance with Wordsworth and Coleridge drew him to the Lake District in 1809; he moved to Edinburgh in 1829. He won instant fame with his *Confessions of an English Opium Eater* (1822), a study of his addiction and its psychological effects from the euphoric early reveries to the appalling nightmares of the later stages. His work, mainly journalism written under pressure to support his family, included 'On the knocking on the Gate in "Macbeth"' (1827), 'Suspiria de Profundis' (1845), and 'The English Mail Coach' (1849), in which he traced how childhood experiences are crystallized in dreams into symbols which can form the dreamer's personality. His writing is distinguished by eclectic learning, pungent black humour, and a stately singular style.

deracinate /diːˈræsɪˌneɪt/ *v.tr. literary* **1** tear up by the roots. **2** obliterate, expunge. □□ **deracination** /-ˈneɪʃ(ə)n/ *n.* [F *déraciner* (as DE-, *racine* f. LL *radicina* dimin. of *radix* root)]

derail /dɪˈreɪl, diː-/ *v.tr.* (usu. in *passive*) cause (a train etc.) to leave the rails. □□ **derailment** *n.* [F *dérailler* (as DE-, RAIL¹)]

Derain /dəˈræ̃/, André (1880–1954), French painter, sculptor, and graphic artist. He was one of the creators of fauvism, and

an early adherent of cubism, but after about 1920 he based his work increasingly on that of the Old Masters and it became rather dry and academic.

derange /dɪˈreɪndʒ/ *v.tr.* **1** throw into confusion; disorganize; cause to act irregularly. **2** (esp. as **deranged** *adj.*) make insane (*deranged by the tragic events*). **3** disturb; interrupt. □□ **derangement** *n.* [F *déranger* (as DE-, *rang* RANK¹)]

derate /diːˈreɪt/ *v.* **1** *tr.* remove part or all of the burden of rates from. **2** *intr.* diminish or remove rates.

deration /diːˈræʃ(ə)n/ *v.tr.* free (food etc.) from rationing.

Derbent /dəˈbent/ a city of Dagestan, on the western shore of the Caspian Sea; pop. (1985) 80,000. The city, formerly on an important land route for trade between Europe and Asia, is approached from the west through a pass known as the Derbent Gateway. A great wall, said to have been built in the 6th c. and named the Caspian Gates, once defended the city against the attacks of nomadic tribes.

Derby¹ /ˈdɑːbɪ/ *n.* (pl. **-ies**) **1 a** an annual horse-race for three-year-olds, founded in 1780 by the 12th Earl of Derby (d. 1834), run on Epsom Downs in England on the last Wednesday in May or the first Wednesday in June. **b** a similar race elsewhere (*Kentucky Derby*). **2** any important sporting contest. **3** (**derby**) *US* a bowler hat. □ **Derby Day** the day on which the Derby is run. **local Derby** a match between two teams from the same district.

Derby² /ˈdɑːbɪ/, Edward George Geoffrey Smith Stanley, 14th Earl of (1799–1869), British statesman, Prime Minister in 1852, 1858–9, and 1866–8. In his last ministry he carried the Reform Act of 1867 through Parliament. This act redistributed the parliamentary seats and more than doubled the electorate, giving the vote to many working men in the towns.

Derby. *abbr.* Derbyshire.

Derbyshire /ˈdɑːbɪʃɪə(r)/ a north midland county of England; pop. (1981) 914,200; county town, Matlock.

deregister /diːˈredʒɪstə(r)/ *v.tr.* remove from a register. □□ **deregistration** /-ˈstreɪʃ(ə)n/ *n.*

de règle /də ˈregl/ *predic.adj.* customary; proper. [F, = of rule]

derelict /ˈderəlɪkt, ˈderɪ-/ *adj. & n.* —*adj.* **1** abandoned, ownerless (esp. of a ship at sea or an empty decrepit property). **2** (esp. of property) ruined; dilapidated. **3** *US* negligent (of duty etc.). —*n.* **1** a social outcast; a person without a home, a job, or property. **2** abandoned property, esp. a ship. [L *derelictus* past part. of *derelinquere* (as DE-, *relinquere* leave)]

dereliction /ˌderɪˈlɪkʃ(ə)n/ *n.* **1** (usu. foll. by *of*) **a** neglect; failure to carry out one's obligations (*dereliction of duty*). **b** an instance of this. **2** the act or an instance of abandoning; the process of being abandoned. **3 a** the retreat of the sea exposing new land. **b** the land so exposed. [L *derelictio* (as DERELICT)]

derequisition /diːˌrekwɪˈzɪʃ(ə)n/ *v.tr.* return (requisitioned property) to its former owner.

derestrict /ˌdiːrɪˈstrɪkt/ *v.tr.* **1** remove restrictions from. **2** remove speed restrictions from (a road, area, etc.). □□ **derestriction** *n.*

deride /dɪˈraɪd/ *v.tr.* laugh scornfully at; mock. □□ **derider** *n.* **deridingly** *adv.* [L *deridēre* (as DE-, *ridēre ris-* laugh)]

de rigueur /də rɪˈɡɜː(r)/ *predic.adj.* required by custom or etiquette (*evening dress is de rigueur*). [F, = of strictness]

derision /dɪˈrɪʒ(ə)n/ *n.* ridicule; mockery (*bring into derision*). □ **hold** (or **have**) **in derision** *archaic* mock at. □□ **derisible** /dɪˈrɪzɪb(ə)l/ *adj.* [ME f. OF f. LL *derisio -onis* (as DERIDE)]

derisive /dɪˈraɪsɪv/ *adj.* = DERISORY. □□ **derisively** *adv.* **derisiveness** *n.*

derisory /dɪˈraɪsərɪ/ *adj.* **1** scoffing; ironical; scornful (*derisory cheers*). **2** so small or unimportant as to be ridiculous (*derisory offer; derisory costs*). [LL *derisorius* (as DERISION)]

derivation /ˌderɪˈveɪʃ(ə)n/ *n.* **1** the act or an instance of deriving or obtaining from a source; the process of being derived. **2 a** the formation of a word from another word or from a root. **b** a derivative. **c** the tracing of the origin of a word. **d** a statement or account of this. **3** extraction, descent. **4** *Math.* a sequence of statements showing that a formula, theorem, etc., is a consequence of previously accepted statements. □□ **derivational** adj. [F *dérivation* or L *derivatio* (as DERIVE)]

derivative /dəˈrɪvətɪv, dɪ-/ adj. & n. —adj. derived from another source; not original (*his music is derivative and uninteresting*). —n. **1** something derived from another source, esp.: **a** a word derived from another or from a root (e.g. *quickly* from *quick*). **b** *Chem.* a chemical compound that is derived from another. **2** *Math.* a quantity measuring the rate of change of another. □□ **derivatively** adv. [F *dérivatif -ive* f. L *derivativus* (as DERIVE)]

derive /dɪˈraɪv/ v. **1** tr. (usu. foll. by *from*) get, obtain, or form (*derived satisfaction from work*). **2** intr. (foll. by *from*) arise from, originate in, be descended or obtained from (*happiness derives from many things*). **3** tr. gather or deduce (*derived the information from the clues*). **4** tr. **a** trace the descent of (a person). **b** show the origin of (a thing). **5** tr. (usu. foll. by *from*) show or state the origin or formation of (a word etc.) (*derived the word from Latin*). **6** tr. *Math.* obtain (a function) by differentiation. □□ **derivable** adj. [ME f. OF *deriver* or f. L *derivare* (as DE-, *rivus* stream)]

derm (also **derma**) var. of DERMIS.

dermatitis /ˌdɜːməˈtaɪtɪs/ n. inflammation of the skin. [Gk *derma -atos* skin + -ITIS]

dermatoglyphics /ˌdɜːmətəʊˈɡlɪfɪks/ n. the science or study of skin markings or patterns, esp. of the fingers, hands, and feet. □□ **dermatoglyphic** adj. **dermatoglyphically** adv. [as DERMATITIS + Gk *gluphē* carving: see GLYPH]

dermatology /ˌdɜːməˈtɒlədʒɪ/ n. the study of the diagnosis and treatment of skin disorders. □□ **dermatological** /-təˈlɒdʒɪk(ə)l/ adj. **dermatologist** n. [as DERMATITIS + -LOGY]

dermis /ˈdɜːmɪs/ n. (also **derm** /dɜːm/ or **derma** /ˈdɜːmə/) **1** (in general use) the skin. **2** *Anat.* the true skin, the thick layer of living tissue below the epidermis. □□ **dermal** adj. **dermic** adj. [mod.L, after EPIDERMIS]

dernier cri /ˌdɜːnjeɪ ˈkriː/ n. the very latest fashion. [F, = last cry]

derogate /ˈderəˌɡeɪt/ v.intr. (foll. by *from*) *formal* **1** take away a part from; detract from (a merit, a right, etc.). **2** deviate from (correct behaviour etc.). □□ **derogative** /dɪˈrɒɡətɪv/ adj. [L *derogare* (as DE-, *rogare* ask)]

derogation /ˌderəˈɡeɪʃ(ə)n/ n. **1** (foll. by *of*) a lessening or impairment of (a law, authority, position, dignity, etc.). **2** deterioration; debasement. [ME f. F *dérogation* or L *derogatio* (as DEROGATE)]

derogatory /dɪˈrɒɡətərɪ/ adj. (often foll. by *to*) involving disparagement or discredit; insulting, depreciatory (*made a derogatory remark*; *derogatory to my position*). □□ **derogatorily** adv. [LL *derogatorius* (as DEROGATE)]

derrick /ˈderɪk/ n. **1** a kind of crane for moving or lifting heavy weights, having a movable pivoted arm. **2** the framework over an oil well or similar excavation, holding the drilling machinery. [obs. senses *hangman, gallows*, f. the name of a London hangman *c.*1600]

derrière /ˌderɪˈeə(r)/ n. *colloq. euphem.* the buttocks. [F, = behind]

derring-do /ˌderɪŋˈduː/ n. *literary joc.* heroic courage or action. [ME, = *daring to do*, misinterpreted by Spenser and by Scott]

derringer /ˈderɪndʒə(r)/ n. a small large-bore pistol. [H. *Deringer*, Amer. inventor d. 1868]

derris /ˈderɪs/ n. **1** any woody tropical climbing leguminous plant of the genus *Derris*, bearing leathery pods. **2** an insecticide made from the powdered root of some kinds of derris. [mod.L f. Gk, = leather covering (with ref. to its pod)]

Derry /ˈderɪ/ see LONDONDERRY.

derry /ˈderɪ/ n. □ **have a derry on** *Austral.* & *NZ colloq.* be prejudiced against (a person). [app. f. the song-refrain *derry down*]

derv /dɜːv/ n. *Brit.* diesel oil for road vehicles. [f. diesel-engined road-vehicle]

dervish /ˈdɜːvɪʃ/ n. a member of any of several Sufi religious groups, vowed to poverty and austerity and holding esoteric beliefs. Some of the orders perform ecstatic rituals (such as dancing or ritual chanting), and are known as *dancing, whirling,* or *howling* dervishes according to the practice of their order. The order of whirling dervishes, founded in Anatolia in the 13th c. by the poet and mystic Mevlana, was dissolved in 1925 by order of Atatürk. **whirling** (or **dancing** or **howling**) **dervish** a dervish performing a wild dance, or howling, according to which sect he belongs to. [Turk. *derviş* f. Pers. *darvēsh* poor, a mendicant]

DES abbr. (in the UK) Department of Education and Science.

desalinate /diːˈsælɪˌneɪt/ v.tr. remove salt from (esp. sea water). □□ **desalination** /-ˈneɪʃ(ə)n/ n.

desalt /diːˈsɔːlt/ v.tr. = DESALINATE.

descale /diːˈskeɪl/ v.tr. remove the scale from.

descant /ˈdeskænt/ n. & v. —n. **1** *Mus.* an independent treble melody usu. sung or played above a basic melody, esp. of a hymn tune. **2** *poet.* a melody; a song. —v.intr. /dɪsˈkænt/ **1** (foll. by *on, upon*) talk lengthily and prosily, esp. in praise of. **2** *Mus.* sing or play a descant. □ **descant recorder** the most common size of recorder, with a range of two octaves. [ME f. OF *deschant* f. med.L *discantus* (as DIS-, *cantus* song, CHANT)]

Descartes /deɪˈkɑːt/, René (1596–1650), French philosopher, mathematician, and man of science, often called the father of modern philosophy. Aiming to reach totally secure foundations for knowledge he began by attacking all his beliefs with sceptical doubts. What was left was the certainty of his own conscious experience, and with it of his existence: '*Cogito, ergo sum*' (I think, therefore I exist). From this certainty he proceeded by arguing for the existence of God (as the first cause) and the reality of the physical world, and developed a dualistic theory: the world was composed of mind (conscious experience) and matter; their interaction remained unsolved. His approach set the agenda for the part of modern philosophy called theory of knowledge. In mathematics his name is attached to the Cartesian method whereby points in the plane are located by their coordinates with respect to rectangular axes fixed in the plane, and lines or curves may then be described by giving the value of the *y*-coordinates of their points as functions of the *x*-coordinates. By this method algebraic techniques, and, later, the techniques of calculus, could be used to solve geometrical problems. A cautious man and a practising Catholic, Descartes suppressed his heretical doctrines of the Earth's rotation and the infinity of the universe; fragments of his work in this field were published after his death. From 1628 to 1649 he lived in Holland, then departed for Sweden at the invitation of Queen Christina, a passionate and learned lady who required daily lessons from him at five o'clock in the morning; the unaccustomed early rising and the bitter Scandinavian winter brought on the pneumonia from which he died.

descend /dɪˈsend/ v. **1** tr. & intr. go or come down (a hill, stairs, etc.). **2** intr. (of a thing) sink, fall (*rain descended heavily*). **3** intr. slope downwards, lie along a descending slope (*fields descended to the beach*). **4** intr. (usu. foll. by *on*) **a** make a sudden attack. **b** make an unexpected and usu. unwelcome visit (*hope they don't descend on us at the weekend*). **5** intr. (usu. foll. by *from, to*) (of property, qualities, rights, etc.) be passed by inheritance (*the house descends from my grandmother; the property descended to me*). **6** intr. **a** sink in rank, quality, etc. **b** (foll. by *to*) degrade oneself morally to (an unworthy act) (*descend to violence*). **7** intr. *Mus.* (of sound) become lower in pitch. **8** intr. (usu. foll. by *to*) proceed (in discourse or writing): **a** in time (to a subsequent event etc.). **b** from the general (to the particular) (*now let's descend to details*). **9** tr. go along (a river etc.) to the sea etc. **10** intr. *Printing* (of a letter) have its tail below the line. □ **be descended from** have as an ancestor. □□ **descendent** adj. [ME f. OF *descendre* f. L *descendere* (as DE-, *scandere* climb)]

descendant /dɪˈsend(ə)nt/ n. (often foll. by *of*) a person or thing descended from another (*a descendant of Charles I*). [F, part. of *descendre* (as DESCEND)]

descender /dɪˈsendə(r)/ n. *Printing* a part of a letter that extends below the line.

descendible /dɪˈsendɪb(ə)l, -dəb(ə)l/ adj. **1** (of a slope etc.) that may be descended. **2** *Law* capable of descending by inheritance. [OF *descendable* (as DESCEND)]

descent /dɪˈsent/ *n.* **1 a** the act of descending. **b** an instance of this. **c** a downward movement. **2 a** a way or path etc. by which one may descend. **b** a downward slope. **3 a** being descended; lineage, family origin (*traces his descent from William the Conqueror*). **b** the transmission of qualities, property, privileges, etc., by inheritance. **4 a** a decline; a fall. **b** a lowering (of pitch, temperature, etc.). **5** a sudden violent attack. [ME f. OF *descente* f. *descendre* DESCEND]

descramble /diːˈskræmb(ə)l/ *v.tr.* **1** convert or restore (a signal) to intelligible form. **2** counteract the effects of (a scrambling device). **3** recover an original signal from (a scrambled signal). □□ **descrambler** *n.*

describe /dɪˈskraɪb/ *v.tr.* **1 a** state the characteristics, appearance, etc. of, in spoken or written form (*described the landscape*). **b** (foll. by *as*) assert to be; call (*described him as a habitual liar*). **2 a** mark out or draw (esp. a geometrical figure) (*described a triangle*). **b** move in (a specified way, esp. a curve) (*described a parabola through the air*). □□ **describable** *adj.* **describer** *n.* [L *describere* (as DE-, *scribere* *script-* write)]

description /dɪˈskrɪpʃ(ə)n/ *n.* **1 a** the act or an instance of describing; the process of being described. **b** a spoken or written representation (of a person, object, or event). **2** a sort, kind, or class (*no food of any description*). □ **answers** (or **fits**) **the description** has the qualities specified. [ME f. OF f. L *descriptio -onis* (as DESCRIBE)]

descriptive /dɪˈskrɪptɪv/ *adj.* **1** serving or seeking to describe (*a descriptive writer*). **2** describing or classifying without expressing feelings or judging (*a purely descriptive account*). **3** *Linguistics* describing a language without comparing, endorsing, or condemning particular usage, vocabulary, etc. **4** *Gram.* (of an adjective) describing the noun, rather than its relation, position, etc., e.g. *blue* as distinct from *few*. □□ **descriptively** *adv.* **descriptiveness** *n.* [LL *descriptivus* (as DESCRIBE)]

descriptor /dɪˈskrɪptə(r)/ *n. Linguistics* a word or expression etc. used to describe or identify. [L, = describer (as DESCRIBE)]

descry /dɪˈskraɪ/ *v.tr.* (**-ies**, **-ied**) *literary* catch sight of; discern (*descried him in the crowd*; *descries no glimmer of light in her situation*). [ME (earlier senses 'proclaim, DECRY') f. OF *descrier*: prob. confused with var. of obs. *descrive* f. OF *descrivre* DESCRIBE]

desecrate /ˈdesɪˌkreɪt/ *v.tr.* **1** violate (a sacred place or thing) with violence, profanity, etc. **2** deprive (a church, a sacred object, etc.) of sanctity; deconsecrate. □□ **desecration** /-ˈkreɪʃ(ə)n/ *n.* **desecrator** *n.* [DE- + CONSECRATE]

deseed /diːˈsiːd/ *v.tr.* remove the seeds from (a plant, vegetable, etc.).

desegregate /diːˈsegrɪˌgeɪt/ *v.tr.* abolish racial segregation in (schools etc.) or of (people etc.). □□ **desegregation** /-ˈgeɪʃ(ə)n/ *n.*

deselect /ˌdiːsɪˈlekt/ *v.tr. Polit.* decline to select or retain as a constituency candidate in an election. □□ **deselection** *n.*

desensitize /diːˈsensɪˌtaɪz/ *v.tr.* (also **-ise**) reduce or destroy the sensitiveness of (photographic materials, an allergic person, etc.). □□ **desensitization** /-ˈzeɪʃ(ə)n/ *n.* **desensitizer** *n.*

desert[1] /dɪˈzɜːt/ *v.* **1** *tr.* abandon, give up, leave (*deserted the sinking ship*). **2** *tr.* forsake or abandon (a cause or a person, people, etc., having claims on one) (*deserted his wife and children*). **3** *tr.* fail (*his presence of mind deserted him*). **4** *intr. Mil.* run away (esp. from military service). **5** *tr.* (as **deserted** *adj.*) empty, abandoned (*a deserted house*). □□ **deserter** *n.* (in sense 4 of *v.*). **desertion** /-ˈzɜːʃ(ə)n/ *n.* [F *déserter* f. LL *desertare* f. L *desertus* (as DESERT[2])]

desert[2] /ˈdezət/ *n. & adj.* —*n.* a dry barren often sand-covered area of land, characteristically desolate, waterless, and without vegetation; an uninteresting or barren subject, period, etc. (*a cultural desert*). —*adj.* **1** uninhabited, desolate. **2** uncultivated, barren. □ **desert boot** a suede etc. boot reaching to or extending just above the ankle. **desert island** a remote (usu. tropical) island presumed to be uninhabited. **Desert Rat** *Brit. colloq.* a soldier of the 7th British armoured division (with the jerboa as a badge), orig. in the N. African desert campaign of

1941–2. [ME f. OF f. L *desertus*, eccl.L *desertum* (n.), past part. of *deserere* leave, forsake]

desert[3] /dɪˈzɜːt/ *n.* **1** (in *pl.*) **a** acts or qualities deserving reward or punishment. **b** such reward or punishment (*has got his deserts*). **2** the fact of being worthy of reward or punishment; deservingness. [ME f. OF f. *deservir* DESERVE]

desertification /dɪˌzɜːtɪfɪˈkeɪʃ(ə)n/ *n.* the process of making or becoming a desert.

deserve /dɪˈzɜːv/ *v.tr.* (often foll. by *to* + infin.) show conduct or qualities worthy of (reward, punishment, etc.) (*deserves to be imprisoned*; *deserves a prize*). □ **deserve well** (or **ill**) **of** be worthy of good (or bad) treatment at the hands of (*deserves well of the electorate*). □□ **deservedly** /-vɪdlɪ/ *adv.* **deservedness** /-vɪdnɪs/ *n.* **deserver** *n.* [ME f. OF *deservir* f. L *deservire* (as DE-, *servire* serve)]

deserving /dɪˈzɜːvɪŋ/ *adj.* meritorious. □ **deserving of** showing conduct or qualities worthy of (praise, blame, help, etc.). □□ **deservingly** *adv.* **deservingness** *n.*

desex /diːˈseks/ *v.tr.* **1** castrate or spay (an animal). **2** deprive of sexual qualities or attractions.

desexualize /diːˈseksjʊəˌlaɪz/ *v.tr.* (also **-ise**) deprive of sexual character or of the distinctive qualities of a sex.

déshabillé /ˌdezæˈbiːeɪ/ *n.* (also ***déshabille*** /ˌdeɪzæˈbiːl/, ***dishabille*** /ˌdɪsæˈbiːl/) a state of being only partly or carelessly clothed. [F, = undressed]

De Sica /də ˈsiːkə/, Vittorio (1901–74), Italian film director and actor. He acted in over 150 films, including some in English, but in 1940 began also to direct. His first notable production, *The Children Are Watching Us* (1942), inaugurated the collaboration with the scriptwriter Cesare Zavattini which was to create four neo-realist masterpieces: *Shoeshine* (1946), *Bicycle Thieves* (1948)—De Sica's best-known work—*Miracle in Milan* (1951), and *Umberto D* (1952). The last marked the end of his most creative directing, and of his numerous later films only a few—including *Two Women* (1960) and especially *The Garden of the Finzi-Continis* (1971)—revealed signs of his former brilliance.

desiccant /ˈdesɪkənt/ *n. Chem.* a hygroscopic substance used as a drying agent.

desiccate /ˈdesɪˌkeɪt/ *v.tr.* remove the moisture from, dry (esp. food for preservation) (*desiccated coconut*). □□ **desiccation** /-ˈkeɪʃ(ə)n/ *n.* **desiccative** /-kətɪv/ *adj.* [L *desiccare* (as DE-, *siccus* dry)]

desiccator /ˈdesɪˌkeɪtə(r)/ *n.* **1** an apparatus for desiccating. **2** *Chem.* an apparatus containing a drying agent to remove the moisture from specimens.

desiderate /dɪˈzɪdəˌreɪt, -ˈsɪdəˌreɪt/ *v.tr. archaic* feel to be missing; regret the absence of; wish to have. [L *desiderare* (as DE-, *siderare* as in CONSIDER)]

desiderative /dɪˈzɪdərətɪv, -ˈsɪdərətɪv/ *adj. & n.* —*adj.* **1** *Gram.* (of a verb, conjugation, etc.) formed from another verb etc. and denoting a desire to perform the action of that verb etc. **2** desiring. —*n. Gram.* a desiderative verb, conjugation, etc. [LL *desiderativus* (as DESIDERATE)]

desideratum /dɪˌzɪdəˈrɑːtəm, dɪˌsɪd-/ *n.* (*pl.* **desiderata** /-tə/) something lacking but needed or desired. [L neut. past part.: see DESIDERATE]

design /dɪˈzaɪn/ *n. & v.* —*n.* **1 a** a preliminary plan or sketch for the making or production of a building, machine, garment, etc. **b** the art of producing these. **2** a scheme of lines or shapes forming a pattern or decoration. **3** a plan, purpose, or intention. **4 a** the general arrangement or layout of a product. **b** an established version of a product (*one of our most popular designs*). —*v.* **1** *tr.* produce a design for (a building, machine, picture, garment, etc.). **2** *tr.* intend, plan, or purpose (*the remark was designed to offend*; *a course designed for beginners*; *designed an attack*). **3** *absol.* be a designer. □ **argument from design** *Theol.* the argument that God's existence is provable by the evidence of design in the universe. **by design** on purpose. **have designs on** plan to harm or appropriate. [F *désigner* appoint or obs. F *desseing* ult. f. L *designare* DESIGNATE]

designate *v. & adj.* —*v.tr.* /ˈdezɪɡˌneɪt/ **1** (often foll. by *as*) appoint to an office or function (*designated him as postmaster* general; *designated his own successor*). **2** specify or particularize (*receives guests at designated times*). **3** (often foll. by *as*) describe as; entitle, style. **4** serve as the name or distinctive mark of (*English uses French words to designate ballet steps*). —*adj.* /ˈdezɪgnət/ (placed after noun) appointed to an office but not yet installed (*bishop designate*). □□ **designator** /-ˌneɪtə(r)/ *n.* [L *designare*, past part. *designatus* (as DE-, *signare* f. *signum* mark)]

designation /ˌdezɪgˈneɪʃ(ə)n/ *n.* **1** a name, description, or title. **2** the act or process of designating. [ME f. OF *designation* or L *designatio* (as DESIGNATE)]

designedly /dɪˈzaɪnɪdlɪ/ *adv.* by design; on purpose.

designer /dɪˈzaɪnə(r)/ *n.* **1** a person who makes artistic designs or plans for construction, e.g. for clothing, machines, theatre sets; a draughtsman. **2** (*attrib.*) (of clothing etc.) bearing the name or label of a famous designer; prestigious. □ **designer drug** a synthetic analogue, not itself illegal, of an illegal drug.

designing /dɪˈzaɪnɪŋ/ *adj.* crafty, artful, or scheming. □□ **designingly** *adv.*

desirable /dɪˈzaɪərəb(ə)l/ *adj.* **1** worth having or wishing for (*it is desirable that nobody should smoke*). **2** arousing sexual desire; very attractive. □□ **desirability** /-ˈbɪlɪtɪ/ *n.* **desirableness** *n.* **desirably** *adv.* [ME f. OF (as DESIRE)]

desire /dɪˈzaɪə(r)/ *n. & v.* —*n.* **1 a** an unsatisfied longing or craving. **b** an expression of this; a request (*expressed a desire to rest*). **2** lust. **3** something desired (*achieved his heart's desire*). —*v.tr.* **1** (often foll. by *to* + infin., or *that* + clause) long for; crave. **2** request (*desires a cup of tea*). **3** *archaic* pray, entreat, or command (*desire him to wait*). [ME f. OF *desir* f. *desirer* f. L *desiderare* DESIDERATE]

desirous /dɪˈzaɪərəs/ *predic.adj.* **1** (usu. foll. by *of*) ambitious, desiring (*desirous of stardom; desirous of doing well*). **2** (usu. foll. by *to* + infin., or *that* + clause) wishful; hoping (*desirous to do the right thing*). [ME f. AF *desirous*, OF *desireus* f. Rmc (as DESIRE)]

desist /dɪˈzɪst/ *v.intr.* (often foll. by *from*) *literary* abstain; cease (*please desist from interrupting; when requested, he desisted*). [OF *desister* f. L *desistere* (as DE-, *sistere* stop, redupl. f. *stare* stand)]

desk /desk/ *n.* **1** a piece of furniture or a portable box with a flat or sloped surface for writing on, and often drawers. **2** a counter in a hotel, bank, etc., which separates the customer from the assistant. **3** a section of a newspaper office etc. dealing with a specified topic (*the sports desk; the features desk*). **4** *Mus.* a music stand in an orchestra regarded as a unit of two players. □ **desk-bound** obliged to remain working at a desk. [ME f. med.L *desca* f. L DISCUS disc]

desktop /ˈdesktɒp/ *n.* **1** the working surface of a desk. **2** (*attrib.*) (esp. of a microcomputer) suitable for use at an ordinary desk. □ **desktop publishing** the production of printed matter by means of a printer (such as a laser printer) linked to a desk-top computer, with special software. The system enables reports, advertising matter, company magazines, etc. to be produced with a print quality similar to that of typeset books and in quantities that would not be commercially viable by traditional printing methods.

desman /ˈdesmən/ *n.* (*pl.* **desmans**) any aquatic flesh-eating shrewlike mammal of two species, one originating in Russia (*Desmana moschata*) and one in the Pyrenees (*Galemys pyrenaicus*). [F & G f. Sw. *desman-råtta* musk-rat]

Des Moines /dɪ ˈmɔɪn/ the capital and largest city of Iowa, on the Des Moines River; pop. (1980) 191,000.

desolate *adj. & v.* —*adj.* /ˈdesələt/ **1** left alone; solitary. **2** (of a building or place) uninhabited, ruined, neglected, barren, dreary, empty (*a desolate moor*). **3** forlorn; wretched; miserable (*was left desolate and weeping*). —*v.tr.* /ˈdesəˌleɪt/ **1** depopulate or devastate; lay waste to. **2** (esp. as **desolated** *adj.*) make wretched or forlorn (*desolated by grief; inconsolable and desolated*). □□ **desolately** /-lətlɪ/ *adv.* **desolateness** /-lətnɪs/ *n.* **desolator** /-ˌleɪtə(r)/ *n.* [ME f. L *desolatus* past part. of *desolare* (as DE-, *solare* f. *solus* alone)]

desolation /ˌdesəˈleɪʃ(ə)n/ *n.* **1 a** the act of desolating. **b** the process of being desolated. **2** loneliness, grief, or wretchedness, esp. caused by desertion. **3** a neglected, ruined, barren, or empty state. [ME f. LL *desolatio* (as DESOLATE)]

desorb /diːˈzɔːb/ *v.* **1** *tr.* cause the release of (an adsorbed substance) from a surface. **2** *intr.* (of an adsorbed substance) become released. □□ **desorbent** *adj. & n.* **desorption** *n.* [DE-, after ADSORB]

despair /dɪˈspeə(r)/ *n. & v.* —*n.* the complete loss or absence of hope. —*v.intr.* **1** (often foll. by *of*) lose or be without hope (*despaired of ever seeing her again*). **2** (foll. by *of*) lose hope about (*his life is despaired of*). □ **be the despair of** be the cause of despair by badness or unapproachable excellence (*he's the despair of his parents*). □□ **despairingly** *adv.* [ME f. OF *desespeir*, *desperer* f. L *desperare* (as DE-, *sperare* hope)]

despatch var. of DISPATCH.

desperado /ˌdespəˈrɑːdəʊ/ *n.* (*pl.* **-oes** or *US* **-os**) a desperate or reckless person, esp. a criminal. [after DESPERATE (obs. n.) & words in -ADO]

desperate /ˈdespərət/ *adj.* **1** reckless from despair; violent and lawless. **2 a** extremely dangerous or serious (*a desperate situation*). **b** staking all on a small chance (*a desperate remedy*). **3** very bad (*a desperate night; desperate poverty*). **4** (usu. foll. by *for*) needing or desiring very much (*desperate for recognition*). □□ **desperately** *adv.* **desperateness** *n.* **desperation** /-ˈreɪʃ(ə)n/ *n.* [ME f. L *desperatus* past part. of *desperare* (as DE-, *sperare* hope)]

despicable /ˈdespɪkəb(ə)l, dɪˈspɪk-/ *adj.* vile; contemptible, esp. morally. □□ **despicably** *adv.* [LL *despicabilis* f. *despicari* (as DE-, *specere* look at)]

despise /dɪˈspaɪz/ *v.tr.* look down on as inferior, worthless, or contemptible. □□ **despiser** *n.* [ME f. *despis-* pres. stem of OF *despire* f. L *despicere* (as DE-, *specere* look at)]

despite /dɪˈspaɪt/ *prep. & n.* —*prep.* in spite of. —*n. archaic* or *literary* **1** outrage, injury. **2** malice, hatred (*died of mere despite*). □ **despite** (or **in despite**) **of** *archaic* in spite of. □□ **despiteful** *adj.* [ME f. OF *despit* f. L *despectus* noun f. *despicere* (as DESPISE)]

despoil /dɪˈspɔɪl/ *v.tr. literary* (often foll. by *of*) plunder; rob; deprive (*despoiled the roof of its lead*). □□ **despoiler** *n.* **despoilment** *n.* **despoliation** /dɪˌspəʊlɪˈeɪʃ(ə)n/ *n.* [ME f. OF *despoill(i)er* f. L *despoliare* (as DE-, *spoliare* SPOIL)]

despond /dɪˈspɒnd/ *v. & n.* —*v.intr.* lose heart or hope; be dejected. —*n. archaic* despondency. [L *despondēre* give up, abandon as DE-, *spondēre* promise)]

despondent /dɪˈspɒnd(ə)nt/ *adj.* in low spirits, dejected. □□ **despondence** *n.* **despondency** *n.* **despondently** *adv.*

despot /ˈdespɒt/ *n.* **1** an absolute ruler. **2** a tyrant or oppressor. □□ **despotic** /-ˈspɒtɪk/ *adj.* **despotically** /-ˈspɒtɪkəlɪ/ *adv.* [F *despote* f. med.L *despota* f. Gk *despotēs* master, lord]

despotism /ˈdespəˌtɪz(ə)m/ *n.* **1 a** rule by a despot. **b** a country ruled by a despot. **2** absolute power or control; tyranny.

des Prez /de ˈpreɪ/, Josquin (*c.*1440–1521), the leading composer of the early Renaissance. Best known for his Italian song 'El grillo', with its imitations of the chirrup of the cricket, he composed both secular and sacred music prolifically.

desquamate /ˈdeskwəˌmeɪt/ *v.intr. Med.* (esp. of the skin) come off in scales (as in some diseases). □□ **desquamation** /-ˈmeɪʃ(ə)n/ *n.* **desquamative** /-ˈskwæmətɪv/ *adj.* **desquamatory** /-ˈskwæmətərɪ/ *adj.* [L *desquamare* (as DE-, *squama* scale)]

des res /dez ˈrez/ *n. sl.* a desirable residence. [abbr.]

Dessau /ˈdesaʊ/ an industrial city in Germany, on the River Mulde, about 112 km (70 miles) south-west of Berlin; pop. (1986) 103,500.

dessert /dɪˈzɜːt/ *n.* **1** the sweet course of a meal, served at or near the end. **2** *Brit.* a course of fruit, nuts, etc., served after a meal. □ **dessert wine** usu. sweet wine drunk with or following dessert. [F, past part. of *desservir* clear the table (as DIS-, *servir* SERVE)]

dessertspoon /dɪˈzɜːtspuːn/ *n.* **1** a spoon used for dessert, smaller than a tablespoon and larger than a teaspoon. **2** the amount held by this. □□ **dessertspoonful** *n.* (*pl.* **-fuls**).

destabilize /diːˈsteɪbɪˌlaɪz/ *v.tr.* (also **-ise**) **1** render unstable. **2** subvert (esp. a foreign government). □□ **destabilization** /-ˈzeɪʃ(ə)n/ *n.*

De Stijl see STIJL.

destination /ˌdestɪˈneɪʃ(ə)n/ n. a place to which a person or thing is going. [OF *destination* or L *destinatio* (as DESTINE)]

destine /ˈdestɪn/ v.tr. (often foll. by *to*, *for*, or *to* + infin.) set apart; appoint; preordain; intend (*destined him for the navy*). □ **be destined** to be fated or preordained to (*was destined to become a great man*). [ME f. F *destiner* f. L *destinare* (as DE-, *stanare* (unrecorded) settle f. *stare* stand)]

destiny /ˈdestɪnɪ/ n. (pl. **-ies**) **1 a** the predetermined course of events; fate. **b** this regarded as a power. **2** what is destined to happen to a particular person etc. (*it was their destiny to be rejected*). [ME f. OF *destinée* f. Rmc, past part. of *destinare*: see DESTINE]

destitute /ˈdestɪˌtjuːt/ adj. **1** without food, shelter, etc.; completely impoverished. **2** (usu. foll. by *of*) lacking (*destitute of friends*). □□ **destitution** /-ˈtjuːʃ(ə)n/ n. [ME f. L *destitutus* past part. of *destituere* forsake (as DE-, *statuere* place)]

destrier /ˈdestrɪə(r)/ n. hist. a war-horse. [ME f. AF *destrer*, OF *destrier* ult. f. L DEXTER[1] right (as the knight's horse was led by the squire with the right hand)]

destroy /dɪˈstrɔɪ/ v.tr. **1** pull or break down; demolish (*destroyed the bridge*). **2** end the existence of (*the accident destroyed her confidence*). **3** kill (esp. a sick or savage animal). **4** make useless; spoil utterly. **5** ruin financially, professionally, or in reputation. **6** defeat (*destroyed the enemy*). [ME f. OF *destruire* ult. f. L *destruere* (as DE-, *struere* *struct-* build)]

destroyer /dɪˈstrɔɪə(r)/ n. **1** a person or thing that destroys. **2** Naut. a fast warship with guns and torpedoes used to protect other ships.

destruct /dɪˈstrʌkt/ v. & n. US esp. Astronaut. —v. **1** tr. destroy (one's own rocket etc.) deliberately, esp. for safety reasons. **2** intr. be destroyed in this way. —n. an act of destructing. [L *destruere* (as DESTROY) or as back-form. f. DESTRUCTION]

destructible /dɪˈstrʌktɪb(ə)l/ adj. able to be destroyed. □□ **destructibility** /-ˈbɪlɪtɪ/ n. [F *destructible* or LL *destructibilis* (as DESTROY)]

destruction /dɪˈstrʌkʃ(ə)n/ n. **1** the act or an instance of destroying; the process of being destroyed. **2** a cause of ruin; something that destroys (*greed was their destruction*). [ME f. OF f. L *destructio -onis* (as DESTROY)]

destructive /dɪˈstrʌktɪv/ adj. **1** (often foll. by *to*, *of*) destroying or tending to destroy (*destructive of her peace of mind; is destructive to organisms; a destructive child*). **2** negative in attitude or criticism; refuting without suggesting, helping, amending, etc. (opp. CONSTRUCTIVE) (*has only destructive criticism to offer*). □□ **destructively** adv. **destructiveness** n. [ME f. OF *destructif -ive* f. LL *destructivus* (as DESTROY)]

destructor /dɪˈstrʌktə(r)/ n. Brit. a refuse-burning furnace.

desuetude /dɪˈsjuːɪˌtjuːd, ˈdeswɪ-/ n. a state of disuse (*the custom fell into desuetude*). [F *désuétude* or L *desuetudo* (as DE-, *suescere suet-* be accustomed)]

desultory /ˈdezəltərɪ/ adj. **1** going constantly from one subject to another, esp. in a half-hearted way. **2** disconnected; unmethodical; superficial. □□ **desultorily** adv. **desultoriness** n. [L *desultorius* superficial f. *desultor* vaulter f. *desult-* (as DE-, *salt-* past part. stem of *salire* leap)]

detach /dɪˈtætʃ/ v.tr. **1** (often foll. by *from*) unfasten or disengage and remove (*detached the buttons; detached himself from the group*). **2** Mil. send (a ship, regiment, officer, messenger, etc.) on a separate mission. **3** (as **detached** adj.) **a** impartial; unemotional (*a detached viewpoint*). **b** (esp. of a house) not joined to another or others; separate. □□ **detachable** adj. **detachedly** /dɪˈtætʃɪdlɪ/ adv. [F *détacher* (as DE-, ATTACH)]

detachment /dɪˈtætʃmənt/ n. **1 a** a state of aloofness from or indifference to other people, one's surroundings, public opinion, etc. **b** disinterested independence of judgement. **2 a** the act or process of detaching or being detached. **b** an instance of this. **3** Mil. a separate group or unit of an army etc. used for a specific purpose. [F *détachement* (as DETACH)]

detail /ˈdiːteɪl/ n. & v. —n. **1 a** a small or subordinate particular; an item. **b** such a particular, considered (ironically) to be unimportant (*the truth of the statement is just a detail*). **2 a** small items or particulars (esp. in an artistic work) regarded collectively (*has an eye for detail*). **b** the treatment of them (*the detail was insufficient and unconvincing*). **3** (often in pl.) a number of particulars; an aggregate of small items (*filled in the details on the form*). **4 a** a minor decoration on a building, in a picture, etc. **b** a small part of a picture etc. shown alone. **5** Mil. **a** the distribution of orders for the day. **b** a small detachment of soldiers etc. for special duty. —v.tr. **1** give particulars of (*detailed the plans*). **2** relate circumstantially (*detailed the anecdote*). **3** Mil. assign for special duty. **4** (as **detailed** adj.) **a** (of a picture, story, etc.) having many details. **b** itemized (*a detailed list*). □ **go into detail** give all the items or particulars. **in detail** item by item, minutely. [F *détail*, *détailler* (as DE-, *tailler* cut, formed as TAIL[2])]

detain /dɪˈteɪn/ v.tr. **1** keep in confinement or under restraint. **2** keep waiting; delay. □□ **detainment** n. [ME f. OF *detenir* ult. f. L *detinēre detent-* (as DE-, *tenēre* hold)]

detainee /ˌdiːteɪˈniː/ n. a person detained in custody, esp. for political reasons.

detainer /dɪˈteɪnə(r)/ n. Law **1** the wrongful detaining of goods taken from the owner for distraint etc. **2** the detention of a person in prison etc. [AF *detener* f. OF *detenir* (as DETAIN)]

detect /dɪˈtekt/ v.tr. **1 a** (often foll. by *in*) reveal the guilt of; discover (*detected him in his crime*). **b** discover (a crime). **2** discover or perceive the existence or presence of (*detected a smell of burning; do I detect a note of sarcasm?*). **3** Physics use an instrument to observe (a signal, radiation, etc.). □□ **detectable** adj. **detectably** adv. [L *detegere detect-* (as DE-, *tegere* cover)]

detection /dɪˈtekʃ(ə)n/ n. **1 a** the act or an instance of detecting; the process of being detected. **b** an instance of this. **2** the work of a detective. **3** Physics the extraction of a desired signal; a demodulation. [LL *detectio* (as DETECT)]

detective /dɪˈtektɪv/ n. & adj. —n. (often *attrib.*) a person, esp. a member of a police force, employed to investigate crime. —adj. serving to detect. □ **detective story** etc. one describing a crime and the detection of criminals. (See below.) **private detective** a usu. freelance detective carrying out investigations for a private employer. [DETECT]

The first detective stories in English literature are generally reckoned to be Poe's 'The Murders in the Rue Morgue' (1841) and Wilkie Collins's *The Moonstone* (1868). Conan Doyle's 'Sherlock Holmes' stories achieved worldwide popularity; other outstanding examples are G. K. Chesterton's 'Father Brown' stories, and E. C. Bentley's *Trent's Last Case* (1913), which set the pattern for the next quarter-century of detective novels, generally regarded as the Golden Age of that genre. Among the classics are the works of Agatha Christie and D. L. Sayers, with their tradition of giving the reader full information presented so as to mislead, and ultimate vindication of law and order. From *c.*1950 the American school of tough detective fiction began to erode but never destroyed the classic British formula.

detector /dɪˈtektə(r)/ n. **1** a person or thing that detects. **2** Physics a device for the detection or demodulation of signals.

detent /dɪˈtent/ n. **1** a catch by the removal of which machinery is allowed to move. **2** (in a clock etc.) a catch that regulates striking. [F *détente* f. OF *destente* f. *destendre* slacken (as DE-, L *tendere*)]

détente /deɪˈtɑːt/ n. an easing of strained relations esp. between States. [F, = relaxation]

detention /dɪˈtenʃ(ə)n/ n. **1** detaining or being detained. **2 a** being kept in school after hours as a punishment. **b** an instance of this. **3** custody; confinement. □ **detention centre** Brit. an institution for the brief detention of young offenders. [F *détention* or LL *detentio* (as DETAIN)]

deter /dɪˈtɜː(r)/ v.tr. (**deterred**, **deterring**) **1** (often foll. by *from*) discourage or prevent (a person) through fear or dislike of the consequences. **2** discourage, check, or prevent (a thing, process, etc.). □□ **determent** n. [L *deterrēre* (as DE-, *terrēre* frighten)]

detergent /dɪˈtɜːdʒ(ə)nt/ n. & adj. —n. a cleansing agent, esp. a synthetic substance (usu. other than soap) used with water as a means of removing dirt etc. —adj. cleansing, esp. in the manner of a detergent. [L *detergēre* (as DE-, *tergēre ters-* wipe)]

deteriorate /dɪ'tɪərɪə,reɪt/ v.tr. & intr. make or become bad or worse (food deteriorates in hot weather; his condition deteriorated after the operation). □□ **deterioration** /-'reɪʃ(ə)n/ n. **deteriorative** /-rətɪv/ adj. [LL deteriorare deteriorat- f. L deterior worse]

determinant /dɪ'tɜ:mɪnənt/ adj. & n. —adj. serving to determine or define. —n. 1 a determining factor, element, word, etc. 2 Math. a quantity obtained by the addition of products of the elements of a square matrix according to a given rule. [L determinare (as DETERMINE)]

determinate /dɪ'tɜ:mɪnət/ adj. 1 limited in time, space, or character. 2 of definite scope or nature. □□ **determinacy** n. **determinately** adv. **determinateness** n. [ME f. L determinatus past part. (as DETERMINE)]

determination /dɪ,tɜ:mɪ'neɪʃ(ə)n/ n. 1 firmness of purpose; resoluteness. 2 the process of deciding, determining, or calculating. 3 a the conclusion of a dispute by the decision of an arbitrator. b the decision reached. 4 Law the cessation of an estate or interest. 5 Law a judicial decision or sentence. 6 archaic a tendency to move in a fixed direction. [ME (in sense 4) f. OF f. L determinatio -onis (as DETERMINE)]

determinative /dɪ'tɜ:mɪnətɪv/ adj. & n. —adj. serving to define, qualify, or direct. —n. a determinative thing or circumstance. □□ **determinatively** adv. [F déterminatif -ive (as DETERMINE)]

determine /dɪ'tɜ:mɪn/ v. 1 tr. find out or establish precisely (have to determine the extent of the problem). 2 tr. decide or settle (determined who should go). 3 tr. be a decisive factor in regard to (demand determines supply). 4 intr. & tr. make or cause (a person) to make a decision (we determined to go at once; what determined you to do it?). 5 tr. & intr. esp. Law bring or come to an end. 6 tr. Geom. fix or define the position of. □ **be determined** be resolved (was determined not to give up). □□ **determinable** adj. [ME f. OF determiner f. L determinare (as DE-, terminus end)]

determined /dɪ'tɜ:mɪnd/ adj. showing determination; resolute, unflinching. □□ **determinedly** adv. **determinedness** n.

determiner /dɪ'tɜ:mɪnə(r)/ n. 1 a person or thing that determines. 2 Gram. any of a class of words (e.g. a, the, every) that determine the kind of reference a noun or noun-substitute has.

determinism /dɪ'tɜ:mɪ,nɪz(ə)m/ n. Philos. the doctrine that all events, including human action, are determined by causes regarded as external to the will. □□ **determinist** n. **deterministic** /-'nɪstɪk/ adj. **deterministically** /-'nɪstɪkəlɪ/ adv.

deterrent /dɪ'terənt/ adj. & n. —adj. that deters. —n. a deterrent thing or factor, esp. a nuclear weapon regarded as deterring an enemy from attack. □□ **deterrence** n.

detest /dɪ'test/ v.tr. hate, loathe. □□ **detester** n. [L detestari (as DE-, testari call to witness f. testis witness)]

detestable /dɪ'testəb(ə)l/ adj. intensely disliked; hateful. □□ **detestably** adv.

detestation /,di:te'steɪʃ(ə)n/ n. 1 intense dislike, hatred. 2 a detested person or thing. [ME f. OF f. L detestatio -onis (as DETEST)]

dethrone /di:'θrəʊn/ v.tr. 1 remove from the throne, depose. 2 remove from a position of authority or influence. □□ **dethronement** n.

detonate /'detə,neɪt/ v.intr. & tr. explode with a loud noise. □□ **detonative** adj. [L detonare detonat- (as DE-, tonare thunder)]

detonation /,detə'neɪʃ(ə)n/ n. 1 a the act or process of detonating. b a loud explosion. 2 the premature combustion of fuel in an internal-combustion engine, causing it to pink. [F détonation f. détoner (as DETONATE)]

detonator /'detə,neɪtə(r)/ n. 1 a device for detonating an explosive. 2 a fog-signal that detonates, e.g. as used on railways.

detour /'di:tʊə(r)/ n. & v. —n. a divergence from a direct or intended route; a roundabout course. —v.intr. & tr. make or cause to make a detour. [F détour change of direction f. détourner turn away (as DE-, TURN)]

detoxicate /di:'tɒksɪ,keɪt/ v.tr. = DETOXIFY. □□ **detoxication** /-'keɪʃ(ə)n/ n. [DE- + L toxicum poison, after intoxicate]

detoxify /di:'tɒksɪ,faɪ/ v.tr. remove the poison from. □□ **detoxification** /-fɪ'keɪʃ(ə)n/ n. [DE- + L toxicum poison]

detract /dɪ'trækt/ v.tr. (usu. foll. by from) take away (a part of something); reduce, diminish (self-interest detracted nothing from their achievement). □□ **detraction** n. **detractive** adj. **detractor** n. [L detrahere detract- (as DE-, trahere draw)]

detrain /di:'treɪn/ v.intr. & tr. alight or cause to alight from a train. □□ **detrainment** n.

detribalize /di:'traɪbə,laɪz/ v.tr. (also -ise) 1 make (a person) no longer a member of a tribe. 2 destroy the tribal habits of. □□ **detribalization** /-'zeɪʃ(ə)n/ n.

detriment /'detrɪmənt/ n. 1 harm, damage. 2 something causing this. [ME f. OF detriment or L detrimentum (as DE-, terere trit- rub, wear)]

detrimental /,detrɪ'ment(ə)l/ adj. harmful; causing loss. □□ **detrimentally** adv.

detrition /dɪ'trɪʃ(ə)n/ n. wearing away by friction. [med.L detritio (as DETRIMENT)]

detritus /dɪ'traɪtəs/ n. matter produced by erosion, such as gravel, sand, silt, rock-debris, etc.; debris. □□ **detrital** /dɪ'traɪt(ə)l/ adj. [after F détritus f. L detritus (n.) = wearing down (as DETRIMENT)]

Detroit /dɪ'trɔɪt/ a major industrial city and Great Lakes shipping centre in NE Michigan; pop. (1982) 1,138,700. It is the centre of the US automobile industry, containing the headquarters of Ford, Chrysler, and General Motors — whence its nickname 'Motown' (short for 'motor town'). It was a famous centre for jazz and later for rock and soul music.

de trop /də 'trəʊ/ predic.adj. not wanted, unwelcome, in the way. [F, = excessive]

detumescence /,di:tju:'mes(ə)ns/ n. subsidence from a swollen state. [L detumescere (as DE-, tumescere swell)]

Deucalion /dju:'keɪlɪən/ Gk Mythol. the Greek Noah, son of Prometheus. When Zeus flooded the earth in wrath at the impiety of mankind, Deucalion and his wife Pyrrha took refuge on the top of Parnassus (or built an ark in which they were carried there). After the flood had subsided, to repopulate the world they were advised by Zeus (or by an oracle) to throw stones over their shoulders; those thrown by Deucalion became men, and those thrown by Pyrrha women.

deuce[1] /dju:s/ n. 1 the two on dice or playing cards. 2 (in lawn tennis) the score of 40 all, at which two consecutive points are needed to win. [OF deus f. L duo (accus. duos) two]

deuce[2] /dju:s/ n. misfortune, the Devil, used esp. colloq. as an exclamation of surprise or annoyance (who the deuce are you?). □ **a** (or **the**) **deuce of a** very bad or remarkable (a deuce of a problem; a deuce of a fellow). **the deuce to pay** trouble to be expected. [LG duus, formed as DEUCE[1], two aces at dice being the worst throw]

deuced /'dju:sɪd, dju:st/ adj. & adv. archaic damned, confounded (a deuced liar). □□ **deucedly** /'dju:sɪdlɪ/ adv.

deus ex machina /,deɪʊs eks 'mækɪnə, ,di:əs/ n. an unexpected power or event saving a seemingly hopeless situation, esp. in a play or novel. [mod.L transl. of Gk theos ek mēkhanēs, = god from the machinery (by which in the Greek theatre the gods were suspended above the stage)]

Deut. abbr. Deuteronomy (Old Testament).

deuteragonist /,dju:tə'rægənɪst/ n. the person second in importance to the protagonist in a drama. [Gk deuteragōnistēs (as DEUTERO-, agōnistēs actor)]

deuterate /'dju:tə,reɪt/ v.tr. replace the usual isotope of hydrogen in (a substance) by deuterium. □□ **deuteration** /-'reɪʃ(ə)n/ n.

deuterium /dju:'tɪərɪəm/ n. Chem. a stable isotope of hydrogen with a mass about double that of the usual isotope, differing from this in having a neutron as well as a proton in the nucleus. It is present to about 1 part in 6,000 in naturally occurring hydrogen. Discovered in 1931, it is used as a moderator in nuclear reactors and a fuel in thermonuclear bombs. [mod.L, formed as DEUTERO- + -IUM]

deutero- /'dju:tərəʊ/ comb. form second. [Gk deuteros second]

Deutero-Isaiah /ˌdjuːtərəʊaɪˈzaɪə/ n. the supposed later author of Isaiah 40–55, who wrote in the later years of the Babylonian Exile (549–538 BC).

deuteron /ˈdjuːtəˌrɒn/ n. Physics the nucleus of a deuterium atom, consisting of a proton and a neutron. [DEUTERIUM + -ON]

Deuteronomy /ˌdjuːtəˈrɒnəmɪ/ the fifth book of the Old Testament, containing a repetition, with hortatory comments, of the Ten Commandments and most of the laws in Exod. 21–4. [LL Deuteronomium f. Gk (deuteros nomos second law), from a mistranslation of Hebrew words (Deut. 17: 18) meaning 'a copy or duplicate of this law']

Deutschmark /ˈdɔɪtʃmɑːk/ n. (also **Deutsche Mark** /ˈdɔɪtʃə mɑːk/) the chief monetary unit of Germany. [G, = German mark (see MARK²)]

deutzia /ˈdjuːtsɪə, ˈdɔɪtsɪə/ n. any ornamental shrub of the genus Deutzia, with usu. white flowers. [J. Deutz 18th-c. Du. patron of botany]

deva /ˈdeɪvə/ n. a member of a class of divine beings in the Vedic period, which in Indian mythology are benevolent and in Zoroastrianism are evil. (Cf. ASURA.) [Skr., = god]

de Valera /də vəˈlɛərə/, Eamon (1882–1975), Irish statesman, one of the leaders of the Easter 1916 uprising against the British, condemned to death but eventually released a year later. He led Sinn Fein 1917–26 and was President of the provisional government in 1919–22. He founded the Fianna Fáil party in 1926 and served as President of the Irish Free State 1932–7. After the formation of the Irish Republic, de Valera served as Prime Minister on three separate occasions before ending his political career as President (1959–73).

devalue /diːˈvæljuː/ v.tr. (**devalues, devalued, devaluing**) 1 reduce the value of. 2 Econ. reduce the value of (a currency) in relation to other currencies or to gold (opp. REVALUE). □□ **devaluation** /-ˈeɪʃ(ə)n/ n.

Devanagari /ˌdeɪvəˈnɑːɡərɪ/ n. the alphabet used for Sanskrit, Hindi, and other Indian languages. [Skr., = divine town script]

devastate /ˈdevəˌsteɪt/ v.tr. 1 lay waste; cause great destruction to. 2 (often in passive) overwhelm with shock or grief; upset deeply. □□ **devastation** /-ˈsteɪʃ(ə)n/ n. **devastator** n. [L devastare devastat- (as DE-, vastare lay waste)]

devastating /ˈdevəˌsteɪtɪŋ/ adj. crushingly effective; overwhelming. □□ **devastatingly** adv.

develop /dɪˈveləp/ v. (**developed, developing**) 1 tr. & intr. **a** make or become bigger or fuller or more elaborate or systematic (the new town developed rapidly). **b** bring or come to an active or visible state or to maturity (developed a plan of action). 2 tr. begin to exhibit or suffer from (developed a rattle). 3 tr. **a** construct new buildings on (land). **b** convert (land) to a new purpose so as to use its resources more fully. 4 tr. treat (photographic film etc.) to make the latent image visible. 5 tr. Mus. elaborate (a theme) by modification of the melody, harmony, rhythm, etc. 6 tr. Chess bring (a piece) into position for effective use. □ **developing country** a poor or primitive country that is developing better economic and social conditions. □□ **developer** n. [F développer f. Rmc (as DIS-, orig. of second element unknown)]

developable /dɪˈveləpəb(ə)l/ adj. that can be developed. □ **developable surface** Geom. a surface that can be flattened into a plane without overlap or separation, e.g. a cylinder.

development /dɪˈveləpmənt/ n. 1 the act or an instance of developing; the process of being developed. 2 **a** a stage of growth or advancement. **b** a thing that has developed, esp. an event or circumstance (the latest developments). 3 a full-grown state. 4 the process of developing a photograph. 5 a developed area of land. 6 Mus. the elaboration of a theme or themes, esp. in the middle section of a sonata movement. 7 Chess the developing of pieces from their original position. □ **development area** Brit. one where new industries are encouraged in order to counteract unemployment.

developmental /dɪˌveləpˈment(ə)l/ adj. 1 incidental to growth (developmental diseases). 2 evolutionary. □□ **developmentally** adv.

Devi /ˈdeɪvɪ/ Hinduism the supreme goddess, often identified with Parvati. [Skr., = goddess]

deviant /ˈdiːvɪənt/ adj. & n. —adj. that deviates from the normal, esp. with reference to sexual practices. —n. a deviant person or thing. □□ **deviance** n. **deviancy** n. [ME (as DEVIATE)]

deviate /ˈdiːvɪˌeɪt/ v. & n. —v.intr. (often foll. by from) turn aside or diverge (from a course of action, rule, truth, etc.); digress. —n. /-vɪət/ a deviant, esp. a sexual pervert. □□ **deviator** n. **deviatory** /-vɪətərɪ/ adj. [LL deviare deviat- (as DE-, via way)]

deviation /ˌdiːvɪˈeɪʃ(ə)n/ n. 1 **a** deviating, digressing. **b** an instance of this. 2 Polit. a departure from accepted (esp. Communist) party doctrine. 3 Statistics the amount by which a single measurement differs from the mean. 4 Naut. the deflection of a ship's compass-needle caused by iron in the ship etc. □ **standard deviation** Statistics a quantity calculated to indicate the extent of deviation for a group as a whole. □□ **deviational** adj. **deviationism** n. **deviationist** n. [F déviation f. med.L deviatio -onis (as DEVIATE)]

device /dɪˈvaɪs/ n. 1 a thing made or adapted for a particular purpose, esp. a mechanical contrivance. 2 a plan, scheme, or trick. 3 **a** an emblematic or heraldic design. **b** a drawing or design. 4 archaic make, look (things of rare device). □ **leave a person to his** or **her own devices** leave a person to do as he or she wishes. [ME f. OF devis ult. f. L (as DIVIDE)]

devil /ˈdev(ə)l/ n. & v. —n. 1 (usu. **the Devil**) (in Christian and Jewish belief) the supreme spirit of evil; Satan. (See below.) 2 **a** an evil spirit; a demon; a superhuman malignant being. **b** a personified evil force or attribute. 3 **a** a wicked or cruel person. **b** a mischievously energetic, clever, or self-willed person. 4 colloq. a person, a fellow (lucky devil). 5 fighting spirit, mischievousness (the devil is in him tonight). 6 colloq. something difficult or awkward (this door is a devil to open). 7 (**the devil** or **the Devil**) colloq. used as an exclamation of surprise or annoyance (who the devil are you?). 8 a literary hack exploited by an employer. 9 Brit. a junior legal counsel. 10 = Tasmanian devil. 11 applied to various instruments and machines, esp. when used for destructive work. 12 S.Afr. = dust devil. —v. (**devilled, devilling**; US **deviled, deviling**) 1 tr. cook (food) with hot seasoning. 2 intr. act as a devil for an author or barrister. 3 tr. US harass, worry. □ **between the devil and the deep blue sea** in a dilemma. **devil-may-care** cheerful and reckless. **a devil of** colloq. a considerable, difficult, or remarkable. **devil a one** not even one. **devil ray** any cartilaginous fish of the family Mobulidae, esp. the manta. **devil's advocate** a person who tests a proposition by arguing against it. **devil's bit** any of various plants whose roots look bitten off, esp. a kind of scabious (Succisa pratensis). **devil's coach-horse** Brit. a large rove-beetle, Staphylinus olens. **devil's darning-needle** a dragonfly or damselfly. **devil's dozen** thirteen. **devils-on-horseback** a savoury of prune or plum wrapped in slices of bacon. **devil's own** colloq. very difficult or unusual (the devil's own job). **devil take the hindmost** a motto of selfish competition. **the devil to pay** trouble to be expected. **go to the devil** 1 be damned. 2 (in imper.) depart at once. **like the devil** with great energy. **play the devil with** cause severe damage to. **printer's devil** hist. an errand-boy in a printing office. **speak** (or **talk**) **of the devil** said when a person appears just after being mentioned. **the very devil** (predic.) colloq. a great difficulty or nuisance. [OE dēofol f. LL diabolus f. Gk diabolos accuser, slanderer f. dia across + ballō to throw]

The Devil is the supreme spirit of evil in Jewish and Christian theology, enemy of God and tempter of mankind. In theological tradition he was regarded as the chief of the fallen angels, cast out of heaven for rebellion against God, but there was no fixed teaching on the exact nature of his sin; known also as Satan, he was held to preside over those condemned to eternal fire (see HELL). In the narrative of the Fall, the serpent which tempted Eve has traditionally been regarded as his embodiment, and in Rev. 12: 7–9 he is identified with the dragon cast out by Michael and his angels.

devilfish /ˈdev(ə)lfɪʃ/ n. (pl. same or **-fishes**) 1 = devil ray. 2 any of various fish, esp. the stonefish. 3 hist. an octopus.

devilish /ˈdevəlɪʃ/ adj. & adv. —adj. **1** of or like a devil; wicked. **2** mischievous. —adv. colloq. very, extremely. □□ **devilishly** adv. **devilishness** n.

devilment /ˈdevəlmənt/ n. mischief, wild spirits.

devilry /ˈdevɪlrɪ/ n. (also **deviltry**) (pl. **-ies**) **1 a** wickedness; reckless mischief. **b** an instance of this. **2 a** black magic. **b** the Devil and his works. [OF diablerie: -try wrongly after harlotry etc.]

Devil's Island a rocky island off the coast of French Guiana. From 1852 it was part of a penal settlement, originally for prisoners suffering from contagious diseases, especially leprosy; later it was used largely for political prisoners, of whom the most famous was Albert Dreyfus, and became notorious for its harsh conditions. No prisoners were sent there after 1938, and the last one was released in 1953. The island is now chiefly a tourist attraction.

devious /ˈdiːvɪəs/ adj. **1** (of a person etc.) not straightforward, underhand. **2** winding, circuitous. **3** erring, straying. □□ **deviously** adv. **deviousness** n. [L devius f. DE- + via way]

devise /dɪˈvaɪz/ v. & n. —v.tr. **1** plan or invent by careful thought. **2** Law leave (real estate) by the terms of a will (cf. BEQUEATH). —n. **1** the act or an instance of devising. **2** Law a devising clause in a will. □□ **devisable** adj. **devisee** /-ˈziː/ n. (in sense 2 of v.). **deviser** n. **devisor** n. (in sense 2 of v.). [ME f. OF deviser ult. f. L dividere divis- DIVIDE: (n.) f. OF devise f. med.L divisa fem. past part. of dividere]

devitalize /diːˈvaɪtəˌlaɪz/ v.tr. (also **-ise**) take away strength and vigour from. □□ **devitalization** /-ˈzeɪʃ(ə)n/ n.

devitrify /diːˈvɪtrɪˌfaɪ/ v.tr. (**-ies**, **-ied**) deprive of vitreous qualities; make (glass or vitreous rock) opaque and crystalline. □□ **devitrification** /-fɪˈkeɪʃ(ə)n/ n.

devoid /dɪˈvɔɪd/ predic.adj. (foll. by of) quite lacking or free from (a book devoid of all interest). [ME, past part. of obs. devoid f. OF devoidier (as DE-, VOID)]

devoir /deˈvwɑː(r)/ n. archaic **1** duty, one's best (do one's devoir). **2** (in pl.) courteous or formal attentions; respects (pay one's devoirs to). [ME f. AF dever = OF deveir f. L debēre owe]

devolute /ˈdiːvəˌluːt, -ˌljuːt/ v.tr. transfer by devolution. [as DEVOLVE]

devolution /ˌdiːvəˈluːʃ(ə)n, -ˈljuːʃ(ə)n/ n. **1** the delegation of power, esp. by central government to local or regional administration. **2 a** descent or passing on through a series of stages. **b** descent by natural or due succession from one to another of property or qualities. **3** the lapse of an unexercised right to an ultimate owner. **4** Biol. degeneration. □□ **devolutionary** adj. **devolutionist** n. [LL devolutio (as DEVOLVE)]

devolve /dɪˈvɒlv/ v. **1** (foll. by on, upon, etc.) **a** tr. pass (work or duties) to (a deputy etc.). **b** intr. (of work or duties) pass to (a deputy etc.). **2** intr. (foll. by on, to, upon) Law (of property etc.) descend or fall by succession to. □□ **devolvement** n. [ME f. L devolvere devolut- (as DE-, volvere roll)]

Devon /ˈdevən/ a county of SW England; pop. (1981) 965,400; county town, Exeter.

Devonian /dɪˈvəʊnɪən/ adj. & n. —adj. **1** of or relating to Devon. **2** Geol. of or relating to the fourth period of the Palaeozoic era, following the Silurian and preceding the Carboniferous, lasting from about 408 to 360 million years ago. During this period fish became abundant, the first amphibians evolved, and the first forests appeared. —n. **1** this period or system. **2** a native of Devon. [med.L Devonia Devonshire]

Devonshire /ˈdevənʃɪə(r)/ = DEVON.

dévot /deɪˈvəʊ/ n. (fem. **dévote** /-ˈvəʊt/) a devotee. [F f. OF (as DEVOUT)]

devote /dɪˈvəʊt/ v.tr. & refl. **1** (foll. by to) apply or give over (resources etc. or oneself) to (a particular activity or purpose or person) (devoted their time to reading; devoted himself to his guests). **2** archaic doom to destruction. □□ **devotement** n. [L devovēre devot- (as DE-, vovēre vow)]

devoted /dɪˈvəʊtɪd/ adj. very loving or loyal (a devoted husband). □□ **devotedly** adv. **devotedness** n.

devotee /ˌdevəˈtiː/ n. **1** (usu. foll. by of) a zealous enthusiast or supporter. **2** a zealously pious or fanatical person.

devotion /dɪˈvəʊʃ(ə)n/ n. **1** (usu. foll. by to) enthusiastic attachment or loyalty (to a person or cause); great love. **2 a** religious worship. **b** (in pl.) prayers. **c** devoutness, religious fervour. □□ **devotional** adj. [ME f. OF devotion or L devotio (as DEVOTE)]

devour /dɪˈvaʊə(r)/ v.tr. **1** eat hungrily or greedily. **2** (of fire etc.) engulf, destroy. **3** take in greedily with the eyes or ears (devoured book after book). **4** absorb the attention of (devoured by anxiety). □□ **devourer** n. **devouringly** adv. [ME f. OF devorer f. L devorare (as DE-, vorare swallow)]

devout /dɪˈvaʊt/ adj. **1** earnestly religious. **2** earnestly sincere (devout hope). □□ **devoutly** adv. **devoutness** n. [ME f. OF devot f. L devotus past part. (as DEVOTE)]

DEW abbr. distant early warning.

dew /djuː/ n. & v. —n. **1** atmospheric vapour condensing in small drops on cool surfaces at night. **2** beaded or glistening moisture resembling this, e.g. tears. **3** freshness, refreshing quality. —v.tr. wet with or as with dew. □ **dew-claw 1** a rudimentary inner toe found on some dogs. **2** a false hoof on a deer etc. **dew-fall 1** the time when dew begins to form. **2** evening. **dew-point** the temperature at which dew forms. **dew-pond** a shallow usu. artificial pond once supposed to have been fed by atmospheric condensation. [OE dēaw f. Gmc]

dewan /dɪˈwɑːn/ n. the prime minister or finance minister of an Indian state. [Arab. & Pers. diwān fiscal register]

dewar /ˈdjuːə(r)/ n. Physics a double-walled flask with a vacuum between the walls to reduce the transfer of heat. [Sir James Dewar, Brit. physicist d. 1923]

dewberry /ˈdjuːbərɪ/ n. (pl. **-ies**) **1** a bluish fruit like the blackberry. **2** the shrub, Rubus caesius, bearing this.

dewdrop /ˈdjuːdrɒp/ n. a drop of dew.

Dewey[1] /ˈdjuːɪ/, John (1859–1952), American philosopher and educationist. His pragmatic philosophy (called instrumentalism) holds that thought is an instrument, producing theories designed to solve practical problems over a wide range (in logic, metaphysics, morals, art, etc.); truth is not final and static but changes as these problems change. In education, he observed that most schools were proceeding along traditional lines and failing to take account of the findings of child psychologists or of the needs of a changing and democratic social environment, and argued strongly for learning by experience and necessity rather than through authoritarian instruction: education should meet and develop the child's own interests and abilities. In the 1930s he was a prominent campaigner in favour of civil liberties and against militarism.

Dewey[2] /ˈdjuːɪ/, Melville (1851–1931), American librarian who devised the decimal system, named after him, of classifying books by their subject-matter.

dewlap /ˈdjuːlæp/ n. **1** a loose fold of skin hanging from the throat of cattle, dogs, etc. **2** similar loose skin round the throat of an elderly person. [ME f. DEW + LAP[1], perh. after ON (unrecorded) döggleppr]

dewy /ˈdjuːɪ/ adj. (**dewier**, **dewiest**) **1 a** wet with dew. **b** moist as if with dew. **2** of or like dew. □ **dewy-eyed** innocently trusting; naïvely sentimental. □□ **dewily** adv. **dewiness** n. [OE dēawig (as DEW, -Y[1])]

dexter[1] /ˈdekstə(r)/ adj. esp. Heraldry on or of the right-hand side (the observer's left) of a shield etc. [L, = on the right]

dexter[2] /ˈdekstə(r)/ n. **1** an animal of a small hardy breed of Irish cattle. **2** this breed. [19th c.: perh. f. the name of a breeder]

dexterity /dekˈsterɪtɪ/ n. **1** skill in handling. **2** manual or mental adroitness. **3** right-handedness, using the right hand. [F dextérité f. L dexteritas (as DEXTER[1])]

dexterous /ˈdekstrəs/ adj. (also **dextrous**) having or showing dexterity. □□ **dexterously** adv. **dexterousness** n. [L DEXTER[1] + -OUS]

dextral /ˈdekstr(ə)l/ adj. & n. —adj. **1** (of a person) right-handed. **2** of or on the right. **3** Zool. (of a spiral shell) with whorls rising to the right and coiling in an anticlockwise direction. **4** *Zool.* (of a flat-fish) with the right side uppermost. —*n.* a right-handed person. □□ **dextrality** /-ˈstrælɪtɪ/ *n.* **dextrally** *adv.* [med.L *dextralis* f. L *dextra* right hand]

dextran /ˈdekstræn/ *n. Chem. & Pharm.* **1** an amorphous gum formed by the fermentation of sucrose etc. **2** a degraded form of this used as a substitute for blood-plasma. [G (as DEXTRO- + -*an* as in Chem. names)]

dextrin /ˈdekstrɪn/ *n. Chem.* a soluble gummy substance obtained from starch and used as an adhesive. [F *dextrine* f. L *dextra*: see DEXTRO-, -IN]

dextro- /ˈdekstrəʊ/ *comb. form* on or to the right (*dextrorotatory*; *dextrose*). [L *dexter*, *dextra* on or to the right]

dextrorotatory /ˌdekstrəʊrəʊˈteɪtərɪ/ *adj. Chem.* having the property of rotating the plane of a polarized light ray to the right (cf. LAEVOROTATORY). □□ **dextrorotation** *n.*

dextrorse /ˈdekstrɔːs/ *adj.* rising towards the right, esp. of a spiral stem. [L *dextrorsus* (as DEXTRO-)]

dextrose /ˈdekstrəʊs/ *n. Chem.* the dextrorotatory form of glucose. [formed as DEXTRO- + -OSE²]

dextrous var. of DEXTEROUS.

DF *abbr.* **1** Defender of the Faith. **2** direction-finder. [in sense 1 f. L *Defensor Fidei*]

DFC *abbr. Brit.* Distinguished Flying Cross.

DFM *abbr. Brit.* Distinguished Flying Medal.

DG *abbr.* **1** *Dei gratia.* **2** *Deo gratias.* **3** director-general.

Dhaka /ˈdækə/ (also **Dacca**) the capital of Bangladesh, on the Ganges delta; pop. (1981) 3,440,150.

dhal /dɑːl/ *n.* (also **dal**) **1** a kind of split pulse, a common foodstuff in India. **2** a dish made with this. [Hindi]

Dhanbad /ˈdɑːnbɑːd/ a city in Bihar in NE India; pop. (1981) 677,000.

dharma /ˈdɑːmə/ *n.* the eternal law of the Hindu cosmos, inherent in the very nature of things, upheld (but neither created nor controlled) by the gods. The concept is both descriptive and prescriptive: what is and what should be. In the context of individual action, it denotes the social rules codified in the lawbooks (e.g. The Laws of Manu); in Buddhism, it is the true doctrine as preached by the Buddha; in Jainism, it is both virtue and a fundamental substance, the medium of motion. [Skr., = law, custom]

Dhelfoí see DELPHI.

dhobi /ˈdəʊbɪ/ *n.* (*pl.* **dhobis**) *Ind.* etc. a washerman or washerwoman. □ **dhobi** (or **dhobi's**) **itch** a tropical skin disease; an allergic dermatitis. [Hindi *dhobī* f. *dhob* washing]

Dhofar /dəʊˈfɑː(r)/ the fertile southern province of Oman. Its chief town is the port of Salalah (pop. est. 10,000).

dhoti /ˈdəʊtɪ/ *n.* (*pl.* **dhotis**) the loincloth worn by male Hindus. [Hindi *dhotī*]

dhow /daʊ/ *n.* a lateen-rigged ship used on the Arabian sea. [19th c.: orig. unkn.]

DHSS *abbr. hist.* (in the UK) Department of Health and Social Security (cf. DoH, DSS).

dhurra var. of DURRA.

DI *abbr. Brit.* Defence Intelligence. **D.I.5** was formerly (and is still often) called M.I.5; **D.I.6** is the technical (though seldom used) name for M.I.6, and is also known as the SIS.

di-¹ /daɪ/ *comb. form* **1** twice, two-, double. **2** *Chem.* containing two atoms, molecules, or groups of a specified kind (*dichromate*; *dioxide*). [Gk f. *dis* twice]

di-² /daɪ, dɪ/ *prefix* form of DIS- occurring before *l, m, n, r, s* (foll. by a consonant), *v,* usu. *g*, and sometimes *j*. [L var. of *dis*-]

di-³ /daɪ/ *prefix* form of DIA- before a vowel.

dia. *abbr.* diameter.

dia- /ˈdaɪə/ *prefix* (also **di-** before a vowel) **1** through (*diaphanous*). **2** apart (*diacritical*). **3** across (*diameter*). [Gk f. *dia* through]

diabetes /ˌdaɪəˈbiːtiːz/ *n.* **1** any disorder of the metabolism with excessive thirst and the production of large amounts of urine. **2** (in full **diabetes mellitus**) the commonest form of diabetes in which sugar and starch are not properly metabolized by the

body. In 1922, as a result of the work of F. G. Banting and others, it was discovered that the disease is due to a deficiency in the production or effectiveness of the hormone insulin, which is produced in certain cells of the pancreas. Diabetes is characterized by thirst, emaciation, excessive production of urine containing glucose, and abnormally high levels of sugar in the blood. It is one of the earliest known diseases, being recorded in an Egyptian papyrus of *c*.1500 BC. The word *mellitus* (L, = sweet) was added to distinguish this disease from the much rarer diabetes insipidus (see below). □ **diabetes insipidus** a rare metabolic disorder due to a pituitary deficiency, with excessive urination and thirst but not involving sugar metabolism. [orig. = siphon: L f. Gk f. *diabainō* go through]

diabetic /ˌdaɪəˈbetɪk/ *adj. & n.* —*adj.* **1** of or relating to or having diabetes. **2** for use by diabetics. —*n.* a person suffering from diabetes.

diablerie /daɪˈɑːblərɪ/ *n.* **1** the devil's work; sorcery. **2** wild recklessness. **3** the realm of devils; devil-lore. [F f. *diable* f. L *diabolus* DEVIL]

diabolic /ˌdaɪəˈbɒlɪk/ *adj.* (also **diabolical** /-ˈbɒlɪk(ə)l/) **1** of the Devil. **2** devilish; inhumanly cruel or wicked. **3** fiendishly clever or cunning or annoying. □□ **diabolically** *adv.* [ME f. OF *diabolique* or LL *diabolicus* f. L *diabolus* (as DEVIL)]

diabolism /daɪˈæbəˌlɪz(ə)m/ *n.* **1 a** belief in or worship of the Devil. **b** sorcery. **2** devilish conduct or character. □□ **diabolist** *n.* [Gk *diabolos* DEVIL]

diabolize /daɪˈæbəˌlaɪz/ *v.tr.* (also **-ise**) make into or represent as a devil.

diabolo /dɪˈæbələʊ, daɪ-/ *n.* (*pl.* **-os**) **1** a game in which a two-headed top is thrown up and caught with a string stretched between two sticks. **2** the top itself. [It., = DEVIL: formerly called *devil on two sticks*]

diachronic /ˌdaɪəˈkrɒnɪk/ *adj. Linguistics* etc. concerned with the historical development of a subject (esp. a language) (opp. SYNCHRONIC). □□ **diachronically** *adv.* **diachronism** /daɪˈækrəˌnɪz(ə)m/ *n.* **diachronistic** /daɪˌækrəˈnɪstɪk/ *adj.* **diachronous** /daɪˈækrənəs/ *adj.* **diachrony** /daɪˈækrənɪ/ *n.* [F *diachronique* (as DIA-, CHRONIC)]

diaconal /daɪˈækən(ə)l/ *adj.* of a deacon. [eccl.L *diaconalis* f. *diaconus* DEACON]

diaconate /daɪˈækəˌneɪt, -nət/ *n.* **1 a** the office of deacon. **b** a person's time as deacon. **2** a body of deacons. [eccl.L *diaconatus* (as DIACONAL)]

diacritic /ˌdaɪəˈkrɪtɪk/ *n. & adj.* —*n.* a sign (e.g. an accent, diaeresis, cedilla) used to indicate different sounds or values of a letter. —*adj.* = DIACRITICAL. [Gk *diakritikos* (as DIA-, CRITIC)]

diacritical /ˌdaɪəˈkrɪtɪk(ə)l/ *adj. & n.* —*adj.* distinguishing, distinctive. —*n.* (in full **diacritical mark** or **sign**) = DIACRITIC.

diadelphous /ˌdaɪəˈdelfəs/ *adj. Bot.* with the stamens united in two bundles (cf. MONADELPHOUS, POLYADELPHOUS). [DI-¹ + Gk *adelphos* brother]

diadem /ˈdaɪəˌdem/ *n. & v.* —*n.* **1** a crown or headband worn as a sign of sovereignty. **2** a wreath of leaves or flowers worn round the head. **3** sovereignty. **4** a crowning distinction or glory. —*v.tr.* (esp. as **diademed** *adj.*) adorn with or as with a diadem. [ME f. OF *diademe* f. L *diadema* f. Gk *diadēma* (as DIA-, *deō* bind)]

Diadochi /daɪˈædəkɪ/ *n.pl.* the Macedonian generals of Alexander the Great (Antigonus, Antipater, Cassander, Lysimachus, Ptolemy, and Seleucus) among whom his empire was eventually divided after his death in 323 BC. [Gk *diadokhoi* successors]

diaeresis /daɪˈɪərəsɪs/ *n.* (US **dieresis**) (*pl.* **-ses** /-ˌsiːz/) **1** a mark (as in *naïve*) over a vowel to indicate that it is sounded separately. **2** *Prosody* a break where a foot ends at the end of a word. [L f. Gk, = separation]

diagenesis /ˌdaɪəˈdʒenɪsɪs/ *n. Geol.* the transformation occurring during the conversion of sedimentation to sedimentary rock.

Diaghilev /dɪˈæɡɪˌlef/, Serge Pavlovich (1872–1929), Russian ballet impresario. After the closure of his magazine *The World of Art* (1899–1904) he began taking opera and ballet productions to Paris, bringing about the gradual formation of his Ballets Russes, which he directed until his death. Initially with Nijinsky as his star performer, and later with Massine, he effected a complete reformation of the European ballet scene, becoming a catalyst of the most important artistic trends during the 1910s and 1920s, though not himself a choreographer. The company never performed in Russia.

diagnose /'daɪəgˌnəʊz/ v.tr. make a diagnosis of (a disease, a mechanical fault, etc.) from its symptoms. □□ **diagnosable** adj.

diagnosis /ˌdaɪəg'nəʊsɪs/ n. (pl. **diagnoses** /-ˌsiːz/) **1 a** the identification of a disease by means of a patient's symptoms. **b** an instance or formal statement of this. **2 a** the identification of the cause of a mechanical fault etc. **b** an instance of this. **3 a** the distinctive characterization in precise terms of a genus, species, etc. **b** an instance of this. [mod.L f. Gk (as DIA-, *gignōskō* recognize)]

diagnostic /ˌdaɪəg'nɒstɪk/ adj. & n. —adj. of or assisting diagnosis. —n. a symptom. □□ **diagnostically** adv. **diagnostician** /-nɒ'stɪʃ(ə)n/ n. [Gk *diagnōstikos* (as DIAGNOSIS)]

diagnostics /ˌdaɪəg'nɒstɪks/ n. **1** (treated as pl.) Computing programs and other mechanisms used to detect and identify faults in hardware or software. **2** (treated as sing.) the science or study of diagnosing disease.

diagonal /daɪ'æg ən(ə)l/ adj. & n. —adj. **1** crossing a straight-sided figure from corner to corner. **2** slanting, oblique. —n. a straight line joining two non-adjacent corners. □□ **diagonally** adv. [L *diagonalis* f. Gk *diagōnios* (as DIA-, *gōnia* angle)]

diagram /'daɪəˌgræm/ n. & v. —n. **1** a drawing showing the general scheme or outline of an object and its parts. **2** a graphic representation of the course or results of an action or process. **3** Geom. a figure made of lines used in proving a theorem etc. —v.tr. (**diagrammed, diagramming**; US **diagramed, diagraming**) represent by means of a diagram. □□ **diagrammatic** /-grə'mætɪk/ adj. **diagrammatically** /-grə'mætɪkəlɪ/ adv. [L *diagramma* f. Gk (as DIA-, -GRAM)]

diagrid /'daɪəgrɪd/ n. Archit. a supporting structure of diagonally intersecting ribs of metal etc. [DIAGONAL + GRID]

diakinesis /ˌdaɪəkɪ'niːsɪs, -kaɪ'niːsɪs/ n. (pl. **diakineses** /-siːz/) Biol. a stage during the prophase of meiosis when the separation of homologous chromosomes is complete and crossing over has occurred. [mod.L f. G *Diakinese* (as DIA-, Gk *kinēsis* motion)]

dial /'daɪ(ə)l/ n. & v. —n. **1** the face of a clock or watch, marked to show the hours etc. **2** a similar flat plate marked with a scale for measuring weight, volume, pressure, consumption, etc., indicated by a pointer. **3** a movable disc on a telephone, with finger-holes and numbers for making a connection. **4 a** a plate or disc etc. on a radio or television set for selecting wavelength or channel. **b** a similar selecting device on other equipment, e.g. a washing machine. **5** Brit. sl. a person's face. —v. (**dialled, dialling**; US **dialed, dialing**) **1** tr. (also absol.) select (a telephone number) by means of a dial or set of buttons (*dialled 999*). **2** tr. measure, indicate, or regulate by means of a dial. □ **dialling code** a sequence of numbers dialled to connect a telephone with the exchange of the telephone being called. **dialling tone** (US **dial tone**) a sound indicating that a caller may start to dial. □□ **dialler** n. [ME, = sundial, f. med.L *diale* clock-dial ult. f. L *dies* day]

dialect /'daɪəˌlekt/ n. **1** a form of speech peculiar to a particular region. **2** a subordinate variety of a language with non-standard vocabulary, pronunciation, or grammar. □□ **dialectal** /-'lekt(ə)l/ adj. **dialectology** /-'tɒlədʒɪ/ n. **dialectologist** /-'tɒlədʒɪst/ n. [F *dialecte* or L *dialectus* f. Gk *dialektos* discourse f. *dialegomai* converse]

dialectic /ˌdaɪə'lektɪk/ n. & adj. Philos. —n. **1 a** the art of investigating the truth of opinions; the testing of truth by discussion. **b** logical disputation. **2 a** inquiry into metaphysical contradictions and their solutions, esp. in the thought of Kant and Hegel. **b** the existence or action of opposing social forces etc. —adj. **1** of or relating to logical disputation. **2** fond of or skilled in logical disputation. [ME f. OF *dialectique* or L *dialectica* f. Gk *dialektikē* (*tekhnē*) (art) of debate (as DIALECT)]

dialectical /ˌdaɪə'lektɪk(ə)l/ adj. of dialectic or dialectics. □ **dialectical materialism** the theory propagated by Marx and Engels according to which political events or social phenomena are to be interpreted as a conflict of social forces (the 'class struggle') produced by the operation of economic causes, and history is to be interpreted as a series of contradictions and their solutions (the thesis, antithesis, and synthesis of Hegel's philosophy). [f. prec.] □□ **dialectically** adv.

dialectician /ˌdaɪəlek'tɪʃ(ə)n/ n. a person skilled in dialectic. [F *dialecticien* f. L *dialecticus*]

dialectics /ˌdaɪə'lektɪks/ n. (treated as sing. or pl.) = DIALECTIC n. 1.

dialogic /ˌdaɪə'lɒdʒɪk/ adj. of or in dialogue. [LL *dialogicus* f. Gk *dialogikos* (as DIALOGUE)]

dialogist /daɪ'ælədʒɪst/ n. a speaker in or writer of dialogue. [LL *dialogista* f. Gk *dialogistēs* (as DIALOGUE)]

dialogue /'daɪəˌlɒg/ n. (US **dialog**) **1 a** conversation. **b** conversation in written form; this as a form of composition. **2 a** a discussion, esp. one between representatives of two political groups. **b** a conversation, a talk (*long dialogues between the two main characters*). [ME f. OF *dialoge* f. L *dialogus* f. Gk *dialogos* f. *dialegomai* converse]

dialyse /'daɪəˌlaɪz/ v.tr. (US **dialyze**) separate by means of dialysis.

dialysis /daɪ'ælɪsɪs/ n. (pl. **dialyses** /-ˌsiːz/) **1** Chem. the separation of particles in a liquid by differences in their ability to pass through a membrane into another liquid. **2** Med. the process of allowing blood to flow past such a membrane on the other side of which is another liquid, so that certain dissolved substances in the blood may pass through the membrane and the blood itself be purified or cleansed in cases of renal failure, poisoning, etc.; an occasion of undergoing this process. The dialysis may take place outside the body in an artificial kidney or inside it using a natural membrane such as the peritoneum. □□ **dialytic** /ˌdaɪə'lɪtɪk/ adj. [L f. Gk *dialusis* (as DIA-, *luō* set free)]

diamagnetic /ˌdaɪəmæg'netɪk/ adj. & n. —adj. tending to become magnetized in a direction at right angles to the applied magnetic field. —n. a diamagnetic body or substance. □□ **diamagnetically** adv. **diamagnetism** /-'mægnɪˌtɪz(ə)m/ n.

diamanté /dɪə'mɒteɪ/ adj. & n. —adj. decorated with powdered crystal or another sparkling substance. —n. fabric or costume jewellery so decorated. [F, past part. of *diamanter* set with diamonds f. *diamant* DIAMOND]

diamantiferous /ˌdaɪəmæn'tɪfərəs/ adj. diamond-yielding. [F *diamantifère* f. *diamant* DIAMOND]

diamantine /ˌdaɪə'mæntaɪn/ adj. of or like diamonds. [F *diamantin* (as DIAMANTIFEROUS)]

diameter /daɪ'æmɪtə(r)/ n. **1 a** a straight line passing from side to side through the centre of a body or figure, esp. a circle or sphere. **b** the length of this line. **2** a transverse measurement; width, thickness. **3** a unit of linear measurement of magnifying power (*a lens magnifying 2000 diameters*). □□ **diametral** adj. [ME f. OF *diametre* f. L *diametrus* f. Gk *diametros* (*grammē*) (line) measuring across f. *metron* measure]

diametrical /ˌdaɪə'metrɪk(ə)l/ adj. (also **diametric**) **1** of or along a diameter. **2** (of opposition, difference, etc.) complete, like that between opposite ends of a diameter. □□ **diametrically** adv. [Gk *diametrikos* (as DIAMETER)]

diamond /'daɪəmənd/ n., adj., & v. —n. **1** a precious stone of pure carbon crystallized in octahedrons etc., the hardest naturally-occurring substance. **2** a figure shaped like the cross-section of a diamond; a rhombus. **3 a** a playing-card of a suit denoted by a red rhombus. **b** (in pl.) this suit. **4** a glittering particle or point (of frost etc.). **5** a tool with a small diamond for glass-cutting. **6** Baseball **a** the space delimited by the bases. **b** the entire field. —adj. **1** made of or set with diamonds or a diamond. **2** rhombus-shaped. —v.tr. adorn with or as with diamonds. □ **diamond cut diamond** wit or cunning is met by its like. **diamond jubilee** the 60th (or 75th) anniversary of an event, esp. a sovereign's accession. **diamond wedding** a 60th (or 75th) wedding anniversary. □□ **diamondiferous** /-'dɪfərəs/ adj. [ME f. OF *diamant* f. med.L *diamas diamant-* var. of L *adamas* ADAMANT f. Gk]

æ cat ɑː arm e bed ɜː her ɪ sit iː see ɒ hot ɔː saw ʌ run ʊ put uː too ə ago aɪ my

diamondback /ˈdaɪəmənd₁bæk/ n. **1** an edible freshwater terrapin, *Malaclemys terrapin*, native to N. America, with lozenge-shaped markings on its shell. **2** any rattlesnake of the genus *Crotalus*, native to N. America, with diamond-shaped markings.

Diamond Head a volcanic crater overlooking the port of Honolulu on the Hawaiian island of Oahu.

Diana /daɪˈænə/ *Rom. Mythol.* an early Italian goddess anciently identified with Artemis. There is no real evidence that she was a moon-goddess, though she often occurs in English literature in this character. [prob. = bright one]

diandrous /daɪˈændrəs/ adj. having two stamens. [DI-¹ + Gk *anēr andr-* man]

dianthus /daɪˈænθəs/ n. any flowering plant of the genus *Dianthus*, e.g. a carnation or pink. [Gk *Dios* of Zeus + *anthos* flower]

diapason /₁daɪəˈpeɪz(ə)n, -ˈpeɪs(ə)n/ n. *Mus.* **1** the compass of a voice or musical instrument. **2** a fixed standard of musical pitch. **3** (in full **open** or **stopped diapason**) either of two main organ-stops extending through the organ's whole compass. **4 a** a combination of notes or parts in a harmonious whole. **b** a melodious succession of notes, esp. a grand swelling burst of harmony. **5** an entire compass, range, or scope. [ME in sense 'octave' f. L *diapason* f. Gk *dia pasōn (khordōn)* through all (notes)]

diapause /ˈdaɪə₁pɔːz/ n. a period of retarded or suspended development in some insects.

diaper /ˈdaɪəpə(r)/ n. & v. —n. **1** US a baby's nappy. **2 a** a linen or cotton fabric with a small diamond pattern. **b** this pattern. **3** a similar ornamental design of diamonds etc. for panels, walls, etc. —v.tr. decorate with a diaper pattern. [ME f. OF *diapre* f. med.L *diasprum* f. med.Gk *diaspros* (adj.) (as DIA-, *aspros* white)]

diaphanous /daɪˈæfənəs/ adj. (of fabric etc.) light and delicate, and almost transparent. □□ **diaphanously** adv. [med.L *diaphanus* f. Gk *diaphanes* (as DIA-, *phainō* show)]

diaphoresis /₁daɪəfəˈriːsɪs/ n. *Med.* sweating, esp. artificially induced. [LL f. Gk f. *diaphoreō* carry through]

diaphoretic /₁daɪəfəˈretɪk/ adj. & n. —adj. inducing perspiration. —n. an agent inducing perspiration. [LL *diaphoreticus* f. Gk *diaphorētikos* (formed as DIAPHORESIS)]

diaphragm /ˈdaɪə₁fræm/ n. **1** a muscular partition separating the thorax from the abdomen in mammals. **2** a partition in animal and plant tissues. **3** a disc pierced by one or more holes in optical and acoustic systems etc. **4** a device for varying the effective aperture of the lens in a camera etc. **5** a thin contraceptive cap fitting over the cervix. **6** a thin sheet of material used as a partition etc. □ **diaphragm pump** a pump using a flexible diaphragm in place of a piston. □□ **diaphragmatic** /-frægˈmætɪk/ adj. [ME f. LL *diaphragma* f. Gk (as DIA-, *phragma -atos* f. *phrassō* fence in)]

diapositive /₁daɪəˈpɒzɪtɪv/ n. a positive photographic slide or transparency.

diarchy /ˈdaɪɑːkɪ/ n. (also **dyarchy**) (pl. **-ies**) **1** government by two independent authorities (esp. in India 1921–37). **2** an instance of this. □□ **diarchal** /daɪˈɑːk(ə)l/ adj. **diarchic** /daɪˈɑːkɪk/ adj. [DI-¹ + Gk *-arkhia* rule, after *monarchy*]

diarist /ˈdaɪərɪst/ n. a person who keeps a diary. □□ **diaristic** /-ˈrɪstɪk/ adj.

diarize /ˈdaɪə₁raɪz/ v. (also **-ise**) **1** intr. keep a diary. **2** tr. enter in a diary.

diarrhoea /₁daɪəˈrɪə/ n. (esp. US **diarrhea**) a condition of excessively frequent and loose bowel movements. □□ **diarrhoeal** adj. **diarrhoeic** adj. [ME f. LL f. Gk *diarrhoia* (as DIA-, *rheō* flow)]

diary /ˈdaɪərɪ/ n. (pl. **-ies**) **1** a daily record of events or thoughts. **2** a book for this or for noting future engagements, usu. printed and with a calendar and other information. [L *diarium* f. *dies* day]

Dias /ˈdiːæs/, Bartolomeu (c.1450–1500), Portuguese navigator and explorer, the first European to round the Cape of Good Hope (1488), thereby establishing a sea route from the Atlantic to Asia round the southernmost point of Africa.

diascope /ˈdaɪə₁skəʊp/ n. an optical projector giving images of transparent objects.

Diaspora /daɪˈæspərə/ n. **1** (prec. by *the*) **a** the dispersion of the Jews among the Gentiles mainly in the 8th–6th c. BC. **b** Jews dispersed in this way. **2** (also **diaspora**) **a** any group of people similarly dispersed. **b** their dispersion. [Gk f. *diaspeirō* (as DIA-, *speirō* scatter)]

diastase /ˈdaɪə₁steɪz/ n. *Biochem.* = AMYLASE. □□ **diastasic** /-ˈsteɪzɪk/ adj. **diastatic** /-ˈstætɪk/ adj. [F f. Gk *diastasis* separation (as DIA-, *stasis* placing)]

diastole /daɪˈæstəlɪ/ n. *Physiol.* the period between two contractions of the heart when the heart muscle relaxes and allows the chambers to fill with blood (cf. SYSTOLE). □□ **diastolic** /₁daɪəˈstɒlɪk/ adj. [LL f. Gk *diastellō* (as DIA-, *stellō* place)]

diathermancy /₁daɪəˈθɜːmənsɪ/ n. the quality of transmitting radiant heat. □□ **diathermic** adj. **diathermous** adj. [F *diathermansie* f. Gk *dia* through + *thermansis* heating: assim. to -ANCY]

diathermy /ˈdaɪə₁θɜːmɪ/ n. the application of high-frequency electric currents to produce heat in the deeper tissues of the body. In medical use the tissues are warmed but not sufficiently to change their nature; in surgical use there is sufficient heating to produce a local change such as destruction of tissue or coagulation of bleeding vessels. [G *Diathermie* f. Gk *dia* through + *thermon* heat]

diathesis /daɪˈæθɪsɪs/ n. *Med.* a constitutional predisposition to a certain state, esp. a diseased one. [mod.L f. Gk *diatithēmi* arrange]

diatom /ˈdaɪətəm/ n. a microscopic unicellular alga with a siliceous cell-wall, found as plankton and forming fossil deposits. □□ **diatomaceous** /-ˈmeɪʃəs/ adj. [mod.L *Diatoma* (genus-name) f. Gk *diatomos* (as DIA-, *temnō* cut)]

diatomic /₁daɪəˈtɒmɪk/ adj. consisting of two atoms. [DI-¹ + ATOM]

diatomite /daɪˈætə₁maɪt/ n. a deposit composed of the siliceous skeletons of diatoms.

diatonic /₁daɪəˈtɒnɪk/ adj. *Mus.* **1** (of a scale, interval, etc.) involving only notes proper to the prevailing key without chromatic alteration. **2** (of a melody or harmony) constructed from such a scale. [F *diatonique* or LL *diatonicus* f. Gk *diatonikos* at intervals of a tone (as DIA-, TONIC)]

diatribe /ˈdaɪə₁traɪb/ n. a forceful verbal attack; a piece of bitter criticism. [F f. L *diatriba* f. Gk *diatribē* spending of time, discourse f. *diatribō* (as DIA-, *tribō* rub)]

diazepam /daɪˈæzɪ₁pæm/ n. a tranquillizing muscle-relaxant drug with anticonvulsant properties used to relieve anxiety, tension, etc. [benzodiazepine + am]

diazo /daɪˈeɪzəʊ/ n. (in full **diazotype**) a copying or colouring process using a diazo compound decomposed by light. □ **diazo compound** *Chem.* a chemical compound containing two usu. multiply-bonded nitrogen atoms, often highly coloured and used as dyes. [DI-¹ + AZO-]

dib /dɪb/ v.intr. (**dibbed**, **dibbing**) = DAP. [var. of DAB¹]

dibasic /daɪˈbeɪsɪk/ adj. *Chem.* having two replaceable protons. [DI-¹ + BASE¹ 6]

dibber /ˈdɪbə(r)/ n. = DIBBLE.

dibble /ˈdɪb(ə)l/ n. & v. —n. a hand-tool for making holes in the ground for seeds or young plants. —v. **1** tr. sow or plant with a dibble. **2** tr. prepare (soil) with a dibble. **3** intr. use a dibble. [ME: perh. rel. to DIB]

dibs /dɪbz/ n.pl. sl. money. [earlier sense 'pebbles for game', also *dib-stones*, perh. f. DIB]

dice /daɪs/ n. & v. —n.pl. **1 a** small cubes with faces bearing 1–6 spots used in games of chance. **b** (treated as *sing.*) one of these cubes (see DIE²). **2** a game played with one or more such cubes. —v. **1 a** intr. play dice. **b** intr. take great risks; gamble (*dicing with death*). **c** tr. (foll. by *away*) gamble away. **2** tr. cut (food) into small cubes. **3** tr. *Austral. sl.* reject; leave alone. **4** tr. chequer, mark with squares. □ **no dice** sl. no success or prospect of it. □□ **dicer** n. (in sense 1 of v.). [pl. of DIE²]

dicey /ˈdaɪsɪ/ adj. (**dicier, diciest**) sl. risky, unreliable. [DICE + -Y¹]

dichotomy /daɪˈkɒtəmɪ/ n. (pl. **-ies**) **1 a** a division into two, esp.

a sharply defined one. **b** the result of such a division. **2** binary classification. **3** *Bot.* & *Zool.* repeated bifurcation. □□ **dichotomic** /-kə'tɒmɪk/ *adj.* **dichotomize** *v.* **dichotomous** *adj.* [mod.L *dichotomia* f. Gk *dikhotomia* f. *dikho-* apart + -TOMY]

dichroic /daɪ'krəʊɪk/ *adj.* (esp. of doubly refracting crystals) showing two colours. □□ **dichroism** *n.* [Gk *dikhroos* (as DI-[1], *khrōs* colour)]

dichromatic /ˌdaɪkrəʊ'mætɪk/ *adj.* **1** two-coloured. **2 a** (of animal species) having individuals that show different colorations. **b** having vision sensitive to only two of the three primary colours. □□ **dichromatism** /daɪ'krəʊməˌtɪz(ə)m/ *n.* [DI-[1] + Gk *khrōmatikos* f. *khrōma -atos* colour]

dick[1] /dɪk/ *n.* **1** *Brit. colloq.* (in certain set phrases) fellow; person (*clever dick*). **2** *coarse sl.* the penis. ¶ In sense 2 usually considered a taboo word. [pet form of the name *Richard*]

dick[2] /dɪk/ *n. sl.* a detective. [perh. abbr.]

dick[3] /dɪk/ *n.* □ **take one's dick** (often foll. by *that* + clause) *sl.* swear, affirm. [abbr. of *declaration*]

dicken /'dɪkən/ *int. Austral. sl.* an expression of disgust or disbelief. [usu. assoc. with DICKENS or the name *Dickens*]

Dickens /'dɪkɪnz/, Charles Huffam (1812–70), English novelist, son of an improvident Royal Navy pay clerk (the model for Micawber in *David Copperfield*). In 1824 his father was imprisoned for debt, and Charles worked briefly in a London blacking factory. This boyhood degradation deeply affected him, prompting him to write on themes such as the Poor Law (*Oliver Twist*, 1837–8), the ill-treatment of schoolchildren (*Nicholas Nickleby*, 1838–9), the dehumanizing effect of business ethics (*Dombey and Son*, 1847–8), the outdated legal system (*Bleak House*, 1852–3), industrialism (*Hard Times*, 1854), imprisonment for debt (*Little Dorrit*, 1855), and class distinction (*Great Expectations*, 1860–1). A master of laughter and tears, with a gift for satirical humour that is never absent from his works, Dickens created the greatest gallery of characters in English fiction, many of them grotesques (e.g. Fagin, Scrooge, Mrs Gamp, Uriah Heep). He enjoyed immense popularity, his reading tours in England and America receiving tumultuous acclaim, though *Martin Chuzzlewit* (1843–4) upset the Americans in its portrayal of American stereotypes. Serial publication helped him to monitor audience reaction, which strongly influenced his art. Through his works, public readings, and speeches Dickens aroused the Victorian conscience and captured the popular imagination as no other novelist has done.

dickens /'dɪkɪnz/ *n.* (usu. prec. by *how, what, why,* etc., *the*) *colloq.* (esp. in exclamations) deuce; the Devil (*what the dickens are you doing here?*). [16th c.: prob. a use of the surname *Dickens*]

Dickensian /dɪ'kenzɪən/ *adj.* & *n.* —*adj.* **1** of or relating to Charles Dickens or his work. **2** resembling or reminiscent of the situations, poor social conditions, or comically repulsive characters described in Dickens's work. —*n.* an admirer or student of Dickens or his work. □□ **Dickensianly** *adv.*

dicker /'dɪkə(r)/ *v.* & *n. esp. US* —*v.* **1 a** *intr.* bargain, haggle. **b** *tr.* barter, exchange. **2** *intr.* dither, hesitate. —*n.* a deal, a barter. □□ **dickerer** *n.* [perh. f. *dicker* set of ten (hides), as a unit of trade]

Dickinson /'dɪkɪns(ə)n/, Emily Elizabeth (1830–86), American poet who lived in seclusion in Amherst, Massachussets. Her withdrawal and inner struggle is reflected in her mystical poems, expressed in her own elliptical language. Of her nearly 2,000 poems only seven were published in her lifetime; the first selection appeared in 1890. At first regarded as an eccentric minor poet, she is now considered a writer of unusual originality.

dicky[1] /'dɪkɪ/ *n.* (also **dickey**) (pl. **-ies** or **-eys**) *colloq.* **1** a false shirt-front. **2** (in full **dicky-bird**) a child's word for a little bird. **3** *Brit.* a driver's seat in a carriage. **4** *Brit.* an extra folding seat at the back of a vehicle. **5** (in full **dicky bow**) *Brit.* a bow-tie. [some senses f. *Dicky* (as DICK[1])]

dicky[2] /'dɪkɪ/ *adj.* (**dickier, dickiest**) *Brit. sl.* unsound, likely to collapse or fail. [19th c.: perh. f. 'as queer as Dick's hatband']

dicot /'daɪkɒt/ *n.* = DICOTYLEDON. [abbr.]

dicotyledon /ˌdaɪkɒtɪ'liːd(ə)n/ *n.* any flowering plant having

two cotyledons. □□ **dicotyledonous** *adj.* [mod.L *dicotyledones* (as DI-[1], COTYLEDON)]

dicrotic /daɪ'krɒtɪk/ *adj.* (of the pulse) having a double beat. [Gk *dikrotos*]

dicta *pl.* of DICTUM.

Dictaphone /'dɪktəˌfəʊn/ *n. propr.* a machine for recording and playing back dictated words. [DICTATE + PHONE]

dictate /dɪk'teɪt/ *v.* & *n.* —*v.* **1** *tr.* say or read aloud (words to be written down or recorded). **2 a** *tr.* prescribe or lay down authoritatively (terms, things to be done). **b** *intr.* lay down the law; give orders. —*n.* /'dɪk-/ (usu. in *pl.*) an authoritative instruction (*dictates of conscience*). [L *dictare dictat-* frequent. of *dicere dict-* say]

dictation /dɪk'teɪʃ(ə)n/ *n.* **1 a** the saying of words to be written down or recorded. **b** an instance of this, esp. as a school exercise. **c** the material that is dictated. **2 a** authoritative prescription. **b** an instance of this. **c** a command. □ **dictation speed** a slow rate of speech suitable for dictation.

dictator /dɪk'teɪtə(r)/ *n.* **1** a ruler with (often usurped) unrestricted authority. **2** a person with supreme authority in any sphere. **3** a domineering person. **4** a person who dictates for transcription. **5** *Rom. Hist.* a chief magistrate with absolute power, appointed in an emergency. [ME f. L (as DICTATE)]

dictatorial /ˌdɪktə'tɔːrɪəl/ *adj.* **1** of or like a dictator. **2** imperious, overbearing. □□ **dictatorially** *adv.* [L *dictatorius* (as DICTATOR)]

dictatorship /dɪk'teɪtəʃɪp/ *n.* **1** a State ruled by a dictator. **2 a** the position, rule, or period of rule of a dictator. **b** rule by a dictator. **3** absolute authority in any sphere.

diction /'dɪkʃ(ə)n/ *n.* **1** the manner of enunciation in speaking or singing. **2** the choice of words or phrases in speech or writing. [F *diction* or L *dictio* f. *dicere dict-* say]

dictionary /'dɪkʃənrɪ, -nərɪ/ *n.* (pl. **-ies**) **1** a book that lists (usu. in alphabetical order) and explains the words of a language or gives equivalent words in another language. (See below.) **2** a reference book on any subject, the items of which are arranged in alphabetical order (*dictionary of architecture*). [med.L *dictionarium* (*manuale* manual) & *dictionarius* (*liber* book) f. L *dictio* (as DICTION)]

Dictionaries are of two kinds: those in which the meanings of the words of one language or dialect are given in another, and those in which the words of a language are treated in this language itself; the former are the earlier. The tradition of making (and subsequently collecting) glossaries arose when the language or dialect used in literary works was no longer intelligible. It began among the Greeks, especially of the 1st–5th c. AD, and continued in medieval times. In the 16th c. the market was for 'bilingual' dictionaries, especially Latin-English. In 1604 schoolmaster Robert Cawdrey produced *A Table Alphabetical of English Words* (based on an earlier word-list); it was written to help 'Ladies . . . or other unskilful persons'. Dictionaries contained only words regarded as 'difficult' until Kersey broke with this tradition in 1702 by including the common words of the language and discarding some of the more fantastic formations. Bailey's dictionary (1721) of about 40,000 words, giving great attention to etymology, was extremely popular in the 18th c. and his great folio dictionary (1730) was used by Samuel Johnson as the basis of his own work, the most famous of all time, which remained the authoritative English dictionary for over a century (see JOHNSON). The 19th c. saw the publication of Noah Webster's *An American Dictionary of the English Language* (1878), containing about 70,000 words, and the initiation of the great *Oxford English Dictionary* (see MURRAY), which remains the supreme achievement in lexicography. (See also GRIMM, LITTRÉ.) In the 20th c. small dictionaries have multiplied and find a ready market.

dictum /'dɪktəm/ *n.* (pl. **dicta** /-tə/ or **dictums**) **1** a formal utterance or pronouncement. **2** a saying or maxim. **3** *Law* = OBITER DICTUM. [L, = neut. past part. of *dicere* say]

dicty /'dɪktɪ/ *adj. US sl.* **1** conceited, snobbish. **2** elegant, stylish. [20th c.: orig. unkn.]

did *past* of DO[1].

didactic /daɪ'dæktɪk, dɪ-/ *adj.* **1** meant to instruct. **2** (of a person) tediously pedantic. □□ **didactically** *adv.* **didacticism** /-tɪˌsɪz(ə)m/ *n.* [Gk *didaktikos* f. *didaskō* teach]

didakai var. of DIDICOI.

diddicoy var. of DIDICOI.

diddle /ˈdɪd(ə)l/ *v. colloq.* **1** *tr.* cheat, swindle. **2** *intr. US* waste time. □□ **diddler** *n.* [prob. back-form. f. Jeremy *Diddler* in Kenney's 'Raising the Wind' (1803)]

diddums /ˈdɪdəmz/ *int.* expressing commiseration esp. to a child. [= *did 'em,* i.e. did they (tease you etc.)?]

Diderot /ˈdiːdəˌrəʊ/, Denis (1713–84), French philosopher and man of letters, a leading member of the Enlightenment and principal director of the *Encyclopédie* through which he disseminated and popularized scientific knowledge and philosophic doctrines. His major philosophic writings include *Lettre sur les aveugles* (1749), a philosophic treatise tending to atheism which caused his temporary imprisonment, and *Pensées sur l'interpretation de la nature* (1754), anticipating evolutionary ideas on the nature and origin of life. His *Salons* (1759–81) inaugurated the genre of art criticism in France.

didgeridoo /ˌdɪdʒərɪˈduː/ *n.* (also **didjeridoo**) an Australian Aboriginal musical wind instrument of long tubular shape. [imit.]

didicoi /ˈdɪdɪˌkɔɪ/ *n.* (also **didakai, diddicoy**) *sl.* a gypsy; an itinerant tinker. [Romany]

didn't /ˈdɪd(ə)nt/ *contr.* did not.

Dido /ˈdaɪdəʊ/ (in the *Aeneid*) the queen of Carthage who fell in love with the shipwrecked Aeneas and killed herself when he deserted her. According to ancient tradition, which may be founded on fact, she was the daughter of a king of Tyre (where she was known as Elissa) and granddaughter of Ithobaal (= Ethbaal, father of Jezebel), and left Tyre with a group of Phoenicians, afterwards founding the city of Carthage.

dido /ˈdaɪdəʊ/ *n.* (*pl.* **-oes** or **-os**) *US colloq.* an antic, a caper, a prank. □ **cut** (or **cut up**) **didoes** play pranks. [19th c.: orig. unkn.]

didst /dɪdst/ *archaic 2nd sing. past of* DO¹.

Didyma /ˈdɪdɪmə/ an ancient sanctuary of Apollo, site of one of the most famous oracles of the Aegean region, close to the west coast of Asia Minor. After the area was conquered by Alexander the Great, work began (*c.*300 BC) on a massive new temple, which was never completed.

didymium /dɪˈdɪmɪəm/ *n.* a mixture of praesodymium and neodymium, orig. regarded as an element. [mod.L f. Gk *didumos* twin (from being closely associated with lanthanum)]

die¹ /daɪ/ *v.* (**dies, died, dying** /ˈdaɪɪŋ/) **1** *intr.* (often foll. by *of*) (of a person, animal, or plant) cease to live; expire, lose vital force (*died of hunger*). **2** *intr.* **a** come to an end, cease to exist, fade away (*the project died within six months*). **b** cease to function; break down (*the engine died*). **c** (of a flame) go out. **3** *intr.* (foll. by *on*) die or cease to function while in the presence or charge of (a person). **4** *intr.* (usu. foll. by *of, from, with*) be exhausted or tormented (*nearly died of boredom; was dying from the heat*). **5** *tr.* suffer (a specified death) (*died a natural death*). □ **be dying** (foll. by *for,* or *to* + infin.) wish for longingly or intently (*was dying for a drink; am dying to see you*). **die away** become weaker or fainter to the point of extinction. **die-away** *adj.* languishing. **die back** (of a plant) decay from the tip towards the root. **die down** become less loud or strong. **die hard** die reluctantly, not without a struggle (*old habits die hard*). **die-hard** *n.* a conservative or stubborn person. **die out** become extinct, cease to exist. **never say die** keep up courage, not give in. [ME, prob. f. ON *deyja* f. Gmc]

die² /daɪ/ *n.* **1** *sing.* of DICE *n.* 1a. ¶ *Dice* is now standard in general use in this sense. **2** (*pl.* **dies**) **a** an engraved device for stamping a design on coins, medals, etc. **b** a device for stamping, cutting, or moulding material into a particular shape. **3** (*pl.* **dice** /daɪs/) *Archit.* the cubical part of a pedestal between the base and the cornice; a dado or plinth. □ **as straight** (or **true**) **as a die 1** quite straight. **2** entirely honest or loyal. **die-cast** (hot metal) in a die or mould. **die-casting** the process or product of casting from metal moulds. **the die is cast** an irrevocable step has been taken. **die-sinker** an engraver of dies. **die-stamping**

embossing paper etc. with a die. [ME f. OF *de* f. L *datum* neut. past part. of *dare* give, play]

Diego Garcia /dɪˌeɪgəʊ gɑːˈsiːə/ the largest island of the Chagos Archipelago, site of a strategic Anglo-American naval base established in 1973.

Diekirch /ˈdiːkɜːx, -kɜːk/ a resort town in Luxembourg, on the River Sûre; pop. (1981) 5,600.

dieldrin /dɪˈeldrɪn/ *n.* a crystalline insecticide produced by the oxidation of aldrin. [O. *Diels,* Ger. chemist d. 1954 + ALDRIN]

dielectric /ˌdaɪɪˈlektrɪk/ *adj.* & *n. Electr.* —*adj.* insulating. —*n.* an insulating medium or substance. □ **dielectric constant** permittivity. □□ **dielectrically** *adv.* [DI-³ + ELECTRIC = through which electricity is transmitted (without conduction)]

diene /ˈdaɪiːn/ *n. Chem.* any organic compound possessing two double bonds between carbon atoms. [DI-¹ + -ENE]

Dieppe /dɪˈep/ a channel port in northern France, from which ferries run to Newhaven and elsewhere; pop. (1982) 26,000.

dieresis *US* var. of DIAERESIS.

diesel /ˈdiːz(ə)l/ *n.* **1** (in full **diesel engine**) an internal-combustion engine in which the heat produced by the compression of air in the cylinder ignites the fuel. (See below.) **2** a vehicle driven by a diesel engine. **3** fuel for a diesel engine. □ **diesel-electric** *n.* a vehicle driven by the electric current produced by a diesel-engined generator. —*adj.* of or powered by this means. **diesel oil** a heavy petroleum fraction used as fuel in diesel engines. □□ **dieselize** *v.tr.* (also **-ise**). [R. *Diesel,* Ger. engineer d. 1913]

The diesel engine was patented by the German engineer Dr Rudolf Diesel (d. 1913) in 1892, though a similar engine was already being made in England to the design of Herbert Ackroyd-Stuart. Air is compressed alone, inside the engine, causing its temperature to rise; fuel oil is sprayed into the combustion chamber when the compressed air is at a high enough temperature to ignite the fuel, which then burns and raises the temperature and pressure of the mixture to very high values at the start of the expansion process. The advantage of compression-ignition over conventional spark-ignition is that a high compression ratio can be employed, since there is no danger of the explosive combustion of a fuel/air mixture as with a petrol engine. The consequent high expansion ratio gives the diesel engine a higher thermal efficiency, over 40% in large engines. Hence the diesel engine is widely used in ships, in railway locomotives, for stationary uses such as electricity generation, and for road vehicles, particularly commercial vehicles, and recently for taxis and private cars.

Dies irae /ˌdiːeɪz ˈɪəraɪ/ *n.* a Latin hymn sung in a Mass for the dead. [L (its first words), = day of wrath]

dies non /ˌdaɪiːz ˈnɒn/ *n. Law* **1** a day on which no legal business can be done. **2** a day that does not count for legal purposes. [L, short for *dies non juridicus* non-judicial day]

diet¹ /ˈdaɪət/ *n.* & *v.* —*n.* **1** the kinds of food that a person or animal habitually eats. **2** a special course of food to which a person is restricted, esp. for medical reasons or to control weight. **3** a regular occupation or series of activities to which one is restricted or which form one's main concern, usu. for a purpose (*a diet of light reading and fresh air*). —*v.* (**dieted, dieting**) **1** *intr.* restrict oneself to small amounts or special kinds of food, esp. to control one's weight. **2** *tr.* restrict (a person or animal) to a special diet. □□ **dieter** *n.* [ME f. OF *diete* (n.), *dieter* (v.) f. L *diaeta* f. Gk *diaita* a way of life]

diet² /ˈdaɪət/ *n.* **1** a legislative assembly in certain countries. **2** *hist.* a national or international conference, esp. of a federal State or confederation. **3** *Sc. Law* a meeting or session of a court. [ME f. med.L *dieta* day's work, wages, etc.]

dietary /ˈdaɪətrɪ/ *adj.* & *n.* —*adj.* of or relating to a diet. —*n.* (*pl.* **-ies**) a regulated or restricted diet. [ME f. med.L *dietarium* (as DIET¹)]

dietetic /ˌdaɪəˈtetɪk/ *adj.* of or relating to diet. □□ **dietetically** *adv.* [L *dieteticus* f. Gk *diaitētikos* (as DIET¹)]

dietetics /ˌdaɪəˈtetɪks/ *n.pl.* (usu. treated as *sing.*) the scientific study of diet and nutrition.

diethyl ether /daɪˈiːθaɪl/ *n. Chem.* = ETHER 1.

dietitian /ˌdaɪəˈtɪʃ(ə)n/ n. (also **dietician**) an expert in dietetics.

Dietrich /ˈdiːtrɪk/, Marlene (real name Maria Magdelene von Losch, 1901–90), German-born American film actress and singer, whose long career in films began in about 1922. Instantly famous after her part in *The Blue Angel* (1930), her image was that of an aloof, sultry, perverse, and sophisticated beauty, with a huskily distinctive voice. In her later career, in the 1950s, she was outstandingly successful in international cabaret.

dif- /dɪf/ prefix assim. form of DIS- before f. [L var. of DIS-]

differ /ˈdɪfə(r)/ v.intr. **1** (often foll. by *from*) be unlike or distinguishable. **2** (often foll. by *with*) disagree; be at variance (with a person). [ME f. OF *differer* f. L *differre*, differ, DEFER¹, (as DIS-, *ferre* bear, tend)]

difference /ˈdɪfrəns/ n. & v. —n. **1** the state or condition of being different or unlike. **2** a point in which things differ; a distinction. **3** a degree of unlikeness. **4 a** the quantity by which amounts differ; a deficit (*will have to make up the difference*). **b** the remainder left after subtraction. **5 a** a disagreement, quarrel, or dispute. **b** the grounds of disagreement (*put aside their differences*). **6** *Heraldry* an alteration in a coat of arms distinguishing members of a family. —v.tr. *Heraldry* alter (a coat of arms) to distinguish members of a family. □ **make a** (or **all the** etc.) **difference** (often foll. by *to*) have a significant effect or influence (on a person, situation, etc.). **make no difference** (often foll. by *to*) have no effect (on a person, situation, etc.). **with a difference** having a new or unusual feature. [ME f. OF f. L *differentia* (as DIFFERENT)]

different /ˈdɪfrənt/ adj. **1** (often foll. by *from, to, than*) unlike, distinguishable in nature, form, or quality (from another). ¶ *Different from* is generally regarded as the most acceptable collocation; *to* is common in less formal use; *than* is established in US use and also found in British use, esp. when followed by a clause, e.g. *I am a different person than I was a year ago.* **2** distinct, separate; not the same one (as another). **3** *colloq.* unusual (*wanted to do something different*). □□ **differently** adv. **differentness** n. [ME f. OF *different* f. L *different-* (as DIFFER)]

differentia /ˌdɪfəˈrenʃɪə/ n. (pl. **differentiae** /-ʃɪˌiː/) a distinguishing mark, esp. between species within a genus. [L: see DIFFERENCE]

differential /ˌdɪfəˈrenʃ(ə)l/ adj. & n. —adj. **1 a** of, exhibiting, or depending on a difference. **b** varying according to circumstances. **2** *Math.* relating to infinitesimal differences. **3** constituting a specific difference; distinctive; relating to specific differences (*differential diagnosis*). **4** *Physics & Mech.* concerning the difference of two or more motions, pressures, etc. —n. **1 a** difference between individuals or examples of the same kind. **2** *Brit.* a difference in wage or salary between industries or categories of employees in the same industry. **3** a difference between rates of interest etc. **4** *Math.* **a** an infinitesimal difference between successive values of a variable. **b** a function expressing this as a rate of change with respect to another variable. **5** (in full **differential gear**) a gear allowing a vehicle's driven wheels to revolve at different speeds in cornering. □ **differential calculus** *Math.* a method of calculating rates of change, maximum or minimum values, etc. (cf. INTEGRAL). **differential coefficient** *Math.* = DERIVATIVE. **differential equation** *Math.* an equation involving differentials among its quantities. □□ **differentially** adv. [med. & mod.L *differentialis* (as DIFFERENCE)]

differentiate /ˌdɪfəˈrenʃɪˌeɪt/ v. **1** tr. constitute a difference between or in. **2** tr. & (often foll. by *between*) intr. find differences (between); discriminate. **3** tr. & intr. make or become different in the process of growth or development (species, word-forms, etc.). **4** tr. *Math.* transform (a function) into its derivative. □□ **differentiation** /-ˈeɪʃ(ə)n/ n. **differentiator** n. [med.L *differentiare* *differentiat-* (as DIFFERENCE)]

difficult /ˈdɪfɪkəlt/ adj. **1 a** needing much effort or skill. **b** troublesome, perplexing. **2** (of a person): **a** not easy to please or satisfy. **b** uncooperative, troublesome. **3** characterized by hardships or problems (*a difficult period in his life*). □□ **difficultly** adv. **difficultness** n. [ME, back-form. f. DIFFICULTY]

difficulty /ˈdɪfɪkəltɪ/ n. (pl. **-ies**) **1** the state or condition of being

difficult. **2 a** a difficult thing; a problem or hindrance. **b** (often in *pl.*) a cause of distress or hardship (*in financial difficulties; there was someone in difficulties in the water*). □ **make difficulties** be intransigent or unaccommodating. **with difficulty** not easily. [ME f. L *difficultas* (as DIS-, *facultas* FACULTY)]

diffident /ˈdɪfɪd(ə)nt/ adj. **1** shy, lacking self-confidence. **2** excessively modest and reticent. □□ **diffidence** n. **diffidently** adv. [L *diffidere* (as DIS-, *fidere* trust)]

diffract /dɪˈfrækt/ v.tr. *Physics* (of the edge of an opaque body, a narrow slit, etc.) break up (a beam of light) into a series of dark or light bands or coloured spectra, or (a beam of radiation or particles) into a series of alternately high and low intensities. □□ **diffraction** n. **diffractive** adj. **diffractively** adv. [L *diffringere diffract-* (as DIS-, *frangere* break)]

diffractometer /ˌdɪfrækˈtɒmɪtə(r)/ n. an instrument for measuring diffraction, esp. in crystallographic work.

diffuse adj. & v. —adj. /dɪˈfjuːs/ **1** (of light, inflammation, etc.) spread out, diffused, not concentrated. **2** (of prose, speech, etc.) not concise, long-winded, verbose. —v.tr. & intr. /dɪˈfjuːz/ **1** disperse or be dispersed from a centre. **2** spread or be spread widely; reach a large area. **3** *Physics* (esp. of fluids) intermingle by diffusion. □□ **diffusely** /dɪˈfjuːslɪ/ adv. **diffuseness** /dɪˈfjuːsnɪs/ n. **diffusible** /dɪˈfjuːzɪb(ə)l/ adj. **diffusive** /dɪˈfjuːsɪv/ adj. [ME f. F *diffus* or L *diffusus* extensive (as DIS-, *fusus* past part. of *fundere* pour)]

diffuser /dɪˈfjuːzə(r)/ n. (also **diffusor**) **1** a person or thing that diffuses, esp. a device for diffusing light. **2** *Engin.* a duct for broadening an airflow and reducing its speed.

diffusion /dɪˈfjuːʒ(ə)n/ n. **1** the act or an instance of diffusing; the process of being diffused. **2** *Physics & Chem.* the interpenetration of substances by the natural movement of their particles. **3** *Anthropol.* the spread of elements of culture etc. to another region or people. □□ **diffusionist** n. [ME f. L *diffusio* (as DIFFUSE)]

dig /dɪg/ v. & n. —v. (**digging**; past and past part. **dug** /dʌg/) **1** intr. break up and remove or turn over soil, ground, etc., with a tool, one's hands, (of an animal) claws, etc. **2** tr. **a** break up and displace (the ground etc.) in this way. **b** (foll. by *up*) break up the soil of (fallow land). **3** tr. make (a hole, grave, tunnel, etc.) by digging. **4** tr. (often foll. by *up, out*) **a** obtain or remove by digging. **b** find or discover after searching. **5** tr. (also *absol.*) excavate (an archaeological site). **6** tr. *sl.* like, appreciate, or understand. **7** tr. & intr. (foll. by *in, into*) thrust or poke into or down into. **8** intr. make one's way by digging (*dug through the mountainside*). —n. **1** a piece of digging. **2** a thrust or poke (a *dig in the ribs*). **3** *colloq.* (often foll. by *at*) a pointed or critical remark. **4** an archaeological excavation. **5** (in *pl.*) *Brit. colloq.* lodgings. □ **dig one's feet** (or **heels** or **toes**) **in** be obstinate. **dig in** *colloq.* begin eating. **dig oneself in 1** prepare a defensive trench or pit. **2** establish one's position. [ME *digge*, of uncert. orig.: cf. OE *dīc* ditch]

digamma /daɪˈgæmə/ n. the sixth letter (Ϝ, ϝ) of the early Greek alphabet (prob. pronounced w), later disused. [L f. Gk (as DI-¹, GAMMA)]

digastric /daɪˈgæstrɪk/ adj. & n. *Anat.* —adj. (of a muscle) having two wide parts with a tendon between. —n. the muscle that opens the jaw. [mod.L *digastricus* (as DI-¹, Gk *gastēr* belly)]

digest v. & n. —v.tr. /daɪˈdʒest, dɪ-/ **1** assimilate (food) in the stomach and bowels. **2** understand and assimilate mentally. **3** *Chem.* treat (a substance) with heat, enzymes, or a solvent in order to decompose it, extract the essence, etc. **4 a** reduce to a systematic or convenient form; classify; summarize. **b** think over; arrange in the mind. —n. /ˈdaɪdʒest/ **1 a** a methodical summary esp. of a body of laws. **b** (**the Digest**) the compendium of Roman law compiled in the reign of Justinian (6th c. AD). **2** a regular or occasional synopsis of current literature or news. □□ **digester** n. **digestible** adj. **digestibility** /-ˈbɪlɪtɪ/ n. [ME f. L *digerere digest-* distribute, dissolve, digest (as DI-², *gerere* carry)]

digestion /daɪˈdʒestʃ(ə)n/ n. **1** the process of digesting. **2** the capacity to digest food (*has a weak digestion*). **3** digesting a substance by means of heat, enzymes, or a solvent. [ME f. OF f. L *digestio -onis* (as DIGEST)]

digestive /dɪˈdʒestɪv, daɪ-/ *adj. & n.* —*adj.* **1** of or relating to digestion. **2** aiding or promoting digestion. —*n.* **1** a substance that aids digestion. **2** (in full **digestive biscuit**) *Brit.* a usu. round semi-sweet wholemeal biscuit. □□ **digestively** *adv.* [ME f. OF *digestif -ive* or L *digestivus* (as DIGEST)]

digger /ˈdɪɡə(r)/ *n.* **1** a person or machine that digs, esp. a mechanical excavator. **2** a miner, esp. a gold-digger. **3** *colloq.* an Australian or New Zealander, esp. a private soldier. **4** *Austral. & NZ colloq.* (as a form of address) mate, fellow.

diggings /ˈdɪɡɪŋz/ *n.pl.* **1 a** a mine or goldfield. **b** material dug out of a mine etc. **2** *Brit. colloq.* lodgings, accommodation.

dight /daɪt/ *adj. archaic* clothed, arrayed. [past part. of *dight* (v.) f. OE *dihtan* f. L *dictare* DICTATE]

digit /ˈdɪdʒɪt/ *n.* **1** any numeral from 0 to 9, esp. when forming part of a number. **2** *Anat. & Zool.* a finger, thumb, or toe. [ME f. L *digitus*]

digital /ˈdɪdʒɪt(ə)l/ *adj.* **1** of or using a digit or digits. **2** (of a clock, watch, etc.) that gives a reading by means of displayed digits instead of hands. **3** (of a computer) operating on data represented as a series of usu. binary digits or in similar discrete form. **4 a** (of a recording) with sound-information represented in digits for more reliable transmission. **b** (of a recording medium) using this process. □ **digital audio tape** magnetic tape on which sound is recorded digitally. **digital to analog converter** *Computing* a device for converting digital values to analog form. □□ **digitalize** *v.tr.* (also **-ise**). **digitally** *adv.* [L *digitalis* (as DIGIT)]

digitalin /ˌdɪdʒɪˈteɪlɪn/ *n.* the pharmacologically active constituent(s) of the foxglove. [DIGITALIS + -IN]

digitalis /ˌdɪdʒɪˈteɪlɪs/ *n.* a drug prepared from the dried leaves of foxgloves and containing substances that stimulate the heart muscle. [mod.L, genus-name of foxglove after G *Fingerhut* thimble: see DIGITAL]

digitate /ˈdɪdʒɪteɪt/ *adj.* **1** *Zool.* having separate fingers or toes. **2** *Bot.* having deep radiating divisions. □□ **digitately** *adv.* **digitation** /-ˈteɪʃ(ə)n/ *n.* [L *digitatus* (as DIGIT)]

digitigrade /ˈdɪdʒɪtɪˌɡreɪd/ *adj. & n. Zool.* —*adj.* (of an animal) walking on its toes and not touching the ground with its heels, e.g. dogs, cats, and rodents. —*n.* a digitigrade animal (cf. PLANTIGRADE). [F f. L *digitus* + -*gradus* -walking]

digitize /ˈdɪdʒɪˌtaɪz/ *v.tr.* (also **-ise**) convert (data etc.) into digital form, esp. for processing by a computer. □□ **digitization** /-ˈzeɪʃ(ə)n/ *n.*

dignified /ˈdɪɡnɪˌfaɪd/ *adj.* having or expressing dignity; noble or stately in appearance or manner. □□ **dignifiedly** *adv.*

dignify /ˈdɪɡnɪˌfaɪ/ *v.tr.* (**-ies, -ied**) **1** give dignity or distinction to. **2** ennoble; make worthy or illustrious. **3** give the form or appearance of dignity to (*dignified the house with the name of mansion*). [obs. F *dignifier* f. OF *dignefier* f. LL *dignificare* f. *dignus* worthy]

dignitary /ˈdɪɡnɪtəri/ *n.* (pl. **-ies**) a person holding high rank or office. [DIGNITY + -ARY¹, after PROPRIETARY]

dignity /ˈdɪɡnɪti/ *n.* (pl. **-ies**) **1** a composed and serious manner or style. **2** the state of being worthy of honour or respect. **3** worthiness, excellence (*the dignity of work*). **4** a high or honourable rank or position. **5** high regard or estimation. □ **beneath one's dignity** not considered worthy enough for one to do. **stand on one's dignity** insist (esp. by one's manner) on being treated with due respect. [ME f. OF *digneté*, *dignité* f. L *dignitas -tatis* f. *dignus* worthy]

digraph /ˈdaɪɡrɑːf/ *n.* a group of two letters representing one sound, as in *ph* and *ey*. □□ **digraphic** /-ˈɡræfɪk/ *adj.*

digress /daɪˈɡres/ *v.intr.* depart from the main subject temporarily in speech or writing. □□ **digresser** *n.* **digression** *n.* **digressive** *adj.* **digressively** *adv.* **digressiveness** *n.* [L *digredi digress-* (as DI-², *gradi* walk)]

digs see DIG *n.* 5.

dihedral /daɪˈhiːdr(ə)l/ *adj. & n.* —*adj.* having or contained by two plane faces. —*n.* = *dihedral angle*. □ **dihedral angle** an angle formed by two plane surfaces, esp. by an aircraft wing with the horizontal. [*dihedron* f. DI-¹ + -HEDRON]

dihydric /daɪˈhaɪdrɪk/ *adj. Chem.* containing two hydroxyl groups. [DI-¹ + HYDRIC]

Dijon /ˌdiːˈʒɒ̃/ an industrial city in east central France, the former capital of Burgundy; pop. (1983) 150,500.

dik-dik /ˈdɪkdɪk/ *n.* any dwarf antelope of the genus *Madoqua*, native to Africa. [name in E. Africa and in Afrik.]

dike¹ var. of DYKE¹.

dike² var. of DYKE².

diktat /ˈdɪktæt/ *n.* a categorical statement or decree, esp. terms imposed after a war by a victor. [G, = DICTATE]

dilapidate /dɪˈlæpɪˌdeɪt/ *v.intr. & tr.* fall or cause to fall into disrepair or ruin. [L *dilapidare* demolish, squander (as DI-², *lapis lapid-* stone)]

dilapidated /dɪˈlæpɪˌdeɪtɪd/ *adj.* in a state of disrepair or ruin, esp. as a result of age or neglect.

dilapidation /dɪˌlæpɪˈdeɪʃ(ə)n/ *n.* **1 a** the process of dilapidating. **b** a state of disrepair. **2** (in pl.) repairs required at the end of a tenancy or lease. **3** *Eccl.* a sum charged against an incumbent for wear and tear during a tenancy. [ME f. LL *dilapidatio* (as DILAPIDATE)]

dilatation /ˌdaɪləˈteɪʃ(ə)n/ *n.* **1** the widening or expansion of a hollow organ or cavity. **2** the process of dilating. □ **dilatation and curettage** an operation in which the cervix is expanded and the womb-lining scraped off with a curette.

dilate /daɪˈleɪt/ *v.* **1** *tr. & intr.* make or become wider or larger (esp. of an opening in the body) (*dilated pupils*). **2** *intr.* (often foll. by *on, upon*) speak or write at length. □□ **dilatable** *adj.* **dilation** *n.* [ME f. OF *dilater* f. L *dilatare* spread out (as DI-², *latus* wide)]

dilator /daɪˈleɪt(ə)r/ *n.* **1** *Anat.* a muscle that dilates an organ. **2** *Surgery* an instrument for dilating a tube or cavity in the body.

dilatory /ˈdɪlətəri/ *adj.* given to or causing delay. □□ **dilatorily** *adv.* **dilatoriness** *n.* [LL *dilatorius* (as DI-², *dilat-* past part. stem of *differre* DEFER¹)]

dildo /ˈdɪldəʊ/ *n.* (pl. **-os**) an object shaped like an erect penis and used, esp. by women, for sexual stimulation. [17th c.: orig. unkn.]

dilemma /daɪˈlemə, dɪ-/ *n.* **1** a situation in which a choice has to be made between two equally undesirable alternatives. **2** a state of indecision between two alternatives. **3** *disp.* a difficult situation. **4** an argument forcing an opponent to choose either of two unfavourable alternatives. [L f. Gk (as DI-¹, *lēmma* premiss)]

dilettante /ˌdɪlɪˈtænti/ *n. & adj.* —*n.* (pl. **dilettanti** /-tɪ/ or **dilettantes**) **1** a person who studies a subject or area of knowledge superficially. **2** a person who enjoys the arts. —*adj.* trifling, not thorough; amateurish. □□ **dilettantish** *adj.* **dilettantism** *n.* [It. f. pres. part. of *dilettare* delight f. L *delectare*]

Dili /ˈdɪli/ a seaport on the island of Timor that was (until 1975) the capital of the former Portuguese colony of East Timor; pop. (1980) 60,150.

diligence¹ /ˈdɪlɪdʒ(ə)ns/ *n.* **1** careful and persistent application or effort. **2** (as a characteristic) industriousness. [ME f. OF f. L *diligentia* (as DILIGENT)]

diligence² /ˈdɪlɪdʒ(ə)ns, ˌdiːliːˈʒɑ̃s/ *n. hist.* a public stagecoach, esp. in France. [F, for *carrosse de diligence* coach of speed]

diligent /ˈdɪlɪdʒ(ə)nt/ *adj.* **1** careful and steady in application to one's work or duties. **2** showing care and effort. □□ **diligently** *adv.* [ME f. OF f. L *diligens* assiduous, part. of *diligere* love, take delight in (as DI-², *legere* choose)]

dill¹ /dɪl/ *n.* **1** an umbelliferous herb, *Anethum graveolens*, with yellow flowers and aromatic seeds. **2** the leaves or seeds of this plant used for flavouring and medicinal purposes. □ **dill pickle** pickled cucumber etc. flavoured with dill. **dill-water** a distillate of dill used as a carminative. [OE *dile*]

dill² /dɪl/ *n. Austral. sl.* **1** a fool or simpleton. **2** the victim of a trickster. [app. back-form. f. DILLY²]

dilly¹ /ˈdɪli/ *n.* (pl. **-ies**) esp. *US sl.* a remarkable or excellent person or thing. [*dilly* (adj.) f. DELIGHTFUL or DELICIOUS]

dilly² /ˈdɪli/ *adj. Austral. sl.* **1** odd or eccentric. **2** foolish, stupid, mad. [perh. f. DAFT, SILLY]

dillybag /ˈdɪliˌbæɡ/ *n. Austral.* a small bag or basket. [Aboriginal *dilly* + BAG]

dilly-dally /ˌdɪlɪˈdælɪ/ v.intr. (-ies, -ied) colloq. **1** dawdle, loiter. **2** vacillate. [redupl. of DALLY]

diluent /ˈdɪljʊənt/ adj. & n. Chem. & Biochem. —adj. that serves to dilute. —n. a diluting agent. [L diluere diluent- DILUTE]

dilute /daɪˈljuːt/ v. & adj. —v.tr. **1** reduce the strength of (a fluid) by adding water or another solvent. **2** weaken or reduce the strength or forcefulness of, esp. by adding something. —adj. /also ˈdaɪ-/ **1** (esp. of a fluid) diluted, weakened. **2** (of a colour) washed out; low in saturation. **3** Chem. **a** (of a solution) having relatively low concentration of solute. **b** (of a substance) in solution (dilute sulphuric acid). □□ **diluter** n. **dilution** n. [L diluere dilut- (as DI-², luere wash)]

diluvial /daɪˈluːvɪəl, dɪ-, -ˈljuːvɪəl/ adj. **1** of a flood, esp. of the Flood in Genesis. **2** Geol. of the Glacial Drift formation (see DRIFT n. 8). [LL diluvialis f. diluvium DELUGE]

diluvium /daɪˈluːvɪəm, dɪ-, -ˈljuːvɪəm/ n. (pl. **diluvia** /-vɪə/) Geol. = DRIFT n. 8. [L: see DILUVIAL]

dim /dɪm/ adj. & v. —adj. (**dimmer, dimmest**) **1 a** only faintly luminous or visible; not bright. **b** obscure; ill-defined. **2** not clearly perceived or remembered. **3** colloq. stupid; slow to understand. **4** (of the eyes) not seeing clearly. —v. (**dimmed, dimming**) **1** tr. & intr. make or become dim or less bright. **2** tr. US dip (headlights). □ **dim-wit** colloq. a stupid person. **dim-witted** colloq. stupid, unintelligent. **take a dim view of** colloq. **1** disapprove of. **2** feel gloomy about. □□ **dimly** adv. **dimmish** adj. **dimness** n. [OE dim, dimm, of unkn. orig.]

dim. abbr. diminuendo.

DiMaggio /dɪˈmædʒɪəʊ/, Joseph Paul ('Joe') (1914–), American baseball player, star of the New York Yankees team from 1936 to 1951, renowned for his outstanding batting ability and for his outfield play. His second wife, to whom he was married for nine months in 1954, was the film actress Marilyn Monroe.

Dimbleby /ˈdɪmbəlbɪ/, Richard (1913–65), English broadcaster, the first to be commemorated in Westminster Abbey (in Poets' Corner). He is noted for his broadcast commentaries on royal, national, and international events, and for reports on current affairs, on radio and television.

dime /daɪm/ n. US & Can. colloq. **1** a ten-cent coin. **2** a small amount of money. □ **a dime a dozen** very cheap or commonplace. **dime novel** a cheap popular novel. **turn on a dime** US colloq. make a sharp turn in a vehicle. [ME (orig. = tithe) f. OF disme f. L decima pars tenth part]

dimension /daɪˈmenʃ(ə)n, dɪ-/ n. & v. —n. **1** a measurable extent of any kind, as length, breadth, depth, area, and volume. **2** (in pl.) size, scope, extent. **3** an aspect or facet of a situation, problem, etc. **4** Algebra one of a number of unknown or variable quantities contained as factors in a product (x^3, x^2y, xyz, are all of three dimensions). **5** Physics the product of mass, length, time, etc., raised to the appropriate power, in a derived physical quantity. —v.tr. (usu. as **dimensioned** adj.) mark the dimensions on (a diagram etc.). □□ **dimensional** adj. (also in comb.). **dimensionless** adj. [ME f. OF f. L dimensio -onis (as DI-², metiri mensus measure)]

dimer /ˈdaɪm(ə)r/ n. Chem. a compound consisting of two identical molecules linked together (cf. MONOMER). □□ **dimeric** /-ˈmerɪk/ adj. [DI-¹ + -mer after POLYMER]

dimerous /ˈdaɪmərəs/ adj. (of a plant) having two parts in a whorl etc. [mod.L dimerus f. Gk dimerēs bipartite]

dimeter /ˈdɪmɪtə(r)/ n. Prosody a line of verse consisting of two metrical feet. [LL dimetrus f. Gk dimetros (as DI-¹, METER)]

diminish /dɪˈmɪnɪʃ/ v. **1** tr. & intr. make or become smaller or less. **2** tr. lessen the reputation or influence of (a person). □ **law of diminishing returns** Econ. the fact that the increase of expenditure, investment, taxation, etc., beyond a certain point ceases to produce a proportionate yield. □□ **diminishable** adj. [ME, blending of earlier minish f. OF menusier (formed as MINCE) and diminue f. OF diminuer f. L diminuere diminut- break up small]

diminished /dɪˈmɪnɪʃt/ adj. **1** reduced; made smaller or less. **2** Mus. (of an interval, usu. a seventh or fifth) less by a semitone than the corresponding minor or perfect interval. □ **diminished responsibility** Law the limitation of criminal responsibility on the ground of mental weakness or abnormality.

diminuendo /dɪˌmɪnjʊˈendəʊ/ adv. & n. Mus. —adv. with a gradual decrease in loudness. —n. (pl. **-os**) a passage to be played in this way. [It., part. of diminuire DIMINISH]

diminution /ˌdɪmɪˈnjuːʃ(ə)n/ n. **1 a** the act or an instance of diminishing. **b** the amount by which something diminishes. **2** Mus. the repetition of a passage in notes shorter than those originally used. [ME f. OF f. L diminutio -onis (as DIMINISH)]

diminutive /dɪˈmɪnjʊtɪv/ adj. & n. —adj. **1** remarkably small; tiny. **2** Gram. (of a word or suffix) implying smallness, either actual or imputed in token of affection, scorn, etc. (e.g. -let, -kins). —n. Gram. a diminutive word or suffix. □□ **diminutival** /-ˈtaɪv(ə)l/ adj. **diminutively** adv. **diminutiveness** n. [ME f. OF diminutif, -ive f. LL diminutivus (as DIMINISH)]

dimissory /dɪˈmɪsərɪ/ adj. **1** ordering or permitting to depart. **2** Eccl. granting permission for a candidate to be ordained outside the bishop's own see (dimissory letters). [ME f. LL dimissorius f. dimittere dimiss- send away (as DI-², mittere send)]

dimity /ˈdɪmɪtɪ/ n. (pl. **-ies**) a cotton fabric woven with stripes or checks. [ME f. It. dimito or med.L dimitum f. Gk dimitos (as DI-¹, mitos warp-thread)]

dimmer /ˈdɪmə(r)/ n. **1** a device for varying the brightness of an electric light. **2** US **a** (in pl.) small parking lights on a motor vehicle. **b** a headlight on low beam.

dimorphic /daɪˈmɔːfɪk/ adj. (also **dimorphous** /daɪˈmɔːfəs/) Biol., Chem., & Mineral. exhibiting, or occurring in, two distinct forms. □□ **dimorphism** n. [Gk dimorphos (as DI-¹, morphē form)]

dimple /ˈdɪmp(ə)l/ n. & v. —n. a small hollow or dent in the flesh, esp. in the cheeks or chin. —v. **1** intr. produce or show dimples. **2** tr. produce dimples in (a cheek etc.). □□ **dimply** adj. [ME prob. f. OE dympel (unrecorded) f. a Gmc root dump-, perh. a nasalized form rel. to DEEP]

dim sum /dɪm ˈsʌm/ n. (also **dim sim** /ˈsɪm/) **1** a meal or course of savoury Cantonese-style snacks. **2** (usu. **dim sim**) Austral. a dish of Cantonese origin, consisting of steamed or fried meat cooked in thin dough. [Cantonese dim-sām, lit. 'dot of the heart']

DIN /dɪn/ n. any of a series of technical standards originating in Germany and used internationally, esp. to designate electrical connections, film speeds, and paper sizes. [G, f. Deutsche Industrie-Norm]

din /dɪn/ n. & v. —n. a prolonged loud and distracting noise. —v. (**dinned, dinning**) **1** tr. (foll. by into) instil (something to be learned) by constant repetition. **2** intr. make a din. [OE dyne, dynn, dynian f. Gmc]

dinar /ˈdiːnɑː(r)/ n. **1** the chief monetary unit of Yugoslavia. **2** the chief monetary unit of certain countries of the Middle East and N. Africa. [Arab. & Pers. dīnār f. Gk dēnarion f. L denarius: see DENIER]

Dinaric Alps /dɪˈnærɪk/ an Alpine range running parallel to the Adriatic coast of Yugoslavia and NW Albania. The range, which includes the limestone Karst region, rises to a height of 2,522 m (8,274 ft.) at Durmitor.

dine /daɪn/ v. **1** intr. eat dinner. **2** tr. give dinner to. □ **dine out 1** dine away from home. **2** (foll. by on) be entertained to dinner etc. on account of (one's ability to relate an interesting event, story, etc.). **dining-car** a railway carriage equipped as a restaurant. **dining-room** a room in which meals are eaten. [ME f. OF diner, disner, ult. f. dis- + LL jejunare f. jejunus fasting]

diner /ˈdaɪnə(r)/ n. **1** a person who dines, esp. in a restaurant. **2** a railway dining-car. **3** US a small restaurant. **4** a small dining-room.

dinette /daɪˈnet/ n. a small room or part of a room used for eating meals.

ding¹ /dɪŋ/ v. & n. —v.intr. make a ringing sound. —n. a ringing sound, as of a bell. [imit.: infl. by DIN]

ding² /dɪŋ/ n. Austral. sl. a party or celebration, esp. a wild one. [perh. f. DING-DONG or WINGDING]

Ding an sich /ˌdɪŋ æn ˈzɪx/ n. Philos. a thing in itself. [G]

dingbat /ˈdɪŋbæt/ n. sl. **1** US & Austral. a stupid or eccentric person. **2** (in *pl.*) *Austral.* & *NZ* **a** madness. **b** discomfort, unease (*gives me the dingbats*). [19th c.: perh. f. *ding* to beat + BAT¹]

ding-dong /ˈdɪŋdɒŋ/ *n., adj.,* & *adv.* —*n.* **1** the sound of alternate chimes, as of two bells. **2** *colloq.* an intense argument or fight. **3** *colloq.* a riotous party. —*adj.* (of a contest etc.) evenly matched and intensely waged; thoroughgoing. —*adv.* with vigour and energy (*hammer away at it ding-dong*). [16th c.: imit.]

dinge /dɪndʒ/ *n.* & *v.* —*n.* a dent or hollow caused by a blow. —*v.tr.* make such a dent in. [17th c.: orig. unkn.]

dinghy /ˈdɪŋɪ, ˈdɪŋgɪ/ *n.* (*pl.* **-ies**) **1** a small boat carried by a ship. **2** a small pleasure-boat. **3** a small inflatable rubber boat (esp. for emergency use). [orig. a rowing-boat used on Indian rivers, f. Hindi *ḍiṅgī, ḍeṅgī*]

dingle /ˈdɪŋg(ə)l/ *n.* a deep wooded valley or dell. [ME: orig. unkn.]

dingo /ˈdɪŋgəʊ/ *n.* (*pl.* **-oes**) **1** a wild or half-domesticated Australian dog, *Canis dingo*. **2** *Austral. sl.* a coward or scoundrel. [Aboriginal]

dingy /ˈdɪndʒɪ/ *adj.* (**dingier, dingiest**) dirty-looking, drab, dull-coloured. □□ **dingily** *adv.* **dinginess** *n.* [perh. ult. f. OE *dynge* DUNG]

dinkum /ˈdɪŋkəm/ *adj.* & *n. Austral.* & *NZ colloq.* —*adj.* genuine, right. —*n.* work, toil. □ **dinkum oil** the honest truth. [19th c.: orig. unkn.]

dinky¹ /ˈdɪŋkɪ/ *adj.* (**dinkier, dinkiest**) *colloq.* **1** *Brit. colloq.* (esp. of a thing) neat and attractive; small, dainty. **2** *US* trifling, insignificant. [Sc. *dink* neat, trim, of unkn. orig.]

dinky² /ˈdɪŋkɪ/ *n.* (*pl.* **-ies**) **1** a well-off young working couple with no children. **2** either partner of this. [contr. of *double income no kids* + -Y²]

dinner /ˈdɪnə(r)/ *n.* **1** the main meal of the day, taken either at midday or in the evening. **2** a formal evening meal, often in honour of a person or event. □ **dinner-dance** a formal dinner followed by dancing. **dinner-jacket** a man's short usu. black formal jacket for evening wear. **dinner lady** a woman who supervises children's lunch in a school. **dinner service** a set of usu. matching crockery for serving a meal. [ME f. OF *diner, disner*: see DINE]

dinosaur /ˈdaɪnəˌsɔː(r)/ *n.* **1** an extinct reptile of the Mesozoic era, often of enormous size. Some dinosaurs were herbivores, others carnivores; all died out (for reasons which are still in dispute) at the end of the Cretaceous period. **2** a large unwieldy system or organization, esp. one not adapting to new conditions. □□ **dinosaurian** /-ˈsɔːrɪən/ *adj.* & *n.* [mod.L *dinosaurus* f. Gk *deinos* terrible + *sauros* lizard]

dinothere /ˈdaɪnəˌθɪə(r)/ *n.* any elephant-like animal of the extinct genus *Deinotherium*, having downward curving tusks. [mod.L *dinotherium* f. Gk *deinos* terrible + *thērion* wild beast]

dint /dɪnt/ *n.* & *v.* —*n.* **1** a dent. **2** *archaic* a blow or stroke. —*v.tr.* mark with dints. □ **by dint of** by force or means of. [ME f. OE *dynt*, and partly f. cogn. ON *dyntr*: ult. orig. unkn.]

diocesan /daɪˈɒsɪs(ə)n/ *adj.* & *n.* —*adj.* of or concerning a diocese. —*n.* the bishop of a diocese. [ME f. F *diocésain* f. LL *diocesanus* (as DIOCESE)]

diocese /ˈdaɪəsɪs/ *n.* a district under the pastoral care of a bishop. [ME f. OF *diocise* f. LL *diocesis* f. L *dioecesis* f. Gk *dioikēsis* administration (as DI-³, *oikeō* inhabit)]

Diocletian /ˌdaɪəˈkliːʃ(ə)n/ (Gaius Aurelius Valerius Diocletianus, d. 316) Roman emperor 284–305, a low-born Dalmatian, elevated to the throne by the army. Faced with military problems on many frontiers and insurrection in the provinces, in 293 he divided the empire between himself (in the east) and Maximian (in the west). His genius was as an organizer, and many of his administrative measures lasted for centuries. An enthusiast for what he believed was the old Roman religion, tradition, and discipline, which he held could reinforce imperial unity, he insisted on maintenance of Roman law in the provinces, and it was against this background that the persecution of the Christians began in 303, probably on the insistence of his assistant, Galerius. In 304 he suffered a collapse in health and abdicated in the following year, retiring to Dalmatia;

the remains of his palace survive at Split, on the coast of Yugoslavia.

diode /ˈdaɪəʊd/ *n. Electronics* **1** a semiconductor allowing the flow of current in one direction only and having two terminals. **2** a thermionic valve having two electrodes. [DI-¹ + ELECTRODE]

dioecious /daɪˈiːʃəs/ *adj.* **1** *Bot.* having male and female organs on separate plants. **2** *Zool.* having the two sexes in separate individuals (cf. MONOECIOUS). [DI-¹ + Gk *-oikos* -housed]

Diogenes /daɪˈɒdʒɪˌniːz/ (*c.*400–*c.*325 BC) the founder of the Cynics. He lived at Athens in extreme poverty (legend says in a tub) and with an ostentatious disregard for social conventions that led to his being nicknamed *Kuōn* (the dog). His main principles were that happiness is attained by satisfying only one's basic natural needs (and in the cheapest and easiest way), practising self-sufficiency, and that what is natural cannot be dishonourable or indecent and should be done in public. His originality apparently consisted more in the way he applied his philosophy in everyday life than in his theories as such. He became a legendary figure, and among the many stories told of him is that he took a lantern in daylight, saying that he was seeking an honest man.

diol /ˈdaɪɒl/ *n. Chem.* any alcohol containing two hydroxyl groups in each molecule. [DI-¹ + -OL¹]

Dionysiac /ˌdaɪəˈnɪsɪˌæk/ *adj.* (also **Dionysian** /-sɪən/) **1** wildly sensual; unrestrained. **2** (in Greek mythology) of or relating to Dionysus, the Greek god of wine, or his worship. [LL *Dionysiacus* f. L *Dionysus* f. Gk *Dionusos*]

Dionysius /ˌdaɪəˈnɪsɪəs/ I ('the Elder') (*c.*430–367 BC), ruler of Syracuse, who fought the Carthaginians with varying success for control of part of Sicily and the Greek cities of southern Italy. His son, Dionysius II ('the Younger'), who succeeded him, lacked his father's military ambitions and welcomed philosophers to his court, but the attempt by Plato to turn him into a philosopher-king miscarried. He was eventually overthrown by rebels.

Dionysius Exiguus /ˌdaɪəˈnɪsɪəs ɪgˈzɪgjʊəs/ a Scythian monk who lived at Rome *c.*500–550, famous for his contributions to ecclesiastical chronology and his corpus of canon law. He introduced the system of the 'Christian era' that is still in use, (wrongly) accepting 753 AUC as the year of the Incarnation. He is said to have dubbed himself 'Exiguus' (little) owing to his extreme humility.

Dionysius of Halicarnassus /ˌdaɪəˈnɪsɪəs, ˌhælɪkɑːˈnæsəs/ (1st c. BC), Greek historian, literary critic, and writer on oratory, who lived at Rome for many years from 30 BC. He wrote (in Greek) a detailed history of Rome from legendary times down to the outbreak of the First Punic War (264 BC), but only the part down to 441 BC has survived.

Dionysius the Areopagite /ˌdaɪəˈnɪsɪəs, ˌærɪˈɒpəˌgaɪt/, St (1st c.), traditionally the first bishop of Athens, whose conversion by St Paul is recorded in Acts 17: 34. He was later confused with St Denis and with a 5th-c. mystical theologian, 'Dionysius the pseudo-Areopagite', whose writings on the soul's journey towards unity with God, combining Christianity with Neoplatonism, exercised a profound influence on medieval theology. Feast day, 9 Oct.

Dionysus /ˌdaɪəˈnaɪsəs/ *Gk Mythol.* a Greek god, also known as Bacchus, son of Zeus and Semele, a god of the fertility of nature, associated with emotional religious rites, and (though not originally) a god of wine who loosens care and inspires to music and poetry.

Diophantine equation /ˌdaɪəˈfæntɪn, -taɪn/ *n. Math.* an equation with integral coefficients for which integral solutions are required. [DIOPHANTUS]

Diophantus /ˌdaɪəˈfæntəs/ (date uncertain; prob. between 150 BC and AD 280) Greek mathematician of Alexandria, the first to attempt an algebraical notation. In his *Arithmetica* he shows how to solve simple and quadratic equations. It was Diophantus' work which led Fermat to take up the theory of numbers, in which he made his world-famous discoveries.

dioptre /daɪˈɒptə(r)/ *n.* (*US* **diopter**) *Optics* a unit of refractive power of a lens, equal to the reciprocal of its focal length in metres. [F *dioptre* f. L *dioptra* f. Gk *dioptra*: see DIOPTRIC]

dioptric /daɪˈɒptrɪk/ *adj. Optics* **1** serving as a medium for sight; assisting sight by refraction (*dioptric glass*; *dioptric lens*). **2** of refraction; refractive. [Gk *dioptrikos* f. *dioptra* a kind of theodolite]

dioptrics /daɪˈɒptrɪks/ *n. Optics* the part of optics dealing with refraction.

Dior /ˈdiːɔː(r)/, Christian (1905–57), French couturier, famous for introducing the 'new look' in 1947, with skirts longer and fuller than those recently worn.

diorama /ˌdaɪəˈrɑːmə/ *n.* **1** a scenic painting in which changes in colour and direction of illumination simulate a sunrise etc. **2** a small representation of a scene with three-dimensional figures, viewed through a window etc. **3** a small-scale model or film-set. □□ **dioramic** /-ˈræmɪk/ *adj.* [DI-³ + Gk *horama -atos* f. *horaō* see]

diorite /ˈdaɪəraɪt/ *n.* a coarse-grained plutonic igneous rock containing quartz. □□ **dioritic** /-ˈrɪtɪk/ *adj.* [F f. Gk *diorizō* distinguish]

Dioscuri /daɪˈɒskjʊərɪ/ *Gk Mythol.* the title of Castor and Polydeuces (latinized as *Pollux*), brothers of Helen, born to Leda after her seduction by Zeus. Castor was mortal, the son of Tyndareus and Leda; his twin, Pollux, was immortal, the son of Zeus and Leda; at Pollux's request they shared his immortality between them, spending half their time below the earth and the other half in Olympus. It is an unsettled controversy whether they are in origin heroes or 'faded' gods. They are often identified with the constellation Gemini, and were the patrons of mariners. [Gk, = sons of Zeus]

dioxan /daɪˈɒks(ə)n/ *n.* (also **dioxane** /-eɪn/) *Chem.* a colourless toxic liquid used as a solvent. ¶ *Chem.* formula: $C_4H_8O_2$.

dioxide /daɪˈɒksaɪd/ *n. Chem.* an oxide containing two atoms of oxygen which are not linked together (*carbon dioxide*).

DIP /dɪp/ *n. Computing* a form of integrated circuit consisting of a small plastic or ceramic slab with two parallel rows of pins. □ **DIP-switch** an arrangement of switches on a printer for selecting a printing mode. [abbr. of dual in-line package]

Dip. *abbr.* Diploma.

dip /dɪp/ *v. & n.* —*v.* (**dipped, dipping**) **1** *tr.* put or let down briefly into liquid etc.; immerse. **2** *intr.* **a** go below a surface or level (*the sun dipped below the horizon*). **b** (of a level of income, activity, etc.) decline slightly, esp. briefly (*profits dipped in May*). **3** *intr.* extend downwards; take or have a downward slope (*the road dips after the bend*). **4** *intr.* go under water and emerge quickly. **5** *intr.* (foll. by *into*) **a** read briefly from (a book etc.). **b** take a cursory interest in (a subject). **6** (foll. by *into*) **a** *intr.* put a hand, ladle, etc., into a container to take something out. **b** *tr.* put (a hand etc.) into a container to do this. **c** *intr.* spend from or make use of one's resources (*dipped into our savings*). **7** *tr. & intr.* lower or be lowered, esp. in salute. **8** *tr. Brit.* lower the beam of (a vehicle's headlights) to reduce dazzle. **9** *tr.* colour (a fabric) by immersing it in dye. **10** *tr.* wash (sheep) by immersion in a vermin-killing liquid. **11** *tr.* make (a candle) by immersing a wick briefly in hot tallow. **12** *tr.* baptize by immersion. **13** *tr.* (often foll. by *up, out of*) remove or scoop up (liquid, grain, etc., or something from liquid). —*n.* **1** an act of dipping or being dipped. **2** a liquid into which something is dipped. **3** a brief bathe in the sea, river, etc. **4** a brief downward slope, followed by an upward one, in a road etc. **5** a sauce or dressing into which food is dipped before eating. **6** a depression in the skyline. **7** *Astron. & Surveying* the apparent depression of the horizon from the line of observation, due to the curvature of the earth. **8** *Physics* the angle made with the horizontal at any point by the earth's magnetic field. **9** *Geol.* the angle a stratum makes with the horizon. **10** *sl.* a pickpocket. **11** a quantity dipped up. **12** a candle made by dipping. □ **dip-switch** a switch for dipping a vehicle's headlight beams. [OE *dyppan* f. Gmc: rel. to DEEP]

Dip. A.D. *abbr. Brit.* Diploma in Art and Design.

Dip. Ed. *abbr.* Diploma in Education.

dipeptide /daɪˈpeptaɪd/ *n. Biochem.* a peptide formed by the combination of two amino acids.

Dip. H.E. *abbr. Brit.* Diploma of Higher Education.

diphtheria /dɪfˈθɪərɪə, *disp.* dɪp-/ *n.* an acute infectious bacterial disease with inflammation of a mucous membrane esp. of the throat, resulting in the formation of a false membrane causing difficulty in breathing and swallowing. □□ **diphtherial** *adj.* **diphtheric** /-ˈθerɪk/ *adj.* **diphtheritic** /-θəˈrɪtɪk/ *adj.* **diphtheroid** /ˈdɪfθərɔɪd/ *adj.* [mod.L f. F *diphthérie*, earlier *diphthérite* f. Gk *diphthera* skin, hide]

diphthong /ˈdɪfθɒŋ/ *n.* **1** a speech sound in one syllable in which the articulation begins as for one vowel and moves as for another (as in *coin, loud*, and *side*). **2 a** a digraph representing the sound of a diphthong or single vowel (as in *feat*). **b** a compound vowel character; a ligature (as *æ*). □□ **diphthongal** /-ˈθɒŋg(ə)l/ *adj.* [F *diphtongue* f. LL *diphthongus* f. Gk *diphthoggos* (as DI-¹, *phthoggos* voice)]

diphthongize /ˈdɪfθɒŋaɪz/ *v.tr.* (also **-ise**) pronounce as a diphthong. □□ **diphthongization** /-ˈzeɪʃ(ə)n/ *n.*

diplo- /ˈdɪpləʊ/ *comb. form* double. [Gk *diplous* double]

diplococcus /ˌdɪpləˈkɒkəs/ *n.* (*pl.* **diplococci** /-kaɪ/) *Biol.* any coccus that occurs mainly in pairs.

diplodocus /dɪpˈlɒdəkəs, ˌdɪpləʊˈdəʊkəs/ *n.* a giant plant-eating dinosaur of the order Sauropoda, with a long neck and tail. [DIPLO- + Gk *dokos* wooden beam]

diploid /ˈdɪplɔɪd/ *adj. & n. Biol.* —*adj.* (of an organism or cell) having two complete sets of chromosomes per cell. —*n.* a diploid cell or organism. [G (as DIPLO-, -OID)]

diploidy /ˈdɪplɔɪdɪ/ *n. Biol.* the condition of being diploid.

diploma /dɪˈpləʊmə/ *n.* **1** a certificate of qualification awarded by a college etc. **2** a document conferring an honour or privilege. **3** a State paper; an official document; a charter. □□ **diplomaed** /-məd/ *adj.* (also **diploma'd**). [L f. Gk *diplōma -atos* folded paper f. *diploō* to fold f. *diplous* double]

diplomacy /dɪˈpləʊməsɪ/ *n.* **1 a** the management of international relations. **b** expertise in this. **2** adroitness in personal relations; tact. [F *diplomatie* f. *diplomatique* DIPLOMATIC after *aristocratie*]

diplomat /ˈdɪpləmæt/ *n.* **1** an official representing a country abroad; a member of a diplomatic service. **2** a tactful person. [F *diplomate*, back-form. f. *diplomatique*: see DIPLOMATIC]

diplomate /ˈdɪpləmeɪt/ *n.* esp. *US* a person who holds a diploma, esp. in medicine.

diplomatic /ˌdɪpləˈmætɪk/ *adj.* **1 a** of or involved in diplomacy. **b** skilled in diplomacy. **2** tactful; adroit in personal relations. **3** (of an edition etc.) exactly reproducing the original. □ **diplomatic bag** a container in which official mail etc. is dispatched to or from an embassy, not usu. subject to customs inspection. **diplomatic corps** the body of diplomats representing other countries at a seat of government. **diplomatic immunity** the exemption of diplomatic staff abroad from arrest, taxation, etc. **diplomatic service** *Brit.* the branch of public service concerned with the representation of a country abroad. □□ **diplomatically** *adv.* [mod.L *diplomaticus* and F *diplomatique* f. L DIPLOMA]

diplomatist /dɪˈpləʊmətɪst/ *n.* = DIPLOMAT.

diplont /ˈdɪplɒnt/ *n. Biol.* an animal or plant which has a diploid number of chromosomes in its somatic cells. [DIPLO- + Gk *ont-* stem of *ōn* being]

diplotene /ˈdɪpləʊtiːn/ *n. Biol.* a stage during the prophase of meiosis where paired chromosomes begin to separate. [DIPLO- + Gk *tainia* band]

dipolar /daɪˈpəʊlə(r)/ *adj.* having two poles, as in a magnet.

dipole /ˈdaɪpəʊl/ *n.* **1** *Physics* two equal and oppositely charged or magnetized poles separated by a distance. **2** *Chem.* a molecule in which a concentration of positive charges is separated from a concentration of negative charges. **3** an aerial consisting of a horizontal metal rod with a connecting wire at its centre.

dipper /ˈdɪpə(r)/ *n.* **1** a diving bird, *Cinclus cinclus*. Also called *water ouzel*. **2** a ladle. **3** *colloq.* an Anabaptist or Baptist.

dippy /ˈdɪpɪ/ *adj.* (**dippier, dippiest**) *sl.* crazy, silly. [20th c.: orig. uncert.]

dipso /ˈdɪpsəʊ/ *n.* (*pl.* **-os**) *colloq.* a dipsomaniac. [abbr.]

dipsomania /ˌdɪpsəˈmeɪnɪə/ n. an abnormal craving for alcohol. □□ **dipsomaniac** /-ˈmeɪnɪˌæk/ n. [Gk dipso- f. dipsa thirst + -MANIA]

dipstick /ˈdɪpstɪk/ n. a graduated rod for measuring the depth of a liquid, esp. in a vehicle's engine.

dipteral /ˈdɪptər(ə)l/ adj. Archit. having a double peristyle. [L dipteros f. Gk (as DI-¹, pteron wing)]

dipteran /ˈdɪptərən/ n. & adj. —n. a dipterous insect. —adj. = DIPTEROUS 1. [mod.L diptera f. Gk diptera neut. pl. of dipterous two-winged (as DI-², pteron wing)]

dipterous /ˈdɪptərəs/ adj. 1 (of an insect) of the order Diptera, having two membranous wings, e.g. the fly, gnat, or mosquito. 2 Bot. having two winglike appendages. [mod.L dipterus f. Gk dipteros: see DIPTERAN]

diptych /ˈdɪptɪk/ n. 1 a painting, esp. an altarpiece, on two hinged usu. wooden panels which may be closed like a book. 2 an ancient writing-tablet consisting of two hinged leaves with waxed inner sides. [LL diptycha f. Gk diptukha (as DI-¹, ptukhē fold)]

Dirac /dɪˈræk/, Paul Adrian Maurice (1902–84), English theoretical physicist. He applied Einstein's theory of relativity to quantum mechanics in order to describe the behaviour of the electron, including its spin, and later predicted the existence of a short-lived fundamental particle, the positive electron or positron, discovered by Carl David Anderson in 1932. He also developed a quantum theory of radiation, and was the co-inventor of the Fermi–Dirac statistics, which describe the behaviour of a class of sub-atomic particles, later called fermions. Dirac shared with Schrödinger the 1933 Nobel Prize for physics, for their contribution to wave mechanics.

dire /ˈdaɪə(r)/ adj. 1 a calamitous, dreadful (in dire straits). b ominous (dire warnings). 2 urgent (in dire need). □□ **direly** adv. **direness** n. [L dirus]

direct /daɪˈrekt, dɪ-/ adj., adv., & v. —adj. 1 extending or moving in a straight line or by the shortest route; not crooked or circuitous. 2 a straightforward; going straight to the point. b frank; not ambiguous. 3 without intermediaries or the intervention of other factors (direct rule; the direct result; made a direct approach). 4 (of descent) lineal, not collateral. 5 exact, complete, greatest possible (esp. where contrast is implied) (the direct opposite). 6 Mus. (of an interval or chord) not inverted. 7 Astron. (of planetary etc. motion) proceeding from East to West; not retrograde. —adv. 1 in a direct way or manner; without an intermediary or intervening factor (dealt with them direct). 2 frankly; without evasion. 3 by a direct route (send it direct to London). —v.tr. 1 control, guide; govern the movements of. 2 (foll. by to + infin., or that + clause) give a formal order or command to. 3 (foll. by to) a address or give indications for the delivery of (a letter etc.). b tell or show (a person) the way to a destination. 4 (foll. by at, to, towards) a point, aim, or cause (a blow or missile) to move in a certain direction. b point or address (one's attention, a remark, etc.). 5 guide as an adviser, as a principle, etc. (I do as duty directs me). 6 a (also absol.) supervise the performing, staging, etc., of (a film, play, etc.). b supervise the performance of (an actor etc.). 7 (also absol.) guide the performance of (a group of musicians), esp. as a participant. □ **direct access** the facility of retrieving data immediately from any part of a computer file. **direct action** action such as a strike or sabotage directly affecting the community and meant to reinforce demands on a government, employer, etc. **direct address** Computing an address (see ADDRESS n. 1c) which specifies the location of data to be used in an operation. **direct current** an electric current flowing in one direction only. ¶ Abbr.: **DC**, **d.c. direct debit** an arrangement for the regular debiting of a bank account at the request of the payee. **direct-grant school** hist. (in the UK) a school receiving funds from the Government and not from a local authority. **direct method** a system of teaching a foreign language using only that language and without the study of formal grammar. **direct object** Gram. the primary object of the action of a transitive verb. **direct proportion** a relation between quantities whose ratio is constant. **direct speech** (or **oration**) words actually spoken, not reported in the third person. **direct tax** a tax levied on the person who ultimately bears the burden of it, esp. on income. □□ **directness**

n. [ME f. L directus past part. of dirigere direct- (as DI-², regere put straight)]

direction /daɪˈrekʃ(ə)n, dɪ-/ n. 1 the act or process of directing; supervision. 2 (usu. in pl.) an order or instruction, esp. each of a set guiding use of equipment etc. 3 a the course or line along which a person or thing moves or looks, or which must be taken to reach a destination (sailed in an easterly direction). b (in pl.) guidance on how to reach a destination. c the point to or from which a person or thing moves or looks. 4 the tendency or scope of a theme, subject, or inquiry. □ **direction-finder** a device for determining the source of radio waves, esp. as an aid in navigation. □□ **directionless** adj. [ME f. F direction or L directio (as DIRECT)]

directional /daɪˈrekʃən(ə)l, dɪ-/ adj. 1 of or indicating direction. 2 Electronics a concerned with the transmission of radio or sound waves in a particular direction. b (of equipment) designed to receive radio or sound waves most effectively from a particular direction or directions and not others. □□ **directionality** /-ˈnælɪtɪ/ n. **directionally** adv.

directive /daɪˈrektɪv, dɪ-/ n. & adj. —n. a general instruction from one in authority. —adj. serving to direct. [ME f. med.L directivus (as DIRECT)]

directly /daɪˈrektlɪ, dɪ-/ adv. & conj. —adv. 1 a at once; without delay. b presently, shortly. 2 exactly, immediately (directly opposite; directly after lunch). 3 in a direct manner. —conj. colloq. as soon as (will tell you directly they come).

Directoire /dɪrekˈtwɑː(r)/ n. & adj. —n. the French Directory. —adj. Needlework & Art in imitation of styles prevalent during the French Directory. □ **Directoire drawers** (or **knickers**) knickers which are straight, full, and knee-length. [F (as DIRECTORY)]

director /daɪˈrektə(r), dɪ-/ n. 1 a person who directs or controls something. 2 a member of the managing board of a commercial company. 3 a person who directs a film, play, etc., esp. professionally. 4 a person acting as spiritual adviser. 5 esp. US = CONDUCTOR 1. □ **director-general** the chief executive of a large (esp. public) organization. **director of public prosecutions** Brit. = public prosecutor. □□ **directorial** /-ˈtɔːrɪəl/ adj. **directorship** n. (esp. in sense 2). [AF directour f. LL director governor (as DIRECT)]

directorate /daɪˈrektərət, dɪ-/ n. 1 a board of directors. 2 the office of director.

Directory /daɪˈrektərɪ, dɪ-/ n. the executive of the French Revolutionary National Convention, constituted in 1795. The Directory was composed of five members, elected at the rate of one a year, and represented an attempt to avoid the one-man dictatorship previously achieved by Robespierre. It maintained an aggressive foreign policy, but proved too weak to control events at home and was overthrown by Napoleon in 1799.

directory /daɪˈrektərɪ, dɪ-/ n. (pl. **-ies**) 1 a book listing alphabetically or thematically a particular group of individuals (e.g. telephone subscribers) or organizations with various details. 2 a book of rules, esp. for the order of private or public worship. [LL directorium (as DIRECT)]

directress /daɪˈrektrɪs, dɪ-/ n. (also **directrice**) a woman director. [DIRECTOR, F directrice (as DIRECTRIX)]

directrix /daɪˈrektrɪks, dɪ-/ n. (pl. **directrices** /-trɪˌsiːz/) Geom. a fixed line used in describing a curve or surface. [med.L f. LL director: see DIRECTOR, -TRIX]

direful /ˈdaɪəˌfʊl/ adj. literary terrible, dreadful. □□ **direfully** adv. [DIRE + -FUL]

dirge /dɜːdʒ/ n. 1 a lament for the dead, esp. forming part of a funeral service. 2 any mournful song or lament. □□ **dirgeful** adj. [ME f. L dirige (imper.) direct, the first word in the Latin antiphon (from Ps. 5: 8) in the Matins part of the Office for the Dead]

dirham /ˈdɜːhæm/ n. the principal monetary unit of Morocco and the United Arab Emirates. [Arab. f. L DRACHMA]

dirigible /ˈdɪrɪdʒɪb(ə)l, dɪˈrɪdʒ-/ adj. & n. —adj. capable of being guided. —n. a dirigible balloon or airship. [L dirigere arrange, direct: see DIRECT]

diriment /ˈdɪrɪmənt/ adj. Law nullifying. □ **diriment imped-**

iment a factor (e.g. the existence of a prior marriage) rendering a marriage null and void from the beginning. [L *dirimere* f. *dir-* = DIS- + *emere* take]

dirk /dɜːk/ *n.* a long dagger, esp. as formerly worn by Scottish Highlanders. [17th-c. *durk*, of unkn. orig.]

dirndl /ˈdɜːnd(ə)l/ *n.* **1** a woman's dress styled in imitation of Alpine peasant costume, with close-fitting bodice, tight waistband, and full skirt. **2** a full skirt of this kind. [G dial., dimin. of *Dirne* girl]

dirt /dɜːt/ *n.* **1** unclean matter that soils. **2 a** earth, soil. **b** earth, cinders, etc., used to make a surface for a road etc. (usu. *attrib.*: *dirt track*; *dirt road*). **3** foul or malicious words or talk. **4** excrement. **5** a dirty condition. **6** a person or thing considered worthless. □ **dirt bike** a motor cycle designed for use on unmade roads and tracks, esp. in scrambling. **dirt cheap** *colloq.* extremely cheap. **dirt-track** a course made of rolled cinders, soil, etc., for motor-cycle racing or flat racing. **do a person dirt** *sl.* harm or injure a person's reputation maliciously. **eat dirt 1** suffer insults etc. without retaliating. **2** *US* make a humiliating confession. **treat like dirt** treat (a person) contemptuously; abuse. [ME f. ON *drit* excrement]

dirty /ˈdɜːtɪ/ *adj., adv., & v.* —*adj.* (**dirtier, dirtiest**) **1** soiled, unclean. **2** causing one to become dirty (*a dirty job*). **3** sordid, lewd; morally illicit or questionable (*dirty joke*). **4** unpleasant, nasty. **5** dishonest, dishonourable, unfair (*dirty play*). **6** (of weather) rough, squally. **7** (of a colour) not pure or clear, dingy. **8** *colloq.* (of a nuclear weapon) producing considerable radioactive fallout. —*adv. sl.* (with adjectives expressing magnitude) very (*a dirty great diamond*). —*v.tr. & intr.* (**-ies, -ied**) make or become dirty. □ **dirty dog** *colloq.* a scoundrel; a despicable person. **the dirty end of the stick** *colloq.* the difficult or unpleasant part of an undertaking, situation, etc. **dirty linen** (or **washing**) *colloq.* intimate secrets, esp. of a scandalous nature. **dirty look** *colloq.* a look of disapproval, anger, or disgust. **dirty money** extra money paid to those who handle dirty materials. **dirty trick 1** a dishonourable and deceitful act. **2** (in *pl.*) underhand political activity, esp. to discredit an opponent. **dirty weekend** *colloq.* a weekend spent clandestinely with a lover. **dirty word 1** an offensive or indecent word. **2** a word for something which is disapproved of (*profit is a dirty word*). **dirty work** dishonourable or illegal activity, esp. done clandestinely. **do the dirty on** *colloq.* play a mean trick on. □□ **dirtily** *adv.* **dirtiness** *n.*

dis- /dɪs/ *prefix* forming nouns, adjectives, and verbs: **1** expressing negation (*dishonest*). **2** indicating reversal or absence of an action or state (*disengage*; *disbelieve*). **3** indicating removal of a thing or quality (*dismember*; *disable*). **4** indicating separation (*distinguish*; *dispose*). **5** indicating completeness or intensification of the action (*disembowel*; *disgruntled*). **6** indicating expulsion from (*disbar*). [L *dis-*, sometimes through OF *des-*]

disability /dɪsəˈbɪlɪtɪ/ *n.* (pl. **-ies**) **1** physical incapacity, either congenital or caused by injury, disease, etc. **2** a lack of some asset, quality, or attribute, that prevents one's doing something. **3** a legal disqualification.

disable /dɪsˈeɪb(ə)l/ *v.tr.* **1** render unable to function; deprive of an ability. **2** (often as **disabled** *adj.*) deprive of or reduce the power of to walk or do other normal activities, esp. by crippling. □□ **disablement** *n.*

disabuse /dɪsəˈbjuːz/ *v.tr.* **1** (foll. by *of*) free from a mistaken idea. **2** disillusion, undeceive.

disaccord /dɪsəˈkɔːd/ *n. & v.* —*n.* disagreement, disharmony. —*v.intr.* (usu. foll. by *with*) disagree; be at odds. [ME f. F *désaccorder* (as ACCORD)]

disadvantage /dɪsədˈvɑːntɪdʒ/ *n. & v.* —*n.* **1** an unfavourable circumstance or condition. **2** damage to one's interest or reputation. —*v.tr.* cause disadvantage to. □ **at a disadvantage** in an unfavourable position or aspect. [ME f. OF *desavantage*: see ADVANTAGE]

disadvantaged /dɪsədˈvɑːntɪdʒd/ *adj.* placed in unfavourable circumstances (esp. of a person lacking the normal social opportunities).

disadvantageous /ˌdɪsˌædvənˈteɪdʒəs/ *adj.* **1** involving disadvantage or discredit. **2** derogatory. □□ **disadvantageously** *adv.*

disaffected /dɪsəˈfektɪd/ *adj.* **1** disloyal, esp. to one's superiors. **2** estranged; no longer friendly; discontented. □□ **disaffectedly** *adv.* [past part. of *disaffect* (v.), orig. = dislike, disorder (as DIS-, AFFECT)]

disaffection /dɪsəˈfekʃ(ə)n/ *n.* **1** disloyalty. **2** political discontent.

disaffiliate /dɪsəˈfɪlɪeɪt/ *v.* **1** *tr.* end the affiliation of. **2** *intr.* end one's affiliation. **3** *tr. & intr.* detach. □□ **disaffiliation** /-ˈeɪʃ(ə)n/ *n.*

disaffirm /dɪsəˈfɜːm/ *v.tr. Law* **1** reverse (a previous decision). **2** repudiate (a settlement). □□ **disaffirmation** /dɪsˌæfəˈmeɪʃ(ə)n/ *n.*

disafforest /dɪsəˈfɒrɪst/ *v.tr. Brit.* **1** clear of forests or trees. **2** reduce from the legal status of forest to that of ordinary land. □□ **disafforestation** /-ˈsteɪʃ(ə)n/ *n.* [ME f. AL *disafforestare* (as DIS-, AFFOREST)]

disagree /dɪsəˈɡriː/ *v.intr.* (**-agrees, -agreed, -agreeing**) (often foll. by *with*) **1** hold a different opinion. **2** quarrel. **3** (of factors or circumstances) not correspond. **4** have an adverse effect upon (a person's health, digestion, etc.). □□ **disagreement** *n.* [ME f. OF *desagreer* (as DIS-, AGREE)]

disagreeable /dɪsəˈɡriːəb(ə)l/ *adj.* **1** unpleasant, not to one's liking. **2** quarrelsome; rude or bad-tempered. □□ **disagreeableness** *n.* **disagreeably** *adv.* [ME f. OF *desagreable* (as DIS-, AGREEABLE)]

disallow /dɪsəˈlaʊ/ *v.tr.* refuse to allow or accept as valid; prohibit. □□ **disallowance** *n.* [ME f. OF *desalouer* (as DIS-, ALLOW)]

disambiguate /dɪsæmˈbɪɡjʊeɪt/ *v.tr.* remove ambiguity from. □□ **disambiguation** /-ˈeɪʃ(ə)n/ *n.*

disamenity /dɪsəˈmiːnɪtɪ, -ˈmenɪtɪ/ *n.* (pl. **-ies**) an unpleasant feature (of a place etc.); a disadvantage.

disappear /dɪsəˈpɪə(r)/ *v.intr.* **1** cease to be visible; pass from sight. **2** cease to exist or be in circulation or use (*trams had all but disappeared*). □□ **disappearance** *n.*

disappoint /dɪsəˈpɔɪnt/ *v.tr.* **1** (also *absol.*) fail to fulfil a desire or expectation of (a person). **2** frustrate (hopes etc.); cause the failure of (a plan etc.). □ **be disappointed** (foll. by *with*, *at*, *in*, or *to* + infin., or *that* + clause) fail to have one's expectation etc. fulfilled in some regard (*was disappointed with you*; *disappointed at the result*; *am disappointed to be last*). □□ **disappointedly** *adv.* **disappointing** *adj.* **disappointingly** *adv.* [ME f. F *désappointer* (as DIS-, APPOINT)]

disappointment /dɪsəˈpɔɪntmənt/ *n.* **1** an event, thing, or person that disappoints. **2** a feeling of distress, vexation, etc., resulting from this (*I cannot hide my disappointment*).

disapprobation /dɪsˌæprəˈbeɪʃ(ə)n/ *n.* strong (esp. moral) disapproval.

disapprove /dɪsəˈpruːv/ *v.* **1** *intr.* (usu. foll. by *of*) have or express an unfavourable opinion. **2** *tr.* be displeased with. □□ **disapproval** *n.* **disapprover** *n.* **disapproving** *adj.* **disapprovingly** *adv.*

disarm /dɪsˈɑːm/ *v.* **1** *tr.* **a** take weapons away from (a person, State, etc.) (often foll. by *of*: *were disarmed of their rifles*). **b** *Fencing* etc. deprive of a weapon. **2** *tr.* deprive (a ship etc.) of its means of defence. **3** *intr.* (of a State etc.) disband or reduce its armed forces. **4** *tr.* remove the fuse from (a bomb etc.). **5** *tr.* deprive of the power to injure. **6** *tr.* pacify or allay the hostility or suspicions of; mollify; placate. □□ **disarmer** *n.* **disarming** *adj.* (esp. in sense 6). **disarmingly** *adv.* [ME f. OF *desarmer* (as DIS-, ARM²)]

disarmament /dɪsˈɑːməmənt/ *n.* the reduction by a State of its military forces and weapons.

disarrange /dɪsəˈreɪndʒ/ *v.tr.* bring into disorder. □□ **disarrangement** *n.*

disarray /dɪsəˈreɪ/ *n. & v.* —*n.* (often prec. by *in*, *into*) disorder, confusion (esp. among people). —*v.tr.* throw into disorder.

disarticulate /dɪsɑːˈtɪkjʊleɪt/ *v.tr. & intr.* separate at the joints. □□ **disarticulation** /-ˈleɪʃ(ə)n/ *n.*

disassemble /ˌdɪsəˈsemb(ə)l/ v.tr. take (a machine etc.) to pieces. □□ **disassembly** n.

disassociate /ˌdɪsəˈsəʊʃɪeɪt, -sɪˌeɪt/ v.tr. & intr. = DISSOCIATE. □□ **disassociation** /-ˈeɪʃ(ə)n/ n.

disaster /dɪˈzɑːstə(r)/ n. 1 a great or sudden misfortune. 2 a a complete failure. b a person or enterprise ending in failure. □□ **disastrous** adj. **disastrously** adv. [orig. 'unfavourable aspect of a star', f. F désastre or It. disastro (as DIS-, astro f. L astrum star)]

disavow /ˌdɪsəˈvaʊ/ v.tr. disclaim knowledge of, responsibility for, or belief in. □□ **disavowal** n. [ME f. OF desavouer (as DIS-, AVOW)]

disband /dɪsˈbænd/ v. 1 intr. (of an organized group etc.) cease to work or act together; disperse. 2 tr. cause (such a group) to disband. □□ **disbandment** n. [obs. F desbander (as DIS-, BAND¹ 6)]

disbar /dɪsˈbɑː(r)/ v.tr. (**disbarred**, **disbarring**) deprive (a barrister) of the right to practise; expel from the Bar. □□ **disbarment** n.

disbelieve /ˌdɪsbɪˈliːv/ v. 1 tr. be unable or unwilling to believe (a person or statement). 2 intr. have no faith. □□ **disbelief** n. **disbeliever** n. **disbelievingly** adv.

disbound /dɪsˈbaʊnd/ adj. (of a pamphlet etc.) removed from a bound volume.

disbud /dɪsˈbʌd/ v.tr. (**disbudded**, **disbudding**) remove (esp. superfluous) buds from.

disburden /dɪsˈbɜːd(ə)n/ v.tr. 1 relieve (a person, one's mind, etc.) of a burden (often foll. by of: was disburdened of all worries). 2 get rid of, discharge (a duty, anxiety, etc.).

disburse /dɪsˈbɜːs/ v. 1 tr. expend (money). 2 tr. defray (a cost). 3 intr. pay money. □□ **disbursal** n. **disbursement** n. **disburser** n. [OF desbourser (as DIS-, BOURSE)]

disc /dɪsk/ n. (also **disk** esp. US and in sense 4) 1 a a flat thin circular object. b a round flat or apparently flat surface (the sun's disc). c a mark of this shape. 2 a layer of cartilage between vertebrae. 3 a gramophone record. 4 a (usu. **disk**; in full **magnetic disk**) a computer storage device consisting of several flat circular magnetically coated plates formed into a rotatable disc. b (in full **optical disc**) a smooth non-magnetic disc with large storage capacity for data recorded and read by laser. 5 a device with a pointer or rotating disc indicating time of arrival or latest permitted time of departure, for display in a parked motor vehicle. □ **disc brake** a brake employing the friction of pads against a disc. **disk drive** Computing a mechanism for rotating a disk and reading or writing data from or to it. **disc harrow** a harrow with cutting edges consisting of a row of concave discs set at an oblique angle. **disc jockey** the presenter of a selection of gramophone records of popular music, esp. in a broadcast. [F disque or L discus: see DISCUS]

discalced /dɪsˈkælst/ adj. (of a friar or a nun) barefoot or wearing only sandals. [var. of discalceated (after F déchaux) f. L discalceatus (as DIS-, calceatus f. calceus shoe)]

discard v. & n. —v.tr. /dɪsˈkɑːd/ 1 reject or get rid of as unwanted or superfluous. 2 (also absol.) Cards remove or put aside (a card) from one's hand. —n. /ˈdɪskɑːd/ a discarded item, esp. a card in a card-game. □□ **discardable** /-ˈkɑːdəb(ə)l/ adj. [DIS- + CARD¹]

discarnate /dɪsˈkɑːnət/ adj. having no physical body; separated from the flesh. [DIS-, L caro carnis flesh]

discern /dɪˈsɜːn/ v.tr. 1 perceive clearly with the mind or the senses. 2 make out by thought or by gazing, listening, etc. □□ **discerner** n. **discernible** adj. **discernibly** adv. [ME f. OF discerner f. L (as DIS-, cernere cret- separate)]

discerning /dɪˈsɜːnɪŋ/ adj. having or showing good judgement or insight. □□ **discerningly** adv.

discernment /dɪˈsɜːnmənt/ n. good judgement or insight.

discerptible /dɪˈsɜːptɪb(ə)l/ adj. literary able to be plucked apart; divisible. □□ **discerptibility** /-ˈbɪlɪtɪ/ n. [L discerpere discerpt- (as DIS-, carpere pluck)]

discerption /dɪˈsɜːpʃ(ə)n/ n. archaic 1 a pulling apart; severance. b an instance of this. 2 a severed piece. [LL discerptio (as DISCERPTIBLE)]

discharge v. & n. —v. /dɪsˈtʃɑːdʒ/ 1 tr. a let go, release, esp. from a duty, commitment, or period of confinement. b relieve (a bankrupt) of residual liability. 2 tr. dismiss from office, employment, army commission, etc. 3 tr. a fire (a gun etc.). b (of a gun etc.) fire (a bullet etc.). 4 a tr. (also absol.) pour out or cause to pour out (pus, liquid, etc.) (the wound was discharging). b tr. throw; eject (discharged a stone at the cat). c tr. utter (abuse etc.). d intr. (foll. by into) (of a river etc.) flow into (esp. the sea). 5 tr. a carry out, perform (a duty or obligation). b relieve oneself of (a financial commitment) (discharged his debt). 6 tr. Law cancel (an order of court). 7 tr. Physics release an electrical charge from. 8 tr. a relieve (a ship etc.) of its cargo. b unload (a cargo) from a ship. —n. /ˈdɪstʃɑːdʒ, dɪsˈtʃɑːdʒ/ 1 the act or an instance of discharging; the process of being discharged. 2 a dismissal, esp. from the armed services. 3 a a release, exemption, acquittal, etc. b a written certificate of release etc. 4 an act of firing a gun etc. 5 a an emission (of pus, liquid, etc.). b the liquid or matter so discharged. 6 (usu. foll. by of) a the payment (of a debt). b the performance (of a duty etc.). 7 Physics a the release of a quantity of electric charge from an object. b a flow of electricity through the air or other gas esp. when accompanied by the emission of light. c the conversion of chemical energy in a cell into electrical energy. 8 the unloading (of a ship or a cargo). □□ **dischargeable** adj. **discharger** n. (in sense 7 of v.). [ME f. OF descharger (as DIS-, CHARGE)]

disciple /dɪˈsaɪp(ə)l/ n. 1 a follower or pupil of a leader, teacher, philosophy, etc. (a disciple of Zen Buddhism). 2 any early believer in Christ, esp. one of the twelve Apostles. □□ **discipleship** n. **discipular** /dɪˈsɪpjʊlə(r)/ adj. [OE discipul f. L discipulus f. discere learn]

disciplinarian /ˌdɪsɪplɪˈneərɪən/ n. a person who upholds or practises firm discipline (a strict disciplinarian).

disciplinary /ˈdɪsɪplɪnərɪ, -ˈplɪnərɪ/ adj. of, promoting, or enforcing discipline. [med.L disciplinarius (as DISCIPLINE)]

discipline /ˈdɪsɪplɪn/ n. & v. —n. 1 a control or order exercised over people or animals, esp. children, prisoners, military personnel, church members, etc. b the system of rules used to maintain this control. c the behaviour of groups subjected to such rules (poor discipline in the ranks). 2 a mental, moral, or physical training. b adversity as used to bring about such training (left the course because he couldn't take the discipline). 3 a branch of instruction or learning (philosophy is a hard discipline). 4 punishment. 5 Eccl. mortification by physical self-punishment, esp. scourging. —v.tr. 1 punish, chastise. 2 bring under control by training in obedience; drill. □□ **disciplinable** adj. **disciplinal** /ˌdɪsɪˈplaɪn(ə)l, ˈdɪsɪplɪn(ə)l/ adj. [ME f. OF discipliner or LL & med.L disciplinare, disciplina f. discipulus DISCIPLE]

disclaim /dɪsˈkleɪm/ v.tr. 1 deny or disown (disclaim all responsibility). 2 (often absol.) Law renounce a legal claim to (property etc.). [ME f. AF desclaim- stressed stem of desclamer (as DIS-, CLAIM)]

disclaimer /dɪsˈkleɪmə(r)/ n. a renunciation or disavowal, esp. of responsibility. [ME f. AF (= DISCLAIM as noun)]

disclose /dɪsˈkləʊz/ v.tr. 1 make known; reveal (disclosed the truth). 2 remove the cover from; expose to view. □□ **discloser** n. [ME f. OF desclos- stem of desclore f. Gallo-Roman (as DIS-, CLOSE²)]

disclosure /dɪsˈkləʊʒə(r)/ n. 1 the act or an instance of disclosing; the process of being disclosed. 2 something disclosed; a revelation. [DISCLOSE + -URE after closure]

disco /ˈdɪskəʊ/ n. & v. colloq. —n. (pl. **-os**) = DISCOTHÈQUE. —v.intr. (**-oes**, **-oed**) 1 attend a discothèque. 2 dance to disco music (discoed the night away). □ **disco music** popular dance music characterized by a heavy bass rhythm. [abbr.]

discobolus /dɪsˈkɒbələs/ n. (pl. **discoboli** /-ˌlaɪ/) 1 a discus-thrower in ancient Greece. 2 a statue of a discobolus. A noted statue was made by the Greek sculptor Myron (5th c. BC), several copies of which survive. [L f. Gk diskobolos f. diskos DISCUS + -bolos -throwing f. ballō to throw]

discography /dɪsˈkɒgrəfɪ/ n. (pl. **-ies**) 1 a descriptive catalogue of gramophone records, esp. of a particular performer or composer. 2 the study of gramophone records. □□ **discographer** n. [DISC + -GRAPHY after biography]

discoid /ˈdɪskɔɪd/ adj. disc-shaped. [Gk diskoeidēs (as DISCUS, -OID)]

discolour /dɪsˈkʌlə(r)/ v.tr. & intr. (US discolor) spoil or cause to spoil the colour of; stain; tarnish. □□ **discoloration** /-ˈreɪʃ(ə)n/ n. (also **discolouration**). [ME f. OF descolorer or med.L discolorare (as DIS-, COLOUR)]

discombobulate /ˌdɪskəmˈbɒbjʊˌleɪt/ v.tr. US joc. disturb; disconcert. [prob. based on discompose or discomfit]

discomfit /dɪsˈkʌmfɪt/ v.tr. (**discomfited, discomfiting**) 1 a disconcert or baffle. b thwart. 2 archaic defeat in battle. □□ **discomfiture** n. [ME f. discomfit f. OF past part. of desconfire f. Rmc (as DIS-, L conficere put together: see CONFECTION)]

discomfort /dɪsˈkʌmfət/ n. & v. —n. 1 a a lack of ease; slight pain (tight collar caused discomfort). b mental uneasiness (his presence caused her discomfort). 2 a lack of comfort. —v.tr. make uneasy. [ME f. OF desconfort(er) (as DIS-, COMFORT)]

discommode /ˌdɪskəˈməʊd/ v.tr. inconvenience (a person etc.). □□ **discommodious** adj. [obs. F discommoder var. of incommoder (as DIS-, INCOMMODE)]

discompose /ˌdɪskəmˈpəʊz/ v.tr. disturb the composure of; agitate; disturb. □□ **discomposure** /-ˈpəʊzə(r)/ n.

disconcert /ˌdɪskənˈsɜːt/ v.tr. 1 disturb the composure of; agitate; fluster (disconcerted by his expression). 2 spoil or upset (plans etc.). □□ **disconcertedly** adv. **disconcerting** adj. **disconcertingly** adv. **disconcertion** /-ˈsɜːʃ(ə)n/ n. **disconcertment** n. [obs. F desconcerter (as DIS-, CONCERT)]

disconfirm /ˌdɪskənˈfɜːm/ v.tr. formal disprove or tend to disprove (a hypothesis etc.). □□ **disconfirmation** /-ˌkɒnfəˈmeɪʃ(ə)n/ n.

disconformity /ˌdɪskənˈfɔːmɪtɪ/ n. (pl. **-ies**) 1 a lack of conformity. b an instance of this. 2 Geol. a difference of plane between two parallel, approximately horizontal sets of strata.

disconnect /ˌdɪskəˈnekt/ v.tr. 1 (often foll. by from) break the connection of (things, ideas, etc.). 2 put (an electrical device) out of action by disconnecting the parts, esp. by pulling out the plug.

disconnected /ˌdɪskəˈnektɪd/ adj. (of speech, writing, argument, etc.) incoherent and illogical. □□ **disconnectedly** adv. **disconnectedness** n.

disconnection /ˌdɪskəˈnekʃ(ə)n/ n. (also **disconnexion**) the act or an instance of disconnecting; the state of being disconnected.

disconsolate /dɪsˈkɒnsələt/ adj. 1 forlorn or inconsolable. 2 unhappy or disappointed. □□ **disconsolately** adv. **disconsolateness** n. **disconsolation** /-ˈleɪʃ(ə)n/ n. [ME f. med.L disconsolatus (as DIS-, consolatus past part. of L consolari console)]

discontent /ˌdɪskənˈtent/ n., adj., & v. —n. lack of contentment; restlessness, dissatisfaction. —adj. dissatisfied (was discontent with his lot). —v.tr. (esp. as **discontented** adj.) make dissatisfied. □□ **discontentedly** adv. **discontentedness** n. **discontentment** n.

discontinue /ˌdɪskənˈtɪnjuː/ v. (**-continues, -continued, -continuing**) 1 intr. & tr. cease or cause to cease to exist or be made (a discontinued line). 2 tr. give up, cease from (discontinued his visits). 3 tr. cease taking or paying (a newspaper, a subscription, etc.). □□ **discontinuance** n. **discontinuation** /-ˈeɪʃ(ə)n/ n. [ME f. OF discontinuer f. med.L discontinuare (as DIS-, CONTINUE)]

discontinuous /ˌdɪskənˈtɪnjʊəs/ adj. lacking continuity in space or time; intermittent. □□ **discontinuity** /-ˌkɒntɪˈnjuːɪtɪ/ n. **discontinuously** adv. [med.L discontinuus (as DIS-, CONTINUOUS)]

discord n. & v. —n. /ˈdɪskɔːd/ 1 disagreement; strife. 2 harsh clashing noise; clangour. 3 Mus. a a lack of harmony between notes sounding together. b an unpleasing or unfinished chord needing to be completed by another. c any interval except unison, an octave, a perfect fifth and fourth, a major and minor third and sixth, and their octaves. d a single note dissonant with another. —v.intr. /dɪsˈkɔːd/ 1 (usu. foll. by with) a disagree or quarrel. b be different or inconsistent. 2 jar, clash, be dissonant. [ME f. OF descord, (n.), descorder (v.) f. L discordare f. discors discordant (as DIS-, cor cord- heart)]

discordant /dɪsˈkɔːd(ə)nt/ adj. (usu. foll. by to, from, with) 1 disagreeing; at variance. 2 (of sounds) not in harmony;

dissonant. □□ **discordance** n. **discordancy** n. **discordantly** adv. [ME f. OF, part. of discorder: see DISCORD]

discothèque /ˈdɪskəˌtek/ n. 1 a club etc. for dancing to recorded popular music. 2 a the professional lighting and sound equipment used at a discothèque. b a business that provides this. 3 a party with dancing to popular music, esp. using such equipment. [F, = record-library]

discount n. & v. —n. /ˈdɪskaʊnt/ 1 a deduction from a bill or amount due given esp. in consideration of prompt or advance payment or to a special class of buyers. 2 a deduction from the amount of a bill of exchange etc. by a person who gives value for it before it is due. 3 the act or an instance of discounting. —v.tr. /dɪˈskaʊnt/ 1 disregard as being unreliable or unimportant (discounted his story). 2 reduce the effect of (an event etc.) by previous action. 3 detract from; lessen; deduct (esp. an amount from a bill etc.). 4 give or get the present worth of (a bill not yet due). □ **at a discount** 1 below the nominal or usual price (cf. PREMIUM). 2 not in demand; depreciated. **discount house** 1 Brit. a firm that discounts bills. 2 US = discount store. **discount rate** US the minimum lending rate. **discount store** esp. US a shop etc. that sells goods at less than the normal retail price. □□ **discountable** /-ˈskaʊntəb(ə)l/ adj. **discounter** /-ˈskaʊntə(r)/ n. [obs. F descompte, -conte, descompter or It. (di)scontare (as DIS-, COUNT[1])]

discountenance /dɪˈskaʊntɪnəns/ v.tr. 1 (esp. in passive) disconcert (was discountenanced by his abruptness). 2 refuse to countenance; show disapproval of.

discourage /dɪˈskʌrɪdʒ/ v.tr. 1 deprive of courage, confidence, or energy. 2 (usu. foll. by from) dissuade (discouraged him from going). 3 show disapproval of (smoking is discouraged). □□ **discouragement** n. **discouragingly** adv. [ME f. OF descouragier (as DIS-, COURAGE)]

discourse n. & v. —n. /ˈdɪskɔːs, -ˈskɔːs/ 1 literary a conversation; talk. b a dissertation or treatise on an academic subject. c a lecture or sermon. 2 Linguistics a connected series of utterances; a text. —v. /dɪˈskɔːs/ 1 intr. talk; converse. 2 intr. (usu. foll. by of, on, upon) speak or write learnedly or at length (on a subject). 3 tr. archaic give forth (music etc.). [ME f. L discursus (as DIS-, COURSE): (v.) partly after F discourir]

discourteous /dɪsˈkɜːtɪəs/ adj. impolite; rude. □□ **discourteously** adv. **discourteousness** n.

discourtesy /dɪsˈkɜːtəsɪ/ n. (pl. **-ies**) 1 bad manners; rudeness. 2 an impolite act or remark.

discover /dɪˈskʌvə(r)/ v.tr. 1 (often foll. by that + clause) a find out or become aware of, whether by research or searching or by chance (discovered a new entrance; discovered that they had been overpaid). b be the first to find or find out (who discovered America?). 2 give (check) in a game of chess by removing one's own obstructing piece. 3 (in show business) find and promote as a new singer, actor, etc. 4 archaic a make known. b exhibit; manifest. c disclose; betray. □□ **discoverable** adj. **discoverer** n. [ME f. OF descovrir f. LL discooperire (as DIS-, COVER)]

discovery /dɪˈskʌvərɪ/ n. (pl. **-ies**) 1 a the act or process of discovering or being discovered. b an instance of this (the discovery of a new planet). 2 a person or thing discovered. 3 Law the compulsory disclosure, by a party to an action, of facts or documents on which the other party wishes to rely. [DISCOVER after recover, recovery]

discredit /dɪsˈkredɪt/ n. & v. —n. 1 harm to reputation (brought discredit on the enterprise). 2 a person or thing causing this (he is a discredit to his family). 3 lack of credibility; doubt (throws discredit on her story). 4 the loss of commercial credit. —v.tr. (**-credited, -crediting**) 1 harm the good reputation of. 2 cause to be disbelieved. 3 refuse to believe.

discreditable /dɪsˈkredɪtəb(ə)l/ adj. bringing discredit; shameful. □□ **discreditably** adv.

discreet /dɪˈskriːt/ adj. (**discreeter, discreetest**) 1 a circumspect in speech or action, esp. to avoid social disgrace or embarrassment. b tactful; trustworthy. 2 unobtrusive (a discreet touch of rouge). □□ **discreetly** adv. **discreetness** n. [ME f. OF discret -ete f. L discretus separate (as DIS-, cretus past part. of cernere sift), with LL sense f. its derivative discretio discernment]

discrepancy /dɪsˈkrepənsɪ/ n. (pl. **-ies**) **1** difference; failure to correspond; inconsistency. **2** an instance of this. □□ **discrepant** adj. [L discrepare be discordant (as DIS-, crepare creak)]

discrete /dɪˈskriːt/ adj. individually distinct; separate, discontinuous. □□ **discretely** adv. **discreteness** n. [ME f. L discretus: see DISCREET]

discretion /dɪˈskreʃ(ə)n/ n. **1** being discreet; discreet behaviour (treats confidences with discretion). **2** prudence; self-preservation. **3** the freedom to act and think as one wishes, usu. within legal limits (it is within his discretion to leave). **4** Law a court's freedom to decide a sentence etc. □ **at discretion** as one pleases. **at the discretion of** to be settled or disposed of according to the judgement or choice of. **discretion is the better part of valour** reckless courage is often self-defeating. **use one's discretion** act according to one's own judgement. **years** (or **age**) **of discretion** the esp. legal age at which a person is able to manage his or her own affairs. □□ **discretionary** adj. [ME f. OF f. L discretio -onis (as DISCREET)]

discriminate /dɪˈskrɪmɪˌneɪt/ v. **1** intr. (often foll. by between) make or see a distinction; differentiate (cannot discriminate between right and wrong). **2** intr. make a distinction, esp. unjustly and on the basis of race, colour, or sex. **3** intr. (foll. by against) select for unfavourable treatment. **4** tr. (usu. foll. by from) make or see or constitute a difference in or between (many things discriminate one person from another). **5** intr. observe distinctions carefully; have good judgement. **6** tr. mark as distinctive; be a distinguishing feature of. □□ **discriminately** /-nɒtlɪ/ adv. **discriminative** /-nɒtɪv/ adj. **discriminator** n. **discriminatory** /-nɒtərɪ/ adj. [L discriminare f. discrimen -minis distinction f. discernere DISCERN]

discriminating /dɪˈskrɪmɪˌneɪtɪŋ/ adj. **1** able to discern, esp. distinctions. **2** having good taste. □□ **discriminatingly** adv.

discrimination /dɪˌskrɪmɪˈneɪʃ(ə)n/ n. **1** unfavourable treatment based on prejudice, esp. regarding race, colour, or sex. **2** good taste or judgement in artistic matters etc. **3** the power of discriminating or observing differences. **4** a distinction made with the mind or in action.

discursive /dɪˈskɜːsɪv/ adj. **1** rambling or digressive. **2** Philos. proceeding by argument or reasoning (opp. INTUITIVE). □□ **discursively** adv. **discursiveness** n. [med.L discursivus f. L discurrere discurs- (as DIS-, currere run)]

discus /ˈdɪskəs/ n. (pl. **discuses**) **1** a heavy thick-centred disc thrown in ancient Greek games. **2** a similar disc thrown in modern athletic field events. [L f. Gk diskos]

discuss /dɪˈskʌs/ v.tr. **1** hold a conversation about (discussed their holidays). **2** examine by argument; examine. □□ **discussable** adj. **discussant** n. **discusser** n. **discussible** adj. [ME f. L discutere discuss- disperse (as DIS-, quatere shake)]

discussion /dɪˈskʌʃ(ə)n/ n. **1** a conversation, esp. on specific subjects; a debate (had a discussion about what they should do). **2** an examination by argument, written or spoken. [ME f. OF f. LL discussio -onis (as DISCUSS)]

disdain /dɪsˈdeɪn/ n. & v. —n. scorn; contempt. —v.tr. **1** regard with disdain. **2** think oneself superior to; reject (disdained his offer; disdained to answer; disdained answering). [ME f. OF desdeign(ier) ult. f. L dedignari (as DE-, dignari f. dignus worthy)]

disdainful /dɪsˈdeɪnfʊl/ adj. showing disdain or contempt. □□ **disdainfully** adv. **disdainfulness** n.

disease /dɪˈziːz/ n. **1** an unhealthy condition of the body (or a part of it) or the mind; illness, sickness. **2** a corresponding physical condition of plants. **3** a particular kind of disease with special symptoms or location. [ME f. OF desaise]

diseased /dɪˈziːzd/ adj. **1** affected with disease. **2** abnormal, disordered. [ME, past part. of disease (v.) f. OF desaisier (as DISEASE)]

diseconomy /ˌdɪsɪˈkɒnəmɪ/ n. Econ. the absence or reverse of economy, esp. the increase of costs in a large-scale operation.

disembark /ˌdɪsɪmˈbɑːk/ v.tr. & intr. put or go ashore or land from a ship or an aircraft. □□ **disembarkation** /-ˈkeɪʃ(ə)n/ n. [F désembarquer (as DIS-, EMBARK)]

disembarrass /ˌdɪsɪmˈbærəs/ v.tr. **1** (usu. foll. by of) relieve (of a load etc.). **2** free from embarrassment. □□ **disembarrassment** n.

disembody /ˌdɪsɪmˈbɒdɪ/ v.tr. (**-ies**, **-ied**) **1** separate or free (esp. the soul) from the body or a concrete form (disembodied spirit). **2** archaic disband (troops). □□ **disembodiment** n.

disembogue /ˌdɪsɪmˈbəʊɡ/ v.tr. & intr. (**disembogues**, **disembogued**, **disemboguing**) (of a river etc.) pour forth (waters) at the mouth. [Sp. desembocar (as DIS-, en in, boca mouth)]

disembowel /ˌdɪsɪmˈbaʊəl/ v.tr. (**-embowelled**, **embowelling**; US **-emboweled**, **-emboweling**) remove the bowels or entrails of. □□ **disembowelment** n.

disembroil /ˌdɪsɪmˈbrɔɪl/ v.tr. extricate from confusion or entanglement.

disenchant /ˌdɪsɪnˈtʃɑːnt/ v.tr. free from enchantment; disillusion. □□ **disenchantingly** adv. **disenchantment** n. [F désenchanter (as DIS-, ENCHANT)]

disencumber /ˌdɪsɪnˈkʌmbə(r)/ v.tr. free from encumbrance.

disendow /ˌdɪsɪnˈdaʊ/ v.tr. strip (esp. the Church) of endowments. □□ **disendowment** n.

disenfranchise /ˌdɪsɪnˈfræntʃaɪz/ v.tr. (also **disfranchise** /dɪsˈfræntʃaɪz/) **1 a** deprive (a person) of the right to vote. **b** deprive (a place) of the right to send a representative to parliament. **2** deprive (a person) of rights as a citizen or of a franchise held. □□ **disenfranchisement** n.

disengage /ˌdɪsɪnˈɡeɪdʒ/ v. & n. —v. **1** tr. detach, free, loosen, or separate (parts etc.) (disengaged the clutch). **2** tr. Mil. remove (troops) from a battle or a battle area. **3** intr. become detached. **4** intr. Fencing pass the point of one's sword to the other side of one's opponent's. **5** intr. (as **disengaged** adj.) **a** unoccupied; free; vacant. **b** uncommitted, esp. politically. —n. Fencing a disengaging movement.

disengagement /ˌdɪsɪnˈɡeɪdʒmənt/ n. **1 a** the act of disengaging. **b** an instance of this. **2** freedom from ties; detachment. **3** the dissolution of an engagement to marry. **4** ease of manner or behaviour. **5** Fencing = DISENGAGE.

disentail /ˌdɪsɪnˈteɪl/ v.tr. Law free (property) from entail; break the entail of.

disentangle /ˌdɪsɪnˈtæŋɡ(ə)l/ v. **1** tr. **a** unravel, untwist. **b** free from complications; extricate (disentangled her from the difficulty). **2** intr. become disentangled. □□ **disentanglement** n.

disenthral /ˌdɪsɪnˈθrɔːl/ v.tr. (US **disenthrall**) (**-enthralled**, **-enthralling**) literary free from enthralment. □□ **disenthralment** n.

disentitle /ˌdɪsɪnˈtaɪt(ə)l/ v.tr. (usu. foll. by to) deprive of any rightful claim.

disentomb /ˌdɪsɪnˈtuːm/ v.tr. literary **1** remove from a tomb; disinter. **2** unearth. □□ **disentombment** /-ˈtuːmmənt/ n.

disequilibrium /ˌdɪsiːkwɪˈlɪbrɪəm/ n. a lack or loss of equilibrium; instability.

disestablish /ˌdɪsɪˈstæblɪʃ/ v.tr. **1** deprive (a Church) of State support. **2** depose from an official position. **3** terminate the establishment of. □□ **disestablishment** n.

disesteem /ˌdɪsɪˈstiːm/ v. & n. —v.tr. have a low opinion of; despise. —n. low esteem or regard.

diseuse /diːˈzɜːz/ n. (masc. ***diseur*** /diːˈzɜː(r)/) a female artiste entertaining with spoken monologues. [F, = talker f. dire dissay]

disfavour /dɪsˈfeɪvə(r)/ n. & v. (US **disfavor**) —n. **1** disapproval or dislike. **2** the state of being disliked (fell into disfavour). —v.tr. regard or treat with disfavour.

disfigure /dɪsˈfɪɡə(r)/ v.tr. spoil the beauty of; deform; deface. □□ **disfigurement** n. [ME f. OF desfigurer f. Rmc (as DIS-, FIGURE)]

disforest /dɪsˈfɒrɪst/ v.tr. Brit. = DISAFFOREST. □□ **disforestation** /-ˈsteɪʃ(ə)n/ n.

disfranchise var. of DISENFRANCHISE.

disfrock /dɪsˈfrɒk/ v.tr. unfrock.

disgorge /dɪsˈɡɔːdʒ/ v.tr. **1** eject from the throat or stomach. **2** pour forth, discharge (contents, ill-gotten gains, etc.). □□ **disgorgement** n. [ME f. OF desgorger (as DIS-, GORGE)]

disgrace /dɪsˈɡreɪs/ n. & v. —n. **1** the loss of reputation; shame; ignominy (brought disgrace on his family). **2** a dishonourable, inefficient, or shameful person, thing, state of affairs, etc. (the bus service is a disgrace). —v.tr. **1** bring shame or discredit on; be a disgrace to. **2** degrade from a position of honour; dismiss from favour. □ **in disgrace** having lost respect or reputation; out of favour. [F disgrâce, disgracier f. It. disgrazia, disgraziare (as DIS-, GRACE)]

disgraceful /dɪsˈgreɪsfʊl/ adj. shameful; dishonourable; degrading. □□ **disgracefully** adv.

disgruntled /dɪsˈgrʌnt(ə)ld/ adj. discontented; moody; sulky. □□ **disgruntlement** n. [DIS- + gruntle obs. frequent. of GRUNT]

disguise /dɪsˈgaɪz/ v. & n. —v.tr. **1** (often foll. by as) alter the appearance, sound, smell, etc., of so as to conceal the identity; make unrecognizable (disguised herself as a policewoman; disguised the taste by adding sugar). **2** misrepresent or cover up (disguised the truth; disguised their intentions). —n. **1 a** a costume, false beard, make-up, etc., used to alter the appearance so as to conceal or deceive. **b** any action, manner, etc., used for deception. **2 a** the act or practice of disguising; the concealment of reality. **b** an instance of this. □ **in disguise 1** wearing a concealing costume etc. **2** appearing to be the opposite (a blessing in disguise). □□ **disguisement** n. [ME f. OF desguis(i)er (as DIS-, GUISE)]

disgust /dɪsˈgʌst/ n. & v. —n. (usu. foll. by at, for) **1** strong aversion; repugnance. **2** indignation. —v.tr. cause disgust in (their behaviour disgusts me; was disgusted to find a slug). □ **in disgust** as a result of disgust (left in disgust). □□ **disgustedly** adv. [OF degoust, desgouster, or It. disgusto, disgustare (as DIS-, GUSTO)]

disgustful /dɪsˈgʌstfʊl/ adj. **1** disgusting; repulsive. **2** (of curiosity etc.) caused by disgust.

disgusting /dɪsˈgʌstɪŋ/ adj. arousing aversion or indignation (disgusting behaviour). □□ **disgustingly** adv. **disgustingness** n.

dish /dɪʃ/ n. & v. —n. **1 a** a shallow, usu. flat-bottomed container for cooking or serving food, made of glass, ceramics, metal, etc. **b** the food served in a dish (all the dishes were delicious). **c** a particular kind of food (a meat dish). **2** (in pl.) dirty plates, cutlery, cooking pots, etc. after a meal. **3 a** a dish-shaped receptacle, object, or cavity. **b** = satellite dish. **4** sl. a sexually attractive person. —v.tr. **1** put (food) into a dish ready for serving. **2** colloq. **a** outmanœuvre. **b** Brit. destroy (one's hopes, chances, etc.). **3** make concave or dish-shaped. □ **dish out** sl. distribute, esp. carelessly or indiscriminately. **dish up 1** serve or prepare to serve (food). **2** colloq. seek to present (facts, argument, etc.) attractively. □□ **dishful** n. (pl. **-fuls**). **dishlike** adj. [OE disc plate, bowl (with Gmc and ON cognates) f. L discus DISC]

dishabille var. of DÉSHABILLÉ.

disharmony /dɪsˈhɑːmənɪ/ n. a lack of harmony; discord. □□ **disharmonious** /-ˈməʊnɪəs/ adj. **disharmoniously** /-ˈməʊnɪəslɪ/ adv. **disharmonize** /-ˌnaɪz/ v.tr.

dishcloth /ˈdɪʃklɒθ/ n. a usu. open-weave cloth for washing dishes. □ **dishcloth gourd** a loofah.

dishearten /dɪsˈhɑːt(ə)n/ v.tr. cause to lose courage or confidence; make despondent. □□ **dishearteningly** adv. **disheartenment** n.

dishevelled /dɪˈʃev(ə)ld/ adj. (US **disheveled**) (of the hair, a person, etc.) untidy; ruffled; disordered. □□ **dishevel** v.tr. (**dishevelled, dishevelling**; US **disheveled, disheveling**). **dishevelment** n. [ME f. OF deschevelee f. OF descheveler past part. (as DIS-, chevel hair f. L capillus)]

dishonest /dɪsˈɒnɪst/ adj. (of a person, act, or statement) fraudulent or insincere. □□ **dishonestly** adv. [ME f. OF deshoneste (as DIS-, HONEST)]

dishonesty /dɪsˈɒnɪstɪ/ n. (pl. **-ies**) **1 a** a lack of honesty. **b** deceitfulness, fraud. **2** a dishonest or fraudulent act. [ME f. OF deshon(n)esté (as DISHONEST)]

dishonour /dɪsˈɒnə(r)/ n. & v. (US **dishonor**) —n. **1** a state of shame or disgrace; discredit. **2** something that causes dishonour (a dishonour to his profession). —v.tr. **1** treat without honour or respect. **2** disgrace (dishonoured his name). **3** refuse to accept or pay (a cheque or a bill of exchange). **4** archaic violate the chastity of; rape. [ME f. OF deshonor, deshonorer f. med.L dishonorare (as DIS-, HONOUR)]

dishonourable /dɪsˈɒnərəb(ə)l/ adj. (US **dishonorable**) **1** causing disgrace; ignominious. **2** unprincipled. □□ **dishonourableness** n. **dishonourably** adv.

dishrag /ˈdɪʃræg/ n. = DISHCLOTH.

dishwasher /ˈdɪʃˌwɒʃə(r)/ n. **1** a machine for automatically washing dishes. **2** a person employed to wash dishes.

dishwater /ˈdɪʃˌwɔːtə(r)/ n. water in which dishes have been washed.

dishy /ˈdɪʃɪ/ adj. (**dishier, dishiest**) Brit. colloq. sexually attractive. [DISH n. 4 + -Y¹]

disillusion /ˌdɪsɪˈluːʒ(ə)n, -ˈljuːʒ(ə)n/ n. & v. —n. freedom from illusions; disenchantment. —v.tr. rid of illusions; disenchant. □□ **disillusionize** v.tr. (also **-ise**). **disillusionment** n.

disincentive /ˌdɪsɪnˈsentɪv/ n. & adj. —n. **1** something that tends to discourage a particular action etc. **2** Econ. a source of discouragement to productivity or progress. —adj. tending to discourage.

disinclination /ˌdɪsɪnklɪˈneɪʃ(ə)n/ n. (usu. foll. by for, or to + infin.) the absence of willingness; a reluctance (a disinclination for work; disinclination to go).

disincline /ˌdɪsɪnˈklaɪn/ v.tr. (usu. foll. by to + infin. or for) make unwilling or reluctant.

disincorporate /ˌdɪsɪnˈkɔːpəˌreɪt/ v.tr. dissolve (a corporate body).

disinfect /ˌdɪsɪnˈfekt/ v.tr. cleanse (a wound, a room, clothes, etc.) of infection, esp. with a disinfectant. □□ **disinfection** n. [F désinfecter (as DIS-, INFECT)]

disinfectant /ˌdɪsɪnˈfekt(ə)nt/ n. & adj. —n. a usu. commercially produced chemical liquid that destroys germs etc. —adj. causing disinfection.

disinfest /ˌdɪsɪnˈfest/ v.tr. rid (a person, a building, etc.) of vermin, infesting insects, etc. □□ **disinfestation** /-ˈsteɪʃ(ə)n/ n.

disinflation /ˌdɪsɪnˈfleɪʃ(ə)n/ n. Econ. a policy designed to counteract inflation without causing deflation. □□ **disinflationary** adj.

disinformation /ˌdɪsɪnfəˈmeɪʃ(ə)n/ n. false information, intended to mislead.

disingenuous /ˌdɪsɪnˈdʒenjʊəs/ adj. having secret motives; insincere. □□ **disingenuously** adv. **disingenuousness** n.

disinherit /ˌdɪsɪnˈherɪt/ v.tr. (**disinherited, disinheriting**) reject as one's heir; deprive of the right of inheritance. □□ **disinheritance** n. [ME f. DIS- + INHERIT in obs. sense 'make heir']

disintegrate /dɪsˈɪntɪˌgreɪt/ v. **1** tr. & intr. **a** separate into component parts or fragments. **b** lose or cause to lose cohesion. **2** intr. colloq. deteriorate mentally or physically. **3** intr. & tr. Physics undergo or cause to undergo disintegration. □□ **disintegrator** n.

disintegration /dɪsˌɪntɪˈgreɪʃ(ə)n/ n. **1** the act or an instance of disintegrating. **2** Physics any process in which a nucleus emits a particle or particles or divides into smaller nuclei.

disinter /ˌdɪsɪnˈtɜː(r)/ v.tr. (**disinterred, disinterring**) **1** remove (esp. a corpse) from the ground; unearth; exhume. **2** find after a protracted search (disinterred the letter from the back of the drawer). □□ **disinterment** n. [F désenterrer (as DIS-, INTER)]

disinterest /dɪsˈɪntrɪst/ n. **1** impartiality. **2** disp. lack of interest; unconcern.

disinterested /dɪsˈɪntrɪstɪd/ adj. **1** not influenced by one's own advantage; impartial. **2** disp. uninterested. □□ **disinterestedly** adv. **disinterestedness** n. [past part. of disinterest (v.) divest of interest]

disinvest /ˌdɪsɪnˈvest/ v.intr. (foll. by from, or absol.) reduce or dispose of one's investment (in a place, company, etc.). □□ **disinvestment** n.

disjecta membra /dɪsˌdʒektə ˈmembrə/ n.pl. scattered remains; fragments, esp. of written work. [L, alt. of disjecti membra poetae (Horace) limbs of a dismembered poet]

disjoin /dɪsˈdʒɔɪn/ v.tr. separate or disunite; part. [ME f. OF desjoindre f. L disjungere (as DIS-, jungere junct- join)]

disjoint /dɪsˈdʒɔɪnt/ v. & adj. —v.tr. **1** take apart at the joints.

2 (as **disjointed** adj.) (esp. of conversation) incoherent; desultory. **3** disturb the working or connection of; dislocate. —adj. (of two or more sets) having no elements in common. □□ **disjointedly** adv. **disjointedness** n. [ME f. obs. disjoint (adj.) f. past part. of OF desjoindre (as DISJOIN)]

disjunction /dɪsˈdʒʌŋkʃ(ə)n/ n. **1** the process of disjoining; separation. **2** an instance of this. [ME f. OF disjunction or L disjunctio (as DISJOIN)]

disjunctive /dɪsˈdʒʌŋktɪv/ adj. & n. —adj. **1** involving separation; disjoining. **2** Gram. (esp. of a conjunction) expressing a choice between two words etc., e.g. or in asked if he was going or staying (cf. COPULATIVE). **3** Logic (of a proposition) expressing alternatives. —n. **1** Gram. a disjunctive conjunction or other word. **2** Logic a disjunctive proposition. □□ **disjunctively** adv. [ME f. L disjunctivus (as DISJOIN)]

disk var. of DISC (esp. US & Computing).

diskette /dɪˈsket/ n. Computing = floppy disk.

Disko /ˈdɪskəʊ/ an island with extensive coal rersources on the west coast of Greenland. Its chief settlement is Godhavn.

dislike /dɪsˈlaɪk/ v. & n. —v.tr. have an aversion or objection to; not like. —n. **1** a feeling of repugnance or not liking. **2** an object of dislike. □□ **dislikable** adj. (also **dislikeable**).

dislocate /ˈdɪsləˌkeɪt/ v.tr. **1** disturb the normal connection of (esp. a joint in the body). **2** disrupt; put out of order. **3** displace. [prob. back-form. f. DISLOCATION]

dislocation /ˌdɪsləˈkeɪʃ(ə)n/ n. **1** the act or result of dislocating. **2** Crystallog. the displacement of part of a crystal lattice structure. [ME f. OF dislocation or med.L dislocatio f. dislocare (as DIS-, locare place)]

dislodge /dɪsˈlɒdʒ/ v.tr. remove from an established or fixed position (was dislodged from his directorship). □□ **dislodgement** n. (also **dislodgment**). [ME f. OF dislog(i)er (as DIS-, LODGE)]

disloyal /dɪsˈlɔɪəl/ adj. (often foll. by to) **1** not loyal; unfaithful. **2** untrue to one's allegiance; treacherous to one's government etc. □□ **disloyalist** n. **disloyally** adv. **disloyalty** n. [ME f. OF desloial (as DIS-, LOYAL)]

dismal /ˈdɪzm(ə)l/ adj. **1** causing or showing gloom; miserable. **2** dreary or sombre (dismal brown walls). **3** colloq. feeble or inept (a dismal performance). □ **the dismals** colloq. melancholy. **the dismal science** joc. economics. □□ **dismally** adv. **dismalness** n. [orig. noun = unlucky days: ME f. AF dis mal f. med.L dies mali two days in each month held to be unpropitious]

Dismal Swamp a vast area of swamp land in SE Virginia and NE Carolina.

dismantle /dɪsˈmænt(ə)l/ v.tr. **1** take to pieces; pull down. **2** deprive of defences or equipment. **3** (often foll. by of) strip of covering or protection. □□ **dismantlement** n. **dismantler** n. [OF desmanteler (as DIS-, MANTLE)]

dismast /dɪsˈmɑːst/ v.tr. deprive (a ship) of masts; break down the mast or masts of.

dismay /dɪsˈmeɪ/ v. & n. —v.tr. fill with consternation or anxiety; discourage or depress; reduce to despair. —n. **1** consternation or anxiety. **2** depression or despair. [ME f. OF desmaïer (unrecorded) ult. f. a Gmc root = deprive of power (as DIS-, MAY)]

dismember /dɪsˈmembə(r)/ v.tr. **1** tear or cut the limbs from. **2** partition or divide up (an empire, country, etc.). □□ **dismemberment** n. [ME f. OF desmembrer f. Rmc (as DIS-, L membrum limb)]

dismiss /dɪsˈmɪs/ v. **1 a** tr. send away, cause to leave one's presence, disperse; disband (an assembly or army). **b** intr. (of an assembly etc.) disperse; break ranks. **2** tr. discharge from employment, office, etc., esp. dishonourably. **3** tr. put out of one's thoughts; cease to feel or discuss (dismissed him from memory). **4** tr. treat (a subject) summarily (dismissed his application). **5** tr. Law refuse further hearing to (a case); send out of court. **6** tr. Cricket put (a batsman or a side) out (was dismissed for 75 runs). **7** intr. (in imper.) Mil. a word of command at the end of drilling. □□ **dismissal** n. **dismissible** adj. **dismission** n. [ME, orig. as past part. after OF desmis f. med.L dismissus (as DIS-, L mittere miss- send)]

dismissive /dɪsˈmɪsɪv/ adj. tending to dismiss from consideration; disdainful. □□ **dismissively** adv. **dismissiveness** n.

dismount /dɪsˈmaʊnt/ v. **1 a** intr. alight from a horse, bicycle, etc. **b** tr. (usu. in passive) throw from a horse, unseat. **2** tr. remove (a thing) from its mounting (esp. a gun from its carriage).

Disney /ˈdɪznɪ/, Walter Elias ('Walt') (1901–66), American animator and film producer. He became famous with the creation of Mickey Mouse in 1928, followed by the Silly Symphony series (1929) involving the Three Little Pigs. In 1934 he began to produce the first feature-length cartoon with sound and colour, Snow White and the Seven Dwarfs (1937). Later came Pinocchio (1940), Dumbo (1941), Bambi (1943), and many others, as well as Fantasia (1940), which combined pieces of classical music with appropriate animation. Treasure Island (1950) was the first of many live-action features, of which the musical Mary Poppins (1964) was the most successful. He also produced nature documentaries, beginning with Seal Island (1949) and including The Living Desert (1953). Disneyland in California and Walt Disney World in Florida are amusement parks incorporating all the elements of Disney fantasy.

disobedient /ˌdɪsəˈbiːdɪənt/ adj. disobeying; rebellious, rule-breaking. □□ **disobedience** n. **disobediently** adv. [ME f. OF desobedient (as DIS-, OBEDIENT)]

disobey /ˌdɪsəˈbeɪ/ v.tr. (also absol.) fail or refuse to obey; disregard (orders); break (rules) (disobeyed his mother; how dare you disobey!). □□ **disobeyer** n. [ME f. OF desobeir f. Rmc (as DIS-, OBEY)]

disoblige /ˌdɪsəˈblaɪdʒ/ v.tr. **1** refuse to consider the convenience or wishes of. **2** (as **disobliging** adj.) uncooperative. [F désobliger f. Rmc (as DIS-, OBLIGE)]

disorder /dɪsˈɔːdə(r)/ n. & v. —n. **1** a lack of order; confusion. **2** a riot; a commotion. **3** Med. a usu. minor ailment or disease. —v.tr. **1** throw into confusion; disarrange. **2** Med. put out of good health; upset. [ME, alt. after ORDER v. of earlier disordain f. OF desordener (as DIS-, ORDAIN)]

disorderly /dɪsˈɔːdəlɪ/ adj. **1** untidy; confused. **2** irregular; unruly; riotous. **3** Law contrary to public order or morality. □ **disorderly house** Law a brothel. □□ **disorderliness** n.

disorganize /dɪsˈɔːgəˌnaɪz/ v.tr. (also **-ise**) **1** destroy the system or order of; throw into confusion. **2** (as **disorganized** adj.) lacking organization or system. □□ **disorganization** /-ˈzeɪʃ(ə)n/ n. [F désorganiser (as DIS-, ORGANIZE)]

disorient /dɪsˈɔːrɪənt/ v.tr. = DISORIENTATE. [F dés- orienter (as DIS-, ORIENT v.)]

disorientate /dɪsˈɔːrɪənˌteɪt/ v.tr. **1** confuse (a person) as to his or her whereabouts or bearings. **2** confuse (a person) (disorientated by his unexpected behaviour). □□ **disorientation** /-ˈteɪʃ(ə)n/ n.

disown /dɪsˈəʊn/ v.tr. **1** refuse to recognize; repudiate; disclaim. **2** renounce one's connection with or allegiance to. □□ **disowner** n.

disparage /dɪˈspærɪdʒ/ v.tr. **1** speak slightingly of; depreciate. **2** bring discredit on. □□ **disparagement** n. **disparagingly** adv. [ME f. OF desparagier marry unequally (as DIS-, parage equality of rank ult. f. L par equal)]

disparate /ˈdɪspərət/ adj. & n. —adj. essentially different in kind; without comparison or relation. —n. (in pl.) things so unlike that there is no basis for their comparison. □□ **disparately** adv. **disparateness** n. [L disparatus separated (as DIS-, paratus past part. of parare prepare), infl. in sense by L dispar unequal]

disparity /dɪˈspærɪtɪ/ n. (pl. **-ies**) **1** inequality; difference; incongruity. **2** an instance of this. [F disparité f. LL disparitas -tatis (as DIS-, PARITY)]

dispassionate /dɪˈspæʃənət/ adj. free from passion; calm; impartial. □□ **dispassionately** adv. **dispassionateness** n.

dispatch /dɪˈspætʃ/ v. & n. (also **despatch**) —v.tr. **1** send off to a destination or for a purpose (dispatched him with the message). **2** perform (business, a task, etc.) promptly; finish off. **3** kill, execute (dispatched him with the revolver). **4** colloq. eat (food, a meal, etc.) quickly. —n. **1** the act or an instance of sending (a messenger, letter, etc.). **2** the act or an instance of killing; execution. **3 a** an official written message on State or esp. military affairs. **b** a report sent in by a newspaper's correspondent, usu. from a foreign country. **4** promptness, efficiency

(*done with dispatch*). □ **dispatch-box** (or **-case**) a container for esp. official State or military documents or dispatches.
dispatch-rider a motor cyclist or rider on horseback carrying military dispatches. □□ **dispatcher** n. [It. *dispacciare* or Sp. *despachar* expedite (as DIS-, It. *impacciare* and Sp. *empachar* hinder, of uncert. orig.)]

dispel /dɪˈspel/ v.tr. (**dispelled, dispelling**) dissipate; disperse; scatter (*the dawn dispelled their fears*). □□ **dispeller** n. [L *dispellere* (as DIS-, *pellere* drive)]

dispensable /dɪˈspensəb(ə)l/ adj. **1** able to be done without; unnecessary. **2** (of a law etc.) able to be relaxed in special cases. □□ **dispensability** /-ˈbɪlɪtɪ/ n. [med.L *dispensabilis* (as DISPENSE)]

dispensary /dɪˈspensərɪ/ n. (pl. **-ies**) **1** a place where medicines etc. are dispensed. **2** a public or charitable institution for medical advice and the dispensing of medicines. [med.L *dispensarius* (as DISPENSE)]

dispensation /ˌdɪspenˈseɪʃ(ə)n/ n. **1 a** the act or an instance of dispensing or distributing. **b** (foll. by *with*) the state of doing without (a thing). **c** something distributed. **2** (usu. foll. by *from*) **a** exemption from a penalty or duty; an instance of this. **b** exemption from a religious observance; an instance of this. **3** a religious or political system obtaining in a nation etc. (*the Christian dispensation*). **4 a** the ordering or management of the world by Providence. **b** a specific example of such ordering (of a community, a person, etc.). □□ **dispensational** adj. [ME f. OF *dispensation* or L *dispensatio* (as DISPENSE)]

dispense /dɪˈspens/ v. **1** tr. distribute; deal out. **2** tr. administer (a sacrament, justice, etc.). **3** tr. make up and give out (medicine etc.) according to a doctor's prescription. **4** tr. (usu. foll. by *from*) grant a dispensation to (a person) from an obligation, esp. a religious observance. **5** intr. (foll. by *with*) **a** do without; render needless. **b** give exemption from (a rule). □ **dispensing chemist** a chemist qualified to make up and give out medicine etc. [ME f. OF *despenser* f. L *dispensare* frequent. of *dispendĕre* weigh or pay out (as DIS-, *pendĕre pens-* weigh)]

dispenser /dɪˈspensə(r)/ n. **1** a person or thing that dispenses something, e.g. medicine, good advice. **2** an automatic machine that dispenses an item or a specific amount of something (e.g. cash).

dispersant /dɪˈspɜːs(ə)nt/ n. *Chem.* an agent used to disperse small particles in a medium.

disperse /dɪˈspɜːs/ v. **1** intr. & tr. go, send, drive, or distribute in different directions or over a wide area. **2 a** intr. (of people at a meeting etc.) leave and go their various ways. **b** tr. cause to do this. **3** tr. send to or station at separate points. **4** tr. put in circulation; disseminate. **5** tr. *Chem.* distribute (small particles) uniformly in a medium. **6** tr. *Physics* divide (white light) into its coloured constituents. □□ **dispersable** adj. **dispersal** n. **disperser** n. **dispersible** adj. **dispersive** adj. [ME f. L *dispergere dispers-* (as DIS-, *spargere* scatter)]

dispersion /dɪˈspɜːʃ(ə)n/ n. **1** the act or an instance of dispersing; the process of being dispersed. **2** *Chem.* a mixture of one substance dispersed in another. **3** *Physics* the separation of white light into colours or of any radiation according to wavelength. **4** *Statistics* the extent to which values of a variable differ from the mean. **5** (**the Dispersion**) the Jews dispersed among the Gentiles after the Captivity in Babylon. [ME f. LL *dispersio* (as DISPERSE), transl. Gk *diaspora*: see DIASPORA]

dispirit /dɪˈspɪrɪt/ v.tr. **1** (esp. as **dispiriting** adj.) make despondent; discourage. **2** (as **dispirited** adj.) dejected; discouraged. □□ **dispiritedly** adv. **dispiritedness** n. **dispiritingly** adv.

displace /dɪsˈpleɪs/ v.tr. **1** shift from its accustomed place. **2** remove from office. **3** take the place of; oust. □ **displaced person** a person who is forced to leave his or her home country because of war, persecution, etc.; a refugee.

displacement /dɪsˈpleɪsmənt/ n. **1 a** the act or an instance of displacing; the process of being displaced. **b** an instance of this. **2** *Physics* the amount of a fluid displaced by a solid floating or immersed in it (*a ship with a displacement of 11,000 tons*). **3** *Psychol.* **a** the substitution of one idea or impulse for another. **b** the unconscious transfer of strong unacceptable emotions from one

object to another. **4** the amount by which a thing is shifted from its place.

display /dɪˈspleɪ/ v. & n. —v.tr. **1** expose to view; exhibit; show. **2** show ostentatiously. **3** allow to appear; reveal; betray (*displayed his ignorance*). —n. **1** the act or an instance of displaying. **2** an exhibition or show. **3** ostentation; flashiness. **4** the distinct behaviour of some birds and fish, esp. used to attract a mate. **5 a** the presentation of signals or data on a visual display unit etc. **b** the information so presented. **6** *Printing* the arrangement and choice of type in order to attract attention. □□ **displayer** n. [ME f. OF *despleier* f. L *displicare* (as DIS-, *plicare* fold): cf. DEPLOY]

displease /dɪsˈpliːz/ v.tr. make indignant or angry; offend; annoy. □ **be displeased** (often foll. by *at*, *with*) be indignant or dissatisfied; disapprove. □□ **displeasing** adj. **displeasingly** adv. [ME f. OF *desplaisir* (as DIS-, L *placēre* please)]

displeasure /dɪsˈpleʒə(r)/ n. & v. —n. disapproval; anger; dissatisfaction. —v.tr. *archaic* cause displeasure to; annoy. [ME f. OF (as DISPLEASE): assim. to PLEASURE]

disport /dɪˈspɔːt/ v. & n. —v.intr. & refl. frolic; gambol; enjoy oneself (*disported on the sand*; *disported themselves in the sea*). —n. *archaic* **1** relaxation. **2** a pastime. [ME f. AF & OF *desporter* (as DIS-, *porter* carry f. L *portare*)]

disposable /dɪˈspəʊzəb(ə)l/ adj. & n. —adj. **1** intended to be used once and then thrown away (*disposable nappies*). **2** that can be got rid of, made over, or used. **3** (esp. of financial assets) at the owner's disposal. —n. a thing designed to be thrown away after one use. □ **disposable income** income after tax etc. □□ **disposability** /-ˈbɪlɪtɪ/ n.

disposal /dɪˈspəʊz(ə)l/ n. (usu. foll. by *of*) **1** the act or an instance of disposing of something. **2** the arrangement, disposition, or placing of something. **3** control or management (of a person, business, etc.). **4** (esp. as **waste disposal**) the disposing of rubbish. □ **at one's disposal 1** available for one's use. **2** subject to one's orders or decisions.

dispose /dɪˈspəʊz/ v. **1** tr. (usu. foll. by *to*, or to + infin.) **a** make willing; incline (*disposed him to the idea*; *was disposed to release them*). **b** give a tendency to (*the wheel was disposed to buckle*). **2** tr. place suitably or in order (*disposed the pictures in sequence*). **3** tr. (as **disposed** adj.) have a specified mental inclination (usu. in comb.: *ill-disposed*). **4** intr. determine the course of events (*man proposes, God disposes*). □ **dispose of 1** a deal with. **b** get rid of. **c** finish. **d** kill. **2** sell. **3** prove (a claim, an argument, an opponent, etc.) to be incorrect. **4** consume (food). □□ **disposer** n. [ME f. OF *disposer* (as DIS-, POSE¹) after L *disponere disposit-*]

disposition /ˌdɪspəˈzɪʃ(ə)n/ n. **1** (often foll. by *to*) a natural tendency; an inclination; a person's temperament (*a happy disposition*; *a disposition to overeat*). **2 a** a setting in order; arranging. **b** the relative position of parts; an arrangement. **3** (usu. in pl.) **a** *Mil.* the stationing of troops ready for attack or defence. **b** preparations; plans. **4 a** a bestowal by deed or will. **b** control; the power of disposing. **5** ordinance, dispensation. [ME f. OF f. L *dispositio* (as DIS-, *ponere posit-* place)]

dispossess /ˌdɪspəˈzes/ v.tr. **1** dislodge; oust (a person). **2** (usu. foll. by *of*) deprive. □□ **dispossession** /-ˈzeʃ(ə)n/ n. [OF *despossesser* (as DIS-, POSSESS)]

dispraise /dɪsˈpreɪz/ v. & n. —v.tr. express disapproval or censure of. —n. disapproval, censure. [ME f. OF *despreisier* ult. f. LL *depretiare* DEPRECIATE]

disproof /dɪsˈpruːf/ n. **1** something that disproves. **2 a** a refutation. **b** an instance of this.

disproportion /ˌdɪsprəˈpɔːʃ(ə)n/ n. **1** a lack of proportion. **2** an instance of this. □□ **disproportional** adj. **disproportionally** adv.

disproportionate /ˌdɪsprəˈpɔːʃənət/ adj. **1** lacking proportion. **2** relatively too large or small, long or short, etc. □□ **disproportionately** adv. **disproportionateness** n.

disprove /dɪsˈpruːv/ v.tr. prove false; refute. □□ **disprovable** adj. **disproval** n. [ME f. OF *desprover* (as DIS-, PROVE)]

disputable /dɪˈspjuːtəb(ə)l/, ˈdɪspjʊ-/ adj. open to question; uncertain. □□ **disputably** adv. [F or f. L *disputabilis* (as DISPUTE)]

disputation /ˌdɪspjuːˈteɪʃ(ə)n/ n. **1 a** disputing, debating. **b** an argument; a controversy. **2** a formal debate. [ME f. F *disputation* or L *disputatio* (as DISPUTE)]

disputatious /ˌdɪspjuːˈteɪʃ(ə)s/ *adj.* fond of or inclined to argument. □□ **disputatiously** *adv.* **disputatiousness** *n.*

dispute *v. & n.* —*v.* /dɪˈspjuːt/ **1** *intr.* (usu. foll. by *with, against*) **a** debate, argue (*was disputing with them about the meaning of life*). **b** quarrel. **2** *tr.* discuss, esp. heatedly (*disputed whether it was true*). **3** *tr.* question the truth or correctness or validity of (a statement, alleged fact, etc.) (*I dispute that number*). **4** *tr.* contend for; strive to win (*disputed the crown; disputed the field*). **5** *tr.* resist (a landing, advance, etc.). —*n.* /dɪˈspjuːt, ˈdɪspjuːt/ **1** a controversy; a debate. **2** a quarrel. **3** a disagreement between management and employees, esp. one leading to industrial action. □ **beyond** (or **past** or **without**) **dispute** certainly; indisputably. **in dispute 1** being argued about. **2** (of a workforce) involved in industrial action. □□ **disputant** /-ˈspjuːt(ə)nt/ *n.* **disputer** *n.* [ME f. OF *desputer* f. L *disputare* estimate (as DIS-, *putare* reckon)]

disqualification /dɪsˌkwɒlɪfɪˈkeɪʃ(ə)n/ *n.* **1** the act or an instance of disqualifying; the state of being disqualified. **2** something that disqualifies.

disqualify /dɪsˈkwɒlɪˌfaɪ/ *v.tr.* (**-ies, -ied**) **1** (often foll. by *from*) debar from a competition or pronounce ineligible as a winner because of an infringement of the rules etc. (*disqualified from the race for taking drugs*). **2** (often foll. by *for, from*) make or pronounce ineligible or unsuitable (*his age disqualifies him for the job; a criminal record disqualified him from applying*). **3** (often foll. by *from*) incapacitate legally; pronounce unqualified (*disqualified from practising as a doctor*).

disquiet /dɪsˈkwaɪət/ *v. & n.* —*v.tr.* deprive of peace; worry. —*n.* anxiety; unrest. □□ **disquieting** *adj.* **disquietingly** *adv.*

disquietude /dɪsˈkwaɪəˌtjuːd/ *n.* a state of uneasiness; anxiety.

disquisition /ˌdɪskwɪˈzɪʃ(ə)n/ *n.* a long or elaborate treatise or discourse on a subject. □□ **disquisitional** *adj.* [F f. L *disquisitio* (as DIS-, *quaerere quaesit-* seek)]

Disraeli /dɪzˈreɪlɪ/, Benjamin, 1st Earl of Beaconsfield (1804–81), British statesman of Italian–Jewish descent, Prime Minister 1868 and 1874–80. A novelist of some distinction in early life, Disraeli first sat in Parliament in 1837, taking a central part in the reconstruction of the Conservative Party after Peel, slowly reuniting it and educating it out of protectionism and into parliamentary reform, arousing its interest in the working man and enthusiasm for the Empire. He was largely responsible for the Second Reform Act of 1867 which doubled the electorate. As Prime Minister between 1874 and 1880 he enacted a useful series of social reforms, involved Britain in the purchase of the Suez Canal, and made Queen Victoria Empress of India. On the Continent the prestige of Britain was revived and her influence in international affairs increased. Against the handicaps of belonging to the wrong race, religion, social class, and educational background, Disraeli made his way by force of genius, energy, and quick imagination. His career is one of the most remarkable in the 19th c.

disrate /dɪsˈreɪt/ *v.tr.* *Naut.* reduce (a sailor) to a lower rating or rank.

disregard /ˌdɪsrɪˈɡɑːd/ *v. & n.* —*v.tr.* **1** pay no attention to; ignore. **2** treat as of no importance. —*n.* (often foll. by *of, for*) indifference; neglect. □□ **disregardful** *adj.* **disregardfully** *adv.*

disrelish /dɪsˈrelɪʃ/ *n. & v.* —*n.* dislike; distaste. —*v.tr.* regard with dislike or distaste.

disremember /ˌdɪsrɪˈmembə(r)/ *v.tr. & intr.* esp. *US* or *dial.* fail to remember; forget.

disrepair /ˌdɪsrɪˈpeə(r)/ *n.* poor condition due to neglect (*in disrepair; in a state of disrepair*).

disreputable /dɪsˈrepjʊtəb(ə)l/ *adj.* **1** of bad reputation; discreditable. **2** not respectable in appearance; dirty, untidy. □□ **disreputableness** *n.* **disreputably** *adv.*

disrepute /ˌdɪsrɪˈpjuːt/ *n.* a lack of good reputation or respectability; discredit (esp. *fall into disrepute*).

disrespect /ˌdɪsrɪˈspekt/ *n.* a lack of respect; discourtesy. □□ **disrespectful** *adj.* **disrespectfully** *adv.*

disrobe /dɪsˈrəʊb/ *v.tr. & refl.* (also *absol.*) **1** divest (oneself or another) of a robe or a garment; undress. **2** divest (oneself or another) of office, authority, etc.

disrupt /dɪsˈrʌpt/ *v.tr.* **1** interrupt the flow or continuity of (a meeting, speech, etc.); bring disorder to. **2** separate forcibly; shatter. □□ **disrupter** *n.* (also **disruptor**). **disruption** *n.* **disruptive** *adj.* **disruptively** *adv.* **disruptiveness** *n.* [L *disrumpere disrupt-* (as DIS-, *rumpere* break)]

dissatisfy /dɪˈsætɪsˌfaɪ/ *v.tr.* (**-ies, -ied**) make discontented; fail to satisfy (*dissatisfied with the accommodation; dissatisfied to find him gone*). □□ **dissatisfaction** /-ˈfækʃ(ə)n/ *n.* **dissatisfactory** /-ˈfæktərɪ/ *adj.* **dissatisfiedly** *adv.*

dissect /dɪˈsekt/ *v.tr.* **1** cut into pieces. **2** cut up (a plant or animal) to examine its parts, structure, etc., or (a corpse) for a post mortem. **3** analyse; criticize or examine in detail. □□ **dissection** *n.* **dissector** *n.* [L *dissecare dissect-* (as DIS-, *secare* cut)]

dissemble /dɪˈsemb(ə)l/ *v.* **1** *intr.* conceal one's motives; talk or act hypocritically. **2** *tr.* **a** disguise or conceal (a feeling, intention, act, etc.). **b** simulate (*dissembled grief in public*). □□ **dissemblance** *n.* **dissembler** *n.* **dissemblingly** *adv.* [ME, alt. after *semblance* of obs. *dissimule* f. OF *dissimuler* f. L *dissimulare* (as DIS-, SIMULATE)]

disseminate /dɪˈsemɪˌneɪt/ *v.tr.* scatter about, spread (esp. ideas) widely. □ **disseminated sclerosis** = SCLEROSIS 2. □□ **dissemination** /-ˈneɪʃ(ə)n/ *n.* **disseminator** *n.* [L *disseminare* (as DIS-, *semen -inis* seed)]

dissension /dɪˈsenʃ(ə)n/ *n.* disagreement giving rise to discord. [ME f. OF f. L *dissensio* (as DIS-, *sentire sens-* feel)]

dissent /dɪˈsent/ *v. & n.* —*v.intr.* (often foll. by *from*) **1** think differently, disagree; express disagreement. **2** differ in religious opinion, esp. from the doctrine of an established or orthodox church. —*n.* **1 a** a difference of opinion. **b** an expression of this. **2** the refusal to accept the doctrines of an established or orthodox church; nonconformity. □□ **dissenting** *adj.* **dissentingly** *adv.* [ME f. L *dissentire* (as DIS-, *sentire* feel)]

dissenter /dɪˈsentə(r)/ *n.* **1** a person who dissents. **2** (**Dissenter**) *Brit.* a member of a non-established church; a Nonconformist.

dissentient /dɪˈsenʃ(ə)nt/ *adj. & n.* —*adj.* disagreeing with a majority or official view. —*n.* a person who dissents. [L *dissentire* (as DIS-, *sentire* feel)]

dissertation /ˌdɪsəˈteɪʃ(ə)n/ *n.* a detailed discourse on a subject, esp. one submitted in partial fulfilment of the requirements of a degree or diploma. □□ **dissertational** *adj.* [L *dissertatio* f. *dissertare* discuss, frequent. of *disserere dissert-* examine (as DIS-, *serere* join)]

disservice /dɪsˈsɜːvɪs/ *n.* an ill turn; an injury, esp. done when trying to help. □□ **disserve** *v.tr.* archaic.

dissever /dɪˈsevə(r)/ *v.tr. & intr.* sever; divide into parts. □□ **disseverance** *n.* **disseverment** *n.* [ME f. AF *dis(c)everer*, OF *desseverer* f. LL *disseparare* (as DIS-, SEPARATE)]

dissidence /ˈdɪsɪd(ə)ns/ *n.* disagreement; dissent. [F *dissidence* or L *dissidentia* (as DISSIDENT)]

dissident /ˈdɪsɪd(ə)nt/ *adj. & n.* —*adj.* disagreeing, esp. with an established government, system, etc. —*n.* a dissident person. [F or f. L *dissidēre* disagree (as DIS-, *sedēre* sit)]

dissimilar /dɪˈsɪmɪlə(r)/ *adj.* (often foll. by *to*) unlike, not similar. □□ **dissimilarity** /-ˈlærɪtɪ/ *n.* (pl. **-ies**) **dissimilarly** *adv.*

dissimilate /dɪˈsɪmɪˌleɪt/ *v.* (often foll. by *to*) *Phonet.* **1** *tr.* change (a sound or sounds in a word) to another when the word originally had the same sound repeated, as in *cinnamon*, orig. *cinnamom*. **2** *intr.* (of a sound) be changed in this way. □□ **dissimilation** /-ˈleɪʃ(ə)n/ *n.* **dissimilatory** /-lətərɪ/ *adj.* [L *dissimilis* (as DIS-, *similis* like), after *assimilate*]

dissimilitude /ˌdɪsɪˈmɪlɪˌtjuːd/ *n.* unlikeness, dissimilarity. [L *dissimilitudo* (as DISSIMILATE)]

dissimulate /dɪˈsɪmjʊˌleɪt/ *v.tr. & intr.* dissemble. □□ **dissimulation** /-ˈleɪʃ(ə)n/ *n.* **dissimulator** *n.* [L *dissimulare* (as DIS-, SIMULATE)]

dissipate /ˈdɪsɪˌpeɪt/ *v.* **1 a** *tr.* cause (a cloud, vapour, fear, darkness, etc.) to disappear or disperse. **b** *intr.* disperse, scatter, disappear. **2** *intr. & tr.* break up; bring or come to nothing. **3** *tr.* squander or fritter away (money, energy, etc.). **4** *intr.* (as **dissipated** *adj.*) given to dissipation, dissolute. □□ **dissipater**

n. **dissipative** *adj.* **dissipator** *n.* [L *dissipare dissipat-* (as DIS-, *sipare* (unrecorded) throw)]

dissipation /ˌdɪsɪˈpeɪʃ(ə)n/ *n.* **1** intemperate, dissolute, or debauched living. **2** (usu. foll. by *of*) wasteful expenditure (*dissipation of resources*). **3** scattering, dispersion, or disintegration. **4** a frivolous amusement. [F *dissipation* or L *dissipatio* (as DISSIPATE)]

dissociate /dɪˈsəʊʃɪˌeɪt, -sɪˌeɪt/ *v.* **1** *tr.* & *intr.* (usu. foll. by *from*) disconnect or become disconnected; separate (*dissociated her from their guilt*). **2** *tr. Chem.* decompose, esp. reversibly. **3** *tr. Psychol.* cause (a person's mind) to develop more than one centre of consciousness. □ **dissociated personality** *Psychol.* the pathological coexistence of two or more distinct personalities in the same person. **dissociate oneself from 1** declare oneself unconnected with. **2** decline to support or agree with (a proposal etc.). □□ **dissociative** /-ətɪv/ *adj.* [L *dissociare* (as DIS-, *socius* companion)]

dissociation /dɪˌsəʊsɪˈeɪʃ(ə)n, -ʃɪˈeɪʃ(ə)n/ *n.* **1** the act or an instance of dissociating. **2** *Psychol.* the state of suffering from dissociated personality.

dissoluble /dɪˈsɒljʊb(ə)l/ *adj.* able to be disintegrated, loosened, or disconnected; soluble. □□ **dissolubility** /-ˈbɪlɪtɪ/ *n.* **dissolubly** *adv.* [F *dissoluble* or L *dissolubilis* (as DIS-, SOLUBLE)]

dissolute /ˈdɪsəˌluːt, -ˌljuːt/ *adj.* lax in morals; licentious. □□ **dissolutely** *adv.* **dissoluteness** *n.* [ME f. L *dissolutus* past part. of *dissolvere* DISSOLVE]

dissolution /ˌdɪsəˈluːʃ(ə)n, -ˈljuːʃ(ə)n/ *n.* **1** disintegration; decomposition. **2** (usu. foll. by *of*) the undoing or relaxing of a bond, esp.: **a** a marriage. **b** a partnership. **c** an alliance. **3** the dismissal or dispersal of an assembly, esp. of a parliament at the end of its term. **4** death. **5** bringing or coming to an end; fading away; disappearance. **6** dissipation; debauchery. □ **Dissolution of the Monasteries** the abolition of monasteries in England by Henry VIII under two Acts (1536, 1539) by which they were suppressed and their assets vested in the Crown. Though monasteries were much criticized in the later Middle Ages for their wealth, moral laxity, and stress on the contemplative life, Henry's motives were personal: to replenish his treasury, and to establish royal supremacy in ecclesiastical affairs. [ME f. OF *dissolution* or L *dissolutio* (as DISSOLVE)]

dissolve /dɪˈzɒlv/ *v.* & *n.* —*v.* **1** *tr.* & *intr.* make or become liquid, esp. by immersion or dispersion in a liquid. **2** *intr.* & *tr.* disappear or cause to disappear gradually. **3 a** *tr.* dismiss or disperse (an assembly, esp. parliament). **b** *intr.* (of an assembly) be dissolved (cf. DISSOLUTION). **4** *tr.* annul or put an end to (a partnership, marriage, etc.). **5** *intr.* (of a person) become enfeebled or emotionally overcome (*completely dissolved when he saw her*; *dissolved into tears*). **6** *intr.* (often foll. by *into*) *Cinematog.* change gradually (from one picture into another). —*n. Cinematog.* the act or process of dissolving a picture. □□ **dissolvable** *adj.* [ME f. L *dissolvere dissolut-* (as DIS-, *solvere* loosen)]

dissolvent /dɪˈzɒlv(ə)nt/ *adj.* & *n.* —*adj.* tending to dissolve or dissipate. —*n.* a dissolvent substance. [L *dissolvere* (as DISSOLVE)]

dissonant /ˈdɪsənənt/ *adj.* **1** *Mus.* harsh-toned; unharmonious. **2** incongruous; clashing. □□ **dissonance** *n.* **dissonantly** *adv.* [ME f. OF *dissonant* or L *dissonare* (as DIS-, *sonare* sound)]

dissuade /dɪˈsweɪd/ *v.tr.* (often foll. by *from*) discourage (a person); persuade against (*dissuaded him from continuing*; *was dissuaded from his belief*). □□ **dissuader** *n.* **dissuasion** /-ˈsweɪʒ(ə)n/ *n.* **dissuasive** /-ˈsweɪsɪv/ *adj.* [L *dissuadēre* (as DIS-, *suadēre suas-* persuade)]

dissyllable var. of DISYLLABLE.

dissymmetry /dɪˈsɪmɪtrɪ/ *n.* (pl. **-ies**) **1 a** lack of symmetry. **b** an instance of this. **2** symmetry as of mirror images or the left and right hands (esp. of crystals with two corresponding forms). □□ **dissymmetrical** /-ˈmetrɪk(ə)l/ *adj.*

distaff /ˈdɪstɑːf/ *n.* **1 a** a cleft stick holding wool or flax wound for spinning by hand. **b** the corresponding part of a spinning-wheel. **2** women's work. □ **distaff side** the female branch of a family. [OE *distæf* (as STAFF¹), the first element being app. rel. to LG *diesse*, MLG *dise(ne)* bunch of flax]

distal /ˈdɪst(ə)l/ *adj. Anat.* situated away from the centre of the body or point of attachment; terminal. □□ **distally** *adv.* [DISTANT + -AL]

distance /ˈdɪst(ə)ns/ *n.* & *v.* —*n.* **1** the condition of being far off; remoteness. **2 a** a space or interval between two things. **b** the length of this (*a distance of twenty miles*). **3** a distant point or place (*came from a distance*). **4** the avoidance of familiarity; aloofness; reserve (*there was a certain distance between them*). **5** a remoter field of vision (*saw him in the distance*). **6** an interval of time (*can't remember what happened at this distance*). **7 a** the full length of a race etc. **b** *Brit. Racing* a length of 240 yards from the winning-post on a racecourse. **c** *Boxing* the scheduled length of a fight. —*v.tr.* (often *refl.*) **1** place far off (*distanced herself from them*; *distanced the painful memory*). **2** leave far behind in a race or competition. □ **at a distance** far off. **distance-post** *Racing* a post at the distance on a racecourse, used to disqualify runners who have not reached it by the end of the race. **distance runner** an athlete who competes in long- or middle-distance races. **go the distance 1** *Boxing* complete a fight without being knocked out. **2** complete, esp. a hard task; endure an ordeal. **keep one's distance** maintain one's reserve. **middle distance** see MIDDLE. **within hailing** (or **walking**) **distance** near enough to reach by hailing or walking. [ME f. OF *distance, destance* f. L *distantia* f. *distare* stand apart (as DI-², *stare* stand)]

distant /ˈdɪst(ə)nt/ *adj.* **1 a** far away in space or time. **b** (usu. predic.; often foll. by *from*) at a specified distance (*three miles distant from them*). **2** remote or far apart in position, time, resemblance, etc. (*a distant prospect*; *a distant relation*; *a distant likeness*). **3** not intimate; reserved; cool (*a distant bow*). **4** remote; abstracted (*a distant stare*). **5** faint, vague (*he was a distant memory to her*). □ **distant early warning** *US* a radar system for the early detection of a missile attack. **distant signal** *Railways* a railway signal preceding a home signal to give warning. □□ **distantly** *adv.* [ME f. OF *distant* or L *distant-* part. stem of *distare*: see DISTANCE]

distaste /dɪsˈteɪst/ *n.* (usu. foll. by *for*) dislike; repugnance; aversion, esp. slight (*a distaste for prunes*; *a distaste for polite company*). □□ **distasteful** *adj.* **distastefully** *adv.* **distastefulness** *n.*

Di Stefano /di: ˈstefəˌnəʊ/, Alfredo (1926–), Brazilian-born footballer, noted especially for his play at centre forward for Real Madrid in international competitions.

distemper¹ /dɪˈstempə(r)/ *n.* & *v.* —*n.* **1** a kind of paint using glue or size instead of an oil-base, for use on walls or for scene-painting. **2** a method of mural and poster painting using this. —*v.tr.* paint (walls etc.) with distemper. [earlier as verb, f. OF *destremper* or LL *distemperare* soak, macerate: see DISTEMPER²]

distemper² /dɪˈstempə(r)/ *n.* **1** a disease of some animals, esp. dogs, causing fever, coughing, and catarrh. **2** *archaic* political disorder. [earlier as verb, = upset, derange: ME f. LL *distemperare* (as DIS-, *temperare* mingle correctly)]

distend /dɪˈstend/ *v.tr.* & *intr.* swell out by pressure from within (*distended stomach*). □□ **distensible** /-ˈstensɪb(ə)l/ *adj.* **distensibility** /-ˈbɪlɪtɪ/ *n.* **distension** /-ˈstenʃ(ə)n/ *n.* [ME f. L *distendere* (as DIS-, *tendere tens-* stretch)]

distich /ˈdɪstɪk/ *n. Prosody* a pair of verse lines; a couplet. [L *distichon* f. Gk *distikhon* (as DI-¹, *stikhos* line)]

distichous /ˈdɪstɪkəs/ *adj. Bot.* arranged in two opposite vertical rows. [L *distichus* (as DISTICH)]

distil /dɪˈstɪl/ *v.* (*US* **distill**) (**distilled, distilling**) **1** *tr. Chem.* purify (a liquid) by vaporizing it with heat, then condensing it with cold and collecting the result. **2** *tr.* **a** *Chem.* extract the essence of (a plant etc.) usu. by heating it in a solvent. **b** extract the essential meaning or implications of (an idea etc.). **3** *tr.* make (whisky, essence, etc.) by distilling raw materials. **4** *tr.* (foll. by *off, out*) *Chem.* drive (the volatile constituent) off or out by heat. **5** *tr.* & *intr.* come as or give forth in drops; exude. **6** *intr.* undergo distillation. □□ **distillatory** *adj.* [ME f. L *distillare* f. *destillare* (as DE-, *stilla* drop)]

distillate /ˈdɪstɪˌleɪt/ *n.* a product of distillation.

distillation /ˌdɪstɪˈleɪʃ(ə)n/ *n.* **1** the process of distilling or being distilled (in various senses). **2** something distilled.

distiller /dɪˈstɪlə(r)/ *n.* a person who distils, esp. a manufacturer of alcoholic liquor.

distillery /dɪˈstɪləri/ n. (pl. **-ies**) a place where alcoholic liquor is distilled.

distinct /dɪˈstɪŋkt/ adj. **1** (often foll. by *from*) **a** not identical; separate; individual. **b** different in kind or quality; unlike. **2 a** clearly perceptible; plain. **b** clearly understandable; definite. **3** unmistakable, decided (*had a distinct impression of being watched*). □□ **distinctly** adv. **distinctness** n. [ME f. L *distinctus* past part. of *distinguere* DISTINGUISH]

distinction /dɪˈstɪŋkʃ(ə)n/ n. **1 a** the act or an instance of discriminating or distinguishing. **b** an instance of this. **c** the difference made by distinguishing. **2 a** something that differentiates, e.g. a mark, name, or title. **b** the fact of being different. **3** special consideration or honour. **4** distinguished character; excellence; eminence (*a film of distinction; shows distinction in his bearing*). **5** a grade in an examination denoting great excellence (*passed with distinction*). □ **distinction without a difference** a merely nominal or artificial distinction. [ME f. OF f. L *distinctio -onis* (as DISTINGUISH)]

distinctive /dɪˈstɪŋktɪv/ adj. distinguishing, characteristic. □□ **distinctively** adv. **distinctiveness** n.

distingué /dɪˈstæŋɡeɪ, dɪstæˈɡeɪ/ adj. (*fem.* **distinguée** *pronunc.* same) having a distinguished air, features, manner, etc. [F, past part. of *distinguer*: see DISTINGUISH]

distinguish /dɪˈstɪŋɡwɪʃ/ v. **1** tr. (often foll. by *from*) **a** see or point out the difference of; draw distinctions (*cannot distinguish one from the other*). **b** constitute such a difference (*the mole distinguishes him from his twin*). **c** draw distinctions between; differentiate. **2** tr. be a mark or property of; characterize (*distinguished by his greed*). **3** tr. discover by listening, looking, etc. (*could distinguish two voices*). **4** tr. (usu. *refl.*; often foll. by *by*) make prominent or noteworthy (*distinguished himself by winning first prize*). **5** tr. (often foll. by *into*) divide; classify. **6** intr. (foll. by *between*) make or point out a difference between. □□ **distinguishable** adj. [F *distinguer* or L *distinguere* (as DIS-, *stinguere stinct-* extinguish): cf. EXTINGUISH]

distinguished /dɪˈstɪŋɡwɪʃt/ adj. **1** (often foll. by *for*, *by*) of high standing; eminent; famous. **2** = DISTINGUÉ.

distort /dɪˈstɔːt/ v.tr. **1 a** put out of shape; make crooked or unshapely. **b** distort the appearance of, esp. by curved mirrors etc. **2** misrepresent (motives, facts, statements, etc.). □□ **distortedly** adv. **distortedness** n. [L *distorquēre distort-* (as DIS-, *torquēre* twist)]

distortion /dɪˈstɔːʃ(ə)n/ n. **1** the act or an instance of distorting; the process of being distorted. **2** *Electronics* a change in the form of a signal during transmission etc. usu. with some impairment of quality. □□ **distortional** adj. **distortionless** adj. [L *distortio* (as DISTORT)]

distract /dɪˈstrækt/ v.tr. **1** (often foll. by *from*) draw away the attention of (a person, the mind, etc.). **2** bewilder, perplex. **3** (as **distracted** adj.) mad or angry (*distracted by grief; distracted with worry*). **4** amuse, esp. in order to take the attention from pain or worry. □□ **distractedly** adv. [ME f. L *distrahere distract-* (as DIS-, *trahere* draw)]

distraction /dɪˈstrækʃ(ə)n/ n. **1 a** the act of distracting, esp. the mind. **b** something that distracts; an interruption. **2** a relaxation from work; an amusement. **3** a lack of concentration. **4** confusion; perplexity. **5** frenzy; madness. □ **to distraction** almost to a state of madness. [ME f. OF *distraction* or L *distractio* (as DISTRACT)]

distrain /dɪˈstreɪn/ v.intr. *Law* (usu. foll. by *upon*) impose distraint (on a person, goods, etc.). □□ **distrainee** /-ˈniː/ n. **distrainer** n. **distrainment** n. **distrainor** n. [ME f. OF *destreindre* f. L *distringere* (as DIS-, *stringere strict-* draw tight)]

distraint /dɪˈstreɪnt/ n. *Law* the seizure of chattels to make a person pay rent etc. or meet an obligation, or to obtain satisfaction by their sale. [DISTRAIN, after *constraint*]

distrait /dɪˈstreɪ/ adj. (*fem.* **distraite** /-ˈstreɪt/) not paying attention; absent-minded; distraught. [ME f. OF *destrait* past part. of *destraire* (as DISTRACT)]

distraught /dɪˈstrɔːt/ adj. distracted with worry, fear, etc.; extremely agitated. [ME, alt. of obs. *distract* (adj.) (as DISTRACT), after *straught* obs. past part. of STRETCH]

distress /dɪˈstres/ n. & v. —n. **1** severe pain, sorrow, anguish, etc. **2** the lack of money or comforts. **3** *Law* = DISTRAINT. **4** breathlessness; exhaustion. —v.tr. **1** subject to distress; exhaust, afflict. **2** cause anxiety to; make unhappy; vex. □ **distress-signal** a signal from a ship in danger. **distress-warrant** *Law* a warrant authorizing distraint. **in distress 1** suffering or in danger. **2** (of a ship, aircraft, etc.) in danger or damaged. □□ **distressful** adj. **distressingly** adv. [ME f. OF *destresse* etc., AF *destresser*, OF *-ecier* f. Gallo-Roman (as DISTRAIN)]

distressed /dɪˈstrest/ adj. **1** suffering from distress. **2** impoverished (*distressed gentlefolk; in distressed circumstances*). **3** (of furniture, leather, etc.) having simulated marks of age and wear. □ **distressed area** *Brit.* a region of high unemployment and poverty.

distributary /dɪˈstrɪbjʊtəri/ n. (pl. **-ies**) a branch of a river or glacier that does not return to the main stream after leaving it (as in a delta).

distribute /dɪˈstrɪbjuːt, ˈdɪ-/ v.tr. **1** give shares of; deal out. **2** spread about; scatter (*distributed the seeds evenly over the garden*). **3** divide into parts; arrange; classify. **4** *Printing* separate (type that has been set up) and return the characters to their separate boxes. **5** *Logic* use (a term) to include every individual of the class to which it refers. □□ **distributable** adj. [ME f. L *distribuere distribut-* (as DIS-, *tribuere* assign)]

distribution /ˌdɪstrɪˈbjuːʃ(ə)n/ n. **1** the act or an instance of distributing; the process of being distributed. **2** *Econ.* **a** the dispersal of goods etc. among consumers, brought about by commerce. **b** the extent to which different groups, classes, or individuals share in the total production or wealth of a community. **3** *Statistics* the way in which a characteristic is spread over members of a class. □□ **distributional** adj. [ME f. OF *distribution* or L *distributio* (as DISTRIBUTE)]

distributive /dɪˈstrɪbjʊtɪv/ adj. & n. —adj. **1** of, concerned with, or produced by distribution. **2** *Logic & Gram.* (of a pronoun etc.) referring to each individual of a class, not to the class collectively (e.g. *each*, *either*). —n. *Gram.* a distributive word. □□ **distributively** adv. [ME f. F *distributif -ive* or LL *distributivus* (as DISTRIBUTE)]

distributor /dɪˈstrɪbjʊtə(r)/ n. **1** a person or thing that distributes. **2** an agent who supplies goods. **3** *Electr.* a device in an internal-combustion engine for passing current to each spark-plug in turn.

district /ˈdɪstrɪkt/ n. & v. —n. **1 a** (often *attrib.*) a territory marked off for special administrative purposes. **b** *Brit.* a division of a county or region electing its own councillors. **2** an area which has common characteristics; a region (*the wine-growing district*). —v.tr. *US* divide into districts. □ **district attorney** (in the US) the prosecuting officer of a district. **district court** (in the US) the Federal court of first instance. **district heating** a supply of heat or hot water from one source to a district or a group of buildings. **district nurse** *Brit.* a peripatetic nurse serving a rural or urban area. **district visitor** *Brit.* a person working for a member of the clergy in a section of a parish. [F f. med.L *districtus* (territory of) jurisdiction (as DISTRAIN)]

District of Colombia /kəˈlɒmbɪə/ a federal district of the US, coextensive with the city of Washington.

distrust /dɪsˈtrʌst/ n. & v. —n. a lack of trust; doubt; suspicion. —v.tr. have no trust or confidence in; doubt. □□ **distruster** n. **distrustful** adj. **distrustfully** adv.

disturb /dɪˈstɜːb/ v.tr. **1** break the rest, calm, or quiet of; interrupt. **2** agitate; worry (*your story disturbs me*). **3** move from a settled position, disarrange (*the papers had been disturbed*). **4** (as **disturbed** adj.) *Psychol.* emotionally or mentally unstable or abnormal. □□ **disturber** n. **disturbing** adj. **disturbingly** adv. [ME f. OF *desto(u)rber* f. L *disturbare* (as DIS-, *turbare* f. *turba* tumult)]

disturbance /dɪˈstɜːbəns/ n. **1** the act or an instance of disturbing; the process of being disturbed. **2** a tumult; an uproar. **3** agitation; worry. **4** an interruption. **5** *Law* interference with rights or property; molestation. [ME f. OF *desto(u)rbance* (as DISTURB)]

w we   z zoo   ʃ she   ʒ decision   θ thin   ð this   ŋ ring   x loch   tʃ chip   dʒ jar   (*see over for vowels*)

disulphide /daɪˈsʌlfaɪd/ n. (US **disulfide**) Chem. a binary chemical containing two atoms of sulphur in each molecule.

disunion /dɪsˈjuːnɪən/ n. a lack of union; separation; dissension. □□ **disunite** /-ˈnaɪt/ v.tr. & intr. **disunity** n.

disuse n. & v. —n. /dɪsˈjuːs/ **1** lack of use or practice; discontinuance. **2** a disused state. —v.tr. /-ˈjuːz/ cease to use. □ **fall into disuse** cease to be used. [ME f. OF desuser (as DIS-, USE)]

disutility /ˌdɪsjuːˈtɪlɪtɪ/ n. (pl. **-ies**) **1** harmfulness, injuriousness. **2** a factor tending to nullify the utility of something; a drawback.

disyllable /dɪˈsɪləb(ə)l, ˈdaɪ-/ n. (also **dissyllable** /dɪˈsɪl-/) Prosody a word or metrical foot of two syllables. □□ **disyllabic** /-ˈlæbɪk/ adj. [F disyllabe f. L disyllabus f. Gk disullabos (as DI-¹, SYLLABLE)]

dit /dɪt/ n. Telegraphy (in the Morse system) = DOT (cf. DAH). [imit.]

ditch /dɪtʃ/ n. & v. —n. **1** a long narrow excavated channel esp. for drainage or to mark a boundary. **2** a watercourse, stream, etc. —v. **1** make or repair ditches (hedging and ditching). **2** tr. provide with ditches; drain. **3** tr. sl. leave in the lurch; abandon. **4** tr. colloq. **a** bring (an aircraft) down on the sea in an emergency. **b** drive (a vehicle) into a ditch. **5** intr. colloq. (of an aircraft) make a forced landing on the sea. **6** tr. sl. defeat; frustrate. **7** tr. US derail (a train). □ **ditch-water** stagnant water in a ditch. **dull as ditch-water** extremely dull. **last ditch** a place of final desperate defence (fight to the last ditch). □□ **ditcher** n. [OE dīc, of unkn. orig.: cf. DIKE¹]

ditheism /ˈdaɪθiːˌɪz(ə)m/ n. Theol. **1** a belief in two gods; dualism. **2** a belief in equal independent ruling principles of good and evil. □□ **ditheist** n.

dither /ˈdɪðə(r)/ v. & n. —v.intr. **1** hesitate; be indecisive. **2** dial. tremble; quiver. —n. colloq. **1** a state of agitation or apprehension. **2** a state of hesitation; indecisiveness. □ **all of a dither** colloq. in a state of extreme agitation or vacillation. □□ **ditherer** n. **dithery** adj. [var. of didder, DODDER¹]

dithyramb /ˈdɪθɪˌræm, -ˌræmb/ n. **1 a** a wild choral hymn in ancient Greece, esp. to Dionysus. **b** a Bacchanalian song. **2** any passionate or inflated poem, speech, etc. □□ **dithyrambic** /-ˈræmbɪk/ adj. [L dithyrambus f. Gk dithurambos, of unkn. orig.]

dittany /ˈdɪtənɪ/ n. (pl. **-ies**) any herb of the genus Dictamnus, formerly used medicinally. [ME f. OF dita(i)n f. med.L dictamus f. L dictamnus f. Gk diktamnon perh. f. Diktē, a mountain in Crete]

ditto /ˈdɪtəʊ/ n. & v. —n. (pl. **-os**) **1** (in accounts, inventories, lists, etc.) the aforesaid, the same. ¶ Often represented by " under the word or sum to be repeated. **2** colloq. (replacing a word or phrase to avoid repetition) the same (came in late last night and ditto the night before). **3** a similar thing; a duplicate. —v.tr. (**-oes**, **-oed**) repeat (another's action or words). □ **ditto marks** inverted commas etc. representing 'ditto'. **say ditto to** colloq. agree with; endorse. [It. dial. f. L dictus past part. of dicere say]

dittography /dɪˈtɒɡrəfɪ/ n. (pl. **-ies**) **1** a copyist's mistaken repetition of a letter, word, or phrase. **2** an example of this. □□ **dittographic** /-ˈɡræfɪk/ adj. [Gk dittos double + -GRAPHY]

ditty /ˈdɪtɪ/ n. (pl. **-ies**) a short simple song. [ME f. OF dité composition f. L dictatum neut. past part. of dictare DICTATE]

ditty-bag /ˈdɪtɪˌbæɡ/ n. (also **ditty-box** /-ˌbɒks/) a sailor's or fisherman's receptacle for odds and ends. [19th c.: orig. unkn.]

Diu /ˈdiːuː/ an island of the NW coast of India (see DAMAN AND DIU).

diuresis /ˌdaɪjʊˈriːsɪs/ n. Med. an increased excretion of urine. [mod.L f. Gk (as DI-³, ourēsis urination)]

diuretic /ˌdaɪjʊˈretɪk/ adj. & n. —adj. causing increased output of urine. —n. a diuretic drug. [ME f. OF diuretique or LL diureticus f. Gk diourētikos f. dioureō urinate]

diurnal /daɪˈɜːn(ə)l/ adj. **1** of or during the day; not nocturnal. **2** daily; of each day. **3** Astron. occupying one day. **4** Zool. (of animals) active in the daytime. **5** Bot. (of plants) open only during the day. □□ **diurnally** adv. [ME f. LL diurnalis f. L diurnus f. dies day]

Div. abbr. Division.

diva /ˈdiːvə/ n. (pl. **divas**) a great or famous woman singer; a prima donna. [It. f. L, = goddess]

divagate /ˈdaɪvəˌɡeɪt/ v.intr. literary stray; digress. □□ **divagation** /-ˈɡeɪʃ(ə)n/ n. [L divagari (as DI-², vagari wander)]

divalent /daɪˈveɪlənt, ˈdaɪ-/ adj. Chem. **1** having a valency of two; bivalent. **2** having two valencies. □□ **divalency** n. [DI-¹ + valent-part. stem (as VALENCY)]

divan /dɪˈvæn, daɪ-, ˈdaɪ-/ n. **1 a** a long, low, padded seat set against a room-wall; a backless sofa. **b** a bed consisting of a base and mattress, usu. with no board at either end. **2** an oriental State legislative body, council-chamber, or court of justice. **3** archaic **a** a cigar-shop. **b** a smoking-room attached to such a shop. [F divan or It. divano f. Turk. dīvān f. Arab. dīwān f. Pers. dīvān anthology, register, court, bench]

divaricate /daɪˈværɪˌkeɪt, dɪ-/ v.intr. diverge, branch; separate widely. □□ **divaricate** /-kət/ adj. **divarication** /-ˈkeɪʃ(ə)n/ n. [L divaricare (as DI-², varicus straddling)]

dive /daɪv/ v. & n. —v. (**dived** or US **dove** /dəʊv/) **1** intr. plunge head first into water, esp. as a sport. **2** intr. **a** Aeron. (of an aircraft) plunge steeply downwards at speed. **b** Naut. (of a submarine) submerge. **c** (of a person) plunge downwards. **3** intr. (foll. by into) colloq. **a** put one's hand into (a pocket, handbag, vessel, etc.) quickly and deeply. **b** occupy oneself suddenly and enthusiastically with (a subject, meal, etc.). **4** tr. (foll. by into) plunge (a hand etc.) into. —n. **1** an act of diving; a plunge. **2 a** the submerging of a submarine. **b** the steep descent of an aircraft. **3** a sudden darting movement. **4** colloq. a disreputable nightclub etc.; a drinking-den (found themselves in a low dive). **5** Boxing sl. a pretended knockout (took a dive in the second round). □ **dive-bomb** bomb (a target) while diving in an aircraft. **dive-bomber** an aircraft designed to dive-bomb. **dive in** colloq. help oneself (to food). **diving-bell** an open-bottomed box or bell, supplied with air, in which a person can descend into deep water. **diving-board** an elevated board used for diving from. **diving-suit** a watertight suit usu. with a helmet and an air-supply, worn for working under water. [OE dūfan (v.intr.) dive, sink, and dȳfan (v.tr.) immerse, f. Gmc: rel. to DEEP, DIP]

diver /ˈdaɪvə(r)/ n. **1** a person who dives. **2 a** a person who wears a diving-suit to work under water for long periods. **b** a pearl-diver etc. **3** any of various diving birds, esp. large waterbirds of the family Gaviidae.

diverge /daɪˈvɜːdʒ/ v. **1** intr. **a** proceed in a different direction or in different directions from a point (diverging rays; the path diverges here). **b** take a different course or different courses (their interests diverged). **2** intr. **a** (often foll. by from) depart from a set course (diverged from the track; diverged from his parents' wishes). **b** differ markedly (they diverged as to the best course). **3** tr. cause to diverge; deflect. **4** intr. Math. (of a series) increase indefinitely as more of its terms are added. [med.L divergere (as DI-², L vergere incline)]

divergent /daɪˈvɜːdʒ(ə)nt/ adj. **1** diverging. **2** Psychol. (of thought) tending to reach a variety of possible solutions when analysing a problem. **3** Math. (of a series) increasing indefinitely as more of its terms are added; not convergent. □□ **divergence** n. **divergency** n. **divergently** adv.

divers /ˈdaɪvəz/ adj. archaic or literary more than one; sundry; several. [ME f. OF f. L diversus DIVERSE (as DI-², versus past part. of vertere turn)]

diverse /daɪˈvɜːs, ˈdaɪ-, dɪ-/ adj. unlike in nature or qualities; varied. □□ **diversely** adv. [ME (as DIVERS)]

diversify /daɪˈvɜːsɪˌfaɪ/ v. (**-ies**, **-ied**) **1** tr. make diverse; vary; modify. **2** tr. Commerce **a** spread (investment) over several enterprises or products, esp. to reduce the risk of loss. **b** introduce a spread of investment in (an enterprise etc.). **3** intr. (often foll. by into) esp. Commerce (of a firm etc.) expand the range of products handled. □□ **diversification** /-fɪˈkeɪʃ(ə)n/ n. [ME f. OF diversifier f. med.L diversificare (as DIVERS)]

diversion /daɪˈvɜːʃ(ə)n, dɪ-/ n. **1 a** the act of diverting; deviation. **b** an instance of this. **2 a** the diverting of attention deliberately. **b** a stratagem for this purpose (created a diversion to secure their escape). **3** a recreation or pastime. **4** Brit. an alternative route when a road is temporarily closed to traffic. □□ **diversional** adj. **diversionary** adj. [LL diversio (as DIVERT)]

diversionist /daɪˈvɜːʃənɪst/ n. **1** a person who engages in disruptive or subversive activities. **2** Polit. (esp. used by communists) a conspirator against the State; a saboteur.

diversity /daɪˈvɜːsɪtɪ, dɪ-/ n. (pl. **-ies**) **1** being diverse; variety. **2** a different kind; a variety. [ME f. OF diversité f. L diversitas -tatis (as DIVERS)]

divert /daɪˈvɜːt, dɪ-/ v.tr. **1** (often foll. by from, to) **a** turn aside; deflect. **b** draw the attention of; distract. **2** (often as **diverting** adj.) entertain; amuse. □□ **divertingly** adv. [ME f. F divertir f. L divertere (as DI-², vertere turn)]

diverticular /ˌdaɪvɜːˈtɪkjʊlə(r)/ adj. Med. of or relating to a diverticulum. □ **diverticular disease** a condition with abdominal pain as a result of muscle spasms in the presence of diverticula.

diverticulitis /ˌdaɪvɜːˌtɪkjʊˈlaɪtɪs/ n. Med. inflammation of a diverticulum.

diverticulum /ˌdaɪvɜːˈtɪkjʊləm/ n. (pl. **diverticula** /-lə/) Anat. a blind tube forming at weak points in a cavity or passage esp. of the alimentary tract. □□ **diverticulosis** /-ˈləʊsɪs/ n. [med.L, var. of L deverticulum byway f. devertere (as DE-, vertere turn)]

divertimento /dɪˌvɜːtɪˈmentəʊ, dɪˌveə-/ n. (pl. **divertimenti** /-tɪ/ or **-os**) Mus. a light and entertaining composition, often in the form of a suite for chamber orchestra. [It., = diversion]

divertissement /ˌdiːveəˈtiːsmɑ̃/ n. **1** a diversion; an entertainment. **2** a short ballet etc. between acts or longer pieces. [F, f. divertiss- stem of divertir DIVERT]

Dives /ˈdaɪviːz/ n. a rich man. [L, in Vulgate transl. of Luke 16, whence commonly taken for the name of the rich man in that parable]

divest /daɪˈvest/ v.tr. **1** (usu. foll. by of; often refl.) unclothe; strip (divested himself of his jacket). **2** deprive, dispossess; free, rid (cannot divest himself of the idea). □□ **divestiture** n. **divestment** n. **divesture** n. [earlier devest f. OF desvestir etc. (as DIS-, L vestire f. vestis garment)]

divi var. of DIVVY.

divide /dɪˈvaɪd/ v. & n. —v. **1** tr. & intr. (often foll. by in, into) separate or be separated into parts; break up; split (the river divides into two; the road divides; divided them into three groups). **2** tr. & intr. (often foll. by out) distribute; deal; share (divided it out between them). **3** tr. **a** cut off; separate; part (divide the sheep from the goats). **b** mark out into parts (a ruler divided into inches). **c** specify different kinds of, classify (people can be divided into two types). **4** tr. cause to disagree; set at variance (religion divided them). **5** Math. **a** tr. find how many times (a number) contains another (divide 20 by 4). **b** intr. (of a number) be contained in (a number) without a remainder (4 divides into 20). **c** tr. be susceptible of division (10 divides by 2 and 5). **d** tr. find how many times (a number) is contained in another (divide 4 into 20). **6** intr. Math. do division (can divide well). **7** Parl. **a** intr. (of a legislative assembly etc.) part into two groups for voting (the House divided). **b** tr. so divide (a Parliament etc.) for voting. —n. **1** a dividing or boundary line (the divide between rich and poor). **2** a watershed. □ **divided against itself** formed into factions. **divided highway** US a dual carriageway. **divided skirt** culottes. **the Great Divide 1** the Continental Divide (see entry). **2** the Great Dividing Range (see entry) of Australia. **3** the boundary between life and death. [ME f. L dividere divis- (as DI-², vid- separate)]

dividend /ˈdɪvɪˌdend/ n. **1 a** a sum of money to be divided among a number of persons, esp. that paid by a company to shareholders. **b** a similar sum payable to winners in a football pool, to members of a cooperative, or to creditors of an insolvent estate. **c** an individual's share of a dividend. **2** Math. a number to be divided by a divisor. **3** a benefit from any action (their long training paid dividends). □ **dividend stripping** the evasion of tax on dividends by arrangement between the company liable to pay tax and another able to claim repayment of tax. **dividend warrant** Brit. the documentary authority for a shareholder to receive a dividend. **dividend yield** a dividend expressed as a percentage of a current share price. [AF dividende f. L dividendum (as DIVIDE)]

divider /dɪˈvaɪdə(r)/ n. **1** a screen, piece of furniture, etc., dividing a room into two parts. **2** (in pl.) a measuring-compass, esp. with a screw for setting small intervals.

divi-divi /ˈdɪvɪˌdɪvɪ/ n. (pl. **divi-divis**) **1** a small tree, Caesalpinia coriaria, native to tropical Africa, bearing curved pods. **2** this pod used as a source of tannin. [Carib]

divination /ˌdɪvɪˈneɪʃ(ə)n/ n. **1** supposed insight into the future or the unknown gained by supernatural means. **2 a** a skilful and accurate forecast. **b** a good guess. □□ **divinatory** adj. [ME f. OF divination or L divinatio (as DIVINE)]

divine /dɪˈvaɪn/ adj., v., & n. —adj. (**diviner, divinest**) **1 a** of, from, or like God or a god. **b** devoted to God; sacred (divine service). **2 a** more than humanly excellent, gifted, or beautiful. **b** colloq. excellent; delightful. —v. **1** tr. discover by guessing, intuition, inspiration, or magic. **2** tr. foresee, predict, conjecture. **3** intr. practise divination. —n. **1** a cleric, usu. an expert in theology. **2** (**the Divine**) providence or God. □ **divine office** see OFFICE. **divine right of kings** the doctrine that a monarch in the hereditary line of succession has authority derived directly from God, independently of the subjects' will, and that rebellion is the worst of political crimes. Enunciated in the 16th c., under the Stuarts it was upheld by almost all the leading Anglican divines, but many of its strenuous upholders found no difficulty in accommodating themselves to the Revolution of 1688, by which the Stuart dynasty was expelled from the throne. **divining-rod** = dowsing-rod (see DOWSE¹). □□ **divinely** adv. **divineness** n. **diviner** n. **divinize** /ˈdɪvɪ-/ v.tr. (also **-ise**). [ME f. OF devin -ine f. L divinus f. divus godlike]

divinity /dɪˈvɪnɪtɪ/ n. (pl. **-ies**) **1** the state or quality of being divine. **2 a** a god; a divine being. **b** (as **the Divinity**) God. **3** the study of religion; theology. [ME f. OF divinité f. L divinitas -tatis (as DIVINE)]

divisible /dɪˈvɪzɪb(ə)l/ adj. **1** capable of being divided, physically or mentally. **2** (foll. by by) Math. containing (a number) a number of times without a remainder (15 is divisible by 3 and 5). □□ **divisibility** /-ˈbɪlɪtɪ/ n. [F divisible or LL divisibilis (as DIVIDE)]

division /dɪˈvɪʒ(ə)n/ n. **1** the act or an instance of dividing; the process of being divided. **2** Math. the process of dividing one number by another (see also long division (see LONG¹), short division). **3** disagreement or discord (division of opinion). **4** Parl. the separation of members of a legislative body into two sets for counting votes for and against. **5** one of two or more parts into which a thing is divided. **6** a major unit of administration or organization, esp.: **a** a group of army brigades or regiments. **b** Sport a grouping of teams within a league, usu. by ability. **7 a** a district defined for administrative purposes. **b** Brit. a part of a county or borough returning a Member of Parliament. **8 a** Bot. a major taxonomic grouping. **b** Zool. a subsidiary category between major levels of classification. **9** Logic a classification of kinds, parts, or senses. □ **division of labour** the improvement of efficiency by giving different parts of a manufacturing process etc. to different people. **division sign** the sign ($\div$) indicating that one quantity is to be divided by another. □□ **divisional** adj. **divisionally** adv. **divisionary** adj. [ME f. OF divisiun f. L divisio -onis (as DIVIDE)]

divisive /dɪˈvaɪsɪv/ adj. tending to divide, esp. in opinion; causing disagreement. □□ **divisively** adv. **divisiveness** n. [LL divisivus (as DIVIDE)]

divisor /dɪˈvaɪzə(r)/ n. Math. **1** a number by which another is to be divided. **2** a number that divides another without a remainder. [ME f. F diviseur or L divisor (as DIVIDE)]

divorce /dɪˈvɔːs/ n. & v. —n. **1 a** the legal dissolution of a marriage. **b** a legal decree of this. **2** a severance or separation (a divorce between thought and feeling). —v. **1 a** tr. (usu. as **divorced** adj.) (often foll. by from) legally dissolve the marriage of (a divorced couple; he wants to get divorced from her). **b** intr. separate by divorce (they divorced last year). **c** tr. end one's marriage with (divorced him for neglect). **2** tr. (often foll. by from) detach, separate (divorced from reality). **3** tr. archaic dissolve (a union). □□ **divorcement** n. [ME f. OF divorce (n.), divorcer (v.) f. LL divortiare f. L divortium f. divortere (as DI-², vertere turn)]

divorcee /ˌdɪvɔːˈsiː/ n. (also masc. **divorcé**, fem. **divorcée** /-ˈseɪ/) a divorced person.

divot /ˈdɪvət/ n. **1** a piece of turf cut out by a golf club in making a stroke. **2** esp. Sc. a piece of turf; a sod. [16th c.: orig. unkn.]

divulge /daɪˈvʌldʒ, dɪ-/ v.tr. disclose; reveal (a secret etc.). □□ **divulgation** /-ˈgeɪʃ(ə)n/ n. **divulgement** n. **divulgence** n. [L divulgare (as DI-², vulgare publish f. vulgus common people)]

divvy /ˈdɪvɪ/ n. & v. (also **divi**) colloq. —n. (pl. **-ies**) **1** Brit. a dividend; a share, esp. of profits earned by a cooperative. **2** a distribution. —v.tr. (**-ies, -ied**) (often foll. by up) share out; divide. [abbr. of DIVIDEND]

Diwali /diːˈwɑːlɪ/ n. a Hindu festival with illuminations, held between September and November in honour of the goddess of wealth (Lakshmi). [Hind. dīwalī f. Skr. dīpāvalī row of lights f. dīpa lamp]

Dixie /ˈdɪksɪ/ n. the southern States of the US. The name is used in the song Dixie (1859) by Daniel D. Emmett, a popular marching-song sung by Confederate soldiers in the American Civil War. [19th c.: orig. uncert.]

dixie /ˈdɪksɪ/ n. a large iron cooking pot used by campers etc. [Hind. degchī cooking pot f. Pers. degcha dimin. of deg pot]

Dixieland /ˈdɪksɪˌlænd/ n. **1** = DIXIE. **2** a kind of jazz with a strong two-beat rhythm and collective improvisation. [DIXIE]

DIY abbr. Brit. do-it-yourself.

dizzy /ˈdɪzɪ/ adj. & v. —adj. (**dizzier, dizziest**) **1 a** giddy, unsteady. **b** feeling confused. **2** causing giddiness (dizzy heights; dizzy speed). —v.tr. **1** make dizzy. **2** bewilder. □□ **dizzily** adv. **dizziness** n. [OE dysig f. WG]

DJ abbr. **1** Brit. dinner-jacket. **2** disc jockey.

Djakarta /dʒəˈkɑːtə/ (also **Jakarta**) the capital of Indonesia, situated in NW Java; pop. (1950) 6,503,400.

djellaba /ˈdʒeləbə/ n. (also **djellabah, jellaba**) a loose hooded woollen cloak worn or as worn by Arab men. [Arab. jallaba, jallābīya]

Djerba /ˈdʒɜːbə/ (also **Jerba**) a resort island in the Gulf of Gabès off the coast of Tunisia.

djibba (also **djibbah**) var. of JIBBA.

Djibouti /dʒɪˈbuːtɪ/ (also **Jibuti**) **1** a country on the NE coast of Africa, formerly known as French Somaliland and then as the French Territory of the Afars and Issas, becoming independent in 1977; pop. (est. 1988) 484,000. **2** its capital city; pop. (est. 1988) 290,000. □□ **Djiboutian** adj. & n.

djinn var. of JINNEE.

DL abbr. Deputy Lieutenant.

dl abbr. decilitre(s).

D-layer /ˈdiːˌleɪə(r)/ n. the lowest layer of the ionosphere able to reflect low-frequency radio waves. [D (arbitrary)]

D.Litt. abbr. Doctor of Letters. [L Doctor Litterarum]

DM abbr. (also **D-mark**) Deutschmark.

dm abbr. decimetre(s).

D.Mus. abbr. Doctor of Music.

DMZ abbr. US demilitarized zone.

DNA abbr. deoxyribonucleic acid, the self-replicating material present in nearly all living organisms, esp. as a constituent of chromosomes. DNA molecules carry the genetic information necessary for the organization and functioning of most living cells and control the inheritance of characteristics (see MENDELISM). The structure of a DNA molecule was first proposed by J. D. Watson and F. H. Crick in 1953: each consists of two strands coiled round each other to form a double helix, a structure like a spiral ladder; it is the 'rungs' of the ladder that carry the information. Each rung consists of a pair of chemical groups called bases (of which there are four types). The different rungs function rather like different letters of the alphabet, which are without meaning in themselves but in sequences produce meaningful words, and long sequences of bases similarly 'spell out' genetic information. These control the manufacture of proteins needed by the cell; genes are 'copied' in the nucleus into the similar RNA, which then passes out into the cytoplasm and forms a template for the synthesis of particular proteins, especially enzymes. The DNA molecule also has the special property of self-replication: the strands separate and each provides a template for the synthesis of a new complementary strand with which it recombines, thus producing two identical copies of the original double helix.

DNB abbr. Dictionary of National Biography.

Dnepropetrovsk /ˌdniːprəpeˈtrɒfsk/ (formerly Ekaterinoslav) an industrial port in Ukraine, on the River Dnieper; pop. (est. 1987) 1,182,000.

Dnieper /ˈdniːpə(r)/ a river of the USSR flowing some 2,200 km (1,370 miles) through Belorussia and Ukraine to the Black Sea. The cities of Kiev and Dnepropetrovsk are situated on it. Dams have been built at a number of points to provide hydroelectric power and water for Ukraine's industries.

Dniester /ˈdniːstə(r)/ a river of the USSR flowing 1,410 km (876 miles) from the Carpathian Mountains through Moldavia to the Black Sea.

D-notice /ˈdiːˌnəʊtɪs/ n. Brit. a government notice to news editors not to publish items on specified subjects, for reasons of security. [defence + NOTICE]

do¹ /duː, də/ v. & n. —v. (3rd sing. present **does** /dʌz/; past **did** /dɪd/; past part. **done** /dʌn/) **1** tr. perform, carry out, achieve, complete (work etc.) (did his homework; there's a lot to do; he can do anything). **2** tr. **a** produce, make (she was doing a painting; I did a translation; decided to do a casserole). **b** provide (do you do lunches?). **3** tr. bestow, grant; have a specified effect on (a walk would do you good; do me a favour). **4** intr. act, behave, proceed (do as I do; she would do well to accept the offer). **5** tr. work at, study; be occupied with (what does your father do?; he did chemistry at university; we're doing Chaucer next term). **6 a** intr. be suitable or acceptable; suffice (this dress won't do for a wedding; a sandwich will do until we get home; that will never do). **b** tr. satisfy; be suitable for (that hotel will do me nicely). **7** tr. deal with; put in order (the garden needs doing; the barber will do you next; I must do my hair before we go). **8** intr. fare; get on (the patients were doing excellently; he did badly in the test). **b** perform, work (could do better). **9** tr. **a** solve; work out (we did the puzzle). **b** (prec. by can or be able to) be competent at (can you do cartwheels?; I never could do maths). **10** tr. **a** traverse (a certain distance) (we did fifty miles today). **b** travel at a specified speed (he overtook us doing about eighty). **11** tr. colloq. **a** act or behave like (did a Houdini). **b** play the part of (she was asked to do hostess). **12** intr. **a** colloq. finish (have you done annoying me?; I've done in the bathroom). **b** (as **done** adj.) be over (the day is done). **13** tr. produce or give a performance of (the school does many plays and concerts; we've never done 'Pygmalion'). **14** tr. cook, esp. to the right degree (do it in the oven; the potatoes aren't done yet). **15** intr. be in progress (what's doing?). **16** tr. colloq. visit; see the sights of (we did all the art galleries). **17** tr. colloq. **a** (often as **done** adj.) exhaust; tire out (the climb has completely done me). **b** beat up, defeat, kill. **c** ruin (now you've done it). **18** tr. (foll. by into) translate or transform (the book was done into French). **19** tr. colloq. (with qualifying adverb) provide food etc. for in a specified way (they do one very well here). **20** tr. sl. **a** rob (they did a shop in Soho). **b** swindle (I was done at the market). **21** tr. sl. prosecute, convict (they were done for shoplifting). **22** tr. sl. undergo (a specified term of imprisonment) (he did two years for fraud). **23** tr. coarse sl. have sexual intercourse with. **24** tr. sl. take (a drug). —v.aux. **1 a** (except with be, can, may, ought, shall, will) in questions and negative statements (do you understand?; I don't smoke). **b** (except with can, may, ought, shall, will) in negative commands (don't be silly; do not come tomorrow). **2** ellipt. or in place of verb or verb and object (you know her better than I do; I wanted to go and I did so; tell me, do!). **3** forming emphatic present and past tenses (I do want to; do tell me; they did go but she was out). **4** in inversion for emphasis (rarely does it happen; did he but know it). —n. (pl. **dos** or **do's**) **1** colloq. an elaborate event, party, or operation. **2** Brit. sl. a swindle or hoax. □ **be done with** see DONE. **be nothing to do with 1** be no business or concern of (his financial situation is nothing to do with me). **2** be unconnected with (his depression is nothing to do with his father's death). **be to do with** be concerned or connected with (the argument was to do with money). **do about** see ABOUT prep. 1d. **do away with** colloq. **1** abolish. **2** kill. **do battle** enter into combat. **do one's best** see BEST. **do one's bit** see BIT. **do by** treat or deal with in a specified way (do as you would be done by). **do credit to** see CREDIT. **do down** colloq. **1** cheat, swindle. **2** get the better of; overcome. **do for 1** be satisfactory or sufficient for. **2** *colloq.* (esp. as **done for** *adj.*) destroy, ruin, kill (*he knew he was done for*). **3** *colloq.* act as housekeeper for. **do one's head** (or **nut**) *sl.* be extremely angry or agitated. **do the honours** see HONOUR. **do in 1** *sl.* **a** kill. **b** ruin, do injury to. **2** *colloq.* exhaust, tire out. **do-it-yourself** *adj.* (of work, esp. building, painting, decorating, etc.) done or to be done by an amateur at home. —*n.* such work. **do justice to** see JUSTICE. **do nothing for** (or to) *colloq.* detract from the appearance or quality of (*such behaviour does nothing for our reputation*). **do or die** persist regardless of danger. **do out** *colloq.* clean or redecorate (a room). **do a person out of** *colloq.* unjustly deprive a person of; swindle out of (*he was done out of his holiday*). **do over 1** *sl.* attack; beat up. **2** *colloq.* redecorate, refurbish. **3** *US colloq.* do again. **do proud** see PROUD. **dos and don'ts** rules of behaviour. **do something for** (or **to**) *colloq.* enhance the appearance or quality of (*that carpet does something for the room*). **do one's stuff** see STUFF. **do to** (*archaic* **unto**) = *do by*. **do to death** see DEATH. **do the trick** see TRICK. **do up 1** fasten, secure. **2** *colloq.* **a** refurbish, renovate. **b** adorn, dress up. **3** *sl.* **a** ruin, get the better of. **b** beat up. **do well for oneself** prosper. **do well out of** profit by. **do with** (prec. by *could*) would be glad to have; would profit by (*I could do with a rest; you could do with a wash*). **do without** manage without; forgo (also *absol.*: *we shall just have to do without*). **have nothing to do with 1** have no connection or dealings with (*our problem has nothing to do with the latest news; after the disagreement he had nothing to do with his father*). **2** be no business or concern of (*the decision has nothing to do with him*). **have to do** (or **something to do**) **with** be connected with (*his limp has to do with a car accident*). [OE *dōn* f. Gmc: rel. to Skr. *dádhami* put, Gk *tithemi* place, L *facere* do]

do² var. of DOH.

do. *abbr.* ditto.

DOA *abbr.* dead on arrival (at hospital etc.).

doable /ˈduːəb(ə)l/ *adj.* that can be done.

dob /dɒb/ *v.tr.* (**dobbed**, **dobbing**) (foll. by *in*) *Austral. sl.* inform against; implicate; betray. [var. of DAB¹]

dobbin /ˈdɒbɪn/ *n.* a draught-horse; a farm horse. [pet-form of the name *Robert*]

dobe /ˈdəʊbɪ/ *n. US colloq.* adobe. [abbr.]

Dobell /dəʊˈbel/, Sir William (1899–1970), Australian painter, noted for his portraits, who combined a mastery of Renaissance tradition with a profound insight into the character and values of 20th-c. Australians. In 1943/4 he won the Archibald Prize, awarded by the Art Gallery of New South Wales, for a portrait of his fellow artist Joshua Smith. The award, which was contested in the courts by two of the unsuccessful competitors on the grounds that it was not a portrait but a caricature, created a *cause célèbre* for modernism in Australia.

Dobermann /ˈdəʊbəmən/ *n.* (in full **Dobermann pinscher** /ˈpɪnʃə(r)/) **1** a large dog of a German breed with a smooth coat. **2** this breed. [L *Dobermann*, 19th-c. Ger. dog-breeder + G *Pinscher* terrier]

Dobruja /ˈdɒbrejə/ a district in SE Romania and NE Bulgaria, bounded on the east by the Black Sea and on the north and west by the Danube.

doc /dɒk/ *n. colloq.* doctor. [abbr.]

Docetist /dəˈsiːtɪst/ *n.* a member of the Docetae, a sect of early Christian heretics who held that Christ's body was not human but a phantom or of celestial substance. □□ **Docetism** *n.* [med. L *Docetae* f. Gk *Dokētai* f. *dokeō* seem, appear]

doch an dorris var. of DEOCH AN DORIS.

docile /ˈdəʊsaɪl/ *adj.* **1** submissive, easily managed. **2** *archaic* teachable. □□ **docilely** /ˈdəʊsaɪllɪ/ *adv.* **docility** /-ˈsɪlɪtɪ/ *n.* [ME f. L *docilis* f. *docēre* teach]

dock¹ /dɒk/ *n. & v.* —*n.* **1** an artificially enclosed body of water for the loading, unloading, and repair of ships. **2** (in *pl.*) a range of docks with wharves and offices; a dockyard. **3** *US* a ship's berth, a wharf. **4** = *dry dock.* **5** *Theatr.* = *scene-dock.* —*v.* **1** *tr. & intr.* bring or come into a dock. **2 a** *tr.* join (spacecraft) together in space. **b** *intr.* (of spacecraft) be joined. **3** *tr.* provide with a dock or docks. □ **dock-glass** a large glass for wine-tasting. **in**

dock *Brit. colloq.* in hospital or (of a vehicle) laid up for repairs. [MDu. *docke*, of unkn. orig.]

dock² /dɒk/ *n.* the enclosure in a criminal court for the accused. □ **dock brief** a brief handed direct to a barrister selected by a prisoner in the dock. **in the dock** on trial. [16th c.: prob. orig. cant = Flem. *dok* cage, of unkn. orig.]

dock³ /dɒk/ *n.* any weed of the genus *Rumex*, with broad leaves. [OE *docce*]

dock⁴ /dɒk/ *v. & n.* —*v.tr.* **1 a** cut short (an animal's tail). **b** cut short the tail of (an animal). **2 a** (often foll. by *from*) deduct (a part) from wages, supplies, etc. **b** reduce (wages etc.) in this way. —*n.* **1** the solid bony part of an animal's tail. **2** the crupper of a saddle or harness. □ **dock-tailed** having a docked tail. [ME, of uncert. orig.]

dockage /ˈdɒkɪdʒ/ *n.* **1** the charge made for using docks. **2** dock accommodation. **3** the berthing of vessels in docks.

docker /ˈdɒkə(r)/ *n.* a person employed to load and unload ships.

docket /ˈdɒkɪt/ *n. & v.* —*n.* **1** *Brit.* **a** a document or label listing goods delivered or the contents of a package, or recording payment of customs dues etc. **b** a voucher; an order form. **2** *US* a list of causes for trial or persons having causes pending. **3** *US* a list of things to be done. —*v.tr.* (**docketed**, **docketing**) label with a docket. [15th c.: orig. unkn.]

dockland /ˈdɒklənd/ *n.* a district near docks. [DOCK¹]

dockyard /ˈdɒkjɑːd/ *n.* an area with docks and equipment for building and repairing ships, esp. for naval use.

doctor /ˈdɒktə(r)/ *n. & v.* —*n.* **1 a** a qualified practitioner of medicine; a physician. **b** *US* a qualified dentist or veterinary surgeon. **2** a person who holds a doctorate (*Doctor of Civil Law*). **3** *colloq.* a person who cures or repairs. **4** *archaic* a teacher or learned man. **5** *sl.* a cook on board a ship or in a camp. **6** (in full **doctor-blade**) *Printing* a blade for removing surplus ink etc. **7** an artificial fishing-fly. —*v. colloq.* **1 a** *tr.* treat medically. **b** *intr.* (esp. as **doctoring** *n.*) practise as a physician. **2** *tr.* castrate or spay. **3** *tr.* patch up (machinery etc.); mend. **4** *tr.* adulterate. **5** *tr.* tamper with, falsify. **6** *tr.* confer a degree of doctor on. □ **Doctor of the Church** any of several early Christian theologians, originally Gregory the Great, Ambrose, Augustine, and Jerome. **Doctor of Philosophy** a doctorate in any faculty except law, medicine, or sometimes theology. **go for the doctor** *Austral. sl.* **1** make an all-out effort. **2** bet all one has. **what the doctor ordered** *colloq.* something beneficial or desirable. □□ **doctorhood** *n.* **doctorial** /-ˈtɔːrɪəl/ *adj.* **doctorly** *adj.* **doctorship** *n.* [ME f. OF *doctour* f. L *doctor* f. *docēre doct-* teach]

doctoral /ˈdɒktər(ə)l/ *adj.* of or for a degree of doctor.

doctorate /ˈdɒktərət/ *n.* the highest university degree in any faculty, often honorary.

doctrinaire /ˌdɒktrɪˈneə(r)/ *adj. & n.* —*adj.* seeking to apply a theory or doctrine in all circumstances without regard to practical considerations; theoretical and impractical. —*n.* a doctrinaire person; a pedantic theorist. □□ **doctrinairism** *n.* **doctrinarian** *n.* [F f. *doctrinaire* DOCTRINE + *-aire* -ARY¹]

doctrinal /dɒkˈtraɪn(ə)l, ˈdɒktrɪn(ə)l/ *adj.* of or inculcating a doctrine or doctrines. □□ **doctrinally** *adv.* [LL *doctrinalis* (as DOCTRINE)]

doctrine /ˈdɒktrɪn/ *n.* **1** what is taught; a body of instruction. **2 a** a principle of religious or political etc. belief. **b** a set of such principles; dogma. □□ **doctrinism** *n.* **doctrinist** *n.* [ME f. OF f. L *doctrina* teaching (as DOCTOR)]

docudrama /ˈdɒkjʊˌdrɑːmə/ *n.* a dramatized television film based on real events. [DOCUMENTARY + DRAMA]

document /ˈdɒkjʊmənt/ *n. & v. Law* —*n.* a piece of written or printed matter that provides a record or evidence of events, an agreement, ownership, identification, etc. —*v.tr.* /ˈdɒkjʊˌment/ **1** prove by or provide with documents or evidence. **2** record in a document. □□ **documental** /-ˈment(ə)l/ *adj.* [ME f. OF f. L *documentum* proof f. *docēre* teach]

documentalist /ˌdɒkjʊˈmentəlɪst/ *n.* a person engaged in documentation.

documentary /ˌdɒkjʊˈmentərɪ/ *adj. & n.* —*adj.* **1** consisting of documents (*documentary evidence*). **2** providing a factual record or report. —*n.* (*pl.* **-ies**) a documentary film etc. (See below.) □□ **documentarily** *adv.*

Documentaries are factual films depicting real people, events, or landscapes either lyrically or as a means of social comment. The lyrical vein was first seen in Robert Flaherty's study of Eskimo life *Nanook of the North* (1922), but the social purpose emerged most strongly in the 1930s, notably in Britain under the influence of John Grierson. Such films were used as propaganda by both sides in the Second World War, but after the war their production sharply declined until the growth of television provided a new outlet; they are now made mainly for this medium.

documentation /ˌdɒkjʊmenˈteɪʃ(ə)n/ *n.* **1** the accumulation, classification, and dissemination of information. **2** the material collected or disseminated. **3** the collection of documents relating to a process or event, esp. the written specification and instructions accompanying a computer program.

DOD *abbr.* US Department of Defense.

dodder[1] /ˈdɒdə(r)/ *v.intr.* tremble or totter, esp. from age. □ **dodder-grass** quaking-grass. □□ **dodderer** *n.* [17th c.: var. of obs. dial. *dadder*]

dodder[2] /ˈdɒdə(r)/ *n.* any climbing parasitic plant of the genus *Cuscuta*, with slender leafless threadlike stems. [ME f. Gmc]

doddered /ˈdɒdəd/ *adj.* (of a tree, esp. an oak) having lost its top or branches. [prob. f. obs. *dod* poll, lop]

doddery /ˈdɒdərɪ/ *adj.* tending to tremble or totter, esp. from age. □□ **dodderiness** *n.* [DODDER[1] + -Y[1]]

doddle /ˈdɒd(ə)l/ *n.* Brit. colloq. an easy task. [perh. f. *doddle* = TODDLE]

dodeca- /ˈdəʊdekə/ *comb. form* twelve. [Gk *dōdeka* twelve]

dodecagon /dəʊˈdekəgən/ *n.* a plane figure with twelve sides.

dodecahedron /ˌdəʊdekəˈhiːdrən/ *n.* a solid figure with twelve faces. □□ **dodecahedral** *adj.*

Dodecanese /ˌdəʊdɪkəˈniːz/ a group of twelve islands in the SE Aegean, of which the largest is Rhodes, which were occupied by Italy in 1912 during the war with Turkey and ceded to Greece in 1947; capital, Rhodes. [Gk (*dōdeka* twelve, *nēsos* island)]

dodecaphonic /ˌdəʊdekəˈfɒnɪk/ *adj.* Mus. = *twelve-note*.

dodge /dɒdʒ/ *v. & n.* —*v.* **1** *intr.* (often foll. by *about, behind, round*) move quickly to one side or quickly change position, to elude a pursuer, blow, etc. (*dodged behind the chair*). **2** *tr.* **a** evade by cunning or trickery (*dodged paying the fare*). **b** elude (a pursuer, opponent, blow, etc.) by a sideward movement etc. **3** *tr.* Austral. *sl.* acquire dishonestly. **4** *intr.* (of a bell in change-ringing) move one place contrary to the normal sequence. —*n.* **1** a quick movement to avoid or evade something. **2** a clever trick or expedient. **3** the dodging of a bell in change-ringing. □ **dodge the column** see COLUMN. [16th c.: orig. unkn.]

Dodge City /dɒdʒ/ a city in SW Kansas; pop. (1980) 18,000. Established in 1872 as a railhead on the Santa Fe Trail, it gained a reputation as a rowdy frontier town.

dodgem /ˈdɒdʒəm/ *n.* each of a number of small electrically-driven cars in an enclosure at a funfair, driven round and bumped into each other. [DODGE + 'EM]

dodger /ˈdɒdʒə(r)/ *n.* **1** a person who dodges, esp. an artful or elusive person. **2** a screen on a ship's bridge etc. as protection from spray etc. **3** US a small handbill. **4** US a maize-flour cake. **5** *sl.* a sandwich; bread; food.

Dodgson, Charles Lutwidge, see Lewis CARROLL.

dodgy /ˈdɒdʒɪ/ *adj.* (**dodgier**, **dodgiest**) **1** colloq. awkward, unreliable, tricky. **2** Brit. cunning, artful.

dodo /ˈdəʊdəʊ/ *n.* (*pl.* **-os** or **-oes**) **1** any large flightless bird of the extinct family Raphidae, formerly native to Mauritius. **2** an old-fashioned, stupid, or inactive person. □ **as dead as the** (or **a**) **dodo 1** completely or unmistakably dead. **2** entirely obsolete. [Port. *doudo* simpleton]

Dodoma /dəˈdəʊmə/ the capital of Tanzania; pop. 45,700.

DoE *abbr.* (in the UK) Department of the Environment.

doe /dəʊ/ *n.* a female fallow deer, reindeer, hare, or rabbit. [OE *dā*]

doek /dʊk/ *n.* S.Afr. a cloth, esp. a head-cloth. [Afrik.]

doer /ˈduːə(r)/ *n.* **1** a person who does something. **2** one who acts rather than merely talking or thinking. **3** (in full **hard doer**) Austral. an eccentric or amusing person.

does 3rd sing. present of DO[1].

doeskin /ˈdəʊskɪn/ *n.* **1 a** the skin of a doe fallow deer. **b** leather made from this. **2** a fine cloth resembling it.

doesn't /ˈdʌz(ə)nt/ contr. does not.

doest /ˈduːɪst/ archaic 2nd sing. present of DO[1].

doeth /ˈduːɪθ/ archaic = DOTH.

doff /dɒf/ *v.tr.* literary take off (one's hat, clothing). [ME, = *do off*]

dog /dɒg/ *n. & v.* —*n.* **1** any four-legged flesh-eating animal of the genus *Canis*, of many breeds domesticated and wild, kept as pets or for work or sport. **2** the male of the dog, or of the fox (also **dog-fox**) or wolf (also **dog-wolf**). **3** colloq. **a** a despicable person. **b** a person or fellow of a specified kind (*a lucky dog*). **c** US & Austral. *sl.* an informer; a traitor. **d** *sl.* a horse that is difficult to handle. **4** a mechanical device for gripping. **5** US *sl.* something poor; a failure. **6** = FIREDOG. **7** (in *pl.*; prec. by *the*) Brit. colloq. greyhound-racing. —*v.tr.* (**dogged, dogging**) **1** follow closely and persistently; pursue, track. **2** Mech. grip with a dog. □ **die like a dog** die miserably or shamefully. **dog-biscuit** a hard thick biscuit for feeding dogs. **dog-box** Austral. *sl.* 'a compartment in a railway carriage without a corridor. **dog-clutch** Mech. a device for coupling two shafts in the transmission of power, one member having teeth which engage with slots in another. **dog-collar 1** a collar for a dog. **2 a** colloq. a clerical collar. **b** a straight high collar. **dog days** the hottest period of the year (reckoned in antiquity from the heliacal rising of the dog-star). **dog-eared** (of a book etc.) with the corners worn or battered with use. **dog-eat-dog** colloq. ruthlessly competitive. **dog-end** *sl.* a cigarette-end. **dog-fall** a fall in which wrestlers touch the ground together. **dog in the manger** a person who prevents others from using something, although that person has no use for it. **dog-leg** (or **-legged**) bent like a dog's hind leg. **dog-leg hole** Golf a hole at which a player cannot aim directly at the green from the tee. **dog-paddle** *n.* an elementary swimming-stroke like that of a dog. —*v.intr.* swim using this stroke. **dog-rose** a wild hedge-rose, *Rosa canina*: also called *brier-rose*. **dog's breakfast** (or **dinner**) colloq. a mess. **dog's disease** Austral. *sl.* influenza. **dog's life** a life of misery or harassment. **dog's meat** horse's or other flesh as food for dogs; carrion. **dogs of war** poet. the havoc accompanying war. **dog's-** (or **dog-**) **tail** any grass of the genus *Cynosurus*, esp. *C. cristatus*, a common pasture grass. **dog-star** the chief star of the constellation Canis Major or Minor, esp. Sirius. **dog's tooth** (in full **dog's tooth violet**) **1** any liliaceous plant of the genus *Erythronium*, esp. *E. dens-canis* with speckled leaves, purple flowers, and a toothed perianth. **2** = *dog-tooth* 2. **dog-tired** tired out. **dog-tooth 1** a small pointed ornament or moulding esp. in Norman and Early English architecture. **2** a broken check pattern used esp. in cloth for suits. **dog trials** Austral. & NZ a public competitive display of the skills of sheepdogs. **dog-violet** any of various scentless wild violets, esp. *Viola riviniana*. **go to the dogs** *sl.* deteriorate, be ruined. **hair of the dog** further drink to cure the effects of drink. **like a dog's dinner** colloq. smartly or flashily (dressed, arranged, etc.). **not a dog's chance** no chance at all. **put on dog** colloq. behave pretentiously. □□ **doglike** *adj.* [OE *docga*, of unkn. orig.]

dogberry /ˈdɒgbərɪ/ *n.* (*pl.* **-ies**) the fruit of the dogwood.

dogcart /ˈdɒgkɑːt/ *n.* a two-wheeled driving-cart with cross seats back to back.

doge /dəʊdʒ/ *n.* hist. the chief magistrate of the former republic of Venice or Genoa. [F f. It. f. Venetian *doze* f. L *dux ducis* leader]

dogfight /ˈdɒgfaɪt/ *n.* **1** a close combat between fighter aircraft. **2** uproar; a fight like that between dogs.

dogfish /ˈdɒgfɪʃ/ *n.* (*pl.* same or **dogfishes**) any of various small sharks esp. of the families Scyliorhinidae or Squalidae.

dogged /ˈdɒgɪd/ *adj.* tenacious; grimly persistent. □ **it's dogged as does it** colloq. persistence succeeds. □□ **doggedly** *adv.* **doggedness** *n.* [ME f. DOG + -ED[1]]

dogger[1] /ˈdɒgə(r)/ *n.* a two-masted bluff-bowed Dutch fishing-boat. [ME f. MDu., = fishing-boat]

dogger[2] /ˈdɒgə(r)/ n. Geol. a large spherical concretion occurring in sedimentary rock. [dial., = kind of iron-stone, perh. f. DOG]

Dogger Bank /ˈdɒgə(r)/ a submerged sandbank in the North Sea, about 115 km (70 miles) off the NE coast of England.

doggerel /ˈdɒgər(ə)l/ n. poor or trivial verse. [ME, app. f. DOG: cf. -REL]

Doggett's Coat and Badge /ˈdɒgɪt/ a rowing contest held each year among Thames watermen for an orange livery with a silver badge. It was instituted in 1715 by an Irish comedian, Thomas Doggett, and is now the oldest sculling race in the world.

doggie var. of DOGGY n.

doggish /ˈdɒgɪʃ/ adj. 1 of or like a dog. 2 currish, malicious, snappish. □□ **doggishly** adv. **doggishness** n.

doggo /ˈdɒgəʊ/ adv. □ **lie doggo** sl. lie motionless or hidden, making no sign. [prob. f. DOG: cf. -o]

doggone /ˈdɒgɒn/ adj., adv., & int. esp. US sl. —adj. & adv. damned. —int. expressing annoyance. [prob. f. dog on it = God damn it]

doggy /ˈdɒgɪ/ adj. & n. —adj. 1 of or like a dog. 2 devoted to dogs. —n. (also **doggie**) (pl. **-ies**) a little dog; a pet name for a dog. □ **doggy bag** a bag given to a customer in a restaurant or to a guest at a party etc. for putting leftovers in to take home. □□ **dogginess** n.

doghouse /ˈdɒghaʊs/ n. US a dog's kennel. □ **in the doghouse** sl. in disgrace or disfavour.

dogie /ˈdəʊgɪ/ n. US a motherless or neglected calf. [19th c.: orig. unkn.]

dogma /ˈdɒgmə/ n. 1 a a principle, tenet, or system of these, esp. as laid down by the authority of a Church. b such principles collectively. 2 an arrogant declaration of opinion. [L f. Gk dogma -matos opinion f. dokeō seem]

dogman /ˈdɒgmən/ n. (pl. **-men**) Austral. a person giving directional signals to the operator of a crane, often while sitting on the crane's load.

dogmatic /dɒgˈmætɪk/ adj. 1 a (of a person) given to asserting or imposing personal opinions; arrogant. b intolerantly authoritative. 2 a of or in the nature of dogma; doctrinal. b based on a priori principles, not on induction. □□ **dogmatically** adv. [LL dogmaticus f. Gk dogmatikos (as DOGMA)]

dogmatics /dɒgˈmætɪks/ n. 1 the study of religious dogmas; dogmatic theology. 2 a system of dogma. [DOGMATIC]

dogmatism /ˈdɒgmə₁tɪz(ə)m/ n. a tendency to be dogmatic. □□ **dogmatist** n. [F dogmatisme f. med.L dogmatismus (as DOGMA)]

dogmatize /ˈdɒgmə₁taɪz/ v. (also **-ise**) 1 intr. make positive unsupported assertions; speak dogmatically. 2 tr. express (a principle etc.) as a dogma. [F dogmatiser or f. LL dogmatizare f. Gk (as DOGMA)]

do-gooder /duːˈgʊdə(r)/ n. a well-meaning but unrealistic philanthropist or reformer. □□ **do-good** /ˈduːgʊd/ adj. & n. **do-goodery** n. **do-goodism** n.

dogsbody /ˈdɒgz₁bɒdɪ/ n. (pl. **-ies**) 1 colloq. a drudge. 2 Naut. sl. a junior officer.

dogshore /ˈdɒgʃɔː(r)/ n. a temporary wooden support for a ship just before launching.

dogskin /ˈdɒgskɪn/ n. leather made of or imitating dog's skin, used for gloves.

dogtrot /ˈdɒgtrɒt/ n. a gentle easy trot.

dogwatch /ˈdɒgwɒtʃ/ n. Naut. either of two short watches (4–6 or 6–8 p.m.).

dogwood /ˈdɒgwʊd/ n. 1 any of various shrubs of the genus Cornus, esp. the wild cornel with dark red branches, greenish-white flowers, and purple berries, found in woods and hedgerows. 2 any of various similar trees. 3 the wood of the dogwood.

DoH abbr. (in the UK) Department of Health.

doh /dəʊ/ n. (also **do**) Mus. 1 (in tonic sol-fa) the first and eighth note of a major scale. 2 the note C in the fixed-doh system. [18th c.: f. It. do]

Doha /ˈdəʊhə/ the capital of Qatar; pop. (1986) 217,300.

doily /ˈdɔɪlɪ/ n. (also **doyley**) (pl. **-ies** or **-eys**) a small ornamental mat of paper, lace, etc., on a plate for cakes etc. [orig. the name of a fabric: f. Doiley, the name of a draper]

doing /ˈduːɪŋ/ n. 1 a an action; the performance of a deed (famous for his doings; it was my doing). b activity, effort (it takes a lot of doing). 2 colloq. a scolding; a beating. 3 (in pl.) sl. things needed; adjuncts; things whose names are not known (have we got all the doings?).

doit /dɔɪt/ n. archaic a very small amount of money. [MLG doyt, MDu. duit, of unkn. orig.]

dojo /ˈdəʊdʒəʊ/ n. (pl. **-os**) 1 a room or hall in which judo and other martial arts are practised. 2 a mat on which judo etc. is practised. [Jap.]

dol. abbr. dollar(s).

Dolby /ˈdɒlbɪ/ n. propr. an electronic noise-reduction system used esp. in tape-recording to reduce hiss. [R. M. Dolby, US inventor]

dolce far niente /₁dɒltʃeɪ ₁fɑː niːˈentɪ/ n. pleasant idleness. [It., = sweet doing nothing]

dolce vita /₁dɒltʃeɪ ˈviːtə/ n. a life of pleasure and luxury. [It., = sweet life]

doldrums /ˈdɒldrəmz/ n.pl. (usu. prec. by the) 1 low spirits; a feeling of boredom or depression. 2 a period of inactivity or state of stagnation. 3 an equatorial ocean region of calms, sudden storms, and light unpredictable winds. [prob. after dull and tantrum]

dole[1] /dəʊl/ n. & v. —n. 1 (usu. prec. by the) Brit. colloq. benefit claimable by the unemployed from the State. 2 a a charitable distribution. b a charitable (esp. sparing, niggardly) gift of food, clothes, or money. 3 archaic one's lot or destiny. —v.tr. (usu. foll. by out) deal out sparingly. □ **dole-bludger** Austral. sl. one who allegedly prefers the dole to work. **on the dole** Brit. colloq. receiving State benefit for the unemployed. [OE dāl f. Gmc]

dole[2] /dəʊl/ n. poet. grief, woe; lamentation. [ME f. OF do(e)l etc. f. pop.L dolus f. L dolēre grieve]

doleful /ˈdəʊlfʊl/ adj. 1 mournful, sad. 2 dreary, dismal. □□ **dolefully** adv. **dolefulness** n. [ME f. DOLE[2] + -FUL]

dolerite /ˈdɒlə₁raɪt/ n. a coarse basaltic rock. [F dolérite f. Gk doleros deceptive (because it is difficult to distinguish from diorite)]

dolichocephalic /₁dɒlɪ₁kəʊsɪˈfælɪk/ adj. (also **dolichocephalous** /-ˈsefələs/) having a skull that is longer than it is wide, with a cephalic index of less than or equal to 75.9. Examples of dolichocephalic populations occur in the peoples of the Iberian Peninsula, Sardinia, Corsica, Sicily, south Italy, parts of France, the British Isles, Norway, and Sweden. □□ **dolichocephalism** /-ˈsefəlɪz(ə)m/ n. **dolichocephaly** /-ˈsefəlɪ/ n. [Gk dolikhos long + -CEPHALIC, -CEPHALOUS]

Dolin /ˈdəʊlɪn, ˈdɒl-/, Anton (1904–83), real name Sydney Francis Patrick Chippendall Healey-Kay, British dancer, choreographer, teacher, actor, and writer. In 1935 he founded with Markova the Markova–Dolin Ballet, which toured until 1938, and in 1940 he joined the Ballet Theatre in New York. From another troupe newly formed with Markova the London Festival Ballet emerged in 1950, of which he became artistic director and first soloist until 1961. Later he pursued a worldwide freelance career as a teacher.

dolina /dɒˈliːnə/ n. (also **doline** /dɒˈliːn/) Geol. an extensive depression or basin. [Russ. dolina valley]

doll /dɒl/ n. & v. —n. 1 a small model of a human figure, esp. a baby or a child, as a child's toy. 2 a colloq. a pretty but silly young woman. b sl. a young woman, esp. an attractive one. 3 a ventriloquist's dummy. —v.tr. & intr. (foll. by up) dress up smartly. □ **doll's house** 1 a miniature toy house for dolls. 2 a very small house. [pet form of the name Dorothy]

dollar /ˈdɒlə(r)/ n. 1 the chief monetary unit in the US, Canada, and Australia. (See below.) 2 the chief monetary unit of certain countries in the Pacific, West Indies, SE Asia, Africa, and S. America. □ **dollar area** the area in which currency is linked to the US dollar. **dollar diplomacy** diplomatic activity aimed at advancing a country's international influence by furthering its financial and commercial interests abroad. **dollar gap** the excess of a country's import trade with the dollar area over the corresponding export trade. **dollar mark** (or **sign**) the sign $, representing a dollar. **dollar spot 1** a fungal disease of lawns etc. **2** a discoloured patch caused by this. [LG *daler* f. G *Taler*, short for *Joachimstaler*, a coin from the silver-mine of *Joachimstal* in what is now Czechoslovakia]

The dollar's ancestors were the Spanish peso (widely used as currency in North and South America in the 17th–18th c.) and the Bohemian *Joachimsthaler* of the early 16th c. The Spanish 'dollar' was formally retained as the standard unit of currency (with decimal subdivisions) in 1785. The first true American dollar was minted in 1794, but Spanish dollars continued in use and remained legal tender until 1857. The origin of the dollar sign $ is uncertain. It may be a modification of the figure 8 (representing 8 reals, the value of the peso), with upright strokes symbolizing the two architectural columns (representing the Pillars of Hercules) which for several centuries were conspicuous on the obverse of the Spanish peso; there are other less plausible suggestions.

Dollfuss /ˈdɒlfʊs/, Engelbert (1892–1934), Chancellor of Austria. After coming to power in 1932, Dollfuss attempted to govern without parliament in order better to oppose Nazi attempts to force Anschluss (union) with Germany. During an attempted Nazi coup in July 1934, he was assassinated by German SS troops dressed as Austrian soldiers, but his successor was able to prevent Anschluss until 1938.

dollhouse /ˈdɒlhaʊs/ n. US = *doll's house* (see DOLL).

dollop /ˈdɒləp/ n. & v. —n. a shapeless lump of food etc. —v.tr. (**dolloped, dolloping**) (usu. foll. by *out*) serve out in large shapeless quantities. [perh. f. Scand.]

dolly /ˈdɒlɪ/ n., v., & adj. —n. (pl. **-ies**) **1** a child's name for a doll. **2** a movable platform for a cine-camera. **3** *Cricket colloq.* an easy catch or hit. **4** a stick for stirring in clothes-washing. **5** = *corn dolly* (see CORN[1]). **6** *colloq.* = *dolly-bird*. —v. (**-ies, -ied**) **1** *tr.* (foll. by *up*) dress up smartly. **2** *intr.* (foll. by *in, up*) move a cine-camera in or up to a subject, or out from it. —adj. (**dollier, dolliest**) **1** *Brit. colloq.* (esp. of a girl) attractive, stylish. **2** *Cricket colloq.* easily hit or caught. □ **dolly-bird** *Brit. colloq.* an attractive and stylish young woman. **dolly mixture** any of a mixture of small variously shaped and coloured sweets.

Dolly Varden /ˌdɒlɪ ˈvɑːd(ə)n/ n. **1** a woman's large hat with one side drooping and with a floral trimming. **2** a brightly spotted char, *Salvelinus malma*, of western N. America. [a character in Dickens's *Barnaby Rudge*]

dolma /ˈdɒlmə/ n. (pl. **dolmas** or **dolmades** /-ˈmɑːðez/) an E. European delicacy of spiced rice or meat etc. wrapped in vine or cabbage leaves. [Turk. f. *dolmak* fill: be filled: *dolmades* f. mod.Gk]

dolman /ˈdɒlmən/ n. **1** a long Turkish robe open in front. **2** a hussar's jacket worn with the sleeves hanging loose. **3** a woman's mantle with capelike or dolman sleeves. □ **dolman sleeve** a loose sleeve cut in one piece with the body of the coat etc. [ult. f. Turk. *dolama*]

dolmen /ˈdɒlmən/ n. a megalithic tomb with a large flat stone laid on upright ones. [F, perh. f. Cornish *tolmên* hole of stone]

dolomite /ˈdɒləmaɪt/ n. a mineral or rock of calcium magnesium carbonate. □□ **dolomitic** /ˌdɒləˈmɪtɪk/ adj. [F f. D. de *Dolomieu*, Fr. geologist d. 1801]

Dolomite Mountains /ˈdɒləmaɪt/ (also **Dolomites**) a range of the Alps in northern Italy, so named because the characteristic rock of the region is dolomitic limestone.

dolorous /ˈdɒlərəs/ adj. *literary* or *joc.* **1** distressing, painful; doleful, dismal. **2** distressed, sad. □□ **dolorously** adv. [ME f. OF *doleros* f. LL *dolorosus* (as DOLOUR)]

dolour /ˈdɒlə(r)/ n. (US **dolor**) *literary* sorrow, distress. [ME f. OF f. L *dolor -oris* pain, grief]

dolphin /ˈdɒlfɪn/ n. **1** any of various porpoise-like sea mammals of the family Delphinidae having a slender beaklike snout. There are many ancient (and some modern) stories of the dolphin's intelligence and friendliness towards people. **2** (in general use) = DORADO 1. **3** a bollard, pile, or buoy for mooring. **4** a structure for protecting the pier of a bridge. **5** a curved fish in heraldry, sculpture, etc. [ME, also *delphin* f. L *delphinus* f. Gk *delphis -inos*]

dolphinarium /ˌdɒlfɪˈneərɪəm/ n. (pl. **dolphinariums**) an aquarium for dolphins, esp. one open to the public.

dolt /dəʊlt/ n. a stupid person. □□ **doltish** adj. **doltishly** adv. **doltishness** n. [app. related to *dol, dold*, obs. var. of DULL]

Dom /dɒm/ n. **1** a title prefixed to the names of some Roman Catholic dignitaries, and Benedictine and Carthusian monks. **2** the Portuguese equivalent of Don (see DON[1]). [L *dominus* master: sense 2 through Port.]

-dom /dəm/ suffix forming nouns denoting: **1** state or condition (*freedom*). **2** rank or status (*earldom*). **3** domain (*kingdom*). **4** a class of people (or the attitudes etc. associated with them) regarded collectively (*officialdom*). [OE *-dōm*, orig. = DOOM]

domain /dəˈmeɪn/ n. **1** an area under one rule; a realm. **2** an estate or lands under one control. **3** a sphere of control or influence. **4** *Math.* the set of possible values of an independent variable. **5** *Physics* a discrete region of magnetism in ferromagnetic material. □□ **domanial** /dəˈmeɪnɪəl/ adj. [ME f. F *domaine*, OF *demeine* DEMESNE, assoc. with L *dominus* lord]

domaine /dəˈmeɪn/ n. a vineyard. [F: see DOMAIN]

dome /dəʊm/ n. & v. —n. **1 a** a rounded vault as a roof, with a circular, elliptical, or polygonal base; a large cupola. **b** the revolving openable hemispherical roof of an observatory. **2 a** a natural vault or canopy (of the sky, trees, etc.). **b** the rounded summit of a hill etc. **3** *Geol.* a dome-shaped structure. **4** *sl.* the head. **5** *poet.* a stately building. —v.tr. (usu. as **domed** adj.) cover with or shape as a dome. □□ **domelike** adj. [F *dôme* f. It. *duomo* cathedral, dome f. L *domus* house]

Dome of the Rock an Islamic shrine in Jerusalem, surrounding the sacred rock on which, according to tradition, Abraham prepared to sacrifice his son (Gen. 22: 9) and from which the Prophet Muhammad made his miraculous midnight ascent into heaven. Built in the area of Solomon's Temple and dating from the end of the 7th c., to Muslims it is the third most holy place, after Mecca and Medina. The expanse of rough irregular rock that forms its centre contrasts starkly with the strict Byzantine geometry and ornate decoration of the surrounding structure, while the exterior is of rich mosaic work capped by a golden dome.

Domesday /ˈduːmzdeɪ/ n. (in full **Domesday Book**) a survey of the lands of England, excluding only London, Winchester, and the four northern counties, compiled on the orders of William the Conqueror in 1086 'to find out what and how much each landholder held in land and livestock, and what it was worth' in order to provide a proper basis for taxation. The most comprehensive survey of property carried out in medieval times, it caused much popular discontent at the time of its compilation, and was given its name because, like the Day of Judgement, there could be no appeal against it. [ME var. of doomsday, as being a book of final authority]

domestic /dəˈmestɪk/ adj. & n. —adj. **1** of the home, household, or family affairs. **2 a** of one's own country, not foreign or international. **b** home-grown or home-made. **3** (of an animal) kept by or living with man. **4** fond of home life. —n. a household servant. □ **domestic science** the study of household management. □□ **domestically** adv. [F *domestique* f. L *domesticus* f. *domus* home]

domesticate /dəˈmestɪˌkeɪt/ v.tr. **1** tame (an animal) to live with humans. **2** accustom to home life and management. **3** naturalize (a plant or animal). □□ **domesticable** /-kəb(ə)l/ adj. **domestication** /-ˈkeɪʃ(ə)n/ n. [med.L *domesticare* (as DOMESTIC)]

domesticity /ˌdɒmeˈstɪsɪtɪ, ˌdəʊ-/ n. **1** the state of being domestic. **2** domestic or home life.

domicile /ˈdɒmɪˌsaɪl, -sɪl/ n. & v. (also **domicil** /-sɪl/) —n. **1** a dwelling-place; one's home. **2** *Law* **a** a place of permanent residence. **b** the fact of residing. **3** the place at which a bill of exchange is made payable. —v.tr. **1** (usu. as **domiciled** adj.) (usu. foll. by *at, in*) establish or settle in a place. **2** (usu. foll. by *at*) make (a bill of exchange) payable at a certain place. [ME f. OF f. L *domicilium* f. *domus* home]

domiciliary /ˌdɒmɪˈsɪlɪərɪ/ adj. of a dwelling-place (esp. of a doctor's, official's, etc., visit to a person's home). [F *domiciliaire* f. med.L *domiciliarius* (as DOMICILE)]

dominance /ˈdɒmɪnəns/ n. 1 the state of being dominant. 2 control, authority.

dominant /ˈdɒmɪnənt/ adj. & n. —adj. 1 dominating, prevailing, most influential. 2 (of a high place) prominent, overlooking others. 3 a (of an allele) expressed even when inherited from only one parent. b (of an inherited characteristic) appearing in an individual even when its allelic counterpart is also inherited (cf. RECESSIVE). —n. Mus. the fifth note of the diatonic scale of any key. □□ **dominantly** adv. [F f. L dominari (as DOMINATE)]

dominate /ˈdɒmɪˌneɪt/ v. 1 tr. & (foll. by over) intr. have a commanding influence on; exercise control over (fear dominated them for years; dominates over his friends). 2 intr. (of a person, sound, feature of a scene, etc.) be the most influential or conspicuous. 3 tr. & (foll. by over) intr. (of a building etc.) have a commanding position over; overlook. □□ **dominator** n. [L dominari dominat- f. dominus lord]

domination /ˌdɒmɪˈneɪʃ(ə)n/ n. 1 command, control. 2 the act or an instance of dominating; the process of being dominated. 3 (in pl.) angelic beings of the fourth order of the celestial hierarchy. [ME f. OF f. L dominatio -onis (as DOMINATE)]

domineer /ˌdɒmɪˈnɪə(r)/ v.intr. (often as **domineering** adj.) behave in an arrogant and overbearing way. □□ **domineeringly** adv. [Du. domineren f. F dominer]

Domingo /dɒˈmɪŋgəʊ/ Placido (1941–), Spanish tenor, an outstanding exponent of lyrical and heroic roles especially in the operas of Verdi and Puccini.

Dominic /ˈdɒmɪnɪk/, St (c.1170–1221), Spanish priest, founder of the order named after him (see DOMINICAN). In 1203 he began his mission to convert the heretics known as the Albigenses, who were flourishing in SW Europe. In this he met with little success, but from it arose his foundation of a religious order dedicated to preaching and teaching. An austere figure and less popular than St Francis of Assisi, his contemporary, Dominic was a man of great integrity, humility, and courage. He is traditionally, but erroneously, held to have instituted the rosary. Feast day (now) 8 Aug.

Dominica /ˌdɒmɪˈniːkə/ a mountainous island in the West Indies, the loftiest of the Lesser Antilles; pop. (est. 1988) 97,800; official language, English; capital, Roseau. It was named by Columbus who discovered it on a Sunday (L dies domenica the Lord's day) in 1493, and after much Anglo-French rivalry came into British possession at the end of the 18th c., becoming an independent republic within the Commonwealth in 1978. □□ **Dominican** adj. & n.

dominical /dəˈmɪnɪk(ə)l/ adj. 1 of the Lord's day, of Sunday. 2 of the Lord (Jesus Christ). □ **dominical letter** the one of the seven letters A–G indicating the dates of Sundays in a year. [F dominical or L dominicalis f. L dominicus f. dominus lord]

Dominican /dəˈmɪnɪkən/ adj. & n. —adj. 1 of or relating to St Dominic or the order of preaching friars which he founded. (See below.) 2 of or relating to either of the two orders of female religious founded on Dominican principles. —n. a Dominican friar, nun, or sister (see also Black Friar). [med.L Dominicanus f. Dominicus L name of Domingo de Guzmán (St Dominic)]

The Dominican order was founded by St Dominic in 1215–16, and followed the established rule of St Augustine. It is known also as Black Friars (from the black cloak worn over a white habit) or in France as Jacobins. Its members are specially devoted to preaching and study, and their chief interest was, and is, educational. During the Middle Ages they supplied many leaders of European thought, including Albertus Magnus and St Thomas Aquinas; the popes used them for preaching crusades and for staffing the Inquisition. They followed the Portuguese and Spanish explorers, and though with the rise of new orders at the Reformation (especially the Jesuits, often their rivals) they fell into the background, they remain one of the most influential orders and retain their original characteristics as champions of learning and orthodoxy.

Dominican Republic /dəˈmɪnɪkən/ a country in the Caribbean, the Spanish-speaking eastern portion of the island named Hispaniola by Columbus, who discovered it in 1492; pop. (est. 1988) 7,136,750; official language, Spanish; capital, Santo Domingo. The Republic is the former Spanish colony of Santo Domingo, the part of Hispaniola which Spain retained when she ceded the western portion (now Haiti) to France in 1697. After the colony of Santo Domingo had itself been made over to France in 1795 and twice been overrun by Haiti, a Republic was proclaimed in 1844. The history of the Republic has been turbulent, culminating in the ruthless dictatorship (1930–61) of Rafael Trujillo Molina. An unsettled period followed, with civil war and US military intervention; a new constitution was introduced in 1966. The country occupies a strategic position on major sea routes leading from both Europe and the US to the Panama Canal. □□ **Dominican** adj. & n.

dominie /ˈdɒmɪnɪ/ n. Sc. a schoolmaster. [later spelling of domine sir, voc. of L dominus lord]

dominion /dəˈmɪnɪən/ n. 1 sovereignty, control. 2 the territory of a sovereign or government; a domain. 3 hist. the title of each of the self-governing territories of the British Commonwealth. [ME f. OF f. med.L dominio -onis f. L dominium f. dominus lord]

domino /ˈdɒmɪˌnəʊ/ n. (pl. -oes) 1 a any of 28 small oblong pieces marked with 0–6 pips in each half. b (in pl., usu. treated as sing.) a game played with these. It was played anciently in China but was unknown in Europe (where it may have arisen independently) before the 18th c., and was introduced to England possibly by French prisoners by about 1800. 2 a loose cloak with a mask for the upper part of the face, worn at masquerades. □ **domino theory** the theory that a political event etc. in one country will cause similar events in neighbouring countries, like a row of falling dominoes. [F, prob. f. L dominus lord, but unexplained]

Domitian /dəˈmɪʃ(ə)n/ (Titus Flavius Domitianus 51–96), Roman emperor 81–96, son of Vespasian. An energetic but autocratic ruler, his assassination ended the Reign of Terror of his last few years. His absolutism found expression in large building programmes, including monumental palace-buildings on the Palatine Hill in Rome.

Don /dɒn/ a river of the southern USSR, rising south-east of Moscow and flowing for a distance of 1,958 km (1,224 miles) to the Sea of Azov.

don[1] /dɒn/ n. 1 a university teacher, esp. a senior member of a college at Oxford or Cambridge. 2 (**Don**) a a Spanish title prefixed to a forename. b a Spanish gentleman; a Spaniard. [Sp. f. L dominus lord]

don[2] /dɒn/ v.tr. (**donned, donning**) put on (clothing). [= do on]

dona /ˈdəʊnə/ n. (also **donah**) Brit. sl. a woman; a sweetheart. [Sp. doña or Port. dona f. L (as DONNA)]

Donald Duck /ˈdɒnəld/ a Disney cartoon character, a duck with a rubbery rear, twistable neck, and a big mouth, who first appeared in 1934. His lines were quacked by Clarence Nash (d. 1985).

donate /dəʊˈneɪt/ v.tr. give or contribute (money etc.), esp. voluntarily to a fund or institution. □□ **donator** n. [back-form. f. DONATION]

Donatello /ˌdɒnəˈteləʊ/, Donato di Niccolo (1386–1466), Florentine sculptor, one of the pioneers of scientific perspective. He is famous especially for his lifelike sculptures, including the bronze David, his most classical work. He was in Padua from 1443 to 1453, where he made the Gattamelata, the first equestrian statue to be created since antiquity. On his return to Florence he reacted somewhat against classical principles, evolving a very moving late style in which distortion is used to convey dramatic and emotional intensity, e.g. his John the Baptist and the carved wooden statue St Mary Magdalene.

donation /dəʊˈneɪʃ(ə)n/ n. 1 the act or an instance of donating. 2 something, esp. an amount of money, donated. [ME f. OF f. L donatio -onis f. donare give f. donum gift]

Donatist /ˈdəʊnətɪst/ n. a member of a Christian sect which arose in North Africa in 311 out of a dispute about the election of the bishop of Carthage, and which maintained that it was the only true and pure Church and that the ordinations of others were invalid. □□ **Donatism** n. [LL Donatista follower of Donatus, bishop of Carthage, or a schismatic leader of the same name]

donative /'dɔʊnətɪv, 'dɒn-/ *n. & adj.* —*n.* a gift or donation, esp. one given formally or officially as a largess. —*adj.* **1** given as a donation or bounty. **2** *hist.* (of a benefice) given directly, not presentative. [ME f. L *donativum* gift, largess f. *donare*: see DONATION]

Donatus /də'neɪtəs/, Aelius (4th c.) Roman grammarian. His two grammatical treatises, the *Ars Minor* (*Lesser Art*) and the *Ars Maior* (*Major Art*) were favourite school-books in the Middle Ages.

Donau see DANUBE.

Donbas, Donbass see DONETS BASIN.

done /dʌn/ *past part.* of DO¹. —*adj.* **1** *colloq.* socially acceptable (*the done thing; it isn't done*). **2** (often with *in, up*) *colloq.* tired out. **3** (esp. as *int.* in reply to an offer etc.) accepted. □ **be done with** have finished with, be finished with. **done for** *colloq.* in serious trouble. **have done** have ceased or finished. **have done with** be rid of; have finished dealing with.

donee /dəʊ'niː/ *n.* the recipient of a gift. [DONOR + -EE]

Donegal /ˌdɒnɪ'ɡɔːl/ a county in the province of Ulster in the extreme north-west of the Republic of Ireland; pop. (est. 1986) 129,400; capital, Lifford.

Donets Basin /dɒ'njets/ (also **Donbas, Donbass** /dɒn'bæs/) a coalmining region of the USSR, in the valley of the Donets and lower Dnieper Rivers.

Donetsk /dɒ'njetsk/ the leading industrial city of the Donbas mining region of Ukraine; pop. (est. 1987) 1,090,000.

dong¹ /dɒŋ/ *v. & n.* —*v.* **1** *intr.* make the deep sound of a large bell. **2** *tr. Austral. & NZ colloq.* hit, punch. —*n.* **1** the deep sound of a large bell. **2** *Austral. & NZ colloq.* a heavy blow. [imit.]

dong² /dɒŋ/ *n.* the chief monetary unit of Vietnam. [Vietnamese]

donga /'dɒŋɡə/ *n. S.Afr. & Austral.* **1** a dry watercourse. **2** a ravine caused by erosion. [Zulu]

dongle /'dɒŋɡ(ə)l/ *n. Computing* a security attachment required by a computer to enable protected software to be used. [arbitrary form.]

Donizetti /ˌdɒnɪ'tsetɪ/, Gaetano (1797–1848), the leading Italian composer between the death of Bellini (1835) and Verdi's first great success in 1842. His tragedies—*Anna Bolena* (1830), *Maria Stuarda* (1835), and *Lucia di Lammermoor* (1835)—all reveal the prevailing taste for librettos set in the wild and romantic north, and his comedies *L'elisir d'amore* (1832) and *La fille du régiment* (1840) reveal him as a master rivalling Rossini.

donjon /'dɒndʒ(ə)n, 'dʌn-/ *n.* the great tower or innermost keep of a castle. [archaic spelling of DUNGEON]

Don Juan /ˌdɒn 'dʒuːən, ˌdɒn 'wɑːn/ a legendary Spanish nobleman of dissolute life. According to a Spanish story first dramatized by Gabriel Tellez (d. 1641) and subsequently by Molière and in Mozart's opera *Don Giovanni*, he was Don Juan Tenorio of Seville. The name is used allusively of a heartless seducer of women, a libertine.

donkey /'dɒŋkɪ/ *n.* (*pl.* -**eys**) **1** a domestic ass. **2** *colloq.* a stupid or foolish person. □ **donkey engine** a small auxiliary engine. **donkey jacket** a thick weatherproof jacket worn by workers and as a fashion garment. **donkey's years** *colloq.* a very long time. **donkey-work** the laborious part of a job; drudgery. [earlier with pronunc. as *monkey*: perh. f. DUN¹, or the Christian name *Duncan*]

Donkin /'dɒŋkɪn/, Bryan (1768–1855), English engineer who made pioneering contributions in several fields, including paper-making and printing, patenting (with Richard Bacon) the first rotary press. Following the work of Nicholas Appert in France he successfully developed the method of food preservation by heat sterilization and sealing the food inside a container made of sheet steel—the ubiquitous tin can (see TIN).

donna /'dɒnə/ *n.* **1** an Italian, Spanish, or Portuguese lady. **2** (**Donna**) the title of such a lady. [It. f. L *domina* mistress fem. of *dominus*: cf. DON¹]

Donne /dʌn/, John (1572–1631), English poet and divine, who was born into a devout Catholic family but renounced his faith *c.*1593. After troubled early years, when his prospects of worldly advancement were ruined by his secret marriage to his patron's niece, he turned to a successful career in the Church, becoming

dean of St Paul's in 1621 and one of the most celebrated of the metaphysical poets; his love poetry (*Song and Sonnets*), satires, and divine poems all display his brilliant wit, passionate temperament, verbal ingenuity, and creative vigour. Out of fashion in the 18th–19th c., his works are now widely admired, interest having been aroused partly by T. S. Eliot's reappraisal.

donnée /'dɒneɪ/ *n.* (also **donné**) **1** the subject or theme of a story etc. **2** a basic fact or assumption. [F, fem. or masc. past part. of *donner* give]

donnish /'dɒnɪʃ/ *adj.* like or resembling a college don, esp. in supposed pedantry. □□ **donnishly** *adv.* **donnishness** *n.*

donor /'dəʊnə(r)/ *n.* **1** a person who gives or donates something (e.g. to a charity). **2** one who provides blood for a transfusion, semen for insemination, or an organ or tissue for transplantation. **3** *Chem.* an atom or molecule that provides a pair of electrons in forming a coordinate bond. **4** *Physics* an impurity atom in a semiconductor which contributes a conducting electron to the material. □ **donor card** an official card authorizing use of organs for transplant, carried by the donor. [ME f. AF *donour*, OF *doneur* f. L *donator -oris* f. *donare* give]

Don Quixote see QUIXOTE.

don't /dəʊnt/ *contr.* do not. —*n.* a prohibition (*dos and don'ts*).

donut *US var.* of DOUGHNUT.

doodad /'duːdæd/ *n. US* = DOODAH. [20th c.: orig. unkn.]

doodah /'duːdɑː/ *n.* **1** a fancy article; a trivial ornament. **2** a gadget or 'thingummy'. □ **all of a doodah** excited, dithering. [from the refrain of the song *Camptown Races*]

doodle /'duːd(ə)l/ *v. & n.* —*v.intr.* scribble or draw, esp. absent-mindedly. —*n.* a scrawl or drawing made. □ **doodle-bug 1** *US* any of various insects, esp. the larva of an ant-lion. **2** *US* an unscientific device for locating minerals. **3** *colloq.* a flying bomb. □□ **doodler** *n.* [orig. = foolish person; cf. LG *dudelkopf*]

doohickey /'duːˌhɪkɪ/ *n.* (*pl.* -**eys**) *US colloq.* a small object, esp. mechanical. [DOODAD + HICKEY]

doom /duːm/ *n. & v.* —*n.* **1 a** a grim fate or destiny. **b** death or ruin. **2 a** a condemnation; a judgement or sentence. **b** the Last Judgement (*the crack of doom*). **3** *hist.* a statute, law, or decree. —*v.tr.* **1** (usu. foll. by *to*) condemn or destine (*a city doomed to destruction*). **2** (esp. as **doomed** *adj.*) consign to misfortune or destruction. [OE *dōm* statute, judgement f. Gmc: rel. to DO¹]

doomsday /'duːmzdeɪ/ *n.* the day of the Last Judgement. □ **till doomsday** for ever (cf. DOMESDAY). [OE *dōmes dæg*: see DOOM]

doomwatch /'duːmwɒtʃ/ *n.* organized vigilance or observation to avert danger, esp. from environmental pollution. □□ **doomwatcher** *n.*

door /dɔː(r)/ *n.* **1 a** a hinged, sliding, or revolving barrier for closing and opening an entrance to a building, room, cupboard, etc. **b** this as representing a house etc. (*lives two doors away*). **2 a** an entrance or exit; a doorway. **b** a means of access or approach. □ **close the door to** exclude the opportunity for. **door-case** (or -**frame**) the structure into which a door is fitted. **door-head** the upper part of a door-case. **door-keeper** = DOORMAN. **door-plate** a plate on the door of a house or room bearing the name of the occupant. **door-to-door** (of selling etc.) done at each house in turn. **lay** (or **lie**) **at the door of** impute (or be imputable) to. **leave the door open** ensure that an option remains available. **next door** in or to the next house or room. **next door to 1** in the next house to. **2** nearly, almost, near to. **open the door to** create an opportunity for. **out of doors** in or into the open air. □□ **doored** *adj.* (also in *comb.*). [OE *duru*, *dor* f. Gmc]

doorbell /'dɔːbel/ *n.* a bell in a house etc. rung by visitors outside to signal their arrival.

doorknob /'dɔːnɒb/ *n.* a knob for turning to release the latch of a door.

doorman /'dɔːmən/ *n.* (*pl.* -**men**) a person on duty at the door to a large building; a janitor or porter.

doormat /'dɔːmæt/ *n.* **1** a mat at an entrance for wiping mud etc. from the shoes. **2** a feebly submissive person.

doornail /'dɔːneɪl/ *n.* a nail with which doors were studded for strength or ornament. □ **dead as a doornail** completely or unmistakably dead.

Doornik see TOURNAI.

doorpost /'dɔːpəʊst/ n. each of the uprights of a door-frame, on one of which the door is hung.

doorstep /'dɔːstep/ n. & v. —n. **1** a step leading up to the outer door of a house etc. **2** sl. a thick slice of bread. —v.intr. (**-stepped, -stepping**) go from door to door selling, canvassing, etc. □ **on one's (or the) doorstep** very close.

doorstop /'dɔːstɒp/ n. a device for keeping a door open or to prevent it from striking a wall etc. when opened.

doorway /'dɔːweɪ/ n. an opening filled by a door.

dooryard /'dɔːjɑːd/ n. US a yard or garden near a house-door.

dop /dɒp/ n. S.Afr. **1** a cheap kind of brandy. **2** a tot of liquor. [Afrik.]

dopa /'dəʊpə/ n. Pharm. a crystalline amino acid derivative used in the treatment of Parkinsonism. The weakness and tremor of this disease are thought to be caused by a lack of the chemical dopamine; this deficiency is corrected by treatment with levodopa, which is converted to dopamine within the body. [G f. Dioxyphenylalanine, former name of the compound]

dopant /'dəʊpənt/ n. Electronics a substance used in doping a semiconductor.

dope /dəʊp/ n. & v. —n. **1** a varnish applied to the cloth surface of aeroplane parts to strengthen them, keep them airtight, etc. **2** a thick liquid used as a lubricant etc. **3** a substance added to petrol etc. to increase its effectiveness. **4 a** sl. a narcotic; a stupefying drug. **b** a drug etc. given to a horse or greyhound, or taken by an athlete, to affect performance. **5** sl. a stupid person. **6** sl. **a** information about a subject, esp. if not generally known. **b** misleading information. —v. **1** tr. administer dope to, drug. **2** tr. Electronics add an impurity to (a semiconductor) to produce a desired electrical characteristic. **3** tr. smear, daub; apply dope to. **4** intr. take addictive drugs. □ **dope out** sl. discover. □□ **doper** n. [Du. doop sauce f. doopen to dip]

dopey /'dəʊpɪ/ adj. (also **dopy**) (**dopier, dopiest**) colloq. **1 a** half asleep. **b** stupefied by or as if by a drug. **2** stupid, silly. □□ **dopily** adv. **dopiness** n.

doppelgänger /'dɒp(ə)lˌɡeŋə(r)/ n. an apparition or double of a living person. [G, = double-goer]

Dopper /'dɒpə(r)/ n. S.Afr. a member of the Gereformeerde Kerk, a strictly orthodox Calvinistic denomination, usu. regarded as old-fashioned in ideas etc.

Doppler effect /'dɒplə(r)/ n. (also **Doppler shift**) Physics an increase (or decrease) in the frequency of sound, light, or other waves as the source and observer move towards (or away) from each other. [C. J. Doppler, Austrian physicist d. 1853]

dopy var. of DOPEY.

dorado /də'rɑːdəʊ/ n. (pl. **-os**) **1** a blue and silver marine fish, Coryphaena hippurus, showing brilliant colours when dying out of water. **2** a brightly coloured freshwater-fish, Salminus maxillosus, native to S. America. [Sp. f. LL deauratus gilt f. aurum gold]

Dordogne /dɔː'dɔɪn/ an inland department of SW France containing numerous caves and rock-shelters that have yielded abundant remains of early humans and their artefacts and art. Fossils of both Neanderthal and Cro-Magnon man have been recovered from its caves and rock-shelters. The walls and ceilings of many of the caves and shelters have served as surfaces upon which the people of the upper palaeolithic expressed their artistic representations of animals, 'hunting magic', and abstract designs. The cave and shelter fillings have also yielded engraved and sculpted bones, antlers, ivory, and clay that have been produced by the populations responsible for the murals. The cave at Lascaux is but a single example of the vast richness of the department's art and archaeology.

Dordrecht /'dɔːdrext/ (abbr. **Dort** /dɔːt/) an industrial city and river port near the mouth of the Rhine, 20 km (12 miles) southeast of Rotterdam in the Dutch province of South Holland; pop. (1987) 107,871. Situated on one of the busiest river junctions in the world, it was the wealthiest town in The Netherlands until surpassed by Rotterdam in the 18th c.

Doré /'dɔːreɪ/, Gustave (1832–83), the most popular and successful French book illustrator of the mid 19th c. He was widely known for his illustrations to books such as Dante's *Inferno* (1861), *Don Quixote* (1862), and the Bible, and was so prolific that at one time he employed more than forty blockcutters. His style often shows a rather naïve but highly spirited love of the grotesque. Drawings of London done in 1869–71 were more sober studies of the poorer quarters of the city and captured the attention of van Gogh.

Dorian /'dɔːrɪən/ n. & adj. —n. (in pl.) the tribes speaking the Doric dialect of Greek who probably entered Greece from the north c.1100–1000 BC and by the 8th c. BC had settled most of the Peloponnese, the southernmost Aegean islands, and the SW corner of Asia Minor. While culturally distinct in architecture and dialect, the Dorians retained their political system only in Sparta and Crete where the ruling military class subjected the local peoples as serfs and dependants. (See DARK AGES.) —adj. of or relating to the Dorians or to Doris in Central Greece. □ **Dorian mode** Mus. the mode represented by the natural diatonic scale D–D. [L Dorius f. Gk Dōrios f. Dōros, the mythical ancestor]

Doric /'dɒrɪk/ adj. & n. —adj. **1** (of a dialect) broad, rustic. **2** Archit. of the oldest, sturdiest, and simplest of the Greek orders. —n. **1** rustic English or esp. Scots. **2** Archit. the Doric order. **3** the dialect of the Dorians in ancient Greece. [L Doricus f. Gk Dōrikos (as DORIAN)]

dorm /dɔːm/ n. colloq. dormitory. [abbr.]

dormant /'dɔːmənt/ adj. **1** lying inactive as in sleep; sleeping. **2 a** (of a volcano etc.) temporarily inactive. **b** (of potential faculties etc.) in abeyance. **3** (of plants) alive but not actively growing. **4** Heraldry (of a beast) lying with its head on its paws. □□ **dormancy** n. [ME f. OF, pres. part. of dormir f. L dormire sleep]

dormer /'dɔːmə(r)/ n. (in full **dormer window**) a projecting upright window in a sloping roof. [OF dormëor (as DORMANT)]

dormitory /'dɔːmɪtərɪ/ n. (pl. **-ies**) **1** a sleeping-room with several beds, esp. in a school or institution. **2** (in full **dormitory town** etc.) a small town or suburb from which people travel to work in a city etc. **3** US a university or college hall of residence or hostel. [ME f. L dormitorium f. dormire dormit- sleep]

Dormobile /'dɔːməˌbiːl/ n. propr. a type of motor caravan with a rear compartment convertible for sleeping and eating in. [blend of DORMITORY, AUTOMOBILE]

dormouse /'dɔːmaʊs/ n. (pl. **dormice**) any small mouselike hibernating rodent of the family Gliridae, having a long bushy tail. [ME: orig. unkn.]

dormy /'dɔːmɪ/ adj. Golf (of a player or side) ahead by as many holes as there are holes left to play (dormy five). [19th c.: orig. unkn.]

doronicum /də'rɒnɪkəm/ n. = leopard's bane (see LEOPARD). [mod.L (Linnaeus) ult. f. Arab. dārānaj]

dorp /dɔːp/ n. S.Afr. a village or small township. [Du. (as THORP)]

dorsal /'dɔːs(ə)l/ adj. Anat., Zool., & Bot. **1** of, on, or near the back (cf. VENTRAL). **2** ridge-shaped. □□ **dorsally** adv. [F dorsal or LL dorsalis f. L dorsum back]

Dorset /'dɔːsɪt/ a county of SW England; pop. (1981) 598,400; county town, Dorchester.

Dort see DORDRECHT.

Dortmund /'dɔːtmʊnd/ an industrial city in NW Germany, the southern terminus of the Dortmund-Ems Canal which links the Ruhr industrial area with the North Sea; pop. (1987) 568,700.

dory[1] /'dɔːrɪ/ n. (pl. **-ies**) any of various marine fish having a compressed body and flat head, esp. the John Dory, used as food. [ME f. F dorée fem. past part. of dorer gild (as DORADO)]

dory[2] /'dɔːrɪ/ n. (pl. **-ies**) US a flat-bottomed fishing-boat with high sides. [Miskito dóri dugout]

DOS /dɒs/ n. Computing a program for manipulating information on a disk. [abbr. of disk operating system]

dos-à-dos /ˌdəʊzɑː'dəʊ/ adj. & n. —adj. (of two books) bound together with a shared central board and facing in opposite directions. —n. (pl. same) a seat, carriage, etc., in which the occupants sit back to back (cf. DO-SE-DO). [F, = back to back]

dosage /'dəʊsɪdʒ/ n. **1** the giving of medicine in doses. **2** the size of a dose.

dose /dəʊs/ n. & v. —n. **1** an amount of a medicine or drug for taking or taken at one time. **2** a quantity of something administered or allocated (e.g. work, praise, punishment, etc.). **3** the amount of ionizing radiation received by a person or thing. **4** sl. a venereal infection. —v.tr. **1** treat (a person or animal) with doses of medicine. **2** give a dose or doses to. **3** adulterate or blend (esp. wine with spirit). □ **like a dose of salts** colloq. very fast and efficiently. [F f. LL dosis f. Gk dosis gift f. didōmi give]

do-se-do /ˌdəʊzɪˈdəʊ, ˌdəʊsɪ-/ n. (also **do-si-do**) (pl. **-os**) a figure in which two dancers pass round each other back to back and return to their original positions. [corrupt. of DOS-À-DOS]

dosh /dɒʃ/ n. sl. money. [20th c.: orig. unkn.]

dosimeter /dəʊˈsɪmɪtə(r)/ n. a device used to measure an absorbed dose of ionizing radiation. □□ **dosimetric** /-ˈmetrɪk/ adj. **dosimetry** n.

Dos Passos /dɒs ˈpæsɒs/, John Roderigo (1896–1970), American novelist, who also wrote poetry, essays, memoirs, and plays. His first important novel Three Soldiers (1921) has war as its subject. He is remembered chiefly for his novels of American life, Manhattan Transfer (1925) and U.S.A. (1938).

doss /dɒs/ v. & n. Brit. sl. —v.intr. (often foll. by down) sleep, esp. roughly or in cheap lodgings. —n. a bed, esp. in cheap lodgings. □ **doss-house** a cheap lodging-house, esp. for vagrants. [prob. = doss ornamental covering for a seat-back etc. f. OF dos ult. f. L dorsum back]

dossal /'dɒs(ə)l/ n. a hanging cloth behind an altar or round a chancel. [med.L dossale f. LL dorsalis DORSAL]

dosser /'dɒsə(r)/ n. Brit. sl. **1** a person who dosses. **2** = doss-house.

dossier /'dɒsɪə(r), -ɪˌeɪ/ n. a set of documents, esp. a collection of information about a person, event, or subject. [F, so called from the label on the back, f. dos back f. L dorsum]

dost /dʌst/ archaic 2nd sing. present of DO[1].

Dostoevsky /ˌdɒstɔɪˈefskɪ/, Fedor Mikhailovich (1821–81), Russian novelist who was arrested in 1849 as a member of the socialist Petrashevsky Circle and after a macabre mock execution sent to Siberia for four years, followed by four years as a private soldier. During his imprisonment he suffered a spiritual crisis and rejected his early socialist ideals, replacing them with orthodox religion and a faith in the Russian people; this period is reflected in Notes from the House of the Dead (1860–1). He made visits abroad during the 1860s, including one to London, which he saw as the centre of the capitalist world, and used this image to express the corruption of the modern scientific world in Notes from Underground (1864). The series of novels that are most admired include Crime and Punishment (1866), The Idiot (1868), The Devils (1872), and The Brothers Karamazov (1880). In these he reveals his genius for character analysis and conveys his religious and political ideas and basic philosophy—that human beings are morally improved by having to undergo physical pain and public humiliation. He influenced the development of the Russian novel through the use of urban settings and by powerful narrative tension.

DoT abbr. (in the UK) Department of Transport.

dot[1] /dɒt/ n. & v. —n. **1 a** a small spot, speck, or mark. **b** such a mark written or printed as part of an i or j, as a diacritical mark, as one of a series of marks to signify omission, or as a full stop. **c** a decimal point. **2** Mus. a dot used to denote the lengthening of a note or rest, or to indicate staccato. **3** the shorter signal of the two used in Morse code (cf. DASH n. 6). **4** a tiny or apparently tiny object (a dot on the horizon). —v.tr. (**dotted, dotting**) **1 a** mark with a dot or dots. **b** place a dot over (a letter). **2** Mus. mark (a note or rest) to show that the time value is increased by half. **3** (often foll. by about) scatter like dots. **4** partly cover as with dots (a sea dotted with ships). **5** sl. hit (dotted him one in the eye). □ **dot the i's and cross the t's** colloq. **1** be minutely accurate, emphasize details. **2** add the final touches to a task, exercise, etc. **dot matrix printer** Computing a printer with characters formed from dots printed by configurations of the tips of small wires. **dotted line** a line of dots on a document, esp. to show a place left for a signature. **on the dot** exactly on

time. **the year dot** Brit. colloq. far in the past. □□ **dotter** n. [OE dott head of a boil, perh. infl. by Du. dot knot]

dot[2] /dɒt/ n. a woman's dowry. [F f. L dos dotis]

dotage /'dəʊtɪdʒ/ n. feeble-minded senility (in his dotage).

dotard /'dəʊtəd/ n. a person who is feeble-minded, esp. from senility. [ME f. DOTE + -ARD]

dote /dəʊt/ v.intr. **1** (foll. by on, upon) be foolishly or excessively fond of. **2** be silly or feeble-minded, esp. from old age. □□ **doter** n. **dotingly** adv. [ME, corresp. to MDu. doten be silly]

doth /dʌθ/ archaic 3rd sing. present of DO[1].

dotterel /'dɒtərəl/ n. a small migrant plover, Eudromias morinellus. [ME f. DOTE + -REL, named from the ease with which it is caught, taken to indicate stupidity]

dottle /'dɒt(ə)l/ n. a remnant of unburnt tobacco in a pipe. [DOT[1] + -LE[1]]

dotty /'dɒtɪ/ adj. (**dottier, dottiest**) colloq. **1** feeble-minded, silly. **2** eccentric. **3** absurd. **4** (foll. by about, on) infatuated with; obsessed by. □□ **dottily** adv. **dottiness** n. [earlier = unsteady: f. DOT[1] + -Y[1]]

Douala /duːˈɑːlə/ the chief port and largest city of Cameroon; pop. (est. 1984) 784,000.

douane /duːˈɑːn/ n. a foreign custom-house. [F f. It. do(g)ana f. Turk. duwan, Arab. dīwān: cf. DIVAN]

Douay Bible /'duːeɪ, 'daʊeɪ/ n. (also **Douay version**) an English translation of the Bible formerly used in the Roman Catholic Church, completed at Douai in France early in the 17th c.

double /'dʌb(ə)l/ adj., adv., n., & v. —adj. **1 a** consisting of two usu. equal parts or things; twofold. **b** consisting of two identical parts. **2** twice as much or many (double the amount; double the number; double thickness). **3** having twice the usual size, quantity, strength, etc. (double whisky). **4** designed for two people (double bed). **5 a** having some part double. **b** (of a flower) having more than one circle of petals. **c** (of a domino) having the same number of pips on each half. **6** having two different roles or interpretations, esp. implying confusion or deceit (double meaning; leads a double life). **7** Mus. lower in pitch by an octave (double bassoon). —adv. **1** at or to twice the amount etc. (counts double). **2** two together (sleep double). —n. **1 a** a double quantity or thing; twice as much or many. **b** colloq. a double measure of spirits. **2 a** a counterpart of a person or thing; a person who looks exactly like another. **b** an understudy. **c** a wraith. **3** (in pl.) Sport (in lawn tennis) a game between two pairs of players. **4** Sport a pair of victories over the same team, a pair of championships at the same game, etc. **5** a system of betting in which the winnings and stake from the first bet are transferred to a second. **6** Bridge the doubling of an opponent's bid. **7** Darts a hit on the narrow ring enclosed by the two outer circles of a dartboard, scoring double. **8** a sharp turn, esp. of the tracks of a hunted animal, or the course of a river. —v. **1** tr. & intr. make or become twice as much or many; increase twofold; multiply by two. **2** tr. amount to twice as much as. **3 a** tr. fold or bend (paper, cloth, etc.) over on itself. **b** intr. become folded. **4 a** tr. (of an actor) play (two parts) in the same piece. **b** intr. (often foll. by for) be understudy etc. **5** intr. (usu. foll. by as) play a twofold role. **6** intr. turn sharply in flight or pursuit; take a tortuous course. **7** tr. Naut. sail round (a headland). **8** tr. Bridge make a call increasing the value of the points to be won or lost on (an opponent's bid). **9** Mus. **a** intr. (often foll. by on) play two or more musical instruments (the clarinettist doubles on tenor sax). **b** tr. add the same note in a higher or lower octave to (a note). **10** tr. clench (a fist). **11** intr. move at twice the usual speed; run. **12** Billiards **a** intr. rebound. **b** tr. cause to rebound. □ **at the double** running, hurrying. **bent double** folded, stooping. **double acrostic** see ACROSTIC. **double agent** one who spies simultaneously for two rival countries etc. **double axe** an axe with two blades, especially as a characteristic Minoan and Mycenaean tool and one of the most common Minoan religious symbols. **double back** take a new direction opposite to the previous one. **double-banking 1** double-parking. **2** Austral. & NZ riding two on a horse etc. **double-barrelled 1** (of a gun) having two barrels. **2** Brit. (of a surname) having two parts joined by a hyphen. **3** twofold. **double-bass 1** the largest and lowest-pitched instrument of the violin family, now possessing four strings (formerly three) and sounding an octave below the cello, with a range of nearly three octaves. **2** its player. **double bill** a programme with two principal items. **double bind** a dilemma. **double-blind** *adj.* (of a test or experiment) in which neither the tester nor the subject has knowledge of identities etc. that might lead to bias. —*n.* such a test or experiment. **double bluff** an action or statement intended to appear as a bluff, but in fact genuine. **double boiler** a saucepan with a detachable upper compartment heated by boiling water in the lower one. **double bond** *Chem.* a pair of bonds between two atoms in a molecule. **double-book** accept two reservations simultaneously for (the same seat, room, etc.). **double-breasted** (of a coat etc.) having two fronts overlapping across the body. **double-check** verify twice or in two ways. **double chin** a chin with a fold of loose flesh below it. **double-chinned** having a double chin. **double concerto** a concerto for two solo instruments. **double cream** thick cream with a high fat-content. **double-cross** *v.tr.* deceive or betray (a person one is supposedly helping). —*n.* an act of doing this. **double-crosser** a person who double-crosses. **double dagger** *Printing* = double obelus. **double-dealer** a deceiver. **double-dealing** *n.* deceit, esp. in business. —*adj.* deceitful; practising deceit. **double-decker 1** esp. *Brit.* a bus having an upper and lower deck. **2** *colloq.* anything consisting of two layers. **double-declutch** see DECLUTCH. **double decomposition** *Chem.* a chemical reaction involving exchange of radicals between two reactants: also called METATHESIS. **double density** *Computing* designating a storage device, esp. a disk, having twice the basic capacity. **double dummy** *Bridge* play with two hands exposed, allowing every card to be located. **double Dutch** *Brit. colloq.* incomprehensible talk. **double-dyed** deeply affected with guilt. **double eagle 1** a figure of a two-headed eagle. **2** *US Golf* = ALBATROSS. **3** *US* a coin worth twenty dollars. **double-edged 1** having two functions or (often contradictory) applications. **2** (of a knife etc.) having two cutting-edges. **double entry** a system of bookkeeping in which each transaction is entered as a debit in one account and a credit in another. **double exposure** *Photog.* the accidental or deliberate repeated exposure of a plate, film, etc. **double-faced 1** insincere. **2** (of a fabric or material) finished on both sides so that either may be used as the right side. **double fault** (in lawn tennis) two consecutive faults in serving. **double feature** a cinema programme with two full-length films. **double figures** the numbers from 10 to 99. **double first** *Brit.* **1** first-class honours in two subjects or examinations at a university. **2** a person achieving this. **double-fronted** (of a house) with principal windows on either side of the front door. **double-ganger** = DOPPELGÄNGER. **double glazing 1** a window consisting of two layers of glass with a space between them, designed to reduce loss of heat and exclude noise. **2** the provision of this. **double Gloucester** a kind of hard cheese orig. made in Gloucestershire. **double header 1** a train pulled by two locomotives coupled together. **2** *US* two games etc. in succession between the same opponents. **3** *Austral. colloq.* a coin with a head on both sides. **double helix** a pair of parallel helices with a common axis, esp. in the structure of the DNA molecule. **double-jointed** having joints that allow unusual bending of the fingers, limbs, etc. **double-lock** lock by a double turn of the key. **double negative** *Gram.* a negative statement containing two negative elements (e.g. *didn't say nothing*). ¶ Considered ungrammatical in standard English. **double obelus** (or **obelisk**) *Printing* a sign (‡) used to introduce a reference. **double or quits** a gamble to decide whether a player's loss or debt be doubled or cancelled. **double-park** park (a vehicle) alongside one that is already parked at the roadside. **double play** *Baseball* putting out two runners. **double pneumonia** pneumonia affecting both lungs. **double-quick** very quick or quickly. **double refraction** *Optics* refraction forming two separate rays from a single incident ray. **double rhyme** a rhyme including two syllables. **double salt** *Chem.* a salt composed of two simple salts and having different crystal properties from either. **double saucepan** *Brit.* = double boiler. **double shuffle** *Dancing* a shuffle executed twice with one foot and then twice with the other. **double standard 1** a rule or principle applied more strictly to some people than to others (or to oneself). **2** bimetallism.

double star two stars actually or apparently very close together. **double-stopping** *Mus.* the sounding of two strings at once on a violin etc. **double take** a delayed reaction to a situation etc. immediately after one's first reaction. **double-talk** verbal expression that is (usu. deliberately) ambiguous or misleading. **double-think** the mental capacity to accept contrary opinions or beliefs at the same time esp. as a result of political indoctrination. **double time 1** payment of an employee at twice the normal rate. **2** *Mil.* the regulation running-pace. **double-tonguing** rapid articulation in playing a wind instrument. **double top** *Darts* a score of double twenty. **double up 1 a** bend or curl up. **b** cause to do this, esp. by a blow. **2** be overcome with pain or laughter. **3** share or assign to a room, quarters, etc., with another or others. **4** fold or become folded. **5** use winnings from a bet as stake for another. □□ **doubler** *n.* **doubly** *adv.* [ME f. OF *doble, duble* (n.), *dobler, dubler* (v.) f. L *duplus* DUPLE]

double entendre /ˌduːˈb(ə)l ɑːnˈtɑːndrə/ *n.* **1** a word or phrase open to two interpretations, one usu. *risqué* or indecent. **2** humour using such words or phrases. [obs. F, = double understanding]

doublet /ˈdʌblɪt/ *n.* **1** either of a pair of similar things, esp. either of two words of the same derivation but different sense (e.g. *fashion* and *faction*, *cloak* and *clock*). **2** *hist.* a man's short close-fitting jacket, with or without sleeves, worn in the 15th–17th c. **3** a historical or biblical account occurring twice in differing contexts, usu. traceable to different sources. **4** (in *pl.*) the same number on two dice thrown at once. **5** a pair of associated lines close together in a spectrum. **6** a combination of two simple lenses. [ME f. OF f. *double*: see DOUBLE]

doubloon /dʌˈbluːn, dəb-/ *n.* **1** *hist.* a Spanish gold coin. **2** (in *pl.*) *sl.* money. [F *doublon* or Sp. *doblón* (as DOUBLE)]

doublure /duːˈbljʊə(r)/ *n.* an ornamental lining, usu. leather, inside a book-cover. [F, = lining (*doubler* to line)]

doubt /daʊt/ *n. & v.* —*n.* **1** a feeling of uncertainty; an undecided state of mind (*be in no doubt about; have no doubt that*). **2** (often foll. by *of, about*) an inclination to disbelieve (*have one's doubts about*). **3** an uncertain state of things. **4** a lack of full proof or clear indication (*benefit of the doubt*). —*v.* **1** *tr.* (often foll. by *whether, if, that* + clause; also foll. (after *neg.* or *interrog.*) by *but, but that*) feel uncertain or undecided about (*I doubt that you are right; I do not doubt but that you are wrong*). **2** *tr.* hesitate to believe or trust. **3** *intr.* (often foll. by *of*) feel uncertain or undecided; have doubts (*never doubted of success*). **4** *tr.* call in question. **5** *tr. Brit. archaic* or *dial.* rather think that; suspect or fear that (*I doubt we are late*). □ **beyond doubt** certainly. **doubting Thomas** see THOMAS[3]. **in doubt** uncertain; open to question. **no doubt** certainly; probably; admittedly. **without doubt** (or **a doubt**) certainly. □□ **doubtable** *adj.* **doubter** *n.* **doubtingly** *adv.* [ME *doute* f. OF *doute* (n.), *douter* (v.) f. L *dubitare* hesitate; mod. spelling after L]

doubtful /ˈdaʊtfʊl/ *adj.* **1** feeling doubt or misgivings; unsure or guarded in one's opinion. **2** causing doubt; ambiguous; uncertain in meaning etc. **3** unreliable (*a doubtful ally*). □□ **doubtfully** *adv.* **doubtfulness** *n.*

doubtless /ˈdaʊtlɪs/ *adv.* (often qualifying a sentence) **1** certainly; no doubt. **2** probably. □□ **doubtlessly** *adv.*

douce /duːs/ *adj. Sc.* sober, gentle, sedate. [ME f. OF *dous douce* f. L *dulcis* sweet]

douche /duːʃ/ *n. & v.* —*n.* **1** a jet of liquid applied to part of the body for cleansing or medicinal purposes. **2** a device for producing such a jet. —*v.* **1** *tr.* treat with a douche. **2** *intr.* use a douche. [F f. It. *doccia* pipe f. *docciare* pour by drops ult. f. L *ductus*: see DUCT]

dough /dəʊ/ *n.* **1** a thick mixture of flour etc. and liquid (usu. water), for baking into bread, pastry, etc. **2** *sl.* money. [OE *dāg* f. Gmc]

doughboy /ˈdəʊbɔɪ/ *n.* **1** a boiled dumpling. **2** *US colloq.* a United States infantryman, esp. in the First World War.

doughnut /ˈdəʊnʌt/ *n.* (*US* **donut**) **1** a small fried cake of sweetened dough, usu. in the shape of a ball or ring. **2** a ring-shaped object, esp. *Physics* a vacuum chamber for acceleration of particles in a betatron or synchrotron.

doughty /ˈdaʊtɪ/ *adj.* (**doughtier, doughtiest**) *archaic* or *joc.* valiant, stout-hearted. □□ **doughtily** *adv.* **doughtiness** *n.* [OE *dohtig* var. of *dyhtig* f. Gmc]

doughy /ˈdəʊɪ/ *adj.* (**doughier, doughiest**) **1** having the form or consistency of dough. **2** pale and sickly in colour. □□ **doughiness** *n.*

Douglas /ˈdʌɡləs/ the capital of the Isle of Man; pop. (1981) 19,900.

Douglas fir /ˈdʌɡləs/ *n.* (also **Douglas pine** or **spruce**) any large conifer of the genus *Pseudotsuga*, of Western N. America. [D. *Douglas*, Sc. botanist d. 1834]

doum /daʊm, duːm/ *n.* (in full **doum-palm**) a palm-tree, *Hyphaene thebaica*, with edible fruit. [Arab. *dawm, dūm*]

dour /dʊə(r)/ *adj.* severe, stern, or sullenly obstinate in manner or appearance. □□ **dourly** *adv.* **dourness** *n.* [ME (orig. Sc.), prob. f. Gael. *dúr* dull, obstinate, perh. f. L *durus* hard]

Douro /ˈdʊərəʊ/ (Spanish **Duero** /ˈdʊərəʊ/) a river of the Iberian peninsula, rising in central Spain and flowing west for 900 km (556 miles) through Portugal to the Atlantic Ocean near Oporto. In its valley in Portugal grow the grapes from which port wine is made.

douroucouli /ˌdʊərʊˈkuːlɪ/ *n.* (pl. **douroucoulis**) any nocturnal monkey of the genus *Aotus*, native to S. America, having large staring eyes. [Indian name]

douse /daʊs/ *v.tr.* (also **dowse**) **1 a** throw water over. **b** plunge into water. **2** extinguish (a light). **3** *Naut.* a lower (a sail). **b** close (a porthole). [16th c.: perh. rel. to MDu., LG *dossen* strike]

dove[1] /dʌv/ *n.* **1** any bird of the family Columbidae, with short legs, small head, and large breast. **2** a gentle or innocent person. **3** *Polit.* an advocate of peace or peaceful policies (cf. HAWK[1]). **4** (**Dove**) *Relig.* a representation of the Holy Spirit (John 1: 32). **5** a soft grey colour. □ **dove's-foot** a cranesbill, *Geranium molle*. **dove-tree** a tree with dovelike flowers, *Davidia involucrata*, native to China. □□ **dovelike** *adj.* [ME f. ON *dúfa* f. Gmc]

dove[2] *US past* and *past part.* of DIVE.

dovecote /ˈdʌvkɒt/ *n.* (also **dovecot**) a shelter with nesting-holes for domesticated pigeons.

Dover[1] /ˈdəʊvə(r)/ a ferry port in Kent, the largest of the Cinque Ports, on the coast of the English Channel; pop. (1981) 34,300. It is mainland Britain's nearest point to the Continent, being only 35 km (21 miles) from Calais.

Dover[2] /ˈdəʊvə(r)/ the capital of Delaware; pop. (1980) 23,510.

dovetail /ˈdʌvteɪl/ *n. & v.* —*n.* **1** a joint formed by a mortise with a tenon shaped like a dove's spread tail or a reversed wedge. **2** such a tenon. —*v.* **1** *tr.* join together by means of a dovetail. **2** *tr. & intr.* (often foll. by *into, with*) fit readily together; combine neatly or compactly.

dowager /ˈdaʊədʒə(r)/ *n.* **1** a widow with a title or property derived from her late husband (*Queen dowager; dowager duchess*). **2** *colloq.* a dignified elderly woman. [OF *douag(i)ere* f. *douage* (as DOWER)]

dowdy /ˈdaʊdɪ/ *adj. & n.* —*adj.* (**dowdier, dowdiest**) **1** (of clothes) unattractively dull; unfashionable. **2** (of a person, esp. a woman) dressed in dowdy clothes. —*n.* (pl. **-ies**) a dowdy woman. □□ **dowdily** *adv.* **dowdiness** *n.* [ME *dowd* slut, of unkn. orig.]

dowel /ˈdaʊəl/ *n. & v.* —*n.* a headless peg of wood, metal, or plastic for holding together components of a structure. —*v.tr.* (**dowelled, dowelling**; *US* **doweled, doweling**) fasten with a dowel or dowels. [ME f. MLG *dovel*: cf. THOLE[1]]

dowelling /ˈdaʊəlɪŋ/ *n.* (*US* **doweling**) round rods for cutting into dowels.

dower /ˈdaʊə(r)/ *n. & v.* —*n.* **1** a widow's share for life of her husband's estate. **2** *archaic* a dowry. **3** a natural gift or talent. —*v.tr.* **1** *archaic* give a dowry to. **2** (foll. by *with*) endow with talent etc. □ **dower house** *Brit.* a smaller house near a big one, forming part of a widow's dower. □□ **dowerless** *adj.* [ME f. OF *douaire* f. med.L *dotarium* f. L *dos dotis*]

Dow–Jones index /daʊˈdʒəʊnz/ *n.* (also **Dow–Jones average**) a figure based on the average price of selected stocks, indicating the relative price of shares on the New York Stock Exchange. Dow Jones & Co. compiled the first average of US stock prices in 1884, and this developed in 1897 into computation of a daily average of (originally 12) industrial stocks; it was reorganized in 1928. [C. H. *Dow* d. 1902 & E. D. *Jones* d. 1920, Amer. economists]

Down /daʊn/ a county of Northern Ireland; pop. (1981) 339,200; county town, Downpatrick.

down[1] /daʊn/ *adv., prep., adj., v., & n.* —*adv.* (*superl.* **downmost**) **1** into or towards a lower place, esp. to the ground (*fall down; knelt down*). **2** in a lower place or position (*blinds were down*). **3** to or in a place regarded as lower, esp.: **a** southwards. **b** *Brit.* away from a major city or a university. **4 a** into a low or weaker position or condition (*hit a man when he's down; many down with colds*). **b** *Brit.* in a position of lagging or loss (*our team was three goals down; £5 down on the transaction*). **c** (of a computer system) out of action or unavailable for use (esp. temporarily). **5** from an earlier to a later time (*customs handed down; down to 1600*). **6** to a finer or thinner consistency or a smaller amount or size (*grind down; water down; boil down*). **7** cheaper; lower in price or value (*bread is down; shares are down*). **8** into a more settled state (*calm down*). **9** in writing; in or into recorded or listed form (*copy it down; I got it down on tape; you are down to speak next*). **10** (of part of a larger whole) paid, dealt with (*£5 down, £20 to pay; three down, six to go*). **11** *Naut.* **a** with the current or wind. **b** (of a ship's helm) with the rudder to windward. **12** inclusively of the lower limit in a series (*read down to the third paragraph*). **13** (as *int.*) lie down, put (something) down, etc. **14** (of a crossword clue or answer) read vertically (*cannot do five down*). **15** downstairs, esp. after rising (*is not down yet*). **16** swallowed (*could not get the pill down*). **17** *Amer. Football* (of the ball) out of play. —*prep.* **1** downwards along, through, or into. **2** from top to bottom of. **3** along (*walk down the road; cut down the middle*). **4** at or in a lower part of (*situated down the river*). —*adj.* (*superl.* **downmost**) **1** directed downwards. **2** *Brit.* of travel away from a capital or centre (*the down train; the down platform*). —*v.tr. colloq.* **1** knock or bring down. **2** swallow (a drink). —*n.* **1** an act of putting down (esp. an opponent in wrestling, or the ball in American football). **2** a reverse of fortune (*ups and downs*). **3** *colloq.* a period of depression. **4** the play of the first piece in dominoes. □ **be** (or **have a**) **down on** *colloq.* disapprove of; show animosity towards. **be down to 1** be attributable to. **2** be the responsibility of. **3** have used up everything except (*down to their last tin of rations*). **down and out 1** penniless, destitute. **2** *Boxing* unable to resume the fight. **down-and-out** *n.* a destitute person. **down at heel 1** (of a shoe) with the heel worn down. **2** (of a person) wearing such shoes; shabby, slovenly. **down draught** a downward draught, esp. one down a chimney into a room. **down grade 1** a descending slope of a road or railway. **2** a deterioration (see also DOWNGRADE). **down in the mouth** *colloq.* looking unhappy. **down-market** *adj. & adv. colloq.* towards or relating to the cheaper or less affluent sector of the market. **down on one's luck** *colloq.* **1** temporarily unfortunate. **2** dispirited by misfortune. **down payment** a partial payment made at the time of purchase. **down stage** *Theatr.* at or to the front of the stage. **down-stroke** a stroke made or written downwards. **down time** time during which a machine, esp. a computer, is out of action or unavailable for use. **down-to-earth** practical, realistic. **down to the ground** *colloq.* completely. **down tools** *colloq.* cease work, esp. to go on strike. **down town 1** into a town from a higher or outlying part. **2** *US* to or in the business part of a city (see also DOWNTOWN). **down under** *colloq.* in the antipodes, esp. Australia. **down wind** in the direction in which the wind is blowing (see also DOWNWIND). **down with** *int.* expressing strong disapproval or rejection of a specified person or thing. [OE *dūn(e)* f. *adūne* ADOWN]

down[2] /daʊn/ *n.* **1 a** the first covering of young birds. **b** a bird's under-plumage, used in cushions etc. **c** a layer of fine soft feathers. **2** fine soft hair esp. on the face. **3** short soft hairs on some leaves, fruit, seeds, etc. **4** a fluffy substance, e.g. thistle-down. [ME f. ON *dúnn*]

down[3] /daʊn/ *n.* **1** an area of open rolling land. **2** (in *pl.*) usu.

prec. by *the*) **a** undulating chalk and limestone uplands esp. in
S. England, with few trees and used mainly for pasture. **b**
(**Downs**) a part of the sea (opposite the North Downs) off E.
Kent. □□ **downy** *adj.* [OE *dūn* perh. f. OCelt.]

downbeat /ˈdaʊnbiːt/ *n.* & *adj.* —*n. Mus.* an accented beat, usu.
the first of the bar. —*adj.* **1** pessimistic, gloomy. **2** relaxed.

downcast /ˈdaʊnkɑːst/ *adj.* & *n.* —*adj.* **1** (of eyes) looking downwards. **2** (of a person) dejected. —*n.* a shaft dug in a mine for
extra ventilation.

downcomer /ˈdaʊnˌkʌmə(r)/ *n.* a pipe for downward transport
of water or gas.

downer /ˈdaʊnə(r)/ *n. sl.* **1 a** depressant or tranquillizing drug,
esp. a barbiturate. **2** a depressing person or experience; a failure.
3 = DOWNTURN.

downfall /ˈdaʊnfɔːl/ *n.* **1 a** a fall from prosperity or power. **b**
the cause of this. **2** a sudden heavy fall of rain etc.

downfold /ˈdaʊnfəʊld/ *n. Geol.* a syncline.

downgrade /ˈdaʊngreɪd/ *v.* & *n.* —*v.tr.* **1** make lower in rank
or status. **2** speak disparagingly of. —*n. US* a downward grade.
□ **on the downgrade** *US* in decline.

downhearted /daʊnˈhɑːtɪd/ *adj.* dejected; in low spirits. □□
downheartedly *adv.* **downheartedness** *n.*

downhill *adv., adj.,* & *n.* —*adv.* /daʊnˈhɪl/ in a descending direction, esp. towards the bottom of an incline. —*adj.* /ˈdaʊnhɪl/
1 sloping down, descending. **2** declining; deteriorating. —*n.*
/ˈdaʊnhɪl/ **1** *Skiing* a downhill race. **2** a downward slope. **3** a
decline. □ **go downhill** *colloq.* decline, deteriorate (in health,
state of repair, moral state, etc.).

Downing Street /ˈdaʊnɪŋ/ a street in Westminster, London,
between Whitehall and St James's Park. It was built by the
diplomat Sir George Downing (d. 1684), described by Pepys as 'a
most ungrateful villain'. His friend and benefactor Colonel Okey
was one of the people who had signed the death warrant of
Charles I; Downing betrayed him to the Royalists (who then
executed Okey), and the street now named after him was his
reward. In 1732 No. 10 was acquired on a Crown lease by Sir
Robert Walpole, Britain's first Prime Minister, who accepted it
on behalf of all future Lords of the Treasury (still the formal
title of the Prime Minister). This house is the official town
residence of the Prime Minister, No. 11 that of the Chancellor
of the Exchequer, and the Foreign and Commonwealth Office is
also situated in this street, whence the allusive use of its name
to refer to the British government, Prime Minister, etc.

downland /ˈdaʊnlənd/ *n.* = DOWN³.

download /daʊnˈləʊd/ *v.tr. Computing* transfer (data) from one
storage device or system to another (esp. smaller remote one).

downmost /ˈdaʊnməʊst/ *adj.* & *adv.* the furthest down.

downpipe /ˈdaʊnpaɪp/ *n. Brit.* a pipe to carry rainwater from a
roof to a drain or ground level.

downplay /daʊnˈpleɪ/ *v.tr.* play down; minimize the importance
of.

downpour /ˈdaʊnpɔː(r)/ *n.* a heavy fall of rain.

downright /ˈdaʊnraɪt/ *adj.* & *adv.* —*adj.* **1** plain, definite,
straightforward, blunt. **2** utter, complete (*a downright lie; downright nonsense*). —*adv.* thoroughly, completely, positively (*downright rude*). □□ **downrightness** *n.*

downscale /ˈdaʊnskeɪl/ *v.* & *adj. US* —*v.tr.* reduce or restrict in
size, scale, or extent. —*adj.* at the lower end of a scale, esp. a
social scale; inferior.

downside /ˈdaʊnsaɪd/ *n.* a downward movement of share prices
etc.

downspout /ˈdaʊnspaʊt/ *n. US* = DOWNPIPE.

Down's syndrome /daʊnz/ *n. Med.* a congenital disorder due
to a chromosome defect, in which a person has a broad flattened
skull, slanting eyes, and mental deficiency (also called *mongolism*
from some physical resemblance to Mongoloid peoples). [J. L.
H. *Down*, Engl. physician d. 1896]

downstairs *adv., adj.,* & *n.* —*adv.* /daʊnˈsteəz/ **1** down a flight
of stairs. **2** to or on a lower floor. —*adj.* /ˈdaʊnsteəz/ (also
downstair) situated downstairs. —*n.* /daʊnˈsteəz/ the lower
floor.

downstate /ˈdaʊnsteɪt/ *adj., n.,* & *adv. US* —*adj.* of or in a part
of a state remote from large cities, esp. the southern part. —*n.*
a downstate area. —*adv.* in a downstate area.

downstream /ˈdaʊnstriːm/ *adv.* & *adj.* —*adv.* in the direction
of the flow of a stream etc. —*adj.* moving downstream.

downthrow /ˈdaʊnθrəʊ/ *n. Geol.* a downward dislocation of
strata.

downtown /ˈdaʊntaʊn/ *adj., n.,* & *adv. US* —*adj.* of or in the
lower or more central part, or the business part, of a town or
city. —*n.* a downtown area. —*adv.* in or into a downtown area.

downtrodden /ˈdaʊnˌtrɒd(ə)n/ *adj.* oppressed; badly treated;
kept under.

downturn /ˈdaʊntɜːn/ *n.* a decline, esp. in economic or business
activity.

downward /ˈdaʊnwəd/ *adv.* & *adj.* —*adv.* (also **downwards**)
towards what is lower, inferior, less important, or later.
—*adj.* moving, extending, pointing, or leading downward. □□
downwardly *adv.*

downwarp /ˈdaʊnwɔːp/ *n. Geol.* a broad surface depression; a
syncline.

downwind /ˈdaʊnwɪnd/ *adj.* & *adv.* in the direction in which
the wind is blowing.

downy /ˈdaʊnɪ/ *adj.* (**downier, downiest**) **1 a** of, like, or covered
with down. **b** soft and fluffy. **2** *Brit. sl.* aware, knowing. □□
downily *adv.* **downiness** *n.*

dowry /ˈdaʊərɪ/ *n.* (*pl.* **-ies**) **1** property or money brought by a
bride to her husband. **2** a talent, a natural gift. [ME f. AF *dowarie,*
OF *douaire* DOWER]

dowse¹ /daʊz/ *v.intr.* search for underground water or minerals
by holding a Y-shaped stick or rod which dips abruptly when
over the right spot. □ **dowsing-rod** such a stick or rod. □□
dowser *n.* [17th c.: orig. unkn.]

dowse² var. of DOUSE.

doxology /dɒkˈsɒlədʒɪ/ *n.* (*pl.* **-ies**) a liturgical formula of praise
to God. □□ **doxological** /-səˈlɒdʒɪk(ə)l/ *adj.* [med.L *doxologia* f. Gk
doxologia f. *doxa* glory + -LOGY]

doxy /ˈdɒksɪ/ *n.* (*pl.* **-ies**) *literary* **1** a lover or mistress. **2** a
prostitute. [16th-c. cant: orig. unkn.]

doyen /ˈdɔɪən, ˈdwɑːjæ̃/ *n.* (*fem.* **doyenne** /dɔɪˈen, dwɑːˈjen/) the
senior member of a body of colleagues, esp. the senior ambassador at a court. [F (as DEAN¹)]

Doyle /dɔɪl/, Sir Arthur Conan (1859–1930), Scottish-born novelist, who qualified in medicine at Edinburgh, creator of the
archetypal private detective Sherlock Holmes and his friend and
foil the ingenuous Dr Watson, who are embodied in a cycle of
stories. The first of these, *A Study in Scarlet* (1887) was followed
by a series of historical and other romances for half a century.
Notable among them are *Micah Clarke* (1889), *The White Company*
(1891), *The Exploits of Brigadier Gerard* (1896), and *Rodney Stone*
(1896). *The Lost World* (1912), an early work of science fiction,
introduced the scientist-explorer Professor Challenger, for
whose photograph the author himself posed wearing a false
beard and whiskers. Doyle's patriotism was shown in his
defence of British policy in the second Boer War (in which he
served), for which he was knighted. During his later years,
following the death of his son in the First World War, he became
much interested in spiritualism.

doyley var. of DOILY.

D'Oyly Carte /ˌdɔɪlɪ ˈkɑːt/, Richard (1844–1901), English
impresario and producer of light operas, who brought together
the librettist Gilbert and the Composer Sullivan. The partnership was so successful that he built the Savoy theatre in London
to house these productions; it opened in 1881.

doz. *abbr.* dozen.

doze /dəʊz/ *v.* & *n.* —*v.intr.* sleep lightly; be half asleep. —*n.* a
short light sleep. □ **doze off** fall lightly asleep. □□ **dozer** *n.*
[17th c.: cf. Da. *døse* make drowsy]

dozen /ˈdʌz(ə)n/ *n.* **1** (prec. by *a* or a number) (*pl.* **dozen**) twelve,
regarded collectively (*a dozen eggs; two dozen packets; ordered three
dozen*). **2** a set or group of twelve (*packed in dozens*). **3** *colloq.* about
twelve, a fairly large indefinite number. **4** (in *pl.*; usu. foll. by *of*)

colloq. very many (*made dozens of mistakes*). **5 (the dozens)** a Black American game or ritualized exchange of verbal insults. □ **by the dozen** in large quantities. **talk nineteen to the dozen** *Brit.* talk incessantly. □□ **dozenth** *adj.* & *n.* [ME f. OF *dozeine*, ult. f. L *duodecim* twelve]

dozer /ˈdəʊzə(r)/ *n. colloq.* = BULLDOZER. [abbr.]

dozy /ˈdəʊzɪ/ *adj.* (**dozier, doziest**) **1** drowsy; tending to doze. **2** *Brit. colloq.* stupid or lazy. □□ **dozily** *adv.* **doziness** *n.*

DP *abbr.* **1** data processing. **2** displaced person.

D.Phil. *abbr.* Doctor of Philosophy.

DPP *abbr.* (in the UK) Director of Public Prosecutions.

Dr *abbr.* **1** Doctor. **2** Drive. **3** debtor.

dr. *abbr.* **1** drachm(s). **2** drachma(s). **3** dram(s).

drab[1] /dræb/ *adj.* & *n.* —*adj.* (**drabber, drabbest**) **1** dull, uninteresting. **2** of a dull brownish colour. —*n.* **1** drab colour. **2** monotony. □□ **drably** *adv.* **drabness** *n.* [prob. f. obs. *drap* cloth f. OF f. LL *drappus*, perh. of Celt. orig.]

drab[2] see DRIBS AND DRABS.

drab[3] /dræb/ *n.* **1** a slut; a slattern. **2** a prostitute. [perh. rel. to LG *drabbe* mire, Du. *drab* dregs]

Drabble /ˈdræb(ə)l/, Margaret (1939–), English novelist, whose early works, such as *The Garrick Year* (1964) and *The Millstone* (1966) are much concerned with the conflicts of career and motherhood. Her later novels (e.g. *The Needle's Eye*, 1972, and *The Ice Age*, 1977) have a larger canvas and a more documentary approach to English social life.

drabble /ˈdræb(ə)l/ *v.intr.* & *tr.* become or make dirty and wet with water or mud. [ME f. LG *drabbelen* paddle in water or mire: cf. DRAB[3]]

drachm /dræm/ *n. Brit.* a weight or measure formerly used by apothecaries, equivalent to 60 grains or one eighth of an ounce, or (in fluid **fluid drachm**) 60 minims, one eighth of a fluid ounce. [ME *dragme* f. OF *dragme* or LL *dragma* f. L *drachma* f. Gk *drakhmē* Attic weight and coin]

drachma /ˈdrækmə/ *n.* (*pl.* **drachmas** or **drachmae** /-miː/) **1** the chief monetary unit of Greece. **2** a silver coin of ancient Greece. [L f. Gk *drakhmē*]

drack /dræk/ *adj. Austral. sl.* **1** (esp. of a woman) unattractive. **2** dismal, dull. [20th c.: orig. unkn.]

dracone /ˈdrækəʊn/ *n.* a large flexible container for liquids, towed on the surface of the sea. [L *draco -onis* (as DRAGON)]

Draconian /drəˈkəʊnɪən, dreɪ-/ *adj.* (also **Draconic** /-ˈkɒnɪk/) very harsh or severe (esp. of laws and their application). [*Drakōn*, 7th-c. BC, said to have established very severe laws in ancient Athens]

Dracula /ˈdrækjʊlə/ the chief of the vampires in Bram Stoker's novel *Dracula* (1897), partly set in a lonely castle in Transylvania. Vlad Tepeş (Vlad the Impaler), also known as Dracula, was a 15th-c. prince of Wallachia, renowned for his cruelty, and the novelist has woven this name into a sinister tale of a region with which vampires and werewolves were traditionally associated.

draff /dræf, drɑːf/ *n.* **1** dregs, lees. **2** refuse. [ME, perh. repr. OE *dræf* (unrecorded)]

draft /drɑːft/ *n.* & *v.* —*n.* **1 a** a preliminary written version of a speech, document, etc. **b** a rough preliminary outline of a scheme. **c** a sketch of work to be carried out. **2 a** a written order for payment of money by a bank. **b** the drawing of money by means of this. **3** (foll. by *on*) a demand made on a person's confidence, friendship, etc. **4 a** a party detached from a larger group for a special duty or purpose. **b** the selection of this. **5** *US* compulsory military service. **6** a reinforcement. **7** *US* = DRAUGHT. —*v.tr.* **1** prepare a draft of (a document, scheme, etc.). **2** select for a special duty or purpose. **3** *US* conscript for military service. □□ **draftee** /-ˈtiː/ *n.* **drafter** *n.* [phonetic spelling of DRAUGHT]

draftsman /ˈdrɑːftsmən/ *n.* (*pl.* **-men**) **1** a person who drafts documents. **2** = DRAUGHTSMAN 1. [phonetic spelling of DRAUGHTSMAN]

drafty *US* var. of DRAUGHTY.

drag /dræg/ *v.* & *n.* —*v.* (**dragged, dragging**) **1** *tr.* pull along with effort or difficulty. **2 a** *tr.* allow (one's feet, tail, etc.) to trail along the ground. **b** *intr.* trail along the ground. **c** *intr.* (of time etc.) go or pass heavily or slowly or tediously. **3 a** *intr.* (usu. foll. by *for*) use a grapnel or drag (to find a drowned person or lost object). **b** *tr.* search the bottom of (a river etc.) with grapnels, nets, or drags. **4** *tr.* (often foll. by *to*) *colloq.* take (a person to a place etc., esp. against his or her will). **5** *intr.* (foll. by *on, at*) draw on (a cigarette etc.). **6** *intr.* (often foll. by *on*) continue at tedious length. —*n.* **1 a** an obstruction to progress. **b** *Aeron.* the longitudinal retarding force exerted by air. **c** slow motion; impeded progress. **d** an iron shoe for retarding a horse-drawn vehicle downhill. **2** *colloq.* a boring or dreary person, duty, performance, etc. **3 a** a strong-smelling lure drawn before hounds as a substitute for a fox. **b** a hunt using this. **4** an apparatus for dredging or recovering drowned persons etc. from under water. **5** = *drag-net*. **6** *sl.* a draw on a cigarette etc. **7** *sl.* **a** women's clothes worn by men. **b** a party at which these are worn. **c** clothes in general. **8** an act of dragging. **9 a** *sl.* a motor car. **b** (in full **drag race**) an acceleration race between cars usu. for a quarter of a mile. **10** *US sl.* influence, pull. **11** *US sl.* a street or road (*the main drag*). **12** *hist.* a private vehicle like a stagecoach, drawn by four horses. □ **drag anchor** (of a ship) move from a moored position when the anchor fails to hold. **drag-anchor** *n.* = *sea anchor*. **drag one's feet** (or **heels**) be deliberately slow or reluctant to act. **drag-hound** a hound used to hunt with a drag. **drag in** introduce (a subject) irrelevantly. **drag-line** an excavator with a bucket pulled in by a wire rope. **drag-net** **1** a net drawn through a river or across ground to trap fish or game. **2** a systematic hunt for criminals etc. **drag out** protract. **drag queen** *sl.* a male homosexual transvestite. **drag up** *colloq.* **1** deliberately mention (an unwelcome subject). **2** rear (a child) roughly and without proper training. [ME f. OE *dragan* or ON *draga* DRAW]

dragée /ˈdrɑːʒeɪ/ *n.* **1** a sugar-coated almond etc. **2** a small silver ball for decorating a cake. **3** a chocolate-coated sweet. [F: see DREDGE[2]]

draggle /ˈdræg(ə)l/ *v.* **1** *tr.* make dirty or wet or limp by trailing. **2** *intr.* hang trailing. **3** *intr.* lag; straggle in the rear. □ **draggle-tailed** (of a woman) with untidily trailing skirts. [DRAG + -LE[4]]

draggy /ˈdrægɪ/ *adj.* (**draggier, draggiest**) *colloq.* **1** tedious. **2** unpleasant.

dragoman /ˈdrægəmən/ *n.* (*pl.* **dragomans** or **dragomen**) an interpreter or guide, esp. in countries speaking Arabic, Turkish, or Persian. [F f. It. *dragomano* f. med.Gk *dragomanos* f. Arab. *tarjumān* f. *tarjama* interpret, f. Aram. *targēm* f. Assyr. *targumānu* interpreter]

dragon /ˈdrægən/ *n.* **1** a mythical monster like a reptile, usu. with wings and claws and able to breathe out fire. (See below.) **2** a fierce person, esp. a woman. **3** (in full **flying dragon**) a lizard, *Draco volans*, with a long tail and membranous winglike structures. Also called *flying lizard*. □ **dragon's blood** a red gum that exudes from the fruit of some palms and the dragon-tree. **dragon's teeth** *Mil. colloq.* obstacles resembling teeth pointed upwards, used esp. against tanks. **dragon-tree** a tree, *Dracaena draco*, native to the Canary Isles. [ME f. OF f. L *draco -onis* f. Gk *drakōn* serpent]

The dragon is probably the commonest emblem in Far Eastern art, and the most ancient. A form with five claws on each foot (Oriental dragons normally have four) was adopted as the chief imperial emblem in China. Fundamentally the dragon represented fertilizing power, cosmic energy revealing itself in nature. It resided especially in water, in rivers, lakes, and the sea; in springtime it moved in heaven among the clouds. In the art of the West the dragon appears in such contexts as St George slaying the dragon as a symbol of threat and destruction, and is used as a heraldic emblem.

dragonet /ˈdrægənɪt/ *n.* any marine spiny fish of the family Callionymidae, the males of which are brightly coloured. [ME f. F, dimin. of DRAGON]

dragonfish /ˈdrægənfɪʃ/ *n.* (*pl.* same or **-fishes**) any marine deep-water fish of the family Stomiatidae, having a long slender body and a barbel on the chin with luminous tissue, serving to attract prey.

b *but* d *dog* f *few* g *get* h *he* j *yes* k *cat* l *leg* m *man* n *no* p *pen* r *red* s *sit* t *top* v *voice*

dragonfly /'drægən,flaɪ/ n. (pl. -ies) any of various insects of the order Odonata, having a long slender body and two pairs of large transparent wings usu. spread while resting.

dragonnade /,drægə'neɪd/ n. & v. —n. a persecution by use of troops, esp. (in pl.) of French Protestants under Louis XIV by quartering dragoons on them. —v.tr. subject to a dragonnade. [F f. dragon: see DRAGOON]

dragoon /drə'gu:n/ n. & v. —n. 1 a cavalryman (orig. a mounted infantryman armed with a carbine). 2 a rough fierce fellow. 3 a variety of pigeon. —v.tr. 1 (foll. by into) coerce into doing something, esp. by use of strong force. 2 persecute, esp. with troops. [orig. = carbine (thought of as breathing fire) f. F dragon DRAGON]

dragster /'drægstə(r)/ n. a car built or modified to take part in drag races.

drail /dreɪl/ n. a fish-hook and line weighted with lead for dragging below the surface of the water. [app. var. of TRAIL]

drain /dreɪn/ v. & n. —v. 1 tr. draw off liquid from, esp.: **a** make (land etc.) dry by providing an outflow for moisture. **b** (of a river) carry off the superfluous water of (a district). **c** remove purulent matter from (an abscess). 2 tr. (foll. by off, away) draw off (liquid) esp. by a pipe. 3 intr. (foll. by away, off, through) flow or trickle away. 4 intr. (of a wet cloth, a vessel, etc.) become dry as liquid flows away (put it there to drain). 5 tr. (often foll. by of) exhaust or deprive (a person or thing) of strength, resources, property, etc. 6 tr. **a** drink (liquid) to the dregs. **b** empty (a vessel) by drinking the contents. —n. 1 **a** a channel, conduit, or pipe carrying off liquid, esp. an artificial conduit for water or sewage. **b** a tube for drawing off the discharge from an abscess etc. 2 a constant outflow, withdrawal, or expenditure (a great drain on my resources). □ **down the drain** colloq. lost, wasted. **laugh like a drain** laugh copiously; guffaw. [OE drē(a)hnian f. Gmc]

drainage /'dreɪnɪdʒ/ n. 1 the process or means of draining (the land has poor drainage). 2 a system of drains, artificial or natural. 3 what is drained off, esp. sewage.

drainboard /'dreɪnbɔːd/ n. US = DRAINING-BOARD.

drainer /'dreɪnə(r)/ n. 1 a device for draining; anything on which things are put to drain, e.g. a draining-board. 2 a person who drains.

draining-board /'dreɪnɪŋbɔːd/ n. a sloping usu. grooved surface beside a sink, on which washed dishes etc. are left to drain.

drainpipe /'dreɪnpaɪp/ n. 1 a pipe for carrying off water, sewage, etc., from a building. 2 (attrib.) (of trousers etc.) very narrow. 3 (in pl.) very narrow trousers.

Drake /dreɪk/, Sir Francis (c.1540–96), Elizabethan sailor and explorer, the most daring and successful of English privateers in the Spanish West Indies. In 1577 he was backed by Elizabeth I in an enterprise of circumnavigation with the prospect of loot in Spanish seas. Having passed through the Magellan Straits he plundered the South American settlements before sailing his ship, the Golden Hind, up the Californian coast. From there he traversed the Pacific, sailed round the Cape of Good Hope, and arrived back in Plymouth in 1580 a rich man, being knighted in the following year. His successful raid on Cadiz in 1587 (the operation known as 'singeing the king of Spain's beard') delayed the sailing of the Armada for a year by destroying its supply-ships, and the next year he played an important part in its defeat in the Channel. Like his cousin, Sir John Hawkins, Drake died at sea during their unsuccessful expedition to the West Indies.

drake /dreɪk/ n. a male duck. [ME prob. f. Gmc]

Drakensberg Mountains /'drɑːkənz,bɜːg/ a range of mountains at the southern edge of the African plateau, stretching in a NE–SW direction for a distance of 1,126 km (700 miles) through Lesotho and the South African provinces of Natal, Orange Free State, and Transvaal. The highest peak is Thabana Ntlenyana (3,482 m, 11,425 ft.).

Drake Passage a channel separating the southern tip of South America from the Antarctic Peninsula and connecting the South Atlantic with the South Pacific Oceans. It is named after Sir Francis Drake.

Dralon /'dreɪlɒn/ n. propr. 1 a synthetic acrylic fibre used in textiles. 2 a fabric made from this. [after NYLON]

dram /dræm/ n. 1 a small drink of spirits. 2 = DRACHM. [ME f. OF drame or med.L drama, dragma: cf. DRACHM]

drama /'drɑːmə/ n. 1 a play for acting on stage or for broadcasting. 2 (often prec. by the) the art of writing and presenting plays. 3 an exciting or emotional event, set of circumstances, etc. 4 dramatic quality (the drama of the situation). [LL f. Gk drama -atos f. draō do]

dramatic /drə'mætɪk/ adj. 1 of drama or the study of drama. 2 (of an event, circumstance, etc.) sudden and exciting or unexpected. 3 vividly striking. 4 (of a gesture etc.) theatrical, overdone, absurd. □ **dramatic irony** = tragic irony. □□ **dramatically** adv. [LL dramaticus f. Gk dramatikos (as DRAMA)]

dramatics /drə'mætɪks/ n.pl. (often treated as sing.) 1 the production and performance of plays. 2 exaggerated or showy behaviour.

dramatis personae /,dræmətɪs pɜː'səʊnaɪ, -niː/ n.pl. (often treated as sing.) 1 the characters in a play. 2 a list of these. [L, = persons of the drama]

dramatist /'dræmətɪst/ n. a writer of dramas.

dramatize /'dræmə,taɪz/ v. (also -ise) 1 **a** tr. adapt (a novel etc.) to form a stage play. **b** intr. admit of such adaptation. 2 tr. make a drama or dramatic scene of. 3 tr. (also absol.) express or react to in a dramatic way. □□ **dramatization** /-'zeɪʃ(ə)n/ n.

dramaturge /'dræmə,tɜːdʒ/ n. 1 a specialist in theatrical production. 2 a dramatist. [F f. Gk dramatourgos (as DRAMA, -ergos worker)]

dramaturgy /'dræmə,tɜːdʒɪ/ n. 1 the art of theatrical production; the theory of dramatics. 2 the application of this. □□ **dramaturgic** /-'tɜːdʒɪk/ adj. **dramaturgical** /-'tɜːdʒɪk(ə)l/ adj.

Drambuie /dræm'bjuːɪ, -'buːɪ/ n. propr. a Scotch whisky liqueur. [Gael. dram buidheach satisfying drink]

Drammen /'drɑːmən/ a seaport in SE Norway; pop. (1988) 51,840.

drank past of DRINK.

drape /dreɪp/ v. & n. —v.tr. 1 hang, cover loosely, or adorn with cloth etc. 2 arrange (clothes or hangings) carefully in folds. —n. 1 (often in pl.) a curtain or drapery. 2 a piece of drapery. 3 the way in which a garment or fabric hangs. [ME f. OF draper f. drap f. LL drappus cloth]

draper /'dreɪpə(r)/ n. Brit. a retailer of textile fabrics. [ME f. AF, OF drapier (as DRAPE)]

drapery /'dreɪpərɪ/ n. (pl. -ies) 1 clothing or hangings arranged in folds. 2 (often in pl.) a curtain or hanging. 3 Brit. cloth; textile fabrics. 4 Brit. the trade of a draper. 5 the arrangement of clothing in sculpture or painting. [ME f. OF draperie f. drap cloth]

drastic /'dræstɪk, 'drɑː-/ adj. having a strong or far-reaching effect; severe. □□ **drastically** adv. [Gk drastikos f. draō do]

drat /dræt/ v. & int. colloq. —v.tr. (**dratted, dratting** (usu. as an exclam.)) curse, confound (drat the thing!). —int. expressing anger or annoyance. □□ **dratted** adj. [for 'od (= God) rot]

draught /drɑːft/ n. & v. (US **draft**) —n. 1 a current of air in a confined space (e.g. a room or chimney). 2 pulling, traction. 3 Naut. the depth of water needed to float a ship. 4 the drawing of liquor from a cask etc. 5 **a** a single act of drinking. **b** the amount drunk in this. **c** a dose of liquid medicine. 6 (in pl.; usu. treated as sing.) Brit. a game for two played with 12 pieces each on a draughtboard. 7 **a** the drawing in of a fishing-net. **b** the fish taken at one draught. 8 = DRAFT. —v.tr. = DRAFT. □ **draught beer** beer drawn from a cask, not bottled. **draught-horse** a horse used for pulling heavy loads, esp. a cart or plough. **feel the draught** colloq. suffer from adverse (usu. financial) conditions. [ME draht, perh. f. ON drahtr, dráttr f. Gmc, rel. to DRAW]

draughtboard /'drɑːftbɔːd/ n. a chequered board, identical to a chessboard, used in draughts.

draughtsman /'drɑːftsmən/ n. (pl. -men) 1 a person who makes drawings, plans, or sketches. 2 /'drɑːftsmæn/ a piece in the game of draughts. 3 = DRAFTSMAN. □□ **draughtsmanship** n. [draught's + MAN]

draughty /ˈdrɑːftɪ/ *adj.* (*US* **drafty**) (**-ier, -iest**) (of a room etc.) letting in sharp currents of air. □□ **draughtily** *adv.* **draughtiness** *n.*

Dravidian /drəˈvɪdɪən/ *n. & adj.* —*n.* **1** a member of a dark-skinned aboriginal people of S. India and Sri Lanka (including the Tamils and Kanarese). **2** any of the group of languages spoken by this people, including Tamil, Telugu, and Kanarese. It is thought that before the arrival of speakers of Indo-Aryan languages *c.*1000 BC the Dravidian languages were spoken over much of India. —*adj.* of or relating to this people or group of languages. [Skr. *Dravida*, a province of S. India]

draw /drɔː/ *v. & n.* —*v.* (*past* **drew** /druː/; *past part.* **drawn** /drɔːn/) **1** *tr.* pull or cause to move towards or after one. **2** *tr.* pull (a thing) up, over, or across. **3** *tr.* pull (curtains etc.) open or shut. **4** *tr.* take (a person) aside, esp. to talk to. **5** *tr.* attract; bring to oneself or to something; take in (*drew a deep breath*; *I felt drawn to her*; *drew my attention to the matter*; *draw him into conversation*; *the match drew large crowds*). **6** *intr.* (foll. by *at, on*) suck smoke from (a cigarette, pipe, etc.). **7** *tr.* (also *absol.*) take out; remove (e.g. a tooth, a gun from a holster, etc.). **8** *tr.* obtain or take from a source (*draw a salary*; *draw inspiration*; *drew £100 from my account*). **9** *tr.* trace (a line, mark, furrow, or figure). **10 a** *tr.* produce (a picture) by tracing lines and marks. **b** *tr.* represent (a thing) by this means. **c** *absol.* make a drawing. **11** *tr.* (also *absol.*) finish (a contest or game) with neither side winning. **12** *intr.* make one's or its way, proceed, move, come (*drew near the bridge*; *draw to a close*; *the second horse drew level*; *drew ahead of the field*; *the time draws near*). **13** *tr.* infer, deduce (a conclusion). **14** *tr.* **a** elicit, evoke. **b** bring about, entail (*draw criticism*; *draw ruin upon oneself*). **c** induce (a person) to reveal facts, feelings, or talent (*refused to be drawn*). **d** (foll. by *to* + *infin.*) induce (a person) to do something. **e** *Cards* cause to be played (*drew all the trumps*). **15** *tr.* haul up (water) from a well. **16** *tr.* bring out (liquid from a vessel or blood from a wound). **17** *tr.* extract a liquid essence from. **18** *intr.* (of a chimney or pipe) promote or allow a draught. **19** *intr.* (of tea) infuse. **20 a** *tr.* obtain by lot (*drew the winner*). **b** *absol.* draw lots. **21** *intr.* (foll. by *on*) make a demand on a person, a person's skill, memory, imagination, etc. **22** *tr.* write out (a bill, cheque, or draft) (*drew a cheque on the bank*). **23** *tr.* frame (a document) in due form, compose. **24** *tr.* formulate or perceive (a comparison or distinction). **25** *tr.* (of a ship) require (a specified depth of water) to float in. **26** *tr.* disembowel (*hang, draw, and quarter*; *draw the fowl before cooking it*). **27** *tr. Hunting* search (cover) for game. **28** *tr.* drag (a badger or fox) from a hole. **29** *tr.* **a** protract, stretch, elongate (*long-drawn agony*). **b** make (wire) by pulling a piece of metal through successively smaller holes. **30** *tr.* **a** *Golf* drive (the ball) to the left (or, of a left-handed player, the right) esp. purposely. **b** *Bowls* cause (a bowl) to travel in a curve to the desired point. **31** *intr.* (of a sail) swell tightly in the wind. —*n.* **1** an act of drawing. **2 a** a person or thing that draws custom, attention, etc. **b** the power to attract attention. **3** the drawing of lots, esp. a raffle. **4** a drawn game. **5** a suck on a cigarette etc. **6** the act of removing a gun from its holster in order to shoot (*quick on the draw*). **7** strain, pull. **8** *US* the movable part of a drawbridge. □ **draw back** withdraw from an undertaking. **draw a bead on** see BEAD. **draw bit** = *draw rein*. **draw a blank** see BLANK. **draw bridle** = *draw rein*. **draw a person's fire** attract hostility, criticism, etc., away from a more important target. **draw in 1 a** (of successive days) become shorter because of the changing seasons. **b** (of a day) approach its end. **c** (of successive evenings or nights) start earlier because of the changing seasons. **2** persuade to join, entice. **3** (of a train etc.) arrive at a station. **draw in one's horns** become less assertive or ambitious; draw back. **draw the line at** set a limit (of tolerance etc.) at. **draw lots** see LOT. **draw off** withdraw (troops). **draw on 1** approach, come near. **2** lead to, bring about. **3** allure. **4** put (gloves, boots, etc.) on. **draw out 1** prolong. **2** elicit. **3** induce to talk. **4** (of successive days) become longer because of the changing seasons. **5** (of a train etc.) leave a station etc. **6** write out in proper form. **7** lead out, detach, or array (troops). **draw rein** see REIN. **draw-sheet** a sheet that can be taken from under a patient without remaking the bed. **draw-string** a string that can be pulled to tighten the mouth of a bag, the waist of a garment, etc. **draw stumps** *Cricket* take the stumps out of the ground at the close of play. **draw one's sword against** attack. **draw up 1** compose or draft (a document etc.). **2** bring or come into regular order. **3** come to a halt. **4** make (oneself) stiffly erect. **5** (foll. by *with, to*) gain on or overtake. **draw-well** a deep well with a rope and a bucket. **quick on the draw** quick to act or react. [OE *dragan* f. Gmc]

drawback /ˈdrɔːbæk/ *n.* **1** a thing that impairs satisfaction; a disadvantage. **2** (foll. by *from*) a deduction. **3** an amount of excise or import duty paid back or remitted on goods exported. □ **drawback lock** a lock with a spring bolt that can be drawn back by an inside knob.

drawbridge /ˈdrɔːbrɪdʒ/ *n.* a bridge, esp. over water, hinged at one end so that it may be raised to prevent passage or to allow ships etc. to pass.

drawee /drɔːˈiː/ *n.* the person on whom a draft or bill is drawn.

drawer /ˈdrɔːə(r)/ *n.* **1** a person or thing that draws, esp. a person who draws a cheque etc. **2** /drɔː(r), ˈdrɔːə(r)/ a boxlike storage compartment without a lid, sliding in and out of a frame, table, etc. (*chest of drawers*). **3** (in *pl.*) an undergarment worn next to the body below the waist. □□ **drawerful** *n.* (*pl.* **-fuls**).

drawing /ˈdrɔːɪŋ/ *n.* **1 a** the art of representing by line. **b** delineation without colour or with a single colour. **c** the art of representing with pencils, pens, crayons, etc., rather than paint. **2** a picture produced in this way. □ **drawing-board** a board for spreading drawing-paper on. **drawing-paper** stout paper for drawing pictures etc. on. **drawing-pin** *Brit.* a flat-headed pin for fastening paper etc. (orig. drawing-paper) to a surface. **out of drawing** incorrectly depicted.

drawing-room /ˈdrɔːɪŋˌruːm, -ˌrʊm/ *n.* **1** a room for comfortable sitting or entertaining in a private house. **2** (*attrib.*) restrained; observing social proprieties (*drawing-room conversation*). **3** *US* a private compartment in a train. **4** *hist.* a levee, a formal reception esp. at court. [earlier *withdrawing-room*, because orig. used for women to withdraw to after dinner]

drawl /drɔːl/ *v. & n.* —*v.* **1** *intr.* speak with drawn-out vowel sounds. **2** *tr.* utter in this way. —*n.* a drawling utterance or way of speaking. □□ **drawler** *n.* [16th c.: prob. orig. cant, f. LG, Du. *dralen* delay, linger]

drawn /drɔːn/ *past part.* of DRAW. —*adj.* **1** looking strained from fear, anxiety, or pain. **2** (of butter) melted. **3** (of a position in chess etc.) that will result in a draw if both players make the best moves available. □ **drawn-work** (or **drawn-thread-work**) ornamental work on linen etc., done by drawing out threads, usu. with additional needlework.

dray[1] /dreɪ/ *n.* **1** a low cart without sides for heavy loads, esp. beer-barrels. **2** *Austral. & NZ* a two-wheeled cart. □ **dray-horse** a large, powerful horse. [ME f. OE *drᴂge* drag-net, *dragan* DRAW]

dray[2] var. of DREY.

drayman /ˈdreɪmən/ *n.* (*pl.* **-men**) a brewer's driver.

dread /dred/ *v., n., & adj.* —*v.tr.* **1** (foll. by *that*, or *to* + *infin.*) fear greatly. **2** shrink from; look forward to with great apprehension. **3** be in great fear of. —*n.* **1** great fear, apprehension, awe. **2** an object of fear or awe. —*adj.* **1** dreaded. **2** *archaic* awe-inspiring, revered. [OE *ādrᴂdan*, *ondrᴂdan*]

dreadful /ˈdredfʊl/ *adj.* **1** terrible; inspiring fear or awe. **2** *colloq.* troublesome, disagreeable; very bad. □□ **dreadfully** *adv.* **dreadfulness** *n.*

dreadlocks /ˈdredlɒks/ *n.pl.* **1** a Rastafarian hairstyle in which the hair is twisted into tight braids or ringlets hanging down on all sides. **2** hair dressed in this way.

dreadnought /ˈdrednɔːt/ *n.* **1** (usu. **Dreadnought**) *hist.* a type of battleship greatly superior in armament to all its predecessors (from the name of the first, launched in 1906). Dreadnoughts revolutionized naval warfare. Powered by steam turbine engines, their speed of 21 knots and their heavy firepower enabled them to fight from outside the range of enemy torpedoes. **2** *archaic* a fearless person. **3** *archaic* **a** a thick coat for stormy weather. **b** the cloth used for such coats.

dream /driːm/ *n. & v.* —*n.* **1 a** a series of pictures or events in the mind of a sleeping person. **b** the act or time of seeing this. **c** (in full **waking dream**) a similar experience of one awake. **2**

a day-dream or fantasy. **3** an ideal, aspiration, or ambition, esp. of a nation. **4** a beautiful or ideal person or thing. **5** a state of mind without proper perception of reality (*goes about in a dream*). —*v.* (*past* and *past part.* **dreamt** /dremt, drempt/ or **dreamed**) **1** *intr.* experience a dream. **2** *tr.* imagine in or as if in a dream. **3** (usu. with *neg.*) **a** *intr.* (foll. by *of*) contemplate the possibility of, have any conception or intention of (*would not dream of upsetting them*). **b** *tr.* (often foll. by *that* + clause) think of as a possibility (*never dreamt that he would come*). **4** *tr.* (foll. by *away*) spend (time) unprofitably. **5** *intr.* be inactive or unpractical. **6** *intr.* fall into a reverie. □ **dream-time** *Austral.* the alcheringa. **dream up** imagine, invent. **like a dream** *colloq.* easily, effortlessly. □□ **dreamful** *adj.* **dreamless** *adj.* **dreamlike** *adj.* [ME f. OE *drēam* joy, music]

dreamboat /'dri:mbəʊt/ *n. colloq.* **1** a very attractive or ideal person, esp. of the opposite sex. **2** a very desirable or ideal thing.

dreamer /'dri:mə(r)/ *n.* **1** a person who dreams. **2** a romantic or unpractical person.

dreamland /'dri:mlænd/ *n.* an ideal or imaginary land.

dreamy /'dri:mɪ/ *adj.* (**dreamier**, **dreamiest**) **1** given to day-dreaming; fanciful; unpractical. **2** dreamlike; vague; misty. **3** *colloq.* delightful; marvellous. **4** *poet.* full of dreams. □□ **dreamily** *adv.* **dreaminess** *n.*

drear /'drɪə(r)/ *adj. poet.* = DREARY. [abbr.]

dreary /'drɪərɪ/ *adj.* (**drearier**, **dreariest**) dismal, dull, gloomy. □□ **drearily** *adv.* **dreariness** *n.* [OE *drēorig* f. *drēor* gore: rel. to *drēosan* to drop f. Gmc]

dredge[1] /dredʒ/ *v.* & *n.* —*v.* **1** *tr.* **a** (often foll. by *up*) bring up (lost or hidden material) as if with a dredge (*don't dredge all that up again*). **b** (often foll. by *away*, *up*, *out*) bring up or clear (mud etc.) from a river, harbour, etc. with a dredge. **2** *tr.* clean (a harbour, river, etc.) with a dredge. **3** *intr.* use a dredge. —*n.* an apparatus used to scoop up oysters, specimens, etc., or to clear mud etc., from a river or sea bed. [15th-c. Sc. *dreg*, perh. rel. to MDu. *dregghe*]

dredge[2] /dredʒ/ *v.tr.* **1** sprinkle with flour, sugar, etc. **2** (often foll. by *over*) sprinkle (flour, sugar, etc.) on. [obs. *dredge* sweetmeat f. OF *dragie*, *dragee*, perh. f. L *tragemata* f. Gk *tragēmata* spices]

dredger[1] /'dredʒə(r)/ *n.* **1** a machine used for dredging rivers etc.; a dredge. **2** a boat containing this.

dredger[2] /'dredʒə(r)/ *n.* a container with a perforated lid used for sprinkling flour, sugar, etc.

dree /dri:/ *v.tr.* (**drees**, **dreed**, **dreeing**) *Sc.* or *archaic* endure. □ **dree one's weird** submit to one's destiny. [OE *drēogan* f. Gmc]

dreg /dreg/ *n.* **1** (usu. in *pl.*) **a** a sediment; grounds, lees, etc. **b** a worthless part; refuse (*the dregs of humanity*). **2** a small remnant (*not a dreg*). □ **drain** (or **drink**) **to the dregs** consume leaving nothing (*drained life to the dregs*). □□ **dreggy** *adj. colloq.* [ME prob. f. ON *dreggjar*]

Dreiser /'draɪsə(r)/, Theodore Herman Albert (1871–1945), American novelist, whose works include *Sister Carrie* (1900), *An American Tragedy* (1925), and *America is Worth Saving* (1941). His later works express a growing faith in socialism that replaces the nihilistic naturalism and pessimism of his earlier writings.

drench /drentʃ/ *v.* & *n.* —*v.tr.* **1 a** wet thoroughly (*was drenched by the rain*). **b** saturate; soak (in liquid). **2** force (an animal) to take medicine. **3** *archaic* cause to drink. —*n.* **1** a soaking; a downpour. **2** medicine administered to an animal. **3** *archaic* a medicinal or poisonous draught. [OE *drencan*, *drenc* f. Gmc: rel. to DRINK]

Drenthe /'drentə/ a sparsely populated agricultural province in NE Netherlands; pop. (1988) 436,586; capital, Assen.

Dresden /'drezd(ə)n/ a city in east Germany, the capital of Saxony, on the River Elbe; pop. (1986) 519,700. —*n.* **1** (also **Dresden china** etc.) china of a kind made originally at Dresden but from 1710 at nearby Meissen, with elaborate decoration and delicate colourings. **2** (*attrib.*) delicately pretty.

dress /dres/ *v.* & *n.* —*v.* **1 a** *tr.* clothe; array (*dressed in rags*; *dressed her quickly*). **b** *intr.* wear clothes of a specified kind or in a specified way (*dresses well*). **2** *intr.* **a** put on clothes. **b** put on

formal or evening clothes, esp. for dinner. **3** *tr.* decorate or adorn. **4** *tr. Med.* **a** treat (a wound) with ointment etc. **b** apply a dressing to (a wound). **5** *tr.* trim, comb, brush, or smooth (the hair). **6** *tr.* **a** clean and prepare (poultry, a crab, etc.) for cooking or eating. **b** add a dressing to (a salad etc.). **7** *tr.* apply manure etc. to a field, garden, etc. **8** *tr.* finish the surface of (fabric, building-stone, etc.). **9** *tr.* groom (a horse). **10** *tr.* curry (leather etc.). **11** *Mil.* **a** *tr.* correct the alignment of (troops etc.). **b** *intr.* (of troops) come into alignment. **12** *tr.* make (an artificial fly) for use in fishing. —*n.* **1** a one-piece woman's garment consisting of a bodice and skirt. **2** clothing, esp. a whole outfit etc. (*fussy about his dress*; *wore the dress of a highlander*). **3** formal or ceremonial costume (*evening dress*; *morning dress*). **4** an external covering; the outward form (*birds in their winter dress*). □ **dress circle** the first gallery in a theatre, in which evening dress was formerly required. **dress coat** a man's swallow-tailed evening coat. **dress down** *colloq.* reprimand or scold. **dress length** a piece of material sufficient to make a dress. **dress out** attire conspicuously. **dress parade 1** *Mil.* a military parade in full dress uniform. **2** a display of clothes worn by models. **dress rehearsal** the final rehearsal of a play etc., wearing costume. **dress-shield** (or **-preserver**) a piece of waterproof material fastened in the armpit of a dress to protect it from sweat. **dress-shirt** a man's usu. starched white shirt worn with evening dress. **dress up 1** dress (oneself or another) elaborately for a special occasion. **2** dress in fancy dress. **3** disguise (unwelcome facts) by embellishment. [ME f. OF *dresser* ult. f. L *directus* DIRECT]

dressage /'dresɑːʒ, -sɑːdʒ/ *n.* the training of a horse in obedience and deportment, esp. for competition. [F f. *dresser* to train]

dresser[1] /'dresə(r)/ *n.* **1** a kitchen sideboard with shelves above for displaying plates etc. **2** *US* a dressing-table or chest of drawers. [ME f. OF *dresseur* f. *dresser* prepare: cf. med.L *directorium*]

dresser[2] /'dresə(r)/ *n.* **1** a person who assists actors to dress, takes care of their costumes, etc. **2** *Med.* a surgeon's assistant in operations. **3** a person who dresses elegantly or in a specified way (*a snappy dresser*).

dressing /'dresɪŋ/ *n.* **1** in senses of DRESS *v.* **2 a** an accompaniment to salads, usu. a mixture of oil with other ingredients; a sauce or seasoning (*French dressing*). **b** *US* stuffing. **3 a** a bandage for a wound. **b** ointment etc. used to dress a wound. **4** size or stiffening used to finish fabrics. **5** compost etc. spread over land (*a top dressing of peat*). □ **dressing-case** a case containing toiletries etc. **dressing-down** *colloq.* a scolding; a severe reprimand. **dressing-gown** a loose usu. belted robe worn over nightwear or while resting. **dressing-room 1** a room for changing the clothes etc. in a theatre, sports-ground, etc. **2** a small room attached to a bedroom, containing clothes. **dressing-station** esp. *Mil.* a place for giving emergency treatment to wounded people. **dressing-table** a table with a mirror, drawers, etc., used while applying make-up etc.

dressmaker /'dres,meɪkə(r)/ *n.* a woman who makes clothes professionally. □□ **dressmaking** *n.*

dressy /'dresɪ/ *adj.* (**dressier**, **dressiest**) **1 a** fond of smart clothes. **b** overdressed. **c** (of clothes) stylish or elaborate. **2** over-elaborate (*the design is rather dressy*). □□ **dressiness** *n.*

drew *past of* DRAW.

drey /dreɪ/ *n.* (also **dray**) a squirrel's nest. [17th c.: orig. unkn.]

Dreyfus /'dreɪfəs/, Alfred (1859–1935), French army officer whose trial on charges of spying for Germany caused a major political crisis in the Third Republic. Falsely accused of providing military secrets to the Germans in 1894, the trial, imprisonment, and eventual rehabilitation of the Jewish Dreyfus polarized deep-set anti-militarist and anti-Semitic trends in a society still coming to terms with defeat and revolution in 1870–1. Notable among the Dreyfusards, as supporters of the supposed spy were known, was the novelist Émile Zola, whose *J'accuse*, published in 1898, ruthlessly exposed attempts to cover up official mistakes.

dribble /'drɪb(ə)l/ *v.* & *n.* —*v.* **1** *intr.* allow saliva to flow from the mouth. **2** *intr.* & *tr.* flow or allow to flow in drops or a trickling stream. **3** *tr.* (also *absol.*) esp. *Football* & *Hockey* move (the ball) forward with slight touches of the feet, the stick, etc.

—*n.* **1** the act or an instance of dribbling. **2** a small trickling stream. □□ **dribbler** *n.* **dribbly** *adj.* [frequent. of obs. *drib*, var. of DRIP]

driblet /ˈdrɪblɪt/ *n.* **1 a** a small quantity. **b** a petty sum. **2** a thin stream; a dribble. [*drib* (see DRIBBLE) + -LET]

dribs and drabs /ˌdrɪbz ənd ˈdræbz/ *n.pl. colloq.* small scattered amounts (*did the work in dribs and drabs*). [as DRIBBLE + *drab* redupl.]

dried *past* and *past part.* of DRY.

drier[1] *compar.* of DRY.

drier[2] /ˈdraɪə(r)/ *n.* (also **dryer**) **1** a machine for drying the hair, laundry, etc. **2** a substance mixed with oil-paint or ink to promote drying.

driest *superl.* of DRY.

drift /drɪft/ *n.* & *v.* —*n.* **1 a** slow movement or variation. **b** such movement caused by a slow current. **2** the intention, meaning, scope, etc. of what is said etc. (*didn't understand his drift*). **3** a large mass of snow, sand, etc., accumulated by the wind. **4** esp. *derog.* a state of inaction. **5 a** *Naut.* a ship's deviation from its course, due to currents. **b** *Aeron.* an aircraft's deviation due to side winds. **c** a projectile's deviation due to its rotation. **d** a controlled slide of a racing car etc. **6** *Mining* a horizontal passage following a mineral vein. **7** a large mass of esp. flowering plants (*a drift of bluebells*). **8** *Geol.* **a** material deposited by the wind, a current of water, etc. **b** (**Drift**) Pleistocene ice detritus, e.g. boulder clay. **9** the movement of cattle, esp. a gathering on an appointed day to determine ownership etc. **10** a tool for enlarging or shaping a hole in metal. **11** *S.Afr.* a ford. —*v.* **1** *intr.* be carried by or as if by a current of air or water. **2** *intr.* move or progress passively, casually, or aimlessly (*drifted into teaching*). **3 a** *tr.* & *intr.* pile or be piled by the wind into drifts. **b** *tr.* cover (a field, a road, etc.) with drifts. **4** *tr.* form or enlarge (a hole) with a drift. **5** *tr.* (of a current) carry. □ **drift-ice** ice driven or deposited by water. **drift-net** a large net for herrings etc., allowed to drift with the tide. □□ **driftage** *n.* [ME f. ON & MDu., MHG *trift* movement of cattle: rel. to DRIVE]

drifter /ˈdrɪftə(r)/ *n.* **1** an aimless or rootless person. **2** a boat used for drift-net fishing.

driftwood /ˈdrɪftwʊd/ *n.* wood etc. driven or deposited by water or wind.

drill[1] /drɪl/ *n.* & *v.* —*n.* **1** a pointed, esp. revolving, steel tool or machine used for boring cylindrical holes, sinking wells, etc. **2 a** esp. *Mil.* instruction or training in military exercises. **b** rigorous discipline or methodical instruction, esp. when learning or performing tasks. **c** routine procedure to be followed in an emergency (*fire-drill*). **d** a routine or exercise (*drills in irregular verb patterns*). **3** *colloq.* a recognized procedure (*I expect you know the drill*). **4** any of various molluscs, esp. *Urosalpinx cinera*, that bore into the shells of young oysters. —*v.* **1** *tr.* (also *absol.*) **a** (of a person or a tool) make a hole with a drill through or into (wood, metal, etc.). **b** make (a hole) with a drill. **2** *tr.* & *intr.* esp. *Mil.* subject to or undergo discipline by drill. **3** *tr.* impart (knowledge etc.) by a strict method. **4** *tr. sl.* shoot with a gun (*drilled him full of holes*). □□ **driller** *n.* [earlier as verb, f. MDu. *drillen* bore, of unkn. orig.]

drill[2] /drɪl/ *n.* & *v.* —*n.* **1** a machine used for making furrows, sowing, and covering seed. **2** a small furrow for sowing seed in. **3** a ridge with such furrows on top. **4** a row of plants so sown. —*v.tr.* **1** sow (seed) with a drill. **2** plant (the ground) in drills. [perh. f. obs. *drill* rill (17th c., of unkn. orig.)]

drill[3] /drɪl/ *n.* a W. African baboon, *Papio leucophaeus*, related to the mandrill. [prob. a native name: cf. MANDRILL]

drill[4] /drɪl/ *n.* a coarse twilled cotton or linen fabric. [earlier *drilling* f. G *Drillich* f. L *trilix -licis* f. *tri-* three + *licium* thread]

drily /ˈdraɪlɪ/ *adv.* (also **dryly**) **1** (said) in a dry manner; humorously. **2** in a dry way or condition.

drink /drɪŋk/ *v.* & *n.* —*v.* (*past* **drank** /dræŋk/; *past part.* **drunk** /drʌŋk/) **1 a** *tr.* swallow (a liquid). **b** *tr.* swallow the liquid contents of (a vessel). **c** *intr.* swallow liquid, take draughts (*drank from the stream*). **2** *intr.* take alcohol, esp. to excess (*I have heard that he drinks*). **3** *tr.* (of a plant, porous material, etc.) absorb (moisture). **4** *refl.* bring (oneself etc.) to a specified condition by drinking

(*drank himself into a stupor*). **5** *tr.* (usu. foll. by *away*) spend (wages etc.) on drink (*drank away the money*). **6** *tr.* wish (a person's good health, luck, etc.) by drinking (*drank his health*). —*n.* **1 a** a liquid for drinking (*milk is a sustaining drink*). **b** a draught or specified amount of this (*had a drink of milk*). **2 a** alcoholic liquor (*got the drink in for Christmas*). **b** a portion, glass, etc. of this (*have a drink*). **c** excessive indulgence in alcohol (*drink is his vice*). **3** (as **the drink**) *colloq.* the sea. □ **drink deep** take a large draught or draughts. **drink-driver** a person who drives a vehicle with an excess of alcohol in the blood. **drink-driving** the act or an instance of this. **drink in** listen to closely or eagerly (*drank in his every word*). **drinking-song** a song sung while drinking, usu. concerning drink. **drinking-up time** *Brit.* a short period legally allowed for finishing drinks bought before closing time in a public house. **drinking-water** water pure enough for drinking. **drink off** drink the whole (contents) of at once. **drink to** toast; wish success to. **drink a person under the table** remain sober longer than one's drinking companion. **drink up** drink the whole of; empty. **in drink** drunk. **strong drink** alcohol, esp. spirits. □□ **drinkable** *adj.* **drinker** *n.* [OE *drincan* (v.), *drinc*(a) (n.) f. Gmc]

drip /drɪp/ *v.* & *n.* —*v.* (**dripped**, **dripping**) **1** *intr.* & *tr.* fall or let fall in drops. **2** *intr.* (often foll. by *with*) be so wet as to shed drops (*dripped with blood*). —*n.* **1 a** the act or an instance of dripping (*the steady drip of rain*). **b** a drop of liquid (*a drip of paint*). **c** a sound of dripping. **2** *colloq.* a stupid, dull, or ineffective person. **3** (*Med.* **drip-feed**) the drip-by-drip intravenous administration of a solution of salt, sugar, etc. **4** *Archit.* a projection, esp. from a window-sill, keeping the rain off the walls. □ **drip-dry** *v.* (**-dries**, **-dried**) **1** *intr.* (of fabric etc.) dry crease-free when hung up to drip. **2** *tr.* leave (a garment etc.) hanging up to dry. —*adj.* able to be drip-dried. **drip-mat** a small mat under a glass. **drip-moulding** (or **-stone**) *Archit.* a stone etc. projection that deflects rain etc. from walls. **dripping wet** very wet. [MDa. *drippe* f. Gmc (cf. DROP)]

dripping /ˈdrɪpɪŋ/ *n.* **1** fat melted from roasted meat and used for cooking or as a spread. **2** (in *pl.*) water, grease, etc., dripping from anything.

drippy /ˈdrɪpɪ/ *adj.* (**drippier**, **drippiest**) **1** tending to drip. **2** *sl.* (of a person) ineffectual; sloppily sentimental. □□ **drippily** *adv.* **drippiness** *n.*

drive /draɪv/ *v.* & *n.* —*v.* (*past* **drove** /drəʊv/; *past part.* **driven** /ˈdrɪv(ə)n/) **1** *tr.* (usu. foll. by *away*, *back*, *in*, *out*, *to*, etc.) urge in some direction, esp. forcibly (*drove back the wolves*). **2** *tr.* **a** (usu. foll. by *to* + infin., or *to* + verbal noun) compel or constrain forcibly (*was driven to complain*; *drove her to stealing*). **b** (often foll. by *to*) force into a specified state (*drove him mad*; *driven to despair*). **c** (often *refl.*) urge to overwork (*drives himself too hard*). **3 a** *tr.* (also *absol.*) operate and direct the course of (a vehicle, a locomotive, etc.) (*drove a sports car*; *drives well*). **b** *tr.* & *intr.* convey or be conveyed in a vehicle (*drove them to the station*; *drove to the station in a bus*) (cf. RIDE). **c** *tr.* (also *absol.*) be licensed or competent to drive (a vehicle) (*does he drive?*). **d** *tr.* (also *absol.*) urge and direct the course of (an animal drawing a vehicle or plough). **4** *tr.* (of wind, water, etc.) carry along, propel, send, or cause to go in some direction (*pure as the driven snow*). **5** *tr.* **a** (often foll. by *into*) force (a stake, nail, etc.) into place by blows (*drove the nail home*). **b** *Mining* bore (a tunnel, horizontal cavity, etc.). **6** *tr.* effect or conclude forcibly (*drove a hard bargain*; *drove his point home*). **7** *tr.* (of steam or other power) set or keep (machinery) going. **8** *intr.* (usu. foll. by *at*) work hard; dash, rush, or hasten. **9** *tr. Cricket* & *Tennis* hit (the ball) hard from a freely swung bat or racket. **10** *tr.* (often *absol.*) *Golf* strike (a ball) with a driver from the tee. **11** *tr.* chase or frighten (game, wild beasts, an enemy in warfare, etc.) from a large area to a smaller, to kill or capture; corner. **12** *tr. Brit.* hold a drift in (a forest etc.) (see DRIFT *n.* 9). —*n.* **1** an act of driving in a motor vehicle; a journey or excursion in such a vehicle (*went for a pleasant drive*; *lives an hour's drive from us*). **2 a** the capacity for achievement; motivation and energy (*lacks the drive needed to succeed*). **b** *Psychol.* an inner urge to attain a goal or satisfy a need (*unconscious emotional drives*). **3 a** a usu. landscaped street or road. **b** a usu. private road through a garden or park to a house. **4** *Cricket, Golf,* & *Tennis* a driving stroke of the bat etc. **5** an organized effort to achieve a usu. charitable purpose (*a famine-relief drive*). **6 a** the transmission of power to machinery, the wheels of a motor vehicle, etc. (*belt drive; front-wheel drive*). **b** the position of a steering-wheel in a motor vehicle (*left-hand drive*). **c** *Computing* = disk drive (see DISC). **7** *Brit.* an organized competition, for many players, of whist, bingo, etc. **8** an act of driving game or an enemy. **9** *Austral.* & *NZ* a line of partly cut trees on a hillside felled when the top one topples on the others. □ **drive at** seek, intend, or mean (*what is he driving at?*). **drive-in** *attrib.adj.* (of a bank, cinema, etc.) able to be used while sitting in one's car. —*n.* such a bank, cinema, etc. **drive-on** (of a ship) on to which motor vehicles may be driven. **drive out** take the place of; oust; exorcize, cast out (*evil spirits etc.*). **driving-licence** a licence permitting a person to drive a motor vehicle. **driving rain** an excessive windblown downpour. **driving-range** *Golf* an area for practising drives. **driving test** an official test of a motorist's competence which must be passed to obtain a driving licence. **driving-wheel 1** the large wheel of a locomotive. **2** a wheel communicating motive power in machinery. **let drive** aim a blow or missile. □□ **drivable** *adj.* [OE *drīfan* f. Gmc]

drivel /ˈdrɪv(ə)l/ *n.* & *v.* —*n.* silly nonsense; twaddle. —*v.* (**drivelled**, **drivelling**; *US* **driveled**, **driveling**) **1** *intr.* run at the mouth or nose; dribble. **2** *intr.* talk childishly or idiotically. **3** *tr.* (foll. by *away*) fritter; squander away. □□ **driveller** *n.* (*US* **driveler**). [OE *dreflian* (v.)]

driven *past part.* of DRIVE.

driver /ˈdraɪvə(r)/ *n.* **1** (often in *comb.*) a person who drives a vehicle (*bus-driver; engine-driver*). **2** *Golf* a club with a flat face and wooden head, used for driving from the tee. **3** *Electr.* a device or part of a circuit providing power for output. **4** *Mech.* a wheel etc. receiving power directly and transmitting motion to other parts. □ **in the driver's seat** in charge. □□ **driverless** *adj.*

driveway /ˈdraɪvweɪ/ *n.* = DRIVE *n.* 3b.

drizzle /ˈdrɪz(ə)l/ *n.* & *v.* —*n.* very fine rain. —*v.intr.* (esp. of rain) fall in very fine drops (*it's drizzling again*). □□ **drizzly** *adj.* [prob. f. ME *drēse*, OE *drēosan* fall]

drogue /drəʊg/ *n.* **1** *Naut.* **a** a buoy at the end of a harpoon line. **b** a sea anchor. **2** *Aeron.* a truncated cone of fabric used as a brake, a target for gunnery, a wind-sock, etc. [18th c.: orig. unkn.]

droit /drɔɪt/ *n. Law* a right or due. [ME f. OF f. L *directum* (n.) f. *directus* DIRECT]

droit de seigneur /ˌdrwɑː də senˈjɜː(r)/ *n. hist.* the alleged right of a feudal lord to have sexual intercourse with a vassal's bride on her wedding night. [F, = lord's right]

droll /drəʊl/ *adj.* & *n.* —*adj.* **1** quaintly amusing. **2** strange; odd; surprising. —*n. archaic* **1** a jester; an entertainer. **2** a quaintly amusing person. □□ **drollery** *n.* (pl. **-ies**). **drolly** /ˈdrəʊllɪ/ *adv.* **drollness** *n.* [F *drôle*, perh. f. MDu. *drolle* little man]

drome /drəʊm/ *n. colloq. archaic* aerodrome. [abbr.]

-drome /drəʊm/ *comb. form* forming nouns denoting: **1** a place for running, racing, or other forms of movement (*aerodrome; hippodrome*). **2** a thing that runs or proceeds in a certain way (*palindrome; syndrome*). [Gk *dromos* course, running]

dromedary /ˈdrɒmɪdərɪ, ˈdrʌm-/ *n.* (pl. **-ies**) a one-humped camel, *Camelus dromedarius*, bred for riding and racing. Also called *Arabian camel*. [ME f. OF *dromedaire* or LL *dromedarius* ult. f. Gk *dromas -ados* runner]

dromond /ˈdrɒmənd, ˈdrʌm-/ *n. hist.* a large medieval ship used for war or commerce. [ME f. OF *dromon(t)* f. LL *dromo -onis* f. late Gk *dromōn* light vessel]

drone /drəʊn/ *n.* & *v.* —*n.* **1** a non-working male of the honey-bee, whose sole function is to mate with fertile females. **2** an idler. **3** a deep humming sound. **4** a monotonous speech or speaker. **5 a** a pipe, esp. of a bagpipe, sounding a continuous note of fixed low pitch. **b** the note emitted by this. **6** a remote-controlled pilotless aircraft or missile. —*v.* **1** *intr.* make a deep humming sound. **2** *intr.* & *tr.* speak or utter monotonously. **3 a** *intr.* be idle. **b** *tr.* (often foll. by *away*) idle away (one's time etc.). [OE *drān, drǣn* prob. f. WG]

drongo /ˈdrɒŋgəʊ/ *n.* (pl. **-os** or **-oes**) **1** any black bird of the

family Dicruridae, native to India, Africa, and Australia, having a long forked tail. **2** *Austral.* & *NZ sl. derog.* a simpleton. [Malagasy]

droob /druːb/ *n. Austral. sl.* a hopeless-looking ineffectual person. [perh. f. DROOP]

drool /druːl/ *v.* & *n.* —*v.intr.* **1** drivel; slobber. **2** (often foll. by *over*) show much pleasure or infatuation. —*n.* slobbering; drivelling. [contr. of *drivel*]

droop /druːp/ *v.* & *n.* —*v.* **1** *intr.* & *tr.* hang or allow to hang down; languish, decline, or sag, esp. from weariness. **2** *intr.* **a** (of the eyes) look downwards. **b** *poet.* (of the sun) sink. **3** *intr.* lose heart; be dejected; flag. —*n.* **1** a drooping attitude. **2** a loss of spirit or enthusiasm. □ **droop-snoot** *colloq.* —*adj.* (of an aircraft) having an adjustable nose or leading-edge flap. —*n.* such an aircraft. [ME f. ON *drúpa* hang the head f. Gmc: cf. DROP]

droopy /ˈdruːpɪ/ *adj.* (**droopier**, **droopiest**) **1** drooping. **2** dejected, gloomy. □□ **droopily** *adv.* **droopiness** *n.*

drop /drɒp/ *n.* & *v.* —*n.* **1 a** a small round or pear-shaped portion of liquid that hangs or falls or adheres to a surface (*drops of dew; tears fell in large drops*). **b** a very small amount of usu. drinkable liquid (*just a drop left in the glass*). **c** a glass etc. of alcoholic liquor (*take a drop with us*). **2 a** an abrupt fall or slope. **b** the amount of this (*a drop of fifteen feet*). **c** an act of falling or dropping (*had a nasty drop*). **d** a reduction in prices, temperature, etc. **e** a deterioration or worsening (*a drop in status*). **3** something resembling a drop, esp.: **a** a pendant or earring. **b** a crystal ornament on a chandelier etc. **c** (often in *comb.*) a sweet or lozenge (*pear-drop; cough drop*). **4** something that drops or is dropped, esp.: **a** *Theatr.* a painted curtain or scenery let down on to the stage. **b** a platform or trapdoor on a gallows, the opening of which causes the victim to fall. **5** *Med.* **a** the smallest separable quantity of a liquid. **b** (in *pl.*) liquid medicine to be measured in drops (*eye drops*). **6** a minute quantity (*not a drop of pity*). **7** *sl.* **a** a hiding-place for stolen or illicit goods. **b** a secret place where documents etc. may be left or passed on in espionage. **8** *sl.* a bribe. **9** *US* a box for letters etc. —*v.* (**dropped**, **dropping**) **1** *intr.* & *tr.* fall or let fall in drops (*tears dropped on to the book; dropped the soup down his shirt*). **2** *intr.* & *tr.* fall or allow to fall; relinquish; let go (*dropped the box; the egg dropped from my hand*). **3 a** *intr.* & *tr.* sink or cause to sink or fall to the ground from exhaustion, a blow, a wound, etc. **b** *intr.* die. **4 a** *intr.* & *tr.* cease or cause to cease; lapse or let lapse; abandon (*the connection dropped; dropped the friendship; drop everything and come at once*). **b** *tr. colloq.* cease to associate with. **5** *tr.* set down (a passenger etc.) (*drop me at the station*). **6** *tr.* & *intr.* utter or be uttered casually (*dropped a hint; the remark dropped into the conversation*). **7** *tr.* send casually (*drop me a postcard*). **8 a** *intr.* & *tr.* fall or allow to fall in direction, amount, condition, degree, pitch, etc. (*his voice dropped; the wind dropped; we dropped the price by £20; the road dropped southwards*). **b** *intr.* (of a person) jump down lightly; let oneself fall. **c** *tr.* remove (clothes, esp. trousers) rapidly, allowing them to fall to the ground. **9** *tr. colloq.* lose (money, esp. in gambling). **10** *tr.* omit (a letter, esp. aitch, a syllable etc.) in speech. **11** *tr.* (as **dropped** *adj.*) in a lower position than usual (*dropped handlebars; dropped waist*). **12** *tr.* give birth to (esp. a lamb, a kitten, etc.). **13 a** *intr.* (of a card) be played in the same trick as a higher card. **b** *tr.* play or cause (a card) to be played in this way. **14** *tr. Sport* lose (a game, a point, a contest, a match, etc.). **15** *tr. Aeron.* deliver (supplies etc.) by parachute. **16** *tr. Football* **a** send (a ball) by a drop-kick. **b** score (a goal) by a drop-kick. **17** *tr. colloq.* dismiss or omit (*was dropped from the team*). □ **at the drop of a hat** given the slightest excuse. **drop anchor** anchor ship. **drop asleep** fall gently asleep. **drop away** decrease or depart gradually. **drop back** (or **behind** or **to the rear**) fall back; get left behind. **drop back into** return to (a habit etc.). **drop a brick** *colloq.* make an indiscreet or embarrassing remark. **drop-curtain** (or **-scene**) *Theatr.* a painted curtain or scenery (cf. sense 4 of *n.*). **drop a curtsy** make a curtsy. **drop dead!** *sl.* an exclamation of intense scorn. **drop down** descend a hill etc. **drop-forging** a method of forcing white-hot metal through an open-ended die by a heavy weight. **drop-hammer** a heavy weight raised mechanically and allowed to drop, as used in drop-forging and pile-driving. **drop-head** *Brit.* the adjustable fabric roof of a car. **drop in** (or **by**) *colloq.* call casually as a visitor. **drop-in centre** a meeting-place where people may call casually for advice, conversation, etc. **a drop in the ocean** (or **a bucket**) a very small amount, esp. compared with what is needed or expected. **drop into** colloq. **1** call casually at (a place). **2** fall into (a habit etc.). **drop it!** sl. stop that! **drop-kick** Football a kick made by dropping the ball and kicking it on the bounce. **drop-leaf** (of a table etc.) having a hinged flap. **drop off 1** decline gradually. **2** colloq. fall asleep. **3** = sense 5 of v. **drop on** reprimand or punish. **drop out** colloq. cease to participate, esp. in a race, a course of study, or in conventional society. **drop-out** n. **1** colloq. a person who has dropped out. **2** the restarting of a game by a drop-kick. **drop scone** Brit. a small thick pancake made by dropping batter into a frying pan etc. **drop-shot** (in lawn tennis) a shot dropping abruptly over the net. **drop a stitch** let a stitch fall off the end of a knitting-needle. **drop-test** Engin. n. a test done by dropping under standard conditions. —v.tr. carry out a drop-test on. **drop to** sl. become aware of. **fit (or ready) to drop** extremely tired. **have the drop on** colloq. have the advantage over. **have had a drop too much** colloq. be slightly drunk. □□ **droplet** n. [OE dropa, drop(p)ian ult. f. Gmc: cf. DRIP, DROOP]

dropper /ˈdrɒpə(r)/ n. **1** a device for administering liquid, esp. medicine, in drops. **2** Austral., NZ, & S.Afr. a light vertical stave in a fence.

droppings /ˈdrɒpɪŋz/ n.pl. **1** the dung of animals or birds. **2** something that falls or has fallen in drops, e.g. wax from candles.

dropsy /ˈdrɒpsɪ/ n. (pl. **-ies**) **1** = OEDEMA. **2** sl. a tip or bribe. □□ **dropsical** adj. (in sense 1). [ME f. idrop(e)sie f. OF idropesie ult. f. L hydropisis f. Gk hudrōps dropsy (as HYDRO-)]

dropwort /ˈdrɒpwɜːt/ n. a plant, Filipendula vulgaris, with tuberous root fibres.

droshky /ˈdrɒʃkɪ/ n. (pl. **-ies**) a Russian low four-wheeled open carriage. [Russ. drozhki dimin. of drogi wagon f. droga shaft]

drosophila /drəˈsɒfɪlə/ n. any fruit fly of the genus Drosophila, used extensively in genetic research. [mod.L f. Gk drosos dew, moisture + philos loving]

dross /drɒs/ n. **1** rubbish, refuse. **2 a** the scum separated from metals in melting. **b** foreign matter mixed with anything; impurities. □□ **drossy** adj. [OE drōs: cf. MLG drōsem, OHG truosana]

Drottningholm /ˈdrɒtnɪŋˌhɒm/ a town in eastern Sweden, near which is the 17th-c. winter palace of the Swedish kings.

drought /draʊt/ n. **1** the continuous absence of rain; dry weather. **2** the prolonged lack of something. **3** archaic a lack of moisture; thirst; dryness. □□ **droughty** adj. [OE drūgath f. drȳge DRY]

drouth /draʊθ/ n. Sc., Ir., US, & poet. var. of DROUGHT.

Drouzhba /ˈdruːʒbə/ (also **Druzba**) a resort town on the Black Sea coast of Bulgaria.

drove[1] past of DRIVE.

drove[2] /drəʊv/ n. **1 a** a large number (of people etc.) moving together; a crowd; a multitude; a shoal. **b** (in pl.) colloq. a great number (people arrived in droves). **2** a herd or flock being driven or moving together. □ **drove-road** an ancient cattle track. [OE drāf f. drīfan DRIVE]

drover /ˈdrəʊvə(r)/ n. a person who drives herds to market; a cattle-dealer. □□ **drove** v.tr. **droving** n.

drown /draʊn/ v. **1** tr. & intr. kill or be killed by submersion in liquid. **2** tr. submerge; flood; drench (drowned the fields in six feet of water). **3** tr. (often foll. by in) deaden (grief etc.) with drink (drowned his sorrows in drink). **4** tr. (often foll. by out) make (a sound) inaudible by means of a louder sound. □ **drowned valley** a valley partly or wholly submerged by a change in land-levels. **drown out** drive out by flood. **like a drowned rat** colloq. extremely wet and bedraggled. [ME (orig. north.) drun(e), droun(e), perh. f. OE drūnian (unrecorded), rel. to DRINK]

drowse /draʊz/ v. & n. —v. **1** intr. be dull and sleepy or half asleep. **2** tr. **a** (often foll. by away) pass (the time) in drowsing. **b** make drowsy. **3** intr. archaic be sluggish. —n. a condition of sleepiness. [back-form. f. DROWSY]

drowsy /ˈdraʊzɪ/ adj. (**drowsier, drowsiest**) **1** half asleep; dozing. **2** soporific; lulling. **3** sluggish. □□ **drowsily** adv. **drowsiness** n. [prob. rel. to OE drūsian be languid or slow, drēosan fall: cf. DREARY]

drub /drʌb/ v.tr. (**drubbed, drubbing**) **1** thump; belabour. **2** beat in a fight. **3** (usu. foll. by into, out of) beat (an idea, attitude, etc.) into or out of a person. □□ **drubbing** n. [ult. f. Arab. ḍaraba beat]

drudge /drʌdʒ/ n. & v. —n. a servile worker, esp. at menial tasks; a hack. —v.intr. (often foll. by at) work slavishly (at menial, hard, or dull work). □□ **drudgery** /ˈdrʌdʒərɪ/ n. [15th c.: perh. rel. to DRAG]

drug /drʌg/ n. & v. —n. **1** a medicinal substance. **2** a narcotic, hallucinogen, or stimulant, esp. one causing addiction. —v. (**drugged, drugging**) **1** tr. add a drug to (food or drink). **2** tr. **a** administer a drug to. **b** stupefy with a drug. **3** intr. take drugs as an addict. □ **drug addict** a person who is addicted to a narcotic drug. **drug on the market** a commodity that is plentiful but no longer in demand. **drug peddler** (colloq. **pusher**) a person who sells esp. addictive drugs illegally. **drug squad** a division of a police force investigating crimes involving illegal drugs. [ME drogges, drouges f. OF drogue, of unkn. orig.]

drugget /ˈdrʌgɪt/ n. **1** a coarse woven fabric used as a floor or table covering. **2** such a covering. [F droguet, of unkn. orig.]

druggist /ˈdrʌgɪst/ n. esp. US a pharmacist. [F droguiste (as DRUG)]

druggy /ˈdrʌgɪ/ n. & adj. colloq. —n. (also **druggie**) (pl. **-ies**) a drug addict. —adj. of or associated with narcotic drugs.

drugstore /ˈdrʌgstɔː(r)/ n. US a chemist's shop also selling light refreshments and other articles.

Druid /ˈdruːɪd/ n. (fem. **Druidess**) **1** an ancient Celtic priest, magician, or soothsayer of Gaul, Britain, or Ireland. (See below.) **2** a member of any of various movements seeking to revive Druid practices. **3** an officer of the Gorsedd. □□ **Druidism** n. **Druidic** /-ˈɪdɪk/ adj. **Druidical** /-ˈɪdɪk(ə)l/ adj. [F druide or L pl. druidae, -des, Gk druidai f. Gaulish druides]

Our picture of the Druids is based chiefly on the hostile account of them in the writings of Julius Caesar and Tacitus. Caesar reports that they had judicial and priestly functions, were proficient in natural philosophy, and held responsibility for the education of young Gaulish nobles, a duty which they carried on in oral poetry; they worshipped in 'groves' (clearings in the forest) and cut mistletoe from the sacred oak with a golden sickle. The religion was stamped out by the Romans with unrelenting ferocity, either because of the human sacrifices that it involved or lest it should become a focus for resistance to Roman rule. Druidism of the Roman period may well contain elements of older faiths. Its association with Stonehenge, however, is now rejected (there is no mention of any constructed temple in the classical accounts), but the modern Druidical order seeks to make ceremonial use of the site.

drum[1] /drʌm/ n. & v. —n. **1 a** a percussion instrument or toy made of a hollow cylinder or hemisphere covered at one or both ends with stretched skin or parchment and sounded by striking (bass drum; kettledrum). **b** (often in pl.) a drummer or a percussion section (the drums are playing too loud). **c** a sound made by or resembling that of a drum. **2** something resembling a drum in shape, esp.: **a** a cylindrical container or receptacle for oil, dried fruit, etc. **b** a cylinder or barrel in machinery on which something is wound etc. **c** Archit. the solid part of a Corinthian or composite capital. **d** Archit. a stone block forming a section of a shaft. **e** Austral. & NZ swag, a bundle. **3** Zool. & Anat. the membrane of the middle ear; the eardrum. **4** sl. **a** a house. **b** a nightclub. **c** a brothel. **5** (in full **drum-fish**) any marine fish of the family Sciaenidae, having a swim-bladder that produces a drumming sound. **6** hist. an evening or afternoon tea party. **7** Austral. sl. a piece of reliable information, esp. a racing tip. —v. (**drummed, drumming**) **1** intr. & tr. play on a drum. **2** tr. & intr. beat, tap, or thump (knuckles, feet, etc.) continuously (on something) (drummed on the table; drummed his feet; drumming at the window). **3** intr. (of a bird or an insect) make a loud, hollow noise with quivering wings. **4** tr. Austral. sl. provide with reliable information. □ **drum brake** a brake in which shoes on a vehicle press against the drum on a wheel. **drum into** drive (a lesson) into (a person) by persistence. **drum machine** an electronic device that imitates the sound of percussion instruments. **drum major 1** the leader of a marching band. **2** *archaic* an NCO commanding the drummers of a regiment. **drum majorette** esp. *US* a member of a female baton-twirling parading group. **drum out** *Mil.* cashier (a soldier) by the beat of a drum; dismiss with ignominy. **drum up** summon, gather, or call up (*needs to drum up more support*). [obs. *drombslade, drombyllsclad*, f. LG *trommelslag* drum-beat f. *trommel* drum + *slag* beat]

drum² /drʌm/ *n.* (also **drumlin** /ˈdrʌmlɪn/) *Geol.* a long oval mound of boulder clay moulded by glacial action. □□ **drumlinoid** *n.* [Gael. & Ir. *druim* ridge: *-lin* perh. for -LING¹]

drumfire /ˈdrʌmˌfaɪə(r)/ *n.* **1** *Mil.* heavy continuous rapid artillery fire, usu. heralding an infantry attack. **2** a barrage of criticism etc.

drumhead /ˈdrʌmhed/ *n.* **1** the skin or membrane of a drum. **2** an eardrum. **3** the circular top of a capstan. **4** (*attrib.*) improvised (*drumhead court martial*).

drumlin var. of DRUM².

drummer /ˈdrʌmə(r)/ *n.* **1** a person who plays a drum or drums. **2** esp. *US colloq.* a commercial traveller. **3** *sl.* a thief.

drumstick /ˈdrʌmstɪk/ *n.* **1** a stick used for beating a drum. **2** the lower joint of the leg of a cooked chicken, turkey, etc.

drunk /drʌŋk/ *adj.* & *n.* —*adj.* **1** rendered incapable by alcohol (*blind drunk; dead drunk; drunk as a lord*). **2** (often foll. by *with*) overcome or elated with joy, success, power, etc. —*n.* **1** a habitually drunk person. **2** *sl.* a drinking-bout; a period of drunkenness. [past part. of DRINK]

drunkard /ˈdrʌŋkəd/ *n.* a person who is drunk, esp. habitually.

drunken /ˈdrʌŋkən/ *adj.* (usu. *attrib.*) **1** = DRUNK. **2** caused by or exhibiting drunkenness (*a drunken brawl*). **3** fond of drinking; often drunk. □□ **drunkenly** *adv.* **drunkenness** *n.*

drupe /druːp/ *n.* any fleshy or pulpy fruit enclosing a stone containing one or a few seeds, e.g. an olive, plum, or peach. □□ **drupaceous** /-ˈpeɪʃəs/ *adj.* [L *drupa* f. Gk *druppa* olive]

drupel /ˈdruːp(ə)l/ *n.* (also **drupelet** /ˈdruːplɪt/) a small drupe usu. in an aggregate fruit, e.g. a blackberry or raspberry.

Drury Lane /ˈdrʊərɪ/, **Theatre Royal**, London's most famous theatre. The first theatre on the site opened in 1663 (see PATENT THEATRE), the second—notable for David Garrick's association with it—in 1674, and the third in 1794. The present theatre, dating from 1812, was not particularly successful until the 1880s, when it became famous for its melodramas and spectacles. Since the 1920s it has staged musicals, including *The Desert Song* (1927), *Glamorous Night* (1935), *Oklahoma!* (1947), *My Fair Lady* (1958), and *Hello, Dolly!* (1965).

Druse /druːz/ *n.* (often *attrib.*) a member of a political and religious sect of Muslim origin, concentrated in Lebanon, with smaller groups in Syria and Israel. The sect broke away from Ismaili Shiite Islam in the 11th c. over a disagreement about the succession to the imamate (leadership), a position in which spiritual and political leadership were and are indissolubly linked. The Druses followed the seventh caliph of the Fatimid dynasty, al-Hakim b'illah (996–1021), who is claimed to have disappeared and whose return is expected. They regard al-Hakim as a deity, and thus are considered heretics by the Muslim community at large. [F f. Arab. *durūz* (pl.), prob. f. their founder *al-Darazī* (11th c.)]

druse /druːz/ *n.* **1** a crust of crystals lining a rock-cavity. **2** a cavity lined with this. [F f. G, = weathered ore]

Druzba see DROUZHBA.

dry /draɪ/ *adj., v.,* & *n.* —*adj.* (**drier** /ˈdraɪə(r)/; **driest** /ˈdraɪɪst/) **1** free from moisture, not wet, esp.: **a** with any moisture having evaporated, drained, or been wiped away (*the clothes are not dry yet*). **b** (of the eyes) free from tears. **c** (of a climate etc.) with insufficient rainfall; not rainy (*a dry spell*). **d** (of a river, well, etc.) dried up; not yielding water. **e** (of a liquid) having disappeared by evaporation etc. **f** not connected with or for use without moisture (*dry shampoo*). **g** (of a shave) with an electric razor. **2** (of wine etc.) not sweet (*dry sherry*). **3 a** meagre, plain, or bare (*dry facts*). **b** uninteresting; dull (*dry as dust*). **4** (of a sense of humour, a joke, etc.) subtle, ironic, and quietly expressed; not

obvious. **5** (of a country, of legislation, etc.) prohibiting the sale of alcoholic drink. **6** (of toast, bread, etc.) without butter, margarine, etc. **7** (of provisions, groceries, etc.) solid, not liquid (*dry goods*). **8** impassive, unsympathetic; hard; cold. **9** (of a cow etc.) not yielding milk. **10** *colloq.* thirsty or thirst-making (*feel dry; this is dry work*). **11** *Polit. colloq.* of or being a political 'dry'. —*v.* (**dries, dried**) **1** *tr.* make or become dry by wiping, evaporation, draining, etc. **2** *tr.* (usu. as **dried** *adj.*) preserve (food etc.) by removing the moisture (*dried egg; dried fruit; dried flowers*). **3** *intr.* (often foll. by *up*) *Theatr. colloq.* forget one's lines. **4** *tr.* & *intr.* (often foll. by *off*) cease or cause (a cow etc.) to cease yielding milk. —*n.* (pl. **dries**) **1** the process or an instance of drying. **2** *sl.* a politician, esp. a Conservative, who advocates individual responsibility, free trade, and economic stringency, and opposes high government spending. **3 a** (prec. by *the*) esp. *Austral. colloq.* the dry season. **b** *Austral.* a desert area, waterless country. **4 a** dry ginger ale. **b** dry wine, sherry, etc. □ **dry battery** *Electr.* an electric battery consisting of dry cells. **dry cell** *Electr.* a cell in which the electrolyte is absorbed in a solid and cannot be spilled. **dry-clean** clean (clothes etc.) with organic solvents without using water. **dry-cleaner** a firm that specializes in dry-cleaning. **dry cough** a cough not producing phlegm. **dry-cure** cure (meat etc.) without pickling in liquid. **dry dock** an enclosure for the building or repairing of ships, from which water can be pumped out. **dry-fly** *adj.* (of fishing) with an artificial fly floating on the surface. —*v.intr.* (**-flies, -flied**) fish by such a method. **dry ice** solid carbon dioxide. **dry land** land as opposed to the sea, a river, etc. **dry measure** a measure of capacity for dry goods. **dry milk** *US* dried milk. **dry-nurse** a nurse for young children, not required to breast-feed. **dry out 1** become fully dry. **2** (of a drug addict, alcoholic, etc.) undergo treatment to cure addiction. **dry painting** see SAND-PAINTING. **dry-plate** *Photog.* a photographic plate with sensitized film hard and dry for convenience of keeping, developing at leisure, etc. **dry-point 1** a needle for engraving on a bare copper plate without acid. **2** an engraving produced with this. **dry rot 1** a decayed state of wood when not ventilated, caused by certain fungi. **2** these fungi. **dry run** *colloq.* a rehearsal. **dry-salt** = *dry-cure*. **dry-salter** a dealer in dyes, gums, drugs, oils, pickles, tinned meats, etc. **dry-shod** without wetting the shoes. **dry up 1** make utterly dry. **2** dry dishes. **3** (of moisture) disappear utterly. **4** (of a well etc.) cease to yield water. **5** *colloq.* (esp. in *imper.*) cease talking. **go dry** enact legislation for the prohibition of alcohol. □□ **dryish** *adj.* **dryness** *n.* [OE *drȳge, drygan*, rel. to MLG *dröge*, MDu. *dröghe*, f. Gmc]

dryad /ˈdraɪæd, ˈdraɪəd/ *n. Mythol.* a nymph inhabiting a tree; a wood nymph. [ME f. OF *dryade* f. L f. Gk *druas -ados* f. *drus* tree]

Dryden /ˈdraɪd(ə)n/, John (1631–1700), English poet, critic, and dramatist. He wrote his first major poem *Heroique Stanzas* (1658) on the death of Cromwell, and later celebrated Charles II's return with two panegyrics. During 1663–81 Dryden wrote almost a play a year (the theatres had been reopened), of which the greatest was the blank verse *All for Love* (1678), based on Shakespeare's *Antony and Cleopatra*. His verse satires, including *Absalom and Achitophel* (1681) and *MacFlecknoe* (1682), demonstrate his developing mastery of the heroic couplet. Following James II's accession Dryden became a Catholic, and lost the position of Poet Laureate, which he had held since 1668, on the accession of the Protestant William III. Dr Johnson, with justification, described Dryden as the 'father of English criticism'. His major critical work is *Of Dramatic Poesie* (1668) but much of his criticism is found in his Prefaces and Prologues. His splendid achievements as a translator include a version of Virgil's *Georgics*, and *Fables Ancient and Modern* (1699).

dryer var. of DRIER².

dryly var. of DRILY.

Dryopithecus /ˌdraɪəˈpɪθɪkəs/ *n.* a genus of fossil anthropoid apes that existed in Europe, Asia, and Africa from the early Miocene to early Pliocene periods (*c.*23–10 million years ago). It is believed that the family to which mankind belongs diverged from these between about 20 and 10 million years ago, through an as yet unspecified species of Dryopithecus. □□ **dryopithecine** /-saɪn/ *adj.* [mod.L f. Gk *drus* tree + *pithēkos* ape]

Drysdale /ˈdraɪzdeɪl/, Sir Russell (1912–81), Australian painter, born in England, whose work became well known throughout Australia during the 1940s. An exhibition of his paintings held in London in 1950 aroused a new interest in Australian art. His subject-matter is the Australian bush and its associated hardship, tragedy, and melancholy, and the plight of Aborigines in contact with White settlement.

drystone /ˈdraɪstəʊn/ adj. (of a wall etc.) built without mortar.

DS abbr. **1** dal segno. **2** disseminated sclerosis.

DSC abbr. Distinguished Service Cross.

D.Sc. abbr. Doctor of Science.

DSM abbr. Distinguished Service Medal.

DSO abbr. (in the UK) Distinguished Service Order.

DSS abbr. (in the UK) Department of Social Security (formerly DHSS).

DT abbr. (also **DT's** /diːˈtiːz/) delirium tremens.

DTI abbr. (in the UK) Department of Trade and Industry.

dual /ˈdjuːəl/ adj., n., & v. —adj. **1** of two; twofold. **2** divided in two; double (dual ownership). **3** Gram. (in some languages) denoting two persons or things (additional to singular and plural). —n. (also **dual number**) Gram. a dual form of a noun, verb, etc. —v.tr. (**dualled, dualling**) Brit. convert (a road) into a dual carriageway. □ **dual carriageway** Brit. a road with a dividing strip between the traffic in opposite directions. **dual control** (of a vehicle or an aircraft) having two sets of controls, one of which is used by the instructor. **dual in-line package** Computing see DIP. **dual-purpose** (of a vehicle) usable for passengers or goods. □□ **duality** /-ˈælɪtɪ/ n. **dualize** v.tr. (also **-ise**). **dually** adv. [L dualis f. duo two]

dualism /ˈdjuːəlɪz(ə)m/ n. **1** being twofold; duality. **2** Philos. the theory that in any domain of reality there are two independent underlying principles, e.g. mind and matter, form and content (cf. IDEALISM, MATERIALISM). **3** Theol. **a** the theory that the forces of good and evil are equally balanced in the universe. **b** the theory of the dual (human and divine) personality of Christ. □□ **dualist** n. **dualistic** /-ˈlɪstɪk/ adj. **dualistically** /-ˈlɪstɪkəlɪ/ adv.

dub[1] /dʌb/ v.tr. (**dubbed, dubbing**) **1** make (a person) a knight by touching his shoulders with a sword. **2** give (a person) a name, nickname, or title (dubbed him a crank). **3** Brit. dress (an artificial fishing-fly). **4** smear (leather) with grease. [OE f. AF duber, aduber, OF adober equip with armour, repair, of unkn. orig.]

dub[2] /dʌb/ v.tr. (**dubbed, dubbing**) **1** provide (a film etc.) with an alternative soundtrack, esp. in a different language. **2** add (sound effects or music) to a film or a broadcast. **3** combine (soundtracks) into one. **4** transfer or make a copy of (a soundtrack). [abbr. of DOUBLE]

dub[3] /dʌb/ n. esp. US sl. an inexperienced or unskilful person. [perh. f. DUB[1] in sense 'beat flat']

dub[4] /dʌb/ v.intr. (**dubbed, dubbing**) sl. (foll. by in, up) pay up; contribute money. [19th c.: orig. uncert.]

Dubai /duːˈbaɪ/ **1** one of the seven member States of the United Arab Emirates; pop. (1980) 419,100. **2** its capital city; pop. (1980) 265,700.

dubbin /ˈdʌbɪn/ n. & v. —n. (also **dubbing** /ˈdʌbɪŋ/) prepared grease for softening and waterproofing leather. —v.tr. (**dubbined, dubbining**) apply dubbin to (boots etc.). [see DUB[1] 4]

dubbing /ˈdʌbɪŋ/ n. an alternative soundtrack to a film etc.

Dubček /ˈdʊbtʃek/, Alexander (1921–), Czechoslovak Communist statesman, who became First Secretary of the Communist Party and leader of his country in 1968. In what came to be known as the 'Prague Spring' he and other liberal members of the government set about freeing the country from rigid political and economic controls and began to pursue a foreign policy independent of the Soviet Union. This led to the invasion of Czechoslovakia by Warsaw Pact forces in August 1968 (see BREZHNEV), and Dubček was removed from office. After the abandonment of Communism at the end of 1989 he was able to return to public life, and was elected Chairman of the Parliament in a new democratic regime.

dubiety /djuːˈbaɪətɪ/ n. (pl. **-ies**) literary **1** a feeling of doubt. **2** a doubtful matter. [LL dubietas f. dubium doubt]

dubious /ˈdjuːbɪəs/ adj. **1** hesitating or doubting (dubious about going). **2** of questionable value or truth (a dubious claim). **3** unreliable; suspicious (dubious company). **4** of doubtful result (a dubious undertaking). □□ **dubiously** adv. **dubiousness** n. [L dubiosus f. dubium doubt]

dubitation /ˌdjuːbɪˈteɪʃ(ə)n/ n. literary doubt, hesitation. [ME f. OF dubitation or L dubitatio f. dubitare DOUBT]

dubitative /ˈdjuːbɪtətɪv/ adj. literary of, expressing, or inclined to doubt or hesitation. □□ **dubitatively** adv. [F dubitatif -ive or LL dubitativus (as DUBITATION)]

Dublin /ˈdʌblɪn/ the capital of the Republic of Ireland, situated at the mouth of the River Liffey; pop. (est. 1986) 502,300. □ **Dublin Bay prawn 1** the Norway lobster. **2** (in pl.) scampi.

Dubonnet /djuːˈbɒneɪ/ n. propr. **1** a sweet French aperitif. **2** a glass of this. [name of a family of French wine-merchants]

Dubrovnik /doˈbrɒvnɪk/ (Italian **Ragusa** /ræˈɡuːzə/) a port and resort on the Adriatic coast of Yugoslavia; pop. (1981) 66,100.

ducal /ˈdjuːk(ə)l/ adj. of, like, or bearing the title of a duke. [F f. duc DUKE]

ducat /ˈdʌkət/ n. **1** hist. a gold coin, formerly current in most European countries. **2 a** a coin. **b** (in pl.) money. [ME f. It. ducato or med.L ducatus DUCHY]

Duccio di Buoninsegna /ˈduːtʃɪəʊ dɪ ˌbwɒnɪnˈseɪnjə/ (active 1278–1319), the leading painter of Siena in the late 13th and early 14th c., who makes the transition from Byzantine to Gothic. The only fully documented surviving work by him is the great Virgin in Majesty (the Maestà) for the high altar of Siena cathedral (completed 1311). Duccio was a master of pictorial narrative, conveying emotion through facial expression, sequence of colour, and arrangement of scenery, yet keeping the composition within Byzantine conventions. After him, even far into the 15th c., Sienese painting was influenced by his sensitive line, his resplendent colours, and his tenderness.

Duce /ˈduːtʃeɪ/ n. a leader, esp. (**Il Duce**) the title assumed by Mussolini. [It., = leader]

Duchamp /duːˈʃɑ̃/, Marcel (1887–1968), French artist and art theorist. He produced few works but is regarded as one of the most influential figures of 20th-c. art, though he recognized that he failed in his attempt to destroy the concept of aesthetic beauty. He was a leader of the New York Dada movement, and in 1912 invented the 'ready-made' (see entry). His most famous provocative gesture was the adding of a moustache and goatee beard to a reproduction of the Mona Lisa. Duchamp was a skilled chess-player, and represented France in four international contests.

duchess /ˈdʌtʃɪs/ n. (as a title usu. **Duchess**) **1** a duke's wife or widow. **2** a woman holding the rank of duke in her own right. [ME f. OF duchesse f. med.L ducissa (as DUKE)]

duchesse /duːˈʃes, ˈdʌtʃɪs/ n. **1** a soft heavy kind of satin. **2** a dressing-table with a pivoting mirror. □ **duchesse lace** a kind of Brussels pillow-lace. **duchesse potatoes** mashed potatoes mixed with egg, baked or fried, and served as small cakes. **duchesse set** a cover or a set of covers for a dressing-table. [F, = DUCHESS]

duchy /ˈdʌtʃɪ/ n. (pl. **-ies**) **1** the territory of a duke or duchess; a dukedom. **2** (often as **the Duchy**) the royal dukedom of Cornwall or Lancaster, each with certain estates, revenues, and jurisdiction of its own. [ME f. OF duché(e) f. med.L ducatus f. L dux ducis leader]

duck[1] /dʌk/ n. (pl. same or **ducks**) **1 a** any of various swimming-birds of the family Anatidae, esp. the domesticated form of the mallard or wild duck. **b** the female of this (opp. DRAKE). **c** the flesh of a duck as food. **2** Cricket (in full **duck's-egg**) the score of a batsman dismissed for nought. **3** (also **ducks**) Brit. colloq. (esp. as a form of address) dear, darling. □ **duck-hawk 1** Brit. a marsh-harrier. **2** US a peregrine. **ducks and drakes** a game of making a flat stone skim along the surface of water. **duck's arse** sl. a haircut with the hair on the back of the head shaped like a duck's tail. **duck soup** US sl. an easy task. **like a duck to water** adapting very readily. **like water off a duck's back**

colloq. (of remonstrances etc.) producing no effect. **play ducks and drakes with** *colloq.* squander. [OE *duce, dūce*: rel. to DUCK²]

duck² /dʌk/ v. & n. —v. **1** *intr.* & *tr.* plunge, dive, or dip under water and emerge (*ducked him in the pond*). **2** *intr.* & *tr.* bend (the head or the body) quickly to avoid a blow or being seen, or as a bow or curtsy; bob (*ducked out of sight; ducked his head under the beam*). **3** *tr.* & *intr. colloq.* avoid or dodge; withdraw (from) (*ducked out of the engagement; ducked the meeting*). **4** *intr. Bridge* lose a trick deliberately by playing a low card. —n. **1** a quick dip or swim. **2** a quick lowering of the head etc. □ **ducking-stool** *hist.* a chair fastened to the end of a pole, which could be plunged into a pond, used formerly for ducking scolds etc. □□ **ducker** *n.* [OE *dūcan* (unrecorded) f. Gmc]

duck³ /dʌk/ n. **1** a strong untwilled linen or cotton fabric used for small sails and the outer clothing of sailors. **2** (in *pl.*) trousers made of this (*white ducks*). [MDu. *doek*, of unkn. orig.]

duck⁴ /dʌk/ n. *colloq.* an amphibious landing-craft. [DUKW, its official designation]

duckbill /ˈdʌkbɪl/ n. (also **duck-billed platypus**) = PLATYPUS.

duckboard /ˈdʌkbɔːd/ n. (usu. in *pl.*) a path of wooden slats placed over muddy ground or in a trench.

duckling /ˈdʌklɪŋ/ n. **1** a young duck. **2** its flesh as food.

duckweed /ˈdʌkwiːd/ n. any of various aquatic plants, esp. of the genus *Lemna*, growing on the surface of still water.

ducky /ˈdʌkɪ/ n. & adj. *Brit. colloq.* —n. (*pl.* **-ies**) darling, dear. —adj. sweet, pretty; splendid.

duct /dʌkt/ n. & v. —n. **1** a channel or tube for conveying fluid, cable, etc. **2 a** a tube in the body conveying secretions such as tears etc. **b** *Bot.* a tube formed by cells that have lost their intervening end walls, holding air, water, etc. —v.tr. convey through a duct. [L *ductus* leading, aqueduct f. *ducere duct-* lead]

ductile /ˈdʌktaɪl/ adj. **1** (of a metal) capable of being drawn into wire; pliable, not brittle. **2** (of a substance) easily moulded. **3** (of a person) docile, gullible. □□ **ductility** /-ˈtɪlɪtɪ/ n. [ME f. OF *ductile* or L *ductilis* f. *ducere duct-* lead]

ducting /ˈdʌktɪŋ/ n. **1** a system of ducts. **2** material in the form of a duct or ducts.

ductless /ˈdʌktlɪs/ adj. lacking or not using a duct or ducts. □ **ductless gland** a gland secreting directly into the bloodstream: also called *endocrine gland*.

dud /dʌd/ n. & adj. *sl.* —n. **1** a futile or ineffectual person or thing (*a dud at the job*). **2** a counterfeit article. **3** a shell etc. that fails to explode. **4** (in *pl.*) clothes. —adj. **1** useless, worthless, unsatisfactory or futile. **2** counterfeit. [ME: orig. unkn.]

dude /djuːd, duːd/ n. *US sl.* **1** a fastidious aesthetic person, usu. male; a dandy. **2** a holiday-maker on a ranch in the western US, esp. when unused to ranch life. **3** a fellow; a guy. □ **dude ranch** a cattle ranch converted to a holiday centre for tourists etc. □□ **dudish** adj. [19th c.: prob. f. G dial. *dude* fool]

dudgeon /ˈdʌdʒ(ə)n/ n. a feeling of offence; resentment. □ **in high dudgeon** very angry or angrily. [16th c.: orig. unkn.]

due /djuː/ adj., n., & adv. —adj. **1** (*predic.*) owing or payable as a debt or an obligation (*our thanks are due to him; £500 was due on the 15th*). **2** (often foll. by *to*) merited; appropriate; fitting (*his due reward; received the applause due to a hero*). **3** rightful; proper; adequate (*after due consideration*). **4** (*predic.*; foll. by *to*) to be ascribed to (a cause, an agent, etc.) (*the discovery was due to Newton*). **5** (*predic.*) intended to arrive at a certain time (*a train is due at 7.30*). **6** (foll. by *to* + infin.) under an obligation or agreement to do something (*due to speak tonight*). —n. **1** a person's right; what is owed to a person (*a fair hearing is my due*). **2** (in *pl.*) **a** what one owes (*pays his dues*). **b** a legally demandable toll or fee (*harbour dues; university dues*). —adv. (of a point of the compass) exactly, directly (*went due east; a due north wind*). □ **due to** *disp.* because of, owing to (*was late due to an accident*) (cf. sense 4 of *adj.*). **fall** (or **become**) **due** (of a bill etc.) be immediately payable. **in due course 1** at about the appropriate time. **2** in the natural order. [ME f. OF *deü* ult. f. L *debitus* past part. of *debēre* owe]

duel /ˈdjuː(ə)l/ n. & v. —n. **1** *hist.* a contest with deadly weapons between two people, in the presence of two seconds, to settle a point of honour. **2** any contest between two people, parties,

causes, animals, etc. (*a duel of wits*). —v.intr. (**duelled, duelling**; *US* **dueled, dueling**) fight a duel or duels. □□ **dueller** *n.* (*US* **dueler**). **duellist** *n.* (*US* **duelist**). [It. *duello* or L *duellum* (archaic form of *bellum* war), in med.L = single combat]

duende /duˈendɪ/ n. **1** an evil spirit. **2** inspiration. [Sp.]

duenna /djuːˈenə/ n. an older woman acting as a governess and companion in charge of girls, esp. in a Spanish family; a chaperon. [Sp. *dueña* f. L *domina* mistress]

Duero see DOURO.

duet /djuːˈet/ n. **1** *Mus.* **a** a performance by two voices, instrumentalists, etc. **b** a composition for two performers. **2** a dialogue. □□ **duettist** *n.* [G *Duett* or It. *duetto* dimin. of *duo* duet f. L *duo* two]

Dufay /ˈduːfaɪ/, Guillaume (c.1400–74), Franco-Flemish composer and singer, who spent much of his life in Italy and Savoy. A noted teacher, he was one of the first great Renaissance composers. His works include much church music (his own Requiem Mass, now lost, was sung at his funeral), motets, and 84 songs.

duff¹ /dʌf/ n. a boiled pudding. [N.Engl. form of DOUGH]

duff² /dʌf/ adj. *Brit. sl.* **1** worthless, counterfeit. **2** useless, broken. [perh. = DUFF¹]

duff³ /dʌf/ v.tr. *sl.* **1** *Brit. Golf* mishit (a shot, a ball); bungle. **2** *Austral.* steal and alter brands on (cattle). □ **duff up** *sl.* beat; thrash. [perh. back-form. f. DUFFER]

duffer /ˈdʌfə(r)/ n. *sl.* **1** an inefficient, useless, or stupid person. **2** *Austral.* a person who duffs cattle. **3** *Austral.* an unproductive mine. [perh. f. Sc. *doofart* stupid person f. *douf* spiritless]

duffle /ˈdʌf(ə)l/ n. (also **duffel**) **1** a coarse woollen cloth with a thick nap. **2** *US* a sportsman's or camper's equipment. □ **duffle bag** a cylindrical canvas bag closed by a draw-string and carried over the shoulder. **duffle-coat** a hooded overcoat of duffle, usu. fastened with toggles. [*Duffel* in Belgium]

Dufy /ˈduːfiː/, Raoul (1877–1953), French painter and textile designer. His mature style shows deft outline drawings of forms on brilliant background washes evocative of Mediterranean sunlight. His favourite subjects were racing scenes, boating scenes, and the glitter and sparkle of the Riviera, London, or Nice—drawing-room art of splendid attractiveness.

dug¹ past and past part. of DIG.

dug² /dʌg/ n. **1** the udder, breast, teat, or nipple of a female animal. **2** *derog.* the breast of a woman. [16th c.: orig. unkn.]

dugong /ˈduːgɒŋ/ n. (*pl.* same or **dugongs**) a marine mammal, *Dugong dugon*, of Asian seas and coasts. Also called *sea cow*. [ult. f. Malay *dūyong*]

dugout /ˈdʌgaʊt/ n. **1 a** a roofed shelter esp. for troops in trenches. **b** an underground air-raid or nuclear shelter. **2** a canoe made from a hollowed tree-trunk. **3** *sl.* a retired officer etc. recalled to service.

duiker /ˈdaɪkə(r)/ n. **1** (also **duyker**) any African antelope of the genus *Cephalophus*, usu. having a crest of long hair between its horns. **2** *S.Afr.* the long-tailed cormorant, *Phalacrocorax africanus*. [Du. *duiker* diver: in sense 1, from plunging through bushes when pursued]

Duisburg /ˈduːsbʊəg/ the largest inland port in Europe, situated at the junction of the Rhine and Ruhr rivers, in NW Germany; pop. (1987) 514,600.

duke /djuːk/ n. (as a title usu. **Duke**) **1 a** a person holding the highest hereditary title of the nobility. The title was introduced into England by Edward III, who in 1337 created his eldest son Edward (the Black Prince) Duke of Cornwall. **b** a sovereign prince ruling a duchy or small State. **2** (usu. in *pl.*) *sl.* the hand; the fist (*put up your dukes!*). **3** *Bot.* a kind of cherry, neither very sweet nor very sour. □ **royal duke** a duke who is also a royal prince. [ME f. OF *duc* f. L *dux ducis* leader, the term for a provincial military commander under the later Roman emperors]

dukedom /ˈdjuːkdəm/ n. **1** a territory ruled by a duke. **2** the rank of duke.

dulcet /ˈdʌlsɪt/ adj. (esp. of sound) sweet and soothing. [ME, earlier *doucet* f. OF dimin. of *doux* f. L *dulcis* sweet]

dulcify /ˈdʌlsɪˌfaɪ/ v.tr. (**-ies, -ied**) *literary* **1** make gentle. **2**

sweeten. □□ **dulcification** /-fɪˈkeɪʃ(ə)n/ n. [L *dulcificare* f. *dulcis* sweet]

dulcimer /ˈdʌlsɪmə(r)/ n. **1** a musical instrument consisting of a shallow closed box over which metal strings of graduated length are stretched to be struck by wood, cane, or wire hammers, the prototype of the piano. **2** a musical instrument of the zither type, fretted and with steel strings which are stopped with one hand and plucked with a plectrum by the other, played in Kentucky and Alabama as an accompaniment to songs and dances. [OF *doulcemer*, said to repr. L *dulce* sweet, *melos* song]

dulcitone /ˈdʌlsɪˌtəʊn/ n. Mus. a keyboard instrument with steel tuning-forks which are struck by hammers. [L *dulcis* sweet + TONE]

dulia /ˈdjuːlɪə/ n. RC Ch. the reverence accorded to saints and angels. [med.L f. Gk *douleia* servitude f. *doulos* slave]

dull /dʌl/ adj. & v. —adj. **1** slow to understand; stupid. **2** tedious; boring. **3** (of the weather) overcast; gloomy. **4 a** (esp. of a knife edge etc.) blunt. **b** (of colour, light, sound, or taste) not bright, vivid, or keen. **5** (of a pain etc.) usu. prolonged and indistinct; not acute (*a dull ache*). **6 a** (of a person, an animal, trade, etc.) sluggish, slow-moving, or stagnant. **b** (of a person) listless; depressed (*he's a dull fellow since the accident*). **7** (of the ears, eyes, etc.) without keen perception. —v.tr. & intr. make or become dull. □ **dull the edge of** make less sensitive, interesting, effective, amusing, etc.; blunt. □□ **dullish** adj. **dullness** n. (also **dulness**). **dully** /ˈdʌllɪ/ adv. [ME f. MLG, MDu. *dul*, corresp. to OE *dol* stupid]

dullard /ˈdʌləd/ n. a stupid person.

Dulles /ˈdʌlɪs/, John Foster (1888–1959), American international lawyer and statesman. He was adviser to the US delegation at the San Francisco conference (1945) which set up the United Nations, and was chief author of the Japanese Peace Treaty (1951). As Secretary of State under Eisenhower (1953–9) he became a protagonist of the Cold War. Advancing beyond the Truman policy of containment, he urged that the US should prepare a build-up of nuclear arms to deter Soviet aggression, and gave clear indications that the US was prepared to defend West Berlin against any encroachment.

dulse /dʌls/ n. an edible seaweed, *Rhodymenia palmata*, with red wedge-shaped fronds. [Ir. & Gael. *duileasg*]

duly /ˈdjuːlɪ/ adv. **1** in due time or manner. **2** rightly, properly, fitly.

duma /ˈduːmə/ n. hist. a Russian council of State, esp. the elected body existing between 1905 and 1917 introduced by Tsar Nicholas II in 1905 in response to popular unrest. In practice the Duma had little effective power. [Russ.: orig. an elective municipal council]

Dumas /ˈdjuːmɑː/, Alexandre (1802–70), French novelist and dramatist, known as 'Dumas *père*', a pioneer of the Romantic theatre in France. He achieved great popularity with his swiftly moving dramas, mostly on historical subjects, such as *Henry III et sa cour* (1829), *Antony* (1831), and *La Tour de Nesle* (1832). Even more successful were his historical novels on which his reputation now rests, including *The Three Musketeers* (1844–5) and its sequels following the adventures of d'Artagnan, and *The Count of Monte Cristo* (1844–5), a masterpiece of mystery and adventure. His son Alexandre Dumas (1824–95), 'Dumas *fils*', also a novelist and dramatist, won fame with his novel *La Dame aux camélias* (1848) which formed the basis of Verdi's opera *La Traviata* (1853).

Du Maurier[1] /du: ˈmɒrɪˌeɪ/, Dame Daphne (1907–89), English novelist, granddaughter of George du Maurier. Many of her popular novels and period romances are set in the West Country, where she spent most of her life. Her most famous novel is *Rebecca* (1938), successfully filmed by Alfred Hitchcock (1940).

Du Maurier[2] /du: ˈmɒrɪˌeɪ/, George Louis Palmella Busson (1834–96), French-born cartoonist, illustrator, and novelist, remembered for his novel *Trilby* (1894).

dumb /dʌm/ adj. **1 a** (of a person) unable to speak, usu. because of a congenital defect or deafness. **b** (of an animal) naturally unable to speak (*our dumb friends*). **2** silenced by surprise, shyness, etc. (*struck dumb by this revelation*). **3** taciturn or reticent, esp. insultingly (*dumb insolence*). **4** (of an action etc.) performed without speech. **5** (often in *comb.*) giving no sound; without voice or some other property normally belonging to things of the name (*a dumb piano*). **6** *colloq.* esp. US stupid; ignorant. **7** (usu. of a class, population, etc.) having no voice in government; inarticulate (*the dumb masses*). **8** (of a computer terminal etc.) able only to transmit data to or receive data from a computer; not programmable (opp. INTELLIGENT). □ **dumb animals** animals, esp. as objects of pity. **dumb-bell 1** a short bar with a weight at each end, used for exercise, muscle-building, etc. **2** sl. a stupid person, esp. a woman. **dumb blonde** a pretty but stupid blonde woman. **dumb cluck** sl. a stupid person. **dumb crambo** see CRAMBO. **dumb-iron** the curved side-piece of a motor-vehicle chassis, joining it to the front springs. **dumb piano** Mus. a silent or dummy keyboard. **dumb show 1** significant gestures or mime, used when words are inappropriate. **2** a part of a play in early drama, acted in mime. **dumb waiter 1** a small lift for carrying food, plates, etc., between floors. **2** a movable table, esp. with revolving shelves, used in a dining-room. □□ **dumbly** /ˈdʌmlɪ/ adv. **dumbness** /ˈdʌmnɪs/ n. [OE: orig. unkn.: sense 6 f. G *dumm*]

dumbfound /dʌmˈfaʊnd/ v.tr. (also **dumfound**) strike dumb; confound; nonplus. [DUMB, CONFOUND]

dumbhead /ˈdʌmhed/ n. esp. US sl. a stupid person.

dumbo /ˈdʌmbəʊ/ n. (pl. **-os**) sl. a stupid person; a fool. [DUMB + -o]

dumbstruck /ˈdʌmstrʌk/ adj. greatly shocked or surprised and so lost for words.

dumdum /ˈdʌmdʌm/ n. (in full **dumdum bullet**) a kind of soft-nosed bullet that expands on impact and inflicts laceration. [*Dum-Dum* in India, where it was first produced]

Dumfries and Galloway /ˌdʌmfriːs, ˈgæləˌweɪ/ a local government region in SW Scotland; pop. (1981) 147,000; capital, Dumfries.

dummy /ˈdʌmɪ/ n., adj., & v. —n. (pl. **-ies**) **1** a model of a human being, esp.: **a** a ventriloquist's doll. **b** a figure used to model clothes in a shop window etc. **c** a target used for firearms practice. **2** (often *attrib.*) **a** a counterfeit object used to replace or resemble a real or normal one. **b** a prototype, esp. in publishing. **3** colloq. a stupid person. **4** a person taking no significant part; a figurehead. **5** Brit. a rubber or plastic teat for a baby to suck on. **6** an imaginary fourth player at whist, whose hand is turned up and played by a partner. **7** Bridge **a** the partner of the declarer, whose cards are exposed after the first lead. **b** this player's hand. **8** Mil. a blank round of ammunition. **9** colloq. a dumb person. —adj. sham; counterfeit. —v.intr. (**-ies**, **-ied**) Football make a pretended pass or swerve etc. □ **dummy run 1** a practice attack, etc.; a trial run. **2** a rehearsal. **dummy up** US sl. keep quiet; give no information. **sell the** (or a) **dummy** Rugby Football colloq. deceive (an opponent) by pretending to pass the ball. [DUMB + -Y²]

dump /dʌmp/ n. & v. —n. **1 a** a place for depositing rubbish. **b** a heap of rubbish. **2** colloq. an unpleasant or dreary place. **3** Mil. a temporary store of ammunition, provisions, etc. **4** an accumulated pile of ore, earth, etc. **5** Computing **a** a printout of stored data. **b** the process or result of dumping data. —v.tr. **1** put down firmly or clumsily (*dumped the shopping on the table*). **2** shoot or deposit (rubbish etc.). **3** colloq. abandon, desert. **4** Mil. leave (ammunition etc.) in a dump. **5** Econ. send (goods unsaleable at a high price in the home market) to a foreign market for sale at a low price, to keep up the price at home, and to capture a new market. **6** Computing **a** copy (stored data) to a different location. **b** reproduce the contents of (a store) externally. □ **dump on** esp. US criticize or abuse; get the better of. **dump truck** a truck with a body that tilts or opens at the back for unloading. [ME perh. f. Norse; cf. Da. *dumpe*, Norw. *dumpa* fall suddenly]

dumper /ˈdʌmpə(r)/ n. **1** a person or thing that dumps. **2** Austral. & NZ a large wave that breaks and hurls the swimmer or surfer on to the beach.

dumpling /ˈdʌmplɪŋ/ n. **1 a** a small ball of usu. suet, flour, and water, boiled in stew or water, and eaten. **b** a pudding consisting of apple or other fruit enclosed in dough and baked. **2** a small fat person. [app. dimin., of *dump* small round object, but recorded much earlier]

dumps /dʌmps/ *n.pl. colloq.* depression; melancholy (*in the dumps*). [prob. f. LG or Du., fig. use of MDu. *domp* exhalation, haze, mist: rel. to DAMP]

dumpy /'dʌmpɪ/ *adj.* (**dumpier, dumpiest**) short and stout. □□ **dumpily** *adv.* **dumpiness** *n.* [*dump* (cf. DUMPLING) + -Y¹]

dun¹ /dʌn/ *adj. & n.* —*adj.* **1** dull greyish-brown. **2** *poet.* dark, dusky. —*n.* **1** a dun colour. **2** a dun horse. **3** a dark fishing-fly. □ **dun-bird** a pochard. **dun diver** a female or young male goosander. [OE *dun, dunn*]

dun² /dʌn/ *n. & v.* —*n.* **1** a debt-collector; an importunate creditor. **2** a demand for payment. —*v.tr.* (**dunned, dunning**) importune for payment of a debt; pester. [abbr. of obs. *dunkirk* privateer, f. *Dunkirk* in France]

Duna, Dunarea, Dunav see DANUBE.

Dunbar /dʌn'bɑː(r)/, William (?1456–?1513), Scottish poet and priest, awarded a royal pension by James IV. His first great poem 'The Thrissill and the Rois' (1503), a political satire, celebrated the marriage of James IV to Mary Tudor, while his best-known poem, the 'Lament for the Makaris', is a powerful elegy on the deaths of Chaucer and other fellow poets. A versatile craftsman, Dunbar wrote in a variety of stanza forms with much humour and satirical power; his vitality and originality were in sharp contrast to much poetry of the preceeding century.

Duncan /'dʌŋkən/, Isadora (1878–1927), American dancer and teacher. Clad appropriately in a loosely falling tunic, she developed a form of 'free' barefoot dancing akin to that of classical Greece and based on natural impulses. Though not popular in America she was much admired in Europe, where she settled, founding a school in Berlin and making many visits to Russia, where she may have influenced Fokine. She had several well-publicized love affairs, lost her two children by drowning, and herself died through strangulation when her trailing scarf became entangled in the wheels of a car.

dunce /dʌns/ *n.* a person slow at learning; a dullard. □ **dunce's cap** a paper cone formerly put on the head of a dunce at school as a mark of disgrace. [John *Duns* Scotus (see entry), whose followers were ridiculed by 16th-c. humanists and reformers as enemies of learning]

Dundee /dʌn'diː/ a city in eastern Scotland, on the north side of the Firth of Tay; pop. (est. 1987) 175,750. □ **Dundee cake** esp. *Brit.* a rich fruit cake usu. decorated with almonds.

dunderhead /'dʌndəˌhed/ *n.* a stupid person. □□ **dunderheaded** *adj.* [17th c.: perh. rel. to dial. *dunder* resounding noise]

dune /djuːn/ *n.* a mound or ridge of loose sand etc. formed by the wind, esp. beside the sea or in a desert. □ **dune buggy** = *beach buggy*. [F f. MDu. *düne*: cf. DOWN³]

Dunedin /dʌ'niːdɪn/ a city and port of South Island, New Zealand, at the head of Otago Harbour; pop. (1988) 106,600. It was founded in 1848 by Scottish settlers; its name reflects the Gaelic word (*Duneideann*) for Edinburgh.

Dunfermline /dʌn'fɜːmlɪn/ an industrial city of Scotland, near the Firth of Forth; pop. (1981) 52,000. A number of Scottish kings, including Robert the Bruce, are buried in its Benedictine abbey. The philanthropist Andrew Carnegie was born in the city in 1835, and it is the headquarters of all the Carnegie trusts.

dung /dʌŋ/ *n. & v.* —*n.* the excrement of animals; manure. —*v.tr.* apply dung to; manure (land). □ **dung-beetle** any of a family of beetles whose larvae develop in dung. **dung-fly** any of various flies feeding on dung. **dung-worm** any of various worms found in cow-dung and used as bait. [OE, rel. to OHG *tunga*, Icel. *dyngja*, and G *dung*: orig. uncert.]

dungaree /ˌdʌŋɡə'riː/ *n.* **1** a coarse Indian calico. **2** (in *pl.*) **a** overalls etc. made of dungaree or similar material, worn esp. by workers. **b** trousers with a bib worn by children or as a fashion garment. [Hindi *dungrī*]

dungeon /'dʌndʒ(ə)n/ *n. & v.* —*n.* **1** a strong underground cell for prisoners. **2** *archaic* a donjon. —*v.tr. archaic* (usu. foll. by *up*)

imprison in a dungeon. [orig. = *donjon*: ME f. OF *donjon* ult. f. L *dominus* lord]

dunghill /'dʌŋhɪl/ *n.* a heap of dung or refuse, esp. in a farmyard.

dunk /dʌŋk/ *v.tr.* **1** dip (bread, a biscuit, etc.) into soup, coffee, etc. while eating. **2** immerse, dip (*was dunked in the river*). [Pennsylvanian G *dunke* to dip f. G *tunken*]

Dunkirk /dʌn'kɜːk/ (French **Dunquerque**) French Channel port, scene of the evacuation of the British Expeditionary Force in 1940. Forced to retreat to the Channel by the German breakthrough at Sedan, 225,000 British troops, as well as 110,000 of their French allies, were evacuated from Dunkirk between 27 May and 2 June by warships, requisitioned civilian ships, and a host of small boats, under constant attack from the air. No British soldiers were left on the beach (although large quantities of arms and equipment had to be left behind), and it is remembered as a success rather than a retreat—'snatching glory out of defeat'.

dunlin /'dʌnlɪn/ *n.* a long-billed sandpiper, *Calidris alpina*. [prob. f. DUN¹ + -LING¹]

Dunlop /'dʌnlɒp/, John Boyd (1840–1921), Scottish veterinary surgeon, working in Belfast, the first person to devise a successful pneumatic tyre (1888), which was manufactured by the company named after him (see PNEUMATIC).

Dunmow Flitch /'dʌnməʊ/ a flitch of bacon awarded in a contest on Whit Monday, according to an ancient custom of Great Dunmow in Essex, to a married couple who will go to the priory and, kneeling on two sharp-pointed stones, swear that they have not quarrelled or repented of their marriage within a year and a day after its celebration. The prize is said to have been offered in 1244 (though its origin may have been earlier).

dunnage /'dʌnɪdʒ/ *n. Naut.* **1** mats, brushwood, etc., stowed under or among cargo to prevent wetting or chafing. **2** *colloq.* miscellaneous baggage. [AL *dennagium*, of unkn. orig.]

Dunne /dʌn/, John William (1875–1949), English philosopher. His theory that all time exists simultaneously (*serialism*) was an attempt to explain the phenomenon of precognition in dreams etc.

Dunnet Head /'dʌnɪt/ the most northerly point on the British mainland.

dunno /də'nəʊ/ *colloq.* (I) do not know. [corrupt.]

dunnock /'dʌnək/ *n. Brit.* the hedge sparrow. [app. f. DUN¹ + -OCK, from its brown and grey plumage]

dunny /'dʌnɪ/ *n.* (*pl.* **-ies**) **1** *Sc.* an underground passage or cellar, esp. in a tenement. **2** esp. *Austral. & NZ sl.* an earth-closet; an outdoor privy. [20th c.: orig. uncert.]

Dunquerque see DUNKIRK.

Duns Scotus /dʌnz 'skəʊtəs/, John (*c.*1260–1308), Scottish-born Franciscan philosopher whose reasoning earned him the title of the 'Subtle Doctor'. In opposition to the teaching of Aquinas he argued that faith was a matter of will, not dependent on logical proofs; his conception of form (i.e. the nature of things, by which they are what they are) and matter differed from that of Aquinas; and he was the first great theologian to defend the theory of the Immaculate Conception. His system was accepted by the Franciscans as their doctrinal basis and exercised a profound influence in the Middle Ages. In the Renaissance his followers were ridiculed by humanists and reformers for the subtleties of their reasoning; they, in turn, hurled abuse at the 'new learning', and the term *Duns* or *Dunce*, soon passed into the sense of 'dull obstinate person impervious to the new learning' and of 'blockhead incapable of learning'.

Dunstable /'dʌnstəb(ə)l/, John (*c.*1390–1453), the leading English composer of the early 15th c., also an astrologer and mathematician. His works include masses and motets.

Dunstan /'dʌnst(ə)n/, St (*c.*909–988), a monk and later abbot at Glastonbury who insisted on full observance of the Benedictine rule, and under whom the monastery became famous for its learning. He was appointed archbishop of Canterbury by King Edgar in 960, and together they carried through a reform of Church and State. The restoration of monastic life, which seems to have been virtually extinct in England by the mid-10th c., was almost wholly Dunstan's work. He zealously supported the cause of learning and himself achieved fame as a musician, illuminator, and metal-worker. Feast day, 19 May.

duo /ˈdjuːəʊ/ n. (pl. **-os**) **1** a pair of actors, entertainers, singers, etc. (*a comedy duo*). **2** *Mus.* a duet. [It. f. L, = two]

duodecimal /ˌdjuːəʊˈdesɪm(ə)l/ adj. & n. —adj. relating to or using a system of numerical notation that has 12 as a base. —n. **1** the duodecimal system. **2** duodecimal notation. □□ **duodecimally** adv. [L *duodecimus* twelfth f. *duodecim* twelve]

duodecimo /ˌdjuːəʊˈdesɪˌməʊ/ n. (pl. **-os**) *Printing* **1** a book-size in which each leaf is one-twelfth of the size of the printing-sheet. **2** a book of this size. [L (*in*) *duodecimo* in a twelfth (as DUODECIMAL)]

duodenary /ˌdjuːəʊˈdiːnərɪ/ adj. proceeding by twelves or in sets of twelve. [L *duodenarius* f. *duodeni* distrib. of *duodecim* twelve]

duodenum /ˌdjuːəʊˈdiːnəm/ n. *Anat.* the first part of the small intestine immediately below the stomach. □□ **duodenal** adj. **duodenitis** /-ˈnaɪtɪs/ n. [ME f. med.L f. *duodeni* (see DUODENARY) from its length of about 12 fingers' breadth]

duologue /ˈdjuːəˌlɒɡ/ n. **1** a conversation between two people. **2** a play or part of a play for two actors. [irreg. f. L *duo* or Gk *duo* two, after *monologue*]

duomo /ˈdwəʊməʊ/ n. (pl. **-os**) an Italian cathedral. [It., = DOME]

duopoly /djuːˈɒpəlɪ/ n. (pl. **-ies**) *Econ.* the possession of trade in a commodity etc. by only two sellers. [Gk *duo* two + *pōleō* sell, after *monopoly*]

duotone /ˈdjuːəˌtəʊn/ n. & adj. *Printing* —n. **1** a half-tone illustration in two colours from the same original with different screen angles. **2** the process of making a duotone. —adj. in two colours. [L *duo* two + TONE]

dupe /djuːp/ n. & v. —n. a victim of deception. —v.tr. make a fool of; cheat; gull. □□ **dupable** adj. **duper** n. **dupery** n. [F f. dial. F *dupe* hoopoe, from the bird's supposedly stupid appearance]

dupion /ˈdjuːpɪən/ n. **1** a rough silk fabric woven from the threads of double cocoons. **2** an imitation of this with other fibres. [F *doupion* f. It. *doppione* f. *doppio* double]

duple /ˈdjuːp(ə)l/ adj. of two parts. □ **duple ratio** *Math.* a ratio of 2 to 1. **duple time** *Mus.* that with two beats to the bar. [L *duplus* f. *duo* two]

duplex /ˈdjuːpleks/ n. & adj. —n. esp. *US* **1** a flat or maisonette on two levels. **2** a house subdivided for two families. —adj. **1** having two elements; twofold. **2** esp. *US* **a** (of a flat) two-storeyed. **b** (of a house) for two families. **3** *Computing* (of a circuit) allowing the transmission of signals in both directions simultaneously (opp. SIMPLEX). □ **half-duplex** *Computing* (of a circuit) allowing the transmission of signals in both directions but not simultaneously. [L *duplex duplicis* f. *duo* two + *plic-* fold]

duplicate adj., n., & v. —adj. /ˈdjuːplɪkət/ **1** exactly like something already existing; copied (esp. in large numbers). **2 a** having two corresponding parts. **b** existing in two examples; paired. **c** twice as large or many; doubled. —n. /ˈdjuːplɪkət/ **1 a** one of two identical things, esp. a copy of an original. **b** one of two or more specimens of a thing exactly or almost identical. **2** *Law* a second copy of a letter or document. **3** (in full **duplicate bridge** or **whist**) a form of bridge or whist in which the same hands are played successively by different players. **4** *archaic* a pawnbroker's ticket. —v.tr. /ˈdjuːplɪˌkeɪt/ **1** multiply by two; double. **2 a** make or be an exact copy of. **b** make or supply copies of (*duplicated the leaflet for distribution*). **3** repeat (an action etc.), esp. unnecessarily. □ **duplicate ratio** *Math.* the proportion of the squares of two numbers. **in duplicate** consisting of two exact copies. □□ **duplicable** /-kəb(ə)l/ adj. **duplication** /-ˈkeɪʃ(ə)n/ n. [L *duplicatus* past part. of *duplicare* (as DUPLEX)]

duplicator /ˈdjuːplɪˌkeɪtə(r)/ n. **1** a machine for making copies of a document, leaflet, etc. **2** a person or thing that duplicates.

duplicity /djuːˈplɪsɪtɪ/ n. **1** double-dealing; deceitfulness. **2** *archaic* doubleness. □□ **duplicitous** adj. [ME f. OF *duplicité* or LL *duplicitas* (as DUPLEX)]

duppy /ˈdʌpɪ/ n. (pl. **-ies**) *W.Ind.* a malevolent spirit or ghost. [perh. of Afr. orig.]

Du Pré /djuː ˈpreɪ/, Jacqueline (1945–87), English cellist, most famous for her performances of Elgar's cello concerto. Her performing career was halted in 1972 by multiple sclerosis.

dura var. of DURRA.

durable /ˈdjʊərəb(ə)l/ adj. & n. —adj. **1** capable of lasting; hard-wearing. **2** (of goods) not for immediate consumption; able to be kept. —n. (in pl.) durable goods. □□ **durability** /-ˈbɪlɪtɪ/ n. **durableness** n. **durably** adv. [ME f. OF f. L *durabilis* f. *durare* endure f. *durus* hard]

Duralumin /djʊəˈræljʊmɪn/ n. *propr.* a light hard alloy of aluminium with copper etc. [perh. f. *Düren* in the Rhineland or L *durus* hard + ALUMINIUM]

dura mater /ˌdjʊərə ˈmeɪtə(r)/ n. *Anat.* the tough outermost membrane enveloping the brain and spinal cord (see MENINX). [med.L = hard mother, transl. Arab. *al-'umm al-jāfiya* ('mother' in Arab. indicating the relationship of things)]

duramen /djʊəˈreɪmen/ n. = HEARTWOOD. [L f. *durare* harden]

durance /ˈdjʊərəns/ n. *archaic* imprisonment (*in durance vile*). [ME f. F f. *durer* last f. L *durare*: see DURABLE]

Durango /dʊəˈræŋɡəʊ/ a State of north central Mexico; pop. (est. 1988) 1,384,500. Its capital is the mining town of Victoria de Durango.

duration /djʊəˈreɪʃ(ə)n/ n. **1** the length of time for which something continues. **2** a specified length of time (*after the duration of a minute*). □ **for the duration 1** until the end of the war. **2** for a very long time. □□ **durational** adj. [ME f. OF f. med.L *duratio -onis* (as DURANCE)]

durative /ˈdjʊərətɪv/ adj. *Gram.* denoting continuing action.

Durban /ˈdɜːbən/ a seaport and resort of the Republic of South Africa, on the coast of Natal province; pop. (1985) 634,300. Formerly known as Port Natal, it was renamed in 1835 after Sir Benjamin d'Urban, then governor of Cape Colony.

durbar /ˈdɜːbɑː(r)/ n. *hist.* **1** the court of an Indian ruler. **2** a public levee of an Indian prince or an Anglo-Indian governor or viceroy. [Urdu f. Pers. *darbār* court]

durchkomponiert /ˈdʊəxˌkɒmpɒˌniːət/ adj. *Mus.* (of a song) having different music for each verse. [G f. *durch* through + *komponiert* composed]

Dürer /ˈdjʊərə(r)/, Albrecht (1471–1528) German painter from Nuremberg, deeply influenced by the forms and ideas of Italian Renaissance art. Dürer was fascinated by scientific problems such as perspective and proportion, and wrote a treatise on the latter (1528), partly inspired by the studies of Leonardo. His interest in ideal form, however, was combined with meticulous attention to detail and with a feeling for individual nature which reflects the realism of the northern tradition. He travelled in Germany in 1490–4, and then set up a workshop at Nuremberg where he produced his great series of woodcuts and engravings, including the *Apocalypse* (1498), *The Great Passion* (1510), and *The Life of the Virgin* (1510). From *c.*1512 he was court painter to the Emperor Maximilian; his graphic works were influential throughout Europe, including Italy. His landscape watercolours, apparently done for his own pleasure, are remarkably advanced for their time in their treatment of light and atmosphere.

duress /djʊəˈres, ˈdjʊə-/ n. **1** compulsion, esp. imprisonment, threats, or violence, illegally used to force a person to act against his or her will (*under duress*). **2** forcible restraint or imprisonment. [ME f. OF *duresse* f. L *duritia* f. *durus* hard]

Durex /ˈdjʊəreks/ n. *propr.* a contraceptive sheath; a condom. [20th c.: orig. uncert.]

Durey /djʊəˈreɪ/, Louis (1888–1979), French composer, a member of 'Les Six' (see SIX) until 1921. His works include chamber music and songs. After 1945 he was one of a group of French composers who wrote music of a deliberate mass appeal, in accordance with Communist doctrines on art.

Durga /ˈdʊəɡə/ *Hinduism* a fierce goddess, wife of Siva (see PARVATI), often identified with Kali. She is usually depicted riding a tiger or lion and slaying the buffalo demon, and with eight or ten arms. [Skr., = inaccessible]

Durham /ˈdʌrəm/ **1** a county of NE England; pop. (1981) 611,400. **2** its county town; pop. (1981) 41,180.

durian /ˈdʊərɪən/ n. **1** a large tree, *Durio zibethinus*, native to SE Asia, bearing oval spiny fruits containing a creamy pulp with a fetid smell and an agreeable taste. **2** this fruit. [Malay *durian* f. *dūrī* thorn]

during /'djʊərɪŋ/ *prep.* **1** throughout the course or duration of (*read during the meal*). **2** at some point in the duration of (*came in during the evening*). [ME f. OF *durant* ult. f. L *durare* last, continue]

Durkheim /'dʊəkhaɪm/, Émile (1858–1917), French philosopher, a founder of modern sociology. He stressed the collective consciousness and the common values of society as the source of religion, morality, and social order.

durmast /'dɜːmɑːst/ *n.* an oak tree, *Quercus petraea*, having sessile flowers. [*dur-* (perh. erron. for DUN¹) + MAST²]

durn *US* var. of DARN².

durned *US* var. of DARNED.

durra /'dʌrə/ *n.* (also **dura, dhurra**) a kind of sorghum, *Sorghum vulgare*, native to Asia, Africa, and the US. [Arab. *ḏura, ḏurra*]

Durrell /djʊə'rel/, Lawrence George (1912–90), English novelist and poet. Born in India, he travelled widely, living in Paris in the 1930s and thereafter mainly in the Eastern Mediterranean. First recognized as a poet, Durrell produced several verse collections before achieving fame with his *Alexandria Quartet* (*Justine*, 1957; *Balthazar*, 1958; *Mountolive*, 1958; *Clea*, 1960), the central topic of which is 'an investigation of modern love'. Set in Alexandria before the Second World War, the novels are bound together in a web of political and sexual intrigue, and written in an ornate lyrical and sensual style. His travel books include *Prospero's Cell* (1945) on Corfu and *Bitter Lemons* (1957) on Cyprus.

Durrës /'dʊres/ a port and resort of Albania, on the Adriatic coast; pop. (1983) 72,000.

durst /dɜːst/ *archaic past* of DARE.

durum /'djʊərəm/ *n.* a kind of wheat, *Triticum turgidum*, having hard seeds and yielding a flour used in the manufacture of spaghetti etc. [L, neut. of *durus* hard]

durzi /'dɜːzɪ/ *n.* (*pl.* **durzis**) an Indian tailor. [Hindi f. Pers. *darzī* f. *darz* sewing]

Dushanbe /duːˈʃænbeɪ/ the capital of the Soviet republic of Tadjikistan; pop. (est. 1987) 582,000. The city was known as Stalinabad from 1929 to 1961.

dusk /dʌsk/ *n.*, *adj.*, & *v.* —*n.* **1** the darker stage of twilight. **2** shade; gloom. —*adj. poet.* shadowy; dim; dark-coloured. —*v.tr.* & *intr. poet.* make or become shadowy or dim. [ME *dosk, dusk* f. OE *dox* dark, swarthy, *doxian* darken in colour]

dusky /'dʌskɪ/ *adj.* (**duskier, duskiest**) **1** shadowy; dim. **2** dark-coloured, darkish. □□ **duskily** *adv.* **duskiness** *n.*

Düsseldorf /'dʊsəlˌdɔːf/ an industrial city of NW Germany, on the Rhine; pop. (1987) 560,600.

dust /dʌst/ *n.* & *v.* —*n.* **1 a** finely powdered earth, dirt, etc., lying on the ground or on surfaces, and blown about by the wind. **b** fine powder of any material (*pollen dust; gold-dust*). **c** a cloud of dust. **2** a dead person's remains (*honoured dust*). **3** confusion or turmoil (*raised quite a dust*). **4** *archaic* or *poet.* the mortal human body (*we are all dust*). **5** the ground; the earth (*kissed the dust*). —*v.* **1** *tr.* (also *absol.*) clear (furniture etc.) of dust etc. by wiping, brushing, etc. **2** *tr.* **a** sprinkle (esp. a cake) with powder, dust, sugar, etc. **b** sprinkle or strew (sugar, powder, etc.). **3** *tr.* make dusty. **4** *intr. archaic* (of a bird) take a dust-bath. □ **dust and ashes** something very disappointing. **dust-bath** a bird's rolling in dust to freshen its feathers. **dust bowl** see separate entry. **dust cover 1** = *dust-sheet*. **2** = *dust-jacket*. **dust devil** (in Africa) a whirlwind visible as a column of dust. **dust down 1** dust the clothes of (a person). **2** *colloq.* reprimand. **3** = *dust off*. **dusting-powder 1** talcum powder. **2** any dusting or drying powder. **dust-jacket** a usu. decorated paper cover used to protect a book from dirt etc. **dust off 1** remove the dust from (an object on which it has long been allowed to settle). **2** use and enjoy again after a long period of neglect. **dust-sheet** *Brit.* a cloth put over furniture to protect it from dust. **dust-shot** the smallest size of shot. **dust-storm** a storm with clouds of dust carried in the air. **dust-trap** something on, in, or under which dust gathers. **dust-up** *colloq.* a fight. **dust-wrapper** = *dust-jacket*. **in the dust 1** humiliated. **2** dead. **when the dust**

settles when things quieten down. □□ **dustless** *adj.* [OE *dūst*: cf. LG *dunst* vapour]

dustbin /'dʌstbɪn, 'dʌsbɪn/ *n. Brit.* a container for household refuse, esp. one kept outside.

dust bowl *n.* an arid or unproductive dry region. The term is applied specifically to an area in the prairie States of the US that was subject to dust storms and drought in the 1930s when the land was returned to grazing after having been cultivated since the First World War, and the hooves of livestock pulverized the unprotected soil. A graphic and moving description is given in John Steinbeck's novel *The Grapes of Wrath* (1939). Increased rainfall, re-grassing, and erosion-preventing measures such as contour ploughing have since reduced the area.

dustcart /'dʌstkɑːt/ *n. Brit.* a vehicle used for collecting household refuse.

duster /'dʌstə(r)/ *n.* **1 a** a cloth for dusting furniture etc. **b** a person or contrivance that dusts. **2** a woman's light, loose, full-length coat.

dustman /'dʌstmən, 'dʌsmən/ *n.* (*pl.* **-men**) *Brit.* **1** a man employed to clear household refuse. **2** the sandman.

dustpan /'dʌstpæn/ *n.* a small pan into which dust etc. is brushed from the floor.

dusty /'dʌstɪ/ *adj.* (**dustier, dustiest**) **1** full of, covered with, or resembling dust. **2** dry as dust; uninteresting. **3** (of a colour) dull or muted. □ **dusty answer** a curt rejection of a request. **dusty miller 1** any of various plants, esp. *Artemisia stelleriana*, having white dust on the leaves and flowers. **2** an artificial fishing-fly. **not so dusty** *Brit. sl.* fairly good. □□ **dustily** *adv.* **dustiness** *n.* [OE *dūstig* (as DUST)]

Dutch /dʌtʃ/ *adj.* & *n.* —*adj.* **1** of, relating to, or associated with The Netherlands or its people or language (see the etymology below). **2** *US sl.* German. **3** *S.Afr.* of Dutch descent. **4** *archaic* of Germany including The Netherlands. —*n.* **1 a** the Dutch language, which belongs to the Germanic language group and is most closely related to German and English. It is spoken by the 13 million inhabitants of The Netherlands and is also the official language of Suriname in South America and the Netherlands Antilles in the Caribbean. The same language is also spoken in parts of Belgium where it is called Flemish. An offshoot of Dutch is Afrikaans which was taken to Africa by Dutch settlers in the 17th c. **b** *S.Afr.* usu. *derog.* Afrikaans. **2** (prec. by *the*; treated as *pl.*) **a** the people of The Netherlands. **b** *S.Afr.* Afrikaans-speakers. **3** *archaic* the language of Germany including the Netherlands. □ **beat the Dutch** *US colloq.* do something remarkable. **Dutch auction** see AUCTION. **Dutch bargain** a bargain concluded by drinking together. **Dutch barn** *Brit.* a barn roof over hay etc., set on poles and having no walls. **Dutch cap 1** a contraceptive diaphragm. **2** a woman's lace cap with triangular flaps on each side. **Dutch courage** false courage gained from alcohol. **Dutch doll** a jointed wooden doll. **Dutch door** a door divided into two parts horizontally allowing one part to be shut and the other open. **Dutch elm disease** a disease affecting elms caused by the fungus *Ceratocystis ulmi*, first found in The Netherlands. **Dutch hoe** a hoe pushed forward by the user. **Dutch interior** a painting of Dutch domestic life, esp. by P. de Hooch (d. 1683). **Dutch metal** a copper-zinc alloy imitating gold leaf. **Dutch oven 1** a metal box the open side of which is turned towards a fire. **2** a covered cooking pot for braising etc. **Dutch treat** a party, outing, etc. to which each person makes a contribution. **Dutch uncle** a person giving advice with benevolent firmness. **Dutch wife** a framework of cane etc., or a bolster, used for resting the legs in bed. **go Dutch** share expenses equally. [MDu. *dutsch* etc. Hollandish, Netherlandish, German, OHG *diutisc* national. In Germany the adj. was used (in the 9th c.) as a rendering of L *vulgaris* to distinguish the 'vulgar tongue' from the Latin of the Church and the learned; hence it came to be applied to any dialect, and generically to German as a whole. From the language, it was naturally extended to those who spoke it, whence arose the name of the country, *Deutschland* = Germany. In the 15th and 16th c. in England 'Dutch' included the language and people of The Netherlands as part of the 'Low Dutch' or Low German domain. After the United Provinces became an independent

State, using the Low German of Holland as the national language, the term 'Dutch' was gradually restricted in England to The Netherlands.]

dutch /dʌtʃ/ n. Brit. sl. a wife (esp. old dutch). [abbr. of duchess (also in this sense)]

Dutch Guiana see SURINAME.

Dutchman /'dʌtʃmən/ n. (pl. **-men**; fem. **Dutchwoman**, pl. **-women**) **1 a** a native or national of The Netherlands. **b** a person of Dutch descent. **2** a Dutch ship. **3** US sl. a German. □ **Dutchman's breeches** US a plant, Dicentra cucullaria, with white flowers and finely divided leaves. **Flying Dutchman 1** a ghostly ship. **2** its captain. **I'm a Dutchman** expression of disbelief or refusal.

duteous /'djuːtɪəs/ adj. literary (of a person or conduct) dutiful; obedient. □□ **duteously** adv. **duteousness** n. [DUTY + -OUS: cf. beauteous]

dutiable /'djuːtɪəb(ə)l/ adj. liable to customs or other duties.

dutiful /'djuːtɪˌfʊl/ adj. doing or observant of one's duty; obedient. □□ **dutifully** adv. **dutifulness** n.

duty /'djuːtɪ/ n. (pl. **-ies**) **1 a** a moral or legal obligation; a responsibility (his duty to report it). **b** the binding force of what is right (strong sense of duty). **c** what is required of one (do one's duty). **2** payment to the public revenue, esp.: **a** that levied on the import, export, manufacture, or sale of goods (customs duty). **b** that levied on the transfer of property, licences, the legal recognition of documents, etc. (death duty; probate duty). **3** a job or function (his duties as caretaker). **4** the behaviour due to a superior; deference, respect. **5** the measure of an engine's effectiveness in units of work done per unit of fuel. **6** Eccl. the performance of church services. □ **do duty for** serve as or pass for (something else). **duty-bound** obliged by duty. **duty-free** (of goods) on which duty is not leviable. **duty-free shop** a shop at an airport etc. at which duty-free goods can be bought. **duty-officer** the officer currently on duty. **duty-paid** (of goods) on which duty has been paid. **duty visit** a visit paid from obligation, not from pleasure. **on** (or **off**) **duty** engaged (or not engaged) in one's work. [AF deweté, dueté (as DUE)]

duumvir /djuː'ʌmvə(r), 'djuː:əm-/ n. Rom.Hist. one of two coequal magistrates or officials. □□ **duumvirate** /-vɪrət/ n. [L f. duum virum of the two men]

duvet /'duːveɪ/ n. a thick soft quilt with a detachable cover, used instead of an upper sheet and blankets. [F]

dux /dʌks/ n. Sc., NZ, & S.Afr. etc. the top pupil in a class or in a school. [L, = leader]

duyker var. of DUIKER 1.

DV abbr. Deo volente.

Dvořák /'dvɔːʒæk/, Antonin (1841–1904), Czech composer, brought up in Bohemia at a time of strong national consciousness, who combined the idioms of folk-dances and songs (not only Czech but also American) with the central German and Austrian tradition from Haydn and Mozart to Brahms and Wagner. His widely popular 'New World' (Ninth) Symphony dates from a period (1892–5) spent in the US as director of the National Conservatory of Music, New York, and contains reminiscences of Negro spirituals, including 'Swing low, sweet chariot', as well as Bohemian melodies. Dvořák's chamber music, the Cello Concerto (1895), and the operas The Jacobin (1887–8), and Rusalka (1900) are now beginning to receive the recognition they deserve.

Dvr. abbr. Driver.

dwale /dweɪl/ n. = BELLADONNA 1. [prob. f. Scand.]

dwarf /dwɔːf/ n. & v. —n. (pl. **dwarfs** or **dwarves** /dwɔːvz/) **1 a** a person of abnormally small stature, esp. one with a normal-sized head and body but short limbs. ¶ The term person of restricted growth is now often preferred. **b** an animal or plant much below the ordinary size for the species. **2** a small mythological being with supernatural powers. **3** (in full **dwarf star**) a small usu. dense star. **4** (attrib.) **a** of a kind very small in size (dwarf bean). **b** puny, stunted. —v.tr. **1** stunt in growth. **2** cause (something similar or comparable) to seem small or insignificant (efforts dwarfed by their rivals' achievements). □□ **dwarfish** adj. [OE dweorg f. Gmc]

dwarfism /'dwɔːfɪz(ə)m/ n. the condition of being a dwarf.

dwell /dwel/ v. & n. —v.intr. (past and past part. **dwelt** or **dwelled**) **1** literary (usu. foll. by in, at, near, on, etc.) live, reside (dwelt in the forest). **2** (of a horse) be slow in raising its feet; pause before taking a fence. —n. a slight, regular pause in the motion of a machine. □ **dwell on** (or **upon**) **1** spend time on, linger over; write, brood, or speak at length on (a specified subject) (always dwells on his grievances). **2** prolong (a note, a syllable, etc.). □□ **dweller** n. [OE dwellan lead astray, later 'continue in a place', f. Gmc]

dwelling /'dwelɪŋ/ n. (also **dwelling-place**) formal a house; a residence; an abode. □ **dwelling-house** a house used as a residence, not as an office etc.

dwindle /'dwɪnd(ə)l/ v.intr. **1** become gradually smaller; shrink; waste away. **2** lose importance; decline; degenerate. [dwine fade away f. OE dwīnan, ON dvina]

dwt. abbr. hist. pennyweight.

d.w.t. abbr. dead-weight tonnage.

Dy symb. Chem. the element dysprosium.

dyad /'daɪæd/ n. Math. an operator which is a combination of two vectors. □□ **dyadic** /-'ædɪk/ adj. [LL dyas dyad- f. Gk duas duados f. duo two]

Dyak /'daɪæk/ n. (also **Dayak**) **1** a member of the indigenous non-Muslim inhabitants of Borneo. (See below.) **2** their language, = Iban. [Malay dayak up-country]

The Dyak peoples are subdivided into several named groups including the Land Dyak of SW Borneo and the Sea Dyak of Sarawak. Reckoned to be early inhabitants of the island, forced inland by subsequent migrations of Malays to the coasts, the people live in long-house communities, and intertribal warfare and head-hunting were formerly characteristic of Dyak society. The term 'Sea Dyak' is a misnomer, since the population to which it is applied is primarily a riverine hill-dwelling people whose economy is based on rice cultivation; it was introduced originally to distinguish the more aggressive peoples of the interior, who carried out raids on their coastal neighbours by going down to the sea and then mounting expeditions, from the more passive Land Dyaks of the coast.

dyarchy var. of DIARCHY.

dybbuk /'dɪbʊk/ n. (pl. **dybbukim** /-kɪm/ or **dybbuks**) (in Jewish folklore) the malevolent spirit of a dead person that enters and controls the body of a living person until exorcized. [Heb. dibbūk f. dābaq cling]

dye /daɪ/ n. & v. —n. **1 a** a substance used to change the colour of hair, fabric, wood, etc. **b** a colour produced by this. **2** (in full **dyestuff**) a substance yielding a dye, esp. for colouring materials in solution. —v.tr. (**dyeing**) **1** impregnate with dye. **2** make (a thing) a specified colour with dye (dyed it yellow). □ **dyed in the wool** (or **grain**) **1** out and out; unchangeable, inveterate. **2** (of a fabric) made of yarn dyed in its raw state. **dye-line** a print made by the diazo process. □□ **dyeable** adj. [OE deag, deagian]

dyer /'daɪə(r)/ n. a person who dyes cloth etc. □ **dyer's broom** (or **greenweed** or **oak** etc.) names of plants yielding dyes.

Dyfed /'dʌvɪd/ a county of SW Wales; pop. (1981) 333,400; county town, Carmarthen.

dying /'daɪɪŋ/ adj. connected with, or at the time of, death (his dying words). □ **dying oath** an oath made at, or with the solemnity proper to, death. **to one's dying day** for the rest of one's life. [pres. part. of DIE¹]

dyke¹ /daɪk/ n. & v. (also **dike**) —n. **1** a long wall or embankment built to prevent flooding, esp. from the sea. **2 a** a ditch or artificial watercourse. **b** Brit. a natural watercourse. **3 a** a low wall, esp. of turf. **b** a causeway. **4** a barrier or obstacle; a defence. **5** Geol. an intrusion of igneous rock across sedimentary strata. **6** esp. Austral. sl. a lavatory. —v.tr. provide or defend with a dyke or dykes. [ME f. ON dík or MLG dīk dam, MDu. dijc ditch, dam: cf. DITCH]

dyke² /daɪk/ n. (also **dike**) sl. a lesbian. [20th c.: orig. unkn.]

Dylan /'dɪlən/, Bob (real name Robert Allen Zimmerman, 1941–), American rock singer and songwriter, leader of the urban folk-music revival in the 1960s and 1970s. Some of his themes are associated with protest (e.g. 'The Times They are A-changin'', 1964), others are abstract. After his conversion to Christianity in 1979 he produced religious albums, and later experimented with reggae rhythms.

dyn *abbr.* dyne.

dynamic /daɪˈnæmɪk/ *adj.* & *n.* —*adj.* (also **dynamical) 1** energetic; active; potent. **2** *Physics* **a** concerning motive force (opp. STATIC). **b** concerning force in actual operation. **3** of or concerning dynamics. **4** *Mus.* relating to the volume of sound. **5** *Philos.* relating to dynamism. **6** (as **dynamical)** *Theol.* (of inspiration) endowing with divine power, not impelling mechanically. —*n.* **1** an energizing or motive force. **2** *Mus.* = DYNAMICS 3. □ **dynamic equilibrium** see EQUILIBRIUM. **dynamic viscosity** see VISCOSITY. □□ **dynamically** *adv.* [F *dynamique* f. Gk *dunamikos* f. *dunamis* power]

dynamics /daɪˈnæmɪks/ *n.pl.* **1** (usu. treated as *sing.*) **a** *Mech.* the branch of mechanics concerned with the motion of bodies under the action of forces (cf. STATICS). **b** the branch of any science in which forces or changes are considered (*aerodynamics; population dynamics*). **2** the motive forces, physical or moral, affecting behaviour and change in any sphere. **3** *Mus.* the varying degree of volume of sound in musical performance. □□ **dynamicist** /-sɪst/ *n.* (in sense 1).

dynamism /ˈdaɪnəˌmɪz(ə)m/ *n.* **1** energizing or dynamic action or power. **2** *Philos.* the theory that phenomena of matter or mind are due to the action of forces (rather than to motion or matter). □□ **dynamist** *n.* [Gk *dunamis* power + -ISM]

dynamite /ˈdaɪnəˌmaɪt/ *n.* & *v.* —*n.* **1** a high explosive consisting of nitroglycerine mixed with an absorbent. (See below.) **2** a potentially dangerous person, thing, or situation. **3** *sl.* a narcotic, esp. heroin. —*v.tr.* charge or shatter with dynamite. □□ **dynamiter** *n.* [formed as DYNAMISM + -ITE¹]

Dynamite is a plastic high explosive introduced by Alfred B. Nobel in 1866, consisting of nitroglycerine absorbed by a solid substance to improve handling quality. The solid may be inert (e.g. kieselguhr, a form of silicon dioxide), or active (e.g. a mixture of sodium nitrate and wood pulp). In particular ammonium nitrate may be added to improve safety during handling, and to reduce cost. Minor ingredients include calcium carbonate to neutralize acidity, and a freezing-point depressant to prevent freezing during cold weather. Dynamite is chiefly used for commercial blasting.

dynamo /ˈdaɪnəˌməʊ/ *n.* (*pl.* **-os) 1** a machine converting mechanical into electrical energy, esp. by rotating coils of copper wire in a magnetic field. **2** *colloq.* an energetic person. [abbr. of *dynamo-electric machine* f. Gk *dunamis* power, force]

dynamometer /ˌdaɪnəˈmɒmɪtə(r)/ *n.* an instrument measuring energy expended. [F *dynamomètre* f. Gk *dunamis* power, force]

dynast /ˈdɪnæst, ˈdaɪ-/ *n.* **1** a ruler. **2** a member of a dynasty. [L f. Gk *dunastēs* f. *dunamai* be able]

dynasty /ˈdɪnəstɪ/ *n.* (*pl.* **-ies) 1** a line of hereditary rulers. **2** a succession of leaders in any field. □□ **dynastic** /-ˈnæstɪk/ *adj.* **dynastically** /-ˈnæstɪkəlɪ/ *adv.* [F *dynastie* or LL *dynastia* f. Gk *dunasteia* lordship (as DYNAST)]

dynatron /ˈdaɪnəˌtrɒn/ *n.* *Electronics* a thermionic valve, used to generate continuous oscillations. [Gk *dunamis* power + -TRON]

dyne /daɪn/ *n.* *Physics* a unit of force that, acting on a mass of one gram, increases its velocity by one centimetre per second every second along the direction that it acts. ¶ Abbr.: **dyn.** [F f. Gk *dunamis* force, power]

dys- /dɪs/ *comb. form* esp. *Med.* bad, difficult. [Gk *dus-* bad]

dysentery /ˈdɪsəntərɪ, -trɪ/ *n.* a disease with inflammation of the intestines, causing severe diarrhoea with blood and mucus. □□ **dysenteric** /-ˈterɪk/ *adj.* [OF *dissenterie* or L *dysenteria* f. Gk *dusenteria* (as DYS-, *enteria* f. *entera* bowels)]

dysfunction /dɪsˈfʌŋkʃ(ə)n/ *n.* an abnormality or impairment of function. □□ **dysfunctional** *adj.*

dysgraphia /dɪsˈgræfɪə/ *n.* an inability to write coherently. □□ **dysgraphic** [DYS- + Gk *graphia* writing]

dyslexia /dɪsˈleksɪə/ *n.* an abnormal difficulty in reading and spelling, caused by a condition of the brain. □□ **dyslexic** *adj.* & *n.* **dyslectic** /-ˈlektɪk/ *adj.* & *n.* [G *Dyslexie* (as DYS-, Gk *lexis* speech)]

dysmenorrhoea /ˌdɪsmenəˈrɪə/ *n.* painful or difficult menstruation.

dyspepsia /dɪsˈpepsɪə/ *n.* indigestion. [L *dyspepsia* f. Gk *duspepsia* (as DYS-, *peptos* cooked, digested)]

dyspeptic /dɪsˈpeptɪk/ *adj.* & *n.* —*adj.* of or relating to dyspepsia or the resulting depression. —*n.* a person suffering from dyspepsia.

dysphasia /ˌdɪsˈfeɪzɪə/ *n.* *Med.* lack of coordination in speech, owing to brain damage. □□ **dysphasic** *adj.* [Gk *dusphatos* hard to utter (as DYS-, PHATIC)]

dysphoria /dɪsˈfɔːrɪə/ *n.* a state of unease or mental discomfort. □□ **dysphoric** /-ˈfɒrɪk/ *adj.* [Gk *dusphoria* f. *dusphoros* hard to bear (as DYS-, *pherō* bear)]

dysplasia /dɪsˈpleɪzɪə/ *n.* *Med.* abnormal growth of tissues etc. □□ **dysplastic** /-ˈplæstɪk/ *adj.* [mod.L, formed as DYS- + Gk *plasis* formation]

dyspnoea /dɪspˈniːə/ *n.* (US **dyspnea)** *Med.* difficult or laboured breathing. □□ **dyspnoeic** *adj.* [L f. Gk *duspnoia* (as DYS-, *pneō* breathe)]

dysprosium /dɪsˈprəʊzɪəm/ *n.* *Chem.* a naturally occurring soft metallic element of the lanthanide series, discovered in 1886. Purified dysprosium has various specialized uses, including as a component in certain magnetic alloys. ¶ Symb.: **Dy**; atomic number 66. [mod.L f. Gk *dusprositos* hard to get at + -IUM]

dystocia /dɪsˈtəʊʃə/ *n.* *Med.* difficult or prolonged childbirth. [DYS- + Gk *tokos* childbirth]

dystrophy /ˈdɪstrəfɪ/ *n.* defective nutrition. □ **muscular dystrophy** a hereditary progressive weakening and wasting of the muscles. □□ **dystrophic** /dɪsˈtrɒfɪk/ *adj.* [mod.L *dystrophia* formed as DYS- + Gk *-trophia* nourishment]

dysuria /dɪsˈjʊərɪə/ *n.* painful or difficult urination. [LL f. Gk *dusouria* (as DYS-, *ouron* urine)]

Dzaoudzi /ˈdzaʊdzi/ the capital of the French island of Mahore in the Indian Ocean; pop. (1985) 5,675.

Dzerzhinsky /dzəˈʒɪnski/, Feliks Edmundovich (1877–1926), Russian Bolshevik leader, of Polish noble family, who was the organizer and first head of the post-revolutionary security police, the Cheka (see entry) and of the agencies that immediately succeeded it.

dzho /zəʊ/ *n.* (also **dzo, zho)** (*pl.* same or **-os)** a hybrid of a cow and a yak. [Tibetan *mdso*]

Dzongkha /ˈzɒŋkə/ *n.* a Tibetan dialect that is the official language of Bhutan. [Tibetan, = language of the fortress]

E

E¹ /iː/ *n.* (also **e**) (*pl.* **Es** or **E's**) **1** the fifth letter of the alphabet. **2** *Mus.* the third note of the diatonic scale of C major.

E² *abbr.* (also **E.**) **1** East, Eastern. **2** Egyptian (*£E*). **3** Engineering (*M.I.Mech.E.* etc.). **4** see E-NUMBER.

e *symb.* **1** *Math.* the base of natural logarithms, equal to approx. 2.71828. **2** used on packaging (in conjunction with specification of weight, size, etc.) to indicate compliance with EEC regulations.

e- /ɪ, e/ *prefix* form of EX-¹ 1 before some consonants.

ea. *abbr.* each.

each /iːtʃ/ *adj. & pron.* —*adj.* every one of two or more persons or things, regarded separately (*each person; five in each class*). —*pron.* each person or thing (*each of us; have two books each; cost a penny each*). □ **each and every** every single. **each other** one another (used as a compound reciprocal pron.: *they hate each other; they wore each other's hats*). **each way** *Brit.* (of a bet) backing a horse etc. for both a win and a place. [OE *ǣlc* f. WG (as AYE, ALIKE)]

eager /ˈiːgə(r)/ *adj.* **1 a** full of keen desire, enthusiastic. **b** (of passions etc.) keen, impatient. **2** keen, impatient, strongly desirous (*eager to learn; eager for news*). □ **eager beaver** *colloq.* a very or excessively diligent person. □□ **eagerly** *adv.* **eagerness** *n.* [ME f. AF *egre*, OF *aigre* keen, ult. f. L *acer acris*]

eagle /ˈiːg(ə)l/ *n.* **1 a** any of various large birds of prey of the family Accipitridae, with keen vision and powerful flight. **b** a figure of an eagle, esp. as a symbol of the US, or formerly as a Roman or French ensign. **2** *Golf* a score of two strokes under par at any hole. **3** *US* a coin worth ten dollars. □ **eagle eye** keen sight, watchfulness. **eagle-eyed** keen-sighted, watchful. **eagle owl** any large owl of the genus *Bubo*, with long ear tufts. [ME f. AF *egle*, OF *aigle* f. L *aquila*]

eaglet /ˈiːglɪt/ *n.* a young eagle.

eagre /ˈeɪgə(r), ˈiːgə(r)/ *n.* = BORE³. [17th c.: orig. unkn.]

Eakins /ˈiːkɪnz/, Thomas (1844–1916), American painter, photographer, and sculptor, regarded by most critics as the outstanding American painter of the 19th c. and by many as the greatest artist his country has yet produced. He was particularly influenced by Velázquez and Ribera and applied an uncompromising realism to portraiture and genre pictures of the life of his native city Philadelphia; boating and bathing were favourite themes. His most famous picture *The Gross Clinic* (1875) aroused controversy because of its unsparing depiction of surgery. His wife Susan (1851–1938) was also a painter and photographer, as well as an accomplished pianist.

-ean /ˈiːən, ɪən/ *suffix* var. of -AN.

E. & O. E. *abbr.* errors and omissions excepted.

ear¹ /ɪə(r)/ *n.* **1 a** the organ of hearing and balance in man and vertebrates, esp. the external part of this. **b** an organ sensitive to sound in other animals. **2** the faculty for discriminating sounds (*an ear for music*). **3** an ear-shaped thing, esp. the handle of a jug. **4** listening, attention. □ **all ears** listening attentively. **bring about one's ears** bring down upon oneself. **ear-drops 1** medicinal drops for the ear. **2** hanging earrings. **ear lobe** the lower soft pendulous external part of the ear. **ear-piercing** loud and shrill. **ear-splitting** excessively loud. **ear-trumpet** a trumpet-shaped device formerly used as a hearing-aid. **give ear to** listen to. **have a person's ear** receive a favourable hearing. **have** (or **keep**) **an ear to the ground** be alert to rumours or the trend of opinion. **in one ear and out the other** heard but disregarded or quickly forgotten. **out on one's ear** dismissed ignominiously. **up to one's ears** (often foll. by *in*) *colloq.* deeply involved or occupied. □□ **eared** *adj.* (also in *comb.*). **earless** *adj.* [OE *ēare* f. Gmc: rel. to L *auris*, Gk *ous*]

ear² /ɪə(r)/ *n.* the seed-bearing head of a cereal plant. [OE *ēar* f. Gmc]

earache /ˈɪəreɪk/ *n.* a (usu. prolonged) pain in the ear.

earbash /ˈɪəbæʃ/ *v.tr.* esp. *Austral. sl.* talk inordinately to; harangue. □□ **earbasher** *n.* **earbashing** *n.*

eardrum /ˈɪədrʌm/ *n.* the membrane of the middle ear (= *tympanic membrane*).

earful /ˈɪəfʊl/ *n.* (*pl.* **-fuls**) *colloq.* **1** a copious or prolonged amount of talking. **2** a strong reprimand.

earl /ɜːl/ *n.* a British nobleman ranking between a marquess and a viscount (cf. COUNT²). The title was first used in England under the Danish king Cnut of the viceroy or governor of one of the great divisions of England (Wessex, Mercia, Northumbria, etc.). After the Norman Conquest it was regarded as equivalent to the Latin *comes* = count, and implied the governorship or feudal lordship of a county; as a title of rank it corresponds to that of *count* in the nobility of other European nations. It is therefore the oldest title and rank of English nobles, and was the highest until 1337 when that of *duke* was created (see DUKE 1a). □ **Earl Marshal** (in the UK) the officer presiding over the College of Heralds, with ceremonial duties on various royal occasions. **Earl Palatine** *hist.* an earl having royal authority within his country or domain. □□ **earldom** *n.* [OE *eorl*, of unkn. orig.]

early /ˈɜːlɪ/ *adj., adv., & n.* —*adj. & adv.* (**earlier**, **earliest**) **1** before the due, usual, or expected time (*was early for my appointment; the train arrived early*). **2 a** not far on in the day or night, or in time (*early evening; at the earliest opportunity*). **b** prompt (*early payment appreciated; at your earliest convenience*). **3 a** not far on in a period, development, or process of evolution; being the first stage (*Early English architecture; the early Christians; early Spring*). **b** of the distant past (*early man*). **c** not far on in a sequence or serial order (*the early chapters; appears early in the list*). **4 a** of childhood, esp. the preschool years (*early learning*). **b** (of a piece of writing, music, etc.) immature, youthful (*an early work*). **5** forward in flowering, ripening, etc. (*early peaches*). —*n.* (*pl.* **-ies**) (usu. in *pl.*) an early fruit or vegetable, esp. potatoes. □ **at the earliest** (often placed after a specified time) not before (*will arrive on Monday at the earliest*). **early bird** *colloq.* one who arrives, gets up, etc. early. **early closing** *Brit.* the shutting of business premises on the afternoon of one particular day of the week. **early days** early in time for something to happen etc. **early grave** an untimely or premature death. **early hours** the very early morning, usu. before dawn. **early** (or **earlier**) **on** at an early (or earlier) stage. **early warning** advance warning of an imminent (esp. nuclear) attack. □□ **earliness** *n.* [orig. as *adv.*, f. OE *ǣrlīce*, *ārlīce* (*ǣr* ERE)]

earmark /ˈɪəmɑːk/ *n. & v.* —*n.* **1** an identifying mark. **2** an owner's mark on the ear of an animal. —*v.tr.* **1** set aside (money etc.) for a special purpose. **2** mark (sheep etc.) with such a mark.

earmuff /ˈɪəmʌf/ *n.* a wrap or cover for the ears, protecting them from cold, noise, etc.

earn /ɜːn/ *v.tr.* **1** (also *absol.*) **a** (of a person) obtain (income) in the form of money in return for labour or services (*earn a weekly wage; happy to be earning at last*). **b** (of capital invested) bring in as interest or profit. **2 a** deserve; be entitled to; obtain as the reward for hard work or merit (*have earned a holiday; earned our admiration; earn one's keep*). **b** incur (a reproach, reputation, etc.). □ **earned income** income derived from wages etc. (opp. *unearned income*). [OE *earnian* f. WG, rel. to Gmc roots assoc. with reaping]

earner /ˈɜːnə(r)/ *n.* **1** a person or thing that earns (often in *comb.*: *wage-earner*). **2** *sl.* a lucrative job or enterprise.

earnest¹ /ˈɜːnɪst/ *adj. & n.* —*adj.* ardently or intensely serious; zealous; not trifling or joking. —*n.* seriousness. □ **in** (or **in real**) **earnest** serious(ly), not joking(ly); with determination. □□ **earnestly** *adv.* **earnestness** *n.* [OE *eornust*, *eornost* (with Gmc cognates): cf. ON *ern* vigorous]

---

b *but* d *dog* f *few* g *get* h *he* j *yes* k *cat* l *leg* m *man* n *no* p *pen* r *red* s *sit* t *top* v *voice*

earnest[2] /'ɜːnɪst/ n. **1** money paid as an instalment, esp. to confirm a contract etc. **2** a token or foretaste (*in earnest of what is to come*). [ME *ernes*, prob. var. of *erles, arles* prob. f. med.L *arrhula* (unrecorded) f. *arr(h)a* pledge]

earnings /'ɜːnɪŋz/ n.pl. money earned. □ **earnings-related** (of benefit, a pension, etc.) calculated on the basis of past or present income.

earphone /'ɪəfəʊn/ n. a device applied to the ear to aid hearing or receive radio or telephone communications.

earpiece /'ɪəpiːs/ n. the part of a telephone etc. applied to the ear during use.

earplug /'ɪəplʌg/ n. a piece of wax etc. placed in the ear to protect against cold air, water, or noise.

earring /'ɪərɪŋ/ n. a piece of jewellery worn in or on (esp. the lobe of) the ear.

earshot /'ɪəʃɒt/ n. the distance over which something can be heard (esp. *within* or *out of earshot*).

earth /ɜːθ/ n. & v. —n. **1 a** (also **Earth**) one of the planets of the solar system orbiting about the sun between Venus and Mars; the planet on which we live. (See below.) **b** land and sea, as distinct from sky. **2 a** dry land; the ground (*fell to earth*). **b** soil, clay, mould. **c** bodily matter (*earth to earth*). **3** *Relig.* the present abode of mankind, as distinct from heaven or hell; the world. **4** *Brit. Electr.* the connection to the earth as an arbitrary reference voltage in an electrical circuit. **5** the hole of a badger, fox, etc. **6** (prec. by *the*) *colloq.* a huge amount; everything (*cost the earth; want the earth*). —v. **1** *tr.* (foll. by *up*) cover (the roots and lower stems of plants) with heaped-up earth. **2 a** *tr.* drive (a fox) to its earth. **b** *intr.* (of a fox etc.) run to its earth. **3** *tr. Brit. Electr.* connect to the earth. □ **come back** (or **down**) **to earth** return to realities. **earth-closet** a lavatory with dry earth used to cover excreta. **earth-hog** (or **-pig**) = AARDVARK. **earth mother 1** *Mythol.* a spirit or deity symbolizing the earth. **2** a sensual and maternal woman. **earth-nut** any of various plants, or its edible roundish tuber, esp.: **1** an umbelliferous woodland plant, *Conopodium majus*. **2** the peanut. **earth sciences** the sciences concerned with the earth or part of it, or its atmosphere (e.g. geology, oceanography, meteorology). **earth-shattering** *colloq.* having a traumatic or devastating effect. **earthshatteringly** *colloq.* devastatingly, remarkably. **earth tremor** see TREMOR n. 3. **gone to earth** in hiding. **on earth** *colloq.* existing anywhere; emphatically (*the happiest man on earth; looked like nothing on earth; what on earth?*). □□ **earthward** adj. & adv. **earthwards** adv. [OE *eorthe* f. Gmc]

Earth is the third-closest planet to the sun in the solar system and has one natural satellite, the moon. It has an equatorial radius of 6,378 km (3,963 miles), an average density 5.5 times that of water, and is believed to have formed about 4,600 million years ago. Internally it consists of three concentric layers: core, mantle, and crust. The crust, which forms the surface of the solid earth, is only a few kilometres thick, although thicker beneath the continents than beneath the oceans. The mantle consists mainly of silicate rocks, and constitutes the bulk of the earth's volume. Beneath it is the core, which extends to the centre of the earth, consisting largely of iron and nickel; its outer part is liquid and is thought to be the seat of the earth's magnetic field. According to the theory of plate tectonics (see entry) the crust and upper part of the mantle are divided into a series of rigid plates, which lie on top of a more plastic region. Earth, which is three-quarters covered by oceans and has a dense atmosphere of nitrogen and oxygen, is the only planet known to support life.

earthbound /'ɜːθbaʊnd/ adj. **1** attached to the earth or earthly things. **2** moving towards the earth.

earthen /'ɜːθ(ə)n/ adj. **1** made of earth. **2** made of baked clay.

earthenware /'ɜːθ(ə)nˌweə(r)/ n. & adj. —n. pottery, vessels, etc., made of clay fired to a porous state which can be made impervious to liquids by the use of a glaze (cf. PORCELAIN). —adj. made of fired clay. [EARTHEN + WARE[1]]

earthling /'ɜːθlɪŋ/ n. an inhabitant of the earth, esp. as regarded in fiction by outsiders.

earthly /'ɜːθlɪ/ adj. **1** of the earth or human life on earth;

terrestrial. **2** (usu. with *neg.*) *colloq.* remotely possible or conceivable (*is no earthly use; there wasn't an earthly reason*). □ **not an earthly** *colloq.* no chance whatever. □□ **earthliness** n.

earthquake /'ɜːθkweɪk/ n. **1** a convulsion of the superficial parts of the earth due to the release of accumulated stress as a result of faults in strata or volcanic action. While gentle earth tremors can occur in any region of the globe, the more severe ones usually occur near the edges of the major 'plates' that make up the earth's crust. The point at which an earthquake shock originates is called the focus and the point immediately above this on the earth's surface is the epicentre. The intensity of the earthquake is reported as measured by the Richter scale. Major earthquakes generally measure between about 7 and 9, though in theory there is no upper limit on the scale. **2** a social etc. disturbance.

earthshine /'ɜːθʃaɪn/ n. *Astron.* **1** the unilluminated portion of a crescent moon shining faintly because of sunlight reflected from the earth on to the moon. **2** illumination on the moon's surface caused by this.

earthstar /'ɜːθstɑː(r)/ n. any woodland fungus of the genus *Geastrum*, esp. *G. triplex*, with a spherical spore-containing fruit body surrounded by a fleshy star-shaped structure.

earthwork /'ɜːθwɜːk/ n. **1** an artificial bank of earth in fortification or road-building etc. **2** the process of excavating soil in civil engineering work.

earthworm /'ɜːθwɜːm/ n. any of various annelid worms, esp. of the genus *Lumbricus* or *Allolobophora*, living and burrowing in the ground.

earthy /'ɜːθɪ/ adj. (**earthier, earthiest**) **1** of or like earth or soil. **2** somewhat coarse or crude; unrefined (*earthy humour*). □□ **earthily** adv. **earthiness** n.

earwax /'ɪəwæks/ n. a yellow waxy secretion produced by the ear, = CERUMEN.

earwig /'ɪəwɪg/ n. & v. —n. **1** any small elongate insect of the order Dermaptera, with a pair of terminal appendages in the shape of forceps. **2** *US* a small centipede. —v.tr. (**earwigged, earwigging**) *archaic* influence (a person) by secret communication. [OE *ēarwicga* f. *ēare* EAR[1] + *wicga* earwig, prob. rel. to *wiggle*: once thought to enter the head through the ear]

ease /iːz/ n. & v. —n. **1** absence of difficulty; facility, effortlessness (*did it with ease*). **2 a** freedom or relief from pain, anxiety, or trouble. **b** freedom from embarrassment or awkwardness. **c** freedom or relief from constraint or formality. —v. **1** *tr.* relieve from pain or anxiety etc. (often foll. by *of*: *eased my mind; eased me of the burden*). **2** *intr.* (often foll. by *off, up*) **a** become less painful or burdensome. **b** relax; begin to take it easy. **c** slow down; moderate one's behaviour, habits, etc. **3** *tr. joc.* rob or extract money etc. from (*let me ease you of your loose change*). **4** *intr. Meteorol.* become less severe (*the wind will ease tonight*). **5 a** *tr.* relax; slacken; make a less tight fit. **b** *tr. & intr.* (foll. by *through, into, etc.*) move or be moved carefully into place (*eased it into the hole*). **6** *intr.* (often foll. by *off*) *Stock Exch.* (of shares etc.) descend in price or value. □ **at ease 1** free from anxiety or constraint. **2** *Mil.* **a** in a relaxed attitude, with the feet apart. **b** the order to stand in this way. **at one's ease** free from embarrassment, awkwardness, or undue formality. **ease away** (or **down** or **off**) *Naut.* slacken (a rope, sail, etc.). □□ **easer** n. [ME f. AF *ese*, OF *eise*, ult. f. L *adjacens* ADJACENT]

easel /'iːz(ə)l/ n. **1** a standing frame, usu. of wood, for supporting an artist's work, a blackboard, etc. **2** an artist's work collectively. [Du. *ezel* = G *Esel* ASS[1]]

easement /'iːzmənt/ n. *Law* a right of way or a similar right over another's land. [ME f. OF *aisement*]

easily /'iːzɪlɪ/ adv. **1** without difficulty. **2** by far (*easily the best*). **3** very probably (*it could easily snow*).

east /iːst/ n., adj., & adv. —n. **1 a** the point of the horizon where the sun rises at the equinoxes (cardinal point 90° to the right of north). **b** the compass point corresponding to this. **c** the direction in which this lies. **2** (usu. **the East**) **a** the regions or countries lying to the east of Europe. **b** the Communist States of eastern Europe. **3** the eastern part of a country, town, etc. **4** (**East**) *Bridge* a player occupying the position designated 'east'.

—*adj.* **1** towards, at, near, or facing east. **2** coming from the east (*east wind*). —*adv.* **1** towards, at, or near the east. **2** (foll. by *of*) further east than. □ **East End** the part of London east of the City as far as the River Lea. **East Ender** an inhabitant of the East End. **East Indiaman** *hist.* a large ship engaged in trade with the East Indies. **east-north** (or **-south**)-**east** the direction or compass point midway between east and north-east (or south-east). **East Side** the eastern part of Manhattan. **to the east** (often foll. by *of*) in an easterly direction. [OE *ēast-* f. Gmc]

East Anglia /ˈæŋglɪə/ an ancient division of England, now a region of eastern England consisting of the counties of Norfolk, Suffolk, and parts of Essex and Cambridgeshire.

eastbound /ˈiːstbaʊnd/ *adj.* travelling or leading eastwards.

East Cape a peninsula on the east coast of North Island, New Zealand, forming an administrative region; pop. (1986) 55,000; chief town, Gisborne.

East China Sea see CHINA SEA.

Easter /ˈiːstə(r)/ *n.* **1** (also **Easter Day** or **Sunday**) the festival of the Resurrection of Christ, the greatest and oldest festival of the Christian Church, celebrated on the first Sunday after the first full moon after the vernal equinox (21 March). The derivation of the name is uncertain. According to Bede, it was connected with an Anglo-Saxon goddess Eostre whose festival was in spring; at any rate it seems clear that the Christian feast superseded an old pagan festival. **2** the season in which this occurs, esp. the weekend from Good Friday to Easter Monday. □ **Easter egg** an edible artificial (usually chocolate) egg given as a gift at Easter. The egg is an ancient symbol of renewed life. Easter eggs, originally called 'pace eggs' (*Pasch* = Easter; see PASCHAL), were known as early as the 13th c. They were ordinary hard-boiled eggs, with the shells dyed different colours. **Easter rising** the insurrection in Dublin and other cities in Ireland against British rule, Easter 1916. It ended with the surrender of the insurgents, some of whose leaders were subsequently executed. **Easter week** the week beginning on Easter Sunday. [OE *ēastre* app. f. *Ēostre*, a goddess associated with spring, f. Gmc]

Easter Island an island in the SE Pacific west of Chile, named by the Dutch navigator Roggeveen who visited it on Easter Day, 1722; pop. (est. 1988) 2,000. It is administered by Chile and is famous for its many monolithic statues of human heads (up to 10 metres high).

easterly /ˈiːstəlɪ/ *adj.*, *adv.*, & *n.* —*adj.* & *adv.* **1** in an eastern position or direction. **2** (of a wind) blowing from the east. —*n.* (*pl.* **-ies**) a wind blowing from the east.

eastern /ˈiːst(ə)n/ *adj.* **1** of or in the east; inhabiting the east. **2** lying or directed towards the east. **3** (**Eastern**) of or in the Far, Middle, or Near East. □ **Eastern Church** the Orthodox Church. **Eastern Empire** see ROMAN EMPIRE. **Eastern hemisphere** the half of the earth containing Europe, Asia, and Africa. **Eastern Time** standard time used in eastern Canada and the US or in eastern Australia. □□ **easternmost** *adj.* [OE *ēasterne* (as EAST, -ERN)]

Eastern Desert (also called the *Arabian Desert*) a desert in eastern Egypt, lying between the Nile and the Red Sea.

easterner /ˈiːstənə(r)/ *n.* a native or inhabitant of the east.

Eastertide /ˈiːstətaɪd/ *n.* the period including Easter.

East India Company a trading company formed in 1600 to develop commerce in the newly discovered East Indies (formerly called East India). In the second half of the 18th c., after a series of victories over local princes, the Company took over the administration of British India, maintaining its own army and political service. Government remained in the hands of the company until 1858 when the British Crown took over in the wake of the Indian Mutiny.

East Indies the many islands off the SE coast of Asia, now often called the Malay Archipelago.

easting /ˈiːstɪŋ/ *n. Naut.* etc. the distance travelled or the angle of longitude measured eastward from either a defined north–south grid line or a meridian.

East London a port and resort on the SE coast of Cape Province in the Republic of South Africa; pop. (1985) 193,800.

Eastman /ˈiːstmən/, George (1854–1932), American inventor of

the hand-held Kodak camera (1888) designed to use a flexible roll-film coated with light-sensitive emulsion, and of the film itself—inventions which did much to popularize amateur photography.

East Sussex /ˈsʌsɪks/ a county of SE England; pop. (1981) 665,500; county town, Lewes.

eastward /ˈiːstwəd/ *adj.*, *adv.*, & *n.* —*adj.* & *adv.* (also **eastwards**) towards the east. —*n.* an eastward direction or region. □□ **eastwardly** *adj.* & *adv.*

Eastwood /ˈiːstwʊd/, Clint (1930–), American film actor, remembered chiefly for his part in westerns such as *For a Fistful of Dollars* (1964).

easy /ˈiːzɪ/ *adj.*, *adv.*, & *int.* (**easier**, **easiest**) —*adj.* **1** not difficult; achieved without great effort. **2 a** free from pain, discomfort, anxiety, etc. **b** comfortably off, affluent (*easy circumstances*). **3** free from embarrassment, awkwardness, constraint, etc.; relaxed and pleasant (*an easy manner*). **4** compliant, obliging; easily persuaded (*an easy touch*). **5** Stock Exch. (of goods, money on loan, etc.) not much in demand. —*adv.* with ease; in an effortless or relaxed manner. —*int.* go carefully; move gently. □ **easy as pie** see PIE¹. **easy chair** a large comfortable chair, usu. an armchair. **easy come easy go** *colloq.* what is easily got is soon lost or spent. **easy does it** *colloq.* go carefully. **easy money** money got without effort (esp. of dubious legality). **easy of access** easily entered or approached. **easy on the eye** (or **ear** etc.) *colloq.* pleasant to look at (or listen to etc.). **easy-peasy** *sl.* very simple. **Easy Street** *colloq.* affluence. **easy terms** payment by instalments. **go easy** (foll. by *with*, *on*) be sparing or cautious. **I'm easy** *colloq.* I have no preference. **of easy virtue** (of a woman) sexually promiscuous. **stand easy!** *Brit. Mil.* permission to a squad standing at ease to relax their attitude further. **take it easy 1** proceed gently or carefully. **2** relax; avoid overwork. □□ **easiness** *n.* [ME f. AF *aisé*, OF *aisié* past part. of *aisier* EASE]

easygoing /ˌiːziˈɡəʊɪŋ/ *adj.* **1** placid and tolerant; relaxed in manner; accepting things as they are. **2** (of a horse) having an easy gait.

eat /iːt/ *v.* (*past* **ate** /et, eɪt/; *past part.* **eaten** /ˈiːt(ə)n/) **1 a** *tr.* take into the mouth, chew, and swallow (food). **b** *intr.* consume food; take a meal. **c** *tr.* devour (*eaten by a lion*). **2** *intr.* (foll. by (*away*) *at*, *into*) **a** destroy gradually, esp. by corrosion, erosion, disease, etc. **b** begin to consume or diminish (resources etc.). **3** *tr. colloq.* trouble, vex (*what's eating you?*). □ **eat dirt** see DIRT. **eat one's hat** *colloq.* admit one's surprise in being wrong (only as a proposition unlikely to be fulfilled: *said he would eat his hat*). **eat one's heart out** suffer from excessive longing or envy. **eat humble pie** see HUMBLE. **eat out** have a meal away from home, esp. in a restaurant. **eat out of a person's hand** be entirely submissive to a person. **eat salt with** see SALT. **eat up 1** (also *absol.*) eat or consume completely. **2** use or deal with rapidly or wastefully (*eats up petrol*; *eats up the miles*). **3** encroach upon or annex (*eating up the neighbouring States*). **4** absorb, preoccupy (*eaten up with pride*). **eat one's words** admit that one was wrong. [OE *etan* f. Gmc]

eatable /ˈiːtəb(ə)l/ *adj.* & *n.* —*adj.* that is in a condition to be eaten (cf. EDIBLE). —*n.* (usu. in *pl.*) food.

eater /ˈiːtə(r)/ *n.* **1** a person who eats (*a big eater*). **2** *Brit.* an eating apple etc.

eatery /ˈiːtərɪ/ *n. US* (*pl.* **-ies**) *colloq.* a restaurant or eating-place.

eating /ˈiːtɪŋ/ *adj.* **1** suitable for eating (*eating apple*). **2** used for eating (*eating-house*).

eats /iːts/ *n.pl. colloq.* food.

eau-de-Cologne /ˌəʊdəkəˈləʊn/ *n.* an alcohol-based perfume of a kind made orig. at Cologne. [F, lit. 'water of Cologne']

eau-de-Nil /ˌəʊdəˈniːl/ *n.* a pale greenish colour. [F, lit. 'water of the Nile' (from the supposed resemblance)]

eau-de-vie /ˌəʊdəˈviː/ *n.* spirits, esp. brandy. [F, lit. 'water of life']

eaves /iːvz/ *n.pl.* the underside of a projecting roof. [orig. sing., f. OE *efes*: prob. rel. to OVER]

eavesdrop /ˈiːvzdrɒp/ *v.intr.* (**-dropped**, **-dropping**) listen

æ cat ɑː arm e bed ɜː her ɪ sit iː see ɒ hot ɔː saw ʌ run ʊ put uː too ə ago aɪ my

secretly to a private conversation. □□ **eavesdropper** n. [*eaves-dropper* orig. 'one who listens under walls' prob. f. ON *upsardropi* (cf. OE *yfæsdrypæ*): *eavesdrop* by back-form.]

ebb /eb/ n. & v. —n. **1** the movement of the tide out to sea (also *attrib.*: *ebb tide*). **2** the process of draining away of flood-water etc. —*v.intr.* (often foll. by *away*) **1** (of tidewater) flow out to sea; recede; drain away. **2** decline; run low (*his life was ebbing away*). □ **at a low ebb** in a poor condition or state of decline. **ebb and flow** a continuing process of decline and upturn in circumstances. **on the ebb** in decline. [OE *ebba*, *ebbian*]

E-boat /ˈiːbəʊt/ n. *hist.* a German torpedo-boat in the Second World War. [*enemy* + BOAT]

ebonite /ˈebənaɪt/ n. = VULCANITE. [EBONY + -ITE¹]

ebony /ˈebənɪ/ n. & adj. —n. (pl. **-ies**) **1** a heavy hard dark wood used for furniture. **2** any of various trees of the genus *Diospyros* producing this. —*adj.* **1** made of ebony. **2** black like ebony. [earlier *hebeny* f. (h)*eben(e)* = *ebon*, perh. after *ivory*]

Ebro /ˈiːbrəʊ, ˈe-/ the principal river of NE Spain, rising in the Cantabrian Mountains and flowing south-east for 910 km (570 miles) into the Mediterranean Sea.

ebullient /ɪˈbʌlɪənt, *disp.* ɪˈbʊlɪənt/ adj. **1** exuberant, high-spirited. **2** *Chem.* boiling. □□ **ebullience** n. **ebulliency** n. **ebulliently** adv. [L *ebullire ebullient-* bubble out (as E-, *bullire* boil)]

EC abbr. **1** East Central (London postal district). **2** executive committee. **3 a** European Community. **b** European Commission.

ecad /ˈiːkæd/ n. *Ecol.* an organism modified by its environment. [Gk *oíkos* house + -AD]

écarté /eɪˈkɑːteɪ/ n. **1** a card-game for two persons in which cards from a player's hand may be exchanged for others from the pack. **2** a position in classical ballet with one arm and leg extended. [F, past part. of *écarter* discard]

Ecce Homo /ˌekeɪ ˈhɒməʊ/ n. *Art* one of the subjects of the Passion cycle: in Renaissance painting typically a depiction of Christ wearing the crown of thorns. [L, = 'behold the man', the words of Pilate to the Jews after the crowning with thorns (John 19: 5)]

eccentric /ɪkˈsentrɪk, ek-/ adj. & n. —*adj.* **1** odd or capricious in behaviour or appearance; whimsical. **2 a** not placed, not having its axis etc. placed centrally. **b** (often foll. by *to*) (of a circle) not concentric (to another). **c** (of an orbit) not circular. —n. **1** an eccentric person. **2** *Mech.* an eccentric contrivance for changing rotatory into backward-and-forward motion, e.g. the cam used in an internal-combustion engine. □□ **eccentrically** adv. **eccentricity** /-ˈtrɪsɪtɪ/ n. (pl. **-ies**). [LL *eccentricus* f. Gk *ekkentros* f. *ek* out of + *kentros* CENTRE]

Eccles. abbr. Ecclesiastes (Old Testament).

Eccles cake /ˈek(ə)lz/ n. a round flat cake made of pastry filled with currants etc. [*Eccles* in N. England]

ecclesial /ɪˈkliːzjəl/ adj. of or relating to a Church. [Gk *ekklesia* assembly, church f. *ekklētos* summoned out f. *ek* out + *kaleō* call]

ecclesiastic /ɪˌkliːzɪˈæstɪk/ n. & adj. —n. a priest or clergyman. —*adj.* = ECCLESIASTICAL. □□ **ecclesiasticism** /-ˌsɪz(ə)m/ n. [F *ecclésiastique* or LL *ecclesiasticus* f. Gk *ekklēsiastikos* f. *ekklēsia* assembly, church: see ECCLESIAL]

ecclesiastical /ɪˌkliːzɪˈæstɪk(ə)l/ adj. of the Church or the clergy. □□ **ecclesiastically** adv.

Ecclesiasticus /ɪˌkliːzɪˈæstɪkəs/ a book of the Apochrypha, also called 'The Wisdom of Jesus the son of Sirach', containing moral and practical maxims and probably composed or compiled in the early 2nd c. BC. The origin of its name is uncertain; the theory that it represents the Latin *Liber ecclesiasticus* (= book of the Church), so called owing to its use as a book of instruction in the early Church, is untenable.

ecclesiology /ɪˌkliːzɪˈɒlədʒɪ/ n. **1** the study of churches, esp. church building and decoration. **2** theology as applied to the nature and structure of the Christian Church. □□ **ecclesiological** /-zɪəˈlɒdʒɪk(ə)l/ adj. **ecclesiologist** n. [Gk *ekklēsia* assembly, church (see ECCLESIAL) + -LOGY]

Ecclus. /ˈeklʌs/ abbr. Ecclesiasticus (Apocrypha).

eccrine /ˈekriːn/ adj. (of a gland, e.g. a sweat gland) secreting without loss of cell material. [Gk *ek* out of + *krinō* sift]

ecdysis /ˈekdaɪsɪs/ n. the action of casting off skin or shedding an exoskeleton etc. [mod.L f. Gk *ekdusis* f. *ekduō* put off]

ECG abbr. electrocardiogram.

echelon /ˈeʃəlɒn, ˈeɪʃəlɔ̃/ n. & v. —n. **1** a level or rank in an organization, in society, etc.; those occupying it (often in *pl.*: *the upper echelons*). **2** *Mil.* a formation of troops, ships, aircraft, etc., in parallel rows with the end of each row projecting further laterally than the one in front (*in echelon*). —*v.tr.* arrange in an echelon. [F *échelon* f. *échelle* ladder f. L *scala*]

echeveria /ˌetʃəˈvɪərɪə/ n. any succulent plant of the genus *Echeveria*, native to Central and S. America. [M. *Echeveri*, 19th-c. Mex. botanical draughtsman]

echidna /ɪˈkɪdnə/ n. any of several egg-laying pouch-bearing mammals native to Australia and New Guinea, with a covering of spines, and having a long snout and long claws. Also called *spiny anteater*. [mod.L f. Gk *ekhidna* viper]

echinoderm /ɪˈkaɪnədɜːm, ˈekɪn-/ n. any marine invertebrate of the phylum Echinodermata, a group of marine invertebrates including starfish and sea urchins, many of which have spiny skins. As well as the characteristic symmetry of their bodies, echinoderms are notable for possessing a unique system of hydraulic tubes used to extend numerous small saclike organs ('tube feet') for locomotion, feeding, etc. Echinoderms are well represented as fossils, and are first found in the Cambrian period. Their embryological development indicates that they are distantly related to the vertebrates. [ECHINUS + Gk *derma -atos* skin]

echinoid /ɪˈkaɪnɔɪd/ n. a sea urchin.

echinus /ɪˈkaɪnəs/ n. **1** any sea urchin of the genus *Echinus*, including the common European edible urchin, *E. esculentus*. **2** *Archit.* a rounded moulding below an abacus on a Doric or Ionic capital. [ME f. L f. Gk *ekhinos* hedgehog, sea urchin]

echo /ˈekəʊ/ n. & v. —n. (pl. **-oes**) **1 a** the repetition of a sound by the reflection of sound waves. **b** the secondary sound produced. (See below.) **2** a reflected radio or radar beam. **3** a close imitation or repetition of something already done. **4** a person who slavishly repeats the words or opinions of another. **5** (often in *pl.*) circumstances or events reminiscent of or remotely connected with earlier ones. **6** *Bridge* etc. a conventional mode of play to show the number of cards held in the suit led etc. —v. (**-oes, -oed**) **1** *intr.* **a** (of a place) resound with an echo. **b** (of a sound) be repeated; resound. **2** *tr.* repeat (a sound) by an echo. **3** *tr.* **a** repeat (another's words). **b** imitate the words, opinions, or actions of (a person). □ **echo chamber** an enclosure with sound-reflecting walls. **echo location** the location of objects by reflected sound. **echo-sounder** sounding apparatus for determining the depth of the sea beneath a ship by measuring the time taken for an echo to be received. **echo-sounding** the use of an echo-sounder. **echo verse** a verse form in which a line repeats the last syllables of the previous line. □□ **echoer** n. **echoless** adj. [ME f. OF or L f. Gk *ēkhō*, rel. to *ēkhē* a sound]

There are two mythological explanations of echoes. (i) Echo was a nymph vainly loved by the god Pan, who finally sent the shepherds mad and they tore her to pieces; but Earth hid the fragments which can still sing and imitate other sounds. (ii) According to Ovid, Hera had deprived Echo of speech in order to stop her chatter, and Echo could only repeat what others had said. On being repulsed by Narcissus she wasted away with grief until there was nothing left of her but her voice.

echocardiogram /ˌekəʊˈkɑːdɪəˌgræm/ n. *Med.* a record produced by echocardiography.

echocardiography /ˌekəʊˌkɑːdɪˈɒgrəfɪ/ n. *Med.* the use of ultrasound waves to investigate the action of the heart. □□ **echocardiograph** /ˌekəʊˈkɑːdɪəˌgrɑːf/ n. **echocardiographer** n.

echoencephalogram /ˌekəʊenˈsefələʊˌgræm/ n. *Med.* a record produced by echoencephalography.

echoencephalography /ˌekəʊenˌsefəˈlɒgrəfɪ/ n. *Med.* the use of ultrasound waves to investigate intracranial structures.

echogram /ˈekəʊˌgræm/ n. a record made by an echo-sounder.

echograph /ˈekəʊˌgrɑːf/ n. a device for automatically recording echograms.

echoic /eˈkəʊɪk/ adj. Phonet. (of a word) imitating the sound it represents; onomatopoeic. □□ **echoically** adv.

echoism /ˈekəʊˌɪz(ə)m/ n. = ONOMATOPOEIA.

echolalia /ˌekəʊˈleɪlɪə/ n. **1** the meaningless repetition of another person's spoken words. **2** the repetition of speech by a child learning to talk. [mod.L f. Gk ēkhō echo + lalia talk]

echovirus /ˈekəʊˌvaɪərəs/ n. (also **ECHO virus**) any of a group of enteroviruses sometimes causing mild meningitis, encephalitis, etc. [f. enteric cytopathogenic human orphan (because not originally assignable to any known disease) + VIRUS]

echt /ext/ adj. authentic, genuine, typical. [G]

éclair /eɪˈkleə(r), ɪˈkleə(r)/ n. a small elongated cake of choux pastry filled with cream and iced with chocolate or coffee icing. [F, lit. lightning, flash]

éclaircissement /ˌeɪkleəˈsiːsmɑ̃/ n. archaic an enlightening explanation of something hitherto inexplicable (e.g. conduct etc.). [F f. éclaircir clear up]

eclampsia /ɪˈklæmpsɪə/ n. a condition involving convulsions leading to coma, occurring esp. in pregnant women. □□ **eclamptic** adj. [mod.L f. F eclampsie f. Gk eklampsis sudden development f. eklampō shine forth]

éclat /eɪˈklɑː, ˈeɪklɑː/ n. **1** brilliant display; dazzling effect. **2** social distinction; conspicuous success; universal approbation (with great éclat). [F f. éclater burst out]

eclectic /ɪˈklektɪk/ adj. & n. —adj. **1** deriving ideas, tastes, style, etc., from various sources. **2** Philos. & Art selecting one's beliefs etc. from various sources; attached to no particular school of philosophy. —n. **1** an eclectic person. **2** a person who subscribes to an eclectic school of thought. □□ **eclectically** adv. **eclecticism** /-ˌsɪz(ə)m/ n. [Gk eklektikos f. eklegō pick out]

Eclipse /ɪˈklɪps/ (1764–89) the most famous racehorse of the 18th c., one of the three who are the ancestors in the direct male line of all thoroughbred racehorses throughout the world. He began racing when he was five years old and then won easily all the races in which he took part. The Eclipse Stakes, a horse-race founded in 1886, is named in his honour; it is a weight-for-age race run annually in July at Sandown Park near London.

eclipse /ɪˈklɪps/ n. & v. —n. **1** the obscuring of the reflected light from one celestial body by the passage of another between it and the eye or between it and its source of illumination. An eclipse may be annular, partial, or total (see these words). **2** a deprivation of light or the period of this. **3** a rapid or sudden loss of importance or prominence, esp. in relation to another or a newly-arrived person or thing. —v.tr. **1** (of a celestial body) obscure the light from or to (another). **2** intercept (light, esp. of a lighthouse). **3** deprive of prominence or importance; outshine, surpass. □ **in eclipse 1** surpassed; in decline. **2** (of a bird) having lost its courting plumage. □□ **eclipser** n. [ME f. OF f. L f. Gk ekleipsis f. ekleipō fail to appear, be eclipsed f. leipō leave]

ecliptic /ɪˈklɪptɪk/ n. & adj. —n. the sun's apparent path among the stars during the year, so called because lunar and solar eclipses will occur only when the moon crosses this path. —adj. of an eclipse or the ecliptic. [ME f. L f. Gk ekleiptikos (as ECLIPSE)]

eclogue /ˈeklɒg/ n. a short poem, esp. a pastoral dialogue. [L ecloga f. Gk eklogē selection f. eklegō pick out]

eclosion /ɪˈkləʊʒ(ə)n/ n. the emergence of an insect from a pupa-case or of a larva from an egg. [F éclosion f. éclore hatch (as EX-1, L claudere to close)]

eco- /ˈiːkəʊ/ comb. form ecology, ecological.

ecoclimate /ˈiːkəʊˌklaɪmɪt, -mət/ n. climate considered as an ecological factor.

ecology /ɪˈkɒlədʒɪ/ n. **1** the branch of biology dealing with the relations of organisms to one another and to their physical surroundings. **2** (in full **human ecology**) the study of the interaction of people with their environment. □□ **ecological** /ˌiːkəˈlɒdʒɪk(ə)l/ adj. **ecologically** /ˌiːkəˈlɒdʒɪkəlɪ/ adv. **ecologist** n. [G Ökologie f. Gk oikos house]

Econ. abbr. Economics.

econometrics /ɪˌkɒnəˈmetrɪks/ n.pl. (usu. treated as sing.) a branch of economics concerned with the application of mathematical economics to economic data by the use of statistics. (See TINBERGEN1.) □□ **econometric** adj. **econometrical** adj. **econometrician** /-məˈtrɪʃ(ə)n/ n. **econometrist** n. [ECONOMY + METRIC]

economic /ˌiːkəˈnɒmɪk, ˌek-/ adj. **1** of or relating to economics. **2** maintained for profit; on a business footing. **3** adequate to repay or recoup expenditure with some profit (not economic to run buses on Sunday; an economic rent). **4** practical; considered or studied with regard to human needs (economic geography). □□ **economically** adv. [ME f. OF economique or L oeconomicus f. Gk oikonomikos (as ECONOMY)]

economical /ˌiːkəˈnɒmɪk(ə)l, ˌek-/ adj. sparing in the use of resources; avoiding waste. □□ **economically** adv.

Economic and Social Committee a consultative body of the European Communities, set up in 1957 to represent the interests of the Community's citizens and composed of representatives of employers, workers, consumers, farmers, professional people, etc. of the member States. It meets in Brussels.

economics /ˌiːkəˈnɒmɪks, ˌek-/ n.pl. (treated as sing.) **1 a** the science of the production and distribution of wealth. **b** the application of this to a particular subject (the economics of publishing). **2** the condition of a country etc. as regards material prosperity.

economist /ɪˈkɒnəmɪst/ n. **1** an expert in or student of economics. **2** a person who manages financial or economic matters. [Gk oikonomos (as ECONOMY) + -IST]

economize /ɪˈkɒnəˌmaɪz/ v.intr. (also **-ise**) **1** be economical; make economies; reduce expenditure. **2** (foll. by on) use sparingly; spend less on. □□ **economization** /-ˈzeɪʃ(ə)n/ n. **economizer** n.

economy /ɪˈkɒnəmɪ/ n. (pl. **-ies**) **1 a** the wealth and resources of a community, esp. in terms of the production and consumption of goods and services. **b** a particular kind of this (a capitalist economy). **c** the administration or condition of an economy. **2 a** the careful management of (esp. financial) resources; frugality. **b** (often in pl.) an instance of this (made many economies). **3** sparing or careful use (economy of language). **4** (also **economy class**) the cheapest class of air travel. **5** (attrib.) (also **economy-size**) (of goods) consisting of a large quantity for a proportionally lower cost. [F économie or L oeconomia f. Gk oikonomia household management f. oikos house + nemō manage]

ecosphere /ˈiːkəʊˌsfɪə(r)/ n. the region of space including planets where conditions are such that living things can exist.

écossaise /ˌeɪkɒˈseɪz/ n. **1** an energetic dance in duple time. **2** the music for this. [F, fem. of écossais Scottish]

ecosystem /ˈiːkəʊˌsɪstəm/ n. a biological community of interacting organisms and their physical environment.

ecru /ˈeɪkruː/ n. the colour of unbleached linen; light fawn. [F écru unbleached]

ECSC abbr. European Coal and Steel Community.

ecstasize /ˈekstəˌsaɪz/ v.tr. & intr. (also **-ise**) throw or go into ecstasies.

ecstasy /ˈekstəsɪ/ n. (pl. **-ies**) **1** an overwhelming feeling of joy or rapture. **2** Psychol. an emotional or religious frenzy or trancelike state. **3** sl. methylenedioxymethamphetamine, a powerful stimulant and hallucinatory drug (see MDMA). [ME f. OF extasie f. LL extasis f. Gk ekstasis standing outside oneself f. ek out + histēmi to place]

ecstatic /ɪkˈstætɪk/ adj. & n. —adj. **1** in a state of ecstasy. **2** very enthusiastic or excited (was ecstatic about his new job). **3** producing ecstasy; sublime (an ecstatic embrace). —n. a person subject to (usu. religious) ecstasy. □□ **ecstatically** adv. [F extatique f. Gk ekstatikos (as ECSTASY)]

ECT abbr. electroconvulsive therapy.

ecto- /ˈektəʊ/ comb. form outside. [Gk ekto- stem of ektos outside]

ectoblast /ˈektəʊˌblæst/ n. = ECTODERM. □□ **ectoblastic** /-ˈblæstɪk/ adj.

ectoderm /ˈektəʊˌdɜːm/ n. Biol. the outermost layer of an animal embryo in early development. □□ **ectodermal** /-ˈdɜːm(ə)l/ adj.

ectogenesis /ˌektəʊˈdʒenɪsɪs/ n. Biol. the production of structures outside the organism. □□ **ectogenetic** /-dʒɪˈnetɪk/ adj. **ectogenic** /-ˈdʒenɪk/ adj. **ectogenous** /ekˈtɒdʒɪnəs/ adj. [mod.L (as ECTO-, GENESIS)]

ectomorph /ˈektəʊˌmɔːf/ n. a person with a lean and delicate build of body and large skin surface in comparison with weight (one of W. H. Sheldon's three constitutional types: cf. ENDOMORPH, MESOMORPH). □□ **ectomorphic** /-ˈmɔːfɪk/ adj. **ectomorphy** n. [ECTO- + Gk morphē form]

-ectomy /ˈektəmɪ/ comb. form denoting a surgical operation in which a part of the body is removed (appendectomy). [Gk ektomē excision f. ek out + temnō cut]

ectopic /ˈektɒpɪk/ adj. Med. in an abnormal place or position. □ **ectopic pregnancy** a pregnancy occurring outside the womb. [mod.L ectopia f. Gk ektopos out of place]

ectoplasm /ˈektəʊˌplæz(ə)m/ n. 1 the dense outer layer of the cytoplasm (cf. ENDOPLASM). 2 the supposed viscous substance exuding from the body of a spiritualistic medium during a trance. □□ **ectoplasmic** /-ˈplæzmɪk/ adj.

ectozoon /ˌektəʊˈzəʊɒn/ n. Biol. a parasite that lives on the outside of its host.

Ecu /ˈeɪkjuː, ˈiː-/ n. (also **ecu**) European currency unit. [abbr.]

Ecuador /ˈekwədɔː(r)/ an equatorial country in South America, on the Pacific coast, pop. (est. 1988) 10,231,600; official language, Spanish; capital, Quito. Ranges and plateaux of the Andes separate the coastal plain from the tropical jungles of the Amazon basin. The economy remains backward and largely agricultural despite some improvement due to oil exports after major oilfields were discovered in 1972. Incorporated in the late 16th c. into the Inca empire, Ecuador was conquered by the Spanish in 1534 and remained part of Spain's American empire until independence was won in 1822. The country has remained independent since leaving the Federation of Grand Colombia in 1830, but has since lost territory in border disputes with its more powerful neighbours. □□ **Ecuadorean** adj. & n.

ecumenical /ˌiːkjuːˈmenɪk(ə)l, ˈek-/ adj. 1 of or representing the whole Christian world. 2 seeking or promoting worldwide Christian unity. □□ **ecumenically** adv. [LL oecumenicus f. Gk oikoumenikos of the inhabited earth (oikoumenē)]

ecumenicalism /ˌiːkjuːˈmenɪkəˌlɪz(ə)m, ˌek-/ n. (also **ecumenism** /iːˈkjuːməˌnɪz(ə)m/) the principle or aim of the unity of Christians worldwide.

eczema /ˈeksɪmə/ n. inflammation of the skin, with itching and discharge from blisters. □□ **eczematous** /ekˈziːmətəs, ekˈzem-/ adj. [mod.L f. Gk ekzema -atos f. ek out + zeō boil]

ed. abbr. 1 edited by. 2 edition. 3 editor. 4 educated; education.

-ed¹ /əd, ɪd/ suffix forming adjectives: 1 from nouns, meaning 'having, wearing, affected by, etc.' (talented; trousered; diseased). 2 from phrases of adjective and noun (good-humoured; three-cornered). [OE -ede]

-ed² /əd, ɪd/ suffix forming: 1 the past tense and past participle of weak verbs (needed; risked). 2 participial adjectives (escaped prisoner; a pained look). [OE -ed, -ad, -od]

Edam /ˈiːdæm/ a market town in The Netherlands, in the province of North Holland; pop. (1987) 24,400 (with Volendam). —n. a round Dutch cheese, usu. pale yellow with a red rind.

edaphic /ɪˈdæfɪk/ adj. 1 Bot. of the soil. 2 Ecol. produced or influenced by the soil. [G edaphisch f. Gk edaphos floor]

Edda /ˈedə/ n. a body of ancient Icelandic literature contained in two 13th-c. books, the Elder or Poetic Edda, a collection of Old Norse poems on mythical or traditional subjects, and the Younger or Prose Edda (attributed to the Icelandic historian Snorri Sturluson), a handbook to Icelandic poetry with prosodic and grammatical treatises and quotations and prose paraphrases from old poems. The Eddas are the chief source of our knowledge of Scandinavian mythology. [perh. a name in a Norse poem or f. ON óthr poetry]

Eddington /ˈedɪŋt(ə)n/, Sir Arthur Stanley (1882–1944), founder of the modern science of astrophysics. His book The Internal Constitution of the Stars (1930) established the fundamental principles of stellar structure and gave some hint of the nature of the energy sources within stars (not fully understood until the discovery of nuclear fusion). He is renowned also for his observations of star positions during the solar eclipse of 1919, which demonstrated the bending of light by gravity and triumphantly vindicated Einstein's recently formulated theory of General Relativity.

eddo /ˈedəʊ/ n. (pl. **-oes**) = TARO. [Afr. word]

Eddy /ˈedɪ/, Mrs Mary Baker (1821–1910), foundress of the Church of Christ Scientist (see CHRISTIAN SCIENCE). Long a victim to various ailments, she believed herself cured by a mesmerist, P. P. Quimby. After his death (1866) she evolved her own system of spiritual healing, set out in her book Science and Health (1875).

eddy /ˈedɪ/ n. & v. —n. (pl. **-ies**) 1 a circular movement of water causing a small whirlpool. 2 a movement of wind, fog, or smoke resembling this. —v.tr. & intr. (**-ies, -ied**) whirl round in eddies. □ **eddy current** Electr. a localized current induced in a conductor by a varying magnetic field. [prob. OE ed- again, back, perh. of Scand. orig.]

edelweiss /ˈeɪd(ə)lˌvaɪs/ n. an Alpine plant, Leontopodium alpinum, with woolly white bracts around the flower-heads, growing in rocky places. [G f. edel noble + weiss white]

edema US var. of OEDEMA.

Eden¹ /ˈiːd(ə)n/ n. (also **Garden of Eden**) a place or state of great happiness; paradise (with reference to the abode of Adam and Eve in the biblical account of the Creation, from which they were expelled for disobedience). [ME f. LL f. Gk Ēdēn f. Heb. ʿēden, orig. = delight]

Eden² /ˈiːd(ə)n/, (Robert) Anthony, 1st Earl of Avon (1897–1977), British statesman, Prime Minister 1955–7, having been Foreign Secretary 1935–8, 1940–5, and 1951–5. His premiership was dominated by the Suez Crisis of 1956; widespread opposition to Britain's role in this, together with his own failing health, led to his resignation.

edentate /iːˈdenteɪt/ adj. & n. —adj. having no or few teeth. —n. any mammal, esp. of the order Edentata, having no or few teeth, e.g. an anteater or sloth. [L edentatus (as E-, dens dentis tooth)]

Edgar /ˈedɡə(r)/ (c.944–75), king of England 959–75. He became king of Northumbria and Mercia in 957 when these regions renounced their allegiance to his elder brother Edwy, and succeeded to the throne of England on Edwy's death two years later. One of the strongest of the Anglo-Saxon kings of England, Edgar was renowned for his support of organized religion, playing a decisive part in the growth of monasticism.

edge /edʒ/ n. & v. —n. 1 a boundary line or margin of an area or surface. 2 a narrow surface of a thin object. 3 the meeting-line of two surfaces of a solid. 4 a the sharpened side of the blade of a cutting instrument or weapon. b the sharpness of this (the knife has lost its edge). 5 the area close to a steep drop (along the edge of the cliff). 6 anything compared to an edge, esp. the crest of a ridge. 7 a (as a personal attribute) incisiveness, excitement. b keenness, excitement (esp. as an element in an otherwise routine situation). —v. 1 tr. & intr. (often foll. by in, into, out, etc.) move gradually or furtively towards an objective (edged it into the corner; they all edged towards the door). 2 tr. a provide with an edge or border. b form a border to. c trim the edge of. 3 tr. sharpen (a knife, tool, etc.). 4 tr. Cricket strike (the ball) with the edge of the bat. □ **have the edge on** (or **over**) have a slight advantage over. **on edge** 1 tense and restless or irritable. 2 eager, excited. **on the edge of** almost involved in or affected by. **set a person's teeth on edge** (of a taste or sound) cause an unpleasant nervous sensation. **take the edge off** dull, weaken; make less effective or intense. □□ **edgeless** adj. **edger** n. [OE ecg f. Gmc]

Edgehill /edʒˈhɪl/ the first pitched battle of the English Civil War (1642), fought at the village of Edgehill in the West Midlands. The royal army failed to exploit a chance of decisive victory through the failure of its cavalry commanders to control their victorious troopers, and the Parliamentary army under the Earl of Essex was able to stay between the King and London. The missed opportunity denied Charles I his chance to win a quick victory in that year.

edgeways /ˈedʒweɪz/ adv. (also **edgewise** /-waɪz/) **1** with the edge uppermost or towards the viewer. **2** edge to edge. □ **get a word in edgeways** contribute to a conversation when the dominant speaker pauses briefly.

Edgeworth /ˈedʒwɜːθ/, Maria (1767–1849), Anglo-Irish novelist. Her humorous but sympathetic portrayal of Irish life in novels such as *Castle Rackrent* (1800) won her the friendship of Sir Walter Scott.

edging /ˈedʒɪŋ/ n. **1** something forming an edge or border, e.g. a fringe or lace. **2** the process of making an edge. □ **edging-shears** shears for trimming the edges of a lawn.

edgy /ˈedʒɪ/ adj. (**edgier**, **edgiest**) **1** irritable; nervously anxious. **2** disjointed (*edgy rhythms*). □□ **edgily** adv. **edginess** n.

edh var. of ETH.

edible /ˈedɪb(ə)l/ adj. & n. —adj. fit or suitable to be eaten (cf. EATABLE). —n. (in pl.) food. □□ **edibility** /-ˈbɪlɪtɪ/ n. [LL *edibilis* f. *edere* eat]

edict /ˈiːdɪkt/ n. an order proclaimed by authority. □□ **edictal** /ɪˈdɪkt(ə)l/ adj. [ME f. L *edictum* f. *edicere* proclaim]

edifice /ˈedɪfɪs/ n. **1 a** building, esp. a large imposing one. **2 a** complex organizational or conceptual structure. [ME f. OF f. L *aedificium* f. *aedis* dwelling + *-ficium* f. *facere* make]

edify /ˈedɪˌfaɪ/ v.tr. (**-ies**, **-ied**) (of a circumstance, experience, etc.) instruct and improve morally or intellectually. □□ **edification** /-fɪˈkeɪʃ(ə)n/ n. **edifying** adj. **edifyingly** adv. [ME f. OF *edifier* f. L *aedificare* (as EDIFICE)]

Edinburgh /ˈedɪnbərə/ the capital of Scotland from 1437, lying close to the southern shore of the Firth of Forth; pop. (est. 1987) 438,700. The city grew up round the 11th-c. castle built by Malcolm III on a rocky ridge which dominates the landscape.

Edison /ˈedɪs(ə)n/, Thomas Alva (1847–1931), the archetypal American inventor. Starting from the humblest beginnings, with three months of school education, he was employed at the age of 12 as a newsboy and at 15 as a telegraph operator, from which he developed an interest in electricity and its applications. He took out the first of over 1,000 patents at the age of 21; his most important inventions were automatic telegraph systems, the mimeograph, the carbon microphone for telephones, the phonograph (precursor of the gramophone), the carbon filament lamp, the nickel-iron or NIFE accumulator (one of the few alternatives to the ubiquitous lead–acid battery), and discovered the 'Edison effect', the passage of electricity from the filament to a metal plate inside an incandescent lamp globe, thus the precursor of the thermionic valve. His development of electric lighting led him to devise complete systems for generating and distributing electricity, originally with direct current. Perhaps his most significant invention was that of the industrial laboratory employing teams of scientists and engineers, though ironically this led to the demise of the individual inventor so splendidly typified by Edison himself.

edit /ˈedɪt/ v. & n. —v.tr. (**edited**, **editing**) **1 a** assemble, prepare, or modify (written material, esp. the work of another or others) for publication. **b** prepare an edition of (an author's work). **2** be in overall charge of the content and arrangement of (a newspaper, journal, etc.). **3** take extracts from and collate (films, tape-recordings, etc.) to form a unified sequence. **4 a** prepare (data) for processing by a computer. **b** alter (a text entered in a word processor etc.). **5 a** reword to correct, or to alter the emphasis. **b** (foll. by *out*) remove (part) from a text etc. —n. **1 a** a piece of editing. **b** an edited item. **2** a facility for editing. [F *éditer* (as EDITION): partly a back-form. f. EDITOR]

edition /ɪˈdɪʃ(ə)n/ n. **1 a** one of the particular forms in which a literary work etc. is published (*paperback edition*; *pocket edition*). **b** a copy of a book in a particular form (*a first edition*). **2** a whole number of copies of a book, newspaper, etc., issued at one time. **3** a particular version or instance of a broadcast, esp. of a regular programme or feature. **4** a person or thing similar to or resembling another (*a miniature edition of her mother*). [F *édition* f. L *editio -onis* f. *edere* edit- put out (as E-, *dare* give)]

editio princeps /ɪˌdɪʃɪəʊ ˈprɪnseps/ n. (pl. **editiones principes** /-ˌəʊniːz -sɪˌpiːz/) the first printed edition of a book, text, etc. [L]

editor /ˈedɪtə(r)/ n. **1** a person who edits material for publication or broadcasting. **2** a person who directs the preparation of a newspaper or periodical, or a particular section of one (*sports editor*). **3** a person who selects or commissions material for publication. **4** a person who edits film, sound track, etc. **5** a computer program for modifying data. □□ **editorship** n. [LL, = producer (of games), publisher (as EDIT)]

editorial /ˌedɪˈtɔːrɪəl/ adj. & n. —adj. **1** of or concerned with editing or editors. **2** written or approved by an editor. —n. a newspaper article written by or on behalf of an editor, esp. one giving an opinion on a topical issue. □□ **editorialist** n. **editorialize** v.intr. (also **-ise**). **editorially** adv.

-edly /ɪdlɪ/ suffix forming adverbs from verbs, meaning 'in a manner characterized by performance of or undergoing of the verbal action' (*allegedly*; *disgustedly*; *hurriedly*).

Edmonton /ˈedmənt(ə)n/ the capital of Alberta; pop. (1986) 574,000 (metropolitan area pop. 785,500).

Edmund¹ /ˈedmənd/ 'the Martyr' (841–69), king of East Anglia from some time before 865. After the defeat of his army by the invading Danes he was captured, and then put to death for refusing to reject the Christian faith or to share power with his pagan conqueror. His body was eventually interred at what is now called Bury St Edmunds and remained there until the Reformation, when it was reburied on a site at present unknown. Feast day, 20 Nov.

Edmund² /ˈedmənd/ (921–46), king of England 939–46. Soon after Athelstan's death (939) a Norse army returned under Olaf Guthfrithson, who took control of York and its dependent territories. On Olaf's death (941) Edmund set about recovering the northern Danelaw, but after his own death York fell again to a Norse king.

Edmund³ /ˈedmənd/, St (Edmund Rich, c.1175–1240), English churchman. He became Archbishop of Canterbury in 1233, and while in office resisted both royal interference and papal exactions. In his earlier years he had taught at Oxford, and he was the first Oxford master to be officially canonized. St Edmund Hall at Oxford University takes its name from him and is traditionally supposed to have been built on the site of his residence. Feast day, 16 Nov.

Edmund Ironside /ˈedmənd ˈaɪənˌsaɪd/ (c.980–1016), son of Ethelred the Unready. Edmund led the resistance to Cnut's forces in 1015 and on his father's death was proclaimed king. After some initial success he was defeated at Ashingdon in Essex (1016), and was forced to divide the kingdom with Cnut, retaining only Wessex. On Edmund's death Cnut became king of all England.

Edomite /ˈiːdəˌmaɪt/ adj. & n. —adj. of Edom, an ancient region south of the Dead Sea, or its people. —n. a member of an ancient people traditionally descended from Esau, living in Edom.

EDP abbr. electronic data processing.

EDT abbr. US Eastern Daylight Time.

educate /ˈedjʊˌkeɪt/ v.tr. (also absol.) **1** give intellectual, moral, and social instruction to (a pupil, esp. a child), esp. as a formal and prolonged process. **2** provide education for. **3** (often foll. by *in*, or *to* + infin.) train or instruct for a particular purpose. **4** advise; give information to. □□ **educable** /-kəb(ə)l/ adj. **educability** /-kəˈbɪlɪtɪ/ n. **educatable** adj. **educative** /-kətɪv/ adj. **educator** n. [L *educare educat-*, rel. to *educere* EDUCE]

educated /ˈedjʊˌkeɪtɪd/ adj. **1** having had an education, esp. to a higher level than average. **2** resulting from a (good) education (*an educated accent*). **3** based on experience or study (*an educated guess*).

education /ˌedjʊˈkeɪʃ(ə)n/ n. **1** the act or process of educating or being educated; systematic instruction. **2** a particular kind of or stage in education (*further education*; *a classical education*). **3 a** development of character or mental powers. **b** a stage in or aspect of this (*travel will be an education for you*). □□ **educational** adj. **educationalist** n. **educationally** adv. **educationist** n. [F *éducation* or L *educatio* (as EDUCATE)]

educe /ɪˈdjuːs/ v.tr. **1** bring out or develop from latent or potential existence; elicit. **2** infer; elicit a principle, number, etc., from data. □□ **educible** adj. **eduction** /ɪˈdʌkʃ(ə)n/ n. **eductive** /ɪˈdʌktɪv/ adj. [ME f. L *educere educt-* lead out (as E-, *ducere* lead)]

Edw. *abbr.* Edward.

Edward[1] /ˈedwəd/ the name of six kings of England since the Conquest and two of the United Kingdom:

Edward I (1239–1307), son of Henry III, reigned 1272–1307, nicknamed 'the Hammer of the Scots'. After coming to the throne Edward did much to solidify the central administration weakened by Henry's fecklessness, but soon became involved in the wars which were eventually to impose a dangerous financial burden on the realm. His campaign against the Welsh prince Llewelyn ended with the annexation of Wales in 1284, but from 1291 onwards Edward became increasingly preoccupied with his attempt to impose feudal superiority on Scotland. There he dealt successfully with a revolt in 1296 but a second uprising dragged on from 1297 until 1305. On his way north to deal with a third revolt, led this time by Robert the Bruce, he died, leaving his weak son Edward II to deal with a situation which was to prove beyond him.

Edward II (1284–1327), son of Edward I, reigned 1307–27. He was the first English Prince of Wales, but the story that as an infant he was presented to the Welsh crowd by his father as their future sovereign, a native prince who could speak no English, is apocryphal. A weak and foolish monarch, Edward soon proved unequal to the problems left him by his more military father. Early trouble with his barons led to civil war, and two years later his defeat by the Scots at Bannockburn further weakened his position and he temporarily lost power to Thomas, Earl of Lancaster. With the help of new favourites, the Despensers, Edward eventually managed to overthrow and kill Lancaster, but his wife, Isobel of France, allied herself with the exiled Roger de Mortimer, who invaded England and deposed Edward in favour of his son. Edward died in Berkeley Castle in Gloucestershire soon after his deposition, almost certainly at the hands of murderers.

Edward III (1312–77), son of Edward II, reigned 1327–77. Edward assumed personal control of his kingdom in 1330, executing Roger de Mortimer who had deposed his father Edward II. He restored order and reconciled the baronial opposition, but was soon involved in the wars which were to dominate much of his reign. Edward resumed his grandfather's policy of undermining Scottish independence by supporting the pretender to the Scottish throne Edward de Baliol, and started the Hundred Years War with France by advancing his claim to the French throne. Although he won dramatic victories in both theatres, final victory eluded him, and following his premature decline into senility, effective government fell into the hands of his unpopular fourth son, John of Gaunt.

Edward IV (1442–83), son of Richard Duke of York, reigned 1461–83. Following his father's death in the early stages of the Wars of the Roses, Edward inherited the Yorkist claim to the throne, and after defeating his opponents in two battles deposed the Lancastrian king Henry VI and reigned in his place as Edward IV. The early years of his reign were troubled by Lancastrian plots, but the most serious threat arose in 1470–1 as a result of an alliance between his old Lancastrian enemies and his disaffected former lieutenant, the Earl of Warwick. Edward was briefly forced into exile, but returned to crush his opponents, thereafter ruling in relative peace until his death. His rule was characterized by vigorous and successful attempts to reform royal government, although in his last few years he seems to have given way to some extent to personal pleasure.

Edward V (1470–*c*.1483), son of Edward IV, reigned 1483 but was not crowned. Illegitimized following his father's death, on debatable evidence of the illegality of Edward IV's marriage, the youthful prince's throne was taken by his uncle Richard III. (See Princes in the Tower.)

Edward VI (1537–53), son of Henry VIII, reigned 1547–53. During his brief reign as a minor England was effectively ruled by two Protectors, the Duke of Somerset and the Duke of Northumberland. Although the young and sickly king had little direct influence over the policies pursued by his guardians, his Protestant beliefs contributed significantly to the establishment of Protestantism as the State religion, a development which was to survive the Catholic reaction which followed under his elder sister and successor, Mary I.

Edward VII (1841–1910), son of Victoria, reigned 1901–10, known as 'the Peacemaker' for no very good reason. His reign, however, was a period of peace. An extrovert and something of a playboy, Edward was kept away from the serious conduct of royal affairs during the long reign of his mother, but although he played little part in government upon finally coming to the throne, his popularity and interest in public appearances generally increased the prestige of the monarchy. He died suddenly in 1910 before his attitude to the then current crisis over the government's plans to create a large number of new peers could have any impact on events.

Edward VIII (1894–1972), son of George V, reigned 1936 but was not crowned. A popular Prince of Wales, Edward abdicated eleven months after coming to the throne in order to marry the American divorcee Mrs Wallis Simpson. Created Duke of Windsor, he served as Governor-General of the Bahamas during the Second World War before spending the rest of his life in France.

Edward[2] /ˈedwəd/, **Lake** a lake on the Zaïre-Uganda frontier in the rift valley running north–south in east central Africa. Discovered by H. M. Stanley in 1889, it was originally called the Albert Edward Nyanza; from 1973 to 1979 it was known as Lake Idi Amin Dada, after President Amin of Uganda.

Edwardian /edˈwɔːdɪən/ *adj. & n.* —*adj.* of, characteristic of, or associated with the reign of King Edward VII (1901–10). —*n.* a person belonging to this period.

Edward the Confessor (*c*.1003–66), king of England 1042–66, son of Ethelred the Unready. Famed for his piety, Edward was dominated through much of his reign by his wife's father Earl Godwin, and in later years took less and less interest in affairs of State, effective control falling to Godwin's son, who eventually succeeded Edward as Harold II. Edward was buried in Westminster Abbey and canonized in 1161.

Edward the Martyr (*c*.963–78), king of England 975–8. Although he successfully succeeded his father Edgar in 975, the youthful Edward was soon faced by a challenge for the throne from his half-brother Ethelred, who eventually had him murdered at Corfe in 978. Edward was subsequently made a saint and became the subject of a considerable medieval cult.

Edwy /ˈedwɪ/ (died 959), king of England 955–9. An ineffective monarch, Edwy alienated a large part of his kingdom during his short reign, and, after Mercia and Northumbria had renounced him in favour of his brother Edgar in 957, he ruled only over the lands south of the Thames.

-ee /iː/ *suffix* forming nouns denoting: **1** the person affected by the verbal action (*addressee; employee; lessee*). **2** a person concerned with or described as (*absentee; bargee; refugee*). **3** an object of smaller size (*bootee*). [from or after AF past part. in *-é* f. L *-atus*]

EEC *abbr.* European Economic Community.

EEG *abbr.* electroencephalogram.

eel /iːl/ *n.* **1** any of various snakelike fish, with slender body and poorly developed fins. **2** a slippery or evasive person or thing. □ **eel-grass 1** any marine plant of the genus *Zostera*, with long ribbon-like leaves. **2** any submerged freshwater plant of the genus *Vallisneria*. □□ **eel-like** *adj.* **eely** *adj.* [OE ǽl f. Gmc]

Eelam /ˈiːləm/ the homeland of the Tamil people of Sri Lanka, named after Elara, the last Tamil king of Anuradhapura. Although the Tamil history of Sri Lanka refers to the whole of the island as Eelam, present-day demands for a separate Tamil State of Eelam extend only to the northern and eastern provinces of Sri Lanka.

eelpout /ˈiːlpaʊt/ *n.* **1** any fish of the family Zoarcidae, with slender body and dorsal and anal fins meeting to fuse with the tail. Also called Pout[2]. **2** = burbot. [OE ǽleputa (as eel, pout[2])]

eelworm /ˈiːlwɜːm/ *n.* any of various small nematode worms infesting plant roots.

e'en[1] /iːn/ *archaic* or *poet.* var. of even[1].

e'en[2] /iːn/ *Sc.* var. of even[2].

-een /iːn/ *suffix Ir.* forming diminutive nouns (*colleen*). [Ir. *-ín* dimin. suffix]

e'er /eə(r)/ *poet.* var. OF EVER.

-eer /ɪə(r)/ *suffix* forming: **1** nouns meaning 'person concerned with or engaged in' (*auctioneer; mountaineer; profiteer*). **2** verbs meaning 'be concerned with' (*electioneer*). [from or after F *-ier* f. L *-arius*: cf. -IER, -ARY¹]

eerie /ˈɪərɪ/ *adj.* (**eerier, eeriest**) gloomy and strange; weird, frightening (*an eerie silence*). □□ **eerily** *adv.* **eeriness** *n.* [orig. N.Engl. and Sc. *eri*, of obscure orig.: cf. OE *earg* cowardly]

EETPU *abbr.* (in the UK) Electrical, Electronic, Tele-communications, and Plumbing Union.

ef- /ɪf, ef/ *prefix* assim. form of EX-¹ 1 before *f*.

eff /ef/ *v. sl. euphem.* **1** *tr. & intr.* (often foll. by *off*) = FUCK (in expletive use). **2** *intr.* say *fuck* or similar coarse slang words. □ **effing and blinding** using coarse slang. [name of the letter *F*, as a euphemistic abbr.]

efface /ɪˈfeɪs/ *v.* **1** *tr.* rub or wipe out (a mark etc.). **2** *tr.* (in abstract senses) obliterate; wipe out (*effaced it from his memory*). **3** *tr.* utterly surpass; eclipse (*success has effaced all previous attempts*). **4** *refl.* treat or regard oneself as unimportant (*self-effacing*). □□ **effacement** *n.* [F *effacer* (as EX-¹, FACE)]

effect /ɪˈfekt/ *n. & v.* —*n.* **1** the result or consequence of an action etc. **2** efficacy (*had little effect*). **3** an impression produced on a spectator, hearer, etc. (*lights had a pretty effect; my words had no effect*). **4** (in *pl.*) property, luggage. **5** (in *pl.*) the lighting, sound, etc., used to accompany a play, film, broadcast, etc. **6** *Physics* a physical phenomenon, usually named after its discoverer (*Doppler effect*). **7** the state of being operative. —*v.tr.* **1** bring about; accomplish. **2** cause to exist or occur. □ **bring** (or **carry**) **into effect** accomplish. **for effect** to create an impression. **give effect to** make operative. **in effect** for practical purposes; in reality. **take effect** become operative. **to the effect that** the general substance or gist being. **to that effect** having that result or implication. **with effect from** coming into operation at or on (a stated time or day). [ME f. OF *effect* or L *effectus* (as EX-¹, *facere* make)]

effective /ɪˈfektɪv/ *adj. & n.* —*adj.* **1** having a definite or desired effect. **2** powerful in effect; impressive. **3 a** actual; existing in fact rather than officially or theoretically (*took effective control in their absence*). **b** actually usable; realizable; equivalent in its effect (*effective money; effective demand*). **4** coming into operation (*effective as from 1 May*). **5** (of manpower) fit for work or service. —*n.* a soldier available for service. □□ **effectively** *adv.* **effectiveness** *n.* [ME f. L *effectivus* (as EFFECT)]

effector /ɪˈfektə(r)/ *adj. & n. Biol.* —*adj.* acting in response to a stimulus. —*n.* an effector organ.

effectual /ɪˈfektʃʊəl, -tjʊəl/ *adj.* **1** capable of producing the required result or effect; answering its purpose. **2** valid. □□ **effectuality** /-ˈælɪtɪ/ *n.* **effectually** *adv.* **effectualness** *n.* [ME f. med.L *effectualis* (as EFFECT)]

effectuate /ɪˈfektjʊˌeɪt/ *v.tr.* cause to happen; accomplish. □□ **effectuation** /-ˈeɪʃ(ə)n/ *n.* [med.L *effectuare* (as EFFECT)]

effeminate /ɪˈfemɪnət/ *adj.* (of a man) feminine in appearance or manner; unmasculine. □□ **effeminacy** *n.* **effeminately** *adv.* [ME f. L *effeminatus* past part. of *effeminare* (as EX-¹, *femina* woman)]

effendi /eˈfendɪ/ *n.* (*pl.* **effendis**) **1** a man of education or standing in Eastern Mediterranean or Arab countries. **2** a former title of respect or courtesy in Turkey. [f. Turk. *efendi* f. mod. Gk *aféntēs* f. Gk *authentēs* lord, master: see AUTHENTIC]

efferent /ˈefərənt/ *adj. Physiol.* conducting outwards (*efferent nerves; efferent vessels*) (opp. AFFERENT). □□ **efference** *n.* [L *efferre* (as EX-¹, *ferre* carry)]

effervesce /ˌefəˈves/ *v.intr.* **1** give off bubbles of gas; bubble. **2** (of a person) be lively or energetic. □□ **effervescence** *n.* **effervescency** *n.* **effervescent** *adj.* [L *effervescere* (as EX-¹, *fervēre* be hot)]

effete /ɪˈfiːt/ *adj.* **1** feeble and incapable. **2** worn out; exhausted of its essential quality or vitality. □□ **effeteness** *n.* [L *effetus* worn out by bearing young (as EX-¹, FOETUS)]

efficacious /ˌefɪˈkeɪʃəs/ *adj.* (of a thing) producing or sure to produce the desired effect. □□ **efficaciously** *adv.* **efficaciousness** *n.* **efficacy** /ˈefɪkəsɪ/ *n.* [L *efficax* (as EFFICIENT)]

efficiency /ɪˈfɪʃənsɪ/ *n.* (*pl.* **-ies**) **1** the state or quality of being efficient. **2** *Mech. & Physics* the ratio of useful work performed to the total energy expended or heat taken in. □ **efficiency bar** a point on a salary scale requiring evidence of efficiency for further promotion. [L *efficientia* (as EFFICIENT)]

efficient /ɪˈfɪʃ(ə)nt/ *adj.* **1** productive with minimum waste or effort. **2** (of a person) capable; acting effectively. □ **efficient cause** *Philos.* an agent that brings a thing into being or initiates a change. □□ **efficiently** *adv.* [ME f. L *efficere* (as EX-¹, *facere* make, accomplish)]

effigy /ˈefɪdʒɪ/ *n.* (*pl.* **-ies**) a sculpture or model of a person. □ **in effigy** in the form of a (usu. crude) representation of a person. [L *effigies* f. *effingere* to fashion]

effleurage /ˌeflɜːˈrɑːʒ/ *n. & v.* —*n.* a form of massage involving a circular inward stroking movement made with the palm of the hand, used esp. during childbirth. —*v.intr.* massage with a circular stroking movement. [F f. *effleurer* to skim]

effloresce /ˌefləˈres/ *v.intr.* **1** burst out into flower. **2** *Chem.* **a** (of a substance) turn to a fine powder on exposure to air. **b** (of salts) come to the surface and crystallize on it. **c** (of a surface) become covered with salt particles. □□ **efflorescence** *n.* **efflorescent** *adj.* [L *efflorescere* (as EX-¹, *florēre* to bloom f. *flos floris* flower)]

effluence /ˈeflʊəns/ *n.* **1** a flowing out (of light, electricity, etc.). **2** that which flows out. [F *effluence* or med.L *effluentia* f. L *effluere efflux-* flow out (as EX-¹, *fluere* flow)]

effluent /ˈeflʊənt/ *adj. & n.* —*adj.* flowing forth or out. —*n.* **1** sewage or industrial waste discharged into a river, the sea, etc. **2** a stream or lake flowing from a larger body of water.

effluvium /ɪˈfluːvɪəm/ *n.* (*pl.* **effluvia** /-vɪə/) an unpleasant or noxious odour or exhaled substance affecting the lungs or the sense of smell etc. [L (as EFFLUENT)]

efflux /ˈeflʌks/ *n.* = EFFLUENCE. □□ **effluxion** /eˈflʌkʃ(ə)n/ *n.* [med.L *effluxus* (as EFFLUENT)]

effort /ˈefət/ *n.* **1** strenuous physical or mental exertion. **2** a vigorous or determined attempt. **3** *Mech.* a force exerted. **4** *colloq.* the result of an attempt; something accomplished (*not bad for a first effort*). □□ **effortful** *adj.* [F f. OF *esforcier* ult. f. L *fortis* strong]

effortless /ˈefətlɪs/ *adj.* **1** seemingly without effort; natural, easy. **2** requiring no effort (*effortless contemplation*). □□ **effortlessly** *adv.* **effortlessness** *n.*

effrontery /ɪˈfrʌntərɪ/ *n.* (*pl.* **-ies**) **1** shameless insolence; impudent audacity (esp. *have the effrontery to*). **2** an instance of this. [F *effronterie* f. *effronté* ult. f. LL *effrons -ontis* shameless (as EX-¹, *frons* forehead)]

effulgent /ɪˈfʌldʒ(ə)nt/ *adj. literary* radiant; shining brilliantly. □□ **effulgence** *n.* **effulgently** *adv.* [L *effulgēre* shine forth (as EX-¹, *fulgēre* shine)]

effuse *adj. & v.* —*adj.* /ɪˈfjuːs/ *Bot.* (of an inflorescence etc.) spreading loosely. —*v.tr.* /ɪˈfjuːz/ **1** pour forth (liquid, light, etc.). **2** give out (ideas etc.). [ME f. L *effusus* past part. of *effundere effus-* pour out (as EX-¹, *fundere* pour)]

effusion /ɪˈfjuːʒ(ə)n/ *n.* **1** a copious outpouring. **2** usu. *derog.* an unrestrained flow of speech or writing. [ME f. OF *effusion* or L *effusio* (as EFFUSE)]

effusive /ɪˈfjuːsɪv/ *adj.* **1** gushing, demonstrative, exuberant (*effusive praise*). **2** *Geol.* (of igneous rock) poured out when molten and later solidified, volcanic. □□ **effusively** *adv.* **effusiveness** *n.*

EFL *abbr.* English as a foreign language.

eft /eft/ *n.* a newt. [OE *efeta*, of unkn. orig.]

Efta /ˈeftə/ *n.* (also **EFTA**) European Free Trade Association. [abbr.]

e.g. *abbr.* for example. [L *exempli gratia*]

egad /iːˈgæd/ *int. archaic* or *joc.* by God. [prob. orig. *a ah* + GOD]

egalitarian /ɪˌgælɪˈteərɪən/ *adj. & n.* —*adj.* **1** of or relating to the principle of equal rights and opportunities for all (*an egalitarian society*). **2** advocating this principle. —*n.* a person who advocates or supports egalitarian principles. □□ **egalitarianism** *n.* [F *égalitaire* f. *égal* EQUAL]

Egbert /ˈegbɜːt/ (d. 839), king of Wessex from 802. In 825 he won a decisive victory near Swindon, bringing Mercian supremacy to an end, and annexed Kent, Essex, Surrey, and Sussex. In 829 Mercia itself fell to Egbert, and Northumbria acknowledged his rule. By his death in 839 Mercia became independent again, but his reign foreshadowed the supremacy that Wessex later secured over all England.

Eger /ˈegə(r)/ a spa town in the north of Hungary, noted for its red 'Bull's Blood' wine; pop. (1988) 67,000.

egg[1] /eg/ n. **1 a** the spheroidal reproductive body produced by females of animals such as birds, reptiles, fish, etc., enclosed in a protective layer and capable of developing into a new individual. **b** the egg of the domestic hen, used for food. **2** *Biol.* the female reproductive cell in animals and plants. **3** *colloq.* a person or thing qualified in some way (*a tough egg*). **4** anything resembling or imitating an egg, esp. in shape or appearance. □ **as sure as eggs is** (or **are**) **eggs** *colloq.* without any doubt. **egg-beater 1** a device for beating eggs. **2** *US sl.* a helicopter. **egg-custard** = CUSTARD[1]. **egg-flip** (or **-nog**) a drink of alcoholic spirit with beaten egg, milk, etc. **eggs** (or **egg**) **and bacon** any of various yellow- and orange-shaded plants, esp. the snapdragon or toad-flax. **egg-spoon** a small spoon for eating a boiled egg. **egg-timer** a device for timing the cooking of an egg. **egg-tooth** a projection of an embryo bird or reptile used for breaking out of the shell. **egg-white** the white of an egg. **have** (or **put**) **all one's eggs in one basket** *colloq.* risk everything on a single venture. **with egg on one's face** *colloq.* made to look foolish. □□ **eggless** adj. **eggy** adj. (**eggier, eggiest**). [ME f. ON, rel. to OE ǣg]

egg[2] /eg/ v.tr. (foll. by on) urge (*egged us on to it*; *egged them on to do it*). [ME f. ON *eggja* = EDGE]

eggcup /ˈegkʌp/ n. a cup for holding a boiled egg.

egger /ˈegə(r)/ n. (also **eggar**) any of various large moths of the family Lasiocampidae, esp. *Lasiocampa quercus*, with an egg-shaped cocoon. [prob. f. EGG[1] + -ER[1]]

egghead /ˈeghed/ n. *colloq.* an intellectual; an expert.

eggplant /ˈegplɑːnt/ n. = AUBERGINE.

eggshell /ˈegʃel/ n. & adj. —n. **1** the shell of an egg. **2** anything very fragile. —adj. **1** (of china) thin and fragile. **2** (of paint) with a slight gloss finish.

eglantine /ˈeglənˌtaɪn/ n. sweet-brier. [ME f. F *églantine* f. OF *aiglent* ult. f. L *acus* needle]

Egmont /ˈegmənt/, **Mount** (Maori **Taranaki**) a volcanic peak rising to a height of 2,518 m (8,260 ft.) at the centre of North Island, New Zealand.

ego /ˈiːgəʊ/ n. (pl. **-os**) **1** *Metaphysics* a conscious thinking subject. **2** *Psychol.* the part of the mind that reacts to reality and has a sense of individuality. **3** self-esteem. □ **ego-ideal 1** *Psychol.* the part of the mind developed from the ego by an awareness of social standards. **2** (in general use) idealization of oneself. **ego-trip** *colloq.* activity etc. devoted entirely to one's own interests or feelings. [L, = I]

egocentric /ˌiːgəʊˈsentrɪk/ adj. **1** centred in the ego. **2** self-centred, egoistic. □□ **egocentrically** adv. **egocentricity** /-ˈtrɪsɪtɪ/ n. [EGO + -CENTRIC after *geocentric* etc.]

egoism /ˈiːgəʊˌɪz(ə)m/ n. **1** an ethical theory that treats self-interest as the foundation of morality. **2** systematic selfishness. **3** self-opinionatedness. **4** = EGOTISM. □□ **egoist** n. **egoistic** /-ˈɪstɪk/ adj. **egoistical** /-ˈɪstɪk(ə)l/ adj. [F *égoïsme* ult. f. mod.L *egoismus* (as EGO)]

egomania /ˌiːgəʊˈmeɪnɪə/ n. morbid egotism. □□ **egomaniac** /-ˈmeɪnɪˌæk/ n. **egomaniacal** /-məˈnaɪək(ə)l/ adj.

egotism /ˈiːgəˌtɪz(ə)m/ n. **1** excessive use of 'I' and 'me'. **2** the practice of talking about oneself. **3** an exaggerated opinion of oneself. **4** selfishness. □□ **egotist** n. **egotistic** /-ˈtɪstɪk/ adj. **egotistical** /-ˈtɪstɪk(ə)l/ adj. **egotistically** /-ˈtɪstɪkəlɪ/ adv. **egotize** v.intr. (also **-ise**). [EGO + -ISM with intrusive -t-]

egregious /ɪˈgriːdʒəs/ adj. **1** outstandingly bad; shocking (*egregious folly*; *an egregious ass*). **2** *archaic* or *joc.* remarkable. □□ **egregiously** adv. **egregiousness** n. [L *egregius* illustrious, lit. 'standing out from the flock' f. *grex gregis* flock]

egress /ˈiːgres/ n. **1 a** going out. **b** the right of going out. **2** an exit; a way out. **3** *Astron.* the end of an eclipse or transit. □□ **egression** /iːˈgreʃ(ə)n/ n. (in senses 1, 2). [L *egressus* f. *egredi egress-* (as E-, *gradi* to step)]

egret /ˈiːgrɪt/ n. any of various herons of the genus *Egretta* or *Bulbulcus*, usu. having long white feathers in the breeding season. [ME, var. of AIGRETTE]

Egypt /ˈiːdʒɪpt/ a country in NE Africa bordering on the Mediterranean Sea, consisting largely of desert, with its population concentrated chiefly along the fertile valley of the River Nile; pop. (est. 1988) 53,347,700; official language, Arabic; capital, Cairo. The chief cash crop is cotton, and Egypt is self-sufficient in energy, having considerable reserves of petroleum and natural gas as well as hydroelectric power produced by the Aswan High Dam. Its antiquities make tourism a major industry.

Egypt's history spans 5,000 years, dating back to the neolithic period when nomadic hunters settled in the Nile valley. The ancient kingdoms of Upper and Lower Egypt became united, according to tradition, under Menes (c.3000 BC), founder of the first of the 31 dynasties which successively ruled ancient Egypt. The period of the Old Kingdom (c.2575–2134 BC, 4th–8th Dynasty), the 'Pyramid Age', was characterized by strong central government, with the political and religious centre at Memphis. The Middle Kingdom (c.2040–1640 BC, 11th–14th Dynasty) is considered to be the classical age of ancient Egyptian culture; its collapse was brought about by infiltration of Asiatics, culminating in the Hyksos usurpation. The New Kingdom (c.1550–1070 BC, 18th–20th Dynasty), the 'empire' period, with its capital at Thebes, begins with the expulsion of the Hyksos. Egyptian claims in Syria and Palestine became definitive and involved direct confrontation with her principal rivals, Mitanni and the Hittites; Nubia was administered directly from Egypt. These foreign interests brought Egypt considerable wealth as well as technological and cultural innovations, but by the end of the period a decline in the power of the pharaohs and an increase in that of the priests resulted in a weakening of the central government. Egypt fell successively to Libyans, Ethiopians, Assyrians, and Persians, and indigenous rule was finally ended by Alexander the Great, who took Egypt in 332 BC. From then until AD 1922 someone other than the Egyptians ruled Egypt. On Alexander's death the Macedonian Ptolemy I acquired Egypt, and for three centuries the country was the centre of Hellenistic culture because of the considerable role played by Alexandria, home of a cosmopolitan Greek-speaking population who cultivated the arts and sciences, until on the death of Cleopatra it became a Roman province. After the Arab conquest in 642 Egypt was an Islamic country. From 1517 it formed part of the Ottoman empire except for a brief period (1798–1801) under French rule following Napoleon's invasion. The opening of the Suez Canal in 1869 made Egypt strategically important, and when the Turks became allies of Germany in the First World War the British (who had installed themselves following an Egyptian nationalist revolt in 1882) declared the country a British protectorate. Independence was granted in 1922 and a kingdom was established, becoming a republic after the overthrow of the monarchy in 1953.

Egyptian /ɪˈdʒɪpʃ(ə)n/ adj. & n. —adj. **1** of or relating to Egypt. **2** of or for Egyptian antiquities (e.g. in a museum) (*Egyptian room*). —n. **1** a native of ancient or modern Egypt; a national of the Arab Republic of Egypt. **2** the Hamitic language used in ancient Egypt, represented in its oldest stages by hieroglyphic inscriptions and in its latest form by Coptic. □□ **Egyptianize** v.tr. (also **-ise**) **Egyptianization** /-ˈzeɪʃ(ə)n/ n.

Egyptology /ˌiːdʒɪpˈtɒlədʒɪ/ n. the study of the language, history, and culture of ancient Egypt. □□ **Egyptologist** n.

eh /eɪ/ int. *colloq.* **1** expressing enquiry or surprise. **2** inviting assent. **3** asking for something to be repeated or explained. [ME *ey*, instinctive exclam.]

Ehrlich /ˈɜːlɪk/, **Paul** (1854–1915), German scientist who was one of the founders of immunology, developed techniques for staining tissues, and was a pioneer of chemotherapy, convinced that each disease could be killed off by an appropriate 'magic bullet'. Success in this last field came in 1911 when a synthetic compound of arsenic, Salvarsan, proved effective against syphilis.

-eian /ɪən/ *suffix* corresp. to *-ey* (or *-y*) + *-an* (*Bodleian*; *Rugbeian*).

Eichmann /ˈaɪxmən/, Karl Adolf (1906–62), Austrian Nazi administrator who played a leading part in the dispatching of Jews to concentration camps during the Second World War, and in the use of gas chambers for mass murder. After the war he went into hiding in Argentina but was traced and abducted by the Israelis, and was executed after trial in Israel.

Eid /iːd/ *n.* a Muslim week-long festival celebrating the end of the fast of Ramadan. [Arab. *īd* feast]

eider /ˈaɪdə(r)/ *n.* **1** (in full **eider duck**) any of various large northern ducks, esp. of the genus *Somateria*. **2** (in full **eider-down**) small soft feathers from the breast of the eider duck. [Icel. *aethr*]

eiderdown /ˈaɪdədaʊn/ *n.* a quilt stuffed with down (orig. from the eider) or some other soft material, esp. as the upper layer of bedclothes.

eidetic /aɪˈdetɪk/ *adj. & n.* —*adj.* *Psychol.* (of a mental image) having unusual vividness and detail, as if actually visible. —*n.* a person able to see eidetic images. □□ **eidetically** *adv.* [G *eidetisch* f. Gk *eidētikos* f. *eidos* form]

eidolon /aɪˈdəʊlɒn/ *n.* (*pl.* **eidolons** or **eidola** /-lə/) **1** a spectre; a phantom. **2** an idealized figure. [Gk *eidōlon*: see IDOL]

Eiffel /ˈaɪf(ə)l/, Alexandre Gustave (1832–1923), French engineer best known as the designer and builder of the **Eiffel Tower**, a wrought-iron structure erected in Paris for the exhibition of 1889 and still a famous landmark, though at first greatly disliked. Before that he had built several notable wrought-iron arch bridges, including one over the River Douro in Portugal. In 1885 he designed the inner structure of the Statue of Liberty in New York harbour. The Eiffel Tower, with a height of 300 metres (984 ft.) was the tallest man-made structure for many years. Eiffel later used it for experiments in aerodynamics, and built one of the first wind tunnels in 1912.

eigen- /ˈaɪgən/ *comb. form* *Math. & Physics* proper, characteristic. [G *eigen* OWN]

eigenfrequency /ˈaɪgənˌfriːkwənsɪ/ *n.* (*pl.* **-ies**) *Math. & Physics* one of the natural resonant frequencies of a system.

eigenfunction /ˈaɪgənˌfʌŋkʃ(ə)n/ *n.* *Math. & Physics* that function which under a given operation generates some multiple of itself.

eigenvalue /ˈaɪgənˌvæljuː/ *n.* *Math. & Physics* that value by which an eigenfunction of an operation is multiplied after the eigenfunction has been subjected to that operation.

Eiger /ˈaɪgə(r)/ a mountain peak in the Alps in central Switzerland, height 3,970 m (13,101 ft.).

eight /eɪt/ *n. & adj.* —*n.* **1** one more than seven, or two less than ten; the product of two units and four units. **2** a symbol for this (8, viii, VIII). **3** a figure resembling the form of 8. **4** a size etc. denoted by eight. **5** an eight-oared rowing-boat or its crew. **6** the time of eight o'clock (*is it eight yet?*). **7** a card with eight pips. —*adj.* that amount to eight. □ **the Eight** a group of American painters who exhibited together in 1908, united by opposition to the National Academy of Design and what they saw as its academic dreariness. They mainly painted scenes of contemporary urban life but were not unified stylistically. The dominant personality was Robert Henri. **have one over the eight** *sl.* get slightly drunk. [OE *ehta, eahta*]

eighteen /eɪˈtiːn/ *n. & adj.* —*n.* **1** one more than seventeen, or eight more than ten; the product of two units and nine units. **2** a symbol for this (18, xviii, XVIII). **3** a size etc. denoted by eighteen. **4** a set or team of eighteen individuals. **5** (**18**) *Brit.* (of films) classified as suitable for persons of 18 years and over. —*adj.* that amount to eighteen. □□ **eighteenth** *adj. & n.* [OE *ehtatēne, eaht-*]

eighteenmo /eɪˈtiːnməʊ/ *n.* = OCTODECIMO.

eightfold /ˈeɪtfəʊld/ *adj. & adv.* **1** eight times as much or as many. **2** consisting of eight parts. **3** amounting to eight.

eighth /eɪtθ/ *n. & adj.* —*n.* **1** the position in a sequence corresponding to the number 8 in the sequence 1–8. **2** something

occupying this position. **3** one of eight equal parts of a thing. —*adj.* that is the eighth. □ **eighth note** esp. *US Mus.* = QUAVER. □□ **eighthly** *adv.*

eightsome /ˈeɪtsəm/ *n.* **1** (in full **eightsome reel**) a lively Scottish reel for eight dancers. **2** the music for this.

8vo *abbr.* octavo.

eighty /ˈeɪtɪ/ *n. & adj.* —*n.* (*pl.* **-ies**) **1** the product of eight and ten. **2** a symbol for this (80, lxxx, LXXX). **3** (in *pl.*) the numbers from 80 to 89, esp. the years of a century or of a person's life. —*adj.* that amount to eighty. □ **eighty-first, -second**, etc. the ordinal numbers between eightieth and ninetieth. **eighty-one, -two**, etc. the cardinal numbers between eighty and ninety. □□ **eightieth** *adj. & n.* **eightyfold** *adj. & adv.* [OE *-eahtatig* (as EIGHT, -TY²)]

Eilat /eɪˈlæt/ (also **Elat**) the southernmost town in Israel, a port at the head of the Gulf of Aqaba; pop. (est. 1982) 19,500. Founded in 1949 near the ruins of biblical Elath, it is Israel's only outlet to the Red Sea.

Eindhoven /ˈaɪnthəʊv(ə)n/ the chief industrial city of the Dutch province of North Brabant, on the Dommel, 88 km (55 miles) south-east of Rotterdam; pop. (1987) 191,000. The city is a major producer of electrical and electronic goods.

einkorn /ˈaɪnkɔːn/ *n.* a kind of wheat (*Triticum monococcum*). [G f. *ein* one + *Korn* seed]

Einstein /ˈaɪnstaɪn/, Albert (1879–1955), German-born theoretical physicist, founder of the theory of relativity, and perhaps the greatest scientist of the 20th c. In 1905 he published several remarkable papers: one dealt with the photoelectric emission in terms of Planck's quantum theory of light, for which he was awarded the 1921 Nobel Prize for physics, another dealt with the Brownian motion in liquids and demonstrated that this effect was caused by the action of molecules, and a third described his Special Theory of Relativity, postulating a constant velocity of light which led to his famous equation relating mass and energy ($E = mc^2$), the basis of atomic energy. After several academic posts he moved, in 1914, to Berlin as a member of the Prussian Academy of Sciences and to direct the Kaiser Wilhelm Institute for Physics. For ten years he tried to incorporate gravitation into his theory, and achieved success at last with his General Theory of Relativity published in 1915. Einstein became a household name when one of the predictions of his theory, the bending of light when passing close to the sun, was observed during the solar eclipse of 1919. A Jew, a Zionist, and a pacifist, he was attacked by the Nazis, and when Hitler came to power in 1933 he settled in the US and joined the Institute for Advanced Study at Princeton. He spent the remainder of his life searching without success for a unified field theory which would combine electromagnetism, gravitation, relativity, and quantum mechanics. In 1939 he wrote a letter to President Roosevelt, at the request of several prominent physicists, outlining the military potential of nuclear energy and the dangers of a Nazi lead in this field. His letter greatly influenced the decision to build an atomic bomb, though he took no part in the Manhattan Project. After the war he spoke out passionately against nuclear weapons and repression. The artificial element einsteinium has been named in his honour.

einsteinium /aɪnˈstaɪnɪəm/ *n.* *Chem.* a transuranic radioactive metallic element produced artificially from plutonium, identified in 1952 in debris from the first hydrogen bomb explosion. ¶ Symb.: **Es**; atomic number 99. [A. EINSTEIN]

Eire /ˈeərə/ the former name of the Republic of Ireland (see IRELAND), still often used in newspapers etc. to distinguish the country from Northern Ireland and from the island as a whole. [Gaelic *Éire*]

eirenic var. of IRENIC.

eirenicon /aɪˈriːnɪˌkɒn/ *n.* (also **irenicon**) a proposal made as a means of achieving peace. [Gk, neut. of *eirēnikos* (adj.) f. *eirēnē* peace]

Eisenhower /ˈaɪzənˌhaʊə(r)/, Dwight David (1890–1969), American general and statesman, 34th President of the US 1953–61. In the Second World War he was Commander-in-Chief of Allied forces in North Africa and Italy 1942–3 and Supreme Commander of Allied Expeditionary Forces in western Europe 1943–5.

Eisenstadt /ˈaɪzənˌʃtɑːt/ the capital (since 1925) of the province of Burgenland in eastern Austria; pop. (1981) 10,100. It was a Hungarian city until ceded to Austria in 1920, and in the 17th–18th c. was the principal seat of the Esterházy princes, patrons of the composer Joseph Haydn who himself lived here for many years.

Eisenstein /ˈaɪzənˌstaɪn/, Sergei Mikhailovich (1898–1948), Russian film director, one of the great innovators of the cinema, particularly in his use of montage in which he presented images, perhaps independent of the main action, to create maximum psychological impact. Chosen by the Russian authorities to direct a film commemorating the revolution of 1905, Eisenstein's response was *The Battleship Potemkin* (1925), about the mutiny on a battleship of the Black Sea fleet, considered one of the greatest films ever made. *Alexander Nevsky* (1938) was an immediate success in the Soviet Union, though in spite of its dramatic power, striking imagery, and imaginative use of Prokofiev's music it could not compare with the stimulating experimentalism of his earlier work and was less well received abroad. His last completed work was *Ivan the Terrible*, Part I (1944), Part II (1946, not released until 1958 because of Stalin's disapproval of the presentation of Ivan's character).

eisteddfod /aɪˈsteðvɒd, -ˈstedfəd/ n. (pl. **eisteddfods** or **eisteddfodau** /-ˌdaɪ/) a congress of Welsh bards; a national or local festival for musical competitions etc. □□ **eisteddfodic** /-ˈfɒdɪk/ adj. [Welsh, lit. = session, f. *eistedd* sit]

either /ˈaɪðə(r), ˈiːðə(r)/ adj., pron., adv., & conj. —adj. & pron. **1** one or the other of two (*either of you can go; you may have either book*). **2** each of two (*houses on either side of the road; either will do*). —adv. & conj. **1** as one possibility (*is either black or white*). **2** as one choice or alternative; which way you will (*either come in or go out*). **3** (with neg. or interrog.) **a** any more than the other (*I didn't like it either; if you do not go, I shall not either*). **b** moreover (*there is no time to lose, either*). □ **either-or** n. an unavoidable choice between alternatives. —adj. involving such a choice. **either way** in either case or event. [OE *ǣgther* f. Gmc]

ejaculate v. & n. —v.tr. /ɪˈdʒækjʊˌleɪt/ (also absol.) **1** utter suddenly (words esp. of prayer or other emotion). **2** eject (fluid etc., esp. semen) from the body. —n. /ɪˈdʒækjʊlət/ semen that has been ejaculated from the body. □□ **ejaculation** /-ˈleɪʃ(ə)n/ n. **ejaculator** /ɪˈdʒækjʊˌleɪtə(r)/ n. **ejaculatory** /ɪˈdʒækjʊˌleɪtərɪ/ adj. [L *ejaculari* to dart (as E-, *jaculum* javelin)]

eject /ɪˈdʒekt/ v.tr. **1** send or drive out precipitately or by force, esp. from a building or other property; compel to leave. **2 a** cause (the pilot etc.) to be propelled from an aircraft or spacecraft in an emergency. **b** (absol.) (of the pilot etc.) be ejected in this way (*they both ejected at 1,000 feet*). **3** cause to be removed or drop out (e.g. a spent cartridge from a gun). **4** dispossess (a tenant etc.) by legal process. **5** dart forth; emit. □□ **ejective** adj. **ejectment** n. [L *ejicere eject-* (as E-, *jacere* throw)]

ejection /ɪˈdʒekʃ(ə)n/ n. the act or an instance of ejecting; the process of being ejected. □ **ejection seat** = *ejector seat*.

ejector /ɪˈdʒektə(r)/ n. a device for ejecting. □ **ejector seat** a device for the automatic ejection of the pilot etc. of an aircraft or spacecraft in an emergency.

Ekaterinburg see SVERDLOVSK.

eke /iːk/ v.tr. □ **eke out 1** (foll. by *with*, *by*) supplement; make the best use of (defective means etc.). **2** contrive to make (a livelihood) or support (an existence). [OE *ēacan*, rel. to L *augēre* increase]

ekka /ˈekə/ n. Ind. a small one-horse vehicle. [Hindi *ekkā* unit]

-el var. of -LE².

El Aaiún see LAˈYOUN.

elaborate adj. & v. —adj. /ɪˈlæbərət/ **1** carefully or minutely worked out. **2** highly developed or complicated. —v.tr. /ɪˈlæbəˌreɪt/ **1 a** work out or explain in detail. **b** (absol.) go into details (*I need not elaborate*). **2** produce by labour. **3** (of a natural agency) produce (a substance etc.) from its elements or sources. □□ **elaborately** /-rətlɪ/ adv. **elaborateness** /-rətnɪs/ n.

elaboration /-ˈreɪʃ(ə)n/ n. **elaborative** /-rətɪv/ adj. **elaborator** /-ˌreɪtə(r)/ n. [L *elaboratus* past part. of *elaborare* (as E-, *labor* work)]

Elagabalus /ˌiːləˈgæbələs/ (born Varius Avitus Bassianus, 204–22) Roman emperor 218–22. He took his name from Elah-Gabal, the sun-god of Emesa in Syria, whose hereditary priest he was. In his fifteenth year he was raised to power under the title of Marcus Aurelius Antoninus, his mother alleging he was the son of Caracalla. He promoted the worship of the sun-god in Rome, in the form of a black stone, and celebrated the midsummer festival with a ceremonial no less ludicrous than obscene, leading a dissipated life and ignoring State affairs. Both he and his mother were murdered in 222 after complicated intrigues.

El Alamein /el ˈæləˌmeɪn/ the site of the decisive British victory in the North African campaign of 1940–3, 90 km (60 miles) west of Alexandria, where the German Afrika Korps under Rommel was checked in its advance towards the Nile by the British Eighth Army under Montgomery.

Elam /ˈiːləm/ an ancient kingdom east of the Tigris, established in the 4th millennium BC, with its capital at Susa. □□ **Elamite** /ˈiːləˌmaɪt/ adj. & n.

élan /eɪˈlɑ̃/ n. vivacity, dash. [F f. *élancer* launch]

eland /ˈiːlənd/ n. any antelope of the genus *Taurotragus*, native to Africa, having spirally twisted horns, esp. the largest of living antelopes *T. derbianus*. [Du., = elk]

elapse /ɪˈlæps/ v.intr. (of time) pass by. [L *elabor elaps-* slip away]

elasmobranch /ɪˈlæzməˌbræŋk/ n. Zool. any cartilaginous fish of the subclass Chondrichthyes, e.g. sharks, skates, rays. [mod.L *elasmobranchii* f. Gk *elasmos* beaten metal + *bragkhia* gills]

elasmosaurus /ɪˌlæzməˈsɔːrəs/ n. a large extinct marine reptile with paddle-like limbs and tough crocodile-like skin. [mod.L f. Gk *elasmos* beaten metal + *sauros* lizard]

elastic /ɪˈlæstɪk, ɪˈlɑːstɪk/ adj. & n. —adj. **1** able to resume its normal bulk or shape spontaneously after contraction, dilatation, or distortion. **2** springy. **3** (of a person or feelings) buoyant. **4** flexible, adaptable (*elastic conscience*). **5** Econ. (of demand) variable according to price. **6** Physics (of a collision) involving no decrease of kinetic energy. —n. elastic cord or fabric, usu. woven with strips of rubber. □ **elastic band** = *rubber band* (see RUBBER¹). □□ **elastically** adv. **elasticity** /ɪlæsˈtɪsɪtɪ/ n. **elasticize** /ɪˈlæstɪˌsaɪz/ v.tr. (also -**ise**). [mod.L *elasticus* f. Gk *elastikos* propulsive f. *elaunō* drive]

elasticated /ɪˈlæstɪˌkeɪtɪd, ɪˈlɑːst-/ adj. (of a fabric) made elastic by weaving with rubber thread.

elastomer /ɪˈlæstəmə(r)/ n. a natural or synthetic rubber or rubber-like plastic. □□ **elastomeric** /-ˈmerɪk/ adj. [ELASTIC, after *isomer*]

Elat see EILAT.

elate /ɪˈleɪt/ v. & adj. —v.tr. **1** (esp. as **elated** adj.) inspirit, stimulate. **2** make proud. —adj. archaic in high spirits; exultant, proud. □□ **elatedly** adv. **elatedness** n. **elation** n. [ME f. L *efferre* elat- raise]

elater /ˈelətə(r)/ n. a click beetle. [mod.L f. Gk *elatēr* driver f. *elaunō* drive]

E-layer /ˈiːˌleɪə(r)/ n. a layer of the ionosphere able to reflect medium-frequency radio waves. [E (arbitrary) + LAYER]

Elba /ˈelbə/ a small island off the west coast of Italy, famous as the place of Napoleon's first exile (1814–15); pop. (1971) 26,830.

Elbasan /ˌelbəˈsɑːn/ an industrial town in central Albania; pop. (1983) 70,000.

Elbe /elb/ a river of Germany flowing 1,159 km (720 miles) from Czechoslovakia to the North Sea. Major cities upon it are Dresden, Magdeburg, and Hamburg.

elbow /ˈelbəʊ/ n. & v. —n. **1 a** the joint between the forearm and the upper arm. **b** the part of the sleeve of a garment covering the elbow. **2** an elbow-shaped bend or corner; a short piece of piping bent through a right angle. —v.tr. (foll. by *in*, *out*, *aside*, etc.) **1** thrust or jostle (a person or oneself). **2** make (one's way) by thrusting or jostling. □ **at one's elbow** close at hand. **elbow-grease** colloq. vigorous polishing; hard work. **elbow-room** plenty of room to move or work in. **give a person the elbow** colloq. send a person away; dismiss or reject a person.

out at elbows 1 (of a coat) worn out. **2** (of a person) ragged, poor. [OE *elboga, elnboga*, f. Gmc (as ELL, BOW¹)]

Elburz Mountains /el'bʊəz/ a mountain range in NW Iran, close to the southern shore of the Caspian Sea. Its highest peak, Damavand, rises to a height of 5,604 m (18,386 ft.).

eld /eld/ *n. archaic* or *poet.* **1** old age. **2** olden time. [OE (*i*)*eldu* f. Gmc: cf. OLD]

elder¹ /'eldə(r)/ *adj. & n.* —*attrib.adj.* (of two indicated persons, esp. when related) senior; of a greater age (*my elder brother*). —*n.* (often prec. by *the*) **1** the older or more senior of two indicated (esp. related) persons (*which is the elder?; is my elder by ten years*). **2** (in *pl.*) **a** persons of greater age or seniority (*respect your elders*). **b** persons venerable because of age. **3** a person advanced in life. **4** *hist.* a member of a senate or governing body. **5** an official in the early Christian Church or in the Presbyterian or Mormon Churches. □ **elder brother** (*pl.* **elder brethren**) *Brit.* each of thirteen senior members of Trinity House. **elder hand** *Cards* the first player. **elder statesman** an influential experienced person, esp. a politician, of advanced age. □□ **eldership** *n.* [OE *eldra*, rel. to OLD]

elder² /'eldə(r)/ *n.* any shrub or tree of the genus *Sambucus*, with white flowers and usu. blue-black or red berries. [OE *ellærn*]

elderberry /'eldəbərɪ/ *n.* (*pl.* **-ies**) the berry of the elder, esp. common elder (*Sambucus nigra*) used for making jelly, wine, etc.

elderly /'eldəlɪ/ *adj.* **1** somewhat old. **2** (of a person) past middle age. □□ **elderliness** *n.*

eldest /'eldɪst/ *adj. & n.* —*adj.* first-born or oldest surviving (member of a family, son, daughter, etc.). —*n.* (often prec. by *the*) the eldest of three or more indicated (*who is the eldest?*). □ **eldest hand** *Cards* the first player. [OE (as ELDER¹)]

El Djem /el 'dʒem/ a town in eastern Tunisia, noted for its vast well-preserved Roman amphitheatre.

El Dorado /el də'rɑːdəʊ/ the name of a fictitious country (according to some, a city) abounding in gold, believed by the Spanish and by Sir Walter Raleigh to exist upon the Amazon. The origin of the belief, which led Spanish conquistadors to converge on the area in search of treasure, appears to have been rumours of an Indian ruler, in what is now Colombia, who ritually coated his body with gold dust and then plunged into a sacred lake while his subjects threw in gold and jewels. [Sp., = the gilded]

eldorado /ˌeldə'rɑːdəʊ/ *n.* (*pl.* **-os**) **1** any imaginary country or city abounding in gold. **2** a place of great abundance. [EL DORADO]

eldritch /'eldrɪtʃ/ *adj.* Sc. **1** weird. **2** hideous. [16th c.: perh. f. OE *elfrīce* (unrecorded) 'fairy realm']

Eleanor Cross /'elɪnə(r)/ any of the stone crosses erected by Edward I to mark the stopping-places of the cortège that brought the body of his queen, Eleanor of Castile, from Nottinghamshire to London in 1290. Three of the twelve crosses survive.

Eleanor of Aquitaine /'elɪnə(r)/ (*c.*1122–1204), the daughter of the Duke of Aquitaine. She became Queen of France (1137–51), having married Louis VII, and after that marriage was annulled she married Henry of Anjou, who became King of England in 1154. Her ten children included Richard and John, future kings of England, whose accession she acted zealously to secure.

Eleanor of Castile /'elɪnə(r)/ (*c.*1244–90), the daughter of Ferdinand III of Castile. She married Edward I of England in 1254. (See ELEANOR CROSS.)

Eleatic /ˌelɪ'ætɪk/ *adj. & n.* —*adj.* of Elea, an ancient Greek city in SW Italy, or the school of philosophers there about the 6th c. BC, especially Xenophanes, Parmenides, and Zeno. —*n.* an Eleatic philosopher.

elecampane /ˌelɪkæm'peɪn/ *n.* **1** a sunflower-like plant, *Inula helenium*, with bitter aromatic leaves and roots, used in herbal medicine and cookery. **2** an esp. candied sweetmeat flavoured with this. [corrupt. of med.L *enula* (for L *inula* f. Gk *helenion*) *campana* (prob. = of the fields)]

elect /ɪ'lekt/ *v. & adj.* —*v.tr.* (usu. foll. by *to* + infin.) **1** choose

(*the principles they elected to follow*). **2** choose (a person) by vote (*elected a new chairman*). **3** *Theol.* (of God) choose (persons) in preference to others for salvation. (See ELECTION 3.) —*adj.* **1** chosen. **2** select, choice. **3** *Theol.* chosen by God. **4** (after a noun designating office) chosen but not yet in office (*president elect*). [ME f. L *electus* past part. of *eligere elect*- (as E-, *legere* pick)]

election /ɪ'lekʃ(ə)n/ *n.* **1** the process of electing or being elected, esp. of members of a political body. **2** the act or an instance of electing. **3** *Theol.* God's choice of some persons in preference to others for salvation. In medieval times the nature and conditions of election were much disputed, and formed a fundamental issue in the teaching of Calvin, who held that God's choice was wholly without relation to faith or good works. [ME f. OF f. L *electio -onis* (as ELECT)]

electioneer /ɪˌlekʃə'nɪə(r)/ *v. & n.* —*v.intr.* take part in an election campaign. —*n.* a person who electioneers.

elective /ɪ'lektɪv/ *adj. & n.* —*adj.* **1 a** (of an office or its holder) filled or appointed by election. **b** (of authority) derived from election. **2** (of a body) having the power to elect. **3** having a tendency to act on or be concerned with some things rather than others (*elective affinity*). **4** (of a course of study) chosen by the student; optional. **5** (of a surgical operation etc.) optional; not urgently necessary. —*n. US* an elective course of study. □□ **electively** *adv.* [F *électif -ive* f. LL *electivus* (as ELECT)]

elector /ɪ'lektə(r)/ *n.* **1** a person who has the right of voting to elect an MP etc. **2** (**Elector**) *hist.* a German prince entitled to take part in the election of the Emperor. **3** *US* a member of an electoral college. □□ **electorship** *n.* [ME f. F *électeur* f. L *elector* (as ELECT)]

electoral /ɪ'lektər(ə)l/ *adj.* relating to or ranking as electors. □ **electoral college 1** a body of persons representing the States of the US, who cast votes for the election of the President. **2** a body of electors. □□ **electorally** *adv.*

electorate /ɪ'lektərət/ *n.* **1** a body of electors. **2** *Austral. & NZ* an area represented by one member of parliament. **3** *hist.* the office or territories of the German Elector.

Electra /ɪ'lektrə/ *Gk legend* the daughter of Agamemnon and Clytemnestra. She urged her brother Orestes to kill Clytemnestra and Aegisthus in revenge for the murder of Agamemnon. The development of her story is due to the Greek dramatists and poets, not to tradition. □ **Electra complex** *Psychol.* a daughter's subconscious sexual attraction to her father and hostility towards her mother, corresponding to the Oedipus complex in a son.

electret /ɪ'lektrɪt/ *n. Physics* a permanently polarized piece of dielectric material, analogous to a permanent magnet. [ELECTRICITY + MAGNET]

electric /ɪ'lektrɪk/ *adj. & n.* —*adj.* **1** of, worked by, or charged with electricity; producing or capable of generating electricity. **2** causing or charged with sudden and dramatic excitement (*the news had an electric effect; the atmosphere was electric*). —*n.* **1** an electric light, vehicle, etc. **2** (in *pl.*) electrical equipment. □ **electric blanket** a blanket that can be heated electrically by an internal element. **electric blue** a steely or brilliant light blue. **electric chair** (in the US) an electrified chair used for capital punishment. **electric eel** an eel-like freshwater fish, *Electrophorus electricus*, native to S. America, that kills its prey by electric shock. **electric eye** *colloq.* a photoelectric cell operating a relay when the beam of light illuminating it is obscured. **electric fence** a fence charged with electricity, often consisting of one strand. **electric field** a region of electrical influence. **electric fire** an electrically operated incandescent or convector heater, usu. portable and for domestic use. **electric guitar** a guitar with a built-in electrical sound pick-up rather than a soundbox. **electric light** a light produced by electricity in any of various devices (e.g. an incandescent lamp, fluorescent lamp, arc lamp). The first successful electric lamps were developed almost simultaneously by Joseph Swan in England and Thomas Edison in America in 1879. **electric organ 1** *Biol.* the organ in some fishes giving an electric shock. **2** *Mus.* an electrically-operated organ. **electric ray** any of several rays which can give an electric shock (see RAY²). **electric shaver** (or **razor**) an electrical device for shaving, with oscillating blades behind a metal guard. **electric shock** the effect of a sudden discharge of electricity on a person or animal, usually with stimulation of the nerves and contraction of the muscles. **electric storm** a violent disturbance of the electrical condition of the atmosphere. □□ **electrically** adv. [mod.L electricus f. L electrum f. Gk ēlektron amber, the rubbing of which causes electrostatic phenomena]

electrical /ɪˈlektrɪk(ə)l/ adj. **1** of or concerned with or of the nature of electricity. **2** operating by electricity. **3** suddenly or dramatically exciting (the effect was electrical).

electrician /ˌɪlekˈtrɪʃ(ə)n/ n. a person who installs or maintains electrical equipment, esp. professionally.

electricity /ˌɪlekˈtrɪsɪtɪ, ˌel-/ n. **1** a form of energy resulting from the existence of charged particles (electrons, protons, etc.), either statically as an accumulation of charge or dynamically as a current. (See below.) **2** the branch of physics dealing with electricity. **3** a supply of electric current for heating, lighting, etc.

When a piece of dry amber is rubbed with cloth it develops the power of attracting small pieces of paper. This manifestation of electricity has been known from antiquity, but the scientific elucidation of the nature of electricity proved to be an extraordinarily difficult problem. William Gilbert (1544–1603) showed that many substances other than amber could be electrified by friction, and seems to have been the first to use the Latin word electrum to refer to the phenomenon, in his treatise De Magnete (1600). In the 18th c. it was discovered that there are two opposite kinds of electricity: like electricities repel each other and unlike electricities attract. Benjamin Franklin named these positive and negative electric. Some of the mystery surrounding electricity was resolved late last century when J. J. Thomson located the seat of negative electricity in subatomic particles called electrons; that of positive electricity was found to lie in larger particles, protons, in the atomic nucleus. All electrical and magnetic phenomena are due ultimately to protons and electrons. Electric current in the wires of domestic appliances, for example, consists in the slow drift of electrons (back and forth if it is an alternating current). Electric forces are responsible for binding protons and electrons together in atoms, binding atoms together to form matter, and for many other natural phenomena.

The town of Godalming in Surrey, England, was the first in the world to have electricity supplied for public and private usage, in a three-year experiment from 1881 (a few private schemes were inaugurated a little earlier), after which the town reverted to gas lighting; the electricity supply was generated at first by water-power, then by a steam engine. Use of electrical power in homes and factories did not become common until the years between the two World Wars.

electrify /ɪˈlektrɪˌfaɪ/ v.tr. (-ies, -ied) **1** charge (a body) with electricity. **2** convert (machinery or the place or system employing it) to the use of electric power. **3** cause dramatic or sudden excitement in. □□ **electrification** /-fɪˈkeɪʃ(ə)n/ n. **electrifier** n.

electro /ɪˈlektrəʊ/ n. & v. —n. (pl. -os) **1** = ELECTROTYPE n. **2** = ELECTROPLATE n. —v.tr. (-oes, -oed) colloq. **1** = ELECTROTYPE v. **2** = ELECTROPLATE v. [abbr.]

electro- /ɪˈlektrəʊ/ comb. form Electr. of, relating to, or caused by electricity (electrocute; electromagnet). [Gk ēlektron amber: see ELECTRIC]

electrobiology /ɪˌlektrəʊbaɪˈɒlədʒɪ/ n. the study of the electrical phenomena of living things.

electrocardiogram /ɪˌlektrəʊˈkɑːdɪəˌgræm/ n. a record of the heartbeat traced by an electrocardiograph. [G Elektrocardiogramm (as ELECTRO-, CARDIO-, -GRAM)]

electrocardiograph /ɪˌlektrəʊˈkɑːdɪəˌgrɑːf/ n. an instrument recording the electric currents generated by a person's heartbeat, receiving these as they vary during the cardiac cycle and transforming them into a graphic record. When the heart muscle contracts and relaxes, changes in potential are produced, which can be picked up from the skin surface by electrodes applied to various parts of the body. The electrocardiograph contains a delicate galvanometer consisting essentially of a silvered wire connected to the electrodes, which

vibrates in a magnetic field in response to the change in potential. While it vibrates, an electrographic record is obtained upon a moving photographic plate or a tape. The electrical activity of the heartbeat was first recorded by the Dutch physiologist William Einthoven in 1903. □□ **electrocardiographic** /-ˈgræfɪk/ adj. **electrocardiography** /-ˈɒgrəfɪ/ n.

electrochemical /ɪˌlektrəʊˈkemɪk(ə)l/ adj. involving electricity as applied to or occurring in chemistry. □□ **electrochemist** n. **electrochemistry** n.

electroconvulsive /ɪˌlektrəʊkənˈvʌlsɪv/ adj. (of a therapy) employing the use of the convulsive response to the application of electric shocks.

electrocute /ɪˈlektrəˌkjuːt/ v.tr. **1** kill by electricity (as a form of capital punishment). **2** cause death of by electric shock. □□ **electrocution** /-ˈkjuːʃ(ə)n/ n. [ELECTRO-, after EXECUTE]

electrode /ɪˈlektrəʊd/ n. a conductor through which electricity enters or leaves an electrolyte, gas, vacuum, etc. [ELECTRIC + Gk hodos way]

electrodialysis /ɪˌlektrəʊdaɪˈælɪsɪs/ n. dialysis in which electrodes are placed on either side of a semi-permeable membrane, as used in obtaining pure water from salt water.

electrodynamics /ɪˌlektrəʊdaɪˈnæmɪks/ n.pl. (usu. treated as sing.) the branch of mechanics concerned with electric current applied to motive forces. □□ **electrodynamic** adj.

electroencephalogram /ɪˌlektrəʊɪnˈsefələˌgræm/ n. a record of the brain's activity traced by an electroencephalograph. [G Elektrenkephalogramm (as ELECTRO-, ENCEPHALO-, -GRAM)]

electroencephalograph /ɪˌlektrəʊɪnˈsefələˌgrɑːf/ n. an instrument recording the electrical activity of the brain introduced in 1929 by Dr J. Berger of Jena in Germany. □□ **electroencephalography** /-ˈɒgrəfɪ/ n.

electroluminescence /ɪˌlektrəʊˌluːmɪˈnes(ə)ns/ n. Chem. luminescence produced electrically, esp. by the application of a voltage. □□ **electroluminescent** adj.

electrolyse /ɪˈlektrəˌlaɪz/ v.tr. (US -yze) subject to or treat by electrolysis. □□ **electrolyser** n. [ELECTROLYSIS after analyse]

electrolysis /ˌɪlekˈtrɒlɪsɪs, ˌel-/ n. **1** Chem. the decomposition of a substance by the application of an electric current. **2** Surgery this process applied to the destruction of tumours, hair-roots, etc. □□ **electrolytic** /ɪˌlektrəʊˈlɪtɪk/ adj. **electrolytical** /-ˈlɪtɪk(ə)l/ adj. **electrolytically** /-ˈlɪtɪkəlɪ/ adv. [ELECTRO- + -LYSIS]

electrolyte /ɪˈlektrəˌlaɪt/ n. **1** a substance which conducts electricity when molten or in solution, esp. in an electric cell or battery. **2** a solution of this. [ELECTRO- + Gk lutos released f. luō loosen]

electromagnet /ɪˌlektrəʊˈmægnɪt/ n. a soft metal core made [into a magnet by the passage of electric current through a coil surrounding it. The first simple electromagnet capable of supporting its own weight was made by William Sturgeon of Manchester, a self-taught electrical engineer, in 1825. □□ **electromagnetically** /-ˈnetɪkəlɪ/ adv.

electromagnetic /ɪˌlektrəʊmægˈnetɪk/ adj. having both an electrical and a magnetic character or properties. □ **electromagnetic radiation** a kind of radiation including visible light, radio waves, gamma rays, X-rays, etc., in which electric and magnetic fields vary simultaneously. **electromagnetic spectrum** the range of wavelengths over which electromagnetic radiation extends. **electromagnetic units** a system of units derived primarily from the magnetic properties of electric currents.

electromagnetism /ɪˌlektrəʊˈmægnɪˌtɪz(ə)m/ n. **1** the magnetic forces produced by electricity. **2** the study of this. Hans Christian Oersted in 1820 was the first to establish that a flow of electricity in a conductor affects a nearby magnetic compass exactly as an ordinary magnet does. Electromagnetism now has an enormous variety of applications. Electric motors are usually driven by electromagnets. Electric bells and automatic switches of various sorts, certain kinds of loudspeakers and television tubes, magnetic tapes, certain kinds of current-measuring instruments and certain navigational systems, all make use of electromagnetism as their most important principle of operation. (See also FIELD.)

electromechanical /ɪˌlektrəʊmɪˈkænɪk(ə)l/ *adj.* relating to the application of electricity to mechanical processes, devices, etc.

electrometer /ɪlekˈtrɒmɪtə(r), ˌel-/ *n.* an instrument for measuring electrical potential without drawing any current from the circuit. □□ **electrometric** /-ˈmetrɪk/ *adj.* **electrometry** *n.*

electromotive /ɪˌlektrəʊˈməʊtɪv/ *adj.* producing or tending to produce an electric current. □ **electromotive force** a force set up in an electric circuit by a difference in potential.

electron /ɪˈlektrɒn/ *n.* a stable elementary particle with a charge of negative electricity, found in all atoms and acting as the primary carrier of electricity in solids, with mass of approximately 9×10^{-31}kg. (See below.) □ **electron beam** a stream of electrons in a gas or vacuum. **electron diffraction** the diffraction of a beam of electrons by atoms or molecules, used for determining crystal structures etc. **electron gun** a device for producing a narrow stream of electrons from a heated cathode. **electron lens** a device for focusing a stream of electrons by means of electric or magnetic fields. **electron microscope** see separate entry. **electron pair** an electron and a positron. **electron spin resonance** a spectroscopic method of locating electrons within the molecules of a paramagnetic substance. ¶ Abbr.: **ESR**. [ELECTRIC + -ON]
Electrons, which orbit the nucleus in atoms, are responsible for an enormous variety of natural phenomena: electric currents in metals and in semiconductors consist of a flow of electrons; light, radio waves, X-rays, and a large proportion of heat radiation are all produced by accelerating and decelerating electrons; electrons are chiefly responsible for the binding together of atoms in molecules, for magnetism, and for the conduction of heat through metals. Electronics and electrical engineering are largely concerned with harnessing the forces and energies of electrons.

electronegative /ɪˌlektrəʊˈnegətɪv/ *adj.* **1** electrically negative. **2** *Chem.* (of an element) tending to acquire electrons.

electronic /ˌɪlekˈtrɒnɪk, ˌel-/ *adj.* **1 a** produced by or involving the flow of electrons. **b** of or relating to electrons or electronics. **2** (of a device) using electronic components. **3 a** (of music) produced by electronic means and usu. recorded on tape. **b** (of a musical instrument) producing sounds by electronic means. □ **electronic flash** a flash from a gas-discharge tube, used in photography. **electronic mail** messages distributed by electronic means esp. from one computer system to one or more recipients: also called EMAIL. □□ **electronically** *adv.*

electronics /ˌɪlekˈtrɒnɪks, ˌel-/ *n.pl.* (treated as *sing.*) **1** a branch of physics and technology concerned with the behaviour and movement of electrons in a vacuum, gas, semiconductor, etc. **2** the circuits used in this.

electron microscope *n.* a type of microscope (first developed in the early 1930s) giving high magnification and resolution by employing a beam of electrons instead of light and focusing it by means of magnetic or electrostatic fields. Because the de Broglie wavelength of a high-speed electron is very much shorter than that of light, a correspondingly greater resolving power is possible, so that magnifications of up to one million can be achieved. In one type of instrument the electron beam is focused on to a very thin specimen and the transmitted beam is made to impinge on a fluorescent screen to give a visible image representing the electron-stopping power of different parts of the specimen. Other types use reflection from the specimen or a scanning beam that is measured electrically and the signal fed to a television monitor.

electronvolt /ɪˈlektrɒnˌvɒlt/ *n.* a unit of energy equal to the work done on an electron in accelerating it through a potential difference of one volt. ¶ Abbr.: **eV**.

electrophilic /ɪˌlektrəʊˈfɪlɪk/ *adj. Chem.* having an affinity for electrons. □□ **electrophile** /ɪˈlektrəʊˌfaɪl/ *n.*

electrophoresis /ɪˌlektrəʊfɔːˈriːsɪs/ *n. Physics & Chem.* the movement of colloidal particles in a fluid under the influence of an electric field. □□ **electrophoretic** /-fəˈretɪk/ *adj.* [ELECTRO- + Gk *phorēsis* being carried]

electrophorus /ˌɪlekˈtrɒfərəs, el-/ *n.* a device for repeatedly

generating static electricity by induction. [mod.L f. ELECTRO- + Gk *-phoros* bearing]

electroplate /ɪˈlektrəˌpleɪt/ *v. & n.* —*v.tr.* coat (a utensil etc.) by electrolytic deposition with chromium, silver, etc. The commercial use of this process dates from the mid-19th c. —*n.* electroplated articles. □□ **electroplater** *n.*

electroplexy /ɪˈlektrəˌpleksɪ/ *n. Brit.* electroconvulsive therapy. [ELECTRO- + APOPLEXY]

electropositive /ɪˌlektrəʊˈpɒzɪtɪv/ *adj.* **1** electrically positive. **2** *Chem.* (of an element) tending to lose electrons.

electroscope /ɪˈlektrəˌskəʊp/ *n.* an instrument for detecting and measuring electricity, esp. as an indication of the ionization of air by radioactivity. □□ **electroscopic** /-ˈskɒpɪk/ *adj.*

electro-shock /ɪˈlektrəˌʃɒk/ *attrib.adj.* (of medical treatment) by means of electric shocks.

electrostatic /ɪˌlektrəʊˈstætɪk/ *adj.* of electricity at rest. □ **electrostatic units** a system of units based primarily on the forces between electric charges. [ELECTRO- + STATIC after *hydrostatic*]

electrostatics /ɪˌlektrəʊˈstætɪks/ *n.pl.* (treated as *sing.*) the study of electricity at rest.

electrotechnology /ɪˌlektrəʊtekˈnɒlədʒɪ/ *n.* the science of the application of electricity in technology. □□ **electrotechnic** /-ˈteknɪk/ *adj.* **electrotechnical** /-ˈteknɪk(ə)l/ *adj.* **electrotechnics** /-ˈteknɪks/ *n.*

electrotherapy /ɪˌlektrəʊˈθerəpɪ/ *n.* the treatment of diseases by the use of electricity. □□ **electrotherapeutic** /-ˈpjuːtɪk/ *adj.* **electrotherapeutical** /-ˈpjuːtɪk(ə)l/ *adj.* **electrotherapist** *n.*

electrothermal /ɪˌlektrəʊˈθɜːm(ə)l/ *adj.* relating to heat electrically derived.

electrotype /ɪˈlektrəʊˌtaɪp/ *v. & n.* —*v.tr.* copy by the electrolytic deposition of copper on a mould, esp. for printing. —*n.* a copy so formed. □□ **electrotyper** *n.*

electrovalent /ɪˌlektrəʊˈveɪlənt/ *adj. Chem.* linking ions by a bond resulting from electrostatic attraction. □□ **electrovalence** *n.* **electrovalency** *n.* [ELECTRO- + -valent after *trivalent* etc.]

electrum /ɪˈlektrəm/ *n.* **1** an alloy of silver and gold used in ancient times. **2** native argentiferous gold ore. [ME f. L f. Gk *ēlektron* amber, electrum]

electuary /ɪˈlektjʊərɪ/ *n.* (*pl.* **-ies**) medicinal powder etc. mixed with honey or other sweet substance. [ME f. LL *electuarium*, prob. f. Gk *ekleikton* f. *ekleikhō* lick up]

eleemosynary /ˌeliːˈmɒsɪnərɪ, -ˈmɒzɪnərɪ/ *adj.* **1** of or dependent on alms. **2** charitable. **3** gratuitous. [med.L *eleemosynarius* f. LL *eleemosyna*: see ALMS]

elegant /ˈelɪɡənt/ *adj.* **1** graceful in appearance or manner. **2** tasteful, refined. **3** (of a mode of life etc.) of refined luxury. **4** ingeniously simple and pleasing. **5** *US* excellent. □□ **elegance** *n.* **elegantly** *adv.* [F *élégant* or L *elegant-*, rel. to *eligere*: see ELECT]

elegiac /ˌelɪˈdʒaɪək/ *adj. & n.* —*adj.* **1** (of a metre) used for elegies. **2** mournful. —*n.* (in *pl.*) verses in an elegiac metre. □ **elegiac couplet** a pair of lines consisting of a dactylic hexameter and a pentameter, esp. in Greek and Latin verse. □□ **elegiacally** *adv.* [F *élégiaque* or f. LL *elegiacus* f. Gk *elegeiakos*: see ELEGY]

elegize /ˈelɪˌdʒaɪz/ *v.* (also **-ise**) **1** *intr.* (often foll. by *upon*) write an elegy. **2** *intr.* write in a mournful strain. **3** *tr.* write an elegy upon. □□ **elegist** *n.*

elegy /ˈelɪdʒɪ/ *n.* (*pl.* **-ies**) **1** a song of lament, esp. for the dead (sometimes vaguely used of other poems). **2** a poem in elegiac metre. [F *élégie* or L *elegia* f. Gk *elegeia* f. *elegos* mournful poem]

element /ˈelɪmənt/ *n.* **1** a component part; a contributing factor or thing. **2** *Chem. & Physics* any of the substances (numbering more than 100) that cannot be resolved by chemical means into simpler substances and whose atoms are now known to be of the same atomic number. (See below.) **3 a** any of the four substances (earth, water, air, and fire) in ancient and medieval philosophy. **b** any of these as a being's natural abode or environment. **4** *Electr.* a resistance wire that heats up in an electric heater, cooker, etc.; an electrode. **5** (in *pl.*) atmospheric agencies, esp. wind and storm. **6** (in *pl.*) the rudiments of learning or of a branch of knowledge. **7** (in *pl.*) the bread and wine of the Eucharist. **8** *Math.* & *Logic* an entity that is a single member of a set. □ **in** (or **out of**) **one's element** in (or out of) one's accustomed or preferred surroundings. **reduced to its elements** analysed. [ME f. OF f. L *elementum*]

All stable matter consists of elements (of which 105 are currently known) either individually or in combination. Each element is a substance composed of atoms all of which have the same atomic number and therefore the same number of electrons orbiting the nucleus; this number differs for each element, a fact which accounts for their different chemical properties. Electrons can be regarded as occupying definite orbits or 'shells' surrounding the nucleus, and it is the number in the outermost shell that determines how an atom of a particular element interacts and forms bonds with other atoms to form molecules and compounds. Certain elements of widely differing atomic number (e.g. halogens, noble gases) are similar chemically because the outermost 'shells' contain the same number of electrons, and this configuration of outer electrons makes possible the general classification in the periodic table. Elements are often classified into metals (comprising the majority) and non-metals. Uranium and almost all of the elements with a smaller atomic number than this occur naturally, but most of the thirteen heavier ones are known only from having been synthesized in nuclear reactions. (For the origin of the elements in the universe see NUCLEOSYNTHESIS.)

elemental /ˌelɪˈment(ə)l/ *adj.* & *n.* —*adj.* **1** of the four elements. **2** of the powers of nature (*elemental worship*). **3** comparable to a force of nature (*elemental grandeur*; *elemental tumult*). **4** uncompounded (*elemental oxygen*). **5** essential. —*n.* an entity or force thought to be physically manifested by occult means. □□ **elementalism** *n.* (in senses 1, 2). [med.L *elementalis* (as ELEMENT)]

elementary /ˌelɪˈmentərɪ/ *adj.* **1 a** dealing with or arising from the simplest facts of a subject; rudimentary, introductory. **b** simple. **2** *Chem.* not decomposable. □ **elementary particle** see separate entry. **elementary school** a school in which elementary subjects are taught to young children. □□ **elementarily** *adv.* **elementariness** *n.* [ME f. L *elementarius* (as ELEMENT)]

elementary particle *n.* *Physics* any of several subatomic particles which are not known to be composed of simpler particles and which are characterized by having a definite mass, a lifetime that is long compared with the interaction time, and well-defined electromagnetic properties, and are capable of an independent existence.

The discovery of the electron in 1897 and the subsequent discoveries of the photon, the atomic nucleus, the proton, and the neutron led to the recognition that the atom itself is composed of more elementary particles, and also that there are other elementary particles, such as the photon, which do not exist in atoms, and which can exist independently of atoms. Theoretical and experimental research from the 1930s to the present has led to the discovery of numerous other 'elementary' particles, most of which are unstable with very short half-lives. The best known of these are the neutrino, which is a stable neutral particle of very small or even zero rest mass; the positron, which is a positively charged electron; and the mesons, which are responsible for the strong interactions between the particles of the nucleus.

Elementary particles are classified into four major groups: quanta, leptons (which include electrons and neutrinos), mesons, and baryons (which include protons and neutrons). There has been an enormous investment of theoretical and experimental effort to establish the properties of these particles, to classify them, and to fit them into a coherent theoretical framework. This effort has led to the postulation of many new hypothetical particles such as 'quarks' and 'gluons', and to the identification of a range of new but poorly understood particle properties including those termed 'parity', 'strangeness', 'isospin number', 'helicity', 'charm', and 'colour' (no connection with visual colour).

elenchus /ɪˈleŋkəs/ *n.* (*pl.* **elenchi** /-kaɪ/) *Logic* logical refutation.

□ **Socratic elenchus** an attempted refutation of an opponent's position by short question and answer. □□ **elenctic** *adj.* [L f. Gk *elegkhos*]

elephant /ˈelɪfənt/ *n.* (*pl.* same or **elephants**) **1** the largest living land animal, with a trunk and ivory tusks. Of several species once distributed over the world, including Britain, only two survive, the Indian elephant (*Elephas maximus*) and the African (*Loxodonta africana*). The African elephant is larger than the Indian, though there is a smaller variety of it (which may be a different species) in parts of Africa. The Indian elephant is used for heavy work and as a beast of burden in India and some countries of SE Asia. **2** a size of paper (711 × 584 mm). □ **elephant grass** any of various tall African grasses, esp. *Pennisetum purpureum*. **elephant seal** = *sea elephant*. **elephant shrew** any small insect-eating mammal of the family Macroscelididae, native to Africa, having a long snout and long hind limbs. □□ **elephantoid** /-ˈfæntɔɪd/ *adj.* [ME *olifaunt* etc. f. OF *oli-*, *elefant* ult. f. L *elephantus*, *elephans* f. Gk *elephas -antos* ivory, elephant (ivory was known to the Greeks long before the elephant)]

elephantiasis /ˌelɪfənˈtaɪəsɪs/ *n.* gross enlargement of the body, esp. the limbs, due to lymphatic obstruction esp. by a nematode parasite. [L f. Gk (as ELEPHANT)]

elephantine /ˌelɪˈfæntaɪn/ *adj.* **1** of elephants. **2 a** huge. **b** clumsy, unwieldy (*elephantine movements*; *elephantine humour*). [L *elephantinus* f. Gk *elephantinos* (as ELEPHANT)]

Elephant Pass a narrow strip of land linking the Jaffna peninsula with the mainland at the north of Sri Lanka.

Eleusinian /ˌeljuːˈsɪnɪən/ *adj.* of or relating to Eleusis near Athens. □ **Eleusinian mysteries** *Gk Hist.* the annual celebrations held at ancient Eleusis in honour of Demeter. [L *Eleusinius* f. Gk *Eleusinios*]

elevate /ˈelɪveɪt/ *v.tr.* **1** bring to a higher position. **2** *Eccl.* hold up (the Host or the chalice) for adoration. **3** raise, lift (one's eyes etc.). **4** raise the axis of (a gun). **5** raise (a railway etc.) above ground level. **6** exalt in rank etc. **7** (usu. as **elevated** *adj.*) raise morally or intellectually (*elevated style*). **8** (as **elevated** *adj.*) *colloq.* slightly drunk. □□ **elevatory** *adj.* [L *elevare* raise (as E-, *levis* light)]

elevation /ˌelɪˈveɪʃ(ə)n/ *n.* **1 a** the process of elevating or being elevated. **b** the angle with the horizontal, esp. of a gun or of the direction of a heavenly body. **c** the height above a given level, esp. sea level. **d** a high place or position. **2 a** a drawing or diagram made by projection on a vertical plane (cf. PLAN). **b** a flat drawing of the front, side, or back of a house etc. **3** *Ballet* **a** the capacity of a dancer to attain height in springing movements. **b** the action of tightening the muscles and uplifting the body. □□ **elevational** *adj.* (in sense 2). [ME f. OF *elevation* or L *elevatio*: see ELEVATE]

elevator /ˈelɪveɪtə(r)/ *n.* **1** a hoisting machine. **2** *Aeron.* the movable part of a tailplane for changing the pitch of an aircraft. **3** *US* **a** = LIFT *n.* 3. **b** a place for lifting and storing quantities of grain. **4** that which elevates, esp. a muscle that raises a limb. [mod.L (as ELEVATE)]

eleven /ɪˈlev(ə)n/ *n.* & *adj.* —*n.* **1** one more than ten; the sum of six units and five units. **2** a symbol for this (11, xi, XI). **3** a size etc. denoted by eleven. **4** a set or team of eleven individuals. **5** the time of eleven o'clock (*is it eleven yet?*). —*adj.* that amount to eleven. □ **eleven-plus** esp. *hist.* (in the UK) an examination taken at the age of 11–12 to determine the type of secondary school a child should enter. [OE *endleofon* f. Gmc]

elevenfold /ɪˈlev(ə)nˌfəʊld/ *adj.* & *adv.* **1** eleven times as much or as many. **2** consisting of eleven parts.

elevenses /ɪˈlevənzɪz/ *n.* (usu. in *pl.*) *Brit. colloq.* light refreshment, usu. with tea or coffee, taken about 11 a.m.

eleventh /ɪˈlevənθ/ *n.* & *adj.* —*n.* **1** the position in a sequence corresponding to the number 11 in the sequence 1–11. **2** something occupying this position. **3** one of eleven equal parts of a thing. **4** *Mus.* **a** an interval or chord spanning an octave and a fourth in the diatonic scale. **b** a note separated from another by this interval. —*adj.* that is the eleventh. □ **the eleventh hour** the last possible moment.

aʊ how eɪ day əʊ no eə hair ɪə near ɔɪ boy ʊə poor aɪə fire aʊə sour (*see over for consonants*)

elevon /ˈelɪˌvɒn/ n. Aeron. the movable part of the trailing edge of a delta wing. [ELEVATOR + AILERON]

elf /elf/ n. (pl. **elves** /elvz/) **1** a mythological being, esp. one that is small and mischievous. **2** a sprite or little creature. □ **elf-lock** a tangled mass of hair. □□ **elfish** adj. **elvish** adj. [OE f. Gmc]

elfin /ˈelfɪn/ adj. & n. —adj. of elves; elflike. —n. archaic a dwarf; a child. [ELF, perh. infl. by ME elvene genit. pl. of elf, and by Elphin in Arthurian romance]

Elgar /ˈelgɑː(r)/, Sir Edward William (1857–1934), the strongest creative personality to appear in British music for nearly two hundred years. A self-taught provincial from Worcester—he always remained a countryman at heart—he learnt more from the scores of Liszt and Wagner than he could have done at any Victorian school of music. He applied their techniques first in the then fashionable form of the cantata; he was in his forties before he made his mark with a novel orchestral work, a set of variations on an 'Enigma' theme dedicated to 'my friends pictured within'. But Elgar's pictures are portraits in a mirror; each variation may suggest a friend but it also reflects the man himself—sensitive, emotional, playful, but also (in the finale) the face of a late Victorian imperialist. He went on to breathe life into the dying form of oratorio, but the essential Elgar was later more perfectly embodied in his symphonies and concertos.

Elgin Marbles /ˈelgɪn/ a collection of marble sculptures and architectural fragments, chiefly from the frieze and pediment of the Parthenon, executed under the supervision of Phidias from 447 BC, which Lord Elgin acquired from the occupying Turkish authorities in 1801–3 and which he sold to the British nation in 1816 for £35,000. Their original exhibition in London had an enormous impact, it being the first time authentic classical Greek sculpture had been on public display. They are regarded as a classical masterpiece, housed in the British Museum, and at the centre of a widely publicized repatriation request from the Greek government, who do not accept the legality of the Turkish sale.

Elgon /ˈelgɒn/, **Mount** an extinct volcano on the Kenya–Uganda frontier, rising to a height of 4,321 m (14,178 ft.).

El Greco /el ˈɡrekəʊ/ (Sp., = the Greek) (1541–1614), Spanish painter of Greek origin whose real name was Domenikos Theotokopoulos. Trained as an icon painter in Crete, he travelled to Venice, where it is believed he became a pupil of Titian. After being in Rome 1570–6 he settled finally in Toledo in 1577, where he remained for the rest of his life. His portraits and religious works, with their distorted perspective, elongated figures, and psychological tension, can have an unnerving effect. His colours can be both bright and discordant, and his works capture the religious fervour and mysticism of the Counter-Reformation in Spain with a sensitive expressionism outreaching his contemporaries.

Elia /ˈiːlɪə/ the pseudonym adopted by Charles Lamb in his Essays of Elia (1823).

elicit /ɪˈlɪsɪt, eˈlɪsɪt/ v.tr. (**elicited**, **eliciting**) **1** draw out, evoke (an admission, response, etc.). **2** draw forth (what is latent). □□ **elicitation** /-ˈteɪʃ(ə)n/ n. **elicitor** n. [L elicere elicit- (as E-, lacere entice)]

elide /ɪˈlaɪd/ v.tr. omit (a vowel or syllable) by elision. [L elidere elis- crush out (as E-, laedere knock)]

eligible /ˈelɪdʒɪb(ə)l/ adj. **1** (often foll. by for) fit or entitled to be chosen (eligible for a rebate). **2** desirable or suitable, esp. as a partner in marriage. □□ **eligibility** /-ˈbɪlɪtɪ/ n. **eligibly** adv. [F éligible f. LL eligibilis (as ELECT)]

Elijah /ɪˈlaɪdʒə/ (9th c. BC) a Hebrew prophet in the time of Jezebel, who maintained the worship of Jehovah against that of Baal and other pagan gods. Legends say that he was miraculously fed by ravens, raised a widow's son from the dead, and was carried to heaven in a chariot of fire (1 Kings 17–2 Kings 2).

eliminate /ɪˈlɪmɪˌneɪt/ v.tr. **1** remove, get rid of. **2** exclude from consideration; ignore as irrelevant. **3** exclude from further participation in a competition etc. on defeat. **4** Physiol. discharge (waste matter). **5** Chem. remove (a simpler substance) from a compound. **6** Algebra remove (a quantity) by combining equations. □□ **eliminable** /-nəb(ə)l/ adj. **elimination** /-ˈneɪʃ(ə)n/

n. **eliminator** n. **eliminatory** /-nətərɪ/ adj. [L eliminare (as E-, limen liminis threshold)]

Eliot¹ /ˈelɪət/, George (pseudonym of Mary Ann Evans, 1819–80), English novelist. Early influenced by Evangelicalism she later adopted agnostic views, but her lofty moral concepts of love and duty retained a religious authority. She became assistant editor of the Westminster Review (1851) and joined George Henry Lewes in a union without marriage until his death in 1878. Her first work of fiction, Scenes of Clerical Life (1858), was praised for its domestic realism, pathos, and humour and Adam Bede (1859) established her as a leading novelist, a reputation she consolidated in The Mill on the Floss (1860), Silas Marner (1861), and other writings. Her masterpiece is Middlemarch (1871–2); its brilliant depiction of provincial Victorian intellect and society has made it one of the greatest English novels.

Eliot² /ˈelɪət/, Thomas Stearns (1888–1965), Anglo-American poet, critic, and dramatist, who was greatly encouraged by Ezra Pound. His early verse collections, Prufrock and other Observations (1917) and Poems (1919) struck a new note in modern poetry. In his newly founded quarterly The Criterion he published The Waste Land (1922), which established him as the voice of a disillusioned generation. In 1927 he became a British subject and an Anglican, describing himself as 'classical in literature, royalist in politics, and Anglo-Catholic in religion'; the same preoccupation with tradition was expressed in his influential critical works. Four Quartets (1943) communicated in modern idiom the fundamentals of Christian faith. His attempts to revive poetic drama resulted in Murder in the Cathedral (1935), The Family Reunion (1939), and The Cocktail Party (1959). Old Possum's Book of Practical Cats (1939) was his classic children's verse collection; it achieved stage success in a musical adaptation Cats in 1981. He was awarded the Nobel Prize for literature in 1947.

Elisabethville /ɪˈliːzəbəθˌvɪl/ the former name (until 1966) of Lubumbashi in SE Zaïre.

Elisha /ɪˈlaɪʃə/ (9th c. BC) a Hebrew prophet, disciple and successor of Elijah.

elision /ɪˈlɪʒ(ə)n/ n. **1** the omission of a vowel or syllable in pronouncing (as in I'm, let's, e'en). **2** the omission of a passage in a book etc. [LL elisio (as ELIDE)]

élite /eɪˈliːt, ɪ-/ n. **1** (prec. by the) the best or choice part of a larger body or group. **2** a select group or class. **3** a size of letter in typewriting (12 per inch). [F f. past part. of élire f. Rmc: rel. to ELECT]

élitism /eɪˈliːtɪz(ə)m, ɪ-/ n. **1** advocacy of or reliance on leadership or dominance by a select group. **2** a sense of belonging to an élite. □□ **élitist** n. & adj.

elixir /ɪˈlɪksɪə(r)/ n. **1** Alchemy **a** a preparation supposedly able to change metals into gold. **b** (in full **elixir of life**) a preparation supposedly able to prolong life indefinitely. **c** a supposed remedy for all ills. **2** Pharm. an aromatic solution used as a medicine or flavouring. [ME f. med.L f. Arab. al-iksīr f. al the + iksīr prob. f. Gk xērion powder for drying wounds f. xēros dry]

Elizabeth I /ɪˈlɪzəbəθ/ (1533–1603), daughter of Henry VIII, queen of England and Ireland 1558–1603. Succeeding her Catholic sister Mary, Elizabeth was successful in uniting a deeply divided nation and re-establishing a moderate form of Protestantism as the religion of the State. Although frequently courted, Elizabeth never married and indeed owed much of her popularity and success to the cult of the Virgin Queen created around her. Her reign was dominated by the threat of a Catholic restoration (eventually leading to the execution of Mary Queen of Scots) and by war with Spain, during which the country was saved from invasion by the defeat of the Armada in 1588. Her reign also witnessed a great flowering of national culture, particularly in the field of literature, in which Shakespeare, Marlowe, and Spenser were all active.

Elizabeth II /ɪˈlɪzəbəθ/ (1926–), daughter of George VI, queen of the United Kingdom from 1952. While strictly adhering to the convention of the British constitution, she has always held a weekly audience with her Prime Minister and shown a strong personal commitment to the Commonwealth. She has done much to maintain the popularity of the monarchy at home and abroad through an extensive series of royal tours and public appearances.

Elizabethan /ɪˌlɪzəˈbiːθ(ə)n/ *adj.* & *n.* —*adj.* of the time of Queen Elizabeth I or II. —*n.* a person, esp. a writer, of the time of Queen Elizabeth I or II.

elk /elk/ *n.* (*pl.* same or **elks**) **1** a large deer, *Alces alces*, of N. Europe and Asia, with palmate antlers and a growth of skin hanging from the neck; a moose. **2** *US* a wapiti. □ **elk-hound** a large Scandinavian hunting dog with a shaggy coat. [ME, prob. repr. OE *elh, eolh*]

ell /el/ *n.* *hist.* a former measure of length, about 45 inches. [OE *eln*, rel. to L *ulna*: see ULNA]

Ellesmere Island /ˈelzmɪə(r)/ the northernmost island of the Canadian Arctic. Discovered in 1616 by William Baffin, the island was eventually named after the statesman and poet Francis Egerton, Earl of Ellesmere (1800–57).

Ellice Islands /ˈelɪs/ see TUVALU.

Ellington /ˈelɪŋt(ə)n/, Edward Kennedy ('Duke') (1899–1974), American composer, pianist, and band-leader, the most distinctive and influential figure in the history of jazz. His band established its fame in the early 1930s, and some of its members remained with him for over 30 years. Ellington wrote over 900 compositions; his first worldwide success was *Mood Indigo* (1930).

ellipse /ɪˈlɪps/ *n.* a regular oval, traced by a point moving in a plane so that the sum of its distances from two other points is constant, or resulting when a cone is cut by a plane which does not intersect the base and makes a smaller angle with the base than the side of the cone makes (cf. HYPERBOLA). [F f. L *ellipsus* f. Gk *elleipsis* f. *elleipō* come short f. *en* in + *leipō* leave]

ellipsis /ɪˈlɪpsɪs/ *n.* (also **ellipse**) (*pl.* **ellipses** /-siːz/) **1** the omission from a sentence of words needed to complete the construction or sense. **2** the omission of a sentence at the end of a paragraph. **3** a set of three dots etc. indicating an omission.

ellipsoid /ɪˈlɪpsɔɪd/ *n.* a solid of which all the plane sections normal to one axis are circles and all the other plane sections are ellipses. □□ **ellipsoidal** /ˌelɪpˈsɔɪd(ə)l/ *adj.*

elliptic /ɪˈlɪptɪk/ *adj.* (also **elliptical**) of, relating to, or having the form of an ellipse or ellipsis. □□ **elliptically** *adv.* **ellipticity** /ˌelɪpˈtɪsɪtɪ/ *n.* [Gk *elleiptikos* defective f. *elleipō* (as ELLIPSE)]

Ellis Island /ˈelɪs/ an island in New York Bay. Long used as an arsenal and a fort, from 1892 until 1943 it served as an entry centre for immigrants to the US, then (until 1954) as a detention centre for aliens and those awaiting deportation. In 1965 it became part of the Statue of Liberty National Monument, open to sightseers. The island is named after Samuel Ellis, a Manhattan merchant who owned it in the 1770s.

elm /elm/ *n.* **1** any tree of the genus *Ulmus*, esp. *U. procera* with rough serrated leaves. **2** (in full **elmwood**) the wood of the elm. □□ **elmy** *adj.* [OE, rel. to L *ulmus*]

Elmo /ˈelməʊ/, St, the popular name of St Peter González (c.1190–1246), a Dominican preacher who worked among seafaring folk on the coasts of Spain, and after his death was canonized as the patron saint of seamen. □ **St Elmo's fire** see CORPOSANT.

elocution /ˌeləˈkjuːʃ(ə)n/ *n.* **1** the art of clear and expressive speech, esp. of distinct pronunciation and articulation. **2** a particular style of speaking. □□ **elocutionary** *adj.* **elocutionist** *n.* [L *elocutio* f. *eloqui elocut-* speak out (as E-, *loqui* speak)]

Elohist /ˈeləʊɪst/ *n.* the postulated author or authors of parts of the Hexateuch in which God is regularly named *Elohim.* (Cf. YAHWIST.) [heb. *ĕlōhīm* god(s) + -IST]

elongate /ˈiːlɒŋˌɡeɪt/ *v.* & *adj.* —*v.* **1** *tr.* lengthen, prolong. **2** *intr. Bot.* be of slender or tapering form. —*adj. Bot.* & *Zool.* long in proportion to width. [LL *elongare* (as E-, L *longus* long)]

elongation /ˌiːlɒŋˈɡeɪʃ(ə)n/ *n.* **1** the act or an instance of lengthening; the process of being lengthened. **2** a part of a line etc. formed by lengthening. **3** *Mech.* the amount of extension under stress. **4** *Astron.* the angular separation of a planet from the sun or of a satellite from a planet. [ME f. LL *elongatio* (as ELONGATE)]

elope /ɪˈləʊp/ *v.intr.* **1** run away to marry secretly, esp. without

parental consent. **2** run away with a lover. □□ **elopement** *n.* **eloper** *n.* [AF *aloper* perh. f. a ME form *alope*, rel. to LEAP]

eloquence /ˈeləkwəns/ *n.* **1** fluent and effective use of language. **2** rhetoric. [ME f. OF f. L *eloquentia* f. *eloqui* speak out (as E-, *loqui* speak)]

eloquent /ˈeləkwənt/ *adj.* **1** possessing or showing eloquence. **2** (often foll. by *of*) clearly expressive or indicative. □□ **eloquently** *adv.* [ME f. OF f. L *eloqui* (as ELOQUENCE)]

El Paso /el ˈpæsəʊ/ an industrial city in western Texas, on the Rio Grande; pop. (1982) 445,000.

El Salvador /el ˈsælvəˌdɔː(r)/ a country in Central America, on the Pacific coast; pop. (est. 1988) 5,388,600; official language, Spanish; capital, San Salvador. Its economy is mainly agricultural, coffee, cotton, and sugar-cane being the chief crops. Conquered by the Spanish in 1524, El Salvador gained its independence in 1821 and joined the Central American Federation in 1824, before finally emerging as an independent republic in 1839. In the late 1970s and early 1980s the country has fallen into increasingly severe internal unrest, characterized by guerrilla warfare, harsh repressive measures, and a large refugee problem.

Elsan /ˈelsæn/ *n. Brit. propr.* a type of transportable chemical lavatory. [app. f. E. L. Jackson (its manufacturer) + SANITATION]

else /els/ *adv.* **1** (prec. by indef. or interrog. pron.) besides; in addition (*someone else; nowhere else; who else*). **2** instead; other, different (*what else could I say?; he did not love her, but someone else*). **3** otherwise; if not (*run, (or) else you will be late*). [OE *elles*, rel. to L *alius*, Gk *allos*]

elsewhere /ˈelsweə(r), elsˈweə(r)/ *adv.* in or to some other place. [OE *elles hwǣr* (as ELSE, WHERE)]

Elsinore /ˈelsɪˌnɔː(r)/ (Danish Helsingør /ˈhelsɪŋˌɜː(r)/) a port on the NE coast of the island of Zealand, Denmark. The 16th-c. Kronborg Castle here is the setting for Shakespeare's *Hamlet*.

eluant var. of ELUENT.

eluate /ˈeljuˌeɪt/ *n. Chem.* a solution or gas stream obtained by elution. [formed as ELUENT]

elucidate /ɪˈluːsɪdeɪt, ɪˈljuːs-/ *v.tr.* throw light on; explain. □□ **elucidation** /-ˈdeɪʃ(ə)n/ *n.* **elucidative** *adj.* **elucidator** *n.* **elucidatory** *adj.* [LL *elucidare* (as E-, LUCID)]

elude /ɪˈluːd, ɪˈljuːd/ *v.tr.* **1** escape adroitly from (a danger, difficulty, pursuer, etc.); dodge. **2** avoid compliance with (a law, request, etc.) or fulfilment of (an obligation). **3** (of a fact, solution, etc.) escape from or baffle (a person's memory or understanding). □□ **elusion** /-ʒ(ə)n/ *n.* **elusory** *adj.* [L *eludere elus-* (as E-, *ludere* play)]

eluent /ˈeljuːənt/ *n.* (also **eluant**) *Chem.* a fluid used for elution. [L *eluere* wash out (as E-, *luere lut-* wash)]

elusive /ɪˈluːsɪv, ɪˈljuːsɪv/ *adj.* **1** difficult to find or catch; tending to elude. **2** difficult to remember or recall. **3** (of an answer etc.) avoiding the point raised; seeking to elude. □□ **elusively** *adv.* **elusiveness** *n.*

elute /ɪˈljuːt/ *v.tr. Chem.* remove (an adsorbed substance) by washing. □□ **elution** *n.* [G *eluieren* (as ELUENT)]

elutriate /ɪˈluːtrɪˌeɪt/ *v.tr. Chem.* separate (lighter and heavier particles in a mixture) by suspension in an upward flow of liquid or gas. □□ **elutriation** /-ˈeɪʃ(ə)n/ *n.* [L *elutriare elutriat-* (as E-, *lutriare* wash)]

elver /ˈelvə(r)/ *n.* a young eel. [var. of *eel-fare* (see FARE) = a brood of young eels]

elves *pl.* of ELF.

elvish see ELF.

Elysium /ɪˈlɪzɪəm/ *n.* **1** (also **Elysian Fields**) *Gk Mythol.* the fields at the ends of the earth to where (according to Homer and Hesiod) certain favoured heroes, exempted from death, were translated by the gods. This concept appears to be a survival from Minoan religion. When a later age concerned itself with the fate of the blessed *dead*, Elysium was transferred to the nether regions, in conformity with Greek ideas and the Homeric picture of the House of Hades. **2** a place or state of ideal happiness. □□ **Elysian** *adj.* [L f. Gk *Elusion (pedion* plain)]

elytron /ˈelɪˌtrɒn/ *n.* (*pl.* **elytra** /-trə/) the outer hard usu. brightly coloured wing-case of a coleopterous insect. [Gk *elutron* sheath]

Elzevir /ˈelzəvɪə(r)/ a family of Dutch printers, 15 of whom were active 1583–1712. Louis (1542–1617), born at Louvain, founded the business at Leiden *c*.1580. Their fame depends largely on their elegant editions of the works of classical authors (1634–6).

em /em/ *n. Printing* **1** a unit for measuring the amount of printed matter in a line, usually equal to the nominal width of capital M. **2** a unit of measurement equal to 12 points. □ **em rule** (or **dash**) a long dash used in punctuation. [name of the letter M]

em- /ɪm, em/ *prefix* assim. form of EN-¹, EN-² before *b*, *p*.

'em /əm/ *pron. colloq.* them (*let 'em all come*). [orig. a form of ME *hem*, dative and accus. 3rd pers. pl. pron.: now regarded as an abbr. of THEM]

emaciate /ɪˈmeɪsɪˌeɪt, ɪˈmeɪʃɪˌeɪt/ *v.tr.* (esp. as **emaciated** *adj.*) make abnormally thin or feeble. □□ **emaciation** /-ˈeɪʃ(ə)n/ *n.* [L *emaciare emaciat-* (as E-, *macies* leanness)]

email /ˈiːmeɪl/ *n.* (also **e-mail**) = *electronic mail*.

emanate /ˈeməˌneɪt/ *v.* **1** *intr.* (usu. foll. by *from*) (of an idea, rumour, etc.) issue, originate (from a source). **2** *intr.* (usu. foll. by *from*) (of gas, light, etc.) proceed, issue. **3** *tr.* emit; send forth. [L *emanare* flow out]

emanation /ˌeməˈneɪʃ(ə)n/ *n.* **1** the act or process of emanating. **2** something that emanates from a source (esp. of virtues, qualities, etc.). **3** *Chem.* a radioactive gas formed by radioactive decay. □□ **emanative** *adj.* [LL *emanatio* (as EMANATE)]

emancipate /ɪˈmænsɪˌpeɪt/ *v.tr.* **1** free from restraint, esp. legal, social, or political. **2** (usu. as **emancipated** *adj.*) cause to be less inhibited by moral or social convention. **3** free from slavery. □□ **emancipation** /-ˈpeɪʃ(ə)n/ *n.* **emancipator** *n.* **emancipatory** *adj.* [L *emancipare* transfer property (as E-, *manus* hand + *capere* take)]

emasculate *v. & adj.* —*v.tr.* /ɪˈmæskjʊˌleɪt/ **1** deprive of force or vigour; make feeble or ineffective. **2** castrate. —*adj.* /ɪˈmæskjʊlət/ **1** deprived of force or vigour. **2** castrated. **3** effeminate. □□ **emasculation** /-ˈleɪʃ(ə)n/ *n.* **emasculator** *n.* **emasculatory** /-lətərɪ/ *adj.* [L *emasculatus* past part. of *emasculare* (as E-, *masculus* dimin. of *mas* male)]

embalm /ɪmˈbɑːm/ *v.tr.* **1** preserve (a corpse) from decay orig. with spices, now by means of arterial injection. **2** preserve from oblivion. **3** endue with balmy fragrance. □□ **embalmer** *n.* **embalmment** *n.* [ME f. OF *embaumer* (as EN-¹, BALM)]

embank /ɪmˈbæŋk/ *v.tr.* shut in or confine (a river etc.) with an artificial bank.

embankment /ɪmˈbæŋkmənt/ *n.* an earth or stone bank for keeping back water, or for carrying a road or railway.

embargo /emˈbɑːɡəʊ, ɪm-/ *n. & v.* —*n.* (pl. **-oes**) **1** an order of a State forbidding foreign ships to enter, or any ships to leave, its ports. **2** an official suspension of commerce or other activity (*be under an embargo*). **3** an impediment. —*v.tr.* (**-oes, -oed**) **1** place (ships, trade, etc.) under embargo. **2** seize (a ship, goods) for State service. [Sp. f. *embargar* arrest f. Rmc (as IN-², BAR¹)]

embark /ɪmˈbɑːk/ *v.* **1** *tr. & intr.* (often foll. by *for*) put or go on board a ship or aircraft (to a destination). **2** *intr.* (foll. by *on*, *upon*) engage in an activity or undertaking. □□ **embarkation** /ˌembɑːˈkeɪʃ(ə)n/ *n.* (in sense 1). [F *embarquer* (as IN-², BARK³)]

embarras de choix /ˌɑ̃bæˌrɑː də ˈʃwɑː/ *n.* (also **embarras de richesse(s)** /riːˈʃes/) more choices than one needs or can deal with. [F, = embarrassment of choice, riches]

embarrass /ɪmˈbærəs/ *v.tr.* **1** cause (a person) to feel awkward or self-conscious or ashamed. **2** (as **embarrassed** *adj.*) encumbered with debts. **3** encumber, impede. **4** complicate (a question etc.). **5** perplex. □□ **embarrassedly** *adv.* **embarrassingly** *adv.* **embarrassment** *n.* [F *embarrasser* (orig. = hamper) f. Sp. *embarazar* f. It. *imbarrare* bar in (as IN-², BAR¹)]

embassy /ˈembəsɪ/ *n.* (pl. **-ies**) **1 a** the residence or offices of an ambassador. **b** the ambassador and staff attached to an embassy. **2** a deputation or mission to a foreign country. [earlier *ambassy* f. OF *ambassée* etc. f. med.L *ambasciata* f. Rmc (as AMBASSADOR)]

embattle /ɪmˈbæt(ə)l/ *v.tr.* **1 a** set (an army etc.) in battle array. **b** fortify against attack. **2** provide (a building or wall) with

battlements. **3** (as **embattled** *adj.*) **a** prepared or arrayed for battle. **b** involved in a conflict or difficult undertaking. **c** *Heraldry* like battlements in form. [ME f. OF *embataillier* (as EN-¹, BATTLE): see BATTLEMENT]

embay /ɪmˈbeɪ/ *v.tr.* **1** enclose in or as in a bay; shut in. **2** form (a coast) into bays. □□ **embayment** *n.*

embed /ɪmˈbed/ *v.tr.* (also **imbed**) (**-bedded, -bedding**) **1** (esp. as **embedded** *adj.*) fix firmly in a surrounding mass (*embedded in concrete*). **2** (of a mass) surround so as to fix firmly. **3** place in or as in a bed. □□ **embedment** *n.*

embellish /ɪmˈbelɪʃ/ *v.tr.* **1** beautify, adorn. **2** add interest to (a narrative) with fictitious additions. □□ **embellisher** *n.* **embellishment** *n.* [ME f. OF *embellir* (as EN-¹, *bel* handsome f. L *bellus*)]

ember¹ /ˈembə(r)/ *n.* **1** (usu. in *pl.*) a small piece of glowing coal or wood in a dying fire. **2** an almost extinct residue of a past activity, feeling, etc. [OE *æmyrge* f. Gmc]

ember² /ˈembə(r)/ *n.* (in full **ember-goose**) = *great northern diver*. [Norw. *emmer*]

ember days /ˈembə/ *n.pl.* a group of three days in each season, observed as days of fasting and prayer in some Churches. Their early history and original purpose is obscure; at first there were apparently only three groups, perhaps taken over from pagan religious observances connected with seed-time, harvest, and autumn vintage. They are now associated almost entirely with the ordination of ministers. [OE *ymbren* (n.), perh. f. *ymbryne* period f. *ymb* about + *ryne* course]

embezzle /ɪmˈbez(ə)l/ *v.tr.* (also *absol.*) divert (money etc.) fraudulently to one's own use. □□ **embezzlement** *n.* **embezzler** *n.* [AF *embesiler* (as EN-¹, OF *besillier* maltreat, ravage, of unkn. orig.)]

embitter /ɪmˈbɪtə(r)/ *v.tr.* **1** arouse bitter feelings in (a person). **2** make more bitter or painful. **3** render (a person or feelings) hostile. □□ **embitterment** *n.*

emblazon /ɪmˈbleɪz(ə)n/ *v.tr.* **1 a** portray conspicuously, as on a heraldic shield. **b** adorn (a shield) with heraldic devices. **2** adorn brightly and conspicuously. **3** celebrate, extol. □□ **emblazonment** *n.*

emblem /ˈembləm/ *n.* **1** a symbol or representation typifying or identifying an institution, quality, etc. **2** (foll. by *of*) (of a person) the type (*the very emblem of courage*). **3** a heraldic device or symbolic object as a distinctive badge. □□ **emblematic** /-ˈmætɪk/ *adj.* **emblematical** /-ˈmætɪk(ə)l/ *adj.* **emblematically** /-ˈmætɪkəlɪ/ *adv.* [ME f. L *emblema* f. Gk *emblēma -matos* insertion f. *emballō* throw in (as EN-¹, *ballō* throw)]

emblematize /ɪmˈblemaˌtaɪz/ *v.tr.* (also **-ise**) **1** serve as an emblem of. **2** represent by an emblem.

emblements /ˈemblmənts/ *n.pl. Law* crops normally harvested annually, regarded as personal property. [ME f. OF *emblaement* f. *emblaier* (as EN-¹, *blé* corn)]

embody /ɪmˈbɒdɪ/ *v.tr.* (**-ies, -ied**) **1** give a concrete or discernible form to (an idea, concept, etc.). **2** (of a thing or person) be an expression of (an idea etc.). **3** express tangibly (*courage embodied in heroic actions*). **4** form into a body. **5** include, comprise. **6** provide (a spirit) with bodily form. □□ **embodiment** *n.*

embolden /ɪmˈbəʊld(ə)n/ *v.tr.* (often foll. by *to* + infin.) make bold; encourage.

embolism /ˈembəˌlɪz(ə)m/ *n.* an obstruction of any artery by a clot of blood, air-bubble, etc. [ME, = 'intercalation' f. LL *embolismus* f. Gk *embolismos* f. *emballō* (as EMBLEM)]

embolus /ˈembələs/ *n.* (pl. **emboli** /-ˌlaɪ/) an object causing an embolism. [L, = piston, f. Gk *embolos* peg, stopper]

embonpoint /ˌɑ̃bɔ̃ˈpwæ̃/ *n.* plumpness (of a person). [F *en bon point* in good condition]

embosom /ɪmˈbʊz(ə)m/ *v.tr. literary* **1** embrace. **2** enclose, surround.

emboss /ɪmˈbɒs/ *v.tr.* **1** carve or mould in relief. **2** form figures etc. so that they stand out on (a surface). **3** make protuberant. □□ **embosser** *n.* **embossment** *n.* [ME, f. OF (as EN-¹, BOSS²)]

embouchure /ˈɒmbuˌʃʊə(r)/ *n.* **1** *Mus.* **a** the mode of applying the mouth to the mouthpiece of a brass or wind instrument. **b** the mouthpiece of some instruments. **2** the mouth of a river. **3**

the opening of a valley. [F f. *s'emboucher* discharge itself by the mouth (as EN-1, *bouche* mouth)]

embowel /ɪmˈbaʊəl/ *v.tr.* (**embowelled, embowelling**; US **emboweled, emboweling**) *archaic* = DISEMBOWEL. [OF *emboweler* f. *esboueler* (as EX-1, BOWEL)]

embower /ɪmˈbaʊə(r)/ *v.tr. literary* enclose as in a bower.

embrace /ɪmˈbreɪs/ *v. & n.* —*v.tr.* **1 a** hold (a person) closely in the arms, esp. as a sign of affection. **b** (*absol.*, of two people) hold each other closely. **2** clasp, enclose. **3** accept eagerly (an offer, opportunity, etc.). **4** adopt (a course of action, doctrine, cause, etc.). **5** include, comprise. **6** take in with the eye or mind. —*n.* an act of embracing; holding in the arms. □□ **embraceable** *adj.* **embracement** *n.* **embracer** *n.* [ME f. OF *embracer*, ult. f. L *in-* IN-1 + *bracchium* arm]

embranchment /ɪmˈbrɑːntʃmənt/ *n.* a branching-out (of the arm of a river etc.). [F *embranchement* BRANCH (as EN-1, BRANCH)]

embrasure /ɪmˈbreɪʒə(r)/ *n.* **1** the bevelling of a wall at the sides of a door or window; splaying. **2** a small opening in a parapet of a fortified building, splayed on the inside. □□ **embrasured** *adj.* [F f. *embraser* splay, of unkn. orig.]

embrittle /ɪmˈbrɪt(ə)l/ *v.tr.* make brittle. □□ **embrittlement** *n.*

embrocation /ˌembrəʊˈkeɪʃ(ə)n/ *n.* a liquid used for rubbing on the body to relieve muscular pain etc. [F *embrocation* or med.L *embrocatio* ult. f. Gk *embrokhē* lotion]

embroider /ɪmˈbrɔɪdə(r)/ *v.tr.* **1** (also *absol.*) **a** decorate (cloth etc.) with needlework. **b** create (a design) in this way. **2** add interest to (a narrative) with fictitious additions. □□ **embroiderer** *n.* [ME f. AF *enbrouder* (as EN-1, OF *brouder, broisder* f. Gmc)]

embroidery /ɪmˈbrɔɪdərɪ/ *n.* (*pl.* **-ies**) **1** the art of embroidering. **2** embroidered work; a piece of this. **3** unnecessary or extravagant ornament. [ME f. AF *enbrouderie* (as EMBROIDER)]

embroil /ɪmˈbrɔɪl/ *v.tr.* **1** (often foll. by *with*) involve (a person) in conflict or difficulties. **2** bring (affairs) into a state of confusion. □□ **embroilment** *n.* [F *embrouiller* (as EN-1, BROIL2)]

embryo /ˈembrɪəʊ/ *n.* (*pl.* **-os**) **1 a** an unborn or unhatched offspring. **b** a human offspring in the first eight weeks from conception. **2** a rudimentary plant contained in a seed. **3** a thing in a rudimentary stage. **4** (*attrib.*) undeveloped, immature. □ **in embryo** undeveloped. □□ **embryoid** *adj.* **embryonal** /ˈembrɪən(ə)l/ *adj.* **embryonic** /ˌembrɪˈɒnɪk/ *adj.* **embryonically** /-ˈɒnɪkəlɪ/ *adv.* [LL *embryo -onis* f. Gk *embruon* foetus (as EN-2, *bruō* swell, grow)]

embryo- /ˈembrɪəʊ/ *comb. form* embryo.

embryogenesis /ˌembrɪəʊˈdʒenɪsɪs/ *n.* the formation of an embryo.

embryology /ˌembrɪˈɒlədʒɪ/ *n.* the study of embryos. □□ **embryologic** /-brɪəˈlɒdʒɪk/ *adj.* **embryological** /-brɪəˈlɒdʒɪk(ə)l/ *adj.* **embryologically** /-brɪəˈlɒdʒɪkəlɪ/ *adv.* **embryologist** *n.*

embus /ɪmˈbʌs/ *v.* (**embused, embusing** or **embussed, embussing**) *Mil.* **1** *tr.* put (persons or equipment) into a motor vehicle. **2** *intr.* board a motor vehicle.

emcee /emˈsiː/ *n. & v. colloq.* —*n.* a master of ceremonies or compère. —*v.tr. & intr.* (**emcees, emceed**) compère. [the letters MC]

-eme /iːm/ *suffix Linguistics* forming nouns denoting units of structure etc. (*grapheme; morpheme*). [F *-ème* unit f. Gk *-ēma*]

emend /ɪˈmend/ *v.tr.* edit (a text etc.) to remove errors and corruptions. □□ **emendation** /ˌiːmenˈdeɪʃ(ə)n/ *n.* **emendator** /ˈiːmenˌdeɪtə(r)/ *n.* **emendatory** *adj.* [ME f. L *emendare* (as E-, *menda* fault)]

emerald /ˈemər(ə)ld/ *n.* **1** a bright-green precious stone, a variety of beryl. **2** (also **emerald green**) the colour of this. □ **Emerald Isle** *literary* Ireland. □□ **emeraldine** /-ˌdaɪn, -dɪn/ *adj.* [ME f. OF *emeraude, esm-*, ult. f. Gk *smaragdos*]

emerge /ɪˈmɜːdʒ/ *v.intr.* (often foll. by *from*) **1** come up or out into view, esp. when formerly concealed. **2** come up out of a liquid. **3** (of facts, circumstances, etc.) come to light, become known, esp. as a result of inquiry etc. **4** become recognized or prominent (*emerged as a leading contender*). **5** (of a question,

difficulty, etc.) become apparent. **6** survive (an ordeal etc.) with a specified result (*emerged unscathed*). □□ **emergence** *n.* [L *emergere emers-* (as E-, *mergere* dip)]

emergency /ɪˈmɜːdʒənsɪ/ *n.* (*pl.* **-ies**) **1** a sudden state of danger, conflict, etc., requiring immediate action. **2 a** a medical condition requiring immediate treatment. **b** a patient with such a condition. **3** (*attrib.*) characterized by or for use in an emergency. **4** *Austral. Sport* a reserve player. □ **state of emergency** a condition of danger or disaster affecting a country, esp. with normal constitutional procedures suspended. [med.L *emergentia* (as EMERGE)]

emergent /ɪˈmɜːdʒ(ə)nt/ *adj.* **1** becoming apparent; emerging. **2** (of a nation) newly formed or made independent.

emeritus /ɪˈmerɪtəs/ *adj.* **1** retired and retaining one's title as an honour (*emeritus professor; professor emeritus*). **2** honourably discharged from service. [L, past part. of *emerēri* (as E-, *merēri* earn)]

emersion /ɪˈmɜːʃ(ə)n/ *n.* **1** the act or an instance of emerging. **2** *Astron.* the reappearance of a celestial body after its eclipse or occultation. [LL *emersio* (as EMERGE)]

Emerson /ˈeməs(ə)n/, Ralph Waldo (1803–82), American philosopher and poet, who was ordained and became a pastor in Boston, but owing to his sceptical views on the nature of the sacraments resigned and left for Europe (1832). In England he met Coleridge, Wordsworth, and Carlyle through whom he became associated with German idealism. On his return he evolved the new quasi-religious concept of transcendentalism which found expression in his essay *Nature* (1836); his mystic idealism and reverence for nature was immensely influential in American life and thought. He was involved in the anti-slavery campaign and continued to write poems and prose until his last decade, when his mental faculties sharply declined.

emery /ˈemərɪ/ *n.* **1** a coarse rock of corundum and magnetite or haematite used for polishing metal or other hard materials. **2** (*attrib.*) covered with emery. □ **emery-board** a strip of thin wood or board coated with emery or another abrasive, used as a nail-file. **emery-paper** cloth or paper covered with emery, used for polishing or cleaning metals etc. [F *émeri(l)* f. It. *smeriglio* ult. f. Gk *smuris, smēris* polishing powder]

emetic /ɪˈmetɪk/ *adj. & n.* —*adj.* that causes vomiting. —*n.* an emetic medicine. [Gk *emetikos* f. *emeō* vomit]

EMF *abbr.* electromotive force.

-emia *US var.* of -AEMIA.

emigrant /ˈemɪgrənt/ *n. & adj.* —*n.* a person who emigrates. —*adj.* emigrating.

emigrate /ˈemɪgreɪt/ *v.* **1** *intr.* leave one's own country to settle in another. **2** *tr.* assist (a person) to emigrate. □□ **emigration** /-ˈgreɪʃ(ə)n/ *n.* **emigratory** *adj.* [L *emigrare emigrat-* (as E-, *migrare* depart)]

émigré /ˈemɪˌgreɪ/ *n.* an emigrant, esp. a political exile. [F, past part. of *émigrer* EMIGRATE]

Emilia-Romagna /eˌmiːljəʊˈmænjə/ a region of north Italy; pop. (1981) 3,957,500; capital, Bologna.

eminence /ˈemɪnəns/ *n.* **1** distinction; recognized superiority. **2** a piece of rising ground. **3** (**Eminence**) a title used in addressing or referring to a cardinal (*Your Eminence; His Eminence*). **4** an important person. [L *eminentia* (as EMINENT)]

éminence grise /ˌeɪmɪˌnãs ˈgriːz/ *n.* **1** a person who exercises power or influence without holding office. **2** a confidential agent. [F, = grey cardinal (see EMINENCE): orig. applied to Cardinal Richelieu's private secretary, Père Joseph d. 1638]

eminent /ˈemɪnənt/ *adj.* **1** distinguished, notable. **2** (of qualities) remarkable in degree. □ **eminent domain** sovereign control over all property in a State, with the right of expropriation. □□ **eminently** *adv.* [ME f. L *eminēre eminent-* jut]

emir /eˈmɪə(r)/ *n.* **1** a title of various Muslim rulers. **2** *archaic* a male descendant of Muhammad. [F *émir* f. Arab. ʾamīr: cf. AMIR]

emirate /ˈemɪrət/ *n.* the rank, domain, or reign of an emir.

emissary /ˈemɪsərɪ/ *n.* (*pl.* **-ies**) a person sent on a special mission (usu. diplomatic, formerly usu. odious or underhand). [L *emissarius* scout, spy (as EMIT)]

emission /ɪˈmɪʃ(ə)n/ n. **1** (often foll. by of) the process or an act of emitting. **2** a thing emitted. [L emissio (as EMIT)]

emissive /ɪˈmɪsɪv/ adj. having the power to radiate light, heat, etc. □□ **emissivity** /ˌiːmɪˈsɪvɪtɪ/ n.

emit /ɪˈmɪt/ v.tr. (**emitted**, **emitting**) **1 a** send out (heat, light, vapour, etc.). **b** discharge from the body. **2** utter (a cry etc.). [L emittere emiss- (as E-, mittere send)]

emitter /ɪˈmɪtə(r)/ n. that which emits, esp. a region in a transistor producing carriers of current.

Emmental /ˈemənˌtɑːl/ n. (also **Emmenthal**) a kind of hard Swiss cheese with many holes in it, similar to Gruyère. [G Emmentaler f. Emmental in Switzerland]

emmer /ˈemə(r)/ n. a kind of wheat, Triticum dicoccum, grown mainly for fodder. [G dial.]

emmet /ˈemɪt/ n. archaic or dial. an ant. [OE ǣmete: see ANT]

Emmy /ˈemɪ/ n. (pl. **-ies**) (in the US) any of several statuettes awarded by the American Academy of Television Arts and Sciences to an outstanding television programme or performer. Such awards have been made annually since 1949. [perh. f. Immy = image orthicon tube]

emollient /ɪˈmɒlɪənt/ adj. & n. —adj. that softens or soothes the skin. —n. an emollient agent. □□ **emollience** n. [L emollire (as E-, mollis soft)]

emolument /ɪˈmɒljʊmənt/ n. a salary, fee, or profit from employment or office. [ME f. OF emolument or L emolumentum, orig. prob. 'payment for corn-grinding', f. emolere (as E-, molere grind)]

emote /ɪˈməʊt/ v.intr. colloq. show excessive emotion. □□ **emoter** n. [back-form. f. EMOTION]

emotion /ɪˈməʊʃ(ə)n/ n. a strong mental or instinctive feeling such as love or fear. [earlier = agitation, disturbance of the mind, f. F émotion f. émouvoir excite]

emotional /ɪˈməʊʃən(ə)l/ adj. **1** of or relating to the emotions. **2** (of a person) liable to excessive emotion. **3** expressing or based on emotion (an emotional appeal). **4** likely to excite emotion (an emotional issue). □□ **emotionalism** n. **emotionalist** n. **emotionality** /-ˈnælɪtɪ/ n. **emotionalize** v.tr. (also **-ise**). **emotionally** adv.

emotive /ɪˈməʊtɪv/ adj. **1** of or characterized by emotion. **2** tending to excite emotion. **3** arousing feeling; not purely descriptive. □□ **emotively** adv. **emotiveness** n. **emotivity** /ˌiːməʊˈtɪvɪtɪ/ n. [L emovēre emot- (as E-, movēre move)]

empanel /ɪmˈpæn(ə)l/ v.tr. (also **impanel**) (**-panelled**, **-panelling**; US **-paneled**, **-paneling**) enrol or enter on a panel (those eligible for jury service). □□ **empanelment** n. [AF empaneller (as EN-¹, PANEL)]

empathize /ˈempəˌθaɪz/ v. Psychol. **1** intr. (usu. foll. by with) exercise empathy. **2** tr. treat with empathy.

empathy /ˈempəθɪ/ n. Psychol. the power of identifying oneself mentally with (and so fully comprehending) a person or object of contemplation. □□ **empathetic** /-ˈθetɪk/ adj. **empathetically** /-ˈθetɪkəlɪ/ adv. **empathic** /emˈpæθɪk/ adj. **empathically** /emˈpæθ-/ adv. **empathist** n. [transl. G Einfühlung f. ein in + Fühlung feeling, after Gk empatheia: see SYMPATHY]

Empedocles /emˈpedəˌkliːz/ (c.493–c.433 BC) Greek philosopher from Sicily, whose theory of matter was a step on the road towards atomism. His hexameter poem On Nature teaches that the universe is composed of the four imperishable elements of fire, air, water, and earth, which mingle and separate under the influence of the opposing principles of Love and Strife. He was also a religious teacher, miracle-worker, statesman, and orator. According to legend he leapt into the crater of Mount Etna in Sicily in order that he might be thought a god.

empennage /emˈpenɪdʒ/ n. Aeron. an arrangement of stabilizing surfaces at the tail of an aircraft. [F f. empenner to feather (an arrow)]

emperor /ˈempərə(r)/ n. **1** the sovereign of an empire. **2** a sovereign of higher rank than a king. □ **emperor moth** a large moth, Saturnia pavonia, of the silk-moth family, with eye-spots on all four wings. **emperor penguin** the largest known penguin,

Aptenodytes forsteri, of the Antarctic. □□ **emperorship** n. [ME f. OF emperere, empereor f. L imperator -oris f. imperare command]

emphasis /ˈemfəsɪs/ n. (pl. **emphases** /-ˌsiːz/) **1** special importance or prominence attached to a thing, fact, idea, etc. (emphasis on economy). **2** stress laid on a word or words to indicate special meaning or importance. **3** vigour or intensity of expression, feeling, action, etc. **4** prominence, sharpness of contour. [L f. Gk f. emphainō exhibit (as EN-², phainō show)]

emphasize /ˈemfəˌsaɪz/ v.tr. (also **-ise**) **1** bring (a thing, fact, etc.) into special prominence. **2** lay stress on (a word in speaking).

emphatic /ɪmˈfætɪk/ adj. **1** (of language, tone, or gesture) forcibly expressive. **2** of words: **a** bearing the stress. **b** used to give emphasis. **3** expressing oneself with emphasis. **4** (of an action or process) forcible, significant. □□ **emphatically** adv. [LL emphaticus f. Gk emphasukos (as EMPHASIS)]

emphysema /ˌemfɪˈsiːmə/ n. **1** enlargement of the air sacs of the lungs causing breathlessness. **2** a swelling caused by the presence of air in the connective tissues of the body. [LL f. Gk emphusēma f. emphusaō puff up]

empire /ˈempaɪə(r)/ n. **1** an extensive group of States or countries under a single supreme authority, esp. an emperor. **2 a** supreme dominion. **b** (often foll. by over) archaic absolute control. **3** a large commercial organization etc. owned or directed by one person or group. **4** (**the Empire**) hist. **a** the British Empire. **b** the Holy Roman Empire. **c** the period of the reign of Napoleon I as Emperor of the French (1804–15), also called 'First Empire' to distinguish it from the 'Second Empire' of Napoleon III (1852–70). **5** a type or period of government in which the sovereign is called emperor. **6** (**Empire**) (attrib.) **a** see EMPIRE STYLE. **b** Brit. denoting produce from the Commonwealth. □ **empire-builder** a person who deliberately acquires extra territory, authority, etc., esp. unnecessarily. **Empire Day** hist. the former name of Commonwealth Day, orig. 24 May. [ME f. OF f. L imperium rel. to imperare: see EMPEROR]

Empire State Building a skyscraper in Fifth Avenue, New York City, which was for long the tallest building in the world. When first erected, in 1930–1, it measured 381 m (1,250 ft.); the addition of a television mast in 1951 brought its height to 449 m (1,472 ft.). It is named after New York, the Empire State.

Empire style a style of furniture, interior decoration, and dress which started in Paris after the French Revolution and spread through Europe, corresponding to the Regency style in England. Basically the style is neoclassical but with an increment of archaeological interest, an attempt to copy what was known of ancient furniture and motifs, with particular affectation of Egyptian motifs probably reflecting interest in Napoleon's Egyptian campaigns. In women's dress there was a distinctive high-waisted fashion embellished with dazzling embroidery.

empiric /ɪmˈpɪrɪk/ adj. & n. —adj. = EMPIRICAL. —n. archaic **1** a person relying solely on experiment. **2** a quack doctor. □□ **empiricism** n. **empiricist** n. [L empiricus f. Gk empeirikos f. empeiria experience f. empeiros skilled]

empirical /ɪmˈpɪrɪk(ə)l/ adj. **1** based or acting on observation or experiment, not on theory. **2** Philos. regarding sense-data as valid information. **3** deriving knowledge from experience alone. □ **empirical formula** Chem. a formula showing the constituents of a compound but not their configuration. □□ **empirically** adv.

emplacement /ɪmˈpleɪsmənt/ n. **1** the act or an instance of putting in position. **2** a platform or defended position where a gun is placed for firing. **3** situation, position. [F (as EN-¹, PLACE)]

emplane /ɪmˈpleɪn/ v.intr. & tr. (also **enplane** /ɪn-/) go or put on board an aeroplane.

employ /ɪmˈplɔɪ/ v. & n. —v.tr. **1** use the services of (a person) in return for payment; keep (a person) in one's service. **2** (often foll. by for, in, on) use (a thing, time, energy, etc.) esp. to good effect. **3** (often foll. by in) keep (a person) occupied. —n. the state of being employed, esp. for wages. □ **in the employ of** employed by. □□ **employable** adj. **employability** /-ˈbɪlɪtɪ/ n. **employer** n. [ME f. OF employer ult. f. L implicari be involved f. implicare enfold: see IMPLICATE]

employee /ˌemplɔɪˈiː, -ˈplɔɪ/ n. (US also **employe**) a person employed for wages or salary, esp. at non-executive level.

employment /ɪmˈplɔɪmənt/ n. **1** the act of employing or the state of being employed. **2** a person's regular trade or profession. □ **employment agency** a business that finds employers or employees for those seeking them. **employment office** (formerly **employment exchange**) Brit. any of a number of government offices concerned with advising and finding work for the unemployed.

empolder var. of IMPOLDER.

emporium /emˈpɔːrɪəm/ n. (pl. **emporia** /-rɪə/ or **-ums**) **1** a large retail store selling a wide variety of goods. **2** a centre of commerce, a market. [L f. Gk emporion f. emporos merchant]

empower /ɪmˈpaʊə(r)/ v.tr. (foll. by to + infin.) **1** authorize, license. **2** give power to; make able. □□ **empowerment** n.

empress /ˈemprɪs/ n. **1** the wife or widow of an emperor. **2** a woman emperor. [ME f. OF emperesse fem. of emperere EMPEROR]

Empson /ˈemps(ə)n/, Sir William (1906–84), English poet, whose intricate closely reasoned poems reflect his training as a mathematician. His Seven Types of Ambiguity (1930) was an influential piece of literary criticism.

empty /ˈemptɪ/ adj., v., & n. —adj. (**emptier**, **emptiest**) **1** containing nothing. **2** (of a house etc.) unoccupied or unfurnished. **3** (of a transport vehicle etc.) without a load, passengers, etc. **4 a** meaningless, hollow, insincere (empty threats; an empty gesture). **b** without substance or purpose (an empty existence). **5** colloq. hungry. **6** (foll. by of) devoid, lacking. —v. (**-ies**, **-ied**) **1** tr. **a** make empty; remove the contents of. **b** (foll. by of) deprive of certain contents (emptied the room of its chairs). **2** tr. (often foll. by into) transfer (the contents of a container). **3** intr. become empty. **4** intr. (usu. foll. by into) (of a river) discharge itself (into the sea etc.). —n. (pl. **-ies**) colloq. a container (esp. a bottle) left empty of its contents. □ **empty-handed 1** bringing or taking nothing. **2** having achieved or obtained nothing. **empty-headed** foolish; lacking common sense. **empty-nester** US either of a couple whose children have grown up and left home. **on an empty stomach** see STOMACH. □□ **emptily** adv. **emptiness** n. [OE ǣmtig, ǣmetig f. ǣmetta leisure]

Empty Quarter see GREAT SANDY DESERT.

empurple /ɪmˈpɜːp(ə)l/ v.tr. **1** make purple or red. **2** make angry.

empyema /ˌempaɪˈiːmə, ˌempɪ-/ n. a collection of pus in a cavity, esp. in the pleura. [LL f. Gk empyēma f. empyeō suppurate (as EN-², puon pus)]

empyrean /ˌempaɪˈriːən, ˌempɪ-/ n. & adj. —n. **1** the highest heaven, as the sphere of fire in ancient cosmology or as the abode of God in early Christianity. **2** the visible heavens. —adj. of the empyrean. □□ **empyreal** /ˌempaɪˈriːəl, ˌempɪ-, emˈpɪr-/ adj. [med.L empyreus f. Gk empyrios (as EN-², pur fire)]

EMS abbr. European Monetary System.

EMU abbr. economic and monetary union, a programme for full economic unity in the EC, based on the phased introduction of a common currency.

emu /ˈiːmjuː/ n. a large flightless bird, Dromaius novaehollandiae, native to Australia, and capable of running at high speed. [earlier emia, eme f. Port. ema]

e.m.u. abbr. electromagnetic unit(s).

emulate /ˈemjʊˌleɪt/ v.tr. **1** try to equal or excel. **2** imitate zealously. **3** rival. □□ **emulation** /-ˈleɪʃ(ə)n/ n. **emulative** /-lətɪv/ adj. **emulator** n. [L aemulari (as EMULOUS)]

emulous /ˈemjʊləs/ adj. **1** (usu. foll. by of) seeking to emulate. **2** actuated by a spirit of rivalry. □□ **emulously** adv. [ME f. L aemulus rival]

emulsifier /ɪˈmʌlsɪˌfaɪə(r)/ n. **1** any substance that stabilizes an emulsion, esp. a food additive used to stabilize processed foods. **2** an apparatus used for producing an emulsion.

emulsify /ɪˈmʌlsɪˌfaɪ/ v.tr. (**-ies**, **-ied**) convert into an emulsion. □□ **emulsifiable** adj. **emulsification** /-fɪˈkeɪʃ(ə)n/ n.

emulsion /ɪˈmʌlʃ(ə)n/ n. **1** a fine dispersion of one liquid in another, esp. as paint, medicine, etc. **2** a mixture of a silver compound suspended in gelatin etc. for coating plates or films. □ **emulsion paint** a water-thinned paint containing a non-volatile substance, e.g. synthetic resin, as its binding medium. □□ **emulsionize** v.tr. (also **-ise**). **emulsive** adj. [F émulsion or mod.L emulsio f. emulgēre (as E-, mulgēre muls- to milk)]

en /en/ n. Printing a unit of measurement equal to half an em. □ **en rule** (or **dash**) a short dash used in punctuation. [name of the letter N]

en-¹ /en, ɪn/ prefix (also **em-** before b, p) forming verbs, = IN-¹: **1** from nouns, meaning 'put into or on' (engulf; entrust; embed). **2** from nouns or adjectives, meaning 'bring into the condition of' (enslave); often with the suffix -en (enlighten). **3** from verbs: **a** in the sense 'in, into, on' (enfold). **b** as an intensive (entangle). [from or after F en- f. L in-]

en-² /en, ɪn/ prefix (also **em-** before b, p) in, inside (energy; enthusiasm). [Gk]

-en¹ /ən/ suffix forming verbs: **1** from adjectives, usu. meaning 'make or become so or more so' (deepen; fasten; moisten). **2** from nouns (happen; strengthen). [OE -nian f. Gmc]

-en² /ən/ suffix (also **-n**) forming adjectives from nouns, meaning: **1** made or consisting of (often with extended and figurative senses) (wooden). **2** resembling or of the nature of (golden; silvern). [OE f. Gmc]

-en³ /ən/ suffix (also **-n**) forming past participles of strong verbs: **1** as a regular inflection (spoken; sworn). **2** with restricted sense (drunken). [OE f. Gmc]

-en⁴ /ən/ suffix forming the plural of a few nouns (children; brethren; oxen). [ME reduction of OE -an]

-en⁵ /ən/ suffix forming diminutives of nouns (chicken; maiden). [OE f. Gmc]

-en⁶ /ən/ suffix **1** forming feminine nouns (vixen). **2** forming abstract nouns (burden). [OE f. Gmc]

enable /ɪˈneɪb(ə)l/ v.tr. **1** (foll. by to + infin.) give (a person etc.) the means or authority to do something. **2** make possible. **3** esp. Computing make (a device) operational; switch on. □ **enabling act 1** a statute empowering a person or body to take certain action. **2** US a statute legalizing something otherwise unlawful. □□ **enabler** n.

enact /ɪˈnækt/ v.tr. **1 a** (often foll. by that + clause) ordain, decree. **b** make (a bill etc.) law. **2** play (a part or scene on stage or in life). □□ **enactable** adj. **enaction** n. **enactive** adj. **enactor** n. **enactory** adj.

enactment /ɪˈnæktmənt/ n. **1** a law enacted. **2** the process of enacting.

enamel /ɪˈnæm(ə)l/ n. & v. —n. **1** a glasslike opaque or semi-transparent coating on metallic or other hard surfaces for ornament or as a preservative lining. **2 a** a smooth hard coating. **b** a cosmetic simulating this. **3** the hard glossy natural coating over the crown of a tooth. **4** painting done in enamel. **5** poet. a smooth bright surface colouring, verdure, etc. —v.tr. (**enamelled**, **enamelling**; US **enameled**, **enameling**) **1** inlay or encrust (a metal etc.) with enamel. **2** portray (figures etc.) with enamel. **3** archaic adorn with varied colours. □ **enamel paint** a paint that dries to give a smooth hard coat. □□ **enameller** n. **enamelwork** n. [ME f. AF enameler, enamailler (as EN-¹, OF esmail f. Gmc)]

enamelware /ɪˈnæm(ə)lˌweə(r)/ n. enamelled kitchenware.

enamour /ɪˈnæmə(r)/ v.tr. (US **enamor**) (usu. in passive; foll. by of) **1** inspire with love or liking. **2** charm, delight. [ME f. OF enamourer f. amourer (as EN-¹, AMOUR)]

enanthema /ˌenænˈθiːmə/ n. Med. an eruption occurring on a mucus-secreting surface such as the inside of the mouth. [mod.L f. Gk enanthēma eruption (as EN-¹, EXANTHEMA)]

enantiomer /enˈæntɪəmə(r)/ n. Chem. a molecule with a mirror image. □□ **enantiomeric** /-ˈmerɪk/ adj. [Gk enantios opposite + -MER]

enantiomorph /enˈæntɪəˌmɔːf/ n. a mirror image; a form (esp. of a crystal structure etc.) related to another as an object is to its mirror image. □□ **enantiomorphic** /-ˈmɔːfɪk/ adj. **enantiomorphism** /-ˈmɔːfɪz(ə)m/ n. **enantiomorphous** /-ˈmɔːfəs/ adj. [G f. Gk enantios opposite + morphē form]

enarthrosis /ˌenɑːˈθrəʊsɪs/ n. (pl. **enarthroses** /-siːz/) Anat. a ball-and-socket joint. [Gk f. *enarthros* jointed (as EN-², *arthron* joint)]

en bloc /ã ˈblɒk/ *adv.* in a block; all at the same time; wholesale. [F]

en brosse /ã ˈbrɒs/ *adj.* (of hair) cut short and bristly. [F]

encaenia /enˈsiːnɪə/ *n.* **1** (at Oxford University) an annual celebration in memory of founders and benefactors. **2** a dedication festival. [L f. Gk *egkainia* (as EN-², *kainos* new)]

encage /ɪnˈkeɪdʒ/ *v.tr.* confine in or as in a cage.

encamp /ɪnˈkæmp/ *v.tr.* & *intr.* **1** settle in a military camp. **2** lodge in the open in tents.

encampment /ɪnˈkæmpmənt/ *n.* **1** a place where troops etc. are encamped. **2** the process of setting up a camp.

encapsulate /ɪnˈkæpsjʊˌleɪt/ *v.tr.* **1** enclose in or as in a capsule. **2** summarize; express the essential features of. **3** isolate. □□ **encapsulation** /-ˈleɪʃ(ə)n/ *n.* [EN-¹ + L *capsula* CAPSULE]

encase /ɪnˈkeɪs/ *v.tr.* (also **incase**) **1** put into a case. **2** surround as with a case. □□ **encasement** *n.*

encash /ɪnˈkæʃ/ *v.tr. Brit.* **1** convert (bills etc.) into cash. **2** receive in the form of cash; realize. □□ **encashable** *adj.* **encashment** *n.*

encaustic /ɪnˈkɔːstɪk/ *adj.* & *n.* —*adj.* **1** (in painting, ceramics, etc.) using pigments mixed with hot wax, which are burned in as an inlay. **2** (of bricks and tiles) inlaid with differently coloured clays burnt in. —*n.* **1** the art of encaustic painting. **2** a painting done with this technique. [L *encausticus* f. Gk *egkaustikos* (as EN-², CAUSTIC)]

-ence /əns/ *suffix* forming nouns expressing: **1** a quality or state or an instance of one (*patience*; *an impertinence*). **2** an action (*reference*; *reminiscence*). [from or after F *-ence* f. L *-entia, -antia* (cf. -ANCE) f. pres. part. stem *-ent-, -ant-*]

enceinte /ãˈsæt/ *n.* & *adj.* —*n.* an enclosure, esp. in fortification. —*adj.* archaic pregnant. [F, ult. f. L *cingere cinct-* gird: see CINCTURE]

encephalic /ˌenkɪˈfælɪk, ˌens-/ *adj.* of or relating to the brain. [Gk *egkephalos* brain (as EN-², *kephalē* head)]

encephalin var. of ENKEPHALIN.

encephalitis /ˌenˌkefəˈlaɪtɪs, enˌsef-/ *n.* inflammation of the brain. □ **encephalitis lethargica** /lɪˈθɑːdʒɪkə/ an infectious encephalitis caused by a virus, with headache and drowsiness leading to coma; sleepy sickness. □□ **encephalitic** /-ˈlɪtɪk/ *adj.*

encephalo- /enˈkefələʊ, enˈsef-/ *comb. form* brain. [Gk *egkephalos* brain]

encephalogram /enˈkefələʊˌgræm, enˈsef-/ *n.* an X-ray photograph of the brain.

encephalograph /enˈkefələʊˌɡrɑːf, enˈsef-/ *n.* an instrument for recording the electrical activity of the brain.

encephalon /enˈkefəˌlɒn, enˈsef-/ *n. Anat.* the brain.

encephalopathy /enˌkefəˈlɒpəθɪ, enˌsef-/ *n.* disease of the brain.

enchain /ɪnˈtʃeɪn/ *v.tr.* **1** chain up, fetter. **2** hold fast (the attention, emotions, etc.). □□ **enchainment** *n.* [ME f. F *enchaîner* ult. f. L *catena* chain]

enchant /ɪnˈtʃɑːnt/ *v.tr.* **1** charm, delight. **2** bewitch. □□ **enchantedly** *adv.* **enchanting** *adj.* **enchantingly** *adv.* **enchantment** *n.* [ME f. F *enchanter* f. L *incantare* (as IN-², *canere cant-* sing)]

enchanter /ɪnˈtʃɑːntə(r)/ *n.* (*fem.* **enchantress**) a person who enchants, esp. by supposed use of magic. □ **enchanter's nightshade** a small plant, *Circaea lutetiana*, with white flowers.

enchase /ɪnˈtʃeɪs/ *v.tr.* **1** (foll. by *in*) place (a jewel) in a setting. **2** (foll. by *with*) set (gold etc.) with gems. **3** inlay with gold etc. **4** adorn with figures in relief. **5** engrave. [ME f. F *enchâsser* (as EN-¹, CHASE³)]

enchilada /ˌentʃɪˈlɑːdə/ *n.* a tortilla with chilli sauce and usu. a filling, esp. meat. [Amer. Sp., fem. past part. of *enchilar* season with chilli]

enchiridion /ˌenkaɪˈrɪdɪən/ *n.* (*pl.* **enchiridions** or **enchiridia** /-dɪə/) *formal* a handbook. [LL f. Gk *egkheiridion* (as EN-², *kheir* hand, *-idion* dimin. suffix)]

encipher /ɪnˈsaɪfə(r)/ *v.tr.* **1** write (a message etc.) in cipher. **2** convert into coded form using a cipher. □□ **encipherment** *n.*

encircle /ɪnˈsɜːk(ə)l/ *v.tr.* **1** (usu. foll. by *with*) surround, encompass. **2** form a circle round. □□ **encirclement** *n.*

encl. *abbr.* **1** enclosed. **2** enclosure.

en clair /ã ˈkleə(r)/ *adj.* & *adv.* (of a telegram, official message, etc.) in ordinary language (not in code or cipher). [F, lit. 'in clear']

enclasp /ɪnˈklɑːsp/ *v.tr.* hold in a clasp or embrace.

enclave /ˈenkleɪv/ *n.* **1** a portion of territory of one State surrounded by territory of another or others, as viewed by the surrounding territory (cf. EXCLAVE). **2** a group of people who are culturally, intellectually, or socially distinct from those surrounding them. [F f. *enclaver* ult. f. L *clavis* key]

enclitic /enˈklɪtɪk/ *adj.* & *n. Gram.* —*adj.* (of a word) pronounced with so little emphasis that it forms part of the preceding word. —*n.* such a word, e.g. *not* in *cannot*. □□ **enclitically** *adv.* [LL *encliticus* f. Gk *egklitikos* (as EN-², *klinō* lean)]

enclose /ɪnˈkləʊz/ *v.tr.* (also **inclose**) **1** (often foll. by *with, in*) **a** surround with a wall, fence, etc. **b** shut in on all sides. **2** fence in (common land) so as to make it private property. **3** put in a receptacle (esp. in an envelope together with a letter). **4** (usu. as **enclosed** *adj.*) seclude (a religious community) from the outside world. **5** esp. *Math.* bound on all sides; contain. **6** hem in on all sides. [ME f. OF *enclos* past part. of *enclore* ult. f. L *includere* (as INCLUDE)]

enclosure /ɪnˈkləʊʒə(r)/ *n.* (also **inclosure**) **1** the act of enclosing, esp. of common land. (See below.) **2** *Brit.* an enclosed space or area, esp. for a special class of persons at a sporting event. **3** a thing enclosed with a letter. **4** an enclosing fence etc. [AF & OF (as ENCLOSE)]

The conversion from the traditional medieval system of open-field farming to that of enclosed fields caused considerable unrest at various times, most notably in the mid-16th c. when the enclosure of much common land for sheep-farming resulted in widespread deprivation in large parts of the English countryside. The pressures of an expanding population, along with the advances made in the Agrarian Revolution, hastened the pace of enclosures during the 18th c., and by the early 19th c. the available agricultural land had been almost completely enclosed.

encode /ɪnˈkəʊd/ *v.tr.* put (a message etc.) into code or cipher. □□ **encoder** *n.*

encomiast /enˈkəʊmɪˌæst/ *n.* **1** the composer of an encomium. **2** a flatterer. □□ **encomiastic** /-ˈæstɪk/ *adj.* [Gk *egkōmiastēs* (as ENCOMIUM)]

encomium /enˈkəʊmɪəm/ *n.* (*pl.* **encomiums** or **encomia** /-mɪə/) a formal or high-flown expression of praise. [L f. Gk *egkōmion* (as EN-², *kōmos* revelry)]

encompass /ɪnˈkʌmpəs/ *v.tr.* **1** surround or form a circle about, esp. to protect or attack. **2** contain. □□ **encompassment** *n.*

encore /ˈɒŋkɔː(r)/ *n., v.,* & *int.* —*n.* **1** a call by an audience or spectators for the repetition of an item, or for a further item. **2** such an item. —*v.tr.* **1** call for the repetition of (an item). **2** call back (a performer) for this. —*int.* /also -ˈkɔː(r)/ again, once more. [F, = once again]

encounter /ɪnˈkaʊntə(r)/ *v.* & *n.* —*v.tr.* **1** meet by chance or unexpectedly. **2** meet as an adversary. —*n.* **1** a meeting by chance. **2** a meeting in conflict. **3** participation in an encounter group. □ **encounter group** a group of persons seeking psychological benefit through close contact with one another. [ME f. OF *encontrer, encontre* ult. f. L *contra* against]

encourage /ɪnˈkʌrɪdʒ/ *v.tr.* **1** give courage, confidence, or hope to. **2** (foll. by *to* + infin.) urge, advise. **3** stimulate by help, reward, etc. **4** promote or assist (an enterprise, opinion, etc.). □□ **encouragement** *n.* **encourager** *n.* **encouraging** *adj.* **encouragingly** *adv.* [ME f. F *encourager* (as EN-¹, COURAGE)]

encroach /ɪnˈkrəʊtʃ/ *v.intr.* **1** (foll. by *on, upon*) intrude, esp. on another's territory or rights. **2** advance gradually beyond due limits. □□ **encroacher** *n.* **encroachment** *n.* [ME f. OF *encrochier* (as EN-¹, *crochier* f. *croc* hook: see CROOK)]

encrust /ɪnˈkrʌst/ *v.* (also **incrust**) **1** *tr.* cover with a crust. **2** *tr.*

overlay with an ornamental crust of precious material. **3** *intr.* form a crust. □□ **encrustment** *n.* [F *incruster* f. L *incrustare* (as IN-², *crustare* f. *crusta* CRUST)]

encrustation var. of INCRUSTATION.

encrypt /ɪnˈkrɪpt/ *v.tr.* **1** convert (data) into code, esp. to prevent unauthorized access. **2** conceal by this means. □□ **encryption** *n.* [EN-¹ + Gk *kruptos* hidden]

encumber /ɪnˈkʌmbə(r)/ *v.tr.* **1** be a burden to. **2** hamper, impede. **3** burden (a person or estate) with debts, esp. mortgages. **4** fill or block (a place) esp. with lumber. □□ **encumberment** *n.* [ME f. OF *encombrer* block up f. Rmc]

encumbrance /ɪnˈkʌmbrəns/ *n.* **1** a burden. **2** an impediment. **3** a mortgage or other charge on property. **4** an annoyance. □ **without encumbrance** having no children. [ME f. OF *encombrance* (as ENCUMBER)]

-ency /ənsɪ/ *suffix* forming nouns denoting a quality (*efficiency*; *fluency*) or state (*presidency*) but not action (cf. -ENCE). [L *-entia* (cf. -ANCY)]

encyclical /enˈsɪklɪk(ə)l/ *n. & adj.* —*n.* a papal letter sent to all bishops of the Roman Catholic Church. —*adj.* (of a letter) for wide circulation. [LL *encyclicus* f. Gk *egkuklios* (as EN-², *kuklos* circle)]

encyclopedia /enˌsaɪkləˈpiːdɪə, ɪn-/ *n.* (also **encyclopaedia**) a book, often in several volumes, giving information on many subjects, or on many aspects of one subject, usu. arranged alphabetically. (See below.) [mod.L f. spurious Gk *egkuklopaideia* for *egkuklios paideia* all-round education: cf. ENCYCLICAL]

The word 'encyclopedia' comes from a Greek phrase meaning 'all-round education', the circle of arts and sciences considered by the ancient Greeks as essential to a liberal education, but their emphasis was on the spoken word and it was left to the Romans to record their knowledge in readable form. Roman encyclopedic works include those of Cato, Varro, Celsus (1st c. AD), and Pliny the Elder, with articles grouped under main topics, as were the Latin medieval compilations such as those of Isidore of Seville and Francis Bacon (1620). The first known use of the word 'encyclopedia' as the title of a book occurs in 1559, in a Latin compilation by the German writer Paul Scaliger. After the Renaissance similar works were produced in vernacular languages and an alphabetical arrangement became adopted. The 18th c. saw the publication of the *Cyclopaedia* of Ephraim Chambers (1728) and the great French *Encyclopédie* (1751–76), under the direction of Diderot, whose contributors included Voltaire, Rousseau, and other brilliant but controversial writers; F. A. Brockhaus produced a successful German encyclopedia (1796–1811); Larousse's *Grand Dictionnaire Universel* was published in 1866–76. The *Encyclopaedia Britannica* began in 1768–71 as a dictionary of the arts and sciences issued by a 'Society of Gentlemen in Scotland'; its second edition, in ten volumes, added history and biography; the current edition is the largest encyclopedia in the English language.

encyclopedic /enˌsaɪkləˈpiːdɪk, ɪn-/ *adj.* (also **encyclopaedic**) (of knowledge or information) comprehensive.

encyclopedism /enˌsaɪkləˈdiːz(ə)m, ɪn-/ *n.* (also **encyclopaedism**) encyclopedic learning.

encyclopedist /enˌsaɪkləˈpiːdɪst, ɪn-/ *n.* (also **encyclopaedist**) a person who writes, edits, or contributes to an encyclopedia.

encyst /ɪnˈsɪst/ *v.tr. & intr. Biol.* enclose or become enclosed in a cyst. □□ **encystation** /-ˈteɪʃ(ə)n/ *n.* **encystment** *n.*

end /end/ *n. & v.* —*n.* **1 a** the extreme limit; the point beyond which a thing does not continue. **b** an extremity of a line, or of the greatest dimension of an object. **c** the furthest point (*to the ends of the earth*). **2** the surface bounding a thing at either extremity; an extreme part (*a strip of wood with a nail in one end*). **3 a** conclusion, finish (*no end to his misery*). **b** the latter or final part. **c** death, destruction, downfall (*met an untimely end*). **d** result, outcome. **e** an ultimate state or condition. **4 a** a thing one seeks to attain; a purpose (*will do anything to achieve his ends*; *to what end?*). **b** the object for which a thing exists. **5** a remnant; a piece left over (*cigarette-end*). **6** (*prec. by the*) *colloq.* the limit of endurability. **7** the half of a sports pitch or court occupied by one team or player. **8** the part or share with which a person is

concerned (*no problem at my end*). **9** *Bowls* a unit of play in which play is from one side of the green towards the other. **10** *US Football* a player at the extremity of a line or team. —*v.* **1** *tr. & intr.* bring or come to an end. **2** *tr.* put an end to; destroy. **3** *intr.* (foll. by *in*) have as its result (*will end in tears*). **4** *intr.* (foll. by *by*) do or achieve eventually (*ended by marrying an heiress*). □ **all ends up** completely. **at an end** exhausted or completed. **at the end of one's tether** see TETHER. **come to a bad** (or **sticky**) **end** meet with ruin or disgrace. **come to an end 1** be completed or finished. **2** become exhausted. **end-around** *n. US Football* an offensive play in which an end carries the ball round the opposite end. —*adj. Computing* involving the transfer of a digit from one end of a register to the other. **end-game** the final stage of a game (esp. chess), when few pieces remain. **end it all** (or **end it**) *colloq.* commit suicide. **end of the road** the point at which a hope or endeavour has to be abandoned. **end of the world** the cessation of mortal life. **end on** with the end facing one, or with the end adjoining the end of the next object. **end-play** *Bridge* a method of play in the last few tricks to force an opponent to make a disadvantageous lead. **end-point** the final stage of a process, esp. the point at which an effect is observed in titration, dilution, etc. **end-product** the final product of manufacture, radioactive decay, etc. **end result** final outcome. **end run** *US* **1** *Football* an attempt by the ball-carrier to run round his or her own end. **2** an evasive tactic esp. in war or politics. **end standard** a standard of length in the form of a metal bar or block with the end faces the standard distance apart. **end-stopped** (of verse) having a pause at the end of each line. **end to end** with the end of each of a series adjoining the end of the next. **end up** reach a specified state, action, or place eventually (*ended up a drunkard*; *ended up making a fortune*). **end-user** the person, customer, etc., who is the ultimate user of a product. **in the end** finally; after all. **keep one's end up** do one's part despite difficulties. **make an end of** put a stop to. **make ends** (or **both ends**) **meet** live within one's income. **no end** *colloq.* to a great extent, very much. **no end of** *colloq.* much or many of. **on end 1** upright (*hair stood on end*). **2** continuously (*for three weeks on end*). **put an end to 1** stop (an activity etc.). **2** abolish, destroy. □□ **ender** *n.* [OE *ende*, *endian*, f. Gmc]

-end /end, ənd/ *suffix* forming nouns in the sense 'person or thing to be treated in a specified way' (*dividend*; *reverend*). [L gerundive ending *-endus*]

endanger /ɪnˈdeɪndʒə(r)/ *v.tr.* place in danger. □ **endangered species** a species in danger of extinction in the wild. □□ **endangerment** *n.*

endear /ɪnˈdɪə(r)/ *v.tr.* (usu. foll. by *to*) make dear to or beloved by.

endearing /ɪnˈdɪərɪŋ/ *adj.* inspiring affection. □□ **endearingly** *adv.*

endearment /ɪnˈdɪəmənt/ *n.* **1** an expression of affection. **2** liking, affection.

endeavour /ɪnˈdevə(r)/ *v. & n.* (*US* **endeavor**) —*v.* **1** *tr.* (foll. by *to* + infin.) try earnestly. **2** *intr.* (foll. by *after*) *archaic* strive. —*n.* (often foll. by *at*, or *to* + infin.) an earnest attempt. [ME f. *put oneself in* DEVOIR]

endemic /enˈdemɪk/ *adj. & n.* —*adj.* regularly or only found among a particular people or in a certain region. —*n.* an endemic disease or plant. □□ **endemically** *adv.* **endemicity** /ˌendɪˈmɪsɪtɪ/ *n.* **endemism** /ˈendɪˌmɪz(ə)m/ *n.* [F *endémique* or mod.L *endemicus* f. Gk *endēmos* native (as EN-², *dēmos* the people)]

Enderby Land /ˈendəbɪ/ a part of Antarctica, claimed by Australia. Its coast was discovered in 1831–2 by the English navigator John Biscoe, sailing for the London whaling firm of Enderby Brothers; he named it after his employers.

endermic /enˈdɜːmɪk/ *adj.* acting on or through the skin. □□ **endermically** *adv.* [EN-² + Gk *derma* skin]

ending /ˈendɪŋ/ *n.* **1** an end or final part, esp. of a story. **2** an inflected final part of a word. [OE (as END, -ING¹)]

endive /ˈendaɪv, -dɪv/ *n.* **1** a curly-leaved plant, *Cichorium endivia*, used in salads. **2** *US* a chicory crown. [ME f. OF f. LL *endivia* ult. f. Gk *entubon*]

endless /ˈendlɪs/ *adj.* **1** infinite; without end; eternal. **2**

continual, incessant (*tired of their endless complaints*). **3** *colloq.* innumerable. **4** (of a belt, chain, etc.) having the ends joined for continuous action over wheels etc. □ **endless screw** a short length of screw revolving to turn a cog-wheel. □□ **endlessly** *adv.* **endlessness** *n.* [OE *endelēas* (as END, -LESS)]

endmost /ˈendməʊst/ *adj.* nearest the end.

endnote /ˈendnəʊt/ *n.* a note printed at the end of a book or section of a book.

endo- /ˈendəʊ/ *comb. form* internal. [Gk *endon* within]

endocarditis /ˌendəʊkɑːˈdaɪtɪs/ *n.* inflammation of the endocardium. □□ **endocarditic** /-ˈdɪtɪk/ *adj.*

endocardium /ˌendəʊˈkɑːdɪəm/ *n.* the lining membrane of the heart. [ENDO- + Gk *kardia* heart]

endocarp /ˈendəʊˌkɑːp/ *n.* the innermost layer of the pericarp. □□ **endocarpic** /-ˈkɑːpɪk/ *adj.* [ENDO- + PERICARP]

endocrine /ˈendəʊˌkraɪn, -ˌkrɪn/ *adj.* (of a gland) secreting directly into the blood; ductless. [ENDO- + Gk *krinō* sift]

endocrinology /ˌendəʊkrɪˈnɒlədʒɪ/ *n.* the study of the structure and physiology of endocrine glands. □□ **endocrinological** /-nəˈlɒdʒɪk(ə)l/ *adj.* **endocrinologist** *n.*

endoderm /ˈendəʊdɜːm/ *n. Biol.* the innermost layer of an animal embryo in early development. □□ **endodermal** /-ˈdɜːm(ə)l/ *adj.* **endodermic** /-ˈdɜːmɪk/ *adj.* [ENDO- + Gk *derma* skin]

endogamy /enˈdɒgəmɪ/ *n.* **1** *Anthropol.* marrying within the same tribe. **2** *Bot.* pollination from the same plant. □□ **endogamous** *adj.* [ENDO- + Gk *gamos* marriage]

endogenous /enˈdɒdʒɪnəs/ *adj.* growing or originating from within. □□ **endogenesis** /ˌendəˈdʒenɪsɪs/ *n.* **endogeny** /enˈdɒdʒɪnɪ/ *n.*

endolymph /ˈendəʊlɪmf/ *n.* the fluid in the membranous labyrinth of the ear.

endometrium /ˌendəʊˈmiːtrɪəm/ *n. Anat.* the membrane lining the womb. □□ **endometritis** /ˌendəʊmɪˈtraɪtɪs/ *n.* [ENDO- + Gk *mētra* womb]

endomorph /ˈendəʊˌmɔːf/ *n.* **1** a person with a soft round build of body and a high proportion of fat tissue (cf. ECTOMORPH, MESOMORPH). **2** *Mineral.* a mineral enclosed within another. □□ **endomorphic** /-ˈmɔːfɪk/ *adj.* **endomorphy** *n.* [ENDO- + Gk *morphē* form]

endoparasite /ˌendəʊˈpærəˌsaɪt/ *n.* a parasite that lives on the inside of its host. Also called ENTOPARASITE.

endoplasm /ˈendəʊˌplæz(ə)m/ *n.* the inner fluid layer of the cytoplasm.

endoplasmic reticulum /ˌendəʊˈplæzmɪk/ *n. Biol.* a system of membranes within the cytoplasm of a eukaryotic cell forming a link between the cell and nuclear membranes and usu. having ribosomes attached to its surface.

endorphin /enˈdɔːfɪn/ *n. Biochem.* any of a group of peptide neurotransmitters occurring naturally in the brain and having pain-relieving properties. [F *endorphine* f. *endogène* endogenous + MORPHINE]

endorse /ɪnˈdɔːs/ *v.tr.* (also **indorse**) **1 a** confirm (a statement or opinion). **b** declare one's approval of. **2** sign or write on the back of (a document), esp. the back of (a bill, cheque, etc.) as the payee or to specify another as payee. **3** write (an explanation or comment) on the back of a document. **4** *Brit.* enter details of a conviction for a motoring offence on (a driving licence). □□ **endorsable** *adj.* **endorsee** /ˌendɔːˈsiː/ *n.* **endorser** *n.* [med.L *indorsare* (as IN-², L *dorsum* back)]

endorsement /ɪnˈdɔːsmənt/ *n.* **1** the act or an instance of endorsing. **2** something with which a document etc. is endorsed, esp. a signature. **3** a record in a driving licence of a conviction for a motoring offence.

endoscope /ˈendəʊˌskəʊp/ *n. Surgery* an instrument for viewing the internal parts of the body. □□ **endoscopic** /-ˈskɒpɪk/ *adj.* **endoscopically** /-ˈskɒpɪkəlɪ/ *adv.* **endoscopist** /enˈdɒskəpɪst/ *n.* **endoscopy** /enˈdɒskəpɪ/ *n.*

endoskeleton /ˈendəʊˌskelɪt(ə)n/ *n.* an internal skeleton, as found in vertebrates.

endosperm /ˈendəʊˌspɜːm/ *n.* albumen enclosed with the germ in seeds.

endospore /ˈendəʊˌspɔː(r)/ *n.* **1** a spore formed by certain bacteria. **2** the inner coat of a spore.

endothelium /ˌendəʊˈθiːlɪəm/ *n. Anat.* a layer of cells lining the blood-vessels, heart, and lymphatic vessels. [ENDO- + Gk *thēlē* teat]

endothermic /ˌendəʊˈθɜːmɪk/ *adj.* occurring or formed with the absorption of heat.

endow /ɪnˈdaʊ/ *v.tr.* **1** bequeath or give a permanent income to (a person, institution, etc.). **2** (esp. as **endowed** *adj.*) (usu. foll. by *with*) provide (a person) with talent, ability, etc. □□ **endower** *n.* [ME f. AF *endouer* (as EN-¹, OF *douer* f. L *dotare* f. *dos dotis* DOWER)]

endowment /ɪnˈdaʊmənt/ *n.* **1** the act or an instance of endowing. **2** assets, esp. property or income with which a person or body is endowed. **3** (usu. in *pl.*) skill, talent, etc., with which a person is endowed. **4** (*attrib.*) denoting forms of life insurance involving payment by the insurer of a fixed sum on a specified date, or on the death of the insured person if earlier. □ **endowment mortgage** a mortgage linked to endowment insurance of the mortgagor's life, the capital being paid from the sum insured.

endpaper /ˈendˌpeɪpə(r)/ *n.* a usu. blank leaf of paper at the beginning and end of a book, fixed to the inside of the cover.

endue /ɪnˈdjuː/ *v.tr.* (also **indue**) (foll. by *with*) invest or provide (a person) with qualities, powers, etc. [earlier = induct, put on clothes: ME f. OF *enduire* f. L *inducere* lead in, assoc. in sense with L *induere* put on (clothes)]

endurance /ɪnˈdjʊərəns/ *n.* **1** the power or habit of enduring (*beyond endurance*). **2** the ability to withstand prolonged strain (*endurance test*). **3** the act of enduring. [OF f. *endurer*: see ENDURE]

endure /ɪnˈdjʊə(r)/ *v.* **1** *tr.* undergo (a difficulty, hardship, etc.). **2** *tr.* **a** tolerate (a person) (*cannot endure him*). **b** (esp. with neg.; foll. by *to* + infin.) bear. **3** *intr.* remain in existence; last. **4** *tr.* submit to. □□ **endurable** *adj.* **endurability** /-ˈbɪlɪtɪ/ *n.* **enduringly** *adv.* [ME f. OF *endurer* f. L *indurare* harden (as IN-², *durus* hard)]

enduro /ɪnˈdjʊərəʊ/ *n.* (*pl.* **-os**) a long-distance race for motor vehicles, designed to test endurance.

endways /ˈendweɪz/ *adv.* **1** with its end uppermost or foremost or turned towards the viewer. **2** end to end.

endwise /ˈendwaɪz/ *adv.* = ENDWAYS.

Endymion /enˈdɪmɪən/ *Gk Mythol.* a remarkably beautiful young man, either a king of Elis in the NE Peloponnese or a Carian. Of the various tales told about him the most celebrated is that he was loved by the Moon (Selene) who caused him to sleep everlastingly so that she could enjoy his beauty for ever. According to another version he obtained from Zeus eternal youth and the gift of sleeping as long as he wished.

ENE *abbr.* east-north-east.

-ene /iːn/ *suffix* **1** forming names of inhabitants of places (*Nazarene*). **2** *Chem.* forming names of unsaturated hydrocarbons containing a double bond (*benzene; ethylene*). [from or after Gk *-ēnos*]

enema /ˈenɪmə/ *n.* (*pl.* **enemas** or **enemata** /ɪˈnemətə/) **1** the injection of liquid or gas into the rectum, esp. to expel its contents. **2** a fluid or syringe used for this. [LL f. Gk *enema* f. *eniēmi* inject (as EN-², *hiēmi* send)]

enemy /ˈenəmɪ/ *n.* (*pl.* **-ies**) **1** a person or group actively opposing or hostile to another, or to a cause etc. **2 a** a hostile nation or army, esp. in war. **b** a member of this. **c** a hostile ship or aircraft. **3** (usu. foll. by *of, to*) an adversary or opponent. **4** a thing that harms or injures. **5** (*attrib.*) of or belonging to an enemy (*destroyed by enemy action*). [ME f. OF *enemi* f. L *inimicus* (as IN-¹, *amicus* friend)]

energetic /ˌenəˈdʒetɪk/ *adj.* **1** strenuously active. **2** forcible, vigorous. **3** powerfully operative. □□ **energetically** *adv.* [Gk *energētikos* f. *energeō* (as EN-², *ergon* work)]

energetics /ˌenəˈdʒetɪks/ *n.pl.* the science of energy.

energize /ˈenəˌdʒaɪz/ *v.tr.* (also **-ise**) **1** infuse energy into (a person or work). **2** provide energy for the operation of (a device). □□ **energizer** *n.*

energumen /ˌenɜːˈgjuːmen/ *n.* an enthusiast or fanatic. [LL *energumenus* f. Gk *energoumenos* passive part. of *energeō*: see ENERGETIC]

energy /'enədʒɪ/ n. (pl. **-ies**) **1** force, vigour; capacity for activity. **2** (in pl.) individual powers in use (*devote your energies to this*). **3** *Physics* the capacity of matter or radiation to do work. (See below.) **4** the means of doing work by utilizing matter or radiation. [F *énergie* or LL *energia* f. Gk *energeia* f. *ergon* work]

The modern scientific concept of energy was formulated in the 19th c. mainly through the study of the generation of mechanical power by means of heat engines and electrical machines, which were increasingly supplementing the more traditional agencies such as wind and flowing water as alternatives to human labour. Energy can be neither created nor destroyed, but only changed from one form into another. These forms include kinetic energy (energy of motion), potential energy (the energy an object has by virtue of its position), heat energy, electrical energy, and so on. Einstein (among others) showed that matter can also be regarded as a form of energy, as the two are in principle interconvertible. The standard unit of energy is the joule.

enervate v. & adj. —v.tr. /'enəˌveɪt/ deprive of vigour or vitality. —adj. /ɪ'nɜːvət/ enervated. □□ **enervation** /ˌenə'veɪʃ(ə)n/ n. [L *enervatus* past part. of *enervare* (as E-, *nervus* sinew)]

en famille /ˌ ̃ɑ fæ'miːj/ adv. **1** in or with one's family. **2** at home. [F, = in family]

enfant gâté /ˌ ̃ɑfɑ̃ gæ'teɪ/ n. a person given undue flattery or indulgence. [F, = spoilt child]

enfant terrible /ˌ ̃ɑfɑ̃ te'riːbl/ n. a person who causes embarrassment by indiscreet or unruly behaviour. [F, = terrible child]

enfeeble /ɪn'fiːb(ə)l/ v.tr. make feeble. □□ **enfeeblement** n. [ME f. OF *enfeblir* (as EN-¹, FEEBLE)]

en fête /ɑ̃ 'feɪt/ adv. & predic.adj. holding or ready for a holiday or celebration. [F, = in festival]

enfetter /ɪn'fetə(r)/ v.tr. *literary* **1** bind in or as in fetters. **2** (foll. by *to*) enslave.

enfilade /ˌenfɪ'leɪd/ n. & v. —n. gunfire directed along a line from end to end. —v.tr. direct an enfilade at (troops, a road, etc.). [F f. *enfiler* (as EN-¹, *fil* thread)]

enfold /ɪn'fəʊld/ v.tr. (also **infold**) **1** (usu. foll. by *in*, *with*) wrap up; envelop. **2** clasp, embrace.

enforce /ɪn'fɔːs/ v.tr. **1** compel observance of (a law etc.). **2** (foll. by *on*, *upon*) impose (an action, conduct, one's will). **3** persist in (a demand or argument). □□ **enforceable** adj. **enforceability** /-səˈbɪlɪtɪ/ n. **enforcedly** /-sɪdlɪ/ adv. **enforcer** n. [ME f. OF *enforcir*, *-ier* ult. f. L *fortis* strong]

enforcement /ɪn'fɔːsmənt/ n. the act or an instance of enforcing. □ **enforcement notice** *Brit.* an official notification to remedy a breach of planning legislation. [ME f. OF, as ENFORCE + -MENT]

enfranchise /ɪn'fræntʃaɪz/ v.tr. **1** give (a person) the right to vote. **2** give (a town) municipal rights, esp. that of representation in parliament. **3** *hist.* free (a slave, villein, etc.). □□ **enfranchisement** /-ɪzmənt/ n. [OF *enfranchir* (as EN-¹, *franc franche* FRANK)]

ENG abbr. electronic news gathering.

engage /ɪn'geɪdʒ/ v. **1** tr. employ or hire (a person). **2** tr. **a** (usu. in passive) employ busily; occupy (*are you engaged tomorrow?*). **b** hold fast (a person's attention). **3** tr. (usu. in passive) bind by a promise, esp. of marriage. **4** tr. (usu. foll. by *to* + infin.) bind by a contract. **5** tr. arrange beforehand to occupy (a room, seat, etc.). **6** (usu. foll. by *with*) *Mech.* **a** tr. interlock (parts of a gear etc.); cause (a part) to interlock. **b** intr. (of a part, gear, etc.) interlock. **7 a** intr. (usu. foll. by *with*) (of troops etc.) come into battle. **b** tr. bring (troops) into battle. **c** tr. come into battle with (an enemy etc.). **8** intr. take part (*engage in politics*). **9** intr. (foll. by *that* + clause or *to* + infin.) pledge oneself. **10** tr. (usu. as **engaged** adj.) *Archit.* attach (a column) to a wall. **11** tr. (of fencers etc.) interlock (weapons). □□ **engager** n. [F *engager*, rel. to GAGE¹]

engagé /ˌ ̃ɑˈgæʒeɪ/ adj. (of a writer etc.) morally committed. [F, past part. of *engager*: see ENGAGE]

engaged /ɪn'geɪdʒd/ adj. **1** under a promise to marry. **2 a** occupied, busy. **b** reserved, booked. **3** *Brit.* (of a telephone line)

unavailable because already in use. □ **engaged signal** (or **tone**) *Brit.* a sound indicating that a telephone line is engaged.

engagement /ɪn'geɪdʒmənt/ n. **1** the act or state of engaging or being engaged. **2** an appointment with another person. **3** a betrothal. **4** an encounter between hostile forces. **5** a moral commitment. □ **engagement ring** a finger-ring given by a man to a woman when they promise to marry. [F f. *engager*: see ENGAGE]

engaging /ɪn'geɪdʒɪŋ/ adj. attractive, charming. □□ **engagingly** adv. **engagingness** n.

Engels /'eŋglz/, Friedrich (1820–95), German socialist, founder with Karl Marx of modern Communism. Engels collaborated with Marx in the writing of the *Communist Manifesto* (1848), but was forced to flee abroad after involvement in the revolution in Baden in 1848–9. He lived the rest of his life in England, making a career as a manufacturer in Manchester before moving to London in 1869. An influential author in his own right, Engels was perhaps more important as the publicist and patron of his colleague Marx.

engender /ɪn'dʒendə(r)/ v.tr. **1** give rise to; bring about (a feeling etc.). **2** *archaic* beget. [ME f. OF *engendrer* f. L *ingenerare* (as IN-², *generare* GENERATE)]

engine /'endʒɪn/ n. **1** a mechanical contrivance consisting of several parts working together, esp. as a source of power. **2 a** a railway locomotive. **b** = *fire-engine*. **c** = *steam engine*. **3** *archaic* a machine or instrument, esp. a contrivance used in warfare. □ **engine-driver** the driver of an engine, esp. a railway locomotive. **engine-room** a room containing engines (esp. in a ship). □□ **engined** adj. (also in comb.). **engineless** adj. [OF *engin* f. L *ingenium* talent, device: cf. INGENIOUS]

engineer /ˌendʒɪ'nɪə(r)/ n. & v. —n. **1** a person qualified in a branch of engineering, esp. as a professional. **2** = *civil engineer*. **3** a person who makes or is in charge of engines. **4** *US* an engine-driver. **5** a person who designs and constructs military works; a soldier trained for this purpose. **6** (foll. by *of*) a skilful or artful contriver. —v. **1** tr. arrange, contrive, or bring about, esp. artfully. **2** intr. act as an engineer. **3** tr. construct or manage as an engineer. □□ **engineership** n. [ME f. OF *engineor* f. med.L *ingeniator -oris* f. *ingeniare* (as ENGINE)]

engineering /ˌendʒɪ'nɪərɪŋ/ n. the application of science to the design, building, and use of machines, constructions, etc. □ **engineering science** engineering as a field of study.

enginery /'endʒɪnrɪ/ n. engines and machinery generally.

engird /ɪn'gɜːd/ v.tr. surround with or as with a girdle.

engirdle /ɪn'gɜːd(ə)l/ v.tr. engird.

England /'ɪŋglənd/ a part of Great Britain and the United Kingdom, largely made up of the area south of the River Tweed and containing the capital, London; pop. (1981) 46,362,836. There were settlements in England from at least palaeolithic times, and considerable remains exist of neolithic and Bronze Age cultures. These were followed by the arrival of the Celtic peoples whose civilization spread over the whole country. The Romans under Julius Caesar raided the south of Britain in 55 and 54 BC, but full-scale invasion did not take place until a century later; the country was then administered as a Roman province until the Teutonic conquest of Gaul in the early 5th c. and the subsequent withdrawal of the last Roman garrison. In the 3rd–7th c. Germanic-speaking tribes, traditionally known as Angles, Saxons, and Jutes, raided and then settled, establishing independent kingdoms, and when that of Wessex became dominant in the 9th c. England emerged as a distinct political entity before being conquered by William, Duke of Normandy, in 1066. The neighbouring principality of Wales was gradually conquered during the Middle Ages and politically incorporated in the 16th c. During the period of Tudor rule (1485–1603) England emerged as a Protestant State with a strong stable monarchy and as a naval power. Scotland and England have been ruled by one monarch from 1603, and the two crowns were formally united in 1707. (See GREAT BRITAIN.)

English /'ɪŋglɪʃ/ adj. & n. —adj. of or relating to England or its people or language. —n. **1** the language of England; its literary or standard form. (See below.) **2** (prec. by *the*; treated as pl.) the people of England. **3** *US Billiards* = SIDE *n.* 10. □ **English bond** *Building* a bond of brickwork arranged in alternate courses of stretchers and headers. **English horn** = COR ANGLAIS. **the Queen's** (or **King's**) **English** the English language as correctly written or spoken in Britain. □□ **Englishness** *n.* [OE *englisc, ænglisc* (as ANGLE, -ISH¹)]

English is the principal language of Great Britain, the US, Ireland, Australia, and many other countries. There are some 300 million native speakers, and it is the medium of communication for many millions more in all parts of the world. Its history can be divided into three stages: Old English (up to 1150), Middle English (1150–1500), and Modern English (1500 onwards). Old English is usually said to have begun with the settlement of Germanic-speaking tribes (Angles, Saxons, and Jutes) in Britain in the mid-5th c. It was an inflected language, and the gradual decay of these endings is one of the chief changes that took place over the centuries, until by the 15th c. most of them had been lost. Old English was essentially a spoken language, but by the time of Alfred the Great something like a standard literary language was emerging, and by the late 10th c. the dialect of Wessex was becoming dominant. In addition to native Celtic elements and words surviving from the period of Roman rule, extension of vocabulary was brought by the spread of Christian culture, with some words adopted or translated from Latin, and by Scandinavian invaders in the 9th–10th c. After the Norman Conquest, Anglo-Norman was the language of the ruling classes, but from the 14th c. English again became the standard. Despite the influence of French, the Germanic nature of English has been maintained in its syntax and morphology. All changes were gradual, including those in pronunciation; by the 16th c. many vowels were sounded much as they are today.

The spread of the language has its origins in colonization from the Middle Ages onwards and the consolidation of the British Empire particularly in the 19th c. It developed locally (as it has in the British Isles) into many different varieties. Even since the break-up of the Empire, English has gained in influence largely through its use as a medium of international communication and now probably ranks as the world's unofficial lingua franca.

English Channel the sea channel separating southern England from northern France. It is 35 km (22 miles) wide at its narrowest point.

Englishman /ˈɪŋglɪʃmən/ *n.* (*pl.* **-men**) a man who is English by birth or descent.

Englishwoman /ˈɪŋglɪʃˌwʊmən/ *n.* (*pl.* **-women**) a woman who is English by birth or descent.

engorge /ɪnˈgɔːdʒ/ *v.tr.* **1** (in *passive*) **a** be crammed. **b** *Med.* be congested with blood. **2** devour greedily. □□ **engorgement** *n.* [F *engorger* (as EN-¹, GORGE)]

engraft /ɪnˈgrɑːft/ *v.tr.* (also **ingraft**) **1** *Bot.* (usu. foll. by *into, upon*) insert (a scion of one tree into another). **2** (usu. foll. by *in*) implant (principles etc.) in a person's mind. **3** (usu. foll. by *into*) incorporate permanently. □□ **engraftment** *n.*

engrail /ɪnˈgreɪl/ *v.tr.* (usu. as **engrailed** *adj.*) esp. *Heraldry* indent the edge of; give a serrated appearance to. [ME f. OF *engresler* (as EN-¹, *gresle* hail)]

engrain /ɪnˈgreɪn/ *v.tr.* **1** implant (a habit, belief, or attitude) ineradicably in a person (see also INGRAINED). **2** cause (dye etc.) to sink deeply into a thing. [ME f. OF *engrainer* dye in grain (*en graine*): see GRAIN]

engrained /ɪnˈgreɪnd/ *adj.* inveterate (see also INGRAINED).

engram /ˈengræm/ *n.* a memory-trace, a supposed permanent change in the brain accounting for the existence of memory. □□ **engrammatic** /-grəˈmætɪk/ *adj.* [G *Engramm* f. Gk *en* in + *gramma* letter of the alphabet]

engrave /ɪnˈgreɪv/ *v.tr.* **1** (often foll. by *on*) inscribe, cut, or carve (a text or design) on a hard surface. **2** (often foll. by *with*) inscribe or ornament (a surface) in this way. **3** cut (a design) as lines on a metal plate for printing. **4** (often foll. by *on*) impress deeply on a person's memory etc. □□ **engraver** *n.* [EN-¹ + GRAVE³]

engraving /ɪnˈgreɪvɪŋ/ *n.* a print made from an engraved plate.

engross /ɪnˈgrəʊs/ *v.tr.* **1** absorb the attention of; occupy fully

(*engrossed in studying*). **2** make a fair copy of a legal document. **3** reproduce (a document etc.) in larger letters or larger format. **4** *archaic* monopolize (a conversation etc.). □□ **engrossing** *adj.* (in sense 1). **engrossment** *n.* [ME f. AF *engrosser*: senses 2 and 3 f. *en* in + *grosse* large writing: senses 1 and 4 f. *en gros* wholesale]

engulf /ɪnˈgʌlf/ *v.tr.* (also **ingulf**) **1** flow over and swamp; overwhelm. **2** swallow or plunge into a gulf. □□ **engulfment** *n.*

enhance /ɪnˈhɑːns/ *v.tr.* heighten or intensify (qualities, powers, value, etc.); improve (something already of good quality). □□ **enhancement** *n.* **enhancer** *n.* [ME f. AF *enhauncer*, prob. alt. f. OF *enhaucier* f. L *altus* high]

enharmonic /ˌenhɑːˈmɒnɪk/ *adj. Mus.* of or having intervals smaller than a semitone (esp. such intervals as that between G sharp and A flat, these notes being made the same in a scale of equal temperament). □□ **enharmonically** *adv.* [LL *enharmonicus* f. Gk *enarmonikos* (as EN-², *harmonia* HARMONY)]

enigma /ɪˈnɪgmə/ *n.* **1** a puzzling thing or person. **2** a riddle or paradox. □□ **enigmatic** /ˌenɪgˈmætɪk/ *adj.* **enigmatical** /ˌenɪgˈmætɪk(ə)l/ *adj.* **enigmatically** /ˌenɪgˈmætɪkəli/ *adv.* **enigmatize** *v.tr.* (also **-ise**). [L *aenigma* f. Gk *ainigma -matos* f. *ainissomai* speak allusively f. *ainos* fable]

enjambment /enˈdʒæmmənt/ *n.* (also **enjambement**) *Prosody* the continuation of a sentence without a pause beyond the end of a line, couplet, or stanza. [F *enjambement* f. *enjamber* (as EN-¹, *jambe* leg)]

enjoin /ɪnˈdʒɔɪn/ *v.tr.* **1 a** (foll. by *to* + infin.) command or order (a person). **b** (foll. by *that* + clause) issue instructions. **2** (often foll. by *on*) impose or prescribe (an action or conduct). **3** (usu. foll. by *from*) *Law* prohibit (a person) by order. □□ **enjoinment** *n.* [ME f. OF *enjoindre* f. L *injungere* (as IN-², *jungere* join)]

enjoy /ɪnˈdʒɔɪ/ *v.tr.* **1** take delight or pleasure in. **2** have the use or benefit of. **3** experience (*enjoy poor health*). □ **enjoy oneself** experience pleasure. □□ **enjoyer** *n.* **enjoyment** *n.* [ME f. OF *enjoier* give joy to or *enjoïr* enjoy, ult. f. L *gaudēre* rejoice]

enjoyable /ɪnˈdʒɔɪəb(ə)l/ *adj.* pleasant; giving enjoyment. □□ **enjoyability** /-ˈbɪlɪti/ *n.* **enjoyableness** *n.* **enjoyably** *adv.*

enkephalin /enˈkefəlɪn/ *n.* (also **encephalin** /enˈsef-/) *Biochem.* either of two morphine-like peptides occurring naturally in the brain and thought to control levels of pain. [Gk *egkephalos* brain]

enkindle /ɪnˈkɪnd(ə)l/ *v.tr. literary* **1 a** cause (flames) to flare up. **b** stimulate (feeling, passion, etc.). **2** inflame with passion.

enlace /ɪnˈleɪs/ *v.tr.* **1** encircle tightly. **2** entwine. **3** enfold. □□ **enlacement** *n.* [ME f. OF *enlacier* ult. f. L *laqueus* noose]

enlarge /ɪnˈlɑːdʒ/ *v.* **1** *tr.* & *intr.* make or become larger or wider. **2 a** *tr.* describe in greater detail. **b** *intr.* (usu. foll. by *upon*) expatiate. **3** *tr. Photog.* produce an enlargement of (a negative). [ME f. OF *enlarger* (as EN-¹, LARGE)]

enlargement /ɪnˈlɑːdʒmənt/ *n.* **1** the act or an instance of enlarging; the state of being enlarged. **2** *Photog.* a print that is larger than the negative from which it is produced.

enlarger /ɪnˈlɑːdʒə(r)/ *n. Photog.* an apparatus for enlarging or reducing negatives or positives.

enlighten /ɪnˈlaɪt(ə)n/ *v.tr.* **1** (often foll. by *on*) instruct or inform (about a subject). **2** (esp. as **enlightened** *adj.*) free from prejudice or superstition. **3** *rhet.* or *poet.* **a** shed light on (an object). **b** give spiritual insight to (a person). □□ **enlightener** *n.*

enlightenment /ɪnˈlaɪtənmənt/ *n.* **1** the act or an instance of enlightening; the state of being enlightened. **2** (**the Enlightenment**) the 18th-c. philosophy emphasizing reason and individualism rather than tradition.

enlist /ɪnˈlɪst/ *v.* **1** *intr.* & *tr.* enrol in the armed services. **2** *tr.* secure as a means of help or support. □ **enlisted man** *US* a soldier or sailor below the rank of officer. □□ **enlister** *n.* **enlistment** *n.*

enliven /ɪnˈlaɪv(ə)n/ *v.tr.* **1** give life or spirit to. **2** make cheerful, brighten (a picture or scene). □□ **enlivener** *n.* **enlivenment** *n.*

en masse /ɑ̃ ˈmæs/ *adv.* **1** all together. **2** in a mass. [F]

enmesh /ɪnˈmeʃ/ *v.tr.* entangle in or as in a net. □□ **enmeshment** *n.*

enmity /ˈenmɪti/ *n.* (*pl.* **-ies**) **1** the state of being an enemy. **2** a feeling of hostility. [ME f. OF *enemitié* f. Rmc (as ENEMY)]

ennead /ˈenɪˌæd/ n. a group of nine. [Gk *enneas enneados* f. *ennea* nine]

Enniskillen /ˌenɪsˈkɪlɪn/ the county town of Fermanagh; pop. (1981) 10,400. In 1987 the explosion of a bomb, planted by the IRA, killed or injured a number of civilians at a Remembrance Day ceremony.

Ennius /ˈenjəs/, Quintus (239–169 BC), Roman writer, originally from Calabria in SW Italy. Brought to Rome by Cato the Censor he was largely responsible for the creation of a native Roman literature based on Greek models. Of his many works (surviving only in fragments) the most important was the *Annals*, a hexameter epic on the history of Rome, which was a major influence on such poets as Lucretius and Virgil.

ennoble /ɪˈnəʊb(ə)l/ v.tr. **1** make (a person) a noble. **2** make noble; elevate. □□ **ennoblement** n. [F *ennoblir* (as EN-1, NOBLE)]

ennui /ɒˈnwiː/ n. mental weariness from lack of occupation or interest; boredom. [F f. L *in odio*: cf. ODIUM]

Enoch /ˈiːnɒk/ **1** the eldest son of Cain. **2** the first city, built by Cain and named after Enoch (Gen. 4: 17). **3** a Hebrew patriarch (said to have 'walked with God'), father of Methuselah. Two works ascribed to him, the *Book of Enoch* and the *Book of the Secrets of Enoch*, date from the 2nd–1st c. BC and 1st c. AD respectively. A third treatise likewise dates from the Christian era.

enology US var. of OENOLOGY.

enormity /ɪˈnɔːmɪtɪ/ n. (pl. **-ies**) **1** extreme wickedness. **2** an act of extreme wickedness. **3** a serious error. **4** disp. great size; enormousness. [ME f. F *énormité* f. L *enormitas -tatis* f. *enormis* (as ENORMOUS)]

enormous /ɪˈnɔːməs/ adj. very large; huge (*enormous animals; an enormous difference*). □□ **enormously** adv. **enormousness** n. [L *enormis* (as E-, *norma* pattern, standard)]

enosis /ˈenəʊsɪs/ n. the political union of Cyprus and Greece, as an ideal or proposal. [mod. Gk *enōsis* f. *ena* one]

enough /ɪˈnʌf/ adj., n., adv., & int. —adj. as much or as many as required (*we have enough apples; we do not have enough sugar; earned enough money to buy a house*). —n. an amount or quantity that is enough (*we have enough of everything now; enough is as good as a feast*). —adv. **1** to the required degree, adequately (*are you warm enough?*). **2** fairly (*she sings well enough*). **3** very, quite (*you know well enough what I mean; oddly enough*). —int. that is enough (in various senses, esp. to put an end to an action, thing said, etc.). □ **have had enough of** want no more of; be satiated with or tired of. [OE *genog* f. Gmc]

en passant /ˌɑ̃ pæˈsɑ̃/ adv. **1** by the way. **2** Chess used with reference to the permitted capture of an opponent's pawn that has just advanced two squares in its first move with a pawn that could have taken it if it had advanced only one square. [F, = in passing]

en pension /ˌɑ̃ pɑ̃ˈsjɔ̃/ adv. as a boarder or resident. [F: see PENSION2]

enplane var. of EMPLANE.

enprint /ˈenprɪnt/ n. a standard-sized photographic print. [*enlarged print*]

enquire /ɪnˈkwaɪə(r), ɪŋ-/ v. **1** intr. (often foll. by *of*) seek information; ask a question (of a person). **2** intr. = INQUIRE. **3** intr. (foll. by *after, for*) ask about a person, a person's health, etc. **4** intr. (foll. by *for*) ask about the availability of. **5** tr. ask for information as to (*enquired my name; enquired whether we were coming*). □□ **enquirer** n. [ME *enquere* f. OF *enquerre* ult. f. L *inquirere* (as IN-2, *quaerere quaesit-* seek)]

enquiry /ɪnˈkwaɪərɪ, ɪŋ-/ n. (pl. **-ies**) **1** the act or an instance of asking or seeking information. **2** = INQUIRY.

enrage /ɪnˈreɪdʒ/ v.tr. (often foll. by *at, by, with*) make furious. □□ **enragement** n. [F *enrager* (as EN-1, RAGE)]

en rapport /ˌɑ̃ ræˈpɔː(r)/ adv. (usu. foll. by *with*) in harmony or rapport. [F: see RAPPORT]

enrapture /ɪnˈræptʃə(r)/ v.tr. give intense delight to.

enrich /ɪnˈrɪtʃ/ v.tr. **1** make rich or richer. **2** make richer in quality, flavour, nutritive value, etc. **3** add to the contents of (a collection, museum, or book). **4** increase the content of an

isotope in (material) esp. enrich uranium with isotope U-235. □□ **enrichment** n. [ME f. OF *enrichir* (as EN-1, RICH)]

enrobe /ɪnˈrəʊb/ v.intr. put on a robe, vestment, etc.

enrol /ɪnˈrəʊl/ v. (US **enroll**) (**enrolled, enrolling**) **1** intr. enter one's name on a list, esp. as a commitment to membership. **2** tr. **a** write the name of (a person) on a list. **b** (usu. foll. by *in*) incorporate (a person) as a member of a society etc. **3** tr. hist. enter (a deed etc.) among the rolls of a court of justice. **4** tr. record. □□ **enrollee** /-ˈliː/ n. **enroller** n. [ME f. OF *enroller* (as EN-1, *rolle* ROLL)]

enrolment /ɪnˈrəʊlmənt/ n. (US **enrollment**) **1** the act or an instance of enrolling; the state of being enrolled. **2** US the number of persons enrolled, esp. at a school or college.

en route /ɑ̃ ˈruːt/ adv. (usu. foll. by *to, for*) on the way. [F]

Enschede /ˈenskədeɪ/ a university city in The Netherlands, in the province of Overijssel; pop. (1987) 144,700. Since its founding (1325) it has been the focal point of the Dutch textile industry.

ensconce /ɪnˈskɒns/ v.tr. (usu. refl. or in passive) establish or settle comfortably, safely, or secretly.

ensemble /ɒnˈsɒmb(ə)l/ n. **1 a** a thing viewed as the sum of its parts. **b** the general effect of this. **2** a set of clothes worn together; an outfit. **3** a group of actors, dancers, musicians, etc., performing together, esp. subsidiary dancers in ballet etc. **4** Mus. **a** a concerted passage for an ensemble. **b** the manner in which this is performed (*good ensemble*). **5** Math. a group of systems with the same constitution but possibly in different states. [F, ult. f. L *insimul* (as IN-2, *simul* at the same time)]

enshrine /ɪnˈʃraɪn/ v.tr. **1** enclose in or as in a shrine. **2** serve as a shrine for. **3** preserve or cherish. □□ **enshrinement** n.

enshroud /ɪnˈʃraʊd/ v.tr. literary **1** cover with or as with a shroud. **2** cover completely; hide from view.

ensign /ˈensaɪn, -s(ə)n/ n. **1 a** a banner or flag, esp. the military or naval flag of a nation. **b** Brit. a flag with the union in the corner. **2** a standard-bearer. **3 a** hist. the lowest commissioned infantry officer. **b** US the lowest commissioned officer in the navy. □ **blue ensign** the ensign of government departments and formerly of the naval reserve etc. **red ensign** the ensign of the merchant service. **white ensign** the ensign of the Royal Navy and the Royal Yacht Squadron. □□ **ensigncy** n. [ME f. OF *enseigne* f. L *insignia*: see INSIGNIA]

ensilage /ˈensɪlɪdʒ/ n. & v. —n. = SILAGE. —v.tr. treat (fodder) by ensilage. [F (as ENSILE)]

ensile /ɪnˈsaɪl/ v.tr. **1** put (fodder) into a silo. **2** preserve (fodder) in a silo. [F *ensiler* f. Sp. *ensilar* (as EN-1, SILO)]

enslave /ɪnˈsleɪv/ v.tr. make (a person) a slave. □□ **enslavement** n. **enslaver** n.

ensnare /ɪnˈsneə(r)/ v.tr. catch in or as in a snare; entrap. □□ **ensnarement** n.

ensue /ɪnˈsjuː/ v.intr. **1** happen afterwards. **2** (often foll. by *from, on*) occur as a result. [ME f. OF *ensuivre* ult. f. L *sequi* follow]

en suite /ɑ̃ ˈswiːt/ adv. forming a single unit (*bedroom with bathroom en suite*). [F, = in sequence]

ensure /ɪnˈʃʊə(r)/ v.tr. **1** (often foll. by *that* + clause) make certain. **2** (usu. foll. by *to, for*) secure (a thing for a person etc.). **3** (usu. foll. by *against*) make safe. □□ **ensurer** n. [ME f. AF *enseürer* f. OF *aseürer* ASSURE]

enswathe /ɪnˈsweɪð/ v.tr. bind or wrap in or as in a bandage. □□ **enswathement** n.

ENT abbr. ear, nose, and throat.

-ent /ənt, ent/ suffix **1** forming adjectives denoting attribution of an action (*consequent*) or state (*existent*). **2** forming nouns denoting an agent (*coefficient; president*). [from or after F *-ent* or L *-ent-* pres. part. stem of verbs (cf. -ANT)]

entablature /ɪnˈtæblətʃə(r)/ n. Archit. the upper part of a classical building supported by columns or a colonnade, comprising architrave, frieze, and cornice. [It. *intavolatura* f. *intavolare* board up (as IN-2, *tavola* table)]

entablement /ɪnˈteɪb(ə)lmənt/ n. a platform supporting a statue, above the dado and base. [F, f. *entabler* (as EN-1, TABLE)]

entail /ɪnˈteɪl, en-/ v. & n. —v.tr. **1** necessitate or involve unavoidably (*the work entails much effort*). **2** *Law* bequeath (property etc.) so that it remains within a family. **3** (usu. foll. by *on*) bestow (a thing) inalienably. —*n. Law* **1** an entailed estate. **2** the succession to such an estate. □□ **entailment** *n.* [ME, f. EN-¹ + AF *taile* TAIL²]

entangle /ɪnˈtæŋg(ə)l/ *v.tr.* **1** cause to get caught in a snare or among obstacles. **2** cause to become tangled. **3** involve in difficulties or illicit activities. **4** make (a thing) tangled or intricate; complicate.

entanglement /ɪnˈtæŋg(ə)lmənt/ *n.* **1** the act or condition of entangling or being entangled. **2 a** a thing that entangles. **b** *Mil.* an extensive barrier erected to obstruct an enemy's movements (esp. one made of stakes and interlaced barbed wire). **3** a compromising (esp. amorous) relationship.

entasis /ˈentəsɪs/ *n. Archit.* a slight convex curve in a column shaft to correct the visual illusion that straight sides give of curving inwards. [mod.L f. Gk f. *enteinō* to stretch]

Entebbe /enˈtebɪ/ a town in Uganda, on the north shore of Lake Victoria; pop. (1980) 20,500.

entellus /ɪnˈteləs/ *n.* = HANUMAN. [name of a Trojan in Virgil's *Aeneid*]

entente /ɒnˈtɒnt/ *n.* **1** = ENTENTE CORDIALE. **2** a group of States in such a relation. [F, = understanding (as INTENT)]

entente cordiale /ã,tãt kɔːdɪˈɑːl/ *n.* a friendly understanding between States, esp. (often **Entente Cordiale**) that reached in 1904 between Britain and France. Although not an alliance in its own right, this entente did draw Britain away from a position of isolation *vis-à-vis* the rest of Europe and towards a common policy with France and Russia. (See also TRIPLE ENTENTE.) [F, = cordial understanding: see ENTENTE]

enter /ˈentə(r)/ *v.* **1 a** *intr.* (often foll. by *into*) go or come in. **b** *tr.* go or come into. **c** *intr.* come on stage (as a direction: *enter Macbeth*). **2** *tr.* penetrate; go through (*a bullet entered his chest*). **3** *tr.* (often foll. by *up*) write (a name, details, etc.) in a list, book, etc. **4 a** *intr.* register or announce oneself as a competitor (*entered for the long jump*). **b** *tr.* become a competitor in (an event). **c** *tr.* record the name of (a person etc.) as a competitor (*entered two horses for the Derby*). **5** *tr.* **a** become a member of (a society etc.). **b** enrol as a member or prospective member of a society, school, etc.; admit or obtain admission for. **6** *tr.* make known; present for consideration (*entered a protest*). **7** *tr.* put into an official record. **8** *intr.* (foll. by *into*) **a** engage in (conversation, relations, an undertaking, etc.). **b** subscribe to; bind oneself by (an agreement etc.). **c** form part of (one's calculations, plans, etc.). **d** sympathize with (feelings etc.). **9** *intr.* (foll. by *on, upon*) **a** begin, undertake; begin to deal with (a subject). **b** assume the functions of (an office). **c** assume possession of (property). **10** *intr.* (foll. by *up*) complete a series of entries in (account-books etc.). □□ **enterer** *n.* [ME f. OF *entrer* f. L *intrare*]

enteric /enˈterɪk/ *adj. & n.* —*adj.* of the intestines. —*n.* (in full **enteric fever**) typhoid. □□ **enteritis** /ˌentəˈraɪtɪs/ *n.* [Gk *enterikos* (as ENTERO-)]

entero- /ˈentərəʊ/ *comb. form* intestine. [Gk *enteron* intestine]

enterostomy /ˌentəˈrɒstəmɪ/ *n.* (*pl.* **-ies**) *Surgery* a surgical operation in which the small intestine is brought through the abdominal wall and opened, in order to bypass the stomach or the colon.

enterotomy /ˌentəˈrɒtəmɪ/ *n.* (*pl.* **-ies**) *Surgery* the surgical cutting open of the intestine.

enterovirus /ˌentərəʊˈvaɪərəs/ *n.* a virus infecting the intestines and sometimes spreading to other parts of the body, esp. the central nervous system.

enterprise /ˈentəpraɪz/ *n.* **1** an undertaking, esp. a bold or difficult one. **2** (as a personal attribute) readiness to engage in such undertakings (*has no enterprise*). **3** a business firm. □ **enterprise zone** *Brit.* a depressed (usu. urban) area where State incentives such as tax concessions are designed to encourage investment. □□ **enterpriser** *n.* [ME f. OF *entreprise* fem. past part. of *entreprendre* var. of *emprendre* ult. f. L *prendere*, *prehendere* take]

enterprising /ˈentəpraɪzɪŋ/ *adj.* **1** ready to engage in enterprises. **2** resourceful, imaginative, energetic. □□ **enterprisingly** *adv.*

entertain /ˌentəˈteɪn/ *v.tr.* **1** amuse; occupy agreeably. **2 a** receive or treat as a guest. **b** (*absol.*) receive guests (*they entertain a great deal*). **3** give attention or consideration to (an idea, feeling, or proposal). [ME f. F *entretenir* ult. f. L *tenēre* hold]

entertainer /ˌentəˈteɪnə(r)/ *n.* a person who entertains, esp. professionally on stage etc.

entertaining /ˌentəˈteɪnɪŋ/ *adj.* amusing, diverting.

entertainment /ˌentəˈteɪnmənt/ *n.* **1** the act or an instance of entertaining; the process of being entertained. **2** a public performance or show. **3** diversions or amusements for guests etc. **4** amusement (*much to my entertainment*). **5** hospitality.

enthalpy /ˈenθəlpɪ, enˈθælpɪ/ *n. Physics* the total thermodynamic heat content of a system. [Gk *enthalpō* warm in (as EN-¹, *thalpō* to heat)]

enthral /ɪnˈθrɔːl/ *v.tr.* (US **enthrall**, **inthrall**) (**-thralled**, **-thralling**) **1** captivate, please greatly. **2** enslave. □□ **enthralment** *n.* (US **enthrallment**). [EN-¹ + THRALL]

enthrone /ɪnˈθrəʊn/ *v.tr.* **1** install (a king, bishop, etc.) on a throne, esp. ceremonially. **2** exalt. □□ **enthronement** *n.*

enthuse /ɪnˈθjuːz, -ˈθuːz/ *v.intr. & tr. colloq.* be or make enthusiastic. [back-form. f. ENTHUSIASM]

enthusiasm /ɪnˈθjuːzɪˌæz(ə)m, -ˈθuːzɪˌæz(ə)m/ *n.* **1** (often foll. by *for, about*) **a** strong interest or admiration. **b** great eagerness. **2** an object of enthusiasm. **3** *archaic* extravagant religious emotion. [F *enthousiasme* or LL *enthusiasmus* f. Gk *enthousiasmos* f. *entheos* possessed by a god, inspired (as EN-², *theos* god)]

enthusiast /ɪnˈθjuːzɪˌæst, -ˈθuːzɪˌæst/ *n.* **1** (often foll. by *for*) a person who is full of enthusiasm. **2** a visionary; a self-deluded person. [F *enthousiaste* or eccl.L *enthusiastes* f. Gk (as ENTHUSIASM)]

enthusiastic /ɪnˌθjuːzɪˈæstɪk, -ˌθuːzɪˈæstɪk/ *adj.* having or showing enthusiasm. □□ **enthusiastically** *adv.* [Gk *enthousiastikos* (as ENTHUSIASM)]

enthymeme /ˈenθɪˌmiːm/ *n. Logic* a syllogism in which one premiss is not explicitly stated. [L *enthymema* f. Gk *enthumēma* f. *enthumeomai* consider (as EN-², *thumos* mind)]

entice /ɪnˈtaɪs/ *v.tr.* (often foll. by *from, into, or to* + *infin.*) persuade by the offer of pleasure or reward. □□ **enticement** *n.* **enticer** *n.* **enticingly** *adv.* [ME f. OF *enticier* prob. f. Rmc]

entire /ɪnˈtaɪə(r)/ *adj. & n.* —*adj.* **1** whole, complete. **2** not broken or decayed. **3** unqualified, absolute (*an entire success*). **4** in one piece; continuous. **5** not castrated. **6** *Bot.* without indentation. **7** pure, unmixed. —*n.* an uncastrated animal. [ME f. AF *enter*, OF *entier* f. L *integer* (as IN-², *tangere* touch)]

entirely /ɪnˈtaɪəlɪ/ *adv.* **1** wholly, completely (*the stock is entirely exhausted*). **2** solely, exclusively (*did it entirely for my benefit*).

entirety /ɪnˈtaɪərətɪ/ *n.* (*pl.* **-ies**) **1** completeness. **2** (usu. foll. by *of*) the sum total. □ **in its entirety** in its complete form; completely. [ME f. OF *entiereté* f. L *integritas* *-tatis* f. *integer*: see ENTIRE]

entitle /ɪnˈtaɪt(ə)l/ *v.tr.* **1 a** (usu. foll. by *to*) give (a person etc.) a just claim. **b** (foll. by *to* + *infin.*) give (a person etc.) a right. **2 a** give (a book etc.) the title of. **b** *archaic* give (a person) the title of (*entitled him sultan*). □□ **entitlement** *n.* [ME f. AF *entitler*, OF *entiteler* f. LL *intitulare* (as IN-², TITLE)]

entity /ˈentɪtɪ/ *n.* (*pl.* **-ies**) **1** a thing with distinct existence, as opposed to a quality or relation. **2** a thing's existence regarded distinctly. □□ **entitative** /-tətɪv/ *adj.* [F *entité* or med.L *entitas* f. LL *ens* being]

ento- /ˈentəʊ/ *comb. form* within. [Gk *entos* within]

entomb /ɪnˈtuːm/ *v.tr.* **1** place in or as in a tomb. **2** serve as a tomb for. □□ **entombment** *n.* [OF *entomber* (as EN-¹, TOMB)]

entomo- /ˈentəməʊ/ *comb. form* insect. [Gk *entomos* cut up (in neut. = INSECT) f. EN-² + *temnō* cut]

entomology /ˌentəˈmɒlədʒɪ/ *n.* the study of the forms and behaviour of insects. □□ **entomological** /-məˈlɒdʒɪk(ə)l/ *adj.* **entomologist** *n.* [F *entomologie* or mod.L *entomologia* (as ENTOMO-, -LOGY)]

entomophagous /ˌentəˈmɒfəgəs/ *adj. Zool.* insect-eating.

b but d dog f few g get h he j yes k cat l leg m man n no p pen r red s sit t top v voice

entomophilous /ˌentəˈmɒfɪləs/ adj. Biol. pollinated by insects.

entoparasite /ˌentəʊˈpærəˌsaɪt/ n. Biol. = ENDOPARASITE.

entophyte /ˈentəʊˌfaɪt/ n. Bot. a plant growing inside a plant or animal.

entourage /ˌɒntʊəˈrɑːʒ/ n. 1 people attending an important person. 2 surroundings. [F f. entourer surround]

entr'acte /ˈɒntrækt/ n. 1 an interval between two acts of a play. 2 a piece of music or a dance performed during this. [F f. entre between + acte act]

entrails /ˈentreɪlz/ n.pl. 1 the bowels and intestines of a person or animal. 2 the innermost parts (entrails of the earth). [ME f. OF entrailles f. med.L intralia alt. f. L interaneus internal f. inter among]

entrain[1] /ɪnˈtreɪn/ v.intr. & tr. go or put on board a train. □□ **entrainment** n.

entrain[2] /ɪnˈtreɪn/ v.tr. 1 (of a fluid) carry (particles etc.) along in its flow. 2 drag along. □□ **entrainment** n. [F entraîner (as EN-[1], traîner drag, formed as TRAIN)]

entrain[3] /ɑ̃ˈtræ/ n. enthusiasm, animation. [F]

entrammel /ɪnˈtræm(ə)l/ v.tr. (**entrammelled, entrammelling**; US **entrammeled, entrammeling**) entangle, hamper.

entrance[1] /ˈentrəns/ n. 1 the act or an instance of going or coming in. 2 a door, passage, etc., by which one enters. 3 right of admission. 4 the coming of an actor on stage. 5 Mus. = ENTRY 8. 6 (foll. by into, upon) entering into office etc. 7 (in full **entrance fee**) a fee paid for admission to a society, club, exhibition, etc. [OF (as ENTER, -ANCE)]

entrance[2] /ɪnˈtrɑːns/ v.tr. 1 enchant, delight. 2 put into a trance. 3 (often foll. by with) overwhelm with strong feeling. □□ **entrancement** n. **entrancing** adj. **entrancingly** adv.

entrant /ˈentrənt/ n. a person who enters (esp. an examination, profession, etc.). [F, part. of entrer: see ENTER]

entrap /ɪnˈtræp/ v.tr. (**entrapped, entrapping**) 1 catch in or as in a trap. 2 (often foll. by into + verbal noun) beguile or trick (a person). □□ **entrapper** n. [OF entraper (as EN-[1], TRAP[1])]

entrapment /ɪnˈtræpmənt/ n. 1 the act or an instance of entrapping; the process of being entrapped. 2 Law inducement to commit a crime, esp. by the authorities to secure a prosecution.

entreat /ɪnˈtriːt/ v.tr. 1 a (foll. by to + infin. or that + clause) ask (a person) earnestly. b ask earnestly for (a thing). 2 archaic treat; act towards (a person). □□ **entreatingly** adv. [ME f. OF entraiter (as EN-[1], traiter TREAT)]

entreaty /ɪnˈtriːtɪ/ n. (pl. -**ies**) an earnest request; a supplication. [ENTREAT, after TREATY]

entrechat /ˌɒntrəˈʃɑː/ n. a leap in ballet, with one or more crossings of the legs while in the air. [F f. It. (capriola) intrecciata complicated (caper)]

entrecôte /ˈɒntrəˌkəʊt/ n. a boned steak cut off the sirloin. [F f. entre between + côte rib]

entrée /ˈɑ̃ntreɪ, ˈɒtreɪ/ n. 1 Cookery a Brit. a dish served between the fish and meat courses. b esp. US the main dish of a meal. 2 the right or privilege of admission, esp. at Court. [F, = ENTRY]

entremets /ˌɒntrəˈmeɪ/ n. 1 a sweet dish. 2 any light dish served between two courses. [F f. entre between + mets dish]

entrench /ɪnˈtrentʃ/ v. (also **intrench**) 1 tr. establish firmly (in a defensible position, in office, etc.). 2 tr. surround (a post, army, town, etc.) with a trench as a fortification. 3 tr. apply extra safeguards to (rights etc. guaranteed by legislation). 4 intr. entrench oneself. 5 intr. (foll. by upon) encroach, trespass. □ **entrench oneself** adopt a well-defended position. □□ **entrenchment** n.

entre nous /ˌɒntrə ˈnuː/ adv. 1 between you and me. 2 in private. [F, = between ourselves]

entrepôt /ˈɒntrəˌpəʊ/ n. 1 a warehouse for temporary storage of goods in transit. 2 a commercial centre for import and export, and for collection and distribution. [F f. entreposer store f. entre-INTER- + poser place]

entrepreneur /ˌɒntrəprəˈnɜː(r)/ n. 1 a person who undertakes an enterprise or business, with the chance of profit or loss. 2 a contractor acting as an intermediary. 3 the person in effective control of a commercial undertaking. □□ **entrepreneurial** /-ˈnɜːrɪəl, -ˈnjʊərɪəl/ adj. **entrepreneurialism** /-ˈnɜːrɪəˌlɪz(ə)m, -ˈnjʊərɪəˌlɪz(ə)m/ n. (also **entrepreneurism**). **entrepreneurially** /-ˈnɜːrɪəlɪ, -ˈnjʊərɪəlɪ/ adv. **entrepreneurship** n. [F f. entreprendre undertake: see ENTERPRISE]

entresol /ˈɒntrəˌsɒl/ n. a low storey between the first and the ground floor; a mezzanine floor. [F f. entre between + sol ground]

entrism var. of ENTRYISM.

entropy /ˈentrəpɪ/ n. 1 Physics a measure of the unavailability of a system's thermal energy for conversion into mechanical work. (See below.) 2 Physics a measure of the disorganization or degradation of the universe. 3 a measure of the rate of transfer of information in a message etc. □□ **entropic** /-ˈtrɒpɪk/ adj. **entropically** /-ˈtrɒpɪkəlɪ/ adv. [G Entropie (as EN-[2], Gk tropē transformation)]

The concept of entropy first arose in the 19th c. as a mathematical quantity in thermodynamics. It was later given a physical interpretation as representing the degree of disorder of the constituents of any physical system. Thermodynamic theory indicates that the entropy of an isolated system can increase but will never decrease, and that the universe therefore appears to be steadily running down and may eventually reach a 'heat death' where the temperature is even throughout the whole universe.

entrust /ɪnˈtrʌst/ v.tr. (also **intrust**) 1 (foll. by to) give responsibility for (a person or a thing) to a person in whom one has confidence. 2 (foll. by with) assign responsibility for a thing to (a person). □□ **entrustment** n.

entry /ˈentrɪ/ n. (pl. -**ies**) 1 a the act or an instance of going or coming in. b the coming of an actor on stage. c ceremonial entrance. 2 liberty to go or come in. 3 a a place of entrance; a door, gate, etc. b a lobby. 4 Brit. a passage between buildings. 5 the mouth of a river. 6 a an item entered in a diary, list, account-book, etc. b the recording of this. 7 a a person or thing competing in a race, contest, etc. b a list of competitors. 8 the start or resumption of music for a particular instrument in an ensemble. 9 Law the act of taking possession. 10 Bridge a the transfer of the lead to one's partner's hand. b a card providing this. □ **entry form** an application form for a competition. **entry permit** an authorization to enter a particular country etc. [ME f. OF entree ult. f. L intrare ENTER]

entryism /ˈentrɪˌɪz(ə)m/ n. (also **entrism**) infiltration into a political organization to change or subvert its policies or objectives. □□ **entrist** n. **entryist** n.

Entryphone /ˈentrɪˌfəʊn/ n. propr. an intercom device at an entrance to a building by which callers may identify themselves to gain admission.

entwine /ɪnˈtwaɪn/ v.tr. (also **intwine**) 1 (foll. by with, about, round) twine together (a thing with or round another). 2 interweave. □□ **entwinement** n.

enucleate /ɪˈnjuːklɪˌeɪt/ v.tr. Surgery extract (a tumour etc.). □□ **enucleation** /-ˈeɪʃ(ə)n/ n. [L enucleare (as E-, NUCLEUS)]

E-number /ˈiːˌnʌmbə(r)/ n. the letter E followed by a code number, designating food additives according to EEC directives.

enumerate /ɪˈnjuːməˌreɪt/ v.tr. 1 specify (items); mention one by one. 2 count; establish the number of. □□ **enumerable** adj. **enumeration** /-ˈreɪʃ(ə)n/ n. **enumerative** /-rətɪv/ adj. [L enumerare (as E-, NUMBER)]

enumerator /ɪˈnjuːməˌreɪtə(r)/ n. 1 a person who enumerates. 2 a person employed in census-taking.

enunciate /ɪˈnʌnsɪˌeɪt/ v.tr. 1 pronounce (words) clearly. 2 express (a proposition or theory) in definite terms. 3 proclaim. □□ **enunciation** /-ˈeɪʃ(ə)n/ n. **enunciative** /-sɪətɪv/ adj. **enunciator** n. [L enuntiare (as E-, nuntiare announce f. nuntius messenger)]

enure /ɪˈnjʊə(r)/ v.intr. Law take effect. [var. of INURE]

enuresis /ˌenjʊəˈriːsɪs/ n. Med. involuntary urination. □□ **enuretic** /-ˈretɪk/ adj. & n. [mod.L f. Gk enoureō urinate in (as EN-[2], ouron urine)]

envelop /ɪnˈveləp/ v.tr. (**enveloped, enveloping**) 1 (often foll. by in) a wrap up or cover completely. b make obscure; conceal (*was enveloped in mystery*). **2** *Mil.* completely surround (an enemy). □□ **envelopment** *n.* [ME f. OF *envoluper* (as EN-¹: cf. DEVELOP)]

envelope /ˈenvəˌləʊp, ˈɒn-/ *n.* **1** a folded paper container, usu. with a sealable flap, for a letter etc. **2** a wrapper or covering. **3** the structure within a balloon or airship containing the gas. **4** the outer metal or glass housing of a vacuum tube, electric light, etc. **5** *Electr.* a curve joining the successive peaks of a modulated wave. **6** *Bot.* any enveloping structure esp. the calyx or corolla (or both). **7** *Math.* a line or curve tangent to each line or curve of a given family. [F *enveloppe* (as ENVELOP)]

envenom /ɪnˈvenəm/ *v.tr.* **1** put poison on or into; make poisonous. **2** infuse venom or bitterness into (feelings, words, or actions). [ME f. OF *envenimer* (as EN-¹, *venim* VENOM)]

enviable /ˈenviəb(ə)l/ *adj.* (of a person or thing) exciting or likely to excite envy. □□ **enviably** *adv.*

envious /ˈenviəs/ *adj.* (often foll. by *of*) feeling or showing envy. □□ **enviously** *adv.* [ME f. AF *envious*, OF *envieus* f. *envie* ENVY]

environ /ɪnˈvaɪərən/ *v.tr.* encircle, surround (esp. hostilely or protectively). [ME f. OF *environer* f. *environ* surroundings f. *en* in + *viron* circuit f. *virer* turn, VEER¹]

environment /ɪnˈvaɪərənmənt/ *n.* **1** physical surroundings and conditions, esp. as affecting people's lives. **2** conditions or circumstances of living. **3** *Ecol.* external conditions affecting the growth of plants and animals. **4** a structure designed to be experienced from inside as a work of art. □□ **environmental** /-ˈment(ə)l/ *adj.* **environmentally** /-ˈmentəlɪ/ *adv.*

environmentalist /ɪnˌvaɪərənˈmentəlɪst/ *n.* **1** a person who is concerned with or advocates the protection of the environment. **2** a person who considers that environment has the primary influence on the development of a person or group. □□ **environmentalism** *n.*

environs /ɪnˈvaɪərənz, ˈenvɪrənz/ *n.pl.* a surrounding district, esp. round an urban area.

envisage /ɪnˈvɪzɪdʒ/ *v.tr.* **1** have a mental picture of (a thing or conditions not yet existing). **2** contemplate or conceive, esp. as possible or desirable. **3** *archaic* **a** face (danger, facts, etc.). **b** look in the face of. □□ **envisagement** *n.* [F *envisager* (as EN-¹, VISAGE)]

envision /ɪnˈvɪʒ(ə)n/ *v.tr.* envisage, visualize.

envoy¹ /ˈenvɔɪ/ *n.* **1** a messenger or representative, esp. on a diplomatic mission. **2** (in full **envoy extraordinary**) a minister plenipotentiary, ranking below ambassador and above chargé d'affaires. □□ **envoyship** *n.* [F *envoyé*, past part. of *envoyer* send f. *en voie* on the way f. L *via*]

envoy² /ˈenvɔɪ/ *n.* (also **envoi**) **1** a short stanza concluding a ballade etc. **2** *archaic* an author's concluding words. [ME f. OF *envoi* f. *envoyer* (as ENVOY¹)]

envy /ˈenvɪ/ *n.* & *v.* —*n.* (pl. **-ies**) **1** a feeling of discontent or resentful longing aroused by another's better fortune etc. **2** the object or ground of this feeling (*their house is the envy of the neighbourhood*). —*v.tr.* (**-ies**, **-ied**) feel envy of (a person, circumstances, etc.) (*I envy you your position*). □□ **envier** *n.* [ME f. OF *envie* f. L *invidia* f. *invidēre* envy (as IN-¹, *vidēre* see)]

enweave var. of INWEAVE.

enwrap /ɪnˈræp/ *v.tr.* (also **inwrap**) (**-wrapped**, **-wrapping**) (often foll. by *in*) *literary* wrap or enfold.

enwreathe /ɪnˈriːð/ *v.tr.* (also **inwreathe**) *literary* surround with or as with a wreath.

Enzed /enˈzed/ *n. Austral. & NZ colloq.* a popular written form of: **1** New Zealand. **2** a New Zealander. □□ **Enzedder** *n.* [pronunc. of *NZ*]

enzootic /ˌenzəʊˈɒtɪk/ *adj.* & *n.* —*adj.* regularly affecting animals in a particular district or at a particular season (cf. ENDEMIC, EPIZOOTIC). —*n.* an enzootic disease. [Gk *en* in + *zōion* animal]

enzyme /ˈenzaɪm/ *n. Biochem.* any of a class of large molecules, consisting entirely or chiefly of protein, found in all cells and essential to life, that act as catalysts of biochemical reactions in all living organisms. They may work within a cell or (as with digestive enzymes) outside it. The shape of each enzyme is such that it catalyses only a specific type of reaction. □□ **enzymatic** /-ˈmætɪk/ *adj.* **enzymic** /-ˈzaɪmɪk/ *adj.* **enzymology** /-ˈmɒlədʒɪ/ *n.* [G *Enzym* f. med. Gk *enzumos* leavened f. Gk *en* in + *zumē* leaven]

EOC *abbr.* Equal Opportunities Commission.

Eocene /ˈiːəʊˌsiːn/ *adj.* & *n. Geol.* —*adj.* of or relating to the second epoch of the Tertiary period, following the Palaeocene and preceding the Oligocene, lasting from about 54.9 to 38 million years ago. It was a time of rising world temperatures. There is evidence of an abundance of mammals, including horses, bats, and whales. —*n.* this epoch or system. [Gk *ēōs* dawn + *kainos* new]

EOKA /eɪˈɒkə/ *n.* (also **Eoka**) a Greek-Cypriot liberation movement of the 1950s. [Gk abbr., = National Organization of Cypriot Struggle (for the furthering of the Greek cause in Cyprus)]

eolian *US* var. of AEOLIAN.

eolith /ˈiːəlɪθ/ *n. Archaeol.* any of various flint objects found in Tertiary strata and thought to be early artefacts. [Gk *ēōs* dawn + *lithos* stone]

eolithic /ˌiːəˈlɪθɪk/ *adj. Archaeol.* of the period preceding the palaeolithic age, thought to include the earliest use of flint tools. [F *éolithique* (as EOLITH)]

eon var. of AEON.

Eos /ˈiːɒs/ see AURORA. [Gk, = dawn]

eosin /ˈiːəsɪn/ *n.* a red fluorescent dyestuff used esp. as a stain in optical microscopy. [Gk *ēōs* dawn + -IN]

eosinophil /ˌiːəˈsɪnəfɪl/ *n.* a white blood cell readily stained by eosin.

-eous /ɪəs/ *suffix* forming adjectives meaning 'of the nature of' (*erroneous*; *gaseous*).

EP *abbr.* **1** electroplate. **2** extended-play (gramophone record).

Ep. *abbr.* Epistle.

ep- /ep, ɪp, iːp/ *prefix* form of EPI- before a vowel or *h*.

e.p. *abbr.* (in chess) *en passant*.

EPA *abbr.* (in the US) Environmental Protection Agency.

epact /ˈiːpækt/ *n.* the number of days by which the solar year exceeds the lunar year. [F *épacte* f. LL *epactae* f. Gk *epaktai* (*hēmerai*) intercalated (days) f. *epagō* intercalate (as EPI-, *agō* bring)]

eparch /ˈepɑːk/ *n.* the chief bishop of an eparchy. [Gk *eparkhos* (as EPI-, *arkhos* ruler)]

eparchy /ˈepɑːkɪ/ *n.* (pl. **-ies**) a province of the Orthodox Church. [Gk *eparkhia* (as EPARCH)]

epaulette /ˈepələt, ˈepɔːˌlet, ˈepəʊˌlet, ˌepəˈlet/ *n.* (*US* **epaulet**) an ornamental shoulder-piece on a coat, dress, etc., esp. on a uniform. [F *épaulette* dimin. of *épaule* shoulder f. L *spatula*: see SPATULA]

épée /eɪˈpeɪ/ *n.* a sharp-pointed duelling-sword, used (with the end blunted) in fencing. □□ **épéeist** *n.* [F, = sword, f. OF *espee*: see SPAY]

epeirogenesis /eɪˌpaɪərəʊˈdʒenɪsɪs/ *n.* (also **epeirogeny** /-ˈrɒdʒənɪ/) *Geol.* the regional uplift of extensive areas of the earth's crust. □□ **epeirogenic** /-ˈdʒenɪk/ *adj.* [Gk *ēpeiros* mainland + -GENESIS, -GENY]

epenthesis /eˈpenθɪsɪs, ɪ-/ *n.* (pl. **epentheses** /-siːz/) the insertion of a letter or sound within a word, e.g. *b* in *thimble*. □□ **epenthetic** /ˌepenˈθetɪk/ *adj.* [LL f. Gk f. *epentithēmi* insert (as EPI- + EN-² + *tithēmi* place)]

epergne /ɪˈpɜːn/ *n.* an ornament (esp. in branched form) for the centre of a dinner-table, holding flowers or fruit. [18th c.: perh. a corrupt. of F *épargne* saving, economy]

epexegesis /eˌpeksɪˈdʒiːsɪs/ *n.* (pl. **epexegeses** /-siːz/) **1** the addition of words to clarify meaning (e.g. *to do* in *difficult to do*). **2** the words added. □□ **epexegetic** /-ˈdʒetɪk/ *adj.* **epexegetical** /-ˈdʒetɪk(ə)l/ *adj.* **epexegetically** /-ˈdʒetɪkəlɪ/ *adv.* [Gk *epexēgēsis* (as EPI-, EXEGESIS)]

Eph. *abbr.* Ephesians (New Testament).

ephebe /ˈefiːb/ *n. Gk Hist.* a young man of 18–20 undergoing military training. □□ **ephebic** /eˈfiːbɪk/ *adj.* [L *ephebus* f. Gk *ephēbos* (as EPI-, *hēbē* early manhood)]

ephedra /ɪˈfedrə/ *n.* any evergreen shrub of the genus *Ephedra*, with trailing stems and scalelike leaves. [mod.L f. Gk *ephedra* sitting upon]

ephedrine /ˈefədrɪn/ *n.* an alkaloid drug found in some ephedras, causing constriction of the blood-vessels and widening of the bronchial passages, used to relieve asthma, etc. [EPHEDRA + -INE⁴]

ephemera¹ /ɪˈfemərə, ɪˈfiːm-/ n. (pl. **ephemeras** or **ephemerae** /-ˌriː/) **1 a** an insect living only a day or a few days. **b** any insect of the order Ephemeroptera, e.g. the mayfly. **2** = EPHEMERON. [mod.L f. Gk *ephēmeros* lasting only a day (as EPI-, *hēmera* day)]

ephemera² pl. of EPHEMERON 1.

ephemeral /ɪˈfemər(ə)l, ɪˈfiːm-/ adj. **1** lasting or of use for only a short time; transitory. **2** lasting only a day. **3** (of an insect, flower, etc.) lasting a day or a few days. □□ **ephemerality** /-ˈrælɪtɪ/ n. **ephemerally** adv. **ephemeralness** n. [Gk *ephēmeros*: see EPHEMERA]

ephemeris /ɪˈfemərɪs, ɪˈfiːm-/ n. (pl. **ephemerides** /ˌefɪˈmerɪˌdiːz/) Astron. an astronomical almanac or table of the predicted positions of celestial bodies. [L f. Gk *ephēmeris* diary (as EPHEMERAL)]

ephemerist /ɪˈfemərɪst/ n. a collector of ephemera.

ephemeron /ɪˈfemərɒn, ɪˈfiːm-/ n. **1** (pl. **ephemera** /-rə/) (usu. in pl.) **a** a thing (esp. a printed item) of short-lived interest or usefulness. **b** a short-lived thing. **2** (pl. **ephemerons**) = EPHEMERA¹ 1. [as EPHEMERA¹]

Ephesians /ɪˈfiːʒ(ə)nz/ **Epistle to the Ephesians** a book of the New Testament ascribed to St Paul, an epistle to the Church at Ephesus.

Ephesus /ˈefɪsəs/ an ancient Greek city and seaport on the west coast of Asia Minor (modern Turkey), site of the temple of Artemis that was one of the Seven Wonders of the World, and an important centre of early Christianity. St Paul visited it several times (cf. Acts 19) and St John is said to be buried here. Because of silting the remains of the city are now more than 5 km (3 miles) inland.

ephod /ˈiːfɒd, ˈefɒd/ n. a Jewish priestly vestment. [ME f. Heb. *'ēpôd*]

ephor /ˈefɔː(r)/ n. Gk Hist. any of five senior magistrates in ancient Sparta. □□ **ephorate** n. [Gk *ephoros* overseer (as EPI-, *horaō* see)]

epi- /ˈepɪ-/ prefix (usu. **ep-** before a vowel or h) **1** upon (epicycle). **2** above (epicotyl). **3** in addition (epiphenomenon). [Gk *epi* (prep.)]

epiblast /ˈepɪˌblæst/ n. Biol. the outermost layer of a gastrula etc.; the ectoderm. [EPI- + -BLAST]

epic /ˈepɪk/ n. & adj. —n. **1** a long poem narrating the adventures or deeds of one or more heroic or legendary figures, e.g. the *Iliad*, *Paradise Lost*. **2** an imaginative work of any form, embodying a nation's conception of its past history. **3** a book or film based on an epic narrative or heroic in type or scale. **4** a subject fit for recital in an epic. —adj. **1** of or like an epic. **2** grand, heroic. □□ **epical** adj. **epically** adv. [L *epicus* f. Gk *epikos* f. *epos* word, song]

epicarp /ˈepɪˌkɑːp/ n. Bot. the outermost layer of the pericarp. [EPI- + Gk *karpos* fruit]

epicedium /ˌepɪˈsiːdɪəm/ n. (pl. **epicedia** /-dɪə/) a funeral ode. □□ **epicedian** adj. [L f. Gk *epikēdeion* (as EPI-, *kēdos* care)]

epicene /ˈepɪˌsiːn/ adj. & n. —adj. **1** Gram. denoting either sex without change of gender. **2** of, for, or used by both sexes. **3** having characteristics of both sexes. **4** having no characteristics of either sex. **5** effete, effeminate. —n. an epicene person. [ME f. LL *epicoenus* f. Gk *epikoinos* (as EPI-, *koinos* common)]

epicentre /ˈepɪˌsentə(r)/ n. (US **epicenter**) **1** Geol. the point at which an earthquake reaches the earth's surface. **2** the central point of a difficulty. □□ **epicentral** /-ˈsentr(ə)l/ adj. [Gk *epikentros* (adj.) (as EPI-, CENTRE)]

epicontinental /ˌepɪˌkɒntɪˈnent(ə)l/ adj. (of the sea) over the continental shelf.

epicotyl /ˌepɪˈkɒtɪl/ n. Bot. the region of an embryo or seedling stem above the cotyledon(s).

Epictetus /ˌepɪkˈtiːtəs/ (c.55–c.135) Stoic philosopher, originally a slave, who taught in Rome and later in Epirus in NW Greece. He addressed himself to the multitude, preaching the common brotherhood of man and advocating indifference to the blows of fortune and submission to the workings of Providence. Post-humous publications of his teaching, including the *Manual* (*Enchiridion*), had a great influence on Marcus Aurelius.

epicure /ˈepɪˌkjʊə(r)/ n. a person with refined tastes, esp. in food and drink. □□ **epicurism** n. [med.L *epicurus* one preferring sensual enjoyment: see EPICUREAN]

epicurean /ˌepɪkjʊəˈriːən/ adj. & n. —adj. fond of refined sensuous pleasure and luxury. —n. a person with epicurean tastes. [F *épicurien* or L *epicureus* f. Gk *epikoureios* f. *Epikouros* EPICURUS]

Epicurus /ˌepɪˈkjʊərəs/ (341–270 BC) Greek philosopher who taught in his garden at Athens (whence the sect named after him is known as the 'Garden'). His physics (later expounded by the Roman writer Lucretius) is based on the theory of a materialist universe, unregulated by divine Providence, composed of indestructible atoms moving in a void. From this follows his moral theory (later misrepresented as licence for indulgence of the appetites), a hedonism seeking the minimization of pain by avoidance of unnecessary fears and desires in private and public life, leading to the quietist ideal of freedom from disturbance. □□ **Epicurean** /-ˈriːən/ adj. & n., **Epicureanism** /-ˈriːənɪz(ə)m/ n.

epicycle /ˈepɪˌsaɪk(ə)l/ n. Geom. a small circle moving round the circumference of a larger one. □□ **epicyclic** /-ˈsaɪklɪk, -ˈsɪklɪk/ adj. [ME f. OF or LL *epicyclus* f. Gk *epikuklos* (as EPI-, *kuklos* circle)]

epicycloid /ˌepɪˈsaɪklɔɪd/ n. Math. a curve traced by a point on the circumference of a circle rolling on the exterior of another circle. □□ **epicycloidal** /-ˈklɔɪd(ə)l/ adj.

Epidaurus /ˌepɪˈdɔːrəs/ an ancient Greek city and port on the NE coast of the Peloponnese, famous for its temple of Asclepius and site of a well-preserved Greek theatre dating from the 4th c. BC.

epideictic /ˌepɪˈdaɪktɪk/ adj. meant for effect or display, esp. in speaking. [Gk *epideiktikos* (as EPI-, *deiknumi* show)]

epidemic /ˌepɪˈdemɪk/ n. & adj. —n. **1** a widespread occurrence of a disease in a community at a particular time. **2** such a disease. **3** (foll. by *of*) a wide prevalence of something usu. undesirable. —adj. in the nature of an epidemic (cf. ENDEMIC). □□ **epidemically** adv. [F *épidémique* f. *épidémie* f. LL *epidemia* f. Gk *epidēmia* prevalence of disease f. *epidēmios* (adj.) (as EPI-, *dēmos* the people)]

epidemiology /ˌepɪdiːmɪˈɒlədʒɪ/ n. the study of the incidence and distribution of diseases, and of their control and prevention. □□ **epidemiological** /-mɪəˈlɒdʒɪk(ə)l/ adj. **epidemiologist** n.

epidermis /ˌepɪˈdɜːmɪs/ n. **1** the outer cellular layer of the skin. **2** Bot. the outer layer of cells of leaves, stems, roots, etc. □□ **epidermal** adj. **epidermic** adj. **epidermoid** adj. [LL f. Gk (as EPI-, DERMIS)]

epidiascope /ˌepɪˈdaɪəˌskəʊp/ n. an optical projector capable of giving images of both opaque and transparent objects. [EPI- + DIA- + -SCOPE]

epididymis /ˌepɪˈdɪdɪmɪs/ n. (pl. **epididymides** /-ˈdɪmɪˌdiːz/) Anat. a convoluted duct behind the testis, along which sperm passes to the vas deferens. [Gk *epididumis* (as EPI-, *didumoi* testicles)]

epidural /ˌepɪˈdjʊər(ə)l/ adj. & n. —adj. **1** Anat. on or around the dura mater. **2** (of an anaesthetic) introduced into the space around the dura mater of the spinal cord. —n. an epidural anaesthetic, used esp. in childbirth to produce loss of sensation below the waist. [EPI- + DURA (MATER)]

epifauna /ˈepɪˌfɔːnə/ n. animals living on the seabed, either attached to animals, plants, etc., or free-living. [Da. (as EPI-, FAUNA)]

epigastrium /ˌepɪˈgæstrɪəm/ n. (pl. **epigastria** /-rɪə/) Anat. the part of the abdomen immediately over the stomach. □□ **epigastric** adj. [LL f. Gk *epigastrion* (neut. adj.) (as EPI-, *gastēr* belly)]

epigeal /ˌepɪˈdʒiːəl/ adj. Bot. **1** having one or more cotyledons above the ground. **2** growing above the ground. [Gk *epigeios* (as EPI-, *gē* earth)]

epigene /ˈepɪˌdʒiːn/ adj. Geol. produced on the surface of the earth. [F *épigène* f. Gk *epigenēs* (as EPI-, *genēs* born)]

epiglottis /ˌepɪˈglɒtɪs/ n. Anat. a flap of cartilage at the root of the tongue, which is depressed during swallowing to cover the windpipe. □□ **epiglottal** adj. **epiglottic** adj. [Gk *epiglōttis* (as EPI-, *glōtta* tongue)]

aʊ how eɪ day əʊ no eə hair ɪə near ɔɪ boy ʊə poor aɪə fire aʊə sour   (*see over for consonants*)

epigone /ˈepɪˌgəʊn/ n. (pl. **epigones** or **epigoni** /eˈpɪgəˌnaɪ/) one of a later (and less distinguished) generation. [pl. f. F *épigones* f. L *epigoni* f. Gk *epigonoi* those born afterwards (as EPI-, root of *gignomai* be born)]

epigram /ˈepɪˌgræm/ n. **1** a short poem with a witty ending. **2** a pointed saying. **3** a pointed mode of expression. □□ **epigrammatic** /-grəˈmætɪk/ adj. **epigrammatically** /-grəˈmætɪkəlɪ/ adv. **epigrammatist** /-ˈgræmətɪst/ n. **epigrammatize** /-ˈgræməˌtaɪz/ v.tr. & intr. (also **-ise**). [F *épigramme* or L *epigramma* f. Gk *epigramma -atos* (as EPI-, -GRAM)]

epigraph /ˈepɪˌgrɑːf/ n. an inscription on a statue or coin, at the head of a chapter, etc. [Gk *epigraphē* f. *epigraphō* (as EPI-, *graphō* write)]

epigraphy /eˈpɪgrəfɪ/ n. the study of (esp. ancient) inscriptions. □□ **epigraphic** /-ˈgræfɪk/ adj. **epigraphical** /-ˈgræfɪk(ə)l/ adj. **epigraphically** /-ˈgræfɪkəlɪ/ adv. **epigraphist** n.

epilate /ˈepɪˌleɪt/ v.tr. remove hair from. □□ **epilation** /-ˈleɪʃ(ə)n/ n. [F *épiler* (cf. DEPILATE)]

epilepsy /ˈepɪˌlepsɪ/ n. a nervous disorder with seizures accompanied by changes in the rhythm of the electrical currents of the brain. There are several different forms: *grand mal* involves loss of consciousness, and convulsions; *petit mal* lasts for only a few seconds, with partial loss of consciousness. [F *épilepsie* or LL *epilepsia* f. Gk *epilēpsia* f. *epilambanō* attack (as EPI-, *lambanō* take)]

epileptic /ˌepɪˈleptɪk/ adj. & n. —adj. of or relating to epilepsy. —n. a person with epilepsy. [F *épileptique* f. LL *epilepticus* f. Gk *epilēptikos* (as EPILEPSY)]

epilimnion /ˌepɪˈlɪmnɪən/ n. (pl. **epilimnia** /-nɪə/) the upper layer of water in a stratified lake. [EPI- + Gk *limnion* dimin. of *limnē* lake]

epilogist /ɪˈpɪlədʒɪst/ n. the writer or speaker of an epilogue.

epilogue /ˈepɪˌlɒg/ n. **1 a** the concluding part of a literary work. **b** an appendix. **2** a speech or short poem addressed to the audience by an actor at the end of a play. **3** Brit. a short piece at the end of a day's broadcasting (cf. PROLOGUE). [ME f. F *épilogue* f. L *epilogus* f. Gk *epilogos* (as EPI-, *logos* speech)]

epimer /ˈepɪmə(r)/ n. Chem. either of two isomers with different configurations of atoms about one of several asymmetric carbon atoms present. □□ **epimeric** /-ˈmerɪk/ adj. **epimerism** /eˈpɪm-/ n. [G (as EPI-, -MER)]

epimerize /eˈpɪməˌraɪz/ v.tr. (also **-ise**) Chem. convert (one epimer) into the other.

epinasty /ˈepɪˌnæstɪ/ n. Bot. a tendency in plant-organs to grow more rapidly on the upper side. [EPI- + Gk *nastos* pressed]

epinephrine /ˌepɪˈnefrɪn/ n. Biochem. = ADRENALIN. [Gk *epi* upon + *nephros* kidney]

epiphany /eˈpɪfənɪ, ɪˈpɪf-/ n. (pl. **-ies**) **1** (**Epiphany**) **a** the manifestation of Christ to the Magi according to the biblical account. **b** the festival of the Church kept on 6 Jan., having originated in the East where it has been celebrated from the 3rd c. in honour of Christ's baptism. It was introduced into the Western Church in the 4th c. where it became associated with the manifestation of Christ to the Gentiles in the persons of the Magi. **2** any manifestation of a god or demigod. □□ **epiphanic** /ˌepɪˈfænɪk/ adj. [ME f. Gk *epiphaneia* manifestation f. *epiphainō* reveal (as EPI-, *phainō* show): sense 1 through OF *epiphanie* and eccl.L *epiphania*]

epiphenomenon /ˌepɪfɪˈnɒmɪnən/ n. (pl. **epiphenomena** /-nə/) **1** a secondary symptom, which may occur simultaneously with a disease etc. but is not regarded as its cause or result. **2** Psychol. consciousness regarded as a by-product of brain activity. □□ **epiphenomenal** adj.

epiphysis /eˈpɪfɪsɪs/ n. (pl. **epiphyses** /-ˌsiːz/) Anat. **1** the end part of a long bone, initially growing separately from the shaft. **2** = *pineal body*. [mod.L f. Gk *epiphusis* (as EPI-, *phusis* growth)]

epiphyte /ˈepɪˌfaɪt/ n. a plant growing but not parasitic on another, e.g. a moss. □□ **epiphytal** /-ˈfaɪt(ə)l/ adj. **epiphytic** /ˌepɪˈfɪtɪk/ adj. [EPI- + Gk *phuton* plant]

Epirus /ɪˈpaɪrəs/ (Greek **Ípiros** /ˈiːpɪˌrɒs/) **1** an ancient country located in the coastal region of NW Greece and southern Albania. Its most famous ruler was Pyrrhus (see entry). **2** an administrative region of NW Greece; pop. (1981) 324,500; capital, Ioánnina.

episcopacy /ɪˈpɪskəpəsɪ/ n. (pl. **-ies**) **1** government of a Church by bishops. **2** (prec. by the) the bishops.

episcopal /ɪˈpɪskəp(ə)l/ adj. **1** of a bishop or bishops. **2** (of a Church) constituted on the principle of government by bishops. □ **Episcopal Church** the Anglican Church in Scotland and the US, with elected bishops. □□ **episcopalism** n. **episcopally** adv. [ME f. F *épiscopal* or eccl.L *episcopalis* f. *episcopus* BISHOP]

episcopalian /ɪˌpɪskəˈpeɪlɪən/ adj. & n. —adj. **1** of or advocating government of a Church by bishops. **2** of or belonging to an episcopal Church or (**Episcopalian**) the Episcopal Church. —n. **1** an adherent of episcopacy. **2** (**Episcopalian**) a member of the Episcopal Church. □□ **episcopalianism** n.

episcopate /ɪˈpɪskəpət/ n. **1** the office or tenure of a bishop. **2** (prec. by the) the bishops collectively. [eccl.L *episcopatus* f. *episcopus* BISHOP]

episcope /ˈepɪˌskəʊp/ n. an optical projector giving images of opaque objects.

episematic /ˌepɪsɪˈmætɪk/ adj. Zool. (of coloration, markings, etc.) serving to help recognition by animals of the same species. [EPI- + Gk *sēma sēmatos* sign]

episiotomy /eˌpɪsɪˈɒtəmɪ, eˌpiːz-/ n. (pl. **-ies**) a surgical cut made at the opening of the vagina during childbirth, to aid delivery. [Gk *epision* pubic region]

episode /ˈepɪˌsəʊd/ n. **1** one event or a group of events as part of a sequence. **2** each of the parts of a serial story or broadcast. **3** an incident or set of incidents in a narrative. **4** an incident that is distinct but contributes to a whole (*a romantic episode in her life*). **5** Mus. a passage containing distinct material or introducing a new subject. **6** the part between two choric songs in Greek tragedy. [Gk *epeisodion* (as EPI- + *eisodos* entry f. *eis* into + *hodos* way)]

episodic /ˌepɪˈsɒdɪk/ adj. (also **episodical** /-ˈsɒdɪk(ə)l/) **1** in the nature of an episode. **2** sporadic; occurring at irregular intervals. □□ **episodically** adv.

epistaxis /ˌepɪˈstæksɪs/ n. Med. a nosebleed. [mod.L f. Gk (as EPI-, *stazō* drip)]

epistemic /ˌepɪˈstiːmɪk, -ˈstemɪk/ adj. Philos. relating to knowledge or to the degree of its validation. □□ **epistemically** adv. [Gk *epistēmē* knowledge]

epistemology /ɪˌpɪstɪˈmɒlədʒɪ/ n. the theory of knowledge, esp. with regard to its methods and validation. □□ **epistemological** /-məˈlɒdʒɪk(ə)l/ adj. **epistemologically** /-məˈlɒdʒɪkəlɪ/ adv. **epistemologist** n.

epistle /ɪˈpɪs(ə)l/ n. **1** formal or joc. a letter, esp. a long one on a serious subject. **2** (**Epistle**) **a** any of the letters of the apostles in the New Testament. **b** an extract from an Epistle read in a church service. **3** a poem or other literary work in the form of a letter or series of letters. [ME f. OF f. L *epistola* f. Gk *epistolē* f. *epistellō* send news (as EPI-, *stellō* send)]

epistolary /ɪˈpɪstələrɪ/ adj. **1** in the style or form of a letter or letters. **2** of, carried by, or suited to letters. [F *épistolaire* or L *epistolaris* (as EPISTLE)]

epistrophe /ɪˈpɪstrəfɪ/ n. the repetition of a word at the end of successive clauses. [Gk (as EPI-, *strophē* turning)]

epistyle /ˈepɪˌstaɪl/ n. Archit. = ARCHITRAVE. [F *épistyle* or L *epistylium* f. Gk *epistulion* (as EPI-, *stulos* pillar)]

epitaph /ˈepɪˌtɑːf/ n. words written in memory of a person who has died, esp. as a tomb inscription. [ME f. OF *epitaphe* f. L *epitaphium* f. Gk *epitaphion* funeral oration (as EPI-, *taphos* tomb)]

epitaxy /ˈepɪˌtæksɪ/ n. Crystallog. the growth of a thin layer on a single-crystal substrate that determines the lattice-structure of the layer. □□ **epitaxial** /-ˈtæksɪəl/ adj. [F *épitaxie* (as EPI-, Gk *taxis* arrangement)]

epithalamium /ˌepɪθəˈleɪmɪəm/ n. (pl. **epithalamiums** or **epithalamia** /-mɪə/) a song or poem celebrating a marriage. □□ **epithalamial** adj. **epithalamic** /-ˈlæmɪk/ adj. [L f. Gk *epithalamion* (as EPI-, *thalamos* bridal chamber)]

epithelium /ˌepɪˈθiːlɪəm/ n. (pl. **epitheliums** or **epithelia** /-lɪə/) the tissue forming the outer layer of the body surface and lining many hollow structures. □□ **epithelial** adj. [mod.L f. EPI- + Gk *thēlē* teat]

epithet /ˈɛpɪˌθɛt/ n. **1** an adjective or other descriptive word expressing a quality or attribute, esp. used with or as a name. **2** such a word as a term of abuse. □□ **epithetic** /-ˈθɛtɪk/ adj. **epithetical** /-ˈθɛtɪk(ə)l/ adj. **epithetically** /-ˈθɛtɪkəlɪ/ adv. [F épithète or L epitheton f. Gk epitheton f. epitithēmi add (as EPI-, tithēmi place)]

epitome /ɪˈpɪtəmɪ/ n. **1** a person or thing embodying a quality, class, etc. **2** a thing representing another in miniature. **3** a summary of a written work; an abstract. □□ **epitomist** n. [L f. Gk epitomē f. epitemnō abridge (as EPI-, temnō cut)]

epitomize /ɪˈpɪtəˌmaɪz/ v.tr. (also **-ise**) **1** be a perfect example of (a quality etc.); typify. **2** make an epitome of (a work). □□ **epitomization** /-ˈzeɪʃ(ə)n/ n.

epizoon /ˌɛpɪˈzəʊɒn/ n. (pl. **epizoa** /-ˈzəʊə/) an animal living on another animal. [mod.L (as EPI-, Gk zōion animal)]

epizootic /ˌɛpɪzəʊˈɒtɪk/ adj. & n. —adj. (of a disease) temporarily prevalent among animals (cf. ENZOOTIC). —n. an outbreak of such a disease. [F épizootique f. épizootie (as EPIZOON)]

EPNS abbr. electroplated nickel silver.

epoch /ˈiːpɒk/ n. **1** a period of history or of a person's life marked by notable events. **2** the beginning of an era. **3** Geol. a division of a period, corresponding to a set of strata. □ **epoch-making** remarkable, historic; of major importance. □□ **epochal** /ˈɛpɒk(ə)l/ adj. [mod.L epocha f. Gk epokhē stoppage]

epode /ˈɛpəʊd/ n. **1** a form of lyric poem written in couplets each of a long line followed by a shorter one. **2** the third section of an ancient Greek choral ode or of one division of it. [F épode or L epodos f. Gk epōidos (as EPI-, ODE)]

eponym /ˈɛpənɪm/ n. **1** a person (real or imaginary) after whom a discovery, invention, place, institution, etc., is named or thought to be named. **2** the name given. □□ **eponymous** /ɪˈpɒnɪməs/ adj. [Gk epōnumos (as EPI-, -ōnumos f. onoma name)]

EPOS /ˈiːpɒs/ abbr. electronic point-of-sale (of retail outlets recording information electronically).

epoxide /ɪˈpɒksaɪd/ n. Chem. a compound containing an oxygen atom bonded in a triangular arrangement to two carbon atoms. [EPI- + OXIDE]

epoxy /ɪˈpɒksɪ/ adj. Chem. relating to or derived from an epoxide. □ **epoxy resin** a synthetic thermosetting resin containing epoxy groups. [EPI- + OXY-²]

epsilon /ˈɛpsɪˌlɒn/ n. the fifth letter of the Greek alphabet (E, ε). [ME f. Gk, = bare E f. psilos bare]

Epsom salts /ˈɛpsəm/ n. a preparation of magnesium sulphate used as a purgative etc. [Epsom in Surrey, where it was first found occurring naturally]

Epstein /ˈɛpstaɪn/, Sir Jacob (1880–1959), sculptor. New York born, but established in London from 1905, he introduced the language of 20th-c. art, evolved in part from cubism, into the academic traditions of British sculpture, causing initially (even into the 1930s) public scandal and uproar. His Rima in Hyde Park was tarred and feathered, but his most successful and original work was the early Rock Drill (1913–15), a key-piece of vorticism. Later, he developed a forceful highly personal and expressive style, modelled not carved, in portraiture of the famous: his Einstein is a superb example.

epyllion /eˈpɪlɪən/ n. (pl. **epyllia** /-lɪə/) a miniature epic poem. [Gk epullion dimin. of epos word, song]

equable /ˈɛkwəb(ə)l/ adj. **1** even; not varying. **2** uniform and moderate (an equable climate). **3** (of a person) not easily disturbed or angered. □□ **equability** /-ˈbɪlɪtɪ/ n. **equably** adv. [L aequabilis (as EQUATE)]

equal /ˈiːkw(ə)l/ adj., n., & v. —adj. **1** (often foll. by to, with) the same in quantity, quality, size, degree, rank, level, etc. **2** evenly balanced (an equal contest). **3** having the same rights or status (human beings are essentially equal). **4** uniform in application or effect (equal opportunities). —n. a person or thing equal to another, esp. in rank, status, or characteristic quality (their treatment of the subject has no equal; is the equal of any man). —v.tr. (**equalled, equalling**; US **equaled, equaling**) **1** be equal to in number, quality, etc. **2** achieve something that is equal to (an achievement) or to the achievement of (a person). □ **be equal**

to have the ability or resources for. **equal opportunity** (often in pl.) the opportunity or right to be employed, paid, etc., without discrimination on grounds of sex, race, etc. **equal** (or **equals**) **sign** the symbol =. [ME f. L aequalis f. aequus even]

equalitarian /iːˌkwɒlɪˈtɛərɪən/ n. = EGALITARIAN. □□ **equalitarianism** n. [EQUALITY, after humanitarian etc.]

equality /ɪˈkwɒlɪtɪ/ n. the state of being equal. [ME f. OF equalité f. L aequalitas -tatis (as EQUAL)]

equalize /ˈiːkwəˌlaɪz/ v. (also **-ise**) **1** tr. & intr. make or become equal. **2** intr. reach one's opponent's score in a game, after being behind. □□ **equalization** /-ˈzeɪʃ(ə)n/ n.

equalizer /ˈiːkwəˌlaɪzə(r)/ n. **1** an equalizing score or goal etc. in a game. **2** sl. a weapon, esp. a gun. **3** Electr. a connection in a system which compensates for any undesirable frequency or phase response with the system.

equally /ˈiːkwəlɪ/ adv. **1** in an equal manner (treated them all equally). **2** to an equal degree (is equally important). ¶ In sense 2 construction with as (equally as important) is often found, but is disp.

equanimity /ˌɛkwəˈnɪmɪtɪ, ˌiːk-/ n. mental composure, evenness of temper, esp. in misfortune. □□ **equanimous** /ɪˈkwænɪməs/ adj. [L aequanimitas f. aequanimis f. aequus even + animus mind]

equate /ɪˈkweɪt/ v. **1** tr. (usu. foll. by to, with) regard as equal or equivalent. **2** intr. (foll. by with) **a** be equal or equivalent to. **b** agree or correspond. □□ **equatable** adj. [ME f. L aequare aequat- f. aequus equal]

equation /ɪˈkweɪʒ(ə)n/ n. **1** the process of equating or making equal; the state of being equal. **2** Math. a statement that two mathematical expressions are equal (indicated by the sign =). **3** Chem. a formula indicating a chemical reaction by means of symbols for the elements taking part. □ **equation of the first order, second order**, etc. an equation involving only the first derivative, second derivative, etc. □□ **equational** adj. [ME f. OF equation or L aequatio (as EQUATE)]

equator /ɪˈkweɪtə(r)/ n. **1** an imaginary line round the earth or other body, equidistant from the poles. **2** Astron. = celestial equator. [ME f. OF equateur or med.L aequator (as EQUATION)]

equatorial /ˌɛkwəˈtɔːrɪəl, ˌiːk-/ adj. of or near the equator. □ **equatorial telescope** a telescope attached to an axis perpendicular to the plane of the equator. □□ **equatorially** adv.

Equatorial Guinea /ˈgɪnɪ/ a small country of West Africa on the Gulf of Guinea, comprising several offshore islands and a coastal settlement between Cameroon and Gabon; pop. (est. 1988) 346,800; official language, Spanish; capital, Malabo (on the island of Bioco). Formerly a Spanish colony, the country became fully independent in 1968. It is the only independent Spanish-speaking State in the continent of Africa.

equerry /ˈɛkwərɪ, ɪˈkwɛrɪ/ n. (pl. **-ies**) **1** an officer of the British royal household attending members of the royal family. **2** hist. an officer of a prince's or noble's household having charge over the horses. [earlier esquiry f. OF esquierie company of squires, prince's stables, f. OF esquier ESQUIRE: perh. assoc. with L equus horse]

equestrian /ɪˈkwɛstrɪən/ adj. & n. —adj. **1** of or relating to horses and horse-riding. **2** on horseback. —n. (fem. **equestrienne** /-trɪˈɛn/) a rider or performer on horseback. □□ **equestrianism** n. [L equestris f. eques horseman, knight, f. equus horse]

equi- /ˈiːkwɪ/ comb. form equal. [L aequi- f. aequus equal]

equiangular /ˌiːkwɪˈæŋɡjʊlə(r)/ adj. having equal angles.

equidistant /ˌiːkwɪˈdɪst(ə)nt/ adj. at equal distances. □□ **equidistantly** adv.

equilateral /ˌiːkwɪˈlætər(ə)l/ adj. having all its sides equal in length.

equilibrate /ɪˈkwɪlɪˌbreɪt, ˌiːkwɪˈlaɪbreɪt/ v. **1** tr. cause (two things) to balance. **2** intr. be in equilibrium; balance. □□ **equilibration** /-ˈbreɪʃ(ə)n/ n. **equilibrator** /ɪˈkwɪlɪˌbreɪtə(r)/ n. [LL aequilibrare aequilibrat- (as EQUI-, libra balance)]

equilibrist /ɪˈkwɪlɪbrɪst/ n. an acrobat, esp. on a high rope.

equilibrium /ˌiːkwɪˈlɪbrɪəm/ n. (pl. **equilibria** /-rɪə/ or **equilibriums**) **1** a state of physical balance. **2** a state of mental or emotional equanimity. **3** a state in which the energy in a system is evenly distributed and forces, influences, etc., balance each other. [L (as EQUI-, *libra* balance)]

equine /ˈiːkwaɪn, ˈek-/ *adj.* of or like a horse. [L *equinus* f. *equus* horse]

equinoctial /ˌiːkwɪˈnɒkʃ(ə)l, ˌek-/ *adj. & n.* —*adj.* **1** happening at or near the time of an equinox (*equinoctial gales*). **2** of or relating to equal day and night. **3** at or near the (terrestrial) equator. —*n.* (in full **equinoctial line**) = *celestial equator.* □ **equinoctial point** the point at which the ecliptic cuts the celestial equator (twice each year at an equinox). **equinoctial year** see YEAR. [ME f. OF *equinoctial* or L *aequinoctialis* (as EQUINOX)]

equinox /ˈiːkwɪˌnɒks, ˈek-/ *n.* **1** the time or date (twice each year) at which the sun crosses the celestial equator, when day and night are of equal length. **2** = *equinoctial point.* □ **autumn** (or **autumnal**) **equinox** about 22 Sept. **spring** (or **vernal**) **equinox** about 20 March. [ME f. OF *equinoxe* or med.L *equinoxium* for L *aequinoctium* (as EQUI-, *nox noctis* night)]

equip /ɪˈkwɪp/ *v.tr.* (**equipped, equipping**) supply with what is needed. □□ **equipper** *n.* [F *équiper*, prob. f. ON *skipa* to man (a ship) f. *skip* SHIP]

equipage /ˈekwɪpɪdʒ/ *n.* **1 a** requisites for an undertaking. **b** an outfit for a special purpose. **2** a carriage and horses with attendants. [F *équipage* (as EQUIP)]

equipment /ɪˈkwɪpmənt/ *n.* **1** the necessary articles, clothing, etc., for a purpose. **2** the process of equipping or being equipped. [F *équipement* (as EQUIP)]

equipoise /ˈekwɪˌpɔɪz, ˈiː-/ *n. & v.* —*n.* **1** equilibrium; a balanced state. **2** a counterbalancing thing. —*v.tr.* counterbalance.

equipollent /ˌiːkwɪˈpɒlənt/ *adj. & n.* —*adj.* **1** equal in power, force, etc. **2** practically equivalent. —*n.* an equipollent thing. □□ **equipollence** *n.* **equipollency** *n.* [ME f. OF *equipolent* f. L *aequipollens -entis* of equal value (as EQUI-, *pollēre* be strong)]

equipotential /ˌiːkwɪpəˈtenʃ(ə)l/ *adj. & n. Physics* —*adj.* (of a surface or line) having the potential of a force the same or constant at all its points. —*n.* an equipotential line or surface.

equiprobable /ˌiːkwɪˈprɒbəb(ə)l/ *adj. Logic* equally probable. □□ **equiprobability** /-ˈbɪlɪtɪ/ *n.*

equitable /ˈekwɪtəb(ə)l/ *adj.* **1** fair, just. **2** *Law* valid in equity as distinct from law. □□ **equitableness** *n.* **equitably** *adv.* [F *équitable* (as EQUITY)]

equitation /ˌekwɪˈteɪʃ(ə)n/ *n.* the art and practice of horsemanship and horse-riding. [F *équitation* or L *equitatio* f. *equitare* ride a horse f. *eques equitis* horseman f. *equus* horse]

equity /ˈekwɪtɪ/ *n.* (pl. **-ies**) **1** fairness. **2** the application of the principles of justice to correct or supplement the law. **3 a** the value of the shares issued by a company. **b** (in pl.) stocks and shares not bearing fixed interest. **4** the net value of a mortgaged property after the deduction of charges. **5** (**Equity**) *Brit.* the actors' trade union. [ME f. OF *equité* f. L *aequitas -tatis* f. *aequus* fair]

equivalent /ɪˈkwɪvələnt/ *adj. & n.* —*adj.* **1** (often foll. by *to*) equal in value, amount, importance, etc. **2** corresponding. **3** (of words) having the same meaning. **4** having the same result. **5** *Chem.* (of a substance) equal in combining or displacing capacity. —*n.* **1** an equivalent thing, amount, word, etc. **2** (in full **equivalent weight**) *Chem.* the weight of a substance that can combine with or displace one gram of hydrogen or eight grams of oxygen. □□ **equivalence** *n.* **equivalency** *n.* **equivalently** *adv.* [ME f. OF f. LL *aequivalēre* (as EQUI-, *valēre* be worth)]

equivocal /ɪˈkwɪvək(ə)l/ *adj.* **1** of double or doubtful meaning; ambiguous. **2** of uncertain nature. **3** (of a person, character, etc.) questionable, suspect. □□ **equivocality** /-ˈkælɪtɪ/ *n.* **equivocally** *adv.* **equivocalness** *n.* [LL *aequivocus* (as EQUI-, *vocare* call)]

equivocate /ɪˈkwɪvəˌkeɪt/ *v.intr.* use ambiguity to conceal the truth. □□ **equivocation** /-ˈkeɪʃ(ə)n/ *n.* **equivocator** *n.* **equivocatory** *adj.* [ME f. LL *aequivocare* (as EQUIVOCAL)]

equivoque /ˈekwɪˌvəʊk, ˈiː-/ *n.* (also **equivoke**) a pun or ambiguity. [ME in the sense 'equivocal' f. OF *equivoque* or LL *aequivocus* EQUIVOCAL]

ER *abbr.* **1** Queen Elizabeth. **2** King Edward. [L *Elizabetha Regina, Edwardus Rex*]

Er *symb. Chem.* the element erbium.

er /ɜː(r)/ *int.* expressing hesitation or a pause in speech. [imit.]

-er[1] /ə(r)/ *suffix* forming nouns from nouns, adjectives, and many verbs, denoting: **1** a person, animal, or thing that performs a specified action or activity (*cobbler; lover; executioner; poker; computer; eye-opener*). **2** a person or thing that has a specified attribute or form (*foreigner; four-wheeler; second-rater*). **3** a person concerned with a specified thing or subject (*hatter; geographer*). **4** a person belonging to a specified place or group (*villager; New Zealander; sixth-former*). [orig. 'one who has to do with': OE *-ere* f. Gmc]

-er[2] /ə(r)/ *suffix* forming the comparative of adjectives (*wider; hotter*) and adverbs (*faster*). [OE *-ra* (adj.), *-or* (adv.) f. Gmc]

-er[3] /ə(r)/ *suffix* used in slang formations usu. distorting the root word (*rugger; soccer*). [prob. an extension of -ER[1]]

-er[4] /ə(r)/ *suffix* forming iterative and frequentative verbs (*blunder; glimmer; twitter*). [OE *-erian, -rian* f. Gmc]

-er[5] /ə(r)/ *suffix* **1** forming nouns and adjectives through OF or AF, corresponding to: **a** L *-aris* (*sampler*) (cf. -AR[1]). **b** L *-arius, -arium* (*butler; carpenter; danger*). **c** (through OF *-eüre*) L *-atura* or (through OF *-eör*) L *-atorium* (see COUNTER[1], FRITTER[2]). **2** = -OR.

-er[6] /ə(r)/ *suffix esp. Law* forming nouns denoting verbal action or a document effecting this (*cesser; disclaimer; misnomer*). ¶ The same ending occurs in *dinner* and *supper*. [AF infin. ending of verbs]

era /ˈɪərə/ *n.* **1** a system of chronology reckoning from a noteworthy event (*the Christian era*). **2** a large distinct period of time, esp. regarded historically (*the pre-Roman era*). **3** a date at which an era begins. **4** *Geol.* a major division of time. [LL *aera* number expressed in figures (pl. of *aes aeris* money, treated as fem. sing.)]

eradicate /ɪˈrædɪˌkeɪt/ *v.tr.* root out; destroy completely; get rid of. □□ **eradicable** *adj.* **eradication** /-ˈkeɪʃ(ə)n/ *n.* **eradicator** *n.* [ME f. L *eradicare* tear up by the roots (as E-, *radix -icis* root)]

erase /ɪˈreɪz/ *v.tr.* **1** rub out; obliterate. **2** remove all traces of (*erased it from my memory*). **3** remove recorded material from (a magnetic tape or medium). □□ **erasable** *adj.* **erasure** *n.* [L *eradere eras-* (as E-, *radere* scrape)]

eraser /ɪˈreɪzə(r)/ *n.* a thing that erases, esp. a piece of rubber or plastic used for removing pencil and ink marks.

Erasmus /ɪˈræzməs/, Desiderius (c.1469–1536), Dutch Christian humanist, during his lifetime the most famous scholar in Europe, and the first best-selling author in printing history. He was a man of vast if not always deep erudition, of uncommon intellectual powers, averse to metaphysical speculation. Though he had himself paved the way for the Reformation by his merciless satires on the Church, his scholarly character, which abhorred violence and sought tranquillity, prevented him from joining the Protestants and threw him back on the tradition of the Church as the safeguard of stability. In the later years of his life he became suspect to both parties.

Erastus /ɪˈræstəs/ the latinized name of the Swiss physician and writer Thomas Lieber or Liebler or Lüber (1524–83), to whom the theory of State supremacy in ecclesiastical affairs has been wrongly attributed. His actual efforts were directed mainly against the use of excommunication, which was exercised tyrannically by the Calvinistic Churches. The Anglican churchman Richard Hooker defended the supremacy of the secular power in his *Ecclesiastical Polity* (1594), and the principle remains in a modified form in Britain, where Parliament, though its members may profess any or no religion, asserts its right to legislate on religious matters concerning the Established Church. □□ **Erastian** /ɪˈræstɪən/ *adj.* **Erastianism** *n.*

Erato /eˈrɑːtəʊ/ *Gk & Rom. Mythol.* the Muse of lyric poetry and hymns. [Gk, = lovely]

Eratosthenes /ˌerəˈtɒsθəˌniːz/ (c.275–194 BC) Hellenistic scholar and geographer, pupil of Callimachus and head of the library at Alexandria. Active in the fields of literary criticism and chronology, he was also the first systematic geographer of antiquity; he calculated the circumference of the earth to a high degree of accuracy and (with much less accuracy) the magnitude and distance of the sun and of the moon.

erbium /'ɜːbɪəm/ n. Chem. a soft silvery metallic element of the lanthanide series, occurring naturally in apatite and xenotine. ¶ Symb.: **Er**; atomic number 68. [mod.L f. Ytterby in Sweden]

ere /eə(r)/ prep. & conj. poet. or archaic before (of time) (ere noon; ere they come). [OE ǣr f. Gmc]

Erechtheum /ɪ'rekθɪəm/ a marble temple built on the Acropolis in Athens in c.421–c.406 BC, with shrines to Athene, Poseidon, and Erechtheus, a legendary king of Athens. A masterpiece of the Ionic order, it is most famous for its southern portico in which the entablature is supported by six caryatids.

erect /ɪ'rekt/ adj. & v. —adj. 1 upright, vertical. 2 (of the penis, clitoris, or nipples) enlarged and rigid, esp. in sexual excitement. 3 (of hair) bristling, standing up from the skin. —v.tr. 1 raise; set upright. 2 build. 3 establish (erect a theory). □□ **erectable** adj. **erectly** adv. **erectness** n. **erector** n. [ME f. L erigere erect- set up (as E-, regere direct)]

erectile /ɪ'rektaɪl/ adj. that can be erected or become erect. □ **erectile tissue** Physiol. animal tissue that is capable of becoming rigid, esp. with sexual excitement. [F érectile (as ERECT)]

erection /ɪ'rekʃ(ə)n/ n. 1 the act or an instance of erecting; the state of being erected. 2 a building or structure. 3 Physiol. an enlarged and erect state of erectile tissue, esp. of the penis. [F érection or L erectio (as ERECTILE)]

E-region var. of E-LAYER.

eremite /'erɪˌmaɪt/ n. a hermit or recluse (esp. Christian). □□ **eremitic** /-'mɪtɪk/ adj. **eremitical** /-'mɪtɪk(ə)l/ adj. **eremitism** n. [ME f. OF, var. of hermite, ermite HERMIT]

erethism /'erɪˌθɪz(ə)m/ n. 1 an excessive sensitivity to stimulation of any part of the body, esp. the sexual organs. 2 a state of abnormal mental excitement or irritation. [F éréthisme f. Gk erethismos f. erethizō irritate]

Erfurt /'eəfʊət/ an industrial city in central Germany, the capital of Thuringia; pop. (1986) 216,600.

erg[1] /ɜːg/ n. Physics a unit of work or energy, equal to the work done by a force of one dyne when its point of application moves one centimetre in the direction of action of the force. [Gk ergon work]

erg[2] /ɜːg/ n. (pl. **ergs** or **areg** /'ɑːreg/) an area of shifting sand-dunes in the Sahara. [F f. Arab. 'irj]

ergo /'ɜːgəʊ/ adv. therefore. [L]

ergocalciferol /ˌɜːgəʊkæl'sɪfəˌrɒl/ n. = CALCIFEROL. [ERGOT + CALCIFEROL]

ergonomics /ˌɜːgə'nɒmɪks/ n. the study of the efficiency of persons in their working environment. □□ **ergonomic** adj. **ergonomist** /ɜː'gɒnəmɪst/ n. [Gk ergon work: cf. ECONOMICS]

ergosterol /ɜː'gɒstəˌrɒl/ n. Biochem. a plant sterol that is converted to vitamin D_2 when irradiated with ultraviolet light. [ERGOT, after CHOLESTEROL]

ergot /'ɜːgət/ n. 1 a disease of rye and other cereals caused by the fungus Claviceps purpurea. 2 a this fungus. b the dried spore-containing structures of this, used as a medicine to aid childbirth. 3 a horny protuberance on the inner side of a horse's fetlock. [F f. OF argot cock's spur, from the appearance produced]

ergotism /'ɜːgəˌtɪz(ə)m/ n. poisoning produced by eating food affected by ergot.

erica /'erɪkə/ n. any shrub or heath of the genus Erica, with small leathery leaves and bell-like flowers. □□ **ericaceous** /-'keɪʃəs/ adj. [L f. Gk ereikē heath]

Ericsson[1] /'erɪks(ə)n/, John (1803–89), versatile Swedish engineer who worked also in Britain and America. His successful invention of the marine screw propeller (1836) led to his move to the US, where he achieved fame by building the ironclad Monitor, the first ship to have a revolving armoured turret, which fought an inconclusive battle on the Union side in the American Civil War. Ericsson was also a pioneer of solar energy, constructing a steam pump supplied from a boiler heated by a concentrating mirror.

Ericsson[2] /'erɪks(ə)n/, Leif (c.1000), Norwegian explorer, son of Eric the Red. He sailed westward from Greenland in about 1000, discovering land (variously identified as Labrador, Newfoundland, or New England) which he named Vinland because of the vines he found growing there.

Eric the Red /'erɪk/ (10th c.) Norwegian explorer who left Iceland in 982 in search of land to the west, exploring Greenland and establishing a Norse settlement there in 986. His explorations were later continued by his son Leif Ericsson.

Erie /'ɪərɪ/, **Lake** one of the five Great Lakes of North America.

erigeron /ɪ'rɪgəˌrɒn/ n. any hardy composite herb of the genus Erigeron, with daisy-like flowers. [Gk ērigerōn f. ēri early + gerōn old man, because some species bear grey down]

Erin /'erɪn, 'ɪərɪn/ n. archaic or poet. Ireland. [Ir.]

Erinys /e'rɪnɪs/ n. (pl. **Erinyes** /e'rɪnɪˌiːz/) Gk Mythol. a Fury. [Gk]

eristic /e'rɪstɪk/ adj. & n. —adj. 1 of or characterized by disputation. 2 (of an argument or arguer) aiming at winning rather than at reaching the truth. —n. 1 the practice of disputation. 2 an exponent of disputation. □□ **eristically** adv. [Gk eristikos f. erizō wrangle f. eris strife]

Eritrea /ˌerɪ'treɪə/ a province of Ethiopia, on the Red Sea. An Italian colony from 1890, it federated with Ethiopia in 1952 and was integrated as a province in 1962; since then secessionist rebels have engaged in a guerrilla war against the government of Ethiopia. □□ **Eritrean** adj. & n.

erk /ɜːk/ n. Brit. sl. 1 a naval rating. 2 an aircraftman. 3 a disliked person. [20th c.: orig. unkn.]

Erlang /'ɜːlæŋ/, Agner Krarup (1878–1929), Danish mathematician whose name is used to designate various formulae, functions, etc., derived by him or arising out of his work.

erl-king /'ɜːlkɪŋ/ n. Germanic Mythol. a bearded giant or goblin who lures little children to the land of death. [G Erlkönig alderking, a mistransl. of Da. ellerkonge king of the elves]

ERM abbr. exchange rate mechanism (see EXCHANGE).

ermine /'ɜːmɪn/ n. (pl. same or **ermines**) 1 the stoat, esp. when in its white winter fur. 2 its white fur, used as trimming for the robes of judges, peers, etc. 3 Heraldry a white fur marked with black spots. □□ **ermined** adj. [ME f. OF (h)ermine prob. f. med.L (mus) Armenius Armenian (mouse)]

ern US var. of ERNE.

-ern /ən/ suffix forming adjectives (northern). [OE -erne f. Gmc]

erne /ɜːn/ n. (US ern) poet. a sea eagle. [OE earn f. Gmc]

Ernie /'ɜːnɪ/ n. (in the UK) a device used (from 1956) for drawing prize-winning numbers of Premium Bonds. [initial letters of electronic random number indicator equipment]

Ernst /ɜːnst/, Max (1891–1976), German-born artist, one of the major figures of surrealism. He studied philosophy and psychology at Bonn University, and became fascinated by the art of psychotics. In 1919 he made himself the leader of the Cologne Dada group, and was responsible for adapting the techniques of collage and photomontage to surrealist uses. He settled in Paris in 1922, was in the US 1941–8, then returned to France, becoming a French citizen in 1958.

erode /ɪ'rəʊd/ v. 1 tr. & intr. wear away, destroy or be destroyed gradually. 2 tr. Med. (of ulcers etc.) destroy (tissue) little by little. □□ **erodible** adj. [F éroder or L erodere eros- (as E-, rodere ros- gnaw)]

erogenous /ɪ'rɒdʒɪnəs/ adj. 1 (esp. of a part of the body) sensitive to sexual stimulation. 2 giving rise to sexual desire or excitement. [as EROTIC + -GENOUS]

Eros /'ɪərɒs/ 1 Gk Mythol. the god of love (see CUPID). 2 (Astron.) an asteroid, discovered in 1898, that comes at times nearer to Earth than any heavenly body except the moon. 3 the name given to the winged figure of an archer over the fountain in Piccadilly Circus made by Sir Alfred Gilbert, erected as a memorial to the Earl of Shaftesbury, the philanthropist, and unveiled in 1899. [Gk erōs, = sexual love]

erosion /ɪ'rəʊʒ(ə)n/ n. 1 Geol. the wearing away of the earth's surface by the action of water, wind, etc. 2 the act or an instance of eroding; the process of being eroded. □□ **erosional** adj. **erosive** adj. [F érosion f. L erosio (as ERODE)]

erotic /ɪ'rɒtɪk/ adj. of or causing sexual love, esp. tending to arouse sexual desire or excitement. □□ **erotically** adv. [F érotique f. Gk erōtikos f. erōs erōtos sexual love]

erotica /ɪ'rɒtɪkə/ n.pl. erotic literature or art.

eroticism /ɪ'rɒtɪˌsɪz(ə)m/ n. 1 erotic nature or character. 2 the use of or response to erotic images or stimulation.

erotism /ˈerəˌtɪz(ə)m/ n. sexual desire or excitement; eroticism.

eroto- /ɪˌrɒtəʊ, ɪˌraʊt-/ comb. form erotic, eroticism. [Gk erōs erōtos sexual love]

erotogenic /ɪˌrɒtəˈdʒenɪk/ adj. (also **erotogenous** /ˌerəˈtɒdʒɪnəs/) = EROGENOUS.

erotology /ˌerəˈtɒlədʒɪ/ n. the study of sexual love.

erotomania /ɪˌrəʊtəˈmeɪnɪə/ n. **1** excessive or morbid erotic desire. **2** a preoccupation with sexual passion. □□ **erotomaniac** /-nɪæk/ n.

err /ɜː(r)/ v.intr. **1** be mistaken or incorrect. **2** do wrong; sin. □ **err on the right side** act so that the least harmful of possible errors is the most likely to occur. **err on the side of** act with a specified bias (errs on the side of generosity). [ME f. OF errer f. L errare stray: rel. to Goth. airzei error, airzjan lead astray]

errand /ˈerənd/ n. **1** a short journey, esp. on another's behalf, to take a message, collect goods, etc. **2** the object of such a journey. □ **errand of mercy** a journey to relieve suffering etc. [OE ǣrende f. Gmc]

errant /ˈerənt/ adj. **1** erring; deviating from an accepted standard. **2** literary or archaic travelling in search of adventure (knight errant). □□ **errancy** n. (in sense 1). **errantry** n. (in sense 2). [ME: sense 1 formed as ERR: sense 2 f. OF errer ult. f. LL itinerare f. iter journey]

erratic /ɪˈrætɪk/ adj. **1** inconsistently variable in conduct, opinions, etc. **2** uncertain in movement. □ **erratic block** Geol. a large rock carried from a distance by glacial action. □□ **erratically** adv. [ME f. OF erratique f. L erraticus (as ERR)]

erratum /ɪˈrɑːtəm/ n. (pl. **errata** /-tə/) an error in printing or writing, esp. (in pl.) a list of corrected errors attached to a book etc. [L, neut. past part. (as ERR)]

erroneous /ɪˈrəʊnɪəs/ adj. incorrect; arising from error. □□ **erroneously** adv. **erroneousness** n. [ME f. OF erroneus or L erroneus f. erro -onis vagabond (as ERR)]

error /ˈerə(r)/ n. **1** a mistake. **2** the condition of being wrong in conduct or judgement (led into error). **3** a wrong opinion or judgement. **4** the amount by which something is incorrect or inaccurate in a calculation or measurement. □□ **errorless** adj. [ME f. OF errour f. L error -oris (as ERR)]

ersatz /ˈɜːzæts, ˈeə-/ adj. & n. —adj. substitute, imitation (esp. of inferior quality). —n. an ersatz thing. [G, = replacement]

Erse /ɜːs/ adj. & n. —adj. Irish or Highland Gaelic. —n. the Erse language. [early Sc. form of IRISH]

erst /ɜːst/ adv. archaic formerly; of old. [OE ǣrest superl. of ǣr: see ERE]

erstwhile /ˈɜːstwaɪl/ adj. & adv. —adj. former, previous. —adv. archaic = ERST.

erubescent /ˌeruːˈbes(ə)nt/ adj. reddening, blushing. [L erubescere (as E-, rubescere f. rubēre be red)]

eructation /ˌiːrʌkˈteɪʃ(ə)n/ n. the act or an instance of belching. [L eructatio f. eructare (as E-, ructare belch)]

erudite /ˈeruːˌdaɪt/ adj. **1** (of a person) learned. **2** (of writing etc.) showing great learning. □□ **eruditely** adv. **erudition** /-ˈdɪʃ(ə)n/ n. [ME f. L eruditus past part. of erudire instruct, train (as E-, rudis untrained)]

erupt /ɪˈrʌpt/ v.intr. **1** break out suddenly or dramatically. **2** (of a volcano) become active and eject lava etc. **3 a** (of a rash, boil, etc.) appear on the skin. **b** (of the skin) produce a rash etc. **4** (of the teeth) break through the gums in normal development. □□ **eruption** n. **eruptive** adj. [L erumpere erupt- (as E-, rumpere break)]

-ery /ərɪ/ suffix forming nouns denoting: **1** a class or kind (greenery; machinery; citizenry). **2** employment; state or condition (archery; dentistry; slavery; bravery). **3** a place of work or cultivation or breeding (brewery; orangery; rookery). **4** behaviour (mimicry). **5** often derog. all that has to do with (knavery; popery; tomfoolery). [ME, from or after F -erie, -ere ult. f. L -ario-, -ator]

erysipelas /ˌerɪˈsɪpɪləs/ n. Med. a streptococcal infection producing inflammation and a deep red colour on the skin, esp. of the face and scalp. [ME f. L f. Gk erusipelas, perh. rel. to eruthros red + a root pel- skin]

erythema /ˌerɪˈθiːmə/ n. a superficial reddening of the skin,

usu. in patches. □□ **erythemal** adj. **erythematic** /ˌeɪrɪθɪˈmætɪk/ adj. [mod.L f. Gk eruthēma f. eruthainō be red f. eruthros red]

erythro- /ɪˈrɪθrəʊ/ comb. form red. [Gk eruthros red]

erythroblast /ɪˈrɪθrəʊˌblæst/ n. an immature erythrocyte. [G]

erythrocyte /ɪˈrɪθrəʊˌsaɪt/ n. a red blood cell, which contains the pigment haemoglobin and transports oxygen and carbon dioxide to and from the tissues. □□ **erythrocytic** /-ˈsɪtɪk/ adj.

erythroid /ˈerɪˌθrɔɪd/ adj. of or relating to erythrocytes.

Erzgebirge see ORE MOUNTAINS.

Erzurum /ˈeəzʊˌrʊm/ the largest city of eastern Anatolia in NE Turkey; pop. (1985) 252,650.

Es symb. Chem. the element einsteinium.

-es[1] /ɪz/ suffix forming plurals of nouns ending in sibilant sounds (such words in -e dropping the e) (kisses; cases; boxes; churches). [var. of -s[1]]

-es[2] /ɪz, z/ suffix forming the 3rd person sing. present of verbs ending in sibilant sounds (such words in -e dropping the e) and ending in -o (but not -oo) (goes; places; pushes). [var. of -s[2]]

ESA abbr. European Space Agency.

Esau /ˈiːsɔː/ the elder son of Isaac and Rebecca, who sold his birthright to his brother Jacob (Gen. 25). He is the traditional ancestor of the Edomites.

Esbjerg /ˈesbjɜːɡ/ a ferry port and oil exploration centre in Denmark, on the SW coast of Jutland; pop. (1988) 81,385.

ESC abbr. Economic and Social Committee.

escadrille /ˌeskəˈdrɪl/ n. a French squadron of aeroplanes. [F]

escalade /ˌeskəˈleɪd/ n. the scaling of fortified walls with ladders, as a military attack. [F f. Sp. escalada, -ado f. med.L scalare f. scala ladder]

escalate /ˈeskəˌleɪt/ v. **1** intr. & tr. increase or develop (usu. rapidly) by stages. **2** tr. cause (an action, activity, or process) to become more intense. □□ **escalation** /-ˈleɪʃ(ə)n/ n. [back-form. f. ESCALATOR]

escalator /ˈeskəˌleɪtə(r)/ n. a moving staircase consisting of a circulating belt forming steps. The name was first applied (originally as a proprietary term) to a moving stairway at the Paris Exposition of 1900. A similar device had been invented earlier by J. W. Reno of the US, and by 1896–8 such staircases were being installed in department stores. [f. the stem of escalade 'climb a wall by ladder' + -ATOR]

escallonia /ˌeskəˈləʊnɪə/ n. any evergreen shrub of the genus Escallonia, bearing rose-red flowers. [Escallon, 18th-c. Sp. traveller]

escallop /ɪˈskæləp/ n. **1** = SCALLOP 1, 2. **2** = ESCALOPE. **3** (in pl.) = SCALLOP 3. **4** Heraldry a scallop shell as a device. [formed as ESCALOPE]

escalope /ˈeskəˌlɒp/ n. a thin slice of meat without any bone, esp. from a leg of veal. [F (in OF = shell): see SCALLOP]

escapade /ˈeskəˌpeɪd, ˌeskəˈpeɪd/ n. a piece of daring or reckless behaviour. [F f. Prov. or Sp. escapada (as ESCAPE)]

escape /ɪˈskeɪp/ v. & n. —v. **1** intr. (often foll. by from) get free of the restriction or control of a place, person, etc. **2** intr. (of a gas, liquid, etc.) leak from a container or pipe etc. **3** intr. succeed in avoiding danger, punishment, etc.; get off safely. **4** tr. get completely free of (a person, grasp, etc.). **5** tr. avoid or elude (a commitment, danger, etc.). **6** tr. elude the notice or memory of (nothing escapes you; the name escaped me). **7** tr. (of words etc.) issue unawares from (a person, a person's lips). —n. **1** the act or an instance of escaping; avoidance of danger, injury, etc. **2** the state of having escaped (was a narrow escape). **3** a means of escaping (often attrib.: escape hatch). **4** a leakage of gas etc. **5** a temporary relief from reality or worry. **6** a garden plant running wild. □ **escape clause** Law a clause specifying the conditions under which a contracting party is free from an obligation. **escape road** a road for a vehicle to turn into if unable to negotiate a bend, descent, etc., safely (esp. on a racetrack). **escape velocity** the minimum velocity needed to escape from the gravitational field of a body. **escape wheel** a toothed wheel in the escapement of a watch or clock. □□ **escapable** adj. **escaper** n. [ME f. AF, ONF escaper ult. f. med.L (as EX-[1], cappa cloak)]

escapee /ɪskeɪˈpiː/ n. a person, esp. a prisoner, who has escaped.

escapement /ɪˈskeɪpmənt/ n. **1** the part of a clock or watch that connects and regulates the motive power. **2** the part of the mechanism in a piano that enables the hammer to fall back immediately it has struck the string. **3** archaic a means of escape. [F échappement f. échapper ESCAPE]

escapism /ɪˈskeɪpɪz(ə)m/ n. the tendency to seek distraction and relief from reality, esp. in the arts or through fantasy. □□ **escapist** n. & adj.

escapology /ˌeskəˈpɒlədʒɪ/ n. the methods and techniques of escaping from confinement, esp. as a form of entertainment. □□ **escapologist** n.

escargot /eˈskɑːgəʊ/ n. an edible snail. [F]

escarpment /ɪˈskɑːpmənt/ n. (also **escarp**) Geol. a long steep slope at the edge of a plateau etc. [F escarpement f. escarpe SCARP]

Escaut see SCHELDT.

-esce /es/ suffix forming verbs, usu. initiating action (effervesce; fluoresce). [from or after L -escere]

-escent /ˈes(ə)nt/ suffix forming adjectives denoting the beginning of a state or action (effervescent; fluorescent). □□ **-escence** suffix forming nouns. [from or after F -escent or L -escent-, pres. part. stem of verbs in -escere]

eschatology /ˌeskəˈtɒlədʒɪ/ n. **1** the part of theology concerned with death and final destiny. **2 a** beliefs about the destiny of mankind and of the world. **b** the study of these. □□ **eschatological** /-təˈlɒdʒɪk(ə)l/ adj. **eschatologist** n. [Gk eskhatos last + -LOGY]

escheat /ɪsˈtʃiːt/ n. & v. hist. —n. **1** the reversion of property to the State, or (in feudal law) to a lord, on the owner's dying without legal heirs. **2** property affected by this. —v. **1** tr. hand over (property) as an escheat. **2** tr. confiscate. **3** intr. revert by escheat. [ME f. OF eschete, ult. f. L excidere (as EX-¹, cadere fall)]

eschew /ɪsˈtʃuː/ v.tr. literary avoid; abstain from. □□ **eschewal** n. [ME f. OF eschiver, ult. f. Gmc: rel. to SHY¹]

eschscholtzia /ɪsˈkɒlʃə, eˈʃɒltsɪə/ n. any yellow-flowering plant of the genus Eschscholtzia, esp. the Californian poppy (see POPPY). [J. F. von Eschscholtz, Ger. botanist d. 1831]

Esch-sur-Alzette /ˌeʃsʊəræˈlzet/ the second-largest town in Luxembourg, situated at the centre of a mining region; pop. (1987) 23,720.

Escoffier /esˈkɒfɪeɪ/, Georges-Auguste (1846–1935), French chef, who gained an international reputation while working in London at the Savoy Hotel (1890–9) and later at the Carlton. He invented a number of dishes, including 'peach Melba' (see entry).

escort n. & v. —n. /ˈeskɔːt/ **1** one or more persons, vehicles, ships, etc., accompanying a person, vehicle, etc., esp. for protection or security or as a mark of rank or status. **2** a person accompanying a person of the opposite sex socially. —v.tr. /ɪˈskɔːt/ act as an escort to. [F escorte, escorter f. It. scorta fem. past part. of scorgere conduct]

escritoire /ˌeskrɪˈtwɑː(r)/ n. a writing-desk with drawers etc. [F f. L scriptorium writing-room: see SCRIPTORIUM]

escrow /eˈskrəʊ/ n. & v. Law —n. **1** money, property, or a written bond, kept in the custody of a third party until a specified condition has been fulfilled. **2** the status of this (in escrow). —v.tr. place in escrow. [AF escrowe, OF escroe scrap, scroll, f. med.L scroda f. Gmc]

escudo /eˈskjuːdəʊ/ n. (pl. -os) the principal monetary unit of Portugal and Chile. [Sp. & Port. f. L scutum shield]

esculent /ˈeskjʊlənt/ adj. & n. —adj. fit to eat; edible. —n. an edible substance. [L esculentus f. esca food]

escutcheon /ɪˈskʌtʃ(ə)n/ n. **1** a shield or emblem bearing a coat of arms. **2** the middle part of a ship's stern where the name is placed. **3** the protective plate around a keyhole or door-handle. □□ **escutcheoned** adj. [AF & ONF escuchon ult. f. L scutum shield]

Esd. abbr. Esdras (Apocrypha).

Esdras /ˈezdrəs/ **1** either of two books of the Apocrypha, of which the first is mainly a compilation from Chronicles, Nehemiah, and Ezra, and the second is a record of angelic revelations, envisaging a new epoch of world history with a promise of national restoration, purportedly written in 557 BC and (illogically) attributed to Ezra (see entry), but actually written in about AD 100, 30 years after the destruction of Jerusalem by Titus. **2** (in the Vulgate) the books of Ezra and Nehemiah.

ESE abbr. east-south-east.

-ese /iːz/ suffix forming adjectives and nouns denoting: **1** an inhabitant or language of a country or city (Japanese; Milanese; Viennese). ¶ Plural forms are the same. **2** often derog. character or style, esp. of language (officialese). [OF -eis ult. f. L -ensis]

Esfahan see ISFAHAN.

esker /ˈeskə(r)/ n. (also **eskar**) Geol. a long ridge of post-glacial gravel in river valleys. [Ir. eiscir]

Eskimo /ˈeskɪˌməʊ/ n. & adj. —n. (pl. same or -os) **1** a member of a people inhabiting N. Canada, Alaska, Greenland, and E. Siberia. (See below.) **2** the language of this people. —adj. of or relating to the Eskimos or their language. ¶ The term Inuit is preferred by the people themselves. [Da. f. F Esquimaux (pl.) f. Algonquian, lit. = eaters of raw flesh]

This North American aboriginal people formerly occupied the habitable coasts and islands of the Arctic western hemisphere from east Greenland and north Newfoundland to Alaska and the westernmost Aleutian Islands, with a small number extending across the Bering Strait to the east coast of Siberia. A semi-nomadic hunting-and-gathering people, they are noted for their adaptation to a harsh environment and for the low level of social integration they effect (with cooperation being limited to very narrowly defined kinship units: the nuclear family).

The Eskimo languages belong to the Eskimo-Aleut family and are divided into two main branches: the Inupik or Inuk (spoken in Greenland, Labrador, the Arctic coast of Canada, and northern Alaska) and the Yupik or Yuk (spoken in southern Alaska and Siberia). There are approximately 40,000 Eskimo-speakers in Greenland, 25,000 in Alaska, 15,000 in Canada, and several hundred in Siberia.

Esky /ˈeskɪ/ n. (pl. -ies) Austral. propr. a portable insulated container for keeping food or drink cool. [prob. f. ESKIMO, with ref. to their cold climate]

ESN abbr. educationally subnormal.

esophagus US var. of OESOPHAGUS.

esoteric /ˌiːsəˈʊterɪk, ˌe-/ adj. **1** intelligible only to those with special knowledge. **2** (of a belief etc.) intended only for the initiated. □□ **esoterical** adj. **esoterically** adv. **esotericism** /-ˌsɪz(ə)m/ n. **esotericist** /-sɪst/ n. [Gk esōterikos f. esōterō compar. of esō within]

ESP abbr. extrasensory perception.

espadrille /ˌespəˈdrɪl/ n. a light canvas shoe with a plaited fibre sole. [F f. Prov. espardillo f. espart ESPARTO]

espalier /ɪˈspælɪə(r)/ n. **1** a lattice-work along which the branches of a tree or shrub are trained to grow flat against a wall etc. **2** a tree or shrub trained in this way. [F f. It. spalliera f. spalla shoulder]

esparto /eˈspɑːtəʊ/ n. (pl. -os) (in full **esparto grass**) a coarse grass, Stipa tenacissima, native to Spain and N. Africa, with tough narrow leaves, used to make ropes, wickerwork, and good-quality paper. [Sp. f. L spartum f. Gk sparton rope]

especial /ɪˈspeʃ(ə)l/ adj. **1** notable, exceptional. **2** attributed or belonging chiefly to one person or thing (your especial charm). [ME f. OF f. L specialis special]

especially /ɪˈspeʃəlɪ, -ʃlɪ/ adv. chiefly; much more than in other cases.

Esperanto /ˌespəˈræntəʊ/ n. an artificial language devised in 1887 by L. L. Zamenhof, Polish physician, as a medium of communication for persons of all languages. Its words are based mainly on roots commonly found in Romance and other European languages, and while it has the advantage of grammatical regularity and ease of pronunciation it retains the structure of these languages, which makes Esperanto no easier than any other European language for a speaker whose native tongue falls outside this group. □□ **Esperantist** n. [the pen-name (f. L sperare hope) of its inventor]

espial /ɪˈspaɪəl/ n. **1** the act or an instance of catching sight of or of being seen. **2** archaic spying. [ME f. OF espiaille f. espier: see ESPY]

espionage /ˈespɪəˌnɑːʒ/ n. the practice of spying or of using spies, esp. by governments. [F espionnage f. espionner f. espion SPY]

esplanade /ˌespləˈneɪd/ n. 1 a long open level area for walking on, esp. beside the sea. 2 a level space separating a fortress from a town. [F f. Sp. esplanada f. esplanar make level f. L explanare (as EX-¹, planus level)]

espousal /ɪˈspaʊz(ə)l/ n. 1 (foll. by of) the espousing of a cause etc. 2 archaic a marriage or betrothal. [ME f. OF espousailles f. L sponsalia neut. pl. of sponsalis (as ESPOUSE)]

espouse /ɪˈspaʊz/ v.tr. 1 adopt or support (a cause, doctrine, etc.). 2 archaic a (usu. of a man) marry. b (usu. foll. by to) give (a woman) in marriage. □□ **espouser** n. [ME f. OF espouser f. L sponsare f. sponsus past part. of spondēre betroth]

espresso /eˈspresəʊ/ n. (also **expresso** /ekˈspresəʊ/) (pl. **-os**) 1 strong concentrated black coffee made under steam pressure. 2 a machine for making this. [It., = pressed out]

esprit /eˈspriː, ˈespriː/ n. sprightliness, wit. □ **esprit de corps** /də ˈkɔː(r)/ a feeling of devotion to and pride in the group one belongs to. **esprit de l'escalier** /də leˈskæljeɪ/ an apt retort or clever remark that comes to mind after the chance to make it is gone. [F f. L spiritus SPIRIT (+ corps body, escalier stairs)]

espy /ɪˈspaɪ/ v.tr. (**-ies**, **-ied**) literary catch sight of; perceive. [ME f. OF espier: see SPY]

Esq. abbr. Esquire.

-esque /esk/ suffix forming adjectives meaning 'in the style of' or 'resembling' (romanesque; Schumannesque; statuesque). [F f. It. -esco f. med.L -iscus]

Esquimau /ˈeskɪˌməʊ/ n. (pl. **-aux** /-əʊz/) = ESKIMO. [F]

Esquipulas /ˌeskiˈpuːlæs/ a town in SE Guatemala, near the frontier with Honduras; pop. (1981) 18,840. Its church contains a black image of Christ (the 'Black Christ') which is a symbol of peace, visited by pilgrims from all over Central America. In 1983 the town was the venue for a summit of Central American presidents who assembled to endorse the Contadora peace process.

esquire /ɪˈskwaɪə(r)/ n. 1 (usu. as abbr. **Esq.**) Brit. a title appended to a man's surname when no other form of address is used, esp. as a form of address for letters. 2 archaic = SQUIRE. [ME f. OF esquier f. L scutarius shield-bearer f. scutum shield]

ESR abbr. Physics electron spin resonance.

-ess¹ /ɪs/ suffix forming nouns denoting females (actress; lioness; mayoress). [from or after F -esse f. LL -issa f. Gk -issa]

-ess² /es/ suffix forming abstract nouns from adjectives (duress). [ME f. F -esse f. L -itia; cf. -ICE]

essay n. & v. —n. /ˈeseɪ/ 1 a composition, usu. short and in prose, on any subject. 2 (often foll. by at, in) formal an attempt. —v.tr. /eˈseɪ/ formal attempt, try. □□ **essayist** n. [ME f. ASSAY, assim. to F essayer ult. f. LL exagium weighing f. exigere weigh: see EXACT]

Essen /ˈes(ə)n/ a city in NW Germany, the administrative centre of the Ruhr; pop. (1987) 615,400.

essence /ˈes(ə)ns/ n. 1 the indispensable quality or element identifying a thing or determining its character; fundamental nature or inherent characteristics. 2 a an extract obtained by distillation etc., esp. a volatile oil. b a perfume or scent, esp. made from a plant or animal substance. 3 the constituent of a plant that determines its chemical properties. 4 an abstract entity; the reality underlying a phenomenon or all phenomena. □ **in essence** fundamentally. **of the essence** indispensable, vital. [ME f. OF f. L essentia f. esse be]

Essene /ˈesiːn, eˈsiːn/ n. a member of an ancient Jewish ascetic sect of the 2nd c. BC–2nd c. AD in Palestine, who lived in highly organized groups and held property in common. The suggestion that St John the Baptist and even Christ himself were Essenes is highly improbable. [L pl. Esseni f. Gk pl. Essēnoi]

essential /ɪˈsenʃ(ə)l/ adj. & n. —adj. 1 absolutely necessary; indispensable. 2 fundamental, basic. 3 of or constituting the essence of a person or thing. 4 (of a disease) with no known external stimulus or cause; idiopathic. —n. (esp. in pl.) a basic or indispensable element or thing. □ **essential element** any of various elements required by living organisms for normal growth. **essential oil** see OIL. □□ **essentiality** /-ʃɪˈælɪtɪ/ n. **essentially** adv. **essentialness** n. [ME f. LL essentialis (as ESSENCE)]

Essequibo /ˌesɪˈkiːbəʊ/ the longest river of Guyana, rising in the Guiana Highlands and flowing c.965 km (600 miles) northwards to the Atlantic Ocean.

Essex /ˈesɪks/ a county of eastern England; pop. (1981) 1,483,200; county town, Chelmsford.

EST abbr. 1 US Eastern Standard Time. 2 electro-shock treatment.

-est¹ /ɪst/ suffix forming the superlative of adjectives (widest; nicest; happiest) and adverbs (soonest). [OE -ost-, -ust-, -ast-]

-est² /ɪst/ suffix (also **-st**) archaic forming the 2nd person sing. of verbs (canst; findest; gavest). [OE -est, -ast, -st]

establish /ɪˈstæblɪʃ/ v.tr. 1 set up or consolidate (a business, system, etc.) on a permanent basis. 2 (foll. by in) settle (a person or oneself) in some capacity. 3 (esp. as **established** adj.) achieve permanent acceptance for (a custom, belief, practice, institution, etc.). 4 validate; place beyond dispute (a fact etc.). □ **Established Church** the Church recognized by the State as the national Church. □□ **establisher** n. [ME f. OF establir (stem establiss-) f. L stabilire f. stabilis STABLE¹]

establishment /ɪˈstæblɪʃmənt/ n. 1 the act or an instance of establishing; the process of being established. 2 a a business organization or public institution. b a place of business. c a residence. 3 a the staff or equipment of an organization. b a household. 4 any organized body permanently maintained for a purpose. 5 a Church system organized by law. 6 (**the Establishment**) a the group in a society exercising authority or influence, and seen as resisting change. b any influential or controlling group (the literary Establishment).

establishmentarian /ɪˌstæblɪʃmənˈteərɪən/ adj. & n. —adj. adhering to or advocating the principle of an established Church. —n. a person adhering to or advocating this. □□ **establishmentarianism** n.

estaminet /eˈstæmɪˌneɪ/ n. a small French café etc. selling alcoholic drinks. [F f. Walloon staminé byre f. stamo a pole for tethering a cow, prob. f. G Stamm stem]

estate /ɪˈsteɪt/ n. 1 a property consisting of an extensive area of land usu. with a large house. 2 Brit. a modern residential or industrial area with integrated design or purpose. 3 all of a person's assets and liabilities, esp. at death. 4 a property where rubber, tea, grapes, etc., are cultivated. 5 (in full **estate of the realm**) an order or class forming (or regarded as) a part of the body politic. 6 archaic or literary a state or position in life (the estate of holy matrimony; poor man's estate). 7 colloq. = estate car. □ **estate agent** Brit. 1 a person whose business is the sale or lease of buildings and land on behalf of others. 2 the steward of an estate. **estate car** Brit. a car with the passenger area extended and combined with space for luggage, usu. with an extra door at the rear. **estate duty** Brit. hist. death duty levied on property. ¶ Replaced in 1975 by capital transfer tax and in 1986 by inheritance tax. **the Three Estates** Lords Spiritual (the heads of the Church), Lords Temporal (the peerage), and the Commons. [ME f. OF estat (as STATUS)]

esteem /ɪˈstiːm/ v. & n. —v.tr. 1 (usu. in passive) have a high regard for; greatly respect; think favourably of. 2 formal consider, deem (esteemed it an honour). —n. high regard; respect; favour (held them in esteem). [ME f. OF estimer f. L aestimare fix the price of]

ester /ˈestə(r)/ n. Chem. any of a class of organic compounds produced by replacing the hydrogen of an acid by an alkyl, aryl, etc. radical, many of which occur naturally as oils and fats. □□ **esterify** /eˈsterɪˌfaɪ/ v.tr. (**-ies**, **-ied**). [G, prob. f. Essig vinegar + Äther ether]

Esth. abbr. Esther (Old Testament & Apocrypha).

Esther /ˈestə(r)/ 1 a Jewish woman who was chosen on account of her beauty by King Ahasuerus (generally supposed to be Xerxes) to be his queen. 2 the book of the Old Testament containing an account of this, with further material in a book of the Apocrypha.

esthete US var. of AESTHETE.

esthetic *US* var. of AESTHETIC.

estimable /ˈestɪməb(ə)l/ *adj.* worthy of esteem. □□ **estimably** *adv.* [F f. L *aestimabilis* (as ESTEEM)]

estimate *n.* & *v.* —*n.* /ˈestɪmət/ **1** an approximate judgement, esp. of cost, value, size, etc. **2** a price specified as that likely to be charged for work to be undertaken. —*v.tr.* (also *absol.*) /ˈestɪˌmeɪt/ **1** form an estimate or opinion of. **2** (foll. by *that* + clause) make a rough calculation. **3** (often foll. by *at*) form an estimate; adjudge. **4** fix (a price etc.) by estimate. □□ **estimative** /-ˌmətɪv/ *adj.* **estimator** /-ˌmeɪtə(r)/ *n.* [L *aestimare aestimat-* fix the price of]

estimation /ˌestɪˈmeɪʃ(ə)n/ *n.* **1** the process or result of estimating. **2** judgement or opinion of worth (*in my estimation*). **3** *archaic* esteem (*hold in estimation*). [ME f. OF *estimation* or L *aestimatio* (as ESTIMATE)]

estival *US* var. of AESTIVAL.

estivate *US* var. of AESTIVATE.

Estonia /ɪˈstəʊnɪə/ a territory on the south coast of the Gulf of Finland, under Danish and then Swedish rule until ceded to Russia in 1721. It was proclaimed an independent republic in 1918 but was annexed by the USSR in 1940 as a constituent republic, the Estonian SSR; pop. (est. 1987) 1,556,000; capital, Tallinn. Growth of a nationalist movement in the 1980s led to demands for independence.

Estonian /ɪˈstəʊnɪən/ *n.* & *adj* —*n.* **1 a** a native of Estonia. **b** a person of Estonian descent. **2** the Finno-Ugric language of Estonia, most closely related to Finnish and spoken by about a million people. —*adj.* of or relating to Estonia or its people or language.

estop /ɪˈstɒp/ *v.tr.* (**estopped, estopping**) (foll. by *from*) *Law* bar or preclude, esp. by estoppel. □□ **estoppage** *n.* [ME f. AF, OF *estoper* f. LL *stuppare* stop up f. L *stuppa* tow: cf. STOP, STUFF]

estoppel /ɪˈstɒp(ə)l/ *n. Law* the principle which precludes a person from asserting something contrary to what is implied by a previous action or statement of that person or by a previous pertinent judicial determination. [OF *estouppail* bung f. *estoper* (as ESTOP)]

Estoril /ˌeʃtəˈrɪl/ a resort on the Atlantic coast of Portugal, west of Lisbon; pop. (1981) 16,000.

estovers /ɪˈstəʊvəz/ *n.pl. hist.* necessaries allowed by law to a tenant (esp. fuel, or wood for repairs). [AF *estover*, OF *estoveir* be necessary, f. L *est opus*]

estrange /ɪˈstreɪndʒ/ *v.tr.* (usu. in *passive*; often foll. by *from*) cause (a person or group) to turn away in feeling or affection; alienate. □□ **estrangement** *n.* [ME f. AF *estraunger*, OF *estranger* f. L *extraneare* treat as a stranger f. *extraneus* stranger]

estreat /ɪˈstriːt/ *n.* & *v. Law* —*n.* **1** a copy of a court record of a fine etc. for use in prosecution. **2** the enforcement of a fine or forfeiture of a recognizance. —*v.tr.* enforce the forfeit of (a fine etc., esp. surety for bail). [ME f. AF *estrete*, OF *estraite* f. *estraire* f. L *extrahere* EXTRACT]

Estremadura /ˌeʃtremaˈduərə/ a region of west central Portugal stretching northwards from the mouth of the River Tagus. Its name is derived from Latin *extrema Durii* = farthest (land) on the Douro.

estrogen *US* var. of OESTROGEN.

estrus etc. *US* var. of OESTRUS etc.

estuary /ˈestjʊərɪ/ *n.* (pl. **-ies**) a wide tidal mouth of a river. □□ **estuarine** /-ˌraɪn/ *adj.* [L *aestuarium* tidal channel f. *aestus* tide]

e.s.u. *abbr.* electrostatic unit(s).

esurient /ɪˈsjʊərɪənt/ *adj. archaic or joc.* **1** hungry. **2** impecunious and greedy. □□ **esuriently** *adv.* [L *esurire* (v.) hunger f. *edere es-* eat]

Esztergom /ˌestəˈɡɒm/ a town and river port in Hungary, on the Danube 40 km (25 miles) north-west of Budapest; pop. (est. 1984) 31,000. From the 10th c. until *c.*1300 it was the capital of Hungary.

ET *abbr.* extraterrestrial.

-et[1] /ɪt/ *suffix* forming nouns (orig. diminutives) (*baronet; bullet; sonnet*). [OF *-et -ete*]

-et[2] /ɪt/ *suffix* (also **-ete** /iːt/) forming nouns usu. denoting persons (*comet; poet; athlete*). [Gk *-ētēs*]

ETA[1] *abbr.* estimated time of arrival.

ETA[2] /ˈetə/ *n.* a Basque separatist movement. [Basque abbr., f. *Euzkadi ta Azkatasuna* Basque homeland and liberty]

eta /ˈiːtə/ *n.* the seventh letter of the Greek alphabet (H, η). [Gk]

et al. /et ˈæl/ *abbr.* and others. [L *et alii, et alia,* etc.]

etalon /ˈetəˌlɒn/ *n. Physics* a device consisting of two reflecting plates, for producing interfering light-beams. [F *étalon* standard]

etc. *abbr.* = ET CETERA.

et cetera /et ˈsetərə, ˈsetrə/ *adv.* & *n.* (also **etcetera**) —*adv.* **1 a** and the rest; and similar things or people. **b** or similar things or people. **2** and so on. —*n.* (in *pl.*) the usual sundries or extras. [ME f. L]

etch /etʃ/ *v.* & *n.* —*v.* **1 a** *tr.* reproduce (a picture etc.) by engraving a design on a metal plate with acid (esp. to print copies). **b** *tr.* engrave (a plate) in this way. **2** *intr.* practise this craft. **3** *tr.* (foll. by *on, upon*) impress deeply (esp. on the mind). —*n.* the action or process of etching. □□ **etcher** *n.* [Du. *etsen* f. G *ätzen* etch f. OHG *azzen* cause to eat or to be eaten f. Gmc]

etchant /ˈetʃ(ə)nt/ *n.* a corrosive used in etching.

etching /ˈetʃɪŋ/ *n.* **1** a print made from an etched plate. **2** the art of producing these plates. The first etchings date from the early 16th c., though the basic principle, that of corroding a design into a metal plate, had been utilized earlier for the decoration of armour.

-ete *suffix* var. of -ET[2].

eternal /ɪˈtɜːn(ə)l/ *adj.* **1** existing always; without an end or (usu.) beginning in time. **2** essentially unchanging (*eternal truths*). **3** *colloq.* constant; seeming not to cease (*your eternal nagging*). □ **the Eternal** God. **Eternal City** Rome. **eternal triangle** a complex of emotional relationships involving two people of one sex and one of the other sex. □□ **eternality** /-ˈnælɪtɪ/ *n.* **eternalize** *v.tr.* (also **-ise**). **eternally** *adv.* **eternalness** *n.* **eternize** *v.tr.* (also **-ise**). [ME f. OF f. LL *aeternalis* f. L *aeternus* f. *aevum* age]

eternity /ɪˈtɜːnɪtɪ/ *n.* (pl. **-ies**) **1** infinite or unending (esp. future) time. **2** *Theol.* endless life after death. **3** the state of being eternal. **4** *colloq.* (often prec. by *an*) a very long time. **5** (in *pl.*) eternal truths. □ **eternity ring** a finger-ring set with gems all round, usu. given as a token of lasting affection. [ME f. OF *eternité* f. L *aeternitas -tatis* f. *aeternus*: see ETERNAL]

Etesian /ɪˈtiːʒ(ə)n/ *adj.* □ **Etesian winds** NW winds blowing each summer in the E. Mediterranean. [L *etesius* f. Gk *etēsios* annual f. *etos* year]

eth /eθ/ *n.* (also **edh** /eð/) the name of an Old English and Icelandic letter, = th. [Icel.]

-eth[1] var. of -TH[1].

-eth[2] /ɪθ/ *suffix* (also **-th**) *archaic* forming the 3rd person sing. present of verbs (*doeth; saith*). [OE *-eth, -ath, -th*]

ethanal /ˈeθəˌnæl/ *n.* = ACETALDEHYDE. [ETHANE + ALDEHYDE]

ethane /ˈeθeɪn, ˈiːθ-/ *n. Chem.* a gaseous hydrocarbon of the alkane series, occurring in natural gas. ¶ Chem. formula: C_2H_6. [ETHER + -ANE[2]]

ethanediol /ˈeθeɪnˌdaɪɒl, ˈiːθ-/ *n. Chem.* = ethylene glycol. [ETHANE + DIOL]

ethanol /ˈeθəˌnɒl/ *n. Chem.* = ALCOHOL 1. [ETHANE + ALCOHOL]

Ethelred /ˈeθəlˌred/ 'the Unready' (= lacking good advice, rash) (*c.*969–1016), king of England 978–1016. Succeeding his murdered half-brother Edward the Martyr, Ethelred proved quite unequal to the task of confronting the Danes, resorting to the payment of tribute (Danegeld) to keep them from attacking, and losing his throne briefly (1013–14) to the Danish king Sven Forkbeard.

ethene /ˈeθiːn, ˈiːθ-/ *n. Chem.* = ETHYLENE. [ETHER + -ENE]

ether /ˈiːθə(r)/ *n.* **1** *Chem.* **a** a colourless volatile organic liquid used as an anaesthetic or solvent. Also called DIETHYL ETHER, ETHOXYETHANE. ¶ Chem. formula: $C_2H_5OC_2H_5$. **b** any of a class of organic compounds with a similar structure to this, having an oxygen joined to two alkyl etc. groups. **2** a clear sky; the upper regions of air beyond the clouds. **3** *hist.* **a** a medium formerly assumed to permeate space and fill the interstices between particles of matter. **b** a medium through which electromagnetic waves were formerly thought to be transmitted. □□ **etheric** /iːˈθerɪk/ adj. [ME f. OF ether or L aether f. Gk aithēr f. root of aithō burn, shine]

ethereal /ɪˈθɪərɪəl/ adj. (also **etherial**) **1** light, airy. **2** highly delicate, esp. in appearance. **3** heavenly, celestial. **4** Chem. of or relating to ether. □□ **ethereality** /-ˈælɪtɪ/ n. **ethereally** adv. [L aethereus, -ius f. Gk aitherios (as ETHER)]

etherial var. of ETHEREAL.

etherize /ˈiːθəˌraɪz/ v.tr. (also **-ise**) hist. treat or anaesthetize with ether. □□ **etherization** /-ˈzeɪʃ(ə)n/ n.

ethic /ˈeθɪk/ n. & adj. —n. a set of moral principles (the Quaker ethic). —adj. = ETHICAL. [ME f. OF éthique or L ethicus f. Gk ēthikos (as ETHOS)]

ethical /ˈeθɪk(ə)l/ adj. **1** relating to morals, esp. as concerning human conduct. **2** morally correct; honourable. **3** (of a medicine or drug) not advertised to the general public, and usu. available only on a doctor's prescription. □□ **ethicality** /-ˈkælɪtɪ/ n. **ethically** adv.

ethics /ˈeθɪks/ n.pl. (also treated as sing.) **1** the science of morals in human conduct. **2 a** moral principles; rules of conduct. **b** a set of these (medical ethics). □□ **ethicist** /-sɪst/ n.

Ethiopia /ˌiːθɪˈəʊpɪə/ a country in NE Africa, bordering on the Red Sea; pop. (est. 1988) 48,264,500; official language, Amharic; capital, Addis Ababa. Its earliest recorded civilization, known to the ancient Egyptians as Punt, dates from the 2nd millennium BC. In ancient times Ethiopians (= 'burnt-faced men') were often confused with Indians. Christianized in the 4th c., Ethiopia was isolated by Muslim conquests to the north three centuries later, remaining remote and little known until the late 19th c. It successfully resisted Italian attempts at colonization in the 1890s but was conquered by Italy in 1935. The Emperor Haile Selaisse was restored by the British in 1941 and ruled until overthrown in a Marxist coup in 1975. In recent years the military government has been faced with serious opposition in the eastern province of Eritrea (originally integrated into the country in 1962). Ethiopia is one of the poorest countries in the world. Agriculture is chiefly at subsistence level, and serious crop failures have resulted in widespread famines. International help was organized on a massive scale following publicity in 1984 about the plight of refugees.

Ethiopian /ˌiːθɪˈəʊpɪən/ n. & adj. —n. **1 a** a native or national of Ethiopia. **b** a person of Ethiopian descent. **2** archaic a Black person. —adj. of or relating to Ethiopia. [Ethiopia f. L Aethiops f. Gk Aithiops f. aithō burn + ōps face]

Ethiopic /ˌiːθɪˈɒpɪk, -ˈəʊpɪk/ n. & adj. —n. the liturgical language of the Coptic Church of Ethiopia. (See GEˈEZ.) —adj. of or in this language. [L aethiopicus f. Gk aithiopikos: see ETHIOPIAN]

ethmoid /ˈeθmɔɪd/ adj. sievelike. □ **ethmoid bone** a square bone at the root of the nose, with many perforations through which the olfactory nerves pass to the nose. □□ **ethmoidal** /-ˈmɔɪd(ə)l/ adj. [Gk ēthmoeidēs f. ēthmos sieve]

ethnic /ˈeθnɪk/ adj. & n. —adj. **1 a** (of a social group) having a common national or cultural tradition. **b** (of clothes etc.) resembling those of a non-European exotic people. **2** denoting origin by birth or descent rather than nationality (ethnic Turks). **3** relating to race or culture (ethnic group; ethnic origins). **4** archaic pagan, heathen. —n. **1** US a member of an (esp. minority) ethnic group. **2** (in pl., usu. treated as sing.) = ETHNOLOGY. □ **ethnic minority** a (usu. identifiable) group differentiated from the main population of a community by racial origin or cultural background. □□ **ethnically** adv. **ethnicity** /-ˈnɪsɪtɪ/ n. [ME f. eccl.L ethnicus f. Gk ethnikos heathen f. ethnos nation]

ethnical /ˈeθnɪk(ə)l/ adj. relating to ethnology.

ethno- /ˈeθnəʊ/ comb. form ethnic, ethnological. [Gk ethnos nation]

ethnoarchaeology /ˌeθnəʊˌɑːkɪˈɒlədʒɪ/ n. the study of a society's institutions based on examination of its material attributes. □□ **ethnoarchaeological** /-kɪəˈlɒdʒɪk(ə)l/ adj. **ethnoarchaeologist** n.

ethnocentric /ˌeθnəʊˈsentrɪk/ adj. evaluating other races and

cultures by criteria specific to one's own. □□ **ethnocentrically** adv. **ethnocentricity** /-ˈtrɪsɪtɪ/ n. **ethnocentrism** n.

ethnography /eθˈnɒɡrəfɪ/ n. the scientific description of races and cultures of mankind. □□ **ethnographer** n. **ethnographic** /-nəˈɡræfɪk/ adj. **ethnographical** /-nəˈɡræfɪk(ə)l/ adj.

ethnology /eθˈnɒlədʒɪ/ n. the comparative scientific study of human peoples. □□ **ethnologic** /-nəˈlɒdʒɪk/ adj. **ethnological** /-nəˈlɒdʒɪk(ə)l/ adj. **ethnologist** n.

ethnomusicology /ˌeθnəʊˌmjuːzɪˈkɒlədʒɪ/ n. the study of the music of one or more (esp. non-European) cultures. □□ **ethnomusicologist** n.

ethogram /ˈiːθəˌɡræm/ n. Zool. a list of the kinds of behaviour or activity observed in an animal. [Gk ētho- (see ETHOS) + -GRAM]

ethology /iːˈθɒlədʒɪ/ n. **1** the science of animal behaviour. **2** the science of character-formation in human behaviour. □□ **ethological** /ˌiːθəˈlɒdʒɪk(ə)l/ adj. **ethologist** n. [L ethologia f. Gk ēthologia (as ETHOS)]

ethos /ˈiːθɒs/ n. the characteristic spirit or attitudes of a community, people, or system, or of a literary work etc. [mod.L f. Gk ēthos nature, disposition]

ethoxyethane /iːˌθɒksɪˈiːθeɪn/ n. Chem. = ETHER 1a. [ETHER + OXY-² + ETHANE]

ethyl /ˈiːθaɪl, ˈeθɪl/ n. (attrib.) Chem. the univalent radical derived from ethane by removal of a hydrogen atom (ethyl alcohol). [G (as ETHER, -YL)]

ethylene /ˈeθɪˌliːn/ n. Chem. a gaseous hydrocarbon of the alkene series, occurring in natural gas and used in the manufacture of polythene. Also called ETHENE. ¶ Chem. formula: C_2H_4. □ **ethylene glycol** Chem. a colourless viscous hygroscopic liquid used as an antifreeze and in the manufacture of polyesters. ¶ Chem. formula: $C_2H_6O_2$: also called ETHANEDIOL. □□ **ethylenic** /-ˈliːnɪk/ adj.

-etic /ˈetɪk/ suffix forming adjectives and nouns (ascetic; emetic; genetic; synthetic). [Gk -ētikos or -ētikos: cf. -IC]

etiolate /ˈiːtɪəʊˌleɪt/ v.tr. **1** make (a plant) pale by excluding light. **2** give a sickly hue to (a person). □□ **etiolation** /-ˈleɪʃ(ə)n/ n. [F étioler f. Norman F étieuler make into haulm f. éteule ult. f. L stipula straw]

etiology US var. of AETIOLOGY.

etiquette /ˈetɪˌket, -ˈket/ n. **1** the conventional rules of social behaviour. **2 a** the customary behaviour of members of a profession towards each other. **b** the unwritten code governing this (medical etiquette). [F étiquette label, etiquette]

Etna /ˈetnə/ a volcano in Sicily, the highest European volcano (3,323 m, 10,902 ft.). It has a long history of eruptions.

Eton College /ˈiːt(ə)n/ a public school near Windsor, Berks., founded in 1440 by Henry VI to prepare scholars for King's College, Cambridge. □ **Eton collar** a broad stiff collar worn outside the coat-collar, esp. of an Eton jacket. **Eton jacket** a short jacket reaching only to the waist, as formerly worn by pupils of Eton College. **Eton wall game** one of the oldest forms of football in existence, played only on a site at Eton College where a red brick wall (built in 1717) separates a playing field from the Slough road. The game consists chiefly of 'bullies' or scrimmages against the wall; the player with the ball attempts to force a way through the opposition, keeping the ball against the wall. Progress is slow, and although points are scored in various ways goals are a rarity. The famous wall game between scholars (or Collegers) and non-scholars (or Oppidans) on St Andrew's Day (30 Nov.) dates back to at least 1820.

Etonian /iːˈtəʊnɪən/ n. a past or present member of Eton College.

Etosha Pan /ɪˈtəʊʃə/ a depression of the great African plateau, filled with salt water and having no outlets, extending over an area of 4,800 sq. km (1,854 sq. miles) in northern Namibia.

étrier /ˈeɪtrɪˌeɪ/ n. Mountaineering a short rope ladder with a few rungs of wood or metal. [F, = stirrup]

Etruscan /ɪˈtrʌskən/ adj. & n. —adj. of ancient Etruria (see below) or its people or language. —n. **1** a native of Etruria. **2** the language of Etruria, which is not of the Indo-European family and has never been satisfactorily deciphered. □□ **Etruscology** /-ˈkɒlədʒɪ/ n. [L Etruscus]

The Etruscans were the earliest historical inhabitants of the area (Etruria) between the Arno and the Tiber (roughly the modern Tuscany). Their empire in Italy was at its height c.500 BC, and their sophisticated civilization was an important influence on the Romans, who completely subdued them by the end of the 3rd c. BC.

et seq. abbr. (also **et seqq.**) and the following (pages etc.). [L et sequentia]

-ette /et/ suffix forming nouns meaning: **1** small (kitchenette; cigarette). **2** imitation or substitute (leatherette; flannelette). **3** female (usherette; suffragette). [from or after OF -ette, fem. of -ET¹]

étude /'eɪtjuːd, -'tjuːd/ n. a short musical composition or exercise, usu. for one instrument, designed to improve the technique of the player. [F, = study]

étui /e'twiː/ n. a small case for needles etc. [F étui f. OF estui prison]

-etum /'iːtəm/ suffix forming nouns denoting a collection of trees or other plants (arboretum; pinetum). [L]

etymologize /ˌetɪ'mɒlədʒaɪz/ v. (also **-ise**) **1** tr. give or trace the etymology of. **2** intr. study etymology. [med.L etymologizare f. L etymologia (as ETYMOLOGY)]

etymology /ˌetɪ'mɒlədʒɪ/ n. (pl. **-ies**) **1 a** the historically verifiable sources of the formation of a word and the development of its meaning. **b** an account of these. **2** the branch of linguistic science concerned with etymologies. □□ **etymological** /-mə'lɒdʒɪk(ə)l/ adj. **etymologically** /-mə'lɒdʒɪkəlɪ/ adv. **etymologist** n. [OF ethimologie f. L etymologia f. Gk etumologia (as ETYMON, -LOGY)]

etymon /'etɪmən/ n. (pl. **etyma** /-mə/) the word that gives rise to a derivative or a borrowed or later form. [L f. Gk etumon (neut. of etumos true), the literal sense or original form of a word]

Eu symb. Chem. the element europium.

eu- /juː/ comb. form well, easily. [Gk]

Euboea /juː'biːə/ (Greek **Évvoia** /'eɪvɪə/) an island of Greece, in the western Aegean Sea, almost parallel to the mainland, from which it is separated by only a narrow channel for most of its length; pop. (1981) 185,600; capital, Chalcis (Khalkis).

eucalyptus /ˌjuːkə'lɪptəs/ n. (also **eucalypt**) (pl. **eucalyptuses** or **eucalypti** /-taɪ/ or **eucalypts**) **1** any tree of the genus Eucalyptus, native to Australasia, cultivated for its timber and for the oil from its leaves. **2** (in full **eucalyptus oil**) this oil used as an antiseptic etc. [mod.L f. EU- + Gk kaluptos covered f. kaluptō to cover, the unopened flower being protected by a cap]

eucaryote var. of EUKARYOTE.

eucharis /'juːkərɪs/ n. any bulbous plant of the genus Eucharis, native to S. America, with white umbellate flowers. [Gk eukharis pleasing (as EU-, kharis grace)]

Eucharist /'juːkərɪst/ n. **1** the Christian sacrament commemorating the Last Supper, in which bread and wine are consecrated and consumed. (See below.) **2** the consecrated elements, esp. the bread (receive the Eucharist). □□ **Eucharistic** /-'rɪstɪk/ adj. **Eucharistical** /-'rɪstɪk(ə)l/ adj. [ME f. OF eucariste, ult. f. eccl.Gk eukharistia thanksgiving f. Gk eukharistos grateful (as EU-, kharizomai offer willingly)]

The origins of the Eucharist are found in the synoptic Gospels and 1 Cor. 10, 11. From the first it was accepted that the Eucharist conveyed to the believer the body and blood of Christ, but there were different interpretations of the sense in which Christ was present (see CONSUBSTANTIATION, TRANSUBSTANTIATION).

euchre /'juːkə(r)/ n. & v. —n. an American card-game for two, three, or four persons, played with a pack of 32 cards (the 2, 3, 4, 5, 6 of each suit being rejected), from which each player is dealt 5 cards. A player may 'pass' or decline to play; if he plays he must take three tricks to win the point, losing two points to his opponent(s) if he fails to do so. —v.tr. **1** (in euchre) gain the advantage over (another player) when that player fails to take three tricks. **2** deceive, outwit. **3** Austral. exhaust, ruin. [19th c.: orig. unkn.]

Euclid /'juːklɪd/ (c.300 BC) Greek mathematician who taught at Alexandria in Egypt, famous for his great textbook, entitled Elements, on plane geometry, the theory of numbers, irrationals,

and solid geometry, which was the standard work on geometry until recent times.

Euclidean /juː'klɪdɪən/ adj. of or relating to Euclid. □ **Euclidean geometry** that of ordinary experience, based on the postulates used by Euclid (that parallel lines meet, that the sum of the angles of a triangle is 180°). **Euclidean space** space for which Euclidean geometry is valid. [L Euclideus f. Gk Eukleideios]

eudemonic /ˌjuːdɪ'mɒnɪk/ adj. (also **eudaemonic**) conducive to happiness. [Gk eudaimonikos (as EUDEMONISM)]

eudemonism /juː'diːmənɪz(ə)m/ n. (also **eudaemonism**) a system of ethics that bases moral obligation on the likelihood of actions producing happiness. □□ **eudemonist** n. **eudemonistic** /-'nɪstɪk/ adj. [Gk eudaimonismos system of happiness f. eudaimōn happy (as EU-, daimōn guardian spirit)]

eudiometer /ˌjuːdɪ'ɒmɪtə(r)/ n. Chem. a graduated glass tube in which gases may be chemically combined by an electric spark, used to measure changes in volume of gases during chemical reactions. □□ **eudiometric** /-dɪə'metrɪk/ adj. **eudiometrical** /-dɪə'metrɪk(ə)l/ adj. **eudiometry** n. [Gk eudios clear (weather): orig. used to measure the amount of oxygen, thought to be greater in clear air]

eugenics /juː'dʒenɪks/ n.pl. (also treated as sing.) the science of improving the (esp. human) population by controlled breeding for desirable inherited characteristics. (See GALTON.) □□ **eugenic** adj. **eugenically** adv. **eugenicist** /juː'dʒenɪsɪst/ n. **eugenist** /'juːdʒɪnɪst/ n.

Eugénie /ɜː'ʒeɪnɪ/ (1826–1920), empress of the French and wife of Napoleon III. Throughout her husband's reign she contributed much to the brilliance of his court, and acted as regent on three occasions.

eukaryote /juː'kærɪɒt/ n. (also **eucaryote**) Biol. an organism consisting of a cell or cells in which the genetic material is contained within a distinct nucleus (cf. PROKARYOTE). □□ **eukaryotic** /-'ɒtɪk/ adj. [EU- + KARYO- + -ote as in ZYGOTE]

Euler /'ɔɪlə(r)/, Leonhard (1707–83), Swiss-born mathematician, who worked in St Petersburg and Berlin for most of his life. He wrote on all branches of mathematics and made significant discoveries in most. His work is characterized by a vigorous originality and an innocent but harmless lack of rigour. Nevertheless, it was his attempts to elucidate the nature of functions and his successful though logically dubious study of infinite series which led his successors, notably Abel, Bolzano, and Cauchy, to introduce ideas of convergence and rigorous argument into mathematics. Perhaps his best-known and best-loved theorem is his startling discovery of a connection between the most important constants in mathematics, the equation $e^{i\pi} = -1$. His enormous output of books and articles, and his extensive correspondence with scientists all over Europe, were scarcely affected by the blindness which afflicted him from 1771.

eulogium /juː'ləʊdʒɪəm/ n. (pl. **eulogia** /-dʒɪə/ or **-ums**) = EULOGY. [med.L: see EULOGY]

eulogize /'juːlədʒaɪz/ v.tr. (also **-ise**) praise in speech or writing. □□ **eulogist** n. **eulogistic** /-'dʒɪstɪk/ adj. **eulogistically** /-'dʒɪstɪkəlɪ/ adv.

eulogy /'juːlədʒɪ/ n. (pl. **-ies**) **1 a** a speech or writing in praise of a person. **b** an expression of praise. **2** US a funeral oration in praise of a person. [med.L eulogium f. (app. by confusion with L elogium epitaph) LL eulogia praise f. Gk]

Eumenides /juː'menɪdiːz/ Gk Mythol. kindly powers sending fertility, but who, being of the earth, were often confused with the Erinyes or Furies. [Gk, = kindly ones]

eunuch /'juːnək/ n. **1** a castrated man, esp. one formerly employed at an oriental harem or court. **2** a person lacking effectiveness (political eunuch). [ME f. L eunuchus f. Gk eunoukhos lit. bedchamber attendant f. eunē bed + second element rel. to ekhō hold]

euonymus /juː'ɒnɪməs/ n. any tree of the genus Euonymus, e.g. the spindle tree. [L f. Gk euōnumos of lucky name (as EU-, onoma name)]

eupeptic /juː'peptɪk/ adj. of or having good digestion. [Gk eupeptos (as EU-, peptō digest)]

euphemism /ˈjuːfɪˌmɪz(ə)m/ n. **1** a mild or vague expression substituted for one thought to be too harsh or direct (e.g. *pass over* for *die*). **2** the use of such expressions. □□ **euphemist** n. **euphemistic** /-ˈmɪstɪk/ adj. **euphemistically** /-ˈmɪstɪkəlɪ/ adv. **euphemize** v.tr. & intr. (also **-ise**). [Gk *euphēmismos* f. *euphēmos* (as EU-, *phēmē* speaking)]

euphonious /juːˈfəʊnɪəs/ adj. **1** sounding pleasant, harmonious. **2** concerning euphony. □□ **euphoniously** adv.

euphonium /juːˈfəʊnɪəm/ n. a brass wind instrument of the tuba family. [mod.L f. Gk *euphōnos* (as EUPHONY)]

euphony /ˈjuːfənɪ/ n. (pl. **-ies**) **1 a** pleasantness of sound, esp. of a word or phrase; harmony. **b** a pleasant sound. **2** the tendency to make a phonetic change for ease of pronunciation. □□ **euphonic** /-ˈfɒnɪk/ adj. **euphonize** v.tr. (also **-ise**). [F *euphonie* f. LL *euphonia* f. Gk *euphōnia* (as EU-, *phōnē* sound)]

euphorbia /juːˈfɔːbɪə/ n. any plant of the genus *Euphorbia*, including spurges. [ME f. L *euphorbea* f. *Euphorbus*, 1st-c. Gk physician]

euphoria /juːˈfɔːrɪə/ n. a feeling of well-being, esp. one based on over-confidence or over-optimism. □□ **euphoric** /-ˈfɒrɪk/ adj. **euphorically** /-ˈfɒrɪkəlɪ/ adv. [Gk f. *euphoros* well-bearing (as EU-, *pherō* bear)]

euphoriant /juːˈfɔːrɪənt/ adj. & n. —adj. inducing euphoria. —n. a euphoriant drug.

Euphrates /juːˈfreɪtiːz/ a river of SW Asia, length about 2,430 km (1,510 miles), that rises in the mountains of eastern Turkey and flows through Syria and Iraq to join the Tigris, forming the Shatt al-Arab which flows into the Persian Gulf.

euphuism /ˈjuːfjuːˌɪz(ə)m/ n. an affected or high-flown style of writing or speaking. □□ **euphuist** n. **euphuistic** /-ˈɪstɪk/ adj. **euphuistically** /-ˈɪstɪkəlɪ/ adv. [Gk *euphuēs* well endowed by nature: orig. of writing imitating Lyly's *Euphues* (1578–80)]

Eurasian /jʊəˈreɪʒ(ə)n/ adj. & n. —adj. **1** of mixed European and Asian (esp. Indian) parentage. **2** of Europe and Asia. —n. a Eurasian person.

Euratom /jʊəˈrætəm/ n. European Atomic Energy Community. [abbr.]

eureka /jʊəˈriːkə/ int. & n. —int. I have found it! (announcing a discovery etc.). —n. the exultant cry of 'eureka'. [Gk *heurēka* 1st pers. sing. perfect of *heuriskō* find: attributed to Archimedes]

eurhythmic /jʊəˈrɪðmɪk/ adj. of or in harmonious proportion (esp. of architecture). [*eurhythmy* harmony of proportions f. L *eur(h)ythmia* f. Gk *eurhuthmia* (as EU-, *rhuthmos* proportion, rhythm)]

eurhythmics /jʊəˈrɪðmɪks/ n.pl. (also treated as *sing.*) (US **eurythmics**) harmony of bodily movement, esp. as developed (originaly by the Swiss composer Émile Jaques-Dalcroze) with music and dance into a system of education.

Euripides /jʊəˈrɪpɪˌdiːz/ (c.485–c.406 BC) Greek dramatist, the latest (after Aeschylus and Sophocles) of the three great tragedians. His 19 surviving plays show important innovations in the handling of the traditional myths, reflecting the contemporary Athenian intellectual enlightenment. He was notorious for introducing a low realism into grand subject-matter, had a deep interest in feminine psychology (e.g. in the *Medea*), was a penetrating portrayer of abnormal and irrational states of mind (e.g. in the *Bacchae* and *Hippolytus*), and had a fondness for involved adventure-plots (e.g. the rescue of Iphigenia from Tauris). The influence of the developing art of rhetoric is pervasive, and his use of the traditional chorus displays an increasing lyricism and detachment from the main action.

Euro- /ˈjʊərəʊ/ comb. form Europe, European. [abbr.]

euro /ˈjʊərəʊ/ n. (pl. **-os**) *Austral.* a large reddish kangaroo. [Aboriginal]

Eurocommunism /ˌjʊərəʊˈkɒmjʊˌnɪz(ə)m/ n. a form of Communism in Western European countries that is independent of the Soviet Communist Party. □□ **Eurocommunist** adj. & n.

Eurocrat /ˈjʊərəʊˌkræt/ n. usu. *derog.* a bureaucrat in the administration of the European Economic Community.

Eurodollar /ˈjʊərəʊˌdɒlə(r)/ n. a dollar held in a bank in Europe.

Europa /jʊəˈrəʊpə/ Gk Mythol. the daughter of Agenor king of Tyre, or of Phoenix (= 'the Phoenician'). Wooed by Zeus in the form of a bull, she was carried off to Crete, where she bore him three sons: Minos, Rhadamanthus, and Sarpedon.

Europe /ˈjʊərəp/ **1** a continent of the northern hemisphere consisting of the western part of the land mass of which Asia forms the eastern (and greater) part, and including Scandinavia and the British Isles. It contains approximately 20 per cent of the world's population. The western part of Europe was consolidated within the Roman Empire, but the subsequent barbarian invasions brought political chaos which was only gradually resolved in the medieval and post-medieval periods, the last modern European nation States emerging in the 19th c. Politically and economically pre-eminent in the 18th and 19th centuries, Europe has been overshadowed as a result of the rise of the superpowers in the 20th c., but it still maintains a general standard of living and political stability well in advance of that of most of the Third World. **2** the European (Economic) Community.

European /ˌjʊərəˈpɪən/ adj. & n. —adj. **1** of or in Europe. **2 a** descended from natives of Europe. **b** originating in or characteristic of Europe. **3 a** happening in or extending over Europe. **b** concerning Europe as a whole rather than its individual countries. **4** of or relating to the European (Economic) Community. —n. **1 a** a native or inhabitant of Europe. **b** a person descended from natives of Europe. **c** a White person. **2** a person concerned with European matters. □ **European plan** US a system of charging for a hotel room only without meals. □□ **Europeanism** n. **Europeanize** v.tr. & intr. (also **-ise**). **Europeanization** /-ˈzeɪʃ(ə)n/ n. [F *européen* f. L *europaeus* f. L *Europa* f. Gk *Eurōpē* Europe]

European Atomic Energy Community an institution established in 1957 by members of the European Coal and Steel Community to create within a short period the technical and industrial conditions needed to utilize nuclear discoveries and especially to produce nuclear energy on a large scale. The UK, Denmark, and Ireland joined in 1973, Greece in 1981, and Spain and Portugal in 1986.

European Bank for Reconstruction and Development a bank established in London in April 1991 with the aim of assisting formerly State-controlled economies in what were the Communist countries of Eastern Europe, and in the Soviet Union, to make the transition to a free-market economy.

European Coal and Steel Community the first of the European Communities (the others are the EEC and Euratom, established in 1952 to regulate pricing, transport, tariffs, etc. for coal, iron ore, and scrap within the Community. The original members were France, West Germany, Italy, Belgium, The Netherlands, and Luxembourg.

European Commission a group of persons, appointed by agreement among the governments of the European Community since 1987, who act as the initiator of Community action and the guardian of its treaties. Its members are pledged to independence of the governments and of national or other particular interests. The Commission meets in Brussels.

European Community an organization of Western European countries, which came into being in 1967 through the merger of the European Economic Community, Euratom, and the European Coal and Steel Community, and was committed to economic and political integration as envisaged by the Treaties of Rome. Its membership is identical with that of the EEC.

European Convention see COUNCIL OF EUROPE.

European Court of Human Rights an institution of the Council of Europe, planned by the European Convention on Human Rights in 1950 but not finally set up until 1959. Under the Convention the task of protecting human rights is shared by this Court and the European Commission of Human Rights; both are based in Strasbourg. The Commission's role is to examine complaints of alleged breaches of the Convention; the Court is called to give judgment in cases where the Commission has failed to secure a settlement.

European Court of Justice an institution of the European Community, with 13 judges appointed by its member governments, meeting in Luxembourg. It was established in 1958, and exists to safeguard the law in the interpretation and application of Community treaties and to determine violations of these. Cases may be brought to it by member States, Community institutions, firms, or individuals.

European currency unit a monetary unit used to evaluate, on a common basis, the exchange rates and reserves of members of the European Monetary System. It was introduced in 1979.

European Economic Community an economic association of Western European countries set up under the terms of the ECSC Treaty of 1952; its authority was extended by the Treaty of Rome (1957) to cover also the EEC and Euratom. The original members were Belgium, France, West Germany, Italy, Luxembourg, and The Netherlands; Denmark, Ireland, and the UK joined in 1973, Greece in 1981, and Spain and Portugal in 1986; Greenland withdrew in 1986. Its aims include the free movement of labour and capital between member countries, especially by the abolition of customs barriers and cartels, and the fostering of common agricultural and trading policies.

European Free Trade Association a customs union of Western European countries, established in 1960, created by a British initiative as a trade grouping unencumbered by the political implications of the EEC. In 1973 Britain and Denmark entered the EEC and left EFTA. Free trade between its original members was achieved by the end of 1966, and all tariffs between EFTA and EEC countries were finally abolished in 1984.

European Investment Bank a bank set up in 1958 by the Treaty of Rome to finance capital investment projects promoting the balanced development of the European Community. It is based in Luxembourg.

European Monetary System a monetary system inaugurated by the EEC in 1979 to coordinate and stabilize the exchange rates of the currencies of member countries. it involves (1) use of the exchange rate mechanism (see entry), (2) a system for supporting a country's balance-of-payments account when necessary.

European Parliament the parliament of the European Community, originally established in 1952. From 1958 to 1979 it was composed of representatives drawn from the parliaments of member countries, but since 1979 quinquennial direct elections have taken place. Treaties signed in 1970, 1975, and 1986 gave it important powers over budgetary and constitutional matters, and through the Single European Act (1986) it assumed a degree of sovereignty over national parliaments. The European Parliament meets (about 12 times a year) in Strasbourg and its committees in Brussels.

European Recovery Program the Marshall Plan, which established Marshall Aid (see MARSHALL).

European Space Agency an organization set up in 1975 and based in Paris, formed from two earlier organizations (the European Space Research Organization and the European Launcher Development Organization), to advance space research and technology, implement a long-term European space technology, and coordinate national space programmes.

europium /joʊˈrəʊpɪəm/ n. Chem. a soft silvery metallic element of the lanthanide series, occurring naturally in small quantities. Europium was first purified (as europium oxide) in 1901. The oxide is used together with yttrium oxide as a red phosphor in colour television screens. ¶ Symb.: **Eu**; atomic number 63. [mod.L f. Europe]

Eurovision /ˈjʊərəʊˌvɪʒ(ə)n/ n. a network of European television production administered by the European Broadcasting Union.

Eurydice /jʊəˈrɪdɪsɪ/ Gk Mythol. the wife of Orpheus.

eurythmics US var. of EURHYTHMICS.

Eusebius /juːˈsiːbɪəs/ (c.260–c.340) bishop of Caesarea on the coast of Palestine, and Church historian. His Ecclesiastical History is the principal source for the history of Christianity (especially in the Eastern Church) from the Apostolic age until his own day.

Eustachian tube /juːˈsteɪʃ(ə)n/ n. Anat. a tube leading from the pharynx to the cavity of the middle ear and equalizing the pressure on each side of the eardrum. [L Eustachius = B. Eustachio, It. anatomist d. 1574]

eustasy /ˈjuːstəsɪ/ n. a change in sea level throughout the world caused by tectonic movements, melting of glaciers, etc. □□ **eustatic** /-ˈstætɪk/ adj. [back-form. f. G eustatisch (adj.) (as EU-, STATIC)]

eutectic /juːˈtektɪk/ adj. & n. Chem. —adj. (of a mixture, alloy, etc.) having the lowest freezing-point of any possible proportions of its constituents. —n. a eutectic mixture. □ **eutectic point** (or **temperature**) the minimum freezing-point for a eutectic mixture. [Gk eutēktos (as EU-, tēkō melt)]

Euterpe /juːˈtɜːpɪ/ Gk & Rom. Mythol. the Muse of flutes. [Gk, = well-pleasing]

euthanasia /ˌjuːθəˈneɪzɪə/ n. 1 the bringing about of a gentle and easy death in the case of incurable and painful disease. 2 such a death. [Gk (as EU-, thanatos death)]

eutherian /juːˈθɪərɪən/ n. & adj. —n. any mammal of the infraclass Eutheria, giving nourishment to its young through a placenta. —adj. of or relating to this infraclass. [EU- + Gk thēr wild beast]

eutrophic /juːˈtrɒfɪk, -ˈtrəʊfɪk/ adj. (of a lake etc.) rich in nutrients and therefore supporting a dense plant population, which kills animal life by depriving it of oxygen. □□ **eutrophicate** v.tr. **eutrophication** /-ˈkeɪʃ(ə)n/ n. **eutrophy** /ˈjuːtrəfɪ/ n. [eutrophy f. Gk eutrophia (as EU-, trephō nourish)]

eV abbr. electronvolt.

EVA abbr. Astronaut. extravehicular activity.

evacuate /ɪˈvækjʊˌeɪt/ v.tr. 1 a remove (people) from a place of danger to stay elsewhere for the duration of the danger. b empty (a place) in this way. 2 make empty (a vessel of air etc.). 3 (of troops) withdraw from (a place). 4 a empty (the bowels or other bodily organ). b discharge (faeces etc.). □□ **evacuant** n. & adj. **evacuation** /-ˈeɪʃ(ə)n/ n. **evacuative** /-kjʊətɪv/ adj. & n. **evacuator** n. [L evacuare (as E-, vacuus empty)]

evacuee /ɪˌvækjuːˈiː/ n. a person evacuated from a place of danger.

evade /ɪˈveɪd/ v.tr. 1 a escape from, avoid, esp. by guile or trickery. b avoid doing (one's duty etc.). c avoid answering (a question) or yielding to (an argument). 2 a fail to pay (tax due). b defeat the intention of (a law etc.), esp. while complying with its letter. 3 (of a thing) elude or baffle (a person). □□ **evadable** adj. **evader** n. [F évader f. L evadere (as E-, vadere vas- go)]

evaginate /ɪˈvædʒɪˌneɪt/ v.tr. Med. & Physiol. turn (a tubular organ) inside out. □□ **evagination** /-ˈneɪʃ(ə)n/ n. [L evaginare (as E-, vaginare as VAGINA)]

evaluate /ɪˈvæljʊˌeɪt/ v.tr. 1 assess, appraise. 2 a find or state the number or amount of. b find a numerical expression for. □□ **evaluation** /-ˈeɪʃ(ə)n/ n. **evaluative** /-ətɪv/ adj. **evaluator** n. [back-form. f. evaluation f. F évaluation f. évaluer (as E-, VALUE)]

evanesce /ˌiːvəˈnes, ˌe-/ v.intr. 1 fade from sight; disappear. 2 become effaced. [L evanescere (as E-, vanus empty)]

evanescent /ˌiːvəˈnes(ə)nt, ˌe-/ adj. (of an impression or appearance etc.) quickly fading. □□ **evanescence** n. **evanescently** adv.

evangel /ɪˈvændʒ(ə)l/ n. 1 archaic a the gospel. b any of the four Gospels. 2 a basic doctrine or set of principles. 3 US = EVANGELIST. [ME f. OF evangile f. eccl.L evangelium f. Gk euaggelion good news (as EU-, ANGEL)]

evangelic /ˌiːvænˈdʒelɪk/ adj. = EVANGELICAL.

evangelical /ˌiːvænˈdʒelɪk(ə)l/ adj. & n. —adj. 1 of the Protestant Churches, as basing their claim pre-eminently on the gospel. 2 (formerly, in Germany and Switzerland) the Lutheran Churches as contrasted with the Calvinist (Reformed) Churches. 3 (in the Church of England) of the school (originating in the 18th c.) that lays special stress on personal conversion and salvation by faith in the Atonement. —n. a member of the evangelical school. □□ **evangelicalism** n. **evangelically** adv. [eccl.L evangelicus f. eccl.Gk euaggelikos (as EVANGEL)]

evangelism /ɪˈvændʒəˌlɪz(ə)m/ n. 1 the preaching or promulgation of the gospel. 2 evangelicalism.

evangelist /ɪˈvændʒəlɪst/ n. 1 any of the writers of the four Gospels (Matthew, Mark, Luke, John). 2 a preacher of the gospel. 3 a lay person doing missionary work.

---

aʊ how   eɪ day   əʊ no   eə hair   ɪə near   ɔɪ boy   ʊə poor   aɪə fire   aʊə sour   (see over for consonants)

evangelistic /ɪˌvændʒəˈlɪstɪk/ adj. **1** = EVANGELICAL. **2** of preachers of the gospel. **3** of the four evangelists.

evangelize /ɪˈvændʒəˌlaɪz/ v.tr. (also **-ise**) **1** (also absol.) preach the gospel to. **2** convert (a person) to Christianity. □□ **evangelization** /-ˈzeɪʃ(ə)n/ n. **evangelizer** n. [ME f. eccl.L evangelizare f. Gk euaggelizomai (as EVANGEL)]

Evans /ˈev(ə)nz/, Sir Arthur John (1851–1941), British archaeologist, best known for his excavations at Knossos in Crete, which lasted intermittently from 1900 to 1935, and the resulting discovery of the Bronze Age civilization of Crete, which he termed Minoan.

Evans-Pritchard /ˌevənzˈprɪtʃəd/, Sir Edward Evan (1902–73), English anthropologist, noted especially for his studies of African tribal life and cultures, which are among the classics of social anthropology. His most important books include Witchcraft, Oracles and Magic among the Azande (1937) and the trilogy of studies on the Nuer (1940–56).

evaporate /ɪˈvæpəˌreɪt/ v. **1** intr. turn from solid or liquid into vapour. **2** intr. & tr. lose or cause to lose moisture as vapour. **3** intr. & tr. disappear or cause to disappear (our courage evaporated). □ **evaporated milk** milk concentrated by partial evaporation. □□ **evaporable** adj. **evaporation** /-ˈreɪʃ(ə)n/ n. **evaporative** /-rətɪv/ adj. **evaporator** n. [L evaporare (as E-, vaporare as VAPOUR)]

evasion /ɪˈveɪʒ(ə)n/ n. **1** the act or a means of evading. **2 a** a subterfuge or prevaricating excuse. **b** an evasive answer. [ME f. OF f. L evasio -onis (as EVADE)]

evasive /ɪˈveɪsɪv/ adj. **1** seeking to evade something. **2** not direct in one's answers etc. **3** enabling or effecting evasion (evasive action). **4** (of a person) tending to evasion; habitually practising evasion. □□ **evasively** adv. **evasiveness** n.

Eve /iːv/ (in the Biblical tradition) the first woman, wife of Adam. According to Genesis 3: 20 she was so named because she was the mother of all living beings, but the Hebrew name may have meant 'serpent' and so she became associated with the primitive myth that all life originated in a primeval serpent. It was a common medieval conceit that the Latin form of her name (Eva) spelt backwards was the first word of the angel's address to Mary (Ave) at the Annunciation, symbolizing the reversal, through the Incarnation, of Eve's fall.

eve /iːv/ n. **1** the evening or day before a church festival or any date or event (Christmas Eve; the eve of the funeral). **2** the time just before anything (the eve of the election). **3** archaic evening. [ME, = EVEN²]

evection /ɪˈvekʃ(ə)n/ n. Astron. a perturbation of the moon's motion caused by the sun's attraction. [L evectio (as E-, vehere vect- carry)]

Evelyn /ˈiːvlɪn/, John (1620–1706), English writer, traveller, connoisseur of the arts, pioneer of English forestry and gardening, humanist, and Christian, a man of means and of untiring curiosity and energy, and a friend of Samuel Pepys. In his diaries he recorded in great detail the extraordinary variety of his life. He was a main founder of the Royal Society, through which he met Robert Boyle and Isaac Newton. Surviving both the plague and the Great Fire of London he saw his country governed by six monarchies and one republic.

even¹ /ˈiːv(ə)n/ adj., adv., & v. —adj. (**evener, evenest**) **1** level; flat and smooth. **2 a** uniform in quality; constant. **b** equal in number or amount or value etc. **c** equally balanced. **3** (usu. foll. by with) in the same plane or line. **4** (of a person's temper etc.) equable, calm. **5 a** (of a number such as 4, 6) divisible by two without a remainder. **b** bearing such a number (no parking on even dates). **c** not involving fractions; exact (in even dozens). —adv. **1** used to invite comparison of the stated assertion, negation, etc., with an implied one that is less strong or remarkable (never even opened [let alone read] the letter; does he even suspect [not to say realize] the danger?; ran even faster [not just as fast as before]; even if my watch is right we shall be late [later if it is slow]). **2** used to introduce an extreme case (even you must realize it; it might even cost £100). —v. **1** tr. & intr. (often foll. by up) make or become even. **2** tr. (often foll. by to) archaic treat as equal or comparable. □ **even as** at the very moment that. **even break** colloq. an equal chance. **even chance** an equal chance of success

or failure. **even money 1** betting odds offering the gambler the chance of winning the amount he or she staked. **2** equally likely to happen or not (it's even money he'll fail to arrive). **even now 1** now as well as before. **2** at this very moment. **even so 1** notwithstanding that; nevertheless. **2** quite so. **3** in that case as well as in others. **get** (or **be**) **even with** have one's revenge on. **of even date** Law & Commerce of the same date. **on an even keel 1** (of a ship or aircraft) not listing. **2** (of a plan or person) untroubled. □□ **evenly** adv. **evenness** n. [OE efen, efne]

even² /ˈiːv(ə)n/ n. poet. evening. [OE æfen]

even-handed /ˌiːv(ə)nˈhændɪd/ adj. impartial, fair. □□ **even-handedly** adv. **even-handedness** n.

evening /ˈiːvnɪŋ/ n. & int. —n. **1** the end part of the day, esp. from about 6 p.m. to bedtime (this evening; during the evening; evening meal). **2** this time spent in a particular way (had a lively evening). **3** a time compared with this, esp. the last part of a person's life. —int. = good evening (see GOOD adj. 14). □ **evening dress** formal dress for evening wear. **evening primrose** any plant of the genus Oenothera with pale yellow flowers that open in the evening. **evening star** a planet, esp. Venus, conspicuous in the west after sunset. [OE æfnung, rel. to EVEN²]

evens /ˈiːv(ə)nz/ n.pl. Brit. = even money.

evensong /ˈiːv(ə)nˌsɒŋ/ n. a service of evening prayer in the Church of England. [EVEN² + SONG]

event /ɪˈvent/ n. **1** a thing that happens or takes place, esp. one of importance. **2 a** the fact of a thing's occurring. **b** a result or outcome. **3** an item in a sports programme, or the programme as a whole. **4** Physics a single occurrence of a process, e.g. the ionization of one atom. **5** something on the result of which money is staked. □ **at all events** (or **in any event**) whatever happens. **event horizon** Astron. the gravitational boundary enclosing a black hole, from which no light escapes. **in the event** as it turns (or turned) out. **in the event of** if (a specified thing) happens. **in the event that** disp. if it happens that. [L eventus f. evenire event- happen (as E-, venire come)]

eventful /ɪˈventfʊl/ adj. marked by noteworthy events. □□ **eventfully** adv. **eventfulness** n.

eventide /ˈiːv(ə)nˌtaɪd/ n. archaic or poet. = EVENING. □ **eventide home** a home for the elderly, orig. one run by the Salvation Army. [OE æfentīd (as EVEN², TIDE)]

eventing /ɪˈventɪŋ/ n. Brit. participation in equestrian competitions, esp. dressage and showjumping, known as a one-, two-, or three-day event.

eventless /ɪˈventlɪs/ adj. without noteworthy or remarkable events. □□ **eventlessly** adv.

eventual /ɪˈventjʊəl/ adj. occurring or existing in due course or at last; ultimate. □□ **eventually** adv. [as EVENT, after actual]

eventuality /ɪˌventjʊˈælɪtɪ/ n. (pl. **-ies**) a possible event or outcome.

eventuate /ɪˈventjʊˌeɪt/ v.intr. formal **1** turn out in a specified way as the result. **2** (often foll. by in) result. □□ **eventuation** /-ˈeɪʃ(ə)n/ n. [as EVENT, after actuate]

ever /ˈevə(r)/ adv. **1** at all times; always (ever hopeful; ever after). **2** at any time (have you ever been to Paris?; nothing ever happens; as good as ever). **3** as an emphatic word: **a** in any way; at all (how ever did you do it?; when will they ever learn?). **b** (prec. by as) in any manner possible (be as quick as ever you can). **4** (in comb.) constantly (ever-present; ever-recurring). **5** (foll. by so, such) Brit. colloq. very; very much (is ever so easy; was ever such a nice man; thanks ever so). **6** (foll. by compar.) constantly, increasingly (grew ever larger). □ **did you ever?** colloq. did you ever hear or see the like? **ever since** throughout the period since. **for ever 1** for all future time. **2** colloq. for a long time (cf. FOREVER). [OE æfre]

Everest /ˈevərɪst/, Mount the highest mountain in the world (8,848 m, 29,028 ft.), in the Himalayas on the border of Nepal and Tibet. It is named after Sir George Everest (1790–1866), surveyor-general of India, and was first climbed in 1953 by the New Zealand mountaineer and explorer (Sir) Edmund Hillary and the Sherpa mountaineer Tenzing Norgay.

Everglades /ˈevəˌɡleɪdz/, **The** a vast area of marshland and coastal mangrove in south Florida, extending from Lake Okeechobee southwards to Florida Bay. A national park established in 1947 protects endangered species which include the alligator, bald eagle, and egret.

evergreen /ˈevəˌgriːn/ *adj.* & *n.* —*adj.* **1** always green or fresh. **2** (of a plant) retaining green leaves throughout the year. —*n.* an evergreen plant (cf. DECIDUOUS).

everlasting /ˌevəˈlɑːstɪŋ/ *adj.* & *n.* —*adj.* **1** lasting for ever. **2** lasting for a long time, esp. so as to become unwelcome. **3** (of flowers) keeping their shape and colour when dried. —*n.* **1** eternity. **2** = IMMORTELLE. □□ **everlastingly** *adv.* **everlastingness** *n.*

evermore /ˌevəˈmɔː(r)/ *adv.* for ever; always.

evert /ɪˈvɜːt/ *v.tr. Physiol.* turn (an organ etc.) outwards or inside out. □□ **eversion** *n.* [L *evertere* (as E-, *vertere vers-* turn)]

every /ˈevrɪ/ *adj.* **1** each single (*heard every word; watched her every movement*). **2** each at a specified interval in a series (*take every third one; comes every four days*). **3** all possible; the utmost degree of (*there is every prospect of success*). □ **every bit as** *colloq.* (in comparisons) quite as (*every bit as good*). **every now and again** (or **now and then**) from time to time. **every one** each one (see also EVERYONE). **every other** each second in a series (*every other day*). **every so often** at intervals; occasionally. **every time** *colloq.* **1** without exception. **2** without hesitation. **every which way** *US colloq.* **1** in all directions. **2** in a disorderly manner. [OE *ǣfre ǣlc* ever each]

everybody /ˈevrɪˌbɒdɪ/ *pron.* every person.

everyday /ˈevrɪdeɪ, -ˈdeɪ/ *adj.* **1** occurring every day. **2** suitable for or used on ordinary days. **3** commonplace, usual.

Everyman /ˈevrɪˌmæn/ *n.* the ordinary or typical human being; the 'man in the street'. [the principal character in a 15th-c. morality play]

everyone /ˈevrɪˌwʌn/ *pron.* every person; everybody.

everything /ˈevrɪθɪŋ/ *pron.* **1** all things; all the things of a group or class. **2** *colloq.* a great deal (*gave me everything*). **3** an essential consideration (*speed is everything*). □ **have everything** *colloq.* possess all the desired attributes etc.

everywhere /ˈevrɪˌweə(r)/ *adv.* **1** in every place. **2** *colloq.* in many places.

evict /ɪˈvɪkt/ *v.tr.* expel (a tenant) from a property by legal process. □□ **eviction** *n.* **evictor** *n.* [L *evincere evict-* (as E-, *vincere* conquer)]

evidence /ˈevɪd(ə)ns/ *n.* & *v.* —*n.* **1** (often foll. by *for*, *of*) the available facts, circumstances, etc. supporting or otherwise a belief, proposition, etc., or indicating whether or not a thing is true or valid. **2** *Law* **a** information given personally or drawn from a document etc. and tending to prove a fact or proposition. **b** statements or proofs admissible as testimony in a lawcourt. **3** clearness, obviousness. —*v.tr.* be evidence of; attest. □ **call in evidence** *Law* summon (a person) as a witness. **in evidence** noticeable, conspicuous. **Queen's** (or **King's** or **State's**) **evidence** *Law* evidence for the prosecution given by a participant in or accomplice to the crime at issue. [ME f. OF f. L *evidentia* (as EVIDENT)]

evident /ˈevɪd(ə)nt/ *adj.* **1** plain or obvious (visually or intellectually); manifest. **2** seeming, apparent (*his evident anxiety*). [ME f. OF *evident* or L *evidēre evident-* (as E-, *vidēre* see)]

evidential /ˌevɪˈdenʃ(ə)l/ *adj.* of or providing evidence. □□ **evidentially** *adv.*

evidentiary /ˌevɪˈdenʃərɪ/ *adj.* = EVIDENTIAL.

evidently /ˈevɪdəntlɪ/ *adv.* **1** as shown by evidence. **2** seemingly; as it appears (*was evidently unwilling to go*).

evil /ˈiːv(ə)l, -ɪl/ *adj.* & *n.* —*adj.* **1** morally bad; wicked. **2** harmful or tending to harm, esp. intentionally or characteristically. **3** disagreeable or unpleasant (*has an evil temper*). **4** unlucky; causing misfortune (*evil days*). —*n.* **1** an evil thing; an instance of something evil. **2** evil quality; wickedness, harm. □ **evil eye** a gaze or stare superstitiously believed to be able to cause material harm. **speak evil of** slander. □□ **evilly** *adv.* **evilness** *n.* [OE *yfel* f. Gmc]

evince /ɪˈvɪns/ *v.tr.* **1** indicate or make evident. **2** show that one has (a quality). □□ **evincible** *adj.* **evincive** *adj.* [L *evincere*: see EVICT]

eviscerate /ɪˈvɪsəˌreɪt/ *v.tr. formal* **1** disembowel. **2** empty or deprive of essential contents. □□ **evisceration** /-ˈreɪʃ(ə)n/ *n.* [L *eviscerare eviscerat-* (as E-, VISCERA)]

evocative /ɪˈvɒkətɪv/ *adj.* tending to evoke (esp. feelings or memories). □□ **evocatively** *adv.* **evocativeness** *n.*

evoke /ɪˈvəʊk/ *v.tr.* **1** inspire or draw forth (memories, feelings, a response, etc.). **2** summon (a supposed spirit from the dead). □□ **evocation** /ˌevəˈkeɪʃ(ə)n/ *n.* **evoker** *n.* [L *evocare* (as E-, *vocare* call)]

evolute /ˈiːvəˌljuːt, ˈev-, -ˌluːt/ *n.* (in full **evolute curve**) *Math.* a curve which is the locus of the centres of curvature of another curve that is its involute. [L *evolutus* past part. (as EVOLVE)]

evolution /ˌiːvəˈluːʃ(ə)n, -ˈljuːʃ(ə)n/ *n.* **1** gradual development, esp. from a simple to a more complex form. **2** a process by which species develop from earlier forms, not by special creation, as an explanation of their origins. (See below.) **3** the appearance or presentation of events etc. in due succession (*the evolution of the plot*). **4** a change in the disposition of troops or ships. **5** the giving off or evolving of gas, heat, etc. **6** an opening out. **7** the unfolding of a curve. **8** *Math.* the extraction of a root from any given power (cf. INVOLUTION). □□ **evolutional** *adj.* **evolutionally** *adv.* **evolutionary** *adj.* **evolutionarily** *adv.* [L *evolutio* unrolling (as EVOLVE)]

The philosophical speculation that primitive organisms may become more complex, change into one another, ascend some imaginary hierarchy, a ladder of life, a great chain of being (often with bouts of spontaneous generation along the way) is an idea that may be traced back to the ancient Greeks. The forebears of the modern scientific concept, however, are Erasmus Darwin in England and Lamarck in France. Species transformation by the inheritance of acquired characteristics (the single-minded neck-stretching giraffe in pursuit of the tender topmost leaves of bushes bequeaths his hard-won muscles to his offspring) was at least a serious secular attempt to understand apparent relationships in the plant and animal kingdom, but it was Charles Lyell's *Principles of Geology* (1830–3), which demonstrated that the structure of the surface of the earth could be explained as the product of slow small changes accumulating in vertiginous stretches of a time almost without end, that gave Charles Darwin the idea of nature which he needed to discover the principle of evolution by natural selection. *On the Origin of Species* (1859) proposed that, once isolated from each other in some way, pre-existent varieties within a population might give rise to new species by differential adaptation to their new surroundings; combined with recent genetical theory, and the new understanding of the role of DNA, this is the great unifying concept in modern biology. (See also SOCIOBIOLOGY.)

evolutionist /ˌiːvəˈluːʃənɪst, -ˈljuːʃənɪst/ *n.* a person who believes in evolution as explaining the origin of species. □□ **evolutionism** *n.* **evolutionistic** /-ˈnɪstɪk/ *adj.*

evolve /ɪˈvɒlv/ *v.* **1** *intr.* & *tr.* develop gradually by a natural process. **2** *tr.* work out or devise (a theory, plan, etc.). **3** *intr.* & *tr.* unfold; open out. **4** *tr.* give off (gas, heat, etc.). □□ **evolvable** *adj.* **evolvement** *n.* [L *evolvere evolut-* (as E-, *volvere* roll)]

Évvoia see EUBOEA.

evzone /ˈevzəʊn/ *n.* a member of a select Greek infantry regiment. [mod. Gk *euzōnos* f. Gk, = dressed for exercise (as EU-, *zōnē* belt)]

ewe /juː/ *n.* a female sheep. □ **ewe lamb** one's most cherished possession (2 Sam. 12). **ewe-necked** (of a horse) having a thin concave neck. [OE *ēowu* f. Gmc]

ewer /ˈjuːə(r)/ *n.* a large pitcher or water-jug with a wide mouth. [ME f. ONF *eviere*, OF *aiguiere*, ult. f. L *aquarius* of water f. *aqua* water]

ex¹ /eks/ *prep.* **1** (of goods) sold from (*ex-works*). **2** (of stocks or shares) without, excluding. [L, = out of]

ex² /eks/ *n. colloq.* a former husband or wife. [absol. use of EX-¹ 2]

ex-¹ /eks/ *prefix* (also **e-** before some consonants, **ef-** before *f*) **1** forming verbs meaning: **a** out, forth (*exclude; exit*). **b** upward (*extol*). **c** thoroughly (*excruciate*). **d** bring into a state (*exasperate*). **e** remove or free from (*expatriate; exonerate*). **2** forming nouns from titles of office, status, etc., meaning 'formerly' (*ex-convict*; *ex-president*; *ex-wife*). [L f. *ex* out of]

ex-[2] /eks/ *prefix* out (*exodus*). [Gk f. *ex* out of]

exa- /'eksə/ *comb. form* denoting a factor of 10[18]. [perh. f. HEXA-]

exacerbate /ek'sæsə₁beɪt, ɪg-/ *v.tr.* **1** make (pain, anger, etc.) worse. **2** irritate (a person). □□ **exacerbation** /-'beɪʃ(ə)n/ *n.* [L *exacerbare* (as EX-[1], *acerbus* bitter)]

exact /ɪg'zækt/ *adj. & v.* —*adj.* **1** accurate; correct in all details (*an exact description*). **2 a** precise. **b** (of a person) tending to precision. —*v.tr.* (often foll. by *from, of*) **1** demand and enforce payment of (money, fees, etc.) from a person. **2 a** demand; insist on. **b** (of circumstances) require urgently. □ **exact science** a science admitting of absolute or quantitative precision. □□ **exactable** *adj.* **exactitude** *n.* **exactness** *n.* **exactor** *n.* [L *exigere exact-* (as EX-[1], *agere* drive)]

exacting /ɪg'zæktɪŋ/ *adj.* **1** making great demands. **2** calling for much effort. □□ **exactingly** *adv.* **exactingness** *n.*

exaction /ɪg'zækʃ(ə)n/ *n.* **1** the act or an instance of exacting; the process of being exacted. **2 a** an illegal or exorbitant demand; an extortion. **b** a sum or thing exacted. [ME f. L *exactio* (as EXACT)]

exactly /ɪg'zæktlɪ/ *adv.* **1** accurately, precisely; in an exact manner (*worked it out exactly*). **2** in exact terms (*exactly when did it happen?*). **3** (said in reply) quite so; I quite agree. □ **not exactly** *colloq.* **1** by no means. **2** not precisely.

exaggerate /ɪg'zædʒə₁reɪt/ *v.tr.* **1** (also *absol.*) give an impression of (a thing), esp. in speech or writing, that makes it seem larger or greater etc. than it really is. **2** enlarge or alter beyond normal or due proportions (*spoke with exaggerated politeness*). □□ **exaggeratedly** *adv.* **exaggeratingly** *adv.* **exaggeration** /-'reɪʃ(ə)n/ *n.* **exaggerative** /-rətɪv/ *adj.* **exaggerator** *n.* [L *exaggerare* (as EX-[1], *aggerare* heap up f. *agger* heap)]

exalt /ɪg'zɔːlt/ *v.tr.* **1** raise in rank or power etc. **2** praise highly. **3** (usu. as **exalted** *adj.*) make lofty or noble (*exalted aims*; *an exalted style*). □□ **exaltedly** *adv.* **exaltedness** *n.* **exalter** *n.* [ME f. L *exaltare* (as EX-[1], *altus* high)]

exaltation /₁egzɔːl'teɪʃ(ə)n/ *n.* **1** the act or an instance of exalting; the state of being exalted. **2** elation; rapturous emotion. [ME f. OF *exaltation* or LL *exaltatio* (as EXALT)]

exam /ɪg'zæm/ *n.* = EXAMINATION 3.

examination /ɪg₁zæmɪ'neɪʃ(ə)n/ *n.* **1** the act or an instance of examining; the state of being examined. **2** a detailed inspection. **3** the testing of the proficiency or knowledge of students or other candidates for a qualification by oral or written questions. **4** an instance of examining or being examined medically. **5** *Law* the formal questioning of the accused or of a witness in court. □ **examination paper 1** the printed questions in an examination. **2** a candidate's set of answers. □□ **examinational** *adj.* [ME f. OF f. L *examinatio -onis* (as EXAMINE)]

examine /ɪg'zæmɪn/ *v.* **1** *tr.* inquire into the nature or condition etc. of. **2** *tr.* look closely or analytically at. **3** *tr.* test the proficiency of, esp. by examination (see EXAMINATION 3). **4** *tr.* check the health of (a patient) by inspection or experiment. **5** *tr. Law* formally question (the accused or a witness) in court. **6** *intr.* (foll. by *into*) inquire. □□ **examinable** *adj.* **examinee** /-'niː/ *n.* **examiner** *n.* [ME f. OF *examiner* f. L *examinare* weigh, test f. *examen* tongue of a balance, ult. f. *exigere* examine, weigh: see EXACT]

example /ɪg'zɑːmp(ə)l/ *n. & v.* —*n.* **1** a thing characteristic of its kind or illustrating a general rule. **2** a person, thing, or piece of conduct, regarded in terms of its fitness to be imitated (*must set him an example*; *you are a bad example*). **3** a circumstance or treatment seen as a warning to others; a person so treated (*shall make an example of you*). **4** a problem or exercise designed to illustrate a rule —*v.tr.* (usu. in *passive*) serve as an example of. □ **for example** by way of illustration. [ME f. OF f. L *exemplum* (as EXEMPT)]

exanthema /₁eksæn'θiːmə/ *n. Med.* a skin rash accompanying any eruptive disease or fever. [LL f. Gk *exanthēma* eruption f. *exantheō* (as EX-[2], *antheō* blossom)]

exarch /'eksɑːk/ *n.* in the Orthodox Church, a bishop lower in rank than a patriarch and having jurisdiction wider than the metropolitan of a diocese. □□ **exarchate** *n.* [eccl.L f. Gk *exarkhos* (as EX-[2], *arkhos* ruler)]

exasperate /ɪg'zɑːspə₁reɪt/ *v.tr.* **1** (often as **exasperated** *adj.* or **exasperating** *adj.*) irritate intensely. **2** make (a pain, ill feeling, etc.) worse. □□ **exasperatedly** *adv.* **exasperatingly** *adv.* **exasperation** /-'reɪʃ(ə)n/ *n.* [L *exasperare exasperat-* (as EX-[1], *asper* rough)]

Excalibur /eks'kælɪbə(r)/ (in Arthurian legend) the name of King Arthur's magic sword.

ex cathedra /₁eks kə'θiːdrə/ *adj. & adv.* with full authority (esp. of a papal pronouncement, implying infallibility as doctrinally defined). [L, = from the (teacher's) chair]

excavate /'ekskə₁veɪt/ *v.tr.* **1 a** make (a hole or channel) by digging. **b** dig out material from (the ground). **2** reveal or extract by digging. **3** (also *absol.*) *Archaeol.* dig systematically into the ground to explore (a site). □□ **excavation** /-'veɪʃ(ə)n/ *n.* **excavator** *n.* [L *excavare* (as EX-[1], *cavus* hollow)]

exceed /ɪk'siːd/ *v.tr.* **1** (often foll. by *by* an amount) be more or greater than (in number, extent, etc.). **2** go beyond or do more than is warranted by (a set limit, esp. of one's instructions or rights). **3** surpass, excel (a person or achievement). [ME f. OF *exceder* f. L *excedere* (as EX-[1], *cedere cess-* go)]

exceeding /ɪk'siːdɪŋ/ *adj. & adv.* —*adj.* **1** surpassing in amount or degree. **2** pre-eminent. —*adv. archaic* = EXCEEDINGLY 2.

exceedingly /ɪk'siːdɪŋlɪ/ *adv.* **1** very; to a great extent. **2** surpassingly, pre-eminently.

excel /ɪk'sel/ *v.* (**excelled, excelling**) (often foll. by *in, at*) **1** *tr.* be superior to. **2** *intr.* be pre-eminent or the most outstanding (*excels at games*). □ **excel oneself** surpass one's previous performance. [ME f. L *excellere* (as EX-[1], *celsus* lofty)]

excellence /'eksələns/ *n.* **1** the state of excelling; surpassing merit or quality. **2** the activity etc. in which a person excels. [ME f. OF *excellence* or L *excellentia* (as EXCEL)]

Excellency /'eksələnsɪ/ *n.* (*pl.* **-ies**) (usu. prec. by *Your, His, Her, Their*) a title used in addressing or referring to certain high officials, e.g. ambassadors and governors, and (in some countries) senior Church dignitaries. [ME f. L *excellentia* (as EXCEL)]

excellent /'eksələnt/ *adj.* extremely good; pre-eminent. □□ **excellently** *adv.* [ME f. OF (as EXCEL)]

excelsior /ɪk'selsɪ₁ɔː(r)/ *int. & n.* —*int.* higher, outstanding (esp. as a motto or trade mark). —*n.* soft wood shavings used for stuffing, packing, etc. [L, compar. of *excelsus* lofty]

excentric var. of ECCENTRIC (in technical senses).

except /ɪk'sept/ *v., prep., & conj.* —*v.tr.* (often as **excepted** *adj.* placed after object) exclude from a general statement, condition, etc. (*excepted him from the amnesty*; *present company excepted*). —*prep.* (often foll. by *for*) not including; other than (*all failed except him*; *all here except for John*; *is all right except that it is too long*). —*conj. archaic* unless (*except he be born again*). [ME f. L *excipere except-* (as EX-[1], *capere* take)]

excepting /ɪk'septɪŋ/ *prep. & conj.* —*prep.* = EXCEPT *prep.* —*conj. archaic* = EXCEPT *conj.*

exception /ɪk'sepʃ(ə)n/ *n.* **1** the act or an instance of excepting; the state of being excepted (*made an exception in my case*). **2** a thing that has been or will be excepted. **3** an instance that does not follow a rule. □ **take exception** (often foll. by *to*) object; be resentful (about). **with the exception of** except; not including. [ME f. OF f. L *exceptio -onis* (as EXCEPT)]

exceptionable /ɪk'sepʃənəb(ə)l/ *adj.* open to objection. □□ **exceptionably** *adv.*

exceptional /ɪk'sepʃən(ə)l/ *adj.* **1** forming an exception. **2** unusual; not typical (*exceptional circumstances*). **3** unusually good; outstanding. □□ **exceptionality** /-'nælɪtɪ/ *n.* **exceptionally** *adv.*

excerpt *n. & v.* —*n.* /'eksɜːpt/ a short extract from a book, film, piece of music, etc. —*v.tr.* /ɪk'sɜːpt/ (also *absol.*) **1** take an excerpt or excerpts from (a book etc.). **2** take (an extract) from a book etc. □□ **excerptible** /-'sɜːptɪb(ə)l/ *adj.* **excerption** /-'sɜːpʃ(ə)n/ *n.* [L *excerpere excerpt-* (as EX-[1], *carpere* pluck)]

excess /ɪk'ses, 'ekses/ *n. & adj.* —*n.* **1** the state or an instance of exceeding. **2** the amount by which one quantity or number exceeds another. **3** exceeding of a proper or permitted limit. **4**

a the overstepping of the accepted limits of moderation, esp. intemperance in eating or drinking. **b** (in *pl.*) outrageous or immoderate behaviour. **5** an extreme or improper degree or extent (*an excess of cruelty*). **6** part of an insurance claim to be paid by the insured, esp. by prior agreement. —*attrib.adj.* /usu. ˈekses/ **1** that exceeds a limited or prescribed amount (*excess weight*). **2** required as extra payment (*excess postage*). □ **excess baggage** (or **luggage**) that exceeding a weight allowance and liable to an extra charge. **in** (or **to**) **excess** exceeding the proper amount or degree. **in excess of** more than; exceeding. [ME f. OF *exces* f. L *excessus* (as EXCEED)]

excessive /ɪkˈsesɪv/ *adj.* **1** too much or too great. **2** more than what is normal or necessary. □□ **excessively** *adv.* **excessiveness** *n.*

exchange /ɪksˈtʃeɪndʒ/ *n. & v.* —*n.* **1** the act or an instance of giving one thing and receiving another in its place. **2 a** the giving of money for its equivalent in the money of the same or another country. **b** the fee or percentage charged for this. **3** the central telephone office of a district, where connections are effected. **4** a place where merchants, bankers, etc. gather to transact business. **5 a** an office where certain information is given or a service provided, usu. involving two parties. **b** an employment office. **6** a system of settling debts between persons (esp. in different countries) without the use of money, by bills of exchange (see BILL¹). **7 a** a short conversation, esp. a disagreement or quarrel. **b** a sequence of letters between correspondents. **8** *Chess* the capture of an important piece (esp. a rook) by one player at the loss of a minor piece to the opposing player. **9** (*attrib.*) forming part of an exchange, e.g. of personnel between institutions (*an exchange student*). —*v.* **1** *tr.* (often foll. by *for*) give or receive (one thing) in place of another. **2** *tr.* give and receive as equivalents (e.g. things or people, blows, information, etc.); give one and receive another of. **3** *intr.* (often foll. by *with*) make an exchange. □ **exchange rate** the value of one currency in terms of another. **exchange rate mechanism** a system for allowing the value of certain currencies to fluctuate only slightly in relation to each other. **in exchange** (often foll. by *for*) as a thing exchanged (for). □□ **exchangeable** *adj.* **exchangeability** /-ˈbɪlɪtɪ/ *n.* **exchanger** *n.* [ME f. OF *eschangier* f. Rmc (as EX-¹, CHANGE)]

exchequer /ɪksˈtʃekə(r)/ *n.* **1** (**Exchequer**) *Brit.* the former government department in charge of national revenue. (See below). **2** a royal or national treasury. **3** the money of a private individual or group. [ME f. AF *escheker*, OF *eschequier* f. med.L *scaccarium* chessboard (its orig. sense, with ref. to keeping accounts on a chequered cloth)]

The Normans created two departments dealing with finance. One was the Treasury, which received and paid out money on behalf of the monarch, the other was the Exchequer which was itself divided into two parts, lower and upper. The lower Exchequer was an office for receiving money and was connected to the Treasury (see entry); the upper Exchequer was a court of law dealing with cases related to revenue, and was merged with the High Court of Justice in 1880. The Exchequer now denotes the account at the Bank of England into which tax receipts and other public monies are paid, the balance of which forms the Consolidated Fund. Its name survives also in the title 'Chancellor of the Exchequer'.

excise¹ /ˈeksaɪz/ *n. & v.* —*n.* **1 a** a duty or tax levied on goods and commodities produced or sold within the country of origin. **b** a tax levied on certain licences. **2** *Brit.* a former government office collecting excise. ¶ Now the *Board of Customs and Excise*. —*v.tr.* **1** charge excise on (goods). **2** force (a person) to pay excise. [MDu. *excijs, accijs*, perh. f. Rmc: rel. to CENSUS]

excise² /ɪkˈsaɪz, ek-/ *v.tr.* **1** remove (a passage of a book etc.). **2** cut out (an organ etc.) by surgery. □□ **excision** /ɪkˈsɪʒ(ə)n/ *n.* [L *excidere excis-* (as EX-¹, *caedere* cut)]

exciseman /ˈeksaɪzˌmæn/ *n.* (*pl.* **-men**) *Brit. hist.* an officer responsible for collecting excise duty.

excitable /ɪkˈsaɪtəb(ə)l/ *adj.* **1** (esp. of a person) easily excited. **2** (of an organism, tissue, etc.) responding to a stimulus, or susceptible to stimulation. □□ **excitability** /-ˈbɪlɪtɪ/ *n.* **excitably** *adv.*

excitation /ˌeksɪˈteɪʃ(ə)n/ *n.* **1 a** the act or an instance of exciting. **b** the state of being excited; excitement. **2** the action of an organism, tissue, etc., resulting from stimulation. **3** *Electr.* **a** the process of applying current to the winding of an electromagnet to produce a magnetic field. **b** the process of applying a signal voltage to the control electrode of an electron tube or the base of a transistor. **4** *Physics* the process in which an atom etc. acquires a higher energy state.

excite /ɪkˈsaɪt/ *v.tr.* **1 a** rouse the feelings or emotions of (a person). **b** bring into play; rouse up (feelings, faculties, etc.). **c** arouse sexually. **2** provoke; bring about (an action or active condition). **3** promote the activity of (an organism, tissue, etc.) by stimulus. **4** *Electr.* **a** cause (a current) to flow in the winding of an electromagnet. **b** supply a signal. **5** *Physics* **a** cause the emission of (a spectrum). **b** cause (a substance) to emit radiation. **c** put (an atom etc.) into a state of higher energy. □□ **excitant** /ˈeksɪt(ə)nt, ɪkˈsaɪt(ə)nt/ *adj. & n.* **excitative** /-tətɪv/ *adj.* **excitatory** /-tətərɪ/ *adj.* **excitedly** *adv.* **excitedness** *n.* **excitement** *n.* **exciter** *n.* (esp. in senses 4, 5). [ME f. OF *exciter* or L *excitare* frequent. of *exciēre* (as EX-¹, *ciēre* set in motion)]

exciting /ɪkˈsaɪtɪŋ/ *adj.* arousing great interest or enthusiasm. □□ **excitingly** *adv.* **excitingness** *n.*

exciton /ekˈsaɪtɒn, ˈeksɪˌtɒn/ *n. Physics* a combination of an electron with a hole in a crystalline solid. [EXCITATION + -ON]

exclaim /ɪkˈskleɪm/ *v.* **1** *intr.* cry out suddenly, esp. in anger, surprise, pain, etc. **2** *tr.* (foll. by *that*) utter by exclaiming. [F *exclamer* or L *exclamare* (as EX-¹: cf. CLAIM)]

exclamation /ˌekskləˈmeɪʃ(ə)n/ *n.* **1** the act or an instance of exclaiming. **2** words exclaimed; a strong sudden cry. □ **exclamation mark** (*US* **point**) a punctuation mark (!) indicating an exclamation. [ME f. OF *exclamation* or L *exclamatio* (as EXCLAIM)]

exclamatory /ɪkˈsklæmətərɪ/ *adj.* of or serving as an exclamation.

exclave /ˈekskleɪv/ *n.* a portion of territory of one State completely surrounded by territory of another or others, as viewed by the home territory (cf. ENCLAVE). [EX-¹ + ENCLAVE]

exclosure /ekˈskləʊʒə(r)/ *n. Forestry* etc. an area from which unwanted animals are excluded. [EX-¹ + ENCLOSURE]

exclude /ɪkˈskluːd/ *v.tr.* **1** shut or keep out (a person or thing) from a place, group, privilege, etc. **2** expel and shut out. **3** remove from consideration (*no theory can be excluded*). **4** prevent the occurrence of; make impossible (*excluded all doubt*). □ **excluded middle** *Logic* the principle that of two contradictory propositions one must be true. □□ **excludable** *adj.* **excluder** *n.* [ME f. L *excludere exclus-* (as EX-¹, *claudere* shut)]

exclusion /ɪkˈskluːʒ(ə)n/ *n.* the act or an instance of excluding; the state of being excluded. □ **exclusion order** *Brit.* an official order preventing a person (esp. a suspected terrorist) from entering the UK. **exclusion principle** *Physics* see PAULI EXCLUSION PRINCIPLE. **to the exclusion of** so as to exclude. □□ **exclusionary** *adj.* [L *exclusio* (as EXCLUDE)]

exclusionist /ɪkˈskluːʒənɪst/ *adj. & n.* —*adj.* favouring exclusion, esp. from rights or privileges. —*n.* **1** a person favouring exclusion. **2** *Austral. hist.* an Australian settler opposed to the emancipation of ex-convicts.

exclusive /ɪkˈskluːsɪv/ *adj. & n.* —*adj.* **1** excluding other things. **2** (*predic.*; foll. by *of*) not including; except for. **3** tending to exclude others, esp. socially; select. **4** catering for few or select customers; high-class. **5 a** (of a commodity) not obtainable elsewhere. **b** (of a newspaper article) not published elsewhere. **6** (*predic.*; foll. by *to*) restricted or limited to; existing or available only in. **7** (of terms etc.) excluding all but what is specified. **8** employed or followed or held to the exclusion of all else (*my exclusive occupation; exclusive rights*). —*n.* an article or story published by only one newspaper or periodical. □ **Exclusive Brethren** a more exclusive section of the Plymouth Brethren. □□ **exclusively** *adv.* **exclusiveness** *n.* **exclusivity** /-ˈsɪvɪtɪ/ *n.* [med.L *exclusivus* (as EXCLUDE)]

excogitate /eksˈkɒdʒɪˌteɪt/ *v.tr.* think out; contrive. □□ **excogitation** /-ˈteɪʃ(ə)n/ *n.* [L *excogitare excogitat-* (as EX-¹, *cogitare* COGITATE)]

excommunicate v., adj., & n. Eccl. —v.tr. /ˌekskəˈmjuːnɪˌkeɪt/ officially exclude (a person) from participation in the sacraments, or from formal communion with the Church. —adj. /ˌekskəˈmjuːnɪkət/ excommunicated. —n. /ˌekskəˈmjuːnɪkət/ an excommunicated person. □□ **excommunication** /-ˈkeɪʃ(ə)n/ n. **excommunicative** /-kətɪv/ adj. **excommunicator** n. **excommunicatory** /-ˈkeɪtəri/ adj. [L excommunicare -atus (as EX-¹, communis COMMON)]

ex-con /eksˈkɒn/ n. colloq. an ex-convict; a former inmate of a prison. [abbr.]

excoriate /eksˈkɔːriˌeɪt/ v.tr. **1 a** remove part of the skin of (a person etc.) by abrasion. **b** strip or peel off (skin). **2** censure severely. □□ **excoriation** /-ˈeɪʃ(ə)n/ n. [L excoriare excoriat- (as EX-¹, corium hide)]

excrement /ˈekskrɪmənt/ n. (in sing. or pl.) faeces. □□ **excremental** /-ˈment(ə)l/ adj. [F excrément or L excrementum (as EXCRETE)]

excrescence /ɪkˈskres(ə)ns/ n. **1** an abnormal or morbid outgrowth on the body or a plant. **2** an ugly addition. □□ **excrescent** adj. **excrescential** /ˌekskrɪˈsenʃ(ə)l/ adj. [L excrescentia (as EX-¹, crescere grow)]

excreta /ekˈskriːtə/ n.pl. waste discharged from the body, esp. faeces and urine. [L neut. pl.: see EXCRETE]

excrete /ɪkˈskriːt/ v.tr. (of an animal or plant) separate and expel waste matter as a result of metabolism. □□ **excreter** n. **excretion** n. **excretive** adj. **excretory** adj. [L excernere excret- (as EX-¹, cernere sift)]

excruciate /ɪkˈskruːʃɪˌeɪt/ v.tr. (esp. as **excruciating** adj.) torment acutely (a person's senses); torture mentally. □□ **excruciatingly** adv. **excruciation** /-ˈeɪʃ(ə)n/ n. [L excruciare excruciat- (as EX-¹, cruciare torment f. crux crucis cross)]

exculpate /ˈekskʌlˌpeɪt/ v.tr. formal **1** free from blame. **2** (foll. by from) clear (a person) of a charge. □□ **exculpation** /-ˈpeɪʃ(ə)n/ n. **exculpatory** /-ˈkʌlpətəri/ adj. [med.L exculpare exculpat- (as EX-¹, culpa blame)]

excursion /ɪkˈskɜːʃ(ə)n/ n. **1** a short journey or ramble for pleasure, with return to the starting-point. **2** a digression. **3** Astron. a deviation from a regular path. **4** archaic a sortie (see ALARUM). □□ **excursional** adj. **excursionary** adj. **excursionist** n. [L excursio f. excurrere excurs- (as EX-¹, currere run)]

excursive /ɪkˈskɜːsɪv/ adj. digressive; diverse. □□ **excursively** adv. **excursiveness** n.

excursus /ekˈskɜːsəs, ɪk-/ n. **1** a detailed discussion of a special point in a book, usu. in an appendix. **2** a digression in a narrative. [L, verbal noun formed as EXCURSION]

excuse v. & n. —v.tr. /ɪkˈskjuːz/ **1** attempt to lessen the blame attaching to (a person, act, or fault). **2** (of a fact or circumstance) serve in mitigation of (a person or act). **3** obtain exemption for (a person or oneself). **4** (foll. by from) release (a person) from a duty etc. (excused from supervision duties). **5** overlook or forgive (a fault or offence). **6** (foll. by for) forgive (a person) for a fault. **7** not insist upon (what is due). **8** refl. apologize for leaving. —n. /ɪkˈskjuːs, ek-/ **1** a reason put forward to mitigate or justify an offence, fault, etc. **2** an apology (made my excuses). **3** (foll. by for) a poor or inadequate example of. □ **be excused** be allowed to leave a room etc., e.g. to go to the lavatory. **excuse me** a polite apology for lack of ceremony, for an interruption etc., or for disagreeing. **excuse-me** a dance in which dancers may interrupt other pairs to change partners. □□ **excusable** /-ˈkjuːzəb(ə)l/ adj. **excusably** /-ˈkjuːzəbli/ adv. **excusatory** /-ˈkjuːzətəri/ adj. [ME f. OF escuser f. L excusare (as EX-¹, causa CAUSE, accusation)]

ex-directory /ˌeksdaɪˈrektəri/ adj. Brit. not listed in a telephone directory, at the wish of the subscriber.

ex div. abbr. ex dividend.

ex dividend /eks ˈdɪvɪˌdend/ adj. & adv. (of stocks or shares) not including the next dividend.

exeat /ˈeksɪˌæt/ n. Brit. permission granted to a student by a college for temporary absence or permission granted to a priest by a bishop to move to another diocese. [L, 3rd sing. pres. subjunctive of exire go out (as EX-¹, ire go)]

exec /ɪkˈzek/ n. an executive. [abbr.]

execrable /ˈeksɪkrəb(ə)l/ adj. abominable, detestable. □□ **execrably** adv. [ME f. OF f. L execrabilis (as EXECRATE)]

execrate /ˈeksɪˌkreɪt/ v. **1** tr. express or feel abhorrence for. **2** tr. curse (a person or thing). **3** intr. utter curses. □□ **execration** /-ˈkreɪʃ(ə)n/ n. **execrative** adj. **execratory** adj. [L exsecrare (as EX-¹, sacrare devote f. sacer sacred, accursed)]

executant /ɪɡˈzekjʊt(ə)nt/ n. formal **1** a performer, esp. of music. **2** one who carries something into effect. [F exécutant pres. part. (as EXECUTE)]

execute /ˈeksɪˌkjuːt/ v.tr. **1 a** carry out a sentence of death on (a condemned person). **b** kill as a political act. **2** carry into effect, perform (a plan, duty, command, operation, etc.). **3 a** carry out a design for (a product of art or skill). **b** perform (a musical composition, dance, etc.). **4** make (a legal instrument) valid by signing, sealing, etc. **5** put into effect (a judicial sentence, the terms of a will, etc.). □□ **executable** adj. [ME f. OF executer f. med.L executare f. L exsequi exsecut- (as EX-¹, sequi follow)]

execution /ˌeksɪˈkjuːʃ(ə)n/ n. **1** the carrying out of a sentence of death. **2** the act or an instance of carrying out or performing something. **3** technique or style of performance in the arts, esp. music. **4 a** seizure of the property or person of a debtor in default of payment. **b** a judicial writ enforcing a judgement. □□ **executionary** adj. [ME f. OF f. L executio -onis (as EXECUTE)]

executioner /ˌeksɪˈkjuːʃənə(r)/ n. an official who carries out a sentence of death.

executive /ɪɡˈzekjʊtɪv/ n. & adj. —n. **1** a person or body with managerial or administrative responsibility in a business organization etc.; a senior businessman. **2** a branch of a government or organization concerned with executing laws, agreements, etc., or with other administration or management. —adj. **1** concerned with executing laws, agreements, etc., or with other administration or management. **2** relating to or having the function of executing. □ **executive session** US a usu. private meeting of a legislative body for executive business. □□ **executively** adv. [med.L executivus (as EXECUTE)]

executor /ɪɡˈzekjʊtə(r)/ n. (fem. **executrix** /-trɪks/) a person appointed by a testator to carry out the terms of his or her will. □ **literary executor** a person entrusted with a writer's papers, unpublished works, etc. □□ **executorial** /-ˈtɔːrɪəl/ adj. **executorship** n. **executory** adj. [ME f. AF executor, -our f. L executor -oris (as EXECUTE)]

exegesis /ˌeksɪˈdʒiːsɪs/ n. (pl. **exegeses** /-siːz/) critical explanation of a text, esp. of Scripture. □□ **exegete** /ˈeksɪˌdʒiːt/ n. **exegetic** /-ˈdʒetɪk/ adj. **exegetical** /-ˈdʒetɪk(ə)l/ adj. **exegetist** /-ˈdʒiːtɪst/ n. [Gk exēgēsis f. exēgeomai interpret (as EX-², hēgeomai lead)]

exemplar /ɪɡˈzemplə(r), -plɑː(r)/ n. **1** a model or pattern. **2** a typical instance of a class of things. **3** a parallel instance. [ME f. OF exemplaire f. LL exemplarium (as EXAMPLE)]

exemplary /ɪɡˈzempləri/ adj. **1** fit to be imitated; outstandingly good. **2 a** serving as a warning. **b** Law (of damages) exceeding the amount needed for simple compensation. **3** illustrative, representative. □□ **exemplarily** adv. **exemplariness** n. [LL exemplaris (as EXAMPLE)]

exemplify /ɪɡˈzemplɪˌfaɪ/ v.tr. (-ies, -ied) **1** illustrate by example. **2** be an example of. **3** Law make an attested copy of (a document) under an official seal. □□ **exemplification** /-fɪˈkeɪʃ(ə)n/ n. [ME f. med.L exemplificare (as EXAMPLE)]

exemplum /ɪɡˈzempləm/ n. (pl. **exempla** /-plə/) an example or model, esp. a moralizing or illustrative story. [L: see EXAMPLE]

exempt /ɪɡˈzempt/ adj., n., & v. —adj. **1** free from an obligation or liability etc. imposed on others. **2** (foll. by from) not liable to. —n. **1** a person who is exempt, esp. from payment of tax. **2** Brit. = EXON. —v.tr. (foll. by from) free from an obligation, esp. one imposed on others. □□ **exemption** n. [ME f. L exemptus past part. of eximere exempt- (as EX-¹, emere take)]

exequies /ˈeksɪkwɪz/ n.pl. formal funeral rites. [ME f. OF f. L exsequiae (as EX-¹, sequi follow)]

exercise /ˈeksəˌsaɪz/ n. & v. —n. **1** activity requiring physical effort, done esp. as training or to sustain or improve health. **2** mental or spiritual activity, esp. as practice to develop a skill. **3** (often in pl.) a particular task or set of tasks devised as exercise, practice in a technique, etc. **4 a** the use or application of a mental faculty, right, etc. **b** practice of an ability, quality, etc. **5** (often in *pl.*) military drill or manoeuvres. **6** (foll. by *in*) a process directed at or concerned with something specified (*was an exercise in public relations*). —*v.* **1** *tr.* use or apply (a faculty, right, influence, restraint, etc.). **2** *tr.* perform (a function). **3 a** *intr.* take (esp. physical) exercise; do exercises. **b** *tr.* provide (an animal) with exercise. **c** *tr.* train (a person). **4** *tr.* **a** tax the powers of. **b** perplex, worry. □ **exercise book 1** a book containing exercises. **2** a book for writing school work, notes, etc., in. □□ **exercisable** *adj.* **exerciser** *n.* [ME f. OF *exercice* f. L *exercitium* f. *exercere exercit*-keep at work (as EX-¹, *arcēre* restrain)]

exergue /eg'zɜːg, 'ek-/ *n.* **1** a small space usu. on the reverse of a coin or medal, below the principal device. **2** an inscription on this space. [F f. med.L *exergum* f. Gk *ex*- (as EX-²) + *ergon* work]

exert /ɪg'zɜːt/ *v.tr.* **1** exercise, bring to bear (a quality, force, influence, etc.). **2** *refl.* (often foll. by *for*, or *to* + infin.) use one's efforts or endeavours; strive. □□ **exertion** *n.* [L *exserere exsert*-put forth (as EX-¹, *serere* bind)]

exeunt /'eksɪˌʌnt/ *v.intr.* (as a stage direction) (actors) leave the stage. □ **exeunt omnes** all leave the stage. [L, = they go out: 3rd pl. pres. of *exire* go out: see EXIT]

exfiltrate /'eksfɪlˌtreɪt/ *v.tr.* (also *absol.*) withdraw (troops, spies, etc.) surreptitiously, esp. from danger. □□ **exfiltration** /-'treɪʃ(ə)n/ *n.*

exfoliate /eks'fəʊlɪˌeɪt/ *v.intr.* **1** (of bone, the skin, a mineral, etc.) come off in scales or layers. **2** (of a tree) throw off layers of bark. □□ **exfoliation** /-'eɪʃ(ə)n/ *n.* **exfoliative** /-lɪətɪv/ *adj.* [LL *exfoliare exfoliat*- (as EX-¹, *folium* leaf)]

ex gratia /eks 'greɪʃə/ *adv. & adj.* —*adv.* as a favour rather than from an (esp. legal) obligation. —*adj.* granted on this basis. [L, = from favour]

exhalation /ˌekshə'leɪʃ(ə)n/ *n.* **1 a** an expiration of air. **b** a puff of breath. **2** a mist, vapour. **3** an emanation or effluvium. [ME f. L *exhalatio* (as EXHALE)]

exhale /eks'heɪl, ɪgz-/ *v.* **1** *tr.* breathe out (esp. air or smoke) from the lungs. **2** *tr. & intr.* give off or be given off in vapour. □□ **exhalable** *adj.* [ME f. OF *exhaler* f. L *exhalare* (as EX-¹, *halare* breathe)]

exhaust /ɪg'zɔːst/ *v. & n.* —*v.tr.* **1** consume or use up the whole of. **2** (often as **exhausted** *adj.* or **exhausting** *adj.*) use up the strength or resources of; tire out. **3** study or expound on (a subject) completely. **4** (often foll. by *of*) empty (a vessel etc.) of its contents. —*n.* **1 a** waste gases etc. expelled from an engine after combustion. **b** (also **exhaust-pipe**) the pipe or system by which these are expelled. **c** the process of expulsion of these gases. **2 a** the production of an outward current of air by the creation of a partial vacuum. **b** an apparatus for this. □□ **exhauster** *n.* **exhaustible** *adj.* **exhaustibility** /-'bɪlɪtɪ/ *n.* **exhaustibly** *adv.* [L *exhaurire exhaust*- (as EX-¹, *haurire* draw (water), drain)]

exhaustion /ɪg'zɔːstʃ(ə)n/ *n.* **1** the act or an instance of exhausting; the state of being exhausted. **2** a total loss of strength. **3** the process of establishing a conclusion by eliminating alternatives. [LL *exhaustio* (as EXHAUST)]

exhaustive /ɪg'zɔːstɪv/ *adj.* **1** thorough, comprehensive. **2** tending to exhaust a subject. □□ **exhaustively** *adv.* **exhaustiveness** *n.*

exhibit /ɪg'zɪbɪt/ *v. & n.* —*v.tr.* (**exhibited, exhibiting**) **1** show or reveal publicly (for amusement, in competition, etc.). **2 a** show, display. **b** manifest (a quality). **3** submit for consideration. —*n.* **1** a thing or collection of things forming part or all of an exhibition. **2** a document or other item or object produced in a lawcourt as evidence. □□ **exhibitory** *adj.* [L *exhibēre exhibit*- (as EX-¹, *habēre* hold)]

exhibition /ˌeksɪ'bɪʃ(ə)n/ *n.* **1** a display (esp. public) of works of art, industrial products, etc. **2** the act or an instance of exhibiting; the state of being exhibited. **3** *Brit.* a scholarship, esp. from the funds of a school, college, etc. □ **make an exhibition of oneself** behave so as to appear silly or foolish. [ME f. OF f. LL *exhibitio -onis* (as EXHIBIT)]

exhibitioner /ˌeksɪ'bɪʃənə(r)/ *n. Brit.* a student who has been awarded an exhibition.

exhibitionism /ˌeksɪ'bɪʃəˌnɪz(ə)m/ *n.* **1** a tendency towards display or extravagant behaviour. **2** *Psychol.* a mental condition characterized by the compulsion to display one's genitals indecently in public. □□ **exhibitionist** *n.* **exhibitionistic** /-'nɪstɪk/ *adj.* **exhibitionistically** /-'nɪstɪkəlɪ/ *adv.*

exhibitor /ɪg'zɪbɪtə(r)/ *n.* a person who provides an item or items for an exhibition.

exhilarate /ɪg'zɪləˌreɪt/ *v.tr.* (often as **exhilarating** *adj.* or **exhilarated** *adj.*) affect with great liveliness or joy; raise the spirits of. □□ **exhilarant** *adj. & n.* **exhilaratingly** *adv.* **exhilaration** /-'reɪʃ(ə)n/ *n.* **exhilarative** /-rətɪv/ *adj.* [L *exhilarare* (as EX-¹, *hilaris* cheerful)]

exhort /ɪg'zɔːt/ *v.tr.* (often foll. by *to* + infin.) urge or advise strongly or earnestly. □□ **exhortative** /-tətɪv/ *adj.* **exhortatory** /-tətərɪ/ *adj.* **exhorter** *n.* [ME f. OF *exhorter* or L *exhortari* (as EX-¹, *hortari* exhort)]

exhortation /ˌegzɔː'teɪʃ(ə)n, ˌeks-/ *n.* **1** the act or an instance of exhorting; the state of being exhorted. **2** a formal or liturgical address. [ME f. OF *exhortation* or L *exhortatio* (as EXHORT)]

exhume /eks'hjuːm, ɪg'zjuːm/ *v.tr.* dig out, unearth (esp. a buried corpse). □□ **exhumation** /-'meɪʃ(ə)n/ *n.* [F *exhumer* f. med.L *exhumare* (as EX-¹, *humus* ground)]

ex hypothesi /ˌeks haɪ'pɒθəsɪ/ *adv.* according to the hypothesis proposed. [mod.L]

exigency /'eksɪdʒənsɪ, ɪg'zɪdʒ-/ *n.* (*pl.* **-ies**) (also **exigence** /'eksɪdʒ(ə)ns/) **1** an urgent need or demand. **2** an emergency. [F *exigence* & LL *exigentia* (as EXIGENT)]

exigent /'eksɪdʒ(ə)nt/ *adj.* **1** requiring much; exacting. **2** urgent, pressing. [ME f. L *exigere* EXACT]

exiguous /eg'zɪgjʊəs, ɪg-/ *adj.* scanty, small. □□ **exiguity** /-'gjuːɪtɪ/ *n.* **exiguously** *adv.* **exiguousness** *n.* [L *exiguus* scanty f. *exigere* weigh exactly: see EXACT]

exile /'eksaɪl, 'egz-/ *n. & v.* —*n.* **1** expulsion, or the state of being expelled, from one's native land or (**internal exile**) native town etc. **2** long absence abroad, esp. enforced. **3** a person expelled or long absent from his or her native country. **4** (**the Exile**) the captivity of the Jews in Babylon in the 6th c. BC. —*v.tr.* (foll. by *from*) officially expel (a person) from his or her native country or town etc. □□ **exilic** /-'sɪlɪk, -'zɪlɪk/ *adj.* (esp. in sense 4 of *n.*). [ME f. OF *exil, exiler* f. L *exilium* banishment]

exist /ɪg'zɪst/ *v.intr.* **1** have a place as part of objective reality. **2 a** have being under specified conditions. **b** (foll. by *as*) exist in the form of. **3** (of circumstances etc.) occur; be found. **4** live with no pleasure under adverse conditions (*felt he was merely existing*). **5** continue in being; maintain life (*can hardly exist on this salary*). **6** be alive, live. [prob. back-form. f. EXISTENCE; cf. LL *existere*]

existence /ɪg'zɪst(ə)ns/ *n.* **1** the fact or condition of being or existing. **2** the manner of one's existing or living, esp. under adverse conditions (*a wretched existence*). **3** an existing thing. **4** all that exists. [ME f. OF *existence* or LL *existentia* f. L *exsistere* (as EX-¹, *stare* stand)]

existent /ɪg'zɪst(ə)nt/ *adj.* existing, actual, current.

existential /ˌegzɪ'stenʃ(ə)l/ *adj.* **1** of or relating to existence. **2** *Logic* (of a proposition etc.) affirming or implying the existence of a thing. **3** *Philos.* concerned with existence, esp. with human existence as viewed by existentialism. □□ **existentially** *adv.* [LL *existentialis* (as EXISTENCE)]

existentialism /ˌegzɪ'stenʃəˌlɪz(ə)m/ *n.* a philosophical theory emphasizing the existence of the individual person as a free and responsible agent determining his or her own development through acts of the will (which, in the Christian form of the theory, leads to God). The term denotes recurring themes in modern philosophy and literature rather than a single school of thought. Kierkegaard is generally taken to be the first existentialist philosopher, and the theory was developed chiefly in continental Europe. □□ **existentialist** *n.* [G *Existentialismus* (as EXISTENTIAL)]

exit /'eksɪt, 'egzɪt/ *n. & v.* —*n.* **1** a passage or door by which to leave a room, building, etc. **2 a** the act of going out. **b** the right to go out. **3** a place where vehicles can leave a motorway or major road. **4** the departure of an actor from the stage. **5** death.

—*v.intr.* (**exited**, **exiting**) **1** go out of a room, building, etc. **2** (as a stage direction) (an actor) leaves the stage (*exit Macbeth*). **3** die. □ **exit permit** (or **visa** etc.) authorization to leave a particular country. [L, 3rd sing. pres. of *exire* go out (as EX-¹, *ire* go): cf. L *exitus* going out]

ex-libris /eks'li:brɪs/ *n.* (*pl.* same) a usu. decorated bookplate or label bearing the owner's name, pasted into the front of a book. [L *ex libris* among the books of]

Exmoor /'eksmʊə(r)/ an area of moorland in north Devon and west Somerset, rising to a height of 520 m (1,706 ft.) at Dunkery Beacon. Together with the adjacent coastline of the Bristol Channel it was designated a National Park in 1954.

ex nihilo /eks 'naɪhɪˌləʊ/ *adv.* out of nothing (*creation ex nihilo*). [L]

exo- /'eksəʊ/ *comb. form* external. [Gk *exō* outside]

exobiology /ˌeksəʊbaɪˈɒlədʒɪ/ *n.* the study of life outside the earth. □□ **exobiologist** *n.*

Exocet /'eksəˌset/ *n. propr.* a short-range guided missile used esp. in sea warfare. [F *exocet* flying fish]

exocrine /'eksəʊˌkraɪn/ *adj.* (of a gland) secreting through a duct (cf. ENDOCRINE). [EXO- + Gk *krīnō* sift]

Exod. *abbr.* Exodus (Old Testament).

exoderm /'eksəʊˌdɜːm/ *n. Biol.* = ECTODERM.

Exodus /'eksədəs/ a book of the Old Testament relating the departure of the Israelites under Moses from their bondage in Egypt. —*n.* **1** this departure, ascribed by scholars to any of various dates within the limits *c.*1580–*c.*1200 BC. Although there is a strong and fervent tradition about the events, the variety of sources and purpose of the narrative make it impossible to treat this as a straightforward historical account, though such considerations have never inhibited speculation about the date and the route involved. **2** (**exodus**) a mass departure of people (esp. emigrants). [eccl.L f. Gk *exodos* (as EX-², *hodos* way)]

ex officio /ˌeks əˈfɪʃɪəʊ/ *adv. & adj.* by virtue of one's office or status. [L]

exogamy /ekˈsɒɡəmɪ/ *n.* **1** *Anthropol.* marriage of a man outside his own tribe. **2** *Biol.* the fusion of reproductive cells from distantly related or unrelated individuals. □□ **exogamous** *adj.*

exogenous /ekˈsɒdʒɪnəs/ *adj. Biol.* growing or originating from outside. □□ **exogenously** *adv.*

exon /'ekson/ *n. Brit.* each of the four officers acting as commanders of the Yeomen of the Guard. [repr. F pronunc. of EXEMPT]

exonerate /ɪɡˈzɒnəˌreɪt/ *v.tr.* (often foll. by *from*) **1** free or declare free from blame etc. **2** release from a duty etc. □□ **exoneration** /-ˈreɪʃ(ə)n/ *n.* **exonerative** /-rətɪv/ *adj.* [L *exonerare exonerat-* (as EX-¹, *onus, oneris* burden)]

exophthalmos /ˌeksɒfˈθælmɒs/ *n.* (also **exophthalmus**, **exophthalmia** /-mɪə/) *Med.* abnormal protrusion of the eyeball. □□ **exophthalmic** *adj.* [mod.L f. Gk *exophthalmos* having prominent eyes (as EX-², *ophthalmos* eye)]

exoplasm /'eksəʊˌplæz(ə)m/ *n. Biol.* = ECTOPLASM.

exorbitant /ɪɡˈzɔːbɪt(ə)nt/ *adj.* (of a price, demand, etc.) grossly excessive. □□ **exorbitance** *n.* **exorbitantly** *adv.* [LL *exorbitare* (as EX-¹, *orbita* ORBIT)]

exorcize /'eksɔːˌsaɪz/ *v.tr.* (also **-ise**) **1** expel (a supposed evil spirit) by invocation or by use of a holy name. **2** (often foll. by *of*) free (a person or place) of a supposed evil spirit. □□ **exorcism** *n.* **exorcist** *n.* **exorcization** /-ˈzeɪʃ(ə)n/ *n.* [F *exorciser* or eccl.L *exorcizare* f. Gk *exorkizō* (as EX-², *horkos* oath)]

exordium /ekˈsɔːdɪəm/ *n.* (*pl.* **exordiums** or **exordia** /-dɪə/) the beginning or introductory part, esp. of a discourse or treatise. □□ **exordial** *adj.* **exordially** *adv.* [L f. *exordiri* (as EX-¹, *ordiri* begin)]

exoskeleton /ˌeksəʊˈskelɪt(ə)n/ *n.* a rigid external covering for the body in certain animals, esp. arthropods, providing support and protection. □□ **exoskeletal** *adj.*

exosphere /'eksəʊˌsfɪə(r)/ *n.* the layer of atmosphere furthest from the earth.

exothermic /ˌeksəʊˈθɜːmɪk/ *adj.* (also **exothermal** /-m(ə)l/) esp.

Chem. occurring or formed with the evolution of heat. □□ **exothermally** *adv.* **exothermically** *adv.*

exotic /ɪɡˈzɒtɪk/ *adj. & n.* —*adj.* **1** introduced from or originating in a foreign (esp. tropical) country (*exotic fruits*). **2** attractively or remarkably strange or unusual; bizarre. **3** (of a fuel, metal, etc.) of a kind newly brought into use. —*n.* an exotic person or thing. □ **exotic dancer** a striptease dancer. □□ **exotically** *adv.* **exoticism** /-tɪˌsɪz(ə)m/ *n.* [L *exoticus* f. Gk *exōtikos* f. *exō* outside]

exotica /ɪɡˈzɒtɪkə/ *n.pl.* remarkably strange or rare objects. [L, neut. pl. of *exoticus*: see EXOTIC]

expand /ɪkˈspænd/ *v.* **1** *tr. & intr.* increase in size or bulk or importance. **2** *intr.* (often foll. by *on*) give a fuller description or account. **3** *intr.* become more genial or effusive; discard one's reserve. **4** *tr.* set or write out in full (something condensed or abbreviated). **5** *tr. & intr.* spread out flat. □ **expanded metal** sheet metal slit and stretched into a mesh, used to reinforce concrete and other brittle materials. □□ **expandable** *adj.* **expander** *n.* **expansible** *adj.* **expansibility** /-ˈbɪlɪtɪ/ *n.* [ME f. L *expandere expans-* spread out (as EX-¹, *pandere* spread)]

expanse /ɪkˈspæns/ *n.* **1** a wide continuous area or extent of land, space, etc. **2** an amount of expansion. [mod.L *expansum* neut. past part. (as EXPAND)]

expansile /ɪkˈspænsaɪl/ *adj.* **1** of expansion. **2** capable of expansion.

expansion /ɪkˈspænʃ(ə)n/ *n.* **1** the act or an instance of expanding; the state of being expanded. **2** enlargement of the scale or scope of (esp. commercial) operations. **3** increase in the amount of a State's territory or area of control. **4** an increase in the volume of fuel etc. on combustion in the cylinder of an engine. □□ **expansionary** *adj.* **expansionism** *n.* **expansionist** *n.* **expansionistic** /-ˈnɪstɪk/ *adj.* (all in senses 2, 3). [LL *expansio* (as EXPAND)]

expansive /ɪkˈspænsɪv/ *adj.* **1** able or tending to expand. **2** extensive, wide-ranging. **3** (of a person, feelings, or speech) effusive, open. □□ **expansively** *adv.* **expansiveness** *n.* **expansivity** /-ˈsɪvɪtɪ/ *n.*

ex parte /eks 'pɑːtɪ/ *adj. & adv. Law* in the interests of one side only or of an interested outside party. [L]

expat /eksˈpæt/ *n. & adj. colloq.* = EXPATRIATE. [abbr.]

expatiate /ɪkˈspeɪʃɪˌeɪt/ *v.intr.* (usu. foll. by *on*, *upon*) speak or write at length or in detail. □□ **expatiation** /-ˈeɪʃ(ə)n/ *n.* **expatiatory** /-ʃɪətərɪ/ *adj.* [L *exspatiari* digress (as EX-¹, *spatium* SPACE)]

expatriate *adj.*, *n.*, *& v.* —*adj.* /eksˈpætrɪət, -ˈpeɪtrɪət/ **1** living abroad, esp. for a long period. **2** expelled from one's country; exiled. —*n.* /eksˈpætrɪət, -ˈpeɪtrɪət/ an expatriate person. —*v.tr.* /eksˈpætrɪˌeɪt/ **1** expel or remove (a person) from his or her native country. **2** *refl.* withdraw (oneself) from one's citizenship or allegiance. □□ **expatriation** /-ˈeɪʃ(ə)n/ *n.* [med.L *expatriare* (as EX-¹, *patria* native country)]

expect /ɪkˈspekt/ *v.tr.* **1** (often foll. by *to* + infin., or *that* + clause) **a** regard as likely; assume as a future event or occurrence. **b** (often foll. by *of*) look for as appropriate or one's due (from a person) (*I expect cooperation; expect you to be here; expected better of you*). **2** *colloq.* (often foll. by *that* + clause) think, suppose (*I expect we'll be on time*). **3** be shortly to have a (baby) (*is expecting twins*). □ **be expecting** *colloq.* be pregnant. □□ **expectable** *adj.* [L *expectare* (as EX-¹, *spectare* look, frequent. of *specere* see)]

expectancy /ɪkˈspektənsɪ/ *n.* (*pl.* **-ies**) **1** a state of expectation. **2** a prospect, esp. of future possession. **3** (foll. by *of*) a prospective chance. [L *expectantia, exp-* (as EXPECT)]

expectant /ɪkˈspekt(ə)nt/ *adj. & n.* —*adj.* **1** (often foll. by *of*) expecting. **2** having the expectation of possession, status, etc. **3** expecting a baby (said of the mother or father). —*n.* **1** one who expects. **2** a candidate for office etc. □□ **expectantly** *adv.*

expectation /ˌekspekˈteɪʃ(ə)n/ *n.* **1** the act or an instance of expecting or looking forward. **2** something expected or hoped for. **3** (foll. by *of*) the probability of an event. **4** (in *pl.*) one's prospects of inheritance. [L *expectatio* (as EXPECT)]

expectorant /ekˈspektərənt/ *adj. & n.* —*adj.* causing the coughing out of phlegm etc. —*n.* an expectorant medicine.

expectorate /ek'spektə,reɪt/ v.tr. (also absol.) cough or spit out (phlegm etc.) from the chest or lungs. □□ **expectoration** /-'reɪʃ(ə)n/ n. **expectorator** n. [L expectorare expectorat- (as EX-¹, pectus -oris breast)]

expedient /ɪk'spiːdɪənt/ adj. & n. —adj. 1 advantageous; advisable on practical rather than moral grounds. 2 suitable, appropriate. —n. a means of attaining an end; a resource. □□ **expedience** n. **expediency** n. **expediently** adv. [ME f. L expedire: see EXPEDITE]

expedite /'ekspɪ,daɪt/ v.tr. 1 assist the progress of; hasten (an action, process, etc.). 2 accomplish (business) quickly. □□ **expediter** n. [L expedire expedit- extricate, put in order (as EX-¹, pes pedis foot)]

expedition /,ekspɪ'dɪʃ(ə)n/ n. 1 a journey or voyage for a particular purpose, esp. exploration, scientific research, or war. 2 the personnel or ships etc. undertaking this. 3 promptness, speed. □□ **expeditionist** n. [ME f. OF f. L expeditio -onis (as EXPEDITE)]

expeditionary /,ekspɪ'dɪʃənərɪ/ adj. of or used in an expedition, esp. military.

expeditious /,ekspɪ'dɪʃəs/ adj. 1 acting or done with speed and efficiency. 2 suited for speedy performance. □□ **expeditiously** adv. **expeditiousness** n. [EXPEDITION + -OUS]

expel /ɪk'spel/ v.tr. (**expelled, expelling**) (often foll. by from) 1 deprive (a person) of the membership of or involvement in (a school, society, etc.). 2 force out or eject (a thing from its container etc.). 3 order or force to leave a building etc. □□ **expellable** adj. **expellee** /-'liː/ n. **expellent** adj. **expeller** n. [ME f. L expellere expuls- (as EX-¹, pellere drive)]

expend /ɪk'spend/ v.tr. spend or use up (money, time, etc.). [ME f. L expendere expens- (as EX-¹, pendere weigh)]

expendable /ɪk'spendəb(ə)l/ adj. 1 that may be sacrificed or dispensed with, esp. to achieve a purpose. 2 a not regarded as worth preserving or saving. b unimportant, insignificant. 3 not normally reused. □□ **expendability** /-'bɪlɪtɪ/ n. **expendably** adv.

expenditure /ɪk'spendɪtʃə(r)/ n. 1 the process or an instance of spending or using up. 2 a thing (esp. a sum of money) expended. [EXPEND, after obs. expenditor officer in charge of expenditure, f. med.L f. expenditus irreg. past part. of L expendere]

expense /ɪk'spens/ n. 1 cost incurred; payment of money. 2 (usu. in pl.) a costs incurred in doing a particular job. (will pay your expenses). b an amount paid to reimburse this (offered me £40 per day expenses). 3 a thing that is a cause of much expense (the house is a real expense to run). □ **at the expense of** so as to cause loss or damage or discredit to. **expense account** a list of an employee's expenses payable by the employer. [ME f. AF, alt. of OF espense f. LL expensa (money) spent, past part. of L expendere EXPEND]

expensive /ɪk'spensɪv/ adj. 1 costing much. 2 making a high charge. 3 causing much expense (has expensive tastes). □□ **expensively** adv. **expensiveness** n.

experience /ɪk'spɪərɪəns/ n. & v. —n. 1 actual observation of or practical acquaintance with facts or events. 2 knowledge or skill resulting from this. 3 a an event regarded as affecting one (an unpleasant experience). b the fact or process of being so affected (learnt by experience). —v.tr. 1 have experience of; undergo. 2 feel or be affected by (an emotion etc.). □□ **experienceable** adj. [ME f. OF f. L experientia f. experiri expert- try]

experienced /ɪk'spɪərɪənst/ adj. 1 having had much experience. 2 skilled from experience (an experienced driver).

experiential /ɪk,spɪərɪ'enʃ(ə)l/ adj. involving or based on experience. □ **experiential philosophy** a philosophy that treats all knowledge as based on experience. □□ **experientialism** n. **experientially** adv.

experiment /ɪk'sperɪmənt, -,ment/ n. & v. —n. 1 a procedure adopted on the chance of its succeeding, for testing a hypothesis etc., or to demonstrate a known fact. 2 (foll. by of) a test or trial of. —v.intr. (often foll. by on, with) make an experiment. □□ **experimentation** /-men'teɪʃ(ə)n/ n. **experimenter** n. [ME f. OF experiment or L experimentum (as EXPERIENCE)]

experimental /ɪk,sperɪ'ment(ə)l/ adj. 1 based on or making use of experiment (experimental psychology). 2 a used in experiments. b serving or resulting from (esp. incomplete) experiment; tentative, provisional. 3 based on experience, not on authority or conjecture. □□ **experimentalism** n. **experimentalist** n. **experimentalize** v.intr. (also **-ise**). **experimentally** adv. [ME f. med.L experimentalis (as EXPERIMENT)]

expert /'eksp3ːt/ adj. & n. —adj. 1 (often foll. by at, in) having special knowledge or skill in a subject. 2 involving or resulting from this (expert evidence; an expert piece of work). —n. (often foll. by at, in) a person having special knowledge or skill. □□ **expertly** adv. **expertness** n. [ME f. OF f. L expertus past part. of experiri: see EXPERIENCE]

expertise /,eksp3ː'tiːz/ n. expert skill, knowledge, or judgement. [F (as EXPERT)]

expertize /'eksp3ː,taɪz/ v. (also **-ise**) 1 intr. give an expert opinion. 2 tr. give an expert opinion concerning.

expiate /'ekspɪ,eɪt/ v.tr. 1 pay the penalty for (wrongdoing). 2 make amends for. □□ **expiable** /'ekspɪəb(ə)l/ adj. **expiatory** /-pɪətərɪ, -pɪ,eɪtərɪ/ adj. **expiation** /-'eɪʃ(ə)n/ n. **expiator** n. [L expiare expiat- (as EX-¹, pius devout)]

expiration /,ekspɪ'reɪʃ(ə)n/ n. 1 breathing out. 2 expiry. [L expiratio (as EXPIRE)]

expire /ɪk'spaɪə(r)/ v. 1 intr. (of a period of time, validity, etc.) come to an end. 2 intr. (of a document, authorization, etc.) cease to be valid; become void. 3 intr. (of a person) die. 4 tr. (usu. foll. by from; also absol.) exhale (air etc.) from the lungs. □□ **expiratory** adj. (in sense 4). [ME f. OF expirer f. L exspirare (as EX-¹, spirare breathe)]

expiry /ɪk'spaɪərɪ/ n. 1 the end of the validity or duration of something. 2 death.

explain /ɪk'spleɪn/ v.tr. 1 make clear or intelligible with detailed information etc. (also absol.: let me explain). 2 (foll. by that + clause) say by way of explanation. 3 account for (one's conduct etc.). □ **explain away** minimize the significance of (a difficulty or mistake) by explanation. **explain oneself 1** make one's meaning clear. 2 give an account of one's motives or conduct. □□ **explainable** adj. **explainer** n. [L explanare (as EX-¹, planus flat, assim. to PLAIN¹)]

explanation /,eksplə'neɪʃ(ə)n/ n. 1 the act or an instance of explaining. 2 a statement or circumstance that explains something. 3 a declaration made with a view to mutual understanding or reconciliation. [ME f. L explanatio (as EXPLAIN)]

explanatory /ɪk'splænətərɪ/ adj. serving or intended to serve to explain. □□ **explanatorily** adv. [LL explanatorius (as EXPLAIN)]

explant /eks'plɑːnt/ v. & n. Biol. —v.tr. transfer (living cells, tissues, or organs) from animals or plants to a nutrient medium. —n. a piece of explanted tissue etc. □□ **explantation** /-'teɪʃ(ə)n/ n. [mod.L explantare (as EX-¹, plantare PLANT)]

expletive /ɪk'spliːtɪv/ n. & adj. —n. 1 an oath, swear-word, or other expression, used in an exclamation. 2 a word used to fill out a sentence etc., esp. in verse. —adj. serving to fill out (esp. a sentence, line of verse, etc.). [LL expletivus (as EX-¹, plēre plet- fill)]

explicable /ɪk'splɪkəb(ə)l, 'ek-/ adj. that can be explained.

explicate /'eksplɪ,keɪt/ v.tr. 1 develop the meaning or implication of (an idea, principle, etc.). 2 make clear, explain (esp. a literary text). □□ **explication** /-'keɪʃ(ə)n/ n. **explicator** n. **explicatory** /ek'splɪkətɪv, 'eksplɪ,keɪtɪv/ adj. **explicator** n. **explicatory** /ek'splɪkətərɪ, 'eksplɪ,keɪtərɪ/ adj. [L explicare explicat- unfold (as EX-¹, plicare plicat- or plicit- fold)]

explicit /ɪk'splɪsɪt/ adj. 1 expressly stated, leaving nothing merely implied; stated in detail. 2 (of knowledge, a notion, etc.) definite, clear. 3 (of a person, book, etc.) expressing views unreservedly; outspoken. □□ **explicitly** adv. **explicitness** n. [F explicite or L explicitus (as EXPLICATE)]

explode /ɪk'spləʊd/ v. 1 a intr. (of gas, gunpowder, a bomb, a boiler, etc.) expand suddenly with a loud noise owing to a release of internal energy. b tr. cause (a bomb etc.) to explode. 2 intr. give vent suddenly to emotion, esp. anger. 3 intr. (of a population etc.) increase suddenly or rapidly. 4 tr. show (a theory etc.) to be false or baseless. 5 tr. (as **exploded** adj.) (of a drawing etc.)

showing the components of a mechanism as if separated by an explosion but in the normal relative positions. □□ **exploder** n. [earliest in sense 4: L *explodere* hiss off the stage (as EX-[1], *plodere plos-* = *plaudere* clap)]

exploit n. & v. —n. /ˈeksplɔɪt/ a bold or daring feat. —v.tr. /ɪkˈsplɔɪt/ 1 make use of (a resource etc.); derive benefit from. 2 usu. *derog.* utilize or take advantage of (esp. a person) for one's own ends. □□ **exploitable** /ɪkˈsplɔɪtəb(ə)l/ adj. **exploitation** /ˌeksplɔɪˈteɪʃ(ə)n/ n. **exploitative** /ɪkˈsplɔɪtətɪv/ adj. **exploiter** n. **exploitive** /ɪkˈsplɔɪtɪv/ adj. [ME f. OF *esploit*, *exploiter* ult. f. L *explicare*: see EXPLICATE]

exploration /ˌeksploˈreɪʃ(ə)n/ n. 1 an act or instance of exploring. 2 the process of exploring. □□ **explorational** adj.

exploratory /ɪkˈsplɒrətərɪ/ adj. 1 (of discussion etc.) preliminary, serving to establish procedure etc. 2 of or concerning exploration or investigation (*exploratory surgery*).

explore /ɪkˈsplɔː(r)/ v.tr. 1 travel extensively through (a country etc.) in order to learn or discover about it. 2 inquire into; investigate thoroughly. 3 *Surgery* examine (a part of the body) in detail. □□ **explorative** /ɪkˈsplɒrətɪv/ adj. [F *explorer* f. L *explorare*]

explorer /ɪkˈsplɔːrə(r)/ n. a traveller into undiscovered or uninvestigated territory, esp. to get scientific information.

explosion /ɪkˈspləʊʒ(ə)n/ n. 1 the act or an instance of exploding. 2 a loud noise caused by something exploding. 3 a a sudden outburst of noise. b a sudden outbreak of feeling, esp. anger. 4 a rapid or sudden increase, esp. of population. [L *explosio* scornful rejection (as EXPLODE)]

explosive /ɪkˈspləʊsɪv/ adj. & n. —adj. 1 able or tending or likely to explode. 2 likely to cause a violent outburst etc.; (of a situation etc.) dangerously tense. —n. an explosive substance. □□ **explosively** adv. **explosiveness** n.

Expo /ˈekspəʊ/ n. (also **expo**) (pl. **-os**) a large international exhibition. [abbr. of EXPOSITION 4]

exponent /ɪkˈspəʊnənt/ n. & adj. —n. 1 a person who favours or promotes an idea etc. 2 a representative or practitioner of an activity, profession, etc. 3 a person who explains or interprets something. 4 an executant (of music etc.). 5 a type or representative. 6 *Math.* a raised symbol or expression beside a numeral indicating how many times it is to be multiplied by itself (e.g. $2^3 = 2 \times 2 \times 2$). —adj. that sets forth or interprets. [L *exponere* (as EX-[1], *ponere posit-* put)]

exponential /ˌekspəˈnenʃ(ə)l/ adj. 1 *Math.* of or indicated by a mathematical exponent. 2 (of an increase etc.) more and more rapid. □ **exponential function** *Math.* a function which increases as a quantity raised to a power determined by the variable on which the function depends. **exponential growth** *Biol.* a form of population growth in which the rate of growth is related to the number of individuals present. [F *exponentiel* (as EXPONENT)]

export v. & n. —v.tr. /ekˈspɔːt, ˈek-/ send out (goods or services) esp. for sale in another country. —n. /ˈekspɔːt/ 1 the process of exporting. 2 a an exported article or service. b (in pl.) an amount exported (*exports exceeded £50m.*). 3 (*attrib.*) suitable for export, esp. of better quality. □ **export reject** an article sold in its country of manufacture, as being below the standard for export. □□ **exportable** adj. **exportability** /-ˈbɪlɪtɪ/ n. **exportation** /-ˈteɪʃ(ə)n/ n. **exporter** /-ˈspɔːtə(r)/ n. [L *exportare* (as EX-[1], *portare* carry)]

expose /ɪkˈspəʊz/ v.tr. 1 leave uncovered or unprotected, esp. from the weather. 2 (foll. by *to*) cause to be liable to or in danger of (*was exposed to great danger*). 3 (as **exposed** adj.) a (foll. by *to*) open to; unprotected from (*exposed to the east*). b vulnerable, risky. 4 *Photog.* subject (a film) to light, esp. by operation of a camera. 5 reveal the identity or fact of (esp. a person or thing disapproved of or guilty of crime etc.). 6 disclose; make public. 7 exhibit, display. 8 put up for sale. □ **expose oneself** display one's body, esp. the genitals, publicly and indecently. □□ **exposer** n. [ME f. OF *exposer* after L *exponere*: see EXPONENT, POSE[1]]

exposé /ekˈspəʊzeɪ/ n. 1 an orderly statement of facts. 2 the act or an instance of revealing something discreditable. [F, past part. of *exposer* (as EXPOSE)]

exposition /ˌekspəˈzɪʃ(ə)n/ n. 1 an explanatory statement or account. 2 an explanation or commentary. 3 *Mus.* the part of a movement, esp. in sonata form, in which the principal themes are first presented. 4 a large public exhibition. 5 *archaic* exposure. □□ **expositional** adj. **expositive** /-ˈspɒzɪtɪv/ adj. [ME f. OF *exposition*, or L *expositio* (as EXPONENT)]

expositor /ɪkˈspɒzɪtə(r)/ n. an expounder or interpreter. □□ **expository** adj.

ex post facto /ˌeks pəʊst ˈfæktəʊ/ adj. & adv. with retrospective action or force. [L *ex postfacto* in the light of subsequent events]

expostulate /ɪkˈspɒstjʊˌleɪt/ v.intr. (often foll. by *with* a person) make a protest; remonstrate earnestly. □□ **expostulation** /-ˈleɪʃ(ə)n/ n. **expostulatory** /-lətərɪ/ adj. [L *expostulare expostulat-* (as EX-[1], *postulare* demand)]

exposure /ɪkˈspəʊʒə(r)/ n. (foll. by *to*) 1 the act or condition of exposing or being exposed (to air, cold, danger, etc.). 2 the condition of being exposed to the elements, esp. in severe conditions (*died from exposure*). 3 the revelation of an identity or fact, esp. when concealed or likely to find disapproval. 4 *Photog.* a the action of exposing a film etc. to the light. b the duration of this action. c the area of film etc. affected by it. 5 an aspect or outlook (*has a fine southern exposure*). □ **exposure meter** *Photog.* a device for measuring the strength of the light to determine the correct duration of exposure. [EXPOSE after *enclosure* etc.]

expound /ɪkˈspaʊnd/ v.tr. 1 set out in detail (a doctrine etc.). 2 explain or interpret (esp. Scripture). □□ **expounder** n. [ME f. OF *espondre* (as EXPONENT)]

express[1] /ɪkˈspres/ v.tr. 1 represent or make known (thought, feelings, etc.) in words or by gestures, conduct, etc. 2 *refl.* say what one thinks or means. 3 esp. *Math.* represent by symbols. 4 squeeze out (liquid or air). □□ **expresser** n. **expressible** adj. [ME f. OF *expresser* f. Rmc (as EX-[1], PRESS[1])]

express[2] /ɪkˈspres/ adj., adv., n., & v. —adj. 1 operating at high speed. 2 /also ˈekspres/ a definitely stated, not merely implied. b *archaic* (of a likeness) exact. 3 a done, made, or sent for a special purpose. b (of messages or goods) delivered by a special messenger or service. —adv. 1 at high speed. 2 by express messenger or train. —n. 1 a an express train or messenger. b an express rifle. 2 *US* a company undertaking the transport of parcels etc. —v.tr. send by express messenger or delivery. □ **express rifle** a rifle that discharges a bullet at high speed. **express train** a fast train, stopping at few intermediate stations. □□ **expressly** adv. (in sense 2 of adj.). [ME f. OF *expres* f. L *expressus* distinctly shown, past part. of *exprimere* (as EX-[1], *premere* press)]

expression /ɪkˈspreʃ(ə)n/ n. 1 the act or an instance of expressing. 2 a word or phrase expressed. 3 *Math.* a collection of symbols expressing a quantity. 4 a person's facial appearance or intonation of voice, esp. as indicating feeling. 5 depiction of feeling, movement, etc., in art. 6 conveying of feeling in the performance of a piece of music. □ **expression-mark** *Mus.* a sign or word indicating the required manner of performance. □□ **expressional** adj. **expressionless** adj. **expressionlessly** adv. **expressionlessness** n. [ME f. OF *expression* or L *expressio* f. *exprimere*: see EXPRESS[1]]

expressionism /ɪkˈspreʃˌnɪz(ə)m/ n. a style of painting, music, drama, etc., in which an artist or writer seeks to express emotional experience rather than impressions of the external world. (See below.) □□ **expressionist** n. & adj. **expressionistic** /-ˈnɪstɪk/ adj. **expressionistically** /-ˈnɪstɪkəlɪ/ adv.

The beginnings of expressionism can be traced to Van Gogh, Gauguin, and Munch in the 1880s and 1890s, but the term was not used until the early 20th c., when it was applied to the fauves and early cubists. Major expressionist painters include Soutine, Chagall, and Roualt in France, Nolde in Germany, Kokoschka in Austria. The word has been used as a synonym for modernism, identified with whatever is thought best in modern art; it can also be applied to earlier art, such as that of El Greco, in which non-naturalistic distortions have an expressive effect. In the theatre, the term has been associated with the works of Ernst Toller, Strindberg, Wedekind, and early Brecht, and embraces a wide variety of moods—satirical, grotesque, visionary, exclamatory, violent, but always anti-naturalistic. The epitome of expressionism in German cinema was Robert Heine's

The Cabinet of Dr. Caligari (1919). Expressionism took little root in Britain, though traces of its influence can be found in the verse dramas of Auden and Isherwood, and later in the cinema (e.g. Carol Reed's version of Graham Greene's *The Third Man*, 1949).

expressive /ɪkˈsprɛsɪv/ *adj.* **1** full of expression (*an expressive look*). **2** (foll. by *of*) serving to express (*words expressive of contempt*). □□ **expressively** *adv.* **expressiveness** *n.* **expressivity** /-ˈsɪvɪtɪ/ *n.* [ME f. F *expressif -ive* or med.L *expressivus* (as EXPRESSION)]

expresso var. of ESPRESSO.

expressway /ɪkˈsprɛsweɪ/ *n.* US an urban motorway.

expropriate /ɛksˈprəʊprɪˌeɪt/ *v.tr.* **1** (esp. of the State) take away (property) from its owner. **2** (foll. by *from*) dispossess. □□ **expropriation** /-ˈeɪʃ(ə)n/ *n.* **expropriator** *n.* [med.L *expropriare expropriat-* (as EX-¹, *proprium* property: see PROPER)]

expulsion /ɪkˈspʌlʃ(ə)n/ *n.* the act or an instance of expelling; the process of being expelled. □□ **expulsive** /-sɪv/ *adj.* [ME f. L *expulsio* (as EXPEL)]

expunge /ɪkˈspʌndʒ/ *v.tr.* (foll. by *from*) erase, remove (esp. a passage from a book or a name from a list). □□ **expunction** /ɪkˈspʌŋkʃ(ə)n/ *n.* **expunger** *n.* [L *expungere expunct-* (as EX-¹, *pungere* prick)]

expurgate /ˈɛkspəˌgeɪt/ *v.tr.* **1** remove matter thought to be objectionable from (a book etc.). **2** remove (such matter). □□ **expurgation** /-ˈgeɪʃ(ə)n/ *n.* **expurgator** *n.* **expurgatorial** /ˌɛkspɜːgəˈtɔːrɪəl/ *adj.* **expurgatory** /ɛkˈspɜːgətərɪ/ *adj.* [L *expurgare expurgat-* (as EX-¹, *purgare* cleanse)]

exquisite /ˈɛkskwɪzɪt, ɛkˈskwɪzɪt/ *adj. & n.* —*adj.* **1** extremely beautiful or delicate. **2** acute; keenly felt (*exquisite pleasure*). **3** keen; highly sensitive or discriminating (*exquisite taste*). —*n.* a person of refined (esp. affected) tastes. □□ **exquisitely** *adv.* **exquisiteness** *n.* [ME f. L *exquirere exquisit-* (as EX-¹, *quaerere* seek)]

exsanguinate /ɛksˈsæŋɡwɪˌneɪt/ *Med.* *v.tr.* drain of blood. □□ **exsanguination** /-ˈneɪʃ(ə)n/ *n.* [L *exsanguinatus* (as EX-¹, *sanguis -inis* blood)]

exsert /ɪkˈsɜːt/ *v.tr.* *Biol.* put forth. [L *exserere*: see EXERT]

ex-service /ɛksˈsɜːvɪs/ *adj.* **1** having formerly been a member of the armed forces. **2** relating to former servicemen and -women.

ex-serviceman /ɛksˈsɜːvɪsmən/ *n.* (*pl.* **-men**) a former member of the armed forces.

ex-servicewoman /ɛksˈsɜːvɪsˌwʊmən/ *n.* (*pl.* **-women**) a former woman member of the armed forces.

ex silentio /ˌɛks sɪˈlɛnʃɪəʊ/ *adv.* by the absence of contrary evidence. [L = from silence]

ext. *abbr.* **1** exterior. **2** external.

extant /ɛkˈstænt, ɪkˈst-, ˈɛkst(ə)nt/ *adj.* (esp. of a document etc.) still existing, surviving. [L *exstare exstant-* (as EX-¹, *stare* stand)]

extemporaneous /ɪkˌstɛmpəˈreɪnɪəs/ *adj.* spoken or done without preparation. □□ **extemporaneously** *adv.* **extemporaneousness** *n.*

extemporary /ɪkˈstɛmpərərɪ/ *adj.* = EXTEMPORANEOUS. □□ **extemporarily** *adv.* **extemporariness** *n.*

extempore /ɪkˈstɛmpərɪ/ *adj. & adv.* **1** without preparation. **2** offhand. [L *ex tempore* on the spur of the moment, lit. out of the time f. *tempus* time]

extemporize /ɪkˈstɛmpəˌraɪz/ *v.tr.* (also **-ise**) (also *absol.*) compose or produce (music, a speech, etc.) without preparation; improvise. □□ **extemporization** /-ˈzeɪʃ(ə)n/ *n.*

extend /ɪkˈstɛnd/ *v.* **1** *tr. & intr.* lengthen or make larger in space or time. **2** *tr.* stretch or lay out at full length. **3** *intr. & tr.* (foll. by *to, over*) reach or be or make continuous over a certain area. **4** *intr.* (foll. by *to*) have a certain scope (*the permit does not extend to camping*). **5** *tr.* offer or accord (an invitation, hospitality, kindness, etc.). **6** *tr.* (usu. *refl.* or in *passive*) tax the powers of (an athlete, horse, etc.) to the utmost. □ **extended family** a family including relatives living near. **extended-play** (of a gramophone record) playing for longer than most singles, usu. at 45 r.p.m. □□ **extendable** *adj.* **extendability** /-dəˈbɪlɪtɪ/ *n.* **extendible** *adj.* **extendibility** /-dɪˈbɪlɪtɪ/ *n.* **extensible** /-sɪb(ə)l/ *adj.* **extensibility** /-sɪˈbɪlɪtɪ/ *n.* [ME f. L *extendere extens-* or *extent-* stretch out (as EX-¹, *tendere* stretch)]

extender /ɪkˈstɛndə(r)/ *n.* **1** a person or thing that extends. **2** a substance added to paint, ink, glue, etc., to dilute its colour or increase its bulk.

extensile /ɪkˈstɛnsaɪl/ *adj.* capable of being stretched out or protruded.

extension /ɪkˈstɛnʃ(ə)n/ *n.* **1** the act or an instance of extending; the process of being extended. **2** prolongation; enlargement. **3** a part enlarging or added on to a main structure or building. **4** an additional part of anything. **5 a** a subsidiary telephone on the same line as the main one. **b** its number. **6 a** an additional period of time, esp. extending allowance for a project etc. **b** permission for the sale of alcoholic drinks until later than usual, granted to licensed premises on special occasions. **7** extramural instruction by a university or college (*extension course*). **8** extent, range. **9** *Logic* a group of things denoted by a term. □□ **extensional** *adj.* [ME f. LL *extensio* (as EXTEND)]

extensive /ɪkˈstɛnsɪv/ *adj.* **1** covering a large area in space or time. **2** having a wide scope; far-reaching, comprehensive (*an extensive knowledge of music*). **3** *Agriculture* involving cultivation from a large area, with a minimum of special resources (cf. INTENSIVE). □□ **extensively** *adv.* **extensiveness** *n.* [F *extensif -ive* or LL *extensivus* (as EXTENSION)]

extensometer /ˌɛkstɛnˈsɒmɪtə(r)/ *n.* **1** an instrument for measuring deformation of metal under stress. **2** an instrument using such deformation to record elastic strains in other materials. [L *extensus* (as EXTEND) + -METER]

extensor /ɪkˈstɛnsə(r)/ *n.* (in full **extensor muscle**) *Anat.* a muscle that extends or straightens out part of the body (cf. FLEXOR). [mod.L (as EXTEND)]

extent /ɪkˈstɛnt/ *n.* **1** the space over which a thing extends. **2** the width or limits of application; scope (*to a great extent; to the full extent of their power*). [ME f. AF *extente* f. med.L *extenta* past part. of L *extendere*: see EXTEND]

extenuate /ɪkˈstɛnjʊˌeɪt/ *v.tr.* (often as **extenuating** *adj.*) lessen the seeming seriousness of (guilt or an offence) by reference to some mitigating factor. □□ **extenuatingly** *adv.* **extenuation** /-ˈeɪʃ(ə)n/ *n.* **extenuatory** /-jʊətərɪ/ *adj.* [L *extenuare extenuat-* (as EX-¹, *tenuis* thin)]

exterior /ɪkˈstɪərɪə(r)/ *adj. & n.* —*adj.* **1 a** of or on the outer side (opp. INTERIOR). **b** (foll. by *to*) situated on the outside of (a building etc.). **c** coming from outside. **2** *Cinematog.* outdoor. —*n.* **1** the outward aspect or surface of a building etc. **2** the outward or apparent behaviour or demeanour of a person. **3** *Cinematog.* an outdoor scene. □ **exterior angle** the angle between the side of a rectilinear figure and the adjacent side extended outward. □□ **exteriority** /-ˈɒrɪtɪ/ *n.* **exteriorize** *v.tr.* (also **-ise**). **exteriorly** *adv.* [L, compar. of *exterus* outside]

exterminate /ɪkˈstɜːmɪˌneɪt/ *v.tr.* **1** destroy utterly (esp. something living). **2** get rid of; eliminate (a pest, disease, etc.). □□ **extermination** /-ˈneɪʃ(ə)n/ *n.* **exterminator** *n.* **exterminatory** /-nətərɪ/ *adj.* [L *exterminare exterminat-* (as EX-¹, *terminus* boundary)]

external /ɪkˈstɜːn(ə)l/ *adj. & n.* —*adj.* **1 a** of or situated on the outside or visible part (opp. INTERNAL). **b** coming or derived from the outside or an outside source. **2** relating to a country's foreign affairs. **3** outside the conscious subject (*the external world*). **4** (of medicine etc.) for use on the outside of the body. **5** for or concerning students taking the examinations of a university without attending it. —*n.* (in *pl.*) **1** the outward features or aspect. **2** external circumstances. **3** inessentials. □ **external evidence** evidence derived from a source independent of the thing discussed. □□ **externality** /ˌɛkstɜːˈnælɪtɪ/ *n.* (*pl.* **-ies**). **externally** *adv.* [med.L f. L *externus* f. *exterus* outside]

externalize /ɪkˈstɜːnəˌlaɪz/ *v.tr.* (also **-ise**) give or attribute external existence to. □□ **externalization** /-ˈzeɪʃ(ə)n/ *n.*

exteroceptive /ˌɛkstərəʊˈsɛptɪv/ *adj.* *Biol.* relating to stimuli produced outside an organism. [irreg. f. L *externus* exterior + RECEPTIVE]

exterritorial /ˌɛkstɛrɪˈtɔːrɪəl/ *adj.* = EXTRATERRITORIAL. □□ **exterritoriality** /-ˈælɪtɪ/ *n.*

extinct /ɪkˈstɪŋkt/ *adj.* **1** (of a family, class, or species) that has died out. **2 a** (of fire etc.) no longer burning. **b** (of a volcano) that no longer erupts. **3** (of life, hope, etc.) terminated, quenched. **4**

(of an office etc.) obsolete. **5** (of a title of nobility) having no qualified claimant. [ME f. L *exstinguere exstinct-* (as EX-¹, *stinguere* quench)]

extinction /ɪk'stɪŋkʃ(ə)n/ *n.* **1** the act of making extinct; the state of being or process of becoming extinct. **2** the act of extinguishing; the state of being extinguished. **3** total destruction or annihilation. **4** the wiping out of a debt. **5** *Physics* a reduction in the intensity of radiation by absorption, scattering, etc. □□ **extinctive** *adj.* [L *extinctio* (as EXTINCT)]

extinguish /ɪk'stɪŋgwɪʃ/ *v.tr.* **1** cause (a flame, light, etc.) to die out; put out. **2** make extinct; annihilate, destroy (*a programme to extinguish disease*). **3** put an end to; terminate; obscure utterly (a feeling, quality, etc.). **4 a** abolish; wipe out (a debt). **b** *Law* render void. **5** *colloq.* reduce to silence (*the argument extinguished the opposition*). □□ **extinguishable** *adj.* **extinguishment** *n.* [irreg. f. L *extinguere* (as EXTINCT): cf. *distinguish*]

extinguisher /ɪk'stɪŋgwɪʃə(r)/ *n.* a person or thing that extinguishes, esp. = *fire extinguisher.*

extirpate /'ekstə,peɪt/ *v.tr.* root out; destroy completely. □□ **extirpation** /-'peɪʃ(ə)n/ *n.* **extirpator** *n.* [L *exstirpare exstirpat-* (as EX-¹, *stirps* stem)]

extol /ɪk'stəʊl, ɪk'stɒl/ *v.tr.* (**extolled, extolling**) praise enthusiastically. □□ **extoller** *n.* **extolment** *n.* [L *extollere* (as EX-¹, *tollere* raise)]

extort /ɪk'stɔːt/ *v.tr.* obtain by force, threats, persistent demands, etc. □□ **extorter** *n.* **extortive** *adj.* [L *extorquēre extort-* (as EX-¹, *torquēre* twist)]

extortion /ɪk'stɔːʃ(ə)n/ *n.* **1** the act or an instance of extorting, esp. money. **2** illegal exaction. □□ **extortioner** *n.* **extortionist** *n.* [ME f. LL *extortio* (as EXTORT)]

extortionate /ɪk'stɔːʃənət/ *adj.* **1** (of a price etc.) exorbitant. **2** using or given to extortion (*extortionate methods*). □□ **extortionately** *adv.*

extra /'ekstrə/ *adj., adv., & n.* —*adj.* additional; more than is usual or necessary or expected. —*adv.* **1** more than usually. **2** additionally (*was charged extra*). —*n.* **1** an extra thing. **2** a thing for which an extra charge is made. **3** a person engaged temporarily to fill out a scene in a film or play, esp. as one of a crowd. **4** a special issue of a newspaper etc. **5** *Cricket* a run scored other than from a hit with the bat. □ **extra cover** *Cricket* **1** a fielding position on a line between cover-point and mid-off, but beyond these. **2** a fielder at this position. **extra size** outsize. **extra time** *Sport* a further period of play at the end of a match when the scores are equal. [prob. a shortening of EXTRAORDINARY]

extra- /'ekstrə/ *comb. form* **1** outside, beyond (*extragalactic*). **2** beyond the scope of (*extracurricular*). [med.L f. L *extra* outside]

extracellular /,ekstrə'seljʊlə(r)/ *adj.* situated or taking place outside a cell or cells.

extract *v. & n.* —*v.tr.* /ɪk'strækt/ **1** remove or take out, esp. by effort or force (anything firmly rooted). **2** obtain (money, an admission, etc.) with difficulty or against a person's will. **3** obtain (a natural resource) from the earth. **4** select or reproduce for quotation or performance (a passage of writing, music, etc.). **5** obtain (juice etc.) by suction, pressure, distillation, etc. **6** derive (pleasure etc.). **7** *Math.* find (the root of a number). **8** *archaic* deduce (a principle etc.). —*n.* /'ekstrækt/ **1** a short passage taken from a book, piece of music, etc.; an excerpt. **2** a preparation containing the active principle of a substance in concentrated form (*malt extract*). □□ **extractable** *adj.* **extractability** /-'bɪlɪtɪ/ *n.* [L *extrahere extract-* (as EX-¹, *trahere* draw)]

extraction /ɪk'strækʃ(ə)n/ *n.* **1** the act or an instance of extracting; the process of being extracted. **2** the removal of a tooth. **3** origin, lineage, descent (*of Indian extraction*). [ME f. F f. LL *extractio -onis* (as EXTRACT)]

extractive /ɪk'stræktɪv/ *adj.* of or involving extraction, esp. extensive extracting of natural resources without provision for their renewal.

extractor /ɪk'stræktə(r)/ *n.* **1** a person or machine that extracts. **2** (*attrib.*) (of a device) that extracts bad air etc. or ventilates a room (*extractor fan; extractor hood*).

extracurricular /,ekstrəkə'rɪkjʊlə(r)/ *adj.* (of a subject of study) not included in the normal curriculum.

extraditable /'ekstrə,daɪtəb(ə)l/ *adj.* **1** liable to extradition. **2** (of a crime) warranting extradition.

extradite /'ekstrə,daɪt/ *v.tr.* hand over (a person accused or convicted of a crime) to the foreign State etc. in which the crime was committed.

extradition /,ekstrə'dɪʃ(ə)n/ *n.* **1** the extraditing of a person accused or convicted of a crime. **2** *Psychol.* the localizing of a sensation at a distance from the centre of sensation. [F (as EX-¹, TRADITION)]

extrados /ek'streɪdɒs/ *n. Archit.* the upper or outer curve of an arch (opp. INTRADOS). [EXTRA- + *dos* back f. L *dorsum*]

extragalactic /,ekstrəgə'læktɪk/ *adj.* occurring or existing outside the Galaxy.

extrajudicial /,ekstrədʒuː'dɪʃ(ə)l/ *adj.* **1** not legally authorized. **2** (of a confession) not made in court. □□ **extrajudicially** *adv.*

extramarital /,ekstrə'mærɪt(ə)l/ *adj.* (esp. of sexual relations) occurring outside marriage. □□ **extramaritally** *adv.*

extramundane /,ekstrə'mʌndeɪn/ *adj.* outside or beyond the physical world.

extramural /,ekstrə'mjʊər(ə)l/ *adj. & n.* —*adj.* **1** taught or conducted off the premises of a university, college, or school. **2** additional to normal teaching or studies, esp. for non-resident students. **3** outside the walls or boundaries of a town or city. —*n.* an extramural lesson, course, etc. □□ **extramurally** *adv.* [L *extra muros* outside the walls]

extraneous /ɪk'streɪnɪəs/ *adj.* **1** of external origin. **2** (often foll. by *to*) **a** separate from the object to which it is attached etc. **b** external to; irrelevant or unrelated to. □□ **extraneously** *adv.* **extraneousness** *n.* [L *extraneus*]

extraordinary /ɪk'strɔːdɪnərɪ, ,ekstrə'ɔːdɪnərɪ/ *adj.* **1** unusual or remarkable; out of the usual course. **2** unusually great (*an extraordinary talent*). **3 a** (of an official etc.) additional; specially employed (*envoy extraordinary*). **b** (of a meeting) specially convened. □□ **extraordinarily** *adv.* **extraordinariness** *n.* [L *extraordinarius* f. *extra ordinem* outside the usual order]

extrapolate /ɪk'stræpə,leɪt/ *v.tr.* (also *absol.*) **1** *Math. & Philos.* a calculate approximately from known values, data, etc. (others which lie outside the range of those known). **b** calculate on the basis of (known facts) to estimate unknown facts, esp. extend (a curve) on a graph. **2** infer more widely from a limited range of known facts. □□ **extrapolation** /-'leɪʃ(ə)n/ *n.* **extrapolative** /-lətɪv/ *adj.* **extrapolator** *n.* [EXTRA- + INTERPOLATE]

extrasensory /,ekstrə'sensərɪ/ *adj.* regarded as derived by means other than the known senses, e.g. by telepathy, clairvoyance, etc. □ **extrasensory perception** a person's supposed faculty of perceiving by such means.

extraterrestrial /,ekstrətɪ'restrɪəl/ *adj. & n.* —*adj.* **1** outside the earth or its atmosphere. **2** (in science fiction) from outer space. —*n.* (in science fiction) a being from outer space.

extraterritorial /,ekstrəterɪ'tɔːrɪəl/ *adj.* **1** situated or (of laws etc.) valid outside a country's territory. **2** (of an ambassador etc.) free from the jurisdiction of the territory of residence. □□ **extraterritoriality** /-'ælɪtɪ/ *n.* [L *extra territorium* outside the territory]

extravagance /ɪk'strævəgəns/ *n.* **1** excessive spending or use of resources; being extravagant. **2** an instance or item of this. □□ **extravagancy** *n.* (*pl.* -**ies**). [F (as EXTRAVAGANT)]

extravagant /ɪk'strævəgənt/ *adj.* **1** spending (esp. money) excessively; immoderate or wasteful in use of resources. **2** exorbitant; costing much. **3** exceeding normal restraint or sense; unreasonable, absurd (*extravagant claims*). □□ **extravagantly** *adv.* [ME f. med.L *extravagari* (as EXTRA-, *vagari* wander)]

extravaganza /ɪk,strævə'gænzə/ *n.* **1** a fanciful literary, musical, or dramatic composition. **2** a spectacular theatrical or television production, esp. of light entertainment. [It. *estravaganza* extravagance]

extravasate /ɪk'strævə,seɪt/ *v.* **1** *tr.* force out (a fluid, esp. blood) from its proper vessel. **2** *intr.* (of blood, lava, etc.) flow out. □□ **extravasation** /-'seɪʃ(ə)n/ *n.* [L *extra* outside + *vas* vessel]

extravehicular /ˌekstrəviːˈhɪkjʊlə(r)/ *adj.* outside a vehicle, esp. a spacecraft.

extrema *pl.* of EXTREMUM.

Extremadura /ˌekstreɪməˈdʊərə,ˌes-/ an autonomous region of western Spain; pop. (1986) 1,088,500; capital, Mérida.

extreme /ɪkˈstriːm/ *adj.* & *n.* —*adj.* **1** reaching a high or the highest degree; exceedingly great or intense (*extreme old age*; *in extreme danger*). **2 a** severe, stringent; lacking restraint or moderation (*take extreme measures*; *an extreme reaction*). **b** (of a person, opinion, etc.) going to great lengths; advocating immoderate measures. **3** outermost; furthest from the centre; situated at either end (*the extreme edge*). **4** *Polit.* on the far left or right of a party. **5** utmost; last. —*n.* **1** (often in *pl.*) one or other of two things as remote or as different as possible. **2** a thing at either end of anything. **3** the highest degree of anything. **4** *Math.* the first or the last term of a ratio or series. **5** *Logic* the subject or predicate in a proposition; the major or the minor term in a syllogism. □ **extreme unction** the last rites in the Roman Catholic and Orthodox Churches. **go to extremes** take an extreme course of action. **go to the other extreme** take a diametrically opposite course of action. **in the extreme** to an extreme degree. □□ **extremely** *adv.* **extremeness** *n.* [ME f. OF f. L *extremus* superl. of *exterus* outward]

extremist /ɪkˈstriːmɪst/ *n.* (also *attrib.*) a person who holds extreme or fanatical political or religious views and esp. resorts to or advocates extreme action. □□ **extremism** *n.*

extremity /ɪkˈstremɪtɪ/ *n.* (*pl.* **-ies**) **1** the extreme point; the very end. **2** (in *pl.*) the hands and feet. **3** a condition of extreme adversity or difficulty. [ME f. OF *extremité* or L *extremitas* (as EXTREME)]

extremum /ekˈstriːməm/ *n.* (*pl.* **extremums** or **extrema** /-mə/) *Math.* the maximum or minimum value of a function. □□ **extremal** *adj.* [L, neut. of *extremus* EXTREME]

extricate /ˈekstrɪˌkeɪt/ *v.tr.* (often foll. by *from*) free or disentangle from a constraint or difficulty. □□ **extricable** *adj.* **extrication** /-ˈkeɪʃ(ə)n/ *n.* [L *extricare extricat-* (as EX-[1], *tricae* perplexities)]

extrinsic /ekˈstrɪnsɪk/ *adj.* **1** not inherent or intrinsic; not essential (opp. INTRINSIC). **2** (often foll. by *to*) extraneous; lying outside; not belonging (to). **3** originating or operating from without. □□ **extrinsically** *adv.* [LL *extrinsicus* outward f. L *extrinsecus* (adv.) f. *exter* outside + *secus* beside]

extrovert /ˈekstrəˌvɜːt/ *n.* & *adj.* —*n.* **1** *Psychol.* a person predominantly concerned with external things or objective considerations. **2** an outgoing or sociable person. —*adj.* typical or characteristic of an extrovert. □□ **extroversion** /-ˈvɜːʃ(ə)n/ *n.* **extroverted** *adj.* [*extro-* = EXTRA- (after *intro-*) + L *vertere* turn]

extrude /ɪkˈstruːd/ *v.tr.* **1** (foll. by *from*) thrust or force out. **2** shape metal, plastics, etc. by forcing them through a die. □□ **extrusion** /-ʒ(ə)n/ *n.* **extrusile** /-saɪl/ *adj.* **extrusive** /-sɪv/ *adj.* [L *extrudere extrus-* (as EX-[1], *trudere* thrust)]

exuberant /ɪgˈzjuːbərənt/ *adj.* **1** lively, high-spirited. **2** (of a plant etc.) prolific; growing copiously. **3** (of feelings etc.) abounding, lavish, effusive. □□ **exuberance** *n.* **exuberantly** *adv.* [F *exubérant* f. L *exuberare* (as EX-[1], *uberare* be fruitful f. *uber* fertile)]

exuberate /ɪgˈzjuːbəˌreɪt/ *v.intr.* be exuberant.

exude /ɪgˈzjuːd/ *v.* **1** *tr.* & *intr.* (of a liquid, moisture, etc.) escape or cause to escape gradually; ooze out; give off. **2** *tr.* emit (a smell). **3** *tr.* display (an emotion etc.) freely or abundantly (*exuded displeasure*). □□ **exudate** /ˈegzjʊˌdeɪt/ *n.* **exudation** /-ˈdeɪʃ(ə)n/ *n.* **exudative** /ɪgˈzjuːdətɪv/ *adj.* [L *exsudare* (as EX-[1], *sudare* sweat)]

exult /ɪgˈzʌlt/ *v.intr.* (often foll. by *at, in, over*, or *to* + infin.) **1** be greatly joyful. **2** (often foll. by *over*) have a feeling of triumph (over a person). □□ **exultancy** *n.* **exultation** /-ˈteɪʃ(ə)n/ *n.* **exultant** *adj.* **exultantly** *adv.* **exultingly** *adv.* [L *exsultare* (as EX-[1], *saltare* frequent. of *salire salt-* leap)]

Exumas /ekˈsuːməz/ a group of islands in the Bahamas, comprising Great Exuma, Little Exuma, and numerous small cays.

exurb /ˈeksɜːb/ *n.* a district outside a city or town, esp. a prosperous area beyond the suburbs. □□ **exurban** /ekˈsɜːbən/ *adj.* **exurbanite** /ekˈsɜːbəˌnaɪt/ *n.* [L *ex* out of + *urbs* city, or backform. f. *exurban* (as EX-[1] + URBAN, after *suburban*)]

exurbia /eksˈɜːbɪə/ *n.* the exurbs collectively; the region beyond the suburbs. [EX-[1], after *suburbia*]

exuviae /ɪgˈzjuːvɪiː/ *n.pl.* (also treated as *sing.*) an animal's cast skin or covering. □□ **exuvial** *adj.* [L, = animal's skins, spoils of the enemy, f. *exuere* divest oneself of]

exuviate /ɪgˈzjuːvɪˌeɪt/ *v.tr.* shed (a skin etc.). □□ **exuviation** /-ˈeɪʃ(ə)n/ *n.*

ex voto /eks ˈvəʊtəʊ/ *n.* (*pl.* **-os**) an offering made in pursuance of a vow. [L, = out of a vow]

-ey /ɪ/ *suffix* var. of -Y[2].

eyas /ˈaɪəs/ *n.* a young hawk, esp. one taken from the nest for training in falconry. [orig. *nyas* f. F *niais* ult. f. L *nidus* nest: for loss of *n-* cf. ADDER]

eye /aɪ/ *n.* & *v.* —*n.* **1 a** the organ of sight in man and other animals. **b** the light-detecting organ in some invertebrates. **2** the eye characterized by the colour of the iris (*has blue eyes*). **3** the region round the eye (*eyes red from weeping*). **4** a glass or plastic ball serving as an artificial eye (*his eye fell out*). **5** (in *sing.* or *pl.*) sight; the faculty of sight (*demonstrate to the eye*; *need perfect eyes to be a pilot*). **6** a particular visual faculty or talent; visual appreciation (*a straight eye*; *cast an expert eye over*). **7** (in *sing.* or *pl.*) a look, gaze, or glance, esp. as indicating the disposition of the viewer (*a friendly eye*). **8** mental awareness; consciousness. **9** a person or animal etc. that sees on behalf of another. **10 a** = *electric eye*. **b** = *private eye*. **11** a thing like an eye, esp.: **a** a spot on a peacock's tail (cf. EYELET *n.* 3). **b** the leaf bud of a potato. **12** the centre of something circular, e.g. a flower or target. **13** the relatively calm region at the centre of a storm or hurricane. **14** an aperture in an implement, esp. a needle, for the insertion of something, e.g. thread. **15** a ring or loop for a bolt or hook etc. to pass through. —*v.tr.* (**eyes, eyed, eyeing** or **eying**) watch or observe closely, esp. admiringly or with curiosity or suspicion. □ **all eyes 1** watching intently. **2** general attention (*all eyes were on us*). **before one's** (or **one's very**) **eyes** right in front of one. **do a person in the eye** *colloq.* defraud or thwart a person. **eye-bolt** a bolt or bar with an eye at the end for a hook etc. **eye-catching** *colloq.* striking, attractive. **eye contact** looking directly into another person's eyes. **an eye for an eye** retaliation in kind (Exodus 21: 24). **eye language** the process of communication by the expression of the eyes. **eye-level** the level seen by the eyes looking horizontally (*eye-level grill*). **eye-liner** a cosmetic applied as a line round the eye. **eye mask 1** a covering of soft material saturated with a lotion for refreshing the eyes. **2** a covering for the eyes. **eye-opener** *colloq.* **1** an enlightening experience; an unexpected revelation. **2** *US* an alcoholic drink taken on waking up. **eye-rhyme** a correspondence of words in spelling but not in pronunciation (e.g. *love* and *move*). **eyes front** (or **left** or **right**) *Mil.* a command to turn the head in the direction stated. **eye-shade** a device to protect the eyes, esp. from strong light. **eye-shadow** a coloured cosmetic applied to the skin round the eyes. **eye-spot 1 a** a light-sensitive area on the bodies of some invertebrate animals, e.g. flatworms, starfish, etc.; an ocellus. **b** *Bot.* an area of light-sensitive pigment found in some algae etc. **2** any of several fungus diseases of plants characterized by yellowish oval spots on the leaves and stems. **eye-stalk** *Zool.* a movable stalk carrying the eye, esp. in crabs, shrimps, etc. **eye strain** fatigue of the (internal or external) muscles of the eye. **eye-tooth** a canine tooth just under or next to the eye, esp. in the upper jaw. **eye-worm** a nematode worm, *Loa loa*, parasitic on man and other primates in Central and West Africa. **get** (or **keep**) **one's eye in** *Sport* accustom oneself (or keep oneself accustomed) to the conditions of play so as to judge speed, distance, etc. **have an eye for** be capable of perceiving or appreciating. **have one's eye on** wish or plan to procure. **have eyes for** be interested in; wish to acquire. **have an eye to** have as one's objective; prudently consider. **hit a person in the eye** (or **between the eyes**) *colloq.* be very obvious or impressive. **keep an eye on 1** pay attention to. **2** look after; take care of. **keep an eye open** (or **out**) (often foll. by *for*) watch carefully. **keep one's eyes open** (or **peeled** or **skinned**) watch out; be on the alert. **lower one's eyes** look modestly or sheepishly down or away. **make eyes** (or **sheep's eyes**) (foll. by *at*) look amorously or flirtatiously at. **my**

(or **all my**) **eye** sl. nonsense. **one in the eye** (foll. by for) a disappointment or setback. **open a person's eyes** be enlightening or revealing to a person. **raise one's eyes** look upwards. **see eye to eye** (often foll. by of. **take one's eyes off** (usu. in neg.) stop watching; stop paying attention to. **under the eye of** under the supervision or observation of. **up to the** (or **one's**) **eyes in 1** deeply engaged or involved in; inundated with (up to the eyes in work). **2** to the utmost limit (mortgaged up to the eyes). **with one's eyes open** deliberately; with full awareness. **with one's eyes shut** (or **closed**) **1** easily; with little effort. **2** without awareness; unobservant (goes around with his eyes shut). **with an eye to** with a view to; prudently considering. **with a friendly** (or **jealous** etc.) **eye** with a feeling of friendship, jealousy, etc. **with one eye on** directing one's attention partly to. **with one eye shut** colloq. easily; with little effort (could do this with one eye shut). □□ **eyed** adj. (also in comb.). **eyeless** adj. [OE ēage f. Gmc]

eyeball /ˈaɪbɔːl/ n. & v. —n. the ball of the eye within the lids and socket. —v. US sl. **1** tr. look or stare at. **2** intr. look or stare. □ **eyeball to eyeball** colloq. confronting closely. **to** (or **up to**) **the eyeballs** colloq. completely (permeated, soaked, etc.).

eyebath /ˈaɪbɑːθ/ n. (also **eyecup** /ˈaɪkʌp/) a small glass or vessel for applying lotion etc. to the eye.

eyeblack /ˈaɪblæk/ n. = MASCARA.

eyebright /ˈaɪbraɪt/ n. any plant of the genus Euphrasia, formerly used as a remedy for weak eyes.

eyebrow /ˈaɪbraʊ/ n. the line of hair growing on the ridge above the eye-socket. □ **raise one's eyebrows** show surprise, disbelief, or mild disapproval.

eyeful /ˈaɪfʊl/ n. (pl. **-fuls**) colloq. **1** a long steady look. **2** a visually striking person or thing. **3** anything thrown or blown into the eye.

eyeglass /ˈaɪglɑːs/ n. **1 a** a lens for correcting or assisting defective sight. **b** (in pl.) a pair of these held in the hand or kept in position on the nose by means of a frame or a spring. **2** a small glass vessel for applying lotion etc. to the eye.

eyehole /ˈaɪhəʊl/ n. a hole to look through.

eyelash /ˈaɪlæʃ/ n. each of the hairs growing on the edges of the eyelids. □ **by an eyelash** by a very small margin.

eyelet /ˈaɪlɪt/ n. & v. —n. **1** a small hole in paper, leather, cloth, etc., for string or rope etc. to pass through. **2** a metal ring reinforcement for this. **3** a small eye, esp. the ocellus on a butterfly's wing (cf. EYE n. 11a). **4** a form of decoration in embroidery. **5** a small hole for observation, shooting through, etc. —v.tr. (**eyeleted**, **eyeleting**) provide with eyelets. [ME f. OF oillet dimin. of oil eye f. L oculus]

eyelid /ˈaɪlɪd/ n. the upper or lower fold of skin closing to cover the eye.

eyepiece /ˈaɪpiːs/ n. the lens or lenses to which the eye is applied at the end of a microscope, telescope, etc.

eyeshot /ˈaɪʃɒt/ n. seeing-distance (out of eyeshot).

eyesight /ˈaɪsaɪt/ n. the faculty or power of seeing.

eyesore /ˈaɪsɔː(r)/ n. a visually offensive or ugly thing, esp. a building.

Eyetie /ˈaɪtaɪ/ n. & adj. sl. offens. Italian. [joc. pronunc. of Italian]

eyewash /ˈaɪwɒʃ/ n. **1** lotion for the eye. **2** sl. nonsense, bunkum; pretentious or insincere talk.

eyewitness /ˈaɪˌwɪtnɪs/ n. a person who has personally seen a thing done or happen and can give evidence of it.

eyot var. of AIT.

eyra /ˈeərə/ n. Zool. a red form of jaguarundi. [Tupi (e)irara]

Eyre[1] /eə(r)/, Edward John (1815–1901), English explorer and colonial statesman. Having emigrated to Australia at the age of 17, Eyre established himself as a sheep-farmer and in 1840–1 undertook explorations in the interior deserts of the continent. He later served as Lieutenant-Governor of New Zealand (1846–53) and Governor of St Vincent (1854–60) and Jamaica (1864–6). He was recalled from the last post for putting down a native revolt with undue severity but was eventually cleared of all charges.

Eyre[2] /eə(r)/, **Lake** a lake in South Australia, named after E. J. Eyre. It is Australia's largest salt lake.

eyrie /ˈaɪərɪ, ˈɪərɪ, ˈɜːrɪ/ n. (also **aerie**) **1** a nest of a bird of prey, esp. an eagle, built high up. **2** a house etc. perched high up. [med.L aeria, aerea, etc., prob. f. OF aire lair ult. f. L agrum piece of ground]

Eysenck /ˈaɪzeŋk/, Hans Jürgen (1916–   ), British psychologist, born in Germany, who argued strongly against Freudian-style theories and questioned the efficacy of traditional psychoanalysis that concerns itself with interpreting symptoms in terms of unconscious motives and childhood experiences. Instead of this he introduced 'behaviour therapy', which involves practical efforts to change behaviour that the patient regards as undesirable. His most controversial work has been in IQ testing, where he claimed that intelligence (as well as personality and social behaviour) is considerably influenced by genetic and racial factors.

Ezek. abbr. Ezekiel (Old Testament).

Ezekiel /ɪˈziːkɪəl/ **1** a Hebrew major prophet of the 6th c. BC who prophesied the forthcoming destruction of Jerusalem and the Jewish nation, and inspired hope for the future well-being of a restored State. **2** a book of the Old Testament containing his prophecies.

Ezra /ˈezrə/ **1** a Jewish priest and scribe who played a central part in the reform of Judaism in the 5th or 4th c. BC, following Nehemiah in taking measures to secure the racial purity of the Jews. **2** a book of the Old Testament dealing with the return of the Jews from Babylon and the rebuilding of the Temple.

F

F abbr. Electr. faraday.

F¹ /ef/ n. (also **f**) (pl. **Fs** or **F's**) **1** the sixth letter of the alphabet. **2** Mus. the fourth note of the diatonic scale of C major.

F² abbr. (also **F.**) **1** Fahrenheit. **2** farad(s). **3** female. **4** fine (pencil-lead). **5** Biol. filial generation (as F_1 for the first filial generation, F_2 for the second, etc.).

F³ symb. Chem. the element fluorine.

f abbr. (also **f.**) **1** female. **2** feminine. **3** following page etc. **4** Mus. forte. **5** folio. **6** focal length (cf. F-NUMBER). **7** femto-. **8** filly. **9** foreign. **10** frequency.

FA abbr. **1** (in the UK) Football Association. **2** = FANNY ADAMS 1.

fa var. of FAH.

FAA abbr. Fleet Air Arm.

fab /fæb/ adj. colloq. fabulous, marvellous. [abbr.]

Fabergé /ˈfɑːberʒeɪ/, Peter Carl (1846–1920), Russian jeweller, famed for his small intricate ornaments.

Fabian /ˈfeɪbɪən/ n. & adj. —n. a member or supporter of the Fabian Society, an organization of socialists founded in 1884, numbering among its members Sidney and Beatrice Webb and George Bernard Shaw, advocating social change through gradual reform rather than by violent revolutionary action. —adj. **1** relating to or characteristic of the Fabians. **2** employing a cautiously persistent and dilatory strategy to wear out an enemy (Fabian tactics). □□ **Fabianism** n. **Fabianist** n. [L Fabianus of FABIUS].

Fabius /ˈfeɪbɪəs/ (Quintus Fabius Maximus Verrucosus Cunctator, d. 203 BC) Roman general and statesman. After Hannibal's defeat of the Roman army at Cannae in 216 BC, he successfully pursued a strategy of caution and delay in order to wear down the Carthaginian invaders, whence his nickname Cunctator ('the Delayer').

fable /ˈfeɪb(ə)l/ n. & v. —n. **1 a** a story, esp. a supernatural one, not based on fact. **b** a tale, esp. with animals as characters, conveying a moral. **2** (collect.) myths and legendary tales (in fable). **3 a** a false statement; a lie. **b** a thing only supposed to exist. —v. **1** intr. tell fictitious tales. **2** tr. describe fictitiously. **3** tr. (as **fabled** adj.) celebrated in fable; famous, legendary. □□ **fabler** /ˈfeɪblə(r)/ n. [ME f. OF fabler f. L fabulari f. fabula discourse f. fari speak]

fabliau /ˈfæblɪəʊ/ n. (pl. **fabliaux** /-əʊz/) a metrical tale in early French poetry, often coarsely humorous. [F f. OF dialect fabliaux, -ax pl. of fablel dimin. (as FABLE)]

fabric /ˈfæbrɪk/ n. **1 a** a woven material; a textile. **b** other material resembling woven cloth. **2** a structure or framework, esp. the walls, floor, and roof of a building. **3** (in abstract senses) the essential structure or essence of a thing (the fabric of society). [ME f. F fabrique f. L fabrica f. faber metal-worker etc.]

fabricate /ˈfæbrɪˌkeɪt/ v.tr. **1** construct or manufacture, esp. from prepared components. **2** invent or concoct (a story, evidence, etc.). **3** forge (a document). □□ **fabrication** /-ˈkeɪʃ(ə)n/ n. **fabricator** n. [L fabricare fabricat- (as FABRIC)]

fabulist /ˈfæbjʊlɪst/ n. **1** a composer of fables. **2** a liar. [F fabuliste f. L fabula: see FABLE]

fabulous /ˈfæbjʊləs/ adj. **1** incredible, exaggerated, absurd (fabulous wealth). **2** colloq. marvellous (looking fabulous). **3 a** celebrated in fable. **b** legendary, mythical. □□ **fabulosity** /-ˈlɒsɪtɪ/ n. **fabulously** adv. **fabulousness** n. [F fabuleux or L fabulosus (as FABLE)]

façade /fəˈsɑːd/ n. **1** the face of a building, esp. its principal front. **2** an outward appearance or front, esp. a deceptive one. [F (as FACE)]

face /feɪs/ n. & v. —n. **1** the front of the head from the forehead to the chin. **2** the expression of the facial features (had a happy face). **3** composure, coolness, effrontery. **4** the surface of a thing, esp. as regarded or approached, esp.: **a** the visible part of a celestial body. **b** a side of a mountain etc. (the north face). **c** the (usu. vertical) surface of a coal-seam. **d** Geom. each surface of a solid. **e** the façade of a building. **f** the plate of a clock or watch bearing the digits, hands, etc. **5 a** the functional or working side of a tool etc. **b** the distinctive side of a playing card. **c** the obverse of a coin. **6** = TYPEFACE. **7** the outward appearance or aspect (the unacceptable face of capitalism). **8** a person, esp. conveying some quality or association (a face from the past; some young faces for a change). —v. **1** tr. & intr. look or be positioned towards or in a certain direction (face towards the window; facing the window; the room faces north). **2** tr. be opposite (facing page 20). **3** tr. **a** (often foll. by out) meet resolutely or defiantly; confront (face one's critics). **b** not shrink from (face the facts). **4** tr. present itself to; confront (the problem that faces us; faces us with a problem). **5** tr. **a** cover the surface of (a thing) with a coating, extra layer, etc. **b** put a facing on (a garment). **6** intr. & tr. turn or cause to turn in a certain direction. □ **face-ache 1** neuralgia. **2** sl. a mournful-looking person. **face-card** = court-card. **face-cloth 1** a cloth for washing one's face. **2** a smooth-surfaced woollen cloth. **face-cream** a cosmetic cream applied to the face to improve the complexion. **face down** (or **downwards**) with the face or surface turned towards the ground, floor, etc. **face facts** (or **the facts**) recognize the truth. **face-flannel** = face-cloth 1. **face-lift 1** (also **face-lifting**) cosmetic surgery to remove wrinkles etc. by tightening the skin of the face. **2** a procedure to improve the appearance of a thing. **face the music** colloq. put up with or stand up to unpleasant consequences, esp. criticism. **face-pack** a preparation beneficial to the complexion, spread over the face and removed when dry. **face-powder** a cosmetic powder for reducing the shine on the face. **face-saving** preserving one's reputation, credibility, etc. **face to face** (often foll. by with) facing; confronting each other. **face up** (or **upwards**) with the face or surface turned upwards to view. **face up to** accept bravely; confront; stand up to. **face value 1** the nominal value as printed or stamped on money. **2** the superficial appearance or implication of a thing. **face-worker** a miner who works at the coalface. **have the face** be shameless enough. **in one's** (or **the**) **face 1** straight against one; as one approaches. **2** confronting. **in face** (or **the face**) **of 1** despite. **2** confronted by. **let's face it** colloq. we must be honest or realistic about it. **on the face of it** as it would appear. **put a bold** (or **brave**) **face on it** accept difficulty etc. cheerfully or with courage. **put one's face on** colloq. apply make-up to one's face. **put a good face on** make (a matter) look well. **put a new face on** alter the aspect of. **save face** preserve esteem; avoid humiliation. **save a person's face** enable a person to save face; forbear from humiliating a person. **set one's face against** oppose or resist with determination. **to a person's face** openly in a person's presence. □□ **faced** adj. (also in comb.). **facing** adj. (also in comb.). [ME f. OF ult. f. L facies]

faceless /ˈfeɪslɪs/ adj. **1** without identity; purposely not identifiable. **2** lacking character. **3** without a face. □□ **facelessly** adv. **facelessness** n.

facer /ˈfeɪsə(r)/ n. colloq. **1** a sudden difficulty or obstacle. **2** a blow in the face.

facet /ˈfæsɪt/ n. **1** a particular aspect of a thing. **2** one side of a many-sided body, esp. of a cut gem. **3** one segment of a compound eye. □□ **faceted** adj. (also in comb.). [F facette dimin. (as FACE, -ETTE)]

facetiae /fəˈsiːʃɪˌiː/ n.pl. **1** pleasantries, witticisms. **2** (in bookselling) pornography. [L, pl. of facetia jest f. facetus witty]

facetious /fəˈsiːʃəs/ adj. **1** characterized by flippant or inopportune humour. **2** (of a person) intending to be amusing, esp.

w we z zoo ʃ she ʒ decision θ thin ð this ŋ ring x loch tʃ chip dʒ jar (see over for vowels)

inopportunely. □□ **facetiously** *adv.* **facetiousness** *n.* [F *facétieux* f. *facétie* f. L *facetia* jest]

facia var. of FASCIA.

facial /ˈfeɪʃ(ə)l/ *adj.* & *n.* —*adj.* of or for the face. —*n.* a beauty treatment for the face. □□ **facially** *adv.* [med.L *facialis* (as FACE)]

-facient /ˈfeɪʃ(ə)nt/ *comb. form* forming adjectives and nouns indicating an action or state produced (*abortifacient*). [from or after L *-faciens -entis* part. of *facere* make]

facies /ˈfeɪʃiːz/ *n.* (*pl.* same) **1** *Med.* the appearance or facial expression of an individual. **2** *Geol.* the character of rock etc. expressed by its composition, fossil content, etc. [L, = FACE]

facile /ˈfæsaɪl/ *adj.* usu. *derog.* **1** easily achieved but of little value. **2** (of speech, writing, etc.) fluent, ready, glib. □□ **facilely** *adv.* **facileness** *n.* [F *facile* or L *facilis* f. *facere* do]

facilitate /fəˈsɪlɪˌteɪt/ *v.tr.* make easy or less difficult or more easily achieved. □□ **facilitation** /-ˈteɪʃ(ə)n/ *n.* **facilitative** /-tətɪv/ *adj.* **facilitator** *n.* [F *faciliter* f. It. *facilitare* f. *facile* easy f. L *facilis*]

facility /fəˈsɪlɪtɪ/ *n.* (*pl.* **-ies**) **1** ease; absence of difficulty. **2** fluency, dexterity, aptitude (*facility of expression*). **3** (esp. in *pl.*) an opportunity, the equipment, or the resources for doing something. **4** *US* a plant, installation, or establishment. [F *facilité* or L *facilitas* (as FACILE)]

facing /ˈfeɪsɪŋ/ *n.* **1 a** a layer of material covering part of a garment etc. for contrast or strength. **b** (in *pl.*) the cuffs, collar, etc., of a military jacket. **2** an outer layer covering the surface of a wall etc.

facsimile /fækˈsɪmɪlɪ/ *n.* & *v.* —*n.* **1** an exact copy, esp. of writing, printing, a picture, etc. (often *attrib.: facsimile edition*). **2 a** production of an exact copy of a document etc. by electronic scanning and transmission of the resulting data (see also FAX). (See below.) **b** a copy produced in this way. —*v.tr.* (**facsimiled**, **facsimileing**) make a facsimile of. □ **in facsimile** as an exact copy. [mod.L f. L *fac* imper. of *facere* make + *simile* neut. of *similis* like]

Most systems of facsimile transmission (fax) involve the scanning of the original image by a device which converts each unit area of it into a specified amount of electric current and transmits this as a signal, over a telephone line or other telecommunications link, to a receiver which produces an image that is a copy of the original. The basic principles were described by the Scottish inventor Alexander Bain in 1843 in his patent for producing copies, at distant places, of surfaces (e.g. printer's types) composed of conducting and non-conducting materials; his device used a frame containing short parallel wires as electrical conductors in contact with the printing surface. Not only printed matter but drawings, maps, photographs, and other graphic matter (e.g. radiographs) can be transmitted by modern techniques.

fact /fækt/ *n.* **1** a thing that is known to have occurred, to exist, or to be true. **2** a datum of experience (often foll. by an explanatory clause or phrase: *the fact that fire burns; the fact of my having seen them*). **3** (usu. in *pl.*) an item of verified information; a piece of evidence. **4** truth, reality. **5** a thing assumed as the basis for argument or inference. □ **before** (or **after**) **the fact** before (or after) the committing of a crime. **a fact of life** something that must be accepted. **facts and figures** precise details. **fact-sheet** a paper setting out relevant information. **the facts of life** information about sexual functions and practices. **in** (or **in point of**) **fact 1** in reality; as a matter of fact. **2** (in summarizing) in short. [L *factum* f. *facere* do]

factice /ˈfæktɪs/ *n.* *Chem.* a rubber-like substance obtained by vulcanizing unsaturated vegetable oils. [G *Faktis* f. L *facticius* FACTITIOUS]

faction[1] /ˈfækʃ(ə)n/ *n.* **1** a small organized dissentient group within a larger one, esp. in politics. **2** a state of dissension within an organization. [F f. L *factio -onis* f. *facere* fact- do, make]

faction[2] /ˈfækʃ(ə)n/ *n.* a book, film, etc., using real events as a basis for a fictional narrative or dramatization. [blend of FACT and FICTION]

-faction /ˈfækʃ(ə)n/ *comb. form* forming nouns of action from verbs in *-fy* (*petrifaction; satisfaction*). [from or after L *-factio -factionis* f. *facere* do, make]

factional /ˈfækʃən(ə)l/ *adj.* **1** of or characterized by faction. **2** belonging to a faction. □□ **factionalism** *n.* **factionalize** *v.tr.* & *intr.* (also **-ise**). **factionally** *adv.* [FACTION[1]]

factious /ˈfækʃəs/ *adj.* of, characterized by, or inclined to faction. □□ **factiously** *adv.* **factiousness** *n.*

factitious /fækˈtɪʃəs/ *adj.* **1** specially contrived, not genuine (*factitious value*). **2** artificial, not natural (*factitious joy*). □□ **factitiously** *adv.* **factitiousness** *n.* [L *facticius* f. *facere* fact- do, make]

factitive /ˈfæktɪtɪv/ *adj.* *Gram.* (of a verb) having a sense of regarding or designating, and taking a complement as well as an object (e.g. *appointed me captain*). [mod.L *factitivus*, irreg. f. L *factitare* frequent. of *facere* fact- do, make]

factoid /ˈfæktɔɪd/ *n.* & *adj.* —*n.* an assumption or speculation that is reported and repeated so often that it becomes accepted as fact; a simulated or imagined fact. —*adj.* being or having the character of a factoid; containing factoids.

factor /ˈfæktə(r)/ *n.* & *v.* —*n.* **1** a circumstance, fact, or influence contributing to a result. **2** *Math.* a whole number etc. that when multiplied with another produces a given number or expression. **3** *Biol.* a gene etc. determining hereditary character. **4** (foll. by identifying number) *Med.* any of several substances in the blood contributing to coagulation (*factor eight*). **5 a** a business agent; a merchant buying and selling on commission. **b** *Sc.* a land-agent or steward. **c** an agent or a deputy. **6** a company that buys a manufacturer's invoices and takes responsibility for collecting the payments due on them. —*v.tr.* **1** *Math.* resolve into factors or components. **2** *tr.* sell (one's receivable debts) to a factor. □ **factor analysis** *Statistics* a process by which the relative importance of variables in the study of a sample is assessed by mathematical techniques. □□ **factorable** *adj.* [F *facteur* or L *factor* f. *facere* fact- do, make]

factorage /ˈfæktərɪdʒ/ *n.* commission or charges payable to a factor.

factorial /fækˈtɔːrɪəl/ *n.* & *adj.* *Math.* —*n.* **1** the product of a number and all the whole numbers below it (*factorial four = 4 × 3 × 2 × 1*). ¶ Symb.: ! (as in 4!). **2** the product of a series of factors in an arithmetical progression. —*adj.* of a factor or factorial. □□ **factorially** *adv.*

factorize /ˈfæktəˌraɪz/ *v.* (also **-ise**) *Math.* **1** *tr.* resolve into factors. **2** *intr.* be capable of resolution into factors. □□ **factorization** /-ˈzeɪʃ(ə)n/ *n.*

factory /ˈfæktərɪ/ *n.* (*pl.* **-ies**) **1** a building or buildings containing plant or equipment for manufacturing machinery or goods. **2** *hist.* a merchant company's foreign trading station. □ **Factory Acts** legislation regulating the operation of factories in order to improve the working conditions of employees. The first effective Act was that of 1833, which provided for the use of inspectors. **factory farm** a farm employing factory farming. **factory farming** a system of rearing livestock using industrial or intensive methods. **factory floor** workers in industry as distinct from management. **factory ship** *Brit.* a fishing ship with facilities for immediate processing of the catch. [Port. *feitoria* and LL *factorium*]

factotum /fækˈtəʊtəm/ *n.* (*pl.* **factotums**) an employee who does all kinds of work. [med.L f. L *fac* imper. of *facere* do, make + *totum* neut. of *totus* whole]

factual /ˈfæktjʊəl/ *adj.* **1** based on or concerned with fact or facts. **2** actual, true. □□ **factuality** /-ˈælɪtɪ/ *n.* **factually** *adv.* **factualness** *n.* [FACT, after *actual*]

factum /ˈfæktəm/ *n.* (*pl.* **factums** or **facta** /-tə/) *Law* **1** an act or deed. **2** a statement of the facts. [F f. L: see FACT]

facture /ˈfæktʃə(r)/ *n.* the quality of execution esp. of the surface of a painting. [ME f. OF f. L *factura* f. *facere* fact- do, make]

facula /ˈfækjʊlə/ *n.* (*pl.* **faculae** /-ˌliː/) *Astron.* a bright spot or streak on the sun. □□ **facular** *adj.* **faculous** *adj.* [L, dimin. of *fax facis* torch]

facultative /ˈfækəltətɪv/ *adj.* **1** *Law* enabling an act to take place. **2** that may occur. **3** *Biol.* not restricted to a particular function, mode of life, etc. **4** of a faculty. □□ **facultatively** *adv.* [F *facultatif -ive* (as FACULTY)]

faculty /ˈfækəltɪ/ *n.* (*pl.* **-ies**) **1** an aptitude or ability for a particular activity. **2** an inherent mental or physical power. **3 a** a group of university departments concerned with a major division of knowledge (*faculty of modern languages*). **b** *US* the staff of a university or college. **c** a branch of art or science; those qualified to teach it. **4** the members of a particular profession, esp. medicine. **5** authorization, esp. by a Church authority. □ **Faculty of Advocates** *Law* the society constituting the Scottish Bar. [ME f. OF *faculté* f. L *facultas -tatis* f. *facilis* easy]

FAD *abbr.* flavin adenine dinucleotide.

fad /fæd/ *n.* **1** a craze. **2** a peculiar notion or idiosyncrasy. □□ **faddish** *adj.* **faddishly** *adv.* **faddishness** *n.* **faddism** *n.* **faddist** *n.* [19th c. (orig. dial.): prob. f. *fidfad* f. FIDDLE-FADDLE]

faddy /'fædɪ/ *adj.* (**faddier**, **faddiest**) having arbitrary likes and dislikes, esp. about food. □□ **faddily** *adv.* **faddiness** *n.*

fade /feɪd/ *v. & n.* —*v.* **1** *intr. & tr.* lose or cause to lose colour. **2** *intr.* lose freshness or strength; (of flowers etc.) droop, wither. **3** *intr.* **a** (of colour, light, etc.) disappear gradually; grow pale or dim. **b** (of sound) grow faint. **4** *intr.* (of a feeling etc.) diminish. **5** *intr.* (foll. by *away, out*) (of a person etc.) disappear or depart gradually. **6** *tr.* (foll. by *in, out*) *Cinematog. & Broadcasting* **a** cause (a picture) to come gradually in or out of view on a screen, or to merge into another shot. **b** make (the sound) more or less audible. **7** *intr.* (of a radio signal) vary irregularly in intensity. **8** *intr.* (of a brake) temporarily lose effectiveness. **9** *Golf* **a** *intr.* (of a ball) deviate from a straight course, esp. in a deliberate slice. **b** *tr.* cause (a ball) to fade. —*n.* the action or an instance of fading. □ **do a fade** *sl.* depart. **fade away** *colloq.* languish, grow thin. **fade-in** *Cinematog. & Broadcasting* the action or an instance of fading in a picture or sound. **fade-out** **1** *colloq.* disappearance, death. **2** *Cinematog. & Broadcasting* the action or an instance of fading out a picture or sound. □□ **fadeless** *adj.* **fader** *n.* (in sense 6 of *v.*). [ME f. OF *fader* f. *fade* dull, insipid prob. ult. f. L *fatuus* silly + *vapidus* VAPID]

fadge /fædʒ/ *n.* *Austral. & NZ* **1** a limp package of wool. **2** a loosely packed wool bale. [16th-c. Engl. dial.: orig. uncert.]

faeces /'fiːsiːz/ *n.pl.* (*US* **feces**) waste matter discharged from the bowels. □□ **faecal** /'fiːk(ə)l/ *adj.* [L, pl. of *faex* dregs]

Faenza /faːˈentsə/ a town in northern Italy, on the Lamone River, that gave its name to the type of pottery known as 'faience'; pop. (1981) 54,900.

faerie /'feɪərɪ/ *n.* (also **faery**) *archaic* **1** Fairyland; the fairies esp. as represented by Spenser (*the Faerie Queene*). **2** (*attrib.*) visionary, fancied. [var. of FAIRY]

Faeroe Islands /'feərəʊ/ (also **Faeroes**) a group of islands in the North Atlantic between Iceland and the Shetlands, belonging to Denmark but partly autonomous; pop. (est. 1986) 46,300; capital, Thorshavn.

Faeroese /ˌfeərəʊˈiːz/ *adj. & n.* (also **Faroese**) —*adj.* of or relating to the Faeroes. —*n.* (*pl.* same) **1** a native of the Faeroes; a person of Faeroese descent. **2** the Norse language of this people.

faff /fæf/ *v. & n.* *Brit. colloq.* —*v.intr.* (often foll. by *about, around*) fuss, dither. —*n.* a fuss. [imit.]

fag[1] /fæg/ *n. & v.* —*n.* **1** esp. *Brit. colloq.* a piece of drudgery; a wearisome or unwelcome task. **2** *sl.* a cigarette. **3** *Brit.* (at public schools) a junior pupil who runs errands for a senior. —*v.* (**fagged**, **fagging**) **1 a** *tr.* (often foll. by *out*) tire out; exhaust. **b** *intr.* toil. **2** *intr. Brit.* (in public schools) act as a fag. **3** *tr. Naut.* (often foll. by *out*) fray (the end of a rope etc.). □ **fag-end** *sl.* **1** *Brit.* a cigarette-end. **2** an inferior or useless remnant. [orig. unkn.: cf. FLAG[1]]

fag[2] /fæg/ *n.* *US sl.* often *offens.* a male homosexual. [abbr. of FAGGOT]

Fagatogo /ˌfæŋgəˈtəʊŋgəʊ/ the capital of American Samoa.

faggot /'fægət/ *n. & v.* (*US* **fagot**) —*n.* **1** (usu. in *pl.*) a ball or roll of seasoned chopped liver etc., baked or fried. **2** a bundle of sticks or twigs bound together as fuel. **3** a bundle of iron rods for heat treatment. **4** a bunch of herbs. **5** *sl. derog.* **a** an unpleasant woman. **b** *US* often *offens.* a male homosexual. —*v.tr.* (**faggoted**, **faggoting**) **1** bind in or make into faggots. **2** join by faggoting (see FAGGOTING). □□ **faggoty** *adj.* [ME f. OF *fagot*, of uncert. orig.]

faggoting /'fægətɪŋ/ *n.* **1** embroidery in which threads are

fastened together like a faggot. **2** the joining of materials in a similar manner.

fagot *US* var. of FAGGOT.

fah /fɑː/ *n.* (also **fa**) *Mus.* **1** (in tonic sol-fa) the fourth note of a major scale. **2** the note F in the fixed-doh system. [ME *fa* f. L *famuli*: see GAMUT]

Fahr. *abbr.* Fahrenheit.

Fahrenheit /'færənˌhaɪt/ *adj.* of or measured on a scale of temperature on which water freezes at 32° and boils at 212° under standard conditions. [G. *Fahrenheit*, Ger. physicist d. 1736]

faience /'faɪɑ̃s/ *n.* decorated and glazed earthenware and porcelain, e.g. delft or majolica. [F *faience* f. FAENZA]

fail /feɪl/ *v. & n.* —*v.* **1** *intr.* not succeed (*failed in persuading; failed to qualify; tried but failed*). **2 a** *tr. & intr.* be unsuccessful in (an examination, test, interview, etc.); be rejected as a candidate. **b** *tr.* (of a commodity etc.) not pass (a test of quality). **c** *tr.* reject (a candidate etc.); adjudge unsuccessful. **3** *intr.* be unable to; neglect to; choose not to (*I fail to see the reason; he failed to appear*). **4** *tr.* disappoint; let down; not serve when needed. **5** *tr.* (of supplies, crops, etc.) be or become lacking or insufficient. **6** *intr.* become weaker; cease functioning; break down (*her health is failing; the engine has failed*). **7** *intr.* **a** (of an enterprise) collapse; come to nothing. **b** become bankrupt. —*n.* a failure in an examination or test. □ **fail-safe** reverting to a safe condition in the event of a breakdown etc. **without fail** for certain, whatever happens. [ME f. OF *faillir* (v.), *fail(l)e* (n.) ult. f. L *fallere* deceive]

failed /feɪld/ *adj.* **1** unsuccessful; not good enough (*a failed actor*). **2** weak, deficient; broken down (*a failed crop; a failed battery*).

failing /'feɪlɪŋ/ *n. & prep.* —*n.* a fault or shortcoming; a weakness, esp. in character. —*prep.* in default of; if not.

failure /'feɪljə(r)/ *n.* **1** lack of success; failing. **2** an unsuccessful person, thing, or attempt. **3** non-performance, non-occurrence. **4** breaking down or ceasing to function (*heart failure; engine failure*). **5** running short of supply etc. **6** bankruptcy, collapse. [earlier *failer* f. AF, = OF *faillir* FAIL]

fain /feɪn/ *adj. & adv.* *archaic* —*predic.adj.* (foll. by *to* + infin.) **1** willing under the circumstances to. **2** left with no alternative but to. —*adv.* gladly (esp. *would fain*). [OE *fægen* f. Gmc]

fainéant /'feɪneɪˌɑ̃/ *n. & adj.* —*n.* an idle or ineffective person. —*adj.* idle, inactive. [F f. *fait* does + *néant* nothing]

faint /feɪnt/ *adj., v., & n.* —*adj.* **1** indistinct, pale, dim; not clearly perceived. **2** (of a person) weak or giddy; inclined to faint. **3** slight, remote, inadequate (*a faint chance*). **4** feeble, half-hearted (*faint praise*). **5** timid (*a faint heart*). **6** (also **feint**) (of ruled paper) with inconspicuous lines to guide writing. —*v.intr.* **1** lose consciousness. **2** become faint. —*n.* a sudden loss of consciousness; fainting. □ **faint-hearted** cowardly, timid. **faint-heartedly** in a faint-hearted manner. **faint-heartedness** cowardliness, timidity. **not have the faintest** *colloq.* have no idea. □□ **faintness** *n.* [ME f. OF, past part. of *faindre* FEIGN]

faintly /'feɪntlɪ/ *adv.* **1** very slightly (*faintly amused*). **2** indistinctly, feebly.

fair[1] /feə(r)/ *adj., adv., n., & v.* —*adj.* **1** just, unbiased, equitable; in accordance with the rules. **2** blond; light or pale in colour or complexion. **3 a** of (only) moderate quality or amount; average. **b** considerable, satisfactory (*a fair chance of success*). **4** (of weather) fine and dry; (of the wind) favourable. **5** clean, clear, unblemished (*fair copy*). **6** beautiful, attractive. **7** *archaic* kind, gentle. **8 a** specious (*fair speeches*). **b** complimentary (*fair words*). **9** *Austral. & NZ* complete, unquestionable. —*adv.* **1** in a fair manner (*play fair*). **2** exactly, completely (*was hit fair on the jaw*). —*n.* **1** a fair thing. **2** *archaic* a beautiful woman. —*v.* **1** *tr.* make (the surface of a ship, aircraft, etc.) smooth and streamlined. **2** *intr. dial.* (of the weather) become fair. □ **fair and square** *adv. & adj.* **1** exactly. **2** straightforward, honest, above-board. **fair crack of the whip** see CRACK. **a fair deal** equitable treatment. **fair dos** /duːz/ *colloq.* fair shares. **fair enough** *colloq.* that is reasonable or acceptable. **fair game** a thing or person one may legitimately pursue, exploit, etc. **fair-minded** just, impartial. **fair-mindedly** justly, impartially. **fair-mindedness** a sense of justice; impartiality. **fair name** a good reputation. **fair play** reasonable treatment or behaviour. **fair rent** the amount of rent which a tenant may reasonably be expected to pay according to established guidelines. **the fair sex** women. **fair's fair** *colloq.* all involved should act fairly. **fair-spoken** courteous. **a fair treat** *colloq.* a very enjoyable or attractive thing or person. **fair-weather friend** a friend or ally who is unreliable in times of difficulty. **for fair** *US sl.* completely. **in a fair way to** likely to. □□ **fairish** *adj.* **fairness** *n.* [OE *fæger* f. Gmc]

fair² /feə(r)/ *n.* **1** a gathering of stalls, amusements, etc., for public (usu. outdoor) entertainment. **2** a periodical gathering for the sale of goods, often with entertainments. **3** an exhibition, esp. to promote particular products. [ME f. OF *feire* f. LL *feria* sing. f. L *feriae* holiday]

Fairbanks /ˈfeəˌbæŋks/, Douglas (Elton) (real name Julius Ullman, 1883–1939), American film actor. With Charlie Chaplin, Mary Pickford (whom he married in 1920), and D. W. Griffith he founded the production and distribution company United Artists Corporation (1919), and embarked on the series of 'spectaculars' that made him a celebrity; they include *The Mark of Zorro* (1920), *Robin Hood* (1922), and *The Thief of Baghdad* (1924). His son Douglas Fairbanks Jr (1909–   ), also a film actor, played roles similar to those of his father, including that of Rupert of Hentzan in *The Prisoner of Zenda* (1937).

fairground /ˈfeəɡraʊnd/ *n.* an outdoor area where a fair is held.

fairing¹ /ˈfeərɪŋ/ *n.* **1** a streamlining structure added to a ship, aircraft, vehicle, etc. **2** the process of streamlining. [FAIR¹ *v.* 1 + -ING¹]

fairing² /ˈfeərɪŋ/ *n. Brit. archaic* a present bought at a fair.

Fair Isle an island about half-way between the Orkneys and Shetlands, noted for the characteristic coloured designs in knitting which are named after it. There is a legend that a Spanish galleon was wrecked there after the defeat of the Armada in 1588, and that the designs were learnt from its survivors.

fairlead /ˈfeəliːd/ *n. Naut.* a device to guide rope etc., e.g. to prevent cutting or chafing.

fairly /ˈfeəlɪ/ *adv.* **1** in a fair manner; justly. **2** moderately, acceptably (*fairly good*). **3** to a noticeable degree (*fairly narrow*). **4** utterly, completely (*fairly beside himself*). **5** actually (*fairly jumped for joy*). □ **fairly and squarely** = *fair and square* (see FAIR¹).

fairwater /ˈfeəˌwɔːtə(r)/ *n.* a structure on a ship etc. assisting its passage through water.

fairway /ˈfeəweɪ/ *n.* **1** a navigable channel; a regular course or track of a ship. **2** the part of a golf-course between a tee and its green, kept free of rough grass.

fairy /ˈfeərɪ/ *n. & adj.* —*n.* (pl. **-ies**) **1** a small imaginary being with magical powers. **2** *sl. derog.* a male homosexual. —*adj.* of fairies, fairy-like, delicate, small. □ **fairy cake** a small individual iced sponge cake. **fairy cycle** a small bicycle for a child. **fairy godmother** a benefactress. **fairy lights** small coloured lights esp. for outdoor decoration. **fairy ring** a ring of darker grass caused by fungi. **fairy story** (or **tale**) **1** a tale about fairies. **2** an incredible story; a fabrication. □□ **fairy-like** *adj.* [ME f. OF *faerie* f. *fae* FAY]

fairyland /ˈfeərɪˌlænd/ *n.* **1** the imaginary home of fairies. **2** an enchanted region.

Faisal /ˈfaɪs(ə)l/ the name of two kings of Iraq:
    Faisal I (1885–1933), reigned 1921–33, British-sponsored ruler, supported also by fervent Arab nationalists. Under his rule Iraq achieved full independence in 1932.
    Faisal II (1935–58), reigned 1939–58, grandson of Faisal I. He was assassinated in a military coup, after which a republic was established.

Faisalabad /ˌfaɪsæləˈbæd/ an industrial city of Pakistan, in Punjab province; pop. (1981) 1,092,000.

fait accompli /ˌfeɪt əˈkɒmpliː, əˈkɔ̃pliː/ *n.* a thing that has been done and is past arguing against or altering. [F]

faith /feɪθ/ *n.* **1** complete trust or confidence. **2** firm belief, esp. without logical proof. **3 a** a system of religious belief (*the Christian faith*). **b** belief in religious doctrines. **c** spiritual apprehension of divine truth apart from proof. **d** things believed or to be believed. **4** duty or commitment to fulfil a trust, promise, etc. (*keep faith*). **5** (*attrib.*) concerned with a supposed ability to cure by faith rather than treatment (*faith-healing*). □ **bad faith**

intent to deceive. **good faith** honesty or sincerity of intention. [ME f. AF *fed* f. OF *feid* f. L *fides*]

faithful /ˈfeɪθfʊl/ *adj.* **1** showing faith. **2** (often foll. by *to*) loyal, trustworthy, constant. **3** accurate; true to fact (*a faithful account*). **4** (**the Faithful**) the believers in a religion, esp. Muslims and Christians. □□ **faithfulness** *n.*

faithfully /ˈfeɪθfʊlɪ/ *adv.* in a faithful manner. □ **yours faithfully** a formula for ending a business or formal letter.

faithless /ˈfeɪθlɪs/ *adj.* **1** false, unreliable, disloyal. **2** without religious faith. □□ **faithlessly** *adv.* **faithlessness** *n.*

fake¹ /feɪk/ *n., adj., & v.* —*n.* **1** a thing or person that is not genuine. **2** a trick. —*adj.* counterfeit; not genuine. —*v.tr.* **1** make (a false thing) appear genuine; forge, counterfeit. **2** make a pretence of having (a feeling, illness, etc.). □□ **faker** *n.* **fakery** *n.* [obs. *feak, feague* thrash f. G *fegen* sweep, thrash]

fake² /feɪk/ *n. & v. Naut.* —*n.* one round of a coil of rope. —*v.tr.* coil (rope). [ME: cf. Scottish *faik* fold]

fakir /ˈfeɪkɪə(r), fəˈkɪə(r)/ *n.* (also **faquir**) a Muslim or (rarely) Hindu religious mendicant or ascetic. [Arab. *faḳīr* needy man]

falafel var. of FELAFEL.

Falange /fæˈlændʒ/ *n.* a Spanish political group, founded in 1933 as a Fascist movement by J. A. Primo de Rivera and merged in 1937 with traditional right-wing elements to form the ruling party, the Falange Española Tradicionalista, under General Franco. It was formally abolished in 1977. □□ **Falangism** *n.* **Falangist** *n.* [Sp., = PHALANX]

Falasha /fæˈlɑːʃə/ *n.* (pl. same) a member of a group of people in Ethiopia holding the Jewish faith. After much persecution they were airlifted to Israel in 1984–5. [Amharic, = exile, immigrant]

falcate /ˈfælkeɪt/ *adj. Anat.* curved like a sickle. [L *falcatus* f. *falx falcis* sickle]

falchion /ˈfɔːltʃ(ə)n/ *n. hist.* a broad curved sword with a convex edge. [ME *fauchoun* f. OF *fauchon* ult. f. L *falx falcis* sickle]

falciform /ˈfælsɪˌfɔːm/ *adj. Anat.* curved like a sickle. [L *falx falcis* sickle]

falcon /ˈfɔːlkən, ˈfɒlkən/ *n.* **1** any diurnal bird of prey of the family Falconidae, having long pointed wings, and sometimes trained to hunt small game for sport. **2** (in falconry) a female falcon (cf. TERCEL). [ME f. OF *faucon* f. LL *falco -onis*, perh. f. L *falx* scythe or f. Gmc]

falconer /ˈfɔːlkənə(r), ˈfɒl-/ *n.* **1** a keeper and trainer of hawks. **2** a person who hunts with hawks. [ME f. AF *fauconer*, OF *fauconier* (as FALCON)]

falconet /ˈfɔːlkənɪt, ˈfɒl-/ *n.* **1** *hist.* a light cannon. **2** *Zool.* a small falcon. [sense 1 f. It. *falconetto* dimin. of *falcone* FALCON: sense 2 f. FALCON + -ET¹]

falconry /ˈfɔːlkənrɪ, ˈfɒl-/ *n.* the breeding and training of hawks; the sport of hawking. [F *fauconnerie* (as FALCON)]

falderal /ˈfældəˌræl/ *n.* (also **folderol** /ˈfɒldəˌrɒl/) **1** a gewgaw or trifle. **2** a nonsensical refrain in a song. [perh. f. *falbala* trimming on a dress]

Faldo /ˈfældəʊ/, Nicholas Alexander ('Nick') (1957–   ), British golfer, who won many amateur and (from 1976) professional tournaments, including the British Open championship in 1987 and 1990 and the US Masters Tournament in 1990.

faldstool /ˈfɔːldstuːl/ *n.* **1** a bishop's backless folding chair. **2** *Brit.* a small movable desk for kneeling at prayer. [OE *fældestōl* f. med.L *faldistolium* f. WG (as FOLD¹, STOOL)]

Falkland Islands /ˈfɔːlklənd, ˈfɒl-/ (also **Falklands**) a group of two main islands and nearly 100 smaller ones in the South Atlantic, about 500 km (300 miles) east of the Magellan Strait. The climate is bleak, with long winters and much snow; the moors are the home of many species of bird. Most of the islanders are occupied in sheep-farming. First visited by European explorers in the late 16th c., the Falklands were successively colonized by the French and Spanish before final occupation by Britain in 1832–3, following the expulsion of an Argentinian garrison. Argentina has since refused to recognize British sovereignty and has continued to refer to the islands by their old Spanish name—the Malvinas. In 1982 an Argentinian invasion led to a two-month war ending in a successful British reoccupation.

fall /fɔːl/ v. & n. —v.intr. (past **fell** /fel/; past part. **fallen** /ˈfɔːlən/) **1 a** go or come down freely; descend rapidly from a higher to a lower level (*fell from the top floor; rain was falling*). **b** drop or be dropped (*supplies fell by parachute; the curtain fell*). **2 a** (often foll. by *over*) cease to stand; come suddenly to the ground from loss of balance etc. **b** collapse forwards or downwards esp. of one's own volition (*fell into my arms; fell over the chair*). **3** become detached and descend or disappear. **4** take a downward direction: **a** (of hair, clothing, etc.) hang down. **b** (of ground etc.) slope. **c** (foll. by *into*) (of a river etc.) discharge into. **5 a** find a lower level; sink lower. **b** subside, abate. **6** (of a barometer, thermometer, etc.) show a lower reading. **7** occur; become apparent or present (*darkness fell*). **8** decline, diminish (*demand is falling; standards have fallen*). **9 a** (of the face) show dismay or disappointment. **b** (of the eyes or a glance) look downwards. **10 a** lose power or status (*the government will fall*). **b** lose esteem, moral integrity, etc. **11** commit sin; yield to temptation. **12** take or have a particular direction or place (*his eye fell on me; the accent falls on the first syllable*). **13 a** find a place; be naturally divisible (*the subject falls into three parts*). **b** (foll. by *under, within*) be classed among. **14** occur at a specified time (*Easter falls early this year*). **15** come by chance or duty (*it fell to me to answer*). **16 a** pass into a specified condition (*fall into decay; fell ill*). **b** become (*fall asleep*). **17 a** (of a position etc.) be overthrown or captured; succumb to attack. **b** be defeated; fail. **18** die (*fall in battle*). **19** (foll. by *on, upon*) **a** attack. **b** meet with. **c** embrace or embark on avidly. **20** (foll. by *to* + verbal noun) begin (*fell to wondering*). **21** (foll. by *to*) lapse, revert (*revenues fall to the Crown*). —n. **1** the act or an instance of falling; a sudden rapid descent. **2** that which falls or has fallen, e.g. snow, rocks, etc. **3** the recorded amount of rainfall etc. **4** a decline or diminution. **5** overthrow, downfall (*the fall of Rome*). **6 a** succumbing to temptation. **b** (**the Fall**) the first act of disobedience by Adam and Eve (Gen. 2 ff.) whereby mankind lost its primal innocence and happiness and entered upon an actual condition of sin and toil. This belief was, from the first, part of the background against which the Christian doctrine of redemption was expounded. **7** (of material, land, light, etc.) a downward direction; a slope. **8** (also **Fall**) US autumn. **9** (esp. in *pl.*) a waterfall, cataract, or cascade. **10** *Mus.* a cadence. **11 a** a wrestling-bout; a throw in wrestling which keeps the opponent on the ground for a specified time. **b** a controlled act of falling, esp. as a stunt or in judo etc. **12 a** the birth of young of certain animals. **b** the number of young born. **13** a rope of a hoisting-tackle. □ **fall about** *colloq.* be helpless, esp. with laughter. **fall apart** (or **to pieces**) **1** break into pieces. **2** (of a situation etc.) disintegrate; be reduced to chaos. **3** lose one's capacity to cope. **fall away 1** (of a surface) incline abruptly. **2** become few or thin; gradually vanish. **3** desert, revolt; abandon one's principles. **fall back** retreat. **fall-back** (*attrib.*) emergency, esp. (of wages) the minimum paid when no work is available. **fall back on** have recourse to in difficulty. **fall behind 1** be outstripped by one's competitors etc.; lag. **2** be in arrears. **fall down** (often foll. by *on*) *colloq.* fail; perform poorly; fail to deliver (payment etc.). **fall for** *colloq.* **1** be captivated or deceived by. **2** admire; yield to the charms or merits of. **fall foul of** come into conflict with; quarrel with. **fall guy** *sl.* **1** an easy victim. **2** a scapegoat. **fall in 1 a** take one's place in military formation. **b** (as *int.*) the order to do this. **2** collapse inwards. **falling star** a meteor. **fall in love** see LOVE. **fall into line 1** take one's place in the ranks. **2** conform or collaborate with others. **fall into place** begin to make sense or cohere. **fall in with 1** meet by chance. **2** agree with; accede to; humour. **3** coincide with. **fall off 1** (of demand etc.) decrease, deteriorate. **2** withdraw. **fall-off** n. a decrease, deterioration, withdrawal, etc. **fall out 1** quarrel. **2** (of the hair, teeth, etc.) become detached. **3** *Mil.* come out of formation. **4** result; come to pass; occur. **fall out of** gradually discontinue (a habit etc.). **fall over oneself** *colloq.* **1** be eager or competitive. **2** be awkward, stumble through haste, confusion, etc. **fall-pipe** a downpipe. **fall short 1** be or become deficient or inadequate. **2** (of a missile etc.) not reach its target. **fall short of** fail to reach or obtain. **fall through** fail; come to nothing;

miscarry. **fall to** begin an activity, e.g. eating or working. [OE *fallan, feallan* f. Gmc]

Falla /ˈfæljə/, Manuel de (1876–1946), Spanish composer and pianist. He received his musical education in his home town, Cádiz, and in Madrid, and in 1907 went to Paris, remaining until the outbreak of the First World War and becoming friends with Ravel and Debussy. In 1939, after the Spanish Civil War, during which he proclaimed himself a pacifist, he settled in Argentina. He was one of the most important representatives of Spanish nationalism abroad and his works remain popular, especially the ballet *The Three-cornered Hat* (produced by Diaghilev in 1919 with designs by Picasso).

fallacy /ˈfæləsɪ/ n. (pl. **-ies**) **1** a mistaken belief, esp. based on unsound argument. **2** faulty reasoning; misleading or unsound argument. **3** *Logic* a flaw that vitiates an argument. □□ **fallacious** /fəˈleɪʃəs/ adj. **fallaciously** /fəˈleɪʃəslɪ/ adv. **fallaciousness** /fəˈleɪʃəsnɪs/ n. [L *fallacia* f. *fallax -acis* deceiving f. *fallere* deceive]

fallen past part. of FALL v. —adj. **1** (*attrib.*) having lost one's honour or reputation. **2** killed in war. □□ **fallenness** n.

fallfish /ˈfɔːlfɪʃ/ n. US a N. American freshwater fish like the chub.

fallible /ˈfæltb(ə)l/ adj. **1** capable of making mistakes. **2** liable to be erroneous. □□ **fallibility** /-ˈbɪlɪtɪ/ n. **fallibly** adv. [med.L *fallibilis* f. L *fallere* deceive]

Fallopian tube /fəˈləʊpɪən/ n. *Anat.* either of two tubes in female mammals along which ova travel from the ovaries to the uterus. [*Fallopius*, Latinized name of G. *Fallopio*, It. anatomist d. 1562]

fallout /ˈfɔːlaʊt/ n. **1** radioactive debris caused by a nuclear explosion or accident. **2** the adverse side-effects of a situation etc.

fallow[1] /ˈfæləʊ/ adj., n., & v. —adj. **1 a** (of land) ploughed and harrowed but left unsown for a year. **b** uncultivated. **2** (of an idea etc.) potentially useful but not yet in use. **3** inactive. **4** (of a sow) not pregnant. —n. fallow or uncultivated land. —v.tr. break up (land) for sowing or to destroy weeds. □□ **fallowness** n. [ME f. OE *fealh* (n.), *fealgian* (v.)]

fallow[2] /ˈfæləʊ/ adj. of a pale brownish or reddish yellow. □ **fallow deer** any small deer of the genus *Dama*, having a white-spotted reddish-brown coat in the summer. [OE *falu, fealu* f. Gmc]

false /fɒls, fɔːls/ adj. & adv. —adj. **1** not according with fact; wrong, incorrect (*a false idea*). **2 a** spurious, sham, artificial (*false gods; false teeth; false modesty*). **b** acting as such; appearing to be such, esp. deceptively (*a false lining*). **3** illusory; not actually so (*a false economy*). **4** improperly so called (*false acacia*). **5** deceptive. **6** (foll. by *to*) deceitful, treacherous, or unfaithful. **7** illegal (*false imprisonment*). —adv. in a false manner (esp. *play false*). □ **false acacia** see ACACIA. **false alarm** an alarm given needlessly. **false bedding** *Geol.* = CROSS-BEDDING. **false colours** deceitful pretence. **false dawn** a transient light in the east before dawn. **false gharial** see GHARIAL. **false pretences** misrepresentations made with intent to deceive (esp. *under false pretences*). **false rib** = *floating rib*. **false start 1** an invalid or disallowed start in a race. **2** an unsuccessful attempt to begin something. **false step** a slip; a mistake. **false topaz** = CITRINE. □□ **falsely** adv. **falseness** n. **falsity** n. (pl. **-ies**). [OE *fals* and OF *fals, faus* f. L *falsus* past part. of *fallere* deceive]

falsehood /ˈfɒlshʊd, ˈfɔːls-/ n. **1** the state of being false, esp. untrue. **2** a false or untrue thing. **3 a** the act of lying. **b** a lie or lies.

falsetto /fɒlˈsetəʊ, fɔːl-/ n. (pl. **-os**) **1** a method of voice production used by male singers, esp. tenors, to sing notes higher than their normal range. **2** a singer using this method. [It., dimin. of *falso* FALSE]

falsework /ˈfɒlswɜːk/ n. a temporary framework or support used during building to form arches etc.

falsies /ˈfɒlsɪz, ˈfɔːls-/ n.pl. *colloq.* padded material to increase the apparent size of the breasts.

falsify /ˈfɒlsɪfaɪ, ˈfɔːls-/ v.tr. (**-ies**, **-ied**) **1** fraudulently alter or make false (a document, evidence, etc.). **2** misrepresent. **3** make wrong; pervert. **4** show to be false. **5** disappoint (a hope, fear, etc.). □□ **falsifiable** *adj.* **falsifiability** /-,faɪə'bɪlɪtɪ/ *n.* **falsification** /-fɪ'keɪʃ(ə)n/ *n.* [ME f. F *falsifier* or med.L *falsificare* f. L *falsificus* making false f. *falsus* false]

Falster /'fɑːlstə(r)/ a Danish island in the Baltic Sea, south of Zealand. Its southern tip is the most southerly point of Denmark.

falter /'fɒltə(r), 'fɔːl-/ *v.* **1** *intr.* stumble, stagger; go unsteadily. **2** *intr.* waver; lose courage. **3** *tr.* & *intr.* stammer; speak hesitatingly. □□ **falterer** *n.* **falteringly** *adv.* [ME: orig. uncert.]

fame /feɪm/ *n.* **1** renown; the state of being famous. **2** reputation. **3** *archaic* public report; rumour. □ **house of ill fame** *archaic* a brothel. **ill fame** disrepute. [ME f. OF f. L *fama*]

famed /feɪmd/ *adj.* **1** (foll. by *for*) famous; much spoken of (*famed for its good food*). **2** *archaic* currently reported.

familial /fə'mɪlɪəl/ *adj.* of, occurring in, or characteristic of a family or its members. [F f. L *familia* FAMILY]

familiar /fə'mɪlɪə(r)/ *adj.* & *n.* —*adj.* **1 a** (often foll. by *to*) well known; no longer novel. **b** common, usual; often encountered or experienced. **2** (foll. by *with*) knowing a thing well or in detail (*am familiar with all the problems*). **3** (often foll. by *with*) **a** well acquainted (with a person); in close friendship; intimate. **b** sexually intimate. **4** excessively informal; impertinent. **5** unceremonious, informal. —*n.* **1** a close friend or associate. **2** *RC Ch.* a person rendering certain services in a pope's or bishop's household. **3** (in full **familiar spirit**) a demon supposedly attending and obeying a witch etc. □□ **familiarly** *adv.* [ME f. OF *familier* f. L *familiaris* (as FAMILY)]

familiarity /fə,mɪlɪ'ærɪtɪ/ *n.* (*pl.* -**ies**) **1** the state of being well known (*the familiarity of the scene*). **2** (foll. by *with*) close acquaintance. **3** a close relationship. **4 a** sexual intimacy. **b** (in *pl.*) acts of physical intimacy. **5** familiar or informal behaviour, esp. excessively so. [ME f. OF *familiarité* f. L *familiaritas -tatis* (as FAMILIAR)]

familiarize /fə'mɪlɪə,raɪz/ *v.tr.* (also -**ise**) **1** (foll. by *with*) make (a person) conversant or well acquainted. **2** make (a thing) well known. □□ **familiarization** /-'zeɪʃ(ə)n/ *n.* [F *familiariser* f. *familiaire* (as FAMILIAR)]

famille /fæ'miːj/ *n.* a Chinese enamelled porcelain with a predominant colour: (*famille jaune* /ʒəʊn/) yellow, (*famille noire* /nwɑː(r)/) black, (*famille rose* /rəʊz/) red, (*famille verte* /veət/) green. [F, = family]

family /'fæmɪlɪ, 'fæmlɪ/ *n.* (*pl.* -**ies**) **1** a set of parents and children, or of relations, living together or not. **2 a** the members of a household, esp. parents and their children. **b** a person's children. **c** (*attrib.*) serving the needs of families (*family butcher*). **3 a** all the descendants of a common ancestor. **b** a race or group of peoples from a common stock. **4** all the languages ultimately derived from a particular early language, regarded as a group. **5** a brotherhood of persons or nations united by political or religious ties. **6** a group of objects distinguished by common features. **7** *Math.* a group of curves etc. obtained by varying one quantity. **8** *Biol.* a group of related genera of organisms within an order in taxonomic classification. □ **family allowance** *Brit.* a former name for *child benefit*. **family credit** (or **income supplement**) (in the UK) a regular payment by the State to a family with an income below a certain level. **Family Division** (in the UK) a division of the High Court dealing with adoption, divorce, etc. **family man** a man having a wife and children, esp. one fond of family life. **family name** a surname. **family planning** birth control. **family tree** a chart showing relationships and lines of descent. **in the family way** *colloq.* pregnant. [ME f. L *familia* household f. *famulus* servant]

famine /'fæmɪn/ *n.* **1 a** extreme scarcity of food. **b** a shortage of something specified (*water famine*). **2** *archaic* hunger, starvation. [ME f. OF f. *faim* f. L *fames* hunger]

famish /'fæmɪʃ/ *v.tr.* & *intr.* (usu. in *passive*) **1** reduce or be reduced to extreme hunger. **2** *colloq.* feel very hungry. [ME f. obs. *fame* f. OF *afamer* ult. f. L *fames* hunger]

famous /'feɪməs/ *adj.* **1** (often foll. by *for*) celebrated; well known. **2** *colloq.* excellent. □□ **famousness** *n.* [ME f. AF, OF *fameus* f. L *famosus* f. *fama* fame]

famously /'feɪməslɪ/ *adv.* **1** *colloq.* excellently (*got on famously*). **2** notably.

famulus /'fæmjʊləs/ *n.* (*pl.* **famuli** /-,laɪ/) *hist.* an attendant on a magician or scholar. [L, = servant]

fan¹ /fæn/ *n.* & *v.* —*n.* **1** an apparatus, usu. with rotating blades, giving a current of air for ventilation etc. **2** a device, usu. folding and forming a semicircle when spread out, for agitating the air to cool oneself. **3** anything spread out like a fan, e.g. a bird's tail or kind of ornamental vaulting (*fan tracery*). **4** a device for winnowing grain. **5** a fan-shaped deposit of alluvium esp. where a stream begins to descend a gentler slope. **6** a small sail for keeping the head of a windmill towards the wind. —*v.* (**fanned**, **fanning**) **1** *tr.* **a** blow a current of air on, with or as with a fan. **b** agitate (the air) with a fan. **2** *tr.* (of a breeze) blow gently on; cool. **3** *tr.* **a** winnow (grain). **b** winnow away (chaff). **4** *tr.* sweep away by or as by the wind from a fan. **5** *intr.* & *tr.* (usu. foll. by *out*) spread out in the shape of a fan. □ **fan belt** a belt that drives a fan to cool the radiator in a motor vehicle. **fan dance** a dance in which the dancer is (apparently) naked and partly concealed by fans. **fan heater** an electric heater in which a fan drives air over an element. **fan-jet** = TURBOFAN. **fan palm** a palm-tree with fan-shaped leaves. □□ **fanlike** *adj.* **fanner** *n.* [OE *fann* (in sense 4 of *n.*) f. L *vannus* winnowing-fan]

fan² /fæn/ *n.* a devotee of a particular activity, performer, etc. (*film fan; football fan*). □ **fan club** an organized group of devotees. **fan mail** letters from fans. □□ **fandom** *n.* [abbr. of FANATIC]

fanatic /fə'nætɪk/ *n.* & *adj.* —*n.* a person filled with excessive and often misguided enthusiasm for something. —*adj.* excessively enthusiastic. □□ **fanatical** *adj.* **fanatically** *adv.* **fanaticism** /-tɪ,sɪz(ə)m/ *n.* **fanaticize** /-tɪ,saɪz/ *v.intr.* & *tr.* (also -**ise**). [F *fanatique* or L *fanaticus* f. *fanum* temple (orig. in religious sense)]

fancier /'fænsɪə(r)/ *n.* a connoisseur or follower of some activity or thing (*dog-fancier*).

fanciful /'fænsɪfʊl/ *adj.* **1** existing only in the imagination or fancy. **2** indulging in fancies; whimsical, capricious. **3** fantastically designed, ornamented, etc.; odd-looking. □□ **fancifully** *adv.* **fancifulness** *n.*

fancy /'fænsɪ/ *n.*, *adj.*, & *v.* —*n.* (*pl.* -**ies**) **1** an individual taste or inclination (*take a fancy to*). **2** a caprice or whim. **3** a thing favoured, e.g. a horse to win a race. **4** an arbitrary supposition. **5 a** the faculty of using imagination or of inventing imagery. **b** a mental image. **6** delusion; unfounded belief. **7** (prec. by *the*) those who have a certain hobby; fanciers, esp. patrons of boxing. —*adj.* (usu. *attrib.*) (**fancier**, **fanciest**) **1** ornamental; not plain. **2** capricious, whimsical, extravagant (*at a fancy price*). **3** based on imagination, not fact. **4** *US* (of foods etc.) above average quality. **5** (of flowers etc.) particoloured. **6** (of an animal) bred for particular points of beauty etc. —*v.tr.* (-**ies**, -**ied**) **1** (foll. by *that* + clause) be inclined to suppose; rather think. **2** *Brit. colloq.* feel a desire for (*do you fancy a drink?*). **3** *Brit. colloq.* find sexually attractive. **4** *colloq.* have an unduly high opinion of (oneself, one's ability, etc.). **5** (in *imper.*) an exclamation of surprise (*fancy their doing that!*). **6** picture to oneself; conceive, imagine. □ **catch** (or **take**) **the fancy of** please; appeal to. **fancy dress** fanciful costume, esp. for masquerading as a different person or as an animal etc. at a party. **fancy-free** without (esp. emotional) commitments. **fancy goods** ornamental novelties etc. **fancy man** *sl. derog.* **1** a woman's lover. **2** a pimp. **fancy woman** *sl. derog.* a mistress. **fancy-work** ornamental sewing etc. □□ **fanciable** *adj.* (in sense 3 of *v.*). **fancily** *adv.* **fanciness** *n.* [contr. of FANTASY]

fandangle /fæn'dæŋg(ə)l/ *n.* **1** a fantastic ornament. **2** nonsense, tomfoolery. [perh. f. FANDANGO after *newfangle*]

fandango /fæn'dæŋgəʊ/ *n.* (*pl.* -**oes** or -**os**) **1 a** a lively Spanish dance for two. **b** the music for this. **2** nonsense, tomfoolery. [Sp.: orig. unkn.]

fane /feɪn/ *n.* *poet.* = TEMPLE¹. [ME f. L *fanum*]

fanfare /'fænfeə(r)/ *n.* **1** a short showy or ceremonious sounding of trumpets, bugles, etc. **2** an elaborate welcome. [F, imit.]

fanfaronade /,fænfærə'neɪd/ *n.* **1** arrogant talk; brag. **2** a fanfare. [F *fanfaronnade* f. *fanfaron* braggart (as FANFARE)]

fang /fæŋ/ n. **1** a canine tooth, esp. of a dog or wolf. **2** the tooth of a venomous snake, by which poison is injected. **3** the root of a tooth or its prong. **4** Brit. colloq. a person's tooth. □□ **fanged** adj. (also in comb.). **fangless** adj. [OE f. ON fang f. a Gmc root = to catch]

Fangio /ˈfændʒɪˌəʊ/, Juan Manuel (1911–), Argentine-born racing-driver who won the world championship in 1951 and 1954–7, as well as a number of other titles, before retiring from racing in 1958.

fanlight /ˈfænlaɪt/ n. a small, orig. semicircular window over a door or another window.

fanny /ˈfænɪ/ n. (pl. **-ies**) **1** Brit. coarse sl. the female genitals. **2** US sl. the buttocks. ¶ Usually considered a taboo word in Brit. use. [20th c.: orig. unkn.]

Fanny Adams /ˌfænɪ ˈædəmz/ n. Brit. sl. **1** (also **sweet Fanny Adams**) nothing at all. ¶ Sometimes understood as a euphemism for fuck all. **2** Naut. **a** tinned meat. **b** stew. [name of a murder victim c.1870]

fantail /ˈfænteɪl/ n. **1** a pigeon with a broad-shaped tail. **2** any flycatcher of the genus Rhipidura, with a fan-shaped tail. **3** a fan-shaped tail or end. **4** the fan of a windmill. **5** the projecting part of a boat's stern. □□ **fantailed** adj.

fan-tan /ˈfæntæn/ n. **1** a Chinese gambling game in which players try to guess the remainder after the banker has divided a number of hidden objects into four groups. **2** a card-game in which players build on sequences of sevens. [Chin., = repeated divisions]

fantasia /fænˈteɪzɪə, ˌfæntəˈzɪə/ n. a musical or other composition free in form and often in improvisatory style, or which is based on several familiar tunes. [It., = FANTASY]

fantasize /ˈfæntəsaɪz/ v. (also **phantasize, -ise**) **1** intr. have a fantasy or fanciful vision. **2** tr. imagine; create a fantasy about. □□ **fantasist** n.

fantast /ˈfæntæst/ n. (also **phantast**) a visionary; a dreamer. [med.L f. Gk phantastēs boaster f. phantazomai make a show f. phainō show]

fantastic /fænˈtæstɪk/ adj. (also **fantastical**) **1** colloq. excellent, extraordinary. **2** extravagantly fanciful; capricious, eccentric. **3** grotesque or quaint in design etc. □□ **fantasticality** /-ˈkælɪtɪ/ n. **fantastically** adv. [ME f. OF fantastique f. med.L fantasticus f. LL phantasticus f. Gk phantastikos (as FANTAST)]

fantasticate /fænˈtæstɪˌkeɪt/ v.tr. make fantastic. □□ **fantastication** /-ˈkeɪʃ(ə)n/ n.

fantasy /ˈfæntəsɪ, -zɪ/ n. & v. (also **phantasy**) —n. (pl. **-ies**) **1** the faculty of inventing images, esp. extravagant or visionary ones. **2** a fanciful mental image; a day-dream. **3** a whimsical speculation. **4** a fantastic invention or composition; a fantasia. —v.tr. (**-ies, -ied**) imagine in a visionary manner. [ME f. OF fantasie f. L phantasia appearance f. Gk (as FANTAST)]

Fanti /ˈfæntɪ/ n. & adj. (also **Fante** /ˈfæntɪ/) —n. (pl. same or **Fantis**) **1** a member of a Black tribe native to Ghana. **2** the language of this tribe. —adj. of the Fanti or their language. [native name]

FAO abbr. Food and Agriculture Organization (of the United Nations).

far /fɑː(r)/ adv. & adj. (**further, furthest** or **farther, farthest**) —adv. **1** at or to or by a great distance (far away; far off; far out). **2** a long way (off) in space or time (are you travelling far?; we talked far into the night). **3** to a great extent or degree; by much (far better; far the best; far too early). —adj. **1** situated at or extending over a great distance in space or time; remote (a far cry; a far country). **2** more distant (the far end of the hall). □ **as far as 1** to the distance of (a place). **2** to the extent that (travel as far as you like). **by far** by a great amount. **far and away** by a very large amount. **far and near** everywhere. **far and wide** over a large area. **far-away 1** remote; long-past. **2** (of a look) dreamy. **3** (of a voice) sounding as if from a distance. **far be it from me** (foll. by to + infin.) I am reluctant to (esp. express criticism etc.). **far cry** a long way. the **Far East** China, Japan, and other countries of East and SE Asia. **Far Eastern** of or in the Far East. **far-fetched** (of an explanation etc.) strained, unconvincing. **far-flung** extending far; widely distributed. **far from** very

different from being; tending to the opposite of (the problem is far from being solved). **far gone 1** advanced in time. **2** colloq. in an advanced state of illness, drunkenness, etc. **far-off** remote. **far-out 1** distant. **2** avant-garde, unconventional, excellent. **far-reaching 1** widely applicable. **2** having important consequences or implications. **far-seeing** shrewd in judgement; prescient. **Far West** the regions of North America in the Rocky Mountains and along the Pacific coast; hist. the area west of the earliest European settlements (now called the Middle West). **go far 1** achieve much. **2** contribute greatly. **3** be adequate. **go too far** go beyond the limits of what is reasonable, polite, etc. **how far** to what extent. **so far 1** to such an extent or distance; to this point. **2** until now. **so** (or **in so**) **far as** (or **that**) to the extent that. **so far so good** progress has been satisfactory up to now. □□ **farness** n. [OE feorr]

farad /ˈfærəd/ n. Electr. the SI unit of capacitance, such that one coulomb of charge causes a potential difference of one volt. ¶ Abbr.: **F**. [shortening of FARADAY]

faradaic /ˌfærəˈdeɪɪk/ adj. (also **faradic** /fəˈrædɪk/) Electr. inductive, induced. [see FARADAY]

Faraday /ˈfærəˌdeɪ/, Michael (1791–1867), English physicist and chemist, discoverer of electromagnetic induction and the concept of the classical field theory. The son of a blacksmith, he came from a poor but closely-knit family and was largely self-educated. At the age of 14 he was apprenticed to a London bookbinder and bookseller, but in 1812 he was appointed by Sir Humphry Davy as his laboratory assistant at the Royal Institution. Initially, he concentrated on analytical chemistry, liquefied chlorine in 1823, discovered benzene in 1825, and studied the composition of optical glass. However, his most important work was to be in electromagnetism, a study begun in 1821 when he demonstrated electromagnetic rotation (the rotation of a wire carrying an electric current round a permanent magnet). In 1831 he discovered electromagnetic induction, the condition under which a permanent magnet could generate electricity, and the key to the development of the electric dynamo and motor. Similar investigations were performed in America by Joseph Henry (1797–1878). Central to these discoveries was Faraday's concept of magnetic lines of force, the basis of the classical field theory of electromagnetic behaviour which Clerk Maxwell was to express in mathematical form. He also discovered the two laws of electrolysis named after him, which established the relationship between electric force and matter (chemical affinity) at the molecular level, and demonstrated the connection between magnetism and light by rotating the plane of polarization of polarized light by means of a powerful electromagnet (the Faraday effect). He retired in 1862 to a house at Hampton Court provided by Queen Victoria.

faraday /ˈfærəˌdeɪ/ n. (also **Faraday's constant**) Electr. the quantity of electric charge carried by one mole of electrons . ¶ Abbr.: **F**. □ **Faraday cage** Electr. an earthed metal screen used for excluding electrostatic influences. **Faraday effect** Physics the rotation of the plane of polarization of electromagnetic waves in certain substances in a magnetic field. [M. FARADAY]

farandole /ˌfærənˈdɒl/ n. **1** a lively Provençal dance. **2** the music for this. [F f. mod. Prov. farandoulo]

farce /fɑːs/ n. **1 a** a coarsely comic dramatic work based on ludicrously improbable events. **b** this branch of drama. **2** absurdly futile proceedings; pretence, mockery. [F, orig. = stuffing, f. OF farsir f. L farcire to stuff, used metaph. of interludes etc.]

farceur /fɑːˈsɜː(r)/ n. **1** a joker or wag. **2** an actor or writer of farces. [F f. farcer act farces]

farcical /ˈfɑːsɪk(ə)l/ adj. **1** extremely ludicrous or futile. **2** of or like farce. □□ **farcicality** /-ˈkælɪtɪ/ n. **farcically** adv.

farcy /ˈfɑːsɪ/ n. glanders with inflammation of the lymph vessels. □ **farcy bud** (or **button**) a small lymphatic tumour as a result of farcy. [ME f. earlier & OF farcin f. LL farciminum f. farcire to stuff]

farded /ˈfɑːdɪd/ adj. archaic (of a face etc.) painted with cosmetics. [past part. of obs. fard f. OF farder]

fare /feə(r)/ n. & v. —n. **1 a** the price a passenger has to pay to be conveyed by bus, train, etc. **b** a passenger paying to travel in a public vehicle. **2** a range of food provided by a restaurant etc. —*v.intr. literary* **1** progress; get on (*how did you fare?*). **2** happen; turn out. **3** journey, go, travel. □ **fare-stage** *Brit.* **1** a section of a bus etc. route for which a fixed fare is charged. **2** a stop marking this. [OE *fær, faru* journeying, *faran* (v.), f. Gmc]

Farewell /feə'wel/, **Cape 1** (Danish *Kap Farvel* /kæp fɑː'vel/ the southernmost point of Greenland. **2** the northernmost point of South Island, New Zealand.

farewell /feə'wel/ *int.* & *n.* —*int.* goodbye, adieu. —*n.* **1** leave-taking, departure (also *attrib.*: *a farewell kiss*). **2** parting good wishes. [ME f. imper. of FARE + WELL[1]]

Fargo, William, see WELLS, FARGO & Co.

farina /fə'raɪnə, -'riːnə/ *n.* **1** the flour or meal of cereal, nuts, or starchy roots. **2** a powdery substance. **3** *Brit.* starch. □□ **farinaceous** /,færɪ'neɪʃəs/ *adj.* [L f. *far* corn]

farl /fɑːl/ *n. Sc.* a thin cake, orig. quadrant-shaped, of oatmeal or flour. [obs. *fardel* quarter (as FOURTH, DEAL[1])]

farm /fɑːm/ *n.* & *v.* —*n.* **1** an area of land and its buildings used under one management for growing crops, rearing animals, etc. **2** a place or establishment for breeding a particular type of animal, growing fruit, etc. (*trout-farm*; *mink-farm*). **3** = FARMHOUSE. **4** a place for the storage of oil or oil products. **5** = *sewage farm*. —*v.* **1 a** *tr.* use (land) for growing crops, rearing animals, etc. **b** *intr.* be a farmer; work on a farm. **2** *tr.* breed (fish etc.) commercially. **3** *tr.* (often foll. by *out*) **a** delegate or subcontract (work) to others. **b** contract (the collection of taxes) to another for a fee. **c** arrange for (a person, esp. a child) to be looked after by another, with payment. **4** *tr.* let the labour of (a person) for hire. **5** *tr.* contract to maintain and care for (a person, esp. a child) for a fixed sum. □ **farm-hand** a worker on a farm. □□ **farmable** *adj.* **farming** *n.* [ME f. OF *ferme* f. med.L *firma* fixed payment f. L *firmus* FIRM[1]: orig. applied only to leased land]

farmer /'fɑːmə(r)/ *n.* **1** a person who cultivates a farm. **2** a person to whom the collection of taxes is contracted for a fee. **3** a person who looks after children for payment. [ME f. AF *fermer*, OF *fermier* f. med.L *firmarius, firmator* f. *firma* FIRM[2]]

farmhouse /'fɑːmhaʊs/ *n.* a dwelling-place (esp. the main one) attached to a farm.

farmstead /'fɑːmsted/ *n.* a farm and its buildings regarded as a unit.

farmyard /'fɑːmjɑːd/ *n.* a yard or enclosure attached to a farmhouse.

Farnese /fɑː'neɪseɪ/ the name of an Italian ducal family, rulers of Parma from 1545 to 1731, who were notable humanists and patrons of the arts. They rose to importance when Cardinal Alessandro Farnese became Pope Paul III (see entry) in 1534. The family also had connections with Spain. Alessandro Farnese (1545–92), regarded as the greatest military expert of his time, served Philip II of Spain, was appointed governor-general of The Netherlands on the death of Don John of Austria (1578), and by the capture of Antwerp in 1585 secured the southern Netherlands for Spain.

Faro /'fɑːru:/ a seaport of southern Portugal, capital of the Algarve region; pop. (1981) 28,200.

faro /'feərəʊ/ *n.* a gambling card-game in which bets are placed on the order of appearance of the cards. [F *pharaon* PHARAOH (said to have been the name of the king of hearts)]

Faroese var. of FAEROESE.

farouche /fə'ruːʃ/ *adj.* sullen, shy. [F f. OF *faroche, forache* f. med.L *forasticus* f. L *foras* out of doors]

Farouk /fæ'ruːk/ (1920–65), king of Egypt 1936–52, an autocratic ruler. His inability to prevent British intervention in Egyptian affairs, his defeat in the Arab-Israeli conflict (1948), and the general corruption of his reign led to a military coup in 1952, headed by Nasser. Farouk was forced to abdicate in favour of his infant son, Faud, who was deposed in 1953.

Farquhar /'fɑːkə(r)/, George (1678–1707), Irish writer of comedies, of which the best are *The Recruiting Officer* (1706) and *The Beaux' Stratagem* (1707). The atmosphere of realism and genial merriment in his plays contrasts markedly with the artificial comedy of the period.

farrago /fə'rɑːgəʊ/ *n.* (*pl.* **-os** or *US* **-oes**) a medley or hotchpotch. □□ **farraginous** /-'rɑːdʒɪnəs/ *adj.* [L *farrago farraginis* mixed fodder f. *far* corn]

Farrell[1] /'fær(ə)l/, James Gordon (1935–79), English novelist. His first substantial novel, *Troubles* (1970), is set in Ireland against a background of Sinn Fein violence; *The Siege of Krishnapur* (1973) deals with events of the Indian Mutiny; and *The Singapore Grip* (1978) describes the fall of Singapore to the Japanese. These works reflect a sense of the end of the Empire and the stubborn refusal of the characters to recognize the course of history. He was accidentally drowned and left unfinished *The Hill Station* (1981).

Farrell[2] /'fær(ə)l/, James Thomas (1904–79), American novelist, best known in Britain for his trilogy (1932–5) about Studs Lonigan, a young Chicago Catholic of Irish descent.

farrier /'færɪə(r)/ *n. Brit.* **1** a smith who shoes horses. **2** a horse-doctor. □□ **farriery** *n.* [OF *ferrier* f. L *ferrarius* f. *ferrum* iron, horseshoe]

farrow /'færəʊ/ *n.* & *v.* —*n.* **1** a litter of pigs. **2** the birth of a litter. —*v.tr.* (also *absol.*) (of a sow) produce (pigs). [OE *fearh, færh* pig f. WG]

farruca /fə'ruːkə/ *n.* a type of flamenco dance. [Sp.]

Farsi /'fɑːsi:/ *n.* the modern Persian language. (See PERSIAN.) [Pers.: cf. PARSEE]

far-sighted /fɑː'saɪtɪd, 'fɑː-/ *adj.* **1** having foresight, prudent. **2** esp. *US* = LONG-SIGHTED. □□ **far-sightedly** *adv.* **far-sightedness** *n.*

fart /fɑːt/ *v.* & *n. coarse sl.* —*v.intr.* **1** emit wind from the anus. **2** (foll. by *about, around*) behave foolishly; waste time. —*n.* **1** an emission of wind from the anus. **2** an unpleasant person. ¶ Usually considered a taboo word. [OE (recorded in *feorting* verbal noun) f. Gmc]

farther var. of FURTHER (esp. with ref. to physical distance).

farthest var. of FURTHEST (esp. with ref. to physical distance).

farthing /'fɑːðɪŋ/ *n.* **1** (in the UK) a coin and monetary unit formerly worth a quarter of an old penny. ¶ Withdrawn in 1961. **2** the least possible amount (*it doesn't matter a farthing*). [OE *feorthing* f. *feortha* fourth]

farthingale /'fɑːðɪŋgeɪl/ *n. hist.* a hooped petticoat or a stiff curved roll to extend a woman's skirt. [earlier *vardingale, verd-* f. F *verdugale* f. Sp. *verdugado* f. *verdugo* rod]

fartlek /'fɑːtlek/ *n. Athletics* a method of training for middle- and long-distance running, mixing fast with slow work. [Sw. f. *fart* speed + *lek* play]

Farvel, Kap see Cape FAREWELL.

fasces /'fæsiːz/ *n.pl.* **1** *Rom.Hist.* a bundle of rods with a projecting axe-blade, carried by a lictor as a symbol of a magistrate's power. **2** *hist.* (in Fascist Italy) emblems of authority. [L, pl. of *fascis* bundle]

fascia /'feɪʃə/ *n.* (also **facia**) **1** *Brit.* **a** the instrument panel of a motor vehicle. **b** any similar panel or plate for operating machinery. **2** the upper part of a shop-front with the proprietor's name etc. **3** *Archit.* **a** a long flat surface between mouldings on the architrave in classical architecture. **b** a flat surface, usu. of wood, covering the ends of rafters. **4** a stripe or band. **5** /'fæʃə/ *Anat.* a thin sheath of fibrous tissue. □□ **fascial** *adj.* [L, = band, door-frame, etc.]

fasciate /'fæʃɪeɪt/ *adj.* (also **fasciated**) **1** *Bot.* (of contiguous parts) compressed or growing into one. **2** striped or banded. □□ **fasciation** /-'eɪʃ(ə)n/ *n.* [L *fasciatus* past part. of *fasciare* swathe (as FASCIA)]

fascicle /'fæsɪk(ə)l/ *n.* **1** (also **fascicule** /-,kjuːl/) a separately published instalment of a book, usu. not complete in itself. **2** a bunch or bundle. **3** (also **fasciculus** /fæ'sɪkjʊləs/) *Anat.* a bundle of fibres. □□ **fascicled** *adj.* **fascicular** /-'sɪkjʊlə(r)/ *adj.* **fasciculate** /-'sɪkjʊlət/ *adj.* **fasciculation** /-'leɪʃ(ə)n/ *n.* [L *fasciculus* bundle, dimin. of *fascis*: see FASCES]

fascinate /'fæsɪneɪt/ *v.tr.* **1** capture the interest of; attract irresistibly. **2** (esp. of a snake) paralyse (a victim) with fear. □□ **fascinated** *adj.* **fascinating** *adj.* **fascinatingly** *adv.*

fascination /-ˈneɪʃ(ə)n/ n. **fascinator** n. [L *fascinare* f. *fascinum* spell]

fascine /fæˈsiːn/ n. a long faggot used for engineering purposes and (esp. in war) for lining trenches, filling ditches, etc. [F f. L *fascina* f. *fascis* bundle: see FASCES]

Fascism /ˈfæʃɪz(ə)m/ n. **1** the totalitarian principles and organization of an extreme right-wing nationalist movement, originally as prevailing in Italy (1922–43) where it was founded by Mussolini. It spread to other European countries (Hitler developed a more racialist brand of authoritarianism in Germany) and to South America. It has remained a latent, if minimal, force in most countries of the western world. **2** (also **fascism**) **a** any similar nationalist and authoritarian movement. **b** *disp.* any system of extreme right-wing or authoritarian views. □□ **Fascist** n. & adj. (also **fascist**). **Fascistic** /-ˈʃɪstɪk/ adj. (also **fascistic**). [It. *fascismo* f. *fascio* political group f. L *fascis* bundle: see FASCES]

fashion /ˈfæʃ(ə)n/ n. & v. —n. **1** the current popular custom or style, esp. in dress or social conduct. **2** a manner or style of doing something (*in a peculiar fashion*). **3** (in *comb.*) in a specified manner (*walk crab-fashion*). **4** fashionable society (*a woman of fashion*). —v.tr. (often foll. by *into*) make into a particular or the required form. □ **after** (or **in**) **a fashion** as well as is practicable, though not satisfactorily. **in** (or **out of**) **fashion** fashionable (or not fashionable) at the time in question. □□ **fashioner** n. [ME f. AF *fasun*, OF *façon*, f. L *factio -onis* f. *facere fact-* do, make]

fashionable /ˈfæʃnəb(ə)l/ adj. **1** following, suited to, or influenced by the current fashion. **2** characteristic of or favoured by those who are leaders of social fashion. □□ **fashionableness** n. **fashionably** adv.

fast¹ /fɑːst/ adj. & adv. —adj. **1** rapid, quick-moving. **2** capable of high speed (*a fast car*). **3** enabling or causing or intended for high speed (*a fast road; fast lane*). **4** (of a clock etc.) showing a time ahead of the correct time. **5** (of a pitch or ground etc. in a sport) likely to make the ball bounce or run quickly. **6 a** (of a photographic film) needing only a short exposure. **b** (of a lens) having a large aperture. **7 a** firmly fixed or attached. **b** secure; firmly established (*a fast friendship*). **8** (of a colour) not fading in light or when washed. **9** (of a person) immoral, dissipated. —adv. **1** quickly; in quick succession. **2** firmly, fixedly, tightly, securely (*stand fast; eyes fast shut*). **3** soundly, completely (*fast asleep*). □ **fast breeder** (or **fast breeder reactor**) a reactor using fast neutrons to produce the same fissile material as it uses. **fast buck** see BUCK². **fast food** food that can be prepared and served quickly and easily, esp. in a snack bar or restaurant. **fast neutron** a neutron with high kinetic energy, esp. not slowed by a moderator etc. **fast reactor** a nuclear reactor using mainly fast neutrons. **fast-talk** US *colloq.* persuade by rapid or deceitful talk. **fast-wind** wind (magnetic tape) rapidly backwards or forwards. **fast worker** *colloq.* a person who achieves quick results, esp. in love affairs. **pull a fast one** *colloq.* try to deceive or gain an unfair advantage. [OE *fæst* f. Gmc]

fast² /fɑːst/ v. & n. —v.intr. abstain from all or some kinds of food or drink, esp. as a religious observance. —n. an act or period of fasting. □□ **faster** n. [ON *fasta* f. Gmc (as FAST¹)]

fastback /ˈfɑːstbæk/ n. **1** a motor car with the rear sloping continuously down to the bumper. **2** such a rear.

fasten /ˈfɑːs(ə)n/ v. **1** tr. make or become fixed or secure. **2** tr. (foll. by *in, up*) lock securely; shut in. **3** tr. **a** (foll. by *on, upon*) direct (a look, thoughts, etc.) fixedly or intently. **b** focus or direct the attention fixedly upon (*fastened him with her eyes*). **4** tr. (foll. by *on, upon*) fix (a designation or imputation etc.). **5** intr. (foll. by *on, upon*) **a** take hold of. **b** single out. □□ **fastener** n. [OE *fæstnian* f. Gmc]

fastening /ˈfɑːsnɪŋ/ n. a device that fastens something; a fastener.

fastidious /fæˈstɪdɪəs/ adj. **1** very careful in matters of choice or taste; fussy. **2** easily disgusted; squeamish. □□ **fastidiously** adv. **fastidiousness** n. [ME f. L *fastidiosus* f. *fastidium* loathing]

fastigiate /fæˈstɪdʒət/ adj. *Bot.* **1** having a conical or tapering outline. **2** having parallel upright branches. [L *fastigium* gable-top]

fastness /ˈfɑːstnɪs/ n. **1** a stronghold or fortress. **2** the state of being secure. [OE *fæstnes* (as FAST¹)]

Fastnet /ˈfɑːs(t)net/ a rocky islet off the SW coast of the Republic of Ireland.

fat /fæt/ n., adj., & v. —n. **1** a natural oily or greasy substance occurring esp. in animal bodies. **2** the part of anything containing this. **3** excessive presence of fat in a person or animal; corpulence. **4** *Chem.* any of a group of natural esters of glycerol and various fatty acids existing as solids at room temperature. —adj. (**fatter, fattest**) **1** (of a person or animal) having excessive fat; corpulent. **2** (of an animal) made plump for slaughter; fatted. **3** containing much fat. **4** greasy, oily, unctuous. **5** (of land or resources) fertile, rich; yielding abundantly. **6 a** thick, substantial in content (*a fat book*). **b** substantial as an asset or opportunity (*a fat cheque; was given a fat part in the play*). **7 a** (of coal) bituminous. **b** (of clay etc.) sticky. **8** *colloq. iron.* very little; not much (*a fat chance; a fat lot*). —v.tr. & intr. (**fatted, fatting**) make or become fat. □ **fat cat** *sl.* **1** US a wealthy person, esp. as a benefactor. **2** *Austral.* a highly paid executive or official. **fat-head** *colloq.* a stupid person. **fat-headed** stupid. **fat-headedness** stupidity. **fat hen** the white goosefoot, *Chenopodium album.* **the fat is in the fire** trouble is imminent. **kill the fatted calf** celebrate, esp. at a prodigal's return (Luke 15). **live off** (or **on**) **the fat of the land** have the best of everything. □□ **fatless** adj. **fatly** adv. **fatness** n. **fattish** adj. [OE *fæt* (adj.), *fættian* (v.) f. Gmc]

fatal /ˈfeɪt(ə)l/ adj. **1** causing or ending in death (*a fatal accident*). **2** (often foll. by *to*) destructive; ruinous; ending in disaster (*was fatal to their chances; made a fatal mistake*). **3** fateful, decisive. □□ **fatally** adv. **fatalness** n. [ME f. OF *fatal* or L *fatalis* (as FATE)]

fatalism /ˈfeɪtəˌlɪz(ə)m/ n. **1** the belief that all events are predetermined and therefore inevitable. **2** a submissive attitude to events as being inevitable. □□ **fatalist** n. **fatalistic** /-ˈlɪstɪk/ adj. **fatalistically** /-ˈlɪstɪkəlɪ/ adv.

fatality /fəˈtælətɪ/ n. (pl. **-ies**) **1 a** an occurrence of death by accident or in war etc. **b** a person killed in this way. **2** a fatal influence. **3** a predestined liability to disaster. **4** subjection to or the supremacy of fate. [F *fatalité* or LL *fatalitas* f. L *fatalis* FATAL]

Fata Morgana /ˈfɑːtə mɔːˈɡɑːnə/ a kind of mirage most frequently seen in the Strait of Messina between Italy and Sicily, attributed in early times to fairy agency. [It., = fairy Morgan, sister of King Arthur, whose legend was carried to Sicily by Norman settlers, where her reputation as an enchantress survived so that by the 19th c. the mirages were attributed to her agency]

fate /feɪt/ n. & v. —n. **1** a power regarded as predetermining events unalterably. **2 a** the future regarded as determined by such a power. **b** an individual's appointed lot. **c** the ultimate condition or end of a person or thing (*that sealed our fate*). **3** death, destruction. **4** (usu. **Fate**) a goddess of destiny, esp. one of the Fates or Norns (see entries). —v.tr. **1** (usu. in *passive*) preordain (*was fated to win*). **2** (as **fated** adj.) doomed to destruction. □ **fate worse than death** see DEATH. [ME f. It. *fato* & L *fatum* that which is spoken, f. *fari* speak]

fateful /ˈfeɪtfʊl/ adj. **1** important, decisive; having far-reaching consequences. **2** controlled as if by fate. **3** causing or likely to cause disaster. **4** prophetic. □□ **fatefully** adv. **fatefulness** n.

Fates /feɪts/ n.pl. *Gk Mythol.* the goddesses who presided over the birth and life of men. The gods were thought of as spinning, with a thread, the great realities—death, trouble, riches, homecoming—around a man, as if he were a spindle. From this image come the 'harsh spinners', usually three: Clotho who presided over the moment of a man's birth and held a distaff, Lachesis who with her spindle spun out the events and actions of his life, and Atropos who cut the thread of human life with her shears.

father /ˈfɑːðə(r)/ n. & v. —n. **1 a** a man in relation to a child or children born from his fertilization of an ovum. **b** (in full **adoptive father**) a man who has continuous care of a child, esp. by adoption. **2** any male animal in relation to its offspring. **3** (usu. in *pl.*) a progenitor or forefather. **4** an originator, designer, or early leader. **5** a person who deserves special respect (*the father of his country*). **6 (Fathers** or **Fathers of the Church)** early Christian theologians, esp. of the first five centuries, whose writings are regarded as especially authoritative. **7** (also **Father**) **a** (often as a title or form of address) a priest, esp. of a religious order. **b** a religious leader. **8 (the Father)** (in Christian belief) the first person of the Trinity. **9 (Father)** a venerable person, esp. as a title in personifications (*Father Time*). **10** the oldest member or doyen (*Father of the House*, see below). **11** (usu. in *pl.*) the leading men or elders in a city or State (*city fathers*). —*v.tr.* **1** beget; be the father of. **2** behave as a father towards. **3** originate (a scheme etc.). **4** appear as or admit that one is the father or originator of. **5** (foll. by *on*) assign the paternity of (a child, book) to a person. □ **father-figure** an older man who is respected like a father; a trusted leader. **father-in-law** (*pl.* **fathers-in-law**) the father of one's husband or wife. **father of chapel** see CHAPEL. **Father of the House** the member of the House of Commons with the longest continuous service. **Father's Day** a day (usu. the third Sunday in June) established for a special tribute to fathers. **Father Time** see TIME. □□ **fatherhood** *n.* **fatherless** *adj.* **fatherlessness** *n.* **fatherlike** *adj.* & *adv.* **fathership** *n.* [OE *fæder* with many Gmc cognates: rel. to L *pater*, Gk *patēr*]

Father Christmas the personification of Christmas as a benevolent old man with a flowing white beard, wearing a red gown and hood trimmed with white fur, and carrying a sack of Christmas presents. Traditionally he arrives from the far north, but his origin is obscure and his attributes are comparatively recent. In late medieval Europe he became associated with St Nicholas (Santa Claus). In England Father Christmas was not St Nicholas but a personification of Christmas, a genial red-robed old man, who appeared in many 16th-c. masques and in mumming plays. He was not then a gift-bringer, but acquired that attribute from St Nicholas in the 19th c. when there was a great revival of Christmas festivities.

fatherland /ˈfɑːðəˌlænd/ *n.* one's native country.

fatherly /ˈfɑːðəlɪ/ *adj.* **1** like or characteristic of a father in affection, care, etc. (*fatherly concern*). **2** of or proper to a father. □□ **fatherliness** *n.*

fathom /ˈfæð(ə)m/ *n.* & *v.* —*n.* (*pl.* often **fathom** when prec. by a number) **1** a measure of six feet, esp. used in taking depth soundings. **2** *Brit.* a quantity of wood six feet square in cross-section —*v.tr.* **1** grasp or comprehend (a problem or difficulty). **2** measure the depth of (water) with a sounding-line. □□ **fathomable** *adj.* **fathomless** *adj.* [OE *fæthm* outstretched arms f. Gmc]

Fathometer /fəˈðɒmɪtə(r)/ *n.* a type of echo-sounder.

fatigue /fəˈtiːg/ *n.* & *v.* —*n.* **1** extreme tiredness after exertion. **2** weakness in materials, esp. metal, caused by repeated variations of stress. **3** a reduction in the efficiency of a muscle, organ, etc., after prolonged activity. **4** an activity that causes fatigue. **5 a** a non-military duty in the army, often as a punishment. **b** (in full **fatigue-party**) a group of soldiers ordered to do fatigues. —*v.tr.* (**fatigues, fatigued, fatiguing**) cause fatigue in; tire, exhaust. □□ **fatiguable** *adj.* (also **fatigable**). **fatiguability** /-gəˈbɪlɪtɪ/ *n.* (also **fatigability**). **fatigueless** *adj.* [F *fatigue, fatiguer* f. L *fatigare* tire out]

Fatiha /ˈfɑːtɪˌhɑː/ *n.* (also **Fatihah**) the short first sura of the Koran, used by Muslims as a prayer. [Arab. *fātiḥa* opening f. *fataḥa* to open]

Fatima /ˈfætɪmə/ (d. 632) the daughter of the Prophet Muhammad and wife of Ali ibn Abi Talib, fourth caliph of the Muslim community. The descendants of Muhammad all trace their lineage through her, and she is revered especially by Shiite Muslims as the mother of the imams Hasan and Husayn.

Fatimid /ˈfætɪmɪd/ *n.* & *adj.* (also **Fatimite** /-ˌmaɪt/) —*n.* **1** a descendant of Fatima, the daughter of Muhammad. **2** a member of an Arabian dynasty claiming descent from Fatima which ruled in parts of northern Africa from 908 to 1171, and during some of that period in Egypt and Syria. —*adj.* of this dynasty.

fatling /ˈfætlɪŋ/ *n.* a young fatted animal.

fatso /ˈfætsəʊ/ *n.* (*pl.* **-oes**) *sl. joc.* or *offens.* a fat person. [prob. f. FAT or the designation *Fats*]

fatstock /ˈfætstɒk/ *n.* livestock fattened for slaughter.

fatten /ˈfæt(ə)n/ *v.* **1** *tr.* & *intr.* (esp. with ref. to meat-producing animals) make or become fat. **2** *tr.* enrich (soil).

fatty /ˈfætɪ/ *adj.* & *n.* —*adj.* (**fattier, fattiest**) **1** like fat; oily, greasy. **2** consisting of or containing fat; adipose. **3** marked by abnormal deposition of fat, esp. in fatty degeneration. —*n.* (*pl.* **-ies**) *colloq.* a fat person (esp. as a nickname). □ **fatty acid** *Chem.* any of a class of organic compounds consisting of a hydrocarbon chain and a terminal carboxyl group, esp. those occurring as constituents of lipids. **fatty oil** = *fixed oil.* □□ **fattily** *adv.* **fattiness** *n.*

fatuous /ˈfætjʊəs/ *adj.* vacantly silly; purposeless, idiotic. □□ **fatuity** /fəˈtjuːɪtɪ/ *n.* (*pl.* **-ies**). **fatuously** *adv.* **fatuousness** *n.* [L *fatuus* foolish]

fatwa /ˈfætwɑː/ *n.* (in Islamic countries) an authoritative ruling on a religious matter. [Arab. *fatwa*]

faubourg /ˈfəʊbʊəg/ *n.* a suburb, esp. of Paris. [F: cf. med.L *falsus burgus* not the city proper]

fauces /ˈfɔːsiːz/ *n.pl. Anat.* a cavity at the back of the mouth. □□ **faucial** /ˈfɔːʃ(ə)l/ *adj.* [L, = throat]

faucet /ˈfɔːsɪt/ *n.* esp. *US* a tap. ¶ In Brit. use only in special applications. [ME f. OF *fausset* vent-peg f. Prov. *falset* f. *falsar* to bore]

Faulkner /ˈfɔːknə(r)/, William (1897–1962), American novelist, born in Mississippi. The history and legends of the South and of his own family provided material for his greatest books. Among his novels set in Jefferson in the mythical county of Yoknapatawpha County (Mississippi) are *Sartoris* (1929) and his tour-de-force, *The Sound and the Fury* (1929), in which Faulkner views the decline of the South through the eyes of 33-year-old 'idiot' Benjay. This work displays a technical brilliance which he further demonstrated in *As I Lay Dying* (1930), and with *Absalom, Absalom!* (1936) he confirmed his reputation as one of the finest of modern novelists. His several volumes of short stories were collected in 1950. He was awarded the Nobel Prize for literature in 1949.

fault /fɒlt, fɔːlt/ *n.* & *v.* —*n.* **1** a defect or imperfection of character or structure, appearance, etc. **2** a break or other defect in an electric circuit. **3** a transgression, offence, or thing wrongly done. **4 a** *Tennis* etc. a service of the ball not in accordance with the rules. **b** (in showjumping) a penalty for an error. **5** responsibility for wrongdoing, error, etc. (*it will be your own fault*). **6** a defect regarded as the cause of something wrong (*the fault lies in the teaching methods*). **7** *Geol.* an extended break in the continuity of strata or a vein. —*v.* **1** *tr.* find fault with; blame. **2** *tr.* declare to be faulty. **3** *tr. Geol.* break the continuity of (strata or a vein). **4** *intr.* commit a fault. **5** *intr. Geol.* show a fault. □ **at fault** guilty; to blame. **fault-finder** a person given to continually finding fault. **fault-finding** continual criticism. **find fault** (often foll. by *with*) make an adverse criticism; complain. **to a fault** (usu. of a commendable quality etc.) excessively (*generous to a fault*). [ME *faut(e)* f. OF ult. f. L *fallere* FAIL]

faultless /ˈfɒltlɪs, ˈfɔːlt-/ *adj.* without fault; free from defect or error. □□ **faultlessly** *adv.* **faultlessness** *n.*

faulty /ˈfɒltɪ, ˈfɔːltɪ/ *adj.* (**faultier, faultiest**) *adj.* having faults; imperfect, defective. □□ **faultily** *adv.* **faultiness** *n.*

faun /fɔːn/ *n.* a Latin rural deity with a human face and torso and a goat's horns, legs, and tail. [ME f. OF *faune* or L FAUNUS]

fauna /ˈfɔːnə/ *n.* (*pl.* **faunae** /-niː/ or **faunas**) **1** the animal life of a region or geological period (cf. FLORA). **2** a treatise on or list of this. □□ **faunal** *adj.* **faunist** *n.* **faunistic** /-ˈnɪstɪk/ *adj.* [mod.L f. the name of a rural goddess, sister of FAUNUS]

Fauntleroy /ˈfɔːntlˌrɔɪ/ the gentle hero of Francis Hodgson Burnett's novel *Little Lord Fauntleroy* (1885). The name is applied to the style of dress (velvet suits with lace collars and cuffs) which the book popularized.

Faunus /ˈfɔːnəs/ *Rom. Mythol.* an ancient Italian pastoral god, grandson of Saturn. His association with wooded places caused him to be identified with Pan.

Fauré /ˈfɔːreɪ/, Gabriel (1845–1924), French composer and organist, director of the Conservatoire in Paris until increasing deafness forced him to retire in 1920. He composed songs throughout his career, creating delicate miniatures in 'Lydia' and 'Clair de lune' and an elegiac masterpiece in the song cycle *La bonne Chanson* (1892–4). He was also successful with large-scale works, such as the Requiem Mass (1887–9) and the opera *Pénélope* (1913), but his restrained style and general lack of interest in dramatic effect prevented his recognition as a great French composer until after the Second World War.

Faust /faʊst/ a wandering astronomer and necromancer who lived in Germany *c*.1488–1541 and was reputed to have sold his soul to the Devil. He was the hero of dramas by Marlowe and Goethe and of an opera by Gounod. □□ **Faustian** *adj.*

faute de mieux /ˌfəʊt də ˈmjɜː/ *adv.* for want of a better alternative. [F]

fauteuil /fəʊˈtɜːɪ/ *n.* a kind of wooden seat in the form of an armchair with open sides and upholstered arms. [F f. OF *faudestuel, faldestoel* FALDSTOOL]

fauve /fəʊv/ *n.* a member of a movement in painting, chiefly associated with Matisse, which flourished in Paris from 1905, characterized mainly by a vivid and arbitrary use of colour, with strident dissonances to express feelings and emotions. The name was coined by the French art critic Louis Vauxcelles at the Autumn Salon of 1905; coming across a quattrocento-like statue in the midst of works by Matisse and his associates, he remarked, 'Donatello au milieu des fauves!' Fauvism was one of the reactions against impressionism; its adherents included Dufy, Derain, and Vlaminck. The movement petered out *c*.1909, but had an important influence on the use of colour by subsequent artists. □□ **fauvism** *n.* **fauvist** *n.* [F, = wild beast]

faux pas /fəʊ ˈpɑː/ *n.* (*pl.* same /ˈpɑːz/) **1** a tactless mistake; a blunder. **2** a social indiscretion. [F, = false step]

fave /feɪv/ *n.* & *adj. sl.* = FAVOURITE (esp. in show business). [abbr.]

favela /fəˈvelə/ *n.* a Brazilian shack, slum, or shanty town. [Port.]

favour /ˈfeɪvə(r)/ *n.* & *v.* (*US* **favor**) —*n.* **1** an act of kindness beyond what is due or usual (*did it as a favour*). **2** esteem, liking, approval, goodwill; friendly regard (*gained their favour; look with favour on*). **3** partiality; too lenient or generous treatment. **4** aid, support (*under favour of night*). **5** a thing given or worn as a mark of favour or support, e.g. a badge or a knot of ribbons. **6** *archaic* leave, pardon (*by your favour*). **7** *Commerce archaic* a letter (*your favour of yesterday*). —*v.tr.* **1** regard or treat with favour or partiality. **2** give support or approval to; promote, prefer. **3 a** be to the advantage of (a person). **b** facilitate (a process etc.). **4** tend to confirm (an idea or theory). **5** (foll. by *with*) oblige (*favour me with a reply*). **6** (as **favoured** *adj.*) having special advantages. **7** *colloq.* resemble in features. □ **in favour 1** meeting with approval. **2** (foll. by *of*) **a** in support of. **b** to the advantage of. **out of favour** lacking approval. □□ **favourer** *n.* [ME f. OF f. L *favor -oris* f. *favēre* show kindness to]

favourable /ˈfeɪvərəb(ə)l/ *adj.* (*US* **favorable**) **1 a** well-disposed; propitious. **b** commendatory, approving. **2** giving consent (*a favourable answer*). **3** promising, auspicious, satisfactory (*a favourable aspect*). **4** (often foll. by *to*) helpful, suitable. □□ **favourableness** *n.* **favourably** *adv.* [ME f. OF *favorable* f. L *favorabilis* (as FAVOUR)]

favourite /ˈfeɪvərɪt/ *adj.* & *n.* (*US* **favorite**) —*adj.* preferred to all others (*my favourite book*). —*n.* **1** a specially favoured person. **2** *Sport* a competitor thought most likely to win. □ **favourite son** *US* a person preferred as the presidential candidate by delegates from the candidate's home State. [obs. F *favorit* f. It. *favorito* past part. of *favorire* favour]

favouritism /ˈfeɪvərɪˌtɪz(ə)m/ *n.* (*US* **favoritism**) the unfair favouring of one person or group at the expense of another.

Fawkes /fɔːks/, Guy (1570–1606), a conspirator in the Gunpowder Plot of 1605, recruited for his ability to deal with gunpowder.

fawn[1] /fɔːn/ *n., adj.,* & *v.* —*n.* **1** a young deer in its first year. **2** a light yellowish brown. —*adj.* fawn-coloured. —*v.tr.* (also *absol.*) (of a deer) bring forth (young). □ **in fawn** (of a deer) pregnant. [ME f. OF *faon* etc. ult. f. L *fetus* offspring: cf. FOETUS]

fawn[2] /fɔːn/ *v.intr.* **1** (often foll. by *on, upon*) (of a person) behave servilely, cringe. **2** (of an animal, esp. a dog) show extreme

affection. □□ **fawner** *n.* **fawning** *adj.* **fawningly** *adv.* [OE *fagnian, fægnian* (as FAIN)]

fax /fæks/ *n.* & *v.* —*n.* **1** facsimile transmission (see FACSIMILE *n.* 2). **2** a copy produced by this —*v.tr.* transmit (a document) in this way. [abbr. of FACSIMILE]

fay /feɪ/ *n. literary* a fairy. [ME f. OF *fae, faie* f. L *fata* (pl.) the Fates]

faze /feɪz/ *v.tr.* (often as **fazed** *adj.*) *colloq.* disconcert, perturb, disorientate. [var. of *feeze* drive off, f. OE *fēsian*, of unkn. orig.]

FBA *abbr.* Fellow of the British Academy.

FBI *abbr.* (in the US) Federal Bureau of Investigation.

FC *abbr.* Football Club.

FCC *abbr.* (in the US) Federal Communications Commission.

FCO *abbr.* (in the UK) Foreign and Commonwealth Office.

fcp. *abbr.* foolscap.

FD *abbr.* Defender of the Faith. [L *Fidei Defensor*]

FDA *abbr.* **1** (in the US) Food and Drugs Administration. **2** (in the UK) First Division (Civil Servants) Association (cf. AFDCS).

Fe *symb. Chem.* the element iron.

fealty /ˈfiːəltɪ/ *n.* (*pl.* **-ies**) **1** *hist.* **a** a feudal tenant's or vassal's fidelity to a lord. **b** an acknowledgement of this. **2** allegiance. [ME f. OF *feaulté* f. L *fidelitas -tatis* f. *fidelis* faithful f. *fides* faith]

fear /fɪə(r)/ *n.* & *v.* —*n.* **1 a** an unpleasant emotion caused by exposure to danger, expectation of pain, etc. **b** a state of alarm (*be in fear*). **2** a cause of fear (*all fears removed*). **3** (often foll. by *of*) dread or fearful respect (towards) (*had a fear of heights*). **4** anxiety for the safety of (*in fear of their lives*). **5** danger; likelihood (of something unwelcome) (*there is little fear of failure*). —*v.* **1 a** *tr.* feel fear about or towards (a person or thing). **b** *intr.* feel fear. **2** *intr.* (foll. by *for*) feel anxiety or apprehension about (*feared for my life*). **3** *tr.* apprehend; have uneasy expectation of (*fear the worst*). **4** *tr.* (usu. foll. by *that* + clause) apprehend with fear or regret (*I fear that you are wrong*). **5** *tr.* **a** (foll. by *to* + infin.) hesitate. **b** (foll. by verbal noun) shrink from; be apprehensive about (*he feared meeting his ex-wife*). **6** *tr.* show reverence towards. □ **for fear of** (or **that**) to avoid the risk of (or that). **never fear** there is no danger of that. **no fear** *colloq.* expressing strong denial or refusal. **without fear or favour** impartially. [OE f. Gmc]

fearful /ˈfɪəfʊl/ *adj.* **1** (usu. foll. by *of*, or *that* + clause) afraid. **2** terrible, awful. **3** *colloq.* extremely unwelcome or unpleasant (*a fearful row*). □□ **fearfully** *adv.* **fearfulness** *n.*

fearless /ˈfɪəlɪs/ *adj.* **1** courageous, brave. **2** (foll. by *of*) without fear. □□ **fearlessly** *adv.* **fearlessness** *n.*

fearsome /ˈfɪəsəm/ *adj.* appalling or frightening, esp. in appearance. □□ **fearsomely** *adv.* **fearsomeness** *n.*

feasibility /ˌfiːzɪˈbɪlɪtɪ/ *n.* the state or degree of being feasible. □ **feasibility study** a study of the practicability of a proposed project.

feasible /ˈfiːzɪb(ə)l/ *adj.* **1** practicable, possible; easily or conveniently done. **2** *disp.* likely, probable (*it is feasible that it will rain*). □□ **feasibly** *adv.* [ME f. OF *faisable, -ible* f. *fais-* stem of *faire* f. L *facere* do, make]

feast /fiːst/ *n.* & *v.* —*n.* **1** a large or sumptuous meal. **2** a gratification to the senses or mind. **3 a** an annual religious celebration. **b** a day dedicated to a particular saint. **4** an annual village festival. —*v.* **1** *intr.* partake of a feast; eat and drink sumptuously. **2** *tr.* **a** regale. **b** pass (time) in feasting. □ **feast-day** a day on which a feast (esp. in sense 3) is held. **feast one's eyes on** take pleasure in beholding. **feast of reason** intellectual talk. □□ **feaster** *n.* [ME f. OF *feste, fester* f. L *festus* joyous]

feat /fiːt/ *n.* a noteworthy act or achievement. [ME f. OF *fait, fet* (as FACT)]

feather /ˈfeðə(r)/ *n.* & *v.* —*n.* **1** any of the appendages growing from a bird's skin, with a horny hollow stem and fine strands. **2** one or more of these as decoration etc. **3** (*collect.*) **a** plumage. **b** game-birds. —*v.* **1** *tr.* cover or line with feathers. **2** *tr. Rowing* turn (an oar) so that it passes through the air edgeways. **3** *tr. Aeron.* & *Naut.* **a** cause (the propeller blades) to rotate in such a way as to lessen the air or water resistance. **b** vary the angle of incidence of (helicopter blades). **4** *intr.* float, move, or wave like feathers. □ **feather bed** a bed with a mattress stuffed with feathers. **feather-bed** v.tr. (**-bedded, -bedding**) provide with (esp. financial) advantages. **feather-bedding** the employment of excess staff. **feather-brain** (or **-head**) a silly or absent-minded person. **feather-brained** (or **-headed**) silly, absent-minded. **feather-edge** the fine edge of a wedge-shaped board. **a feather in one's cap** an achievement to one's credit. **feather one's nest** enrich oneself. **feather-stitch** ornamental zigzag sewing. **in fine** (or **high**) **feather** colloq. in good spirits. □□ **feathered** adj. (also in comb.). **featherless** adj. **feathery** adj. **featheriness** n. [OE fether, gefithrian, f. Gmc]

feathering /ˈfeðərɪŋ/ n. **1** bird's plumage. **2** the feathers of an arrow. **3** a feather-like structure in an animal's coat. **4** Archit. cusps in tracery.

featherweight /ˈfeðəˌweɪt/ n. **1 a** a weight in certain sports intermediate between bantamweight and lightweight, in the amateur boxing scale 54–7 kg but differing for professionals, wrestlers, and weightlifters. **b** a sportsman of this weight. **2 a** very light person or thing. **3** (usu. attrib.) a trifling or unimportant thing.

feature /ˈfiːtʃə(r)/ n. & v. —n. **1** a distinctive or characteristic part of a thing. **2** (usu. in pl.) a distinctive part of the face, esp. with regard to shape and visual effect. **3** a distinctive or regular article in a newspaper or magazine. **4 a** (in full **feature film**) a full-length film intended as the main item in a cinema programme. **b** (in full **feature programme**) a broadcast devoted to a particular topic. —v. **1** tr. make a special display or attraction of; give special prominence to. **2** tr. & intr. have as or be an important actor, participant, or topic in a film, broadcast, etc. **3** intr. be a feature. □□ **featured** adj. (also in comb.). **featureless** adj. [ME f. OF feture, faiture form f. L factura formation: see FACTURE]

Feb. abbr. February.

febrifuge /ˈfebrɪˌfjuːdʒ/ n. a medicine or treatment that reduces fever; a cooling drink. □□ **febrifugal** /fɪˈbrɪfjʊg(ə)l, ˌfebrɪˈfjuːg(ə)l/ adj. [F fébrifuge f. L febris fever + -FUGE]

febrile /ˈfiːbraɪl/ adj. of or relating to fever; feverish. □□ **febrility** /fɪˈbrɪlɪtɪ/ n. [F fébrile or med.L febrilis f. L febris fever]

February /ˈfebrʊərɪ/ n. (pl. **-ies**) the second month of the year. □ **February Revolution** a revolutionary movement in Russia in 1917 (see REVOLUTION 1). [ME f. OF feverier ult. f. L februarius f. februa a purification feast held in this month]

feces US var. of FAECES.

Fechner /ˈfexnə(r)/, Gustav Theodor (1801–87), German poet, physicist, and psychologist, who sought to define the quantitative relationship between degrees of physical stimulation and the resulting sensation, the study of which he termed 'psychophysics' (1859). By associating sensations with numerical values, he hoped to make psychology a truly objective science.

feckless /ˈfeklɪs/ adj. **1** feeble, ineffective. **2** unthinking, irresponsible (feckless gaiety). □□ **fecklessly** adv. **fecklessness** n. [Sc. feck f. effeck var. of EFFECT]

feculent /ˈfekjʊlənt/ adj. **1** murky; filthy. **2** containing sediments or dregs. □□ **feculence** n. [F féculent or L faeculentus (as FAECES)]

fecund /ˈfiːkənd, ˈfek-/ adj. **1** prolific, fertile. **2** fertilizing. □□ **fecundability** /fiˌkʌndəˈbɪlɪtɪ/ n. **fecundity** /fɪˈkʌndɪtɪ/ n. [ME f. F fécond or L fecundus]

fecundate /ˈfiːkənˌdeɪt, ˈfek-/ v.tr. **1** make fruitful. **2** = FERTILIZE. □□ **fecundation** /-ˈdeɪʃ(ə)n/ n. [L fecundare f. fecundus fruitful]

Fed /fed/ n. US sl. a federal official, esp. a member of the FBI. [abbr. of FEDERAL]

fed past and past part. of FEED. □ **fed up** (or **fed to death**) (often foll. by with) discontented or bored, esp. from a surfeit of something (am fed up with the rain). **fed-upness** the state of being fed up.

fedayeen /ˌfedəˈjiːn/ n.pl. Arab guerrillas operating esp. against Israel. [colloq. Arab. fidā'iyīn pl. f. Arab. fidā'ī adventurer]

federal /ˈfedər(ə)l/ adj. **1** of a system of government in which several States form a unity but remain independent in internal affairs. **2** relating to or affecting such a federation (federal laws).

3 relating to or favouring centralized government. **4** (**Federal**) US of the Northern States in the Civil War. **5** comprising an association of largely independent units. □□ **federalism** n. **federalist** n. **federalize** v.tr. (also **-ise**). **federalization** /-ˈzeɪʃ(ə)n/ n. **federally** adv. [L foedus -eris league, covenant]

Federal Bureau of Investigation the agency of the US federal government, established in 1908 within the Department of Justice, that conducts investigations in federal law enforcement and other matters.

Federal Reserve System the banking authority, created in 1913, that performs the functions of a central bank in the US and is used to implement the country's monetary policy. The system consists of twelve Federal Reserve Districts, each having a Federal Reserve Bank that is controlled from Washington by the Federal Reserve Board.

federate v. & adj. —v.tr. & intr. /ˈfedəˌreɪt/ organize or be organized on a federal basis. —adj. /ˈfedərət/ having a federal organization. □□ **federative** /ˈfedərətɪv/ adj. [LL foederare foederat- (as FEDERAL)]

federation /ˌfedəˈreɪʃ(ə)n/ n. **1** a federal group of States. **2** a federated society or group. **3** the act or an instance of federating. □□ **federationist** n. [F fédération f. LL foederatio (as FEDERAL)]

fedora /fɪˈdɔːrə/ n. a low soft felt hat with a crown creased lengthways. [Fédora, drama by V. Sardou (1882)]

fee /fiː/ n. & v. —n. **1** a payment made to a professional person or to a professional or public body in exchange for advice or services. **2** money paid as part of a special transaction, for a privilege, admission to a society, etc. (enrolment fee). **3** (in pl.) money regularly paid (esp. to a school) for continuing services. **4** Law an inherited estate, unlimited (**fee simple**) or limited (**fee tail**) as to the category of heir. **5** hist. a fief; a feudal benefice. —v.tr. (**fee'd** or **feed**) **1** pay a fee to. **2** engage for a fee. [ME f. AF, = OF feu, fieu, etc. f. med.L feodum, feudum, perh. f. Frank.: cf. FEUD², FIEF]

feeble /ˈfiːb(ə)l/ adj. **1** weak, infirm. **2** lacking energy, force, or effectiveness. **3** dim, indistinct. **4** deficient in character or intelligence. □□ **feebleness** n. **feeblish** adj. **feebly** adv. [ME f. AF & OF feble, fieble, fleible f. L flebilis lamentable f. flēre weep]

feeble-minded /ˌfiːb(ə)lˈmaɪndɪd/ adj. **1** unintelligent. **2** mentally deficient. □□ **feeble-mindedly** adv. **feeble-mindedness** n.

feed /fiːd/ v. & n. —v. (past and past part. **fed** /fed/) **1** tr. **a** supply with food. **b** put food into the mouth of. **2** tr. **a** give as food, esp. to animals. **b** graze (cattle). **3** tr. serve as food for. **4** intr. (usu. foll. by on) (esp. of animals, or colloq. of people) take food; eat. **5** tr. nourish; make grow. **6 a** tr. maintain supply of raw material, fuel, etc., to (a fire, machine, etc.). **b** tr. (foll. by into) supply (material) to a machine etc. **c** intr. (often foll. by into) (of a river etc.) flow into another body of water. **d** tr. insert further coins into (a meter) to continue its function, validity, etc. **7** intr. (foll. by on) **a** be nourished by. **b** derive benefit from. **8** tr. use (land) as pasture. **9** tr. Theatr. sl. supply (an actor etc.) with cues. **10** tr. Sport send passes to (a player) in a ball-game. **11** tr. gratify (vanity etc.). **12** tr. provide (advice, information, etc.) to. —n. **1** an amount of food, esp. for animals or infants. **2** the act or an instance of feeding; the giving of food. **3** colloq. a meal. **4** pasturage; green crops. **5 a** a supply of raw material to a machine etc. **b** the provision of this or a device for it. **6** the charge of a gun. **7** Theatr. sl. an actor who supplies another with cues. □ **feed back** produce feedback. **feed the fishes 1** meet one's death by drowning. **2** be seasick. **feeding-bottle** a bottle with a teat for feeding infants. **feed up 1** fatten. **2** satiate (cf. fed up (see FED)). □□ **feedable** adj. [OE fēdan f. Gmc]

feedback /ˈfiːdbæk/ n. **1** information about the result of an experiment etc.; response. **2** Electronics **a** the return of a fraction of the output signal from one stage of a circuit, amplifier, etc., to the input of the same or a preceding stage. **b** a signal so returned. **3** Biol. etc. the modification or control of a process or system by its results or effects, esp. by the difference between the desired and the actual result.

feeder /ˈfiːdə(r)/ n. **1** a person or thing that feeds. **2** a person who eats in a specified manner. **3** a child's feeding-bottle. **4** Brit.

a bib for an infant. **5** a tributary stream. **6** a branch road, railway line, etc., linking outlying districts with a main communication system. **7** *Electr.* a main carrying electricity to a distribution point. **8** a hopper or feeding apparatus in a machine.

feel /fiːl/ v. & n. —v. (*past* and *past part.* **felt** /felt/) **1** *tr.* **a** examine or search by touch. **b** (*absol.*) have the sensation of touch (*was unable to feel*). **2** *tr.* perceive or ascertain by touch; have a sensation of (*could feel the warmth; felt that it was cold*). **3** *tr.* **a** undergo, experience (*shall feel my anger*). **b** exhibit or be conscious of (an emotion, sensation, conviction, etc.). **4 a** *intr.* have a specified feeling or reaction (*felt strongly about it*). **b** *tr.* be emotionally affected by (*felt the rebuke deeply*). **5** *tr.* (foll. by *that* + clause) have a vague or unreasoned impression (*I feel that I am right*). **6** *tr.* consider, think (*I feel it useful to go*). **7** *intr.* seem; give an impression of being; be perceived as (*the air feels chilly*). **8** *intr.* be consciously; consider oneself (*I feel happy; do not feel well*). **9** *intr.* **a** (foll. by *with*) have sympathy with. **b** (foll. by *for*) have pity or compassion for. **10** *tr.* (often foll. by *up*) *sl.* fondle the genitals of. —n. **1** the act or an instance of feeling; testing by touch. **2** the sensation characterizing a material, situation, etc. **3** the sense of touch. □ **feel free** (often foll. by *to* + infin.) not be reluctant or hesitant (*do feel free to criticize*). **feel like** have a wish for; be inclined towards. **feel one's oats** see OAT. **feel oneself** be fit or confident etc. **feel out** investigate cautiously. **feel strange** see STRANGE. **feel up to** be ready to face or deal with. **feel one's way** proceed carefully; act cautiously. **get the feel of** become accustomed to using. **make one's influence** (or **presence** etc.) **felt** assert one's influence; make others aware of one's presence etc. [OE *fēlan* f. WG]

feeler /ˈfiːlə(r)/ n. **1** an organ in certain animals for testing things by touch or for searching for food. **2** a tentative proposal or suggestion, esp. to elicit a response (*put out feelers*). **3** a person or thing that feels. □ **feeler gauge** a gauge equipped with blades for measuring narrow gaps etc.

feeling /ˈfiːlɪŋ/ n. & adj. —n. **1 a** the capacity to feel; a sense of touch (*lost all feeling in his arm*). **b** a physical sensation. **2 a** (often foll. by *of*) a particular emotional reaction (*a feeling of despair*). **b** (in pl.) emotional susceptibilities or sympathies (*hurt my feelings; had strong feelings about it*). **3** a particular sensitivity (*had a feeling for literature*). **4 a** an opinion or notion, esp. a vague or irrational one (*my feelings on the subject; had a feeling she would be there*). **b** vague awareness (*had a feeling of safety*). **c** sentiment (*the general feeling was against it*). **5** readiness to feel sympathy or compassion. **6 a** the general emotional response produced by a work of art, piece of music, etc. **b** emotional commitment or sensibility in artistic execution (*played with feeling*). —adj. **1** sensitive, sympathetic. **2** showing emotion or sensitivity. □□ **feelingless** adj. **feelingly** adv.

feet pl. of FOOT.

feign /feɪn/ v. **1** *tr.* simulate; pretend to be affected by (*feign madness*). **2** *tr. archaic* invent (an excuse etc.). **3** *intr.* indulge in pretence. [ME f. *feign-* stem of OF *feindre* f. L *fingere* mould, contrive]

feijoa /feɪˈdʒəʊə, faɪ-/ n. **1** any evergreen shrub or tree of the genus *Feijoa*, bearing edible guava-like fruit. **2** this fruit. [mod.L f. J. da Silva Feijo, 19th-c. Sp. naturalist]

feint¹ /feɪnt/ n. & v. —n. **1** a sham attack or blow etc. to divert attention or fool an opponent or enemy. **2** pretence. —v.intr. make a feint. [F *feinte*, fem. past part. of *feindre* FEIGN]

feint² /feɪnt/ adj. esp. *Printing* = FAINT adj. 6 (*feint lines*). [ME f. OF (as FEINT¹): see FAINT]

feisty /ˈfaɪstɪ/ adj. (**feistier, feistiest**) US sl. **1** aggressive, exuberant. **2** touchy. □□ **feistiness** n. [*feist* (= fist) small dog]

felafel /feˈlɑːf(ə)l/ n. (also **falafel**) (in Near Eastern countries) a spicy dish of fried rissoles made from mashed chick peas or beans. [Arab. *falāfil*]

feldspar /ˈfeldspɑː(r)/ n. (also **felspar** /ˈfelspɑː(r)/) *Mineral.* any of a group of aluminium silicates of potassium, sodium, or calcium, which are the most abundant minerals in the earth's crust. □□ **feldspathic** /-ˈspæθɪk/ adj. **feldspathoid** /ˈfeldspəˌθɔɪd/ n. [G *Feldspat*, *-spath* f. *Feld* FIELD + *Spat*, *Spath* SPAR³: *felspar* by false assoc. with G *Fels* rock]

felicitate /fəˈlɪsɪˌteɪt/ v.tr. (usu. foll. by *on*) congratulate. □□ **felicitation** /-ˈteɪʃ(ə)n/ n. (usu. in pl.). [LL *felicitare* make happy f. L *felix -icis* happy]

felicitous /fəˈlɪsɪtəs/ adj. (of an expression, quotation, civilities, or a person making them) strikingly apt; pleasantly ingenious. □□ **felicitously** adv. **felicitousness** n.

felicity /fəˈlɪsɪtɪ/ n. (pl. **-ies**) **1** intense happiness; being happy. **2** a cause of happiness. **3 a** a capacity for apt expression; appropriateness. **b** an appropriate or well-chosen phrase. **4** a fortunate trait. [ME f. OF *felicité* f. L *felicitas -tatis* f. *felix -icis* happy]

feline /ˈfiːlaɪn/ adj. & n. —adj. **1** of or relating to the cat family. **2** catlike, esp. in beauty or slyness. —n. an animal of the cat family Felidae. □□ **felinity** /fɪˈlɪnɪtɪ/ n. [L *felinus* f. *feles* cat]

fell¹ past of FALL v.

fell² /fel/ v. & n. —v.tr. **1** cut down (esp. a tree). **2** strike or knock down (a person or animal). **3** stitch down (the edge of a seam) to lie flat. —n. an amount of timber cut. □□ **feller** n. [OE *fellan* f. Gmc, rel. to FALL]

fell³ /fel/ n. N.Engl. **1** a hill. **2** a stretch of hills or moorland. [ME f. ON *fjall*, *fell* hill]

fell⁴ /fel/ adj. poet. or rhet. **1** fierce, ruthless. **2** terrible, destructive. □ **at** (or **in**) **one fell swoop** in a single (orig. deadly) action. [ME f. OF *fel* f. Rmc FELON¹]

fell⁵ /fel/ n. an animal's hide or skin with its hair. [OE *fel*, *fell* f. Gmc]

fellah /ˈfelə/ n. (pl. **fellahin** /-əˈhiːn/) an Egyptian peasant. [Arab. *fallāḥ* husbandman f. *falaḥa* till the soil]

fellatio /fɪˈleɪʃɪəʊ, feˈlɑːtɪəʊ/ n. oral stimulation of the penis. □□ **fellate** /fɪˈleɪt/ v.tr. **fellator** /fɪˈleɪtə(r)/ n. [mod.L f. L *fellare* suck]

feller /ˈfelə(r)/ n. = FELLOW 1, 2. [repr. an affected or sl. pronunc.]

felloe /ˈfeləʊ/ n. (also **felly** /ˈfelɪ/) (pl. **-oes** or **-ies**) the outer circle (or a section of it) of a wheel, to which the spokes are fixed. [OE *felg*, of unkn. orig.]

fellow /ˈfeləʊ/ n. **1** *colloq.* a man or boy (*poor fellow!; my dear fellow*). **2** *derog.* a person regarded with contempt. **3** (usu. in pl.) a person associated with another; a comrade (*were separated from their fellows*). **4** a counterpart or match; the other of a pair. **5** an equal; one of the same class. **6** a contemporary. **7 a** an incorporated senior member of a college. **b** an elected graduate receiving a stipend for a period of research. **c** a member of the governing body in some universities. **8** a member of a learned society. **9** (attrib.) belonging to the same class or activity (*fellow soldier; fellow-countryman*). □ **fellow-feeling** sympathy from common experience. **fellow-traveller 1** a person who travels with another. **2** a sympathizer with, or a secret member of, the Communist Party. [OE *fēolaga* f. ON *félagi* f. *fé* cattle, property, money: see LAY¹]

fellowship /ˈfeləʊʃɪp/ n. **1** companionship, friendliness. **2** participation, sharing; community of interest. **3** a body of associates; a company. **4** a brotherhood or fraternity. **5** a guild or corporation. **6** the status or emoluments of a fellow of a college or society.

felly var. of FELLOE.

felon¹ /ˈfelən/ n. & adj. —n. a person who has committed a felony. —adj. archaic cruel, wicked. □□ **felonry** n. [ME f. OF f. med.L *felo -onis*, of unkn. orig.]

felon² /ˈfelən/ n. an inflammatory sore on the finger near the nail. [ME, perh. as FELON¹: cf. med.L *felo*, *fello* in the same sense]

felonious /fɪˈləʊnɪəs/ adj. **1** criminal. **2** *Law* **a** of or involving felony. **b** who has committed felony. □□ **feloniously** adv.

felony /ˈfelənɪ/ n. (pl. **-ies**) any of a class of crimes which may loosely be said to have been regarded by the law as of graver character than those called misdemeanours. The class (which included murder, wounding, arson, rape, and robbery) comprised those offences the penalty of which formerly included forfeiture of land and goods, together with others added to the list by statute. Forfeiture was abolished in 1870, but procedural differences applied until 1967 when (in English law) all distinctions between felonies and misdemeanours were removed; the distinction never existed in Scotland. In the US most jurisdictions distinguish between felonies and misdemeanours, the distinction usually depending on the penalties or consequences attaching to the crime. [ME f. OF *felonie* (as FELON¹)]

felspar var. of FELDSPAR.

felt¹ /felt/ *n. & v.* —*n.* **1** a kind of cloth made by rolling and pressing wool etc., or by weaving and shrinking it. **2** a similar material made from other fibres. —*v.* **1** *tr.* make into felt; mat together. **2** *tr.* cover with felt. **3** *intr.* become matted. □ **felt-tipped** (or **felt-tip**) **pen** a pen with a writing-point made of felt or fibre. □□ **felty** *adj.* [OE f. WG]

felt² *past* and *past part.* of FEEL.

felucca /fɪˈlʌkə/ *n.* a small Mediterranean coasting vessel with oars or lateen sails or both. [It. *felucca* f. obs. Sp. *faluca* f. Arab. *fulk*, perh. f. Gk *epholkion* sloop]

felwort /ˈfelwɜːt/ *n.* a purple-flowered gentian, *Gentianella amarella*. [OE *feldwyrt* (as FIELD, WORT)]

female /ˈfiːmeɪl/ *adj. & n.* —*adj.* **1** of the sex that can bear offspring or produce eggs. **2** (of plants or their parts) fruit-bearing; having a pistil and no stamens. **3** of or consisting of women or female animals or female plants. **4** (of a screw, socket, etc.) manufactured hollow to receive a corresponding inserted part. —*n.* a female person, animal, or plant. □ **female impersonator** a male performer impersonating a woman. □□ **femaleness** *n.* [ME f. OF *femelle* (n.) f. L *femella* dimin. of *femina* a woman, assim. to *male*]

feme /fiːm/ *n. Law* a woman or wife. □ **feme covert** a married woman. **feme sole** a woman without a husband (esp. if divorced). [ME f. AF & OF f. L *femina* woman]

feminal /ˈfemɪn(ə)l/ *adj. archaic* womanly. □□ **feminality** /-ˈnælɪtɪ/ *n.* [med.L *feminalis* f. L *femina* woman]

femineity /ˌfemɪˈniːɪtɪ/ *n. archaic* womanliness; womanishness. [L *femineus* womanish f. *femina* woman]

feminine /ˈfemɪnɪn/ *adj. & n.* —*adj.* **1** of or characteristic of women. **2** having qualities associated with women. **3** womanly, effeminate. **4** *Gram.* of or denoting the gender proper to women's names. —*n. Gram.* a feminine gender or word. □□ **femininely** *adv.* **feminineness** *n.* **femininity** /-ˈnɪnɪtɪ/ *n.* [ME f. OF *feminin* -ine or L *femininus* f. *femina* woman]

feminism /ˈfemɪˌnɪz(ə)m/ *n.* **1** the advocacy of women's rights on the ground of the equality of the sexes. **2** *Med.* the development of female characteristics in a male person. □□ **feminist** *n.* (in sense 1). [L *femina* woman (in sense 1 after F *féminisme*)]

feminity /feˈmɪnɪtɪ/ *n.* = FEMININITY (see FEMININE). [ME f. OF *feminité* f. med.L *feminitas -tatis* f. L *femina* woman]

feminize /ˈfemɪˌnaɪz/ *v.tr. & intr.* (also **-ise**) make or become feminine or female. □□ **feminization** /-ˈzeɪʃ(ə)n/ *n.*

femme fatale /ˌfæm fæˈtɑːl/ *n.* (*pl.* **femmes fatales** pronunc. same) a seductively attractive woman. [F]

femto- /ˈfemtəʊ/ *comb. form* denoting a factor of 10^{-15} (*femtometre*). [Da. or Norw. *femten* fifteen]

femur /ˈfiːmə(r)/ *n.* (*pl.* **femurs** or **femora** /ˈfemərə/) **1** *Anat.* the thigh-bone, the thick bone between the hip and the knee. **2** the corresponding part of an insect. □□ **femoral** /ˈfemər(ə)l/ *adj.* [L *femur femoris* thigh]

fen /fen/ *n.* **1** a low marshy or flooded area of land. **2** (**the Fens**) flat low-lying areas of Lincolnshire, Cambridgeshire, and neighbouring counties in eastern England. Formerly marshland, they have been drained for agriculture since the 17th c., originally by Dutch engineers. □ **fen-berry** (*pl.* **-berries**) a cranberry. **fen-fire** will-o'-the-wisp. □□ **fenny** *adj.* [OE *fenn* f. Gmc]

fence /fens/ *n. & v.* —*n.* **1** a barrier or railing or other upright structure enclosing an area of ground, esp. to prevent or control access. **2** a large upright obstacle in steeplechasing or show-jumping. **3** *sl.* a receiver of stolen goods. **4** a guard or guide in machinery. —*v.* **1** *tr.* surround with or as with a fence. **2** *tr.* **a** (foll. by *in, off*) enclose or separate with or as with a fence. **b** (foll. by *up*) seal with or as with a fence. **3** *tr.* (foll. by *from, against*) screen, shield, protect. **4** *tr.* (foll. by *out*) exclude with or as with a fence; keep out. **5** *tr.* (also *absol.*) *sl.* deal in (stolen goods). **6** *intr.* practise the sport of fencing; use a sword. **7** *intr.* (foll. by *with*) evade answering (a person or question). **8** *intr.* (of a horse

etc.) leap fences. □ **sit on the fence** remain neutral or undecided in a dispute etc. □□ **fenceless** *adj.* **fencer** *n.* [ME f. DEFENCE]

fencible /ˈfensɪb(ə)l/ *n. hist.* a soldier liable only for home service. [ME f. DEFENSIBLE]

fencing /ˈfensɪŋ/ *n.* **1** a set or extent of fences. **2** material for making fences. **3** the art or sport of fighting with foils or other kinds of sword. Skilful use of a sword according to established rules and movements was practised by the ancient Egyptians, Persians, Greeks, and Romans not only in war but as a pastime.

fend /fend/ *v.* **1** *intr.* (foll. by *for*) look after (esp. oneself). **2** *tr.* (usu. foll. by *off*) keep away; ward off (an attack etc.). [ME f. DEFEND]

fender /ˈfendə(r)/ *n.* **1** a low frame bordering a fireplace to keep in falling coals etc. **2** *Naut.* a piece of old cable, matting, etc., hung over a vessel's side to protect it against impact. **3 a** a thing used to keep something off, prevent a collision, etc. **b** *US* a bumper or mudguard of a motor vehicle.

fenestella /ˌfenɪˈstelə/ *n. Archit.* a niche in a wall south of an altar, holding the piscina and often the credence. [L, dimin. of *fenestra* window]

fenestra /fɪˈnestrə/ *n.* (*pl.* **fenestrae** /-triː/) **1** *Anat.* a small hole or opening in a bone etc., esp. one of two (**fenestra ovalis**, **fenestra rotunda**) in the inner ear. **2** a perforation in a surgical instrument. **3** a hole made by surgical fenestration. [L, = window]

fenestrate /fɪˈnestreɪt/ *adj. Bot. & Zool.* having small window-like perforations or transparent areas. [L *fenestratus* past part. of *fenestrare* f. *fenestra* window]

fenestrated /fɪˈnestreɪtɪd/ *adj.* **1** *Archit.* having windows. **2** perforated. **3** = FENESTRATE. **4** *Surgery* having fenestrae.

fenestration /ˌfenɪˈstreɪʃ(ə)n/ *n.* **1** *Archit.* the arrangement of windows in a building. **2** *Bot. & Zool.* being fenestrate. **3** a surgical operation in which a new opening is formed, esp. in the bony labyrinth of the inner ear, as a form of treatment in some cases of deafness.

Fenian /ˈfiːnɪən/ *n. & adj.* —*n. hist.* a member of the Irish Republican Brotherhood, a revolutionary nationalist organization founded in the US in 1858 by James Stephens, a veteran of the failed 1848 Irish uprising. The Fenians staged an unsuccessful revolt in Ireland in 1867 and were responsible for isolated revolutionary acts against the British until the early 20th c., when they were gradually eclipsed by the IRA. —*adj.* of or relating to the Fenians. □□ **Fenianism** *n.* [OIr. *féne* name of an ancient Irish people, confused with *fiann* guard of legendary kings]

fennec /ˈfenɪk/ *n.* a small fox, *Vulpes zerda*, native to N. Africa, having large pointed ears. [Arab. *fanak*]

fennel /ˈfen(ə)l/ *n.* **1** a yellow-flowered fragrant umbelliferous plant, *Foeniculum vulgare*, with leaves or leaf-stalks used in salads, soups, etc. **2** the seeds of this used as flavouring. [OE *finugl* etc. & OF *fenoil* f. L *feniculum* f. *fenum* hay]

fenugreek /ˈfenjuˌɡriːk/ *n.* **1** a leguminous plant, *Trigonella foenum-graecum*, having aromatic seeds. **2** these seeds used as flavouring, esp. ground and used in curry powder. [OE *fenogrecum*, superseded in ME f. OF *fenugrec* f. L *faenugraecum* (*fenum graecum* Greek hay), used by the Romans as fodder]

feoffment /ˈfefmənt/ *n. hist.* a mode of conveying a freehold estate by a formal transfer of possession. □□ **feoffee** /feˈfiː/ *n.* **feoffor** *n.* [ME f. AF *feoffement*, rel. to FEE]

feral /ˈfɪər(ə)l, ˈfer(ə)l/ *adj.* **1** (of an animal or plant) wild, untamed, uncultivated. **2 a** (of an animal) in a wild state after escape from captivity. **b** born in the wild of such an animal. **3** brutal. [L *ferus* wild]

fer de lance /ˌfeə də ˈlɑːns/ *n.* a large highly venomous snake, *Bothrops atrox*, native to Central and S. America. [F, = iron (head) of a lance]

Ferdinand /ˈfɜːdɪnənd/ (1452–1516), king of Spain. A prince of the House of Aragon, Ferdinand married Isabella of Castile in 1469 and succeeded to the throne of Castile (as Ferdinand V) with her in 1474. When he became king of Aragon (as Ferdinand II) in 1479 he effectively united Spain as one country. While on the throne he waged the final war against the Moors (1482–92), capturing Granada and ending Muslim rule in the Iberian peninsula. He and his wife earned the title 'the Catholic Kings'.

feretory /'ferɪtərɪ/ n. (pl. **-ies**) **1** a shrine for a saint's relics. **2** a chapel containing such a shrine. [ME f. OF *fiertre* f. L *feretrum* f. Gk *pheretron* f. *pherō* bear]

ferial /'fɪərɪəl, 'fer-/ adj. *Eccl.* **1** (of a day) ordinary; not appointed for a festival or fast. **2** (of a service etc.) for use on a ferial day. [ME f. OF *ferial* or med.L *ferialis* f. L *feriae*: see FAIR²]

Ferm. abbr. Fermanagh.

Fermanagh /fə'mænə/ a county of Northern Ireland; pop. (1981) 51,000; county town, Enniskillen.

Fermat /'feərmɑː/, Pierre de (1601–65), French lawyer and counsellor, whose professional activities were overshadowed by his success and fame as a mathematician. His study of the problems of finding tangents to curves, finding areas under curves, and maxima and minima, led directly to the general methods of the calculus introduced by Newton and Leibnitz. He made many beautiful discoveries about integers, for which he is seen as the founder of the theory of numbers. His most famous assertion is that if n is greater than 2 then there is no integer whose nth power can be expressed as the sum of two smaller nth powers. This statement, known as Fermat's Last Theorem, attracts more attention from both professionals and amateurs than any other mathematical problem, but after more than 300 years it has still been neither proved nor disproved.

fermata /fə'mɑːtə/ n. (pl. **fermatas**) *Mus.* **1** an unspecified prolongation of a note or rest. **2** a sign indicating this. [It.]

ferment n. & v. —n. /'fɜːment/ **1** agitation, excitement, tumult. **2 a** fermenting, fermentation. **b** a fermenting-agent or leaven. —v. /fə'ment/ **1** intr. & tr. undergo or subject to fermentation. **2** intr. & tr. effervesce or cause to effervesce. **3** tr. excite; stir up; foment. □□ **fermentable** /-'mentəb(ə)l/ adj. **fermenter** /'mentə(r)/ n. [ME f. OF *ferment* or L *fermentum* f. L *fervēre* boil]

fermentation /ˌfɜːmen'teɪʃ(ə)n/ n. **1** the breakdown of a substance by micro-organisms, such as yeasts and bacteria, usu. in the absence of oxygen, esp. of sugar to ethyl alcohol in making beers, wines, and spirits. **2** agitation, excitement. □□ **fermentative** /-'mentətɪv/ adj. [ME f. LL *fermentatio* (as FERMENT)]

Fermi /'fɜːmɪ/, Enrico (1901–54), Italian-born American atomic physicist, a key figure in the development of the atomic bomb and nuclear energy. Working at first in his native Italy, he established the statistical laws—found independently by Paul Dirac—which apply to the particles forming the atom, a mathematical tool of great value in atomic, nuclear, and solid-state physics. In 1934 he began work on artificial radioactivity, predicted the existence of the neutrino, and produced radioactive isotopes by bombarding the atomic nuclei of elements with neutrons; this work was to culminate in the discovery of nuclear fission by Hahn and Fritz Strassmann in 1938. In that year Fermi was awarded the Nobel Prize for physics, and left Italy to escape Fascist persecution, settling in the US. He directed the first controlled nuclear chain reaction at the University of Chicago in December 1942, joined the Manhattan Project, and worked on the atomic bomb at Los Alamos. The artificial element fermium and a class of sub-atomic particles, the fermions, are named after him.

fermi /'fɜːmɪ/ n. (pl. **fermis**) a unit of length equal to 10^{-15} metre, formerly used in nuclear physics. [E. FERMI]

fermion /'fɜːmɪˌɒn/ n. *Physics* any of several elementary particles with half-integral spin, e.g. nucleons (cf. BOSON). [as FERMI + -ON]

fermium /'fɜːmɪəm/ n. *Chem.* a transuranic radioactive metallic element produced artificially; identified in 1953 from the debris of the first hydrogen bomb explosion. ¶ Symb.: **Fm**; atomic number 100. [as FERMI + -IUM]

fern /fɜːn/ n. (pl. same or **ferns**) any flowerless plant of the order Filicales, reproducing by spores and usu. having feathery fronds. □□ **fernery** n. (pl. **-ies**). **fernless** adj. **ferny** adj. [OE *fearn* f. WG]

Fernando Póo /fə'nændəʊ 'pəʊ/ the former name (until 1973) of Bioko.

ferocious /fə'rəʊʃəs/ adj. fierce, savage; wildly cruel. □□ **ferociously** adv. **ferociousness** n. [L *ferox -ocis*]

ferocity /fə'rɒsɪtɪ/ n. (pl. **-ies**) a ferocious nature or act. [F *férocité* or L *ferocitas* (as FEROCIOUS)]

-ferous /fərəs/ comb. form (usu. **-iferous**) forming adjectives with the sense 'bearing', 'having' (*auriferous*; *odoriferous*). □□ **-ferously** suffix **-ferousness** suffix [from or after F *-fère* or L *-fer* producing f. *ferre* bear]

Ferranti /fə'ræntɪ/, Sebastian Ziani de (1864–1930), English electrical engineer, one of the great pioneers of electricity generation and distribution in Britain, his particular contribution being the use of high voltages for economical transmission over a distance.

ferrate /'fereɪt/ n. *Chem.* a salt of (the hypothetical) ferric acid. [L *ferrum* iron]

ferrel var. of FERRULE.

ferret /'ferɪt/ n. & v. —n. **1** a small half-domesticated polecat, *Mustela putorius furo*, used in catching rabbits, rats, etc. **2** a person who searches assiduously. —v. **1** intr. hunt with ferrets. **2** intr. rummage; search about. **3** tr. (often foll. by *about, away, out*, etc.) **a** clear out (holes or an area of ground) with ferrets. **b** take or drive away (rabbits etc.) with ferrets. **4** tr. (foll. by *out*) search out (secrets, criminals, etc.). □□ **ferreter** n. **ferrety** adj. [ME f. OF *fu(i)ret* alt. f. *fu(i)ron* f. LL *furo -onis* f. L *fur* thief]

ferri- /'ferɪ/ comb. form *Chem.* containing iron, esp. in ferric compounds. [L *ferrum* iron]

ferriage /'ferɪɪdʒ/ n. **1** conveyance by ferry. **2** a charge for using a ferry.

ferric /'ferɪk/ adj. **1** of iron. **2** *Chem.* containing iron in a trivalent form (cf. FERROUS).

Ferrier /'ferɪə(r)/, Kathleen (1912–53), English contralto singer. After her London début in Handel's *Messiah* she rose rapidly to a leading position among British singers. She made her opera début as Lucretia in the first performance of Britten's *The Rape of Lucretia* (1946), and became a noted exponent of Mahler's *Das Lied von der Erde*. The beauty of her voice, combined with a warm and humorous personality, endeared her to audiences.

ferrimagnetism /ˌferɪ'mægnɪˌtɪz(ə)m/ n. *Physics* a form of ferromagnetism with non-parallel alignment of neighbouring atoms or ions. □□ **ferrimagnetic** /-mæg'netɪk/ adj. [F *ferrimagnétisme* (as FERRI-, MAGNETISM)]

Ferris wheel /'ferɪs/ n. a fairground ride consisting of a tall revolving vertical wheel with passenger cars suspended on its outer edge. [G. W. G. *Ferris*, Amer. engineer d. 1896]

ferrite /'ferɪt/ n. *Chem.* **1** a salt of (the hypothetical) ferrous acid $H_2Fe_2O_4$, often with magnetic properties. **2** an allotrope of pure iron occurring in low-carbon steel. □□ **ferritic** /fe'rɪtɪk/ adj. [L *ferrum* iron]

ferro- /'ferəʊ/ comb. form *Chem.* **1** iron, esp. in ferrous compounds. **2** (of alloys) containing iron (*ferrocyanide*; *ferromanganese*). [L *ferrum* iron]

ferroconcrete /ˌferəʊ'kɒnkriːt/ n. & adj. —n. concrete reinforced with steel. —adj. made of reinforced concrete.

ferroelectric /ˌferəʊɪ'lektrɪk/ adj. & n. *Physics* —adj. exhibiting permanent electric polarization which varies in strength with the applied electric field. —n. a ferroelectric substance. □□ **ferroelectricity** /-'trɪsɪtɪ/ n. [ELECTRIC after *ferromagnetic*]

ferromagnetism /ˌferəʊ'mægnɪˌtɪz(ə)m/ n. *Physics* a phenomenon in which there is a high susceptibility to magnetization, the strength of which varies with the applied magnetizing field, and which may persist after removal of the applied field. □□ **ferromagnetic** /-mæg'netɪk/ adj.

ferrous /'ferəs/ adj. **1** containing iron (*ferrous and non-ferrous metals*). **2** *Chem.* containing iron in a divalent form (cf. FERRIC). [L *ferrum* iron]

ferruginous /fə'ruːdʒɪnəs/ adj. **1** of or containing iron-rust, or iron as a chemical constituent. **2** rust-coloured; reddish-brown. [L *ferrugo -ginis* rust f. *ferrum* iron]

ferrule /'feruːl/ n. (also **ferrel** /'fer(ə)l/) **1** a ring or cap strengthening the end of a stick or tube. **2** a band strengthening or forming a joint. [earlier *verrel* etc. f. OF *virelle*, *virol(e)*, f. L *viriola* dimin. of *viriae* bracelet: assim. to L *ferrum* iron]

ferry /ˈferɪ/ *n. & v.* —*n.* (*pl.* **-ies**) **1** a boat or aircraft etc. for conveying passengers and goods, esp. across water and as a regular service. **2** the service itself or the place where it operates. —*v.* (**-ies, -ied**) **1** *tr. & intr.* convey or go in a boat etc. across water. **2** *intr.* (of a boat etc.) pass to and fro across water. **3** *tr.* transport from one place to another, esp. as a regular service. □□ **ferryman** *n.* (*pl.* **-men**). [ME f. ON *ferja* f. Gmc]

fertile /ˈfɜːtaɪl/ *adj.* **1 a** (of soil) producing abundant vegetation or crops. **b** fruitful. **2 a** (of a seed, egg, etc.) capable of becoming a new individual. **b** (of animals and plants) able to conceive young or produce fruit. **3** (of the mind) inventive. **4** (of nuclear material) able to become fissile by the capture of neutrons. □ **Fertile Crescent** a crescent-shaped area of cultivable land extending from the eastern Mediterranean via the fertile steppe between the Arabian Desert and the mountains of Asia Minor to the Tigris-Euphrates valley and the Persian Gulf. □□ **fertility** /-ˈtɪlɪtɪ/ *n.* [ME f. F f. L *fertilis*]

fertilization /ˌfɜːtɪlaɪˈzeɪʃ(ə)n/ *n.* (also **-isation**) **1** *Biol.* the fusion of male and female gametes during sexual reproduction to form a zygote. **2 a** the act or an instance of fertilizing. **b** the process of being fertilized.

fertilize /ˈfɜːtɪˌlaɪz/ *v.tr.* (also **-ise**) **1** make (soil etc.) fertile or productive. **2** cause (an egg, female animal, or plant) to develop a new individual by introducing male reproductive material. □□ **fertilizable** *adj.*

fertilizer *n.* a chemical or natural substance added to soil to make it more fertile.

ferula /ˈferʊlə/ *n.* **1** any plant of the genus *Ferula*, esp. the giant fennel (*F. communis*), having a tall sticklike stem and thick roots. **2** = FERULE. [ME f. L, = giant fennel, rod]

ferule /ˈferuːl/ *n. & v.* —*n.* a flat ruler with a widened end formerly used for beating children. —*v.tr.* beat with a ferule. [ME (as FERULA)]

fervent /ˈfɜːv(ə)nt/ *adj.* **1** ardent, impassioned, intense (*fervent admirer; fervent hatred*). **2** hot, glowing. □□ **fervency** *n.* **fervently** *adv.* [ME f. OF f. L *fervēre* boil]

fervid /ˈfɜːvɪd/ *adj.* **1** ardent, intense. **2** *poet.* hot, glowing. □□ **fervidly** *adv.* [L *fervidus* (as FERVENT)]

fervour /ˈfɜːvə(r)/ *n.* (US **fervor**) **1** vehemence, passion, zeal. **2** a glowing condition; intense heat. [ME f. OF f. L *fervor -oris* (as FERVENT)]

Fès see FEZ.

fescue /ˈfeskjuː/ *n.* any grass of the genus *Festuca*, valuable for pasture and fodder. [ME *festu(e)* f. OF *festu* ult. f. L *festuca* stalk, straw]

fess /fes/ *n.* (also **fesse**) *Heraldry* a horizontal stripe across the middle of a shield. □ **fess point** a point at the centre of a shield. **in fess** arranged horizontally. [ME f. OF f. L *fascia* band]

festal /ˈfest(ə)l/ *adj.* **1** joyous, merry. **2** engaging in holiday activities. **3** of a feast. □□ **festally** *adv.* [OF f. LL *festalis* (as FEAST)]

fester /ˈfestə(r)/ *v.* **1** *tr. & intr.* make or become septic. **2** *intr.* cause continuing annoyance. **3** *intr.* rot, stagnate. [ME f. obs. *fester* (n.) or OF *festrir*, f. OF *festre* f. L *fistula*: see FISTULA]

festival /ˈfestɪv(ə)l/ *n. & adj.* —*n.* **1** a day or period of celebration, religious or secular. **2** a concentrated series of concerts, plays, etc., held regularly in a town etc. (*Bath Festival*). —*attrib.adj.* of or concerning a festival. [earlier as adj.: ME f. OF f. med.L *festivalis* (as FESTIVE)]

festive /ˈfestɪv/ *adj.* **1** of or characteristic of a festival. **2** joyous. **3** fond of feasting, jovial. □□ **festively** *adv.* **festiveness** *n.* [L *festivus* f. *festum* (as FEAST)]

festivity /feˈstɪvɪtɪ/ *n.* (*pl.* **-ies**) **1** gaiety, rejoicing. **2 a** a festive celebration. **b** (in *pl.*) festive proceedings. [ME f. OF *festivité* or L *festivitas* (as FESTIVE)]

festoon /feˈstuːn/ *n. & v.* —*n.* **1** a chain of flowers, leaves, ribbons, etc., hung in a curve as a decoration. **2** a carved or moulded ornament representing this. —*v.tr.* (often foll. by *with*) adorn with or form into festoons; decorate elaborately. □□ **festoonery** *n.* [F *feston* f. It. *festone* f. *festa* FEAST]

Festschrift /ˈfestʃrɪft/ *n.* (also **festschrift**) (*pl.* **-schriften** or **-schrifts**) a collection of writings published in honour of a scholar. [G f. *Fest* celebration + *Schrift* writing]

feta /ˈfetə/ *n.* (also **fetta**) a soft white ewe's-milk or goat's-milk cheese made esp. in Greece. [mod.Gk *pheta*]

fetch¹ /fetʃ/ *v. & n.* —*v.tr.* **1** go for and bring back (a person or thing) (*fetch a doctor*). **2** be sold for; realize (a price) (*fetched £10*). **3** cause (blood, tears, etc.) to flow. **4** draw (breath), heave (a sigh). **5** *colloq.* give (a blow, slap, etc.) (usu. with recipient stated: *fetched him a slap on the face*). **6** excite the emotions of, delight or irritate. —*n.* **1** an act of fetching. **2** a dodge or trick. **3** *Naut.* **a** the distance travelled by wind or waves across open water. **b** the distance a vessel must sail to reach open water. □ **fetch and carry** run backwards and forwards with things, be a mere servant. **fetch up** *colloq.* **1** arrive, come to rest. **2** vomit. □□ **fetcher** *n.* [OE *fecc(e)an* var. of *fetian*, prob. rel. to a Gmc root = grasp]

fetch² /fetʃ/ *n.* a person's wraith or double. [18th c.: orig. unkn.]

fetching /ˈfetʃɪŋ/ *adj.* attractive. □□ **fetchingly** *adv.*

fête /feɪt/ *n. & v.* —*n.* **1** an outdoor function with the sale of goods, amusements, etc., esp. to raise funds for charity. **2** a great entertainment; a festival. **3** a saint's day. —*v.tr.* honour or entertain lavishly. [F *fête* (as FEAST)]

fête champêtre /feɪt ʃãˈpeɪtr/ *n.* an outdoor entertainment; a rural festival. [F (as FÊTE, *champêtre* rural)]

fetid /ˈfetɪd, ˈfiːtɪd/ *adj.* (also **foetid**) stinking. □□ **fetidly** *adv.* **fetidness** *n.* [L *fetidus* f. *fetēre* stink]

fetish /ˈfetɪʃ/ *n.* **1** *Psychol.* a thing abnormally stimulating or attracting sexual desire. **2 a** an inanimate object worshipped by primitive peoples for its supposed inherent magical powers or as being inhabited by a spirit. **b** a thing evoking irrational devotion or respect. □□ **fetishism** *n.* **fetishist** *n.* **fetishistic** /-ˈʃɪstɪk/ *adj.* [F *fétiche* f. Port. *feitiço* charm: orig. adj. = made by art, f. L *factitius* FACTITIOUS]

fetlock /ˈfetlɒk/ *n.* part of the back of a horse's leg above the hoof where a tuft of hair grows. [ME *fetlak* etc. rel. to G *Fessel* fetlock f. Gmc]

fetor /ˈfiːtə(r)/ *n.* a stench. [L (as FETID)]

fetta var. of FETA.

fetter /ˈfetə(r)/ *n. & v.* —*n.* **1 a** a shackle for holding a prisoner by the ankles. **b** any shackle or bond. **2** (in *pl.*) captivity. **3** a restraint or check. —*v.tr.* **1** put into fetters. **2** restrict, restrain, impede. [OE *feter* f. Gmc]

fetterlock /ˈfetəˌlɒk/ *n.* **1** a D-shaped fetter for tethering a horse by the leg. **2** a heraldic representation of this.

fettle /ˈfet(ə)l/ *n. & v.* —*n.* condition or trim (*in fine fettle*). —*v.tr.* trim or clean (the rough edge of a metal casting, pottery before firing, etc.). [earlier as verb, f. dial. *fettle* (n.) = girdle, f. OE *fetel* f. Gmc]

fettler /ˈfetlə(r)/ *n.* **1** *Brit. & Austral.* a railway maintenance worker. **2** a person who fettles.

fetus US var. of FOETUS.

feu /fjuː/ *n. & v. Sc.* —*n.* **1** a perpetual lease at a fixed rent. **2** a piece of land so held. —*v.tr.* (**feus, feued, feuing**) grant (land) on feu. [OF: see FEE]

feud¹ /fjuːd/ *n. & v.* —*n.* **1** prolonged mutual hostility, esp. between two families, tribes, etc., with murderous assaults in revenge for a previous injury (*a family feud; be at feud with*). **2** a prolonged or bitter quarrel or dispute. —*v.intr.* conduct a feud. [ME *fede* f. OF *feide, fede* f. MDu., MLG *vēde* f. Gmc, rel. to FOE]

feud² /fjuːd/ *n.* a piece of land held under the feudal system or in fee; a fief. [med.L *feudum*: see FEE]

feudal /ˈfjuːd(ə)l/ *adj.* **1** of, according to, or resembling the feudal system. **2** of a feud or fief. **3** outdated (*had a feudal attitude*). □ **feudal system** a medieval European politico-economic system based on the relation of vassal and superior arising from the holding of lands on condition of homage and military service or labour. The nobility held lands from the Crown in exchange for a specified amount of military service; the peasantry lived on their lord's land and had to provide him with labour or a share of his own produce in exchange for protection. The feudal system began to break down in England in the 13th and 14th c., although feudal tenures were not actually abolished by statute until 1666. □□ **feudalism** *n.* **feudalist** *n.* **feudalistic** /-'lɪstɪk/ *adj.* **feudalize** *v.tr.* (also **-ise**). **feudalization** /-'zeɪʃ(ə)n/ *n.* **feudally** *adv.* [med.L *feudalis*, *feodalis* f. *feudum*, *feodum* FEE, perh. f. Gmc]

feudality /fjuː'dælɪtɪ/ *n.* (*pl.* **-ies**) **1** the feudal system or its principles. **2** a feudal holding, a fief. [F *féodalité* f. *féodal* (as FEUDAL)]

feudatory /'fjuːdətərɪ/ *adj. & n.* —*adj.* (often foll. by *to*) feudally subject, under overlordship. —*n.* (*pl.* **-ies**) a feudal vassal. [med.L *feudatorius* f. *feudare* enfeoff (as FEUD²)]

feu de joie /ˌfɜː də 'ʒwɑː/ *n.* (*pl.* **feux** *pronunc.* same) a salute by firing rifles etc. on a ceremonial occasion. [F, = fire of joy]

feudist /'fjuːdɪst/ *n.* US a person who is conducting a feud.

feuilleton /ˌfɜːjə'tõ/ *n.* **1** a part of a newspaper etc. devoted to fiction, criticism, light literature, etc. **2** an item printed in this. [F, = leaflet]

fever /'fiːvə(r)/ *n. & v.* —*n.* **1 a** an abnormally high body temperature, often with delirium etc. **b** a disease characterized by this (*scarlet fever; typhoid fever*). **2** nervous excitement; agitation. —*v.tr.* (esp. as **fevered** *adj.*) affect with fever or excitement. □ **fever pitch** a state of extreme excitement. [OE *fēfor* & AF *fevre*, OF *fievre* f. L *febris*]

feverfew /'fiːvəˌfjuː/ *n.* an aromatic bushy plant, *Tenacetum parthenium*, with feathery leaves and white daisy-like flowers, formerly used to reduce fever. [OE *feferfuge* f. L *febrifuga* (as FEBRIFUGE)]

feverish /'fiːvərɪʃ/ *adj.* **1** having the symptoms of a fever. **2** excited, fitful, restless. **3** (of a place) infested by fever; feverous. □□ **feverishly** *adv.* **feverishness** *n.*

feverous /'fiːvərəs/ *adj.* **1** infested with or apt to cause fever. **2** *archaic* feverish.

few /fjuː/ *adj. & n.* —*adj.* not many (*few doctors smoke; visitors are few*). —*n.* (as *pl.*) **1** (prec. by *a*) some but not many (*a few words should be added; a few of his friends were there*). **2** a small number, not many (*many are called but few are chosen*). **3** (prec. by *the*) **a** the minority. **b** the elect. **4** (**the Few**) *colloq.* the RAF pilots who took part in the Battle of Britain. □ **every few** once in every small group of (*every few days*). **few and far between** scarce. **a good few** *colloq.* a fairly large number. **have a few** *colloq.* take several alcoholic drinks. **no fewer than** as many as (a specified number). **not a few** a considerable number. **some few** some but not at all many. □□ **fewness** *n.* [OE *fēawe*, *fēawa* f. Gmc]

fey /feɪ/ *adj.* **1 a** strange, other-worldly; elfin; whimsical. **b** clairvoyant. **2** *Sc.* **a** fated to die soon. **b** overexcited or elated, as formerly associated with the state of mind of a person about to die. □□ **feyly** *adv.* **feyness** *n.* [OE *fǣge* f. Gmc]

Fez /fez/ (also **Fès**) the oldest of the four imperial cities of Morocco, founded in 808; pop. (1982) 448,800.

fez /fez/ *n.* (*pl.* **fezzes**) a flat-topped conical red cap with a tassel, worn by men in some Muslim countries. □□ **fezzed** *adj.* [Turk., perh. f. FEZ]

ff *abbr. Mus.* fortissimo.

ff. *abbr.* **1** following pages etc. **2** folios.

fiacre /fɪ'ɑːkr/ *n. hist.* a small four-wheeled cab. [the Hôtel de St Fiacre, Paris]

fiancé /fɪ'ɒnseɪ, fɪ'ɑ̃seɪ/ *n.* (*fem.* **fiancée** *pronunc.* same) a person to whom another is engaged to be married. [F, past part. of *fiancer* betroth f. OF *fiance* a promise, ult. f. L *fidere* to trust]

fianchetto /ˌfɪən'tʃetəʊ/ *n. & v. Chess* —*n.* (*pl.* **-oes**) the development of a bishop to a long diagonal of the board. —*v.tr.* (**-oes**, **-oed**) develop (a bishop) in this way. [It., dimin. of *fianco* FLANK]

Fianna Fáil /ˌfɪ:ənə'fɔɪl/ *n.* an Irish political party, traditionally more republican than its rival Fine Gael. It was formed by De Valera in 1926 from moderate members of Sinn Fein. [Ir. *fianna* bands of hunters, *fál* of the defensive fortification. The term *fál* was applied to the rampart of mountains surrounding the central plain of Ireland. The phrase *Fianna Fáil* was used in 15th-c. poetry in the neutral sense 'people of Ireland', but the founders of the political party interpreted it to mean 'soldiers of destiny'.]

fiasco /fɪ'æskəʊ/ *n.* (*pl.* **-os**) a ludicrous or humiliating failure or breakdown (orig. in a dramatic or musical performance); an ignominious result. [It., = bottle (with unexplained allusion): see FLASK]

fiat /'faɪæt, 'faɪət/ *n.* **1** an authorization. **2** a decree or order. □ **fiat money** US inconvertible paper money made legal tender by a Government decree. [L, = let it be done]

fib /fɪb/ *n. & v.* —*n.* a trivial or venial lie. —*v.intr.* (**fibbed**, **fibbing**) tell a fib. □□ **fibber** *n.* **fibster** *n.* [perh. f. obs. *fible-fable* nonsense, redupl. of FABLE]

fiber US var. of FIBRE.

Fibonacci /ˌfiːbə'nɑːtʃɪ/, Leonardo (*c.*1200), Italian mathematician (also called Leonardo Pisano) after whom is named the series of numbers 1, 1, 2, 3, 5, 8, 13, etc., in which each number after the first two is the sum of the two preceding numbers.

fibre /'faɪbə(r)/ *n.* (US **fiber**) **1** *Biol.* any of the threads or filaments forming animal or vegetable tissue and textile substances. **2** a piece of glass in the form of a thread. **3 a** a substance formed of fibres. **b** a substance that can be spun, woven, or felted. **4** the structure, grain, or character of something (*lacks moral fibre*). **5** dietary material that is resistant to the action of digestive enzymes; roughage. □ **fibre optics** see separate entry. □□ **fibred** *adj.* (also in *comb.*). **fibreless** *adj.* **fibriform** /'faɪbrɪˌfɔːm/ *adj.* [ME f. F f. L *fibra*]

fibreboard /'faɪbəˌbɔːd/ *n.* (US **fiberboard**) a building material made of wood or other plant fibres compressed into boards.

fibreglass /'faɪbəˌɡlɑːs/ *n.* (US **fiberglass**) glass in fibrous form; material made from this (e.g. fabric for curtains, matter for use in thermal insulation); plastic containing such glass, used as a structural material e.g. for boat-hulls. Fibreglass was developed commercially in the US in the 1930s; the word was originally a proprietary term.

fibre optics *n.* the use of thin flexible fibres of glass or other transparent solids to transmit light-signals, using the total internal reflection of light, developed and named by Dr Narinder Singh Kapany in the mid 1950s. The fibres, which may be used singly or in bundles, and which need not be straight, are less than 1 mm in thickness and have a high refractive index. Early applications included their use in the medical practice of endoscopy, for inspection of internal organs. In optical communications, a system consists of a transmitter, a length of fibre, and a receiver. The transmitter converts an electrical signal into optical energy by modulation of a light-source, which can be a semiconductor laser or a light-emitting diode. The modulated light is passed into the fibre, propagated through it by a series of total internal reflections at the fibre walls, and received by a light-detector which converts the optical signal back into electrical form; the receiver then converts this back into the original form. Because of the high frequencies employed nearly 2,000 channels can be used in one fibre to carry that number of signals simultaneously.

fibril /'faɪbrɪl/ *n.* **1** a small fibre. **2** a subdivision of a fibre. □□ **fibrillar** *adj.* **fibrillary** *adj.* [mod.L *fibrilla* dimin. of L *fibra* fibre]

fibrillate /'fɪbrɪˌleɪt, 'faɪ-/ *v.* **1** *intr.* **a** (of a fibre) split up into fibrils. **b** (of a muscle, esp. in the heart) undergo a quivering movement in fibrils. **2** *tr.* break (a fibre) into fibrils. □□ **fibrillation** /-'leɪʃ(ə)n/ *n.*

fibrin /'faɪbrɪn/ *n.* an insoluble protein formed during blood-clotting from fibrinogen. □□ **fibrinoid** *adj.* [FIBRE + -IN]

fibrinogen /faɪ'brɪnədʒ(ə)n/ *n.* a soluble blood-plasma protein which produces fibrin when acted upon by the enzyme thrombin.

fibro /'faɪbrəʊ/ *n.* (*pl.* **-os**) *Austral.* **1** fibro-cement. **2** a house constructed mainly of this. [abbr.]

fibro- /'faɪbrəʊ/ *comb. form* fibre.

fibro-cement /ˌfaɪbrəʊsɪ'ment/ *n.* a mixture of any of various fibrous materials, such as glass fibre, cellulose fibre, etc. and cement, used in sheets for building etc.

fibroid /'faɪbrɔɪd/ *adj. & n.* —*adj.* **1** of or characterized by fibrous tissue. **2** resembling or containing fibres. —*n.* a benign

tumour of muscular and fibrous tissues, one or more of which
may develop in the wall of the womb.

fibroin /ˈfaɪbrəʊɪn/ n. a protein which is the chief constituent
of silk. [FIBRO- + -IN]

fibroma /faɪˈbrəʊmə/ n. (pl. **fibromas** or **fibromata** /-mətə/) a
fibrous tumour. [mod.L f. L fibra fibre + -OMA]

fibrosis /faɪˈbrəʊsɪs/ n. Med. a thickening and scarring of connective tissue, usu. as a result of injury. □□ **fibrotic** /-ˈbrɒtɪk/
adj. [mod.L f. L fibrosus fibrous + -OSIS]

fibrositis /ˌfaɪbrəˈsaɪtɪs/ n. an inflammation of fibrous connective tissue, usu. rheumatic and painful. □□ **fibrositic** /-ˈsɪtɪk/
adj. [mod.L f. L fibrosus fibrous + -ITIS]

fibrous /ˈfaɪbrəs/ adj. consisting of or like fibres. □□ **fibrously**
adv. **fibrousness** n.

fibula /ˈfɪbjʊlə/ n. (pl. **fibulae** /-ˌliː/ or **fibulas**) 1 Anat. the smaller
and outer of the two bones between the knee and the ankle in
terrestrial vertebrates. 2 Antiq. a brooch or clasp. □□ **fibular**
adj. [L, perh. rel. to figere fix]

-fic /fɪk/ suffix (usu. as **-ific**) forming adjectives meaning 'producing', 'making' (prolific; pacific). □□ **-fically** suffix forming
adverbs. [from or after F -fique or L -ficus f. facere do, make]

-fication /fɪˈkeɪʃ(ə)n/ suffix (usu. as **-ification**) forming nouns
of action from verbs in -fy (acidification; purification; simplification).
[from or after F -fication or L -ficatio -onis f. -ficare: see -FY]

fiche /fiːʃ/ n. (pl. same or **fiches**) a microfiche. [F, = slip of paper]

Fichte /ˈfɪxtə/, Johann Gottlieb (1762–1814), German philosopher, a pupil of Kant from whose dualism he later dissented.
His philosophy is a pure idealism: the thinking self or ego is
the only basic reality; the world around it, comprehensively
classified as the 'non-ego', is posited by the ego in defining and
limiting itself. In his later writings he sought reality not in the
ego but in the 'divine idea which lies at the base of all experience', and of which the world of the senses is a manifestation.
Fichte preached moral virtues and was an eloquent patriot; his
political addresses had some influence on the development of
German nationalism and the overthrow of Napoleon.

fichu /ˈfiːʃuː, ˈfiːʃuː/ n. a woman's small triangular shawl of lace
etc. for the shoulders and neck. [F]

fickle /ˈfɪk(ə)l/ adj. inconstant, changeable, esp. in loyalty. □□
fickleness n. **fickly** adv. [OE ficol: cf. befician deceive, fæcne
deceitful]

fictile /ˈfɪktaɪl/ adj. 1 made of earth or clay by a potter. 2 of
pottery. [L fictilis f. fingere fict- fashion]

fiction /ˈfɪkʃ(ə)n/ n. 1 an invented idea or statement or narrative;
an imaginary thing. 2 literature, esp. novels, describing imaginary events and people. 3 a conventionally accepted falsehood
(legal fiction; polite fiction). 4 the act or process of inventing imaginary things. □□ **fictional** adj. **fictionality** /-ˈzeɪʃ(ə)n/ n.
fictionalize v.tr. (also **-ise**). **fictionalization** /-ˈzeɪʃ(ə)n/ n.
fictionally adv. **fictionist** n. [ME f. OF f. L fictio -onis (as FICTILE)]

fictitious /fɪkˈtɪʃəs/ adj. 1 imaginary, unreal. 2 counterfeit; not
genuine. 3 (of a name or character) assumed. 4 of or in novels.
5 regarded as what it is called by a legal or conventional fiction.
□□ **fictitiously** adv. **fictitiousness** n. [L ficticius (as FICTILE)]

fictive /ˈfɪktɪv/ adj. 1 creating or created by imagination. 2 not
genuine. □□ **fictively** adv. **fictiveness** n. [F fictif -ive or med.L
fictivus (as FICTILE)]

fid /fɪd/ n. 1 a small thick piece or wedge or heap of anything. 2
Naut. **a** a square wooden or iron bar to support the topmast. **b**
a conical wooden pin used in splicing. [17th c.: orig. unkn.]

Fid. Def. abbr. Brit. Defender of the Faith. [L Fidei Defensor]

fiddle /ˈfɪd(ə)l/ n. & v. —n. 1 colloq. or derog. a stringed instrument played with a bow, esp. a violin. 2 colloq. an instance of
cheating or fraud. 3 Naut. a contrivance for stopping things
from rolling or sliding off a table in bad weather. —v. 1 intr. **a**
(often foll. by with, at) play restlessly. **b** (often foll. by about) move
aimlessly. **c** act idly or frivolously. **d** (usu. foll. by with) make
minor adjustments; tinker (esp. in an attempt to make improvements). 2 tr. sl. **a** cheat, swindle. **b** falsify. **c** get by cheating. 3
a intr. play the fiddle. **b** tr. play (a tune etc.) on the fiddle. □ **as
fit as a fiddle** in very good health. **face as long as a fiddle** a

dismal face. **fiddle-back** a fiddle-shaped back of a chair or front
of a chasuble. **fiddle-head** a scroll-like carving at a ship's bows.
fiddle pattern the pattern of spoons and forks with
fiddle-shaped handles. **play second** (or **first**) **fiddle** take a subordinate (or leading) role. [OE fithele f. Gmc f. a Rmc root rel. to
VIOL]

fiddle-de-dee /ˌfɪdəldɪˈdiː/ int. & n. nonsense.

fiddle-faddle /ˈfɪd(ə)lˌfæd(ə)l/ n., v., int., & adj. —n. trivial matters. —v.intr. fuss, trifle. —int. nonsense! —adj. (of a person
or thing) petty, fussy. [redupl. of FIDDLE]

fiddler /ˈfɪdlə(r)/ n. 1 a fiddle-player. 2 sl. a swindler, a cheat. 3
any small N. American crab of the genus Uca, the male having
one of its claws held in a position like a violinist's arm. [OE
fithelere (as FIDDLE)]

Fiddler's Green the sailor's Elysium, in which wine, women,
and song figure prominently.

fiddlestick /ˈfɪd(ə)lstɪk/ n. 1 (usu. in pl.; as int.) nonsense! 2
colloq. a bow for a fiddle.

fiddling /ˈfɪdlɪŋ/ adj. 1 **a** petty, trivial. **b** contemptible, futile. 2
colloq. = FIDDLY. 3 that fiddles.

fiddly /ˈfɪdlɪ/ adj. (**fiddlier**, **fiddliest**) colloq. intricate, awkward,
or tiresome to do or use.

fideism /ˈfaɪdɪˌɪz(ə)m, ˈfɪdeɪ-/ n. the doctrine that all or some
knowledge depends on faith or revelation. □□ **fideist** n.
fideistic /-ˈɪstɪk/ adj. [L fides faith + -ISM]

fidelity /fɪˈdelɪtɪ/ n. 1 (often foll. by to) faithfulness, loyalty. 2
strict conformity to truth or fact. 3 exact correspondence to the
original. 4 precision in reproduction of sound (high fidelity). □
fidelity insurance insurance taken out by an employer against
losses incurred through an employee's dishonesty etc. [F fidélité
or L fidelitas (as FEALTY)]

fidget /ˈfɪdʒɪt/ v. & n. —v. (**fidgeted**, **fidgeting**) 1 intr. move or
act restlessly or nervously, usu. while maintaining basically the
same posture. 2 intr. be uneasy, worry. 3 tr. make (a person)
uneasy or uncomfortable. —n. 1 a person who fidgets. 2 (usu. in
pl.) **a** bodily uneasiness seeking relief in spasmodic movements;
such movements. **b** a restless mood. □□ **fidgety** adj. **fidgetiness**
n. [obs. or dial. fidge to twitch]

Fido /ˈfaɪdəʊ/ n. a device enabling aircraft to land by dispersing
fog by means of petrol-burners on the ground. [initials of Fog
Intensive Dispersal Operation]

fiducial /fɪˈdjuːʃ(ə)l/ adj. Surveying, Astron., etc. (of a line, point,
etc.) assumed as a fixed basis of comparison. [LL fiducialis f.
fiducia trust f. fidere to trust]

fiduciary /fɪˈdjuːʃərɪ/ adj. & n. —adj. 1 **a** of a trust, trustee, or
trusteeship. **b** held or given in trust. 2 (of a paper currency)
depending for its value on public confidence or securities. —n.
(pl. **-ies**) a trustee. [L fiduciarius (as FIDUCIAL)]

fidus Achates /ˌfaɪdəs əˈkeɪtiːz/ n. a faithful friend; a devoted
follower. [L, = faithful Achates (a companion of Aeneas in
Virgil's Aeneid)]

fie /faɪ/ int. expressing disgust, shame, or a pretence of outraged
propriety. [ME f. OF f. L fi exclam. of disgust at a stench]

fief /fiːf/ n. 1 a piece of land held under the feudal system or in
fee. 2 a person's sphere of operation or control. [F (as FEE)]

fiefdom /ˈfiːfdəm/ n. a fief.

field /fiːld/ n. & v. —n. 1 an area of open land, esp. one used for
pasture or crops, often bounded by hedges, fences, etc. 2 an area
rich in some natural product (gas field; diamond field). 3 a piece
of land for a specified purpose, esp. an area marked out for
games (football field). 4 **a** the participants in a contest or sport.
b all the competitors in a race or all except those specified. 5
Cricket **a** the side fielding. **b** a fielder. 6 an expanse of ice, snow,
sea, sky, etc. 7 **a** the ground on which a battle is fought; a
battlefield (left his rival in possession of the field). **b** the scene of a
campaign. **c** (attrib.) (of artillery etc.) light and mobile for use
on campaign. **d** a battle. 8 an area of operation or activity; a
subject of study (each supreme in his own field). 9 **a** the region in
which a force is effective (gravitational field; magnetic field). **b** the
force exerted in such an area. (See below.) 10 a range of perception (field of view; wide field of vision; filled the field of the telescope).

11 *Math.* a system subject to two operations analogous to those for the multiplication and addition of real numbers. **12** (*attrib.*) **a** (of an animal or plant) found in the countryside, wild (*field mouse*). **b** carried out or working in the natural environment, not in a laboratory etc. (*field test*). **13 a** the background of a picture, coin, flag, etc. **b** *Heraldry* the surface of an escutcheon or of one of its divisions. **14** *Computing* a part of a record, representing an item of data. —*v.* **1** *Cricket, Baseball,* etc. **a** *intr.* act as a fieldsman. **b** *tr.* stop (and return) (the ball). **2** *tr.* select (a team or individual) to play in a game. **3** *tr.* deal with (a succession of questions etc.). □ **field-book** a book used in the field by a surveyor for technical notes. **field-cornet** *S.Afr. hist.* a minor magistrate. **field-day 1** wide scope for action or success; a time occupied with exciting events (*when crowds form, pickpockets have a field-day*). **2** *Mil.* an exercise, esp. in manoeuvring; a review. **3** a day spent in exploration, scientific investigation, etc., in the natural environment. **field events** athletic sports other than races (e.g. shot-putting, jumping, discus-throwing). **field-glasses** binoculars for outdoor use. **field goal** *US Football & Basketball* a goal scored when the ball is in normal play. **field hockey** *US* = HOCKEY[1]. **field hospital** a temporary hospital near a battlefield. **Field Marshal** *Brit.* an army officer of the highest rank. **field mouse** a small rodent, *Apodemus sylvaticus*, with beady eyes, prominent ears, and a long tail. **field mushroom** the edible fungus *Agaricus campestris*. **field mustard** charlock. **field officer** an army officer of field rank. **field of honour** the place where a duel or battle is fought. **field rank** any rank in the army above captain and below general. **field sports** outdoor sports, esp. hunting, shooting, and fishing. **field telegraph** a movable telegraph for use on campaign. **hold the field** not be superseded. **in the field 1** campaigning. **2** working etc. away from one's laboratory, headquarters, etc. **keep the field** continue a campaign. **play the field** *colloq.* avoid exclusive attachment to one person or activity etc. **take the field 1** begin a campaign. **2** (of a sports team) go on to a pitch to begin a game. [OE *feld* f. WG]

The means by which a magnet attracts a piece of iron or another magnet some distance away, even when wood or stone is interposed, has perplexed natural philosophers from antiquity and is still poorly understood. The explanation most widely accepted today was originally proposed by Michael Faraday. According to present theory a magnet produces an intermediate 'condition' in space, called a magnetic field, which in turn acts directly on iron objects or on other magnets placed in the field; this condition can exist even in the absence of any material medium and is not directly affected by the presence of any such medium. Electric fields are similar hypothetical 'conditions' in space introduced to explain the action of one stationary electric charge upon another. It is now known that the magnetism of any body is due to tiny electric currents circulating in that body, and that electric charges in motion are responsible for all magnetic fields. When electric charges accelerate, a third type of field is produced, the electromagnetic radiation field. Light, radiowaves, microwaves, infrared and ultraviolet radiation, and X-rays are all electromagnetic radiation produced by accelerating electric charges. To summarize: stationary electric charges produce electric fields, steadily moving charges produce in addition a magnetic field, and accelerating charges produce electromagnetic radiation.

fielder /ˈfiːldə(r)/ *n.* = FIELDSMAN.

fieldfare /ˈfiːldfeə(r)/ *n.* a thrush, *Turdus pilaris*, having grey plumage with a speckled breast. [ME *feldefare*, perh. as FIELD + FARE]

Fielding /ˈfiːldɪŋ/, Henry (1707–54), English novelist. After he had written several comedies and farces including *Tom Thumb* (1730), his fierce political satire *The Historical Register for 1736* provoked the introduction of censorship in the Licensing Act of 1737 and ended his career as a playwright. He subsequently turned to political journalism and fiction. His first major novel, *Joseph Andrews* (1742), begins as a parody of his rival Richardson's *Pamela*. His greatest achievement, *Tom Jones* (1749), with its ingeniously constructed plot, traces the fortunes of the highly sexed hero while presenting a vivid panorama of 18th-c. London

society. Fielding attempted, in these comic epics in prose, 'to laugh mankind out of their follies and vices'; they were significant contributions to the development of the English novel. In 1748 Fielding became JP for Westminster; he wrote several pamphlets on the suppression of crime and established the Bow Street Runners, predecessors of the London police. *A Journal of a Voyage to Lisbon* (1755) was written in Portugal where he died.

Field of the Cloth of Gold a meeting-place of Henry VIII of England and Francis I of France near Calais in 1520, so called because of the magnificent display made by the rival monarchs. Little of importance was achieved at the meeting which was most significant as a symbol of Henry's determination to play a full part in European dynastic politics.

Fields[1] /fiːldz/, Dame Gracie (real name Grace Stansfield, 1898–1979), English music-hall singer and comedienne. Her films include *Sing as We Go* (1934), written by the novelist J. B. Priestley, but in spite of her legendary popularity in Britain her appeal was ineffective abroad.

Fields[2] /fiːldz/, W. C. (real name William Claude Dukinfield, 1880–1946), American comedian who made his name as a comedy juggler and became a star of vaudeville and musical comedy. Fields was eccentric in public and in private, with a gravelly voice and an intolerance of sentimentality. His films include *The Bank Dick* and *My Little Chickadee* (both 1940).

fieldsman /ˈfiːldzmən/ *n.* (*pl.* **-men**) *Cricket, Baseball,* etc. a member (other than the bowler or pitcher) of the side that is fielding.

fieldstone /ˈfiːldstəʊn/ *n.* stone used in its natural form.

fieldwork /ˈfiːldwɜːk/ *n.* **1** the practical work of a surveyor, collector of scientific data, sociologist, etc., conducted in the natural environment rather than a laboratory, office, etc. **2** a temporary fortification. □□ **fieldworker** *n.*

fiend /fiːnd/ *n.* **1 a** an evil spirit, a demon. **b** (prec. by *the*) the Devil. **2 a** a very wicked or cruel person. **b** a person causing mischief or annoyance. **3** (with a qualifying word) *sl.* a devotee or addict (*a fitness fiend*). **4** something difficult or unpleasant. □□ **fiendish** *adj.* **fiendishly** *adv.* **fiendishness** *n.* **fiendlike** *adj.* [OE *feond* f. Gmc]

fierce /fɪəs/ *adj.* (**fiercer, fiercest**) **1** vehemently aggressive or frightening in temper or action, violent. **2** eager, intense, ardent. **3** unpleasantly strong or intense; uncontrolled (*fierce heat*). **4** (of a mechanism) not smooth or easy in action. □□ **fiercely** *adv.* **fierceness** *n.* [ME f. AF *fers*, OF *fiers fier* proud f. L *ferus* savage]

fieri facias /ˌfaɪəraɪ ˈfeɪʃɪˌæs/ *n. Law* a writ to a sheriff for executing a judgement. [L, = cause to be made or done]

fiery /ˈfaɪərɪ/ *adj.* (**fierier, fieriest**) **1 a** consisting of or flaming with fire. **b** (of an arrow etc.) fire-bearing. **2** like fire in appearance, bright red. **3 a** hot as fire. **b** acting like fire; producing a burning sensation. **4 a** flashing, ardent (*fiery eyes*). **b** eager, pugnacious, spirited, irritable (*fiery temper*). **c** (of a horse) mettlesome. **5** (of gas, a mine, etc.) inflammable; liable to explosions. **6** *Cricket* (of a pitch) making the ball rise dangerously. □ **fiery cross** a wooden cross charred or set on fire as a symbol. □□ **fierily** *adv.* **fieriness** *n.*

fiesta /fɪˈestə/ *n.* **1** a holiday or festivity. **2** a religious festival in Spanish-speaking countries. [Sp., = feast]

FIFA /ˈfiːfə/ *abbr.* International Football Federation. [F *Fédération Internationale de Football Association*]

fi. fa. *abbr.* fieri facias.

Fife /faɪf/ a local government region in east central Scotland; pop. (1981) 344,600.

fife /faɪf/ *n. & v.* —*n.* **1** a kind of small shrill flute used with the drum in military music. **2** its player. —*v.* **1** *intr.* play the fife. **2** *tr.* play (an air etc.) on the fife. □□ **fifer** *n.* [G *Pfeife* PIPE, or F *fifre* f. Swiss G *Pfifre* piper]

fife-rail /ˈfaɪfreɪl/ *n. Naut.* a rail round the mainmast with belaying-pins. [18th c.: orig. unkn.]

fifteen /fɪfˈtiːn, ˈfɪf-/ *n. & adj.* —*n.* **1** one more than fourteen, or five more than ten; the product of three units and five units. **2** a symbol for this (15, xv, XV). **3** a size etc. denoted by fifteen. **4** a team of fifteen players, esp. in Rugby football. **5** (**the Fifteen**) *hist.* the Jacobite rebellion of 1715. **6** (**15**) *Brit.* (of films) classified as suitable for persons of 15 years and over. —*adj.* that amount to fifteen. □□ **fifteenth** *adj.* & *n.* [OE *fīftēne* (as FIVE, -TEEN)]

fifth /fɪfθ/ *n.* & *adj.* —*n.* **1** the position in a sequence corresponding to that of the number 5 in the sequence 1–5. **2** something occupying this position. **3** the fifth person etc. in a race or competition. **4** any of five equal parts of a thing. **5** *Mus.* **a** an interval or chord spanning five consecutive notes in the diatonic scale (e.g. C to G). **b** a note separated from another by this interval. **6** *US colloq.* **a** a fifth of a gallon of liquor. **b** a bottle containing this. —*adj.* that is the fifth. □ **fifth column** a group working for an enemy within a country at war etc. The term dates from the Spanish Civil War when General Mola, leading four columns of troops towards Madrid, declared that he had a fifth column inside the city. **fifth-columnist** a member of a fifth column; a traitor or spy. **Fifth Monarchy** the last of the five great kingdoms predicted in Daniel 2: 44. **Fifth-monarchy-man** *hist.* a 17th-c. zealot expecting the immediate second coming of Christ and repudiating all other government. **fifth part** = sense 4 of *n.* **fifth wheel 1** an extra wheel of a coach. **2** a superfluous person or thing. **3** a horizontal turntable over the front axle of a carriage as an extra support to prevent its tipping. **take the fifth** (in the US) exercise the right guaranteed by the Fifth Amendment to the Constitution of refusing to answer questions in order to avoid incriminating oneself. □□ **fifthly** *adv.* [earlier and dial. *fift* f. OE *fīfta* f. Gmc, assim. to FOURTH]

fifty /fɪftɪ/ *n.* & *adj.* —*n.* (*pl.* **-ies**) **1** the product of five and ten. **2** a symbol for this (50, l, L). **3** (in *pl.*) the numbers from 50 to 59, esp. the years of a century or of a person's life. **4** a set of fifty persons or things. **5** a large indefinite number (*have fifty things to tell you*). —*adj.* that amount to fifty. □ **fifty-fifty** *adj.* equal, with equal shares or chances (*on a fifty-fifty basis*). —*adv.* equally, half and half (*go fifty-fifty*). **fifty-first, -second**, etc. the ordinal numbers between fiftieth and sixtieth. **fifty-one, -two**, etc. the cardinal numbers between fifty and sixty. □□ **fiftieth** *adj.* & *n.* **fiftyfold** *adj.* & *adv.* [OE *fīftig* (as FIVE, -TY²)]

fig¹ /fɪg/ *n.* **1 a** a soft pear-shaped fruit with many seeds, eaten fresh or dried. **b** (in full **fig-tree**) any deciduous tree of the genus *Ficus*, esp. *F. carica*, having broad leaves and bearing figs. **2** a valueless thing (*don't care a fig for*). □ **fig-leaf 1** a leaf of a fig-tree. **2** a device for concealing something, esp. the genitals (Gen. 3: 7). [ME f. OF *figue* f. Prov. *fig(u)a* ult. f. L *ficus*]

fig² /fɪg/ *n.* & *v.* —*n.* **1** dress or equipment (*in full fig*). **2** condition or form (*in good fig*). —*v.tr.* (**figged, figging**) **1** (foll. by *out*) dress up (a person). **2** (foll. by *out, up*) make (a horse) lively. [var. of obs. *feague* (v.) f. G *fegen*: see FAKE¹]

fig. *abbr.* figure.

fight /faɪt/ *v.* & *n.* —*v.* (*past* and *past part.* **fought** /fɔːt/) **1** *intr.* (often foll. by *against, with*) contend or struggle in war, battle, single combat, etc. **2** *tr.* contend with (an opponent) in this way. **3** *tr.* take part or engage in (a battle, war, duel, etc.). **4** *tr.* contend about (an issue, an election); maintain (a lawsuit, cause, etc.) against an opponent. **5** *intr.* campaign or strive determinedly to achieve something. **6** *tr.* strive to overcome (disease, fire, fear, etc.). **7** *tr.* make (one's way) by fighting. **8** *tr.* cause (cocks or dogs) to fight. **9** *tr.* handle (troops, a ship, etc.) in battle. —*n.* **1 a** a combat, esp. unpremeditated, between two or more persons, animals, or parties. **b** a boxing-match. **c** a battle. **2** a conflict or struggle; a vigorous effort in the face of difficulty. **3** power or inclination to fight (*has no fight left; showed fight*). □ **fight back 1** counter-attack. **2** suppress (one's feelings, tears, etc.). **fight down** suppress (one's feelings, tears, etc.). **fight for 1** fight on behalf of. **2** fight to secure (a thing). **fighting chair** *US* a fixed chair on a boat for use when catching large fish. **fighting chance** an opportunity of succeeding by great effort. **fighting fish** (in full **Siamese fighting fish**) a freshwater fish, *Betta splendens*, native to Thailand, the males of which sometimes kill each other during fights for territory. **fighting fit** fit enough to fight; at the peak of fitness. **fighting fund** money raised to support a campaign. **fighting-top** *Naut.* a circular gun-platform high on a warship's mast. **fighting words** *colloq.* words indicating a willingness to fight. **fight off** repel with effort. **fight out** (usu. **fight it out**) settle (a dispute etc.) by fighting. **fight shy**

of avoid; be unwilling to approach (a person, task, etc.). **make a fight of it** (or **put up a fight**) offer resistance. [OE *feohtan*, *feoht(e)*, f. WG]

fighter /faɪtə(r)/ *n.* **1** a person or animal that fights. **2** a fast military aircraft designed for attacking other aircraft. □ **fighter-bomber** an aircraft serving as both fighter and bomber.

figment /fɪgmənt/ *n.* a thing invented or existing only in the imagination. [ME f. L *figmentum*, rel. to *fingere* fashion]

figura /fɪˈgjʊərə/ *n.* **1** a person or thing representing or symbolizing a fact etc. **2** *Theol.* a type of a person etc. [mod.L f. L, = FIGURE]

figural /fɪgjʊr(ə)l/ *adj.* **1** figurative. **2** relating to figures or shapes. **3** *Mus.* florid in style. [OF *figural* or LL *figuralis* f. *figura* FIGURE]

figurant /fɪgjʊrənt/ *n.* (*fem.* **figurante** pronunc. same) a ballet-dancer appearing only in a group. [F, pres. part. of *figurer* FIGURE]

figurante /ˌfɪgjʊˈrænti/ *n.* (*pl.* **figuranti** /-tiː/) = FIGURANT. [It., pres. part. of *figurare* FIGURE]

figuration /ˌfɪgjʊˈreɪʃ(ə)n/ *n.* **1 a** the act of formation. **b** a mode of formation; a form. **c** a shape or outline. **2 a** ornamentation by designs. **b** *Mus.* ornamental patterns of scales, arpeggios, etc., often derived from an earlier motif. **3** allegorical representation. [ME f. F or f. L *figuratio*]

figurative /fɪgjʊrətɪv, fɪgər-/ *adj.* **1 a** metaphorical, not literal. **b** metaphorically so called. **2** characterized by or addicted to figures of speech. **3** of pictorial or sculptural representation. **4** emblematic, serving as a type. □□ **figuratively** *adv.* **figurativeness** *n.* [ME f. LL *figurativus* (as FIGURE)]

figure /fɪgə(r)/ *n.* & *v.* —*n.* **1 a** the external form or shape of a thing. **b** bodily shape (*has a well-developed figure*). **2 a** a person as seen in outline but not identified (*saw a figure leaning against the door*). **b** a person as contemplated mentally (*a public figure*). **3** appearance as giving a certain impression (*cut a poor figure*). **4 a** a representation of the human form in drawing, sculpture, etc. **b** an image or likeness. **c** an emblem or type. **5** *Geom.* a two-dimensional space enclosed by a line or lines, or a three-dimensional space enclosed by a surface or surfaces; any of the classes of these, e.g. the triangle, the sphere. **6 a** a numerical symbol, esp. any of the ten in Arabic notation. **b** a number so expressed. **c** an amount of money, a value (*cannot put a figure on it*). **d** (in *pl.*) arithmetical calculations. **7** a diagram or illustrative drawing. **8** a decorative pattern. **9 a** a division of a set dance, an evolution. **b** (in skating) a prescribed pattern of movements from a stationary position. **10** *Mus.* a short succession of notes producing a single impression, a brief melodic or rhythmic formula out of which longer passages are developed. **11** (in full **figure of speech**) a recognized form of rhetorical expression giving variety, force, etc., esp. metaphor or hyperbole. **12** *Gram.* a permitted deviation from the usual rules of construction, e.g. ellipsis. **13** *Logic* the form of a syllogism, classified according to the position of the middle term. **14** a horoscope. —*v.* **1** *intr.* appear or be mentioned, esp. prominently. **2** *tr.* represent in a diagram or picture. **3** *tr.* imagine; picture mentally. **4** *tr.* **a** embellish with a pattern (*figured satin*). **b** *Mus.* embellish with figures. **5** *tr.* mark with numbers (*figured bass*) or prices. **6 a** *tr.* calculate. **b** *intr.* do arithmetic. **7** *tr.* be a symbol of, represent typically. **8** esp. *US* **a** *tr.* understand, ascertain, consider. **b** *intr. colloq.* be likely or understandable (*that figures*). □ **figured bass** *Mus.* = CONTINUO. **figure of fun** a ridiculous person. **figure on** *US* count on, expect. **figure out 1** work out by arithmetic or logic. **2** estimate. **3** understand. **figure-skater** a person who practises figure-skating. **figure-skating** skating in prescribed patterns from a stationary position. □□ **figureless** *adj.* [ME f. OF *figure* (n.), *figurer* (v.) f. L *figura*, *figurare*, rel. to *fingere* fashion]

figurehead /fɪgəhed/ *n.* **1** a nominal leader or head without real power. **2** a carving, usu. a bust or a full-length figure, at a ship's prow.

figurine /ˌfɪgjʊˈriːn, fɪg-/ *n.* a statuette. [F f. It. *figurina* dimin. of *figura* FIGURE]

figwort /fɪgwɜːt/ *n.* any aromatic green-flowered plant of the genus *Scrophularia*, once believed to be useful against scrofula.

Fiji /'fi:dʒɪ/ a group of some 840 islands, of which about 100 are inhabited, in the South Pacific (the International Date Line has been diverted to the east of the island group); pop. (est. 1988) 740,760; official language, English; capital, Suva. The population, which is mostly engaged in agriculture and fishing, contains an almost equal mix of native Pacific islanders and Indians, the latter being descendants of those brought in to work the sugar plantations in the 19th c. Discovered by Tasman in 1643 and visited by Captain Cook in 1774, the Fiji Islands became a British Crown Colony in 1874 and an independent State, a member of the Commonwealth, in 1970. □□ **Fijian** adj. & n.

filagree var. of FILIGREE.

filament /'fɪləmənt/ n. **1** a slender threadlike body or fibre (esp. in animal or vegetable structures). **2** a conducting wire or thread with a high melting-point in an electric bulb or thermionic valve, heated or made incandescent by an electric current. **3** Bot. the part of the stamen that supports the anther. **4** archaic (of air, light, etc.) a notional train of particles following each other. □□ **filamentary** /-'mentərɪ/ adj. **filamented** adj. **filamentous** /-'mentəs/ adj. [F filament or mod.L filamentum f. LL filare spin f. L filum thread]

filaria /fɪ'leərɪə/ n. (pl. **filariae** /-rɪ,i:/) any threadlike parasitic nematode worm of the family Filariidae introduced into the blood by certain biting flies and mosquitoes. □□ **filarial** adj. [mod.L f. L filum thread]

filariasis /,fɪlə'raɪəsɪs, fɪ,leərɪ'eɪsɪs/ n. a disease common in the tropics, caused by the presence of filarial worms in the lymph vessels.

filature /'fɪlətʃə(r)/ n. an establishment for or the action of reeling silk from cocoons. [F f. It. filatura f. filare spin]

filbert /'fɪlbət/ n. **1** the cultivated hazel, Corylus maxima, bearing edible ovoid nuts. **2** this nut. [ME philliberd etc. f. AF philbert, dial. F noix de filbert, a nut ripe about St Philibert's day (20 Aug.)]

filch /fɪltʃ/ v.tr. pilfer, steal. □□ **filcher** n. [16th-c. thieves' sl.: orig. unkn.]

file[1] /faɪl/ n. & v. —n. **1** a folder, box, etc., for holding loose papers, esp. arranged for reference. **2** a set of papers kept in this. **3** Computing a collection of (usu. related) data stored under one name. **4** a series of issues of a newspaper etc. in order. **5** a stiff pointed wire on which documents etc. are impaled for keeping. —v.tr. **1** place (papers) in a file or among (esp. public) records. **2** submit (a petition for divorce, an application for a patent, etc.) to the appropriate authority. **3** (of a reporter) send (a story, information, etc.) to a newspaper. □ **filing cabinet** a case with drawers for storing documents. □□ **filer** n. [F fil f. L filum thread]

file[2] /faɪl/ n. & v. —n. **1** a line of persons or things one behind another. **2** (foll. by of) Mil. a small detachment of men (now usu. two). **3** Chess a line of squares from player to player (cf. RANK[1]). —v.intr. walk in a file. □ **file off** (or **away**) Mil. go off by files. [F file f. LL filare spin or L filum thread]

file[3] /faɪl/ n. & v. —n. a tool with a roughened surface or surfaces, usu. of steel, for smoothing or shaping metal, wood, fingernails, etc. —v.tr. **1** smooth or shape with a file. **2** elaborate or improve (a thing, esp. a literary work). □ **file away** remove (roughness etc.) with a file. **file-fish** any fish of the family Ostracionidae, with sharp dorsal fins and usu. bright coloration. □□ **filer** n. [OE fíl f. WG]

filet /'fɪlɪt/ n. **1** a kind of net or lace with a square mesh. **2** a fillet of meat. □ **filet mignon** /'mi:njɔ̃/ a small tender piece of beef from the end of the undercut. [F, = thread]

filial /'fɪlɪəl/ adj. **1** of or due from a son or daughter. **2** Biol. bearing the relation of offspring (cf. F[2] 5). □□ **filially** adv. [ME f. OF filial or LL filialis f. filius son, filia daughter]

filiation /,fɪlɪ'eɪʃ(ə)n/ n. **1** being the child of one or two specified parents. **2** (often foll. by from) descent or transmission. **3** the formation of offshoots. **4** a branch of a society or language. **5** a genealogical relation or arrangement. [F f. LL filiatio -onis f. L filius son]

filibeg /'fɪlɪ,beg/ n. (also **philabeg** /'fɪlə-/) Sc. a kilt. [Gael. feileadh-beag little fold]

filibuster /'fɪlɪ,bʌstə(r)/ n. & v. —n. **1 a** the obstruction of progress in a legislative assembly, esp. by prolonged speaking. **b** esp. US a person who engages in a filibuster. **2** esp. hist. a person engaging in unauthorized warfare against a foreign State —v. **1** intr. act as a filibuster. **2** tr. act in this way against (a motion etc.). □□ **filibusterer** n. [ult. f. Du. vrijbuiter FREEBOOTER, infl. by F flibustier, Sp. filibustero]

filigree /'fɪlɪ,gri:/ n. (also **filagree** /'fɪlə,gri:/) **1** ornamental work of gold or silver or copper as fine wire formed into delicate tracery; fine metal openwork. **2** anything delicate resembling this. □□ **filigreed** adj. [earlier filigreen, filigrane f. F filigrane f. It. filigrana f. L filum thread + granum seed]

filing /'faɪlɪŋ/ n. (usu. in pl.) a particle rubbed off by a file.

Filioque /,fɪlɪ'əʊkwi:/ the word (L, = and from the Son) inserted in the Western version of the Nicene Creed to assert the doctrine of the procession of the Holy Ghost from the Son as well as from the Father, which is not admitted by the Eastern Church. It was one of the central issues in the Great Schism of 1054.

Filipino /,fɪlɪ'pi:nəʊ/ n. & adj. —n. (pl. **-os**; fem. **Filipina** /-nə/) a native or national of the Philippines. —adj. of or relating to the Philippines or the Filipinos. [Sp., = Philippine]

fill /fɪl/ v. & n. —v. **1** tr. & intr. (often foll. by with) make or become full. **2** tr. occupy completely; spread over or through; pervade. **3** tr. block up (a cavity or hole in a tooth) with cement, amalgam, gold, etc.; drill and put a filling into (a decayed tooth). **4** tr. appoint a person to hold (a vacant post). **5** tr. hold (a position); discharge the duties of (an office). **6** tr. carry out or supply (an order, commission, etc.). **7** tr. occupy (vacant time). **8** intr. (of a sail) be distended by wind. **9** tr. (usu. as **filling** adj.) (esp. of food) satisfy, satiate. **10** tr. Poker etc. complete (a holding) by drawing the necessary cards. **11** tr. stock abundantly. —n. **1** (prec. by possessive) as much as one wants or can bear (eat your fill). **2** enough to fill something (a fill of tobacco). **3** earth etc. used to fill a cavity. □ **fill the bill** be suitable or adequate. **fill in 1** add information to complete (a form, document, blank cheque, etc.). **2 a** complete (a drawing etc.) within an outline. **b** fill (an outline) in this way. **3** fill (a hole etc.) completely. **4** (often foll. by for) act as a substitute. **5** occupy oneself during (time between other activities). **6** colloq. inform (a person) more fully. **7** sl. thrash, beat. **fill out 1** enlarge to the required size. **2** become enlarged or plump. **3** US fill in (a document etc.). **fill up 1** make or become completely full. **2** fill in (a document etc.). **3** fill the petrol tank of (a car etc.). **4** provide what is needed to occupy vacant parts or places or deal with deficiencies in. **5** do away with (a pond etc.) by filling. **fill-up** n. a thing that fills something up. [OE fyllan f. Gmc, rel. to FULL[1]]

fille de joie /,fi:j də 'zwa:/ n. a prostitute. [F, lit. 'daughter of joy']

filler /'fɪlə(r)/ n. **1** material or an object used to fill a cavity or increase bulk. **2** an item filling space in a newspaper etc. **3** a person or thing that fills. □ **filler cap** a cap closing the filling-pipe leading to the petrol tank of a motor vehicle.

fillet /'fɪlɪt/ n. & v. —n. **1 a** a fleshy boneless piece of meat from near the loins or the ribs. **b** (in full **fillet steak**) the undercut of a sirloin. **c** a boned longitudinal section of a fish. **2 a** a headband, ribbon, string, or narrow band, for binding the hair or worn round the head. **b** a band or bandage. **3 a** a thin narrow strip of anything. **b** a raised rim or ridge on any surface. **4** Archit. **a** a narrow flat band separating two mouldings. **b** a small band between the flutes of a column. **5** Carpentry an added triangular piece of wood to round off an interior angle. **6 a** a plain line impressed on the cover of a book. **b** a roller used to impress this. **7** Heraldry a horizontal division of a shield, a quarter of the depth of a chief. —v.tr. (**filleted, filleting**) **1 a** remove bones from (fish or meat). **b** divide (fish or meat) into fillets. **2** bind or provide with a fillet or fillets. **3** encircle with an ornamental band. □□ **filleter** n. [ME f. OF filet f. Rmc dimin. of L filum thread]

filling /'fɪlɪŋ/ n. **1** any material that fills or is used to fill, esp.: **a** a piece of material used to fill a cavity in a tooth. **b** the edible substance between the bread in a sandwich or between the pastry in a pie. **2** US weft. □ **filling-station** an establishment selling petrol etc. to motorists.

fillip /'fɪlɪp/ n. & v. —n. **1** a stimulus or incentive. **2 a** a sudden release of a finger or thumb when it has been bent and checked by a thumb or finger. **b** a slight smart stroke given in this way. —*v.* (**filliped, filliping**) **1** *tr.* stimulate (*fillip one's memory*). **2** *tr.* strike slightly and smartly. **3** *tr.* propel (a coin, marble, etc.) with a fillip. **4** *intr.* make a fillip. [imit.]

fillis /ˈfɪlɪs/ *n. Hort.* loosely-twisted string used as a tying material. [F *filasse* tow]

fillister /ˈfɪlɪstə(r)/ *n.* a rabbet or rabbet plane for window-sashes etc. [19th c.: perh. f. F *feuilleret*]

Fillmore /ˈfɪlmɔː(r)/, Millard (1800–74), 13th President of the US, who succeeded to the Presidency on the death of Zachary Taylor.

filly /ˈfɪlɪ/ *n.* (*pl.* **-ies**) **1** a young female horse, usu. before it is four years old. **2** *colloq.* a girl or young woman. [ME, prob. f. ON *fylja* f. Gmc (as FOAL)]

film /fɪlm/ *n.* & *v.* —*n.* **1** a thin coating or covering layer. **2** *Photog.* a strip or sheet of plastic or other flexible base coated with light-sensitive emulsion for exposure in a camera, either as individual visual representations or as a sequence which form the illusion of movement when shown in rapid succession. **3 a** a representation of a story, episode, etc., on a film, with the illusion of movement. **b** a story represented in this way. **c** (in *pl.*) the cinema industry. **4** a slight veil or haze etc. **5** a dimness or morbid growth affecting the eyes. **6** a fine thread or filament. —*v.* **1 a** *tr.* make a photographic film of (a scene, person, etc.). **b** *tr.* (also *absol.*) make a cinema or television film of (a book etc.). **c** *intr.* be (well or ill) suited for reproduction on film. **2** *tr.* & *intr.* cover or become covered with or as with a film. □ **film-goer** a person who frequents the cinema. **film star** a celebrated actor or actress in films. **film-strip** a series of transparencies in a strip for projection. [OE *filmen* membrane f. WG, rel. to FELL⁵]

filmic /ˈfɪlmɪk/ *adj.* of or relating to films or cinematography.

filmography /fɪlˈmɒgrəfɪ/ *n.* (*pl.* **-ies**) a list of films by one director etc. or on one subject. [FILM + -GRAPHY after *bibliography*]

filmset /ˈfɪlmset/ *v.tr.* (**-setting**; *past* and *past part.* **-set**) *Printing* set (material for printing) by filmsetting. □□ **filmsetter** *n.*

filmsetting /ˈfɪlmˌsetɪŋ/ *n. Printing* typesetting using characters on photographic film.

filmy /ˈfɪlmɪ/ *adj.* (**filmier, filmiest**) **1** thin and translucent. **2** covered with or as with a film. □□ **filmily** *adv.* **filminess** *n.*

Filofax /ˈfaɪləʊˌfæks/ *n. propr.* a portable loose-leaf filing system for personal or office use. [FILE¹ + *facts* pl. of FACT]

filoplume /ˈfaɪləˌpluːm/ *n.* a slender feather of a type found between and beneath the flight feathers of some birds. [mod. L *filopluma* f. L *filum* thread, *pluma* feather]

filoselle /ˈfɪləˌsel/ *n.* floss silk. [F]

fils /fiːs/ *n.* (added to a surname to distinguish a son from a father) the son, junior (cf. PÈRE). [F, = son]

filter /ˈfɪltə(r)/ *n.* & *v.* —*n.* **1** a porous device for removing impurities or solid particles from a liquid or gas passed through it. **2** = *filter tip*. **3** a screen or attachment for absorbing or modifying light, X-rays, etc. **4** a device for suppressing electrical or sound waves of frequencies not required. **5** *Brit.* **a** an arrangement for filtering traffic. **b** a traffic-light signalling this. —*v.intr.* & *tr.* **1** pass or cause to pass through a filter. **2** (foll. by *through, into,* etc.) make way gradually. **3** (foll. by *out*) leak or cause to leak. **4** *Brit.* allow (traffic) or (of traffic) be allowed to pass to the left or right at a junction while traffic going straight ahead is halted (esp. at traffic lights). □ **filter-bed** a tank or pond containing a layer of sand etc. for filtering large quantities of liquid. **filter-paper** porous paper for filtering. **filter tip 1** a filter attached to a cigarette for removing impurities from the inhaled smoke. **2** a cigarette with this. **filter-tipped** having a filter tip. [F *filtre* f. med.L *filtrum* felt used as a filter, f. WG]

filterable /ˈfɪltərəb(ə)l/ *adj.* (also **filtrable** /ˈfɪltrəb(ə)l/) **1** *Med.* (of a virus) able to pass through a filter that retains bacteria. **2** that can be filtered.

filth /fɪlθ/ *n.* **1** repugnant or extreme dirt. **2** vileness, corruption, obscenity. **3** foul or obscene language. **4** (prec. by *the*) *sl.* the police. [OE *fȳlth* (as FOUL, -TH²)]

filthy /ˈfɪlθɪ/ *adj.* & *adv.* —*adj.* (**filthier, filthiest**) **1** extremely or disgustingly dirty. **2** obscene. **3** *colloq.* (of weather) very unpleasant. **4** vile. —*adv.* **1** filthily (*filthy dirty*). **2** *colloq.* extremely (*filthy rich*). □ **filthy lucre 1** dishonourable gain (Tit. 1: 11). **2** *joc.* money. □□ **filthily** *adv.* **filthiness** *n.*

filtrable var. of FILTERABLE.

filtrate /ˈfɪltreɪt/ *v.* & *n.* —*v.tr.* filter. —*n.* filtered liquid. □□ **filtration** /-ˈtreɪʃ(ə)n/ *n.* [mod.L *filtrare* (as FILTER)]

fimbriate /ˈfɪmbrɪˌeɪt/ *adj.* (also **fimbriated**) **1** *Bot.* & *Zool.* fringed or bordered with hairs etc. **2** *Heraldry* having a narrow border. [L *fimbriatus* f. *fimbriae* fringe]

fin /fɪn/ *n.* & *v.* —*n.* **1** an organ on various parts of the body of many aquatic vertebrates and some invertebrates, including fish and cetaceans, for propelling, steering, and balancing (*dorsal fin; anal fin*). **2** a small projecting surface or attachment on an aircraft, rocket, or motor car for ensuring aerodynamic stability. **3** an underwater swimmer's flipper. **4** a sharp lateral projection on the share or coulter of a plough. **5** a finlike projection on any device, for improving heat transfer etc. —*v.* (**finned, finning**) **1** *tr.* provide with fins. **2** *intr.* swim under water. □ **fin-back** (or **fin whale**) a rorqual, *Balaenoptera physalus.* □□ **finless** *adj.* **finned** *adj.* (also in *comb.*). [OE *fin(n)*]

finable see FINE².

finagle /fɪˈneɪg(ə)l/ *v.intr.* & *tr. colloq.* act or obtain dishonestly. □□ **finagler** *n.* [dial. *fainaigue* cheat]

final /ˈfaɪn(ə)l/ *adj.* & *n.* —*adj.* **1** situated at the end, coming last. **2** conclusive, decisive, unalterable, putting an end to doubt. **3** concerned with the purpose or end aimed at. —*n.* **1** the last or deciding heat or game in sports or in a competition (*Cup Final*). **2** the edition of a newspaper published latest in the day. **3** (usu. in *pl.*) the series of examinations at the end of a degree course. **4** *Mus.* the principal note in any mode. □ **final cause** *Philos.* the end towards which a thing naturally develops or at which an action aims. **final clause** *Gram.* a clause expressing purpose, introduced by *in order that, lest,* etc. **final drive** the last part of the transmission system in a motor vehicle. **final solution** the Nazi policy (1941–5) of exterminating European Jews. □□ **finally** *adv.* [ME f. OF or f. L *finalis* f. *finis* end]

finale /fɪˈnɑːlɪ, -leɪ/ *n.* **1 a** the last movement of an instrumental composition. **b** a piece of music closing an act in an opera. **2** the close of a drama etc. **3** a conclusion. [It. (as FINAL)]

finalism /ˈfaɪnəˌlɪz(ə)m/ *n.* the doctrine that natural processes (e.g. evolution) are directed towards some goal. □□ **finalistic** /-ˈlɪstɪk/ *adj.*

finalist /ˈfaɪnəlɪst/ *n.* a competitor in the final of a competition etc.

finality /faɪˈnælɪtɪ/ *n.* (*pl.* **-ies**) **1** the quality or fact of being final. **2** the belief that something is final. **3** a final act, state, or utterance. **4** the principle of final cause viewed as operative in the universe. [F *finalité* f. LL *finalitas -tatis* (as FINAL)]

finalize /ˈfaɪnəˌlaɪz/ *v.tr.* (also **-ise**) **1** put into final form. **2** complete; bring to an end. **3** approve the final form or details of. □□ **finalization** /-ˈzeɪʃ(ə)n/ *n.*

finance /ˈfaɪnæns, fɪˈnæns, faɪˈnæns/ *n.* & *v.* —*n.* **1** the management of (esp. public) money. **2** monetary support for an enterprise. **3** (in *pl.*) the money resources of a State, company, or person. —*v.tr.* provide capital for (a person or enterprise). □ **finance company** (or **house**) a company concerned mainly with providing money for hire-purchase transactions. [ME f. OF f. *finer* settle a debt f. *fin* end: see FINE²]

financial /faɪˈnænʃ(ə)l, fɪ-/ *adj.* **1** of finance. **2** *Austral.* & *NZ sl.* possessing money. □ **financial year** a year as reckoned for taxing or accounting (e.g. the British tax year, reckoned from 6 April). □□ **financially** *adv.*

financier *n.* & *v.* —*n.* /faɪˈnænsɪə(r), ˌfɪ-/ a person engaged in large-scale finance. —*v.intr.* /ˌfaɪnænˈsɪə(r), fɪ-/ usu. *derog.* conduct financial operations. [F (as FINANCE)]

finch /fɪntʃ/ *n.* any small seed-eating passerine bird of the family Fringillidae (esp. one of the genus *Fringilla*), including crossbills, canaries, and chaffinches. [OE *finc* f. WG]

find /faɪnd/ *v.* & *n.* —*v.tr.* (*past* and *past part.* **found** /faʊnd/) **1 a**

discover by chance or effort (*found a key*). **b** become aware of. **c** (*absol.*) discover game, esp. a fox. **2 a** get possession of by chance (*found a treasure*). **b** obtain, receive (*idea found acceptance*). **c** succeed in obtaining (*cannot find the money; can't find time to read*). **d** summon up (*found courage to protest*). **e** *sl.* steal. **3 a** seek out and provide (*will find you a book*). **b** supply, furnish (*each finds his own equipment*). **4** ascertain by study or calculation or inquiry (*could not find the answer*). **5 a** perceive or experience (*find no sense in it; find difficulty in breathing*). **b** (often in *passive*) recognize or discover to be present (*the word is not found in Shakespeare*). **c** regard or discover from experience (*finds England too cold; you'll find it pays; find it impossible to reply*). **6** *Law* (of a jury, judge, etc.) decide and declare (*found him guilty; found that he had done it; found it murder*). **7** reach by a natural or normal process (*water finds its own level*). **8 a** (of a letter) reach (a person). **b** (of an address) be adequate to enable a letter etc. to reach (a person). **9** *archaic* reach the conscience of. —*n.* **1 a** a discovery of treasure, minerals, etc. **b** *Hunting* the finding of a fox. **2** a thing or person discovered, esp. when of value. □ **all found** (of an employee's wages) with board and lodging provided free. **find against** *Law* decide against (a person), judge to be guilty. **find fault** see FAULT. **find favour** prove acceptable. **find one's feet 1** become able to walk. **2** develop one's independent ability. **find for** *Law* decide in favour of (a person), judge to be innocent. **find it in one's heart** (esp. with *neg.*; foll. by *to* + infin.) prevail upon oneself, be willing. **find oneself 1** discover that one is (*woke to find myself in hospital; found herself agreeing*). **2** discover one's vocation. **3** provide for one's own needs. **find out 1** discover or detect (a wrongdoer etc.). **2** (often foll. by *about*) get information (*find out about holidays abroad*). **3** discover (*find out where we are*). **4** (often foll. by *about*) discover the truth, a fact, etc. (*he never found out*). **5** devise. **6** solve. **find-spot** *Archaeol.* the place where an object is found. **find one's way 1** (often foll. by *to*) manage to reach a place. **2** (often foll. by *into*) be brought or get. □□ **findable** *adj.* [OE *findan* f. Gmc]

finder /ˈfaɪndə(r)/ *n.* **1** a person who finds. **2** a small telescope attached to a large one to locate an object for observation. **3** the viewfinder of a camera. □ **finders keepers** *colloq.* whoever finds a thing is entitled to keep it.

fin de siècle /ˌfæ̃ də ˈsjekl/ *adj.* **1** characteristic of the end of the nineteenth century. **2** decadent. [F, = end of century]

finding /ˈfaɪndɪŋ/ *n.* **1** (often in *pl.*) a conclusion reached by an inquiry. **2** (in *pl.*) *US* small parts or tools used by workmen.

fine¹ /faɪn/ *adj., n., adv., & v.* —*adj.* **1** of high quality. **2 a** excellent; of notable merit (*a fine painting*). **b** good, satisfactory (*that will be fine*). **c** fortunate (*has been a fine thing for him*). **d** well conceived or expressed (*a fine saying*). **3 a** pure, refined. **b** (of gold or silver) containing a specified proportion of pure metal. **4** of handsome appearance or size; imposing, dignified (*fine buildings; a person of fine presence*). **5** in good health (*I'm fine, thank you*). **6** (of weather etc.) bright and clear with sunshine; free from rain. **7 a** thin; sharp. **b** in small particles. **c** worked in slender thread. **d** (esp. of print) small. **e** (of a pen) narrow-pointed. **8** *Cricket* behind the wicket and near the line of flight of the ball. **9** tritely complimentary; euphemistic (*say fine things about a person; call things by fine names*). **10** ornate, showy, smart. **11** fastidious, dainty, pretending refinement; (of speech or writing) affectedly ornate. **12 a** capable of delicate perception or discrimination. **b** perceptible only with difficulty (*a fine distinction*). **13 a** delicate, subtle, exquisitely fashioned. **b** (of feelings) refined, elevated. **14** (of wine or other goods) of a high standard; conforming to a specified grade. —*n.* **1** fine weather (*in rain or fine*). **2** (in *pl.*) very small particles in mining, milling, etc. —*adv.* **1** finely. **2** *colloq.* very well (*suits me fine*). —*v.* **1** (often foll. by *down*) **a** tr. make (beer or wine) clear. **b** intr. (of liquid) become clear. **2** tr. & intr. (often foll. by *away, down, off*) make or become finer, thinner, or less coarse; dwindle or taper, or cause to do so. □ **cut** (or **run**) **it fine** allow very little margin of time etc. **fine arts** those appealing to the mind or to the sense of beauty, as poetry, music, and esp. painting, sculpture, and architecture. **fine chemicals** see CHEMICAL. **fine-draw** sew together (two pieces of cloth, edges of a tear, parts of a garment) so that the join is imperceptible. **fine-drawn 1** extremely thin. **2** subtle. **fine**

print detailed printed information, esp. in legal documents, instructions, etc. **fine-spun 1** delicate. **2** (of a theory etc.) too subtle, unpractical. **fine-tooth comb** a comb with narrow close-set teeth. **fine-tune** make small adjustments to (a mechanism etc.) in order to obtain the best possible results. **fine up** *Austral. colloq.* (of the weather) become fine. **go over with a fine-tooth comb** check or search thoroughly. **not to put too fine a point on it** (as a parenthetic remark) to speak bluntly. □□ **finely** *adv.* **fineness** *n.* [ME f. OF *fin* ult. f. L *finire* finish]

fine² /faɪn/ *n. & v.* —*n.* **1** a sum of money exacted as a penalty. **2** *hist.* a sum of money paid by an incoming tenant in return for the rent's being small. —*v.tr.* punish by a fine (*fined him £5*). □ **in fine** to sum up; in short. □□ **finable** /ˈfaɪnəb(ə)l/ *adj.* [ME f. OF *fin* f. med.L *finis* sum paid on settling a lawsuit f. L *finis* end]

fine³ /fiːn/ *n.* = FINE CHAMPAGNE. [abbr.]

fine champagne /ˌfiːn ʃãˈpɑːnj/ *n.* old liqueur brandy. [F, = fine (brandy from) Champagne (vineyards in Charente)]

Fine Gael /ˌfiːnəˈɡeɪl/ *n.* one of the major political parties in the Republic of Ireland. Founded in 1923 as Cumann na nGaedheal, it changed its name in 1933. It has advocated the concept of a united Ireland achieved by peaceful means.

finery¹ /ˈfaɪnərɪ/ *n.* showy dress or decoration. [FINE¹ + -ERY, after BRAVERY]

finery² /ˈfaɪnərɪ/ *n.* (*pl.* **-ies**) *hist.* a hearth where pig iron was converted into wrought iron. [F *finerie* f. *finer* refine, FINE¹]

fines herbes /fiːnz ˈɛəb/ *n.pl.* mixed herbs used in cooking, esp. chopped as omelette-flavouring. [F, = fine herbs]

finesse /fɪˈnes/ *n. & v.* —*n.* **1** refinement. **2** subtle or delicate manipulation. **3** artfulness, esp. in handling a difficulty tactfully. **4** *Cards* an attempt to win a trick with a card that is not the highest held. —*v.* **1** intr. & tr. use or achieve by finesse. **2** *Cards* **a** intr. make a finesse. **b** tr. play (a card) by way of finesse. **3** tr. evade or trick by finesse. [F, rel. to FINE¹]

Fingal /ˈfɪŋɡ(ə)l/ a character in an epic poem by the Scottish poet James Macpherson (1736–96). The legendary Irish hero Finn (see FINN¹) is fictionally transformed into the Scottish Fingal, and depicted as fighting both the Norse invaders and the Romans (under Caracalla) from an invented kingdom in NW Scotland. □ **Fingal's Cave** a cave on Staffa Island in the Inner Hebrides, famous for the clustered basaltic pillars that are its cliffs. It is said to have been the inspiration of Mendelssohn's overture *The Hebrides*, but in fact he noted down the principal theme before his visit to Staffa (1829).

finger /ˈfɪŋɡə(r)/ *n. & v.* —*n.* **1** any of the terminal projections of the hand (including or excluding the thumb). **2** the part of a glove etc. intended to cover a finger. **3 a** a finger-like object (*fish finger*). **b** a long narrow structure. **4** *colloq.* a measure of liquor in a glass, based on the breadth of a finger. **5** *sl.* **a** an informer. **b** a pickpocket. **c** a policeman. —*v.tr.* **1** touch, feel, or turn about with the fingers. **2** *Mus.* **a** play (a passage) with fingers used in a particular way. **b** mark (music) with signs showing which fingers are to be used. **c** play upon (an instrument) with the fingers. **3** *US sl.* indicate (a victim, or a criminal to the police). □ **all fingers and thumbs** clumsy. **finger alphabet** a form of sign language using the fingers. **finger-board** a flat strip at the top end of a stringed instrument, against which the strings are pressed to determine tones. **finger-bowl** (or **-glass**) a small bowl for rinsing the fingers during a meal. **finger language** language expressed by means of the finger alphabet. **finger-mark** a mark left on a surface by a finger. **finger-paint** *n.* paint that can be applied with the fingers. —*v.intr.* apply paint with the fingers. **finger-plate** a plate fixed to a door above the handle to prevent finger-marks. **finger-post** a signpost at a road junction. **one's fingers itch** (often foll. by *to* + infin.) one is longing or impatient. **finger-stall** a cover to protect a finger, esp. when injured. **get** (or **pull**) **one's finger out** *sl.* cease prevaricating and start to act. **have a finger in the pie** be (esp. officiously) concerned in the matter. **lay a finger on** touch however slightly. **put one's finger on** locate or identify exactly. **put the finger on** *sl.* **1** inform against. **2** identify (an intended victim). **twist** (or **wind**) **round one's finger** (or **little finger**) persuade (a person) without difficulty, dominate (a person)

aʊ how eɪ day əʊ no eə hair ɪə near ɔɪ boy ʊə poor aɪə fire aʊə sour (*see over for consonants*)

completely. **work one's fingers to the bone** see BONE. □□ **fingered** *adj.* (also in *comb.*). **fingerless** *adj.* [OE f. Gmc]

fingering[1] /ˈfɪŋgərɪŋ/ *n.* **1** a manner or technique of using the fingers, esp. to play an instrument. **2** an indication of this in a musical score.

fingering[2] /ˈfɪŋgərɪŋ/ *n.* fine wool for knitting. [earlier *fingram*, perh. f. F *fin grain*, as GROGRAM f. *gros grain*]

fingerling /ˈfɪŋgəlɪŋ/ *n.* a parr.

fingernail /ˈfɪŋgəˌneɪl/ *n.* the nail at the tip of each finger.

fingerprint /ˈfɪŋgəprɪnt/ *n. & v.* —*n.* **1** an impression made on a surface by the fingertips, esp. as used for identifying individuals. **2** a distinctive characteristic. —*v.tr.* record the fingerprints of (a person). No two persons in the world have exactly the same pattern of ridges and marks on these parts, and the patterns can be classified and recorded systematically. Sir William Herschel (1833–1917) had introduced the use of fingerprints for identification purposes in India in the late 1870s. It was adopted in Britain, as a means of identifying criminals, in 1901.

fingertip /ˈfɪŋgətɪp/ *n.* the tip of a finger. □ **have at one's fingertips** be thoroughly familiar with (a subject etc.).

finial /ˈfɪnɪəl/ *n. Archit.* **1** an ornament finishing off the apex of a roof, pediment, gable, tower-corner, canopy, etc. **2** the topmost part of a pinnacle. [ME f. OF *fin* f. L *finis* end]

finical /ˈfɪnɪk(ə)l/ *adj.* = FINICKY. □□ **finicality** /-ˈkælɪtɪ/ *n.* **finically** *adv.* **finicalness** *n.* [16th c.: prob. orig. university sl. f. FINE[1] + -ICAL]

finicking /ˈfɪnɪkɪŋ/ *adj.* = FINICKY. [FINICAL + -ING[2]]

finicky /ˈfɪnɪkɪ/ *adj.* **1** over-particular, fastidious. **2** needing much attention to detail; fiddly. □□ **finickiness** *n.*

finis /ˈfɪnɪs, ˈfiːnɪs, ˈfaɪnɪs/ *n.* **1** (at the end of a book) the end. **2** the end of anything, esp. of life. [L]

finish /ˈfɪnɪʃ/ *v. & n.* —*v.* **1** *tr.* **a** (often foll. by *off*) bring to an end; come to the end of; complete. **b** (usu. foll. by *off*) *colloq.* kill; overcome completely. **c** (often foll. by *off*, *up*) consume or get through the whole or the remainder of (food or drink) (*finish up your dinner*). **2** *intr.* **a** come to an end, cease. **b** reach the end, esp. of a race. **c** = *finish up*. **3** *tr.* **a** complete the manufacture of (cloth, woodwork, etc.) by surface treatment. **b** put the final touches to; make perfect or highly accomplished (*finished manners*). **c** prepare (a girl) for entry into fashionable society. —*n.* **1 a** the end, the last stage. **b** the point at which a race etc. ends. **c** the death of a fox in a hunt (*be in at the finish*). **2** a method, material, or texture used for surface treatment of wood, cloth, etc. (*mahogany finish*). **3** what serves to give completeness. **4** an accomplished or completed state. □ **fight to a finish** fight till one party is completely beaten. **finishing-school** a private college where girls are prepared for entry into fashionable society. **finish off** provide with an ending. **finish up** (often foll. by *in*, *by*) end in something, end by doing something (*he finished up last in the race; the plan finished up in the waste-paper basket; finished up by apologizing*). **finish with** have no more to do with, complete one's use of or association with. [ME f. OF *fenir* f. L *finire* f. *finis* end]

finisher /ˈfɪnɪʃə(r)/ *n.* **1** a person who finishes something. **2** a worker or machine doing the last operation in manufacture. **3** *colloq.* a discomfiting thing, a crushing blow, etc.

Finisterre /ˌfɪnɪˈsteə(r)/ the westernmost point of mainland Spain, a promontory on its NW coast.

finite /ˈfaɪnaɪt/ *adj.* **1** limited, bounded; not infinite. **2** *Gram.* (of a part of a verb) having a specific number and person. **3** not infinitely small. □□ **finitely** *adv.* **finiteness** *n.* **finitude** /ˈfɪnɪˌtjuːd/ *n.* [L *finitus* past part. of *finire* FINISH]

finitism /ˈfaɪnaɪˌtɪz(ə)m/ *n.* belief in the finiteness of the world, God, etc. □□ **finitist** *n.*

fink /fɪŋk/ *n. & v. US sl.* —*n.* **1** an unpleasant person. **2** an informer. **3** a strikebreaker; a blackleg. —*v.intr.* (foll. by *on*) inform on. [20th c.: orig. unkn.]

Finland /ˈfɪnlənd/ a Scandinavian country with a coastline on the Baltic Sea and an extensive network of inland waterways; pop. (est. 1988) 4,949,700; official languages, Finnish and Swedish; capital, Helsinki. The country is highly industrialized, principal export earnings being from timber and the paper industry, shipbuilding, and engineering. Converted to Christianity by Eric IX of Sweden in the 12th c., Finland became an area of Swedish–Russian rivalry. A Grand Duchy from the 16th c., it was ceded to Russia in 1809, regaining full independence after the Russian Revolution. Wars with the USSR in 1939–40 and 1941–4 cost Finland Karelia and Petsamo, and although Finland has been neutral since the war, she has remained, at least partially, under Soviet influence.

Finn[1] /fɪn/ the principal hero of a cycle of Irish legends, father of Ossian. He is supposed to have lived in the 3rd c. AD.

Finn[2] /fɪn/ *n.* a native or national of Finland; a person of Finnish descent. [OE *Finnas* pl.]

finnan /ˈfɪnən/ *n.* (in full **finnan haddock**) a haddock cured with the smoke of green wood, turf, or peat. [*Findhorn* or *Findon* in Scotland]

finnesko /ˈfɪnəˌskəʊ/ *n.* (*pl.* same) a boot of tanned reindeer-skin with the hair on the outside. [Norw. *finnsko* (as FINN, *sko* SHOE)]

Finnic /ˈfɪnɪk/ *adj.* **1** of the group of peoples related to the Finns. **2** of the group of languages related to Finnish.

Finnish /ˈfɪnɪʃ/ *adj. & n.* —*adj.* of the Finns or their language. —*n.* the language spoken by some five and a half million people in Finland (where it is one of the two official languages), the NW Soviet Union, and Sweden, belonging to the Finno-Ugric group and closely related to Estonian. It is noted for its complexity; a Finnish noun has 15 different case-forms.

Finno-Ugric /ˌfɪnəʊˈuːgrɪk, -ˈjuːgrɪk/ *adj. & n.* (also **FinnoUgrian** /-ˈuːgrɪən/) —*adj.* belonging to the group of Ural-Altaic languages, divided into Finnic languages (of which the most important are Finnish and Estonian), and Ugric languages (of which the most important is Hungarian). The languages are also spoken in scattered areas of central Russia, which is thought to be the original homeland of their speakers. —*n.* this group.

finny /ˈfɪnɪ/ *adj.* **1** having fins; like a fin. **2** *poet.* of or teeming with fish.

fino /ˈfiːnəʊ/ *n.* (*pl.* **-os**) a light-coloured dry sherry. [Sp., = fine]

fiord /fjɔːd/ *n.* (also **fjord**) a long narrow inlet of sea between high cliffs, as in Norway. [Norw. f. ON *fjörthr* f. Gmc: cf. FIRTH, FORD]

fioritura /fiˌɔːrɪˈtʊərə/ *n.* (*pl.* **fioriture** *pronunc.* same) *Mus.* the usu. improvised decoration of a melody. [It., = flowering f. *fiorire* to flower]

fipple /ˈfɪp(ə)l/ *n.* a plug at the mouth-end of a wind instrument. □ **fipple flute** a flute played by blowing endwise, e.g. a recorder. [17th c.: orig. unkn.]

fir /fɜː(r)/ *n.* **1** (in full **fir-tree**) any evergreen coniferous tree, esp. of the genus *Abies*, with needles borne singly on the stems (cf. PINE[1]). **2** the wood of the fir. □ **fir-cone** the fruit of the fir. □□ **firry** *adj.* [ME, prob. f. ON *fyri-* f. Gmc]

fire /ˈfaɪə(r)/ *n. & v.* —*n.* **1 a** the state or process of combustion, in which substances combine chemically with oxygen from the air and usu. give out bright light and heat. **b** the active principle operative in this. **c** flame or incandescence. The earliest evidence for the use of fire dates from about 500,000 years ago (see PEKING MAN). **2** a conflagration, a destructive burning (*forest fire*). **3** a burning fuel in a grate, furnace, etc. **b** = *electric fire*. **c** = *gas fire*. **4** firing of guns. **5 a** fervour, spirit, vivacity. **b** poetic inspiration, lively imagination. **c** vehement emotion. **6** burning heat, fever. **7** luminosity, glow (*St Elmo's fire*). —*v.* **1 a** *tr.* discharge (a gun etc.). **b** *tr.* propel (a missile) from a gun etc. **c** *intr.* (often foll. by *at*, *into*, *on*) fire a gun or missile. **d** *tr.* produce (a broadside, salute, etc.) by discharge of guns. **e** *intr.* (of a gun etc.) be discharged. **2** *tr.* cause (explosive) to explode. **3** *tr.* deliver or utter in rapid succession (*fired insults at us*). **4** *tr. sl.* dismiss (an employee) from a job. **5** *tr.* **a** set fire to with the intention of destroying. **b** kindle (explosives). **6** *intr.* catch fire. **7** *intr.* (of an internal-combustion engine, or a cylinder in one) undergo ignition of its fuel. **8** *tr.* supply (a furnace, engine, boiler, or power station) with fuel. **9** *tr.* **a** stimulate (the imagination). **b**

fill (a person) with enthusiasm. **10** *tr.* **a** bake or dry (pottery, bricks, etc.). **b** cure (tea or tobacco) by artificial heat. **11** *intr.* become heated or excited. **12** *tr.* cause to glow or redden. □ **catch fire** begin to burn. **fire-alarm** a device for giving warning of fire. **fire and brimstone** the supposed torments of hell. **fire away** *colloq.* begin; go ahead. **fire-ball 1** a large meteor. **2** a ball of flame, esp. from a nuclear explosion. **3** an energetic person. **4** ball lightning. **5** *Mil. hist.* a ball filled with combustibles. **fire-balloon** a balloon made buoyant by the heat of a fire burning at its mouth. **fire-blight** a disease of plants, esp. hops and fruit trees, causing a scorched appearance. **fire-bomb** an incendiary bomb. **fire-break** an obstacle to the spread of fire in a forest etc., esp. an open space. **fire-brick** a fireproof brick used in a grate. **fire brigade** esp. *Brit.* an organized body of firemen trained and employed to extinguish fires. **fire-bug** *colloq.* a pyromaniac. **fire company 1** = *fire brigade.* **2** a fire-insurance company. **fire-control** a system of regulating the fire of a ship's or a fort's guns. **fire department** US = *fire brigade.* **fire door** a fire-resistant door to prevent the spread of fire. **fire-drake** (in Germanic mythology) a fiery dragon. **fire-drill 1** a rehearsal of the procedures to be used in case of fire. **2** a primitive device for kindling fire with a stick and wood. **fire-eater 1** a conjuror who appears to swallow fire. **2** a person fond of quarrelling or fighting. **fire-engine** a vehicle carrying equipment for fighting large fires. **fire-escape** an emergency staircase or apparatus for escape from a building on fire. **fire extinguisher** an apparatus with a jet for discharging liquid chemicals, water, or foam to extinguish a fire. **fire-fighter** a person whose task is to extinguish fires. **fire-guard 1** a protective screen or grid placed in front of a fireplace. **2** US a fire-watcher. **3** US a fire-break. **fire-hose** a hose-pipe used in extinguishing fires. **fire-irons** tongs, poker, and shovel, for tending a domestic fire. **fire-lighter** *Brit.* a piece of inflammable material to help start a fire in a grate. **fire-office** a fire-insurance company. **Fire of London** see GREAT FIRE. **fire-opal** girasol. **fire-plug** a hydrant for a fire-hose. **fire-power 1** the destructive capacity of guns etc. **2** financial, intellectual, or emotional strength. **fire-practice** a fire-drill. **fire-raiser** *Brit.* an arsonist. **fire-raising** *Brit.* arson. **fire-screen 1** a screen to keep off the direct heat of a fire. **2** a fire-guard. **3** an ornamental screen for a fireplace. **fire-ship** *hist.* a ship loaded with combustibles and sent adrift to ignite an enemy's ships etc. **fire station** the headquarters of a fire brigade. **fire-step** = *firing-step.* **fire-stone** stone that resists fire, used for furnaces etc. **fire-storm** a high wind or storm following a fire caused by bombs. **fire-tongs** tongs for picking up pieces of coal etc. in tending a fire. **fire-trap** a building without proper provision for escape in case of fire. **fire up** show sudden anger. **fire-walking** the (often ceremonial) practice of walking barefoot over white-hot stones, wood-ashes, etc. **fire warden** US a person employed to prevent or extinguish fires. **fire-watcher** a person keeping watch for fires, esp. those caused by bombs. **fire-water** *colloq.* strong alcoholic liquor. **go on fire** *Sc. & Ir.* catch fire. **go through fire and water** face all perils. **on fire 1** burning. **2** excited. **set fire to** (or **set on fire**) ignite, kindle, cause to burn. **set the world** (or **Thames**) **on fire** do something remarkable or sensational. **take fire** catch fire. **under fire 1** being shot at. **2** being rigorously criticized or questioned. □□ **fireless** *adj.* **firer** *n.* [OE *fȳr*, *fȳrian*, f. WG]

firearm /ˈfaɪərˌɑːm/ *n.* (usu. in *pl.*) a gun, esp. a pistol or rifle.

fireback /ˈfaɪəˌbæk/ *n.* **1 a** the back wall of a fireplace. **b** an iron sheet for this. **2** a SE Asian pheasant of the genus *Lophura.*

firebox /ˈfaɪəˌbɒks/ *n.* the fuel-chamber of a steam engine or boiler.

firebrand /ˈfaɪəˌbrænd/ *n.* **1** a piece of burning wood. **2** a cause of trouble, esp. a person causing unrest.

fireclay /ˈfaɪəˌkleɪ/ *n.* clay capable of withstanding high temperatures, often used to make fire-bricks.

firecracker /ˈfaɪəˌkrækə(r)/ *n.* US an explosive firework.

firecrest /ˈfaɪəˌkrest/ *n.* a warbler, *Regulus ignicapillus*, with red and orange crown feathers which may be erected.

firedamp /ˈfaɪəˌdæmp/ *n.* a miners' name for methane, which is explosive when mixed in certain proportions with air.

firedog /ˈfaɪəˌdɒg/ *n.* a metal support for burning wood or for a grate or fire-irons.

firefly /ˈfaɪəˌflaɪ/ *n.* (*pl.* **-flies**) any soft-bodied beetle of the family Lampyridae, emitting phosphorescent light, including glow-worms.

firehouse /ˈfaɪəˌhaʊs/ *n.* US a fire station.

firelight /ˈfaɪəˌlaɪt/ *n.* light from a fire in a fireplace. [OE *fȳr-leoht* (as FIRE, LIGHT[1])]

firelock /ˈfaɪəˌlɒk/ *n. hist.* a musket in which the priming was ignited by sparks.

fireman /ˈfaɪəmən/ *n.* (*pl.* **-men**) **1** a member of a fire brigade; a person employed to extinguish fires. **2** a person who tends a furnace or the fire of a steam engine or steamship.

Firenze see FLORENCE.

fireplace /ˈfaɪəˌpleɪs/ *n. Archit.* **1** a place for a domestic fire, esp. a grate or hearth at the base of a chimney. **2** a structure surrounding this. **3** the area in front of this.

fireproof /ˈfaɪəˌpruːf/ *adj. & v.* —*adj.* able to resist fire or great heat. —*v.tr.* make fireproof.

fireside /ˈfaɪəˌsaɪd/ *n.* **1** the area round a fireplace. **2** a person's home or home-life. □ **fireside chat** an informal talk.

firewood /ˈfaɪəˌwʊd/ *n.* wood for use as fuel.

firework /ˈfaɪəˌwɜːk/ *n.* **1** a device containing combustible chemicals that cause explosions or spectacular effects. **2** (in *pl.*) **a** an outburst of passion, esp. anger. **b** a display of wit or brilliance.

firing /ˈfaɪərɪŋ/ *n.* **1** the discharging of guns. **2** material for a fire, fuel. **3** the heating process which hardens clay into pottery etc. □ **firing-line 1** the front line in a battle. **2** the leading part in an activity etc. **firing-party** a group detailed to fire the salute at a military funeral. **firing-squad 1** a group detailed to shoot a condemned person. **2** a firing-party. **firing-step** a step on which soldiers in a trench stand to fire.

firkin /ˈfɜːkɪn/ *n.* **1** a small cask for liquids, butter, fish, etc. **2** *Brit.* (as a measure) half a kilderkin (8 or 9 gallons). [ME *ferdekyn*, prob. f. MDu. *vierdekijn* (unrecorded) dimin. of *vierde* fourth]

firm¹ /fɜːm/ *adj., adv., & v.* —*adj.* **1 a** of solid or compact structure. **b** fixed, stable. **c** steady; not shaking. **2 a** resolute, determined. **b** not easily shaken (*firm belief*). **c** steadfast, constant (*a firm friend*). **3 a** (of an offer etc.) not liable to cancellation after acceptance. **b** (of a decree, law, etc.) established, immutable. **4** *Commerce* (of prices or goods) maintaining their level or value. —*adv.* firmly (*stand firm; hold firm to*). —*v.* **1** *tr. & intr.* make or become firm, secure, compact, or solid. **2** *tr.* fix (plants) firmly in the soil. □□ **firmly** *adv.* **firmness** *n.* [ME f. OF *ferme* f. L *firmus*]

firm² /fɜːm/ *n.* **1 a** a business concern. **b** the partners in such a concern. **2** a group of persons working together, esp. of hospital doctors and assistants. [earlier = signature, style: Sp. & It. *firma* f. med.L, f. L *firmare* confirm f. *firmus* FIRM¹]

firmament /ˈfɜːməmənt/ *n. literary* the sky regarded as a vault or arch. □□ **firmamental** /-ˈment(ə)l/ *adj.* [ME f. OF f. L *firmamentum* f. *firmare* (as FIRM²)]

firman /fɜːˈmɑːn, ˈfɜːmən/ *n.* **1** an oriental sovereign's edict. **2** a grant or permit. [Pers. *fermān*, Skr. *pramāṇam* right measure]

firmware /ˈfɜːmweə(r)/ *n. Computing* a permanent kind of software programmed into a read-only memory.

firry see FIR.

first /fɜːst/ *adj., n., & adv.* —*adj.* **1 a** earliest in time or order. **b** coming next after a specified or implied time (*shall take the first train; the first cuckoo*). **2** foremost in position, rank, or importance (*First Lord of the Treasury; first mate*). **3** *Mus.* performing the highest or chief of two or more parts for the same instrument or voice. **4** most willing or likely (*should be the first to admit the difficulty*). **5** basic or evident (*first principles*). —*n.* **1** (prec. by *the*) the person or thing first mentioned or occurring. **2** the first occurrence of something notable. **3 a** a place in the first class in an examination. **b** a person having this. **4** the first day of a month. **5** first gear. **6 a** first place in a race. **b** the winner of this. **7** (in *pl.*) goods of the best quality. —*adv.* **1** before any other person or thing (*first of all; first and foremost; first come first served*). **2** before someone or something else (*must get this done first*). **3** for the first time (*when did you first see her?*). **4** in preference; rather (*will see him damned first*). **5** first-class (*I usually travel first*). □ **at first** at the beginning. **at first hand** directly from the original source. **first aid** help given to an injured person until proper medical treatment is available. **first and last** taking one thing with another, on the whole. **first blood** see BLOOD. **first-born** *adj.* eldest. —*n.* the eldest child of a person. **First Cause** the Creator of the universe. **first class 1** a set of persons or things grouped together as the best. **2** the best accommodation in a train, ship, etc. **3** the class of mail given priority in handling. **4 a** the highest division in an examination list. **b** a place in this. **first-class** *adj.* **1** belonging to or travelling by the first class. **2** of the best quality; very good. —*adv.* by the first class (*travels first-class*). **first cousin** see COUSIN. **first-day cover** an envelope with stamps postmarked on their first day of issue. **first-degree** *Med.* denoting burns that affect only the surface of the skin, causing reddening. **first finger** the finger next to the thumb. **first floor** see FLOOR. **first-foot** *Sc. n.* the first person to cross a threshold in the New Year. —*v.intr.* be a first-foot. **first-fruit** (usu. in *pl.*) **1** the first agricultural produce of a season, esp. as offered to God. **2** the first results of work etc. **3** *hist.* a payment to a superior by the new holder of an office. **first gear** see GEAR. **first intention** see INTENTION. **First Lady** (in the US) the wife of the President. **first lesson** the first of several passages from the Bible read at a service in the Church of England. **first lieutenant** *US* an army or air force officer next below captain. **first light** the time when light first appears in the morning. **first mate** (on a merchant ship) the officer second in command to the master. **first name** a personal or Christian name. **first night** the first public performance of a play etc. **first-nighter** a habitual attender of first nights. **first off** *US colloq.* at first, first of all. **first offender** a criminal against whom no previous conviction is recorded. **first officer** the mate on a merchant ship. **first or last** sooner or later. **first past the post 1** winning a race etc. by being the first to reach the finishing line. **2** (of an electoral system) selecting a candidate or party by simple majority (see also *proportional representation, single transferable vote*). **first person** see PERSON. **first post** see POST³. **first-rate** *adj.* of the highest class, excellent. —*adv. colloq.* **1** very well (*feeling first-rate*). **2** excellently. **first reading** the occasion when a Bill is presented to a legislature to permit its introduction. **first refusal** see REFUSAL. **first school** *Brit.* a school for children from 5 to 9 years old. **first sergeant** *US* the highest-ranking non-commissioned officer in a company. **first-strike** denoting a first aggressive attack with nuclear weapons. **first thing** *colloq.* before anything else; very early in the morning (*shall do it first thing*). **the first thing** even the most elementary fact or principle (*does not know the first thing about it*). **first things first** the most important things before any others (*we must do first things first*). **first up** *Austral.* first of all; at the first attempt. **First World War** see WORLD WAR. **from the first** from the beginning. **from first to last** throughout. **get to first base** *US* achieve the first step towards an objective. **in the first place** as the first consideration. **of the first water** see WATER. [OE *fyrst* f. Gmc]

firsthand /fɜːstˈhænd, *attrib.* ˈfɜːst-/ *adj. & adv.* from the original source; direct.

firstling /ˈfɜːstlɪŋ/ *n.* (usu. in *pl.*) **1** the first result of anything; first-fruits. **2** the first offspring; the first born in a season.

firstly /ˈfɜːstlɪ/ *adv.* (in enumerating topics, arguments, etc.) in the first place, first (cf. FIRST *adv.*).

firth /fɜːθ/ *n.* (also **frith** /frɪθ/) **1** a narrow inlet of the sea. **2** an estuary. □ **Firth of Forth** see FORTH. [ME (orig. Sc.) f. ON *fjörthr* FIORD]

fisc /fɪsk/ *n. Rom.Hist.* the public treasury; the emperor's privy purse. [F *fisc* or L *fiscus* rush-basket, purse, treasury]

fiscal /ˈfɪsk(ə)l/ *adj. & n.* —*adj.* of public revenue. —*n.* **1** a legal official in some countries. **2** *Sc.* = *procurator fiscal.* □ **fiscal year** = *financial year.* □□ **fiscally** *adv.* [F *fiscal* or L *fiscalis* (as FISC)]

fiscality /fɪˈskælɪtɪ/ *n.* (pl. **-ies**) **1** (in pl.) fiscal matters. **2** excessive regard for these.

Fischer /ˈfɪʃə(r)/, Robert James ('Bobby') (1943–), American chess-player, world champion 1972–5.

fish¹ /fɪʃ/ *n. & v.* —*n.* (*pl.* same or **fishes**) **1** a vertebrate cold-blooded animal with gills and fins living wholly in water. (See below.) **2** any animal living wholly in water, e.g. cuttlefish, shellfish, jellyfish. **3** the flesh of fish as food. **4** *colloq.* a person remarkable in some way (usu. unfavourable) (*an odd fish*). **5** (**the Fish** or **Fishes**) the zodiacal sign or constellation Pisces. **6** *Naut. sl.* a torpedo; a submarine. —*v.* **1** *intr.* try to catch fish, esp. with a line or net. **2** *tr.* fish for (a certain kind of fish) or in (a certain stretch of water). **3** *intr.* (foll. by *for*) **a** search for in water or a concealed place. **b** seek by indirect means (*fishing for compliments*). **4** *tr.* (foll. by *up, out,* etc.) retrieve with careful or awkward searching. □ **drink like a fish** drink excessively. **fish-bowl** a usu. round glass bowl for keeping pet fish in. **fish cake** a cake of shredded fish and mashed potato, usu. eaten fried. **fish eagle 1** any large eagle of the genus *Haliaeetus*, with long broad wings, strong legs, and a strong tail. **2** any of several other eagles catching and feeding on fish. **fish-eye lens** a very wide-angle lens with a curved front. Its field of vision covers nearly 180°, and it reduces the scale of the image more at the edges than in the centre. **fish farm** a place where fish are bred for food. **fish finger** *Brit.* a small oblong piece of fish in batter or breadcrumbs. **fish-glue** isinglass. **fish-hawk** an osprey, *Pandion haliaeetus*. **fish-hook** a barbed hook for catching fish. **fish-kettle** an oval pan for boiling fish. **fish-knife** a knife for eating or serving fish. **fish-meal** ground dried fish used as fertilizer or animal feed. **fish out of water** a person in an unsuitable or unwelcome environment or situation. **fish-pond** (or **-pool**) a pond or pool in which fish are kept. **fish-slice** a flat utensil for lifting fish and fried foods during and after cooking. **other fish to fry** other matters to attend to. [OE *fisc, fiscian* f. Gmc]

Fish represent a form of life rather than a single related group. The most primitive class are the jawless fishes, which first appeared about 500 million years ago and are represented today by the lampreys. Jawed fishes appeared about 100 million years later, and present-day forms can be divided into two main classes: cartilaginous fish and bony fish. The former includes sharks, dogfish, skates, and rays. As their name suggests, they have a skeleton of cartilage rather than bone, and they also lack a swim-bladder to give them buoyancy, so that they must remain in motion constantly in order not to sink to the sea bottom. Bony fish, which constitute the great majority of the 30,000 or so living fish species, typically have a swim-bladder and also possess fins with much greater manoeuvrability than those of cartilaginous forms.

fish² /fɪʃ/ *n. & v.* —*n.* **1** a flat plate of iron, wood, etc., to strengthen a beam or joint. **2** *Naut.* a piece of wood, convex and concave, used to strengthen a mast etc. —*v.tr.* **1** mend or strengthen (a spar etc.) with a fish. **2** join (rails) with a fish-plate. □ **fish-bolt** a bolt used to fasten fish-plates and rails together. **fish-plate a** a flat piece of iron etc. connecting railway rails. **b** a flat piece of metal with ends like a fish's tail, used to position masonry. □□ **fishlike** *adj.* [orig. as verb: f. F *ficher* fix ult. f. L *figere*]

fish³ /fɪʃ/ *n.* a piece of ivory etc. used as a counter in games. [F *fiche* (*ficher*; see FISH²)]

Fisher¹ /ˈfɪʃə(r)/, Sir Ronald Aylmer (1890–1962), English statistician and geneticist, who made major contributions to the development of statistics in the 20th c. He published influential books on statistical theory, the design of experiments, statistical methods for research workers, and the relationship between Mendelian genetics and evolutionary theory. He himself also carried out experimental work in agriculture and on the genetics of blood groups.

Fisher² /ˈfɪʃə(r)/, St John (1469–1535), English churchman, one of the greatest scholars of his day, a noted Chancellor of Cambridge University, where he appreciated and encouraged the work of Erasmus. In 1504 he became bishop of Rochester, and earned the disfavour of Henry VIII by opposing the King's divorce from Catherine of Aragon and by refusing to accept him as supreme head of the English Church. Fisher was condemned to death on a trumped-up charge; the fact that the Pope, in recognition of his merits, created him a cardinal increased the King's fury. Feast day, 22 June (the anniversary of his execution).

fisher /ˈfiʃə(r)/ n. **1** an animal that catches fish, esp. a pekan. **2** archaic a fisherman. [OE fiscere f. Gmc (as FISH¹)]

fisherman /ˈfiʃəmən/ n. (pl. **-men**) **1** a person who catches fish as a livelihood or for sport. **2** a fishing-boat.

fishery /ˈfiʃərɪ/ n. (pl. **-ies**) **1** a place where fish are caught or reared. **2** the occupation or industry of catching or rearing fish.

fishing /ˈfiʃɪŋ/ n. the activity of catching fish, esp. for food or as a sport. □ **fishing-line** a long thread of silk etc. with a baited hook, sinker, float, etc., used for catching fish. **fishing-rod** a long tapering usu. jointed rod to which a fishing-line is attached.

fishmonger /ˈfiʃˌmʌŋgə(r)/ n. esp. Brit. a dealer in fish.

fishnet /ˈfiʃnet/ n. (often attrib.) an open-meshed fabric (fishnet stockings).

fishpot /ˈfiʃpɒt/ n. a wicker trap for eels, lobsters, etc.

fishtail /ˈfiʃteɪl/ n. & v. —n. a device etc. shaped like a fish's tail. —v.intr. move the tail of a vehicle from side to side. □ **fishtail burner** a kind of burner producing a broadening jet of flame.

fishwife /ˈfiʃwaɪf/ n. (pl. **-wives**) **1** a coarse-mannered or noisy woman. **2** a woman who sells fish.

fishy /ˈfiʃɪ/ adj. (**fishier**, **fishiest**) **1 a** smelling or tasting like fish. **b** like that of a fish. **c** (of an eye) dull, vacant-looking. **d** consisting of fish (a fishy repast). **e** joc. or poet. abounding in fish. **2** sl. of dubious character, questionable, suspect. □□ **fishily** adv. **fishiness** n.

fisk /fisk/ n. Sc. the State treasury, the exchequer. [var. of FISC]

fissile /ˈfisaɪl/ adj. **1** capable of undergoing nuclear fission. **2** cleavable; tending to split. □□ **fissility** /-ˈsɪlɪtɪ/ n. [L fissilis (as FISSURE)]

fission /ˈfiʃ(ə)n/ n. & v. —n. **1** Physics the spontaneous or impact-induced splitting of a heavy atomic nucleus, accompanied by a release of energy. **2** Biol. the division of a cell etc. into new cells etc. as a mode of reproduction. —v.intr. & tr. undergo or cause to undergo fission. □ **fission bomb** an atomic bomb. □□ **fissionable** adj. [L fissio (as FISSURE)]

fissiparous /fiˈsɪpərəs/ adj. **1** Biol. reproducing by fission. **2** tending to split. □□ **fissiparity** /-ˈpærɪtɪ/ n. **fissiparously** adv. **fissiparousness** n. [L fissus past part. (as FISSURE) after viviparous]

fissure /ˈfiʃə(r)/ n. & v. —n. **1** an opening, usu. long and narrow, made esp. by cracking, splitting, or separation of parts. **2** Bot. & Anat. a narrow opening in an organ etc., esp. a depression between convolutions of the brain. **3** a cleavage. —v.tr. & intr. split or crack. [ME f. OF fissure or L fissura f. findere fiss- cleave]

fist /fist/ n. & v. —n. **1** a tightly closed hand. **2** sl. handwriting (writes a good fist; I know his fist). **3** a hand (give us your fist). —v.tr. **1** strike with the fist. **2** Naut. handle (a sail, an oar, etc.). □ **make a good** (or **poor** etc.) **fist** (foll. by at, of) colloq. make a good (or poor etc.) attempt at. □□ **fisted** adj. (also in comb.). **fistful** n. (pl. **-fuls**). [OE fŷst f. WG]

fistic /ˈfistɪk/ adj. (also **fistical**) joc. pugilistic.

fisticuffs /ˈfistɪˌkʌfs/ n.pl. fighting with the fists. [prob. obs. fisty adj. = FISTIC, + CUFF²]

fistula /ˈfistjʊlə/ n. (pl. **fistulas** or **fistulae** /-ˌliː/) **1** an abnormal or surgically made passage between a hollow organ and the body surface or between two hollow organs. **2** a natural pipe or spout in whales, insects, etc. □□ **fistular** adj. **fistulous** adj. [L, = pipe, flute]

fit¹ /fit/ adj., v., n., & adv. —adj. (**fitter**, **fittest**) **1 a** (usu. foll. by for, or to + infin.) well adapted or suited. **b** (foll. by to + infin.) qualified, competent, worthy. **c** (foll. by for, or to + infin.) in a suitable condition, ready. **d** (foll. by for) good enough (a dinner fit for a king). **e** (foll. by to + infin.) sufficiently exhausted, troubled, or angry (fit to drop). **2** in good health or athletic condition. **3** proper, becoming, right (it is fit that). —v. (**fitted**, **fitting**) **1 a** tr. (also absol.) be of the right shape and size for (the dress fits her; the key doesn't fit the lock; these shoes don't fit). **b** tr. make, fix, or insert (a thing) so that it is of the right size or shape (fitted shelves in the alcoves). **c** intr. (often foll. by in, into) (of a component) be correctly positioned (that bit fits here). **d** tr. find room for (can't fit another person on the bench). **2** tr. (foll. by for, or to + infin.) **a** make suitable; adapt. **b** make competent (fitted

him to be a priest). **3** tr. (usu. foll. by with) supply, furnish (fitted the boat with a new rudder). **4** tr. fix in place (fit a lock on the door). **5** tr. = fit on. **6** tr. be in harmony with, befit, become (it fits the occasion; the punishment fits the crime). —n. the way in which a garment, component, etc., fits (a bad fit; a tight fit). —adv. (foll. by to + infin.) colloq. in a suitable manner, appropriately (was laughing fit to bust). □ **fit the bill** = fill the bill. **fit in 1** (often foll. by with) be (esp. socially) compatible or accommodating (doesn't fit in with the rest of the group; tried to fit in with their plans). **2** find space or time for (an object, engagement, etc.) (the dentist fitted me in at the last minute). **fit on** try on (a garment). **fit out** (or **up**) (often foll. by with) equip. **fit-up** Theatr. sl. **1** a temporary stage etc. **2** a travelling company. **see** (or **think**) **fit** (often foll. by to + infin.) decide or choose (a specified course of action). □□ **fitly** adv. **fitness** n. [ME: orig. unkn.]

fit² /fit/ n. **1** a sudden seizure of epilepsy, hysteria, apoplexy, fainting, or paralysis, with unconsciousness or convulsions. **2** a sudden brief attack of an illness or of symptoms (fit of coughing). **3** a sudden short bout or burst (fit of energy; fit of giggles). **4** colloq. an attack of strong feeling (fit of rage). **5** a capricious impulse; a mood (when the fit was on him). □ **by** (or **in**) **fits and starts** spasmodically. **give a person a fit** colloq. surprise or outrage him or her. **have a fit** colloq. be greatly surprised or outraged. **in fits** laughing uncontrollably. [ME, = position of danger, perh. = OE fitt conflict (?)]

fit³ /fit/ n. (also **fytte**) archaic a section of a poem. [OE fitt]

fitch /fitʃ/ n. **1** a polecat. **2 a** the hair of a polecat. **b** a brush made from this or similar hair. [MDu. fisse etc.: cf. FITCHEW]

fitchew /ˈfitʃuː/ n. a polecat. [14th c. f. OF ficheau, fissel dimin. of MDu. fisse]

fitful /ˈfitfʊl/ adj. active or occurring spasmodically or intermittently. □□ **fitfully** adv. **fitfulness** n.

fitment /ˈfitmənt/ n. (usu. in pl.) a fixed item of furniture.

fitted /ˈfitɪd/ adj. **1** made or shaped to fill a space or cover something closely or exactly (a fitted carpet). **2** provided with appropriate equipment, fittings, etc. (a fitted kitchen). **3** built-in; filling an alcove etc. (fitted cupboards).

fitter /ˈfitə(r)/ n. **1** a person who supervises the cutting, fitting, altering, etc. of garments. **2** a mechanic who fits together and adjusts machinery.

fitting /ˈfitɪŋ/ n. & adj. —n. **1** the process or an instance of having a garment etc. fitted (needed several fittings). **2 a** (in pl.) the fixtures and fitments of a building. **b** a piece of apparatus or furniture —adj. proper, becoming, right. □ **fitting-shop** a place where machine parts are put together. □□ **fittingly** adv. **fittingness** n.

Fitzgerald¹ /fitsˈdʒer(ə)ld/, Edward (1809–83), English scholar, famous for his English poetic version of the Rubáiyát of Omar Khayyám.

Fitzgerald² /fitsˈdʒerəld/, Ella (1918–), American jazz singer, noted for her interpretations of songs by George Gershwin and Cole Porter.

Fitzgerald³ /fitsˈdʒer(ə)ld/, (Francis) Scott (Key) (1896–1940), American novelist. His first novel This side of Paradise (1920) made him instantly famous, and shortly afterwards he married the glamorous Zelda Sayre; together they embarked on a high-living, big-spending, party-going 'jazz-age' life. His short stories, which chronicled the mood and manners of the times, were collected in Flappers and Philosophers (1920) and Tales of the Jazz Age (1922; containing 'The Diamond as Big as the Ritz'). Probably his finest novel was The Great Gatsby (1925), a tale of romantic and destructive passion played against a backdrop of Long Island glamour and New York squalor. By now Zelda was suffering from a nervous breakdown, Scott from the effects of their violent lives, and Tender is the Night (1934) reflects his own sense of impending disaster. His unfinished The Last Tycoon (1941) analyses his own deterioration.

FitzGerald /fitsˈdʒer(ə)ld/, George Francis (1851–1901), Irish physicist, who suggested that length, time, and mass depended on the relative motion of the observer, while the speed of light was constant. This hypothesis, postulated independently by Lorentz (see entry), prepared the way for Einstein's special theory of relativity.

Fiume see RIJEKA.

five /faɪv/ n. & adj. —n. **1** one more than four or one half of ten; the sum of three units and two units. **2** a symbol for this (5, v, V). **3** a size etc. denoted by five. **4** a set or team of five individuals. **5** the time of five o'clock (*is it five yet?*). **6** a card with five pips. **7** *Cricket* a hit scoring five runs. —adj. that amount to five. □ **bunch of fives** *Brit. sl.* a hand or fist. **five-corner** (or **-corners**) *Austral.* **1** a shrub of the genus *Styphelia*. **2** the pentagonal fruit of this. **five-eighth** *Austral.* & *NZ Rugby Football* either of two players between the scrum-half and the centre three-quarter. **five-finger exercise 1** an exercise on the piano involving all the fingers. **2** an easy task. **five hundred** a form of euchre in which 500 points make a game. **five o'clock shadow** beard-growth visible on a man's face in the latter part of the day. **five-star** of the highest class. **five-year plan 1** (in the USSR) a government plan for economic development over five years, inaugurated in 1928 (and later repeated). **2** a similar plan in another country. [OE *fíf* f. Gmc]

fivefold /ˈfaɪvfəʊld/ adj. & adv. **1** five times as much or as many. **2** consisting of five parts. **3** amounting to five.

fiver /ˈfaɪvə(r)/ n. *colloq.* **1** *Brit.* a five-pound note. **2** *US* a five-dollar bill.

fives /faɪvz/ n. a game in which a ball is hit with a gloved hand or a bat against the walls of a court with three walls (**Eton fives**) or four walls (**Rugby fives**). [*pl.* of FIVE used as *sing.* The significance of the word *fives* is unknown; its slang use to mean 'a hand' is not found until the early 19th c., whereas forms of the game date from much earlier.]

fivestones /ˈfaɪvstəʊnz/ n. *Brit.* jacks played with five pieces of metal etc. and usu. without a ball.

fix /fɪks/ v. & n. —v. **1** tr. make firm or stable; fasten, secure (*fixed a picture to the wall*). **2** tr. decide, settle, specify (a price, date, etc.). **3** tr. mend, repair. **4** tr. implant (an idea or memory) in the mind (*couldn't get the rules fixed in his head*). **5** tr. **a** (foll. by *on*, *upon*) direct steadily, set (one's eyes, gaze, attention, or affection). **b** attract and hold (a person's attention, eyes, etc.). **c** (foll. by *with*) single out with one's eyes etc. **6** tr. place definitely or permanently, establish, station. **7** tr. determine the exact nature, position, etc., of; refer (a thing or person) to a definite place or time; identify, locate. **8 a** tr. make (eyes, features, etc.) rigid. **b** intr. (of eyes, features, etc.) become rigid. **9** tr. *US colloq.* prepare (food or drink) (*fixed me a drink*). **10 a** tr. deprive of fluidity or volatility; congeal. **b** intr. lose fluidity or volatility, become congealed. **11** tr. *colloq.* punish, kill, silence, deal with (a person). **12** tr. *colloq.* **a** secure the support of (a person) fraudulently, esp. by bribery. **b** arrange the result of (a race, match, etc.) fraudulently (*the competition was fixed*). **13** *sl.* **a** tr. inject (a person, esp. oneself) with a narcotic. **b** intr. take an injection of a narcotic. **14** tr. make (a colour, photographic image, or microscope-specimen) fast or permanent. **15** tr. (of a plant or micro-organism) assimilate (nitrogen or carbon dioxide) by forming a non-gaseous compound. **16** tr. castrate or spay (an animal). **17** tr. arrest changes or development in (a language or literature). **18** tr. determine the incidence of (liability etc.). **19** intr. *archaic* take up one's position. —n. *colloq.* **1** a position hard to escape from; a dilemma or predicament. **2 a** the act of finding one's position by bearings or astronomical observations. **b** a position found in this way. **3** *sl.* a dose of a narcotic drug to which one is addicted. **4** *US sl.* bribery. □ **be fixed** (usu. foll. by *for*) be disposed or affected (regarding) (*how is he fixed for money?*; *how are you fixed for Friday?*). **fixed capital** machinery etc. that remains in the owner's use. **fixed-doh** *Mus.* applied to a system of sight-singing in which C is called 'doh', D is called 'ray', etc., irrespective of the key in which they occur (cf. *movable-doh*). **fixed focus** a camera focus at a distance from a lens that is not adjustable. **fixed idea** = IDÉE FIXE. **fixed income** income deriving from a pension, investment at fixed interest, etc. **fixed odds** predetermined odds in racing etc. (opp. *starting price*). **fixed oil** see OIL. **fixed point** *Physics* a well-defined reproducible temperature. **fixed star** *Astron.* a star so far from Earth as

to appear motionless except for the diurnal revolution of the heavens (opp. *planet*, *comet*, etc.). **fix on** (or **upon**) choose, decide on. **fix up 1** arrange, organize, prepare. **2** accommodate. **3** (often foll. by *with*) provide (a person) (*fixed me up with a job*). □□ **fixable** adj. **fixedly** /ˈfiksɪdlɪ/ adv. **fixedness** /ˈfiksɪdnɪs/ n. [ME, partly f. obs. *fix* fixed f. OF *fix* or L *fixus* past part. of *figere* fix, fasten, partly f. med.L *fixare* f. *fixus*]

fixate /fik'seɪt/ v.tr. **1** direct one's gaze on. **2** *Psychol.* **a** (usu. in *passive*; often foll. by *on*, *upon*) cause (a person) to acquire an abnormal attachment to persons or things (*was fixated on his son*). **b** arrest (part of the libido) at an immature stage, causing such attachment. [L *fixus* (see FIX) + -ATE[3]]

fixation /fik'seɪʃ(ə)n/ n. **1** the act or an instance of being fixated. **2** an obsession, concentration on a single idea. **3** fixing or being fixed. **4** the process of rendering solid; coagulation. **5** the process of assimilating a gas to form a solid compound. [ME f. med.L *fixatio* f. *fixare*: see FIX]

fixative /ˈfiksətɪv/ adj. & n. —adj. tending to fix or secure. —n. a substance used to fix colours, hair, microscope-specimens, etc.

fixer /ˈfiksə(r)/ n. **1** a person or thing that fixes. **2** *Photog.* a substance used for fixing a photographic image. **3** *colloq.* a person who makes arrangements, esp. of an illicit kind.

fixings /ˈfiksɪŋz/ n.pl. *US* **1** apparatus or equipment. **2** the trimmings for a dish. **3** the trimmings of a dress etc.

fixity /ˈfiksɪtɪ/ n. **1** a fixed state. **2** stability; permanence. [obs. *fix* fixed: see FIX]

fixture /ˈfikstʃə(r)/ n. **1 a** something fixed or fastened in position. **b** (usu. *predic.*) *colloq.* a person or thing confined to or established in one place (*he seems to be a fixture*). **2 a** a sporting event, esp. a match, race, etc. **b** the date agreed for this. **3** (in *pl.*) *Law* articles attached to a house or land and regarded as legally part of it. [alt. of obs. *fixure* f. LL *fixura* f. L *figere* *fix-* fix]

fizgig /ˈfizgɪg/ n. & adj. *archaic* —n. **1** a silly or flirtatious young woman. **2** a kind of small firework; a cracker. **3** *Austral. sl.* a police informer. —adj. flighty. [prob. f. FIZZ + obs. *gig* flighty girl]

fizz /fiz/ v. & n. —v.intr. **1** make a hissing or spluttering sound. **2** (of a drink) make bubbles; effervesce. —n. **1** effervescence. **2** *colloq.* an effervescent drink, esp. champagne. [imit.]

fizzle /ˈfiz(ə)l/ v. & n. —v.intr. make a feeble hissing or spluttering sound. —n. such a sound. □ **fizzle out** end feebly (*the party fizzled out at 10 o'clock*). [formed as FIZZ + -LE[4]]

fizzy /ˈfizɪ/ adj. (**fizzier**, **fizziest**) effervescent. □□ **fizzily** adv. **fizziness** n.

FJI abbr. Fellow of the Institute of Journalists.

fjord var. of FIORD.

FL abbr. *US* Florida (in official postal use).

fl. abbr. **1** floor. **2** floruit. **3** fluid.

Fla. abbr. Florida.

flab /flæb/ n. *colloq.* fat; flabbiness. [imit., or back-form. f. FLABBY]

flabbergast /ˈflæbəˌgɑːst/ v.tr. (esp. as **flabbergasted** adj.) *colloq.* overwhelm with astonishment; dumbfound. [18th c.: perh. f. FLABBY + AGHAST]

flabby /ˈflæbɪ/ adj. (**flabbier**, **flabbiest**) **1** (of flesh etc.) hanging down; limp; flaccid. **2** (of language or character) feeble. □□ **flabbily** adv. **flabbiness** n. [alt. of earlier *flappy* f. FLAP]

flaccid /ˈflæksɪd, ˈflæsɪd/ adj. **1 a** (of flesh etc.) hanging loose or wrinkled; limp, flabby. **b** (of plant tissue) soft; less rigid. **2** relaxed, drooping. **3** lacking vigour; feeble. □□ **flaccidity** /-ˈsɪdɪtɪ/ n. **flaccidly** adv. [F *flaccide* or L *flaccidus* f. *flaccus* flabby]

flack[1] /flæk/ n. *US sl.* a publicity agent. [20th c.: orig. unkn.]

flack[2] var. of FLAK.

flag[1] /flæg/ n. & v. —n. **1 a** a piece of cloth, usu. oblong or square, attachable by one edge to a pole or rope and used as a country's emblem or as a standard, signal, etc. **b** a small toy, device, etc., resembling a flag. **2** *Brit.* an oblong strip of metal etc. that can be raised or lowered to indicate whether a taxi is for hire or occupied. **3** *Naut.* a flag carried by a flagship as an emblem of an admiral's rank afloat. —v. (**flagged**, **flagging**) **1** intr. **a** grow tired; lose vigour; lag (*his energy flagged after the first* *lap*). **b** hang down; droop; become limp. **2** *tr.* **a** place a flag on or over. **b** mark out with or as if with a flag or flags. **3** *tr.* (often foll. by *that*) **a** inform (a person) by flag-signals. **b** communicate (information) by flagging. □ **black flag 1** a pirate's ensign. **2** *hist.* a flag hoisted outside a prison to announce an execution. **flag-boat** a boat serving as a mark in sailing-matches. **flag-captain** the captain of a flagship. **flag-day** *Brit.* a day on which money is raised for a charity by the sale of small paper flags etc. in the street. **Flag Day** *US* 14 June, the anniversary of the adoption of the Stars and Stripes in 1777. **flag down** signal to (a vehicle or driver) to stop. **flag-lieutenant** *Naut.* an admiral's ADC. **flag-list** *Naut.* a roll of flag-officers. **flag of convenience** a foreign flag under which a ship is registered, usu. to avoid financial charges etc. **flag-officer** *Naut.* an admiral, vice admiral, or rear admiral, or the commodore of a yacht-club. **flag of truce** a white flag indicating a desire for a truce. **flag-pole** = FLAGSTAFF. **flag-rank** *Naut.* the rank attained by flag-officers. **flag-station** a station at which trains stop only if signalled. **flag-wagging** *sl.* **1** signalling with hand-held flags. **2** = *flag-waving*. **flag-waver** a populist agitator; a chauvinist. **flag-waving** populist agitation, chauvinism. **keep the flag flying** continue the fight. **put the flag out** celebrate victory, success, etc. **show the flag 1** make an official visit to a foreign port etc. **2** ensure that notice is taken of one's country, oneself, etc.; make a patriotic display. □□ **flagger** *n.* [16th c.: perh. f. obs. *flag* drooping]

flag² /flæg/ *n.* & *v.* —*n.* (also **flagstone**) **1** a flat usu. rectangular stone slab used for paving. **2** (in *pl.*) a pavement made of these. —*v.tr.* (**flagged, flagging**) pave with flags. [ME, = sod: cf. Icel. *flag* spot from which a sod has been cut out, ON *flaga* slab of stone, and FLAKE¹]

flag³ /flæg/ *n.* **1** any plant with a bladed leaf (esp. several of the genus *Iris*) growing on moist ground. **2** the long slender leaf of such a plant. [ME: cf. MDu. *flag*, Da. *flæg*]

flag⁴ /flæg/ *n.* (in full **flag-feather**) a quill-feather of a bird's wing. [perh. rel. to obs. *fag* loose flap: cf. FLAG¹ *v.*]

flagellant /ˈflædʒələnt, fləˈdʒelənt/ *n.* & *adj.* —*n.* **1** a person who scourges himself or herself or others as a religious discipline. **2** a person who engages in flogging as a sexual stimulus. —*adj.* of or concerning flagellation. [L *flagellare* to whip f. FLAGELLUM]

flagellate¹ /ˈflædʒəˌleɪt/ *v.tr.* scourge, flog (cf. FLAGELLANT). □□ **flagellation** /-ˈleɪʃ(ə)n/ *n.* **flagellator** *n.* **flagellatory** /-lətərɪ/ *adj.*

flagellate² /ˈflædʒɪlɪt/ *adj.* & *n.* —*adj.* having flagella (see FLAGELLUM). —*n.* a protozoan having one or more flagella.

flagellum /fləˈdʒeləm/ *n.* (*pl.* **flagella** /-lə/) **1** *Biol.* a long lashlike appendage found principally on microscopic organisms. **2** *Bot.* a runner; a creeping shoot. □□ **flagellar** *adj.* **flagelliform** *adj.* [L, = whip, dimin. of *flagrum* scourge]

flageolet¹ /ˌflædʒəˈlet, ˈflædʒ-/ *n.* **1** a small flute blown at the end, like a recorder but with two thumb-holes. **2** an organ stop having a similar sound. [F, dimin. of OF *flag(e)ol* f. Prov. *flajol*, of unkn. orig.]

flageolet² /ˌflædʒəʊˈlet, -ˈlet/ *n.* a kind of French kidney bean. [F]

flagitious /fləˈdʒɪʃəs/ *adj.* deeply criminal; utterly villainous. □□ **flagitiously** *adv.* **flagitiousness** *n.* [ME f. L *flagitiosus* f. *flagitium* shameful crime]

flagman /ˈflægmən/ *n.* (*pl.* **-men**) a person who signals with or as with a flag, e.g. at races.

flagon /ˈflægən/ *n.* **1** a large bottle in which wine, cider, etc., are sold, usu. holding 1.13 litres. **2 a** a large vessel usu. with a handle, spout, and lid, to hold wine etc. **b** a similar vessel used for the Eucharist. [ME *flakon* f. OF *flacon* ult. f. LL *flasco -onis* FLASK]

flagrant /ˈfleɪgrənt/ *adj.* (of an offence or an offender) glaring; notorious; scandalous. □□ **flagrancy** /-grənsɪ/ *n.* **flagrantly** *adv.* [F *flagrant* or L *flagrant-* part. stem of *flagrare* blaze]

flagship /ˈflægʃɪp/ *n.* **1** a ship having an admiral on board. **2** something that is held to be the best or most important of its kind; a leader.

flagstaff /ˈflægstɑːf/ *n.* a pole on which a flag may be hoisted.

flagstone /ˈflægstəʊn/ *n.* = FLAG².

flail /fleɪl/ *n.* & *v.* —*n.* a threshing-tool consisting of a wooden staff with a short heavy stick swinging from it. —*v.* **1** *tr.* beat or strike with or as if with a flail. **2** *intr.* wave or swing wildly or erratically (*went into the fight with arms flailing*). [OE prob. f. L FLAGELLUM]

flair /fleə(r)/ *n.* **1** an instinct for selecting or performing what is excellent, useful, etc.; a talent (*has a flair for knowing what the public wants; has a flair for languages*). **2** talent or ability, esp. artistic or stylistic. [F *flairer* to smell ult. f. L *fragrare*: see FRAGRANT]

flak /flæk/ *n.* (also **flack**) **1** anti-aircraft fire. **2** adverse criticism; abuse. □ **flak jacket** a protective jacket of heavy camouflage fabric reinforced with metal, worn by soldiers etc. [abbr. of G *Fliegerabwehrkanone*, lit. aviator-defence-gun]

flake¹ /fleɪk/ *n.* & *v.* —*n.* **1 a** a small thin light piece of snow. **b** a similar piece of another material. **2** a thin broad piece of material peeled or split off. **3** *Archaeol.* a piece of hard stone chipped off and used as a tool. **4** a natural division of the flesh of some fish. **5** the dogfish or other shark as food. —*v.tr.* & *intr.* (often foll. by *away, off*) **1** take off or come away in flakes. **2** sprinkle with or fall in snowlike flakes. □ **flake out** *colloq.* fall asleep or drop from exhaustion; faint. [ME: orig. unkn.: cf. ON *flakna* flake off]

flake² /fleɪk/ *n.* **1** a stage for drying fish etc. **2** a rack for storing oatcakes etc. [ME, perh. f. ON *flaki, fleki* wicker shield]

flaky /ˈfleɪkɪ/ *adj.* (**flakier, flakiest**) **1** of or like flakes; separating easily into flakes. **2** esp. *US sl.* crazy, eccentric. □ **flaky pastry** pastry consisting of thin light layers. □□ **flakily** *adv.* **flakiness** *n.*

flambé /ˈflɒmbeɪ/ *adj.* (of food) covered with alcohol and set alight briefly. [F, past part. of *flamber* singe (as FLAMBEAU)]

flambeau /ˈflæmbəʊ/ *n.* (*pl.* **flambeaus** or **flambeaux** /-əʊz/) **1** a flaming torch, esp. composed of several thick waxed wicks. **2** a branched candlestick. [F f. *flambe* f. L *flammula* dimin. of *flamma* flame]

flamboyant /flæmˈbɔɪənt/ *adj.* **1** ostentatious; showy. **2** floridly decorated. **3** gorgeously coloured. **4** *Archit.* (of decoration) marked by wavy flamelike lines. □□ **flamboyance** *n.* **flamboyancy** *n.* **flamboyantly** *adv.* [F (in Archit. sense), pres. part. of *flamboyer* f. *flambe*: see FLAMBEAU]

flame /fleɪm/ *n.* & *v.* —*n.* **1 a** ignited gas (*the fire burnt with a steady flame*). **b** one portion of this (*the flame flickered and died*). **c** (usu. in *pl.*) visible combustion (*burst into flames*). **2 a** a bright light; brilliant colouring. **b** a brilliant orange-red colour. **3 a** strong passion, esp. love (*fan the flame*). **b** *colloq.* a boyfriend or girlfriend. —*v.* **1** *intr.* (often foll. by *away, forth, out, up*) emit or cause to emit flames. **2** *intr.* (often foll. by *out, up*) **a** (of passion) break out. **b** (of a person) become angry. **3** *intr.* shine or glow like flame (*leaves flamed in the autumn sun*). **4** *intr. poet.* move like flame. **5** *tr.* send (a signal) by means of flame. **6** *tr.* subject to the action of flame. □ **flame gun** a device for throwing flames to destroy weeds etc. **flame out** (of a jet engine) lose power through the extinction of the flame in the combustion chamber. **flame-proof** (esp. of a fabric) treated so as to be non-flammable. **flame-thrower** (or **-projector**) a weapon for throwing a spray of flame. **flame-tree** any of various trees with brilliant red flowers esp. flame-of-the-forest, *Delonix regia*. **go up in flames** be consumed by fire. □□ **flameless** *adj.* **flamelike** *adj.* **flamy** *adj.* [ME f. OF *flame, flam(m)e* f. L *flamma*]

flamen /ˈfleɪmən/ *n. Rom.Hist.* a priest serving a particular deity. [ME f. L]

flamenco /fləˈmeŋkəʊ/ *n.* (*pl.* **-os**) **1** a style of music played (esp. on the guitar) and sung by Spanish gypsies. **2** a dance performed to this music. [Sp., = Flemish]

flaming /ˈfleɪmɪŋ/ *adj.* **1** emitting flames. **2** very hot (*flaming June*). **3** *colloq.* **a** passionate; intense (*a flaming row*). **b** expressing annoyance, or as an intensifier (*that flaming dog*). **4** bright-coloured (*flaming red hair*).

flamingo /fləˈmɪŋgəʊ/ *n.* (*pl.* **-os** or **-oes**) any tall long-necked web-footed wading bird of the family Phoenicopteridae, with crooked bill and pink, scarlet, and black plumage. [Port. *flamengo* f. Prov. *flamenc* f. *flama* flame + *-enc* = -ING³]

---

w *we* z *zoo* ʃ *she* ʒ *decision* θ *thin* ð *this* ŋ *ring* x *loch* tʃ *chip* dʒ *jar* (*see over for vowels*)

flammable /ˈflæməb(ə)l/ *adj.* inflammable. ¶ Often used because *inflammable* can be mistaken for a negative (the true negative being *non-flammable*). □□ **flammability** /-ˈbɪlɪtɪ/ *n.* [L *flammare* f. *flamma* flame]

flan /flæn/ *n.* **1 a** a pastry case with a savoury or sweet filling. **b** a sponge base with a sweet topping. **2** a disc of metal from which a coin etc. is made. [F (orig. = round cake) f. OF *flaon* f. med.L *flado -onis* f. Frank.]

flanch /flɑːntʃ/ *v.tr.* & *intr.* (also **flaunch** /flɔːntʃ/) (esp. with ref. to a chimney) slope inwards or cause to slope inwards towards the top. □□ **flanching** *n.* [perh. f. OF *flanchir* f. *flanche, flanc* FLANK]

Flanders /ˈflɑːndəz/ a medieval principality in the SW part of the Low Countries, now divided between Belgium, France, and The Netherlands. The area was the scene of considerable military activity during the First World War when British troops held the sector of the Western Front round the town of Ypres. □ **Flanders poppy 1** a red poppy used as an emblem of the soldiers of the Allies who fell in the First World War. **2** an artificial red poppy made for wearing on Remembrance Sunday, sold in aid of needy ex-service people.

flânerie /flɑːnˈriː/ *n.* idling, idleness. [F f. *flâner* lounge]

flâneur /flæˈnɜː/ *n.* an idler; a lounger. [F (as FLÂNERIE)]

flange /flændʒ/ *n.* & *v. Engin.* —*n.* a projecting flat rim, collar, or rib, used for strengthening or attachment. —*v.tr.* provide with a flange. □□ **flangeless** *n.* [17th c.: perh. f. *flange* widen out f. OF *flangir* (as FLANCH)]

flank /flæŋk/ *n.* & *v.* —*n.* **1 a** the side of the body between the ribs and the hip. **b** the side of an animal carved as meat (*flank of beef*). **2** the side of a mountain, building, etc. **3** the right or left side of an army or other body of persons. —*v.tr.* **1** (often in *passive*) be situated at both sides of (*a road flanked by mountains*). **2** *Mil.* **a** a guard or strengthen on the flank. **b** menace the flank of. **c** rake with sweeping gunfire; enfilade. □ **flank forward** *Rugby Football* a wing forward. **in flank** at the side. [ME f. OF *flanc* f. Frank.]

flanker /ˈflæŋkə(r)/ *n.* **1** *Mil.* a fortification guarding or menacing the flank. **2** anything that flanks another thing. **3** (in Rugby and American Football) a flank forward. **4** *sl.* a trick; a swindle (*pulled a flanker*).

flannel /ˈflæn(ə)l/ *n.* & *v.* —*n.* **1 a** a kind of woven woollen fabric, usu. without a nap. **b** (in *pl.*) flannel garments, esp. trousers. **2** *Brit.* a small usu. towelling cloth, used for washing oneself. **3** *Brit. sl.* nonsense; flattery. —*v.* (**flannelled**, **flannelling**; *US* **flanneled, flanneling**) **1** *Brit. sl.* **a** *tr.* flatter. **b** *intr.* use flattery. **2** *tr.* wash or clean with a flannel. □ **flannel-mouth** *US sl.* a flatterer; a braggart. □□ **flannelly** *adj.* [perh. f. Welsh *gwlanen* f. *gwlân* wool]

flannelboard /ˈflæn(ə)l,bɔːd/ *n.* a piece of flannel as a base for paper or cloth cut-outs, used as a toy or a teaching aid.

flannelette /ˌflænəˈlet/ *n.* a napped cotton fabric imitating flannel. [FLANNEL]

flannelgraph /ˈflæn(ə)l,grɑːf/ *n.* = FLANNELBOARD.

flannelled /ˈflæn(ə)ld/ *adj.* (*US* also **flanneled**) wearing flannel trousers. [FLANNEL]

flap /flæp/ *v.* & *n.* —*v.* (**flapped, flapping**) **1 a** *tr.* move (wings, the arms, etc.) up and down when flying, or as if flying. **b** *intr.* (of wings, the arms, etc.) move up and down; beat. **2** *intr. colloq.* be agitated or panicky. **3** *intr.* (esp. of curtains, loose cloth, etc.) swing or sway about; flutter. **4** *tr.* (usu. foll. by *away, off*) strike (flies etc.) with something broad; drive. **5** *intr. colloq.* (of ears) listen intently. —*n.* **1** a piece of cloth, wood, paper, etc. hinged or attached by one side only and often used to cover a gap, e.g. a pocket-cover, the folded part of an envelope, a table-leaf. **2** one up-and-down motion of a wing, an arm, etc. **3** *colloq.* a state of agitation; panic (*don't get into a flap*). **4** a hinged or sliding section of a wing used to control lift; an aileron. **5** a light blow with something broad. **6** an open mushroom-top. □□ **flappy** *adj.* [ME, prob. imit.]

flapdoodle /flæpˈduːd(ə)l, ˈflæp-/ *n. colloq.* nonsense. [19th c.: orig. unkn.]

flapjack /ˈflæpdʒæk/ *n.* **1** a cake made from oats and golden syrup etc. **2** esp. *US* a pancake. [FLAP + JACK¹]

flapper /ˈflæpə(r)/ *n.* **1** a person or thing that flaps. **2** an instrument that is flapped to kill flies, scare birds, etc. **3** a person who panics easily or is easily agitated. **4** *sl.* (in the 1920s) a young unconventional or lively woman. **5** a young mallard or partridge.

flare /fleə(r)/ *v.* & *n.* —*v.* **1** *intr.* & *tr.* widen or cause to widen gradually towards the top or bottom (*flared trousers*). **2** *intr.* & *tr.* burn or cause to burn suddenly with a bright unsteady flame. **3** *intr.* burst into anger; burst forth. —*n.* **1 a** a dazzling irregular flame or light, esp. in the open air. **b** a sudden outburst of flame. **2 a** a signal light used at sea. **b** a bright light used as a signal. **c** a flame dropped from an aircraft to illuminate a target etc. **3** *Astron.* a sudden burst of radiation from a star. **4 a** a gradual widening, esp. of a skirt or trousers. **b** (in *pl.*) wide-bottomed trousers. **5** an outward bulge in a ship's sides. **6** *Photog.* unnecessary illumination on a lens caused by internal reflection etc. □ **flare-path** an area illuminated to enable an aircraft to land or take off. **flare up 1** burst into a sudden blaze. **2** become suddenly angry or active. **flare-up** *n.* an outburst of flame, anger, activity, etc. [16th c.: orig. unkn.]

flash /flæʃ/ *v., n.,* & *adj.* —*v.* **1** *intr.* & *tr.* emit or reflect or cause to emit or reflect light briefly, suddenly, or intermittently; gleam or cause to gleam. **2** *intr.* break suddenly into flame; give out flame or sparks. **3** *tr.* send or reflect like a sudden flame or blaze (*his eyes flashed fire*). **4** *intr.* **a** burst suddenly into view or perception (*the explanation flashed upon me*). **b** move swiftly (*the train flashed through the station*). **5** *tr.* **a** send (news etc.) by radio, telegraph, etc. (*flashed a message to her*). **b** signal to (a person) by shining lights or headlights briefly. **6** *tr. colloq.* show ostentatiously (*flashed her engagement ring*). **7** *intr.* (of water) rush along; rise and flow. **8** *intr. sl.* indecently expose oneself. —*n.* **1** a sudden bright light or flame, e.g. of lightning. **2** a very brief time; an instant (*all over in a flash*). **3 a** a brief, sudden burst of feeling (*a flash of hope*). **b** a sudden display (of wit, understanding, etc.). **4** = NEWSFLASH. **5** *Photog.* **a** the brief intense bright light produced by a flash bulb or electronic flash, used to provide or supplement illumination. **b** the apparatus for producing this.. **6 a** a rush of water, esp. down a weir to take a boat over shallows. **b** a contrivance for producing this. **7** *Brit. Mil.* a coloured patch of cloth on a uniform etc. as a distinguishing emblem. **8** *vulgar* display, ostentation. **9** a bright patch of colour. **10** *Cinematog.* the momentary exposure of a scene. **11** excess plastic or metal oozing from a mould during moulding. —*adj. colloq.* **1** gaudy; showy; vulgar (*a flash car*). **2** counterfeit (*flash notes*). **3** connected with thieves, the underworld, etc. □ **flash-board** a board used for sending more water from a mill-dam into a mill-race. **flash bulb** *Photog.* a glass bulb operated usu. electrically to produce a brief intense flash of light. **flash burn** a burn caused by sudden intense heat, esp. from a nuclear explosion. **flash card** a card containing a small amount of information, held up for pupils to see, as an aid to learning. **flash-cube** *Photog.* a set of four flash bulbs arranged as a cube and operated in turn. **flash-flood** a sudden local flood due to heavy rain etc. **flash-gun** *Photog.* a device for operating a flash bulb. **flashing-point** = FLASHPOINT. **flash in the pan** a promising start followed by failure (from the priming of old guns). **flash-lamp** a portable flashing electric lamp. **flash out** (or **up**) show sudden passion. **flash over** *Electr.* make an electric circuit by sparking across a gap. **flash-over** *n.* an instance of this. [ME orig. with ref. to the rushing of water: cf. SPLASH]

flashback /ˈflæʃbæk/ *n. Cinematog.* a scene set in a time earlier than the main action.

flasher /ˈflæʃə(r)/ *n.* **1** *Brit. sl.* a man who indecently exposes himself. **2 a** an automatic device for switching lights rapidly on and off. **b** a sign or signal using this. **3** a person or thing that flashes.

flashing /ˈflæʃɪŋ/ *n.* a usu. metallic strip used to prevent water penetration at the junction of a roof with a wall etc. [dial. *flash* seal with lead sheets or obs. *flash* flashing]

flashlight /ˈflæʃlaɪt/ *n.* **1** *Photog.* = FLASH *n.* 5. **2** *US* an electric torch. **3** a flashing light used for signals and in lighthouses.

flashpoint /ˈflæʃpɔɪnt/ n. **1** the temperature at which vapour from oil etc. will ignite in air. **2** the point at which anger, indignation, etc. becomes uncontrollable.

flashy /ˈflæʃɪ/ adj. (**flashier, flashiest**) showy; gaudy; cheaply attractive. □□ **flashily** adv. **flashiness** n.

flask /flɑːsk/ n. **1** a narrow-necked bulbous bottle for wine etc. or as used in chemistry. **2** = hip-flask (see HIP¹). **3** = vacuum flask. **4** hist. = powder-flask. [F flasque & (prob.) It. fiasco f. med.L flasca, flasco: cf. FLAGON]

flat¹ /flæt/ adj., adv., n., & v. —adj. (**flatter, flattest**) **1 a** horizontally level (a flat roof). **b** even; smooth; unbroken; without projection or indentation (a flat stomach). **c** with a level surface and little depth; shallow (a flat cap; a flat heel). **2** unqualified; plain; downright (a flat refusal; a flat denial). **3 a** dull; lifeless; monotonous (spoke in a flat tone). **b** without energy; dejected. **4** (of a fizzy drink) having lost its effervescence. **5** (of an accumulator, a battery, etc.) having exhausted its charge. **6** Mus. **a** below true or normal pitch (the violins are flat). **b** (of a key) having a flat or flats in the signature. **c** (as **B**, **E**, etc. **flat**) a semitone lower than B, E, etc. **7** Photog. lacking contrast. **8 a** (of paint etc.) not glossy; matt. **b** (of a tint) uniform. **9** (of a tyre) punctured; deflated. **10** (of a market, prices, etc.) inactive; sluggish. **11** of or relating to flat-racing. —adv. **1** lying at full length; spread out, esp. on another surface (lay flat on the floor; the ladder was flat against the wall). **2** colloq. **a** completely, absolutely (turned it down flat; flat broke). **b** exactly (in five minutes flat). **3** Mus. below the true or normal pitch (always sings flat). —n. **1** the flat part of anything; something flat (the flat of the hand). **2** level ground, esp. a plain or swamp. **3** Mus. **a** a note lowered a semitone below natural pitch. **b** the sign (♭) indicating this. **4** (as **the flat**) Brit. **a** flat racing. **b** the flat racing season. **5** Theatr. a flat section of scenery mounted on a frame. **6** esp. US colloq. a flat tyre. **7** sl. a foolish person. —v.tr. (**flatted, flatting**) **1** make flat, flatten (esp. in technical use). **2** US Mus. make (a note) flat. □ **fall flat** fail to live up to expectations; not win applause. **flat arch** Archit. an arch with a flat lower or inner curve. **flat** (or **flat-bottomed**) **boat** a boat with a flat bottom for transport in shallow water. **flat-fish** any marine fish of various families having an asymmetric appearance with both eyes on one side of a flattened body, including sole, turbot, plaice, etc. **flat foot** a foot with a less than normal arch. **flat-four** (of an engine) having four cylinders all horizontal, two on each side of the crankshaft. **flat-head 1** any marine fish of the family Platycephalidae, having a flattened body with both eyes on the top side. **2** sl. a foolish person. **flat-iron** hist. an iron heated externally and used for pressing clothes etc. **flat out 1** at top speed. **2** using all one's strength, energy, or resources. **flat race** a horse race over level ground, as opposed to a steeplechase or hurdles. **flat-racing** the racing of horses in flat races. **flat rate** a rate that is the same in all cases, not proportional. **flat spin 1** Aeron. a nearly horizontal spin. **2** colloq. a state of agitation or panic. **flat-top 1** US Aeron. sl. an aircraft-carrier. **2** a man's short flat haircut. **that's flat** colloq. let there be no doubt about it. □□ **flatly** adv. **flatness** n. **flattish** adj. [ME f. ON flatr f. Gmc]

flat² /flæt/ n. & v. —n. a set of rooms, usu. on one floor, used as a residence. —v.intr. (**flatted, flatting**) (often foll. by with) Austral. share a flat with. □□ **flatlet** n. [alt. f. obs. flet floor, dwelling f. Gmc (as FLAT¹)]

flatcar /ˈflætkɑː(r)/ n. a railway wagon without raised sides or ends.

flatfoot /ˈflætfʊt/ n. (pl. **-foots** or **-feet**) sl. a policeman.

flat-footed /ˈflætˌfʊtɪd/ adj. **1** having flat feet. **2** colloq. downright, positive. **3** colloq. unprepared; off guard (was caught flat-footed). □□ **flat-footedly** adv. **flat-footedness** n.

flatmate /ˈflætmeɪt/ n. Brit. a person in relation to one or more others living in the same flat.

flatten /ˈflæt(ə)n/ v. **1** tr. & intr. make or become flat. **2** tr. colloq. **a** humiliate. **b** knock down. □ **flatten out** bring an aircraft parallel to the ground. □□ **flattener** n.

flatter /ˈflætə(r)/ v.tr. **1** compliment unduly; overpraise, esp. for gain or advantage. **2** (usu. refl.; usu. foll. by that + clause) please, congratulate, or delude (oneself etc.) (I flatter myself that I can sing). **3 a** (of a colour, a style, etc.) make (a person) appear to the best advantage (that blouse flatters you). **b** (esp. of a portrait, a painter, etc.) represent too favourably. **4** gratify the vanity of; make (a person) feel honoured. **5** inspire (a person) with hope, esp. unduly (was flattered into thinking himself invulnerable). **6** please or gratify (the ear, the eye, etc.). □ **flattering unction** a salve that one administers to one's own conscience or self-esteem (Shakesp. esp. Hamlet III. iv. 136). □□ **flatterer** n. **flattering** adj. **flatteringly** adv. [ME, perh. rel. to OF flater to smooth]

flattery /ˈflætərɪ/ n. (pl. **-ies**) **1** exaggerated or insincere praise. **2** the act or an instance of flattering.

flattie /ˈflætɪ/ n. (also **flatty**) (pl. **-ies**) colloq. **1** a flat-heeled shoe. **2** a flat-bottomed boat. **3** a policeman.

flatulent /ˈflætjʊlənt/ adj. **1 a** causing formation of gas in the alimentary canal. **b** caused by or suffering from this. **2** (of speech etc.) inflated, pretentious. □□ **flatulence** n. **flatulency** n. **flatulently** adv. [F f. mod.L flatulentus (as FLATUS)]

flatus /ˈfleɪtəs/ n. wind in or from the stomach or bowels. [L, = blowing f. flare blow]

flatware /ˈflætweə(r)/ n. **1** plates, saucers, etc. (opp. HOLLOW-WARE). **2** US domestic cutlery.

flatworm /ˈflætwɜːm/ n. any worm of the phylum Platyhelminthes, having a flattened body and no body-cavity or blood vessels, including turbellaria, flukes, etc.

Flaubert /ˈfləʊbeə(r)/, Gustave (1821–80), French novelist. His first published (and greatest) novel Madame Bovary (1857) relates the adulteries and suicide of a doctor's wife in provincial Normandy and is noted for its rigorous psychological development, a quality which marks all his mature work. This sensational work was judged offensive to public morals, but Flaubert and his printer were acquitted after trial. Flaubert's Correspondence (1887–93), with searching reflections on the art of fiction, shows the novelist as an extravagant romantic, an enthusiastic traveller, and the lover of the poet Louise Colet (1808–76).

flaunch var. of FLANCH.

flaunt /flɔːnt/ v. —v.tr. & intr. **1** (often refl.) display ostentatiously (oneself or one's finery); show off; parade (liked to flaunt his gold cuff-links; flaunted themselves before the crowd). ¶ Often confused with flout. **2** wave or cause to wave proudly (flaunted the banner). —n. an act or instance of flaunting. □□ **flaunter** n. **flaunty** adj. [16th c.: orig. unkn.]

flautist /ˈflɔːtɪst/ n. a flute-player. [It. flautista f. flauto FLUTE]

flavescent /fləˈves(ə)nt/ adj. turning yellow; yellowish. [L flavescere f. flavus yellow]

Flavian /ˈfleɪvɪən/ adj. & n. —adj. of the dynasty of Roman emperors including Vespasian and his sons Titus and Domitian. —n. a member of this dynasty. [L Flavianus f. Flavius name of family]

flavin /ˈfleɪvɪn/ n. (also **flavine** /-viːn/) **1** the chemical compound forming the nucleus of various natural yellow pigments. **2** a yellow dye obtained from dyer's oak. □ **flavin adenine dinucleotide** a coenzyme derived from riboflavin, important in various biochemical reactions. ¶ Abbr.: **FAD**. [L flavus yellow + -IN]

flavine /ˈfleɪviːn/ n. Pharm. an antiseptic derived from acridine. [as FLAVIN + -INE⁴]

flavone /ˈfleɪvəʊn/ n. Biochem. any of a group of naturally occurring white or yellow pigments found in plants. [as FLAVINE + -ONE]

flavoprotein /ˌfleɪvəʊˈprəʊtiːn/ n. Biochem. any of a group of conjugated proteins containing flavin that are involved in oxidation reactions in cells. [FLAVINE + PROTEIN]

flavorous /ˈfleɪvərəs/ adj. having a pleasant or pungent flavour.

flavour /ˈfleɪvə(r)/ n. & v. (US **flavor**) —n. **1** a distinctive mingled sensation of smell and taste (has a cheesy flavour). **2** an indefinable characteristic quality (music with a romantic flavour). **3** (usu. foll. by of) a slight admixture of a usu. undesirable quality (the flavour of failure hangs over the enterprise). **4** esp. US = FLAVOURING. —v.tr. give flavour to; season. □ **flavour of the month** (or **week**) a temporary trend or fashion. □□ **flavourful** adj. **flavourless** adj. **flavoursome** adj. [ME f. OF flaor perh. f. L flatus blowing & foetor stench: assim. to savour]

flavouring /ˈfleɪvərɪŋ/ n. a substance used to flavour food or drink.

flaw[1] /flɔː/ n. & v. —n. 1 an imperfection; a blemish (has a character without a flaw). 2 a crack or similar fault (the cup has a flaw). 3 Law an invalidating defect in a legal matter. —v.tr. & intr. crack; damage; spoil. □□ **flawless** adj. **flawlessly** adv. **flawlessness** n. [ME perh. f. ON flaga slab f. Gmc: cf. FLAKE[1], FLAG[2]]

flaw[2] /flɔː/ n. a squall of wind; a short storm. [prob. f. MDu. vlāghe, MLG vlāge, perh. = stroke]

flax /flæks/ n. 1 a a blue-flowered plant, Linum usitatissimum, cultivated for its textile fibre and its seeds (see LINSEED). b a plant resembling this. 2 a dressed or undressed flax fibres. b archaic linen, cloth of flax. □ **flax-lily** (pl. -ies) NZ any plant of the genus Phormium, yielding valuable fibre. **flax-seed** linseed. [OE flæx f. WG]

flaxen /ˈflæks(ə)n/ adj. 1 of flax. 2 (of hair) coloured like dressed flax; pale yellow.

Flaxman /ˈflæksmən/, John (1755–1826), English neoclassical sculptor. He worked for the potter, Josiah Wedgwood, 1775–87, designing medallion portraits and plaques, and was in Rome 1787–94 studying the antique and Italian medieval art. In 1793 he published engraved illustrations to Homer, greatly influenced by Greek vase-painting, which won him international fame. On his return to England he became a busy sculptor, executing many church monuments. He is one of the very few English sculptors to have had a European reputation, though this was based largely on his drawings.

flay /fleɪ/ v.tr. 1 strip the skin or hide off, esp. by beating. 2 criticize severely (the play was flayed by the critics). 3 peel off (skin, bark, peel, etc.). 4 strip (a person) of wealth by extortion or exaction. □□ **flayer** n. [OE flēan f. Gmc]

F-layer /ˈefˌleɪə(r)/ n. the highest and most strongly ionized region of the ionosphere. [F (arbitrary) + LAYER]

flea /fliː/ n. 1 a small wingless jumping insect of the order Siphonaptera, feeding on human and other blood. 2 a (in full **flea beetle**) a small jumping beetle infesting hops, cabbages, etc. b (in full **water flea**) daphnia. □ **flea-bite** 1 the bite of a flea. 2 a trivial injury or inconvenience. **flea-bitten** 1 bitten by or infested with fleas. 2 shabby. **flea-bug** US = FLEA 2a. **flea-circus** a show of performing fleas. **flea-collar** an insecticidal collar for pets. **a flea in one's ear** a sharp reproof. **flea market** a street market selling second-hand goods etc. **flea-pit** a dingy dirty place, esp. a run-down cinema. **flea-wort** any of several plants supposed to drive away fleas. [OE flēa, flēah f. Gmc]

fleabag /ˈfliːbæg/ n. sl. a shabby or unattractive person or thing.

fleabane /ˈfliːbeɪn/ n. any of various composite plants of the genus Inula or Pulicaria, supposed to drive away fleas.

flèche /fleɪʃ, fleʃ/ n. a slender spire, often perforated with windows, esp. at the intersection of the nave and the transept of a church. [F, orig. = arrow]

fleck /flek/ n. & v. —n. 1 a small patch of colour or light (eyes with green flecks). 2 a small particle or speck, esp. of dust. 3 a spot on the skin; a freckle. —v.tr. mark with flecks; dapple; variegate. [perh. f. ON flekkr (n.), flekka (v.), or MLG, MDu. vlecke, OHG flec, fleccho]

Flecker /ˈflekə(r)/, (Herman) James Elroy (1884–1915), English poet, whose best-known works are 'The Golden Journey to Samarkand' (1913) and the verse drama Hassan, published posthumously in 1922, for which Delius wrote incidental music.

flection US var. of FLEXION.

fled past and past part. of FLEE.

fledge /fledʒ/ v. 1 intr. (of a bird) grow feathers. 2 tr. provide (an arrow) with feathers. 3 tr. bring up (a young bird) until it can fly. 4 tr. (as **fledged** adj.) a able to fly. b independent; mature. 5 tr. deck or provide with feathers or down. [obs. fledge (adj.) 'fit to fly', f. OE flycge (recorded in unfligge) f. a Gmc root rel. to FLY[1]]

fledgling /ˈfledʒlɪŋ/ n. (also **fledgeling**) 1 a young bird. 2 an inexperienced person. [FLEDGE + -LING[1]]

flee /fliː/ v. (past and past part. **fled** /fled/) 1 intr. (often foll. by from, before) **a** run away. **b** seek safety by fleeing. 2 tr. run away from; leave abruptly; shun (fled the room; fled his attentions). 3 intr. vanish; cease; pass away. □□ **fleer** /ˈfliːə(r)/ n. [OE flēon f. Gmc]

fleece /fliːs/ n. & v. —n. 1 a the woolly covering of a sheep or a similar animal. b the amount of wool sheared from a sheep at one time. 2 something resembling a fleece, esp.: **a** a woolly or rough head of hair. **b** a soft warm fabric with a pile, used for lining coats etc. **c** a white cloud, a blanket of snow, etc. 3 Heraldry a representation of a fleece suspended from a ring. —v.tr. 1 (often foll. by of) strip (a person) of money, valuables, etc.; swindle. 2 remove the fleece from (a sheep etc.); shear. 3 cover as if with a fleece (a sky fleeced with clouds). □ **fleece-picker** Austral. & NZ = FLEECY. **Golden Fleece** see GOLDEN. □□ **fleeceable** adj. **fleeced** adj. (also in comb.). [OE flēos, flēs f. WG]

fleecy /ˈfliːsɪ/ adj. & n. —adj. (**fleecier**, **fleeciest**) 1 of or like a fleece. 2 covered with a fleece. —n. (also **fleecie**) (pl. -ies) Austral. & NZ a person whose job is to pick up fleeces in a shearing shed. □□ **fleecily** adv. **fleeciness** n.

fleer /ˈflɪə(r)/ v. & n. —v.intr. laugh impudently or mockingly; sneer; jeer. —n. a mocking look or speech. [ME, prob. f. Scand.: cf. Norw. & Sw. dial. flira to grin]

fleet[1] /fliːt/ n. 1 **a** a number of warships under one commander-in-chief. **b** (prec. by the) all the warships and merchant-ships of a nation. 2 a number of ships, aircraft, buses, lorries, taxis, etc. operating together or owned by one proprietor. □ **Fleet Admiral** see ADMIRAL. **Fleet Air Arm** hist. the aviation service of the Royal Navy. [OE flēot ship, shipping f. flēotan float, FLEET[5]]

fleet[2] /fliːt/ adj. poet. literary swift; nimble. □□ **fleetly** adv. **fleetness** n. [prob. f. ON fljótr swift f. Gmc: cf. FLEET[5]]

fleet[3] /fliːt/ n. dial. 1 a creek; an inlet. 2 (**the Fleet**) **a** an underground stream running into the Thames east of Fleet St. **b** hist. a prison that stood near it. [OE flēot f. Gmc: cf. FLEET[5]]

fleet[4] /fliːt/ adj. & adv. dial. —adj. (of water) shallow. —adv. at or to a small depth (plough fleet). [orig. uncert.: perh. f. OE flēat (unrecorded), rel. to FLEET[5]]

fleet[5] /fliːt/ v.intr. archaic 1 glide away; vanish; be transitory. 2 (usu. foll. by away) (of time) pass rapidly; slip away. 3 move swiftly; fly. [OE flēotan float, swim f. Gmc]

fleeting /ˈfliːtɪŋ/ adj. transitory; brief. □□ **fleetingly** adv. [FLEET[5] + -ING[2]]

Fleet Street a London street between the Strand and the City, in or near which most of the leading national newspapers formerly (until the mid-1980s) had offices, whence the allusive use of its name to refer to the British press. It is named after the River Fleet, which is now covered in.

Fleming[1] /ˈflemɪŋ/ n. 1 a native of medieval Flanders in the Low Countries. 2 a member of a Flemish-speaking people inhabiting north and west Belgium (see also WALLOON). [OE f. ON Flǣmingi & MDu. Vlāming f. root of Vlaanderen Flanders]

Fleming[2] /ˈflemɪŋ/, Sir Alexander (1881–1955), Scottish doctor and scientist, who spent most of his career at St Mary's Hospital, London, where he investigated the body's defences against bacteriological infection. In 1928 he discovered the effect of penicillin on bacteria, and twelve years later a team of Oxford scientists, led by Florey and Chain, established its therapeutic use. In 1942 Fleming was propelled into the limelight, as a British scientific hero, by a government eager for 'good news', and so achieved fame retrospectively for his work in the 1920s. A string of honours followed: fellowship of the Royal Society (1943), a knighthood (1944), and the award of the Nobel Prize for medicine, jointly with Florey and Chain, in 1945.

Fleming[3] /ˈflemɪŋ/, Ian (Lancaster) (1908–64), English thriller-writer, creator of the fictional secret agent James Bond.

Flemish /ˈflemɪʃ/ adj. & n. —adj. of or relating to Flanders or its people or their language. —n. one of the two official languages of Belgium, the other being French. It is essentially the same language as Dutch; the apparent differences are a matter of spelling convention. □ **Flemish bond** Building a bond in which each course consists of alternate headers and stretchers. [MDu. Vlāmisch (as FLEMING)]

flense /flenz/ v.tr. (also **flench** /flentʃ/, **flinch** /flɪntʃ/) 1 cut up (a whale or seal). 2 flay (a seal). [Da. flense: cf. Norw. flinsa, flunsa flay]

flesh /fleʃ/ n. & v. —n. **1 a** the soft, esp. muscular, substance between the skin and bones of an animal or a human. **b** plumpness; fat (*has put on flesh*). **c** *archaic* meat, esp. excluding poultry, game, and offal. **2** the body as opposed to the mind or the soul, esp. considered as sinful. **3** the pulpy substance of a fruit or a plant. **4 a** the visible surface of the human body with ref. to its colour or appearance. **b** (also **flesh-colour**) a yellowish pink colour. **5** animal or human life. —*v.tr.* **1** embody in flesh. **2** incite (a hound etc.) by the taste of blood. **3** initiate, esp. by aggressive or violent means, esp.: **a** use (a sword etc.) for the first time on flesh. **b** use (wit, the pen, etc.) for the first time. **c** inflame (a person) by the foretaste of success. □ **all flesh** all human and animal creation. **flesh and blood** —n. **1** the body or its substance. **2** humankind. **3** human nature, esp. as being fallible. —*adj.* actually living, not imaginary or supernatural. **flesh-fly** (pl. **-flies**) any fly of the family Sarcophagidae that deposits eggs or larvae in dead flesh. **flesh out** make or become substantial. **flesh side** the side of a hide that adjoined the flesh. **flesh tints** flesh-colours as rendered by a painter. **flesh-wound** a wound not reaching a bone or a vital organ. **in the flesh** in bodily form, in person. **lose** (or **put on**) **flesh** grow thinner or fatter. **make a person's flesh creep** frighten or horrify a person, esp. with tales of the supernatural etc. **one flesh** (of two people) intimately united, esp. by virtue of marriage (Gen. 2: 24). **one's own flesh and blood** near relatives; descendants. **sins of the flesh** unchastity. **the way of all flesh** experience common to all mankind. □□ **fleshless** adj. [OE *flæsc* f. Gmc]

flesher /ˈfleʃə(r)/ n. Sc. a butcher.

fleshings /ˈfleʃɪŋz/ n.pl. an actor's flesh-coloured tights.

fleshly /ˈfleʃlɪ/ adj. (**fleshlier**, **fleshliest**) **1** (of desire etc.) bodily; lascivious; sensual. **2** mortal, not divine. **3** worldly. □□ **fleshliness** n. [OE *flæsclic* (as FLESH)]

fleshpots /ˈfleʃpɒts/ n.pl. luxurious living (Exod. 16: 3).

fleshy /ˈfleʃɪ/ adj. (**fleshier**, **fleshiest**) **1** plump, fat. **2** of flesh, without bone. **3** (of plant or fruit tissue) pulpy. **4** like flesh. □□ **fleshiness** n.

Fletcher /ˈfletʃə(r)/, John (1579–1625), English dramatist. Before dying of the plague he had produced some 15 plays with Beaumont, including *Philaster* (1609), *The Maid's Tragedy* (1610–11), 16 plays of which he was the sole author, such as *The Faithful Shepherdess* (1610) and *The Woman's Prize* (1604–17), and others in collaboration with Massinger, Jonson, Chapman, and with Shakespeare in *The Two Noble Kinsmen* (1612–13) and *Henry VIII* (c.1613). His reputation was at its highest during the Restoration when he ranked with Shakespeare and Jonson.

fletcher /ˈfletʃə(r)/ n. *archaic* a maker or seller of arrows. [ME f. OF *flech(i)er* f. *fleche* arrow]

fleur-de-lis /ˌflɜː.dəˈliː/ n. (also **fleur-de-lys**) (pl. **fleurs-** pronunc. same) **1** the iris flower. **2** *Heraldry* **a** a lily composed of three petals bound together near their bases. **b** the former royal arms of France. [ME f. OF *flour de lys* flower of lily]

fleuret /fluəˈret/ n. an ornament like a small flower. [F *fleurette* f. *fleur* flower]

fleuron /ˈflɜːrɒ̃/ n. a flower-shaped ornament on a building, a coin, a book, etc. [ME f. OF *floron* f. *flour* FLOWER]

fleury /ˈfluərɪ/ adj. (also **flory** /ˈflɔːrɪ/) *Heraldry* decorated with fleurs-de-lis. [ME f. OF *flo(u)ré* (as FLEURON)]

Flevoland /ˈfleɪvəʊˌlɑːnt/ a province of The Netherlands, created in 1986, comprising an area reclaimed from the Zuider Zee in 1950–7 and 1959–68.

flew past of FLY¹.

flews /fluːz/ n.pl. the hanging lips of a bloodhound etc. [16th c.: orig. unkn.]

flex¹ /fleks/ v. **1** tr. & intr. bend (a joint, limb, etc.) or be bent. **2** tr. & intr. move (a muscle) or (of a muscle) be moved to bend a joint. **3** tr. *Geol.* bend (strata). **4** tr. *Archaeol.* place (a corpse) with the legs drawn up under the chin. [L *flectere flex-* bend]

flex² /fleks/ n. Brit. a flexible insulated cable used for carrying electric current to an appliance. [abbr. of FLEXIBLE]

flexible /ˈfleksɪb(ə)l/ adj. **1** able to bend without breaking; pliable; pliant. **2** easily led; manageable; docile. **3** adaptable; versatile; variable (*works flexible hours*). □□ **flexibility** /-ˈbɪlɪtɪ/ n. **flexibly** adv. [ME f. OF *flexible* or L *flexibilis* (as FLEX¹)]

flexile /ˈfleksaɪl/ adj. *archaic* **1** supple; mobile. **2** tractable; manageable. **3** versatile. □□ **flexility** /-ˈsɪlɪtɪ/ n. [L *flexilis* (as FLEX¹)]

flexion /ˈflekʃ(ə)n/ n. (US **flection**) **1 a** the act of bending or the condition of being bent, esp. of a limb or joint. **b** a bent part; a curve. **2** *Gram.* inflection. **3** *Math.* = FLEXURE. □□ **flexional** adj. (in sense 2). **flexionless** adj. (in sense 2). [L *flexio* (as FLEX¹)]

flexitime /ˈfleksɪˌtaɪm/ n. Brit. **1** a system of working a set number of hours with the starting and finishing times chosen within agreed limits by the employee. **2** the hours worked in this way. [FLEXIBLE + TIME]

flexography /flekˈsɒɡrəfɪ/ n. *Printing* a rotary letterpress technique using rubber or plastic plates and synthetic inks or dyes for printing on fabrics, plastics, etc., as well as on paper. □□ **flexographic** /-səˈɡræfɪk/ adj. [L *flexus* a bending f. *flectere* bend + -GRAPHY]

flexor /ˈfleksə(r)/ n. (in full **flexor muscle**) a muscle that bends part of the body (cf. EXTENSOR). [mod.L (as FLEX¹)]

flexuous /ˈfleksjʊəs/ adj. full of bends; winding. □□ **flexuosity** /-ˈɒsɪtɪ/ n. **flexuously** adv. [L *flexuosus* f. *flexus* bending formed as FLEX¹]

flexure /ˈflekʃə(r)/ n. **1 a** the act of bending or the condition of being bent. **b** a bend, curve, or turn. **2** *Math.* the curving of a line, surface, or solid, esp. from a straight line, plane, etc. **3** *Geol.* the bending of strata under pressure. □□ **flexural** adj. [L *flexura* (as FLEX¹)]

flibbertigibbet /ˌflɪbətɪˈdʒɪbɪt, ˈflɪb-/ n. a gossiping, frivolous, or restless person. [imit. of chatter]

flick /flɪk/ n. & v. —n. **1 a** a light, sharp, quickly retracted blow with a whip etc. **b** the sudden release of a bent finger or thumb, esp. to propel a small object. **2** a sudden movement or jerk. **3** a quick turn of the wrist in playing games, esp. in throwing or striking a ball. **4** a slight, sharp sound. **5** Brit. *colloq.* **a** a cinema film. **b** (in pl.; prec. by *the*) the cinema. —v. **1** tr. (often foll. by *away, off*) strike or move with a flick (*flicked the ash off his cigar*; *flicked away the dust*). **2** tr. give a flick with (a whip, towel, etc.). **3** intr. make a flicking movement or sound. □ **flick-knife** a weapon with a blade that springs out from the handle when a button is pressed. **flick through 1** turn over (cards, pages, etc.). **2 a** turn over the pages etc. of, by a rapid movement of the fingers. **b** look cursorily through (a book etc.). [ME, imit.]

flicker¹ /ˈflɪkə(r)/ v. & n. —v.intr. **1** (of light) shine unsteadily or fitfully. **2** (of a flame) burn unsteadily, alternately flaring and dying down. **3 a** (of a flag, a reptile's tongue, an eyelid, etc.) move or wave to and fro; quiver; vibrate. **b** (of the wind) blow lightly and unsteadily. **4** (of hope etc.) increase and decrease unsteadily and intermittently. —n. a flickering movement or light. □ **flicker out** die away after a final flicker. [OE *flicorian, flycerian*]

flicker² /ˈflɪkə(r)/ n. any woodpecker of the genus *Colaptes*, native to N. America. [imit. of its note]

flier var. of FLYER.

flight¹ /flaɪt/ n. & v. —n. **1 a** the act or manner of flying through the air (*studied swallows' flight*). **b** the swift movement or passage of a projectile etc. through the air (*the flight of an arrow*). **2 a** a journey made through the air or in space. **b** a timetabled journey made by an airline. **c** an RAF unit of about six aircraft. **3 a** a flock or large body of birds, insects, etc., esp. when migrating. **b** a migration. **4** (usu. foll. by *of*) a series, esp. of stairs between floors, or of hurdles across a race track (*lives up six flights*). **5** an extravagant soaring, a mental or verbal excursion or sally (of wit etc.) (*a flight of fancy; a flight of ambition*). **6** the trajectory and pace of a ball in games. **7** the distance that a bird, aircraft, or missile can fly. **8** (usu. foll. by *of*) a volley (*a flight of arrows*). **9** the tail of a dart. **10** the pursuit of game by a hawk. **11** swift passage (of time). —v.tr. **1** vary the trajectory and pace of (a cricket-ball etc.). **2** provide (an arrow) with feathers. **3** shoot (wildfowl etc.) in flight. □ **flight bag** a small, zipped, shoulder bag carried by air travellers. **flight control** an internal or

external system directing the movement of aircraft. **flight-deck**
1 the deck of an aircraft-carrier used for take-off and landing. **2**
the accommodation for the pilot, navigator, etc. in an aircraft.
flight-feather a bird's wing or tail feather. **flight lieutenant**
an RAF officer next in rank below squadron leader. **flight officer**
a rank in the WRAF, corresponding to flight lieutenant. **flight**
path the planned course of an aircraft or spacecraft.
flight-recorder a device in an aircraft to record technical
details during a flight, that may be used in the event of an
accident to discover its cause. **flight sergeant** *Mil.* an RAF rank
next above sergeant. **flight-test** test (an aircraft, rocket, etc.)
during flight. **in the first** (or **top**) **flight** taking a leading place.
take (or **wing**) **one's flight** fly. [OE *flyht* f. WG: rel to FLY¹]

flight² /flaɪt/ *n.* **1 a** the act or manner of fleeing. **b** a hasty
retreat. **2** *Econ.* the selling of currency, investments, etc. in
anticipation of a fall in value (*flight from sterling*). □ **put to flight**
cause to flee. **take** (or **take to**) **flight** flee. [OE f. Gmc: rel. to
FLEE]

flightless /ˈflaɪtlɪs/ *adj.* (of a bird etc.) naturally unable to fly.

flighty /ˈflaɪtɪ/ *adj.* (**flightier, flightiest**) **1** (usu. of a girl) frivolous, fickle, changeable. **2** crazy. □□ **flightily** *adv.* **flightiness**
n. [FLIGHT¹ + -Y¹]

flimflam /ˈflɪmflæm/ *n.* & *v.* —*n.* **1** a trifle; nonsense; idle talk.
2 humbug; deception. —*v.tr.* (**flimflammed, flimflamming**)
cheat; deceive. □□ **flimflammer** *n.* **flimflammery** *n.* (*pl.* **-ies**).
[imit. redupl.]

flimsy /ˈflɪmzɪ/ *adj.* & *n.* —*adj.* (**flimsier, flimsiest**) **1** lightly
or carelessly assembled; insubstantial, easily damaged (*a flimsy
structure*). **2** (of an excuse etc.) unconvincing (*a flimsy pretext*). **3**
paltry; trivial; superficial (*a flimsy play*). **4** (of clothing) thin (*a
flimsy blouse*). —*n.* (*pl.* **-ies**) **1 a** very thin paper. **b** a document,
esp. a copy, made on this. **2** a flimsy thing, esp. women's
underwear. □□ **flimsily** *adv.* **flimsiness** *n.* [17th c.: prob. f.
FLIMFLAM: cf. TIPSY]

flinch¹ /flɪntʃ/ *v.* & *n.* —*v.intr.* **1** draw back in pain or expectation
of a blow etc.; wince. **2** (often foll. by *from*) give way; shrink, turn
aside (*flinched from his duty*). —*n.* an act or instance of flinching.
□□ **flincher** *n.* **flinchingly** *adv.* [OF *flenchir, flaînchir* f. WG]

flinch² var. of FLENSE.

Flinders /ˈflɪndəz/, Matthew (1774–1814), English explorer. In
the company of George Bass, Flinders explored the coast of New
South Wales in 1795–1800, before being commissioned by the
Royal Navy to circumnavigate Australia. Between 1801 and 1803
he charted much of the west coast of the continent for the first
time, but was wrecked on his voyage home and imprisoned by
the French on Mauritius until 1810. Flinders Island, the Flinders
Range in South Australia, and Flinders River in Queensland are
named after him.

flinders /ˈflɪndəz/ *n.pl.* fragments; splinters. [ME, prob. f. Scand.]

Flinders Island the largest island in the Furneaux group,
situated in the Bass Strait between Tasmania and mainland
Australia.

fling /flɪŋ/ *v.* & *n.* —*v.* (*past* and *past part.* **flung** /flʌŋ/) **1** *tr.* throw
or hurl (an object) forcefully. **2** *refl.* **a** (usu. foll. by *into*) rush
headlong (into a person's arms, a train, etc.). **b** (usu. foll. by *into*)
embark wholeheartedly (on an enterprise). **c** (usu. foll. by *on*)
throw (oneself) on a person's mercy etc. **3** *tr.* utter (words)
forcefully. **4** *tr.* (usu. foll. by *out*) suddenly spread (the arms). **5**
tr. (foll. by *on, off*) put on or take off (clothes) carelessly or rapidly.
6 *intr.* go angrily or violently; rush (*flung out of the room*). **7** *tr.*
put or send suddenly or violently (*was flung into jail*). **8** *tr.* (foll.
by *away*) discard or put aside thoughtlessly or rashly (*flung away
their reputation*). **9** *intr.* (usu. foll. by *out*) (of a horse etc.) kick and
plunge. **10** *tr.* *archaic* send, emit (sound, light, smell). —*n.* **1** an
act or instance of flinging; a throw; a plunge. **2** a spell of
indulgence or wild behaviour (*he's had his fling*). **3** an impetuous,
whirling Scottish dance, esp. the Highland fling. □ **have a fling**
at 1 make an attempt at. **2** jeer at. □□ **flinger** *n.* [ME, perh. f.
ON]

flint /flɪnt/ *n.* **1 a** a hard grey stone of nearly pure silica occurring
naturally as nodules or bands in chalk. **b** a piece of this esp. as
flaked or ground to form a primitive tool or weapon. **2** a piece

of hard alloy of rare-earth metals used to give an igniting spark
in a cigarette-lighter etc. **3** a piece of flint used with steel
to produce fire, esp. in a flintlock gun. **4** anything hard and
unyielding. □ **flint corn** a variety of maize having hard
translucent grains. see GLASS. □□ **flinty** *adj.* (**flintier,
flintiest**). **flintily** *adv.* **flintiness** *n.* [OE]

flintlock /ˈflɪntlɒk/ *n.* *hist.* **1** an old type of gun fired by a spark
from a flint. **2** the lock producing such a spark.

flip¹ /flɪp/ *v.*, *n.*, & *adj.* —*v.* (**flipped, flipping**) **1** *tr.* **a** flick or
toss (a coin, pellet, etc.) with a quick movement so that it spins
in the air. **b** remove (a small object) from a surface with a flick
of the fingers. **2** *tr.* **a** strike or flick (a person's ear, cheek, etc.)
lightly or smartly. **b** move (a fan, whip, etc.) with a sudden jerk.
3 *tr.* turn (a small object) over. **4** *intr.* **a** make a fillip or flicking
noise with the fingers. **b** (foll. by *at*) strike smartly at. **5** *intr.* move
about with sudden jerks. **6** *intr.* *sl.* become suddenly excited or
enthusiastic. —*n.* **1** a smart light blow; a flick. **2** *colloq.* **a** a
short pleasure flight in an aircraft. **b** a quick tour etc. **3** an act
of flipping over (*gave the stone a flip*). —*adj.* *colloq.* glib; flippant.
□ **flip chart** a large pad erected on a stand and bound so that
one page can be turned over at the top to reveal the next. **flip**
one's lid *sl.* **1** lose self-control. **2** go mad. **flip side** *colloq.* the
less important side of a gramophone record. **flip through** =
flick through. [prob. f. FILLIP]

flip² /flɪp/ *n.* **1** a drink of heated beer and spirit. **2** = *egg-flip*.
[perh. f. FLIP¹ in the sense *whip up*]

flip-flop /ˈflɪpflɒp/ *n.* & *v.* —*n.* **1** a usu. rubber sandal with a
thong between the big and second toe. **2** esp. *US* a backward
somersault. **3** an electronic switching circuit changed from one
stable state to another, or through an unstable state back to its
stable state, by a triggering pulse. —*v.intr.* (**-flopped,
-flopping**) move with a sound or motion suggested by 'flip-flop'.
[imit.]

flippant /ˈflɪpənt/ *adj.* lacking in seriousness; treating serious
things lightly; disrespectful. □□ **flippancy** *n.* **flippantly** *adv.*
[FLIP¹ + -ANT]

flipper /ˈflɪpə(r)/ *n.* **1** a broadened limb of a turtle, penguin, etc.,
used in swimming. **2** a flat rubber etc. attachment worn on the
foot for underwater swimming. **3** *sl.* a hand.

flipping /ˈflɪpɪŋ/ *adj.* & *adv.* *Brit.* *sl.* expressing annoyance, or as
an intensifier (*where's the flipping towel?*; *he flipping beat me*). [FLIP¹
+ -ING²]

flirt /flɜːt/ *v.* & *n.* —*v.* **1** *intr.* (usu. foll. by *with*) behave in a
frivolously amorous or sexually enticing manner. **2** *intr.* (usu.
foll. by *with*) **a** superficially interest oneself (with an idea etc.).
b trifle (with danger etc.) (*flirted with disgrace*). **3** *tr.* wave or move
(a fan, a bird's tail, etc.) briskly. **4** *intr.* & *tr.* move or cause to
move with a jerk. —*n.* **1** a person who indulges in flirting. **2** a
quick movement; a sudden jerk. □□ **flirtation** /-ˈteɪʃ(ə)n/ *n.*
flirtatious /-ˈteɪʃəs/ *adj.* **flirtatiously** /-ˈteɪʃəslɪ/ *adv.*
flirtatiousness /-ˈteɪʃəsnɪs/ *n.* **flirty** *adj.* (**flirtier, flirtiest**).
[imit.]

flit /flɪt/ *v.* & *n.* —*v.intr.* (**flitted, flitting**) **1** move lightly, softly,
or rapidly (*flitted from one room to another*). **2** fly lightly; make
short flights (*flitted from branch to branch*). **3** *Brit.* *colloq.* leave
one's house etc. secretly to escape creditors or obligations. **4**
esp. *Sc.* & *N.Engl.* change one's home; move. —*n.* **1** an act of
flitting. **2** (also **moonlight flit**) a secret change of abode in
order to escape creditors etc. □□ **flitter** *n.* [ME f. ON *flytja*: rel.
to FLEET⁵]

flitch /flɪtʃ/ *n.* **1** a side of bacon. **2** a slab of timber from a
tree-trunk, usu. from the outside. **3** (in full **flitch-plate**) a
strengthening plate in a beam etc. □ **flitch-beam** a compound
beam, esp. of an iron plate between two slabs of wood. [OE *flicce*
f. Gmc]

flitter /ˈflɪtə(r)/ *v.intr.* flit about; flutter. □ **flitter-mouse** = BAT².
[FLIT + -ER⁴]

flivver /ˈflɪvə(r)/ *n.* *US* *sl.* **1** a cheap car or aircraft. **2** a failure.
[20th c.: orig. uncert.]

flixweed /ˈflɪkswiːd/ *n.* a cruciferous plant, *Descurainia sophia*,
formerly thought to cure dysentery. [earlier *fluxweed*]

float /fləʊt/ *v.* & *n.* —*v.* **1** *intr.* & *tr.* **a** rest or move or cause (a buoyant object) to rest or move on the surface of a liquid without sinking. **b** get afloat or set (a stranded ship) afloat. **2** *intr.* move with a liquid or current of air; drift (*the clouds floated high up*). **3** *intr. colloq.* a move in a leisurely or casual way (*floated about humming quietly*). **b** (often foll. by *before*) hover before the eye or mind (*the prospect of lunch floated before them*). **4** *intr.* (often foll. by *in*) move or be suspended freely in a liquid or a gas. **5** *tr.* **a** bring (a company, scheme, etc.) into being; launch. **b** offer (stock, shares, etc.) on the stock market. **6** *Commerce* **a** *intr.* (of currency) be allowed to have a fluctuating exchange rate. **b** *tr.* cause (currency) to float. **c** *intr.* (of an acceptance) be in circulation. **7** *tr.* (of water etc.) support; bear along (a buoyant object). **8** *intr. & tr.* circulate or cause (a rumour or idea) to circulate. **9** *tr.* waft (a buoyant object) through the air. **10** *tr. archaic* cover with liquid; inundate. —*n.* **1** a thing that floats, esp.: **a** a raft. **b** a cork or quill on a fishing-line as an indicator of a fish biting. **c** a cork supporting the edge of a fishing-net. **d** the hollow or inflated part or organ supporting a fish etc. in the water; an air bladder. **e** a hollow structure fixed underneath an aircraft enabling it to float on water. **f** a floating device on the surface of water, petrol, etc., controlling the flow. **2** a small vehicle or cart, esp. one powered by electricity (*milk float*). **3** a platform mounted on a lorry and carrying a display in a procession etc. **4 a** a sum of money used at the beginning of a period of selling in a shop, a fête, etc. to provide change. **b** a small sum of money for minor expenditure; petty cash. **5** *Theatr.* (in *sing.* or *pl.*) footlights. **6** a tool used for smoothing plaster. □ **float-board** one of the boards of a water-wheel or paddle-wheel. **float glass** a kind of glass made by drawing the molten glass continuously on to a surface of molten metal for hardening. **float process** the process used to make float glass. **float-stone** a light, porous stone that floats. □□ **floatable** *adj.* **floatability** /-ˈbɪlɪtɪ/ *n.* [OE *flot, flotian* float, OE *flota* ship, ON *flota, floti* rel. to FLEET⁵: in ME infl. by OF *floter*]

floatage /ˈfləʊtɪdʒ/ *n.* **1** the act or state of floating. **2** *Brit.* **a** floating objects or masses; flotsam. **b** the right of appropriating flotsam. **3 a** ships etc. afloat on a river. **b** the part of a ship above the water-line. **4** buoyancy; floating power.

floatation var. of FLOTATION.

floater /ˈfləʊtə(r)/ *n.* **1** a person or thing that floats. **2** a floating voter. **3** *sl.* a mistake; a gaffe. **4** a person who frequently changes occupation. **5** *Stock Exch.* a government stock certificate etc. recognized as a security.

floating /ˈfləʊtɪŋ/ *adj.* not settled in a definite place; fluctuating; variable (*the floating population*). □ **floating anchor** a sea anchor. **floating bridge 1** a bridge on pontoons etc. **2** a ferry working on chains. **floating debt** a debt repayable on demand, or at a stated time. **floating dock** a floating structure usable as a dry dock. **floating kidney 1** an abnormal condition in which the kidneys are unusually movable. **2** such a kidney. **floating light 1** a lightship. **2** a lifebuoy with a lantern. **floating point** *Computing* a decimal etc. point that does not occupy a fixed position in the numbers processed. **floating rib** any of the lower ribs, which are not attached to the breastbone. **floating voter** a voter without allegiance to any political party. □□ **floatingly** *adv.*

floaty /ˈfləʊtɪ/ *adj.* (esp. of a woman's garment or a fabric) light and airy. [FLOAT]

floc /flɒk/ *n.* a flocculent mass of fine particles. [abbr. of FLOCCULUS]

flocculate /ˈflɒkjʊˌleɪt/ *v.tr. & intr.* form into flocculent masses. □□ **flocculation** /-ˈleɪʃ(ə)n/ *n.*

floccule /ˈflɒkjuːl/ *n.* a small portion of matter resembling a tuft of wool.

flocculent /ˈflɒkjʊlənt/ *adj.* **1** like tufts of wool. **2** consisting of or showing tufts, downy. **3** *Chem.* (of precipitates) loosely massed. □□ **flocculence** *n.* [L *floccus* FLOCK²]

flocculus /ˈflɒkjʊləs/ *n.* (*pl.* **flocculi** /-ˌlaɪ/) **1** a floccule. **2** *Anat.* a small ovoid lobe in the under-surface of the cerebellum. **3** *Astron.* a small cloudy wisp on the sun's surface. [mod.L, dimin. of FLOCCUS]

floccus /ˈflɒkəs/ *n.* (*pl.* **flocci** /ˈflɒksaɪ/) a tuft of woolly hairs or filaments. [L, = FLOCK²]

flock¹ /flɒk/ *n. & v.* —*n.* **1 a** a number of animals of one kind, esp. birds, feeding or travelling together. **b** a number of domestic animals, esp. sheep, goats, or geese, kept together. **2** a large crowd of people. **3 a** a Christian congregation or body of believers, esp. in relation to one minister. **b** a family of children, a number of pupils, etc. —*v.intr.* **1** congregate; mass. **2** (usu. foll. by *to, in, out, together*) go together in a crowd; troop (*thousands flocked to Wembley*). [OE *flocc*]

flock² /flɒk/ *n.* **1** a lock or tuft of wool, cotton, etc. **2 a** (also in *pl.*; often *attrib.*) material for quilting and stuffing made of wool-refuse or torn-up cloth (*a flock pillow*). **b** powdered wool or cloth. □ **flock-paper** (or **-wallpaper**) wallpaper sized and sprinkled with powdered wool to make a raised pattern. □□ **flocky** *adj.* [ME f. OF *floc* f. L *floccus*]

Flodden /ˈflɒd(ə)n/ the scene of the decisive battle of the Anglo-Scottish war of 1513. A Scottish army under James IV was defeated by a smaller but better-led English force under the Earl of Surrey (sent northwards by Henry VIII, who was on campaign in France) near the Northumbrian village of Branxton. The Scottish king and most of his nobles were among the heavy Scots losses.

floe /fləʊ/ *n.* a sheet of floating ice. [prob. f. Norw. *flo* f. ON *fló* layer]

flog /flɒg/ *v.* (**flogged, flogging**) **1** *tr.* **a** beat with a whip, stick, etc. (as a punishment or to urge on). **b** make work through violent effort (*flogged the engine*). **2** *tr. Brit. sl.* sell. **3** *tr.* (usu. foll. by *into, out of*) drive (a quality, knowledge, etc.) into or out of a person, esp. by physical punishment. **4** *intr. & refl. sl.* proceed by violent or painful effort. □ **flog a dead horse** waste energy on something unalterable. **flog to death** *colloq.* talk about or promote at tedious length. □□ **flogger** *n.* [17th-c. cant: prob. imit. or f. L *flagellare* to whip]

flong /flɒŋ/ *n. Printing* prepared paper for making stereotype moulds. [F *flan* FLAN]

flood /flʌd/ *n. & v.* —*n.* **1 a** an overflowing or influx of water beyond its normal confines, esp. over land; an inundation. **b** the water that overflows. **2 a** an outpouring of water; a torrent (*a flood of rain*). **b** something resembling a torrent (*a flood of tears; a flood of relief*). **3** the inflow of the tide (also in *comb.*: *flood-tide*). **4** *colloq.* a floodlight. **5** (**the Flood**) the flood described in Genesis, brought by God upon the earth in the time of Noah (Gen. 6 ff.) to destroy mankind because of the wickedness of the human race. Parallel stories are found in Mesopotamian sources (e.g. the Gilgamesh epic); the flood that forms part of Chinese mythology was not a retribution for sin. Archaeological evidence at Ur and Kish shows that the Tigris–Euphrates valley was subject to periodic inundations but cannot be equated directly with the Biblical narrative. **6** *poet.* a river; a stream; a sea. —*v.* **1 a** cover with or overflow in a flood (*rain flooded the cellar*). **b** overflow as if with a flood (*the market was flooded with foreign goods*). **2** *tr.* irrigate (*flooded the paddy fields*). **3** *tr.* deluge (a burning house, a mine, etc.) with water. **4** *intr.* (often foll. by *in, through*) arrive in great quantities (*complaints flooded in; fear flooded through them*). **5** *intr.* become inundated (*the bathroom flooded*). **6** *tr.* overfill (a carburettor) with petrol. **7** *intr.* experience a uterine haemorrhage. **8** *tr.* (of rain etc.) fill (a river) to overflowing. □ **flood and field** sea and land. **flood out** drive out (of one's home etc.) with a flood. **flood plain** the level area over which a river spreads in flood. **flood-tide** the periodical exceptional rise of the tide because of lunar or solar attraction. [OE *flōd* f. Gmc]

floodgate /ˈflʌdgeɪt/ *n.* **1** a gate opened or closed to admit or exclude water, esp. the lower gate of a lock. **2** (usu. in *pl.*) a last restraint holding back tears, rain, anger, etc.

floodlight /ˈflʌdlaɪt/ *n. & v.* —*n.* **1** a large powerful light (usu. one of several) to illuminate a building, sports ground, stage, etc. **2** the illumination so provided. —*v.tr.* illuminate with floodlight.

floor /flɔː(r)/ *n. & v.* —*n.* **1 a** the lower surface of a room. **b** the boards etc. of which it is made. **2 a** the bottom of the sea, a cave, a cavity, etc. **b** any level area. **3** all the rooms etc. on the same level of a building; a storey (*lives on the ground floor; walked up to the sixth floor*). **4 a** (in a legislative assembly) the part of the house in which members sit and from which they speak. **b** the right to speak next in debate (*gave him the floor*). **5** *Stock Exch.* the large central hall where trading takes place. **6** the minimum of prices, wages, etc. **7** *colloq.* the ground. —*v.tr.* **1** furnish with a floor; pave. **2** bring to the ground; knock (a person) down. **3** *colloq.* confound, baffle (*was floored by the puzzle*). **4** *colloq.* get the better of; overcome. **5** serve as the floor of (*leopard skins floored the hall*). □ **first** (US **second**) **floor** the floor above the ground floor. **floor-lamp** US a standard lamp. **floor-leader** US the leader of a party in a legislative assembly. **floor manager 1** the stage manager of a television production. **2** a shopwalker. **floor plan** a diagram of the rooms etc. on one storey of a building. **floor-polish** a manufactured substance used for polishing floors. **floor show** an entertainment presented on the floor (as opposed to the stage) of a nightclub etc. **floor-walker** US a shopwalker. **from the floor** (of a speech etc.) given by a member of the audience, not by those on the platform etc. **take the floor 1** begin to dance on a dance-floor etc. **2** speak in a debate. □□ **floorless** adj. [OE *flōr* f. Gmc]

floorboard /ˈflɔːbɔːd/ n. a long wooden board used for flooring.

floorcloth /ˈflɔːklɒθ/ n. a cloth for washing the floor.

flooring /ˈflɔːrɪŋ/ n. the boards etc. of which a floor is made.

floozie /ˈfluːzɪ/ n. (also **floozy**) (pl. **-ies**) *colloq.* a girl or a woman, esp. a disreputable one. [20th c.: cf. FLOSSY and dial. *floosy* fluffy]

flop /flɒp/ v., n., & adv. —*v.intr.* (**flopped**, **flopping**) **1** sway about heavily or loosely (*hair flopped over his face*). **2** move in an ungainly way (*flopped along the beach in flippers*). **3** (often foll. by *down*, *on*, *into*) sit, kneel, lie, or fall awkwardly or suddenly (*flopped down on to the bench*). **4** *sl.* (esp. of a play, film, book, etc.) fail; collapse (*flopped on Broadway*). **5** *sl.* sleep. **6** make a dull sound as of a soft body landing, or of a flat thing slapping water. —n. **1 a** a flopping movement. **b** the sound made by it. **2** *sl.* a failure. **3** *sl.* esp. US a bed. —adv. with a flop. □ **flop-house** *sl.* esp. US a doss-house. [var. of FLAP]

floppy /ˈflɒpɪ/ adj. & n. —adj. (**floppier**, **floppiest**) tending to flop; not firm or rigid. —n. (pl. **-ies**) (in full **floppy disk**) *Computing* a flexible removable magnetic disc for the storage of data. □□ **floppily** adv. **floppiness** n.

flor. abbr. floruit.

Flora /ˈflɔːrə/ *Rom. Mythol.* the goddess of flowering plants.

flora /ˈflɔːrə/ n. (pl. **floras** or **florae** /-riː/) **1** the plants of a particular region, geological period, or environment. **2** a treatise on or list of these. [mod.L f. the name of the goddess of flowers f. L *flos floris* flower]

floral /ˈflɔːr(ə)l, ˈflɒ-/ adj. **1** of flowers. **2** decorated with or depicting flowers. **3** of flora or floras. □□ **florally** adv. [L *floralis* or *flos floris* flower]

floreat /ˈflɒrɪæt/ v.intr. may (he, she, or it) flourish. [L, 3rd sing. pres. subj. of *florēre* flourish]

Florence /ˈflɒrəns/ (Italian **Firenze** /fiəˈrentseɪ/) a city of Tuscany in northern Italy; pop. (est. 1981) 453,293. From the 14th to the 16th c., especially under the Medici family, it was the centre of the Italian Renaissance.

Florentine /ˈflɒrəntaɪn/ adj. & n. —adj. **1** of or relating to Florence in Italy. **2** (**florentine** /-ˌtiːn/) (of a dish) served on a bed of spinach. —n. a native or citizen of Florence. [F *Florentin -ine* or L *Florentinus* f. *Florentia* Florence]

Flores /ˈflɔːrez/ the largest island of the Lesser Sunda group in Indonesia.

florescence /flɔːˈres(ə)ns, flɒ-/ n. the process, state, or time of flowering. [mod.L *florescentia* f. L *florescere* f. *florēre* bloom]

floret /ˈflɒrɪt, ˈflɔː-/ n. *Bot.* **1** each of the small flowers making up a composite flower-head. **2** each of the flowering stems making up a head of cauliflower, broccoli, etc. **3** a small flower. [L *flos floris* flower]

Florey /ˈflɔːrɪ/, Howard Walter, Baron (1898–1968), Australian pathologist who, in collaboration with Sir Ernst Chain, isolated and purified penicillin, developed techniques for its large-scale production, and performed the first clinical trials. For their

work Florey and Chain shared a 1945 Nobel Prize with the discoverer of penicillin, Sir Alexander Fleming.

floriate /ˈflɔːrɪeɪt/ v.tr. decorate with flower-designs etc.

floribunda /ˌflɒrɪˈbʌndə, ˌflɔː-/ n. a plant, esp. a rose, bearing dense clusters of flowers. [mod.L f. *floribundus* freely flowering f. L *flos floris* flower, infl. by L *abundus* copious]

floriculture /ˈflɒrɪˌkʌltʃə(r), ˈflɔː-/ n. the cultivation of flowers. □□ **floricultural** /-ˈkʌltʃər(ə)l/ adj. **floriculturist** /-ˈkʌltʃərɪst/ n. [L *flos floris* flower + CULTURE, after *horticulture*]

florid /ˈflɒrɪd/ adj. **1** ruddy; flushed; high-coloured (*a florid complexion*). **2** (of a book, a picture, music, architecture, etc.) elaborately ornate; ostentatious; showy. **3** adorned with or as with flowers; flowery. □□ **floridity** /-ˈrɪdɪtɪ/ n. **floridly** adv. **floridness** n. [F *floride* or L *floridus* f. *flos floris* flower]

Florida /ˈflɒrɪdə/ a State forming a peninsula of the southeastern US; pop. (est. 1985) 9,747,000; capital, Tallahassee. Having been chiefly under Spanish dominion from the 16th c. and purchased from Spain in 1819, it became the 27th State of the Union in 1845.

floriferous /flɔːˈrɪfərəs, flɒ-/ adj. (of a seed or plant) producing many flowers. [L *florifer* f. *flos floris* flower]

florilegium /ˌflɔːrɪˈliːdʒɪəm/ n. (pl. **florilegia** /-ˈliːdʒɪə/ or **florilegiums**) an anthology. [mod.L f. L *flos floris* flower + *legere* gather, transl. of Gk *anthologion* ANTHOLOGY]

florin /ˈflɒrɪn/ n. *hist.* **1 a** a British silver or alloy two-shilling coin of the 19th–20th c. (now worth 10 pence at face value). **b** an English gold coin of the 14th c., worth 6s. 8d. (33 pence). **2** a foreign coin of gold or silver, esp. a Dutch guilder. [ME f. OF f. It. *fiorino* dimin. of *fiore* flower f. L *flos floris*, the orig. coin having a figure of a lily on it]

Florio /ˈflɔːrɪˌəʊ/, John (c.1553–1625), born in London, son of an Italian Protestant refugee. He was reader in Italian to Anne, wife of James I. In 1598 he produced an Italian dictionary entitled *A Worlde of Wordes*. His most important work was the first translation into English of Montaigne's essays, on which Shakespeare drew in *The Tempest* and elsewhere.

florist /ˈflɒrɪst/ n. a person who deals in or grows flowers. □□ **floristry** n. [L *flos floris* flower + -IST]

floristic /flɒˈrɪstɪk/ adj. relating to the study of the distribution of plants. □□ **floristically** adv. **floristics** n.

floruit /ˈflɒrʊɪt, ˈflɔː-/ v. & n. —*v.intr.* (he or she) was alive and working; flourished (used of a person, esp. a painter, a writer, etc., whose exact dates are unknown). —n. the period or date at which a person lived or worked. [L, = he or she flourished]

flory var. of FLEURY.

floscular /ˈflɒskjʊlə(r)/ adj. (also **flosculous** /-kjʊləs/) having florets or composite flowers. [L *flosculus* dimin. of *flos* flower]

floss /flɒs/ n. & v. —n. **1** the rough silk enveloping a silkworm's cocoon. **2** untwisted silk thread used in embroidery. **3** = *dental floss*. —*v.tr.* (also *absol.*) clean (the teeth) with dental floss. □ **floss silk** a rough silk used in cheap goods. [F (*soie*) *floche* floss(-silk) f. OF *flosche* down, nap of velvet]

flossy /ˈflɒsɪ/ adj. (**flossier**, **flossiest**) **1** of or like floss. **2** *colloq.* fancy, showy.

flotation /fləʊˈteɪʃ(ə)n/ n. (also **floatation**) **1** the process of launching or financing a commercial enterprise. **2** the separation of the components of crushed ore etc. by their different capacities to float. **3** the capacity to float. □ **centre of flotation** the centre of gravity in a floating body. [alt. of *floatation* f. FLOAT, after *rotation* etc.]

flotilla /fləˈtɪlə/ n. **1** a small fleet. **2** a fleet of boats or small ships. [Sp., dimin. of *flota* fleet, OF *flote* multitude]

flotsam /ˈflɒtsəm/ n. wreckage found floating. □ **flotsam and jetsam 1** odds and ends; rubbish. **2** vagrants etc. [AF *floteson* f. *floter* FLOAT]

flounce[1] /flaʊns/ v. & n. —*v.intr.* (often foll. by *away*, *about*, *off*, *out*) go or move with an agitated, violent, or impatient motion (*flounced out in a huff*). —n. a flouncing movement. [16th c.: orig. unkn.: perh. imit., as *bounce*, *pounce*]

flounce[2] /flaʊns/ n. & v. —n. a wide ornamental strip of material gathered and sewn to a skirt, dress, etc.; a frill. —*v.tr.* trim with a flounce or flounces. [alt. of earlier *frounce* fold, pleat, f. OF *fronce* f. *froncir* wrinkle]

flounder[1] /ˈflaʊndə(r)/ v. & n. —v.intr. **1** struggle in mud, or as if in mud, or when wading. **2** perform a task badly or without knowledge; be out of one's depth. —n. an act of floundering. □□ **flounderer** n. [imit.: perh. assoc. with *founder, blunder*]

flounder[2] /ˈflaʊndə(r)/ n. **1** an edible flat-fish, *Pleuronectes flesus*, native to European shores. **2** any of various flat-fish native to N. American shores. [ME f. AF *floundre*, OF *flondre*, prob. of Scand. orig.]

flour /ˈflaʊə(r)/ n. & v. —n. **1** a meal or powder obtained by grinding and usu. sifting cereals, esp. wheat. **2** any fine powder. —v.tr. **1** sprinkle with flour. **2** *US* grind into flour. □□ **floury** adj. (**flourier, flouriest**). **flouriness** n. [ME, different. spelling of FLOWER in the sense 'finest part']

flourish /ˈflʌrɪʃ/ v. & n. —v. **1** intr. **a** grow vigorously; thrive. **b** prosper; be successful. **c** be in one's prime. **d** be in good health. **2** intr. (usu. foll. by *in, at, about*) spend one's life; be active (at a specified time) (*flourished in the Middle Ages*) (cf. FLORUIT). **3** tr. show ostentatiously (*flourished his cheque-book*). **4** tr. wave (a weapon, one's limbs, etc.) vigorously. —n. **1** an ostentatious gesture with a weapon, a hand, etc. (*removed his hat with a flourish*). **2** an ornamental curving decoration of handwriting. **3** a florid verbal expression; a rhetorical embellishment. **4** *Mus.* **a** a fanfare played by brass instruments. **b** an ornate musical passage. **c** an extemporized addition played esp. at the beginning or end of a composition. **5** *archaic* an instance of prosperity; a flourishing. □□ **flourisher** n. **flourishy** adj. [ME f. OF *florir* ult. f. L *flōrēre* f. *flos floris* flower]

flout /flaʊt/ v. & n. —v. **1** tr. express contempt for (the law, rules, etc.) by word or action; mock; insult (*flouted convention by shaving her head*). ¶ Often confused with *flaunt*. **2** intr. (often foll. by *at*) mock or scoff at. —n. a flouting speech or act. [perh. f. Du. *fluiten* whistle, hiss: cf. FLUTE]

flow /fləʊ/ v. & n. —v.intr. **1** glide along as a stream (*the Thames flows under London Bridge*). **2 a** (of a liquid, esp. water) gush out; spring. **b** (of blood, liquid, etc.) be spilt. **3** (of blood, money, electric current, etc.) circulate. **4** (of people or things) come or go in large numbers or smoothly (*traffic flowed down the hill*). **5** (of talk, literary style, etc.) proceed easily and smoothly. **6** (of a garment, hair, etc.) hang easily or gracefully; undulate. **7** (often foll. by *from*) result from; be caused by (*his failure flows from his diffidence*). **8** (esp. of the tide) be in flood; run full. **9** (of wine) be poured out copiously. **10** (of a rock or metal) undergo a permanent change of shape under stress. **11** (foll. by *with*) *archaic* be plentifully supplied with (*land flowing with milk and honey*). —n. **1 a** a flowing movement in a stream. **b** the manner in which a thing flows (*a sluggish flow*). **c** a flowing liquid (*couldn't stop the flow*). **d** a copious outpouring; a stream (*a continuous flow of complaints*). **2** the rise of a tide or a river (*ebb and flow*). **3** the gradual deformation of a rock or metal under stress. **4** *Sc.* a bog or morass. □ **flow chart** (or **diagram** or **sheet**) **1** a diagram of the movement or action of things or persons engaged in a complex activity. **2** a graphical representation of a computer program in relation to its sequence of functions (as distinct from the data it processes). **flow of spirits** habitual cheerfulness. **flow-on** *Austral.* a wage or salary adjustment made as a consequence of one already made in a similar or related occupation. [OE *flōwan* f. Gmc, rel. to FLOOD]

flower /ˈflaʊə(r)/ n. & v. —n. **1** the part of a plant from which the fruit or seed is developed. **2** the reproductive organ in a plant containing one or more pistils or stamens or both, and usu. a corolla and calyx. **3** a blossom, esp. on a stem and used in bunches for decoration. **4** a plant cultivated or noted for its flowers. **5** (in pl.) ornamental phrases (*flowers of speech*). —v. **1** intr. (of a plant) produce flowers; bloom or blossom. **2** intr. reach a peak. **3** tr. cause or allow (a plant) to flower. **4** tr. decorate with worked flowers or a floral design. □ **flower-bed** a garden bed in which flowers are grown. **flower-girl** a woman who sells flowers, esp. in the street. **flower-head** = HEAD n. 4d. **the flower of** the best or best part of. **flower people** hippies carrying or wearing flowers as symbols of peace and love. **flower power** the ideas of the flower people regarded as an instrument

in changing the world. **flowers of sulphur** *Chem.* a fine powder produced when sulphur evaporates and condenses. **in flower** with the flowers out. □□ **flowered** adj. (also in *comb.*). **flowerless** adj. **flowerlike** adj. [ME f. AF *flur*, OF *flour, flor*, f. L *flos floris*]

flowerer /ˈflaʊərə(r)/ n. a plant that flowers at a specified time (*a late flowerer*).

floweret /ˈflaʊərɪt/ n. a small flower.

flowering /ˈflaʊərɪŋ/ adj. (of a plant) capable of producing flowers.

flowerpot /ˈflaʊəˌpɒt/ n. a pot in which a plant may be grown.

flowery /ˈflaʊərɪ/ adj. **1** decorated with flowers or floral designs. **2** (of literary style, manner of speech, etc.) high-flown; ornate. **3** full of flowers (*a flowery meadow*). □□ **floweriness** n.

flowing /ˈfləʊɪŋ/ adj. **1** (of literary style etc.) fluent; easy. **2** (of a line, a curve, or a contour) smoothly continuous, not abrupt. **3** (of hair, a garment, a sail, etc.) unconfined. □□ **flowingly** adv.

flown past part. of FLY[1].

flowstone /ˈfləʊstəʊn/ n. rock deposited in a thin sheet by a flow of water.

FLQ abbr. Front de Libération du Québec.

Flt. Lt. abbr. Flight Lieutenant.

Flt. Off. abbr. Flight Officer.

Flt. Sgt. abbr. Flight Sergeant.

flu /fluː/ n. *colloq.* influenza. [abbr.]

flub /flʌb/ v. & n. *US colloq.* —v.tr. & intr. (**flubbed, flubbing**) botch; bungle. —n. something badly or clumsily done. [20th c.: orig. unkn.]

fluctuate /ˈflʌktjʊˌeɪt/ v.intr. vary irregularly; be unstable, vacillate; rise and fall, move to and fro. □□ **fluctuation** /-ˈeɪʃ(ə)n/ n. [L *fluctuare* f. *fluctus* flow, wave f. *fluere fluct-* flow]

flue /fluː/ n. **1** a smoke-duct in a chimney. **2** a channel for conveying heat, esp. a hot-air passage in a wall; a tube for heating water in some kinds of boiler. □ **flue-cure** cure (tobacco) by artificial heat from flues. **flue-pipe** an organ pipe into which the air enters directly, not striking a reed. [16th c.: orig. unkn.]

fluence /ˈfluːəns/ n. *colloq.* influence. □ **put the fluence on** apply hypnotic etc. power to (a person). [shortening of INFLUENCE]

fluency /ˈfluːənsɪ/ n. **1** a smooth, easy flow, esp. in speech or writing. **2** a ready command of words or of a specified foreign language.

fluent /ˈfluːənt/ adj. **1 a** (of speech or literary style) flowing naturally and readily. **b** having command of a foreign language (*is fluent in German*). **c** able to speak quickly and easily. **2** flowing easily or gracefully (*the fluent line of her arabesque*). **3** *archaic* liable to change; unsettled. □□ **fluently** adv. [L *fluere* flow]

fluff /flʌf/ n. & v. —n. **1** soft, light, feathery material coming off blankets etc. **2** soft fur or feathers. **3** *sl.* **a** a mistake in delivering theatrical lines, in playing music, etc. **b** a mistake in playing a game. —v. **1** tr. & intr. (often foll. by *up*) shake into or become a soft mass. **2** tr. & intr. *colloq.* make a mistake in (a theatrical part, a game, playing music, a speech, etc.); blunder (*fluffed his opening line*). **3** tr. make into fluff. **4** tr. put a soft surface on (the flesh side of leather). □ **bit of fluff** *sl. offens.* a woman regarded as an object of sexual desire. [prob. dial. alt. of *flue* fluff]

fluffy /ˈflʌfɪ/ adj. (**fluffier, fluffiest**) **1** of or like fluff. **2** covered in fluff; downy. □□ **fluffily** adv. **fluffiness** n.

flugelhorn /ˈfluːg(ə)lˌhɔːn/ n. a valved brass wind instrument like a cornet but with a broader tone. [G *Flügelhorn* f. *Flügel* wing + *Horn* horn]

fluid /ˈfluːɪd/ n. & adj. —n. **1** a substance, esp. a gas or liquid, lacking definite shape and capable of flowing and yielding to the slightest pressure. **2** a fluid part or secretion. —adj. **1** able to flow and alter shape freely. **2** constantly changing or fluctuating (*the situation is fluid*). **3** (of a clutch, coupling, etc.) in which liquid is used to transmit power. □ **fluid drachm** see DRACHM. **fluid ounce** see OUNCE[1]. □□ **fluidify** /-ˈɪdɪˌfaɪ/ v.tr. (**-ies, -ied**). **fluidity** /-ˈɪdɪtɪ/ n. **fluidly** adv. **fluidness** n. [F *fluide* or L *fluidus* f. *fluere* flow]

fluidics /fluːˈɪdɪks/ n.pl. (usu. treated as *sing.*) the study and technique of using small interacting flows and fluid jets for functions usu. performed by electronic devices. □□ **fluidic** adj.

fluidize /ˈfluːɪˌdaɪz/ v.tr. (also **-ise**) cause (a finely divided solid) to acquire the characteristics of a fluid by passing a current of gas, vapour, or liquid upwards through it. The technique has various applications, e.g. in the transporting of powdered material and in cleaning a catalyst in oil refining. □□ **fluidization** /-ˈzeɪʃ(ə)n/ n.

fluidounce /ˈfluːɪdˌaʊns/ n. US a fluid ounce (see OUNCE[1]).

fluidram /ˈfluːɪˌdræm/ n. US a fluid drachm (see DRACHM).

fluke[1] /fluːk/ n. & v. —n. **1** a lucky accident (won by a fluke). **2** a chance breeze. —v.tr. achieve by a fluke (fluked that shot). [19th c.: perh. f. dial. fluke guess]

fluke[2] /fluːk/ n. **1** any parasitic flatworm of the class Digenea or Monogenea, including liver flukes and blood flukes. **2** a flat-fish, esp. a flounder. [OE flōc]

fluke[3] /fluːk/ n. **1** Naut. a broad triangular plate on the arm of an anchor. **2** the barbed head of a lance, harpoon, etc. **3** Zool. either of the lobes of a whale's tail. [16th c.: perh. f. FLUKE[2]]

fluky /ˈfluːkɪ/ adj. (**flukier, flukiest**) of the nature of a fluke; obtained more by chance than skill. □□ **flukily** adv. **flukiness** n.

flume /fluːm/ n. & v. —n. **1** an artificial channel conveying water etc. for industrial use. **2** a ravine with a stream. —v. **1** intr. build flumes. **2** tr. convey down a flume. [ME f. OF flum, flun f. L flumen river f. fluere flow]

flummery /ˈflʌmərɪ/ n. (pl. **-ies**) **1** empty compliments; trifles; nonsense. **2** a sweet dish made with beaten eggs, sugar, etc. [Welsh llymru, of unkn. orig.]

flummox /ˈflʌməks/ v.tr. colloq. bewilder, confound, disconcert. [19th c.: prob. dial., imit.]

flump /flʌmp/ v. & n. —v. (often foll. by down) **1** intr. fall or move heavily. **2** tr. set or throw down with a heavy thud. —n. the action or sound of flumping. [imit.]

flung past and past part. of FLING.

flunk /flʌŋk/ v. & n. US colloq. —v. **1** tr. **a** fail (an examination etc.). **b** fail (an examination candidate). **2** intr. (often foll. by out) fail utterly; give up. —n. an instance of flunking. □ **flunk out** be dismissed from school etc. after failing an examination. [cf. FUNK[1] and obs. flink be a coward]

flunkey /ˈflʌŋkɪ/ n. (also **flunky**) (pl. **-eys** or **-ies**) usu. derog. **1** a liveried servant; a footman. **2** a toady; a snob. **3** US a cook, waiter, etc. □□ **flunkeyism** n. [18th c. (orig. Sc.): perh. f. FLANK with the sense 'sidesman, flanker']

fluoresce /fluəˈres/ v.intr. be or become fluorescent.

fluorescence /fluəˈres(ə)ns/ n. **1** the visible or invisible radiation produced from certain substances as a result of incident radiation of a shorter wavelength as X-rays, ultraviolet light, etc. **2** the property of absorbing light of short (invisible) wavelength and emitting light of longer (visible) wavelength. [FLUORSPAR (which fluoresces) after opalescence]

fluorescent /fluəˈres(ə)nt/ adj. (of a substance) having or showing fluorescence. □ **fluorescent lamp** (or **bulb**) a lamp or bulb radiating largely by fluorescence, esp. a tubular lamp in which phosphor on the inside surface of the tube is made to fluoresce by ultraviolet radiation from mercury vapour. **fluorescent screen** a screen coated with fluorescent material to show images from X-rays etc.

fluoridate /ˈfluərɪˌdeɪt/ v.tr. add traces of fluoride to (drinking-water etc.).

fluoridation /ˌfluərɪˈdeɪʃ(ə)n/ n. (also **fluoridization** /-daɪˈzeɪʃ(ə)n/) the addition of traces of fluoride to drinking-water in order to prevent or reduce tooth-decay.

fluoride /ˈfluəraɪd/ n. any binary compound of fluorine.

fluorinate /ˈfluərɪˌneɪt/ v.tr. **1** = FLUORIDATE. **2** introduce fluorine into (a compound) (fluorinated hydrocarbons). □□ **fluorination** /-ˈneɪʃ(ə)n/ n.

fluorine /ˈfluəriːn/ n. a poisonous pale-yellow gaseous element of the halogen group occurring naturally in fluorite and cryolite. The most reactive of all elements, fluorine is common in combined form in nature but the element itself was not isolated until 1886. Its compounds are used as catalysts and to protect against dental decay, and hydrocarbons combined with fluorine form an important group of very unreactive substances used to form non-stick surfaces and as lubricants. ¶ Symb.: **F**; atomic number 9. [F (as FLUORSPAR)]

fluorite /ˈfluəraɪt/ n. a mineral form of calcium fluoride. [It. (as FLUORSPAR)]

fluoro- /ˈfluərəʊ/ comb. form **1** fluorine (fluorocarbon). **2** fluorescence (fluoroscope). [FLUORINE, FLUORESCENCE]

fluorocarbon /ˌfluərəʊˈkɑːbən/ n. a compound formed by replacing one or more of the hydrogen atoms in a hydrocarbon with fluorine atoms.

fluoroscope /ˈfluərəˌskəʊp/ n. an instrument with a fluorescent screen on which X-ray images may be viewed without taking and developing X-ray photographs.

fluorosis /fluəˈrəʊsɪs/ n. poisoning by fluorine or its compounds. [F fluorose (as FLUORO- 1)]

fluorspar /ˈfluəspɑː(r)/ n. = FLUORITE. [fluor a flow, any of the minerals used as fluxes, fluorspar, f. L fluor f. fluere flow + SPAR[3]]

flurry /ˈflʌrɪ/ n. & v. —n. (pl. **-ies**) **1** a gust or squall (of snow, rain, etc.). **2** a sudden burst of activity. **3** a commotion; excitement; nervous agitation (a flurry of speculation; the flurry of the city). —v.tr. (**-ies, -ied**) confuse by haste or noise; agitate. [imit.: cf. obs. flurr ruffle, hurry]

flush[1] /flʌʃ/ v. & n. —v. **1** intr. **a** blush, redden (he flushed with embarrassment). **b** glow with a warm colour (sky flushed pink). **2** tr. (usu. as **flushed** adj.) cause to glow or blush (often foll. by with: flushed with pride). **3** tr. **a** cleanse (a drain, lavatory, etc.) by a rushing flow of water. **b** (often foll. by away, down) dispose of (an object) in this way (flushed away the cigarette). **4** intr. rush out, spurt. **5** tr. flood (the river flushed the meadow). **6** intr. (of a plant) throw out fresh shoots. —n. **1 a** a blush. **b** a glow of light or colour. **2 a** a rush of water. **b** the cleansing of a drain, lavatory, etc. by flushing. **3 a** a rush of emotion. **b** the elation produced by a victory etc. (the flush of triumph). **4** sudden abundance. **5** freshness; vigour (in the first flush of womanhood). **6 a** (also **hot flush**) a sudden feeling of heat during the menopause. **b** a feverish temperature. **c** facial redness, esp. caused by fever, alcohol, etc. **7** a fresh growth of grass etc. □□ **flusher** n. [ME, perh. = FLUSH[4] infl. by flash and blush]

flush[2] /flʌʃ/ adj. & v. —adj. **1** (often foll. by with) in the same plane; level; even (the sink is flush with the cooker; fitted it flush with the wall). **2** (usu. predic.) colloq. **a** having plenty of money. **b** (of money) abundant, plentiful. **3** full to overflowing; in flood. —v.tr. **1** make (surfaces) level. **2** fill in (a joint) level with a surface. □□ **flushness** n. [prob. f. FLUSH[1]]

flush[3] /flʌʃ/ n. a hand of cards all of one suit, esp. in poker. □ **royal flush** a straight poker flush headed by an ace. **straight flush** a flush that is a numerical sequence. [OF flus, flux f. L fluxus FLUX]

flush[4] /flʌʃ/ v. **1** tr. cause (esp. a game bird) to fly up. **2** intr. (of a bird) fly up and away. □ **flush out 1** reveal. **2** drive out. [ME, imit.: cf. fly, rush]

fluster /ˈflʌstə(r)/ v. & n. —v. **1** tr. & intr. make or become nervous or confused; flurry (was flustered by the noise; he flusters easily). **2** tr. confuse with drink; half-intoxicate. **3** intr. bustle. —n. a confused or agitated state. [ME: orig. unkn.: cf. Icel. flaustr(a) hurry, bustle]

flute /fluːt/ n. & v. —n. **1 a** a high-pitched woodwind instrument made in silver, stainless steel, or occasionally wood, having holes along it stopped by fingers or (since the 19th c.) keys, and a blow-hole in the side, near the end. The flute has a range of three octaves. Since the 14th c. it has had an association with military music as a marching instrument (fife and drums), and it has been a standard orchestral instrument since the early 18th c. **b** an organ stop having a similar sound. **c** any of various wind instruments resembling a flute. **d** a flute-player. **2 a** Archit. an ornamental vertical groove in a column. **b** a trumpet-shaped frill on a dress etc. **c** any similar cylindrical groove. **3** a tall narrow wineglass. —v. **1** intr. play the flute. **2** intr. speak, sing, or whistle in a fluting way. **3** tr. make flutes or grooves in. **4** tr. play (a tune etc.) on a flute. □□ **flutelike** adj. **fluting** n. **flutist**

n. US (cf. FLAUTIST). **fluty** adj. (in sense 1a of n.). [ME f. OF *fleute, flaute, flahute*, prob. f. Prov. *flaut*]

flutter /ˈflʌtə(r)/ v. & n. —v. **1 a** intr. flap the wings in flying or trying to fly (*butterflies fluttered in the sunshine*). **b** tr. flap (the wings). **2** intr. fall with a quivering motion (*leaves fluttered to the ground*). **3** intr. & tr. move or cause to move irregularly or tremblingly (*the wind fluttered the flag*). **4** intr. go about restlessly; flit; hover. **5** tr. agitate, confuse. **6** intr. (of a pulse or heartbeat) beat feebly or irregularly. **7** intr. tremble with excitement or agitation. —n. **1 a** the act of fluttering. **b** an instance of this. **2** tremulous excitement; a sensation (*was in a flutter; caused a flutter with his behaviour*). **3** Brit. sl. a small bet, esp. on a horse. **4** an abnormally rapid but regular heartbeat. **5** Aeron. an undesired oscillation in a part of an aircraft etc. under stress. **6** Mus. a rapid movement of the tongue (as when rolling one's rs) in playing a wind instrument. **7** Electronics a rapid variation of pitch, esp. of recorded sound (cf. wow²). **8** a vibration. □ **flutter the dovecots** cause alarm among normally imperturbable people. □□ **flutterer** n. **fluttery** adj. [OE *floterian, flotorian*, frequent. form rel. to FLEET⁵]

fluvial /ˈfluːvɪəl/ adj. of or found in a river or rivers. [ME f. L *fluvialis* f. *fluvius* river f. *fluere* flow]

fluviatile /ˈfluːvɪətaɪl/ adj. of, found in, or produced by a river or rivers. [F f. L *fluviatilis* f. *fluviatus* moistened f. *fluvius*]

fluvio- /ˈfluːvɪəʊ/ comb. form river (*fluviometer*). [L *fluvius* river f. *fluere* flow]

fluvioglacial /ˌfluːvɪəʊˈɡleɪsɪəl, -ʃ(ə)l/ adj. of or caused by streams from glacial ice, or the combined action of rivers and glaciers.

fluviometer /ˌfluːvɪˈɒmɪt(ə)r/ n. an instrument for measuring the rise and fall of rivers.

flux /flʌks/ n. & v. —n. **1** a process of flowing or flowing out. **2** an issue or discharge. **3** continuous change (*in a state of flux*). **4** Metallurgy a substance mixed with a metal etc. to promote fusion. **5** Physics **a** the rate of flow of any fluid across a given area. **b** the amount of fluid crossing an area in a given time. **6** Physics the amount of radiation or particles incident on an area in a given time. **7** Electr. the total electric or magnetic field passing through a surface. **8** Med. an abnormal discharge of blood or excrement from the body. —v. **1** tr. & intr. make or become fluid. **2** tr. **a** fuse. **b** treat with a fusing flux. [ME f. OF *flux* or L *fluxus* f. *fluere flux-* flow]

fluxion /ˈflʌkʃ(ə)n/ n. Math. the rate at which a variable quantity changes; a derivative. [F *fluxion* or L *fluxio* (as FLUX)]

fly¹ /flaɪ/ v. & n. —v. (**flies**; past **flew** /fluː/; past part. **flown** /fləʊn/) **1** intr. move through the air under control, esp. with wings. **2** (of an aircraft or its occupants): **a** intr. travel through the air or through space. **b** tr. traverse (a region or distance) (*flew the Channel*). **3** tr. **a** control the flight of (esp. an aircraft). **b** transport in an aircraft. **4 a** tr. cause to fly or remain aloft. **b** intr. (of a flag, hair, etc.) wave or flutter. **5** intr. pass or rise quickly through the air or over an obstacle. **6** intr. go or move quickly; pass swiftly (*time flies*). **7** intr. **a** flee. **b** colloq. depart hastily. **8** intr. be driven or scattered; be forced off suddenly (*sent me flying; the door flew open*). **9** intr. (foll. by at, upon) **a** hasten or spring violently. **b** attack or criticize fiercely. **10** tr. flee from; escape in haste. —n. (pl. **-ies**) **1** (usu. in pl.) **a** a flap on a garment, esp. trousers, to contain or cover a fastening. **b** this fastening. **2** a flap at the entrance of a tent. **3** (in pl.) the space over the proscenium in a theatre. **4** the act or an instance of flying. **5** (pl. usu. **flys**) Brit. hist. a one-horse hackney carriage. **6** a speed-regulating device in clockwork and machinery. □ **fly-away** (of hair etc.) tending to fly out or up; streaming. **fly-by** (pl. **-bys**) a flight past a position, esp. the approach of a spacecraft in a planet for observation. **fly-by-night** adj. unreliable. —n. an unreliable person. **fly-half** Rugby Football a stand-off half. **fly high 1** pursue a high ambition. **2** excel, prosper. **fly in the face of** openly disregard or disobey; conflict roundly with (probability, the evidence, etc.). **fly into a rage** (or **temper** etc.) become suddenly or violently angry. **fly a kite 1** try something out; test public opinion. **2** raise money by an accommodation bill. **fly off the handle** colloq. lose one's temper suddenly and unexpectedly. **fly-past** a ceremonial flight of aircraft past a person or a place. **fly-pitcher**

sl. a street-trader. **fly-pitching** sl. street-trading. **fly-post** display (posters etc.) rapidly in unauthorized places. **fly-tip** illegally dump (waste). **fly-tipper** a person who engages in fly-tipping. □□ **flyable** adj. [OE *fleogan* f. Gmc]

fly² /flaɪ/ n. (pl. **flies**) **1** any insect of the order Diptera with two usu. transparent wings. **2** any other winged insect, e.g. a firefly or mayfly. **3** a disease of plants or animals caused by flies. **4** a natural or artificial fly used as bait in fishing. □ **fly agaric** a poisonous fungus *Amanita Muscaria*, forming bright-red mushrooms with white flecks. **fly-blow** flies' eggs contaminating food, esp. meat. **fly-blown** adj. tainted, esp. by flies. **fly-fish** v.intr. fish with a fly. **fly in the ointment** a minor irritation that spoils enjoyment. **fly on the wall** an unnoticed observer. **fly-paper** sticky treated paper for catching flies. **fly-trap** any of various plants that catch flies, esp. the Venus fly-trap. **like flies** in large numbers (usu. of people dying in an epidemic etc.). **no flies on** colloq. nothing to diminish (a person's) astuteness. [OE *flyge, fleoge* f. WG]

fly³ /flaɪ/ adj. Brit. sl. knowing, clever, alert. □□ **flyness** n. [19th c.: orig. unkn.]

flycatcher /ˈflaɪˌkætʃə(r)/ n. any bird of the families Tyrannidae and Muscicapidae, catching insects esp. in short flights from a perch.

flyer /ˈflaɪə(r)/ n. (also **flier**) colloq. **1** an airman or airwoman. **2** a thing that flies in a specified way (*a poor flyer*). **3** a fast-moving animal or vehicle. **4** an ambitious or outstanding person. **5** US a small handbill. **6** US a speculative investment. **7** a flying jump.

flying /ˈflaɪɪŋ/ adj. & n. —adj. **1** fluttering or waving in the air; hanging loose. **2** hasty, brief (*a flying visit*). **3** designed for rapid movement. **4** (of an animal) able to make very long leaps by using winglike membranes etc. —n. flight, esp. in an aircraft. □ **flying boat** an aircraft that can land on and take off from water and whose main body is a hull which supports it in the water. **flying bomb** a pilotless aircraft with an explosive warhead. **flying buttress** a buttress slanting from a separate column, usu. forming an arch with the wall it supports. **flying doctor** a doctor (esp. in a large sparsely populated area) who visits distant patients by aircraft. **flying fish** any tropical fish of the family Exocoetidae, with winglike pectoral fins for gliding through the air. **flying fox** any of various fruit-eating bats esp. of the genus *Pteropus*, with a fox-like head. **flying lemur** either of two mammals of the genus *Cyanocephalus* of S. Asia, with a lemur-like appearance and having a membrane between the fore and hind limbs for gliding from tree to tree. **flying lizard** any lizard of the genus *Draco*, having membranes on elongated ribs for gliding. **flying officer** the RAF rank next below flight lieutenant. **flying phalanger** any of various phalangers having a membrane between the fore and hind limbs for gliding. **flying picket** an industrial picket that can be moved rapidly from one site to another, esp. to reinforce local pickets. **flying saucer** any unidentified, esp. circular, flying object, popularly supposed to have come from space. **flying squad** a police detachment or other body organized for rapid movement. **flying squirrel** any of various squirrels, esp. of the genus *Pteromys*, with skin joining the fore and hind limbs for gliding from tree to tree. **flying start 1** a start (of a race etc.) in which the starting-point is passed at full speed. **2** a vigorous start giving an initial advantage. **flying wing** an aircraft with little or no fuselage and no tailplane. **with flying colours** with distinction.

Flying Dutchman a legendary spectral ship supposed to be seen in the region of the Cape of Good Hope and presaging disaster. The legend is the basis of a music drama (1843) by Wagner.

flyleaf /ˈflaɪliːf/ n. (pl. **-leaves**) a blank leaf at the beginning or end of a book.

Flynn /flɪn/, Errol (1909–59), American actor, born in Northern Ireland, not, as he alleged, in Tasmania. His usual role was the swashbuckling hero of romantic costume dramas in films such as *Captain Blood* (1935) and *The Adventures of Robin Hood* (1938).

flyover /ˈflaɪˌəʊvə(r)/ n. **1** Brit. a bridge carrying one road or railway over another. **2** US = fly-past (see FLY¹).

flysheet /ˈflaɪʃiːt/ n. **1** a tract or circular of two or four pages. **2**

a canvas cover pitched outside and over a tent to give extra protection against bad weather.

flyweight /ˈflaɪweɪt/ n. **1** a weight in certain sports intermediate between light flyweight and bantamweight, in the amateur boxing scale 48–51 kg but differing for professionals, wrestlers, and weightlifters. **2** a sportsman of this weight. □ **light flyweight 1** a weight in amateur boxing up to 48 kg. **2** an amateur boxer of this weight.

flywheel /ˈflaɪwiːl/ n. a heavy wheel on a revolving shaft used to regulate machinery or accumulate power.

FM abbr. **1** Field Marshal. **2** frequency modulation.

Fm symb. Chem. the element fermium.

fm. abbr. (also **fm**) fathom(s).

f-number /ˈefˌnʌmbə(r)/ n. Photog. the ratio of the focal length to the effective diameter of a lens (e.g. ƒ5, indicating that the focal length is five times the diameter, used to indicate the amount of light passing through the lens). [ƒ (denoting focal length) + NUMBER]

FO abbr. **1** Flying Officer. **2** hist. (in the UK) Foreign Office.

fo. abbr. folio.

foal /fəʊl/ n. & v. —n. the young of a horse or related animal. —v.tr. (of a mare etc.) give birth to (a foal). □ **in** (or **with**) **foal** (of a mare etc.) pregnant. [OE fola f. Gmc: cf. FILLY]

foam /fəʊm/ n. & v. —n. **1** a mass of small bubbles formed on or in liquid by agitation, fermentation, etc. **2** a froth of saliva or sweat. **3** a substance resembling these, e.g. rubber or plastic in a cellular mass. —v.intr. **1** emit foam; froth. **2** run with foam. **3** (of a vessel) be filled and overflow with foam. □ **foam at the mouth** be very angry. □□ **foamless** adj. **foamy** adj. (**foamier, foamiest**). [OE fām f. WG]

fob[1] /fɒb/ n. & v. —n. **1** (in full **fob-chain**) a chain attached to a watch for carrying in a waistcoat or waistband pocket. **2** a small pocket for carrying a watch. **3** a tab on a key-ring. —v.tr. (**fobbed, fobbing**) put in one's fob; pocket. [orig. cant, prob. f. G]

fob[2] /fɒb/ v.tr. (**fobbed, fobbing**) □ **fob off 1** (often foll. by with a thing) deceive into accepting something inferior. **2** (often foll. by on to a person) palm or pass off (an inferior thing). [16th c.: cf. obs. fop to dupe, G foppen to banter]

f.o.b. abbr. free on board.

focal /ˈfəʊk(ə)l/ adj. of, at, or in terms of a focus. □ **focal distance** (or **length**) the distance between the centre of a mirror or lens and its focus. **focal plane** the plane through the focus perpendicular to the axis of a mirror or lens. **focal point** = FOCUS n. 1. [mod.L focalis (as FOCUS)]

focalize /ˈfəʊkəˌlaɪz/ v.tr. (also **-ise**) = FOCUS v. □□ **focalization** /-ˈzeɪʃ(ə)n/ n.

Foch /fɒʃ/, Ferdinand (1851–1929), French military officer, one of the most influential proponents of the doctrine of offensive warfare which was to cost the French dear in the early years of the First World War. During that war Foch rose steadily to become Supreme Commander of all Allied Forces on the Western Front in early 1918, and served as the senior French representative at the Armistice negotiations which ended hostilities.

fo'c's'le var. of FORECASTLE.

focus /ˈfəʊkəs/ n. & v. —n. (pl. **focuses** or **foci** /ˈfəʊsaɪ/) **1** Physics **a** the point at which rays or waves meet after reflection or refraction. **b** the point from which diverging rays or waves appear to proceed. Also called focal point. **2 a** Optics the point at which an object must be situated for an image of it given by a lens or mirror to be well defined (bring into focus). **b** the adjustment of the eye or a lens necessary to produce a clear image (the binoculars were not in focus). **c** a state of clear definition (the photograph was out of focus). **3** the centre of interest or activity (focus of attention). **4** Geom. one of the points from which the distances to any point of a given curve are connected by a linear relation. **5** Med. the principal site of an infection or other disease. **6** Geol. the place of origin of an earthquake. —v. (**focused, focusing** or **focussed, focussing**) **1** tr. bring into focus. **2** tr. adjust the focus of (a lens, the eye, etc.). **3** tr. & intr. (often foll.

by on) concentrate or be concentrated on. **4** intr. & tr. converge or make converge to a focus. □□ **focuser** n. [L, = hearth]

fodder /ˈfɒdə(r)/ n. & v. —n. dried hay or straw etc. for cattle, horses, etc. —v.tr. give fodder to. [OE fōdor f. Gmc, rel. to FOOD]

foe /fəʊ/ n. esp. poet. or formal an enemy or opponent. [OE fāh hostile, rel. to FEUD[1]]

foehn var. of FÖHN.

foetid var. of FETID.

foetus /ˈfiːtəs/ n. (US **fetus**) an unborn or unhatched offspring of a mammal esp. a human one more than eight weeks after conception. □□ **foetal** adj. **foeticide** /-tɪˌsaɪd/ n. [ME f. L fetus offspring]

fog[1] /fɒg/ n. & v. —n. **1 a** a thick cloud of water droplets or smoke suspended in the atmosphere at or near the earth's surface restricting or obscuring visibility. **b** obscurity in the atmosphere caused by this. **2** Photog. cloudiness on a developed negative etc. obscuring the image. **3** an uncertain or confused position or state. —v. (**fogged, fogging**) **1** tr. **a** envelop or cover with fog or condensed vapour. **b** bewilder or confuse as if with a fog. **2** intr. become covered with fog or condensed vapour. **3** tr. Photog. make (a negative etc.) obscure or cloudy. □ **fog-bank** a mass of fog at sea. **fog-bound** unable to proceed because of fog. **fog-bow** a manifestation like a rainbow, produced by light on fog. **fog-lamp** a lamp used to improve visibility in fog. **fog-signal** a detonator placed on a railway line in fog to warn train drivers. **in a fog** puzzled; at a loss. [perh. back-form. f. FOGGY]

fog[2] /fɒg/ n. & v. esp. Brit. —n. **1** a second growth of grass after cutting; aftermath. **2** long grass left standing in winter. —v.tr. (**fogged, fogging**) **1** leave (land) under fog. **2** feed (cattle) on fog. [ME: orig. unkn.]

fogey var. of FOGY.

foggy /ˈfɒgɪ/ adj. (**foggier, foggiest**) **1** (of the atmosphere) thick or obscure with fog. **2** of or like fog. **3** vague, confused, unclear. □ **not have the foggiest** colloq. have no idea at all. □□ **foggily** adv. **fogginess** n.

foghorn /ˈfɒghɔːn/ n. **1** a deep-sounding instrument for warning ships in fog. **2** colloq. a loud penetrating voice.

fogy /ˈfəʊgɪ/ n. (also **fogey**) (pl. **-ies** or **-eys**) a dull old-fashioned person (esp. old fogy). □□ **fogydom** n. **fogyish** adj. [18th c.: rel. to sl. fogram, of unkn. orig.]

föhn /fɜːn/ n. (also **foehn**) **1** a hot southerly wind on the northern slopes of the Alps. **2** a warm dry wind on the lee side of mountains. [G, ult. f. L Favonius mild west wind]

foible /ˈfɔɪb(ə)l/ n. **1** a minor weakness or idiosyncrasy. **2** Fencing the part of a sword-blade from the middle to the point. [F, obs. form of faible (as FEEBLE)]

foie gras /fwɑː ˈgrɑː/ n. colloq. = pâté de foie gras.

foil[1] /fɔɪl/ v. & n. —v.tr. **1** frustrate, baffle, defeat. **2** Hunting **a** run over or cross (ground or a scent) to confuse the hounds. **b** (absol.) (of an animal) spoil the scent in this way. —n. **1** Hunting the track of a hunted animal. **2** archaic a repulse or defeat. [ME, = trample down, perh. f. OF fouler to full cloth, trample, ult. f. L fullo FULLER[1]]

foil[2] /fɔɪl/ n. **1 a** metal hammered or rolled into a thin sheet (tin foil). **b** a sheet of this, or of tin amalgam, attached to mirror glass as a reflector. **c** a leaf of foil placed under a precious stone etc. to brighten or colour it. **2** a person or thing that enhances the qualities of another by contrast. **3** Archit. a leaf-shaped curve formed by the cusping of an arch or circle. [ME f. OF f. L folium leaf, and f. OF foille f. L folia (pl.)]

foil[3] /fɔɪl/ n. a light blunt-edged sword with a button on its point used in fencing. □□ **foilist** n. [16th c.: orig. unkn.]

foil[4] /fɔɪl/ n. = HYDROFOIL. [abbr.]

foist /fɔɪst/ v.tr. (foll. by off) on, (off) upon) **1** present (a thing) falsely as genuine or superior. **2** falsely fix the ownership of. **3** (foll. by in, into) introduce surreptitiously or unwarrantably. [orig. of palming a false die, f. Du. dial. vuisten take in the hand f. vuist FIST]

Fokine /ˈfəʊkiːn/, Mikhail Mikhailovich (in the West he called himself Michel) (1880–1942), Russian dancer and choreographer. Though an excellent, expressive, and technically strong dancer, he was more important as one of the great ballet reformers, striving for a greater dramatic, stylistic, and directional unity. From 1909, as Diaghilev's chief choreographer, he produced such works as *Firebird* (music by Stravinsky, 1910), *Petrushka* (1911), *Daphnis and Chloë* (1912), and *The Golden Cockerel* (1914). He never returned to Russia after 1918, settling in New York in 1923. His *œuvre* comprises over 60 titles, but few of his later ballets compare with his earlier work.

Fokker /ˈfɒkə(r)/, Anthony Herman Gerard (1890–1939), Dutch pioneer aircraft designer and pilot. He built his first aircraft in 1908, the monoplane Eindecker, a type used by Germany as a fighter aircraft in the First World War, and designed the successful Trimotor F-7 airliners (1925), later versions of which provided the backbone of continental airlines in the 1930s.

fol. *abbr.* folio.

folacin /ˈfəʊləsɪn/ *n.* = FOLIC ACID. [*folic acid* + -IN]

fold[1] /fəʊld/ *v. & n.* —*v.* **1** *tr.* **a** bend or close (a flexible thing) over upon itself. **b** (foll. by *back, over, down*) bend a part of (a flexible thing) in the manner specified (*fold down the flap*). **2** *intr.* become or be able to be folded. **3** *tr.* (foll. by *away, up*) make compact by folding. **4** *intr.* (often foll. by *up*) *colloq.* **a** collapse, disintegrate. **b** (of an enterprise) fail; go bankrupt. **5** *tr. poet.* embrace (esp. *fold in the arms* or *to the breast*). **6** *tr.* (foll. by *about, round*) clasp (the arms); wrap, envelop. **7** *tr.* (foll. by *in*) mix (an ingredient with others) using a gentle cutting and turning motion. —*n.* **1** the act or an instance of folding. **2** a line made by or for folding. **3** a folded part. **4** a hollow among hills. **5** *Geol.* a curvature of strata. □ **fold one's arms** place one's arms across the chest, side by side or entwined. **fold one's hands** clasp them. **folding door** a door with jointed sections, folding on itself when opened. **folding money** esp. *US colloq.* banknotes. **fold-out** an oversize page in a book etc. to be unfolded by the reader. □□ **foldable** *adj.* [OE *falden, fealden* f. Gmc]

fold[2] /fəʊld/ *n. & v.* —*n.* **1** = SHEEPFOLD. **2** a body of believers or members of a Church. —*v.tr.* enclose (sheep) in a fold. [OE *fald*]

-fold /fəʊld/ *suffix* forming adjectives and adverbs from cardinal numbers, meaning: **1** in an amount multiplied by (*repaid tenfold*). **2** consisting of so many parts (*threefold blessing*). [OE *-fald, -feald*, rel. to FOLD[1]: orig. sense 'folded in so many layers']

foldaway /ˈfəʊldəweɪ/ *adj.* adapted or designed to be folded away.

folder /ˈfəʊldə(r)/ *n.* **1** a folding cover or holder for loose papers. **2** a folded leaflet.

folderol var. of FALDERAL.

foliaceous /ˌfəʊlɪˈeɪʃəs/ *adj.* **1** of or like leaves. **2** having organs like leaves. **3** laminated. [L *foliaceus* leafy f. *folium* leaf]

foliage /ˈfəʊlɪɪdʒ/ *n.* **1** leaves, leafage. **2** a design in art resembling leaves. □ **foliage leaf** a leaf excluding petals and other modified leaves. [ME f. F *feuillage* f. *feuille* leaf f. OF *foille*: see FOIL[2]]

foliar /ˈfəʊlɪə(r)/ *adj.* of or relating to leaves. □ **foliar feed** feed supplied to leaves of plants. [mod.L *foliaris* f. L *folium* leaf]

foliate *adj. & v.* —*adj.* /ˈfəʊlɪət/ **1** leaflike. **2** having leaves. **3** (in *comb.*) having a specified number of leaflets (*trifoliate*). —*v.* /ˈfəʊlɪeɪt/ **1** *intr.* split into laminae. **2** *tr.* decorate (an arch or door-head) with foils. **3** *tr.* number leaves (not pages) of (a volume) consecutively. □□ **foliation** /-ˈeɪʃ(ə)n/ *n.* [L *foliatus* leaved f. *folium* leaf]

folic acid /ˈfəʊlɪk/ *n.* a vitamin of the B complex, found in leafy green vegetables, liver, and kidney, a deficiency of which causes pernicious anaemia. Also called FOLACIN or PTEROYLGLUTAMIC ACID. [L *folium* leaf (because found esp. in green leaves) + -IC]

Folies-Bergère /ˌfɒlibeəˈʒeə(r)/ a variety theatre in Paris, opened in 1869. In an age of decorum its reputation was for lavish productions and pleasurable impropriety.

folio /ˈfəʊlɪəʊ/ *n. & adj.* —*n.* (*pl.* -os) **1** a leaf of paper etc., esp. one numbered only on the front. **2** a leaf-number of a book. **3** a sheet of paper folded once making two leaves of a book. **4** a book made of such sheets. —*adj.* (of a book) made of folios, of

the largest size. □ **in folio** made of folios. [L, ablat. of *folium* leaf, = *on leaf* (as specified)]

foliole /ˈfəʊlɪˌəʊl/ *n.* a division of a compound leaf; a leaflet. [F f. LL *foliolum* dimin. of L *folium* leaf]

foliot /ˈfəʊlɪət, ˈfɒ-/ *n.* a type of clock escapement consisting of a bar with adjustable weights on the ends [OF, = watch-spring, perh. f. *folier* play the fool, dance about]

folk /fəʊk/ *n.* (*pl.* **folk** or **folks**) **1** (treated as *pl.*) people in general or of a specified class (*few folk about; townsfolk*). **2** (in *pl.*) (usu. **folks**) one's parents or relatives. **3** (treated as *sing.*) a people. **4** (treated as *sing.*) *colloq.* traditional music. **5** (*attrib.*) of popular origin; traditional (*folk art*). □ **folk-dance 1** a dance of popular origin. **2** the music for such a dance. **folk etymology** a popular modifying of the form of a word or phrase to make it seem to be derived from a more familiar word (e.g. *forlorn hope*). **folk memory** recollection of the past persisting among a people. **folk-singer** a singer of folk-songs. **folk-song** a song of popular or traditional origin or style. **folk-tale** a popular or traditional story. **folk-ways** the traditional behaviour of a people. [OE *folc* f. Gmc]

Folkestone /ˈfəʊkst(ə)n/ a seaport and resort in Kent, on the SE coast of England; pop. (1981) 43,998. The English terminal of the Channel Tunnel is at Cheriton, near Folkestone.

folkish /ˈfəʊkɪʃ/ *adj.* of the common people; traditional, unsophisticated.

folklore /ˈfəʊklɔː(r)/ *n.* the traditional beliefs and stories of a people; the study of these. □□ **folkloric** *adj.* **folklorist** *n.* **folkloristic** /-ˈrɪstɪk/ *adj.*

folksy /ˈfəʊksɪ/ *adj.* (**folksier, folksiest**) **1** friendly, sociable, informal. **2 a** having the characteristics of folk art, culture, etc. **b** ostensibly or artificially folkish. □□ **folksiness** *n.*

folkweave /ˈfəʊkwiːv/ *n.* a rough loosely woven fabric.

folky /ˈfəʊkɪ/ *adj.* (**folkier, folkiest**) **1** = FOLKSY **2**. **2** = FOLKISH. □□ **folkiness** *n.*

follicle /ˈfɒlɪk(ə)l/ *n.* **1** a small sac or vesicle. **2** a small sac-shaped secretory gland or cavity. **3** *Bot.* a single-carpelled dry fruit opening on one side only to release its seeds. □□ **follicular** /fɒˈlɪkjʊlə(r)/ *adj.* **folliculate** /fɒˈlɪkjʊlət/ *adj.* **folliculated** /fɒˈlɪkjʊˌleɪtɪd/ *adj.* [L *folliculus* dimin. of *follis* bellows]

follow /ˈfɒləʊ/ *v.* **1** *tr.* or (foll. by *after*) intr. go or come after (a person or thing proceeding ahead). **2** *tr.* go along (a route, path, etc.). **3** *tr. & intr.* come after in order or time (*Nero followed Claudius; dessert followed; my reasons are as follows*). **4** *tr.* take as a guide or leader. **5** *tr.* conform to (*follow your example*). **6** *tr.* practise (a trade or profession). **7** *tr.* undertake (a course of study etc.). **8** *tr.* understand the meaning or tendency of (a speaker or argument). **9** *tr.* maintain awareness of the current state or progress of (events etc. in a particular sphere). **10** *tr.* (foll. by *with*) provide with a sequel or successor. **11** *intr.* happen after something else; ensue. **12** *intr.* **a** be necessarily true as a result of something else. **b** (foll. by *from*) be a result of. **13** *tr.* strive after; aim at; pursue (*followed fame and fortune*). □ **follow-my-leader** a game in which players must do as the leader does. **follow one's nose** trust to instinct. **follow on 1** continue. **2** (of a cricket team) have to bat again immediately after the first innings. **follow-on** *n.* an instance of this. **follow out** carry out; adhere precisely to (instructions etc.). **follow suit 1** *Cards* play a card of the suit led. **2** conform to another person's actions. **follow through 1** continue (an action etc.) to its conclusion. **2** *Sport* continue the movement of a stroke after the ball has been struck. **follow-through** *n.* the action of following through. **follow up** (foll. by *with*) **1** pursue, develop, supplement. **2** make further investigation of. **follow-up** *n.* a subsequent or continued action, measure, experience, etc. [OE *folgian* f. Gmc]

follower /ˈfɒləʊə(r)/ *n.* **1** an adherent or devotee. **2** a person or thing that follows.

following /ˈfɒləʊɪŋ/ *prep., n., & adj.* —*prep.* coming after in time; as a sequel to. —*n.* a body of adherents or devotees. —*adj.* that follows or comes after.

folly /ˈfɒlɪ/ *n.* (*pl.* -ies) **1** foolishness; lack of good sense. **2** a foolish act, behaviour, idea, etc. **3** an ornamental building, usu. a tower or mock Gothic ruin. **4** (in *pl.*) *Theatr.* **a** a revue with glamorous female performers, esp. scantily-clad. **b** the performers. [ME f. OF *folie* f. *fol* mad, FOOL¹]

Folsom /'fəʊlsəm/ the name of a village in NE New Mexico in the US, applied to the remains of a prehistoric industry first found there, and especially to a distinctive type of fluted lanceolate projectile point or spearhead, flaked from stone, found at the site in association with the bones of an extinct bison. These points have now been found throughout much of central North America but are commonest in eastern Colorado and New Mexico. The industry dates from *c.*11,000–10,000 to *c.*8000 BP. It is generally thought that the development of the Folsom industry reflects a change in prehistoric economy from the hunting of mammoth, prevalent during the preceding period, to the hunting of bison. The impact of the initial Folsom site discovery in 1926 cannot be underestimated, for before 1926 it was held that man entered the New World no earlier than 3,000–4,000 years ago. The direct association of the Folsom point with an extinct late Pleistocene bison clearly demonstrated man's presence at an early date and forced a radical rethinking of the date of man's discovery and population of the New World. It is now known that man was in the New World long, perhaps 20,000 years, before the blossoming of the Folsom 'culture'. (See CLOVIS.)

foment /fə'ment, fəʊ-/ *v.tr.* **1** instigate or stir up (trouble, sedition, etc.). **2 a** bathe with warm or medicated liquid. **b** apply warmth to. □□ **fomenter** *n.* [ME f. F *fomenter* f. LL *fomentare* f. L *fomentum* poultice, lotion f. *fovēre* heat, cherish]

fomentation /ˌfəʊmen'teɪʃ(ə)n/ *n.* **1** the act or an instance of fomenting. **2** materials prepared for application to a wound etc. [ME f. OF or LL *fomentatio* (as FOMENT)]

fond /fɒnd/ *adj.* **1** (foll. by *of*) having affection or a liking for. **2** affectionate, loving, doting. **3** (of beliefs etc.) foolishly optimistic or credulous; naïve. □□ **fondly** *adv.* **fondness** *n.* [ME f. obs. *fon* fool, be foolish]

Fonda /'fɒndə/, Henry (1905–82), American film actor and director, noted for his roles as a man of conscience, resisting ignorance and prejudice, as in *The Grapes of Wrath* (1939) and *Twelve Angry Men* (1957), or as the hero of westerns such as *My Darling Clementine* (1946). His daughter Jane (1937–) was a model and stage actress before becoming a screen star; her films include *Cat Ballou* (1965) and *Klute* (1971). His son Peter (1939–) is noted especially for his performance in the film *Easy Rider* (1969), which he also produced.

fondant /'fɒnd(ə)nt/ *n.* a soft sweet of flavoured sugar. [F, pres. part. of *fondre* melt f. L *fundere* pour]

fondle /'fɒnd(ə)l/ *v.tr.* touch or stroke lovingly; caress. □□ **fondler** *n.* [back-form. f. *fondling* fondled person (as FOND, -LING¹)]

fondue /'fɒndju:, -du:/ *n.* a dish of flavoured melted cheese. [F, fem. past part. of *fondre* melt f. L *fundere* pour]

font¹ /fɒnt/ *n.* **1** a receptacle in a church for baptismal water. **2** the reservoir for oil in a lamp. □□ **fontal** *adj.* (in sense 1). [OE *font, fant* f. OIr. *fant, font* f. L *fons fontis* fountain, baptismal water]

font² var. of FOUNT².

fontanel US var. of FONTANELLE.

fontanelle /ˌfɒntə'nel/ *n.* (US **fontanel**) a membranous space in an infant's skull at the angles of the parietal bones. [F *fontanelle* f. mod.L *fontanella* f. OF *fontenelle* dimin. of *fontaine* fountain]

Fonteyn /fɒn'teɪn/, Dame Margot (1919–91), real name Margaret Hookham, British dancer. With her beautiful physique, exquisite line, innate musicality, and refined artistry, she was one of the greatest 20th-c. ballerinas. She created her first major role in Ashton's *Le Baiser de la fée* (1935), later dancing all the ballerina roles of the standard classics and creating many others. Her partnership with Nureyev revivified her career. In 1955 she married Roberto Arias, a Panamanian politician who was later paralysed in an assassination attempt.

Foochow see FUZHOU.

food /fu:d/ *n.* **1** a nutritious substance, esp. solid in form, that can be taken into an animal or a plant to maintain life and growth. **2** ideas as a resource for or stimulus to mental work (*food for thought*). □ **food additive** a substance added to food to enhance its colour, flavour, or presentation, or for any other non-nutritional purpose. **food-chain** *Ecol.* a series of organisms each dependent on the next for food. **food-gatherer** a member of a people at a primitive stage of civilization obtaining food from natural sources not through agriculture. **food-gathering** this practice. **food poisoning** illness due to bacteria or other toxins in food. **food processor** a machine for chopping and mixing food materials. **food value** the relative nourishing power of a food. [OE *fōda* f. Gmc: cf. FEED]

Food and Agriculture Organization, an agency of the United Nations, established in 1945 to secure improvements in the production and distribution of all food and agricultural products and to raise levels of nutrition. Its headquarters are in Rome.

foodie /'fu:dɪ/ *n.* (also **foody**) (*pl.* **-ies**) *colloq.* a person who is particular about food; a gourmet.

foodstuff /'fu:dstʌf/ *n.* any substance suitable as food.

fool¹ /fu:l/ *n.,* *v.,* & *adj.* —*n.* **1** a person who acts unwisely or imprudently; a stupid person. **2** *hist.* a jester; a clown. **3** a dupe. —*v.* **1** *tr.* deceive so as to cause to appear foolish. **2** *tr.* (foll. by *into* + verbal noun, *or out of*) trick; cause to do something foolish. **3** *tr.* play tricks on; dupe. **4** *intr.* act in a joking, frivolous, or teasing way. **5** *intr.* (foll. by *about, around*) behave in a playful or silly way. —*adj.* US *colloq.* foolish, silly. □ **act** (or **play**) **the fool** behave in a silly way. **fool's errand** a fruitless venture. **fool's gold** iron pyrites. **fool's paradise** happiness founded on an illusion. **fool's parsley** a species of hemlock resembling parsley. **make a fool of** make (a person or oneself) look foolish; trick or deceive. **no** (or **nobody's**) **fool** a shrewd or prudent person. [ME f. OF *fol* f. L *follis* bellows, empty-headed person]

fool² /fu:l/ *n.* a dessert of usu. stewed fruit crushed and mixed with cream, custard, etc. [16th c.: perh. f. FOOL¹]

foolery /'fu:lərɪ/ *n.* (*pl.* **-ies**) **1** foolish behaviour. **2** a foolish act.

foolhardy /'fu:lˌhɑ:dɪ/ *adj.* (**foolhardier**, **foolhardiest**) rashly or foolishly bold; reckless. □□ **foolhardily** *adv.* **foolhardiness** *n.* [ME f. OF *folhardi* f. *fol* foolish + *hardi* bold]

foolish /'fu:lɪʃ/ *adj.* (of a person, action, etc.) lacking good sense or judgement; unwise. □□ **foolishly** *adv.* **foolishness** *n.*

foolproof /'fu:lpru:f/ *adj.* (of a procedure, mechanism, etc.) so straightforward or simple as to be incapable of misuse or mistake.

foolscap /'fu:lskæp/ *n. Brit.* a size of paper, about 330 × 200 (or 400) mm. [named from the former watermark representing a fool's cap (jester's cap with bells)]

foot /fʊt/ *n.* & *v.* —*n.* (*pl.* **feet** /fi:t/) **1 a** the lower extremity of the leg below the ankle. **b** the part of a sock etc. covering the foot. **2 a** the lower or lowest part of anything, e.g. a mountain, a page, stairs, etc. **b** the lower end of a table. **c** the end of a bed where the user's feet normally rest. **3** the base, often projecting, of anything extending vertically. **4** a step, pace, or tread; a manner of walking (*fleet of foot*). **5** (*pl.* **feet** or **foot**) a unit of linear measure equal to 12 inches (30.48 cm). **6** *Prosody* **a** a group of syllables (one usu. stressed) constituting a metrical unit. **b** a similar unit of speech etc. **7** *Brit. hist.* infantry (*a regiment of foot*). **8** *Zool.* the locomotive or adhesive organ of invertebrates. **9** *Bot.* the part by which a petal is attached. **10** a device on a sewing-machine for holding the material steady as it is sewn. **11** (*pl.* **foots**) **a** dregs; oil refuse. **b** coarse sugar. —*v.tr.* **1** (usu. as **foot it**) **a** traverse (esp. a long distance) by foot. **b** dance. **2** pay (a bill, esp. one considered large). □ **at a person's feet** as a person's disciple or subject. **feet of clay** a fundamental weakness in a person otherwise revered. **foot-and-mouth disease** a contagious viral disease of cattle etc. **foot-fault** (in lawn tennis) incorrect placement of the feet while serving. **foot-pound** the amount of energy required to raise 1 lb. a distance of 1 foot. **foot-pound-second system** a system of measurement with these as basic units. **foot-rot** a bacterial disease of the feet in sheep and cattle. **foot-rule** a ruler 1 foot long. **foot-soldier** a soldier who fights on foot. **get one's feet wet** begin to participate. **have one's** (or **both**) **feet on the ground** be practical. **have a foot in the door** have a prospect of success. **have one foot in the grave** be near death or very old. **my foot!** int. expressing strong contradiction. **not put a foot wrong** make no mistakes. **off one's feet** so as to be unable to stand, or in a state compared with this (was rushed off my feet). **on foot** walking, not riding etc. **put one's best foot forward** make every effort; proceed with determination. **put one's feet up** colloq. take a rest. **put one's foot down** colloq. **1** be firmly insistent or repressive. **2** accelerate a motor vehicle. **put one's foot in it** colloq. commit a blunder or indiscretion. **set foot on** (or **in**) enter; go into. **set on foot** put (an action, process, etc.) in motion. **under one's feet** in the way. **under foot** on the ground. □□ **footed** adj. (also in comb.). **footless** adj. [OE fōt f. Gmc]

footage /ˈfʊtɪdʒ/ n. **1** length or distance in feet. **2** an amount of film made for showing, broadcasting, etc.

football /ˈfʊtbɔːl/ n. & v. —n. **1** any of several outdoor games between two teams played with a ball on a pitch with goals at each end, esp. = Association Football. (See below.) **2** a large inflated ball of a kind used in these. **3** a topical issue or problem that is the subject of continued argument or controversy. —v.intr. play football. □ **football pool** (or **pools**) a form of gambling on the results of football matches, the winners receiving sums accumulated from entry money. □□ **footballer** n.

There is a strong and natural inclination to kick at a rounded object and propel it. Interpretations of the significance of the procedure involving two teams, a ball, and a goal, have varied: one traces its origin to fertility rites in ancient Egypt, another regards it as a symbolic hunt. A form of football was played at an early date in China (c.300 BC) and in ancient Greece and Rome; the ball was handled as well as kicked. In medieval England it was a rowdy game, played in the streets, and attempts were made to ban it; in Tudor times it caused 'fighting, brawling . . . murder, and great effusion of blood'; in 1624 James I banned it by Act of Parliament because it interfered with the practice of archery, which was of practical use in warfare, but still it persisted, with no rules except those agreed locally and no limit on the number of participants. By the 19th c. forms of football were played regularly in the public schools, but it was not until the middle of the century that the establishment of common rules made it possible to hold matches between different schools, clubs, and (eventually) countries. (See also AMERICAN FOOTBALL, RUGBY FOOTBALL.)

footboard /ˈfʊtbɔːd/ n. **1** a board to support the feet or a foot. **2** an upright board at the foot of a bed.

footbrake /ˈfʊtbreɪk/ n. a brake operated by the foot in a motor vehicle.

footbridge /ˈfʊtbrɪdʒ/ n. a bridge for use by pedestrians.

footer[1] /ˈfʊtə(r)/ n. (in comb.) a person or thing of so many feet in length or height (six-footer).

footer[2] /ˈfʊtə(r)/ n. Brit. colloq. = FOOTBALL 1.

footfall /ˈfʊtfɔːl/ n. the sound of a footstep.

foothill /ˈfʊthɪl/ n. (often in pl.) any of the low hills around the base of a mountain.

foothold /ˈfʊthəʊld/ n. **1** a place, esp. in climbing, where a foot can be supported securely. **2** a secure initial position or advantage.

footing /ˈfʊtɪŋ/ n. **1** a foothold; a secure position (lost his footing). **2** the basis on which an enterprise is established or operates; the position or status of a person in relation to others (on an equal footing). **3** the foundations of a wall, usu. with a course of brickwork wider than the base of the wall.

footle /ˈfuːt(ə)l/ v.intr. (usu. foll. by about) colloq. behave foolishly or trivially. [19th c.: perh. f. dial. footer idle]

footlights /ˈfʊtlaɪts/ n.pl. a row of lights along the front of a stage at the level of the actors' feet.

footling /ˈfuːtlɪŋ/ adj. colloq. trivial, silly.

footloose /ˈfʊtluːs/ adj. free to go where or act as one pleases.

footman /ˈfʊtmən/ n. (pl. **-men**) **1** a liveried servant attending at the door, at table, or on a carriage. **2** hist. an infantryman.

footmark /ˈfʊtmɑːk/ n. a footprint.

footnote /ˈfʊtnəʊt/ n. & v. —n. a note printed at the foot of a page. —v.tr. supply with a footnote or footnotes.

footpad /ˈfʊtpæd/ n. hist. an unmounted highwayman.

footpath /ˈfʊtpɑːθ/ n. a path for pedestrians; a pavement.

footplate /ˈfʊtpleɪt/ n. esp. Brit. the platform in the cab of a locomotive for the crew.

footprint /ˈfʊtprɪnt/ n. **1** the impression left by a foot or shoe. **2** Computing the area of desk space etc. occupied by a microcomputer or other piece of hardware.

footrest /ˈfʊtrest/ n. a support for the feet or a foot.

Footsie /ˈfʊtsɪ/ n. (also **Footsie index** or **footsie**) Stock Exch. colloq. the Financial Times–Stock Exchange 100 share index, an index based on the share values of Britain's hundred largest public companies, set up in 1984. [repr. pronunc. of FT-SE (abbr.)]

footsie /ˈfʊtsɪ/ n. colloq. amorous play with the feet. [joc. dimin. of FOOT]

footslog /ˈfʊtslɒɡ/ v. & n. —v.intr. (**-slogged**, **-slogging**) walk or march, esp. laboriously for a long distance. —n. a laborious walk or march. □□ **footslogger** n.

footsore /ˈfʊtsɔː(r)/ adj. having sore feet, esp. from walking.

footstalk /ˈfʊtstɔːk/ n. **1** Bot. a stalk of a leaf or peduncle of a flower. **2** Zool. an attachment of a barnacle etc.

footstep /ˈfʊtstep/ n. **1** a step taken in walking. **2** the sound of this. □ **follow** (or **tread**) **in a person's footsteps** do as another person did before.

footstool /ˈfʊtstuːl/ n. a stool for resting the feet on when sitting.

footway /ˈfʊtweɪ/ n. a path or way for pedestrians.

footwear /ˈfʊtweə(r)/ n. shoes, socks, etc.

footwork /ˈfʊtwɜːk/ n. the use of the feet, esp. skilfully, in sports, dancing, etc.

fop /fɒp/ n. an affectedly elegant or fashionable man; a dandy. □□ **foppery** n. **foppish** adj. **foppishly** adv. **foppishness** n. [17th c.: perh. f. earlier fop fool]

for /fə, fɔː(r)/ prep. & conj. —prep. **1** in the interest or to the benefit of; intended to go to (these flowers are for you; wish to see it for myself; did it all for my country; silly for you to go). **2** in defence, support, or favour of (fight for one's rights). **3** suitable or appropriate to (a dance for beginners; not for me to say). **4** in respect of or with reference to; regarding; so far as concerns (usual for ties to be worn; don't care for him at all; ready for bed; MP for Lincoln). **5** representing or in place of (here for my uncle). **6** in exchange against (swopped it for a bigger one). **7 a** as the price of (give me £5 for it). **b** at the price of (bought it for £5). **c** to the amount of (a bill for £100; all out for 45). **8** as the penalty of (fined them heavily for it). **9** in requital of (that's for upsetting my sister). **10** as a reward for (here's £5 for your trouble). **11 a** with a view to; in the hope or quest of; in order to get (go for a walk; run for a doctor; did it for the money). **b** on account of (could not speak for laughing). **12** corresponding to (word for word). **13** to reach; in the direction of; towards (left for Rome; ran for the end of the road). **14** conducive or conducively to; in order to achieve (take the pills for a sound night's sleep). **15** so as to start promptly at (the meeting is at seven-thirty for eight). **16** through or over (a distance or period); during (walked for miles; sang for two hours). **17** in the character of; as being (for the last time; know it for a lie; I for one refuse). **18** because of; on account of (could not see for tears). **19** in spite of; notwithstanding (for all we know; for all your fine words). **20** considering or making due allowance in respect of (good for a beginner). **21** in order to be (gone for a soldier). —conj. because, since, seeing that. □ **be for it** Brit. colloq. be in imminent danger of punishment or other trouble. **for ever** see EVER; (cf. FOREVER). **o** (or **oh**) **for** I wish I had. [OE, prob. a reduction of Gmc fora (unrecorded) BEFORE (of place and time)]

for- /fɔː, fə/ prefix forming verbs and their derivatives meaning: **1** away, off, apart (forget; forgive). **2** prohibition (forbid). **3** abstention or neglect (forgo; forsake). **4** excess or intensity (forlorn). [OE for-, fær-]

f.o.r. abbr. free on rail.

forage /ˈfɒrɪdʒ/ n. & v. —n. **1** food for horses and cattle. **2** the act or an instance of searching for food. —v. **1** intr. go searching; rummage (esp. for food). **2** tr. collect food from; ravage. **3** tr. **a**

get by foraging. **b** supply with food. □ **forage cap** an infantry undress cap. □□ **forager** n. [ME f. OF fourrage, fourrager, rel. to FODDER]

foramen /fɒˈreɪmen/ n. (pl. **foramina** /-ˈræmɪnə/) Anat. an opening, hole, or passage, esp. in a bone. □□ **foraminate** /-ˈræmɪnət/ adj. [L foramen -minis f. forare bore a hole]

foraminifer /ˌfɒrəˈmɪnɪfə(r)/ n. (also **foraminiferan** /-ˈnɪfərən/) any protozoan of the order Foraminifera, having a perforated shell through which amoeba-like pseudopodia emerge. □□ **foraminiferous** /-ˈnɪfərəs/ adj.

foraminiferan var. of FORAMINIFER.

forasmuch as /ˌfɒrəzˈmʌtʃ/ conj. archaic because, since. [= for as much]

foray /ˈfɒreɪ/ n. & v. —n. a sudden attack; a raid or incursion. —v.intr. make or go on a foray. [ME, prob. earlier as verb: back-form. f. forayer f. OF forrier forager, rel. to FODDER]

forbade (also **forbad**) past of FORBID.

forbear[1] /fɔːˈbeə(r)/ v.intr. & tr. (past **forbore** /-ˈbɔː(r)/; past part. **forborne** /-ˈbɔːn/) (often foll. by from, or to + infin.) literary abstain or desist (from) (could not forbear (from) speaking out; forbore to mention it). [OE forberan (as FOR-, BEAR[1])]

forbear[2] var. of FOREBEAR.

forbearance /fɔːˈbeərəns/ n. patient self-control; tolerance.

forbid /fəˈbɪd/ v.tr. (**forbidding**; past **forbade** /-ˈbæd, -ˈbeɪd/ or **forbad** /-ˈbæd/; past part. **forbidden** /-ˈbɪd(ə)n/) **1** (foll. by to + infin.) order not (I forbid you to go). **2** refuse to allow (a thing, or a person to have a thing) (I forbid it; was forbidden any wine). **3** refuse a person entry to (the gardens are forbidden to children). □ **Forbidden City** a name applied to Lhasa (see entry) and Peking, to the central part of which foreigners are still not freely admitted. **forbidden degrees** see DEGREE. **forbidden fruit** something desired or enjoyed all the more because not allowed. **God forbid!** may it not happen! [OE forbēodan (as FOR-, BID)]

forbidding /fəˈbɪdɪŋ/ adj. uninviting, repellent, stern. □□ **forbiddingly** adv.

forbore past of FORBEAR[1].

forborne past part. of FORBEAR[1].

forbye /fɔːˈbaɪ/ prep. & adv. archaic or Sc. —prep. besides. —adv. in addition.

force[1] /fɔːs/ n. & v. —n. **1** power; exerted strength or impetus; intense effort. **2** coercion or compulsion, esp. with the use or threat of violence. **3 a** military strength. **b** (in pl.) troops; fighting resources. **c** an organized body of people, esp. soldiers, police, or workers. **4** binding power; validity. **5** effect; precise significance (the force of their words). **6 a** mental or moral strength; influence, efficacy (force of habit). **b** vividness of effect (described with much force). **7** Physics **a** an influence tending to cause the motion of a body. (See below.) **b** the intensity of this equal to the mass of the body and its acceleration. **8** a person or thing regarded as exerting influence (is a force for good). —v. **1** tr. constrain (a person) by force or against his or her will. **2** tr. make a way through or into by force; break open by force. **3** tr. (usu. with prep. or adv.) drive or propel violently or against resistance (forced it into the hole; the wind forced them back). **4** tr. (foll. by on, upon) impose or press (on a person) (forced their views on us). **5** tr. **a** cause or produce by effort (forced a smile). **b** attain by strength or effort (forced an entry; must force a decision). **6** tr. strain or increase to the utmost; overstrain. **7** tr. artificially hasten the development or maturity of (a plant). **8** tr. seek or demand quick results from; accelerate the process of (force the pace). **9** intr. Cards make a play that compels another particular play. □ **by force of** by means of. **force the bidding** (at an auction) make bids to raise the price rapidly. **forced labour** compulsory labour, esp. under harsh conditions. **forced landing** the unavoidable landing of an aircraft in an emergency. **forced march** a long and vigorous march esp. by troops. **force-feed** force (esp. a prisoner) to take food. **force field** (in science fiction) an invisible barrier of force. **force a person's hand** make a person act prematurely or unwillingly. **force the issue** render an immediate decision necessary. **force-land** land an aircraft in an emergency. **force-pump** a pump that forces water under pressure. **in force 1** valid, effective. **2** in great

strength or numbers. **join forces** combine efforts. □□ **forceable** adj. **forceably** adv. **forcer** n. [ME f. OF force, forcer ult. f. L fortis strong]

Force in physics is that which causes a mass to undergo acceleration or deformation, or the quantity 'mass times acceleration' itself. In a static entity such as a building opposing forces may be equally balanced so that there is no net acceleration, but some deformation of the material will still occur. Force was first described mathematically by Newton in his laws of motion, and the present-day standard unit of force, the newton, is named after him. Newton's first law, the principle of inertia, states that a moving body will naturally tend to maintain its present motion for ever in a straight line. A force is not, therefore, as earlier thinkers had supposed, necessary for maintaining motion itself; its effect is rather to cause a body to tend to accelerate (or decelerate). This is the substance of Newton's second law of motion, that force equals mass times acceleration. In the everyday world, impacts of bodies, tensions in wires, and air and water pressures, all constitute forces. Physicists, however, consider that such phenomena are ultimately dependent on four fundamental forces that govern the interaction between all particles of matter: the strong nuclear force which binds protons and neutrons to one another in the atomic nucleus; the weak nuclear force responsible for some radioactive phenomena; the electromagnetic force acting between charged particles; and the gravitational force.

force[2] /fɔːs/ n. N.Engl. a waterfall. [ON fors]

forceful /ˈfɔːsfʊl/ adj. **1** vigorous, powerful. **2** (of speech) compelling, impressive. □□ **forcefully** adv. **forcefulness** n.

force majeure /ˌfɔːs mæˈʒɜː(r)/ n. **1** irresistible compulsion or coercion. **2** an unforeseeable course of events excusing a person from the fulfilment of a contract. [F, = superior strength]

forcemeat /ˈfɔːsmiːt/ n. meat etc. chopped and seasoned for use as a stuffing or a garnish. [obs. force, farce stuff f. OF farsir: see FARCE]

forceps /ˈfɔːseps/ n. (pl. same) **1** surgical pincers, used for grasping and holding. **2** Bot. & Zool. an organ or structure resembling forceps. □□ **forcipate** /-sɪpət/ adj. [L forceps forcipis]

forcible /ˈfɔːsɪb(ə)l/ adj. done by or involving force; forceful. □□ **forcibleness** n. **forcibly** adv. [ME f. AF & OF (as FORCE[1])]

Ford[1] /fɔːd/, Ford Madox (formerly Ford Hermann Hueffer 1873–1939), English novelist, grandson of the Pre-Raphaelite painter Ford Madox Brown. He collaborated with Conrad on The Inheritors (1901) and Romance (1903). His own major works were the novel The Good Soldier (1915) and the tetralogy Parade's End (1924–8), a remarkable record in fiction of the change and disruption caused by the First World War. As founder of the English Review (1908) and the Paris-based Translantic Review (1924) he published works by the most prominent authors of his day (e.g. Hemingway, Joyce, Pound, and Wells), exerting an important influence on the course of 20th-c. literature.

Ford[2] /fɔːd/, Gerald Rudolph (1913–), 38th President of the US 1974–7, who became President on the resignation of Richard Nixon (see entry).

Ford[3] /fɔːd/, Henry (1863–1947), American pioneer of mass-production for motor vehicles, who had a profound influence on their widespread use by making them available so cheaply. He was brought up on a farm but was more interested in mechanical matters. By 1903 he had evolved a reliable car and founded his own firm, making several different models. In 1909 Ford produced his famous Model T of which 15 million were made over the next 19 years at gradually reducing prices that were due to large-scale manufacture of a standard model, to a succession of simple tasks performed by unskilled or semi-skilled labour, and to the use of a conveyor belt for assembly. Ford went on to produce in 1917 a cheap and effective farm tractor, the Fordson, which had a great effect on agricultural mechanization. It can fairly be said that Henry Ford was a philanthropist, for his aim was to provide cheap transport and cheap food for the millions, while with his profits he endowed the Ford Foundation, a major charitable trust.

ford /fɔːd/ n. & v. —n. a shallow place where a river or stream may be crossed by wading or in a vehicle. —*v.tr.* cross (water) at a ford. □□ **fordable** *adj.* **fordless** *adj.* [OE f. WG]

fore /fɔː(r)/ *adj., n., int.,* & *prep.* —*adj.* situated in front. —*n.* the front part, esp. of a ship; the bow. —*int.* *Golf* a warning to a person in the path of a ball. —*prep.* *archaic* (in oaths) in the presence of (*fore God*). □ **come to the fore** take a leading part. **fore and aft** at bow and stern; all over the ship. **fore-and-aft** *adj.* (of a sail or rigging) set lengthwise, not on the yards. **to the fore** in front; conspicuous. [OE f. Gmc.: (adj. & n.) ME f. compounds with FORE-]

fore- /fɔː(r)/ *prefix* forming: **1** verbs meaning: **a** in front (*foreshorten*). **b** beforehand; in advance (*foreordain; forewarn*). **2** nouns meaning: **a** situated in front of (*forecourt*). **b** the front part of (*forehead*). **c** of or near the bow of a ship (*forecastle*). **d** preceding (*forerunner*).

forearm[1] /ˈfɔːrɑːm/ *n.* **1** the part of the arm from the elbow to the wrist or the fingertips. **2** the corresponding part in a foreleg or wing.

forearm[2] /fɔːrˈɑːm/ *v.tr.* prepare or arm beforehand.

forebear /ˈfɔːbeə(r)/ *n.* (also **forbear**) (usu. in *pl.*) an ancestor. [FORE + obs. *bear, beer* (as BE, -ER[1])]

forebode /fɔːˈbəʊd/ *v.tr.* **1** betoken; be an advance warning of (an evil or unwelcome event). **2** have a presentiment of (usu. evil).

foreboding /fɔːˈbəʊdɪŋ/ *n.* an expectation of trouble or evil; a presage or omen. □□ **forebodingly** *adv.*

forecast /ˈfɔːkɑːst/ *v.* & *n.* —*v.tr.* (*past* and *past part.* -**cast** or -**casted**) predict; estimate or calculate beforehand. —*n.* a calculation or estimate of something future, esp. coming weather. □□ **forecaster** *n.*

forecastle /ˈfəʊks(ə)l/ *n.* (also **fo'c's'le**) *Naut.* **1** the forward part of a ship where the crew has quarters. **2** *hist.* a short raised deck at the bow.

foreclose /fɔːˈkləʊz/ *v.tr.* **1** (also *absol.*; foll. by *on*) stop (a mortgage) from being redeemable or (a mortgager) from redeeming, esp. as a result of defaults in payment. **2** exclude; prevent. **3** shut out; bar. □□ **foreclosure** *n.* [ME f. OF *forclos* past part. of *forclore* f. *for-* out f. L *foras* + CLOSE[2]]

forecourt /ˈfɔːkɔːt/ *n.* **1** an enclosed space in front of a building. **2** the part of a filling-station where petrol is supplied. **3** (in lawn tennis) the part of a tennis-court between the service line and the net.

foredoom /fɔːˈduːm/ *v.tr.* (often foll. by *to*) doom or condemn beforehand.

fore-edge /ˈfɔːredʒ/ *n.* (also **foredge**) the front or outer edge (esp. of the pages of a book).

forefather /ˈfɔːfɑːðə(r)/ *n.* (usu. in *pl.*) **1** an ancestor. **2** a member of a past generation of a family or people.

forefinger /ˈfɔːfɪŋɡə(r)/ *n.* the finger next to the thumb.

forefoot /ˈfɔːfʊt/ *n.* (*pl.* -**feet**) **1** either of the front feet of a four-footed animal. **2** *Naut.* the foremost section of a ship's keel.

forefront /ˈfɔːfrʌnt/ *n.* **1** the foremost part. **2** the leading position.

foregather var. of FORGATHER.

forego[1] /fɔːˈɡəʊ/ *v.tr.* & *intr.* (-**goes**; *past* -**went** /-ˈwent/; *past part.* -**gone** /-ˈɡɒn/) precede in place or time. □□ **foregoer** *n.* [OE *foregān*]

forego[2] var. of FORGO.

foregoing /fɔːˈɡəʊɪŋ, ˈfɔː-/ *adj.* preceding; previously mentioned.

foregone /fɔːˈɡɒn/ *past part.* of FOREGO[1]. —*attrib.adj.* /ˈfɔːɡɒn/ previous, preceding, completed. □ **foregone conclusion** an easily foreseen or predictable result.

foreground /ˈfɔːɡraʊnd/ *n.* **1** the part of a view, esp. in a picture, that is nearest the observer. **2** the most conspicuous position. [Du. *voorgrond* (as FORE-, GROUND[1])]

forehand /ˈfɔːhænd/ *n.* **1** *Tennis* etc. **a** a stroke played with the palm of the hand facing the opponent. **b** (*attrib.*) (also **forehanded**) of or made with a forehand. **2** the part of a horse in front of the seated rider.

forehead /ˈfɒrɪd, ˈfɔːhed/ *n.* the part of the face above the eyebrows. [OE *forhēafod* (as FORE-, HEAD)]

forehock /ˈfɔːhɒk/ *n.* a foreleg cut of pork or bacon.

foreign /ˈfɒrɪn, ˈfɒrən/ *adj.* **1** of or from or situated in or characteristic of a country or a language other than one's own. **2** dealing with other countries (*foreign service*). **3** of another district, society, etc. **4** (often foll. by *to*) unfamiliar, strange, uncharacteristic (*his behaviour is foreign to me*). **5** coming from outside (*a foreign body lodged in my eye*). □ **foreign aid** money, food, etc. given or lent by one country to another. **Foreign and Commonwealth Office** the UK government department dealing with foreign affairs. **foreign exchange 1** the currency of other countries. **2** dealings in these. **foreign legion** a body of foreign volunteers in an army (esp. the French army). (See separate entry.) **foreign minister** (or **secretary**) a government minister in charge of his or her country's relations with other countries. **foreign office** a government department dealing with other countries. □□ **foreignness** *n.* [ME f. OF *forein, forain* ult. f. L *foras, -is* outside for -g- cf. *sovereign*]

foreigner /ˈfɒrɪnə(r), ˈfɒrənə(r)/ *n.* **1** a person born in or coming from a foreign country or place. **2** *dial.* a non-native of a place. **3 a** a foreign ship. **b** an imported animal or article.

Foreign Legion a military formation of foreign volunteers was founded in the 1830s to fight France's colonial wars and composed, except for the higher ranks, of non-Frenchmen. Most of the Legion's most famous campaigns were in French North Africa in the late 19th and early 20th c., although it also fought in both World Wars, in various 19th-c. colonial wars, and most recently in the unsuccessful French resistance to the Vietnamese and Algerian independence movements. Although its original purpose has been lost, the Legion is still in existence, in greatly reduced form.

forejudge /fɔːˈdʒʌdʒ/ *v.tr.* judge or determine before knowing the evidence.

foreknow /fɔːˈnəʊ/ *v.tr.* (*past* -**knew** /-ˈnjuː/; *past part.* -**known** /-ˈnəʊn/) know beforehand; have prescience of. □□ **foreknowledge** /fɔːˈnɒlɪdʒ/ *n.*

forelady /ˈfɔːleɪdɪ/ *n.* (*pl.* -**ies**) *US* = FOREWOMAN.

foreland /ˈfɔːlænd/ *n.* **1** a cape or promontory. **2** a piece of land in front of something.

foreleg /ˈfɔːleɡ/ *n.* each of the front legs of a quadruped.

forelimb /ˈfɔːlɪm/ *n.* any of the front limbs of an animal.

forelock /ˈfɔːlɒk/ *n.* a lock of hair growing just above the forehead. □ **take time by the forelock** seize an opportunity.

foreman /ˈfɔːmən/ *n.* (*pl.* -**men**) **1** a worker with supervisory responsibilities. **2** the member of a jury who presides over its deliberations and speaks on its behalf.

foremast /ˈfɔːmɑːst, -məst/ *n.* the forward (lower) mast of a ship.

foremost /ˈfɔːməʊst/ *adj.* & *adv.* —*adj.* **1** the chief or most notable. **2** the most advanced in position; the front. —*adv.* before anything else in position; in the first place (*first and foremost*). [earlier *formost, formest*, superl. of OE *forma* first, assim. to FORE, MOST]

forename /ˈfɔːneɪm/ *n.* a first or Christian name.

forenoon /ˈfɔːnuːn/ *n.* *Naut.* or *Law* or *archaic* the part of the day before noon.

forensic /fəˈrensɪk/ *adj.* of or used in connection with courts of law (*forensic science*). □ **forensic medicine** the application of medical knowledge to legal problems. □□ **forensically** *adv.* [L *forensis* f. FORUM]

foreordain /ˌfɔːrɔːˈdeɪn/ *v.tr.* predestinate; ordain beforehand. □□ **foreordination** /-dɪˈneɪʃ(ə)n/ *n.*

forepaw /ˈfɔːpɔː/ *n.* either of the front paws of a quadruped.

forepeak /ˈfɔːpiːk/ *n.* *Naut.* the end of the forehold in the angle of the bows.

foreplay /ˈfɔːpleɪ/ *n.* stimulation preceding sexual intercourse.

forerun /fɔːˈrʌn/ *v.tr.* (-**running**; *past* -**ran** /-ˈræn/; *past part.* -**run**) **1** go before. **2** indicate the coming of; foreshadow.

forerunner /ˈfɔːˌrʌnə(r)/ *n.* **1** a predecessor. **2** an advance messenger.

foresail /ˈfɔːseɪl, -s(ə)l/ *n.* *Naut.* the principal sail on a foremast (the lowest square sail, or the fore-and-aft bent on the mast, or the triangular before the mast).

foresee /fɔː'siː/ v.tr. (past **-saw** /-'sɔː/; past part. **-seen** /-'siːn/) (often foll. by that + clause) see or be aware of beforehand. □□ **foreseeable** adj. **foreseeability** /-'bɪlɪtɪ/ n. **foreseer** /-'siːə(r)/ n. [OE foresēon (as FORE- + SEE[1])]

foreshadow /fɔː'ʃædəʊ/ v.tr. be a warning or indication of (a future event).

foresheets /'fɔːʃiːts/ n.pl. Naut. the inner part of the bows of a boat with gratings for the bowman to stand on.

foreshore /'fɔːʃɔː(r)/ n. the part of the shore between high- and low-water marks, or between the water and cultivated or developed land.

foreshorten /fɔː'ʃɔːt(ə)n/ v.tr. show or portray (an object) with the apparent shortening due to visual perspective.

foreshow /fɔː'ʃəʊ/ v.tr. (past part. **-shown** /-'ʃəʊn/) 1 foretell. 2 foreshadow, portend, prefigure.

foresight /'fɔːsaɪt/ n. 1 regard or provision for the future. 2 the process of foreseeing. 3 the front sight of a gun. 4 Surveying a sight taken forwards. □□ **foresighted** /-'saɪtɪd/ adj. **foresightedly** /-'saɪtɪdlɪ/ adv. **foresightedness** /-'saɪtɪdnɪs/ n. [ME, prob. after ON forsjá, forsjó (as FORE-, SIGHT)]

foreskin /'fɔːskɪn/ n. the fold of skin covering the end of the penis. Also called PREPUCE.

forest /'fɒrɪst/ n. & v. —n. 1 a (often attrib.) a large area covered chiefly with trees and undergrowth. b the trees growing in it. c a large number or dense mass of vertical objects (a forest of masts). 2 a district formerly a forest but now cultivated (Sherwood Forest). 3 hist. an area usu. owned by the sovereign and kept for hunting. —v.tr. 1 plant with trees. 2 convert into a forest. □ **forest-tree** a large tree suitable for a forest. [ME f. OF f. LL forestis silva wood outside the walls of a park f. L foris outside]

forestall /fɔː'stɔːl/ v.tr. 1 act in advance of in order to prevent. 2 anticipate (the action of another, or an event). 3 anticipate the action of. 4 deal with beforehand. 5 hist. buy up (goods) in order to profit by an enhanced price. □□ **forestaller** n. **forestalment** n. [ME in sense 5: cf. AL forestallare f. OE foresteall an ambush (as FORE-, STALL)]

forestay /'fɔːsteɪ/ n. Naut. a stay from the head of the foremast to the ship's deck to support the foremast.

Forester /'fɒrɪstə(r)/, Cecil Scott (pseudonym of Cecil Lewis Troughton Smith, 1899–1966), English author, remembered for his seafaring novels set during the Napoleonic Wars and featuring Horatio Hornblower. His other works include The African Queen (1935).

forester /'fɒrɪstə(r)/ n. 1 a person in charge of a forest or skilled in forestry. 2 a person or animal living in a forest. 3 (**Forester**) a member of the Ancient Order of Foresters (a friendly society). [ME f. OF forestier (as FOREST)]

forestry /'fɒrɪstrɪ/ n. 1 the science or management of forests. 2 wooded country; forests.

foretaste n. & v. —n. /'fɔːteɪst/ partial enjoyment or suffering in advance; anticipation. —v.tr. /fɔː'teɪst/ taste beforehand; anticipate the experience of.

foretell /fɔː'tel/ v.tr. (past and past part. **-told** /-'təʊld/) 1 tell of (an event etc.) before it takes place; predict, prophesy. 2 presage; be a precursor of. □□ **foreteller** n.

forethought /'fɔːθɔːt/ n. 1 care or provision for the future. 2 previous thinking or devising. 3 deliberate intention.

foretoken n. & v. —n. /'fɔːtəʊkən/ a sign of something to come. —v.tr. /fɔː'təʊkən/ portend; indicate beforehand. [OE foretācn (as FORE-, TOKEN)]

foretold past and past part. of FORETELL.

foretop /'fɔːtɒp/ n. Naut. a platform at the top of a foremast (see TOP[1] n. 9). □ **foretop-gallant mast** the mast above the fore-topmast. **foretop-gallant-sail** the sail above the fore-topsail.

fore-topmast /fɔː'tɒpmɑːst/ n. Naut. the mast above the foremast.

fore-topsail /fɔː'tɒpseɪl, -s(ə)l/ n. Naut. the sail above the foresail.

forever /fə'revə(r)/ adv. continually, persistently (is forever complaining) (cf. for ever).

forevermore /fə,revə'mɔː(r)/ adv. esp. US an emphatic form of FOREVER or for ever (see EVER).

forewarn /fɔː'wɔːn/ v.tr. warn beforehand. □□ **forewarner** n.

forewent past of FOREGO[1], FOREGO[2].

forewoman /'fɔː,wʊmən/ n. (pl. **-women**) 1 a female worker with supervisory responsibilities. 2 a woman who presides over a jury's deliberations and speaks on its behalf.

foreword /'fɔːwɜːd/ n. introductory remarks at the beginning of a book, often by a person other than the author. [FORE- + WORD after G Vorwort]

foreyard /'fɔːjɑːd/ n. Naut. the lowest yard on a foremast.

forfeit /'fɔːfɪt/ n., adj., & v. —n. 1 a penalty for a breach of contract or neglect; a fine. 2 a a trivial fine for a breach of rules in clubs etc. or in games. b (in pl.) a game in which forfeits are exacted. 3 something surrendered as a penalty. 4 the process of forfeiting. 5 Law property or a right or privilege lost as a legal penalty. —adj. lost or surrendered as a penalty. —v.tr. (**forfeited, forfeiting**) lose the right to, be deprived of, or have to pay as a penalty. □□ **forfeitable** adj. **forfeiter** n. **forfeiture** n. [ME (= crime) f. OF forfet, forfait past part. of forfaire transgress (f. L foris outside) + faire f. L facere do]

forfend /fɔː'fend/ v.tr. 1 US protect by precautions. 2 archaic avert; keep off.

forgather /fɔː'gæðə(r)/ v.intr. (also **foregather**) assemble; meet together; associate. [16th-c. Sc. f. Du. vergaderen, assim. to FOR-, GATHER]

forgave past of FORGIVE.

forge[1] /fɔːdʒ/ v. & n. —v.tr. 1 a make (money etc.) in fraudulent imitation. b write (a document or signature) in order to pass it off as written by another. 2 fabricate, invent. 3 shape (esp. metal) by heating in a fire and hammering. —n. 1 a blacksmith's workshop; a smithy. 2 a a furnace or hearth for melting or refining metal. b a workshop containing this. □□ **forgeable** adj. **forger** n. [ME f. OF forge (n.), forger (v.) f. L fabricare FABRICATE]

forge[2] /fɔːdʒ/ v.intr. move forward gradually or steadily. □ **forge ahead** 1 take the lead in a race. 2 move forward or make progress rapidly. [18th c.: perh. an aberrant pronunc. of FORCE[1]]

forgery /'fɔːdʒərɪ/ n. (pl. **-ies**) 1 the act or an instance of forging, counterfeiting, or falsifying a document etc. 2 a forged or spurious thing, esp. a document or signature.

forget /fə'get/ v. (**forgetting**; past **forgot** /-'gɒt/; past part. **forgotten** /-'gɒt(ə)n/ or esp. US **forgot**) 1 tr. & (often foll. by about) intr. lose the remembrance of; not remember (a person or thing). 2 tr. (foll. by clause or to + infin.) not remember; neglect (forgot to come; forgot how to do it). 3 tr. inadvertently omit to bring or mention or attend to. 4 tr. (also absol.) put out of mind; cease to think of (forgive and forget). □ **forget-me-not** any plant of the genus Myosotis, esp. M. alpestris with small yellow-eyed bright blue flowers. **forget oneself** 1 neglect one's own interests. 2 act unbecomingly or unworthily. □□ **forgettable** adj. **forgetter** n. [OE forgietan f. WG (as FOR-, GET)]

forgetful /fə'getful/ adj. 1 apt to forget, absent-minded. 2 (often foll. by of) forgetting, neglectful. □□ **forgetfully** adv. **forgetfulness** n.

forgive /fə'gɪv/ v.tr. (also absol. or with double object) (past **forgave**; past part. **forgiven**) 1 cease to feel angry or resentful towards; pardon (an offender or offence) (forgive us our mistakes). 2 remit or let off (a debt or debtor). □□ **forgivable** adj. **forgivably** adv. **forgiver** n. [OE forgiefan (as FOR-, GIVE)]

forgiveness /fə'gɪvnɪs/ n. the act of forgiving; the state of being forgiven. [OE forgiefenes (as FORGIVE)]

forgiving /fə'gɪvɪŋ/ adj. inclined readily to forgive. □□ **forgivingly** adv.

forgo /fɔː'gəʊ/ v.tr. (also **forego**) (**-goes**; past **-went** /-'went/; past part. **-gone** /-'gɒn/) 1 abstain from; go without; relinquish. 2 omit or decline to take or use (a pleasure, advantage, etc.). [OE forgān (as FOR-, GO[1])]

forgot past of FORGET.

forgotten past part. of FORGET.

forint /ˈfɒrɪnt/ n. the chief monetary unit of Hungary. [Magyar f. It. *fiorino*: see FLORIN]

fork /fɔːk/ n. & v. —n. **1** an instrument with two or more prongs used in eating or cooking. **2** a similar much larger instrument used for digging, lifting, etc. **3** any pronged device or component (*tuning-fork*). **4** a forked support for a bicycle wheel. **5 a** a divergence of anything, e.g. a stick or road, or *US* a river, into two parts. **b** the place where this occurs. **c** either of the two parts (*take the left fork*). **6** a flash of forked lightning. **7** *Chess* a simultaneous attack on two pieces by one. —v. **1** *intr.* form a fork or branch by separating into two parts. **2** *intr.* take one or other road etc. at a fork (*fork left for Banbury*). **3** *tr.* dig or lift etc. with a fork. **4** *tr. Chess* attack (two pieces) simultaneously with one. □ **fork-lift truck** a vehicle with a horizontal fork in front for lifting and carrying loads. **fork lunch** (or **supper** etc.) a light meal eaten with a fork at a buffet etc. **fork out** (or **up**) *sl.* hand over or pay, usu. reluctantly. [OE *forca*, *force* f. L *furca*]

forked /fɔːkt/ adj. **1** having a fork or forklike end or branches. **2** divergent, cleft. **3** (in *comb.*) having so many prongs (*three-forked*). □ **forked lightning** a lightning-flash in the form of a zigzag or branching line.

forlorn /fəˈlɔːn/ adj. **1** sad and abandoned or lonely. **2** in a pitiful state; of wretched appearance. **3** desperate, hopeless, forsaken. □ **forlorn hope 1** a faint remaining hope or chance. **2** a desperate enterprise. □□ **forlornly** adv. **forlornness** n. [past part. of obs. *forlese* f. OE *forlēosan* (as FOR-, LOSE): forlorn hope f. Du. *verloren hoop* lost troop, orig. of a storming-party etc.]

form /fɔːm/ n. & v. —n. **1 a** a shape; an arrangement of parts. **b** the outward aspect (esp. apart from colour) or shape of a body. **2** a person or animal as visible or tangible (*the familiar form of the postman*). **3** the mode in which a thing exists or manifests itself (*took the form of a book*). **4** a species, kind, or variety. **5 a** a printed document with blank spaces for information to be inserted. **b** a regularly drawn document. **6** esp. *Brit.* a class in a school. **7** a customary method; what is usually done (*common form*). **8** a set order of words; a formula. **9** behaviour according to a rule or custom. **10** (prec. by *the*) correct procedure (*knows the form*). **11 a** (of an athlete, horse, etc.) condition of health and training (*is in top form*). **b** *Racing* details of previous performances. **12** general state or disposition (*was in great form*). **13** *sl.* a criminal record. **14** formality or mere ceremony. **15** *Gram.* **a** one of the ways in which a word may be spelt or pronounced or inflected. **b** the external characteristics of words apart from meaning. **16** arrangement and style in literary or musical composition. **17** *Philos.* the essential nature of a species or thing. **18** a long bench without a back. **19** esp. *US Printing* = FORME. **20** a hare's lair. **21** = FORMWORK. —v. **1** *tr.* make or fashion into a certain shape or form. **2** *intr.* take a certain shape; be formed. **3** *tr.* be the material of; make up or constitute (*together form a unit; forms part of the structure*). **4** *tr.* train or instruct. **5** *tr.* develop or establish as a concept, institution, or practice (*form an idea; formed an alliance; form a habit*). **6** *tr.* (foll. by *into*) embody, organize. **7** *tr.* articulate (a word). **8** *tr. & intr.* (often foll. by *up*) esp. *Mil.* bring or be brought into a certain arrangement or formation. **9** *tr.* construct (a new word) by derivation, inflection, etc. □ **bad form** an offence against current social conventions. **form class** *Linguistics* a class of linguistic forms with grammatical or syntactical features in common. **form criticism** textual analysis of the Bible etc. by tracing the history of its content by forms (e.g. proverbs, myths). **form letter** a standardized letter to deal with frequently occurring matters. **good form** what complies with current social conventions. **in form** fit for racing etc. **off form** not playing or performing well. **on form** playing or performing well. **out of form** not fit for racing etc. [ME f. OF *forme* f. L *forma* mould, form]

-form /fɔːm/ comb. form (usu. as **-iform**) forming adjectives meaning: **1** having the form of (*cruciform; cuneiform*). **2** having such a number of (*uniform; multiform*). [from or after F *-forme* f. L *-formis* f. *forma* FORM]

formal /ˈfɔːm(ə)l/ adj. & n. —adj. **1** used or done or held in accordance with rules, convention, or ceremony (*formal dress; a formal occasion*). **2** ceremonial; required by convention (*a formal call*). **3** precise or symmetrical (*a formal garden*). **4** prim or stiff in manner. **5** perfunctory, having the form without the spirit. **6** valid or correctly so called because of its form; explicit and definite (*a formal agreement*). **7** in accordance with recognized forms or rules. **8** of or concerned with (outward) form or appearance, esp. as distinct from content or matter. **9** *Logic* concerned with the form and not the matter of reasoning. **10** *Philos.* of the essence of a thing; essential not material. —n. *US* **1** evening dress. **2** an occasion on which evening dress is worn. □□ **formally** adv. **formalness** n. [ME f. L *formalis* (as FORM)]

formaldehyde /fɔːˈmældɪˌhaɪd/ n. a colourless pungent gas used as a disinfectant and preservative and in the manufacture of synthetic resins. ¶ Chem. formula: CH_2O. Also called METHANAL. [FORMIC (ACID) + ALDEHYDE]

formalin /ˈfɔːməlɪn/ n. a colourless solution of formaldehyde in water used as a preservative for biological specimens etc.

formalism /ˈfɔːməˌlɪz(ə)m/ n. **1 a** excessive adherence to prescribed forms. **b** the use of forms without regard to inner significance. **2** *derog.* an artist's concentration on form at the expense of content. **3** the treatment of mathematics as a manipulation of meaningless symbols. **4** *Theatr.* a symbolic and stylized manner of production. **5** *Physics & Math.* the mathematical description of a physical situation etc. □□ **formalist** n. **formalistic** /-ˈlɪstɪk/ adj.

formality /fɔːˈmælɪtɪ/ n. (pl. **-ies**) **1 a** a formal or ceremonial act, requirement of etiquette, regulation, or custom (often with an implied lack of real significance). **b** a thing done simply to comply with a rule. **2** the rigid observance of rules or convention. **3** ceremony; elaborate procedure. **4** being formal; precision of manners. **5** stiffness of design. [F *formalité* or med.L *formalitas* (as FORMAL)]

formalize /ˈfɔːməlaɪz/ v.tr. (also **-ise**) **1** give definite shape or legal formality to. **2** make ceremonious, precise, or rigid; imbue with formalism. □□ **formalization** /-ˈzeɪʃ(ə)n/ n.

formant /ˈfɔːmənt/ n. **1** the characteristic pitch-constituent of a vowel. **2** a morpheme occurring only in combination in a word or word-stem. [G f. L *formare formant-* to form]

format /ˈfɔːmæt/ n. & v. —n. **1** the shape and size of a book, periodical, etc. **2** the style or manner of an arrangement or procedure. **3** *Computing* a defined structure for holding data etc. in a record for processing or storage. —v.tr. (**formatted**, **formatting**) **1** arrange or put into a format. **2** *Computing* prepare (a storage medium) to receive data. [F f. G f. L *formatus* (*liber*) shaped (book), past part. of *formare* FORM]

formate see FORMIC ACID.

formation /fɔːˈmeɪʃ(ə)n/ n. **1** the act or an instance of forming; the process of being formed. **2** a thing formed. **3** a structure or arrangement of parts. **4** a particular arrangement, e.g. of troops, aircraft in flight, etc. **5** *Geol.* an assemblage of rocks or series of strata having some common characteristic. □□ **formational** adj. [ME f. OF *formation* or L *formatio* (as FORM)]

formative /ˈfɔːmətɪv/ adj. & n. —adj. **1** serving to form or fashion; of formation. **2** *Gram.* (of a flexional or derivative suffix or prefix) used in forming words. —n. *Gram.* a formative element. □□ **formatively** adv. [ME f. OF *formatif -ive* or med.L *formativus* (as FORM)]

forme /fɔːm/ n. (*US* **form**: see FORM n. 19) *Printing* **1** a body of type secured in a chase for printing at one impression. **2** a quantity of film arranged for making a plate etc. [var. of FORM]

former¹ /ˈfɔːmə(r)/ attrib.adj. **1** of or occurring in the past or an earlier period (*in former times*). **2** having been previously (*her former husband*). **3** (prec. by *the*; often *absol.*) the first or first mentioned of two (opp. LATTER). [ME f. *forme* first, after FOREMOST]

former² /ˈfɔːmə(r)/ n. **1** a person or thing that forms. **2** *Electr.* a frame or core for winding a coil on. **3** *Aeron.* a transverse strengthening member in a wing or fuselage. **4** (in *comb.*) a pupil of a specified form in a school (*fourth-former*).

formerly /ˈfɔːməlɪ/ adv. in the past; in former times.

Formica /fɔːˈmaɪkə/ n. propr. a hard durable plastic laminate used for working surfaces, cupboard doors, etc. [20th c.: orig. uncert.]

formic acid /ˈfɔːmɪk/ n. a colourless irritant volatile acid

aʊ how eɪ day əʊ no eə hair ɪə near ɔɪ boy ʊə poor aɪə fire aʊə sour (see over for consonants)

(HCOOH) contained in the fluid emitted by some ants. Also called METHANOIC ACID. □□ **formate** /-meɪt/ n. [L formica ant]

formication /ˌfɔːmɪˈkeɪʃ(ə)n/ n. a sensation as of ants crawling over the skin. [L formicatio f. formica ant]

formidable /ˈfɔːmɪdəb(ə)l, disp. fɔːˈmɪd-/ adj. **1** inspiring fear or dread. **2** inspiring respect or awe. **3** likely to be hard to overcome, resist, or deal with. □□ **formidableness** n. **formidably** adv. [F formidable or L formidabilis f. formidare fear]

formless /ˈfɔːmlɪs/ adj. shapeless; without determinate or regular form. □□ **formlessly** adv. **formlessness** n.

Formosa /fɔːˈməʊsə/ the former name (from Portuguese formosa the beautiful) of Taiwan.

formula /ˈfɔːmjʊlə/ n. (pl. **formulas** or (esp. in senses 1, 2) **formulae** /-ˌliː/) **1** Chem. a set of chemical symbols showing the constituents of a substance and their relative proportions. **2** Math. a mathematical rule expressed in symbols. **3 a** a fixed form of words, esp. one used on social or ceremonial occasions. **b** a rule unintelligently or slavishly followed; an established or conventional usage. **c** a form of words embodying or enabling agreement, resolution of a dispute, etc. **4 a** a list of ingredients; a recipe. **b** US an infant's food made up from a recipe. **5** a classification of racing car, esp. by the engine capacity. □□ **formulaic** /-ˈleɪɪk/ adj. **formularize** v.tr. (also **-ise**). **formulize** v.tr. (also **-ise**). [L, dimin. of forma form]

formulary /ˈfɔːmjʊlərɪ/ n. & adj. —n. (pl. **-ies**) **1** a collection of formulas or set forms, esp. for religious use. **2** Pharm. a compendium of formulae used in the preparation of medicinal drugs. —adj. **1** using formulae. **2** in or of formulae. [(n.) F formulaire or f. med.L formularius (liber book) f. L (as FORMULA): (adj.) f. FORMULA]

formulate /ˈfɔːmjʊˌleɪt/ v.tr. **1** express in a formula. **2** express clearly and precisely. □□ **formulation** /-ˈleɪʃ(ə)n/ n.

formulism /ˈfɔːmjʊˌlɪz(ə)m/ n. adherence to or dependence on conventional formulas. □□ **formulist** n. **formulistic** /-ˈlɪstɪk/ adj.

formwork /ˈfɔːmwɜːk/ n. = SHUTTERING 1.

fornicate /ˈfɔːnɪˌkeɪt/ v.intr. archaic or joc. (of people not married or not married to each other) have sexual intercourse voluntarily. □□ **fornication** /-ˈkeɪʃ(ə)n/ n. **fornicator** n. [eccl.L fornicari f. L fornix -icis brothel]

forrader /ˈfɒrədə(r)/ colloq. compar. of FORWARD.

Forrest /ˈfɒrɪst/, Sir John (1847–1918), Australian explorer and statesman, one of the principal explorers of Western Australia. He did much to secure the colony's self-government and became its first Premier and Colonial Treasurer (1890–1901).

forsake /fəˈseɪk, fɔː-/ v.tr. (past **forsook** /-ˈsʊk/; past part. **forsaken** /-ˈseɪkən/) **1** give up; break off from; renounce. **2** withdraw one's help, friendship, or companionship from; desert, abandon. □□ **forsakenness** n. **forsaker** n. [OE forsacan deny, renounce, refuse, f. WG; cf. OE sacan quarrel]

forsooth /fəˈsuːθ, fɔː-/ adv. archaic or joc. truly; in truth; no doubt. [OE forsōth (as FOR, SOOTH)]

Forster /ˈfɔːstə(r)/, Edward Morgan (1879–1970), English novelist, a master of social comedy, sometimes with pagan supernatural elements, contrasting British (and Christian) inhibition and philistinism with passionate Mediterranean culture and, in his last novel A Passage to India (1924), with Hindu religious sensibility. A homosexual, Forster felt conventional narrow-mindedness acutely. Maurice (finished in 1914) and some other homosexual stories appeared posthumously. Forster exerted, through essays and journalism, a humane civilizing influence.

forswear /fɔːˈsweə(r)/ v.tr. (past **forswore** /-ˈswɔː(r)/; past part. **forsworn** /-ˈswɔːn/) **1** abjure; renounce on oath. **2** (as **forsworn** adj.) perjured. □ **forswear oneself** swear falsely; perjure oneself. [OE forswerian (as FOR-, SWEAR)]

Forsyth /fɔːˈsaɪθ/, Frederick (1938–), English author of political documentary thrillers, including The Day of the Jackal (1971), The Odessa File (1972), and The Fourth Protocol (1984), written with great narrative power and a wealth of circumstantial detail.

forsythia /fɔːˈsaɪθɪə/ n. any ornamental shrub of the genus Forsythia bearing bright-yellow flowers in early spring. [mod.L f. W. Forsyth, Engl. botanist d. 1804]

fort /fɔːt/ n. **1** a fortified building or position. **2** hist. a trading-station, orig. fortified. [F fort or It. forte f. L fortis strong]

Fort-de-France /ˌfɔːdəˈfrɑːs/ the capital of Martinique; pop. (1982) 99,800.

forte[1] /ˈfɔːteɪ/ n. **1** a person's strong point; a thing in which a person excels. **2** Fencing the part of a sword-blade from the hilt to the middle (cf. FOIBLE 2). [F fort strong f. L fortis]

forte[2] /ˈfɔːtɪ/ adj., adv., & n. Mus. —adj. performed loudly. —adv. loudly. —n. a passage to be performed loudly. □ **forte piano** adj. & adv. loud and then immediately soft. [It., = strong, loud]

fortepiano /ˌfɔːtɪˈpiːænəʊ/ n. (pl. **-os**) Mus. = PIANOFORTE esp. with ref. to an instrument of the 18th to early 19th c. [FORTE[2] + PIANO[2]]

Forth /fɔːθ/ a river of SE Scotland, rising on Ben Lomond and flowing into the North Sea. □ **Firth of Forth** its estuary, separating Fife from the Lothians. It is spanned by a railway bridge (1890) and a road bridge (1964).

forth /fɔːθ/ adv. archaic except in set phrases and after certain verbs, esp. bring, come, go, and set **1** forward; into view. **2** onwards in time (from this time forth; henceforth). **3** forwards. **4** out from a starting-point (set forth). □ **and so forth** and so on; and the like. [OE f. Gmc]

forthcoming /fɔːθˈkʌmɪŋ, attrib. ˈfɔːθ-/ adj. **1 a** about or likely to appear or become available. **b** approaching. **2** produced when wanted (no reply was forthcoming). **3** (of a person) informative, responsive. □□ **forthcomingness** n.

forthright adj. & adv. —adj. /ˈfɔːθraɪt/ **1** direct and outspoken; straightforward. **2** decisive, unhesitating. —adv. /fɔːθˈraɪt/ in a direct manner; bluntly. □□ **forthrightly** adv. **forthrightness** n. [OE forthriht (as FORTH, RIGHT)]

forthwith /fɔːθˈwɪθ, -ˈwɪð/ adv. immediately; without delay. [earlier forthwithal (as FORTH, WITH, ALL)]

fortification /ˌfɔːtɪfɪˈkeɪʃ(ə)n/ n. **1** the act or an instance of fortifying; the process of being fortified. **2** Mil. **a** the art or science of fortifying. **b** (usu. in pl.) defensive works fortifying a position. [ME f. F f. LL fortificatio -onis act of strengthening (as FORTIFY)]

fortify /ˈfɔːtɪˌfaɪ/ v.tr. (**-ies, -ied**) **1** provide or equip with defensive works so as to strengthen against attack. **2** strengthen or invigorate mentally or morally; encourage. **3** strengthen the structure of. **4** strengthen (wine) with alcohol. **5** increase the nutritive value of (food, esp. with vitamins). □□ **fortifiable** adj. **fortifier** n. [ME f. OF fortifier f. LL fortificare f. L fortis strong]

fortissimo /fɔːˈtɪsɪˌməʊ/ adj., adv., & n. Mus. —adj. performed very loudly. —adv. very loudly. —n. (pl. **-os** or **fortissimi** /-ˌmiː/) a passage to be performed very loudly. [It., superl. of FORTE[2]]

fortitude /ˈfɔːtɪˌtjuːd/ n. courage in pain or adversity. [ME f. F f. L fortitudo -dinis f. fortis strong]

Fort Knox /nɒks/ a US military reservation in Kentucky, famous as the site of the US Depository (built in 1936) which holds the bulk of the nation's gold bullion in its vaults.

Fort Lamy /læˈmiː/ the former name (until 1973) of N'Djamena.

fortnight /ˈfɔːtnaɪt/ n. **1** a period of two weeks. **2** (prec. by a specified day) two weeks after (that day) (Tuesday fortnight). [OE fēowertiene niht fourteen nights]

fortnightly /ˈfɔːtˌnaɪtlɪ/ adj., adv., & n. —adj. done, produced, or occurring once a fortnight. —adv. every fortnight. —n. (pl. **-ies**) a magazine etc. issued every fortnight.

Fortran /ˈfɔːtræn/ n. (also **FORTRAN**) Computing a high-level programming language used esp. for scientific calculations. [formula translation]

fortress /ˈfɔːtrɪs/ n. a military stronghold, esp. a strongly fortified town fit for a large garrison. [ME f. OF forteresse, ult. f. L fortis strong]

fortuitous /fɔːˈtjuːɪtəs/ adj. due to or characterized by chance; accidental, casual. □□ **fortuitously** adv. **fortuitousness** n. [L fortuitus f. forte by chance]

fortuity /fɔːˈtjuːɪtɪ/ n. (pl. **-ies**) **1** a chance occurrence. **2** accident or chance; fortuitousness.

fortunate /ˈfɔːtjʊnət, -tʃənət/ adj. **1** favoured by fortune; lucky, prosperous. **2** auspicious, favourable. [ME f. L fortunatus (as FORTUNE)]

fortunately /ˈfɔːtjʊnətlɪ, -tʃənətlɪ/ adv. **1** luckily, successfully. **2** (qualifying a whole sentence) it is fortunate that.

fortune /ˈfɔːtjuːn, -tʃuːn/ n. **1 a** chance or luck as a force in human affairs. **b** a person's destiny. **2** (**Fortune**) this force personified, often as a deity. **3** (in sing. or pl.) luck (esp. favourable) that befalls a person or enterprise. **4** good luck. **5** prosperity; a prosperous condition. **6** (also colloq. **small fortune**) great wealth; a huge sum of money. □ **fortune-hunter** colloq. a person seeking wealth by marriage. **fortune-teller** a person who claims to predict future events in a person's life. **fortune-telling** the practice of this. **make a** (or **one's**) **fortune** acquire wealth or prosperity. **tell a person's fortune** make predictions about a person's future. [ME f. OF f. L fortuna luck, chance]

Fort Worth /wɜːθ/ an oil-refining city in northern Texas; pop. (1982) 401,400. Before oil was discovered (1919) the city was a meat-packing and cattle-shipping centre.

forty /ˈfɔːtɪ/ n. & adj. —n. (pl. **-ies**) **1** the product of four and ten. **2** a symbol for this (40, xl, XL). **3** (in pl.) the numbers from 40 to 49, esp. the years of a century or of a person's life. **4** (**the Forties**) Brit. the sea area between the NE coast of Scotland and the SW coast of Norway (so called from its depth of forty fathoms or more). —adj. that amount to forty. □ **forty-first**, **-second**, etc. the ordinal numbers between fortieth and fiftieth. **forty-five** a gramophone record played at 45 r.p.m. **the Forty-five** the Jacobite rebellion of 1745. **forty-niner** US a seeker for gold etc., esp. in the Californian gold-rush of 1849. **forty-one**, **-two**, etc. the cardinal numbers between forty and fifty. **forty winks** colloq. a short sleep. □□ **fortieth** adj. & n. **fortyfold** adj. & adv. [OE féowertig (as FOUR, -TY²)]

forum /ˈfɔːrəm/ n. **1** a place of or meeting for public discussion. **2** a periodical etc. giving an opportunity for discussion. **3** a court or tribunal. **4** hist. a public square or market-place in an ancient Roman city used for judicial and other business. [L, in sense 4]

forward /ˈfɔːwəd/ adj., n., adv., & v. —adj. **1** lying in one's line of motion. **2 a** onward or towards the front. **b** Naut. belonging to the fore part of a ship. **3** precocious; bold in manner; presumptuous. **4** Commerce relating to future produce, delivery, etc. (forward contract). **5 a** advanced; progressing towards or approaching maturity or completion. **b** (of a plant etc.) well advanced or early. —n. an attacking player positioned near the front of a team in football, hockey, etc. —adv. **1** to the front; into prominence (come forward; move forward). **2** in advance; ahead (sent them forward). **3** onward so as to make progress (not getting any further forward). **4** towards the future; continuously onwards (from this time forward). **5** (also **forwards**) **a** towards the front in the direction one is facing. **b** in the normal direction of motion or of traversal. **c** with continuous forward motion (backwards and forwards; rushing forward). **6** Naut. & Aeron. in, near, or towards the bow or nose. —v.tr. **1 a** send (a letter etc.) on to a further destination. **b** dispatch (goods etc.) (forwarding agent). **2** help to advance; promote. □ **forward-looking** progressive; favouring change. □□ **forwarder** n. **forwardly** adv. **forwardness** n. (esp. in sense 3 of adj.). [OE forweard, var. of forthweard (as FORTH, -WARD)]

forwards var. of FORWARD adv. 5.

forwent past of FORGO.

Fosbury /ˈfɒzbərɪ/, Richard (1947–), American high jumper, who originated the style of jumping that came to be known as the 'Fosbury flop'. In 1968 he won the Olympic gold medal with a height of 2.24 metres (7 ft. 4¼ in.), using his novel head-first face-upwards technique and landing on his back.

fossa /ˈfɒsə/ n. (pl. **fossae** /-siː/) Anat. a shallow depression or cavity. [L, = ditch, fem. past part. of fodere dig]

fosse /fɒs/ n. **1** a long narrow trench or excavation, esp. in a fortification. **2** Anat. = FOSSA. [ME f. OF f. L fossa: see FOSSA]

Fosse Way /fɒs/ an ancient road in Britain, so called from the fosse or ditch on each side. It probably ran from Axminster to Lincoln, via Bath and Leicester (about 300 km, 200 miles), and

marked the limit of the first stage of the Roman occupation (mid-1st c. AD).

fossick /ˈfɒsɪk/ v.intr. Austral. & NZ colloq. **1** (foll. by about, around) rummage, search. **2** search for gold etc. in abandoned workings. □□ **fossicker** n. [19th c.: cf. dial. fossick bustle about]

fossil /ˈfɒs(ə)l/ n. **1** the remains or impression of a (usu. prehistoric) plant or animal hardened in rock (often attrib.: fossil bones; fossil shells). (See below.) **2** colloq. an antiquated or unchanging person or thing. **3** a word that has become obsolete except in set phrases or forms, e.g. hue in hue and cry. —adj. **1** of or like a fossil. **2** antiquated; out of date. □ **fossil fuel** a natural fuel such as coal or gas formed in the geological past from the remains of living organisms. **fossil ivory** see IVORY. □□ **fossiliferous** /ˌfɒsɪˈlɪfərəs/ adj. **fossilize** v.tr. & intr. (also **-ise**). **fossilization** /-ˈzeɪʃ(ə)n/ n. [F fossile f. L fossilis f. fodere fossdig]

Fossils are usually the hard parts of organisms, the bones or shells, preserved as moulds or casts in rock. Rarely, the fossils of organisms such as jellyfish, which do not have a bony component, are preserved in fine-grained rocks such as shales. The study of fossils and the fossil record has provided much of the information upon which the present subdivisions of the geological time-scale are based.

fossorial /fɒˈsɔːrɪəl/ adj. **1** (of animals) burrowing. **2** (of limbs etc.) used in burrowing. [med.L fossorius f. fossor digger (as FOSSIL)]

Foster /ˈfɒstə(r)/, Stephen Collins (1826–64), American composer, who wrote more than 200 songs, several of which capture the Southern plantation spirit though he himself was a Northerner. Among the most famous are 'Oh! Susannah' (1848), 'Camptown Races' (1850), 'Old Folks at Home' (1851), 'My Old Kentucky Home' (1853), and 'Beautiful Dreamer' (1864).

foster /ˈfɒstə(r)/ v. & adj. —v.tr. **1 a** promote the growth or development of. **b** encourage or harbour (a feeling). **2** (of circumstances) be favourable to. **3 a** bring up (a child that is not one's own by birth). **b** Brit. (of a local authority etc.) assign (a child) to be fostered. **4** cherish; have affectionate regard for (an idea, scheme, etc.). —adj. **1** having a family connection by fostering and not by birth (foster-brother; foster-child; foster-parent). **2** involving or concerned with fostering a child (foster care; foster home). □□ **fosterage** n. (esp. in sense 3 of v.). **fosterer** n. [OE fóstrian, fóster, rel. to FOOD]

fosterling /ˈfɒstəlɪŋ/ n. a foster-child; a nursling or protégé. [OE fósterling (as FOSTER)]

Foucault /ˈfuːkəʊ/, Jean Bernard Léon (1819–68), French physicist, inventor of the gyroscope. He is chiefly remembered for the huge pendulum which he hung from the roof of the Panthéon in Paris in 1851: as the pendulum swung, the path of its swing slowly rotated, demonstrating the rotation of the Earth beneath it. He obtained the first reasonably accurate determination of the velocity of light by using the rotating mirror technique developed by Wheatstone in the 1830s, introduced the modern technique of silvering glass for the reflecting telescope, pioneered astronomical photography, discovered eddy currents (the Foucault currents induced in cores of electrical equipment such as generators and transformers), and improved a host of devices such as the arc lamp and the induction coil.

fouetté /fweˈteɪ/ n. Ballet a quick whipping movement of the raised leg. [F, past part. of fouetter whip]

fought past and past part. of FIGHT.

foul /faʊl/ adj., n., adv., & v. —adj. **1** offensive to the senses; loathsome, stinking. **2** dirty, soiled, filthy. **3** colloq. revolting, disgusting. **4 a** containing or charged with noxious matter (foul air). **b** clogged, choked. **5** morally polluted; disgustingly abusive or offensive (foul language; foul deeds). **6** unfair; against the rules of a game etc. (by fair means or foul). **7** (of the weather) wet, rough, stormy. **8** (of a rope etc.) entangled. **9** (of a ship's bottom) overgrown with weeds, barnacles, etc. —n. **1** Sport an unfair or invalid stroke or piece of play. **2** a collision or entanglement, esp. in riding, rowing, or running. **3** a foul thing. —adv. unfairly; contrary to the rules. —v. **1** tr. & intr. make or become foul or dirty. **2** tr. (of an animal) make dirty with excrement. **3 a** tr. Sport commit a foul against (a player). **b** intr. commit a foul. **4 a**

tr. (often foll. by *up*) cause (an anchor, cable, etc.) to become entangled or muddled. **b** *intr.* become entangled. **5** *tr.* jam or block (a crossing, railway line, or traffic). **6** *tr.* (usu. foll. by *up*) *colloq.* spoil or bungle. **7** *tr.* run foul of; collide with. **8** *tr.* pollute with guilt; dishonour. □ **foul brood** a fatal disease of larval bees caused by bacteria. **foul mouth** a person who uses foul language. **foul play 1** unfair play in games. **2** treacherous or violent activity, esp. murder. **foul-up** a muddled or bungled situation. □□ **foully** *adv.* **foulness** *n.* [OE *fūl* f. Gmc]

foulard /fuːˈlɑːd/ *n.* **1 a** thin soft material of silk or silk and cotton. **2** an article made of this. [F]

foumart /ˈfuːmɑːt/ *n.* a polecat. [ME *fulmert* etc. (as FOUL, *mart* MARTEN)]

found[1] *past* and *past part.* of FIND.

found[2] /faʊnd/ *v.* **1** *tr.* **a** establish (esp. with an endowment). **b** originate or initiate (an institution). **2** *tr.* be the original builder or begin the building of (a town etc.). **3** *tr.* lay the base of (a building etc.). **4** (foll. by *on*, *upon*) **a** *tr.* construct or base (a story, theory, rule, etc.) according to a specified principle or ground. **b** *intr.* have a basis in. □ **founding father** a person associated with a founding, esp. an American statesman at the time of the Revolution. [ME f. OF *fonder* f. L *fundare* f. *fundus* bottom]

found[3] /faʊnd/ *v.tr.* **1 a** melt and mould (metal). **b** fuse (materials for glass). **2** make by founding. □□ **founder** *n.* [ME f. OF *fondre* f. L *fundere fus-* pour]

foundation /faʊnˈdeɪʃ(ə)n/ *n.* **1 a** the solid ground or base, natural or artificial, on which a building rests. **b** (usu. in *pl.*) the lowest load-bearing part of a building, usu. below ground level. **2** a body or ground on which other parts are overlaid. **3** a basis or underlying principle; groundwork (*the report has no foundation*). **4 a** the act or an instance of establishing or constituting (esp. an endowed institution) on a permanent basis. **b** such an institution, e.g. a monastery, college, or hospital. **5** (in full **foundation garment**) a woman's supporting undergarment, e.g. a corset. □ **foundation cream** a cream used as a base for applying cosmetics. **foundation-stone 1** a stone laid with ceremony to celebrate the founding of a building. **2** the main ground or basis of something. □□ **foundational** *adj.* [ME f. OF *fondation* f. L *fundatio -onis* (as FOUND[2])]

founder[1] /ˈfaʊndə(r)/ *n.* a person who founds an institution. □□ **foundership** *n.*

founder[2] /ˈfaʊndə(r)/ *v.* & *n.* —*v.* **1 a** *intr.* (of a ship) fill with water and sink. **b** *tr.* cause (a ship) to founder. **2** *intr.* (of a plan etc.) fail. **3** *intr.* (of earth, a building, etc.) fall down or in, give way. **4 a** *intr.* (of a horse or its rider) fall to the ground, fall from lameness, stick fast in mud etc. **b** *tr.* cause (a horse) to break down, esp. with founder. —*n.* **1** inflammation of a horse's foot from overwork. **2** rheumatism of the chest-muscles in horses. [ME f. OF *fondrer, esfondrer* submerge, collapse, ult. f. L *fundus* bottom]

foundling /ˈfaʊndlɪŋ/ *n.* an abandoned infant of unknown parentage. [ME, perh. f. obs. *funding* (as FIND, -ING[3]), assim. to -LING[1]]

foundry /ˈfaʊndrɪ/ *n.* (*pl.* **-ies**) a workshop for or a business of casting metal.

fount[1] /faʊnt/ *n. poet.* a spring or fountain; a source. [back-form. f. FOUNTAIN after MOUNT[2]]

fount[2] /faʊnt, fɒnt/ *n.* (also **font** /fɒnt/) *Printing* a set of type of one face or size. [F *fonte* f. *fondre* FOUND[3]]

fountain /ˈfaʊntɪn/ *n.* **1 a** a jet or jets of water made to spout for ornamental purposes or for drinking. **b** a structure provided for this. **2** a structure for the constant public supply of drinking-water. **3** a natural spring of water. **4** a source (in physical or abstract senses). **5** = *soda-fountain*. **6** a reservoir for oil, ink, etc. □ **fountain-head** an original source. **fountain-pen** a pen with a reservoir or cartridge holding ink. □□ **fountained** *adj.* (also in *comb.*). [ME f. OF *fontaine* f. LL *fontana* fem. of L *fontanus* (adj.) f. *fons fontis* a spring]

four /fɔː(r)/ *n.* & *adj.* —*n.* **1** one more than three, or six less than ten; the product of two units and two units. **2** a symbol for this (4, iv, IV, rarely iiii, IIII). **3** a size etc. denoted by four. **4 a** four-oared rowing-boat or its crew. **5** the time of four o'clock (*is it four yet?*). **6** a card with four pips. **7** a hit at cricket scoring four runs. —*adj.* that amount to four. □ **four-eyes** *sl.* a person wearing glasses. **four-flush** *US Cards* a poker hand of little value, having four cards of the same suit and one of another. **four-flusher** *US* a bluffer or humbug. **four freedoms** see FREEDOM. **four hundred** *US* the social élite of a community. **four-in-hand 1** a vehicle with four horses driven by one person. **2** *US* a necktie worn with a knot and two hanging ends superposed. **four-leaf** (or **-leaved**) **clover** a clover leaf with four leaflets thought to bring good luck. **four-letter word** any of several short words referring to sexual or excretory functions, regarded as coarse or offensive. **four o'clock** = *marvel of Peru*. **four-part** *Mus.* arranged for four voices to sing or instruments to play. **four-poster** a bed with a post at each corner supporting a canopy. **four-square** *adj.* **1** solidly based. **2** steady, resolute; forthright. **3** square-shaped. —*adv.* steadily, resolutely. **four-stroke** (of an internal-combustion engine) having a cycle of four strokes (intake, compression, combustion, and exhaust). **four-wheel drive** drive acting on all four wheels of a vehicle. **on all fours** on hands and knees. [OE *fēower* f. Gmc]

fourchette /fʊəˈʃet/ *n. Anat.* a thin fold of skin at the back of the vulva. [F, dimin. of *fourche* (as FORK)]

fourfold /ˈfɔːfəʊld/ *adj.* & *adv.* **1** four times as much or as many. **2** consisting of four parts. **3** amounting to four.

Fourier /ˈfʊərɪˌeɪ/, Jean Baptiste Joseph (1768–1830), French public servant and mathematician whose theory of the diffusion of heat involved him in the solution of partial differential equations by the method of separation of variables and superposition. This led him to study the series and integrals that are now known by his name. Fourier's belief, controversial at the time, that a wide class of periodic phenomena could be described by means of series of trigonometrical functions was substantially vindicated by the results of later mathematicians, who had to invent extremely delicate techniques of mathematical analysis for that purpose. The theory of Fourier series now provides one of the most important methods for solving many partial differential equations that occur in physics and engineering. □ **Fourier analysis** *Math.* the resolution of periodic data into harmonic functions using a Fourier series. **Fourier series** an expansion of a periodic function as a series of trigonometric functions.

fourpence /ˈfɔːpəns/ *n. Brit.* the sum of four pence, esp. before decimalization.

fourpenny /ˈfɔːpənɪ/ *adj. Brit.* costing four pence, esp. before decimalization. □ **fourpenny one** *colloq.* a hit or blow.

fourscore /fɔːˈskɔː(r)/ *n. archaic* eighty.

foursome /ˈfɔːsəm/ *n.* **1** a group of four persons. **2** a golf match between two pairs with partners playing the same ball.

fourteen /fɔːˈtiːn/ *n.* & *adj.* —*n.* **1** one more than thirteen, or four more than ten; the product of two units and seven units. **2** a symbol for this (14, xiv, XIV). **3** a size etc. denoted by fourteen. —*adj.* that amount to fourteen. □□ **fourteenth** *adj.* & *n.* [OE *fēowertīene* (as FOUR, -TEEN)]

fourth /fɔːθ/ *n.* & *adj.* —*n.* **1** the position in a sequence corresponding to that of the number 4 in the sequence 1–4. **2** something occupying this position. **3** the fourth person etc. in a race or competition. **4** each of four equal parts of a thing; a quarter. **5** the fourth (and often highest) in a sequence of gears. **6** *Mus.* **a** an interval or chord spanning four consecutive notes in the diatonic scale (e.g. C to F). **b** a note separated from another by this interval. —*adj.* that is the fourth. □ **fourth dimension 1** a postulated dimension additional to those determining area and volume. **2** time regarded as equivalent to linear dimensions. **fourth estate** *joc.* the press; journalism. □□ **fourthly** *adv.* [OE *fēortha, fēowertha* f. Gmc]

4to *abbr.* quarto.

fovea /ˈfəʊvɪə/ *n.* (*pl.* **foveae** /-vɪˌiː/) *Anat.* a small depression or pit, esp. the pit in the retina of the eye for focusing images. □□ **foveal** *adj.* **foveate** /-vɪˌeɪt/ *adj.* [L]

fowl /faʊl/ *n.* & *v.* (*pl.* same or **fowls**) —*n.* **1** any domestic cock or hen of various gallinaceous birds, kept for eggs and flesh. **2** the flesh of birds, esp. a domestic cock or hen, as food. **3** *archaic* (except in *comb.* or *collect.*) a bird (*guineafowl; wildfowl*). —*v.intr.*

catch or hunt wildfowl. □ **fowl cholera** see CHOLERA. **fowl pest** an infectious virus disease of fowls. **fowl-run 1** a place where fowls may run. **2** a breeding establishment for fowls. □□ **fowler** *n.* **fowling**. [OE *fugol* f. Gmc]

Fowler /ˈfaʊlə(r)/, Henry Watson (1858–1933), English lexicographer and author of prescriptive works on style and idiom. With his brother Francis George Fowler (1870–1918) he compiled the *Concise Oxford Dictionary* (1911), adopting certain principles which continued to be followed in the smaller Oxford dictionaries for more than half a century. In 1926 his most famous work appeared, *Modern English Usage* (still known affectionately as 'Fowler'), in which major hazards of English were pointed out and recommendations made with 'a cheerful attitude of infallibility'. In isolation from the current linguistic controversies and from the growing support for a 'descriptive' approach, he displayed such acknowledged and respected sensitivity to all aspects of the English language that those departing from his recommendations knew that they risked censure.

Fowles /faʊlz/, John Robert (1926–   ), English writer, some of whose novels have an element of fantasy and a mythological dimension faintly suggestive of 'magic realism' (see entry). *The French Lieutenant's Woman* (1969) is a semi-historical novel set largely in the seaside town Lyme Regis in 1867.

Fox /fɒks/, George (1624–91), founder of the Society of Friends. The son of a Leicestershire weaver, he began his life of preaching in 1647, teaching that truth is the inner voice of God speaking to the soul. Despite frequent imprisonment he attracted followers ('Friends of the Truth') whom he formed into a stable organization.

fox /fɒks/ *n.* & *v.* —*n.* **1 a** any of various wild flesh-eating mammals of the dog family, esp. of the genus *Vulpes*, with a sharp snout, bushy tail, and red or grey fur. **b** the fur of a fox. **2** a cunning or sly person. **3** *US sl.* an attractive young woman. —*v.* **1 a** *intr.* act craftily. **b** *tr.* deceive, baffle, trick. **2** *tr.* (usu. as **foxed** *adj.*) discolour (the leaves of a book, engraving, etc.) with brownish marks. □ **fox-terrier 1** a terrier of a short-haired breed originally used for unearthing foxes. **2** this breed. □□ **foxing** *n.* (in sense 2 of *v.*). **foxlike** *adj.* [OE f. WG]

Foxe /fɒks/, John (1516–87), English religious writer and martyrologist, who relinquished his fellowship at Magdalen College, Oxford, in 1545 because he was unwilling to conform to the religious statutes. He fled to the Continent on the accession of Catholic Mary I, and published in Strasbourg an early draft of his *Actes and Monuments*, popularly known as *The Book of Martyrs*, which appeared in England in 1563. This passionate account of suffering and persecution under Bloody Mary inspired hatred towards Catholicism for generations.

foxglove /ˈfɒksglʌv/ *n.* any tall plant of the genus *Digitalis*, with erect spikes of purple or white flowers like glove-fingers.

foxhole /ˈfɒkshəʊl/ *n.* **1** *Mil.* a hole in the ground used as a shelter against enemy fire or as a firing-point. **2** a place of refuge or concealment.

foxhound /ˈfɒkshaʊnd/ *n.* a kind of hound bred and trained to hunt foxes.

fox-hunt /ˈfɒkshʌnt/ *n.* & *v.* —*n.* **1** the hunting of foxes with hounds. **2** a particular group of people engaged in this. —*v.intr.* engage in a fox-hunt. □□ **fox-hunter** *n.* **fox-hunting** *n.* & *adj.*

Foxhunter /ˈfɒkshʌntə(r)/ (1940–59), British show-jumping horse, owned by Lt.-Col. (Sir) Henry Llewellyn (1911–   ), who won 78 international competitions between 1947 and 1953. Horse and owner were part of the British team that won a bronze medal in the Olympic Games of 1948 and a gold medal in 1952.

foxtail /ˈfɒksteɪl/ *n.* any of several grasses of the genus *Alopecurus*, with brushlike spikes.

foxtrot /ˈfɒkstrɒt/ *n.* & *v.* —*n.* **1** a ballroom dance with slow and quick steps. **2** the music for this. —*v.intr.* (**foxtrotted**, **foxtrotting**) perform this dance.

foxy /ˈfɒksɪ/ *adj.* (**foxier**, **foxiest**) **1** of or like a fox. **2** sly or cunning. **3** reddish-brown. **4** (of paper) damaged, esp. by mildew. **5** *US sl.* (of a woman) sexually attractive. □□ **foxily** *adv.* **foxiness** *n.*

foyer /ˈfɔɪeɪ/ *n.* the entrance hall or other large area in a hotel, theatre, etc. [F, = hearth, home, ult. f. L *focus* fire]

FP *abbr.* freezing-point.

fp *abbr.* forte piano.

FPA *abbr.* (in the UK) Family Planning Association.

FPS *abbr.* Fellow of the Pharmaceutical Society of Great Britain.

fps *abbr.* (also **f.p.s.**) **1** feet per second. **2** foot-pound-second.

Fr *symb. Chem.* the element francium.

Fr. *abbr.* (also **Fr**) **1** Father. **2** French.

fr. *abbr.* franc(s).

Fra /frɑː/ *n.* a prefixed title given to an Italian monk or friar. [It., abbr. of *frate* brother]

frabjous /ˈfræbdʒəs/ *adj.* delightful, joyous. □□ **frabjously** *adv.* [devised by Lewis Carroll, app. to suggest *fair* and *joyous*]

fracas /ˈfrækɑː/ *n.* (pl. same /-kɑːz/) a noisy disturbance or quarrel. [F f. *fracasser* f. It. *fracassare* make an uproar]

fraction /ˈfrækʃ(ə)n/ *n.* **1** a numerical quantity that is not a whole number (e.g. ½, 0.5). **2** a small, esp. very small, part, piece, or amount. **3** a portion of a mixture separated by distillation etc. **4** *Polit.* any organized dissentient group, esp. a group of communists in a non-communist organization. **5** the division of the Eucharistic bread. □□ **fractionary** *v.tr.* (also **-ise**). [ME f. OF f. LL *fractio -onis* f. L *frangere fract-* break]

fractional /ˈfrækʃən(ə)l/ *adj.* **1** of or relating to or being a fraction. **2** very slight; incomplete. **3** *Chem.* relating to the separation of parts of a mixture by making use of their different physical properties (*fractional crystallization*; *fractional distillation*). □□ **fractionalize** *v.tr.* (also **-ise**). **fractionally** *adv.* (esp. in sense 2).

fractionate /ˈfrækʃəˌneɪt/ *v.tr.* **1** break up into parts. **2** separate (a mixture) by fractional distillation etc. □□ **fractionation** /-ˈneɪʃ(ə)n/ *n.*

fractious /ˈfrækʃəs/ *adj.* **1** irritable, peevish. **2** unruly. □□ **fractiously** *adv.* **fractiousness** *n.* [FRACTION in obs. sense 'brawling', prob. after *factious* etc.]

fracto- /ˈfræktəʊ/ *comb. form Meteorol.* (of a cloud form) broken or fragmentary (*fracto-cumulus*; *fracto-nimbus*). [L *fractus* broken: see FRACTION]

fracture /ˈfræktʃə(r)/ *n.* & *v.* —*n.* **1** a breakage or breaking, esp. of a bone or cartilage. **b** the result of breaking; a crack or split. **2** the surface appearance of a freshly broken rock or mineral. **3** *Linguistics* **a** the substitution of a diphthong for a simple vowel owing to an influence esp. of a following consonant. **b** a diphthong substituted in this way. —*v.intr.* & *tr.* **1** *Med.* undergo or cause to undergo a fracture. **2** break or cause to break. [ME f. F *fracture* or f. L *fractura* (as FRACTION)]

fraenulum /ˈfriːnjʊləm/ *n.* (also **frenulum**) (pl. **-la** /-lə/) *Anat.* a small fraenum. [mod.L, dimin. of FRAENUM]

fraenum /ˈfriːnəm/ *n.* (also **frenum**) (pl. **-na** /-nə/) *Anat.* a fold of mucous membrane or skin esp. under the tongue, checking the motion of an organ. [L, = bridle]

fragile /ˈfrædʒaɪl, -dʒɪl/ *adj.* **1** easily broken; weak. **2** of delicate frame or constitution; not strong. □□ **fragilely** *adv.* **fragility** /frəˈdʒɪlɪtɪ/ *n.* [F *fragile* or L *fragilis* f. *frangere* break]

fragment *n.* & *v.* —*n.* /ˈfrægmənt/ **1** a part broken off; a detached piece. **2** an isolated or incomplete part. **3** the remains of an otherwise lost or destroyed whole, esp. the extant remains or unfinished portion of a book or work of art. —*v.tr.* & *intr.* /frægˈment/ break or separate into fragments. □□ **fragmental** /-ˈment(ə)l/ *adj.* **fragmentize** /ˈfrægmənˌtaɪz/ *v.tr.* (also **-ise**). [ME f. F *fragment* or L *fragmentum* (as FRAGILE)]

fragmentary /ˈfrægməntərɪ/ *adj.* **1** consisting of fragments. **2** disconnected. **3** *Geol.* composed of fragments of previously existing rocks. □□ **fragmentarily** *adv.*

fragmentation /ˌfrægmənˈteɪʃ(ə)n/ *n.* the process or an instance of breaking into fragments. □ **fragmentation bomb** a bomb designed to break up into small rapidly-moving fragments when exploded.

Fragonard /ˌfrægɒˈnɑː/, Jean-Honoré (1732–1806), French painter, whose scenes of frivolity and gallantry embody the rococo spirit. His paintings include landscapes, gardens, and family scenes, but he is most famous for erotic canvases such as *The Swing* (c.1766) and *The Progress of Love* (1771–3). He was ruined by the Revolution and died in poverty.

fragrance /'freɪgrəns/ n. **1** sweetness of smell. **2** a sweet scent. [F *fragrance* or L *fragrantia* (as FRAGRANT)]

fragrancy /'freɪgrənsɪ/ n. (pl. **-ies**) = FRAGRANCE.

fragrant /'freɪgrənt/ adj. sweet-smelling. □□ **fragrantly** adv. [ME f. F *fragrant* or L *fragrare* smell sweet]

frail /freɪl/ adj. & n. —adj. **1** fragile, delicate. **2** in weak health. **3** morally weak; unable to resist temptation. **4** transient, insubstantial. —n. *US sl.* a woman. □□ **frailly** adv. **frailness** n. [ME f. OF *fraile, frele* f. L *fragilis* FRAGILE]

frailty /'freɪltɪ/ n. (pl. **-ies**) **1** the condition of being frail. **2** liability to err or yield to temptation. **3** a fault, weakness, or foible. [ME f. OF *fraileté* f. L *fragilitas -tatis* (as FRAGILE)]

Fraktur /'fræktʊə(r)/ n. a German style of black-letter type. [G]

framboesia /fræm'biːzɪə/ n. (US **frambesia**) *Med.* = YAWS. [mod.L f. F *framboise* raspberry f. L *fraga ambrosia* ambrosial strawberry]

frame /freɪm/ n. & v. —n. **1** a case or border enclosing a picture, window, door, etc. **2** the basic rigid supporting structure of anything, e.g. of a building, motor vehicle, or aircraft. **3** (in *pl.*) the structure of spectacles holding the lenses. **4** a human or animal body, esp. with reference to its size or structure (*his frame shook with laughter*). **5** a framed work or structure (*the frame of heaven*). **6** an established order, plan, or system (*the frame of society*). **b** construction, constitution, build. **7** a temporary state (esp. in **frame of mind**). **8** a single complete image or picture on a cinema film or transmitted in a series of lines by television. **9 a** a triangular structure for positioning the balls in snooker etc. **b** the balls positioned in this way. **c** a round of play in snooker etc. **10** *Hort.* a boxlike structure of glass etc. for protecting plants. **11** a removable box of slats for the building of a honeycomb in a beehive. **12** *US sl.* = frame-up. —v.tr. **1 a** set in or provide with a frame. **b** serve as a frame for. **2** construct by a combination of parts or in accordance with a design or plan. **3** formulate or devise the essentials of (a complex thing, idea, theory, etc.). **4** (foll. by *to, into*) adapt or fit. **5** *colloq.* concoct a false charge or evidence against; devise a plot with regard to. **6** articulate (words). □ **frame-house** a house constructed of a wooden skeleton covered with boards etc. **frame of reference 1** a set of standards or principles governing behaviour, thought, etc. **2** *Geom.* a system of geometrical axes for defining position. **frame-saw** a saw stretched in a frame to make it rigid. **frame-up** *colloq.* a conspiracy, esp. to make an innocent person appear guilty. □□ **framable** adj. **frameless** adj. **framer** n. [OE *framian* be of service f. *fram* forward: see FROM]

framework /'freɪmwɜːk/ n. **1** an essential supporting structure. **2** a basic system.

framing /'freɪmɪŋ/ n. a framework; a system of frames.

franc /fræŋk/ n. the chief monetary unit of France, Belgium, Switzerland, Luxembourg, and several other countries. [ME f. OF f. *Francorum Rex* king of the Franks, the legend on the earliest gold coins so called (14th c.): see FRANK]

France[1] /frɑːns/ a country in western Europe, with coastlines on the Atlantic Ocean, the English Channel, and the Mediterranean Sea; pop. (1982) 54,335,000; official language, French; capital, Paris. Although it is an industrial country agriculture remains important, and many regions are famous for their wines. Prehistoric remains, cave paintings, and megalithic monuments attest the long history of human habitation. Julius Caesar subdued the area in the 1st c. BC and it became the Roman province of Gaul. It was politically splintered by barbarian invasions from the 3rd c. onwards and, although briefly united under the Merovingian and Carolingian kings, did not emerge as a permanently unified State until the ejection of the English and Burgundians at the end of the Middle Ages. Under the Valois and Bourbon dynasties France rose to contest European hegemony in the 16th–18th c., and after the overthrow of the monarchy in the French Revolution briefly dominated Europe under Napoleon. Defeated in the Franco–Prussian war (1870–1), severely handled in the First World War and occupied by the Germans in the Second, France has revived in the post-war era as a major European power.

France[2] /frɑːs/, Anatole (pseudonym of Jacques-Anatole-François Thibault, 1844–1922), French novelist and man of letters. He wrote poems and criticism, developed wide interests in journalism and radical politics, and achieved success as a novelist with *Le Crime de Sylvestre Bonnard* (1881). *L'Histoire contemporaine* (1897–1901), a social and political satire, introduced the disenchanted provincial professor Bergeret. The Dreyfus case had aroused France's sympathies of which *L'Île des pingouins* (1908) contains an ironic account with clear Marxist overtones. *Les dieux ont soif* (1912) is a study of fanaticism during the French Revolution. Qualities of graceful erudition and clarity of thought are displayed in all his works and notably in his short stories. He was awarded the Nobel Prize for literature in 1921.

Franche-Comté /ˌfrɑ̃ʃkɒn'teɪ/ a region of eastern France in the northern foothills of the Jura Mountains; pop. (1982) 1,084,000; capital, Besançon.

franchise /'fræntʃaɪz/ n. & v. —n. **1 a** the right to vote at State (esp. parliamentary) elections. **b** the principle of qualification for this. **2** full membership of a corporation or State; citizenship. **3** authorization granted to an individual or group by a company to sell its goods or services in a particular way. **4** *hist.* legal immunity or exemption from a burden or jurisdiction. **5** a right or privilege granted to a person or corporation. —v.tr. grant a franchise to. □□ **franchisee** /-'ziː/ n. **franchiser** n. (also **franchisor**). [ME f. OF f. *franc, franche* free: see FRANK]

Francis[1] /'frɑːnsɪs/, Richard Stanley ('Dick') (1920–), Welshborn author of numerous thrillers with a background of horseracing. He was champion jockey 1953–4, and began writing after his retirement in 1957. His works include *Forfeit* (1969), *Whip Hand* (1980), and *Reflex* (1981); all three of these won literary awards.

Francis[2] /'frɑːnsɪs/, St, of Assisi (1181/2–1226), founder of the Franciscan order. Born of a rich family, he became dissatisfied with his worldly life, and in 1208, hearing read in church Christ's words bidding his disciples to leave all (Matt. 10: 7–19), understood them as a personal call and set out to save souls. Before long he had gathered a band of like-minded followers, and he drew up for them a simple rule of life based on sayings from the Gospels. He was the first person known to have shown the stigmata (1224). His generosity, simple faith, deep humility, and love of nature have made him one of the most cherished saints. Feast day, 4 Oct.

Franciscan /fræn'sɪskən/ n. & adj. —n. a monk, nun, or sister of an order founded in 1209 by St Francis of Assisi. (See below.) —adj. of St Francis or his order. [F *franciscain* f. mod.L *Franciscanus* f. *Franciscus* Francis]

The Franciscan order of friars minor or Grey Friars was founded by St Francis of Assisi (1209). His ideal of complete poverty proved incompatible with the organization of a large membership, and the original simple rule was modified, to his great regret (1221 and 1223), and successive laxities and reforms led to the formation of separate branches. The nuns are known as Poor Clares, after their founder, St Clare (1215). There is also an order of tertiaries or lay brothers (founded 1221). The friars have been important preachers and missionaries.

Francis de Sales /'frɑːnsɪs də 'sɑːl/, St (1567–1622), bishop of Geneva from 1602, one of the leaders of the Counter-Reformation, and co-founder of the Order of the Visitation, an order of nuns. The Salesian order is named after him. Feast day, 29 Jan.

Francis Xavier, St, see XAVIER.

francium /'fræŋkɪəm/ n. *Chem.* a radioactive metallic element, discovered in 1939, that is the heaviest member of the alkali-metal group and is chemically similar to caesium. All its isotopes have short half-lives (the most stable about 22 minutes) and only one occurs naturally, produced by the radioactive decay of actinium 227. ¶ Symb.: **Fr**; atomic number 87. [mod.L f. FRANCE[1], the country of its discoverer (M. Perey)]

Franck /frɑ̃k/, César (1822–90), Belgian composer. In 1836 he moved to Paris, where he became one of the most influential figures in French musical life. He was a noted organist, and the sonorities of that instrument found their way into his orchestral works. He is at his best when formal considerations restrict a tendency to massiveness and over-chromaticism, and it is his instrumental works that have proved most durable, particularly the Piano Quintet (1879), the Symphonic Variations for piano and orchestra (1885), the hugely popular Violin Sonata (1886), the D minor Symphony (1886–8), and the String Quartet (1889).

Franco /ˈfræŋkəʊ/, Francisco (1892–1975), Spanish general and head of State. After service in Morocco, where he helped to form the Spanish Foreign Legion, Franco was among the leaders of the military uprising against the republican government which led to the Spanish Civil War. In October 1936 he became leader of the Nationalist forces, and when the last loyalist strongholds finally surrendered in early 1939 he assumed dictatorial powers and set up a Fascist regime. Despite pressure from Germany and Italy, Franco kept Spain neutral during the Second World War, and continued to rule until his death in 1975. In 1969 he named Prince Juan Carlos (1938), grandson of Alfonso XIII, not only as his successor but as heir to the reconstituted Spanish throne.

Franco- /ˈfræŋkəʊ/ comb. form **1** French; French and (Franco-German). **2** regarding France or the French (Francophile). [med.L Francus FRANK]

francolin /ˈfræŋkəʊlɪn/ n. any medium-sized partridge of the genus Francolinus. [F f. It. francolino]

Francophile /ˈfræŋkəˌfaɪl/ n. a person who is fond of France or the French.

francophone /ˈfræŋkəˌfəʊn/ n. & adj. —n. a French-speaking person. —adj. French-speaking. [FRANCO- + Gk phōnē voice]

Franco-Prussian war the war of 1870–1 between France (under Napoleon III) and Prussia, in which Prussian troops advanced into France and were decisively defeated at Sedan. The defeat marked the end of the French Second Empire. For Prussia, the proclamation of the German Second Empire at Versailles was the climax of Bismarck's ambitions to unite Germany.

frangible /ˈfrændʒɪb(ə)l/ adj. breakable, fragile. [OF frangible or med.L frangibilis f. L frangere to break]

frangipane /ˈfrændʒɪˌpeɪn/ n. **1 a** an almond-flavoured cream or paste. **b** a flan filled with this. **2** = FRANGIPANI. [F prob. f. Marquis Frangipani, 16th-c. It. inventor of the perfume]

frangipani /ˌfrændʒɪˈpɑːnɪ/ n. (pl. **frangipanis**) **1** any tree or shrub of the genus Plumeria, native to tropical America, esp. P. rubra with clusters of fragrant white, pink, or yellow flowers. **2** the perfume from this plant. [var. of FRANGIPANE]

franglais /ˈfrɑ̃gleɪ/ n. a corrupt version of French using many words and idioms borrowed from English. [F f. français French + anglais English]

Frank[1] /fræŋk/ n. **1** a member of the Germanic nation or coalition that conquered Gaul in the 6th c. **2** (in the Levant) a person of Western nationality. □□ **Frankish** adj. [OE Franca, OHG Franko, perh. f. the name of a weapon: cf. OE franca javelin]

Frank[2] /fræŋk/, Anne (1929–45), German-Jewish girl, whose diary records the experiences of her family living for two years in hiding from the Nazis in Amsterdam. They were eventually betrayed, and she died in a concentration camp.

frank /fræŋk/ adj., v., & n. —adj. **1** candid, outspoken (a frank opinion). **2** undisguised, avowed (frank admiration). **3** ingenuous, open (a frank face). **4** Med. unmistakable. —v.tr. **1** stamp (a letter) with an official mark (esp. other than a normal postage stamp) to record the payment of postage. **2** hist. superscribe (a letter etc.) with a signature ensuring conveyance without charge; send without charge. **3** archaic facilitate the coming and going of (a person). —n. **1** a franking signature or mark. **2** a franked cover. □□ **frankable** adj. **franker** n. **frankness** n. [ME f. OF franc f. med.L francus free, f. FRANK[1] (since only Franks had full freedom in Frankish Gaul)]

Frankenstein /ˈfræŋkənˌstaɪn/ n. (in full **Frankenstein's monster**) a thing that becomes terrifying to its maker; a monster. [Baron Frankenstein, a character in Mary Shelley's novel Frankenstein (1818), who constructed a human monster and

endowed it with life. It became filled with hatred for its creator and eventually killed him.]

Frankfort /ˈfræŋkfəːt/ the capital of Kentucky; pop. (1980) 25,970.

Frankfurt /ˈfræŋkfəːt/ (in full **Frankfurt am Main** /æm ˈmaɪn/) a port and commercial city on the River Main in western Germany; pop. (1987) 592,400. It was the birthplace of Goethe, and is the headquarters of the Bundesbank.

frankfurter /ˈfræŋkˌfəːtə(r)/ n. a seasoned smoked sausage made of beef and pork. [G Frankfurter Wurst Frankfurt sausage]

frankincense /ˈfræŋkɪnˌsens/ n. an aromatic gum resin obtained from trees of the genus Boswellia, used for burning as incense. [ME f. OF franc encens pure incense]

Franklin /ˈfræŋklɪn/, Benjamin (1706–90), American statesman, one of the signatories to the peace between the US and Great Britain after the War of American Independence, inventor, and scientist. He became a wealthy printer and publisher and published, amongst other things, the Pennsylvania Gazette and Poor Richard's Almanack. His main scientific achievements were the formulation of a theory of electrical (electrostatic) action based on the concept of a single electric 'fluid' which was widely used in the second half of the 18th c., and a demonstration of the electrical nature of lightning (his suggestion was first taken up in France by Jean François d'Alibard), which led to the invention of the lightning conductor. His inventions include the Pennsylvanian fireplace or Franklin stove, and bifocal spectacles.

franklin /ˈfræŋklɪn/ n. hist. a landowner of free but not noble birth in the 14th and 15th c. in England. [ME francoleyn etc. f. AL francalanus f. francalis held without dues f. francus free: see FRANK[1]]

frankly /ˈfræŋklɪ/ adv. **1** in a frank manner. **2** (qualifying a whole sentence) to be frank.

frantic /ˈfræntɪk/ adj. **1** wildly excited; frenzied. **2** characterized by great hurry or anxiety; desperate, violent. **3** colloq. extreme; very great. □□ **frantically** adv. **franticly** adv. **franticness** n. [ME frentik, frantik f. OF frenetique f. L phreneticus: see PHRENETIC]

Franz Joseph Land /frænts ˈdʒəʊsef/ a group of islands in the Arctic Ocean, discovered in 1873 by an Austrian expedition and named after the Austrian emperor. The islands were annexed by the USSR in 1928.

frap /fræp/ v.tr. (**frapped, frapping**) Naut. bind tightly. [F frapper bind, strike]

frappé /ˈfræpeɪ/ adj. & n. —adj. (esp. of wine) iced, cooled. —n. **1** an iced drink. **2** a soft water-ice. [F, past part. of frapper strike, ice (drinks)]

frass /fræs/ n. **1** a fine powdery refuse left by insects boring. **2** the excrement of insect larvae. [G f. fressen devour (as FRET[1])]

fraternal /frəˈtɜːn(ə)l/ adj. **1** of a brother or brothers. **2** suitable to a brother; brotherly. **3** (of twins) developed from separate ova and not necessarily closely similar. **4** US of or concerning a fraternity (see FRATERNITY 3). □□ **fraternalism** n. **fraternally** adv. [med.L fraternalis f. L fraternus f. frater brother]

fraternity /frəˈtɜːnɪtɪ/ n. (pl. **-ies**) **1** a religious brotherhood. **2** a group or company with common interests, or of the same professional class. **3** US a male students' society in a university or college. **4** being fraternal; brotherliness. [ME f. OF fraternité f. L fraternitas -tatis (as FRATERNAL)]

fraternize /ˈfrætəˌnaɪz/ v.intr. (also **-ise**) (often foll. by with) **1** associate; make friends; behave as intimates. **2** (of troops) enter into friendly relations with enemy troops or the inhabitants of an occupied country. □□ **fraternization** /-ˈzeɪʃ(ə)n/ n. [F fraterniser & med.L fraternizare f. L fraternus: see FRATERNAL]

fratricide /ˈfrætrɪˌsaɪd/ n. **1** the killing of one's brother or sister. **2** a person who does this. □□ **fratricidal** /-ˈsaɪd(ə)l/ adj. [F fratricide or LL fratricidium, L fratricida, f. frater fratris brother]

Frau /frau/ n. (pl. **Frauen** /ˈfrauən/) (often as a title) a married or widowed German woman. [G]

fraud /frɔːd/ n. **1** criminal deception; the use of false representations to gain an unjust advantage. **2** a dishonest artifice or trick. **3** a person or thing not fulfilling what is claimed or expected of it. [ME f. OF fraude f. L fraus fraudis]

fraudulent /ˈfrɔːdjʊlənt/ adj. **1** characterized or achieved by fraud. **2** guilty of fraud; intending to deceive. □□ **fraudulence** n. **fraudulently** adv. [ME f. OF fraudulent or L fraudulentus (as FRAUD)]

fraught /frɔːt/ adj. **1** (foll. by with) filled or attended with (fraught with danger). **2** colloq. causing or affected by great anxiety or distress. [ME, past part. of obs. fraught (v.) load with cargo f. MDu. vrachten f. vracht FREIGHT]

Fräulein /ˈfrɔɪlaɪn/ n. (often as a title or form of address) an unmarried (esp. young) German woman. [G, dimin. f. FRAU]

Fraunhofer /ˈfraʊnˌhoʊfə(r)/, Joseph von (1787–1826), German skilled optician and pioneer in spectroscopy. He observed and mapped a large number of fine dark lines in the solar spectrum and plotted their wavelengths. These lines, named after him, had already been observed by Wollaston in 1802. They were explained by Bunsen and Gustav Kirchhoff in 1859, and were used to determine the chemical elements present in the spectra of the sun and stars. He became noted for his finely ruled diffraction gratings, used by him to determine the wavelengths of specific colours of light and of the major spectral lines.

fraxinella /ˌfræksɪˈnelə/ n. an aromatic plant Dictamnus albus, having foliage that emits an ethereal inflammable oil. Also called DITTANY, gas plant, burning bush. [mod.L, dimin. of L fraxinus ash-tree]

fray[1] /freɪ/ v. **1** tr. & intr. wear through or become worn, esp. (of woven material) unweave at the edges. **2** intr. (of nerves, temper, etc.) become strained; deteriorate. [F frayer f. L fricare rub]

fray[2] /freɪ/ n. **1** conflict, fighting (eager for the fray). **2** a noisy quarrel or brawl. [ME f. fray to quarrel f. affray (v.) (as AFFRAY)]

Fray Bentos /fraɪ ˈbentɒs/ a port and meat-packing centre on the Uruguay River in western Uruquay; pop. (1985) 20,000.

Frazer /ˈfreɪzə(r)/, Sir James George (1854–1941), Scottish classicist and a founder of British social anthropology and ethnology. The first chair in anthropology (at Liverpool University) was created for him in 1907. Born five years before the publication of Darwin's Origin of Species, Frazer's work throughout his lifetime reflected his pre-eminent position as an intellectualist evolutionist. Nowhere is this more clearly seen than in his twelve-volume series of essays The Golden Bough: A Study in Magic and Religion (1890–1915) in which he proposed a theory of evolutionary development in human modes of thought from the magical and religious to the scientific through which, he believed, all societies pass. Although his evolutionary sequence is now disregarded, his important distinction between magic (the attempt to manipulate events by technical means based upon misconceived or pseudo-scientific natural laws) and religion (the appeal to the supernatural for help) continues to underlie much contemporary anthropology. While Frazer's lasting contribution to anthropology (and more widely: it caught the literary imagination and influenced D. H. Lawrence, T. S. Eliot, and others) was The Golden Bough, he was a prolific writer in other fields as well, and within his own lifetime he was highly regarded as a biblical scholar and classicist.

frazil /ˈfreɪzɪl/ n. US ice crystals that form in a stream or on its bed. [Can.F frasil snow floating in the water; cf. F fraisil cinders]

frazzle /ˈfræz(ə)l/ n. & v. colloq. —n. a worn or exhausted state (burnt to a frazzle). —v.tr. (usu. as **frazzled** adj.) wear out; exhaust. [orig. uncert.]

freak /friːk/ n. & v. —n. **1** (also **freak of nature**) a monstrosity; an abnormally developed individual or thing. **2** (often attrib.) an abnormal, irregular, or bizarre occurrence (a freak storm). **3** colloq. **a** an unconventional person. **b** a person with a specified enthusiasm or interest (health freak). **c** a person who undergoes hallucinations or (see sense 2 of v.). **4 a** a caprice or vagary. **b** capriciousness. —v. (often foll. by out) colloq. **1** intr. & tr. become or make very angry. **2** intr. & tr. undergo or cause to undergo hallucinations or a strong emotional experience, esp. from use of narcotics. **3** intr. adopt a wildly unconventional lifestyle. □ **freak-out** colloq. an act of freaking out; a hallucinatory or strong emotional experience. [16th c.: prob. f. dial.]

freakish /ˈfriːkɪʃ/ adj. **1** of or like a freak. **2** bizarre, unconventional. □□ **freakishly** adv. **freakishness** n.

freaky /ˈfriːkɪ/ adj. (**freakier**, **freakiest**) = FREAKISH. □□ **freakily** adv. **freakiness** n.

freckle /ˈfrek(ə)l/ n. & v. —n. (often in pl.) a light brown spot on the skin, usu. caused by exposure to the sun. —v. **1** tr. (usu. as **freckled** adj.) spot with freckles. **2** intr. be spotted with freckles. □□ **freckly** adj. [ME fracel etc. f. dial. freken f. ON freknur (pl.)]

Frederick[1] /ˈfredrɪk/ (German Friedrich) the name of three Holy Roman Emperors:

Frederick I 'Barbarossa' (= 'Redbeard'), (c.1123–90), emperor 1152–90. One of the strongest rulers of his age, Barbarossa made a sustained attempt to bring Italy and the papacy under military subjugation but was eventually checked at the Battle of Legnano in 1176. He was drowned while crossing the River Calycadnus (modern Göksu) in SE Asia Minor on his way to the Third Crusade, but legend says that he still sleeps in a cavern in the Kyffhäuser mountains until the needs of his country shall summon him forth.

Frederick[2] /ˈfredrɪk/ (German Friedrich) the name of three kings of Prussia:

Frederick II 'the Great' (1712–86), reigned 1740–86. On his succession to the throne Frederick promptly claimed Silesia, launching Europe into the War of the Austrian Succession. He soon proved to be a brilliant soldier, building the Prussian army into the best fighting force in Europe. During the Seven Years War (1756–63) he fought against a coalition of France, Russia, Austria, Sweden, and Saxony, and despite some setbacks successfully brought his country out of the war in a better position than it had enjoyed at the outset. The most famous soldier of his age, Frederick also made his name as a patron of culture and enacted a series of legal and administrative reforms in his kingdom.

Fredericton /ˈfredərɪkt(ə)n/ the capital of New Brunswick, Canada; pop. (1986) 44,350. The city was founded in 1785 by United Empire Loyalists who named it after Frederick Augustus, son of George III.

free /friː/ adj., adv., & v. —adj. (**freer** /ˈfriːə(r)/; **freest** /ˈfriːɪst/) **1** not in bondage to or under the control of another; having personal rights and social and political liberty. **2** (of a State, or its citizens or institutions) subject neither to foreign domination nor to despotic government; having national and civil liberty (a free press; a free society). **3 a** unrestricted, unimpeded; not restrained or fixed. **b** at liberty; not confined or imprisoned. **c** released from ties or duties; unimpeded. **d** unrestrained as to action; independent (set free). **4** (foll. by of, from) **a** not subject to; exempt from (free of tax). **b** not containing or subject to a specified (usu. undesirable) thing (free of preservatives; free from disease). **5** (foll. by to + infin.) able or permitted to take a specified action (you are free to choose). **6** unconstrained (free gestures). **7 a** available without charge; costing nothing. **b** not subject to tax, duty, trade-restraint, or fees. **8 a** clear of engagements or obligations (are you free tomorrow?). **b** not occupied or in use (the bathroom is free now). **c** clear of obstructions. **9** spontaneous, unforced (free compliments). **10** open to all comers. **11** lavish, profuse; using or used without restraint (very free with their money). **12** frank, unreserved. **13** (of a literary style) not observing the strict laws of form. **14** (of a translation) conveying the broad sense; not literal. **15** forward, familiar, impudent. **16** (of talk, stories, etc.) slightly indecent. **17** Physics a not modified by an external force. **b** not bound in an atom or molecule. **18** Chem. not combined (free oxygen). **19** (of power or energy) disengaged or available. —adv. **1** in a free manner. **2** without cost or payment. **3** Naut. not close-hauled. —v.tr (**frees**, **freed**). **1** make free; set at liberty. **2** (foll. by of, from) relieve from (something undesirable). **3** disengage, disentangle. □ **free agent** a person with freedom of action. **free and easy** informal, unceremonious. **free association** Psychol. a method of investigating a person's unconscious by eliciting from him or her spontaneous associations with ideas proposed by the examiner. **free-born** inheriting a citizen's rights and liberty. **Free Church** a Church dissenting or seceding from an established

Church. **Free Church of Scotland** that which seceded from the Presbyterian establishment 1843–1929. **free enterprise** a system in which private business operates in competition and largely free of State control. **free fall** movement under the force of gravity only, esp.: **1** the part of a parachute descent before the parachute opens. **2** the movement of a spacecraft in space without thrust from the engines. **free fight** a general fight in which all present join. **free-for-all** a free fight, unrestricted discussion, etc. **free-form** (*attrib.*) of an irregular shape or structure. **Free French** (in the Second World War) the members of a movement, led by General Charles de Gaulle, consisting of French troops and volunteers who continued fighting against the Axis powers after the surrender of France in the summer of 1940. **free hand** freedom to act at one's own discretion (see also FREEHAND). **free-handed** generous. **free-handedly** generously. **free-handedness** generosity. **free house** *Brit.* an inn or public house not controlled by a brewery and therefore not restricted to selling particular brands of beer or liquor. **free kick** *Football* a set kick allowed to be taken by one side without interference from the other. **free labour** the labour of workmen not in a trade union. **free-living 1** indulgence in pleasures, esp. that of eating. **2** *Biol.* living freely and independently; not attached to a substrate. **free love** sexual relations according to choice and unrestricted by marriage. **free market** a market in which prices are determined by unrestricted competition. **free on board** (or **rail**) without charge for delivery to a ship or railway wagon. **free pass** an authorization of free admission, travel, etc. **free port 1** a port area where goods in transit are exempt from customs duty. **2** a port open to all traders. **free radical** *Chem.* an unchanged atom or group of atoms with one or more unpaired electrons. **free-range** esp. *Brit.* (of hens etc.) kept in natural conditions with freedom of movement. **free rein** see REIN. **free school 1** a school for which no fees are charged. **2** a school run on the basis of freedom from restriction for the pupils. **free speech** the right to express opinions freely. **free-spoken** speaking candidly; not concealing one's opinions. **free-standing** not supported by another structure. **free-style** (of a swimming-race) in which any stroke may be used; (of wrestling) with few restrictions on the holds permitted. **free trade** international trade left to its natural course without restriction on imports or exports. **free verse** = VERS LIBRE. **free vote** a Parliamentary vote not subject to party discipline. **free wheel** the driving wheel of a bicycle, able to revolve with the pedals at rest. **free-wheel** *v.intr.* **1** ride a bicycle with the pedals at rest, esp. downhill. **2** move or act without constraint or effort. **free will 1** the power of acting without the constraint of necessity or fate. **2** the ability to act at one's own discretion (*I did it of my own free will*). **free world** esp. *US* the non-Communist countries' name for themselves. □□ **freely** *adv.* **freeness** *n.* [OE *frēo, frēon* f. Gmc]

-free /friː/ *comb. form* free of or from (*duty-free; fancy-free*).

freebase /ˈfriːbeɪs/ *n. & v. sl.* —*n.* cocaine that has been purified by heating with ether, and is taken by inhaling the fumes or smoking the residue. —*v.tr.* purify (cocaine) for smoking or inhaling.

freebie /ˈfriːbɪ/ *n.* esp. *US colloq.* a thing provided free of charge. [arbitrary f. FREE]

freeboard /ˈfriːbɔːd/ *n.* the part of a ship's side between the water-line and the deck.

freebooter /ˈfriːbuːtə(r)/ *n.* a pirate or lawless adventurer. □□ **freeboot** *v.intr.* [Du. *vrijbuiter* (as FREE, BOOTY): cf. FILIBUSTER]

freedman /ˈfriːdmən/ *n.* (*pl.* **-men**) an emancipated slave.

freedom /ˈfriːdəm/ *n.* **1** the condition of being free or unrestricted. **2** personal or civic liberty; absence of slave status. **3** the power of self-determination; independence of fate or necessity. **4** the state of being free to act (often foll. by *to* + infin.: *we have the freedom to leave*). **5** frankness, outspokenness; undue familiarity. **6** (foll. by *from*) the condition of being exempt from or not subject to (a defect, burden, etc.). **7** (foll. by *of*) **a** full or honorary participation in (membership, privileges, etc.). **b** unrestricted use of (facilities etc.). **8** a privilege possessed by a city or corporation. **9** facility or ease in action. **10** boldness of conception. □ **the four freedoms** four essential human

freedoms propounded by Franklin D. Roosevelt in 1941: freedom of speech and expression, freedom of worship, freedom from want, and freedom from fear. **freedom fighter** a person who takes part in violent resistance to an established political system etc. **Freedom Trail** a historic route through Boston, Massachusetts, which begins and ends at the Faneuil Hall where Bostonians met to protest against British 'taxation without representation' in the months preceding the War of American Independence. [OE *frēodōm* (as FREE, -DOM)]

Freefone /ˈfriːfəʊn/ *n.* (also **Freephone**) the name of a system operated in the UK by British Telecom whereby a person can make a telephone call free of charge to certain organizations, especially to obtain information or make use of a service.

freehand /ˈfriːhænd/ *adj. & adv.* —*adj.* (of a drawing or plan etc.) done by hand without special instruments or guides. —*adv.* in a freehand manner.

freehold /ˈfriːhəʊld/ *n. & adj.* —*n.* **1** tenure of land or property in fee simple or fee tail or for life. **2** land or property or an office held by such tenure. —*adj.* held by or having the status of freehold. □□ **freeholder** *n.*

freelance /ˈfriːlɑːns/ *n., v., & adv.* —*n.* **1 a** (also **freelancer**) a person, usu. self-employed, offering services on a temporary basis, esp. to several businesses etc. for particular assignments. **b** (*attrib.*) (*a freelance editor*). **2** (usu. **free lance**) *hist.* a medieval mercenary. —*v.intr.* act as a freelance. —*adv.* as a freelance. [19th c.: orig. in sense 2 of *n.*]

freeloader /ˈfriːˌləʊdə(r)/ *n.* *US sl.* a person who eats or drinks at others' expense; a sponger. □□ **freeload** /-ˈləʊd/ *v.intr.*

freeman /ˈfriːmən/ *n.* (*pl.* **-men**) **1** a person who has the freedom of a city, company, etc. **2** a person who is not a slave or serf.

freemartin /ˈfriːˌmɑːtɪn/ *n.* a hermaphrodite or imperfect female calf of oppositely sexed twins. [17th c.: orig. unkn.]

Freemason /ˈfriːˌmeɪs(ə)n/ *n.* a member of an international fraternity for mutual help and fellowship (the *Free and Accepted Masons*), with an elaborate ritual and system of secret signs. The original *free masons* were probably emancipated skilled itinerant stonemasons who (in and after the 14th c.) found work wherever important buildings were being erected, the *accepted masons* being honorary members (originally supposed to be eminent for architectural or antiquarian learning) who began to be admitted early in the 17th c., all of whom recognized their fellow craftsmen by secret signs. The distinction of being an 'accepted mason' became a fashionable object of ambition, and before the end of the 17th c. the purpose of the fraternities seems to have been chiefly social and convivial. In 1717 four of these societies or 'lodges' in London united to form a 'grand lodge', with a new constitution and ritual, and a new objective of mutual help and fellowship among members. The London 'grand lodge' became the parent of other 'lodges' in Britain and around the world, and there are now bodies of Freemasons in many countries of the world.

Freemasonry /ˈfriːˌmeɪsənrɪ/ *n.* **1** the system and institutions of the Freemasons. **2** (**freemasonry**) instinctive sympathy or understanding.

freepost /ˈfriːpəʊst/ *n.* a system of sending business post using printed envelopes or cards with postage paid by the issuing firm.

freer *compar.* of FREE.

freesia /ˈfriːzjə, -ʒə/ *n.* any bulbous plant of the genus *Freesia*, native to Africa, having fragrant coloured flowers. [mod.L f. F. H. T. *Freese*, Ger. physician d. 1876]

freest *superl.* of FREE.

freestone /ˈfriːstəʊn/ *n.* **1** any fine-grained stone which can be cut easily, esp. sandstone or limestone. **2** a stone-fruit, esp. a peach, in which the stone is loose when the fruit is ripe (cf. CLINGSTONE).

freestyle /ˈfriːstaɪl/ *adj.* (of a race or contest) in which all styles are allowed, esp.: **1** *Swimming* in which any stroke may be used. **2** *Wrestling* with few restrictions on the holds permitted.

freethinker /friːˈθɪŋkə(r)/ *n.* a person who rejects dogma or authority, esp. in religious belief. □□ **freethinking** *n. & adj.*

Freetown /ˈfriːtaʊn/ the capital and chief port of Sierra Leone; pop. (est. 1988) 469,800.

freeway /ˈfriːweɪ/ n. US 1 an express highway, esp. with controlled access. 2 a toll-free highway.

freeze /friːz/ v. & n. —v. (past froze /frəʊz/; past part. frozen /ˈfrəʊz(ə)n/) 1 tr. & intr. a turn or be turned into ice or another solid by cold. b (often foll. by over, up) make or become rigid or solid as a result of the cold. 2 intr. be or feel very cold. 3 tr. & intr. cover or become covered with ice. 4 intr. (foll. by to, together) adhere or be fastened by frost (the curtains froze to the window). 5 tr. preserve (food) by refrigeration below freezing-point. 6 tr. & intr. a make or become motionless or powerless through fear, surprise, etc. b react or cause to react with sudden aloofness or detachment. 7 tr. stiffen or harden, injure or kill, by chilling (frozen to death). 8 tr. make (credits, assets, etc.) temporarily or permanently unrealizable. 9 tr. fix or stabilize (prices, wages, etc.) at a certain level. 10 tr. arrest (an action) at a certain stage of development. 11 tr. arrest (a movement in a film) by repeating a frame or stopping the film at a frame. —n. 1 a state of frost; a period or the coming of frost or very cold weather. 2 the fixing or stabilization of prices, wages, etc. 3 a film-shot in which movement is arrested by the repetition of a frame. □ **freeze-dry** (-dries, -dried) freeze and dry by the sublimation of ice in a high vacuum. **freeze-frame** = sense 3 of n. **freeze on to** colloq. take or keep tight hold of. **freeze out** US colloq. exclude from business, society, etc. by competition or boycott etc. **freeze up** obstruct or be obstructed by the formation of ice. **freeze-up** n. a period or conditions of extreme cold. **freezing-mixture** salt and snow or some other mixture used to freeze liquids. **freezing-point** the temperature at which a liquid, esp. water, freezes. **freezing works** Austral. & NZ a place where animals are slaughtered and carcasses frozen for export. **frozen mitt** colloq. a cool reception. □□ **freezable** adj. **frozenly** adv. [OE frēosan f. Gmc]

freezer /ˈfriːzə(r)/ n. a refrigerated cabinet or room for preserving food at very low temperatures; = DEEP-FREEZE n.

Frege /ˈfreɪgə/, Gottlob (1848–1925), German philosopher and mathematician, founder of modern logic. His aim was to introduce rigour into mathematical proofs and establish the certainty of mathematical truth, and he developed a logical system for the expression of mathematics which was a vast improvement on the syllogistic logic which it replaced; he also worked on general questions of philosophical logic and semantics. His theory of meaning, based on his use of a distinction between what a linguistic term refers to and what it expresses, is still influential. Frege tried to provide a rigorous foundation for mathematics on the basis of purely logical principles, but abandoned the attempt when Bertrand Russell pointed out that his system was inconsistent.

freight /freɪt/ n. & v. —n. 1 the transport of goods in containers or by water or air or US by land. 2 goods transported; cargo. 3 a charge for transportation of goods. 4 the hire of a ship or aircraft for transporting goods. 5 a load or burden. —v.tr. 1 transport (goods) as freight. 2 load with freight. 3 hire or let out (a ship) for the carriage of goods and passengers. □ **freight ton** see TON¹. [MDu., MLG vrecht var. of vracht: cf. FRAUGHT]

freightage /ˈfreɪtɪdʒ/ n. 1 a the transportation of freight. b the cost of this. 2 freight transported.

freighter /ˈfreɪtə(r)/ n. 1 a ship or aircraft designed to carry freight. 2 US a wagon for freight. 3 a person who loads or charters and loads a ship. 4 a person who consigns goods for carriage inland. 5 a person whose business is to receive and forward freight.

freightliner /ˈfreɪtˌlaɪnə(r)/ n. a train carrying goods in containers.

Fremantle /ˈfriːmænt(ə)l/ the principal port of Western Australia; pop. (est. 1987) 24,000.

Frémont /ˈfriːmɒnt/, John Charles (1813–90), American explorer and statesman. Known as the Pathfinder for his efforts at opening up the American West, Frémont was responsible for exploring several viable routes to the Pacific across the Rockies in the 1840s. His public career, however, was stormy, involving two resignations from the army (one from a high position during the American Civil War), an unsuccessful bid for the Presidency in 1856, and a scandal over railway speculation which lost him his fortune in the 1870s. He served as Governor of Arizona in 1878–83 before eventually dying in New York.

French /frentʃ/ adj. & n. —adj. 1 of or relating to France or its people or language. 2 having the characteristics attributed to the French people. —n. 1 the language of France, also used in Belgium, Switzerland, Canada, and elsewhere. (See below.) 2 (the French) (pl.) the people of France. 3 colloq. bad language (excuse my French). 4 colloq. dry vermouth (gin and French). □ **French bean** Brit. 1 a beanplant, Phaseolus vulgaris, having many varieties cultivated for their pods and seeds. 2 a the pod used as food. b the seed used as food: also called HARICOT, kidney bean. **French bread** white bread in a long crisp loaf. **French Canadian** n. a Canadian whose principal language is French. —adj. of or relating to French-speaking Canadians. **French chalk** a kind of steatite used for marking cloth and removing grease and as a dry lubricant. **French cricket** an informal type of cricket without stumps and played with a soft ball. **French cuff** a cuff of double thickness. **French curve** a template used for drawing curved lines. **French door** = French window. **French dressing** a salad dressing of vinegar and oil, usu. seasoned. **French fried potatoes** (US **French fries**) potato chips. **French horn** a coiled brass wind instrument with a wide bell. **French kiss** a kiss with one partner's tongue inserted in the other's mouth. **French knickers** wide-legged knickers. **French leave** absence without permission. **French letter** Brit. colloq. a condom. **French mustard** Brit. a mild mustard mixed with vinegar. **French polish** shellac polish for wood. **French-polish** v.tr. polish with this. **French roof** a mansard. **French seam** a seam with the raw edges enclosed. **French toast** 1 Brit. bread buttered on one side and toasted on the other. 2 bread dipped in egg and milk and fried. **French vermouth** dry vermouth. **French window** a glazed door in an outside wall, serving as a window and door. □□ **Frenchness** n. [OE frencisc f. Gmc]

French is spoken as a native language by some 75 million people in France and neighbouring countries and also in Canada, and is the official language of a number of African States, having spread as a result of French colonization. It is a Romance language which has developed from the version of the Latin spoken in Gaul after its conquest in 58–51 BC. A number of dialects of French arose, but in recent centuries, since Paris became the French capital, the northern dialects have gained the ascendancy. A feature of French which began in the Middle Ages is the nasal pronunciation of certain vowels, found in no other living West European speeches except Portuguese. From the 11th to the 14th c. France was the leading country in Europe. Its influence and language spread, and in most European countries it became customary for the upper classes to learn French. From the 13th c. until well into the 20th c. it was the language of diplomacy, used for international negotiations. In 1635 the French Academy was founded (see ACADÉMIE FRANÇAISE), determining what should be considered correct French, and although modern writers continue to experiment with the language modern literary French remains much the same as the language of the 17th c.

French is the international postal language (whence the use of aérogramme on air-letter forms)—a status that it has held since a decision of the Universal Postal Union on its foundation in 1875.

French Guiana /gɪˈɑːnə/ an overseas department of France, in the north of South America; pop. (est. 1988) 90,500; capital, Cayenne.

Frenchify /ˈfrentʃɪˌfaɪ/ v.tr. (-ies, -ied) (usu. as **Frenchified** adj.) make French in form, character, or manners.

Frenchman /ˈfrentʃmən/ n. (pl. -men) a man who is French by birth or descent.

French Polynesia an overseas territory of France in the South Pacific, comprising five groups of islands (Windward, Leeward, Tuamotu, Tubuai, and Marquesas); pop. (est. 1988) 191,400; capital, Papeete (on the island of Tahiti).

b but d dog f few g get h he j yes k cat l leg m man n no p pen r red s sit t top v voice

French Revolution the overthrow of the Bourbon monarchy in France. It was the first of a series of European political upheavals, in which various groups in French society found common cause in opposing the feudal structure of the State, with its privileged Establishment and discredited monarchy. It began with the meeting of the legislative assembly in May 1789, when the French government was already in crisis. The Bastille was stormed in July of the same year and thereafter the Revolution became steadily more radical, with the rise of orators such as Robespierre in Paris, and attempts at intervention from abroad resulting in the execution of Louis XVI (Jan. 1793) and the Reign of Terror (Sept. 1793–July 1794). The Revolution failed to produce a stable form of republican government, and after several different forms of administration had been tried, the last, the Directory, was overthrown by Napoleon in 1799.

French Somaliland /səˈmɑːlɪˌlænd/ the former name (until 1967) of Djibouti.

Frenchwoman /ˈfrentʃˌwʊmən/ n. (pl. **-women**) a woman who is French by birth or descent.

frenetic /frəˈnetɪk/ adj. **1** frantic, frenzied. **2** fanatic. □□ **frenetically** adv. [ME f. OF frenetique f. L phreneticus f. Gk phrenitikos f. phrenitis delirium f. phrēn phrenos mind]

frenulum var. of FRAENULUM.

frenum var. of FRAENUM.

frenzy /ˈfrenzɪ/ n. & v. —n. (pl. **-ies**) **1** mental derangement; wild excitement or agitation. **2** delirious fury. —v.tr. (**-ies**, **-ied**) (usu. as **frenzied** adj.) drive to frenzy; infuriate. □□ **frenziedly** adv. [ME f. OF frenesie f. med.L phrenesia f. L phrenesis f. Gk phrēn mind]

Freon /ˈfriːɒn/ n. propr. any of a group of halogenated hydrocarbons containing fluorine, chlorine, and sometimes bromine, used in aerosols, refrigerants, etc. (see also CFC).

frequency /ˈfriːkwənsɪ/ n. (pl. **-ies**) **1** commonness of occurrence. **2 a** the state of being frequent; frequent occurrence. **b** the process of being repeated at short intervals. **3** Physics the rate of recurrence of a vibration, oscillation, cycle, etc.; the number of repetitions in a given time, esp. per second. ¶ Abbr.: f. **4** Statistics the ratio of the number of actual to possible occurrences of an event. □ **frequency band** Electronics = BAND¹ 3a. **frequency distribution** Statistics a measurement of the frequency of occurrence of the values of a variable. **frequency modulation** Electronics a modulation in which the frequency of the carrier wave is varied. (See ARMSTRONG¹.) ¶ Abbr.: FM. **frequency response** Electronics the dependence on signal-frequency of the output–input ratio of an amplifier etc. [L frequentia (as FREQUENT)]

frequent adj. & v. —adj. /ˈfriːkwənt/ **1** occurring often or in close succession. **2** habitual, constant (a frequent caller). **3** found near together; numerous, abundant. **4** (of the pulse) rapid. —v.tr. /frɪˈkwent/ attend or go to habitually. □□ **frequentation** /ˌfriːkwenˈteɪʃ(ə)n/ n. **frequenter** /frɪˈkwentə(r)/ n. **frequently** /ˈfriːkwəntlɪ/ adv. [F fréquent or L frequens -entis crowded]

frequentative /frɪˈkwentətɪv/ adj. & n. Gram. —adj. expressing frequent repetition or intensity of action. —n. a verb or verbal form or conjugation expressing this (e.g. chatter, twinkle). [F fréquentatif -ive or L frequentativus (as FREQUENT)]

fresco /ˈfreskəʊ/ n. (pl. **-os** or **-oes**) **1** a painting done in watercolour on a wall or ceiling while the plaster is still wet. **2** this method of painting (esp. in fresco), in which pure powdered pigments, mixed only in water, are applied to a wet freshly laid lime-plaster ground. The colours penetrate into the surface and as it dries they become fixed and insoluble in water as the paint becomes chemically bonded to the plaster that holds it. The fresco painter has to work rapidly, before the plaster dries, and corrections are almost impossible; but, once completed, the fresco will last as long as the wall itself. Fresco was used in the wall-paintings at Pompeii, and by the great masters of the Italian Renaissance, Giotto, Masaccio, Piero della Francesca, Raphael, and Michelangelo. It works best in dry climates, and has been used chiefly in Italy (except Venice) and rarely in northern Europe, although attempts were made to revive it by the German Nazarenes and English Pre-Raphaelites in the 19th c. □ **fresco secco** = SECCO. □□ **frescoed** adj. [It., = cool, fresh]

fresh /freʃ/ adj., adv., & n. —adj. **1** newly made or obtained (fresh sandwiches). **2 a** other, different; not previously known or used (start a fresh page; we need fresh ideas). **b** additional (fresh supplies). **3** (foll. by from) lately arrived from (a specified place or situation). **4** not stale or musty or faded (fresh flowers; fresh memories). **5** (of food) not preserved by salting, tinning, freezing, etc. **6** not salty (fresh water). **7 a** pure, untainted, refreshing, invigorating (fresh air). **b** bright and pure in colour (a fresh complexion). **8** (of the wind) brisk; of fair strength. **9** alert, vigorous, fit (never felt fresher). **10** colloq. **a** cheeky, presumptuous. **b** amorously impudent. **11** young and inexperienced. —adv. newly, recently (esp. in comb.: fresh-baked; fresh-cut). —n. the fresh part of the day, year, etc. (in the fresh of the morning). □□ **freshly** adv. **freshness** n. [ME f. OF freis fresche ult. f. Gmc]

freshen /ˈfreʃ(ə)n/ v. **1** tr. & intr. make or become fresh or fresher. **2** intr. & tr. (foll. by up) **a** wash, change one's clothes, etc. **b** revive, refresh, renew.

fresher /ˈfreʃə(r)/ n. Brit. colloq. = FRESHMAN.

freshet /ˈfreʃɪt/ n. **1** a rush of fresh water flowing into the sea. **2** the flood of a river from heavy rain or melted snow. [prob. f. OF freschete f. frais FRESH]

freshman /ˈfreʃmən/ n. (pl. **-men**) a first-year student at university or US at high school.

freshwater /ˈfreʃˌwɔːtə(r)/ adj. **1** of or found in fresh water; not of the sea. **2** US (esp. of a school or college) rustic or provincial. □ **freshwater flea** = DAPHNIA.

Fresnel /frəˈnel/, Augustin Jean (1788–1827), French physicist and civil engineer. He took up the study of polarized light in 1814 and postulated that light moved in a wave-like motion, which had already been suggested by, among others, Huygens and Thomas Young (1773–1829). They, however, assumed the waves to be longitudinal, while by 1821 Fresnel was sure that they vibrated transversely to the direction of propagation, and he used this to explain successfully the phenomenon of double refraction. He invented a large lens, made up of a series of concentric rings, for lighthouses and searchlights.

fret¹ /fret/ v. & n. —v. (**fretted, fretting**) **1** intr. **a** be greatly and visibly worried or distressed. **b** be irritated or resentful. **2** tr. **a** cause anxiety or distress to. **b** irritate, annoy. **3** tr. wear or consume by gnawing or rubbing. **4** tr. form (a channel or passage) by wearing away. **5** intr. (of running water) flow or rise in little waves. —n. irritation, vexation, querulousness (esp. in a fret). [OE fretan f. Gmc, rel. to EAT]

fret² /fret/ n. & v. —n. **1** an ornamental pattern made of continuous combinations of straight lines joined usu. at right angles. **2** Heraldry a device of narrow bands and a diamond interlaced. —v.tr. (**fretted, fretting**) **1** embellish or decorate with a fret. **2** adorn (esp. a ceiling) with carved or embossed work. [ME f. OF frete trellis-work and freter (v.)]

fret³ /fret/ n. each of a sequence of bars or ridges on the finger-board of some stringed musical instruments (esp. the guitar) fixing the positions of the fingers to produce the desired notes. □□ **fretless** adj. [15th c.: orig. unkn.]

fretful /ˈfretfʊl/ adj. visibly anxious, distressed, or irritated. □□ **fretfully** adv. **fretfulness** n.

fretsaw /ˈfretsɔː/ n. a saw consisting of a narrow blade stretched on a frame, for cutting thin wood in patterns.

fretwork /ˈfretwɜːk/ n. ornamental work in wood, done with a fretsaw.

Freud /frɔɪd/, Sigmund (1856–1939), Austrian neurologist and psychotherapist, the first to draw attention to the significance of unconscious processes in normal and neurotic behaviour, and founder of psychoanalysis as both a theory of personality and a therapeutic practice (see PSYCHOANALYSIS). The study of neurotic ailments led him to various conclusions relating to mental processes in general, such as the existence of an unconscious element in the mind which influences consciousness, and of conflicts in it between various sets of forces (including repression); he emphasized the importance of a child's semi-consciousness of sex as a factor in mental development, while his theory of the sexual origin of neuroses drew wide publicity and aroused great controversy. Born of a Jewish family, he left

Vienna after the German annexation of Austria in 1938 and joined his son in London, where he lived for the rest of his life. His publications include *The Interpretation of Dreams* (1899), *The Psychopathology of Everyday Life* (1904), and *Totem and Taboo* (1913).

Freudian /ˈfrɔɪdɪən/ *adj.* & *n. Psychol.* —*adj.* of or relating to Sigmund Freud or his methods of psychoanalysis, esp. with reference to the importance of sexuality in human behaviour. —*n.* a follower of Freud or his methods. □ **Freudian slip** an unintentional error regarded as revealing subconscious feelings. □□ **Freudianism** *n.*

Frey /freɪ/ (also **Freyr** /ˈfreɪə(r)/) *Scand. Mythol.* the god of fertility and dispenser of rain and sunshine.

Freya /ˈfreɪə/ *Scand. Mythol.* the goddess of love and of the night, the northern Venus, sister of Frey. She is sometimes indistinguishable from Frigga.

Freyberg /ˈfraɪbɜːɡ/, Bernard Cecil, 1st Baron (1889–1963), New Zealand soldier, who served in both World Wars and was Governor-General of New Zealand 1946–52.

Fri. *abbr.* Friday.

friable /ˈfraɪəb(ə)l/ *adj.* easily crumbled. □□ **friability** /-ˈbɪlɪtɪ/ *n.* **friableness** *n.* [F *friable* or L *friabilis* f. *friare* crumble]

friar /ˈfraɪə(r)/ *n.* a member of any of certain religious orders of men, esp. the four mendicant orders (Augustinians, Carmelites, Dominicans, and Franciscans). □ **friar's** (or **friars'**) **balsam** a tincture of benzoin etc. used esp. as an inhalant. □□ **friarly** *adj.* [ME & OF *frere* f. L *frater fratris* brother]

friary /ˈfraɪərɪ/ *n.* (*pl.* **-ies**) a convent of friars.

fricandeau /ˈfrɪkəndəʊ/ *n.* & *v.* —*n.* (*pl.* **fricandeaux** /-ˌdəʊz/) 1 a cushion-shaped piece of meat, esp. veal, cut from the leg. 2 a dish made from this, usu. fried or stewed and served with a sauce. —*v.tr.* (**fricandeaus, fricandeaued, fricandeauing**) make into fricandeaux. [F]

fricassee /ˈfrɪkəsiː, -ˈsiː/ *n.* & *v.* —*n.* a dish of stewed or fried pieces of meat served in a thick white sauce. —*v.tr.* (**fricassees, fricasseed**) make a fricassee of. [F, fem. past part. of *fricasser* (v.)]

fricative /ˈfrɪkətɪv/ *adj.* & *n. Phonet.* —*adj.* made by the friction of breath in a narrow opening. —*n.* a consonant made in this way, e.g. *f* and *th*. [mod.L *fricativus* f. L *fricare* rub]

friction /ˈfrɪkʃ(ə)n/ *n.* 1 the action of one object rubbing against another. 2 the resistance an object encounters in moving over another. 3 a clash of wills, temperaments, or opinions; mutual animosity arising from disagreement. 4 (in *comb.*) of devices that transmit motion by frictional contact (*friction-clutch; friction-disc*). □ **friction-ball** a ball used in bearings to lessen friction. □□ **frictional** *adj.* **frictionless** *adj.* [F f. L *frictio -onis* f. *fricare frict-* rub]

Friday /ˈfraɪdeɪ, -dɪ/ *n.* & *adv.* —*n.* the sixth day of the week, following Thursday. —*adv. colloq.* 1 on Friday. 2 (**Fridays**) on Fridays; each Friday. □ **girl** (or **man**) **Friday** a helper or follower (after *Man Friday* in Defoe's *Robinson Crusoe*). [OE *frigedæg* f. Gmc, (named after FRIGGA wife of Odin (cf. WEDNESDAY); the Latin name was *Veneris dies* day of Venus]

fridge /frɪdʒ/ *n. Brit. colloq.* = REFRIGERATOR. □ **fridge-freezer** an upright unit comprising a refrigerator and a freezer, each self-contained. [abbr.]

Friedman /ˈfriːdmən/, Milton (1912–), American economist, the principal exponent of monetarism (see entry). He was awarded the Nobel Prize for economics in 1976.

Friedrich /ˈfriːdrɪx/, Caspar David (1774–1840), German Romantic painter of landscapes, in which he saw a spiritual significance. His *The Cross in the Mountains* (1808) caused great controversy because it was painted as an altarpiece, and the use of a landscape in this unprecedented way was considered sacrilege by some critics.

friend /frend/ *n.* & *v.* —*n.* 1 a person with whom one enjoys mutual affection and regard (usu. exclusive of sexual or family bonds). 2 a sympathizer, helper, or patron (*no friend to virtue; a friend of order*). 3 a person who is not an enemy or who is on the same side (*friend or foe?*). 4 a a person already mentioned or under discussion (*my friend at the next table then left the room*). b a

person known by sight. c used as a polite or ironic form of address. 5 (usu. in *pl.*) a regular contributor of money or other assistance to an institution. 6 (**Friend**) a member of the Society of Friends (see entry), a Quaker. 7 (in *pl.*) one's near relatives, those responsible for one. 8 a helpful thing or quality. —*v.tr.* archaic or *poet.* befriend, help. □ **be** (or **keep**) **friends with** be friendly with. **friend at court** a friend whose influence may be made use of. **Friends of the Earth** a pressure group established in 1971 to campaign for a better awareness of and response to environmental problems. **my honourable friend** *Brit.* used in the House of Commons to refer to another member of one's own party. **my learned friend** used by a lawyer in court to refer to another lawyer. **my noble friend** *Brit.* used in the House of Lords to refer to another member of one's own party. □□ **friended** *adj.* **friendless** *adj.* [OE *frēond* f. Gmc]

friendly /ˈfrendlɪ/ *adj.*, *n.*, & *adv.* —*adj.* (**friendlier, friendliest**) 1 acting as or like a friend, well-disposed, kindly. 2 a (often foll. by *with*) on amicable terms. b not hostile. 3 characteristic of friends, showing or prompted by kindness. 4 favourably disposed, ready to approve or help. 5 a (of a thing) serviceable, convenient, opportune. b = *user-friendly*. —*n.* (*pl.* **-ies**) = *friendly match*. —*adv.* in a friendly manner. □ **friendly action** *Law* an action brought merely to get a point decided. **friendly match** a match played for enjoyment and not in competition for a cup etc. **Friendly Society** see separate entry. □□ **friendlily** *adv.* **friendliness** *n.*

Friendly Islands see TONGA.

Friendly Society any of a number of mutual-aid associations in Britain whose members pay regular contributions and in return recieve financial aid in sickness or old age, and provision for their families when they die. Such societies arose in the 17th and 18th centuries and became numerous in the 19th and early 20th centuries; many closed after 1946 when the welfare State was established, but some developed into life insurance companies. 'Friendly Society' was originally the name of a particular fire insurance company operating *c.*1700.

friendship /ˈfrendʃɪp/ *n.* 1 being friends, the relationship between friends. 2 a friendly disposition felt or shown. [OE *frēondscipe* (AS FRIEND, -SHIP)]

frier var. of FRYER.

Friesian /ˈfriːʒ(ə)n, -zɪən/ *n.* & *adj. Brit.* —*n.* 1 a large animal of a usu. black and white breed of dairy cattle orig. from Friesland. 2 this breed. —*adj.* of or concerning Friesians. [var. of FRISIAN]

Friesland /ˈfriːzlənd/ a northern province of The Netherlands, bounded to the north and west by the Zuider Zee; pop. (1988) 599,100; capital, Leeuwarden.

frieze¹ /friːz/ *n.* 1 the part of an entablature between the architrave and the cornice. 2 a horizontal band of sculpture filling this. 3 a band of decoration elsewhere, esp. along a wall near the ceiling. [F *frise* f. med.L *frisium, frigium* f. L *Phrygium* (*opus*) (work) of Phrygia]

frieze² /friːz/ *n.* coarse woollen cloth with a nap, usu. on one side only. [ME f. F *frise*, prob. rel. to FRISIAN]

frig¹ /frɪg/ *v.* & *n. coarse sl.* —*v.* (**frigged, frigging**) 1 *tr.* & *intr.* a have sexual intercourse (with). b masturbate. 2 *tr.* (usu. as an exclamation) = FUCK *v.* 3 *intr.* (foll. by *about, around*) mess about; fool around. 4 *intr.* (foll. by *off*) go away. —*n.* an act of frigging. ¶ Usually considered a taboo word. [perh. imit.: orig. senses 'move about, rub']

frig² /frɪdʒ/ *n. Brit. colloq.* = REFRIGERATOR. [abbr.]

frigate /ˈfrɪgɪt/ *n.* 1 a *Brit.* a naval escort-vessel between a corvette and a destroyer in size. b *US* a similar ship between a destroyer and a cruiser in size. 2 *hist.* a warship next in size to ships of the line. □ **frigate-bird** any marine bird of the family Fregatidae, found in tropical seas, with a wide wingspan and deeply forked tail: also called *hurricane-bird*. [F *frégate* f. It. *fregata*, of unkn. orig.]

Frigga /ˈfrɪgə/ *Scand. Mythol.* the wife of Odin and goddess of married love and of the hearth. (See FREYA.) Friday is named after her.

fright /fraɪt/ *n.* & *v.* —*n.* 1 a sudden or extreme fear. b an instance of this (*gave me a fright*). 2 a person or thing looking grotesque or ridiculous. —*v.tr. poet.* frighten. □ **take fright** become frightened. [OE *fryhto*, metathetic form of *fyrhto*, f. Gmc]

frighten /ˈfraɪt(ə)n/ *v.tr.* **1** fill with fright; terrify (*was frightened at the bang; is frightened of dogs*). **2** (foll. by *away, off, out of, into*) drive or force by fright (*frightened it out of the room; frightened them into submission; frightened me into agreeing*). □□ **frightening** *adj.* **frighteningly** *adv.*

frightener /ˈfraɪtənə(r)/ *n.* a person or thing that frightens. □ **put the frighteners on** *sl.* intimidate.

frightful /ˈfraɪtful/ *adj.* **1 a** dreadful, shocking, revolting. **b** ugly, hideous. **2** *colloq.* extremely bad (*a frightful idea*). **3** *colloq.* very great, extreme. □□ **frightfully** *adv.*

frightfulness /ˈfraɪtfulnɪs/ *n.* **1** being frightful. **2** (transl. G *Schrecklichkeit*) the terrorizing of a civilian population as a military resource.

frigid /ˈfrɪdʒɪd/ *adj.* **1 a** lacking friendliness or enthusiasm; apathetic, formal, forced. **b** dull, flat, insipid. **c** chilling, depressing. **2** (of a woman) sexually unresponsive. **3** (esp. of climate or air) cold. □ **frigid zones** the parts of the earth north of the Arctic Circle and south of the Antarctic Circle. □□ **frigidity** /-ˈdʒɪdɪtɪ/ *n.* **frigidly** *adv.* **frigidness** *n.* [L *frigidus* f. *frigēre* be cold f. *frigus* (n.) cold]

frijoles /friːˈhəʊleɪs/ *n.pl.* beans. [Sp., pl. of *frijol* bean ult. f. L *phaseolus*]

frill /frɪl/ *n. & v.* —*n.* **1 a** a strip of material with one side gathered or pleated and the other left loose with a fluted appearance, used as an ornamental edging. **b** a similar paper ornament on a ham-knuckle, chop, etc. **c** a natural fringe of feathers, hair, etc., on an animal (esp. a bird) or a plant. **2** (in *pl.*) **a** unnecessary embellishments or accomplishments. **b** airs, affectation (*put on frills*). —*v.tr.* **1** decorate with a frill. **2** form into a frill. □ **frill** (or **frilled**) **lizard** a large N. Australian lizard, *Chlamydosaurus kingii*, with a erectile membrane round the neck. □□ **frilled** *adj.* **frillery** *n.* [16th c.: orig. unkn.]

frilling /ˈfrɪlɪŋ/ *n.* **1** a set of frills. **2** material for frills.

frilly /ˈfrɪlɪ/ *adj. & n.* —*adj.* (**frillier, frilliest**) **1** having a frill or frills. **2** resembling a frill. —*n.* (*pl.* **-ies**) (in *pl.*) *colloq.* women's underwear. □□ **frilliness** *n.*

fringe /frɪndʒ/ *n. & v.* —*n.* **1** an ornamental bordering of threads left loose or formed into tassels or twists. **b** such a bordering made separately. **c** any border or edging. **2 a** a portion of the front hair hanging over the forehead. **b** a natural border of hair etc. in an animal or plant. **3** an outer edge or margin; the outer limit of an area, population, etc. (often *attrib.*: *fringe theatre*). **4** a thing, part, or area of secondary or minor importance. **5 a** a band of contrasting brightness or darkness produced by diffraction or interference of light. **b** a strip of false colour in an optical image. **6** *US* a fringe benefit —*v.tr.* **1** adorn or encircle with a fringe. **2** serve as a fringe to. □ **fringe benefit** an employee's benefit supplementing a money wage or salary. **fringe medicine** systems of treatment of disease etc. not regarded as orthodox by the medical profession. **fringing reef** a coral reef that fringes the shore. □□ **fringeless** *adj.* **fringy** *adj.* [ME & OF *frenge* ult. f. LL *fimbria* (earlier only in pl.) fibres, fringe]

fringing /ˈfrɪndʒɪŋ/ *n.* material for a fringe or fringes.

frippery /ˈfrɪpərɪ/ *n. & adj.* —*n.* (*pl.* **-ies**) **1** showy, tawdry, or unnecessary finery or ornament, esp. in dress. **2** empty display in speech, literary style, etc. **3 a** knick-knacks, trifles. **b** a knick-knack or trifle. —*adj.* **1** frivolous. **2** contemptible. [F *friperie* f. OF *freperie* f. *frepe* rag]

frippet /ˈfrɪpɪt/ *n. sl.* a frivolous or showy young woman. [20th c.: orig. unkn.]

Frisbee /ˈfrɪzbɪ/ *n. propr.* a concave plastic disc for skimming through the air as an outdoor game. [perh. f. *Frisbie* bakery (Bridgeport, Conn.), whose pie-tins could be used similarly]

Frisch[1] /frɪʃ/, Karl von (1886–1982), Austrian zoologist, noted for his work on animal behaviour, and especially his conclusion that honey bees perform an elaborate 'dance' to show others the direction and distance of a source of nectar. He shared a Nobel Prize in 1973 with Lorenz and Tinbergen.

Frisch[2] /frɪʃ/, Otto Robert (1904–79), Austrian physicist, who in 1938, with his aunt Lise Meitner (see HAHN) recognized that

Hahn's experiments with uranium had produced a new type of nuclear reaction. Frisch named it nuclear fission, and indicated the explosive potential of its chain reaction. During the Second World War he continued his research in England, becoming a British subject, and worked on nuclear weapons in the US at the Los Alamos laboratory.

Frisch[3] /frɪʃ/, Ragnar Anton Kittil (1895–1973), Norwegian economist, pioneer of econometrics. He shared with Jan Tinbergen the first Nobel Prize to be awarded for economics (1969).

Frisian /ˈfrɪzɪən/ *adj. & n.* —*adj.* of Friesland or its people or language. —*n.* **1** a native or inhabitant of Friesland. **2** the Germanic language of Friesland, most closely related to English and Dutch, with about 300,000 speakers. [L *Frisii* pl. f. OFris. *Frīsa, Frēsa*]

Frisian Islands a line of islands off the coast of Denmark, Germany, and The Netherlands, stretching from the Zuider Zee to Jutland.

frisk /frɪsk/ *v. & n.* —*v.* **1** *intr.* leap or skip playfully. **2** *tr. sl.* feel over or search (a person) for a weapon etc. (usu. rapidly). —*n.* **1** a playful leap or skip. **2** *sl.* the frisking of a person. □□ **frisker** *n.* [obs. *frisk* (adj.) f. OF *frisque* lively, of unkn. orig.]

frisket /ˈfrɪskɪt/ *n. Printing* a thin iron frame keeping the sheet in position during printing on a hand-press. [F *frisquette* f. Prov. *frisqueto* f. Sp. *frasqueta*]

frisky /ˈfrɪskɪ/ *adj.* (**friskier, friskiest**) lively, playful. □□ **friskily** *adv.* **friskiness** *n.*

frisson /ˈfriːsɒn, -sɔ̃/ *n.* an emotional thrill. [F, = shiver]

frit /frɪt/ *n. & v.* —*n.* **1** a calcined mixture of sand and fluxes as material for glass-making. **2** a vitreous composition from which soft porcelain, enamel, etc., are made. —*v.tr.* (**fritted, fritting**) make into frit, partially fuse, calcine. [It. *fritta* fem. past part. of *friggere* FRY[1]]

frit-fly /ˈfrɪtflaɪ/ *n.* (*pl.* **-flies**) a small fly, *Oscinella frit*, of which the larvae are destructive to cereals. [19th c.: orig. unkn.]

Frith /frɪθ/, William Powell (1819–1909), English painter, best known for his panoramic scenes of Victorian middle-class life, executed in fine detail with great technical dexterity.

frith var. of FIRTH.

fritillary /frɪˈtɪlərɪ, ˈfrɪ-/ *n.* (*pl.* **-ies**) **1** any liliaceous plant of the genus *Fritillaria*, esp. snake's head, having pendent bell-like flowers. **2** any of various butterflies, esp. of the genus *Argynnis*, having red-brown wings chequered with black. [mod.L *fritillaria* f. L *fritillus* dice-box]

fritter[1] /ˈfrɪtə(r)/ *v.tr.* **1** (usu. foll. by *away*) waste (money, time, energy, etc.) triflingly, indiscriminately, or on divided aims. **2** *archaic* subdivide. [obs. n. *fritter(s)* fragments = obs. *fitters* (n.pl.), perh. rel. to MHG *vetze* rag]

fritter[2] /ˈfrɪtə(r)/ *n.* a piece of fruit, meat, etc., coated in batter and deep-fried (*apple fritter*). [ME f. OF *friture* ult. f. L *frigere* frict- FRY[1]]

fritto misto /ˌfrɪtəʊ ˈmɪstəʊ/ *n.* a mixed grill. [It., = mixed fry]

fritz /frɪts/ *n.* □ **on the fritz** *US sl.* out of order, unsatisfactory. [20th c.: orig. unkn.]

Friuli-Venezia Giulia /frɪˌuːlɪveˈnetsɪə ˈdʒuːlɪə/ an autonomous region of NE Italy, on the Yugoslavian frontier; pop. (1981) 1,234,000; capital, Trieste.

frivol /ˈfrɪv(ə)l/ *v.* (**frivolled, frivolling**; *US* **frivoled, frivoling**) **1** *intr.* be a trifler; trifle. **2** *tr.* (foll. by *away*) spend (money or time) foolishly. [back-form. f. FRIVOLOUS]

frivolous /ˈfrɪvələs/ *adj.* **1** paltry, trifling, trumpery. **2** lacking seriousness; given to trifling; silly. □□ **frivolity** /-ˈvɒlɪtɪ/ *n.* (*pl.* **-ies**). **frivolously** *adv.* **frivolousness** *n.* [L *frivolus* silly, trifling]

frizz /frɪz/ *v. & n.* —*v.tr.* **1** form (hair) into a mass of small curls. **2** dress (wash-leather etc.) with pumice or a scraping-knife. —*n.* **1 a** a frizzed hair. **b** a row of curls. **2** a frizzed state. [F *friser*, perh. f. the stem of *frire* FRY[1]]

frizzle[1] /ˈfrɪz(ə)l/ *v.intr. & tr.* **1** fry, toast, or grill, with a sputtering noise. **2** (often foll. by *up*) burn or shrivel. [*frizz* (in the same sense) f. FRY[1], with imit. ending + -LE[4]]

frizzle[2] /ˈfrɪz(ə)l/ *v. & n.* —*v.* **1** *tr.* form (hair) into tight curls. **2**

intr. (often foll. by *up*) (of hair etc.) curl tightly. —*n.* frizzled hair. [16th c.: orig. unkn. (earlier than FRIZZ)]

frizzly /ˈfrɪzlɪ/ *adj.* in tight curls.

frizzy /ˈfrɪzɪ/ *adj.* (**frizzier, frizziest**) in a mass of small curls. □□ **frizziness** *n.*

Frl. *abbr.* Fräulein.

fro /frəʊ/ *adv.* back (now only in *to and fro*: see TO). [ME f. ON *frá* FROM]

Frobisher /ˈfrəʊbɪʃə(r)/, Sir Martin (*c.*1535–94), English sailor and explorer. Having first gone to sea as a boy, he went on to lead an expedition in search of the Northwest Passage, discovering what became called Frobisher Bay and landing in Labrador before returning safely despite the loss of one of his three tiny ships and the desertion of another (1576). He returned to Canada in each of the following two years in a fruitless search for gold, before serving in Drake's West Indies expedition of 1585–6 and playing a prominent part in the defeat of the Spanish Armada (for which he was knighted). He died in Plymouth from wounds received in the siege of the Spanish fort at Crozon in Brittany.

frock /frɒk/ *n.* & *v.* —*n.* **1** a woman's or girl's dress. **2 a** a monk's or priest's long gown with loose sleeves. **b** priestly office. **3** a smock. **4 a** a frock-coat. **b** a military coat of similar shape. **5** a sailor's woollen jersey. —*v.tr.* invest with priestly office (cf. UNFROCK). □ **frock-coat** a man's long-skirted coat not cut away in front. [ME f. OF *froc* f. Frank.]

froe /frəʊ/ *n.* (also **frow**) *US* a cleaving tool with a handle at right angles to the blade. [abbr. of *frower* f. FROWARD 'turned away']

Froebel /ˈfrəʊb(ə)l, ˈfrɜːb(ə)l/, Friedrich Wilhelm (1782–1852), German educationist, founder of the kindergarten system. Believing that play materials, practical occupations, and songs were needed to develop a child's real nature, when his two brothers died he undertook the education of their children, opening a school in his native Thuringia to put his theories into practice. In 1837 he opened a school for younger children, naming it the Kindergarten (= children's garden), and later developed a system of specialized training for teachers. In the reactionary period after the 1848 uprisings, however, his reforms fell into disfavour, with the result that his schools were closed by Prussian authorities in 1851. □□ **Froebelian** /-ˈbiːlɪən/ *adj.* **Froebelism** *n.* [F. W. A. *Fröbel*, Ger. teacher d. 1852]

frog¹ /frɒg/ *n.* **1** any of various small amphibians of the order Anura, having a tailless smooth-skinned body with legs developed for jumping. **2** (**Frog**) *Brit. sl. offens.* a Frenchman. **3** a hollow in the top face of a brick for holding the mortar. **4** the nut of a violin-bow etc. □ **frog-fish** = *angler-fish.* **frog in the** (or **one's**) **throat** *colloq.* hoarseness. **frog-spawn** the spawn of a frog. [OE *frogga* f. Gmc]

frog² /frɒg/ *n.* an elastic horny substance in the sole of a horse's foot. [17th c.: orig. uncert. (perh. a use of FROG¹)]

frog³ /frɒg/ *n.* **1** an ornamental coat-fastening of a spindle-shaped button and loop. **2** an attachment to a waist-belt to support a sword, bayonet, etc. □□ **frogged** *adj.* **frogging** *n.* [18th c.: orig. unkn.]

frog⁴ /frɒg/ *n.* a grooved piece of iron at a place in a railway where tracks cross. [19th c.: orig. unkn.]

froggy /ˈfrɒgɪ/ *adj.* & *n.* —*adj.* **1** of or like a frog or frogs. **2 a** cold as a frog. **b** abounding in frogs. **3** *Brit. sl. offens.* French. —*n.* (**Froggy**) (*pl.* **-ies**) *sl. derog.* a Frenchman.

froghopper /ˈfrɒgˌhɒpə(r)/ *n.* any jumping insect of the family Cercopidae, sucking sap and as larvae producing a protective mass of froth (see *cuckoo-spit*).

frogman /ˈfrɒgmən/ *n.* (*pl.* **-men**) a person equipped with a rubber suit, flippers, and an oxygen supply for underwater swimming.

frogmarch /ˈfrɒgmɑːtʃ/ *v.* & *n.* esp. *Brit.* —*v.tr.* **1** hustle (a person) forward forcibly, esp. holding and pinning the arms from behind. **2** carry (a person) face downwards by four persons each holding a limb. —*n.* the process of frogmarching a person.

frogmouth /ˈfrɒgmaʊθ/ *n.* any of various birds of Australia and SE Asia, esp. of the family Podargidae, having large wide mouths.

frolic /ˈfrɒlɪk/ *v., n.,* & *adj.* —*v.intr.* (**frolicked, frolicking**) play about cheerfully, gambol. —*n.* **1** cheerful play. **2** a prank. **3** a merry party. **4** an outburst of gaiety. **5** merriment. —*adj. archaic* **1** full of pranks, sportive. **2** joyous, mirthful. □□ **frolicker** *n.* [Du. *vrolijk* (adj.) f. *vro* glad + -LY¹]

frolicsome /ˈfrɒlɪksəm/ *adj.* merry, playful. □□ **frolicsomely** *adv.* **frolicsomeness** *n.*

from /frəm, frɒm/ *prep.* expressing separation or origin, followed by: **1** a person, place, time, etc., that is the starting-point of motion or action, or of extent in place or time (*rain comes from the clouds; repeated from mouth to mouth; dinner is served from 8; from start to finish*). **2** a place, object, etc. whose distance or remoteness is reckoned or stated (*ten miles from Rome; I am far from admitting it; absent from home; apart from its moral aspect*). **3 a** a source (*dig gravel from a pit; a man from Italy; draw a conclusion from premisses; quotations from Shaw*). **b** a giver or sender (*presents from Father Christmas; have not heard from her*). **4 a** a thing or person avoided, escaped, lost, etc. (*released him from prison; cannot refrain from laughing; dissuaded from folly*). **b** a person or thing deprived (*took his gun from him*). **5** a reason, cause, or motive (*died from fatigue; suffering from mumps; did it from jealousy; from his looks you might not believe it*). **6** a thing distinguished or unlike (*know black from white*). **7** a lower limit (*saw from 10 to 20 boats; tickets from £5*). **8** a state changed for another (*from being the victim he became the attacker; raised the penalty from a fine to imprisonment*). **9** an adverb or preposition of time or place (*from long ago; from abroad; from under the bed*). **10** the position of a person who observes or considers (*saw it from the roof; from his point of view*). **11** a model (*painted it from nature*). □ **from a child** since childhood. **from day to day** (or **hour to hour** etc.) daily (or hourly etc.); as the days (or hours etc.) pass. **from home** out, away. **from now on** henceforward. **from time to time** occasionally. **from year to year** each year; as the years pass. [OE *fram, from* f. Gmc]

frond /frɒnd/ *n.* **1** *Bot.* **a** a large usu. divided foliage leaf in various flowerless plants, esp. ferns and palms. **b** the leaflike thallus of some algae. **2** *Zool.* a leaflike expansion. □□ **frondage** *n.* **frondose** *adj.* [L *frons frondis* leaf]

frondeur /frɒnˈdɜː(r)/ *n.* a political rebel. [F, = slinger, applied to a party (the Fronde) rebelling during the minority of Louis XIV of France]

front /frʌnt/ *n., adj.,* & *v.* —*n.* **1** the side or part normally nearer or towards the spectator or the direction of motion (*the front of the car; the front of the chair; the front of the mouth*). **2** any face of a building, esp. that of the main entrance. **3** *Mil.* **a** the foremost line or part of an army etc. **b** line of battle. **c** the part of the ground towards a real or imaginary enemy. **d** a scene of actual fighting (*go to the front*). **e** the direction in which a formed line faces (*change front*). **4 a** a sector of activity regarded as resembling a military front. **b** an organized political group. **5 a** demeanour, bearing (*show a bold front*). **b** outward appearance. **6** a forward or conspicuous position (*come to the front*). **7 a** a bluff. **b** a pretext. **8** a person etc. serving to cover subversive or illegal activities. **9** (prec. by *the*) the promenade of a seaside resort. **10** *Meteorol.* the forward edge of an advancing mass of cold or warm air. **11** (prec. by *the*) the auditorium of a theatre. **12 a** a face. **b** *poet.* or *rhet.* a forehead. **13 a** the breast of a man's shirt. **b** a false shirt-front. **14** impudence. —*attrib.adj.* **1** of the front. **2** situated in front. **3** *Phonet.* formed at the front of the mouth. —*v.* **1** *intr.* (foll. by *on, to, towards, upon*) have the front facing or directed. **2** *intr.* (foll. by *for*) *sl.* act as a front or cover for. **3** *tr.* furnish with a front (*fronted with stone*). **4** *tr.* lead (a band). **5** *tr.* a stand opposite to, front towards. **b** have its front on the side of (a street etc.). **6** *tr. archaic* confront, meet, oppose. □ **front bench** *Brit.* the foremost seats in Parliament, occupied by leading members of the government and opposition. **front-bencher** *Brit.* such a member. **front door 1** the chief entrance of a house. **2** a chief means of approach or access to a place, situation, etc. **front line** *Mil.* = sense 3 of *n.* **front-line States** countries in southern Africa bordering on and opposed to South Africa. **front man** a person acting as a front or cover. **front matter** *Printing* the title-page, preface, etc. preceding the text proper. **front office** a main office, esp. police headquarters. **front page** the first page of a newspaper, esp. as containing important or remarkable news. **front passage** *colloq.* the vagina. **front runner 1** the contestant most likely to succeed. **2** an athlete or horse running best when in the lead. **in front 1** in an advanced position. **2** facing the spectator. **in front of 1** ahead of, in advance of. **2** in the presence of, confronting. **on the front burner** see BURNER. □□ **frontless** *adj.* **frontward** *adj. & adv.* **frontwards** *adv.* [ME f. OF *front* (n.), *fronter* (v.) f. L *frons frontis*]

frontage /ˈfrʌntɪdʒ/ *n.* **1** the front of a building. **2 a** land abutting on a street or on water. **b** the land between the front of a building and the road. **3** extent of front (*a shop with little frontage*). **4 a** the way a thing faces. **b** outlook. □ **frontage road** US a service road. □□ **frontager** *n.*

frontal[1] /ˈfrʌnt(ə)l/ *adj.* **1 a** of, at, or on the front (*a frontal attack*). **b** of the front as seen by an onlooker (*a frontal view*). **2** of the forehead or front part of the skull (*frontal bone*). □□ **frontally** *adv.* [mod.L *frontalis* (as FRONT)]

frontal[2] /ˈfrʌnt(ə)l/ *n.* **1** a covering for the front of an altar. **2** the façade of a building. [ME f. OF *frontel* f. L *frontale* (as FRONT)]

frontier /ˈfrʌntɪə(r), -ˈtɪə(r)/ *n.* **1 a** the border between two countries. **b** the district on each side of this. **2** the limits of attainment or knowledge in a subject. **3** US the borders between settled and unsettled country. □□ **frontierless** *adj.* [ME f. AF *frounter*, OF *frontiere* ult. f. L *frons frontis* FRONT]

frontiersman /ˈfrʌntɪəzmən, -ˈtɪəzmən/ *n.* (*pl.* **-men**) a person living in the region of a frontier, esp. between settled and unsettled country.

frontispiece /ˈfrʌntɪsˌpiːs/ *n.* **1** an illustration facing the title-page of a book or of one of its divisions. **2** *Archit.* **a** the principal face of a building. **b** a decorated entrance. **c** a pediment over a door etc. [F *frontispice* or LL *frontispicium* façade f. L *frons frontis* FRONT + *-spicium* f. *specere* look: assim. to PIECE]

frontlet /ˈfrʌntlɪt/ *n.* **1** a piece of cloth hanging over the upper part of an altar frontal. **2** a band worn on the forehead. **3** a phylactery. **4** an animal's forehead. [OF *frontelet* (as FRONTAL[2])]

fronton /ˈfrʌnt(ə)n/ *n.* a pediment. [F f. It. *frontone* f. *fronte* forehead]

frore /frɔː(r)/ *adj. poet.* frozen, frosty. [archaic past part. of FREEZE]

Frost /frɒst/, Robert Lee (1874–1963), American poet, whose work is deeply expressive of the farm country in which he had lived. But beneath the 'simple woodland philosophy' lay a more troubled and combative spirit, expressed in such poems as 'Fire and Ice' (1923) and 'Bereft' (1928).

frost /frɒst/ *n. & v.* —*n.* **1 a** (also **white frost**) a white frozen dew coating esp. the ground at night (*windows covered with frost*). **b** a consistent temperature below freezing-point causing frost to form. **2** a chilling dispiriting atmosphere. **3** *sl.* a failure. —*v.* **1** *intr.* (usu. foll. by *over*, *up*) become covered with frost. **2** *tr.* **a** cover with or as if with frost, powder, etc. **b** injure (a plant etc.) with frost. **3** *tr.* give a roughened or finely granulated surface to (glass, metal) (*frosted glass*). **4** *tr.* US cover or decorate (a cake etc.) with icing. □ **black frost** a frost without white dew. **degrees of frost** *Brit.* degrees below freezing-point (*ten degrees of frost tonight*). **frost-work** tracery made by frost on glass etc. □□ **frostless** *adj.* [OE f. Gmc]

frostbite /ˈfrɒstbaɪt/ *n.* injury to body tissues, esp. the nose, fingers, or toes, due to freezing and often resulting in gangrene.

frosting /ˈfrɒstɪŋ/ *n.* **1** US icing. **2** a rough surface on glass etc.

frosty /ˈfrɒstɪ/ *adj.* (**frostier, frostiest**) **1** cold with frost. **2** covered with or as with hoar-frost. **3** unfriendly in manner, lacking in warmth of feeling. □□ **frostily** *adv.* **frostiness** *n.*

froth /frɒθ/ *n. & v.* —*n.* **1 a** a collection of small bubbles in liquid, caused by shaking, fermenting, etc.; foam. **b** impure matter on liquid; scum. **2 a** idle talk or ideas. **b** anything unsubstantial or of little worth. —*v.* **1** *intr.* emit or gather froth (*frothing at the mouth*). **2** *tr.* cause (beer etc.) to foam. □ **froth-blower** *Brit. joc.* a beer-drinker (esp. as a designation of a member of a charitable organization). □□ **frothily** *adv.* **frothiness** *n.* **frothy** *adj.* (**frothier, frothiest**). [ME f. ON *frotha*, *frauth* f. Gmc]

frottage /frɒˈtɑːʒ/ *n.* **1** *Psychol.* an abnormal desire for contact between the clothed bodies of oneself and another. **2** *Art* the

technique or process of taking a rubbing from an uneven surface to form the basis of a work of art. [F, = rubbing f. *frotter* rub f. OF *froter*]

frou-frou /ˈfruːfruː/ *n.* a rustling, esp. of a dress. [F, imit.]

frow[1] /fraʊ/ *n.* **1** a Dutchwoman. **2** a housewife. [ME f. Du. *vrouw* woman]

frow[2] var. of FROE.

froward /ˈfrəʊəd/ *adj. archaic* perverse; difficult to deal with. □□ **frowardly** *adv.* **frowardness** *n.* [ME f. FRO + -WARD]

frown /fraʊn/ *v. & n.* —*v.* **1** *intr.* wrinkle one's brows, esp. in displeasure or deep thought. **2** *intr.* (foll. by *at*, *on*, *upon*) express disapproval. **3** *intr.* (of a thing) present a gloomy aspect. **4** *tr.* compel with a frown (*frowned them into silence*). **5** *tr.* express (defiance etc.) with a frown. —*n.* **1** an action of frowning; a vertically furrowed or wrinkled state of the brow. **2** a look expressing severity, disapproval, or deep thought. □□ **frowner** *n.* **frowningly** *adv.* [ME f. OF *frongnier*, *froignier* f. *froigne* surly look f. Celt.]

frowst /fraʊst/ *n. & v. Brit. colloq.* —*n.* fusty warmth in a room. —*v.intr.* stay in or enjoy frowst. □□ **frowster** *n.* [back-form. f. FROWSTY]

frowsty /ˈfraʊstɪ/ *adj. Brit.* (**frowstier, frowstiest**) fusty, stuffy. □□ **frowstiness** *n.* [var. of FROWZY]

frowzy /ˈfraʊzɪ/ *adj.* (also **frowsy**) (**-ier, -iest**) **1** fusty, musty, ill-smelling, close. **2** slatternly, unkempt, dingy. □□ **frowziness** *n.* [17th c.: orig. unkn.: cf. earlier *frowy*]

froze *past* of FREEZE.

frozen *past part.* of FREEZE.

FRS *abbr.* (in the UK) Fellow of the Royal Society.

FRSE *abbr.* Fellow of the Royal Society of Edinburgh.

fructiferous /frʌkˈtɪfərəs/ *adj.* bearing fruit. [L *fructifer* f. *fructus* FRUIT]

fructification /ˌfrʌktɪfɪˈkeɪʃ(ə)n/ *n. Bot.* **1** the process of fructifying. **2** any spore-bearing structure esp. in ferns, fungi, and mosses. [LL *fructificatio* (as FRUCTIFY)]

fructify /ˈfrʌktɪfaɪ/ *v.* (**-ies, -ied**) **1** *intr.* bear fruit. **2** *tr.* make fruitful; impregnate. [ME f. OF *fructifier* f. L *fructificare* f. *fructus* FRUIT]

fructose /ˈfrʌktəʊz, -əʊs, ˈfrʊk-/ *n. Chem.* a simple sugar found in honey and fruits. Also called LAEVULOSE, *fruit sugar*. [L *fructus* FRUIT + -OSE 2]

fructuous /ˈfrʌktjʊəs/ *adj.* full of or producing fruit. [ME f. OF *fructuous* or L *fructuosus* (as FRUIT)]

frugal /ˈfruːg(ə)l/ *adj.* **1** (often foll. by *of*) sparing or economical, esp. as regards food. **2** sparingly used or supplied, meagre, costing little. □□ **frugality** /-ˈgælɪtɪ/ *n.* **frugally** *adv.* **frugalness** *n.* [L *frugalis* f. *frugi* economical]

frugivorous /fruːˈdʒɪvərəs/ *adj.* feeding on fruit. [L *frux frugis* fruit + -VOROUS]

fruit /fruːt/ *n. & v.* —*n.* **1 a** the usu. sweet and fleshy edible product of a plant or tree, containing seed. **b** (in *sing.*) these in quantity (*eats fruit*). **2** the seed of a plant or tree with its covering, e.g. an acorn, pea pod, cherry, etc. **3** (usu. in *pl.*) vegetables, grains, etc. used for food (*fruits of the earth*). **4** (usu. in *pl.*) the result of action etc., esp. as financial reward (*fruits of his labours*). **5** *sl.* US a male homosexual. **6** *Bibl.* an offspring (*the fruit of the womb; the fruit of his loins*). —*v.intr.* bear or cause to bear fruit. □ **fruit bar** a piece of dried and pressed fruit. **fruit-bat** any large bat of the suborder Megachiroptera, feeding on fruit. **fruit- (or fruiting-) body** (*pl.* **-ies**) the spore-bearing part of a fungus. **fruit cake 1** a cake containing dried fruit. **2** *sl.* an eccentric or mad person. **fruit cocktail** a finely-chopped usu. tinned fruit salad. **fruit fly** (*pl.* **flies**) any of various flies, esp. of the genus *Drosophila*, having larvae that feed on fruit. **fruit machine** *Brit.* a coin-operated gaming machine giving random combinations of symbols often representing fruit. **fruit salad 1** various fruits cut up and served in syrup, juice, etc. **2** *sl.* a display of medals etc. **fruit sugar** fructose. **fruit-tree** a tree grown for its fruit. **fruit-wood** the wood of a fruit-tree, esp. when used in furniture. □□ **fruitage** *n.* **fruited** *adj.* (also in comb.). [ME f. OF f. L *fructus* fruit, enjoyment f. *frui* enjoy]

fruitarian /fruːˈtɛərɪən/ n. a person who eats only fruit. [FRUIT, after *vegetarian*]

fruiter /ˈfruːtə(r)/ n. 1 a tree producing fruit, esp. with reference to its quality (*a poor fruiter*). 2 Brit. a fruit grower. 3 a ship carrying fruit. [ME f. OF *fruitier* (as FRUIT, -ER⁵): later f. FRUIT + -ER¹]

fruiterer /ˈfruːtərə(r)/ n. esp. Brit. a dealer in fruit.

fruitful /ˈfruːtfʊl/ adj. 1 producing much fruit; fertile; causing fertility. 2 producing good results, successful; beneficial, remunerative. 3 producing offspring, esp. prolifically. □□ **fruitfully** adv. **fruitfulness** n.

fruition /fruːˈɪʃ(ə)n/ n. 1 a the bearing of fruit. b the production of results. 2 the realization of aims or hopes. 3 enjoyment. [ME f. OF f. LL *fruitio -onis* f. *frui* enjoy, erron. assoc. with FRUIT]

fruitless /ˈfruːtlɪs/ adj. 1 not bearing fruit. 2 useless, unsuccessful, unprofitable. □□ **fruitlessly** adv. **fruitlessness** n.

fruitlet /ˈfruːtlɪt/ n. = DRUPEL.

fruity /ˈfruːtɪ/ adj. (**fruitier, fruitiest**) 1 a of fruit. b tasting or smelling like fruit, esp. (of wine) tasting of the grape. 2 (of a voice etc.) of full rich quality. 3 colloq. full of rough humour or (usu. scandalous) interest; suggestive. □□ **fruitily** adv. **fruitiness** n.

frumenty /ˈfruːmənti/ n. (also **furmety** /ˈfɜːmɪti/) hulled wheat boiled in milk and seasoned with cinnamon, sugar, etc. [ME f. OF *frumentee* f. *frument* f. L *frumentum* corn]

frump /frʌmp/ n. a dowdy unattractive old-fashioned woman. □□ **frumpish** adj. **frumpishly** adv. [16th c.: perh. f. dial. *frumple* (v.) wrinkle f. MDu. *verrompelen* (as FOR-, RUMPLE)]

frumpy /ˈfrʌmpi/ adj. (**frumpier, frumpiest**) dowdy, unattractive, and old-fashioned. □□ **frumpily** adv. **frumpiness** n.

Frunze /ˈfruːnzjə/ (formerly **Pishpek** /pɪʃˈpek/) the capital of Kirghizia; pop. (est. 1987) 632,000.

frustrate v. & adj. —v.tr. /frʌˈstreɪt, ˈfrʌs-/ 1 make (efforts) ineffective. 2 prevent (a person) from achieving a purpose. 3 (as **frustrated** adj.) a discontented because unable to achieve one's desire. b sexually unfulfilled. 4 disappoint (a hope). —adj. /ˈfrʌstreɪt/ archaic frustrated. □□ **frustratedly** adv. **frustrater** n. **frustrating** adj. **frustratingly** adv. **frustration** n. [ME f. L *frustrari frustrat-* f. *frustra* in vain]

frustule /ˈfrʌstjuːl/ n. Bot. the siliceous cell wall of a diatom. [F f. L *frustulum* (as FRUSTUM)]

frustum /ˈfrʌstəm/ n. (pl. **frusta** /-tə/ or **frustums**) Geom. 1 the remainder of a cone or pyramid whose upper part has been cut off by a plane parallel to its base. 2 the part of a cone or pyramid intercepted between two planes. [L, = piece cut off]

frutescent /fruːˈtes(ə)nt/ adj. Bot. of the nature of a shrub. [irreg. f. L *frutex* bush]

frutex /ˈfruːteks/ n. (pl. **frutices** /-tɪˌsiːz/) Bot. a woody-stemmed plant smaller than a tree; a shrub. [L *frutex fruticis*]

fruticose /ˈfruːtɪˌkəʊz, -ˌkəʊs/ adj. Bot. resembling a shrub. [L *fruticosus* (as FRUTEX)]

Fry¹ /fraɪ/, Christopher Harris (1907–), English writer of poetic dramas. His mystical and religious plays (e.g. *The Boy with a Cart*, 1939; *A Sleep of Prisoners*, 1951) were often compared to those of T. S. Eliot, though his comedies, which include *A Phoenix too Frequent* (1946), *The Lady's not for Burning* (1949), and *Venus Observed* (1950) were more popular with the general public. Fry also wrote several screenplays and made successful translations and adaptations of Anouilh (e.g. *Ring round the Moon*, 1950).

Fry² /fraɪ/, Elizabeth (1780–1845), English Quaker prison reformer who was in the forefront of the early 19th-c. campaign for penal reform, concerning herself with conditions in English prisons, the lot of convicts transported to Australia, and the large vagrant population in London and the south-east.

fry¹ /fraɪ/ v. & n. —v. (**fries, fried**) 1 tr. & intr. cook or be cooked in hot fat. 2 tr. & intr. sl. electrocute or be electrocuted. 3 tr. (as **fried** adj.) sl. drunk. —n. (pl. **fries**) 1 various internal parts of animals usu. eaten fried (*lamb's fry*). 2 a dish of fried food, esp. meat. 3 US a social gathering to eat fried food. □ **frying-** (US **fry-**) **pan** a shallow pan used in frying. **fry up** heat or reheat

(food) in a frying-pan. **fry-up** n. Brit. colloq. a dish of miscellaneous fried food. **out of the frying-pan into the fire** from a bad situation to a worse one. [ME f. OF *frire* f. L *frigere*]

fry² /fraɪ/ n.pl. 1 young or newly hatched fishes. 2 the young of other creatures produced in large numbers, e.g. bees or frogs. □ **small fry** people of little importance; children. [ME f. ON *frjó*]

Frye /fraɪ/, (Herman) Northrop (1912–91), Canadian literary critic. His first major work was *Fearful Symmetry* (1947), which studies not only the poet William Blake but the role of myth and symbol in various literary genres. *The Bush Garden* (1971) is a collection of his writings about Canadian literature and its creators.

fryer /ˈfraɪə(r)/ n. (also **frier**) 1 a person who fries. 2 a vessel for frying esp. fish. 3 US a chicken suitable for frying.

FSA abbr. Fellow of the Society of Antiquaries.

FSH abbr. follicle-stimulating hormone.

Ft. abbr. Fort.

ft. abbr. foot, feet.

FTC abbr. US Federal Trade Commission.

Fuad /ˈfuːæd/ the name of two kings of Egypt:

Fuad I (1868–1936), sultan of Egypt from 1917 and its first king (reigned 1922–36) when it became independent.

Fuad II (1952–), grandson of Fuad I, was named as king (as an infant) in 1952 on the abdication of his father Farouk, but in the following year Egypt became a republic.

fubsy /ˈfʌbzi/ adj. (**fubsier, fubsiest**) Brit. fat or squat. [obs. *fubs* small fat person + -Y¹]

Fuchs¹ /fʊks/, (Emil) Klaus Julius (1911–88), German physicist, a Communist who came to England to escape Nazi persecution and became a British citizen. During the 1940s he passed to the USSR secret information acquired while working in the UK, where he was involved in the development of the Allied atom bomb, and in Britain, where he held a senior post in the atomic energy research establishment at Harwell; his motives were idealistic. He was imprisoned 1950–9, and on his release he returned to East Germany.

Fuchs² /fʊks/, Sir Vivian Ernest (1908–), English geologist and explorer, leader of the Falkland Islands Dependencies Survey (Antarctica) 1947–50. In 1957–8 he led the Commonwealth Trans-Antarctic Expedition in which his party successfully met that of Sir Edmund Hillary, which had started from New Zealand and approached from the opposite direction, at the South Pole, thus completing the first land journey across Antarctica. The expedition's survey confirmed the existence of a single continent beneath the polar ice sheet.

fuchsia /ˈfjuːʃə/ n. any shrub of the genus *Fuchsia*, with drooping red or purple or white flowers. [mod.L f. L. *Fuchs*, Ger. botanist d. 1566]

fuchsine /ˈfuːksiːn, -ɪn/ n. a deep red aniline dye used in the pharmaceutical and textile-processing industries, rosaniline. [FUCHSIA (from its resemblance to the colour of the flower)]

fuck /fʌk/ v., int., & n. coarse sl. —v. 1 tr. & intr. have sexual intercourse (with). 2 intr. (foll. by about, around) mess about; fool around. 3 tr. (usu. as an exclam.) curse, confound (*fuck the thing!*). 4 intr. (as **fucking** adj., adv.) used as an intensive to express annoyance etc. —int. expressing anger or annoyance. —n. 1 a an act of sexual intercourse. b a partner in sexual intercourse. 2 the slightest amount (*don't give a fuck*). □ **fuck all** nothing. **fuck off** go away. **fuck up** make a mess of. **fuck-up** n. a mess or muddle. ¶ A highly taboo word. □□ **fucker** n. (often as a term of abuse). [16th c.: orig. unkn.]

fucus /ˈfjuːkəs/ n. (pl. **fuci** /ˈfjuːsaɪ/) any seaweed of the genus *Fucus*, with flat leathery fronds. □□ **fucoid** adj. [L, = rock-lichen, f. Gk *phukos*, of Semitic orig.]

fuddle /ˈfʌd(ə)l/ v. & n. —v. 1 tr. confuse or stupefy, esp. with alcoholic liquor. 2 intr. tipple, booze. —n. 1 confusion. 2 intoxication. 3 a spell of drinking (*on the fuddle*). [16th c.: orig. unkn.]

fuddy-duddy /ˈfʌdiˌdʌdi/ adj. & n. sl. —adj. old-fashioned or quaintly fussy. —n. (pl. **-ies**) a fuddy-duddy person. [20th c.: orig. unkn.]

fudge /fʌdʒ/ n., v., & int. —n. 1 a soft toffee-like sweet made with milk, sugar, butter, etc. **2** nonsense. **3** a piece of dishonesty or faking. **4** a piece of late news inserted in a newspaper page. —*v.* **1** *tr.* put together in a makeshift or dishonest way; fake. **2** *tr.* deal with incompetently. **3** *intr.* practise such methods. —*int.* expressing disbelief or annoyance. [perh. f. obs. *fadge* (v.) fit]

fuehrer var. of FÜHRER.

fuel /ˈfjuːəl/ *n. & v.* —*n.* **1** material, esp. coal, wood, oil, etc., burnt or used as a source of heat or power. **2** food as a source of energy. **3** material used as a source of nuclear energy. **4** anything that sustains or inflames emotion or passion. —*v.* (**fuelled, fuelling;** US **fueled, fueling**) **1** *tr.* supply with fuel. **2** *tr.* sustain or inflame (an argument, feeling, etc.) (*drink fuelled his anger*). **3** *intr.* take in or get fuel. □ **fuel cell** a cell producing an electric current direct from a chemical reaction. **fuel element** an element of nuclear fuel etc. for use in a reactor. **fuel injection** the direct introduction of fuel under pressure into the combustion units of an internal-combustion engine. **fuel oil** oil used as fuel in an engine or furnace. [ME f. AF *fuaille, fewaile,* OF *fouaille,* ult. f. L *focus* hearth]

Fuentes /ˈfwenteɪs/, Carlos (1928–), Mexican novelist, screenwriter, scholar, and diplomat, an outspoken critic of US policies in Latin America. His first novel, *Where the Air is Clear* (1958), was an immediate success and was translated from Spanish into many languages; its theme, like that of several of his works, is Mexico City. Other novels include his magnum opus *Terra Nostra* (1975), which explores the Spanish heritage in Mexico.

fug /fʌg/ *n. & v. colloq.* —*n.* stuffiness or fustiness of the air in a room. —*v.intr.* (**fugged, fugging**) stay in or enjoy a fug. □□ **fuggy** *adj.* [19th c.: orig. unkn.]

fugacious /fjuːˈɡeɪʃəs/ *adj. literary* fleeting, evanescent, hard to capture or keep. □□ **fugaciously** *adv.* **fugaciousness** *n.* **fugacity** /-ˈɡæsɪtɪ/ *n.* [L *fugax fugacis* f. *fugere* flee]

fugal /ˈfjuːɡ(ə)l/ *adj.* of the nature of a fugue. □□ **fugally** *adv.*

-fuge /fjuːdʒ/ *comb. form* forming adjectives and nouns denoting expelling or dispelling (*febrifuge; vermifuge*). [from or after mod.L *-fugus* f. L *fugare* put to flight]

fugitive /ˈfjuːdʒɪtɪv/ *adj. & n.* —*adj.* **1** fleeing; that runs or has run away. **2** transient, fleeting; of short duration. **3** (of literature) of passing interest, ephemeral. **4** flitting, shifting. —*n.* **1** (often foll. by *from*) a person who flees, esp. from justice, an enemy, danger, or a master. **2** an exile or refugee. □□ **fugitively** *adv.* [ME f. OF *fugitif -ive* f. L *fugitivus* f. *fugere fugit-* flee]

fugle /ˈfjuːɡ(ə)l/ *v.intr.* act as a fugleman. [back-form. f. FUGLEMAN]

fugleman /ˈfjuːɡ(ə)lmən/ *n.* (pl. **-men**) **1** *hist.* a soldier placed in front of a regiment etc. while drilling to show the motions and time. **2** a leader, organizer, or spokesman. [G *Flügelmann* f. *Flügel* wing + *Mann* man]

fugue /fjuːɡ/ *n. & v.* —*n.* **1** *Mus.* a piece of music in which three or more parts or 'voices' (described thus whether vocal or instrumental) enter successively in imitation of each other. The first voice enters with a short melody (the *subject*) and is 'answered' by the second voice transposing the subject up a perfect fifth or down a perfect fourth. Subject and voice continue to alternate in this way until all the voices have entered. This 'exposition' is followed by an 'episode' introducing new material or developing existing motives. Further entries of the subject may be made in different keys, but the piece will end with its appearance in the original key. **2** *Psychol.* loss of awareness of one's identity, often coupled with flight from one's usual environment. —*v.intr.* (**fugues, fugued, fuguing**) *Mus.* compose or perform a fugue. □□ **fuguist** *n.* [F or It. f. L *fuga* flight]

fugued /fjuːɡd/ *adj.* in the form of a fugue.

führer /ˈfjʊərə(r)/ *n.* (also **fuehrer**) a leader, esp. a tyrannical one. [G, = leader: part of the title assumed in 1934 by Hitler (see HITLER)]

Fujairah /fuːˈdʒaɪrə/ **1** one of the seven member States of the United Arab Emirates; pop. (1980) 54,400. **2** its capital city.

Fujian /ˌfuːdʒiˈæn/ (formerly **Fukien** /fuːˈkjen/) a province of SE China; pop. (est. 1986) 27,490,000; capital, Fuzhou.

Fujiyama /ˈfuːdʒiˈjɑːmə/ a dormant (or perhaps extinct) volcano which is Japan's highest peak (3,776 m, 12,385 ft.). It has a snow-capped cone of exceptional beauty. Its last eruption was in 1707. Its Japanese name means 'Mount Fuji'.

Fukuoka /ˌfuːkuˈəʊkə/ a commercial and industrial city and port of Japan, the chief city of Kyushu.

-ful /fʊl/ *comb. form* forming: **1** adjectives from nouns, meaning: **a** full of (*beautiful*). **b** having the qualities of (*masterful*). **2** adjectives from adjectives or Latin stems with little change of sense (*direful; grateful*). **3** adjectives from verbs, meaning 'apt to', 'able to', 'accustomed to' (*forgetful; mournful; useful*). **4** nouns (pl. **-fuls**) meaning 'the amount needed to fill' (*handful; spoonful*).

Fulbright /ˈfʊlbraɪt/, (James) William (1905–), US senator, whose name designates grants etc. awarded under the Fulbright Act of 1 August 1946, which authorized funds from the sale of surplus war materials overseas to be used for financing higher learning by exchange of students and teachers between the US and other countries. The programme was later supported by grants from the US government.

fulcrum /ˈfʊlkrəm, ˈfʌl-/ *n.* (pl. **fulcra** /-rə/ or **fulcrums**) **1** the point against which a lever is placed to get a purchase or on which it turns or is supported. **2** the means by which influence etc. is brought to bear. [L, = post of a couch, f. *fulcire* to prop]

fulfil /fʊlˈfɪl/ *v.tr.* (US **fulfill**) (**fulfilled, fulfilling**) **1** bring to consummation, carry out (a prophecy or promise). **2** satisfy (a desire or prayer). **3 a** execute, obey (a command or law). **b** perform, carry out (a task). **4** comply with (conditions). **5** answer (a purpose). **6** bring to an end, finish, complete (a period or piece of work). □ **fulfil oneself** develop one's gifts and character to the full. □□ **fulfillable** *adj.* **fulfiller** *n.* **fulfilment** *n.* (US **fulfillment**) [OE *fullfyllan* (as FULL[1], FILL)]

fulgent /ˈfʌldʒ(ə)nt/ *adj. poet. or rhet.* shining, brilliant. [ME f. L *fulgēre* shine]

fulguration /ˌfʌlɡjʊˈreɪʃ(ə)n/ *n. Surgery* the destruction of tissue by means of high-voltage electric sparks. [L *fulguratio* sheet lightning f. *fulgur* lightning]

fulgurite /ˈfʌlɡjʊˌraɪt/ *n. Geol.* a rocky substance of sand fused or vitrified by lightning. [L *fulgur* lightning]

fuliginous /fjuːˈlɪdʒɪnəs/ *adj.* sooty, dusky. [LL *fuliginosus* f. *fuligo -ginis* soot]

full[1] /fʊl/ *adj., adv., n., & v.* —*adj.* **1** (often foll. by *of*) holding all its limits will allow (*the bucket is full; full of water*). **2** having eaten to one's limits or satisfaction. **3** abundant, copious, satisfying, sufficient (*a full programme of events; led a full life; turned it to full account; give full details; the book is very full on this point*). **4** (foll. by *of*) having or holding an abundance of, showing marked signs of (*full of vitality; full of interest; full of mistakes*). **5** (foll. by *of*) **a** engrossed in thinking about (*full of himself; full of his work*). **b** unable to refrain from talking about (*full of the news*). **6 a** complete, perfect, reaching the specified or usual or utmost limit (*full membership; full daylight; waited a full hour; it was full summer; in full bloom*). **b** *Bookbinding* used for the entire cover (*full leather*). **7 a** (of tone or colour) deep and clear, mellow. **b** (of light) intense. **c** (of motion etc.) vigorous (*a full pulse; at full gallop*). **8** plump, rounded, protuberant (*a full figure*). **9** (of clothes) made of much material arranged in folds or gathers. **10** (of the heart etc.) overcharged with emotion. **11** *sl.* drunk. **12** (foll. by *of*) *archaic* having had plenty of (*full of years and honours*). —*adv.* **1** very (*you know full well*). **2** quite, fully (*full six miles; full ripe*). **3** exactly (*hit him full on the nose*). **4** more than sufficiently (*full early*). —*n.* **1** height, acme (*season is past the full*). **2** the state or time of full moon. **3** the whole (*cannot tell you the full of it*). —*v.intr. & tr.* be or become or make (esp. clothes) full. □ **at full length 1** lying stretched out. **2** without abridgement. **come full circle** see CIRCLE. **full age** adult status (esp. with ref. to legal rights and duties). **full and by** *Naut.* close-hauled but with sails filling. **full back** a defensive player, or a position near the goal, in football, hockey, etc. **full blood** pure descent. **full-blooded 1** vigorous, hearty, sensual. **2** not hybrid. **full-bloodedly** forcefully, wholeheartedly. **full-bloodedness** being full-blooded. **full-blown** fully developed, complete, (of flowers) quite open. **full board** provision of accommodation and all meals at a hotel etc. **full-bodied** rich in quality, tone, etc. **full-bottomed** (of a wig) long at the back. **full brother** a brother born of the same parents. **full-cream** of or made from unskimmed milk. **full dress** formal clothes worn on great occasions. **full-dress** adj. (of a debate etc.) of major importance. **full employment 1** the condition in which there is no idle capital or labour of any kind that is in demand. **2** the condition in which virtually all who are able and willing to work are employed. **full face** with all the face visible to the spectator. **full-fashioned** = fully-fashioned. **full-fledged** mature. **full-frontal 1** (of nudity or a nude figure) with full exposure at the front. **2** unrestrained, explicit; with nothing concealed. **full-grown** having reached maturity. **full hand** Poker a hand with three of a kind and a pair. **full-hearted** full of feeling; confident, zealous. **full-heartedly** in a full-hearted manner. **full-heartedness** fullness of feeling, ardour, zeal. **full house 1** a maximum or large attendance at a theatre, in Parliament, etc. **2** = full hand. **full-length 1** not shortened or abbreviated. **2** (of a mirror, portrait, etc.) showing the whole height of the human figure. **full lock** see LOCK[1]. **full marks** the maximum award in an examination, in assessment of a person, etc. **full measure** not less than the professed amount. **full moon 1** the moon with its whole disc illuminated. **2** the time when this occurs. **full-mouthed 1** (of cattle or sheep) having a full set of teeth. **2** (of a dog) baying loudly. **3** (of oratory etc.) sonorous, vigorous. **full out 1** Printing flush with the margin. **2** at full power. **3** complete. **full page** an entire page of a newspaper etc. **full pitch** = full toss. **full point** = full stop 1. **full professor** a professor of the highest grade in a university etc. **full-scale** not reduced in size, complete. **full score** Mus. a score giving the parts for all performers on separate staves. **full service** a church service performed by a choir without solos, or performed with music wherever possible. **full sister** a sister born of the same parents. **full speed** (or **steam**) **ahead!** an order to proceed at maximum speed or to pursue a course of action energetically. **full stop 1** a punctuation mark (.) used at the end of a sentence or an abbreviation. **2** a complete cessation. **full term** the completion of a normal pregnancy. **full tilt** see TILT. **full time 1** the total normal duration of work etc. **2** the end of a football etc. match. **full-time** adj. occupying or using the whole of the available working time. **full-timer** a person who does a full-time job. **full toss** Cricket n. a ball pitched right up to the batsman. —adv. without the ball's having touched the ground. **full up** colloq. completely full. **in full 1** without abridgement. **2** to or for the full amount (paid in full). **in full swing** at the height of activity. **in full view** entirely visible. **on a full stomach** see STOMACH. **to the full** to the utmost extent. [OE f. Gmc]

full[2] /fʊl/ v.tr. cleanse and thicken (cloth). [ME, back-form. f. FULLER[1]: cf. OF fouler (FOIL[1])]

Fuller[1] /ˈfʊlə(r)/, Richard Buckminster (1895–1983), American designer and architect, best known for his invention of the geodesic dome (see entry).

Fuller[2] /ˈfʊlə(r)/, Thomas (1608–61), English cleric, preacher, and historian, whose best-known and most characteristic work, The Worthies of England (a description of the counties, with short biographies of local personages) appeared in 1662, after his death. His writings are marked with humour and a quaint wit that is sometimes a little incongruous with the subject.

fuller[1] /ˈfʊlə(r)/ n. a person who fulls cloth. □ **fuller's earth** a type of clay used for many centuries in fulling (see FULL[2]). It possesses the ability to absorb water, grease, oil, and colouring matter, and now has a variety of industrial uses, especially in the purification of oils and as an absorbent and a bleaching agent. [OE fullere f. L fullo]

fuller[2] /ˈfʊlə(r)/ n. & v. —n. **1** a grooved or rounded tool on which iron is shaped. **2** a groove made by this esp. in a horseshoe. —v.tr. stamp with a fuller. [19th c.: orig. unkn.]

fullness /ˈfʊlnɪs/ n. (also **fulness**) **1** being full. **2** (of sound, colour, etc.) richness, volume, body. **3** all that is contained (in the world etc.). □ **the fullness of the heart** emotion, genuine feelings. **the fullness of time** the appropriate or destined time.

fully /ˈfʊlɪ/ adv. **1** completely, entirely (am fully aware). **2** no less or fewer than (fully 60). □ **fully-fashioned** (of women's clothing)

shaped to fit the body. **fully-fledged** mature. [OE fullīce (as FULL[1], -LY[2])]

-fully /ˈfʊlɪ/ comb. form forming adverbs corresp. to adjectives in -ful.

fulmar /ˈfʊlmə(r)/ n. any medium-sized sea bird of the genus Fulmarus, with stout body, robust bill, and rounded tail. [orig. Hebridean dial.: perh. f. ON fúll FOUL (with ref. to its smell) + már gull (cf. MEW[2])]

fulminant /ˈfʌlmɪnənt, ˈfʊl-/ adj. **1** fulminating. **2** Med. (of a disease or symptom) developing suddenly. [F fulminant or L fulminant- (as FULMINATE)]

fulminate /ˈfʌlmɪneɪt, ˈfʊl-/ v. & n. —v.intr. **1** (often foll. by against) express censure loudly and forcefully. **2** explode violently; flash like lightning (fulminating mercury). **3** Med. (of a disease or symptom) develop suddenly. —n. Chem. a salt or ester of fulminic acid. □□ **fulmination** /-ˈneɪʃ(ə)n/ n. **fulminatory** adj. [L fulminare fulminat- f. fulmen -minis lightning]

fulminic acid /fʌlˈmɪnɪk, fʊl-/ n. Chem. an isomer of cyanic acid that is stable only in solution. ¶ Chem. formula: HONC. [L fulmen: see FULMINATE]

fulness var. of FULLNESS.

fulsome /ˈfʊlsəm/ adj. **1** disgusting by excess of flattery, servility, or expressions of affection; excessive, cloying. **2** disp. copious. ¶ In fulsome praise, fulsome means 'excessive', not 'generous'. □□ **fulsomely** adv. **fulsomeness** n. [ME f. FULL[1] + -SOME]

Fulton /ˈfʊlt(ə)n/, Robert (1765–1815), American pioneer of the steamship. He came to England at an early age and in London studied painting under Benjamin West. Urged by James Watt and others, he turned to engineering and invented an apparatus for raising and lowering canal boats, a device for sawing marble, and a machine for twisting hemp into rope. During the Napoleonic Wars he spent some time in France and proposed both torpedoes and submarines, constructing a steam-propelled 'diving-boat' which in 1801 submerged to a depth of 7.6 m (25 ft.). Unable to obtain support for his ideas in Europe he returned to America in 1806 and built the Clermont, a paddle-steamer powered by a steam engine. This made a successful trip in 1807, and 18 other steamships were subsequently built (including some for Russia), inaugurating the era of commercial steam navigation.

fulvous /ˈfʌlvəs/ adj. reddish-yellow, tawny. □□ **fulvescent** /-ˈves(ə)nt/ adj. [L fulvus]

fumarole /ˈfjuːməˌrəʊl/ n. an opening in or near a volcano, through which hot vapours emerge. □□ **fumarolic** /-ˈrɒlɪk/ adj. [F fumarolle]

fumble /ˈfʌmb(ə)l/ v. & n. —v. **1** intr. (often foll. by at, with, for, after) use the hands awkwardly, grope about. **2** tr. a deal with clumsily or nervously. **b** Sport fail to stop (a ball) cleanly. —n. an act of fumbling. □□ **fumbler** n. **fumblingly** adv. [LG fummeln, fommeln, Du. fommelen]

fume /fjuːm/ n. & v. —n. **1** (usu. in pl.) exuded gas or smoke or vapour, esp. when harmful or unpleasant. **2** a fit of anger (in a fume). —v. **1** a intr. emit fumes. **b** tr. give off as fumes. **2** intr. (often foll. by at) be affected by (esp. suppressed) anger (was fuming at their inefficiency). **3** tr. a fumigate. **b** subject to fumes esp. those of ammonia (to darken tints in oak, photographic film, etc.). **4** tr. perfume with incense. □ **fume cupboard** (or **chamber** etc.) a ventilated structure in a laboratory, for storing or experimenting with noxious chemicals. □□ **fumeless** adj. **fumingly** adv. **fumy** adj. (in sense 1 of n.). [ME f. OF fum f. fumus smoke & OF fume f. fumer f. L fumare to smoke]

fumigate /ˈfjuːmɪˌɡeɪt/ v.tr. **1** disinfect or purify with fumes. **2** apply fumes to. □□ **fumigant** n. **fumigation** /-ˈɡeɪʃ(ə)n/ n. **fumigator** n. [L fumigare fumigat- f. fumus smoke]

fumitory /ˈfjuːmɪtərɪ/ n. any plant of the genus Fumaria, esp. F. officinalis, formerly used against scurvy. [ME f. OF fumeterre f. med.L fumus terrae earth-smoke]

fun /fʌn/ n. & adj. —n. **1** amusement, esp. lively or playful. **2** a source of this. **3** (in full **fun and games**) exciting or amusing goings-on. —adj. disp. colloq. amusing, entertaining, enjoyable (a fun thing to do). □ **for fun** (or **for the fun of it**) not for a

b but d dog f few g get h he j yes k cat l leg m man n no p pen r red s sit t top v voice

serious purpose. **fun run** *colloq.* an uncompetitive run, esp. for sponsored runners in support of a charity. **have fun** enjoy oneself. **in fun** as a joke, not seriously. **is great** (or **good**) **fun** is very amusing. **like fun 1** vigorously, quickly. **2** much. **3** *iron.* not at all. **what fun!** how amusing! [obs. *fun* (v.) var. of *fon* befool: cf. FOND]

Funafuti /ˌfuːnəˈfuːtɪ/ the capital of Tuvalu, situated on the island of Funafuti.

funambulist /fjuːˈnæmbjʊlɪst/ *n.* a rope-walker. [F *funambule* or L *funambulus* f. *funis* rope + *ambulare* walk]

Funchal /fʊnˈʃɑːl/ the capital and chief port of Madeira, on the south coast of the island; pop. (1981) 119,500.

function /ˈfʌŋkʃ(ə)n/ *n. & v.* —*n.* **1 a** an activity proper to a person or institution. **b** a mode of action or activity by which a thing fulfils its purpose. **c** an official or professional duty; an employment, profession, or calling. **2 a** a public ceremony or occasion. **b** a social gathering, esp. a large, formal, or important one. **3** *Math.* a variable quantity regarded in relation to another or others in terms of which it may be expressed or on which its value depends (*x is a function of y and z*). **4** a part of a program that corresponds to a single value. —*v.intr.* fulfil a function, operate; be in working order. □□ **functionless** *adj.* [F *fonction* f. L *functio -onis* f. *fungi funct-* perform]

functional /ˈfʌŋkʃən(ə)l/ *adj.* **1** of or serving a function. **2** (esp. of buildings) designed or intended to be practical rather than attractive; utilitarian. **3** *Physiol.* **a** (esp. of disease) of or affecting only the functions of an organ etc., not structural or organic. **b** (of mental disorder) having no discernible organic cause. **c** (of an organ) having a function, not functionless or rudimentary. **4** *Math.* of a function. □ **functional group** *Chem.* a group of atoms that determine the reactions of a compound containing the group. □□ **functionality** /-ˈnælɪtɪ/ *n.* **functionally** *adv.*

functionalism /ˈfʌŋkʃənəˌlɪz(ə)m/ *n.* belief in or stress on the practical application of a thing. The idea that beauty results from or is identical to function is found in Xenophon (4th c. BC) and in 18th-c. aesthetic theory, but has had its greatest impact in architecture, whose language it entered at least as early as the 1840s. In 1901 Louis Sullivan originated the phrase 'form follows function' and Frank Lloyd Wright amplified this as 'form and function are one'. Functionalism was preached as a new aesthetic creed by Le Corbusier (*Towards a New Architecture*, 1927), who defined a house as a machine for living in, and it became popular also in the severely utilitarian furniture design of the 1930s. By the mid-20th c., however, functionalism was seen as one element in the aesthetic basis of the practical arts but no longer preached as the sole principle of beauty. □□ **functionalist** *n.*

functionary /ˈfʌŋkʃənərɪ/ *n.* (pl. **-ies**) a person who has to perform official functions or duties; an official.

fund /fʌnd/ *n. & v.* —*n.* **1** a permanent stock of something ready to be drawn upon (*a fund of knowledge; a fund of tenderness*). **2** a stock of money, esp. one set apart for a purpose. **3** (in *pl.*) money resources. **4** (in *pl.*; prec. by *the*) *Brit.* the stock of the National Debt (as a mode of investment). —*v.tr.* **1** provide with money. **2** convert (a floating debt) into a more or less permanent debt at fixed interest. **3** put into a fund. □ **fund-raiser** a person who seeks financial support for a cause, enterprise, etc. **fund-raising** the seeking of financial support. **in funds** *colloq.* having money to spend. [L *fundus* bottom, piece of land]

fundament /ˈfʌndəmənt/ *n. joc.* the buttocks. [ME f. OF *fondement* f. L *fundamentum* (as FOUND²)]

fundamental /ˌfʌndəˈment(ə)l/ *adj. & n.* —*adj.* of, affecting, or serving as a base or foundation, essential, primary, original (*a fundamental change; the fundamental rules; the fundamental form*). —*n.* **1** (usu. in *pl.*) a fundamental rule, principle, or article. **2** *Mus.* a fundamental note or tone. □ **fundamental note** *Mus.* the lowest note of a chord in its original (uninverted) form. **fundamental particle** an elementary particle. **fundamental tone** *Mus.* the tone produced by vibration of the whole of a sonorous body (opp. HARMONIC). □□ **fundamentality** /-ˈtælɪtɪ/ *n.* **fundamentally** *adv.* [ME f. F *fondamental* or LL *fundamentalis* (as FUNDAMENT)]

fundamentalism /ˌfʌndəˈmentəˌlɪz(ə)m/ *n.* **1** strict maintenance of traditional orthodox religious beliefs, as in a religious movement which developed among various Protestant bodies in the US after the First World War, based on strict adherence to certain tenets (e.g. the literal inerrancy of Scripture) held to be fundamental to the Christian faith. **2** strict maintenance of ancient or fundamental doctrines of any religion, esp. Islam. □□ **fundamentalist** *n.*

fundus /ˈfʌndəs/ *n.* (pl. **fundi** /-daɪ/) *Anat.* the base of a hollow organ; the part furthest from the opening. [L, = bottom]

Fundy /ˈfʌndɪ/, **Bay of** an inlet of the Atlantic Ocean between the Canadian Provinces of new Brunswick and Nova Scotia. It is subject to fast-running tides, the highest in the world, reaching 12–15 m (50–80 ft.) and now used to generate electricity.

funeral /ˈfjuːnər(ə)l/ *n. & adj.* —*n.* **1 a** the burial or cremation of a dead person with its ceremonies. **b** a burial or cremation procession. **c** *US* a burial or cremation service. **2** *sl.* one's (usu. unpleasant) concern (*that's your funeral*). —*attrib.adj.* of or used etc. at a funeral (*funeral oration*). □ **funeral director** an undertaker. **funeral parlour** (*US* **home**) an establishment where the dead are prepared for burial or cremation. **funeral pile** (or **pyre**) a pile of wood etc. on which a corpse is burnt. **funeral urn** an urn holding the ashes of a cremated body. [ME f. OF *funeraille* f. med.L *funeralia* neut. pl. of LL *funeralis* f. L *funus -eris* funeral: (adj.) OF f. L *funeralis*]

funerary /ˈfjuːnərərɪ/ *adj.* of or used at a funeral or funerals. [LL *funerarius* (as FUNERAL)]

funereal /fjuːˈnɪərɪəl/ *adj.* **1** of or appropriate to a funeral. **2** gloomy, dismal, dark. □□ **funereally** *adv.* [L *funereus* (as FUNERAL)]

funfair /ˈfʌnfeə(r)/ *n. Brit.* a fair, or part of one, consisting of amusements and sideshows.

fungi *pl.* of FUNGUS.

fungible /ˈfʌndʒɪb(ə)l/ *adj. Law* (of goods etc. contracted for, when an individual specimen is not meant) that can serve for, or be replaced by, another answering to the same definition. □□ **fungibility** /-ˈbɪlɪtɪ/ *n.* [med.L *fungibilis* f. *fungi* (*vice*) serve (in place of)]

fungicide /ˈfʌndʒɪˌsaɪd/ *n.* a fungus-destroying substance. □□ **fungicidal** /-ˈsaɪd(ə)l/ *adj.*

fungistatic /ˌfʌndʒɪˈstætɪk/ *adj.* inhibiting the growth of fungi. □□ **fungistatically** *adv.*

fungoid /ˈfʌŋɡɔɪd/ *adj. & n.* —*adj.* **1** resembling a fungus in texture or in rapid growth. **2** *Brit.* of a fungus or fungi. —*n.* a fungoid plant.

fungous /ˈfʌŋɡəs/ *adj.* **1** having the nature of a fungus. **2** springing up like a mushroom; transitory. [ME f. L *fungosus* (as FUNGUS)]

fungus /ˈfʌŋɡəs/ *n.* (pl. **fungi** /-ɡaɪ, -dʒaɪ/ or **funguses**) **1** any of a group of unicellular, multicellular, or multinucleate nonphotosynthetic organisms feeding on organic matter, which include moulds, yeast, mushrooms, and toadstools. (See below.) **2** anything similar usu. growing suddenly and rapidly. **3** *Med.* a spongy morbid growth. **4** *sl.* a beard. □□ **fungal** *adj.* **fungiform** /ˈfʌndʒɪˌfɔːm/ *adj.* **fungivorous** /-ˈdʒɪvərəs/ *adj.* [L, perh. f. Gk *sp(h)oggos* SPONGE]

Fungi lack chlorophyll and are therefore incapable of photosynthesis; most live either on dead matter or as parasites, but some form associations with other plants, notably growing with algae to form lichens. Many species play an ecologically vital role in breaking down dead organic matter, others are an important source of antibiotics, others cause disease in plants, animals, and humans. Although believed to be an ancient group, fungi are scarce as fossils, and their relationship with other plants is obscure; they are sometimes classified as a separate kingdom, distinct from the green plants.

funicular /fjuːˈnɪkjʊlə(r)/ *adj. & n.* —*adj.* **1** (of a railway, esp. on a mountainside) operating by cable with ascending and descending cars counterbalanced. **2** of a rope or its tension. —*n.* a funicular railway. [L *funiculus* f. *funis* rope]

funk¹ /fʌŋk/ *n. & v. sl.* —*n.* **1** fear, panic. **2** a coward. —*v. Brit.* **1** *intr.* flinch, shrink, show cowardice. **2** *tr.* try to evade (an undertaking), shirk. **3** *tr.* be afraid of. [18th-c. Oxford sl.: perh. f. sl. FUNK² = tobacco-smoke]

funk² /fʌŋk/ *n. sl.* **1** funky music. **2** *US* a strong smell. [*funk* blow smoke on, perh. f. F dial. *funkier* f. L (as FUMIGATE)]

funkia /ˈfʌŋkɪə/ *n.* = HOSTA. [mod.L f. H. C. *Funck*, Prussian botanist d. 1839]

funky¹ /ˈfʌŋkɪ/ *adj.* (**funkier**, **funkiest**) *sl.* **1** (esp. of jazz or rock music) earthy, bluesy, with a heavy rhythmical beat. **2** fashionable. **3** *US* having a strong smell. □□ **funkily** *adv.* **funkiness** *n.*

funky² /ˈfʌŋkɪ/ *adj.* (**funkier**, **funkiest**) *sl.* **1** terrified. **2** cowardly.

funnel /ˈfʌn(ə)l/ *n. & v.* — *n.* **1** a narrow tube or pipe widening at the top, for pouring liquid, powder, etc., into a small opening. **2** a metal chimney on a steam engine or ship. **3** something resembling a funnel in shape or use. — *v.tr. & intr.* (**funnelled**, **funnelling**; *US* **funneled**, **funneling**) guide or move through or as through a funnel. □□ **funnel-like** *adj.* [ME f. Prov. *fonilh* f. LL *fundibulum* f. L *infundibulum* f. *infundere* (as IN-², *fundere* pour)]

funniosity /ˌfʌnɪˈɒsɪtɪ/ *n.* (pl. **-ies**) *joc.* **1** comicality. **2** a comical thing. [FUNNY + -OSITY]

funny /ˈfʌnɪ/ *adj. & n.* (**funnier**, **funniest**) **1** amusing, comical. **2** strange, perplexing, hard to account for. **3** *colloq.* slightly unwell, eccentric, etc. — *n.* (pl. **-ies**) (usu. in *pl.*) *colloq.* **1** a comic strip in a newspaper. **2** a joke. □ **funny-bone** the part of the elbow over which the ulnar nerve passes. **funny business 1** *sl.* misbehaviour or deception. **2** comic behaviour, comedy. **funny-face** *joc. colloq.* an affectionate form of address. **funny farm** *sl.* a mental hospital. **funny-ha-ha** *colloq.* = sense 1 of *adj.* **funny man** a clown or comedian, esp. a professional. **funny money** *colloq.* inflated currency. **funny paper** a newspaper etc. containing humorous matter. **funny-peculiar** *colloq.* = senses 2, 3 of *adj.* □□ **funnily** *adv.* **funniness** *n.* [FUN + -Y¹]

fur /fɜː(r)/ *n. & v.* — *n.* **1 a** the short fine soft hair of certain animals, distinguished from the longer hair. **b** the skin of such an animal with the fur on it; a pelt. **2 a** the coat of certain animals as material for making, trimming, or lining clothes. **b** a trimming or lining made of the dressed coat of such animals, or of material imitating this. **c** a garment made of or trimmed or lined with fur. **3** (*collect.*) furred animals. **4 a** a coating formed on the tongue in sickness. **b** *Brit.* a coating formed on the inside surface of a pipe, kettle, etc., by hard water. **c** a crust adhering to a surface, e.g. a deposit from wine. **5** *Heraldry* a representation of tufts on a plain ground. — *v.* (**furred**, **furring**) **1** *tr.* (esp. as **furred** *adj.*) **a** line or trim (a garment) with fur. **b** provide (an animal) with fur. **c** clothe (a person) with fur. **d** coat (a tongue, the inside of a kettle) with fur. **2** *intr.* (often foll. by *up*) (of a kettle etc.) become coated with fur. **3** *tr.* level (floor-timbers) by inserting strips of wood. □ **fur and feather** game animals and birds. **fur-seal** a sea lion with a valuable undercoat. **make the fur fly** *colloq.* cause a disturbance, stir up trouble. □□ **furless** *adj.* [ME (earlier as *v.*) f. OF *forrer* f. *forre, fuerre* sheath f. Gmc]

fur. *abbr.* furlong(s).

furbelow /ˈfɜːbɪˌləʊ/ *n. & v.* — *n.* **1** a gathered strip or pleated border of a skirt or petticoat. **2** (in *pl.*) *derog.* showy ornaments. — *v.tr.* adorn with a furbelow or furbelows. [18th-c. var. of *falbala* flounce, trimming]

furbish /ˈfɜːbɪʃ/ *v.tr.* (often foll. by *up*) **1** remove rust from, polish, burnish. **2** give a new look to, renovate, revive (something antiquated). □□ **furbisher** *n.* [ME f. OF *forbir* f. Gmc]

furcate /ˈfɜːkeɪt/ *adj. & v.* — *adj.* /also ˈfɜːkət/ forked, branched. — *v.intr.* form a fork, divide. □□ **furcation** /fɜːˈkeɪʃ(ə)n/ *n.* [L *furca* fork: (adj.) f. LL *furcatus*]

furfuraceous /ˌfɜːfəˈreɪʃəs/ *adj.* **1** *Med.* (of skin) resembling bran or dandruff; scaly. **2** *Bot.* covered with branlike scales. [*furfur* scurf f. L *furfur* bran]

Furies /ˈfjʊərɪz/ *n.pl. Gk Mythol.* spirits of punishment (esp. Allecto, Megaera, and Tisiphone) who executed the curses pronounced upon criminals, tortured the guilty with stings of conscience, or inflicted famines and pestilences. They were anciently confused with the Eumenides. [pl. of FURY]

furious /ˈfjʊərɪəs/ *adj.* **1** extremely angry. **2** full of fury. **3** raging, violent, intense. □ **fast and furious** *adv.* **1** rapidly. **2** eagerly,

uproariously. — *adj.* (of mirth etc.) eager, uproarious. □□ **furiously** *adv.* **furiousness** *n.* [ME f. OF *furieus* f. L *furiosus* (as FURY)]

furl /fɜːl/ *v.* **1** *tr.* roll up and secure (a sail, umbrella, flag, etc.). **2** *intr.* become furled. **3** *tr.* **a** close (a fan). **b** fold up (wings). **c** draw away (a curtain). **d** relinquish (hopes). □□ **furlable** *adj.* [F *ferler* f. OF *fer(m)* FIRM¹ + *lier* bind f. L *ligare*]

furlong /ˈfɜːlɒŋ/ *n.* one-eighth of a mile, 220 yards. The term originally meant the length of the furrow in the common field, which was theoretically regarded as a square containing ten acres; as a lineal measure the furlong therefore varied according to the extent assigned at various times and places to the acre. As early as the 9th c. it was regarded as the equivalent of the Roman *stadium*, which was one-eighth of a Roman mile, and hence *furlong* has always been used as a name for the eighth part of an English mile, whether this coincided with the agricultural measure or not. [OE *furlang* f. *furh* FURROW + *lang* LONG¹: orig. = length of a furrow in a common field]

furlough /ˈfɜːləʊ/ *n. & v.* — *n.* leave of absence, esp. granted to a member of the services or to a missionary. — *v.* *US* **1** *tr.* grant furlough to. **2** *intr.* spend furlough. [Du. *verlof* after G *Verlaub* (as FOR-, LEAVE²)]

furmety var. of FRUMENTY.

furnace /ˈfɜːnɪs/ *n.* **1** an enclosed structure for intense heating by fire, esp. of metals or water. **2** a very hot place. [ME f. OF *fornais* f. L *fornax -acis* f. *fornus* oven]

furnish /ˈfɜːnɪʃ/ *v.tr.* **1** provide (a house, room, etc.) with all necessary contents, esp. movable furniture. **2** (foll. by *with*) cause to have possession or use of. **3** provide, afford, yield. [OF *furnir* ult. f. WG]

furnished /ˈfɜːnɪʃt/ *adj.* (of a house, flat, etc.) let with furniture.

furnisher /ˈfɜːnɪʃə(r)/ *n.* **1** a person who sells furniture. **2** a person who furnishes.

furnishings /ˈfɜːnɪʃɪŋz/ *n.pl.* the furniture and fitments in a house, room, etc.

furniture /ˈfɜːnɪtʃə(r)/ *n.* **1** the movable equipment of a house, room, etc., e.g. tables, chairs, and beds. **2** *Naut.* a ship's equipment, esp. tackle etc. **3** accessories, e.g. the handles and lock of a door. **4** *Printing* pieces of wood or metal placed round or between type to make blank spaces and fasten the matter in the chase. □ **furniture beetle** a beetle, *Anobium punctatum*, the larvae of which bore into wood (see WOODWORM). **furniture van** a large van used to move furniture from one house to another. **part of the furniture** *colloq.* a person or thing taken for granted. [F *fourniture* f. *fournir* (as FURNISH)]

furore /fjʊəˈrɔːrɪ/ *n.* (*US* **furor** /ˈfjʊərɔː(r)/) **1** an uproar; an outbreak of fury. **2** a wave of enthusiastic admiration, a craze. [It. f. L *furor -oris* f. *furere* be mad]

furphy /ˈfɜːfɪ/ *n.* (pl. **-ies**) *Austral. sl.* **1** a false report or rumour. **2** an absurd story. [water and sanitary *Furphy* carts of the war of 1914–18, made at a foundry set up by the Furphy family]

furrier /ˈfʌrɪə(r)/ *n.* a dealer in or dresser of furs. [ME *furrour* f. OF *forreor* f. *forrer* trim with fur, assim. to -IER]

furriery /ˈfʌrɪərɪ/ *n.* the work of a furrier.

furrow /ˈfʌrəʊ/ *n. & v.* — *n.* **1** a narrow trench made in the ground by a plough. **2** a rut, groove, or deep wrinkle. **3** a ship's track. — *v.tr.* **1** plough. **2 a** make furrows, grooves, etc. in. **b** mark with wrinkles. □ **furrow-slice** the slice of earth turned up by the mould-board of a plough. □□ **furrowless** *adj.* **furrowy** *adj.* [OE *furh* f. Gmc]

furry /ˈfɜːrɪ/ *adj.* (**furrier**, **furriest**) **1** of or like fur. **2** covered with or wearing fur. □□ **furriness** *n.*

further /ˈfɜːðə(r)/ *adv., adj., & v.* — *adv.* (also **farther** /ˈfɑːðə(r)/) esp. with ref. to physical distance) **1** to or at a more advanced point in space or time (*unsafe to proceed further*). **2** at a greater distance (*nothing was further from his thoughts*). **3** to a greater extent, more (*will enquire further*). **4** in addition; furthermore (*I may add further*). — *adj.* (also **farther** /ˈfɑːðə(r)/) **1** more distant or advanced (*on the further side*). **2** more, additional, going beyond what exists or has been dealt with (*threats of further punishment*).

—v.tr. promote, favour, help on (a scheme, undertaking, movement, or cause). □ **further education** Brit. education for persons above school age but usu. below degree level. **further to** formal following on from (esp. an earlier letter etc.). **till further notice** (or **orders**) to continue until explicitly changed. □□ **furtherer** n. **furthermost** adj. [OE furthor (adv.), furthra (adj.), fyrthrian (v.), formed as FORTH, -ER³]

furtherance /ˈfɜːðərəns/ n. furthering or being furthered; the advancement of a scheme etc.

furthermore /ˌfɜːðəˈmɔː(r)/ adv. in addition, besides (esp. introducing a fresh consideration in an argument).

furthest /ˈfɜːðɪst/ adj. & adv. (also **farthest** /ˈfɑːðɪst/ esp. with ref. to physical distance) —adj. most distant. —adv. to or at the greatest distance. □ **at the furthest** (or **at furthest**) at the greatest distance; at the latest; at most. [ME, superl. f. FURTHER]

furtive /ˈfɜːtɪv/ adj. **1** done by stealth, clandestine, meant to escape notice. **2** sly, stealthy. **3** stolen, taken secretly. **4** thievish, pilfering. □□ **furtively** adv. **furtiveness** n. [F furtif -ive or L furtivus f. furtum theft]

Furtwängler /ˈfʊərtˌveŋglə(r)/, Wilhelm (1886–1954), German conductor and composer, noted especially for his interpretations of Wagner and Beethoven.

furuncle /ˈfjʊərʌŋk(ə)l/ n. Med. = BOIL². □□ **furuncular** /-ˈrʌŋkjʊlə(r)/ adj. **furunculous** /-ˈrʌŋkjʊləs/ adj. [L furunculus f. fur thief]

furunculosis /fjʊˌrʌŋkjʊˈləʊsɪs/ n. **1** a diseased condition in which boils appear. **2** a bacterial disease of salmon and trout. [mod.L (as FURUNCLE)]

fury /ˈfjʊəri/ n. (pl. **-ies**) **1 a** wild and passionate anger, rage. **b** a fit of rage (in a blind fury). **c** impetuosity in battle etc. **2** violence of a storm, disease, etc. **3** (**Fury**) (usu. in pl.) Gk Mythol. any of the FURIES. **4** an avenging spirit. **5** an angry or malignant woman, a virago. □ **like fury** colloq. with great force or effect. [ME f. OF furie f. L furia f. furere be mad]

furze /fɜːz/ n. Brit. = GORSE. □□ **furzy** /ˈfɜːzi/ adj. [OE fyrs, of unkn. orig.]

fuscous /ˈfʌskəs/ adj. sombre, dark-coloured. [L fuscus dusky]

fuse¹ /fjuːz/ v. & n. —v. **1** tr. & intr. melt with intense heat; liquefy. **2** tr. & intr. blend or amalgamate into one whole by or as by melting. **3** tr. provide (a circuit, plug, etc.) with a fuse. **4 a** intr. (of an appliance) cease to function when a fuse blows. **b** tr. cause (an appliance) to do this. —n. a device or component for protecting an electric circuit, containing a strip of wire of easily melted metal and placed in the circuit so as to break it by melting when an excessive current passes through. □ **fuse-box** a box housing the fuses for circuits in a building. [L fundere fus-pour, melt]

fuse² /fjuːz/ n. & v. (also **fuze**) —n. **1** a device for igniting a bomb or explosive charge, consisting of a tube or cord etc. filled or saturated with combustible matter. **2** a component in a shell, mine, etc., designed to detonate an explosive charge on impact, after an interval, or when subjected to a magnetic or vibratory stimulation. —v.tr. fit a fuse to. □□ **fuseless** adj. [It. fuso f. L fusus spindle]

fusee /fjuːˈziː/ n. (US **fuzee**) **1** a conical pulley or wheel esp. in a watch or clock. **2** a large-headed match for lighting a cigar or pipe in a wind. **3** US a railway signal-flare. [F fusée spindle ult. f. L fusus]

fuselage /ˈfjuːzəˌlɑːʒ, -lɪdʒ/ n. the body of an aeroplane. [F f. fuseler cut into a spindle f. fuseau spindle f. OF fusel ult. f. L fusus]

fusel oil /ˈfjuːz(ə)l/ n. a mixture of several alcohols, chiefly amyl alcohol, produced usu. in small amounts during alcoholic fermentation. [G Fusel bad brandy etc.: cf. fuseln to bungle]

fusible /ˈfjuːzɪb(ə)l/ adj. that can be easily fused or melted. □□ **fusibility** /-ˈbɪlɪti/ n.

fusiform /ˈfjuːzɪˌfɔːm/ adj. Bot. & Zool. shaped like a spindle or cigar, tapering at both ends. [L fusus spindle + -FORM]

fusil /ˈfjuːzɪl/ n. hist. a light musket. [F ult. f. L focus hearth, fire]

fusilier /ˌfjuːzɪˈlɪə(r), -zəˈlɪə(r)/ n. (US **fusileer**) **1** a member of any of several British regiments formerly armed with fusils. **2** hist. a soldier armed with a fusil. [F (as FUSIL)]

fusillade /ˌfjuːzɪˈleɪd/ n. & v. —n. **1 a** a continuous discharge of firearms. **b** a wholesale execution by this means. **2** a sustained outburst of criticism etc. —v.tr. **1** assault (a place) by a fusillade. **2** shoot down (persons) with a fusillade. [F f. fusiller shoot]

fusion /ˈfjuːʒ(ə)n/ n. **1** the act or an instance of fusing or melting. **2** a fused mass. **3** the blending of different things into one. **4** a coalition. **5** Physics = nuclear fusion. □ **fusion bomb** a bomb involving nuclear fusion, esp. a hydrogen bomb. □□ **fusional** adj. [F fusion or L fusio (as FUSE¹)]

fuss /fʌs/ n. & v. —n. **1** excited commotion, bustle, ostentatious or nervous activity. **2 a** excessive concern about a trivial thing. **b** abundance of petty detail. **3** a sustained protest or dispute. **4** a person who fusses. —v. **1** intr. **a** make a fuss. **b** busy oneself restlessly with trivial things. **c** (often foll. by about, up and down) move fussily. **2** tr. agitate, worry. □ **make a fuss** complain vigorously. **make a fuss of** (or **over**) treat (a person or animal) with great or excessive attention. □□ **fusser** n. [18th c.: perh. Anglo-Ir.]

fusspot /ˈfʌspɒt/ n. colloq. a person given to fussing.

fussy /ˈfʌsi/ adj. (**fussier**, **fussiest**) **1** inclined to fuss. **2** full of unnecessary detail or decoration. **3** fastidious. □□ **fussily** adv. **fussiness** n.

fustanella /ˌfʌstəˈnelə/ n. a man's stiff white kilt worn in Albania and Greece. [It. dimin. of mod. Gk phoustani prob. f. It. fustagno FUSTIAN]

fustian /ˈfʌstɪən/ n. & adj. —n. **1** thick twilled cotton cloth with a short nap, usu. dyed in dark colours. **2** turgid speech or writing, bombast. —adj. **1** made of fustian. **2** bombastic. **3** worthless. [ME f. OF fustaigne f. med.L fustaneus (adj.) relating to cloth from Fostat a suburb of Cairo]

fustic /ˈfʌstɪk/ n. a yellow dye obtained from either of two kinds of wood, esp. old fustic. □ **old fustic 1** a tropical tree, Chlorophora tinctoria, native to America. **2** the wood of this tree. **young fustic 1** a sumac, Cotinus coggyria, native to Europe (also called Venetian sumac). **2** the wood of this tree. [F f. Sp. fustoc f. Arab. fustuķ f. Gk pistakē pistachio]

fusty /ˈfʌsti/ adj. (**fustier**, **fustiest**) **1** stale-smelling, musty, mouldy. **2** stuffy, close. **3** antiquated, old-fashioned. □□ **fustily** adv. **fustiness** n. [ME f. OF fusté smelling of the cask f. fust cask, tree-trunk, f. L fustis cudgel]

futhorc /ˈfuːθɔːk/ n. the Scandinavian runic alphabet. [its first six letters f, u, th, ö, r, k]

futile /ˈfjuːtaɪl/ adj. **1** useless, ineffectual, vain. **2** frivolous, trifling. □□ **futilely** adv. **futility** /-ˈtɪlɪti/ n. [L futilis leaky, futile, rel. to fundere pour]

futon /ˈfuːtɒn/ n. a Japanese quilted mattress rolled out on the floor for use as a bed. [Jap.]

futtock /ˈfʌtək/ n. each of the middle timbers of a ship's frame, between the floor and the top timbers. [ME votekes etc. pl. f. MLG f. fōt FOOT + -ken -KIN]

future /ˈfjuːtʃə(r)/ adj. & n. —adj. **1 a** going or expected to happen or be or become (his future career). **b** that will be something specified (my future wife). **c** that will be after death (a future life). **2 a** of time to come (future years). **b** Gram. (of a tense or participle) describing an event yet to happen. —n. **1** time to come (past, present, and future). **2** what will happen in the future (the future is uncertain). **3** the future condition of a person, country, etc. **4** a prospect of success etc. (there's no future in it). **5** Gram. the future tense. **6** (in pl.) Stock Exch. **a** goods and stocks sold for future delivery. **b** contracts for these. □ **for the future** = in future. **future perfect** Gram. a tense giving the sense will have done. **future shock** inability to cope with rapid progress. **in future** from now onwards. □□ **futureless** adj. [ME f. OF futur -ure f. L futurus future part. of esse be f. stem fu- be]

futurism /ˈfjuːtʃəˌrɪz(ə)m/ n. a movement in art, literature, music, etc., with violent departure from traditional forms so as to express movement and growth. Launched by the Italian poet Filippo Marinetti in 1909, futurism was designed to shake the public out of their cultural torpor. Its participants demanded the incorporation in art of 20th-c. experience, particularly the celebration of new technology, dynamism, and the altered sensibilities of modern mankind. The use of manifestos and public demonstrations to publicize the movement ensured the wide dissemination over Europe of its art and theory, with important repercussions particularly in Russia. Although effectively ended by the First World War, the group's attitude to art and its techniques of propaganda had a lasting influence on Dada and other new artistic groupings. [FUTURE + -ISM, after It. *futurismo*, F *futurisme*]

futurist /ˈfjuːtʃərɪst/ *n.* (often *attrib.*) **1** an adherent of futurism. **2** a believer in human progress. **3** a student of the future. **4** *Theol.* one who believes that biblical prophecies, esp. those of the Apocalypse, are still to be fulfilled.

futuristic /ˌfjuːtʃəˈrɪstɪk/ *adj.* **1** suitable for the future; ultra-modern. **2** of futurism. **3** relating to the future. □□ **futuristically** *adv.*

futurity /fjuːˈtjʊərɪtɪ/ *n.* (*pl.* -**ies**) **1** future time. **2** (in *sing.* or *pl.*) future events. **3** future condition; existence after death. □ **futurity stakes** US stakes raced for long after entries or nominations are made.

futurology /ˌfjuːtʃəˈrɒlədʒɪ/ *n.* systematic forecasting of the future esp. from present trends in society. □□ **futurologist** *n.*

fuze var. of FUSE².

fuzee US var. of FUSEE.

Fuzhou /fuːˈdʒəʊ/ (also **Foochow**) the capital of Fujian province in east China; pop. (est. 1986) 1,190,000.

fuzz /fʌz/ *n.* **1** fluff. **2** fluffy or frizzled hair. **3** *sl.* **a** the police. **b** a policeman. □ **fuzz-ball** a puff-ball fungus. [17th c.: prob. f. LG or Du.: sense 3 perh. a different word]

fuzzy /ˈfʌzɪ/ *adj.* (**fuzzier, fuzziest**) **1 a** like fuzz. **b** frayed, fluffy. **c** frizzy. **2** blurred, indistinct. □ **fuzzy-wuzzy** (*pl.* -**ies**) *offens.* **1** *colloq. hist.* a Sudanese soldier. **2** *sl.* a Coloured native of any country. □□ **fuzzily** *adv.* **fuzziness** *n.*

fwd *abbr.* forward.

f.w.d. *abbr.* **1** four-wheel drive. **2** front-wheel drive.

f.y. *abbr.* US fiscal year.

-fy /faɪ/ *suffix* forming: **1** verbs from nouns, meaning: **a** make, produce (*pacify; satisfy*). **b** make into (*deify; petrify*). **2** verbs from adjectives, meaning 'bring or come into such a state' (*Frenchify; solidify*). **3** verbs in causative sense (*horrify; stupefy*). [from or after F -*fier* f. L -*ficare, -facere* f. *facere* do, make]

fylfot /ˈfɪlfɒt/ *n.* a swastika. [perh. f. *fill-foot*, pattern to fill the foot of a painted window]

fyrd /fɜːd/ *n. hist.* **1** the English militia before 1066. **2** the duty to serve in this. [OE f. Gmc (as FARE)]

fytte var. of FIT³.

G

G¹ /dʒiː/ n. (also **g**) (pl. **Gs** or **G's**) **1** the seventh letter of the alphabet. **2** *Mus.* the fifth note in the diatonic scale of C major.

G² *abbr.* (also **G.**) **1** gauss. **2** giga-. **3** gravitational constant. **4** *US sl.* = GRAND *n.* 2. **5** group (as in G5 'Group of Five'; see GROUP).

g *abbr.* (also **g.**) **1** gelding. **2** gram(s). **3 a** gravity. **b** acceleration due to gravity.

GA *abbr.* US Georgia (in official postal use).

Ga *symb. Chem.* the element gallium.

Ga. *abbr.* Georgia (US).

gab /gæb/ n. *colloq.* talk, chatter, twaddle. □ **gift of the gab** the facility of speaking eloquently or profusely. □□ **gabber** n. [17th-c. var. of GOB¹]

gabardine /ˈgæbəˌdiːn, -ˈdiːn/ n. (also **gaberdine**) **1** a smooth durable twill-woven cloth esp. of worsted or cotton. **2** a garment made of this, esp. a raincoat. [var. of GABERDINE]

gabble /ˈgæb(ə)l/ v. & n. —v. **1** *intr.* **a** talk volubly or inarticulately. **b** read aloud too fast. **2** *tr.* utter too fast, esp. in reading aloud. —n. fast unintelligible talk. □□ **gabbler** n. [MDu. *gabbelen* (imit.)]

gabbro /ˈgæbrəʊ/ n. (pl. **-os**) a dark granular plutonic rock of crystalline texture. □□ **gabbroic** /-ˈbrəʊɪk/ adj. **gabbroid** adv. [It. f. *Gabbro* in Tuscany]

gabby /ˈgæbɪ/ adj. (**gabbier, gabbiest**) *colloq.* talkative. [GAB + -Y¹]

gaberdine /ˈgæbəˌdiːn, -ˈdiːn/ n. **1** var. of GABARDINE. **2** *hist.* a loose long upper garment worn esp. by Jews and almsmen. [OF *gauvardine* perh. f. MHG *wallevart* pilgrimage]

Gabès /ˈgɑːbez/ an industrial seaport in eastern Tunisia; pop. (1984) 92,250.

gabion /ˈgeɪbɪən/ n. a cylindrical wicker or metal basket for filling with earth or stones, used in engineering or (formerly) in fortification. □□ **gabionage** n. [F f. It. *gabbione* f. *gabbia* CAGE]

Gable /ˈgeɪb(ə)l/, Clark (1901–60), American actor, whose air of tough arrogant masculinity combined with a straightforward easy going manner appealed to both men and women. In 1934 he topped the poll for the title 'King of Hollywood', and was known as 'The King' for the rest of his life. The film *Gone with the Wind* (1939) gave him his greatest role, as Rhett Butler.

gable /ˈgeɪb(ə)l/ n. **1 a** the triangular upper part of a wall at the end of a ridged roof. **b** (in full **gable-end**) a gable-topped wall. **2** a gable-shaped canopy over a window or door. □□ **gabled** adj. (also in *comb.*). [ME *gable* f. ON *gafl*]

Gabo /ˈgɑːbəʊ/, Naum (born Naum Neemia Pevsner, 1890–1977), Russian-born sculptor, who became an American citizen in 1952 and was the most influential exponent of constructivism (see entry).

gad¹ /gæd/ v. & n. —v.intr. (**gadded, gadding**) (foll. by *about, abroad, around*) go about idly or in search of pleasure. —n. idle wandering or adventure (esp. in **on the gad**). [back-form. f. obs. *gadling* companion f. OE *gædeling* f. *gæd* fellowship]

gad² /gæd/ int. (also **by gad**) an expression of surprise or emphatic assertion. [= *God*]

gadabout /ˈgædəˌbaʊt/ n. a person who gads about; an idle pleasure-seeker.

Gadaffi /gəˈdɑːfɪ/, Muammar al- (1942–), head of the State of Libya since 1970 after leading the coup which overthrew King Idris in 1969. Formerly an officer in the Libyan army, he established himself as the leader of a socialist republic, acquiring a reputation for unpredictability in his dealings with the West and with his Arab neighbours.

Gadarene /ˈgædəˌriːn/ adj. involving or engaged in headlong or suicidal rush or flight. [LL *Gadarenus* f. Gk *Gadarēnos* of Gadara in anc. Palestine, with ref. to Matthew 8: 28–32]

gadfly /ˈgædflaɪ/ n. (pl. **-flies**) **1** a cattle-biting fly, esp. a warble fly, horsefly, or bot-fly. **2** an irritating or harassing person. [obs. *gad* goad, spike f. ON *gaddr*, rel. to YARD¹]

gadget /ˈgædʒɪt/ n. any small and usu. ingenious mechanical device or tool. □□ **gadgeteer** /-ˈtɪə(r)/ n. **gadgetry** n. **gadgety** adj. [19th-c. Naut.: orig. unkn.]

gadoid /ˈgeɪdɔɪd/ n. & adj. —n. any marine fish of the cod family Gadidae, including haddock and whiting. —adj. belonging to or resembling the Gadidae. [mod.L *gadus* f. Gk *gados* cod + -OID]

gadolinite /ˈgædəlɪˌnaɪt/ n. a dark crystalline mineral consisting of ferrous silicate of beryllium. [J. *Gadolin*, Finnish mineralogist d. 1852]

gadolinium /ˌgædəˈlɪnɪəm/ n. *Chem.* a soft silvery metallic element of the lanthanide series, occurring naturally in gadolinite. It resembles steel in appearance and is strongly magnetic below room temperature. First isolated in pure form (as the oxide) in 1886, it is now used as a phosphor in colour television sets. ¶ Symb.: **Gd**; atomic number 64. [mod.L f. GADOLINITE]

gadroon /gəˈdruːn/ n. a decoration on silverware etc., consisting of convex curves in a series forming an ornamental edge like inverted fluting. [F *godron*: cf. *goder* pucker]

gadwall /ˈgædwɔːl/ n. a brownish-grey freshwater duck, *Anas strepera*. [17th c.: orig. unkn.]

gadzooks /gædˈzuːks/ int. *archaic* an expression of asseveration etc. [GAD² + *zooks* of unkn. orig.]

Gaea var. of GAIA.

Gael /geɪl/ n. **1** a Scottish Celt. **2** a Gaelic-speaking Celt. □□ **Gaeldom** n. [Gael. *Gaidheal*]

Gaelic /ˈgeɪlɪk, ˈgæ-/ n. & adj. —n. a language spoken in Ireland and Scotland in two distinct varieties, referred to also as Irish (or Erse; see IRISH) and Scots Gaelic respectively, forming, together with Manx, the Goidelic group of the Celtic language group. From about the 5th c. AD the language was carried to Scotland by settlers from Ireland (see DALRIADA) and became the language of most of the Highlands and islands; in time the Scottish variety diverged to the point where it was clearly a different dialect. Scots Gaelic, however, has no official status and now is spoken by only about 75,000 people in the far west of Scotland; there is a small but flourishing literary movement. A number of English words are taken from it, e.g. *bog, cairn, slogan, whisky*. —adj. of or relating to Gaelic or the Gaels.

Gaeltacht /ˈgeɪltəxt/ n. any of the regions in Ireland where the vernacular language is Irish. [Ir.]

gaff¹ /gæf/ n. & v. **1 a** a stick with an iron hook for landing large fish. **b** a barbed fishing-spear. **2** a spar to which the head of a fore-and-aft sail is bent. —v.tr. seize (a fish) with a gaff. [ME f. Prov. *gaf* hook]

gaff² /gæf/ n. *Brit. sl.* □ **blow the gaff** let out a plot or secret. [19th c., = nonsense: orig. unkn.]

gaffe /gæf/ n. a blunder; an indiscreet act or remark. [F]

gaffer /ˈgæfə(r)/ n. **1** an old fellow; an elderly rustic. **2** *Brit. colloq.* a foreman or boss. **3** *colloq.* the chief electrician in a film or television production unit. [prob. contr. of GODFATHER]

Gafsa /ˈgæfsə/ an industrial town in central Tunisia; pop. (1984) 61,000.

gag /gæg/ n. & v. —n. **1** a piece of cloth etc. thrust into or held over the mouth to prevent speaking or crying out, or to hold it open in surgery. **2** a joke or comic scene in a play, film, etc., or as part of a comedian's act. **3** an actor's interpolation in a dramatic dialogue. **4** a thing or circumstance restricting free speech. **5 a** a joke or hoax. **b** a humorous action or situation. **6** an imposture or deception. **7** *Parl.* a closure or guillotine. —v. (**gagged, gagging**) **1** *tr.* apply a gag to. **2** *tr.* silence; deprive of free speech. **3** *tr.* apply a gag-bit to (a horse). **4 a** *intr.* choke or retch. **b** *tr.* cause to do this. **5** *intr. Theatr.* make gags. □ **gag-bit**

a specially powerful bit for horse-breaking. **gag man** a deviser or performer of theatrical gags. [ME, orig. as verb: orig. uncert.]

gaga /ˈɡɑːɡɑː/ adj. sl. **1** senile. **2** fatuous; slightly crazy. [F, = senile]

Gagarin /ɡəˈɡɑːrɪn/, Yuri Alekseevich (1934–68), Russian cosmonaut, who in 1961 made the first manned space flight. He was killed when a plane that he was testing crashed.

gage¹ /ɡeɪdʒ/ n. & v. —n. **1** a pledge; a thing deposited as security. **2 a** a challenge to fight. **b** a symbol of this, esp. a glove thrown down. —v.tr. archaic stake, pledge; offer as a guarantee. [ME f. OF gage (n.), F gager (v.) ult. f. Gmc, rel. to WED]

gage² US var. of GAUGE.

gage³ /ɡeɪdʒ/ n. = GREENGAGE. [abbr.]

gaggle /ˈɡæɡ(ə)l/ n. & v. —n. **1** a flock of geese. **2** colloq. a disorderly group of people. —v.intr. (of geese) cackle. [ME, imit.: cf. gabble, cackle]

gagster /ˈɡæɡstə(r)/ n. = gag man.

Gaia /ˈɡeɪə,ˈɡaɪə/ (also **Gaea, Ge**) Gk Mythol. the Earth, personified as a goddess, daughter of Chaos. She was the mother and wife of Uranus (Heaven); their offspring included the Titans and the Cyclopes. □ **Gaia hypothesis** the theory, put forward by the British scientist James Lovelock in 1969, that the entire range of living matter on Earth defines the material conditions needed for its survival, functioning as a vast organism (which he named after the goddess Gaia) capable of modifying the biosphere, atmosphere, oceans, and soil to produce the physical and chemical environment that suits its needs.

gaiety /ˈɡeɪətɪ/ n. (US **gayety**) **1** the state of being light-hearted or merry; mirth. **2** merrymaking, amusement. **3** a bright appearance. □ **gaiety of nations** the cheerfulness or pleasure of numerous people. [F gaieté (as GAY)]

gaillardia /ɡeɪˈlɑːdɪə/ n. any composite plant of the genus Gaillardia, with showy flowers. [mod.L f. Gaillard de Marentoneau, 18th-c. Fr. botanist]

gaily /ˈɡeɪlɪ/ adv. **1** in a gay or light-hearted manner. **2** with a bright or colourful appearance.

gain /ɡeɪn/ v. & n. —v. **1** tr. obtain or secure (usu. something desired or favourable) (gain an advantage; gain recognition). **2** tr. acquire (a sum) as profits or as a result of changed conditions; earn. **3** tr. obtain as an increment or addition (gain momentum; gain weight). **4** tr. **a** win (a victory). **b** reclaim (land from the sea). **5** intr. (foll. by in) make a specified advance or improvement (gained in stature). **6** intr. & tr. (of a clock etc.) become fast, or be fast by (a specified amount of time). **7** intr. (often foll. by on, upon) come closer to a person or thing pursued. **8** tr. **a** bring over to one's interest or views. **b** (foll. by over) win by persuasion etc. **9** tr. reach or arrive at (a desired place). —n. **1** something gained, achieved, etc. **2** an increase of possessions etc.; a profit, advance, or improvement. **3** the acquisition of wealth. **4** (in pl.) sums of money acquired by trade etc., emoluments, winnings. **5** an increase in amount. **6** Electronics **a** the factor by which power etc. is increased. **b** the logarithm of this. □ **gain ground** see GROUND¹. **gain time** improve one's chances by causing or accepting delay. □□ **gainable** adj. **gainer** n. **gainings** n.pl. [OF gaigner, gaaignier to till, acquire, ult. f. Gmc]

gainful /ˈɡeɪnfʊl/ adj. **1** (of employment) paid. **2** lucrative, remunerative. □□ **gainfully** adv. **gainfulness** n.

gainsay /ɡeɪnˈseɪ/ v.tr. (past and past part. **gainsaid** /-ˈsed/) archaic or literary deny, contradict. □□ **gainsayer** n. [ME f. obs. gain-against f. ON gegn straight f. Gmc + SAY]

Gainsborough /ˈɡeɪnzbərə/, Thomas (1727–88), English painter of portraits and landscapes. Born in Suffolk, he worked there 1746–60, thereafter in fashionable Bath (1760–74), and finally in London (1774–88). Landscape was always his greatest love, and his mature landscapes are poetic and broadly painted, reflecting the influence of Rubens: in the 1780s he found a lucrative way to combine them with peasant figures in his 'fancy pictures'. His light rapid brushwork was especially suited to the depiction of effects of light, whether in twilight landscapes or in shimmering silks and satins; in his later years he painted by candle-light, so that such effects became even more delicate and subtle.

'gainst /ɡenst/ prep. poet. = AGAINST. [abbr.]

gait /ɡeɪt/ n. **1** a manner of walking; one's bearing or carriage as one walks. **2** the manner of forward motion of a runner, horse, vehicle, etc. □ **go one's** (or **one's own**) **gait** pursue one's own course. [var. of GATE²]

gaiter /ˈɡeɪtə(r)/ n. a covering of cloth, leather, etc. for the leg below the knee, for the ankle, for part of a machine, etc. □□ **gaitered** adj. [F guêtre, prob. rel. to WRIST]

Gaitskell /ˈɡeɪtsk(ə)l/, Hugh Todd Naylor (1906–63), British Labour politician, who succeeded Clement Attlee as leader of the Labour Party in 1955 and held this post until his death. His party was defeated in the general election of 1959.

Gaius /ˈɡaɪəs/ Gaius Julius Caesar Germanicus (12–41), also known as Caligula, Roman emperor 37–41. His short and autocratic reign, which ended with his assassination, has become a byword for tyrannical excess. The story that he appointed his horse as consul appears to be without foundation.

Gal. abbr. Galatians (New Testament).

gal¹ /ɡæl/ n. sl. a girl. [repr. var. pronunc.]

gal² /ɡæl/ n. Physics a unit of acceleration for a gravitational field, equal to one centimetre per second per second. [Galileo: see GALILEAN¹]

gal. abbr. gallon(s).

gala /ˈɡɑːlə/ n. **1** a festive occasion. **2** Brit. a festive gathering for sports, esp. swimming. [F or It. f. Sp. f. OF gale rejoicing f. Gmc]

galactagogue /ɡəˈlæktəˌɡɒɡ/ adj. & n. —adj. inducing a flow of milk. —n. a galactagogue substance. [Gk gala galaktos milk, + agōgos leading]

galactic /ɡəˈlæktɪk/ adj. of or relating to a galaxy or galaxies, esp. the Galaxy. [Gk galaktias, var. of galaxias: see GALAXY]

galago /ɡəˈleɪɡəʊ/ n. (pl. **-os**) any small tree-climbing primate of the genus Galago, found in southern Africa, with large eyes and ears and a long tail. Also called bush-baby. [mod.L]

galah /ɡəˈlɑː/ n. Austral. **1** a small rose-breasted grey-backed cockatoo, Cacatua roseicapilla. **2** sl. a fool or simpleton. [Aboriginal]

Galahad /ˈɡæləˌhæd/ (in Arthurian legend) a knight of immaculate purity, destined to retrieve the Holy Grail. —n. a person characterized by nobility, integrity, courtesy, etc.

galantine /ˈɡæləntiːn/ n. white meat or fish boned, cooked, pressed, and served cold in aspic etc. [ME f. OF, alt. f. galatine jellied meat f. med.L galatina]

galanty show /ˈɡæləntɪ/ n. see SHADOW-SHOW. [perh. f. It. galanti gallants]

Galapagos Islands /ɡəˈlæpəɡəs/ a Pacific archipelago on the Equator, about 1,045 km (650 miles) west of Ecuador, to which it belongs; pop. (1982) 6,100. The abundant wildlife of the islands includes giant tortoises, flightless cormorants, and many other endemic species. The observations made here by Charles Darwin in 1835, when official naturalist on HMS Beagle, helped him to form his theory of natural selection. Fragments of pottery found there, made by the Chimu Indians, indicate that the islands were visited by people who travelled from the mainland of South America before the Spanish conquest. [Sp., = tortoises]

Galatea /ˌɡæləˈtiːə/ Gk Mythol. **1** a sea-nymph courted by the Cyclops Polyphemus, who in jealousy killed his rival Acis. **2** the name given to the statue fashioned by Pygmalion and brought to life (see PYGMALION).

Galatia /ɡəˈleɪʃə/ **1** the ancient name for the region in central Asia Minor, centred on Ankara, settled by invading Celts (the Galatians) in the 3rd c. BC. **2** a Roman province formed in 25 BC including Galatia proper and additional territories. □□ **Galatian** adj. & n.

Galatians /ɡəˈleɪʃ(ə)nz/ **Epistle to the Galatians** a book of the New Testament, an epistle of St Paul to the Church at Galatia.

Galatz /ɡæˈlæts/ an industrial city on the lower Danube in eastern Romania; pop. (1985) 292,800.

galaxy /ˈɡæləksɪ/ n. (pl. **-ies**) **1** any of many independent systems of gas, dust, and millions or billions of stars, bound together by gravity, in form either elliptical, irregular, or disc-shaped (usually with well-defined spiral arms). **2 (the Galaxy)** the galaxy of which the solar system is a part. (See below.) **3 (the Galaxy)** the Milky Way (see entry). **4** (foll. by *of*) a brilliant company or gathering. [ME f. OF *galaxie* f. med.L *galaxia*, LL *galaxias* f. Gk f. *gala galaktos* milk]

The Galaxy in which the Earth is located is a collection of approximately 100,000 million stars. It has two main components: the halo, 100,000 light-years in diameter, containing a relatively sparse population of cool dim stars and the globular clusters (see CLUSTER), and the disc, a few thousand light-years thick, rich in gas, dust, and young stars, where the spiral arms denote regions of most recent star formation. Our sun is located slightly above the mid-plane of the disc, and about two-thirds of the way out from the centre. The centre of the disc exhibits a thickening, called the nuclear bulge, in which high-velocity gas motions seem to be occurring. The central few light-years of the Galaxy contain energetic radio and infrared sources, associated apparently with disturbed complexes of ionized hydrogen. These streaming gas-clouds behave as if ejected explosively from something not yet understood, perhaps a massive black hole, at the precise centre.

Galba /ˈgælbə/ Servius Sulpicius Galba (*c*.3 BC–AD 69), Roman emperor AD 68–9. He had had a distinguished career and was a governor in Spain when invited to succeed the murdered emperor Nero in AD 68, quickly obtaining the allegiance of all the Roman military forces. Once in power, however, he lacked the cool judgement that his task required, aroused hostility by his notorious parsimony, and alienated the legions in Germany by removing their commander. In mid-January AD 69 he was murdered in a conspiracy organized by Otho, who succeeded him.

galbanum /ˈgælbənəm/ *n*. a bitter aromatic gum resin produced from kinds of ferula. [ME f. L f. Gk *khalbanē*, prob. of Semitic orig.]

gale[1] /geɪl/ *n*. **1** a very strong wind, esp. (on the Beaufort scale) one of 32–54 m.p.h. **2** *Naut.* a storm. **3** an outburst, esp. of laughter. [16th c.: orig. unkn.]

gale[2] /geɪl/ *n*. (in full **sweet-gale**) bog myrtle. [OE *gagel(le)*, MDu. *gaghel*]

galea /ˈgeɪlɪə/ *n*. (*pl*. **galeae** /-lɪˌiː/ or **-as**) *Bot.* & *Zool.* a structure like a helmet in shape, form, or function. □□ **galeate** /-ɪət/ *adj.* **galeated** /-ɪˌeɪtɪd/ *adj.* [L, = helmet]

Galen /ˈgeɪlɪn/ (129–199) Greek physician from Pergamum in Asia Minor (where he tended the gladiators) who became court-physician in Rome. He was the author of numerous works which attempt to systematize the whole of medicine. His pathology was founded on Hippocrates' doctrine of the four humours, but he was especially productive as a practical anatomist and experimental physiologist. He demonstrated that the arteries carry blood not (as had been thought) air, but postulated the presence of minute pores in the wall between the ventricles of the heart, allowing blood to pass through, a theory which was accepted until medieval times. His works reached Europe in the 12th c. in Latin translations from Arabic texts, and were widely influential.

galena /gəˈliːnə/ *n*. a bluish, grey or black mineral ore of lead sulphide. ¶ *Chem.* formula: PbS. [L, = lead ore (in a partly purified state)]

galenic /gəˈlenɪk/ *adj.* & *n*. (also **galenical** /-ˈlenɪk(ə)l/) —*adj.* **1** of or relating to Galen or his methods. **2** made of natural as opposed to synthetic components. —*n*. a drug or medicament produced directly from animal or vegetable tissues.

galenical var. of GALENIC.

Galicia /gəˈlɪsɪə/ an autonomous region of NW Spain; pop. (1986) 2,785,400; capital, Santiago de Compostella. □□ **Galician** *adj.* & *n*.

Galilean[1] /ˌgælɪˈliːən/ *adj.* of or relating to Galileo, Italian astronomer d. 1642, or his methods. □ **Galilean satellites** the four largest moons of Jupiter, discovered by Galileo in 1610 and independently by Simon Marius. Visible through almost any small telescope, they are worlds in their own right, airless but with individual geological features: Io has many volcanoes

which erupt frequently to cover the surface in bright sulphurous lava, the others have rocky cores topped by a mantle of ice, heavily marked by either grooves (Ganymede), criss-crossing lines (Europa), or craters (Callisto and Ganymede). **Galilean telescope** the first type of astronomical telescope, used by Galileo, with a biconvex objective and biconcave eyepiece.

Galilean[2] /ˌgælɪˈliːən/ *adj.* & *n*. —*adj*. **1** of Galilee in Palestine. **2** Christian. —*n*. **1** a native of Galilee. **2** a Christian. **3** (prec. by *the*) *derog.* Christ.

Galilee /ˈgælɪlɪ/ the northern part of ancient Palestine, west of the Jordan, now in Israel. □ **Sea of Galilee** (also called Lake Tiberias) a lake in northern Israel. The River Jordan flows through it from north to south.

Galileo /ˌgælɪˈleɪəʊ/ a space probe bound for the planet Jupiter in a six-year journey, launched in October 1989.

Galileo Galilei /ˌgælɪlˈeɪəʊ ˌgælɪˈleɪɪ/ (1564–1642), Italian astronomer and physicist, one of the founding fathers of modern science. His important discoveries include the constancy of the time of a pendulum's swing, later applied to the regulation of clocks. He formulated the law of uniform acceleration for falling bodies, and described the parabolic trajectory of projectiles, important to the development of classical mechanics. In 1609 he improved the primitive telescope, applied it to astronomy, and made a number of startling observations, including mountains on the moon, sunspots, the stars of the Milky Way, the four satellites of Jupiter, and the phases of Venus. His acceptance (and supporting evidence) of the Copernican system with the Earth and other planets moving round the sun was rejected by the Catholic Church and led to his appearing before the Inquisition in 1633. Under threat of torture he publicly recanted his heretical views and was released into permanent house arrest; he spent his last days blind but still working on problems of astronomy and physics.

galingale /ˈgælɪŋˌgeɪl/ *n*. **1** an aromatic rhizome of an E. Asian plant of the genus *Alpinia*, formerly used in cookery and medicine. **2** (in full **English galingale**) a sedge (*Cyperus longus*) having a root with similar properties. [OE *gallengar* OF *galingal* f. Arab. *ḳalanjān* f. Chin. *ge-liang-jiang* mild ginger from Ge in Canton]

galiot var. of GALLIOT.

galipot /ˈgælɪˌpɒt/ *n*. a hardened deposit of resin formed on the stem of the cluster pine. [F: orig. unkn.]

gall[1] /gɔːl/ *n*. **1** *sl.* impudence. **2** asperity, rancour. **3** bitterness; anything bitter (*gall and wormwood*). **4** the bile of animals. **5** the gall-bladder and its contents. □ **gall-bladder** the vessel storing bile after its secretion by the liver and before release into the intestine. [ON, corresp. to OE *gealla*, f. Gmc]

gall[2] /gɔːl/ *n*. & *v*. —*n*. **1** a sore on the skin made by chafing. **2 a** mental soreness or vexation. **b** a cause of this. **3** a place rubbed bare. —*v.tr.* **1** rub sore; injure by rubbing. **2** vex, annoy, humiliate. □□ **gallingly** *adv.* [ME f. LG or Du. *galle*, corresp. to OE *gealla* sore on a horse]

gall[3] /gɔːl/ *n*. **1** a growth produced by insects or fungus etc. on plants and trees, esp. on oak. **2** (*attrib.*) of insects producing galls (*gall-fly*). [ME f. OF *galle* f. L *galla*]

gall. *abbr.* gallon(s).

gallant *adj.*, *n.*, & *v.* —*adj.* /ˈgælənt/ **1** brave, chivalrous. **2 a** (of a ship, horse, etc.) grand, fine, stately. **b** *archaic* finely dressed. **3** /ˈgælənt, gəˈlænt/ **a** markedly attentive to women. **b** concerned with sexual love; amatory. —*n.* /ˈgælənt, gəˈlænt/ **1** a ladies' man; a lover or paramour. **2** *archaic* a man of fashion; a fine gentleman. —*v.* /gəˈlænt/ **1** *tr.* flirt with. **2** *tr.* escort; act as a cavalier to (a lady). **3** *intr.* **a** play the gallant. **b** (foll. by *with*) flirt. □□ **gallantly** /ˈgæləntlɪ/ *adv.* [ME f. OF *galant* part. of *galer* make merry]

gallantry /ˈgæləntrɪ/ *n*. (*pl*. **-ies**) **1** bravery; dashing courage. **2** courtliness; devotion to women. **3** a polite act or speech. **4** the conduct of a gallant; sexual intrigue; immorality. [F *galanterie* (as GALLANT)]

Galle /ˈgɑːlə/ a seaport on the SW coast of Sri Lanka; pop. (1981) 76,800.

galleon /ˈgælɪən/ *n*. *hist.* a type of ship that was a development of the carrack, following the successful experiments of Sir John

Hawkins in 1570 in eliminating the high forecastle (which caught the wind), with which all large ships were then built, and so producing a ship that was more weatherly and manœuvrable. This new design reached Spain c.1587 and the resulting galleon, originally designed as a warship, over the next 30–40 years became the principal type of trading ship. Although the design was essentially English the name was never adopted for ships of England or northern Europe. [MDu. *galjoen* f. F *galion* f. *galie* galley, or f. Sp. *galeón*]

gallery /'gælərɪ/ n. (pl. **-ies**) **1** a room or building for showing works of art. **2** a balcony, esp. a platform projecting from the inner wall of a church, hall, etc., providing extra room for spectators etc. or reserved for musicians etc. (*minstrels' gallery*). **3 a** the highest balcony in a theatre. **b** its occupants. **4 a** a covered space for walking in, partly open at the side; a portico or colonnade. **b** a long narrow passage in the thickness of a wall or supported on corbels, open towards the interior of the building. **5** a long narrow room, passage, or corridor. **6** *Mil. & Mining* a horizontal underground passage. **7** a group of spectators at a golf-match etc. □ **play to the gallery** seek to win approval by appealing to popular taste. □□ **galleried** adj. [F *galerie* f. It. *galleria* f. med.L *galeria*]

galleryite /'gælərɪˌaɪt/ n. a person occupying a seat in a gallery; a playgoer.

galley /'gælɪ/ n. (pl. **-eys**) **1** *hist.* **a** a low flat single-decked vessel using sails and oars, and usu. rowed by slaves or criminals. **b** an ancient Greek or Roman warship with one or more banks of oars. (See below.) **c** a large open rowing-boat, e.g. that used by the captain of a man-of-war. **2** a ship's or aircraft's kitchen. **3** *Printing* **a** an oblong tray for set type. **b** the corresponding part of a composing-machine. **c** (in full **galley proof**) a proof in the form of long single-column strips from type in a galley, not in sheets or pages. □ **galley-slave 1** *hist.* a person condemned to row in a galley. **2** a drudge. [ME f. OF *galie* f. med.L *galea*, med.Gk *galaia*]

The galley was the oared fighting-ship of the Mediterranean, dating from about 3000 BC and lasting into the 18th c. AD. Such ships may have had up to three banks of oars (see TRIREME), or angled benches with several men to each oar, but firm evidence is lacking. The weapon was the ram, a pointed spur fixed to the bow of the galley on or just below the waterline; the ancient Greek technique of fighting was to ram and then depart at speed; the Romans preferred to grapple and fight on deck, or use catapult weapons. Galleys were fitted with one or two masts, which were lowered or beached before action. With its slim light-draught design the galley was an unstable vessel suitable only for calm waters.

galliard /'gælɪˌɑːd/ n. *hist.* **1** a lively dance usu. in triple time for two persons. **2** the music for this. [ME f. OF *gaillard* valiant]

Gallic /'gælɪk/ adj. **1** French or typically French. **2** of the Gauls; Gaulish. □□ **Gallicize** /-ˌsaɪz/ v.tr. & intr. (also **-ise**). [L *Gallicus* f. *Gallus* a Gaul]

gallic acid /'gælɪk/ n. *Chem.* an acid extracted from gallnuts etc., formerly used in making ink. [F *gallique* f. *galle* GALL³]

Gallican /'gælɪkən/ adj & n. —*adj.* **1** of the ancient church of Gaul or France. **2** of a doctrine (reaching its peak in the 17th c.) asserting the freedom of the Roman Catholic Church, especially in France, from the ecclesiastical authority of the papacy (cf. ULTRAMONTANE). —*n.* an adherent of this doctrine. □□ **Gallicanism** n. [as GALLIC.]

gallice /'gælɪˌsiː/ adv. in French. [L, = in Gaulish]

Gallicism /'gælɪˌsɪz(ə)m/ n. a French idiom, esp. one adopted in another language. [F *gallicisme* (as GALLIC)]

galligaskins /ˌgælɪˈgæskɪnz/ n.pl. *hist.* or *joc.* breeches, trousers. [orig. wide hose of the 16th–17th c., f. obs. F *garguesque* for *greguesque* f. It. *grechesca* fem. of *grechesco* Greek]

gallimaufry /ˌgælɪˈmɔːfrɪ/ n. (pl. **-ies**) a heterogeneous mixture; a jumble or medley. [F *galimafrée*, of unkn. orig.]

gallinaceous /ˌgælɪˈneɪʃəs/ adj. of or relating to the order Galliformes, which includes domestic poultry, pheasants, partridges, etc. [L *gallinaceus* f. *gallina* hen f. *gallus* cock]

gallinule /'gælɪˌnjuːl/ n. **1** a moorhen. **2** any of various similar birds of the genus *Porphyrula* or *Porphyrio*. [mod.L *gallinula*, dimin. of L *gallina* hen f. *gallus* cock]

galliot /'gælɪət/ n. (also **galiot**) **1** a Dutch cargo-boat or fishing-vessel. **2** a small (usu. Mediterranean) galley. [ME f. OF *galiote* f. It. *galeotta* f. med.L *galea* galley]

Gallipoli /gəˈlɪpəlɪ/ a peninsula on the European side of the Dardanelles, the scene of heavy fighting during the First World War. In early 1915, after a naval attempt to force the Dardanelles had failed, the Allies decided to invade the Gallipoli peninsula, hoping thereby to remove Turkey from the war and open supply lines to Russia's Black Sea ports. Although the Turks were caught at a severe disadvantage, the Allies failed to take their opportunity and the campaign bogged down in trench warfare. After each side had suffered a quarter of a million casualties, the Allies successfully evacuated the peninsula without further loss in January 1916.

gallipot /'gælɪˌpɒt/ n. a small pot of earthenware, metal, etc., used for ointments etc. [prob. GALLEY + POT¹, because brought in galleys from the Mediterranean]

gallium /'gælɪəm/ n. *Chem.* a soft bluish-white metallic element occurring naturally in zinc blende, bauxite, and kaolin. Discovered in 1875, gallium now has a number of uses, e.g. in thermometers designed for high temperatures, and as a semiconductor in electronic components. ¶ Symb.: **Ga**; atomic number 31. [mod.L f. L *Gallia* France (so named patriotically by its discoverer Lecoq de Boisbaudran d. 1912)]

gallivant /'gælɪˌvænt/ v.intr. *colloq.* **1** gad about. **2** flirt. [orig. uncert.]

galliwasp /'gælɪˌwɒsp/ n. a W. Indian lizard, *Diploglossus monotropis*. [18th c.: orig. unkn.]

gallnut /'gɔːlnʌt/ n. = GALL³.

Gallo- /'gæləʊ/ comb. form **1** French; French and. **2** Gaul (*Gallo-Roman*). [L *Gallus* a Gaul]

gallon /'gælən/ n. **1 a** (in full **imperial gallon**) *Brit.* a measure of capacity equal to eight pints and equivalent to 4546 cc, used for liquids and corn etc. **b** *US* a measure of capacity equivalent to 3785 cc, used for liquids. **2** (usu. in *pl.*) *colloq.* a large amount. □□ **gallonage** n. [ME f. ONF *galon*, OF *jalon*, f. base of med.L *galleta*, *galletum*, perh. of Celtic orig.]

galloon /gəˈluːn/ n. a narrow close-woven braid of gold, silver, silk, cotton, nylon, etc., for binding dresses etc. [F *galon* f. *galonner* trim with braid, of unkn. orig.]

gallop /'gæləp/ n. & v. —*n.* **1** the fastest pace of a horse or other quadruped, with all the feet off the ground together in each stride. **2** a ride at this pace. **3** a track or ground for this. —*v.* (**galloped, galloping**) **1 a** intr. (of a horse etc. or its rider) go at the pace of a gallop. **b** tr. make (a horse etc.) gallop. **2** intr. (foll. by *through, over*) read, recite, or talk at great speed. **3** intr. move or progress rapidly (*galloping inflation*). □ **at a gallop** at the pace of a gallop. □□ **galloper** n. [OF *galop, galoper*: see WALLOP]

galloway /'gæləˌweɪ/ n. **1** an animal of a breed of hornless black beef cattle from Galloway in SW Scotland. **2** this breed.

gallows /'gæləʊz/ n.pl. (usu. treated as *sing.*) **1** a structure, usu. of two uprights and a crosspiece, for the hanging of criminals. **2** (prec. by *the*) execution by hanging. □ **gallows humour** grim and ironical humour. [ME f. ON *gálgi*]

gallstone /'gɔːlstəʊn/ n. a small hard mass forming in the gall-bladder.

Gallup poll /'gæləp/ n. an assessment of public opinion by questioning a representative sample, esp. as the basis for forecasting the results of voting. [G. H. *Gallup*, Amer. statistician d. 1984, who devised such assessment]

galluses /'gæləsɪz/ n.pl. *dial.* & *US* trouser-braces. [pl. of *gallus* var. of GALLOWS]

Galois /ˈɡɑːlwɑː/, Évariste (1811–32), French mathematician, whose name is used to designate various concepts in algebra that arose out of his work. His bids for recognition were dogged by lost and rejected manuscripts; his memoir on the conditions for solubility of polynomial equations was highly innovative and unappreciated by his contemporaries, and was not published until fourteen years after his death. Having made fundamental discoveries in mathematics at the age of 18, he was imprisoned for his republican activities aged 19, and died aged 20 of wounds received in a mysterious early-morning duel.

galoot /gə'luːt/ n. colloq. a person, esp. a strange or clumsy one. [19th-c. Naut. sl.: orig. unkn.]

galop /'gæləp/ n. & v. —n. 1 a lively dance in duple time. 2 the music for this. —v.intr. (**galoped, galoping**) perform this dance. [F: see GALLOP]

galore /gə'lɔː(r)/ adv. in abundance (placed after noun: flowers galore). [Ir. go leór to sufficiency]

galosh /gə'lɒʃ/ n. (also **golosh**) (usu. in pl.) a waterproof overshoe, usu. of rubber. [ME f. OF galoche f. LL gallicula small Gallic shoe]

Galsworthy /'gɔːlzwɜːðɪ/, John (1867–1933), English novelist and dramatist. A severe and humourless writer, he wrote several plays on social and moral themes, notably The Silver Box (1906) and Strife (1909), but is remembered chiefly for his sequence of novels known collectively as The Forsyte Saga (1922), tracing the declining fortunes of an affluent Victorian middle-class family. Galsworthy was caricatured by his contemporaries for his superficial and limited vision of social phenomena, but the Forsyte novels have a history of continuing success. He was awarded the Nobel Prize for literature in 1932.

Galton /'gɔːlt(ə)n/, Sir Francis (1822–1911), English scientist. A man of wide interests and a cousin of Charles Darwin, he is remembered chiefly for his advocacy of eugenics (a word coined by him) as a method of improving the human race as a whole. To this end he introduced methods of measuring human mental and physical abilities, and developed statistical techniques to analyse his data. Galton also carried out important work in meteorology and pioneered the use of fingerprints as a means of identification. Eugenics, a widely supported idea in the early decades of the 20th c., fell into disfavour after the perversion of its doctrines by the Nazis.

galumph /gə'lʌmf/ v.intr. colloq. 1 move noisily or clumsily. 2 go prancing in triumph. [coined by Lewis Carroll in Through the Looking-glass (in sense 2), perh. f. GALLOP + TRIUMPH]

Galvani /gæl'vɑːnɪ/, Luigi (1737–98), Italian anatomist. He studied the structure of the kidneys and ears of birds, the irritability of tissue, and the physiology of muscles and nerves, but he is best remembered for his chance discovery in the 1780s of the twitching of frogs' legs in an electric field produced by his electrostatic generator. He concluded that these convulsions were caused by 'animal electricity' found in the body. This was disputed by Volta who, in the course of this argument, invented his electrochemical cell. The current produced by this device was, for many years, called 'galvanic electricity', and the terms galvanize and galvanometer etc. embody his name.

galvanic /gæl'vænɪk/ adj. 1 a sudden and remarkable (had a galvanic effect). b stimulating; full of energy. 2 of or producing an electric current by chemical action. □□ **galvanically** adv.

galvanism /'gælvə̩nɪz(ə)m/ n. hist. 1 electricity produced by chemical action. 2 the use of electricity for medical purposes. □□ **galvanist** n. [F galvanisme f. GALVANI]

galvanize /'gælvə̩naɪz/ v.tr. (also **-ise**) 1 (often foll. by into) rouse forcefully, esp. by shock or excitement (was galvanized into action). 2 stimulate by or as if by electricity. 3 coat (iron) with zinc (usu. without the use of electricity) as a protection against rust. □□ **galvanization** /-'zeɪʃ(ə)n/ n. **galvanizer** n. [F galvaniser: see GALVANISM]

galvanometer /̩gælvə'nɒmɪtə(r)/ n. an instrument for detecting and measuring small electric currents. □□ **galvanometric** /-nə'metrɪk/ adj.

Galway /'gɔːlweɪ/ 1 a county on the west coast of the Republic of Ireland, in the county of Connaught; pop. (est. 1986) 131,200. 2 its capital city, a seaport at the head of Galway Bay; pop. (1981) 41,681.

Gama /'gɑːmə/, Vasco da (c.1469–1524), Portuguese explorer. Da Gama led a Portuguese expedition round the Cape of Good Hope in 1497–9 (the first European to do so), crossing the Indian Ocean to Calicut. Ennobled on his return, he led a second expedition in 1502–3, forcing the Raja of Calicut (who had massacred settlers left behind earlier) to make peace and establishing colonies at Mozambique and Sofala. After 20 years in retirement, da Gama was sent east again to restore Portuguese authority in the East Indies but died soon after his arrival.

gambade /gæm'bɑːd/ n. (also **gambado** /-'bɑːdəʊ/) (pl. **gambades; -os** or **-oes**) 1 a horse's leap or bound. 2 a fantastic movement. 3 an escapade. [F gambade & Sp. gambado f. It. & Sp. gamba leg]

Gambia /'gæmbɪə/ (also **the Gambia**) a picturesque but poor country of West Africa, consisting of a narrow strip on either side of the River Gambia upstream from its mouth, forming an enclave in Senegal; pop. (est. 1988) 779,500; official language, English; capital, Banjul. A British trading post from the 17th c., Gambia was created a colony in 1843. It became an independent member of the Commonwealth in 1965, and a republic in 1970. The economy is mainly agricultural, the chief product being groundnuts. □□ **Gambian** adj. & n.

gambier /'gæmbɪə(r)/ n. an astringent extract of an Eastern plant used in tanning etc. [Malay gambir name of the plant]

Gambier Islands /'gæmbɪə(r)/ a group of coral islands in the Tuamoutu Archipelago in French Polynesia; pop. (1986) 582.

gambit /'gæmbɪt/ n. 1 a chess opening in which a player sacrifices a piece or pawn to secure an advantage. 2 an opening move in a discussion etc. 3 a trick or device. [earlier gambett f. It. gambetto tripping up f. gamba leg]

gamble /'gæmb(ə)l/ v. & n. —v. 1 intr. play games of chance for money, esp. for high stakes. 2 tr. a bet (a sum of money) in gambling. b (often foll. by away) lose (assets) by gambling. 3 intr. take great risks in the hope of substantial gain. 4 intr. (foll. by on) act in the hope or expectation of (gambled on fine weather). —n. 1 a risky undertaking or attempt. 2 a spell of gambling. □□ **gambler** n. [obs. gamel to sport, gamene GAME¹]

gamboge /gæm'bəʊʒ, -'buːʒ/ n. a gum resin produced by various E. Asian trees and used as a yellow pigment and as a purgative. [mod.L gambaugium f. Cambodia in SE Asia]

gambol /'gæmb(ə)l/ v. & n. —v.intr. (**gambolled, gambolling**; US **gamboled, gamboling**) skip or frolic playfully. —n. a playful frolic. [GAMBADE]

gambrel /'gæmbr(ə)l/ n. (in full **gambrel roof**) 1 Brit. a roof like a hipped roof but with gable-like ends. 2 US = curb roof. [ONF gamberel f. gambier forked stick f. gambe leg (from the resemblance to the shape of a horse's hind leg)]

game¹ /geɪm/ n., adj., & v. —n. 1 a form or spell of play or sport, esp. a competitive one played according to rules and decided by skill, strength, or luck. 2 a single portion of play forming a scoring unit in some contests, e.g. bridge or tennis. 3 (in pl.) a athletics or sports as organized in a school etc. b a meeting for athletic etc. contests (Olympic Games). 4 a winning score in a game; the state of the score in a game (the game is two all). 5 the equipment for a game. 6 one's level of achievement in a game, as specified (played a good game). 7 a a piece of fun; a jest (was only playing a game with you). b (in pl.) dodges, tricks (none of your games!). 8 a scheme or undertaking etc. regarded as a game (so that's your game). 9 a policy or line of action. 10 (collect.) a wild animals or birds hunted for sport or food. b the flesh of these. 11 a hunted animal; a quarry or object of pursuit or attack. 12 a kept flock of swans. —adj. 1 spirited; eager and willing. 2 (foll. by for, or to + infin.) having the spirit or energy; eagerly prepared. —v. intr. play at games of chance for money; gamble. □ **the game is up** the scheme is revealed or foiled. **game plan** esp. US 1 a winning strategy worked out in advance for a particular match. 2 a plan of campaign, esp. in politics. **game point** Tennis etc. a point which, if won, would win the game. **game (or games) theory** the branch of mathematics that deals with the selection of best strategies for participants in conflict. The theory was founded by John von Neumann in 1928 and was expanded in collaboration with Oskar Morgenstern in their book Theory of games and economic behavior (1944) etc. **game-warden** an official locally supervising game and hunting. **gaming-house** a place frequented for gambling; a casino. **gaming-table** a table used for gambling. **make game (or a game) of** mock, taunt. **off** (or **on**) one's game playing badly (or well). **on the game** *Brit. sl.* involved in prostitution or thieving. **play the game** behave fairly or according to the rules. □□ **gamely** *adv.* **gameness** *n.* **gamester** *n.* [OE *gamen*]

game² /geɪm/ *adj.* (of a leg, arm, etc.) lame, crippled. [18th-c. dial.: orig. unkn.]

gamebook /ˈgeɪmbʊk/ *n.* a book for recording game killed by a sportsman.

gamecock /ˈgeɪmkɒk/ *n.* (also **gamefowl** /-faʊl/) a cock bred and trained for cock-fighting.

gamekeeper /ˈgeɪmˌkiːpə(r)/ *n.* a person employed to breed and protect game.

gamelan /ˈgæməˌlæn/ *n.* **1** the standard instrumental ensemble of Indonesia, comprising sets of tuned gongs, gong-chimes, and other percussion instruments as well as string and woodwind instruments. Sir Francis Drake heard the 'pleasant and delightful' sound of the gamelan during his visit to Java in 1580, and in 1889 a Javanese gamelan formed one of the attractions of the Paris World Exhibition, where it was heard by Debussy and had a marked influence on his music. **2** a kind of xylophone used in this. [Jav.]

gamesman /ˈgeɪmzmən/ *n.* (*pl.* **-men**) an exponent of gamesmanship.

gamesmanship /ˈgeɪmzmənʃɪp/ *n.* the art or practice of winning games or other contests by gaining a psychological advantage over an opponent.

gamesome /ˈgeɪmsəm/ *adj.* merry, sportive. □□ **gamesomely** *adv.* **gamesomeness** *n.*

gametangium /ˌgæmɪˈtændʒɪəm/ *n.* (*pl.* **gametangia** /-dʒɪə/) *Bot.* an organ in which gametes are formed. [as GAMETE + *aggeion* vessel]

gamete /ˈgæmiːt, gəˈmiːt/ *n.* *Biol.* a mature germ cell able to unite with another in sexual reproduction. □□ **gametic** /gəˈmetɪk/ *adj.* [mod.L *gameta* f. Gk *gametē* wife f. *gamos* marriage]

gameto- /gəˈmiːtəʊ/ *comb. form Biol.* gamete.

gametocyte /gəˈmiːtəʊˌsaɪt/ *n.* *Biol.* any cell that is in the process of developing into one or more gametes.

gametogenesis /gəˌmiːtəʊˈdʒenɪsɪs/ *n.* *Biol.* the process by which cells undergo meiosis to form gametes.

gametophyte /gəˈmiːtəʊˌfaɪt/ *n.* the gamete-producing form of a plant that has alternation of generations between this and the asexual form. □□ **gametophytic** /-ˈfɪtɪk/ *adj.*

gamin /ˈgæmɪn/ *n.* **1** a street urchin. **2** an impudent child. [F]

gamine /gæˈmiːn/ *n.* **1** a girl gamin. **2** a girl with mischievous or boyish charm. [F]

gamma /ˈgæmə/ *n.* **1** the third letter of the Greek alphabet (Γ, γ). **2** a third-class mark given for a piece of work or in an examination. **3** *Astron.* the third brightest star in a constellation. **4** the third member of a series. □ **gamma radiation** (or **rays**) electromagnetic radiation of very short wavelength emitted by some radioactive substances. [ME f. Gk]

gammer /ˈgæmə(r)/ *n.* *archaic* an old woman, esp. as a rustic name. [prob. contr. of GODMOTHER: cf. GAFFER]

gammon¹ /ˈgæmən/ *n.* & *v.* —*n.* **1** the bottom piece of a flitch of bacon including a hind leg. **2** the ham of a pig cured like bacon. —*v.tr.* cure (bacon). [ONF *gambon* f. *gambe* leg: cf. JAMB]

gammon² /ˈgæmən/ *n.* & *v.* —*n.* a kind of victory scoring two games at backgammon. —*v.tr.* defeat in this way. [app. = ME *gamen* GAME¹]

gammon³ /ˈgæmən/ *n.* & *v.* *colloq.* —*n.* humbug, deception. —*v.* **1** *intr.* **a** talk speciously. **b** pretend. **2** *tr.* hoax, deceive. [18th c.: orig. uncert.]

gammy /ˈgæmɪ/ *adj.* (**gammier, gammiest**) *Brit. sl.* (esp. of a leg) lame; permanently injured. [dial. form of GAME²]

gamp /gæmp/ *n.* *Brit. colloq.* an umbrella, esp. a large unwieldy one. [Mrs *Gamp* in Dickens's *Martin Chuzzlewit*]

gamut /ˈgæmət/ *n.* **1** the whole series or range or scope of anything (*the whole gamut of crime*). **2** *Mus.* **a** the whole series of notes used in medieval or modern music. **b** a major diatonic scale. **c** a people's or a period's recognized scale. **d** a voice's or instrument's compass. **3** *Mus.* the lowest note in the medieval sequence of hexachords, = modern G on the lowest line of the

bass staff. [med.L *gamma ut* f. GAMMA taken as the name for a note one tone lower than A of the classical scale + *ut* the first of six arbitrary names of notes forming the hexachord, being syllables (*ut, re, mi, fa, so, la*) of the 7th-c. Latin hymn: *Ut queant laxis resonare fibris Mira gestorum famuli tuorum, Solve polluti labii reatum, Sancte Ioannes*]

gamy /ˈgeɪmɪ/ *adj.* (**gamier, gamiest**) **1** having the flavour or scent of game kept till it is high. **2** *US* scandalous, sensational. **3** = GAME¹ *adj.* □□ **gamily** *adv.* **gaminess** *n.*

Ganapati /ˈgʌnəpʌtɪ/ = GANESHA. [as GANESHA]

Gand see GHENT.

gander /ˈgændə(r)/ *n.* & *v.* —*n.* **1** a male goose. **2** *sl.* a look, a glance (*take a gander*). —*v.intr.* look or glance. [OE *gandra*, rel. to GANNET]

Gandhi¹ /ˈgɑːndɪ/, Indira (1917–84), Indian stateswoman, who sought to establish a secular State and to lead her country out of poverty. Daughter of an independent India's first Prime Minister, Jawaharlal Nehru, she was herself Prime Minister 1966–77 and again from 1980, dominating Indian politics for nearly twenty years before her assassination.

Gandhi² /ˈgɑːndɪ/, Mohandas Karamchand, called 'Mahatma' (1869–1948), Indian statesman. After early civil rights activities as a lawyer in South Africa, Gandhi returned to India in 1914 and after 1918 began to take an increasingly important part in the opposition to British rule, utilizing policies of passive resistance and civil disobedience. President of the Indian National Congress 1925–34, Gandhi was at once the leader and the symbol of the nationalist movement. He was assassinated by a Hindu fanatic at the very time when independence had finally been achieved.

Gandzhe /ˈgɑːndʒə/ an industrial city in Azerbaijan; pop. (est. 1987) 270,000. The city was formerly named Elizavetpol (1804–1918) and Kirovabad (1935–89).

Ganesha /gəˈneɪʃə/ *Hinduism* an elephant-headed deity, also called Ganapati, son of Siva and Parvati. Worshipped as the remover of obstacles and patron of learning, he is invoked at the beginning of literary works, rituals, or any new undertaking. He is usually depicted coloured red, with a pot belly and one broken tusk, riding a rat. [Skr., = lord of ganas (Siva's attendants)]

gang¹ /gæŋ/ *n.* & *v.* —*n.* **1 a** a band of persons acting or going about together, esp. for criminal purposes. **b** *colloq.* such a band pursuing a purpose causing disapproval. **2** a set of workers, slaves, or prisoners. **3** a set of tools arranged to work simultaneously. —*v.tr.* arrange (tools etc.) to work in coordination. □ **gang-bang** *sl.* an occasion on which several men successively have sexual intercourse with one woman. **gang up** *colloq.* **1** (often foll. by *with*) act in concert. **2** (foll. by *on*) combine against. [orig. = going, journey, f. ON *gangr, ganga* GOING, corresp. to OE *gang*]

gang² /gæŋ/ *v.intr. Sc.* go. □ **gang agley** (of a plan etc.) go wrong. [OE *gangan*: cf. GANG¹]

Ganga /ˈgʌŋgə/ the name in India of the Ganges.

gangboard /ˈgæŋbɔːd/ *n.* = GANGPLANK.

ganger /ˈgæŋə(r)/ *n.* *Brit.* the foreman of a gang of workers, esp. navvies.

Ganges /ˈgændʒiːz/ a river in the north of India, held sacred by the Hindus who seek to wash away their sins in its waters. It flows some 2,700 km (1,678 miles) from the Himalayas southeast to Bangladesh, where it reaches the Bay of Bengal in the world's largest delta.

gangle /ˈgæŋg(ə)l/ *v.intr.* move ungracefully. [back-form. f. GANGLING]

gangling /ˈgæŋglɪŋ/ *adj.* (of a person) loosely built; lanky. [frequent. of GANG²]

ganglion /ˈgæŋglɪən/ *n.* (*pl.* **ganglia** /-lɪə/ or **ganglions**) **1 a** an enlargement or knot on a nerve etc. containing an assemblage of nerve-cells. **b** a mass of grey matter in the central nervous system forming a nerve-nucleus. **2** *Med.* a cyst, esp. on a tendon sheath. **3** a centre of activity or interest. □□ **gangliar** *adj.* **gangliform** *adj.* **ganglionated** *adj.* **ganglionic** /-ˈɒnɪk/ *adj.* [Gk *gagglion*]

gangly /ˈgæŋglɪ/ adj. (**ganglier, gangliest**) = GANGLING.

gangplank /ˈgæŋplæŋk/ n. a movable plank usu. with cleats nailed on it for boarding or disembarking from a ship etc.

gangrene /ˈgæŋgriːn/ n. & v. —n. **1** Med. death and decomposition of a part of the body tissue, usu. resulting from obstructed circulation. **2** moral corruption. —v.tr. & intr. affect or become affected with gangrene. □□ **gangrenous** /ˈgæŋgrɪnəs/ adj. [F gangrène f. L gangraena f. Gk gaggraina]

gangster /ˈgæŋstə(r)/ n. a member of a gang of violent criminals. □□ **gangsterism** n.

gangue /gæŋ/ n. valueless earth etc. in which ore is found. [F f. G Gang lode = GANG¹]

gangway /ˈgæŋweɪ/ n. & int. —n. **1** Brit. a passage, esp. between rows of seats. **2 a** an opening in the bulwarks by which a ship is entered or left. **b** a bridge laid from ship to shore. **c** a passage on a ship, esp. a platform connecting the quarterdeck and forecastle. **3** a temporary bridge on a building site etc. —int. make way!

ganister /ˈgænɪstə(r)/ n. a close-grained hard siliceous stone found in the coal measures of northern England, and used for furnace-linings. [19th c.: orig. unkn.]

ganja /ˈgændʒə/ n. marijuana. [Hindi gānjhā]

gannet /ˈgænɪt/ n. **1** any sea bird of the genus Sula, esp. Sula bassana, catching fish by plunge-diving. **2** sl. a greedy person. □□ **gannetry** n. (pl. **-ies**). [OE ganot f. Gmc, rel. to GANDER]

ganoid /ˈgænɔɪd/ adj. & n. —adj. **1** (of fish scales) enamelled; smooth and bright. **2** having ganoid scales. —n. a fish having ganoid scales. [F ganoïde f. Gk ganos brightness]

Gansu /gænˈsuː/ (also **Kansu**) a province of north central China, in the upper Yellow River valley; pop. (est. 1986) 20,710,000; capital, Lanzhou (Lanchow).

gantlet US var. of GAUNTLET².

gantry /ˈgæntrɪ/ n. (pl. **-ies**) **1** an overhead structure with a platform supporting a travelling crane, or railway or road signals. **2** a structure supporting a space rocket prior to launching. **3** (also **gauntry** /ˈgɔːntrɪ/) a wooden stand for barrels. [prob. f. gawn, dial. form of GALLON + TREE]

Ganymede /ˈgænɪˌmiːd/ **1** Gk Mythol. a Trojan youth who was so beautiful that he was carried off (in one version, by an eagle) to be Zeus' cup-bearer. **2** Astron. the largest satellite of the planet Jupiter.

gaol Brit. var. of JAIL.

gaoler Brit. var. of JAILER.

gap /gæp/ n. **1** an unfilled space or interval; a blank; a break in continuity. **2** a breach in a hedge, fence, or wall. **3** a wide (usu. undesirable) divergence in views, sympathies, development, etc. (generation gap). **4** a gorge or pass. □ **fill** (or **close** etc.) **a gap** make up a deficiency. **gap-toothed** having gaps between the teeth. □□ **gapped** adj. **gappy** adj. [ME f. ON, = chasm, rel. to GAPE]

gape /geɪp/ v. & n. —v.intr. **1 a** open one's mouth wide, esp. in amazement or wonder. **b** be or become wide open. **2** (foll. by at) gaze curiously or wondrously. **3** split; part asunder. **4** yawn. —n. **1** an open-mouthed stare. **2** a yawn. **3** (in pl.; prec. by the) **a** a disease of birds with gaping as a symptom, caused by infestation with gapeworm. **b** joc. a fit of yawning. **4 a** an expanse of open mouth or beak. **b** the part of a beak that opens. **5** a rent or opening. □□ **gapingly** adv. [ME f. ON gapa]

gaper /ˈgeɪpə(r)/ n. **1** any bivalve mollusc of the genus Mya, with the shell open at one or both ends. **2** the comber fish, which gapes when dead. **3** a person who gapes.

gapeworm /ˈgeɪpwɜːm/ n. a nematode worm, Syngamus tracheae, that infests the trachea and bronchi of birds and causes the gapes.

gar /gɑː(r)/ n. = GARFISH 2.

garage /ˈgærɑːdʒ, -rɑːʒ, -rɪdʒ/ n. & v. —n. **1** a building or shed for the storage of a motor vehicle or vehicles. **2** an establishment selling petrol etc., or repairing and selling motor vehicles. —v.tr. put or keep (a motor vehicle) in a garage. □ **garage sale** US a sale of miscellaneous household goods, usu. for charity, held in the garage of a private house. [F f. garer shelter]

garb /gɑːb/ n. & v. —n. **1** clothing, esp. of a distinctive kind. **2** the way a person is dressed. —v.tr. **1** (usu. in passive or refl.) put (esp. distinctive) clothes on (a person). **2** attire. [obs. F garbe f. It. garbo f. Gmc, rel. to GEAR]

garbage /ˈgɑːbɪdʒ/ n. **1 a** a refuse, filth. **b** domestic waste. **2** foul or rubbishy literature etc. □ **garbage can** US a dustbin. [AF: orig. unkn.]

garble /ˈgɑːb(ə)l/ v.tr. **1** unintentionally distort or confuse (facts, messages, etc.). **2 a** mutilate in order to misrepresent. **b** make (usu. unfair or malicious) selections from (facts, statements, etc.). □□ **garbler** n. [It. garbellare f. Arab. ġarbala sift, perh. f. LL cribellare to sieve f. L cribrum sieve]

Garbo /ˈgɑːbəʊ/, Greta (1905–90), real name Greta Gustafsson, Swedish film actress. Her first important Swedish film, Gösta Berlings Saga (1924), led to a Hollywood contract, and her beauty and compelling screen presence received instant recognition in The Torrent (1925). After a number of silent films she made a successful transition to sound in Anna Christie (1930). She played a number of tragic heroines including Queen Christina (1934), Anna Karenina (1935), and Camille (1936), and in 1939 made her first comedy, Ninotchka. After another comedy, Two Faced Woman (1941), she abruptly announced her retirement. She is considered by many the greatest of all film actresses.

garboard /ˈgɑːbəd/ n. (in full **garboard strake**) the first range of planks or plates laid on a ship's bottom next to the keel. [Du. gaarboord, perh. f. garen GATHER + boord BOARD]

García Lorca see LORCA.

García Márquez /ˈgɑːsɪə (-θɪə) ˈmɑːkes/, Gabriel (1928–), Colombian writer, whose most famous novel is Cien años de soledad (One Hundred Years of Solitude, 1967, 1970), a classic work of 'magic realism'. He was awarded the Nobel Prize for literature in 1982.

garçon /ˈgɑːsɔ̃/ n. a waiter in a French restaurant, hotel, etc. [F, lit. 'boy']

Garda¹ /ˈgɑːdə/ n. **1** the State police force of the Irish Republic. **2** (also **garda**) (pl. **-daí** /-diː/) a member of this. [Ir. Garda Síochána Civic Guard]

Garda² /ˈgɑːdə/, **Lake** the largest lake in Italy, situated on the frontier between the northern regions of Lombardy and Venetia.

garden /ˈgɑːd(ə)n/ n. & v. —n. **1** esp. Brit. a piece of ground, usu. partly grassed and adjoining a private house, used for growing flowers, fruit, or vegetables, and as a place of recreation. **2** (esp. in pl.) ornamental grounds laid out for public enjoyment (botanical gardens). **3** a similar place with the service of refreshments (tea garden). **4** (attrib.) **a** (of plants) cultivated, not wild. **b** for use in a garden (garden seat). **5** (usu. in pl. prec. by a name) Brit. a street, square, etc. (Onslow Gardens). **6** an especially fertile region. **7** US a large public hall. **8** (**the Garden**) the philosophy or school of Epicurus. —v.intr. cultivate or work in a garden. □ **garden centre** an establishment where plants and garden equipment etc. are sold. **garden city** an industrial or other town laid out systematically with spacious surroundings, parks, etc. **garden cress** a cruciferous plant, Lepidium sativum, used in salads. **garden party** a social event held on a lawn or in a garden. **garden suburb** Brit. a suburb laid out spaciously with open spaces, parks, etc. **garden warbler** a European woodland songbird, Sylvia borin. □□ **gardenesque** /-ˈnesk/ adj. **gardening** n. [ME f. ONF gardin (OF jardin) ult. f. Gmc: cf. YARD²]

gardener /ˈgɑːdnə(r)/ n. a person who gardens or is employed to tend a garden. □ **gardener-bird** a bowerbird making a 'garden' of moss etc. in front of a bower. [ME ult. f. OF jardinier (as GARDEN)]

gardenia /gɑːˈdiːnɪə/ n. any tree or shrub of the genus Gardenia, with large white or yellow flowers and usu. a fragrant scent. [mod.L f. Dr A. Garden, Sc. naturalist d. 1791]

Gardner /ˈgɑːdnə(r)/, Erle Stanley (1899–1970), American author of detective novels, who had practised as a lawyer in California. Many of his stories end with a dramatic courtroom scene featuring his famous hero the lawyer-detective Perry Mason.

Garfield /ˈgɑːfiːld/, James Abram (1831–81), 20th President of the US (1881), who was assassinated within months of taking office.

garfish /'gɑːfɪʃ/ n. (pl. same) **1** any mainly marine fish of the family Belonidae, esp. Belone belone, having long beaklike jaws with sharp teeth. Also called NEEDLEFISH. **2** US any similar freshwater fish of the genus Lepisosteus, with ganoid scales. Also called GAR or GARPIKE. **3** NZ & Austral. either of two marine fish of the genus Hemiramphus. Also called HALFBEAK. [app. f. OE gār spear + fisc FISH¹]

garganey /'gɑːgənɪ/ n. (pl. -eys) a small duck, Anas querquedula, the drake of which has a white stripe from the eye to the neck. [It., dial. var. of garganello]

gargantuan /gɑːˈgæntjʊən/ adj. enormous, gigantic. [the name of a giant in Rabelais' book Gargantua (1534)]

garget /'gɑːgɪt/ n. **1** inflammation of a cow's or ewe's udder. **2** US pokeweed. [perh. f. obs. garget throat f. OF gargate, -guete]

gargle /'gɑːg(ə)l/ v. & n. —v. **1** tr. (also absol.) wash (one's mouth and throat), esp. for medicinal purposes, with a liquid kept in motion by breathing through it. **2** intr. make a sound as when doing this. —n. **1** a liquid used for gargling. **2** sl. an alcoholic drink. [F gargouiller f. gargouille: see GARGOYLE]

gargoyle /'gɑːgɔɪl/ n. a grotesque carved human or animal face or figure projecting from the gutter of (esp. a Gothic) building usu. as a spout to carry water clear of a wall. [OF gargouille throat, gargoyle]

gargoylism /'gɑːgɔɪˌlɪz(ə)m/ n. Med. = HURLER'S SYNDROME.

Garibaldi /ˌgærɪˈbɔːldɪ/, Giuseppe (1807–82), Italian patriot and military leader, one of the heroes of the Risorgimento. After involvement in the early struggles against Austrian rule in the 1830s and 1840s he commanded a volunteer force on the Sardinian side in the campaign of 1859, and successfully led his 'Red Shirts' to victory in Sicily and southern Italy in 1860–1, thus playing a vital part in the establishment of a united kingdom of Italy. Subsequent independent attempts to conquer the papal territories around French-held Rome failed in 1862 and 1867, and Garibaldi proved no more successful in French service during the Franco-Prussian War in 1870–1. In the last years of his life, his health ruined by years of soldiering, he served as a Deputy in the Italian Parliament.

garibaldi /ˌgærɪˈbɔːldɪ/ n. (pl. garibaldis) **1** a kind of loose blouse worn by a woman or a child, orig. of bright red material imitating the shirts worn by Garibaldi and his followers. **2** Brit. a biscuit containing a layer of currants. **3** US a small red Californian dish, Hypsypops rubicundus. [GARIBALDI]

garish /'geərɪʃ/ adj. **1** obtrusively bright; showy. **2** gaudy; over-decorated. □□ **garishly** adv. **garishness** n. [16th-c. gaurish app. f. obs. gaure stare]

Garland /'gɑːlənd/, Judy (1922–69), real name Frances Gumm, American singer and film actress. Her films include The Wizard of Oz (1939) in which she sang 'Over the Rainbow', and A Star is Born (1954).

garland /'gɑːlənd/ n. & v. —n. **1** a wreath of flowers, leaves, etc., worn on the head or hung as a decoration. **2** a prize or distinction. **3** a literary anthology or miscellany. —v.tr. **1** adorn with garlands. **2** crown with a garland. [ME f. OF garlande, of unkn. orig.]

garlic /'gɑːlɪk/ n. **1** any of various alliaceous plants, esp. Allium sativum. **2** the strong-smelling pungent-tasting bulb of this plant, used as a flavouring in cookery. □□ **garlicky** adj. [OE gārlēac f. gār spear + lēac LEEK]

garment /'gɑːmənt/ n. & v. —n. **1 a** an article of dress. **b** (in pl.) clothes. **2** the outward and visible covering of anything. —v.tr. (usu. in passive) rhet. attire. [ME f. OF garnement (as GARNISH)]

garner /'gɑːnə(r)/ v. & n. —v.tr. **1** collect. **2** store, deposit. —n. literary a storehouse or granary. [ME (orig. as noun) f. OF gernier f. L granarium GRANARY]

garnet /'gɑːnɪt/ n. a vitreous silicate mineral, esp. a transparent deep-red kind used as a gem. [ME f. OF grenat f. med.L granatum POMEGRANATE, from its resemblance to the pulp of the fruit]

garnish /'gɑːnɪʃ/ v. & n. —v.tr. **1** decorate or embellish (esp.

food). **2** Law **a** serve notice on (a person) for the purpose of legally seizing money belonging to a debtor or defendant. **b** summon (a person) as a party to litigation started between others. —n. (also **garnishing**) a decoration or embellishment, esp. to food. □□ **garnishment** n. (in sense 2). [ME f. OF garnir f. Gmc]

garnishee /ˌgɑːnɪˈʃiː/ n. & v. Law —n. a person garnished. —v.tr. (**garnishees, garnisheed**) **1** garnish (a person). **2** attach (money etc.) by way of garnishment.

garniture /'gɑːnɪtʃə(r)/ n. **1** decoration or trimmings, esp. of food. **2** accessories, appurtenances. [F (as GARNISH)]

Garonne /gæˈrɒn/ a river of SW France, which rises in the Pyrenees and flows 645 km (400 miles) before joining the Dordogne to form the Gironde estuary.

garotte var. of GAROTTE.

garpike /'gɑːpaɪk/ n. a gar or garfish (see GARFISH 2). [OE gār spear + PIKE¹]

garret /'gærɪt/ n. **1** a top-floor or attic room, esp. a dismal one. **2** an attic. [ME f. OF garite watch-tower f. Gmc]

Garrick /'gærɪk/, David (1717–79), one of the greatest English actors, who replaced formal declamation with an easy natural manner of speech, of whom Burke said that 'he raised the character of his profession to the rank of a liberal art'. In 1747 he became involved in the management, later becoming sole manager, of Drury Lane theatre. Unsurpassed as the tragic heroes of contemporary works as well as Hamlet, Macbeth, and Lear, he proved his versatility with successes in comedy roles such as Benedick in Much Ado About Nothing and Abel Drugger in Jonson's The Alchemist, and was also a prolific dramatist. He is buried in Westminster Abbey.

garrison /'gærɪs(ə)n/ n. & v. —n. **1** the troops stationed in a fortress, town, etc., to defend it. **2** the building occupied by them. —v.tr. **1** provide (a place) with or occupy as a garrison. **2** place on garrison duty. □ **garrison town** a town having a permanent garrison. [ME f. OF garison f. garir defend, furnish f. Gmc]

garrotte /gəˈrɒt/ v. & n. (also **garotte**; US **garrote**) —v.tr. **1** execute or kill by strangulation, esp. with an iron collar or a length of wire or cord etc. **2** throttle in order to rob. —n. **1 a** a Spanish method of execution by garrotting. **b** the apparatus used for this. **2** highway robbery in which the victim is throttled. [F garrotter or Sp. garrotear f. garrote a cudgel, of unkn. orig.]

garrulous /'gærʊləs/ adj. **1** talkative, esp. on trivial matters. **2** loquacious, wordy. □□ **garrulity** /gəˈruːlɪtɪ/ n. **garrulously** adv. **garrulousness** n. [L garrulus f. garrire chatter]

garter /'gɑːtə(r)/ n. & v. —n. **1** a band worn to keep a sock or stocking up. **2** (**the Garter**) Brit. **a** the highest order of English knighthood. (See below.) **b** the badge of this. **c** membership of this. **3** US a suspender for a sock or stocking. —v.tr. fasten (a stocking) or encircle (a leg) with a garter. □ **garter-belt** US a suspender belt. **Garter King of Arms** see King of Arms. **garter-snake** any water-snake of the genus Thamnophis, native to N. America, having lengthwise stripes. **garter stitch** a plain knitting stitch or pattern, forming ridges in alternate rows. [ME f. OF gartier f. garet bend of the knee]

The Order of the Garter was founded by Edward III c.1344. The traditional story of the order's founding is that the garter was that of the Countess of Salisbury, which the king placed on his own leg after it fell off while she was dancing with him. The king's comment to those present, 'Honi soit qui mal y pense', became the motto of the order, which became the highest in English knighthood and the model for others founded by other late medieval kings. The Garter as the badge of the order is a ribbon of dark-blue velvet, edged and buckled with gold, bearing the motto embroidered in gold, and is worn below the left knee; garters also form part of the ornament of the collar worn by the Knights.

garth /gɑːθ/ n. Brit. **1** an open space within cloisters. **2** archaic **a** a close or yard. **b** a garden or paddock. [ME f. ON garthr = OE geard YARD²]

gas /gæs/ n. & v. —n. (pl. **gases**) **1 a** any substance which is compressible, expands to fill any space in which it is enclosed, and consists of molecules which are not bound together but move about relatively independently. (See below, and cf. KINETIC THEORY.) **b** a substance which is a gas at normal temperatures and pressures. **c** a gas which at a given temperature cannot be liquefied by pressure alone (other gases generally being known as 'vapours' in this context). **2 a** such a substance (esp. found naturally or extracted from coal) used as a domestic or industrial fuel (also *attrib.*: *gas cooker*; *gas fire*). **b** an explosive mixture of firedamp with air. **3** nitrous oxide or another gas used as an anaesthetic (esp. in dentistry). **4** a gas or vapour used as a poisonous agent to disable an enemy in warfare. **5** *US colloq.* petrol, gasoline. **6** *sl.* pointless idle talk; boasting. **7** *sl.* an enjoyable, attractive, or amusing thing or person. —*v.* (**gases, gassed, gassing**) **1** *tr.* expose to gas, esp. to kill or make unconscious. **2** *intr.* give off gas. **3** *tr.* (usu. foll. by *up*) *US colloq.* fill (the tank of a motor vehicle) with petrol. **4** *intr. colloq.* talk idly or boastfully. □ **gas chamber** an airtight chamber that can be filled with poisonous gas to kill people or animals. **gas chromatography** chromatography employing gas as the eluent. **gas-cooled** (of a nuclear reactor etc.) cooled by a current of gas. **gas fire** a domestic fire using gas as its fuel. **gas-fired** using gas as the fuel. **gas gangrene** a rapidly spreading gangrene of injured tissue infected by a soil bacterium and accompanied by the evolution of gas. **gas mask** a respirator used as a defence against poison gas. **gas meter** an apparatus recording the amount of gas consumed. **gas oil** a type of fuel oil distilled from petroleum and heavier than paraffin oil. **gas plant** *Bot.* fraxinella. **gas-proof** impervious to gas. **gas ring** a hollow ring perforated with gas jets, used esp. for cooking. **gas station** *US* a filling-station. **gas-tight** proof against the leakage of gas. **gas turbine** a turbine driven by a flow of gas or by gas from combustion. [word coined by J. B. van Helmont, Belgian chemist d. 1644, after Gk *khaos* chaos]

Different 'airs', vapours, and exhalations were recognized in antiquity and classified with the element 'air', distinguishing them from the other Aristotelian elements earth, water, and fire. It was not until the second half of the 18th c. that different chemical species of gases were clearly distinguished and identified, and recognized as elements in their own right. During the same period the four Aristotelian elements were definitively replaced by three states of matter—solid, liquid, and gas.

The technical founder of the modern gas industry was William Murdock, a Scotsman, who experimented with the distillation of gas from coal (as an Irish clergyman named Clayton had done, for frivolous purposes, nearly a century before him), and in 1792 succeeded in lighting his office with the new gas. In 1807 the first street in London was lit with it, and the Gas Light and Coke Company came into being three years later. In the early years rival companies competed for business, but soon after 1850 many amalgamated and 'zoning' arrangements were established whereby a single company was responsible for supplies in an allotted district. Gas for lighting was followed by the use of gas for cooking and (from 1863) for heating water. The British gas industry was nationalized in 1949 and denationalized by the Gas Act of 1986. Early in the 1960s oil began to replace coal as the primary raw material, but from 1965 great natural gas deposits were discovered under the North Sea, creating a rapidly expanding market for gas in western Europe. Natural gas reserves are found also in the USSR (which supplies Eastern Europe), the US, Algeria, Iran, The Netherlands, Saudi Arabia, and Kuwait.

gasbag /ˈgæsbæg/ *n.* **1** a container of gas, esp. for holding the gas for a balloon or airship. **2** *sl.* an idle talker.

Gascon /ˈgæskən/ *n.* **1** a native of Gascony. **2** (**gascon**) a braggart. [F f. L *Vasco -onis*]

Gascony /ˈgæskənɪ/ (French **Gascogne** /gæsˈkɒnjə/) a former region of SW France, in the northern foothills of the Pyrenees.

gaseous /ˈgæsɪəs/ *adj.* of or like gas. □□ **gaseousness** *n.*

gash[1] /gæʃ/ *n. & v.* —*n.* **1** a long and deep slash, cut, or wound. **2 a** a cleft such as might be made by a slashing cut. **b** the act of making such a cut. —*v.tr.* make a gash in; cut. [var. of ME *garse* f. OF *garcer* scarify, perh. ult. f. Gk *kharassō*]

gash[2] /gæʃ/ *adj. Brit. sl.* spare, extra. [20th-c. Naut. sl.: orig. unkn.]

gasholder /ˈgæsˌhəʊldə(r)/ *n.* a large receptacle for storing gas; a gasometer.

gasify /ˈgæsɪˌfaɪ/ *v.tr. & intr.* (**-ies, -ied**) convert or be converted into gas. □□ **gasification** /-fɪˈkeɪʃ(ə)n/ *n.*

Gaskell /ˈgæsk(ə)l/, Mrs Elizabeth Cleghorn (1810–65), English novelist, whose father and husband were Unitarian ministers. Her first novel, *Mary Barton* (1848), was admired by Dickens, and much of her subsequent works appeared in his *Household Words*, including *Cranford* (1851–3), drawn from childhood experiences in Cheshire. Mrs Gaskell was an active humanitarian; the message in several of her novels is the need for social reconciliation, notably in *North and South* (1855); she also wrote a celebrated biography of her friend Charlotte Brontë (1857).

gasket /ˈgæskɪt/ *n.* **1** a sheet or ring of rubber etc., shaped to seal the junction of metal surfaces. **2** a small cord securing a furled sail to a yard. □ **blow a gasket** *sl.* lose one's temper. [perh. f. F *garcette* thin rope (orig. little girl)]

gaskin /ˈgæskɪn/ *n.* the hinder part of a horse's thigh. [perh. erron. f. GALLIGASKINS]

gaslight /ˈgæslaɪt/ *n.* **1** a jet of burning gas, usu. heating a mantle, to provide light. **2** light emanating from this.

gasman /ˈgæsmən/ *n.* (*pl.* **-men**) a man who instals or services gas appliances, or reads gas meters.

gasolene var. of GASOLINE.

gasoline /ˈgæsəˌliːn/ *n.* (also **gasolene**) **1** a volatile inflammable liquid distilled from petroleum and used for heating and lighting. **2** *US* petrol. [GAS + -OL[2] + -INE[4], -ENE]

gasometer /gæˈsɒmɪtə(r)/ *n.* a large tank in which gas is stored for distribution by pipes to users. [F *gazomètre* f. *gaz* gas + -*mètre* -METER]

gasp /gɑːsp/ *v. & n.* —*v.* **1** *intr.* catch one's breath with an open mouth as in exhaustion or astonishment. **2** *intr.* (foll. by *for*) strain to obtain by gasping (*gasped for air*). **3** *tr.* (often foll. by *out*) utter with gasps. —*n.* a convulsive catching of breath. □ **at one's last gasp 1** at the point of death. **2** exhausted. [ME f. ON *geispa*: cf. *geip* idle talk]

gasper /ˈgɑːspə(r)/ *n.* **1** a person who gasps. **2** *Brit. sl.* a cigarette.

gasser /ˈgæsə(r)/ *n.* **1** *colloq.* an idle talker. **2** *sl.* a very attractive or impressive person or thing.

gassy /ˈgæsɪ/ *adj.* (**gassier, gassiest**) **1 a** of or like gas. **b** full of gas. **2** *colloq.* (of talk etc.) pointless, verbose. □□ **gassiness** *n.*

gasteropod var. of GASTROPOD.

gasthaus /ˈgæsthaʊs/ *n.* a small inn or hotel in German-speaking countries. [G f. *Gast* GUEST + *Haus* HOUSE]

gastrectomy /gæˈstrektəmɪ/ *n.* (*pl.* **-ies**) a surgical operation in which the whole or part of the stomach is removed. [GASTRO- + -ECTOMY]

gastric /ˈgæstrɪk/ *adj.* of the stomach. □ **gastric flu** a popular name for an intestinal disorder of unknown cause. **gastric juice** a thin clear virtually colourless acid fluid secreted by the stomach glands and active in promoting digestion. [mod.L *gastricus* f. Gk *gastēr gast(e)ros* stomach]

gastritis /gæˈstraɪtɪs/ *n.* inflammation of the lining of the stomach.

gastro- /ˈgæstrəʊ/ *comb. form* (also **gastr-** before a vowel) stomach. [Gk *gastēr gast(e)ros* stomach]

gastro-enteric /ˌgæstrəʊənˈterɪk/ *adj.* of or relating to the stomach and intestines.

gastro-enteritis /ˌgæstrəʊˌentəˈraɪtɪs/ *n. Med.* inflammation of the stomach and intestines.

gastronome /ˈgæstrəˌnəʊm/ *n.* a gourmet. [F f. *gastronomie* GASTRONOMY]

gastronomy /gæˈstrɒnəmɪ/ *n.* the practice, study, or art of eating and drinking well. □□ **gastronomic** /ˌgæstrəˈnɒmɪk/ *adj.* **gastronomical** /ˌgæstrəˈnɒmɪk(ə)l/ *adj.* **gastronomically** /ˌgæstrəˈnɒmɪkəlɪ/ *adv.* [F *gastronomie* f. Gk *gastronomia* (as GASTRO-, -*nomia* f. *nomos* law)]

gastropod /ˈgæstrəˌpɒd/ *n.* (also **gasteropod**) any mollusc of the class Gastropoda that moves along by means of a large muscular foot, e.g. a snail, slug, etc. □□ **gastropodous**

/gæ'strɒpədəs/ adj. [F gastéropode f. mod.L gasteropoda (as GASTRO-, Gk pous podos foot)]

gastroscope /'gæstrə,skəʊp/ n. an optical instrument used for inspecting the interior of the stomach.

gastrula /'gæstrʊlə/ n. (pl. **gastrulae** /-,li:/) Zool. an embryonic stage developing from the blastula. [mod.L f. Gk gastēr gast(e)ros belly]

gasworks /'gæswɜ:ks/ n. a place where gas is manufactured and processed.

gat¹ /gæt/ n. sl. a revolver or other firearm. [abbr. of GATLING]

gat² /gæt/ archaic past of GET v.

gate¹ /geɪt/ n. & v. —n. **1** a barrier, usu. hinged, used to close an opening made for entrance and exit through a wall, fence, etc. **2** such an opening, esp. in the wall of a city, enclosure, or large building. **3** a means of entrance or exit. **4** a numbered place of access to aircraft at an airport. **5** a mountain pass. **6** an arrangement of slots into which the gear lever of a motor vehicle moves to engage the required gear. **7** a device for holding the frame of a cine film momentarily in position behind the lens of a camera or projector. **8 a** an electrical signal that causes or controls the passage of other signals. **b** an electrical circuit with an output which depends on the combination of several inputs. **9** a device regulating the passage of water in a lock etc. **10 a** the number of people entering by payment at the gates of a sports ground etc. **b** (in full **gate-money**) the proceeds taken for admission. **11** sl. the mouth. **12** US sl. dismissal. **13** = starting-gate. —v.tr. **1** Brit. confine to college or school entirely or after certain hours. **2** (as **gated** adj.) (of a road) having a gate or gates to control the movement of traffic or animals. [OE gæt, geat, pl. gatu, f. Gmc]

gate² /geɪt/ n. (prec. or prefixed by a name) Brit. a street (Westgate). [ME f. ON gata, f. Gmc]

gateau /'gætəʊ/ n. (pl. **gateaus** or **gateaux**) any of various rich cakes, usu. containing cream or fruit. [F gâteau cake]

gatecrasher /'geɪt,kræʃə(r)/ n. an uninvited guest at a party etc. □□ **gatecrash** v.tr. & intr.

gatefold /'geɪtfəʊld/ n. a page in a book or magazine etc. that folds out to be larger than the page-format.

gatehouse /'geɪthaʊs/ n. **1** a house standing by a gateway, esp. to a large house or park. **2** hist. a room over a city gate, often used as a prison.

gatekeeper /'geɪt,ki:pə(r)/ n. **1** an attendant at a gate, controlling entrance and exit. **2** any of several large brown species of butterfly, esp. Maniola tithonus, frequenting hedgerows and woodland.

gateleg /'geɪtleg/ n. (in full **gateleg table**) a table with folding flaps supported by legs swung open like a gate. □□ **gatelegged** adj.

gateman /'geɪtmən/ n. (pl. **-men**) = GATEKEEPER 1.

gatepost /'geɪtpəʊst/ n. a post on which a gate is hung or against which it shuts. □ **between you and me and the gatepost** in strict confidence.

gateway /'geɪtweɪ/ n. **1** an entrance with or opening for a gate. **2** a frame or structure built over a gate.

gather /'gæðə(r)/ v. & n. —v. **1** tr. & intr. bring or come together; assemble, accumulate. **2** tr. (usu. foll. by up) **a** bring together from scattered places or sources. **b** take up together from the ground, a surface, etc. **c** draw into a smaller compass. **3** tr. acquire by gradually collecting; amass. **4** tr. **a** pick a quantity of (flowers etc.). **b** collect (grain etc.) as a harvest. **5** tr. (often foll. by that + clause) infer or understand. **6** tr. be subjected to or affected by the accumulation or increase of (unread books gathering dust; gather speed; gather strength). **7** tr. (often foll. by up) summon up (one's thoughts, energy, etc.) for a purpose. **8** tr. gain or recover (one's breath). **9** tr. **a** draw (material, or one's brow) together in folds or wrinkles. **b** pucker or draw together (part of a dress) by running a thread through. **10** intr. come to a head; develop a purulent swelling. —n. (in pl.) a part of a garment that is gathered or drawn in. □ **gather way** (of a ship) begin to move. □□ **gatherer** n. [OE gaderian f. WG]

gathering /'gæðərɪŋ/ n. **1** an assembly or meeting. **2** a purulent swelling. **3** a group of leaves taken together in bookbinding.

Gatling /'gætlɪŋ/, Richard Jordan (1818–1903), American inventor, remembered for his rapid-fire crank-driven gun (the Gatling or Gatling gun) that was the first practical machine-gun. It was officially adopted by the US Army in 1866, too late to be much used in the American Civil War. The weapon was superseded by the Maxim.

GATT /gæt/ abbr. (also **Gatt**) General Agreement on Tariffs and Trade, a treaty to which about 100 countries are party (others apply it de facto) in operation since 1948, to promote trade and economic development).

Gatwick /'gætwɪk/ an international airport in SE England, near Crawley in West Sussex.

gauche /gəʊʃ/ adj. **1** lacking ease or grace; socially awkward. **2** tactless. □□ **gauchely** adv. **gaucheness** n. [F, = left-handed, awkward]

gaucherie /'gəʊʃə,ri:/ n. **1** gauche manners. **2** a gauche action. [F]

gaucho /'gaʊtʃəʊ/ n. (pl. **-os**) a cowboy from the S. American pampas. [Sp. f. Quechua]

gaud /gɔ:d/ n. **1** a gaudy thing; a showy ornament. **2** (in pl.) showy ceremonies. [perh. through AF f. OF gaudir rejoice f. L gaudēre]

Gaudier-Brzeska /,gəʊdɪəɪ'bʒeskə/, Henri (1891–1915), French vorticist sculptor, whose stylistically advanced work was appreciated by only a small circle during his short lifetime but has achieved recognition since his death. In addition to his sculptures he made some splendid animal drawings.

gaudy¹ /'gɔ:dɪ/ adj. (**gaudier, gaudiest**) tastelessly or extravagantly bright or showy. □□ **gaudily** adv. **gaudiness** n. [prob. f. GAUD + -Y¹]

gaudy² /'gɔ:dɪ/ n. (pl. **-ies**) Brit. an annual feast or entertainment, esp. a college dinner for old members etc. [L gaudium joy or gaude imper. of gaudēre rejoice]

gauge /geɪdʒ/ n. & v. (US **gage**: see also sense 7) —n. **1** a standard measure to which certain things must conform, esp.: **a** the measure of the capacity or contents of a barrel. **b** the fineness of a textile. **c** the diameter of a bullet. **d** the thickness of sheet metal. **2** any of various instruments for measuring or determining this, or for measuring length, thickness, or other dimensions or properties. **3** the distance between a pair of rails or the wheels on one axle. **4** the capacity, extent, or scope of something. **5** a means of estimating; a criterion or test. **6** a graduated instrument measuring the force or quantity of rainfall, stream, tide, wind, etc. **7** (usu. **gage**) Naut. a relative position with respect to the wind. —v.tr. **1** measure exactly (esp. objects of standard size). **2** determine the capacity or content of. **3** estimate or form a judgement of (a person, temperament, situation, etc.). **4** make uniform; bring to a standard size or shape. □ **gauge pressure** the amount by which a pressure exceeds that of the atmosphere. **take the gauge of** estimate. □□ **gaugeable** adj. **gauger** n. [ME f. ONF gauge, gauger, of unkn. orig.]

Gauguin /'gəʊgæ̃/, Paul (1848–1903), French painter, son of a French father and a Peruvian Creole mother, who was a stock-broker, collector, and amateur artist before becoming a professional artist in 1883. In 1891 he left France for Tahiti, and remained in the tropics until his death, apart from two years in Europe in 1893–5. Gauguin yearned for the simple life of nature and regarded civilization as a disease; he found inspiration in primitive art (e.g. pre-Columbian Peruvian pottery). Reacting against the realism of the impressionists, he freed colour from its representational function, using it in flat contrasting areas to emphasize its decorative or emotional effect, and introduced emphatic outlines, suggestive of Japanese prints or stained glass. Both the Nabis and the symbolist movements were formed under the inspiration of Gauguin's ideas.

Gaul /gɔ:l/ an ancient region of Europe, divided by the Romans into Cisalpine Gaul (northern Italy, = 'Gaul on this side of the Alps') and Transalpine Gaul (= 'Gaul beyond the Alps'), an area corresponding roughly to modern France and Belgium. Tribal groups of Celts had spread from across the Rhine over Transalpine Gaul perhaps as early as 900 BC. From c.400 BC some migrated south of the Alps in successive waves, gradually ousting the Etruscans, and waging long and ultimately unsuccessful wars against Rome; before 100 BC the area had been made into a Roman province. Transalpine Gaul was conquered by Julius Caesar in 58–51 BC and remained under Roman rule, extensively romanized, until the withdrawal of the garrisons in the 5th c. AD. —*n.* a native or inhabitant of Gaul. □□ **Gaulish** *adj.* & *n.* [F f. Gmc, = foreigners]

gauleiter /ˈgaʊˌlaɪtə(r)/ *n.* **1** an official governing a district under Nazi rule. **2** a local or petty tyrant. [G f. *Gau* administrative district + *Leiter* leader]

Gaulle /gəʊl/, Charles Joseph de (1890–1970), French general and statesman. A career soldier with extensive service in the First World War behind him, de Gaulle became the leading French advocate of mechanized warfare in the 1920s and 1930s and commanded a French armoured division in the early days of the Second World War. In Britain at the time of France's surrender, he refused to recognize the capitulation and organized the Free French forces to fight alongside the Allies. After the war he became interim President of the new French Republic, but resigned after he was refused wide presidential powers and retired to his country home to await the recall he was sure must come. He returned as President in 1959 and extracted France from the Algerian crisis, going on to stamp his own highly individualistic mark on the government, withdrawing French forces from NATO command, and blocking British entry into the EEC. He resigned in 1969 after proposed political reforms had been rejected by a referendum, and died suddenly shortly afterwards.

Gaullism /ˈgəʊlɪz(ə)m/ *n.* **1** the principles and policies of Charles de Gaulle, characterized by their conservatism, nationalism, and advocacy of centralized government. **2** adherence to these. □□ **Gaullist** *n.* [F *Gaullisme*]

gault /gɔːlt/ *n. Geol.* **1** a series of clay and marl beds between the upper and lower greensand in S. England. **2** clay obtained from these beds. [16th c.: orig. unkn.]

Gaunt /gɔːnt/ the former English name of Ghent.

gaunt /gɔːnt/ *adj.* **1** lean, haggard. **2** grim or desolate in appearance. □□ **gauntly** *adv.* **gauntness** *n.* [ME: orig. unkn.]

gauntlet[1] /ˈgɔːntlɪt/ *n.* **1** a stout glove with a long loose wrist. **2** *hist.* an armoured glove. **3** the part of a glove covering the wrist. **4** a challenge (esp. in **throw down the gauntlet**). [ME f. OF *gantelet* dimin. of *gant* glove f. Gmc]

gauntlet[2] /ˈgɔːntlɪt/ *n.* (US **gantlet** /ˈgænt-/) □ **run the gauntlet** **1** be subjected to harsh criticism. **2** pass between two rows of people and receive blows from them, as a punishment or ordeal. [earlier *gantlope* f. Sw. *gatlopp* f. *gata* lane, *lopp* course, assim. to GAUNTLET[1]]

gauntry var. of GANTRY 3.

gaur /ˈgaʊə(r)/ *n.* a wild species of Indian cattle, *Bos gaurus*. [Hind.]

Gauss /gaʊs/, Karl Friedrich (1777–1855), German mathematician, astronomer, and physicist. Regarded as the 'prince of mathematics', he laid the foundations of number theory, producing the first major book on this subject in 1801. In the same year he rediscovered the lost asteroid, Ceres, using computational techniques too advanced for most astronomers. He contributed to many areas of mathematics (his name is attached to a number of important results), and refused to distinguish between pure and applied mathematics, applying his rigorous mathematical analysis to such subjects as geometry, geodesy, electrostatics, and electromagnetism. He was involved in the first worldwide survey of the earth's magnetic field. Two of Gauss's most interesting discoveries, which he did not pursue, were non-Euclidean geometry and quaternions (a kind of complex number later developed by the mathematician W. R. Hamilton, 1805–65).

gauss /gaʊs/ *n.* (*pl.* same or **gausses**) a unit of magnetic induction, equal to one ten-thousandth of a tesla. ¶ Abbr.: **G**. [GAUSS]

Gaussian distribution /ˈgaʊsɪən/ *n. Statistics* = *normal distribution.* [as GAUSS]

Gautama /ˈgaʊtəmə/ the family name of the Buddha. [Skr.]

gauze /gɔːz/ *n.* **1** a thin transparent fabric of silk, cotton, etc. **2** a fine mesh of wire etc. **3** a slight haze. [F *gaze* f. *Gaza* in Palestine]

gauzy /ˈgɔːzɪ/ *adj.* (**gauzier, gauziest**) **1** like gauze; thin and translucent. **2** flimsy, delicate. □□ **gauzily** *adv.* **gauziness** *n.*

Gavaskar /gəˈvæskɑː(r)/, Sunil Manohar (1949–), Indian cricketer, who achieved several world batting records and became the most prolific scorer of runs in Indian test-match history.

gave past of GIVE.

gavel /ˈgæv(ə)l/ *n.* & *v.* —*n.* a small hammer used by an auctioneer, or for calling a meeting to order. —*v.* (**gavelled, gavelling**; US **gaveled, gaveling**) **1** *intr.* use a gavel. **2** *tr.* (often foll. by *down*) end (a meeting) or dismiss (a speaker) by use of a gavel. [19th c.: orig. unkn.]

gavial var. of GHARIAL.

gavotte /gəˈvɒt/ *n.* **1** an old French dance in common time beginning on the third beat of the bar. **2** the music for this, or a piece of music in the rhythm of this as a movement in a suite. [F f. Prov. *gavoto* f. *Gavot* native of a region in the Alps]

gawk /gɔːk/ *v.* & *n.* —*v.intr. colloq.* stare stupidly. —*n.* an awkward or bashful person. □□ **gawkish** *adj.* [rel. to obs. *gaw* gaze f. ON *gá* heed]

gawky /ˈgɔːkɪ/ *adj.* (**gawkier, gawkiest**) awkward or ungainly. □□ **gawkily** *adv.* **gawkiness** *n.*

gawp /gɔːp/ *v.intr. Brit. colloq.* stare stupidly or obtrusively. □□ **gawper** *n.* [earlier *gaup, galp* f. ME *galpen* yawn, rel. to YELP]

Gay /geɪ/, John (1685–1732), English poet and dramatist, who achieved success with his *Fables* (1727) but is now best known for *The Beggar's Opera* (1728), a ballad opera dealing with life in low society, adapted by Brecht in *The Threepenny Opera* (1928). This with its sequel *Polly* (1729) contained some of his best-known ballads. In 'Mr Pope's Welcome from Greece' (1776) he vividly portrays members of the Scriblerus Club, including Pope and Arbuthnot with whom he collaborated in *Three Hours after Marriage* (1717).

gay /geɪ/ *adj.* & *n.* —*adj.* **1** light-hearted and carefree; mirthful. **2** characterized by cheerfulness or pleasure (*a gay life*). **3** brightly coloured; showy, brilliant (*a gay scarf*). **4** *colloq.* **a** homosexual. **b** intended for or used by homosexuals (*a gay bar*). ¶ Generally informal in use, but favoured by homosexuals with ref. to themselves. **5** *colloq.* dissolute, immoral. —*n. colloq.* a homosexual, esp. male. □ **Gay Liberation** the advocacy of homosexuals' freedom from social discrimination. □□ **gayness** *n.* [ME f. OF *gai*, of unkn. orig.]

gayal /gəˈjæl/ *n.* a wild species of Indian cattle, *Bos fontalis.* [Hindi]

gayety US var. of GAIETY.

Gay-Lussac /geɪˈluːsæk/, Joseph Louis (1778–1850), French chemist and physicist, best known for his careful work on gases. In 1802 he re-established a law of gas expansion suggested c.1787 by Jacques Charles (1746–1823): at constant pressure the volume of a gas is proportional to the temperature. Six years later he formulated the law usually known by his name, that gases which combine chemically do so in volumes which are in a simple ratio to each other. His discovery was an important step towards an understanding of the nature of molecules. He developed techniques of quantitative chemical analysis, notably that of titration, identified iodine as an element and the gas, cyanogen, improved the process for manufacturing sulphuric acid, prepared with the chemist Louis-Jacques Thenard (1777–1857) potassium and boron, and made two balloon ascents in 1804 to study the composition of air, atmospheric electricity, and terrestrial magnetism at high altitudes.

gazania /gəˈzeɪnɪə/ *n.* any herbaceous plant of the genus *Gazania*, with showy yellow or orange daisy-shaped flowers. [18th c.: f. Theodore of *Gaza*, Greek scholar d. 1478]

Gazankulu /ˌgæzənˈkuːluː/ a tribal homeland (a self-governing State) of the Tsonga people, in the province of Transvaal; pop. (1985) 495,000.

Gaza Strip /ˈgɑːzə/ a strip of coastal territory in the SE

Mediterranean, including the town of Gaza; pop. (est. 1988) 564,000. Administered by Egypt from 1949, it was occupied by Israel in 1967.

gaze /geɪz/ v. & n. —v.intr. (foll. by at, into, on, upon, etc.) look fixedly. —n. a fixed or intent look. □□ **gazer** n. [ME: orig. unkn.; cf. obs. gaw GAWK]

gazebo /gəˈziːbəʊ/ n. (pl. **-os** or **-oes**) a small building or structure such as a summer-house or turret, designed to give a wide view. [perh. joc. f. GAZE, in imitation of L futures in -ēbo: cf. LAVABO]

gazelle /gəˈzel/ n. any of various small graceful soft-eyed antelopes of Asia or Africa, esp. of the genus Gazella. [F prob. f. Sp. gacela f. Arab. ġazāl]

gazette /gəˈzet/ n. & v. —n. 1 a newspaper, esp. the official one of an organization or institution (University Gazette). 2 hist. a news-sheet; a periodical publication giving current events. 3 Brit. an official journal with a list of government appointments, bankruptcies, and other public notices (London Gazette). —v.tr. Brit. announce or publish in an official gazette. [F f. It. gazzetta f. gazeta, a Venetian small coin]

gazetteer /ˌgæzɪˈtɪə(r)/ n. a geographical index or dictionary. [earlier = journalist, for whom such an index was provided: f. F gazettier f. It. gazzettiere (as GAZETTE)]

gazpacho /gæˈspætʃəʊ/ n. (pl. **-os**) a Spanish soup made with oil, garlic, onions, etc., and served cold. [Sp.]

gazump /gəˈzʌmp/ v.tr. (also absol.) Brit. colloq. 1 (of a seller) raise the price of a property after having accepted an offer by (an intending buyer). 2 swindle. □□ **gazumper** n. [20th c.: orig. uncert.]

gazunder /gəˈzʌndə(r)/ v.tr. (also absol.) Brit. colloq. (of a buyer) lower the amount of an offer made to (the seller for a property), esp. just before exchange of contracts. [GAZUMP + UNDER]

GB abbr. Great Britain.

GBE abbr. (in the UK) Knight (or Dame) Grand Cross (of the Order) of the British Empire.

GBH abbr. grievous bodily harm.

GC abbr. (in the UK) George Cross.

GCB abbr. (in the UK) Knight (or Dame) Grand Cross (of the Order) of the Bath.

GCE abbr. (in the UK) General Certificate of Education.

GCHQ abbr. (in the UK) Government Communications Headquarters.

GCMG abbr. (in the UK) Knight (or Dame) Grand Cross (of the Order) of St Michael & St George.

GCSE abbr. (in the UK) General Certificate of Secondary Education.

GCVO abbr. (in the UK) Knight (or Dame) Grand Cross (of the Royal Victorian Order.

Gd symb. Chem. the element gadolinium.

Gdańsk /gdænsk/ (German **Danzig** /ˈdæntsɪg/) an industrial port and shipbuilding centre in northern Poland, on an inlet of the Baltic Sea; pop. (1985) 467,000. Poland's refusal to cede Gdańsk to Germany occasioned the German invasion of Poland in Sept. 1939, which precipitated the Second World War.

Gdn. abbr. Garden.

Gdns. abbr. Gardens.

GDP abbr. gross domestic product.

GDR abbr. hist. German Democratic Republic.

Ge[1] symb. Chem. the element germanium.

Ge[2] /geɪ/ Gk Mythol. = GAIA. [Gk, = earth]

gear /gɪə(r)/ n. & v. —n. 1 (often in pl.) **a** a set of toothed wheels that work together to transmit and control motion from an engine, esp. to the road wheels of a vehicle. **b** a mechanism for doing this. 2 a particular function or state of adjustment of engaged gears (low gear; second gear). 3 a mechanism of wheels, levers, etc., usu. for a special purpose (winding-gear). 4 a particular apparatus or mechanism, as specified (landing-gear). 5 equipment or tackle for a special purpose. 6 colloq. clothing, esp. when modern or fashionable. 7 goods; household utensils. 8 rigging. 9 a harness for a draught animal. —v. 1 tr. (foll. by to)

adjust or adapt to suit a special purpose or need. 2 tr. (often foll. by up) equip with gears. 3 tr. (foll. by up) make ready or prepared. 4 tr. put (machinery) in gear. 5 intr. **a** be in gear. **b** (foll. by with) work smoothly with. □ **be geared** (or **all geared**) **up** (often foll. by for, or to + infin.) colloq. be ready or enthusiastic. **first** (or **bottom**) **gear** the lowest gear in a series. **gear down** (or **up**) provide with a low (or high) gear. **gear lever** (or **shift**) a lever used to engage or change gear, esp. in a motor vehicle. **high** (or **low**) **gear** a gear such that the driven end of a transmission revolves faster (or slower) than the driving end. **in gear** with a gear engaged. **out of gear** 1 with no gear engaged. 2 out of order. **top gear** the highest gear in a series. [ME f. ON gervi f. Gmc]

gearbox /ˈgɪəbɒks/ n. 1 the casing that encloses a set of gears. 2 a set of gears with its casing, esp. in a motor vehicle.

gearing /ˈgɪərɪŋ/ n. 1 a set or arrangement of gears in a machine. 2 Brit. Commerce **a** the allocation of part of a dividend to preferred recipients. **b** the amount of this part.

gearwheel /ˈgɪəwiːl/ n. 1 a toothed wheel in a set of gears. 2 (in a bicycle) the cog-wheel driven directly by the chain.

gecko /ˈgekəʊ/ n. (pl. **-os** or **-oes**) any of various house lizards found in warm climates, with adhesive feet for climbing vertical surfaces. [Malay chichak etc., imit. of its cry]

gee[1] /dʒiː/ int. (also **gee whiz** /wɪz/) US colloq. a mild expression of surprise, discovery, etc. [perh. abbr. of JESUS]

gee[2] /dʒiː/ int. (often foll. by up) a command to a horse etc., esp. to go faster. [17th c.: orig. unkn.]

gee[3] /dʒiː/ n. US sl. (usu. in pl.) a thousand dollars. [the letter G, as initial of GRAND]

gee-gee /ˈdʒiːdʒiː/ n. Brit. colloq. a horse. [orig. a child's word, f. GEE[2]]

geek /giːk/ n. Austral. sl. a look. [E dial.]

Geelong /dʒiːˈlɒŋ/ a port and oil-refining centre on the south coast of Australia, in the State of Victoria; pop. (1986) 148,300.

geese pl. of GOOSE.

gee-string var. of G-STRING 2.

Ge'ez /ˈgiːez/ n. the classical literary language of Ethiopia, a Semitic language thought to have been introduced from Arabia in the 1st c. BC. It is the ancestor of all the modern Ethiopian languages such as Amharic, and survives in the liturgical language of the Coptic Church in Ethiopia. [Ethiopic]

geezer /ˈgiːzə(r)/ n. sl. a person, esp. an old man. [dial. pronunc. of guiser mummer]

Gehenna /gɪˈhenə/ n. 1 (in the New Testament) hell. 2 a place of burning, torment, or misery. [eccl.L f. Gk f. Heb. gē' hinnōm hell, orig. the name of the valley of Hinnom near Jerusalem, where children were burnt in ancient times in sacrifice to pagan gods]

Geiger /ˈgaɪgə(r)/, Hans (Johann) Wilhelm (1882–1945), German nuclear physicist who developed the first radiation counter. He worked with Rutherford at Manchester on radioactivity, and in 1908 developed his prototype counter for detecting alpha particles. In 1925 he was appointed professor of physics at Kiel, where he improved the sensitivity of his device with Walther Müller (hence, it is often referred to as the 'Geiger-Müller counter'), and it was used for measuring all kinds of radiation, including cosmic ray showers for the first time in 1928. □ **Geiger counter** a device for measuring radioactivity by detecting and counting ionizing particles.

geisha /ˈgeɪʃə/ n. (pl. same or **geishas**) 1 a Japanese hostess trained in entertaining men with dance and song. 2 a Japanese prostitute. [Jap.]

Geissler tube /ˈgaɪslə/ n. a sealed tube of glass or quartz with a central constriction, filled with vapour for the production of a luminous electrical discharge. [H. Geissler, Ger. mechanic d. 1879]

gel /dʒel/ n. & v. —n. a semi-solid colloidal suspension or jelly, of a solid dispersed in a liquid. (**gelled, gelling**) form a gel. □□ **gelation** /-ˈleɪʃ(ə)n/ n. [abbr. of GELATIN]

gelatin /ˈdʒelətɪn/ n. (also **gelatine** /-ˌtiːn/) a virtually colourless tasteless transparent water-soluble protein derived from collagen and used in food preparation, photography, etc. □ **gelatin paper** a paper coated with sensitized gelatin for photography. □□ **gelatinize** /dʒɪˈlætɪˌnaɪz/ v.tr. & intr. (also **-ise**). **gelatinization** /dʒɪˌlætɪnaɪˈzeɪʃ(ə)n/ n. [F *gélatine* f. It. *gelatina* f. *gelata* JELLY]

gelatinous /dʒɪˈlætɪnəs/ adj. **1** of or like gelatin. **2** of a jelly-like consistency. □□ **gelatinously** adv.

gelation /dʒɪˈleɪʃ(ə)n/ n. solidification by freezing. [L *gelatio* f. *gelare* freeze]

geld /geld/ v.tr. **1** deprive (usu. a male animal) of the ability to reproduce. **2** castrate or spay; excise the testicles or ovaries of. [ME f. ON *gelda* f. *geldr* barren f. Gmc]

gelding /ˈgeldɪŋ/ n. a gelded animal, esp. a male horse. [ME f. ON *geldingr*: see GELD]

Geldof /ˈgeldɒf/, Bob (1954–), Irish rock musician, who instigated charity events such as Band Aid and Live Aid (1984–6) which raised millions of pounds for the relief of famine, especially that in Ethiopia.

gelid /ˈdʒelɪd/ adj. **1** icy, ice-cold. **2** chilly, cool. [L *gelidus* f. *gelu* frost]

gelignite /ˈdʒelɪgˌnaɪt/ n. a plastic high explosive (also known as gelatine dynamite) consisting of nitroglycerine which is at least partially gelatinized by means of gun cotton. It is favoured for its good handling properties, water resistance, and low fume emission, and is a preferred explosive for rock-blasting under wet conditions. [GELATIN + L *ignis* fire + -ITE¹]

gelly /ˈdʒelɪ/ n. Brit. sl. gelignite. [abbr.]

gem /dʒem/ n. & v. —n. **1** a precious stone, esp. when cut and polished or engraved. **2** an object or person of great beauty or worth. —v.tr. (**gemmed**, **gemming**) adorn with or as with gems. □□ **gemlike** adj. **gemmy** adj. [ME f. OF *gemme* f. L *gemma* bud, jewel]

Gemara /gɪˈmɑːrə/ n. a rabbinical commentary on the Mishnah, written in Aramaic and forming the second part of the Talmud. [Aram. *gᵉmārâ* completion]

geminal /ˈdʒemɪn(ə)l/ adj. Chem. (of molecules) having two functional groups attached to the same atom. □□ **geminally** adv. [as GEMINATE + -AL]

geminate adj. & v. —adj. /ˈdʒemɪnət/ combined in pairs. —v.tr. /ˈdʒemɪˌneɪt/ **1** double, repeat. **2** arrange in pairs. □□ **gemination** /-ˈneɪʃ(ə)n/ n. [L *geminatus* past part. of *geminare* f. *geminus* twin]

Gemini /ˈdʒemɪˌnaɪ, -ˌniː/ **1** a constellation, traditionally regarded as contained in the figures of twins. **2** the third sign of the zodiac (the Twins; see DIOSCURI), which the sun enters about 21 May. —n. a person born when the sun is in this sign. □□ **Geminean** /ˌdʒemɪˈniːən/ n. & adj. [ME f. L, = twins]

gemma /ˈdʒemə/ n. (pl. **gemmae** /-miː/) a small cellular body in cryptogams that separates from the mother-plant and starts a new one; an asexual spore. [L: see GEM]

gemmation /dʒeˈmeɪʃ(ə)n/ n. reproduction by gemmae. [F f. *gemmer* to bud, *gemme* bud]

gemmiferous /dʒeˈmɪfərəs/ adj. **1** producing precious stones. **2** bearing buds. [L *gemmifer* (as GEMMA, -FEROUS)]

gemmiparous /dʒeˈmɪpərəs/ adj. of or propagating by gemmation. [mod.L *gemmiparus* f. L *gemma* bud + *parere* bring forth]

gemmology /dʒeˈmɒlədʒɪ/ n. the study of gems. □□ **gemmologist** n. [L *gemma* gem + -LOGY]

gemmule /ˈdʒemjuːl/ n. an encysted embryonic cell-cluster in sponges. [F *gemmule* or L *gemmula* little bud (as GEM)]

gemstone /ˈdʒemstəʊn/ n. a precious stone used as a gem.

gemütlich /gəˈmuːtlɪx/ adj. **1** pleasant and comfortable. **2** genial, agreeable. [G]

Gen. abbr. **1** General. **2** Genesis (Old Testament).

gen /dʒen/ n. & v. Brit. sl. —n. information. —v.tr. & intr. (**genned**, **genning**) (foll. by *up*) provide with or obtain information. [perh. f. first syll. of *general information*]

-gen /dʒ(ə)n/ comb. form **1** Chem. that which produces (*hydrogen*; *antigen*). **2** Bot. growth (*endogen*; *exogen*; *acrogen*). [F *-gène* f. Gk

-genēs -born, of a specified kind f. *gen-* root of *gignomai* be born, become]

gendarme /ˈʒɒndɑːm/ n. **1** a soldier, mounted or on foot, employed in police duties esp. in France. **2** a rock-tower on a mountain, occupying and blocking an arête. [F f. *gens d'armes* men of arms]

gendarmerie /ʒɒnˈdɑːmərɪ/ n. **1** a force of gendarmes. **2** the headquarters of such a force.

gender /ˈdʒendə(r)/ n. **1 a** the grammatical classification of nouns and related words, found mainly in Indo-European and Semitic languages roughly corresponding to the two sexes and sexlessness. **b** each of the classes of nouns (see MASCULINE, FEMININE, NEUTER, COMMON adj. 6). **2** (of nouns and related words) the property of belonging to such a class. **3** colloq. a person's sex. [ME f. OF *gendre* ult. f. L GENUS]

gene /dʒiːn/ n. a unit of heredity composed of DNA or RNA and forming part of a chromosome etc., that determines a particular characteristic of an individual. The word has been defined in a number of ways since its coinage (in German) in 1909; genes were originally regarded as inherited factors each controlling one feature (e.g. eye colour) of an organism, but are now usually regarded as lengths of DNA (or in certain viruses RNA) which determine the synthesis of protein molecules needed by living cells (see DNA). [G *Gen*: see -GEN]

genealogical /ˌdʒiːnɪəˈlɒdʒɪk(ə)l/ adj. **1** of or concerning genealogy. **2** tracing family descent. □ **genealogical tree** a chart like an inverted branching tree showing the descent of a family or of an animal species. □□ **genealogically** adv. [F *généalogique* f. Gk *genealogikos* (as GENEALOGY)]

genealogy /ˌdʒiːnɪˈælədʒɪ/ n. (pl. **-ies**) **1 a** a line of descent traced continuously from an ancestor. **b** an account or exposition of this. **2** the study and investigation of lines of descent. **3** a plant's or animal's line of development from earlier forms. □□ **genealogist** n. **genealogize** v.tr. & intr. (also **-ise**). [ME f. OF *genealogie* f. LL *genealogia* f. Gk *genealogia* f. *genea* race]

genera pl. of GENUS.

general /ˈdʒenər(ə)l/ adj. & n. —adj. **1 a** completely or almost universal. **b** including or affecting all or nearly all parts or cases of things. **2** prevalent, widespread, usual. **3** not partial, particular, local, or sectional. **4** not limited in application; relating to whole classes or all cases. **5** including points common to the individuals of a class and neglecting the differences (*a general term*). **6** not restricted or specialized (*general knowledge*). **7 a** roughly corresponding or adequate. **b** sufficient for practical purposes. **8** not detailed (*a general resemblance; a general idea*). **9** vague, indefinite (*spoke only in general terms*). **10** chief or principal; having overall authority (*general manager*; *Secretary-General*). —n. **1 a** an army officer ranking next below Field Marshal or above lieutenant-general. **b** US = lieutenant-general, major-general. **2** a commander of an army. **3** a tactician or strategist of specified merit (*a great general*). **4** the head of a religious order, e.g. of the Jesuits or Dominicans or the Salvation Army. **5** (prec. by *the*) archaic the public. □ **as a general rule** in most cases. **General American** a form of US speech not markedly dialectal or regional. **General Certificate of Education 1** an examination set esp. for secondary-school pupils at advanced level in England and Wales. **2** the certificate gained by passing it. **General Certificate of Secondary Education** an examination replacing and combining the GCE ordinary level and CSE examinations. **general delivery** US the delivery of letters to callers at a post office. **general election** the election of representatives to a legislature (esp. in the UK to the House of Commons) from constituencies throughout the country. **general headquarters** the headquarters of a military commander. **general meeting** a meeting open to all the members of a society etc. **general of the army** (or **air force**) US the officer of the highest rank in the army or air force. **general practice** the work of a general practitioner. **general practitioner** a doctor working in the community and treating cases of all kinds in the first instance, as distinct from a consultant or specialist. **general staff** the staff assisting a military commander in planning and administration. **general strike** a strike of workers in all or most trades. **General Synod** the highest governing body in the Church of England. **in general 1** as a normal rule; usually. **2** for the most part. □□ **generalness** n. [ME f. OF f. L *generalis* (as GENUS)]

generalissimo /ˌdʒenərəˈlɪsɪˌməʊ/ n. (pl. **-os**) the commander of a combined military force consisting of army, navy, and air-force units. [It., superl. of *generale* GENERAL]

generalist /ˈdʒenərəlɪst/ n. a person competent in several different fields or activities (opp. SPECIALIST).

generality /ˌdʒenəˈrælɪtɪ/ n. (pl. **-ies**) **1** a statement or principle etc. having general validity or force. **2** applicability to a whole class of instances. **3** vagueness; lack of detail. **4** the state of being general. **5** (foll. by *of*) the main body or majority. [F *généralité* f. LL *generalitas -tatis* (as GENERAL)]

generalization /ˌdʒenərəlaɪˈzeɪʃ(ə)n/ n. (also **-isation**) **1** a general notion or proposition obtained by inference from (esp. limited or inadequate) particular cases. **2** the act or an instance of generalizing. [F *généralisation* (as GENERALIZE)]

generalize /ˈdʒenərəˌlaɪz/ v. (also **-ise**) **1** intr. **a** speak in general or indefinite terms. **b** form general principles or notions. **2** tr. reduce to a general statement, principle, or notion. **3** tr. **a** give a general character to. **b** call by a general name. **4** tr. infer (a law or conclusion) by induction. **5** tr. Math. & Philos. express in a general form; extend the application of. **6** tr. (in painting) render only the typical characteristics of. **7** tr. bring into general use. □□ **generalizable** adj. **generalizability** /-zəˈbɪlɪtɪ/ n. **generalizer** n. [F *généraliser* (as GENERAL)]

generally /ˈdʒenərəlɪ/ adv. **1** usually; in most cases. **2** in a general sense; without regard to particulars or exceptions (*generally speaking*). **3** for the most part; extensively (*not generally known*). **4** in most respects (*they were generally well-behaved*).

generalship /ˈdʒenər(ə)lʃɪp/ n. **1** the art or practice of exercising military command. **2** military skill; strategy. **3** skilful management; tact, diplomacy.

generate /ˈdʒenəˌreɪt/ v.tr. **1** bring into existence; produce, evolve. **2** produce (electricity). **3** Math. (of a point or line or surface conceived as moving) make (a line or surface or solid). **4** Math. & Linguistics produce (a set or sequence of items) by the formulation and application of precise criteria. □□ **generable** /-rəb(ə)l/ adj. [L *generare* beget (as GENUS)]

generation /ˌdʒenəˈreɪʃ(ə)n/ n. **1** all the people born at a particular time, regarded collectively (*my generation; the rising generation*). **2** a single step in descent or pedigree (*have known them for three generations*). **3** a stage in (esp. technological) development (*fourth-generation computers*). **4** the average time in which children are ready to take the place of their parents (usu. reckoned at about 30 years). **5** production by natural or artificial process, esp. the production of electricity or heat. **6 a** procreation; the propagation of species. **b** the act of begetting or being begotten. □ **generation gap** differences of outlook or opinion between those of different generations. □□ **generational** adj. [ME f. OF f. L *generatio -onis* (as GENERATE)]

generative /ˈdʒenərətɪv/ adj. **1** of or concerning procreation. **2** able to produce, productive. □ **generative grammar** see GRAMMAR. [ME f. OF *generatif* or LL *generativus* (as GENERATE)]

generator /ˈdʒenəˌreɪtə(r)/ n. **1** a machine for converting mechanical into electrical energy; a dynamo. **2** an apparatus for producing gas, steam, etc. **3** a person who generates an idea etc.; an originator.

generic /dʒɪˈnerɪk/ adj. **1** characteristic of or relating to a class; general, not specific or special. **2** Biol. characteristic of or belonging to a genus. **3** (of goods, esp. a drug) having no brand name; not protected by a registered trade mark. □□ **generically** adv. [F *générique* f. L GENUS]

generous /ˈdʒenərəs/ adj. **1** giving or given freely. **2** magnanimous, noble-minded, unprejudiced. **3 a** ample, abundant, copious (*a generous portion*). **b** (of wine) rich and full. □□ **generosity** /-ˈrɒsɪtɪ/ n. **generously** adv. **generousness** n. [OF *genereus* f. L *generosus* noble, magnanimous (as GENUS)]

genesis /ˈdʒenɪsɪs/ n. **1** the origin, or mode of formation or generation, of a thing. **2** (**Genesis**) the first book of the Old Testament, containing an account of the creation of the universe and of the early history of mankind. (See PENTATEUCH.) [L f. Gk f. *gen-* be produced, root of *gignomai* become]

Genet /ʒəˈneɪ/, Jean (1910–86), French novelist and dramatist. Much of the earlier part of his life was spent in reformatories or in prison, and his literary work is marked by those experiences. His novels include *Notre-Dame des Fleurs* (1944, written while in prison); his plays include *Le Balcon* (1956) and *Les Nègres* (1958).

genet /ˈdʒenɪt/ n. (also **genette** /dʒɪˈnet/) **1** any catlike mammal of the genus *Genetta*, native to Africa and S. Europe, with spotted fur and a long ringed bushy tail. **2** the fur of the genet. [ME f. OF *genete* f. Arab. *ǰarnait*]

genetic /dʒɪˈnetɪk/ adj. **1** of genetics or genes; inherited. **2** of, in, or concerning origin; causal. □ **genetic code** Biochem. the system by which DNA and RNA molecules carry genetic information. Particular sequences of bases in these molecules represent particular sequences of amino acids (the building blocks of proteins) and thereby embody 'instructions' for the making of individual types of proteins (see DNA). **genetic engineering** the deliberate modification of the characters of an organism by the manipulation of DNA and the transformation of certain genes. □□ **genetically** adv. [GENESIS after *antithetic*]

genetic fingerprinting n. (also **genetic profiling**) the analysis of characteristic patterns in DNA. Genetic material (DNA) varies enormously from one individual to another. This material can be analysed to produce patterns on an X-ray which somewhat resemble supermarket bar-codes and which (except for those of identical twins) are completely specific to an individual; such patterns are called a 'DNA fingerprint'. They have uses in forensic analysis (e.g. to establish possible links—or exclusions—between a forensic sample and a suspected person), in the determination of parentage, and to establish whether twins are identical or not.

genetics /dʒɪˈnetɪks/ n.pl. (treated as *sing.*) the study of heredity and the variation of inherited characteristics. □□ **geneticist** /-tɪsɪst/ n.

genette var. of GENET.

Geneva /dʒɪˈniːvə/ a city of SW Switzerland, on the Lake of Geneva; pop. (1987) 160,900. In the 16th c. it was a stronghold of John Calvin, who rewrote its laws and constitution. More recently it has become the headquarters of international bodies such as the Red Cross, the League of Nations (1920–46), and the World Health Organization. □ **Geneva Bible** an English translation of the Bible prepared by Protestant exiles at Geneva and printed there in 1560, the 'Breeches Bible'. **Geneva bands** two white cloth strips attached to the collar of some Protestants' clerical dress (orig. worn by Calvinists in Geneva). **Geneva Conventions** a series of international agreements concluded at Geneva between 1846 and 1949 with the object of mitigating the harm done by war to both service personnel and civilians. They govern the status of hospitals, ambulances, the wounded, etc.

geneva /dʒɪˈniːvə/ n. Hollands gin. [Du. *genever* f. OF *genevre* f. L *juniperus*, with assim. GENEVA]

Genghis Khan /ˌɡeŋɡɪs ˈkɑːn, ˌdʒe-/ (1162–1227), the founder of the Mongol empire, one of the greatest conquerors in history. Originally named Temujin, he took the name Genghis Khan (= ruler of all) in 1206 after uniting the nomadic Mongol tribes under his command and becoming master of both eastern and western Mongolia. He then attacked China, and captured Peking in 1215. By the time of his death his empire extended from the shores of the Pacific to the northern shores of the Black Sea, won through brilliant generalship, iron discipline, and unimaginable cruelty particularly towards conquered peoples. A good administrator, he organized his empire into States. His grandson Kublai Khan carried on his empire and completed the conquest of China.

genial[1] /ˈdʒiːnɪəl/ adj. **1** jovial, sociable, kindly, cheerful. **2** (of the climate) mild and warm; conducive to growth. **3** cheering, enlivening. □□ **geniality** /-ˈælɪtɪ/ n. **genially** adv. [L *genialis* (as GENIUS)]

genial[2] /dʒɪˈniːəl/ adj. Anat. of or relating to the chin. [Gk geneion chin f. genus jaw]

genic /ˈdʒiːnɪk/ adj. of or relating to genes.

-genic /ˈdʒɛnɪk/ comb. form forming adjectives meaning: **1** producing (carcinogenic; pathogenic). **2** well suited to (photogenic; radiogenic). **3** produced by (iatrogenic). □□ **-genically** suffix forming adverbs. [-GEN + -IC]

genie /ˈdʒiːnɪ/ n. (pl. usu. **genii** /ˈdʒiːnɪˌaɪ/) a jinnee, goblin, or familiar spirit of Arabian folklore. [F génie f. L GENIUS: cf. JINNEE]

genii pl. of GENIE, GENIUS.

genista /dʒɪˈnɪstə/ n. any almost leafless shrub of the genus Genista, with a profusion of flowers shaped like those of the pea plant, e.g. dyer's broom. [L]

genital /ˈdʒɛnɪt(ə)l/ adj. & n. —adj. of or relating to animal reproduction. —n. (in pl.) the external reproductive organs. [OF génital or L genitalis f. gignere genit- beget]

genitalia /ˌdʒɛnɪˈteɪlɪə/ n.pl. the genitals. [L, neut. pl. of genitalis: see GENITAL]

genitive /ˈdʒɛnɪtɪv/ n. & adj. Gram. —n. the case of nouns and pronouns (and words in grammatical agreement with them) corresponding to of, from, and other prepositions and indicating possession or close association. —adj. of or in the genitive. □□ **genitival** /-ˈtaɪv(ə)l/ adj. **genitivally** /-ˈtaɪvəlɪ/ adv. [ME f. OF genetif, -ive or L genitivus f. gignere genit- beget]

genito- /ˈdʒɛnɪtəʊ/ comb. form genital.

genito-urinary /ˌdʒɛnɪtəʊˈjʊərɪnərɪ/ adj. of the genital and urinary organs.

genius /ˈdʒiːnɪəs/ n. (pl. **geniuses** or **genii** /-nɪˌaɪ/) **1** (pl. **geniuses**) **a** an exceptional intellectual or creative power or other natural ability or tendency. **b** a person having this. **2** the tutelary spirit of a person, place, institution, etc. **3** a person or spirit regarded as powerfully influencing a person for good or evil. **4** the prevalent feeling or associations etc. of a nation, age, etc. [L (in sense 2) f. the root of gignere beget]

genizah /dʒeˈniːzə/ n. a room attached to a synagogue and housing damaged, discarded, or heretical books etc., and sacred relics. The term is used with specific reference of the genizah of an ancient synagogue in Cairo, dating from AD 882, where vast quantities of fragments of biblical and other Jewish MSS (liturgical, legal, commercial, and literary documents) were discovered in 1896–8. [Heb. gĕnīzāh, lit. hiding-place f. gānaz hide, set aside]

Genoa /ˈdʒɛnəʊə/ (Italian **Genova** /ˈdʒɛnəvə/) a city and seaport of NW Italy, on the Ligurian coast; pop. (1983) 188,000. □ **Genoa cake** a rich fruit cake with almonds on top. **Genoa jib** a large jib or foresail used esp. on yachts.

genocide /ˈdʒɛnəˌsaɪd/ n. the deliberate extermination of a people or nation. □□ **genocidal** /-ˈsaɪd(ə)l/ adj. [Gk genos race + -CIDE]

genome /ˈdʒiːnəʊm/ n. **1** the haploid set of chromosomes of an organism. **2** the genetic material of an organism. [GENE + CHROMOSOME]

genotype /ˈdʒiːnəˌtaɪp/ n. Biol. the genetic constitution of an individual. □□ **genotypic** /-ˈtɪpɪk/ adj. [G Genotypus (as GENE, TYPE)]

-genous /ˈdʒɛnəs/ comb. form forming adjectives meaning 'produced' (endogenous).

genre /ˈʒɑ̃rə/ n. **1** a kind or style, esp. of art or literature (e.g. novel, drama, satire). **2** (in full **genre painting**) the painting of scenes from ordinary life,. especially the type of subject-matter favoured by Dutch artists of the 17th c. (e.g. Pieter Bruegel the Elder and Vermeer). [F, = a kind (as GENDER)]

gens /dʒɛnz/ n. (pl. **gentes** /-tiːz/) **1** Rom.Hist. a group of families sharing a name and claiming a common origin. **2** Anthropol. a number of people sharing descent through the male line. [L, f. the root of gignere beget]

Gent see GHENT.

gent /dʒɛnt/ n. colloq. (often joc.) **1** a gentleman. **2** (in pl.) (in shop titles) men (gents' outfitters). **3** (**the Gents**) Brit. colloq. a men's public lavatory. [abbr. of GENTLEMAN]

genteel /dʒɛnˈtiːl/ adj. **1** affectedly or ostentatiously refined or stylish. **2** often iron. of or appropriate to the upper classes. □□ **genteelly** adv. **genteelness** n. [earlier gentile, readoption of F gentil GENTLE]

genteelism /dʒɛnˈtiːlɪz(ə)m/ n. a word used because it is thought to be less vulgar than the commoner word (e.g. perspire for sweat).

gentes pl. of GENS.

gentian /ˈdʒɛnʃ(ə)n, -ʃɪən/ n. **1** any plant of the genus Gentiana or Gentianella, found esp. in mountainous regions, and having usu. vivid blue flowers. **2** (in full **gentian bitter**) a liquor extracted from the root of the gentian. □ **gentian violet** a violet dye used as an antiseptic, esp. in the treatment of burns. [OE f. L gentiana f. Gentius king of Illyria]

gentile /ˈdʒɛntaɪl/ adj. & n. —adj. **1** (**Gentile**) not Jewish; heathen. **2** of or relating to a nation or tribe. **3** Gram. (of a word) indicating nationality. —n. **1** (**Gentile**) a person who is not Jewish. **2** Gram. a word indicating nationality. [ME f. L gentilis f. gens gentis family: see GENS]

Gentile da Fabriano /dʒɛnˈtiːleɪ dɑː ˌfæbrɪˈɑːnəʊ/ (c.1370–1427), Florentine painter, named after his birthplace (Fabriano). Most of the work on which his great contemporary reputation was based has been destroyed. His major surviving work, the altarpiece Adoration of the Magi (1423), is remarkable for its decorative beauty and for the naturalistic treatment of light.

gentility /dʒɛnˈtɪlɪtɪ/ n. **1** social superiority. **2** good manners; habits associated with the nobility. **3** people of noble birth. [ME f. OF gentilité (as GENTLE)]

Genting Highlands /ˈdʒɛntɪŋ/ a recreational hill resort in Malaysia, on the border between the States of Pahang and Selangor, built at an altitude of 1,700 m (5,520 ft.) in 1971.

gentle /ˈdʒɛnt(ə)l/ adj., v., & n. —adj. (**gentler**, **gentlest**) **1** not rough; mild or kind, esp. in temperament. **2** moderate; not severe or drastic (a gentle rebuke; a gentle breeze). **3** (of birth, pursuits, etc.) honourable, of or fit for people of good social position. **4** quiet; requiring patience (gentle art). **5** archaic generous, courteous. —v.tr. **1** make gentle or docile. **2** handle (a horse etc.) firmly but gently. —n. a maggot, the larva of the meat-fly or bluebottle used as fishing-bait. □□ **gentleness** n. **gently** adv. [ME f. OF gentil f. L gentilis: see GENTILE]

gentlefolk /ˈdʒɛnt(ə)lˌfəʊk/ n.pl. literary people of good family.

gentleman /ˈdʒɛnt(ə)lmən/ n. (pl. **-men**) **1** a man (in polite or formal use). **2** a chivalrous or well-bred man. **3** a man of good social position or of wealth and leisure (country gentleman). **4** a man of gentle birth attached to a royal household (gentleman in waiting). **5** (in pl. as a form of address) a male audience or the male part of an audience. □ **gentleman-at-arms** one of a sovereign's bodyguard. **gentleman farmer** a country gentleman who farms. **gentleman's** (or **-men's**) **agreement** one which is binding in honour but not legally enforceable. [GENTLE + MAN after OF gentilz hom]

gentlemanly /ˈdʒɛnt(ə)lmənlɪ/ adj. like a gentleman in looks or behaviour; befitting a gentleman. □□ **gentlemanliness** n.

gentlewoman /ˈdʒɛnt(ə)lˌwʊmən/ n. (pl. **-women**) archaic a woman of good birth or breeding.

gentoo /ˈdʒɛntuː/ n. a penguin, Pygoscelis papua, esp. abundant in the Falkland Islands. [perh. f. Anglo-Ind. Gentoo = Hindu, f. Port. gentio GENTILE]

gentrification /ˌdʒɛntrɪfɪˈkeɪʃ(ə)n/ n. the social advancement of an inner urban area by the arrival of affluent middle-class residents. □□ **gentrify** /-ˌfaɪ/ v.tr. (**-ies**, **-ied**)

gentry /ˈdʒɛntrɪ/ n.pl. **1** the people next below the nobility in position and birth. **2** derog. people (these gentry). [prob. f. obs. gentrice f. OF genterise var. of gentelise nobility f. gentil GENTLE]

genuflect /ˈdʒɛnjʊˌflɛkt/ v.intr. bend the knee, esp. in worship or as a sign of respect. □□ **genuflection** /-ˈflɛkʃ(ə)n/ n. (also **genuflexion**). **genuflector** n. [eccl.L genuflectere genuflex- f. L genu the knee + flectere bend]

genuine /ˈdʒɛnjʊɪn/ adj. **1** really coming from its stated, advertised, or reputed source. **2** properly so called; not sham. **3** pure-bred. □□ **genuinely** adv. **genuineness** n. [L genuinus f. genu knee, with ref. to a father's acknowledging a new-born child by placing it on his knee: later associated with GENUS]

genus /ˈdʒiːnəs, ˈdʒenəs/ n. (pl. **genera** /ˈdʒenərə/) **1** Biol. a taxonomic grouping of organisms having common characteristics distinct from those of other genera, usu. containing several or many species and being one of a series constituting a taxonomic family. **2** a kind or class having common characteristics. **3** Logic kinds of things including subordinate kinds or species. [L genus -eris birth, race, stock]

-geny /dʒənɪ/ comb. form forming nouns meaning 'mode of production or development of' (anthropogeny; ontogeny; pathogeny). [F -génie (as -GEN, -Y³)]

Geo. abbr. George.

geo- /ˈdʒiːəʊ/ comb. form earth. [Gk geō- f. gē earth]

geobotany /ˌdʒiːəʊˈbɒtənɪ/ n. the study of the geographical distribution of plants. □□ **geobotanist** n.

geocentric /ˌdʒiːəʊˈsentrɪk/ adj. **1** considered as viewed from the centre of the earth. **2** having or representing the earth as the centre; not heliocentric. □ **geocentric latitude** the latitude at which a planet would appear if viewed from the centre of the earth. □□ **geocentrically** adv.

geochemistry /ˌdʒiːəʊˈkemɪstrɪ/ n. the chemistry of the earth and its rocks, minerals, etc. □□ **geochemical** adj. **geochemist** n.

geochronology /ˌdʒiːəʊkrəˈnɒlədʒɪ/ n. **1** the study and measurement of geological time by means of geological events. **2** the ordering of geological events. □□ **geochronological** /-ˌkrɒnəˈlɒdʒɪk(ə)l/ adj. **geochronologist** n.

geode /ˈdʒiːəʊd/ n. **1** a small cavity lined with crystals or other mineral matter. **2** a rock containing such a cavity. □□ **geodic** /dʒiːˈɒdɪk/ adj. [L geodes f. Gk geōdēs earthy f. gē earth]

geodesic /ˌdʒiːəʊˈdiːzɪk/ adj. (also **geodetic** /-ˈdetɪk/) **1** of or relating to geodesy. **2** of, involving, or consisting of a geodesic line. □ **geodesic dome** a dome constructed of short struts along geodesic lines. The principles of its construction were declared by the American designer and architect R. Buckminster Fuller (1895–1983). It combines the structural advantages of the sphere and the tetrahedron; the sphere encloses the most space within the least surface and is strongest against internal pressure; the tetrahedron encloses the least space with the most surface and has the greatest stiffness against external pressure. **geodesic line** the shortest possible line between two points on a curved surface.

geodesy /dʒiːˈɒdɪsɪ/ n. the branch of mathematics dealing with the figures and areas of the earth or large portions of it. □□ **geodesist** n. [mod.L f. Gk geōdaisia (as GEO-, daiō divide)]

geodetic var. of GEODESIC.

Geoffrey of Monmouth /ˌdʒefrɪ, ˈmɒnməθ/ (1100?–1155), British chronicler. His Historia Regum Britanniae (first printed in 1508), a purported account, in Latin, of the kings of Britain, is highly suspect as history but was a major source of Arthurian legend.

geographic var. of GEOGRAPHICAL.

geographical /ˌdʒiːəˈgræfɪk(ə)l/ adj. (also **geographic** /-ˈgræfɪk/) of or relating to geography. □ **geographical latitude** the angle made with the plane of the equator by a perpendicular to the earth's surface at any point. **geographical mile** a distance equal to one minute of longitude or latitude at the equator (about 1850 metres). □□ **geographically** adv. [geographic f. F géographique or LL geographicus f. Gk geōgraphikos (as GEO-, -GRAPHIC)]

geography /dʒɪˈɒgrəfɪ/ n. **1** the study of the earth's physical features, resources, and climate, and the physical aspects of its population. **2** the main physical features of an area. **3** the layout or arrangement of rooms in a building. □□ **geographer** n. [F géographie or L geographia f. Gk geōgraphia (as GEO-, -GRAPHY)]

geoid /ˈdʒiːɔɪd/ n. **1** the shape of the earth. **2** a shape formed by the mean sea level and its imagined extension under land areas. **3** an oblate spheroid. [Gk geōeidēs (as GEO-, -OID)]

geology /dʒɪˈɒlədʒɪ/ n. **1** the science of the earth, including the composition, structure, and origin of its rocks. (See below.) **2** this science applied to any other planet or celestial body. **3** the geological features of a district. □□ **geologic** /ˌdʒiːəˈlɒdʒɪk/ adj.

geological /ˌdʒiːəˈlɒdʒɪk(ə)l/ adj. **geologically** /ˌdʒiːəˈlɒdʒɪkəlɪ/ adv. **geologist** n. **geologize** v.tr. & intr. (also **-ise**). [med.L geologia (as GEO-, -LOGY)]

The medieval Latin word geologia was used by Bishop Richard de Bury (14th c.) in the sense of 'science of earthly things', applied to the study of law as distinguished from the arts and sciences which are concerned with the works of God. In 1687 Geologia appears as the title of an Italian work intended to prove that the 'influence' ascribed by astrologers to the stars really proceeded from the earth itself. Use of the term geology to mean study of the earth, and specifically of its crust, dates from the 18th c. in English.

geomagnetism /ˌdʒiːəʊˈmægnɪˌtɪz(ə)m/ n. the study of the magnetic properties of the earth. □□ **geomagnetic** /-mægˈnetɪk/ adj. **geomagnetically** /-mægˈnetɪkəlɪ/ adv.

geomancy /ˈdʒiːəʊˌmænsɪ/ n. divination from the configuration of a handful of earth or random dots. □□ **geomantic** /-ˈmæntɪk/ adj.

geometer /dʒɪˈɒmɪtə(r)/ n. **1** a person skilled in geometry. **2** any moth, esp. of the family Geometridae, having twiglike larvae which move in a looping fashion, seeming to measure the ground. [ME f. LL geometra f. L geometres f. Gk geōmetrēs (as GEO-, metrēs measurer)]

geometric /ˌdʒiːəˈmetrɪk/ adj. (also **geometrical**) **1** of, according to, or like geometry. **2** (of a design, architectural feature, etc.) characterized by or decorated with regular lines and shapes. □ **geometric mean** the central number in a geometric progression, also calculable as the nth root of a product of n numbers (as 9 from 3 and 27). **geometric progression** a progression of numbers with a constant ratio between each number and the one before (as 1, 3, 9, 27, 81). **geometric tracery** tracery with openings of geometric form. □□ **geometrically** adv. [F géométrique f. L geometricus f. Gk geōmetrikos (as GEOMETER)]

geometry /dʒɪˈɒmɪtrɪ/ n. **1** the branch of mathematics concerned with the properties and relations of points, lines, surfaces, and solids. For 2,000 years geometry was based on the teachings of the thirteen books of Euclid but since the early 19th c. mathematics has embraced successful theories describing non-Euclidean geometry, higher dimensional geometry, and many other related topics. **2** the relative arrangement of objects or parts. □□ **geometrician** /ˌdʒiːəmɪˈtrɪʃ(ə)n/ n. [ME f. OF geometrie f. L geometria f. Gk (as GEO-, -METRY)]

geomorphology /ˌdʒiːəʊmɔːˈfɒlədʒɪ/ n. the study of the physical features of the surface of the earth and their relation to its geological structures. □□ **geomorphological** /-fəˈlɒdʒɪk(ə)l/ adj. **geomorphologist** n.

geophagy /dʒɪˈɒfədʒɪ/ n. the practice of eating earth. [GEO- + Gk phagō eat]

geophysics /ˌdʒiːəʊˈfɪzɪks/ n. the physics of the earth. □□ **geophysical** adj. **geophysicist** /-sɪst/ n.

geopolitics /ˌdʒiːəʊˈpɒlɪtɪks/ n. **1** the politics of a country as determined by its geographical features. **2** the study of this. □□ **geopolitical** /-pəˈlɪtɪk(ə)l/ adj. **geopolitically** /-pəˈlɪtɪkəlɪ/ adv. **geopolitician** /-ˈtɪʃ(ə)n/ n.

Geordie /ˈdʒɔːdɪ/ n. Brit. colloq. a native of Tyneside. [the name George + -IE]

George¹ /dʒɔːdʒ/ the name of six kings of Great Britain and Ireland:

George I (1660–1727), great-grandson of James I, reigned 1714–27. Elector of Hanover from 1698, George succeeded to the British throne on the death of Anne, as a result of the Act of Settlement. Unpopular in England, the language of which he never learnt, he left the administration of his new kingdom to his ministers and devoted himself to diplomacy and the interests of Hanover, but despite all this the relatively easy suppression of the Jacobite uprisings of 1715 and 1719 demonstrated that he was generally preferred to the Catholic Old Pretender.

George II (1683–1760), son of George I, reigned 1727–60. While Prince of Wales, George quarrelled openly with his father and became the centre of opposition to the administration. Like George I, he depended heavily on his ministers, but took an active part in Britain's entry into the War of Austrian Succession and successfully led his army against the French at Dettingen in 1743, the last occasion on which a British king was present on the field of battle. In the latter years of his reign, George largely withdrew from active politics, allowing advances in the development of constitutional monarchy which his successor George III was unable to reverse permanently.

George III (1738–1820), grandson of George II, reigned 1760–1820. Unlike his two predecessors George III took great interest in domestic politics and attempted to exercise royal control of government to the fullest possible extent. His determination to suppress the War of American Independence dominated British war policy 1775–83, but in 1788 he suffered a serious bout of insanity and thereafter his political influence declined. This insanity became permanently incapacitating in 1811 and his son, later George IV, was made regent.

George IV (1762–1830), son of George III, reigned 1820–30, known as 'the First Gentleman of Europe'. As Prince of Wales, George IV was prince regent during his father's final bout of insanity (1811–20), by which time his dissolute lifestyle had already gained him an unsavoury reputation. His attempt to divorce his estranged wife Caroline of Brunswick just after coming to the throne caused a great scandal and further damaged his reputation.

George V (1865–1936), son of Edward VII, reigned 1910–36. He proved to be one of Britain's most popular sovereigns, winning great respect for his punctilious attitude towards royal duties and responsibilities, especially during the First World War. He exercised restrained but none the less important influence over British politics, playing an especially significant role in the formation of the National Government in 1931.

George VI (1894–1952), son of George V, reigned 1936–52. He came to the throne on the abdication of his elder brother Edward VIII, and despite a retiring disposition became a popular and respected monarch, playing an important part in the Second World War as a symbol of the nation's determination to resist Nazi aggression.

George² /dʒɔːdʒ/, St, patron saint of England. Little is known of his life, but his historical existence is now generally accepted. He may have been martyred near Lydda in Palestine some time before the reign of Constantine (d. 337), but his cult did not become popular until the 6th c. and the slaying of the dragon (possibly derived from the legend of Perseus) was not attributed to him until the 12th c. His rank as patron saint of England (in place of Edward the Confessor) probably dates from the reign of Edward III, who founded the Order of the Garter (c.1344) under the patronage of St George who by that time was honoured as the ideal of chivalry.

George³ /dʒɔːdʒ/ n. Brit. sl. the automatic pilot of an aircraft. [the name George]

George Cross, George Medal decorations for gallantry, chiefly in civilian life, instituted in 1940 by King George VI.

Georgetown /ˈdʒɔːdʒtaʊn/ the capital and a port of Guyana, at the mouth of the Demerara River; pop. (1983) 188,000.

George Town¹ the capital of the Cayman Islands, on the island of Grand Cayman; pop. (est. 1988) 12,000.

George Town² (also called *Penang*) the chief port of Malaysia and capital of the State of Penang, on Penang Island; pop. (1980) 250,500.

georgette /dʒɔːˈdʒet/ n. a thin silk or crêpe dress-material. [*Georgette* de la Plante, Fr. dressmaker]

Georgia¹ /ˈdʒɔːdʒɪə/ a district of the Caucasus that was an independent kingdom in medieval times until divided between Persia and Turkey in 1555 and acquired by the Russian Empire in the 19th c. It is now the Georgian SSR, a constituent republic of the USSR; pop. (est. 1987) 5,266,000; capital, Tbilisi (Tiflis). In April 1991 the Georgian parliament voted for independence from Moscow.

Georgia² /ˈdʒɔːdʒɪə/ a State of the south-eastern US, bordering on the Atlantic; pop. (est. 1985) 5,462,000; capital, Atlanta. Originally an English colony, founded in 1733 and named after George II, it was one of the original 13 States of the US (1788).

Georgian¹ /ˈdʒɔːdʒ(ə)n/ adj. **1** of or characteristic of the time of

Kings George I–IV (1714–1830). **2** of or characteristic of the time of Kings George V and VI (1910–52), esp. of the literature of 1910–20.

Georgian² /ˈdʒɔːdʒ(ə)n/ adj. & n. —adj. of or relating to Georgia in the Caucasus (USSR). —n. **1** a native of Georgia; a person of Georgian descent. **2** the language of Georgia, a Caucasian language spoken by some 3 million people. The origin of the characteristic Georgian alphabet is obscure but it is known to have been invented in the 5th c. AD.

Georgian³ /ˈdʒɔːdʒ(ə)n/ adj. & n. —adj. of or relating to Georgia in the US. —n. a native of Georgia.

geosphere /ˈdʒiːə,sfɪə(r)/ n. **1** the solid surface of the earth. **2** any of the almost spherical concentric regions of the earth and its atmosphere.

geostationary /,dʒiːəʊˈsteɪʃənərɪ/ adj. Electronics (of an artificial satellite of the earth) moving in such an orbit as to remain above the same point on the earth's surface (see also GEOSYNCHRONOUS).

geostrophic /,dʒiːəʊˈstrɒfɪk/ adj. Meteorol. depending upon the rotation of the earth. [GEO- + Gk strophē a turning f. strephō to turn]

geosynchronous /,dʒiːəʊˈsɪŋkrənəs/ adj. (of an artificial satellite of the earth) moving in an orbit equal to the earth's period of rotation (see also GEOSTATIONARY).

geothermal /,dʒiːəʊˈθɜːm(ə)l/ adj. relating to, originating from, or produced by the internal heat of the earth.

geotropism /dʒɪˈɒtrə,pɪz(ə)m/ n. plant growth in relation to gravity. □ **negative geotropism** the tendency of stems etc. to grow away from the centre of the earth. **positive geotropism** the tendency of roots to grow towards the centre of the earth. □□ **geotropic** /,dʒiːəʊˈtrɒpɪk/ adj. [GEO- + Gk tropikos f. tropē a turning f. trepō to turn]

Ger. abbr. German.

Geraldton /ˈdʒerəldt(ə)n/ a seaport and resort to the north of Perth on the west coast of Australia; pop. (est. 1987) 20,150.

geranium /dʒəˈreɪnɪəm/ n. **1** any herb or shrub of the genus Geranium bearing fruit shaped like the bill of a crane, e.g. cranesbill. **2** (in general use) a cultivated pelargonium. **3** the colour of the scarlet geranium. [L f. Gk geranion f. geranos crane]

gerbera /ˈdʒɜːbərə/ n. any composite plant of the genus Gerbera of Africa or Asia, esp. the Transvaal daisy. [T. Gerber, Ger. naturalist d. 1743]

gerbil /ˈdʒɜːbɪl/ n. (also **jerbil**) a mouselike desert rodent of the subfamily Gerbillinae, with long hind legs. [F gerbille f. mod.L gerbillus dimin. of gerbo JERBOA]

gerenuk /ˈdʒerə,nʊk/ n. an antelope, Litocranius walleri, native to E. Africa, with a very long neck and small head. [Somali]

gerfalcon var. of GYRFALCON.

geriatric /,dʒerɪˈætrɪk/ adj. & n. —adj. **1** of or relating to old people. **2** colloq. old, outdated. —n. **1** an old person, esp. one receiving special care. **2** colloq. a person or thing considered as relatively old or outdated. [Gk gēras old age + iatros doctor]

geriatrics /,dʒerɪˈætrɪks/ n.pl. (usu. treated as sing.) a branch of medicine or social science dealing with the health and care of old people. □□ **geriatrician** /-əˈtrɪʃ(ə)n/ n.

Géricault /ˈʒerɪ,kəʊ/, Théodore (1791–1824), French Romantic painter. His most famous work, The Raft of the Medusa (1819), depicts the ordeal of the survivors of a shipwreck in 1816, with realistic treatment of the macabre. A passionate horseman, he enjoyed painting jockeys and horseraces with their stirring action and swirling movement.

germ /dʒɜːm/ n. **1** a micro-organism, esp. one which causes disease. **2 a** a portion of an organism capable of developing into a new one; the rudiment of an animal or plant. **b** an embryo of a seed (wheat germ). **3** an original idea etc. from which something may develop; an elementary principle. □ **germ-cell 1** a cell containing half the number of chromosomes of a somatic cell and able to unite with one from the opposite sex to form a new individual; a gamete. **2** any embryonic cell with the potential of developing into a gamete. **germ warfare** the systematic spreading of micro-organisms to cause disease in an enemy population. **in germ** not yet developed. □□ **germy** adj. [F germe f. L germen germinis sprout]

German /ˈdʒɜ:mən/ n. & adj. —n. **1** a native or national of Germany; a person of German descent. **2** the language of Germany, a Germanic language spoken by some 100 million people mainly in Germany, Austria, and Switzerland, although there are large German-speaking communities in the US. It is the official language of Germany and of Austria, and one of the official languages of Switzerland. —adj. of or relating to Germany or its people or language. □ **German measles** a contagious disease, rubella, with symptoms like mild measles. **German shepherd** (or **shepherd dog**) an Alsatian. **German silver** a white alloy of nickel, zinc, and copper. **High German** the variety of Teutonic speech, originally confined to 'High' or southern Germany, now accepted as the literary language of the whole country. Its chief distinctive characteristic is that certain consonants have been altered from their original Teutonic sounds which the other dialects in the main preserve. The spread of this form of the language owes much to the biblical translations of Martin Luther in the 16th c. **Low German** the general name for the dialects of Germany which are not High German. It is spoken in the lowland areas of northern Germany, and is most closely related to Dutch and Friesian. [L Germanus with ref. to related peoples of Central and N. Europe, a name perh. given by Celts to their neighbours: cf. OIr. gair neighbour]

german /ˈdʒɜ:mən/ adj. (placed after brother, sister, or cousin) **1** having both parents the same (brother german). **2** having both grandparents the same on one side (cousin german). **3** archaic germane. [ME f. OF germain f. L germanus genuine, of the same parents]

germander /dʒɜ:ˈmændə(r)/ n. any plant of the genus Teucrium. □ **germander speedwell** a creeping plant, Veronica chamaedrys, with germander-like leaves and blue flowers. [ME f. med.L germandra ult. f. Gk khamaidrus f. khamai on the ground + drus oak]

germane /dʒɜ:ˈmeɪn/ adj. (usu. foll. by to) relevant (to a subject under consideration). □□ **germanely** adv. **germaneness** n. [var. of GERMAN]

Germanic /dʒɜ:ˈmænɪk/ adj. & n. —adj. **1** having German characteristics. **2** hist. of the Germans. **3** of the Scandinavians, Anglo-Saxons, or Germans. **4** of the languages or language group called Germanic. —n. **1** the branch of Indo-European languages including English, German, Dutch, and the Scandinavian languages. These different languages reflect an original dialectal split into West Germanic (English and German), North Germanic (the Scandinavian languages for which the oldest evidence is that of Old Norse), and East Germanic, which has died out but for which Gothic provided the oldest evidence. **2** the (unrecorded) early language from which other Germanic languages developed. □ **East Germanic** an extinct group including Gothic. **North Germanic** the Scandinavian languages. **West Germanic** a group including High and Low German, English, Frisian, and Dutch. [L Germanicus (as GERMAN)]

germanic /dʒɜ:ˈmænɪk/ adj. Chem. of or containing germanium, esp. in its quadrivalent state.

Germanist /ˈdʒɜ:mənɪst/ n. an expert in or student of the language, literature, and civilization of Germany, or Germanic languages.

germanium /dʒɜ:ˈmeɪnɪəm/ n. Chem. a lustrous brittle semi-metallic element occurring naturally in sulphide ores and used in semiconductors. A rare element, first isolated in 1886, germanium became very important after the Second World War in the making of transistors and other semiconductor devices, but more recently it has been largely displaced by silicon for this purpose. ¶ Symb.: **Ge**; atomic number 32. [mod.L f. Germanus GERMAN]

Germanize /ˈdʒɜ:mənaɪz/ v.tr. & intr. (also **-ise**) make or become German; adopt or cause to adopt German customs etc. □□ **Germanization** /-ˈzeɪʃ(ə)n/ n. **Germanizer** n.

Germano- /dʒɜ:ˈmænəʊ/ comb. form German; German and.

germanous /dʒɜ:ˈmeɪnəs/ adj. Chem. containing germanium in the bivalent state.

Germany /ˈdʒɜ:mənɪ/ a country in central Europe, divided after the Second World War into the Federal Republic of Germany (West Germany; pop. (est. 1988) 60,980,200; capital, Bonn) and the German Democratic Republic (East Germany; pop. (est. 1988) 16,596,900; seat of government, East Berlin); official language, German. German tribes came repeatedly into conflict with the Romans, and after the collapse of the Roman Empire they overran the Rhine which had been its northern frontier. Loosely unified upon the Holy Roman Empire during the Middle Ages, the multiplicity of small German States achieved real unity only with the rise of Prussia and the formation of the German empire in the mid-19th c. Defeated in the First World War, in the 1930s Germany was taken over by the Nazi dictatorship which led her into a policy of expansionism and eventually complete defeat in the Second World War. After the partition of Germany, the West emerged as a European industrial power incorporated within the western defence and economic community, while the East remained to a considerable extent under Soviet domination. After the general collapse of Communism in eastern Europe towards the end of 1989, East and West Germany reunited on 3 Oct. 1990; capital, Berlin; seat of goverment, Bonn.

germicide /ˈdʒɜ:mɪˌsaɪd/ n. a substance destroying germs, esp. those causing disease. □□ **germicidal** /-ˈsaɪd(ə)l/ adj.

germinal /ˈdʒɜ:mɪn(ə)l/ adj. **1** relating to or of the nature of a germ or germs (see GERM 1). **2** in the earliest stage of development. **3** productive of new ideas. □□ **germinally** adv. [L germen germin- sprout: see GERM]

germinate /ˈdʒɜ:mɪˌneɪt/ v. **1 a** intr. sprout, bud, or put forth shoots. **b** tr. cause to sprout or shoot. **2 a** tr. cause (ideas etc.) to originate or develop. **b** intr. come into existence. □□ **germination** /-ˈneɪʃ(ə)n/ n. **germinative** /-nətɪv/ adj. **germinator** n. [L germinare germinat- (as GERM)]

germon /ˈdʒɜ:mən/ n. = ALBACORE 1. [F]

Geronimo /dʒəˈrɒnɪˌməʊ/ (c.1829–1909), an American Indian Apache chief, who led his people in resistance to White settlement in Arizona. For twelve years he waged war against US troops, leading brutal raids, before surrendering in 1886. His name is used as a war cry by US paratroops going into action.

gerontology /ˌdʒerɒnˈtɒlədʒɪ/ n. the scientific study of old age, the process of ageing, and the special problems of old people. □□ **gerontological** /-təˈlɒdʒɪk(ə)l/ adj. **gerontologist** n. [Gk gerōn -ontos old man + -LOGY]

-gerous /dʒərəs/ comb. form forming adjectives meaning 'bearing' (lanigerous).

gerrymander /ˌdʒerɪˈmændə(r)/ v. & n. (also **jerrymander**) —v.tr. **1** manipulate the boundaries of (a constituency etc.) so as to give undue influence to some party or class. **2** manipulate (a situation etc.) to gain advantage. —n. this practice. □□ **gerrymanderer** n. [the name of Governor Gerry of Massachusetts (who rearranged boundaries for this purpose) + (SALA)MANDER, from the shape of a district on a political map drawn when he was in office (1812)]

Gershwin /ˈgɜ:ʃwɪn/, George (1898–1937), American composer and pianist, of Russian-Jewish family (Gershovitz). He had early experience of popular music, gained from working in Tin Pan Alley, but no formal musical training. His works made an immediate impact in the US. Gershwin composed many popular songs, mainly with lyrics by his elder brother Ira (Israel, d. 1983), the opera Porgy and Bess, and works for piano and orchestra, including Rhapsody in Blue and Concerto in F. His mixture of the primitive and sophisticated gives his works individuality and an appeal which shows no sign of diminishing.

gerund /ˈdʒerənd/ n. Gram. a form of a verb functioning as a noun, orig. in Latin ending in -ndum (declinable), in English ending in -ing and used distinctly as a part of a verb (e.g. do you mind my asking you?). [LL gerundium f. gerundum var. of gerendum, the gerund of L gerere do]

gerundive /dʒeˈrʌndɪv/ n. Gram. a form of a Latin verb, ending in -ndus (declinable) and functioning as an adjective meaning 'that should or must be done' etc. [LL gerundivus (modus mood) f. gerundium: see GERUND]

gesso /ˈdʒesəʊ/ n. (pl. **-oes**) plaster of Paris or gypsum as used in painting or sculpture. [It. f. L gypsum: see GYPSUM]

æ cat ɑ: arm e bed ɜ: her ɪ sit i: see ɒ hot ɔ: saw ʌ run ʊ put u: too ə ago aɪ my

gestalt /gə'stɑ:lt/ n. Psychol. an organized whole that is perceived as more than the sum of its parts. □ **gestalt psychology** a movement in psychology founded in 1912 by three German psychologists, Wertheimer, Köhler, and Koffka, as a reaction to the analytic approach of Wundt's structuralism. Its essential tenet was that perceptions, reactions, etc., are gestalts. The job of the psychologist is then to analyse the conditions under which the gestalt is experienced and understood. □□ **gestaltism** n. **gestaltist** n. [G, = form, shape]

Gestapo /ge'stɑ:pəʊ/ n. 1 the German secret police under Nazi rule. 2 derog. an organization compared to this. [G, f. Geheime Staatspolizei]

gestate /dʒe'steɪt/ v.tr. 1 carry (a foetus) in gestation. 2 develop (an idea etc.).

gestation /dʒe'steɪʃ(ə)n/ n. 1 **a** the process of carrying or being carried in the womb between conception and birth. **b** this period. 2 the private development of a plan, idea, etc. [L gestatio f. gestare frequent. of gerere carry]

gesticulate /dʒe'stɪkjʊˌleɪt/ v. 1 intr. use gestures instead of or in addition to speech. 2 tr. express with gestures. □□ **gesticulation** /-'leɪʃ(ə)n/ n. **gesticulative** /-lətɪv/ adj. **gesticulator** n. **gesticulatory** /-lətərɪ/ adj. [L gesticulari f. gesticulus dimin. of gestus GESTURE]

gesture /'dʒestʃə(r)/ n. & v. —n. 1 a significant movement of a limb or the body. 2 the use of such movements esp. to convey feeling or as a rhetorical device. 3 an action to evoke a response or convey intention, usu. friendly. —v.tr. & intr. gesticulate. □□ **gestural** adj. **gesturer** n. [ME f. med.L gestura f. L gerere gest-wield]

gesundheit /gə'zʊnthaɪt/ int. expressing a wish of good health, esp. before drinking or to a person who has sneezed. [G, = health]

get /get/ v. & n. —v. (**getting**; past **got** /gɒt/; past part. **got** or US (and in comb.) **gotten** /'gɒt(ə)n/) 1 tr. come into the possession of; receive or earn (get a job; got £200 a week; got first prize). 2 tr. fetch, obtain, procure, purchase (get my book for me; got a new car). 3 tr. go to reach or catch (a bus, train, etc.). 4 tr. prepare (a meal etc.). 5 intr. & tr. reach or cause to reach a certain state or condition; become or cause to become (get rich; get one's feet wet; get to be famous; got them ready; got him into trouble; cannot get the key into the lock). 6 tr. obtain as a result of calculation. 7 tr. contract (a disease etc.). 8 tr. establish or be in communication with via telephone or radio; receive (a radio signal). 9 tr. experience or suffer; have inflicted on one; receive as one's lot or penalty (got four years in prison). 10 **a** tr. succeed in bringing, placing, etc. (get it round the corner; get it on the agenda; flattery will get you nowhere). **b** intr. & tr. succeed or cause to succeed in coming or going (will get you there somehow; got absolutely nowhere). 11 tr. (prec. by have) **a** possess (have not got a penny). **b** (foll. by to + infin.) be bound or obliged (have got to see you). 12 tr. (foll. by to + infin.) induce; prevail upon (got them to help me). 13 tr. colloq. understand (a person or an argument) (have you got that?; I get your point; do you get me?). 14 tr. colloq. inflict punishment or retribution on, esp. in retaliation (I'll get you for that). 15 tr. colloq. **a** annoy. **b** move; affect emotionally. **c** attract, obsess. **d** amuse. 16 tr. (foll. by to + infin.) develop an inclination as specified (am getting to like it). 17 intr. (foll. by verbal noun) begin (get going). 18 tr. (esp. in past or perfect) catch in an argument; corner, puzzle. 19 tr. establish (an idea etc.) in one's mind. 20 intr. sl. be off; go away. 21 tr. archaic beget. 22 tr. archaic learn; acquire (knowledge) by study. —n. 1 **a** an act of begetting (of animals). **b** an offspring (of animals). 2 sl. a fool or idiot. □ **get about** (or **around**) 1 travel extensively or fast; go from place to place. 2 manage to walk, move about, etc. (esp. after illness). 3 (of news) be circulated, esp. orally. **get across** 1 manage to communicate (an idea etc.). 2 (of an idea etc.) be communicated successfully. 3 colloq. annoy, irritate. **get along** (or **on**) 1 (foll. by together, with) live harmoniously, accord. 2 be off! nonsense! **get at** 1 reach; get hold of. 2 colloq. imply (what are you getting at?). **get away** 1 escape. 2 (as imper.) colloq. expressing disbelief or scepticism. 3 (foll. by with) escape blame or punishment for. **get back at** colloq. retaliate against. **get by** colloq. 1 just manage, even with difficulty. 2 be acceptable. **get down** 1 alight, descend (from a

vehicle, ladder, etc.). 2 record in writing. **get a person down** depress or deject him or her. **get down to** begin working on or discussing. **get even** (often foll. by with) 1 achieve revenge; act in retaliation. 2 equalize the score. **get his** (or **hers** etc.) sl. be killed. **get hold of** 1 grasp (physically). 2 grasp (intellectually); understand. 3 make contact with (a person). 4 acquire. **get in** 1 enter. 2 be elected. **get into** become interested or involved in. **get it** sl. be punished or in trouble. **get it into one's head** (foll. by that + clause) firmly believe or maintain; realize. **get off** 1 colloq. be acquitted; escape with little or no punishment. 2 start. 3 alight; alight from (a bus etc.). 4 go, or cause to go, to sleep. 5 (foll. by with, together) Brit. colloq. form an amorous or sexual relationship, esp. abruptly or quickly. **get off on** colloq. cause a person to be acquitted. **get on** 1 make progress; manage. 2 enter (a bus etc.). 3 = get along 1. **get on to** colloq. 1 make contact with. 2 understand; become aware of. **get out** 1 leave or escape. 2 manage to go outdoors. 3 alight from a vehicle. 4 transpire; become known. 5 succeed in uttering, publishing, etc. 6 solve or finish (a puzzle etc.). 7 Cricket be dismissed. **get-out** n. a means of avoiding something. **get a person out** 1 help a person to leave or escape. 2 Cricket dismiss (a batsman). **get out of** 1 avoid or escape (a duty etc.). 2 abandon (a habit) gradually. **get a thing out of** manage to obtain it from (a person) esp. with difficulty. **get outside** (or **outside of**) sl. eat or drink. **get over** 1 recover from (an illness, upset, etc.). 2 overcome (a difficulty). 3 manage to communicate (an idea etc.). **get a thing over** (or **over with**) complete (a tedious task) promptly. **get one's own back** colloq. have one's revenge. **get-rich-quick** adj. designed to make a lot of money fast. **get rid of** see RID. **get round** (US **around**) 1 successfully coax or cajole (a person) esp. to secure a favour. 2 evade (a law etc.). **get round to** deal with (a task etc.) in due course. **get somewhere** make progress; be initially successful. **get there** colloq. 1 succeed. 2 understand what is meant. **get through** 1 pass or assist in passing (an examination, an ordeal, etc.). 2 finish or use up (esp. resources). 3 make contact by telephone. 4 (foll. by to) succeed in making (a person) listen or understand. **get a thing through** cause it to overcome obstacles, difficulties, etc. **get to** 1 reach. 2 = get down to. **get together** gather, assemble. **get-together** n. colloq. a social gathering. **get up** 1 rise or cause to rise from sitting etc., or from bed after sleeping or an illness. 2 ascend or mount, e.g. on horseback. 3 (of fire, wind, or the sea) begin to be strong or agitated. 4 prepare or organize. 5 enhance or refine one's knowledge of (a subject). 6 work up (a feeling, e.g. anger). 7 produce or stimulate (get up steam; get up speed). 8 (often refl.) dress or arrange elaborately; make presentable; arrange the appearance of. 9 (foll. by to) colloq. indulge or be involved in (always getting up to mischief). **get-up** n. colloq. a style or arrangement of dress etc., esp. an elaborate one. **get-up-and-go** colloq. energy, vim, enthusiasm. **get the wind up** see WIND[1]. **get with child** archaic make pregnant. **have got it bad** (or **badly**) sl. be obsessed or affected emotionally. □□ **gettable** adj. [ME f. ON geta obtain, beget, guess, corresp. to OE gietan (recorded only in compounds), f. Gmc]

get-at-able /get'ætəb(ə)l/ adj. colloq. accessible.

getaway /'getəˌweɪ/ n. an escape, esp. after committing a crime.

Gethsemane /geθ'semənɪ/, **Garden of** the garden to which Christ went with his disciples after the Last Supper, and which was the scene of his agony and betrayal. It lies in the valley between Jerusalem and the Mount of Olives. [Heb. gath-shemen oil-press]

getter /'getə(r)/ n. & v. —n. 1 in senses of GET v. 2 Physics a substance used to remove residual gas from an evacuated vessel. —v.tr. Physics remove (gas) or evacuate (a vessel) with a getter.

Getty /'getɪ/, Jean Paul (1892–1976), American industrialist, who made his immense fortune in the oil industry and was also a noted art collector. He founded the museum which bears his name at Malibu in California.

Gettysburg /'getɪzˌbɜːg/ a small town in Pennsylvania, scene of a decisive battle of the American Civil War, fought in the first three days of July 1863. The Confederate Army of Northern Virginia, commanded by General Lee, was repulsed in a bloody engagement by the Union Army of the Potomac, commanded by General Meade, forcing Lee to abandon his invasion of the north. □ **Gettysburg address** a speech delivered on 18 Nov. 1863 by President Abraham Lincoln at the dedication of the national cemetery on the battlefield.

geum /ˈdʒiːəm/ n. any rosaceous plant of the genus *Geum* including herb bennet, with rosettes of leaves and yellow, red, or white flowers. [mod.L, var. of L *gaeum*]

GeV abbr. gigaelectronvolt (equivalent to 10⁹ electronvolts).

gewgaw /ˈgjuːgɔː/ n. a gaudy plaything or ornament; a bauble. [ME: orig. unkn.]

geyser /ˈgaɪzə(r), ˈgiː-/ n. **1** an intermittently gushing hot spring that throws up a tall column of water. **2** /ˈgiːzə(r)/ Brit. an apparatus for heating water rapidly for domestic use. [Icel. *Geysir*, the name of a particular spring in Iceland, rel. to *geysa* to gush]

Ghana /ˈgɑːnə/ a country of West Africa, with its southern coastline bordering on the Atlantic Ocean; pop. (est. 1988) 14,360,100; official language, English; capital, Accra. The country's principal crop is cocoa, of which it is world's chief producer. In the 15th c. it was visited by Portuguese and other European traders, who called it the Gold Coast, and it became a centre of the slave trade until the 19th c. Britain established control over the area and it became the British colony of Gold Coast in 1874. In 1957 it gained independence as a member State of the Commonwealth, the first British colony to do so, under the leadership of Dr Kwame Nkrumah, taking the name of Ghana from an important kingdom (said to date from the 4th c.) that had flourished in that region in medieval times. Ghana became a republic in 1960. □□ **Ghanaian** /gɑːˈneɪən/ adj. & n.

gharial /ˈgeərɪəl, ˈgærɪəl/ n. (also **gavial** /ˈgeɪvɪəl/) a large Indian crocodile, *Gavialis gangeticus*, having a long narrow snout widening at the nostrils. □ **false gharial** a similar crocodile, *Tomistoma schlegelii*, of Indonesia and Malaya. [Hind.]

ghastly /ˈgɑːstlɪ/ adj. & adv. —adj. (**ghastlier**, **ghastliest**) **1** horrible, frightful. **2** colloq. objectionable, unpleasant. **3** death-like, pallid. —adv. in a ghastly or sickly way (*ghastly pale*). □□ **ghastlily** adv. **ghastliness** n. [ME *gastlich* f. obs. *gast* terrify: gh after *ghost*]

ghat /gæt, gɔːt/ n. (also **ghaut** /gɔːt/) in India: **1** steps leading down to a river. **2** a landing-place. **3** a defile or mountain pass. □ **burning-ghat** a level area at the top of a river ghat where Hindus burn their dead. **Eastern Ghats, Western Ghats** mountain chains parallel to the east and west coasts in southern India. [Hindi *ghāt*]

Ghazi /ˈgɑːzɪ/ n. (pl. **Ghazis**) a Muslim fighter against non-Muslims. [Arab. *al-gāzī* part. of *gazā* raid]

ghee /giː/ n. (also **ghi**) Indian clarified butter esp. from the milk of a buffalo or cow. [Hindi *ghī* f. Skr. *ghṛitá-* sprinkled]

Ghent /gent/ (Flemish **Gent**, French **Gand** /gɑ̃/) Belgian city and port, the capital of East Flanders; pop. (1988) 232,620. In English it was formerly called Gaunt.

gherao /geˈraʊ/ n. (pl. **-os**) (in India and Pakistan) coercion of employers, by which their workers prevent them from leaving the premises until certain demands are met. [Hind. *gherna* besiege]

gherkin /ˈgɜːkɪn/ n. **1** a small variety of cucumber, or a young green cucumber, used for pickling. **2 a** a trailing plant, *Cucumis sativus*, with cucumber-like fruits used for pickling. **b** this fruit. [Du. *gurkkijn* (unrecorded), dimin. of *gurk*, f. Slavonic, ult. f. med. Gk *aggourion*]

ghetto /ˈgetəʊ/ n. & v. —n. (pl. **-os**) **1** a part of a city, esp. a slum area, occupied by a minority group or groups. **2** hist. the Jewish quarter in a city. **3** a segregated group or area. —v.tr. (**-oes, -oed**) put or keep (people) in a ghetto. □ **ghetto-blaster** sl. a large portable radio, esp. used to play loud pop music. [perh. f. It. *getto* foundry (applied to the site of the first ghetto in Venice in 1516)]

ghi var. of GHEE.

Ghibelline /ˈgɪbɪlaɪn/ n. a member of one of the two great political factions in Italian medieval politics, traditionally supporting the Holy Roman Emperor against the pope and his supporters, the Guelphs, during the long struggle between the papacy and the Empire. [It. *Ghibellino* perh. f. G *Waiblingen* estate belonging to Hohenstaufen emperors]

Ghiberti /gɪˈbeətɪ/, Lorenzo (1378–1455), Florentine sculptor, who spent most of his career working on two successive pairs of bronze doors for the Baptistery of Florence. The second, more famous, pair (1425–52), dubbed by Michelangelo the 'Gates of Paradise', represent episodes from the Old Testament laid out on carefully constructed perspective stages.

ghillie var. of GILLIE.

Ghirlandaio /ˌgɪrlænˈdaɪəʊ/ the popular name of Domenico Bigordi (c. 1448–94), Italian painter in fresco, who established a flourishing workshop in Florence with his two younger brothers. He is noted for his naturalism and for his detailed religious frescos, into which he introduced portraits of many leading citizens in contemporary dress.

ghost /gəʊst/ n. & v. —n. **1** the supposed apparition of a dead person or animal; a disembodied spirit. **2** a shadow or mere semblance (*not a ghost of a chance*). **3** an emaciated or pale person. **4** a secondary or duplicated image produced by defective television reception or by a telescope. **5** archaic a spirit or soul. —v. **1** intr. (often foll. by *for*) act as ghost-writer. **2** tr. act as ghost-writer of (a work). □ **ghost town** a deserted town with few or no remaining inhabitants. **ghost-write** v.tr. & intr. act as ghost-writer (of). **ghost-writer** a person who writes on behalf of the credited author of a work. □□ **ghostlike** adj. [OE *gāst* f. WG: gh- occurs first in Caxton, prob. infl. by Flem. *gheest*]

ghosting /ˈgəʊstɪŋ/ n. the appearance of a 'ghost' (see GHOST n. 4) or secondary image in a television picture.

ghostly /ˈgəʊstlɪ/ adj. (**ghostlier**, **ghostliest**) like a ghost; spectral. □□ **ghostliness** n. [OE *gāstlic* (as GHOST)]

ghoul /guːl/ n. **1** a person morbidly interested in death etc. **2** an evil spirit or phantom. **3** (in Muslim folklore) a spirit preying on corpses. □□ **ghoulish** adj. **ghoulishly** adv. **ghoulishness** n. [Arab. *gūl* protean desert demon]

GHQ abbr. General Headquarters.

ghyll Brit. var. of GILL³.

GI /dʒiːˈaɪ/ n. & adj. —n. a private soldier in the US Army. —adj. of or for US servicemen. [abbr. of *government* (or *general*) *issue*]

Giacometti /ˌdʒɑːkəˈmetɪ/, Alberto (1901–66), Swiss sculptor and painter. He experimented with naturalistic sculpture and surrealism, but his most characterisitc style features human figures, sometimes disposed in groups, that are notable for their emaciated, extremely elongated, and nervous character.

giant /ˈdʒaɪənt/ n. & adj. —n. **1** an imaginary or mythical being of human form but superhuman size. **2** (in pl., **Giants** Gk Mythol.) a race of monstrous appearance and great strength, sons of Gaia or Ge (Earth) who tried to overthrow the Olympian gods and were defeated with the help of Hercules. **3** an abnormally tall or large person, animal, or plant. **4** a person of exceptional ability, integrity, courage, etc. **5** a star of relatively great luminosity arising from either high surface temperatures (**blue giants,** young massive stars with a high rate of consumption of hydrogen at their centres) or very extended atmospheres (**red giants,** whose energy is generated by nuclear reactions in regions of the star outside its centre). —attrib.adj. **1** of extraordinary size or force, gigantic; monstrous. **2** colloq. extra large (*giant packet*). **3** (of a plant or animal) of a very large kind. □ **giant-killer** a person who defeats a seemingly much more powerful opponent. □□ **giantism** n. **giant-like** adj. [ME *geant* (later infl. by L) f. OF, ult. f. L *gigas gigant-* f. Gk]

Giant's Causeway a formation of basalt columns dating from the Tertiary period on the coast of Antrim, Northern Ireland. It was once believed to be the end of a road made by a legendary giant to Staffa in the Inner Hebrides, where there is a similar formation.

giaour /ˈdʒaʊə(r)/ n. derog. or literary a non-Muslim, esp. a Christian (orig. a Turkish name). [Pers. *gaur, gōr*]

Gib. /dʒɪb/ colloq. Gibraltar. [abbr.]

gib /dʒɪb, gɪb/ n. a wood or metal bolt, wedge, or pin for holding a machine part etc. in place. [18th c.: orig. unkn.]

gibber[1] /ˈdʒɪbə(r)/ v. & n. —v.intr. speak fast and inarticulately; chatter incoherently. —n. such speech or sound. [imit.]

gibber[2] /ˈɡɪbə(r)/ n. Austral. a boulder or large stone. [Aboriginal]

gibberellin /ˌdʒɪbəˈrelɪn/ n. one of a group of plant hormones that stimulate the growth of leaves and shoots. [Gibberella a genus of fungi, dimin. of genus-name Gibbera f. L gibber hump]

gibberish /ˈdʒɪbərɪʃ/ n. unintelligible or meaningless speech; nonsense. [perh. f. GIBBER[1] (but attested earlier) + -ISH[1] as used in Spanish, Swedish, etc.]

gibbet /ˈdʒɪbɪt/ n. & v. —n. hist. **1 a** a gallows. **b** an upright post with an arm on which the bodies of executed criminals were hung up. **2** (prec. by the) death by hanging. —v.tr. (**gibbeted**, **gibbeting**) **1** put to death by hanging. **2 a** expose on a gibbet. **b** hang up as on a gibbet. **3** hold up to contempt. [ME f. OF gibet gallows dimin. of gibe club, prob. f. Gmc]

Gibbon /ˈɡɪbən/, Edward (1737–94), English historian. He became a Catholic convert at 16, was sent to Lausanne and soon reconverted to Protestantism. In Rome in 1764, while musing amid the ruins of the Capitol, he formed the plan for his The History of the Decline and Fall of the Roman Empire (1776–88), the greatest historical work in English literature, marked by its eloquent prose and sustained by a lively dramatic style. His remarkable Memoirs (1796) reveal Gibbon's sense of vocation as a historian; anti-clerical, rational, he was one of the last great Augustans.

gibbon /ˈɡɪbən/ n. any small ape of the genus Hylobates, native to SE Asia, having a slender body and long arms. [F f. a native name]

Gibbons /ˈɡɪbənz/, Grinling (1648–1721), English sculptor, born in Rotterdam, famous for his decorative carvings (chiefly in wood) of fruit and flowers, small animals, and cherubs' heads. Examples may be seen at Windsor, Hampton Court, and in the choir stalls of St Paul's Cathedral.

gibbous /ˈɡɪbəs/ adj. **1** convex or protuberant. **2** (of a moon or planet) having the bright part greater than a semicircle and less than a circle. **3** humped or humpbacked. □□ **gibbosity** /-ˈbɒsɪtɪ/ n. **gibbously** adv. **gibbousness** n. [ME f. LL gibbosus f. gibbus hump]

Gibbs /ɡɪbz/, James (1682–1754), Scottish architect who settled in London in 1709. An admirer of Wren, he developed the ideas of Wren's city churches, especially in his masterpiece St Martin's-in-the-Fields (1722–6); its combination of steeple and portico was very influential.

gibe /dʒaɪb/ v. & n. (also **jibe**) —v.intr. (often foll. by at) jeer, mock. —n. an instance of gibing; a taunt. □□ **giber** n. [perh. f. OF giber handle roughly]

giblets /ˈdʒɪblɪts/ n.pl. the liver, gizzard, neck, etc., of a bird, usu. removed and kept separate when the bird is prepared for cooking. [OF gibelet game stew, perh. f. gibier game]

Gibraltar /dʒɪˈbrɔːltə(r)/ a fortified town and rocky headland (the Rock of Gibraltar) at the southern tip of the Iberian peninsula on the Strait of Gibraltar that forms the only outlet of the Mediterranean Sea to the Atlantic. It is a British naval and air base of great strategic importance; pop. (est. 1988) 29,140; official languages, English and Spanish. The site has been in British hands since it was captured during the War of the Spanish Succession in 1704 and formally ceded to Britain by the Treaty of Utrecht (1713), and is now a British dependency with Britain responsible for defence, external affairs, and internal security. Since the Second World War Spain has forcefully urged her claim to the territory. Remains of what was later called Neanderthal man were first discovered in Gibraltar in 1848, but were not recognized to be of this species until the discovery of other remains in the Neander Valley in 1857. □□ **Gibraltarian** /ˌdʒɪbrɔːlˈteərɪən/ adj. & n. [Arab. gebel-al-Tarik hill of Tarik (8th-c. Saracen commander)]

Gibson Desert /ˈɡɪbs(ə)n/ a desert region in Western Australia, situated between the Nullarbor Plain and the Great Sandy Desert.

giddy /ˈɡɪdɪ/ adj. & v. —adj. (**giddier**, **giddiest**) **1** having a sensation of whirling and a tendency to fall, stagger, or spin round. **2 a** overexcited as a result of success, pleasurable emotion, etc.; mentally intoxicated. **b** excitable, frivolous. **3** tending to make one giddy. —v.tr. & intr. (**-ies**, **-ied**) make or become giddy. □□ **giddily** adv. **giddiness** n. [OE gidig insane, lit. 'possessed by a god']

Gide /ʒiːd/, André (1869–1951), French novelist and critic, whose early works were influenced by symbolism. After a visit to Algeria in the mid-1890s Gide reacted against the restraints of his Protestant upbringing and Les Nourritures terrestres (Fruits of the Earth, 1897) reflects his subsequent emancipation. Homosexuality, and the conflict between desire and strict morality, are recurrent themes in his works, notably in the autobiographical Si le grain ne meurt (1926). Gide experimented in many literary genres but is best known for his two short works L'Immoraliste (1902) and La Porte étroite (Strait is the Gate, 1909), for which his cousin Madeleine Rondeaux, whom he married in 1895, was the inspiration, for the longer Les Caves du Vatican (1914), and for his novel Les Faux-Monnayeurs (The Counterfeiters, 1926). In his works, and as co-founder of the literary journal Nouvelle Revue française, he influenced the aesthetic and moral values of the inter-war generation. He was awarded the Nobel Prize for literature in 1947.

Gideon /ˈɡɪdɪən/ **1** an Israelite leader (see Judges 6:11 ff.). **2 a** member of a Christian organization of American commercial travellers, founded in 1899. □□ **Gideon Bible** a Bible purchased by this organization and placed in a hotel room etc.

gie /ɡiː/ v.tr. & intr. Sc. = GIVE.

Gielgud /ˈɡiːlɡʊd/, Sir (Arthur) John (1904–), English actor, famous for his Shakespearian roles, especially for his interpretation of Hamlet.

gift /ɡɪft/ n. & v. —n. **1** a thing given; a present. **2** a natural ability or talent. **3** the power to give (in his gift). **4** the act or an instance of giving. **5** colloq. an easy task. —v.tr. **1** endow with gifts. **2 a** (foll. by with) give to as a gift. **b** bestow as a gift. □ **gift of tongues** see TONGUE. **gift token** (or **voucher**) a voucher used as a gift and exchangeable for goods. **gift-wrap** (**-wrapped**, **-wrapping**) wrap attractively as a gift. **look a gift-horse in the mouth** (usu. neg.) find fault with what has been given. [ME f. ON gipt f. Gmc, rel. to GIVE]

gifted /ˈɡɪftɪd/ adj. exceptionally talented or intelligent. □□ **giftedly** adv. **giftedness** n.

gig[1] /ɡɪɡ/ n. **1** a light two-wheeled one-horse carriage. **2** a light ship's boat for rowing or sailing. **3** a rowing-boat esp. for racing. [ME in var. senses: prob. imit.]

gig[2] /ɡɪɡ/ n. & v. colloq. —n. an engagement of an entertainer, esp. of musicians to play jazz or dance music, usu. for a single appearance. —v.intr. (**gigged**, **gigging**) perform a gig. [20th c.: orig. unkn.]

gig[3] /ɡɪɡ/ n. a kind of fishing-spear. [short for fizgig, fishgig: cf. Sp. fisga harpoon]

giga- /ˈɡaɪɡə, ˈɡɪɡə/ comb. form denoting a factor of 10^9. [Gk gigas giant]

gigametre /ˈɡɪɡəˌmiːtə(r)/ n. a metric unit equal to 10^9 metres.

gigantic /dʒaɪˈɡæntɪk/ adj. **1** very large; enormous. **2** like or suited to a giant. □□ **gigantesque** /-ˈtesk/ adj. **gigantically** adv. [L gigas gigantis GIANT]

gigantism /ˈdʒaɪɡənˌtɪz(ə)m/ n. abnormal largeness, esp. Med. excessive growth due to hormonal imbalance, or to polyploidy in plants.

Gigantopithecus /dʒaɪˌɡæntəˈpɪθɪkəs/ n. a genus of large fossil primates, sometimes considered hominids, known from bones found in China. [mod.L, f. Gk gigas giant + pithēkos ape]

giggle /ˈɡɪɡ(ə)l/ v. & n. —v.intr. laugh in half-suppressed spasms, esp. in an affected or silly manner. —n. **1** such a laugh. **2** colloq. an amusing person or thing; a joke. □□ **giggler** n. **giggly** adj. (**gigglier**, **giggliest**). **giggliness** n. [imit.: cf. Du. gichelen, G gickeln]

Gigli /ˈdʒiːliː/, Beniamino (1890–1957), Italian operatic tenor singer, who excelled as Rodolfo in La Bohème, the Duke of Mantua in Rigoletto, and Cavaradossi in Tosca. He made his Milan début with Toscanini in 1918, and still sang superbly in his tour of the US in 1955.

gigolo /'ʒɪgə,ləʊ, 'dʒɪg-/ n. (pl. **-os**) **1** a young man paid by an older woman to be her escort or lover. **2** a professional male dancing-partner or escort. [F, formed as masc. of *gigole* dance-hall woman]

gigot /'dʒɪgət/ n. a leg of mutton or lamb. □ **gigot sleeve** a leg-of-mutton sleeve. [F, dimin. of dial. *gigue* leg]

gigue /ʒiːg/ n. **1** = JIG 1. **2** *Mus.* a lively dance usu. in a dotted rhythm with two sections each repeated. [F: see JIG¹]

Gijón /hiː'hɔʊn/ a port and industrial city in northern Spain, on the Bay of Biscay; pop. (1986) 259,200.

Gila¹ /'hiːlə/ n. (in full **Gila monster**) a large venomous lizard, *Heloderma suspectum*, found in the southwestern US. [name of river in New Mexico and Arizona]

Gilbert¹ /'gɪlbət/, Sir Humphrey (c.1537–83), English explorer. After an active and distinguished career as a soldier in Ireland and The Netherlands Gilbert led an unsuccessful attempt to colonize the New World in 1578–9. On a second such voyage in 1583 he claimed Newfoundland for Elizabeth I and established a colony at St John's, but was lost on the trip homewards when his tiny vessel *The Squirrel* foundered in a storm off Nova Scotia.

Gilbert² /'gɪlbət/, Sir William Schwenck (1836–1911), English comic dramatist. He excelled as a writer of humorous verse, and his *Bab Ballads* (1866–73) were extremely popular. Between 1871 and 1896 he collaborated with the composer Sir Arthur Sullivan, writing the libretti for 14 comic operas.

Gilbert Islands /'gɪlbət/ a group of islands in the central Pacific, forming part of Kiribati.

gild¹ /gɪld/ v.tr. (*past part.* **gilded** or as adj. in sense 1 **gilt**) **1** cover thinly with gold. **2** tinge with a golden colour or light. **3** give a specious or false brilliance to. □ **gilded cage** luxurious but restrictive surroundings. **gilded youth** young people of wealth, fashion, and flair. **gild the lily** try to improve what is already beautiful or excellent. □□ **gilder** n. [OE *gyldan* f. Gmc]

gild² var. of GUILD.

gilding /'gɪldɪŋ/ n. **1** the act or art of applying gilt. **2** material used in applying gilt.

gilet /dʒɪ'leɪ/ n. a light often padded waistcoat, usu. worn for warmth by women. [F, = waistcoat]

gilgai /'gɪlgaɪ/ n. *Austral.* a saucer-like natural reservoir for rainwater. [Aboriginal]

Gilgamesh /'gɪlgə,meʃ/ a legendary king of the Sumerian city-state of Uruk in southern Mesopotamia some time during the first half of the 3rd millennium BC, and hero of the Gilgamesh epic, one of the best-known works of ancient literature. This epic, the latest version of which is mostly preserved on twelve tablets, inscribed in Akkadian, from the library of Ashurbanipal at Nineveh, recounts Gilgamesh's exploits in his ultimately unsuccessful quest for immortality. It contains an account of a flood that has close parallels with the biblical story of Noah.

Gilgit /'gɪlgɪt/ the chief town of the Gilgit region in the part of Kashmir that is ruled by Pakistan.

Gill /gɪl/, (Arthur) Eric (Rowton) (1882–1940), English sculptor, engraver, and typographer, whose best-known sculptures are the relief carvings *Stations of the Cross* (1914–18) at Westminster Cathedral and the *Prospero and Ariel* on Broadcasting House in London. He illustrated many books for the Golden Cockerell Press, and designed printing types for the Monotype Corporation.

gill¹ /gɪl/ n. & v. —n. (usu. in *pl.*) **1** the respiratory organ in fishes and other aquatic animals. **2** the vertical radial plates on the underside of mushrooms and other fungi. **3** the flesh below a person's jaws and ears (*green about the gills*). **4** the wattles or dewlap of fowls. —v.tr. **1** gut (a fish). **2** cut off the gills of (a mushroom). **3** catch in a gill-net. □ **gill-cover** a bony case protecting a fish's gills; an operculum. **gill-net** a net for entangling fishes by the gills. □□ **gilled** adj. (also in *comb.*). [ME f. ON *gil* (unrecorded) f. Gmc]

gill² /dʒɪl/ n. **1** a unit of liquid measure, equal to a quarter of a pint. **2** *Brit. dial.* half a pint. [ME f. OF *gille*, med.L *gillo* f. LL *gello*, *gillo* water-pot]

gill³ /gɪl/ n. (also **ghyll**) *Brit.* **1** a deep usu. wooded ravine. **2** a narrow mountain torrent. [ME f. ON *gil* glen]

gill⁴ /dʒɪl/ n. (also **Gill**, **jill**, **Jill**) **1** *derog.* a young woman. **2** *colloq.* or *dial.* a female ferret. [ME, abbr. of *Gillian* f. OF *Juliane* f. L *Juliana* (*Julius*)]

Gillespie /gɪ'lespɪ/, John Birks ('Dizzy') (1917–), American jazz trumpet-player, a leading exponent of the 'bop' style. After working with various other groups he formed his own in New York in 1944.

gillie /'gɪlɪ/ n. (also **ghillie**) *Sc.* **1** a man or boy attending a person hunting or fishing. **2** *hist.* a Highland chief's attendant. [Gael. *gille* lad, servant]

gillion /'dʒɪlɪən/ n. **1** a thousand million. **2** a large number. ¶ Mainly used to avoid the ambiguity of *billion*. [GIGA- + MILLION]

gillyflower /'dʒɪlɪ,flaʊə(r)/ n. **1** (in full **clove gillyflower**) a clove-scented pink (see CLOVE 2). **2** any of various similarly scented flowers such as the wallflower or white stock. [ME *gilofre*, *gerofle* f. OF *gilofre*, *girofle*, f. med.L f. Gk *karuophullon* clove-tree f. *karuon* nut + *phullon* leaf, assim. to FLOWER]

gilt¹ /gɪlt/ adj. & n. —adj. **1** covered thinly with gold. **2** gold-coloured. —n. **1** gold or a goldlike substance applied in a thin layer to a surface. **2** (often in *pl.*) a gilt-edged security. □ **gilt-edged 1** (of securities, stocks, etc.) having a high degree of reliability as an investment. **2** having a gilded edge. [past part. of GILD¹]

gilt² /gɪlt/ n. a young unbred sow. [ME f. ON *gyltr*]

gimbals /'dʒɪmb(ə)lz/ n.pl. a contrivance, usu. of rings and pivots, for keeping instruments such as a compass and chronometer horizontal at sea, in the air, etc. [var. of earlier *gimmal* f. OF *gemel* double finger-ring f. L *gemellus* dimin. of *geminus* twin]

gimcrack /'dʒɪmkræk/ adj. & n. —adj. showy but flimsy and worthless. —n. a cheap showy ornament; a knick-knack. □□ **gimcrackery** n. **gimcracky** adj. [ME *gibecrake* a kind of ornament, of unkn. orig.]

gimlet /'gɪmlɪt/ n. **1** a small tool with a screw-tip for boring holes. **2** a cocktail usu. of gin and lime-juice. □ **gimlet eye** an eye with a piercing glance. [ME f. OF *guimbelet*, dimin. of *guimble*]

gimmick /'gɪmɪk/ n. *colloq.* a trick or device, esp. to attract attention, publicity, or trade. □□ **gimmickry** n. **gimmicky** adj. [20th-c. US: orig. unkn.]

gimp¹ /gɪmp/ n. (also **guimp**, **gymp**) **1** a twist of silk etc. with cord or wire running through it, used esp. as trimming. **2** fishing-line of silk etc. bound with wire. **3** a coarser thread outlining the design of lace. [Du.: orig. unkn.]

gimp² /gɪmp/ n. *sl.* a lame person or leg.

gin¹ /dʒɪn/ n. an alcoholic spirit distilled from grain or malt and flavoured with juniper berries. (See below.) □ **gin rummy** a form of the card-game rummy. [abbr. of GENEVA]

The origin of gin is attributed to a professor of medicine, François de la Boë (d. 1672), at the university of Leyden in Holland: he distilled the juniper berry with spirits to produce a cheap diuretic medicine. The beverage became popular, and was brought to Britain by soldiers returning from the Low Countries. By the late 18th c. its excessive consumption had made it the scourge of the poor in London, until heavy taxation removed it from what they could afford. Netherlands gin has a strong grain flavour; English and US gins are based on spirit that is almost without flavour or aroma, to which flavouring agents are added.

gin² /dʒɪn/ n. & v. —n. **1** a snare or trap. **2** a machine for separating cotton from its seeds, first devised by the American inventor Eli Whitney in 1792. **3** a kind of crane and windlass. —v.tr. (**ginned**, **ginning**) **1** treat (cotton) in a gin. **2** trap. □□ **ginner** n. [ME f. OF *engin* ENGINE]

gin³ /dʒɪn/ n. *Austral.* an Aboriginal woman. [Aboriginal]

ginger /'dʒɪndʒə(r)/ n., adj., & v. —n. **1 a** a hot spicy root usu. powdered for use in cooking, or preserved in syrup, or candied. **b** the plant, *Zingiber officinale*, of SE Asia, having this root. **2** a light reddish-yellow colour. **3** spirit, mettle. **4** stimulation. —adj. of a ginger colour. —v.tr. **1** flavour with ginger. **2** (foll. by *up*) rouse or enliven. □ **black ginger** unscraped ginger. **ginger ale** an effervescent non-alcoholic clear drink flavoured with ginger extract. **ginger beer** an effervescent mildly alcoholic cloudy drink, made by fermenting a mixture of ginger and syrup. **ginger group** *Brit.* a group within a party or movement that presses for stronger or more radical policy or action. **ginger-nut** a ginger-flavoured biscuit. **ginger-pop** *colloq.* = *ginger ale.* **ginger-snap** a thin brittle biscuit flavoured with ginger. **ginger wine** a drink of fermented sugar, water, and bruised ginger. □□ **gingery** *adj.* [ME f. OE *gingiber* & OF *gingi(m)bre*, both f. med.L *gingiber* ult. f. Skr. *śṛṅgaveram* f. *śṛṅgam* horn + *-vera* body, with ref. to the antler-shape of the root]

gingerbread /'dʒɪndʒəˌbred/ *n.* **1** a cake made with treacle or syrup and flavoured with ginger. **2** (often *attrib.*) a gaudy or tawdry decoration or ornament.

gingerly /'dʒɪndʒəlɪ/ *adv. & adj.* —*adv.* in a careful or cautious manner. —*adj.* showing great care or caution. □□ **gingerliness** *n.* [perh. f. OF *gensor* delicate, compar. of *gent* graceful f. L *genitus* (well-)born]

gingham /'gɪŋəm/ *n.* a plain-woven cotton cloth esp. striped or checked. [Du. *gingang* f. Malay *ginggang* (orig. adj. = striped)]

gingili /'dʒɪndʒɪlɪ/ *n.* **1** sesame. **2** sesame oil. [Hindi *jinjalī* f. Arab. *juljulān*]

gingiva /'dʒɪndʒɪvə/ *n.* (*pl.* **gingivae** /-ˌviː/) the gum. □□ **gingival** /-ˈdʒaɪv(ə)l/ *adj.* [L]

gingivitis /ˌdʒɪndʒɪ'vaɪtɪs/ *n.* inflammation of the gums.

gingko var. of GINKGO.

ginglymus /'dʒɪŋglɪməs/ *n.* (*pl.* **ginglymi** /-ˌmaɪ/) *Anat.* a hinge-like joint in the body with motion in one plane only, e.g. the elbow or knee. [mod.L f. Gk *gigglumos* hinge]

gink /gɪŋk/ *n. sl.* often *derog.* a fellow; a man. [20th-c. US: orig. unkn.]

ginkgo /'gɪŋkgəʊ/ *n.* (also **gingko** /'gɪŋkəʊ/) (*pl.* **-os** or **-oes**) an orig. Chinese and Japanese tree, *Ginkgo biloba*, with fan-shaped leaves and yellow flowers. Also called *maidenhair tree*. [Jap. *ginkyo* f. Chin. *yinxing* silver apricot]

ginormous /dʒaɪ'nɔːməs/ *adj. Brit. sl.* very large; enormous. [GIANT + ENORMOUS]

ginseng /'dʒɪnseŋ/ *n.* **1** any of several medicinal plants of the genus *Panax*, found in E. Asia and N. America. **2** the root of this. [Chin. *renshen* perh. = man-image, with allusion to its forked root]

Giorgione /ˌdʒɔːdʒɪ'əʊnɪ/, Giorgio Barbarelli or Giorgio del Castelfranco (*c.*1478–1510), Venetian painter, a pivotal figure in the Renaissance in Venice, though the definite details of his life and work are tantalizingly few. According to Vasari he developed a new method of painting, without preliminary drawing; many of his works were easel pictures for private collectors, enigmatic in subject and mood. His pupils included Titian and Sebastiano del Piombo, who are said to have completed some of his works when he died suddenly, of plague, in 1510. Many 'Giorgionesque' paintings were produced after his death, as a result of the unsatisfied demand for his work, and there is now a great discrepancy between the many paintings attributed to him and the few that are undoubtedly of his hand.

Giotto di Bondone /ˌdʒɒtəʊ dɪ bɒn'dəʊnɪ/ (*c.*1267–1337), Florentine painter, an important figure in the birth of modern painting, since he moved away from the stylized two-dimensional stereotypes of Italo-Byzantine art in the direction of naturalism and human expression. The frescos of the *Life of St Francis* in Assisi (1297–*c.*1305), long thought to be by Giotto, are now considered of doubtful attribution, but the cycle in the Arena Chapel, Padua (1305–8), with its revolutionary rejection of medieval formulae in composition, is unchallenged. Giotto was famous in his own day, was court painter in Naples 1329–33, and in 1334 was made overseer of works for the cathedral in Florence.

gippy tummy /'dʒɪpɪ/ *n.* (also **gyppy tummy**) *colloq.* diarrhoea affecting visitors to hot countries. [abbr. of EGYPTIAN]

gipsy var. of GYPSY.

giraffe /dʒɪ'rɑːf, -'ræf/ *n.* (*pl.* same or **giraffes**) a ruminant mammal, *Giraffa camelopardalis* of Africa, the tallest living animal, with a long neck and forelegs and a skin of dark patches separated by lighter lines. [F *girafe*, It. *giraffa*, ult. f. Arab. *zarāfa*]

girandole /'dʒɪrənˌdəʊl/ *n.* **1** a revolving cluster of fireworks. **2** a branched candle-bracket or candlestick. **3** an earring or pendant with a large central stone surrounded by small ones. [F f. It. *girandola* f. *girare* GYRATE]

girasol /'dʒɪrəˌsɒl/ *n.* (also **girasole** /-ˌsəʊl/) a kind of opal reflecting a reddish glow; a fire-opal. [orig. = sunflower, f. F *girasol* or It. *girasole* f. *girare* (as GIRANDOLE) + *sole* sun]

gird[1] /gɜːd/ *v.tr.* (*past* and *past part.* **girded** or **girt**) *literary* **1** encircle, attach, or secure with a belt or band. **2** secure (clothes) on the body with a girdle or belt. **3** enclose or encircle. **4 a** (foll. by *with*) equip with a sword in a belt. **b** fasten (a sword) with a belt. **5** (foll. by *round*) place (cord etc.) round. □ **gird** (or **gird up**) **one's loins** prepare for action. [OE *gyrdan* f. Gmc (as GIRTH)]

gird[2] /gɜːd/ *v. & n.* —*v.intr.* (foll. by *at*) jeer or gibe. —*n.* a gibe or taunt. [ME, = strike etc.: orig. unkn.]

girder /'gɜːdə(r)/ *n.* a large iron or steel beam or compound structure for bearing loads, esp. in bridge-building. [GIRD[1] + -ER[1]]

girdle[1] /'gɜːd(ə)l/ *n. & v.* —*n.* **1** a belt or cord worn round the waist. **2** a woman's corset extending from waist to thigh. **3** a thing that surrounds like a girdle. **4** the bony support for a limb (*pelvic girdle*). **5** the part of a cut gem dividing the crown from the base and embraced by the setting. **6** a ring round a tree made by the removal of bark. —*v.tr.* **1** surround with a girdle. **2** remove a ring of bark from (a tree), esp. to make it more fruitful. [OE *gyrdel* f. *gyrd* GIRD[1]]

girdle[2] /'gɜːd(ə)l/ *n. Sc. & N.Engl.* a circular iron plate placed over a fire or otherwise heated for baking, toasting, etc. [var. of GRIDDLE]

girl /gɜːl/ *n.* **1** a female child or youth. **2** *colloq.* a young (esp. unmarried) woman. **3** *colloq.* a girlfriend or sweetheart. **4** a female servant. □ **girl Friday** see FRIDAY. **Girl Scout** a member of the American organization corresponding to the Girl Guides Association (see entry). □□ **girlhood** *n.* [ME *gurle*, *girle*, *gerle*, perh. rel. to LG *gör* child]

girlfriend /'gɜːlfrend/ *n.* **1** a regular female companion or lover. **2** a female friend.

Girl Guides Association an organization for girls, corresponding to the Scout Association, established in 1910 by (Sir) Robert Baden-Powell and his sister Agnes (1858–1945). The three sections into which it is divided, originally Brownies, Guides, and Rangers, are now called Brownie Guides (7–11 years), Guides (10–16 years), and Ranger Guides (14–19 years). In the US, where they were formed in 1912, members are known as Girl Scouts.

girlie /'gɜːlɪ/ *adj. colloq.* (of a magazine etc.) depicting nude or partially nude young women in erotic poses.

girlish /'gɜːlɪʃ/ *adj.* of or like a girl. □□ **girlishly** *adv.* **girlishness** *n.*

giro /'dʒaɪrəʊ/ *n. & v.* —*n.* (*pl.* **-os**) **1** a system of credit transfer between banks, post offices, etc. **2** a cheque or payment by giro. —*v.tr.* (**-oes**, **-oed**) pay by giro. [G f. It., = circulation (of money)]

Gironde /ʒɪ'rɒnd/ a river estuary in SW France, formed at the junction of the Garonne and Dordogne rivers.

Girondist /dʒɪ'rɒndɪst/ *n.* a member of the moderate republican party in the French Assembly 1791–3. Its leaders were the deputies from the department of the Gironde. [F *Girondiste* (now *Girondin*)]

girt[1] *past part.* of GIRD[1].

girt[2] var. of GIRTH.

girth /gɜːθ/ *n. & v.* (also **girt** /gɜːt/) —*n.* **1** the distance around a thing. **2** a band round the body of a horse to secure the saddle etc. —*v.* **1** *tr.* **a** secure (a saddle etc.) with a girth. **b** put a girth on (a horse). **2** *tr.* surround, encircle. **3** *intr.* measure (an amount) in girth. [ME f. ON *gjörth*, Goth. *gairda* f. Gmc]

Gisborne /'gɪzbəːn/ a seaport and resort on the East Cape of North Island, New Zealand; pop. (1988) 32,000.

Gish /gɪʃ/, Lillian (1896–), American stage and film actress. She and her sister Dorothy (1898–1968) appeared in a number of D. W. Griffith's films, including *Hearts of the World* (1918) and *Orphans of the Storm* (1922).

gismo /'gɪzməʊ/ *n.* (also **gizmo**) (*pl.* **-os**) *sl.* a gadget. [20th c.: orig. unkn.]

Gissing /'gɪsɪŋ/, George Robert (1857–1903), English writer, whose own experiences of poverty and failure provided material for his stories. His most famous novels are *New Grub Street* (1891), *Born in Exile* (1892), and *The Private Papers of Henry Ryecroft* (1903).

gist /dʒɪst/ *n.* **1** the substance or essence of a matter. **2** *Law* the real ground of an action etc. [OF, 3rd sing. pres. of *gesir* lie f. L *jacēre*]

git /gɪt/ *n. Brit. sl.* a silly or contemptible person. [var. of GET *n.*]

gîte /ʒiːt/ *n.* a furnished holiday house in France, usu. small and in a rural district. [orig. = lodging: F f. OF *giste*, rel. to *gésir* lie]

Gitega /gɪˈteɪgə/ a city of Burundi, formerly a royal residence of the Tutsi kingdom; pop. (1986) 95,300.

gittern /ˈgɪt(ə)n/ *n.* a medieval stringed instrument, a forerunner of the guitar. [ME f. OF *guiterne*: cf. CITTERN, GUITAR]

give /gɪv/ *v. & n.* —*v.* (*past* **gave** /geɪv/; *past part.* **given** /ˈgɪv(ə)n/) **1** *tr.* (also *absol.*; often foll. by *to*) transfer the possession of freely; hand over as a present (*gave them her old curtains*; *gives to cancer research*). **2** *tr.* **a** transfer the ownership of with or without actual delivery; bequeath (*gave him £200 in her will*). **b** transfer, esp. temporarily or for safe keeping; hand over; provide with (*gave him the dog to hold*; *gave them a drink*). **c** administer (medicine). **d** deliver (a message) (*give her my best wishes*). **3** *tr.* (usu. foll. by *for*) make over in exchange or payment; pay; sell (*gave him £30 for the bicycle*). **4** *tr.* **a** confer; grant (a benefit, an honour, etc.). **b** accord; bestow (one's affections, confidence, etc.). **c** award; administer (one's approval, blame, etc.); tell, offer (esp. something unpleasant) (*gave him a talking-to*; *gave me my blessing*; *gave him the sack*). **d** pledge, assign as a guarantee (*gave his word*). **5** *tr.* **a** effect or perform (an action etc.) (*gave him a kiss*; *gave a jump*). **b** utter (*gave a shriek*). **6** *tr.* allot; assign; grant (*was given the contract*). **7** *tr.* (in *passive*; foll. by *to*) be inclined to or fond of (*is given to speculation*). **8** *tr.* yield as a product or result (*the lamp gives a bad light*; *the field gives fodder for twenty cows*). **9** *intr.* **a** yield to pressure; become relaxed; lose firmness (*this elastic doesn't give properly*). **b** collapse (*the roof gave under the pressure*). **10** *intr.* (usu. foll. by *of*) grant; bestow (*gave freely of his time*). **11** *tr.* **a** commit, consign, or entrust (*gave him into custody*; *give her into your care*). **b** sanction the marriage of (a daughter etc.). **12** *tr.* devote; dedicate (*gave his life to table tennis*; *shall give it my attention*). **13** *tr.* (usu. *absol.*) *colloq.* tell what one knows (*What happened? Come on, give!*). **14** *tr.* present; offer; show; hold out (*gives no sign of life*; *gave her his arm*; *give him your ear*). **15** *tr. Theatr.* read, recite, perform, act, etc. (*gave them Hamlet's soliloquy*). **16** *tr.* impart; be a source of (*gave him my sore throat*; *gave its name to the battle*; *gave me much pain*; *gives him a right to complain*). **17** *tr.* allow (esp. a fixed amount of time) (*can give you five minutes*). **18** *tr.* (usu. foll. by *for*) value (something) (*gives nothing for their opinions*). **19** *tr.* concede; yield (*I give you the victory*). **20** *tr.* deliver (a judgement etc.) authoritatively (*gave his verdict*). **21** *tr. Cricket* (of an umpire) declare (a batsman) out or not out. **22** *tr.* toast (a person, cause, etc.) (*I give you our President*). **23** *tr.* provide (a party, meal, etc.) as host (*gave a banquet*). —*n.* **1** capacity to yield or bend under pressure; elasticity (*there is no give in a stone floor*). **2** ability to adapt or comply (*no give in his attitudes*). □ **give and take** *v.tr.* exchange (words, blows, or concessions). —*n.* an exchange of words etc.; a compromise. **give as good as one gets** retort adequately in words or blows. **give away 1** transfer as a gift. **2** hand over (a bride) ceremonially to a bridegroom. **3** betray or expose to ridicule or detection. **4** *Austral.* abandon, desist from, give up, lose faith or interest in. **give-away** *n. colloq.* **1** an inadvertent betrayal or revelation. **2** an act of giving away. **3** a free gift; a low price. **give back** return (something) to its previous owner or in exchange. **give a person the best** see BEST. **give birth (to)** see BIRTH. **give chase** pursue a person, animal, etc.; hunt. **give down** (often *absol.*) (of a cow) let (milk) flow. **give forth** emit; publish; report. **give the game (or show) away** reveal a secret or intention. **give a hand** see HAND. **give a person (or the devil) his or her due** acknowledge, esp. grudgingly, a person's rights, abilities, etc. **give in 1** cease fighting or arguing; yield. **2** hand in (a document etc.) to an official etc. **give in marriage** sanction the marriage of (one's daughter etc.). **give it to a person** *colloq.* scold or punish. **give me** I prefer or admire (*give me the Greek islands*). **give off** emit (vapour etc.). **give oneself** (of a woman) yield sexually. **give oneself airs** act pretentiously or snobbishly. **give oneself up to 1** abandon oneself to an emotion, esp. despair. **2** addict oneself to. **give on to** (or **into**) (of a window, corridor, etc.) overlook or lead into. **give or take** *colloq.* add or subtract (a specified amount or number) in estimating. **give out 1** announce; emit; distribute. **2** cease or break down from exhaustion etc. **3** run short. **give over 1** *colloq.* cease from doing; abandon (a habit etc.); desist (*give over sniffing*). **2** hand over. **3** devote. **give rise to** cause, induce, suggest. **give tongue 1** speak one's thoughts. **2** (of hounds) bark, esp. on finding a scent. **give a person to understand** inform authoritatively. **give up 1** resign; surrender. **2** part with. **3** deliver (a wanted person etc.). **4** pronounce incurable or insoluble; renounce hope of. **5** renounce or cease (an activity). **give up the ghost** *archaic* or *colloq.* die. **give way** see WAY. **give a person what for** *colloq.* punish or scold severely. **give one's word** (or **word of honour** etc.) promise solemnly. **not give a damn** (or **monkey's** or **toss** etc.) *colloq.* not care at all. **what gives?** *colloq.* what is the news?; what's happening? **would give the world** (or **one's ears**, **eyes**, etc.) **for** covet or wish for desperately. □□ **giveable** *adj.* **giver** *n.* [OE *g(i)efan* f. Gmc]

given /ˈgɪv(ə)n/ *adj. & n.* —*adj.* **1** as previously stated or assumed; granted; specified (*given that he is a liar, we cannot trust him*; *a given number of people*). **2** *Law* (of a document) signed and dated (*given this day the 30th June*). —*n.* a known fact or situation. □ **given name** *US* a name given at, or as if at, baptism; a Christian name. [past part. of GIVE]

Giza /ˈgiːzə/, **El** a city south-west of Cairo in northern Egypt, on the west bank of the Nile, site of the pyramids of Khufu, Khephren, and Menkaure, and of the great sphinx; pop. (est. 1986) 1,670,800.

gizmo var. of GISMO.

gizzard /ˈgɪzəd/ *n.* **1** the second part of a bird's stomach, for grinding food usu. with grit. **2** a muscular stomach of some fish, insects, molluscs, and other invertebrates. □ **stick in one's gizzard** *colloq.* be distasteful. [ME *giser* f. OF *giser, gesier* etc., ult. f. L *gigeria* cooked entrails of fowl]

glabella /gləˈbelə/ *n.* (*pl.* **glabellae** /-liː/) the smooth part of the forehead above and between the eyebrows. □□ **glabellar** *adj.* [mod.L f. L *glabellus* (adj.) dimin. of *glaber* smooth]

glabrous /ˈgleɪbrəs/ *adj.* free from hair or down; smooth skinned. [L *glaber glabri* hairless]

glacé /ˈglæseɪ/ *adj.* **1** (of fruit, esp. cherries) preserved in sugar, usu. resulting in a glossy surface. **2** (of cloth, leather, etc.) smooth; polished. □ **glacé icing** icing made with icing sugar and water. [F, past part. of *glacer* to ice, gloss f. *glace* ice: see GLACIER]

glacial /ˈgleɪʃ(ə)l, -sɪəl/ *adj.* **1** of ice; icy. **2** *Geol.* characterized or produced by the presence or agency of ice. **3** *Chem.* forming icelike crystals upon freezing (*glacial acetic acid*). □□ **glacially** *adv.* [F *glacial* or L *glacialis* icy f. *glacies* ice]

glacial period *n.* a period in the earth's history characterized by an unusual extension of polar and mountain ice-sheets over the earth's surface. The Pleistocene and the preceding Pliocene epoch included a number of such periods, interrupted by warmer phases called interglacials, and it may be that the climate of the present day represents such a warm phase and that another ice age is to follow. During the coldest time, about 18,000 years ago, extensive ice-sheets covered much of Europe, North America, and Asia, and sea levels were up to 200 metres lower than they are today. In the southern hemisphere glaciation was less extensive owing to the isolation of the Antarctic ice-sheet from the other southern continents. Although the glacial periods of the Pleistocene epoch are the most important in terms of their effect upon present-day topography, there is evidence of earlier glaciations in Palaeozoic and Precambrian times. Their causes are not fully understood but it is thought that their onset may be affected by the position of the continents relative to the pole and by small variations in the brightness of the sun.

glaciated /ˈgleɪsɪˌeɪtɪd, ˈglæs-/ *adj.* **1** marked or polished by the action of ice. **2** covered or having been covered by glaciers or

b but d dog f few g get h he j yes k cat l leg m man n no p pen r red s sit t top v voice

ice sheets. □□ **glaciation** /-'eɪʃ(ə)n/ n. [past part. of *glaciate* f. L *glaciare* freeze f. *glacies* ice]

glacier /'glæsɪə(r)/ n. a mass of land ice formed by the accumulation of snow on high ground. [F f. *glace* ice ult. f. L *glacies*]

glaciology /ˌgleɪsɪ'ɒlədʒɪ/ n. the science of the internal dynamics and effects of glaciers. □□ **glaciological** /-ə'lɒdʒɪk(ə)l/ adj. **glaciologist** n. [L *glacies* ice + -LOGY]

glacis /'glæsɪs, -siː/ n. (pl. same /-sɪz, -siːz/) a bank sloping down from a fort, on which attackers are exposed to the defenders' missiles etc. [F f. OF *glacier* to slip f. *glace* ice: see GLACIER]

glad[1] /glæd/ adj. & v. —adj. (**gladder, gladdest**) **1** (predic.; usu. foll. by *of, about,* or *to* + infin.) pleased; willing (*shall be glad to come; would be glad of a chance to talk about it*). **2 a** marked by, filled with, or expressing, joy (*a glad expression*). **b** (of news, events, etc.) giving joy (*glad tidings*). **3** (of objects) bright; beautiful. —v.tr. (**gladded, gladding**) *archaic* make glad. □ **the glad eye** *colloq.* an amorous glance. **glad hand** the hand of welcome. **glad-hand** v.tr. greet cordially; welcome. **glad rags** *colloq.* best clothes; evening dress. □□ **gladly** adv. **gladness** n. **gladsome** adj. *poet.* [OE *glæd* f. Gmc]

glad[2] /glæd/ n. (also *Austral.* **gladdie** /'glædɪ/) *colloq.* a gladiolus. [abbr.]

gladden /'glæd(ə)n/ v.tr. & intr. make or become glad. □□ **gladdener** n.

gladdie *Austral.* var. of GLAD[2].

glade /gleɪd/ n. an open space in a wood or forest. [16th c.: orig. unkn.]

gladiator /'glædɪˌeɪtə(r)/ n. **1** *hist.* a man trained to fight with a sword or other weapons at ancient Roman shows. **2** a person defending or opposing a cause; a controversialist. □□ **gladiatorial** /-ɪə'tɔːrɪəl/ adj. [L f. *gladius* sword]

gladiolus /ˌglædɪ'əʊləs/ n. (pl. **gladioli** /-laɪ/ or **gladioluses**) any iridaceous plant of the genus *Gladiolus* with sword-shaped leaves and usu. brightly coloured flower-spikes. [L, dimin. of *gladius* sword]

Gladstone /'glædst(ə)n/, William Ewart (1809–98), British statesman. After an early career as a Conservative minister, Gladstone joined the Liberal Party and succeeded Russell as its leader in 1867. Prime Minister on four separate occasions (1868–74, 1880–5, 1886, and 1892–4), Gladstone dominated British political life in the second half of the 19th c. His career was particularly notable for his rivalry with his Conservative opposite number, Disraeli, the long series of social and political reforms he was responsible for introducing (of which Cardwell's army reforms, the Irish Land Acts, and the third Reform Act are important examples) and for his conversion to Home Rule for Ireland, which led to the defection of the Unionists from the Liberal Party.

Gladstone bag /'glædst(ə)n/ n. a bag having two equal compartments joined by a hinge. [W. E. GLADSTONE]

Glagolitic /ˌglægə'lɪtɪk/ adj. of or relating to an alphabet, based largely on Greek minuscules, formerly used in writing some Slavonic languages. It was introduced about the same time as Cyrillic (9th c.), and may have been devised by St Cyril, but its origin is obscure. [mod.L *glagoliticus* f. Serbo-Croatian *glagolica* Glagolitic alphabet f. OSlav. *glagol* word]

glair /gleə(r)/ n. (also **glaire**) **1** white of egg. **2** an adhesive preparation made from this, used in bookbinding etc. □□ **glaireous** adj. **glairy** adj. [ME f. OF *glaire,* ult. f. L *clara* fem. of *clarus* clear]

glaire var. of GLAIR.

glaive /gleɪv/ n. *archaic poet.* **1** a broadsword. **2** any sword. [ME f. OF, app. f. L *gladius* sword]

Glam. *abbr.* Glamorgan.

glam /glæm/ adj., n., & v. *colloq.* —adj. glamorous. —n. glamour. —v.tr. (**glammed, glamming**) glamorize. [abbr.]

glamorize /'glæməˌraɪz/ v.tr. (also **glamourize, -ise**) make glamorous or attractive. □□ **glamorization** /-'zeɪʃ(ə)n/ n.

glamour /'glæmə(r)/ n. & v. (*US* **glamor**) —n. **1** physical attractiveness, esp. when achieved by make-up etc. **2** alluring or exciting beauty or charm (*the glamour of New York*). —v.tr. **1** *poet.* affect

with glamour; bewitch; enchant. **2** *colloq.* make glamorous. □ **cast a glamour over** enchant. **glamour girl** (or **boy**) an attractive young woman (or man), esp. a model etc. □□ **glamorous** adj. **glamorously** adv. [18th c.: var. of GRAMMAR in obs. sense 'magic', with ref. to the occult practices associated with learning in the Middle Ages]

glance[1] /glɑːns/ v. & n. —v. **1** *intr.* (often foll. by *down, up,* etc.) cast a momentary look (*glanced up at the sky*). **2** *intr.* (often foll. by *off*) (esp. of a weapon) glide or bounce (off an object). **3** *intr.* (usu. foll. by *over, off, from*) (of talk or a talker) pass quickly over a subject or subjects (*glanced over the question of payment*). **4** *intr.* (of a bright object or light) flash, dart, or gleam; reflect (*the sun glanced off the knife*). **5** *tr.* (esp. of a weapon) strike (an object) obliquely. **6** *tr. Cricket* deflect (the ball) with an oblique stroke. —n. **1** (usu. foll. by *at, into, over,* etc.) a brief look (*took a glance at the paper; threw a glance over her shoulder*). **2 a** a flash or gleam (*a glance of sunlight*). **b** a sudden movement producing this. **3** a swift oblique movement or impact. **4** *Cricket* a stroke with the bat's face turned slantwise to deflect the ball. □ **at a glance** immediately upon looking. **glance at 1** give a brief look at. **2** make a passing and usu. sarcastic allusion to. **glance one's eye** (foll. by *at, over,* etc.) look at briefly (esp. a document). **glance over** (or **through**) read cursorily. □□ **glancingly** adv. [ME *glence* etc., prob. a nasalized form of obs. *glace* in the same sense, f. OF *glacier* to slip: see GLACIS]

glance[2] /glɑːns/ n. any lustrous sulphide ore (*copper glance; lead glance*). [G *Glanz* lustre]

gland[1] /glænd/ n. **1 a** an organ in an animal body secreting substances for use in the body or for ejection. **b** a structure resembling this, such as a lymph gland. **2** *Bot.* a secreting cell or group of cells on the surface of a plant-structure. [F *glande* f. OF *glandre* f. L *glandulae* throat-glands]

gland[2] /glænd/ n. a sleeve used to produce a seal round a moving shaft. [19th c.: perh. var. of *glam, glan* a vice, rel. to CLAMP[1]]

glanders /'glændəz/ n.pl. (also treated as *sing.*) **1** a contagious disease of horses, caused by a bacterium and characterized by swellings below the jaw and mucous discharge from the nostrils. **2** this disease in humans or other animals. □□ **glandered** adj. **glanderous** adj. [OF *glandre:* see GLAND[1]]

glandular /'glændjʊlə(r)/ adj. of or relating to a gland or glands. □ **glandular fever** an infectious viral disease characterized by swelling of the lymph glands and prolonged lassitude, infectious mononucleosis (see MONONUCLEOSIS). [F *glandulaire* (as GLAND[1])]

glans /glænz/ n. (pl. **glandes** /'glændiːz/) the rounded part forming the end of the penis or clitoris. [L, = acorn]

glare[1] /gleə(r)/ v. & n. —v. **1** *intr.* (usu. foll. by *at, upon*) look fiercely or fixedly. **2** *intr.* shine dazzlingly or disagreeably. **3** *tr.* express (hate, defiance, etc.) by a look. **4** *intr.* be over-conspicuous or obtrusive. —n. **1 a** a strong fierce light, esp. sunshine. **b** oppressive public attention (*the glare of fame*). **2** a fierce or fixed look (*a glare of defiance*). **3** tawdry brilliance. □□ **glary** adj. [ME, prob. ult. rel. to GLASS: cf. MDu. and MLG *glaren* gleam, glare]

glare[2] /gleə(r)/ adj. *US* (esp. of ice) smooth and glassy. [perh. f. *glare* frost (16th c., of uncert. orig.)]

glaring /'gleərɪŋ/ adj. **1** obvious, conspicuous (*a glaring error*). **2** shining oppressively. **3** staring fiercely. □□ **glaringly** adv. **glaringness** n.

Glasgow /'glæsgəʊ/ the largest city in Scotland; pop. (est. 1987) 715,600. Situated on the River Clyde, the city owes its growth successively to the tobacco, cotton, iron and steel, and shipbuilding industries. Although these industries are no longer of major significance, Glasgow has remained an important commercial centre.

glasnost /'glæznɒst, 'glɑːs-/ n. the policy or practice of more open consultative government and wider dissemination of information, esp. in the Soviet Union since 1985. [Russ. *glasnost',* lit. = publicity, openness]

glass /glɑːs/ n., v., & adj. —n. **1 a** (often *attrib.*) a hard, brittle, usu. transparent, translucent, or shiny substance, made by fusing sand with soda and lime and sometimes other ingredients (*a glass jug*). (See below; also *crown glass, flint glass, plate glass.*) **b** a substance of similar properties or composition. **2** (often *collect.*)

an object or objects made from, or partly from, glass, esp.: **a** a drinking vessel. **b** a mirror; a looking-glass. **c** an hour- or sand-glass. **d** a window. **e** a greenhouse (*rows of lettuce under glass*). **f** glass ornaments. **g** a barometer. **h** a glass disc covering a watch-face. **i** a magnifying lens. **j** a monocle. **3** (in *pl.*) **a** spectacles. **b** field-glasses; opera-glasses. **4** the amount of liquid contained in a glass; a drink (*he likes a glass*). —*v.tr.* **1** (usu. as **glassed** *adj.*) fit with glass; glaze. **2** *poet.* reflect as in a mirror. **3** *Mil.* look at or for with field-glasses. —*adj.* of or made from glass. □ **crown glass** glass which contains no lead or iron, was formerly used in windows and is now used as an optical glass of low refractive index. **flint glass** a pure and lustrous glass, originally made with flint, invented in 1674 by George Ravenscroft. **glass-blower** a person who blows semi-molten glass to make glassware. **glass-blowing** this occupation. **glass case** an exhibition display case made mostly from glass. **glass-cloth 1** a linen cloth for drying glasses. **2** a cloth covered with powdered glass or abrasive, like glass-paper. **glass cloth** a woven fabric of fine-spun glass. **glass-cutter 1** a worker who cuts glass. **2** a tool used for cutting glass. **glass eye** a false eye made from glass. **glass fibre 1** a filament or filaments of glass made into fabric. **2** such filaments embedded in plastic as reinforcement. **glass-gall** = SANDIVER. **glass-making** the manufacture of glass. **glass-paper** paper covered with glass-dust or abrasive and used for smoothing and polishing. **glass snake** any snakelike lizard of the genus *Ophisaurus*, with a very brittle tail. **glass wool** glass in the form of fine fibres used for packing and insulation. **has had a glass too much** is rather drunk. **plate glass** thick fine-quality glass used for shop windows, originally cast in plates, rolled through heated rollers, then ground and polished, until about 1959 when the float process was introduced (saving labour and space but introducing a rich variety of technological and scientific problems), in which the glass is drawn in a continuous sheet from the melting-tank and made to float on the surface of molten metal while it hardens. Its surface has a brilliant finish and is perfectly true because it has not been in contact, when soft, with anything but a liquid. □□ **glassful** *n.* (*pl.* -**fuls**). **glassless** *adj.* **glasslike** *adj.* [OE *glæs* f. Gmc: cf. GLAZE]

Glass has the property of being smoothly and reversibly converted to a liquid by the application of heat. The art of producing a vitreous surface on stone or clay was known in ancient Egypt. Objects composed entirely of glass paste begin to appear there *c.*1500 BC, when two allied processes seem to have been in use: modelling molten glass about a removable core of sand, and pressing it into an open mould. The invention of glass-blowing in the 1st c. BC (probably in Syria) wrought a profound change in the glass industry which, hitherto limited to luxury articles, now became capable of cheap mass production. Window glass, made by a primitive process of rolling, was known at Pompeii and later became common. Because of its special properties of transparency and resistance to corrosion glass has found widespread uses for windows, food containers, chemical apparatus, and optical lenses.

glasshouse /ˈglɑːshaʊs/ *n.* **1** a greenhouse. **2** *Brit. sl.* a military prison. **3** a building where glass is made.

glassie var. of GLASSY *n.*

glassine /ˈglɑːsiːn/ *n.* a glossy transparent paper. [GLASS]

glassware /ˈglɑːsweə(r)/ *n.* articles made from glass, esp. drinking glasses, tableware, etc.

glasswort /ˈglɑːswɜːt/ *n.* any plant of the genus *Salicornia* or *Salsola* formerly burnt for use in glass-making.

glassy /ˈglɑːsɪ/ *adj.* & *n.* —*adj.* (**glassier, glassiest**) **1** of or resembling glass, esp. in smoothness. **2** (of the eye, the expression, etc.) abstracted; dull; fixed (*fixed her with a glassy stare*). —*n.* (also **glassie**) *Austral.* a glass marble. □ **the** (or **just the**) **glassy** *Austral.* the most excellent person or thing. □□ **glassily** *adv.* **glassiness** *n.*

Glastonbury /ˈglæstənbərɪ/ the site in Somerset of the abbey supposed to have been founded by Joseph of Arimathea, and of the legendary resting-place of King Arthur and his queen Guinevere. It was also identified in medieval times with the legendary Avalon.

Glaswegian /glæzˈwiːdʒ(ə)n, glɑː-/ *adj.* & *n.* —*adj.* of or relating to Glasgow. —*n.* a native or citizen of Glasgow. [*Glasgow* after *Norwegian* etc.]

Glauber's salt /ˈglaʊbə(r)z, ˈglɔː-/ *n.* (also **Glauber's salts**) a crystalline hydrated form of sodium sulphate used esp. as a laxative. [J. R. *Glauber*, Ger. chemist d. 1668]

glaucoma /glɔːˈkəʊmə/ *n.* an eye-condition with increased pressure within the eyeball, causing gradual loss of sight. □□ **glaucomatous** *adj.* [L f. Gk *glaukōma* -*atos*, ult. f. *glaukos*: see GLAUCOUS]

glaucous /ˈglɔːkəs/ *adj.* **1** of a dull greyish green or blue. **2** covered with a powdery bloom as of grapes. [L *glaucus* f. Gk *glaukos*]

glaze /gleɪz/ *v.* & *n.* —*v.* **1** *tr.* **a** fit (a window, picture, etc.) with glass. **b** provide (a building) with glass windows. **2** *tr.* **a** cover (pottery etc.) with a glaze. **b** fix (paint) on pottery with a glaze. **3** *tr.* cover (pastry, meat, etc.) with a glaze. **4** *intr.* (often foll. by *over*) (of the eyes) become fixed or glassy (*his eyes glazed over*). **5** *tr.* cover (cloth, paper, leather, a painted surface, etc.) with a glaze. **6** *tr.* give a glassy surface to, e.g. by rubbing. —*n.* **1** a vitreous substance, usu. a special glass, used to glaze pottery. **2** a smooth shiny coating of milk, sugar, gelatine, etc., on food. **3** a thin topcoat of transparent paint used to modify the tone of the underlying colour. **4** a smooth surface formed by glazing. **5** *US* a thin coating of ice. □ **glazed frost** a glassy coating of ice caused by frozen rain or a sudden thaw succeeded by a frost. **glaze in** enclose (a building, a window frame, etc.) with glass. □□ **glazer** *n.* **glazy** *adj.* [ME f. an oblique form of GLASS]

glazier /ˈgleɪzjə(r)/ *n.* a person whose trade is glazing windows etc. □□ **glaziery** *n.*

glazing /ˈgleɪzɪŋ/ *n.* **1** the act or an instance of glazing. **2** windows (see also *double glazing*). **3** material used to produce a glaze.

Glazunov /ˈglæzʊˌnɒf/, Alexander Konstantinovich (1865–1936), Russian composer, a pupil of Rimsky-Korsakov 1880–1. His works were influenced by Liszt and Wagner; they include orchestral and chamber music, songs, and the ballet *The Seasons* (1901).

GLC *abbr. hist.* (in the UK) Greater London Council (1963–86).

gleam /gliːm/ *n.* & *v.* —*n.* **1** a faint or brief light (*a gleam of sunlight*). **2** a faint, sudden, intermittent, or temporary show (*not a gleam of hope*). —*v.intr.* **1** emit gleams. **2** shine with a faint or intermittent brightness. **3** (of a quality) be indicated (*fear gleamed in his eyes*). □□ **gleamingly** *adv.* **gleamy** *adj.* [OE *glǣm*: cf. GLIMMER]

glean /gliːn/ *v.* **1** *tr.* collect or scrape together (news, facts, gossip, etc.) in small quantities. **2 a** *tr.* (also *absol.*) gather (ears of corn etc.) after the harvest. **b** *tr.* strip (a field etc.) after a harvest. □□ **gleaner** *n.* [ME f. OF *glener* f. LL *glennare*, prob. of Celt. orig.]

gleanings /ˈgliːnɪŋz/ *n.pl.* things gleaned, esp. facts.

glebe /gliːb/ *n.* **1** a piece of land serving as part of a clergyman's benefice and providing income. **2** *poet.* earth; land; a field. [ME f. L *gl(a)eba* clod, soil]

glee /gliː/ *n.* **1** mirth; delight (*watched the enemy's defeat with glee*). **2** a song for three or more, esp. adult male, voices, singing different parts simultaneously, usu. unaccompanied. □ **glee club** a society for singing part-songs. □□ **gleesome** *adj.* [OE *glīo*, *glēo* minstrelsy, jest f. Gmc]

gleeful /ˈgliːfʊl/ *adj.* joyful. □□ **gleefully** *adv.* **gleefulness** *n.*

Gleichschaltung /ˈglaɪxˌʃæltʊŋ/ *n.* the standardization of political, economic, and social institutions in authoritarian States. [G]

glen /glen/ *n.* a narrow valley. [Gael. & Ir. *gleann*]

Glencoe /glenˈkəʊ/ a glen in the Scottish Highlands, scene of the massacre in 1692 of Jacobite MacDonald clansmen by Campbell soldiers acting for the government of William III. While this massacre has often been considered a particularly foul violation of the rules of Highland hospitality in continuation of the long-standing feud between the Campbells and the MacDonalds, it was in fact a deliberate government attempt to make an example of one of the most notorious Jacobite clans, badly botched by the men on the spot (who killed less than a third of about 140 intended victims).

Glendower /glenˈdauə(r)/, Owen (c.1355–c.1417), the last independent prince of Wales. Leader first of guerrilla resistance to English overlordship and then of a national uprising against Henry IV, which by 1404 had progressed sufficiently for him to hold his own parliament, Glendower benefited considerably from supporting Henry's English opponents, notably the Percy family. Although Welsh independence collapsed soon after Glendower's death, he rapidly became a legendary symbol of Welsh nationalism.

glengarry /glenˈgærɪ/ n. (pl. **-ies**) a brimless Scottish hat with a cleft down the centre and usu. two ribbons hanging at the back. [*Glengarry* in Scotland]

glenoid cavity /ˈgliːnɔɪd/ n. a shallow depression on a bone, esp. the scapula and temporal bone, receiving the projection of another bone to form a joint. [F *glénoïde* f. Gk *glēnoeidēs* f. *glēnē* socket]

gley /gleɪ/ n. a tacky waterlogged soil grey to blue in colour. [Ukrainian, = sticky blue clay, rel. to CLAY]

glia /ˈglaɪə/ n. = NEUROGLIA. □□ **glial** adj. [Gk, = glue]

glib /glɪb/ adj. (**glibber**, **glibbest**) 1 (of a speaker, speech, etc.) fluent and voluble but insincere and shallow. 2 *archaic* smooth; unimpeded. □□ **glibly** adv. **glibness** n. [rel. to obs. *glibbery* slippery f. Gmc: perh. imit.]

glide /glaɪd/ v. & n. —v. 1 intr. (of a stream, bird, snake, ship, train, skater, etc.) move with a smooth continuous motion. 2 intr. (of an aircraft, esp. a glider) fly without engine-power. 3 intr. of time etc.: **a** pass gently and imperceptibly. **b** (often foll. by *into*) pass and change gradually and imperceptibly (*night glided into day*). 4 intr. move quietly or stealthily. 5 tr. cause to glide (*breezes glided the ship on its course*). 6 tr. cross in a glider. —n. 1 **a** the act of gliding. **b** an instance of this. 2 *Phonet.* a gradually changing sound made in passing from one position of the speech-organs to another. 3 a gliding dance or dance-step. 4 a flight in a glider. 5 *Cricket* = GLANCE n. 4. □ **glide clip** *Austral.* a paper fastener made of bent wire. **glide path** an aircraft's line of descent to land, esp. as indicated by ground radar. □□ **glidingly** adv. [OE *glīdan* f. WG]

glider /ˈglaɪdə(r)/ n. 1 **a** a fixed-wing aircraft that is not power-driven when in flight. It is launched by being towed from an aircraft, winch, or car, or by catapult; some gliders are fitted with a small retractable engine and propeller to enable them to be self-launched and dispense with this. The first glider to fly in free flight was devised by Sir George Cayley (see entry). **b** a glider pilot. 2 a person or thing that glides.

glim /glɪm/ n. 1 a faint light. 2 *archaic sl.* a candle; a lantern. [17th c.: perh. abbr. of GLIMMER or GLIMPSE]

glimmer /ˈglɪmə(r)/ v. & n. —v.intr. shine faintly or intermittently. —n. 1 a feeble or wavering light. 2 (usu. foll. by *of*) a faint gleam (of hope, understanding, etc.). 3 a glimpse. □□ **glimmeringly** adv. [ME prob. f. Scand. f. WG: see GLEAM]

glimmering /ˈglɪmərɪŋ/ n. 1 = GLIMMER n. 2 an act of glimmering.

glimpse /glɪmps/ n. & v. —n. (often foll. by *of*) 1 a momentary or partial view (*caught a glimpse of her*). 2 a faint and transient appearance (*glimpses of the truth*). —v. 1 tr. see faintly or partly (*glimpsed his face in the crowd*). 2 intr. (often foll. by *at*) cast a passing glance. 3 intr. **a** shine faintly or intermittently. **b** *poet.* appear faintly; dawn. [ME *glimse* corresp. to MHG *glimsen* f. WG (as GLIMMER)]

glint /glɪnt/ v. & n. —v.intr. & tr. flash or cause to flash; glitter; sparkle; reflect (*eyes glinted with amusement; the sword glinted fire*). —n. a brief flash of light; a sparkle. [alt. of ME *glent*, prob. of Scand. orig.]

glissade /glɪˈsɑːd, -ˈseɪd/ n. & v. —n. 1 an act of sliding down a steep slope of snow or ice, usu. on the feet with the support of an ice-axe etc. 2 a gliding step in ballet. —v.intr. perform a glissade. [F f. *glisser* slip, slide]

glissando /glɪˈsændəʊ/ n. (pl. **glissandi** /-dɪ/ or **-os**) *Mus.* a continuous slide of adjacent notes upwards or downwards. [It. f. F *glissant* sliding (as GLISSADE)]

glissé /gliːˈseɪ/ n. (also **pas glissé** /pɑː/) *Ballet* a sliding step in which the flat of the foot is often used. [F, past part. of *glisser*: see GLISSADE]

glisten /ˈglɪs(ə)n/ v. & n. —v.intr. shine, esp. like a wet object, snow, etc.; glitter. —n. a glitter; a sparkle. [OE *glisnian* f. *glisian* shine]

glister /ˈglɪstə(r)/ v. & n. *archaic* —v.intr. sparkle; glitter. —n. a sparkle; a gleam. [ME f. MLG *glistern*, MDu *glisteren*, rel. to GLISTEN]

glitch /glɪtʃ/ n. *colloq.* a sudden irregularity or malfunction (of equipment etc.). [20th c.: orig. unkn.]

glitter /ˈglɪtə(r)/ v. & n. —v.intr. 1 shine, esp. with a bright reflected light; sparkle. 2 (usu. foll. by *with*) **a** be showy or splendid (*glittered with diamonds*). **b** be ostentatious or flashily brilliant (*glittering rhetoric*). —n. 1 a gleam; a sparkle. 2 showiness; splendour. 3 tiny pieces of sparkling material as on Christmas-tree decorations. □□ **glitteringly** adv. **glittery** adj. [ME f. ON *glitra* f. Gmc]

glitterati /ˌglɪtəˈrɑːtɪ/ n.pl. *sl.* the fashionable set of literary or show-business people. [GLITTER + LITERATI]

Glittertind /ˈglɪtəˌtɪn/ the highest mountain in Norway, a peak in the Jotunheim range, rising to a height of 2,470 m (8,104 ft.).

glitz /glɪts/ n. *sl.* extravagant but superficial display; show-business glamour. [back-form. f. GLITZY]

glitzy /ˈglɪtsɪ/ adj. (**glitzier**, **glitziest**) *sl.* extravagant, ostentatious; tawdry; gaudy. □□ **glitzily** adv. **glitziness** n. [GLITTER, after RITZY: cf. G *glitzerig* glittering]

gloaming /ˈgləʊmɪŋ/ n. *poet.* twilight; dusk. [OE *glōmung* f. *glōm* twilight, rel. to GLOW]

gloat /gləʊt/ v. & n. —v.intr. (often foll. by *on, upon, over*) consider or contemplate with lust, greed, malice, triumph, etc. (*gloated over his collection*). —n. 1 the act of gloating. 2 a look or expression of triumphant satisfaction. □□ **gloater** n. **gloatingly** adv. [16th c.: orig. unkn., but perh. rel. to ON *glotta* grin, MHG *glotzen* stare]

glob /glɒb/ n. a mass or lump of semi-liquid substance, e.g. mud. [20th c.: perh. f. BLOB and GOB¹]

global /ˈgləʊb(ə)l/ adj. 1 worldwide (*global conflict*). 2 relating to or embracing a group of items etc.; total. □ **global warming** an increase in temperature of the earth's atmosphere attributed to the greenhouse effect. □□ **globally** adv. [F (as GLOBE)]

globe /gləʊb/ n. & v. —n. 1 **a** (prec. by *the*) the planet Earth. **b** a planet, star, or sun. **c** any spherical body; a ball. 2 a spherical representation of the earth or of the constellations with a map on the surface. 3 a golden sphere as an emblem of sovereignty; an orb. 4 any spherical glass vessel, esp. a fish bowl, a lamp, etc. 5 the eyeball. —v.tr. & intr. make (usu. in *passive*) or become globular. □ **globe artichoke** the partly edible head of the artichoke plant. **globe-fish** any tropical fish of the family Tetraodontidae, able to inflate itself into a spherical form: also called PUFFER-FISH. **globe-flower** any ranunculaceous plant of the genus *Trollius* with globular usu. yellow flowers. **globe lightning** = ball lightning (see BALL¹). **globe-trotter** a person who travels widely. **globe-trotting** such travel. □□ **globelike** adj. **globoid** adj. & n. **globose** adj. [F *globe* or L *globus*]

Globe Theatre the Burbages' theatre at Bankside in Southwark, London, erected in 1599 with materials from the old Theatre on the north side of the river. It was a large thatched circular building, with the centre open to the sky, and was used only during the summer months. The thatch caught fire in 1613 from a discharge of stage gunfire during a play, and the whole building was destroyed. It was rebuilt in 1614 and was in constant use until all the London theatres were closed on the outbreak of the Civil War in 1642. Shakespeare had a share in the theatre and acted there.

globigerina /glɒuˌbɪdʒəˈraɪnə, -ˈriːnə/ n. any planktonic protozoan of the genus *Globigerina*, living near the surface of the sea. [mod.L f. L *globus* globe + *-ger* carrying + -INA]

globular /ˈglɒbjʊlə(r)/ adj. 1 globe-shaped, spherical. 2 composed of globules. □□ **globularity** /-ˈlærɪtɪ/ n. **globularly** adv.

globule /ˈglɒbjuːl/ n. 1 a small globe or round particle; a drop. 2 a pill. □□ **globulous** adj. [F *globule* or L *globulus* (as GLOBE)]

globulin /ˈglɒbjʊlɪn/ n. any of a group of proteins found in plant and animal tissues and esp. responsible for the transport of molecules etc.

glockenspiel /ˈglɒkənˌspiːl, -ˌʃpiːl/ n. a percussion instrument formed from a set of tuned metal bars each supported at two points but with both ends free and struck in the centre with small hand-held hammers. It has a range of about two-and-a-half octaves, and became a fairly regular member of the orchestra only in the 19th c. [G, = bell-play]

glom /glɒm/ v. US sl. (**glommed, glomming**) 1 tr. steal; grab. 2 intr. (usu. foll. by on to) steal; grab. [var. of Sc. glaum (18th c., of unkn. orig.)]

glomerate /ˈglɒmərət/ adj. Bot. & Anat. compactly clustered. [L glomeratus past part. of glomerare f. glomus -eris ball]

glomerule /ˈglɒməˌruːl/ n. a clustered flower-head.

glomerulus /glɒˈmerʊləs/ n. (pl. **glomeruli** /-ˌlaɪ/) a cluster of small organisms, tissues, or blood vessels, esp. of the capillaries of the kidney. □□ **glomerular** adj. [mod.L, dimin. of L glomus -eris ball]

gloom /gluːm/ n. & v. —n. 1 darkness; obscurity. 2 melancholy; despondency. 3 poet. a dark place. —v. 1 intr. be gloomy or melancholy; frown. 2 intr. (of the sky etc.) be dull or threatening; lour. 3 intr. appear darkly or obscurely. 4 tr. cover with gloom; make dark or dismal. [ME gloum(b)e, of unkn. orig.: cf. GLUM]

gloomy /ˈgluːmɪ/ adj. (**gloomier, gloomiest**) 1 dark; unlighted. 2 depressed; sullen. 3 dismal; depressing. □□ **gloomily** adv. **gloominess** n.

glop /glɒp/ n. US sl. a liquid or sticky mess, esp. inedible food. [imit.: cf. obs. glop swallow greedily]

Gloria /ˈglɔːrɪə/ n. 1 any of various doxologies beginning with Gloria, esp. the hymn beginning with Gloria in excelsis Deo (Glory be to God in the highest). 2 an aureole. [L, = glory]

Gloriana /ˌglɒrɪˈɑːnə/ the nickname of Elizabeth I of England.

glorify /ˈglɔːrɪˌfaɪ/ v.tr. (**-ies, -ied**) 1 exalt to heavenly glory; make glorious. 2 transform into something more splendid. 3 extol; praise. 4 (as **glorified** adj.) seeming or pretending to be more splendid than in reality (just a glorified office boy). □□ **glorification** /-fɪˈkeɪʃ(ə)n/ n. **glorifier** n. [ME f. OF glorifier f. eccl.L glorificare f. LL glorificus f. L gloria glory]

gloriole /ˈglɔːrɪˌəʊl/ n. an aureole; a halo. [F f. L gloriola dimin. of gloria glory]

glorious /ˈglɔːrɪəs/ adj. 1 possessing glory; illustrious. 2 conferring glory; honourable. 3 colloq. splendid; magnificent; delightful (a glorious day; glorious fun). 4 iron. intense; unmitigated (a glorious muddle). 5 colloq. happily intoxicated. □ **Glorious Revolution** the events that led to the removal of James II from the English throne and his replacement by his daughter Mary and her husband William of Orange (1688), with their acceptance of the conditions laid down in the Bill of Rights. □□ **gloriously** adv. **gloriousness** n. [ME f. AF glorious, OF glorios, -eus f. L gloriosus (as GLORY)]

glory /ˈglɔːrɪ/ n. & v. —n. (pl. **-ies**) 1 high renown or fame; honour. 2 adoring praise and thanksgiving (Glory to the Lord). 3 resplendent majesty or magnificence; great beauty (the glory of Versailles; the glory of the rose). 4 a thing that brings renown or praise; a distinction. 5 the bliss and splendour of heaven. 6 colloq. a state of exaltation, prosperity, happiness, etc. (is in his glory playing with his trains). 7 an aureole, a halo. 8 an anthelion. —v.intr. (often foll. by in, or to + infin.) pride oneself; exult (glory in their skill). □ **glory be!** 1 a devout ejaculation. 2 colloq. an exclamation of surprise or delight. **glory-box** Austral. & NZ a box for women's clothes etc., stored in preparation for marriage. **glory-hole** 1 colloq. an untidy room, drawer, or receptacle. 2 US an open quarry. **glory-of-the-snow** = CHIONODOXA. **go to glory** sl. die; be destroyed. [ME f. AF & OF glorie f. L gloria]

Glos. /glɒs/ abbr. Gloucestershire.

gloss¹ /glɒs/ n. & v. —n. 1 **a** surface shine or lustre. **b** an instance of this; a smooth finish. 2 **a** deceptively attractive appearance. **b** an instance of this. 3 (in full **gloss paint**) paint formulated to give a hard glossy finish (cf. MATT). —v.tr. make

glossy. □ **gloss over** 1 seek to conceal beneath a false appearance. 2 conceal or evade by mentioning briefly or misleadingly. □□ **glosser** n. [16th c.: orig. unkn.]

gloss² /glɒs/ n. & v. —n. 1 **a** an explanatory word or phrase inserted between the lines or in the margin of a text. **b** a comment, explanation, interpretation, or paraphrase. 2 a misrepresentation of another's words. 3 **a** a glossary. **b** an interlinear translation or annotation. —v. 1 tr. **a** add a gloss or glosses to (a text, word, etc.). **b** read a different sense into; explain away. 2 intr. (often foll. by on) make (esp. unfavourable) comments. 3 intr. write or introduce glosses. □□ **glosser** n. [alt. of GLOZE after med.L glossa]

glossal /ˈglɒs(ə)l/ adj. Anat. of the tongue; lingual. [Gk glōssa tongue]

glossary /ˈglɒsərɪ/ n. (pl. **-ies**) 1 (also **gloss**) an alphabetical list of terms or words found in or relating to a specific subject or text, esp. dialect, with explanations; a brief dictionary. 2 a collection of glosses. □□ **glossarial** /glɒˈseərɪəl/ adj. **glossarist** n. [L glossarium f. glossa GLOSS²]

glossator /glɒˈseɪtə(r)/ n. 1 a writer of glosses. 2 hist. a commentator on, or interpreter of, medieval law-texts. [ME f. med.L f. glossare f. glossa GLOSS²]

glosseme /ˈglɒsiːm/ n. any meaningful feature of a language that cannot be analysed into smaller meaningful units. [Gk glōssēma f. glōssa GLOSS²]

glossitis /glɒˈsaɪtɪs/ n. inflammation of the tongue. [Gk glōssa tongue + -ITIS]

glossographer /glɒˈsɒgrəfə(r)/ n. a writer of glosses or commentaries. [GLOSS² + -GRAPHER]

glossolalia /ˌglɒsəˈleɪlɪə/ n. = gift of tongues (see TONGUE). [mod.L f. Gk glōssa tongue + -lalia speaking]

glosso-laryngeal /ˌglɒsəʊlæˈrɪndʒɪəl/ adj. of the tongue and larynx. [Gk glōssa tongue + LARYNGEAL]

glossy /ˈglɒsɪ/ adj. & n. —adj. (**glossier, glossiest**) 1 having a shine; smooth. 2 (of paper etc.) smooth and shiny. 3 (of a magazine etc.) printed on such paper. —n. (pl. **-ies**) colloq. 1 a glossy magazine. 2 a photograph with a glossy surface. □□ **glossily** adv. **glossiness** n.

glottal /ˈglɒt(ə)l/ adj. of or produced by the glottis. □ **glottal stop** a sound produced by the sudden opening or shutting of the glottis.

glottis /ˈglɒtɪs/ n. the space at the upper end of the windpipe and between the vocal cords, affecting voice modulation through expansion or contraction. □□ **glottic** adj. [mod.L f. Gk glōttis f. glōtta var. of glōssa tongue]

Gloucester /ˈglɒstə(r)/ n. (usu. **double Gloucester**, orig. a richer kind) a kind of hard cheese orig. made in Gloucestershire.

Gloucestershire /ˈglɒstəˌʃɪə(r)/ a county of SW England; pop. (1981) 506,000; county town, Gloucester.

glove /glʌv/ n. & v. —n. 1 a covering for the hand, of wool, leather, cotton, etc., worn esp. for protection against cold or dirt, and usu. having separate fingers. 2 a padded protective glove, esp.: **a** a boxing glove. **b** a wicket-keeper's glove. —v.tr. cover or provide with a glove or gloves. □ **fit like a glove** fit exactly. **glove box** 1 a box for gloves. 2 a closed chamber with sealed-in gloves for handling radioactive material etc. 3 = glove compartment. **glove compartment** a recess for small articles in the dashboard of a motor vehicle. **glove puppet** a small cloth puppet fitted on the hand and worked by the fingers. **throw down** (or **take up**) **the glove** issue (or accept) a challenge. **with the gloves off** mercilessly; unfairly; with no compunction. □□ **gloveless** adj. **glover** n. [OE glōf, corresp. to ON glófi, perh. f. Gmc]

glow /gləʊ/ v. & n. —v.intr. 1 **a** throw out light and heat without flame; be incandescent. **b** shine like something heated in this way. 2 (of the cheeks) redden, esp. from cold or exercise. 3 (often foll. by with) **a** (of the body) be heated, esp. from exertion; sweat. **b** express or experience strong emotion (glowed with pride; glowing with indignation). 4 show a warm colour (the painting glows with warmth). 5 (as **glowing** adj.) expressing pride or satisfaction (a glowing report). —n. 1 a glowing state. 2 a bright warm colour, esp. the red of cheeks. 3 ardour; passion. 4 a feeling induced by good health, exercise, etc.; well-being. □ **glow discharge** a luminous sparkless electrical discharge from a pointed conductor in a gas at low pressure. **glow-worm** any beetle of the genus *Lampyris* whose wingless female emits light from the end of the abdomen. **in a glow** *colloq.* hot or flushed; sweating. □□ **glowingly** *adv.* [OE *glōwan* f. Gmc]

glower /ˈglaʊə(r)/ *v. & n.* —*v.intr.* (often foll. by *at*) stare or scowl, esp. angrily. —*n.* a glowering look. □□ **gloweringly** *adv.* [orig. uncert.: perh. Sc. var. of ME *glore* f. LG or Scand., or f. obs. (ME) *glow* stare + -ER⁴]

gloxinia /glɒkˈsɪnɪə/ *n.* any tropical plant of the genus *Gloxinia*, native to S. America, with large bell flowers of various colours. [mod.L f. B. P. *Gloxin*, 18th-c. Ger. botanist]

gloze /gləʊz/ *v.* **1** *tr.* (also **gloze over**) explain away; extenuate; palliate. **2** *intr. archaic* **a** (usu. foll. by *on*, *upon*) comment. **b** talk speciously; fawn. [ME f. OF *gloser* f. *glose* f. med.L *glosa*, *gloza* f. L *glossa* tongue, GLOSS²]

glucagon /ˈgluːkəgɒn/ *n.* a polypeptide hormone formed in the pancreas, which aids the breakdown of glycogen. [Gk *glukus* sweet + *agōn* leading]

Gluck /glʊk/, Christoph Willibald von (1714–87), composer who was born in Germany and died in Vienna, having travelled widely. From early operas in the Italian style he went on to seek a balance of music and drama in his 'reform' operas, discarding the claims of the star singer and attempting a continuous musical unfolding of the narrative. He had a lyrical gift which can be seen at its best in his operas, and the simplicity and sublimity of his melodies, supported by a vivid dramatic sense, have ensured the survival of a large proportion of his music.

glucose /ˈgluːkəʊs, -kəʊz/ *n.* **1** a simple sugar containing six carbon atoms, found mainly in its dextrorotatory form (see DEXTROSE), which is an important energy source in living organisms and obtainable from some carbohydrates by hydrolysis. ¶ Chem. formula: $C_6H_{12}O_6$. **2** a syrup containing glucose sugars from the incomplete hydrolysis of starch. [F f. Gk *gleukos* sweet wine, rel. to *glukus* sweet]

glucoside /ˈgluːkəsaɪd/ *n.* a compound giving glucose and other products upon hydrolysis. □□ **glucosidic** /-ˈsɪdɪk/ *adj.*

glue /gluː/ *n. & v.* —*n.* an adhesive substance used for sticking objects or materials together. —*v.tr.* (**glues**, **glued**, **gluing** or **glueing**) **1** fasten or join with glue. **2** keep or put very close (*an eye glued to the keyhole*). □ **glue-pot 1** a pot with an outer vessel holding water to heat glue. **2** *colloq.* an area of sticky mud etc. **glue-sniffer** a person who inhales the fumes from adhesives as a drug. □□ **gluelike** *adj.* **gluer** *n.* **gluey** /ˈgluːɪ/ *adj.* (**gluier**, **gluiest**). **glueyness** *n.* [ME f. OF *glu* (n.), *gluer* (v.), f. LL *glus glutis* f. L *gluten*]

glum /glʌm/ *adj.* (**glummer**, **glummest**) looking or feeling dejected; sullen; displeased. □□ **glumly** *adv.* **glumness** *n.* [rel. to dial. *glum* (v.) frown, var. of *gloume* GLOOM v.]

glume /gluːm/ *n.* **1** a membranous bract surrounding the spikelet of grasses or the florets of sedges. **2** the husk of grain. □□ **glumaceous** /-ˈmeɪʃəs/ *adj.* **glumose** *adj.* [L *gluma* husk]

gluon /ˈgluːɒn/ *n. Physics* any of a group of elementary particles that are thought to bind quarks together. [GLUE + -ON]

glut /glʌt/ *v. & n.* —*v.tr.* (**glutted**, **glutting**) **1** feed (a person, one's stomach, etc.) or indulge (an appetite, a desire, etc.) to the full; satiate; cloy. **2** fill to excess; choke up. **3** *Econ.* overstock (a market) with goods. —*n.* **1** *Econ.* supply exceeding demand; a surfeit (*a glut in the market*). **2** full indulgence; one's fill. [ME prob. f. OF *gloutir* swallow f. L *gluttire*: cf. GLUTTON]

glutamate /ˈgluːtəmeɪt/ *n.* any salt or ester of glutamic acid, esp. a sodium salt used to enhance the flavour of food.

glutamic acid /gluːˈtæmɪk/ *n.* a naturally occurring amino acid, a constituent of many proteins. [GLUTEN + AMINE + -IC]

gluten /ˈgluːt(ə)n/ *n.* **1** a mixture of proteins present in cereal grains. **2** *archaic* a sticky substance. [F f. L *gluten glutinis* glue]

gluteus /ˈgluːtɪəs/ *n.* (pl. **glutei** /-tɪˌaɪ/) any of the three muscles in each buttock. □□ **gluteal** *adj.* [mod.L f. Gk *gloutos* buttock]

glutinous /ˈgluːtɪnəs/ *adj.* sticky; like glue. □□ **glutinously** *adv.* **glutinousness** *n.* [F *glutineux* or L *glutinosus* (as GLUTEN)]

glutton /ˈglʌt(ə)n/ *n.* **1** an excessively greedy eater. **2** (often foll. by *for*) *colloq.* a person insatiably eager (*a glutton for work*). **3** an animal of the weasel family, also called WOLVERINE. □ **a glutton for punishment** a person eager to take on hard or unpleasant tasks. □□ **gluttonize** *v.intr.* (also **-ise**). **gluttonous** *adj.* **gluttonously** *adv.* [ME f. OF *gluton*, *gloton* f. L *glutto -onis* f. *gluttire* swallow, *gluttus* greedy]

gluttony /ˈglʌtənɪ/ *n.* habitual greed or excess in eating. [OF *glutonie* (as GLUTTON)]

glyceride /ˈglɪsəraɪd/ *n.* any fatty-acid ester of glycerol.

glycerine /ˈglɪsəˌriːn/ *n.* (US **glycerin** /-rɪn/) = GLYCEROL. [F *glycerin* f. Gk *glukeros* sweet]

glycerol /ˈglɪsəˌrɒl/ *n.* a colourless sweet viscous liquid formed as a by-product in the manufacture of soap, used as an emollient and laxative, in explosives, etc. ¶ Chem. formula: $C_3H_8O_3$. Also called GLYCERINE. [GLYCERINE + -OL¹]

glycine /ˈglaɪsiːn/ *n.* the simplest naturally occurring amino acid, a general constituent of proteins. [G *Glycin* f. Gk *glukus* sweet]

glyco- /ˈglaɪkəʊ/ *comb. form* sugar. [Gk *glukus* sweet]

glycogen /ˈglaɪkədʒ(ə)n/ *n.* a polysaccharide serving as a store of carbohydrates, esp. in animal tissues, and yielding glucose on hydrolysis. □□ **glycogenic** /-ˈdʒenɪk/ *adj.*

glycogenesis /ˌglaɪkəʊˈdʒenɪsɪs/ *n. Biochem.* the formation of glycogen from sugar.

glycol /ˈglaɪkɒl/ *n.* a diol, esp. ethylene glycol. □□ **glycolic** /-ˈkɒlɪk/ *adj.* **glycollic** /-ˈkɒlɪk/ *adj.* [GLYCERINE + -OL¹, orig. as being intermediate between glycerine and alcohol]

glycolysis /glaɪˈkɒlɪsɪs/ *n. Biochem.* the breakdown of glucose by enzymes in most living organisms to release energy and pyruvic acid.

glycoprotein /ˌglaɪkəʊˈprəʊtiːn/ *n.* any of a group of compounds consisting of a protein combined with a carbohydrate.

glycoside /ˈglaɪkəˌsaɪd/ *n.* any compound giving sugar and other products on hydrolysis. □□ **glycosidic** /-ˈsɪdɪk/ *adj.* [GLYCO-, after GLUCOSIDE]

glycosuria /ˌglaɪkəˈsjʊərɪə/ *n.* a condition characterized by an excess of sugar in the urine, associated with diabetes, kidney disease, etc. □□ **glycosuric** *adj.* [F *glycose* glucose + -URIA]

Glyndebourne /ˈglaɪndbɔːn/ an estate near Lewes in Sussex, England, where an annual festival of opera is held. The opera house was built by the owner of the estate, John Christie (d. 1962), who founded the festival in 1934 to stage ideal performances in a beautiful setting. The inspiration for the enterprise was his wife, the soprano Audrey Mildmay.

glyph /glɪf/ *n.* **1** a sculptured character or symbol. **2** a vertical groove, esp. that on a Greek frieze. □□ **glyphic** *adj.* [F *glyphe* f. Gk *gluphē* carving f. *gluphō* carve]

glyptal /ˈglɪptæl/ *n.* an alkyd resin, esp. one formed from glycerine and phthalic acid or anhydride. [perh. f. *glycerol* + *phthalic*]

glyptic /ˈglɪptɪk/ *adj.* of or concerning carving, esp. on precious stones. [F *glyptique* or Gk *gluptikos* f. *gluptēs* carver f. *gluphō* carve]

glyptodont /ˈglɪptəˌdɒnt/ *n.* any extinct armadillo-like edentate animal of the genus *Glyptodon* native to S. America, having fluted teeth and a body covered in a hard thick bony shell. [mod.L f. Gk *gluptos* carved + *odous odontos* tooth]

glyptography /glɪpˈtɒgrəfɪ/ *n.* the art or scientific study of gem-engraving. [Gk *gluptos* carved + -GRAPHY]

GM *abbr.* **1** (in the UK) George Medal. **2** (in the US) General Motors. **3** general manager.

gm *abbr.* gram(s).

G-man /ˈdʒiːmæn/ *n.* (pl. **G-men**) **1** *US colloq.* a federal criminal-investigation officer. **2** *Ir.* a political detective. [Government + MAN]

GMT *abbr.* Greenwich Mean Time.

GMWU *abbr.* (in the UK) General & Municipal Workers' Union.

gnamma /ˈnæmə/ *n.* (also **namma**) *Austral.* a natural hole in a rock, containing water; a waterhole. [Aboriginal]

w we   z zoo   ʃ she   ʒ decision   θ thin   ð this   ŋ ring   x loch   tʃ chip   dʒ jar   (*see over for vowels*)

gnarled /nɑːld/ adj. (also **gnarly** /'nɑːlɪ/) (of a tree, hands, etc.) knobbly, twisted, rugged. [var. of knarled, rel. to KNURL]

gnash /næʃ/ v. & n. —v. **1** tr. grind (the teeth). **2** intr. (of the teeth) strike together; grind. —n. an act of grinding the teeth. [var. of obs. gnacche or gnast, rel. to ON gnastan a gnashing (imit.)]

gnat /næt/ n. **1** any small two-winged biting fly of the genus Culex, esp. C. pipiens. **2** an insignificant annoyance. **3** a tiny thing. [OE gnætt]

gnathic /'næθɪk/ adj. of or relating to the jaws. [Gk gnathos jaw]

gnaw /nɔː/ v. (past part. **gnawed** or **gnawn**) **1 a** tr. (usu. foll. by away, off, in two, etc.) bite persistently; wear away by biting. **b** intr. (often foll. by at, into) bite, nibble. **2 a** intr. (often foll. by at, into) (of a destructive agent, pain, fear, etc.) corrode; waste away; consume; torture. **b** tr. corrode, consume, torture, etc. with pain, fear, etc. (was gnawed by doubt). **3** tr. (as **gnawing** adj.) persistent; worrying. □□ **gnawingly** adv. [OE gnagan, ult. imit.]

gneiss /naɪs/ n. a usu. coarse-grained metamorphic rock foliated by mineral layers, principally of feldspar, quartz, and ferromagnesian minerals. □□ **gneissic** adj. **gneissoid** adj. **gneissose** adj. [G]

gnocchi /'nɒkɪ, 'njɒkɪ/ n.pl. an Italian dish of small dumplings usu. made from potato, semolina flour, etc., or from spinach and cheese. [It., pl. of gnocco f. nocchio knot in wood]

gnome[1] /nəʊm/ n. **1 a** a dwarfish legendary creature supposed to guard the earth's treasures underground; a goblin. **b** a figure of a gnome, esp. as a garden ornament. **2** (esp. in pl.) colloq. a person with secret influence, esp. financial (gnomes of Zurich). □□ **gnomish** adj. [F f. mod.L gnomus (word invented by Paracelsus)]

gnome[2] /'nəʊmɪ, nəʊm/ n. a maxim; an aphorism. [Gk gnōmē opinion f. gignōskō know]

gnomic /'nəʊmɪk/ adj. **1** of, consisting of, or using gnomes or aphorisms; sententious (see GNOME[2]). **2** Gram. (of a tense) used without the implication of time to express a general truth, e.g. men were deceivers ever. □□ **gnomically** adv. [Gk gnōmikos (as GNOME[2])]

gnomon /'nəʊmɒn/ n. **1** the rod or pin etc. on a sundial that shows the time by the position of its shadow. **2** Geom. the part of a parallelogram left when a similar parallelogram has been taken from its corner. **3** Astron. a column etc. used in observing the sun's meridian altitude. □□ **gnomonic** /-'mɒnɪk/ adj. [F or L gnomon f. Gk gnōmōn indicator etc. f. gignōskō know]

gnosis /'nəʊsɪs/ n. knowledge of spiritual mysteries. [Gk gnōsis knowledge (as GNOMON)]

gnostic /'nɒstɪk/ adj. & n. —adj. **1** relating to knowledge, esp. esoteric mystical knowledge. **2** (**Gnostic**) concerning the Gnostics; occult; mystic. —n. (**Gnostic**) (usu. in pl.) a Christian heretic of the 1st–3rd c. claiming gnosis. (See below.) □□ **Gnosticism** /-ˌsɪz(ə)m/ n. **gnosticize** /-ˌsaɪz/ v.tr. & intr. [eccl.L gnosticus f. Gk gnōstikos (as GNOSIS)]

Gnosticism was a movement, in part at least of pre-Christian origin and with ideas drawn from Greek philosophy and other pagan sources, prominent in the Christian Church in the 2nd c. It took many different forms, some of which are wild amalgams of mythology and magical rites with only an admixture of Christian terminology. Gnostics emphasized the power of gnosis, the supposed revealed knowledge of God, to redeem the spiritual element in man; they contrasted the supreme remote Divine Being with the 'Demiurge' or 'creator god', who controlled the world and was antagonistic to all that was purely spiritual. Christ came as an emissary from the supreme god, bringing gnosis. Gnostic teaching for long was known only from antiheretical writers, such as Irenaeus and Tertullian, until in 1945–6 a collection of Gnostic texts was found at Nag Hammadi in Upper Egypt.

GNP abbr. gross national product.

Gnr. abbr. Brit. Gunner.

gns. abbr. Brit. hist. guineas.

gnu /nuː, njuː/ n. any antelope of the genus Connochaetes, native to S. Africa, with a large erect head and brown stripes on the neck and shoulders. Also called WILDEBEEST. [Bushman nqu, prob. through Du. gnoe]

go[1] /gəʊ/ v., n., & adj. —v. (3rd sing. present **goes** /gəʊz/; past **went** /went/; past part. **gone** /gɒn/) —v. **1** intr. **a** start moving or be moving from one place or point in time to another; travel, proceed. **b** (foll. by to + infin., or and + verb) proceed in order to (went to find him; go and buy some bread). **c** (foll. by and + verb) colloq. expressing annoyance (you went and told him; they've gone and broken it; she went and won). **2** intr. (foll. by verbal noun) make a special trip for; participate in; proceed to do (went skiing; then went shopping; often goes running). **3** intr. lie or extend in a certain direction (the road goes to London). **4** intr. leave; depart (they had to go). **5** intr. move, act, work, etc. (the clock doesn't go; his brain is going all the time). **6** intr. **a** make a specified movement (go like this with your foot). **b** make a sound (often of a specified kind) (the gun went bang; the door bell went). **c** colloq. say (so he goes to me 'Why didn't you like it?'). **d** (of an animal) make (its characteristic cry) (the cow went 'moo'). **7** intr. be in a specified state (go hungry; went in fear of his life). **8** intr. **a** pass into a specified condition (gone bad; went mad; went to sleep). **b** colloq. die. **c** proceed or escape in a specified condition (the poet went unrecognized; the crime went unnoticed). **9** intr. (of time or distance) pass, elapse; be traversed (ten days to go before Easter; the last mile went quickly). **10** intr. **a** (of a document, verse, song, etc.) have a specified content or wording; run (the tune goes like this). **b** be current or accepted (so the story goes). **c** be suitable; fit; match (the shoes don't go with the hat). **d** be regularly kept or put (the forks go here). **e** find room; fit (this won't go into the cupboard). **11** intr. **a** turn out, proceed; take a course or view (things went well; Liverpool went Labour). **b** be successful (make the party go; went like a bomb). **c** progress (we've still a long way to go). **12** intr. **a** be sold (went for £1; went cheap). **b** (of money) be spent (£200 went on a new jacket). **13** intr. **a** be relinquished, dismissed, or abolished (the car will have to go). **b** fail, decline; give way, collapse (his sight is going; the bulb has gone). **14** intr. be acceptable or permitted; be accepted without question (anything goes; what I say goes). **15** intr. (often foll. by by, with, on, upon) be guided by; judge or act on or in harmony with (have nothing to go on; a good rule to go by). **16** intr. attend or visit or travel to regularly (goes to church; goes to school; this train goes to Bristol). **17** intr. (foll. by pres. part.) colloq. proceed (often foolishly) to do (went running to the police; don't go making him angry). **18** intr. act or proceed to a certain point (will go so far and no further; went as high as £100). **19** intr. (of a number) be capable of being contained in another (6 into 12 goes twice; 6 into 5 won't go). **20** tr. Cards bid; declare (go nap; has gone two spades). **21** intr. (usu. foll. by to) be allotted or awarded; pass (first prize went to the girl; the job went to his rival). **22** intr. (foll. by to, towards) amount to; contribute to (12 inches go to make a foot; this will go towards your holiday). **23** intr. (in imper.) begin motion (a starter's order in a race) (ready, steady, go!). **24** intr. (usu. foll. by to) refer or appeal (go to him for help). **25** intr. (often foll. by on) take up a specified profession (went on the stage; gone soldiering; went to sea). **26** intr. (usu. foll. by by, under) be known or called (goes by the name of Droopy). **27** tr. colloq. proceed to (go jump in the lake). **28** intr. (foll. by for) apply to; have relevance to (that goes for me too). —n. (pl. **goes**) **1** the act or an instance of going. **2** mettle; spirit; dash; animation (she has a lot of go in her). **3** vigorous activity (it's all go). **4** colloq. a success (made a go of it). **5** colloq. a turn; an attempt (I'll have a go; it's my go; all in one go). **6** colloq. a state of affairs (a rum go). **7** colloq. an attack of illness (a bad go of flu). **8** colloq. a quantity of liquor, food, etc. served at one time. —adj. colloq. **1** functioning properly (all systems are go). **2** fashionable; progressive. □ **all the go** colloq. in fashion. **as** (or **so**) **far as it goes** an expression of caution against taking a statement too positively (the work is good as far as it goes). **as** (**a person or thing**) **goes** as the average is (a good actor as actors go). **from the word go** colloq. from the very beginning. **give it a go** colloq. make an effort to succeed. **go about 1** busy oneself with; set to work at. **2** be socially active. **3** (foll. by pres. part.) make a habit of doing (goes about telling lies). **4** Naut. change to an opposite tack. **go ahead** proceed without hesitation. **go-ahead** n. permission to proceed. —adj. enterprising. **go along with** agree to; take the same view as. **go around 1** (foll. by with) be regularly in the company of. **2** = go about 3. **go-as-you-please** untrammelled; free. **go at** take in hand energetically; attack. **go away** depart, esp. from home for a holiday etc. **go back on** fail to keep (one's word, promise, etc.). **go bail** see BAIL¹. **go begging** see BEG. **go-between** an intermediary; a negotiator. **go by 1** pass. **2** be dependent on; be guided by. **go-by** *colloq.* a snub; a slight (*gave it the go-by*). **go by default** see DEFAULT. **go-cart 1** a handcart; a pushchair. **2** = *go-kart*. **3** *archaic* a baby-walker. **go-devil** *US* an instrument used to clean the inside of pipes etc. **go down 1 a** (of an amount) become less (*the coffee has gone down a lot*). **b** subside (*the flood went down*). **c** decrease in price; lose value. **2 a** (of a ship) sink. **b** (of the sun) set. **3** (usu. foll. by *to*) be continued to a specified point. **4** deteriorate; fail; (of a computer network etc.) cease to function. **5** be recorded in writing. **6** be swallowed. **7** (often foll. by *with*) find acceptance. **8** *Brit. colloq.* leave university. **9** *colloq.* be sent to prison (*went down for ten years*). **10** (often foll. by *before*) fall (before a conqueror). **go down with** *Brit.* begin to suffer from (a disease). **go Dutch** see DUTCH. **go far** be very successful. **go for 1** go to fetch. **2** be accounted as or achieve (*went for nothing*). **3** prefer; choose (*that's the one I go for*). **4** *colloq.* strive to attain (*go for it!*). **5** *colloq.* attack (*the dog went for him*). **go-getter** *colloq.* an aggressively enterprising person, esp. a businessman. **go-go** *colloq.* **1** (of a dancer, music, etc.) in modern style, lively and rhythmic. **2** unrestrained; energetic. **3** (of investment) speculative. **go great guns** see GUN. **go halves** (or **shares**) (often foll. by *with*) share equally. **go in 1** enter a room, house, etc. **2** (usu. foll. by *for*) enter as a competitor. **3** *Cricket* take or begin an innings. **4** (of the sun etc.) become obscured by cloud. **go in for** take as one's object, style, pursuit, principle, etc. **going!, gone!** an auctioneer's announcement that bidding is closing or closed. **go into 1** enter (a profession, Parliament, etc.). **2** take part in; be a part of. **3** investigate. **4** allow oneself to pass into (hysterics etc.). **5** dress oneself in (mourning etc.). **6** frequent (society). **go it** *colloq.* **1** act vigorously, furiously, etc. **2** indulge in dissipation. **go it alone** see ALONE. **go it strong** *colloq.* go to great lengths; exaggerate. **go-kart** = KART. **go a long way 1** (often foll. by *towards*) have a great effect. **2** (of food, money, etc.) last a long time, buy much. **3** = *go far*. **go off 1** explode. **2** leave the stage. **3** gradually cease to be felt. **4** (esp. of foodstuffs) deteriorate; decompose. **5** go to sleep; become unconscious. **6** begin. **7** die. **8** be got rid of by sale etc. **9** *Brit. colloq.* begin to dislike (*I've gone off him*). **go-off** *colloq.* a start (*at the first go-off*). **go off at** *Austral. & NZ sl.* reprimand, scold. **go off well** (or **badly** etc.) (of an enterprise etc.) be received or accomplished well (or badly etc.). **go on 1** (often foll. by pres. part.) continue, persevere (*decided to go on with it; went on trying; unable to go on*). **2** *colloq.* **a** talk at great length. **b** (foll. by *at*) admonish (*went on and on at him*). **3** (foll. by *to* + infin.) proceed (*went on to become a star*). **4** happen. **5** conduct oneself (*shameful, the way they went on*). **6** *Theatr.* appear on stage. **7** *Cricket* begin bowling. **8** (of a garment) be large enough for its wearer. **9** take one's turn to do something. **10** (also **go upon**) *colloq.* use as evidence (*police don't have anything to go on*). **11** *colloq.* (esp. in neg.) **a** concern oneself about. **b** care for (*don't go much on red hair*). **12** become chargeable to (the parish etc.). **go on!** *colloq.* an expression of encouragement or disbelief. **go out 1** leave a room, house, etc. **2** be broadcast. **3** be extinguished. **4** (often foll. by *with*) be courting. **5** (of a government) leave office. **6** cease to be fashionable. **7** (usu. foll. by *to*) depart, esp. to a colony etc. **8** *colloq.* lose consciousness. **9** (of workers) strike. **10** (usu. foll. by *to*) (of the heart etc.) expand with sympathy etc. towards (*my heart goes out to them*). **11** *Golf* play the first nine holes in a round. **12** *Cards* be the first to dispose of one's hand. **13** (of a tide) turn to low tide. **go over 1** inspect the details of; rehearse; retouch. **2** (often foll. by *to*) change one's allegiance or religion. **3** (of a play etc.) be successful (*went over well in Dundee*). **go round 1** spin, revolve. **2** be long enough to encompass. **3** (of food etc.) suffice for everybody. **4** (usu. foll. by *to*) visit informally. **5** = *go around*. **go slow** work slowly, as a form of industrial action. **go-slow** *Brit.* such industrial action. **go through 1** be dealt with or completed. **2** discuss in detail; scrutinize in sequence. **3** perform (a ceremony, a recitation, etc.). **4** undergo. **5** *colloq.* use up; spend (money etc.). **6** make holes in. **7** (of a book) be successively published (in so many editions). **8** *Austral. sl.* abscond. **go through with** not leave unfinished; complete. **go to!** *archaic* an exclamation of disbelief, impatience, admonition, etc. **go to the bar** become a barrister. **go to blazes** (or **hell** or

Jericho etc.) *sl.* an exclamation of dismissal, contempt, etc. **go to the country** see COUNTRY. **go together 1** match; fit. **2** be courting. **go to it!** *colloq.* begin work! **go-to-meeting** (of a hat, clothes, etc.) suitable for going to church in. **go to show** (or **prove**) serve to demonstrate (or prove). **go under** sink; fail; succumb. **go up 1** increase in price. **2** *Brit. colloq.* enter university. **3** be consumed (in flames etc.); explode. **go well** (or **ill** etc.) (often foll. by *with*) turn out well, (or ill etc.). **go with 1** be harmonious with; match. **2** agree to; take the same view as. **3 a** be a pair with. **b** be courting. **4** follow the drift of. **go without** manage without; forgo (also *absol.*: *we shall just have to go without*). **go with the tide** (or **times**) do as others do; follow the drift. **have a go at 1** attack, criticize. **2** attempt, try. **on the go** *colloq.* **1** in constant motion. **2** constantly working. **to go** *US* (of refreshments etc.) to be eaten or drunk off the premises. **who goes there?** a sentry's challenge. [OE *gān* f. Gmc: *went* orig. past of WEND]

go² /gəʊ/ *n.* a Japanese board game of territorial possession and capture. [Jap.]

Goa /ˈgəʊə/ a State on the west coast of India; pop. (1981) 1,003,136; capital, Panaji. Formerly a Portuguese territory, it was seized by India in 1961, and together with two other Portuguese territories, Daman and Diu, formed a Union Territory of India until it achieved statehood in 1987. □□ **Goan** *adj. & n.* **Goanese** /ˌgəʊəˈniːz/ *adj. & n.*

goad /gəʊd/ *n. & v.* —*n.* **1** a spiked stick used for urging cattle forward. **2** anything that torments, incites, or stimulates. —*v.tr.* **1** urge on with a goad. **2** (usu. foll. by *on, into*) irritate; stimulate (*goaded him into retaliating; goaded me on to win*). [OE *gād*, rel. to Lombard *gaida* arrowhead f. Gmc]

goal /gəʊl/ *n.* **1** the object of a person's ambition or effort; a destination; an aim (*fame is his goal; London was our goal*). **2 a** *Football* a pair of posts with a crossbar between which the ball has to be sent to score. **b** a cage or basket used similarly in other games. **c** a point won (*scored 3 goals*). **3** a point marking the end of a race. □ **goal average** *Football* the ratio of the numbers of goals scored for and against a team in a series of matches. **goal difference** *Football* the difference of goals scored for and against. **goal-kick 1** *Assoc. Football* a kick by the defending side after attackers send the ball over the goal-line without scoring. **2** *Rugby Football* an attempt to kick a goal. **goal-line** *Football* a line between each pair of goalposts, extended to form the end-boundary of a field of play (cf. *touch-line*). **goal-minder** (or **-tender**) *US* a goalkeeper at ice hockey. **goal-mouth** *Football* the space between or near the goalposts. **in goal** in the position of goalkeeper. □□ **goalless** *adj.* [16th c.: orig. unkn.: perh. identical with ME *gol* goal]

goalball /ˈgəʊlbɔːl/ *n.* a team ball game for blind and visually handicapped players.

goalie /ˈgəʊlɪ/ *n. colloq.* = GOALKEEPER.

goalkeeper /ˈgəʊlˌkiːpə(r)/ *n.* a player stationed to protect the goal in various sports.

goalpost /ˈgəʊlpəʊst/ *n.* either of the two upright posts of a goal. □ **move the goalposts** alter the basis or scope of a procedure during its course, so as to fit adverse circumstances encountered.

goanna /gəʊˈænə/ *n. Austral.* a monitor lizard. [corrupt. of IGUANA]

goat /gəʊt/ *n.* **1 a** a hardy lively frisky short-haired domesticated mammal, *Capra aegagrus*, having horns and (in the male) a beard, and kept for its milk and meat. **b** either of two similar mammals, the mountain goat and the Spanish goat. **2** any other mammal of the genus *Capra*, including the ibex. **3** a lecherous man. **4** *colloq.* a foolish person. **5** (**the Goat**) the zodiacal sign or constellation Capricorn. **6** *US* a scapegoat. □ **get a person's goat** *colloq.* irritate a person. **goat-antelope** any antelope-like member of the goat family, including the chamois and goral. **goat-god** Pan. **goat moth** any of various large moths of the family Cossidae. **goat's-beard 1** a meadow plant, *Tragopogon pratensis*. **2** a herbaceous plant, *Aruncus dioicus*, with long plumes of white flowers. □□ **goatish** *adj.* **goaty** *adj.* [OE *gāt* she-goat f. Gmc]

goatee /gəʊˈtiː/ n. a small pointed beard like that of a goat.

goatherd /ˈgəʊthɜːd/ n. a person who tends goats.

goatskin /ˈgəʊtskɪn/ n. **1** the skin of a goat. **2** a garment or bottle made out of goatskin.

goatsucker /ˈgəʊtˌsʌkə(r)/ n. = NIGHTJAR.

gob[1] /gɒb/ n. esp. Brit. sl. the mouth. □ **gob-stopper** a very large hard sweet. [perh. f. Gael. & Ir., = beak, mouth]

gob[2] /gɒb/ n. & v. Brit. sl. —n. a clot of slimy matter. —v.intr. (**gobbed, gobbing**) spit. [ME f. OF go(u)be mouthful]

gob[3] /gɒb/ n. sl. a US sailor. [20th c.: cf. GOBBY]

gobbet /ˈgɒbɪt/ n. **1** a piece or lump of raw meat, flesh, food, etc. **2** an extract from a text, esp. one set for translation or comment in an examination. [ME f. OF gobet (as GOB[2])]

gobble[1] /ˈgɒb(ə)l/ v.tr. & intr. eat hurriedly and noisily. □□ **gobbler** n. [prob. dial. f. GOB[2]]

gobble[2] /ˈgɒb(ə)l/ v.intr. **1** (of a turkeycock) make a characteristic swallowing sound in the throat. **2** make such a sound when speaking, esp. when excited, angry, etc. [imit.: perh. based on GOBBLE[1]]

gobbledegook /ˈgɒb(ə)ldɪˌguːk, -ˌgʊk/ n. (also **gobbledygook**) colloq. pompous or unintelligible jargon. [prob. imit. of a turkeycock]

gobbler /ˈgɒblə(r)/ n. colloq. a turkeycock.

gobby /ˈgɒbɪ/ n. (pl. **-ies**) sl. **1** a coastguard. **2** an American sailor. [perh. f. GOB[2] + -Y[1]]

Gobelins /ˈgəʊbəlɪnz, gɒbˈlæ/ the most important tapestry factory of the late 17th and early 18th c., producing work of unrivalled excellence. It originated as a family dyeing workshop, founded by Gilles and Jean Gobelins c.1440, and was taken over by the French Crown in 1662; in the 18th c. leading French painters provided cartoons, and tapestry panels became an alternative to oil painting. The leaders of the Revolution condemned its productions as frivolous, but it was revived by Napoleon. The factory still exists, and now works exclusively for the State.

gobemouche /ˈgɒbmuːʃ/ n. (pl. **gobemouches** pronunc. same) a gullible listener. [F gobe-mouches, = fly-catcher f. gober swallow + mouches flies]

Gobi Desert /ˈgəʊbɪ/ a barren plateau of southern Mongolia and northern China.

goblet /ˈgɒblɪt/ n. **1** a drinking-vessel with a foot and a stem, usu. of glass. **2** archaic a metal or glass bowl-shaped drinking-cup without handles, sometimes with a foot and a cover. **3** poet. a drinking-cup. [ME f. OF gobelet dimin. of gobel cup, of unkn. orig.]

goblin /ˈgɒblɪn/ n. a mischievous ugly dwarflike creature of folklore. [ME prob. f. AF gobelin, med.L gobelinus, prob. f. name dimin. of Gobel, rel. to G Kobold: see COBALT]

goby /ˈgəʊbɪ/ n. (pl. **-ies**) any small marine fish of the family Gabiidae, having ventral fins joined to form a sucker or disc. [L gobius, cobius f. Gk kōbios GUDGEON[1]]

GOC abbr. General Officer Commanding.

god /gɒd/ n. **1 a** (in many religions) a superhuman being or spirit worshipped as having power over nature, human fortunes, etc.; a deity. **b** an image, idol, animal, or other object worshipped as divine or symbolizing a god. **2** (**God**) (in Christian and other monotheistic religions) the creator and ruler of the universe; the supreme being. **3 a** an adored, admired, or influential person. **b** something worshipped like a god (makes a god of success). **4** Theatr. (in pl.) **a** the gallery. **b** the people sitting in it. **5** (**God!**) an exclamation of surprise, anger, etc. □ **by God!** an exclamation of surprise etc. **for God's sake!** see SAKE[1]. **God-awful** sl. extremely unpleasant, nasty, etc. **God bless** an expression of good wishes on parting. **God bless me** (or **my soul**) see BLESS. **God damn** (**you, him,** etc.) may (you etc.) be damned. **god-damn** (or **-dam** or **-damned**) sl. accursed, damnable. **god-daughter** a female godchild. **God the Father, Son, and Holy Ghost** (in the Christian tradition) the Persons of the Trinity. **God-fearing** earnestly religious. **God forbid** (foll. by that + clause, or absol.) may it not happen! **God-forsaken** devoid of all merit; dismal; dreary. **God grant** (foll. by that + clause) may it happen. **God help** (**you, him,** etc.) an expression of concern for or sympathy with a person. **God knows 1** it is beyond all knowledge (God knows what will become of him). **2** I call God to witness that (God knows we tried hard enough). **God's Acre** a churchyard. **God's book** the Bible. **God Save the King** or **Queen** the British national anthem. The origins of both words and tune are obscure. The phrase 'God save the king' occurs in various passages in the Old Testament, while as early as 1545 it was a watchword in the Navy, with 'long to reign over us' as a counter-sign. The anthem probably arose from a series of common loyal phrases being gradually combined into one national hymn, and evidence points to the 17th c. for both the words and the tune of this. **God's gift** often iron. a godsend. **God's own country** an earthly paradise, esp. the United States. **God squad** sl. **1** a religious organization, esp. an evangelical Christian group. **2** its members. **God's truth** the absolute truth. **God willing** if Providence allows. **good God!** an exclamation of surprise, anger, etc. **in God's name** an appeal for help. **my** (or **oh**) **God!** an exclamation of surprise, anger, etc. **play God** assume importance or superiority. **thank God!** an exclamation of pleasure or relief. **with God** dead and in Heaven. □□ **godhood** n. **godship** n. **godward** adj. & adv. **godwards** adv. [OE f. Gmc]

Godavari /gəʊˈdɑːvərɪ/ a river in central India which rises in the State of Maharashtra and flows south-east across the Deccan plateau to the Bay of Bengal.

godchild /ˈgɒdtʃaɪld/ n. (pl. **-children**) a person in relation to a godparent.

goddess /ˈgɒdɪs/ n. **1** a female deity. **2** a woman who is adored, esp. for her beauty.

Gödel /ˈgɜːd(ə)l/, Kurt (1906–78), Austrian mathematician who emigrated to the US in 1938. He made several contributions to mathematical logic, the greatest of which is his incompleteness theorem (1931): that in any sufficiently powerful, logically consistent formulation of the logic of mathematics there must be true formulas which are neither provable nor disprovable, thus making mathematics essentially incomplete, and also the corollary that the consistency of such a system as arithmetic cannot be proved within that system.

godet /ˈgəʊdeɪ/ n. a triangular piece of material inserted in a dress, glove, etc. [F]

godetia /gəˈdiːʃə/ n. any plant of the genus Godetia, having showy rose-purple or reddish flowers. [mod.L f. C. H. Godet, Swiss botanist d. 1879]

godfather /ˈgɒdˌfɑːðə(r)/ n. **1** a male godparent. **2** esp. US a person directing an illegal organization, esp. the Mafia. □ **my godfathers!** euphem. my God!

Godhavn /ˈgəʊdhaʊn, ˈgɒ-/ a town in western Greenland, on the south coast of Disko island.

godhead /ˈgɒdhed/ n. (also **Godhead**) **1 a** the state of being God or a god. **b** divine nature. **2** a deity. **3** (**the Godhead**) God.

Godiva /gəˈdaɪvə/ the wife of an 11th-c. Earl of Mercia, who (according to a 13th-c. legend) agreed to her husband's proposition that he would remit some particularly unpopular taxes only if she rode naked on horseback through Coventry.

godless /ˈgɒdlɪs/ adj. **1** impious; wicked. **2** without a god. **3** not recognizing God. □□ **godlessness** n.

godlike /ˈgɒdlaɪk/ adj. **1** resembling God or a god in some quality, esp. in physical beauty. **2** befitting or appropriate to a god.

godly /ˈgɒdlɪ/ adj. religious, pious, devout. □□ **godliness** n.

godmother /ˈgɒdˌmʌðə(r)/ n. a female godparent.

godown /gəʊˈdaʊn/ n. a warehouse in parts of E. Asia, esp. in India. [Port. gudão f. Malay godong perh. f. Telugu gidangi place where goods lie f. kidu lie]

godparent /ˈgɒdˌpeərənt/ n. a person who presents a child at baptism and responds on the child's behalf.

godsend /ˈgɒdsend/ n. an unexpected but welcome event or acquisition.

godson /ˈgɒdsʌn/ n. a male godchild.

Godspeed /gɒdˈspiːd/ int. an expression of good wishes to a person starting a journey.

Godthåb /'gɒthɔːb/ (Eskimo **Nuuk** /nuːk/) the capital of Greenland; pop. (1986) 11,200.

Godunov /'gɒduˌnɒf/, Boris (1550–1605), tsar of Russia 1598–1605. A noble of Tartar descent, Boris Godunov rose to prominence as a counsellor of Ivan the Terrible and eventually succeeded Ivan's son as tsar. His brief reign was overshadowed by famine, doubts over his involvement in the earlier death of Ivan's eldest son, and the appearance of a pretender, the so-called False Dmitry. His position was seriously undermined by the intrigues of several influential noble families (notably the Romanovs who were later to gain the throne), and Boris died suddenly at a time when his army was trying to defeat an invasion by the Pretender. His family was murdered during the period of anarchy that followed, thus bringing the Ruril dynasty to an end. He was the subject of a play by Pushkin and an opera (based on this) by Mussorgsky.

Godwin /'gɒdwɪn/, William (1756–1836), English philosopher and novelist, who began as a dissenting minister but became an atheist and anarchical philosopher. His propagandist novel *Caleb Williams* (1794), which exposes the perfidiousness of the ruling classes, was an early example of the crime and detection novel. Godwin married Mary Wollstonecraft (1759–97), author of *A Vindication of the Rights of Women* (1792); their daughter, Mary, married the poet Shelley.

Godwin-Austen /ˌgɒdwɪn 'ɔːstɪn/, **Mount** see K2.

godwit /'gɒdwɪt/ n. any wading bird of the genus *Limosa*, with long legs and a long straight or slightly upcurved bill. [16th c.: of unkn. orig.]

Godwottery /gɒd'wɒtəri/ n. joc. affected, archaic, or excessively elaborate speech or writing, esp. regarding gardens. [*God wot* (in a poem on gardens, by T. E. Brown 1876)]

Goebbels /'gɜːb(ə)lz/, (Paul) Joseph (1897–1945), German Nazi leader and politician. In 1933 he became Hitler's minister of propaganda, with control of the press, radio, and all aspects of culture, and manipulated these in order to further Nazi aims.

goer /'gəʊə(r)/ n. **1** a person or thing that goes (*a slow goer*). **2** (often in comb.) a person who attends, esp. regularly (*a churchgoer*). **3** colloq. **a** a lively or persevering person. **b** a sexually promiscuous person. **4** *Austral. colloq.* a project likely to be accepted or to succeed.

Goering /'gɜːrɪŋ/, Hermann Wilhelm (1893–1946), German Nazi leader. In 1934 he became commander of the German air force, and was responsible for the German rearmament programme. Until 1936 Goering headed the Gestapo, which he had founded; from then until 1943 he directed the German economy. He held other senior posts but became increasingly dependent on narcotics; in 1943 he was deprived of all authority and finally dismissed (1945) after unauthorized attempts to make peace with the Western Allies. Sentenced to death at the Nuremberg trials, he committed suicide in his cell.

Goes /guːs/, Hugo van der (active c.1467–82), Flemish painter, born in Ghent and mainly working there, though his best-known work is the large-scale *Portinari Altarpiece* commissioned for a church in Florence.

goes 3rd sing. present of GO[1].

goest /'gəʊɪst/ archaic 2nd sing. present of GO[1].

goeth /'gəʊɪθ/ archaic 3rd sing. present of GO[1].

Goethe /'gɜːtə/, Johann Wolfgang von (1749–1832), German writer, scholar, and statesman who spent most of his life at the court of the Duke of Saxe-Weimar where he was Prime Minister until 1785 as well as being director of the Weimar court theatre from 1791 and head of various scientific institutions, for his wide-ranging interests included not only philosophy but physics, biology, and astrology. He was raised to the nobility in 1782. Goethe's literary achievements cover many forms and closely relate to the social and emotional events of his life. His first important work was an epic drama *Götz von Berlichingen* (1773), inspired by his discovery of Shakespeare. *The Sorrows of Young Werther* (1774), an epistolary novel ending in the hero's death, caused a European sensation. After a visit to Italy, recorded in *Italian Journey* (1816–17), Goethe turned to the classicism which is demonstrated in his dramas *Iphigenia in Tauris* (1787)

and *Tasso* (1790). His 'Wilhelm Meister' novels are the prototype of the German *Bildungsroman*. Goethe was a poet of great genius but outside Germany is celebrated for his major work, *Faust* (1808–32). Among his friends was the dramatist Schiller. He has emerged as the major force that created a national literature of Germany.

Goethean /'gɜːtɪən/ adj. & n. (also **Goethian**) —adj. of, relating to, or characteristic of the German writer J. W. von Goethe. —n. an admirer or follower of Goethe.

gofer /'gəʊfə(r)/ n. esp. *US sl.* a person who runs errands, esp. on a film set or in an office; a dogsbody. [*go for* (see GO[1])]

goffer /'gəʊfə(r), 'gɒf-/ v. & n. —v.tr. **1** make wavy, flute, or crimp (a lace edge, a trimming, etc.) with heated irons. **2** (as **goffered** adj.) (of the edges of a book) embossed. —n. **1** an iron used for goffering. **2** ornamental plaiting used for frills etc. [F *gaufrer* stamp with a patterned tool f. *gaufre* honeycomb, rel. to WAFER, WAFFLE[2]]

Gog and Magog /gɒg, 'meɪgɒg/ **1** the names of various people and lands in the Old Testament. **2** nations under the dominion of Satan (Rev. 20: 8), opposed to the people of God. **3** (in medieval legend) opponents of Alexander the Great, living north of the Caucasus. **4** the names given to two giant statues standing in Guildhall, London, from the time of Henry V (destroyed in 1666 and 1940; replaced in 1953), either (according to Caxton) the last two survivors of a race of giants inhabiting Britain before Roman times, or (in another account) Gogmagog, chief of the giants, and Corineus, a Roman invader.

goggle /'gɒg(ə)l/ v., adj., & n. —v. **1** intr. **a** (often foll. by *at*) look with wide-open eyes. **b** (of the eyes) be rolled about; protrude. **2** tr. turn (the eyes) sideways or from side to side. —adj. (usu. attrib.) (of the eyes) protuberant or rolling. —n. **1** (in pl.) **a** spectacles for protecting the eyes from glare, dust, water, etc. **b** colloq. spectacles. **2** (in pl.) a sheep disease, the staggers. **3** a goggling expression. □ **goggle-box** *Brit. colloq.* a television set. **goggle-dive** an underwater dive in goggles. **goggle-eyed** having staring or protuberant eyes. [ME, prob. from a base *gog* (unrecorded) expressive of oscillating movement]

Gogh /gɒf/, Vincent Willem van, see VAN GOGH.

goglet /'gɒglɪt/ n. *Ind.* a long-necked usu. porous earthenware vessel used for keeping water cool. [Port. *gorgoleta*]

Gogol /'gəʊgɒl/, Nikolai Vasilievich (1809–52), Russian writer, born in the Ukraine, which provided the background for his early writings. His play *The Inspector General* (1836) is a savagely satirical picture of life in a provincial Russian town. His St Petersburg stories (including *Notes of a Madman*, 1835; *The Portrait*, 1835; and *The Greatcoat*, 1842) are set in a mad city where nothing is what it seems. Living mainly abroad from 1836 to 1848, mostly in Rome, he produced his masterpiece, the comic epic *Dead Souls* (1842), but after a spiritual crisis burnt the manuscript of the second part. His fictional world is unique and fantastic, and his prose is marked by an intense imaginative power and linguistic originality.

Goidel /'gɔɪd(ə)l/ n. a member of the Gaelic people that comprise the Scots, Irish, and Manx Celts. □□ **Goidelic** /-'delɪk/ n. [OIr. *Góidel*]

going /'gəʊɪŋ/ n. & adj. —n. **1 a** the act or process of going. **b** an instance of this; a departure. **2 a** the condition of the ground for walking, riding, etc. **b** progress affected by this (*found the going hard*). —adj. **1** in or into action (*set the clock going*). **2** existing, available; to be had (*there's cold beef going; one of the best fellows going*). **3** current, prevalent (*the going rate*). □ **get going** start steadily talking, working, etc. (*can't stop him when he gets going*). **going away** a departure, esp. on a honeymoon. **going concern** a thriving business. **going for one** colloq. acting in one's favour (*he has got a lot going for him*). **going on fifteen** etc. esp. *US* approaching one's fifteenth etc. birthday. **going on for** approaching (a time, an age, etc.) (*must be going on for 6 years*). **going-over 1** colloq. an inspection or overhaul. **2** sl. a thrashing. **3** *US colloq.* a scolding. **goings-on** /ˌgəʊɪŋz'ɒn/ behaviour, esp. morally suspect. **going to** intending or intended to; about to; likely to (*it's going to sink!*). **heavy going** slow or difficult to progress with (*found Proust heavy going*). **to be going on with** to start with; for the time being. **while the going is good** while conditions are favourable. [GO¹: in some senses f. earlier *a-going*: see A²]

goitre /'gɔɪtə(r)/ *n.* (*US* **goiter**) *Med.* a swelling of the neck resulting from enlargement of the thyroid gland. □□ **goitred** *adj.* **goitrous** *adj.* [F, back-form. f. *goitreux* or f. Prov. *goitron*, ult. f. L *guttur* throat]

Golan Heights /gəʊ'lɑːn/ a range of hills in SE Syria, on the border with Israel north-east of the Sea of Galilee. The area was occupied by Israel in 1967 and annexed in 1981; some Jewish settlements have been built; pop. (1983) 19,700.

Golconda /gɒl'kɒndə/ *n.* a mine or source of wealth, advantages, etc. [city near Hyderabad, India]

gold /gəʊld/ *n. & adj.* —*n.* **1** a yellow malleable ductile high density metallic element resistant to chemical reaction, occurring naturally in quartz veins and gravel, and precious as a monetary medium, in jewellery, etc. (See below.) ¶ Symb.: Au; atomic number 79. **2** the colour of gold. **3 a** coins or articles made of gold. **b** money in large sums, wealth. **4** something precious, beautiful, or brilliant (*all that glitters is not gold*). **5** = *gold medal*. **6** gold used for coating a surface or as a pigment, gilding. **7** the bull's-eye of an archery target (usu. gilt). —*adj.* **1** made wholly or chiefly of gold. **2** coloured like gold. □ **age of gold** = *golden age*. **gold amalgam** an easily-moulded combination of gold with mercury. **gold-beater** a person who beats gold out into gold leaf. **gold-beater's skin** a membrane used to separate leaves of gold during beating, or as a covering for slight wounds. **gold bloc** a bloc of countries having a gold standard. **gold brick** *sl.* **1** a thing with only a surface appearance of value, a sham or fraud. **2** *US* a lazy person. **gold-digger 1** *sl.* a woman who wheedles money out of men. **2** a person who digs for gold. **gold-dust 1** gold in fine particles as often found naturally. **2** a plant, *Alyssum saxatile*, with many small yellow flowers. **gold-field** a district in which gold is found as a mineral. **gold foil** gold beaten into a thin sheet. **gold leaf** gold beaten into a very thin sheet. **gold medal** a medal of gold, usu. awarded as first prize. **gold-mine 1** a place where gold is mined. **2** *colloq.* a source of wealth. **gold of pleasure** an annual yellow-flowered plant, *Camelina sativa*. **gold plate 1** vessels made of gold. **2** material plated with gold. **gold-plate** *v.tr.* plate with gold. **gold reserve** a reserve of gold coins or bullion held by a central bank etc. **gold-rush** a rush to a newly-discovered gold-field, esp. the transcontinental journey to California after the discovery of gold there in 1848. **gold standard** a system by which the value of a currency is defined in terms of gold, for which the currency may be exchanged. Most countries held to this from 1900 until it was suspended during the First World War. It was reintroduced in 1925 but abandoned in 1931. **Gold Stick 1** (in the UK) a gilt rod carried on State occasions by the colonel of the Life Guards or the captain of the gentlemen-at-arms. **2** the officer carrying this rod. **gold thread 1** a thread of silk etc. with gold wire wound round it. **2** a bitter plant, *Coptis tinfolia*. [OE f. Gmc]

Gold is quite widely distributed in nature. It occurs in minute quantities in almost all rocks and in sea water, but its extraction from these is not economically feasible and most gold is collected from lodes or rock veins and the alluvial deposits that represent the disintegration of auriferous rocks; it exists in association with most copper and lead deposits, and some gold is recovered in the refining of these. It occurs naturally in the metallic state, never quite pure but alloyed with silver, copper, platinum, or certain other elements; in world production of gold South Africa is dominant, while the USSR has considerable resources. Gold has been known from ancient times and valued for its colour and brightness, rareness, and durability; in normal conditions it does not corrode or tarnish. Its most important uses are for jewellery and other decorative purposes and as currency or to guarantee its value; it is also used in electrical contacts and (in some countries) as a filling for teeth. The relative purity of gold is measured in carats.

Gold Coast 1 the name given by European traders to a coastal area of West Africa, on the Gulf of Guinea, that was an important source of gold. (See GHANA.) **2** a resort region on the east coast of Australia between Brisbane and Sydney; pop. (1986) 219,300.

Gold Collar a classic greyhound race, inaugurated in 1933, run annually at the Catford track in south London, originally in May, now in September.

goldcrest /'gəʊldkrest/ *n.* a small bird, *Regulus regulus*, with a golden crest.

golden /'gəʊld(ə)n/ *adj.* **1 a** made or consisting of gold (*golden sovereign*). **b** yielding gold. **2** coloured or shining like gold (*golden hair*). **3** precious; valuable; excellent; important (*a golden memory; a golden opportunity*). □ **golden age 1** a supposed past age when people were happy and innocent. **2** the period of a nation's greatest prosperity, literary merit, etc. **golden-ager** *US* an old person. **golden balls** a pawnbroker's sign. **golden boy** (or **girl**) *colloq.* a popular or successful person. **golden calf** wealth as an object of worship (Exod. 32). **golden chain** the laburnum. **golden delicious** a variety of dessert apple. **golden disc** an award given to a performer after the sale of 500,000 copies of a record. **golden eagle** a large eagle, *Aquila chrysaetos*, with yellow-tipped head-feathers. **golden-eye** any marine duck of the genus *Bucephala*. **Golden Fleece** *Gk legend* the fleece of gold taken from the ram, given by Hermes, that bore Phrixus through the air to Colchis. It was guarded by a sleepless dragon until secured by Jason with the help of Medea. (See ARGONAUTS.) **Golden Gate** a deep channel connecting San Francisco Bay with the Pacific Ocean, spanned by a suspension bridge (1937). **golden goose** a continuing source of wealth or profit. **golden hamster** a usu. tawny hamster, *Mesocricetus auratus*, kept as a pet or laboratory animal. **golden handshake** *colloq.* a payment given on redundancy or early retirement. **golden hello** *colloq.* a payment made by an employer to a keenly sought recruit. **Golden Horde** the Mongol-Tartar horde that overran Asia and part of eastern Europe in the 13th c., and maintained an empire of varying size in the centre of the continent until the end of the 15th c. **Golden Horn** a curved inlet of the Bosporus, forming the harbour of Istanbul. **golden jubilee 1** the fiftieth anniversary of a sovereign's accession. **2** any other fiftieth anniversary. **golden mean 1** the principle of moderation, as opposed to excess. **2** = *golden section*. **golden number** the number of a year in the Metonic lunar cycle, used to fix the date of Easter. **golden oldie** *colloq.* an old hit record or film etc. that is still well known and popular. **golden opinions** high regard. **golden oriole** a European oriole, *Oriolus oriolus*, of which the male has yellow and black plumage and the female has mainly green plumage. **golden perch** *Austral.* = CALLOP. **golden retriever** a retriever with a thick golden-coloured coat. **golden rod** any plant of the genus *Solidago* with a rodlike stem and a spike of small bright-yellow flowers. **golden rule** a basic principle of action, esp. 'do as you would be done by'. **golden section** the division of a line so that the whole is to the greater part as that part is to the smaller part. **Golden State** *US* California. **golden syrup** *Brit.* a pale treacle. **golden wedding** the fiftieth anniversary of a wedding. □□ **goldenly** *adv.* **goldenness** *n.*

Golden Hind /haɪnd/ the ship in which, in 1577–80, Francis Drake circumnavigated the globe and was knighted on his return. She was originally the *Pelican*, but Drake changed the name en route in honour of his patron, Sir Christopher Hatton, whose crest was a golden hind.

goldfinch /'gəʊldfɪntʃ/ *n.* any of various bright-coloured songbirds of the genus *Carduelis*, esp. the Eurasian *C. carduelis*, with a yellow band across each wing. [OE *goldfinc* (as GOLD, FINCH)]

goldfish /'gəʊldfɪʃ/ *n.* a small reddish-golden Chinese carp kept for ornament, *Carassius auratus*. □ **goldfish bowl 1** a globular glass container for goldfish. **2** a situation lacking privacy.

goldilocks /'gəʊldɪˌlɒks/ *n.* **1** a person with golden hair. **2 a** a kind of buttercup, *Ranunculus auricomus*. **b** a composite plant, *Aster linosyris*, like the golden rod. [*goldy* f. GOLD + LOCK²]

Golding /'gəʊldɪŋ/, Sir William Gerald (1911–), English novelist, who achieved literary success with his first novel *Lord of the Flies* (1954) about a group of boys who revert to savagery when stranded on a desert island. The intrinsic cruelty of man is at the heart of many of his novels, including *The Inheritors* (1955) and *Rites of Passage* (1980). In presenting man in his basic condition, in extreme situations, and 'gripped by original sin', Golding creates the quality of a fable. He was awarded the Nobel Prize for literature in 1983.

Goldsmith /'gəʊldsmɪθ/, Oliver (?1730–74), Anglo-Irish novelist, poet, essayist, and dramatist. After studying medicine at Edinburgh and Leyden and wandering on the Continent he arrived destitute in London in 1756 where he practised as a physician and began his literary career as a reviewer and hackwriter. His first substantial work was *An Enquiry into the Present State of Polite Learning* (1759). His masterpieces are *The Citizen of the World* (1762), a collection of satirical letters written by an imaginary Chinese philosopher, his novel *The Vicar of Wakefield* (1766), and his poem *The Deserted Village* (1770). His most successful plays were *She Stoops to Conquer* (1773) and *The Good-Natur'd Man* (1768). Goldsmith was admired by Samuel Johnson for the charm and elegance of his writing.

goldsmith /'gəʊldsmɪθ/ n. a worker in gold, a manufacturer of gold articles. [OE (as GOLD, SMITH)]

Goldwyn /'gəʊldwɪn/, Samuel (?1882–1974), born Schmuel Gelbfisz (changed to Goldfish then Goldwyn), American film producer. He became independent by 1925, producing films of high quality in his own studio, including *Wuthering Heights* (1939), *The Little Foxes* (1941), and *The Best Years of Our Lives* (1946). He also produced some notable musicals, such as *Guys and Dolls* (1955), and the opera *Porgy and Bess* (1959). Goldwynisms such as 'Include me out' became common usage.

golem /'gəʊləm/ n. 1 (in Jewish legend) a clay figure supposedly brought to life. 2 an automaton; a robot. [Yiddish *goylem* f. Heb. *gōlem* shapeless mass]

golf /gɒlf/ n. & v. —n. a game played on a course set in open country, in which a small hard ball is struck with various clubs into a series of small cylindrical holes (now usually 18 or 9) on smooth greens at varying distances apart and separated by fairways, rough ground, hazards, etc. The aim is to drive the ball into any one hole, or into all the holes successively, with the fewest possible strokes, with two persons or two couples playing against each other. (See below.) —v.intr. play golf. □ **golf-bag** a bag used for carrying clubs and balls. **golf ball 1** a ball used in golf. **2** *colloq.* a small ball used in some electric typewriters to carry the type. **golf cart 1** a trolley used for carrying clubs in golf. **2** a motorized cart for golfers and equipment. **golf club 1** a club used in golf. **2** an association for playing golf. **3** the premises used by a golf club. **golf-course** (or **-links**) the course on which golf is played. [15th-c. Sc.: orig. unkn.]

The game of golf is of considerable antiquity in Scotland (the word is attested in the 15th c.) and in Holland. James II banned the game in 1457 because (like football) it interfered with the practice of archery, but royal patronage after the peace treaty of 1502 stimulated the growth of the game, and James VI of Scotland brought it south with him when he succeeded to the English throne. In early days it was played on the common links land bordering the sea.

golfer /'gɒlfə(r)/ n. 1 a golf-player. 2 a cardigan.

Golgi /'gɒldʒɪ/, Camillo (1844–1926), Italian anatomist noted for his study of the minute structure of the nervous system. He devised a method of staining tissue with silver salts which revealed details of the cells and enabled individual nerve fibres to be traced, classified types of nerve cell, and described a complex structure in the cytoplasm of most cells, the 'Golgi body' or 'Golgi apparatus', that is now believed to be involved in secretion. Golgi was awarded the Nobel Prize for medicine, jointly with Ramón y Cajal, in 1906.

Golgotha /'gɒlgəθə/ the Aramaic name of Calvary (Mark 15: 22). [LL f. Gk. f. Heb. *gulgoleth* skull]

Goliath /gə'laɪəθ/ a Philistine giant, according to legend slain by David (1 Sam. 17), but according to another tradition slain by Elhanan (2 Sam. 21: 19). □ **Goliath beetle** any large beetle of the genus *Goliathus*, esp. *G. giganteus* native to Africa.

golliwog /'gɒlɪˌwɒg/ n. a black-faced brightly dressed soft doll with fuzzy hair. [19th c.: perh. f. GOLLY¹ + POLLIWOG]

gollop /'gɒləp/ v. & n. *colloq.* —v.tr. (**golloped, golloping**) swallow hastily or greedily. —n. a hasty gulp. [perh. f. GULP, infl. by GOBBLE¹]

golly¹ /'gɒlɪ/ int. expressing surprise. [euphem. for GOD]

golly² /'gɒlɪ/ n. (pl. **-ies**) *colloq.* = GOLLIWOG. [abbr.]

golosh Brit. var. of GALOSH.

GOM abbr. Grand Old Man (name orig. applied to W. E. Gladstone).

gombeen /gɒm'biːn/ n. Ir. usury. □ **gombeen-man** a moneylender. [Ir. *gaimbín* perh. f. the same OCelt. source as med.L *cambire* CHANGE]

Gomorrah /gə'mɒrə/ a town of ancient Palestine, probably south of the Dead Sea, destroyed by fire from heaven (according to Genesis 19: 24), along with Sodom, for the wickedness of its inhabitants.

-gon /gən/ *comb. form* forming nouns denoting plane figures with a specified number of angles (*hexagon*; *polygon*; *n-gon*). [Gk *-gōnos* -angled]

gonad /'gəʊnæd/ n. an animal organ producing gametes, e.g. the testis or ovary. □□ **gonadal** /gəʊ'neɪd(ə)l/ adj. [mod.L *gonas gonad-* f. Gk *gonē, gonos* generation, seed]

gonadotrophic hormone /ˌgəʊnədəʊ'trəʊfɪk/ n. (also **gonadotropic** /-'trɒpɪk, -'trəʊpɪk/) Biochem. any of various hormones stimulating the activity of the gonads.

gonadotrophin /ˌgəʊnədəʊ'trəʊfɪn/ n. = GONADOTROPHIC HORMONE.

Goncourt /'gɔ̃kuːr/, Edmond and Jules de (1822–96 and 1830–70), French authors, brothers, who wrote in close collaboration. Their early work included art criticism and social history. *Soeur Philomène* (1861), *Germinie Lacerteux* (1864), and *Madame Gervaisais* (1869) are among their painstakingly documented novels often cited as examples of 19th-c. realism and naturalism. The *Journal des Goncourt* is their detailed record of literary and artistic life in Paris between 1851 and 1896. The Académie Goncourt which awards the annual *Prix Goncourt* for imaginative prose was founded under the will of Edmond de Goncourt.

gondola /'gɒndələ/ n. 1 a light flat-bottomed pleasure-boat, much ornamented, with a high rising and curving stem and stern-post, used on the canals of Venice and worked by one man with a single oar, standing near the stern. Its origin is unknown but it is mentioned as early as 1094. 2 a car suspended from an airship or dirigible balloon. 3 an island of shelves used to display goods in a supermarket. 4 (also **gondola car**) US a flat-bottomed open railway goods wagon. 5 a car attached to a ski-lift. [Venetian It., of obscure orig.]

gondolier /ˌgɒndə'lɪə(r)/ n. the oarsman on a gondola. [F f. It. *gondoliere* (as GONDOLA)]

Gondwana /gɒn'dwɑːnə/ (also **Gondwanaland**) a vast continental area thought to have once existed in the southern hemisphere and to have broken up in Mesozoic or late Palaeozoic times to form Arabia, Africa, South America, Antarctica, Australia, and the peninsula of India. [*Gondwana* land of the Gonds, a Dravidian people of central India]

gone /gɒn/ adj. 1 (of time) past (*not until gone nine*). 2 a lost; hopeless. b dead. 3 *colloq.* pregnant for a specified time (*already three months gone*). 4 *sl.* completely enthralled or entranced, esp. by rhythmic music, drugs, etc. □ **be gone** depart; leave temporarily (cf. BEGONE). **gone away!** a huntsman's cry, indicating that a fox has been started. **gone goose** (or **gosling**) *colloq.* a person or thing beyond hope. **gone on** *sl.* infatuated with. [past part. of GO¹]

goner /'gɒnə(r)/ n. *sl.* a person or thing that is doomed, ended, irrevocably lost, etc.; a dead person.

gonfalon /'gɒnfələn/ n. 1 a banner, often with streamers, hung from a crossbar. 2 *hist.* such a banner as the standard of some Italian republics. □□ **gonfalonier** /ˌgɒnfələ'nɪə(r)/ n. [It. *gonfalone* f. Gmc (cf. VANE)]

gong /gɒŋ/ n. & v. —n. 1 a a metal disc with a turned rim, giving a resonant note when struck, esp. one used as a signal for meals. b a percussion instrument which exists in widely varying shapes and sizes, generally comprising a large hanging bronze disc with a bossed centre which is struck in the middle with a soft-headed drumstick. Today the name 'tam-tam' refers to a gong of indefinite pitch, and 'gong' to one which may be tuned to a specific pitch. The ancient gong dates from at least the 6th c. AD in an area extending from Tibet to Indonesia (in the latter, for example, forming an important part of the gamelan); in the West it began to appear in orchestral music towards the end of the 19th c. **2** a saucer-shaped bell. **3** *Brit. sl.* a medal; a decoration. —*v.tr.* **1** summon with a gong. **2** (of traffic police) sound a gong etc. to direct (a motorist) to stop. [Malay *gong, gung* of imit. orig.]

goniometer /ˌgəʊnɪˈɒmɪtə(r)/ *n.* an instrument for measuring angles. □□ **goniometry** *n.* **goniometric** /-əˈmetrɪk/ *adj.* **goniometrical** /-əˈmetrɪk(ə)l/ *adj.* [F *goniomètre* f. Gk *gōnia* angle]

gonococcus /ˌgɒnəˈkɒkəs/ *n.* (pl. **gonococci** /-kaɪ/) a bacterium causing gonorrhoea. □□ **gonococcal** *adj.* [Gk *gonos* generation, semen + COCCUS]

gonorrhoea /ˌgɒnəˈrɪə/ *n.* (US **gonorrhea**) a venereal disease with inflammatory discharge from the urethra or vagina. □□ **gonorrhoeal** *adj.* [LL f. Gk *gonorrhoia* f. *gonos* semen + *rhoia* flux]

goo /guː/ *n.* **1** a sticky or slimy substance. **2** sickly sentiment. [20th c.: perh. f. *burgoo* (Naut. sl.) = porridge]

good /gʊd/ *adj., n., & adv.* —*adj.* (**better, best**) **1** having the right or desired qualities; satisfactory, adequate. **2 a** (of a person) efficient, competent (*good at French; a good driver*). **b** (of a thing) reliable, efficient (*good brakes*). **c** (of health etc.) strong (*good eyesight*). **3 a** kind, benevolent (*good of you to come*). **b** morally excellent; virtuous (*a good deed*). **c** charitable (*good works*). **d** well-behaved (*a good child*). **4** enjoyable, agreeable (*a good party; good news*). **5** thorough, considerable (*gave it a good wash*). **6 a** not less than (*waited a good hour*). **b** considerable in number, quality, etc. (*a good many people*). **7** healthy, beneficial (*milk is good for you*). **8 a** valid, sound (*a good reason*). **b** financially sound (*his credit is good*). **9** in exclamations of surprise (*good heavens!*). **10** right, proper, expedient (*thought it good to have a try*). **11** fresh, eatable, untainted (*is the meat still good?*). **12** (sometimes patronizing) commendable, worthy (*good old George; your good lady wife; good men and true; my good man*). **13** well shaped, attractive (*has good legs; good looks*). **14** in courteous greetings and farewells (*good afternoon*). —*n.* **1** (only in *sing.*) that which is good; what is beneficial or morally right (*only good can come of it; did it for your own good; what good will it do?*). **2** (only in *sing.*) a desirable end or object; a thing worth attaining (*sacrificing the present for a future good*). **3** (in *pl.*) **a** movable property or merchandise. **b** *Brit.* things to be transported, as distinct from passengers. **c** (prec. by *the*) *colloq.* what one has undertaken to supply (esp. *deliver the goods*). **d** (prec. by *the*) *sl.* the real thing; the genuine article. **4** (as *pl.*; prec. by *the*) virtuous people. —*adv.* US *colloq.* well (*doing pretty good*). □ **as good as** practically (*he as good as told me*). **be so good as** (or **be good enough**) **to** (often in a request) be kind and do (a favour) (*be so good as to open the window*). **be (a certain amount) to the good** have as net profit or advantage. **do good** show kindness, act philanthropically. **do a person good** be beneficial to. **for good (and all)** finally, permanently. **good and** *colloq.* used as an intensifier before an adj. or adv. (*raining good and hard; was good and angry*). **the good book** the Bible. **good breeding** correct or courteous manners. **good faith** see FAITH. **good for 1** beneficial to; having a good effect on. **2** able to perform; inclined for (*good for a ten-mile walk*). **3** able to be trusted to pay (*is good for £100*). **good form** see FORM. **good-for-nothing** (or **-nought**) *adj.* worthless. —*n.* a worthless person. **good for you!** (or **him!, her!,** etc.) exclamation of approval towards a person. **Good Friday** the Friday before Easter Sunday, commemorating the Crucifixion of Christ. **good-hearted** kindly, well-meaning. **good humour** a genial mood. **a good job** a fortunate state of affairs (*it's a good job you came early*). **good-looker** a handsome or attractive person. **good-looking** handsome; attractive. **good luck 1** good fortune, happy chance. **2** exclamation of well-wishing. **good money 1** genuine money; money that might usefully have been spent elsewhere. **2** *colloq.* high wages. **good nature** a friendly disposition. **good oil** *Austral. sl.* reliable information. **good on you!** (or **him!** etc.)

= *good for you!* **goods and chattels** see CHATTEL. **good-time** recklessly pursuing pleasure. **good-timer** a person who recklessly pursues pleasure. **good times** a period of prosperity. **good will** the intention and hope that good will result (see also GOODWILL). **a good word** (often in phr. **put in a good word for**) words in recommendation or defence of a person. **good works** charitable acts. **have a good mind** see MIND. **have the goods on a person** *sl.* have advantageous information about a person. **have a good time** enjoy oneself. **in a person's good books** see BOOK. **in good faith** with honest or sincere intentions. **in good time 1** with no risk of being late. **2** (also **all in good time**) in due course but without haste. **make good 1** make up for, compensate (for, pay (an expense). **2** fulfil (a promise); effect (a purpose or an intended action). **3** demonstrate the truth of (a statement); substantiate (a charge). **4** gain and hold (a position). **5** replace or restore (a thing lost or damaged). **6** (*absol.*) accomplish what one intended. **no good 1** mischief (*is up to no good*). **2** useless; to no advantage (*it is no good arguing*). **no-good** —*adj.* useless. —*n.* a useless thing or person. **take in good part** not be offended by. **to the good** having as profit or benefit. □□ **goodish** *adj.* [OE *gōd* f. Gmc]

goodbye /gʊdˈbaɪ/ *int. & n.* (US **goodby**) —*int.* expressing good wishes on parting, ending a telephone conversation, etc., or said with reference to a thing got rid of or irrevocably lost. —*n.* (pl. **goodbyes** or US **goodbys**) the saying of 'goodbye'; a parting; a farewell. [contr. of *God be with you!* with *good* substituted after *good night* etc.]

good-humoured /gʊdˈhjuːməd/ *adj.* genial, cheerful, amiable. □□ **good-humouredly** *adv.*

goodie var. of GOODY¹ *n.*

goodly /ˈgʊdlɪ/ *adj.* (**goodlier, goodliest**) **1** comely, handsome. **2** of imposing size etc. □□ **goodliness** *n.* [OE *gōdlic* (as GOOD, -LY¹)]

Goodman /ˈgʊdmən/, Benjamin David ('Benny') (1909–86), American clarinettist and jazz musician, who formed his own big band in 1934. He was known as the 'King of Swing' and his style started a new era in the history of jazz. His skill as a clarinettist was not confined to jazz: Bartók, Hindemith, and Copland all composed solo works for him, and he also gave distinguished performances of classical works.

goodman /ˈgʊdmən/ *n.* (pl. **-men**) *Sc. archaic* the head of a household.

good-natured /gʊdˈneɪtʃəd/ *adj.* kind, patient; easygoing. □□ **good-naturedly** *adv.*

goodness /ˈgʊdnɪs/ *n. & int.* —*n.* **1** virtue; excellence, esp. moral. **2** kindness (*had the goodness to wait*). **3** what is good or beneficial in a thing (*vegetables with all the goodness boiled out*). —*int.* (as a substitution for 'God') expressing surprise, anger, etc. (*goodness me!; goodness knows; for goodness' sake!*). [OE *gōdnes* (as GOOD, -NESS)]

goodo /ˈgʊdəʊ/ *adj. Austral. & NZ* = GOOD *adj.* 10.

good-tempered /gʊdˈtempəd/ *adj.* having a good temper; not easily annoyed. □□ **good-temperedly** *adv.*

goodwife /ˈgʊdwaɪf/ *n.* (pl. **-wives**) *Sc. archaic* the mistress of a household.

goodwill /gʊdˈwɪl/ *n.* **1** kindly feeling. **2** the established reputation of a business etc. as enhancing its value. **3** cheerful consent or acquiescence; readiness, zeal.

goody¹ /ˈgʊdɪ/ *n. & int.* —*n.* (also **goodie**) (pl. **-ies**) **1** *colloq.* a good or favoured person, esp. a hero in a story, film, etc. **2** (usu. in *pl.*) something good or attractive, esp. to eat. **3** = GOODY-GOODY *n.* —*int.* expressing childish delight.

goody² /ˈgʊdɪ/ *n.* (pl. **goodies**) *archaic* (often as a title prefixed to a surname) an elderly woman of humble station (*Goody Blake*). [for GOODWIFE: cf. HUSSY]

goody-goody /ˈgʊdɪˌgʊdɪ/ *n. & adj. colloq.* —*n.* a smug or obtrusively virtuous person. —*adj.* obtrusively or smugly virtuous.

gooey /ˈguːɪ/ *adj.* (**gooier, gooiest**) *sl.* **1** viscous, sticky. **2** sickly, sentimental. □□ **gooeyness** *n.* (also **gooiness**). [GOO + -Y²]

goof /guːf/ *n. & v. sl.* —*n.* **1** a foolish or stupid person. **2** a mistake. —v. 1 tr. bungle, mess up. 2 intr. blunder, make a mistake. 3 intr. (often foll. by off) idle. 4 tr. (as **goofed** adj.) stupefied with drugs. [var. of dial. goff f. F goffe f. It. goffo f. med.L gufus coarse]

goofy /ˈguːfɪ/ adj. (**goofier, goofiest**) colloq. 1 stupid, silly, daft. 2 having protruding or crooked front teeth. □□ **goofily** adv. **goofiness** n. [sense 2 from the Disney cartoon character with this name]

goog /gʊg/ n. Austral. sl. an egg. □ **full as a goog** very drunk. [20th c.: orig. unkn.]

googly /ˈguːglɪ/ n. (pl. **-ies**) Cricket an off-break ball bowled with apparent leg-break action. (See BOSANQUET.) [20th c.: orig. unkn.]

googol /ˈguːgɒl/ n. ten raised to the hundredth power (10^{100}). ¶ Not in formal use. [arbitrary formation]

gook /guːk, gʊk/ n. US sl. offens. a foreigner, esp. a coloured person from E. Asia. [20th c.: orig. unkn.]

goolie /ˈguːlɪ/ n. (also **gooly**) (pl. **-ies**) 1 (usu. in pl.) sl. a testicle. 2 Austral. sl. a stone or pebble. [app. f. Ind. orig.; cf. Hind. golí bullet, ball, pill]

goon /guːn/ n. sl. 1 a stupid or playful person. 2 esp. US a person hired by racketeers etc. to terrorize political or industrial opponents. [perh. f. dial. gooney booby; infl. by the subhuman cartoon character 'Alice the Goon']

goop /guːp/ n. sl. a stupid or fatuous person. [20th c.: cf. GOOF]

goopy /ˈguːpɪ/ adj. sl. (**goopier, goopiest**) stupid, fatuous. □□ **goopiness** n.

goosander /guːˈsændə(r)/ n. a large diving duck, Mergus merganser, with a narrow serrated bill. [prob. f. GOOSE + -ander in bergander sheldrake]

goose /guːs/ n. & v. —n. (pl. **geese** /giːs/) 1 a any of various large water-birds of the family Anatidae, with short legs, webbed feet, and a broad bill. b the female of this (opp. GANDER). c the flesh of a goose as food. 2 colloq. a simpleton. 3 (pl. **gooses**) a tailor's smoothing-iron, having a handle like a goose's neck. —v.tr. sl. poke (a person) in the bottom. □ **goose bumps** US = goose-flesh. **goose-egg** US a zero score in a game. **goose-flesh** (or **-pimples** or **-skin**) a bristling state of the skin produced by cold or fright. **goose-step** a military marching step in which the knees are kept stiff. [OE gōs f. Gmc]

gooseberry /ˈgʊzbərɪ/ n. (pl. **-ies**) 1 a round edible yellowish-green berry with a thin usu. translucent skin enclosing seeds in a juicy flesh. 2 the thorny shrub, Ribes grossularia, bearing this fruit. □ **play gooseberry** Brit. colloq. be an unwanted extra (usu. third) person. [perh. f. GOOSE + BERRY]

goosefoot /ˈguːsfʊt/ n. (pl. **-foots**) any plant of the genus Chenopodium, having leaves shaped like the foot of a goose.

goosegog /ˈgʊzgɒg/ n. Brit. colloq. a gooseberry. [joc. corrupt.]

goosegrass /ˈguːsgrɑːs/ n. cleavers.

Goossens /ˈguːsənz/, Sir (Aynsley) Eugene (1893–1962), English conductor, violinist, and composer. He came of a Belgian musical family: his father and grandfather were conductors, his brother Leon was a virtuoso oboist (for whom Goossens, Elgar, and Vaughan Williams all wrote works), and his sister Marie was a harpist. From 1947 until 1956 Goossens directed both the Sydney Symphony Orchestra and the New South Wales Conservatorium, and was thus able to exert a marked influence on the emergence of a distinctively Australian music.

GOP abbr. US Grand Old Party (the Republican Party).

gopher¹ /ˈgəʊfə(r)/ n. 1 (in full **pocket gopher**) any burrowing rodent of the family Geomyidae, native to N. America, having external cheek pouches and sharp front teeth. 2 a N. American ground-squirrel. 3 a tortoise, Gopherus polyphemus, native to the southern US, that excavates tunnels as shelter from the sun. □ **gopher snake** a cribo. [18th c.: orig. uncert.]

gopher² /ˈgəʊfə(r)/ n. 1 Bibl. a tree from the wood of which Noah's ark was made. 2 (in full **gopher-wood**) a tree, Cladrastis lutea, yielding yellowish timber. [Heb. gōper]

goral /ˈgɔːr(ə)l/ n. a goat-antelope, Nemorhaedus goral, native to mountainous regions of N. India, having short horns curving to the rear. [native name]

Gorbachev /ˈgɔːbəˌtʃɒf/, Mikhail Sergeevich (1931–), Soviet statesman, General Secretary of the Communist Party of the USSR from 1985, President from 1988 (later with increased powers). Abroad, he negotiated arms control treaties with the West; at home, he introduced a policy of openness (glasnost) and restructuring (perestroika), but later became accused of replacing reform with repression. His policies reshaped the socialist ideals of the USSR (though opposed by traditionalists who resisted reform and radicals who sought for it to be more rapid), and unleashed both the energy of political change in a number of countries of eastern Europe and initiatives towards independence in the constituent republics of his own country. He was awarded a Nobel Peace Prize in 1990.

gorblimey /gɔːˈblaɪmɪ/ int. & n. Brit. colloq. —int. an expression of surprise, indignation, etc. —n. (pl. **-eys**) a soft service cap. [corrupt. of God blind me]

gorcock /ˈgɔːkɒk/ n. Sc. & N.Engl. the male of the red grouse. [gor- (of unkn. orig.) + COCK¹]

Gordian knot /ˈgɔːdɪən/ n. 1 an intricate knot. 2 a difficult problem or task. □ **cut the Gordian knot** solve a problem by force or by evasion. [Gordius, king of ancient Phrygia, who tied an intricate knot that remained tied until cut by Alexander the Great]

Gordimer /ˈgɔːdɪmə(r)/, Nadine (1923–), South African writer of novels and short stories. Most of her work is concerned with the political situation in her country, and her protests against apartheid and censorship have been outspoken. Her novels include A Guest of Honour (1970) and The Conservationist (1974).

Gordon /ˈgɔːd(ə)n/, Charles George (1833–85), British general and colonial administrator, known as 'Chinese Gordon' after service against the Taiping rebels in 1863–4. Sent to rescue the Egyptian garrisons in the Sudan from the Dervishes, he was trapped at Khartoum and killed before a relieving force could reach him.

Gordon riots /ˈgɔːd(ə)n/ a series of anti-Catholic riots in London on 2–9 June 1780, in which about 300 people were killed. The riots were provoked by a petition presented to Parliament by Lord George Gordon against the relaxation of restrictions on the holding of landed property by Roman Catholics.

Gordon setter /ˈgɔːd(ə)n/ n. 1 a setter of a black and tan breed, used as a gun dog. 2 this breed. [4th Duke of Gordon, d. 1827, promoter of the breed]

gore¹ /gɔː(r)/ n. blood shed and clotted. [OE gor dung, dirt]

gore² /gɔː(r)/ v.tr. pierce with a horn, tusk, etc. [ME: orig. unkn.]

gore³ /gɔː(r)/ n. & v. —n. 1 a wedge-shaped piece in a garment. 2 a triangular or tapering piece in an umbrella etc. —v.tr. shape with a gore. [OE gāra triangular piece of land, rel. to OE gār spear, a spearhead being triangular]

Göreme /ˈɡɜːrɪmɪ/ a valley in Cappadocia in central Turkey, noted for its cave-dwellings. Originally the name was applied to a larger area which was a major centre of early Christianity; in the Byzantine era it contained hermits' cells, monasteries, and over 400 churches, all hollowed out of the soft tufa rock.

gorge /gɔːdʒ/ n. & v. —n. 1 a narrow opening between hills or a rocky ravine, often with a stream running through it. 2 an act of gorging; a feast. 3 the contents of the stomach; what has been swallowed. 4 the neck of a bastion or other outwork; the rear entrance to a work. 5 US a mass of ice etc. blocking a narrow passage. —v. 1 intr. feed greedily. 2 tr. a (often refl.) satiate, glut. b swallow, devour greedily. □ **cast the gorge at** reject with loathing. **one's gorge rises at** one is sickened by. □□ **gorger** n. [ME f. OF gorge throat ult. f. L gurges whirlpool]

gorgeous /ˈgɔːdʒəs/ adj. 1 richly coloured, sumptuous, magnificent. 2 colloq. very pleasant, splendid (gorgeous weather). 3 colloq. strikingly beautiful. □□ **gorgeously** adv. **gorgeousness** n. [earlier gorgayse, -yas f. OF gorgias fine, elegant, of unkn. orig.]

gorget /ˈgɔːgɪt/ n. 1 hist. a a piece of armour for the throat. b a woman's wimple. 2 a patch of colour on the throat of a bird, insect, etc. [OF gorgete (as GORGE)]

Gorgio /ˈgɔːdʒɪˌəʊ/ n. (pl. **-os**) the Gypsy name for a non-Gypsy. [Romany]

gorgon /ˈgɔːgən/ n. 1 (**gorgon**) Gk Mythol. any of three sisters, Stheno, Euryale, and Medusa (the only mortal one), with snakes for hair, who had the power to turn anyone who looked at them to stone. **2** a frightening or repulsive person, esp. a woman. □□ **gorgonian** /gɔːˈɡəʊnɪən/ *adj*. [L *Gorgo -onis* f. Gk *Gorgō* f. *gorgos* terrible]

gorgonian /gɔːˈɡəʊnɪən/ *n*. & *adj*. —*n*. a usu. brightly coloured horny coral of the order Gorgonacea, having a treelike skeleton bearing polyps, e.g. a sea fan. —*adj*. of or relating to the Gorgonacea. [mod.L (as GORGON), with ref. to its petrifaction]

gorgonize /ˈɡɔːɡənaɪz/ *v.tr.* (also **-ise**) **1** stare at like a gorgon. **2** paralyse with terror etc.

Gorgonzola /ˌɡɔːɡənˈzəʊlə/ *n*. a type of rich cheese with bluish-green veins. [*Gorgonzola* in N. Italy]

gorilla /ɡəˈrɪlə/ *n*. the largest anthropoid ape, *Gorilla gorilla*, native to Central Africa, having a large head, short neck, and prominent mouth. [adopted as the specific name in 1847 f. Gk *Gorillai* an African tribe noted for hairiness]

Gorky[1] /ˈɡɔːkɪ/ a river port on the Volga in the USSR, formerly called Nizhny Novgorod and renamed after Maxim Gorky in 1932; pop. (est. 1987) 1,425,000.

Gorky[2] /ˈɡɔːkɪ/, Maxim (pseudonym of Alexei Maximovich Peshkov, 1868–1936) Russian novelist, playwright, and revolutionary, who was largely self-educated, being obliged to earn his living from the age of eight. His childhood experiences of wanderings all over Russia are related in his autobiographical masterpieces *Childhood* (1913), *Among People* (1915), and *My Universities* (1923). Gorky became famous for the short realistic stories that he published in 1895–1900, and followed these with novels and plays including *The Mother* (1906–7, the story of the radicalization of an uneducated woman, which became a model for the socialist-realist novel), and *The Lower Depths* (1902), but suffered for his radical views. From 1906 to 1913 and again from 1921 to 1928 he lived abroad, then returning to Russia as an enthusiastic supporter of the government and Stalinism. Officially lionized as the father of the new socialist art, he was partly responsible for the doctrine of socialist realism, and became president of the Union of Soviet Writers in 1934. His last years and the circumstances of his death are shrouded in mystery.

gormandize /ˈɡɔːmənˌdaɪz/ *v*. & *n*. (also **-ise**) —*v*. **1** *intr.* & *tr.* eat or devour voraciously. **2** *intr.* indulge in good eating. —*n*. = GOURMANDISE. □□ **gormandizer** *n*. [as GOURMANDISE]

gormless /ˈɡɔːmlɪs/ *adj*. esp. *Brit. colloq.* foolish, lacking sense. □□ **gormlessly** *adv*. **gormlessness** *n*. [orig. *gaumless* f. dial. *gaum* understanding]

gorse /ɡɔːs/ *n*. any spiny yellow-flowered shrub of the genus *Ulex*, esp. growing on European wastelands. Also called FURZE. □□ **gorsy** *adj*. [OE *gors(t)* rel. to OHG *gersta*, L *hordeum*, barley]

Gorsedd /ˈɡɔːseð/ *n*. a meeting of Welsh etc. bards and druids (esp. as a daily preliminary to the eisteddfod). [Welsh, lit. 'throne']

gory /ˈɡɔːrɪ/ *adj*. (**gorier, goriest**) **1** involving bloodshed; bloodthirsty (*a gory film*). **2** covered in gore. □□ **gorily** *adv*. **goriness** *n*.

gosh /ɡɒʃ/ *int.* expressing surprise. [euphem. for GOD]

goshawk /ˈɡɒshɔːk/ *n*. a large short-winged hawk, *Accipiter gentilis*. [OE *gōs-hafoc* (as GOOSE, HAWK[1])]

gosling /ˈɡɒzlɪŋ/ *n*. a young goose. [ME, orig. *gesling* f. ON *gǣslingr*]

gospel /ˈɡɒsp(ə)l/ *n*. **1** the teaching or revelation of Christ. **2** (**Gospel**) **a** the record of Christ's life and teaching in the first four books of the New Testament. **b** each of these books (the use probably originated from the occurrence of the word in the opening sentence at Mark 1: 1), attributed to Matthew, Mark, Luke, and John. **c** a portion from one of them read at a service. **3** a thing regarded as absolutely true (*take my word as gospel*). **4** a principle one acts on or advocates. **5** (in full **gospel music**) Black American evangelical religious singing. □ **Gospel side** the north side of the altar, at which the Gospel is read. **gospel truth** something as true as the Gospel. [OE *gōdspel* (as GOOD, *spel* news, SPELL[1]), rendering eccl.L *bona annuntiatio, bonus nuntius* = *evangelium* EVANGEL: assoc. with GOD]

gospeller /ˈɡɒspələ(r)/ *n*. the reader of the Gospel in a Communion service. □ **hot gospeller** a zealous puritan; a rabid propagandist.

gossamer /ˈɡɒsəmə(r)/ *n*. & *adj*. —*n*. **1** a filmy substance of small spiders' webs. **2** delicate filmy material. **3** a thread of gossamer. —*adj*. light and flimsy as gossamer. □□ **gossamered** *adj*. **gossamery** *adj*. [ME *gos(e)somer(e)*, app. f. GOOSE + SUMMER[1] (*goose summer* = St Martin's summer, i.e. early November when geese were eaten, gossamer being common then)]

gossip /ˈɡɒsɪp/ *n*. & *v*. —*n*. **1 a** easy or unconstrained talk or writing esp. about persons or social incidents. **b** idle talk; groundless rumour. **2** an informal chat, esp. about persons or social incidents. **3** a person who indulges in gossip. —*v.intr.* (**gossiped, gossiping**) talk or write gossip. □ **gossip column** a section of a newspaper devoted to gossip about well-known people. **gossip columnist** a regular writer of gossip columns. **gossip-monger** a perpetrator of gossip. □□ **gossiper** *n*. **gossipy** *adj*. [earlier sense 'godparent': f. OE *godsibb* person related to one in GOD: see SIB]

gossoon /ɡɒˈsuːn/ *n*. Ir. a lad. [earlier *garsoon* f. F *garçon* boy]

got *past* and *past part.* of GET.

Göteborg see GOTHENBURG.

Goth /ɡɒθ/ *n*. **1** a member of a Germanic tribe that invaded the Roman Empire from the east between the 3rd and 5th centuries. The eastern half of the tribe, the Ostrogoths, eventually founded a kingdom in Italy, while the Visigoths, their western cousins, went on to found one in Spain. **2** an uncivilized or ignorant person. [LL *Gothi* (pl.) f. Gk *Go(t)thoi* f. Goth.]

Gothenburg /ˈɡɒθənˌbɜːɡ/ (Swedish **Göteborg** /ˈjɜːtəˌbɔːr/) a seaport in SW Sweden; pop. (1987) 431,500.

Gothic /ˈɡɒθɪk/ *adj*. & *n*. —*adj*. **1** of the Goths or their language. **2** in the style of architecture prevalent in W. Europe in the 12th–16th c., characterized by pointed arches. **3** barbarous, uncouth. **4** *Printing* (of type) old-fashioned German, black letter, or sanserif. —*n*. **1** the Gothic language which constitutes the oldest manuscript evidence for the Germanic language group. It belongs to the East Germanic group and was spoken in the area to the north and west of the Black Sea. The evidence is fragmentary, the main text being part of a Gothic translation of the Greek Bible written in the 4th c. by Bishop Wulfila. **2** Gothic architecture. **3** *Printing* Gothic type. □ **Gothic novel** etc., an English genre of fiction, popular in the 18th–early 19th c., characterized by an atmosphere of mystery and horror and with a pseudo-medieval ('Gothic') setting. Examples include Horace Walpole's *Castle of Otranto* (1765) and Ann Radcliffe's *The Mysteries of Udolpho* (1794). **Gothic revival** the reintroduction in England of Gothic architecture towards the middle of the 19th c. □□ **Gothically** *adv*. **Gothicism** /-ˌsɪz(ə)m/ *n*. **Gothicize** /-ˌsaɪz/ *v.tr.* & *intr.* (also **-ise**). [F *gothique* or LL *gothicus* f. Gothi: see GOTH]

Gotland /ˈɡɒtlənd/ an island of Sweden, in the Baltic Sea; pop. (1987) 56,300; capital, Visby.

gotta /ˈɡɒtə/ *colloq.* have got a; have got to (*I gotta pain; we gotta go*). [corrupt.]

gotten US *past part.* of GET.

Götterdämmerung /ˌɡɜːtəˈdeməˌrʊŋ/ *n*. **1** the twilight (i.e. downfall) of the gods (see TWILIGHT). **2** the complete downfall of a regime etc. [G, esp. as the title of an opera by Wagner]

gouache /ɡuˈɑːʃ, gwɑːʃ/ *n*. **1** a method of painting in opaque pigments ground in water and thickened with a gluelike substance. **2** these pigments. **3** a picture painted in this way. [F f. It. *guazzo*]

Gouda /ˈɡaʊdə/ a market town of The Netherlands, 15 km (9 miles) north-east of Rotterdam, noted for its cheese and its stained-glass windows. —*n*. a flat round cheese with a yellow rind, orig. made at Gouda.

gouge /ɡaʊdʒ/ *n*. & *v*. —*n*. **1 a** a chisel with a concave blade, used in carpentry, sculpture, and surgery. **b** an indentation or groove made with or as with this. **2** US *colloq.* a swindle. —*v*. **1** *tr.* cut with or as with a gouge. **2** *tr.* **a** (foll. by *out*) force out (esp. an eye with the thumb) with or as with a gouge. **b** force out the eye of (a person). **3** *tr.* US *colloq.* swindle; extort money from. **4**

intr. Austral. dig for opal. □□ **gouger** n. [F f. LL gubia, perh. of Celt. orig.]

goulash /ˈguːlæʃ/ n. **1** a highly-seasoned Hungarian dish of meat and vegetables, usu. flavoured with paprika. **2** (in contract bridge) a re-deal, several cards at a time, of the four hands (unshuffled, but with each hand arranged in suits and order of value) when no player has bid. [Magyar gulyás-hús f. gulyás herdsman + hús meat]

Gounod /ˈguːnəʊ/, Charles François (1818–93), French composer, conductor, and organist, a Parisian born and bred. He wrote his first opera in 1851 but did not achieve success in the opera house until 1859 with Faust, a grand opera in the French tradition but with a lyrical grace and an easy naturalism quite new to the genre. Gounod's later operas have not maintained their popularity to the extent that Faust—translated into over 25 languages—has, but Roméo et Juliette (1867) is still heard and several of his songs remain in the French repertory.

gourami /ˈɡʊərəmɪ, -ˈrɑːmɪ/ n. **1 a** a large freshwater fish, Osphronemus goramy, native to SE Asia, used as food. **b** any small fish of the family Osphronemidae, usu. kept in aquariums. **2** any small brightly coloured freshwater fish of the family Belontiidae, usu. kept in aquariums. Also called LABYRINTH FISH. [Malay gurāmi]

gourd /ɡʊəd/ n. **1 a** any of various fleshy usu. large fruits with a hard skin, often used as containers, ornaments, etc. **b** any of various climbing or trailing plants of the family Cucurbitaceae bearing this fruit. Also called CUCURBIT. **2** the hollow hard skin of the gourd-fruit, dried and used as a drinking-vessel, water container, etc. □□ **gourdful** n. (pl. **-fuls**). [ME f. AF gurde, OF gourde ult. f. L cucurbita]

gourmand /ˈɡʊəmænd/ n. & adj. —n. **1** a glutton. **2** disp. a gourmet. —adj. gluttonous; fond of eating, esp. to excess. □□ **gourmandism** n. [ME f. OF, of unkn. orig.]

gourmandise /ˈɡʊəmɑ̃ˌdiːz/ n. the habits of a gourmand; gluttony. [F (as GOURMAND)]

gourmet /ˈɡʊəmeɪ/ n. a connoisseur of good or delicate food. [F, = wine-taster: sense infl. by GOURMAND]

gout /ɡaʊt/ n. **1** a disease with inflammation of the smaller joints, esp. the toe, as a result of excess uric acid salts in the blood. **2** archaic a drop, esp. of blood. **b** a splash or spot. □□ **gouty** adj. **goutily** adv. **goutiness** n. [ME f. OF goute f. L gutta drop, with ref. to the medieval theory of the flowing down of humours]

Gov. abbr. **1** Government. **2** Governor.

gov. abbr. governor.

govern /ˈɡʌv(ə)n/ v. **1 a** tr. rule or control (a State, subject, etc.) with authority; conduct the policy and affairs of (an organization etc.). **b** intr. be in government. **2 a** tr. influence or determine (a person or a course of action). **b** intr. be the predominating influence. **3** tr. be a standard or principle for; constitute a law for; serve to decide (a case). **4** tr. check or control (esp. passions). **5** tr. Gram. (esp. of a verb or preposition) have (a noun or pronoun or its case) depending on it. **6** tr. be in military command of (a fort, town). □ **governing body** the managers of an institution. □□ **governable** adj. **governability** /-nəˈbɪlɪtɪ/ n. **governableness** n. [ME f. OF governer f. L gubernare steer, rule f. Gk kubernaō]

governance /ˈɡʌvənəns/ n. **1** the act or manner of governing. **2** the office or function of governing. **3** sway, control. [ME f. OF (as GOVERN)]

governess /ˈɡʌvənɪs/ n. a woman employed to teach children in a private household. [earlier governeress f. OF governeresse (as GOVERNOR)]

governessy /ˈɡʌvənɪsɪ/ adj. characteristic of a governess; prim.

government /ˈɡʌvənmənt/ n. **1** the act or manner of governing. **2** the system by which a State or community is governed. **3 a** a body of persons governing a State. **b** (usu. **Government**) a particular ministry in office. **4** the State as an agent. **5** Gram. the relation between a governed and a governing word. □ **Government House** the official residence of a governor. **government issue** US (of equipment) provided by the government. **government paper** (or **securities**) bonds etc.

issued by the government. **government surplus** unused equipment sold by the government. □□ **governmental** /-ˈment(ə)l/ adj. **governmentally** /-ˈmentəlɪ/ adv. [ME f. OF governement (as GOVERN)]

governor /ˈɡʌvənə(r)/ n. **1** a person who governs; a ruler. **2 a** an official governing a province, town, etc. **b** a representative of the Crown in a colony. **3** the executive head of each State of the US. **4** an officer commanding a fortress or garrison. **5** the head or a member of a governing body of an institution. **6** the official in charge of a prison. **7 a** sl. one's employer. **b** sl. one's father. **c** colloq. (as a form of address) sir. **8** Mech. an automatic regulator controlling the speed of an engine etc. □ **Governor-General** the representative of the Crown in a Commonwealth country that regards the Queen as Head of State. □□ **governorate** /-rət/ n. **governorship** n. [ME f. AF gouvernour, OF governeǒ(u)r f. L gubernator -oris (as GOVERN)]

Govt. abbr. Government.

gowan /ˈɡaʊən/ n. Sc. **1** a daisy. **2** any white or yellow field-flower. [prob. var. of dial. gollan ranunculus etc., and rel. to gold in marigold]

gowk /ɡaʊk/ n. dial. **1** a cuckoo. **2** an awkward or halfwitted person; a fool. [ME f. ON gaukr f. Gmc]

gown /ɡaʊn/ n. & v. —n. **1** a loose flowing garment, esp. a long dress worn by a woman. **2** the official robe of an alderman, judge, cleric, member of a university, etc. **3** a surgeon's overall. **4** the members of a university as distinct from the permanent residents of the university town (cf. TOWN). —v.tr. (usu. as **gowned** adj.) attire in a gown. [ME f. OF goune, gon(n)e f. LL gunna fur garment: cf. med. Gk gouna fur]

goy /ɡɔɪ/ n. (pl. **goyim** /ˈɡɔɪɪm/ or **goys**) sl. derog. a Jewish name for a non-Jew. □□ **goyish** adj. (also **goyisch**). [Heb. gŏy people, nation]

Goya y Lucientes /ˈɡɔɪə iː ˌluːˈθiˈentɪz/, Francisco José de (1746–1828), Spanish painter and etcher, whose early tapestry cartoons (1776–91) presented idyllic and everyday scenes with rococo lightness and charm, contributing to his appointment as court painter in 1789. An illness, 1792–4, left him stone deaf, and from this time darker themes of fantasy, terror, and menace predominate. In his day, Goya was celebrated for his portraits, such as The Family of Charles IV (1800), which reveals the weaknesses of the royal family with unsparing realism. Most admired today, however, are the works which express his reaction to the French occupation of Spain 1808–14: The Shootings of May 3rd 1808 (1814), and the set of 65 etchings Los Desastres de la Guerra (1810–14), a savage nightmarish attack on the cruelty and horror of war. In 1824 he settled in Bordeaux, where he took up the new medium of lithography. His work was an important influence on the impressionists, especially Manet.

Gozo /ˈɡəʊzəʊ/ one of the three main islands of Malta.

GP abbr. **1** general practitioner. **2** Grand Prix.

Gp. Capt. abbr. (in the RAF) Group Captain.

GPI abbr. general paralysis of the insane.

GPO abbr. **1** General Post Office. **2** US Government Printing Office.

GPU n. the Ogpu (see entry). [Russ. abbr.]

GR abbr. King George. [L Georgius Rex]

gr abbr. (also **gr.**) **1** gram(s). **2** grains. **3** gross. **4** grey.

Graafian follicle /ˈɡrɑːfɪən/ n. a follicle in the mammalian ovary in which an ovum develops prior to ovulation. [R. de Graaf, Du. anatomist d. 1673]

grab /ɡræb/ v. & n. —v. (**grabbed, grabbing**) **1** tr. **a** seize suddenly. **b** capture, arrest. **2** tr. take greedily or unfairly. **3** tr. sl. attract the attention of, impress. **4** intr. (foll. by at) make a sudden snatch at. **5** intr. (of the brakes of a motor vehicle) act harshly or jerkily. —n. **1** a sudden clutch or attempt to seize. **2** a mechanical device for clutching. **3** the practice of grabbing; rapacious proceedings esp. in politics and commerce. **4** a children's card-game in which certain cards may be snatched from the table. □ **grab-bag** US a lucky dip. **grab handle** (or **rail** etc.) a handle or rail etc. to steady passengers in a moving vehicle. **up for grabs** sl. easily obtainable; inviting capture. □□ **grabber** n. [MLG, MDu. grabben: cf. GRIP, GRIPE, GROPE]

grabble /ˈgræb(ə)l/ v.intr. **1** grope about, feel for something. **2** (often foll. by for) sprawl on all fours, scramble (for something). [Du. & LG grabbeln scramble for a thing (as GRAB)]

grabby /ˈgræbɪ/ adj. colloq. tending to grab; greedy, grasping.

graben /ˈgrɑːbən/ n. (pl. same or **grabens**) Geol. a depression of the earth's surface between faults. [G, orig. = ditch]

Gracchus /ˈgrækəs/, Tiberius Sempronius (d. 133 BC), the elder of two aristocratic Roman brothers who, as tribunes of the people, pushed through revolutionary social and economic legislation against the wishes of the senatorial class. He was killed by his opponents after the passing of his agrarian bill (133 BC) which aimed at a redistribution of land by limiting the amount that could be held and dividing the surplus amongst poorer citizens. Gaius Sempronius Gracchus continued his brother's programme and instituted other reforms to relieve poverty, but was killed in a riot in 121 BC over the proposal to grant Roman citizenship to the people of Latium.

Grace /greɪs/, Dr William Gilbert (1848–1915), English cricketer, the best-known of all in the history of the game, who was supreme amongst his contemporaries. He began playing at the highest level while still a youth, and played in his last test match at the age of 50.

grace /greɪs/ n. & v. —n. **1** attractiveness, esp. in elegance of proportion or manner or movement; gracefulness. **2** courteous good will (had the grace to apologize). **3** an attractive feature; an accomplishment (social graces). **4 a** (in Christian belief) the unmerited favour of God; a divine saving and strengthening influence. The nature and conditions of divine grace were a subject of controversy between St Augustine and the adherents of Pelagianism, and between Calvin and his opponents at the Reformation. **b** the state of receiving this. **c** a divinely given talent. **5** goodwill, favour (fall from grace). **6** delay granted as a favour (a year's grace). **7** a short thanksgiving before or after a meal. **8** (**Grace**) Gk Mythol. any of the Graces (see entry). **9** (**Grace**) (prec. by His, Her, Your) forms of description or address for a duke, duchess, or archbishop. —v.tr. (often foll. by with) add grace to; enhance; confer honour or dignity on (graced us with his presence). □ **days of grace** the time allowed by law for payment of a sum due. **grace and favour house** etc. Brit. a house etc. occupied by permission of a sovereign etc. **grace-note** Mus. an extra note as an embellishment not essential to the harmony or melody. **in a person's good** (or **bad**) **graces** regarded by a person with favour (or disfavour). **with good** (or **bad**) **grace** as if willingly (or reluctantly). [ME f. OF f. L gratia f. gratus pleasing: cf. GRATEFUL]

graceful /ˈgreɪsfʊl/ adj. having or showing grace or elegance. □□ **gracefully** adv. **gracefulness** n.

graceless /ˈgreɪslɪs/ adj. lacking grace or elegance or charm. □□ **gracelessly** adv. **gracelessness** n.

Graces /ˈgreɪsɪz/ n.pl. Gk Mythol. beautiful goddesses, usually three (Aglaia, Thalia, Euphrosyne), daughters of Zeus, personifying charm, grace, and beauty, which they bestowed as physical, intellectual, artistic, and moral qualities.

Gracias a Dios /ˈgrɑːsɪˌɑːs ɑː ˈdiːɒs/, **Cape** the easternmost extremity of the Mosquito Coast in Central America, on the frontier between Nicaragua and Honduras. The cape was named by Columbus who had been becalmed off the coast but was able to continue his voyage with the arrival of a following wind. [Sp., = thanks (be) to God]

gracile /ˈgræsaɪl, -sɪl/ adj. slender; gracefully slender. [L gracilis slender]

gracility /grəˈsɪlɪtɪ/ n. **1** slenderness. **2** (of literary style) unornamented simplicity.

gracious /ˈgreɪʃəs/ adj. & int. —adj. **1** kind; indulgent and beneficent to inferiors. **2** (of God) merciful, benign. **3** poet. kindly, courteous. **4** a polite epithet used of royal persons or their acts (the gracious speech from the throne). —int. expressing surprise. □ **gracious living** an elegant way of life. □□ **graciosity** /ˌgreɪsɪˈɒsɪtɪ/ n. **graciously** adv. **graciousness** n. [ME f. OF f. L gratiosus (as GRACE)]

grackle /ˈgræk(ə)l/ n. **1** any of various orioles, esp. of the genus Quiscalus, native to America, the males of which are shiny black with a blue-green sheen. Also called BLACKBIRD. **2** any of various minas, esp. of the genus Gracula, native to Asia. [mod.L Gracula f. L graculus jackdaw]

grad /græd/ n. colloq. = GRADUATE n. 1. [abbr.]

gradate /grəˈdeɪt/ v. **1** v.intr. & tr. pass or cause to pass by gradations from one shade to another. **2** tr. arrange in steps or grades of size etc. [back-form. f. GRADATION]

gradation /grəˈdeɪʃ(ə)n/ n. (usu. in pl.) **1** a stage of transition or advance. **2 a** a certain degree in rank, intensity, merit, divergence, etc. **b** such a degree; an arrangement in such degrees. **3** (of paint etc.) the gradual passing from one shade, tone, etc., to another. **4** Philol. ablaut. □□ **gradational** adj. **gradationally** adv. [L gradatio f. gradus step]

grade /greɪd/ n. & v. —n. **1 a** a certain degree in rank, merit, proficiency, quality, etc. **b** a class of persons or things of the same grade. **2 a** a mark indicating the quality of a student's work. **b** an examination, esp. in music. **3** US a class in school, concerned with a particular year's work and usu. numbered from the first upwards. **4 a** a gradient or slope. **b** the rate of ascent or descent. **5 a** a variety of cattle produced by crossing native stock with a superior breed. **b** a group of animals at a similar level of development. **6** Philol. a relative position in a series of forms involving ablaut. —v. **1** tr. arrange in or allocate to grades; class, sort. **2** intr. (foll. by up, down, off, into, etc.) pass gradually between grades, or into a grade. **3** tr. give a grade to (a student). **4** tr. blend so as to affect the grade of colour with tints passing into each other. **5** tr. reduce (a road etc.) to easy gradients. **6** tr. (often foll. by up) cross (livestock) with a better breed. □ **at grade** US on the same level. **grade crossing** US = level crossing. **grade school** US elementary school. **make the grade** colloq. succeed; reach the desired standard. [F grade or L gradus step]

grader /ˈgreɪdə(r)/ n. **1** a person or thing that grades. **2** a wheeled machine for levelling the ground, esp. in road-making. **3** (in comb.) US a pupil of a specified grade in a school.

gradient /ˈgreɪdɪənt/ n. **1 a** a stretch of road, railway, etc., that slopes from the horizontal. **b** the amount of such a slope. **2** the rate of rise or fall of temperature, pressure, etc., in passing from one region to another. [prob. formed on GRADE after salient]

gradine /ˈgreɪdiːn/ n. (also **gradin** /-dɪn/) **1** each of a series of low steps or a tier of seats. **2** a ledge at the back of an altar. [It. gradino dimin. of grado GRADE]

gradual /ˈgrædjʊəl/ adj. & n. —adj. **1** taking place or progressing slowly or by degrees. **2** not rapid or steep or abrupt. —n. Eccl. **1** a response sung or recited between the Epistle and Gospel in the Mass. **2** a book of music for the sung Mass service. □□ **gradually** adv. **gradualness** n. [med.L gradualis, -ale f. L gradus step, the noun referring to the altar-steps on which the response is sung]

gradualism /ˈgrædjʊəˌlɪz(ə)m/ n. a policy of gradual reform rather than sudden change or revolution. □□ **gradualist** n. **gradualistic** /-ˈlɪstɪk/ adj.

graduand /ˈgrædjʊˌænd/ n. Brit. a person about to receive an academic degree. [med.L graduandus gerundive of graduare GRADUATE]

graduate n. & v. —n. /ˈgrædjʊət/ **1** a person who has been awarded an academic degree (also attrib.: graduate student). **2** US a person who has completed a school course. —v. /ˈgrædjʊˌeɪt/ **1 a** intr. take an academic degree. **b** tr. US admit to an academic degree or a certificate of completion of School Studies. **2** intr. **a** (foll. by from) be a graduate of a specified university. **b** (foll. by in) be a graduate in a specified subject. **3** tr. US send out as a graduate from a university etc. **4** intr. **a** (foll. by to) move up to (a higher grade of activity etc.). **b** (foll. by as, in) gain specified qualifications. **5** tr. mark out in degrees or parts. **6** tr. arrange in gradations; apportion (e.g. tax) according to a scale. **7** intr. (foll. by into, away) pass by degrees. □ **graduated pension** (in the UK) a system of pension contributions by employees in proportion to their wages or salary. **graduate school** a department of a university for advanced work by graduates. □□ **graduator** n. [med.L graduari take a degree f. L gradus step]

graduation /ˌgrædjʊˈeɪʃ(ə)n/ n. **1** the act or an instance of graduating or being graduated. **2** a ceremony at which degrees are conferred. **3** each or all of the marks on a vessel or instrument indicating degrees of quantity etc.

Graecism /'griːkɪz(ə)m, -sɪz(ə)m/ n. (also **Grecism**) **1** a Greek idiom, esp. as imitated in another language. **2 a** the Greek spirit, style, mode of expression, etc. **b** the imitation of these. [F *grécisme* or med.L *Graecismus* f. *Graecus* GREEK]

Graecize /'griːkaɪz/ v.tr. (also **Grecize, -ise**) give a Greek character or form to. [L *Graecizare* (as GRAECISM)]

Graeco- /'griːkəʊ/ comb. form (also **Greco-**) Greek; Greek and. [L *Graecus* GREEK]

Graeco-Roman /ˌgriːkəʊ'rəʊmən/ adj. **1** of or relating to the Greeks and Romans. **2** *Wrestling* denoting a style attacking only the upper part of the body.

Graf /grɑːf/, Stephanie ('Steffi') (1969–), German tennis player, who in 1988 won the Australian, French, and US open championships as well as the Wimbledon trophy and an Olympic gold medal.

graffito /grə'fiːtəʊ/ n. (pl. **graffiti** /-tiː/) **1** (usu. in pl.) a piece of writing or drawing scribbled, scratched, or sprayed on a surface. ¶ Not a mass noun in this sense, and so a plural construction is needed, e.g. *graffiti are* (not *is*) *an art form*. **2** *Art* a form of decoration made by scratches on wet plaster, showing a different-coloured under-surface. [It. f. *graffio* a scratch]

graft[1] /grɑːft/ n. & v. —n. **1** *Bot.* **a** a shoot or scion inserted into a slit of stock, from which it receives sap. **b** the place where a graft is inserted. **2** *Surgery* a piece of living tissue, organ, etc., transplanted surgically. **3** sl. hard work. —v. **1** tr. **a** (often foll. by *into, on, together,* etc.) insert (a scion) as a graft. **b** insert a graft on (a stock). **2** intr. insert a graft. **3** tr. *Surgery* transplant (living tissue). **4** tr. (foll. by *in, on*) insert or fix (a thing) permanently to another. **5** intr. sl. work hard. □ **grafting-clay** (or **-wax**) a substance for covering the united parts of a graft and stock. □□ **grafter** n. [ME (earlier *graff*) f. OF *grafe, grefe* f. L *graphium* f. Gk *graphion* stylus f. *graphō* write]

graft[2] /grɑːft/ n. & v. colloq. —n. **1** practices, esp. bribery, used to secure illicit gains in politics or business. **2** such gains. —v.intr. seek or make such gains. □□ **grafter** n. [19th c.: orig. unkn.]

Grafton /'grɑːft(ə)n/, Augustus Henry Fitzroy, 3rd Duke of (1735–1811), British statesman, Prime Minister 1768–70.

Graham[1] /'greɪəm/, Martha (1893–1991), American ballet dancer and choreographer, one of the most influential teachers of modern dance (see BALLET). Her most famous ballets include *Frontier* (1935).

Graham[2] /'greɪəm/, William Franklin ('Billy') (1918–), American evangelistic preacher, who has conducted large theatrically staged religious meetings throughout the world.

Grahame /'greɪəm/, Kenneth (1859–1932), Scottish-born writer. His most famous book *The Wind in the Willows* is based largely on bedtime stories and letters to his son; Grahame never intended it to become a published work. Its reception on publication in 1908 was muted, and it was some years before the story of Rat, Mole, Badger, and Toad, and their life by the river, became established as a children's classic. The book was dramatized as *Toad of Toad Hall* by A. A. Milne in 1929.

Graham Land /'greɪəm/ the northern part of the Antarctic Peninsula, the only part of the Antarctic continent lying outside the Antarctic Circle. It was annexed for Great Britain by John Biscoe in 1831–2 and now forms part of British Antarctic Territory, but is claimed also by Chile and Argentina.

Grail /greɪl/ n. (in full **Holy Grail**) **1** an object of quest in medieval legend, conferring mystical benefits. Its origin, nature, and significance are unknown. From the late 12th c. onwards it was given a Christian significance (though no Church authority has ever recognized the legend), and was supposed to be the vessel from which Christ drank at the Last Supper and in which Joseph of Arimathea, who acquired it and brought it to England, had caught some of the blood of the crucified Christ; in other legends it was the dish used at the Last Supper. By the early 13th c. it had become attached to the Arthurian cycle of legends as a symbol of perfection sought by the knights of the Round

Table. The three principal ways of explaining its origin and motivation are (1) as a Christian legend, which altered only in detail through its history; (2) as an ancient pagan fertility ritual, 'the horn of plenty'; (3) as a Celtic story, already mythological in its origins in Irish, transmitted through Welsh and Breton to the French romance tradition and gradually Christianized. **2** any object of a quest. [ME f. OF *graal* etc. f. 1med.L *gradalis* dish, of unkn. orig.]

grain /greɪn/ n. & v. —n. **1** a fruit or seed of a cereal. **2 a** (collect.) wheat or any allied grass used as food, corn. **b** (collect.) their fruit. **c** any particular species of corn. **3 a** a small hard particle of salt, sand, etc. **b** a discrete particle or crystal, usu. small, in a rock or metal. **c** a piece of solid propellant for use in a rocket engine. **4** the smallest unit of weight in the troy system (equivalent to $\frac{1}{480}$ of an ounce), and in the avoirdupois system (equivalent to $\frac{1}{437.5}$ of an ounce). **5** the smallest possible quantity (not *a grain of truth in it*). **6 a** roughness of surface. **b** *Photog.* a granular appearance on a photograph or negative. **7** the texture of skin, wood, stone, etc.; the arrangement and size of constituent particles. **8 a** a pattern of lines of fibre in wood or paper. **b** lamination or planes of cleavage in stone, coal, etc. **9** nature, temper, tendency. **10 a** *hist.* kermes or cochineal, or dye made from either of these. **b** *poet.* dye; colour. —v. **1** tr. paint in imitation of the grain of wood or marble. **2** tr. give a granular surface to. **3** tr. dye in grain. **4** tr. & intr. form into grains. **5** tr. remove hair from (hides). □ **against the grain** contrary to one's natural inclination or feeling. **grain-leather** leather dressed with grain-side out. **grain-side** the side of a hide on which the hair was. **grains of Paradise** capsules of a W. African plant (*Aframomum melegueta*), used as a spice and a drug. **in grain** thorough, genuine, by nature, downright, indelible. □□ **grained** adj. (also in comb.). **grainer** n. **grainless** adj. [ME f. OF f. L *granum*]

Grainger /'greɪndʒə(r)/, (George) Percy Aldridge (1882–1961), Australian-born composer and pianist, who lived in London 1900–15 and thereafter in the US. He became a friend of Grieg and Delius, and collected, edited, and arranged English folksongs. As a composer he is best known for his lighter tunes, including *Shepherd's Hey, Country Gardens*, and *Handel in the Strand*.

grainy /'greɪnɪ/ adj. (**grainier, grainiest**) **1** granular. **2** resembling the grain of wood. **3** *Photog.* having a granular appearance. □□ **graininess** n.

grallatorial /ˌgrælə'tɔːrɪəl/ adj. *Zool.* of or relating to long-legged wading birds, e.g. storks, flamingos, etc. [mod.L *grallatorius* f. L *grallator* stilt-walker f. *grallae* stilts]

Gram /græm/, Hans Christian Joachim (1853–1938), Danish physician and bacteriologist, who invented a technique of staining bacteria and discovered that certain species (called Gram-positive) retained the colour, while others lost it (Gram-negative). This became a useful technique for classifying micro-organisms.

gram[1] /græm/ n. (also **gramme**) a metric unit of mass equal to one-thousandth of a kilogram. □ **gram-atom** *Chem.* the quantity of a chemical element equal to its relative atomic mass in grams (see MOLE[4]). **gram-equivalent** *Chem.* the quantity of a substance equal to its equivalent weight in grams. **gram-molecule** *Chem.* the quantity of a substance equal to its relative molecular mass in grams. [F *gramme* f. Gk *gramma* small weight]

gram[2] /græm/ n. any of various pulses used as food. [Port. *grão* f. L *granum* grain]

-gram /græm/ comb. form forming nouns denoting a thing written or recorded (often in a certain way) (*anagram; epigram; monogram; telegram*). □□ **-grammatic** /grə'mætɪk/ comb. form forming adjectives. [from or after Gk *gramma -atos* thing written, letter of the alphabet, f. *graphō* write]

graminaceous /ˌgræmɪ'neɪʃəs/ adj. of or like grass; grassy. [L *gramen -inis* grass]

gramineous /grə'mɪnɪəs/ adj. = GRAMINACEOUS. [L *gramineus* f. *gramen -inis* grass]

graminivorous /ˌgræmɪ'nɪvərəs/ adj. feeding on grass, cereals, etc. [L *gramen -inis* grass + -VOROUS]

grammalogue /'græməˌlɒg/ n. **1** a word represented by a single shorthand sign. **2** a logogram. [irreg. f. Gk *gramma* letter of the alphabet + *logos* word]

grammar /ˈgræmə(r)/ n. **1 a** the study of the main elements of a language, including its sounds, inflections or other means of showing the relation between words as used in speech or writing, and the established rules for using these (often limited to phonology, morphology, and syntax, and excluding vocabulary, stylistics, etc.; see LINGUISTICS). **b** a body of form and usages in a specified language (*Latin grammar*). **2** a person's manner or quality of observance or application of the rules of grammar (*bad grammar*). **3** a book on grammar. **4** the elements or rudiments of an art or science. **5** *Brit. colloq.* = *grammar school.* □ **generative grammar** a theory which aims at formulating for each language a set of rules capable of 'generating' all the infinite sentences of that language and providing them with the correct structural description. The theory, which was obviously influenced by mathematics, is best known in the many versions which it had in the US from the 1960s onwards. **grammar school** see separate entry. **transformational grammar** a form of generative grammar which makes use of operations called 'transformations' which systematically indicate the links between various types of sentences (e.g. declarative and interrogative, active and passive) and derive one type from the other. The use of transformations in linguistics started with the American linguist Z. S. Harris (1909–), but transformational grammar is more commonly associated with the name of N. Chomsky. □□ **grammarless** *adj.* [ME f. AF *gramere*, OF *gramaire* f. L *grammatica* f. Gk *grammatikē* (*tekhnē*) (art) of letters f. *gramma -atos* letter of the alphabet]

grammarian /grəˈmeəriən/ n. an expert in grammar or linguistics; a philologist. [ME f. OF *gramarien*]

grammar school n. **1** *Brit.* any of a class of (usually endowed) schools founded in the 16th c. or earlier for teaching Latin, with some instruction also in literature and elementary mathematics. By the end of the 19th c. they had become secondary schools with a curriculum including languages, literature, history, and science, and under the Education Act of 1947 offered a similar curriculum for pupils with academic ability. Since 1965 many have been absorbed into or replaced by comprehensive schools. **2** *US* a school intermediate between primary and high school.

grammatical /grəˈmætɪk(ə)l/ *adj.* **1 a** of or relating to grammar. **b** determined by grammar, esp. by form or inflection (*grammatical gender*). **2** conforming to the rules of grammar, or to the formal principles of an art, science, etc. □□ **grammatically** *adv.* **grammaticalness** n. [F *grammatical* or LL *grammaticalis* f. L *grammaticus* f. Gk *grammatikos* (as GRAMMAR)]

gramme var. of GRAM¹.

gramophone /ˈgræməˌfəʊn/ n. an instrument for reproducing recorded sounds such as music or speech. The sound wave is defined by a pattern of lateral waves moulded into a fine spiral groove in a thin plastic disc, the 'record'. A fine stylus is used under a pick-up to sense the lateral vibrations as the disc is rotated about its centre at a steady speed of revolution. Formerly the stylus acted directly on a diaphragm, creating sound waves which were amplified by a divergent horn, but modern pick-ups use a variable magnetic circuit and coil to induce a varying voltage, which is amplified electronically and passed to a loudspeaker. The gramophone evolved from the earlier phonograph, invented by Thomas Edison in 1877, which used a rotating wax cylinder to record and reproduce sound waves. The flat gramophone disc, with a needle moving in a groove, was the invention of the German-American Emile Berliner (1851–1929) in 1888. ¶ Now more usually called *record-player*. □□ **gramophonic** /-ˈfɒnɪk/ *adj.* [formed by inversion of PHONOGRAM]

Grampian /ˈgræmpɪən/ a local government region in NE Scotland; pop. (1981) 502,850; capital, Aberdeen. It includes part of the Grampian Mountains which extend SW–NE across Scotland; their southern edge forms the natural boundary between the Highlands and the Lowlands.

Grampians /ˈgræmpɪənz/ **1** the Grampian Mountains in Scotland. **2** a mountain range in Australia in SW central Victoria, a spur of the Great Dividing Range.

grampus /ˈgræmpəs/ n. (pl. **grampuses**) **1** a dolphin, *Grampus griseus*, with a blunt snout and long pointed black flippers. **2** a person breathing heavily and loudly. [earlier *graundepose, grapeys* f. OF *grapois* etc. f. med.L *craspiscis* f. L *crassus piscis* fat fish]

gran /græn/ n. *colloq.* grandmother (cf. GRANNY). [abbr.]

Granada¹ /grəˈnɑːdə/ a city in Andalusia in southern Spain; pop. (1986) 280,600. Founded in the 8th c., it became the capital of the Moorish kingdom of Granada in 1238. The poet Federico Garcia de Lorca was born here in 1898.

Granada² /grəˈnɑːdə/ a city in Nicaragua, on the NW shore of Lake Nicaragua, founded in the Spanish colonial period; pop. (1985) 88,600.

granadilla /ˌgrænəˈdɪlə/ n. (also **grenadilla** /ˌgren-/) a passion-fruit. [Sp., dimin. of *granada* pomegranate]

granary /ˈgrænəri/ n. (pl. **-ies**) **1** a storehouse for threshed grain. **2** a region producing, and esp. exporting, much corn. [L *granarium* f. *granum* grain]

Gran Chaco /græn ˈtʃɑːkəʊ/ a vast sparsely populated lowland plain in central South America, forming part of Bolivia, Paraguay, and Argentina. The discovery of oil in the Chaco Boreal to the north of the Pilcomayo River precipitated the Chaco War (1932–5) between Paraguay and Bolivia in a dispute about the interstate boundary. [Sp., = great hunting-ground or riches]

grand /grænd/ *adj. & n.* —*adj.* **1 a** splendid, magnificent, imposing, dignified. **b** solemn or lofty in conception, execution, or expression; noble. **2** main; of chief importance (*grand staircase*; *grand entrance*). **3** (**Grand**) of the highest rank, esp. in official titles (*Grand Cross; grand vizier; Grand Inquisitor*). **4** *colloq.* excellent, enjoyable (*had a grand time; in grand condition*). **5** belonging to high society; wealthy (*the grand folk at the big house*). **6** (in *comb.*) in names of family relationships, denoting the second degree of ascent or descent (*granddaughter*). **7** (**Grand**) (in French phrases or imitations) great (*grand army; Grand Monarch; Grand Hotel*). **8** *Law* serious, important (*grand larceny*) (cf. COMMON, PETTY). —*n.* **1** = *grand piano.* **2** (pl. same) (usu. in pl.) esp. *US sl.* a thousand dollars or pounds. □ **grand aunt** a great-aunt (see GREAT *adj.* 11). **grand duchy** a State ruled by a grand duke or duchess. **grand duke** (or **duchess**) **1** a prince (or princess) or noble person ruling over a territory. **2** (**Grand Duke**) *hist.* the son or grandson of a Russian tsar. **grand jury** esp. *US Law* a jury selected to examine the validity of an accusation prior to trial. **grand master 1** a chess-player of the highest class. **2** the head of a military order of knighthood, of Freemasons, etc. **Grand National** see separate entry. **grand nephew** (or **niece**) a great-nephew or -niece (see GREAT *adj.* 11). **grand opera** opera on a serious theme, or in which the entire libretto (including dialogue) is sung. **grand piano** a large full-toned piano standing on three legs, with the body, strings, and soundboard arranged horizontally and in line with the keys. **grand slam 1** *Sport* the winning of all of a group of championships. **2** *Bridge* the winning of 13 tricks. **grand total** the final amount after everything is added up; the sum of other totals. **grand tour** *hist.* a cultural tour of Europe, esp. in the 18th c. for educational purposes. □□ **grandly** *adv.* **grandness** n. [ME f. AF *graunt*, OF *grant* f. L *grandis* full-grown]

grandad /ˈgrændæd/ n. (also **grand-dad**) *colloq.* **1** grandfather. **2** an elderly man.

grandam /ˈgrændæm/ n. **1** (also **grandame**) *archaic* grandmother. **2** an old woman. **3** an ancestress. [ME f. AF *graund dame* (as GRAND, DAME)]

Grand Canal 1 a series of waterways in north China. it was started in 486 BC with a link between the Huai and Yangtze rivers, and over many centuries canal and riverine sections were added until by AD 1327 it linked Peking and Hangchow, 1,700 km (1,060 miles) apart. Its original purpose was to transport rice grain from the river valleys to the cities. **2** the main waterway of Venice in Italy, that divides the city into two parts. It is lined on each side by many of the finest Venetian palaces and other public buildings in a variety of architectural styles.

Grand Canyon a deep gorge about 350 km (217 miles) long, formed by the Colorado River in Arizona, US. It is 8–24 km (5–15 miles) wide and, in places, 1,800 m (6,000 ft.) deep.

grandchild /'græntʃaɪld, 'grænd-/ n. (pl. **-children**) a child of one's son or daughter.

granddaughter /'grænˌdɔːtə(r)/ n. a female grandchild.

grande dame /grãd 'daːm/ n. a dignified lady of high rank. [F]

grandee /græn'diː/ n. **1** a Spanish or Portuguese nobleman of the highest rank. **2** a person of high rank or eminence. [Sp. & Port. *grande*, assim. to -EE]

grandeur /'grændjə(r), -ndʒə(r)/ n. **1** majesty, splendour; dignity of appearance or bearing. **2** high rank, eminence. **3** nobility of character. [F f. *grand* great, GRAND]

grandfather /'grænˌfaːðə(r), 'grænd-/ n. a male grandparent. □ **grandfather clock** a clock in a tall wooden case, driven by weights. □□ **grandfatherly** adj.

Grand Guignol see GUIGNOL.

grandiflora /ˌgrændɪ'flɔːrə/ adj. bearing large flowers. [mod.L (often used in specific names of large-flowered plants) f. L *grandis* great + FLORA]

grandiloquent /græn'dɪləkwənt/ adj. **1** pompous or inflated in language. **2** given to boastful talk. □□ **grandiloquence** n. **grandiloquently** adv. [L *grandiloquus* (as GRAND, -loquus -speaking f. *loqui* speak), after *eloquent* etc.]

grandiose /'grændɪˌəʊs/ adj. **1** producing or meant to produce an imposing effect. **2** planned on an ambitious or magnificent scale. □□ **grandiosely** adv. **grandiosity** /-'ɒsɪtɪ/ n. [F f. It. *grandioso* (as GRAND, -OSE¹)]

grandma /'grænmaː, 'grænd-/ n. colloq. grandmother.

grand mal /grã 'mæl/ n. a serious form of epilepsy with loss of consciousness (cf. PETIT MAL). [F, = great sickness]

grandmama /'grænməˌmaː, 'grænd-/ n. archaic colloq. = GRANDMA.

grandmother /'grænˌmʌðə(r), 'grænd-/ n. a female grandparent. □ **grandmother clock** a clock like a grandfather clock but in a smaller case. **teach one's grandmother to suck eggs** presume to advise a more experienced person. □□ **grandmotherly** adj.

Grand National a steeplechase established in 1839, run annually over a course of 4 miles 856 yds (about 7,200 metres) with 30 jumps at Aintree, Liverpool, in late March or early April.

grandpa /'grænpaː, 'grænd-/ n. colloq. grandfather.

grandpapa /'grænpəˌpaː, 'grænd-/ n. archaic colloq. = GRANDPA.

grandparent /'grænˌpeərənt, 'grænd-/ n. a parent of one's father or mother.

Grand Prix /grã 'priː/ **1** (in full **Grand Prix de Paris**) an international horse-race for three-year-olds, founded in 1863 and run annually in June at Longchamp near Paris. **2** any of various important motor-racing contests, governed by international rules. [F, = great or chief prize]

grand siècle /grã sɪ'eklə/ n. the classical or golden age, esp. the 17th c. in France. [F, = great century or age]

grandsire /'grænˌsaɪə(r)/ n. archaic **1** grandfather, old man, ancestor. **2** Bell-ringing a method of change-ringing.

grandson /'grænsʌn, 'grænd-/ n. a male grandchild.

grandstand /'grænstænd, 'grænd-/ n. the main stand, usu. roofed, for spectators at a racecourse etc. □ **grandstand finish** a close and exciting finish to a race etc.

grange /greɪndʒ/ n. **1** a country house with farm-buildings. **2** archaic a barn. [ME f. AF *graunge*, OF *grange* f. med.L *granica* (*villa*) ult. f. L *granum* GRAIN]

graniferous /grə'nɪfərəs/ adj. producing grain or a grainlike seed. □□ **graniform** /'grænɪˌfɔːm/ adj. [L *granum* GRAIN]

granite /'grænɪt/ n. **1** a granular crystalline igneous rock of quartz, mica, feldspar, etc., used for building. **2** a determined or resolute quality, attitude, etc. □□ **granitic** /grə'nɪtɪk/ adj. **granitoid** adj. & n. [It. *granito*, lit. grained f. *grano* f. L *granum* GRAIN]

graniteware /'grænɪtˌweə(r)/ n. **1** a speckled form of earthenware imitating the appearance of granite. **2** a kind of enamelled ironware.

granivorous /grə'nɪvərəs/ adj. feeding on grain. □□ **granivore** /'grænɪˌvɔː(r)/ n. [L *granum* GRAIN]

granny /'grænɪ/ n. (also **grannie**) (pl. **-ies**) colloq. grandmother. □ **granny bond** Brit. colloq. a form of National Savings certificate orig. available only to pensioners. **granny flat** (or **annexe**) Brit. part of a house made into self-contained accommodation for an elderly relative. **granny knot** a reef-knot crossed the wrong way and therefore insecure. [obs. *grannam* for GRANDAM + -Y²]

Granny Smith /ˌgrænɪ 'smɪθ/ n. an Australian green variety of apple. [Maria Ann ('Granny') Smith d. 1870]

Grant¹ /graːnt/, Cary (real name Alexander Archibald Leach, 1904–   ), American film actor, born in England, noted for his sophisticated and amiable assurance. He has acted in more than 70 films, including *Holiday* (1938) and *The Philadelphia Story* (1940), in both of which he partnered Katherine Hepburn.

Grant² /graːnt/, Ulysses Simpson (1822–85), Union general and later President of the US (1869–77). Having made his reputation through a series of victories in the western theatre of the American Civil War (most notably the capture of Vicksburg in 1863), Grant was made supreme commander of the northern armies. By pursuing a policy of attrition he was eventually able to wear down the Confederate Army of Northern Virginia and bring the war to an end. He was elected President in 1868 but proved unequal to the post and was unable to check widespread political corruption and inefficiency.

grant /graːnt/ v. & n. —v.tr. **1 a** consent to fulfil (a request, wish, etc.) (*granted all he asked*). **b** allow (a person) to have (a thing) (*granted me my freedom*). **c** (as **granted**) colloq. apology accepted; pardon given. **2** give (rights, property, etc.) formally; transfer legally. **3** (often foll. by *that* + clause) admit as true; concede, esp. as a basis for argument. —n. **1** the process of granting or a thing granted. **2** a sum of money given by the State for any of various purposes, esp. to finance education. **3** Law **a** a legal conveyance by written instrument. **b** formal conferment. □ **grant-in-aid** (pl. **grants-in-aid**) a grant by central government to local government or an institution. **take for granted 1** assume something to be true or valid. **2** cease to appreciate through familiarity. □□ **grantable** adj. **grantee** /-'tiː/ n. (esp. in sense 2 of v.). **granter** n. **grantor** /-'tɔː(r)/ n. (esp. in sense 2 of v.). [ME f. OF *gr(e)anter* var. of *creanter* ult. f. part. of L *credere* entrust]

Granth /grʌnt/ n. (also **Grunth**) = ADI GRANTH.

Grantha /'grʌntə/ n. a South Indian alphabet dating from the 5th c. AD, used by the Tamil brahmins for the Sanskrit transcriptions of their sacred books. [Skr., = tying, literary composition]

gran turismo /ˌgræn tuː'rɪzməʊ/ n. (pl. **-os**) a touring-car. [It., = great touring]

granular /'grænjʊlə(r)/ adj. **1** of or like grains or granules. **2** having a granulated surface or structure. □□ **granularity** /-'lærɪtɪ/ n. **granularly** adv. [LL *granulum* GRANULE]

granulate /'grænjʊˌleɪt/ v. **1** tr. & intr. form into grains (*granulated sugar*). **2** tr. roughen the surface of. **3** intr. (of a wound etc.) form small prominences as the beginning of healing; heal, join. □□ **granulation** /-'leɪʃ(ə)n/ n. **granulator** n.

granule /'grænjuːl/ n. a small grain. [LL *granulum*, dimin. of L *granum* grain]

granulocyte /'grænjʊləˌsaɪt/ n. Physiol. any of various white blood cells having granules in their cytoplasm. □□ **granulocytic** /-'sɪtɪk/ adj.

granulometric /ˌgrænjʊlə'metrɪk/ adj. relating to the distribution of grain sizes in sand etc. [F *granulométrique* (as GRANULE, METRIC)]

grape /greɪp/ n. **1** a berry (usu. green, purple, or black) growing in clusters on a vine, used as fruit and in making wine. **2** (prec. by *the*) colloq. wine. **3** = GRAPESHOT. **4** (in pl.) a diseased growth like a bunch of grapes on the pastern of a horse etc., or on a pleura in cattle. □ **grape hyacinth** any liliaceous plant of the genus *Muscari*, with clusters of usu. blue flowers. **grape-sugar** dextrose. □□ **grapey** adj. (also **grapy**). [ME f. OF *grape* bunch of grapes prob. f. *graper* gather (grapes) f. *grap(p)e* hook, ult. f. Gmc]

grapefruit /'greɪpfruːt/ n. (pl. same) **1** a large round yellow citrus fruit with an acid juicy pulp. **2** the tree, *Citrus paradisi*, bearing this fruit.

grapeshot /ˈgreɪpʃɒt/ *n. hist.* small balls used as charge in a cannon and scattering when fired.

grapevine /ˈgreɪpvaɪn/ *n.* **1** any of various vines of the genus *Vitis*, esp. *Vitis vinifera*. **2** *colloq.* the means of transmission of unofficial information or rumour (*heard it through the grapevine*).

graph[1] /grɑːf, græf/ *n. & v.* —*n.* **1** a diagram showing the relation between variable quantities, usu. of two variables, each measured along one of a pair of axes at right angles. **2** *Math.* a collection of points whose coordinates satisfy a given relation. —*v.tr.* plot or trace on a graph. □ **graph paper** paper printed with a network of lines as a basis for drawing graphs. [abbr. of *graphic formula*]

graph[2] /grɑːf, græf/ *n. Linguistics* a visual symbol, esp. a letter or letters, representing a unit of sound or other feature of speech. [Gk *graphē* writing]

-graph /grɑːf/ *comb. form* forming nouns and verbs meaning: **1** a thing written or drawn etc. in a specified way (*autograph*; *photograph*). **2** an instrument that records (*heliograph*; *seismograph*; *telegraph*).

grapheme /ˈgræfiːm/ *n. Linguistics* **1** a class of letters etc. representing a unit of sound. **2** a feature of a written expression that cannot be analysed into smaller meaningful units. □□ **graphematic** /-ˈmætɪk/ *adj.* **graphemic** /grəˈfiːmɪk/ *adj.* **graphemically** /grəˈfiːmɪkəlɪ/ *adv.* [GRAPH[2] + -EME]

-grapher /grəfə(r)/ *comb. form* forming nouns denoting a person concerned with a subject (*geographer*; *radiographer*). [from or after Gk -*graphos* writer + -ER[1]]

graphic /ˈgræfɪk/ *adj. & n.* —*adj.* **1** of or relating to the visual or descriptive arts, esp. writing and drawing. **2** vividly descriptive. **3** (of minerals) showing marks like writing on the surface or in a fracture. **4** = GRAPHICAL. —*n.* a product of the graphic arts (cf. GRAPHICS). □ **graphic arts** the visual and technical arts involving design, writing, drawing, printing, etc. **graphic equalizer** a device for the separate control of the strength and quality of selected frequency bands. □□ **graphically** *adv.* **graphicness** *n.* [L *graphicus* f. Gk *graphikos* f. *graphē* writing]

-graphic /ˈgræfɪk/ *comb. form* (also **-graphical**) forming adjectives corresponding to nouns in -*graphy* (see -GRAPHY). □□ **-graphically** *comb. form* forming adverbs. [from or after Gk -*graphikos* (as GRAPHIC)]

graphicacy /ˈgræfɪkəsɪ/ *n.* the ability to read a map, graph, etc., or to present information by means of diagrams. [GRAPHIC, after *literacy*, *numeracy*]

graphical /ˈgræfɪk(ə)l/ *adj.* **1** of or in the form of graphs (see GRAPH[1]). **2** graphic. □□ **graphically** *adv.*

graphics /ˈgræfɪks/ *n.pl.* (usu. treated as *sing.*) **1** the products of the graphic arts, esp. commercial design or illustration. **2** the use of diagrams in calculation and design. **3** (in full **computer graphics**) *Computing* a mode of processing and output in which a significant part of the information is in pictorial form.

graphite /ˈgræfaɪt/ *n.* a crystalline allotropic form of carbon used as a solid lubricant, in pencils, and as a moderator in nuclear reactors etc. Also called PLUMBAGO, *black lead*. □□ **graphitic** /-ˈfɪtɪk/ *adj.* **graphitize** /-fɪˌtaɪz/ *v.tr. & intr.* (also **-ise**). [G *Graphit* f. Gk *graphō* write]

graphology /grəˈfɒlədʒɪ/ *n.* **1** the study of handwriting esp. as a supposed guide to character. **2** a system of graphic formulae; notation for graphs (see GRAPH[1]). **3** *Linguistics* the study of systems of writing. □□ **graphological** /-fəˈlɒdʒɪk(ə)l/ *adj.* **graphologist** *n.* [Gk *graphē* writing]

-graphy /grəfɪ/ *comb. form* forming nouns denoting: **1** a descriptive science (*bibliography*; *geography*). **2** a technique of producing images (*photography*; *radiography*). **3** a style or method of writing, drawing, etc. (*calligraphy*). [from or after F or G -*graphie* f. L -*graphia* f. Gk -*graphia* writing]

grapnel /ˈgræpn(ə)l/ *n.* **1** a device with iron claws, attached to a rope and used for dragging or grasping. **2** a small anchor with several flukes. [ME f. AF f. OF *grapon* f. Gmc: cf. GRAPE]

grappa /ˈgræpə/ *n.* a brandy distilled from the fermented residue of grapes after they have been pressed in wine-making. [It.]

grapple /ˈgræp(ə)l/ *v. & n.* —*v.* **1** *intr.* (often foll. by *with*) fight at close quarters or in close combat. **2** *intr.* (foll. by *with*) try to manage or overcome a difficult problem etc. **3** *tr.* **a** grip with the hands; come to close quarters with. **b** seize with or as with a grapnel; grasp. —*n.* **1 a** a hold or grip in or as in wrestling. **b** a contest at close quarters. **2** a clutching-instrument; a grapnel. □ **grappling-iron** (or **-hook**) = GRAPNEL. □□ **grappler** *n.* [OF *grapil* (n.) f. Prov., dimin. of *grapa* hook (as GRAPNEL)]

graptolite /ˈgræptəˌlaɪt/ *n.* an extinct marine invertebrate animal found as a fossil in lower Palaeozoic rocks. [Gk *graptos* marked with letters + -LITE]

grasp /grɑːsp/ *v. & n.* —*v.* **1** *tr.* **a** clutch at; seize greedily. **b** hold firmly; grip. **2** *intr.* (foll. by *at*) try to seize; accept avidly. **3** *tr.* understand or realize (a fact or meaning). —*n.* **1 a** firm hold; a grip. **2** (foll. by *of*) **a** mastery or control (*a grasp of the situation*). **b** a mental hold or understanding (*a grasp of the facts*). **3** mental agility (*a quick grasp*). □ **grasp at a straw** see STRAW. **grasp the nettle** tackle a difficulty boldly. **within one's grasp** capable of being grasped or comprehended by one. □□ **graspable** *adj.* **grasper** *n.* [ME *graspe*, *grapse* perh. f. OE *græpsan* (unrecorded) f. Gmc, rel. to GROPE: cf. LG *grapsen*]

grasping /ˈgrɑːspɪŋ/ *adj.* avaricious, greedy. □□ **graspingly** *adv.* **graspingness** *n.*

Grass /grɑːs/, Günter Wilhelm (1927–), German novelist, a committed and outspoken socialist, born in Danzig. His long humorous novels portray modern Germany, during and after the Third Reich; they include *Die Blechtrommel* (*The Tin Drum*, 1959, which won international acclaim), *Hundejahre* (*Dog Years*, 1963), and *Der Butt* (*The Flounder*, 1978).

grass /grɑːs/ *n. & v.* —*n.* **1 a** vegetation belonging to a group of small plants with green blades that are eaten by cattle, horses, sheep, etc. **b** any species of this. **c** any plant of the family Gramineae, which includes cereals, reeds, and bamboos. **2** pasture land. **3** grass-covered ground, a lawn (*keep off the grass*). **4** grazing (*out to grass*; *be at grass*). **5** *sl.* marijuana. **6** *Brit. sl.* an informer, esp. a police informer. **7** the earth's surface above a mine; the pit-head. **8** *sl.* asparagus. —*v.* **1** *tr.* cover with turf. **2** *tr.* *US* provide with pasture. **3** *Brit. sl.* **a** betray, esp. to the police. **b** *intr.* inform the police. **4** *tr.* knock down; fell (an opponent). **5** *tr.* **a** bring (a fish) to the bank. **b** bring down (a bird) by a shot. □ **at grass** out of work, on holiday, etc. **grass bird** *Austral.* any of various warblers, esp. of the genus *Megalurus*, living among reeds. **grass-box** a receptacle for cut grass on a lawnmower. **grass-cloth** a linen-like cloth woven from ramie etc. **grass court** a grass-covered lawn-tennis court. **grass of Parnassus** a herbaceous plant, *Parnassia palustris*. **grass parakeet** *Austral.* a parakeet, esp. of the genus *Neophema*, frequenting grassland. **grass roots 1** a fundamental level or source. **2** ordinary people, esp. as voters; the rank and file of an organization, esp. a political party. **grass skirt** a skirt made of long grass and leaves fastened to a waistband. **grass snake 1** *Brit.* the common ringed snake, *Natrix natrix*. **2** *US* the common greensnake, *Opheodrys vernalis*. **grass tree** = BLACKBOY. **grass widow** (or **widower**) a person whose husband (or wife) is away for a prolonged period. **grass-wrack** eel-grass. **not let the grass grow under one's feet** be quick to act or to seize an opportunity. □□ **grassless** *adj.* **grasslike** *adj.* [OE *græs* f. Gmc, rel. to GREEN, GROW]

Grasse /grɑːs/ a town near Cannes in SE France, centre of the French perfume-making industry; pop. (1982) 38,360.

grasshopper /ˈgrɑːsˌhɒpə(r)/ *n.* a jumping and chirping plant-eating insect of the order Saltatoria.

grassland /ˈgrɑːslænd/ *n.* a large open area covered with grass, esp. one used for grazing.

grassy /ˈgrɑːsɪ/ *adj.* (**grassier**, **grassiest**) **1** covered with or abounding in grass. **2** resembling grass. **3** of grass. □□ **grassiness** *n.*

grate[1] /greɪt/ *v.* **1** *tr.* reduce to small particles by rubbing on a serrated surface. **2** *intr.* (often foll. by *against, on*) rub with a harsh scraping sound. **3** *tr.* utter in a harsh tone. **4** *intr.* (often foll. by *on*) **a** sound harshly or discordantly. **b** have an irritating effect. **5** *tr.* grind (one's teeth). **6** *intr.* (of a hinge etc.) creak. [ME f. OF *grater* ult. f. WG]

grate[2] /greɪt/ *n.* **1** the recess of a fireplace or furnace. **2** a metal frame confining fuel in a grate. [ME, = grating f. OF ult. f. L *cratis* hurdle]

grateful /ˈgreɪtfʊl/ *adj.* **1** thankful; feeling or showing gratitude (*am grateful to you for helping*). **2** pleasant, acceptable. □□ **gratefully** *adv.* **gratefulness** *n.* [obs. *grate* (adj.) f. L *gratus* + -FUL]

grater /ˈgreɪtə(r)/ *n.* a device for reducing cheese or other food to small particles.

graticule /ˈgrætɪˌkjuːl/ *n.* **1** fine lines or fibres incorporated in a telescope or other optical instrument as a measuring scale or as an aid in locating objects. **2** *Surveying* a network of lines on paper representing meridians and parallels. [F f. med.L *graticula* for *craticula* gridiron f. L *cratis* hurdle]

gratify /ˈgrætɪˌfaɪ/ *v.tr.* (**-fies, -fied**) **1 a** please, delight. **b** please by compliance; assent to the wish of. **2** indulge in or yield to (a feeling or desire). □□ **gratification** /-fɪˈkeɪʃ(ə)n/ *n.* **gratifier** *n.* **gratifying** *adj.* **gratifyingly** *adv.* [F *gratifier* or L *gratificari* do a favour to, make a present of, f. *gratus* pleasing]

grating[1] /ˈgreɪtɪŋ/ *adj.* **1** sounding harsh or discordant (*a grating laugh*). **2** having an irritating effect. □□ **gratingly** *adv.*

grating[2] /ˈgreɪtɪŋ/ *n.* **1** a framework of parallel or crossed metal bars. **2** *Optics* a set of parallel wires, lines ruled on glass, etc., for producing spectra by diffraction.

gratis /ˈgrɑːtɪs, ˈgreɪ-/ *adv.* & *adj.* free; without charge. [L, contracted ablat. pl. of *gratia* favour]

gratitude /ˈgrætɪˌtjuːd/ *n.* being thankful; readiness to show appreciation for and to return kindness. [F *gratitude* or med.L *gratitudo* f. *gratus* thankful]

gratuitous /grəˈtjuːɪtəs/ *adj.* **1** given or done free of charge. **2** uncalled for; unwarranted; lacking good reason (*a gratuitous insult*). □□ **gratuitously** *adv.* **gratuitousness** *n.* [L *gratuitus* spontaneous: cf. *fortuitous*]

gratuity /grəˈtjuːɪtɪ/ *n.* (*pl.* **-ies**) money given in recognition of services; a tip. [OF *gratuité* or med.L *gratuitas* gift f. L *gratus* grateful]

gratulatory /ˈgrætjʊlətərɪ/ *adj.* expressing congratulation. [LL *gratulatorius* f. *gratus* grateful]

graunch /grɔːntʃ/ *v.intr.* & *tr.* make or cause to make a crunching or grinding sound. [imit.]

gravamen /grəˈveɪmen/ *n.* (*pl.* **gravamens** or **gravamina** /-mɪnə/) **1** the essence or most serious part of an argument. **2** a grievance. [LL, = inconvenience, f. L *gravare* to load f. *gravis* heavy]

grave[1] /greɪv/ *n.* **1 a** a trench dug in the ground to receive a coffin on burial. **b** a mound or memorial stone placed over this. **2** (prec. by *the*) death, esp. as indicating mortal finality. **3** something compared to or regarded as a grave. □ **turn in one's grave** (of a dead person) be thought of in certain circumstances as likely to have been shocked or angry when alive. □□ **graveless** *adj.* **graveward** *adv.* & *adj.* [OE *græf* f. WG]

grave[2] /greɪv/ *adj.* & *n.* —*adj.* **1 a** serious, weighty, important (*a grave matter*). **b** dignified, solemn, sombre (*a grave look*). **2** extremely serious or threatening (*grave danger*). **3** /grɑːv/ (of sound) low-pitched, not acute. —*n.* /grɑːv/ = *grave accent*. □ **grave accent** /grɑːv/ a mark (`) placed over a vowel in some languages to denote pronunciation, length, etc., orig. indicating low or falling pitch. □□ **gravely** *adv.* **graveness** *n.* [F *grave* or L *gravis* heavy, serious]

grave[3] /greɪv/ *v.tr.* (*past part.* **graven** or **graved**) **1** (foll. by *in, on*) fix indelibly (on one's memory). **2** *archaic* engrave, carve. □ **graven image** an idol. [OE *grafan* dig, engrave f. Gmc: cf. GROOVE]

grave[4] /greɪv/ *v.tr.* clean (a ship's bottom) by burning off accretions and by tarring. □ **graving dock** = *dry dock*. [perh. F dial. *grave* = OF *greve* shore]

gravedigger /ˈgreɪvˌdɪgə(r)/ *n.* **1** a person who digs graves. **2** (in full **gravedigger beetle**) a sexton beetle.

gravel /ˈgræv(ə)l/ *n.* & *v.* —*n.* **1 a** a mixture of coarse sand and small water-worn or pounded stones, used for paths and roads and as an aggregate. **b** *Geol.* a stratum of this. **2** *Med.* aggregations of crystals formed in the urinary tract. —*v.tr.* (**gravelled, gravelling;** *US* **graveled, graveling**) **1** lay or strew with gravel. **2** perplex, puzzle, nonplus (from an obs. sense 'run (a ship) aground'). □ **gravel-blind** *literary* almost completely blind ('more than sand-blind', in Shakesp. *Merchant of Venice* II. ii. 33). [ME f. OF *gravel(e)* dimin. of *grave* (as GRAVE[4])]

gravelly /ˈgrævəlɪ/ *adj.* **1** of or like gravel. **2** having or containing gravel. **3** (of a voice) deep and rough-sounding.

graven *past part.* of GRAVE[3].

graver /ˈgreɪvə(r)/ *n.* **1** an engraving tool; a burin. **2** *archaic* an engraver; a carver.

Graves[1] /grɑːv/ *n.* a light usu. white wine from Graves in the Bordeaux region in France.

Graves[2] /greɪvz/, Robert (Ranke) (1895–1985), English poet, who also wrote unconventional historical novels such as *I, Claudius* (1934), an autobiography *Good-bye to all That* (1929), recounting his experiences in the trenches, and an idiosyncratic mythological study *The White Goddess* (1948). All his work is strongly individualistic and often drily humorous.

Graves' disease /greɪvz/ *n.* exophthalmic goitre with characteristic swelling of the neck and protrusion of the eyes, resulting from an overactive thyroid gland. [R. J. *Graves*, Ir. physician d. 1853]

gravestone /ˈgreɪvstəʊn/ *n.* a stone (usu. inscribed) marking a grave.

Gravettian /grəˈvetɪən/ *adj.* & *n.* —*adj.* of an upper palaeolithic industry in Europe, following the Aurignacian, named after the type-site at La Gravette in the Dordogne, France. —*n.* this industry.

graveyard /ˈgreɪvjɑːd/ *n.* a burial-ground, esp. by a church.

gravid /ˈgrævɪd/ *adj.* *literary* or *Zool.* pregnant. [L *gravidus* f. *gravis* heavy]

gravimeter /grəˈvɪmɪtə(r)/ *n.* an instrument for measuring the difference in the force of gravity from one place to another. [F *gravimètre* f. L *gravis* heavy]

gravimetric /ˌgrævɪˈmetrɪk/ *adj.* **1** of or relating to the measurement of weight. **2** denoting chemical analysis based on weight.

gravimetry /grəˈvɪmɪtrɪ/ *n.* the measurement of weight.

gravitas /ˈgrævɪˌtæs, -ˌtɑːs/ *n.* solemn demeanour; seriousness. [L f. *gravis* serious]

gravitate /ˈgrævɪˌteɪt/ *v.* **1** *intr.* (foll. by *to, towards*) move or be attracted to some source of influence. **2** *tr.* & *intr.* **a** move or tend by force of gravity towards. **b** sink by or as if by gravity. [mod.L *gravitare* GRAVITAS]

gravitation /ˌgrævɪˈteɪʃ(ə)n/ *n.* *Physics* **1** a force of attraction between any particle of matter in the universe and any other. **2** the effect of this, esp. the falling of bodies to the earth. (See below.) [mod.L *gravitatio* (as GRAVITY)]

In Plato's cosmology gravity was a tendency of like bodies to cluster together. In Aristotle's theory it was a self-propelling force that urged a body towards the centre of the universe, which coincided with the centre of the earth. In Newton's theory all bodies in the universe attract each other gravitationally with a force which depends directly on the mass of each body and which is also inversely proportional to the square of the distance between both bodies. Long thought to be conclusively established, Newton's theory gave way to Einstein's after 1916, when the latter's theory of gravity, also called the general theory of relativity (see RELATIVITY), was published, according to which gravitational force is the consequence of space-time being 'curved' in the vicinity of matter. For most terrestrial events the predictions of the Newtonian theory and that of Einstein do not differ significantly, but evidence in support of the latter has come from a number of astronomical observations.

gravitational /ˌgrævɪˈteɪʃən(ə)l/ *adj.* of or relating to gravitation. □ **gravitational constant** the constant in Newton's law of gravitation relating gravity to the masses and separation of particles. ¶ Symb.: **G. gravitational field** the region of space surrounding a body in which another body experiences a force of attraction. □□ **gravitationally** *adv.*

gravity /ˈgrævɪtɪ/ *n.* **1 a** the force that attracts a body to the centre of the earth or other celestial body. (See GRAVITATION.) **b** the degree of intensity of this measured by acceleration. **c** gravitational force. **2** the property of having weight. **3 a** importance, seriousness; the quality of being grave. **b** solemnity, sobriety; serious demeanour. □ **gravity feed** the supply of material by its fall under gravity. [F *gravité* or L *gravitas* f. *gravis* heavy]

gravure /grəˈvjʊə(r)/ *n.* = PHOTOGRAVURE. [abbr.]

gravy /ˈgreɪvɪ/ *n.* (*pl.* **-ies**) **1 a** the juices exuding from meat during and after cooking. **b** a dressing or sauce for food, made from these or from other materials, e.g. stock. **2** *sl.* unearned or unexpected money. □ **gravy-boat** a boat-shaped vessel for serving gravy. **gravy train** *sl.* a source of easy financial benefit. [ME, perh. from a misreading as *gravé* of OF *grané*, prob. f. *grain* spice: see GRAIN]

Gray[1] /greɪ/, Asa (1810–88), American botanist, author of many textbooks which greatly popularized botany. Finding no conflict between evolution and his view of divine design in nature, he supported Darwin's theories at a time when they were anathema to many.

Gray[2] /greɪ/, Thomas (1716–71), English poet, who spent most of his life in Cambridge. The popularity of his first major poem *Elegy Written in a Country Church-Yard* (1751) led to the general recognition of Gray as the foremost poet of the day and (in 1757) to the offer of the laureateship—which he declined. Two Pindaric odes, *The Bard* (1757) and *The Progress of Poesy* (1757), published by his friend Horace Walpole, mark a clear transition from neoclassical lucidity towards the obscure and the sublime. His letters reveal his character and humorous spirit.

gray[1] /greɪ/ *n.* Physics the SI unit of the absorbed dose of ionizing radiation, corresponding to one joule per kilogram. ¶ Abbr.: **Gy**. [L. H. *Gray*, Engl. radiobiologist d. 1965]

gray[2] US var. of GREY.

grayling /ˈgreɪlɪŋ/ *n.* **1** any silver-grey freshwater fish of the genus *Thymallus*, with a long high dorsal fin. **2** a butterfly, *Hipparchia semele*, having wings with grey undersides and bright eye-spots on the upper side. [*gray* var. of GREY + -LING[2]]

graywacke US var. of GREYWACKE.

Graz /grɑːts/ the second-largest city in Austria, the industrial capital of Styria province, situated on the River Mur; pop. (1981) 243,000.

graze[1] /greɪz/ *v.* **1** *intr.* (of cattle, sheep, etc.) eat growing grass. **2** *tr.* **a** feed (cattle etc.) on growing grass. **b** feed on (grass). **3** *intr.* pasture cattle. □□ **grazer** *n.* [OE *grasian* f. *græs* GRASS]

graze[2] /greɪz/ *v. & n.* —*v.* **1** *tr.* rub or scrape (a part of the body, esp. the skin) so as to break the surface without causing bleeding. **2 a** *tr.* touch lightly in passing. **b** *intr.* (foll. by *against*, *along*, etc.) move with a light passing contact. —*n.* an act or instance of grazing. [perh. a specific use of GRAZE[1], as if 'take off the grass close to the ground' (of a shot etc.)]

grazier /ˈgreɪzɪə(r)/ *n.* **1** a person who feeds cattle for market. **2** *Austral.* a large-scale sheep-farmer or cattle-farmer. □□ **graziery** *n.* [GRASS + -IER]

grazing /ˈgreɪzɪŋ/ *n.* grassland suitable for pasturage.

grease /griːs/ *n. & v.* —*n.* **1** oily or fatty matter esp. as a lubricant. **2** the melted fat of a dead animal. **3** oily matter in unprocessed wool. —*v.tr.* /griːs, griːz/ smear or lubricate with grease. □ **grease-gun** a device for pumping grease under pressure to a particular point. **grease the palm of** *colloq.* bribe. **like greased lightning** *colloq.* very fast. □□ **greaseless** *adj.* [ME f. AF *grece, gresse*, OF *graisse* ult. f. L *crassus* (adj.) fat]

greasepaint /ˈgriːspeɪnt/ *n.* a waxy composition used as make-up for actors.

greaseproof /ˈgriːspruːf/ *adj.* impervious to the penetration of grease.

greaser /ˈgriːsə(r)/ *n.* **1** a person or thing that greases. **2** *sl.* a

member of a gang of youths with long hair and riding motor cycles. **3** *US sl. offens.* a Mexican or Spanish-American. **4** *sl.* a gentle landing of an aircraft.

greasy /ˈgriːsɪ, -zɪ/ *adj.* (**greasier, greasiest**) **1 a** of or like grease. **b** smeared or covered with grease. **c** containing or having too much grease. **2 a** slippery. **b** (of a person or manner) unpleasantly unctuous, smarmy. **c** objectionable. □□ **greasily** *adv.* **greasiness** *n.*

great /greɪt/ *adj. & n.* —*adj.* **1 a** of a size, amount, extent, or intensity considerably above the normal or average; big (*made a great hole; take great care; lived to a great age*). **b** also with implied surprise, admiration, contempt, etc., esp. in exclamations (*you great idiot!; great stuff!; look at that great wasp*). **c** reinforcing other words denoting size, quantity, etc. (*a great big hole; a great many*). **2** important, pre-eminent; worthy or most worthy of consideration (*the great thing is not to get caught*). **3** grand, imposing (*a great occasion; the great hall*). **4 a** (esp. of a public or historic figure) distinguished; prominent. **b** (**the Great**) as a title denoting the most important of the name (*Alfred the Great*). **5 a** (of a person) remarkable in ability, character, achievement, etc. (*great men; a great thinker*). **b** (of a thing) outstanding of its kind (*the Great Fire*). **6** (foll. by *at, on*) competent, skilled, well-informed. **7** fully deserving the name of; doing a thing habitually or extensively (*a great reader; a great believer in tolerance; not a great one for travelling*). **8** (also **greater**) the larger of the name, species, etc. (*great auk; greater celandine*). **9** (**Greater**) (of a city etc.) including adjacent urban areas (*Greater Manchester*). **10** *colloq.* **a** very enjoyable or satisfactory; attractive, fine (*had a great time; it would be great if we won*). **b** (as an exclam.) fine, very good. **11** (in *comb.*) (in names of family relationships) denoting one degree further removed upwards or downwards (*great-uncle; great-great-grandmother*). —*n.* **1** a great or outstanding person or thing. **2** (in *pl.*) (**Greats**) *colloq.* (at Oxford University) an honours course or final examinations in classics and philosophy. □ **great and small** all classes or types. **great circle** see CIRCLE. **great deal** see DEAL[1]. **great-hearted** magnanimous; having a noble or generous mind. **great-heartedness** magnanimity. **the great majority** by far the most. **Great Mother** see MOTHER GODDESS. **great northern diver** a diving sea bird, *Gavia immer*, of the northern hemisphere. **great organ** the chief manual in a large organ, with its related pipes and mechanism. **great tit** a Eurasian songbird, *Parus major*, with black and white head markings. **great toe** the big toe. **to a great extent** largely. □□ **greatness** *n.* [OE *grēat* f. WG]

Great Australian Bight a wide bay (part of the Southern Ocean) on the south coast of Australia.

Great Barrier Reef the largest coral reef in the world, stretching for about 2,000 km (1,250 miles) roughly parallel to the NE coast of Australia.

Great Bear the constellation Ursa Major.

Great Bear Lake the largest lake in Canada and fourth-largest in North America; area *c.*31,795 sq. km (12,275 sq. miles). Situated in the Northwest Territories, it drains into the Mackenzie River via the Great Bear River.

Great Bible the edition of the English Bible which Thomas Cromwell ordered in 1538 to be set up in every parish church. It was the work of Martin Coverdale, and was first issued in 1539.

Great Britain England, Wales, and Scotland considered as a unit (see BRITAIN). Wales was politically incorporated with England in the 16th c., and the Act of Union formally united Scotland with England in 1707. (See ENGLAND, SCOTLAND, WALES.) Constitutional monarchy was established by the 'Glorious Revolution' of 1688, with parliamentary supremacy guaranteed by the passing of the Bill of Rights (1689). Although the American colonies broke away in 1783, in the 18th c. Britain was the leading naval and colonial power in the world, while the Industrial Revolution which was then beginning made it the first industrialized country, with improvements also in agriculture and communications (see INDUSTRIAL REVOLUTION). During Queen Victoria's long reign the monarchy regained the esteem and affection of the people, and the last quarter of the 19th c. saw a new wave of imperial expansion. The Commonwealth system replaced the Empire in the 20th c., and one country after another gained independence. After the Second World War the newly elected Labour government initiated a programme of nationalization, established a National Health Service, and laid the foundations of the Welfare State. In the following decades immigration from Commonwealth countries made Britain a multiracial society. Manufacturing is the largest industry, though most of the raw materials needed must be imported. New methods of farming have greatly reduced the numbers employed in this, but productivity has increased. Coal (which was of crucial importance during the Industrial Revolution) is mined in large quantities, and the revenue from North Sea oil wells, where production began in 1975, is an important factor in the economy.

greatcoat /ˈɡreɪtkəʊt/ n. a long heavy overcoat.

Great Dane see DANE.

Great Dividing Range the crest of the eastern highlands of Australia, curving roughly parallel to the coast for almost its entire north–south length.

Great Elector Frederick William, Elector of Brandenburg (1620–88).

Greater London an administrative area comprising London and the surrounding regions.

Greater Manchester a metropolitan county of NW England; pop. (1981) 2,618,900.

Great Exhibition the first international exhibition of the products of industry, promoted by Prince Albert and held in the Crystal Palace in London in 1851.

Great Fire (of London) the fire which destroyed some 13,000 houses over 400 acres in London between 2 and 6 Sept. 1666 after starting in a bakery in Pudding Lane east of the City of London.

Great Indian Desert see THAR DESERT.

Great Lakes five large interconnected lakes (Superior, Michigan, Huron, Erie, and Ontario) in North America. Except for Lake Michigan, which is wholly within the US, they lie on the Canada–US border. They are connected to the Atlantic Ocean by the St Lawrence Seaway and form an important commercial waterway.

greatly /ˈɡreɪtlɪ/ adv. by a considerable amount; much (greatly admired; greatly superior).

Great Plains a vast area of plains in Canada and the US, between the Rocky Mountains and the Mississippi valley.

Great Rebellion the Royalist name for the English Civil War of 1642–51.

Great Rift Valley the most extensive rift valley system in the earth's surface, running from the Jordan valley in Syria, along the Red Sea into Ethiopia, and through Kenya, Tanzania, and Malawi into Mozambique. It is marked by a chain of steep-sided lakes and a series of volcanoes, including Mount Kilimanjaro.

Great Russian n. & adj. —n. a member or the language of the principal ethnic group in the USSR; Russian. —adj. of or relating to this people or language.

Great Salt Lake a heavily saline lake in northern Utah.

Great Sand Sea the northern part of the Libyan Desert in NE Africa.

Great Sandy Desert 1 a large tract of desert in the north central part of Western Australia. 2 a vast desert stretching from the Nejd of central Saudi Arabia to the Hadhramaut of Yemen.

Great Schism 1 the breach between the Eastern and the Western Church, traditionally dated 1054, when, in an attempt to assert the primacy of the papacy, Cardinal Humbert excommunicated the Patriarch of Constantinople and the latter excommunicated the Western legates. (See also FILIOQUE.) Negotiations to restore unity continued over a long period but the breach became final in 1472. 2 the period 1378–1417, when the Western Church was divided by the creation of anti-popes. The Council of Constance ended the schism by the election of Martin V in 1417.

Great Seal a seal used to authenticate important documents issued in the name of the sovereign or highest executive authority. In Britain the Great Seal is held by the Lord Chancellor, who was formerly sometimes also referred to as the Lord Keeper (of the Seal); the analogous Great Seal of the US is held by the Secretary of State.

Great Slave Lake a lake in the Northwest Territories in Canada, the deepest lake in North America, with a depth of 615 m (2,015 ft.).

Great Trek the northward migration in 1835–7 of large numbers of Boers, discontented with British rule in the Cape, to the areas where they eventually founded the Transvaal Republic and the Orange Free State.

Great Victoria Desert a vast arid region straddling the boundary between Western Australia and South Australia.

Great Wall of China a defensive wall in northern China, extending some 2,400 km (1,500 miles) from Kansu province to the Yellow Sea north of Peking. Its origin dates from c.210 BC when the country was unified under one ruler, and the northern walls of existing rival States were linked to form a continuous protection against nomad invaders. It was rebuilt in medieval times largely against the Mongols, and the present wall dates from the Ming dynasty. Although principally a defensive wall it served also as a means of communication: for most of its length it was wide enough to allow five horses to travel abreast. It has the distinction of being the only man-made structure on earth that is visible from the moon.

Great War the First World War.

Great White Way Broadway in New York City, in reference to its brilliant street illuminations.

Great Zimbabwe see ZIMBABWE.

greave /ɡriːv/ n. (usu. in pl.) armour for the shin. [ME f. OF greve shin, greave, of unkn. orig.]

grebe /ɡriːb/ n. any diving bird of the family Podicipedidae, with a long neck, lobed toes, and almost no tail. □ **little grebe** a small water bird of the grebe family, Tachybaptus ruficollis. [F grèbe, of unkn. orig.]

Grecian /ˈɡriːʃ(ə)n/ adj. (of architecture or facial outline) following Greek models or ideals. □ **Grecian nose** a straight nose that continues the line of the forehead without a dip. [OF grecien or med.L graecianus (unrecorded) f. L Graecia Greece]

Grecism var. of GRAECISM.

Grecize var. of GRAECIZE.

Greco- var. of GRAECO-.

Greece /ɡriːs/ a country in SE Europe comprising a peninsula bounded by the Ionian, Mediterranean, and Aegean Seas, and numerous outlying islands; pop. (est. 1988) 10,015,000; official language, Greek; capital, Athens. Agriculture remains important to the economy, though there has been a substantial increase in industrialization; tobacco, fresh fruit, and currants are among the main exports. The chief industries include textiles, chemicals, metallurgy, and electrical equipment. Greece became a full member of the EEC in 1981.
  The country was invaded by Greek-speaking peoples c.2000–1700 BC, and thereafter enjoyed settled conditions which allowed the Mycenaean civilization to develop and flourish until the arrival in the 12th c. of the Dorians (see DARK AGE). Village settlements developed into city-states, of which the most prominent were Athens and Sparta, and rising populations and expanding trade led to overseas colonization, especially in Ionia. Although the city-states showed themselves able to combine in a crisis, as against the Persian expeditionary force which they unexpectedly defeated in 480 BC, they were weakened by rivalries and conflicts with each other and by internal political turmoil. In 338 BC they fell to the superior military power of Philip II of Macedon, and formed part of the empire of his successor Alexander the Great. Towards the end of the 3rd c. BC Macedonia came into conflict with the expanding power of Rome, and in 146 BC Greece was made a Roman province; the liberties of the Greek city-states were at an end.
  In AD 395 the Roman Empire was divided and Greece became part of the Eastern Empire, centred on Constantinople. It was

conquered by the Ottoman Turks (1466) and remained under Turkish rule until the successful war of independence (1821–30), after which it became a monarchy and then in 1973 a republic.

greed /griːd/ n. an excessive desire, esp. for food or wealth. [back-form. f. GREEDY]

greedy /'griːdɪ/ adj. (**greedier**, **greediest**) **1** having or showing an excessive appetite for food or drink. **2** wanting wealth or pleasure to excess. **3** (foll. by for, or to + infin.) very keen or eager; needing intensely (greedy for affection; greedy to learn). □□ **greedily** adv. **greediness** n. [OE grǣdig f. Gmc]

Greek /griːk/ n. & adj. —n. **1 a** a native or national of modern Greece; a person of Greek descent. **b** a native or citizen of any of the ancient States of Greece; a member of the Greek people. **2** the Indo-European language of Greece. (See below.) —adj. of Greece or its people or language; Hellenic. □ **Greek** (or **Greek Orthodox**) **Church** the national Church of Greece (see also Orthodox Church). **Greek cross** a cross with four equal arms. **Greek fire** hist. a combustible composition for setting fire to an enemy's ships, works, etc., emitted by a flame-throwing weapon, so called from being first used by the Greeks besieged in Constantinople (673–8). **Greek to me** colloq. incomprehensible to me. □□ **Greekness** n. [OE Grēcas (pl.) f. Gmc f. L Graecus Greek f. Gk Graikoi, the prehistoric name of the Hellenes (in Aristotle)]

Greek belongs to the Indo-European family of languages. Its ancient form was spoken in the Balkan peninsula from the 2nd millennium BC; the earliest evidence is to be found in the Linear B tablets dating from 1500 BC. Like Latin, it was a highly inflected language with strict rules and rather complicated grammar. The alphabet normally used was adapted from the Phoenician c.1000 BC; the capitals have remained unaltered, and the lower-case letters have developed from them. There were four main dialects, but with the rise of Athens the dialect of that city (Attic) predominated and formed the basis of the koine which became the standard dialect from the 3rd c. BC onwards. It was the official language of the Byzantine empire, but in the four centuries when Greece was under Turkish rule oral speech and dialects developed unchallenged. Today Greek is spoken by some 10 million people in mainland Greece and the Aegean archipelago, and is the official language of Greece. Modern Greek has changed from ancient Greek in various ways: some vowels, diphthongs, and consonants have changed or modified their sounds, there are fewer grammatical forms, and the structure is simpler. Two forms of the language are in use: demotic, the common language, and katharevousa, an imitation of classical Greek which has been revived for literary purposes. Demotic is gaining ground not only for conversation but also in literature.

green /griːn/ adj., n., & v. —adj. **1** of the colour between blue and yellow in the spectrum; coloured like grass, emeralds, etc. **2 a** covered with leaves or grass. **b** mild and without snow (a green Christmas). **3** (of fruit etc. or wood) unripe or unseasoned. **4** not dried, smoked, or tanned. **5** inexperienced, naïve, gullible. **6 a** (of the complexion) pale, sickly-hued. **b** jealous, envious. **7** young, flourishing. **8** not withered or worn out (a green old age). **9** vegetable (green food; green salad). **10** (also **Green**) concerned with or supporting protection of the environment as a political principle. **11** archaic fresh; not healed (a green wound). —n. **1** a green colour or pigment. **2** green clothes or material (dressed in green). **3 a** a piece of public or common grassy land (village green). **b** a grassy area used for a special purpose (putting-green; bowling-green). **c** Golf a putting-green. **d** Golf a fairway. **4** (in pl.) green vegetables. **5** vigour, youth, virility (in the green). **6** a green light. **7** a green ball, piece, etc., in a game or sport. **8** (also **Green**) a member or supporter of an environmentalist group or party, formed largely in the 1970s. **9** (in pl.) sl. sexual intercourse. **10** sl. low-grade marijuana. **11** sl. money. **12** green foliage or growing plants. —v. **1** tr. & intr. make or become green. **2** tr. sl. hoax; take in. □ **green belt** an area of open land round a city, designated for preservation. **Green Beret** colloq. a British or American commando. **green card** an international insurance document for motorists. **green cheese 1** cheese coloured green with sage. **2** whey cheese. **3** unripened cheese. **Green**

Cloth (in full **Board of Green Cloth**) (in the UK) the Lord Steward's department of the Royal Household. **green crop** a crop used as fodder in a green state rather than as hay etc. **green drake** the common mayfly. **green earth** a hydrous silicate of potassium, iron, and other metals. **green-eyed** jealous. **the green-eyed monster** jealousy. **green fat** part of a turtle, highly regarded by gourmets. **green-fee** Golf a charge for playing one round on a course. **green fingers** skill in growing plants. **green goose** a goose killed under four months old and eaten without stuffing. **green in a person's eye** a sign of gullibility (do you see any green in my eye?). **green leek** any of several green-faced Australian parakeets. **green light 1** a signal to proceed on a road, railway, etc. **2** colloq. permission to go ahead with a project. **green linnet** = GREENFINCH. **green manure** growing plants ploughed into the soil as fertilizer. **green meat** grass and green vegetables as food. **Green Paper** (in the UK) a preliminary report of Government proposals, for discussion. **green plover** a lapwing. **green pound** the exchange rate for the pound for payments for agricultural produce in the EEC. **green revolution** greatly increased crop production in the developing countries by improvement of soil fertility, pest control, increased mechanization, etc. **green-room** a room in a theatre for actors and actresses who are off stage. **green-stick fracture** a bone-fracture, esp. in children, in which one side of the bone is broken and one only bent. **green tea** tea made from steam-dried, not fermented, leaves. **green thumb** = green fingers. **green turtle** a green-shelled sea turtle, Chelonia mydas, highly regarded as food. **green vitriol** ferrous sulphate crystals. □□ **greenish** adj. **greenly** adv. **greenness** n. [OE grēne (adj. & n.), grēnian (v.), f. Gmc, rel. to GROW]

Greenaway /'griːnəˌweɪ/, Catherine ('Kate') (1846–1901), English artist, known especially for her book-illustrations of children in early 19th-c. dress.

greenback /'griːnbæk/ n. US **1** a US legal-tender note. **2** any of various green-backed animals.

greenbottle /'griːnˌbɒt(ə)l/ n. any fly of the genus Lucilia, esp. L. sericata which lays eggs in the flesh of sheep.

Greene /griːn/, (Henry) Graham (1904–91), English novelist. He became a Roman Catholic in 1926, and from 1930 was a full-time writer. Among his major novels are The Power and the Glory (1940), set in Mexico, which combines a conspicuous religious theme with elements of a thriller, The Heart of the Matter (1948), and The End of the Affair (1951). Other fictional works classed as 'entertainments' include Brighton Rock (1938) which paradoxically introduced a strong Catholic message foreshadowing the religious complexity and ambiguities of his later work, and The Third Man (1950), originally written as a screenplay and filmed by Carol Reed in 1949. He has also written plays, travel books, essays, and two volumes of autobiography. His skilful variations of popular forms (e.g. the thriller, the detective story), his preoccupations with moral dilemmas (personal, religious, and political), and his choice of seedy locations give his work a highly distinctive quality.

greenery /'griːnərɪ/ n. green foliage or growing plants.

greenfeed /'griːnfiːd/ n. Austral. & NZ forage grown to be fed fresh to livestock.

greenfield /'griːnfiːld/ n. (attrib.) (of a site, in terms of its potential development) having no previous building development on it.

greenfinch /'griːnfɪntʃ/ n. a finch, Carduelis chloris, with green and yellow plumage.

greenfly /'griːnflaɪ/ n. (pl. **-flies**) Brit. **1** a green aphid. **2** these collectively.

greengage /'griːnɡeɪdʒ/ n. a roundish green fine-flavoured variety of plum. [Sir W. Gage d. 1727]

greengrocer /'griːnˌɡrəʊsə(r)/ n. Brit. a retailer of fruit and vegetables.

greengrocery /'griːnˌɡrəʊsərɪ/ n. (pl. **-ies**) Brit. **1** the business of a greengrocer. **2** goods sold by a greengrocer.

greenhead /'griːnhed/ n. **1** any biting fly of the genus Chrysops. **2** an Australian ant, Chalcoponera metallica, with a painful sting.

greenheart /'griːnhɑːt/ n. **1** any of several tropical American trees, esp. *Ocotea rodiaei*. **2** the hard greenish wood of one of these.

greenhorn /ˈgriːnhɔːn/ *n.* an inexperienced or foolish person; a new recruit.

greenhouse /ˈgriːnhaʊs/ *n.* a light structure with the sides and roof mainly of glass, for rearing delicate plants or hastening the growth of plants. □ **greenhouse effect** the trapping of the sun's warmth in the lower atmosphere of the earth caused by an increase in carbon dioxide, which is more transparent to solar radiation than to the reflected radiation from the earth. **greenhouse gas** any of various gases, esp. carbon dioxide, that contribute to the greenhouse effect.

greening /ˈgriːnɪŋ/ *n.* a variety of apple that is green when ripe. [prob. f. MDu. *groeninc* (as GREEN)]

greenkeeper /ˈgriːnˌkiːpə(r)/ *n.* the keeper of a golf-course.

Greenland /ˈgriːnlənd/ an island, the largest in the world, lying to the NE of North America and mostly within the Arctic Circle; pop. (est. 1988) 54,800, mostly Eskimos; capital, Godthåb. It was discovered and named by the Norse explorer Eric the Red in 986 and settled by Norse colonists. From 1721 onwards it was resettled by the Danes, and became part of Denmark in 1953, with internal autonomy from 1979; it withdrew from the EEC in 1985. □□ **Greenlander** *n.*

greenlet /ˈgriːnlɪt/ *n.* = VIREO.

Greenock /ˈgriːnək, ˈgreɪ-/ a port in western Scotland, on the Firth of Clyde; pop. (1981) 57,300. The engineer James Watt was born here in 1736.

Greenpeace /ˈgriːnpiːs/ an international organization that campaigns actively in support of general conservation and protection of the environment and the preservation of endangered species of animals. It was first active in Brtitish Columbia in 1971, opposing US testing of nuclear weapons in Alaska.

greensand /ˈgriːnsænd/ *n.* **1** a greenish kind of sandstone, often imperfectly cemented. **2** a stratum largely formed of this sandstone.

greenshank /ˈgriːnʃæŋk/ *n.* a large sandpiper, *Tringa nebularia.*

greensick /ˈgriːnsɪk/ *adj.* affected with chlorosis. □□ **greensickness** *n.*

greenstone /ˈgriːnstəʊn/ *n.* **1** a greenish igneous rock containing feldspar and hornblende. **2** a variety of jade found in New Zealand, used for tools, ornaments, etc.

greenstuff /ˈgriːnstʌf/ *n.* vegetation; green vegetables.

greensward /ˈgriːnswɔːd/ *n.* **1** grassy turf. **2** an expanse of this.

greenweed /ˈgriːnwiːd/ *n.* (**dyer's greenweed**) a bushy plant, *Genista tinctoria*, with deep yellow flowers.

Greenwich /ˈgrenɪtʃ, ˈgrɪnɪdʒ/ a London borough, site of the Royal Observatory, founded in 1675 by Charles II, in a building designed by Sir Christopher Wren. Soon after the Second World War, the observatory was moved to Herstmonceux in East Sussex; to preserve its links with the past it is called the Royal Greenwich Observatory. The buildings at Greenwich itself, together with many of the old instruments, now form part of the National Maritime Museum. The Greenwich Meridian, which was defined to pass through the Airy Transit Circle at Greenwich, was adopted internationally as the zero of longitude at a conference in Washington in 1884. Its acceptance was facilitated by the overwhelming use of the Greenwich Meridian in navigation and the adoption, in the US and Canada, of time zones based on Greenwich. Originally, different towns in Great Britain kept their own local time, varying according to longitude. In the mid-19th c. Greenwich time was adopted by railways throughout Britain for the sake of uniformity. However, it was only in 1880 that Greenwich Mean Time, mean solar time on the Greenwich Meridian, became the legal time throughout Great Britain. The international reference time-scale for civil use is now based on atomic clocks but is subject to step adjustments (leap seconds) to keep it close to mean solar time on the Greenwich meridian. The formal name of this time-scale is UTC (a language-independent abbreviation of coordinated universal time) but it is still widely known as Greenwich Mean Time.

greenwood /ˈgriːnwʊd/ *n.* a wood in summer, esp. as the scene of outlaw life.

greeny /ˈgriːnɪ/ *adj.* greenish (*greeny-yellow*).

greenyard /ˈgriːnjɑːd/ *n. Brit.* an enclosure for stray animals, a pound.

Greer /grɪə(r)/, Germaine (1939–), Australian feminist writer, noted especially for her influential book *The Female Eunuch* (1970), an analysis of women's sexual stereotypes.

greet[1] /griːt/ *v.tr.* **1** address politely or welcomingly on meeting or arrival. **2** receive or acknowledge in a specified way (*was greeted with derision*). **3** (of a sight, sound, etc.) become apparent to or noticed by. □□ **greeter** *n.* [OE *grētan* handle, attack, salute f. WG]

greet[2] /griːt/ *v.intr. Sc.* weep. [OE *grētan*, *grēotan*, of uncert. orig.]

greeting /ˈgriːtɪŋ/ *n.* **1** the act or an instance of welcoming or addressing politely. **2** words, gestures, etc., used to greet a person. **3** (often in *pl.*) an expression of goodwill. □ **greetings card** a decorative card sent to convey greetings.

gregarious /grɪˈgeərɪəs/ *adj.* **1** fond of company. **2** living in flocks or communities. **3** growing in clusters. □□ **gregariously** *adv.* **gregariousness** *n.* [L *gregarius* f. *grex gregis* flock]

Gregorian calendar /grɪˈgɔːrɪən/ *n.* the modified calendar, also known as the 'New Style', introduced by Pope Gregory XIII in 1582, adopted in Great Britain in 1752, and now in use throughout most of the Christian world. It is a modification of the Julian calendar, which was adapted to bring it into closer conformity with astronomical data and in order to correct errors which had accumulated because the Julian year of 365¼ days was 11 min. 10 sec. too long, 10 days were suppressed in 1582 and in Great Britain 11 in 1752, and to prevent further displacement Gregory provided that of the centenary years (1600, 1700, etc.) only those exactly divisible by 400 should be counted as leap years. [med.L *Gregorianus* f. LL *Gregorius* f. Gk *Grēgorios* Gregory]

Gregorian chant /grɪˈgɔːrɪən/ *n.* plainsong ritual music, named after Pope Gregory I. (See PLAINSONG.)

Gregorian telescope /grɪˈgɔːrɪən/ *n.* a reflecting telescope in which light reflected from a secondary mirror passes through a hole in a primary mirror. [J. *Gregory*, Sc. mathematician d. 1675, who devised it]

Gregory[1] /ˈgregərɪ/, St (329–89), Doctor of the Church, born at Nazianzus in Cappadocia. With St Basil and Gregory of Nyssa he was an upholder of orthodoxy against the Arian and Apollinarian heresies, and influential in restoring the Nicene faith. Feast day, (in the East) 25 and 30 Jan., (in the West) formerly 9 May but since 1969, with St Basil, 2 Jan.

Gregory[2] /ˈgregərɪ/, St (*c*.330–*c*.395), Doctor of the Church, bishop of Nyssa in Cappadocia, brother of St Basil, and an orthodox follower of Origen. (See GREGORY[1].) Feast day, 9 March.

Gregory[3] /ˈgregərɪ/, St, 'the Great' (*c.* 540–604), pope (as Gregory I) from 590 and Doctor of the Church. When he became pope Italy was in an alarming state, devastated by floods, famine, and the Lombard invasions, and the position of the Church was threatened by the imperial power at Constantinople; it was owing to Gregory that many of these evils were conquered. He made a separate peace with the Lombards in 592–3, and (acting independently of the imperial authorities) appointed governors to the Italian cities, thus establishing the temporal power of the papacy. One of his great achievements was the conversion of England, for which he selected St Augustine as head of the mission. He was a prolific author, promoted monasticism, made important changes in the liturgy and fostered the development of liturgical music, and is credited with the invention of Gregorian chant (see PLAINSONG). Feast day, 12 March.

Gregory of Tours /ˈgregərɪ, tʊə(r)/, St (*c.*540–94), bishop of Tours, whose writings are our chief authority for the early Merovingian period of French history.

gregory-powder /ˈgregərɪ/ *n. hist.* a compound powder of rhubarb, magnesia, and ginger, used as a laxative. [J. *Gregory*, Sc. physician d. 1822]

gremlin /ˈgremlɪn/ *n. colloq.* **1** an imaginary mischievous sprite regarded as responsible for mechanical faults, esp. in aircraft. **2** any similar cause of trouble. [20th c.: orig. unkn., but prob. after *goblin*]

Grenada /grəˈneɪdə/ a State in the West Indies, consisting of the island of Grenada (the southernmost of the Windward

Islands) and the southern Grenadines; pop. (est. 1988) 84,455; official language, English; capital, St George's. The island was sighted in 1498 by Columbus on 15 Aug., which is now Grenada's national day. Colonized by the French, it was ceded to Britain in 1763, recaptured by the French, and restored to Britain in 1783. It became an independent State within the Commonwealth in 1974. Seizure of power by a left-wing military group in 1983 prompted an invasion by US and some Caribbean countries, fearful of instability and Communist influence in the region; they withdrew in 1985. □□ **Grenadian** *adj.* & *n.*

grenade /grɪˈneɪd/ *n.* **1** a small bomb thrown by hand (**hand-grenade**) or shot from a rifle. **2** a glass receptacle containing chemicals which disperse on impact, for testing drains, extinguishing fires, etc. [F f. OF *grenate* and Sp. *granada* POMEGRANATE]

grenadier /ˌgrenəˈdɪə(r)/ *n.* **1 a** *Brit.* (**Grenadiers** or **Grenadier Guards**) the first regiment of the royal household infantry. **b** *hist.* a soldier armed with grenades. **2** any deep-sea fish of the family Macrouridae, with a long tapering body and pointed tail, and secreting luminous bacteria when disturbed. [F (as GRENADE)]

grenadilla var. of GRANADILLA.

grenadine[1] /ˈgrenəˌdiːn/ *n.* a French cordial syrup of pomegranates etc. [F f. *grenade*: see GRENADE]

grenadine[2] /ˈgrenəˌdiːn/ *n.* a dress-fabric of loosely woven silk or silk and wool. [F, earlier *grenade* grained silk f. *grenu* grained]

Grenadine Islands /ˈgrenəˌdiːn/ (also **Grenadines**) a chain of small islands in the West Indies, divided between St Vincent and Grenada.

Grenoble /grəˈnəʊbl/ an industrial city in the Dauphiné Alps of SE France; pop. (1982) 159,500. The novelist Stendhal was born here in 1783.

Grenville /ˈgrenvɪl/, George (1712–70). British statesman, Prime Minister 1763–5.

Gresham /ˈgreʃəm/, Sir Thomas (*c.*1519–79), English financier who founded the Royal Exchange in 1566 and served as the chief financial adviser to the Elizabethan government. □ **Gresham's law** the tendency for money of lower intrinsic value to circulate more freely than money of higher intrinsic and equal nominal value (pithily expressed as 'Bad money drives out good'). Formulation of this principle is attributed to Gresham.

gressorial /greˈsɔːrɪəl/ *adj.* Zool. **1** walking. **2** adapted for walking. [mod.L *gressorius* f. L *gradi gress-* walk]

Gretna Green /ˈgretnə/ a village just north of the Scottish/English border near Carlisle, formerly a popular place for runaway couples from England to be married according to Scots law without the parental consent required in England for those who had not attained their majority. A valid marriage could be contracted in Scotland merely by a declaration of consent by the two parties before a witness (traditionally the village blacksmith, who also read the marriage service to couples for sentiment's sake). The practice began after 1753, when English law made it impossible to conduct a marriage clandestinely, and lapsed after 1857 when Scots law prescribed certain conditions for 'irregular' marriages, though it recognized such marriages until 1939.

Greuze /grɜːz/, Jean-Baptiste (1725–1805), French painter. He had a great success in 1755 with his *Father Reading the Bible to his Children*, and won popularity with similar sentimental and melodramatic scenes, but was unsuccessful in his history painting. Much of his later work consisted of vaguely erotic pictures of young women.

grew past of GROW.

Grey[1] /greɪ/, Charles, 2nd Earl (1764–1845), British statesman, Prime Minister 1830–4. he was an advocate of electoral reform, and his government passed the first great parliamentary Reform Act (1832) as well as important factory legislation and the Act abolishing slavery throughout the British Empire.

Grey[2] /greɪ/, Sir George (1812–98), British statesman and colonial administrator, who was appointed as governor in South Australia (1840), New Zealand (1845, 1861), and Cape Colony (1854), in each case at a time of conflict between the native peoples and European settlers. In New Zealand he also served as Prime Minister (1877–9), and is regarded as one of the outstanding

personalities in its political history. He brought peace to the country and established good relations with the Maoris, learning their language and studying their mythology and culture in order to understand their intentions and problems.

Grey[3] /greɪ/, Lady Jane (1537–54), queen of England for nine days. The granddaughter of Henry VIII's sister, Jane fell victim to the dynastic ambitions of the Duke of Northumberland, who, in 1553, married her against her will to his son and then persuaded the dying Edward VI to name her as his successor. Jane was deposed after nine days on the throne by forces loyal to Edward's elder sister Mary. She was initially spared, but after Wyatt's Rebellion in 1554 was executed because she was seen as a potential focal point for Protestant opposition to Mary's Catholic regime.

grey /greɪ/ *adj., n.,* & *v.* (US **gray**) —*adj.* **1** of a colour intermediate between black and white, as of ashes or lead. **2 a** (of the weather etc.) dull, dismal; heavily overcast. **b** bleak, depressing; (of a person) depressed. **3 a** (of hair) turning white with age etc. **b** (of a person) having grey hair. **4** anonymous, nondescript, unidentifiable. —*n.* **1 a** a grey colour or pigment. **b** grey clothes or material (*dressed in grey*). **2** a cold sunless light. **3** a grey or white horse. —*v.tr.* & *intr.* make or become grey. □ **grey area 1** a situation or topic sharing features of more than one category and not clearly attributable to any one category. **2** *S.Afr.* an area where Black and Coloured people live (usu. illicitly) alongside White. **3** *Brit.* an area in economic decline. **grey eminence** = ÉMINENCE GRISE. **Grey Friar** a Franciscan friar, so called from the grey cloak worn. **grey goose** = GREYLAG. **grey-hen** the female of the black grouse (cf. BLACKCOCK). **grey matter 1** the darker tissues of the brain and spinal cord consisting of nerve-cell bodies and branching dendrites. **2** *colloq.* intelligence. **grey squirrel** an American squirrel, *Sciurus carolinensis*, brought to Europe in the 19th c. □□ **greyish** *adj.* **greyly** *adv.* **greyness** *n.* [OE *græg* f. Gmc]

greybeard /ˈgreɪbɪəd/ *n. archaic* **1** an old man. **2** a large stoneware jug for spirits. **3** *Brit.* clematis in seed.

greyhound /ˈgreɪhaʊnd/ *n.* **1** a dog of a tall slender breed having keen sight and capable of high speed, used in racing and coursing. **2** this breed. Dogs of greyhound type are depicted on murals of ancient Egypt dating from the 2nd millennium BC and were valued in the east for hunting in deserts and plains, where speed is crucial. In England greyhounds were used to hunt small game, especially hares, and in the Middle Ages ownership was restricted by law to the aristocracy. By the early 19th c. hare-coursing had become an organized sport, and the sport of dog-racing, with an electrically propelled lure, developed from this in the early 20th c., originally in the US. [OE *grīghund* f. *grīeg* bitch (unrecorded: cf. ON *grey*) + *hund* dog, rel. to HOUND]

greylag /ˈgreɪlæg/ *n.* (in full **greylag goose**) a wild goose, *Anser anser*, native to Europe. [GREY + LAG[1] (because of its late migration)]

Greymouth /ˈgreɪmaʊθ/ the capital of West Coast region, South Island, New Zealand; pop. (1986) 7,600.

greywacke /ˈgreɪˌwækə, -wæk/ *n.* (US **graywacke**) *Geol.* a dark and coarse-grained sandstone, usu. with an admixture of clay. [Anglicized f. G *Grauwacke* f. *grau* grey: see WACKE]

grid /grɪd/ *n.* **1** a framework of spaced parallel bars; a grating. **2** a system of numbered squares printed on a map and forming the basis of map references. **3** a network of lines, electric-power connections, gas-supply lines, etc. **4** a pattern of lines marking the starting-places on a motor-racing track. **5** the wire network between the filament and the anode of a thermionic valve etc. **6** an arrangement of town streets in a rectangular pattern. □ **grid bias** *Electr.* a fixed voltage applied between the cathode and the control grid of a thermionic valve which determines its operating conditions. □□ **gridded** *adj.* [back-form. f. GRIDIRON]

griddle /ˈgrɪd(ə)l/ *n.* & *v.* —*n.* **1** = GIRDLE[2]. **2** a miner's wire-bottomed sieve. —*v.tr.* **1** cook with a griddle; grill. **2** sieve with a griddle. [ME f. OF *gredil*, *gridil* gridiron ult. f. L *craticula* dimin. of *cratis* hurdle; cf. GRATE[2], GRILL[1]]

gridiron /ˈgrɪdˌaɪən/ *n.* **1** a cooking utensil of metal bars for broiling or grilling. **2** a frame of parallel beams for supporting a ship in dock. **3** *US* a football field (with parallel lines marking out the area of play). **4** *Theatr.* a plank structure over a stage supporting the mechanism for drop-scenes etc. **5** = GRID 6. [ME *gredire*, var. of *gredil* GRIDDLE, later assoc. with IRON]

grief /griːf/ *n*. **1** deep or intense sorrow or mourning. **2** the cause of this. □ **come to grief** meet with disaster; fail. **good** (or **great**) **grief!** an exclamation of surprise, alarm, etc. [ME f. AF *gref*, OF *grief* f. *grever* GRIEVE¹]

Grieg /griːg/, Edvard (1843–1907), Norwegian composer, conductor, and violinist. He married his cousin, the soprano Nina Hagerup, in 1867, she being the inspiration and interpreter of many of his songs. His compositions earned the admiration of Liszt, whom he met in Rome (1870) where Liszt played the piano concerto, from manuscript, at sight. In 1874 he was asked by Ibsen to write the incidental music to *Peer Gynt*, and its performance (1876) made Grieg a national figure. His music eschews the larger forms of opera and symphony, but within his chosen scale it is deeply poetic, superbly fashioned, and (in the songs especially) emotionally passionate. His nationalist idiom transcends local boundaries by reason of the strong individuality of his work.

grievance /ˈgriːv(ə)ns/ *n*. a real or fancied cause for complaint. [ME, = injury, f. OF *grevance* (as GRIEF)]

grieve¹ /griːv/ *v*. **1** *tr*. cause grief or great distress to. **2** *intr*. suffer grief, esp. at another's death. □□ **griever** *n*. [ME f. OF *grever* ult. f. L *gravare* f. *gravis* heavy]

grieve² /griːv/ *n*. *Sc*. a farm-bailiff; an overseer. [OE *grǽfa*: cf. REEVE¹]

grievous /ˈgriːvəs/ *adj*. **1** (of pain etc.) severe. **2** causing grief or suffering. **3** injurious. **4** flagrant, heinous. □ **grievous bodily harm** *Law* serious injury inflicted intentionally on a person. □□ **grievously** *adv*. **grievousness** *n*. [ME f. OF *grevos* (as GRIEVE¹)]

griffin /ˈgrifin/ *n*. (also **gryphon** /-f(ə)n/) a fabulous creature with an eagle's head and wings and a lion's body. [ME f. OF *grifoun* ult. f. LL *gryphus* f. L *gryps* f. Gk *grups*]

Griffith /ˈgrifiθ/, D(avid) W(ark) (1875–1948), American film director, one of the most significant figures in the history of film. He began to discover the elements of cinematic expression in his early one-reel films, and he is responsible for introducing the techniques of flashback and fade-out. His most memorable films included his epic of the American Civil War *The Birth of a Nation* (1915), *Intolerance* (1916), which incorporated four separate stories to illustrate the theme, and *Broken Blossoms* (1919). He made only two sound films, in 1930 and 1931, and then had a long and lonely retirement virtually forgotten.

griffon /ˈgrif(ə)n/ *n*. **1 a** a dog of a small terrier-like breed with coarse or smooth hair. **b** this breed. **2** (in full **griffon vulture**) a large vulture, *Gyps fulvus*. **3** = GRIFFIN. [F (in sense 1) or var. of GRIFFIN]

grig /grig/ *n*. **1** a small eel. **2** a grasshopper or cricket. □ **merry** (or **lively**) **as a grig** full of fun; extravagantly lively. [ME, orig. = dwarf: orig. unkn.]

grill¹ /gril/ *n*. & *v*. —*n*. **1 a** a device on a cooker for radiating heat downwards. **b** = GRIDIRON 1. **2** a dish of food cooked on a grill. **3** (in full **grill room**) a restaurant serving grilled food. —*v*. **1** *tr*. & *intr*. cook or be cooked under a grill or on a gridiron. **2** *tr*. & *intr*. subject or be subjected to extreme heat, esp. from the sun. **3** *tr*. subject to severe questioning or interrogation. □□ **griller** *n*. **grilling** *n*. (in sense 3 of *v*.). [F *gril* (*n*.), *griller* (*v*.), f. OF forms of GRILLE]

grill² var. of GRILLE.

grillage /ˈgrilidʒ/ *n*. a heavy framework of cross-timbering or metal beams forming a foundation for building on difficult ground. [F (as GRILLE)]

grille /gril/ *n*. (also **grill**) **1** a grating or latticed screen, used as a partition or to allow discreet vision. **2** a metal grid protecting the radiator of a motor vehicle. **3** (in real tennis) a square opening in the wall at the end of the hazard side (a ball entering it scores a point). [F f. OF *graille* f. med.L *graticula*, *craticula*: see GRIDDLE]

grilse /grils/ *n*. a young salmon that has returned to fresh water from the sea for the first time. [ME: orig. unkn.]

grim /grim/ *adj*. (**grimmer**, **grimmest**) **1** of a stern or forbidding appearance. **2** harsh, merciless, severe. **3** ghastly, joyless, sinister (*has a grim truth in it*). **4** unpleasant, unattractive. □ **like grim death** with great determination. □□ **grimly** *adv*. **grimness** *n*. [OE f. Gmc]

grimace /ˈgriməs, griˈmeis/ *n*. & *v*. —*n*. a distortion of the face made in disgust etc. or to amuse. —*v.intr*. make a grimace. □□ **grimacer** *n*. [F f. Sp. *grimazo* f. *grima* fright]

Grimaldi¹ /griˈmældi/, Francesco Maria (1618–63), Italian Jesuit physicist and astronomer, who discovered the diffraction of light. He verified Galileo's law of falling bodies, drew a detailed map of the moon, based on many telescopic observations, and began the practice of naming lunar regions after astronomers and physicists.

Grimaldi² /griˈmældi/, Joseph (1779–1837), English actor, the creator of the English clown, in whose honour all later clowns were nicknamed Joey. He performed at Covent Garden from 1806 until his retirement in 1823. His inventive comic genius could make a man out of vegetables and a coach out of four cheeses, and he designed a number of trick scenes. Making Clown a rustic booby, Grimaldi gave him his traditional costume. His acrobatics were characterized by dynamic energy which finally wore him out.

grimalkin /griˈmælkin, -ˈmɔːlkin/ *n. archaic* (esp. in fiction) **1** an old she-cat. **2** a spiteful old woman. [GREY + *Malkin* dimin. of the name *Matilda*]

grime /graim/ *n*. & *v*. —*n*. soot or dirt ingrained in a surface, esp. of buildings or the skin. —*v.tr*. blacken with grime; befoul. [orig. as verb: f. MLG & MDu.]

Grimm /grim/, Jacob Ludwig Carl (1785–1863) and Wilhelm Carl (1786–1859), German linguistics scholars. Jacob produced a historical and descriptive German grammar (1819, 1822) and the brothers jointly inaugurated a dictionary of German on historical principles; begun in 1852, it was continued by other scholars and completed in 1960. They are remembered also for the anthology of German fairy-tales which they compiled. □ **Grimm's law** a statement of the regular consonantal differences between related words in the different Indo-European languages, first fully formulated by Jacob Grimm in the second edition of his German grammar (1822).

grimy /ˈgraimi/ *adj*. (**grimier**, **grimiest**) covered with grime; dirty. □□ **grimily** *adv*. **griminess** *n*.

grin /grin/ *v*. & *n*. —*v*. (**grinned**, **grinning**) **1** *intr*. **a** smile broadly, showing the teeth. **b** make a forced, unrestrained, or stupid smile. **2** *tr*. express by grinning (*grinned his satisfaction*). —*n*. the act or action of grinning. □ **grin and bear it** take pain or misfortune stoically. □□ **grinner** *n*. **grinningly** *adv*. [OE *grennian* f. Gmc]

grind /graind/ *v*. & *n*. —*v*. (*past* and *past part*. **ground** /graund/) **1 a** *tr*. reduce to small particles or powder by crushing esp. by passing through a mill. **b** *intr*. (of a mill, machine, etc.) move with a crushing action. **2 a** *tr*. reduce, sharpen, or smooth by friction. **b** *tr*. & *intr*. rub or rub together gratingly (*grind one's teeth*). **3** *tr*. (often foll. by *down*) oppress; harass with exactions (*grinding poverty*). **4** *intr*. **a** (often foll. by *away*) work or study hard. **b** (foll. by *out*) produce with effort (*grinding out verses*). **c** (foll. by *on*) (of a sound) continue gratingly or monotonously. **5** *tr*. turn the handle of e.g. a coffee-mill, barrel-organ, etc. **6** *intr*. *sl*. (of a dancer) rotate the hips. **7** *intr. coarse sl*. have sexual intercourse. —*n*. **1** the act or an instance of grinding. **2** *colloq*. hard dull work; a laborious task (*the daily grind*). **3** the size of ground particles. **4** *sl*. a dancer's rotary movement of the hips. **5** *coarse sl*. an act of sexual intercourse. □ **grind to a halt** stop laboriously. **ground glass 1** glass made non-transparent by grinding etc. **2** glass ground to a powder. □□ **grindingly** *adv*. [OE *grindan*, of unkn. orig.]

grinder /ˈgraində(r)/ *n*. **1** a person or thing that grinds, esp. a machine (often in *comb*.: *coffee-grinder*; *organ-grinder*). **2** a molar tooth.

grindstone /ˈgraindstəʊn/ *n*. **1** a thick revolving disc used for grinding, sharpening, and polishing. **2** a kind of stone used for this. □ **keep one's nose to the grindstone** work hard and continuously.

gringo /ˈɡrɪŋɡəʊ/ n. (pl. **-os**) colloq. a foreigner, esp. a British or N. American person, in a Spanish-speaking country. [Sp., = gibberish]

grip /ɡrɪp/ v. & n. —v. (**gripped, gripping**) **1 a** tr. grasp tightly; take a firm hold of. **b** intr. take a firm hold, esp. by friction. **2** tr. (of a feeling or emotion) deeply affect (a person) (was gripped by fear). **3** tr. compel the attention or interest of (a gripping story). —n. **1 a** a firm hold; a tight grasp or clasp. **b** a manner of grasping or holding. **2** the power of holding attention. **3 a** mental or intellectual understanding or mastery. **b** effective control of a situation or one's behaviour etc. (lose one's grip). **4 a** a part of a machine that grips or holds something. **b** a part or attachment by which a tool, implement, weapon, etc., is held in the hand. **5** = HAIRGRIP. **6** a travelling bag. **7** an assistant in a theatre, film studio, etc. **8** Austral. sl. a job or occupation. □ **come** (or **get**) **to grips with** approach purposefully; begin to deal with. **in the grip of** dominated or affected by (esp. an adverse circumstance or unpleasant sensation). □□ **gripper** n. **grippingly** adv. [OE gripe, gripa handful (as GRIPE)]

gripe /ɡraɪp/ v. & n. —v. **1** intr. colloq. complain, esp. peevishly. **2** tr. affect with gastric or intestinal pain. **3** tr. archaic clutch, grip. **4** Naut. **a** tr. secure with gripes. **b** intr. turn to face the wind in spite of the helm. —n. **1** (usu. in pl.) gastric or intestinal pain; colic. **2** colloq. **a** a complaint. **b** the act of griping. **3** a grip or clutch. **4** (in pl.) Naut. lashings securing a boat in its place. □ **Gripe Water** propr. a carminative solution to relieve colic and stomach ailments in infants. □□ **griper** n. **gripingly** adv. [OE grīpan f. Gmc: cf. GROPE]

grippe /ɡrɪp/ n. archaic or colloq. influenza. [F f. gripper seize]

grisaille /ɡrɪˈzaɪl, -ˈzaɪl/ n. **1** a method of painting in grey monochrome, often to imitate sculpture. **2** a painting or stained-glass window of this kind. [F f. gris grey]

griseofulvin /ˌɡrɪzɪəʊˈfʊlvɪn/ n. an antibiotic used against fungal infections of the hair and skin. [mod.L griseofulvum f. med.L griseus grey + L fulvus reddish-yellow]

grisette /ɡriːˈzet/ n. a young working-class Frenchwoman. [F, orig. a grey dress-material, f. gris grey]

grisly /ˈɡrɪzlɪ/ adj. (**grislier, grisliest**) causing horror, disgust, or fear. □□ **grisliness** n. [OE grislic terrifying]

grison /ˈɡrɪz(ə)n/ n. any weasel-like mammal of the genus Galictis, with dark fur and a white stripe across the forehead. [F, app. f. grison grey]

grist /ɡrɪst/ n. **1** corn to grind. **2** malt crushed for brewing. □ **grist to the** (or **a person's**) **mill** a source of profit or advantage. [OE f. Gmc, rel. to GRIND]

gristle /ˈɡrɪs(ə)l/ n. tough flexible tissue in vertebrates; cartilage. □□ **gristly** /-slɪ/ adj. [OE gristle]

grit /ɡrɪt/ n. & v. —n. **1** particles of stone or sand, esp. as causing discomfort, clogging machinery, etc. **2** coarse sandstone. **3** colloq. pluck, endurance; strength of character. —v. (**gritted, gritting**) **1** tr. spread grit on (icy roads etc.). **2** tr. clench (the teeth). **3** intr. make or move with a grating sound. □□ **gritter** n. **gritty** adj. (**grittier, grittiest**). **grittily** adv. **grittiness** n. [OE grēot f. Gmc: cf. GRITS, GROATS]

grits /ɡrɪts/ n.pl. **1** coarsely ground grain, esp. oatmeal. **2** oats that have been husked but not ground. [OE grytt(e): cf. GRIT, GROATS]

grizzle /ˈɡrɪz(ə)l/ v.intr. Brit. colloq. **1** (esp. of a child) cry fretfully. **2** complain whiningly. □□ **grizzler** n. **grizzly** adj. [19th c.: orig. unkn.]

grizzled /ˈɡrɪz(ə)ld/ adj. having, or streaked with, grey hair. [grizzle grey f. OF grisel f. gris grey]

grizzly /ˈɡrɪzlɪ/ adj. & n. —adj. (**grizzlier, grizzliest**) grey, greyish, grey-haired. —n. (pl. **-ies**) (in full **grizzly bear**) a large variety of brown bear, found in N. America and the northern USSR.

groan /ɡrəʊn/ v. & n. —v. **1 a** intr. make a deep sound expressing pain, grief, or disapproval. **b** tr. utter with groans. **2** intr. complain inarticulately. **3** intr. (usu. foll. by under, beneath, with) be loaded or oppressed. —n. the sound made in groaning. □ **groan inwardly** be distressed. □□ **groaner** n. **groaningly** adv. [OE grānian f. Gmc, rel. to GRIN]

groat /ɡrəʊt/ n. hist. **1** a silver coin worth four old pence. **2** archaic a small sum (don't care a groat). [ME f. MDu. groot, orig. = great, i.e. thick (penny): cf. GROSCHEN]

groats /ɡrəʊts/ n.pl. hulled or crushed grain, esp. oats. [OE grotan (pl.): cf. grot fragment, grēot GRIT, grytt bran]

grocer /ˈɡrəʊsə(r)/ n. a dealer in food and household provisions. [ME & AF grosser, orig. one who sells in the gross, f. OF grossier f. med.L grossarius (as GROSS)]

grocery /ˈɡrəʊsərɪ/ n. (pl. **-ies**) **1** a grocer's trade or shop. **2** (in pl.) provisions, esp. food, sold by a grocer.

grockle /ˈɡrɒk(ə)l/ n. dial. & sl. a visitor or holiday-maker, esp. from the North or Midlands to SW England. [20th c.: orig. uncert.]

grog /ɡrɒɡ/ n. **1** a drink of spirit (orig. rum) and water. **2** Austral. & NZ colloq. alcoholic liquor, esp. beer. [said to be from 'Old Grog', the reputed nickname (f. his GROGRAM cloak) of Admiral Vernon, who in 1740 first had diluted instead of neat rum served out to sailors]

groggy /ˈɡrɒɡɪ/ adj. (**groggier, groggiest**) incapable or unsteady from being dazed or semi-conscious. □□ **groggily** adv. **grogginess** n.

grogram /ˈɡrɒɡrəm/ n. a coarse fabric of silk, mohair, and wool, or a mixture of these, often stiffened with gum. [F gros grain coarse grain (as GROSS, GRAIN)]

groin[1] /ɡrɔɪn/ n. & v. —n. **1** the depression between the belly and the thigh. **2** Archit. **a** an edge formed by intersecting vaults. **b** an arch supporting a vault. —v.tr. Archit. build with groins. [ME grynde, perh. f. OE grynde depression]

groin[2] US var. of GROYNE.

grommet /ˈɡrɒmɪt/ n. (also **grummet** /ˈɡrʌmɪt/) **1** a metal, plastic, or rubber eyelet placed in a hole to protect or insulate a rope or cable etc. passed through it. **2** a tube passed through the eardrum in surgery to make a communication with the middle ear. [obs. F grommette f. gourmer to curb, of unkn. orig.]

gromwell /ˈɡrɒmw(ə)l/ n. any of various plants of the genus Lithospermum, with hard seeds formerly used in medicine. [ME f. OF gromil, prob. f. med.L gruinum milium (unrecorded) crane's millet]

Gromyko /ɡrəˈmiːkəʊ/, Andrei Andreievich (1909–), Soviet statesman, Foreign Minister 1957–85, President of the USSR (Chairman of the Presidium of the Supreme Soviet) 1985–8.

Groningen /ˈɡrəʊnɪŋən/ **1** an agricultural province of NE Netherlands; pop. (1988) 556,757. **2** its capital city; pop. (1984) 206,610.

groom /ɡruːm/ n. & v. —n. **1** a person employed to take care of horses. **2** = BRIDEGROOM. **3** Brit. Mil. any of certain officers of the Royal Household. —v.tr. **1 a** curry or tend (a horse). **b** give a neat appearance to (a person etc.). **2** (of an ape or monkey etc.) clean and comb the fur of (its fellow) with the fingers. **3** prepare or train (a person) for a particular purpose or activity (was groomed for the top job). [ME, orig. = boy: orig. unkn.]

groove /ɡruːv/ n. & v. —n. **1 a** a channel or hollow, esp. one made to guide motion or receive a corresponding ridge. **b** a spiral track cut in a gramophone record. **2** an established routine or habit, esp. a monotonous one. —v. **1** tr. make a groove or grooves in. **2** intr. sl. **a** enjoy oneself. **b** (often foll. by with) make progress; get on well. ¶ Often with ref. to popular music or jazz; now largely disused in general contexts. □ **in the groove** sl. **1** doing or performing well. **2** fashionable. [ME, = mine-shaft, f. obs. Du. groeve furrow f. Gmc]

groovy /ˈɡruːvɪ/ adj. (**groovier, grooviest**) **1** sl. fashionable and exciting; enjoyable, excellent. **2** of or like a groove. □□ **groovily** adv. **grooviness** n.

grope /ɡrəʊp/ v. & n. —v. **1** intr. (usu. foll. by for) feel about or search blindly or uncertainly with the hands. **2** intr. (foll. by for, after) search mentally (was groping for the answer). **3** tr. feel (one's way) towards something. **4** tr. sl. fondle clumsily for sexual pleasure. —n. the process or an instance of groping. □□ **groper** n. **gropingly** adv. [OE grāpian f. Gmc]

groper /ˈgrəʊpə(r)/ n. esp. Austral. & NZ = GROUPER. [var. of GROUPER]

Gropius /ˈgrəʊpɪəs/, Walter (1883–1969), German architect, director of the Bauhaus School of Design 1919–28, one of the leading personalities in modern architecture, both as teacher and as designer. His special contribution was to bring architecture into closer relationship firstly with social needs and secondly with the industrial techniques on which it was increasingly coming to rely. In 1934, finding his ideas unpalatable to the Nazi regime, he came to England, and in 1938 moved to Harvard University, where he was an influential teacher.

grosbeak /ˈgrəʊsbiːk/ n. any of various finches of the families Cardinalidae and Fringillidae, having stout conical bills and usu. brightly coloured plumage. [F grosbec (as GROSS)]

groschen /ˈgrɒʃ(ə)n/ n. 1 an Austrian coin and monetary unit, one hundredth of a schilling. 2 colloq. a German 10-pfennig piece. 3 hist. a small German silver coin. [G f. MHG gros, grosse f. med.L (denarius) grossus thick (penny): cf. GROAT]

grosgrain /ˈgrəʊgreɪn/ n. a corded fabric of silk etc. [F, = coarse grain (as GROSS, GRAIN)]

gros point /grəʊ ˈpwæ̃/ n. cross-stitch embroidery on canvas. [F (as GROSS, POINT)]

gross /grəʊs/ adj., v., & n. —adj. 1 overfed, bloated; repulsively fat. 2 (of a person, manners, or morals) noticeably coarse, unrefined, or indecent. 3 flagrant; conspicuously wrong (gross negligence). 4 total; without deductions; not net (gross tonnage; gross income). 5 a luxuriant, rank. b thick, solid, dense. 6 (of the senses etc.) dull; lacking sensitivity. —v.tr. produce or earn as gross profit or income. —n. (pl. same) an amount equal to twelve dozen. □ **by the gross** in large quantities; wholesale. **gross domestic product** the total value of goods produced and services provided in a country in one year. **gross national product** the gross domestic product plus the total of net income from abroad. **gross out** US sl. disgust, esp. by repulsive or obscene behaviour. **gross up** increase (a net amount) to its value before deductions. □□ **grossly** adv. **grossness** n. [ME f. OF gros grosse large f. LL grossus: (n.) f. F grosse douzaine large dozen]

Grosseteste /ˈgrɒstest/, Robert (c.1175–1253), English churchman and scholar. He studied and taught at Oxford before becoming bishop of Lincoln (1235), where his opposition to clerical laxity in his diocese and to nepotism in church appointments set him at variance with his dean and chapter and with the papacy. Grosseteste's interests covered a wide range of subjects, and his experimental science, especially optics and mathematics, inspired his pupil Roger Bacon. His writings include translations of Aristotle and the Church Fathers, philosophical treatises, and devotional works.

Grossglockner /ˈgrəʊsglɒknə(r)/ the highest mountain in Austria, in the eastern Tyrolean Alps, rising to a height of 3,797 m (12,457 ft.).

Grosz /grəʊs/, George (1893–1959), German-born painter and draughtsman, an American citizen from 1938. He is famous for his satirical drawings and paintings, some anti-war, others denouncing a decaying society in which gluttony and depraved sensuality are placed beside money and disease.

grot /grɒt/ n. & adj. Brit. sl. —n. rubbish, junk. —adj. dirty. [back-form. f. GROTTY]

grotesque /grəʊˈtesk/ adj. & n. —adj. 1 comically or repulsively distorted; monstrous, unnatural. 2 incongruous, ludicrous, absurd. —n. 1 a decorative form interweaving human and animal features. 2 a comically distorted figure or design. 3 Printing a family of sanserif typefaces. □□ **grotesquely** adv. **grotesqueness** n. **grotesquerie** /-ˈteskərɪ/ n. [earlier crotesque f. F crotesca f. It. grottesca grotto-like (painting etc.) fem. of grottesco (as GROTTO, -ESQUE)]

Grotius /ˈgrəʊʃəs/, Hugo (1583–1645), Dutch jurist. He led an interesting life, serving as a diplomat, escaping from life imprisonment in Holland, and eventually dying in the service of Queen Christina of Sweden, but his fame rests on the legal treatise De Jure Belli et Pacis, written in exile in Paris and published in 1625, which established the basis of modern international law.

grotto /ˈgrɒtəʊ/ n. (pl. **-oes** or **-os**) 1 a small picturesque cave. 2

an artificial ornamental cave, e.g. in a park or large garden. □□ **grottoed** adj. [It. grotta ult. f. L crypta f. Gk kruptē CRYPT]

grotty /ˈgrɒtɪ/ adj. (**grottier, grottiest**) Brit. sl. unpleasant, dirty, shabby, unattractive. □□ **grottiness** n. [shortening of GROTESQUE + -Y¹]

grouch /graʊtʃ/ v. & n. colloq. —v.intr. grumble. —n. 1 a discontented person. 2 a fit of grumbling or the sulks. 3 a cause of discontent. [var. of grutch: see GRUDGE]

grouchy /ˈgraʊtʃɪ/ adj. (**grouchier, grouchiest**) colloq. discontented, grumpy. □□ **grouchily** adv. **grouchiness** n.

ground¹ /graʊnd/ n. & v. —n. 1 a the surface of the earth, esp. as contrasted with the air around it. b a part of this specified in some way (low ground). 2 the substance of the earth's surface; soil, earth (stony ground; dug deep into the ground). 3 a a position, area, or distance on the earth's surface. b the extent of activity etc. achieved or of a subject dealt with (the book covers a lot of ground). 4 (often in pl.) a foundation, motive, or reason (there is ground for concern; there are grounds for believing; excused on the grounds of ill-health). 5 an area of a special kind or designated for special use (often in comb.: cricket-ground; fishing-grounds). 6 (in pl.) an area of usu. enclosed land attached to a house etc. 7 an area or basis for consideration, agreement, etc. (common ground; on firm ground). 8 a (in painting) the prepared surface giving the predominant colour or tone. b (in embroidery, ceramics, etc.) the undecorated surface. 9 (in full **ground bass**) Mus. a short theme in the bass constantly repeated with the upper parts of the music varied. 10 (in pl.) solid particles, esp. of coffee, forming a residue. 11 Electr. = EARTH. 12 the bottom of the sea (the ship touched ground). 13 Brit. the floor of a room etc. 14 a piece of wood fixed to a wall as a base for boards, plaster, or joinery. 15 (attrib.) a (of animals) living on or in the ground; (of fish) living at the bottom of water; (of plants) dwarfish or trailing. b relating to or concerned with the ground (ground staff). —v. 1 refuse authority for (a pilot or an aircraft) to fly. 2 a tr. run (a ship) aground; strand. b intr. (of a ship) run aground. 3 tr. (foll. by in) instruct thoroughly (in a subject). 4 tr. (often as **grounded** adj.) (foll. by on) base (a principle, conclusion, etc.) on. 5 tr. Electr. = EARTH v. 6 intr. alight on the ground. 7 tr. place or lay (esp. weapons) on the ground. □ **break new** (or **fresh**) **ground** treat a subject previously not dealt with. **cut the ground from under a person's feet** anticipate and pre-empt a person's arguments, plans, etc. **down to the ground** Brit. colloq. thoroughly; in every respect. **fall to the ground** (of a plan etc.) fail. **gain** (or **make**) **ground** 1 advance steadily; make progress. 2 (foll. by on) catch (a person) up. **get in on the ground floor** become part of an enterprise in its early stages. **get off the ground** colloq. make a successful start. **give** (or **lose**) **ground** 1 retreat, decline. 2 lose the advantage or one's position in an argument, contest, etc. **go to ground** 1 (of a fox etc.) enter its earth or burrow etc. 2 (of a person) become inaccessible for a prolonged period. **ground-bait** bait thrown to the bottom of a fishing-ground. **ground control** the personnel directing the landing etc. of aircraft or spacecraft. **ground cover** plants covering the surface of the earth, esp. low-growing spreading plants that inhibit the growth of weeds. **ground elder** a garden weed, Aegopodium podagraria, spreading by means of underground stems. **ground floor** the floor of a building at ground level. **ground frost** frost on the surface of the ground or in the top layer of soil. **ground level 1** the level of the ground; the ground floor. **2** Physics the lowest energy state of an atom etc. **ground-plan 1** the plan of a building at ground level. **2** the general outline of a scheme. **ground-rent** rent for land leased for building. **ground rule** a basic principle. **ground speed** an aircraft's speed relative to the ground. **ground-squirrel 1** a squirrel-like rodent, e.g. a chipmunk, gopher, etc. **2** any squirrel of the genus Spermophilus living in burrows. **ground staff** the non-flying personnel of an airport or airbase. **ground state** Physics = ground level 2. **ground stroke** Tennis a stroke played near the ground after the ball has bounced. **ground swell 1** a heavy sea caused by a distant or past storm or an earthquake. **2** an increasingly forceful presence (esp. of public opinion). **ground zero** the point on the ground under an exploding (usu. nuclear) bomb. **hold one's ground** not retreat or give way. **on the ground** at the point of production or operation; in practical conditions. **on one's own ground** on one's own territory or subject; on one's own terms. **thin on the ground** not numerous. **work** (or **run** etc.) **oneself into the ground** colloq. work etc. to the point of exhaustion. □□ **grounder** n. [OE grund f. Gmc]

ground² past and past part. of GRIND.

groundage /ˈgraʊndɪdʒ/ n. Brit. duty levied on a ship entering a port or lying on a shore.

groundhog /ˈgraʊndhɒg/ n. **1** = AARDVARK. **2** US a marmot; a woodchuck. □ **Groundhog Day** US 2 Feb., when the groundhog is said to come out of his hole at the end of hibernation. (If he sees his shadow—i.e. if the weather is sunny—there are supposed to be six weeks more of winter weather.)

grounding /ˈgraʊndɪŋ/ n. basic training or instruction in a subject.

groundless /ˈgraʊndlɪs/ adj. without motive or foundation. □□ **groundlessly** adv. **groundlessness** n. [OE grundlēas (as GROUND¹, -LESS)]

groundling /ˈgraʊndlɪŋ/ n. **1 a** a creeping or dwarf plant. **b** an animal that lives near the ground, at the bottom of a lake, etc., esp. a ground-fish. **2** a person on the ground as opposed to one in an aircraft. **3** a spectator or reader of inferior taste (with ref. to Shakesp. Hamlet III. ii. 11).

groundnut /ˈgraʊndnʌt/ n. **1** Brit. = PEANUT. **2 a** a N. American wild bean. **b** its edible tuber.

groundsel /ˈgraʊns(ə)l/ n. any composite plant of the genus Senecio, esp. S. vulgaris, used as a food for cage-birds. [OE grundeswylige, gundæswelgiæ (perh. = pus-absorber f. gund pus, with ref. to use for poultices)]

groundsheet /ˈgraʊndʃiːt/ n. a waterproof sheet for spreading on the ground, esp. in a tent.

groundsman /ˈgraʊndzmən/ n. (pl. **-men**) a person who maintains a sports ground.

groundwater /ˈgraʊndˌwɔːtə(r)/ n. water found in soil or in pores, crevices, etc., in rock.

groundwork /ˈgraʊndwɜːk/ n. **1** preliminary or basic work. **2** a foundation or basis.

group /gruːp/ n. & v. —n. **1** a number of persons or things located close together, or considered or classed together. **2** (attrib.) concerning or done by a group (a group photograph; group sex). **3** a number of people working together or sharing beliefs, e.g. part of a political party. **4** a number of commercial companies under common ownership. **5** an ensemble playing popular music. **6** a division of an air force or air-fleet. **7** Math. a set of elements, together with an associative binary operation, which contains an inverse for each element and an identity element. **8** Chem. **a** a set of ions or radicals giving a characteristic qualitative reaction. **b** a set of elements having similar properties. **c** a combination of atoms having a recognizable identity in a number of compounds. —v. **1** tr. & intr. form or be formed into a group. **2** tr. (often foll. by with) place in a group or groups. **3** tr. form (colours, figures, etc.) into a well-arranged and harmonious whole. **4** tr. classify. □ **group captain** an RAF officer next below air commodore. **group dynamics** Psychol. the field of social psychology concerned with the nature, development, and interactions of human groups. **Group of Five** the five countries of France, Japan, the US, and (West) Germany, whose financial representatives, at a meeting in New York in Sept. 1985, agreed to take measures to establish greater stability of international currency. **Group of Seven** see separate entry. **Group of Seventy-Seven** the developing countries of the world. **Group of Ten** the ten relatively prosperous industrial countries (Belgium, Canada, France, Italy, Japan, The Netherlands, Sweden, (West) Germany, the UK, and the US) who agreed in 1962 to lend money to the IMF to be used to give financial assistance to other members of the group. **Group of Three** the three largest western industrialized economies (the US, Germany, and Japan). **group practice** a medical practice in which several doctors are associated. **group therapy** therapy in which patients with a similar condition are brought together to assist one another psychologically. **group velocity** the speed

of travel of the energy of a wave or wave-group. □□ **groupage** n. [F groupe f. It. gruppo f. Gmc, rel. to CROP]

grouper /ˈgruːpə(r)/ n. any marine fish of the family Serranidae, with heavy body, big head, and wide mouth. [Port. garupa, prob. f. native name in S. America]

groupie /ˈgruːpɪ/ n. sl. an ardent follower of touring pop groups, esp. a young woman seeking sexual relations with them.

grouping /ˈgruːpɪŋ/ n. a process or system of allocation to groups.

Group of Seven 1 a Canadian art movement, officially formed in 1920 by seven artists, that found inspiration in the landscapes of northern Ontario to represent the unique character of Canada. A gallery dedicated to the Group was opened in Kleinburg, Ontario, in 1966. **2** the seven leading industrial nations outside the Communist bloc, i.e. the US, Japan, Germany, France, the UK, Italy, and Canada.

grouse¹ /graʊs/ n. (pl. same) **1** any of various game-birds of the family Tetraonidae, with a plump body and feathered legs. **2** the flesh of a grouse used as food. [16th c.: orig. uncert.]

grouse² /graʊs/ v. & n. colloq. —v.intr. grumble or complain pettily. —n. a complaint. □□ **grouser** n. [19th c.: orig. unkn.]

grout¹ /graʊt/ n. & v. —n. a thin fluid mortar for filling gaps in tiling etc. —v.tr. provide or fill with grout. □□ **grouter** n. [perh. f. GROUT², but cf. F dial. grouter grout a wall]

grout² /graʊt/ n. sediment, dregs. [OE grūt, rel. to GRITS, GROATS]

grouter /ˈgraʊtə(r)/ n. Austral. sl. an unfair advantage. [20th c.: orig. uncert.]

Grove /grəʊv/, Sir George (1820–1900), English writer on music, founder and first editor of a Dictionary of Music and Musicians (1879–89). Among his other activities were building lighthouses in the West Indies (he had trained as a civil engineer), founding the Palestine Exploration Fund, and helping to edit a biblical dictionary.

grove /grəʊv/ n. a small wood or group of trees. □□ **grovy** adj. [OE grāf, rel. to grǣfa brushwood]

grovel /ˈgrɒv(ə)l/ v.intr. (**grovelled, grovelling**; US **groveled, groveling**) **1** behave obsequiously in seeking favour or forgiveness. **2** lie prone in abject humility. □□ **groveller** n. **grovelling** adj. **grovellingly** adv. [back-form. f. obs. grovelling (adv.) f. gruf face down f. on grufe f. ON á grúfu, later taken as pres. part.]

grow /grəʊ/ v. (past **grew** /gruː/; past part. **grown** /grəʊn/) **1** intr. increase in size, height, quantity, degree, or in any way regarded as measurable (e.g. authority or reputation) (often foll. by in: grew in stature). **2** intr. **a** develop or exist as a living plant or natural product. **b** develop in a specific way or direction (began to grow sideways). **c** germinate, sprout; spring up. **3** intr. be produced; come naturally into existence; arise. **4** intr. (as **grown** adj.) fully matured; adult. **5** intr. **a** become gradually (grow rich; grow less). **b** (foll. by to + infin.) come by degrees (grew to like it). **6** intr. (foll. by into) **a** become, having grown or developed (the acorn has grown into a tall oak; will grow into a fine athlete). **b** become large enough for or suited to (will grow into the coat; grew into her new job). **7** intr. (foll. by on) become gradually more favoured by. **8** tr. **a** produce (plants, fruit, wood, etc.) by cultivation. **b** bring forth. **c** cause (a beard etc.) to develop. **9** tr. (in passive; foll. by over, up) be covered with a growth. □ **growing bag** a bag containing peat-based potting compost in which plants may be grown. **growing pains 1** early difficulties in the development of an enterprise etc. **2** neuralgic pain in children's legs due to fatigue etc. **grown-up** adj. adult. —n. an adult person. **grow out of 1** become too large to wear (a garment). **2** become too mature to retain (a childish habit etc.). **3** be the result or development of. **grow together** coalesce. **grow up 1 a** advance to maturity. **b** (esp. in imper.) begin to behave sensibly. **2** (of a custom) arise, become common. □□ **growable** adj. [OE grōwan f. Gmc, rel. to GRASS, GREEN]

grower /ˈgrəʊə(r)/ n. **1** (often in comb.) a person growing produce (fruit-grower). **2** a plant that grows in a specified way (a fast grower).

growl /graʊl/ v. & n. —v. **1** intr. **a** (often foll. by at) (esp. of a dog) make a low guttural sound, usu. of anger. **b** murmur angrily. **2** intr. rumble. **3** tr. (often foll. by out) utter with a growl. —n. **1** a growling sound, esp. made by a dog. **2** an angry murmur; complaint. **3** a rumble. □□ **growlingly** adv. [prob. imit.]

growler /'graʊlə(r)/ n. **1** a person or thing that growls, esp. sl. a dog. **2** a small iceberg.

grown past part. of GROW.

growth /grəʊθ/ n. **1** the act or process of growing. **2** an increase in size or value. **3** something that has grown or is growing. **4** Med. a morbid formation. **5** the cultivation of produce. **6** a crop or yield of grapes. □ **full growth** the size ultimately attained; maturity. **growth hormone** Biol. a substance which stimulates the growth of a plant or animal. **growth industry** an industry that is developing rapidly. **growth stock** etc. stock etc. that tends to increase in capital value rather than yield high income.

groyne /grɔɪn/ n. (US **groin**) a timber framework or low broad wall built out from a shore to check erosion of a beach. [dial. groin snout f. OF groign f. LL grunium pig's snout]

grub /grʌb/ n. & v. —n. **1** the larva of an insect, esp. of a beetle. **2** colloq. food. —v. (**grubbed**, **grubbing**) **1** tr. & intr. dig superficially. **2** tr. **a** clear (the ground) of roots and stumps. **b** clear away (roots etc.). **3** tr. (foll. by up, out) **a** fetch by digging (grubbing up weeds). **b** extract (information etc.) by searching in books etc. **4** intr. search, rummage. **5** intr. (foll. by on, along, away) toil, plod. □ **grub-screw** a small headless screw, esp. used to attach a handle etc. to a spindle. □□ **grubber** n. (also in comb.). [ME, (v.) perh. corresp. to OE grybban (unrecorded) f. Gmc]

grubby /'grʌbɪ/ adj. (**grubbier**, **grubbiest**) **1** dirty, grimy, slovenly. **2** of or infested with grubs. □□ **grubbily** adv. **grubbiness** n.

grubstake /'grʌbsteɪk/ n. & v. US colloq. —n. material or provisions supplied to an enterprise in return for a share in the resulting profits (orig. in prospecting for ore). —v.tr. provide with a grubstake. □□ **grubstaker** n.

Grub Street /'grʌb striːt/ n. (often attrib.) the world or class of literary hacks and impoverished authors. [name of a street (later Milton St.) in Moorgate, London, inhabited by these in the 17th c.]

grudge /grʌdʒ/ n. & v. —n. a persistent feeling of ill will or resentment, esp. one due to an insult or injury (bears a grudge against me). —v.tr. **1** be resentfully unwilling to give, grant, or allow (a thing). **2** (foll. by verbal noun or to + infin.) be reluctant to do (a thing) (grudged paying so much). □□ **grudger** n. [ME grutch f. OF grouchier murmur, of unkn. orig.]

grudging /'grʌdʒɪŋ/ adj. reluctant; not willing. □□ **grudgingly** adv. **grudgingness** n.

gruel /'gruːəl/ n. a liquid food of oatmeal etc. boiled in milk or water chiefly for invalids. [ME f. OF, ult. f. Gmc, rel. to GROUT¹]

gruelling /'gruːəlɪŋ/ adj. & n. (US **grueling**) —adj. extremely demanding, severe, or tiring. —n. a harsh or exhausting experience; punishment. □□ **gruellingly** adv. [GRUEL as verb, = exhaust, punish]

gruesome /'gruːsəm/ adj. horrible, grisly, disgusting. □□ **gruesomely** adv. **gruesomeness** n. [Sc. grue to shudder f. Scand. + -SOME¹]

gruff /grʌf/ adj. **1 a** (of a voice) low and harsh. **b** (of a person) having a gruff voice. **2** surly, laconic, rough-mannered. □□ **gruffly** adv. **gruffness** n. [Du., MLG grof coarse f. WG (rel. to ROUGH)]

grumble /'grʌmb(ə)l/ v. & n. —v. **1** intr. **a** (often foll. by at, about, over) complain peevishly. **b** be discontented. **2** intr. **a** utter a dull inarticulate sound; murmur, growl faintly. **b** rumble. **3** tr. (often foll. by out) utter complainingly. **4** intr. (as **grumbling** adj.) colloq. giving intermittent discomfort without causing illness (a grumbling appendix). —n. **1** a complaint. **2 a** a dull inarticulate sound; a murmur. **b** a rumble. □□ **grumbler** n. **grumbling** adj. **grumblingly** adv. **grumbly** adj. [obs. grumme; cf. MDu. grommen, MLG grommelen f. Gmc]

grummet var. of GROMMET.

grump /grʌmp/ n. colloq. **1** a grumpy person. **2** (in pl.) a fit of sulks. □□ **grumpish** adj. **grumpishly** adv. [imit.]

grumpy /'grʌmpɪ/ adj. (**grumpier**, **grumpiest**) morosely irritable; surly. □□ **grumpily** adv. **grumpiness** n.

Grundy /'grʌndɪ/ n. (pl. **-ies**) (in full **Mrs Grundy**) a person embodying conventional propriety and prudery. □□ **Grundyism** n. [a person repeatedly mentioned ('What will Mrs Grundy say?') in T. Morton's comedy Speed the Plough (1798)]

Grünewald /'gruːnəvɑːlt/, Mathias, properly Mathis Neithart, called Gothart (c.1460–1528), German painter. His early life is obscure, but he may have been apprenticed in Augsburg since his style resembles that of the elder Holbein. In 1501–25 he worked near Frankfurt, from 1511 for successive archbishops of Mainz, but lost their patronage because of his sympathy for the doctrines of Luther and involvement in the Peasants' Rising of 1525. His masterpiece, the Isenheim Altar, is an intensely moving work and exemplifies his characteristic style: twisted limbs, contorted postures, and highly expressive heads, painted in glowing colour against a dark background. He was the subject of a symphony and of an opera (Mathis der Maler, 1933–8) by Hindemith, in which an artist leads a rebellion against authority—a theme unpopular with the Nazi regime.

grunion /'grʌnjən/ n. a slender Californian marine fish, Leuresthes tenuis, that comes ashore to spawn. [prob. f. Sp. gruñón grunter]

grunt /grʌnt/ n. & v. —n. **1** a low guttural sound made by a pig. **2** a sound resembling this. **3** any fish of the genus Haemulon that grunts when caught. —v. **1** intr. (of a pig) make a grunt or grunts. **2** intr. (of a person) make a low inarticulate sound resembling this, esp. to express discontent, dissent, fatigue, etc. **3** tr. utter with a grunt. [OE grunnettan, prob. orig. imit.]

grunter /'grʌntə(r)/ n. **1** a person or animal that grunts, esp. a pig. **2** a grunting fish, esp. = GRUNT n. 3.

Grunth var. of GRANTH.

Gruyère /'gruːjeə(r)/ n. a firm pale cheese made from cow's milk. [Gruyère, a district in Switzerland where it was first made]

gryphon var. of GRIFFIN.

grysbok /'grɪsbɒk/ n. any small antelope of the genus Raphicerus, native to S. Africa. [S.Afr. Du. f. Du. grijs grey + bok BUCK¹]

Grytviken /'grɪtvɪk(ə)n/ the chief settlement on the island of South Georgia in the South Atlantic. A whaling station established in 1904 was abandoned in 1966 but the site was reoccupied by British military personnel during the Falklands War of 1982.

gs. abbr. Brit. hist. guineas.

Gstaad /gə'ʃtɑːt/ a winter-sports resort in western Switzerland.

G-string /'dʒiːstrɪŋ/ n. **1** Mus. a string sounding the note G. **2** (also **gee-string**) a narrow strip of cloth etc. covering only the genitals and attached to a string round the waist, as worn esp. by striptease artistes.

G-suit /'dʒiːsuːt, -sjuːt/ n. a garment with inflatable pressurized pouches, worn by pilots and astronauts to enable them to withstand high acceleration. [g = gravity + SUIT]

GT /dʒiː'tiː/ n. a high-performance saloon car. [abbr. f. It. gran turismo great touring]

Gt. abbr. Great.

guacamole /ˌɡwɑːkə'məʊlɪ/ n. a dish of mashed avocado pears mixed with chopped onion, tomatoes, chilli peppers, and seasoning. [Amer. Sp. f. Nahuatl ahuacamolli f. ahuacatl avocado + molli sauce]

guacharo /'ɡwɑːtʃərəʊ/ n. (pl. **-os**) a nocturnal bird, Steatornis caripensis, native to S. America and feeding on fruit. Also called oil-bird. [S.Amer. Sp.]

Guadalajara /ˌɡwædələ'hɑːrə/ the second-largest city in Mexico; pop. (1980) 2,244,700.

Guadalcanal /ˌɡwædəlkə'næl/ the largest of the Solomon Islands; pop. (est. 1987) 71,300. During the Second World War it was the scene of the first major US offensive against the Japanese (Aug. 1942).

Guadalquivir /ˌɡwædəlkwɪ'vɪə(r)/ a river of Andalusia in southern Spain, flowing west and south-west into the Atlantic.

Guadeloupe /ˌɡwɑːdə'luːp/ a group of islands in the Lesser Antilles, forming an overseas department of France; pop. (est. 1988) 338,730; capital, Basse-Terre. □□ **Guadeloupian** adj. & n.

guaiac var. of GUAIACUM 2.

guaiacum /'ɡwaɪəkəm/ n. **1** any tree of the genus Guaiacum, native to tropical America. **2** (also **guaiac** /'ɡwaɪæk/) **a** the hard dense oily timber of some of these, esp. *G. officinale*. Also called LIGNUM VITAE. **b** the resin from this used medicinally. [mod.L f. Sp. *guayaco* of Haitian orig.]

Guam /gwɑːm/ the largest and southernmost of the Mariana Islands, administered as an unincorporated territory of the US; pop. (1980) 106,000; capital, Agaña. Discovered by Magellan in 1521, Guam was ceded to the US by Spain in 1898.

guan /gwɑːn/ *n.* any of various game-birds of the family Cracidae, of tropical America. [prob. f. a native name]

guanaco /gwəˈnɑːkəʊ/ *n.* (*pl.* **-os**) a llama-like camelid, *Lama guanicoe*, with a coat of soft pale-brown hair used for wool. [Quechua *huanaco*]

Guanajuato /ˌgwænəˈhwɑːtəʊ/ **1** a State of central Mexico; pop. (est. 1988) 3,542,100. **2** its capital city, a resort situated at an altitude of 2,025 m (6,600 ft.) above sea level; pop. (est. 1983) 45,000.

Guangdong /gwæŋˈdʊŋ/ (also **Kwangtung** /kwæŋˈtʊŋ/) a province of southern China; pop. (est. 1986) 63,640,000; capital, Canton.

Guangxi /ˈgwæŋʃiː/ (also **Kwangsi** /ˈkwæŋsiː/) an autonomous region of southern China; pop. (est. 1986) 39,460,000; capital, Manning.

guanine /ˈgwɑːniːn/ *n. Biochem.* a purine derivative found in all living organisms as a component base of DNA and RNA. [GUANO + -INE⁴]

guano /ˈgwɑːnəʊ/ *n. & v.* (*pl.* **-os**) —*n.* **1** the excrement of sea-fowl, found esp. in the islands off Peru and used as manure. **2** an artificial manure, esp. that made from fish. —*v.tr.* (**-oes, -oed**) fertilize with guano. [Sp. f. Quechua *huanu* dung]

Guarani /ˌgwɑːrəˈniː/ *n.* **1 a** a member of a S. American Indian people. **b** the language of this people. **2** (**guarani**) the monetary unit of Paraguay. [Sp.]

guarantee /ˌgærənˈtiː/ *n. & v.* —*n.* **1 a** a formal promise or assurance, esp. that an obligation will be fulfilled or that something is of a specified quality and durability. **b** a document giving such an undertaking. **2** = GUARANTY. **3** a person making a guaranty or giving a security. —*v.tr.* (**guarantees, guaranteed**) **1 a** give or serve as a guarantee for; answer for the due fulfilment of (a contract etc.) or the genuineness of (an article). **b** assure the permanence etc. of. **c** provide with a guarantee. **2** (foll. by *that* + clause, or *to* + infin.) give a promise or assurance. **3 a** (foll. by *to*) secure the possession of (a thing) for a person. **b** make (a person) secure against a risk or in possession of a thing. □ **guarantee fund** a sum pledged as a contingent indemnity for loss. [earlier *garante*, perh. f. Sp. *garante* = F *garant* WARRANT; later infl. by F *garantie* guaranty]

guarantor /ˌgærənˈtɔː(r), ˈgærəntə(r)/ *n.* a person who gives a guarantee or guaranty.

guaranty /ˈgærəntɪ/ *n.* (*pl.* **-ies**) **1** a written or other undertaking to answer for the payment of a debt or for the performance of an obligation by another person liable in the first instance. **2** a thing serving as security for a guaranty. [AF *guarantie*, var. of *warantie* WARRANTY]

guard /gɑːd/ *v. & n.* —*v.* **1** *tr.* (often foll. by *from, against*) watch over and defend or protect from harm. **2** *tr.* keep watch by (a door etc.) so as to control entry or exit. **3** *tr.* supervise (prisoners etc.) and prevent from escaping. **4** *tr.* provide (machinery) with a protective device. **5** *tr.* keep (thoughts or speech) in check. **6** *tr.* provide with safeguards. **7** *intr.* (foll. by *against*) take precautions. **8** *tr.* (in various games) protect (a piece, card, etc.) with set moves. —*n.* **1** a state of vigilance or watchfulness. **2** a person who protects or keeps watch. **3** a body of soldiers etc. serving to protect a place or person; an escort. **4** US a prison warder. **5** a part of an army detached for some purpose (*advance guard*). **6** (in *pl.*) (usu. **Guards**) any of various bodies of troops nominally employed to guard a monarch. **7** a thing that protects or defends. **8** (often in *comb.*) a device fitted to a machine, vehicle, weapon, etc., to prevent injury or accident to the user (*fire-guard*). **9** *Brit.* an official who rides with and is in general charge of a train. **10** in some sports: **a** a protective or defensive player. **b** a defensive posture or motion. □ **be on** (or **keep** or **stand**) **guard** (of a sentry etc.) keep watch. **guard cell** *Bot.* either of a pair of cells

surrounding the stomata in plants. **guard-rail** a rail, e.g. a handrail, fitted as a support or to prevent an accident. **guard ring** *Electronics* a ring-shaped electrode used to limit the extent of an electric field, esp. in a capacitor. **guard's van** *Brit.* a coach or compartment occupied by a guard. **lower one's guard** reduce vigilance against attack. **off** (or **off one's**) **guard** unprepared for some surprise or difficulty. **on** (or **on one's**) **guard** prepared for all contingencies; vigilant. **raise one's guard** become vigilant against attack. □□ **guarder** *n.* **guardless** *adj.* [ME f. OF *garde, garder* ult. f. WG, rel. to WARD *n.*]

guardant /ˈgɑːd(ə)nt/ *adj. Heraldry* depicted with the body sideways and the face towards the viewer.

guarded /ˈgɑːdɪd/ *adj.* (of a remark etc.) cautious, avoiding commitment. □□ **guardedly** *adv.* **guardedness** *n.*

guardhouse /ˈgɑːdhaʊs/ *n.* a building used to accommodate a military guard or to detain prisoners.

Guardi /ˈgwɑːdɪ/ the name of a family of Venetian painters. Giacomo (1678–1716) founded the workshop, and was followed by his sons, Giannantonio (1699–1760) and Francesco (1712–93). Francesco is famous as a painter of views, but was never as successful as his contemporary, Canaletto, and was not elected to the Venetian Academy until 1784, in spite of being brother-in-law to its first president, Tiepolo. His reputation has risen in the 20th c., and his broken touch and feeling for light and atmosphere now appear to anticipate the impressionists.

guardian /ˈgɑːdɪən/ *n.* **1** a defender, protector, or keeper. **2** a person having legal custody of another person and his or her property when that person is incapable of managing his or her own affairs. **3** the superior of a Franciscan convent. □ **guardian angel** a spirit conceived as watching over a person or place. □□ **guardianship** *n.* [ME f. AF *gardein*, OF *garden* f. Frank., rel. to WARD, WARDEN]

guardroom /ˈgɑːdruːm, -rʊm/ *n.* a room with the same purpose as a guardhouse.

guardsman /ˈgɑːdzmən/ *n.* (*pl.* **-men**) **1** a soldier belonging to a body of guards. **2** (in the UK) a soldier of a regiment of Guards.

Guarneri 'del Gesù' /gwɑːˈneərɪ del ˈjeɪsuː/, Giuseppe (1687–1744), the most celebrated of a family of violin-makers based in Cremona, noted for the attention he gave to the tone quality of his instruments, which do not conform to any standard details of shape or size. Paganini owned a 'del Gesù', which he bequeathed to his native city, Genoa.

Guatemala /ˌgwætɪˈmɑːlə/ a country in the north of Central America, bordering on the Pacific Ocean and with a short coastline on the Caribbean Sea; pop. (est. 1988) 8,831,100; official language, Spanish; capital, Guatemala City (pop. (est. 1988) 1,500,000). The land is fertile, with numerous rivers, but is subject to frequent earthquakes. The principal export is coffee; oil was discovered in the 1970s. A former centre of Mayan civilization, Guatemala was conquered by the Spanish in 1523–4. After independence it formed the core of the short-lived Central American Federation (1828–38) before becoming an independent republic in its own right. Its history since then has frequently been characterized by dictatorship and revolution, and in modern times it has not escaped the unrest and guerrilla activity which paralyses the general area. Guatemala still claims the territory on its NE frontier, despite the establishment of this as the independent republic of Belize in 1981. □□ **Guatemalan** *adj. & n.*

guava /ˈgwɑːvə/ *n.* **1** a small tropical American tree, *Psidium guajava*, bearing an edible pale yellow fruit with pink juicy flesh. **2** this fruit. [Sp. *guayaba* prob. f. a S.Amer. name]

Guayaquil /ˌgwaɪəˈkiːl/ the principal Pacific seaport and second-largest city of Ecuador, situated at the mouth of the Guayas River; pop. (1982) 1,300,900.

guayule /gwaɪˈjuːlɪ/ *n.* **1** a silver-leaved shrub, *Parthenium argentatum*, native to Mexico. **2** a rubber substitute made from the sap of this plant. [Amer. Sp. f. Nahuatl *cuauhuli*]

gubbins /ˈgʌbɪnz/ *n. Brit.* **1** a set of equipment or paraphernalia. **2** a gadget. **3** something of little value. **4** *colloq.* a foolish person (often with ref. to oneself). [orig. = fragments, f. obs. *gobbon*: perh. rel. to GOBBET]

gubernatorial /ˌgjuːbənəˈtɔːriəl/ adj. esp. US of or relating to a governor. [L gubernator governor]

gudgeon[1] /ˈgʌdʒ(ə)n/ n. **1** a small European freshwater fish, Gobio gobio, often used as bait. **2** a credulous or easily fooled person. [ME f. OF goujon f. L gobio -onis GOBY]

gudgeon[2] /ˈgʌdʒ(ə)n/ n. **1** any of various kinds of pivot working a wheel, bell, etc. **2** the tubular part of a hinge into which the pin fits to effect the joint. **3** a socket at the stern of a boat, into which a rudder is fitted. **4** a pin holding two blocks of stone etc. together. □ **gudgeon-pin** (in an internal-combustion engine) a pin holding a piston-rod and a connecting-rod together. [ME f. OF goujon dimin. of gouge GOUGE]

guelder rose /ˈgeldə(r)/ n. a deciduous shrub, Viburnum opulus, with round bunches of creamy-white flowers. Also called snowball tree. [Du. geldersch f. Gelderland a province in the Netherlands]

Guelph /gwelf/ n. **1** a member of one of the two great factions in Italian medieval politics (see GHIBELLINE). **2** a member of a princely family of Swabian origin from which the British royal house is descended through George I (the name is often given as the surname of the House of Hanover, although D'Este is equally accurate). [It. Guelfo f. MHG Welf name of German noble family]

guenon /gəˈnɒn/ n. any African monkey of the genus Cercopithecus, having a characteristic long tail, e.g. the vervet. [F: orig. unkn.]

guerdon /ˈgɜːd(ə)n/ n. & v. poet. —n. a reward or recompense. —v.tr. give a reward to. [ME f. OF guerdon f. med.L widerdonum f. WG widarlōn (as WITH, LOAN[1]), assim. to L donum gift]

Guernica /gɜːˈniːkə, ˈgɜːnɪkə/ a town in the Basque provinces of northern Spain; pop. (1981) 17,800. It was bombed in 1937 by German planes in support of Franco during the Spanish Civil War; a painting by Picasso expresses horror and indignation at its destruction.

Guernsey /ˈgɜːnzɪ/ the second-largest of the Channel Islands; pop. (1981) 54,380; capital, St Peter Port. —n. (pl. -eys) **1 a** an animal of a breed of dairy cattle from Guernsey. **b** this breed. **2** (**guernsey**) **a** a thick (usu. blue) woollen sweater of a distinctive pattern. **b** Austral. a football shirt. □ **get a guernsey** Austral. colloq. **1** be selected for a football team. **2** gain recognition. **guernsey lily** a kind of nerine orig. from S. Africa, with large pink lily-like flowers.

Guerrero /geˈrɛərəʊ/ a State of SW central Mexico, on the Pacific Coast; pop. (est. 1988) 2,560,250; capital, Chilpancingo.

guerrilla /gəˈrɪlə/ n. (also **guerilla**) a member of a small independently acting (usu. political) group taking part in irregular fighting, esp. against larger regular forces. □ **guerrilla war** (or **warfare**) fighting by or with guerrillas. [Sp. guerrilla, dimin. of guerra war]

guess /ges/ v. & n. —v. **1** tr. (often absol.) estimate without calculation or measurement, or on the basis of inadequate data. **2** tr. (often foll. by that etc. + clause, or to + infin.) form a hypothesis or opinion about; conjecture; think likely (cannot guess how you did it; guess them to be Italian). **3** tr. conjecture or estimate correctly by guessing (you have to guess the weight). **4** intr. (foll. by at) make a conjecture about. —n. an estimate or conjecture reached by guessing. □ **anybody's** (or **anyone's**) **guess** something very vague or difficult to determine. **I guess** colloq. I think it likely; I suppose. **keep a person guessing** colloq. withhold information. □□ **guessable** adj. **guesser** n. [ME gesse, of uncert. orig.: cf. OSw. gissa, MLG, MDu. gissen: f. the root of GET v.]

guess-rope var. of GUEST-ROPE.

guesswork /ˈgeswɜːk/ n. the process of or results got by guessing.

guest /gest/ n. & v. —n. **1** a person invited to visit another's house or have a meal etc. at the expense of the inviter. **2** a person lodging at a hotel, boarding-house, etc. **3 a** an outside performer invited to take part with a regular body of performers. **b** a person who takes part by invitation in a radio or television programme (often attrib.: guest artist). **4** (attrib.) **a** serving or set aside for guests (guest-room; guest-night). **b** acting as a guest (guest speaker).

5 an organism living in close association with another. —v.intr. be a guest on a radio or television show or in a theatrical performance etc. □ **be my guest** colloq. make what use you wish of the available facilities. **guest-house** a private house offering accommodation for payment. **guest of honour** the most important guest at an occasion. □□ **guestship** n. [ME f. ON gestr f. Gmc]

guestimate /ˈgestɪmət/ n. (also **guesstimate**) colloq. an estimate based on a mixture of guesswork and calculation. [GUESS + ESTIMATE]

guest-rope /ˈgestrəʊp, ˈgesrəʊp/ n. (also **guess-rope**) **1** a second rope fastened to a boat in tow to steady it. **2** a rope slung outside a ship to give a hold for boats coming alongside. [17th c.: orig. uncert.]

Guevara /gəˈvɑːrə/, Ernesto (known as 'Che Guevara') (1928–67), Argentinian-born revolutionary and guerrilla leader, a principal supporter of Fidel Castro. He played a major role in the transfer of Cuba's traditional economic ties from the US to the Communist bloc. In 1967 he moved to Bolivia where he trained guerrillas for a planned uprising against the military government, and was captured and executed. His refusal to commit himself to either capitalism or orthodox Communism made him an archetypal figurehead for radical students in the 1960s and early 1970s.

guff /gʌf/ n. sl. empty talk; nonsense. [19th c., orig. = 'puff': imit.]

guffaw /gʌˈfɔː/ n. & v. —n. a coarse or boisterous laugh. —v. **1** intr. utter a guffaw. **2** tr. say with a guffaw. [orig. Sc.: imit.]

Guggenheim /ˈgʊgənˌhaɪm/, Meyer (1828–1905), American industrialist, born in Switzerland, who with his sons established vast enterprises in the mining and processing of metals. His sons created the Foundations that beat the family name, including that of Daniel (1856–1930), set up for philanthropic purposes, and that of Simon (1867–1941), named for his son (the John Simon Guggenheim Memorial Foundation, established in 1925, often called simply 'the Guggenheim Foundation'), to provide financial support for scholars, artists, and writers. In 1937 his fourth son, Solomon, established a foundation for the advancement of art; it now operates the Guggenheim Museum in New York and directs the Guggenheim Collection in Venice.

Guiana /giˈɑːnə/ a region in the north of South America bounded by the Orinoco, Negro, and Amazon rivers and the Atlantic Ocean. It now comprises Suriname, Guyana, French Guiana, and part of Venezuela and of Brazil. □ **Guiana Highlands** a mountainous tableland situated between the Orinoco and Amazon river basins. Its highest peak is Roraima (see entry).

guidance /ˈgaɪd(ə)ns/ n. **1** advice or information aimed at resolving a problem, difficulty, etc. **2** the process of guiding or being guided.

guide /gaɪd/ n. & v. —n. **1** a person who leads or shows the way, or directs the movements of a person or group. **2** a person who conducts travellers on tours etc. **3** a professional mountain-climber in charge of a group. **4** an adviser. **5** a directing principle or standard (one's feelings are a bad guide). **6** a book with essential information on a subject, esp. = GUIDEBOOK. **7** a thing marking a position or guiding the eye. **8** a soldier, vehicle, or ship whose position determines the movements of others. **9** Mech. **a** a bar, rod, etc., directing the motion of something. **b** a gauge etc. controlling a tool. **10** (**Guide**) Brit. a member of the Girl Guides Association (see entry). —v.tr. **1 a** act as guide to; lead or direct. **b** arrange the course of (events). **2** be the principle, motive, or ground of (an action, judgement, etc.). **3** direct the affairs of (a State etc.). □ **guided missile** a missile directed to its target by remote control or by equipment within itself. **guide-dog** a dog trained to guide a blind person. **guide-rope** a rope guiding the movement of a crane, airship, etc. **Queen's** (or **King's**) **Guide** a Guide (sense 10) who has reached the highest rank of proficiency. □□ **guidable** adj. **guider** n. [ME f. OF guide (n.), guider (v.), earlier guier ult. f. Gmc, rel. to WIT[2]]

guidebook /ˈgaɪdbʊk/ n. a book of information about a place for visitors, tourists, etc.

guideline /ˈgaɪdlaɪn/ n. a principle or criterion guiding or directing action.

guidepost /ˈgaɪdpəʊst/ n. = SIGNPOST.

Guider /ˈgaɪdə(r)/ n. an adult leader of Guides (see GUIDE n. 10).

w we z zoo ʃ she ʒ decision θ thin ð this ŋ ring x loch tʃ chip dʒ jar (see over for vowels)

guideway /ˈgaɪdweɪ/ n. a groove or track that guides movement.

guidon /ˈgaɪd(ə)n/ n. a pennant narrowing to a point or fork at the free end, esp. one used as the standard of a regiment of dragoons. [F f. It. *guidone* f. *guida* GUIDE]

Guignol /giːˈnjɒl/ the chief character in a French puppet-show of that name, similar to 'Punch and Judy'. The term is also used for the theatre where the show is performed. □ **Grand Guignol** /grɑ̃/, a theatre presenting a succession of short plays of gruesome character (in this respect resembling 'Punch and Judy').

guild /gɪld/ n. (also **gild** an association of people for mutual aid or the pursuit of a common goal. Such associations are first recorded in England in pre-Conquest times and resembled the later burial and benefit societies but always with a strong religious element; their meetings were convivial. Merchant guilds were formed from the 11th c. (earlier on the Continent), and many became powerful in local government. Trade guilds (associations of persons exercising the same craft) came into prominence in England in the 14th c. and became powerful there and elsewhere in medieval Europe, effectively controlling trade and commerce in many countries, particularly in large cities. Their monopolistic policies generally brought them into conflict with strengthening central governments and their powers were gradually curtailed. [ME prob. f. MLG, MDu. *gilde* f. Gmc: rel. to OE *gild* payment, sacrifice]

guilder /ˈgɪldə(r)/ n. **1** the chief monetary unit of the Netherlands. **2** *hist.* a gold coin of the Netherlands and Germany. [ME, alt. of Du. *gulden*: see GULDEN]

guildhall /gɪldˈhɔːl, ˈgɪld-/ n. **1** the meeting-place of a guild or corporation; a town hall. **2** (**Guildhall**) the hall of the Corporation of the City of London, used for ceremonial occasions.

guildsman /ˈgɪldzmən/ n. (pl. **-men**; fem. **guildswoman**, pl. **-women**) a member of a guild.

guile /gaɪl/ n. treachery, deceit; cunning or sly behaviour. □□ **guileful** adj. **guilefully** adv. **guilefulness** n. **guileless** adj. **guilelessly** adv. **guilelessness** n. [ME f. OF, prob. f. Gmc]

Guilin /gweɪˈlɪn/ (also **Kweilin** /kweɪˈlɪn/) a city in southern China, on the Li River in Guangxi province; pop. (est. 1984) 446,900. The surrounding limestone hills are a tourist attraction.

guillemot /ˈgɪlɪˌmɒt/ n. any fast-flying sea bird of the genus *Uria* or *Cepphus*, nesting on cliffs or islands. [F f. *Guillaume* William]

guilloche /gɪˈlɒʃ/ n. an architectural or metalwork ornament imitating braided ribbons. [F *guillochis* (or *guilloche* the tool used)]

guillotine /ˈgɪləˌtiːn/ n. & v. —n. **1** a machine with a heavy knife-blade sliding vertically in grooves, used for beheading. **2** a device for cutting paper, metal, etc. **3** a surgical instrument for excising the uvula etc. **4** *Parl.* a method of preventing delay in the discussion of a legislative bill by fixing times at which various parts of it must be voted on. —v.tr. **1** use a guillotine on. **2** *Parl.* end discussion of (a bill) by applying a guillotine. □□ **guillotiner** n. [F f. J.-I. *Guillotin*, Fr. physician d. 1814, who recommended its use for executions in 1789]

guilt /gɪlt/ n. **1** the fact of having committed a specified or implied offence. **2 a** culpability. **b** the feeling of this. □ **guilt complex** *Psychol.* a mental obsession with the idea of having done wrong. [OE *gylt*, of unkn. orig.]

guiltless /ˈgɪltlɪs/ adj. **1** (often foll. by *of* an offence) innocent. **2** (foll. by *of*) not having knowledge or possession of. □□ **guiltlessly** adv. **guiltlessness** n. [OE *gyltlēas* (as GUILT, -LESS)]

guilty /ˈgɪltɪ/ adj. (**guiltier, guiltiest**) **1** culpable of or responsible for a wrong. **2** conscious of or affected by guilt (*a guilty conscience*; *a guilty look*). **3** concerning guilt (*a guilty secret*). **4 a** (often foll. by *of*) having committed a (specified) offence. **b** *Law* adjudged to have committed a specified offence, esp. by a verdict in a trial. □□ **guiltily** adv. **guiltiness** n. [OE *gyltig* (as GUILT, -Y¹)]

guimp var. of GIMP¹.

Guinea /ˈgɪnɪ/ a country on the west coast of Africa; pop. (est. 1988) 6,909,300; official language, French; capital, Conakry. Formerly part of French West Africa, Guinea became an independent republic in 1958. The economy is chiefly agricultural; bauxite and iron ore are extensively mined, and alumina is the principal export. □ **Gulf of Guinea** a large inlet of the Atlantic Ocean bordering on the coast of Guinea.

guinea /ˈgɪnɪ/ n. **1** *Brit. hist.* the sum of 21 old shillings (£1.05), used esp. in determining professional fees. **2** *hist.* a former British gold coin worth 21 shillings, first coined for the African trade. □ **guinea-fowl** any African fowl of the family Numididae, esp. *Numida meleagris*, with slate-coloured white-spotted plumage. Its name was given when it was brought from Guinea by the Portuguese. **guinea-pig 1** a domesticated S. American cavy, *Cavia porcellus*, kept as a pet or for research in biology etc. **2** a person or thing used as a subject for experiment. [GUINEA]

Guinea-Bissau /gɪnɪbɪˈsaʊ/ a country on the west coast of Africa, between Senegal and Guinea; pop. (est. 1988) 950,700; official language, Portuguese; capital, Bissau. The area was explored by the Portuguese in the 15th c. and became a colony in 1879. It gained independence, as a republic, in 1974. The economy is chiefly agricultural, groundnuts being the principal crop.

Guinevere /ˈgwɪnɪvɪə(r)/ (in Arthurian legend) the wife of King Arthur and mistress of Lancelot.

Guinness /ˈgɪnɪs/, Sir Alec (1914–), English actor, whose film career has been paralleled by a succession of distinguished stage performances, including Hamlet in modern dress (1938). His most famous film roles include Fagin in *Oliver Twist* (1948), eight noble eccentrics in *Kind Hearts and Coronets* (1949), Coloneal Nicholson in *The Bridge on the River Kwai* (1957), and the spymaster George Smiley in the television production of le Carré's *Tinker Tailor Soldier Spy* (1979).

guipure /giːˈpjʊə(r)/ n. a heavy lace of linen pieces joined by embroidery. [F f. *guiper* cover with silk etc. f. Gmc]

guise /gaɪz/ n. **1** an assumed appearance; a pretence (*in the guise of*; *under the guise of*). **2** external appearance. **3** *archaic* style of attire, garb. [ME f. OF ult. f. Gmc]

guitar /gɪˈtɑː(r)/ n. a usu. six-stringed musical instrument with a fretted finger-board, played by plucking with the fingers or a plectrum or finger-pick. The characteristic form of the instrument, probably of Spanish origin, came in at the end of the 15th c., although there have been from pre-Christian times stringed instruments played with a plectrum; the strings or courses (two or more strings to a note) then numbered four, the present six strings dating from the 1790s. 'Acoustic' (i.e. non-electric) guitars include the Spanish, or classical, with nylon strings; the 'country-and-western', or 'folk', with steel strings; and the Hawaiian guitar, which is played with the strings stopped by a small metal bar. The electric guitar (with built-in microphone) dates back to the 1930s. □□ **guitarist** n. [Sp. *guitarra* (partly through F *guitare*) f. Gk *kithara*: see CITTERN, GITTERN]

guiver /ˈgaɪvə(r)/ n. (also **gyver**) *Austral. & NZ sl.* **1** plausible talk. **2** affectation of speech or manner. [19th c.: orig. unkn.]

Guiyang /gweɪˈjæŋ/ (also **Kweiyang** /kweɪˈjæŋ/) a city in southern China, capital of Guizhou province; pop. (est. 1986) 1,380,000.

Guizhou /gweɪˈdʒəʊ/ (also **Kweichow** /kweɪˈdʒəʊ/) a province of southern China; pop. (est. 1986) 30,080,000; capital, Guiyang.

Gujarat /ˌguːdʒəˈrɑːt/ a State in western India formed from the north part of the former Bombay State; pop. (1981) 33,960,900; capital, Gandhinagar.

Gujarati /ˌguːdʒəˈrɑːtɪ/ n. & adj. —n. (pl. **Gujaratis**) **1** a language descended from Sanskrit and so belonging to the Indo-Iranian language group, spoken by over 25 million people mainly in the State of Gujarat. It is written in a form of the Devanagari script. **2** a native of Gujarat. —adj. of or relating to Gujarat or its language. [Hind.: see -I²]

Gujranwala /ˌgʊdʒrənˈwɑːlə/ a city of Pakistan in Punjab province; pop. (1981) 597,000. It was the birthplace of the Sikh ruler Ranjit Singh, and was his capital city until he occupied Lahore in 1799.

Gujrat /ˈguːdʒrɑːt/ a city of Pakistan, in Punjab province; pop. (1981) 154,000.

Gulag /ˈguːlæg/ n. the system of detention camps in the Soviet Union 1930–55. Besides ordinary criminals, inmates included dissident intellectuals, members of the ethnic groups suspected of disloyalty, and members of political factions who had lost power. A system of forced-labour camps had been introduced in 1919, after the Revolution, and much used by Stalin during the period of mass arrests: it was more economical to put prisoners to work than to let them languish in jail. Although the Gulag was officially disbanded in 1955, a system of 'corrective labour colonies' remained. Alexander Solzhenitsyn's book *The Gulag Archipelago* (1973–5), an epic 'history and geography' of the labour camps, likened these to a chain of islands strung out through the USSR. [Russ. abbr. of *Glavnoe Upravlenie Ispravitel'no-Trudovykh Lagerei* Chief Administration of Corrective Labour Camps]

Gulbenkian /gʊlˈbeŋkɪən/, Calouste Sarkis (1869–1955), British oil magnate and philanthropist, born in Turkey of Armenian family, who endowed the international foundation (named after him) for the advancement of social and cultural projects. Its headquarters are in Lisbon, where he lived from 1942 until his death.

gulch /gʌltʃ/ *n. US* a ravine, esp. one in which a torrent flows. [perh. dial. *gulch* to swallow]

gulden /ˈgʊld(ə)n/ *n.* = GUILDER. [Du. & G, = GOLDEN]

gules /gjuːlz/ *n.* & *adj.* (usu. placed after noun) *Heraldry* red. [ME f. OF *goules* red-dyed fur neck ornaments f. *gole* throat]

gulf /gʌlf/ *n.* & *v.* —*n.* 1 a stretch of sea consisting of a deep inlet with a narrow mouth. 2 a deep hollow; a chasm or abyss. 3 a wide difference of feelings, opinion, etc. —*v.tr.* engulf; swallow up. □ **the Gulf** the Persian Gulf. [ME f. OF *golfe* f. It. *golfo* ult. f. Gk *kolpos* bosom, gulf]

Gulf States 1 the States with a coastline on the Persian Gulf (esp. Bahrain, Kuwait, Oman, Qatar, Saudi Arabia, and the United Arab Emirates; sometimes also including Iran and Iraq). 2 *US* the States bordering on the Gulf of Mexico (Florida, Alabama, Mississippi, Louisiana, and Texas).

Gulf Stream a warm ocean current which flows from the Gulf of Mexico parallel with the American coast towards Newfoundland, continuing (as the North Atlantic Drift) across the Atlantic Ocean and along the coast of NW Europe, where it has a significant effect upon the climate.

Gulf War 1 (also known as the Iran-Iraq war) the war of 1980–8 between Iran and Iraq in the general area of the Persian Gulf. It ended inconclusively. 2 the war of Jan.–Feb. 1991 between Iraq and an international coalition of forces based in Saudi Arabia to compel Iraqi withdrawal from Kuwait, which Iraq had invaded and occupied in Aug. 1990.

gulfweed /ˈgʌlfwiːd/ *n.* = SARGASSO.

gull¹ /gʌl/ *n.* any of various long-winged web-footed sea birds of the family Laridae, usu. having white plumage with a mantle varying from pearly-grey to black, and a bright bill. □□ **gullery** *n.* (*pl.* **-ies**). [ME ult. f. OCelt.]

gull² /gʌl/ *v.tr.* (usu. in *passive*; foll. by *into*) dupe, fool. [perh. f. obs. *gull* yellow f. ON *gulr*]

Gullah /ˈgʌlə/ *n.* 1 a member of a Black people living on the coast of S. Carolina or the nearby sea islands. 2 the Creole language spoken by them. [perh. a shortening of *Angola*, or f. a tribal name *Golas*]

gullet /ˈgʌlɪt/ *n.* 1 the food-passage extending from the mouth to the stomach; the oesophagus. 2 the throat. [ME f. OF dimin. of *go(u)le* throat f. L *gula*]

gullible /ˈgʌlɪb(ə)l/ *adj.* easily persuaded or deceived, credulous. □□ **gullibility** /-ˈbɪlɪtɪ/ *n.* **gullibly** *adv.* [GULL² + -IBLE]

gully /ˈgʌlɪ/ *n.* & *v.* —*n.* (*pl.* **-ies**) 1 a water-worn ravine. 2 a deep artificial channel; a gutter or drain. 3 *Austral.* & *NZ* a river valley. 4 *Cricket* a the fielding position between point and slips. b a fielder in this position. —*v.tr.* (**-ies, -ied**) 1 form (channels) by water action. 2 make gullies in. □ **gully-hole** an opening in a street to a drain or sewer. [F *goulet* bottle-neck (as GULLET)]

gulp /gʌlp/ *v.* & *n.* —*v.* 1 *tr.* (often foll. by *down*) swallow hastily, greedily, or with effort. 2 *intr.* swallow gaspingly or with difficulty; choke. 3 *tr.* (foll. by *down, back*) stifle, suppress (tears). —*n.* 1 an act of gulping (*drained it at one gulp*). 2 an effort to swallow. 3 a large mouthful of a drink. □□ **gulper** *n.* **gulpingly** *adv.* **gulpy** *adj.* [ME prob. f. MDu. *gulpen* (imit.)]

gum¹ /gʌm/ *n.* & *v.* —*n.* 1 a a viscous secretion of some trees and shrubs that hardens on drying but is soluble in water (cf. RESIN). b an adhesive substance made from this. 2 *US* chewing

gum. 3 = GUMDROP. 4 = *gum arabic.* 5 = *gum-tree.* 6 a secretion collecting in the corner of the eye. 7 *US* = GUMBOOT. —*v.* (**gummed, gumming**) 1 *tr.* smear or cover with gum. 2 *tr.* (usu. foll. by *down, together*, etc.) fasten with gum. 3 *intr.* exude gum. □ **gum arabic** a gum exuded by some kinds of acacia and used as glue and in incense. **gum benjamin** benzoin. **gum dragon** tragacanth. **gum juniper** sandarac. **gum resin** a vegetable secretion of resin mixed with gum, e.g. gamboge. **gum-tree** a tree exuding gum, esp. a eucalyptus. **gum up 1** (of a mechanism etc.) become clogged or obstructed with stickiness. 2 *colloq.* interfere with the smooth running of (*gum up the works*). **up a gum-tree** *colloq.* in great difficulties. [ME f. OF *gomme* ult. f. L *gummi, cummi* f. Gk *kommi* f. Egypt. *kemai*]

gum² /gʌm/ *n.* (usu. in *pl.*) the firm flesh around the roots of the teeth. □ **gum-shield** a pad protecting a boxer's teeth and gums. [OE *gōma* rel. to OHG *guomo*, ON *gómr* roof or floor of the mouth]

gum³ /gʌm/ *n. colloq.* (in oaths) God (*by gum!*). [corrupt. of *God*]

gumbo /ˈgʌmbəʊ/ *n.* (*pl.* **-os**) *US* 1 okra. 2 a soup thickened with okra pods. 3 (**Gumbo**) a patois of Blacks and Creoles spoken esp. in Louisiana. [of Afr. orig.]

gumboil /ˈgʌmbɔɪl/ *n.* a small abscess on the gums.

gumboot /ˈgʌmbuːt/ *n.* a rubber boot; a wellington.

gumdrop /ˈgʌmdrɒp/ *n.* a soft coloured sweet made with gelatin or gum arabic.

gumma /ˈgʌmə/ *n.* (*pl.* **gummas** or **gummata** /-mətə/) *Med.* a small soft swelling occurring in the connective tissue of the liver, brain, testes, and heart, and characteristic of the late stages of syphilis. □□ **gummatous** *adj.* [mod.L f. L *gummi* GUM¹]

gummy¹ /ˈgʌmɪ/ *adj.* (**gummier, gummiest**) 1 viscous, sticky. 2 abounding in or exuding gum. □□ **gumminess** *n.* [ME f. GUM¹ + -Y¹]

gummy² /ˈgʌmɪ/ *adj.* & *n.* —*adj.* (**gummier, gummiest**) toothless. —*n.* (*pl.* **-ies**) 1 *Austral.* a small shark, *Mustelus antarcticus*, having rounded teeth with which it crushes hard-shelled prey. 2 *Austral.* & *NZ* a toothless sheep. □□ **gummily** *adv.* [GUM² + -Y¹]

gumption /ˈgʌmpʃ(ə)n/ *n. colloq.* 1 resourcefulness, initiative; enterprising spirit. 2 common sense. [18th-c. Sc.: orig. unkn.]

gumshoe /ˈgʌmʃuː/ *n. US* 1 a galosh. 2 *sl.* a detective.

gun /gʌn/ *n.* & *v.* —*n.* 1 any kind of weapon consisting of a metal tube and often held in the hand with a grip at one end, from which bullets or other missiles are propelled with great force, esp. by a contained explosion. 2 any device imitative of this, e.g. a starting pistol. 3 a device for discharging insecticide, grease, electrons, etc., in the required direction (often in *comb.*: *grease-gun*). 4 a member of a shooting-party. 5 *US* a gunman. 6 the firing of a gun. 7 (in *pl.*) *Naut. sl.* a gunnery officer. —*v.* (**gunned, gunning**) 1 *tr.* **a** (usu. foll. by *down*) shoot (a person) with a gun. **b** shoot at with a gun. 2 *tr. colloq.* accelerate (an engine or vehicle). 3 *intr.* go shooting. 4 *intr.* (foll. by *for*) seek out determinedly to attack or rebuke. □ **go great guns** *colloq.* proceed forcefully or vigorously or successfully. **gun-carriage** a wheeled support for a gun. **gun-cotton** an explosive used for blasting, made by steeping cotton in nitric and sulphuric acids. **gun crew** a team manning a gun. **gun dog** a dog trained to follow sportsmen using guns. **gun-shy** (esp. of a sporting dog) alarmed at the report of a gun. **gun-site** a (usu. fortified) emplacement for a gun. **jump the gun** *colloq.* start before a signal is given, or before an agreed time. **stick to one's guns** *colloq.* maintain one's position under attack. □□ **gunless** *adj.* **gunned** *adj.* [ME *gunne, gonne*, perh. f. the Scand. name *Gunnhildr*]

gunboat /ˈgʌnbəʊt/ *n.* a small vessel of shallow draught and with relatively heavy guns. □ **gunboat diplomacy** political negotiation supported by the use or threat of military force.

gunfight /ˈgʌnfaɪt/ *n. US* a fight with firearms. □□ **gunfighter** *n.*

gunfire /ˈgʌnˌfaɪə(r)/ *n.* 1 the firing of a gun or guns, esp. repeatedly. 2 the noise from this.

gunge /gʌndʒ/ *n.* & *v. Brit. colloq.* —*n.* sticky or viscous matter, esp. when messy or indeterminate. —*v.tr.* (usu. foll. by *up*) clog or obstruct with gunge. □□ **gungy** *adj.* [20th c.: orig. uncert.: cf. GOO, GUNK]

gung-ho /gʌŋˈhəʊ/ *adj.* enthusiastic, eager. [Chin. *gonghe* work together, slogan adopted by US Marines in 1942]

gunk /gʌnk/ *n. sl.* viscous or liquid material. [20th c.: orig. the name of a detergent (propr.)]

gunlock /ˈgʌnlɒk/ *n.* a mechanism by which the charge of a gun is exploded.

gunman /ˈgʌnmən/ *n.* (*pl.* **-men**) a man armed with a gun, esp. in committing a crime.

gun-metal /ˈgʌnˌmet(ə)l/ *n.* **1** a dull bluish-grey colour. **2** an alloy of copper and tin or zinc (formerly used for guns).

Gunn /gʌn/, Thomson William ('Thom') (1929–), English poet who settled permanently in California. His volumes of verse include *Fighting Terms* (1954), *The Sense of Movement* (1959), *My Sad Captains* (1961), *Moly* (1971), and *Jack Straw's Castle* (1976). His works combine a celebration of men of action, a fascination for violence, and a gallery of heroes (ranging from Elvis Presley to Caravaggio), with a low-key, rational, laconic, colloquial manner.

gunnel[1] /ˈgʌn(ə)l/ *n.* any small eel-shaped marine fish of the family Pholidae, esp. *Pholis gunnellus*. Also called BUTTERFISH. [17th c.: orig. unkn.]

gunnel[2] var. of GUNWALE.

gunner /ˈgʌnə(r)/ *n.* **1** an artillery soldier (esp. as an official term for a private). **2** *Naut.* a warrant-officer in charge of a battery, magazine, etc. **3** a member of an aircraft crew who operates a gun. **4** a person who hunts game with a gun.

gunnera /ˈgʌnərə/ *n.* any plant of the genus *Gunnera* from S. America and New Zealand, having large leaves and often grown for ornament. [J. E. *Gunnerus*, Norw. botanist d. 1773]

gunnery /ˈgʌnərɪ/ *n.* **1** the construction and management of large guns. **2** the firing of guns.

gunny /ˈgʌnɪ/ *n.* (*pl.* **-ies**) **1** coarse sacking, usu. of jute fibre. **2** a sack made of this. [Hindi & Marathi *gōnī* f. Skr. *gōṇi* sack]

gunplay /ˈgʌnpleɪ/ *n.* the use of guns.

gunpoint /ˈgʌnpɔɪnt/ *n.* the point of a gun. □ **at gunpoint** threatened with a gun or an ultimatum etc.

gunpowder /ˈgʌnˌpaʊdə(r)/ *n.* **1** the earliest known propellant explosive, a mixture of potassium nitrate, charcoal, and sulphur. It was made by Roger Bacon *c.*1250, though probably discovered much earlier. By the mid-14th c. its military uses were well established (it was used in the battle of Crécy, 1346), and it remained the foremost military explosive for five centuries, having a profound effect on weapons and warfare. **2** a fine green tea of granular appearance.

Gunpowder Plot a conspiracy by a small group of extremist Catholics to blow up James I and his Parliament on 5 Nov. 1605, uncovered when a Catholic MP was sent an anonymous letter telling him to stay away from the House on the appointed day. Guy Fawkes was arrested in the cellars of the Houses of Parliament the day before the scheduled attack and betrayed his colleagues under torture. The leader of the plot, Robert Catesby, was killed resisting arrest and the rest of the conspirators were captured and executed. Controversy continues about whether the episode was a contrived plot against the Catholics (who looked as if they were about to regain power), with Fawkes and others 'framed' to discredit them. The plot is commemorated by the traditional searching of the vaults by the Yeomen of the Guard before the opening of each session of Parliament, and by bonfires and fireworks, with the burning of a 'guy', annually on 5 Nov.

gunpower /ˈgʌnˌpaʊə(r)/ *n.* the strength or quantity of available guns.

gunroom /ˈgʌnruːm, -rʊm/ *n. Brit.* **1** a room in a house for storing sporting-guns. **2** quarters for junior officers (orig. for gunners) in a warship.

gunrunner /ˈgʌnˌrʌnə(r)/ *n.* a person engaged in the illegal sale or importing of firearms. □□ **gunrunning** *n.*

gunship /ˈgʌnʃɪp/ *n.* a heavily-armed helicopter or other aircraft.

gunshot /ˈgʌnʃɒt/ *n.* **1** a shot fired from a gun. **2** the range of a gun (*within gunshot*).

gunslinger /ˈgʌnˌslɪŋə(r)/ *n.* esp. *US sl.* a gunman. □□ **gunslinging** *n.*

gunsmith /ˈgʌnsmɪθ/ *n.* a person who makes, sells, and repairs small firearms.

gunstock /ˈgʌnstɒk/ *n.* the wooden mounting of the barrel of a gun.

Gunter /ˈgʌntə(r)/, Edmund (1581–1626), English mathematician who invented or improved several mathematical instruments. □ **Gunter's chain** a measuring instrument 66 ft. long (80 chains = 1 mile), subdivided into 100 links (1 rod or perch = 25 links; each link was a short section of wire connected to the next link by a loop). It was long used for land-surveying in the English-speaking countries and elsewhere, but has now been superseded by the steel tape and electronic equipment.

Gunther /ˈgʊntə(r)/ (in the Nibelungenlied) the husband of Brunhild and brother of Kriemhild, by whom he was beheaded in revenge for Siegfried's murder.

gunwale /ˈgʌn(ə)l/ *n.* (also **gunnel**) the upper edge of the side of a boat or ship. [GUN + WALE (because formerly used to support guns)]

gunyah /ˈgʌnjɑː/ *n. Austral.* an Aboriginal bush hut. [Aboriginal]

guppy /ˈgʌpɪ/ *n.* (*pl.* **-ies**) a freshwater fish, *Poecilia reticulata*, of the W. Indies and S. America, frequently kept in aquariums, and giving birth to live young. [R. J. L. *Guppy*, 19th-c. Trinidad clergyman who sent the first specimen to the British Museum]

Gupta /ˈgʊptə/ the name of a Hindu dynasty established in 320 by Chandra Gupta I in Bihar. The Gupta empire eventually stretched across most of northern India, but began to disintegrate towards the end of the 5th c., only North Bengal being left by the middle of the 6th c. □□ **Guptan** *adj.*

gurdwara /gɜːˈdwɑːrə/ *n.* a Sikh place of worship, containing a copy of the Adi Granth. [Punjabi *gurduārā* f. Skr. *guru* teacher + *dvāra* door]

gurgle /ˈgɜːg(ə)l/ *v. & n.* —*v.* **1** *intr.* make a bubbling sound as of water from a bottle. **2** *tr.* utter with such a sound. —*n.* a gurgling sound. □□ **gurgler** *n.* [imit., or f. Du. *gorgelen*, G *gurgeln*, or med.L *gurgulare* f. L *gurgulio* gullet]

Gurkha /ˈgɜːkə/ *n.* **1** a member of a military people of Hindu descent and Sanskritic speech, who settled in the province of Gurkha, Nepal, in the 18th c. and made themselves supreme. **2** a member of one of the Gurkha regiments (orig. specifically for Nepalese soldiers) in the British Army. [native name, f. Skr. *gāus* cow + *raksh* protect]

gurnard /ˈgɜːnəd/ *n.* (also **gurnet** /ˈgɜːnɪt/) any marine fish of the family Triglidae, having a large spiny head with mailed sides, and three finger-like pectoral rays used for walking on the sea bed etc. [ME f. OF *gornart* f. *grondir* to grunt f. L *grunnire*]

guru /ˈgʊruː, ˈguːruː/ *n.* **1** a Hindu spiritual teacher or head of a religious sect. **2 a** an influential teacher. **b** a revered mentor. [Hindi *gurū* teacher f. Skr. *gurús* grave, dignified]

gush /gʌʃ/ *v. & n.* —*v.* **1** *tr. & intr.* emit or flow in a sudden and copious stream. **2** *intr.* speak or behave with effusiveness or sentimental affectation. —*n.* **1** a sudden or copious stream. **2** an effusive or sentimental manner. □□ **gushing** *adj.* **gushingly** *adv.* [ME *gosshe, gusche*, prob. imit.]

gusher /ˈgʌʃə(r)/ *n.* **1** an oil well from which oil flows without being pumped. **2** an effusive person.

gushy /ˈgʌʃɪ/ *adj.* (**gushier, gushiest**) excessively effusive or sentimental. □□ **gushily** *adv.* **gushiness** *n.*

gusset /ˈgʌsɪt/ *n.* **1** a piece let into a garment etc. to strengthen or enlarge a part. **2** a bracket strengthening an angle of a structure. □□ **gusseted** *adj.* [ME f. OF *gousset* flexible piece filling up a joint in armour f. *gousse* pod, shell]

gust /gʌst/ *n. & v.* —*n.* **1** a sudden strong rush of wind. **2** a burst of rain, fire, smoke, or sound. **3** a passionate or emotional outburst. —*v.intr.* blow in gusts. [ON *gustr*, rel. to *gjósa* to gush]

gustation /gʌˈsteɪʃ(ə)n/ *n.* the act or capacity of tasting. □□ **gustative** /ˈgʌstətɪv/ *adj.* **gustatory** /ˈgʌstətərɪ/ *adj.* [F *gustation* or L *gustatio* f. *gustare* f. *gustus* taste]

Gustavus Adolphus /gʊˌstɑːvəs əˈdɒlfəs/ (1594–1632), king of Sweden 1611–32. One of the greatest soldiers of his day, Gustavus raised Sweden to the status of a European power by his victories against Denmark, Poland, and Russia in the first decade and a half of his reign. In 1630 he intervened on the Protestant side in the Thirty Years War, revitalizing the anti-Imperialist cause with several brilliant victories and earning himself the title of 'Lion of the North'. His motives are debated, but his own assertion, that he sought security for the Swedish State and Church, was probably part if not the whole of the truth. At home he instituted creative reforms in administration, economic development, and education, laying the foundation of the modern State.

gusto /'gʌstəʊ/ n. (pl. **-oes**) **1** zest; enjoyment or vigour in doing something. **2** (foll. by *for*) *archaic* relish or liking. **3** *archaic* a style of artistic execution. [It. f. L *gustus* taste]

gusty /'gʌstɪ/ adj. (**gustier**, **gustiest**) **1** characterized by or blowing in strong winds. **2** characterized by gusto. □□ **gustily** adv. **gustiness** n.

gut /gʌt/ n. & v. —n. **1** the lower alimentary canal or a part of this; the intestine. **2** (in pl.) the bowel or entrails, esp. of animals. **3** (in pl.) *colloq.* personal courage and determination; vigorous application and perseverance. **4** (in pl.) *colloq.* the belly as the source of appetite. **5** (in pl.) **a** the contents of anything, esp. representing substantiality. **b** the essence of a thing, e.g. of an issue or problem. **6 a** material for violin or racket strings or surgical use made from the intestines of animals. **b** material for fishing-lines made from the silk-glands of silkworms. **7 a** a narrow water-passage; a sound, straits. **b** a defile or narrow passage. **8** (*attrib.*) **a** instinctive (*a gut reaction*). **b** fundamental (*a gut issue*). —v.tr. (**gutted**, **gutting**) **1** remove or destroy (esp. by fire) the internal fittings of (a house etc.). **2** take out the guts of (a fish). **3** extract the essence of (a book etc.). □ **gut-rot** *colloq.* **1** = *rot-gut.* **2** a stomach upset. **hate a person's guts** *colloq.* dislike a person intensely. **sweat** (or **work**) **one's guts out** *colloq.* work extremely hard. [OE *guttas* (pl.), prob. rel. to *gēotan* pour]

Gutenberg /'guːt(ə)nˌbɜːg/, Johann (*c.*1400–68), German inventor of printing using movable type, i.e. individual letters arranged to form words and lines of type (rather than using a solid block for each page), achieving the high degree of accuracy in casting the type which this method of printing requires. By *c.*1456 an edition of the Bible (Vulgate version) had been produced, probably the first book to be printed in Europe, with double columns and 42 lines to the page. It was known as the Mazarin Bible because the copy which first attracted the attention of bibliographers was discovered in the library of Cardinal Mazarin (17th c.).

gutless /'gʌtlɪs/ adj. *colloq.* lacking courage or determination; feeble. □□ **gutlessly** adv. **gutlessness** n.

gutsy /'gʌtsɪ/ adj. (**gutsier**, **gutsiest**) *colloq.* **1** courageous. **2** greedy. □□ **gutsily** adv. **gutsiness** n.

gutta-percha /ˌgʌtə'pɜːtʃə/ n. a tough plastic substance obtained from the latex of various Malaysian trees. [Malay *getah* gum + *percha* name of a tree]

guttate /'gʌteɪt/ adj. *Biol.* having droplike markings. [L *guttatus* speckled f. *gutta* drop]

gutter /'gʌtə(r)/ n. & v. —n. **1** a shallow trough below the eaves of a house, or a channel at the side of a street, to carry off rainwater. **2** (prec. by *the*) a poor or degraded background or environment. **3** an open conduit along which liquid flows out. **4** a groove. **5** a track made by the flow of water. —v. **1** *intr.* flow in streams. **2** *tr.* furrow, channel. **3** *intr.* (of a candle) melt away as the wax forms channels down the side. □ **gutter press** sensational journalism concerned esp. with the private lives of public figures. [ME f. AF *gotere*, OF *goutiere* ult. f. L *gutta* drop]

guttering /'gʌtərɪŋ/ n. **1 a** the gutters of a building etc. **b** a section or length of a gutter. **2** material for gutters.

guttersnipe /'gʌtəˌsnaɪp/ n. a street urchin.

guttural /'gʌtər(ə)l/ adj. & n. —adj. **1** throaty, harsh-sounding. **2 a** *Phonet.* (of a consonant) produced in the throat or by the back of the tongue and palate. **b** (of a sound) coming from the throat. **c** of the throat. —n. *Phonet.* a guttural consonant (e.g. k, g). □□ **gutturally** adv. [F *guttural* or med.L *gutturalis* f. L *guttur* throat]

guv /gʌv/ n. *Brit. sl.* = GOVERNOR 7. [abbr.]

guy¹ /gaɪ/ n. & v. —n. **1** *colloq.* a man; a fellow. **2** (usu. in pl.) *US* a person of either sex. **3** *Brit.* an effigy of Guy Fawkes in ragged clothing, burnt on a bonfire on 5 Nov. **4** *Brit.* a grotesquely

dressed person. —v.tr. **1** ridicule. **2** exhibit in effigy. [*Guy* FAWKES]

guy² /gaɪ/ n. & v. —n. a rope or chain to secure a tent or steady a crane-load etc. —v.tr. secure with a guy or guys. [prob. of LG orig.: cf. LG & Du. *gei* brail etc.]

Guyana /gaɪ'ænə/ a country on the NE coast of South America; pop. (est. 1987) 812,000; official language, English; capital, Georgetown. The Spaniards explored the area in 1499, and the Dutch settled there in the 17th c. It was occupied by the British from 1796 and established, with adjacent areas, as the colony of British Guiana in 1831. In 1966 it gained independence as Guyana (the name is taken from an American Indian word meaning 'land of waters'), and became a Cooperative Republic within the Commonwealth in 1970. Much of the country is covered with dense rain forest. Its economy is dominated by the sugar industry (the province of Demerara has given its name to a type of sugar that originated there), but bauxite-mining is becoming increasingly important. □□ **Guyanese** /ˌgaɪə'niːz/ adj. & n.

Guyenne /giː'en/ a former region of southern France stretching from the Bay of Biscay across Aquitaine to the SW edge of the Massif Central. Its capital was Bordeaux.

guzzle /'gʌz(ə)l/ v.tr. & intr. eat, drink, or consume excessively or greedily. □□ **guzzler** n. [perh. f. OF *gosiller* chatter, vomit f. *gosier* throat]

Gwalior /'gwɑːlɪˌɔː(r)/ a city and former princely State in Madhya Pradesh in central India; pop. (1981) 560,000.

Gwent /gwent/ a county of SE Wales; pop. (1981) 441,600; county town, Cwmbran.

Gwynedd /'gwɪneð/ a county of NW Wales; pop. (1981) 231,400; county town, Caernarfon.

Gwynn /gwɪn/, Nell (1650–87), an actress who became one of Charles II's many mistresses, one of her sons later being created Duke of St Albans.

Gy abbr. = GRAY¹.

gybe /dʒaɪb/ v. & n. (*US* **jibe**) —v. **1** *intr.* (of a fore-and-aft sail or boom) swing across in wearing or running before the wind. **2** *tr.* cause (a sail) to do this. **3** *intr.* (of a ship or its crew) change course so that this happens. —n. a change of course causing gybing. [obs. Du. *gijben*]

gym /dʒɪm/ n. *colloq.* **1** a gymnasium. **2** gymnastics. [abbr.]

gymkhana /dʒɪm'kɑːnə/ n. **1** a meeting for competition or display in sport, esp. horse-riding. **2** a public place with facilities for athletics. [Hind. *gendkhāna* ball-house, racket-court, assim. to GYMNASIUM]

gymnasium /dʒɪm'neɪzɪəm/ n. (pl. **gymnasiums** or **gymnasia** /-zɪə/) **1** a room or building equipped for gymnastics. **2** a school in Germany or Scandinavia that prepares pupils for university entrance. □□ **gymnasial** adj. [L f. Gk *gumnasion* f. *gumnazō* exercise f. *gumnos* naked]

gymnast /'dʒɪmnæst/ n. an expert in gymnastics. [F *gymnaste* or Gk *gumnastēs* athlete-trainer f. *gumnazō*: see GYMNASIUM]

gymnastic /dʒɪm'næstɪk/ adj. of or involving gymnastics. □□ **gymnastically** adv. [L *gymnasticus* f. Gk *gumnastikos* (as GYMNASIUM)]

gymnastics /dʒɪm'næstɪks/ n.pl. (also treated as *sing.*) **1** exercises developing or displaying physical agility and coordination, usu. in competition. **2** other forms of physical or mental agility.

gymno- /'dʒɪmnəʊ/ comb. form *Biol.* bare, naked. [Gk *gumnos* naked]

gymnosophist /dʒɪm'nɒsəfɪst/ n. a member of an ancient Hindu sect wearing little clothing and devoted to contemplation. □□ **gymnosophy** n. [ME f. F *gymnosophiste* f. L *gymnosophistae* (pl.) f. Gk *gumnosophistai*: see GYMNO-, SOPHIST]

gymnosperm /'dʒɪmnəʊˌspɜːm/ n. any of various plants having seeds unprotected by an ovary, including conifers, cycads, and ginkgos (opp. ANGIOSPERM). □□ **gymnospermous** /-'spɜːməs/ adj.

gymp var. of GIMP¹.

gymslip /'dʒɪmslɪp/ n. a sleeveless tunic, usu. belted, worn by schoolgirls.

gynaeceum var. of GYNOECIUM.

gynaeco- /'gaɪnɪkəʊ/ comb. form (*US* **gyneco-**) woman, women; female. [Gk *gunē gunaikos* woman]

gynaecology /ˌgaɪnɪˈkɒlədʒɪ/ n. (US **gynecology**) the science of the physiological functions and diseases of women and girls, esp. those affecting the reproductive system. □□ **gynaecological** /-kəˈlɒdʒɪk(ə)l/ adj. **gynaecologically** /-kəˈlɒdʒɪkəlɪ/ adv. **gynaecologist** n. **gynecologic** /-kəˈlɒdʒɪk/ adj. US.

gynaecomastia /ˌgaɪnɪkəʊˈmæstɪə/ n. (US **gynecomastia**) Med. enlargement of a man's breasts, usu. due to hormone imbalance or hormone therapy.

gynandromorph /gaɪˈnændrəˌmɔːf/ n. Biol. an individual, esp. an insect, having male and female characteristics. □□ **gynandromorphic** /-ˈmɔːfɪk/ adj. **gynandromorphism** /-ˈmɔːfɪz(ə)m/ n. [formed as GYNANDROUS + Gk morphē form]

gynandrous /gaɪˈnændrəs/ adj. Bot. with stamens and pistil united in one column as in orchids. [Gk gunandros of doubtful sex, f. gunē woman + anēr andros man]

gyneco- comb. form US var. of GYNAECO-.

gynoecium /gaɪˈniːsɪəm/ n. (also **gynaecium**) (pl. **-cia** /-sɪə/) Bot. the carpels of a flower taken collectively. [mod.L f. Gk gunaikeion women's apartments (as GYNAECO-, Gk oikos house)]

-gynous /ˈgɪnəs, ˈdʒɪnəs/ comb. form Bot. forming adjectives meaning 'having specified female organs or pistils' (monogynous). [Gk -gunos f. gunē woman]

gyp¹ /dʒɪp/ n. Brit. colloq. **1** pain or severe discomfort. **2** a scolding (gave them gyp). [19th c.: perh. f. gee-up (see GEE²)]

gyp² /dʒɪp/ n. Brit. a college servant at Cambridge and Durham. [perh. f. obs. gippo scullion, orig. a man's short tunic, f. obs. F jupeau]

gyp³ /dʒɪp/ v. & n. sl. —v.tr. (**gypped**, **gypping**) cheat, swindle. —n. an act of cheating; a swindle. [19th c.: perh. f. GYP²]

gyppy tummy var. of GIPPY TUMMY.

gypsophila /dʒɪpˈsɒfɪlə/ n. any plant of the genus Gypsophila, with a profusion of small usu. white composite flowers. [mod.L f. Gk gupsos chalk +

gypsum /ˈdʒɪpsəm/ n. a hydrated form of calcium sulphate occurring naturally and used to make plaster of Paris and in the building industry. □□ **gypseous** adj. **gypsiferous** /-ˈsɪfərəs/ adj. [L f. Gk gupsos]

Gypsy /ˈdʒɪpsɪ/ n. (also **Gipsy**) (pl. **-ies**) **1** a member of a travelling people with dark skin and hair, speaking a language related to Hindi (see ROMANY) and usually living by seasonal work, itinerant trade, and fortune-telling. (See below.) **2** (**gypsy**) a person resembling or living like a Gypsy. □ **gypsy moth** a kind of tussock moth, Lymantria dispar, of which the larvae are very destructive to foliage. □□ **Gypsydom** n. **Gypsyfied** adj. **Gypsyhood** n. **Gypsyish** adj. [earlier gipcyan, gipsen f. EGYPTIAN, from the supposed origin of Gypsies when they appeared in England in the early 16th c.]

Gypsies, who now number approximately one million, are found on most continents. Their primary identifying cultural characteristic is their distinctive language, and it is generally agreed that their original homeland was the Indian subcontinent which they probably left in three separate migrations. With their distinctive language and customs the Gypsies continue to resist assimilation and their dispersion has been accelerated in modern times by prejudice and by persecution. The English began a policy of transportation in 1544 and sent them to the West Indies, the American colonies, and later to Australia. Similar forced migration was practised by the Portuguese (to Brazil and Angola), the Dutch, Germans, etc.; Nazi extermination campaigns directed against the Gypsies reduced their numbers in Europe by 250,000 between 1939 and 1945.

gyrate v. & adj. —v.intr. /ˌdʒaɪəˈreɪt/ go in a circle or spiral; revolve, whirl. —adj. /ˈdʒaɪrət/ Bot. arranged in rings or convolutions. □□ **gyration** /-ˈreɪʃ(ə)n/ n. **gyrator** /ˌdʒaɪəˈreɪtə(r)/ n. **gyratory** /-rətərɪ, -ˈreɪtərɪ/ adj. [L gyrare gyrat- revolve f. gyrus ring f. Gk guros]

gyre /dʒaɪə(r)/ v. & n. esp. poet. —v.intr. whirl or gyrate. —n. a gyration. [L gyrus ring f. Gk guros]

gyrfalcon /ˈdʒɜːˌfɔːlkən/ n. (also **gerfalcon**) a large falcon, Falco rusticolus, of the northern hemisphere. [ME f. OF gerfaucon f. Frank. gērfalco f. ON geirfálki: see FALCON]

gyro /ˈdʒaɪərəʊ/ n. (pl. **-os**) colloq. **1** = GYROSCOPE. **2** = GYROCOMPASS. [abbr.]

gyro- /ˈdʒaɪərəʊ/ comb. form rotation. [Gk guros ring]

gyrocompass /ˈdʒaɪərəʊˌkʌmpəs/ n. a compass giving the true north and bearings from it relative to the earth's rotation and depending on the properties of a gyroscope, independent of earth's magnetism. It is used in ships and provided that the speed of the vessel is comparatively low the axis of the gyroscope, which remains horizontal, aligns itself north/south under the influence of the earth's rotation. The high speed of aircraft renders the gyrocompass less suitable for use in flight.

gyrograph /ˈdʒaɪərəʊˌgrɑːf/ n. an instrument for recording revolutions.

gyromagnetic /ˌdʒaɪərəʊmægˈnetɪk/ adj. **1** Physics of the magnetic and mechanical properties of a rotating charged particle. **2** (of a compass) combining a gyroscope and a normal magnetic compass.

gyropilot /ˈdʒaɪərəʊˌpaɪlət/ n. a gyrocompass used for automatic steering.

gyroplane /ˈdʒaɪərəʊˌpleɪn/ n. a form of aircraft deriving its lift mainly from freely rotating overhead vanes.

gyroscope /ˈdʒaɪərəˌskəʊp/ n. a rotating wheel whose axis is free to change its direction but maintains a fixed direction in the absence of perturbing forces. The most familiar example is the spinning-top, whose axis remains vertical as it spins, but in most of its practical uses the wheel is spun by electric motors. The gyroscope is used in automatic pilots in aircraft and in gyrocompasses. □□ **gyroscopic** /-ˈskɒpɪk/ adj. **gyroscopically** /-ˈskɒpɪkəlɪ/ adv. [F (as GYRO-, SCOPE²)]

gyrostabilizer /ˈdʒaɪərəʊˌsteɪbɪˌlaɪzə(r)/ n. a gyroscopic device for maintaining the equilibrium of a ship, aircraft, platform, etc.

gyrus /ˈdʒaɪərəs/ n. (pl. **gyri** /-rɪ/) a fold or convolution, esp. of the brain. [L f. Gk guros ring]

gyttja /ˈjɪtʃə/ n. Geol. a lake deposit of a usu. black organic sediment. [Sw., = mud, ooze]

gyver var. of GUIVER.

H

H¹ /eɪtʃ/ n. (also **h**) (pl. **Hs** or **H's**) **1** the eighth letter of the alphabet (see AITCH). **2** anything having the form of an H (esp. in comb.: H-girder).

H² abbr. (also **H.**) **1** hardness. **2** (of a pencil-lead) hard. **3** henry, henrys. **4** (water) hydrant. **5** sl. heroin.

H³ symb. Chem. the element hydrogen.

h. abbr. **1** hecto-. **2** height. **3** horse. **4** hot. **5** hour(s). **6** husband. **7** Planck's constant.

Ha symb. Chem. the element hahnium.

ha¹ /hɑː/ int. & v. (also **hah**) —int. expressing surprise, suspicion, triumph, etc. (cf. HA HA). —v. intr. (in **hum and ha**: see HUM¹) [ME]

ha² abbr. hectare(s).

haar /hɑː(r)/ n. a cold sea-fog on the east coast of England or Scotland. [perh. f. ON hárr hoar, hoary]

Haarlem /ˈhɑːləm/ a city in The Netherlands, capital of the province of North Holland and commercial centre of the Dutch bulb industry, 20km (12 miles) west of Amsterdam; pop. (1987) 91,369.

Hab. abbr. Habakkuk (Old Testament).

Habakkuk /ˈhæbəkək, həˈbæ-/ **1** a Hebrew minor prophet probably of the 7th c. BC. **2** a book of the Old Testament bearing his name.

habanera /ˌhæbəˈneərə/ n. **1** a Cuban dance in slow duple time. **2** the music for this. [Sp., fem. of habanero of Havana in Cuba]

habeas corpus /ˌheɪbɪəs ˈkɔːpəs/ n. a writ requiring a person under arrest to be brought before a judge or into court, esp. to investigate the lawfulness of his or her detention, thus ensuring that imprisonment cannot take place without a legal hearing. The right to sue for such a writ was an old common-law right; formulations of it look back to a phrase in Magna Carta, but the right may predate this. It was not actually passed as an Act of Parliament until 1679 and before that date was frequently disregarded. A similar right is recognized in the legal system of the US. [L, = you must have the body]

haberdasher /ˈhæbəˌdæʃə(r)/ n. **1** Brit. a dealer in dress accessories and sewing-goods. **2** US a dealer in men's clothing. □□ **haberdashery** n. (pl. **-ies**). [ME prob. ult. f. AF hapertas perh. the name of a fabric]

habergeon /ˈhæbədʒ(ə)n/ n. hist. a sleeveless coat of mail. [ME f. OF haubergeon (as HAUBERK)]

habiliment /həˈbɪlɪmənt/ n. (usu. in pl.) **1** clothes suited to a particular purpose. **2** joc. ordinary clothes. [ME f. OF habillement f. habiller fit out f. habile ABLE]

habilitate /həˈbɪlɪteɪt/ v.intr. qualify for office (esp. as a teacher in a German university). □□ **habilitation** /-ˈteɪʃ(ə)n/ n. [med.L habilitare (as ABILITY)]

habit /ˈhæbɪt/ n. & v. —n. **1** a settled or regular tendency or practice (often foll. by of´ + verbal noun: has a habit of ignoring me). **2** a practice that is hard to give up. **3** a mental constitution or attitude. **4** Psychol. an automatic reaction to a specific situation. **5** colloq. an addictive practice, esp. of taking drugs. **6 a** the dress of a particular class, esp. of a religious order. **b** (in full **riding-habit**) a woman's riding-dress. **c** archaic dress, attire. **7** a bodily constitution. **8** Biol. & Crystallog. a mode of growth. —v.tr. (usu. as **habited** adj.) clothe. □ **habit-forming** causing addiction. **make a habit of** do regularly. [ME f. OF abit f. L habitus f. habēre habit- have, be constituted]

habitable /ˈhæbɪtəb(ə)l/ adj. that can be inhabited. □□ **habitability** /-ˈbɪlɪtɪ/ n. **habitableness** n. **habitably** adv. [ME f. OF f. L habitabilis (as HABITANT)]

habitant n. **1** /ˈhæbɪt(ə)nt/ an inhabitant. **2** /ˌæbiːˈtɑ̃/ **a** an early French settler in Canada or Louisiana. **b** a descendant of these settlers. [F f. OF habiter f. L habitare inhabit (as HABIT)]

habitat /ˈhæbɪˌtæt/ n. **1** the natural home of an organism. **2** a habitation. [L, = it dwells: see HABITANT]

habitation /ˌhæbɪˈteɪʃ(ə)n/ n. **1** the process of inhabiting (fit for human habitation). **2** a house or home. [ME f. OF f. L habitatio -onis (as HABITANT)]

habitual /həˈbɪtjʊəl/ adj. **1** done constantly or as a habit. **2** regular, usual. **3** given to a (specified) habit (a habitual smoker). □□ **habitually** adv. **habitualness** n. [med.L habitualis (as HABIT)]

habituate /həˈbɪtjʊˌeɪt/ v.tr. (often foll. by to) accustom; make used to something. □□ **habituation** /-ˈeɪʃ(ə)n/ n. [LL habituare (as HABIT)]

habitude /ˈhæbɪˌtjuːd/ n. **1** a mental or bodily disposition. **2** a custom or tendency. [ME f. OF f. L habitudo -dinis f. habēre habit-have]

habitué /həˈbɪtjʊˌeɪ/ n. a habitual visitor or resident. [F, past part. of habituer (as HABITUATE)]

Habsburg /ˈhæbsbɜːg/ var. of HAPSBURG.

háček /ˈhætʃek/ n. a diacritic mark (ˇ) placed over letters to modify the sound in some Slavonic and Baltic languages. [Czech, dimin. of hák hook]

hachures /hæˈʃʊə(r)/ n.pl. parallel lines used in hill-shading on maps, their closeness indicating the steepness of gradient. [F f. hacher HATCH³]

hacienda /ˌhæsɪˈendə/ n. in Spanish-speaking countries: **1** an estate or plantation with a dwelling-house. **2** a factory. [Sp. f. L facienda things to be done]

hack¹ /hæk/ v. & n. —v. **1** tr. cut or chop roughly; mangle. **2** tr. kick the shin of (an opponent at football). **3** intr. (often foll. by at) deliver cutting blows. **4** tr. cut (one's way) through thick foliage etc. **5** tr. colloq. gain unauthorized access to (data in a computer). **6** tr. sl. **a** manage, cope with. **b** tolerate. —n. **1** a kick with the toe of a boot. **2** a gash or wound, esp. from a kick. **3 a** a mattock. **b** a miner's pick. □ **hacking cough** a short dry frequent cough. [OE haccian cut in pieces f. WG]

hack² /hæk/ n., adj., & v. —n. **1 a** a horse for ordinary riding. **b** a horse let out for hire. **c** = JADE² 1. **2** a dull, uninspired writer. **3** a person hired to do dull routine work. **4** US a taxi. —attrib.adj. **1** used as a hack. **2** typical of a hack; commonplace (hack work). —v. **1 a** intr. ride on horseback on a road at an ordinary pace. **b** tr. ride (a horse) in this way. **2** tr. make common or trite. [abbr. of HACKNEY]

hack³ /hæk/ n. **1** a board on which a hawk's meat is laid. **2** a rack holding fodder for cattle. □ **at hack** (of a young hawk) not yet allowed to prey for itself. [var. of HATCH¹]

hackberry /ˈhækbərɪ/ n. (pl. **-ies**) US **1** any tree of the genus Celtis, native to N. America, bearing purple edible berries. **2** the berry of this tree. [var. of hagberry, of Norse orig.]

hacker /ˈhækə(r)/ n. **1** a person or thing that hacks or cuts roughly. **2** colloq. a person who uses computers for a hobby, esp. to gain unauthorized access to data.

hackle /ˈhæk(ə)l/ n. & v. —n. **1** a long feather or series of feathers on the neck or saddle of a domestic cock and other birds. **2** Fishing an artificial fly dressed with a hackle. **3** a feather in a Highland soldier's bonnet. **4** (in pl.) the erectile hairs along the back of a dog, which rise when it is angry or alarmed. **5** a steel comb for dressing flax. —v.tr. dress or comb with a hackle. □ **make one's hackles rise** cause one to be angry or indignant. [ME hechele, hakele, prob. f. OE f. WG]

hackney /ˈhæknɪ/ n. (pl. **-eys**) **1** a horse of average size and quality for ordinary riding. **2** (attrib.) designating any of various vehicles kept for hire. ¶ No longer used except in hackney carriage, still in official use as a term for 'taxi'. Hackney coaches began to ply in London in 1625, and were only 20 in number, but ten years later there were so many that Charles I issued an order restricting them. By the reign of George III the number had been increased to 1,000, operating by licence and paying duty of five shillings a week to the king. Drivers of hackney coaches were required to give way to persons of quality and gentlemen's coaches. [ME, perh. f. *Hackney* (formerly *Hakenei*) in London, where horses were pastured]

hackneyed /ˈhæknɪd/ *adj.* (of a phrase etc.) made commonplace or trite by overuse.

hacksaw /ˈhæksɔː/ *n.* a saw with a narrow blade set in a frame, for cutting metal.

had *past* and *past part.* of HAVE.

haddock /ˈhædək/ *n.* (*pl.* same) a marine fish, *Melanogrammus aeglefinus*, of the N. Atlantic, allied to cod, but smaller. [ME, prob. f. AF *hadoc*, OF (*h*)*adot*, of unkn. orig.]

hade /heɪd/ *n. & v. Geol.* —*n.* an incline from the vertical. —*v.intr.* incline from the vertical. [17th c., perh. dial. form of *head*]

Hades /ˈheɪdiːz/ *Gk Mythol.* one of the sons of Cronus, lord of the lower world (which is known as 'the House of Hades'). In classical Greek the name is always that of a person, not of a place, but later it was transferred to his kingdom. He is represented as grim and unpitying, never as evil (Greek mythology has no Satan). One of his titles is *Pluto*. [Gk *haidēs*, orig. a name of Pluto]

Hadhramaut /ˌhɑːdrəˈmaʊt/ a narrow coastal plain in eastern Yemen, separating the Gulf of Aden and the Arabian Sea from the desert land of the southern Arabian peninsula.

Hadith /ˈhædɪθ/ *n.* any of a number of collections of traditions rendering the sayings of the Prophet Muhammad and, with accounts of his daily practice (see SUNNA), constituting the major source of guidance for Muslims after the Koran. [Arab. *ḥadīt* tradition]

hadj var. of HAJJ.

hadji var. of HAJJI.

Hadlee /ˈhædlɪ/, Sir Richard John (1951–), New Zealand all-round cricketer. As a batsman, he achieved the highest test-match score against the West Indies in 1979–80; as a bowler, he holds the record for the number of test wickets taken. In 1990 he became the first cricketer to be knighted while still playing in test matches.

hadn't /ˈhæd(ə)nt/ *contr.* had not.

Hadrian /ˈheɪdrɪən/ (Publius Aelius Hadrianus, 76–138) Roman emperor 117–38, born in Spain, the adopted successor of Trajan. He spent much of his reign touring the provinces of the empire, promoting good government and loyalty to Rome, and securing the frontiers. An admirer of Greek culture, he was both practitioner and patron of the arts, and erected many buildings in Rome (including the Pantheon) and Athens.

Hadrian's Wall a Roman defensive wall across northern England from the Solway Firth in the west to the mouth of the River Tyne in the east (about 120 km, 74 miles). It was begun in AD 122, after the emperor Hadrian's visit, to defend the province of Britain against invasions of tribes from the north. There were forts and fortified posts at intervals, a ditch on the north and a wider ditch on the south, and the wall itself (2.5–3 m thick) was eventually built of stone throughout its length. After Hadrian's death the frontier was advanced to the Antonine Wall, which the Romans proved unable to hold; after being overrun and restored several times Hadrian's Wall was abandoned *c.* AD 410.

hadron /ˈhædrɒn/ *n. Physics* any strongly interacting elementary particle. □□ **hadronic** /-ˈdrɒnɪk/ *adj.* [Gk *hadros* bulky]

hadst /hædst/ *archaic 2nd sing. past* of HAVE.

haecceity /hekˈsiːɪtɪ/ *n. Philos.* **1** the quality of a thing that makes it unique or describable as 'this (one)'. **2** individuality. [med.L *haecceitas* f. *haec* fem. of *hic* this]

Haeckel /ˈhek(ə)l/, Ernst Heinrich (1834–1919) German biologist and firm supporter of Darwin's theories. His vivid popularizations of Darwinism were best-sellers, and through his works many millions first encountered the theory that man was descended from the ape. For Haeckel the implications of evolution were that Roman Catholicism promoted superstition and that the German empire was the highest evolved form of civilized nation. He upheld the essential unity of mind, organic

life, and inorganic matter, and compared crystals to simple nerve-cells. By careful studies of the earliest stages of embryos he developed his 'recapitulation' theory—that the development of the individual organism reflects the evolutionary history of the species—a theory now discredited.

haem /hiːm/ *n.* (also **heme**) a non-protein compound containing iron, and responsible for the red colour of haemoglobin. [Gk *haima* blood or f. HAEMOGLOBIN]

haemal /ˈhiːm(ə)l/ *adj.* (US **hemal**) *Anat.* **1** of or concerning the blood. **2 a** situated on the same side of the body as the heart and great blood-vessels. **b** ventral. [Gk *haima* blood]

haematic /hiːˈmætɪk/ *adj.* (US **hematic**) *Med.* of or containing blood. [Gk *haimatikos* (as HAEMATIN)]

haematin /ˈhiːmətɪn/ *n.* (US **hematin** /ˈhiːm-, ˈhem-/) *Anat.* a bluish-black derivative of haemoglobin, formed by removal of the protein part and oxidation of the iron atom. [Gk *haima -matos* blood]

haematite /ˈhiːmətaɪt/ *n.* (US **hematite** /ˈhiːm-, ˈhem-/) a ferric oxide ore. [L *haematites* f. Gk *haimatitēs* (*lithos*) bloodlike (stone) (as HAEMATIN)]

haemato- /ˈhiːmətəʊ/ *comb. form* (US **hemato-**) blood. [Gk *haima haimat-* blood]

haematocele /ˈhiːmətəʊˌsiːl/ *n.* (US **hematocele** /ˈhiː-, ˈhe-/) *Med.* a swelling caused by blood collecting in a body cavity.

haematocrit /ˈhiːmətəʊkrɪt/ *n.* (US **hematocrit** /ˈhiː-, ˈhe-/) *Physiol.* **1** the ratio of the volume of red blood cells to the total volume of blood. **2** an instrument for measuring this. [HAEMATO- + Gk *kritēs* judge]

haematology /ˌhiːməˈtɒlədʒɪ/ *n.* (US **hematology** /ˈhiː-, ˈhe-/) the study of the physiology of the blood. □□ **haematologic** /-təˈlɒdʒɪk/ *adj.* **haematological** /-təˈlɒdʒɪk(ə)l/ *adj.* **haematologist** *n.*

haematoma /ˌhiːməˈtəʊmə/ *n.* (US **hematoma** /ˌhiː-, ˌhe-/) *Med.* a solid swelling of clotted blood within the tissues.

haematuria /ˌhiːməˈtjʊərɪə/ *n.* (US **hematuria** /ˌhiː-, ˌhe-/) *Med.* the presence of blood in urine.

-haemia var. of -AEMIA.

haemo- /ˈhiːməʊ/ *comb. form* (US **hemo-**) = HAEMATO-. [abbr.]

haemocyanin /ˌhiːməˈsaɪənɪn/ *n.* (US **hemocyanin** /ˌhiː-, ˌhe-/) an oxygen-carrying substance containing copper, present in the blood plasma of arthropods and molluscs. [HAEMO- + *cyanin* blue pigment (as CYAN)]

haemodialysis /ˌhiːməʊdaɪˈælɪsɪs/ *n.* = DIALYSIS 2.

haemoglobin /ˌhiːməˈɡləʊbɪn/ *n.* (US **hemoglobin** /ˌhiː-, ˌhe-/) a red oxygen-carrying substance containing iron, present in the red blood-cells of vertebrates. [shortened f. *haematoglobin*, compound of HAEMATIN + GLOBULIN]

haemolysis /hiːˈmɒlɪsɪs/ *n.* (US **hemolysis** /hiː-, he-/) the loss of haemoglobin from red blood-cells. □□ **haemolytic** /-məˈlɪtɪk/ *adj.*

haemophilia /ˌhiːməˈfɪlɪə/ *n.* (US **hemophilia** /ˌhiː-, ˌhe-/) *Med.* a usu. hereditary disorder with a tendency to bleed severely from even a slight injury, through the failure of the blood to clot normally. □□ **haemophilic** *adj.* [mod.L (as HAEMO-, -PHILIA)]

haemophiliac /ˌhiːməˈfɪlɪˌæk/ *n.* (US **hemophiliac** /ˌhiː-, ˌhe-/) a person suffering from haemophilia.

haemorrhage /ˈhemərɪdʒ/ *n. & v.* (US **hemorrhage**) —*n.* **1** an escape of blood from a ruptured blood-vessel, esp. when profuse. **2** an extensive damaging loss suffered by a State, organization, etc., esp. of people or assets. —*v.intr.* undergo a haemorrhage. □□ **haemorrhagic** /ˌheməˈrædʒɪk/ *adj.* [earlier *haemorrhagy* f. *hémorr(h)agie* f. L *haemorrhagia* f. Gk *haimorrhagia* f. *haima* blood + stem of *rhēgnumi* burst]

haemorrhoid /ˈhemərɔɪd/ *n.* (US **hemorrhoid**) (usu. in *pl.*) swollen veins at or near the anus; piles. □□ **haemorrhoidal** /-ˈrɔɪd(ə)l/ *adj.* [ME *emeroudis* (Bibl. *emerods*) f. OF *emeroyde* f. L f. Gk *haimorrhoides* (*phlebes*) bleeding (veins) f. *haima* blood, *-rhoos* -flowing]

haemostasis /ˌhiːməʊˈsteɪsɪs/ *n.* (US **hemostasis**) the stopping of the flow of blood. □□ **haemostatic** /ˌhiːməˈstætɪk, ˌhe-/ *adj.*

haere mai /ˈhaɪrə ˌmaɪ/ *int.* NZ welcome. [Maori, lit. 'come hither']

hafiz /ˈhɑːfiz/ *n.* a Muslim who knows the Koran by heart. [Pers. f. Arab. *ḥāfiz* guardian]

hafnium /ˈhæfnɪəm/ *n. Chem.* a silvery lustrous metallic element, chemically similar to zirconium and usually found associated with it. It was discovered in 1923 and is used in control rods of nuclear reactors because of its capacity to absorb neutrons, its resistance to corrosion in hot water, and its adequate strength at the operating temperature of reactors. It is also used in tungsten alloys for filaments and electrodes. ¶ Symb.: Hf; atomic number 72. [mod.L f. *Hafnia* Copenhagen]

haft /hɑːft/ *n.* & *v.* —*n.* the handle of a dagger or knife etc. —*v.tr.* provide with a haft. [OE *hæft* f. Gmc]

Hag. *abbr.* Haggai (Old Testament).

hag[1] /hæg/ *n.* **1** an ugly old woman. **2** a witch. **3** = HAGFISH. □□ **haggish** *adj.* [ME *hegge, hagge*, perh. f. OE *hægtesse*, OHG *hagazissa*, of unkn. orig.]

hag[2] /hæg/ *n. Sc.* & *N.Engl.* **1** a soft place on a moor. **2** a firm place in a bog. [ON *högg* gap, orig. 'cutting blow', rel. to HEW]

hagfish /ˈhægfɪʃ/ *n.* any jawless fish of the family Myxinidae, with a rasp-like tongue used for feeding on dead or dying fish. [HAG[1]]

Haggadah /həˈɡɑːdə/ *n.* **1** a legend etc. used to illustrate a point of the Law in the Talmud; the legendary element of the Talmud. **2** a book recited at the Passover Seder service. □□ **Haggadic** /-ˈɡædɪk, -ˈɡɑːdɪk/ *adj.* [Heb., = tale, f. *higgîḏ* tell]

Haggai /ˈhægɪˌaɪ/ **1** a Hebrew minor prophet of the 6th c. BC. **2** a book of the Old Testament containing his prophecies of a glorious future in the Messianic age.

Haggard /ˈhægəd/, Sir Henry Rider (1856–1925), English writer, a close friend of Kipling, famous for his 34 adventure novels which have been continuously popular (several have been filmed). The most celebrated of these are *King Solomon's Mines* (1886) and *She* (1889), both set in Africa, which vividly convey the author's fascination with the life, landscape, and history of that continent.

haggard /ˈhægəd/ *adj.* & *n.* —*adj.* **1** looking exhausted and distraught, esp. from fatigue, worry, privation, etc. **2** (of a hawk) caught and trained as an adult. —*n.* a haggard hawk. □□ **haggardly** *adv.* **haggardness** *n.* [F *hagard*, of uncert. orig.: later infl. by HAG[1]]

haggis /ˈhægɪs/ *n.* a Scottish dish consisting of a sheep's or calf's offal mixed with suet, oatmeal, etc., and boiled in a bag made from the animal's stomach or in an artificial bag. [ME: orig. unkn.]

haggle /ˈhæg(ə)l/ *v.* & *n.* —*v.intr.* (often foll. by *about, over*) dispute or bargain persistently. —*n.* a dispute or wrangle. □□ **haggler** *n.* [earlier sense 'hack' f. ON *höggva* HEW]

Hagia Sophia /ˌhæɡɪə səˈfiːə/ = ST SOPHIA. [Gk, = holy wisdom]

hagio- /ˈhæɡɪəʊ/ *comb. form* of saints or holiness. [Gk *hagios* holy]

Hagiographa /ˌhæɡɪˈɒɡrəfə/ *n.* the twelve books comprising the last of the three major divisions of the Hebrew Scriptures, additional to the Law and the Prophets.

hagiographer /ˌhæɡɪˈɒɡrəfə(r)/ *n.* **1** a writer of the lives of saints. **2** a writer of any of the Hagiographa.

hagiography /ˌhæɡɪˈɒɡrəfɪ/ *n.* the writing of the lives of saints. □□ **hagiographic** /-ˈɡræfɪk/ *adj.* **hagiographical** /-əˈɡræfɪk(ə)l/ *adj.*

hagiolatry /ˌhæɡɪˈɒlətrɪ/ *n.* the worship of saints.

hagiology /ˌhæɡɪˈɒlədʒɪ/ *n.* literature dealing with the lives and legends of saints. □□ **hagiological** /-ɡɪəˈlɒdʒɪk(ə)l/ *adj.* **hagiologist** *n.*

hagridden /ˈhæɡˌrɪd(ə)n/ *adj.* afflicted by nightmares or anxieties.

Hague /heɪɡ/, **The** (Dutch **'s-Gravenhage** /ˈsxrɑːvənˌhɑːxə/ or **Den Haag** /den ˈhɑːɡ/) the seat of government and administrative centre of The Netherlands, on the North Sea coast in southern Holland; pop. (1987) 444,313. The International Court of Justice is based at The Hague.

hah var. of HA.

ha ha /hɑ: ˈhɑ:/ *int.* repr. laughter. [OE: cf. HA]

ha-ha /ˈhɑːhɑː/ *n.* a ditch with a wall on its inner side below ground level, forming a boundary to a park or garden without interrupting the view. [F, perh. from the cry of surprise on encountering it]

Hahn /hɑːn/, Otto (1879–1968), German chemist, co-discoverer of nuclear fission, for which he shared the 1944 Nobel Prize for chemistry with Fritz Strassmann (1902–80). He started the study of radiochemistry during a brief work period outside Germany to study English, first with Sir William Ramsey in London and then with Rutherford in Manchester, identifying various radioactive isotopes of thorium. His fruitful partnership with Lise Meitner (1878–1968) began shortly after his return to Germany and ended when she, a Jew, fled from the Nazis in 1938. They discovered the new element protoactinium in 1917, but the culmination of their collaboration occurred in 1938 when, with Strassmann, they discovered nuclear fission, so named by Meitner's nephew, the physicist Otto Robert Frisch.

hahnium /ˈhɑːnɪəm/ *n. Chem.* the US name for the chemical element of atomic number 105, a short-lived artificially produced transuranic element (cf. NIELSBOHRIUM). The preferred name for it is now *unnilpentium*. ¶ Symb.: **Ha**. [HAHN + -IUM]

Haifa /ˈhaɪfə/ the chief seaport of Israel, in the north-west of the country on a peninsula jutting into the Mediterranean Sea; pop. (1987) 223,200. It is the site of the Baha'i Shrine.

Haig /heɪɡ/, Douglas, 1st Earl Haig of Bemersyde (1861–1928), commander of British armies in France 1915–18. Firmly believing that the war could be won only by defeating the German army on the Western Front, he maintained a policy of attrition throughout his period of command, despite political pressure to reduce casualties. Although frequently dismissed as a butcher, Haig was among the most competent soldiers of his day, and did at last succeed in winning the war in the way he said he would, by breaking the strength of the main enemy army in the field, albeit at a dreadful cost in British lives. After the war he established the (Royal) British Legion, and organized Poppy Day.

haik /haɪk, heɪk/ *n.* (also **haick**) an outer covering for head and body worn by Arabs. [Moroccan Arab. *ḥā'ik*]

haiku /ˈhaɪkʊ/ *n.* (*pl.* same) **1** a Japanese three-part poem of usu. 17 syllables in lines of 5, 7, 5, syllables. It emerged in the 16th c. and flourished from the 17th c. to the 19th c., and dealt traditionally with images of the natural world; in the 20th c. it has been much imitated in Western literature. **2** an English imitation of this. [Jap.]

hail[1] /heɪl/ *n.* & *v.* —*n.* **1** pellets of frozen rain falling in showers from cumulonimbus clouds. **2** (foll. by *of*) a barrage or onslaught (of missiles, curses, questions, etc.). —*v.* **1** *intr.* (prec. by *it* as subject) hail falls (*it is hailing; if it hails*). **2 a** *tr.* pour down (blows, words, etc.). **b** *intr.* come down forcefully. [OE *hagol, hægl, hagalian* f. Gmc]

hail[2] /heɪl/ *v., int.,* & *n.* —*v.* **1** *tr.* greet enthusiastically. **2** *tr.* signal to or attract the attention of (*hailed a taxi*). **3** *tr.* acclaim (*hailed him king*). **4** *intr.* (foll. by *from*) have one's home or origins in (a place) (*hails from Mauritius*). —*int.* expressing greeting. —*n.* **1** a greeting or act of hailing. **2** distance as affecting the possibility of hailing (*was within hail*). □ **hail-fellow-well-met** intimate, esp. too intimate. **Hail Mary** the Ave Maria (see AVE). □□ **hailer** *n.* [ellipt. use of obs. *hail* (adj.) f. ON *heill* sound, WHOLE]

Haile Selassie /ˌhaɪlɪ səˈlæsɪ/ (1892–1975), emperor of Ethiopia 1930–74. His original name was Tafari Makonnen, and before coming to the throne he was known as Ras (= Prince) Tafari. He became an internationally known figure during his country's heroic but unsuccessful resistance to Italian invasion. After living in exile in Britain during the Italian occupation (1936–41) he returned to his throne, eventually being deposed in a Communist military coup in 1974.

hailstone /ˈheɪlstəʊn/ *n.* a pellet of hail.

hailstorm /ˈheɪlstɔːm/ *n.* a period of heavy hail.

Hainan /haɪˈnæn/ an island in the South China Sea forming an autonomous region of China; pop. (est. 1986) 6,000,000; capital, Haikou.

Haiphong /haɪˈfɒŋ/ a port in north Vietnam, on the delta of the Red River; pop. (est.) 1,279,700.

hair /heə(r)/ n. **1 a** any of the fine threadlike strands growing from the skin of mammals, esp. from the human head. **b** these collectively (his hair is falling out). **2 a** an artificially produced hairlike strand, e.g. in a brush. **b** a mass of such hairs. **3** anything resembling a hair. **4** an elongated cell growing from the epidermis of a plant. **5** a very small quantity or extent (also attrib.: a hair crack). □ **get in a person's hair** colloq. encumber or annoy a person. **hair-drier** (or **-dryer**) an electrical device for drying the hair by blowing warm air over it. **hair-grass** any of various grasses, esp. of the genus Deschampsia, Corynephorus, Aira, etc., with slender stems. **hair of the dog** see DOG. **hair-raising** extremely alarming; terrifying. **hair's breadth** a very small amount or margin. **hair shirt** a shirt of haircloth, worn formerly by penitents and ascetics. **hair-shirt** adj. (attrib.) austere, harsh, self-sacrificing. **hair-slide** Brit. a (usu. ornamental) clip for keeping the hair in position. **hair-splitter** a quibbler. **hair-splitting** adj. & n. making overfine distinctions; quibbling. **hair-trigger** a trigger of a firearm set for release at the slightest pressure. **keep one's hair on** Brit. colloq. remain calm; not get angry. **let one's hair down** colloq. abandon restraint; behave freely or wildly. **make one's hair stand on end** alarm or horrify one. **not turn a hair** remain apparently unmoved or unaffected. □□ **haired** adj. (also in comb.). **hairless** adj. **hairlike** adj. [OE hær f. Gmc]

hairbreadth /ˈheəbredθ/ n. = hair's breadth; (esp. attrib.: a hairbreadth escape).

hairbrush /ˈheəbrʌʃ/ n. a brush for arranging or smoothing the hair.

haircloth /ˈheəklɒθ/ n. stiff cloth woven from hair, used e.g. in upholstery.

haircut /ˈheəkʌt/ n. **1** a cutting of the hair. **2** the style in which the hair is cut.

hairdo /ˈheədu:/ n. (pl. **-dos**) colloq. the style of or an act of styling a woman's hair.

hairdresser /ˈheəˌdresə(r)/ n. **1** a person who cuts and styles hair, esp. professionally. **2** the business or establishment of a hairdresser. □□ **hairdressing** n.

hairgrip /ˈheəgrɪp/ n. Brit. a flat hairpin with the ends close together.

hairline /ˈheəlaɪn/ n. **1** the edge of a person's hair, esp. on the forehead. **2** a very thin line or crack etc.

hairnet /ˈheənet/ n. a piece of fine mesh-work for confining the hair.

hairpiece /ˈheəpi:s/ n. a quantity or switch of detached hair used to augment a person's natural hair.

hairpin /ˈheəpɪn/ n. a U-shaped pin for fastening the hair. □ **hairpin bend** a sharp U-shaped bend in a road.

hairspray /ˈheəspreɪ/ n. a solution sprayed on to the hair to keep it in place.

hairspring /ˈheəsprɪŋ/ n. a fine spring regulating the balance-wheel in a watch.

hairstreak /ˈheəstri:k/ n. a butterfly of the genus Strymonidia etc. with fine streaks or rows of spots on its wings.

hairstyle /ˈheəstaɪl/ n. a particular way of arranging or dressing the hair. □□ **hairstyling** n. **hairstylist** n.

hairy /ˈheərɪ/ adj. (**hairier**, **hairiest**) **1** made of or covered with hair. **2** having the feel of hair. **3** sl. **a** alarmingly unpleasant or difficult. **b** crude, clumsy. □□ **hairily** adv. **hairiness** n.

Haiti /ˈheɪtɪ/ a county in the Caribbean, the French-speaking western portion of the island of Hispaniola; pop. (est. 1988) 6,295,600; official language, French; capital, Port-au-Prince. In 1492 Columbus discovered the island that now comprises Haiti and the Dominican Republic, and named it La Isla Española (the Spanish Island). The native inhabitants were quickly enslaved or killed by the Spaniards, who established some not very successful settlements at the east end of the island, while French pirates were more successful in establishing plantations in the west. In 1697 the eastern area was ceded to the French, who introduced large numbers of slaves from West Africa to work in the sugar-plantations. In 1791, the slaves rose in rebellion; they swept to victory under Black leaders such as Toussaint L'Ouverture and in 1804 the colony was proclaimed an independent State, under the name of Haiti, the first country in Americas (after the US) to achieve freedom from colonial rule. Haiti's West African heritage is shown by the great preponderance of pure Blacks in the population (in contrast to the largely mulatto Dominican Republic) and the practice of voodoo rites. □□ **Haitian** adj. & n.

hajj /hædʒ/ n. (also **hadj**) the Islamic pilgrimage to Mecca. [Arab. ḥājj pilgrimage]

hajji /ˈhædʒɪ/ n. (also **hadji**) (pl. **-is**) a Muslim who has been to Mecca as a pilgrim: also (**Hajji**) used as a title. [Pers. ḥājī (partly through Turk. hacı) f. Arab. ḥajj: see HAJJ]

haka /ˈhɑːkə/ n. NZ **1** a Maori ceremonial war-dance accompanied by chanting. **2** an imitation of this by members of a sports team before a match. [Maori]

hake /heɪk/ n. any marine fish of the genus Merluccius, esp. M. merluccius with an elongate body and large head. [ME perh. ult. f. dial. hake hook + FISH¹]

hakenkreuz /ˈhɑːkənˌkrɔɪts/ n. a swastika, esp. as a Nazi symbol. [G f. Haken hook + Kreuz CROSS]

hakim¹ /hʌˈkiːm/ n. (in India and Muslim countries) a physician. [Arab. ḥakīm wise man, physician]

hakim² /ˈhɑːkɪm/ n. (in India and Muslim countries) a judge, ruler, or governor. [Arab. ḥākim governor]

Hakluyt /ˈhæklu:t/, Richard (c.1552–1616), English geographer. A distinguished scholar and cleric, he was lecturer in geography at Oxford University and Archdeacon of Westminster. His fame, however, was due to his writings on exploration, his most famous work Principal Navigations (1589) being a compilation of accounts of famous voyages of discovery up to his time of writing, which brought to light the hitherto obscure achievements of English navigators and gave great impetus to discovery and colonization.

Halacha /həˈlɑːxə/ n. (also **Halakah**) Jewish law and jurisprudence, based on the Talmud. □□ **Halachic** adj. [Aram. hªlākāh law]

Halafian /hæˈlæfiən/ adj & n. —adj. of a chalcolithic culture (c.5000–4500 BC) identified primarily by the use of polychrome pottery (Halaf ware) which was first noted during excavations at Tell Halaf in NE Syria. Its distribution extends to the Mediterranean coast and the region of Lake Van in eastern Turkey. —n. this culture.

halal /hɑːˈlɑːl/ v. & n. (also **hallal**) —v.tr. (**halalled**, **halalling**) kill (an animal) as prescribed by Muslim law. —n. (often attrib.) meat prepared in this way; lawful food. [Arab. ḥalāl lawful]

halation /hæˈleɪʃ(ə)n/ n. Photog. the spreading of light beyond its proper extent in a developed image, caused by internal reflection in the support of the emulsion. [irreg. f. HALO + -ATION]

halberd /ˈhælbəd/ n. (also **halbert**) hist. a combined spear and battleaxe. [ME f. F hallebarde f. It alabarda f. MHG helmbarde f. helm handle + barde hatchet]

halberdier /ˌhælbəˈdɪə(r)/ n. hist. a man armed with a halberd. [F hallebardier (as HALBERD)]

halcyon /ˈhælsɪən/ adj. & n. —adj. **1** calm, peaceful (halcyon days). **2** (of a period) happy, prosperous. —n. **1** any kingfisher of the genus Halcyon, native to Europe, Africa, and Australasia, with brightly-coloured plumage. **2** Mythol. a bird thought in antiquity to breed in a nest floating at sea at the winter solstice, charming the wind and waves into calm. [ME f. L (h)alcyon f. Gk (h)alkuōn kingfisher]

Haldane /ˈhɔːldeɪn/, John Burdon Sanderson (1892–1964), Scottish mathematical biologist who helped to lay the foundations of population genetics (the genetics of breeding groups of organisms). He also carried out experimental work in biochemistry and on the effects of diving on human physiology. Haldane became well known as a popularizer of science and for

æ cat ɑː arm e bed ɜː her ɪ sit iː see ɒ hot ɔː saw ʌ run ʊ put uː too ə ago aɪ my

his outspoken Marxist political views. He was the brother of the novelist Naomi Mitchison.

hale[1] /heɪl/ adj. (esp. of an old person) strong and healthy (esp. in **hale and hearty**). □□ **haleness** n. [OE hāl WHOLE]

hale[2] /heɪl/ v.tr. drag or draw forcibly. [ME f. OF haler f. ON hala]

half /hɑːf/ n., adj., & adv. —n. (pl. **halves** /hɑːvz/) **1** either of two equal or corresponding parts or groups into which a thing is or might be divided. **2** colloq. = half-back. **3** colloq. half a pint, esp. of beer etc. **4** either of two equal periods of play in sports. **5** colloq. a half-price fare or ticket, esp. for a child. **6** Golf a score that is the same as one's opponent's. —adj. **1** of an amount or quantity equal to a half, or loosely to a part thought of as roughly a half (take half the men; spent half the time reading; half a pint; a half-pint; half-price). **2** forming a half (a half share). —adv. **1** (often in comb.) to the extent of half; partly (only half cooked; half-frozen; half-laughing). **2** to a certain extent; somewhat (esp. in idiomatic phrases: half dead; am half inclined to agree). **3** (in reckoning time) by the amount of half (an hour etc.) (half past two). □ **at half cock** see COCK[1]. **by half** (prec. by too + adj.) excessively (too clever by half). **by halves** imperfectly or incompletely (never does things by halves). **half-and-half** being half one thing and half another. **half-back** (in some sports) a player between the forwards and full backs. **half-baked 1** incompletely considered or planned. **2** (of enthusiasm etc.) only partly committed. **3** foolish. **half the battle** see BATTLE. **half-beak** any fish of the family Hemirhamphidae with the lower jaw projecting beyond the upper. **half-binding** a type of bookbinding in which the spine and corners are bound in one material (usu. leather) and the sides in another. **half-blood 1** a person having one parent in common with another. **2** this relationship. **3** = half-breed. **half-blooded** born from parents of different races. **half-blue** Brit. **1** a person who has represented a university, esp. Oxford or Cambridge, in a sport but who has not received a full blue. **2** this distinction (see BLUE[1] n. 3). **half board** provision of bed, breakfast, and one main meal at a hotel etc. **half-boot** a boot reaching up to the calf. **half-breed** often offens. a person of mixed race. **half-brother** a brother with only one parent in common. **half-caste** often offens. n. a person whose parents are of different races, esp. the offspring of a European father and an Indian mother. —adj. of or relating to such a person. **half a chance** colloq. the slightest opportunity (esp. given half a chance). **half-crown** (or **half a crown**) (in the UK) a former coin and monetary unit worth 2s. 6d. (12½p). **half-cut** Brit. sl. fairly drunk. **half-deck** the quarters of cadets and apprentices on a merchant vessel. **half-dozen** (or **half a dozen**) colloq. six, or about six. **half-duplex** see DUPLEX. **half an eye** the slightest degree of perceptiveness. **half-hardy** (of a plant) able to grow in the open air at all times except in severe frost. **half hitch** a noose or knot formed by passing the end of a rope round its standing part and then through the loop. **half holiday** a day of which half (usu. the afternoon) is taken as a holiday. **half-hour 1** (also **half an hour**) a period of 30 minutes. **2** a point of time 30 minutes after any hour o'clock. **half-hourly** at intervals of 30 minutes. **half-hunter** a watch with a hinged cover in which a small opening allows identification of the approximate position of the hands. **half-inch** n. a unit of length half as large as an inch. —v.tr. rhyming sl. steal (= pinch). **half-integral** equal to half an odd integer. **half-landing** a landing part of the way up a flight of stairs, whose length is twice the width of the flight plus the width of the well. **half-lap** the joining of rails, shafts, etc., by halving the thickness of each at one end and fitting them together. **half-length** a canvas depicting a half-length portrait. **half-life** see separate entry. **half-light** a dim imperfect light. **half-mast** the position of a flag halfway down the mast, as a mark of respect for a person who has died. **half measures** an unsatisfactory compromise or inadequate policy. **half a mind** see MIND. **half moon 1** the moon when only half its illuminated surface is visible from earth. **2** the time when this occurs. **3** a semicircular object. **half nelson** Wrestling see NELSON. **half-note** esp. US Mus. = MINIM 1. **the half of it** colloq. the rest or more important part of something (usu. after neg.: you don't know the half of it). **half pay** reduced income, esp. on retirement. **half-pie** NZ sl. imperfect,

mediocre. **half-plate 1** a photographic plate 16.5 by 10.8 cm. **2** a photograph reproduced from this. **half-seas-over** Brit. sl. partly drunk. **half-sister** a sister with only one parent in common. **half-sole** the sole of a boot or shoe from the shank to the toe. **half-sovereign** a former British gold coin and monetary unit worth ten shillings (50p). **half-step** Mus. a semitone. **half-term** Brit. a period about halfway through a school term, when a short holiday is usually taken. **half-timbered** Archit. having walls with a timber frame and a brick or plaster filling, a structural style common in England in the 15th–16th c. **half-time 1** the time at which half of a game or contest is completed. **2** a short interval occurring at this time. **half the time** see TIME. **half-title 1** the title or short title of a book, printed on the recto of the leaf preceding the title-page. **2** the title of a section of a book printed on the recto of the leaf preceding it. **half-tone 1** a reproduction printed from a block (produced by photographic means) in which the various tones of grey are produced from small and large black dots. **2** US Mus. a semitone. **half-track 1** a propulsion system for land vehicles with wheels at the front and an endless driven belt at the back. **2** a vehicle equipped with this. **half-truth** a statement that (esp. deliberately) conveys only part of the truth. **half-volley** (pl. **-eys**) (in ball games) the playing of a ball as soon as it bounces off the ground. **half-yearly** at intervals of six months. **not half 1** not nearly (not half long enough). **2** colloq. not at all (not half bad). **3** Brit. sl. to an extreme degree (he didn't half get angry). [OE half, healf f. Gmc, orig. = 'side']

half-hearted /hɑːfˈhɑːtɪd/ adj. lacking enthusiasm; feeble. □□ **half-heartedly** adv. **half-heartedness** n.

half-life n. the time taken for half of any sample of a particular radioactive isotope to decay into other materials. (The term is also used in other contexts, e.g. to describe the persistence of a drug in the body after administration.) Half-lives of radioactive isotopes vary enormously from minute fractions of a second to periods longer than the age of the universe. Each isotope, however, has a characteristic half-life which is independent of its physical and chemical environment. Knowlege of the half-lives of radiocarbon and other naturally occuring isotopes forms the basis of their use for dating purposes. For a given initial level of radioactivity, isotopes with long half-lives are more dangerous because their radioactivity persists longer.

halfpenny /ˈheɪpnɪ/ n. (also **ha'penny** /ˈheɪpnɪ/) (pl. **-pennies** or **-pence** /ˈheɪpəns/) (in the UK) a former bronze coin worth half a penny. ¶ Withdrawn in 1984. (cf. FARTHING).

halfpennyworth /ˈheɪpəθ/ n. (also **ha'p'orth** /ˈheɪpəθ/) **1** as much as could be bought for a halfpenny. **2** colloq. a negligible amount (esp. after neg.: doesn't make a halfpennyworth of difference).

halfway /hɑːfˈweɪ, ˈhɑːfweɪ/ adv. & adj. —adv. at a point equidistant between two others (we were halfway to Rome). **2** US to some extent; more or less (is halfway decent). —adj. situated halfway (reached a halfway point). □ **halfway house 1** a compromise. **2** the halfway point in a progression. **3** a centre for rehabilitating ex-prisoners, mental patients, or others unused to normal life. **4** an inn midway between two towns. **halfway line** a line midway between the ends of a pitch, esp. in football.

halfwit /ˈhɑːfwɪt/ n. **1** colloq. an extremely foolish or stupid person. **2** a person who is mentally deficient. □□ **halfwitted** /-ˈwɪtɪd/ adj. **halfwittedly** /-ˈwɪtɪdlɪ/ adv. **halfwittedness** /-ˈwɪtɪdnɪs/ n.

halibut /ˈhælɪbət/ n. (also **holibut** /ˈhɒl-/) (pl. same) a large marine flat-fish, Hippoglossus vulgaris, used as food. [ME f. haly HOLY + BUTT[3] flat-fish, perh. because eaten on holy days]

Halicarnassus /ˌhælɪkɑːˈnæsəs/ (now Bodrum in Turkey) an ancient Greek city on the SW coast of Asia Minor, birthplace of the historian Herodotus and site of the Mausoleum, tomb of the local dynast Mausolus (d. 353 BC), which was one of the Seven Wonders of the World.

halide /ˈhælaɪd, ˈheɪl-/ n. Chem. **1** a binary compound of a halogen with another group or element. **2** any organic compound containing a halogen.

halieutic /ˌhælɪˈjuːtɪk/ adj. formal of or concerning fishing. [L halieuticus f. Gk halieutikos f. halieutēs fisherman]

Halifax /ˈhælɪˌfæks/ the capital of Nova Scotia, and Canada's principal ice-free port on the eastern seaboard; pop. (1986) 113,577; metropolitan area pop. 296,000. Originally a French fishing station, it was settled in 1749 by the English, who named it after the second earl of Halifax, President of the Board of Trade and Plantations.

haliotis /ˌhælɪˈəʊtɪs/ n. any edible gastropod mollusc of the genus *Haliotis* with an ear-shaped shell lined with mother-of-pearl. [Gk *hals hali-* sea + *ous ōt-* ear]

halite /ˈhælaɪt/ n. rock-salt. [mod.L *halites* f. Gk *hals* salt]

halitosis /ˌhælɪˈtəʊsɪs/ n. = *bad breath*. [mod.L f. L *halitus* breath]

hall /hɔːl/ n. **1 a** a space or passage into which the front entrance of a house etc. opens. **b** *US* a corridor or passage in a building. **2 a** a large room or building for meetings, meals, concerts, etc. **b** (in *pl.*) music-halls. **3** a large country house, esp. with a landed estate. **4** (in full **hall of residence**) a university residence for students. **5 a** (in a college etc.) a common dining-room. **b** dinner in this. **6** the building of a guild (*Fishmongers' Hall*). **7 a** a large public room in a palace etc. **b** the principal living-room of a medieval house. □ **Hall of Fame** *US* a building with memorials of celebrated people. **hall porter** *Brit.* a porter who carries baggage etc. in a hotel. **hall-stand** a stand in the hall of a house, with a mirror, pegs, etc. [OE = *hall* f. Gmc, rel. to HELL]

hallal var. of HALAL.

Halle /ˈhælə/ a city in central Germany, on the River Saale; pop. (1986) 234,700. The composer Handel was born here in 1685.

Hallé /ˈhæleɪ/, Sir Charles (original name Karl Halle, 1819–95), German-born pianist and conductor, a friend of Chopin, Liszt, Berloiz, and other major composers. He came to Manchester from Paris in 1848 to escape the revolution and remained there for the rest of his life. In 1858 he founded his own series of orchestral concerts, thereby inaugurating what are still known as the Hallé Orchestra and Hallé Concerts.

hallelujah var. of ALLELUIA.

Halley /ˈhælɪ, ˈhɔlɪ/, Edmond (1656–1742), English astronomer and mathematician, an influential Fellow of the Royal Society and friend of Newton, the publication of whose *Principia* was due largely to him. He became Professor of Geometry at Oxford University in 1703 (he was refused the chair of astronomy owing to a suspicion, which he vainly tried to combat, of his holding materialistic views), and was appointed Astronomer Royal in 1720. Halley was involved in most of the weighty astronomical problems of his day, realizing in particular that the nebulae were clouds of luminous gas among the stars and that the aurora was a phenomenon connected with the Earth's magnetism. He is best known for the prediction, published in 1705, that a bright comet seen in 1531, 1607, and 1682 would reappear in 1758. □ **Halley's comet** a bright comet whose reappearance in 1758 was predicted by Halley. Its orbital period is about 76 years (varying slightly, depending on gravitational perturbations by the planet Jupiter), and earlier appearances can be traced in historical documents. It is first recorded in 240 BC; a representation of its appearance in 1066 is visible on the Bayeux Tapestry.

halliard var. of HALYARD.

hallmark /ˈhɔːlmɑːk/ n. & v. —n. **1** a mark used at Goldsmiths' Hall (and by the UK assay offices) for marking the standard of gold, silver, and (since 1975) platinum. (See below.) **2** any distinctive feature esp. of excellence. —v.tr. **1** stamp with a hallmark. **2** designate as excellent.

In the UK hallmarking dates from a statute of 1300, in the reign of Edward I. The Worshipful Company of Goldsmiths has been responsible for the assaying and marking of plate in London since then, and there are assay offices in certain other towns also. With certain exceptions, all gold, silver, and platinum articles are required by law to be hallmarked before they are offered for sale. The marks impressed include a number of symbols indicating the maker, standard, date, and office. Many countries outside the UK have a system of plate marks. In the US there is no hallmarking; local regulations existed in the 18th and 19th c., but there is no consistent system of symbols. Signatory countries of the International Convention—the UK,

Austria, Finland, Ireland, Portugal, Norway, Sweden, and Switzerland—recognize equivalents to their own hallmarks applied in the others.

hallo var. of HELLO.

halloo /həˈluː/ int., n., & v. —int. **1** inciting dogs to the chase. **2** calling attention. **3** expressing surprise. —n. the cry 'halloo'. —v. (**halloos**, **hallooed**) **1** intr. cry 'halloo', esp. to dogs. **2** intr. shout to attract attention. **3** tr. urge on (dogs etc.) with shouts. [perh. f. *hallow* pursue with shouts f. OF *halloer* (imit.)]

hallow /ˈhæləʊ/ v. & n. —v.tr. **1** make holy, consecrate. **2** honour as holy. —n. *archaic* a saint or holy person. □ **All Hallows** All Saints' Day, 1 Nov. [OE *hālgian*, *hālga* f. Gmc]

Hallowe'en /ˌhæləʊˈiːn/ n. the eve of All Saints' Day, 31 Oct. [HALLOW + EVEN²]

Hallowes /ˈhæləʊz/, Odette Marie Celine (1912–), French-born heroine of the Second World War, who entered occupied France in 1942 and worked secretly as a British agent until captured by the Gestapo in 1943. Imprisoned until 1945, in spite of torture she refused to betray her associates. For her work and her courage she was awarded the George Cross (1946).

Hallstatt /ˈhɑːlʃtɑːt/ adj. of or relating to a phase of the late Bronze–early Iron Age, (c.700–500 BC), preceding the La Tène, named after a village in Austria, site of an ancient necropolis, where remains of the period were found.

halluces pl. of HALLUX.

hallucinate /həˈluːsɪˌneɪt/ v. **1** tr. produce illusions in the mind of (a person). **2** intr. experience hallucinations. □□ **hallucinant** adj. & n. **hallucinator** n. [L (h)*allucinari* wander in mind f. Gk *alussō* be uneasy]

hallucination /həˌluːsɪˈneɪʃ(ə)n/ n. the apparent or alleged perception of an object not actually present. □□ **hallucinatory** /həˈluːsɪnətərɪ/ adj. [L *hallucinatio* (as HALLUCINATE)]

hallucinogen /həˈluːsɪnədʒ(ə)n/ n. a drug causing hallucinations. □□ **hallucinogenic** /-ˈdʒenɪk/ adj.

hallux /ˈhæləks/ n. (pl. **halluces** /-juːˌsiːz/) **1** the big toe. **2** the innermost digit of the hind foot of vertebrates. [mod.L f. L *allex*]

hallway /ˈhɔːlweɪ/ n. an entrance-hall or corridor.

halm var. of HAULM.

halma /ˈhælmə/ n. a game played by two or four persons on a board of 256 squares, with men advancing from one corner to the opposite corner by being moved over other men into vacant squares. It dates from c.1880. [Gk, = leap]

Halmahera /ˌhælməˈhɑːrə/ the largest of the Molucca Islands.

halo /ˈheɪləʊ/ n. & v. —n. (pl. **-oes**) **1** a disc or circle of light shown surrounding the head of a sacred person. **2** the glory associated with an idealized person etc. **3** a circle of white or coloured light round a luminous body, esp. the sun or moon, caused by the refraction of light through vapour. **4** a circle or ring. —v.tr. (**-oes**, **-oed**) surround with a halo. [med.L f. L f. Gk *halōs* threshing-floor, disc of the sun or moon]

halogen /ˈhæləedʒ(ə)n/ n. *Chem.* any of the group of five chemically related non-metallic elements fluorine, chlorine, bromine, iodine, and astatine. Only iodine and astatine are solids at room temperature. All the halogens display a valency of 1 and form simple salts, such as common salt, with alkali metals. Being very reactive, they are not found in the free state in nature. □□ **halogenic** /-ˈdʒenɪk/ adj. [Gk *hals halos* salt]

halogenation /ˌhælədʒɪˈneɪʃ(ə)n/ n. the introduction of a halogen atom into a molecule.

halon /ˈheɪlɒn/ n. *Chem.* any of various gaseous compounds of carbon, bromine, and other halogens, used to extinguish fires. [as HALOGEN + -ON]

Hals /hæls/, Frans (1581/5–1666), Dutch painter who spent his life in Haarlem, specializing in portraits. His early life is obscure, but in 1616 his *Banquet of the Officers of the St George Militia Company* shattered well-established traditions with its unprecedentedly vigorous characterization. By exploiting facial expression and using bold brushwork Hals sought in his portraits to capture the character and vitality of the individual rather than producing a map-like record of the features. His genre pictures, which reflect the influence of the Dutch followers of Caravaggio, also have a

b *but* d *dog* f *few* g *get* h *he* j *yes* k *cat* l *leg* m *man* n *no* p *pen* r *red* s *sit* t *top* v *voice*

portrait-like quality. A late phase of sober restraint culminated in the group portraits of the *Regents* and *Regentesses of the Old Men's Alms House* (Haarlem, 1664) which are among the most moving portraits ever painted. Two of Hals' brothers, Dirk and Joost, and five of his sons, were also artists, but none approached his level.

halt[1] /hɒlt, hɔːlt/ n. & v. —n. 1 a stop (usu. temporary); an interruption of progress (*come to a halt*). 2 a temporary stoppage on a march or journey. 3 *Brit.* a minor stopping-place on a local railway line, usu. without permanent buildings. —v.intr. & tr. stop; come or bring to a halt. □ **call a halt (to)** decide to stop. [orig. in phr. *make halt* f. G *Halt machen* f. *halten* hold, stop]

halt[2] /hɒlt, hɔːlt/ v. & adj. —v.intr. 1 (esp. as **halting** adj.) lack smooth progress. 2 hesitate (*halt between two opinions*). 3 walk hesitatingly. 4 *archaic* be lame. —adj. *archaic* lame or crippled. □□ **haltingly** adv. [OE *halt, healt, healtian* f. Gmc]

halter /ˈhɒltə(r), ˈhɔːl-/ n. & v. —n. 1 a rope or strap with a noose or headstall for horses or cattle. 2 a a strap round the back of a woman's neck holding her dress-top and leaving her shoulders and back bare. b a dress-top held by this. 3 a a rope with a noose for hanging a person. b death by hanging. —v.tr. 1 put a halter on (a horse etc.). 2 hang (a person) with a halter. □ **halter-break** accustom (a horse) to a halter. [OE *hælftre*: cf. HELVE]

halteres /hælˈtɪəriːz/ n.pl. the balancing-organs of dipterous insects. [Gk, = weights used to aid leaping f. *hallomai* to leap]

halva /ˈhælvɑː/ n. (also **halvah**) a sweet confection of sesame flour and honey. [Yiddish f. Turk. *helva* f. Arab. *ḥalwa*]

halve /hɑːv/ v.tr. 1 divide into two halves or parts. 2 reduce by half. 3 share equally (with another person etc.). 4 *Golf* use the same number of strokes as one's opponent in (a hole or match). 5 fit (crossing timbers) together by cutting out half the thickness of each. [ME *halfen* f. HALF]

halves pl. of HALF.

halyard /ˈhæljəd/ n. (also **halliard, haulyard** /ˈhɔːljəd/) *Naut.* a rope or tackle for raising or lowering a sail or yard etc. [ME *halier* f. HALE[2] + -IER, assoc. with YARD[1]]

Ham /hæm/ a son of Noah (Gen. 10: 1), traditional ancestor of the Hamites.

ham /hæm/ n. & v. —n. 1 a the upper part of a pig's leg salted and dried or smoked for food. b the meat from this. 2 the back of the thigh; the thigh and buttock. 3 *sl.* (often *attrib.*) an inexpert or unsubtle actor or piece of acting. 4 (in full **radio ham**) *colloq.* the operator of an amateur radio station. —v.intr. & (often foll. by *up*) tr. (**hammed, hamming**) *sl.* overact; act or treat emotionally or sentimentally. [OE *ham, hom* f. a Gmc root meaning 'be crooked']

Hamada /ˈhæmədə/, Shoji (1894–1978), Japanese potter, designated a 'living national treasure' by his government. His art was based upon natural materials, and his style aimed at an unpretentious simplicity. Hamada was a close friend of Bernard Leach (see entry) with whom he collaborated before returning to Japan in 1923 to set up his own kiln at Mashiko, afterwards continuing to work and lecture with the English potter.

hamadryad /ˌhæməˈdraɪjæd/ n. 1 *Gk & Rom. Mythol.* a nymph who lives in a tree and dies when it dies. 2 the king cobra, *Naja bungarus*. [ME f. L *hamadryas* f. Gk *hamadruas* f. *hama* with + *drus* tree]

hamadryas /ˌhæməˈdraɪəs/ n. a large Arabian baboon, *Papio hamadryas*, with a silvery-grey cape of hair over the shoulders, held sacred in ancient Egypt.

hamamelis /ˌhæməˈmiːlɪs/ n. any shrub of the genus *Hamamelis*, e.g. witch-hazel. [mod.L f. Gk *hamamēlis* medlar]

hamba /ˈhæmbə/ int. *S.Afr.* be off; go away. [Nguni *-hambe* go]

Hamburg /ˈhæmbɜːg/ a city and port of Germany, on the River Elbe, constituting a 'Land' (State); pop. (1987) 1,571,300.

hamburger /ˈhæmˌbɜːgə(r)/ n. a cake of minced beef usu. fried or grilled and eaten in a soft bread roll. [G, = of Hamburg in Germany]

hames /heɪmz/ n.pl. two curved pieces of iron or wood forming the collar or part of the collar of a draught-horse, to which the traces are attached. [ME f. MDu. *hame*]

ham-fisted /hæmˈfɪstɪd/ adj. *colloq.* clumsy, heavy-handed, bungling. □□ **ham-fistedly** adv. **ham-fistedness** n.

ham-handed /hæmˈhændɪd/ adj. *colloq.* = HAM-FISTED. □□ **ham-handedly** adv. **ham-handedness** n.

Hamilcar /ˈhæmɪlˌkɑː(r)/, (d. 229/8 BC) Carthaginian general and father of Hannibal, who fought Rome in the First Punic War and negotiated terms of peace after the Carthaginian defeat of 241 BC, which led to the loss of Sicily to the Romans. From 237 BC he and Hannibal were engaged in the conquest of Spain.

Hamilton[1] /ˈhæmɪlt(ə)n/ the capital of the Bermuda Islands; pop. (1980) 1,617.

Hamilton[2] /ˈhæmɪlt(ə)n/ a port and industrial city of Canada, at the west end of Lake Ontario; pop. (1986) 306,700; metropolitan area pop. 557,000. The city was founded in 1813 by George Hamilton, a local landowner.

Hamilton[3] /ˈhæmɪlt(ə)n/ the largest inland city of New Zealand, situated in Waikato region, North Island; pop. (1988) 103,500.

Hamilton[4] /ˈhæmɪlt(ə)n/, Sir William Rowan (1806–65), Irish mathematician and physicist, who made influential contributions to optics and in the foundations of algebra. His approach to mathematical physics was the only classical approach that met the needs of quantum theory (see entry).

Hamite /ˈhæmaɪt/ n. a member of a group of North African peoples, including the ancient Egyptians and Berbers, supposedly descended from Ham.

Hamitic /həˈmɪtɪk/ n. & adj. —n. a group of African languages including ancient Egyptian, Berber, and Cushitic, probably related in the past to the Semitic languages. adj. 1 of or relating to this group of languages. 2 of or relating to the Hamites.

Hamito-Semitic /ˌhæmɪtəʊsɪˈmɪtɪk/ adj. of or relating to a family of languages (also known as *Afro-Asiatic*) spoken in the Middle East and in northern Africa. They can be divided into five groups: Semitic, Berber, Cushitic (spoken mainly in Ethiopia and Somalia), Chadic (which includes Hausa), and Egyptian.

Hamlet /ˈhæmlɪt/ a legendary prince of Denmark, hero of a tragedy by Shakespeare. □ **Hamlet without the Prince** an entertainment etc. from which the chief personage is absent.

hamlet /ˈhæmlɪt/ n. a small village, esp. one without a church. [ME f. AF *hamelet(t)e*, OF *hamelet* dimin. of *hamel* dimin. of *ham* f. MLG *hamm*]

Hammamet /ˈhæməˌmet/ a resort town in NE Tunisia, on the Cape Bon peninsula.

hammer /ˈhæmə(r)/ n. & v. —n. 1 a a tool with a heavy metal head at right angles to the handle, used for breaking, driving nails, etc. b a machine with a metal block serving the same purpose. c a similar contrivance, as for exploding the charge in a gun, striking the strings of a piano, etc. 2 an auctioneer's mallet, indicating by a rap that an article is sold. 3 a a metal ball of about 7 kg, attached to a wire for throwing in an athletic contest. b the sport of throwing the hammer. 4 a bone of the middle ear; the malleus. —v. 1 a tr. & intr. hit or beat with or as with a hammer. b intr. strike loudly; knock violently (esp. on a door). 2 tr. a drive in (nails) with a hammer. b fasten or secure by hammering (*hammered the lid down*). 3 tr. (often foll. by *in*) inculcate (ideas, knowledge, etc.) forcefully or repeatedly. 4 tr. *colloq.* utterly defeat; inflict heavy damage on. 5 intr. (foll. by *at, away at*) work hard or persistently at. 6 tr. *Stock Exch.* declare (a person or a firm) a defaulter; announce on the International Stock Exchange in London that (a named broker) is unable to comply with his bargains. Until 1970 the announcement was introduced by three blows of a hammer and followed by the broker's name. □ **come under the hammer** be sold at an auction. **hammer and sickle** the symbols of the industrial worker and the peasant used as the emblem of the USSR and of international communism. **hammer and tongs** *colloq.* with great vigour and commotion. **hammer out** 1 make flat or smooth by hammering. 2 work out the details of (a plan, agreement, etc.) laboriously. 3 play (a tune, esp. on the piano) loudly or clumsily. **hammer-toe** a deformity in which the toe is bent permanently downwards. □□ **hammering** n. (esp. in sense 4 of v.). **hammerless** adj. [OE *hamor, hamer*]

hammerbeam /ˈhæməˌbiːm/ n. a wooden beam (often carved)

projecting from a wall to support the principal rafter or the end of an arch.

Hammerfest /ˈhæməˌfest/ a port in NW Norway, on Kvaløy island; pop. (est. 1985) 7,500. It is the northernmost town of Europe.

hammerhead /ˈhæməˌhed/ n. **1** any shark of the family Sphyrinidae, with a flattened head and eyes in lateral extensions of it. **2** a long-legged African marsh-bird, *Scopus umbretta*, with a thick bill and an occipital crest.

hammerlock /ˈhæməˌlɒk/ n. *Wrestling* a hold in which the arm is twisted and bent behind the back.

Hammerstein /ˈhæməˌstaɪn/, Oscar (1895–1960), American librettist and song-writer, who collaborated with the composers Kern (e.g. in *Showboat*, 1927), Romberg, and most notably with Richard Rodgers (see entry). He also wrote the libretto for *Carmen Jones* (1943), the successful adaptation of the opera *Carmen* as a musical.

Hammett /ˈhæmɪt/, (Samuel) Dashiell (1894–1961), American writer of detective fiction, whose tough realistic style, based in part on his own experiences as a detective in San Francisco, influenced Raymond Chandler and other writers. Several of Hammett's stories, including *The Maltese Falcon* (1930) and *The Thin Man* (1932), were made into successful films, and he himself worked as a screenwriter in Hollywood. For many years he lived with the playwright Lillian Hellman (see entry).

hammock /ˈhæmək/ n. a bed of canvas or rope network, suspended by cords at the ends, used esp. on board ship. [earlier *hamaca* f. Sp., of Carib orig.]

Hammurabi /ˌhæmjʊəˈrɑːbɪ/ (d. 1750 BC), the sixth king of the first dynasty of Babylonia. He is best known for his code of laws, drawn up late in his reign, and inscribed in Akkadian on an upright slab (now in the Louvre) originally set up in the temple of the god Marduk in Babylon. The code, in the form of 282 case laws, deals with economic provisions and with family, criminal, and civil law, providing crucial insight into the contemporary social organization.

hammy /ˈhæmɪ/ adj. (**hammier**, **hammiest**) **1** of or like ham. **2** *colloq.* (of an actor or acting) over-theatrical.

hamper¹ /ˈhæmpə(r)/ n. **1** a large basket usu. with a hinged lid and containing food (*picnic hamper*). **2** *Brit.* a selection of food, drink, etc., for an occasion. [ME f. obs. *hanaper*, AF f. OF *hanapier* case for a goblet f. *hanap* goblet]

hamper² /ˈhæmpə(r)/ v. & n. —v.tr. **1** prevent the free movement or activity of. **2** impede, hinder. —n. *Naut.* necessary but cumbersome equipment on a ship. [ME: orig. unkn.]

Hampshire /ˈhæmpʃɪə(r)/ a county of southern England; pop. (1981) 1,488,000; county town, Winchester.

Hampton Court /ˈhæmpt(ə)n/ a palace on the north bank of the Thames in the borough of Richmond, London. It was built by Cardinal Wolsey as his private residence but later presented by him to Henry VIII, and was a favourite royal residence until the reign of George II. William III had part rebuilt by Sir Christopher Wren and the gardens laid out in formal Dutch style.

hamsin var. of KHAMSIN.

hamster /ˈhæmstə(r)/ n. any of various rodents of the subfamily Cricetinae, esp. *Cricetus cricetus*, having a short tail and large cheek pouches for storing food, kept as a pet or laboratory animal. [G f. OHG *hamustro* corn-weevil]

hamstring /ˈhæmstrɪŋ/ n. & v. *Anat.* —n. **1** each of five tendons at the back of the knee in humans. **2** the great tendon at the back of the hock in quadrupeds. —v.tr. (*past* and *past part.* **hamstrung** or **hamstringed**) **1** cripple by cutting the hamstrings of (a person or animal). **2** prevent the activity or efficiency of (a person or enterprise).

hamulus /ˈhæmjʊləs/ n. (pl. **hamuli** /-ˌlaɪ/) *Anat., Zool., & Bot.* a hooklike process. [L, dimin. of *hamus* hook]

Han /hæn/ the name of the Chinese dynasty that ruled from 206 BC until AD 220 with only a brief interruption. During this period the territory was expanded, administration was in the hands of an organized civil service, Confucianism was recognized as the State philosophy, and detailed historical records

were kept. The arts flourished, and technological advances included the invention of paper. It was to this era that later dynasties looked for their model.

hand /hænd/ n. & v. —n. **1 a** the end part of the human arm beyond the wrist, including the fingers and thumb. **b** in other primates, the end part of a forelimb, also used as a foot. **2 a** (often in *pl.*) control, management, custody, disposal (*is in good hands*). **b** agency or influence (*suffered at their hands*). **c** a share in an action; active support. **3** a thing compared with a hand or its functions, esp. the pointer of a clock or watch. **4** the right or left side or direction relative to a person or thing. **5 a** a skill, esp. in something practical (*a hand for making pastry*). **b** a person skilful in some respect. **6** a person who does or makes something, esp. distinctively (*a picture by the same hand*). **7** an individual's writing or the style of this; a signature (*a legible hand; in one's own hand; witness the hand of . . .*). **8** a person etc. as the source of information etc. (*at first hand*). **9** a pledge of marriage. **10** a person as a source of manual labour esp. in a factory, on a farm, or on board ship. **11 a** the playing-cards dealt to a player. **b** the player holding these. **c** a round of play. **12** *colloq.* applause (*got a big hand*). **13** the unit of measure of a horse's height, equal to 4 inches (10.16 cm). **14** a forehock of pork. **15** a bunch of bananas. **16** (*attrib.*) **a** operated or held in the hand (*hand-drill; hand-luggage*). **b** done by hand and not by machine (*hand-knitted*). —v.tr. **1** (foll. by *in, to, over,* etc.) deliver; transfer by hand or otherwise. **2** convey verbally (*handed me a lot of abuse*). **3** *colloq.* give away too readily (*handed them the advantage*). □ **all hands 1** the entire crew of a ship. **2** the entire workforce. **at hand 1** close by. **2** about to happen. **by hand 1** by a person and not a machine. **2** delivered privately and not by the public post. **from hand to mouth** satisfying only one's immediate needs (also *attrib.*: *a hand-to-mouth existence*). **get** (or **have** or **keep**) **one's hand in** become (or be or remain) practised in something. **give** (or **lend**) **a hand** assist in an action or enterprise. **hand and foot** completely; satisfying all demands (*waited on them hand and foot*). **hand-axe** a prehistoric stone implement, normally oval or pear-shaped and bifacially worked, used for cutting and scraping things as well as for chopping. **hand cream** an emollient for the hands. **hand down 1** pass the ownership or use of to another. **2 a** transmit (a decision) from a higher court etc. **b** *US* express (an opinion or verdict). **hand-grenade** see GRENADE. **hand in glove** in collusion or association. **hand in hand** in close association. **hand it to** *colloq.* acknowledge the merit of (a person). **hand-me-down** an article of clothing etc. passed on from another person. **hand off** *Rugby Football* push off (a tackling opponent) with the hand. **hand on** pass (a thing) to the next in a series or succession. **hand out 1** serve, distribute. **2** award, allocate (*the judges handed out stiff sentences*). **hand-out 1** something given free to a needy person. **2** a statement given to the press etc. **hand over** deliver; surrender possession of. **hand-over** n. the act or an instance of handing over. **hand-over-fist** *colloq.* with rapid progress. **hand-pick** choose carefully or personally. **hand-picked** carefully or personally chosen. **hand round** distribute. **hands down** (esp. of winning) with no difficulty. **hands off 1** a warning not to touch or interfere with something. **2** *Computing* etc. not requiring manual use of controls. **hands on** *Computing* of or requiring personal operation at a keyboard. **hands up!** an instruction to raise one's hands in surrender or to signify assent or participation. **hand-to-hand** (of fighting) at close quarters. **have** (or **take**) **a hand in** share or take part in. **have one's hands full** be fully occupied. **have one's hands tied** *colloq.* be unable to act. **hold one's hand** = *stay one's hand* (see HAND). **in hand 1** receiving attention. **2** in reserve; at one's disposal. **3** under one's control. **lay** (or **put**) **one's hands on** see LAY¹. **off one's hands** no longer one's responsibility. **on every hand** (or **all hands**) to or from all directions. **on hand** available. **on one's hands** resting on one as a responsibility. **on the one** (or **the other**) **hand** from one (or another) point of view. **out of hand 1** out of control. **2** peremptorily (*refused out of hand*). **put** (or **set**) **one's hand to** start work on; engage in. **stay one's hand** *archaic* or *literary* refrain from action. **to hand 1** within easy reach. **2** (of a letter) received. **turn one's hand to** undertake (as a new activity). □□ **handed** *adj.* **handless** *adj.* [OE *hand, hond*]

handbag /ˈhændbæg/ *n. & v.* —*n.* a small bag for a purse etc., carried esp. by a woman. —*v.tr.* (of a woman politician) treat (a person, idea, etc.) ruthlessly or insensitively.

handball *n.* 1 /ˈhændbɔːl/ a game with a ball thrown by hand among players or against a wall. Various handball games were played in ancient times (one is mentioned in the *Odyssey*), but the term is now usually applied to one played between two goals or in a walled court. An annual contest, usually on a holiday in spring, is an ancient institution in towns, villages, and parishes in southern Scotland. 2 /hændˈbɔːl/ *Football* intentional touching of the ball with the hand or arm by a player other than the goalkeeper in the goal area, constituting a foul.

handbell /ˈhændbel/ *n.* a small bell, usu. tuned to a particular note and rung by hand, esp. one of a set giving a range of notes.

handbill /ˈhændbɪl/ *n.* a printed notice distributed by hand.

handbook /ˈhændbʊk/ *n.* a short manual or guidebook.

handbrake /ˈhændbreɪk/ *n.* a brake operated by hand.

h. & c. *abbr.* hot and cold (water).

handcart /ˈhændkɑːt/ *n.* a small cart pushed or drawn by hand.

handclap /ˈhændklæp/ *n.* a clapping of the hands.

handcraft /ˈhændkrɑːft/ *n. & v.* —*n.* = HANDICRAFT. —*v.tr.* make by handicraft.

handcuff /ˈhændkʌf/ *n. & v.* —*n.* (in *pl.*) a pair of lockable linked metal rings for securing a prisoner's wrists. —*v.tr.* put handcuffs on.

-handed /ˈhændɪd/ *adj.* (in *comb.*) 1 for or involving a specified number of hands (in various senses) (*two-handed*). 2 using chiefly the hand specified (*left-handed*). □□ **-handedly** *adv.* **-handedness** *n.* (both in sense 2).

Handel /ˈhænd(ə)l/, George Frederick (1685–1759), German-born composer, who settled in London in 1712 and became English by naturalization. His patrons in England included George I, for whom he composed the *Water Music* suite (*c.*1717). Handel stands in complete contrast to his great contemporary, Bach: his way of life was cosmopolitan, he had a natural feeling for the dramatic and the personal in music, and he was in touch with all the modern styles and developments. Like Bach he was a noted organist; most of his works for that instrument are organ concertos, a form invented by him and intended to be performed between the acts of his own oratorios. Superb as are his instrumental compositions it is in the operas and oratorios that the nobility, expressiveness, and captivation of his art are found at their highest degree of development. Handel's English oratorios, perhaps his most original contribution to the art of music, became and have remained an institution in this country. The *Messiah* (1742), by which his name is known throughout the world, takes words directly from the Bible and is without a plot in the usual sense, but more typical of his concept of oratorio as biblical stories expressed in musical drama are *Alexander's Feast* (1736), *Saul* (1739), *Belshazzar* (1745), and *Judas Maccabaeus* (1747). For the last seven years of his life Handel was blind, yet he continued to conduct oratorio performances and to revise his scores. The popularity of his work dominated English music for nearly 150 years. He died a national figure, and so has remained; he is buried in Westminster Abbey.

handful /ˈhændfʊl/ *n.* (*pl.* **-fuls**) 1 a quantity that fills the hand. 2 a small number or amount. 3 *colloq.* a troublesome person or task.

handglass /ˈhændɡlɑːs/ *n.* 1 a magnifying glass held in the hand. 2 a small mirror with a handle.

handgrip /ˈhændɡrɪp/ *n.* 1 a grasp with the hand. 2 a handle designed for easy holding.

handgun /ˈhændɡʌn/ *n.* a small firearm held in and fired with one hand.

handhold /ˈhændhəʊld/ *n.* something for the hands to grip on (in climbing, sailing, etc.).

handicap /ˈhændɪkæp/ *n. & v.* —*n.* 1 a a disadvantage imposed on a superior competitor in order to make the chances more equal. b a race or contest in which this is imposed. 2 the number

of strokes by which a golfer normally exceeds par for the course. 3 a thing that makes progress or success difficult. 4 a physical or mental disability. —*v.tr.* (**handicapped**, **handicapping**) 1 impose a handicap on. 2 place (a person) at a disadvantage. □□ **handicapper** *n.* [prob. from the phrase *hand i'* (= in) *cap* describing a kind of sporting lottery]

handicapped /ˈhændɪˌkæpt/ *adj.* suffering from a physical or mental disability.

handicraft /ˈhændɪˌkrɑːft/ *n.* work that requires both manual and artistic skill. [ME, alt. of earlier HANDCRAFT after HANDIWORK]

handiwork /ˈhændɪˌwɜːk/ *n.* work done or a thing made by hand, or by a particular person. [OE *handgeweorc*]

handkerchief /ˈhæŋkətʃɪf, -ˌtʃiːf/ *n.* (*pl.* **handkerchiefs** or **-chieves** /-ˌtʃiːvz/) a square of cotton, linen, silk, etc., usu. carried in the pocket for wiping one's nose, etc.

handle /ˈhænd(ə)l/ *n. & v.* —*n.* 1 the part by which a thing is held, carried, or controlled. 2 a fact that may be taken advantage of (*gave a handle to his critics*). 3 *colloq.* a personal title. 4 the feel of goods, esp. textiles, when handled. —*v.tr.* 1 touch, feel, operate, or move with the hands. 2 manage or deal with; treat in a particular or correct way (*knows how to handle people; unable to handle the situation*). 3 deal in (goods). 4 discuss or write about (a subject). □ **get a handle on** *colloq.* understand the basis of or reason for a situation, circumstance, etc. □□ **handleable** *adj.* **handleability** /-ˈbɪlɪtɪ/ *n.* **handled** *adj.* (also in *comb.*). [OE *handle, handlian* (as HAND)]

handlebar /ˈhænd(ə)lˌbɑːr/ *n.* (often in *pl.*) the steering bar of a bicycle etc., with a handgrip at each end. □ **handlebar moustache** a thick moustache with curved ends.

handler /ˈhændlə(r)/ *n.* 1 a person who handles or deals in certain commodities. 2 a person who trains and looks after an animal (esp. a police dog).

handlist /ˈhændlɪst/ *n.* a short list of essential reading, reference books, etc.

handmade /hændˈmeɪd/ *adj.* made by hand and not by machine, esp. as designating superior quality.

handmaid /ˈhændmeɪd/ *n.* (also **handmaiden** /-ˌmeɪd(ə)n/) *archaic* a female servant or helper.

handrail /ˈhændreɪl/ *n.* a narrow rail for holding as a support on stairs etc.

handsaw /ˈhændsɔː/ *n.* a saw worked by one hand.

handsel /ˈhæns(ə)l/ *n. & v.* (also **hansel**) —*n.* 1 a gift at the beginning of the new year, or on coming into new circumstances. 2 = EARNEST² 1. 3 a foretaste. —*v.tr.* (**handselled**, **handselling**; *US* **handseled**, **handseling**) 1 give a handsel to. 2 inaugurate. 3 be the first to try. [ME, corresp. to OE *handselen* giving into a person's hands, ON *handsal* giving of the hand (esp. in promise), formed as HAND + OE *sellan* SELL]

handset /ˈhændset/ *n.* a telephone mouthpiece and earpiece forming one unit.

handshake /ˈhændʃeɪk/ *n.* the shaking of a person's hand with one's own as a greeting etc.

handsome /ˈhænsəm/ *adj.* (**handsomer**, **handsomest**) 1 (of a person) good-looking. 2 (of a building etc.) imposing, attractive. 3 a generous, liberal (*a handsome present; handsome treatment*). b (of a price, fortune, etc., as assets gained) considerable. □□ **handsomeness** *n.* [ME, = easily handled, f. HAND + -SOME¹]

handsomely /ˈhænsəmlɪ/ *adv.* 1 generously, liberally. 2 finely, beautifully. 3 *Naut.* carefully.

handspike /ˈhændspaɪk/ *n.* a wooden rod shod with iron, used on board ship and by artillery soldiers.

handspring /ˈhændsprɪŋ/ *n.* a somersault in which one lands first on the hands and then on the feet.

handstand /ˈhændstænd/ *n.* balancing on one's hands with the feet in the air or against a wall.

handwork /ˈhændwɜːk/ *n.* work done with the hands, esp. as opposed to machinery. □□ **handworked** *adj.*

handwriting /ˈhændˌraɪtɪŋ/ *n.* 1 writing with a pen, pencil, etc. 2 a person's particular style of writing. □□ **handwritten** /-ˌrɪt(ə)n/ *adj.*

handy /ˈhændɪ/ adj. (**handier**, **handiest**) **1** convenient to handle or use; useful. **2** ready to hand; placed or occurring conveniently. **3** clever with the hands. □□ **handily** adv. **handiness** n.

handyman /ˈhændɪˌmæn/ n. (pl. **-men**) a person able or employed to do occasional domestic repairs and minor renovations.

hang /hæŋ/ v. & n. —v. (past and past part. **hung** /hʌŋ/ except in sense 7) **1** tr. **a** secure or cause to be supported from above, esp. with the lower part free. **b** (foll. by up, on, on to, etc.) attach loosely by suspending from the top. **2** tr. set up (a door, gate, etc.) on its hinges so that it moves freely. **3** tr. place (a picture) on a wall or in an exhibition. **4** tr. attach (wallpaper) in vertical strips to a wall. **5** tr. (foll. by on) colloq. attach the blame for (a thing) to (a person) (you can't hang that on me). **6** tr. (foll. by with) decorate by hanging pictures or decorations etc. (a hall hung with tapestries). **7** tr. & intr. (past and past part. **hanged**) **a** suspend or be suspended by the neck with a noosed rope until dead, esp. as a form of capital punishment. **b** as a mild oath (hang the expense; let everything go hang). **8** tr. let droop (hang one's head). **9** tr. suspend (meat or game) from a hook and leave it until dry or tender or high. **10** intr. be or remain hung (in various senses). **11** intr. remain static in the air. **12** intr. (often foll. by over) be present or imminent, esp. oppressively or threateningly (a hush hung over the room). **13** intr. (foll. by on) **a** be contingent or dependent on (everything hangs on the discussions). **b** listen closely to (hangs on their every word). —n. **1** the way a thing hangs or falls. **2** a downward droop or bend. □ **get the hang of** colloq. understand the technique or meaning of. **hang about** (or **around**) **1** loiter or dally; not move away. **2** (foll. by with) associate with (a person etc.). **hang back 1** show reluctance to act or move. **2** remain behind. **hang fire** be slow in taking action or in progressing. **hang heavily** (or **heavy**) (of time) pass slowly. **hang in** US colloq. **1** persist, persevere. **2** linger. **hang on** colloq. **1** continue or persevere, esp. with difficulty. **2** (often foll. by to) continue to hold or grasp. **3** (foll. by to) retain; fail to give back. **4 a** wait for a short time. **b** (in telephoning) continue to listen during a pause in the conversation. **hang out 1** hang from a window, clothes-line, etc. **2** protrude or cause to protrude downwards. **3** sl. reside or be often present. **4** (foll. by of) lean out of (a window etc.). **hang-out** n. sl. a place one lives in or frequently visits. **hang together 1** make sense. **2** remain associated. **hang up 1** hang from a hook, peg, etc. **2** (often foll. by on) end a telephone conversation, esp. abruptly (then he hung up on me). **3** cause delay or difficulty to. **4** (usu. in passive, foll. by on) sl. be a psychological or emotional obsession or problem to (is really hung up on her father). **hang-up** n. sl. an emotional problem or inhibition. **hung-over** colloq. suffering from a hangover. **hung parliament** a parliament in which no party has a clear majority. **let it all hang out** sl. be uninhibited or relaxed. **not care** (or **give**) **a hang** colloq. not care at all. [ON hanga (tr.) = OE hōn, & f. OE hangian (intr.), f. Gmc]

hangar /ˈhæŋə(r)/ n. a building with extensive floor area, for housing aircraft etc. □□ **hangarage** n. [F, of unkn. orig.]

hangdog /ˈhæŋdɒg/ adj. having a dejected or guilty appearance; shamefaced.

hanger¹ /ˈhæŋə(r)/ n. **1** a person or thing that hangs. **2** (in full **coat-hanger**) a shaped piece of wood or plastic etc. from which clothes may be hung. □ **hanger-on** (pl. **hangers-on**) a follower or dependant, esp. an unwelcome one.

hanger² /ˈhæŋə(r)/ n. Brit. a wood on the side of a steep hill. [OE hangra f. hangian HANG]

hang-glider /ˈhæŋˌglaɪdə(r)/ n. a frame with a fabric aerofoil stretched over it, from which the operator is suspended and controls flight by body movement. □□ **hang-glide** v.intr. **hang-gliding** n.

hanging /ˈhæŋɪŋ/ n. & adj. —n. **1 a** the practice or an act of executing by hanging a person. **b** (attrib.) meriting or causing this (a hanging offence). **2** (usu. in pl.) draperies hung on a wall etc. —adj. that hangs or is hung; suspended. □ **hanging gardens** gardens laid out on a steep slope. **Hanging Gardens of Babylon,** terraced gardens at Babylon, watered by pumps from the Euphrates, ascribed to Nebuchadnezzar II (c.600 BC). They were one of the Seven Wonders of the World. **hanging valley** a valley, usu. tributary, above the level of the valleys or plains it joins.

hangman /ˈhæŋmən/ n. (pl. **-men**) **1** an executioner who hangs condemned persons. **2** a word-game for two players, in which the tally of failed guesses is kept by drawing a representation of a gallows.

hangnail /ˈhæŋneɪl/ n. = AGNAIL. [alt. of AGNAIL, infl. by HANG and taking nail as = NAIL¹ 2]

hangover /ˈhæŋˌəʊvə(r)/ n. **1** a severe headache or other after-effects caused by drinking an excess of alcohol. **2** a survival from the past.

Hang Seng index /hæŋ sen/ an index based on the average movement in the price of selected securities on the Hong Kong stock exchange. [name of a bank in Honk Kong]

Hangzhou /hæŋˈdʒəʊ/ (also **Hangchow** /hæŋˈʃaʊ/) the capital of Zhejang province in eastern China, situated at the southern end of the Grand Canal; pop. (est. 1986) 1,250,000.

hank /hæŋk/ n. **1** a coil or skein of wool or thread etc. **2** any of several measures of length of cloth or yarn, e.g. 840 yds. for cotton yarn and 560 yds. for worsted. **3** Naut. a ring of rope, iron, etc., for securing the staysails to the stays. [ME f. ON hönk: cf. Sw. hank string, Da. hank handle]

hanker /ˈhæŋkə(r)/ v.intr. (foll. by for, after, or to + infin.) long for; crave. □□ **hankerer** n. **hankering** n. [obs. hank, prob. rel. to HANG]

hanky /ˈhæŋkɪ/ n. (also **hankie**) (pl. **-ies**) colloq. a handkerchief. [abbr.]

hanky-panky /ˌhæŋkɪˈpæŋkɪ/ n. sl. **1** naughtiness, esp. sexual misbehaviour. **2** dishonest dealing; trickery. [orig. unkn.]

Hannibal /ˈhænɪb(ə)l/ (247–183/2 BC), Carthaginian general, one of the world's greatest soldiers, with extraordinary tactical skill, a bold conception of strategy, and a capacity for leadership which commanded the loyalty of mercenary troops amid danger and defeat. He precipitated the Second Punic War by attacking Rome's ally Saguntum in Spain. In 218 BC by a pre-emptive move he led an army of about 30,000 over the Alps into Italy; the perennial problem of his exact route remains unsolved but the achievement still rouses admiration. There he inflicted a series of defeats on the Romans, campaigning for sixteen years undefeated but failing to take Rome itself. Finally recalled to Africa he was defeated at Zama by Scipio in 202 BC, escaped to Carthage, and counselled peace. After a further career as statesman in Carthage he committed suicide in exile in Bithynia to avoid a Roman extradition order.

Hannover see HANOVER.

Hanoi /hæˈnɔɪ/ the capital of Vietnam, and formerly of North Vietnam before the reunification of South and North Vietnam; pop. (1984) 925,000.

Hanover /ˈhænəvə(r)/ (German **Hannover**) **1** a North German town (pop. (est. 1987) 505,700), capital of Lower Saxony and formerly capital of the State of Hanover. **2** a North German State, an electorate of the Empire ruled by the Guelph dynasty, and subsequently a province of Prussia. In 1714 the Elector of Hanover succeeded to the British throne as George I, and from then until 1837 the same monarch ruled both Britain and Hanover. With the accession of Victoria to the British throne, however, Hanover passed to her uncle, Ernest, Duke of Cumberland, the Hanoverian succession being denied to a woman as long as a male member of the Guelph family survived. **3** the name of the British royal house from 1714 to the death of Queen Victoria in 1901. □□ **Hanoverian** /-ˈvɪərɪən/ adj. & n.

Hansa /ˈhænsə/ n. (also **Hanse**) **1 a** a medieval guild of merchants. **b** the entrance fee to a guild. **2** the Hanseatic League. [MHG hanse, OHG, Goth. hansa company]

Hansard /ˈhænsɑːd/ the official verbatim record of the proceedings of the Houses of Parliament, colloquially so called because for most of the 19th c. it was published by Messrs Hansard. The name disappeared from the title-page in 1892 and was restored in the reports on the session of 1942–3; since 1909 publication has been by HMSO.

Hanseatic League /ˌhænsɪˈætɪk/ a medieval association of north German cities, formed in 1241 as a commercial alliance for trade between the eastern and western sides of northern Europe. In the later Middle Ages the League, with about 100 member towns, functioned as an independent political power, with its own army and navy, but it began to collapse in the early 17th c. and only three major cities (Hamburg, Bremen, and Lübeck) remained until it was finally broken up in the 19th c. [HANSA]

hansel var. of HANDSEL.

Hansen's disease /ˈhæns(ə)nz/ n. leprosy. [G. H. A. Hansen, Norw. physician d. 1912, discoverer of the leprosy bacillus]

hansom /ˈhænsəm/ n. (in full **hansom cab**) hist. a two-wheeled horse-drawn cab accommodating two inside, with the driver seated behind. [J. A. Hansom, Engl. architect d. 1882, who designed it]

Hants /hænts/ abbr. Hampshire. [OE Hantescire]

Hanukkah /ˈhɑːnəkə, -xə/ n. (also **Chanukkah**) the eight-day Jewish festival of lights, beginning in December, commemorating the re-dedication of the Temple in 165 BC after its desecration by the Syrian king. [Heb. ḥănukkāh consecration]

hanuman /ˌhænʊˈmɑːn/ n. 1 an Indian langur venerated by Hindus. 2 (**Hanuman**) (in Hindu mythology) a semi-divine monkey-like creature to whom extraordinary powers were attributed, whose exploits are described in the Ramayana. [Hindi]

hap /hæp/ n. & v. archaic —n. 1 chance, luck. 2 a chance occurrence. —v.intr. (**happed, happing**) 1 come about by chance. 2 (foll. by to + infin.) happen to. [ME f. ON happ]

hapax legomenon /ˌhæpæks lɪˈɡɒmɪˌnɒn/ n. (pl. **hapax legomena** /-mɪnə/) a word of which only one instance of use is recorded. [Gk, = a thing said once]

ha'penny var. of HALFPENNY.

haphazard /hæpˈhæzəd/ adj. & adv. —adj. done etc. by chance; random. —adv. at random. □□ **haphazardly** adv. **haphazardness** n. [HAP + HAZARD]

hapless /ˈhæplɪs/ adj. unlucky. □□ **haplessly** adv. **haplessness** n. [HAP + -LESS]

haplography /hæpˈlɒɡrəfɪ/ n. the accidental omission of letters when these are repeated in a word (e.g. philogy for philology). [Gk haplous single + -GRAPHY]

haploid /ˈhæplɔɪd/ adj. & n. —adj. Biol. (of an organism or cell) with a single set of chromosomes. —n. a haploid organism or cell. [G f. Gk haplous single + eidos form]

haplology /hæpˈlɒlədʒɪ/ n. the omission of a sound when this is repeated within a word (e.g. February pronounced /ˈfebrɪ/). [Gk haplous + -LOGY]

ha'p'orth Brit. var. of HALFPENNYWORTH.

happen /ˈhæpən/ v. & adv. —v.intr. 1 occur (by chance or otherwise). 2 (foll. by to + infin.) have the (good or bad) fortune to (I happened to meet her). 3 (foll. by to) be the (esp. unwelcome) fate or experience of (what happened to you?; I hope nothing happens to them). 4 (foll. by on) encounter or discover by chance. —adv. N.Engl. dial. perhaps, maybe (happen it'll rain). □ **as it happens** in fact; in reality (as it happens, it turned out well). [ME f. HAP + -EN¹]

happening /ˈhæpənɪŋ, -pnɪŋ/ n. 1 an event or occurrence. 2 an improvised or spontaneous theatrical etc. performance.

happenstance /ˈhæpənst(ə)ns/ n. US a thing that happens by chance. [HAPPEN + CIRCUMSTANCE]

happi /ˈhæpɪ/ n. (pl. **happis**) (also **happi-coat**) a loose informal Japanese coat. [Jap.]

happy /ˈhæpɪ/ adj. (**happier, happiest**) 1 feeling or showing pleasure or contentment. 2 a fortunate; characterized by happiness. b (of words, behaviour, etc.) apt, pleasing. 3 colloq. slightly drunk. 4 (in comb.) colloq. inclined to use excessively or at random (trigger-happy). □ **happy as a sandboy** see SANDBOY. **happy event** colloq. the birth of a child. **happy families** a card-game the object of which is to acquire four members of the same 'family'. **happy-go-lucky** cheerfully casual. **happy hour** esp. US a period of the day when drinks are sold at reduced prices in bars, hotels, etc. **happy hunting-ground** a place where success or enjoyment is obtained. **happy medium** a

compromise; the avoidance of extremes. □□ **happily** adv. **happiness** n. [ME f. HAP + -Y¹]

Hapsburg /ˈhæpsbɜːɡ/ the name, taken from Castle Hapsburg in Switzerland, of a German family to which belonged rulers of various countries of Europe from 1273, when they first became kings of Germany, until 1918, and various Holy Roman Emperors from 1483. A branch of the family ruled in Spain 1504–1700.

haptic /ˈhæptɪk/ adj. relating to the sense of touch. [Gk haptikos able to touch f. haptō fasten]

hara-kiri /ˌhærəˈkɪrɪ/ n. ritual suicide by disembowelment with a sword, formerly practised by Samurai to avoid dishonour. [colloq. Jap. f. hara belly + kiri cutting]

harangue /həˈræŋ/ n. & v. —n. a lengthy and earnest speech. —v.tr. lecture or make a harangue to. □□ **haranguer** n. [ME f. F f. OF arenge f. med.L harenga, perh. f. Gmc]

Harappa /həˈræpə/ an ancient city of the Indus Valley civilization, in NW Pakistan.

Harare /hɑːˈrɑːrɪ/ (formerly Salisbury) the capital of Zimbabwe; pop. (est. 1982) 656,000.

harass /ˈhærəs, disp. həˈræs/ v.tr. 1 trouble and annoy continually or repeatedly. 2 make repeated attacks on (an enemy or opponent). □□ **harasser** n. **harassingly** adv. **harassment** n. [F harasser f. OF harer set a dog on]

Harbin /ˈhɑːbɪn/ (also **Haerhpin**) the capital of Heilongjiang province in NE China, on the Sungari River; pop. (est. 1986) 2,630,000.

harbinger /ˈhɑːbɪndʒə(r)/ n. 1 a person or thing that announces or signals the approach of another. 2 a forerunner. [earlier = 'one who provides lodging': ME herbergere f. OF f. herberge lodging f. Gmc]

harbour /ˈhɑːbə(r)/ n. & v. (US **harbor**) —n. 1 a place of shelter for ships. 2 a shelter; a place of refuge or protection. —v. 1 tr. give shelter to (esp. a criminal or wanted person). 2 tr. keep in one's mind, esp. resentfully (harbour a grudge). 3 intr. come to anchor in a harbour. □ **harbour-master** an official in charge of a harbour. □□ **harbourless** adj. [OE hereberg perh. f. ON, rel. to HARBINGER]

harbourage /ˈhɑːbərɪdʒ/ n. (US **harborage**) a shelter or place of shelter, esp. for ships.

hard /hɑːd/ adj., adv., & n. —adj. 1 (of a substance, material, etc.) firm and solid; unyielding to pressure; not easily cut. 2 a difficult to understand or explain (a hard problem). b difficult to accomplish (a hard decision). c (foll. by to + infin.) not easy to (hard to believe; hard to please). 3 difficult to bear; entailing suffering (a hard life). 4 (of a person) unfeeling; severely critical. 5 (of a season or the weather) severe, harsh (a hard winter; a hard frost). 6 harsh or unpleasant to the senses (a hard voice; hard colours). 7 a strenuous, enthusiastic, intense (a hard worker; a hard fight). b severe, uncompromising (a hard blow; a hard bargain; hard words). c Polit. extreme; most radical (the hard right). 8 a (of liquor) strongly alcoholic. b (of drugs) potent and addictive. c (of radiation) highly penetrating. d (of pornography) highly suggestive and explicit. 9 (of water) containing mineral salts that make lathering difficult. 10 established; not disputable; reliable (hard facts; hard data). 11 Stock Exch. (of currency, prices, etc.) high; not likely to fall in value. 12 Phonet. (of a consonant) guttural (as c in cat, g in go). —adv. 1 strenuously, intensely, copiously; with one's full effort (try hard; look hard at; is raining hard; hard-working). 2 with difficulty or effort (hard-earned). 3 so as to be hard or firm (hard-baked; the jelly set hard). —n. Brit. 1 a sloping roadway across a foreshore. 2 sl. hard labour (got two years hard). □ **be hard on 1** be difficult for. 2 be severe in one's treatment or criticism of. 3 be unpleasant to (the senses). **be hard put to it** (usu. foll. by to + infin.) find it difficult. **go hard with** turn out to (a person's disadvantage). **hard and fast** (of a rule or a distinction made) definite, unalterable, strict. **hard at it** colloq. busily working or occupied. **hard-boiled 1** (of an egg) boiled until the white and the yolk are solid. 2 (of a person) tough, shrewd. **hard by** near; close by. **a hard case 1** colloq. **a** an intractable person. **b** Austral. & NZ an amusing or eccentric person. 2 a case of hardship. **hard cash** negotiable coins and banknotes. **hard**

coal anthracite. **hard copy** printed material produced by computer, usu. on paper, suitable for ordinary reading. **hard core 1** an irreducible nucleus. **2** *colloq.* **a** the most active or committed members of a society etc. **b** a conservative or reactionary minority. **3** *Brit.* solid material, esp. rubble, forming the foundation of a road etc. **hard-core** *adj.* blatant, uncompromising, esp.: **1** (of pornography) explicit, obscene. **2** (of drug addiction) relating to 'hard' drugs, esp. heroin. **hard disk** *Computing* a large-capacity rigid usu. magnetic storage disk. **hard-done-by** harshly or unfairly treated. **hard error** *Computing* a permanent error. **hard feelings** feelings of resentment. **hard hat** *colloq.* **1** protective headgear worn on building-sites etc. **2** a reactionary person. **hard hit** badly affected. **hard-hitting** aggressively critical. **hard labour** heavy manual work as a punishment, esp. in a prison. **hard landing 1** a clumsy or rough landing of an aircraft. **2** an uncontrolled landing in which a spacecraft is destroyed. **hard line** unyielding adherence to a firm policy. **hard-liner** a person who adheres rigidly to a policy. **hard lines** *Brit. colloq.* = *hard luck.* **hard luck** worse fortune than one deserves. **hard-nosed** *colloq.* realistic, uncompromising. **hard nut** *sl.* a tough, aggressive person. **a hard nut to crack** *colloq.* **1** a difficult problem. **2** a person or thing not easily understood or influenced. **hard of hearing** somewhat deaf. **hard on** (or **upon**) close to in pursuit etc. **hard-on** *n. coarse sl.* an erection of the penis. **hard pad** a form of distemper in dogs etc. **hard palate** the front part of the palate. **hard-paste** denoting a Chinese or 'true' porcelain made of fusible and infusible materials (usu. clay and stone) and fired at a high temperature. **hard-pressed 1** closely pursued. **2** burdened with urgent business. **hard rock** *colloq.* rock music with a heavy beat. **hard roe** see ROE¹. **hard sauce** a sauce of butter and sugar, often with brandy etc. added. **hard sell** aggressive salesmanship or advertising. **hard shoulder** *Brit.* a hardened strip alongside a motorway for stopping on in an emergency. **hard stuff** *sl.* strong alcoholic drink, esp. whisky. **hard tack** ship's biscuit. **hard up 1** short of money. **2** (foll. by *for*) at a loss for; lacking. **hard-wearing** able to stand much wear. **hard wheat** wheat with a hard grain rich in gluten. **hard-wired** involving or achieved by permanently connected circuits designed to perform a specific function. **hard-working** diligent. **put the hard word on** *Austral. & NZ sl.* ask a favour (esp. sexual or financial) of. □□ **hardish** *adj.* **hardness** *n.* [OE *hard, heard* f. Gmc]

hardback /ˈhɑːdbæk/ *adj. & n.* —*adj.* (of a book) bound in stiff covers. —*n.* a hardback book.

hardball /ˈhɑːbɔːl/ *n. & v. US* —*n.* **1** = BASEBALL. **2** *sl.* uncompromising methods or dealings, esp. in politics (*play hardball*). —*v.tr. sl.* pressure or coerce politically.

hardbitten /ˈhɑːdˌbɪt(ə)n/ *adj. colloq.* tough and cynical.

hardboard /ˈhɑːdbɔːd/ *n.* stiff board made of compressed and treated wood pulp.

harden /ˈhɑːd(ə)n/ *v.* **1** *tr. & intr.* make or become hard or harder. **2** *intr. & tr.* become, or make (one's attitude etc.), uncompromising or less sympathetic. **3** *intr.* (of prices etc.) cease to fall or fluctuate. □ **harden off** inure (a plant) to cold by gradual increase of its exposure. □□ **hardener** *n.*

hardening /ˈhɑːdənɪŋ/ *n.* **1** the process or an instance of becoming hard. **2** (in full **hardening of the arteries**) *Med.* = ARTERIOSCLEROSIS.

hard-headed /hɑːdˈhedɪd/ *adj.* practical, realistic; not sentimental. □□ **hard-headedly** *adv.* **hard-headedness** *n.*

hard-hearted /hɑːdˈhɑːtɪd/ *adj.* unfeeling, unsympathetic. □□ **hard-heartedly** *adv.* **hard-heartedness** *n.*

Hardie /ˈhɑːdɪ/, James Keir (1856–1915), Scottish labour leader and politician, first chairman of the Labour Party (1906).

hardihood /ˈhɑːdɪˌhʊd/ *n.* boldness, daring.

Harding /ˈhɑːdɪŋ/, Warren Gamaliel (1865–1923), 29th President of the US, 1921–3. His fondness for his self-seeking friends, whom he took into office, resulted in incompetence and corruption in the administration.

hardly /ˈhɑːdlɪ/ *adv.* **1** scarcely; only just (*we hardly knew them*). **2** only with difficulty (*could hardly speak*). **3** harshly.

hardpan /ˈhɑːdpæn/ *n. Geol.* a hardened layer of clay occurring in or below the soil profile.

hardshell /ˈhɑːʃel/ *adj.* **1** having a hard shell. **2** esp. *US* rigid, orthodox, uncompromising.

hardship /ˈhɑːdʃɪp/ *n.* **1** severe suffering or privation. **2** the circumstance causing this.

hardtop /ˈhɑːdtɒp/ *n.* a motor car with a rigid (usu. detachable) roof.

Hardwar /hɑːˈdwɑː(r)/ a city in northern India, on the Ganges in Uttar Pradesh, a place of Hindu pilgrimage; pop. (est. 1981) 146,190.

hardware /ˈhɑːdweə(r)/ *n.* **1** tools and household articles of metal etc. **2** heavy machinery or armaments. **3** the mechanical and electronic components of a computer etc. (cf. SOFTWARE).

hardwood /ˈhɑːdwʊd/ *n.* the wood from a deciduous broad-leaved tree as distinguished from that of conifers.

Hardy¹, Oliver, see LAUREL AND HARDY.

Hardy² /ˈhɑːdɪ/, Thomas (1840–1928), English novelist and poet, born in Dorset (the son of a stonemason), where he spent most his life, working as an architect until his literary reputation became established. His most popular novels are those set in 'Wessex' (Dorset) with which Hardy is so closely identified, among them *Under the Greenwood Tree* (1872), *Far from the Madding Crowd* (1874), *The Mayor of Casterbridge* (1886), *Tess of the D'Urbervilles* (1891), and *Jude the Obscure* (1896), his most pessimistic. Hardy then turned to poetry and produced eight volumes of poems of great variety and distinction. In all his works, including his epic drama *The Dynasts* (1904–8), the underlying theme is mankind's struggle against the indifferent force that inflicts the sufferings and ironies of life and love, though there is sharp humour in his rustic characters.

hardy /ˈhɑːdɪ/ *adj.* (**hardier, hardiest**) **1** robust; capable of enduring difficult conditions. **2** (of a plant) able to grow in the open air all the year. □ **hardy annual 1** an annual plant that may be sown in the open. **2** *joc.* a subject that comes up at regular intervals. □□ **hardily** *adv.* **hardiness** *n.* [ME f. OF *hardi* past part. of *hardir* become bold, f. Gmc, rel. to HARD]

Hare /heə(r)/, William, see BURKE⁴.

hare /heə(r)/ *n. & v.* —*n.* **1** any of various mammals of the family Leporidae, esp. *Lepus europaeus*, like a large rabbit, with tawny fur, long ears, short tail, and hind legs longer than forelegs, inhabiting fields, hills, etc. **2** (in full **electric hare**) a dummy hare propelled by electricity, used in greyhound racing. —*v.intr.* run with great speed. □ **hare and hounds** a paperchase. **hare-brained** rash, wild. **hare's-foot** (in full **hare's-foot clover**) a clover, *Trifolium arvense*, with soft hair around the flowers. **run with the hare and hunt with the hounds** try to remain on good terms with both sides. **start a hare** raise a topic of conversation. [OE *hara* f. Gmc]

harebell /ˈheəbel/ *n.* **1** a plant, *Campanula rotundifolia*, with slender stems and pale-blue bell-shaped flowers. **2** = BLUEBELL 2.

Hare Krishna /ˌhɑːrɪ ˈkrɪʃnə/ the title of a love-chant or mantra based on the name of the Hindu deity Vishnu, used as an incantation by members of a religious sect in the US and elsewhere. The International Society for Krishna Consciousness was founded in New York in 1966; its principles include strict vegetarianism and prohibit gambling, drugs, and extramarital sex. Members dress in saffron robes, the men have shaved heads, and daily ritual includes dance-marching through the streets to the accompaniment of Oriental instruments and chanting of the Hare Krishna mantra. —*n. pop.* **1** the sect itself. **2** (*pl.* **Hare Krishnas**) a member of this sect. [Hindi, f. Skr. *O Hari!* an epithet of Krishna]

harelip /ˈheəlɪp/ *n.* a congenital fissure of the upper lip. □□ **harelipped** *adj.*

harem /ˈhɑːriːm, hɑːˈriːm/ *n.* **1 a** the women of a Muslim household, living in a separate part of the house. **b** their quarters. **2** a group of female animals sharing a mate. [Arab. *ḥarām, ḥarīm,* orig. = prohibited, prohibited place, f. *ḥarama* prohibit]

harewood /ˈheəwʊd/ *n.* stained sycamore-wood used for making furniture. [G dial. *Ehre* f. L *acer* maple + WOOD]

Hargeisa /haːˈgeɪsə/ a city in NW Somalia, formerly the capital of British Somaliland; pop. 400,000.

Hargreaves /ˈhaːgriːvz/, James (1720–78), English inventor, one of the great pioneers of the cotton industry in Lancashire. He was employed by Robert Peel (grandfather of the statesman) to construct an improved carding-machine (c.1760), and produced one using a roller with multiple pins to comb out the cotton fibres, but is best known for the 'spinning jenny' (the reason for its name is not known) which he patented in 1770. This was the first machine with multiple spindles, enabling one man to work 8 or even 16 spindles simultaneously. The invention was greatly needed: improvements in weaving following the invention of the flying shuttle (1733) meant that the weavers were working more quickly and the spinners could no longer keep pace with them. Unfortunately Hargreaves's success in speeding up the spinning process caused opposition; spinners on the old-fashioned wheels were alarmed at the threat to their employment, and in 1768 a mob broke into his house and destroyed it and the machinery. He failed commercially, though Arkwright later developed the machine successfully and Crompton improved upon it with his 'mule'.

haricot /ˈhærɪˌkəʊ/ n. **1** (in full **haricot bean**) a variety of French bean with small white seeds. **2** the dried seed of this used as a vegetable. [F]

Harijan /ˈhærɪdʒ(ə)n/ n. a member of the class of untouchables in India. [Skr., = a person dedicated to Vishnu, f. *Hari* Vishnu, *jana* person]

hark /haːk/ v.intr. (usu. in *imper.*) *archaic* listen attentively. □ **hark back** revert to a topic discussed earlier. [ME *herkien* f. OE *heorcian* (unrecorded): cf. HEARKEN: *hark back* was orig. a hunting call to retrace steps]

harken var. of HEARKEN.

harl /haːl/ n. (also **harle**, **herl** /haːl/) fibre of flax or hemp. [MLG *herle*, *harle* fibre of flax or hemp]

Harlem /ˈhaːləm/ a district of New York City, situated to the north of 96th Street, having a large Black population.

harlequin /ˈhaːlɪkwɪn/ n. & adj. —n. **1** (**Harlequin**) originally a stock character in Italian comedy, a witty servant, always in love, always in trouble, easily despairing, easily consoled. In English pantomime he is a mute character supposed to be invisible to the clown and pantaloon, the clown's rival in the affections of Columbine, usually wearing a mask and parti-coloured tights. **2** (in full **harlequin duck**) an Icelandic duck, *Histrionicus histrionicus*, with variegated plumage. —adj. in varied colours; variegated. [F f. earlier *Herlequin* leader of a legendary nocturnal troup of demon horsemen]

harlequinade /ˌhaːlɪkwɪˈneɪd/ n. **1** a play or section of a pantomime in which Harlequin plays the leading role. (See below.) **2** a piece of buffoonery. [F *arlequinade* (as HARLEQUIN)]

Harlequinade was an important element, originating in Italy, in the development of the English pantomime. It originally consisted of story-telling dances in which Harlequin, a magical character, played the leading role. In the 19th c. Grimaldi made the purely English character Clown into the chief personage, and to ease the burden on the dancers the harlequinade was preceded by a fairy-tale. As Harlequin's importance lessened and the fairy-tales became longer and more popular, the harlequinade dwindled into a short epilogue to what became the present English pantomime (see entry). It was finally abandoned completely.

Harley Street /ˈhaːlɪ/ a street in London long associated with the premises of eminent physicians and surgeons, whence the allusive use of its name to refer to medical specialists.

harlot /ˈhaːlət/ n. *archaic* a prostitute. □□ **harlotry** n. [ME f. OF *harlot*, *herlot* lad, knave, vagabond]

harm /haːm/ n. & v. —n. hurt, damage. —v.tr. cause harm to. □ **out of harm's way** in safety. [OE *hearm*, *hearmian* f. Gmc]

harmattan /haːˈmæt(ə)n/ n. a parching dusty land-wind of the W. African coast occurring from December to February. [Fanti or Twi *haramata*]

harmful /ˈhaːmfʊl/ adj. causing or likely to cause harm. □□ **harmfully** adv. **harmfulness** n.

harmless /ˈhaːmlɪs/ adj. **1** not able or likely to cause harm. **2** inoffensive. □□ **harmlessly** adv. **harmlessness** n.

harmonic /haːˈmɒnɪk/ adj. & n. —adj. **1** of or characterized by harmony; harmonious. **2** *Mus.* **a** of or relating to harmony. **b** (of a tone) produced by vibration of a string etc. in an exact fraction of its length. **3** *Math.* of or relating to quantities whose reciprocals are in arithmetical progression (*harmonic progression*). —n. **1** *Mus.* an overtone accompanying at a fixed interval (and forming a note with) a fundamental. **2** *Physics* a component frequency of wave motion. □ **harmonic motion** (in full **simple harmonic motion**) oscillatory motion under a retarding force proportional to the amount of displacement from an equilibrium position. **harmonic progression** (or **series**) *Math.* a series of quantities whose reciprocals are in arithmetical progression. □□ **harmonically** adv. [L *harmonicus* f. Gk *harmonikos* (as HARMONY)]

harmonica /haːˈmɒnɪkə/ n. a small rectangular wind instrument with a row of metal reeds along its length, held against the lips and moved from side to side to produce different notes by blowing or sucking. [L, fem. sing. or neut. pl. of *harmonicus*: see HARMONIC]

harmonious /haːˈməʊnɪəs/ adj. **1** sweet-sounding, tuneful. **2** forming a pleasing or consistent whole; concordant. **3** free from disagreement or dissent. □□ **harmoniously** adv. **harmoniousness** n.

harmonist /ˈhaːmənɪst/ n. a person skilled in musical harmony, a harmonizer. □□ **harmonistic** /-ˈnɪstɪk/ adj.

harmonium /haːˈməʊnɪəm/ n. a keyboard instrument in which the notes are produced by air driven through metal reeds by bellows operated by the feet. [F f. L (as HARMONY)]

harmonize /ˈhaːmənaɪz/ v. (also **-ise**) **1** tr. add notes to (a melody) to produce harmony. **2** tr. & intr. (often foll. by *with*) bring into or be in harmony. **3** intr. make or form a pleasing or consistent whole. □□ **harmonization** /-ˈzeɪʃ(ə)n/ n. [f. F *harmoniser* (as HARMONY)]

harmony /ˈhaːmənɪ/ n. (pl. **-ies**) **1 a** a combination of simultaneously sounded musical notes to produce chords and chord progressions, esp. as having a pleasing effect. (See below.) **b** the study of this. **2 a** an apt or aesthetic arrangement of parts. **b** the pleasing effect of this. **3** agreement, concord. **4** a collation of parallel narratives, esp. of the Gospels. □ **in harmony 1** (of singing etc.) producing chords; not discordant. **2** (often foll. by *with*) in agreement. **harmony of the spheres** see SPHERE. [ME f. OF *harmonie* f. L *harmonia* f. Gk *harmonia* joining, concord, f. *harmos* joint]

Harmony gives what is known as 'vertical' music, contrasted with the 'horizontal' music of melody. Chords and chord progressions play an important role, and one melody is usually given prominence, whereas in counterpoint several strands of melody are given equal prominence. The traditional system of harmony became the dominating force in Western music towards the beginning of the 17th c., and the primacy of melody and accompaniment has underpinned much music since. Chromatic harmony was always a means of creating particularly expressive passages, but in the 19th c. it became so pervasive that often the tonal organization of a piece seems lost in dense ambiguous texture. Schoenberg's early music is of this kind, and he was one of the first composers to tip the scales away from tonal thinking towards atonality (called by him 'pantonality') and from there into serial composition.

Harmsworth /ˈhaːmzwɜːθ/, Alfred Charles William (1865–1922), see NORTHCLIFFE.

harness /ˈhaːnɪs/ n. & v. —n. **1** the equipment of straps and fittings by which a horse is fastened to a cart etc. and controlled. **2** a similar arrangement for fastening a thing to a person's body, for restraining a young child, etc. —v.tr. **1 a** put a harness on (esp. a horse). **b** (foll. by *to*) attach by a harness. **2** make use of (natural resources) esp. to produce energy. □ **harness racing** see TROTTING. **in harness** in the routine of daily work. □□ **harnesser** n. [ME f. OF *harneis* military equipment f. ON *hernest* (unrecorded) f. *herr* army + *nest* provisions]

Harold /ˈhær(ə)ld/ the name of two kings of England:

Harold I 'Harefoot' (d. 1040), reigned 1035–40. An illegitimate son of Cnut, Harold first came to the throne when Cnut's legitimate son was absent in Denmark at the time of his father's death. When the other royal claimant, Alfred the Aetheling, was murdered a year later, Harold was formally recognized as king, although Cnut's legitimate son Harthacnut returned to the kingdom when Harold himself died.

Harold II (c.1019–66), reigned 1066, the last Anglo-Saxon king of England. He succeeded Edward the Confessor, having dominated the court in the last years of his predecessor's reign, but was faced with two invasions within months of his accession. He defeated and killed his half-brother Tostig and the Norse king Harald Hardrada at Stamford Bridge, but was himself slain at Hastings by William, Duke of Normandy, who took the throne as William I.

Haroun-al-Raschid see HARŪN AR-RASHĪD.

harp /hɑːp/ n. & v. —n. a large upright roughly triangular musical instrument comprising a set of strings placed over an open frame so that they can be plucked or swept with the fingers from both sides. The standard orchestral harp has a range of about six-and-a-half octaves, but has only seven notes to each octave, further notes being obtained by use of the pedals. The harp may be the oldest stringed instrument: it is depicted in various forms in pre-Christian times, is mentioned in the Old Testament (Gk *psalterion*), and appears in Ireland, Scotland, and France in the 9th and 10th centuries. —v.intr. **1** (foll. by *on*, *on about*) talk repeatedly and tediously about. **2** play on a harp. □ **harp-seal** a Greenland seal, *Phoca groenlandica*, with a harp-shaped dark mark on its back. □□ **harper** n. **harpist** n. [OE *hearpe* f. Gmc]

Harpers Ferry /ˈhɑːpəz/ a small town in Jefferson County in West Virginia, at the junction of the Potamac and Shenandoah rivers. It is famous for a raid in Oct. 1859 in which John Brown and a group of Abolitionists captured a federal arsenal located there.

Harpocrates /hɑːˈpɒkrəˌtiːz/ see HORUS.

harpoon /hɑːˈpuːn/ n. & v. —n. a barbed spearlike missile with a rope attached, for catching whales etc. —v.tr. spear with a harpoon. □ **harpoon-gun** a gun for firing a harpoon. □□ **harpooner** n. [F *harpon* f. *harpe* clamp f. L *harpa* f. Gk *harpē* sickle]

harpsichord /ˈhɑːpsɪˌkɔːd/ n. a wing-shaped keyboard instrument which differs from clavichord and piano in that the strings are plucked by a small leather or quill plectrum. Other instruments of the harpsichord type are the spinet and the oblong-shaped virginal, but the terms were sometimes used interchangeably. The first full description of an instrument of this kind is found in the mid-15th c., and an upright harpsichord (or *clavicytherium*) survives from the same period, but the heyday of the harpsichord was from the late 16th to the mid-18th c. Its tone is crisp and clear, but it is unable to make a gradual progression between loud and soft sounds by pressure on the keys. It was overtaken in popularity by the piano, which can do this, at the end of the 18th c., but enjoyed a revival in the 20th c. □□ **harpsichordist** n. [obs. F *harpechorde* f. LL *harpa* harp, + *chorda* string, the -*s*- being unexplained]

harpy /ˈhɑːpɪ/ n. (pl. **-ies**) **1** Gk & Rom. Mythol. any of the winged beings, apparently winds in origin, who carry off various persons and things. Their names are Aello, Ocypete, and Celoeno. In ancient art they are shown as winged women; Virgil, however, describes them as birds with women's faces, and they were later portrayed in this form. **2** a grasping unscrupulous person. □ **harpy eagle** a S. American crested bird of prey, *Harpia harpyja*, one of the largest of eagles. [F *harpie* or L *harpyia* f. Gk *harpuiai* snatchers (cf. *harpazō* snatch)]

harquebus /ˈhɑːkwɪbəs/ n. (also **arquebus** /ˈɑːk-/) hist. an early type of portable gun supported on a tripod or on a forked rest. [F (h)*arquebuse* ult. f. MLG *hakebusse* or MHG *hakenbühse*, f. *haken* hook + *busse* gun]

harridan /ˈhærɪd(ə)n/ n. a bad-tempered old woman. [17th-c. cant, perhaps f. F *haridelle* old horse]

harrier¹ /ˈhærɪə(r)/ n. a person who harries or lays waste.

harrier² /ˈhærɪə(r)/ n. **1 a** a hound used for hunting hares. **b** (in pl.) a pack of these with huntsmen. **2** a group of cross-country runners. [HARE + -IER, assim. to HARRIER¹]

harrier³ /ˈhærɪə(r)/ n. any bird of prey of the genus *Circus*, with long wings for swooping over the ground. [*harrower* f. *harrow* harry, rob, assim. to HARRIER¹]

Harris /ˈhærɪs/ the southern part of the largest and northernmost island of the Outer Hebrides, off the west coast of Scotland. It is famous for its hand-woven tween (Harris tweed).

Harrisburg /ˈhærɪsˌbɜːg/ the capital of Pennsylvania; pop. (1980) 53,264.

Harrison¹ /ˈhærɪs(ə)n/, Benjamin (1833–1901), 23rd President of the US, 1889–93, grandson of William Henry Harrison.

Harrison² /ˈhærɪs(ə)n/, Sir Rex (Reginald Carey) (1908–90), English stage and film actor. He first appeared on the stage in 1924; his films include *Blithe Spirit* (1944), *The Constant Husband* (1955), and *Cleopatra* in which he played Julius Caesar (1962). His most famous role was as Professor Higgins in the stage and film musical *My Fair Lady* (1956, 1964).

Harrison³ /ˈhærɪs(ə)n/, William Henry (1773–1841), 9th President of the US, 1841. He died one month after his inauguration.

Harrod /ˈhærəd/, Charles Henry (1800–85), English grocer and tea merchant (originally a miller by trade) who in 1853 took over a shop in Knightsbridge, London, which after expansion in the late 19th c. by his son, Charles Digby Harrod (1841–1905), became a prestigious department store.

Harrow /ˈhærəʊ/ (short for **Harrow School**) a public school at Harrow-on-the-Hill, Middlesex, and traditional rival of Eton College. It was founded and endowed by John Lyon under a charter (1572) granted by Queen Elizabeth I.

harrow /ˈhærəʊ/ n. & v. —n. a heavy frame with iron teeth dragged over ploughed land to break up clods, remove weeds, cover seed, etc. —v.tr. **1** draw a harrow over (land). **2** (usu. as **harrowing** adj.) distress greatly. □□ **harrower** n. **harrowingly** adv. [ME f. ON *hervi*]

Harrowing of Hell the medieval term for the defeat of the powers of evil, and the release of its victims, by the descent of Christ into Hell after his death. It is mentioned in the Epistle to the Ephesians 4: 9 and included in certain early creeds (but not the Nicene Creed). In art, it was depicted mainly in the Greek Church, where it superseded the Resurrection; examples in the West are usually those under Greek influence. It was also a subject of medieval mystery plays.

harrumph /həˈrʌmf/ v.intr. US clear the throat or make a similar sound, esp. ostentatiously. [imit.]

harry /ˈhærɪ/ v.tr. (**-ies**, **-ied**) **1** ravage or despoil. **2** harass, worry. [OE *herian*, *hergian* f. Gmc, rel. to OE *here* army]

harsh /hɑːʃ/ adj. **1** unpleasantly rough or sharp, esp. to the senses. **2** severe, cruel. □□ **harshen** v.tr. & intr. **harshly** adv. **harshness** n. [MLG *harsch* rough, lit. 'hairy', f. *haer* HAIR]

harslet var. of HASLET.

hart /hɑːt/ n. the male of the deer (esp. the red deer) usu. over five years old. □ **hart's tongue** a fern, *Phyllitis scolopendrium*, with narrow undivided fronds. [OE *heor(o)t* f. Gmc]

hartal /ˈhɑːt(ə)l/ n. the closing of shops and offices in India as a mark of protest or sorrow. [Hind. *hartāl*, *hattāl* f. Skr. *haṭṭa* shop + *tālaka* lock]

Harte /hɑːt/, (Francis) Bret (1836–1902), American writer, remembered chiefly for his short stories about low life in a gold-mining settlement, inspired by his own brief experience in mining, collected in *The Luck of Roaring Camp* (1870). His humorous-pathetic verse included 'Plain Language from Truthful James' (1870), often referred to as 'The Heathen Chinee'.

hartebeest /ˈhɑːtɪˌbiːst/ n. any large African antelope of the genus *Alcelaphus*, with ringed horns bent back at the tips. [Afrik. f. Du. *hert* HART + *beest* BEAST]

Hartford /ˈhɑːtfəd/ the capital of Connecticut; pop. (1980) 136,392.

Hartley /ˈhɑːtlɪ/, Leslie Poles (1895–1972), English novelist. After years as a fiction reviewer and writer of short stories he published his trilogy *The Shrimp and the Anemone* (1944), *The Sixth Heaven* (1946), and *Eustace and Hilda* (1947), a vivid evocation of childhood and young manhood. His most successful novel *The Go-Between* (1953) records the events of the hot summer of 1900 and gives a spirited account of leisurely Edwardian England.

Hartnell /ˈhɑːtn(ə)l/, Sir Norman (1901–79), English couturier, who was dressmaker to Queen Elizabeth II and the Queen Mother.

hartshorn /ˈhɑːtshɔːn/ *n. archaic* **1** an ammonious substance got from the horns of a hart. **2** (in full **spirit of hartshorn**) an aqueous solution of ammonia. [OE (as HART, HORN¹)]

harum-scarum /ˌheərəmˈskeərəm/ *adj. & n. colloq.* —*adj.* wild and reckless. —*n.* such a person. [rhyming form. on HARE, SCARE]

Harūn ar-Rashīd /hæˈruːn ɑːˈræʃiːd/ (also **Haroun-al-Raschid**) (763–809), a calif of Baghdad, who figures in many tales of the Arabian Nights. He was the most powerful and vigorous of the Abbasid Caliphs, his rule extending from India to Africa, and was on friendly terms with Charlemagne, who was almost his exact contemporary.

haruspex /həˈrʌspeks/ *n.* (*pl.* **haruspices** /-spɪˌsiːz/) a Roman religious official who interpreted omens from the inspection of animals' entrails. □□ **haruspicy** /-spɪsɪ/ *n.* [L]

Harvard /ˈhɑːvəd/ the oldest American university, founded in 1636 at Cambridge, Massachusetts. It is named after John Harvard (d. 1638), an English settler who bequeathed to it his library and half his estate.

harvest /ˈhɑːvɪst/ *n. & v.* —*n.* **1 a** the process of gathering in crops etc. **b** the season when this takes place. **2** the season's yield or crop. **3** the product or result of any action. —*v.tr.* **1** gather as a harvest, reap. **2** experience (consequences). □ **harvest festival** a thanksgiving festival in church for the harvest. **harvest home** the close of harvesting or the festival to mark this. **harvest mite** any arachnid larvae of the genus *Trombicula*, a chigger. **harvest moon** the full moon nearest to the autumn equinox (22 or 23 Sept.). **harvest mouse** a small rodent, *Micromys minutus*, that nests in the stalks of growing grain. □□ **harvestable** *adj.* [OE *hærfest* f. Gmc]

harvester /ˈhɑːvɪstə(r)/ *n.* **1** a reaper. **2** a reaping-machine, esp. with sheaf-binding.

harvestman /ˈhɑːvɪstmən/ *n.* (*pl.* **-men**) any of various arachnids of the family Opilionidae, with very long thin legs, found in humus and on tree trunks.

Harvey /ˈhɑːvɪ/, William (1578–1657), English discoverer of the circulation of the blood, and physician to James I and Charles I. Harvey set himself to provide, on the basis of the Aristotelian technique of sensory observation, a satisfactory account of the motion of the heart, and concluded that it forcibly expelled blood in contraction. He emphasized the quantity of blood emerging from the heart into the arteries, and finding that this quanitity was too great to be absorbed by the body as food, as contemporary theory held, noted that it must therefore pass through the flesh and enter the veins, returning once more to the heart. Harvey also applied his Aristotelianism to a study of insects, the motions of animals, and animal reproduction.

Haryana /hʌrɪˈɑːnə/ a State of northern India, formed in 1966 mostly from the Hindi-speaking part of the former State of Punjab; pop. (1981) 12,850,900.

Harz Mountains /hɑːts/ a range of mountains in Germany, between the Leine and Saale rivers, on the border between former East and West Germany. The mountains rise to a height of 1,142 m (3,747 ft.) at Brocken; the region is the source of many legends.

has *3rd sing. present of* HAVE.

has-been /ˈhæzbiːn/ *n. colloq.* a person or thing that has lost a former importance or usefulness.

Hasdrubal¹ /ˈhæzdrʊb(ə)l/ (d. 221 BC) Carthaginian leader, the son-in-law of Hamilcar whom he accompanied to Spain in 237 BC, succeeding to the command on the latter's death in 229 BC. He advanced to the Ebro, which became recognized as the boundary of Carthaginian and Roman spheres of influence.

Hasdrubal² /ˈhæzdrʊb(ə)l/ (d. 207 BC) Carthaginian leader, the son of Hamilcar and younger brother of Hannibal. In 218 BC he was left in command of Carthaginian forces in Spain after

Hannibal had left for Italy. After a defeat, he campaigned with only moderate success before reaching Gaul and crossing the Alps with the aim of joining Hannibal. he was killed in battle; although a fairly competent soldier his generalship did not match his courage.

hash¹ /hæʃ/ *n. & v.* —*n.* **1** a dish of cooked meat cut into small pieces and recooked. **2 a** a mixture; a jumble. **b** a mess. **3** re-used or recycled material. —*v.tr.* (often foll. by *up*) **1** make (meat etc.) into a hash. **2** recycle (old material). □ **make a hash of** *colloq.* make a mess of; bungle. **settle a person's hash** *colloq.* deal with and subdue a person. [F *hacher* f. *hache* HATCHET]

hash² /hæʃ/ *n. colloq.* hashish. [abbr.]

Hashemite /ˈhæʃɪmaɪt/ *adj. & n.* —*adj.* of or relating to an Arab princely family related to Muhammad. —*n.* a member of this family. [*Hashim* great-grandfather of Muhammad + -ITE¹]

hashish /ˈhæʃiːʃ/ *n.* a resinous product of the top leaves and tender parts of hemp, smoked or chewed for its narcotic effects. [f. Arab. *ḥašīš* dry herb; powdered hemp leaves]

Hasid /ˈhæsɪd/ *n.* (also **Chasid**) (*pl.* **Hasidim**) **1** a member of a strictly orthodox Jewish sect in Palestine in the 2nd–3rd c. BC who opposed Hellenizing influences on their faith and supported the Maccabean revolt. **2** a member of a mystical Jewish sect in Germany in the 12th–13th c. **3** a supporter of Hasidism (see entry). □□ **hasidic** /-ˈsɪdɪk/ *adj.* [Heb. *ḥāsîd* pious (person)]

Hasidism /ˈhæsɪˌdɪz(ə)m/ *n.* (also **Chasidism**) a mystical Jewish movement founded in Poland in the 18th c. in reaction to the rigid academic formation of rabbinical Judaism. Its founder was Israel ben Eliezer (d. 1760), called Bad-Shem-Tov (Heb., = master of the good name) because of his reputation as a miraculous healer. The movement was denounced as heretical in 1781 and declined sharply in the 19th c. with the spread of modernism, but fundamentalist communities developed from it are currently a force in Jewish life, particularly in Israel and New York, where they oppose fellow Jews whom they regard as violating the moral and religious principles of their faith.

haslet /ˈhæzlɪt/ *n.* (also **harslet** /ˈhɑː-/) pieces of (esp. pig's) offal cooked together and usu. compressed into a meat loaf. [ME f. OF *hastelet* dimin. of *haste* roast meat, spit, f. OLG, OHG *harst* roast]

Hasmonean /ˌhæzməˈnɪən/ *adj. & n.* —*adj.* of or relating to a Jewish dynasty or family to which the Maccabees belonged. —*n.* a member of this dynasty. [Gk *Asmōnaios* f. Heb. *ḥašmōnây* Hasmon, name of reputed ancestor]

hasn't /ˈhæz(ə)nt/ *contr.* has not.

hasp /hɑːsp/ *n. & v.* —*n.* a hinged metal clasp that fits over a staple and can be secured by a padlock. —*v.tr.* fasten with a hasp. [OE *hæpse, hæsp*]

Hasselt /ˈhæsɛlt/ a city in NE Belgium, capital of Limbourg province, on the River Demer; pop. (1988) 65,800.

hassle /ˈhæs(ə)l/ *n. & v. colloq.* —*n.* **1** a prolonged trouble or inconvenience. **2** an argument or involved struggle. —*v.* **1** *tr.* harass, annoy; cause trouble to. **2** *intr.* argue, quarrel. [20th c.: orig. dial.]

hassock /ˈhæsək/ *n.* **1** a thick firm cushion for kneeling on, esp. in church. **2** a tuft of matted grass etc. [OE *hassuc*]

hast /hæst/ *archaic 2nd sing. present of* HAVE.

hastate /ˈhæsteɪt/ *adj. Bot.* triangular like the head of a spear. [L *hastatus* f. *hasta* spear]

haste /heɪst/ *n. & v.* —*n.* **1** urgency of movement or action. **2** excessive hurry. —*v.intr. archaic* = HASTEN. □ **in haste** quickly, hurriedly. **make haste** hurry; be quick. [ME f. OF *haste, haster* f. WG]

hasten /ˈheɪs(ə)n/ *v.* **1** *intr.* (often foll. by *to* + infin.) make haste; hurry. **2** *tr.* cause to occur or be ready or be done sooner.

Hastings¹ /ˈheɪstɪŋz/ a town on the coast of East Sussex, scene of William the Conqueror's victory over the Anglo-Saxon king Harold II in 1066. Having invaded England to enforce his claim to the throne, William, Duke of Normandy was confronted by Harold's army drawn up on a hill. The English shield wall withstood Norman attacks through most of the day, but eventually broke after the less disciplined parts of the army had been lured off the hill and destroyed. Harold, along with most of his good fighting men, died in the battle, and William subsequently seized London and the vacant throne.

Hastings² /ˈheɪstɪŋz/, Warren (1732–1818), British colonial administrator who rose from being a clerk in the East India Company to become India's first Governor-General in 1774, and, while holding that post, introduced many of the administrative reforms vital to the successful maintenance of British rule in India, while also overseeing the defence of his territories against invasion. On his return to England in 1785 he was accused, not completely unjustly, of high-handedness and corruption, and was eventually impeached on the latter charge. After a seven-year trial before the House of Lords, he was acquitted in 1795 and retired to private life.

hasty /ˈheɪstɪ/ adj. (**hastier, hastiest**) **1** hurried; acting too quickly or hurriedly. **2** said, made, or done too quickly or too soon; rash, unconsidered. **3** quick-tempered. □□ **hastily** adv. **hastiness** n. [ME f. OF hasti, hastif (as HASTE, -IVE)]

hat /hæt/ n. & v. —n. **1** a covering for the head, often with a brim and worn out of doors. **2** colloq. a person's occupation or capacity, esp. one of several (wearing his managerial hat). —v.tr. (**hatted, hatting**) cover or provide with a hat. □ **hat trick 1** Cricket the taking of three wickets by the same bowler with three successive balls. **2** the scoring of three goals, points, etc. in other sports. **keep it under one's hat** colloq. keep it secret. **out of a hat** by random selection. **pass the hat round** collect contributions of money. **take off one's hat to** colloq. acknowledge admiration for. **throw one's hat in the ring** take up a challenge. □□ **hatful** n. (pl. -**fuls**). **hatless** adj. [OE hætt f. Gmc]

hatband /ˈhætbænd/ n. a band of ribbon etc. round a hat above the brim.

hatbox /ˈhætbɒks/ n. a box to hold a hat, esp. for travelling.

hatch¹ /hætʃ/ n. **1** an opening between two rooms, e.g. between a kitchen and a dining-room for serving food. **2** an opening or door in an aircraft, spacecraft, etc. **3** Naut. **a** = HATCHWAY. **b** a trapdoor or cover for this (often in pl.: batten the hatches). **4** a floodgate. □ **down the hatch** sl. (as a drinking toast) drink up, cheers! **under hatches 1** below deck. **2 a** down out of sight. **b** brought low; dead. [OE hæcc f. Gmc]

hatch² /hætʃ/ v. & n. —v. **1** intr. **a** (often foll. by out) (of a young bird or fish etc.) emerge from the egg. **b** (of an egg) produce a young animal. **2** tr. incubate (an egg). **3** tr. (also foll. by up) devise (a plot etc.). —n. **1** the act or an instance of hatching. **2** a brood hatched. [ME hacche, of unkn. orig.]

hatch³ /hætʃ/ v.tr. mark (a surface, e.g. a map or drawing) with close parallel lines. [ME f. F hacher f. hache HATCHET]

hatchback /ˈhætʃbæk/ n. a car with a sloping back hinged at the top to form a door.

hatchery /ˈhætʃərɪ/ n. (pl. -**ies**) a place for hatching eggs, esp. of fish or poultry.

hatchet /ˈhætʃɪt/ n. a light short-handled axe. □ **hatchet-faced** colloq. sharp-featured or grim-looking. **hatchet job** colloq. a fierce verbal attack on a person, esp. in print. **hatchet man** colloq. **1** a hired killer. **2** a person employed to carry out a hatchet job. [ME f. OF hachette dimin. of hache axe f. med.L hapia f. Gmc]

hatching /ˈhætʃɪŋ/ n. Art & Archit. close parallel lines forming shading esp. on a map or an architectural drawing.

hatchling /ˈhætʃlɪŋ/ n. a bird or fish that has just hatched.

hatchment /ˈhætʃmənt/ n. a large usu. diamond-shaped tablet with a deceased person's armorial bearings, affixed to that person's house, tomb, etc. [contr. of ACHIEVEMENT]

hatchway /ˈhætʃweɪ/ n. an opening in a ship's deck for lowering cargo into the hold.

hate /heɪt/ v. & n. —v.tr. **1** dislike intensely; feel hatred towards. **2** colloq. **a** dislike. **b** (foll. by verbal noun or to + infin.) be reluctant (to do something) (I hate to disturb you). —n. **1** hatred. **2** colloq. a hated person or thing. □□ **hatable** adj. (also **hateable**). **hater** n. [OE hatian f. Gmc]

hateful /ˈheɪtfʊl/ adj. arousing hatred. □□ **hatefully** adv. **hatefulness** n.

hath /hæθ/ archaic 3rd sing. present of HAVE.

Hathaway /ˈhæθəˌweɪ/, Anne (?1557–1623), the wife of Shakespeare, whom she married in 1582. They had three children, a daughter (Susannah) and a twin daughter and son (Judith and Hamnet).

hatha yoga /ˈhæθə/ n. a system of physical exercises and breathing control used in yoga. [Skr. haṭha force: see YOGA]

Hathor /ˈhæːθɔ(r), ˈhæθɔ(r)/ Egyptian Mythol. a sky and cow goddess, the patron of love and joy, represented as a cow or with a cow's head or ears, or with a solar disc between a cow's horns. Her name means 'House of Horus' (= the sky, in which Horus (the sun) rises and sets).

hatpin /ˈhætpɪn/ n. a long pin, often decorative, for securing a hat to the head.

hatred /ˈheɪtrɪd/ n. intense dislike or ill will. [ME f. HATE + -red f. OE ræden condition]

Hatshepsut /hætˈʃepsʊt/ a queen of Egypt (c.1473–1458 BC) of the 18th Dynasty, widow of Tuthmosis II. Initially ruler under her nephew Tuthmosis III, she proclaimed herself co-ruler and dominated the partnership until her death, after which she was vilified by Tuthmosis who defaced her monuments.

hatstand /ˈhætstænd/ n. a stand with hooks on which to hang hats.

hatter /ˈhætə(r)/ n. **1** a maker or seller of hats. **2** Austral. & NZ a person (esp. a miner or bushman) who lives alone.

Hattusas /ˈhætuːsæs/ the capital of the Hittite empire, situated in central Turkey about 35 km (22 miles) east of Ankara.

hauberk /ˈhɔːbɜːk/ n. hist. a coat of mail. [ME f. OF hau(s)berc f. Frank., = neck protection, f. hals neck + berg- f. beorg protection]

haughty /ˈhɔːtɪ/ adj. (**haughtier, haughtiest**) arrogantly self-admiring and disdainful. □□ **haughtily** adv. **haughtiness** n. [extension of haught (adj.), earlier haut f. OF haut f. L altus high]

haul /hɔːl/ v. & n. —v. **1** tr. pull or drag forcibly. **2** tr. transport by lorry, cart, etc. **3** intr. turn a ship's course. **4** tr. colloq. (usu. foll. by up) bring for reprimand or trial. —n. **1** the act or an instance of hauling. **2** an amount gained or acquired. **3** a distance to be traversed (a short haul). □ **haul over the coals** see COAL. [var. of HALE²]

haulage /ˈhɔːlɪdʒ/ n. **1** the commercial transport of goods. **2** a charge for this.

hauler /ˈhɔːlə(r)/ n. **1** a person or thing that hauls. **2** a miner who takes coal from the workface to the bottom of the shaft. **3** a person or firm engaged in the transport of goods.

haulier /ˈhɔːlɪə(r)/ n. Brit. = HAULER.

haulm /hɔːm, hɑːm/ n. (also **halm**) **1** a stalk or stem. **2** the stalks or stems collectively of peas, beans, potatoes, etc., without the pods etc. [OE h(e)alm f. Gmc]

haulyard var. of HALYARD.

haunch /hɔːntʃ/ n. **1** the fleshy part of the buttock with the thigh, esp. in animals. **2** the leg and loin of a deer etc. as food. **3** the side of an arch between the crown and the pier. [ME f. OF hanche, of Gmc orig.: cf. LG hanke hind leg of a horse]

haunt /hɔːnt/ v. & n. —v. **1** tr. (of a ghost) visit (a place) regularly, usu. reputedly giving signs of its presence. **2** tr. (of a person or animal) frequent or be persistently in (a place). **3** tr. (of a memory etc.) be persistently in the mind of. **4** intr. (foll. by with, in) stay habitually. —n. **1** (often in pl.) a place frequented by a person. **2** a place frequented by animals, esp. for food and drink. □□ **haunter** n. [ME f. OF hanter f. Gmc]

haunting /ˈhɔːntɪŋ/ adj. (of a memory, melody, etc.) poignant, wistful, evocative. □□ **hauntingly** adv.

Hauptmann /ˈhaʊptmæn/, Gerhart (1862–1946), German dramatist, who studied sculpture before turning to literature. His first play Vor Sonnenaufgang (Before Sunrise, 1889), and Die Weber (The Weavers, 1892) are important examples of German naturalism, but Hanneles Himmelfahrt (The Ascension of Joan, 1893), with its visionary elements, deviated towards a new symbolism. Though he frequently returned to more realistic drama during his productive career, Hauptmann's reputation rests on his earlier works which significantly influenced German literature by introducing to the theatre the most uncompromising material of daily life. He was awarded the Nobel Prize for literature in 1912.

æ cat ɑː arm e bed ɜː her ɪ sit iː see ɒ hot ɔː saw ʌ run ʊ put uː too ə ago aɪ my

Hausa /ˈhaʊzə/ n. & adj. —n. (pl. same or **Hausas**) **1 a** a widespread Negroid people of the Sudan and northern Nigeria, of the Bantu family with some Hamitic mixture. **b** a member of this people. **2** their language, the most important in West Africa, spoken by some 25 million people mainly in Nigeria and Niger. It belongs to the Chadic branch of the Afro-Asiatic language group. —adj. of or relating to this people or language. [native name]

hausfrau /ˈhaʊsfraʊ/ n. a German housewife. [G f. *Haus* house + *Frau* woman]

hautboy archaic var. of OBOE.

haute couture /ˌəʊt kuːˈtjʊə(r)/ n. high fashion; the leading fashion houses or their products. [F, lit. = high dressmaking]

haute cuisine /ˌəʊt kwɪˈziːn/ n. cookery of a high standard, esp. of the French traditional school. [F, lit. = high cookery]

haute école /ˌəʊt eɪˈkɒl/ n. the art or practice of advanced classical dressage. [F, = high school]

hauteur /əʊˈtɜː(r)/ n. haughtiness of manner. [F f. *haut* high]

haut monde /əʊ ˈmɒːnd/ n. fashionable society. [F, lit. = high world]

Havana /həˈvænə/ the capital of Cuba and chief port of the West Indies, famous for its cigars; pop. (est. 1986) 2,014,800. —n. a cigar made at Havana or elsewhere in Cuba.

have /hæv, həv/ v. & n. —v. (3rd sing. present **has** /hæz, həs/; past and past part. **had** /hæd/) —v.tr. **1** hold in possession as one's property or at one's disposal; be provided with (*has a car; had no time to read; has nothing to wear*). **2** hold in a certain relationship (*has a sister; had no equals*). **3** contain as a part or quality (*house has two floors; has green eyes*). **4 a** undergo, experience, enjoy, suffer (*had a good time; had a shock; has a headache*). **b** be subjected to a specified state (*had my car stolen; the book has a page missing*). **c** cause, instruct, or invite (a person or thing) to be in a particular state or take a particular action (*had him dismissed; had us worried; had my hair cut; had a copy made; had them to stay*). **5 a** engage in (an activity) (*had an argument; had sex*). **b** hold (a meeting, party, etc.). **6** eat or drink (*had a beer*). **7** (usu. in *neg.*) accept or tolerate; permit to (*I won't have it; will not have you say such things*). **8 a** let (a feeling etc.) be present (*have no doubt; has a lot of sympathy for me; have nothing against them*). **b** show or feel (mercy, pity, etc.) towards another person (*have pity on him; have mercy!*). **c** (foll. by *to* + infin.) show by action that one is influenced by a (feeling, quality, etc.) (*have the goodness to leave now*). **9 a** give birth to (offspring). **b** conceive mentally (an idea etc.). **10** receive, obtain (*had a letter from him; not a ticket to be had*). **11** be burdened with or committed to (*has a job to do; have my garden to attend to*). **12 a** have obtained (a qualification) (*has six O levels*). **b** know (a language) (*has no Latin*). **13** *sl.* **a** get the better of (*I had him there*). **b** (usu. in *passive*) Brit. cheat, deceive (*you were had*). **14** coarse *sl.* have sexual intercourse with. —v.aux. (with past part. or ellipt., to form the perfect, pluperfect, and future perfect tenses, and the conditional mood) (*have worked; had seen; will have been; had I known, I would have gone; have you met her? yes, I have*). —n. **1** (usu. in *pl.*) colloq. a person who has wealth or resources. **2** *sl.* a swindle. ▫ **had best** see BEST. **had better** would find it prudent to. **had rather** see RATHER. **have a care** see CARE. **have done**, **have done with** see DONE. **have an eye for, have eyes for, have an eye to** see EYE. **have a good mind to** see MIND. **have got to** colloq. = have to. **have had it** colloq. **1** have missed one's chance. **2** have passed one's prime. **3** have been killed, defeated, etc. **have it 1** (foll. by *that* + clause) express the view that. **2** win a decision in a vote etc. **3** colloq. have found the answer etc. **have it away** (or **off**) Brit. coarse *sl.* have sexual intercourse. **have it both ways** see BOTH. **have it in for** colloq. be hostile or ill-disposed towards. **have it out** (often foll. by *with*) colloq. attempt to settle a dispute by discussion or argument. **have it one's own way** see WAY. **have-not** (usu. in *pl.*) colloq. a person lacking wealth or resources. **have nothing to do with** see DO¹. **have on 1** be wearing (clothes). **2** be committed to (an engagement). **3** colloq. tease, play a trick on. **have out** get (a tooth etc.) extracted (*had her tonsils out*). **have something** (or **nothing**) **on a person 1** know something (or nothing) discreditable or incriminating about a person. **2** have an (or no) advantage or superiority over a person. **have to** be obliged to,

must. **have to do with** see DO¹. **have up** Brit. colloq. bring (a person) before a court of justice, interviewer, etc. [OE *habban* f. Gmc, prob. rel. to HEAVE]

Havel /ˈhɑːvel/, Václav (1936–), Czech writer, whose works include plays, letters, and the essays *Living in Truth*. His *Vanek Trilogy* of plays deals with the problems of reconciling political realities with the demands of honesty. A leading thinker and man of letters, he was imprisoned as a dissident under the Communist regime. Shortly after his release he became President of his country after its peaceful overthrow of bureaucratic communism in 1989.

haven /ˈheɪv(ə)n/ n. **1** a harbour or port. **2** a place of refuge. [OE *hæfen* f. ON *höfn*]

haven't /ˈhæv(ə)nt/ contr. have not.

haver /ˈheɪvə(r)/ v. & n. —v.intr. Brit. **1** talk foolishly; babble. **2** vacillate, hesitate. —n. (usu. in *pl.*) Sc. foolish talk; nonsense. [18th c.: orig. unkn.]

haversack /ˈhævəˌsæk/ n. a stout bag for provisions etc., carried on the back or over the shoulder. [F *havresac* f. G *Habersack* f. *Haber* oats + *Sack* SACK¹]

haversine /ˈhævəˌsaɪn/ n. (also **haversin**) Math. half of a versed sine. [contr.]

havildar /ˈhævɪlˌdɑː(r)/ n. an Indian NCO corresponding to an army sergeant. [Hind. *ḥavildār* f. Pers. *ḥawāldār* trust-holder]

havoc /ˈhævək/ n. & v. —n. widespread destruction; great confusion or disorder. —v.tr. (**havocked, havocking**) devastate. ▫ **play havoc with** colloq. cause great confusion or difficulty to. [ME f. AF *havok* f. OF *havo(t)*, of unkn. orig.]

haw¹ /hɔː/ n. the hawthorn or its fruit. [OE *haga* f. Gmc, rel. to HEDGE]

haw² /hɔː/ n. the nictitating membrane of a horse, dog, etc., esp. when inflamed. [16th c.: orig. unkn.]

haw³ /hɔː/ int. & v. —int. expressing hesitation. —v.intr. (in **hum and haw**: see HUM¹) [imit.: cf. HA]

Hawaii /həˈwaɪiː/ a State of the US comprising a chain of islands (including Hawaii) in the North Pacific, discovered by Captain Cook in 1778; pop. (est. 1985) 964,700; capital, Honolulu. Annexed by the US in 1898, it became the 50th State in 1959. ▫▫ **Hawaiian** adj. & n.

hawfinch /ˈhɔːfɪntʃ/ n. any large stout finch of the genus *Coccothraustes*, with a thick beak for cracking seeds. [HAW¹ + FINCH]

hawk¹ /hɔːk/ n. & v. —n. **1** any of various diurnal birds of prey of the family Accipitridae, having a characteristic curved beak, rounded short wings, and a long tail. **2** Polit. a person who advocates an aggressive or warlike policy, esp. in foreign affairs. **3** a rapacious person. —v. **1** intr. hunt game with a hawk. **2** intr. (often foll. by *at*) & tr. attack, as a hawk does. **3** intr. (of a bird) hunt on the wing for food. ▫ **hawk-eyed** keen-sighted. **hawk moth** any darting and hovering moth of the family Sphingidae, having narrow forewings and a stout body. **hawk-nosed** having an aquiline nose. ▫▫ **hawkish** adj. **hawkishness** n. **hawklike** adj. [OE *h(e)afoc, hæbuc* f. Gmc]

hawk² /hɔːk/ v.tr. **1** carry about or offer around (goods) for sale. **2** (often foll. by *about*) relate (news, gossip, etc.) freely. [back-form. f. HAWKER¹]

hawk³ /hɔːk/ v. **1** intr. clear the throat noisily. **2** tr. (foll. by *up*) bring (phlegm etc.) up from the throat. [prob. imit.]

hawk⁴ /hɔːk/ n. a plasterer's square board with a handle underneath for carrying plaster or mortar. [17th c.: orig. unkn.]

Hawke Bay /hɔːk/ a bay on the east coast of North Island, New Zealand. The port of Napier lies on its southern shore. It was visited in 1769 by Captain James Cook, who named it after Edward Hawke, First Lord of the Admiralty 1766–71.

hawker¹ /ˈhɔːkə(r)/ n. a person who travels about selling goods. [16th c.: prob. f. LG or Du.; cf. HUCKSTER]

hawker² /ˈhɔːkə(r)/ n. a falconer. [OE *hafocere*]

Hawking /ˈhɔːkɪŋ/, Stephen William (1942–), English theoretical physicist, whose work has greatly advanced understanding of space-time and its singularities. His main work has been on quantum mechanics and 'black holes', which he deduced can emit thermal radiation at a steady rate. While still a student he developed a progressive disabling neuromuscular disease that limits movement and speech. Confined to a wheelchair, unable to write, and with severely impaired speech he has carried out his mathematical calculations mentally and communicated them in a developed form. His life and work are a notable triumph over severe physical disability.

Hawkins[1] /ˈhɔːkɪnz/, Coleman Randolph (1904–69), American saxophonist, who was influential in making the tenor saxophone popular as a jazz instrument.

Hawkins[2] /ˈhɔːkɪnz/, Sir John (1532–95), Elizabethan sailor. A former slave-trader (associated with his cousin Sir Francis Drake), Hawkins was involved in the early privateering raids on the Spanish West Indies in the 1560s and 1570s. As first Treasurer and then Comptroller of the Elizabethan navy he played an important part in building up the fleet which defeated the Spanish Armada in 1588, during which time he was third in command of the English forces. Like Drake, he died at sea during an unsuccessful expedition to the West Indies in 1595.

hawksbill /ˈhɔːksbɪl/ n. (in full **hawksbill turtle**) a small turtle, *Eretmochelys imbricata*, yielding tortoiseshell.

Hawksmoor /ˈhɔːksmʊə(r)/, Nicholas (1661–1736), English architect who worked with Wren and with Vanbrugh. His most distinguished works are the six London churches designed under the commission of 1711.

hawkweed /ˈhɔːkwiːd/ n. any composite plant of the genus *Hieracium*, with yellow flowers.

hawse /hɔːz/ n. **1** the part of a ship's bows in which hawse-holes or hawse-pipes are placed. **2** the space between the head of an anchored vessel and the anchors. **3** the arrangement of cables when a ship is moored with port and starboard forward anchors. □ **hawse-hole** a hole in the side of a ship through which a cable or anchor-rope passes. **hawse-pipe** a metal pipe lining a hawse-hole. [ME *halse*, prob. f. ON *háls* neck, ship's bow]

hawser /ˈhɔːzə(r)/ n. *Naut.* a thick rope or cable for mooring or towing a ship. [ME f. AF *haucer*, *hauceour* f. OF *haucier* hoist ult. f. L *altus* high]

hawthorn /ˈhɔːθɔːn/ n. any thorny shrub or tree of the genus *Crataegus*, esp. *C. monogyna*, with white, red, or pink blossom and small dark-red fruit or haws. [OE *hagathorn* (as HAW[1], THORN)]

Hawthorne /ˈhɔːθɔːn/, Nathaniel (1804–64), American novelist, best known as the author of *The Scarlet Letter* (1850), an inquiry into the nature of American Puritanism and the New England conscience, and *The House of Seven Gables* (1851), dealing with hereditary guilt and expiation. He was in England as consul in Liverpool 1853–7, then spent two years in Italy which inspired *The Marble Faun* (1860). Hawthorne is recognized as one of the greatest of American writers, a moralist much preoccupied with the 'transmitted vices of society', reflecting his own sensitivity about his Puritan ancestry.

hay[1] /heɪ/ n. & v. —n. grass mown and dried for fodder. —v. **1** *intr.* make hay. **2** *tr.* put (land) under grass for hay. **3** *tr.* make into hay. □ **hay fever** an allergy with catarrhal and other asthmatic symptoms, caused by pollen or dust. **make hay of** throw into confusion. **make hay (while the sun shines)** seize opportunities for profit or enjoyment. [OE *hēg*, *hīeg*, *hīg* f. Gmc]

hay[2] /heɪ/ n. (also **hey**) **1** a country dance with interweaving steps. **2** a figure in this. [obs. F *haie*]

haybox /ˈheɪbɒks/ n. a box stuffed with hay, in which heated food is left to continue cooking.

haycock /ˈheɪkɒk/ n. a conical heap of hay in a field.

Haydn /ˈhaɪd(ə)n/, Franz Joseph (1732–1809), Austrian-born composer, of German parentage. He has long been regarded as the 'father of the symphony', and although the paternity of that form must remain in doubt his position in musical history is assured by the number and magnitude of his masterpieces. His oratorios *The Creation* (1796–8) and *The Seasons* (1799–1801), with their vivid pictorialism and expansive choruses, have long been favourites with the musical public, but his humour, vitality, and sophisticated strength are equally at home in his vast output of over 100 symphonies, 68 string quartets, 47 firmly attributable keyboard sonatas, and the six great Masses composed in Vienna 1796–1802. Haydn spent 30 years with the Esterházy household,

mostly in Hungary, and this enforced isolation from the musical world meant that, in his own words, he was 'forced to become original'. He became a friend of Mozart, whom he greatly admired, and his later years were crowded with invitations to conduct and compose abroad; when he visited England in 1791–2 and 1794–5 he was fêted, lionized, and entertained by royalty. On his return to Vienna he accepted Beethoven as a pupil, an uneasy relationship for them both. From about 1801 his health began to fail and he died during the French occupation of Vienna.

Hayes /heɪz/, Rutherford Birchard (1822–93), 19th President of the US, 1877–81. He withdrew Federal (Northern) troops from the Southern States where they had been stationed in the process of reconstruction (see entry) after the Civil War.

hayfield /ˈheɪfiːld/ n. a field where hay is being or is to be made.

haymaker /ˈheɪˌmeɪkə(r)/ n. **1** a person who tosses and spreads hay to dry after mowing. **2** an apparatus for shaking and drying hay. **3** *sl.* a forceful blow or punch. □□ **haymaking** n.

haymow /ˈheɪməʊ/ n. hay stored in a stack or barn.

hayrick /ˈheɪrɪk/ n. = HAYSTACK.

hayseed /ˈheɪsiːd/ n. **1** grass seed obtained from hay. **2** *US colloq.* a rustic or yokel.

haystack /ˈheɪstæk/ n. a packed pile of hay with a pointed or ridged top.

haywire /ˈheɪˌwaɪə(r)/ adj. *colloq.* **1** badly disorganized, out of control. **2** (of a person) badly disturbed; erratic. [HAY[1] + WIRE, from the use of hay-baling wire in makeshift repairs]

hazard /ˈhæzəd/ n. & v. —n. **1** a danger or risk. **2** a source of this. **3** chance. **4** a dice game with a complicated arrangement of chances. **5** *Golf* an obstruction in playing a shot, e.g. a bunker, water, etc. **6** each of the winning openings in a real-tennis court. —v.tr. **1** venture on (*hazard a guess*). **2** run the risk of. **3** expose to hazard. [ME f. OF *hasard* f. Sp. *azar* f. Arab. *az-zahr* chance, luck]

hazardous /ˈhæzədəs/ adj. **1** risky, dangerous. **2** dependent on chance. □□ **hazardously** adv. **hazardousness** n. [F *hasardeux* (as HAZARD)]

haze[1] /heɪz/ n. **1** obscuration of the atmosphere near the earth by fine particles of water, smoke, or dust. **2** mental obscurity or confusion. [prob. back-form. f. HAZY]

haze[2] /heɪz/ v.tr. **1** *Naut.* harass with overwork. **2** *US* bully; seek to disconcert. [orig. uncert.: cf. obs. F *haser* tease, insult]

hazel /ˈheɪz(ə)l/ n. **1** any shrub or small tree of the genus *Corylus*, esp. *C. avellana* bearing round brown edible nuts. **2 a** wood from the hazel. **b** a stick made of this. **3** a reddish-brown or greenish-brown colour (esp. of the eyes). □ **hazel-grouse** a woodland grouse, *Tetrastes bonasia*. [OE *hæsel* f. Gmc]

hazelnut /ˈheɪz(ə)lˌnʌt/ n. the fruit of the hazel.

Hazlitt /ˈhæzlɪt/, William (1778–1830), British essayist and critic, the son of a Unitarian minister whose radical views he inherited. Hazlitt began as a painter but, encouraged by Coleridge, chose a literary career. He became a prominent journalist, lecturer, and critic, contributing articles on diverse subjects to many periodicals; some of his best essays are collected in *Table Talk* (1821–2) and *The Plain Speaker* (1826). Among his important critical works are *Lectures on the English Poets* (1818) and *The Spirit of the Age* (1825). His style, marked by clarity and conviction, brought a new vigour to English prose writing.

hazy /ˈheɪzɪ/ adj. (**hazier**, **haziest**) **1** misty. **2** vague, indistinct. **3** confused, uncertain. □□ **hazily** adv. **haziness** n. [17th c. in Naut. use: orig. unkn.]

HB abbr. hard black (pencil-lead).

Hb symb. haemoglobin.

HBM abbr. Her or His Britannic Majesty (or Majesty's).

H-bomb /ˈeɪtʃbɒm/ n. = hydrogen bomb. [H[3] + BOMB]

HC abbr. **1** Holy Communion. **2** (in the UK) House of Commons.

h.c. abbr. honoris causa.

HCF abbr. **1** highest common factor. **2** *Brit.* Honorary Chaplain to the Forces.

HE abbr. **1** His or Her Excellency. **2** His Eminence. **3** high explosive.

He *symb. Chem.* the element helium.

he /hiː, hɪ/ *pron. & n.* —*pron.* (*obj.* **him** /hɪm/; *poss.* **his** /hɪz/; *pl.* **they** /ðeɪ/) **1** the man or boy or male animal previously named or in question. **2** a person etc. of unspecified sex, esp. referring to one already named or identified (*if anyone comes he will have to wait*). —*n.* **1** a male; a man. **2** (in *comb.*) male (*he-goat*). **3** a children's chasing game, with the chaser designated 'he'. □ **he-man** (*pl.* **-men**) a masterful or virile man. [OE f. Gmc]

head /hed/ *n., adj., & v.* —*n.* **1** the upper part of the human body, or the foremost or upper part of an animal's body, containing the brain, mouth, and sense-organs. **2 a** the head regarded as the seat of intellect or repository of comprehended information. **b** intelligence; imagination (*use your head*). **c** mental aptitude or tolerance (usu. foll. by *for: a good head for business; no head for heights*). **3** *colloq.* a headache, esp. resulting from a blow or from intoxication. **4** a thing like a head in form or position, esp.: **a** the operative part of a tool. **b** the flattened top of a nail. **c** the ornamented top of a pillar. **d** a mass of leaves or flowers at the top of a stem. **e** the flat end of a drum. **f** the foam on top of a glass of beer etc. **g** the upper horizontal part of a window frame, door frame, etc. **5** life when regarded as vulnerable (*it cost him his head*). **6 a** a person in charge; a director or leader (esp. the principal teacher at a school or college). **b** a position of leadership or command. **7** the front or forward part of something, e.g. a queue. **8** the upper end of something, e.g. a table or bed. **9** the top or highest part of something, e.g. a page, stairs, etc. **10** a person or individual regarded as a numerical unit (*£10 per head*). **11** (*pl.* same) **a** an individual animal as a unit. **b** (as *pl.*) a number of cattle or game as specified (*20 head*). **12 a** the side of a coin bearing the image of a head. **b** (usu. in *pl.*) this side as a choice when tossing a coin. **13 a** the source of a river or stream etc. **b** the end of a lake at which a river enters it. **14** the height or length of a head as a measure. **15** the component of a machine that is in contact with or very close to what is being processed or worked on, esp.: **a** the component on a tape recorder that touches the moving tape in play and converts the signals. **b** the part of a record-player that holds the playing cartridge and stylus. **c** = PRINTHEAD. **16 a** a confined body of water or steam in an engine etc. **b** the pressure exerted by this. **17** a promontory (esp. in place-names) (*Beachy Head*). **18** *Naut.* **a** the bows of a ship. **b** (often in *pl.*) a ship's latrine. **19** a main topic or category for consideration or discussion. **20** *Journalism* = HEADLINE *n.* **21** a culmination, climax, or crisis. **22** the fully developed top of a boil etc. **23** *sl.* a habitual taker of drugs; a drug addict. —*attrib.adj.* chief or principal (*head gardener; head office*). —*v.* **1** *tr.* be at the head or front of. **2** *tr.* be in charge of (*headed a small team*). **3** *tr.* **a** provide with a head or heading. **b** (of an inscription, title, etc.) be at the top of, serve as a heading for. **4 a** *intr.* face or move in a specified direction or towards a specified result (often foll. by *for: is heading for trouble*). **b** *tr.* direct in a specified direction. **5** *tr. Football* strike (the ball) with the head. **6 a** *tr.* (often foll. by *down*) cut the head off (a plant etc.). **b** *intr.* (of a plant etc.) form a head. □ **above** (or **over**) **one's head** beyond one's ability to understand. **come to a head** reach a crisis. **enter** (or **come into**) **one's head** *colloq.* occur to one. **from head to toe** (or **foot**) all over a person's body. **get one's head down** *sl.* **1** go to bed. **2** concentrate on the task in hand. **give a person his** or **her head** allow a person to act freely. **go out of one's head** go mad. **go to one's head 1** (of liquor) make one dizzy or slightly drunk. **2** (of success) make one conceited. **head and shoulders** *colloq.* by a considerable amount. **head back 1** get ahead of so as to intercept and turn back. **2** return home etc. **head-banger** *sl.* **1** a young person shaking violently to the rhythm of pop music. **2** a crazy or eccentric person. **head-butt** *n.* a forceful thrust with the top of the head into the chin or body of another person. —*v.tr.* attack (another person) with a head-butt. **head-dress** an ornamental covering or band for the head. **head first 1** with the head foremost. **2** precipitately. **head in the sand** refusal to acknowledge an obvious danger or difficulty. **head off 1** get ahead of so as to intercept and turn aside. **2** forestall. **a head of hair** the hair on a person's head, esp. as a distinctive feature. **head-on 1** with the front foremost (*a head-on crash*). **2** in direct confrontation. **head over**

heels 1 turning over completely in forward motion as in a somersault etc. **2** topsy-turvy. **3** utterly, completely (*head over heels in love*). **head-shrinker** *sl.* a psychiatrist. **head start** an advantage granted or gained at an early stage. **heads will roll** *colloq.* people will be disgraced or dismissed. **head-up** (of instrument readings in an aircraft, vehicle, etc.) shown so as to be visible without lowering the eyes. **head-voice** the high register of the voice in speaking or singing. **head wind** a wind blowing from directly in front. **hold up one's head** be confident or unashamed. **in one's head 1** in one's thoughts or imagination. **2** by mental process without use of physical aids. **keep one's head** remain calm. **keep one's head above water** *colloq.* **1** keep out of debt. **2** avoid succumbing to difficulties. **keep one's head down** *colloq.* remain inconspicuous in difficult or dangerous times. **lose one's head** lose self-control; panic. **make head or tail of** (usu. with *neg.* or *interrog.*) understand at all. **off one's head** *sl.* crazy. **off the top of one's head** *colloq.* impromptu; without careful thought or investigation. **on one's** (or **one's own**) **head** as one's sole responsibility. **out of one's head 1** *sl.* crazy. **2** from one's imagination or memory. **over one's head 1** beyond one's ability to understand. **2** without one's knowledge or involvement, esp. when one has a right to this. **3** with disregard for one's own (stronger) claim (*was promoted over their heads*). **put heads together** consult together. **put into a person's head** suggest to a person. **take** (or **get**) **it into one's head** (foll. by *that* + clause or *to* + infin.) form a definite idea or plan. **turn a person's head** make a person conceited. **with one's head in the clouds** see CLOUD. □□ **headed** *adj.* (also in *comb.*). **headless** *adj.* **headward** *adj. & adv.* [OE *hēafod* f. Gmc]

-head /hed/ *suffix* = -HOOD (*godhead; maidenhead*). [ME *-hed, -hede* = -HOOD]

headache /'hedeɪk/ *n.* **1** a continuous pain in the head. **2** *colloq.* **a** a worrying problem. **b** a troublesome person. □□ **headachy** *adj.*

headband /'hedbænd/ *n.* a band worn round the head as decoration or to keep the hair off the face.

headboard /'hedbɔːd/ *n.* an upright panel placed behind the head of a bed.

headcount /'hedkaʊnt/ *n.* **1** a counting of individual people. **2** a total number of people, esp. the number of people employed in a particular organization.

header /'hedə(r)/ *n.* **1** *Football* a shot or pass made with the head. **2** *colloq.* a headlong fall or dive. **3** a brick or stone laid at right angles to the face of a wall. **4** (in full **header-tank**) a tank of water etc. maintaining pressure in a plumbing system.

headgear /'hedgɪə(r)/ *n.* a hat or head-dress.

head-hunting /'hed,hʌntɪŋ/ *n.* **1** the practice among some peoples of collecting the heads of dead enemies as trophies. **2** the practice of filling a (usu. senior) business position by approaching a suitable person employed elsewhere. □□ **head-hunt** *v.tr.* (also *absol.*). **head-hunter** *n.*

heading /'hedɪŋ/ *n.* **1 a** a title at the head of a page or section of a book etc. **b** a division or section of a subject of discourse etc. **2 a** a horizontal passage made in preparation for building a tunnel. **b** *Mining* = DRIFT *n.* 6. **3** material for making caskheads. **4** the extension of the top of a curtain above the tape that carries the hooks or the pocket for a wire.

headlamp /'hedlæmp/ *n.* = HEADLIGHT.

headland *n.* **1** /'hedlənd/ a promontory. **2** /'hedlænd/ a strip left unploughed at the end of a field, for machinery to pass along.

headlight /'hedlaɪt/ *n.* **1** a strong light at the front of a motor vehicle or railway engine. **2** the beam from this.

headline /'hedlaɪn/ *n. & v.* —*n.* **1** a heading at the top of an article or page, esp. in a newspaper. **2** (in *pl.*) the most important items of news in a newspaper or broadcast news bulletin. —*v.tr.* give a headline to. □ **hit** (or **make**) **the headlines** *colloq.* be given prominent attention as news.

headliner /'hed,laɪnə(r)/ *n. US* a star performer.

headlock /'hedlɒk/ *n. Wrestling* a hold with an arm round the opponent's head.

headlong /'hedlɒŋ/ adv. & adj. **1** with head foremost. **2** in a rush. [ME *heading* (as HEAD, -LING²), assim. to -LONG]

headman /'hedmən/ n. (pl. **-men**) the chief man of a tribe etc.

headmaster /hed'mɑ:stə(r)/ n. (fem. **headmistress** /-'mɪstrɪs/) the principal teacher in charge of a school.

headmost /'hedməʊst/ adj. (esp. of a ship) foremost.

headphone /'hedfəʊn/ n. (usu. in pl.) a pair of earphones joined by a band placed over the head, for listening to audio equipment etc.

headpiece /'hedpi:s/ n. **1** an ornamental engraving at the head of a chapter etc. **2** a helmet. **3** archaic intellect.

headquarters /hed'kwɑ:təz/ n. (as sing. or pl.) **1** the administrative centre of an organization. **2** the premises occupied by a military commander and the commander's staff.

headrest /'hedrest/ n. a support for the head, esp. on a seat or chair.

headroom /'hedru:m, -rʊm/ n. **1** the space or clearance between the top of a vehicle and the underside of a bridge etc. which it passes under. **2** the space above a driver's or passenger's head in a vehicle.

headscarf /'hedskɑ:f/ n. a scarf worn round the head and tied under the chin, instead of a hat.

headset /'hedset/ n. a set of headphones, often with a microphone attached, used esp. in telephony and radio communication.

headship /'hedʃɪp/ n. the position of chief or leader, esp. of a headmaster or headmistress.

headsman /'hedzmən/ n. (pl. **-men**) **1** hist. an executioner who beheads. **2** a person in command of a whaling boat.

headspring /'hedsprɪŋ/ n. **1** the main source of a stream. **2** a principal source of ideas etc.

headsquare /'hedskweə(r)/ n. a rectangular scarf for wearing on the head.

headstall /'hedstɔ:l/ n. the part of a halter or bridle that fits round a horse's head.

headstock /'hedstɒk/ n. a set of bearings in a machine, supporting a revolving part.

headstone /'hedstəʊn/ n. a (usu. inscribed) stone set up at the head of a grave.

headstrong /'hedstrɒŋ/ adj. self-willed and obstinate. □□ **headstrongly** adv. **headstrongness** n.

headwater /'hed,wɔ:tə(r)/ n. (in sing. or pl.) streams flowing from the sources of a river.

headway /'hedweɪ/ n. **1** progress. **2** the rate of progress of a ship. **3** = HEADROOM 1.

headword /'hedwɜ:d/ n. a word forming a heading, e.g. of an entry in a dictionary or encyclopedia.

headwork /'hedwɜ:k/ n. mental work or effort.

heady /'hedɪ/ adj. (**headier, headiest**) **1** (of liquor) potent, intoxicating. **2** (of success etc.) likely to cause conceit. **3** (of a person, thing, or action) impetuous, violent. □□ **headily** adv. **headiness** n.

heal /hi:l/ v. **1** intr. (often foll. by up) (of a wound or injury) become sound or healthy again. **2** tr. cause (a wound, disease, or person) to heal or be healed. **3** tr. put right (differences etc.). **4** tr. alleviate (sorrow etc.). □ **heal-all 1** a universal remedy, a panacea. **2** a popular name of various medicinal plants. □□ **healable** adj. **healer** n. [OE hǣlan f. Gmc, rel. to WHOLE]

heald /hi:ld/ n. = HEDDLE. [app. f. OE hefel, hefeld, f. Gmc]

health /helθ/ n. **1** the state of being well in body or mind. **2** a person's mental or physical condition (has poor health). **3** soundness, esp. financial or moral (the health of the nation). **4** a toast drunk in someone's honour. □ **health centre** the headquarters of a group of local medical services. **health certificate** a certificate stating a person's fitness for work etc. **health farm** a residential establishment where people seek improved health by a regime of dieting, exercise, etc. **health food** natural food thought to have health-giving qualities. **health service** a public service providing medical care. **health visitor** Brit. a trained nurse who visits those in need of medical attention in their homes. [OE hǣlth f. Gmc]

healthful /'helθfʊl/ adj. conducive to good health; beneficial. □□ **healthfully** adv. **healthfulness** n.

healthy /'helθɪ/ adj. (**healthier, healthiest**) **1** having, showing, or promoting good health. **2** beneficial, helpful (a healthy respect for experience). □□ **healthily** adv. **healthiness** n.

Heaney /'hi:nɪ/, Seamus Justin (1939–   ), Irish poet. His early poetry is connected with the farmland of his youth; his later works, such as Wintering Out (1972) and Field Work (1979), brood on the cultural and historical implications of words.

heap /hi:p/ n. & v. —n. **1** a collection of things lying haphazardly one on another. **2** (esp. in pl.) colloq. a large number or amount (there's heaps of time; is heaps better). **3** sl. an old or dilapidated thing, esp. a motor vehicle or building. —v. **1** tr. & intr. (foll. by up, together, etc.) collect or be collected in a heap. **2** tr. (foll. by with) load copiously or to excess. **3** tr. (foll. by on, upon) accord or offer copiously to (heaped insults on them). **4** tr. (as **heaped** adj.) (of a spoonful etc.) with the contents piled above the brim. □ **heap coals of fire on a person's head** cause a person remorse by returning good for evil. [OE hēap, hēapian f. Gmc]

hear /hɪə(r)/ v. (past and past part. **heard** /hɜ:d/) **1** tr. (also absol.) perceive (sound etc.) with the ear. **2** tr. listen to (heard them on the radio). **3** tr. listen judicially to and judge (a case, plaintiff, etc.). **4** intr. (foll. by about, of, or that + clause) be told or informed. **5** intr. (foll. by from) be contacted by, esp. by letter or telephone. **6** tr. be ready to obey (an order). **7** tr. grant (a prayer). □ **have heard of** be aware of; know of the existence of. **hear! hear!** int. expressing agreement (esp. with something said in a speech). **hear a person out** listen to all that a person says. **hear say** (or **tell**) (usu. foll. by of, or that + clause) be informed. **will not hear of** will not allow or agree to. □□ **hearable** adj. **hearer** n. [OE hīeran f. Gmc]

Heard and McDonald Islands /hɜ:d, mək'dɒnəld/ a group of uninhabited islands in the south Indian Ocean, administered by Australia since 1947 as an external territory.

hearing /'hɪərɪŋ/ n. **1** the faculty of perceiving sounds. **2** the range within which sounds may be heard; earshot (within hearing; in my hearing). **3** an opportunity to state one's case (give them a fair hearing). **4** the listening to evidence and pleadings in a law court. □ **hearing-aid** a small device to amplify sound, worn by a partially deaf person.

hearken /'hɑ:kən/ v.intr. (also **harken**) archaic or literary (often foll. by to) listen. [OE heorcnian (as HARK)]

hearsay /'hɪəseɪ/ n. rumour, gossip. □ **hearsay evidence** Law evidence given by a witness based on information received from others rather than personal knowledge.

hearse /hɜ:s/ n. a vehicle for conveying the coffin at a funeral. [ME f. OF herse harrow f. med.L herpica ult. f. L hirpex -icis large rake]

Hearst /hɜ:st/, William Randolph (1863–1951), American newspaper publisher, noted for his introduction of large headlines, sensational crime reporting, and other flamboyant features to increase circulation. At the peak of his fortunes in the mid-1930s he had acquired a number of newspapers and magazines, radio stations, and two film companies, but his extravagant purchases and the Depression seriously weakened his financial position. His methods greatly influenced American journalism. The central character of Orson Welles's film Citizen Kane (1941) was modelled on Hearst.

heart /hɑ:t/ n. **1** a hollow muscular organ maintaining the circulation of blood by rhythmic contraction and dilation. (See below.) **2** the region of the heart; the breast. **3 a** the heart regarded as the centre of thought, feeling, and emotion (esp. love). **b** a person's capacity for feeling emotion (has no heart). **4 a** courage or enthusiasm (take heart; lose heart). **b** one's mood or feeling (change of heart). **5 a** the central or innermost part of something. **b** the vital part or essence (the heart of the matter). **6** the close compact head of a cabbage, lettuce, etc. **7 a** a heart-shaped thing. **b** a conventional representation of a heart with two equal curves meeting at a point at the bottom and a cusp at the top. **8 a** a playing-card of a suit denoted by a red figure of a heart. **b** (in *pl.*) this suit. **c** (in *pl.*) a card-game in which players avoid taking tricks containing a card of this suit. **9** condition of land as regards fertility (*in good heart*). □ **after one's own heart** such as one likes or desires. **at heart 1** in one's inmost feelings. **2** basically, essentially. **break a person's heart** overwhelm a person with sorrow. **by heart** in or from memory. **close to** (or **near**) **one's heart 1** dear to one. **2** affecting one deeply. **from the heart** (or **the bottom of one's heart**) sincerely, profoundly. **give** (or **lose**) **one's heart** (often foll. by *to*) fall in love (with). **have a heart** be merciful. **have the heart** (usu. with *neg.*; foll. by *to* + infin.) be insensitive or hard-hearted enough (*didn't have the heart to ask him*). **have** (or **put**) **one's heart in** be keenly involved in or committed to (an enterprise etc.). **have one's heart in one's mouth** be greatly alarmed or apprehensive. **have one's heart in the right place** be sincere or well-intentioned. **heart attack** a sudden occurrence of coronary thrombosis usu. resulting in the death of part of a heart muscle. **heart failure** a gradual failure of the heart to function properly, resulting in breathlessness, oedema, etc. **heart-lung machine** a machine that temporarily takes over the functions of the heart and lungs, esp. in surgery. **heart of gold** a generous nature. **heart of oak** a courageous nature. **heart of stone** a stern or cruel nature. **heart-rending** very distressing. **heart-rendingly** in a heart-rending way. **heart's-blood** lifeblood, life. **heart-searching** thorough examination of one's own feelings and motives. **heart to heart** candidly, intimately. **heart-to-heart** *adj.* (of a conversation etc.) candid, intimate. —*n.* a candid or personal conversation. **heart-warming** emotionally rewarding or uplifting. **in heart** in good spirits. **in one's heart of hearts** in one's inmost feelings. **out of heart** in low spirits. **take to heart** be much affected or distressed by. **to one's heart's content** see CONTENT¹. **wear one's heart on one's sleeve** make one's feelings apparent. **with all one's heart** sincerely; with all goodwill. **with one's whole heart** with enthusiasm; without doubts or reservations. □□ **-hearted** *adj.* [OE *heorte* f. Gmc]

The heart is a four-chambered double-barrelled muscular pump whose function is to drive arterial blood through the body and venous blood through the lungs. The two sides of the heart are quite separate, each consisting of a receiving chamber or atrium and a pumping chamber or ventricle. Venous blood from the body, laden with carbon dioxide, flows into the right atrium, is drawn into the right ventricle, ejected by each contraction or beat of the ventricle into the pulmonary artery, and so to the lungs. Oxygenated blood from the lungs flows into the left atrium, passes to the left ventricle, and is pumped into the large artery (the aorta) and so to all arteries of the body. The heartbeat begins as the spontaneous electrical discharge of clusters of cells in the right atrium, known collectively as the pacemaker. Brief electrical impulses are transmitted to both atria and then to the ventricles, causing these to contract and force the blood to the next stage in its journey round the body; flap valves at the openings between atria and ventricles open to allow its passage and close to prevent it from flowing back. The heart is controlled by two sets of nerves which can make it beat more or less often according to circumstances (during exercise, for example, the tissues need more blood and the heartbeat becomes faster).

The heart has been regarded as the seat of feeling, understanding, and thought (whence phrases such as *a warm heart, knew in his heart*), as the seat of the emotions and distinguished from the intellectual nature (placed in the *head*), or of courage (as in *stout-hearted*). (Cf. LIVER.)

heartache /ˈhɑːteɪk/ *n.* mental anguish or grief.

heartbeat /ˈhɑːtbiːt/ *n.* a pulsation of the heart.

heartbreak /ˈhɑːtbreɪk/ *n.* overwhelming distress. □□ **heartbreaker** *n.* **heartbreaking** *adj.* **heartbroken** *adj.*

heartburn /ˈhɑːtbɜːn/ *n.* a burning sensation in the chest resulting from indigestion; pyrosis.

hearten /ˈhɑːt(ə)n/ *v.tr.* & *intr.* make or become more cheerful. □□ **hearteningly** *adv.*

heartfelt /ˈhɑːtfelt/ *adj.* sincere; deeply felt.

hearth /hɑːθ/ *n.* **1 a** the floor of a fireplace. **b** the area in front

of a fireplace. **2** this symbolizing the home. **3** the bottom of a blast-furnace where molten metal collects. [OE *heorth* f. WG]

hearthrug /ˈhɑːθrʌg/ *n.* a rug laid before a fireplace.

hearthstone /ˈhɑːθstəʊn/ *n.* **1** a flat stone forming a hearth. **2** a soft stone used to whiten hearths, doorsteps, etc.

heartily /ˈhɑːtɪlɪ/ *adv.* **1** in a hearty manner; with goodwill, appetite, or courage. **2** very; to a great degree (esp. with ref. to personal feelings) (*am heartily sick of it; disliked him heartily*).

heartland /ˈhɑːtlənd/ *n.* the central or most important part of an area.

heartless /ˈhɑːtlɪs/ *adj.* unfeeling, pitiless. □□ **heartlessly** *adv.* **heartlessness** *n.*

heartsease /ˈhɑːtsiːz/ *n.* (also **heart's-ease**) a pansy.

heartsick /ˈhɑːtsɪk/ *adj.* very despondent. □□ **heartsickness** *n.*

heartsore /ˈhɑːtsɔː(r)/ *adj.* grieving, heartsick.

heartstrings /ˈhɑːtstrɪŋz/ *n.pl.* one's deepest feelings or emotions.

heartthrob /ˈhɑːtθrɒb/ *n.* **1** beating of the heart. **2** *colloq.* a person for whom one has (esp. immature) romantic feelings.

heartwood /ˈhɑːtwʊd/ *n.* the dense inner part of a tree-trunk yielding the hardest timber.

hearty /ˈhɑːtɪ/ *adj.* & *n.* —*adj.* (**heartier, heartiest**) **1** strong, vigorous. **2** spirited. **3** (of a meal or appetite) large. **4** warm, friendly. —*n.* **1** a hearty person, esp. one ostentatiously so. **2** (usu. in *pl.*) (as a form of address) fellows, esp. fellow sailors. □□ **heartiness** *n.*

heat /hiːt/ *n.* & *v.* —*n.* **1 a** the condition of being hot. **b** the sensation or perception of this. **c** high temperature of the body. **2** *Physics* **a** a form of energy arising from the random motion of the molecules of bodies, which may be transferred by conduction, convection, or radiation. (See below.) **b** the amount of this needed to cause a specific process, or evolved in a process (*heat of formation; heat of solution*). **3** hot weather (*succumbed to the heat*). **4 a** warmth of feeling. **b** anger or excitement (*the heat of the argument*). **5** (foll. by *of*) the most intense part or period of an activity (*in the heat of the battle*). **6 a** (usu. preliminary or trial) round in a race or contest. **7** the receptive period of the sexual cycle, esp. in female mammals. **8** redness of the skin with a sensation of heat (*prickly heat*). **9** pungency of flavour. **10** *sl.* intensive pursuit, e.g. by the police. —*v.* **1** *tr.* & *intr.* make or become hot or warm. **2** *tr.* inflame; excite or intensify. □ **heat barrier** the limitation of the speed of an aircraft etc. by heat resulting from air friction. **heat capacity** thermal capacity. **heat death** *Physics* a state of uniform distribution of energy to which the universe is thought to be tending. **heat engine** a device for producing motive power from heat (e.g. a steam engine, internal-combustion engine, gas turbine). **heat-exchanger** a device for the transfer of heat from one medium to another. **heat pump** see separate entry. **heat-resistant** = HEATPROOF. **heat-seeking** (of a missile etc.) able to detect infra-red radiation to guide it to its target. **heat shield** a device for protection from excessive heat, esp. fitted to a spacecraft. **heat sink** a device or substance for absorbing excessive or unwanted heat. **heat-treat** subject to heat treatment. **heat treatment** the use of heat to modify the properties of a metal etc. **heat wave** a period of very hot weather. **in the heat of the moment** during or resulting from intense activity, without pause for thought. **on heat** (of mammals, esp. females) sexually receptive. **turn the heat on** *colloq.* concentrate an attack or criticism on (a person). [OE *hætu* f. Gmc]

The scientific concept of heat is a development of the ordinary understanding of heat as that which passes into a cold body from a hot body in contact with it. In the late 18th and early 19th c. heat was widely believed to be a kind of fluid substance, called caloric. It is now well established, however, that heat is a form of energy consisting of the motions of the individual molecules that make up all solids, liquids, and gases; temperature is a measure of the average kinetic energy of the molecules in a body.

Addition of heat to a body does not always lead to an increase in temperature, because the body may change state (from solid to liquid, or liquid to gas).

heated /'hiːtɪd/ adj. **1** (of a person, discussions, etc.) angry; inflamed with passion or excitement. **2** made hot. □□ **heatedly** adv.

heater /'hiːtə(r)/ n. **1** a device for supplying heat to its environment. **2** a container with an element etc. for heating the contents (*water-heater*). **3** sl. a gun.

Heath /hiːθ/, Edward Richard George (1916–), British Conservative statesman, Prime Minister 1970–4. During his ministry Britain became a member of the European Economic Community (1973), a move to which Heath had a deep personal commitment. In domestic and economic affairs, however, there were great difficulties: serious problems of inflation and balance of payments were exacerbated by a huge increase in oil prices (1973), and attempts to restrain wage rises led to major strikes. After a national stoppage in the coal industry Heath called an election to strengthen his position, but was defeated. He was replaced as party leader by Margaret Thatcher in 1975.

heath /hiːθ/ n. **1** an area of flattish uncultivated land with low shrubs. **2** a plant growing on a heath, esp. of the genus *Erica* or *Calluna* (e.g. heather). □□ **heathless** adj. **heathlike** adj. **heathy** adj. [OE *hǣth* f. Gmc]

heathen /'hiːð(ə)n/ n. & adj. —n. **1** a person who does not belong to a widely-held religion (esp. who is not Christian, Jew, or Muslim) as regarded by those that do. **2** an unenlightened person; a person regarded as lacking culture or moral principles. **3** (**the heathen**) heathen people collectively. **4** *Bibl.* a Gentile. —adj. **1** of or relating to heathens. **2** having no religion. □□ **heathendom** n. **heathenism** n. [OE *hǣthen* f. Gmc]

heather /'heðə(r)/ n. **1** an evergreen shrub, *Calluna vulgaris*, with purple bell-shaped flowers. **2** any of various shrubs of the genus *Erica* or *Daboecia*, growing esp. on moors and heaths. □ **heather mixture 1** a fabric of mixed hues supposed to resemble heather. **2** the colour of this. □□ **heathery** adj. [ME, Sc., & N.Engl. *hathir* etc., of unkn. orig.: assim. to *heath*]

Heath Robinson /hiːθ 'rɒbɪns(ə)n/ adj. absurdly ingenious and impractical in design or construction. [W. *Heath Robinson*, Engl. cartoonist d. 1944 who drew such contrivances]

Heathrow /hiːθ'rəʊ/ an international airport situated 25 km (15 miles) west of the centre of London.

heating /'hiːtɪŋ/ n. **1** the imparting or generation of heat. **2** equipment or devices used to provide heat, esp. to a building.

heatproof /'hiːtpruːf/ adj. & v. —adj. able to resist great heat. —v.tr. make heatproof.

heat pump n. an engine which (operating as a heat engine in reverse) uses mechanical energy to extract heat from a source (e.g. river water, the earth, or even the air) that is at a slightly higher temperature than its surroundings and transfer a higher level of heat (e.g. to a hot-water system). Its mechanical arrangement, and the principle upon which it works, are exactly those of a large refrigerator. The idea of a heat pump was suggested by Lord Kelvin in 1852, but was not a practical proposition in the 19th c. when fuel (coal) was cheap and the cost of machinery and repairs was expensive.

heatstroke /'hiːtstrəʊk/ n. a feverish condition caused by excessive exposure to high temperature.

heatwave /'hiːtweɪv/ n. a prolonged period of abnormally hot weather.

heave /hiːv/ v. & n. —v. (*past* and *past part.* **heaved** or esp. *Naut.* **hove** /həʊv/) **1** tr. lift or haul (a heavy thing) with great effort. **2** tr. utter with effort or resignation (*heaved a sigh*). **3** tr. *colloq.* throw. **4** *intr.* rise and fall rhythmically or spasmodically. **5** tr. *Naut.* haul by rope. **6** *intr.* retch. —n. **1** an instance of heaving. **2** *Geol.* a sideways displacement in a fault. **3** (in *pl.*) a disease of horses, with laboured breathing. □ **heave-ho** a sailors' cry, esp. on raising the anchor. **heave in sight** *Naut.* or *colloq.* come into view. **heave to** esp. *Naut.* bring or be brought to a standstill. □□ **heaver** n. [OE *hebban* f. Gmc, rel. to L *capere* take]

heaven /'hev(ə)n/ n. **1** a place regarded in some religions as the abode of God and the angels, and of the good after death, often characterized as above the sky. **2** a place or state of supreme bliss. **3** *colloq.* something delightful. **4** (usu. **Heaven**) God, Providence (often, in *sing.* or *pl.* as an exclam. or mild oath: *by Heaven*).

5 (**the heavens**) esp. *poet.* the sky as the abode of the sun, moon, and stars and regarded from earth. □ **heaven-sent** providential; wonderfully opportune. **seventh heaven** see SEVENTH. **move heaven and earth** (foll. by *to* + infin.) make extraordinary efforts. □□ **heavenward** adj. & adv. **heavenwards** adv. [OE *heofon*]

heavenly /'hevənlɪ/ adj. **1** of heaven; divine. **2** of the heavens or sky. **3** *colloq.* very pleasing; wonderful. □ **heavenly bodies** the sun, stars, planets, etc. □□ **heavenliness** n. [OE *heofonlic* (as HEAVEN)]

Heaviside /'hevɪˌsaɪd/, Oliver (1850–1925), English physicist and electrical engineer. Largely self-taught, he began as a telegraph operator, but was forced to retire through deafness. His contributions to telegraphy theory not only improved long-distance telephone communication, but had much broader significance to both cable and wireless telegraphy. He studied inductance, and introduced the concept of impedance and of operational calculus for dealing with transient currents in electrical networks. He suggested in 1902, independently of A. E. Kennelly (1861–1939) of Harvard University, the existence of a layer in the atmosphere responsible for reflecting radio waves back to earth. The Kennelly–Heaviside (or E-) layer was later found by Appleton and others in the ionosphere.

heavy /'hevɪ/ adj., n., & adv. —adj. (**heavier**, **heaviest**) **1** of great or exceptionally high weight; difficult to lift. **2 a** of great density. **b** *Physics* having a greater than the usual mass (esp. of isotopes and compounds containing them). **3** abundant, considerable (*a heavy crop*). **4** severe, intense, extensive, excessive (*heavy fighting*; *a heavy sleep*). **5** doing something to excess (*a heavy drinker*). **6 a** striking or falling with force (*heavy blows*; *heavy rain*). **b** (of the sea) having large powerful waves. **7** (of machinery, artillery, etc.) very large of its kind; large in calibre etc. **8** causing a strong impact (*a heavy fall*). **9** needing much physical effort (*heavy work*). **10** (foll. by *with*) laden. **11** carrying heavy weapons (*the heavy brigade*). **12** (of a person, writing, music, etc.) serious or sombre in tone or attitude; dull, tedious. **13 a** (of food) hard to digest. **b** (of a literary work etc.) hard to read or understand. **14 a** (of temperament) dignified, stern. **b** intellectually slow. **15** (of bread etc.) too dense from not having risen. **16** (of ground) difficult to traverse or work. **17** oppressive; hard to endure (*a heavy fate*; *heavy demands*). **18 a** coarse, ungraceful (*heavy features*). **b** unwieldy. —n. (*pl.* **-ies**) **1** *colloq.* a large violent person; a thug. **2** a villainous or tragic role or actor in a play etc. (usu. in *pl.*). **3** *colloq.* a serious newspaper. **4** anything large or heavy of its kind, e.g. a vehicle. —adv. heavily (esp. in *comb.*: *heavy-laden*). □ **heavier-than-air** (of an aircraft) weighing more than the air it displaces. **heavy chemicals** see CHEMICAL. **heavy-duty** adj. intended to withstand hard use. **heavy-footed** awkward, ponderous. **heavy going** slow or difficult progress. **heavy-hearted** sad, doleful. **heavy hydrogen** = DEUTERIUM. **heavy industry** industry producing metal, machinery, etc. **heavy metal 1** heavy guns. **2** metal of high density. **3** *colloq.* (often *attrib.*) a type of highly-amplified rock music with a strong beat. **heavy petting** erotic fondling between two people, stopping short of intercourse. **heavy sleeper** a person who sleeps deeply. **heavy water** a substance composed entirely or mainly of deuterium oxide. **make heavy weather of** see WEATHER. □□ **heavily** adv. **heaviness** n. **heavyish** adj. [OE *hefig* f. Gmc, rel. to HEAVE]

heavy-handed /hevɪ'hændɪd/ adj. **1** clumsy. **2** overbearing, oppressive. □□ **heavy-handedly** adv. **heavy-handedness** n.

heavyweight /'hevɪˌweɪt/ n. **1 a** a weight in certain sports, in the amateur boxing scale over 81 kg but differing for professional boxers, wrestlers, and weightlifters. **b** a sportsman of this weight. **2** a person, animal, or thing of above average weight. **3** *colloq.* a person of influence or importance. □ **light heavyweight 1** the weight in some sports between middleweight and heavyweight, in the amateur boxing scale 75–81 kg: also called CRUISERWEIGHT. **2** a sportsman of this weight.

Heb. *abbr.* **1** Hebrew. **2** Hebrews (New Testament).

hebdomadal /heb'dɒməd(ə)l/ adj. *formal* weekly, esp. meeting weekly. [LL *hebdomadalis* f. Gk *hebdomas*, *-ados* f. *hepta* seven]

Hebe /ˈhiːbɪ/ **1** *Gk Mythol.* daughter of Hera and Zeus, and cupbearer of the gods. **2** *Astron.* the sixth of the minor planets, discovered in 1847. [Gk *hēbē* = youthful beauty]

hebe /ˈhiːbɪ/ *n.* any flowering shrub of the genus *Hebe*, with usu. overlapping scale-like leaves. [mod.L after the Gk goddess *Hēbē*]

Hebei /həˈbeɪ/ (also **Hopeh** /həˈpeɪ/) a province of NE China; pop. (est. 1986) 56,170,000; capital, Shijiazhuang.

hebetude /ˈhebɪˌtjuːd/ *n. literary* dullness. [LL *hebetudo* f. *hebes*, *-etis* blunt]

Hebraic /hiːˈbreɪɪk/ *adj.* of Hebrew or the Hebrews. □□ **Hebraically** *adv.* [LL f. Gk *Hebraikos* (as HEBREW)]

Hebraism /ˈhiːbreɪˌɪz(ə)m/ *n.* **1** a Hebrew idiom or expression, esp. in the Greek of the Bible. **2** an attribute of the Hebrews. **3** the Hebrew system of thought or religion. □□ **Hebraistic** /-ˈɪstɪk/ *adj.* **Hebraize** *v.tr.* & *intr.* (also **-ise**). [F *hébraïsme* or mod.L *Hebraismus* f. late Gk *Hebraïsmos* (as HEBREW)]

Hebraist /ˈhiːbreɪɪst/ *n.* an expert in Hebrew.

Hebrew /ˈhiːbruː/ *n.* & *adj.* —*n.* **1** a member of a Semitic people orig. centred in ancient Palestine, traditionally from the middle Bronze Age (mid-18th c. BC); an Israelite. **2 a** the language of this people. (See below.) **b** a modern form of this used esp. in the State of Israel. —*adj.* **1** of or in Hebrew. **2** of the Hebrews or the Jews. □ **(Epistle to the) Hebrews** a book of the New Testament, traditionally included among the letters of St Paul but now generally held to be non-Pauline. [ME f. OF *Ebreu* f. med.L *Ebreus* f. L *hebraeus* f. Gk *Hebraios* f. Aram. *'iḇray* f. Heb. *'iḇrî* one from the other side (of the river)]

Hebrew was spoken and written in ancient Palestine for more than a thousand years. It is written from right to left in an alphabet consisting of 22 letters, all consonants; not until the 6th c. AD were vowel signs added to the Hebrew text of the Old Testament to facilitate reading. By *c.*500 BC it had come greatly under the influence of Aramaic, which largely replaced it as a spoken language by *c.*200 AD, but it continued as the religious language of the Jewish people. It was revived as a spoken language in the 19th c., with the modern form having its roots in the ancient language but drawing words from the vocabularies of European languages, and is now the official language of the State of Israel.

Hebrides /ˈhebrɪˌdiːz/ a group of about 500 islands off the NW coast of Scotland. The Inner Hebrides are divided between Highland and Strathclyde regions; the largest of the islands is Skye, others include Mull, Jura, Islay, and Iona. The Outer Hebrides form part of the Western Isles, separated from the Inner group by the Little Minch; the largest is Lewis with Harris, others include North and South Vist and the island group of St Kilda. Until near the end of the 13th c. 'The Hebrides' included also Scottish islands in the Firth of Clyde, the peninsula of Kintyre in SW Scotland, the Isle of Man, and the (Irish) Isle of Rathlin; they formed part of the kingdom of Scotland from 1266, when they were ceded to the Scottish king Alexander III by Magnus of Norway. Norse occupation has influenced the language, customs, and place-names of the islands. The main occupations are farming, fishing, and the manufacture of textiles and woollens. □□ **Hebridean** /-ˈdiːən/ *adj.* & *n.*

Hebron /ˈhebrɒn/ a city lying between Jerusalem and Beersheba, in the West Bank area occupied by Israel since 1967. One of the oldest cities in the country, probably founded in the 18th c. BC, as the home of Abraham it is a holy city of both Judaism and Islam.

Hecate /ˈhekətɪ/ *Gk Mythol.* a goddess, probably of Carian origin, frequently confused with Artemis and also with Selene. She was a powerful and formidable figure, associated with uncanny things, the ghost world, and sorcery, and was worshipped at road junctions, which seem to be haunted the world over.

hecatomb /ˈhekəˌtuːm/ *n.* **1** (in ancient Greece or Rome) a great public sacrifice, orig. of 100 oxen. **2** any extensive sacrifice. [L *hecatombe* f. Gk *hekatombē* f. *hekaton* hundred + *bous* ox]

heck /hek/ *int. colloq.* a mild exclamation of surprise or dismay. [alt. f. HELL]

heckelphone /ˈhekəlˌfəʊn/ *n. Mus.* a bass oboe. [G *Heckelphon* f. W. *Heckel*, 20th-c. Ger. instrument-maker]

heckle /ˈhek(ə)l/ *v.tr.* **1** interrupt and harass (a public speaker). **2** dress (flax or hemp). □□ **heckler** *n.* [ME, northern and eastern form of HACKLE¹]

hectare /ˈhekteə(r), -tɑː(r)/ *n.* a metric unit of square measure, equal to 100 ares (2.471 acres or 10,000 square metres). □□ **hectarage** /ˈhektərɪdʒ/ *n.* [F (as HECTO-, ARE²)]

hectic /ˈhektɪk/ *adj.* & *n.* —*adj.* **1** busy and confused; excited. **2** having a hectic fever; morbidly flushed. —*n.* **1** a hectic fever or flush. **2** a patient suffering from this. □ **hectic fever** (or **flush**) *hist.* a fever which accompanies consumption and similar diseases, with flushed cheeks and hot dry skin. □□ **hectically** *adv.* [ME *etik* f. OF *etique* f. LL *hecticus* f. Gk *hektikos* habitual f. *hexis* habit, assim. to F *hectique* or LL]

hecto- /ˈhektəʊ/ *comb. form* a hundred, esp. of a unit in the metric system. ¶ Abbr.: **ha**. [F, irreg. f. Gk *hekaton* hundred]

hectogram /ˈhektəˌgræm/ *n.* (also **hectogramme**) a metric unit of mass, equal to one hundred grams.

hectograph /ˈhektəˌɡrɑːf/ *n.* an apparatus for copying documents by the use of a gelatin plate which receives an impression of the master copy.

hectolitre /ˈhektəˌliːtə(r)/ *n.* (*US* **hectoliter**) a metric unit of capacity, equal to one hundred litres.

hectometre /ˈhektəˌmiːtə(r)/ *n.* (*US* **hectometer**) a metric unit of length, equal to one hundred metres.

Hector /ˈhektə(r)/ *Gk legend* a Trojan warrior, son of Priam and Hecuba and husband of Andromache. He was killed by Achilles, who dragged his body at the wheels of his chariot three times round the walls of Troy.

hector /ˈhektə(r)/ *v.* & *n.* —*v.tr.* bully, intimidate —*n.* a bully. □□ **hectoringly** *adv.* [*Hector*, L f. Gk *Hektōr* HECTOR, f. its earlier use to mean 'swaggering fellow']

Hecuba /ˈhekjʊbə/ *Gk legend* the wife of Priam, mother of Hector and eighteen others of Priam's fifty sons. The legends about her are many and varied.

he'd /hiːd, hɪd/ *contr.* **1** he had. **2** he would.

heddle /ˈhed(ə)l/ *n.* one of the sets of small cords or wires between which the warp is passed in a loom before going through the reed. [app. f. OE *hefeld*]

hedge /hedʒ/ *n.* & *v.* —*n.* **1** a fence or boundary formed by closely growing bushes or shrubs. **2** a protection against possible loss or diminution. —*v.* **1** *tr.* surround or bound with a hedge. **2** *tr.* (foll. by *in*) enclose. **3 a** *tr.* reduce one's risk of loss on (a bet or speculation) by compensating transactions on the other side. **b** *intr.* avoid a definite decision or commitment. **4** *intr.* make or trim hedges. □ **hedge-hop** fly at a very low altitude. **hedge sparrow** a common grey and brown bird, *Prunella modularis*; the dunnock. □□ **hedger** *n.* [OE *hegg* f. Gmc]

hedgehog /ˈhedʒhɒg/ *n.* **1** any small nocturnal insect-eating mammal of the genus *Erinaceus*, esp. *E. europaeus*, having a piglike snout and a coat of spines, and rolling itself up into a ball for defence. **2** a porcupine or other animal similarly covered with spines. □□ **hedgehoggy** *adj.* [ME f. HEDGE (from its habitat) + HOG (from its snout)]

hedgerow /ˈhedʒrəʊ/ *n.* a row of bushes etc. forming a hedge.

hedonic /hiːˈdɒnɪk, he-/ *adj.* **1** of or characterized by pleasure. **2** *Psychol.* of pleasant or unpleasant sensations. [Gk *hēdonikos* f. *hēdonē* pleasure]

hedonism /ˈhiːdəˌnɪz(ə)m, ˈhe-/ *n.* **1** belief in pleasure as the highest good and mankind's proper aim. **2** behaviour based on this. □□ **hedonist** *n.* **hedonistic** /-ˈnɪstɪk/ *adj.* [Gk *hēdonē* pleasure]

-hedron /ˈhiːdrən, ˈhedrən/ *comb. form* (*pl.* **-hedra**) forming nouns denoting geometrical solids with various numbers or shapes of faces (*dodecahedron*; *rhombohedron*). □□ **-hedral** *comb. form* forming adjectives. [Gk *hedra* seat]

heebie-jeebies /ˌhiːbɪˈjiːbɪz/ *n.pl.* (prec. by *the*) *sl.* a state of nervous depression or anxiety. [20th c.: orig. unkn.]

heed /hiːd/ *v.* & *n.* —*v.tr.* attend to; take notice of. —*n.* careful attention. □□ **heedful** *adj.* **heedfully** *adv.* **heedfulness** *n.* **heedless** *adj.* **heedlessly** *adv.* **heedlessness** *n.* [OE *hēdan* f. WG]

hee-haw /ˈhiːhɔː/ n. & v. —n. the bray of a donkey. —v.intr. (of or like a donkey) emit a braying sound. [imit.]

heel¹ /hiːl/ n. & v. —n. **1** the back part of the foot below the ankle. **2** the corresponding part in vertebrate animals. **3 a** the part of a sock etc. covering the heel. **b** the part of a shoe or boot supporting the heel. **4** a thing like a heel in form or position, e.g. the part of the palm next to the wrist, the end of a violin bow at which it is held, or the part of a golf club near where the head joins the shaft. **5** the crust end of a loaf of bread. **6** colloq. a person regarded with contempt or disapproval. **7** (as int.) a command to a dog to walk close to its owner's heel. —v. **1** tr. fit or renew a heel on (a shoe or boot). **2** intr. touch the ground with the heel as in dancing. **3** intr. (foll. by out) Rugby Football pass the ball with the heel. **4** tr. Golf strike (the ball) with the heel of the club. □ **at heel 1** (of a dog) close behind. **2** (of a person etc.) under control. **at** (or **on**) **the heels of** following closely after (a person or event). **cool** (or **kick**) **one's heels** be kept waiting. **down at heel 1** (of a shoe) with the heel worn down. **2** (of a person) shabby. **take to one's heels** run away. **to heel 1** (of a dog) close behind. **2** (of a person etc.) under control. **turn on one's heel** turn sharply round. **well-heeled** colloq. wealthy. □□ **heelless** adj. [OE hēla, hǣla f. Gmc]

heel² /hiːl/ v. & n. —v. **1** intr. (of a ship etc.) lean over owing to the pressure of wind or an uneven load (cf. LIST²). **2** tr. cause (a ship etc.) to do this —n. the act or amount of heeling. [prob. f. obs. heeld, hield incline, f. OE hieldan, OS -heldian f. Gmc]

heel³ var. of HELE.

heelball /ˈhiːlbɔːl/ n. **1** a mixture of hard wax and lampblack used by shoemakers for polishing. **2** this or a similar mixture used in brass-rubbing.

heeltap /ˈhiːltæp/ n. **1** a layer of leather in a shoe heel. **2** liquor left at the bottom of a glass after drinking.

heft /heft/ v. & n. —v.tr. lift (something heavy), esp. to judge its weight. —n. dial. or US weight, heaviness. [prob. f. HEAVE after cleft, weft]

hefty /ˈhefti/ adj. (**heftier**, **heftiest**) **1** (of a person) big and strong. **2** (of a thing) large, heavy, powerful. □□ **heftily** adv. **heftiness** n.

Hegel /ˈheɪg(ə)l/, Georg Wilhelm Friedrich (1770–1831), German idealist philosopher. Kant's philosophy had left an essential dualism: nature opposed to spirit, object to subject, the outer world composed of isolated unrelated substances. Hegel sought to bridge this gulf, to reduce duality to unity, by finding more reality (and more value) in a whole than in its parts; the apparently separate things of which the world is composed each have a reality which consists in an aspect of the whole. Among his major works is his Philosophy of History, which can be interpreted in different ways. Hegel himself states his view of the direction and destination of human history as 'the development of the idea of freedom', reaching its consummation in the Germanic world of his own time. His influence was greatest in the 1880s and 1890s; his doctrine was broad enough (or contained sufficient ambiguity) to encourage great diversity in its application, having attractions for political thinkers of both right and left (Marx, in his youth, was a disciple of Hegel), and some theologians developed the more spiritualistic aspects of his teaching. □□ **Hegelian** /hɪˈɡeɪlɪən/ adj. & n. **Hegelianism** n.

hegemonic /ˌhedʒɪˈmɒnɪk, ˌheɡɪ-/ adj. ruling, supreme. [Gk hēgemonikos (as HEGEMONY)]

hegemony /hɪˈdʒemənɪ, -ˈɡemənɪ/ n. leadership esp. by one State of a confederacy. [Gk hēgemonia f. hēgemōn leader f. hēgeomai lead]

hegira /ˈhedʒɪrə/ n. (also **hejira**, **hijra** /ˈhɪdʒrə/) **1** (**Hegira**) Muhammad's departure from Mecca to Medina in AD 622, which made possible the consolidation of the first Muslim community. The departure was made necessary by the opposition of the merchant community in Mecca both to Muhammad's preaching and his attempt to achieve a social solidarity that was not tribally based. Its significance to the history of Islam is indicated by the fact that the Islamic calendar (which is based on lunar months) is dated from AD 622 (= 1 AH). **2** a general exodus or departure. [med.L hegira f. Arab. hijra departure from one's country f. hajara separate]

Heidegger /ˈhaɪdeɡə(r)/, Martin (1889–1976), German philosopher, a professor at Freiburg for much of his life and probably the leading Continental philosopher of the 20th c. His early existentialist work (though he did not regard himself as an existentialist) Being and Time (1927) examines the setting of human existence in the world. His picture of mankind's place in nature is a gloomy one: Angst (dread) is a fundamental part of their consciousness, a symptom of the gravity of their situation with its radical freedom of choice and its horizon of death. Consequently we are continually in flight from our destiny, disguising it and distracting our attention from its inevitability. Heidegger's later work addresses the question of Being: human destiny is to seek and be 'the shepherd' of Being through the almost mystical power of language, yet the mediocrity of modern life falls far short of this. His early flirtation with Nazism casts a shadow, in the eyes of some critics, over his entire philosophy.

Heidelberg /ˈhaɪd(ə)lbɜːɡ/ a city in SW Germany on the River Neckar; pop. (1987) 136,200. Its university, which received its charter in 1386, is the oldest in Germany.

heifer /ˈhefə(r)/ n. **1 a** a young cow, esp. one that has not had more than one calf. **b** a female calf. **2** sl. derog. a woman. [OE heahfore]

heigh /heɪ/ int. expressing encouragement or enquiry. □ **heigh-ho** expressing boredom, resignation, etc. [imit.]

height /haɪt/ n. **1** the measurement from base to top or (of a standing person) from head to foot. **2** the elevation above ground or a recognized level (usu. sea level). **3** any considerable elevation (situated at a height). **4 a** a high place or area. **b** rising ground. **5** the top of something. **6** Printing the distance from the foot to the face of type. **7 a** the most intense part or period of anything (the battle was at its height). **b** an extreme instance or example (the height of fashion). □ **height of land** US a watershed. [OE hēhthu f. Gmc]

heighten /ˈhaɪt(ə)n/ v.tr. & intr. make or become higher or more intense.

Heilongjiang /ˌheɪlʊŋdʒɪˈæŋ/ (also **Heilungkiang** /-kɪˈæŋ/) a province of NE China; pop. (est. 1986) 33,320,000; capital, Harbin.

Heine /ˈhaɪnə/, Heinrich (1797–1856), German poet, born in Düsseldorf of Jewish parents. His reputation rests on his lyrics which combine a self-indulgent emotion with sharp self-criticism and deflated irony. The Buch der Lieder (Book of Songs, 1827) is one of the most influential volumes of poetry in Germany (many of these poems were set to music by Schumann and Schubert). Reisebilder (Travel Pictures, 1826–31) contains the satirical-idyllic prose book Die Harzreise. After the expulsion of Napoleon, Heine emigrated to Paris in 1830, where his works became more political; they include Zur Geschichte der Religion und Philosophie in Deutschland (1834), a witty and savage attack on German thought and literature, and his two masterpieces of verse satire Atta Troll (1843) and Deutschland (1844).

heinous /ˈheɪnəs, ˈhiːnəs/ adj. (of a crime or criminal) utterly odious or wicked. □□ **heinously** adv. **heinousness** n. [ME f. OF haïneus ult. f. haïr to hate f. Frank.]

heir /eə(r)/ n. **1** a person entitled to property or rank as the legal successor of its former owner (often foll. by to: heir to the throne). **2** a person deriving or morally entitled to some thing, quality, etc., from a predecessor. □ **heir apparent** an heir whose claim cannot be set aside by the birth of another heir. **heir-at-law** (pl. **heirs-at-law**) an heir by right of blood, esp. to the real property of an intestate. **heir presumptive** an heir whose claim may be set aside by the birth of another heir. □□ **heirdom** n. **heirless** adj. **heirship** n. [ME f. OF eir f. LL herem f. L heres -edis]

heiress /ˈeərɪs/ n. a female heir, esp. to wealth or high title.

heirloom /ˈeəluːm/ n. **1** a piece of personal property that has been in a family for several generations. **2** a piece of property received as part of an inheritance. [HEIR + LOOM¹ in the sense 'tool']

Heisenberg /ˈhaɪz(ə)nˌbɜːɡ/, Werner Karl (1901–76), German mathematical physicist and philosopher, who developed a system of quantum mechanics based on matrix algebra. For this and his discovery of the allotropic forms of hydrogen he was awarded the 1932 Nobel Prize for physics. He announced his famous uncertainty principle (also known as the interdeterminancy principle) in 1927, which overthrew classical physics and has found applications in many other fields of study. According to this, at the atomic level, the position and momentum of a particle cannot be determined with limitless accuracy simultaneously, and follows from the wave property of matter. During the Second World War he was involved with the German atomic energy programme.

heist /haɪst/ n. & v. US sl. —n. a robbery. —v.tr. rob. [repr. a local pronunc. of HOIST]

hei-tiki /heɪˈtɪkɪ/ n. NZ a greenstone neck-ornament worn by Maoris. [Maori f. hei hang, TIKI]

Hejaz /hɪˈdʒæz/ (also **Hijaz**) a coastal region of western Saudi Arabia, extending along the Red Sea.

hejira var. of HEGIRA.

Hekla /ˈheklə/ an active volcano in SW Iceland, rising to a height of 1,491 m (4,840 ft.).

HeLa /ˈhiːlə/ adj. of a strain of human epithelial cells maintained in tissue culture. [early 1950s; Henrietta Lacks, whose cervical carcinoma provided the original cells]

held past and past part. of HOLD.

Heldentenor /ˈheldənteˌnɔː(r)/ n. **1** a powerful tenor voice suitable for heroic roles in opera. **2** a singer with this voice. [G f. Held a hero]

hele /hiːl/ v.tr. (also **heel**) (foll. by in) set (a plant) in the ground and cover its roots. [OE helian f. Gmc]

Helen /ˈhelɪn/ Gk legend the daughter of Zeus and Leda, born from an egg. She has a non-Greek name and is probably an ancient pre-Hellenic goddess connected with vegetation and fertility. In the Homeric poems she is the (human) wife of Menelaus, and her abduction by Paris (to whom she had been promised, as a bribe, by Aphrodite; see PARIS¹) led to the Trojan War.

Helena¹ /ˈhelɪnə/ the capital of Montana; pop. (1980) 23,938.

Helena² /ˈhelɪnə/, St (c.255–c.330), mother of Constantine and a zealous supporter of Christianity. In 326 she visited the Holy Land and founded basilicas on the Mount of Olives and at Bethlehem; later tradition ascribes to her the finding of the Cross on which Christ was crucified. Feast day, in the East (with Constantine) 21 May; in the West, 18 Aug.

helenium /heˈliːnɪəm/ n. any composite plant of the genus Helenium, with daisy-like flowers having prominent central discs. [mod.L f. Gk helenion, possibly commemorating Helen of Troy]

Helgoland see HELIGOLAND.

heli- /ˈhelɪ/ comb. form helicopter (heliport).

heliacal /hɪˈlaɪək(ə)l/ adj. Astron. relating to or near the sun. □ **heliacal rising** (or **setting**) the first rising (or setting) of a star after (or before) a period of invisibility owing to conjunction with the sun. [LL heliacus f. Gk hēliakos f. hēlios sun]

helianthemum /ˌhiːlɪˈænθəməm/ n. any evergreen shrub of the genus Helianthemum, with saucer-shaped flowers. Also called rock rose. [mod.L f. Gk hēlios sun + anthemon flower]

helianthus /ˌhiːlɪˈænθəs/ n. any plant of the genus Helianthus, including the sunflower and Jerusalem artichoke. [mod.L f. Gk hēlios sun + anthos flower]

helical /ˈhelɪk(ə)l/ adj. having the form of a helix. □□ **helically** adv. **helicoid** adj. & n.

helices pl. of HELIX.

helichrysum /ˌhelɪˈkraɪz(ə)m/ n. any composite plant of the genus Helichrysum, with flowers retaining their appearance when dried. [L f. Gk helikhrusos f. helix spiral + khrusos gold]

helicon /ˈhelɪkɒn/ n. a large spiral bass tuba played encircling the player's head and resting on the shoulder. [L f. Gk Helikōn mountain sacred to the Muses: later assoc. with HELIX]

helicopter /ˈhelɪˌkɒptə(r)/ n. & v. —n. a type of aircraft which derives both its lift and its control from one or more powered rotors which rotate about a vertical or near-vertical axis. Addi-

tional directional control may sometimes be provided by a tail-rotor. It differs from an autogiro which, since its rotors were not powered, could not take off vertically. Leonardo da Vinci drew and described an aircraft using its principle of flight. A design was patented in 1861, and the Wright brothers built and tested flying machines of this kind in the early 20th c., but the name chiefly associated with its development is that of Igor Sikorski. —v.tr. & intr. transport or fly by helicopter. [F hélicoptère f. Gk helix (see HELIX) + pteron wing]

Heligoland /ˈhelɪgəˌlænd/ (German **Helgoland** /ˈhelgəˌlɑːnt/ a small island in the North Sea, off the coast of Germany. Originally the home of Frisian seamen, it was Danish from 1714 until seized by the British Navy in 1807 and later ceded officially to Britain. In 1890 it was given to Germany in exchange for Zanzibar and Pemba, and was made into an important German naval base in both World Wars. Its naval installations were demolished in 1947, and it was returned to the Federal Republic of Germany in 1952.

helio- /ˈhiːlɪəʊ/ comb. form the sun. [Gk hēlios sun]

heliocentric /ˌhiːlɪəˈsentrɪk/ adj. **1** regarding the sun as centre. **2** considered as viewed from the sun's centre. □□ **heliocentrically** adv.

Heliogabalus /ˌhiːlɪəˈgæbələs/ var. of ELAGABALUS.

heliogram /ˈhiːlɪəˌgræm/ n. a message sent by heliograph.

heliograph /ˈhiːlɪəˌgrɑːf/ n. & v. —n. **1 a** a signalling apparatus reflecting sunlight in flashes from a movable mirror. **b** a message sent by means of this; a heliogram. **2** an apparatus for photographing the sun. **3** an engraving obtained chemically by exposure to light. —v.tr. send (a message) by heliograph. □□ **heliography** /-ˈɒgrəfɪ/ n.

heliogravure /ˌhiːlɪəʊgrəˈvjʊə(r)/ n. = PHOTOGRAVURE.

heliolithic /ˌhiːlɪəˈlɪθɪk/ adj. (of a civilization) characterized by sun-worship and megaliths.

heliometer /ˌhiːlɪˈɒmɪtə(r)/ n. an instrument used for finding the angular distance between two stars (orig. used for measuring the diameter of the sun).

Helios /ˈhiːlɪɒs/ Gk Mythol. the Sun, personified as a god, father of Phaethon. He is generally represented as a charioteer driving daily from east to west across the sky. In Rhodes he was the chief national god; the Colossus erected by the harbour entrance was a statue to him. [Gk hēlios sun]

heliostat /ˈhiːlɪəˌstæt/ n. an apparatus with a mirror driven by clockwork to reflect sunlight in a fixed direction. □□ **heliostatic** /-ˈstætɪk/ adj.

heliotherapy /ˌhiːlɪəʊˈθerəpɪ/ n. the use of sunlight in treating disease.

heliotrope /ˈhiːlɪəˌtrəʊp, ˈhel-/ n. **1 a** any plant of the genus Heliotropium, with fragrant purple flowers. **b** the scent of these. **2** a light purple colour. **3** bloodstone. [L heliotropium f. Gk hēliotropion plant turning its flowers to the sun, f. hēlios sun + -tropos f. trepō turn]

heliotropism /ˌhiːlɪˈɒtrəˌpɪz(ə)m/ n. the directional growth of a plant in response to sunlight (cf. PHOTOTROPISM). □□ **heliotropic** /ˌhiːlɪəˈtrɒpɪk/ adj.

heliotype /ˈhiːlɪəˌtaɪp/ n. a picture obtained from a sensitized gelatin film exposed to light.

heliport /ˈhelɪˌpɔːt/ n. a place where helicopters take off and land. [HELI-, after airport]

helium /ˈhiːlɪəm/ n. Chem. a colourless odourless element, the lightest of the noble gases. Before it was discovered on earth, helium was detected spectroscopically in the sun (1868), where it is present as the main product of the thermonuclear fusion of hydrogen. On earth it is found most abundantly in natural gas deposits, especially in the US. Because helium is light and chemically inert it is a particularly suitable lifting gas for balloons and airships, and is now used for this purpose and as a coolant. In the 1930s the US had a monopoly of the manufacture of helium, which they would not sell to Germany lest this should bring America within the range of bombing raids by German airships. This embargo gave rise to the Hindenburg disaster since the airship, designed to use helium, was obliged to substitute hydrogen (which is inflammable), with tragic consequences. ¶ Symb.: **He**; atomic number 2. [Gk *hēlios* sun (having been first identified in the sun's atmosphere)]

helix /ˈhiːlɪks/ n. (pl. **helices** /ˈhiːlɪˌsiːz, ˈhel-/) **1** a spiral curve (like a corkscrew) or a coiled curve (like a watch spring). **2** Geom. a curve that cuts a line on a solid cone or cylinder, at a constant angle with the axis. **3** Archit. a spiral ornament. **4** Anat. the rim of the external ear. [L *helix* -icis f. Gk *helix* -ikos]

hell /hel/ n. **1** a place regarded in some religions as the abode of the dead, or of condemned sinners and devils. The popular idea of hell as a dark and fiery pit is derived from texts such as Matt. 25: 41 and Rev. 19: 20. **2** a place or state of misery or wickedness. **3** colloq. used as an exclamation of surprise or annoyance (*who the hell are you?; a hell of a mess*). **4** US colloq. fun; high spirits. □ **beat** (or **knock** etc.) **the hell out of** colloq. beat etc. without restraint. **come hell or high water** no matter what the difficulties. **for the hell of it** colloq. for fun; on impulse. **get** (or **catch**) **hell** colloq. be severely scolded or punished. **give a person hell** colloq. scold or punish or make things difficult for a person. **hell-bent** (foll. by *on*) recklessly determined. **hell-cat** a spiteful violent woman. **hell-fire** the fire or fires regarded as existing in hell. **hell for leather** at full speed. **hell-hole** an oppressive or unbearable place. **hell-hound** a fiend. **like hell** colloq. **1** not at all. **2** recklessly, exceedingly. **not a hope in hell** colloq. no chance at all. **play hell** (or **merry hell**) **with** colloq. be upsetting or disruptive to. **what the hell** colloq. it is of no importance. □□ **hell-like** adj. **hellward** adv. & adj. [OE *hel, hell* f. Gmc]

he'll /hiːl, hɪl/ contr. he will; he shall.

Helladic /heˈlædɪk/ adj. of or belonging to the Bronze Age culture of mainland Greece (c.3000–1050 BC), of which the latest period is equivalent to Mycenaean. [Gk *Helladikos* f. *Hellas* -ados Greece]

Hellas /ˈhelæs/ the ancient and modern Greek name for Greece. [cf. HELLENE]

hellebore /ˈhelɪˌbɔː(r)/ n. **1** any evergreen plant of the genus *Helleborus*, having large white, green, or purplish flowers, e.g. the Christmas rose. **2** a liliaceous plant, *Veratrum album*. **3** hist. any of various plants supposed to cure madness. [ME f. OF *ellebore, elebore* or med.L *eleborus* f. L *elleborus* f. Gk *(h)elleboros*]

helleborine /ˈhelɪbəˌriːn/ n. any orchid of the genus *Epipactis* or *Cephalanthera*. [F or L *helleborine* or L f. Gk *helleborinē* plant like hellebore (as HELLEBORE)]

Hellene /ˈheliːn/ n. **1** a native of modern Greece. **2** an ancient Greek of genuine Greek descent. □□ **Hellenic** /heˈlenɪk, -ˈliːnɪk/ adj. [Gk *Hellēn* eponymous ancestor, son or brother of Deucalion]

Hellenism /ˈhelɪˌnɪz(ə)m/ n. **1** Greek character or culture (esp. of ancient Greece). **2** the study or imitation of Greek culture. □□ **Hellenize** v.tr. & intr. (also **-ise**). **Hellenization** /-naɪˈzeɪʃ(ə)n/ n. [Gk *hellēnismos* f. *hellēnizō* speak Greek, make Greek (as HELLENE)]

Hellenist /ˈhelɪnɪst/ n. an expert on or admirer of Greek language or culture. [Gk *Hellēnistēs* (as HELLENISM)]

Hellenistic /ˌhelɪˈnɪstɪk/ adj. of or relating to Greek history, language, and culture from the death of Alexander the Great in 323 BC until the defeat of Mark Antony and Cleopatra by Roman forces under Octavian at the battle of Actium in 31 BC.

Heller /ˈhelə(r)/, Joseph (1923–), American novelist. His experiences in the air force during the Second World War inspired his first novel *Catch 22* (1961). This grotesque and comic tale of an American bombardier's resistance to his fanatic commander's ambition for promotion at the expense of his squadron satirizes military illogicality. It became enormously popular, particularly among younger readers during the Vietnam era, and its title passed into the language. His subsequent novels include *Something Happened* (1964) and *Good as Gold* (1979).

Hellespont /ˈhelɪsˌpont/ the ancient name for the Dardanelles, named after the legendary Helle who fell into the strait and was drowned while escaping with her brother Phrixus from their stepmother, Ino, on a golden-fleeced ram (see ARGONAUTS). [Gk *Hellēspontos* sea of Helle]

hellgrammite /ˈhelɡrəˌmaɪt/ n. US an aquatic larva of an American fly, *Corydalus cornutus*, often used as fishing bait. [19th c.: orig. unkn.]

hellion /ˈhelɪən/ n. US colloq. a mischievous or troublesome person, esp. a child. [perh. f. dial. *hallion* a worthless fellow, assim. to HELL]

hellish /ˈhelɪʃ/ adj. & adv. —adj. **1** of or like hell. **2** colloq. extremely difficult or unpleasant. —adv. Brit. colloq. (as an intensifier) extremely (*hellish expensive*). □□ **hellishly** adv. **hellishness** n.

Hellman /ˈhelmən/, Lillian (1907–84), American playwright, whose works include *The Children's Hour* (1934), *The Little Foxes* (1939), and *Watch on the Rhine* (1941). For more than thirty years she lived with the detective-story writer Dashiell Hammett; both were blacklisted during the McCarthy era for their left-wing opinions.

hello /həˈləʊ/ int., n., & v. (also **hallo, hullo**) —int. **1 a** an expression of informal greeting, or of surprise. **b** used to begin a telephone conversation. **2** a cry used to call attention. —n. (pl. **-os**) a cry of 'hello'. —v.intr. (**-oes, -oed**) cry 'hello'. [var. of earlier HOLLO]

Hell's Angel a member of a group of lawless usually leather-jacketed motor-cyclists in California in the 1950s, notorious for their disturbances of civil order there, or of a similar group elsewhere. Their culture revolves round the motor cycle, and the winged death's-head is their symbol.

Hells Canyon a chasm cut by the Snake River, Idaho, to form the deepest gorge in the US. Flanked by the Seven Devils Mountains, the canyon drops to a depth of 2,433 m. (7,900 ft.).

helm[1] /helm/ n. & v. —n. **1** a tiller or wheel by which a ship's rudder is controlled. **2** the amount by which this is turned (*more helm needed*). —v.tr. steer or guide as if with a helm. □ **at the helm** in control; at the head (of an organization etc.). [OE *helma*, prob. related to HELVE]

helm[2] /helm/ n. archaic helmet. □□ **helmed** adj. [OE f. Gmc]

Helmand /ˈhelmənd/ the longest river in Afghanistan. Rising in the Hindu Kush, it flows 1,125 km (700 miles) before emptying into the marshland surrounding Lake Saberi on the Iran–Afghanistan frontier.

helmet /ˈhelmɪt/ n. **1** any of various protective head-coverings worn by soldiers, policemen, firemen, divers, motor cyclists, etc. **2** Bot. the arched upper part of the corolla in some flowers. **3** the shell of a gastropod mollusc of the genus *Cassis*, used in jewellery. □□ **helmeted** adj. [ME f. OF, dimin. of *helme* f. WG (as HELM[2])]

Helmholtz /ˈhelmhɔːlts/, Hermann Ludwig Ferdinand von (1821–94), German physiologist and physicist, one of the greatest scientists and teachers of his age, who made fundamental contributions to all the fields he studied. His investigation of animal heat led to his formulation of the principle of the conservation of energy in 1847, central to the subsequent development of thermodynamics. He produced two monumental studies on sense perception: the first dealt with physiological optics (in the course of which he invented the ophthalmoscope), and the second with physiological acoustics, for which he devised the Helmholtz resonators for the analysis of complex sounds in 1856. Other achievements include his attempts to measure the speed of nerve impulses, and his study of vortex motion in hydrodynamics; he also contributed to non-Euclidean geometry. His research into the properties of oscillating electric currents was continued by his assistant, Heinrich Hertz.

helminth /ˈhelmɪnθ/ n. any of various parasitic worms including flukes, tapeworms, and nematodes. □□ **helminthic** /-ˈmɪnθɪk/ adj. **helminthoid** /-ˈmɪnθɔɪd/ adj. **helminthology** /-mɪnˈθɒlədʒɪ/ n. [Gk *helmins* -inthos intestinal worm]

helminthiasis /ˌhelmɪnˈθaɪəsɪs/ n. a disease characterized by the presence of any of several parasitic worms in the body.

helmsman /ˈhelmzmən/ n. (pl. **-men**) a steersman.

Héloïse /ˈeɪləʊˌiːz/ see ABELARD.

helot /ˈhelət/ n. a serf, esp. (**Helot**) of a class in ancient Sparta owned by the State and employed in the service of the Spartans, whom they greatly outnumbered. □□ **helotism** n. **helotry** n. [L *helotes* pl. f. Gk *heilōtes*, -ōtai, erron. taken as = inhabitants of *Helos*, a Laconian town]

help /help/ *v. & n.* —*v.tr.* **1** provide (a person etc.) with the means towards what is needed or sought (*helped me with my work*; *helped me (to) pay my debts*). **2** (foll. by *up*, *down*, etc.) assist or give support to (a person) in moving etc. as specified (*helped her into the chair*; *helped him on with his coat*). **3** (often *absol.*) be of use or service to (a person) (*does that help?*). **4** contribute to alleviating (a pain or difficulty). **5** prevent or remedy (*it can't be helped*). **6** (usu. with *neg.*) **a** *tr.* refrain from (*can't help it*; *could not help laughing*). **b** *refl.* refrain from acting (*couldn't help himself*). **7** *tr.* (often foll. by *to*) serve (a person with food) (*shall I help you to greens?*). —*n.* **1** the act of helping or being helped (*we need your help*; *came to our help*). **2** a person or thing that helps. **3** a domestic servant or employee, or several collectively. **4** a remedy or escape (*there is no help for it*). □ **helping hand** assistance. **help oneself** (often foll. by *to*) **1** serve oneself (with food). **2** take without seeking help or permission. **help a person out** give a person help, esp. in difficulty. **so help me** (or **help me God**) (as an invocation or oath) I am speaking the truth. □□ **helper** *n.* [OE *helpan* f. Gmc]

helpful /ˈhelpfʊl/ *adj.* (of a person or thing) giving help; useful. □□ **helpfully** *adv.* **helpfulness** *n.*

helping /ˈhelpɪŋ/ *n.* a portion of food esp. at a meal.

helpless /ˈhelplɪs/ *adj.* **1** lacking help or protection; defenceless. **2** unable to act without help. □□ **helplessly** *adv.* **helplessness** *n.*

helpline /ˈhelplaɪn/ *n.* a telephone service providing help with problems.

Helpmann /ˈhelpmən/, Sir Robert Murray (1909–86), Australian dancer, choreographer, director, and actor. Having studied with the Pavlova company he came to England in 1933 and joined the Vic-Wells (later Sadler's Wells, now the Royal) Ballet. He partnered Alicia Markova in de Valois's *Haunted Ballroom* (1934), and became the regular partner of Margot Fonteyn; their partnership contributed to the success of the company. Helpmann was noted for his dramatic ability and for his strongly theatrical choreography.

helpmate /ˈhelpmeɪt/ *n.* a helpful companion or partner (usu. a husband or wife).

Helsingborg /ˈhelsɪŋbɔːɡ/ (Swedish **Hälsingborg**) a port in southern Sweden, situated on the Øresund (Sound) opposite Helsingør in Denmark; pop. (1987) 107,000.

Helsingør see ELSINORE.

Helsinki /ˈhelsɪŋkɪ, -ˈsɪŋkɪ/ (Swedish **Helsingfors** /ˈhelsɪŋfɔːʃ/) the capital of Finland; pop. (1987) 490,034.

helter-skelter /ˌheltəˈskeltə(r)/ *adv.*, *adj.*, & *n.* —*adv. & adj.* in disorderly haste. —*n. Brit.* a tall spiral slide round a tower, at a fairground or funfair. [imit., orig. in a rhyming jingle, perh. f. ME *skelte* hasten]

helve /helv/ *n.* the handle of a weapon or a tool. [OE *helfe* f. WG]

Helvetian /helˈviːʃ(ə)n/ *adj. & n.* —*adj.* Swiss. —*n.* a native of Switzerland. [L *Helvetia* Switzerland (*Helvetii* Celtic tribe living there)]

hem¹ /hem/ *n. & v.* —*n.* the border of a piece of cloth, esp. a cut edge turned under and sewn down. —*v.tr.* (**hemmed**, **hemming**) turn down and sew in the edge of (a piece of cloth etc.). □ **hem in** confine; restrict the movement of. [OE, perh. rel. to dial. *ham* enclosure]

hem² /hem, həm/ *int.*, *n.*, & *v.* —*int.* calling attention or expressing hesitation by a slight cough or clearing of the throat. —*n.* an utterance of this. —*v.intr.* (**hemmed**, **hemming**) say *hem*; hesitate in speech. □ **hem and haw** = hum and haw (see HUM¹). [imit.]

hemal etc. *US* var. of HAEMAL etc.

hemato- etc. *US* var. of HAEMATO- etc.

heme var. of HAEM.

hemerocallis /ˌheməˈrəʊkælɪs/ *n.* = day lily. [L *hemerocalles* f. Gk *hēmerokalles* a kind of lily f. *hēmera* day + *kallos* beauty]

hemi- /ˈhemɪ/ *comb. form* half. [Gk *hēmi-* = L *semi-*: see SEMI-]

-hemia *comb. form US* var. of -AEMIA.

hemianopsia /ˌhemɪəˈnɒpsɪə/ *n.* (also **hemianopia** /ˌhemɪəˈnəʊpɪə/) blindness over half the field of vision.

hemicellulose /ˌhemɪˈseljʊˌləʊz/ *n.* any of various polysaccharides forming the matrix of plant cell walls in which cellulose is embedded. [G (as HEMI-, CELLULOSE)]

hemicycle /ˈhemɪˌsaɪk(ə)l/ *n.* a semicircular figure.

hemidemisemiquaver /ˈhemɪˌdemɪˌsemɪˌkweɪvə(r)/ *n. Mus.* a note having the time value of half a demisemiquaver and represented by a large dot with a four-hooked stem. Also called *sixty-fourth note*.

hemihedral /ˌhemɪˈhiːdr(ə)l/ *adj. Crystallog.* having half the number of planes required for symmetry of the holohedral form.

Hemingway /ˈhemɪŋweɪ/, Ernest Miller (1899–1961), American novelist, who settled in Paris among an American expatriate literary group which included Gertrude Stein and Ezra Pound. He achieved success with *The Sun Also Rises* (1926) which catches the postwar mood of disillusion of the 'lost generation', and *A Farewell to Arms* (1929), the story of a love affair between an American lieutenant and an English nurse, confirmed his position as one of the most influential writers of the time. *Death in the Afternoon* (1932), about bullfighting, shows his deliberate cultivation of the brutal and primitive which grew from his dissatisfaction with contemporary culture. Hemingway actively supported the Republicans in the Spanish Civil War and *For Whom the Bell Tolls* (1940) is set against its background. In his later years he lived mostly in Cuba where his passion for deep-sea fishing provided the background for *The Old Man and the Sea* (1952) about mankind's struggle against nature. His fine short stories appeared in *Men without Women* (1927), *Winner Take Nothing*, and other volumes. In 1954 he was awarded the Nobel Prize for literature. He committed suicide after a period of serious illness.

hemiplegia /ˌhemɪˈpliːdʒɪə/ *n. Med.* paralysis of one side of the body. □□ **hemiplegic** *n. & adj.* [mod.L f. Gk *hēmiplēgia* paralysis (as HEMI-, *plēgē* stroke)]

hemipterous /heˈmɪptərəs/ *adj.* of the insect order Hemiptera including aphids, bugs, and cicadas, with piercing or sucking mouthparts. [HEMI- + Gk *pteron* wing]

hemisphere /ˈhemɪˌsfɪə(r)/ *n.* **1** half of a sphere. **2** a half of the earth, esp. as divided by the equator (into *northern* and *southern hemisphere*) or by a line passing through the poles (into *eastern* and *western hemisphere*). □□ **hemispheric** /-ˈsferɪk/ *adj.* **hemispherical** /-ˈsferɪk(ə)l/ *adj.* [OF *emisphere* & L *hemisphaerium* f. Gk *hēmisphaira* (as HEMI, SPHERE)]

hemistich /ˈhemɪstɪk/ *n.* half of a line of verse. [LL *hemistichium* f. Gk *hēmistikhion* (as HEMI, *stikhion* f. *stikhos* line)]

Hemkund Lake /ˈhemkənd/ a holy lake of the Sikhs in northern India, in the Himalayan foothills of Uttar Pradesh.

hemline /ˈhemlaɪn/ *n.* the line or level of the lower edge of a skirt, dress, or coat.

hemlock /ˈhemlɒk/ *n.* **1 a** a poisonous umbelliferous plant, *Conium maculatum*, with fernlike leaves and small white flowers. **b** a poisonous potion obtained from this. **2** (in full **hemlock fir** or **spruce**) **a** any coniferous tree of the genus *Tsuga*, having foliage that smells like hemlock when crushed. **b** the timber or pitch of these trees. [OE *hymlic(e)*]

hemo- *comb. form US* var. of HAEMO-.

hemp /hemp/ *n.* **1** (in full **Indian hemp**) a herbaceous plant, *Cannabis sativa*, native to Asia. **2** its fibre extracted from the stem and used to make rope and stout fabrics. **3** any of several narcotic drugs made from the hemp plant (cf. CANNABIS, MARIJUANA). **4** any of several other plants yielding fibre, including Manila hemp and sunn hemp. □ **hemp agrimony** a composite plant, *Eupatorium cannabinum*, with pale-purple flowers and hairy leaves. **hemp-nettle** any of various nettle-like plants of the genus *Galeopsis*. [OE *henep*, *hænep* f. Gmc, rel. to Gk *kannabis*]

hempen /ˈhempən/ *adj.* made from hemp.

hemstitch /ˈhemstɪtʃ/ *n. & v.* —*n.* a decorative stitch used in sewing hems. —*v.tr.* hem with this stitch.

hen /hen/ *n.* **1 a** a female bird, esp. of a domestic fowl. **b** (in pl.)

domestic fowls of either sex. **2** a female lobster or crab or salmon. □ **hen and chickens** any of several plants esp. the houseleek. **hen-coop** a coop for keeping fowls in. **hen-harrier** a common harrier, *Circus cyaneus*. **hen-house** a small shed for fowls to roost in. **hen-party** *colloq. derog.* a social gathering of women. **hen-roost** a place where fowls roost at night. **hen-run** an enclosure for fowls. [OE *henn* f. WG]

Henan /hə'næn/ (also **Honan**) a province of NE central China; pop. (est. 1986) 78,080,000; capital, Zhengzhou.

henbane /'henbeɪn/ n. **1** a poisonous herbaceous plant, *Hyoscyamus niger*, with sticky hairy leaves and an unpleasant smell. **2** a narcotic drug obtained from this.

hence /hens/ adv. **1** from this time (*two years hence*). **2** for this reason; as a result of inference (*hence we seem to be wrong*). **3** *archaic* from here; from this place. [ME *hens, hennes, henne* f. OE *heonan* f. the root of HE]

henceforth /hens'fɔːθ/ adv. (also **henceforward** /-'fɔːwəd/) from this time onwards.

henchman /'hentʃmən/ n. (pl. **-men**) **1** a trusted supporter or attendant. **2** *hist.* a squire; a page of honour. **3** the principal attendant of a Highland chief. [ME *henxman, hengestman* f. OE *hengst* male horse]

hendeca- /hen'dekə/ comb. form eleven. [Gk *hendeka* eleven]

hendecagon /hen'dekəˌgɒn/ n. a plane figure with eleven sides and angles.

hendiadys /hen'daɪədɪs/ n. the expression of an idea by two words connected with 'and', instead of one modifying the other, e.g. *nice and warm* for *nicely warm*. [med.L f. Gk *hen dia duoin* one thing by two]

henequen /'henɪˌken/ n. **1** a Mexican agave, *Agave fourcroydes*. **2** the sisal-like fibre obtained from this. [Sp. *jeniquen*]

henge /hendʒ/ n. a prehistoric monument consisting of a circle of massive stone or wood uprights. Such monuments are found only in the British Isles and are believed to have served a ritual function. [back-form. f. STONEHENGE, such a monument]

Hengist /'hengɪst/ the reputed leader, along with his brother Horsa, of the Jutes who came to Britain at the invitation of the British King Vortigern in 449 and later revolted and established an independent Anglo-Saxon kingdom in Kent. The historicity of the brothers has been questioned, and they may have been mythological figures (their names mean 'gelding' and 'horse').

Henley /'henlɪ/ Henley Royal Regatta, the oldest rowing regatta in Europe, inaugurated in 1839 at Henley-on-Thames, Oxfordshire, as a direct result of the interest aroused locally by the first Oxford and Cambridge boat race which took place at Henley in 1829. It is held annually in the first week in July.

henna /'henə/ n. **1** a tropical shrub, *Lawsonia inermis*, having small pink, red, or white flowers. **2** the reddish dye from its shoots and leaves esp. used to colour hair. [Arab. *ḥinnā'*]

hennaed /'henəd/ adj. treated with henna.

henotheism /'henəˌθiːɪz(ə)m/ n. belief in or adoption of a particular god in a polytheistic system as the god of a tribe, class, etc. [Gk *heis henos* one + *theos* god]

henpeck /'henpek/ v.tr. (of a woman) constantly harass (a man, esp. her husband).

Henri /'henrɪ/, Robert (1865–1929), American painter, who believed that the artist must be a social force. His sense of the importance of an art in touch with contemporary life was a powerful force in turning young American painters away from academicism and towards the realism that blossomed in the Ash-can School (see entry). His own work has a certain dash but is generally rather superficial.

Henrietta Maria /ˌhenrɪ'etə mə'riːə/ (1609–69), daughter of Henry IV of France. She was Queen consort of Charles I from 1625; her Roman Catholicism heightened public anxieties about the court's religious sympathies and was a contributory cause of the English Civil War. From 1644 she lived mainly in France.

Henry[1] /'henrɪ/ the name of eight kings of England:
    Henry I (1068–1135), youngest son of William I, reigned 1100–35. On the death of his brother William II, Henry was able to seize the throne in the absence of his other brother Robert on crusade. He campaigned successfully in France (1111–13 and 1116–20) after conquering Normandy in 1105. At home his reign was characterized by the development of the royal administration and the restraint of baronial power, but after his only son William drowned in 1120 there were problems with the succession, and although Henry extracted an oath of loyalty to his daughter Matilda from the barons in 1127, his death eight years later was followed almost immediately by the outbreak of civil war.

    Henry II (1133–89), son of Matilda, reigned 1154–89. The first Angevin king, Henry restored order after the anarchy of the disputed reigns of Stephen and Matilda, added Anjou and Aquitaine to the English possessions in France, established his rule in Ireland, and forced the king of Scotland to acknowledge him overlord of that kingdom. These successes were overshadowed by his feud with Thomas Becket, who disagreed with him over the relative rights of Church and Crown and was eventually murdered by some of Henry's knights. In the last years of his reign much trouble was caused by his four sons who intrigued with France in particular to raise rebellion against him.

    Henry III (1207–72), son of John, reigned 1216–72. Until Henry declared himself of age to rule personally in 1227, his regent the Earl of Pembroke kept the rebellious barony in check, but afterwards the King's ineffectual government, characterized by financial mismanagement and a dependence on unpopular foreign favourites, caused widespread discontent, ending in de Montfort's defeat and capture of the King at Lewes in 1264. Although Henry was restored following the defeat of the rebels a year later at Evesham, he was by this time little more than a figurehead, real power resting with his son who eventually succeeded him as Edward I.

    Henry IV (1367–1413), known as Henry Bolingbroke, son of John of Gaunt, reigned 1399–1413. One of the Lords Appellant who opposed Richard II, Henry returned from exile in 1399 to overthrow Richard and establish the Lancastrian dynasty. His reign was scarred by rebellion, both in Wales where Owen Glendower was briefly successful in establishing Welsh independence, and in the north where the powerful Percy family raised several dangerous uprisings. Although Henry defeated and killed Hotspur (Sir Henry Percy) at Shrewsbury in 1403, the Percy threat did not abate until the head of the family was killed at Bramham Moor in 1408.

    Henry V (1387–1422), son of Henry IV, reigned 1413–22. Having shown early military prowess in his father's wars against the Percy family and the Welsh, Henry V renewed the Hundred Years War soon after coming to the throne and won a resounding victory over the French at Agincourt in 1415. By the Treaty of Troyes (1420) Henry was named successor to Charles VI of France and betrothed to his daughter Catherine of Valois. When the Dauphin repudiated the treaty Henry took the field against him but died of dysentery, leaving a difficult inheritance to his infant son Henry VI.

    Henry VI (1421–71), son of Henry V, reigned 1422–61 and 1470–1. Succeeding his father while still an infant, Henry VI proved scholarly and kindly but prone to bouts of madness and unfit to rule effectively on his own. During his reign the Hundred Years War with France was finally lost, and the royal government, in the hands of a series of regents and noble favourites, became increasingly unpopular through corruption and inefficiency. In the 1450s opposition coalesced round the House of York, and, after intermittent civil war (see WARS OF THE ROSES), Henry was deposed in 1461 by Edward IV. He regained his throne briefly in 1470–1 following a Lancastrian uprising, but was deposed once again following Edward's victories at Barnet and Tewkesbury, and died within days of his deposition, almost certainly murdered by the victorious Edward IV.

    Henry VII (1457–1509), the first Tudor king, son of Edmund Tudor, Earl of Richmond, reigned 1485–1509. He inherited the Lancastrian claim to the throne through his grandfather's marriage to the widow of Henry V. After growing up in exile in France and Brittany, Henry eventually returned to England in 1485 and, after defeating and killing the Yorkist king Richard III at Bosworth, ascended the throne as Henry VII. Threatened in the early years of his reign by a series of Yorkist plots, Henry eventually established an unchallenged Tudor dynasty, dealing ruthlessly with other claimants to the throne. As king he continued the modernization and strengthening of royal government commenced by his Yorkist predecessors, although his attempts to increase royal revenues made him increasingly unpopular.

Henry VIII (1491–1547), son of Henry VII, reigned 1509–47. Although most widely known for his six wives, two of whom he had executed and two of whom he divorced, Henry was responsible for some of the most dramatic changes in post-medieval English society. His efforts to divorce his first wife, Catherine of Aragon, led to England's break with the Roman Church and less directly to the establishment of Protestantism. The dissolution of the monasteries, masterminded by his chief minister Thomas Cromwell, not only destroyed most of the remaining vestiges of the old religious establishment but also changed the pattern of land ownership. Though Henry's reign began in a burst of Renaissance splendour, costly wars, internal rebellion, and general mismanagement in his last years left England in a weak and uncertain condition.

Henry[2] /ˈhenrɪ/ (French *Henri*), the name of four kings of France: **Henry IV** of Navarre (1553–1610), reigned 1589–1610. As king of Navarre, Henry was the leader of Huguenot forces in the latter stages of the French Wars of Religion, but upon succeeding the Catholic Henry III he turned Catholic himself in order to guarantee peace. The founder of the Bourbon dynasty, Henry established religious freedom with the Edict of Nantes (1598) and became nationally popular, restoring normality in a country long plagued by civil war. He was eventually assassinated by a Catholic fanatic in Paris in 1610.

Henry[3] /ˈhenrɪ/ (1394–1460), 'the Navigator', Portuguese prince. The third son of John I of Portugal, despite his title he never undertook any explorations himself but was a notable patron of such voyages. He established a school of navigation at Cape St Vincent and spent his life organizing and funding voyages of discovery, most notably south along the African coast. The efforts of his captains, who reached as far south as Cape Verde and the Azores, laid the groundwork for later Portuguese imperial expansion south-east round Africa to the Far East.

henry /ˈhenrɪ/ n. (pl. **-ies** or **henrys**) *Electr.* the SI unit of inductance which gives an electromotive force of one volt in a closed circuit with a uniform rate of change of current of one ampere per second. ¶ Abbr.: **H**. [J. *Henry*, Amer. physicist d. 1878]

Henze /ˈhentsə/, Hans Werner (1926–), German composer and conductor. A committed socialist, his musical style is bewilderingly diverse, reflecting his fertile imaginative gifts and his refusal to be 'tied down' by formulae. Sensuous lyricisim, rich and delicate tone-colours, and easy mastery of choral writing are among the principal features of his works.

heortology /ˌhiːɔːˈtɒlədʒɪ/ n. the study of Church festivals. [G *Heortologie*, F *héortologie* f. Gk *heortē* feast]

hep[1] var. of HIP[3].

hep[2] var. of HIP[2].

heparin /ˈhepərɪn/ n. *Biochem.* a substance found in liver cells etc. which inhibits blood coagulation, and is used as an anticoagulant in the treatment of thrombosis. □□ **heparinize** v.tr. (also **-ise**). [L f. Gk *hēpar* liver]

hepatic /hɪˈpætɪk/ adj. **1** of or relating to the liver. **2** dark brownish-red; liver-coloured. [ME f. L *hepaticus* f. Gk *hēpatikos* f. *hēpar -atos* liver]

hepatica /hɪˈpætɪkə/ n. any plant of the genus *Hepatica*, with reddish-brown lobed leaves resembling the liver. [med.L fem. of *hepaticus*: see HEPATIC]

hepatitis /ˌhepəˈtaɪtɪs/ n. inflammation of the liver. [mod.L: see HEPATIC]

Hepburn /ˈhepbɜːn/, Katherine (1909–), American stage and film actress, who began her career on Broadway in 1929. She is noted for her versatility and for the vivid intelligence of her acting. Her films include *A Bill of Divorcement* (1932), *The Philadelphia Story* (1940), *The African Queen* (1952), *Suddenly Last Summer* (1960), and *On Golden Pond* (1981).

Hephaestus /hɪˈfiːstəs/ *Gk Mythol.* the god of fire (especially the smithy fire), a craftsman's god and himself a divine craftsman, called Vulcan by the Romans.

Hepplewhite /ˈhepəlˌwaɪt/ n. a light and graceful style of furniture made by George Hepplewhite, English cabinet-maker (d. 1786), or according to his designs.

hepta- /ˈheptə/ comb. form seven. [Gk *hepta* seven]

heptad /ˈheptæd/ n. a group of seven. [Gk *heptas -ados* set of seven (*hepta*)]

heptagon /ˈheptəgən/ n. a plane figure with seven sides and angles. □□ **heptagonal** /-ˈtægən(ə)l/ adj. [F *heptagone* or med.L *heptagonum* f. Gk (as HEPTA-, -GON)]

heptahedron /ˌheptəˈhiːdrən/ n. a solid figure with seven faces. □□ **heptahedral** adj. [HEPTA- + -HEDRON after POLYHEDRON]

heptameter /hepˈtæmɪtə(r)/ n. a line or verse of seven metrical feet. [L *heptametrum* f. Gk (as HEPTA-, -METER)]

heptane /ˈhepteɪn/ n. *Chem.* a liquid hydrocarbon of the alkane series, obtained from petroleum. ¶ Chem. formula: C_7H_{16}. [HEPTA- + -ANE]

heptarchy /ˈheptɑːkɪ/ n. (pl. **-ies**) **1 a** a government by seven rulers. **b** an instance of this. **2** *hist.* the supposed seven kingdoms of the Angles and the Saxons in Britain in the 7th–8th c. □□ **heptarchic** /-ˈtɑːkɪk/ adj. **heptarchical** /-ˈtɑːkɪk(ə)l/ adj. [HEPTA-after *tetrarchy*]

Heptateuch /ˈheptəˌtjuːk/ n. the first seven books of the Old Testament. [L f. Gk f. *hepta* seven + *teukhos* book, volume]

heptavalent /ˌheptəˈveɪlənt/ adj. *Chem.* having a valency of seven; septivalent.

Hepworth /ˈhepwəθ/, Dame Jocelyn Barbara (1903–75) English sculptor, winner of international awards for works such as *The Unknown Political Prisoner* (1953), married to the painter Ben Nicholson from 1933 to 1951. She professed an emotional affinity with nature, but from the 1930s her work was entirely abstract, characterized by simple shapes such as the sphere, cylinder, and ovoid. From the 1950s onwards she gave greater attention to bronze, using this medium to express essentially the same structural principles as in her carved sculpture, seeking 'to infuse the formal perfection of geometry with the vital grace of nature'.

her /hɜː(r), hə(r)/ pron. & poss.pron. —pron. **1** objective case of SHE (*I like her*). **2** colloq. she (*it's her all right; am older than her*). **3** archaic herself (*she fell and hurt her*). —poss.pron. (attrib.) **1** of or belonging to her or herself (*her house; her own business*). **2** (**Her**) (in titles) that she is (*Her Majesty*). [OE *hi(e)re* dative & genit. of *hio*, *hēo* fem. of HE]

Hera /ˈhɪərə/ *Gk Mythol.* an ancient pre-Hellenic goddess. The Greeks made her the wife and sister of Zeus, and the daughter of Cronus and Rhea. She was worshipped as the queen of heaven and as a marriage-goddess, and was identified by the Romans with Juno. [Gk *Hēra* (perh. as a title, = lady, fem. of *hērōs* hero)]

Heracles /ˈherəˌkliːz/ the Greek form of HERCULES.

Heraclitus[1] /ˌhɪərəˈklaɪtəs/ (c.500 BC) Greek philosopher from Ephesus, noted for the oracular obscurity of his writings. He regarded the universe as a ceaselessly changing conflict of opposites, all things being in a state of flux, coming into being and passing away, and held that fire, the type of this constant change, is their origin. From the passing impressions of experience the mind derives a false idea of the permanence of the external world, which is really in a harmonious process of constant change; for his melancholy view of the changing and fleeting character of life he was known as the 'weeping philosopher'.

Heraclitus[2] /ˌhɪərəˈklaɪtəs/ (4th c. BC) Greek poet of Halicarnassus, a friend of the poet Callimachus whose epigram on Heraclitus' death was translated by the Victorian schoolmaster W. J. Cory (1823–92), 'They told me, Heraclitus, they told me you were dead'.

Heraklion /hɪˈræklɪən/ (Greek **Iráklion** /ɪˈræklɪən/) a seaport and the administrative centre of Crete, on the north coast of the island; pop. (1981) 110,950.

herald /ˈher(ə)ld/ n. & v. —n. **1** an official messenger bringing news. **2** a forerunner (*spring is the herald of summer*). **3 a** *hist.*

an officer who made State proclamations and bore messages between princes, officiated in the tournament, arranged various State ceremonials, regulated the use of armorial bearings, settled questions of precedence, or recorded the names and pedigrees of those entitled to armorial bearings. **b** *Brit.* an official of the Heralds' College. —*v.tr.* proclaim the approach of; usher in (*the storm heralded trouble*). □ **Heralds' College** *Brit. colloq.* = College of Arms. [ME f. OF herau(l)t, herauder f. Gmc]

heraldic /heˈrældɪk/ *adj.* of or concerning heraldry. □□ **heraldically** *adv.* [HERALD]

heraldist /ˈherəldɪst/ *n.* an expert in heraldry. [HERALD]

heraldry /ˈherəldrɪ/ *n.* **1** the science or art of a herald, esp. in blazoning armorial bearings and settling the right of persons to bear arms. Bearings probably originated as designs on shields at a time when chain-mail was worn and a bold, simple identification device was needed. Such designs are found in western Europe from the 12th c.; Japan is the only country outside this area where a similar system (dating also from the 12th c.) occurs. When such devices were no longer needed in war their design became more intricate and developed into a complex system. The designs were associated originally with the higher social classes, a link which still persists. Armorial bearings are hereditary, and strictly belong to the head of a family, other members being entitled to use them only with some mark of cadency. The use of heraldic devices is now widespread, and they are sought by corporate bodies for reasons of prestige and identification. **2** heraldic pomp. **3** armorial bearings.

Herat /həˈræt/ the largest city of western Afghanistan; pop. (est. 1984) 160,000.

herb /hɜːb/ *n.* **1** any non-woody seed-bearing plant which dies down to the ground after flowering. **2** any plant with leaves, seeds, or flowers used for flavouring, food, medicine, scent, etc. □ **herb bennet** a common yellow-flowered plant, *Geum urbanum.* **herb Christopher** a white-flowered baneberry, *Actaea spicata.* **herb Gerard** a white-flowered plant, *Aegopodium podagraria.* **herb Paris** a plant, *Paris quadrifolia*, with a single flower and four leaves in a cross shape on an unbranched stem. **herb Robert** a common cranesbill, *Geranium robertianum*, with red-stemmed leaves and pink flowers. **herb tea** an infusion of herbs. **herb tobacco** a mixture of herbs smoked as a substitute for tobacco. □□ **herbiferous** /-ˈbɪfərəs/ *adj.* **herblike** *adj.* [ME f. OF *erbe* f. L *herba* grass, green crops, herb; *herb bennet* prob. f. med.L *herba benedicta* blessed herb (thought of as expelling the Devil)]

herbaceous /hɜːˈbeɪʃəs/ *adj.* of or like herbs (see HERB 1). □ **herbaceous border** a garden border containing esp. perennial flowering plants. **herbaceous perennial** a plant whose growth dies down annually but whose roots etc. survive. [L *herbaceus* grassy (as HERB)]

herbage /ˈhɜːbɪdʒ/ *n.* **1** herbs collectively. **2** the succulent part of herbs, esp. as pasture. **3** *Law* the right of pasture on another person's land. [ME f. OF *erbage* f. med.L *herbaticum*, *herbagium* right of pasture, f. L *herba* herb]

herbal /ˈhɜːb(ə)l/ *adj. & n.* —*adj.* of herbs in medicinal and culinary use. —*n.* a book with descriptions and accounts of the properties of these. [med.L *herbalis* (as HERB)]

herbalist /ˈhɜːbəlɪst/ *n.* **1** a dealer in medicinal herbs. **2** a person skilled in herbs, esp. an early botanical writer.

herbarium /hɜːˈbeərɪəm/ *n.* (*pl.* **herbaria** /-rɪə/) **1** a systematically arranged collection of dried plants. **2** a book, room, or building for these. [LL (as HERB)]

Herbert[1] /ˈhɜːbət/, Sir Alan Patrick (1890–1970), English writer of great versatility and humour, who contributed to *Punch* for many years. He campaigned for several causes such as divorce law reform (expressed in *Holy Deadlock*, 1934) and reform in English spelling (in *What a Word*, 1935). *Independent Member* (1950) describes his experiences as MP for Oxford University (1935–50), and *My Life and Times* (1970) is his autobiography.

Herbert[2] /ˈhɜːbət/, George (1593–1633), English poet. Renouncing worldly ambition, he became the saintly vicar of Bemerton, near Salisbury. His devout trustful religious verse is marked by

metrical versatility and homely, if at times far-fetched imagery. An account of his life was written by Izaak Walton (1670).

herbicide /ˈhɜːbɪˌsaɪd/ *n.* a substance toxic to plants and used to destroy unwanted vegetation.

herbivore /ˈhɜːbɪˌvɔː(r)/ *n.* an animal that feeds on plants. □□ **herbivorous** /-ˈbɪvərəs/ *adj.* [L *herba* herb + -VORE (see -VOROUS)]

herby /ˈhɜːbɪ/ *adj.* (**herbier**, **herbiest**) **1** abounding in herbs. **2** of the nature of a culinary or medicinal herb.

Herculaneum /ˌhɜːkjʊˈleɪnɪəm/ a small but luxurious ancient Roman town on the lower slopes of Vesuvius, whose eruption in AD 79 buried it under deep heavy volcanic ash and thus largely preserved it for modern excavators.

Herculean /ˌhɜːkjʊˈliːən, -ˈkjuːlɪən/ *adj.* having or requiring great strength or effort. [L *Herculeus* (as HERCULES)]

Hercules /ˈhɜːkjʊˌliːz/ **1** *Gk & Rom. Mythol.* (Gk *Herakles*) a hero (occasionally worshipped as a god) of prodigious strength and courage who performed twelve immense tasks or labours imposed on him by Eurystheus king of Argos. He is usually shown in art with a lion-skin, club, and bow. **2** *Astron.* a northern constellation, figured as a man kneeling on his right knee. □ **Hercules beetle** *Zool.* a large S. American beetle, *Dynastes hercules*, with two horns extending from the head. **Pillars of Hercules 1** the name given in ancient times to two mountains (Calpe and Abyla) opposite one another at the eastern end of the Strait of Gibraltar, marking the limit of the known world. They are identified as the Rock of Gibraltar and Mount Acho, just south of Ceuta in North Africa, said to have been parted by the arm of Hercules. **2** the ultimate limit. [ME f. L f. Gk *Hēraklēs* (= Hera's glory; *kleos* fame)]

Hercynian /hɜːˈsɪnɪən/ *adj.* *Geol.* of a mountain-forming time in the E. hemisphere in the late Palaeozoic era. [L *Hercynia silva* forested mountains of central Germany]

herd /hɜːd/ *n. & v.* —*n.* **1** a large number of animals, esp. cattle, feeding or travelling or kept together. **2** (*prec. by the*) *derog.* a large number of people; a mob (*prefers not to follow the herd*). **3** (esp. in *comb.*) a keeper of herds; a herdsman (*cowherd*). —*v.* **1** *intr. & tr.* go or cause to go in a herd (*herded together for warmth*; *herded the cattle into the field*). **2** *tr.* tend (sheep, cattle, etc.) (*he herds the goats*). □ **herd-book** a book recording the pedigrees of cattle or pigs. **the herd instinct** the tendency of associating or conforming with one's own kind for support etc. **ride herd on** US keep watch on. □□ **herder** *n.* [OE *heord*, (in sense 3) *hirdi*, f. Gmc]

herdsman /ˈhɜːdzmən/ *n.* (*pl.* **-men**) the owner or keeper of herds (of domesticated animals).

Herdwick /ˈhɜːdwɪk/ *n.* **1** an animal of a hardy breed of mountain sheep from N. England. **2** this breed. [obs. *herdwick* pasture-ground (as HERD, WICK[2]), perh. because this breed originated in Furness Abbey pastures]

here /hɪə(r)/ *adv., n., & int.* —*adv.* **1** in or at or to this place or position (*put it here*; *has lived here for many years*; *comes here every day*). **2** indicating a person's presence or a thing offered (*here is your coat*; *my son here will show you*). **3** at this point in the argument, situation, etc. (*here I have a question*). —*n.* this place (*get out of here*; *lives near here*; *fill it up to here*). —*int.* **1** calling attention: short for *come here, look here*, etc. (*here, where are you going with that?*). **2** indicating one's presence in a roll-call: short for *I am here.* □ **here and now** at this very moment; immediately. **here and there** in various places. **here goes!** *colloq.* an expression indicating the start of a bold act. **here's to** I drink to the health of. **here we are** *colloq.* said on arrival at one's destination. **here we go again** *colloq.* the same, usu. undesirable, events are recurring. **here you are** said on handing something to somebody. **neither here nor there** of no importance or relevance. [OE *hēr* f. Gmc: cf. HE]

hereabouts /ˌhɪərəˈbaʊts/ *adv.* (also **hereabout**) near this place.

hereafter /hɪərˈɑːftə(r)/ *adv. & n.* —*adv.* **1** from now on; in the future. **2** in the world to come (after death). —*n.* **1** the future. **2** life after death.

hereat /hɪərˈæt/ *adv.* *archaic* as a result of this.

hereby /hɪəˈbaɪ/ *adv.* by this means; as a result of this.

hereditable /hɪˈredɪtəb(ə)l/ *adj.* that can be inherited. [obs. F *héréditable* or med.L *hereditabilis* f. eccl.L *hereditare* f. L *heres -edis* heir]

hereditament /ˌherɪˈdɪtəmənt, hɪˈredɪ-/ n. *Law* **1** any property that can be inherited. **2** inheritance. [med.L *hereditamentum* (as HEREDITABLE)]

hereditary /hɪˈredɪtərɪ/ adj. **1** (of disease, instinct, etc.) able to be passed down from one generation to another. **2 a** descending by inheritance. **b** holding a position by inheritance. **3** the same as or resembling what one's parents had (*a hereditary hatred*). **4** of or relating to inheritance. □□ **hereditarily** adv. **hereditariness** n. [L *hereditarius* (as HEREDITY)]

heredity /hɪˈredɪtɪ/ n. **1 a** the passing on of physical or mental characteristics genetically from one generation to another. (See below.) **b** these characteristics. **2** the genetic constitution of an individual. [F *hérédité* or L *hereditas* heirship (as HEIR)]

That 'like begets like' has been recognized since ancient times, but a real understanding of the nature of heredity came slowly and had to await the discovery of the sex cells (gametes), the phenomenon of fertilization, and the existence of genes. Lamarck proposed that characteristics acquired by parents during life could by passed on to their offspring, and Darwin too believed that this was possible, although it is now held not to be the case. It was also widely believed in the 19th c. that sexual reproduction involved 'blending' of the characteristics of the two parents in the offspring, a view which appeared to cause difficulties for the theory of natural selection since it seemed that advantageous variations in one parent would inevitably be 'diluted' in the progeny. It was Mendel who first demonstrated that, on the contrary, the hereditary material consists of discrete hereditary factors now known as genes (see MENDELISM).

Hereford /ˈherɪfəd/ n. **1** an animal of a breed of red and white beef cattle. **2** this breed. [*Hereford* in England, where it originated]

Hereford and Worcester /ˈherɪfəd, ˈwʊstə(r)/ a west midland county of England, bordering on Wales; pop. (1981) 636,800; county town, Worcester.

herein /hɪəˈrɪn/ adv. *formal* in this matter, book, etc.

hereinafter /ˌhɪərɪnˈɑːftə(r)/ adv. esp. *Law formal* in a later part of this document etc.

hereinbefore /ˌhɪərɪnbɪˈfɔː(r)/ adv. esp. *Law formal* in a preceding part of this document etc.

hereof /hɪərˈɒv/ adv. *formal* of this.

heresiarch /heˈriːzɪˌɑːk/ n. the leader or founder of a heresy. [eccl.L *haeresiarcha* f. Gk *hairesiarkhēs* (as HERESY + *arkhēs* ruler)]

heresy /ˈherəsɪ/ n. (pl. **-ies**) **1 a** belief or practice contrary to the orthodox doctrine of the Christian Church. **b** an instance of this. **2 a** opinion contrary to what is normally accepted or maintained (*it's heresy to suggest that instant coffee is as good as the real thing*). **b** an instance of this. □□ **heresiology** /ˌherɪsɪˈɒlədʒɪ/ n. [ME f. OF (h)*eresie*, f. eccl.L *haeresis*, in L = school of thought, f. Gk *hairesis* choice, sect f. *haireomai* choose]

heretic /ˈherətɪk/ n. **1** the holder of an unorthodox opinion. **2** *hist.* a person believing in or practising religious heresy. □□ **heretical** /hɪˈretɪk(ə)l/ adj. **heretically** /hɪˈretɪkəlɪ/ adv. [ME f. OF *heretique* f. eccl.L *haereticus* f. Gk *hairetikos* able to choose (as HERESY)]

hereto /hɪəˈtuː/ adv. *formal* to this matter.

heretofore /ˌhɪətʊˈfɔː(r)/ adv. *formal* before this time.

hereunder /hɪərˈʌndə(r)/ adv. *formal* below (in a book, legal document, etc.).

hereunto /ˌhɪərʌnˈtuː/ adv. *archaic* to this.

hereupon /ˌhɪərəˈpɒn/ adv. after this; in consequence of this.

Hereward the Wake /ˈherɪwəd, weɪk/ a semi-legendary leader of Anglo-Saxon resistance to William the Conqueror. Although little is known of Hereward's life beyond what can be found in unreliable literary accounts, he was apparently responsible for a rising at Ely in 1070 which caused some trouble for William I's new Norman regime.

herewith /hɪəˈwɪð, -ˈwɪθ/ adv. with this (esp. of an enclosure in a letter etc.).

heriot /ˈherɪət/ n. *Brit. hist.* a tribute paid to a lord on the death

of a tenant, consisting of a live animal, a chattel, or, orig., the return of borrowed equipment. [OE *heregeatwa* f. *here* army + *geatwa* trappings]

heritable /ˈherɪtəb(ə)l/ adj. **1** *Law* **a** (of property) capable of being inherited by heirs-at-law (cf. MOVABLE). **b** capable of inheriting. **2** *Biol.* (of a characteristic) transmissible from parent to offspring. □□ **heritability** /-ˈbɪlɪtɪ/ n. **heritably** adv. [ME f. OF *heriter* f. eccl.L *hereditare*: see HEREDITABLE]

heritage /ˈherɪtɪdʒ/ n. **1** anything that is or may be inherited. **2** inherited circumstances, benefits, etc. (*a heritage of confusion*). **3** a nation's historic buildings, monuments, countryside, etc., esp. when regarded as worthy of preservation. **4** *Bibl.* **a** the ancient Israelites. **b** the Church. [ME f. OF (as HERITABLE)]

heritor /ˈherɪtə(r)/ n. (esp. in Scottish Law) a person who inherits. [ME f. AF *heriter*, OF *heritier* (as HEREDITARY), assim. to words in -OR[1]]

herl var. of HARL.

herm /hɜːm/ n. *Gk Antiq.* a squared stone pillar with a head (esp. of Hermes) on top, used as a boundary-marker etc. (cf. TERMINUS 6). [L *Herma* f. Gk *Hermēs* messenger of the gods]

hermaphrodite /hɜːˈmæfrəˌdaɪt/ n. & adj. —n. **1 a** *Zool.* an animal having both male and female sexual organs. **b** *Bot.* a plant having stamens and pistils in the same flower. **2** a human being in which both male and female sex organs are present, or in which the sex organs contain both ovarian and testicular tissue. **3** a person or thing combining opposite qualities or characteristics. —adj. **1** combining both sexes. **2** combining opposite qualities or characteristics. □ **hermaphrodite brig** *hist.* a two-masted sailing ship rigged on the foremast as a brig and on the mainmast as a schooner. □□ **hermaphroditic** /-ˈdɪtɪk/ adj. **hermaphroditical** /-ˈdɪtɪk(ə)l/ adj. **hermaphroditism** n. [L *hermaphroditus* f. Gk *hermaphroditos*, orig. the name of a son of Hermes and Aphrodite in Greek mythology, who became joined in one body with the nymph Salmacis]

hermeneutic /ˌhɜːmɪˈnjuːtɪk/ adj. concerning interpretation, esp. of Scripture or literary texts. □□ **hermeneutical** adj. **hermeneutically** adv. [Gk *hermēneutikos* f. *hermēneuō* interpret]

hermeneutics /ˌhɜːmɪˈnjuːtɪks/ n.pl. (also treated as *sing.*) *Bibl.* interpretation, esp. of Scripture or literary texts.

Hermes /ˈhɜːmiːz/ **1** *Gk Mythol.* the son of Zeus and Maia. He was the messenger of the gods, god of merchants, thieves, oratory, etc.; identified by the Romans with Mercury, was represented in human form as a herald equipped for travelling, with broad-brimmed hat, winged shoes, and a winged rod. But he was also associated with fertility, and from early times is shown as a mere stock or stone (*herm*) having generally a human head carved at the top and a phallus half way up it. **2 Hermes Trismegistus** (= thrice-greatest), a clumsy translation of the Egyptian 'Thoth the very great', regarded by Neoplatonists and others as the author of certain works on astrology, magic, and alchemy. [prob. f. Gk *herma* heap of stones]

hermetic /hɜːˈmetɪk/ adj. (also **hermetical**) **1** with an airtight closure. **2** protected from outside agencies. **3 a** of alchemy or other occult sciences (*hermetic art*). **b** esoteric. □ **hermetic seal** an airtight seal (orig. as used by alchemists). □□ **hermetically** adv. **hermetism** /ˈhɜːmɪˌtɪz(ə)m/ n. [mod.L *hermeticus* irreg. f. *Hermes Trismegistus* (as the founder of alchemy; see HERMES 2)]

hermit /ˈhɜːmɪt/ n. **1** an early Christian recluse. **2** any person living in solitude. □ **hermit-crab** any crab of the family Paguridae that lives in a cast-off mollusc shell for protection. **hermit thrush** a migratory N. American thrush, *Catharus guttatus*. □□ **hermitic** /-ˈmɪtɪk/ adj. [ME f. OF (h)*ermite* or f. LL *eremita* f. Gk *erēmitēs* f. *erēmia* desert f. *erēmos* solitary]

Hermitage /ˈhɜːmɪtɪdʒ/, **the** a leading art museum in Leningrad, containing the collections begun by Catherine the Great, one of the most voracious collectors of all time. It derives its name from the 'retreat' in which she displayed them to her friends.

hermitage /ˈhɜːmɪtɪdʒ/ n. **1** a hermit's dwelling. **2** a monastery. **3** a solitary dwelling. [ME f. OF (h)*ermitage* (as HERMIT)]

hernia /ˈhɜːnɪə/ n. (pl. **hernias** or **herniae** /-nɪˌiː/) the displacement and protrusion of part of an organ through the wall of the cavity containing it, esp. of the abdomen. □□ **hernial** *adj.* **herniary** *adj.* **herniated** *adj.* [L]

Herning /ˈhɜːnɪŋ/ a city of Denmark, in central Jutland; pop. (1988) 56,200.

Hero[1] /ˈhɪərəʊ/ *Gk legend* a beautiful priestess of Aphrodite at Sestos on the European shore of the Hellespont, whose lover Leander, a youth of Abydos on the opposite shore, swam the strait nightly to visit her until one stormy night he was drowned and Hero in grief threw herself into the sea.

Hero[2] /ˈhɪərəʊ/ of Alexandria (1st c.), Greek mathematician and inventor, whose surviving works are important as a source for ancient practical mathematics and mechanics. He describes a number of hydraulic, pneumatic, and other mechanical devices, designed both for utility and amusement, including elementary applications of the power of steam.

hero /ˈhɪərəʊ/ *n.* (*pl.* **-oes**) **1 a** a man noted or admired for nobility, courage, outstanding achievements, etc. (*Newton, a hero of science*). **b** a great warrior. **2** the chief male character in a poem, play, story, etc. **3** *Gk Antiq.* a man of superhuman qualities, favoured by the gods; a demigod. □ **hero's welcome** a rapturous welcome, like that given to a successful warrior. **hero-worship** *n.* **1** idealization of an admired man. **2** *Gk Antiq.* worship of the ancient heroes. —*v.tr.* (**-worshipped**, **-worshipping**; *US* **-worshiped**, **-worshiping**) worship as a hero; idolize. **hero-worshipper** a person engaging in hero-worship. [ME f. L *heros* f. Gk *hērōs*]

Herod /ˈherəd/ the name of 4 rulers in ancient Palestine:

Herod the Great (d. 4 BC), ruled for 37 years; Christ was born during his reign. He rebuilt the Temple, and was an effective and able ruler until illness and mental instability marred the last years of his reign.

Herod Antipas son of Herod the Great, governor (tetrarch) of Galilee and Peraea 4 BC–AD 39. He married Herodias and was responsible for the beheading of John the Baptist.

Herod Agrippa I (called 'Herod' in Acts) grandson of Herod the Great, king of the Jews AD 41–4; he put St James the Apostle to death.

Herod Agrippa II son of Herod Agrippa I, was king of various territories in northern Palestine AD 50–c.93; St Paul appeared before him (Acts 25: 13 ff.).

Herodotus /hɪˈrɒdətəs/ (5th c. BC) Greek historian from Halicarnassus in Asia Minor, the 'Father of History'. His *History* tells of the wars between Greece and Persia in the early 5th c. BC, with an account of the earlier history of the Persian Empire and its relations with the Greeks in order to explain the origins of those wars. He professes to record what he had seen and heard (some on his own extensive travels), and this is supplemented by reading, verified by inquiry, and criticized by common sense, with moral honesty. Explorer, observer, and listener, he combines encyclopaedic interest and curiosity with humane sympathy and goodwill, loves wonders and secrets, enjoys a tale and a joke, and tells them vividly. Devoid of race-prejudice and intolerance he venerates antiquity, without military insight he has recorded a great war, and his narrative is constructed to the rules of literary art.

heroic /hɪˈrəʊɪk/ *adj.* & *n.* —*adj.* **1 a** (of an act or a quality) of or fit for a hero. **b** (of a person) like a hero. **2 a** (of language) grand, high-flown, dramatic. **b** (of a work of art) heroic in scale or subject. **3** (of poetry) dealing with the ancient heroes. —*n.* (in *pl.*) **1 a** high-flown language or sentiments. **b** unduly bold behaviour. **2** = *heroic verse*. □ **the heroic age** the period in Greek history before the return from Troy. **heroic couplet** two lines of rhyming iambic pentameters. **heroic verse** a type of verse used for heroic poetry, esp. the hexameter, the iambic pentameter, or the alexandrine. □□ **heroically** *adv.* [F *héroïque* or L *heroicus* f. Gk *hērōikos* (as HERO)]

heroi-comic /hɪrəʊɪˈkɒmɪk/ *adj.* (also **heroi-comical**) combining the heroic with the comic. [F *héroï-comique* (as HERO, COMIC)]

heroin /ˈherəʊɪn/ *n.* a highly addictive white crystalline analgesic drug derived from morphine, often used as a narcotic. [G (as HERO, from its effects on the user's self-esteem)]

heroine /ˈherəʊɪn/ *n.* **1** a woman noted or admired for nobility,

courage, outstanding achievements, etc. **2** the chief female character in a poem, play, story, etc. **3** *Gk Antiq.* a demigoddess. [F *héroïne* or L *heroina* f. Gk *hērōïnē*, fem. of *hērōs* HERO]

heroism /ˈherəʊˌɪz(ə)m/ *n.* heroic conduct or qualities. [F *héroïsme* f. *héros* HERO]

heroize /ˈherəʊˌaɪz/ *v.* (also **-ise**) **1** *tr.* **a** make a hero of. **b** make heroic. **2** *intr.* play the hero.

heron /ˈherən/ *n.* any of various large wading birds of the family Ardeidae, esp. *Ardea cinerea*, with long legs and a long S-shaped neck. □□ **heronry** *n.* (*pl.* **-ies**). [ME f. OF *hairon* f. Gmc]

herpes /ˈhɜːpiːz/ *n.* a virus disease with outbreaks of blisters on the skin etc. □ **herpes simplex** a viral infection which may produce blisters or conjunctivitis. **herpes zoster** /ˈzɒstə(r)/ = SHINGLES. □□ **herpetic** /-ˈpetɪk/ *adj.* [ME f. L f. Gk *herpēs* -*ētos* shingles f. *herpō* creep: *zoster* f. Gk *zōstēr* belt, girdle]

herpetology /ˌhɜːpɪˈtɒlədʒɪ/ *n.* the study of reptiles. □□ **herpetological** /-təˈlɒdʒɪk(ə)l/ *adj.* **herpetologist** *n.* [Gk *herpeton* reptile f. *herpō* creep]

Herr /heə(r)/ *n.* (*pl.* **Herren** /ˈherən/) **1** the title of a German man; Mr. **2** a German man. [G f. OHG *hērro* compar. of *hēr* exalted]

Herrenvolk /ˈherənˌfɒlk, -ˌfəʊk/ *n.* **1** the German nation characterized by the Nazis as born to mastery. **2** a group regarding itself as naturally superior. [G, = master-race (as HERR, FOLK)]

Herrick /ˈherɪk/, Robert (1591–1674), English poet, who graduated from Cambridge and was ordained priest in 1617. In London he was part of Jonson's literary circle. He was incumbent of Dean Prior in Devon during 1630–47, and again after the Restoration. His poems *Hesperides* (1648) were published together with his religious poems, *Noble Numbers*; the latter are often derided as naïve. His secular poems, which treat such subjects as country rituals, Christian festivals, folklore, and love, are marked with gaiety and grace and show a clear debt to the classical poets, particularly Horace and Catullus.

herring /ˈherɪŋ/ *n.* a N. Atlantic fish, *Clupea harengus*, coming near the coast in large shoals to spawn. □ **herring-gull** a large gull, *Larus argentatus*, with dark wing-tips. [OE *hæring*, *hēring* f. WG]

herring-bone /ˈherɪŋˌbəʊn/ *n.* & *v.* —*n.* **1** a stitch with a zigzag pattern, resembling the pattern of a herring's bones. **2** this pattern, or cloth woven in it. **3** any zigzag pattern, e.g. in building. **4** *Skiing* a method of ascending a slope with the skis pointing outwards. —*v.* **1** *tr.* **a** work with a herring-bone stitch. **b** mark with a herring-bone pattern. **2** *intr. Skiing* ascend a slope using the herring-bone technique.

Herriott /ˈherɪət/, James (pseudonym of James Alfred Wight, 1916–), English veterinary surgeon and writer, whose experiences at his work in North Yorkshire inspired a series of stories, including *If Only They Could Talk* (1970), *All Creatures Great and Small* (1972), and *The Lord God Made Them All* (1981).

Herrnhuter /ˈheənˌhuːtə(r), ˈherən-/ *n.* a member of a Christian Moravian sect (see MORAVIAN). [G f. *Herrnhut* (= the Lord's keeping), name of their first German settlement]

hers /hɜːz/ *poss.pron.* the one or ones belonging to or associated with her (*it is hers; hers are over there*). □ **of hers** of or belonging to her (*a friend of hers*).

Herschel /ˈhɜːʃ(ə)l/, Sir William (1738–1822), German-born astronomer who settled in England and became court astronomer to George III. He is often called the Father of Stellar Astronomy, and was a first-rate observer whose painstaking cataloguing of the skies was rewarded in 1781 by the discovery of the planet Uranus. A skilful telescope maker, his unsuccessful attempts to measure the distances of the stars convinced him of their remoteness, while his mapping of stellar distributions suggested to him that the sun was a member of a great star system forming the disc of the Milky Way. Elected first President of the Royal Astronomical Society in 1820, in his work he was greatly helped by his sister Caroline (1750–1848) who was also an able and careful observer. The family's domination of the science of astronomy was continued into the next generation by his son John (1792–1871).

herself /həˈself/ *pron.* **1 a** *emphat. form* of SHE or HER (*she herself*

æ **cat** ɑː **arm** e **bed** ɜː **her** ɪ **sit** iː **see** ɒ **hot** ɔː **saw** ʌ **run** ʊ **put** uː **too** ə **ago** aɪ **my** *will do it).* **b** *refl. form* of HER (*she has hurt herself*). **2** in her normal state of body or mind (*does not feel quite herself today*). □ **be herself** act in her normal unconstrained manner. **by herself** see *by oneself*. [OE *hire self* (as HER, SELF)]

Hertfordshire /ˈhɑːfədʃɪə(r)/ one of the Home Counties of England; pop. (1981) 965,400; county town, Hertford.

Herts. /hɑːts/ *abbr.* Hertfordshire.

Hertz /hɜːts/, Heinrich Rudolf (1857–94), German physicist and a pioneer of radio communication, who worked for a time as Helmholtz's assistant in Berlin. He began his world-famous study of electromagnetic waves in 1886. Maxwell had predicted the existence of these waves in his electromagnetic theory; Hertz demonstrated this experimentally, and also the fact that these waves behaved like light and radiant heat, thus proving that these phenomena, too, were electromagnetic. In 1889 he was appointed professor of physics at Bonn, where he had more time for research, but he died of blood poisoning at the early age of 37.

hertz /hɜːts/ *n.* (*pl.* same) the SI unit of frequency, equal to one cycle per second. ¶ *Abbr.*: **Hz**. [H. R. HERTZ]

Hertzian wave /ˈhɜːtsɪən/ *n.* an electromagnetic wave of a length suitable for use in radio.

Hertzsprung–Russell diagram /ˈhɜːtsprʌŋ ˈrʌs(ə)l/ *n.* a two-dimensional graph, discovered independently by the Danish astronomer E. Hertzsprung (1911) and the American astronomer H. N. Russell (1913), in which the spectral types and absolute magnitudes of stars may be plotted as points. Stars are found to occupy only certain regions of this diagram, depending on their mass and the stage of their life cycle which they occupy. Most stars fall on a line known as the *main sequence*, which represents a well-defined relationship between the physical properties of a star which is still relying on hydrogen as its energy source; when a star has exhausted its hydrogen and begun to consume other elements, it will occupy a different position on the diagram.

Herzl /ˈhɜːts(ə)l/, Theodor (1860–1904), Zionist writer, a Hungarian-born Jew. He worked for most of his life as a writer and journalist in Vienna, advocating the establishment of a Jewish State in Palestine and building up the Zionist movement of which he was the most influential statesman.

he's /hiːz, hɪz/ *contr.* **1** he is. **2** he has.

Hesiod /ˈhiːsɪəd/ (*c.*700 BC), one of the oldest known Greek poets, often coupled or contrasted with Homer as the other main representative of early epic. His hexameter poem the *Theogony* deals with the origin and genealogies of the gods; his *Works and Days* contains moral and practical advice for living an honest life of (chiefly agricultural) work, and was the chief model for later ancient didactic poetry. Both bear the marks of a distinct personality: a surly conservative countryman, given to reflection, no lover of women or of life, who felt the gods' presence heavy about him.

hesitant /ˈhezɪt(ə)nt/ *adj.* hesitating; irresolute. □□ **hesitance** *n.* **hesitancy** *n.* **hesitantly** *adv.*

hesitate /ˈhezɪˌteɪt/ *v.intr.* **1** (often foll. by *about, over*) show or feel indecision or uncertainty; pause in doubt (*hesitated over her choice*). **2** (often foll. by *to* + infin.) be deterred by scruples; be reluctant (*I hesitate to inform against him*). □□ **hesitater** *n.* **hesitatingly** *adv.* **hesitation** /-ˈteɪʃ(ə)n/ *n.* **hesitative** *adj.* [L *haesitare* frequent. of *haerēre haes-* stick fast]

Hesperian /heˈspɪərɪən/ *adj. poet.* **1** western. **2** of or concerning the Hesperides [L *Hesperius* f. Gk *Hesperios* (as HESPERUS)]

Hesperides /hesˈperɪˌdiːz/ *Gk Mythol.* three, four, or seven nymphs, daughters of Hesperus (or, in earlier versions, of Night and Hades). They were guardians, with the aid of a watchful dragon, of a tree of golden apples in a garden popularly located beyond the Atlas mountains at the western border of Oceanus, the river encircling the world.

hesperidium /ˌhespəˈrɪdɪəm/ *n.* (*pl.* **hesperidia** /-dɪə/) a fruit with sectioned pulp in a separable rind, e.g. an orange or grapefruit. [Gk *Hesperides* daughters of Hesperus, nymphs in Greek mythology who guarded a tree of golden apples]

Hesperus /ˈhespərəs/ *n.* the evening star, Venus. [ME f. L f. Gk *hesperos* (adj. & n.) western, concerning (star)]

Hess¹ /hes/, Dame Myra (1890–1965), English pianist, noted for her performances of the music of Schumann, Beethoven, Mozart, and Bach and for her transcription of a chorale from Bach's church cantata No. 147.

Hess² /hes/, Victor Franz (Francis) (1883–1964), Austrian-born American physicist who divided his academic career between Austria and the US. His research interests in atmospheric electricity and radioactivity culminated in the discovery of cosmic rays, which led to the discovery of the positively-charged electron or positron by the American physicist C. D. Anderson (1905–). They shared the 1936 Nobel Prize for physics.

Hess³ /hes/, Walther Richard Rudolf (1894–1987), German Nazi leader, a close friend of Hitler and his deputy as party leader 1933–8. In 1941, secretly and independently, he parachuted into Scotland to negotiate peace with Britain. He was imprisoned for the duration of the war, and after his conviction at the Nuremberg war trials was sentenced to life imprisonment.

Hesse¹ /ˈhesə/ (German **Hessen** /ˈhes(ə)n/) a 'Land' (State) of western Germany; pop. (1987) 5,552,000; capital, Wiesbaden.

Hesse² /ˈhesə/, Hermann (1877–1962), German novelist and poet, author of several novels of a more or less mystical nature which attracted a revival of interest in the 1960s. His works include *Siddhartha* (1922), *Der Steppenwolf* (1927), and *Das Glasperlenspiel* (*The Glass Bead Game*, 1943). He was awarded the Nobel Prize for literature in 1946.

hessian /ˈhesɪən/ *n. & adj.* —*n.* **1** a strong coarse sacking made of hemp or jute. **2** (**Hessian**) a native of Hesse in Germany. —*adj.* (**Hessian**) of or concerning Hesse. □ **Hessian boot** a tasselled high boot first worn by Hessian troops. **Hessian fly** a midge, *Mayetiola destructor*, whose larva destroys growing wheat (thought to have been brought to America by Hessian troops). [*Hesse* in Germany]

hest /hest/ *n. archaic* behest. [OE *hǣs* (see HIGHT), assim. to ME nouns in -*t*]

hetaera /hɪˈtɪərə/ *n.* (also **hetaira** /-ˈtaɪrə/) (*pl.* **-as, hetaerae** /-ˈtɪəriː/, or **hetairai** /-ˈtaɪraɪ/) a courtesan or mistress, esp. in ancient Greece. [Gk *hetaira*, fem. of *hetairos* companion]

hetaerism /hɪˈtɪərɪzəm/ *n.* (also **hetairism** /-ˈtaɪrɪzəm/) **1** a recognized system of concubinage. **2** communal marriage in a tribe. [Gk *hetairismos* prostitution (as HETAERA)]

hetero /ˈhetərəʊ/ *n.* (*pl.* **-os**) *colloq.* a heterosexual. [abbr.]

hetero- /ˈhetərəʊ/ *comb. form* other, different (often opp. HOMO-). [Gk *heteros* other]

heterochromatic /ˌhetərəʊkrəˈmætɪk/ *adj.* of several colours.

heteroclite /ˈhetərəʊˌklaɪt/ *adj. & n.* —*adj.* **1** abnormal. **2** *Gram.* (esp. of a noun) irregularly declined. —*n.* **1** an abnormal thing or person. **2** *Gram.* an irregularly declined word, esp. a noun. [LL *heteroclitus* f. Gk (as HETERO-, *klitos* f. *klinō* bend, inflect)]

heterocyclic /ˌhetərəʊˈsaɪklɪk, -ˈsɪklɪk/ *adj. Chem.* (of a compound) with a bonded ring of atoms of more than one kind.

heterodox /ˈhetərəʊˌdɒks/ *adj.* (of a person, opinion, etc.) not orthodox. □□ **heterodoxy** *n.* [LL *heterodoxus* f. Gk (as HETERO-, *doxos* f. *doxa* opinion)]

heterodyne /ˈhetərəʊˌdaɪn/ *adj. & v. Radio* —*adj.* relating to the production of a lower frequency from the combination of two almost equal high frequencies. —*v.intr.* produce a lower frequency in this way.

heterogamous /ˌhetəˈrɒɡəməs/ *adj.* **1** *Bot.* irregular as regards stamens and pistils. **2** *Biol.* characterized by heterogamy or heterogony.

heterogamy /ˌhetəˈrɒɡəmɪ/ *n.* **1** the alternation of generations, esp. of a sexual and parthenogenic generation. **2** sexual reproduction by fusion of unlike gametes. **3** *Bot.* a state in which the flowers of a plant are of two types.

heterogeneous /ˌhetərəʊˈdʒiːnɪəs/ *adj.* **1** diverse in character. **2** varied in content. **3** *Math.* incommensurable through being of different kinds or degrees. □□ **heterogeneity** /-dʒɪˈniːɪtɪ/ *n.* **heterogeneously** *adv.* **heterogeneousness** *n.* [med.L *heterogeneus* f. Gk *heterogenēs* (as HETERO-, *genos* kind)]

heterogenesis /ˌhetərəʊˈdʒenɪsɪs/ n. **1** the birth of a living being otherwise than from parents of the same kind. **2** spontaneous generation from inorganic matter. □□ **heterogenetic** /-dʒɪˈnetɪk/ adj.

heterogony /ˌhetəˈrɒɡənɪ/ n. the alternation of generations, esp. of a sexual and hermaphroditic generation. □□ **heterogonous** adj.

heterograft /ˈhetərəʊˌɡrɑːft/ n. living tissue grafted from one individual to another of a different species.

heterologous /ˌhetəˈrɒləɡəs/ adj. not homologous. □□ **heterology** n.

heteromerous /ˌhetəˈrɒmərəs/ adj. not isomerous.

heteromorphic /ˌhetərəʊˈmɔːfɪk/ adj. (also **heteromorphous** /-ˈmɔːfəs/) Biol. **1** of dissimilar forms. **2** (of insects) existing in different forms at different stages in their life cycle.

heteromorphism /ˌhetərəʊˈmɔːfɪz(ə)m/ n. existing in various forms.

heteronomous /ˌhetəˈrɒnəməs/ adj. **1** subject to an external law (cf. AUTONOMOUS). **2** Biol. subject to different laws (of growth etc.).

heteronomy /ˌhetəˈrɒnəmɪ/ n. **1** the presence of a different law. **2** subjection to an external law.

heteropathic /ˌhetərəʊˈpæθɪk/ adj. **1** allopathic. **2** differing in effect.

heterophyllous /ˌhetərəʊˈfɪləs/ adj. bearing leaves of different forms on the same plant. □□ **heterophylly** n. [HETERO- + Gk phullon leaf]

heteropolar /ˌhetərəʊˈpəʊlə(r)/ adj. having dissimilar poles, esp. Electr. with an armature passing north and south magnetic poles alternately.

heteropteran /ˌhetəˈrɒptərən/ n. any insect of the suborder Heteroptera, including bugs, with non-uniform fore-wings having a thickened base and membranous tip (cf. HOMOPTERAN). □□ **heteropterous** adj. [HETERO- + Gk pteron wing]

heterosexual /ˌhetərəʊˈseksjʊəl/ adj. & n. —adj. **1** feeling or involving sexual attraction to persons of the opposite sex. **2** concerning heterosexual relations or people. **3** relating to the opposite sex. —n. a heterosexual person. □□ **heterosexuality** /-ˈælɪtɪ/ n. **heterosexually** adv.

heterosis /ˌhetəˈrəʊsɪs/ n. the tendency of a cross-bred individual to show qualities superior to those of both parents. [Gk f. heteros different]

heterotaxy /ˈhetərəʊˌtæksɪ/ n. the abnormal disposition of organs or parts. [HETERO- + Gk taxis arrangement]

heterotransplant /ˌhetərəʊˈtrænsplɑːnt/ n. = HETEROGRAFT.

heterotrophic /ˌhetərəʊˈtrɒfɪk/ adj. Biol. deriving its nourishment and carbon requirements from organic substances; not autotrophic. [HETERO- + Gk trophos feeder]

heterozygote /ˌhetərəʊˈzaɪɡəʊt/ n. Biol. **1** a zygote resulting from the fusion of unlike gametes. **2** an individual with dominant and recessive alleles determining a particular characteristic. □□ **heterozygous** adj.

hetman /ˈhetmən/ n. (pl. **-men**) a Polish or Cossack military commander. [Pol., prob. f. G Hauptmann captain]

het up /het ˈʌp/ adj. colloq. excited, overwrought. [het dial. past part. of HEAT]

heuchera /ˈhjuːkərə, ˈhɔɪk-/ n. any N. American herbaceous plant of the genus Heuchera, with dark-green round or heart-shaped leaves and tiny flowers. [mod.L f. J. H. von Heucher, Ger. botanist d. 1747]

heuristic /hjʊəˈrɪstɪk/ adj. & n. —adj. **1** allowing or assisting to discover. **2** Computing proceeding to a solution by trial and error. —n. **1** the science of heuristic procedure. **2** a heuristic process or method. **3** (in pl., usu. treated as sing.) Computing the study and use of heuristic techniques in data processing. □ **heuristic method** a system of education under which pupils are trained to find out things for themselves. □□ **heuristically** adv. [irreg. f. Gk heuriskō find]

hevea /ˈhiːvɪə/ n. any S. American tree of the genus Hevea, yielding a milky sap used for making rubber. [mod.L f. native name hevé]

HEW abbr. US Department of Health, Education, and Welfare.

hew /hjuː/ v. (past part. **hewn** /hjuːn/ or **hewed**) **1** tr. **a** (often foll. by down, away, off) chop or cut (a thing) with an axe, a sword, etc. **b** cut (a block of wood etc.) into shape. **2** intr. (often foll. by at, among, etc.) strike cutting blows. **3** intr. US (usu. foll. by to) conform. □ **hew one's way** make a way for oneself by hewing. [OE hēawan f. Gmc]

hewer /ˈhjuːə(r)/ n. **1** a person who hews. **2** a person who cuts coal from a seam. □ **hewers of wood and drawers of water** menial drudges; labourers (Josh. 9: 21).

hex /heks/ v. & n. US —v. **1** intr. practise witchcraft. **2** tr. bewitch. —n. **1** a magic spell. **2** a witch. [Pennsylvanian G hexe (v.), Hex (n.), f. G hexen, Hexe]

hexa- /ˈheksə/ comb. form six. [Gk hex six]

hexachord /ˈheksəˌkɔːd/ n. a diatonic series of six notes with a semitone between the third and fourth, used at three different pitches in medieval music. [HEXA- + CHORD[1]]

hexad /ˈheksæd/ n. a group of six. [Gk hexas -ados f. hex six]

hexadecimal /ˌheksəˈdesɪm(ə)l/ adj. & n. esp. Computing. —adj. relating to or using a system of numerical notation that has 16 rather than 10 as a base. —n. the hexadecimal system; hexadecimal notation. □□ **hexadecimally** adv.

hexagon /ˈheksəɡən/ n. a plane figure with six sides and angles. □□ **hexagonal** /-ˈsæɡən(ə)l/ adj. [LL hexagonum f. Gk (as HEXA-, -GON)]

hexagram /ˈheksəˌɡræm/ n. **1** a figure formed by two intersecting equilateral triangles. **2** a figure of six lines. [HEXA- + Gk gramma line]

hexahedron /ˌheksəˈhiːdrən/ n. a solid figure with six faces. □□ **hexahedral** adj. [Gk (as HEXA-, -HEDRON)]

hexameter /hekˈsæmɪtə(r)/ n. a line or verse of six metrical feet. □ **dactylic hexameter** a hexameter having five dactyls and a spondee or trochee, any of the first four feet, and sometimes the fifth, being replaceable by a spondee. □□ **hexametric** /-səˈmetrɪk/ adj. **hexametrist** n. [ME f. L f. Gk hexametros (as HEXA-, metron measure)]

hexane /ˈhekseɪn/ n. Chem. a liquid hydrocarbon of the alkane series. ¶ Chem. formula: C_6H_{14}. [HEXA- + -ANE]

hexapla /ˈheksəplə/ n. a sixfold text, esp. of the Old Testament, in parallel columns. [Gk neut. pl. of hexaploos (as HEXA-, ploos -fold), orig. of Origen's OT text]

hexapod /ˈheksəˌpɒd/ n. & adj. —n. any arthropod with six legs; an insect. —adj. having six legs. [Gk hexapous, hexapod- (as HEXA-, pous pod- foot)]

hexastyle /ˈheksəˌstaɪl/ n. & adj. —n. a six-columned portico. —adj. having six columns. [Gk hexastulos (as HEXA-, stulos column)]

Hexateuch /ˈheksəˌtjuːk/ n. the first six books of the Old Testament. [Gk hex six + teukhos book]

hexavalent /ˌheksəˈveɪlənt/ adj. having a valency of six; sexivalent.

hexose /ˈheksəʊz/ n. Biochem. a monosaccharide with six carbon atoms in each molecule, e.g. glucose or fructose. [HEXA- + -OSE[2]]

hey[1] /heɪ/ int. calling attention or expressing joy, surprise, inquiry, enthusiasm, etc. □ **hey presto!** a phrase of command, or indicating a successful trick, used by a conjuror etc. [ME: cf. OF hay, Du., G hei]

hey[2] var. of HAY[2].

heyday /ˈheɪdeɪ/ n. the flush or full bloom of youth, vigour, prosperity, etc. [archaic heyday expression of joy, surprise, etc.: cf. LG heidi, heida, excl. denoting gaiety]

Heyer /ˈheɪə(r)/, Georgette (1902–74), English author, noted especially for her historical novels which include numerous Regency romances, such as Devil's Cub (1934), Regency Buck (1935), and Faro's Daughter (1941). She also wrote detective stories in the classic style, including Envious Casca (1941) and Detection Unlimited (1953).

Heyerdahl /ˈheɪəˌdɑːl/, Thor (1914–), Norwegian anthropologist, famous for his practical efforts to demonstrate his theories of cultural diffusion. In 1947, to show that Polynesian peoples could originally have been migrants from South America, he sailed with a small crew in a primitive raft named the *Kon-Tíki* from Peru to the islands east of Tahiti. Later, in similar voyages, he crossed the Atlantic from Morocco towards Central America and travelled from the Tigris to Pakistan and then the Red Sea, but even after these epic journeys much of the scientific world remained sceptical about his conclusions.

Hezbollah /ˌhezbəˈlɑː/ an extreme Shiite Muslim group, active especially in Lebanon. [Pers., f. Arab. *ḥizbullah* Party of God, f. *ḥezb* party + *allāh* ALLAH]

HF *abbr.* high frequency.

Hf *symb. Chem.* the element hafnium.

hf. *abbr.* half.

HG *abbr.* **1** Her or His Grace. **2** Home Guard.

Hg *symb. Chem.* the element mercury. [mod.L *hydrargyrum*].

hg *abbr.* hectogram(s).

HGV *abbr. Brit.* heavy goods vehicle.

HH *abbr.* **1** Her or His Highness. **2** His Holiness. **3** double-hard (pencil-lead).

hh. *abbr.* hands (see HAND *n.* 13).

hhd. *abbr.* hogshead(s).

H-hour /ˈeɪtʃˌaʊə(r)/ *n.* the hour at which an operation is scheduled to begin. [H for *hour* + HOUR]

HI *abbr. US* **1** Hawaii (also in official postal use). **2** the Hawaiian Islands.

hi /haɪ/ *int.* calling attention or as a greeting. [parallel form to HEY[1]]

hiatus /haɪˈeɪtəs/ *n.* (*pl.* **hiatuses**) **1** a break or gap, esp. in a series, account, or chain of proof. **2** *Prosody & Gram.* a break between two vowels coming together but not in the same syllable, as in *though oft the ear.* □□ **hiatal** *adj.* [L, = gaping f. *hiare* gape]

Hiawatha /ˌhaɪəˈwɒθə/ a legendary 16th-c. American Indian teacher and chieftain, hero of a narrative poem (1855) by Longfellow (who took nothing but the name from the historical figure).

hibernate /ˈhaɪbəˌneɪt/ *v.intr.* **1** (of some animals) spend the winter in a dormant state. **2** remain inactive. □□ **hibernation** /-ˈneɪʃ(ə)n/ *n.* **hibernator** *n.* [L *hibernare* f. *hibernus* wintry]

Hibernian /haɪˈbɜːnɪən/ *adj. & n. archaic poet.* —*adj.* of or concerning Ireland. —*n.* a native of Ireland. [L *Hibernia, Iverna* f. Gk *Iernē* f. OCelt.]

Hibernicism /haɪˈbɜːnɪˌsɪz(ə)m/ *n.* an Irish idiom or expression; = BULL[3] 1. [as HIBERNIAN after *Anglicism* etc.]

Hiberno- /haɪˈbɜːnəʊ/ *comb. form* Irish (*Hiberno-British*). [med.L *hibernus* Irish (as HIBERNIAN)]

hibiscus /hɪˈbɪskəs/ *n.* any tree or shrub of the genus *Hibiscus*, cultivated for its large bright-coloured flowers. Also called *rose-mallow.* [L f. Gk *hibiskos* marsh mallow]

hic /hɪk/ *int.* expressing the sound of a hiccup, esp. a drunken hiccup. [imit.]

hiccup /ˈhɪkʌp/ *n. & v.* (also **hiccough**) —*n.* **1 a** an involuntary spasm of the diaphragm and respiratory organs, with sudden closure of the glottis and characteristic coughlike sound. **b** (in *pl.*) an attack of such spasms. **2** a temporary or minor stoppage or difficulty. —*v.* **1** *intr.* make a hiccup or series of hiccups. **2** *tr.* utter with a hiccup. □□ **hiccupy** *adj.* [imit.]

hic jacet /hɪk ˈdʒeɪset, hiːk ˈjæket/ *n.* an epitaph. [L, = here lies]

hick /hɪk/ *n.* esp. *US colloq.* a country dweller; a provincial. [petform of the name *Richard*; cf. DICK[1]]

hickey /ˈhɪkɪ/ *n.* (*pl.* **-eys**) *US colloq.* a gadget (cf. DOOHICKEY). [20th c.; orig. unkn.]

hickory /ˈhɪkərɪ/ *n.* (*pl.* **-ies**) **1** any N. American tree of the genus *Carya*, yielding tough heavy wood and bearing nutlike edible fruits (see PECAN). **2 a** the wood of these trees. **b** a stick made of this. □ **Old Hickory** the nickname of US President Andrew Jackson. [native Virginian *pohickery*]

Hicks /hɪks/, Sir John Richard (1904–89), English economist, whose most important work was in his pioneering contributions to general 'equilibrium' theory (that economic forces

tend to balance one another rather than simply reflect cyclical trends), for which he shared a Nobel Prize with K. J. Arrow in 1972.

hid *past* of HIDE[1].

Hidalgo /hɪˈdælgəʊ/ a State of central Mexico; pop. (est. 1988) 1,822,300; capital, Pachuca de Soto.

hidalgo /hɪˈdælgəʊ/ *n.* (*pl.* **-os**) a Spanish gentleman. [Sp. f. *hijo dalgo* son of something]

hidden *past part.* of HIDE[1]. □□ **hiddenness** *n.*

hide[1] /haɪd/ *v. & n.* —*v.* (*past* **hid**; *past part.* **hidden** /ˈhɪd(ə)n/ or *archaic* **hid**) **1** *tr.* put or keep out of sight (*hid it under the cushion; hid her in the cupboard*). **2** *intr.* conceal oneself. **3** *tr.* (usu. foll. by *from*) keep (a fact) secret (*hid his real motive from her*). **4** *tr.* conceal (a thing) from sight intentionally or not (*trees hid the house*). —*n. Brit.* a camouflaged shelter used for observing wildlife or hunting animals. □ **hidden reserves** extra profits, resources, etc. kept concealed in reserve. **hide-and-seek** a children's game in which one or more players seek a child or children hiding. **2** a process of attempting to find an evasive person or thing. **hide one's head** keep out of sight, esp. from shame. **hide one's light under a bushel** conceal one's merits (Matthew 5: 15). **hide out** (or **up**) remain in concealment. **hide-out** *colloq.* a hiding-place. **hidey-** (or **hidy-**) **hole** *colloq.* a hiding-place. □□ **hider** *n.* [OE *hȳdan* f. WG]

hide[2] /haɪd/ *n. & v.* —*n.* **1** the skin of an animal, esp. when tanned or dressed. **2** *colloq.* the human skin (*saved his own hide; I'll tan your hide*). —*v.tr. colloq.* flog. □□ **hided** *adj.* (also in *comb.*). [OE *hȳd* f. Gmc]

hide[3] /haɪd/ *n.* a former measure of land large enough to support a family and its dependants, usu. between 60 and 120 acres. [OE *hī(gi)d* f. *hīw-, hīg-* household]

hideaway /ˈhaɪdəˌweɪ/ *n.* a hiding-place or place of retreat.

hidebound /ˈhaɪdbaʊnd/ *adj.* **1 a** narrow-minded; bigoted. **b** (of the law, rules, etc.) constricted by tradition. **2** (of cattle) with the skin clinging close as a result of bad feeding. [HIDE[2] + BOUND[4]]

hideosity /ˌhɪdɪˈɒsɪtɪ/ *n.* (*pl.* **-ies**) **1** a hideous object. **2** hideousness.

hideous /ˈhɪdɪəs/ *adj.* **1** frightful, repulsive, or revolting, to the senses or the mind (*a hideous monster; a hideous pattern*). **2** *colloq.* unpleasant. □□ **hideously** *adv.* **hideousness** *n.* [ME *hidous* f. AF *hidous*, OF *hidos*, *-eus*, f. OF *hide, hisde* fear, of unkn. orig.]

hiding[1] /ˈhaɪdɪŋ/ *n. colloq.* a thrashing. □ **on a hiding to nothing** in a position from which there can be no successful outcome. [HIDE[2] + -ING[1]]

hiding[2] /ˈhaɪdɪŋ/ *n.* **1** the act or an instance of hiding. **2** the state of remaining hidden (*go into hiding*). □ **hiding-place** a place of concealment. [ME, f. HIDE[1] + -ING[1]]

hidrosis /hɪˈdrəʊsɪs, haɪ-/ *n. Med.* perspiration. □□ **hidrotic** /-ˈdrɒtɪk/ *adj.* [mod.L f. Gk f. *hidrōs* sweat]

hie /haɪ/ *v.intr. & refl.* (**hies**, **hied**, **hieing** or **hying**) *archaic or poet.* go quickly (*hie to your chamber; hied him to the chase*). [OE *hīgian* strive, pant, of unkn. orig.]

hierarch /ˈhaɪəˌrɑːk/ *n.* **1** a chief priest. **2** an archbishop. □□ **hierarchal** /-ˈrɑːk(ə)l/ *adj.* [med.L f. Gk *hierarkhēs* f. *hieros* sacred + *-arkhēs* ruler]

hierarchy /ˈhaɪəˌrɑːkɪ/ *n.* (*pl.* **-ies**) **1 a** a system in which grades or classes of status or authority are ranked one above the other (*ranks third in the hierarchy*). **b** the hierarchical system (of government, management, etc.). **2 a** a priestly government. **b** a priesthood organized in grades. **3 a** each of the three divisions of angels. **b** the angels. □□ **hierarchic** /-ˈrɑːkɪk/ *adj.* **hierarchical** /-ˈrɑːkɪk(ə)l/ *adj.* **hierarchism** *n.* **hierarchize** *v.tr.* (also **-ise**). [ME f. OF *ierarchie* f. med.L *(h)ierarchia* f. Gk *hierarkhia* (as HIERARCH)]

hieratic /ˌhaɪəˈrætɪk/ *adj. & n.* —*adj.* **1** of or concerning priests. **2** of the ancient Egyptian script that is a form of cursive hieroglyphs used from early times, originally for religious texts, and eventually superseded by demotic. **3** of or concerning Egyptian or Greek traditional styles of art. **4** priestly. —*n.* hieratic script. □□ **hieratically** *adv.* [L f. Gk *hieratikos* f. *hieraomai* be a priest f. *hiereus* priest]

hiero- /'haɪərəʊ/ *comb. form* sacred, holy. [Gk *hieros* sacred + -o-]

hierocracy /ˌhaɪə'rɒkrəsɪ/ *n.* (*pl.* **-ies**) **1** priestly rule. **2** a body of ruling priests. [HIERO- + -CRACY]

hieroglyph /'haɪərəglɪf/ *n.* **1 a** a picture of an object representing a word, sound, or syllable in any of the pictorial systems of writing, especially the ancient Egyptian. (See below.) **b** a writing consisting of characters of this kind. **2** a secret or enigmatic symbol. **3** (in *pl.*) *joc.* writing difficult to read. [back-form. f. HIEROGLYPHIC]
Hieroglyphs were used in ancient Egypt for monumental inscriptions from the end of the 4th millennium BC until the 4th C. AD. Monumental hieroglyphs were an art form; there was no separation between words or phrases, and the direction of the writing varied (vertical, right to left, or left to right), with the purely decorative aspect sometimes having priority. In the classic period there were about 700 signs, but signs were continually invented and modified and became innumerable. Hieroglyphs remained undeciphered until the discovery of the Rosetta stone (see entry).

hieroglyphic /ˌhaɪərə'glɪfɪk/ *adj. & n.* —*adj.* **1** of or written in hieroglyphs. **2** symbolical. —*n.* (in *pl.*) hieroglyphs; hieroglyphic writing. □□ **hieroglyphical** *adj.* **hieroglyphically** *adv.* [F *hiéroglyphique* or LL *hieroglyphicus* f. Gk *hieroglyphikos* (as HIERO-, *gluphikos* f. *gluphē* carving)]

hierogram /'haɪərəʊˌgræm/ *n.* a sacred inscription or symbol.

hierograph /'haɪərəʊˌgrɑːf/ *n.* = HIEROGRAM.

hierolatry /ˌhaɪə'rɒlətrɪ/ *n.* the worship of saints or sacred things.

hierology /ˌhaɪə'rɒlədʒɪ/ *n.* sacred literature or lore.

hierophant /'haɪərəˌfænt/ *n.* **1** *Gk Antiq.* an initiating or presiding priest; an official interpreter of sacred mysteries. **2** an interpreter of sacred mysteries or any esoteric principle. □□ **hierophantic** /-'fæntɪk/ *adj.* [LL *hierophantes* f. Gk *hierophantēs* (as HIERO-, *phantēs* f. *phainō* show)]

hi-fi /'haɪfaɪ/ *adj. & n. colloq.* —*adj.* = high fidelity. —*n.* (*pl.* **hi-fis**) a set of equipment for high-fidelity sound reproduction. [abbr.]

higgle /'hɪg(ə)l/ *v.intr.* dispute about terms; haggle. [var. of HAGGLE]

higgledy-piggledy /ˌhɪgəldɪ'pɪgəldɪ/ *adv., adj., & n.* —*adv. & adj.* in confusion or disorder. —*n.* a state of disordered confusion. [rhyming jingle, prob. with ref. to the irregular herding together of pigs]

high /haɪ/ *adj., n., & adv.* —*adj.* **1 a** of great vertical extent (*a high building*). **b** (*predic.*; often in *comb.*) of a specified height (*one inch high*; *water was waist-high*). **2 a** far above ground or sea level etc. (*a high altitude*). **b** inland, esp. when raised (*High Asia*). **3** extending above the normal or average level (*high boots*; *jersey with a high neck*). **4** of exalted, esp. spiritual, quality (*high minds*; *high principles*; *high art*). **5** of exalted rank (*in high society*; *is high in the Government*). **6 a** great; intense; extreme; powerful (*high praise*; *high temperature*). **b** greater than normal (*high prices*). **c** extreme in religious or political opinion (*high Tory*). **7** (of physical action, esp. athletics) performed at, to, or from a considerable height (*high diving*; *high flying*). **8** *colloq.* (often foll. by *on*) intoxicated by alcohol or esp. drugs. **9** (of a sound or note) of high frequency; shrill; at the top end of the scale. **10** (of a period, an age, a time, etc.) at its peak (*high noon*; *high summer*; *High Renaissance*). **11 a** (of meat) beginning to go bad; off. **b** (of game) well-hung and slightly decomposed. **12** *Geog.* (of latitude) near the North or South Pole. **13** *Phonet.* (of a vowel) close (see CLOSE¹ *adj.* 14). —*n.* **1** a high, or the highest, level or figure. **2** an area of high barometric pressure; an anticyclone. **3** *sl.* a euphoric drug-induced state. **4** top gear in a motor vehicle. **5** *US colloq.* high school. **6** (**the High**) *Brit. colloq.* a High Street, esp. that in Oxford. —*adv.* **1** far up; aloft (*flew the flag high*). **2** in or to a high degree. **3** at a high price. **4** (of a sound) at or to a high pitch (*sang high*). □ **ace** (or **King** or **Queen** etc.) **high** (in card games) having the ace etc. as the highest-ranking card. **from on high** from heaven or a high place. **High Admiral** etc. a chief officer. **high altar** the chief altar of a church. **high and dry 1** out of the current of events; stranded. **2** (of a ship) out of the water.

high and low 1 everywhere (*searched high and low*). **2** (people) of all conditions. **high and mighty 1** *colloq.* arrogant. **2** *archaic* of exalted rank. **high-born** of noble birth. **high camp** sophisticated camp (cf. CAMP²). **high card** a card that outranks others, esp. the ace or a court-card. **high chair** an infant's chair with long legs and a tray, for use at meals. **High Church** *n.* the section of the Church of England which stresses historical continuity with Catholic Christianity and attaches 'high' importance to the authority of the episcopate and the saving grace of the Sacraments. In its modern sense the term dates back to the Oxford Movement. —*adj.* of or relating to this section. **High Churchman** (*pl.* **-men**) an advocate of High Church principles. **high-class** of high quality. **high colour** a flushed complexion. **high command** an army commander-in-chief and associated staff. **High Commission** an embassy from one Commonwealth country to another. **High Commissioner** the head of such an embassy. **High Court** (also in England **High Court of Justice**) a supreme court of justice for civil cases. **high day** a festal day. **High Dutch** see DUTCH. **high enema** an enema delivered into the colon. **higher animal** (or **plant**) an animal or plant evolved to a high degree. **higher court** *Law* a court that can overrule the decision of another. **the higher criticism** see CRITICISM. **higher education** education at university etc., esp. to degree level. **higher mathematics** advanced mathematics as taught at university etc. **higher-up** *colloq.* a person of higher rank. **highest common factor** *Math.* the highest number that can be divided exactly into each of two or more numbers. **high explosive** an extremely explosive substance used in shells, bombs, etc. **high fashion** = HAUTE COUTURE. **high fidelity** the reproduction of sound with little distortion, giving a result very similar to the original. In order to achieve this the system must be able to record all frequencies and their respective intensities within the audible frequency and volume range, and the reverberation and spatial sound-pattern of the original must be reproduced too. **high finance** financial transactions involving large sums. **high-flown** (of language etc.) extravagant, bombastic. **high-flyer** (or **-flier**) **1** an ambitious person. **2** a person or thing with great potential for achievement. **high-flying** reaching a great height; ambitious. **high frequency** a frequency, esp. in radio, of 3 to 30 megahertz. **high gear** see GEAR. **High German** see GERMAN. **high-grade** of high quality. **high hat 1** a tall hat; a top hat. **2** foot-operated cymbals. **3** a snobbish or overbearing person. **high-hat** —*adj.* supercilious; snobbish. —*v.* (**-hatted**, **-hatting**) *US* **1** *tr.* treat superciliously. **2** *intr.* assume a superior attitude. **high holiday** the Jewish New Year or the Day of Atonement. **high jinks** boisterous joking or merrymaking. **high jump 1** an athletic event consisting of jumping as high as possible over a bar of adjustable height. **2** *colloq.* a drastic punishment (*he's for the high-jump*). **high-key** *Photog.* consisting of light tones only. **high kick** a dancer's kick high in the air. **high-level 1** (of negotiations etc.) conducted by high-ranking people. **2** *Computing* (of a programming language) that is not machine-dependent and is usu. at a level of abstraction close to natural language. **high life** (or **living**) a luxurious existence ascribed to the upper classes. **high-lows** *archaic* boots reaching over the ankles. **high mass** see MASS². **high-octane** (of petrol etc.) having good antiknock properties. **high old** *colloq.* most enjoyable (*had a high old time*). **high opinion** of a favourable opinion of. **high-pitched 1** (of a sound) high. **2** (of a roof) steep. **3** (of style etc.) lofty. **high places** the upper ranks of an organization etc. **high point** the maximum or best state reached. **high polymer** a polymer having a high molecular weight. **high-powered 1** having great power or energy. **2** important or influential. **high pressure 1** a high degree of activity or exertion. **2** a condition of the atmosphere with the pressure above average. **high priest 1** a chief priest, esp. Jewish. **2** the head of any cult. **high profile** exposure to attention or publicity. **high-profile** *adj.* (usu. *attrib.*) having a high profile. **high-ranking** of high rank, senior. **high relief** see RELIEF. **high-rise 1** (of a building) having many storeys. **2** such a building. **high-risk** (usu. *attrib.*) involving or exposed to danger (*high-risk sports*). **high road 1** a main road. **2** (usu. foll. by *to*) a direct route (*on the high road to success*). **high roller** *US sl.* a person who gambles large sums or spends freely.

high school 1 *Brit.* a grammar school. **2** *US & Sc.* a secondary school. **high sea** (or **seas**) open seas not within any country's jurisdiction. **high season** the period of the greatest number of visitors at a resort etc. **High Sheriff** see SHERIFF. **high sign** *US colloq.* a surreptitious gesture indicating that all is well or that the coast is clear. **high-sounding** pretentious, bombastic. **high-speed 1** operating at great speed. **2** (of steel) suitable for cutting-tools even when red-hot. **high-spirited** vivacious; cheerful. **high-spiritedness** = *high spirits*. **high spirits** vivacity; energy; cheerfulness. **high spot** *sl.* an important place or feature. **high-stepper 1** a horse that lifts its feet high when walking or trotting. **2** a stately person. **High Steward** see STEWARD *n.* 6. **high street** *Brit.* a main road, esp. the principal shopping street of a town. **high-strung** = *highly-strung.* **high table** a table on a platform at a public dinner or for the fellows of a college. **high tea** *Brit.* a main evening meal usu. consisting of a cooked dish, bread and butter, tea, etc. **high tech** *n.* = *high technology.* —*adj.* **1** (of interior design etc.) imitating styles more usual in industry etc., esp. using steel, glass, or plastic in a functional way. **2** employing, requiring, or involved in high technology. **high technology** advanced technological development, esp. in electronics. **high-tensile** (of metal) having great tensile strength. **high tension** = *high voltage.* **high tide** the time or level of the tide at its flow. **high time** a time that is late or overdue (*it is high time they arrived*). **high-toned** stylish; dignified; superior. **high treason** see TREASON. **high-up** *colloq.* a person of high rank. **high voltage** electrical potential causing some danger of injury or damage. **high water 1** the tide at its fullest. **2** the time of this. **high-water mark 1** the level reached at high water. **2** the maximum recorded value or highest point of excellence. **high, wide, and handsome** *colloq.* in a carefree or stylish manner. **high wire** a high tightrope. **high words** angry talk. **high yellow** *US* a person of mixed race with a palish skin. **in high feather** see FEATHER. **the Most High** God. **on high** in or to heaven or a high place. **on one's high horse** *colloq.* behaving superciliously or arrogantly. **play high 1** play for high stakes. **2** play a card of high value. **run high 1** (of the sea) have a strong current with high tide. **2** (of feelings) be strong. [OE *hēah* f. Gmc]

highball /ˈhaɪbɔːl/ *n.* *US* **1** a drink of spirits and soda etc., served with ice in a tall glass. **2** a railway signal to proceed.

highbinder /ˈhaɪˌbaɪndə(r)/ *n.* *US* a ruffian; a swindler; an assassin.

highboy /ˈhaɪbɔɪ/ *n.* *US* a tall chest of drawers on legs.

highbrow /ˈhaɪbraʊ/ *adj. & n. colloq.* —*adj.* intellectual; cultural. —*n.* an intellectual or cultured person.

highfalutin /ˌhaɪfəˈluːtɪn/ *adj. & n.* (also **highfaluting** /-tɪŋ/) *colloq.* —*adj.* absurdly pompous or pretentious. —*n.* highfalutin speech or writing. [HIGH + -*falutin*, of unkn. orig.]

high-handed /haɪˈhændɪd/ *adj.* disregarding others' feelings; overbearing. □□ **high-handedly** *adv.* **high-handedness** *n.*

Highland /ˈhaɪlənd/ a local government region of northern Scotland; pop. (1981) 200,600.

highland /ˈhaɪlənd/ *n. & adj.* —*n.* (usu. in *pl.*) **1** an area of high land. **2** (**the Highlands**) the mountainous part of Scotland. —*adj.* of or in a highland or the Highlands. □ **Highland cattle 1** cattle of a shaggy-haired breed with long curved widely-spaced horns. **2** this breed. **Highland dress** the kilt etc. **Highland fling** see FLING *n.* 3. □□ **highlander** *n.* (also **Highlander**). **Highlandman** *n.* (*pl.* -**men**) [OE *hēahlond* promontory (as HIGH, LAND)]

highlight /ˈhaɪlaɪt/ *n. & v.* —*n.* **1** (in a painting etc.) a light area, or one seeming to reflect light. **2** a moment or detail of vivid interest; an outstanding feature. **3** (usu. in *pl.*) a bright tint in the hair produced by bleaching. —*v.tr.* **1 a** bring into prominence; draw attention to. **b** mark with a highlighter. **2** create highlights in (the hair).

highlighter /ˈhaɪlaɪtə(r)/ *n.* a marker pen which overlays colour on a printed word etc., leaving it legible and emphasized.

highly /ˈhaɪlɪ/ *adv.* **1** in a high degree (*highly amusing; highly probable; commend it highly*). **2** honourably; favourably (*think highly*

of him). □ **highly-strung** very sensitive or nervous. [OE *hēalīce* (as HIGH)]

high-minded /haɪˈmaɪndɪd/ *adj.* **1** having high moral principles. **2** *archaic* proud. □□ **high-mindedly** *adv.* **high-mindedness** *n.*

high-muck-a-muck /ˈhaɪˌmʌkəˌmʌk/ *n.* *US* a person of great self-importance. [perh. f. Chinook *hiu* plenty + *muckamuck* food]

highness /ˈhaɪnɪs/ *n.* **1** the state of being high (*highness of taxation*) (cf. HEIGHT). **2** (**Highness**) a title used in addressing and referring to a prince or princess (*Her Highness; Your Royal Highness*). [OE *hēanes* (as HIGH)]

hight /haɪt/ *adj. archaic, poet.,* or *joc.* called; named. [past part. (from 14th c.) of OE *hātan* command, call]

hightail /ˈhaɪteɪl/ *v.intr.* *US colloq.* move at high speed.

highway /ˈhaɪweɪ/ *n.* **1 a** a public road. **b** a main route (by land or water). **2** a direct course of action (*on the highway to success*). □ **Highway Code** *Brit.* the official booklet of guidance for road-users. **King's** (or **Queen's**) **highway** a public road, regarded as being under the sovereign's protection.

highwayman /ˈhaɪweɪmən/ *n.* (*pl.* -**men**) *hist.* a robber of passengers, travellers, etc., usu. mounted. [HIGHWAY]

HIH *abbr.* Her or His Imperial Highness.

hijack /ˈhaɪdʒæk/ *v. & n.* —*v.tr.* **1** seize control of (a loaded lorry, an aircraft in flight, etc.), esp. to force it to a different destination. **2** seize (goods) in transit. **3** take over (an organization etc.) by force or subterfuge in order to redirect it. —*n.* an instance of hijacking. □□ **hijacker** *n.* [20th c.: orig. unkn.]

Hijaz see HEJAZ.

hijra var. of HEGIRA.

hike /haɪk/ *n. & v.* —*n.* **1** a long country walk, esp. with rucksacks etc. **2** esp. *US* an increase (of prices etc.). —*v.* **1** *intr.* walk, esp. across country, for a long distance, esp. with boots, rucksack, etc. **2** (usu. foll. by *up*) **a** *tr.* hitch up (clothing etc.); hoist; shove. **b** *intr.* work upwards out of place, become hitched up. **3** *tr.* esp. *US* increase (prices etc.). □□ **hiker** *n.* [19th-c. dial.: orig. unkn.]

hila *pl.* of HILUM.

hilarious /hɪˈleərɪəs/ *adj.* **1** exceedingly funny. **2** boisterously merry. □□ **hilariously** *adv.* **hilariousness** *n.* **hilarity** /-ˈlærɪtɪ/ *n.* [L *hilaris* f. Gk *hilaros* cheerful]

Hilary /ˈhɪlərɪ/, St (*c.*315–*c.*367), bishop of Poitiers, champion of orthodoxy against Arianism, and the leading Latin theologian of his age. His feast day (13 Jan. in the Anglican Church, 14 Jan. in the RC calendar) gives its name to the university and law terms that begin in January.

Hilbert, /ˈhɪlbət/, David (1862–1943), German mathematician who epitomizes, and did more than anyone else to produce, the changes in mathematics that occurred around the turn of the century. He proved fundamental theorems about rings and their ideals, he collected, systematized, and extended all that was then known about algebraic numbers, he reorganized the axiomatic foundations of geometry, he set potential theory and the theory of integral equations on its modern course with his invention of Hilbert space (an infinite-dimensional analogue of Euclidean space), and he formulated the formalist philosophy of mathematics and mathematical logic. At the International Congress of Mathematicians in Paris in 1900 Hilbert proposed 23 problems which, as he had hoped, crystallized mathematical thinking for the next few decades.

Hill /hɪl/, Sir Rowland (1795–1879), British administrator and inventor, who introduced the penny postage-stamp system (see STAMP).

hill /hɪl/ *n. & v.* —*n.* **1 a** a naturally raised area of land, not as high as a mountain. **b** (as **the hills**) Anglo-Ind. = *hill-station.* **2** (often in *comb.*) a heap; a mound (*anthill; dunghill*). **3** a sloping piece of road. —*v.tr.* **1** form into a hill. **2** (usu. foll. by *up*) bank up (plants) with soil. □ **hill and dale** (of a gramophone record) with groove-undulations in a vertical plane. **hill-billy** (*pl.* -**ies**) *US* **1** *colloq.,* often *derog.* a person from a remote rural area in a southern State (cf. HICK). **2** folk music of or like that of the southern US. **hill climb** a race for vehicles up a steep hill. **hill figure** a design (usually either a horse or a human figure) cut into the chalk or limestone hills of southern England and standing out white against the green turf. The oldest of these (the White Horse at Uffington, Oxon.) dates back to the Iron Age (1st or 2nd c. BC), and probably had a religious function. **hill-fort** a fortified place built on a hill-top, with ramparts and ditches, occurring in western Europe from the late Bronze Age until the Roman period. **hill-station** *Anglo-Ind.* a government settlement, esp. for holidays etc. during the hot season, in the low mountains of N. India. **old as the hills** very ancient. **over the hill** *colloq.* **1** past the prime of life; declining. **2** past the crisis. **up hill and down dale** see UP. [OE *hyll*]

Hillary /ˈhɪləri/, Sir Edmund (1919–), New Zealand mountaineer and explorer who, with Sherpa Tenzing Norgay, was the first to reach the summit of Mount Everest (1953). In 1958–9 he participated in the Commonwealth Trans-Antarctic Expedition (see FUCHS²). His son climbed Mt Everest in 1990.

hillock /ˈhɪlək/ n. a small hill or mound. □□ **hillocky** adj.

hillside /ˈhɪlsaɪd/ n. the sloping side of a hill.

hilltop /ˈhɪltɒp/ n. the summit of a hill.

hillwalking /ˈhɪlˌwɔːkɪŋ/ n. the pastime of walking in hilly country. □□ **hillwalker** n.

hilly /ˈhɪli/ adj. (**hillier**, **hilliest**) having many hills. □□ **hilliness** n.

hilt /hɪlt/ n. & v. —n. **1** the handle of a sword, dagger, etc. **2** the handle of a tool. —v.tr. provide with a hilt. □ **up to the hilt** completely. [OE *hilt(e)* f. Gmc]

hilum /ˈhaɪləm/ n. (pl. **hila** /-lə/) **1** Bot. the point of attachment of a seed to its seed-vessel. **2** Anat. a notch or indentation where a vessel enters an organ. [L, = little thing, trifle]

Hilversum /ˈhɪlvəˌsʊm/ a town of The Netherlands, in North Holland province, 20 km (12 miles) south-east of Amsterdam; pop. (1987) 85,150. It is the centre of the Dutch radio and television network.

HIM abbr. Her or His Imperial Majesty.

him /hɪm/ pron. **1** objective case of HE (I saw him). **2** colloq. he (it's him again; is taller than him). **3** archaic himself (fell and hurt himself). [OE, masc. and neut. dative sing. of HE, IT¹]

Himachal Pradesh /hɪˌmɑːtʃ(ə)l prəˈdeʃ/ a State in northern India; pop. (1981) 4,237,550; capital, Simla.

Himalayas /ˌhɪməˈleɪəz/ a system of high mountains which stretches for over 1,600 km (1,000 miles) and forms the NE boundary of the Indian subcontinent. It includes the highest summits in the world with several peaks rising to over 7,700 m (25,000 ft.). □□ **Himalayan** adj. [Skr. f. *hima* snow + *ālaya* abode]

himation /hɪˈmætɪən/ n. hist. the outer garment worn by the ancient Greeks over the left shoulder and under the right. [Gk]

Himmler /ˈhɪmlə(r)/, Heinrich (1900–45), German Nazi leader, chief of the SS from 1929 and of the Gestapo from 1936. He established and oversaw the concentration camps in which he directed the systematic genocide of Jews.

himself /hɪmˈself/ pron. **1 a** emphat. form of HE or HIM (he himself will do it). **b** refl. form of HIM (he has hurt himself). **2** in his normal state of body or mind (does not feel quite himself today). **3** esp. Ir. a third party of some importance; the master of the house. □ **be himself** act in his normal unconstrained manner. **by himself** see by oneself. [OE (as HIM, SELF)]

Hinayana /ˌhiːnəˈjɑːnə/ n. a derogatory name given by the followers of Mahayana Buddhism to denote the other major division of early Buddhism. It died out in India by the 7th c. AD but survived in Ceylon (see THERAVADA) and was taken from there to Burma, Thailand, and other regions of SE Asia. Hinayana was the pristine form of the faith, while Mahayana represents the general one, of the majority of followers. [Skr. f. *hīna* lesser + *yāna* vehicle]

hind¹ /haɪnd/ adj. (esp. of parts of the body) situated at the back, posterior (hind leg) (opp. FORE). □ **on one's hind legs** see LEG. [ME, perh. shortened f. OE *bihindan* BEHIND]

hind² /haɪnd/ n. a female deer (usu. a red deer or sika), esp. in and after the third year. [OE f. Gmc]

hind³ /haɪnd/ n. hist. **1** esp. Sc. a skilled farm-worker, usu. married

and with a tied cottage, and formerly having charge of two horses. **2** a steward on a farm. **3** a rustic, a boor. [ME *hine* f. OE *hīne* (pl.) app. f. *hī(g)na* genit. pl. of *hīgan*, *hīwan* 'members of a family' (cf. HIDE³): for -d cf. SOUND¹]

Hindemith /ˈhɪndəmɪt/, Paul (1895–1963), a successful composer, conductor, and teacher in Germany until the 1930s, when criticisms of his music by the Nazis led him to leave the country and settle in the US, becoming an American citizen in 1946. He is invariably associated with *Gebrauchsmusik* ('music for use'), a term used in the 1920s to describe music with a social purpose; his attitude was that audiences should participate as well as listen. His harmonic idiom was based on well-controlled dissonant tensions, but he remained firmly committed to tonality. The severe reaction against his music eventually slackened, and the best of his prolific works (which include operas, concertos, and orchestral and chamber music) occupy an important place in the history of 20th-c. composition.

Hindenburg /ˈhɪndənˌbɜːg/, Paul von (1847–1934), German general and statesman, recalled from retirement at the outbreak of the First World War, commander-in-chief of German forces from 1916. He was elected President in 1925 and re-elected in 1932, and was persuaded to appoint Hitler as Chancellor in 1933. □ **Hindenburg Line** the shortened and fortified line of defence on the German western front, to which Hindenburg directed retreat and which was not breached until near the end of the war. It was known also as the Siegfried Line (see entry).

hinder¹ /ˈhɪndə(r)/ v.tr. (also absol.) impede; delay; prevent (you will hinder him; hindered me from working). [OE *hindrian* f. Gmc]

hinder² /ˈhaɪndə(r)/ adj. rear, hind (the hinder part). [ME, perh. f. OE *hinderweard* backward: cf. HIND¹]

Hindi /ˈhɪndi/ n. & adj. —n. **1** a literary form of Hindustani with vocabulary based on Sanskrit, written in the Devanagari script, an official language of India. Hindi is the most widely spoken language in India, with some 180 million speakers. **2** a group of spoken dialects of northern India, belonging to the Indo-European family of languages and related to Urdu. —adj. of or concerning Hindi. [Urdu *hindī* f. *Hind* India]

hindmost /ˈhaɪndməʊst/ adj. furthest behind; most remote.

Hindoo archaic var. of HINDU.

hindquarters /haɪndˈkwɔːtəz/ n.pl. the hind legs and adjoining parts of a quadruped.

hindrance /ˈhɪndrəns/ n. **1** the act or an instance of hindering; the state of being hindered. **2** a thing that hinders; an obstacle.

hindsight /ˈhaɪndsaɪt/ n. **1** wisdom after the event (realized with hindsight that they were wrong) (opp. FORESIGHT). **2** the backsight of a gun.

Hindu /ˈhɪnduː, -ˈduː/ n. & adj. —n. **1** a follower of Hinduism. **2** archaic an Indian. —adj. **1** of or concerning Hindus or Hinduism. **2** archaic Indian. [Urdu f. Pers. f. *Hind* India]

Hinduism /ˈhɪnduːˌɪz(ə)m/ n. a system of religious beliefs and social customs, with adherents especially in India, both a way of life and a rigorous system of religious law, developed over a period of about fifty centuries. Unlike most religions, Hinduism requires no one belief concerning the nature of god: it embraces polytheism, monotheism, and monism. More important are the beliefs concerning the nature of the universe and the structure of society. The former is described by the key concepts of *dharma*, the eternal law underlying the whole of existence; *karma*, the law of action by which each cause has its effect in an endless chain reaching from one life to the next; and *moksha*, liberation from this chain of birth, death, and rebirth. The latter is prescribed by the ideals of *varna*, the division of mankind into four classes or types, the forerunner of caste; *ashrama*, the four stages of life; and personal dharma, according to which one's religious duty is defined by birth and circumstance. □□ **Hinduize** v.tr. (also **-ise**).

Hindu Kush /ˌhɪnduː ˈkuːʃ, ˈkʊʃ/ a range of high mountains in northern Pakistan and Afghanistan which forms a westward continuation of the Himalayas. Several peaks exceed 6,150 m (20,000 ft.).

Hindustan /ˌhɪndəˈstɑːn/ (lit. 'the country of the Hindus') (hist.)

b *but*　d *dog*　f *few*　g *get*　h *he*　j *yes*　k *cat*　l *leg*　m *man*　n *no*　p *pen*　r *red*　s *sit*　t *top*　v *voice*

northern India; the Indian subcontinent. [HINDU + Persian- *stān* country]

Hindustani /ˌhɪndʊˈstɑːnɪ/ *n. & adj.* —*n.* **1** a language based on the Western Hindi dialect of the Delhi region with an admixture of Arabic, Persian, etc., current as the standard language and lingua franca in much of northern India and (as colloquial Urdu) Pakistan. —*adj.* of or relating to Hindustan or its people, or Hindustani.

hinge /hɪndʒ/ *n. & v.* —*n.* **1 a** a movable, usu. metal, joint or mechanism such as that by which a door is hung on a side post. **b** *Biol.* a natural joint performing a similar function, e.g. that of a bivalve shell. **2** a central point or principle on which everything depends. —*v.* **1** *intr.* (foll. by *on*) **a** depend (on a principle, an event, etc.) (*all hinges on his acceptance*). **b** (of a door etc.) hang and turn (on a post etc.). **2** *tr.* attach with or as if with a hinge. □ **stamp-hinge** a small piece of gummed transparent paper used for fixing postage stamps in an album etc. □□ **hinged** *adj.* **hingeless** *adj.* **hingewise** *adv.* [ME *heng* etc., rel. to HANG]

hinny[1] /ˈhɪnɪ/ *n.* (*pl.* **-ies**) the offspring of a female donkey and a male horse. [L *hinnus* f. Gk *hinnos*]

hinny[2] /ˈhɪnɪ/ *n.* (also **hinnie**) (*pl.* **-ies**) *Sc. & N.Engl.* (esp. as a form of address) darling, sweetheart. □ **singing hinny** a currant cake baked on a griddle. [var. of HONEY]

hint /hɪnt/ *n. & v.* —*n.* **1** a slight or indirect indication or suggestion (*took the hint and left*). **2** a small piece of practical information (*handy hints on cooking*). **3** a very small trace; a suggestion (*a hint of perfume*). —*v.tr.* (often foll. by *that* + clause) suggest slightly (*hinted the contrary; hinted that they were wrong*). □ **hint at** give a hint of; refer indirectly to. [app. f. obs. *hent* grasp, lay hold of, f. OE *hentan*, f. Gmc, rel. to HUNT]

hinterland /ˈhɪntəˌlænd/ *n.* **1** the often deserted or uncharted areas beyond a coastal district or a river's banks. **2** an area served by a port or other centre. **3** a remote or fringe area. [G f. *hinter* behind + *Land* LAND]

hip[1] /hɪp/ *n.* **1** a projection of the pelvis and upper thigh-bone on each side of the body in human beings and quadrupeds. **2** (often in *pl.*) the circumference of the body at the buttocks. **3** *Archit.* the sharp edge of a roof from ridge to eaves where two sides meet. □ **hip-bath** a portable bath in which a person sits. **hip-bone** a bone forming the hip, esp. the ilium. **hip-flask** a flask for spirits etc., carried in a hip-pocket. **hip-joint** the articulation of the head of the thigh-bone with the ilium. **hip-length** (of a garment) reaching down to the hips. **hip-pocket** a trouser-pocket just behind the hip. **hip-** (or **hipped-**) **roof** a roof with the sides and the ends inclined. **on the hip** *archaic* at a disadvantage. □□ **hipless** *adj.* **hipped** *adj.* (also in comb.). [OE *hype* f. Gmc, rel. to HOP[1]]

hip[2] /hɪp/ *n.* (also **hep** /hep/) the fruit of a rose, esp. a wild kind. [OE *hēope*, *hīope* f. WG]

hip[3] /hɪp/ *adj.* (also **hep** /hep/) (**hipper**, **hippest** or **hepper**, **heppest**) *sl.* **1** following the latest fashion in esp. jazz music, clothes, etc.; stylish. **2** (often foll. by *to*) understanding, aware. □ **hip-cat** a hip person; a devotee of jazz or swing. □□ **hipness** *n.* [20th c.: orig. unkn.]

hip[4] /hɪp/ *int.* introducing a united cheer (*hip, hip, hooray*). [19th c.: orig. unkn.]

Hipparchus /hɪˈpɑːkəs/ (*c.*190–after 126 BC) Greek astronomer, working in Rhodes. His major works are lost, but his astronomical observations were preserved and developed by Ptolemy. He constructed the celestial coordinates of some 800 stars, indicating their relative brightness, but rejected Aristarchus' hypothesis that the sun is the centre of the planetary system. Hipparchus is best known for his discovery of the precission of the equinoxes. His geographical work was a polemic against that of Eratosthenes, criticising descriptive and mathematical data.

hippeastrum /ˌhɪpɪˈæstrəm/ *n.* any S. American bulbous plant of the genus *Hippeastrum* with showy white or red flowers. [mod.L f. Gk *hippeus* horseman (the leaves appearing to ride on one another) + *astron* star (from the flower-shape)]

hipped /hɪpt/ *adj.* (usu. foll. by *on*) esp. *US sl.* obsessed, infatuated. [past part. of *hip* (v.) = make hip (HIP[3])]

hippie /ˈhɪpɪ/ *n.* (also **hippy**) (*pl.* **-ies**) *colloq.* **1** (esp. in the 1960s) a person of unconventional appearance, typically with long hair, jeans, beads, etc., often associated with hallucinogenic drugs and a rejection of conventional values. **2** = HIPSTER[2]. [HIP[3]]

hippo /ˈhɪpəʊ/ *n.* (*pl.* **-os**) *colloq.* a hippopotamus. [abbr.]

hippocampus /ˌhɪpəˈkæmpəs/ *n.* (*pl.* **hippocampi** /-paɪ/) **1** any marine fish of the genus *Hippocampus*, swimming in an upright position and with a head suggestive of a horse; a sea horse. **2** *Anat.* the elongated ridges on the floor of each lateral ventricle of the brain, thought to be the centre of emotion and the autonomic nervous system. [L f. Gk *hippokampos* f. *hippos* horse + *kampos* sea monster]

hippocras /ˈhɪpəˌkræs/ *n. hist.* wine flavoured with spices. [ME f. OF *ipocras* Hippocrates (see HIPPOCRATIC OATH), prob. because strained through a filter called 'Hippocrates' sleeve']

Hippocrates /hɪpˈɒkrəˌtiːz/ (*c.*460–357 BC), the most famous of all physicians, of whom almost nothing is known. Referred to briefly and historically by Plato, his name was attached, probably by later Alexandrian historians, to a body of ancient Greek medical writings of which probably none was written by Hippocrates. This collection is so various in style and content that all subsequent physicians have been able to find within it notions that agreed with their own of what medicine and doctors should be: 'Hippocrates' is a synthesis of history. Thus the Hippocratic oath is Pythagorean in origin, but exerted great influence in medical ethics; Galen, the greatest commentator upon Hippocrates, made his subject an Aristotelian rationalist; and numberless others have found 'true Hippocratism' in an anti-philosophical and observational accumulation of medical data. If there are common features of an agreed Hippocraticism, they might be that nature has an innate power of healing, and that diseases are closely linked to the physical environment.

Hippocratic oath /ˌhɪpəˈkrætɪk/ *n.* an oath stating the obligations and proper conduct of physicians, formerly taken by those beginning medical practice. (See HIPPOCRATES.) [med.L *Hippocraticus* f. *Hippocrates*, Gk physician of the 5th c. BC]

Hippocrene /ˈhɪpəˌkriːn/ *n.* a spring on Mount Helicon, the inspiration of poets. It was fabled to have been produced by a stroke from the hoof of Pegasus. [L f. Gk f. *hippos* horse + *krēnē* fountain]

hippodrome /ˈhɪpəˌdrəʊm/ *n.* **1** a music-hall or dancehall. **2** (in classical antiquity) a course for chariot races etc. **3** a circus. [F *hippodrome* or L *hippodromus* f. Gk *hippodromos* f. *hippos* horse + *dromos* race, course]

hippogriff /ˈhɪpəgrɪf/ *n.* (also **hippogryph**) a mythical griffin-like creature with the body of a horse. [F *hippogriffe* f. It. *ippogrifo* f. Gk *hippos* horse + It. *grifo* GRIFFIN]

hippopotamus /ˌhɪpəˈpɒtəməs/ *n.* (*pl.* **hippopotamuses** or **hippopotami** /-ˌmaɪ/) **1** a large thick-skinned four-legged mammal, *Hippopotamus amphibius*, native to Africa, inhabiting rivers, lakes, etc. **2** (in full **pigmy hippopotamus**) a smaller related mammal, *Choeropsis liberiensis*, native to Africa, inhabiting forests and swamps. [ME f. L f. Gk *hippopotamos* f. *hippos* horse + *potamos* river]

hippy[1] var. of HIPPIE.

hippy[2] /ˈhɪpɪ/ *adj.* having large hips.

hipster[1] /ˈhɪpstə(r)/ *adj. & n. Brit.* —*adj.* (of a garment) hanging from the hips rather than the waist. —*n.* (in *pl.*) trousers hanging from the hips.

hipster[2] /ˈhɪpstə(r)/ *n. sl.* a person who is hip; a hip-cat. □□ **hipsterism** *n.*

hiragana /ˌhɪərəˈɡɑːnə/ *n.* the cursive form of Japanese syllabic writing or kana (cf. KATAKANA). [Jap., = plain kana]

hircine /ˈhɜːsaɪn/ *adj.* goatlike. [L *hircinus* f. *hircus* he-goat]

hire /ˈhaɪə(r)/ *v. & n.* —*v.tr.* **1** (often foll. by *from*) procure the temporary use of (a thing) for an agreed payment (*hired a van from them*). **2** esp. *US* employ (a person) for wages or a fee. **3** *US* borrow (money). —*n.* **1** hiring or being hired. **2** payment for this. □ **for** (or **on**) **hire** ready to be hired. **hire-car** a car available for hire. **hired girl** (or **man**) *US* a domestic servant, esp. on a farm. **hire out** grant the temporary use of (a thing) for an agreed payment. **hire purchase** *Brit.* a system by which a person may purchase a thing by regular payments while having the use of it. □□ **hireable** adj. (US **hirable**). **hirer** n. [OE hȳrian, hȳr f. WG]

hireling /ˈhaɪəlɪŋ/ n. usu. derog. a person who works for hire. [OE hȳrling (as HIRE, -LING¹)]

Hirohito /ˌhɪrəˈhiːtəʊ/ (1901–89), emperor of Japan 1926–89. Supposedly divine and all-powerful, he was venerated but in fact had little authority. He did, however, influence his government to agree to the unconditional surrender which ended the Second World War. Afterwards he renounced his divinity and, as a constitutional monarch, lived to see his country recover and prosper.

Hiroshima /hɪˈrɒʃɪmə/ the capital of Chugoku region on Honshu Island; pop. (1987) 1,034,000. It was the Japanese city, target of the first atomic bomb on 6 Aug. 1945, which resulted in the deaths of about one-third of the city's population of 300,000, and, together with a second attack on Nagasaki three days later, led directly to Japan's surrender and the end of the Second World War.

hirsute /ˈhɜːsjuːt/ adj. 1 hairy, shaggy. 2 untrimmed. □□ **hirsuteness** n. [L hirsutus]

hirsutism /ˈhɜːsjuːˌtɪz(ə)m/ n. the excessive growth of hair on the face and body.

his /hɪz/ poss.pron. 1 (attrib.) of or belonging to him or himself (his house; his own business). 2 (**His**) (attrib.) (in titles) that he is (His Majesty). 3 the one or ones belonging to or associated with him (it is his; his are over there). □ **his and hers** joc. (of matching items) for husband and wife, or men and women. **of his** of or belonging to him (a friend of his). [OE, genit. of HE, IT¹]

Hispanic /hɪˈspænɪk/ adj. & n. —adj. 1 of or relating to Spain or to Spain and Portugal. 2 of Spain and other Spanish-speaking countries. —n. a Spanish-speaking person, esp. one of Latin-American descent, living in the US. □□ **Hispanicize** /-ˌsaɪz/ v.tr. (also **-ise**). [L Hispanicus f. Hispania Spain]

Hispaniola /ˌhɪspænˈjəʊlə/ an island of the Greater Antilles in the West Indies, divided into the States of Haiti and the Dominican Republic. [f. Sp. La Isla Española (the Spanish island), so named by Columbus who discovered it in 1492]

Hispanist /ˈhɪspənɪst/ n. (also **Hispanicist** /hɪˈspænɪsɪst/) an expert in or student of the language, literature, and civilization of Spain.

Hispano- /hɪˈspænəʊ/ comb. form Spanish. [L Hispanus Spanish]

hispid /ˈhɪspɪd/ adj. Bot. & Zool. 1 rough with bristles; bristly. 2 shaggy. [L hispidus]

hiss /hɪs/ v. & n. —v. 1 intr. (of a person, snake, goose, etc.) make a sharp sibilant sound, esp. as a sign of disapproval or derision (audience booed and hissed; the water hissed on the hotplate). 2 tr. express disapproval of (a person etc.) by hisses. 3 tr. whisper (a threat etc.) urgently or angrily ('Where's the door?' he hissed). —n. 1 a sharp sibilant sound as of the letter s. 2 Electronics unwanted interference at audio frequencies. □ **hiss away** (or **down**) drive off etc. by hisses. **hiss off** hiss (actors etc.) so that they leave the stage. [ME: imit.]

hist /hɪst/ int. archaic used to call attention, enjoin silence, incite a dog, etc. [16th c.: natural excl.]

histamine /ˈhɪstəmɪn, ˈhɪstəˌmiːn/ n. Biochem. an organic compound occurring in injured body tissues etc., and also associated with allergic reactions. □□ **histaminic** /-ˈmɪnɪk/ adj. [HISTO- + AMINE]

histidine /ˈhɪstɪˌdiːn/ n. Biochem. an amino acid from which histamine is derived. [Gk histos web, tissue]

histo- /ˈhɪstəʊ/ comb. form (also **hist-** before a vowel) Biol. tissue. [Gk histos web]

histochemistry /ˌhɪstəʊˈkemɪstrɪ/ n. the study of the identification and distribution of the chemical constituents of tissues by means of stains, indicators, and microscopy. □□ **histochemical** adj.

histogenesis /ˌhɪstəʊˈdʒenɪsɪs/ n. the formation of tissues. □□ **histogenetic** /-dʒɪˈnetɪk/ adj.

histogeny /hɪˈstɒdʒɪnɪ/ n. = HISTOGENESIS. □□ **histogenic** /ˌhɪstəˈdʒenɪk/ adj.

histogram /ˈhɪstəˌɡræm/ n. Statistics a chart consisting of rectangles (usu. drawn vertically from a base line) whose areas and positions are proportional to the value or range of a number of variables. [Gk histos mast + -GRAM]

histology /hɪˈstɒlədʒɪ/ n. the study of the structure of tissues. □□ **histological** /ˌhɪstəˈlɒdʒɪk(ə)l/ adj. **histologist** /hɪˈstɒlədʒɪst/ n.

histolysis /hɪˈstɒlɪsɪs/ n. the breaking down of tissues. □□ **histolytic** /-təˈlɪtɪk/ adj.

histone /ˈhɪstəʊn/ n. Biochem. any of a group of proteins found in chromatin. [G Histon perh. f. Gk histamai arrest, or as HISTO-]

histopathology /ˌhɪstəʊpəˈθɒlədʒɪ/ n. 1 changes in tissues caused by disease. 2 the study of these.

historian /hɪˈstɔːrɪən/ n. 1 a writer of history, esp. a critical analyst, rather than a compiler. 2 a person learned in or studying history (English historian; ancient historian). [F historien f. L (as HISTORY)]

historiated /hɪˈstɔːrɪˌeɪtɪd/ adj. = STORIATED. [med.L historiare (as HISTORY)]

historic /hɪˈstɒrɪk/ adj. 1 famous or important in history or potentially so (a historic moment). 2 Gram. (of a tense) normally used in the narration of past events (esp. Latin & Greek imperfect and pluperfect; cf. PRIMARY). 3 archaic or disp. = HISTORICAL. □ **historic infinitive** the infinitive when used instead of the indicative. **historic present** the present tense used instead of the past in vivid narration. [L historicus f. Gk historikos (as HISTORY)]

historical /hɪˈstɒrɪk(ə)l/ adj. 1 of or concerning history (historical evidence). 2 belonging to history, not to prehistory or legend. 3 (of the study of a subject) based on an analysis of its development over a period. 4 belonging to the past, not the present. 5 (of a novel, a film, etc.) dealing or professing to deal with historical events. 6 in connection with history, from the historian's point of view (of purely historical interest). □□ **historically** adv.

historicism /hɪˈstɒrɪˌsɪz(ə)m/ n. 1 a the theory that social and cultural phenomena are determined by history. b the belief that historical events are governed by laws. 2 the tendency to regard historical development as the most basic aspect of human existence. 3 an excessive regard for past styles etc. □□ **historicist** n. [HISTORIC after G Historismus]

historicity /ˌhɪstəˈrɪsɪtɪ/ n. the historical genuineness of an event etc.

historiographer /hɪˌstɔːrɪˈɒɡrəfə(r)/ n. 1 an expert in or student of historiography. 2 a writer of history, esp. an official historian. [ME f. F historiographe or f. LL historiographus f. Gk historiographos (as HISTORY, -GRAPHER)]

historiography /hɪˌstɔːrɪˈɒɡrəfɪ/ n. 1 the writing of history. 2 the study of history-writing. □□ **historiographic** /-ˈɡræfɪk/ adj. **historiographical** /-ˈɡræfɪk(ə)l/ adj. [med.L historiographia f. Gk historiographia (as HISTORY, -GRAPHY)]

history /ˈhɪstərɪ/ n. (pl. **-ies**) 1 a continuous, usu. chronological, record of important or public events. 2 a the study of past events, esp. human affairs. b the total accumulation of past events, esp. relating to human affairs or to the accumulation of developments connected with a particular nation, person, thing, etc. (our island history; the history of astronomy). 3 an eventful past (this house has a history). 4 a a systematic or critical account of or research into a past event or events etc. b a similar record or account of natural phenomena. 5 a historical play. □ **history painting** pictorial representation of an event or series of events. **make history** 1 influence the course of history. 2 do something memorable. [ME f. L historia f. Gk historia finding out, narrative, history f. histōr learned, wise man, rel. to WIT²]

histrionic /ˌhɪstrɪˈɒnɪk/ adj. & n. —adj. 1 of or concerning actors or acting. 2 (of behaviour) theatrical, dramatic. —n. 1 (in pl.) a insincere and dramatic behaviour designed to impress. b theatricals; theatrical art. 2 archaic an actor. □□ **histrionically** adv. [LL histrionicus f. L histrio -onis actor]

hit /hɪt/ v. & n. —v. (**hitting**; past and past part. **hit**) 1 tr. a strike with a blow or a missile. b (of a moving body) strike (the plane hit the ground). c reach (a target, a person, etc.) with a directed missile (hit the window with the ball). 2 tr. cause to suffer or affect adversely; wound (*the loss hit him hard*). **3** *intr.* (often foll. by *at*, *against*, *upon*) direct a blow. **4** *tr.* (often foll. by *against*, *on*) knock (a part of the body) (*hit his head on the door-frame*). **5** *tr.* light upon; get at (a thing aimed at) (*he's hit the truth at last; tried to hit the right tone in his apology*) (see **hit on**). **6** *tr. colloq.* **a** encounter (*hit a snag*). **b** arrive at (*hit an all-time low; hit the town*). **c** indulge in, esp. liquor etc. (*hit the bottle*). **7** *tr. esp. US sl.* rob or kill. **8** *tr.* occur forcefully to (*the seriousness of the situation only hit him later*). **9** *tr. Sport* **a** propel (a ball etc.) with a bat etc. to score runs or points. **b** score (runs etc.) in this way. **c** (usu. foll. by *for*) strike (a ball or a bowler) for so many runs (*hit him for six*). **10** *tr.* represent exactly. —*n.* **1** **a** a blow; a stroke. **b** a collision. **2** a shot etc. that hits its target. **3** *colloq.* a popular success in entertainment. **4** a stroke of sarcasm, wit, etc. **5** a stroke of good luck. **6** *esp. US sl.* **a** a murder or other violent crime. **b** a drug injection etc. **7** a successful attempt. □ **hit and run** cause (accidental or wilful) damage and escape or leave the scene before being discovered. **hit-and-run** *attrib.adj.* relating to or (of a person) committing an act of this kind. **hit back** retaliate. **hit below the belt 1** *esp. Boxing* give a foul blow. **2** treat or behave unfairly. **hit for six** *Brit.* defeat in argument. **hit the hay** (or **sack**) *colloq.* go to bed. **hit the headlines** see HEADLINE. **hit home** make a salutary impression. **hit it off** (often foll. by *with*, *together*) agree or be congenial. **hit list** *sl.* a list of prospective victims. **hit man** (*pl.* **hit men**) *sl.* a hired assassin. **hit the nail on the head** state the truth exactly. **hit on** (or **upon**) find (what is sought), esp. by chance. **hit-or-miss** aimed or done carelessly. **hit out** deal vigorous physical or verbal blows (*hit out at her enemies*). **hit-out** *n. Austral. sl.* a brisk gallop. **hit parade** *colloq.* a list of the current best-selling records of popular music. **hit the road** (*US* **trail**) *sl.* depart. **hit the roof** see ROOF. **hit up** *Cricket* score (runs) energetically. **hit wicket** *Cricket* be out by striking one's wicket with the bat etc. **make a hit** (usu. foll. by *with*) be successful or popular. □□ **hitter** *n.* [ME f. OE *hittan* f. ON *hitta* meet with, of unkn. orig.]

hitch /hɪtʃ/ *v. & n.* —*v.* **1** **a** *tr.* fasten with a loop, hook, etc.; tether (*hitched the horse to the cart*). **b** *intr.* (often foll. by *in*, *on to*, etc.) become fastened in this way (*the rod hitched in to the bracket*). **2** *tr.* move (a thing) with a jerk; shift slightly (*hitched the pillow to a comfortable position*). **3** *colloq.* **a** *intr.* = HITCHHIKE. **b** *tr.* obtain (a lift) by hitchhiking. —*n.* **1** an impediment; a temporary obstacle. **2** an abrupt pull or push; a jerk. **3** a noose or knot of various kinds. **4** *colloq.* a free ride in a vehicle. **5** *US sl.* a period of service. □ **get hitched** *colloq.* marry. **half hitch** a knot formed by passing the end of a rope round its standing part and then through the bight. **hitch up** lift (esp. clothing) with a jerk. **hitch one's wagon to a star** make use of powers higher than one's own. □□ **hitcher** *n.* [ME: orig. uncert.]

Hitchcock /ˈhɪtʃkɒk/, Sir Alfred Joseph (1899–1980), British-born film director, master of the suspense thriller, who liked to make a fleeting personal appearance in his films. He established his reputation in Britain in the 1930s with *The Man Who Knew Too Much* (1934; remade in 1956), *The Thirty-Nine Steps* (1935), and *The Lady Vanishes* (1938). In 1939 he moved to Hollywood, where his first film was *Rebecca* (1940). His numerous later works include *Strangers on a Train* (1951), *Psycho* (1960), and *The Birds* (1963). He could show great technical ingenuity: *Lifeboat* (1944) was shot entirely within the boat; *Rope* (1948) was filmed in one room in one continuous shot. Of Irish-Catholic background in London, son of a greengrocer, Hitchcock was an unhappy, disturbed, and permanently insecure man (almost anyone who crossed him was rejected or humiliated), yet one of the authentic geniuses of the popular cinema.

Hitchens /ˈhɪtʃɪnz/, Ivon (1893–1979), English painter, who in a highly distinctive style used broad fluid areas of vibrant colour, usually on a wide canvas, that evoke but do not pictorially represent the forms of the English countryside which were his main inspiration. He also painted flowers and figures and several large murals.

hitchhike /ˈhɪtʃhaɪk/ *v. & n.* —*v.intr.* travel by seeking free lifts in passing vehicles. —*n.* a journey made by hitchhiking. □□ **hitchhiker** *n.*

hi-tech /ˈhaɪtek/ *n.* = high tech. [abbr.]

hither /ˈhɪðə(r)/ *adv. & adj. formal* —*adv.* to or towards this place. —*adj. archaic* situated on this side; the nearer (of two). □ **hither and thither** (or **yon**) in various directions; to and fro. [OE *hider*: cf. THITHER]

hitherto /ˌhɪðəˈtuː/ *adv.* until this time, up to now.

hitherward /ˈhɪðəwəd/ *adv. archaic* in this direction.

Hitler /ˈhɪtlə(r)/, Adolf (1889–1945), German dictator. An Austrian by birth, Hitler served in the German Army during the First World War before becoming involved in right-wing politics. An attempted *putsch* in 1923 failed and earned him a spell in prison (during which he wrote *Mein Kampf*, an exposition of his political ideas), but after his release his powers as an orator soon won prominence for him and his National Socialist (Nazi) party, and with his appointment as Chancellor in 1933 he was able to overthrow the Weimar Republic and establish a Nazi dictatorship. Hitler succeeded in rescuing the German economy from collapse, but his expansionist foreign policy led eventually to the Second World War, while his racist ideas launched Germany on an attempt to wipe out European Jewry and establish a German super-State. After a series of overwhelming early successes, Germany was eventually defeated by the combined strengths of the Allied powers, and Hitler committed suicide in his Berlin headquarters just as Russian troops were storming the city. □□ **Hitlerite** /-ˌraɪt/ *n. & adj.*

Hitlerism /ˈhɪtləˌrɪz(ə)m/ *n.* the political principles or policy of the Nazi Party in Germany. [HITLER]

Hittite /ˈhɪtaɪt/ *n. & adj.* —*n.* **1** **a** a member of a powerful and widespread ancient (non-Semitic) people whose history can be traced from *c*.1900–700 BC in Asia Minor and Syria. (See below.) **b** a subject of the Hittite empire. **2** the Indo-European language of the Hittites, written in cuneiform and hieroglyphs, deciphered in 1916. **3** (in the Bible) a member of a Canaanite or Syrian tribe, perhaps an offshoot of the peoples described above. —*adj.* of or relating to the Hittites or their language. [Heb. *Ḥittīm*]

The Hittites gained political control of central Anatolia *c*.1800–1200 BC and reached the zenith of their power under the totalitarian rule of Suppiluliuma I (*c*.1380 BC), whose political influence extended from the capital, Hattusas, situated at Boğazkale (about 35 km (22 miles) east of Ankara) west to the Mediterranean coast and SE into northern Syria. In their struggle for power over Syria and Palestine they clashed with the troops of Rameses II of Egypt in a battle (1285 BC) at Kadesh on the River Orontes which seems to have ended indecisively. The subsequent decline of Hittite power resulted from internal and external dissension, probably following an outbreak of famine.

HIV *abbr.* human immunodeficiency virus, either of two retroviruses causing Aids.

hive /haɪv/ *n. & v.* —*n.* **1** **a** a beehive. **b** the bees in a hive. **2** a busy swarming place. **3** a swarming multitude. **4** a thing shaped like a hive in being domed. —*v.* **1** *tr.* **a** place (bees) in a hive. **b** house (people etc.) snugly. **2** *intr.* **a** enter a hive. **b** live together like bees. □ **hive off 1** separate from a larger group. **2** **a** form into or assign (work) to a subsidiary department or company. **b** denationalize or privatize (an industry etc.). **hive up** hoard. [OE *hȳf* f. Gmc]

hives /haɪvz/ *n.pl.* **1** a skin-eruption, esp. nettle-rash. **2** inflammation of the larynx etc. [16th c. (orig. Sc.): orig. unkn.]

hiya /ˈhaɪjə/ *int. colloq.* a word used in greeting. [corrupt. of *how are you?*]

HK *abbr.* Hong Kong.

HL *abbr.* (in the UK) House of Lords.

hl *abbr.* hectolitre(s).

HM *abbr.* **1** Her (or His) Majesty('s). **2** **a** headmaster. **b** headmistress.

hm *abbr.* hectometre(s).

h'm /hm/ *int. & n.* (also **hmm**) = HEM², HUM².

HMG *abbr.* Her or His Majesty's Government.

HMI *abbr.* Her or His Majesty's Inspector (of Schools).

HMS *abbr.* Her or His Majesty's Ship.

HMSO *abbr.* Her or His Majesty's Stationery Office.

HMV *abbr.* (in the UK) His Master's Voice.

HNC *abbr.* (in the UK) Higher National Certificate.

HND *abbr.* (in the UK) Higher National Diploma.

Ho *symb. Chem.* the element holmium.

ho /həʊ/ *int.* **1 a** an expression of surprise, admiration, triumph, or (often repeated as **ho! ho!** etc.) derision. **b** (in *comb.*) (*heigh-ho; what ho*). **2** a call for attention. **3** (in *comb.*) *Naut.* an addition to the name of a destination etc. (*westward ho*). [ME, imit.: cf. ON *hó*]

ho. *abbr.* house.

hoar /hɔː(r)/ *adj. & n. literary* —*adj.* **1** grey-haired with age. **2** greyish-white. **3** (of a thing) grey with age. —*n.* **1** = *hoar-frost*. **2** hoariness. □ **hoar-frost** frozen water vapour deposited in clear still weather on vegetation etc. [OE *hār* f. Gmc]

hoard /hɔːd/ *n. & v.* —*n.* **1** a stock or store (esp. of money) laid by. **2** an amassed store of facts etc. **3** *Archaeol.* an ancient store of treasure etc. —*v.* **1** *tr.* (often *absol.*; often foll. by *up*) amass (money etc.) and put away; store. **2** *intr.* accumulate more than one's current requirements of food etc. in a time of scarcity. **3** *tr.* store in the mind. □□ **hoarder** *n.* [OE *hord* f. Gmc]

hoarding /ˈhɔːdɪŋ/ *n.* **1** *Brit.* a large, usu. wooden, structure used to carry advertisements etc. **2** a board fence erected round a building site etc., often used for displaying posters etc. [obs. *hoard* f. AF h(o)*urdis* f. OF *hourd, hort,* rel. to HURDLE]

hoarhound var. of HOREHOUND.

hoarse /hɔːs/ *adj.* **1** (of the voice) rough and deep; husky; croaking. **2** having such a voice. □□ **hoarsely** *adv.* **hoarsen** *v.tr. & intr.* **hoarseness** *n.* [ME f. ON *hārs* (unrecorded) f. Gmc]

hoarstone /ˈhɔːstəʊn/ *n. Brit.* an ancient boundary stone.

hoary /ˈhɔːrɪ/ *adj.* (**hoarier, hoariest**) **1 a** (of hair) grey or white with age. **b** having such hair; aged. **2** old and trite (*a hoary joke*). **3** *Bot. & Zool.* covered with short white hairs. □□ **hoarily** *adv.* **hoariness** *n.*

hoatzin /hwætˈsiːn/ *n.* a tropical American bird, *Opisthocomus hoatzin,* whose young climb by means of hooked claws on their wings. [native name, imit.]

hoax /həʊks/ *n. & v.* —*n.* a humorous or malicious deception; a practical joke. —*v.tr.* deceive (a person) with a hoax. □□ **hoaxer** *n.* [18th c.: prob. contr. f. HOCUS]

hob[1] /hɒb/ *n.* **1 a** a flat heating surface for a pan on a cooker. **b** a flat metal shelf at the side of a fireplace, having its surface level with the top of the grate, used esp. for heating a pan etc. **2** a tool used for cutting gear-teeth etc. **3** a peg or pin used as a mark in quoits etc. **4** = HOBNAIL. [perh. var. of HUB, orig. = lump]

hob[2] /hɒb/ *n.* **1** a male ferret. **2** a hobgoblin. □ **play** (or **raise**) **hob** *US* cause mischief. [ME, familiar form of *Rob,* short for *Robin* or *Robert*]

Hobart /ˈhəʊbɑːt/ the capital and a port of Tasmania; pop. (1986) 180,300. A penal colony named after Lord Hobart, Secretary of State for the Colonies, was moved to the city's present site in 1804; it became the island's capital in 1812.

Hobbema /ˈhɒbɪmə/, Meindert (1638–1709), the last of the great 17th-c. Dutch painters of landscape, a native of Amsterdam, friend and pupil of Jacob van Ruisdael. He painted a narrow range of favourite subject-matter—water-mills and trees round a pool—over and over again. By the later 1660s, the demand in Holland for this type of landscape had much diminished, and he took up a clerical appointment at the age of 30 and practically ceased to paint. His *Avenue at Middelharnis* (1689) ranks among the best-known achievements of Dutch art.

Hobbes /hɒbz/, Thomas (1588–1679), English philosopher. His philosophy arose from a systematic project of investigating in turn the nature of matter, of man, and of society. He thought that the method of science should be the axiomatic method of geometry. There were two key components in his conception of man: he was fiercely materialist, claiming that there was no more to the mind than the physical motions discovered by science, and he thought that human action was motivated entirely by selfish concerns, notably fear of death. His view of society was expressed in his most famous work, *Leviathan* (1651),

in which he argued, by means of a version of a social contract theory, that given his view of human motivation, simple rationality made social institutions and even absolute monarchy inevitable. His adherence to the axiomatic method led him to give great weight to definition, and this in turn led him to locate philosophical confusions in the misuse of words. In all these respects he was a peculiarly forthright exponent of a distinctive tendency in British philosophy.

hobbit /ˈhɒbɪt/ *n.* a member of an imaginary race of half-sized people in stories by J. R. R. Tolkien. □□ **hobbitry** *n.* [invented by Tolkien and said by him to mean 'hole-dweller']

hobble /ˈhɒb(ə)l/ *v. & n.* —*v.* **1** *intr.* **a** walk lamely; limp. **b** proceed haltingly in action or speech (*hobbled lamely to his conclusion*). **2** *tr.* **a** tie together the legs of (a horse etc.) to prevent it from straying. **b** tie (a horse's etc. legs). **3** *tr.* cause (a person etc.) to limp. —*n.* **1** an uneven or infirm gait. **2** a rope, clog, etc. used for hobbling a horse etc. □ **hobble skirt** a skirt so narrow at the hem as to impede walking. □□ **hobbler** *n.* [ME, prob. f. LG: cf. HOPPLE and Du. *hobbelen* rock from side to side]

hobbledehoy /ˈhɒbəldɪˌhɔɪ/ *n. colloq.* **1** a clumsy or awkward youth. **2** a hooligan. [16th c.: orig. unkn.]

Hobbs /hɒbz/, Sir John Berry ('Jack') (1882–1963), English cricketer, a batsman whose career extended from 1905 to 1934. He holds the record for the greatest number of runs (61,237) and of centuries (197) scored in first-class cricket.

hobby[1] /ˈhɒbɪ/ *n.* (*pl.* **-ies**) **1** a favourite leisure-time activity or occupation. **2** *archaic* a small horse. **3** *hist.* an early type of velocipede. □□ **hobbyist** *n.* [ME *hobyn, hoby,* f. pet-forms of *Robin:* cf. DOBBIN]

hobby[2] /ˈhɒbɪ/ *n.* (*pl.* **-ies**) any of several small long-winged falcons, esp. *Falco subbuteo,* catching prey on the wing. [ME f. OF *hobé, hobet* dimin. of *hobe* small bird of prey]

hobby-horse /ˈhɒbɪˌhɔːs/ *n.* **1** a child's toy consisting of a stick with a horse's head. **2** a preoccupation; a favourite topic of conversation. **3** a model of a horse, esp. of wicker, used in morris dancing etc. **4** a rocking horse. **5** a horse on a merry-go-round.

hobday /ˈhɒbdeɪ/ *v.tr.* operate on (a horse) to improve its breathing. [F. T. *Hobday,* veterinary surgeon d. 1939]

hobgoblin /ˈhɒbˌɡɒblɪn/ *n.* a mischievous imp; a bogy; a bugbear. [HOB[2] + GOBLIN]

hobnail /ˈhɒbneɪl/ *n.* a heavy-headed nail used for boot-soles. □ **hobnail** (or **hobnailed**) **liver** a liver having many small knobbly projections due to cirrhosis. □□ **hobnailed** *adj.* [HOB[1] + NAIL]

hobnob /ˈhɒbnɒb/ *v.intr.* (**hobnobbed, hobnobbing**) **1** (usu. foll. by *with*) mix socially or informally. **2** drink together. [*hob or nob* = give or take, of alternate drinking; earlier *hab nab,* = have or not have]

hobo /ˈhəʊbəʊ/ *n.* (*pl.* **-oes** or **-os**) *US* a wandering worker; a tramp. [19th c.: orig. unkn.]

Hobson's choice /ˈhɒbs(ə)nz/ *n.* a choice of taking the thing offered or nothing. [T. *Hobson,* Cambridge carrier d. 1631, who let out horses on the basis that customers must take the one nearest the door]

Ho Chi Minh /həʊ tʃiː ˈmɪn/ (Nguyen That Thanh, 1890–1969), Vietnamese Communist statesman, who led his country in its struggle for independence from French rule. A founder of what became the Indo-Chinese Communist Party, in 1945, when the Japanese, who had overrun Indo-China, had surrendered to the West, having entered Hanoi with a guerrilla force he proclaimed Vietnamese independence (Viet Minh). Years of guerrilla warfare ended in victory in May 1954, and Vietnam was divided along the 17th parallel into North Vietnam, of which Ho became president, and South Vietnam. His aim of Vietnamese unification was achieved after his death, with victory not only over the French but over the forces of the US.

Ho Chi Minh City (formerly *Saigon*) a city in southern Vietnam; pop. (est.) 4,000,000.

hock[1] /hɒk/ *n.* **1** the joint of a quadruped's hind leg between the knee and the fetlock. **2** a knuckle of pork; the lower joint of a ham. [obs. *hockshin* f. OE *hōhsinu:* see HOUGH]

hock² /hɒk/ n. *Brit.* a German white wine from the Rhineland (properly that of Hochheim on the river Main). [abbr. of obs. *hockamore* f. G *Hochheimer*]

hock³ /hɒk/ v. & n. esp. US *colloq.* —v.tr. pawn; pledge. —n. a pawnbroker's pledge. □ **in hock 1** in pawn. **2** in debt. **3** in prison. [Du. *hok* hutch, prison, debt]

hockey¹ /ˈhɒkɪ/ n. **1** a game played between two teams with a ball on a field or by skaters with a puck on ice (**ice hockey**) with hooked sticks, between two goals. The word *hockie* dates from the 16th c. in an isolated example, but the game has descended from early civilizations (it is depicted on an ancient Egyptian tomb). Forms of it are at least 4,000 years old, but it was not an organized sport until the end of the 19th c. **2** US ice hockey. □□ **hockeyist** n. (in sense 2). [16th c.: orig. unkn.; the name probably belonged originally to the hooked stick]

hockey² var. of OCHE.

Hockney /ˈhɒknɪ/, David (1937–), English painter and draughtsman, often classified as a pop artist (though he himself dislikes the label) who won international success, while still a student, with a set of 16 etchings, *A Rake's Progress*, inspired by a visit to New York in 1961.

Hocktide /ˈhɒktaɪd/ n. *hist.* the time of hock-days (Hock Monday and Hock Tuesday), the second Monday and Tuesday after Easter Day, on which in pre-Reformation times money was collected for church and parish purposes, and various sports and amusements took place. The merrymaking at this season survived in some places until the 19th c. [ME; orig. unkn.]

hocus /ˈhəʊkəs/ v.tr. (**hocussed**, **hocussing**; US **hocused**, **hocusing**) **1** take in; hoax. **2** stupefy (a person) with drugs. **3** drug (liquor). [obs. noun *hocus* = HOCUS-POCUS]

hocus-pocus /ˌhəʊkəsˈpəʊkəs/ n. & v. —n. **1** deception; trickery. **2** a typical verbal formula used in conjuring. —v. (**-pocussed**, **-pocussing**; US **-pocused**, **-pocusing**) **1** intr. (often foll. by *with*) play tricks. **2** tr. play tricks on, deceive. [17th-c. sham L]

hod /hɒd/ n. **1** a V-shaped open trough on a pole used for carrying bricks, mortar, etc. **2** a portable receptacle for coal. [prob. = dial. *hot* f. OF *hotte* pannier, f. Gmc]

hodden /ˈhɒd(ə)n/ n. *Sc.* a coarse woollen cloth. □ **hodden grey** grey hodden; typical rustic clothing. [16th c.: orig. unkn.]

Hodeida /həʊˈdeɪdə/ the chief port of Yemen, on the Red Sea; pop. (1986) 155,100.

Hodge /hɒdʒ/ n. *Brit.* a typical English agricultural labourer. [pet-form of the name *Roger*]

hodgepodge /ˈhɒdʒpɒdʒ/ n. = HOTCHPOTCH 1, 3. [ME, assim. to HODGE]

Hodgkin's disease /ˈhɒdʒkɪnz/ n. a malignant disease of lymphatic tissues usu. characterized by enlargement of the lymph nodes. [T. *Hodgkin*, Engl. physician d. 1866]

hodiernal /ˌhɒdɪˈɜːnəl, ˌhəʊ-/ adj. *formal* of the present day. [L *hodiernus* f. *hodie* today]

hodman /ˈhɒdmæn/ n. (pl. **-men**) **1** a labourer who carries a hod. **2** a literary hack. **3** a person who works mechanically.

hodograph /ˈhɒdəˌɡrɑːf/ n. a curve in which the radius vector represents the velocity of a moving particle. [Gk *hodos* way + -GRAPH]

hodometer /həˈdɒmɪtə(r)/ var. of ODOMETER.

Hoe /həʊ/, Richard March (1812–86), American inventor, the first printer to develop a successful rotary press (in 1846). This greatly increased the speed of printing over that of a flat-bed press; by 1857 *The Times* had a Hoe press printing 20,000 impressions an hour. This machine had still to be fed with individual cut sheets, but by 1871 Hoe had developed a machine fed from a continuous roll.

hoe /həʊ/ n. & v. —n. a long-handled tool with a thin metal blade, used for weeding etc. —v. (**hoes**, **hoed**, **hoeing**) **1** tr. weed (crops); loosen (earth); dig up or cut down with a hoe. **2** intr. use a hoe. □ **hoe-cake** US a coarse cake of maize flour orig. baked on the blade of a hoe. **hoe in** Austral. & NZ sl. eat eagerly. **hoe into** Austral. & NZ sl. attack (food, a person, a task). □□ **hoer** n. [ME *howe* f. OF *houe* f. Gmc]

hoedown /ˈhəʊdaʊn/ n. US a lively dance or dance-party.

Hoek van Holland see HOOK OF HOLLAND.

Hoffmann /ˈhɒfmən/, Ernst Theodor Amadeus (1776–1882), German writer and music critic, whose stories and his wild unhappy life provided the inspiration for Offenbach's *Tales of Hoffmann*. His works include the extravagantly fantastic *Phantasiestücke* (1814–15) and *Elixire des Teufels* (*The Devil's Elixir*, 1815–16).

Hofmannsthal /ˈhɒfmænˌstɑːl/, Hugo von (1874–1929), Austrian dramatist and poet. He wrote the libretti for Strauss's operas *Elektra* (1909), *Der Rosenkavalier* (1911), *Ariadne auf Naxos* (1912), and *Arabella* (1933); his correspondence with Strauss is of literary and musical interest. With Max Reinhardt, they founded the Salzburg Festival; *Jedermann* (*Everyman*, 1912; a modernization of the morality play) was first performed at the opening of the Festival in 1920. This work inaugurated his development away from the aestheticism of the *fin de siècle* towards a social and religious literature completed in his last play *Der Turm* (*The Tower*, 1925).

hog /hɒɡ/ n. & v. —n. **1 a** a domesticated pig, esp. a castrated male reared for slaughter. **b** any of several other pigs of the family Suidae, e.g. a wart-hog. **2** *colloq.* a greedy person. **3** (also **hogg**) *Brit. dial.* a young sheep before the first shearing. —v. (**hogged**, **hogging**) **1** tr. *colloq.* take greedily; hoard selfishly. **2** tr. & intr. raise (the back), or rise in an arch in the centre. □ **go the whole hog** *colloq.* do something completely or thoroughly. **hog-tie** US **1** secure by fastening the hands and feet or all four feet together. **2** restrain, impede. □□ **hogger** n. **hoggery** n. **hoggish** adj. **hoggishly** adv. **hoggishness** n. **hoglike** adj. [OE *hogg, hocg*, perh. of Celt. orig.]

hogan /ˈhəʊɡən/ n. an American Indian hut of logs etc. [Navajo]

Hogarth /ˈhəʊɡɑːθ/, William (1697–1764), English painter and engraver. An important figure in the development of an English school of painting, Hogarth railed against the taste of his time for foreign artists and blackened Old Masters, and was instrumental in the moves to found art institutions in England which culminated after his death in the foundation of the Royal Academy (1769). Many of his works were engraved, most notably the 'modern moral subjects' such as *Marriage à la Mode*, which vividly satirized the vices of both high and low life in 18th-c. England. He was much influenced by the French rococo, despite his pugnacious pride in his nationality. Hogarth attempted history painting, in accordance with the contemporary emphasis given to 'high art', but was at his best in spontaneous sketches such as *A Shrimp Girl*.

hogback /ˈhɒɡbæk/ n. (also **hog's back**) a steep-sided ridge of a hill.

Hogg /hɒɡ/, James (1770–1835), Scottish poet, a shepherd in the Ettrick Forest until his poetic talent was discovered by Scott (whence his nickname 'the Ettrick Shepherd'). He made his reputation as a poet with *The Queen's Wake* (1813) but is better known today for his prose work *The Confessions of a Justified Sinner* (1824).

hogg var. of HOG n. 3.

Hoggar Mountains /ˈhɒɡə(r)/ (also **Ahaggar Mountains** /əˈhæɡə(r)/) a mountain plateau in the central Saharan desert of southern Algeria, rising to a height of more than 3,000 m (9,740 ft.).

hogget /ˈhɒɡɪt/ n. *Brit.* a yearling sheep. [HOG]

hoggin /ˈhɒɡɪn/ n. **1** a mixture of sand and gravel. **2** sifted gravel. [19th c.: orig. unkn.]

hogmanay /ˈhɒɡməˌneɪ, -ˈneɪ/ n. *Sc.* **1** New Year's Eve. **2** a celebration on this day. **3** a gift of cake etc. demanded by children at hogmanay. [17th c.: perh. f. Norman F *hoguinané* f. OF *aguillanneuf* (also = new year's gift)]

hog's back var. of HOGBACK.

hogshead /ˈhɒɡzhed/ n. **1** a large cask. **2** a liquid or dry measure, usu. about 50 imperial gallons. [ME f. HOG, HEAD: reason for the name unkn.]

hogwash /ˈhɒɡwɒʃ/ n. **1** *colloq.* nonsense, rubbish. **2** kitchen swill etc. for pigs.

hogweed /ˈhɒɡwiːd/ n. any of various coarse weeds of the genus *Heracleum*, esp. *H. sphondylium*.

Hohenstaufen /ˌhəʊɪnˈʃtaʊf(ə)n/ the name of a German princely family from which came Holy Roman Emperors from 1138 to 1254.

Hohenzollern /ˌhəʊɪnˈzɒlən/ the name of a German princely family from which came the kings of Prussia from 1701 to 1918 and German emperors from 1871 to 1918.

ho-ho /həʊˈhəʊ/ int. expressing surprise, triumph, or derision. [redupl. of HO]

ho-hum /ˈhəʊhʌm/ int. expressing boredom. [imit. of yawn]

hoick[1] /hɔɪk/ v. & n. *colloq.* —v.tr. (often foll. by *out*) lift or pull, esp. with a jerk. —n. a jerky pull; a jerk. [perh. var. of HIKE]

hoick[2] /hɔɪk/ v.intr. *sl.* spit. [perh. var. of HAWK[3]]

hoicks var. of YOICKS.

hoi polloi /ˌhɔɪ pəˈlɔɪ/ n. (often prec. by *the*: see note below) 1 the masses; the common people. 2 the majority. ¶ Use with *the* is strictly unnecessary, since *hoi* = 'the', but this construction is very common. [Gk, = the many]

hoist /hɔɪst/ v. & n. —v.tr. 1 raise or haul up. 2 raise by means of ropes and pulleys etc. —n. 1 an act of hoisting, a lift. 2 an apparatus for hoisting. 3 a the part of a flag nearest the staff. b a group of flags raised as a signal. □ **hoist the flag** stake one's claim to discovered territory by displaying a flag. **hoist one's flag** signify that one takes command. **hoist with one's own petard** see PETARD. □□ **hoister** n. [16th c.: alt. of *hoise* f. (15th-c.) *hysse*, prob. of LG orig.: cf. LG *hissen*]

hoity-toity /ˌhɔɪtɪˈtɔɪtɪ/ adj., int., & n. —adj. 1 haughty; petulant; snobbish. 2 *archaic* frolicsome. —int. expressing surprised protest at presumption etc. —n. *archaic* riotous or giddy conduct. [obs. *hoit* indulge in riotous mirth, of unkn. orig.]

hokey /ˈhəʊkɪ/ adj. (also **hoky**) (**hokier**, **hokiest**) US *sl.* sentimental, melodramatic, artificial. □□ **hokeyness** n. (also **hokiness**). **hokily** adv. [HOKUM + -Y[2]]

hokey-cokey /ˌhəʊkɪˈkəʊkɪ/ n. a communal dance performed in a circle with synchronized shaking of each limb in turn. [perh. f. HOCUS-POCUS]

hokey-pokey /ˌhəʊkɪˈpəʊkɪ/ n. *colloq.* 1 = HOCUS-POCUS. 2 icecream formerly sold esp. by Italian street vendors. [HOCUS-POCUS: sense 2 of unkn. orig.]

Hokkaido /hɒˈkaɪdəʊ/ the most northerly of the four main islands of Japan; pop. (1986) 5,678,000; capital, Sapporo.

hokku /ˈhɒkʊ/ n. (pl. same) = HAIKU. [Jap.]

hokum /ˈhəʊkəm/ n. esp. US *sl.* 1 sentimental, popular, sensational, or unreal situations, dialogue, etc., in a film or play etc. 2 bunkum; rubbish. [20th c.: orig. unkn.]

Hokusai /ˈhəʊkʊˌsaɪ, -ˈsaɪ/, Katsushika (1760–1849), Japanese painter, one of the most famous of the ukiyo-e designers, who is noted for his landscapes, which influenced the impressionists and post-impressionists. His most famous works include his *Views of Mount Fuji* (1835).

hoky var. of HOKEY.

Holarctic /həˈlɑːktɪk/ adj. of or relating to the geographical distribution of animals in the whole northern or Arctic region. [HOLO- + ARCTIC]

Holbein /ˈhɒlbaɪn/, Hans (1497/8–1543), German painter who worked in Basle 1514–26, where he executed a series of woodcuts, the *Dance of Death* (c.1523–6). In 1526, finding his patronage reduced as a result of the Reformation, he came to England, with an introduction (from Erasmus) to Sir Thomas More. His group portrait of the More family is the first picture to be painted of full-length figures in their own home. By 1536 he had gained the patronage of Henry VIII, but was disappointed by the English court's almost exclusive interest in portraits. His late portraits (*The Ambassadors*, 1533, and *Christina, Duchess of Milan*, 1538) became increasingly detailed, frozen, and spaceless, perhaps in connection with an interest in miniature painting.

hold[1] /həʊld/ v. & n. —v. (past and past part. **held** /held/) 1 tr. a keep fast; grasp (esp. in the hands or arms). b (also *refl.*) keep or sustain (a thing, oneself, one's head, etc.) in a particular position (*hold it to the light; held himself erect*). c grasp so as to control (*hold*

the reins). 2 tr. (of a vessel etc.) contain or be capable of containing (*the jug holds two pints; the hall holds 900*). 3 tr. possess, gain, or have, esp.: a be the owner or tenant of (land, property, stocks, etc.) (*holds the farm from the trust*). b gain or have gained (a degree, record, etc.) (*holds the long-jump record*). c have the position of (a job or office). d have (a specified card) in one's hand. e keep possession of (a place, a person's thoughts, etc.) esp. against attack (*held the fort against the enemy; held his place in her estimation*). 4 intr. remain unbroken; not give way (*the roof held under the storm*). 5 tr. observe; celebrate; conduct (a meeting, festival, conversation, etc.). 6 tr. a keep (a person etc.) in a specified condition, place, etc. (*held him prisoner; held him at arm's length*). b detain, esp. in custody (*hold him until I arrive*). 7 tr. a engross (a person or a person's attention) (*the book held him for hours*). b dominate (*held the stage*). 8 tr. (foll. by *to*) make (a person etc.) adhere to (terms, a promise, etc.). 9 intr. (of weather) continue fine. 10 tr. (often foll. by *to* + infin., or *that* + clause) think; believe (*held it to be self-evident; held that the earth was flat*). 11 tr. regard with a specified feeling (*held him in contempt*). 12 tr. a cease; restrain (*hold your fire*). b US *colloq.* withhold; not use (*a burger please, and hold the onions!*). 13 tr. keep or reserve (*will you hold our seats please?*). 14 tr. be able to drink (liquor) without effect (*can't hold his drink*). 15 tr. (usu. foll. by *that* + clause) (of a judge, a court, etc.) lay down; decide. 16 intr. keep going (*held on his way*). 17 tr. Mus. sustain (a note). 18 intr. *archaic* restrain oneself. —n. 1 a grasp (*catch hold of him; keep a hold on him*). 2 (often in *comb.*) a thing to hold by (*seized the handhold*). 3 (foll. by *on, over*) influence over (*has a strange hold over them*). 4 a manner of holding in wrestling etc. 5 *archaic* a fortress. □ **hold (a thing) against (a person)** resent or regard it as discreditable to (a person). **hold aloof** avoid communication with people etc. **hold back** 1 impede the progress of; restrain. 2 keep (a thing) to or for oneself. 3 (often foll. by *from*) hesitate; refrain. **hold-back** n. a hindrance. **hold one's breath** see BREATH. **hold by** (or **to**) adhere to (a choice, purpose, etc.). **hold cheap** not value highly; despise. **hold the clock on** time (a sporting event etc.). **hold court** preside over one's admirers etc., like a sovereign. **hold dear** regard with affection. **hold down** 1 repress. 2 *colloq.* be competent enough to keep (one's job etc.). **hold everything!** (or **it!**) cease action or movement. **hold the fort** 1 act as a temporary substitute. 2 cope in an emergency. **hold forth** 1 offer (an inducement etc.). 2 usu. *derog.* speak at length or tediously. **hold good** (or **true**) be valid; apply. **hold one's ground** see GROUND[1]. **hold one's hand** see HAND. **hold a person's hand** give a person guidance or moral support. **hold hands** grasp one another by the hand as a sign of affection or for support or guidance. **hold hard!** stop!; wait! **hold harmless** *Law* indemnify. **hold one's head high** behave proudly and confidently. **hold one's horses** *colloq.* stop; slow down. **hold in** keep in check, confine. **hold it good** think it advisable. **hold the line** 1 not yield. 2 maintain a telephone connection. **hold one's nose** compress the nostrils to avoid a bad smell. **hold off** 1 delay; not begin. 2 keep one's distance. **hold on** 1 keep one's grasp on something. 2 wait a moment. 3 (when telephoning) not ring off. **hold out** 1 stretch forth (a hand etc.). 2 offer (an inducement etc.). 3 maintain resistance. 4 persist or last. **hold out for** continue to demand. **hold out on** *colloq.* refuse something to (a person). **hold over** postpone. **hold-over** n. US a relic. **hold something over** threaten (a person) constantly with something. **hold one's own** see OWN. **hold to bail** *Law* bind by bail. **hold to a draw** manage to achieve a draw against (an opponent thought likely to win). **hold together** 1 cohere. 2 cause to cohere. **hold one's tongue** *colloq.* be silent. **hold to ransom** 1 keep (a person) prisoner until a ransom is paid. 2 demand concessions from by threats of damaging action. **hold up** 1 a support; sustain. b maintain (the head etc.) erect. 2 exhibit; display. 3 arrest the progress of; obstruct. 4 stop and rob by violence or threats. **hold-up** n. 1 a stoppage or delay by traffic, fog, etc. 2 a robbery, esp. by the use of threats or violence. **hold water** (of reasoning) be sound; bear examination. **hold with** (usu. with *neg.*) *colloq.* approve of (*don't hold with motor bikes*). **left holding the baby** left with unwelcome responsibility. **take hold** (of a custom or habit) become established. **there is no holding him** (or **her** etc.) he (or she etc.) is restive, high-spirited, determined, etc. **with no holds barred** with no restrictions, all methods being permitted. □□ **holdable** adj. [OE h(e)aldan, heald]

hold² /həʊld/ n. a cavity in the lower part of a ship or aircraft in which the cargo is stowed. [obs. holl f. OE hol (orig. adj. = hollow), rel. to HOLE, assim. to HOLD¹]

holdall /ˈhəʊldɔːl/ n. a portable case for miscellaneous articles.

holder /ˈhəʊldə(r)/ n. **1** (often in comb.) a device or implement for holding something (cigarette-holder). **2 a** the possessor of a title etc. **b** the occupant of an office etc. **3** = SMALLHOLDER.

Hölderlin /ˈhɜːldəlɪn/, Johann Christian Friedrich (1770–1843), German poet who studied for the Church. His early poetry was full of political idealism fostered by the French Revolution, but most of his poems express a hopeless romantic yearning for ancient Greek harmony with nature and beauty. While working as a tutor he fell in love with his employer's wife, who is portrayed in his novel Hyperion (1797–9), and after her death in 1802 he drifted into insanity.

holdfast /ˈhəʊldfɑːst/ n. **1** a firm grasp. **2** a staple or clamp securing an object to a wall etc. **3** the attachment-organ of an alga etc.

holding /ˈhəʊldɪŋ/ n. **1 a** land held by lease (cf. SMALLHOLDING). **b** the tenure of land. **2** stocks, property, etc. held. □ **holding company** a company created to hold the shares of other companies, which it then controls. **holding operation** a manoeuvre designed to maintain the status quo.

hole /həʊl/ n. & v. —n. **1 a** an empty space in a solid body. **b** an aperture in or through something. **2** an animal's burrow. **3 a** cavity or receptacle for a ball in various sports or games. **4** colloq. a small, mean, or dingy abode. **5** colloq. an awkward situation. **6** Golf **a** a point scored by a player who gets the ball from tee to hole with the fewest strokes. **b** the terrain or distance from tee to hole. **7** a position from which an electron is absent, esp. acting as a mobile positive particle in a semiconductor. —v.tr. **1** make a hole or holes in. **2** pierce the side of (a ship). **3** put into a hole. **4** (also absol.; often foll. by out) send (a golf ball) into a hole. □ **hole-and-corner** secret; underhand. **hole in the heart** a congenital defect in the heart septum. **hole in one** Golf a shot that enters the hole from the tee. **hole in the wall** a small dingy place (esp. of business). **hole-proof** (of materials etc.) treated so as to be resistant to wear. **hole up** US colloq. hide oneself. **in holes** worn so much that holes have formed. **make a hole in** use a large amount of. **a round** (or **square**) **peg in a square** (or **round**) **hole** see PEG. □□ **holey** adj. [OE hol, holian (as HOLD²)]

Holi /ˈhəʊliː/ n. a Hindu spring festival celebrated in February or March in honour of Krishna the amorous cowherd. [Hindi f. Skr.]

holibut var. of HALIBUT.

Holiday /ˈhɒlɪˌdeɪ/, Billie (real name Eleanora Fagan, 1915–59), American jazz singer, affectionately known as 'Lady Day', noted for the dramatic intensity of her singing, especially in recordings made with the saxophonist Lester Young. Her autobiography Lady Sings the Blues (1956) was made into a film in 1972.

holiday /ˈhɒlɪˌdeɪ, -dɪ/ n. & v. —n. **1** esp. Brit. (often in pl.) an extended period of recreation, esp. away from home or in travelling; a break from work (cf. VACATION). **2** a day of festivity or recreation when no work is done, esp. a religious festival etc. **3** (attrib.) (of clothes etc.) festive. —v.intr. esp. Brit. spend a holiday. □ **holiday camp** Brit. a camp for holiday-makers with accommodation, entertainment, and facilities on site. **holiday centre** a place with many tourist attractions. **holiday-maker** esp. Brit. a person on holiday. **on holiday** (or **one's holidays**) in the course of one's holiday. **take a** (or **make**) **holiday** have a break from work. [OE hāligdæg (HOLY, DAY)]

holily /ˈhəʊlɪlɪ/ adv. in a holy manner. [OE hāliglīce (as HOLY)]

holiness /ˈhəʊlɪnɪs/ n. **1** sanctity; the state of being holy. **2** (**Holiness**) a title used when referring to or addressing the pope. [OE hālignes (as HOLY)]

Holinshed /ˈhɒlɪnˌʃed/, Raphael (d. ?1580), English chronicler, who planned the Chronicles (1577) which are known by his name though written by several hands (the Historie of England was written by Holinshed himself). In 1587 the work was revised and reissued, and this edition was widely used by Shakespeare and other dramatists.

holism /ˈhɒlɪz(ə)m, ˈhəʊ-/ n. (also **wholism**) **1** Philos. the theory that certain wholes are to be regarded as greater than the sum of their parts (cf. REDUCTIONISM). **2** Med. the treating of the whole person including mental and social factors rather than just the symptoms of a disease. □□ **holistic** /-ˈlɪstɪk/ adj. **holistically** /-ˈlɪstɪkəlɪ/ adv. [as HOLO- + -ISM]

holla /ˈhɒlə/ int., n., & v. —int. calling attention. —n. a cry of 'holla'. —v. (**hollas, hollaed** or **holla'd, hollaing**) **1** intr. shout. **2** tr. call to (hounds). [F holà (as HO, là there)]

Holland /ˈhɒlənd/ n. a former province of The Netherlands, now divided into North and South Holland. Its name is often used interchangeably with The Netherlands as the name of the country. [Du., earlier Holtlant f. Holt wood + -lant land, describing Dordrecht district]

holland /ˈhɒlənd/ n. a smooth hard-wearing linen fabric. □ **brown holland** unbleached holland. [HOLLAND]

hollandaise sauce /ˌhɒlənˈdeɪz, ˈhɒl-/ n. a creamy sauce of melted butter, egg-yolks, vinegar, etc., served esp. with fish. [F, fem. of hollandais Dutch f. Hollande Holland]

Hollander /ˈhɒləndə(r)/ n. **1** a native of Holland (The Netherlands). **2** a Dutch ship.

Hollands /ˈhɒləndz/ n. gin made in Holland. [Du. hollandsch genever Dutch gin]

holler /ˈhɒlə(r)/ v. & n. US colloq. —v. **1** intr. make a loud cry or noise. **2** tr. express with a loud cry or shout. —n. a loud cry, noise, or shout. [var. of HOLLO]

Hollerith /ˈhɒlərɪθ/, Herman (1860–1929), American inventor of a tabulating machine that was an important precursor of the electronic computer.

hollo /ˈhɒləʊ/ int., n., & v. —int. = HOLLA. —n. (pl. **-os**) = HOLLA. —v. (**-oes, -oed**) (also **hollow** pronunc. same) = HOLLA. [rel. to HOLLA]

hollow /ˈhɒləʊ/ adj., n., v., & adv. —adj. **1 a** having a hole or cavity inside; not solid throughout. **b** having a depression; sunken (hollow cheeks). **2** (of a sound) echoing, as though made in or on a hollow container. **3** empty; hungry. **4** without significance; meaningless (a hollow triumph). **5** insincere; cynical; false (a hollow laugh; hollow promises). —n. **1** a hollow place; a hole. **2** a valley; a basin. —v.tr. (often foll. by out) make hollow; excavate. —adv. colloq. completely (beaten hollow). □ **hollow-eyed** with eyes deep sunk. **hollow-hearted** insincere. **hollow square** Mil. hist. a body of infantry drawn up in a square with a space in the middle. **in the hollow of one's hand** entirely subservient to one. □□ **hollowly** adv. **hollowness** n. [ME holg, holu, hol(e)we f. OE holh cave, rel. to HOLE]

hollowware /ˈhɒləʊˌweə(r)/ n. hollow articles of metal, china, etc., such as pots, kettles, jugs, etc. (opp. FLATWARE).

holly /ˈhɒlɪ/ n. (pl. **-ies**) **1** an evergreen shrub, Ilex aquifolium, with prickly usu. dark-green leaves, small white flowers, and red berries. **2** its branches and foliage used as decorations at Christmas. □ **holly oak** a holm-oak. [OE hole(g)n]

hollyhock /ˈhɒlɪˌhɒk/ n. a tall plant, Alcea rosea, with large showy flowers of various colours. [ME (orig. = marsh mallow) f. HOLY + obs. hock mallow, OE hoc, of unkn. orig.]

Hollywood /ˈhɒlɪˌwʊd/ a district of Los Angeles. American film-making was originally based on New York, but Southern California, with its sunshine and scenic variety, appealed to film-makers from as early as 1907. In 1911 the first studio was established in Hollywood and 15 others followed in the same year. The Hollywood studio system reached its peak in the 1930s, but by 1950 television had become a serious competitor, and many films are now made for that medium.

holm¹ /həʊm/ n. (also **holme**) Brit. **1** an islet, esp. in a river or near a mainland. **2** a piece of flat ground by a river, which is submerged in time of flood. [ON holmr]

holm² /həʊm/ n. (in full **holm-oak**) an evergreen oak, Quercus ilex, with holly-like young leaves. [ME alt. of obs. holin (as HOLLY)]

Holmes[1] /ˈhəʊmz/, Oliver Wendell (1809–94), American physician, poet, and essayist, professor and dean of the medical school at Harvard, and father of the eminent Supreme Court Justice of the same name (1841–1935). His example was much prized among medical men as showing an ability to combine scientific and literary interests. In medicine his main contribution was an essay (1843) on contagion as one cause of puerperal fever. As a member of a literary circle in Boston, Holmes published novels, volumes of verse, and a series of 'table talks', beginning with 'The Autocrat of the Breakfast Table' (1857–8). Holmes's opinions were in general more conventional than is implied by many of the much-loved quotations from his writings.

Holmes[2] /ˈhəʊmz/, Sherlock. A private detective, the central figure in a number of detective stories by Conan Doyle. The character was in part based on an eminent Edinburgh surgeon, Dr Joseph Bell, under whom Doyle studied medicine. Holmes was so credited by readers that requests for his help are still received at his fictional address in Baker Street, London.

holmium /ˈhəʊlmɪəm/ n. Chem. a soft silvery metallic element of the lanthanide series occurring naturally in apatite, first discovered in 1878. It has few uses at present. ¶ Symb.: Ho; atomic number 67. [mod.L f. Holmia Stockholm, native city of its discoverer (P. T. Cleve)]

holo- /ˈhɒləʊ/ comb. form whole (Holocene; holocaust). [Gk holos whole]

holocaust /ˈhɒləkɔːst/ n. 1 a case of large-scale destruction, esp. by fire or nuclear war. 2 (the Holocaust) the mass murder of the Jews (and of other disfavoured groups such as Poles and Gypsies) under the Nazi regime, esp. during the Second World War. 3 a sacrifice wholly consumed by fire. [ME f. OF holocauste f. LL holocaustum f. Gk holokauston (as HOLO-, kaustos burnt f. kaiō burn)]

Holocene /ˈhɒləˌsiːn/ adj. & n. Geol. —adj. (also called Recent) of or relating to the second of the two epochs of the Quaternary period, following the Pleistocene and lasting from about 10,000 years ago to the present. The epoch has seen a rise in world temperatures after the last of the Pleistocene ice ages, and coincides with the development of human agricultural settlement and civilization. —n. this period or system. [HOLO- + Gk kainos new]

holoenzyme /ˌhɒləʊˈenzaɪm/ n. Biochem. a complex enzyme consisting of several components.

Holofernes /ˌhɒləˈfɜːniːz/ the Assyrian general of Nebuchadnezzar's forces who was killed by Judith (Judith 4: 1 etc.).

hologram /ˈhɒləˌgræm/ n. Physics 1 a three-dimensional image formed by the interference of light beams from a coherent light source. 2 a photograph of the interference pattern, which when suitably illuminated produces a three-dimensional image.

holograph /ˈhɒləˌɡrɑːf/ adj. & n. —adj. wholly written by hand by the person named as the author. —n. a holograph document. [F holographe or LL holographus f. Gk holographos (as HOLO-, -GRAPH)]

holography /həˈlɒɡrəfɪ/ n. Physics the study or production of holograms. □□ **holographic** /-ləˈɡræfɪk/ adj. **holographically** /-ləˈɡræfɪkəlɪ/ adv.

holohedral /ˌhɒləˈhiːdr(ə)l/ adj. Crystallog. having the full number of planes required by the symmetry of a crystal system.

holophyte /ˈhɒləˌfaɪt/ n. an organism that synthesizes complex organic compounds by photosynthesis. □□ **holophytic** /-ˈfɪtɪk/ adj.

holothurian /ˌhɒləˈθjʊərɪən/ n. & adj. —n. any echinoderm of the class Holothurioidea, with a wormlike body, e.g. a sea cucumber. —adj. of or relating to this class. [mod.L Holothuria (n.pl.) f. Gk holothourion, a zoophyte]

holotype /ˈhɒləˌtaɪp/ n. the specimen used for naming and describing a species.

hols /hɒlz/ n.pl. Brit. colloq. holidays. [abbr.]

Holst /həʊlst/, Gustav (1874–1934), English-born composer of mixed Swedish and Russian descent. Like his friend and contemporary, Vaughan Williams, Holst was deeply interested in English folk-song, but while still a student he took lessons in Hindi, making his own translation of Sanskrit verses from the Rig-Veda and writing several works on Indian subjects. Much of his music has a timeless quality which was unfamiliar to English ears of the time, and Vaughan Williams said of his Choral Symphony (1923–4) that he felt for it only a 'cold admiration'. Holst was bewildered by the immediate popularity of The Planets (first performed in 1919), but here the essence of his style is plainly seen, combining a love for tight rhythmic control with a visionary quality perfectly expressed. He was also an inspiring teacher, with great feeling for the community spirit engendered by music, and played an outstanding part in music-making in the early 20th c.

Holstein /ˈhɒlstiːn/ n. & adj. US = FRIESIAN. [Holstein in NW Germany]

holster /ˈhəʊlstə(r)/ n. a leather case for a pistol or revolver, worn on a belt or under an arm or fixed to a saddle. [17th c., synonymous with Du. holster: orig. unkn.]

holt[1] /həʊlt/ n. 1 an animal's (esp. an otter's) lair. 2 colloq. or dial. grip, hold. [var. of HOLD[1]]

holt[2] /həʊlt/ n. archaic or dial. 1 a wood or copse. 2 a wooded hill. [OE f. Gmc]

holus-bolus /ˌhəʊləsˈbəʊləs/ adv. all in a lump, altogether. [app. sham L]

holy /ˈhəʊlɪ/ adj. (**holier**, **holiest**) 1 morally and spiritually excellent or perfect, and to be revered. 2 belonging to, devoted to, or empowered by, God. 3 consecrated, sacred. 4 used in trivial exclamations (holy cow!; holy mackerel!; holy Moses!; holy smoke!). □ **holier-than-thou** colloq. self-righteous. **Holy City** 1 a city held sacred by the adherents of a religion, esp. Jerusalem. 2 Heaven. **Holy Communion** see COMMUNION. **Holy Cross Day** the festival of the Exaltation of the Cross, 14 Sept. **holy day** a religious festival. **Holy Family** the young Jesus with his mother and St Joseph (often with St John the Baptist, St Anne, etc.) as grouped in pictures etc. **Holy Father** the Pope. **Holy Ghost** = Holy Spirit. **Holy Grail** see GRAIL. **holy Joe** orig. Naut. sl. 1 a clergyman. 2 a pious person. **Holy Name** RC Ch. the name of Jesus as an object of formal devotion. **holy of holies** 1 the inner chamber of the sanctuary in the Jewish temple, separated by a veil from the outer chamber. 2 an innermost shrine. 3 a thing regarded as most sacred. **holy orders** see ORDER. **holy place** 1 (in pl.) places to which religious pilgrimage is made. 2 the outer chamber of the sanctuary in the Jewish temple. **holy roller** sl. a member of a religious group characterized by frenzied excitement or trances. **Holy Rood Day** 1 the festival of the Invention of the Cross, 3 May. 2 = Holy Cross Day. **Holy Sacrament** see SACRAMENT. **Holy Saturday** Saturday in Holy Week. **Holy Scripture** the Bible. **Holy Spirit** the Third Person of the Trinity, God as spiritually acting. **holy terror** see TERROR. **Holy Thursday** 1 Anglican Ch. Ascension Day. 2 RC Ch. Maundy Thursday. **Holy Trinity** see TRINITY. **holy war** a war waged in support of a religious cause. **holy water** water dedicated to holy uses, or blessed by a priest. **Holy Week** the week before Easter. **Holy Writ** holy writings collectively, esp. the Bible. **Holy Year** RC Ch. a period of remission from the penal consequences of sin, granted under certain conditions for a year usu. at intervals of 25 years. [OE hālig f. Gmc, rel. to WHOLE]

Holy Alliance a loose alliance of European powers pledged to uphold the principles of the Christian religion. It was proclaimed at the Congress of Vienna (1815) by the emperors of Austria and Russia and the king of Prussia. All other European leaders were invited to join, except the pope and the Ottoman sultan. Most of them joined, Britain did not. As a diplomatic instrument it was short-lived and never effective, and it became associated with repressive and autocratic regimes.

Holyhead /ˌhɒlɪˈhed/ the chief town and a port on Holyhead Island, off the coast of Anglesey; pop. (1981) 12,652.

Holy Island see LINDISFARNE.

Holy Land 1 the western part of Palestine, esp. Judaea. The name has been applied in the Christian religion since the Middle Ages, with reference both to its having been the scene of the Incarnation and also to the existing sacred sites there, esp. the Holy Sepulchre at Jerusalem. 2 a region similarly revered in non-Christian religions.

Holy League the name given to several European alliances sponsored by the papacy during the 15th, 16th, and 17th c. They include the League of 1511–13, formed by Pope Julius II to expel Louis XII of France from Italy; the French Holy League (also known as the Catholic League) of 1576 and 1584, a Catholic extremist league formed during the French wars of religion; the Holy (or Catholic) League of 1609, a military alliance of the German Catholic princes.

Holy Office an ecclesiastical court established in 1542 (see INQUISITION) as the final court of appeal in trials of heresy. In 1965 it was renamed the Sacred Congregation for the Doctrine of the Faith; its function is to promote as well as to safeguard sound doctrine in the Roman Catholic Church.

Holy Roman Empire the empire set up in the West following the coronation of Charlemagne as emperor, in the year 800. Of the emperors after 1250 only five were crowned as such; the dignity was abolished by Napoleon in 1806. In true apocalyptic style the Empire lasted about 1,000 years. The creation of the medieval popes, it has been called their greatest mistake; for whereas their intention was to appoint a powerful secular deputy to rule Christendom, in fact they generated a rival. The Emperor never ruled the whole of Christendom, nor was there any substantial machinery of imperial government. From Otto I's coronation (962) the Empire was always associated with the German Crown, even after it became a Hapsburg/ Austrian preserve in the 15th c. Its somewhat mystical ideal was formal unity of government, based on coronation in Rome, memories of the old Roman Empire as well as Charlemagne, and devotion to the Roman Church. Perhaps for the very reason that this was generally at odds with the facts of political fragmentation within imperial territories, its ideological appeal remained astonishingly persistent, although as the supposed embodiment of a united Christendom it took a blow in the Reformation.

Holy See the papacy or papal court; those associated with the pope in the government of the Roman Catholic Church at its headquarters in Rome (see VATICAN).

Holy Shroud a relic, preserved at Turin in Italy since 1578, venerated as the winding-sheet in which Christ's body was wrapped for burial. It bears the imprint of the front and back of a human body marked with the traditional stigmata. Scientific tests carried out in 1988 have dated it to the 13th–14th c.

holystone /ˈhəʊliˌstəʊn/ n. & v. Naut. —n. a piece of soft sandstone used for scouring decks. —v.tr. scour with this. [19th c.: prob. f. HOLY + STONE: the stones were called *bibles* etc., perh. because used while kneeling]

hom /həʊm/ n. (also **homa** /ˈhəʊmə/) **1** the soma plant. **2** the juice of this plant as a sacred drink of the Parsees. [Pers. *hōm*, *hūm*, Avestan *haoma*]

homage /ˈhɒmɪdʒ/ n. **1** acknowledgement of superiority, dutiful reverence (*pay homage to; do homage to*). **2** *hist.* formal public acknowledgement of feudal allegiance. [ME f. OF (*h*)*omage* f. med.L *hominaticum* f. L *homo -minis* man]

hombre /ˈɒmbreɪ/ n. US a man. [Sp.]

Homburg /ˈhɒmbɜːg/ n. a man's felt hat with a narrow curled brim and a lengthwise dent in the crown. [*Homburg* in Germany, where first worn]

home /həʊm/ n., adj., adv., & v. —n. **1 a** the place where one lives; the fixed residence of a family or household. **b** a dwelling-house. **2** the members of a family collectively; one's family background (*comes from a good home*). **3** the native land of a person or of a person's ancestors. **4** an institution for persons needing care, rest, or refuge (*nursing home*). **5** the place where a thing originates or is native or most common. **6 a** the finishing-point in a race. **b** (in games) the place where one is free from attack; the goal. **c** *Lacrosse* a player in an attacking position near the opponents' goal. **7** *Sport* a home match or win. —attrib.adj. **1 a** of or connected with one's home. **b** carried on, done, or made, at home. **c** proceeding from home. **2 a** carried on or produced in one's own country (*home industries; the home market*). **b** dealing with the domestic affairs of a country. **3** *Sport* played on one's own ground etc. (*home match; home win*). **4** in the

neighbourhood of home. —adv. **1 a** to one's home or country (*go home*). **b** arrived at home (*is he home yet?*). **c** US at home (*stay home*). **2 a** to the point aimed at (*the thrust went home*). **b** as far as possible (*drove the nail home; pressed his advantage home*). —v. **1** intr. (esp. of a trained pigeon) return home (cf. HOMING 1). **2** intr. (often foll. by *on, in on*) (of a vessel, missile, etc.) be guided towards a destination or target by a landmark, radio beam, etc. **3** tr. send or guide homewards. **4** tr. provide with a home. □ **at home 1** in one's own house or native land. **2** at ease as if in one's own home (*make yourself at home*). **3** (usu. foll. by *in, on, with*) familiar or well informed. **4** available to callers. **at-home** n. a social reception in a person's home. **come home** to become fully realized by. **come home to roost** see ROOST¹. **home and dry** having achieved one's purpose. **home away from home** = *home from home*. **home-bird** a person who likes to stay at home. **home-brew** beer or other alcoholic drink brewed at home. **home-brewed** (of beer etc.) brewed at home. **home-coming** arrival at home. **Home Counties** the counties closest to London. **home economics** the study of household management. **home farm** *Brit.* a farm (one of several on an estate) set aside to provide produce for the owner. **home-felt** felt intimately. **home from home** a place other than one's home where one feels at home; a place providing homelike amenities. **home-grown** grown or produced at home. **Home Guard** *hist.* **1** the British citizen army organized in 1940 to defend the UK against invasion, and disbanded in 1957. **2** a member of this. **home help** *Brit.* a woman employed to help in a person's home, esp. one provided by a local authority. **home, James!** *joc.* drive home quickly! **home-made** made at home. **home-making** creation of a (pleasant) home. **home movie** a film made at home or of one's own activities. **Home Office 1** the British government department dealing with law and order, immigration, etc., in England and Wales. **2** the building used for this. **home of lost causes** Oxford University. **home-owner** a person who owns his or her own home. **home perm** a permanent wave made with domestic equipment. **home plate** *Baseball* a plate beside which the batter stands. **home port** the port from which a ship originates. **home rule** see separate entry. **home run** *Baseball* a hit that allows the batter to make a complete circuit of the bases. **Home Secretary** (in the UK) the Secretary of State in charge of the Home Office. **home signal** a signal indicating whether a train may proceed into a station or to the next section of the line. **home straight** (US **stretch**) the concluding stretch of a racecourse. **home town** the town of one's birth or early life or present fixed residence. **home trade** trade carried on within a country. **home truth** basic but unwelcome information concerning oneself. **home unit** *Austral.* a private residence, usu. occupied by the owner, as one of several in a building. **near home** affecting one closely. □□ **homelike** *adj.* [OE *hām* f. Gmc]

homebody /ˈhəʊmˌbɒdɪ/ n. (pl. **-ies**) a person who likes to stay at home.

homeland /ˈhəʊmlænd/ n. **1** one's native land. **2** an area in S. Africa reserved for a particular African people (the official name for a Bantustan).

homeless /ˈhəʊmlɪs/ adj. lacking a home. □□ **homelessness** n.

homely /ˈhəʊmlɪ/ adj. (**homelier**, **homeliest**) **1 a** simple, plain. **b** unpretentious. **c** primitive. **2** US (of people or their features) not attractive in appearance, ugly. **3** comfortable in the manner of a home, cosy. **4** skilled at housekeeping. □□ **homeliness** n.

homeopath etc. US var. of HOMOEOPATH etc.

homeostasis US var. of HOMOEOSTASIS.

Homer /ˈhəʊmə(r)/ (? c.700 BC) Greek epic poet, traditionally the author of the *Iliad* and the *Odyssey*. Various cities in Ionia claimed him as a son, and he is said to have been blind. Modern scholarship has fully revealed the nature of the Homeric poems as the product of a pre-literate oral tradition, in which a succession of bards elaborated the traditional stories of the heroic age (historically to be placed at the end of the Mycenaean period) in formulaic language in hexameter verse; questions of authorship are thus very difficult to answer. In later antiquity Homer was regarded as the greatest and unsurpassable poet, and his poems were constantly used as a model and source by others.

w we z zoo ʃ she ʒ decision θ thin ð this ŋ ring x loch tʃ chip dʒ jar (*see over for vowels*)

homer /ˈhəʊmə(r)/ n. **1** a homing pigeon. **2** *Baseball* a home run.

Homeric /həʊˈmerɪk, həˈm-/ adj. **1** of, or in the style of, Homer or the epic poems ascribed to him. **2** of Bronze Age Greece as described in these poems. **3** epic, large-scale, titanic (*Homeric conflict*). [L *Homericus* f. Gk *Homērikos* f. *Homēros* HOMER]

home rule n. government of a country or region by its own citizens, especially (usu. **Home Rule**) in a movement campaigning for autonomy for Ireland under the British Crown, 1870–1914. The campaign was one of the dominant forces in British politics in the late 19th and early 20th c., particularly in that the Irish nationalists, under Parnell and later Redmond, frequently held the balance of power in the House of Commons. After Gladstone's conversion in 1885 the Liberal Party supported Home Rule, but the Conservatives, joined by the Unionists, continued to oppose it. The situation was complicated by the opposition to Home Rule of the Ulster Unionists on one side and Sinn Fein on the other. Although a Home Rule Act was finally passed in 1914 it was suspended because of the First World War, the onset of which probably prevented, as least for a time, civil war breaking out in Ireland.

homesick /ˈhəʊmsɪk/ adj. depressed by longing for one's home during absence from it. □□ **homesickness** n.

homespun /ˈhəʊmspʌn/ adj. & n. —adj. **1 a** (of cloth) made of yarn spun at home. **b** (of yarn) spun at home. **2** plain, simple, unsophisticated, homely. —n. **1** homespun cloth. **2** anything plain or homely.

homestead /ˈhəʊmsted, -stɪd/ n. **1** a house, esp. a farmhouse, and outbuildings. **2** *Austral.* & *NZ* the owner's residence on a sheep or cattle station. **3** *US* an area of land (usu. 160 acres) granted to a settler as a home. □□ **homesteader** n. [OE *hāmstede* (as HOME, STEAD)]

homestyle /ˈhəʊmstaɪl/ adj. *US* (esp. of food) of a kind made or done at home, homely.

homeward /ˈhəʊmwəd/ adv. & adj. —adv. (also **homewards** /-wədz/) towards home. —adj. going or leading towards home. □ **homeward-bound** (esp. of a ship) preparing to go, or on the way, home. [OE *hāmweard(es)* (as HOME, -WARD)]

homework /ˈhəʊmwɜːk/ n. **1** work to be done at home, esp. by a school pupil. **2** preparatory work or study.

homey /ˈhəʊmɪ/ adj. (also **homy**) (**homier, homiest**) suggesting home; cosy. □□ **homeyness** n. (also **hominess**).

homicide /ˈhɒmɪˌsaɪd/ n. **1** the killing of a human being by another. **2** a person who kills a human being. □□ **homicidal** /-ˈsaɪd(ə)l/ adj. [ME f. OF f. L *homicidium* (sense 1), *homicida* (sense 2) (HOMO man)]

homiletic /ˌhɒmɪˈletɪk/ adj. & n. —adj. of homilies. —n. (usu. in pl.) the art of preaching. [LL *homileticus* f. Gk *homilētikos* f. *homileō* hold converse, consort (as HOMILY)]

homiliary /həˈmɪlɪərɪ/ n. (pl. **-ies**) a book of homilies. [med.L *homeliarius* (as HOMILY)]

homily /ˈhɒmɪlɪ/ n. (pl. **-ies**) **1** a sermon. **2** a tedious moralizing discourse. □□ **homilist** n. [ME f. OF *omelie* f. eccl.L *homilia* f. Gk *homilia* f. *homilos* crowd]

homing /ˈhəʊmɪŋ/ attrib.adj. **1** (of a pigeon) trained to fly home, bred for long-distance racing. **2** (of a device) for guiding to a target etc. **3** that goes home. □ **homing instinct** the instinct of certain animals to return to the territory from which they have been moved.

hominid /ˈhɒmɪnɪd/ n. & adj. —n. any member of the primate family Hominidae, including humans and their fossil ancestors. —adj. of or relating to this family. [mod.L *Hominidae* f. L *homo hominis* man]

hominoid /ˈhɒmɪˌnɔɪd/ adj. & n. —adj. **1** like a human. **2** hominid or pongid. —n. an animal resembling a human.

hominy /ˈhɒmɪnɪ/ n. esp. *US* coarsely ground maize kernels esp. boiled with water or milk. [Algonquian]

Homo /ˈhəʊməʊ, ˈhɒməʊ/ n. any primate of the genus *Homo* of which we (*Homo sapiens sapiens*) are the modern representatives. The genus *Homo* has now been in existence for c.2 million years, while our species, including the archaic *H. sapiens*, has occupied only the last 80,000 years or so, *H. habilis* 2.1/1.7–c.1.5 million

years BP, *H. erectus* 1.5 million years to c.80,000 years BP, and *H. sapiens* c.80,000 years BP to the present. The genus appears to have begun in East Africa with the advent of *H. habilis*, from Olduvai Gorge, Tanzania, and an as yet undifferentiated species from Koobi Fora, Kenya. It is believed that this or some other early species of *Homo* diverged from the Australopithecines more than two million years ago. This divergence is most readily seen in the fossil record where significant differences in the cranial and post-cranial skeleton can be observed. What is not so easily seen, though of equal significance, is the emergence and/or further development of social and cultural traits that we commonly view as human. With respect to material culture, only members of the genus *Homo* can be confidently shown to have made and used stone and bone tools and to have the controlled use of fire. These extra-personal aids enabled *Homo* (*H. erectus*) to radiate out from East Africa to the more varied environments of the remainder of the Old World to produce a distribution of individuals far greater than that of the earlier Australopithecines. The principal trends within the genus *Homo* through time can be summarized thus: an increase in brain size and complexity, an increase in the complexity of culture and social relationships, and the increasing ability to modify the environment. [L, = man]

homo /ˈhəʊməʊ/ n. (pl. **-os**) *colloq.* a homosexual. [abbr.]

homo- /ˈhəʊməʊ, ˈhɒməʊ/ comb. form same (often opp. HETERO-). [Gk *homos* same]

homocentric /ˌhəʊməʊˈsentrɪk, ˌhɒməʊ-/ adj. having the same centre.

homoeopath /ˈhəʊmɪəʊˌpæθ, ˈhɒmɪ-/ n. (*US* **homeopath**) a person who practises homoeopathy. [G *Homöopath* (as HOMOEOPATHY)]

homoeopathy /ˌhəʊmɪˈɒpəθɪ, ˌhɒmɪ-/ n. (*US* **homeopathy**) the treatment of disease by minute doses of drugs that in a healthy person would produce symptoms like those of the disease (cf. ALLOPATHY). The practice is based on the theory that 'like cures like', an idea known to the Greeks and Romans but first given definite expression by Samuel Hahnemann (1755–1843), a German physician and chemist who had become dissatisfied with orthodox medical teaching. He explained the success of his method by affirming that the drug induced a condition which displaced the disease; some of his followers maintained that the drugs stimulated the body's protective responses to the disease and thereby quickened its natural healing power. Homoeopathy made converts throughout Europe in the early 19th c. and was introduced into the US, but with advances in medicine and related sciences its influence diminished, though the practice still has its supporters. □□ **homoeopathic** /-ˈpæθɪk/ adj. **homoeopathist** n. [G *Homöopathie* f. Gk *homoios* like + *patheia* -PATHY]

homoeostasis /ˌhəʊmɪəʊˈsteɪsɪs, ˌhɒm-/ n. (*US* **homeostasis**) (pl. **-stases** /-siːz/) the tendency towards a relatively stable equilibrium between interdependent elements, esp. as maintained by physiological processes. □□ **homoeostatic** /-ˈstætɪk/ adj. [mod.L f. Gk *homoios* like + -STASIS]

homoeotherm /ˈhɒmɪəʊˌθɜːm/ n. (also **homoiotherm**) an organism that maintains its body temperature at a constant level, usu. above that of the environment, by its metabolic activity; a warm-blooded organism (cf. POIKILOTHERM). □□ **homoeothermal** /-ˈθɜːm(ə)l/ adj. **homoeothermic** /-ˈθɜːmɪk/ adj. **homoeothermy** n. [mod.L f. Gk *homoios* like + *thermē* heat]

homoerotic /ˌhəʊməʊɪˈrɒtɪk, ˌhɒməʊ-/ adj. homosexual.

homogametic /ˌhəʊməʊɡəˈmiːtɪk, ˌhɒməʊ-/ adj. *Biol.* (of a sex or individuals of a sex) producing gametes that carry the same sex chromosome.

homogamy /həˈmɒɡəmɪ/ n. *Bot.* **1** a state in which the flowers of a plant are hermaphrodite or of the same sex. **2** the simultaneous ripening of the stamens and pistils of a flower. □□ **homogamous** adj. [Gk *homogamos* (as HOMO-, *gamos* marriage)]

homogenate /həˈmɒdʒɪˌneɪt/ n. a suspension produced by homogenizing.

homogeneous /ˌhəʊməʊˈdʒiːnɪəs, ˌhɒməʊ-/ adj. **1** of the same kind. **2** consisting of parts all of the same kind; uniform. **3** *Math.*

containing terms all of the same degree. □□ **homogeneity** /-ˈdʒiːˈniːɪtɪ/ n. **homogeneously** adv. **homogeneousness** n. [med.L *homogeneus* f. Gk *homogenēs* (as HOMO-, *genēs* f. *genos* kind)]

homogenetic /ˌhɒʊməʊdʒɪˈnetɪk, ˌhɒmɒʊ-/ adj. Biol. having a common descent or origin.

homogenize /həˈmɒdʒɪˌnaɪz/ v. (also **-ise**) **1** tr. & intr. make or become homogeneous. **2** tr. treat (milk) so that the fat droplets are emulsified and the cream does not separate. □□ **homogenization** /-ˈzeɪʃ(ə)n/ n. **homogenizer** n.

homogeny /həˈmɒdʒɪnɪ/ n. Biol. similarity due to common descent. □□ **homogenous** adj.

homograft /ˈhɒməˌgrɑːft/ n. a graft of living tissue from one to another of the same species but different genotype.

homograph /ˈhɒməˌgrɑːf/ n. a word spelt like another but of different meaning or origin (e.g. POLE[1], POLE[2]).

homoiotherm var. of HOMOEOTHERM.

homoiousian /ˌhɒmɔɪˈuːsɪən, -ˈaʊsɪən/ n. hist. a person who held that God the Father and God the Son are of like but not identical substance (cf. HOMOOUSIAN). [eccl.L f. Gk *homoiousios* f. *homoios* like + *ousia* essence]

homolog US var. of HOMOLOGUE.

homologate /həˈmɒləˌgeɪt/ v.tr. **1** acknowledge, admit. **2** confirm, accept. **3** approve (a car, boat, engine, etc.) for use in a particular class of racing. □□ **homologation** /-ˈgeɪʃ(ə)n/ n. [med.L *homologare* agree f. Gk *homologeō* (as HOMO-, *logos* word)]

homologize /həˈmɒləˌdʒaɪz/ v. (also **-ise**) **1** intr. be homologous; correspond. **2** tr. make homologous.

homologous /həˈmɒləgəs/ adj. **1 a** having the same relation, relative position, etc. **b** corresponding. **2** Biol. (of organs etc.) similar in position and structure but not necessarily in function. **3** Biol. (of chromosomes) pairing at meiosis and having the same structural features and pattern of genes. **4** Chem. (of a series of chemical compounds) having the same functional group but differing in composition by a fixed group of atoms. [med.L *homologus* f. Gk (as HOMO-, *logos* ratio, proportion)]

homologue /ˈhɒməˌlɒg/ n. (US **homolog**) a homologous thing. [F f. Gk *homologon* (neut. adj.) (as HOMOLOGOUS)]

homology /həˈmɒlədʒɪ/ n. a homologous state or relation; correspondence. □□ **homological** /ˌhɒməˈlɒdʒɪk(ə)l/ adj.

homomorphic /ˌhɒʊməʊˈmɔːfɪk, ˌhɒmɒʊ-/ adj. (also **homomorphous**) of the same or similar form. □□ **homomorphically** adv. **homomorphism** n. **homomorphy** n.

homonym /ˈhɒmənɪm/ n. **1** a word of the same spelling or sound as another but of different meaning; a homograph or homophone. **2** a namesake. □□ **homonymic** /-ˈnɪmɪk/ adj. **homonymous** /həˈmɒnɪməs/ adj. [L *homonymum* f. Gk *homōnumon* (neut. adj.) (as HOMO-, *onoma* name)]

homoousian /ˌhɒməʊˈuːsɪən, ˌhɒʊm-, -ˈaʊsɪən/ n. (also **homousian** /hɒˈmuː-, hɒˈmaʊ-/) hist. a person who held that God the Father and God the Son are of the same substance (cf. HOMOIOUSIAN). [eccl.L *homoousianus* f. LL *homousius* f. Gk *homoousios* (as HOMO-, *ousia* essence)]

homophobia /ˌhɒʊməˈfəʊbɪə/ n. a hatred or fear of homosexuals. □□ **homophobe** /ˈhɒʊm-/ n. **homophobic** /-ˈfəʊbɪk/ adj.

homophone /ˈhɒməˌfəʊn/ n. **1** a word having the same sound as another but of different meaning or origin (e.g. *pair*, *pear*). **2** a symbol denoting the same sound as another.

homophonic /ˌhɒməˈfɒnɪk/ adj. Mus. in unison; characterized by movement of all parts to the same melody. □□ **homophonically** adv.

homophonous /həˈmɒfənəs/ adj. **1** (of music) homophonic. **2** (of a word or symbol) that is a homophone. □□ **homophony** n.

homopolar /ˌhɒʊməʊˈpəʊlə(r), ˌhɒmɒʊ-/ adj. **1** electrically symmetrical. **2** Electr. (of a generator) producing direct current without the use of commutators. **3** Chem. (of a covalent bond) in which one atom supplies both electrons.

homopteran /həˈmɒptərən/ n. any insect of the suborder Homoptera, including aphids and cicadas, with wings of uniform texture (cf. HETEROPTERAN). □□ **homopterous** adj. [HOMO- + Gk *pteron* wing]

Homo sapiens /ˌhəʊməʊ ˈsæpɪenz/ n. modern humans regarded as a species. (See HOMO.) [L, = wise man]

homosexual /ˌhəʊməʊˈseksjʊəl, ˌhɒm-/ adj. & n. —adj. **1** feeling or involving sexual attraction only to persons of the same sex. **2** concerning homosexual relations or people. **3** relating to the same sex. —n. a homosexual person. □□ **homosexuality** /-ˈælɪtɪ/ n. **homosexually** adv.

homousian var. of HOMOOUSIAN.

homozygote /ˌhəʊməʊˈzaɪgəʊt, ˌhɒmɒʊ-/ n. Biol. **1** an individual with identical alleles determining a particular characteristic. **2** an individual that is homozygous and so breeds true. □□ **homozygous** adj.

Homs /hɒms, -z/ an industrial city of west central Syria; pop. (1981) 354,500. Known in ancient times as Emesa, it lay at the junction of north–south and east–west trade routes. It was the birthplace of the emperor Elagabalus (see entry), and was the site of Zenobia's defeat by Aurelian (272).

homunculus /həˈmʌŋkjʊləs/ n. (also **homuncule** /-kjuːl/) (pl. **homunculi** /-ˌlaɪ/ or **homuncules**) a little man, a manikin. [L *homunculus* f. *homo* -*minis* man]

homy var. of HOMEY.

Hon. abbr. **1** Honorary. **2** Honourable.

hon /hʌn/ n. colloq. = HONEY 5. [abbr.]

Honan see HENAN.

honcho /ˈhɒntʃəʊ/ n. & v. US sl. —n. (pl. **-os**) **1** a leader or manager, the person in charge. **2** an admirable man. —v.tr. (**-oes, -oed**) be in charge of, oversee. [Jap. *han'chō* group leader]

Honduras /hɒnˈdjʊrəs/ a country of Central America, between Guatemala and Nicaragua; pop. (est. 1988) 4,972,300; official language, Spanish; capital, Tegucigalpa. Discovered by Columbus in 1502, for nearly three centuries until the proclamation of independence in 1821 Honduras was a dependency of Spain. Much of the country is mountainous and there are extensive pine-forests; its principal exports are bananas and coffee. □□ **Honduran** adj. & n.

hone /həʊn/ n. & v. —n. **1** a whetstone, esp. for razors. **2** any of various stones used as material for this. —v.tr. sharpen on or as on a hone. [OE *hān* stone f. Gmc]

Honegger /ˈɒnegə(r)/, Arthur (1892–1955), Swiss composer who lived and worked in Paris, a somewhat uneasy member of the group of advanced composers know as Les Six, since he was influenced as much by the German Romantics as by Satie and Cocteau. His representation of a steam-engine in *Pacific 231* (1923) brought him his first major success, and his dramatic oratorio *Jeanne d'Arc au bûcher* (1934–5) achieves strong emotional power through its combination of speech and song.

honest /ˈɒnɪst/ adj. & adv. —adj. **1** fair and just in character or behaviour, not cheating or stealing. **2** free of deceit and untruthfulness, sincere. **3** fairly earned (an *honest living*). **4** (of an act or feeling) showing fairness. **5** (with patronizing effect) blameless but undistinguished (cf. WORTHY). **6** (of a thing) unadulterated, unsophisticated. —adv. colloq. genuinely, really. □ **earn** (or **turn**) **an honest penny** earn money fairly. **honest broker** a mediator in international, industrial, etc., disputes (orig. of Bismarck). **honest Injun** colloq. genuinely, really. **honest-to-God** (or **-goodness**) colloq. adj. genuine, real. —adv. genuinely, really. **make an honest woman of** colloq. marry (esp. a pregnant woman). [ME f. OF (*h*)*oneste* f. L *honestus* f. *honos* HONOUR]

honestly /ˈɒnɪstlɪ/ adv. **1** in an honest way. **2** really (I *don't honestly know*; *honestly, the cheek of it!*).

honesty /ˈɒnɪstɪ/ n. **1** being honest. **2** truthfulness. **3** a plant of the genus *Lunaria* with purple or white flowers, so called from its flat round semi-transparent seed-pods. [ME f. OF (*h*)*onesté* f. L *honestas* -*tatis* (as HONEST)]

honey /ˈhʌnɪ/ n. (pl. **-eys**) **1** a sweet sticky yellowish fluid made by bees and other insects from nectar collected from flowers. **2** the colour of this. **3 a** sweetness. **b** a sweet thing. **4** a person or thing excellent of its kind. **5** esp. US (usu. as a form of address) darling, sweetheart. □ **honey-badger** a ratel. **honey-bee** any of various bees of the genus *Apis*, esp. the common hive-bee (*A.*

mellifera). **honey-bun** (or **-bunch**) (esp. as a form of address) darling. **honey-buzzard** any bird of prey of the genus *Pernis* feeding on the larvae of bees and wasps. **honey-eater** any Australasian bird of the family Meliphagidae with a long tongue that can take nectar from flowers. **honey-fungus** a parasitic fungus, *Armillaria mellea*, with honey-coloured edible toadstools. **honey-guide** 1 any small bird of the family Indicatoridae which feeds on beeswax and insects. 2 a marking on the corolla of a flower thought to guide bees to nectar. **honey-parrot** a lorikeet. **honey-pot** 1 a pot for honey. 2 a posture with the hands clasped under the hams. 3 something very attractive or tempting. **honey sac** an enlarged part of a bee's gullet where honey is formed. **honey-sweet** sweet as honey. [OE *hunig* f. Gmc]

honeycomb /ˈhʌnɪˌkəʊm/ n. & v. —n. 1 a structure of hexagonal cells of wax, made by bees to store honey and eggs. 2 a a pattern arranged hexagonally. b fabric made with a pattern of raised hexagons etc. 3 tripe from the second stomach of a ruminant. 4 a cavernous flaw in metalwork, esp. in guns. —v.tr. 1 fill with cavities or tunnels, undermine. 2 mark with a honeycomb pattern. [OE *hunigcamb* (as HONEY, COMB)]

honeydew /ˈhʌnɪˌdjuː/ n. 1 a sweet sticky substance found on leaves and stems, excreted by aphids. 2 a variety of melon with smooth pale skin and sweet green flesh. 3 an ideally sweet substance. 4 tobacco sweetened with molasses.

honeyed /ˈhʌnɪd/ adj. (also **honied**) 1 of or containing honey. 2 sweet.

honeymoon /ˈhʌnɪˌmuːn/ n. & v. —n. 1 a holiday spent together by a newly married couple. 2 an initial period of enthusiasm or goodwill. —v.intr. (usu. foll. by *in*, *at*) spend a honeymoon. □□ **honeymooner** n. [HONEY + MOON, orig. with ref. to waning affection, not to a period of a month]

honeysuckle /ˈhʌnɪˌsʌk(ə)l/ n. any climbing shrub of the genus *Lonicera* with fragrant yellow and pink flowers. [ME *hunisucche*, *-soukel*, extension of *hunisuce*, *-souke*, f. OE *hunigsūce*, *-sūge* (as HONEY, SUCK)]

Hong Kong /hɒŋ ˈkɒŋ/ a British dependency on the SE coast of China; pop. (est. 1988) 5,651,200; official languages, English and Chinese. It comprises Hong Kong island, ceded by China in 1841, the Kowloon peninsula, ceded in 1860, and the New Territories, additional areas of the mainland, leased for 99 years in 1898. By an agreement between the British and Chinese governments (signed in 1984), in 1997 China will resume sovereignty over Hong Kong which will then become a Special Administrative Region whose basic law will guarantee present systems and life-styles for a period of 50 years. Hong Kong is a major financial and manufacturing centre. Its container port is the third largest in the world.

Honiara /ˌhəʊnɪˈɑːrə/ the capital of the Solomon Islands, situated on the NW coast of the island of Guadalcanal; pop. (est. 1985) 26,000.

honied var. of HONEYED.

honk /hɒŋk/ n. & v. —n. 1 the cry of a wild goose. 2 the harsh sound of a car horn. —v. 1 intr. emit or give a honk. 2 tr. cause to do this. [imit.]

honky /ˈhɒŋkɪ/ n. (pl. **-ies**) US Black sl. offens. 1 a White person. 2 White people collectively. [20th c.: orig. unkn.]

honky-tonk /ˈhɒŋkɪˌtɒŋk/ n. colloq. 1 ragtime piano music. 2 a cheap or disreputable nightclub, dancehall, etc. [20th c.: orig. unkn.]

honnête homme /ˌɒneɪt ˈɒm/ n. an honest and decent man. [F]

Honolulu /ˌhɒnəˈluːluː/ the capital and principal port of Hawaii, situated on the SE coast of the island of Oahu; pop. (1982) 781,900.

honor US var. of HONOUR.

honorable US var. of HONOURABLE.

honorand /ˈhɒnəˌrænd/ n. a person to be honoured, esp. with an honorary degree. [L *honorandus* (as HONOUR)]

honorarium /ˌɒnəˈreərɪəm/ n. (pl. **honorariums** or **honoraria** /-rɪə/) a fee, esp. a voluntary payment for professional services rendered without the normal fee. [L, neut. of *honorarius*: see HONORARY]

honorary /ˈɒnərərɪ/ adj. 1 a conferred as an honour, without the usual requirements, functions, etc. (*honorary degree*). b holding such a title or position (*honorary colonel*). 2 (of an office or its holder) unpaid (*honorary secretaryship*; *honorary treasurer*). 3 (of an obligation) depending on honour, not legally enforceable. [L *honorarius* (as HONOUR)]

honorific /ˌɒnəˈrɪfɪk/ adj. & n. —adj. 1 conferring honour. 2 (esp. of Oriental forms of speech) implying respect. —n. an honorific form of words. □□ **honorifically** adv. [L *honorificus* (as HONOUR)]

honoris causa /ɒˌnɔːrɪs ˈkaʊzə/ adv. (esp. of a degree awarded without examination) as a mark of esteem. [L, = for the sake of honour]

honour /ˈɒnə(r)/ n. & v. (US **honor**) —n. 1 high respect; glory; credit, reputation, good name. 2 adherence to what is right or to a conventional standard of conduct. 3 nobleness of mind, magnanimity (*honour among thieves*). 4 a thing conferred as a distinction, esp. an official award for bravery or achievement. 5 (foll. by *of* + verbal noun, or *to* + infin.) privilege, special right (*had the honour of being invited*). 6 a exalted position. b (**Honour**) (prec. by *your*, *his*, etc.) a title of a circuit judge, US a mayor, and Ir. or in rustic speech any person of rank. 7 (foll. by *to*) a person or thing that brings honour (*she is an honour to her profession*). 8 a (of a woman) chastity. b the reputation for this. 9 (in *pl.*) a special distinction for proficiency in an examination. b a course of degree studies more specialized than for an ordinary pass. 10 a *Bridge* the ace, king, queen, jack, and ten, esp. of trumps, or the four aces at no trumps. b *Whist* the ace, king, queen, and jack, esp. of trumps. 11 *Golf* the right of driving off first as having won the last hole (*it is my honour*). —v.tr. 1 respect highly. 2 confer honour on. 3 accept or pay (a bill or cheque) when due. 4 acknowledge. □ **do the honours** perform the duties of a host to guests etc. **honour bright** colloq. = *on my honour*. **honour point** *Heraldry* the point halfway between the top of a shield and the fesse point. **honours are even** there is equality in the contest. **honours list** a list of persons awarded honours. **honours of war** privileges granted to a capitulating force, e.g. that of marching out with colours flying. **honour system** a system of examinations etc. without supervision, relying on the honour of those concerned. **honour-trick** = *quick trick*. **in honour bound** = *on one's honour*. **in honour of** as a celebration of. **on one's honour** (usu. foll. by *to* + infin.) under a moral obligation. **on** (or **upon**) **my honour** an expression of sincerity. [ME f. OF (*h*)*onor* (n.), *onorer* (v.) f. L *honor*, *honorare*]

honourable /ˈɒnərəb(ə)l/ adj. (US **honorable**) 1 a worthy of honour. b bringing honour to its possessor. c showing honour, not base. d consistent with honour. e colloq. (of the intentions of a man courting a woman) directed towards marriage. 2 (**Honourable**) a title indicating eminence or distinction, given to certain high officials, the children of certain ranks of the nobility, and MPs. □ **honourable mention** an award of merit to a candidate in an examination, a work of art, etc., not awarded a prize. □□ **honourableness** n. **honourably** adv. [ME f. OF *honorable* f. L *honorabilis* (as HONOUR)]

Hon. Sec. abbr. Honorary Secretary.

Honshu /hɒnˈʃuː/ the largest of the four main islands of Japan; pop. (1986) 97,283,000.

hooch /huːtʃ/ n. (also **hootch**) US colloq. alcoholic liquor, esp. inferior or illicit whisky. [abbr. of Alaskan *hoochinoo*, name of a liquor-making tribe]

Hood /hʊd/, Thomas (1799–1845), English poet and humorist, a friend of Lamb, Hazlitt, de Quincey, and other literary men. His serious poems include 'The Song of the Shirt', 'The Bridge of Sighs', 'The Dream of Eugene Aram', and 'The Plea of the Midsummer Fairies' (which includes 'I remember, I remember').

hood¹ /hʊd/ n. & v. —n. 1 a a covering for the head and neck, whether part of a cloak etc. or separate. b a separate hoodlike garment worn over a university gown or a surplice to indicate the wearer's degree. 2 *Brit.* a folding waterproof top of a motor car, pram, etc. 3 US the bonnet of a motor vehicle. 4 a canopy to protect users of machinery or to remove fumes etc. **5** the hoodlike part of a cobra, seal, etc. **6** a leather covering for a hawk's head. —*v.tr.* cover with a hood. □ **hood-mould** (or **-moulding**) *Archit.* a dripstone. □□ **hoodless** *adj.* **hoodlike** *adj.* [OE *hōd* f. WG, rel. to HAT]

hood[2] /hʊd, huːd/ *n. US sl.* a gangster or gunman. [abbr. of HOODLUM]

-hood /hʊd/ *suffix* forming nouns: **1** of condition or state (*childhood; falsehood*). **2** indicating a collection or group (*sisterhood; neighbourhood*). [OE *-hād*, orig. an independent noun, = person, condition, quality]

hooded /ˈhʊdɪd/ *adj.* having a hood; covered with a hood. □ **hooded crow** a piebald grey and black crow, *Corvus cornix*.

hoodie /ˈhʊdɪ/ *n.* = hooded crow.

hoodlum /ˈhuːdləm/ *n.* **1** a street hooligan, a young thug. **2** a gangster. [19th c.: orig. unkn.]

hoodoo /ˈhuːduː/ *n. & v. esp. US* —*n.* **1 a** bad luck. **b** a thing or person that brings or causes this. **2** voodoo. **3** a fantastic rock pinnacle or column of rock formed by erosion etc. —*v.tr.* (**hoodoos, hoodooed**) **1** make unlucky. **2** bewitch. [alt. of VOODOO]

hoodwink /ˈhʊdwɪŋk/ *v.tr.* deceive, delude. [orig. 'blindfold', f. HOOD[1] n. + WINK]

hooey /ˈhuːɪ/ *n. & int. sl.* nonsense, humbug. [20th c.: orig. unkn.]

hoof /huːf/ *n. & v.* —*n.* (*pl.* **hoofs** or **hooves** /-vz/) the horny part of the foot of a horse, antelope, and other ungulates. —*v.* **1** *tr.* strike with a hoof. **2** *tr.* kick or shove. □ **hoof it** *sl.* **1** go on foot. **2** dance. **on the hoof** (of cattle) not yet slaughtered. □□ **hoofed** *adj.* (also in *comb.*). [OE *hōf* f. Gmc]

hoofer /ˈhuːfə(r)/ *n. sl.* a professional dancer.

Hooghley /ˈhuːglɪ/ (also **Hugli**) the most westerly of the rivers of the Ganges delta, in West Bengal.

hoo-ha /ˈhuːhɑː/ *n. sl.* a commotion, a row; uproar, trouble. [20th c.: orig. unkn.]

hook /hʊk/ *n. & v.* —*n.* **1 a** a piece of metal or other material bent back at an angle or with a round bend, for catching hold of or for hanging things on. **b** (in full **fish-hook**) a bent piece of wire, usu. barbed and baited, for catching fish. **2** a curved cutting instrument (*reaping-hook*). **3 a** a sharp bend, e.g. in a river. **b** a projecting point of land (*Hook of Holland*). **c** a sand-spit with a curved end. **4 a** *Cricket & Golf* a hooking stroke (see sense 5 of *v.*). **b** *Boxing* a short swinging blow with the elbow bent and rigid. **5** a trap, a snare. **6 a** a curved stroke in handwriting, esp. as made in learning to write. **b** *Mus.* an added stroke transverse to the stem in the symbol for a quaver etc. **7** (in *pl.*) *sl.* fingers. —*v.* **1** *tr.* **a** grasp with a hook. **b** secure with a hook or hooks. **2** (often foll. by *on, up*) **a** *tr.* attach with or as with a hook. **b** *intr.* be or become attached with a hook. **3** *tr.* catch with or as with a hook (*he hooked a fish; she hooked a husband*). **4** *tr.* steal. **5** *tr.* **a** *Cricket* play (the ball) round from the off to the on side with an upward stroke. **b** (also *absol.*) *Golf* strike (the ball) so that it deviates towards the striker. **6** *tr. Rugby Football* secure (the ball) and pass it backward with the foot in the scrum. **7** *tr. Boxing* strike (one's opponent) with the elbow bent and rigid. □ **be hooked on** *sl.* be addicted to or captivated by. **by hook or by crook** by one means or another, by fair means or foul. **hook and eye** a small metal hook and loop as a fastener on a garment. **hook it** *sl.* make off, run away. **hook, line, and sinker** entirely. **hook-nose** an aquiline nose. **hook-nosed** having an aquiline nose. **hook-up** a connection, esp. an interconnection of broadcasting equipment for special transmissions. **off the hook 1** *colloq.* no longer in difficulty or trouble. **2** (of a telephone receiver) not on its rest, and so preventing incoming calls. **off the hooks** *sl.* dead. **on one's own hook** *sl.* on one's own account. **sling** (or **take**) **one's hook** *sl.* = hook it. □□ **hookless** *adj.* **hooklet** *n.* **hooklike** *adj.* [OE *hōc*: sense 3 of *n.* prob. influenced by Du. *hoek* corner]

hookah /ˈhʊkə/ *n.* an oriental tobacco-pipe with a long tube passing through water for cooling the smoke as it is drawn through. [Urdu f. Arab. *ḥuḳḳah* casket]

Hooke /hʊk/, Robert (1635–1703), English scientist, one of the most versatile of his age. In 1655 he became Boyle's assistant, and devised an improved air-pump for him. In 1662 he became the first curator of experiments of the recently founded Royal Society; after the Fire of London in 1666 he was made one of the surveyors to the City and also designed several of London's prominent buildings. His scientific achievements are many: he proposed an undulating theory of light, formulated the law of elasticity (Hooke's law—that the strain in a solid is proportional to the applied stress within the elastic limit of that solid), contributed to the study of fossils, introduced the term 'cell' to biology, postulated elliptical orbits for the earth and moon, and proposed the inverse-square of gravitation attraction which helped Newton to formulate his theory of universal gravitation applied to planetary motion. He improved and invented many scientific instruments: he stimulated the improvement of the compound microscope and reflecting telescope and invented, among other things, the wheel barometer, the balance-spring for watches, the universal or Hooke joint, a sounding instrument and sea-water sampler, and several meteorological instruments.

hooked /hʊkt/ *adj.* **1** hook-shaped (*hooked nose*). **2** furnished with a hook or hooks. **3** in senses of HOOK *v.* **4** (of a rug or mat) made by pulling woollen yarn through canvas with a hook.

Hooker /ˈhʊkə(r)/, Sir Joseph Dalton (1817–1911), English botanist who travelled widely and was a pioneer in plant geography. In 1839–43 he joined a voyage to the Antarctic, and concluded that the distribution of plants indicated an ancient joining of land between Australia and South America. From 1847 he spent three years in NE India, from which area he sent home a collection of rhododendrons and (through Kew Gardens) introduced their cultivation. Hooker was a firm friend and admirer of Charles Darwin, whose theories he supported and applied to the development of plants. His many works include *Genera Plantarum* (1862–83), a classification of plants devised jointly with George Bentham. In 1865 he became Director of the Botanic Gardens at Kew near London, succeeding his father Sir William Jackson Hooker (1785–1865), who had greatly extended the royal gardens there, founded a museum, and opened the gardens to the public.

hooker[1] /ˈhʊkə(r)/ *n.* **1** *Rugby Football* the player in the middle of the front row of the scrum who tries to hook the ball. **2** *sl.* a prostitute. **3** a person or thing that hooks.

hooker[2] /ˈhʊkə(r)/ *n.* **1** a small Dutch or Irish fishing-vessel. **2** *derog.* any ship. [Du. *hoeker* f. *hoek* HOOK]

hookey /ˈhʊkɪ/ *n.* (also **hooky**) *US* □ **blind hookey** a gambling guessing-game at cards. **play hookey** *sl.* play truant. [19th c.: orig. unkn.]

Hook of Holland (Dutch **Hoek van Holland**) a cape and port of The Netherlands, 15 km (9 miles) south-east of The Hague, linked by ferry to Harwich, Hull, and Dublin. Its Dutch name means 'corner of Holland'.

hookworm /ˈhʊkwɜːm/ *n.* **1** any of various nematode worms, with hooklike mouthparts for attachment and feeding, infesting humans and animals. **2** a disease caused by one of these, often resulting in severe anaemia.

hooligan /ˈhuːlɪɡən/ *n.* a young ruffian, esp. a member of a gang. □□ **hooliganism** *n.* [19th c.: orig. unkn.]

hoop /huːp/ *n. & v.* —*n.* **1** a circular band of metal, wood, etc., esp. for binding the staves of casks etc. or for forming part of a framework. **2 a** a ring bowled along by a child. **b** a large ring usu. with paper stretched over it for circus performers to jump through. **3** an arch of iron etc. through which the balls are hit in croquet. **4** *hist.* **a** a circle of flexible material for expanding a woman's petticoat or skirt. **b** (in full **hoop petticoat**) a petticoat expanded with this. **5 a** a band in contrasting colour on a jockey's blouse, sleeves, or cap. **b** *Austral. colloq.* a jockey. —*v.tr.* **1** bind with a hoop or hoops. **2** encircle with or as with a hoop. □ **be put** (or **go**) **through the hoop** (or **hoops**) undergo an ordeal. **hoop-iron** iron in long thin strips for binding casks etc. **hoop-la 1** *Brit.* a game in which rings are thrown in an attempt to encircle one of various prizes. **2** *sl.* commotion. **3** *sl.* pretentious nonsense. [OE *hōp* f. WG]

hoop[2] var. of WHOOP.

hoopoe /ˈhuːpuː/ *n.* a salmon-pink bird, *Upupa epops*, with black and white wings and tail, a large erectile crest, and a long decurved bill. [alt. of ME *hoop* f. OF *huppe* f. L *upupa*, imit. of its cry]

hooray /hʊˈreɪ/ *int.* **1** = HURRAH. **2** *Austral.* & *NZ* goodbye. □ **Hooray Henry** /ˈhuːreɪ/ *Brit. sl.* a rich ineffectual young man, esp. one who is fashionable, extroverted, and conventional. [var. of HURRAH]

hoosegow /ˈhuːsɡaʊ/ *n. US sl.* a prison. [Amer. Sp. *juzgao*, Sp. *juzgado* tribunal f. L *judicatum* neut. past part. of *judicare* JUDGE]

hoot /huːt/ *n.* & *v.* —*n.* **1** an owl's cry. **2** the sound made by a motor horn or a steam whistle. **3** a shout expressing scorn or disapproval; an inarticulate shout. **4** *colloq.* laughter. **a** laughter. **b** a cause of this. **5** (also **two hoots**) *sl.* anything at all (*don't care a hoot*; *don't give a hoot*; *doesn't matter two hoots*). —*v.* **1** *intr.* **a** (of an owl) utter its cry. **b** (of a motor horn or steam whistle) make a hoot. **c** (often foll. by *at*) make loud sounds, esp. of scorn or disapproval or *colloq.* merriment (*hooted with laughter*). **2** *tr.* **a** assail with scornful shouts. **b** (often foll. by *out*, *away*) drive away by hooting. **3** *tr.* sound (a motor horn or steam whistle). [ME *hūten* (v.), perh. imit.]

hootch var. of HOOCH.

hootenanny /ˈhuːtəˌnænɪ/ *n.* (*pl.* **-ies**) *US colloq.* an informal gathering with folk music. [orig. dial., = 'gadget']

hooter /ˈhuːtə(r)/ *n.* **1** *Brit.* a siren or steam whistle, esp. as a signal for work to begin or cease. **2** *Brit.* the horn of a motor vehicle. **3** *sl.* a nose. **4** a person or animal that hoots.

hoots /huːts/ *int. Sc.* & *N.Engl.* expressing dissatisfaction or impatience. [natural exclam.: cf. Sw. *hut* begone, Welsh *hwt* away, Ir. *ut* out, all in similar sense]

Hoover[1] /ˈhuːvə(r)/ *n.* & *v.* —*n. propr.* a vacuum cleaner (properly one made by the Hoover company, first patented in 1927). —*v.* (**hoover**) **1** *tr.* (also *absol.*) clean (a carpet etc.) with a vacuum cleaner. **2** (foll. by *up*) **a** *tr.* suck up with or as with a vacuum cleaner (*hoovered up the crumbs*). **b** *absol.* clean a room etc. with a vacuum cleaner (*decided to hoover up before they arrived*). [W. H. Hoover, Amer. manufacturer d. 1932]

Hoover[2] /ˈhuːvə(r)/, Herbert Clark (1874–1964), 31st President of the US, 1929–33. He earned a reputation as a humanitarian, organizing the production and distribution of foodstuffs in the US and Europe during and after the First World War, but during his Presidency he failed to prevent the Great Depression which followed the Stock Market crash of 1929. Long after his electoral defeat in 1932 he was a respected elder statesman, and became coordinator of the European Food Program (1947).

hooves pl. of HOOF.

hop[1] /hɒp/ *v.* & *n.* —*v.* (**hopped**, **hopping**) **1** *intr.* (of a bird, frog, etc.) spring with two or all feet at once. **2** *intr.* (of a person) jump on one foot. **3** *tr.* cross (a ditch etc.) by hopping. **4** *intr. colloq.* **a** make a quick trip. **b** make a quick change of position or location. **5** *tr. colloq.* **a** jump into (a vehicle). **b** obtain (a ride) in this way. **6** *tr.* (usu. as **hopping** n.) (esp. of aircraft) pass quickly from one (place of a specified type) to another (*cloud-hopping*; *hedge-hopping*). —*n.* **1** a hopping movement. **2** *colloq.* an informal dance. **3** a short flight in an aircraft; the distance travelled by air without landing; a stage of a flight or journey. □ **hop in** (or **out**) *colloq.* get into (or out of) a car etc. **hop it** *Brit. sl.* go away. **hopping mad** *colloq.* very angry. **hop, skip** (or **step**), **and jump** = *triple jump*. **hop the twig** (or **stick**) *sl.* **1** depart suddenly. **2** die. **on the hop** *colloq.* **1** unprepared (*caught on the hop*). **2** bustling about. [OE *hoppian*]

hop[2] /hɒp/ *n.* & *v.* —*n.* **1** a climbing plant, *Humulus lupulus*, cultivated for the cones borne by the female. **2** (in pl.) **a** the ripe cones of this, used to give a bitter flavour to beer. **b** *Austral.* & *NZ colloq.* beer. **3** *US sl.* opium or any other narcotic. —*v.* (**hopped**, **hopping**) **1** *tr.* flavour with hops. **2** *intr.* produce or pick hops. **3** *tr. US sl.* (foll. by *up*) stimulate with a drug. (esp. as **hopped up**). □ **hop-bind** (or **-bine**) the climbing stem of the hop. **hop-sack** (or **-sacking**) **1 a** a coarse material made from hemp etc. **b** sacking for hops made from this. **2** a coarse clothing fabric of a loose plain weave. [ME *hoppe* f. MLG, MDu. *hoppe*]

Hope /həʊp/, Bob (real name Leslie Townes Hope, 1903–), American comedian, born in Britain. His dry allusive style gave

him the character of a humorously cowardly incompetent, always cheerfully failing in his attempts to become a romantic hero, particularly in the series of *Road* films (1940–51), in which he starred with Bing Crosby and Dorothy Lamour.

hope /həʊp/ *n.* & *v.* —*n.* **1** (in *sing.* or *pl.*; often foll. by *of*, *that*) expectation and desire combined, e.g. for a certain thing to occur (*hope of getting the job*). **2 a** a person, thing, or circumstance that gives cause for hope. **b** ground of hope, promise. **3** what is hoped for. **4** *archaic* a feeling of trust. —*v.* **1** *intr.* (often foll. by *for*) feel hope. **2** *tr.* expect and desire. **3** *tr.* feel fairly confident. □ **hope against hope** cling to a mere possibility. **hope chest** *US* = *bottom drawer*. **not a** (or **some**) **hope!** *colloq.* no chance at all. □□ **hoper** *n.* [OE *hopa*]

hopeful /ˈhəʊpfʊl/ *adj.* & *n.* —*adj.* **1** feeling hope. **2** causing or inspiring hope. **3** likely to succeed, promising. —*n.* (in full **young hopeful**) **1** a person likely to succeed. **2** *iron.* a person likely to be disappointed. □□ **hopefulness** *n.*

hopefully /ˈhəʊpfʊlɪ/ *adv.* **1** in a hopeful manner. **2** *disp.* (qualifying a whole sentence) it is to be hoped (*hopefully, the car will be ready by then*).

Hopeh see HEBEI.

hopeless /ˈhəʊplɪs/ *adj.* **1** feeling no hope. **2** admitting no hope (*a hopeless case*). **3** inadequate, incompetent (*am hopeless at tennis*). □□ **hopelessly** *adv.* **hopelessness** *n.*

hophead /ˈhɒphed/ *n. sl.* **1** *US* a drug addict. **2** *Austral.* & *NZ* a drunkard.

Hopkins[1] /ˈhɒpkɪnz/, Sir Frederick Gowland (1861–1947), English biochemist, who in 1912 published an important paper giving precision to ideas about the existence of certain substances (now called vitamins) which are essential to the diet. For his work in the development of this concept he shared the Nobel Prize for medicine in 1929.

Hopkins[2] /ˈhɒpkɪnz/, Gerard Manley (1844–89), English poet. At Oxford he became influenced by Newman, was converted to Roman Catholicism in 1866, became a Jesuit, and renounced poetry until 1876. His most ambitious work 'The Wreck of the Deutschland', with 'Windhover' and 'Pied Beauty', is among his best-known poems. Hopkins developed his theories of natural beauty, using the terms 'inscape' (the individual or essential quality of the object) and 'instress' (the force of 'inscape' on the mind of the observer). A skilful innovator, he sought to unite the rhythm of his verse with the flow and varying emphasis of spoken language by using 'sprung rhythm' (a combination of regularity of stress patterns with freely varying numbers of syllables). His *Poems* were all published posthumously by his friend Robert Bridges in 1918. The great impact of his work on 20th-c. poets inspired a revival of poetic energy, seriousness, and originality.

hoplite /ˈhɒplaɪt/ *n.* a heavily-armed foot-soldier of ancient Greece. [Gk *hoplitēs* f. *hoplon* weapon]

hopper[1] /ˈhɒpə(r)/ *n.* **1** a person who hops. **2** a hopping arthropod, esp. a flea or cheese-maggot or young locust. **3 a** a container tapering downward (orig. having a hopping motion) through which grain passes into a mill. **b** a similar contrivance in various machines. **4 a** a barge carrying away mud etc. from a dredging-machine and discharging it. **b** a railway truck able to discharge coal etc. through its floor.

hopper[2] /ˈhɒpə(r)/ *n.* a hop-picker.

hopple /ˈhɒp(ə)l/ *v.* & *n.* —*v.tr.* fasten together the legs of (a horse etc.) to prevent it from straying etc. —*n.* an apparatus for this. [prob. LG: cf. HOBBLE and early Flem. *hoppelen* = MDu. *hobelen* jump, dance]

hopscotch /ˈhɒpskɒtʃ/ *n.* a children's game of hopping over squares or oblongs marked on the ground to retrieve a flat stone etc. [HOP[1] + SCOTCH[1]]

Horace /ˈhɒrəs/ (Quintus Horatius Flaccus, 65–8 BC), Roman poet born in southern Italy, the son of a freedman. Educated in Rome and Athens, he was pardoned after fighting for Brutus at the battle of Philippi, and was subsequently a star in the poetic circle of Maecenas. His works, frequently with an autobiographical element, include two books of hexameter *Satires* presenting the poet's reflections on life, literature, and morality,

æ cat ɑː arm e bed ɜː her ɪ sit iː see ɒ hot ɔː saw ʌ run ʊ put uː too ə ago aɪ my

four books of *Odes* (short lyric poems in a variety of metres), two books of hexameter *Epistles*, essays in a conversational letter form, one book of *Epodes*, and a hexameter didactic, the *Art of Poetry* (*Ars Poetica*).

horary /'hɔːrərɪ/ *adj. archaic* **1** of the hours. **2** occurring every hour, hourly. [med.L *horarius* f. L *hora* HOUR]

horde /hɔːd/ *n.* **1 a** usu. *derog.* a large group, a gang. **b** a moving swarm or pack (of insects, wolves, etc.). **2** a troop of Tartar or other nomads. [Pol. *horda* f. Turki *ordī, ordū* camp: cf. URDU]

horehound /'hɔːhaʊnd/ *n.* (also **hoarhound**) **1 a** a herbaceous plant, *Marrubium vulgare*, with a white cottony covering on its stem and leaves. **b** its bitter aromatic juice used against coughs etc. **2** a herbaceous plant, *Ballota nigra*, with an unpleasant aroma. [OE *hāre hūne* f. *hār* HOAR + *hūne* a plant]

horizon /hə'raɪz(ə)n/ *n.* **1 a** the line at which the earth and sky appear to meet. **b** (in full **apparent** or **sensible** or **visible** **horizon**) the line at which the earth and sky would appear to meet but for irregularities and obstructions; a circle where the earth's surface touches a cone whose vertex is at the observer's eye. **c** (in full **celestial** or **rational** or **true horizon**) a great circle of the celestial sphere, the plane of which passes through the centre of the earth and is parallel to that of the apparent horizon of a place. **2** limit of mental perception, experience, interest, etc. **3** a geological stratum or set of strata, or layer of soil, with particular characteristics. **4** *Archaeol.* the level at which a particular set of remains is found. □ **on the horizon** (of an event) just imminent or becoming apparent. [ME f. OF *orizon(te)* f. LL *horizon -ontis* f. Gk *horizōn* (*kuklos*) limiting (circle)]

horizontal /ˌhɒrɪ'zɒnt(ə)l/ *adj. & n.* —*adj.* **1 a** parallel to the plane of the horizon, at right angles to the vertical (*horizontal plane*). **b** (of machinery etc.) having its parts working in a horizontal direction. **2 a** combining firms engaged in the same stage of production (*horizontal integration*). **b** involving social groups of equal status etc. **3** of or at the horizon. —*n.* a horizontal line, plane, etc. □□ **horizontality** /-'tælɪtɪ/ *n.* **horizontally** *adv.* **horizontalness** *n.* [F *horizontal* or mod.L *horizontalis* (as HORIZON)]

hormone /'hɔːməʊn/ *n.* **1** *Biochem.* a regulatory substance produced in an organism and transported in tissue fluids such as blood or sap to stimulate cells or tissues into action. **2** a synthetic substance with a similar effect. □□ **hormonal** /-'məʊn(ə)l/ *adj.* [Gk *hormōn* part. of *hormaō* impel]

Hormuz /'hɔːmʊz/ an ancient city on an island at the mouth of the Persian Gulf, an important centre of commerce in the Middle Ages. □ **Strait of Hormuz** a strait separating Iran from the Arabian peninsula and linking the Persian Gulf with the Gulf of Oman which leads to the Arabian Sea, of strategic and economic importance as a waterway through which sea traffic to and from the oil-rich States of the Persian Gulf must pass.

horn /hɔːn/ *n. & v.* —*n.* **1 a** a hard permanent outgrowth, often curved and pointed, on the head of cattle, rhinoceroses, giraffes, and other esp. hoofed mammals, found singly, in pairs, or one in front of another. **b** the structure of a horn, consisting of a core of bone encased in keratinized skin. **2** each of two deciduous branched appendages on the head of (esp. male) deer. **3** a hornlike projection on the head of other animals, e.g. a snail's tentacle, the crest of a horned owl, etc. **4** the substance of which horns are composed. **5** anything resembling or compared to a horn in shape. **6** *Mus.* **a** = French horn. **b** a wind instrument played by lip vibration, orig. made of horn, now usu. of brass. (See below.) **c** a horn player. **7** an instrument sounding a warning or other signal (*car horn; foghorn*). **8** a receptacle or instrument made of horn, e.g. a drinking-vessel or powder-flask etc. **9** a horn-shaped projection. **10** the extremity of the moon or other crescent. **11 a** an arm or branch of a river, bay, etc. **b** (**the Horn**) Cape Horn. **12** a pyramidal peak formed by glacial action. **13** *coarse sl.* an erect penis. **14** the hornlike emblem of a cuckold. —*v.tr.* **1** (esp. as **horned** *adj.*) provide with horns. **2** gore with the horns. □ **horn in** *sl.* **1** (usu. foll. by *on*) intrude. **2** interfere. **Horn of Africa** the peninsula of NE Africa separating the Gulf of Aden from the main part of the Indian Ocean. It is also called the Somali Peninsula and comprises Somalia and parts of Ethiopia. **horn of plenty** a cornucopia. **horn-rimmed** (esp. of

spectacles) having rims made of horn or a substance resembling it. **on the horns of a dilemma** faced with a decision involving equally unfavourable alternatives. □□ **hornist** *n.* (in sense 6 of *n.*). **hornless** *adj.* **hornlike** *adj.* [OE f. Gmc, rel. to L *cornu*]

The horn of domesticated cattle, with the tip cut off (or, in Africa, with a central orifice cut) to leave a hole for blowing, has been used by herdsmen, watchmen, and huntsmen from time immemorial. Instruments of this kind were also made of bronze, ivory, and brass. In written music and among musicians the term 'horn' denotes the French horn (see FRENCH).

hornbeam /'hɔːnbiːm/ *n.* any tree of the genus *Carpinus*, with a smooth bark and a hard tough wood.

hornbill /'hɔːnbɪl/ *n.* any bird of the family Bucerotidae, with a hornlike excrescence on its large red or yellow curved bill.

hornblende /'hɔːnblend/ *n.* a dark-brown, black, or green mineral occurring in many igneous and metamorphic rocks, and composed of calcium, magnesium, and iron silicates. [G (as HORN, BLENDE)]

hornbook /'hɔːnbʊk/ *n. hist.* a leaf of paper containing the alphabet, the Lord's Prayer, etc., mounted on a wooden tablet with a handle, and protected by a thin plate of horn.

horned /hɔːnd/ *adj.* having a horn. □ **horned owl** an owl, *Bubo virginianus*, with hornlike feathers over the ears. **horned toad** **1** an American lizard, *Phrynosoma cornutum*, covered with spiny scales. **2** any SE Asian toad of the family Pelobatidae, with horn-shaped extensions over the eyes.

hornet /'hɔːnɪt/ *n.* a large wasp, *Vespa crabro*, with a brown and yellow striped body, and capable of inflicting a serious sting. □ **stir up a hornets' nest** provoke or cause trouble or opposition. [prob. f. MLG, MDu. *horn(e)te*, corresp. to OE *hyrnet*, perh. rel. to HORN]

hornpipe /'hɔːnpaɪp/ *n.* **1** a lively dance, usu. by one person (esp. associated with sailors). **2** the music for this. [name of an obs. wind instrument partly of horn: ME, f. HORN + PIPE]

hornstone /'hɔːnstəʊn/ *n.* a brittle siliceous rock.

hornswoggle /'hɔːnˌswɒg(ə)l/ *v.tr. sl.* cheat, hoax. [19th c.: orig. unkn.]

Hornung /'hɔːnʌŋ/, Ernest William (1866–1921), English novelist and writer of short stories, brother-in-law of Sir Arthur Conan Doyle. He is remembered as the creator of the gentleman burglar Raffles.

hornwort /'hɔːnwɜːt/ *n.* any aquatic rootless plant of the genus *Ceratophyllum*, with forked leaves.

horny /'hɔːnɪ/ *adj.* (**hornier, horniest**) **1** of or like horn. **2** hard like horn, callous (*horny-handed*). **3** *sl.* sexually excited. □□ **horniness** *n.*

horologe /'hɒrəlɒdʒ/ *n. archaic* a timepiece. [ME f. OF *orloge* f. L *horologium* f. Gk *hōrologion* f. *hōra* time + *-logos* -telling]

horology /hə'rɒlədʒɪ/ *n.* the art of measuring time or making clocks, watches, etc.; the study of this. □□ **horologer** *n.* **horologic** /ˌhɒrə'lɒdʒɪk/ *adj.* **horological** /ˌhɒrə'lɒdʒɪk(ə)l/ *adj.* **horologist** *n.* [Gk *hōra* time + -LOGY]

horoscope /'hɒrəskəʊp/ *n. Astrol.* **1** a forecast of a person's future based on a diagram showing the relative positions of the stars and planets at that person's birth. **2** such a diagram (*cast a horoscope*). **3** observation of the sky and planets at a particular moment, esp. at a person's birth. □□ **horoscopic** /-'skɒpɪk/ *adj.* **horoscopical** /-'skɒpɪk(ə)l/ *adj.* **horoscopy** /hə'rɒskəpɪ/ *n.* [F f. L *horoscopus* f. Gk *hōroskopos* f. *hōra* time + *skopos* observer]

Horowhenua /ˌhɔːrəʊhen'uːə/ an administrative region of North Island, New Zealand pop. (1986) 53,600; chief town, Levin.

Horowitz /'hɒrəvɪts/, Vladimir (1904–89), Russian-born pianist, who settled in the US, marrying Toscanini's daughter. His career as an international virtuoso of the highest rank was interrupted by bouts of illness.

horrendous /hə'rendəs/ *adj.* horrifying. □□ **horrendously** *adv.* **horrendousness** *n.* [L *horrendus* gerundive of *horrēre*: see HORRID]

horrent /'hɒrənt/ *adj. poet.* **1** bristling. **2** shuddering. [L *horrēre*: see HORRID]

horrible /'hɒrɪb(ə)l/ *adj.* **1** causing or likely to cause horror;

hideous, shocking. **2** *colloq.* unpleasant, excessive (*horrible weather; horrible noise*). □□ **horribleness** *n.* **horribly** *adv.* [ME f. OF (h)*orrible* f. L *horribilis* f. *horrēre*: see HORRID]

horrid /ˈhɒrɪd/ *adj.* **1** horrible, revolting. **2** *colloq.* unpleasant, disagreeable (*horrid weather; horrid children*). **3** *poet.* rough, bristling. □□ **horridly** *adv.* **horridness** *n.* [L *horridus* f. *horrēre* bristle, shudder]

horrific /həˈrɪfɪk/ *adj.* horrifying. □□ **horrifically** *adv.* [F *horrifique* or L *horrificus* f. *horrēre*: see HORRID]

horrify /ˈhɒrɪfaɪ/ *v.tr.* (**-ies, -ied**) arouse horror in; shock, scandalize. □□ **horrification** /-fɪˈkeɪʃ(ə)n/ *n.* **horrifiedly** /-ˌfaɪdlɪ/ *adv.* **horrifying** *adj.* **horrifyingly** *adv.* [L *horrificare* (as HORRIFIC)]

horripilation /ˌhɒrɪpɪˈleɪʃ(ə)n/ *n.* *literary* = *goose-flesh.* [LL *horripilatio* f. L *horrēre* to bristle + *pilus* hair]

horror /ˈhɒrə(r)/ *n. & adj.* —*n.* **1** a painful feeling of loathing and fear. **2 a** (often foll. by *of*) intense dislike. **b** (often foll. by *at*) *colloq.* intense dismay. **3 a** a person or thing causing horror. **b** *colloq.* a bad or mischievous person etc. **4** (in *pl.*; prec. by *the*) a fit of horror, depression, or nervousness, esp. as in delirium tremens. **5** a terrified and revolted shuddering. **6** (in *pl.*) an exclamation of dismay. —*attrib. adj.* (of literature, films, etc.) designed to attract by arousing pleasurable feelings of horror. □ **Chamber of Horrors** a place full of horrors (orig. a room of criminals etc. in Madame Tussaud's waxworks). **horror-struck** (or **-stricken**) horrified, shocked. [ME f. OF (h)*orrour* f. L *horror -oris* (as HORRID)]

Horsa /ˈhɔːsə/ see HENGIST.

hors concours /ˌɔːr kɔ̃ˈkʊə(r)/ *adj.* **1** unrivalled, unequalled. **2** (of an exhibit or exhibitor) not competing for a prize. [F, lit. 'outside competition']

hors de combat /ˌɔːr də ˈkɔ̃bɑː/ *adj.* out of the fight, disabled. [F]

hors-d'œuvre /ɔːˈdɜːvr, -ˈdɜːv/ *n.* an appetizer served at the beginning of a meal or (occasionally) during a meal. [F, lit. 'outside the work']

horse /hɔːs/ *n. & v.* —*n.* **1 a** a solid-hoofed plant-eating quadruped, *Equus caballus*, with flowing mane and tail, used for riding and to carry and pull loads. (See below.) **b** an adult male horse; a stallion or gelding. **c** any other four-legged mammal of the genus *Equus*, including asses and zebras. **d** (*collect.*; as *sing.*) cavalry. **e** a representation of a horse. **2** a vaulting-block. **3** a supporting frame esp. with legs (*clothes-horse*). **4** *sl.* heroin. **5** *colloq.* a unit of horsepower. **6** *Naut.* any of various ropes and bars. **7** *Mining* an obstruction in a vein. —*v.* **1** *intr.* (foll. by *around*) fool about. **2** *tr.* provide (a person or vehicle) with a horse or horses. **3** *intr.* mount or go on horseback. □ **from the horse's mouth** (of information etc.) from the person directly concerned or another authoritative source. **horse-and-buggy** *US* old-fashioned, bygone. **horse-block** a small platform of stone or wood for mounting a horse. **horse-brass** see BRASS. **horse-breaker** one who breaks in horses. **horse chestnut 1** any large ornamental tree of the genus *Aesculus*, with upright conical clusters of white or pink or red flowers. **2** the dark brown fruit of this (like an edible chestnut, but with a coarse bitter taste). **horse-cloth** a cloth used to cover a horse, or as part of its trappings. **horse-coper** a horse-dealer. **horse-doctor** a veterinary surgeon attending horses. **horse-drawn** (of a vehicle) pulled by a horse or horses. **Horse Guards 1** (in the UK) the cavalry brigade of the household troops. **2** the headquarters of such cavalry, esp. a building in Whitehall. **horse latitudes** a belt of calms in each hemisphere between the trade winds and the westerlies. The origin of the name is uncertain; some hold that it arose from the alleged practice of throwing overboard horses, which were being transported to America or the West Indies, when the ship's passage was unduly prolonged by lack of a favourable wind. **horse-mackerel** any large fish of the mackerel type, e.g. the scad or the tunny. **horse-mushroom** a large edible mushroom, *Agaricus arvensis*. **horse opera** *US sl.* a western film. **horse-pistol** a pistol for use by a horseman. **horse-pond** a pond for watering and washing horses, proverbial as a place for ducking obnoxious persons.

horse-race a race between horses with riders. **horse-racing** see separate entry. **horse sense** *colloq.* plain common sense. **horses for courses** the matching of tasks and talents. **horse's neck** *sl.* a drink of flavoured ginger ale usu. with spirits. **horse-soldier** a soldier mounted on a horse. **horse-trading 1** *US* dealing in horses. **2** shrewd bargaining. **to horse!** (as a command) mount your horses. □□ **horseless** *adj.* **horselike** *adj.* [OE *hors* f. Gmc]

The horse family is thought to have evolved in North America and spread to Asia and into Africa. During the ice age these animals provided human populations in Europe with an abundant source of food, but the effective domestication of horses there did not take place before the Bronze Age, by which time, paradoxically, they had become extinct in their country of origin until reintroduced by European settlers. There is some evidence that the horse was used for riding from *c*.4000 BC in the lands north of the Black Sea, but its most important use from *c*.19th c. BC was to draw the war chariots which gave mounted archers superiority over infantry bowmen. The use of cavalry dates from the Iron Age, when larger breeds of horses, capable of carrying mounted warriors, became available; spurs, and cheek-pieces attached to the bit, were introduced in this period and used to control the speed and direction of horses ridden in combat; stirrups reached Europe in the 6th–8th c. AD, having been known earlier in China and India. The new breeds of heavy horses found a use also in traction, and in medieval times became of economic as well as military importance, very gradually replacing the ox at cart and plough; from the 17th c. they were used to draw public conveyances. These animals were the heavy 'working' horses; introduction of Arab and Barbary blood for race-horses and hunters in the Stuart period changed the appearance of horses in Britain, and royal patronage of Newmarket greatly increased the popularity of horse-racing.

horseback /ˈhɔːsbæk/ *n.* the back of a horse, esp. as sat on in riding. □ **on horseback** mounted on a horse.

horsebean /ˈhɔːsbiːn/ *n.* a broad bean used as fodder.

horsebox /ˈhɔːsbɒks/ *n.* *Brit.* a closed vehicle for transporting a horse or horses.

horseflesh /ˈhɔːsfleʃ/ *n.* **1** the flesh of a horse, esp. as food. **2** horses collectively.

horsefly /ˈhɔːsflaɪ/ *n.* (pl. **-flies**) any of various biting dipterous insects of the family Tabanidae troublesome esp. to horses.

horsehair /ˈhɔːsheə(r)/ *n.* hair from the mane or tail of a horse, used for padding etc.

horseleech /ˈhɔːsliːtʃ/ *n.* **1** a large kind of leech feeding by swallowing not sucking. **2** an insatiable person (cf. Prov. 30: 15).

horseless /ˈhɔːslɪs/ *adj.* without a horse. □ **horseless carriage** *archaic* a motor car.

horseman /ˈhɔːsmən/ *n.* (pl. **-men**) **1** a rider on horseback. **2** a skilled rider.

horsemanship /ˈhɔːsmənʃɪp/ *n.* the art of riding on horseback; skill in doing this.

Horsens /ˈhɔːsənz/ a port of Denmark, situated at the head of Horsens Fiord on the east coast; pop. (1988) 54,800.

horseplay /ˈhɔːspleɪ/ *n.* boisterous play.

horsepower /ˈhɔːsˌpaʊə(r)/ *n.* (pl. same) **1** an imperial unit of power equal to 550 foot-pounds per second (about 750 watts). The term was introduced by James Watt, who modified Savery's method of estimating engine-power in terms of equivalent work done by horses. ¶ Abbr.: **hp**. **2** the power of an engine etc. measured in terms of this.

horse-racing *n.* the sport of conducting races between horses with riders. Its origin is lost in time; racing is attested in ancient Assyria by *c*.1500 BC. The first permanent racecourse with an annual fixture was established at Chester in 1540; by 1660 Charles II made Newmarket the headquarters, and 'Newmarket's glory rose, as Britain's fell'.

horseradish /ˈhɔːsˌrædɪʃ/ *n.* **1** a cruciferous plant, *Armoracia rusticana*, with long lobed leaves. **2** the pungent root of this scraped or grated as a condiment, often made into a sauce.

horseshoe /ˈhɔːʃʃuː, ˈhɔːsʃuː/ *n.* **1** an iron shoe for a horse shaped like the outline of the hard part of the hoof. **2** a thing of this shape; an object shaped like C or U (e.g. a magnet, a table, a Spanish or Islamic arch). □ **horseshoe crab** a large marine arthropod, *Xiphosura polyphemus*, with a horseshoe-shaped shell and a long tail-spine: also called *king-crab*.

horsetail /ˈhɔːsteɪl/ *n.* **1** the tail of a horse (formerly used in Turkey as a standard, or as an ensign denoting the rank of a pasha). **2** any cryptogamous plant of the genus *Equisetum*, like a horse's tail, with a hollow jointed stem and scale-like leaves. **3** = *pony-tail*.

horsewhip /ˈhɔːswɪp/ *n. & v.* —*n.* a whip for driving horses. —*v.tr.* (**-whipped, -whipping**) beat with a horsewhip.

horsewoman /ˈhɔːswʊmən/ *n.* (*pl.* **-women**) **1** a woman who rides on horseback. **2** a skilled woman rider.

horst /hɔːst/ *n. Geol.* a raised elongated block of land bounded by faults on both sides. [G, = heap]

Horst Wessel Song /hɔːst ˈves(ə)l/ the official song of the Nazi party in Germany. The tune was that of a music-hall song popular with the German army in the First World War; the words were written by Horst Wessel (1907–30), a member of Hitler's Storm Troops, killed by political enemies and regarded as a Nazi martyr.

horsy /ˈhɔːsɪ/ *adj.* (also **horsey**) (**horsier, horsiest**) **1** of or like a horse. **2** concerned with or devoted to horses or horse-racing. **3** affectedly using the dress and language of a groom or jockey. □□ **horsily** *adv.* **horsiness** *n.*

hortative /ˈhɔːtətɪv/ *adj.* (also **hortatory** /ˈhɔːtətərɪ/) tending or serving to exhort. □□ **hortation** /hɔːˈteɪʃ(ə)n/ *n.* [L *hortativus* f. *hortari* exhort]

hortensia /hɔːˈtensɪə/ *n.* a kind of hydrangea, *Hydrangea macrophylla*, with large rounded infertile flower heads. [mod.L f. *Hortense* Lepaute, 18th-c. Frenchwoman]

horticulture /ˈhɔːtɪˌkʌltʃə(r)/ *n.* the art of garden cultivation. □□ **horticultural** /-ˈkʌltʃər(ə)l/ *adj.* **horticulturist** /-ˈkʌltʃərɪst/ *n.* [L *hortus* garden, after AGRICULTURE]

hortus siccus /ˌhɔːtəs ˈsɪkəs/ *n.* **1** an arranged collection of dried plants. **2** a collection of uninteresting facts etc. [L, = dry garden]

Horus /ˈhɔːrəs/ *Egyptian Mythol.* originally a sky god (his eyes were the sun and the moon) whose symbol was the hawk ('Horus the Elder'). From early dynastic times he was regarded as the protector of the king and of the monarchy; his name is often added to the royal titles. He is usually depicted as a falcon-headed man. Horus assumed various aspects in different theologies: in the myth of Isis and Osiris he was the posthumous son of the latter, whose murder he avenged, and in this aspect was known to the Greeks as Harpocrates (= 'Horus the Child'), most often represented as a chubby infant with a finger held to his mouth.

Hos. *abbr.* Hosea (Old Testament).

hosanna /həʊˈzænə/ *n. & int.* a shout of adoration (Matt. 21: 9, 15, etc.). [ME f. LL f. Gk *hōsanna* f. Heb. *hôša'nā* for *hôší'a'nnā* save now!]

hose /həʊz/ *n. & v.* —*n.* **1** (also **hose-pipe**) a flexible tube conveying water for watering plants etc., putting out fires, etc. **2 a** (*collect.*; as *pl.*) stockings and socks (esp. in trade use). **b** *hist.* breeches (*doublet and hose*). —*v.tr.* **1** (often foll. by *down*) water or spray or drench with a hose. **2** provide with hose. □ **half-hose** socks. [OE f. Gmc]

Hosea /həʊˈzɪə/ **1** a Hebrew minor prophet of the 8th c. BC. **2** a book of the Old Testament containing his prophecies.

hosier /ˈhəʊzɪə(r), ˈhəʊʒə(r)/ *n.* a dealer in hosiery.

hosiery /ˈhəʊzɪərɪ, ˈhəʊʒərɪ/ *n.* **1** stockings and socks. **2** *Brit.* knitted or woven underwear.

hospice /ˈhɒspɪs/ *n.* **1** *Brit.* a home for people who are ill (esp. terminally) or destitute. **2** a lodging for travellers, esp. one kept by a religious order. [F f. L *hospitium* (as HOST²)]

hospitable /ˈhɒspɪtəb(ə)l, hɒˈspɪt-/ *adj.* giving or disposed to give welcome and entertainment to strangers or guests. □□ **hospitably** *adv.* [F f. *hospiter* f. med.L *hospitare* entertain (as HOST²)]

hospital /ˈhɒspɪt(ə)l/ *n.* **1** an institution providing medical and surgical treatment and nursing care for ill or injured people. **2** *hist.* **a** a hospice. **b** an establishment of the Knights Hospitallers. **3** *Law* a charitable institution (also in proper names, e.g. *Christ's Hospital*). □ **hospital corners** a way of tucking in sheets, used by nurses. **hospital fever** a kind of typhus formerly prevalent in crowded hospitals. **hospital ship** a ship to receive sick and wounded seamen, or to take sick and wounded soldiers home. **hospital train** a train taking wounded soldiers from a battlefield. [ME f. OF f. med.L *hospitale* neut. of L *hospitalis* (adj.) (as HOST²)]

hospitaler US var. of HOSPITALLER.

hospitalism /ˈhɒspɪtəˌlɪz(ə)m/ *n.* the adverse effects of a prolonged stay in hospital.

hospitality /ˌhɒspɪˈtælɪtɪ/ *n.* the friendly and generous reception and entertainment of guests or strangers. [ME f. OF *hospitalité* f. L *hospitalitas -tatis* (as HOSPITAL)]

hospitalize /ˈhɒspɪtəˌlaɪz/ *v.tr.* (also **-ise**) send or admit (a patient) to hospital. □□ **hospitalization** /-ˈzeɪʃ(ə)n/ *n.*

hospitaller /ˈhɒspɪtələ(r)/ *n.* (*US* **hospitaler**) **1** a member of a charitable religious order. (See KNIGHTS HOSPITALLERS.) **2** a chaplain (in some London hospitals). [ME f. OF *hospitalier* f. med.L *hospitalarius* (as HOSPITAL)]

host¹ /həʊst/ *n.* **1** (usu. foll. by *of*) a large number of people or things. **2** *archaic* an army. **3** (in full **heavenly host**) *Bibl.* **a** the sun, moon, and stars. **b** the angels. □ **host** (or **hosts**) **of heaven** = sense 3 of *n.* **is a host in himself** can do as much as several ordinary people. **Lord** (or **Lord God**) **of hosts** God as Lord over earthly or heavenly armies. [ME f. OF f. L *hostis* stranger, enemy, in med.L 'army']

host² /həʊst/ *n. & v.* —*n.* **1** a person who receives or entertains another as a guest. **2** the landlord of an inn (*mine host*). **3** *Biol.* an animal or plant having a parasite or commensal. **4** an animal or person that has received a transplanted organ etc. **5** the compère of a show, esp. of a television or radio programme. —*v.tr.* act as host to (a person) or at (an event). [ME f. OF *oste* f. L *hospes -pitis* host, guest]

host³ /həʊst/ *n.* the bread consecrated in the Eucharist. [ME f. OF (*h*)*oiste* f. L *hostia* victim]

hosta /ˈhɒstə/ *n.* any perennial garden plant of the genus *Hosta* (formerly *Funkia*) with green or variegated ornamental leaves and loose clusters of tubular mauve or white flowers. [mod.L, f. N. T. *Host*, Austrian physician d. 1834]

hostage /ˈhɒstɪdʒ/ *n.* **1** a person seized or held as security for the fulfilment of a condition. **2** a pledge or security. □ **a hostage to fortune** an acquisition, commitment, etc., regarded as endangered by unforeseen circumstances. □□ **hostageship** *n.* [ME f. OF (*h*)*ostage* ult. f. LL *obsidatus* hostageship f. L *obses obsidis* hostage]

hostel /ˈhɒst(ə)l/ *n.* **1** *Brit.* a house of residence or lodging for students, nurses, etc. **2** = *youth hostel*. **3** *archaic* an inn. [ME f. OF (*h*)*ostel* f. med.L (as HOSPITAL)]

hostelling /ˈhɒstəlɪŋ/ *n.* (*US* **hosteling**) the practice of staying in youth hostels, esp. while travelling. □□ **hosteller** *n.*

hostelry /ˈhɒstəlrɪ/ *n.* (*pl.* **-ies**) *archaic* or *literary* an inn. [ME f. OF (*h*)*ostelerie* f. (*h*)*ostelier* innkeeper (as HOSTEL)]

hostess /ˈhəʊstɪs/ *n.* **1** a woman who receives or entertains a guest. **2** a woman employed to welcome and entertain customers at a nightclub etc. **3** a stewardess on an aircraft, train, etc. (*air hostess*). [ME f. OF (*h*)*ostesse* (as HOST²)]

hostile /ˈhɒstaɪl/ *adj.* **1** of an enemy. **2** (often foll. by *to*) unfriendly, opposed. □ **hostile witness** *Law* a witness who appears hostile to the party calling him or her and therefore untrustworthy. □□ **hostilely** *adv.* [F *hostile* or L *hostilis* (as HOST¹)]

hostility /hɒˈstɪlɪtɪ/ *n.* (*pl.* **-ies**) **1** being hostile, enmity. **2** a state of warfare. **3** (in *pl.*) acts of warfare. **4** opposition (in thought etc.). [F *hostilité* or LL *hostilitas* (as HOSTILE)]

hostler /ˈɒslə(r)/ *n.* **1** = OSTLER. **2** *US* a person in charge of vehicles or machines, esp. railway engines, when they are not in use. [ME f. *hosteler* (as OSTLER)]

hot /hɒt/ *adj., v., & adv.* —*adj.* (**hotter, hottest**) **1 a** having a relatively or noticeably high temperature. **b** (of food or drink) prepared by heating and served without cooling. **2** producing the sensation of heat (*hot fever; hot flush*). **3** (of pepper, spices, etc.) pungent. **4** (of a person) feeling heat. **5 a** ardent, passionate, excited. **b** (often foll. by *for, on*) eager, keen (*in hot pursuit*). **c** angry or upset. **d** lustful. **e** exciting. **6 a** (of news etc.) fresh, recent. **b** *Brit. colloq.* (of Treasury bills) newly issued. **7** *Hunting* (of the scent) fresh and strong, indicating that the quarry has passed recently. **8 a** (of a player) very skilful. **b** (of a competitor in a race or other sporting event) strongly fancied to win (*a hot favourite*). **c** (of a hit, return, etc., in ball games) difficult for an opponent to deal with. **9** (of music, esp. jazz) strongly rhythmical and emotional. **10** *sl.* **a** (of goods) stolen, esp. easily identifiable and hence difficult to dispose of. **b** (of a person) wanted by the police. **11** *sl.* radioactive. **12** *colloq.* (of information) unusually reliable (*hot tip*). —*v.* (**hotted, hotting**) (usu. foll. by *up*) *Brit. colloq.* **1** *tr. & intr.* make or become hot. **2** *tr. & intr.* make or become active, lively, exciting, or dangerous. —*adv.* **1** angrily, severely (*give it him hot*). **2** eagerly. □ **go hot and cold** feel alternately hot and cold owing to fear etc. **have the hots for** *sl.* be sexually attracted to. **hot air** *sl.* empty, boastful, or excited talk. **hot-air balloon** a balloon (see BALLOON *n.* 2) consisting of a bag in which air is heated by burners located below it, causing it to rise. **hot blast** a blast of heated air forced into a furnace. **hot-blooded** ardent, passionate. **hot cathode** a cathode heated to emit electrons. **hot cross bun** see BUN. **hot dog** *n. colloq.* a hot sausage sandwiched in a soft roll. —*int.* *US sl.* expressing approval. **hot flush** see FLUSH[1]. **hot gospeller** see GOSPELLER. **hot line** a direct exclusive line of communication, esp. for emergencies. **hot metal** *Printing* using type made from molten metal. **hot money** capital transferred at frequent intervals. **hot potato** *colloq.* a controversial or awkward matter or situation. **hot-press** *n.* a press of glazed boards and hot metal plates for smoothing paper or cloth or making plywood. —*v.tr.* press (paper etc.) in this. **hot rod** a motor vehicle modified to have extra power and speed. **hot seat** *sl.* **1** a position of difficult responsibility. **2** the electric chair. **hot-short** (of metal) brittle in its hot state (cf. COLD-SHORT). **hot spot 1** a small region that is relatively hot. **2** a lively or dangerous place. **hot spring** a spring of naturally hot water. **hot stuff** *colloq.* **1** a formidably capable person. **2** an important person or thing. **3** a sexually attractive person. **4** a spirited, strong-willed, or passionate person. **5** a book, film, etc. with a strongly erotic content. **hot-tempered** impulsively angry. **hot under the collar** angry, resentful, or embarrassed. **hot war** an open war, with active hostilities. **hot water** *colloq.* difficulty, trouble, or disgrace (*be in hot water; get into hot water*). **hot-water bottle** (*US* **bag**) a container, usu. made of rubber, filled with hot water, esp. to warm a bed. **hot well 1** = *hot spring*. **2** a reservoir in a condensing steam engine. **hot-wire** operated by the expansion of heated wire. **like hot cakes** see CAKE. **make it** (or **things**) **hot for a person** persecute a person. **not so hot** *colloq.* only mediocre. □□ **hotly** *adv.* **hotness** *n.* **hottish** *adj.* [OE *hāt* f. Gmc: cf. HEAT]

hotbed /ˈhɒtbed/ *n.* **1** a bed of earth heated by fermenting manure. **2** (foll. by *of*) an environment promoting the growth of something, esp. something unwelcome (*hotbed of vice*).

hotchpotch /ˈhɒtʃpɒtʃ/ *n.* (also (esp. in sense 3) **hotchpot** /-pɒt/) **1** a confused mixture, a jumble. **2** a dish of many mixed ingredients, esp. a mutton broth or stew with vegetables. **3** *Law* the reunion and blending of properties for the purpose of securing equal division (esp. of the property of an intestate parent). [ME f. AF & OF *hochepot* f. OF *hocher* shake + POT[1]: *-potch* by assim.]

hotel /həʊˈtel/ *n.* **1** an establishment providing accommodation and meals for payment. **2** *Austral. & NZ* a public house. [F *hôtel*, later form of HOSTEL]

hotelier /həʊˈtelɪə(r)/ *n.* a hotel-keeper. [F *hôtelier* f. OF *hostelier*: see HOSTELRY]

hotfoot /ˈhɒtfʊt/ *adv., v., & adj.* —*adv.* in eager haste. —*v.tr.* hurry eagerly (esp. *hotfoot it*). —*adj.* acting quickly.

hothead /ˈhɒthed/ *n.* an impetuous person.

hotheaded /hɒtˈhedɪd/ *adj.* impetuous, excitable. □□ **hotheadedly** *adv.* **hotheadedness** *n.*

hothouse /ˈhɒthaʊs/ *n.* **1** a heated building, usu. largely of glass,

for rearing plants out of season or in a climate colder than is natural for them. **2** an environment that encourages the rapid growth or development of something.

hotplate /ˈhɒtpleɪt/ *n.* a heated metal plate etc. (or a set of these) for cooking food or keeping it hot.

hotpot /ˈhɒtpɒt/ *n.* a casserole of meat and vegetables, usu. with a layer of potato on top.

hotshot /ˈhɒtʃɒt/ *n. & adj. esp. US colloq.* —*n.* an important or exceptionally able person. —*adj.* (*attrib.*) important, able, expert, suddenly prominent.

hotspur /ˈhɒtspɜː(r)/ *n.* a rash person. [sobriquet of Sir H. Percy, d. 1403]

Hottentot /ˈhɒtəntɒt/ *n. & adj.* —*n.* (*pl.* same or **Hottentot**) **1** a member of a people now found chiefly in SW Africa, characterized by short stature, yellow-brown skin colour, and tightly curled hair, related to the Bushmen. They formerly occupied the region near the Cape but were largely dispossessed by Dutch settlers. **2** their language (also known as *Nama*), spoken in Namibia by about 50,000 people. It is characterized by a series of 'click' consonants made by drawing air into the mouth and clicking the tongue. —*adj.* of this people. [Afrik., perh. = stammerer, with ref. to their mode of pronunc.]

hottie /ˈhɒtɪ/ *n.* (also **hotty**) (*pl.* **-ies**) *colloq.* a hot-water bottle.

Houdini /huːˈdiːnɪ/, Harry (real name Eric Weiss, 1874–1926), American escapologist.

hough /hɒk/ *n. & v. Brit.* —*n.* **1** = HOCK[1]. **2** a cut of beef etc. from this and the leg above it. —*v.tr.* hamstring. □□ **hougher** *n.* [ME *ho(u)gh* = OE *hōh* (heel) in *hōhsinu* hamstring]

hoummus var. of HUMMUS.

hound /haʊnd/ *n. & v.* —*n.* **1 a** a dog used for hunting, esp. one able to track by scent. **b** (**the hounds**) *Brit.* a pack of foxhounds. **2** *colloq.* a despicable man. **3** a runner who follows a trail in hare and hounds. **4** a person keen in pursuit of something (usu. in *comb.: news-hound*). —*v.tr.* **1** harass or pursue relentlessly. **2** chase or pursue with a hound. **3** (foll. by *at*) set (a dog or person) on (a quarry). **4** urge on or nag (a person). □ **hound's tongue** *Bot.* a tall plant, *Cynoglossum officinale*, with tongue-shaped leaves. **hound's-tooth** a check pattern with notched corners suggestive of a canine tooth. **ride to hounds** go fox-hunting on horseback. □□ **hounder** *n.* **houndish** *adj.* [OE *hund* f. Gmc]

hour /aʊə(r)/ *n.* **1** a twenty-fourth part of a day and night, 60 minutes. **2** a time of day, a point in time (*a late hour; what is the hour?*). **3** (in *pl.* with preceding numerals in form 18.00, 20.30, etc.) this number of hours and minutes past midnight on the 24-hour clock (*will assemble at 20.00 hours*). **4 a** a period set aside for some purpose (*lunch hour; keep regular hours*). **b** (in *pl.*) a fixed period of time for work, use of a building, etc. (*office hours; opening hours*). **5** a short indefinite period of time (*an idle hour*). **6** the present time (*question of the hour*). **7** a time for action etc. (*the hour has come*). **8** the distance traversed in one hour by a means of transport stated or implied (*we are an hour from London*). **9** *RC Ch.* **a** prayers to be said at one of seven fixed times of day (*book of hours*). **b** any of these times. **10** (prec. by *the*) each time o'clock of a whole number of hours (*buses leave on the hour; on the half hour; at quarter past the hour*). **11** *Astron.* 15° of longitude or right ascension. □ **after hours** after closing-time. **hour-hand** the hand on a clock or watch which shows the hour. **hour-long** *adj.* lasting for one hour. —*adv.* for one hour. **till all hours** till very late. [ME *ure* etc. f. AF *ure*, OF *ore, eure* f. L *hora* f. Gk *hōra* season, hour]

hourglass /ˈaʊəˌglɑːs/ *n.* a reversible device with two connected glass bulbs containing sand that takes an hour to pass from the upper to the lower bulb.

houri /ˈhʊərɪ/ *n.* a beautiful young woman, esp. in the Muslim Paradise. [F f. Pers. *ḥūrī* f. Arab. *ḥūr* *pl.* of *ḥawrā'* gazelle-like (in the eyes)]

hourly /ˈaʊəlɪ/ *adj. & adv.* —*adj.* **1** done or occurring every hour. **2** frequent, continual. **3** reckoned hour by hour (*hourly wage*). —*adv.* **1** every hour. **2** frequently, continually.

house *n. & v.* —*n.* /haʊs/ (*pl.* /ˈhaʊzɪz/) **1 a** a building for human habitation. **b** (*attrib.*) (of an animal) kept in, frequenting, or infesting houses (*house-cat; housefly*). **2** a building for a special purpose (*opera-house*; *summer-house*). **3** a building for keeping animals or goods (*hen-house*). **4 a** a religious community. **b** the buildings occupied by it. **5 a** a body of pupils living in the same building at a boarding-school. **b** such a building. **c** a division of a day-school for games, competitions, etc. **6 a** a college of a university. **b** (**the House**) Christ Church, Oxford. **7 a** a family, esp. a royal family; a dynasty (*House of York*). **8 a** a firm or institution. **b** its place of business. **c** (**the House**) *Brit. colloq.* the Stock Exchange. **9 a** a legislative or deliberative assembly. **b** the building where it meets. **c** (**the House**) (in the UK) the House of Commons or Lords; (in the US) the House of Representatives. **10 a** an audience in a theatre, cinema, etc. **b** a performance in a theatre or cinema (*second house starts at 9 o'clock*). **c** a theatre. **11** *Astrol.* a twelfth part of the heavens. **12** (*attrib.*) living in a hospital as a member of staff (*house officer*; *house physician*; *house surgeon*). **13 a** a place of public refreshment, a restaurant or inn (*coffee-house*; *public house*). **b** (*attrib.*) (of wine) selected by the management of a restaurant, hotel, etc. to be offered at a special price. **14** *US* a brothel. **15** *Sc.* a dwelling that is one of several in a building. **16** *Brit. sl.* = HOUSEY-HOUSEY. **17** an animal's den, shell, etc. **18** (**the House**) *Brit. hist. euphem.* the workhouse. **19** (also **House**) house music (see separate entry). —*v.tr.* /haʊz/ **1** provide (a person, a population, etc.) with a house or houses or other accommodation. **2** store (goods etc.). **3** enclose or encase (a part or fitting). **4** fix in a socket, mortise, etc. □ **as safe as houses** thoroughly or completely safe. **house-agent** *Brit.* an agent for the sale and letting of houses. **house and home** (as an emphatic) home. **house arrest** detention in one's own house etc., not in prison. **house-broken** = *house-trained*. **house church 1** a charismatic church independent of traditional denominations. **2** a group meeting in a house as part of the activities of a church. **house-dog** a dog kept to guard a house. **house-father** a man in charge of a house, esp. of a home for children. **house-flag** a flag indicating to what firm a ship belongs. **house guest** a guest staying for some days in a private house. **house-hunting** seeking a house to live in. **house-husband** a husband who carries out the household duties traditionally carried out by a housewife. **house lights** the lights in the auditorium of a theatre. **house magazine** a magazine published by a firm and dealing mainly with its own activities. **house-martin** a black and white swallow-like bird, *Delichon urbica*, which builds a mud nest on house walls etc. **house-mother** a woman in charge of a house, esp. of a home for children. **house of cards 1** an insecure scheme etc. **2** a structure built (usu. by a child) out of playing cards. **House of Commons** (in the UK) the elected chamber of Parliament. **house of God** a church, a place of worship. **house of ill fame** *archaic* a brothel. **House of Keys** (in the Isle of Man) the elected chamber of Tynwald. **House of Lords 1** (in the UK) the chamber of Parliament composed of peers and bishops. **2** a committee of specially qualified members of this appointed as the ultimate judicial appeal court. **House of Representatives** the lower house of the US Congress and other legislatures. **house-parent** a house-mother or house-father. **house party** a group of guests staying at a country house etc. **house-plant** a plant grown indoors. **house-proud** attentive to, or unduly preoccupied with, the care and appearance of the home. **Houses of Parliament 1** the Houses of Lords and Commons regarded together. **2** the buildings where they meet. **house sparrow** a common brown and grey sparrow, *Passer domesticus*, which nests in the eaves and roofs of houses. **house style** a particular printer's or publisher's etc. preferred way of presentation. **house-to-house** performed at or carried to each house in turn. **house-trained** *Brit.* **1** (of animals) trained to be clean in the house. **2** *colloq.* well-mannered. **house-warming** a party celebrating a move to a new home. **keep** (or **make**) **a House** secure the presence of enough members for a quorum in the House of Commons. **keep open house** provide general hospitality. **keep to the house** (or **keep the house**) stay indoors. **like a house on fire 1** vigorously, fast. **2** successfully, excellently. **on the house** at the management's expense, free. **play house** play at being a family in its home. **put** (or **set**) **one's house in order** make necessary reforms. **set**

up house begin to live in a separate dwelling. □□ **houseful** *n.* (*pl.* **-fuls**). **houseless** *adj.* [OE *hūs, hūsian*, f. Gmc]

houseboat /ˈhaʊsbəʊt/ *n.* a boat fitted up for living in.

housebound /ˈhaʊsbaʊnd/ *adj.* unable to leave one's house through illness etc.

houseboy /ˈhaʊsbɔɪ/ *n.* a boy or man as a servant in a house.

housebreaker /ˈhaʊsˌbreɪkə(r)/ *n.* **1** a person guilty of house-breaking. **2** *Brit.* a person who is employed to demolish houses.

housebreaking /ˈhaʊsˌbreɪkɪŋ/ *n.* the act of breaking into a building, esp. in daytime, to commit a crime. ¶ In 1968 replaced as a statutory crime in English law by *burglary*.

housecarl /ˈhaʊskɑːl/ *n.* (also **housecarle**) *hist.* a member of the bodyguard of a Danish or English king or noble. [OE *húscarl* f. ON *húskarl* f. *hús* HOUSE + *karl* man: cf. CARL]

housecoat /ˈhaʊskəʊt/ *n.* a woman's garment for informal wear in the house, usu. a long dresslike coat.

housecraft /ˈhaʊskrɑːft/ *n.* *Brit.* skill in household management.

housefly /ˈhaʊsflaɪ/ *n.* any fly of the family Muscidae, esp. *Musca domestica*, breeding in decaying organic matter and often entering houses.

household /ˈhaʊshəʊld/ *n.* **1** the occupants of a house regarded as a unit. **2** a house and its affairs. **3** (prec. by *the*) (in the UK) the royal household. □ **household gods 1** gods presiding over a household, esp. the lares and penates. **2** the essentials of home life. **household troops** (in the UK) troops nominally employed to guard the sovereign. **household word** (or **name**) **1** a familiar name or saying. **2** a familiar person or thing.

householder /ˈhaʊsˌhəʊldə(r)/ *n.* **1** a person who owns or rents a house. **2** the head of a household.

housekeep /ˈhaʊskiːp/ *v.intr.* (*past* and *past part.* **-kept**) *colloq.* keep house.

housekeeper /ˈhaʊsˌkiːpə(r)/ *n.* **1** a person, esp. a woman, employed to manage a household. **2** a person in charge of a house, office, etc.

housekeeping /ˈhaʊsˌkiːpɪŋ/ *n.* **1** the management of house-hold affairs. **2** money allowed for this. **3** operations of maintenance, record-keeping, etc., in an organization.

houseleek /ˈhaʊsliːk/ *n.* a plant, *Sempervivum tectorum*, with pink flowers, growing on walls and roofs.

housemaid /ˈhaʊsmeɪd/ *n.* a female servant in a house, esp. in charge of reception rooms and bedrooms. □ **housemaid's knee** inflammation of the kneecap, often due to excessive kneeling.

houseman /ˈhaʊsmən/ *n.* (*pl.* **-men**) **1** *Brit.* a resident doctor at a hospital etc. **2** = HOUSEBOY.

housemaster /ˈhaʊsˌmɑːstə(r)/ *n.* (*fem.* **housemistress** /ˈhaʊsˌmɪstrɪs/) the teacher in charge of a house at a boarding-school.

house music *n.* a style of pop music typically featuring the use of drum machines, sampled sound effects, and prominent synthesized bass lines, combined with sparse repetitive vocals and a fast beat. The word *house* in its name is short for *Warehouse*, the name of a nightclub in Chicago where it was first played 1985. Created by disc jockeys and designed for dancing, it does away with meaningful lyrics. Its marked popularity in Britain during the late 1980s led to the proliferation of associated styles.

houseroom /ˈhaʊsruːm, -rʊm/ *n.* space or accommodation in one's house. □ **not give houseroom to** not have in any circumstances.

housetop /ˈhaʊstɒp/ *n.* the roof of a house. □ **proclaim** (or **shout** etc.) **from the housetops** announce publicly.

housewife /ˈhaʊswaɪf/ *n.* (*pl.* **-wives**) **1** a woman (usu. married) managing a household. **2** /ˈhʌzɪf/ a case for needles, thread, etc. □□ **housewifely** *adj.* **housewifeliness** *n.* [ME *hus(e)wif* f. HOUSE + WIFE]

housewifery /ˈhaʊsˌwɪfrɪ/ *n.* **1** housekeeping. **2** skill in this, housecraft.

housework /ˈhaʊswɜːk/ *n.* regular work done in housekeeping, e.g. cleaning and cooking.

housey-housey /ˌhaʊsɪˈhaʊsɪ, ˌhaʊzɪˈhaʊzɪ/ n. (also **housie-housie**) *Brit. sl.* a gambling form of lotto.

housing[1] /ˈhaʊzɪŋ/ n. **1 a** dwelling-houses collectively. **b** the provision of these. **2** shelter, lodging. **3** a rigid casing, esp. for moving or sensitive parts of a machine. **4** the hole or niche cut in one piece of wood to receive some part of another in order to join them. □ **housing estate** a residential area planned as a unit.

housing[2] /ˈhaʊzɪŋ/ n. a cloth covering put on a horse for protection or ornament. [ME = covering, f. obs. *house* f. OF *houce* f. med.L *hultia* f. Gmc]

Housman /ˈhaʊsmən/, Alfred Edward (1859–1936), English poet and classical scholar. Having failed at Oxford and spent ten years in obscurity as a clerk in the Civil Service, he afterwards became Professor of Latin at London University and then at Cambridge. His best poems are found in *A Shropshire Lad* (1896), a series of spare nostalgic verses largely based on ballad forms, and *Last Poems* (1922), in which he combines a classical simplicity with an underlying mood of pessimism and melancholy.

Houston /ˈhjuːst(ə)n/ an inland port of Texas, linked to the Gulf of Mexico by the Houston Ship Canal; pop. (1980) 1,595,138. Since 1961 it has been an important centre for space research and manned space-flight. The city is named after Samuel Houston (1793–1863), American politician and military leader who led the struggle to win control of Texas (1834–6) and make it part of the US.

hove *past* of HEAVE.

hovel /ˈhɒv(ə)l/ n. **1** a small miserable dwelling. **2** a conical building enclosing a kiln. **3** an open shed or outhouse. [ME: orig. unkn.]

hover /ˈhɒvə(r)/ v. & n. —*v.intr.* **1** (of a bird, helicopter, etc.) remain in one place in the air. **2** (often foll. by *about, round*) wait close at hand, linger. **3** remain undecided. —*n.* **1** hovering. **2** a state of suspense. □ **hover-fly** (*pl.* **-flies**) any fly of the family Syrphidae which hovers with rapidly beating wings. □□ **hoverer** n. [ME f. obs. *hove* hover, linger]

hovercraft /ˈhɒvəˌkrɑːft/ n. (*pl.* same) a vehicle or craft that travels over land or water on a cushion of air provided by a downward blast. A design was first patented by the English boat-designer, Christopher Cockerell, in 1955, and a hovercraft crossing of the English Channel was made on 25 July 1959, the 50th anniversary of Blériot's historic flight.

hoverport /ˈhɒvəˌpɔːt/ n. a terminal for hovercraft.

hovertrain /ˈhɒvəˌtreɪn/ n. a train that travels on a cushion of air like a hovercraft.

how[1] /haʊ/ adv., conj., & n. —*interrog. adv.* **1** by what means, in what way (*how do you do it?; tell me how you do it; how could you behave so disgracefully?; but how to bridge the gap?*). **2** in what condition, esp. of health (*how is the patient?; how do things stand?*). **3 a** to what extent (*how far is it?; how would you like to take my place?; how we laughed!*). **b** to what extent good or well, what . . . like (*how was the film?; how did they play?*). —*rel. adv.* in whatever way, as (*do it how you can*). —*conj. colloq.* that (*told us how he'd been in India*). —*n.* the way a thing is done (*the how and why of it*). □ **and how!** *sl.* very much so (chiefly used ironically or intensively). **here's how!** I drink to your good health. **how about 1** would you like (*how about a game of chess?*). **2** what is to be done about. **3** what is the news about. **how are you? 1** what is your state of health? **2** = *how do you do?* **how come?** see COME. **how do?** an informal greeting on being introduced to a stranger. **how do you do?** a formal greeting. **how-do-you-do** (or **how-d'ye-do**) n. (*pl.* **-dos**) an awkward situation. **how many** what number. **how much 1** what amount (*how much do I owe you?; did not know how much to take*). **2** what price (*how much is it?*). **3** (as *interrog.*) *joc.* what? ('*She is a hedonist.*' '*A how much?*'). **how now?** *archaic* what is the meaning of this? **how so?** how can you show that that is so? **how's that? 1** what is your opinion or explanation of that? **2** *Cricket* (said to an umpire) is the batsman out or not? [OE *hū* f. WG]

how[2] /haʊ/ int. a greeting used by N. American Indians. [perh. f. Sioux *háo*, Omaha *hau*]

Howard[1] /ˈhaʊəd/, Catherine (d. 1542), the fifth wife of Henry VIII. Thrust on the ailing and increasingly despotic king by her ambitious Howard relatives, Catherine, a flirtatious girl of nineteen, was soon in trouble over alleged infidelities. She went to the block in 1542 after only two years of marriage.

Howard[2] /ˈhaʊəd/, John (?1726–90), English philanthropist and prison reformer, who travelled all over the country unearthing abuses and scandals in the prison system, and extended his tours to Ireland and the Continent. His great work on the *State of Prisons in England and Wales* (1777) gave the initial impetus to the movement for improvement in the building and management of prisons.

howbeit /haʊˈbiːɪt/ adv. *archaic* nevertheless.

howdah /ˈhaʊdə/ n. a seat for two or more, usu. with a canopy, for riding on the back of an elephant or camel. [Urdu *hawda* f. Arab. *hawdaj* litter]

howdy /ˈhaʊdɪ/ int. *US* = how do you do? [corrupt.]

Howe /haʊ/, (1819–67), American inventor, who in 1846 patented a sewing-machine with an eyed needle to carry the upper thread and a shuttlelike holder for the lower thread. At first it was not a commercial success, but its principles were adapted by Singer and others, in violation of Howe's patent rights, and after litigation he was able to secure royalties. (See SEWING MACHINE.)

however /haʊˈevə(r)/ adv. **1 a** in whatever way (*do it however you want*). **b** to whatever extent, no matter how (*must go however inconvenient*). **2** nevertheless. **3** *colloq.* (as an emphatic) in what way, by what means (*however did that happen?*).

howitzer /ˈhaʊɪtsə(r)/ n. a short gun for high-angle firing of shells at low velocities. [Du. *houwitser* f. G *Haubitze* f. Czech *houfnice* catapult]

howl /haʊl/ n. & v. —*n.* **1** a long loud doleful cry uttered by a dog, wolf, etc. **2** a prolonged wailing noise, e.g. as made by a strong wind. **3** a loud cry of pain or rage. **4** a yell of derision or merriment. **5** *Electronics* a howling noise in a loudspeaker due to electrical or acoustic feedback. —*v.* **1** *intr.* make a howl. **2** *intr.* weep loudly. **3** *tr.* utter (words) with a howl. □ **howl down** prevent (a speaker) from being heard by howls of derision. [ME *houle* (v.), prob. imit.: cf. OWL]

howler /ˈhaʊlə(r)/ n. **1** *colloq.* a glaring mistake. **2** a S. American monkey of the genus *Alouatta*. **3** a person or animal that howls.

howling /ˈhaʊlɪŋ/ adj. **1** that howls. **2** *sl.* extreme (*a howling shame*). **3** *archaic* dreary (*howling wilderness*). □ **howling dervish** see DERVISH.

howsoever /ˌhaʊsəʊˈevə(r)/ adv. (also *poet.* **howsoe'er** /-ˈeə(r)/) **1** in whatsoever way. **2** to whatsoever extent.

Hoxha /ˈhɒdʒə/, Enver (1908–85), Albanian politician. A founder of the Albanian Communist Party, he became Prime Minister (1944–54) and thereafter first secretary of the Central Committee in a regime which he conducted on Stalinist principles.

hoy[1] /hɔɪ/ int. & n. —*int.* used to call attention, drive animals, or *Naut.* hail or call aloft. —*n. Austral.* a game of chance resembling bingo, using playing cards. [ME: natural cry]

hoy[2] /hɔɪ/ n. *hist.* a small vessel, usu. rigged as a sloop, carrying passengers and goods esp. for short distances. [MDu. *hoei, hoede*, of unkn. orig.]

hoy[3] /hɔɪ/ v.tr. *Austral. sl.* throw. [Brit. dial.: orig. unkn.]

hoya /ˈhɔɪə/ n. any climbing shrub of the genus *Hoya*, with pink, white, or yellow waxy flowers. [mod.L f. T. *Hoy*, Engl. gardener d. 1821]

hoyden /ˈhɔɪd(ə)n/ n. a boisterous girl. □□ **hoydenish** adj. [orig. = rude fellow, prob. f. MDu. *heiden* (= HEATHEN)]

Hoyle[1] /hɔɪl/ n. □ **according to Hoyle** adv. correctly, exactly. —*adj.* correct, exact. [E. *Hoyle*, Engl. writer on card-games d. 1769]

Hoyle[2] /hɔɪl/, Sir Fred (1915–), English astrophysicist, one of the proponents of the steady-state theory of the universe (see STEADY STATE). He also formulated theories about the origins of stars, of elements within the stars, and of life itself, for which he suggested an extraterrestrial origin. Hoyle is noted as a theorist and as a writer; his works include many scientific books and papers, works of popular science, and science fiction.

h.p. *abbr.* **1** horsepower. **2** hire purchase. **3** high pressure.

HQ *abbr.* headquarters.

HR *abbr.* US House of Representatives.

hr. *abbr.* hour.

HRH *abbr.* Her or His Royal Highness.

hrs. *abbr.* hours.

HSH *abbr.* Her or His Serene Highness.

HT *abbr.* high tension.

Huallaga /waːˈjɑːgə/ a river of Peru, one of the headwaters of the Amazon, rising near the Andean mining town of Cerro de Pasco. The remote upper river valley is one of the world's chief coca-growing regions.

Huambo /ˈwæmbəʊ/ the second-largest city in Angola, known as Nova Lisboa until 1978; pop. 62,000.

Huang He /wæŋ ˈhəʊ/ (also **Huang Ho**) the Yellow River (see entry).

hub /hʌb/ *n.* **1** the central part of a wheel, rotating on or with the axle, and from which the spokes radiate. **2** a central point of interest, activity, etc. □ **hub-cap** a cover for the hub of a vehicle's wheel. [16th c.: perh. = HOB¹]

Hubble /ˈhʌb(ə)l/, Edwin Powell (1889–1953), American astronomer, who in 1929 demonstrated the statement (known as Hubble's law) that the distance to a distant galaxy is directly proportional to its observed velocity of recession from us. Such a result is a natural consequence of a uniformly expanding universe, as predicted by the 'big bang' theory of cosmology, and implies that the age of the universe is inversely proportional to the constant of proportionality in the mathematical expression of the law. This constant (Hubble's constant) is uncertain to a factor of two, suggesting an age for the universe of between ten and twenty thousand million years.

hubble-bubble /ˈhʌb(ə)l,bʌb(ə)l/ *n.* **1** a rudimentary form of hookah. **2** a bubbling sound. **3** confused talk. [redupl. of BUBBLE]

hubbub /ˈhʌbʌb/ *n.* **1** a confused din, esp. from a crowd of people. **2** a disturbance or riot. [perh. of Ir. orig.: cf. Gael. *ubub* int. of contempt, Ir. *abú*, used in battle-cries]

hubby /ˈhʌbɪ/ *n.* (*pl.* **-ies**) *colloq.* a husband. [abbr.]

Hubei /huːˈbeɪ/ (also **Hupeh**) a province of east central China; pop. (est. 1986) 49,890,000; capital, Wuhan.

hubris /ˈhjuːbrɪs/ *n.* **1** arrogant pride or presumption. **2** (in Greek tragedy) excessive pride towards or defiance of the gods, leading to nemesis. □□ **hubristic** /-ˈbrɪstɪk/ *adj.* [Gk]

huckaback /ˈhʌkəˌbæk/ *n.* a stout linen or cotton fabric with a rough surface, used for towelling. [17th c.: orig. unkn.]

huckleberry /ˈhʌkəlˌberɪ/ *n.* (*pl.* **-ies**) **1** any low-growing N. American shrub of the genus *Gaylussacia*. **2** the blue or black soft fruit of this plant. [prob. alt. of *hurtleberry*, WHORTLEBERRY]

huckster /ˈhʌkstə(r)/ *n.* & *v.* —*n.* **1** a mercenary person. **2** US a publicity agent, esp. for broadcast material. **3** a pedlar or hawker. —*v.* **1** *intr.* bargain, haggle. **2** *tr.* carry on a petty traffic in. **3** *tr.* adulterate. [ME prob. f. LG: cf. dial. *huck* to bargain, HAWKER]

huddle /ˈhʌd(ə)l/ *v.* & *n.* —*v.* **1** *tr.* & *intr.* (often foll. by *up*) crowd together; nestle closely. **2** *intr.* & *refl.* (often foll. by *up*) coil one's body into a small space. **3** *tr. Brit.* heap together in a muddle. —*n.* **1** a confused or crowded mass of people or things. **2** *colloq.* a close or secret conference (esp. in **go into a huddle**). **3** confusion, bustle. [16th c.: perh. f. LG and ult. rel. to HIDE³]

Hudson /ˈhʌds(ə)n/, Henry (d. 1611), English explorer, discoverer of the North American bay, river, and strait which bear his name. He conducted two voyages in 1607–8 for the English Muscovy Company in search of the North-east Passage to Asia, reaching Greenland and Spitzbergen on the first and Novaya Zemlya on the second. In 1609 he explored the NE coast of America for the Dutch East Indies Company, sailing 240 km (150 miles) up the Hudson River to Albany. In 1610 he set out on his last voyage, again under English colours, and reached Hudson('s) Bay in the north of Canada. He attempted to winter in the Bay, but when food ran out his men mutinied and set him adrift in a small boat with a few companions—none of them were ever seen again.

Hudson's Bay Company a British colonial trading company. Created by Royal Charter in 1670, it was granted the lands draining into Hudson's Bay in northern Canada for purposes of commercial exploitation. The Company continued to control these lands, amalgamating with the rival North-West Company in 1821, for two centuries, finally handing them over to the new Canadian government in 1869. It is currently a retail organization with department stores in a number of Canadian cities, and in addition has large wholesale operations and extensive interests in the fur trade and oil trade.

Hué /hweɪ/ a city in central Vietnam; pop. (est.) 209,000.

hue /hjuː/ *n.* **1 a** a colour or tint. **b** a variety or shade of colour caused by the admixture of another. **2** the attribute of a colour by virtue of which it is discernible as red, green, etc. □□ **-hued** *adj.* **hueless** *adj.* [OE *hīew*, *hēw* form, beauty f. Gmc: cf. ON *hý* down on plants]

hue and cry /hjuː/ *n.* **1** a loud clamour or outcry. **2** *hist.* a proclamation for the pursuit and capture of a criminal. In former English law, such an outcry had to be raised by the inhabitants of a hundred in which a robbery had been committed, if they were not to become liable for the damages suffered by the victim. [AF *hu e cri* f. OF *hu* outcry (f. *huer* shout) + *e* and + *cri* cry. There is some ground for thinking that *hue* (as distinct from *cry*) originally meant inarticulate sound, including that of a horn or trumpet as well as of the voice.]

huff /hʌf/ *v.* & *n.* —*v.* **1** *intr.* give out loud puffs of air, steam, etc. **2** *intr.* bluster loudly or threateningly (*huffing and puffing*). **3** *intr.* & *tr.* take or cause to take offence. **4** *tr. Draughts* remove (an opponent's man that could have made a capture) from the board as a forfeit (orig. after blowing on the piece). —*n.* a fit of petty annoyance. □ **in a huff** annoyed and offended. □□ **huffish** *adj.* [imit. of the sound of blowing]

huffy /ˈhʌfɪ/ *adj.* (**huffier**, **huffiest**) **1** apt to take offence. **2** offended. □□ **huffily** *adv.* **huffiness** *n.*

hug /hʌg/ *v.* & *n.* —*v.* (**hugged**, **hugging**) **1** squeeze tightly in one's arms, esp. with affection. **2** (of a bear) squeeze (a person) between its forelegs. **3** keep close to (the shore, kerb, etc.). **4** cherish or cling to (prejudices etc.). **5** *refl.* congratulate or be pleased with (oneself). —*n.* **1** a strong clasp with the arms. **2** a squeezing grip in wrestling. □□ **huggable** *adj.* [16th c.: prob. f. Scand.: cf. ON *hugga* console]

huge /hjuːdʒ/ *adj.* **1** extremely large; enormous. **2** (of immaterial things) very great (*a huge success*). □□ **hugeness** *n.* [ME *huge* f. OF *ahuge*, *ahoge*, of unkn. orig.]

hugely /ˈhjuːdʒlɪ/ *adv.* **1** enormously (*hugely successful*). **2** very much (*enjoyed it hugely*).

hugger-mugger /ˈhʌgəˌmʌgə(r)/ *adj.*, *adv.*, *n.*, & *v.* —*adj.* & *adv.* **1** in secret. **2** confused; in confusion. —*n.* **1** secrecy. **2** confusion. —*v.intr.* proceed in a secret or muddled fashion. [prob. rel. to ME *hoder* huddle, *mokere* conceal: cf. 15th-c. *hoder moder*, 16th-c. *hucker mucker* in the same sense]

Hughes¹ /hjuːz/, Howard Robard (1905–76), American industrialist, aviator, and film producer. While still in his teens he took control of the Hughes Tool Company on his father's death, and in 1926, with an annual income estimated at two million dollars, he moved to Hollywood. His films include *Two Arabian Nights* (1928), *Hell's Angels* (1930), and *The Outlaw* (1941). He founded an aircraft company and used its profits to finance a medical institute, both bearing his family name, and broke a number of aviation records, sometimes while flying an aircraft of his own design. Hughes had bought stock that gave him a controlling interest in the company that became Trans World Airlines (TWA), but sold out in 1966 in the face of litigation. For the last twenty-five years of his life he lived as a recluse.

Hughes² /hjuːz/, Ted (1930–), English poet, whose wife was the American poet Sylvia Plath, whom he met at Cambridge University. His obsession with animals and his sense of the beauty and violence of the natural world appear in his first volume, *The Hawk in the Rain* (1957). In *Crow* (1970) Hughes retells the legends of creation and birth through the dark vision of the predatory, mocking, indestructible crow. His style is rough and forceful; his poetry is vital, original, at times excessively brutal with a stress on the physical and animal. He was appointed Poet Laureate in 1984.

Hugli see HOOGHLY.

Hugo /ˈhjuːgəʊ/, Victor-Marie (1802–85), the greatest French poet of the 19th c., novelist, and dramatist, the central figure of the Romantic movement in France. He spent the years 1851–70 in exile, mainly in Guernsey where he wrote his violent satire against Napoleon (*Les Châtiments*, 1853); after his return to Paris he became a senator of the Third Republic. Hugo brought a new freedom of subject, diction, and versification to French poetry; among his many collections are the spiritual and cosmic *Les Contemplations* (1856), *Les Orientales* (1829), and *Les Chants du crépuscule* (1835). Of his plays, the Preface of *Cromwell* (1827) became a manifesto of the Romantic movement, *Hernani* (1830) broke with dramatic conventions and won the day for the Romantics, and *Ruy Blas* (1838) continued his success in verse drama. *Notre Dame de Paris* (1831) and *Les Misérables* (1862) are among his best-known novels. National recognition came to him in the last years of his life, and he was buried in the Panthéon in Paris.

Huguenot /ˈhjuːgənəʊ, -ˌnɒt/ *n. hist.* a member of the Calvinist French Protestants *c.*1560, who were involved in almost continuous civil war with the Catholic majority and were a disruptive element even after full freedom of worship was granted by the Edict of Nantes (1598). When the edict was revoked in 1685 many Huguenots were forced to apostatize or flee from France. [F, assim. of *eiguenot* (f. Du. *eedgenot* f. Swiss G *Eidgenoss* confederate) to the name of a Geneva burgomaster *Hugues*]

huh /hə/ *int.* expressing disgust, surprise, etc. [imit.]

hula /ˈhuːlə/ *n.* (also **hula-hula**) a Polynesian dance performed by women, with flowing movements of the arms. □ **hula hoop** a large hoop for spinning round the body with hula-like movements. **hula skirt** a long grass skirt. [Hawaiian]

hulk /hʌlk/ *n.* **1 a** the body of a dismantled ship, used as a store vessel etc. **b** (in *pl.*) *hist.* this used as a prison. **2** an unwieldy vessel. **3** *colloq.* a large clumsy-looking person or thing. [OE *hulc* & MLG, MDu. *hulk*: cf. Gk *holkas* cargo ship]

hulking /ˈhʌlkɪŋ/ *adj. colloq.* bulky; large and clumsy.

Hull /hʌl/ (official name **Kingston-upon-Hull**) a city and port in Humberside, situated at the junction of the Hull and Humber rivers; pop. (1981) 268,000. It is linked to the south bank of the estuary by a suspension bridge completed in 1981.

hull[1] /hʌl/ *n. & v.* —*n.* the body or frame of a ship, airship, flying boat, etc. —*v.tr.* pierce the hull of (a ship) with gunshot etc. [ME, perh. rel. to HOLD[2]]

hull[2] /hʌl/ *n. & v.* —*n.* **1** the outer covering of a fruit, esp. the pod of peas and beans, the husk of grain, or the green calyx of a strawberry. **2** a covering. —*v.tr.* remove the hulls from (fruit etc.). [OE *hulu* ult. f. *helan* cover: cf. HELE]

hullabaloo /ˌhʌləbəˈluː/ *n.* (*pl.* **hullabaloos**) an uproar or clamour. [18th c.: redupl. of *hallo, hullo,* etc.]

hullo var. of HELLO.

hum[1] /hʌm/ *v. & n.* —*v.* (**hummed, humming**) **1** *intr.* make a low steady continuous sound like that of a bee. **2** *tr.* (also *absol.*) sing (a wordless tune) with closed lips. **3** *intr.* utter a slight inarticulate sound. **4** *intr. colloq.* be in an active state (*really made things hum*). **5** *intr. Brit. colloq.* smell unpleasantly. —*n.* **1 a** humming sound. **2** an unwanted low-frequency noise caused by variation of electric current, usu. the alternating frequency of the mains, in an amplifier etc. **3** *Brit. colloq.* a bad smell. □ **hum and haw** (or **ha**) hesitate, esp. in speaking. □□ **hummable** *adj.* **hummer** *n.* [ME, imit.]

hum[2] /həm/ *int.* expressing hesitation or dissent. [imit.]

human /ˈhjuːmən/ *adj. & n.* —*adj.* **1** of or belonging to the genus *Homo* (see entry). **2** consisting of human beings (*the human race*). **3** of or characteristic of mankind as opposed to God or animals or machines, esp. susceptible to the weaknesses of mankind (*is only human*). **4** showing (esp. the better) qualities of man (*proved to be very human*). —*n.* a human being. □ **human being** any man or woman or child of the species *Homo sapiens*, distinguished from other animals by superior mental development, power of articulate speech, and upright stance. **human**

chain a line of people formed for passing things along, e.g. buckets of water to the site of a fire. **human engineering 1** the management of industrial labour, esp. as regards man–machine relationships. **2** the study of this. **human equation** a bias or prejudice. **human interest** (in a newspaper story etc.) reference to personal experience and emotions etc. **human nature** the general characteristics and feelings of mankind. **human relations** relations with or between people or individuals. **human rights** rights held to be justifiably belonging to any person. □□ **humanness** *n.* [ME *humain(e)* f. OF f. L *humanus* f. *homo* human being]

humane /hjuːˈmeɪn/ *adj.* **1** benevolent, compassionate. **2** inflicting the minimum of pain. **3** (of a branch of learning) tending to civilize or confer refinement. □ **humane killer** an instrument for the painless slaughter of animals. □□ **humanely** *adv.* **humaneness** *n.* [var. of HUMAN, differentiated in sense in the 18th c.]

humanism /ˈhjuːməˌnɪz(ə)m/ *n.* **1** an outlook or system of thought concerned with human rather than divine or supernatural matters, or with the human race (not the individual), or with mankind as responsible intellectual beings. **2 a** a pragmatic system of thought, introduced by F. C. S. Schiller and William James, which emphasizes that people can comprehend and investigate only with the resources of the human mind, and discounts abstract theorizing. **b** the further theory that technological advance must be guided by awareness of widely understood human needs. **3** (often **Humanism**) literary culture, esp. the cultural movement of the Renaissance which turned away from medieval scholasticism (with its theological bias) to value the human achievement of the language, literature, and antiquities of ancient Rome (later of Greece). **4** humanitarianism.

humanist /ˈhjuːmənɪst/ *n.* **1** an adherent of humanism. **2** a humanitarian. **3** a student (esp. in the 14th–16th c.) of Roman and Greek literature and antiquities. □□ **humanistic** /-ˈnɪstɪk/ *adj.* **humanistically** /-ˈnɪstɪkəlɪ/ *adv.* [F *humaniste* f. It. *umanista* (as HUMAN)]

humanitarian /hjuːˌmænɪˈteərɪən/ *n. & adj.* —*n.* **1** a person who seeks to promote human welfare. **2** a person who advocates or practises humane action; a philanthropist. —*adj.* relating to or holding the views of humanitarians. □□ **humanitarianism** *n.*

humanity /hjuːˈmænɪtɪ/ *n.* (*pl.* **-ies**) **1 a** the human race. **b** human beings collectively. **c** the fact or condition of being human. **2** humaneness, benevolence. **3** (in *pl.*) human attributes. **4** (in *pl.*) learning or literature concerned with human culture, esp. the study of Latin and Greek literature and philosophy. [ME f. OF *humanité* f. L *humanitas -tatis* (as HUMAN)]

humanize /ˈhjuːməˌnaɪz/ *v.tr.* (also **-ise**) **1** make human; give a human character to. **2** make humane. □□ **humanization** /-ˈzeɪʃ(ə)n/ *n.* [F *humaniser* (as HUMAN)]

humankind /ˈhjuːmənˌkaɪnd/ *n.* human beings collectively.

humanly /ˈhjuːmənlɪ/ *adv.* **1** by human means (*I will do it if it is humanly possible*). **2** in a human manner. **3** from a human point of view. **4** with human feelings.

Humberside /ˈhʌmbəˌsaɪd/ a county of NE England; pop. (1981) 857,500; county town, Beverley.

humble /ˈhʌmb(ə)l/ *adj. & v.* —*adj.* **1 a** having or showing a low estimate of one's own importance. **b** offered with or affected by such an estimate (*if you want my humble opinion*). **2** of low social or political rank (*humble origins*). **3** (of a thing) of modest pretensions, dimensions, etc. —*v.tr.* **1** make humble; bring low; abase. **2** lower the rank or status of. □ **eat humble pie** make a humble apology; accept humiliation. □□ **humbleness** *n.* **humbly** *adv.* [ME *umble, humble* f. OF *umble* f. L *humilis* lowly f. *humus* ground: *humble* pie f. UMBLES]

humble-bee /ˈhʌmb(ə)lˌbiː/ *n.* = BUMBLE-BEE. [ME prob. f. MLG *hummelbē,* MDu. *hommel,* OHG *humbal*]

Humboldt /ˈhʌmbəʊlt/, Friedrich Heinrich Alexander, Baron von (1769–1859), German explorer and scientist who travelled for five years in Central and South America (1799–1804) and wrote extensively on natural history, meteorology, and physical

æ cat ɑː arm e bed ɜː her ɪ sit iː see ɒ hot ɔː saw ʌ run ʊ put uː too ə ago aɪ my

geography, financing his expeditions and scientific work out of his own pocket. During his travels in South America, accompanied by the French botanist Bonpland, he proved that the Amazon and Orinoco river systems are connected, and ascended to 5,877 m (19,280 ft.) in the Andes, the highest ascent ever made at that time. Returning to Europe in 1804, he settled in Paris and spent the next 20 years writing up the results of the collections and observations made during his travels. By 1827 Humboldt's private funds had almost run out and he returned to his birthplace, Berlin, serving in various capacities at the Prussian court. Towards the end of his life he wrote a popular work in several volumes, *Kosmos* (1845–62) describing the structure of the universe as it was then known. A kindly and liberal-minded man, Humboldt gave encouragement and financial assistance to students and young scientists and was also an early advocate of international scientific cooperation.

humbug /ˈhʌmbʌg/ n. & v. —n. **1** deceptive or false talk or behaviour. **2** an impostor. **3** *Brit.* a hard boiled sweet usu. flavoured with peppermint. —v. (**humbugged, humbugging**) **1** *intr.* be or behave like an impostor. **2** *tr.* deceive, hoax. □□ **humbuggery** n. [18th c.: orig. unkn.]

humdinger /ˈhʌmˌdɪŋə(r)/ n. *sl.* an excellent or remarkable person or thing. [20th c.: orig. unkn.]

humdrum /ˈhʌmdrʌm/ adj. & n. —adj. **1** commonplace, dull. **2** monotonous. —n. **1** commonplaceness, dullness. **2** a monotonous routine etc. [16th c.: prob. f. HUM¹ by redupl.]

Hume /hjuːm/, David (1711–76), Scottish philosopher and historian. His chief work *A Treatise of Human Nature* (1739/40) was followed by a number of essays and a *History of Great Britain* (1754–61) which was, in spite of its faults, the first great English history, written while he was librarian of the Advocates' Library in Edinburgh. He obtained a literary reputation and, because of that, some well-paid diplomatic appointments, including one in Paris in 1763–5. There he was well received by court and literary society, and befriended and brought back Rousseau to England, but the latter's suspicious and ungrateful nature led to a quarrel. For the rest of his life Hume lived in his native Edinburgh. Hume developed the empirical philosophy of Locke and Berkeley to its logical conclusion, and thereby made it incredible. He rejected the possibility of certainty in knowledge, finding in the mind only a series of sensations ('impressions'), and discounted the existing notion of causation: we are aware of events in pairs, but although we can observe that one constantly follows another we can never be certain that it must follow. A similar scepticism is apparent in his writings on religion.

humectant /hjuːˈmekt(ə)nt/ adj. & n. —adj. retaining or preserving moisture. —n. a substance, esp. a food additive, used to reduce loss of moisture. [L (h)umectant- part. stem of (h)umectare moisten f. umēre be moist]

humeral /ˈhjuːmər(ə)l/ adj. **1** of the humerus or shoulder. **2** worn on the shoulder. [F huméral & LL humeralis (as HUMERUS)]

humerus /ˈhjuːmərəs/ n. (pl. **humeri** /-ˌraɪ/) **1** the bone of the upper arm in man. **2** the corresponding bone in other vertebrates. [L, = shoulder]

humic /ˈhjuːmɪk/ adj. of or consisting of humus.

humid /ˈhjuːmɪd/ adj. (of the air or climate) warm and damp. □□ **humidly** adv. [F humide or L humidus f. umēre be moist]

humidifier /hjuːˈmɪdɪˌfaɪə(r)/ n. a device for keeping the atmosphere moist in a room etc.

humidify /hjuːˈmɪdɪˌfaɪ/ v.tr. (**-ies, -ied**) make (air etc.) humid or damp. □□ **humidification** /-fɪˈkeɪʃ(ə)n/ n.

humidity /hjuːˈmɪdɪtɪ/ n. (pl. **-ies**) **1** a humid state. **2** moisture. **3** the degree of moisture esp. in the atmosphere. □ **relative humidity** the proportion of moisture to the value for saturation at the same temperature. [ME f. OF humidité or L humiditas (as HUMID)]

humidor /ˈhjuːmɪˌdɔː(r)/ n. a room or container for keeping cigars or tobacco moist. [HUMID after cuspidor]

humify /ˈhjuːmɪˌfaɪ/ v.tr. & intr. (**-ies, -ied**) make or be made into humus. □□ **humification** /-fɪˈkeɪʃ(ə)n/ n.

humiliate /hjuːˈmɪlɪˌeɪt/ v.tr. make humble; injure the dignity or self-respect of. □□ **humiliating** adj. **humiliatingly** adv.

humiliation /-ˈeɪʃ(ə)n/ n. **humiliator** n. [LL humiliare (as HUMBLE)]

humility /hjuːˈmɪlɪtɪ/ n. **1** humbleness, meekness. **2** a humble condition. [ME f. OF humilité f. L humilitas -tatis (as HUMBLE)]

hummingbird /ˈhʌmɪŋˌbɜːd/ n. any small nectar-feeding tropical bird of the family Trochilidae that makes a humming sound by the vibration of its wings when it hovers.

humming-top /ˈhʌmɪŋˌtɒp/ n. a child's top which hums as it spins.

hummock /ˈhʌmək/ n. **1** a hillock or knoll. **2** *US* a piece of rising ground, esp. in a marsh. **3** a hump or ridge in an ice-field. □□ **hummocky** adj. [16th c.: orig. unkn.]

hummus /ˈhʊməs/ n. (also **hoummos**) a thick sauce or spread made from ground chick-peas and sesame oil flavoured with lemon and garlic. [Turk. humus mashed chick-peas]

humor *US* var. of HUMOUR.

humoral /ˈhjuːmər(ə)l/ adj. **1** *hist.* of the four bodily humours. **2** *Med.* relating to body fluids, esp. as distinct from cells. [F humoral or med.L humoralis (as HUMOUR)]

humoresque /ˌhjuːməˈresk/ n. a short lively piece of music. [G Humoreske f. Humor HUMOUR]

humorist /ˈhjuːmərɪst/ n. **1** a facetious person. **2** a humorous talker, actor, or writer. □□ **humoristic** /-ˈrɪstɪk/ adj.

humorous /ˈhjuːmərəs/ adj. **1** showing humour or a sense of humour. **2** facetious, comic. □□ **humorously** adv. **humorousness** n.

humour /ˈhjuːmə(r)/ n. & v. (*US* **humor**) —n. **1 a** the condition of being amusing or comic (less intellectual and more sympathetic than wit). **b** the expression of humour in literature, speech, etc. **2** (in full **sense of humour**) the ability to perceive or express humour or take a joke. **3** a mood or state of mind (bad humour). **4** an inclination or whim (in the humour for fighting). **5** (in full **cardinal humour**) *hist.* each of the four chief fluids of the body (blood, phlegm, choler, melancholy), held (in Galen's theory) to determine a person's physical and mental qualities. —v.tr. **1** gratify or indulge (a person or taste etc.). **2** adapt oneself to; make concessions to. □ **aqueous humour** *Anat.* the clear fluid in the eye between the lens and the cornea. **out of humour** displeased. **vitreous humour** (or **body**) *Anat.* a transparent jelly-like tissue filling the eyeball. □□ **-humoured** adj. **humourless** adj. **humourlessly** adv. **humourlessness** n. [ME f. AF umour, humour, OF umor, humor f. L humor moisture (as HUMID)]

humous /ˈhjuːməs/ adj. like or consisting of humus.

hump /hʌmp/ n. & v. —n. **1** a rounded protuberance on the back of a camel etc., or as an abnormality on a person's back. **2** a rounded raised mass of earth etc. **3** a mound over which railway vehicles are pushed so as to run by gravity to the required place in a marshalling yard. **4** a critical point in an undertaking, ordeal, etc. **5** (prec. by the) *Brit. sl.* a fit of depression or vexation (it gives me the hump). —v.tr. **1 a** (often foll. by about) *colloq.* lift or carry (heavy objects etc.) with difficulty. **b** esp. *Austral.* hoist up, shoulder (one's pack etc.). **2** make hump-shaped. **3** annoy, depress. **4** *coarse sl.* have sexual intercourse with. ¶ In sense 4 usually considered a taboo word. □ **hump bridge** = humpback bridge. **live on one's hump** *colloq.* be self-sufficient. **over the hump** over the worst; well begun. □□ **humped** adj. **humpless** adj. [17th c.: perh. rel. to LG humpel hump, LG humpe, Du. homp lump, hunk (of bread)]

humpback /ˈhʌmpbæk/ n. **1 a** a deformed back with a hump. **b** a person having this. **2** a baleen whale, *Megaptera novaeangliae*, with a dorsal fin forming a hump. □ **humpback bridge** *Brit.* a small bridge with a steep ascent and descent. □□ **humpbacked** adj.

Humperdinck /ˈhʌmpədɪŋk/, Engelbert (1854–1921), German composer. He assisted Wagner with the score of *Parsifal*, produced at Bayreuth in 1882. His opera *Hänsel und Gretel* (1893), which uses a Wagnerian idiom for a fairy tale, achieved a success which his other operas failed to emulate.

humph /hʌmf/ int. & n. an inarticulate sound expressing doubt or dissatisfaction. [imit.]

humpty-dumpty /ˌhʌmptɪˈdʌmptɪ/ n. (pl. -ies) 1 a short dumpy person. 2 a person or thing that once overthrown cannot be restored. [the nursery rhyme *Humpty-Dumpty*, perh. ult. f. HUMPY¹, DUMPY]

humpy¹ /ˈhʌmpɪ/ adj. (**humpier, humpiest**) 1 having a hump or humps. 2 humplike.

humpy² /ˈhʌmpɪ/ n. (pl. -ies) *Austral.* a primitive hut. [Aboriginal *oompi*, infl. by HUMP]

humus /ˈhjuːməs/ n. the organic constituent of soil, usu. formed by the decomposition of plants and leaves by soil bacteria. □□ **humusify** v.tr. & intr. (-ies, -ied) [L, = soil]

Hun /hʌn/ n. 1 a member of a warlike Asiatic nomadic people who invaded and ravaged Europe in the 4th–5th c. 2 *offens.* a German (esp. in military contexts). 3 an uncivilized devastator; a vandal. □□ **Hunnish** adj. [OE *Hūne* pl. f. LL *Hunni* f. Gk *Hounnoi* f. Turki *Hun-yü*]

Hunan /huːˈnæn/ a province of east central China; pop. (est. 1986) 56,960,000; capital, Changsha.

hunch /hʌntʃ/ v. & n. —v. 1 tr. bend or arch into a hump. 2 tr. thrust out or up to form a hump. 3 intr. (usu. foll. by up) *US* sit with the body hunched. —n. 1 an intuitive feeling or conjecture. 2 a hint. 3 a hump. 4 a thick piece. [16th c.: orig. unkn.]

hunchback /ˈhʌntʃbæk/ n. = HUMPBACK. □□ **hunchbacked** adj.

hundred /ˈhʌndrəd/ n. & adj. —n. (pl. **hundreds** or (in sense 1) **hundred**) (in *sing.*, prec. by *a* or *one*) 1 the product of ten and ten. 2 a symbol for this (100, c, C). 3 a set of a hundred things. 4 (in *sing.* or *pl.*) *colloq.* a large number. 5 (in *pl.*) the years of a specified century (*the seventeen hundreds*). 6 *Brit. hist.* a subdivision of a county or shire, having its own court. —adj. 1 that amount to a hundred. 2 used to express whole hours in the 24-hour system (*thirteen hundred hours*). □ **a** (or **one**) **hundred per cent** adv. entirely, completely. —adj. 1 entire, complete. 2 (usu. with *neg.*) fully recovered. **hundreds and thousands** tiny coloured sweets used chiefly for decorating cakes etc. □□ **hundredfold** adj. & adv. **hundredth** adj. & n. [OE f. Gmc]

hundredweight /ˈhʌndrədˌweɪt/ n. (pl. same or **-weights**) 1 (in full **long hundredweight**) *Brit.* a unit of weight equal to 112 lb. avoirdupois (about 50.8 kg). 2 (in full **metric hundredweight**) a unit of weight equal to 50 kg. 3 (in full **short hundredweight**) *US* a unit of weight equal to 100 lb. (about 45.4 kg).

Hundred Years War a war between France and England which stretched over more than a century between the 1340s and the 1450s, not as one continuous conflict but rather a series of attempts by English kings to dominate France. Edward III began the war by claiming the throne of France following the death of the last Capetian king (a brother of his mother), but despite an early string of military successes, most notably Crécy and Poitiers, and the occupation of a large part of France, the House of Valois retained its new position on the French throne. The French gradually improved their position, and in the reign of Edward's son Richard II hostilities ceased almost completely. The English claim was revived by the Lancastrian king Henry V, who renewed hostilities in 1415 with a crushing victory at Agincourt and occupied much of northern France. England once again proved unable to consolidate her advantage, however, and following Henry V's early death the regents of his ineffectual son Henry VI gradually lost control of conquered territory to French forces, revitalized in the first instance by Joan of Arc. With the exception of Calais, which did not fall for another century, all English conquests had been lost by 1453 when the war finally ended.

hung past and past part. of HANG.

Hungarian /hʌŋˈgeərɪən/ n. & adj. —n. 1 **a** a native or national of Hungary. **b** a person of Hungarian descent. 2 the official language of Hungary, one of the Finno-Ugric languages, spoken by some 11 million people in Hungary and Romania, the only major language of the Ugric branch. —adj. of or relating to Hungary or its people or language. [med.L *Hungaria* f. *Hungari* Magyar nation]

Hungary /ˈhʌŋgərɪ/ a country in central Europe, bordering on Czechoslovakia in the north and Yugoslavia in the south; pop. (est. 1988) 10,588,300; official language, Hungarian; capital, Budapest. Settled by the Magyars in the 9th c., Hungary emerged as the centre of a strong Magyar kingdom in the late Middle Ages, but was conquered first by the Turks in the 16th c. and then by the Hapsburgs in the 17th c., being incorporated in the Austrian empire thereafter. Nationalist pressure resulted in increased Hungarian power and autonomy within the empire in the 19th c., and following the collapse of Hapsburg power in 1918 Hungary finally achieved independence. After participation in the Second World War on the Axis side, Hungary was occupied by the Soviets and became a Communist State under their strong influence, a liberal reform movement being crushed by Soviet troops in 1956. In recent years the traditionally agricultural Hungarian economy has been progressively industrialized. The Communist system was abandoned towards the end of 1989.

hunger /ˈhʌŋgə(r)/ n. & v. —n. 1 a feeling of pain or discomfort, or (in extremes) an exhausted condition, caused by lack of food. 2 (often foll. by *for, after*) a strong desire. —v.intr. 1 (often foll. by *for, after*) have a craving or strong desire. 2 feel hunger. □ **hunger march** a march undertaken by a body of unemployed etc. to call attention to their condition. Demonstrations of this kind were launched by unemployed workers in Britain between the two World Wars, particularly after the economic collapse of 1929, which took the form of marches from various cities to London. The first took place in 1922 from Glasgow, the most famous from Jarrow in 1936. **hunger marcher** a person who goes on a hunger march. **hunger strike** the refusal of food as a form of protest, esp. by prisoners. **hunger striker** a person who takes part in a hunger strike. [OE *hungor, hyngran* f. Gmc]

hungry /ˈhʌŋgrɪ/ adj. (**hungrier, hungriest**) 1 feeling or showing hunger; needing food. 2 inducing hunger (*a hungry air*). 3 **a** eager, greedy, craving. **b** *Austral.* mean, stingy. 4 (of soil) poor, barren. □□ **hungrily** adv. **hungriness** n. [OE *hungrig* (as HUNGER)]

hunk /hʌŋk/ n. 1 **a** a large piece cut off (*a hunk of bread*). **b** a thick or clumsy piece. 2 *colloq.* **a** a very large person. **b** esp. *US* a sexually attractive man. □□ **hunky** adj. (**hunkier, hunkiest**). [19th c.: prob. f. Flem. *hunke*]

hunkers /ˈhʌŋkəz/ n.pl. the haunches. [orig. Sc., f. *hunker* crouch, squat]

hunky-dory /ˌhʌŋkɪˈdɔːrɪ/ adj. esp. *US colloq.* excellent. [19th c.: orig. unkn.]

Hunt /hʌnt/, William Holman (1827–1910), English painter, co-founder of the Pre-Raphaelite Brotherhood in 1848, who remained true to its aims, which he summarized as seriousness, direct study from nature, and the attempt to envisage events as they must have happened. Many of his works have a didactic emphasis on moral or religious symbolism (e.g. *The Awakening Conscience*, 1852; *The Light of the World*, 1852). From 1854, Hunt made several journeys to Egypt and Palestine and painted biblical scenes with attention to accuracy of local detail. His painting from nature is characterized by minute precision and bright colour.

hunt /hʌnt/ v. & n. —v. 1 tr. (also *absol.*) **a** pursue and kill (wild animals, esp. foxes, or game), esp. on horseback and with hounds, for sport or food. **b** (of an animal) chase (its prey). 2 intr. (foll. by *after, for*) seek, search (*hunting for a pen*). 3 intr. **a** oscillate. **b** (of an engine etc.) run alternately too fast and too slow. 4 tr. (foll. by *away* etc.) drive off by pursuit. 5 tr. scour (a district) in pursuit of game. 6 tr. (as **hunted** adj.) (of a look etc.) expressing alarm or terror as of one being hunted. 7 tr. (foll. by *down, up*) move the place of (a bell) in ringing the changes. —n. 1 the practice of hunting or an instance of this. 2 **a** an association of people engaged in hunting with hounds. **b** an area where hunting takes place. 3 an oscillating motion. □ **hunt down** pursue and capture. **hunt out** find by searching; track down. [OE *huntian*, weak grade of *hentan* seize]

huntaway /ˈhʌntəˌweɪ/ n. *Austral.* & *NZ* a dog trained to drive sheep forward.

Hunter /ˈhʌntə(r)/, John (1728–93), Scottish anatomist, who is regarded as a founder of scientific surgery and made valuable investigations in pathology, physiology, and biology. His elder brother William (1718–83), under whom he studied, became one of London's foremost obstetricians.

hunter /'hʌntə(r)/ n. 1 a (fem. **huntress**) a person or animal that hunts. b a horse used in hunting. 2 a person who seeks something. 3 a watch with a hinged cover protecting the glass. □ **hunter's moon** the next full moon after the harvest moon.

hunting /'hʌntɪŋ/ n. the practice of pursuing and killing wild animals, esp. for sport. □ **hunting-crop** see CROP n. 3. **hunting-ground** 1 a place suitable for hunting. 2 a source of information or object of exploitation likely to be fruitful. **hunting horn** a straight horn used in hunting. **hunting pink** see PINK¹. [OE huntung (as HUNT)]

Huntingdon /'hʌntɪŋd(ə)n/, Selina, Countess of (1707–91). Selina Hastings, foundress of the body of Calvinistic Methodists known as 'the Countess of Huntingdon's Connexion'. On her husband's death in 1746 she gave herself wholly to religious and social work, making herself the chief medium for introducing Methodism to the upper classes.

Huntington's chorea /'hʌntɪŋt(ə)nz/ n. Med. see CHOREA. [G. Huntington, Amer. neurologist, d. 1916]

huntsman /'hʌntsmən/ n. (pl. **-men**) 1 a hunter. 2 a hunt official in charge of hounds.

Hupeh see HUBEI.

hurdle /'hɜːd(ə)l/ n. & v. —n. 1 Athletics a each of a series of light frames to be cleared by athletes in a race. b (in pl.) a hurdle-race. 2 an obstacle or difficulty. 3 a portable rectangular frame strengthened with withes or wooden bars, used as a temporary fence etc. 4 hist. a frame on which traitors were dragged to execution. —v. 1 Athletics a intr. run in a hurdle-race. b tr. clear (a hurdle). 2 tr. fence off etc. with hurdles. 3 tr. overcome (a difficulty). [OE hyrdel f. Gmc]

hurdler /'hɜːdlə(r)/ n. 1 Athletics a person who runs in hurdle-races. 2 a person who makes hurdles.

hurdy-gurdy /'hɜːdɪˌɡɜːdɪ/ n. (pl. **-ies**) 1 a musical instrument with a droning sound, played by turning a handle, esp. one with a rosined wheel turned by the right hand to sound the drone-strings, and keys played by the left hand. The instrument, called 'organistrum', was known in Europe from the early 12th c., used at first in choir schools; today it is mainly heard as a folk instrument, esp. in France. 2 colloq. a barrel-organ. [prob. imit.]

hurl /hɜːl/ v. & n. —v. 1 tr. throw with great force. 2 tr. utter (abuse etc.) vehemently. 3 intr. play hurling. —n. 1 a forceful throw. 2 the act of hurling. [ME, prob. imit., but corresp. in form and partly in sense with LG hurreln]

Hurler's syndrome /'hɜːləz/ n. Med. a defect in metabolism resulting in mental retardation, a protruding abdomen, and deformities of the bones, including an abnormally large head. Also called GARGOYLISM. [G. Hurler, Ger. paediatrician]

hurling /'hɜːlɪŋ/ n. (also **hurley** /'hɜːlɪ/) 1 an Irish game somewhat resembling hockey, played with broad sticks. It is the national game of Ireland, mentioned in folk-tales, in the Irish Annals (relating events of c.1272 BC), and in an Irish legal code dating from centuries BC. 2 a stick used in this.

hurly-burly /'hɜːlɪˌbɜːlɪ/ n. boisterous activity; commotion. [redupl. f. HURL]

Huron /'hjʊərən/ n. 1 a confederation of five Iroquoian tribes formerly inhabiting a region adjacent to Lake Huron. 2 a member of these tribes. 3 their language. □ **Lake Huron** one of the five Great Lakes of North America.

hurrah /hʊˈrɑː/ int., n., & v. (also **hurray** /hʊˈreɪ/) —int. & n. an exclamation of joy or approval. —v.intr. cry or shout 'hurrah' or 'hurray'. [alt. of earlier huzza, perh. orig. a sailor's cry when hauling]

Hurrian /'hʌrɪən/ n. & adj. —n. 1 a member of a widespread non-Semitic people in the Middle East during the 3rd–2nd millennium BC (see MITANNI), sometimes identified with the Horites of the Bible. 2 their language, written in cuneiform, of unknown derivation (it is neither Semitic nor Indo-European). —adj. of the Hurrians or their language. [Hittite & Assyrian Harri, Hurri + -AN]

hurricane /'hʌrɪkən, -ˌkeɪn/ n. 1 a storm with a violent wind, esp. a W. Indian cyclone. 2 Meteorol. a wind of 65 knots (75 m.p.h.) or more, force 12 on the Beaufort scale. 3 a violent commotion. □ **hurricane-bird** a frigate-bird. **hurricane-deck** a light upper deck on a ship etc. **hurricane-lamp** an oil-lamp designed to resist a high wind. [Sp. huracan & Port. furacão of Carib orig.]

hurry /'hʌrɪ/ n. & v. —n. (pl. **-ies**) 1 a great haste. b (with neg. or interrog.) a need for haste (there is no hurry; what's the hurry?). 2 (often foll. by for, or to + infin.) eagerness to get a thing done quickly. —v. (**-ies, -ied**) 1 move or act with great or undue haste. 2 tr. (often foll. by away, along) cause to move or proceed in this way. 3 tr. (as **hurried** adj.) hasty; done rapidly owing to lack of time. □ **hurry along** (or **up**) make or cause to make haste. **in a hurry 1** hurrying; rushed; in a rushed manner. 2 colloq. easily or readily (you will not beat that in a hurry; shall not ask again in a hurry). □□ **hurriedly** adv. **hurriedness** n. [16th c.: imit.]

hurry-scurry /ˌhʌrɪˈskʌrɪ/ n., adj., & adv. —n. disorderly haste. —adj. & adv. in confusion. [jingling redupl. of HURRY]

hurst /hɜːst/ n. 1 a hillock. 2 a sandbank in the sea or a river. 3 a wood or wooded eminence. [OE hyrst, rel. to OS, OHG hurst, horst]

hurt /hɜːt/ v. & n. —v. (past and past part. **hurt**) 1 tr. (also absol.) cause pain or injury to. 2 tr. cause mental pain or distress to (a person, feelings, etc.). 3 intr. suffer pain or harm (my arm hurts). —n. 1 bodily or material injury. 2 harm, wrong. □□ **hurtless** adj. [ME f. OF hurter, hurt ult. perh. f. Gmc]

hurtful /'hɜːtfʊl/ adj. causing (esp. mental) hurt. □□ **hurtfully** adv. **hurtfulness** n.

hurtle /'hɜːt(ə)l/ v. 1 intr. & tr. move or hurl rapidly or with a clattering sound. 2 intr. come with a crash. [HURT in obs. sense 'strike forcibly']

husband /'hʌzbənd/ n. & v. —n. a married man esp. in relation to his wife. —v.tr. manage thriftily; use (resources) economically. □□ **husbander** n. **husbandhood** n. **husbandless** adj. **husbandlike** adj. **husbandly** adj. **husbandship** n. [OE hūsbonda house-dweller f. ON húsbóndi (as HOUSE, bóndi one who has a household)]

husbandry /'hʌzbəndrɪ/ n. 1 farming. 2 a management of resources. b careful management.

hush /hʌʃ/ v., int., & n. —v.tr. & intr. make or become silent or quiet. —int. calling for silence. —n. an expectant stillness or silence. □ **hush money** money paid to prevent the disclosure of a discreditable matter. **hush puppy** US quickly fried maize bread. **hush up** suppress public mention of (an affair). [back-form. f. obs. husht int., = quiet!, taken as a past part.]

hushaby /'hʌʃəˌbaɪ/ int. (also **hushabye**) used to lull a child.

hush-hush /ˌhʌʃˈhʌʃ/ adj. colloq. (esp. of an official plan or enterprise etc.) highly secret or confidential.

husk /hʌsk/ n. & v. —n. 1 the dry outer covering of some fruits or seeds, esp. of a nut or US maize. 2 the worthless outside part of a thing. —v.tr. remove a husk or husks from. [ME, prob. f. LG hūske sheath, dimin. of hūs HOUSE]

husky¹ /'hʌskɪ/ adj. (**huskier, huskiest**) 1 (of a person or voice) dry in the throat; hoarse. 2 of or full of husks. 3 dry as a husk. 4 tough, strong, hefty. □□ **huskily** adv. **huskiness** n.

husky² /'hʌskɪ/ n. (pl. **-ies**) 1 a dog of a powerful breed used in the Arctic for pulling sledges. 2 this breed. [perh. contr. f. ESKIMO]

Huss /hʌs/, John (c.1372–1415), Bohemian reformer. A preacher in Prague and enthusiastic supporter of Wyclif's views, he aroused the hostility of the Church, was excommunicated (1411), tried (1414), and burnt at the stake. By his death he became a national hero and was declared a martyr by the university of Prague. His followers took up arms against the Holy Roman Empire, and, through a combination of religious fervour and innovative military methods, inflicted a dramatic series of defeats on imperialist forces. □□ **Hussite** adj. & n. **Hussitism** n.

huss /hʌs/ n. dogfish as food. [ME husk, of unkn. orig.]

hussar /hʊˈzɑː(r)/ n. **1** a soldier of a light cavalry regiment. **2** a Hungarian light horseman of the 15th c. [Magyar *huszár* f. OSerb. *husar* f. It. *corsaro* CORSAIR]

Hussein[1] /hʊˈseɪn/, ibn Talal (1935–), king of Jordan from 1952. He showed considerable dexterity in maintaining his position in spite of Egyptian intrigues during Nasser's presidency, loss of territory in the Arab–Israeli war of 1967, and the operations of Arab extremists.

Hussein[2] /hʊˈseɪn/, Saddam (in full Saddam bin Hussein at-Takriti) (1937–), Iraqi leader, President from 1979. A member of the Baath Socialist party, he took part in a successful coup in 1968 that brought the party back to power. On becoming President he suppressed opposing parties, built up a formidable army and its weaponry, and made himself the object of an extensive personality cult among the Iraqi people. He led his country into war with Iran (1980–8) after tension and border disputes between the two countries, and in 1990 invaded and occupied Kuwait (see GULF WAR 2).

Husserl /ˈhʊsɜːl/, Edmund (1859–1938), German philosopher. Having originally trained as a mathematician he turned to philosophy and taught in German universities, latterly coming under pressure because of his Jewish ancestry. In his philosophy he sought the clarity and certainty belonging to mathematics and science, and became the leading figure in the movement known as phenomenology. He rejected metaphysical assumptions about what actually exists, and explanations of why it exists, in favour of pure subjective consciousness as the condition for all experience, with the world as the object of this consciousness; the task of philosophy was to describe the fundamental structures of the world which make experience and consciousness possible. Among his pupils was Heidegger, who succeeded him as professor at Freiburg in 1928.

hussy /ˈhʌsɪ/ n. (pl. **-ies**) *derog.* an impudent or immoral girl or woman. [phonetic reduction of HOUSEWIFE (the orig. sense)]

hustings /ˈhʌstɪŋz/ n. **1** parliamentary election proceedings. **2** *Brit. hist.* a platform from which (before 1872) candidates for Parliament were nominated and addressed electors. [late OE *husting* f. ON *hústhing* house of assembly]

hustle /ˈhʌs(ə)l/ v. & n. —v. **1** tr. push roughly; jostle. **2** tr. **a** (foll. by *into, out of,* etc.) force, coerce, or deal with hurriedly or unceremoniously (*hustled them out of the room*). **b** (foll. by *into*) coerce hurriedly (*was hustled into agreeing*). **3** intr. push one's way; hurry, bustle. **4** tr. sl. **a** obtain by forceful action. **b** swindle. **5** intr. sl. engage in prostitution. —n. **1** an act or instance of hustling. **2** *colloq.* a fraud or swindle. [MDu. *husselen* shake, toss, frequent. of *hutsen,* orig. imit.]

hustler /ˈhʌslə(r)/ n. sl. **1** an active, enterprising, or unscrupulous individual. **2** a prostitute.

hut /hʌt/ n. & v. —n. **1** a small simple or crude house or shelter. **2** *Mil.* a temporary wooden etc. house for troops. —v. (**hutted,** **hutting**) **1** tr. provide with huts. **2** tr. *Mil.* place (troops etc.) in huts. **3** intr. lodge in a hut. □□ **hutlike** adj. [F *hutte* f. MHG *hütte*]

hutch /hʌtʃ/ n. **1** a box or cage, usu. with a wire mesh front, for keeping small pet animals. **2** *derog.* a small house. [ME, = coffer, f. OF *huche* f. med.L *hutica,* of unkn. orig.]

hutment /ˈhʌtmənt/ n. *Mil.* an encampment of huts.

Hutton[1] /ˈhʌt(ə)n/, James (1726–97), Scottish geologist who put forward certain views, controversial at the time, that became accepted tenets of modern geology. In opposition to Werner's Neptunian theory he emphasized heat as the principal agent in the formation of land masses, and held that rocks such as granite were igneous in origin. He described the processes of deposition and denudation and proposed that such phenomena, operating with roughly equal intensity over millions of years, would account for the present configuration of the earth's surface; it therefore followed that the earth was very much older than was generally believed at the time. These conclusions were presented in his *Theory of the Earth* (1785), and met with the hostility of those who accepted the biblical account of the creation of the world. Hutton's writing style was poor, however, and his views did not become widely known until a concise account of them was published by his friend Playfair in 1802.

Hutton[2] /ˈhʌt(ə)n/, Sir Leonard ('Len') (1916–90), English cricketer. In a career that lasted from 1934 to 1960 he played for Yorkshire and for England, made a record score of 364 in the 1938 test match against Australia, and became the first professional captain of the England team in 1953.

Huxley[1] /ˈhʌkslɪ/, Aldous Leonard (1894–1963), English novelist and essayist. During the 1920s and 1930s he lived in Italy and France, and there wrote much of his best fiction, notably *Brave New World* (1932) and *Eyeless in Gaza* (1936). Disillusioned with Europe he left for California in 1937, in search of new spiritual direction. There he became interested in mysticism and parapsychology; *The Doors of Perception* (1954) describes his experiments with mescalin. His works, often pessimistic, combine satire and earnestness, brutality and humanity, and shed light on unexplored territory.

Huxley[2] /ˈhʌkslɪ/, Sir Julian (1887–1975), English biologist, grandson of T. H. Huxley. He contributed to the early development of the study of animal behaviour, was an outstanding interpreter of science to the public through writing and broadcasting, and became the first director-general of UNESCO (1946–8).

Huxley[3] /ˈhʌkslɪ/, Thomas Henry (1825–95), English biologist. A qualified surgeon and self-taught naturalist, he made his reputation as a marine biologist during service as ship's surgeon on HMS *Rattlesnake,* reporting his studies of marine species off the coast of northern Australia. Later he studied fossils, especially of fishes and reptiles, and became a firm supporter of Darwin, although he did not accept his theories without qualification. On the basis of a detailed study in anthropology he wrote *Man's Place in Nature* (1863), and coined the word 'agnostic' to describe his position in the face of religious orthodoxy, taking it from St Paul's mention of the altar 'to the Unknown God'. A liberal-minded man, Huxley was a supporter of education for the less privileged and argued for the inclusion of science in the school curriculum.

Huygens /ˈhaɪɡənz/, Christiaan (1629–95), Dutch physicist, mathematician, and astronomer, best known for his pendulum-regulated clock invented in 1656. He improved the lenses of his telescope, discovered a satellite of Saturn, and also the latter's rings, which had foxed Galileo. In dynamics he studied such topics as centrifugal force and the problem of colliding bodies, but his greatest contribution was his wave theory of light, made public in 1678. He formulated what has become known as 'Huygens' principle', that every point on a wave front is the centre of a new wave, and this allowed him to explain the reflection and refraction of light, including its double refraction in Iceland spar.

Hwange /ˈwæŋɡi, ˈhw-/ (until 1982 called **Wankie**) a town in western Zimbabwe, centre of the country's coal-mining industry; pop. (1982) 39,000. Nearby is the Hwange National park, established as a game reserve in 1928 and as a park in 1949.

HWM abbr. high-water mark.

hwyl /ˈhuːɪl/ n. an emotional quality inspiring impassioned eloquence. [Welsh]

Hy. abbr. Henry.

hyacinth /ˈhaɪəsɪnθ/ n. **1** any bulbous plant of the genus *Hyacinthus* with racemes of usu. purplish-blue, pink, or white bell-shaped fragrant flowers. **2** = *grape hyacinth.* **3** the purplish-blue colour of the hyacinth flower. **4** an orange variety of zircon used as a precious stone. **5** *poet.* hair or locks like the hyacinth flower (as a Homeric epithet of doubtful sense). □ **wild** (or **wood**) **hyacinth** = BLUEBELL 1. □□ **hyacinthine** /-ˈsɪnθiːn/ adj. [F *hyacinthe* f. L *hyacinthus* f. Gk *huakinthos,* flower and gem, also the name of a youth loved by Apollo (see HYACINTHUS)]

Hyacinthus /ˌhaɪəˈsɪnθəs/ *Gk Mythol.* a pre-Hellenic god whose cult, in historical times, was subordinate to that of Apollo. He is said to have been a beautiful boy whom the god loved but killed accidentally with a discus. From his blood Apollo caused the flower that bears his name to spring up.

Hyades /ˈhaɪədiːz/ n.pl. a group of stars in Taurus near the Pleiades, whose heliacal rising was once thought to foretell rain.

[ME f. Gk *Huades* (by popular etym. f. *huŏ* rain, but perh. f. *hus* pig, the Latin name being *suculae* little pigs)]

hyaena var. of HYENA.

hyalin /ˈhaɪəlɪn/ *n.* a clear glassy substance produced as a result of the degeneration of certain body tissues. [Gk *hualos* glass + -IN]

hyaline /ˈhaɪəlɪn, -ˌlaɪn, -ˌliːn/ *adj. & n.* —*adj.* glasslike, vitreous, transparent. —*n. literary* a smooth sea, clear sky, etc. □ **hyaline cartilage** *n.* a common type of cartilage. [L *hyalinus* f. Gk *hualinos* f. *hualos* glass]

hyalite /ˈhaɪəˌlaɪt/ *n.* a colourless variety of opal. [Gk *hualos* glass]

hyaloid /ˈhaɪəˌlɔɪd/ *adj. Anat.* glassy. □ **hyaloid membrane** a thin transparent membrane enveloping the vitreous humour of the eye. [F *hyaloïde* f. LL *hyaloides* f. Gk *hualoeidēs* (as HYALITE)]

hybrid /ˈhaɪbrɪd/ *n. & adj.* —*n.* **1** *Biol.* the offspring of two plants or animals of different species or varieties. **2** often *offens.* a person of mixed racial or cultural origin. **3** a thing composed of incongruous elements, e.g. a word with parts taken from different languages. —*adj.* **1** bred as a hybrid from different species or varieties. **2** *Biol.* heterogeneous. □ **hybrid vigour** heterosis. □□ **hybridism** *n.* **hybridity** /-ˈbrɪdɪtɪ/ *n.* [L *hybrida*, (h)*ibrida* offspring of a tame sow and wild boar, child of a freeman and slave, etc.]

hybridize /ˈhaɪbrɪˌdaɪz/ *v.* (also **-ise**) **1** *tr.* subject (a species etc.) to cross-breeding. **2** *intr.* **a** produce hybrids. **b** (of an animal or plant) interbreed. □□ **hybridizable** *adj.* **hybridization** /-ˈzeɪʃ(ə)n/ *n.*

hydatid /ˈhaɪdətɪd/ *n. Med.* **1** a cyst containing watery fluid (esp. one formed by, and containing, a tapeworm larva). **2** a tapeworm larva. □□ **hydatidiform** /-ˈtɪdɪˌfɔːm/ *adj.* [mod.L *hydatis* f. Gk *hudatis -idos* watery vesicle f. *hudōr hudatos* water]

Hyde[1] /haɪd/, Edward, see CLARENDON.

Hyde[2] /haɪd/, Edward, see JEKYLL.

Hyderabad /ˈhaɪdərəˌbæd/ **1** a city of India, capital of Andhra Pradesh; pop. (1981) 2,528,000. **2** *hist.* a former princely State of south central India, divided in 1956 between Maharashtra, Mysore, and Andhra Pradesh. **3** a city of SE Pakistan, in the province of Sind; pop. (1981) 795,000.

Hydra /ˈhaɪdrə/ **1** *Gk Mythol.* a many-headed snake of the marshes of Lerna in the Peloponnese, whose heads grew again as they were cut off, killed by Hercules. **2** *Astron.* a southern constellation represented as a water-snake or sea serpent. [Gk *hudra* water-snake]

hydra /ˈhaɪdrə/ *n.* **1** a freshwater polyp of the genus *Hydra* with tubular body and tentacles around the mouth. **2** any water-snake. **3** something which is hard to destroy. [ME f. L f. Gk *hudra* water-snake, esp. HYDRA]

hydrangea /haɪˈdreɪndʒə/ *n.* any shrub of the genus *Hydrangea* with large white, pink, or blue flowers. [mod.L f. Gk *hudōr* water + *aggos* vessel (from the cup-shape of its seed-capsule)]

hydrant /ˈhaɪdrənt/ *n.* a pipe (esp. in a street) with a nozzle to which a hose can be attached for drawing water from the main. [irreg. f. HYDRO- + -ANT]

hydrate /ˈhaɪdreɪt/ *n. & v.* —*n. Chem.* a compound of water combined with another compound or with an element. —*v.tr.* **1 a** combine chemically with water. **b** (as **hydrated** *adj.*) chemically bonded to water. **2** cause to absorb water. □□ **hydratable** *adj.* **hydration** /-ˈdreɪʃ(ə)n/ *n.* **hydrator** *n.* [F f. Gk *hudōr* water]

hydraulic /haɪˈdrɔːlɪk, -ˈdrɒlɪk/ *adj.* **1** (of water, oil, etc.) conveyed through pipes or channels usu. by pressure. **2** (of a mechanism etc.) operated by liquid moving in this manner (*hydraulic brakes*; *hydraulic lift*). **3** of or concerned with hydraulics (*hydraulic engineer*). **4** hardening under water (*hydraulic cement*). □ **hydraulic press** a device in which the force applied to a fluid creates a pressure which when transmitted to a larger volume of fluid gives rise to a greater force. **hydraulic ram** an automatic pump in which the kinetic energy of a descending column of water raises some of the water above its original level. □□ **hydraulically** *adv.* **hydraulicity** /-ˈlɪsɪtɪ/ *n.* [L *hydraulicus* f. Gk *hudraulikos* f. *hudōr* water + *aulos* pipe]

hydraulics /haɪˈdrɔːlɪks, -ˈdrɒlɪks/ *n.pl.* (usu. treated as *sing.*) the

science of the conveyance of liquids through pipes etc. esp. as motive power.

hydrazine /ˈhaɪdrəˌziːn/ *n. Chem.* a colourless alkaline liquid which is a powerful reducing agent and is used as a rocket propellant. ¶ Chem. formula: N_2H_4. [HYDROGEN + AZO- + -INE[4]]

hydride /ˈhaɪdraɪd/ *n. Chem.* a binary compound of hydrogen with an element, esp. with a metal.

hydriodic acid /ˌhaɪdrɪˈɒdɪk, -aɪˈɒdɪk/ *n. Chem.* a solution of the colourless gas hydrogen iodide in water. ¶ Chem. formula: HI. [HYDROGEN + IODINE]

hydro /ˈhaɪdrəʊ/ *n.* (*pl.* **-os**) *colloq.* **1** a hotel or clinic etc. orig. providing hydropathic treatment. **2** a hydroelectric power plant. [abbr.]

hydro- /ˈhaɪdrəʊ/ *comb. form* (also **hydr-** before a vowel) **1** having to do with water (*hydroelectric*). **2** *Med.* affected with an accumulation of serous fluid (*hydrocele*). **3** *Chem.* combined with hydrogen (*hydrochloric*). [Gk *hudro-* f. *hudōr* water]

hydrobromic acid /ˌhaɪdrəʊˈbrəʊmɪk/ *n. Chem.* a solution of the colourless gas hydrogen bromide in water. ¶ Chem. formula: HBr.

hydrocarbon /ˌhaɪdrəʊˈkɑːbən/ *n. Chem.* a compound of hydrogen and carbon.

hydrocele /ˈhaɪdrəˌsiːl/ *n. Med.* the accumulation of serous fluid in a body sac.

hydrocephalus /ˌhaɪdrəʊˈsefələs/ *n. Med.* an abnormal amount of fluid within the brain, esp. in young children, which makes the head enlarge and can cause mental deficiency. □□ **hydrocephalic** /-sɪˈfælɪk/ *adj.*

hydrochloric acid /ˌhaɪdrəˈklɔːrɪk, -ˈklɒrɪk/ *n. Chem.* a solution of the colourless gas hydrogen chloride in water. ¶ Chem. formula: HCl.

hydrochloride /ˌhaɪdrəˈklɔːraɪd/ *n. Chem.* a compound of an organic base with hydrochloric acid.

hydrocortisone /ˌhaɪdrəˈkɔːtɪˌzəʊn/ *n. Biochem.* a steroid hormone produced by the adrenal cortex, used medicinally to treat inflammation and rheumatism.

hydrocyanic acid /ˌhaɪdrəsaɪˈænɪk/ *n. Chem.* a highly poisonous volatile liquid with a characteristic odour of bitter almonds. ¶ Chem. formula: HCN. Also called *prussic acid.*

hydrodynamics /ˌhaɪdrəʊdaɪˈnæmɪks/ *n.* the science of forces acting on or exerted by fluids (esp. liquids). □□ **hydrodynamic** *adj.* **hydrodynamical** *adj.* **hydrodynamicist** /-sɪst/ *n.* [mod.L *hydrodynamicus* (as HYDRO-, DYNAMIC)]

hydroelectric /ˌhaɪdrəʊɪˈlektrɪk/ *adj.* **1** generating electricity by utilization of water-power. **2** (of electricity) generated in this way. The first public supply of electricity to be generated by water-power was that at Godalming in Surrey (see ELECTRICITY). □□ **hydroelectricity** /-ˈtrɪsɪtɪ/ *n.*

hydrofining /ˈhaɪdrəʊˌfaɪnɪŋ/ *n.* a catalytic process in which a petroleum product is stabilized and its sulphur content reduced by treatment with gaseous hydrogen under relatively mild conditions, so that unsaturated hydrocarbons and sulphur compounds undergo selective hydrogenation. □□ **hydrofined** *adj.* [HYDRO- + REFINING]

hydrofluoric acid /ˌhaɪdrəʊˈfluːərɪk/ *n. Chem.* a solution of the colourless liquid hydrogen fluoride in water. ¶ Chem. formula: HF.

hydrofoil /ˈhaɪdrəˌfɔɪl/ *n.* **1** a boat equipped with a device consisting of planes for lifting its hull out of the water to increase its speed. **2** this device, which provides lift in much the same way as an aerofoil. The first true hydrofoil was probably built by an Italian inventor, Enrico Forlamini, in 1898-1905, but such craft were not widely used until the 1950s. [HYDRO-, after AEROFOIL]

hydrogen /ˈhaɪdrədʒ(ə)n/ *n. Chem.* a colourless gaseous element, without taste or odour, the lightest of the elements, first recognized by Cavendish in 1766 and named by Lavoisier. Its chief isotope has a nucleus consisting of a single proton. Hydrogen is by far the commonest element in the universe (although not on the earth). It combines with oxygen to form water, and is a constituent of nearly all organic compounds. ¶ Symb.: **H**; atomic number 1. □ **hydrogen bomb** an immensely powerful bomb utilizing the explosive fusion of hydrogen nuclei: also called H-BOMB. **hydrogen bond** a weak electrostatic interaction between an electronegative atom and a hydrogen atom bonded to a different electronegative atom. **hydrogen peroxide** a colourless viscous unstable liquid with strong oxidizing properties. ¶ Chem. formula: H_2O_2. **hydrogen sulphide** a colourless poisonous gas with a disagreeable smell, formed by rotting animal matter. ¶ Chem. formula: H_2S. □□ **hydrogenous** /-'drɒdʒɪnəs/ *adj.* [F *hydrogène* (as HYDRO-, -GEN)]

hydrogenase /haɪ'drɒdʒɪˌneɪz, -ˌneɪs/ *n. Biochem.* any enzyme which catalyses the oxidation of hydrogen and the reduction of protons.

hydrogenate /haɪ'drɒdʒɪˌneɪt, 'haɪdrədʒəˌneɪt/ *v.tr.* charge with or cause to combine with hydrogen. □□ **hydrogenation** /-'neɪʃ(ə)n/ *n.*

hydrography /haɪ'drɒgrəfɪ/ *n.* the science of surveying and charting seas, lakes, rivers, etc. □□ **hydrographer** *n.* **hydrographic** /ˌhaɪdrə'græfɪk/ *adj.* **hydrographical** /ˌhaɪdrə'græfɪk(ə)l/ *adj.* **hydrographically** /ˌhaɪdrə'græfɪkəlɪ/ *adv.*

hydroid /'haɪdrɔɪd/ *adj. & n. Zool.* any usu. polypoid hydrozoan of the order Hydroida, including hydra.

hydrolase /'haɪdrəʊˌleɪz, -ˌleɪs/ *n. Biochem.* any enzyme which catalyses the hydrolysis of a substrate.

hydrology /haɪ'drɒlədʒɪ/ *n.* the science of the properties of the earth's water, esp. of its movement in relation to land. □□ **hydrologic** /ˌhaɪdrə'lɒdʒɪk/ *adj.* **hydrological** /ˌhaɪdrə'lɒdʒɪk(ə)l/ *adj.* **hydrologically** /ˌhaɪdrə'lɒdʒɪkəlɪ/ *adv.* **hydrologist** *n.*

hydrolyse /'haɪdrəˌlaɪz/ *v.tr. & intr.* (US **hydrolyze**) subject to or undergo the chemical action of water.

hydrolysis /haɪ'drɒlɪsɪs/ *n.* the chemical reaction of a substance with water, usu. resulting in decomposition. □□ **hydrolytic** /ˌhaɪdrə'lɪtɪk/ *adj.*

hydromagnetic /ˌhaɪdrəmæg'netɪk/ *adj.* involving hydrodynamics and magnetism; magnetohydrodynamic.

hydromania /ˌhaɪdrə'meɪnɪə/ *n.* a craving for water.

hydromechanics /ˌhaɪdrəʊmɪ'kænɪks/ *n.* the mechanics of liquids; hydrodynamics.

hydrometer /haɪ'drɒmɪtə(r)/ *n.* an instrument for measuring the density of liquids. □□ **hydrometric** /ˌhaɪdrə'metrɪk/ *adj.* **hydrometry** *n.*

hydronium ion /haɪ'drəʊnɪəm/ *n. Chem.* = HYDROXONIUM ION. [contr.]

hydropathy /haɪ'drɒpəθɪ/ *n.* the (medically unorthodox) treatment of disease by external and internal application of water. □□ **hydropathic** /ˌhaɪdrə'pæθɪk/ *adj.* **hydropathist** *n.* [HYDRO-, after HOMOEOPATHY etc.]

hydrophil /'haɪdrəfɪl/ *adj.* (also **hydrophile** /-ˌfaɪl/) = HYDROPHILIC. [as HYDROPHILIC]

hydrophilic /ˌhaɪdrə'fɪlɪk/ *adj.* **1** having an affinity for water. **2** wettable by water. [HYDRO- + Gk *philos* loving]

hydrophobia /ˌhaɪdrə'fəʊbɪə/ *n.* **1** a morbid aversion to water, esp. as a symptom of rabies in man. **2** rabies, esp. in man. [LL f. Gk *hudrophobia* (as HYDRO-, -PHOBIA)]

hydrophobic /ˌhaɪdrə'fəʊbɪk/ *adj.* **1** of or suffering from hydrophobia. **2 a** lacking an affinity for water. **b** not readily wettable.

hydrophone /'haɪdrəˌfəʊn/ *n.* an instrument for the detection of sound-waves in water.

hydrophyte /'haɪdrəˌfaɪt/ *n.* an aquatic plant, or a plant which needs much moisture.

hydroplane /'haɪdrəˌpleɪn/ *n. & v.* —*n.* **1** a light fast motor boat designed to skim over the surface of water. **2** a finlike attachment which enables a submarine to rise and fall in water. —*v.intr.* **1** (of a boat) skim over the surface of water with its hull lifted. **2** = AQUAPLANE *v.* 2.

hydroponics /ˌhaɪdrə'pɒnɪks/ *n.* the process of growing plants in sand, gravel, or liquid, without soil and with added nutrients. □□ **hydroponic** *adj.* **hydroponically** *adv.* [HYDRO- + Gk *ponos* labour]

hydroquinone /ˌhaɪdrə'kwɪnəʊn/ *n.* a substance formed by the reduction of quinone, used as a photographic developer.

hydrosphere /'haɪdrəˌsfɪə(r)/ *n.* the waters of the earth's surface.

hydrostatic /ˌhaɪdrə'stætɪk/ *adj.* of the equilibrium of liquids and the pressure exerted by liquid at rest. □ **hydrostatic press** = *hydraulic press.* □□ **hydrostatical** *adj.* **hydrostatically** *adv.* [prob. f. Gk *hudrostatēs* hydrostatic balance (as HYDRO-, STATIC)]

hydrostatics /ˌhaɪdrə'stætɪks/ *n.pl.* (usu. treated as *sing.*) the branch of mechanics concerned with the hydrostatic properties of liquids.

hydrotherapy /ˌhaɪdrə'θerəpɪ/ *n.* the use of water in the treatment of disorders, usu. exercises in swimming pools for arthritic or partially paralysed patients. □□ **hydrotherapist** *n.* **hydrotherapic** *adj.*

hydrothermal /ˌhaɪdrə'θɜːm(ə)l/ *adj.* of the action of heated water on the earth's crust. □□ **hydrothermally** *adv.*

hydrothorax /ˌhaɪdrə'θɔːræks/ *n.* the condition of having fluid in the pleural cavity.

hydrotropism /haɪ'drɒtrəˌpɪz(ə)m/ *adj.* a tendency of plant roots etc. to turn to or from moisture.

hydrous /'haɪdrəs/ *adj. Chem. & Mineral.* containing water. [Gk *hudōr hudro-* water]

hydroxide /haɪ'drɒksaɪd/ *n. Chem.* a metallic compound containing oxygen and hydrogen either in the form of the hydroxide ion (OH-) or the hydroxyl group (-OH).

hydroxonium ion /ˌhaɪdrɒk'səʊnɪəm/ *n. Chem.* the hydrated hydrogen ion, H_3O^+. [HYDRO- + OXY-² + -*onium*]

hydroxy- /haɪ'drɒksɪ/ *comb. form Chem.* having a hydroxide ion (or ions) or a hydroxyl group (or groups) (*hydroxybenzoic acid*). [HYDROGEN + OXYGEN]

hydroxyl /haɪ'drɒksɪl/ *n. Chem.* the univalent group containing hydrogen and oxygen, as -OH. [HYDROGEN + OXYGEN + -YL]

hydrozoan /ˌhaɪdrə'zəʊən/ *n. & adj.* —*n.* any aquatic coelenterate of the class Hydrozoa of mainly marine polyp or medusoid forms, including hydra and Portuguese man-of-war. [mod.L *Hydrozoa* (as HYDRA, Gk *zōion* animal)]

hyena /haɪ'iːnə/ *n.* (also **hyaena**) any flesh-eating mammal of the order Hyaenidae, with hind limbs shorter than forelimbs. □ **laughing hyena** *n.* a hyena, *Crocuta crocuta*, whose howl is compared to a fiendish laugh. [ME f. OF *hyene* & L *hyaena* f. Gk *huaina* fem. of *hus* pig]

hygiene /'haɪdʒiːn/ *n.* **1 a** a study, or set of principles, of maintaining health. **b** conditions or practices conducive to maintaining health. **2** sanitary science. [F *hygiène* f. mod.L *hygieina* f. Gk *hugieinē (tekhnē)* (art) of health f. *hugiēs* healthy]

hygienic /haɪ'dʒiːnɪk/ *adj.* conducive to hygiene; clean and sanitary. □□ **hygienically** *adv.*

hygienics /haɪ'dʒiːnɪks/ *n.pl.* (usu. treated as *sing.*) = HYGIENE 1a.

hygienist /'haɪdʒiːnɪst/ *n.* a specialist in the promotion and practice of cleanliness for the preservation of health.

hygro- /'haɪgrəʊ/ *comb. form* moisture. [Gk *hugro-* f. *hugros* wet, moist]

hygrology /haɪ'grɒlədʒɪ/ *n.* the study of the humidity of the atmosphere etc.

hygrometer /haɪ'grɒmɪtə(r)/ *n.* an instrument for measuring the humidity of the air or a gas. □□ **hygrometric** /ˌhaɪgrə'metrɪk/ *adj.* **hygrometry** *n.*

hygrophilous /haɪ'grɒfɪləs/ *adj.* (of a plant) growing in a moist environment.

hygrophyte /'haɪgrəˌfaɪt/ *n.* = HYDROPHYTE.

hygroscope /'haɪgrəˌskəʊp/ *n.* an instrument which indicates but does not measure the humidity of the air.

hygroscopic /ˌhaɪgrə'skɒpɪk/ *adj.* **1** of the hygroscope. **2** (of a substance) tending to absorb moisture from the air. □□ **hygroscopically** *adv.*

hying *pres. part.* of HIE.

Hyksos /'hɪksɒs/ *n.pl.* a people of mixed Semitic-Asiatic stock who settled in the Nile delta *c*.1640 BC. They formed the 15th and 16th Dynasties of Egypt, and ruled a large part of the country until driven out by the powerful 18th Dynasty *c.*1532 BC. Described as oppressors by later Egyptians they nevertheless upheld many Egyptian traditions. During their reign the composite bow, the horse and chariot, and new military techniques were introduced into Egypt. [Gk *Huksos* (interpreted by Manetho as 'shepherd kings' or 'captive shepherds') f. Egyptian *heqa khoswe* chief of foreign lands]

hylic /ˈhaɪlɪk/ *adj.* of matter; material. [LL *hylicus* f. Gk *hulikos* f. *hulē* matter]

hylo- /ˈhaɪləʊ/ *comb. form* matter. [Gk *hulo-* f. *hulē* matter]

hylomorphism /ˌhaɪləˈmɔːfɪz(ə)m/ *n.* the theory that physical objects are composed of matter and form. [HYLO- + Gk *morphē* form]

hylozoism /ˌhaɪləˈzəʊɪz(ə)m/ *n.* the doctrine that all matter has life. [HYLO- + Gk *zōē* life]

Hymen /ˈhaɪmen/ *int.* a cry (*Hymen Hymenaie*) used at ancient Greek weddings, and understood (rightly or wrongly) as an invocation of a being of that name. Various stories were invented of him, all to the effect that he was a very handsome young man who had either married happily or had something happen to him on his wedding-day.

hymen /ˈhaɪmen/ *n. Anat.* a membrane which partially closes the opening of the vagina and is usu. broken at the first occurrence of sexual intercourse. □□ **hymenal** *adj.* [LL f. Gk *humēn* membrane]

hymeneal /ˌhaɪmɪˈniːəl/ *adj. literary* of or concerning marriage. [*Hymen* (L f. Gk *Humēn*) Greek and Roman god of marriage]

hymenium /haɪˈmiːnɪəm/ *n.* (*pl.* **hymenia** /-nɪə/) the spore-bearing surface of certain fungi. [mod.L f. Gk *humenion* dimin. of *humēn* membrane]

hymenopteran /ˌhaɪmɪˈnɒptərən/ *n.* any insect of the order *Hymenoptera* having four transparent wings, including bees, wasps, and ants. □□ **hymenopterous** *adj.* [mod.L *hymenoptera* f. Gk *humenopteros* membrane-winged (as HYMENIUM, *pteron* wing)]

hymn /hɪm/ *n. & v.* —*n.* **1** a song of praise, esp. to God in Christian worship, usu. a metrical composition sung in a religious service. **2** a song of praise in honour of a god or other exalted being or thing. —*v.* **1** *tr.* praise or celebrate in hymns. **2** *intr.* sing hymns. □ **hymn-book** a book of hymns. □□ **hymnic** /ˈhɪmnɪk/ *adj.* [ME *ymne* etc. f. OF *ymne* f. L *hymnus* f. Gk *humnos*]

hymnal /ˈhɪmn(ə)l/ *n. & adj.* —*n.* a hymn-book. —*adj.* of hymns. [ME f. med.L *hymnale* (as HYMN)]

hymnary /ˈhɪmnərɪ/ *n.* (*pl.* **-ies**) a hymn-book.

hymnody /ˈhɪmnədɪ/ *n.* (*pl.* **-ies**) **1 a** the singing of hymns. **b** the composition of hymns. **2** hymns collectively. □□ **hymnodist** *n.* [med.L *hymnodia* f. Gk *humnōidia* f. *humnos* hymn: cf. PSALMODY]

hymnographer /hɪmˈnɒɡrəfə(r)/ *n.* a writer of hymns. □□ **hymnography** *n.* [Gk *humnographos* f. *humnos* hymn]

hymnology /hɪmˈnɒlədʒɪ/ *n.* (*pl.* **-ies**) **1** the composition or study of hymns. **2** hymns collectively. □□ **hymnologist** *n.*

hyoid /ˈhaɪɔɪd/ *n. & adj. Anat.* —*n.* (in full **hyoid bone**) a U-shaped bone in the neck which supports the tongue. —*adj.* of or relating to this. [F *hyoïde* f. mod.L *hyoïdes* f. Gk *huoeidēs* shaped like the letter upsilon (*hu*)]

hyoscine /ˈhaɪəsiːn/ *n.* a poisonous alkaloid found in plants of the nightshade family, esp. of the genus *Scopolia*, and used as an antiemetic in motion sickness and a preoperative medication for examination of the eye. Also called SCOPOLAMINE.

hyoscyamine /ˌhaɪəˈsaɪəmiːn/ *n.* a poisonous alkaloid obtained from henbane, having similar properties to hyoscine. [mod.L *hyoscyamus* f. Gk *huoskuamos* henbane f. *hus huos* pig + *kuamos* bean]

hypaesthesia /ˌhaɪpiːsˈθiːzɪə/ *n.* (*US* **hypesthesia**) a diminished capacity for sensation, esp. of the skin. □□ **hypaesthetic** /-ˈθetɪk/ *adj.* [mod.L (as HYPO-, Gk *-aisthēsia* f. *aisthanomai* perceive)]

hypaethral /haɪˈpiːθr(ə)l/ *adj.* (also **hypethral**) **1** open to the sky; roofless. **2** open-air. [L *hypaethrus* f. Gk *hupaithros* (as HYPO-, *aithēr* air)]

hypallage /haɪˈpælədʒɪ/ *n. Rhet.* the transposition of the natural relations of two elements in a proposition (e.g. *Melissa shook her doubtful curls*). [LL f. Gk *hupallagē* (as HYPO-, *allassō* exchange)]

hype[1] /haɪp/ *n. & v. sl.* —*n.* **1** extravagant or intensive publicity promotion. **2** cheating; a trick. —*v.tr.* **1** promote (a product) with extravagant publicity. **2** cheat, trick. [20th c.: orig. unkn.]

hype[2] /haɪp/ *n. sl.* **1** a drug addict. **2** a hypodermic needle or injection. □ **hyped up** stimulated by or as if by a hypodermic injection. [abbr. of HYPODERMIC]

hyper- /ˈhaɪpə(r)/ *prefix* meaning: **1** over, beyond, above (*hyperphysical*). **2** exceeding (*hypersonic*). **3** excessively; above normal (*hyperbole*; *hypersensitive*). [Gk *huper* over, beyond]

hyperactive /ˌhaɪpəˈræktɪv/ *adj.* (of a person, esp. a child) abnormally active. □□ **hyperactivity** /-ˈtɪvɪtɪ/ *n.*

hyperaemia /ˌhaɪpəˈriːmɪə/ *n.* (*US* **hyperemia**) an excessive quantity of blood in the vessels supplying an organ or other part of the body. □□ **hyperaemic** *adj.* [mod.L (as HYPER-, -AEMIA]

hyperaesthesia /ˌhaɪpəriːsˈθiːzɪə/ *n.* (*US* **hyperesthesia**) an excessive physical sensibility, esp. of the skin. □□ **hyperaesthetic** /-ˈθetɪk/ *adj.* [mod.L (as HYPER-, Gk *-aisthēsia* f. *aisthanomai* perceive)]

hyperbaric /ˌhaɪpəˈbærɪk/ *adj.* (of a gas) at a pressure greater than normal. [HYPER- + Gk *barus* heavy]

hyperbaton /haɪˈpɜːbəˌtɒn/ *n. Rhet.* the inversion of the normal order of words, esp. for the sake of emphasis (e.g. *this I must see*). [L f. Gk *huperbaton* (as HYPER-, *bainō* go)]

hyperbola /haɪˈpɜːbələ/ *n.* (*pl.* **hyperbolas** or **hyperbolae** /-ˌliː/) *Geom.* the plane curve of two equal branches, produced when a cone is cut by a plane that makes a larger angle with the base than the side of the cone (cf. ELLIPSE). [mod.L f. Gk *huperbolē* excess (as HYPER-, *ballō* to throw)]

hyperbole /haɪˈpɜːbəlɪ/ *n. Rhet.* an exaggerated statement not meant to be taken literally. □□ **hyperbolical** /-ˈbɒlɪk(ə)l/ *adj.* **hyperbolically** /-ˈbɒlɪkəlɪ/ *adv.* **hyperbolism** *n.* [L (as HYPERBOLA)]

hyperbolic /ˌhaɪpəˈbɒlɪk/ *adj. Geom.* of or relating to a hyperbola. □ **hyperbolic function** a function related to a rectangular hyperbola, e.g. a hyperbolic cosine.

hyperboloid /haɪˈpɜːbəˌlɔɪd/ *n. Geom.* a solid or surface having plane sections that are hyperbolas, ellipses, or circles. □□ **hyperboloidal** *adj.*

hyperborean /ˌhaɪpəbɔːˈriːən, -ˈbɔːrɪən/ *n. & adj.* —*n.* **1** an inhabitant of the extreme north of the earth. **2** (**Hyperborean**) *Gk Mythol.* a member of a race worshipping Apollo and living in a land of sunshine and plenty beyond the north wind. —*adj.* of the extreme north of the earth. [LL *hyperboreanus* f. L *hyperboreus* f. Gk *huperboreos* (as HYPER-, *Boreas* god of the north wind)]

hyperconscious /ˌhaɪpəˈkɒnʃəs/ *adj.* (foll. by *of*) acutely or excessively aware.

hypercritical /ˌhaɪpəˈkrɪtɪk(ə)l/ *adj.* excessively critical, esp. of small faults. □□ **hypercritically** *adv.*

hyperemia *US* var. of HYPERAEMIA.

hyperesthesia *US* var. of HYPERAESTHESIA.

hyperfocal distance /ˌhaɪpəˈfəʊk(ə)l/ *n.* the distance on which a camera lens can be focused to bring the maximum range of object-distances into focus.

hypergamy /haɪˈpɜːɡəmɪ/ *n.* marriage to a person of equal or superior caste or class. [HYPER- + Gk *gamos* marriage]

hyperglycaemia /ˌhaɪpəɡlaɪˈsiːmɪə/ *n.* (*US* **hyperglycemia**) an excess of glucose in the bloodstream, often associated with diabetes mellitus. □□ **hyperglycaemic** *adj.* [HYPER- + GLYCO- + -AEMIA]

hypergolic /ˌhaɪpəˈɡɒlɪk/ *adj.* (of a rocket propellant) igniting spontaneously on contact with an oxidant etc. [G *Hypergol* (perh. as HYPO-, ERG[1], -OL)]

hypericum /haɪˈperɪkəm/ *n.* any shrub of the genus *Hypericum* with five-petalled yellow flowers. Also called St JOHN'S WORT. [L f. Gk *hupereikon* (as HYPER-, *ereikē* heath)]

hypermarket /ˈhaɪpəˌmɑːkɪt/ *n. Brit.* a very large self-service store with a wide range of goods and extensive car-parking facilities, usu. outside a town. [transl. F *hypermarché* (as HYPER-, MARKET)]

hypermetropia /ˌhaɪpəmɪˈtrəʊpɪə/ *n.* the condition of having long sight. □□ **hypermetropic** /-ˈtrɒpɪk/ *adj.* [mod.L f. HYPER- + Gk *metron* measure, *ōps* eye]

hyperon /ˈhaɪpəˌrɒn/ *n. Physics* an unstable elementary particle which is classified as a baryon apart from the neutron or proton. [HYPER- + -ON]

hyperopia /ˌhaɪpəˈrəʊpɪə/ *n.* = HYPERMETROPIA. □□ **hyperopic** /-ˈrɒpɪk/ *adj.* [mod.L f. HYPER- + Gk *ōps* eye]

hyperphysical /ˌhaɪpəˈfɪzɪk(ə)l/ *adj.* supernatural. □□ **hyperphysically** *adv.*

hyperplasia /ˌhaɪpəˈpleɪzɪə/ *n.* the enlargement of an organ or tissue from the increased production of cells. [HYPER- + Gk *plasis* formation]

hypersensitive /ˌhaɪpəˈsensɪtɪv/ *adj.* abnormally or excessively sensitive. □□ **hypersensitiveness** *n.* **hypersensitivity** /-ˈtɪvɪtɪ/ *n.*

hypersonic /ˌhaɪpəˈsɒnɪk/ *adj.* **1** relating to speeds of more than five times the speed of sound (Mach 5). **2** relating to sound-frequencies above about a thousand million hertz. □□ **hypersonically** *adv.* [HYPER-, after SUPERSONIC, ULTRASONIC]

hypersthene /ˈhaɪpəˌsθiːn/ *n.* a rock-forming mineral, magnesium iron silicate, of greenish colour. [F *hyperstène* as HYPER-, Gk *sthenos* strength, from its being harder than hornblende]

hypertension /ˌhaɪpəˈtenʃ(ə)n/ *n.* **1** abnormally high blood pressure. **2** a state of great emotional tension. □□ **hypertensive** /-sɪv/ *adj.*

hyperthermia /ˌhaɪpəˈθɜːmɪə/ *n. Med.* the condition of having a body-temperature greatly above normal. □□ **hyperthermic** *adj.* [HYPER- + Gk *thermē* heat]

hyperthyroidism /ˌhaɪpəˈθaɪrɔɪˌdɪz(ə)m/ *n. Med.* overactivity of the thyroid gland, resulting in rapid heartbeat and an increased rate of metabolism. □□ **hyperthyroid** *n.* & *adj.* **hyperthyroidic** *adj.*

hypertonic /ˌhaɪpəˈtɒnɪk/ *adj.* **1** (of muscles) having high tension. **2** (of a solution) having a greater osmotic pressure than another solution. □□ **hypertonia** /-ˈtəʊnɪə/ *n.* (in sense 1). **hypertonicity** /-təˈnɪsɪtɪ/ *n.*

hypertrophy /haɪˈpɜːtrəfɪ/ *n.* the enlargement of an organ or tissue from the increase in size of its cells. □□ **hypertrophic** /ˌhaɪpəˈtrɒfɪk/ *adj.* **hypertrophied** *adj.* [mod.L *hypertrophia* (as HYPER-, Gk *-trophia* nourishment)]

hyperventilation /ˌhaɪpəˌventɪˈleɪʃ(ə)n/ *n.* breathing at an abnormally rapid rate, resulting in an increased loss of carbon dioxide.

hypethral var. of HYPAETHRAL.

hypha /ˈhaɪfə/ *n.* (*pl.* **hyphae** /-fiː/) a filament in the mycelium of a fungus. □□ **hyphal** *adj.* [mod.L f. Gk *huphē* web]

hyphen /ˈhaɪf(ə)n/ *n.* & *v.* —*n.* the sign (-) used to join words semantically or syntactically (as in *fruit-tree*, *pick-me-up*, *rock-forming*), to indicate the division of a word at the end of a line, or to indicate a missing or implied element (as in *man-* and *womankind*). —*v.tr.* **1** write (a compound word) with a hyphen. **2** join (words) with a hyphen. [LL f. Gk *huphen* together f. *hupo* under + *hen* one]

hyphenate /ˈhaɪfəˌneɪt/ *v.tr.* = HYPHEN *v.* □□ **hyphenation** /-ˈneɪʃ(ə)n/ *n.*

hypno- /ˈhɪpnəʊ/ *comb. form* sleep, hypnosis. [Gk *hupnos* sleep]

hypnogenesis /ˌhɪpnəʊˈdʒenəsɪs/ *n.* the induction of a hypnotic state.

hypnology /hɪpˈnɒlədʒɪ/ *n.* the science of the phenomena of sleep. □□ **hypnologist** *n.*

hypnopaedia /ˌhɪpnəʊˈpiːdɪə/ *n.* learning by hearing while asleep.

Hypnos /ˈhɪpnɒs/ *Gk Mythol.* the god of sleep, son of Night. [Gk *hupnos* sleep]

hypnosis /hɪpˈnəʊsɪs/ *n.* **1** a state like sleep in which the subject acts only on external suggestion. **2** artificially produced sleep. Hypnotic techniques were used in ancient times, but it was the experiments of Mesmer in the 18th c. that led to its introduction into Europe; the word 'hypnotism' was first applied by the Scottish surgeon James Braid in 1842. In France the process was

used by the physiologist J.-M. Charcot (1825–93), and one of his students was Sigmund Freud, who from his study of hypnosis began his exploration of the unconscious mind, which he elaborated into his theory of psychoanalysis. Some subjects under hypnosis seem able to recall memories (e.g. of childhood or other experiences) that have been forgotten by the conscious mind. Hypnosis has always been regarded with suspicion arising from its use as a form of stage entertainment, from recognition that the process is not fully understood, and from unwillingness to allow one person to control another's actions in this way. [mod.L f. Gk *hupnos* sleep + -OSIS]

hypnotherapy /ˌhɪpnəʊˈθerəpɪ/ *n.* the treatment of disease by hypnosis.

hypnotic /hɪpˈnɒtɪk/ *adj.* & *n.* —*adj.* **1** of or producing hypnotism. **2** (of a drug) soporific. —*n.* **1** a thing, esp. a drug, that produces sleep. **2** a person under or open to the influence of hypnotism. □□ **hypnotically** *adv.* [F *hypnotique* f. LL *hypnoticus* f. Gk *hupnōtikos* f. *hupnoō* put to sleep]

hypnotism /ˈhɪpnəˌtɪz(ə)m/ *n.* the study or practice of hypnosis. □□ **hypnotist** *n.*

hypnotize /ˈhɪpnəˌtaɪz/ *v.tr.* (also **-ise**) **1** produce hypnosis in. **2** fascinate; capture the mind of (a person). □□ **hypnotizable** *adj.* **hypnotizer** *n.*

hypo[1] /ˈhaɪpəʊ/ *n. Photog.* the chemical sodium thiosulphate (incorrectly called hyposulphite) used as a photographic fixer. [abbr.]

hypo[2] /ˈhaɪpəʊ/ *n.* (*pl.* **-os**) *colloq.* = HYPODERMIC *n.* [abbr.]

hypo- /ˈhaɪpəʊ/ *prefix* (usu. **hyp-** before a vowel or *h*) **1** under (*hypodermic*). **2** below normal (*hypoxia*). **3** slightly (*hypomania*). **4** *Chem.* containing an element combined in low valence (*hypochlorous*). [Gk f. *hupo* under]

hypoblast /ˈhaɪpəˌblæst/ *n. Biol.* = ENDODERM. [mod.L *hypoblastus* (as HYPO-, -BLAST)]

hypocaust /ˈhaɪpəˌkɔːst/ *n.* a hollow space under the floor in ancient Roman houses, into which hot air was sent for heating a room or bath. [L *hypocaustum* f. Gk *hupokauston* place heated from below (as HYPO-, *kaiō*, *kau-* burn)]

hypochondria /ˌhaɪpəˈkɒndrɪə/ *n.* **1** abnormal anxiety about one's health. **2** morbid depression without real cause. [LL f. Gk *hupokhondria* soft parts of the body below the ribs, where melancholy was thought to arise (as HYPO-, *khondros* sternal cartilage)]

hypochondriac /ˌhaɪpəˈkɒndrɪˌæk/ *n.* & *adj.* —*n.* a person suffering from hypochondria. —*adj.* (also **hypochondriacal** /-ˈdraɪək(ə)l/) of or affected by hypochondria. [F *hypocondriaque* f. Gk *hupokhondriakos* (as HYPOCHONDRIA)]

hypocoristic /ˌhaɪpəkɒˈrɪstɪk/ *adj. Gram.* of the nature of a pet name. [Gk *hupokoristikos* f. *hupokorizomai* call by pet names]

hypocotyl /ˌhaɪpəˈkɒtɪl/ *n. Bot.* the part of the stem of an embryo plant beneath the stalks of the seed leaves or cotyledons and directly above the root.

hypocrisy /hɪˈpɒkrɪsɪ/ *n.* (*pl.* **-ies**) **1** the assumption or postulation of moral standards to which one's own behaviour does not conform; dissimulation, pretence. **2** an instance of this. [ME f. OF *ypocrisie* f. eccl.L *hypocrisis* f. Gk *hupokrisis* acting of a part, pretence (as HYPO-, *krinō* decide, judge)]

hypocrite /ˈhɪpəkrɪt/ *n.* a person given to hypocrisy. □□ **hypocritical** /-ˈkrɪtɪk(ə)l/ *adj.* **hypocritically** /-ˈkrɪtɪkəlɪ/ *adv.* [ME f. OF *ypocrite* f. eccl.L f. Gk *hupokritēs* actor (as HYPOCRISY)]

hypocycloid /ˌhaɪpəˈsaɪklɔɪd/ *n. Math.* the curve traced by a point on the circumference of a circle rolling on the interior of another circle. □□ **hypocycloidal** /-ˈklɔɪd(ə)l/ *adj.*

hypodermic /ˌhaɪpəˈdɜːmɪk/ *adj.* & *n.* —*adj. Med.* **1** of or relating to the area beneath the skin. **2 a** (of a drug etc. or its application) injected beneath the skin. **b** (of a needle, syringe, etc.) used to do this. —*n.* a hypodermic injection or syringe. □□ **hypodermically** *adv.* [HYPO- + Gk *derma* skin]

hypogastrium /ˌhaɪpəˈgæstrɪəm/ *n.* (*pl.* **hypogastria** /-strɪə/) the part of the central abdomen which is situated below the region of the stomach. □□ **hypogastric** *adj.* [mod.L f. Gk *hupogastrion* (as HYPO-, *gastēr* belly)]

hypogean /ˌhaɪpəˈdʒiːən/ adj. (also **hypogeal** /-ˈdʒiːəl/) **1** (existing or growing) underground. **2** (of seed germination) with the seed leaves remaining below the ground. [LL hypogeus f. Gk hupogeios (as HYPO-, gē earth)]

hypogene /ˈhaɪpədʒiːn/ adj. Geol. produced under the surface of the earth. [HYPO- + Gk gen- produce]

hypogeum /ˌhaɪpəˈdʒiːəm/ n. (pl. **hypogea** /-ˈdʒiːə/) an underground chamber. [L f. Gk hupogeion neut. of hupogeios: see HYPOGEAL]

hypoglycaemia /ˌhaɪpəʊɡlaɪˈsiːmɪə/ n. (US **hypoglycemia**) a deficiency of glucose in the bloodstream. □□ **hypoglycaemic** adj. [HYPO- + GLYCO- + -AEMIA]

hypoid /ˈhaɪpɔɪd/ n. a gear with the pinion offset from the centre-line of the wheel, to connect non-intersecting shafts. [perh. f. HYPERBOLOID]

hypolimnion /ˌhaɪpəˈlɪmnɪən/ n. (pl. **hypolimnia** /-nɪə/) the lower layer of water in stratified lakes. [HYPO- + Gk limnion dimin. of limnē lake]

hypomania /ˌhaɪpəˈmeɪnɪə/ n. a minor form of mania. □□ **hypomanic** /-ˈmænɪk/ adj. [mod.L f. G Hypomanie (as HYPO-, MANIA)]

hyponasty /ˈhaɪpəˌnæstɪ/ n. Bot. the tendency in plant-organs for growth to be more rapid on the under-side. □□ **hyponastic** /-ˈnæstɪk/ adj. [HYPO- + Gk nastos pressed]

hypophysis /haɪˈpɒfɪsɪs/ n. (pl. **hypophyses** /-ˌsiːz/) Anat. = pituitary gland. □□ **hypophyseal** /ˌhaɪpə ˈfɪzɪəl/ adj. (also **-physial**). [mod.L f. Gk hupophusis offshoot (as HYPO-, phusis growth)]

hypostasis /haɪˈpɒstəsɪs/ n. (pl. **hypostases** /-ˌsiːz/) **1** Med. an accumulation of fluid or blood in the lower parts of the body or organs under the influence of gravity, in cases of poor circulation. **2** Metaphysics an underlying substance, as opposed to attributes or to that which is unsubstantial. **3** Theol. **a** the person of Christ, combining human and divine natures. **b** each of the three persons of the Trinity. □□ **hypostasize** v.tr. (also **-ise**) (in senses 1, 2). [eccl.L f. Gk hupostasis (as HYPO-, STASIS standing, state)]

hypostatic /ˌhaɪpəˈstætɪk/ adj. (also **hypostatical**) Theol. relating to the three persons of the Trinity. □ **hypostatic union** the union of divine and human natures in Christ, a doctrine formally accepted by the Church in 451.

hypostyle /ˈhaɪpəˌstaɪl/ adj. Archit. having a roof supported by pillars. [Gk hupostulos (as HYPO-, STYLE)]

hypotaxis /ˌhaɪpəˈtæksɪs/ n. Gram. the subordination of one clause to another. □□ **hypotactic** /-ˈtæktɪk/ adj. [Gk hupotaxis (as HYPO-, taxis arrangement)]

hypotension /ˌhaɪpəˈtenʃ(ə)n/ n. abnormally low blood pressure. □□ **hypotensive** adj.

hypotenuse /haɪˈpɒtəˌnjuːz/ n. the side opposite the right angle of a right-angled triangle. [L hypotenusa f. Gk hupoteinousa (grammē) subtending (line) fem. part. of hupoteinō (as HYPO-, teinō stretch)]

hypothalamus /ˌhaɪpəˈθæləməs/ n. (pl. **-mi** /-maɪ/) Anat. the region of the brain which controls body-temperature, thirst, hunger, etc. □□ **hypothalamic** adj. [mod.L formed as HYPO-, THALAMUS]

hypothec /ˈhaɪpəθɪk/ n. (in Roman and Scottish law) a right established by law over property belonging to a debtor. □□ **hypothecary** /haɪˈpɒθɪkərɪ/ adj. [F hypothèque f. LL hypotheca f. Gk hupothēkē deposit (as HYPO-, tithēmi place)]

hypothecate /haɪˈpɒθɪˌkeɪt/ v.tr. pledge, mortgage. □□ **hypothecation** /-ˈkeɪʃ(ə)n/ n. [med.L hypothecare (as HYPOTHEC)]

hypothermia /ˌhaɪpəʊˈθɜːmɪə/ n. Med. the condition of having an abnormally low body-temperature. [HYPO- + Gk thermē heat]

hypothesis /haɪˈpɒθɪsɪs/ n. (pl. **hypotheses** /-ˌsiːz/) **1** a proposition made as a basis for reasoning, without the assumption of its truth. **2** a supposition made as a starting-point for further investigation from known facts (cf. THEORY). **3** a groundless assumption. [LL f. Gk hupothesis foundation (as HYPO-, THESIS)]

hypothesize /haɪˈpɒθɪˌsaɪz/ v. (also **-ise**) **1** intr. frame a hypothesis. **2** tr. assume a hypothesis. □□ **hypothesist** /-sɪst/ n. **hypothesizer** n.

hypothetical /ˌhaɪpəˈθetɪk(ə)l/ adj. **1** of or based on or serving as a hypothesis. **2** supposed but not necessarily real or true. □□ **hypothetically** adv.

hypothyroidism /ˌhaɪpəʊˈθaɪrɔɪˌdɪz(ə)m/ n. Med. subnormal activity of the thyroid gland, resulting in cretinism in children, and mental and physical slowing in adults. □□ **hypothyroid** n. & adj. **hypothyroidic** /-ˈrɔɪdɪk/ adj.

hypoventilation /ˌhaɪpəʊˌventɪˈleɪʃ(ə)n/ n. breathing at an abnormally slow rate, resulting in an increased amount of carbon dioxide in the blood.

hypoxaemia /ˌhaɪpɒkˈsiːmɪə/ n. (US **hypoxemia**) Med. an abnormally low concentration of oxygen in the blood. [mod.L (as HYPO-, OXYGEN, -AEMIA)]

hypoxia /haɪˈpɒksɪə/ n. Med. a deficiency of oxygen reaching the tissues. □□ **hypoxic** adj. [HYPO- + OX- + -IA¹]

hypso- /ˈhɪpsəʊ/ comb. form height. [Gk hupsos height]

hypsography /hɪpˈsɒɡrəfɪ/ n. a description or mapping of the contours of the earth's surface. □□ **hypsographic** /-ˈɡræfɪk/ adj. **hypsographical** /-ˈɡræfɪk(ə)l/ adj.

hypsometer /hɪpˈsɒmɪtə(r)/ n. **1** a device for calibrating thermometers at the boiling point of water. **2** this instrument when used to estimate height above sea level. □□ **hypsometric** /-səˈmetrɪk/ adj.

hyrax /ˈhaɪræks/ n. any small mammal of the order Hyracoidea, including rock-rabbit and dassie. [mod.L f. Gk hurax shrew-mouse]

hyson /ˈhaɪs(ə)n/ n. a kind of green China tea. [Chin. xichun, lit. 'bright spring']

hyssop /ˈhɪsəp/ n. **1** any small bushy aromatic herb of the genus Hyssopus, esp. H. officinalis, formerly used medicinally. **2** Bibl. **a** a plant whose twigs were used for sprinkling in Jewish rites. **b** a bunch of this used in purification. [OE (h)ysope (reinforced in ME by OF ysope) f. L hyssopus f. Gk hyssōpos, of Semitic orig.]

hysterectomy /ˌhɪstəˈrektəmɪ/ n. (pl. **-ies**) the surgical removal of the womb. □□ **hysterectomize** v.tr. (also **-ise**). [Gk hustera womb + -ECTOMY]

hysteresis /ˌhɪstəˈriːsɪs/ n. Physics the lagging behind of an effect when its cause varies in amount etc., esp. of magnetic induction behind the magnetizing force. [Gk husterēsis f. hustereō be behind f. husteros coming after]

hysteria /hɪˈstɪərɪə/ n. **1** a wild uncontrollable emotion or excitement. **2** a functional disturbance of the nervous system, of psychoneurotic origin. [mod.L (as HYSTERIC)]

hysteric /hɪˈsterɪk/ n. & adj. —n. **1** (in pl.) **a** a fit of hysteria. **b** colloq. overwhelming mirth or laughter (we were in hysterics). **2** a hysterical person. —adj. = HYSTERICAL. [L f. Gk husterikos of the womb (hustera), hysteria being thought to occur more frequently in women than in men and to be associated with the womb]

hysterical /hɪˈsterɪk(ə)l/ adj. **1** of or affected with hysteria. **2** morbidly or uncontrolledly emotional. **3** colloq. extremely funny or amusing. □□ **hysterically** adv.

hysteron proteron /ˌhɪstərɒn ˈprɒtərɒn/ n. Rhet. a figure of speech in which what should come last is put first; an inversion of the natural order (e.g. I die! I faint! I fail!). [LL f. Gk husteron proteron the latter (put in place of) the former]

Hz abbr. hertz.

I

I¹ /aɪ/ n. (also i) (pl. Is or I's) 1 the ninth letter of the alphabet. 2 (as a Roman numeral) 1. □ I-beam a girder of I-shaped section.

I² /aɪ/ pron. & n. —pron. (obj. me; poss. my, mine; pl. we) used by a speaker or writer to refer to himself or herself. —n. (the I) Metaphysics the ego; the subject or object of self-consciousness. [OE f. Gmc]

I³ symb. Chem. the element iodine.

I⁴ abbr. (also I.) 1 Island(s). 2 Isle(s).

-i¹ /i, aɪ/ suffix forming the plural of nouns from Latin in -us or from Italian in -e or -o (foci; dilettanti; timpani). ¶ Plural in -s or -es is often also possible.

-i² /i/ suffix forming adjectives from names of countries or regions in the Near or Middle East (Israeli; Pakistani). [adj. suffix in Semitic and Indo-Iranian languages]

-i- a connecting vowel esp. forming words in -ana, -ferous, -fic, -form, -fy, -gerous, -vorous (cf. -O-). [from or after F f. L]

IA abbr. US Iowa (in official postal use).

Ia. abbr. Iowa.

-ia¹ /ɪə/ suffix 1 forming abstract nouns (mania; utopia), often in Med. (anaemia; pneumonia). 2 Bot. forming names of classes and genera (dahlia; fuchsia). 3 forming names of countries (Australia; India). [from or after L & Gk]

-ia² /ɪə/ suffix forming plural nouns or the plural of nouns: 1 from Greek in -ion or Latin in -ium (paraphernalia; regalia; amnia; labia). 2 Zool. the names of groups (Mammalia).

IAA abbr. indoleacetic acid.

IAEA abbr. International Atomic Energy Agency.

-ial /ɪəl/ suffix forming adjectives (celestial; dictatorial; trivial). [from or after F -iel or L -ialis: cf. -AL]

iamb /ˈaɪæmb/ n. an iambus. [Anglicized f. IAMBUS]

iambic /aɪˈæmbɪk/ adj. & n. Prosody —adj. of or using iambuses. —n. (usu. in pl.) iambic verse. [F iambique f. LL iambicus f. Gk iambikos (as IAMBUS)]

iambus /aɪˈæmbəs/ n. (pl. iambuses or -bi /-baɪ/) Prosody a foot consisting of one short (or unstressed) followed by one long (or stressed) syllable. [L f. Gk iambos iambus, lampoon, f. iaptō assail in words, from its use by Gk satirists]

-ian /ɪən/ suffix var. of -AN. [from or after F -ien or L -ianus]

Iasi /ˈjæʃɪ/ (German Jassy) a city in eastern Romania, close to the Soviet frontier; pop. (1985) 314,150. Between 1565 and 1859 it was the capital of the principality of Moldavia.

-iasis /ˈaɪəsɪs/ suffix the usual form of -ASIS.

IATA /aɪˈɑːtə, i:-/ abbr. International Air Transport Association.

iatrogenic /aɪˌætrəˈdʒenɪk/ adj. (of a disease etc.) caused by medical examination or treatment. [Gk iatros physician + -GENIC]

ib. var. of IBID.

IBA abbr. (in the UK) Independent Broadcasting Authority, replaced in 1991 by the Independent Television Commission and the Radio Authority.

Ibadan /ˌɪbəˈdɑːn, ɪˈbæd(ə)n/ the second-largest city of Nigeria; pop. (1983) 1,060,000.

Iban /ˈiːbæn/ n. & adj. —n. (pl. same) 1 a member of a group of non-Muslim indigenous peoples from the island of Borneo; a member of the Sea Dyaks. (See DYAK.) 2 their language, spoken by about 303,000 people, belonging to the Indonesian section of the Malayo-Polynesian group of languages. —adj. of the Iban or their language. [native name]

Iberia /aɪˈbɪərɪə/ the ancient name for the country now comprising Spain and Portugal, forming the extreme SW peninsula of Europe. □□ Iberian adj. & n. [L f. Gk Ibēres Spaniards]

Ibero- /ɪˈbeərəʊ/ comb. form Iberian; Iberian and (Ibero-American).

ibex /ˈaɪbeks/ n. (pl. ibexes) a wild goat, Capra ibex, esp. of mountainous areas of Europe, N. Africa, and Asia, with a chin beard and thick curved ridged horns. [L]

ibid. abbr. (also ib.) in the same book or passage etc. [L ibidem in the same place]

-ibility /ɪˈbɪlɪtɪ/ suffix forming nouns from, or corresponding to, adjectives in -ible (possibility; credibility). [F -ibilité or L -ibilitas]

ibis /ˈaɪbɪs/ n. (pl. ibises) any wading bird of the family Threskiornithidae with a curved bill, long neck, and long legs, and nesting in colonies. □ sacred ibis an ibis, Threskiornis aethiopicus, native to Africa and Madagascar, venerated by the ancient Egyptians. [ME f. L f. Gk]

Ibiza /ɪˈbiːθə/ 1 the westernmost of the Balearic Islands; pop. (1981) 40,000. 2 its capital city and port.

-ible /ˈɪb(ə)l/ suffix forming adjectives meaning 'that may or may be' (see -ABLE) (terrible; forcible; possible). [F -ible or L -ibilis]

-ibly /ˈɪblɪ/ suffix forming adverbs corresponding to adjectives in -ible.

IBM abbr. International Business Machines.

Ibn Batuta /ˌɪbən bɑːˈtuːtɑː/ (c.1304–68), Arab explorer who spent 24 years on journeys through North and West Africa, Asia, India, and China, and wrote a vivid description of his travels (the Rihlah).

Ibo /ˈiːbəʊ/ n. & adj. (also Igbo) —n. (pl. same or -os) 1 a member of a Black people of SE Nigeria. 2 the language of this people, which belongs to the Niger–Congo language group and is spoken by some 8 million people, one of the major languages of Nigeria. —adj. of the Ibo or their language. [native name]

IBRD abbr. International Bank for Reconstruction and Development (also known as the World Bank).

Ibsen /ˈɪbs(ə)n/, Henrik (1828–1906), Norwegian dramatist, generally acknowledged as the founder of modern prose drama, who came to fame at a time when the theatre in Europe was at a low ebb. He gave vent to his despondency at his country's attitude to the Danish–German War in two great lyrical dramas, Brand (1866) and Peer Gynt (1867). A series of problem plays followed, dealing mainly with the relation of the individual to his social environment, and particularly the case of woman in marriage; these include A Doll's House (1879), Ghosts (1881), Rosmersholm (1886), and Hedda Gabler (1890) which influenced Shaw who introduced Ibsen's work to English theatre. Ibsen's later works, such as The Master Builder (1892) and When we Dead Awake (1900), deal increasingly with the forces of the unconscious and were of great interest to Freud. The quality of Ibsen's dialogue and his disregarding of traditional theatrical effects demanded a new style of performance.

IC abbr. integrated circuit.

i/c abbr. 1 in charge. 2 in command. 3 internal combustion.

-ic /ɪk/ suffix 1 forming adjectives (Arabic; classic; public) and nouns (critic; epic; mechanic; music). 2 Chem. in higher valence or degree of oxidation (ferric; sulphuric) (see also -OUS). 3 denoting a particular form or instance of a noun in -ics (aesthetic; tactic). [from or after F -ique or L -icus or Gk -ikos: cf. -ATIC, -ETIC, -FIC, -OTIC]

-ical /ˈɪk(ə)l/ suffix 1 forming adjectives corresponding to nouns or adjectives, usu. in -ic (classical; comical; farcical; musical). 2 forming adjectives corresponding to nouns in -y (pathological).

-ically /ˈɪkəlɪ/ suffix forming adverbs corresponding to adjectives in -ic or -ical (comically; musically; tragically).

ICAO abbr. International Civil Aviation Organization.

Icarus /ˈɪkərəs/ Gk legend the son of Daedalus (see entry).

ICBM abbr. intercontinental ballistic missile.

ICE abbr. 1 (in the UK) Institution of Civil Engineers. 2 internal-combustion engine.

ice /aɪs/ n. & v. —n. 1 a frozen water, a brittle transparent

b but d dog f few g get h he j yes k cat l leg m man n no p pen r red s sit t top v voice

crystalline solid. **b** a sheet of this on the surface of water (*fell through the ice*). **2** Brit. a portion of ice-cream or water-ice (*would you like an ice?*). **3** sl. diamonds. —*v.* **1** tr. mix with or cool in ice (*iced drinks*). **2** tr. & intr. (often foll. by *over*, *up*) **a** cover or become covered with ice. **b** freeze. **3** tr. cover (a cake etc.) with icing. □ **ice age** a glacial period (see GLACIAL), esp. in the Pleistocene epoch, which ended about 10,000 years ago. **ice-axe** a tool used by mountain-climbers for cutting footholds. **ice-bag** an ice-filled rubber bag for medical use. **ice-blue** a very pale blue. **ice-boat 1** a boat mounted on runners for travelling on ice. **2** a boat used for breaking ice on a river etc. **ice-bound** confined by ice. **ice-breaker 1** = *ice-boat* 2. **2** something that serves to relieve inhibitions, start a conversation, etc. **ice bucket** a bucket-like container with chunks of ice, used to keep a bottle of wine chilled. **ice-cap** a permanent covering of ice e.g. in polar regions. **ice-cold** as cold as ice. **ice-cream** a sweet creamy frozen food, usu. flavoured. **ice-cube** a small block of ice made in a refrigerator. **ice-fall** a steep part of a glacier like a frozen waterfall. **ice-field** an expanse of ice, esp. in polar regions. **ice-fish** a capelin. **ice floe** = FLOE. **ice hockey** see HOCKEY. **ice house** a building often partly or wholly underground for storing ice. **ice** (or **iced**) **lolly** Brit. a piece of flavoured ice, often with chocolate or ice-cream, on a stick. **ice-pack 1** = *pack ice*. **2** a quantity of ice applied to the body for medical etc. purposes. **ice-pick** a needle-like implement with a handle for splitting up small pieces of ice. **ice-plant** a plant, *Mesembryanthemum crystallinum*, with leaves covered with crystals or vesicles looking like ice specks. **ice-rink** = RINK *n.* 1. **ice-skate** *n.* a skate consisting of a boot with a blade beneath, for skating on ice. —*v.intr.* skate on ice. **ice-skater** a person who skates on ice. **ice station** a meteorological research centre in polar regions. **on ice 1** (of an entertainment, sport, etc.) performed by skaters. **2** colloq. held in reserve; awaiting further attention. **on thin ice** in a risky situation. [OE īs f. Gmc]

-ice /ɪs/ suffix forming (esp. abstract) nouns (*avarice; justice; service*) (cf. -ISE²).

iceberg /'aɪsbɜːg/ *n.* **1** a large floating mass of ice detached from a glacier or ice-sheet and carried out to sea. **2** an unemotional or cold-blooded person. □ **iceberg lettuce** any of various crisp lettuces with a freely blanching head. **the tip of the iceberg** a small perceptible part of something (esp. a difficulty) the greater part of which is hidden. [prob. f. Du. *ijsberg* f. *ijs* ice + *berg* hill]

iceblink /'aɪsblɪŋk/ *n.* a luminous appearance on the horizon, caused by a reflection from ice.

iceblock /'aɪsblɒk/ *n.* Austral. & NZ = *ice lolly*.

icebox /'aɪsbɒks/ *n.* **1** a compartment in a refrigerator for making or storing ice. **2** US a refrigerator.

Iceland /'aɪslənd/ a volcanic island country in the North Atlantic, just south of the Arctic Circle; pop. (est. 1988) 246,500; official language, Icelandic; capital, Reykjavik. First settled by Norse colonists in the 9th c., Iceland was under Norwegian rule from 1262 to 1380 when it passed to Denmark. Granted internal self-government in 1874, it became a fully fledged independent republic in 1944. The Icelandic economy is dominated by fishing, and since the late 1950s there have been periodic disputes with Great Britain over fishing rights around the island. □ **Iceland lichen** (or **moss**) a mountain and moorland lichen, *Cetraria islandica*, with edible branching fronds. **Iceland poppy** an Arctic poppy, *Papaver nudicaule*, with red or yellow flowers. **Iceland spar** a transparent variety of calcite with the optical property of strong double refraction. □□ **Icelander** *n.*

Icelandic /aɪs'lændɪk/ adj & *n.* —adj. of or relating to Iceland or its language. —*n.* the official language of Iceland, spoken by its 250,000 inhabitants, a Scandinavian language which is the purest descendant of Old Norse. Its purity is due partly to the geographical position of Iceland but also to a policy of avoiding the use of loan-words.

iceman /'aɪsmən/ *n.* (pl. **-men**) esp. US **1** a man skilled in crossing ice. **2** a man who sells or delivers ice.

ICFTU abbr. Internationl Confederation of Free Trade Unions.

I.Chem.E. abbr. (in the UK) Institution of Chemical Engineers.

I Ching /iː 'tʃɪŋ/ *n.* an ancient Chinese manual with symbols

known as the eight trigrams and sixty-four hexagrams that were symbolically interpreted in terms of the principles of yin and yang. Originally used for divination, it was later included as one of the 'five classics' of Confucianism. [Chin. *yijing* book of changes]

ichneumon /ɪk'njuːmən/ *n.* **1** (in full **ichneumon wasp**) any small hymenopterous insect of the family Ichneumonidae, depositing eggs in or on the larva of another insect as food for its own larva. **2** a mongoose of N. Africa, *Herpestes ichneumon*, noted for destroying crocodile eggs. [L f. Gk *ikhneumōn* spider-hunting wasp f. *ikhneuō* trace f. *ikhnos* footstep]

ichnography /ɪk'nɒgrəfɪ/ *n.* (pl. **-ies**) **1** the ground-plan of a building, map of a region, etc. **2** a drawing of this. [F *ichnographie* or L *ichnographia* f. Gk *ikhnographia* f. *ikhnos* track: see -GRAPHY]

ichor /'aɪkɔː(r)/ *n.* **1** Gk Mythol. fluid flowing like blood in the veins of the gods. **2** poet. bloodlike fluid. **3** hist. a watery fetid discharge from a wound etc. □□ **ichorous** /'aɪkərəs/ adj. [Gk *ikhōr*]

ichthyo- /'ɪkθɪəʊ/ comb. form fish. [Gk *ikhthus* fish]

ichthyoid /'ɪkθɪˌɔɪd/ adj. & *n.* —adj. fishlike. —*n.* any fishlike vertebrate.

ichthyolite /'ɪkθɪəˌlaɪt/ *n.* a fossil fish.

ichthyology /ˌɪkθɪ'ɒlədʒɪ/ *n.* the study of fishes. □□ **ichthyological** /-ə'lɒdʒɪk(ə)l/ adj. **ichthyologist** *n.*

ichthyophagous /ˌɪkθɪ'ɒfəgəs/ adj. fish-eating. □□ **ichthyophagy** /-fədʒɪ/ *n.*

ichthyosaurus /ˌɪkθɪə'sɔːrəs/ *n.* (also **ichthyosaur** /'ɪkθɪəˌsɔːr/) any extinct marine reptile of the order Ichthyosauria, with long head, tapering body, four flippers, and usu. a large tail. [ICHTHYO- + Gk *sauros* lizard]

ichthyosis /ˌɪkθɪ'əʊsɪs/ *n.* a skin disease which causes the epidermis to become dry and horny like fish scales. □□ **ichthyotic** /-'ɒtɪk/ adj. [Gk *ikhthus* fish + -OSIS]

ICI abbr. Imperial Chemical Industries.

-ician /'ɪʃ(ə)n/ suffix forming nouns denoting persons skilled in or concerned with subjects having nouns (usu.) in -ic or -ics (*magician; politician*). [from or after F -icien (as -IC, -IAN)]

icicle /'aɪsɪk(ə)l/ *n.* a hanging tapering piece of ice, formed by the freezing of dripping water. [ME f. ICE + *ickle* (now dial.) icicle]

icing /'aɪsɪŋ/ *n.* **1** a coating of sugar etc. on a cake or biscuit. **2** the formation of ice on a ship or aircraft. □ **icing on the cake** an attractive though inessential addition or enhancement. **icing sugar** Brit. finely powdered sugar for making icing for cakes etc.

-icist /ɪsɪst/ suffix = -ICIAN (*classicist*). [-IC + -IST]

-icity /'ɪsɪtɪ/ suffix forming abstract nouns esp. from adjectives in -ic (*authenticity; publicity*). [-IC + -ITY]

-ick /ɪk/ suffix archaic var. of -IC.

Icknield Way /'ɪkniːld/ an ancient pre-Roman track crossing England in a wide curve from Wiltshire to Norfolk.

icky /'ɪkɪ/ adj. (also **ikky**) colloq. **1** sweet, sticky, sickly. **2** (as a general term of disapproval) nasty, repulsive. [20th c.: orig. unkn.]

-icle /'ɪk(ə)l/ suffix forming (orig. diminutive) nouns (*article; particle*). [formed as -CULE]

icon /'aɪkɒn/ *n.* (also **ikon**) **1** a devotional painting or carving, usu. on wood, of Christ or another holy figure, esp. in the Eastern Church. **2** an image or statue. **3** Computing a symbol or graphic representation on a VDU screen of a program, option, or window, esp. one of several for selection. **4** Linguistics a sign which has a characteristic in common with the thing it signifies. [L f. Gk *eikōn* image]

iconic /aɪ'kɒnɪk/ adj. **1** of or having the nature of an image or portrait. **2** (of a statue) following a conventional type. **3** Linguistics that is an icon. □□ **iconicity** /-kə'nɪsɪtɪ/ *n.* (esp. in sense 3). [L *iconicus* f. Gk *eikonikos* (as ICON)]

icono- /aɪ'kɒnəʊ/ comb. form an image or likeness. [Gk *eikōn*]

iconoclasm /aɪ'kɒnəˌklæz(ə)m/ *n.* **1** the breaking of images. **2** the assailing of cherished beliefs. [ICONOCLAST after *enthusiasm* etc.]

iconoclast /aɪˈkɒnəˌklæst/ n. **1** a person who attacks cherished beliefs. **2** a person who destroys images used in religious worship, esp. *hist.* one who took part in a movement in the 8th–9th c. against the use of images in religious worship in churches in the Eastern Roman Empire, or a Puritan of the 16th–17th c. □□ **iconoclastic** /-ˈklæstɪk/ adj. **iconoclastically** /-ˈklæstɪkəlɪ/ adv. [med.L iconoclastes f. eccl.Gk eikonoklastēs (as ICONO-, klaō break)]

iconography /ˌaɪkəˈnɒgrəfɪ/ n. (pl. -ies) **1** the illustration of a subject by drawings or figures. **2 a** the study of portraits, esp. of an individual. **b** the study of artistic images or symbols. **3** a treatise on pictures or statuary. **4** a book whose essence is pictures. □□ **iconographer** n. **iconographic** /-nəˈgræfɪk/ adj. **iconographical** /-nəˈgræfɪk(ə)l/ adj. **iconographically** /-nəˈgræfɪkəlɪ/ adv. [Gk eikonographia sketch (as ICONO- + -GRAPHY)]

iconolatry /ˌaɪkəˈnɒlətrɪ/ n. the worship of images. □□ **iconolater** n. [eccl.Gk eikonolatreia (as ICONO-, -LATRY)]

iconology /ˌaɪkəˈnɒlədʒɪ/ n. **1** an artistic theory developed from iconography (see ICONOGRAPHY 2b). **2** symbolism.

iconostasis /ˌaɪkəˈnɒstəsɪs, aɪˌkɒnəˈstæsɪs/ n. (pl. **iconostases** /-ˌsiːz/) (in the Eastern Church) a screen bearing icons and separating the sanctuary from the nave. [mod.Gk eikonostasis (as ICONO-, STASIS)]

icosahedron /ˌaɪkəsəˈhedrən, -ˈhiːdrən/ n. a solid figure with twenty faces. □□ **icosahedral** adj. [LL icosahedrum f. Gk eikosaedron f. eikosi twenty + -HEDRON]

-ics /ɪks/ suffix (treated as sing. or pl.) forming nouns denoting arts or sciences or branches of study or action (athletics; politics) (cf. -IC 3). [from or after F pl. -iques or L pl. -ica or Gk pl. -ika]

icterus /ˈɪktərəs/ n. Med. = JAUNDICE. □□ **icteric** /ɪkˈterɪk/ adj. [L f. Gk ikteros]

Ictinus /ɪkˈtiːnəs/ (5th c. BC) Greek architect. His most famous building was the Parthenon at Athens which he designed with his colleague Callicrates and the sculptor Phidias between 448 and 437 BC.

ictus /ˈɪktəs/ n. (pl. same or **ictuses**) **1** Prosody rhythmical or metrical stress. **2** Med. a stroke or seizure; a fit. [L, = blow f. icere strike]

icy /ˈaɪsɪ/ adj. (**icier, iciest**) **1** very cold. **2** covered with or abounding in ice. **3** (of a tone or manner) unfriendly, hostile (an icy stare). □□ **icily** adv. **iciness** n.

ID abbr. **1** esp. US identification, identity (ID card). **2** US Idaho (in official postal use).

id /ɪd/ n. Psychol. the inherited instinctive impulses of the individual as part of the unconscious. [L, = that, transl. G es]

id. abbr. = IDEM.

i.d. abbr. inner diameter.

I'd /aɪd/ contr. **1** I had. **2** I should; I would.

-id[1] /ɪd/ suffix forming adjectives (arid; rapid). [F -ide f. L -idus]

-id[2] /ɪd/ suffix forming nouns: **1** general (pyramid). **2** Biol. of structural constituents (plastid). **3** Bot. of a plant belonging to a family with a name in -aceae (orchid). [from or after F -ide f. L -is -idis f. Gk -is -ida or -idos]

-id[3] /ɪd/ suffix forming nouns denoting: **1** Zool. an animal belonging to a family with a name in -idae or a class with a name in -ida (canid; arachnid). **2** a member of a person's family (Seleucid from Seleucus). **3** Astron. **a** a meteor in a group radiating from a specified constellation (Leonid from Leo). **b** a star of a class like one in a specified constellation (cepheid). [from or after L -ides, pl. -idae or -ida]

-id[4] /ɪd/ suffix esp. US var. of -IDE.

IDA abbr. International Development Association.

Idaho /ˈaɪdəˌhəʊ/ a State in the north-western US, bordering on British Columbia and containing part of the Rocky Mountains; pop. (est. 1985) 944,100; capital, Boise. It became the 43rd State of the US in 1890.

ide /aɪd/ n. a freshwater fish, Leuciscus idus, used as food. Also called ORFE. [mod.L idus f. Sw. id]

-ide /aɪd/ suffix (also esp. US **-id**) Chem. forming nouns denoting: **1** binary compounds of an element (the suffix -ide being added to the abbreviated name of the more electronegative element etc.) (sodium chloride; lead sulphide; calcium carbide). **2** various other compounds (amide; anhydride; peptide; saccharide). **3** elements of a series in the periodic table (actinide; lanthanide). [orig. in OXIDE]

idea /aɪˈdɪə/ n. **1** a conception or plan formed by mental effort (have you any ideas?; had the idea of writing a book). **2 a** a mental impression or notion; a concept. **b** a vague belief or fancy (had an idea you were married; had no idea where you were). **3** an intention, purpose, or essential feature (the idea is to make money). **4** an archetype or pattern as distinguished from its realization in individual cases. **5** Philos. **a** (in Platonism) an eternally existing pattern of which individual things in any class are imperfect copies. **b** a concept of pure reason which transcends experience. □ **get** (or **have**) **ideas** colloq. be ambitious, rebellious, etc. **have no idea** colloq. **1** not know at all. **2** be completely incompetent. **not one's idea of** colloq. not what one regards as (not my idea of a pleasant evening). **put ideas into a person's head** suggest ambitions etc. he or she would not otherwise have had. **that's an idea** colloq. that proposal etc. is worth considering. **the very idea!** colloq. an exclamation of disapproval or disagreement. □□ **idea'd** adj. **ideaed** adj. **idealess** adj. [Gk idea form, pattern f. stem id- see]

ideal /aɪˈdiːəl/ adj. & n. —adj. **1 a** answering to one's highest conception. **b** perfect or supremely excellent. **2 a** existing only in idea. **b** visionary. **3** embodying an idea. **4** relating to or consisting of ideas; dependent on the mind. —n. **1** a perfect type, or a conception of this. **2** an actual thing as a standard for imitation. □ **ideal gas** a hypothetical gas consisting of molecules occupying negligible space and without attraction for each other, thereby obeying simple laws. □□ **ideally** adv. [ME f. F idéal f. LL idealis (as IDEA)]

idealism /aɪˈdɪəˌlɪz(ə)m/ n. **1** the practice of forming or following after ideals, esp. unrealistically (cf. REALISM). **2** the representation of things in ideal or idealized form. **3** imaginative treatment. **4** Philos. any of various systems of thought in which the objects of knowledge are held to be in some way dependent on the activity of mind (cf. REALISM). □□ **idealist** n. **idealistic** /-ˈlɪstɪk/ adj. **idealistically** /-ˈlɪstɪkəlɪ/ adv. [F idéalisme or G Idealismus (as IDEAL)]

ideality /ˌaɪdɪˈælɪtɪ/ n. (pl. -ies) **1** the quality of being ideal. **2** an ideal thing.

idealize /aɪˈdɪəˌlaɪz/ v.tr. (also **-ise**) **1** regard or represent (a thing or person) in ideal form or character. **2** exalt in thought to ideal perfection or excellence. □□ **idealization** /-ˈzeɪʃ(ə)n/ n. **idealizer** n.

ideate /ˈaɪdɪˌeɪt/ v. Psychol. **1** tr. imagine, conceive. **2** intr. form ideas. □□ **ideation** /-ˈeɪʃ(ə)n/ n. **ideational** /-ˈeɪʃən(ə)l/ adj. **ideationally** /-ˈeɪʃənəlɪ/ adv. [med.L ideare form an idea (as IDEA)]

idée fixe /ˌiːdeɪ ˈfiːks/ n. (pl. **idées fixes** pronunc. same) an idea that dominates the mind; an obsession. [F, lit. 'fixed idea']

idée reçue /iːˌdeɪ rəˈsjuː/ n. (pl. **idées reçues** pronunc. same) a generally accepted notion or opinion. [F]

idem /ˈɪdem/ adv. & n. —adv. in the same author. —n. the same word or author. [ME f. L]

identical /aɪˈdentɪk(ə)l/ adj. **1** (often foll. by with) (of different things) agreeing in every detail. **2** (of one thing viewed at different times) one and the same. **3** (of twins) developed from a single fertilized ovum, therefore of the same sex and usu. very similar in appearance. **4** Logic & Math. expressing an identity. □□ **identically** adv. **identicalness** n. [med.L identicus (as IDENTITY)]

identification /aɪˌdentɪfɪˈkeɪʃ(ə)n/ n. **1** the act or an instance of identifying. **2** a means of identifying a person. **3** (attrib.) serving to identify (esp. the bearer) (identification card). □ **identification parade** an assembly of persons from whom a suspect is to be identified.

identifier /aɪˈdentɪˌfaɪə(r)/ n. **1** a person or thing that identifies. **2** Computing a sequence of characters used to identify or refer to a set of data.

identify /aɪˈdentɪˌfaɪ/ v. (**-ies, -ied**) **1** tr. establish the identity of; recognize. **2** tr. establish or select by consideration or analysis of the circumstances (identify the best method of solving the problem). **3** tr. (foll. by with) associate (a person or oneself) inseparably or very closely (with a party, policy, etc.). **4** *tr.* (often foll. by *with*) treat (a thing) as identical. **5** *intr.* (foll. by *with*) **a** regard oneself as sharing characteristics of (another person). **b** associate oneself. □□ **identifiable** *adj.* [med.L *identificare* (as IDENTITY)]

Identikit /aɪˈdentɪkɪt/ *n.* (often *attrib.*) *propr.* a reconstructed picture of a person (esp. one sought by the police) assembled from transparent strips showing typical facial features according to witnesses' descriptions. [IDENTITY + KIT¹]

identity /aɪˈdentɪtɪ/ *n.* (*pl.* **-ies**) **1 a** the quality or condition of being a specified person or thing. **b** individuality, personality (*felt he had lost his identity*). **2** identification or the result of it (*a case of mistaken identity*; *identity card*). **3** the state of being the same in substance, nature, qualities, etc.; absolute sameness (*no identity of interests between them*). **4** *Algebra* **a** the equality of two expressions for all values of the quantities expressed by letters. **b** an equation expressing this, e.g. $(x + 1)^2 = x^2 + 2x + 1$. **5** *Math.* **a** (in full **identity element**) an element in a set, left unchanged by any operation to it. **b** a transformation that leaves an object unchanged. □ **identity crisis** a phase in which an individual feels a need to establish an identity in relation to society. **identity parade** = *identification parade*. [LL *identitas* f. L *idem* same]

ideogram /ˈɪdɪəˌɡræm/ *n.* a character symbolizing the idea of a thing without indicating the sequence of sounds in its name (e.g. a numeral, and many Chinese characters). [Gk *idea* form + -GRAM]

ideograph /ˈɪdɪəˌɡrɑːf/ *n.* = IDEOGRAM. □□ **ideographic** /-ˈɡræfɪk/ *adj.* **ideography** /ˌɪdɪˈɒɡrəfɪ/ *n.* [Gk *idea* form + -GRAPH]

ideologue /ˈaɪdɪəˌlɒɡ/ *n.* **1** a theorist; a visionary. **2** an adherent of an ideology. [F *idéologue* f. Gk *idea* (see IDEA) + -LOGUE]

ideology /ˌaɪdɪˈɒlədʒɪ/ *n.* (*pl.* **-ies**) **1** the system of ideas at the basis of an economic or political theory (*Marxist ideology*). **2** the manner of thinking characteristic of a class or individual (*bourgeois ideology*). **3** visionary speculation. **4** *archaic* the science of ideas. □□ **ideological** /-əˈlɒdʒɪk(ə)l/ *adj.* **ideologically** /-əˈlɒdʒɪkəlɪ/ *adv.* **ideologist** *n.* [F *idéologie* (as IDEOLOGUE)]

ides /aɪdz/ *n.pl.* the eighth day after the nones in the ancient Roman calendar (the 15th day of March, May, July, October, the 13th of other months). [ME f. OF f. L *idus* (pl.), perh. f. Etruscan]

idiocy /ˈɪdɪəsɪ/ *n.* (*pl.* **-ies**) **1** utter foolishness; idiotic behaviour or an idiotic action. **2** extreme mental imbecility. [ME f. IDIOT, prob. after *lunacy*]

idiolect /ˈɪdɪəˌlekt/ *n.* the form of language used by an individual person. [Gk *idios* own + -*lect* in DIALECT]

idiom /ˈɪdɪəm/ *n.* **1** a group of words established by usage and having a meaning not deducible from those of the individual words (as in *over the moon, see the light*). **2** a form of expression peculiar to a language, person, or group of people. **3 a** the language of a people or country. **b** the specific character of this. **4** a characteristic mode of expression in music, art, etc. [F *idiome* or LL *idioma* f. Gk *idiōma -matos* private property f. *idios* own, private]

idiomatic /ˌɪdɪəˈmætɪk/ *adj.* **1** relating to or conforming to idiom. **2** characteristic of a particular language. □□ **idiomatically** *adv.* [Gk *idiōmatikos* peculiar (as IDIOM)]

idiopathy /ˌɪdɪˈɒpəθɪ/ *n.* *Med.* any disease or condition of unknown cause or that arises spontaneously. □□ **idiopathic** /ˌɪdɪəˈpæθɪk/ *adj.* [mod.L *idiopathia* f. Gk *idiopatheia* f. *idios* own + -PATHY]

idiosyncrasy /ˌɪdɪəˈsɪŋkrəsɪ/ *n.* (*pl.* **-ies**) **1** a mental constitution, view or feeling, or mode of behaviour, peculiar to a person. **2** anything highly individualized or eccentric. **3** a mode of expression peculiar to an author. **4** *Med.* a physical constitution peculiar to a person. □□ **idiosyncratic** /-ˈkrætɪk/ *adj.* **idiosyncratically** /-ˈkrætɪkəlɪ/ *adv.* [Gk *idiosugkrasia* f. *idios* own + *sun* together + *krasis* mixture]

idiot /ˈɪdɪət/ *n.* **1** *colloq.* a stupid person; an utter fool. **2** a person deficient in mind and permanently incapable of rational conduct. □ **idiot board** (or **card**) *colloq.* a board displaying a television script to a speaker as an aid to memory. □□ **idiotic** /-ˈɒtɪk/ *adj.* **idiotically** /-ˈɒtɪkəlɪ/ *adv.* [ME f. OF f. L *idiota* ignorant

person f. Gk *idiōtēs* private person, layman, ignorant person f. *idios* own, private]

idle /ˈaɪd(ə)l/ *adj.* & *v.* —*adj.* (**idler, idlest**) **1** lazy, indolent. **2** not in use; not working; unemployed. **3** (of time etc.) unoccupied. **4** having no special basis or purpose (*idle rumour; idle curiosity*). **5** useless. **6** (of an action, thought, or word) ineffective, worthless, vain. —*v.* **1 a** *intr.* (of an engine) run slowly without doing any work. **b** *tr.* cause (an engine) to idle. **2** *intr.* be idle. **3** *tr.* (foll. by *away*) pass (time etc.) in idleness. □ **idle wheel** an intermediate wheel between two geared wheels, esp. to allow them to rotate in the same direction. □□ **idleness** *n.* **idly** *adv.* [OE *īdel* empty, useless]

idler /ˈaɪdlə(r)/ *n.* **1** a habitually lazy person. **2** = *idle wheel.*

Ido /ˈiːdəʊ/ *n.* an artificial universal language based on Esperanto. [Ido, = offspring, f. Esperanto suffix -*ido* derived from]

idol /ˈaɪd(ə)l/ *n.* **1** an image of a deity etc. used as an object of worship. **2** *Bibl.* a false god. **3** a person or thing that is the object of excessive or supreme adulation (*cinema idol*). **4** *archaic* a phantom. [ME f. OF *idole* f. L *idolum* f. Gk *eidōlon* phantom f. *eidos* form]

idolater /aɪˈdɒlətə(r)/ *n.* (*fem.* **idolatress** /-trɪs/) **1** a worshipper of idols. **2** (often foll. by *of*) a devoted admirer. □□ **idolatrous** *adj.* [ME *idolatrer* f. OF or f. *idolatry* or f. OF *idolâtre*, ult. f. Gk *eidōlolatrēs* (as IDOL, -LATER)]

idolatry /aɪˈdɒlətrɪ/ *n.* **1** the worship of idols. **2** great adulation. [OF *idolatrie* (as IDOLATER)]

idolize /ˈaɪdəˌlaɪz/ *v.* (also **-ise**) **1** *tr.* venerate or love extremely or excessively. **2** *tr.* make an idol of. **3** *intr.* practise idolatry. □□ **idolization** /-ˈzeɪʃ(ə)n/ *n.* **idolizer** *n.*

idyll /ˈɪdɪl/ *n.* (also **idyl**) **1** a short description in verse or prose of a picturesque scene or incident, esp. in rustic life. **2** an episode suitable for such treatment, usu. a love-story. □□ **idyllist** *n.* **idyllize** *v.tr.* (also **-ise**). [L *idyllium* f. Gk *eidullion*, dimin. of *eidos* form]

idyllic /ɪˈdɪlɪk/ *adj.* **1** blissfully peaceful and happy. **2** of or like an idyll. □□ **idyllically** *adv.*

i.e. *abbr.* that is to say. [L *id est*]

-ie /ɪ/ *suffix* **1** var. of -Y² (*dearie; nightie*). **2** *archaic* var. of -Y¹, -Y³ (*litanie; prettie*). [earlier form of -Y]

IEA *abbr.* International Energy Agency.

IEE *abbr.* (in the UK) Institution of Electrical Engineers.

-ier /ɪə(r)/ *suffix* forming personal nouns denoting an occupation or interest: **1** with stress on the preceding element (*grazier*). **2** with stress on the suffix (*cashier; brigadier*). [sense 1 ME of various orig.; sense 2 F -*ier* f. L -*arius*]

IF *abbr.* intermediate frequency.

if /ɪf/ *conj.* & *n.* —*conj.* **1** introducing a conditional clause: **a** on the condition or supposition that; in the event that (*if he comes I will tell him; if you are tired we will rest*). **b** (with past tense) implying that the condition is not fulfilled (*if I were you; if I knew I would say*). **2** even though (*I'll finish it, if it takes me all day*). **3** whenever (*if I am not sure I ask*). **4** whether (*see if you can find it*). **5 a** expressing wish or surprise (*if I could just try!; if it isn't my old hat!*). **b** expressing a request (*if you wouldn't mind opening the door?*). **6** with implied reservation, = and perhaps not (*very rarely if at all*). **7** (with reduction of the protasis to its significant word) if there is or it is etc. (*took little if any*). **8** despite being (*a useful if cumbersome device*). —*n.* a condition or supposition (*too many ifs about it*). □ **if only 1** even if for no other reason than (*I'll come if only to see her*). **2** (often *ellipt.*) an expression of regret (*if only I had thought of it; if only I could swim!*). **if so** if that is the case. [OE *gif*]

IFAD *abbr.* International Fund for Agricultural Development.

IFC *abbr.* International Finance Corporation.

iff /ɪf/ *conj.* *Logic & Math.* = if and only if. [arbitrary extension of *if*]

iffy /ˈɪfɪ/ *adj.* (**iffier, iffiest**) *colloq.* uncertain, doubtful.

Ifni /ˈɪfniː/ a former overseas province of Spain, on the SW coast of Morocco. It was settled by Spain in the late 15th c., then abandoned until reclaimed in 1860, and was formally ceded to Morocco in 1969.

au how ei day əʊ no eə hair ɪə near ɔɪ boy ʊə poor aɪə fire aʊə sour (*see over for consonants*)

Igbo var. of IBO.

igloo /ˈɪɡluː/ n. an Eskimo dome-shaped dwelling, esp. one built of snow. [Eskimo, = house]

Ignatius Loyola /ɪɡˌneɪʃəs ˈlɔɪələ/, St (1491 or 1495–1556), Spanish theologian, founder of the Jesuits and their first superior general. Of noble birth, he entered on a military career, but after reading a Life of Christ and biographies of the saints while convalescing from a wound decided to change his life and become a soldier of Christ, hung up his sword at the altar of Our Lady, and devoted himself to a life of prayer and extreme mortification. His greatest work is the *Spiritual Exercises*, an ordered scheme of meditations on the life of Christ and the truths of the Christian faith, manifesting considerable psychological insight, aimed at bringing the individual to a firm commitment to God and the Church.

igneous /ˈɪɡnɪəs/ adj. 1 of fire; fiery. 2 Geol. (esp. of rocks) produced by solidification of lava or magma (cf. METAMORPHIC, SEDIMENTARY). Igneous rocks are commonly divided into *volcanic* (those which solidified at the earth's surface) and *plutonic* (which solidified below it); they constitute 95 per cent of the known crust of the earth. [L igneus f. ignis fire]

ignis fatuus /ˌɪɡnɪs ˈfætjʊəs/ n. (pl. **ignes fatui** /ˌɪɡniːz ˈfætjʊɪ/) a will-o'-the-wisp. [mod.L, = foolish fire, because of its erratic movement]

ignite /ɪɡˈnaɪt/ v. 1 tr. set fire to; cause to burn. 2 intr. catch fire. 3 tr. Chem. heat to the point of combustion or chemical change. 4 tr. provoke or excite (feelings etc.). □□ **ignitable** adj. **ignitability** /-təˈbɪlɪtɪ/ n. **ignitible** adj. **ignitibility** /-tɪˈbɪlɪtɪ/ n. [L ignire ignit- f. ignis fire]

igniter /ɪɡˈnaɪtə(r)/ n. 1 a device for igniting a fuel mixture in an engine. 2 a device for causing an electric arc.

ignition /ɪɡˈnɪʃ(ə)n/ n. 1 a mechanism for, or the action of, starting the combustion of mixture in the cylinder of an internal-combustion engine. 2 the act or an instance of igniting or being ignited. □ **ignition key** a key to operate the ignition of a motor vehicle. [F ignition or med.L ignitio (as IGNITE)]

ignitron /ɪɡˈnaɪtrɒn/ n. Electr. a mercury-arc rectifier able to carry large currents. [IGNITE + -TRON]

ignoble /ɪɡˈnəʊb(ə)l/ adj. (**ignobler**, **ignoblest**) 1 dishonourable, mean, base. 2 of low birth, position, or reputation. □□ **ignobility** /-nəˈbɪlɪtɪ/ n. **ignobly** adv. [F ignoble or L ignobilis (as IN-¹, nobilis noble)]

ignominious /ˌɪɡnəˈmɪnɪəs/ adj. 1 causing or deserving ignominy. 2 humiliating. □□ **ignominiously** adv. **ignominiousness** n. [ME f. F ignominieux or L ignominiosus]

ignominy /ˈɪɡnəmɪnɪ/ n. 1 dishonour, infamy. 2 archaic infamous conduct. [F ignominie or L ignominia (as IN-¹, nomen name)]

ignoramus /ˌɪɡnəˈreɪməs/ n. (pl. **ignoramuses**) an ignorant person. [L, = we do not know: in legal use (formerly of a grand jury rejecting a bill) we take no notice of it; mod. sense perh. from a character in Ruggle's *Ignoramus* (1615) exposing lawyers' ignorance]

ignorance /ˈɪɡnərəns/ n. (often foll. by of) lack of knowledge (about a thing). [ME f. OF f. L ignorantia (as IGNORANT)]

ignorant /ˈɪɡnərənt/ adj. 1 **a** lacking knowledge. **b** (foll. by of, in) uninformed (about a fact or subject). 2 colloq. ill-mannered, uncouth. □□ **ignorantly** adv. [ME f. OF f. L ignorare ignorant- (as IGNORE)]

ignore /ɪɡˈnɔː(r)/ v.tr. 1 refuse to take notice of or accept. 2 intentionally disregard. □□ **ignorer** n. [F ignorer or L ignorare not know, ignore (as IN-¹, gno- know)]

Iguaçu /ˌiːɡwəˈsuː/ (Spanish **Iguazú**) a river of southern Brazil, famous especially for the Iguaçu Falls, a spectacular series of waterfalls close to the frontier between Brazil and Argentina.

iguana /ɪɡˈwɑːnə/ n. any of various large lizards of the family Iguanidae native to America, the W. Indies, and the Pacific islands, having a dorsal crest and throat appendages. [Sp. f. Carib iwana]

iguanodon /ɪˈɡwɑːnəˌdɒn/ n. a large extinct plant-eating dinosaur of the genus *Iguanodon*, with forelimbs smaller than hind limbs. [IGUANA (from its resemblance to this), after mastodon etc.]

i.h.p. abbr. indicated horsepower.

IHS abbr. Jesus. [ME f. LL, repr. Gk *IHΣ* = *Iēs(ous)* Jesus: often taken as an abbr. of various Latin words]

Ijssel /ˈaɪs(ə)l/ a tributary of the Rhine that flows through the east and central Netherlands, joining the Rhine at Arnhem.

ikebana /ˌɪkɪˈbɑːnə/ n. the art of Japanese flower arrangement, with formal display according to strict rules. [Jap., = living flowers]

Ikhnaton /ɪkˈnɑːt(ə)n/ var. of AKHENATEN.

ikky var. of ICKY.

ikon var. of ICON.

IL abbr. US Illinois (in official postal use).

il- /ɪl/ prefix assim. form of IN-¹, IN-² before l.

-il /ɪl/ suffix (also **-ile** /aɪl/) forming adjectives or nouns denoting relation (civil; utensil) or capability (agile; sessile). [OF f. L -ilis]

ilang-ilang var. of YLANG-YLANG.

ILEA /ˈɪlɪə/ abbr. Inner London Education Authority.

ilea pl. of ILEUM.

Île-de-France /ˌiːldəˈfrɑ̃s/ a region of north central France, incorporating the city of Paris; pop. (1982) 10,073,000.

ileostomy /ˌɪlɪˈɒstəmɪ/ n. (pl. **-ies**) a surgical operation in which the ileum is brought through the abdominal wall to create an artificial opening for the evacuation of the intestinal contents. [ILEUM + Gk stoma mouth]

ileum /ˈɪlɪəm/ n. (pl. **ilea** /ɪlɪə/) Anat. the third and last portion of the small intestine. □□ **ileac** adj. [var. of ILIUM]

ileus /ˈɪlɪəs/ n. Med. any painful obstruction of the intestine, esp. of the ileum. [L f. Gk (e)ileos colic]

ilex /ˈaɪleks/ n. 1 any tree or shrub of the genus *Ilex*, esp. the common holly. 2 the holm-oak. [ME f. L]

ilia pl. of ILIUM.

iliac /ˈɪlɪˌæk/ adj. of the lower body or ilium (iliac artery). [LL iliacus (as ILIUM)]

Iliad /ˈɪlɪəd/ a Greek hexameter epic poem in 24 books, traditionally ascribed to Homer. It tells of the climax of the war at Troy (Ilium) between Greeks and Trojans: the greatest of the Greek heroes, Achilles, retires to his tent enraged at Agamemnon's abduction of his mistress, the captive Briseis; in his absence the Trojan forces under Hector push the Greeks back on their ships; Achilles' close companion Patroclus fights and is killed by Hector; the grief-stricken Achilles takes the field and kills Hector under the walls of Troy.

Ilium /ˈɪlɪəm/ the Homeric city of Troy, or a Greek foundation of the 7th c. BC on the same site.

ilium /ˈɪlɪəm/ n. (pl. **ilia** /ˈɪlɪə/) 1 the bone forming the upper part of each half of the human pelvis. 2 the corresponding bone in animals. [ME f. L]

ilk /ɪlk/ n. 1 colloq. disp. a family, class, or set (not of the same ilk as you). ¶ Usu. derog. and therefore best avoided. 2 (in of that ilk) Sc. of the same (name) (Guthrie of that ilk = of Guthrie). [OE ilca same]

Ill. abbr. Illinois.

ill /ɪl/ adj., adv., & n. —adj. 1 (usu. predic.; often foll. by with) out of health; sick (is ill; was taken ill with pneumonia; mentally ill people). 2 (of health) unsound, disordered. 3 wretched, unfavourable (ill fortune; ill luck). 4 harmful (ill effects). 5 hostile, unkind (ill feeling). 6 archaic morally bad. 7 faulty, unskilful (ill taste; ill management). 8 (of manners or conduct) improper. —adv. 1 badly, wrongly (ill-matched). 2 **a** imperfectly (ill-provided). **b** scarcely (can ill afford to do it). 3 unfavourably (it would have gone ill with them). —n. 1 injury, harm. 2 evil; the opposite of good. □ **do an ill turn to** harm (a person or a person's interests). **ill-advised** 1 acting foolishly or imprudently. 2 (of a plan etc.) not well formed or considered. **ill-advisedly** /-ədˈvaɪzɪdlɪ/ in a foolish or badly considered manner. **ill-affected** (foll. by towards) not well disposed. **ill-assorted** not well matched. **ill at ease** embarrassed, uneasy. **ill-behaved** see BEHAVE. **ill blood** bad feeling; animosity. **ill-bred** badly brought up; rude. **ill breeding** bad manners. **ill-considered** = ill-advised. **ill-defined** not clearly defined. **ill-disposed** 1 (often foll. by towards) unfavourably

b but d dog f few g get h he j yes k cat l leg m man n no p pen r red s sit t top v voice

disposed. **2** disposed to evil; malevolent. **ill-equipped** (often foll. by *to* + infin.) not adequately equipped or qualified. **ill fame** see FAME. **ill-fated** destined to or bringing bad fortune. **ill-favoured** (*US* **-favored**) unattractive, displeasing, objectionable. **ill feeling** bad feeling; animosity. **ill-founded** (of an idea etc.) not well founded; baseless. **ill-gotten** gained by wicked or unlawful means. **ill humour** moroseness, irritability. **ill-humoured** bad-tempered. **ill-judged** unwise; badly considered. **ill-mannered** having bad manners; rude. **ill nature** churlishness, unkindness. **ill-natured** churlish, unkind. **ill-naturedly** churlishly. **ill-omened** attended by bad omens. **ill-starred** unlucky; destined to failure. **ill success** partial or complete failure. **ill temper** moroseness. **ill-tempered** morose, irritable. **ill-timed** done or occurring at an inappropriate time. **ill-treat** (or **-use**) treat badly; abuse. **ill-treatment** (or **ill use**) abuse; bad treatment. **ill will** bad feeling; animosity. **an ill wind** an unfavourable or untoward circumstance (with ref. to the proverb *it's an ill wind that blows nobody good*). **speak ill of** say something unfavourable about. [ME f. ON *illr*, of unkn. orig.]

I'll /aɪl/ *contr.* I shall; I will.

illation /ɪˈleɪʃ(ə)n/ *n.* **1** a deduction or conclusion. **2** a thing deduced. [L *illatio* f. *illatus* past part. of *inferre* INFER]

illative /ɪˈleɪtɪv, ˈɪlətɪv/ *adj.* **1 a** (of a word) stating or introducing an inference. **b** inferential. **2** *Gram.* (of a case) denoting motion into. □□ **illatively** *adv.* [L *illativus* (as ILLATION)]

illegal /ɪˈliːg(ə)l/ *adj.* **1** not legal. **2** contrary to law. □□ **illegality** /-ˈgælɪtɪ/ *n.* (pl. **-ies**). **illegally** *adv.* [F *illégal* or med.L *illegalis* (as IN-¹, LEGAL)]

illegible /ɪˈledʒɪb(ə)l/ *adj.* not legible. □□ **illegibility** /-ˈbɪlɪtɪ/ *n.* **illegibly** *adv.*

illegitimate *adj., n.,* & *v.* —*adj.* /ˌɪlɪˈdʒɪtɪmət/ **1** (of a child) born of parents not married to each other. **2** not authorized by law; unlawful. **3** improper. **4** wrongly inferred. **5** physiologically abnormal. —*n.* /ˌɪlɪˈdʒɪtɪmət/ a person whose position is illegitimate, esp. by birth. —*v.tr.* /ˌɪlɪˈdʒɪtɪˌmeɪt/ declare or pronounce illegitimate. □□ **illegitimacy** *n.* **illegitimately** *adv.* [LL *illegitimus*, after LEGITIMATE]

illiberal /ɪˈlɪbər(ə)l/ *adj.* **1** intolerant, narrow-minded. **2** without liberal culture. **3** not generous; stingy. **4** vulgar, sordid. □□ **illiberality** /-ˈrælɪtɪ/ *n.* (pl. **-ies**). **illiberally** *adv.* [F *illibéral* f. L *illiberalis* mean, sordid (as IN-¹, LIBERAL)]

illicit /ɪˈlɪsɪt/ *adj.* unlawful, forbidden (*illicit dealings*). □□ **illicitly** *adv.* **illicitness** *n.*

illimitable /ɪˈlɪmɪtəb(ə)l/ *adj.* limitless. □□ **illimitability** /-ˈbɪlɪtɪ/ *n.* **illimitableness** *n.* **illimitably** *adv.* [LL *illimitatus* f. L *limitatus* (as IN-¹, L *limitatus* past part. of *limitare* LIMIT)]

Illinois /ɪlɪˈnɔɪ/ a State in the Middle West of the US, ceded to Britain by the French in 1763 and acquired by the US in 1783; pop. (est. 1985) 11,427,400; capital, Springfield. It became the 21st State in 1818.

illiquid /ɪˈlɪkwɪd/ *adj.* (of assets) not easily converted into cash. □□ **illiquidity** /-ˈkwɪdɪtɪ/ *n.*

illiterate /ɪˈlɪtərət/ *adj.* & *n.* —*adj.* **1** unable to read. **2** uneducated. —*n.* an illiterate person. □□ **illiteracy** *n.* **illiterately** *adv.* **illiterateness** *n.* [L *illitteratus* (as IN-¹, *litteratus* LITERATE)]

illness /ˈɪlnɪs/ *n.* **1** a disease, ailment, or malady. **2** the state of being ill.

illogical /ɪˈlɒdʒɪk(ə)l/ *adj.* devoid of or contrary to logic. □□ **illogicality** /-ˈkælɪtɪ/ *n.* (pl. **-ies**). **illogically** *adv.*

illude /ɪˈluːd, ɪˈljuːd/ *v.tr. literary* trick or deceive. [ME, = mock, f. L *illudere* (as ILLUSION)]

illume /ɪˈluːm, ɪˈljuːm/ *v.tr. poet.* light up; make bright. [shortening of ILLUMINE]

illuminant /ɪˈluːmɪnənt, ɪˈljuː-/ *n.* & *adj.* —*n.* a means of illumination. —*adj.* serving to illuminate. □□ **illuminance** *n.* [L *illuminant-* part. stem of *illuminare* ILLUMINATE]

illuminate /ɪˈluːmɪneɪt, ɪˈljuː-/ *v.tr.* **1** light up; make bright. **2** decorate (buildings etc.) with lights as a sign of festivity. **3** decorate (an initial letter, a manuscript, etc.) with gold, silver, or brilliant colours. **4** help to explain (a subject etc.). **5** enlighten

spiritually or intellectually. **6** shed lustre on. □□ **illuminating** *adj.* **illuminatingly** *adv.* **illumination** /-ˈneɪʃ(ə)n/ *n.* **illuminative** /-ˌneɪtɪv, -nətɪv/ *adj.* **illuminator** *n.* [L *illuminare* (as IN-², *lumen luminis* light)]

illuminati /ɪˌluːmɪˈnɑːtɪ, ɪˌljuː-/ *n.pl.* **1** persons claiming to possess special knowledge or enlightenment. **2** (**Illuminati**) *hist.* any of various intellectual movements or societies of illuminati. □□ **illuminism** /ɪˈluːmɪˌnɪz(ə)m, ɪˈljuː-/ *n.* **illuminist** /ɪˈluːmɪnɪst, ɪˈljuː-/ *n.* [pl. of L *illuminatus* or It. *illuminato* past part. (as ILLUMINATE)]

illumine /ɪˈljuːmɪn, ɪˈljuː-/ *v.tr. literary* **1** light up; make bright. **2** enlighten spiritually. [ME f. OF *illuminer* f. L (as ILLUMINATE)]

illusion /ɪˈluːʒ(ə)n, ɪˈljuː-/ *n.* **1** deception, delusion. **2** a misapprehension of the true state of affairs. **3 a** the faulty perception of an external object. **b** an instance of this. **4** a figment of the imagination. **5** = *optical illusion.* □ **be under the illusion** (foll. by *that* + clause) believe mistakenly. □□ **illusional** *adj.* [ME f. F f. L *illusio -onis* f. *illudere* mock (as IN-², *ludere lus-* play)]

illusionist /ɪˈluːʒənɪst, ɪˈljuː-/ *n.* a person who produces illusions; a conjuror. □□ **illusionism** *n.* **illusionistic** /-ˈnɪstɪk/ *adj.*

illusive /ɪˈluːsɪv, ɪˈljuː-/ *adj.* = ILLUSORY. [med.L *illusivus* (as ILLUSION)]

illusory /ɪˈluːsərɪ, ɪˈljuː-/ *adj.* **1** deceptive (esp. as regards value or content). **2** having the character of an illusion. □□ **illusorily** *adv.* **illusoriness** *n.* [eccl.L *illusorius* (as ILLUSION)]

illustrate /ˈɪləstreɪt/ *v.tr.* **1 a** provide (a book, newspaper, etc.) with pictures. **b** elucidate (a description etc.) by drawings or pictures. **2** serve as an example of. **3** explain or make clear, esp. by examples. [L *illustrare* (as IN-², *lustrare* light up)]

illustration /ˌɪləˈstreɪʃ(ə)n/ *n.* **1** a drawing or picture illustrating a book, magazine article, etc. **2** an example serving to elucidate. **3** the act or an instance of illustrating. □□ **illustrational** *adj.* [ME f. OF f. L *illustratio -onis* (as ILLUSTRATE)]

illustrative /ˈɪləstrətɪv/ *adj.* (often foll. by *of*) serving as an explanation or example. □□ **illustratively** *adv.*

illustrator /ˈɪləˌstreɪtə(r)/ *n.* a person who makes illustrations, esp. for magazines, books, advertising copy, etc.

illustrious /ɪˈlʌstrɪəs/ *adj.* distinguished, renowned. □□ **illustriously** *adv.* **illustriousness** *n.* [L *illustris* (as ILLUSTRATE)]

Illyria /ɪˈlɪrɪə/ the country of an ancient Indo-European people, the Illyrians, along the coast of the Adriatic Sea in what is now Yugoslavia and part of Albania. It was subsequently the Roman province of Illyricum. □□ **Illyrian** *adj.* & *n.*

illywhacker /ˈɪlɪˌwækə(r)/ *n. Austral. sl.* a professional trickster. [20th c.: orig. unkn.]

ilmenite /ˈɪlmɪˌnaɪt/ *n.* a black ore of titanium. [*Ilmen* mountains in the Urals]

ILO *abbr.* International Labour Organization.

Iloilo /ˌiːlɔˈwiːləʊ/ a port on the south coast of the island of Panay in the Philippines; pop. (1980) 244,800.

ILR *abbr.* Independent Local Radio.

-ily /ɪlɪ/ *suffix* forming adverbs corresponding to adjectives in *-y* (see -Y¹, -LY²).

im- /ɪm/ *prefix* assim. form of IN-¹, IN-² before *b, m, p.*

I'm /aɪm/ *contr.* I am.

image /ˈɪmɪdʒ/ *n.* & *v.* —*n.* **1** a representation of the external form of an object, e.g. a statue (esp. of a saint etc. as an object of veneration). **2** the character or reputation of a person or thing as generally perceived. **3** an optical appearance or counterpart produced by light or other radiation from an object reflected in a mirror, refracted through a lens, etc. **4** semblance, likeness (*God created man in His own image*). **5** a person or thing that closely resembles another (*is the image of his father*). **6** a typical example. **7** a simile or metaphor. **8 a** a mental representation. **b** an idea or conception. **9** *Math.* a set formed by mapping from another set. —*v.tr.* **1** make an image of; portray. **2** reflect, mirror. **3** describe or imagine vividly. **4** typify. □□ **imageable** *adj.* **imageless** *adj.* [ME f. OF f. L *imago -ginis*, rel. to IMITATE]

imagery /ˈɪmɪdʒərɪ/ *n.* **1** figurative illustration, esp. as used by an author for particular effects. **2** images collectively. **3** statuary, carving. **4** mental images collectively. [ME f. OF *imagerie* (as IMAGE)]

imaginable /ɪˈmædʒɪnəb(ə)l/ *adj.* that can be imagined (*the greatest difficulty imaginable*). □□ **imaginably** *adv.* [ME f. LL *imaginabilis* (as IMAGINE)]

imaginal /ɪˈmædʒɪn(ə)l/ *adj.* **1** of an image or images. **2** *Zool.* of an imago. [L *imago imagin-*: see IMAGE]

imaginary /ɪˈmædʒɪnəri/ *adj.* **1** existing only in the imagination. **2** *Math.* being the square root of a negative quantity, and plotted graphically in a direction usu. perpendicular to the axis of real quantities (see REAL[1]). □□ **imaginarily** *adv.* [ME f. L *imaginarius* (as IMAGE)]

imagination /ɪˌmædʒɪˈneɪʃ(ə)n/ *n.* **1** a mental faculty forming images or concepts of external objects not present to the senses. **2** the ability of the mind to be creative or resourceful. **3** the process of imagining. [ME f. OF f. L *imaginatio -onis* (as IMAGINE)]

imaginative /ɪˈmædʒɪnətɪv/ *adj.* **1** having or showing in a high degree the faculty of imagination. **2** given to using the imagination. □□ **imaginatively** *adv.* **imaginativeness** *n.* [ME f. OF *imaginatif -ive* f. med.L *imaginativus* (as IMAGINE)]

imagine /ɪˈmædʒɪn/ *v.tr.* **1 a** form a mental image or concept of. **b** picture to oneself (something non-existent or not present to the senses). **2** (often foll. by *to* + infin.) think or conceive (*imagined them to be soldiers*). **3** guess (*cannot imagine what they are doing*). **4** (often foll. by *that* + clause) suppose; be of the opinion (*I imagine you will need help*). **5** (in *imper.*) as an exclamation of surprise (*just imagine!*). □□ **imaginer** *n.* [ME f. OF *imaginer* f. L *imaginari* (as IMAGE)]

imagines *pl.* of IMAGO.

imaginings /ɪˈmædʒɪnɪŋz/ *n.pl.* fancies, fantasies.

imagism /ˈɪmɪˌdʒɪz(ə)m/ *n.* a movement in English and American poetry *c.*1910–17 which, in a revolt against romanticism, sought clarity of expression through the use of precise images. The movement derived in part from the aesthetic philosophy of T. E. Hulme and involved Ezra Pound, James Joyce, Amy Lowell, and others. □□ **imagist** *n.* **imagistic** /-ˈdʒɪstɪk/ *adj.*

imago /ɪˈmeɪɡəʊ/ *n.* (*pl.* **-os** or **imagines** /ɪˈmædʒɪˌniːz/) **1** the final and fully developed stage of an insect after all metamorphoses, e.g. a butterfly or beetle. **2** *Psychol.* an idealized mental picture of oneself or others, esp. a parent. [mod.L sense of *imago* IMAGE]

imam /ɪˈmɑːm/ *n.* **1** a leader of prayers in a mosque. **2** a title of various Muslim leaders, esp. of one succeeding Muhammad as leader of Islam. □□ **imamate** /-meɪt/ *n.* [Arab. *'imām* leader f. *'amma* precede]

imbalance /ɪmˈbæləns/ *n.* **1** lack of balance. **2** disproportion.

imbecile /ˈɪmbɪˌsiːl/ *n.* & *adj.* —*n.* **1** a person of abnormally weak intellect, esp. an adult with a mental age of about five. **2** *colloq.* a stupid person. —*adj.* mentally weak; stupid, idiotic. □□ **imbecilely** *adv.* **imbecilic** /-ˈsɪlɪk/ *adj.* **imbecility** /-ˈsɪlɪtɪ/ *n.* (*pl.* **-ies**) [F *imbécil(l)e* f. L *imbecillus* (as IN-[1], *baculum* stick) orig. in sense 'without supporting staff']

imbed *var.* of EMBED.

imbibe /ɪmˈbaɪb/ *v.tr.* **1** (also *absol.*) drink (esp. alcoholic liquor). **2 a** absorb or assimilate (ideas etc.). **b** absorb (moisture etc.). **3** inhale (air etc.). □□ **imbiber** *n.* **imbibition** /ˌɪmbɪˈbɪʃ(ə)n/ *n.* [ME f. L *imbibere* (as IN-[2], *bibere* drink)]

imbricate *v.* & *adj.* —*v.tr.* & *intr.* /ˈɪmbrɪˌkeɪt/ arrange (leaves, the scales of a fish, etc.), or be arranged, so as to overlap like roof-tiles. —*adj.* /ˈɪmbrɪkət/ having scales etc. arranged in this way. □□ **imbrication** /-ˈkeɪʃ(ə)n/ *n.* [L *imbricare imbricat-* cover with rain-tiles f. *imbrex -icis* rain-tile f. *imber* shower]

imbroglio /ɪmˈbrəʊlɪəʊ/ *n.* (*pl.* **-os**) **1** a confused or complicated situation. **2** a confused heap. [It. *imbrogliare* confuse (as EMBROIL)]

Imbros /ˈɪmbrɒs/ (Turkish **Imroz** /ˈɪmrɒz/) a Turkish island in the north-east Aegean Sea, near the entrance to the Dardanelles.

imbrue /ɪmˈbruː/ *v.tr.* (foll. by *in*, *with*) *literary* stain (one's hand, sword, etc.). [OF *embruer* bedabble (as IN-[2], *breu* ult. f. Gmc, rel. to BROTH)]

imbue /ɪmˈbjuː/ *v.tr.* (**imbues**, **imbued**, **imbuing**) (often foll.

by *with*) **1** inspire or permeate (with feelings, opinions, or qualities). **2** saturate. **3** dye. [orig. as past part., f. F *imbu* or L *imbutus* f. *imbuere* moisten]

I.Mech.E. *abbr.* (in the UK) Institution of Mechanical Engineers.

IMF *abbr.* International Monetary Fund.

Imhotep /ɪmˈhəʊtep/ an ancient Egyptian architect and scholar, the probable designer of the step pyramid built at Saqqara for the 3rd-Dynasty pharaoh Djoser (early 3rd millennium BC) and said by Manetho to be the inventor of building in hewn stone. He was later deified: his cult was widespread in Egypt during the Graeco-Roman period, when he was regarded as the patron of architects, scribes, and doctors; the Greeks identified him with Asclepius. Imhotep is represented with a shaven head and seated, with a roll of papyrus on his knees.

imide /ˈɪmaɪd/ *n.* *Chem.* an organic compound containing the group (—CO.NH.CO.—) formed by replacing two of the hydrogen atoms in ammonia by carbonyl groups. [orig. F: arbitrary alt. of AMIDE]

imine /ˈɪmiːn/ *n.* *Chem.* a compound containing the group (—NH—) formed by replacing two of the hydrogen atoms in ammonia by other groups. [G *Imin* arbitrary alt. of *Amin* AMINE]

I.Min.E. *abbr.* (in the UK) Institution of Mining Engineers.

imitate /ˈɪmɪˌteɪt/ *v.tr.* **1** follow the example of; copy the action(s) of. **2** mimic. **3** make a copy of; reproduce. **4** be (consciously or not) like. □□ **imitable** *adj.* **imitator** *n.* [L *imitari imitat-*, rel. to *imago* IMAGE]

imitation /ˌɪmɪˈteɪʃ(ə)n/ *n.* **1** the act or an instance of imitating or being imitated. **2** a copy. **3** counterfeit (often *attrib.*: *imitation leather*). **4** *Mus.* the repetition of a phrase etc., usu. at a different pitch, in another part or voice. [F *imitation* or L *imitatio* (as IMITATE)]

imitative /ˈɪmɪtətɪv/ *adj.* **1** (often foll. by *of*) imitating; following a model or example. **2** counterfeit. **3** of a word: **a** that reproduces a natural sound (e.g. *fizz*). **b** whose sound is thought to correspond to the appearance etc. of the object or action described (e.g. *blob*). □ **imitative arts** painting and sculpture. □□ **imitatively** *adv.* **imitativeness** *n.* [LL *imitativus* (as IMITATE)]

immaculate /ɪˈmækjʊlət/ *adj.* **1** pure, spotless; perfectly clean. **2** perfectly or extremely well executed (*an immaculate performance*). **3** free from fault; innocent. **4** *Biol.* not spotted. □□ **immaculacy** *n.* **immaculately** *adv.* **immaculateness** *n.* [ME f. L *immaculatus* (as IN-[1], *maculatus* f. *macula* spot)]

Immaculate Conception the doctrine that the Virgin Mary was conceived, and remained, free from all stain of original sin. The belief, which sought biblical support from Gen. 3: 15 and Luke 1: 28, was much disputed in the Middle Ages, but was generally accepted by Roman Catholics from the 16th c.; it was defined as a dogma of the RC Church in 1854. The feast is kept on 8 Dec.

immanent /ˈɪmənənt/ *adj.* **1** (often foll. by *in*) indwelling, inherent. **2** (of the supreme being) permanently pervading the universe (opp. TRANSCENDENT). □□ **immanence** *n.* **immanency** *n.* **immanentism** *n.* **immanentist** *n.* [LL *immanēre* (as IN-[2], *manēre* remain)]

Immanuel /ɪˈmænjʊəl/ the name given to Christ as the deliverer of Judah prophesied by Isaiah (Isa. 7: 14, 8: 8; Matt. 1: 23). [Heb., = God with us]

immaterial /ˌɪməˈtɪərɪəl/ *adj.* **1** of no essential consequence; unimportant. **2** not material; incorporeal. □□ **immateriality** /-ˈælɪtɪ/ *n.* **immaterialize** *v.tr.* (also **-ise**). **immaterially** *adv.* [ME f. LL *immaterialis* (as IN-[1], MATERIAL)]

immaterialism /ˌɪməˈtɪərɪəˌlɪz(ə)m/ *n.* the doctrine that matter has no objective existence. □□ **immaterialist** *n.*

immature /ˌɪməˈtjʊə(r)/ *adj.* **1** not mature or fully developed. **2** lacking emotional or intellectual development. **3** unripe. □□ **immaturely** *adv.* **immaturity** *n.* [L *immaturus* (as IN-[1], MATURE)]

immeasurable /ɪˈmeʒərəb(ə)l/ *adj.* not measurable; immense. □□ **immeasurability** /-ˈbɪlɪtɪ/ *n.* **immeasurableness** *n.* **immeasurably** *adv.*

immediate /ɪˈmiːdɪət/ *adj.* **1** occurring or done at once or without delay (*an immediate reply*). **2** nearest, next; not separated by others (*the immediate vicinity; the immediate future; my immediate neighbour*). **3** most pressing or urgent (*our immediate concern was to get him to hospital*). **4** (of a relation or action) having direct effect; without an intervening medium or agency (*the immediate cause of death*). **5** (of knowledge) intuitive, gained without reasoning. □□ **immediacy** *n.* **immediateness** *n.* [ME f. F *immediat* or LL *immediatus* (as IN-¹, MEDIATE)]

immediately /ɪˈmiːdɪətlɪ/ *adj.* & *conj.* —*adv.* **1** without pause or delay. **2** without intermediary. —*conj.* as soon as.

immedicable /ɪˈmedɪkəb(ə)l/ *adj.* that cannot be healed or cured. □□ **immedicably** *adv.* [L *immedicabilis* (as IN-¹, MEDICABLE)]

immemorial /ˌɪmɪˈmɔːrɪəl/ *adj.* **1** ancient beyond memory or record. **2** very old. □□ **immemorially** *adv.* [med.L *immemorialis* (as IN-¹, MEMORIAL)]

immense /ɪˈmens/ *adj.* **1** immeasurably large or great; huge. **2** very great; considerable (*made an immense difference*). **3** *colloq.* very good. □□ **immenseness** *n.* **immensity** *n.* [ME f. F f. L *immensus* immeasurable (as IN-¹, *mensus* past part. of *metiri* measure)]

immensely /ɪˈmenslɪ/ *adv.* **1** very much (*enjoyed myself immensely*). **2** to an immense degree.

immerse /ɪˈmɜːs/ *v.tr.* **1 a** (often foll. by *in*) dip, plunge. **b** cause (a person) to be completely under water. **2** (often *refl.* or in *passive*; often foll. by *in*) absorb or involve deeply. **3** (often foll. by *in*) bury, embed. [L *immergere* (as IN-², *mergere* mers- dip)]

immersion /ɪˈmɜːʃ(ə)n/ *n.* **1** the act or an instance of immersing; the process of being immersed. **2** baptism by immersing the whole person in water. **3** mental absorption. **4** *Astron.* the disappearance of a celestial body behind another or in its shadow. □ **immersion heater** an electric heater designed for direct immersion in a liquid to be heated, esp. as a fixture in a hot-water tank. [ME f. LL *immersio* (as IMMERSE)]

immigrant /ˈɪmɪgrənt/ *n.* & *adj.* —*n.* a person who immigrates. —*adj.* **1** immigrating. **2** of or concerning immigrants.

immigrate /ˈɪmɪˌgreɪt/ *v.* **1** *intr.* come as a permanent resident to a country other than one's native land. **2** *tr.* bring in (a person) as an immigrant. □□ **immigration** /-ˈgreɪʃ(ə)n/ *n.* **immigratory** *adj.* [L *immigrare* (as IN-², MIGRATE)]

imminent /ˈɪmɪnənt/ *adj.* **1** (of an event, esp. danger) impending; about to happen. **2** *archaic* overhanging. □□ **imminence** *n.* **imminently** *adv.* [L *imminēre* imminent- overhang, project]

immiscible /ɪˈmɪsɪb(ə)l/ *adj.* (often foll. by *with*) that cannot be mixed. □□ **immiscibility** /-ˈbɪlɪtɪ/ *n.* **immiscibly** *adv.* [LL *immiscibilis* (as IN-¹, MISCIBLE)]

immitigable /ɪˈmɪtɪgəb(ə)l/ *adj.* that cannot be mitigated. □□ **immitigably** *adv.* [LL *immitigabilis* (as IN-¹, MITIGATE)]

immittance /ɪˈmɪt(ə)ns/ *n.* *Electr.* admittance or impedance (when not distinguished). [impedance + admittance]

immixture /ɪˈmɪkstʃə(r)/ *n.* **1** the process of mixing up. **2** (often foll. by *in*) being involved.

immobile /ɪˈməʊbaɪl/ *adj.* **1** not moving. **2** not able to move or be moved. □□ **immobility** /-ˈbɪlɪtɪ/ *n.* [ME f. OF f. L *immobilis* (as IN-¹, MOBILE)]

immobilize /ɪˈməʊbɪˌlaɪz/ *v.tr.* (also **-ise**) **1** make or keep immobile. **2** make (a vehicle or troops) incapable of being moved. **3** keep (a limb or patient) restricted in movement for healing purposes. **4** restrict the free movement of. **5** withdraw (coins) from circulation to support banknotes. □□ **immobilization** /-ˈzeɪʃ(ə)n/ *n.* **immobilizer** *n.* [F *immobiliser* (as IMMOBILE)]

immoderate /ɪˈmɒdərət/ *adj.* excessive; lacking moderation. □□ **immoderately** *adv.* **immoderateness** *n.* **immoderation** /-ˈreɪʃ(ə)n/ *n.* [ME f. L *immoderatus* (as IN-¹, MODERATE)]

immodest /ɪˈmɒdɪst/ *adj.* **1** lacking modesty; forward, impudent. **2** lacking due decency. □□ **immodestly** *adv.* **immodesty** *n.* [F *immodeste* or L *immodestus* (as IN-¹, MODEST)]

immolate /ˈɪməˌleɪt/ *v.tr.* **1** kill or offer as a sacrifice. **2** *literary* sacrifice (a valued thing). □□ **immolation** /-ˈleɪʃ(ə)n/ *n.* **immolator** *n.* [L *immolare* sprinkle with sacrificial meal (as IN-², *mola* MEAL²)]

immoral /ɪˈmɒr(ə)l/ *adj.* **1** not conforming to accepted standards of morality (cf. AMORAL). **2** morally wrong (esp. in sexual

matters). **3** depraved, dissolute. □□ **immorality** /ˌɪməˈrælɪtɪ/ *n.* (*pl.* **-ies**). **immorally** *adv.*

immortal /ɪˈmɔːt(ə)l/ *adj.* & *n.* —*adj.* **1 a** living for ever; not mortal. **b** divine. **2** unfading, incorruptible. **3** likely or worthy to be famous for all time. —*n.* **1 a** an immortal being. **b** (in *pl.*) the gods of antiquity. **2** a person (esp. an author) of enduring fame. **3** (**Immortal**) a member of the French Academy. □□ **immortality** /ˌɪmɔːˈtælɪtɪ/ *n.* **immortalize** *v.tr.* (also **-ise**). **immortalization** /-ˈzeɪʃ(ə)n/ *n.* **immortally** *adv.* [ME f. L *immortalis* (as IN-¹, MORTAL)]

immortelle /ˌɪmɔːˈtel/ *n.* a composite flower of papery texture retaining its shape and colour after being dried, esp. a helichrysum. [F, fem. of *immortel* IMMORTAL]

immovable /ɪˈmuːvəb(ə)l/ *adj.* & *n.* (also **immoveable**) —*adj.* **1** that cannot be moved. **2** steadfast, unyielding. **3** emotionless. **4** not subject to change (*immovable law*). **5** motionless. **6** *Law* (of property) consisting of land, houses, etc. —*n.* (in *pl.*) *Law* immovable property. □ **immovable feast** a religious feast-day that occurs on the same date each year. □□ **immovability** /-ˈbɪlɪtɪ/ *n.* **immovableness** *n.* **immovably** *adv.*

immune /ɪˈmjuːn/ *adj.* **1 a** (often foll. by *against*, *from*, *to*) protected against an infection owing to the presence of specific antibodies, or through inoculation or inherited or acquired resistance. **b** relating to immunity (*immune mechanism*). **2** (foll. by *from*, *to*) free or exempt from or not subject to (some undesirable factor or circumstance). □ **immune response** the reaction of the body to the introduction into it of an antigen. [ME f. L *immunis* exempt from public service or charge (as IN-¹, *munis* ready for service): sense 1 f. F *immun*]

immunity /ɪˈmjuːnɪtɪ/ *n.* (*pl.* **-ies**) **1** *Med.* the ability of an organism to resist infection, by means of the presence of circulating antibodies and white blood cells. **2** freedom or exemption from an obligation, penalty, or unfavourable circumstance. [ME f. L *immunitas* (as IMMUNE): sense 1 f. F *immunité*]

immunize /ˈɪmjuːˌnaɪz/ *v.tr.* (also **-ise**) make immune, esp. to infection, usu. by inoculation. □□ **immunization** /-ˈzeɪʃ(ə)n/ *n.* **immunizer** *n.*

immuno- /ˈɪmjuːnəʊ/ *comb. form* immunity to infection.

immunoassay /ˌɪmjuːnəʊˈæseɪ/ *n.* *Biochem.* the determination of the presence or quantity of a substance, esp. a protein, through its properties as an antigen or antibody.

immunochemistry /ˌɪmjuːnəʊˈkemɪstrɪ/ *n.* the chemistry of immune systems, esp. in mammalian tissues.

immunodeficiency /ˌɪmjuːˌnəʊdɪˈfɪʃənsɪ/ *n.* a reduction in a person's normal immune defences.

immunogenic /ˌɪmjuːnəʊˈdʒenɪk/ *adj.* *Biochem.* of, relating to, or possessing the ability to elicit an immune response.

immunoglobulin /ˌɪmjuːnəʊˈglɒbjʊlɪn/ *n.* *Biochem.* any of a group of structurally related proteins which function as antibodies.

immunology /ˌɪmjuːˈnɒlədʒɪ/ *n.* the scientific study of immunity. □□ **immunologic** /-nəˈlɒdʒɪk/ *adj.* **immunological** /-nəˈlɒdʒɪk(ə)l/ *adj.* **immunologically** /-nəˈlɒdʒɪkəlɪ/ *adv.* **immunologist** *n.*

immunosuppressed /ˌɪmjuːnəʊsəˈprest/ *adj.* (of an individual) rendered partially or completely unable to react immunologically.

immunosuppression /ˌɪmjuːnəʊsəˈpreʃ(ə)n/ *n.* *Biochem.* the partial or complete suppression of the immune response of an individual, esp. to maintain the survival of an organ after a transplant operation. □□ **immunosuppressant** *n.*

immunosuppressive /ˌɪmjuːnəʊsəˈpresɪv/ *adj.* & *n.* —*adj.* partially or completely suppressing the immune response of an individual. —*n.* an immunosuppressive drug.

immunotherapy /ˌɪmjuːnəʊˈθerəpɪ/ *n.* *Med.* the prevention or treatment of disease with substances that stimulate the immune response.

immure /ɪˈmjʊə(r)/ *v.tr.* **1** enclose within walls; imprison. **2** *refl.* shut oneself away. □□ **immurement** *n.* [F *emmurer* or med.L *immurare* (as IN-², *murus* wall)]

immutable /ɪˈmjuːtəb(ə)l/ *adj.* **1** unchangeable. **2** not subject to variation in different cases. □□ **immutability** /-'bɪlɪtɪ/ n. **immutably** adv. [ME f. L immutabilis (as IN-1, MUTABLE)]

IMO abbr. International Maritime Organization.

imp /ɪmp/ n. & v. —n. **1** a mischievous child. **2** a small mischievous devil or sprite. —v.tr. **1** add feathers to (the wing of a falcon) to restore or improve its flight. **2** archaic enlarge; add by grafting. [OE impa, impe young shoot, scion, impian graft: ult. f. Gk emphutos implanted, past part. of emphuō]

impact n. & v. —n. /'ɪmpækt/ **1** (often foll. by on, against) the action of one body coming forcibly into contact with another. **2** an effect or influence, esp. when strong. —v.tr. /ɪm'pækt/ **1** (often foll. by in, into) press or fix firmly. **2** (as impacted adj.) **a** (of a tooth) wedged between another tooth and the jaw. **b** (of a fractured bone) with the parts crushed together. **c** (of faeces) lodged in the intestine. □□ **impaction** /ɪm'pækʃ(ə)n/ n. [L impact-part. stem of impingere IMPINGE]

impair /ɪm'peə(r)/ v.tr. damage or weaken. □□ **impairment** n. [ME empeire f. OF empeirier (as IN-2, LL pejorare f. L pejor worse)]

impala /ɪm'pɑːlə, -'pælə/ n. (pl. same) a small antelope, Aepyceros melampus, of S. and E. Africa, capable of long high jumps. [Zulu]

impale /ɪm'peɪl/ v.tr. **1** (foll. by on, upon, with) transfix or pierce with a sharp instrument. **2** Heraldry combine (two coats of arms) by placing them side by side on one shield separated by a vertical line down the middle. □□ **impalement** n. [F empaler or med.L impalare (as IN-2, palus stake)]

impalpable /ɪm'pælpəb(ə)l/ adj. **1** not easily grasped by the mind; intangible. **2** imperceptible to the touch. **3** (of powder) very fine; not containing grains that can be felt. □□ **impalpability** /-'bɪlɪtɪ/ n. **impalpably** adv. [F impalpable or LL impalpabilis (as IN-1, PALPABLE)]

impanel var. of EMPANEL.

impark /ɪm'pɑːk/ v.tr. **1** enclose (animals) in a park. **2** enclose (land) for a park. [ME f. AF enparker, OF emparquer (as IN-2, parc PARK)]

impart /ɪm'pɑːt/ v.tr. (often foll. by to) **1** communicate (news etc.). **2** give a share of (a thing). □□ **impartable** adj. **impartation** /ˌɪmpɑː'teɪʃ(ə)n/ n. **impartment** n. [ME f. OF impartir f. L impartire (as IN-2, pars part)]

impartial /ɪm'pɑːʃ(ə)l/ adj. treating all sides in a dispute etc. equally; unprejudiced, fair. □□ **impartiality** /-ʃɪ'ælɪtɪ/ n. **impartially** adv.

impassable /ɪm'pɑːsəb(ə)l/ adj. that cannot be traversed. □□ **impassability** /-'bɪlɪtɪ/ n. **impassableness** n. **impassably** adv.

impasse /'æmpæs, 'ɪm-/ n. a position from which progress is impossible; deadlock. [F (as IN-1, passer PASS1)]

impassible /ɪm'pæsɪb(ə)l/ adj. **1** impassive. **2** incapable of feeling or emotion. **3** incapable of suffering injury. **4** Theol. not subject to suffering. □□ **impassibility** /-'bɪlɪtɪ/ n. **impassibleness** n. **impassibly** adv. [ME f. OF f. eccl.L impassibilis (as IN-1, PASSIBLE)]

impassion /ɪm'pæʃ(ə)n/ v.tr. fill with passion; arouse emotionally. [It. impassionare (as IN-2, PASSION)]

impassioned /ɪm'pæʃ(ə)nd/ adj. deeply felt; ardent (an impassioned plea).

impassive /ɪm'pæsɪv/ adj. **1 a** deficient in or incapable of feeling emotion. **b** undisturbed by passion; serene. **2** without sensation. **3** not subject to suffering. □□ **impassively** adv. **impassiveness** n. **impassivity** /-'sɪvɪtɪ/ n.

impasto /ɪm'pæstəʊ/ n. Art **1** the process of laying on paint thickly. **2** this technique of painting. [It. impastare (as IN-2, pastare paste)]

impatiens /ɪm'peɪʃɪˌenz/ n. any plant of the genus Impatiens, including busy Lizzie and touch-me-not. [mod.L f. IMPATIENT]

impatient /ɪm'peɪʃ(ə)nt/ adj. **1 a** (often foll. by at, with) lacking patience or tolerance. **b** (of an action) showing a lack of patience. **2** (often foll. by for, or to + infin.) restlessly eager. **3** (foll. by of) intolerant. □□ **impatience** n. **impatiently** adv. [ME f. OF f. L impatiens (as IN-1, PATIENT)]

impeach /ɪm'piːtʃ/ v.tr. **1** Brit. charge with a crime against the State, esp. treason. **2** US charge (the holder of a public office) with misconduct. **3** call in question, disparage (a person's integrity etc.). □□ **impeachable** adj. **impeachment** n. [ME f. OF empecher impede f. LL impedicare entangle (as IN-2, pedica fetter f. pes pedis foot)]

impeccable /ɪm'pekəb(ə)l/ adj. **1** (of behaviour, performance, etc.) faultless, exemplary. **2** not liable to sin. □□ **impeccability** /-'bɪlɪtɪ/ n. **impeccably** adv. [L impeccabilis (as IN-1, peccare sin)]

impecunious /ˌɪmpɪ'kjuːnɪəs/ adj. having little or no money. □□ **impecuniosity** /-'ɒsɪtɪ/ n. **impecuniousness** n. [IN-1 + obs. pecunious having money f. L pecuniosus f. pecunia money f. pecu cattle]

impedance /ɪm'piːd(ə)ns/ n. **1** Electr. the total effective resistance of an electric circuit etc. to alternating current, arising from ohmic resistance and reactance. **2** an analogous mechanical property. [IMPEDE + -ANCE]

impede /ɪm'piːd/ v.tr. retard by obstructing; hinder. [L impedire shackle the feet of (as IN-2, pes foot)]

impediment /ɪm'pedɪmənt/ n. **1** a hindrance or obstruction. **2** a defect in speech, e.g. a lisp or stammer. □□ **impedimental** /-'ment(ə)l/ adj. [ME f. L impedimentum (as IMPEDE)]

impedimenta /ɪmˌpedɪ'mentə/ n.pl. **1** encumbrances. **2** travelling equipment, esp. of an army. [L, pl. of impedimentum: see IMPEDIMENT]

impel /ɪm'pel/ v.tr. (**impelled**, **impelling**) **1** drive, force, or urge into action. **2** drive forward; propel. □□ **impellent** adj. & n. **impeller** n. [ME f. L impellere (as IN-2, pellere puls- drive)]

impend /ɪm'pend/ v.intr. **1** be about to happen. **2** (often foll. by over) **a** (of a danger) be threatening. **b** hang; be suspended. □□ **impending** adj. [L impendēre (as IN-2, pendēre hang)]

impenetrable /ɪm'penɪtrəb(ə)l/ adj. **1** that cannot be penetrated. **2** inscrutable, unfathomable. **3** inaccessible to ideas, influences, etc. **4** Physics (of matter) having the property such that a body is incapable of occupying the same place as another body at the same time. □□ **impenetrability** /-'bɪlɪtɪ/ n. **impenetrableness** n. **impenetrably** adv. [ME f. F impénétrable f. L impenetrabilis (as IN-1, PENETRATE)]

impenitent /ɪm'penɪt(ə)nt/ adj. not repentant or penitent. □□ **impenitence** n. **impenitency** n. **impenitently** adv. [eccl.L impaenitens (as IN-1, PENITENT)]

imperative /ɪm'perətɪv/ adj. & n. —adj. **1** urgent. **2** obligatory. **3** commanding, peremptory. **4** Gram. (of a mood) expressing a command (e.g. come here!). —n. **1** Gram. the imperative mood. **2** a command. □□ **imperatival** /ɪmˌperə'taɪv(ə)l/ adj. **imperatively** adv. **imperativeness** n. [LL imperativus f. imperare command (as IN-2, parare make ready)]

imperator /ˌɪmpə'rɑːtɔː(r)/ n. Rom.Hist. commander (a title conferred under the Republic on a victorious general and under the Empire on the emperor). □□ **imperatorial** /ɪmˌperə'tɔːrɪəl/ adj. [L (as IMPERATIVE)]

imperceptible /ˌɪmpə'septɪb(ə)l/ adj. **1** that cannot be perceived. **2** very slight, gradual, or subtle. □□ **imperceptibility** /-'bɪlɪtɪ/ n. **imperceptibly** adv. [F imperceptible or med.L imperceptibilis (as IN-1, PERCEPTIBLE)]

impercipient /ˌɪmpə'sɪpɪənt/ adj. lacking in perception. □□ **impercipience** n.

imperfect /ɪm'pɜːfɪkt/ adj. & n. —adj. **1** not fully formed or done; faulty, incomplete. **2** Gram. (of a tense) denoting a (usu. past) action in progress but not completed at the time in question (e.g. they were singing). **3** Mus. (of a cadence) ending on the dominant chord. —n. the imperfect tense. □ **imperfect rhyme** Prosody a rhyme that only partly satisfies the usual criteria (e.g. love and move). □□ **imperfectly** adv. [ME imparfit etc. f. OF imparfait f. L imperfectus (as IN-1, PERFECT)]

imperfection /ˌɪmpə'fekʃ(ə)n/ n. **1** incompleteness. **2 a** faultiness. **b** a fault or blemish. [ME f. OF imperfection or LL imperfectio (as IMPERFECT)]

imperfective /ˌɪmpə'fektɪv/ adj. & n. Gram. —adj. (of a verb aspect etc.) expressing an action without reference to its completion (opp. PERFECTIVE). —n. an imperfective aspect or form of a verb.

imperforate /ɪm'pɜːfərət/ adj. **1** not perforated. **2** Anat. lacking the normal opening. **3** (of a postage stamp) lacking perforations.

imperial /ɪmˈpɪərɪəl/ *adj.* & *n.* —*adj.* **1** of or characteristic of an empire or comparable sovereign State. **2 a** of or characteristic of an emperor. **b** supreme in authority. **c** majestic, august. **d** magnificent. **3** (of non-metric weights and measures) used or formerly used by statute in the UK (*imperial gallon*). (See below.) —*n.* a former size of paper, 762 × 559 mm (30 × 22 inches). □□ **imperially** *adv.* [ME f. OF f. L *imperialis* f. *imperium* command, authority]

Imperial measures are often of great antiquity, but until defined by Parliament they often varied from place to place. Units of length are the mile and the yard; area of land is measured in acres. The basic unit of capacity is the gallon, divided into 8 pints; 8 gallons = 1 bushel; these units are larger than their counterparts in US measures. The basic unit of weight is the pound, divided into 16 ounces; the hundredweight is 112 pounds, and the ton is 20 hundredweight. A unit peculiar to Britain is the stone (14 pounds).

imperialism /ɪmˈpɪərɪəˌlɪz(ə)m/ *n.* **1** an imperial rule or system. **2** usu. *derog.* a policy of acquiring dependent territories or extending a country's influence over less powerful or less developed countries through trade, diplomacy, etc. □□ **imperialistic** /-ˈlɪstɪk/ *adj.* **imperialistically** /-ˈlɪstɪkəlɪ/ *adv.* **imperialize** *v.tr.* (also **-ise**).

imperialist /ɪmˈpɪərɪəlɪst/ *n.* & *adj.* —*n.* usu. *derog.* an advocate or agent of imperial rule or of imperialism. —*adj.* of or relating to imperialism or imperialists.

imperil /ɪmˈperɪl/ *v.tr.* (**imperilled, imperilling**; US **imperiled, imperiling**) bring or put into danger.

imperious /ɪmˈpɪərɪəs/ *adj.* **1** overbearing, domineering. **2** urgent, imperative. □□ **imperiously** *adv.* **imperiousness** *n.* [L *imperiosus* f. *imperium* command, authority]

imperishable /ɪmˈperɪʃəb(ə)l/ *adj.* that cannot perish. □□ **imperishability** /-ˈbɪlɪtɪ/ *n.* **imperishableness** *n.* **imperishably** *adv.*

imperium /ɪmˈpɪərɪəm, -ˈperɪəm/ *n.* absolute power or authority. [L, = command, authority]

impermanent /ɪmˈpɜːmənənt/ *adj.* not permanent; transient. □□ **impermanence** *n.* **impermanency** *n.* **impermanently** *adv.*

impermeable /ɪmˈpɜːmɪəb(ə)l/ *adj.* **1** that cannot be penetrated. **2** *Physics* that does not permit the passage of fluids. □□ **impermeability** /-ˈbɪlɪtɪ/ *n.* [F *imperméable* or LL *impermeabilis* (as IN-¹, PERMEABLE)]

impermissible /ˌɪmpəˈmɪsɪb(ə)l/ *adj.* not allowable. □□ **impermissibility** /-ˈbɪlɪtɪ/ *n.*

impersonal /ɪmˈpɜːsən(ə)l/ *adj.* **1** having no personality. **2** having no personal feeling or reference. **3** *Gram.* **a** (of a verb) used only with a formal subject (usu. *it*) and expressing an action not attributable to a definite subject (e.g. *it is snowing*). **b** (of a pronoun) = INDEFINITE. □□ **impersonality** /-ˈnælɪtɪ/ *n.* **impersonally** *adv.* [LL *impersonalis* (as IN-¹, PERSONAL)]

impersonate /ɪmˈpɜːsəˌneɪt/ *v.tr.* **1** pretend to be (another person) for the purpose of entertainment or fraud. **2** act (a character). □□ **impersonation** /-ˈneɪʃ(ə)n/ *n.* **impersonator** *n.* [IN-² + L *persona* PERSON]

impertinent /ɪmˈpɜːtɪnənt/ *adj.* **1** rude or insolent; lacking proper respect. **2** out of place; absurd. **3** esp. *Law* irrelevant, intrusive. □□ **impertinence** *n.* **impertinently** *adv.* [ME f. OF or LL *impertinens* (as IN-¹, PERTINENT)]

imperturbable /ˌɪmpəˈtɜːbəb(ə)l/ *adj.* not excitable; calm. □□ **imperturbability** /-ˈbɪlɪtɪ/ *n.* **imperturbableness** *n.* **imperturbably** *adv.* [ME f. LL *imperturbabilis* (as IN-¹, PERTURB)]

impervious /ɪmˈpɜːvɪəs/ *adj.* (usu. foll. by *to*) **1** not responsive to an argument etc. **2** not affording passage to a fluid. □□ **imperviously** *adv.* **imperviousness** *n.* [L *impervius* (as IN-¹, PERVIOUS)]

impetigo /ˌɪmpɪˈtaɪɡəʊ/ *n.* a contagious bacterial skin infection forming pustules and yellow crusty sores. □□ **impetiginous** /ˌɪmpɪˈtɪdʒɪnəs/ *adj.* [ME f. L *impetigo -ginis* f. *impetere* assail]

impetuous /ɪmˈpetjʊəs/ *adj.* **1** acting or done rashly or with sudden energy. **2** moving forcefully or rapidly. □□ **impetuosity** /-ˈɒsɪtɪ/ *n.* **impetuously** *adv.* **impetuousness** *n.* [ME f. OF *impetueux* f. LL *impetuosus* (as IMPETUS)]

impetus /ˈɪmpɪtəs/ *n.* **1** the force or energy with which a body moves. **2** a driving force or impulse. [L, = assault, force, f. *impetere* assail (as IN-², *petere* seek)]

impi /ˈɪmpɪ/ *n.* (*pl.* **impis**) *S.Afr.* **1** a band of armed men. **2** *hist.* an African tribal army or regiment. [Zulu, = regiment, armed band]

impiety /ɪmˈpaɪətɪ/ *n.* (*pl.* **-ies**) **1** a lack of piety or reverence. **2** an act etc. showing this. [ME f. OF *impieté* or L *impietas* (as IN-¹, PIETY)]

impinge /ɪmˈpɪndʒ/ *v.tr.* (usu. foll. by *on, upon*) **1** make an impact; have an effect. **2** encroach. □□ **impingement** *n.* **impinger** *n.* [L *impingere* drive (a thing) at (as IN-², *pangere* fix, drive)]

impious /ˈɪmpɪəs/ *adj.* **1** not pious. **2** wicked, profane. □□ **impiously** *adv.* **impiousness** *n.* [L *impius* (as IN-¹, PIOUS)]

impish /ˈɪmpɪʃ/ *adj.* of or like an imp; mischievous. □□ **impishly** *adv.* **impishness** *n.*

implacable /ɪmˈplækəb(ə)l/ *adj.* that cannot be appeased; inexorable. □□ **implacability** /-ˈbɪlɪtɪ/ *n.* **implacably** *adv.* [ME f. F *implacable* or L *implacabilis* (as IN-¹, PLACABLE)]

implant *v.* & *n.* —*v.tr.* /ɪmˈplɑːnt/ **1** (often foll. by *in*) insert or fix. **2** (often foll. by *in*) instil (a principle, idea, etc.) in a person's mind. **3** plant. **4** *Med.* **a** insert (tissue etc.) in a living body. **b** (in *passive*) (of a fertilized ovum) become attached to the wall of the womb. —*n.* /ˈɪmplɑːnt/ *n.* **1** a thing implanted. **2** a thing implanted in the body, e.g. a piece of tissue or a capsule containing material for radium therapy. □□ **implantation** /-ˈteɪʃ(ə)n/ *n.* [F *implanter* or LL *implantare* engraft (as IN-², PLANT)]

implausible /ɪmˈplɔːzɪb(ə)l/ *adj.* not plausible. □□ **implausibility** /-ˈbɪlɪtɪ/ *n.* **implausibly** *adv.*

implead /ɪmˈpliːd/ *v.tr.* *Law* **1** prosecute or take proceedings against (a person). **2** involve (a person etc.) in a suit. [ME f. AF *empleder*, OF *empleidier* (as EN-¹, PLEAD)]

implement *n.* & *v.* —*n.* /ˈɪmplɪmənt/ **1** a tool, instrument, or utensil. **2** (in *pl.*) equipment; articles of furniture, dress, etc. **3** *Law* performance of an obligation. —*v.tr.* /ˈɪmplɪˌment/ **1 a** put (a decision, plan, etc.) into effect. **b** fulfil (an undertaking). **2** complete (a contract etc.). **3** fill up; supplement. □□ **implementation** /ˌɪmplɪmenˈteɪʃ(ə)n/ *n.* [ME f. med.L *implementa* (pl.) f. *implēre* employ (as IN-², L *plēre plet-* fill)]

implicate *v.* & *n.* —*v.tr.* /ˈɪmplɪˌkeɪt/ **1** (often foll. by *in*) show (a person) to be concerned or involved (in a charge, crime, etc.). **2** (in *passive*; often foll. by *in*) be affected or involved. **3** lead to as a consequence or inference. —*n.* /ˈɪmplɪkət/ a thing implied. □□ **implicative** /ɪmˈplɪkətɪv/ *adj.* **implicatively** /ɪmˈplɪkətɪvlɪ/ *adv.* [L *implicatus* past part. of *implicare* (as IN-², *plicare, plicat-* or *plicit-* fold)]

implication /ˌɪmplɪˈkeɪʃ(ə)n/ *n.* **1** what is involved in or implied by something else. **2** the act of implicating or implying. □ **by implication** by what is implied or suggested rather than by formal expression. [ME f. L *implicatio* (as IMPLICATE)]

implicit /ɪmˈplɪsɪt/ *adj.* **1** implied though not plainly expressed. **2** (often foll. by *in*) virtually contained. **3** absolute, unquestioning, unreserved (*implicit obedience*). **4** *Math.* (of a function) not expressed directly in terms of independent variables. □□ **implicitly** *adv.* **implicitness** *n.* [F *implicite* or L *implicitus* (as IMPLICATE)]

implode /ɪmˈpləʊd/ *v.intr.* & *tr.* burst or cause to burst inwards. □□ **implosion** /ɪmˈpləʊʒ(ə)n/ *n.* **implosive** /-sɪv, -zɪv/ *adj.* [IN-² + L *-plodere*, after EXPLODE]

implore /ɪmˈplɔː(r)/ *v.tr.* **1** (often foll. by *to* + infin.) entreat (a person). **2** beg earnestly for. □□ **imploringly** *adv.* [F *implorer* or L *implorare* invoke with tears (as IN-², *plorare* weep)]

imply /ɪmˈplaɪ/ *v.tr.* (**-ies, -ied**) **1** (often foll. by *that* + clause) strongly suggest the truth or existence of (a thing not expressly asserted). **2** insinuate, hint (*what are you implying?*). **3** signify. □□ **implied** *adj.* **impliedly** *adv.* [ME f. OF *emplier* f. L *implicare* (as IMPLICATE)]

impolder /ɪmˈpəʊldə(r)/ *v.tr.* (also **empolder**) *Brit.* **1** make a polder of. **2** reclaim from the sea. [Du. *inpolderen* (as IN-², POLDER)]

impolite /ˌɪmpəˈlaɪt/ *adj.* (**impolitest**) ill-mannered, uncivil, rude. □□ **impolitely** *adv.* **impoliteness** *n.* [L *impolitus* (as IN-¹, POLITE)]

impolitic /ɪmˈpɒlɪtɪk/ *adj.* **1** inexpedient, unwise. **2** not politic. □□ **impoliticly** *adv.*

imponderable /ɪmˈpɒndərəb(ə)l/ *adj. & n.* —*adj.* **1** that cannot be estimated or assessed in any definite way. **2** very light. **3** *Physics* having no weight. —*n.* (usu. in *pl.*) something difficult or impossible to assess. □□ **imponderability** /-ˈbɪlɪtɪ/ *n.* **imponderably** *adv.*

import *v. & n.* —*v.tr.* /ɪmˈpɔːt, ˈɪm-/ **1** bring in (esp. foreign goods or services) to a country. **2** (often foll. by *that* + clause) **a** imply, indicate, signify. **b** express, make known. —*n.* /ˈɪmpɔːt/ **1** the process of importing. **2 a** an imported article or service. **b** (in *pl.*) an amount imported (*imports exceeded £50m.*). **3** what is implied; meaning. **4** importance. □□ **importable** /ɪmˈpɔːtəb(ə)l/ *adj.* **importation** /ˌɪmpɔːˈteɪʃ(ə)n/ *n.* **importer** /ɪmˈpɔːtə(r)/ *n.* (all in sense 1 of *v.*). [ME f. L *importare* bring in, in med.L = imply, be of consequence (as IN-², *portare* carry)]

importance /ɪmˈpɔːt(ə)ns/ *n.* **1** the state of being important. **2** weight, significance. **3** personal consequence; dignity. [F f. med.L *importantia* (as IMPORT)]

important /ɪmˈpɔːt(ə)nt/ *adj.* **1** (often foll. by *to*) of great effect or consequence; momentous. **2** (of a person) having high rank or status, or great authority. **3** pretentious, pompous. **4** (*absol.* in parenthetic construction) what is a more important point or matter (*they are willing and, more important, able*). ¶ Use of *importantly* here is *disp.* □□ **importantly** *adv.* (see note above). [F f. med.L (as IMPORT)]

importunate /ɪmˈpɔːtjʊnət/ *adj.* **1** making persistent or pressing requests. **2** (of affairs) urgent. □□ **importunately** *adv.* **importunity** /ˌɪmpɔːˈtjuːnɪtɪ/ *n.* [L *importunus* inconvenient (as IN-¹, *portunus* f. *portus* harbour)]

importune /ˌɪmpɔːˈtjuːn, -ˈtjuːn/ *v.tr.* **1** solicit (a person) pressingly. **2** solicit for an immoral purpose. [F *importuner* or med.L *importunari* (as IMPORTUNATE)]

impose /ɪmˈpəʊz/ *v.* **1** *tr.* (often foll. by *on, upon*) require (a tax, duty, charge, or obligation) to be paid or undertaken (by a person etc.). **2** *tr.* enforce compliance with. **3** *intr. & refl.* (foll. by *on, upon,* or *absol.*) demand the attention or commitment of (a person); take advantage of (*I do not want to impose on you any longer; I did not want to impose*). **4** *tr.* (often foll. by *on, upon*) palm (a thing) off on (a person). **5** *tr. Printing* lay (pages of type) in the proper order ready for printing. **6** *intr.* (foll. by *on, upon*) exert influence by an impressive character or appearance. **7** *intr.* (often foll. by *on, upon*) practise deception. **8** *tr. archaic* (foll. by *upon*) place (a thing). [ME f. F *imposer* f. L *imponere imposit-* inflict, deceive (as IN-², *ponere* put)]

imposing /ɪmˈpəʊzɪŋ/ *adj.* impressive, formidable, esp. in appearance. □□ **imposingly** *adv.* **imposingness** *n.*

imposition /ˌɪmpəˈzɪʃ(ə)n/ *n.* **1** the act or an instance of imposing; the process of being imposed. **2** an unfair or resented demand or burden. **3** a tax or duty. **4** *Brit.* work set as a punishment at school. [ME f. OF *imposition* or L *impositio* f. *imponere*: see IMPOSE]

impossibility /ɪmˌpɒsɪˈbɪlɪtɪ/ *n.* (*pl.* **-ies**) **1** the fact or condition of being impossible. **2** an impossible thing or circumstance. [F *impossibilité* or L *impossibilitas* (as IMPOSSIBLE)]

impossible /ɪmˈpɒsɪb(ə)l/ *adj.* **1** not possible; that cannot occur, exist, or be done (*such a thing is impossible; it is impossible to alter them*). **2** (loosely) not easy; not convenient; not easily believable. **3** *colloq.* (of a person or thing) outrageous, intolerable. □□ **impossibly** *adv.* [ME f. OF *impossible* or L *impossibilis* (as IN-¹, POSSIBLE)]

impost¹ /ˈɪmpəʊst/ *n.* **1** a tax, duty, or tribute. **2** a weight carried by a horse in a handicap race. [F f. med.L *impost-* part. stem of L *imponere*: see IMPOSE]

impost² /ˈɪmpəʊst/ *n.* the upper course of a pillar, carrying an arch. [F *imposte* or It. *imposta* fem. past part. of *imporre* f. L *imponere*: see IMPOSE]

impostor /ɪmˈpɒstə(r)/ *n.* (also **imposter**) **1** a person who

assumes a false character or pretends to be someone else. **2** a swindler. □□ **impostorous** *adj.* **impostrous** *adj.* [F *imposteur* f. LL *impostor* (as IMPOST¹)]

imposture /ɪmˈpɒstʃə(r)/ *n.* the act or an instance of fraudulent deception. [F f. LL *impostura* (as IMPOST¹)]

impotent /ˈɪmpət(ə)nt/ *adj.* **1 a** powerless; lacking all strength. **b** helpless, decrepit. **2** (esp. of a male) unable, esp. for a prolonged period, to achieve a sexual erection or orgasm. □□ **impotence** *n.* **impotency** *n.* **impotently** *adv.* [ME f. OF f. L *impotens* (as IN-¹, POTENT¹)]

impound /ɪmˈpaʊnd/ *v.tr.* **1** confiscate. **2** take possession of. **3** shut up (animals) in a pound. **4** shut up (a person or thing) as in a pound. **5** (of a dam etc.) collect or confine (water). □□ **impoundable** *adj.* **impounder** *n.* **impoundment** *n.*

impoverish /ɪmˈpɒvərɪʃ/ *v.tr.* **1** make poor. **2** exhaust the strength or natural fertility of. □□ **impoverishment** *n.* [ME f. OF *empoverir* (as EN-¹, *povre* POOR)]

impracticable /ɪmˈpræktɪkəb(ə)l/ *adj.* **1** impossible in practice. **2** (of a road etc.) impassable. **3** (of a person or thing) unmanageable. □□ **impracticability** /-ˈbɪlɪtɪ/ *n.* **impracticableness** *n.* **impracticably** *adv.*

impractical /ɪmˈpræktɪk(ə)l/ *adj.* **1** not practical. **2** esp. *US* not practicable. □□ **impracticality** /-ˈkælɪtɪ/ *n.* **impractically** *adv.*

imprecate /ˈɪmprɪkeɪt/ *v.tr.* (often foll. by *upon*) invoke, call down (evil). □□ **imprecatory** *adj.* [L *imprecari* (as IN-², *precari* pray)]

imprecation /ˌɪmprɪˈkeɪʃ(ə)n/ *n.* **1** a spoken curse; a malediction. **2** imprecating.

imprecise /ˌɪmprɪˈsaɪs/ *adj.* not precise. □□ **imprecisely** *adv.* **impreciseness** *n.* **imprecision** /-ˈsɪʒ(ə)n/ *n.*

impregnable¹ /ɪmˈpregnəb(ə)l/ *adj.* **1** (of a fortified position) that cannot be taken by force. **2** resistant to attack or criticism. □□ **impregnability** /-ˈbɪlɪtɪ/ *n.* **impregnably** *adv.* [ME f. OF *imprenable* (as IN-¹, *prendre* take)]

impregnable² /ɪmˈpregnəb(ə)l/ *adj.* that can be impregnated.

impregnate *v. & adj.* —*v.tr.* /ˈɪmpregneɪt/ **1** (often foll. by *with*) fill or saturate. **2** (often foll. by *with*) imbue, fill (with feelings, moral qualities, etc.). **3 a** make (a female) pregnant. **b** *Biol.* fertilize (a female reproductive cell or ovum). —*adj.* /ɪmˈpregnət/ **1** pregnant. **2** (often foll. by *with*) permeated. □□ **impregnation** /ˌɪmpregˈneɪʃ(ə)n/ *n.* [LL *impregnare impregnat-* (as IN-², *pregnare* be pregnant)]

impresario /ˌɪmprɪˈsɑːrɪəʊ/ *n.* (*pl.* **-os**) an organizer of public entertainments, esp. the manager of an operatic, theatrical, or concert company. [It. f. *impresa* undertaking]

imprescriptible /ˌɪmprɪˈskrɪptɪb(ə)l/ *adj. Law* (of rights) that cannot be taken away by prescription or lapse of time. [med.L *imprescriptibilis* (as IN-¹, PRESCRIBE)]

impress¹ *v. & n.* —*v.tr.* /ɪmˈpres/ **1** (often foll. by *with*) **a** affect or influence deeply. **b** evoke a favourable opinion or reaction from (a person) (*was most impressed with your efforts*). **2** (often foll. by *on*) emphasize (an idea etc.) (*must impress on you the need to be prompt*). **3** (often foll. by *on*) **a** imprint or stamp. **b** apply (a mark etc.) with pressure. **4** make a mark or design on (a thing) with a stamp, seal, etc. **5** *Electr.* apply (voltage etc.) from outside. —*n.* /ˈɪmpres/ **1** the act or an instance of impressing. **2** a mark made by a seal, stamp, etc. **3** a characteristic mark or quality. **4** = IMPRESSION 1. □□ **impressible** /ɪmˈpresɪb(ə)l/ *adj.* [ME f. OF *empresser* (as EN-¹, PRESS¹)]

impress² /ɪmˈpres/ *v.tr. hist.* **1** force (men) to serve in the army or navy. **2** seize (goods etc.) for public service. □□ **impressment** *n.* [IN-² + PRESS²]

impression /ɪmˈpreʃ(ə)n/ *n.* **1** an effect produced (esp. on the mind or feelings). **2** a notion or belief (esp. a vague or mistaken one) (*my impression is they are afraid*). **3** an imitation of a person or sound, esp. done to entertain. **4 a** the impressing of a mark. **b** a mark impressed. **5** an unaltered reprint from standing type or plates (esp. as distinct from *edition*). **6 a** the number of copies of a book, newspaper, etc., issued at one time. **b** the printing of these. **7** a print taken from a wood engraving. **8** *Dentistry* a negative copy of the teeth or mouth made by pressing them into a soft substance. □□ **impressional** adj. [ME f. OF f. L *impressio -onis* f. *imprimere* impress- (as IN-², PRESS¹)]

impressionable /ɪmˈpreʃənəb(ə)l/ adj. easily influenced; susceptible to impressions. □□ **impressionability** /-ˈbɪlɪtɪ/ n. **impressionably** adv. [F *impressionnable* f. *impressionner* (as IMPRESSION)]

impressionism /ɪmˈpreʃəˌnɪz(ə)m/ n. **1** a style or movement in art concerned with expression of feeling by visual impression, esp. from the effect of light on objects. (See below.) **2** a style of music or writing that seeks to describe a feeling or experience rather than achieve accurate depiction or systematic structure. □□ **impressionist** n. [F *impressionnisme* (see below)]

The name and reputation of this French art movement of the late 19th c. derive from eight exhibitions held in Paris in 1874–86. The title of one of Monet's paintings—*Impression: soleil levant*—prompted the critic Leroy to dub the whole group 'impressionists'. The term was coined in derision but was accepted by the artists as an adequate indicator of at least one significant aspect of their aims. It refers to their free loose brushwork, lack of interest in precise academic draughtsmanship, and the immediacy of the resultant image, the picture's 'unfinished' quality. They painted chiefly out of doors, and the ability to treat nature as light, and light as colour, resulted in a freshness and luminosity, enhanced by the use of bright colours and white grounds. Among the principal members of the group were Monet, Renoir, Pissarro, Cézanne, Degas, and Sisley. In music, the term is applied to a style of composition originating in the 1880s with Debussy, departing from the strong direct structure and themes of the Romantic composers, and also to a type of jazz with similar 'atmospheric' characteristics.

impressionistic /ɪmˌpreʃəˈnɪstɪk/ adj. **1** in the style of impressionism. **2** subjective, unsystematic. □□ **impressionistically** adv.

impressive /ɪmˈpresɪv/ adj. **1** impressing the mind or senses, esp. so as to cause approval or admiration. **2** (of language, a scene, etc.) tending to excite deep feeling. □□ **impressively** adv. **impressiveness** n.

imprest /ˈɪmprest/ n. money advanced to a person for use in State business. [orig. *in prest* f. OF *prest* loan, advance pay: see PRESS²]

imprimatur /ˌɪmprɪˈmeɪtə(r), -ˈmɑːtə(r), -tʊə(r)/ n. **1** RC Ch. an official licence to print (an ecclesiastical or religious book etc.). **2** official approval. [L, = let it be printed]

imprimatura /ˌɪmprɪːˈmɑːtʊərə/ n. (in painting) a coloured transparent glaze as a primer. [It. *imprimitura* f. *imprimere* IMPRESS¹]

imprint v. & n. —v.tr. /ɪmˈprɪnt/ **1** (often foll. by *on*) impress or establish firmly, esp. on the mind. **2 a** (often foll. by *on*) make a stamp or impression of (a figure etc.) on a thing. **b** make an impression on (a thing) with a stamp etc. —n. /ˈɪmprɪnt/ **1** an impression or stamp. **2** the printer's or publisher's name and other details printed in a book. [ME f. OF *empreinter empreint* f. L *imprimere*: see IMPRESSION]

imprinting /ɪmˈprɪntɪŋ/ n. **1** in senses of IMPRINT v. **2** Zool. the development in a young animal of a pattern of recognition and trust for its own species. This type of behaviour was first described by the Austrian zoologist Konrad Lorenz in 1937.

imprison /ɪmˈprɪz(ə)n/ v.tr. **1** put into prison. **2** confine; shut up. □□ **imprisonment** n. [ME f. OF *emprisoner* (as EN-¹, PRISON)]

improbable /ɪmˈprɒbəb(ə)l/ adj. **1** not likely to be true or to happen. **2** difficult to believe. □□ **improbability** /-ˈbɪlɪtɪ/ n. **improbably** adv. [F *improbable* or L *improbabilis* (as IN-¹, PROBABLE)]

improbity /ɪmˈprəʊbɪtɪ/ n. (pl. **-ies**) **1** wickedness; lack of moral integrity. **2** dishonesty. **3** a wicked or dishonest act. [L *improbitas* (as IN-¹, PROBITY)]

impromptu /ɪmˈprɒmptjuː/ adj., adv., & n. —adj. & adv. extempore, unrehearsed. —n. **1** an extempore performance or speech. **2** a short piece of usu. solo instrumental music, often songlike. [F f. L *in promptu* in readiness: see PROMPT]

improper /ɪmˈprɒpə(r)/ adj. **1 a** unseemly; indecent. **b** not

in accordance with accepted rules of behaviour. **2** inaccurate, wrong. **3** not properly so called. □ **improper fraction** a fraction in which the numerator is greater than or equal to the denominator. □□ **improperly** adv. [F *impropre* or L *improprius* (as IN-¹, PROPER)]

impropriate /ɪmˈprəʊprɪˌeɪt/ v.tr. Brit. **1** annex (an ecclesiastical benefice) to a corporation or person as property. **2** place (tithes or ecclesiastical property) in lay hands. □□ **impropriation** /-ˈeɪʃ(ə)n/ n. [AL *impropriare* (as IN-², *proprius* own)]

impropriator /ɪmˈprəʊprɪˌeɪtə(r)/ n. Brit. a person to whom a benefice is impropriated.

impropriety /ˌɪmprəˈpraɪətɪ/ n. (pl. **-ies**) **1** lack of propriety; indecency. **2** an instance of improper conduct etc. **3** incorrectness. **4** unfitness. [F *impropriété* or L *improprietas* (as IN-¹, *proprius* proper)]

improvable /ɪmˈpruːvəb(ə)l/ adj. **1** that can be improved. **2** suitable for cultivation. □□ **improvability** /-ˈbɪlɪtɪ/ n.

improve /ɪmˈpruːv/ v. **1 a** tr. & intr. make or become better. **b** intr. (foll. by *on, upon*) produce something better than. **2** absol. (as **improving** adj.) giving moral benefit (*improving literature*). [orig. *emprowe, improwe* f. AF *emprower* f. OF *emprou* f. *prou* profit, infl. by PROVE]

improvement /ɪmˈpruːvmənt/ n. **1** the act or an instance of improving or being improved. **2** something that improves, esp. an addition or alteration that adds to value. **3** something that has been improved. [ME f. AF *emprowement* (as IMPROVE)]

improver /ɪmˈpruːvə(r)/ n. **1** a person who improves. **2** Brit. a person who works for low wages while acquiring skill and experience in a trade.

improvident /ɪmˈprɒvɪd(ə)nt/ adj. **1** lacking foresight or care for the future. **2** not frugal; thriftless. **3** heedless, incautious. □□ **improvidence** n. **improvidently** adv.

improvise /ˈɪmprəˌvaɪz/ v.tr. (also absol.) **1** compose or perform (music, verse, etc.) extempore. **2** provide or construct (a thing) extempore. □□ **improvisation** /-ˈzeɪʃ(ə)n/ n. **improvisational** /-ˈzeɪʃən(ə)l/ adj. **improvisatorial** /-zəˈtɔːrɪəl/ adj. **improvisatory** /-ˈzeɪtərɪ/ adj. **improviser** n. [F *improviser* or It. *improvvisare* f. *improvviso* extempore, f. L *improvisus* past part. (as IN-¹, PROVIDE)]

imprudent /ɪmˈpruːd(ə)nt/ adj. rash, indiscreet. □□ **imprudence** n. **imprudently** adv. [ME f. L *imprudens* (as IN-¹, PRUDENT)]

impudent /ˈɪmpjʊd(ə)nt/ adj. **1** insolently disrespectful; impertinent. **2** shamelessly presumptuous. **3** unblushing. □□ **impudence** n. **impudently** adv. [ME f. L *impudens* (as IN-¹, *pudēre* be ashamed)]

impudicity /ˌɪmpjʊˈdɪsɪtɪ/ n. shamelessness, immodesty. [F *impudicité* f. L *impudicus* (as IMPUDENT)]

impugn /ɪmˈpjuːn/ v.tr. challenge or call in question (a statement, action, etc.). □□ **impugnable** adj. **impugnment** n. [ME f. L *impugnare* assail (as IN-², *pugnare* fight)]

impuissant /ɪmˈpjuːɪs(ə)nt/ adj. impotent, weak. □□ **impuissance** n. [F (as IN-¹, PUISSANT)]

impulse /ˈɪmpʌls/ n. **1** the act or an instance of impelling; a push. **2** an impetus. **3** Physics **a** an indefinitely large force acting for a very short time but producing a finite change of momentum (e.g. the blow of a hammer). **b** the change of momentum produced by this or any force. **4** a wave of excitation in a nerve. **5** mental incitement. **6** a sudden desire or tendency to act without reflection (*did it on impulse*). □ **impulse buying** the unpremeditated buying of goods as a result of a whim or impulse. [L *impulsus* (as IMPEL)]

impulsion /ɪmˈpʌlʃ(ə)n/ n. **1** the act or an instance of impelling. **2** a mental impulse. **3** impetus. [ME f. OF f. L *impulsio -onis* (as IMPEL)]

impulsive /ɪmˈpʌlsɪv/ adj. **1** (of a person or conduct etc.) apt to be affected or determined by sudden impulse. **2** tending to impel. **3** Physics acting as an impulse. □□ **impulsively** adv. **impulsiveness** n. [ME f. F *impulsif -ive* or LL *impulsivus* (as IMPULSION)]

impunity /ɪmˈpjuːnɪtɪ/ n. exemption from punishment or from the injurious consequences of an action. □ **with impunity** without having to suffer the normal injurious consequences (of an action). [L *impunitas* f. *impunis* (as IN-¹, *poena* penalty)]

impure /ɪmˈpjʊə(r)/ adj. **1** mixed with foreign matter; adulterated. **2** dirty. **3** unchaste. **4** (of a colour) mixed with another colour. □□ **impurely** adv. **impureness** n. [ME f. L *impurus* (as IN-¹, *purus* pure)]

impurity /ɪmˈpjʊərɪtɪ/ n. (pl. **-ies**) **1** the quality or condition of being impure. **2** an impure thing or constituent. [F *impurité* or L *impuritas* (as IMPURE)]

impute /ɪmˈpjuːt/ v.tr. (foll. by *to*) **1** regard (esp. something undesirable) as being done or caused or possessed by. **2** *Theol.* ascribe (righteousness, guilt, etc.) to (a person) by virtue of a similar quality in another. □□ **imputable** adj. **imputation** /-ˈteɪʃ(ə)n/ n. **imputative** /-tətɪv/ adj. [ME f. OF *imputer* f. L *imputare* enter in the account (as IN-², *putare* reckon)]

Imroz see IMBROS.

I.Mun.E. abbr. (in the UK) Institution of Municipal Engineers.

IN abbr. US Indiana (in official postal use).

In symb. Chem. the element indium.

in /ɪn/ prep., adv., & adj. —prep. **1** expressing inclusion or position within limits of space, time, circumstance, etc. (*in England; in bed; in the rain*). **2** during the time of (*in the night; in 1989*). **3** within the time of (*will be back in two hours*). **4 a** with respect to (*blind in one eye; good in parts*). **b** as a kind of (*the latest thing in luxury*). **5** as a proportionate part of (*one in three failed; a gradient of one in six*). **6** with the form or arrangement of (*packed in tens; falling in folds*). **7** as a member of (*in the army*). **8** concerned with (*is in politics*). **9** as or regarding the content of (*there is something in what you say*). **10** within the ability of (*does he have it in him?*). **11** having the condition of; affected by (*in bad health; in danger*). **12** having as a purpose (*in search of; in reply to*). **13** by means of or using as material (*drawn in pencil; modelled in bronze*). **14 a** using as the language of expression (*written in French*). **b** (of music) having as its key (*symphony in C*). **15** (of a word) having as a beginning or ending (*words in un-*). **16** wearing as dress (*in blue; in a suit*). **17** with the identity of (*found a friend in Mary*). **18** (of an animal) pregnant with (*in calf*). **19** into (with a verb of motion or change: *put it in the box; cut it in two*). **20** introducing an indirect object after a verb (*believe in; engage in; share in*). **21** forming adverbial phrases (*in any case; in reality; in short*). —adv. expressing position within limits, or motion to such a position: **1** into a room, house, etc. (*come in*). **2** at home, in one's office, etc. (*is not in*). **3** so as to be enclosed or confined (*locked in*). **4** in a publication (*is the advertisement in?*). **5** in or to the inward side (*rub it in*). **6 a** in fashion, season, or office (*long skirts are in; strawberries are not yet in*). **b** elected (*the Democrat got in*). **7** exerting favourable action or influence (*their luck was in*). **8** *Cricket* (of a player or side) batting. **9** (of transport) at the platform etc. (*the train is in*). **10** (of a season, harvest, order, etc.) having arrived or been received. **11** *Brit.* (of a fire) continuing to burn. **12** denoting effective action (*join in*). **13** (of the tide) at the highest point. **14** (in comb.) *colloq.* denoting prolonged or concerted action, esp. by large numbers (*sit-in; teach-in*). —adj. **1** internal; living in; inside (*in-patient*). **2** fashionable, esoteric (*the in thing to do*). **3** confined to or shared by a group of people (*in-joke*). □ **in all** see ALL. **in at** present at; contributing to (*in at the kill*). **in between** see BETWEEN adv. **in-between** attrib.adj. colloq. intermediate (*at an in-between stage*). **in for 1** about to undergo (esp. something unpleasant). **2** competing in or for. **3** involved in; committed to. **in on** sharing in; privy to (a secret etc.). **ins and outs** (often foll. by *of*) all the details (of a procedure etc.). **in so far as** see FAR. **in that** because; in so far as. **in with** on good terms with. [OE *in, inn*, orig. as adv. with verbs of motion]

in. abbr. inch(es).

in-¹ /ɪn/ prefix (also **il-, im-, ir-**) added to: **1** adjectives, meaning 'not' (*inedible; insane*). **2** nouns, meaning 'without, lacking' (*inaction*). [L]

in-² /ɪn/ prefix (also **il-** before *l*, **im-** before *b, m, p*, **ir-** before *r*) in, on, into, towards, within (*induce; influx; insight; intrude*). [IN, or from or after L in IN prep.]

-in /ɪn/ suffix Chem. forming names of: **1** neutral substances (*gelatin*). **2** antibiotics (*penicillin*). [-INE⁴]

-ina /ˈiːnə/ suffix denoting: **1** feminine names and titles (*Georgina; tsarina*). **2** names of musical instruments (*concertina*). **3** names of zoological classification categories (*globigerina*). [It. or Sp. or L]

inability /ˌɪnəˈbɪlɪtɪ/ n. **1** the state of being unable. **2** a lack of power or means.

in absentia /ˌɪn æbˈsentɪə/ adv. in (his, her, or their) absence. [L]

inaccessible /ˌɪnækˈsesɪb(ə)l/ adj. **1** not accessible; that cannot be reached. **2** (of a person) not open to advances or influence; unapproachable. □□ **inaccessibility** /-ˈbɪlɪtɪ/ n. **inaccessibleness** n. **inaccessibly** adv. [ME f. F *inaccessible* or LL *inaccessibilis* (as IN-¹, ACCESSIBLE)]

inaccurate /ɪnˈækjʊrət/ adj. not accurate. □□ **inaccuracy** n. (pl. **-ies**). **inaccurately** adv.

inaction /ɪnˈækʃ(ə)n/ n. **1** lack of action. **2** sluggishness, inertness.

inactivate /ɪnˈæktɪˌveɪt/ v.tr. make inactive or inoperative. □□ **inactivation** /-ˈveɪʃ(ə)n/ n.

inactive /ɪnˈæktɪv/ adj. **1** not active or inclined to act. **2** passive. **3** indolent. □□ **inactively** adv. **inactivity** /-ˈtɪvɪtɪ/ n.

inadequate /ɪnˈædɪkwət/ adj. (often foll. by *to*) **1** not adequate; insufficient. **2** (of a person) incompetent; unable to deal with a situation. □□ **inadequacy** n. (pl. **-ies**). **inadequately** adv.

inadmissible /ˌɪnədˈmɪsɪb(ə)l/ adj. that cannot be admitted or allowed. □□ **inadmissibility** /-ˈbɪlɪtɪ/ n. **inadmissibly** adv.

inadvertent /ˌɪnədˈvɜːt(ə)nt/ adj. **1** (of an action) unintentional. **2 a** not properly attentive. **b** negligent. □□ **inadvertence** n. **inadvertency** n. **inadvertently** adv. [IN-¹ + obs. *advertent* attentive (as ADVERT²)]

inadvisable /ˌɪnədˈvaɪzəb(ə)l/ adj. not advisable. □□ **inadvisability** /-ˈbɪlɪtɪ/ n. [ADVISABLE]

inalienable /ɪnˈeɪlɪənəb(ə)l/ adj. that cannot be transferred to another; not alienable. □□ **inalienability** /-ˈbɪlɪtɪ/ n. **inalienably** adv.

inalterable /ɪnˈɒltərəb(ə)l/ adj. not alterable; that cannot be changed. □□ **inalterability** /-ˈbɪlɪtɪ/ n. **inalterably** adv. [med.L *inalterabilis* (as IN-¹, *alterabilis* alterable)]

inamorato /ɪnˌæməˈrɑːtəʊ/ n. (pl. **-os**; fem. **inamorata** /-tə/) a lover. [It., past part. of *inamorare* enamour (as IN-², *amore* f. L *amor* love)]

inane /ɪˈneɪn/ adj. **1** silly, senseless. **2** empty, void. □□ **inanely** adv. **inaneness** n. **inanity** /-ˈænɪtɪ/ n. (pl. **-ies**). [L *inanis* empty, vain]

inanimate /ɪnˈænɪmət/ adj. **1** destitute of life. **2** not endowed with animal life. **3** spiritless, dull. □ **inanimate nature** everything other than the animal world. □□ **inanimately** adv. **inanimation** /-ˈmeɪʃ(ə)n/ n. [LL *inanimatus* (as IN-¹, ANIMATE)]

inanition /ˌɪnəˈnɪʃ(ə)n/ n. emptiness, esp. exhaustion from lack of nourishment. [ME f. LL *inanitio* f. L *inanire* make empty (as INANE)]

inappellable /ˌɪnəˈpeləb(ə)l/ adj. that cannot be appealed against. [obs.F *inappelable* (as IN-¹, *appeler* APPEAL)]

inapplicable /ɪnˈæplɪkəb(ə)l, ˌɪnəˈplɪk-/ adj. (often foll. by *to*) not applicable; unsuitable. □□ **inapplicability** /-ˈbɪlɪtɪ/ n. **inapplicably** adv.

inapposite /ɪnˈæpəzɪt/ adj. not apposite; out of place. □□ **inappositely** adv. **inappositeness** n.

inappreciable /ˌɪnəˈpriːʃəb(ə)l/ adj. **1** imperceptible; not worth reckoning. **2** that cannot be appreciated. □□ **inappreciably** adv.

inappreciation /ˌɪnəˌpriːʃɪˈeɪʃ(ə)n/ n. failure to appreciate. □□ **inappreciative** /-ˈpriːʃətɪv/ adj.

inappropriate /ˌɪnəˈprəʊprɪət/ adj. not appropriate. □□ **inappropriately** adv. **inappropriateness** n.

inapt /ɪnˈæpt/ adj. **1** not apt or suitable. **2** unskilful. □□ **inaptitude** n. **inaptly** adv. **inaptness** n.

inarch /ɪnˈɑːtʃ/ v.tr. graft (a plant) by connecting a growing branch without separation from the parent stock. [IN-² + ARCH¹ v.]

inarguable /ɪnˈɑːgjʊəb(ə)l/ adj. that cannot be argued about or disputed. □□ **inarguably** adv.

inarticulate /ˌɪnɑːˈtɪkjʊlət/ adj. **1** unable to speak distinctly or express oneself clearly. **2** (of speech) not articulate; indistinctly pronounced. **3** dumb. **4** esp. Anat. not jointed. □□ **inarticulately** adv. **inarticulateness** n. [LL inarticulatus (as IN-¹, ARTICULATE)]

inartistic /ˌɪnɑːˈtɪstɪk/ adj. **1** not following the principles of art. **2** lacking skill or talent in art; not appreciating art. □□ **inartistically** adv.

inasmuch /ˌɪnəzˈmʌtʃ/ adv. (foll. by as) **1** since, because. **2** to the extent that. [ME, orig. in as much]

inattentive /ˌɪnəˈtentɪv/ adj. **1** not paying due attention; heedless. **2** neglecting to show courtesy. □□ **inattention** n. **inattentively** adv. **inattentiveness** n.

inaudible /ɪnˈɔːdɪb(ə)l/ adj. that cannot be heard. □□ **inaudibility** /-ˈbɪlɪtɪ/ n. **inaudibly** adv.

inaugural /ɪˈnɔːgjʊr(ə)l/ adj. & n. —adj. **1** of inauguration. **2** (of a lecture etc.) given by a person being inaugurated. —n. an inaugural speech etc. [F f. inaugurer (as INAUGURATE)]

inaugurate /ɪˈnɔːgjʊˌreɪt/ v.tr. **1** admit (a person) formally to office. **2** initiate the public use of (a building etc.). **3** begin, introduce. **4** enter with ceremony upon (an undertaking etc.). □□ **inauguration** /-ˈreɪʃ(ə)n/ n. **inaugurator** n. **inauguratory** adj. [L inaugurare (as IN-², augurare take omens: see AUGUR)]

inauspicious /ˌɪnɔːˈspɪʃəs/ adj. **1** ill-omened, unpropitious. **2** unlucky. □□ **inauspiciously** adv. **inauspiciousness** n.

inboard /ˈɪnbɔːd/ adv. & adj. —adv. within the sides of or towards the centre of a ship, aircraft, or vehicle. —adj. situated inboard.

inborn /ˈɪnbɔːn/ adj. existing from birth; implanted by nature.

inbreathe /ɪnˈbriːð/ v.tr. **1** breathe in or absorb. **2** inspire (a person).

inbred /ɪnˈbred, ˈɪn-/ adj. **1** inborn. **2** produced by inbreeding.

inbreeding /ɪnˈbriːdɪŋ/ n. breeding from closely related animals or persons. □□ **inbreed** v.tr. & intr. (past and past part. **inbred**).

inbuilt /ˈɪnbɪlt/ adj. incorporated as part of a structure.

Inc. abbr. US Incorporated.

Inca /ˈɪŋkə/ n. (pl. same or **-s**) a member of an American Indian people of the central Andes before the Spanish conquest. The Inca arrived in the valley of Cuzco c.1250. Their origin and early history are uncertain, but in the first part of the 15th c. they began a series of rapid conquests and a century later their power extended over most of modern Ecuador and Peru, large areas of Bolivia, and parts of Argentina and Chile. Their empire was highly centralized and governed by a despotic monarchy supported by an aristocratic bureaucracy, with Cuzco as its capital city and religious centre. They were skilled engineers, and built a network of roads; technology and architecture were highly developed despite the absence of wheeled vehicles and a system of writing, and many of their palaces, temples, fortifications, and irrigation systems still survive. The empire was weakened by civil war in the early 16th c., and fell to the invading Spaniards in 1532. □□ **Incaic** /ɪŋˈkeɪɪk/ adj. **Incan** adj. [Quechua, = lord, royal person]

incalculable /ɪnˈkælkjʊləb(ə)l/ adj. **1** too great for calculation. **2** that cannot be reckoned beforehand. **3** (of a person, character, etc.) uncertain. □□ **incalculability** /-ˈbɪlɪtɪ/ n. **incalculably** adv.

in camera see CAMERA.

incandesce /ˌɪnkænˈdes/ v.intr. & tr. glow or cause to glow with heat. [back-form. f. INCANDESCENT]

incandescent /ˌɪnkænˈdes(ə)nt/ adj. **1** glowing with heat. **2** shining brightly. **3** (of an electric or other light) produced by a glowing white-hot filament. □□ **incandescence** n. **incandescently** adv. [F f. L incandescere (as IN-², candescere inceptive of candēre be white)]

incantation /ˌɪnkænˈteɪʃ(ə)n/ n. **1 a** a magical formula. **b** the use of this. **2** a spell or charm. □□ **incantational** adj.

incantatory adj. [ME f. OF f. LL incantatio -onis f. incantare chant, bewitch (as IN-², cantare sing)]

incapable /ɪnˈkeɪpəb(ə)l/ adj. **1** (often foll. by of) **a** not capable. **b** lacking the required quality or characteristic (favourable or adverse) (incapable of hurting anyone). **2** not capable of rational conduct or of managing one's own affairs (drunk and incapable). □□ **incapability** /-ˈbɪlɪtɪ/ n. **incapably** adv. [F incapable or LL incapabilis (as IN-¹, capabilis CAPABLE)]

incapacitate /ˌɪnkəˈpæsɪˌteɪt/ v.tr. **1** render incapable or unfit. **2** disqualify. □□ **incapacitant** n. **incapacitation** /-ˈteɪʃ(ə)n/ n.

incapacity /ˌɪnkəˈpæsɪtɪ/ n. (pl. **-ies**) **1** inability; lack of the necessary power or resources. **2** legal disqualification. **3** an instance of incapacity. [F incapacité or LL incapacitas (as IN-¹, CAPACITY)]

incarcerate /ɪnˈkɑːsəˌreɪt/ v.tr. imprison or confine. □□ **incarceration** /-ˈreɪʃ(ə)n/ n. **incarcerator** n. [med.L incarcerare (as IN-², L carcer prison)]

incarnadine /ɪnˈkɑːnəˌdaɪn/ adj. & v. poet. —adj. flesh-coloured or crimson. —v.tr. dye this colour. [F incarnadin -ine f. It. incarnadino (for -tino) f. incarnato INCARNATE adj.]

incarnate adj. & v. —adj. /ɪnˈkɑːnət/ **1** (of a person, spirit, quality, etc.) embodied in flesh, esp. in human form (is the devil incarnate). **2** represented in a recognizable or typical form (folly incarnate). —v.tr. /ˈɪnkɑːˌneɪt, -ˈkɑːneɪt/ **1** embody in flesh. **2** put (an idea etc.) into concrete form; realize. **3** (of a person etc.) be the living embodiment of (a quality). [ME f. eccl.L incarnare incarnat- make flesh (as IN-², L caro carnis flesh)]

incarnation /ˌɪnkɑːˈneɪʃ(ə)n/ n. **1 a** embodiment in (esp. human) flesh. **b** (**the Incarnation**) Theol. the embodiment of God the Son in human flesh as Jesus Christ. **2** (often foll. by of) a living type (of a quality etc.). **3** Med. the process of forming new flesh. [ME f. OF f. eccl.L incarnatio -onis (as INCARNATE)]

incase var. of ENCASE.

incautious /ɪnˈkɔːʃəs/ adj. heedless, rash. □□ **incaution** n. **incautiously** adv. **incautiousness** n.

incendiary /ɪnˈsendɪərɪ/ adj. & n. —adj. **1** (of a substance or device, esp. a bomb) designed to cause fires. **2 a** of or relating to the malicious setting on fire of property. **b** guilty of this. **3** tending to stir up strife; inflammatory. —n. (pl. **-ies**) **1** an incendiary bomb or device. **2** an incendiary person. □□ **incendiarism** n. [ME f. L incendiarius f. incendium conflagration f. incendere incens- set fire to]

incense¹ /ˈɪnsens/ n. & v. —n. **1** a gum or spice producing a sweet smell when burned. **2** the smoke of this, esp. in religious ceremonial. —v.tr. **1** treat or perfume (a person or thing) with incense. **2** burn incense to (a deity etc.). **3** suffuse with fragrance. □□ **incensation** /-ˈseɪʃ(ə)n/ n. [ME f. OF encens, encenser f. eccl.L incensum a thing burnt, incense: see INCENDIARY]

incense² /ɪnˈsens/ v.tr. (often foll. by at, with, against) enrage; make angry. [ME f. OF incenser (as INCENDIARY)]

incensory /ˈɪnsensərɪ/ n. (pl. **-ies**) = CENSER. [med.L incensorium (as INCENSE¹)]

incentive /ɪnˈsentɪv/ n. & adj. —n. **1** (often foll. by to) a motive or incitement, esp. to action. **2** a payment or concession to stimulate greater output by workers. —adj. serving to motivate or incite. [ME f. L incentivus setting the tune f. incinere incent- sing to (as IN-², canere sing)]

incept /ɪnˈsept/ v. **1** tr. Biol. (of an organism) take in (food etc.). **2** intr. Brit. hist. take a master's or doctor's degree at a university. □□ **inceptor** n. (in sense 2). [L incipere incept- begin (as IN-², capere take)]

inception /ɪnˈsepʃ(ə)n/ n. a beginning. [ME f. OF inception or L inceptio (as INCEPT)]

inceptive /ɪnˈseptɪv/ adj. & n. —adj. **1 a** beginning. **b** initial. **2** Gram. (of a verb) that denotes the beginning of an action. —n. an inceptive verb. [LL inceptivus (as INCEPT)]

incertitude /ɪnˈsɜːtɪˌtjuːd/ n. uncertainty, doubt. [F incertitude or LL incertitudo (as IN-¹, CERTITUDE)]

incessant /ɪnˈses(ə)nt/ adj. unceasing, continual, repeated. □□ **incessancy** n. **incessantly** adv. **incessantness** n. [F incessant or LL incessans (as IN-¹, cessans pres. part. of L cessare CEASE)]

incest /ˈɪnsest/ n. sexual intercourse between persons regarded as too closely related to marry each other. [ME f. L incestus (as IN-¹, castus CHASTE)]

incestuous /ɪnˈsestjʊəs/ adj. **1** involving or guilty of incest. **2** (of human relations generally) excessively restricted or resistant to wider influence. □□ **incestuously** adv. **incestuousness** n. [LL incestuosus (as INCEST)]

inch¹ /ɪntʃ/ n. & v. —n. **1** a unit of linear measure equal to one-twelfth of a foot (2.54 cm). **2 a** (as a unit of rainfall) a quantity that would cover a horizontal surface to a depth of 1 inch. **b** (of atmospheric or other pressure) an amount that balances the weight of a column of mercury 1 inch high. **3** (as a unit of map-scale) so many inches representing 1 mile on the ground (a 4-inch map). **4** a small amount (usu. with neg.: would not yield an inch). —v.tr. & intr. move gradually in a specified way (inched forward). □ **every inch 1** entirely (looked every inch a queen). **2** the whole distance or area (combed every inch of the garden). **give a person an inch and he** or **she will take a mile** (or orig. **an ell**) a person once conceded to will demand much. **inch by inch** gradually; bit by bit. **within an inch of** almost to the point of. [OE ynce f. L uncia twelfth part: cf. OUNCE¹]

inch² /ɪntʃ/ n. esp. Sc. a small island (esp. in place-names). [ME f. Gael. innis]

inchoate /ɪnˈkəʊeɪt, ˈɪn-/ adj. & v. —adj. **1** just begun. **2** undeveloped, rudimentary, unformed. —v.tr. begin; originate. □□ **inchoately** adv. **inchoateness** n. **inchoation** /-ˈeɪʃ(ə)n/ n. **inchoative** /-ˈkəʊətɪv/ adj. [L inchoatus past part. of inchoare (as IN-², choare begin)]

Inchon /ɪnˈtʃɒn/ a port of Korea, on the Yellow Sea west of Seoul; pop. (1985) 1,387,500.

inchworm /ˈɪntʃwɜːm/ n. = measuring-worm (see MEASURE).

incidence /ˈɪnsɪd(ə)ns/ n. **1** (often foll. by of) the fact, manner, or rate, of occurrence or action. **2** the range, scope, or extent of influence of a thing. **3** Physics the falling of a line, or of a thing moving in a line, upon a surface. **4** the act or an instance of coming into contact with a thing. □ **angle of incidence** the angle which an incident line, ray, etc., makes with the perpendicular to the surface at the point of incidence. [ME f. OF incidence or med.L incidentia (as INCIDENT)]

incident /ˈɪnsɪd(ə)nt/ n. & adj. —n. **1 a** an event or occurrence. **b** a minor or detached event attracting general attention or noteworthy in some way. **2** a hostile clash, esp. of troops of countries at war (a frontier incident). **3** a distinct piece of action in a play or a poem. **4** Law a privilege, burden, etc., attaching to an obligation or right. —adj. **1 a** (often foll. by to) apt or liable to happen; naturally attaching or dependent. **b** (foll. by to) Law attaching to. **2** (often foll. by on, upon) (of light etc.) falling or striking. [ME f. F incident or L incidere (as IN-², cadere fall)]

incidental /ˌɪnsɪˈdent(ə)l/ adj. **1** (often foll. by to) **a** having a minor role in relation to a more important thing, event, etc. **b** not essential. **2** (foll. by to) liable to happen. **3** (foll. by on, upon) following as a subordinate event. □ **incidental music** music used as a background to the action of a film, broadcast, etc.

incidentally /ˌɪnsɪˈdent(ə)lɪ/ adv. **1** by the way; as an unconnected remark. **2** in an incidental way.

incinerate /ɪnˈsɪnəˌreɪt/ v.tr. **1** consume (a body etc.) by fire. **2** reduce to ashes. □□ **incineration** /-ˈreɪʃ(ə)n/ n. [med.L incinerare (as IN-², cinis -eris ashes)]

incinerator /ɪnˈsɪnəˌreɪtə(r)/ n. a furnace or apparatus for burning esp. refuse to ashes.

incipient /ɪnˈsɪpɪənt/ adj. **1** beginning. **2** in an initial stage. □□ **incipience** n. **incipiency** n. **incipiently** adv. [L incipere incipient- (as INCEPT)]

incise /ɪnˈsaɪz/ v.tr. **1** make a cut in. **2** engrave. [F inciser f. L incidere incis- (as IN-², caedere cut)]

incision /ɪnˈsɪʒ(ə)n/ n. **1** a cut; a division produced by cutting; a notch. **2** the act of cutting into a thing. [ME f. OF incision or LL incisio (as INCISE)]

incisive /ɪnˈsaɪsɪv/ adj. **1** mentally sharp; acute. **2** clear and effective. **3** cutting, penetrating. □□ **incisively** adv. **incisiveness** n. [med.L incisivus (as INCISE)]

incisor /ɪnˈsaɪzə(r)/ n. a cutting-tooth, esp. at the front of the mouth. [med.L, = cutter (as INCISE)]

incite /ɪnˈsaɪt/ v.tr. (often foll. by to) urge or stir up. □□ **incitation** /-ˈteɪʃ(ə)n/ n. **incitement** n. **inciter** n. [ME f. F inciter f. L incitare (as IN-², citare rouse)]

incivility /ˌɪnsɪˈvɪlɪtɪ/ n. (pl. **-ies**) **1** rudeness, discourtesy. **2** a rude or discourteous act. [F incivilité or LL incivilitas (as IN-¹, CIVILITY)]

inclement /ɪnˈklemənt/ adj. (of the weather or climate) severe, esp. cold or stormy. □□ **inclemency** n. (pl. **-ies**). **inclemently** adv. [F inclément or L inclemens (as IN-¹, CLEMENT)]

inclination /ˌɪnklɪˈneɪʃ(ə)n/ n. **1** (often foll. by to) a disposition or propensity. **2** (often foll. by for) a liking or affection. **3** a leaning, slope, or slant. **4** the difference of direction of two lines or planes, esp. as measured by the angle between them. **5** the dip of a magnetic needle. [ME f. OF inclination or L inclinatio (as INCLINE)]

incline v. & n. —v. /ɪnˈklaɪn/ **1** tr. (usu. in passive; often foll. by to, for, or to + infin.) **a** make (a person, feelings, etc.) willing or favourably disposed (am inclined to think so; does not incline me to agree). **b** give a specified tendency to (a thing) (the door is inclined to bang). **2** intr. **a** be disposed (I incline to think so). **b** (often foll. by to, towards) tend. **3** intr. & tr. lean or turn away from a given direction, esp. the vertical. **4** tr. bend (the head, body, or oneself) forward or downward. —n. /ˈɪnklaɪn/ **1** a slope. **2** an inclined plane. □ **inclined plane** a sloping plane (esp. as a means of reducing the force needed to raise a load). **incline one's ear** (often foll. by to) listen favourably. □□ **incliner** n. [ME encline f. OF encliner f. L inclinare (as IN-², clinare bend)]

inclinometer /ˌɪnklɪˈnɒmɪtə(r)/ n. **1** an instrument for measuring the angle between the direction of the earth's magnetic field and the horizontal. **2** an instrument for measuring the inclination of an aircraft or ship to the horizontal. **3** an instrument for measuring a slope. [L inclinare INCLINE v. + -METER]

inclose var. of ENCLOSE.

inclosure var. of ENCLOSURE.

include /ɪnˈkluːd/ v.tr. **1** comprise or reckon in as part of a whole. **2** (as **including** prep.) if we include (six members, including the chairman). **3** treat or regard as comprised. **4** (as **included** adj.) shut in; enclosed. □ **include out** colloq. or joc. specifically exclude. □□ **includable** adj. **includible** adj. **inclusion** /-ʒ(ə)n/ n. [ME f. L includere inclus- (as IN-², claudere shut)]

inclusive /ɪnˈkluːsɪv/ adj. **1** (often foll. by of) including, comprising. **2** with the inclusion of the extreme limits stated (pages 7 to 26 inclusive). **3** including all the normal services etc. (a hotel offering inclusive terms). □□ **inclusively** adv. **inclusiveness** n. [med.L inclusivus (as INCLUDE)]

incog /ɪnˈkɒg/ adj., adv., & n. colloq. = INCOGNITO. [abbr.]

incognito /ˌɪnkɒgˈniːtəʊ/ adj., adv., & n. —adj. & adv. with one's name or identity kept secret (was travelling incognito). —n. (pl. **-os**) **1** a person who is incognito. **2** the pretended identity or anonymous character of such a person. [It., = unknown, f. L incognitus (as IN-¹, cognitus past part. of cognoscere know)]

incognizant /ɪnˈkɒgnɪz(ə)nt/ adj. (foll. by of) unaware; not knowing. □□ **incognizance** n.

incoherent /ˌɪnkəʊˈhɪərənt/ adj. **1** (of a person) unable to speak intelligibly. **2** (of speech etc.) lacking logic or consistency. **3** Physics (of waves) having no definite or stable phase relationship. □□ **incoherence** n. **incoherency** n. (pl. **-ies**). **incoherently** adv.

incombustible /ˌɪnkəmˈbʌstɪb(ə)l/ adj. that cannot be burnt or consumed by fire. □□ **incombustibility** /-ˈbɪlɪtɪ/ n. [ME f. med.L incombustibilis (as IN-¹, COMBUSTIBLE)]

income /ˈɪnkʌm, ˈɪŋkəm/ n. the money or other assets received, esp. periodically or in a year, from one's business, lands, work, investments, etc. □ **income group** a section of the population determined by income. **income tax** see separate entry. [ME (orig. = arrival), prob. f. ON innkoma: in later use f. come in]

incomer /ˈɪnˌkʌmə(r)/ n. **1** a person who comes in. **2** a person who arrives to settle in a place; an immigrant. **3** an intruder. **4** a successor.

-incomer /ˈɪnkʌmə(r), ˈɪŋkʌmə(r)/ comb. form earning a specified kind or level of income (middle-incomer).

income tax *n.* a tax levied on income. Such a tax was first introduced in Britain in 1799 to help pay for the war against Revolutionary France. Through most of the 19th c. it was regarded as a temporary measure to meet extraordinary expenses, and the rate was generally kept below two shillings in the pound. By the end of the century, however, it had become the major source of revenue. The rate of taxation rose dramatically during the two World Wars, and during the Second (1944) the pay-as-you-earn system, deducting tax at the source of income, was introduced.

incoming /ˈɪnˌkʌmɪŋ/ *adj. & n.* —*adj.* **1** coming in (*the incoming tide; incoming telephone calls*). **2** succeeding another person or persons (*the incoming tenant*). **3** immigrant. **4** (of profit) accruing. —*n.* **1** (usu. in *pl.*) revenue, income. **2** the act of arriving or entering.

incommensurable /ˌɪnkəˈmenʃərəb(ə)l, -sjərəb(ə)l/ *adj.* (often foll. by *with*) **1** not comparable in respect of magnitude. **2** incapable of being measured (in comparison with). **3** *Math.* (of a magnitude or magnitudes) having no common factor, integral or fractional. **4** *Math.* irrational. ☐☐ **incommensurability** /-ˈbɪlɪtɪ/ *n.* **incommensurably** *adv.* [LL *incommensurabilis* (as IN-1, COMMENSURABLE)]

incommensurate /ˌɪnkəˈmenʃərət, -sjərət/ *adj.* **1** (often foll. by *with, to*) out of proportion; inadequate. **2** = INCOMMENSURABLE. ☐☐ **incommensurately** *adv.* **incommensurateness** *n.*

incommode /ˌɪnkəˈməʊd/ *v.tr.* **1** hinder, inconvenience. **2** trouble, annoy. [F *incommoder* or L *incommodare* (as IN-1, *commodus* convenient)]

incommodious /ˌɪnkəˈməʊdɪəs/ *adj.* not affording good accommodation; uncomfortable. ☐☐ **incommodiously** *adv.* **incommodiousness** *n.*

incommunicable /ˌɪnkəˈmjuːnɪkəb(ə)l/ *adj.* **1** that cannot be communicated or shared. **2** that cannot be uttered or told. **3** that does not communicate; uncommunicative. ☐☐ **incommunicability** /-ˈbɪlɪtɪ/ *n.* **incommunicableness** *n.* **incommunicably** *adv.* [LL *incommunicabilis* (as IN-1, COMMUNICABLE)]

incommunicado /ˌɪnkəˌmjuːnɪˈkɑːdəʊ/ *adj.* **1** without or deprived of the means of communication with others. **2** (of a prisoner) in solitary confinement. [Sp. *incomunicado* past part. of *incomunicar* deprive of communication]

incommunicative /ˌɪnkəˈmjuːnɪkətɪv/ *adj.* not communicative; taciturn. ☐☐ **incommunicatively** *adv.* **incommunicativeness** *n.*

incommutable /ˌɪnkəˈmjuːtəb(ə)l/ *adj.* **1** not changeable. **2** not commutable. ☐☐ **incommutably** *adv.* [ME f. L *incommutabilis* (as IN-1, COMMUTABLE)]

incomparable /ɪnˈkɒmpərəb(ə)l/ *adj.* **1** without an equal; matchless. **2** (often foll. by *with, to*) not to be compared. ☐☐ **incomparability** /-ˈbɪlɪtɪ/ *n.* **incomparableness** *n.* **incomparably** *adv.* [ME f. OF f. L *incomparabilis* (as IN-1, COMPARABLE)]

incompatible /ˌɪnkəmˈpætɪb(ə)l/ *adj.* **1** opposed in character; discordant. **2** (often foll. by *with*) inconsistent. **3** (of persons) unable to live, work, etc., together in harmony. **4** (of drugs) not suitable for taking at the same time. **5** (of equipment, machinery, etc.) not capable of being used in combination. ☐☐ **incompatibility** /-ˈbɪlɪtɪ/ *n.* **incompatibleness** *n.* **incompatibly** *adv.* [med.L *incompatibilis* (as IN-1, COMPATIBLE)]

incompetent /ɪnˈkɒmpɪt(ə)nt/ *adj. & n.* —*adj.* **1** (often foll. by *to* + infin.) not qualified or able to perform a particular task or function (*an incompetent builder*). **2** showing a lack of skill (*an incompetent performance*). **3** *Med.* (esp. of a valve or sphincter) not able to perform its function. —*n.* an incompetent person. ☐☐ **incompetence** *n.* **incompetency** *n.* **incompetently** *adv.* [F *incompétent* or LL *incompetens* (as IN-1, COMPETENT)]

incomplete /ˌɪnkəmˈpliːt/ *adj.* not complete. ☐☐ **incompletely** *adv.* **incompleteness** *n.* [ME f. LL *incompletus* (as IN-1, COMPLETE)]

incomprehensible /ɪnˌkɒmprɪˈhensɪb(ə)l/ *adj.* (often foll. by *to*) that cannot be understood. ☐☐ **incomprehensibility** /-ˈbɪlɪtɪ/ *n.* **incomprehensibleness** *n.* **incomprehensibly** *adv.* [ME f. L *incomprehensibilis* (as IN-1, COMPREHENSIBLE)]

incomprehension /ɪnˌkɒmprɪˈhenʃ(ə)n/ *n.* failure to understand.

incompressible /ˌɪnkəmˈpresɪb(ə)l/ *adj.* that cannot be compressed. ☐☐ **incompressibility** /-ˈbɪlɪtɪ/ *n.*

inconceivable /ˌɪnkənˈsiːvəb(ə)l/ *adj.* **1** that cannot be imagined. **2** *colloq.* very remarkable. ☐☐ **inconceivability** /-ˈbɪlɪtɪ/ *n.* **inconceivableness** *n.* **inconceivably** *adv.*

inconclusive /ˌɪnkənˈkluːsɪv/ *adj.* (of an argument, evidence, or action) not decisive or convincing. ☐☐ **inconclusively** *adv.* **inconclusiveness** *n.*

incondensable /ˌɪnkənˈdensəb(ə)l/ *adj.* that cannot be condensed, esp. that cannot be reduced to a liquid or solid condition.

incongruous /ɪnˈkɒŋgrʊəs/ *adj.* **1** out of place; absurd. **2** (often foll. by *with*) disagreeing; out of keeping. ☐☐ **incongruity** /-ˈgruːɪtɪ/ *n.* (*pl.* **-ies**). **incongruously** *adv.* **incongruousness** *n.* [L *incongruus* (as IN-1, CONGRUOUS)]

inconsecutive /ˌɪnkənˈsekjʊtɪv/ *adj.* lacking sequence; inconsequent. ☐☐ **inconsecutively** *adv.* **inconsecutiveness** *n.*

inconsequent /ɪnˈkɒnsɪkwənt/ *adj.* **1** not following naturally; irrelevant. **2** lacking logical sequence. **3** disconnected. ☐☐ **inconsequence** *n.* **inconsequently** *adv.* [L *inconsequens* (as IN-1, CONSEQUENT)]

inconsequential /ɪnˌkɒnsɪˈkwenʃ(ə)l, ˌɪnkɒn-/ *adj.* **1** unimportant. **2** = INCONSEQUENT. ☐☐ **inconsequentiality** /-ˈʃɪælɪtɪ/ *n.* (*pl.* **-ies**). **inconsequentially** *adv.* **inconsequentialness** *n.*

inconsiderable /ˌɪnkənˈsɪdərəb(ə)l/ *adj.* **1** of small size, value, etc. **2** not worth considering. ☐☐ **inconsiderableness** *n.* **inconsiderably** *adv.* [obs. F *inconsidérable* or LL *inconsiderabilis* (as IN-1, CONSIDERABLE)]

inconsiderate /ˌɪnkənˈsɪdərət/ *adj.* **1** (of a person or action) thoughtless, rash. **2** lacking in regard for the feelings of others. ☐☐ **inconsiderately** *adv.* **inconsiderateness** *n.* **inconsideration** /-ˈreɪʃ(ə)n/ *n.* [L *inconsideratus* (as IN-1, CONSIDERATE)]

inconsistent /ˌɪnkənˈsɪst(ə)nt/ *adj.* **1** acting at variance with one's own principles or former conduct. **2** (often foll. by *with*) not in keeping; discordant, incompatible. **3** (of a single thing) incompatible or discordant; having self-contradictory parts. ☐☐ **inconsistency** *n.* (*pl.* **-ies**). **inconsistently** *adv.*

inconsolable /ˌɪnkənˈsəʊləb(ə)l/ *adj.* (of a person, grief, etc.) that cannot be consoled or comforted. ☐☐ **inconsolability** /-ˈbɪlɪtɪ/ *n.* **inconsolableness** *n.* **inconsolably** *adv.* [F *inconsolable* or L *inconsolabilis* (as IN-1, *consolabilis* f. *consolari* CONSOLE1)]

inconsonant /ɪnˈkɒnsənənt/ *adj.* (often foll. by *with, to*) not harmonious; not compatible. ☐☐ **inconsonance** *n.* **inconsonantly** *adv.*

inconspicuous /ˌɪnkənˈspɪkjʊəs/ *adj.* **1** not conspicuous; not easily noticed. **2** *Bot.* (of flowers) small, pale, or green. ☐☐ **inconspicuously** *adv.* **inconspicuousness** *n.* [L *inconspicuus* (as IN-1, CONSPICUOUS)]

inconstant /ɪnˈkɒnst(ə)nt/ *adj.* **1** (of a person) fickle, changeable. **2** frequently changing; variable, irregular. ☐☐ **inconstancy** *n.* (*pl.* **-ies**). **inconstantly** *adv.* [ME f. OF f. L *inconstans -antis* (as IN-1, CONSTANT)]

incontestable /ˌɪnkənˈtestəb(ə)l/ *adj.* that cannot be disputed. ☐☐ **incontestability** /-ˈbɪlɪtɪ/ *n.* **incontestably** *adv.* [F *incontestable* or med.L *incontestabilis* (as IN-1, *contestabilis* f. L *contestari* CONTEST)]

incontinent /ɪnˈkɒntɪnənt/ *adj.* **1** unable to control movements of the bowels or bladder or both. **2** lacking self-restraint (esp. in regard to sexual desire). **3** (foll. by *of*) unable to control. ☐☐ **incontinence** *n.* **incontinently** *adv.* [ME f. OF or L *incontinens* (as IN-1, CONTINENT2)]

incontrovertible /ˌɪnkɒntrəˈvɜːtɪb(ə)l/ *adj.* indisputable, indubitable. ☐☐ **incontrovertibility** /-ˈbɪlɪtɪ/ *n.* **incontrovertibly** *adv.*

inconvenience /ˌɪnkənˈviːnɪəns/ *n. & v.* —*n.* **1** lack of suitability to personal requirements or ease. **2** a cause or instance of this. —*v.tr.* cause inconvenience to. [ME f. OF f. LL *inconvenientia* (as INCONVENIENT)]

inconvenient /ˌɪnkənˈviːnɪənt/ adj. **1** unfavourable to ease or comfort; not convenient. **2** awkward, troublesome. □□ **inconveniently** adv. [ME f. OF f. L inconveniens -entis (as IN-¹, CONVENIENT)]

inconvertible /ˌɪnkənˈvɜːtɪb(ə)l/ adj. **1** not convertible. **2** (esp. of currency) not convertible into another form on demand. □□ **inconvertibility** /-ˈbɪlɪtɪ/ n. **inconvertibly** adv. [F inconvertible or LL inconvertibilis (as IN-¹, CONVERTIBLE)]

incoordination /ˌɪnkəʊˌɔːdɪˈneɪʃ(ə)n/ n. lack of coordination, esp. of muscular action.

incorporate v. & adj. —v. /ɪnˈkɔːpəˌreɪt/ **1** tr. (often foll. by in, with) unite; form into one body or whole. **2** intr. become incorporated. **3** tr. combine (ingredients) into one substance. **4** tr. admit as a member of a company etc. **5** tr. **a** constitute a legal corporation. **b** (as **incorporated** adj.) forming a legal corporation. —adj. /ɪnˈkɔːpərət/ **1** (of a company etc.) formed into a legal corporation. **2** embodied. □□ **incorporation** /-ˈreɪʃ(ə)n/ n. **incorporator** n. [ME f. LL incorporare (as IN-², L corpus -oris body)]

incorporeal /ˌɪnkɔːˈpɔːrɪəl/ adj. **1** not composed of matter. **2** of immaterial beings. **3** Law having no physical existence. □□ **incorporeality** /-ˈælɪtɪ/ n. **incorporeally** adv. **incorporeity** /-pəˈriːɪtɪ/ n. [L incorporeus (as INCORPORATE)]

incorrect /ˌɪnkəˈrekt/ adj. **1** not in accordance with fact; wrong. **2** (of style etc.) improper, faulty. □□ **incorrectly** adv. **incorrectness** n. [ME f. OF or L incorrectus (as IN-¹, CORRECT)]

incorrigible /ɪnˈkɒrɪdʒɪb(ə)l/ adj. **1** (of a person or habit) incurably bad or depraved. **2** not readily improved. □□ **incorrigibility** /-ˈbɪlɪtɪ/ n. **incorrigibleness** n. **incorrigibly** adv. [ME f. OF incorrigible or L incorrigibilis (as IN-¹, CORRIGIBLE)]

incorruptible /ˌɪnkəˈrʌptɪb(ə)l/ adj. **1** that cannot be corrupted, esp. by bribery. **2** that cannot decay; everlasting. □□ **incorruptibility** /-ˈbɪlɪtɪ/ n. **incorruptibly** adv. [ME f. OF incorruptible or eccl.L incorruptibilis (as IN-¹, CORRUPT)]

increase v. & n. —v. /ɪnˈkriːs/ **1** tr. & intr. make or become greater in size, amount, etc., or more numerous. **2** intr. advance (in quality, attainment, etc.). **3** tr. intensify (a quality). —n. /ˈɪnkriːs/ **1** the act or process of becoming greater or more numerous; growth, enlargement. **2** (of people, animals, or plants) growth in numbers; multiplication. **3** the amount or extent of an increase. □ **on the increase** increasing, esp. in frequency. □□ **increasable** adj. **increaser** n. **increasingly** adv. [ME f. OF encreiss- stem of encreistre f. L increscere (as IN-², crescere grow)]

incredible /ɪnˈkredɪb(ə)l/ adj. **1** that cannot be believed. **2** colloq. hard to believe; amazing. □□ **incredibility** /-ˈbɪlɪtɪ/ n. **incredibleness** n. **incredibly** adv. [ME f. L incredibilis (as IN-¹, CREDIBLE)]

incredulous /ɪnˈkredjʊləs/ adj. (often foll. by of) unwilling to believe. □□ **incredulity** /ˌɪnkrɪˈdjuːlɪtɪ/ n. **incredulously** adv. **incredulousness** n. [L incredulus (as IN-¹, CREDULOUS)]

increment /ˈɪnkrɪmənt/ n. **1 a** an increase or addition, esp. one of a series on a fixed scale. **b** the amount of this. **2** Math. a small amount by which a variable quantity increases. □□ **incremental** /-ˈment(ə)l/ adj. [ME f. L incrementum f. increscere INCREASE]

incriminate /ɪnˈkrɪmɪˌneɪt/ v.tr. **1** tend to prove the guilt of (incriminating evidence). **2** involve in an accusation. **3** charge with a crime. □□ **incrimination** /-ˈneɪʃ(ə)n/ n. **incriminatory** adj. [LL incriminare (as IN-², L crimen offence)]

incrust var. of ENCRUST.

incrustation /ˌɪnkrʌˈsteɪʃ(ə)n/ n. **1** the process of encrusting or state of being encrusted. **2** a crust or hard coating, esp. of fine material. **3** a concretion or deposit on a surface. **4** a facing of marble etc. on a building. [F incrustation or LL incrustatio (as ENCRUST)]

incubate /ˈɪnkjʊbeɪt/ v. **1** tr. sit on or artificially heat (eggs) in order to bring forth young birds etc. **2** tr. cause the development of (bacteria etc.) by creating suitable conditions. **3** intr. sit on eggs; brood. [L incubare (as IN-², cubare cubit- or cubat- lie)]

incubation /ˌɪnkjʊˈbeɪʃ(ə)n/ n. **1 a** the act of incubating. **b** brooding. **2** Med. **a** a phase through which the germs causing a disease pass before the development of the first symptoms. **b** the period of this. □□ **incubational** adj. **incubative** /ˈɪŋkjʊˌbeɪtɪv/ adj. **incubatory** /ˈɪŋkjʊˌbeɪtərɪ/ adj. [L incubatio (as INCUBATE)]

incubator /ˈɪŋkjʊˌbeɪtə(r)/ n. **1** an apparatus used to provide a suitable temperature and environment for a premature baby or one of low birth-weight. **2** an apparatus used to hatch eggs or grow micro-organisms.

incubus /ˈɪŋkjʊbəs/ n. (pl. **incubuses** or **incubi** /-ˌbaɪ/) **1** an evil spirit supposed to descend on sleeping persons. **2** a nightmare. **3** a person or thing that oppresses like a nightmare. [ME f. LL, = L incubo nightmare (as INCUBATE)]

incudes pl. of INCUS.

inculcate /ˈɪnkʌlˌkeɪt/ v.tr. (often foll. by upon, in) urge or impress (a fact, habit, or idea) persistently. □□ **inculcation** /-ˈkeɪʃ(ə)n/ n. **inculcator** n. [L inculcare (as IN-², calcare tread f. calx calcis heel)]

inculpate /ˈɪnkʌlˌpeɪt/ v.tr. **1** involve in a charge. **2** accuse, blame. □□ **inculpation** /-ˈpeɪʃ(ə)n/ n. **inculpative** /ɪnˈkʌlpətɪv/ adj. **inculpatory** /ɪnˈkʌlpətərɪ/ adj. [LL inculpare (as IN-², culpare blame f. culpa fault)]

incumbency /ɪnˈkʌmbənsɪ/ n. (pl. **-ies**) the office, tenure, or sphere of an incumbent.

incumbent /ɪnˈkʌmbənt/ adj. & n. —adj. **1** (foll. by on, upon) resting as a duty (it is incumbent on you to warn them). **2** (often foll. by on) lying, pressing. —n. the holder of an office or post, esp. an ecclesiastical benefice. [ME f. AL incumbens pres. part. of L incumbere lie upon (as IN-², cubare lie)]

incunable /ɪnˈkjuːnəb(ə)l/ n. = INCUNABULUM 1. [F, formed as INCUNABULUM]

incunabulum /ˌɪnkjuˈnæbjʊləm/ n. (pl. **incunabula** /-lə/) **1** a book printed at an early date, esp. before 1501. **2** (in pl.) the early stages of the development of a thing. [L incunabula swaddling-clothes, cradle (as IN-², cunae cradle)]

incur /ɪnˈkɜː(r)/ v.tr. (**incurred**, **incurring**) suffer, experience, or become subject to (something unpleasant) as a result of one's own behaviour etc. (incurred huge debts). □□ **incurrable** adj. [ME f. L incurrere incurs- (as IN-², currere run)]

incurable /ɪnˈkjʊərəb(ə)l/ adj. & n. —adj. that cannot be cured. —n. a person who cannot be cured. □□ **incurability** /-ˈbɪlɪtɪ/ n. **incurableness** n. **incurably** adv. [ME f. OF incurable or LL incurabilis (as IN-¹, CURABLE)]

incurious /ɪnˈkjʊərɪəs/ adj. **1** lacking curiosity. **2** heedless, careless. □□ **incuriosity** /-ˈɒsɪtɪ/ n. **incuriously** adv. **incuriousness** n. [L incuriosus (as IN-¹, CURIOUS)]

incursion /ɪnˈkɜːʃ(ə)n/ n. an invasion or attack, esp. when sudden or brief. □□ **incursive** /-sɪv/ adj. [ME f. L incursio (as INCUR)]

incurve /ɪnˈkɜːv/ v.tr. **1** bend into a curve. **2** (as **incurved** adj.) curved inwards. □□ **incurvation** /-ˈveɪʃ(ə)n/ n. [L incurvare (as IN-², CURVE)]

incus /ˈɪŋkəs/ n. (pl. **incudes** /-ˈkjuːdiːz/) the small anvil-shaped bone in the middle ear, in contact with the malleus and stapes. [L, = anvil]

incuse /ɪnˈkjuːz/ n., v., & adj. —n. an impression hammered or stamped on a coin. —v.tr. **1** mark (a coin) with a figure by stamping. **2** impress (a figure) on a coin by stamping. —adj. hammered or stamped on a coin. [L incusus past part. of incudere (as IN-², cudere forge)]

Ind. abbr. **1** Independent. **2 a** India. **b** Indian. **3** Indiana.

indaba /ɪnˈdɑːbə/ n. S.Afr. **1** a conference between or with members of S. African native tribes. **2** colloq. one's problem or concern. [Zulu, = business]

indebted /ɪnˈdetɪd/ adj. (usu. foll. by to) **1** owing gratitude or obligation. **2** owing money. □□ **indebtedness** n. [ME f. OF endetté past part. of endetter involve in debt (as EN-¹, detter f. dette DEBT)]

indecent /ɪnˈdiːs(ə)nt/ adj. **1** offending against recognized standards of decency. **2** unbecoming; highly unsuitable (with indecent haste). □ **indecent assault** a sexual attack not involving rape. **indecent exposure** the intentional act of publicly and indecently exposing one's body, esp. the genitals. □□ **indecency** n. (pl. **-ies**). **indecently** adv. [F indécent or L indecens (as IN-¹, DECENT)]

indecipherable /ˌɪndɪˈsaɪfərəb(ə)l/ adj. that cannot be deciphered.

indecision /ˌɪndɪˈsɪʒ(ə)n/ n. lack of decision; hesitation. [F indécision (as IN-¹, DECISION)

indecisive /ˌɪndɪˈsaɪsɪv/ adj. **1** not decisive. **2** undecided, hesitating. □□ **indecisively** adv. **indecisiveness** n.

indeclinable /ˌɪndɪˈklaɪnəb(ə)l/ adj. Gram. **1** that cannot be declined. **2** having no inflexions. [ME f. F indéclinable f. L indeclinabilis (as IN-¹, DECLINE)]

indecorous /ɪnˈdekərəs/ adj. **1** improper. **2** in bad taste. □□ **indecorously** adv. **indecorousness** n. [L indecorus (as IN-¹, decorus seemly)]

indecorum /ˌɪndɪˈkɔːrəm/ n. **1** lack of decorum. **2** improper behaviour. [L, neut. of indecorus: see INDECOROUS]

indeed /ɪnˈdiːd/ adv. & int. —adv. **1** in truth; really (they are, indeed, a remarkable family). **2** expressing emphasis or intensification (I shall be very glad indeed; indeed it is). **3** admittedly (there are indeed exceptions). **4** in point of fact (if indeed such a thing is possible). **5** expressing an approving or ironic echo (who is this Mr Smith?—who is he indeed?). —int. expressing irony, contempt, incredulity, etc.

indefatigable /ˌɪndɪˈfætɪgəb(ə)l/ adj. (of a person, quality, etc.) that cannot be tired out; unwearying, unremitting. □□ **indefatigability** /-ˈbɪlɪtɪ/ n. **indefatigably** adv. [obs. F indéfatigable or L indefatigabilis (as IN-¹, defatigare wear out)

indefeasible /ˌɪndɪˈfiːzɪb(ə)l/ adj. literary (esp. of a claim, rights, etc.) that cannot be lost. □□ **indefeasibility** /-ˈbɪlɪtɪ/ n. **indefeasibly** adv.

indefectible /ˌɪndɪˈfektɪb(ə)l/ adj. **1** unfailing; not liable to defect or decay. **2** faultless. [IN-¹ + defectible f. LL defectibilis (as DEFECT)]

indefensible /ˌɪndɪˈfensɪb(ə)l/ adj. that cannot be defended or justified. □□ **indefensibility** /-ˈbɪlɪtɪ/ n. **indefensibly** adv.

indefinable /ˌɪndɪˈfaɪnəb(ə)l/ adj. that cannot be defined or exactly described. □□ **indefinably** adv.

indefinite /ɪnˈdefɪnɪt/ adj. **1** vague, undefined. **2** unlimited. **3** Gram. not determining the person, thing, time, etc., referred to. □ **indefinite article** see ARTICLE. **indefinite integral** see INTEGRAL. **indefinite pronoun** Gram. a pronoun indicating a person, amount, etc., without being definite or particular, e.g. any, some, anyone. □□ **indefiniteness** n. [L indefinitus (as IN-¹, DEFINITE)]

indefinitely /ɪnˈdefɪnɪtlɪ/ adv. **1** for an unlimited time (was postponed indefinitely). **2** in an indefinite manner.

indehiscent /ˌɪndɪˈhɪs(ə)nt/ adj. Bot. (of fruit) not splitting open when ripe. □□ **indehiscence** n.

indelible /ɪnˈdelɪb(ə)l/ adj. **1** that cannot be rubbed out or (in abstract senses) removed. **2** (of ink etc.) that makes indelible marks. □□ **indelibility** /-ˈbɪlɪtɪ/ n. **indelibly** adv. [F indélébile or L indelebilis (as IN-¹, delebilis f. delēre efface)]

indelicate /ɪnˈdelɪkət/ adj. **1** coarse, unrefined. **2** tactless. **3** tending to indecency. □□ **indelicacy** n. (pl. -ies). **indelicately** adv.

indemnify /ɪnˈdemnɪˌfaɪ/ v.tr. (-ies, -ied) **1** (often foll. by from, against) protect or secure (a person) in respect of harm, a loss, etc. **2** (often foll. by for) secure (a person) against legal responsibility for actions. **3** (often foll. by for) compensate (a person) for a loss, expenses, etc. □□ **indemnification** /-fɪˈkeɪʃ(ə)n/ n. **indemnifier** n. [L indemnis unhurt (as IN-¹, damnum loss, damage)]

indemnity /ɪnˈdemnɪtɪ/ n. (pl. -ies) **1 a** compensation for loss incurred. **b** a sum paid for this, esp. a sum exacted by a victor in war etc. as one condition of peace. **2** security against loss. **3** legal exemption from penalties etc. incurred. [ME f. F indemnité or LL indemnitas -tatis (as INDEMNIFY)]

indemonstrable /ɪnˈdemənstrəb(ə)l/, ˌɪndɪˈmɒn-/ adj. that cannot be proved (esp. of primary or axiomatic truths).

indene /ˈɪndiːn/ n. Chem. a colourless flammable liquid hydrocarbon obtained from coal tar and used in making synthetic resins. [INDOLE + -ENE]

indent¹ v. & n. —v. /ɪnˈdent/ **1** tr. start (a line of print or writing) further from the margin than other lines, e.g. to mark a new paragraph. **2** tr. **a** divide (a document drawn up in duplicate) into its two copies with a zigzag line dividing them and ensuring identification. **b** draw up (usu. a legal document) in exact duplicate. **3** Brit. **a** intr. (often foll. by on, upon a person, for a thing) make a requisition (orig. a written order with a duplicate). **b** tr. order (goods) by requisition. **4** tr. make toothlike notches in. **5** tr. form deep recesses in (a coastline etc.). —n. /ˈɪndent/ **1** Brit. **a** an order (esp. from abroad) for goods. **b** an official requisition for stores. **2** an indented line. **3** indentation. **4** an indenture. □□ **indenter** n. **indentor** n. [ME f. AF endenter f. AL indentare (as IN-², L dens dentis tooth)]

indent² /ɪnˈdent/ v.tr. **1** make a dent in. **2** impress (a mark etc.). [ME f. IN-² + DENT]

indentation /ˌɪndenˈteɪʃ(ə)n/ n. **1** the act or an instance of indenting; the process of being indented. **2** a cut or notch. **3** a zigzag. **4** a deep recess in a coastline etc.

indention /ɪnˈdenʃ(ə)n/ n. **1** the indenting of a line in printing or writing. **2** = INDENTATION.

indenture /ɪnˈdentʃ(ə)r/ n. & v. —n. **1** an indented document (see INDENT¹ v. 2). **2** a sealed agreement or contract (usu. in pl.). **3** a formal list, certificate, etc. —v.tr. hist. bind (a person) by indentures, esp. as an apprentice. □□ **indentureship** n. [ME (orig. Sc.) f. AF endenture (as INDENT¹)]

independence /ˌɪndɪˈpend(ə)ns/ n. **1** (often foll. by of, from) the state of being independent. **2** independent income. □ **Independence Day** a day celebrating the anniversary of national independence, esp. 4 July in the US.

independency /ˌɪndɪˈpendənsɪ/ n. (pl. -ies) **1** an independent State. **2** = INDEPENDENCE.

independent /ˌɪndɪˈpend(ə)nt/ adj. & n. —adj. **1 a** (often foll. by of) not depending on authority or control. **b** self-governing. **2 a** not depending on another person for one's opinion or livelihood. **b** (of income or resources) making it unnecessary to earn one's living. **3** unwilling to be under an obligation to others. **4** Polit. not belonging to or supported by a party. **5** not depending on something else for its validity, efficiency, value, etc. (independent proof). **6** (of broadcasting, a school, etc.) not supported by public funds. **7** (**Independent**) hist. Congregational. —n. **1** a person who is politically independent. **2** (**Independent**) hist. a Congregationalist. □□ **independently** adv.

in-depth see DEPTH.

indescribable /ˌɪndɪˈskraɪbəb(ə)l/ adj. **1** too unusual or extreme to be described. **2** vague, indefinite. □□ **indescribability** /-ˈbɪlɪtɪ/ n. **indescribably** adv.

indestructible /ˌɪndɪˈstrʌktɪb(ə)l/ adj. that cannot be destroyed. □□ **indestructibility** /-ˈbɪlɪtɪ/ n. **indestructibly** adv.

indeterminable /ˌɪndɪˈtɜːmɪnəb(ə)l/ adj. **1** that cannot be ascertained. **2** (of a dispute etc.) that cannot be settled. □□ **indeterminably** adv. [ME f. LL indeterminabilis (as IN-¹, L determinare DETERMINE)]

indeterminate /ˌɪndɪˈtɜːmɪnət/ adj. **1** not fixed in extent, character, etc. **2** left doubtful; vague. **3** Math. (of a quantity) not limited to a fixed value by the value of another quantity. **4** (of a judicial sentence) such that the convicted person's conduct determines the date of release. □ **indeterminate vowel** the obscure vowel /ə/ heard in 'a moment ago'; a schwa. □□ **indeterminacy** n. **indeterminately** adv. **indeterminateness** n. [ME f. LL indeterminatus (as IN-¹, DETERMINATE)]

indetermination /ˌɪndɪˌtɜːmɪˈneɪʃ(ə)n/ n. **1** lack of determination. **2** the state of being indeterminate.

indeterminism /ˌɪndɪˈtɜːmɪˌnɪz(ə)m/ n. the belief that human action is not wholly determined by motives. □□ **indeterminist** n. **indeterministic** /-ˈnɪstɪk/ adj.

index /ˈɪndeks/ n. & v. —n. (pl. **indexes** or esp. in technical use **indices** /ˈɪndɪˌsiːz/) **1** an alphabetical list of names, subjects, etc., with references, usu. at the end of a book. **2** = card index. **3** (in full **index number**) a number showing the variation of prices or wages as compared with a chosen base period (retail price index; Dow-Jones index). **4** Math. **a** the exponent of a number. **b** the power to which it is raised. **5 a** a pointer, esp. on an instrument, showing a quantity, a position on a scale, etc. **b** an indicator of a trend, direction, tendency, etc. **c** (usu. foll. by *of*) a sign, token, or indication of something. **6** *Physics* a number expressing a physical property etc. in terms of a standard (*refractive index*). **7** *Computing* a set of items each of which specifies one of the records of a file and contains information about its address. **8** (**Index**) *RC Ch. hist.* a list of books forbidden to Roman Catholics to read (or to be read only in expurgated editions) as contrary to their faith or morals. The first Index was issued in 1557; it was revised at intervals until abolished in 1966. **9** *Printing* a symbol shaped like a pointing hand, used to draw attention to a note etc. —*v.tr.* **1** provide (a book etc.) with an index. **2** enter in an index. **3** relate (wages etc.) to the value of a price index. □ **index finger** the forefinger. **index-linked** related to the value of a retail price index. □□ **indexation** /-ˈseɪʃ(ə)n/ *n.* **indexer** *n.* **indexible** /ˈɪndeks-, ɪnˈdeks-/ *adj.* **indexical** /ɪnˈdeks-/ *adj.* **indexless** *adj.* [ME f. L *index indicis* forefinger, informer, sign: sense 8 f. L *Index librorum prohibitorum* list of prohibited books]

India /ˈɪndɪə/ a country in South Asia, a member State of the Commonwealth, occupying the greater part of the Indian sub-continent, a peninsula bounded by the Arabian Sea and the Bay of Bengal and on the north by the Himalayas; pop. (est. 1988) 816,828,360; official languages, Hindi and English (another 14 are also recognized by the constitution); capital, New Delhi. India comprises 25 States and 6 Union Territories and is inhabited by brown-skinned peoples following the Hindu, Muslim, and other religions and speaking over 200 languages and dialects, with Hindi being the most widespread in the north and Tamil and Telugu in the south. The economy is heavily dependent on agriculture, but since 1947 the country has built up a substantial industrial base. The textile and jute industries are important; other major industries are based on the exploitation of the country's mineral resources, chiefly coal, oil, and iron. The second most populous country in the world, India faces serious problems arising from poverty and a high rate of illiteracy.

Its history began in the 3rd millennium BC, when the Indus valley was the site of a fully developed civilization. This collapsed *c.*1760 BC when the invading Aryans spread from the west through the northern part of the country. Consolidated first within the Buddhist empire of Asoka and then the Hindu empire of the Gupta dynasty, much of India was united under a Muslim sultanate based on Delhi from the 12th c. until incorporated in the Mughal empire by Babur and Akbar the Great in the 16th c. The decline of Mughal power in the late 17th and early 18th c. coincided with increasing European penetration, with Britain eventually triumphing over her colonial rivals. British interest had begun in the 17th c. with the formation of the East India Company, which in 1765 acquired the right to administer Bengal and afterwards other parts; in 1858, after the Indian Mutiny, the Crown took over the Company's authority, and in 1877 Queen Victoria was proclaimed Empress of India. Rising nationalism, with Mahatma Gandhi a notable leader, resulted in independence and partition in 1947, but the new States of India and Pakistan did not prove good neighbours, going to war several times over the disputed territory of Kashmir and the Pakistani enclave (now Bangladesh) in the north-east.

India ink /ˈɪndɪə/ *n. US* = *Indian ink.*

Indiaman /ˈɪndɪəmən/ *n.* (*pl.* **-men**) *Naut. hist.* a ship engaged in trade with India or the East Indies.

Indian /ˈɪndɪən/ *n. & adj.* —*n.* **1 a** a native or national of India. **b** a person of Indian descent. **2** an American Indian (see entry). **3** any of the languages of the American Indians. —*adj.* **1** of or relating to India, or to the subcontinent comprising India, Pakistan, and Bangladesh. **2** of or relating to American Indians. □ **Indian clubs** a pair of bottle-shaped clubs swung to exercise the arms in gymnastics. **Indian corn** maize. **Indian elephant** the elephant, *Elephas maximus*, of India, which is smaller than the African elephant. **Indian file** = *single file.* **Indian hemp** see HEMP 1. **Indian ink** *Brit.* **1** a black pigment made orig. in China and Japan. **2** a dark ink made from this, used esp. in drawing and technical graphics. **Indian rope-trick** the supposed Indian feat of climbing an upright unsupported length of rope. **Indian summer 1** a period of unusually dry warm weather sometimes occurring in late autumn. **2** a late period of life characterized by comparative calm. [ME f. *India* ult. f. Gk *Indos* the River Indus f. Pers. *Hind*: cf. HINDU]

Indiana /ˌɪndɪˈænə/ a State in the Middle West of the US; pop. (est. 1985) 5,490,200; capital, Indianapolis. Ceded to Britain by the French in 1763 and to the US in 1783, it became the 19th State in 1816.

Indianapolis /ˌɪndɪəˈnæpəlɪs/ the capital of Indiana; pop. (1982) 707,650. The city hosts an annual 500-mile (804.5-km) motor race.

Indian Mutiny a revolt of Indians against British rule, 1857–8. At a time when the number of British troops in India had reached a low point and the ruling East India Company was almost totally dependent on native soldiers (sepoys), discontent with British administration finally resulted in widespread mutinies in British garrison towns with accompanying massacres of white soldiers and inhabitants. After a series of sieges (most notably that of Lucknow) and battles in which British training and discipline triumphed over Indian numbers, order was finally restored. The most important of the reforms enacted in the wake of the mutiny was the institution of direct rule by the British Crown in place of the East India Company administration.

Indian Ocean the ocean to the south of India, extending from the east coast of Africa to the East Indies and Australia.

India paper /ˈɪndɪə/ *n.* **1** a soft absorbent kind of paper orig. imported from China, used for proofs of engravings. **2** a very thin tough opaque printing-paper.

indiarubber /ˌɪndɪəˈrʌbə(r)/ *n.* = RUBBER[1] 2.

Indic /ˈɪndɪk/ *adj. & n.* —*adj.* of the group of Indo-European languages comprising Sanskrit and the modern Indian languages which are its descendants. —*n.* this language-group. [L *Indicus* f. Gk *Indikos* INDIAN]

indicate /ˈɪndɪkeɪt/ *v.tr.* (often foll. by *that* + clause) **1** point out; make known; show. **2** be a sign or symptom of; express the presence of. **3** (often in *passive*) suggest; call for; require or show to be necessary (*stronger measures are indicated*). **4** admit to or state briefly (*indicated his disapproval*). **5** (of a gauge etc.) give as a reading. [L *indicare* (as IN-[2], *dicare* make known)]

indication /ˌɪndɪˈkeɪʃ(ə)n/ *n.* **1** the act or an instance of indicating. **2** something indicated or suggested. **3** a reading given by a gauge or instrument. [F f. L *indicatio* (as INDICATE)]

indicative /ɪnˈdɪkətɪv/ *adj. & n.* —*adj.* **1** (foll. by *of*) suggestive; serving as an indication. **2** *Gram.* (of a mood) denoting simple statement of a fact. —*n. Gram.* **1** the indicative mood. **2** a verb in this mood. □□ **indicatively** *adv.* [ME f. F *indicatif -ive* f. LL *indicativus* (as INDICATE)]

indicator /ˈɪndɪkeɪtə(r)/ *n.* **1** a person or thing that indicates. **2** a device indicating the condition of a machine etc. **3** a recording instrument attached to an apparatus etc. **4** a board in a railway station etc. giving current information. **5** a device (esp. a flashing light) on a vehicle to show that it is about to change direction. **6** a substance which changes colour at a given stage in a chemical reaction. **7** *Physics & Med.* a radioactive tracer.

indicatory /ˈɪndɪkətərɪ, ɪnˈdɪk-/ *adj.* = INDICATIVE *adj.* 1.

indices *pl.* of INDEX.

indicia /ɪnˈdɪʃɪə/ *n.pl.* **1** distinguishing or identificatory marks. **2** signs, indications. [pl. of L *indicium* (as INDEX)]

indicial /ɪnˈdɪʃ(ə)l/ *adj.* **1** of the nature or form of an index. **2** of the nature of indicia; indicative.

indict /ɪnˈdaɪt/ *v.tr.* accuse (a person) formally by legal process. □□ **indictee** /-ˈtiː/ *n.* **indicter** *n.* [ME f. AF *enditer* indict f. OF *enditier* declare f. Rmc *indictare* (unrecorded: as IN-[2], DICTATE)]

indictable /ɪnˈdaɪtəb(ə)l/ *adj.* **1** (of an offence) rendering the person who commits it liable to be charged with a crime. **2** (of a person) so liable.

indictment /ɪnˈdaɪtmənt/ *n.* **1** the act of indicting. **2 a** a formal accusation. **b** a legal process in which this is made. **c** a document containing a charge. **3** something that serves to condemn or censure. [ME f. AF *enditement* (as INDICT)]

indie /ˈɪndɪ/ *n. colloq.* an independent record or film company.

Indies /ˈɪndɪz/ *n.pl.* (prec. by *the*) *archaic* India and adjacent regions. □ **East Indies, West Indies** see separate entries. [pl. of obs. *Indy* India]

indifference /ɪnˈdɪfrəns/ *n.* **1** lack of interest or attention. **2** unimportance (*a matter of indifference*). **3** neutrality. [L *indifferentia* (as INDIFFERENT)]

indifferent /ɪnˈdɪfrənt/ *adj.* **1** neither good nor bad; average, mediocre. **2 a** not especially good. **b** fairly bad. **3** (often prec. by *very*) decidedly inferior. **4** (foll. by *to*) having no partiality for or against; having no interest in or sympathy for. **5** chemically, magnetically, etc., neutral. □□ **indifferently** *adv.* [ME f. OF *indifferent* or L *indifferens* (as IN-¹, DIFFERENT)]

indifferentism /ɪnˈdɪfrəntɪz(ə)m/ *n.* an attitude of indifference, esp. in religious matters. □□ **indifferentist** *n.*

indigenize /ɪnˈdɪdʒɪnaɪz/ *v.tr.* (also **-ise**) **1** make indigenous; subject to native influence. **2** subject to increased use of indigenous people in government etc. □□ **indigenization** /-ˈzeɪʃ(ə)n/ *n.*

indigenous /ɪnˈdɪdʒɪnəs/ *adj.* **1 a** (esp. of flora or fauna) originating naturally in a region. **b** (of people) born in a region. **2** (foll. by *to*) belonging naturally to a place. □□ **indigenously** *adv.* **indigenousness** *n.* [L *indigena* f. *indi-* = IN-² + *gen-* be born]

indigent /ˈɪndɪdʒ(ə)nt/ *adj.* needy, poor. □□ **indigence** *n.* [ME f. OF f. LL *indigēre* f. *indi-* = IN-² + *egēre* need]

indigested /ˌɪndaɪˈdʒestɪd/ *adj.* **1** shapeless. **2** ill-considered. **3** not digested.

indigestible /ˌɪndɪˈdʒestɪb(ə)l/ *adj.* **1** difficult or impossible to digest. **2** too complex or awkward to read or comprehend easily. □□ **indigestibility** /-ˈbɪlɪtɪ/ *n.* **indigestibly** *adv.* [F *indigestible* or LL *indigestibilis* (as IN-¹, DIGEST)]

indigestion /ˌɪndɪˈdʒestʃ(ə)n/ *n.* **1** difficulty in digesting food. **2** pain or discomfort caused by this. □□ **indigestive** *adj.* [ME f. OF *indigestion* or LL *indigestio* (as IN-¹, DIGESTION)]

indignant /ɪnˈdɪgnənt/ *adj.* feeling or showing scornful anger or a sense of injured innocence. □□ **indignantly** *adv.* [L *indignari indignant-* regard as unworthy (as IN-¹, *dignus* worthy)]

indignation /ˌɪndɪgˈneɪʃ(ə)n/ *n.* scornful anger at supposed unjust or unfair conduct or treatment. [ME f. OF *indignation* or L *indignatio* (as INDIGNANT)]

indignity /ɪnˈdɪgnɪtɪ/ *n.* (*pl.* **-ies**) **1** unworthy treatment. **2** a slight or insult. **3** the humiliating quality of something (*the indignity of my position*). [F *indignité* or L *indignitas* (as INDIGNANT)]

indigo /ˈɪndɪgəʊ/ *n.* (*pl.* **-os**) **1 a** a natural blue dye obtained from the indigo plant. **b** a synthetic form of this dye. **2** any plant of the genus *Indigofera*. **3** (in full **indigo blue**) a colour between blue and violet in the spectrum. □□ **indigotic** /-ˈgɒtɪk/ *adj.* [16th-c. *indico* (f. Sp.), *indigo* (f. Port.) f. L *indicum* f. Gk *indikon* INDIAN (dye)]

Indira Gandhi Canal /ɪnˈdɪərə ˈgaːndɪ, ˈɪndərə/ (formerly called *Rajasthan Canal*) a massive canal which brings water to the arid Thar Desert of Rajasthan from the snow-fed Beas and Sutlej rivers which meet at the Harike Barrage in Punjab in NW India. The canal was completed in 1986.

indirect /ˌɪndaɪˈrekt/ *adj.* **1** not going straight to the point. **2** (of a route etc.) not straight. **3** not directly sought or aimed at (*an indirect result*). **4** (of lighting) from a concealed source and diffusely reflected. □ **indirect object** *Gram.* a person or thing affected by a verbal action but not primarily acted on (e.g. *him* in *give him the book*). **indirect question** *Gram.* a question in reported speech (e.g. *they asked who I was*). **indirect speech** (or **oration**) = *reported speech* (see REPORT). **indirect tax** a tax levied on goods and services and not on income or profits. □□ **indirectly** *adv.* **indirectness** *n.* [ME f. OF *indirect* or med.L *indirectus* (as IN-¹, DIRECT)]

indiscernible /ˌɪndɪˈsɜːnɪb(ə)l/ *adj.* that cannot be discerned or distinguished from another. □□ **indiscernibility** /-ˈbɪlɪtɪ/ *n.* **indiscernibly** *adv.*

indiscipline /ɪnˈdɪsɪplɪn/ *n.* lack of discipline.

indiscreet /ˌɪndɪˈskriːt/ *adj.* **1** not discreet; revealing secrets. **2** injudicious, unwary. □□ **indiscreetly** *adv.* [ME f. LL *indiscretus* (as IN-¹, DISCREET)]

indiscrete /ˌɪndɪˈskriːt/ *adj.* not divided into distinct parts. [L *indiscretus* (as IN-¹, DISCRETE)]

indiscretion /ˌɪndɪˈskreʃ(ə)n/ *n.* **1** lack of discretion; indiscreet conduct. **2** an indiscreet action, remark, etc. [ME f. OF *indiscretion* or LL *indiscretio* (as IN-¹, DISCRETION)]

indiscriminate /ˌɪndɪˈskrɪmɪnət/ *adj.* **1** making no distinctions. **2** confused, promiscuous. □□ **indiscriminately** *adv.* **indiscriminateness** *n.* **indiscrimination** /-ˈneɪʃ(ə)n/ *n.* **indiscriminative** *adj.* [IN-¹ + *discriminate* (adj.) f. L *discriminatus* past part. (as DISCRIMINATE)]

indispensable /ˌɪndɪˈspensəb(ə)l/ *adj.* **1** (often foll. by *to, for*) that cannot be dispensed with; necessary. **2** (of a law, duty, etc.) that is not to be set aside. □□ **indispensability** /-ˈbɪlɪtɪ/ *n.* **indispensableness** *n.* **indispensably** *adv.* [med.L *indispensabilis* (as IN-¹, DISPENSABLE)]

indispose /ˌɪndɪˈspəʊz/ *v.tr.* **1** (often foll. by *for*, or *to* + infin.) make unfit or unable. **2** (often foll. by *towards*, *from*, or *to* + infin.) make averse.

indisposed /ˌɪndɪˈspəʊzd/ *adj.* **1** slightly unwell. **2** averse or unwilling.

indisposition /ˌɪndɪspəˈzɪʃ(ə)n/ *n.* **1** ill health, a slight or temporary ailment. **2** disinclination. **3** aversion. [F *indisposition* or IN-¹ + DISPOSITION]

indisputable /ˌɪndɪˈspjuːtəb(ə)l/ *adj.* **1** that cannot be disputed. **2** unquestionable. □□ **indisputability** /-ˈbɪlɪtɪ/ *n.* **indisputableness** *n.* **indisputably** *adv.* [LL *indisputabilis* (as IN-¹, DISPUTABLE)]

indissolubilist /ˌɪndɪˈsɒljʊbɪlɪst/ *n. & adj.* —*n.* a person who believes that the Church should not remarry divorcees. —*adj.* of or holding this belief.

indissoluble /ˌɪndɪˈsɒljʊb(ə)l/ *adj.* **1** that cannot be dissolved or decomposed. **2** lasting, stable (*an indissoluble bond*). □□ **indissolubility** /-ˈbɪlɪtɪ/ *n.* **indissolubly** *adv.* [L *indissolubilis* (as IN-¹, DISSOLUBLE)]

indistinct /ˌɪndɪˈstɪŋkt/ *adj.* **1** not distinct. **2** confused, obscure. □□ **indistinctly** *adv.* **indistinctness** *n.* [ME f. L *indistinctus* (as IN-¹, DISTINCT)]

indistinctive /ˌɪndɪˈstɪŋktɪv/ *adj.* not having distinctive features. □□ **indistinctively** *adv.* **indistinctiveness** *n.*

indistinguishable /ˌɪndɪˈstɪŋgwɪʃəb(ə)l/ *adj.* (often foll. by *from*) not distinguishable. □□ **indistinguishableness** *n.* **indistinguishably** *adv.*

indite /ɪnˈdaɪt/ *v.tr. formal or joc.* **1** put (a speech etc.) into words. **2** write (a letter etc.). [ME f. OF *enditer*: see INDICT]

indium /ˈɪndɪəm/ *n. Chem.* a soft silvery-white metallic element, first discovered by spectrum analysis in 1863, that occurs in association with zinc and other metals. It is used in semiconductor devices and in alloys of low melting-point. ¶ Symb.: **In**; atomic number 49. [L *indicum* indigo with ref. to its characteristic indigo spectral lines]

indivertible /ˌɪndɪˈvɜːtɪb(ə)l/ *adj.* that cannot be turned aside. □□ **indivertibly** *adv.*

individual /ˌɪndɪˈvɪdjʊəl/ *adj. & n.* —*adj.* **1** single. **2** particular, special; not general. **3** having a distinct character. **4** characteristic of a particular person. **5** designed for use by one person. —*n.* **1** a single member of a class. **2** a single human being as distinct from a family or group. **3** *colloq.* a person (*a most unpleasant individual*). [ME, = indivisible, f. med.L *individualis* (as IN-¹, *dividuus* f. *dividere* DIVIDE)]

individualism /ˌɪndɪˈvɪdjʊəlɪz(ə)m/ *n.* **1** the habit or principle of being independent and self-reliant. **2** a social theory favouring the free action of individuals. **3** self-centred feeling or conduct; egoism. □□ **individualist** *n.* **individualistic** /-ˈlɪstɪk/ *adj.* **individualistically** /-ˈlɪstɪkəlɪ/ *adv.*

individuality /ˌɪndɪvɪdjʊˈælɪtɪ/ *n.* (*pl.* **-ies**) **1** individual character, esp. when strongly marked. **2** (in *pl.*) individual tastes etc. **3** separate existence.

individualize /ˌɪndɪˈvɪdjʊəˌlaɪz/ v.tr. (also **-ise**) **1** give an individual character to. **2** specify. □□ **individualization** /-ˈzeɪʃ(ə)n/ n.

individually /ˌɪndɪˈvɪdjʊəlɪ/ adv. **1** personally; in an individual capacity. **2** in a distinctive manner. **3** one by one; not collectively.

individuate /ˌɪndɪˈvɪdjʊˌeɪt/ v.tr. individualize; form into an individual. □□ **individuation** /-ˈeɪʃ(ə)n/ n. [med.L individuare (as INDIVIDUAL)]

indivisible /ˌɪndɪˈvɪzɪb(ə)l/ adj. **1** not divisible. **2** not distributable among a number. □□ **indivisibility** /-ˈbɪlɪtɪ/ n. **indivisibly** adv. [ME f. LL indivisibilis (as IN-¹, DIVISIBLE)]

Indo- /ˈɪndəʊ/ comb. form Indian; Indian and. [L Indus f. Gk Indos]

Indo-Aryan /ˌɪndəʊˈeərɪən/ n. & adj. —n. **1** a member of any of the Aryan peoples of India. **2** the Indic group of languages. —adj. of or relating to the Indo-Aryans or Indo-Aryan.

Indo-China /ˌɪndəʊˈtʃaɪnə/ **1** the peninsula of SE Asia containing Burma, Thailand, Malaya, Laos, Cambodia, and Vietnam. **2** hist. the region that now consists of Laos, Cambodia, and Vietnam. It was formerly a French dependency (French Indo-China). □□ **Indo-Chinese** adj. & n.

indocile /ɪnˈdəʊsaɪl/ adj. not docile. □□ **indocility** /-dəˈsɪlɪtɪ/ n. [F indocile or L indocilis (as IN-¹, DOCILE)]

indoctrinate /ɪnˈdɒktrɪˌneɪt/ v.tr. **1** teach (a person or group) systematically or for a long period to accept (esp. partisan or tendentious) ideas uncritically. **2** teach, instruct. □□ **indoctrination** /-ˈneɪʃ(ə)n/ n. **indoctrinator** n. [IN-² + DOCTRINE + -ATE³]

Indo-European /ˌɪndəʊˌjʊərəˈpɪən/ adj. & n. —adj. **1** of or relating to the family of languages (also called Indo-Germanic or Aryan) spoken for at least the last 3,000 years over the greater part of Europe and extending into Asia as far as northern India. (See below.) —n. **1** the Indo-European family of languages. **2** (usu. in pl.) a speaker of an Indo-European language.

The name has become established as a technical term, but it must not be supposed to include all the languages of India and Europe, some of which (e.g. the Dravidian languages, Finnish, and Hungarian) belong to quite different families. Considerably before 2000 BC there must have existed a relatively small tribe speaking a language which we may call 'Proto-Indo-European'. No records of it survive, nor is there any evidence that it could ever have been written, but its existence can be inferred from a comparison of its daughter languages, and most of its phonology and morphology and some of its vocabulary can be reconstructed with some degree of certainty. The main divisions into which it split up, in the course of time, are the Indo-Iranian or Aryan group, the Hellenic group or Greek, the Italic group (of which the most important member is Latin, together with its daughter languages French and the other Romance languages), the Germanic languages (to which English belongs), the Celtic group, the Baltic languages, and the closely related Slavonic languages. In addition to these, Albanian forms a distinct member of the family and so does Armenian. Two important discoveries of the 20th c. have added to the family the ancient Anatolian languages (from the 2nd millennium BC: Hittite is the oldest attested Indo-European language), and Tocharian, which flourished in Chinese Turkestan more than 1,000 years ago.

Recognition of the breadth of this language family is only relatively recent and was first reached when a number of European scholars started studying Sanskrit in the late 18th and early 19th c. In 1786 the English orientalist Sir William Jones pointed out the strong affinity that Sanskrit bore to Greek and Latin, and spoke of a common origin for these languages, but most of the research on which the language groupings and the reconstruction of the parent language are based was the work of German scholars in the 19th c.

Indo-Germanic /ˌɪndəʊdʒɜːˈmænɪk/ adj. & n. = Indo-European.

Indo-Iranian /ˌɪndəʊɪˈreɪnɪən/ adj. & n. —adj. of or relating to the large group of Indo-European languages spoken chiefly in northern India and Iran. It can be divided into the Indo-Aryan (or Indic) group and the Iranian. —n. this sub-family.

indole /ˈɪndəʊl/ n. Chem. an organic compound with a characteristic odour formed on the reduction of indigo. [INDIGO + L oleum oil]

indoleacetic acid /ˌɪndəʊləˈsiːtɪk/ n. Biochem. any of the several isomeric acetic acid derivatives of indole, esp. one found as a natural growth hormone in plants. ¶ Abbr.: **IAA**. [INDOLE + ACETIC]

indolent /ˈɪndələnt/ adj. **1** lazy; wishing to avoid activity or exertion. **2** Med. causing no pain (an indolent tumour). □□ **indolence** n. **indolently** adv. [LL indolens (as IN-¹, dolēre suffer pain)]

Indology /ɪnˈdɒlədʒɪ/ n. the study of Indian history, literature, etc. □□ **Indologist** n.

indomitable /ɪnˈdɒmɪtəb(ə)l/ adj. **1** that cannot be subdued; unyielding. **2** stubbornly persistent. □□ **indomitability** /-ˈbɪlɪtɪ/ n. **indomitableness** n. **indomitably** adv. [LL indomitabilis (as IN-¹, L domitare tame)]

Indonesia /ˌɪndəˈniːzjə, -ʒə, -ʃə/ a large island group in SE Asia, formerly the Dutch East Indies, composed of Java, Sumatra, South Borneo, West New Guinea, the Moluccas, Sulawesi, and a host of minor islands; pop. (est. 1988) 174,951,000; official language, Indonesian; capital (on Java) Djakarta. Most of the population is engaged in agriculture and the industries based on its products; timber is the second most important export, after oil. Economic and political power is largely centred in Java. Colonized, largely by the Dutch, in the early 17th c., the area was conquered by the Japanese in 1942 and upon liberation was proclaimed a republic by local nationalists. Sovereignty passed formally to the new Indonesian government in 1949 and the last Dutch enclave in the area was finally handed over in 1963. Although the economy has expanded considerably since then, especially under Western and Japanese influence, in terms of per capita income Indonesia remains one of the world's poorest countries.

Indonesian /ˌɪndəˈniːzjən, -ʒ(ə)n, -ʃ(ə)n/ n. & adj. —n. **1 a** a native or national of Indonesia. **b** a person of Indonesian descent. **2** a member of the chief pre-Malay population of the E. Indies. **3** a language of the group spoken in the E. Indies, esp. the official language (also called Bahasa) of Indonesia. —adj. of or relating to Indonesia or its people or language. It is virtually the same language as Malay; the apparent differences are mainly due to the different spelling systems, the Indonesian one having been developed by the Dutch and the Malay by the British. [Indonesia f. INDIES after Polynesia]

indoor /ˈɪndɔː(r)/ adj. situated, carried on, or used within a building or under cover (indoor aerial; indoor games). [earlier within-door: cf. INDOORS]

indoors /ɪnˈdɔːz/ adv. into or within a building. [earlier within doors]

Indore /ɪnˈdɔː(r)/ a manufacturing city of Madhya Pradesh in central India; pop. (1981) 827,000.

indorse var. of ENDORSE.

Indra /ˈɪndrə/ Hinduism the most popular deity of the Rig-Veda, warrior-king of the heavens, god of war and storm. His weapons are the thunderbolt and lightning, his helpers are the Maruts. His role in later Hinduism is small. [Skr., = lord]

indraught /ˈɪndrɑːft/ n. (US **indraft**) **1** the drawing in of something. **2** an inward flow or current.

indrawn /ˈɪndrɔːn/ adj. **1** (of breath etc.) drawn in. **2** aloof.

indri /ˈɪndrɪ/ n. (pl. **indris**) a large lemur, Indri indri, of Madagascar. [Malagasy indry behold, mistaken for its name]

indubitable /ɪnˈdjuːbɪtəb(ə)l/ adj. that cannot be doubted. □□ **indubitably** adv. [F indubitable or L indubitabilis (as IN-¹, dubitare to doubt)]

induce /ɪnˈdjuːs/ v.tr. **1** (often foll. by to + infin.) prevail on; persuade. **2** bring about; give rise to. **3** Med. bring on (labour) artificially, esp. by use of drugs. **4** Electr. produce (a current) by induction. **5** Physics cause (radioactivity) by bombardment. **6** infer; derive as a deduction. □□ **inducer** n. **inducible** adj. [ME f. L inducere induct- (as IN-², ducere lead)]

inducement /ɪnˈdjuːsmənt/ n. **1** (often foll. by to) an attraction that leads one on. **2** a thing that induces.

induct /ɪnˈdʌkt/ v.tr. (often foll. by *to*, *into*) **1** introduce formally into possession of a benefice. **2** install into a room, office, etc. **3** introduce, initiate. **4** *US* enlist (a person) for military service. □□ **inductee** /ˌɪndʌkˈtiː/ n. [ME (as INDUCE)]

inductance /ɪnˈdʌkt(ə)ns/ n. *Electr.* the property of an electric circuit that causes an electromotive force to be generated by a change in the current flowing.

induction /ɪnˈdʌkʃ(ə)n/ n. **1** the act or an instance of inducting or inducing. **2** *Med.* the process of bringing on (esp. labour) by artificial means. **3** *Logic* **a** the inference of a general law from particular instances (cf. DEDUCTION). **b** *Math.* a means of proving a theorem by showing that if it is true of any particular case it is true of the next case in a series, and then showing that it is indeed true in one particular case. **c** (foll. by *of*) the production of (facts) to prove a general statement. **4** (often *attrib.*) a formal introduction to a new job, position, etc. (*attended an induction course*). **5** *Electr.* **a** the production of an electric or magnetic state by the proximity (without contact) of an electrified or magnetized body. **b** the production of an electric current in a conductor by a change of magnetic field. **6** the drawing of a fuel mixture into the cylinders of an internal-combustion engine. **7** *US* enlistment for military service. □ **induction-coil** a coil for generating intermittent high voltage from a direct current. **induction heating** heating by an induced electric current. [ME f. OF *induction* or L *inductio* (as INDUCE)]

inductive /ɪnˈdʌktɪv/ adj. **1** (of reasoning etc.) of or based on induction. **2** of electric or magnetic induction. □□ **inductively** adv. **inductiveness** n. [LL *inductivus* (as INDUCE)]

inductor /ɪnˈdʌktə(r)/ n. **1** *Electr.* a component (in a circuit) which possesses inductance. **2** a person who inducts a member of the clergy. [L (as INDUCE)]

indue var. of ENDUE.

indulge /ɪnˈdʌldʒ/ v. **1** *intr.* (often foll. by *in*) take pleasure freely. **2** *tr.* yield freely to (a desire etc.). **3** *tr.* gratify the wishes of; favour (*indulged them with money*). **4** *intr. colloq.* take alcoholic liquor. □□ **indulger** n. [L *indulgēre indult-* give free rein to]

indulgence /ɪnˈdʌldʒ(ə)ns/ n. **1 a** the act of indulging. **b** the state of being indulgent. **2** something indulged in. **3** *RC Ch.* the remission of temporal punishment in purgatory, still due for sins even after sacramental absolution. The later Middle Ages saw the growth of considerable abuses, such as the unrestricted sale of indulgences by professional 'pardoners', which were an immediate occasion of the Reformation. In the Roman Catholic Church the granting of indulgences is now ordinarily confined to the pope. **4** a privilege granted. □ **Declaration of Indulgence** the proclamation of religious liberties, esp. under Charles II in 1672 and James II in 1687. [ME f. OF f. L *indulgentia* (as INDULGENT)]

indulgent /ɪnˈdʌldʒ(ə)nt/ adj. **1** ready or too ready to overlook faults etc. **2** indulging or tending to indulge. □□ **indulgently** adv. [F *indulgent* or L *indulgere indulgent-* (as INDULGE)]

indumentum /ˌɪndjʊˈmentəm/ n. (pl. **indumenta** /-tə/) *Bot.* the covering of hairs on part of a plant, esp. when dense. [L, = garment]

induna /ɪnˈduːnə/ n. **1** *S.Afr.* a tribal councillor or headman. **2 a** an African foreman. **b** a person in authority. [Nguni *inDuna* captain, councillor]

indurate /ˈɪndjʊəˌreɪt/ v. **1** *tr. & intr.* make or become hard. **2** *tr.* make callous or unfeeling. **3** *intr.* become inveterate. □□ **induration** /-ˈreɪʃ(ə)n/ n. **indurative** adj. [L *indurare* (as IN-2, *durus* hard)]

Indus /ˈɪndəs/ a river of southern Asia, about 2,900 km (1,800 miles) in length, flowing from Tibet through Kashmir and Pakistan to the Arabian Sea. Along its valley an early culture flourished from *c.*2600 to 1760 BC, with important centres at Mohenjo-Daro and Harappa, characterized by towns built to a grid-like plan with granaries, drainage systems, and public buildings, copper–bronze technology, a standard system of weights and measures, and steatite seals with (undeciphered) hieroglyphic inscriptions. Its economic wealth was derived from well-attested sea and land trade with the Indian subcontinent, Afghanistan, the Gulf, Iran, and Mesopotamia. In the early 2nd

millennium its power declined, probably because of incursions by the Aryans.

indusium /ɪnˈdjuːzɪəm/ n. (pl. **indusia** /-zɪə/) **1** a membranous shield covering the fruit-cluster of a fern. **2** a collection of hairs enclosing the stigma of some flowers. **3** the case of a larva. □□ **indusial** adj. [L, = tunic, f. *induere* put on (a garment)]

industrial /ɪnˈdʌstrɪəl/ adj. & n. —adj. **1** of or relating to industry or industries. **2** designed or suitable for industrial use (*industrial alcohol*). **3** characterized by highly developed industries (*the industrial nations*). —n. (in pl.) shares in industrial companies. □ **industrial action** *Brit.* any action, esp. a strike or work to rule, taken by employees as a protest. **industrial archaeology** the study of machines, factories, bridges, etc., formerly used in industry. **industrial estate** *Brit.* an area of land developed for the siting of industrial enterprises. **industrial relations** the relations between management and workers in industries. **the Industrial Revolution** see separate entry. □□ **industrially** adv. [INDUSTRY + -AL: in 19th c. partly f. F *industriel*]

industrialism /ɪnˈdʌstrɪəˌlɪz(ə)m/ n. a social or economic system in which manufacturing industries are prevalent.

industrialist /ɪnˈdʌstrɪəlɪst/ n. a person engaged in the management of industry.

industrialize /ɪnˈdʌstrɪəˌlaɪz/ v. (also **-ise**) **1** *tr.* introduce industries to (a country or region etc.). **2** *intr.* become industrialized. □□ **industrialization** /-ˈzeɪʃ(ə)n/ n.

Industrial Revolution the rapid development of a nation's industry, especially that occurring first in Britain in the second half of the 18th c. and the first half of the 19th c., in which the bulk of the working population changed from agriculture to industry. Preceded by major changes in agricultural methods which freed workers for the factories, it was caused by the rise of modern industrial methods, with steam power replacing the use of muscle, wind, and water, the growth of factories, and the mass production of manufactured goods. The textile industry was the prime example of industrialization, and created a demand for machines, and for tools for their manufacture, which stimulated further mechanization. Improved transport was needed, provided by canals, roads, railways, and steamships; construction of these required a large labour force, and the skills acquired were exported to other countries. It made Britain the most powerful industrial country in the world but radically changed the face of British society, throwing up large cities (particularly in the Midlands) as the population shifted from the countryside, and causing or exacerbating a series of profound social and economic problems, the solution of which dominated domestic politics for more than a century.

Industrial Workers of the World a radical US labour movement, popularly known as the Wobblies, founded in 1905 and dedicated to the overthrow of capitalism. Its popularity declined after the First World War and by 1925 its membership was insignificant.

industrious /ɪnˈdʌstrɪəs/ adj. diligent, hard-working. □□ **industriously** adv. **industriousness** n. [F *industrieux* or LL *industriosus* (as INDUSTRY)]

industry /ˈɪndəstrɪ/ n. (pl. **-ies**) **1 a** a branch of trade or manufacture. **b** trade and manufacture collectively (*incentives to industry*). **2** concerted or copious activity (*the building was a hive of industry*). **3 a** diligence. **b** *colloq.* the diligent study of a particular topic (*the Shakespeare industry*). **4** habitual employment in useful work. [ME, = skill, f. F *industrie* or L *industria* diligence]

indwell /ɪnˈdwel/ v. (past and past part. **indwelt**) *literary* **1** *intr.* (often foll. by *in*) be permanently present as a spirit, principle, etc. **2** *tr.* inhabit spiritually. □□ **indweller** n.

Ine /ˈiːnə/ king of Wessex 688–726. The strongest king of the West Saxons before Alfred, Ine greatly extended the prestige and power of the throne, developing the most extensive legal code of the age. He abdicated in 726 at an advanced age and retired to Rome.

-ine[1] /aɪn, ɪn/ suffix forming adjectives, meaning 'belonging to, of the nature of' (*Alpine; asinine*). [from or after F *-in -ine*, or f. L *-inus*]

-ine[2] /aɪn/ *suffix* forming adjectives esp. from names of minerals, plants, etc. (*crystalline*). [L *-inus* from or after Gk *-inos*]

-ine[3] /ɪn, iːn/ *suffix* forming feminine nouns (*heroine*; *margravine*). [F f. L *-ina* f. Gk *-inē*, or f. G *-in*]

-ine[4] *suffix* **1** /ɪn/ forming (esp. abstract) nouns (*discipline*; *medicine*). **2** /iːn, ɪn/ *Chem*. forming nouns denoting derived substances, esp. alkaloids, halogens, amines, and amino acids. [F f. L *-ina* (fem.) = -INE[1]]

inebriate *v., adj.,* & *n.* —*v.tr.* /ɪˈniːbrɪˌeɪt/ **1** make drunk; intoxicate. **2** excite. —*adj.* /ɪˈniːbrɪət/ drunken. —*n.* /ɪˈniːbrɪət/ a drunken person, esp. a habitual drunkard. □□ **inebriation** /-ˈeɪʃ(ə)n/ *n.* **inebriety** /-ˈbraɪətɪ/ *n.* [ME f. L *inebriatus* past part. of *inebriare* (as IN-[2], *ebrius* drunk)]

inedible /ɪnˈedɪb(ə)l/ *adj.* not edible, esp. not suitable for eating (cf. UNEATABLE). □□ **inedibility** /-ˈbɪlɪtɪ/ *n.*

inedited /ɪnˈedɪtɪd/ *adj.* **1** not published. **2** published without editorial alterations or additions.

ineducable /ɪnˈedjʊkəb(ə)l/ *adj.* incapable of being educated, esp. through mental retardation. □□ **ineducability** /-ˈbɪlɪtɪ/ *n.*

ineffable /ɪnˈefəb(ə)l/ *adj.* **1** unutterable; too great for description in words. **2** that must not be uttered. □□ **ineffability** /-ˈbɪlɪtɪ/ *n.* **ineffably** *adv.* [ME f. OF *ineffable* or L *ineffabilis* (as IN-[1], *effari* speak out, utter)]

ineffaceable /ɪnɪˈfeɪsəb(ə)l/ *adj.* that cannot be effaced. □□ **ineffaceability** /-ˈbɪlɪtɪ/ *n.* **ineffaceably** *adv.*

ineffective /ɪnɪˈfektɪv/ *adj.* **1** not producing any effect or the desired effect. **2** (of a person) inefficient; not achieving results. **3** lacking artistic effect. □□ **ineffectively** *adv.* **ineffectiveness** *n.*

ineffectual /ɪnɪˈfektjʊəl, -ʃʊəl/ *adj.* **1 a** without effect. **b** not producing the desired or expected effect. **2** (of a person) lacking the ability to achieve results (*an ineffectual leader*). □□ **ineffectuality** /-tjʊˈælɪtɪ/ *n.* **ineffectually** *adv.* **ineffectualness** *n.* [ME f. med.L *ineffectualis* (as IN-[1], EFFECTUAL)]

inefficacious /ˌɪnefɪˈkeɪʃəs/ *adj.* (of a remedy etc.) not producing the desired effect. □□ **inefficaciously** *adv.* **inefficaciousness** *n.* **inefficacy** /ɪnˈefɪkəsɪ/ *n.*

inefficient /ɪnɪˈfɪʃ(ə)nt/ *adj.* **1** not efficient. **2** (of a person) not fully capable; not well qualified. □□ **inefficiency** *n.* **inefficiently** *adv.*

inelastic /ˌɪnɪˈlæstɪk/ *adj.* **1** not elastic. **2** unadaptable, inflexible, unyielding. □□ **inelastically** *adv.* **inelasticity** /-ˈtɪsɪtɪ/ *n.*

inelegant /ɪnˈelɪgənt/ *adj.* **1** ungraceful. **2 a** unrefined. **b** (of a style) unpolished. □□ **inelegance** *n.* **inelegantly** *adv.* [F *inélégant* f. L *inelegans* (as IN-[1], ELEGANT)]

ineligible /ɪnˈelɪdʒɪb(ə)l/ *adj.* **1** not eligible. **2** undesirable. □□ **ineligibility** /-ˈbɪlɪtɪ/ *n.* **ineligibly** *adv.*

ineluctable /ˌɪnɪˈlʌktəb(ə)l/ *adj.* **1** against which it is useless to struggle. **2** that cannot be escaped from. □□ **ineluctability** /-ˈbɪlɪtɪ/ *n.* **ineluctably** *adv.* [L *ineluctabilis* (as IN-[1], *eluctari* struggle out)]

inept /ɪˈnept/ *adj.* **1** unskilful. **2** absurd, silly. **3** out of place. □□ **ineptitude** *n.* **ineptly** *adv.* **ineptness** *n.* [L *ineptus* (as IN-[1], APT)]

inequable /ɪnˈekwəb(ə)l/ *adj.* **1** not fairly distributed. **2** not uniform. [L *inaequabilis* uneven (as IN-[1], EQUABLE)]

inequality /ˌɪnɪˈkwɒlɪtɪ/ *n.* (*pl.* **-ies**) **1 a** lack of equality in any respect. **b** an instance of this. **2** the state of being variable. **3** (of a surface) irregularity. **4** *Math.* a formula affirming that two expressions are not equal. [ME f. OF *inequalité* or L *inaequalitas* (as IN-[1], EQUALITY)]

inequitable /ɪnˈekwɪtəb(ə)l/ *adj.* unfair, unjust. □□ **inequitably** *adv.*

inequity /ɪnˈekwɪtɪ/ *n.* (*pl.* **-ies**) unfairness, bias.

ineradicable /ˌɪnɪˈrædɪkəb(ə)l/ *adj.* that cannot be rooted out. □□ **ineradicably** *adv.*

inerrant /ɪnˈerənt/ *adj.* not liable to err. □□ **inerrancy** *n.* [L *inerrans* (as IN-[1], ERR)]

inert /ɪˈnɜːt/ *adj.* **1** without inherent power of action, motion, or resistance. **2** without active chemical or other properties. **3** sluggish, slow. □ **inert gas** = *noble gas*. □□ **inertly** *adv.* **inertness** *n.* [L *iners inert-* (as IN-[1], *ars* ART[1])]

inertia /ɪˈnɜːʃə, -ʃɪə/ *n.* **1** *Physics* a property of matter by which it continues in its existing state of rest or uniform motion in a straight line, unless that state is changed by an external force. (See MASS[1].) **2** inertness, sloth. □ **inertia reel** a reel device which allows a vehicle seat-belt to unwind freely but which locks under force of impact or rapid deceleration. **inertia selling** the sending of unsolicited goods in the hope of making a sale. □□ **inertial** *adj.* **inertialess** *adj.* [L (as INERT)]

inescapable /ˌɪnɪˈskeɪpəb(ə)l/ *adj.* that cannot be escaped or avoided. □□ **inescapability** /-ˈbɪlɪtɪ/ *n.* **inescapably** *adv.*

-iness /ɪnɪs/ *suffix* forming nouns corresponding to adjectives in *-y* (see -Y[1], -LY[2]).

inessential /ˌɪnɪˈsenʃ(ə)l/ *adj.* & *n.* —*adj.* **1** not necessary. **2** dispensable. —*n.* an inessential thing.

inestimable /ɪnˈestɪməb(ə)l/ *adj.* too great, intense, precious, etc., to be estimated. □□ **inestimably** *adv.* [ME f. OF f. L *inaestimabilis* (as IN-[1], ESTIMABLE)]

inevitable /ɪnˈevɪtəb(ə)l/ *adj.* **1 a** unavoidable; sure to happen. **b** that is bound to occur or appear. **2** *colloq.* that is tiresomely familiar. **3** (of character-drawing, the development of a plot, etc.) so true to nature etc. as to preclude alternative treatment or solution; convincing. □□ **inevitability** /-ˈbɪlɪtɪ/ *n.* **inevitableness** *n.* **inevitably** *adv.* [L *inevitabilis* (as IN-[1], *evitare* avoid)]

inexact /ˌɪnɪgˈzækt/ *adj.* not exact. □□ **inexactitude** *n.* **inexactly** *adv.* **inexactness** *n.*

inexcusable /ˌɪnɪkˈskjuːzəb(ə)l/ *adj.* (of a person, action, etc.) that cannot be excused or justified. □□ **inexcusably** *adv.* [ME f. L *inexcusabilis* (as IN-[1], EXCUSE)]

inexhaustible /ˌɪnɪgˈzɔːstɪb(ə)l/ *adj.* that cannot be exhausted or used up. □□ **inexhaustibility** /-ˈbɪlɪtɪ/ *n.* **inexhaustibly** *adv.*

inexorable /ɪnˈeksərəb(ə)l/ *adj.* **1** relentless. **2** (of a person or attribute) that cannot be persuaded by request or entreaty. □□ **inexorability** /-ˈbɪlɪtɪ/ *n.* **inexorably** *adv.* [F *inexorable* or L *inexorabilis* (as IN-[1], *exorare* entreat)]

inexpedient /ˌɪnɪkˈspiːdɪənt/ *adj.* not expedient. □□ **inexpediency** *n.*

inexpensive /ˌɪnɪkˈspensɪv/ *adj.* **1** not expensive, cheap. **2** offering good value for the price. □□ **inexpensively** *adv.* **inexpensiveness** *n.*

inexperience /ˌɪnɪkˈspɪərɪəns/ *n.* lack of experience, or of the resulting knowledge or skill. □□ **inexperienced** *adj.* [F *inexpérience* f. LL *inexperientia* (as IN-[1], EXPERIENCE)]

inexpert /ɪnˈekspɜːt/ *adj.* unskilful; lacking expertise. □□ **inexpertly** *adv.* **inexpertness** *n.* [OF f. L *inexpertus* (as IN-[1], EXPERT)]

inexpiable /ɪnˈekspɪəb(ə)l/ *adj.* (of an act or feeling) that cannot be expiated or appeased. □□ **inexpiably** *adv.* [L *inexpiabilis* (as IN-[1], EXPIATE)]

inexplicable /ˌɪnɪkˈsplɪkəb(ə)l, ɪnˈeks-/ *adj.* that cannot be explained or accounted for. □□ **inexplicability** /-ˈbɪlɪtɪ/ *n.* **inexplicably** *adv.* [F *inexplicable* or L *inexplicabilis* that cannot be unfolded (as IN-[1], EXPLICABLE)]

inexplicit /ˌɪnɪkˈsplɪsɪt/ *adj.* not definitely or clearly expressed. □□ **inexplicitly** *adv.* **inexplicitness** *n.*

inexpressible /ˌɪnɪkˈspresɪb(ə)l/ *adj.* that cannot be expressed in words. □□ **inexpressibly** *adv.*

inexpressive /ˌɪnɪkˈspresɪv/ *adj.* not expressive. □□ **inexpressively** *adv.* **inexpressiveness** *n.*

inexpungible /ˌɪnɪkˈspʌndʒɪb(ə)l/ *adj.* that cannot be expunged or obliterated.

in extenso /ˌɪn ekˈstensəʊ/ *adv.* in full; at length. [L]

inextinguishable /ˌɪnɪkˈstɪŋgwɪʃəb(ə)l/ *adj.* **1** not quenchable; indestructible. **2** (of laughter etc.) irrepressible.

in extremis /ˌɪn ekˈstriːmɪs/ *adj.* **1** at the point of death. **2** in great difficulties. [L]

inextricable /ɪnˈekstrɪkəb(ə)l, ˌɪnɪkˈstrɪk-/ *adj.* **1** (of a circumstance) that cannot be escaped from. **2** (of a knot, problem, etc.) that cannot be unravelled or solved. **3** intricately confused. □□ **inextricability** /-ˈbɪlɪtɪ/ *n.* **inextricably** *adv.* [ME f. L *inextricabilis* (as IN-[1], EXTRICATE)]

infallible /ɪnˈfælɪb(ə)l/ *adj.* **1** incapable of error. **2** (of a method, test, proof, etc.) unfailing; sure to succeed. **3** *RC Ch.* (of the Pope) unable to err in pronouncing dogma as doctrinally defined. □□ **infallibility** /-ˈbɪlɪtɪ/ *n.* **infallibly** *adv.* [ME f. F *infaillible* or LL *infallibilis* (as IN-¹, FALLIBLE)]

infamous /ˈɪnfəməs/ *adj.* **1** notoriously bad; having a bad reputation. **2** abominable. **3** (in ancient law) deprived of all or some rights of a citizen on account of serious crime. □□ **infamously** *adv.* **infamy** /ˈɪnfəmɪ/ *n.* (*pl.* **-ies**). [ME f. med.L *infamosus* f. L *infamis* (as IN-¹, FAME)]

infancy /ˈɪnfənsɪ/ *n.* (*pl.* **-ies**) **1** early childhood; babyhood. **2** an early state in the development of an idea, undertaking, etc. **3** *Law* the state of being a minor. [L *infantia* (as INFANT)]

infant /ˈɪnf(ə)nt/ *n.* **1 a** a child during the earliest period of its life. **b** *Brit.* a schoolchild below the age of seven years. **2** (*esp. attrib.*) a thing in an early stage of its development. **3** *Law* a minor; a person under 18. □ **infant mortality** death before the age of one. [ME f. OF *enfant* f. L *infans* unable to speak (as IN-¹, *fans fantis* pres. part. of *fari* speak)]

infanta /ɪnˈfæntə/ *n. hist.* a daughter of the ruling monarch of Spain or Portugal (usu. the eldest daughter who is not heir to the throne). [Sp. & Port., fem. of INFANTE]

infante /ɪnˈfæntɪ/ *n. hist.* the second son of the ruling monarch of Spain or Portugal. [Sp. & Port. f. L (as INFANT)]

infanticide /ɪnˈfæntɪˌsaɪd/ *n.* **1** the killing of an infant soon after birth. **2** the practice of killing newborn infants. **3** a person who kills an infant. □□ **infanticidal** /-ˈsaɪd(ə)l/ *adj.* [F f. LL *infanticidium, -cida* (as INFANT)]

infantile /ˈɪnfənˌtaɪl/ *adj.* **1 a** like or characteristic of a child. **b** childish, immature (*infantile humour*). **2** in its infancy. □ **infantile paralysis** poliomyelitis. □□ **infantility** /-ˈtɪlɪtɪ/ *n.* (*pl.* **-ies**). [F *infantile* or L *infantilis* (as INFANT)]

infantilism /ɪnˈfæntɪˌlɪz(ə)m/ *n.* **1** childish behaviour. **2** *Psychol.* the persistence of infantile characteristics or behaviour in adult life.

infantry /ˈɪnfəntrɪ/ *n.* (*pl.* **-ies**) a body of soldiers who march and fight on foot; foot-soldiers collectively. [F *infanterie* f. It. *infanteria* f. *infante* youth, infantryman (as INFANT)]

infantryman /ˈɪnfəntrɪmən/ *n.* (*pl.* **-men**) a soldier of an infantry regiment.

infarct /ˈɪnfɑːkt/ *n. Med.* a small localized area of dead tissue caused by an inadequate blood supply. □□ **infarction** /ɪnˈfɑːkʃ(ə)n/ *n.* [mod.L *infarctus* (as IN-², L *farcire farct-* stuff)]

infatuate /ɪnˈfætjʊˌeɪt/ *v.tr.* **1** inspire with intense usu. transitory fondness or admiration. **2** affect with extreme folly. □□ **infatuation** /-ˈeɪʃ(ə)n/ *n.* [L *infatuare* (as IN-², *fatuus* foolish)]

infatuated /ɪnˈfætjʊˌeɪtɪd/ *adj.* (often foll. by *with*) affected by an intense fondness or admiration.

infauna /ˈɪnˌfɔːnə/ *n.* any animals which live just below the surface of the seabed. [Da. *ifauna* (as IN-², FAUNA)]

infeasible /ɪnˈfiːzɪb(ə)l/ *adj.* not feasible; that cannot easily be done. □□ **infeasibility** /-ˈbɪlɪtɪ/ *n.*

infect /ɪnˈfekt/ *v.tr.* **1** contaminate (air, water, etc.) with harmful organisms or noxious matter. **2** affect (a person) with disease etc. **3** instil bad feeling or opinion into (a person). □□ **infector** *n.* [ME f. L *inficere infect-* taint (as IN-², *facere* make)]

infection /ɪnˈfekʃ(ə)n/ *n.* **1 a** the process of infecting or state of being infected. **b** an instance of this; an infectious disease. **2** communication of disease, esp. by the agency of air or water etc. **3 a** moral contamination. **b** the diffusive influence of example, sympathy, etc. [ME f. OF *infection* or LL *infectio* (as INFECT)]

infectious /ɪnˈfekʃəs/ *adj.* **1** infecting with disease. **2** (of a disease) liable to be transmitted by air, water, etc. **3** (of emotions etc.) apt to spread; quickly affecting others. □□ **infectiously** *adv.* **infectiousness** *n.*

infective /ɪnˈfektɪv/ *adj.* **1** capable of infecting with disease. **2** infectious. □□ **infectiveness** *n.* [L *infectivus* (as INFECT)]

infelicitous /ˌɪnfɪˈlɪsɪtəs/ *adj.* not felicitous; unfortunate. □□ **infelicitously** *adv.*

infelicity /ˌɪnfɪˈlɪsɪtɪ/ *n.* (*pl.* **-ies**) **1 a** inaptness of expression

etc. **b** an instance of this. **2 a** unhappiness. **b** a misfortune. [ME f. L *infelicitas* (as IN-¹, FELICITY)]

infer /ɪnˈfɜː(r)/ *v.tr.* (**inferred, inferring**) (often foll. by *that* + clause) **1** deduce or conclude from facts and reasoning. **2** *disp.* imply, suggest. □□ **inferable** *adj.* (also **inferrable**). [L *inferre* (as IN-², *ferre* bring)]

inference /ˈɪnfərəns/ *n.* **1** the act or an instance of inferring. **2** *Logic* **a** the forming of a conclusion from premisses. **b** a thing inferred. □□ **inferential** /-ˈrenʃ(ə)l/ *adj.* **inferentially** /-ˈrenʃəlɪ/ *adv.* [med.L *inferentia* (as INFER)]

inferior /ɪnˈfɪərɪə(r)/ *adj.* & *n.* —*adj.* **1** (often foll. by *to*) **a** lower; in a lower position. **b** of lower rank, quality, etc. **2** poor in quality. **3** (of a planet) having an orbit within the earth's. **4** *Bot.* situated below an ovary or calyx. **5** (of figures or letters) written or printed below the line. —*n.* **1** a person inferior to another, esp. in rank. **2** an inferior letter or figure. □□ **inferiorly** *adv.* [ME f. L, compar. of *inferus* that is below]

inferiority /ɪnˌfɪərɪˈɒrɪtɪ/ *n.* the state of being inferior. □ **inferiority complex** an unrealistic feeling of general inadequacy caused by actual or supposed inferiority in one sphere, sometimes marked by aggressive behaviour in compensation (first described by the Austrian psychiatrist Alfred Adler).

infernal /ɪnˈfɜːn(ə)l/ *adj.* **1 a** of hell or the underworld. **b** hellish, fiendish. **2** *colloq.* detestable, tiresome. □□ **infernally** *adv.* [ME f. OF f. LL *infernalis* f. L *infernus* situated below]

inferno /ɪnˈfɜːnəʊ/ *n.* (*pl.* **-os**) **1** a raging fire. **2** a scene of horror or distress. **3** hell, esp. with ref. to Dante's *Divine Comedy*. [It. f. LL *infernus* (as INFERNAL)]

infertile /ɪnˈfɜːtaɪl/ *adj.* not fertile. □□ **infertility** /-ˈtɪlɪtɪ/ *n.* [F *infertile* or LL *infertilis* (as IN-¹, FERTILE)]

infest /ɪnˈfest/ *v.tr.* (of harmful persons or things, esp. vermin or disease) overrun (a place) in large numbers. □□ **infestation** /-ˈsteɪʃ(ə)n/ *n.* [ME f. F *infester* or L *infestare* assail f. *infestus* hostile]

infidel /ˈɪnfɪd(ə)l/ *n.* & *adj.* —*n.* **1** a person who does not believe in religion or in a particular religion; an unbeliever. **2** *hist.* an adherent of a religion other than Christianity, esp. a Muslim. —*adj.* **1** that is an infidel. **2** of unbelievers. [ME f. F *infidèle* or L *infidelis* (as IN-¹, *fidelis* faithful)]

infidelity /ˌɪnfɪˈdelɪtɪ/ *n.* (*pl.* **-ies**) **1 a** disloyalty or unfaithfulness, esp. to a husband or wife. **b** an instance of this. **2** disbelief in Christianity or another religion. [ME f. F *infidélité* or L *infidelitas* (as INFIDEL)]

infield /ˈɪnfiːld/ *n.* **1** *Cricket* **a** the part of the ground near the wicket. **b** the fielders stationed there. **2** *Baseball* **a** the area between the four bases. **b** the four fielders stationed on its boundaries. **3** farm land around or near a homestead. **4 a** arable land. **b** land regularly manured and cropped. □□ **infielder** *n.* (in sense 2).

infighting /ˈɪnˌfaɪtɪŋ/ *n.* **1** hidden conflict or competitiveness within an organization. **2** boxing at closer quarters than arm's length. □□ **infighter** *n.*

infill /ˈɪnfɪl/ *n.* & *v.* —*n.* **1** material used to fill a hole, gap, etc. **2** the placing of buildings to occupy the space between existing ones. —*v.tr.* fill in (a cavity etc.).

infilling /ˈɪnˌfɪlɪŋ/ *n.* = INFILL *n.*

infiltrate /ˈɪnfɪlˌtreɪt/ *v.* **1** *tr.* **a** gain entrance or access to surreptitiously and by degrees (as spies etc.). **b** cause to do this. **2** *tr.* permeate by filtration. **3** *tr.* (often foll. by *into, through*) introduce (fluid) by filtration. □□ **infiltration** /-ˈtreɪʃ(ə)n/ *n.* **infiltrator** *n.* [IN-² + FILTRATE]

infinite /ˈɪnfɪnɪt/ *adj.* & *n.* —*adj.* **1** boundless, endless. **2** very great. **3** (usu. with *pl.*) innumerable; very many (*infinite resources*). **4** *Math.* **a** greater than any assignable quantity or countable number. **b** (of a series) that may be continued indefinitely. **5** *Gram.* (of a verb part) not limited by person or number, e.g. infinitive, gerund, and participle. —*n.* **1** (**the Infinite**) God. **2** (**the infinite**) infinite space. □□ **infinitely** *adv.* **infiniteness** *n.* [ME f. L *infinitus* (as IN-¹, FINITE)]

infinitesimal /ˌɪnfɪnɪˈtesɪm(ə)l/ *adj.* & *n.* —*adj.* infinitely or very small. —*n.* an infinitesimal amount. □ **infinitesimal calculus** the differential and integral calculuses regarded as one subject. □□ **infinitesimally** *adv.* [mod.L *infinitesimus* f. INFINITE: cf. CENTESIMAL]

infinitive /ɪnˈfɪnɪtɪv/ *n. & adj.* —*n.* a form of a verb expressing the verbal notion without reference to a particular subject, tense, etc. (e.g. *see* in *we came to see, let him see*). —*adj.* having this form. □□ **infinitival** /-ˈtaɪv(ə)l/ *adj.* **infinitivally** /-ˈtaɪvəlɪ/ *adv.* [L *infinitivus* (as IN-¹, *finitivus* definite f. *finire finit-* define)]

infinitude /ɪnˈfɪnɪˌtjuːd/ *n.* **1** the state of being infinite; boundlessness. **2** (often foll. by *of*) a boundless number or extent. [L *infinitus*: see INFINITE, -TUDE]

infinity /ɪnˈfɪnɪtɪ/ *n.* (*pl.* **-ies**) **1** the state of being infinite. **2** an infinite number or extent. **3** infinite distance. **4** *Math.* infinite quantity. ¶ Symb.: ∞. [ME f. OF *infinité* or L *infinitas* (as INFINITE)]

infirm /ɪnˈfɜːm/ *adj.* **1** physically weak, esp. through age. **2** (of a person, mind, judgement, etc.) weak, irresolute. □□ **infirmity** *n.* (*pl.* **-ies**). **infirmly** *adv.* [ME f. L *infirmus* (as IN-¹, FIRM¹)]

infirmary /ɪnˈfɜːmərɪ/ *n.* (*pl.* **-ies**) **1** a hospital. **2** a place for those who are ill in a monastery, school, etc. [med.L *infirmaria* (as INFIRM)]

infix *v. & n.* —*v.tr.* /ɪnˈfɪks/ **1** (often foll. by *in*) **a** fix (a thing in another). **b** impress (a fact etc. in the mind). **2** *Gram.* insert (a formative element) into the body of a word. —*n.* /ˈɪnfɪks/ *Gram.* a formative element inserted in a word. □□ **infixation** /-ˈseɪʃ(ə)n/ *n.* [L *infigere infix-* (as IN-², FIX): (n.) after *prefix, suffix*]

in flagrante delicto /ˌɪn fləˌɡræntɪ dɪˈlɪktəʊ/ *adj.* in the very act of committing an offence. [L, = in blazing crime]

inflame /ɪnˈfleɪm/ *v.* **1** *tr. & intr.* (often foll. by *with, by*) provoke or become provoked to strong feeling, esp. anger. **2** *Med.* **a** *intr.* become hot, reddened, and sore. **b** *tr.* cause inflammation or fever in (a body etc.); make hot. **3** *tr.* aggravate. **4** *intr. & tr.* catch or set on fire. **5** *tr.* light up with or as if with flames. □□ **inflamer** *n.* [ME f. OF *enflammer* f. L *inflammare* (as IN-², *flamma* flame)]

inflammable /ɪnˈflæməb(ə)l/ *adj. & n.* —*adj.* **1** easily set on fire; flammable. **2** easily excited. —*n.* (usu. in *pl.*) an inflammable substance. □□ **inflammability** /-ˈbɪlɪtɪ/ *n.* **inflammableness** *n.* **inflammably** *adv.* [INFLAME after F *inflammable*]

inflammation /ˌɪnfləˈmeɪʃ(ə)n/ *n.* **1** the act or an instance of inflaming. **2** *Med.* a localized physical condition with heat, swelling, redness, and usu. pain, esp. as a reaction to injury or infection. [L *inflammatio* (as INFLAME)]

inflammatory /ɪnˈflæmətərɪ/ *adj.* **1** (esp. of speeches, leaflets, etc.) tending to cause anger etc. **2** of or tending to inflammation of the body.

inflatable /ɪnˈfleɪtəb(ə)l/ *adj. & n.* —*adj.* that can be inflated. —*n.* an inflatable plastic or rubber object.

inflate /ɪnˈfleɪt/ *v.tr.* **1** distend (a balloon etc.) with air. **2** (usu. foll. by *with*; usu. in *passive*) puff up (a person with pride etc.). **3 a** (often *absol.*) bring about inflation (of the currency). **b** raise (prices) artificially. **4** (as **inflated** *adj.*) (esp. of language, sentiments, etc.) bombastic. □□ **inflatedly** *adv.* **inflatedness** *n.* **inflater** *n.* **inflator** *n.* [L *inflare inflat-* (as IN-², *flare* blow)]

inflation /ɪnˈfleɪʃ(ə)n/ *n.* **1 a** the act or condition of inflating or being inflated. **b** an instance of this. **2** *Econ.* **a** a general increase in prices and fall in the purchasing value of money. **b** an increase in available currency regarded as causing this. □□ **inflationary** *adj.* **inflationism** *n.* **inflationist** *n. & adj.* [ME f. L *inflatio* (as INFLATE)]

inflect /ɪnˈflekt/ *v.* **1** *tr.* change the pitch of (the voice, a musical note, etc.). **2** *Gram.* **a** *tr.* change the form of (a word) to express tense, gender, number, mood, etc. **b** *intr.* (of a word, language, etc.) undergo such change. **3** *tr.* bend inwards; curve. □□ **inflective** *adj.* [ME f. L *inflectere inflex-* (as IN-², *flectere* bend)]

inflection /ɪnˈflekʃ(ə)n/ *n.* (also **inflexion**) **1 a** the act or condition of inflecting or being inflected. **b** an instance of this. **2** *Gram.* **a** the process or practice of inflecting words. **b** an inflected form of a word. **c** a suffix etc. used to inflect, e.g. *-ed*. **3** a modulation of the voice. **4** *Geom.* a change of curvature from convex to concave at a particular point on a curve. □□ **inflectional** *adj.* **inflectionally** *adv.* **inflectionless** *adj.* [F *inflection* or L *inflexio* (as INFLECT)]

inflexible /ɪnˈfleksɪb(ə)l/ *adj.* **1** unbendable. **2** stiff; immovable; obstinate (*old and inflexible in his attitudes*). **3** unchangeable; inexorable. □□ **inflexibility** /-ˈbɪlɪtɪ/ *n.* **inflexibly** *adv.* [L *inflexibilis* (as IN-¹, FLEXIBLE)]

inflict /ɪnˈflɪkt/ *v.tr.* (usu. foll. by *on, upon*) **1** administer, deal (a stroke, wound, defeat, etc.). **2** (also *refl.*) often *joc.* impose (suffering, a penalty, oneself, one's company, etc.) on (*shall not inflict myself on you any longer*). □□ **inflictable** *adj.* **inflicter** *n.* **inflictor** *n.* [L *infligere inflict-* (as IN-², *fligere* strike)]

infliction /ɪnˈflɪkʃ(ə)n/ *n.* **1** the act or an instance of inflicting. **2** something inflicted, esp. a troublesome or boring experience. [LL *inflictio* (as INFLICT)]

inflight /ˈɪnflaɪt/ *attrib.adj.* occurring or provided during an aircraft flight.

inflorescence /ˌɪnfləˈres(ə)ns/ *n.* **1** *Bot.* **a** the complete flowerhead of a plant including stems, stalks, bracts, and flowers. **b** the arrangement of this. **2** the process of flowering. [mod.L *inflorescentia* f. LL *inflorescere* (as IN-², FLORESCENCE)]

inflow /ˈɪnfləʊ/ *n.* **1** a flowing in. **2** something that flows in. □□ **inflowing** *n. & adj.*

influence /ˈɪnfluəns/ *n. & v.* —*n.* **1 a** (usu. foll. by *on*) the effect a person or thing has on another. **b** (usu. foll. by *over, with*) moral ascendancy or power. **c** a thing or person exercising such power (*is a good influence on them*). **2** *Astrol.* an ethereal fluid supposedly flowing from the stars and affecting character and destiny. **3** *Electr. archaic* = INDUCTION. —*v.tr.* exert influence on; have an effect on. □ **under the influence** *colloq.* affected by alcoholic drink. □□ **influenceable** *adj.* **influencer** *n.* [ME f. OF *influence* or med.L *influentia* inflow f. L *influere* flow in (as IN-², *fluere* flow)]

influent /ˈɪnfluənt/ *adj. & n.* —*adj.* flowing in. —*n.* a tributary stream. [ME f. L (as INFLUENCE)]

influential /ˌɪnfluˈenʃ(ə)l/ *adj.* having a great influence or power (*influential in the financial world*). □□ **influentially** *adv.* [med.L *influentia* INFLUENCE]

influenza /ˌɪnfluˈenzə/ *n.* a highly contagious virus infection causing fever, severe aching, and catarrh, often occurring in epidemics. □□ **influenzal** *adj.* [It. f. med.L *influentia* INFLUENCE]

influx /ˈɪnflʌks/ *n.* **1** a continual stream of people or things (*an influx of complaints*). **2** (usu. foll. by *into*) a flowing in, esp. of a stream etc. [F *influx* or LL *influxus* (as IN-², FLUX)]

info /ˈɪnfəʊ/ *n. colloq.* information. [abbr.]

infold var. of ENFOLD.

inform /ɪnˈfɔːm/ *v.* **1** *tr.* (usu. foll. by *of, about, on,* or *that, how* + clause) tell (*informed them of their rights; informed us that the train was late*). **2** *intr.* (usu. foll. by *against, on*) make an accusation. **3** *tr.* (usu. foll. by *with*) *literary* inspire or imbue (a person, heart, or thing) with a feeling, principle, quality, etc. **4** *tr.* impart its quality to; permeate. □□ **informant** *n.* [ME f. OF *enfo(u)rmer* f. L *informare* give shape to, fashion, describe (as IN-², *forma* form)]

informal /ɪnˈfɔːm(ə)l/ *adj.* **1** without ceremony or formality (*just an informal chat*). **2** (of language, clothing, etc.) everyday; normal. □ **informal vote** NZ & Austral. an invalid vote or voting paper. □□ **informality** /-ˈmælɪtɪ/ *n.* (*pl.* **-ies**). **informally** *adv.*

informatics /ˌɪnfəˈmætɪks/ *n.pl.* (usu. treated as *sing.*) the science of processing data for storage and retrieval; information science. [transl. Russ. *informatika* (as INFORMATION, -ICS)]

information /ˌɪnfəˈmeɪʃ(ə)n/ *n.* **1 a** something told; knowledge. **b** (usu. foll. by *on, about*) items of knowledge; news (*the latest information on the crisis*). **2** *Law* (usu. foll. by *against*) a charge or complaint lodged with a court or magistrate. **3 a** the act of informing or telling. **b** an instance of this. **4 a** (in technical use) the content of one of two or more alternative sequences etc. that produce different responses in something and that can be stored in, transferred by, or communicated to inanimate things. **b** (in information theory) a mathematically defined quantity that represents the degree of choice exercised in forming one particular symbol-sequence or 'message' out of a number of possible ones. □ **information retrieval** the tracing of information stored in books, computers, etc. **information science** the study of the processes for storing and retrieving information. **information technology** a wide range of modern technologies based on the widespread availability of computing power for recording, transmitting, and disseminating information, and including computing science, telecommunications, printing, and broadcasting. **information theory** see separate entry. □□ **informational** adj. **informationally** adv. [ME f. OF f. L *informatio -onis* (as INFORM)]

information theory n. the mathematical theory of communication that deals with aspects and problems of the coding and transmission of 'information' (see INFORMATION 4). Its aim is to make it possible to find out how much information can be transmitted, and how fast, in any given situation, and it uses statistical concepts, such as probability, to assess the extra information (*redundancy*) needed to compensate for distortion and losses that may occur during transmission. In technological use the information is measured in 'bits' (i.e. binary digits: see BIT[4]), and information theory establishes the capacity of a channel (e.g. a telegraph line) to transmit information, expressed in bits per second. Information theory was developed (but not so named) by the American engineer Claude E. Shannon in the 1940s. It is of central importance in outlining the engineering requirements and limitations of computers and communications systems, and has greatly assisted the understanding of other processes, including thermodynamics and the use of language.

informative /ɪnˈfɔːmətɪv/ adj. (also **informatory** /ɪnˈfɔːmətərɪ/) giving information; instructive. □□ **informatively** adv. **informativeness** n. [med.L *informativus* (as INFORM)]

informed /ɪnˈfɔːmd/ adj. **1** knowing the facts; instructed (*his answers show that he is badly informed*). **2** educated; intelligent. □□ **informedly** /also ɪn ˈfɔːmɪdlɪ/ adv. **informedness** /also ɪnˈfɔːmɪdnɪs/ n.

informer /ɪnˈfɔːmə(r)/ n. **1** a person who informs against another. **2** a person who informs or advises.

infra /ˈɪnfrə/ adv. below, further on (in a book or writing). [L, = below]

infra- /ˈɪnfrə/ comb. form **1** below (opp. SUPRA-). **2** Anat. below or under a part of the body. [from or after L *infra* below, beneath]

infraclass /ˈɪnfrəˌklɑːs/ n. Biol. a taxonomic category below a subclass.

infraction /ɪnˈfrækʃ(ə)n/ n. esp. Law a violation or infringement. □□ **infract** v.tr. **infractor** n. [L *infractio* (as INFRINGE)]

infra dig /ˌɪnfrə ˈdɪg/ predic.adj. colloq. beneath one's dignity; unbecoming. [abbr. of L *infra dignitatem*]

infrangible /ɪnˈfrændʒɪb(ə)l/ adj. **1** unbreakable. **2** inviolable. □□ **infrangibility** /-ˈbɪlɪtɪ/ n. **infrangibleness** n. **infrangibly** adv. [obs.F *infrangible* or med.L *infrangibilis* (as IN-[1], FRANGIBLE)]

infrared /ˌɪnfrəˈred/ adj. **1** having a wavelength just greater than the red end of the visible light spectrum but less than that of radio waves. **2** of or using such radiation.

infrasonic /ˌɪnfrəˈsɒnɪk/ adj. of or relating to sound waves with a frequency below the lower limit of human audibility. □□ **infrasonically** adv.

infrasound /ˈɪnfrəˌsaʊnd/ n. sound waves with frequencies below the lower limit of human audibility.

infrastructure /ˈɪnfrəˌstrʌktʃə(r)/ n. **1 a** the basic structural foundations of a society or enterprise; a substructure or foundation. **b** roads, bridges, sewers, etc., regarded as a country's economic foundation. **2** permanent installations as a basis for military etc. operations. [F (as INFRA-, STRUCTURE)]

infrequent /ɪnˈfriːkwənt/ adj. not frequent. □□ **infrequency** n. **infrequently** adv. [L *infrequens* (as IN-[1], FREQUENT)]

infringe /ɪnˈfrɪndʒ/ v. **1** tr. **a** act contrary to; violate (a law, an oath, etc.). **b** act in defiance of (another's rights etc.). **2** intr. (usu. foll. by *on, upon*) encroach; trespass. □□ **infringement** n. **infringer** n. [L *infringere infract-* (as IN-[2], *frangere* break)]

infula /ˈɪnfjʊlə/ n. (pl. **infulae** /-ˌliː/) Eccl. either of the two ribbons on a bishop's mitre. [L, = woollen fillet worn by priest etc.]

infundibular /ˌɪnfʌnˈdɪbjʊlə(r)/ adj. funnel-shaped. [L *infundibulum* funnel f. *infundere* pour in (as IN-[2], *fundere* pour)]

infuriate v. & adj. —v.tr. /ɪnˈfjʊərɪˌeɪt/ fill with fury; enrage.

—adj. /ɪnˈfjʊərɪət/ literary excited to fury; frantic. □□ **infuriating** /ɪnˈfjʊərɪˌeɪtɪŋ/ adj. **infuriatingly** /ɪnˈfjʊərɪˌeɪtɪŋlɪ/ adv. **infuriation** /-ˈeɪʃ(ə)n/ n. [med.L *infuriare infuriat-* (as IN-[2], L *furia* FURY)]

infuse /ɪnˈfjuːz/ v. **1** tr. (usu. foll. by *with*) imbue; pervade (*anger infused with resentment*). **2** tr. steep (herbs, tea, etc.) in liquid to extract the content. **3** tr. (usu. foll. by *into*) instil (grace, spirit, life, etc.). **4** intr. undergo infusion (*let it infuse for five minutes*). **5** tr. (usu. foll. by *into*) pour (a thing). □□ **infusable** adj. **infuser** n. **infusive** /-sɪv/ adj. [ME f. L *infundere infus-* (as IN-[2], *fundere* pour)]

infusible /ɪnˈfjuːzɪb(ə)l/ adj. not able to be fused or melted. □□ **infusibility** /-ˈbɪlɪtɪ/ n.

infusion /ɪnˈfjuːʒ(ə)n/ n. **1** a liquid obtained by infusing. **2** an infused element; an admixture. **3** Med. a slow injection of a substance into a vein or tissue. **4 a** the act of infusing. **b** an instance of this. [ME f. F *infusion* or L *infusio* (as INFUSE)]

infusorial earth /ˌɪnfjuːˈzɔːrɪəl, -ˈsɔːrɪəl/ n. = KIESELGUHR. [mod.L *infusoria*, formerly a class of protozoa found in decaying animal or vegetable matter (as INFUSE)]

-ing[1] /ɪŋ/ suffix forming gerunds and nouns from verbs (or occas. from nouns), denoting: **1 a** the verbal action or its result (*asking; carving; fighting; learning*). **b** the verbal action as described or classified in some way (*tough going*). **2** material used for or associated with a process etc. (*piping; washing*). **3** an occupation or event (*banking; wedding*). **4** a set or arrangement of (*colouring; feathering*). [OE *-ung, -ing* f. Gmc]

-ing[2] /ɪŋ/ suffix **1** forming the present participle of verbs (*asking; fighting*), often as adjectives (*charming; strapping*). **2** forming adjectives from nouns (*hulking*) and verbs (*balding*). [ME alt. of OE *-ende*, later *-inde*]

-ing[3] /ɪŋ/ suffix forming nouns meaning 'one belonging to' or 'one having the quality of', surviving esp. in names of coins and fractional parts (*farthing; gelding; riding*). [OE f. Gmc]

ingather /ɪnˈgæðə(r)/ v.tr. gather in; assemble.

ingathering /ɪnˈgæðərɪŋ/ n. the act or an instance of gathering in, esp. of a harvest.

ingeminate /ɪnˈdʒemɪˌneɪt/ v.tr. literary repeat; reiterate. □ **ingeminate peace** constantly urge peace. [L *ingeminare ingeminat-* (as IN-[2], GEMINATE)]

ingenious /ɪnˈdʒiːnɪəs/ adj. **1** clever at inventing, constructing, organizing, etc.; skilful; resourceful. **2** (of a machine, theory, etc.) cleverly contrived. □□ **ingeniously** adv. **ingeniousness** n. [ME, = talented, f. F *ingénieux* or L *ingeniosus* f. *ingenium* cleverness: cf. ENGINE]

ingénue /ˌæʒeɪˈnjuː/ n. **1** an innocent or unsophisticated young woman. **2** Theatr. **a** such a part in a play. **b** the actress who plays this part. [F, fem. of *ingénu* INGENUOUS]

ingenuity /ˌɪndʒɪˈnjuːɪtɪ/ n. skill in devising or contriving; ingeniousness. [L *ingenuitas* ingenuousness (as INGENUOUS): Engl. meaning by confusion of INGENIOUS with INGENUOUS]

ingenuous /ɪnˈdʒenjʊəs/ adj. **1** innocent; artless. **2** open; frank. □□ **ingenuously** adv. **ingenuousness** n. [L *ingenuus* free-born, frank (as IN-[2], root of *gignere* beget)]

ingest /ɪnˈdʒest/ v.tr. **1** take in (food etc.); eat. **2** absorb (facts, knowledge, etc.). □□ **ingestion** /ɪnˈdʒestʃ(ə)n/ n. **ingestive** adj. [L *ingerere ingest-* (as IN-[2], *gerere* carry)]

inglenook /ˈɪŋg(ə)lˌnʊk/ n. a space within the opening on either side of a large fireplace. [dial. (orig. Sc.) *ingle* fire burning on a hearth, perh. f. Gael. *aingeal* fire, light, + NOOK]

inglorious /ɪnˈglɔːrɪəs/ adj. **1** shameful; ignominious. **2** not famous. □□ **ingloriously** adv. **ingloriousness** n.

-ingly /ɪŋlɪ/ suffix forming adverbs esp. denoting manner of action or nature or condition (*dotingly; charmingly; slantingly*).

ingoing /ˈɪnˌgəʊɪŋ/ adj. **1** going in; entering. **2** penetrating; thorough.

ingot /ˈɪŋgɒt, -gət/ n. a usu. oblong piece of cast metal, esp. of gold, silver, or steel. [ME: perh. f. IN[1] + *goten* past part. of OE *geotan* cast]

ingraft var. of ENGRAFT.

ingrain /ˈɪngreɪn/ adj. **1** inherent; ingrained. **2** (of textiles) dyed in the fibre, before being woven. □ **ingrain carpet** a reversible carpet, with different colours interwoven.

ingrained /ɪnˈɡreɪnd, attrib. ˈɪn-/ adj. **1** deeply rooted; inveterate. **2** thorough. **3** (of dirt etc.) deeply embedded. □□ **ingrainedly** /-ˈɡreɪnɪdlɪ/ adv. [var. of engrained: see ENGRAIN]

ingrate /ˈɪnɡreɪt, -ˈɡreɪt/ n. & adj. formal or literary —n. an ungrateful person. —adj. ungrateful. [ME f. L ingratus (as IN-[1], gratus grateful)]

ingratiate /ɪnˈɡreɪʃɪˌeɪt/ v.refl. (usu. foll. by with) bring oneself into favour. □□ **ingratiating** adj. **ingratiatingly** adv. **ingratiation** /-ˈeɪʃ(ə)n/ n. [L in gratiam into favour]

ingratitude /ɪnˈɡrætɪˌtjuːd/ n. a lack of due gratitude. [ME f. OF ingratitude or LL ingratitudo (as INGRATE)]

ingravescent /ˌɪnɡrəˈves(ə)nt/ adj. Med. (of a disease etc.) growing worse. □□ **ingravescence** n. [L ingravescere (as IN-[2], gravescere grow heavy f. gravis heavy)]

ingredient /ɪnˈɡriːdɪənt/ n. a component part or element in a recipe, mixture, or combination. [ME f. L ingredi ingress- enter (as IN-[2], gradi step)]

Ingres /ˈæ̃ɡrə/, Jean Auguste Dominique (1780–1867), French painter, David's pupil and successor, the most generally admired of his day, rival of Delacroix, and upholder of classicism. He was a doctrinaire teacher, who forbade his students to look at the works of Rubens, and was fully accepted by the Establishment, becoming a Senator in 1862. Ingres is a puzzling artist: his portraits are sentimental, his nudes have a strong almost cruelly sensuous quality, but as a draughtsman he is supreme. In his feeling for pure form his true heirs are Degas, Matisse, and Picasso.

ingress /ˈɪnɡres/ n. **1** the act or right of going in or entering. **2** Astron. the start of an eclipse or transit. □□ **ingression** /ɪnˈɡreʃ(ə)n/ n. [ME f. L ingressus (as INGREDIENT)]

in-group /ˈɪnɡruːp/ n. a small exclusive group of people with a common interest.

ingrowing /ˈɪnˌɡrəʊɪŋ/ adj. growing inwards, esp. (of a toenail) growing into the flesh. □□ **ingrown** adj. **ingrowth** n.

inguinal /ˈɪnɡwɪn(ə)l/ adj. of the groin. □□ **inguinally** adv. [L inguinalis f. inguen -inis groin]

ingulf var. of ENGULF.

ingurgitate /ɪnˈɡɜːdʒɪˌteɪt/ v.tr. **1** swallow greedily. **2** engulf. □□ **ingurgitation** /-ˈteɪʃ(ə)n/ n. [L ingurgitare ingurgitat- (as IN-[2], gurges gurgitis whirlpool)]

inhabit /ɪnˈhæbɪt/ v.tr. (**inhabited, inhabiting**) (of a person or animal) dwell in; occupy (a region, town, house, etc.). □□ **inhabitability** /-təˈbɪlɪtɪ/ n. **inhabitable** adj. **inhabitant** n. **inhabitation** /-ˈteɪʃ(ə)n/ n. [ME inhabite, enhabite f. OF enhabiter or L inhabitare (as IN-[2], habitare dwell): see HABIT]

inhabitancy /ɪnˈhæbɪtənsɪ/ n. (also **inhabitance** /-t(ə)ns/) residence as an inhabitant, esp. during a specified period so as to acquire rights etc.

inhalant /ɪnˈheɪlənt/ n. a medicinal preparation for inhaling.

inhale /ɪnˈheɪl/ v.tr. (often absol.) breathe in (air, gas, tobacco-smoke, etc.). □□ **inhalation** /-həˈleɪʃ(ə)n/ n. [L inhalare breathe in (as IN-[2], halare breathe)]

inhaler /ɪnˈheɪlə(r)/ n. a portable device used for relieving esp. asthma by inhaling.

inharmonic /ˌɪnhɑːˈmɒnɪk/ adj. esp. Mus. not harmonic.

inharmonious /ˌɪnhɑːˈməʊnɪəs/ adj. esp. Mus. not harmonious. □□ **inharmoniously** adv.

inhere /ɪnˈhɪə(r)/ v.intr. (often foll. by in) **1** exist essentially or permanently in (goodness inheres in that child). **2** (of rights etc.) be vested in (a person etc.). [L inhaerere inhaes- (as IN-[2], haerere to stick)]

inherent /ɪnˈhɪərənt, ɪnˈherənt/ adj. (often foll. by in) **1** existing in something, esp. as a permanent or characteristic attribute. **2** vested in (a person etc.) as a right or privilege. □□ **inherence** n. **inherently** adv. [L inhaerere inhaerent- (as INHERE)]

inherit /ɪnˈherɪt/ v. (**inherited, inheriting**) **1** tr. receive (property, rank, title, etc.) by legal descent or succession. **2** tr. derive (a quality or characteristic) genetically from one's ancestors. **3** absol. succeed as an heir (a younger son rarely inherits). □□

inheritor n. (fem. **inheritress** or **inheritrix**). [ME f. OF enheriter f. LL inhereditare (as IN-[2], L heres heredis heir)]

inheritable /ɪnˈherɪtəb(ə)l/ adj. **1** capable of being inherited. **2** capable of inheriting. □□ **inheritability** /-ˈbɪlɪtɪ/ n. [ME f. AF (as INHERIT)]

inheritance /ɪnˈherɪt(ə)ns/ n. **1** something that is inherited. **2 a** the act of inheriting. **b** an instance of this. □ **inheritance tax** a tax levied on property etc. acquired by gift or inheritance. ¶ Introduced in the UK in 1986 to replace Capital Transfer Tax. [ME f. AF inheritaunce f. OF enheriter: see INHERIT]

inhesion /ɪnˈhiːʒ(ə)n/ n. formal the act or fact of inhering. [LL inhaesio (as INHERE)]

inhibit /ɪnˈhɪbɪt/ v.tr. (**inhibited, inhibiting**) **1** hinder, restrain, or prevent (an action or progress). **2** (as **inhibited** adj.) subject to inhibition. **3 a** (usu. foll. by from + verbal noun) forbid or prohibit (a person etc.). **b** (esp. in ecclesiastical law) forbid (an ecclesiastic) to exercise clerical functions. □□ **inhibitive** adj. **inhibitor** n. **inhibitory** adj. [L inhibēre (as IN-[2], habēre hold)]

inhibition /ˌɪnhɪˈbɪʃ(ə)n/ n. **1** Psychol. a restraint on the direct expression of an instinct. **2** colloq. an emotional resistance to a thought, an action, etc. (has inhibitions about singing in public). **3** Law an order forbidding alteration to property rights. **4 a** the act of inhibiting. **b** the process of being inhibited. [ME f. OF inhibition or L inhibitio (as INHIBIT)]

inhomogeneous /ɪnˌhɒməˈdʒiːnɪəs, ˌɪnˌhəʊm-/ adj. not homogeneous. □□ **inhomogeneity** /-dʒɪˈniːɪtɪ/ n.

inhospitable /ˌɪnhɒˈspɪtəb(ə)l, ɪnˈhɒsp-/ adj. **1** not hospitable. **2** (of a region, coast, etc.) not affording shelter etc. □□ **inhospitableness** n. **inhospitably** adv. [obs. F (as IN-[1], HOSPITABLE)]

inhospitality /ɪnˌhɒspɪˈtælɪtɪ/ n. the act or process of being inhospitable. [L inhospitalitas (as IN-[1], HOSPITALITY)]

in-house /ˈɪnhaʊs, -ˈhaʊs/ adj. & adv. —adj. done or existing within an institution, company, etc. (an in-house project). —adv. internally, without outside assistance.

inhuman /ɪnˈhjuːmən/ adj. **1** (of a person, conduct, etc.) brutal; unfeeling; barbarous. **2** not of a human type. □□ **inhumanly** adv. [L inhumanus (as IN-[1], HUMAN)]

inhumane /ˌɪnhjuːˈmeɪn/ adj. not humane. □□ **inhumanely** adv. [L inhumanus (see INHUMAN) & f. IN-[1] + HUMANE, orig. = INHUMAN]

inhumanity /ˌɪnhjuːˈmænɪtɪ/ n. (pl. **-ies**) **1** brutality; barbarousness; callousness. **2** an inhumane act.

inhume /ɪnˈhjuːm/ v.tr. literary bury. □□ **inhumation** /-ˈmeɪʃ(ə)n/ n. [L inhumare (as IN-[2], humus ground)]

inimical /ɪˈnɪmɪk(ə)l/ adj. (usu. foll. by to) **1** hostile. **2** harmful. □□ **inimically** adv. [LL inimicalis f. L inimicus (as IN-[1], amicus friend)]

inimitable /ɪˈnɪmɪtəb(ə)l/ adj. impossible to imitate. □□ **inimitability** /-ˈbɪlɪtɪ/ n. **inimitableness** n. **inimitably** adv. [F inimitable or L inimitabilis (as IN-[1], imitabilis imitable)]

iniquity /ɪˈnɪkwɪtɪ/ n. (pl. **-ies**) **1** wickedness; unrighteousness. **2** a gross injustice. □□ **iniquitous** adj. **iniquitously** adv. **iniquitousness** n. [ME f. OF iniquité f. L iniquitas -tatis f. iniquus (as IN-[1], aequus just)]

initial /ɪˈnɪʃ(ə)l/ adj., n., & v. —adj. of, existing, or occurring at the beginning (initial stage; initial expenses). —n. **1** = initial letter. **2** (usu. in pl.) the first letter or letters of the words of a (esp. a person's) name or names. —v.tr. (**initialled, initialling**; US **initialed, initialing**) mark or sign with one's initials. □ **initial letter** (or **consonant**) a letter or consonant at the beginning of a word. **initial teaching alphabet** a 44-letter phonetic alphabet used to help those beginning to read and write English. □□ **initially** adv. [L initialis f. initium beginning f. inire init- go in]

initialism /ɪˈnɪʃəˌlɪz(ə)m/ n. a group of initial letters used as an abbreviation for a name or expression, each letter being pronounced separately (e.g. BBC) (cf. ACRONYM).

initialize /ɪˈnɪʃəˌlaɪz/ v.tr. (also **-ise**) (often foll. by to) Computing set to the value or put in the condition appropriate to the start of an operation. □□ **initialization** /-ˈzeɪʃ(ə)n/ n.

initiate v., n., & adj. —v.tr. /ɪˈnɪʃɪˌeɪt/ **1** begin; set going; originate. **2 a** (usu. foll. by *into*) admit (a person) into a society, an office, a secret, etc., esp. with a ritual. **b** (usu. foll. by *in*, *into*) instruct (a person) in science, art, etc. —n. /ɪˈnɪʃɪət/ a person who has been newly initiated. —adj. /ɪˈnɪʃɪət/ (of a person) newly initiated (*an initiate member*). □□ **initiation** /-ˈeɪʃ(ə)n/ n. **initiator** n. **initiatory** /ɪˈnɪʃɪətərɪ, ɪˈnɪʃətərɪ/ adj. [L *initiare* f. *initium*: see INITIAL]

initiative /ɪˈnɪʃətɪv, ɪˈnɪʃɪətɪv/ n. & adj. —n. **1** the ability to initiate things; enterprise (*I'm afraid he lacks all initiative*). **2** a first step; origination (*a peace initiative*). **3** the power or right to begin something. **4** Polit. (esp. in Switzerland and some US States) the right of citizens outside the legislature to originate legislation. —adj. beginning; originating. □ **have the initiative** esp. Mil. be able to control the enemy's movements. **on one's own initiative** without being prompted by others. **take the initiative** (usu. foll. by *in* + verbal noun) be the first to take action. [F (as INITIATE)]

inject /ɪnˈdʒekt/ v.tr. **1** Med. **a** (usu. foll. by *into*) drive or force (a solution, medicine, etc.) by or as if by a syringe. **b** (usu. foll. by *with*) fill (a cavity etc.) by injecting. **c** administer medicine etc. to (a person) by injection. **2** place or insert (an object, a quality, etc.) into something (*may I inject a note of realism?*). □□ **injectable** adj. & n. **injector** n. [L *injicere* (as IN-², *jacere* throw)]

injection /ɪnˈdʒekʃ(ə)n/ n. **1 a** the act of injecting. **b** an instance of this. **2** a liquid or solution (to be) injected (*prepare a morphine injection*). □ **injection moulding** the shaping of rubber or plastic articles by injecting heated material into a mould. [F *injection* or L *injectio* (as INJECT)]

injudicious /ˌɪndʒuːˈdɪʃəs/ adj. unwise; ill-judged. □□ **injudiciously** adv. **injudiciousness** n.

Injun /ˈɪndʒ(ə)n/ n. colloq. US or dial. an American Indian. [corrupt.]

injunction /ɪnˈdʒʌŋkʃ(ə)n/ n. **1** an authoritative warning or order. **2** Law a judicial order restraining a person from an act or compelling redress to an injured party. □□ **injunctive** adj. [LL *injunctio* f. L *injungere* ENJOIN]

injure /ˈɪndʒə(r)/ v.tr. **1** do physical harm or damage to; hurt (*was injured in a road accident*). **2** harm or impair (*illness might injure her chances*). **3** do wrong to. □□ **injurer** n. [back-form. f. INJURY]

injured /ˈɪndʒəd/ adj. **1** harmed or hurt (*the injured passengers*). **2** offended; wronged (*in an injured tone*).

injurious /ɪnˈdʒʊərɪəs/ adj. **1** hurtful. **2** (of language) insulting; libellous. **3** wrongful. □□ **injuriously** adv. **injuriousness** n. [ME f. F *injurieux* or L *injuriosus* (as INJURY)]

injury /ˈɪndʒərɪ/ n. (pl. **-ies**) **1 a** physical harm or damage. **b** an instance of this (*suffered head injuries*). **2** esp. Law a wrongful action or treatment. **b** an instance of this. **3** damage to one's good name etc. □ **injury time** Brit. Football extra playing-time allowed by a referee to compensate for time lost in dealing with injuries. [ME f. AF *injurie* f. L *injuria* a wrong (as IN-¹, *jus juris* right)]

injustice /ɪnˈdʒʌstɪs/ n. **1** a lack of fairness or justice. **2** an unjust act. □ **do a person an injustice** judge a person unfairly. [ME f. OF f. L *injustitia* (as IN-¹, JUSTICE)]

ink /ɪŋk/ n. & v. —n. **1 a** a coloured fluid used for writing with a pen, marking with a rubber stamp, etc. **b** a thick paste used in printing, duplicating, in ball-point pens, etc. (See below.) **2** Zool. a black liquid ejected by a cuttlefish, octopus, etc. to confuse a predator. —v.tr. **1** (usu. foll. by *in*, *over*, etc.) mark with ink. **2** cover (type etc.) with ink before printing. **3** apply ink to. **4** (as **inked** adj.) Austral. sl. drunk. □ **ink-blot test** = RORSCHACH TEST. **ink-cap** any fungus of the genus *Coprinus*. **ink-horn** hist. a small portable horn container for ink. **ink out** obliterate with ink. **ink-pad** an ink-soaked pad, usu. in a box, used for inking a rubber stamp etc. **ink-well** a pot for ink usu. housed in a hole in a desk. □□ **inker** n. [ME *enke*, *inke* f. OF *enque* f. LL *encau(s)tum* f. Gk *egkauston* purple ink used by Roman emperors for signature (as IN-², CAUSTIC)]

The ancient Egyptians and Chinese made ink from lampblack mixed with gum or glue; such inks continued in use in medieval Europe. Plant juices and other substances were also used as colouring-matter, especially an extract of tannin with a soluble iron salt. Oil-based printing inks were developed in the mid-15th c. and used for over three hundred years. Synthetic dyes, developed in the 1860s, provided a better colouring-matter, chemical drying-agents appeared, and by the early 20th c. ink-making for various purposes had become a complicated industrial process. Ball-point pens use an oil-based ink that dries almost instantly.

Inkatha /ɪŋˈkɑːtə/ n. a Zulu organization, first founded in 1928 by the Zulu king Solomon as a cultural and social movement, revived by Chief Buthelezi in 1975. Its current aim is to achieve a single South African State with equality for all. It is supported almost universally by the Zulus, and opposed by the Xhosas who favour the ANC. [Zulu *inKhata* (tribal emblem) crown of woven grass symbolizing the nation's unifying force]

inkling /ˈɪŋklɪŋ/ n. (often foll. by *of*) a slight knowledge or suspicion; a hint. [ME *inkle* utter in an undertone, of unkn. orig.]

inkstand /ˈɪŋkstænd/ n. a stand for one or more ink bottles, often incorporating a pen tray etc.

inky /ˈɪŋkɪ/ adj. (**inkier**, **inkiest**) of, as black as, or stained with ink. □□ **inkiness** n.

INLA abbr. Irish National Liberation Army, a terrorist organization seeking to achieve union between Northern Ireland and the Irish Republic.

inlaid past and past part. of INLAY.

inland /ˈɪnlənd, ˈɪnlænd/ adj., n., & adv. —adj. **1** situated in the interior of a country. **2** esp. Brit. carried on within the limits of a country; domestic (*inland trade*). —n. the parts of a country remote from the sea or frontiers; the interior. —adv. /ɪnˈlænd/ in or towards the interior of a country. □ **inland duty** a tax payable on inland trade. **inland revenue** Brit. revenue consisting of taxes and inland duties. **Inland Revenue** (in the UK) the government department responsible for assessing and collecting such taxes. □□ **inlander** n. **inlandish** adj.

in-law /ˈɪnlɔː/ n. (often in pl.) a relative by marriage.

inlay v. & n. —v.tr. /ɪnˈleɪ/ (past and past part. **inlaid** /ɪnˈleɪd/) **1 a** (usu. foll. by *in*) embed (a thing in another) so that the surfaces are even. **b** (usu. foll. by *with*) ornament (a thing with inlaid work). **2** (as **inlaid** adj.) (of a piece of furniture etc.) ornamented by inlaying. **3** insert (a page, an illustration, etc.) in a space cut in a larger thicker page. —n. /ˈɪnleɪ/ **1** inlaid work. **2** material inlaid. **3** a filling shaped to fit a tooth-cavity. □□ **inlayer** n. [IN-² + LAY¹]

inlet /ˈɪnlet, -lɪt/ n. **1** a small arm of the sea, a lake, or a river. **2** a piece inserted, esp. in dressmaking etc. **3** a way of entry. [ME f. IN + LET¹ v.]

inlier /ˈɪnˌlaɪə(r)/ n. Geol. a structure or area of older rocks completely surrounded by newer rocks. [IN, after *outlier*]

in-line /ˈɪnlaɪn/ adj. **1** having parts arranged in a line. **2** constituting an integral part of a continuous sequence of operations or machines.

in loco parentis /ɪn ˌləʊkəʊ pəˈrentɪs/ adv. in the place or position of a parent (used of a teacher etc. responsible for children). [L]

inly /ˈɪnlɪ/ adv. poet. **1** inwardly; in the heart. **2** intimately; thoroughly. [OE *innlīce* (as IN, -LY²)]

inlying /ˈɪnˌlaɪɪŋ/ adj. situated within, or near a centre.

Inmarsat /ˈɪnmɑːˌsæt/ n. an international organization, founded in 1978 and with headquarters in London, that operates a system of satellites to provide telephone, telex, and data and facsimile transmission, as well as distress and safety telecommunication services to the world's shipping, aviation, and offshore industries. [International Maritime Satellite Organization]

inmate /ˈɪnmeɪt/ n. (usu. foll. by *of*) **1** an occupant of a hospital, prison, institution, etc. **2** an occupant of a house etc., esp. one of several. [prob. orig. INN + MATE¹, assoc. with IN]

in medias res /ɪn ˌmiːdɪæs ˈreɪz/ adv. **1** into the midst of things. **2** into the middle of a story, without preamble. [L]

in memoriam /ɪn mɪˈmɔːrɪˌæm/ prep. & n. —prep. in memory of (a dead person). —*n*. a written article or notice etc. in memory of a dead person; an obituary. [L]

inmost /'ɪnməʊst, -məst/ *adj.* **1** most inward. **2** most intimate; deepest. [OE *innemest* (as IN, -MOST)]

inn /ɪn/ *n.* **1** a public house providing alcoholic liquor for consumption on the premises, and sometimes accommodation etc. **2** *hist.* a house providing accommodation, esp. for travellers. □ **Inn of Court** *Brit. Law* **1** each of the four legal societies having the exclusive right of admitting people to the English bar. Originally there were a number of these societies, the chief being the ones now remaining—Lincoln's Inn, the Inner Temple, the Middle Temple, and Gray's Inn; subordinate to them were a number of Inns of Chancery, all of which have ceased to exist. **2** any of the sets of buildings in London belonging to these societies. **3** a similar society in Ireland. **Inns of Chancery** *Brit. hist.* buildings in London formerly used as hostels for law students. [OE *inn* (as IN)]

innards /'ɪnədz/ *n.pl. colloq.* **1** entrails. **2** works (of an engine etc.). [dial. etc. pronunc. of *inwards*: see INWARD n.]

innate /ɪ'neɪt, 'ɪ-/ *adj.* **1** inborn; natural. **2** *Philos.* originating in the mind. □□ **innately** *adv.* **innateness** *n.* [ME f. L *innatus* (as IN-², *natus* past part. of *nasci* be born)]

inner /'ɪnə(r)/ *adj. & n.* —*adj.* (usu. *attrib.*) **1** further in; inside; interior (*the inner compartment*). **2** (of thoughts, feelings, etc.) deeper; more secret. —*n. Archery* **1** a division of the target next to the bull's-eye. **2** a shot that strikes this. □ **inner bar** *Brit. Law* Queen's or King's Counsel collectively. **inner city** the central most densely populated area of a city (also (with hyphen) *attrib.*: *inner-city housing*). **inner-directed** *Psychol.* governed by standards formed in childhood. **inner man** (or **woman**) **1** the soul or mind. **2** *joc.* the stomach. **inner planet** an inferior planet (see INFERIOR *adj.* 3). **inner space 1** the region between the earth and outer space, or below the surface of the sea. **2** the part of the mind not normally accessible to consciousness. **inner-spring** *US* = *interior-sprung*. **Inner Temple** one of the two Inns of Court on the site of the Temple in London (cf. *Middle Temple*). **inner tube** a separate inflatable tube inside the cover of a pneumatic tyre. □□ **innerly** *adv.* **innermost** *adj.* **innerness** *n.* [OE *innera* (adj.), compar. of IN]

Inner Mongolia an autonomous region of northern China; pop. (est. 1986) 20,290,000; capital, Hohhot.

innervate /'ɪnəˌveɪt, ɪ'nɜː-/ *v.tr.* supply (an organ etc.) with nerves. □□ **innervation** /-'veɪʃ(ə)n/ *n.* [IN-² + L *nervus* nerve + -ATE³]

inning /'ɪnɪŋ/ *n. US* an innings at baseball etc. [in (v.) go in (f. IN)]

innings /'ɪnɪŋz/ *n.* (*pl.* same or *colloq.* **inningses**) **1** *Cricket* **a** the part of a game during which a side is in or batting. **b** the play of or score achieved by a player during a turn at batting. **2** a period during which a government, party, cause, etc. is in office or effective. **3 a** a period during which a person can achieve something. **b** *colloq.* a person's life span (*had a good innings and died at 94*).

innkeeper /'ɪnˌkiːpə(r)/ *n.* a person who keeps an inn.

innocent /'ɪnəs(ə)nt/ *adj. & n.* —*adj.* **1** free from moral wrong; sinless. **2** (usu. foll. by *of*) not guilty (of a crime etc.). **3 a** simple; guileless; naïve. **b** pretending to be guileless. **4** harmless. **5** (foll. by *of*) *colloq.* without, lacking (*appeared, innocent of shoes*). —*n.* **1** an innocent person, esp. a young child. **2** (in *pl.*) the young children killed by Herod after the birth of Jesus (Matt. 2: 16). □ **Innocents'** (or **Holy Innocents'**) **Day** the day, 28 Dec., commemorating the massacre of the innocents. □□ **innocence** *n.* **innocency** *n.* **innocently** *adv.* [ME f. OF *innocent* or L *innocens innocent-* (as IN-¹, *nocēre* hurt)]

innocuous /ɪ'nɒkjʊəs/ *adj.* **1** not injurious; harmless. **2** inoffensive. □□ **innocuity** /ˌɪnəˈkjuːɪtɪ/ *n.* **innocuously** *adv.* **innocuousness** *n.* [L *innocuus* (as IN-¹, *nocuus* formed as INNOCENT)]

innominate /ɪ'nɒmɪnət/ *adj.* unnamed. □ **innominate bone** *n. Anat.* the bone formed from the fusion of the ilium, ischium, and pubis; the hip-bone. [LL *innominatus* (as IN-¹, NOMINATE)]

innovate /'ɪnəˌveɪt/ *v.intr.* **1** bring in new methods, ideas, etc. **2**

(often foll. by *in*) make changes. □□ **innovation** /-'veɪʃ(ə)n/ *n.* **innovational** /-'veɪʃən(ə)l/ *adj.* **innovator** *n.* **innovative** *adj.* **innovatory** /-ˌveɪtərɪ/ *adj.* [L *innovare* make new, alter (as IN-², *novus* new)]

innoxious /ɪ'nɒkʃəs/ *adj.* harmless. □□ **innoxiously** *adv.* **innoxiousness** *n.* [L *innoxius* (as IN-¹, NOXIOUS)]

Innsbruck /'ɪnzbrʊk/ a city of western Austria, a winter sports centre and capital of Tyrol; pop. (1981) 117,300.

innuendo /ˌɪnjuˈendəʊ/ *n. & v.* —*n.* (*pl.* **-oes** or **-os**) **1** an allusive or oblique remark or hint, usu. disparaging. **2** a remark with a double meaning, usu. suggestive. —*v.intr.* (**-oes**, **-oed**) make innuendoes. [L, = by nodding at, by pointing to: ablat. gerund of *innuere* nod at (as IN-², *nuere* nod)]

Innuit var. of INUIT.

innumerable /ɪ'njuːmərəb(ə)l/ *adj.* too many to be counted. □□ **innumerability** /-'bɪlɪtɪ/ *n.* **innumerably** *adv.* [ME f. L *innumerabilis* (as IN-¹, NUMERABLE)]

innumerate /ɪ'njuːmərət/ *adj.* having no knowledge of or feeling for mathematical operations; not numerate. □□ **innumeracy** /-əsɪ/ *n.* [IN-¹, NUMERATE]

innutrition /ˌɪnjuːˈtrɪʃ(ə)n/ *n.* lack of nutrition. □□ **innutritious** *adj.*

inobservance /ˌɪnəbˈzɜːv(ə)ns/ *n.* **1** inattention. **2** (usu. foll. by *of*) non-observance (of a law etc.). [F *inobservance* or L *inobservantia* (as IN-¹, OBSERVANCE)]

inoculate /ɪ'nɒkjʊˌleɪt/ *v.tr.* **1 a** treat (a person or animal) with a small quantity of the agent of a disease, in the form of vaccine or serum, usu. by injection, to promote immunity against the disease. **b** implant (a disease) by means of vaccine. **2** instil (a person) with ideas or opinions. □□ **inoculable** *adj.* **inoculation** /-'leɪʃ(ə)n/ *n.* **inoculative** /-lətɪv/ *adj.* **inoculator** *n.* [orig. in sense 'insert (a bud) into a plant': L *inoculare inoculat-* engraft (as IN-², *oculus* eye, bud)]

inoculum /ɪ'nɒkjʊləm/ *n.* (*pl.* **inocula** /-lə/) any substance used for inoculation. [mod.L (as INOCULATE)]

inodorous /ɪn'əʊdərəs/ *adj.* having no smell; odourless.

in-off /'ɪnɒf/ *n. Billiards* the act of pocketing a ball by bouncing it off another ball.

inoffensive /ˌɪnəˈfensɪv/ *adj.* not objectionable; harmless. □□ **inoffensively** *adv.* **inoffensiveness** *n.*

inoperable /ɪn'ɒpərəb(ə)l/ *adj.* **1** *Surgery* that cannot suitably be operated on (*inoperable cancer*). **2** that cannot be operated; inoperative. □□ **inoperability** /-'bɪlɪtɪ/ *n.* **inoperably** *adv.* [F *inopérable* (as IN-¹, OPERABLE)]

inoperative /ɪn'ɒpərətɪv/ *adj.* not working or taking effect.

inopportune /ɪn'ɒpəˌtjuːn/ *adj.* not appropriate, esp. as regards time; unseasonable. □□ **inopportunely** *adv.* **inopportuneness** *n.* [L *inopportunus* (as IN-¹, OPPORTUNE)]

inordinate /ɪn'ɔːdɪnət/ *adj.* **1** immoderate; excessive. **2** intemperate. **3** disorderly. □□ **inordinately** *adv.* [ME f. L *inordinatus* (as IN-¹, *ordinatus* past part. of *ordinare* ORDAIN)]

inorganic /ˌɪnɔːˈgænɪk/ *adj.* **1** *Chem.* (of a compound) not organic, usu. of mineral origin (opp. ORGANIC). **2** without organized physical structure. **3** not arising by natural growth; extraneous. **4** *Philol.* not explainable by normal etymology. □ **inorganic chemistry** the chemistry of inorganic compounds. □□ **inorganically** *adv.*

inosculate /ɪn'ɒskjʊˌleɪt/ *v.intr. & tr.* **1** join by running together. **2** join closely. □□ **inosculation** /-'leɪʃ(ə)n/ *n.* [IN-² + L *osculare* provide with a mouth f. *osculum* dimin. of *os* mouth]

in-patient /'ɪnˌpeɪʃ(ə)nt/ *n.* a patient who lives in hospital while under treatment.

in propria persona /ɪn ˌprəʊprɪə pɜːˈsəʊnə/ *adv.* in his or her own person. [L]

input /'ɪnpʊt/ *n. & v.* —*n.* **1** what is put in or taken in, or operated on by any process or system. **2** *Electronics* **a** a place where, or a device through which, energy, information, etc., enters a system (*a tape recorder with inputs for microphone and radio*). **b** energy supplied to a device or system; an electrical signal. **3** the information fed into a computer. **4** the action or

b *but* d *dog* f *few* g *get* h *he* j *yes* k *cat* l *leg* m *man* n *no* p *pen* r *red* s *sit* t *top* v *voice*

process of putting in or feeding in. **5** a contribution of information etc. —*v.tr.* (**inputting**; *past* and *past part.* **input** or **inputted**) (often foll. by *into*) **1** put in. **2** *Computing* supply (data, programs, etc., to a computer, program, etc.). □ **input-** (or **input/**) **output** *Computing* etc. of, relating to, or for input and output. □□ **inputter** *n.*

inquest /ˈɪnkwest, ˈɪŋ-/ *n.* **1** *Law* **a** an inquiry by a coroner's court into the cause of a death. **b** a judicial inquiry to ascertain the facts relating to an incident etc. **c** a coroner's jury. **2** *colloq.* a discussion analysing the outcome of a game, an election, etc. [ME f. OF *enqueste* (as ENQUIRE)]

inquietude /ɪnˈkwaɪɪˌtjuːd, ɪŋ-/ *n.* uneasiness of mind or body. [ME f. OF *inquietude* or LL *inquietudo* f. L *inquietus* (as IN-[1], *quietus* quiet)]

inquiline /ˈɪnkwɪˌlaɪn, ˈɪŋk-/ *n.* an animal living in the home of another; a commensal. □□ **inquilinous** /-ˈlaɪnəs/ *adj.* [L *inquilinus* sojourner (as IN-[2], *colere* dwell)]

inquire /ɪnˈkwaɪə(r), ɪŋ-/ *v.* **1** *intr.* seek information formally; make a formal investigation. **2** *intr.* & *tr.* = ENQUIRE. □□ **inquirer** *n.* [var. of ENQUIRE]

inquiry /ɪnˈkwaɪərɪ, ɪŋ-/ *n.* (*pl.* **-ies**) **1** an investigation, esp. an official one. **2** = ENQUIRY. □ **inquiry agent** *Brit.* a private detective.

Inquisition *n.* an ecclesiastical court established *c.*1232 for the detection of heretics, at a time when certain heretical groups threatened not only religion but the institutions of contemporary society. Its officials were chiefly Dominicans and Franciscans, and it became notorious for the use of torture (though at the time this was part of accepted judicial procedure); in grave cases the penalties, inflicted by the civil authorities, included death at the stake. The 'Spanish Inquisition' was a separate body, established in 1479 by the Spanish monarchy (with papal approval), and was a political instrument, directed originally against converts from Judaism and Islam but later also against Protestants, operating with great severity especially under its first inquisitor, Torquemada; it was finally suppressed in 1820. In 1542 the medieval Inquisition was assigned by Pope Paul III to a Church department, the Congregation of the Inquisition or Holy Office. Originally established to combat Protestantism, which threatened Italian religious unity, it became an organ of papal government.

inquisition /ˌɪnkwɪˈzɪʃ(ə)n, ˌɪŋ-/ *n.* **1** usu. *derog.* an intensive search or investigation. **2** a judicial or official inquiry. □□ **inquisitional** *adj.* [ME f. OF f. L *inquisitio -onis* examination (as INQUIRE)]

inquisitive /ɪnˈkwɪzɪtɪv, ɪŋ-/ *adj.* **1** unduly curious; prying. **2** seeking knowledge; inquiring. □□ **inquisitively** *adv.* **inquisitiveness** *n.* [ME f. OF *inquisitif -ive* f. LL *inquisitivus* (as INQUISITION)]

inquisitor /ɪnˈkwɪzɪtə(r), ɪŋ-/ *n.* **1** an official investigator. **2** *hist.* an officer of the Inquisition. □ **Grand Inquisitor** the director of the court of Inquisition in some countries. **Inquisitor-General** the head of the Spanish Inquisition. [F *inquisiteur* f. L *inquisitor -oris* (as INQUIRE)]

inquisitorial /ɪnˌkwɪzɪˈtɔːrɪəl, ɪŋ-/ *adj.* **1** of or like an inquisitor. **2** offensively prying. **3** *Law* (of a trial etc.) in which the judge has a prosecuting role (opp. ACCUSATORIAL). □□ **inquisitorially** *adv.* [med.L *inquisitorius* (as INQUISITOR)]

inquorate /ɪnˈkwɔːreɪt, ɪŋ-/ *adj.* not constituting a quorum.

in re /ɪn ˈriː, ˈreɪ/ *prep.* = RE[1]. [L, = in the matter of]

INRI *abbr.* Jesus of Nazareth, King of the Jews. [L *Iesus Nazarenus Rex Iudaeorum*]

inroad /ˈɪnrəʊd/ *n.* **1** (often in *pl.*; usu. foll. by *on*, *into*) an encroachment; a using up of resources etc. (*makes inroads on my time*). **2** a hostile attack; a raid. [IN + ROAD[1] in sense 'riding']

inrush /ˈɪnrʌʃ/ *n.* a rushing in; an influx. □□ **inrushing** *adj.* & *n.*

ins. *abbr.* **1** inches. **2** insurance.

insalubrious /ˌɪnsəˈluːbrɪəs, -ˈljuːbrɪəs/ *adj.* (of a climate or place) unhealthy. □□ **insalubrity** *n.* [L *insalubris* (as IN-[1], SALUBRIOUS)]

insane /ɪnˈseɪn/ *adj.* **1** not of sound mind; mad. **2** *colloq.* extremely foolish; irrational. □□ **insanely** *adv.* **insaneness** *n.* **insanity** /-ˈsænɪtɪ/ *n.* (*pl.* **-ies**). [L *insanus* (as IN-[1], *sanus* healthy)]

insanitary /ɪnˈsænɪtərɪ/ *adj.* not sanitary; dirty or germ-carrying.

insatiable /ɪnˈseɪʃəb(ə)l/ *adj.* **1** unable to be satisfied. **2** (usu. foll. by *of*) extremely greedy. □□ **insatiability** /-ˈbɪlɪtɪ/ *n.* **insatiably** *adv.* [ME f. OF *insaciable* or L *insatiabilis* (as IN-[1], SATIATE)]

insatiate /ɪnˈseɪʃɪət/ *adj.* never satisfied. [L *insatiatus* (as IN-[1], SATIATE)]

inscape /ˈɪnskeɪp/ *n.* *literary* the unique inner quality or essence of an object etc. as shown in a work of art, esp. a poem. [perh. f. IN-[2] + -SCAPE]

inscribe /ɪnˈskraɪb/ *v.tr.* **1 a** (usu. foll. by *in*, *on*) write or carve (words etc.) on stone, metal, paper, a book, etc. **b** (usu. foll. by *with*) mark (a sheet, tablet, etc.) with characters. **2** (usu. foll. by *to*) write an informal dedication (to a person) in or on (a book etc.). **3** enter the name of (a person) on a list or in a book. **4** *Geom.* draw (a figure) within another so that some or all points of it lie on the boundary of the other (cf. CIRCUMSCRIBE). **5** (esp. as **inscribed** *adj.*) *Brit.* issue (stock etc.) in the form of shares with registered holders. □□ **inscribable** *adj.* **inscriber** *n.* [L *inscribere inscript-* (as IN-[2], *scribere* write)]

inscription /ɪnˈskrɪpʃ(ə)n/ *n.* **1** words inscribed, esp. on a monument, coin, stone, or in a book etc. **2 a** the act of inscribing, esp. the informal dedication of a book etc. **b** an instance of this. □□ **inscriptional** *adj.* **inscriptive** *adj.* [ME f. L *inscriptio* (as INSCRIBE)]

inscrutable /ɪnˈskruːtəb(ə)l/ *adj.* wholly mysterious, impenetrable. □□ **inscrutability** /-ˈbɪlɪtɪ/ *n.* **inscrutableness** *n.* **inscrutably** *adv.* [ME f. eccl.L *inscrutabilis* (as IN-[1], *scrutari* search: see SCRUTINY)]

insect /ˈɪnsekt/ *n.* **1 a** any arthropod of the class Insecta, typically having six legs, two or four wings, and a body divided into three sections: head, thorax, and abdomen. Insects, of which there are over a million species, are abundant on land and in fresh water, but are almost absent from the sea. They display great diversity of form and have a number of roles in nature: some are important in the pollination of crops, some produce useful substances such as honey, beeswax, and silk, others are harmful to plants and animals, and some are carriers of disease. **b** (loosely) any other small segmented invertebrate animal. **2** an insignificant or contemptible person or creature. □□ **insectile** /-ˈsektaɪl/ *adj.* [L *insectum* (*animal*) notched (animal) f. *insecare insect-* (as IN-[2], *secare* cut)]

insectarium /ˌɪnsekˈteərɪəm/ *n.* (also **insectary** /ɪnˈsektərɪ/) (*pl.* **insectariums** or **insectaries**) a place for keeping insects.

insecticide /ɪnˈsektɪˌsaɪd/ *n.* a substance used for killing insects. □□ **insecticidal** /-ˈsaɪd(ə)l/ *adj.*

insectivore /ɪnˈsektɪˌvɔː(r)/ *n.* **1** any mammal of the order Insectivora feeding on insects etc., e.g. a hedgehog or mole. **2** any plant which captures and absorbs insects. □□ **insectivorous** /-ˈtɪvərəs/ *adj.* [F f. mod.L *insectivorus* (as INSECT, -VORE: see -VOROUS)]

insecure /ˌɪnsɪˈkjʊə(r)/ *adj.* **1** (of a person or state of mind) uncertain; lacking confidence. **2 a** unsafe; not firm or fixed. **b** (of ice, ground, etc.) liable to give way. □□ **insecurely** *adv.* **insecurity** /-ˈkjʊərɪtɪ/ *n.*

inselberg /ˈɪns(ə)lˌbɜːg, ˈɪnz-/ *n.* an isolated hill or mountain rising abruptly from its surroundings. [G, = island mountain]

inseminate /ɪnˈsemɪˌneɪt/ *v.tr.* **1** introduce semen into (a female) by natural or artificial means. **2** sow (seed etc.). □□ **insemination** /-ˈneɪʃ(ə)n/ *n.* **inseminator** *n.* [L *inseminare* (as IN-[2], SEMEN)]

insensate /ɪnˈsenseɪt/ *adj.* **1** without physical sensation; unconscious. **2** without sensibility; unfeeling. **3** stupid. □□ **insensately** *adv.* [eccl.L *insensatus* (as IN-[1], *sensatus* f. *sensus* SENSE)]

insensibility /ɪnˌsensɪˈbɪlɪtɪ/ *n.* **1** unconsciousness. **2** a lack of mental feeling or emotion; hardness. **3** (often foll. by *to*) indifference. [F *insensibilité* or LL *insensibilitas* (as INSENSIBLE)]

insensible /ɪnˈsensɪb(ə)l/ *adj.* **1 a** without one's mental faculties;

unconscious. **b** (of the extremities etc.) numb; without feeling. **2** (usu. foll. by *of, to*) unaware; indifferent (*insensible of her needs*). **3** without emotion; callous. **4** too small or gradual to be perceived; inappreciable. □□ **insensibly** *adv.* [ME f. OF *insensible* or L *insensibilis* (as IN-¹, SENSIBLE)]

insensitive /ɪnˈsensɪtɪv/ *adj.* (often foll. by *to*) **1** unfeeling; boorish; crass. **2** not sensitive to physical stimuli. □□ **insensitively** *adv.* **insensitiveness** *n.* **insensitivity** /-ˈtɪvɪti/ *n.*

insentient /ɪnˈsenʃ(ə)nt/ *adj.* not sentient; inanimate. □□ **insentience** *n.*

inseparable /ɪnˈsepərəb(ə)l/ *adj. & n.* —*adj.* **1** (esp. of friends) unable or unwilling to be separated. **2** *Gram.* (of a prefix, or a verb in respect of it) unable to be used as a separate word, e.g.: *dis-, mis-, un-*. —*n.* (usu. in *pl.*) an inseparable person or thing, esp. a friend. □□ **inseparability** /-ˈbɪlɪti/ *n.* **inseparably** *adv.* [ME f. L *inseparabilis* (as IN-¹, SEPARABLE)]

insert *v. & n.* —*v.tr.* /ɪnˈsɜːt/ **1** (usu. foll. by *in, into, between*, etc.) place, fit, or thrust (a thing) into another. **2** (usu. foll. by *in, into*) introduce (a letter, word, article, advertisement, etc.) into a newspaper etc. **3** (as **inserted** *adj.*) *Anat.* etc. (of a muscle etc.) attached (at a specific point). —*n.* /ˈɪnsɜːt/ something inserted, e.g. a loose page in a magazine, a piece of cloth in a garment, a shot in a cinema film. □□ **insertable** *adj.* **inserter** *n.* [L *inserere* (as IN-², *serere sert-* join)]

insertion /ɪnˈsɜːʃ(ə)n/ *n.* **1** the act or an instance of inserting. **2** an amendment etc. inserted in writing or printing. **3** each appearance of an advertisement in a newspaper etc. **4** an ornamental section of needlework inserted into plain material (*lace insertions*). **5** the manner or place of attachment of a muscle, an organ, etc. **6** the placing of a spacecraft in an orbit. [LL *insertio* (as INSERT)]

in-service /ˈɪnˌsɜːvɪs/ *adj.* (of training) intended for those actively engaged in the profession or activity concerned.

inset *n. & v.* —*n.* /ˈɪnset/ **1 a** an extra page or pages inserted in a folded sheet or in a book; an insert. **b** a small map, photograph, etc., inserted within the border of a larger one. **2** a piece let into a dress etc. —*v.tr.* /ɪnˈset/ (**insetting**; *past* and *past part.* **inset** or **insetted**) **1** put in as an inset. **2** decorate with an inset. □□ **insetter** *n.*

inshallah /ɪnˈʃælə/ *int.* if Allah wills it. [Arab. *in šā' Allah*]

inshore /ˈɪnʃɔː(r)/, /ɪnˈ-/ *adv. & adj.* at sea but close to the shore. □ **inshore of** nearer to shore than.

inside *n., adj., adv., & prep.* —*n.* /ɪnˈsaɪd/ **1 a** the inner side or surface of a thing. **b** the inner part; the interior. **2 a** (of a path) the side next to the wall or away from the road. **b** (of a double-decker bus) the lower section. **3** (usu. in *pl.*) *colloq.* the stomach and bowels (*something wrong with my insides*). **4** *colloq.* a position affording inside information (*knows someone on the inside*). —*adj.* /ˈɪnsaɪd/ **1** situated on or in, or derived from, the inside. **2** *Football & Hockey* nearer to the centre of the field (*inside forward; inside left; inside right*). —*adv.* /ɪnˈsaɪd/ **1** on, in, or to the inside. **2** *sl.* in prison. —*prep.* /ɪnˈsaɪd/ **1** on the inner side of; within (*inside the house*). **2** in less than (*inside an hour*). □ **inside country** *Austral.* settled areas near the coast. **inside information** information not accessible to outsiders. **inside job** *colloq.* a crime committed by a person living or working on the premises burgled etc. **inside of** *colloq.* **1** in less than (a week etc.). **2** *Brit.* the middle part of. **inside out** with the inner surface turned outwards. **inside track 1** the track which is shorter, because of the curve. **2** a position of advantage. **know a thing inside out** know a thing thoroughly. **turn inside out 1** turn the inner surface outwards. **2** *colloq.* cause confusion or a mess in. [IN + SIDE]

insider /ɪnˈsaɪdə(r)/ *n.* **1** a person who is within a society, organization, etc. (cf. OUTSIDER). **2** a person privy to a secret, esp. when using it to gain advantage. □ **insider dealing** *Stock Exch.* the illegal practice of trading to one's own advantage through having access to confidential information.

insidious /ɪnˈsɪdɪəs/ *adj.* **1** proceeding or progressing inconspicuously but harmfully (*an insidious disease*). **2** treacherous; crafty. □□ **insidiously** *adv.* **insidiousness** *n.* [L *insidiosus* cunning f. *insidiae* ambush (as IN-², *sedēre* sit)]

insight /ˈɪnsaɪt/ *n.* (usu. foll. by *into*) **1** the capacity of understanding hidden truths etc., esp. of character or situations. **2** an instance of this. □□ **insightful** *adj.* **insightfully** *adv.* [ME, = 'discernment', prob. of Scand. & LG orig. (as IN-², SIGHT)]

insignia /ɪnˈsɪɡnɪə/ *n.* (treated as *sing.* or *pl.*; usu. foll. by *of*) **1** badges (*wore his insignia of office*). **2** distinguishing marks. [L, pl. of *insigne* neut. of *insignis* distinguished (as IN-², *signis* f. *signum* SIGN)]

insignificant /ˌɪnsɪɡˈnɪfɪkənt/ *adj.* **1** unimportant; trifling. **2** (of a person) undistinguished. **3** meaningless. □□ **insignificance** *n.* **insignificancy** *n.* **insignificantly** *adv.*

insincere /ˌɪnsɪnˈsɪə(r)/ *adj.* not sincere; not candid. □□ **insincerely** *adv.* **insincerity** /-ˈserɪti/ *n.* (*pl.* **-ies**) [L *insincerus* (as IN-¹, SINCERE)]

insinuate /ɪnˈsɪnjʊˌeɪt/ *v.tr.* **1** (often foll. by *that* + clause) convey indirectly or obliquely; hint (*insinuated that she was lying*). **2** (often *refl.*; usu. foll. by *into*) **a** introduce (oneself, a person, etc.) into favour, office, etc., by subtle manipulation. **b** introduce (a thing, oneself, etc.) subtly or deviously into a place (*insinuated himself into the Royal Box*). □□ **insinuation** /-ˈeɪʃ(ə)n/ *n.* **insinuative** *adj.* **insinuator** *n.* **insinuatory** /-jʊətəri/ *adj.* [L *insinuare insinuat-* (as IN-², *sinuare* to curve)]

insipid /ɪnˈsɪpɪd/ *adj.* **1** lacking vigour or interest; dull. **2** lacking flavour; tasteless. □□ **insipidity** /-ˈpɪdɪti/ *n.* **insipidly** *adv.* **insipidness** *n.* [F *insipide* or LL *insipidus* (as IN-¹, *sapidus* SAPID)]

insist /ɪnˈsɪst/ *v.tr.* (usu. foll. by *that* + clause; also *absol.*) maintain or demand positively and assertively (*insisted that he was innocent; give me that bag! I insist!*). □ **insist on** demand or maintain (*I insist on being present; insists on his suitability*). □□ **insister** *n.* **insistingly** *adv.* [L *insistere* stand on, persist (as IN-², *sistere* stand)]

insistent /ɪnˈsɪst(ə)nt/ *adj.* **1** (often foll. by *on*) insisting; demanding positively or continually (*is insistent on taking me with him*). **2** obtruding itself on the attention (*the insistent rattle of the window frame*). □□ **insistence** *n.* **insistency** *n.* **insistently** *adv.*

in situ /ɪn ˈsɪtjuː/ *adv.* **1** in its place. **2** in its original place. [L]

insobriety /ˌɪnsəˈbraɪəti/ *n.* intemperance, esp. in drinking.

insofar /ˌɪnsəʊˈfɑː(r)/ *adv.* = in so far (see FAR).

insolation /ˌɪnsəʊˈleɪʃ(ə)n/ *n.* exposure to the sun's rays, esp. for bleaching. [L *insolatio* f. *insolare* (as IN-², *solare* f. *sol* sun)]

insole /ˈɪnsəʊl/ *n.* **1** a removable sole worn in a boot or shoe for warmth etc. **2** the fixed inner sole of a boot or shoe.

insolent /ˈɪnsələnt/ *adj.* offensively contemptuous or arrogant; insulting. □□ **insolence** *n.* **insolently** *adv.* [ME, = 'arrogant', f. L *insolens* (as IN-¹, *solens* pres. part. of *solēre* be accustomed)]

insoluble /ɪnˈsɒljʊb(ə)l/ *adj.* **1** incapable of being solved. **2** incapable of being dissolved. □□ **insolubility** /-ˈbɪlɪti/ *n.* **insolubilize** /-bɪˌlaɪz/ *v.tr.* (also **-ise**). **insolubleness** *n.* **insolubly** *adv.* [ME f. OF *insoluble* or L *insolubilis* (as IN-¹, SOLUBLE)]

insolvable /ɪnˈsɒlvəb(ə)l/ *adj.* = INSOLUBLE.

insolvent /ɪnˈsɒlv(ə)nt/ *adj. & n.* —*adj.* **1** unable to pay one's debts. **2** relating to insolvency (*insolvent laws*). —*n.* a debtor. □□ **insolvency** *n.*

insomnia /ɪnˈsɒmnɪə/ *n.* habitual sleeplessness; inability to sleep. □□ **insomniac** /-ˌæk/ *n. & adj.* [L f. *insomnis* sleepless (as IN-¹, *somnus* sleep)]

insomuch /ˌɪnsəʊˈmʌtʃ/ *adv.* **1** (foll. by *that* + clause) to such an extent. **2** (foll. by *as*) inasmuch. [ME, orig. *in so much*]

insouciant /ɪnˈsuːsɪənt, æ̃ˈsʊsjɑ̃/ *adj.* carefree; unconcerned. □□ **insouciance** *n.* **insouciantly** *adv.* [F (as IN-¹, *souciant* pres. part. of *soucier* care)]

inspan /ɪnˈspæn/ *v.* (**inspanned, inspanning**) *S.Afr.* **1** *tr.* (also *absol.*) **a** yoke (oxen etc.) in a team to a vehicle. **b** harness an animal or animals to (a wagon). **2** *tr.* harness (people or resources) into service. [Du. *inspannen* stretch (as IN-², SPAN²)]

inspect /ɪnˈspekt/ *v.tr.* **1** look closely at or into. **2** examine (a document etc.) officially. □□ **inspection** *n.* [L *inspicere inspect-* (as IN-², *specere* look at), or its frequent. *inspectare*]

inspector /ɪnˈspektə(r)/ *n.* **1** a person who inspects. **2** an official employed to supervise a service, a machine, etc., and make reports. **3** *Brit.* a police officer below a superintendent and above a sergeant in rank. □ **inspector general** a chief inspector.

inspector of taxes (in the UK) an official of the Inland Revenue responsible for collecting taxes. □□ **inspectorate** /-rət/ *n.* **inspectorial** /-ˈtɔːrɪəl/ *adj.* **inspectorship** *n.* [L (as INSPECT)]

inspiration /ˌɪnspɪˈreɪʃ(ə)n/ *n.* **1 a** a supposed creative force or influence on poets, artists, musicians, etc., stimulating the production of works of art. **b** a person, principle, faith, etc. stimulating artistic or moral fervour and creativity. **c** a similar divine influence supposed to have led to the writing of Scripture etc. **2** a sudden brilliant, creative, or timely idea. **3** a drawing in of breath; inhalation. □□ **inspirational** *adj.* **inspirationism** *n.* **inspirationist** *n.* [ME f. OF f. LL *inspiratio -onis* (as INSPIRE)]

inspirator /ˈɪnspɪˌreɪtə(r)/ *n.* an apparatus for drawing in air or vapour. [LL (as INSPIRE)]

inspire /ɪnˈspaɪə(r)/ *v.tr.* **1** stimulate or arouse (a person) to esp. creative activity, esp. by supposed divine or supernatural agency (*your faith inspired him; inspired by God*). **2 a** (usu. foll. by *with*) animate (a person) with a feeling. **b** (usu. foll. by *into*) instil (a feeling) into a person etc. **c** (usu. foll. by *in*) create (a feeling) in a person. **3** prompt; give rise to (*the poem was inspired by the autumn*). **4** (as **inspired** *adj.*) **a** (of a work of art etc.) as if prompted by or emanating from a supernatural source; characterized by inspiration (*an inspired speech*). **b** (of a guess) intuitive but accurate. **5** (also *absol.*) breathe in (air etc.); inhale. □□ **inspiratory** /ɪnˈspɪrətərɪ/ *adj.* **inspiredly** /-rɪdlɪ/ *adv.* **inspirer** *n.* **inspiring** *adj.* **inspiringly** *adv.* [ME f. OF *inspirer* f. L *inspirare* breathe in (as IN-², *spirare* breathe)]

inspirit /ɪnˈspɪrɪt/ *v.tr.* (**inspirited, inspiriting**) **1** put life into; animate. **2** (usu. foll. by *to*, or *to* + infin.) encourage (a person). □□ **inspiriting** *adj.* **inspiritingly** *adv.*

inspissate /ɪnˈspɪseɪt/ *v.tr. literary* thicken; condense. □□ **inspissation** /-ˈseɪʃ(ə)n/ *n.* [LL *inspissare inspissat-* (as IN-², L *spissus* thick)]

inspissator /ˈɪnspɪˌseɪtə(r)/ *n.* an apparatus for thickening serum etc. by heat.

inst. *abbr.* **1** = INSTANT *adj.* 4 (*the 6th inst.*). **2** institute. **3** institution.

instability /ˌɪnstəˈbɪlɪtɪ/ *n.* (*pl.* **-ies**) **1** a lack of stability. **2** *Psychol.* unpredictability in behaviour etc. **3** an instance of instability. [ME f. F *instabilité* f. L *instabilitas -tatis* f. *instabilis* (as IN-¹, STABLE¹)]

install /ɪnˈstɔːl/ *v.tr.* (also **instal**) (**installed, installing**) **1** place (equipment, machinery, etc.) in position ready for use. **2** place (a person) in an office or rank with ceremony (*installed in the office of chancellor*). **3** establish (oneself, a person, etc.) in a place, condition, etc. (*installed herself at the head of the table*). □□ **installant** *adj.* & *n.* **installer** *n.* [med.L *installare* (as IN-², *stallare* f. *stallum* STALL¹)]

installation /ˌɪnstəˈleɪʃ(ə)n/ *n.* **1 a** the act or an instance of installing. **b** the process or an instance of being installed. **2** a piece of apparatus, a machine, etc. installed. [med.L *installatio* (as INSTALL)]

instalment /ɪnˈstɔːlmənt/ *n.* (*US* **installment**) **1** a sum of money due as one of several usu. equal payments for something, spread over an agreed period of time. **2** any of several parts, esp. of a television or radio serial or a magazine story, published or shown in sequence at intervals. □ **instalment plan** payment by instalments, esp. hire purchase. [alt. f. obs. *estallment* f. AF *estalement* f. *estaler* fix: prob. assoc. with INSTALLATION]

instance /ˈɪnst(ə)ns/ *n.* & *v.* —*n.* **1** an example or illustration of (*just another instance of his lack of determination*). **2** a particular case (*that's not true in this instance*). **3** *Law* a suit. —*v.tr.* cite (a fact, case, etc.) as an instance. □ **at the instance of** at the request or suggestion of. **court of first instance** *Law* a court of primary jurisdiction. **for instance** as an example. **in the first** (or **second** etc.) **instance** in the first (or second etc.) place; at the first (or second etc.) stage of a proceeding. [ME f. OF f. L *instantia* (as INSTANT)]

instancy /ˈɪnstənsɪ/ *n.* **1** urgency. **2** pressing nature. [L *instantia*: see INSTANCE]

instant /ˈɪnst(ə)nt/ *adj.* & *n.* —*adj.* **1** occurring immediately (*gives an instant result*). **2 a** (of food etc.) ready for immediate use, with little or no preparation. **b** prepared hastily and with little

effort (*I have no instant solution*). **3** urgent; pressing. **4** *Commerce* of the current month (*the 6th instant*). **5** *archaic* of the present moment. —*n.* **1** a precise moment of time, esp. the present (*come here this instant; went that instant; told you the instant I heard*). **2** a short space of time (*was there in an instant; not an instant too soon*). □ **instant replay** the immediate repetition of part of a filmed sports event, often in slow motion. [ME f. F f. L *instare* *instant-* be present, press upon (as IN-², *stare* stand)]

instantaneous /ˌɪnstənˈteɪnɪəs/ *adj.* **1** occurring or done in an instant or instantly. **2** *Physics* existing at a particular instant. □□ **instantaneity** /-təˈniːɪtɪ/ *n.* **instantaneously** *adv.* **instantaneousness** *n.* [med.L *instantaneus* f. L *instans* (as INSTANT) after eccl.L *momentaneus*]

instanter /ɪnˈstæntə(r)/ *adv. archaic* or *joc.* immediately; at once. [L f. *instans* (as INSTANT)]

instantiate /ɪnˈstænʃɪˌeɪt/ *v.tr.* represent by an instance. □□ **instantiation** /-ˈeɪʃ(ə)n/ *n.* [L *instantia*: see INSTANCE]

instantly /ˈɪnstəntlɪ/ *adv.* **1** immediately; at once. **2** *archaic* urgently; pressingly.

instar /ˈɪnstɑː(r)/ *n.* a stage in the life of an insect etc. between two periods of moulting. [L, = form]

instate /ɪnˈsteɪt/ *v.tr.* (often foll. by *in*) install; establish. [IN-² + STATE]

in statu pupillari /ɪn ˌstætjuː ˌpjuːpɪˈlɑːrɪ/ *adj.* **1** under guardianship, esp. as a pupil. **2** in a junior position at university; not having a master's degree. [L]

instauration /ˌɪnstɔːˈreɪʃ(ə)n/ *n. formal* **1** restoration; renewal. **2** an act of instauration. □□ **instaurator** /ˈɪnstɔːˌreɪtə(r)/ *n.* [L *instauratio* f. *instaurare* (as IN-²; cf. RESTORE)]

instead /ɪnˈsted/ *adv.* **1** (foll. by *of*) as a substitute or alternative to; in place of (*instead of this one; stayed instead of going*). **2** as an alternative (*took me instead*) (cf. STEAD). [ME, f. IN + STEAD]

instep /ˈɪnstep/ *n.* **1** the inner arch of the foot between the toes and the ankle. **2** the part of a shoe etc. fitting over or under this. **3** a thing shaped like an instep. [16th c.: ult. formed as IN-² + STEP, but immed. orig. uncert.]

instigate /ˈɪnstɪˌgeɪt/ *v.tr.* **1** bring about by incitement or persuasion; provoke (*who instigated the inquiry?*). **2** (usu. foll. by *to*) urge on, incite (a person etc.) to esp. an evil act. □□ **instigation** /-ˈgeɪʃ(ə)n/ *n.* **instigative** /-gətɪv/ *adj.* **instigator** *n.* [L *instigare instigat-*]

instil /ɪnˈstɪl/ *v.tr.* (*US* **instill**) (**instilled, instilling**) (often foll. by *into*) **1** introduce (a feeling, idea, etc.) into a person's mind etc. gradually. **2** put (a liquid) into something in drops. □□ **instillation** /-ˈleɪʃ(ə)n/ *n.* **instiller** *n.* **instilment** *n.* [L *instillare* (as IN-², *stillare* drop): cf. DISTIL]

instinct *n.* & *adj.* —*n.* /ˈɪnstɪŋkt/ **1 a** an innate, usu. fixed, pattern of behaviour in most animals in response to certain stimuli. **b** a similar propensity in human beings to act without conscious intention; innate impulsion. **2** (usu. foll. by *for*) unconscious skill; intuition. —*predic.adj.* /ɪnˈstɪŋkt/ (foll. by *with*) imbued, filled (with life, beauty, force, etc.). □□ **instinctual** /-ˈstɪŋktjʊəl/ *adj.* **instinctually** /-ˈstɪŋktjʊəlɪ/ *adv.* [ME, = 'impulse', f. L *instinctus* f. *instinguere* incite (as IN-², *stinguere stinct-* prick)]

instinctive /ɪnˈstɪŋktɪv/ *adj.* **1** relating to or prompted by instinct. **2** apparently unconscious or automatic (*an instinctive reaction*). □□ **instinctively** *adv.*

institute /ˈɪnstɪˌtjuːt/ *n.* & *v.* —*n.* **1 a** a society or organization for the promotion of science, education, etc. **b** a building used by an institute. **2** *Law* (usu. in *pl.*) a digest of the elements of a legal subject (*Institutes of Justinian*). **3** a principle of instruction. **4** *US* a short course of instruction for teachers etc. —*v.tr.* **1** establish; found. **2 a** initiate (an inquiry etc.). **b** begin (proceedings) in a court. **3** (usu. foll. by *to, into*) appoint (a person) as a cleric in a church etc. [ME f. L *institutum* design, precept, neut. past part. of *instituere* establish, arrange, teach (as IN-², *statuere* set up)]

institution /ˌɪnstɪˈtjuːʃ(ə)n/ *n.* **1** the act or an instance of instituting. **2 a** a society or organization founded esp. for charitable, religious, educational, or social purposes. **b** a building used by an institution. **3** an established law, practice, or custom. **4** *colloq.*

(of a person, a custom, etc.) a familiar object. **5** the establishment of a cleric etc. in a church. [ME f. OF f. L *institutio -onis* (as INSTITUTE)]

institutional /ˌɪnstɪˈtjuːʃən(ə)l/ *adj.* **1** of or like an institution. **2** typical of institutions, esp. in being regimented or unimaginative (*the food was dreadfully institutional*). **3** (of religion) expressed or organized through institutions (churches etc.). **4** *US* (of advertising) intended to create prestige rather than immediate sales. □□ **institutionalism** *n.* **institutionally** *adv.*

institutionalize /ˌɪnstɪˈtjuːʃənəˌlaɪz/ *v.tr.* (also **-ise**) **1** (as **institutionalized** *adj.*) (of a prisoner, a long-term patient, etc.) made apathetic and dependent after a long period in an institution. **2** place or keep (a person) in an institution. **3** convert into an institution; make institutional. □□ **institutionalization** /-ˈzeɪʃ(ə)n/ *n.*

Inst.P. *abbr.* (in the UK) Institute of Physics.

INSTRAW *abbr.* International Research and Training Institute for the Advancement of Women.

instruct /ɪnˈstrʌkt/ *v.tr.* **1** (often foll. by *in*) teach (a person) a subject etc. (*instructed her in French*). **2** (usu. foll. by *to* + infin.) direct; command (*instructed him to fill in the hole*). **3** (often foll. by *of,* or *that* etc. + clause) inform (a person) of a fact etc. **4** *Brit.* **a** (of a client or solicitor) give information to (a solicitor or counsel). **b** authorize (a solicitor or counsel) to act for one. [ME f. L *instruere instruct-* build, teach (as IN-², *struere* pile up)]

instruction /ɪnˈstrʌkʃ(ə)n/ *n.* **1** (often in *pl.*) a direction; an order (*gave him his instructions*). **2** teaching; education (*took a course of instruction*). **3** *Law* (in *pl.*) directions to a solicitor or counsel. **4** *Computing* a direction in a computer program defining and effecting an operation. □□ **instructional** *adj.* [ME f. OF f. LL *instructio -onis* (as INSTRUCT)]

instructive /ɪnˈstrʌktɪv/ *adj.* tending to instruct; conveying a lesson; enlightening (*found the experience instructive*). □□ **instructively** *adv.* **instructiveness** *n.*

instructor /ɪnˈstrʌktə(r)/ *n.* (*fem.* **instructress** /-ˈstrʌktrɪs/) **1** a person who instructs; a teacher, demonstrator, etc. **2** *US* a university teacher ranking below professor. □□ **instructorship** *n.*

instrument /ˈɪnstrəmənt/ *n. & v.* —*n.* **1** a tool or implement, esp. for delicate or scientific work. **2** (in full **musical instrument**) a device for producing musical sounds by vibration, wind, percussion, etc. **3 a** a thing used in performing an action (*the meeting was an instrument in his success*). **b** a person made use of (*is merely their instrument*). **4** a measuring-device, esp. in an aeroplane, serving to determine its position in darkness etc. **5** a formal, esp. legal, document. —*v.tr.* **1** arrange (music) for instruments. **2** equip with instruments (for measuring, recording, controlling, etc.). □ **instrument board** (or **panel**) a surface, esp. in a car or aeroplane, containing the dials etc. of measuring-devices. [ME f. OF *instrument* or L *instrumentum* (as INSTRUCT)]

instrumental /ˌɪnstrəˈment(ə)l/ *adj. & n.* —*adj.* **1** (usu. foll. by *to, in,* or *in* + verbal noun) serving as an instrument or means (*was instrumental in finding the money*). **2** (of music) performed on instruments, without singing (cf. VOCAL). **3** of, or arising from, an instrument (*instrumental error*). **4** *Gram.* of or in the instrumental. —*n.* **1** a piece of music performed by instruments, not by the voice. **2** *Gram.* the case of nouns and pronouns (and words in grammatical agreement with them) indicating a means or instrument. □□ **instrumentalist** /-ˈment(ə)lɪst/ *n.* **instrumentality** /-ˈtælɪtɪ/ *n.* **instrumentally** *adv.* [ME f. F f. med.L *instrumentalis* (as INSTRUMENT)]

instrumentation /ˌɪnstrəmenˈteɪʃ(ə)n/ *n.* **1 a** the arrangement or composition of music for a particular group of musical instruments. **b** the instruments used in any one piece of music. **2 a** the design, provision, or use of instruments in industry, science, etc. **b** such instruments collectively. [F f. *instrumenter* (as INSTRUMENT)]

insubordinate /ˌɪnsəˈbɔːdɪnət/ *adj.* disobedient; rebellious. □□ **insubordinately** *adv.* **insubordination** /-ˈneɪʃ(ə)n/ *n.*

insubstantial /ˌɪnsəbˈstænʃ(ə)l, -ˈstɑːnʃ(ə)l/ *adj.* **1** lacking solidity or substance. **2** not real. □□ **insubstantiality** /-ˈælɪtɪ/ *n.* **insubstantially** *adv.* [LL *insubstantialis* (as IN-¹, SUBSTANTIAL)]

insufferable /ɪnˈsʌfərəb(ə)l/ *adj.* **1** intolerable. **2** unbearably arrogant or conceited etc. □□ **insufferableness** *n.* **insufferably** *adv.*

insufficiency /ˌɪnsəˈfɪʃənsɪ/ *n.* **1** the condition of being insufficient. **2** *Med.* the inability of an organ to perform its normal function (*renal insufficiency*). [ME f. LL *insufficientia* (as INSUFFICIENT)]

insufficient /ˌɪnsəˈfɪʃ(ə)nt/ *adj.* not sufficient; inadequate. □□ **insufficiently** *adv.* [ME f. OF f. LL *insufficiens* (as IN-¹, SUFFICIENT)]

insufflate /ˈɪnsəˌfleɪt/ *v.tr.* **1** *Med.* **a** blow or breathe (air, gas, powder, etc.) into a cavity of the body etc. **b** treat (the nose etc.) in this way. **2** *Theol.* blow or breathe on (a person) to symbolize spiritual influence. □□ **insufflation** /-ˈfleɪʃ(ə)n/ *n.* [LL *insufflare insufflat-* (as IN-², *sufflare* blow upon)]

insufflator /ˈɪnsəˌfleɪtə(r)/ *n.* **1** a device for blowing powder on to a surface in order to make fingerprints visible. **2** an instrument for insufflating.

insular /ˈɪnsjʊlə(r)/ *adj.* **1 a** of or like an island. **b** separated or remote, like an island. **2** ignorant of or indifferent to cultures, peoples, etc., outside one's own experience; narrow-minded. **3** of a British variant of Latin handwriting current in the Middle Ages. **4** (of climate) equable. □□ **insularism** *n.* **insularity** /-ˈlærɪtɪ/ *n.* **insularly** *adv.* [LL *insularis* (as INSULATE)]

insulate /ˈɪnsjʊˌleɪt/ *v.tr.* **1** prevent the passage of electricity, heat, or sound from (a thing, room, etc.) by interposing non-conductors. **2** detach (a person or thing) from its surroundings; isolate. **3** *archaic* make (land) into an island. □ **insulating tape** an adhesive tape used to cover exposed electrical wires etc. □□ **insulation** /-ˈleɪʃ(ə)n/ *n.* [L *insula* island + -ATE³]

insulator /ˈɪnsjʊˌleɪtə(r)/ *n.* **1** a thing or substance used for insulation against electricity, heat, or sound. **2** an insulating device to support telegraph wires etc. **3** a device preventing contact between electrical conductors.

insulin /ˈɪnsjʊlɪn/ *n.* *Biochem.* a hormone concerned with carbohydrate metabolism in man and some other vertebrates, produced in the pancreas and having effects that include the removal of sugar from the blood (so that a deficiency of insulin causes diabetes mellitus) and the promotion of protein synthesis and fat storage. (See BANTING.) [L *insula* island (because it is produced by the islets of Langerhans) + -IN]

insult *v. & n.* —*v.tr.* /ɪnˈsʌlt/ **1** speak to or treat with scornful abuse or indignity. **2** offend the self-respect or modesty of. —*n.* /ˈɪnsʌlt/ **1** an insulting remark or action. **2** *colloq.* something so worthless or contemptible as to be offensive. **3** *Med.* **a** an agent causing damage to the body. **b** such damage. □□ **insulter** *n.* **insulting** *adj.* **insultingly** *adv.* [F *insulte* or L *insultare* (as IN-², *saltare* frequent. of *salire* salt- leap)]

insuperable /ɪnˈsuːpərəb(ə)l, ɪnˈsjuː-/ *adj.* **1** (of a barrier) impossible to surmount. **2** (of a difficulty etc.) impossible to overcome. □□ **insuperability** /-ˈbɪlɪtɪ/ *n.* **insuperably** *adv.* [ME f. OF *insuperable* or L *insuperabilis* (as IN-¹, SUPERABLE)]

insupportable /ˌɪnsəˈpɔːtəb(ə)l/ *adj.* **1** unable to be endured. **2** unjustifiable. □□ **insupportableness** *n.* **insupportably** *adv.* [F (as IN-¹, SUPPORT)]

insurance /ɪnˈʃʊərəns/ *n.* **1 a** the act or an instance of insuring. **b** the business of providing this. (See below.) **2 a** a sum paid for this; a premium. **b** a sum paid out as compensation for theft, damage, loss, etc. **3** = *insurance policy*. **4** a measure taken to provide for a possible contingency (*take an umbrella as insurance*). □ **insurance agent** *Brit.* a person employed to collect premiums door to door. **insurance company** *Brit.* a company engaged in the business of insurance. **insurance policy** *Brit.* **1** a contract of insurance. **2** a document detailing such a policy and constituting a contract. **insurance stamp** *hist.* a stamp certifying the payment of a sum, usu. paid weekly, for National Insurance. [earlier *ensurance* f. OF *enseürance* (as ENSURE)]

Insurance was known in ancient Greece and among the maritime peoples with whom they traded. It developed first as a means of spreading the huge risks attendant on early maritime enterprises, and dates as a distinct contract from the 14th c., when it evolved in the commercial cities of Italy. It is found in the Admiralty Court in England in the 16th c.; life and fire insurance developed later. Lloyd's of London began in the 17th c., and the first US company was organized by Benjamin Franklin in 1752. Since the mid-19th c. insurance against other kinds of risk has developed greatly.

insure /ɪnˈʃʊə(r)/ v.tr. **1** (often foll. by *against*; also *absol.*) secure the payment of a sum of money in the event of loss or damage to (property, life, a person, etc.) by regular payments or premiums (*insured the house for £100,000*; *we have insured against flood damage*) (cf. ASSURANCE). **2** (of the owner of a property, an insurance company, etc.) secure the payment of (a sum of money) in this way. **3** (usu. foll. by *against*) provide for (a possible contingency) (*insured themselves against the rain by taking umbrellas*). **4** US = ENSURE. □□ **insurable** *adj.* **insurability** /-ˈbɪlɪtɪ/ *n.* [ME, var. of ENSURE]

insured /ɪnˈʃʊəd/ *adj.* & *n.* —*adj.* covered by insurance. —*n.* (usu. prec. by *the*) a person etc. covered by insurance.

insurer /ɪnˈʃʊərə(r)/ *n.* **1** a person or company offering insurance policies for premiums; an underwriter. **2** a person who takes out insurance.

insurgent /ɪnˈsɜːdʒ(ə)nt/ *adj.* & *n.* —*adj.* **1** rising in active revolt. **2** (of the sea etc.) rushing in. —*n.* a rebel; a revolutionary. □□ **insurgence** *n.* **insurgency** *n.* (*pl.* **-ies**). [F f. L *insurgere insurrect-* (as IN-², *surgere* rise)]

insurmountable /ˌɪnsəˈmaʊntəb(ə)l/ *adj.* unable to be surmounted or overcome. □□ **insurmountably** *adv.*

insurrection /ˌɪnsəˈrekʃ(ə)n/ *n.* a rising in open resistance to established authority; a rebellion. □□ **insurrectional** *adj.* **insurrectionary** *adj.* **insurrectionist** *n.* [ME f. OF f. LL *insurrectio -onis* (as INSURGENT)]

insusceptible /ˌɪnsəˈseptɪb(ə)l/ *adj.* (usu. foll. by *of*, *to*) not susceptible (of treatment, to an influence, etc.). □□ **insusceptibility** /-ˈbɪlɪtɪ/ *n.*

in-swinger /ˈɪnˌswɪŋə(r)/ *n.* **1** *Cricket* a ball bowled with a swing towards the batsman. **2** *Football* a pass or kick that sends the ball curving towards the goal.

int. *abbr.* **1** interior. **2** internal. **3** international.

intact /ɪnˈtækt/ *adj.* **1** entire; unimpaired. **2** untouched. □□ **intactness** *n.* [ME f. L *intactus* (as IN-¹, *tactus* past part. of *tangere* touch)]

intagliated /ɪnˈtælɪˌeɪtɪd/ *adj.* decorated with surface carving. [It. *intagliato* past part. of *intagliare* cut into]

intaglio /ɪnˈtælɪəʊ, -ˈtɑːlɪəʊ/ *n.* & *v.* —*n.* (*pl.* **-os**) **1** a gem with an incised design (cf. CAMEO). **2** an engraved design. **3** a carving, esp. incised, in hard material. **4** a process of printing from an engraved design. —*v.tr.* (**-oes**, **-oed**) **1** engrave (material) with a sunk pattern or design. **2** engrave (such a design). [It. (as INTAGLIATED)]

intake /ˈɪnteɪk/ *n.* **1 a** the action of taking in. **b** an instance of this. **2** a number or the amount taken in or received. **3** a place where water is taken into a channel or pipe from a river, or fuel or air enters an engine etc. **4** an airway into a mine. **5** *N.Engl.* land reclaimed from a moor etc.

intangible /ɪnˈtændʒɪb(ə)l/ *adj.* & *n.* —*adj.* **1** unable to be touched; not solid. **2** unable to be grasped mentally. —*n.* something that cannot be precisely measured or assessed. □□ **intangibility** /-ˈbɪlɪtɪ/ *n.* **intangibly** *adv.* [F *intangible* or med.L *intangibilis* (as IN-¹, TANGIBLE)]

intarsia /ɪnˈtɑːsɪə/ *n.* **1** the craft of using wood inlays, esp. as practised in 15th-c. Italy. **2** work of this kind. [It. *intarsio*]

integer /ˈɪntɪdʒə(r)/ *n.* **1** a whole number. **2** a thing complete in itself. [L (adj.) = untouched, whole: see ENTIRE]

integral /ˈɪntɪgr(ə)l/ *adj.* & *n.* —*adj.* /ˈɪntɪgr(ə)l, *disp.* ɪnˈtegr(ə)l/ **1 a** of a whole or necessary to the completeness of a whole. **b** forming a whole (*integral design*). **c** whole, complete. **2** *Math.* **a** of or denoted by an integer. **b** involving only integers, esp. as coefficients of a function. —*n. Math.* **1** a quantity of which a given function is the derivative, either containing an indeterminate additive constant (**indefinite integral**), or calculated as the difference between its values at specified limits (**definite integral**). **2** a function satisfying a given differential equation. □ **integral calculus** mathematics concerned with finding integrals, their properties and application, etc. (cf. *differential calculus*). (See NEWTON.) □□ **integrality** /-ˈgrælɪtɪ/ *n.* **integrally** *adv.* [LL *integralis* (as INTEGER)]

integrand /ˈɪntɪˌgrænd/ *n. Math.* a function that is to be integrated. [L *integrandus* gerundive of *integrare*: see INTEGRATE]

integrant /ˈɪntəgrənt/ *adj.* (of parts) making up a whole; component. [F *intégrant* f. *intégrer* (as INTEGRATE)]

integrate *v.* & *adj.* —*v.* /ˈɪntɪˌgreɪt/ **1** *tr.* **a** combine (parts) into a whole. **b** complete (an imperfect thing) by the addition of parts. **2** *tr.* & *intr.* bring or come into equal participation in or membership of society, a school, etc. **3** *tr.* desegregate, esp. racially (a school etc). **4** *tr. Math.* **a** find the integral of. **b** (as **integrated** *adj.*) indicating the mean value or total sum of (temperature, an area, etc.). —*adj.* /ˈɪntɪgrət/ **1** made up of parts. **2** whole; complete. □ **integrated circuit** *Electronics* a small chip etc. of material replacing several separate components in a conventional electrical circuit. □□ **integrable** /ˈɪntɪgrəb(ə)l/ *adj.* **integrability** /ˌɪntɪgrəˈbɪlɪtɪ/ *n.* **integrative** /ˈɪntɪgrətɪv/ *adj.* [L *integrare integrat-* make whole (as INTEGER)]

integration /ˌɪntɪˈgreɪʃ(ə)n/ *n.* **1** the act or an instance of integrating. **2** the intermixing of persons previously segregated. **3** *Psychol.* the combination of the diverse elements of perception etc. in a personality. □□ **integrationist** *n.* [L *integratio* (as INTEGRATE)]

integrator /ˈɪntɪˌgreɪtə(r)/ *n.* **1** an instrument for indicating or registering the total amount or mean value of some physical quality, as area, temperature, etc. **2** a person or thing that integrates.

integrity /ɪnˈtegrɪtɪ/ *n.* **1** moral uprightness; honesty. **2** wholeness; soundness. [ME f. F *intégrité* or L *integritas* (as INTEGER)]

integument /ɪnˈtegjʊmənt/ *n.* a natural outer covering, as a skin, husk, rind, etc. □□ **integumental** /-ˈment(ə)l/ *adj.* **integumentary** /-ˈmentərɪ/ *adj.* [L *integumentum* f. *integere* (as IN-², *tegere* cover)]

intellect /ˈɪntɪˌlekt/ *n.* **1 a** the faculty of reasoning, knowing, and thinking, as distinct from feeling. **b** the understanding or mental powers (of a particular person etc.) (*his intellect is not great*). **2 a** a clever or knowledgeable person. **b** the intelligentsia regarded collectively (*the combined intellect of four universities*). [ME f. OF *intellect* or L *intellectus* understanding (as INTELLIGENT)]

intellection /ˌɪntɪˈlekʃ(ə)n/ *n.* the action or process of understanding (opp. IMAGINATION). □□ **intellective** *adj.* [ME f. med.L *intellectio* (as INTELLIGENT)]

intellectual /ˌɪntɪˈlektjʊəl/ *adj.* & *n.* —*adj.* **1** of or appealing to the intellect. **2** possessing a high level of understanding or intelligence; cultured. **3** requiring, or given to the exercise of, the intellect. —*n.* a person possessing a highly developed intellect. □□ **intellectuality** /-ˈælɪtɪ/ *n.* **intellectualize** /-ˈlektjʊəˌlaɪz/ *v.tr.* & *intr.* (also **-ise**). **intellectually** *adv.* [ME f. L *intellectualis* (as INTELLECT)]

intellectualism /ˌɪntɪˈlektjʊəˌlɪz(ə)m/ *n.* **1** the exercise, esp. when excessive, of the intellect at the expense of the emotions. **2** *Philos.* the theory that knowledge is wholly or mainly derived from pure reason. □□ **intellectualist** *n.*

intelligence /ɪnˈtelɪdʒ(ə)ns/ *n.* **1 a** the intellect; the understanding. **b** (of a person or an animal) quickness of understanding; wisdom. **2 a** the collection of information, esp. of military or political value. **b** people employed in this. **c** *archaic* information; news. **3** an intelligent or rational being. □ **intelligence department** a usu. government department engaged in collecting esp. secret information. **intelligence quotient** a number denoting the ratio of a person's intelligence to the normal or average. **intelligence test** a test designed to measure intelligence rather than acquired knowledge. (See BINET.) □□ **intelligential** /-ˈdʒenʃ(ə)l/ *adj.* [ME f. OF f. L *intelligentia* (as INTELLIGENT)]

intelligent /ɪnˈtelɪdʒ(ə)nt/ *adj.* **1** having or showing intelligence, esp. of a high level. **2** quick of mind; clever. **3 a** (of a device or machine) able to vary its behaviour in response to varying situations and requirements and past experience. **b** (esp. of a computer terminal) having its own data-processing capability; incorporating a microprocessor (opp. DUMB). □□ **intelligently** *adv.* [L *intelligere intellect-* understand (as INTER-, *legere* gather, pick out, read)]

intelligentsia /ɪnˌtelɪˈdʒentsɪə/ *n.* **1** the class of intellectuals regarded as possessing culture and political initiative. **2** people doing intellectual work; intellectuals. [Russ. f. Pol. *inteligencja* f. L *intelligentia* (as INTELLIGENT)]

intelligible /ɪnˈtelɪdʒɪb(ə)l/ *adj.* **1** (often foll. by *to*) able to be understood; comprehensible. **2** *Philos.* able to be understood only by the intellect, not by the senses. □□ **intelligibility** /-ˈbɪlɪtɪ/ *n.* **intelligibly** *adv.* [L *intelligibilis* (as INTELLIGENT)]

Intelpost /ˈɪntelˌpəʊst/ *n.* the international electronic transmission of messages and graphics by fax, telex, etc. [*International Electronic Post*]

Intelsat /ˈɪntelˌsæt/ *n.* an international organization of countries, formed in 1964, which owns and operates the worldwide commercial communications satellite system. Its headquarters are in Washington, DC. Each of the 117 national signatories contributes to its cost. [*International Telecommunications Satellite Consortium*]

intemperate /ɪnˈtempərət/ *adj.* **1** (of a person, conduct, or speech) immoderate; unbridled; violent (*used intemperate language*). **2 a** given to excessive indulgence in alcohol. **b** excessively indulgent in one's appetites. □□ **intemperance** *n.* **intemperately** *adv.* **intemperateness** *n.* [ME f. L *intemperatus* (as IN-¹, TEMPERATE)]

intend /ɪnˈtend/ *v.tr.* **1** have as one's purpose; propose (*we intend to go; we intend going; we intend that it shall be done*). **2** (usu. foll. by *for, as*) design or destine (a person or a thing) (*I intend him to go; I intend it as a warning*). **3** mean (*what does he intend by that?*). **4** (in *passive*; foll. by *for*) **a** be meant for a person to have or use etc. (*they are intended for the children*). **b** be meant to represent (*the picture is intended for you*). **5** (as **intending** *adj.*) who intends to be (*an intending visitor*). [ME *entende, intende* f. OF *entendre, intendre* f. L *intendere intent-* or *intens-* strain, direct, purpose (as IN-², *tendere* stretch, tend)]

intendant /ɪnˈtend(ə)nt/ *n.* **1** (esp. as a title of foreign officials) a superintendent or manager of a department of public business etc. **2** the administrator of an opera house or theatre. □□ **intendancy** *n.* [F f. L *intendere* (as INTEND)]

intended /ɪnˈtendɪd/ *adj. & n.* —*adj.* **1** done on purpose; intentional. **2** designed, meant. —*n. colloq.* the person one intends to marry; one's fiancé or fiancée (*is this your intended?*). □□ **intendedly** *adv.*

intense /ɪnˈtens/ *adj.* (**intenser, intensest**) **1** (of a quality etc.) existing in a high degree; violent; forceful (*intense cold*). **2** (of a person) feeling, or apt to feel, strong emotion (*very intense about her music*). **3** (of a feeling or action etc.) extreme (*intense joy; intense thought*). □□ **intensely** *adv.* **intenseness** *n.* [ME f. OF *intens* or L *intensus* (as INTEND)]

intensifier /ɪnˈtensɪˌfaɪə(r)/ *n.* **1** a person or thing that intensifies. **2** *Gram.* = INTENSIVE *n.*

intensify /ɪnˈtensɪˌfaɪ/ *v.* (**-ies, -ied**) **1** *tr. & intr.* make or become intense or more intense. **2** *tr. Photog.* increase the opacity of (a negative). □□ **intensification** /-fɪˈkeɪʃ(ə)n/ *n.*

intension /ɪnˈtenʃ(ə)n/ *n.* **1** *Logic* the internal content of a concept. **2** *formal* the intensity, or high degree, of a quality. **3** *formal* the strenuous exertion of the mind or will. □□ **intensional** *adj.* **intensionally** *adv.* [L *intensio* (as INTEND)]

intensity /ɪnˈtensɪtɪ/ *n.* (pl. **-ies**) **1** the quality or an instance of being intense. **2** esp. *Physics* the measurable amount of some quality, e.g. force, brightness, a magnetic field, etc.

intensive /ɪnˈtensɪv/ *adj. & n.* —*adj.* **1** thorough, vigorous; directed to a single point, area, or subject (*intensive study; intensive bombardment*). **2** of or relating to intensity as opp. to extent; producing intensity. **3** serving to increase production in relation to costs (*intensive farming methods*). **4** (usu. in *comb.*) *Econ.* making much use of (*a labour-intensive industry*). **5** *Gram.* (of an adjective, adverb, etc.) expressing intensity; giving force, as *really* in *my feet are really cold*. —*n. Gram.* an intensive adjective, adverb, etc.

□ **intensive care** medical treatment with constant monitoring etc. of a dangerously ill patient (also (with hyphen) *attrib.*: *intensive-care unit*). □□ **intensively** *adv.* **intensiveness** *n.* [F *intensif -ive* or med.L *intensivus* (as INTEND)]

intent /ɪnˈtent/ *n. & adj.* —*n.* (usu. without article) intention; a purpose (*with intent to defraud; my intent to reach the top; with evil intent*). —*adj.* **1** (usu. foll. by *on*) **a** resolved; bent; determined (*was intent on succeeding*). **b** attentively occupied (*intent on his books*). **2** (esp. of a look) earnest; eager; meaningful. □ **to all intents and purposes** practically; virtually. □□ **intently** *adv.* **intentness** *n.* [ME *entent* f. OF f. L *intentus* (as INTEND)]

intention /ɪnˈtenʃ(ə)n/ *n.* **1** (often foll. by *to* + infin., or *of* + verbal noun) a thing intended; an aim or purpose (*it was not his intention to interfere; have no intention of staying*). **2** the act of intending (*done without intention*). **3** *colloq.* (usu. in *pl.*) a person's, esp. a man's, designs in respect to marriage (*are his intentions strictly honourable?*). **4** *Logic* a conception. □ **first intention** *Med.* the healing of a wound by natural contact of the parts. **first intentions** *Logic* one's primary conceptions of things (e.g. a tree, an oak). **intention tremor** *Med.* a trembling of a part of a body when commencing a movement. **second intention** *Med.* the healing of a wound by granulation. **second intentions** *Logic* one's secondary conceptions (e.g. difference, identity, species). **special** (or **particular**) **intention** *RC Ch.* a special aim or purpose for which a mass is celebrated, prayers are said, etc. □□ **intentioned** *adj.* (usu. in *comb.*). [ME *entencion* f. OF f. L *intentio* stretching, purpose (as INTEND)]

intentional /ɪnˈtenʃən(ə)l/ *adj.* done on purpose. □□ **intentionality** /-ˈnælɪtɪ/ *n.* **intentionally** *adv.* [F *intentionnel* or med.L *intentionalis* (as INTENTION)]

inter /ɪnˈtɜː(r)/ *v.tr.* (**interred, interring**) deposit (a corpse etc.) in the earth, a tomb, etc.; bury. [ME f. OF *enterrer* f. Rmc (as IN-², L *terra* earth)]

inter. *abbr.* intermediate.

inter- /ˈɪntə(r)/ *comb. form* **1** between, among (*intercontinental*). **2** mutually, reciprocally (*interbreed*). [OF *entre-* or L *inter* between, among]

interact /ˌɪntərˈækt/ *v.intr.* act reciprocally; act on each other. □□ **interactant** *adj. & n.*

interaction /ˌɪntərˈækʃ(ə)n/ *n.* **1** reciprocal action or influence. **2** *Physics* the action of atomic and subatomic particles on each other.

interactive /ˌɪntərˈæktɪv/ *adj.* **1** reciprocally active; acting upon or influencing each other. **2** (of a computer or other electronic device) allowing a two-way flow of information between it and a user, responding to the user's input. □□ **interactively** *adv.* [INTERACT, after *active*]

inter alia /ˌɪntər ˈeɪlɪə, ˈælɪə/ *adv.* among other things. [L]

inter-allied /ˌɪntərˈælaɪd/ *adj.* relating to two or more allies (in war etc.).

interarticular /ˌɪntɑːˈtɪkjʊlə(r)/ *adj.* between the contiguous surfaces of a joint.

interatomic /ˌɪntərəˈtɒmɪk/ *adj.* between atoms.

interbank /ˈɪntəˌbæŋk/ *adj.* agreed, arranged, or operating between banks (*interbank loan*).

interbed /ˌɪntəˈbed/ *v.tr.* (**-bedded, -bedding**) embed (one thing) among others.

interblend /ˌɪntəˈblend/ *v.* **1** *tr.* (usu. foll. by *with*) mingle (things) together. **2** *intr.* blend with each other.

interbreed /ˌɪntəˈbriːd/ *v.* (*past* and *past part.* **-bred** /-ˈbred/) **1** *intr. & tr.* breed or cause to breed with members of a different race or species to produce a hybrid. **2** *tr.* breed within one family etc. in order to produce desired characteristics (cf. CROSS-BREED).

intercalary /ɪnˈtɜːkələrɪ, -ˈkælərɪ/ *adj.* **1 a** (of a day or a month) inserted in the calendar to harmonize it with the solar year, e.g. 29 Feb. in leap years. **b** (of a year) having such an addition. **2** interpolated; intervening. [L *intercalari(u)s* (as INTERCALATE)]

intercalate /ɪnˈtɜːkəˌleɪt/ *v.tr.* **1** (also *absol.*) insert (an intercalary day etc.). **2** interpose (anything out of the ordinary course). **3** (as **intercalated** *adj.*) (of strata etc.) interposed. □□

intercalation /-ˈleɪʃ(ə)n/ n. [L intercalare intercalat- (as INTER-, calare proclaim)]

intercede /ˌɪntəˈsiːd/ v.intr. (usu. foll. by with) interpose or intervene on behalf of another; plead (they interceded with the king for his life). □□ **interceder** n. [F intercéder or L intercedere intercess- intervene (as INTER-, cedere go)]

intercellular /ˌɪntəˈseljʊlə(r)/ adj. Biol. located or occurring between cells.

intercensal /ˌɪntəˈsens(ə)l/ adj. between two censuses.

intercept v. & n. —v.tr. /ˌɪntəˈsept/ 1 seize, catch, or stop (a person, message, vehicle, ball, etc.) going from one place to another. 2 (usu. foll. by from) cut off (light etc.). 3 check or stop (motion etc.). 4 Math. mark off (a space) between two points etc. —n. /ˈɪntəˌsept/ Math. the part of a line between two points of intersection with usu. the coordinate axes or other lines. □□ **interception** /-ˈsepʃ(ə)n/ n. **interceptive** /-ˈseptɪv/ adj. [L intercipere intercept- (as INTER-, capere take)]

interceptor /ˌɪntəˈseptə(r)/ n. 1 an aircraft used to intercept enemy raiders. 2 a person or thing that intercepts.

intercession /ˌɪntəˈseʃ(ə)n/ n. 1 the act of interceding, esp. by prayer. 2 an instance of this. 3 a prayer. □□ **intercessional** adj. **intercessor** n. **intercessorial** /-seˈsɔːrɪəl/ adj. **intercessory** adj. [F intercession or L intercessio (as INTERCEDE)]

interchange v. & n. —v.tr. /ˌɪntəˈtʃeɪndʒ/ 1 (of two people) exchange (things) with each other. 2 put each of (two things) in the other's place; alternate. —n. /ˈɪntəˌtʃeɪndʒ/ 1 (often foll. by of) a reciprocal exchange between two people etc. 2 alternation (the interchange of woods and fields). 3 a road junction designed so that traffic streams do not intersect. □□ **interchangeable** adj. **interchangeability** /-ˈbɪlɪtɪ/ n. **interchangeableness** n. **interchangeably** adv. [ME f. OF entrechangier (as INTER-, CHANGE)]

inter-city /ˌɪntəˈsɪtɪ/ adj. existing or travelling between cities.

inter-class /ˌɪntəˈklɑːs/ adj. existing or conducted between different social classes.

intercollegiate /ˌɪntəkəˈliːdʒət/ adj. existing or conducted between colleges or universities.

intercolonial /ˌɪntəkəˈləʊnɪəl/ adj. existing or conducted between colonies.

intercom /ˈɪntəˌkɒm/ n. colloq. a system of intercommunication by radio or telephone between or within offices, aircraft, etc. [abbr.]

intercommunicate /ˌɪntəkəˈmjuːnɪkeɪt/ v.intr. 1 communicate reciprocally. 2 (of rooms etc.) have free passage into each other; have a connecting door. □□ **intercommunication** /-ˈkeɪʃ(ə)n/ n. **intercommunicative** /-kətɪv/ adj.

intercommunion /ˌɪntəkəˈmjuːnɪən/ n. 1 mutual communion. 2 a mutual action or relationship, esp. between Christian denominations.

intercommunity /ˌɪntəkəˈmjuːnɪtɪ/ n. 1 the quality of being common to various groups etc. 2 having things in common.

interconnect /ˌɪntəkəˈnekt/ v.tr. & intr. connect with each other. □□ **interconnection** /-ˈnekʃ(ə)n/ n.

intercontinental /ˌɪntəˌkɒntɪˈnent(ə)l/ adj. connecting or travelling between continents. □□ **intercontinentally** adv.

interconvert /ˌɪntəkənˈvɜːt/ v.tr. & intr. convert into each other. □□ **interconversion** n. **interconvertible** adj.

intercooling /ˈɪntəˌkuːlɪŋ/ n. the cooling of gas between successive compressions, esp. in a car or truck engine. □□ **intercool** v.tr. **intercooler** n.

intercorrelate /ˌɪntəˈkɒrəˌleɪt/ v.tr. & intr. correlate with one another. □□ **intercorrelation** /-ˈleɪʃ(ə)n/ n.

intercostal /ˌɪntəˈkɒst(ə)l/ adj. between the ribs (of the body or a ship). □□ **intercostally** adv.

intercounty /ˌɪntəˈkaʊntɪ/ adj. existing or conducted between counties.

intercourse /ˈɪntəˌkɔːs/ n. 1 communication or dealings between individuals, nations, etc. 2 = sexual intercourse. 3 communion between human beings and God. [ME f. OF entrecours exchange, commerce, f. L intercursus (as INTER-, currere curs- run)]

intercrop /ˌɪntəˈkrɒp/ v.tr. (also absol.) (-cropped, -cropping) raise (a crop) among plants of a different kind, usu. in the space between rows. □□ **intercropping** n.

intercross /ˌɪntəˈkrɒs/ v. 1 tr. & intr. lay or lie across each other. 2 a intr. (of animals) breed with each other. b tr. cause to do this.

intercrural /ˌɪntəˈkrʊər(ə)l/ adj. between the legs.

intercurrent /ˌɪntəˈkʌrənt/ adj. 1 (of a time or event) intervening. 2 Med. a (of a disease) occurring during the progress of another. b recurring at intervals. □□ **intercurrence** n. [L intercurrere intercurrent- (as INTERCOURSE)]

intercut /ˌɪntəˈkʌt/ v.tr. (-cutting; past and past part. -cut) Cinematog. alternate (shots) with contrasting shots by cutting.

interdenominational /ˌɪntədɪˌnɒmɪˈneɪʃən(ə)l/ adj. concerning more than one (religious) denomination. □□ **interdenominationally** adv.

interdepartmental /ˌɪntəˌdiːpɑːtˈment(ə)l/ adj. concerning more than one department. □□ **interdepartmentally** adv.

interdepend /ˌɪntədɪˈpend/ v.intr. depend on each other. □□ **interdependence** n. **interdependency** n. **interdependent** adj.

interdict n. & v. —n. /ˈɪntədɪkt/ 1 an authoritative prohibition. 2 RC Ch. a sentence debarring a person, or esp. a place, from ecclesiastical functions and privileges. 3 Sc. Law an injunction. —v.tr. /ˌɪntəˈdɪkt/ 1 prohibit (an action). 2 forbid the use of. 3 (usu. foll. by from + verbal noun) restrain (a person). 4 (usu. foll. by to) forbid (a thing) to a person. □□ **interdiction** /-ˈdɪkʃ(ə)n/ n. **interdictory** /-ˈdɪktərɪ/ adj. [ME f. OF entredit f. L interdictum past part. of interdicere interpose, forbid by decree (as INTER-, dicere say)]

interdigital /ˌɪntəˈdɪdʒɪt(ə)l/ adj. between the fingers or toes. □□ **interdigitally** adv.

interdigitate /ˌɪntəˈdɪdʒɪteɪt/ v.intr. interlock like clasped fingers. [INTER- + L digitus finger + -ATE³]

interdisciplinary /ˌɪntəˌdɪsɪˈplɪnərɪ/ adj. of or between more than one branch of learning.

interest /ˈɪntrəst, -trɪst/ n. & v. —n. 1 a a concern; curiosity (have no interest in fishing). b a quality exciting curiosity or holding the attention (this magazine lacks interest). 2 a subject, hobby, etc., in which one is concerned (his interests are gardening and sport). 3 advantage or profit, esp. when financial (it is in your interest to go; look after your own interests). 4 money paid for the use of money lent, or for not requiring the repayment of a debt. 5 (usu. foll. by in) a a financial stake (in an undertaking etc.). b a legal concern, title, or right (in property). 6 a a party or group having a common interest (the brewing interest). b a principle in which a party or group is concerned. 7 the selfish pursuit of one's own welfare, self-interest. —v.tr. 1 excite the curiosity or attention of (your story interests me greatly). 2 (usu. foll. by in) cause (a person) to take a personal interest or share (can I interest you in a holiday abroad?). 3 (as **interested** adj.) having a private interest; not impartial or disinterested (an interested party). □ **at interest** (of money borrowed) on the condition that interest is payable. **declare an** (or **one's**) **interest** make known one's financial etc. interests in an undertaking before it is discussed. **in the interest** (or **interests**) **of** as something that is advantageous to. **lose interest** become bored or boring. **with interest** with increased force etc. (returned the blow with interest). □□ **interestedly** adv. **interestedness** n. [ME, earlier interesse f. AF f. med.L, alt. app. after OF interest, both f. L interest, 3rd sing. pres. of interesse matter, make a difference (as INTER-, esse be)]

interesting /ˈɪntrəstɪŋ, -trɪstɪŋ/ adj. causing curiosity; holding the attention. □ **in an interesting condition** archaic pregnant. □□ **interestingly** adv. **interestingness** n.

interface /ˈɪntəˌfeɪs/ n. & v. —n. 1 esp. Physics a surface forming a common boundary between two regions. 2 a point where interaction occurs between two systems, processes, subjects, etc. (the interface between psychology and education). 3 esp. Computing an apparatus for connecting two pieces of equipment so that they can be operated jointly. —v.tr. & intr. (often foll. by with) connect with (another piece of equipment etc.) by an interface.

interfacial /ˌɪntəˈfeɪʃ(ə)l/ adj. 1 included between two faces of a crystal or other solid. 2 of or forming an interface. □□ **interfacially** adv. (esp. in sense 2).

interfacing /ˈɪntəˌfeɪsɪŋ/ n. a stiffish material, esp. buckram, between two layers of fabric in collars etc.

interfemoral /ˌɪntəˈfemər(ə)l/ adj. between the thighs.

interfere /ˌɪntəˈfɪə(r)/ v.intr. 1 (usu. foll. by with) **a** (of a person) meddle; obstruct a process etc. **b** (of a thing) be a hindrance; get in the way. 2 (usu. foll. by in) take part or intervene, esp. without invitation or necessity. 3 (foll. by with) euphem. molest or assault sexually. 4 Physics (of light or other waves) combine so as to cause interference. 5 (of a horse) knock one leg against another. □□ **interferer** n. **interfering** adj. **interferingly** adv. [OF s'entreferir strike each other (as INTER-, ferir f. L ferire strike)]

interference /ˌɪntəˈfɪərəns/ n. 1 (usu. foll. by with) **a** the act of interfering. **b** an instance of this. 2 the fading or disturbance of received radio signals by the interference of waves from different sources, or esp. by atmospherics or unwanted signals. 3 Physics the combination of two or more wave motions to form a resultant wave in which the displacement is reinforced or cancelled. □□ **interferential** /-fəˈrenʃ(ə)l/ adj.

interferometer /ˌɪntəfəˈrɒmɪt(ə)r/ n. an instrument for measuring wavelengths etc. by means of interference phenomena. □□ **interferometric** /-ˌferəˈmetrɪk/ adj. **interferometrically** /-ˌferəˈmetrɪkəli/ adv. **interferometry** n.

interferon /ˌɪntəˈfɪərɒn/ n. Biochem. any of various proteins released by animal cells, usually in response to the entry of a virus, which have the property of inhibiting further development of viruses of any kind in the animal or in others of the same species. The discovery of such a protein by the virologists A. Isaacs and J. Lindenmann was announced in 1957. [INTERFERE + -ON]

interfibrillar /ˌɪntəˈfɪbrɪlə(r)/ adj. between fibrils.

interfile /ˌɪntəˈfaɪl/ v.tr. 1 file (two sequences) together. 2 file (one or more items) into an existing sequence.

interflow /ˈɪntəˌfləʊ/ v. & n. —v.intr. flow into each other. —n. the process or result of this.

interfluent /ˌɪntəˈfluːənt/ adj. flowing into each other. [L interfluere interfluent- (as INTER-, fluere flow)]

interfuse /ˌɪntəˈfjuːz/ v. 1 tr. **a** (usu. foll. by with) mix (a thing) with; intersperse. **b** blend (things) together. 2 intr. (of two things) blend with each other. □□ **interfusion** /-ˈfjuːʒ(ə)n/ n. [L interfundere interfus- (as INTER-, fundere pour)]

intergalactic /ˌɪntəɡəˈlæktɪk/ adj. of or situated between two or more galaxies. □□ **intergalactically** adv.

interglacial /ˌɪntəˈɡleɪʃ(ə)l, -sɪəl/ adj. between glacial periods.

intergovernmental /ˌɪntəˌɡʌvən'ment(ə)l/ adj. concerning or conducted between two or more governments. □□ **intergovernmentally** adv.

intergradation /ˌɪntəɡrəˈdeɪʃ(ə)n/ n. the process of merging together by gradual change of the constituents.

intergrade /ˈɪntəˌɡreɪd/ v. & n. —v.intr. pass into another form by intervening grades. —n. such a grade.

intergrowth /ˈɪntəˌɡrəʊθ/ n. the growing of things into each other.

interim /ˈɪntərɪm/ n., adj., & adv. —n. the intervening time (in the interim he had died). —adj. intervening; provisional, temporary. —adv. archaic meanwhile. □ **interim dividend** a dividend declared on the basis of less than a full year's results. [L, as INTER- + adv. suffix -im]

interior /ɪnˈtɪərɪə(r)/ adj. & n. —adj. 1 inner (opp. EXTERIOR). 2 remote from the coast or frontier; inland. 3 internal; domestic (opp. FOREIGN). 4 (usu. foll. by to) situated further in or within. 5 existing in the mind or soul; inward. 6 drawn, photographed, etc. within a building. 7 coming from inside. —n. 1 the interior part; the inside. 2 the interior part of a country or region. 3 **a** the home affairs of a country. **b** a department dealing with these (Minister of the Interior). 4 a representation of the inside of a building or a room (Dutch interior). 5 the inner nature; the soul. □ **interior angle** the angle between adjacent sides of a rectilinear figure. **interior decoration** (or **design**) the decoration or design of the interior of a building, a room, etc. **interior monologue** a form of writing expressing a character's inner thoughts. **interior-sprung** (of a mattress etc.) with

internal springs. □□ **interiorize** v.tr. (also **-ise**). **interiorly** adv. [L, compar. f. inter among]

interject /ˌɪntəˈdʒekt/ v.tr. 1 utter (words) abruptly or parenthetically. 2 interrupt with. □□ **interjectory** adj. [L interjicere (as INTER-, jacere throw)]

interjection /ˌɪntəˈdʒekʃ(ə)n/ n. an exclamation, esp. as a part of speech (e.g. ah!, dear me!). □□ **interjectional** adj. [ME f. OF f. L interjectio -onis (as INTERJECT)]

interknit /ˌɪntəˈnɪt/ v.tr. & intr. (**-knitting**; past and past part. **-knitted** or **-knit**) knit together; intertwine.

interlace /ˌɪntəˈleɪs/ v. 1 tr. bind intricately together; interweave. 2 tr. mingle, intersperse. 3 intr. cross each other intricately. □□ **interlacement** n. [ME f. OF entrelacier (as INTER-, LACE v.)]

Interlaken /ˈɪntəˌlɑːkən/ the chief town of the Bernese Alps in central Switzerland, situated on the River Aare between Lake Brienz and Lake Thun; pop. (1980) 4,852.

interlanguage /ˈɪntəˌlæŋɡwɪdʒ/ n. a language or use of language having features of two others, often a pidgin or dialect form.

interlap /ˌɪntəˈlæp/ v.intr. (**-lapped, -lapping**) overlap.

interlard /ˌɪntəˈlɑːd/ v.tr. (usu. foll. by with) mix (writing or speech) with unusual words or phrases. [F entrelarder (as INTER-, LARD v.)]

interleaf /ˈɪntəˌliːf/ n. (pl. **-leaves**) an extra (usu. blank) leaf between the leaves of a book.

interleave /ˌɪntəˈliːv/ v.tr. insert (usu. blank) leaves between the leaves of (a book etc.).

interleukin /ˌɪntəˈluːkɪn/ n. Biochem. any of several glycoproteins produced by leucocytes for regulating immune responses. [INTER- + LEUCOCYTE]

interlibrary /ˈɪntəˌlaɪbrəri/ adj. between libraries (esp. interlibrary loan).

interline[1] /ˌɪntəˈlaɪn/ v.tr. 1 insert words between the lines of (a document etc.). 2 insert (words) in this way. □□ **interlineation** /-ˌlɪnɪˈeɪʃ(ə)n/ n. [ME f. med.L interlineare (as INTER-, LINE[1])]

interline[2] /ˌɪntəˈlaɪn/ v.tr. put an extra lining between the ordinary lining and the fabric of (a garment).

interlinear /ˌɪntəˈlɪnɪə(r)/ adj. written or printed between the lines of a text. [ME f. med.L interlinearis (as INTER-, LINEAR)]

interlining /ˈɪntəˌlaɪnɪŋ/ n. material used to interline a garment.

interlink /ˌɪntəˈlɪŋk/ v.tr. & intr. link or be linked together.

interlobular /ˌɪntəˈlɒbjʊlə(r)/ adj. situated between lobes.

interlock /ˌɪntəˈlɒk/ v., adj., & n. —v. 1 intr. engage with each other by overlapping or by the fitting together of projections and recesses. 2 tr. (usu. in passive) lock or clasp within each other. —adj. (of a fabric) knitted with closely interlocking stitches. —n. a device or mechanism for connecting or coordinating the function of different components. □□ **interlocker** n.

interlocutor /ˌɪntəˈlɒkjʊtə(r)/ n. (fem. **interlocutrix** /-trɪks/) a person who takes part in a dialogue or conversation. □□ **interlocution** /-ləˈkjuːʃ(ə)n/ n. (mod.L f. L interloqui interlocut- interrupt in speaking (as INTER-, loqui speak)]

interlocutory /ˌɪntəˈlɒkjʊtəri/ adj. 1 of dialogue or conversation. 2 Law (of a decree etc.) given provisionally in a legal action. [med.L interlocutorius (as INTERLOCUTOR)]

interloper /ˈɪntəˌləʊpə(r)/ n. 1 an intruder. 2 a person who interferes in others' affairs, esp. for profit. □□ **interlope** v.intr. [INTER- + loper as in landloper vagabond f. MDu. landlooper]

interlude /ˈɪntəˌluːd, -ˌljuːd/ n. 1 **a** a pause between the acts of a play. **b** something performed or done during this pause. 2 **a** an intervening time, space, or event that contrasts with what goes before or after. **b** a temporary amusement or entertaining episode. 3 a piece of music played between other pieces, the verses of a hymn, etc. [ME, = a light dramatic item between the acts of a morality play, f. med.L interludium (as INTER-, ludus play)]

intermarriage /ˌɪntəˈmærɪdʒ/ n. 1 marriage between people of different races, castes, families, etc. 2 (loosely) marriage between near relations.

b but d dog f few g get h he j yes k cat l leg m man n no p pen r red s sit t top v voice

intermarry /ˌɪntəˈmærɪ/ v.intr. (-ies, -ied) (foll. by with) (of races, castes, families, etc.) become connected by marriage.

intermediary /ˌɪntəˈmiːdɪərɪ/ n. & adj. —n. (pl. -ies) an intermediate person or thing, esp. a mediator. —adj. acting as mediator; intermediate. [F intermédiaire f. It. intermediario f. L intermedius (as INTERMEDIATE)]

intermediate /ˌɪntəˈmiːdɪət/ adj., n., & v. —adj. coming between two things in time, place, order, character, etc. —n. **1** an intermediate thing. **2** a chemical compound formed by one reaction and then used in another, esp. during synthesis. —v.intr. /-dɪˌeɪt/ (foll. by between) act as intermediary; mediate. □ **intermediate frequency** the frequency to which a radio signal is converted during heterodyne reception. □□ **intermediacy** /-sɪ/ n. **intermediately** adv. **intermediateness** n. **intermediation** /-ˈeɪʃ(ə)n/ n. **intermediator** /-ˌeɪtə(r)/ n. [med.L intermediatus (as INTER-, medius middle)]

interment /ɪnˈtɜːmənt/ n. the burial of a corpse, esp. with ceremony.

intermesh /ˌɪntəˈmeʃ/ v.tr. & intr. make or become meshed together.

intermezzo /ˌɪntəˈmetsəʊ/ n. (pl. **intermezzi** /-tsɪ/ or **-os**) **1 a** a short connecting instrumental movement in an opera or other musical work. **b** a similar piece performed independently. **c** a short piece for a solo instrument. **2** a short light dramatic or other performance inserted between the acts of a play. [It. f. L intermedium interval (as INTERMEDIATE)]

interminable /ɪnˈtɜːmɪnəb(ə)l/ adj. **1** endless. **2** tediously long or habitual. **3** with no prospect of an end. □□ **interminableness** n. **interminably** adv. [ME f. OF interminable or LL interminabilis (as IN-¹, TERMINATE)]

intermingle /ˌɪntəˈmɪŋg(ə)l/ v.tr. & intr. (often foll. by with) mix together; mingle.

intermission /ˌɪntəˈmɪʃ(ə)n/ n. **1** a pause or cessation. **2** an interval between parts of a play, film, concert, etc. **3** a period of inactivity. [F intermission or L intermissio (as INTERMIT)]

intermit /ˌɪntəˈmɪt/ v. (**intermitted, intermitting**) **1** intr. esp. Med. stop or cease activity briefly (e.g. of a fever, or a pulse). **2** tr. suspend; discontinue for a time. [L intermittere intermiss- (as INTER-, mittere let go)]

intermittent /ˌɪntəˈmɪt(ə)nt/ adj. occurring at intervals; not continuous or steady. □□ **intermittence** /-t(ə)ns/ n. **intermittency** /-tənsɪ/ n. **intermittently** adv. [L intermittere intermittent- (as INTERMIT)]

intermix /ˌɪntəˈmɪks/ v.tr. & intr. mix together. □□ **intermixable** adj. **intermixture** n. [back-form. f. intermixed, intermixt f. L intermixtus past part. of intermiscēre mix together (as INTER-, miscēre mix)]

intermolecular /ˌɪntəməˈlekjʊlə(r)/ adj. between molecules.

intern n. & v. —n. /ˈɪntɜːn/ (also **interne**) US a recent graduate or advanced student living in a hospital and acting as an assistant physician or surgeon. —v. **1** tr. /ɪnˈtɜːn/ confine; oblige (a prisoner, alien, etc.) to reside within prescribed limits. **2** intr. /ˈɪntɜːn/ US serve as an intern. □□ **internment** n. **internship** n. [F interne f. L internus internal]

internal /ɪnˈtɜːn(ə)l/ adj. & n. —adj. **1** of or situated in the inside or invisible part. **2** relating or applied to the inside of the body (internal injuries). **3** of a nation's domestic affairs. **4** (of a student) attending a university etc. as well as taking its examinations. **5** used or applying within an organization. **6 a** of the inner nature of a thing; intrinsic. **b** of the mind or soul. —n. (in pl.) intrinsic qualities. □ **internal energy** the energy in a system arising from the relative positions and interactions of its parts. **internal evidence** evidence derived from the contents of the thing discussed. **internal exile** see EXILE n. 1. **internal rhyme** a rhyme involving a word in the middle of a line and another at the end of the line or in the middle of the next. □□ **internality** /-ˈnælɪtɪ/ n. **internalize** v.tr. (also **-ise**). **internalization** /-ˈzeɪʃ(ə)n/ n. **internally** adv. [mod.L internalis (as INTERN)]

internal-combustion engine a form of heat engine in which fuel is burnt inside the cylinder of the engine instead of in a separate boiler (as used in a steam engine). The gases produced attain high values of pressure and temperature, driving the piston outwards as they expand. The exhaust gases are then released and a fresh supply of air (in a diesel engine) or a mixture of air and fuel (in a spark-ignition engine) is admitted and compressed before combustion again takes place. Most engines work on a four-stroke cycle (see OTTO), with four piston-strokes for each explosion, but two-stroke engines are used where lower power is sufficient. The advantage of internal-combustion engines over external combustion is their compactness, with all processes taking place in a single mechanism, giving a high output of power for a low weight, thus making them very suitable for transport purposes; their disadvantage is the need for very specific types of liquid or gaseous fuels, while external-combustion engines can use coal or any other fuel.

Internal-combustion engines originated in the early 19th c. The first reliable one was that of J. J. É. Lenoir in Paris in 1859. It ran slowly, lacked power, and consumed large quantities of fuel, but was the first real challenge to the dominance of steam. In 1862 a French engineer, Alphonse de Rochas, described a four-stroke cycle, but his work remained theoretical and he never made an engine; the principle was reinvented by Otto.

internat. abbr. international.

International n. an international Socialist organization. The First International was formed by Karl Marx in London in 1864 as an international working men's association and was dissolved twelve years later after internal wrangling between Marxists and Anarchists. The Second International was formed in Paris in 1889 and, although gravely weakened by the First World War, still survives as a loose association of Social Democrats. The Third International, also known as the Comintern, was formed by the Bolsheviks in 1919 to further the cause of the world revolution. Active if seldom effective between the wars, it was abolished in 1943 as a gesture towards the Soviet Union's allies. The Fourth International, a body of Trotskyist organizations, was formed in 1938 in opposition to the policies of the Stalin-dominated Third International.

international /ˌɪntəˈnæʃ(ə)n(ə)l/ adj. & n. —adj. **1** existing, involving, or carried on between two or more nations. **2** agreed on or used by all or many nations (international date-line; international driving licence). —n. **1** a contest, esp. in sport, between teams representing different countries. **2** a member of such a team. □ **international law** a body of rules established by custom or treaty and agreed as binding by nations in their relations with one another. **international style** see separate entry. **International System of Units** see separate entry. **international unit** a standard quantity of a vitamin etc. □□ **internationality** /-ˈnælɪtɪ/ n. **internationally** adv.

International Atomic Energy Agency an international organization set up in 1957 to accelerate and increase the contribution of atomic energy to peace, health, and prosperity throughout the world, and to ensure that assistance provided by it is not used for military purposes. Its headquarters are in Vienna.

International Bank for Reconstruction and Development an agency of the United Nations, established in 1945, and together with IDA known as the World Bank (see entry). Its headquarters are in Washington, DC.

International Civil Aviation Organization an agency of the United Nations, founded in 1947 to study problems of international civil aviation and establish standards and regulations etc. Its headquarters are in Montreal.

International Confederation of Free Trade Unions an association formed in 1949 to promote free trade unionism worldwide. Its headquarters are in Brussels.

International Court of Justice a judicial court of the United Nations which replaced the Cour Permanente de Justice in 1945 and meets at The Hague.

International Development Association an affiliate of the International Bank for Reconstruction and Development, established in 1960 to provide assistance primarily in the poorer developing countries. Its headquarters are in Washington, DC.

Internationale /ˌɪntəˌnæʃjəˈnɑːl/ n. **1** (prec. by the) a revolutionary hymn composed by Pierre Degeyter of Lille to words written earlier (1871) by Eugène Pottier, a Parisian transport worker. It was adopted by French socialists and subsequently by others, and was the official anthem of the USSR until 1 Jan. 1944. **2** the International. [F, fem. of *international* (adj.) f. INTERNATIONAL]

International Energy Agency an agency founded in 1974, within the framework of the OECD, to improve energy supply and demand etc. worldwide. Its headquarters are in Paris.

International Finance Corporation an organization established in 1956 as an affiliate of the World Bank to assist developing member countries by promoting the growth of the private sector of their economies.

International Fund for Agricultural Development an agency of the United Nations that began operations in 1977, with headquarters in Rome. Its purpose is to mobilize additional funds for agricultural and rural development in developing countries through programmes that directly benefit the poorest rural populations.

internationalism /ˌɪntəˈnæʃənəˌlɪz(ə)m/ n. **1** the advocacy of a community of interests among nations. **2** (**Internationalism**) the principles of any of the Internationals. □□ **internationalist** n.

internationalize /ˌɪntəˈnæʃənəˌlaɪz/ v.tr. (also **-ise**) **1** make international. **2** bring under the protection or control of two or more nations. □□ **internationalization** /-ˈzeɪʃ(ə)n/ n.

International Labour Organization an organization, established with the League of Nations in 1919, that became in 1946 the first specialized agency associated with the United Nations. Its headquarters are in Geneva. Its aim is to promote lasting peace through social justice, and to this end it works for better economic and social conditions everywhere. The organization was awarded the Nobel Peace Prize in 1969.

International Maritime Association an agency of the United Nations established in 1958 for cooperation and exchange of information among governments on matters relating to international shipping. Its headquarters are in London.

International Maritime Satellite Organization see INMARSAT.

International Monetary Fund an international organization affiliated to the UN, with headquarters in Washington, DC. Established in 1945, it exists to promote international trade and monetary cooperation, and the stabilization of exchange rates. Member countries contribute in gold and in their own currencies to provide a reserve on which they may draw (on certain conditions) to meet foreign obligations during periods of deficit in their international balance of payments.

International Organization for Standardization an organization founded in 1946 to standardize measurements etc. for international industrial, commercial, and scientific purposes. The British Standards Institution is a member.

International Phonetic Alphabet a set of phonetic symbols for international use, introduced in the late 19th c. by the International Phonetic Association, based on the Roman and Greek alphabets with the addition of some special symbols and diacritical marks.

international style n. an architectural style of the 20th c., associated especially with Gropius, Wright, and Le Corbusier, so called because it breached national and cultural barriers. It is characterized by the use of new building materials (especially steel and reinforced concrete), wide windows, uninterrupted interior spaces, simple lines, and strict geometric forms.

International System of Units (tr. F *Système international d'unités*), a system of physical units (together with a set of prefixes indicating multiplication or division by a power of ten) based on the metre, kilogram, second, ampere, kelvin, candela, and mole as independent basic units, with each of the derived units defined in terms of these without any multiplying factor. It was instituted in 1957.

International Telecommunications Satellite Consortium see INTELSAT.

International Telecommunication Union an organization whose purpose is to promote international cooperation in the use and improvement of telecommunications of all kinds. Founded at Paris in 1865 as the International Telegraph Union, it became an agency of the United Nations in 1947; its headquarters are in Geneva.

interne US var. of INTERN n.

internecine /ˌɪntəˈniːsaɪn/ adj. mutually destructive. [orig. = deadly, f. L *internecinus* f. *internecio* massacre f. *internecare* slaughter (as INTER-, *necare* kill)]

internee /ˌɪntɜːˈniː/ n. a person interned.

internist /ɪnˈtɜːnɪst/ n. Med. **1** a specialist in internal diseases. **2** US a general practitioner.

internode /ˈɪntəˌnəʊd/ n. **1** Bot. a part of a stem between two of the knobs from which leaves arise. **2** Anat. a slender part between two joints, esp. the bone of a finger or toe.

internuclear /ˌɪntəˈnjuːklɪə(r)/ adj. between nuclei.

internuncial /ˌɪntəˈnʌnʃ(ə)l/ adj. (of nerves) communicating between different parts of the system. [*internuncio* ambassador f. It. *internunzio*]

interoceanic /ˌɪntərˌəʊsɪˈænɪk/ adj. between or connecting two oceans.

interoceptive /ˌɪntərəʊˈseptɪv/ adj. Biol. relating to stimuli produced within an organism, esp. in the viscera. [irreg. f. L *internus* interior + RECEPTIVE]

interosculate /ˌɪntərˈɒskjʊˌleɪt/ v.intr. = INOSCULATE.

interosseous /ˌɪntərˈɒsɪəs/ adj. between bones.

interparietal /ˌɪntəpəˈraɪət(ə)l/ adj. between the right and left parietal bones of the skull. □□ **interparietally** adv.

interpellate /ɪnˈtɜːpeˌleɪt/ v.tr. (in European parliaments) interrupt the order of the day by demanding an explanation from (the Minister concerned). □□ **interpellation** /-ˈleɪʃ(ə)n/ n. **interpellator** n. [L *interpellare interpellat-* (as INTER-, *pellere* drive)]

interpenetrate /ˌɪntəˈpenɪˌtreɪt/ v. **1** intr. (of two things) penetrate each other. **2** tr. pervade; penetrate thoroughly. □□ **interpenetration** /-ˈtreɪʃ(ə)n/ n. **interpenetrative** /-trətɪv/ adj.

interpersonal /ˌɪntəˈpɜːsən(ə)l/ adj. (of relations) occurring between persons, esp. reciprocally. □□ **interpersonally** adv.

interplait /ˌɪntəˈplæt/ v.tr. & intr. plait together.

interplanetary /ˌɪntəˈplænɪtərɪ/ adj. **1** between planets. **2** relating to travel between planets.

interplay /ˈɪntəˌpleɪ/ n. **1** reciprocal action. **2** the operation of two things on each other.

interplead /ˌɪntəˈpliːd/ v. **1** intr. litigate with each other to settle a point concerning a third party. **2** tr. cause to do this. □□ **interpleader** n. [ME f. AF *enterpleder* (as INTER-, PLEAD)]

Interpol /ˈɪntəˌpɒl/ International Criminal Police Commission, an organization (founded in 1923, with headquarters in Vienna; reconstituted after the Second World War, with headquarters in Paris) that coordinates investigations made by the police forces of member countries into crimes with an international basis. [abbr. *International police*]

interpolate /ɪnˈtɜːpəˌleɪt/ v.tr. **1 a** insert (words) in a book etc., esp. to give false impressions as to its date etc. **b** make such insertions in (a book etc.). **2** interject (a remark) in a conversation. **3** estimate (values) from known ones in the same range. □□ **interpolation** /-ˈleɪʃ(ə)n/ n. **interpolative** /-lətɪv/ adj. **interpolator** n. [L *interpolare* furbish up (as INTER-, *polire* POLISH[1])]

interpose /ˌɪntəˈpəʊz/ v. **1** tr. (often foll. by *between*) place or insert (a thing) between others. **2** tr. say (words) as an interruption. **3** tr. exercise or advance (a veto or objection) so as to interfere. **4** intr. (foll. by *between*) intervene (between parties). [F *interposer* f. L *interponere* put (as INTER-, POSE[1])]

interposition /ˌɪntəpəˈzɪʃ(ə)n/ n. **1** the act of interposing. **2** a thing interposed. **3** an interference. [ME f. OF *interposition* or L *interpositio* (as INTER-, POSITION)]

interpret /ɪnˈtɜːprɪt/ v. (**interpreted, interpreting**) **1** tr. explain the meaning of (foreign or abstruse words, a dream, etc.). **2** tr. make out or bring out the meaning of (creative work). **3** intr. act as an interpreter, esp. of foreign languages. **4** tr.

æ cat ɑː arm e bed ɜː her ɪ sit iː see ɒ hot ɔː saw ʌ run ʊ put uː too ə ago aɪ my

explain or understand (behaviour etc.) in a specified manner (*interpreted his gesture as mocking*). □□ **interpretable** *adj.* **interpretability** /-təˈbɪlɪtɪ/ *n.* **interpretation** /-ˈteɪʃ(ə)n/ *n.* **interpretational** /-ˈteɪʃən(ə)l/ *adj.* **interpretative** /-ˈtətɪv/ *adj.* **interpretive** *adj.* **interpretively** *adv.* [ME f. OF *interpreter* or L *interpretari* explain, translate f. *interpres -pretis* explainer]

interpreter /ɪnˈtɜːprɪtə(r)/ *n.* a person who interprets, esp. one who translates speech orally. [ME f. AF *interpretour*, OF *interpreteur* f. LL *interpretator -oris* (as INTERPRET)]

interprovincial /ˌɪntəprəˈvɪnʃ(ə)l/ *adj.* situated or carried on between provinces.

interracial /ˌɪntəˈreɪʃ(ə)l/ *adj.* existing between or affecting different races. □□ **interracially** *adv.*

interregnum /ˌɪntəˈreɡnəm/ *n.* (*pl.* **interregnums** or **interregna** /-nə/) **1** an interval when the normal government is suspended, esp. between successive reigns or regimes. **2** an interval or pause. [L (as INTER-, *regnum* reign)]

interrelate /ˌɪntərɪˈleɪt/ *v.tr.* relate (two or more things) to each other. □□ **interrelation** *n.* **interrelationship** *n.*

interrogate /ɪnˈterəˌɡeɪt/ *v.tr.* ask questions of (a person) esp. closely, thoroughly, or formally. □□ **interrogator** *n.* [ME f. L *interrogare interrogat-* ask (as INTER-, *rogare* ask)]

interrogation /ɪnˌterəˈɡeɪʃ(ə)n/ *n.* **1** the act or an instance of interrogating; the process of being interrogated. **2** a question or enquiry. □ **interrogation point** (or **mark** etc.) = *question mark*. □□ **interrogational** *adj.* [ME f. F *interrogation* or L *interrogatio* (as INTERROGATE)]

interrogative /ˌɪntəˈrɒɡətɪv/ *adj.* & *n.* —*adj.* **1 a** of or like a question; used in questions. **b** *Gram.* (of an adjective or pronoun) asking a question (e.g. *who?, which?*). **2** having the form or force of a question. **3** suggesting enquiry (*an interrogative tone*). —*n.* an interrogative word (e.g. *what?, why?*). □□ **interrogatively** *adv.* [LL *interrogativus* (as INTERROGATE)]

interrogatory /ˌɪntəˈrɒɡətərɪ/ *adj.* & *n.* —*adj.* questioning; of or suggesting enquiry (*an interrogatory eyebrow*). —*n.* (*pl.* **-ies**) a formal set of questions, esp. *Law* one formally put to an accused person etc. [LL *interrogatorius* (as INTERROGATE)]

interrupt /ˌɪntəˈrʌpt/ *v.tr.* **1** act so as to break the continuous progress of (an action, speech, a person speaking, etc.). **2** obstruct (a person's view etc.). **3** break the continuity of. □□ **interruptible** *adj.* **interruption** /-ˈrʌpʃ(ə)n/ *n.* **interruptive** *adj.* **interruptory** *adj.* [ME f. L *interrumpere interrupt-* (as INTER-, *rumpere* break)]

interrupter /ˌɪntəˈrʌptə(r)/ *n.* (also **interruptor**) **1** a person or thing that interrupts. **2** a device for interrupting, esp. an electric circuit.

intersect /ˌɪntəˈsekt/ *v.* **1** *tr.* divide (a thing) by passing or lying across it. **2** *intr.* (of lines, roads, etc.) cross or cut each other. [L *intersecare intersect-* (as INTER-, *secare* cut)]

intersection /ˌɪntəˈsekʃ(ə)n/ *n.* **1** the act of intersecting. **2** a place where two roads intersect. **3** a point or line common to lines or planes that intersect. □□ **intersectional** *adj.* [L *intersectio* (as INTERSECT)]

interseptal /ˌɪntəˈsept(ə)l/ *adj.* between septa or partitions.

intersex /ˈɪntəˌseks/ *n.* **1** the abnormal condition of being intermediate between male and female. **2** an individual in this condition.

intersexual /ˌɪntəˈseksjʊəl/ *adj.* **1** existing between the sexes. **2** of intersex. □□ **intersexuality** /-ˈælɪtɪ/ *n.* **intersexually** *adv.*

interspace /ˈɪntəˌspeɪs/ *n.* & *v.* —*n.* an interval of space or time. —*v.tr.* put interspaces between.

interspecific /ˌɪntəspəˈsɪfɪk/ *adj.* formed from different species.

intersperse /ˌɪntəˈspɜːs/ *v.tr.* **1** (often foll. by *between, among*) scatter; place here and there. **2** (foll. by *with*) diversify (a thing or things with others so scattered). □□ **interspersion** *n.* [L *interspergere interspers-* (as INTER-, *spargere* scatter)]

interspinal /ˌIntəˈspaɪn(ə)l/ *adj.* (also **interspinous** /-nəs/) between spines or spinous processes.

interstate /ˈɪntəˌsteɪt/ *adj.* & *n.* *US* —*adj.* existing or carried on between States, esp. of the US. —*n.* a motorway, esp. crossing a State boundary.

interstellar /ˌɪntəˈstelə(r)/ *adj.* occurring or situated between stars.

interstice /ɪnˈtɜːstɪs/ *n.* **1** an intervening space. **2** a chink or crevice. [L *interstitium* (as INTER-, *sistere stit-* stand)]

interstitial /ˌɪntəˈstɪʃ(ə)l/ *adj.* of, forming, or occupying interstices. □□ **interstitially** *adv.*

intertextuality /ˌɪntəˌtekstjʊˈælɪtɪ/ *n.* the relationship between esp. literary texts.

intertidal /ˌɪntəˈtaɪd(ə)l/ *adj.* of or relating to the area which is covered at high tide and uncovered at low tide.

intertribal /ˌɪntəˈtraɪb(ə)l/ *adj.* existing or occurring between different tribes.

intertrigo /ˌɪntəˈtraɪɡəʊ/ *n.* (*pl.* **-os**) *Med.* inflammation from the rubbing of one area of skin on another. [L f. *interterere intertrit-* (as INTER-, *terere* rub)]

intertwine /ˌɪntəˈtwaɪn/ *v.* **1** *tr.* (often foll. by *with*) entwine (together). **2** *intr.* become entwined. □□ **intertwinement** *n.*

intertwist /ˌɪntəˈtwɪst/ *v.tr.* twist together.

interval /ˈɪntəv(ə)l/ *n.* **1** an intervening time or space. **2** *Brit.* a pause or break, esp. between the parts of a theatrical or musical performance. **3** the difference in pitch between two sounds. **4** the distance between persons or things in respect of qualities. □ **at intervals** here and there; now and then. □□ **intervallic** /-ˈvælɪk/ *adj.* [ME ult. f. L *intervallum* space between ramparts, interval (as INTER-, *vallum* rampart)]

intervene /ˌɪntəˈviːn/ *v.intr.* (often foll. by *between, in*) **1** occur in time between events. **2** interfere; come between so as to prevent or modify the result or course of events. **3** be situated between things. **4** come in as an extraneous factor or thing. **5** *Law* interpose in a lawsuit as a third party. □□ **intervener** *n.* **intervenient** *adj.* **intervenor** *n.* [L *intervenire* (as INTER-, *venire* come)]

intervention /ˌɪntəˈvenʃ(ə)n/ *n.* **1** the act or an instance of intervening. **2** interference, esp. by a State in another's affairs. **3** mediation. [ME f. F *intervention* or L *interventio* (as INTERVENE)]

interventionist /ˌɪntəˈvenʃənɪst/ *n.* a person who favours intervention.

intervertebral /ˌɪntəˈvɜːtɪbr(ə)l/ *adj.* between vertebrae.

interview /ˈɪntəˌvjuː/ *n.* & *v.* —*n.* **1** an oral examination of an applicant for employment, a college place, etc. **2** a conversation between a reporter etc. and a person of public interest, used as a basis of a broadcast or publication. **3** a meeting of persons face to face, esp. for consultation. —*v.tr.* **1** hold an interview with. **2** question to discover the opinions or experience of (a person). □□ **interviewee** /-vjuːˈiː/ *n.* **interviewer** *n.* [F *entrevue* f. *s'entrevoir* see each other (as INTER-, *voir* f. L *vidēre* see: see VIEW)]

interwar /ˌɪntəˈwɔː(r)/ *adj.* existing in the period between two wars, esp. the two world wars.

interweave /ˌɪntəˈwiːv/ *v.tr.* (*past* **-wove** /-ˈwəʊv/; *past part.* **-woven** /-ˈwəʊv(ə)n/) **1** (often foll. by *with*) weave together. **2** blend intimately.

interwind /ˌɪntəˈwaɪnd/ *v.tr.* & *intr.* (*past and past part.* **-wound** /-ˈwaʊnd/) wind together.

interwork /ˌɪntəˈwɜːk/ *v.* **1** *intr.* work together or interactively. **2** *tr.* interweave.

intestate /ɪnˈtestət/ *adj.* & *n.* —*adj.* (of a person) not having made a will before death. —*n.* a person who has died intestate. □□ **intestacy** /-təsɪ/ *n.* [ME f. L *intestatus* (as IN-¹, *testari testat-* make a will f. *testis* witness)]

intestine /ɪnˈtestɪn/ *n.* (in *sing.* or *pl.*) the lower part of the alimentary canal from the end of the stomach to the anus. □ **large intestine** the caecum, colon, and rectum collectively. **small intestine** the duodenum, jejunum, and ileum collectively. □□ **intestinal** /also ˌɪnteˈstaɪn(ə)l/ *adj.* [L *intestinum* f. *intestinus* internal]

inthrall *US var.* of ENTHRAL.

intifada /ˌɪntɪˈfɑːdə/ *n.* the uprising and unrest amongst Palestinians in the Israeli-occupied West Bank and Gaza Strip, which began towards the end of 1987. [Arab. *intifāda* shake free]

intimacy /ˈɪntɪməsɪ/ *n.* (*pl.* **-ies**) **1** the state of being intimate.

2 an intimate act, esp. sexual intercourse. **3** an intimate remark; an endearment.

intimate[1] /'ıntımət/ adj. & n. —adj. **1** closely acquainted; familiar, close (an intimate friend; an intimate relationship). **2** private and personal (intimate thoughts). **3** (usu. foll. by with) having sexual relations. **4** (of knowledge) detailed, thorough. **5** (of a relationship between things) close. **6** (of mixing etc.) thorough. **7** essential, intrinsic. **8** (of a place etc.) friendly; promoting close personal relationships. —n. a very close friend. □□ **intimately** adv. [L intimus inmost]

intimate[2] /'ıntı,meıt/ v.tr. **1** (often foll. by that + clause) state or make known. **2** imply, hint. □□ **intimater** n. **intimation** /-'meıʃ(ə)n/ n. [LL intimare announce f. L intimus inmost]

intimidate /ın'tımı,deıt/ v.tr. frighten or overawe, esp. to subdue or influence. □□ **intimidation** /-'deıʃ(ə)n/ n. **intimidator** n. [med.L intimidare (as IN-[2], timidare f. timidus TIMID)]

intinction /ın'tıŋkʃ(ə)n/ n. Eccl. the dipping of the Eucharistic bread in the wine so that the communicant receives both together. [LL intinctio f. L intingere intinct- (as IN-[2], TINGE)]

intitule /ın'tıtju:l/ v.tr. Brit. entitle (an Act of Parliament etc.). [OF intituler f. LL intitulare (as IN-[2], titulare f. titulus title)]

into /'ıntʊ, 'ıntə/ prep. **1** expressing motion or direction to a point on or within (walked into a tree; ran into the house). **2** expressing direction of attention or concern (will look into it). **3** expressing a change of state (turned into a dragon; separated into groups; forced into cooperation). **4** colloq. interested in; knowledgeable about (is really into art). [OE intō (as IN, TO)]

intolerable /ın'tɒlərəb(ə)l/ adj. that cannot be endured. □□ **intolerableness** n. **intolerably** adv. [ME f. OF intolerable or L intolerabilis (as IN-[1], TOLERABLE)]

intolerant /ın'tɒlərənt/ adj. not tolerant, esp. of views, beliefs, or behaviour differing from one's own. □□ **intolerance** n. **intolerantly** adv. [L intolerans (as IN-[1], TOLERANT)]

intonate /'ıntə,neıt/ v.tr. intone. [med.L intonare: see INTONE]

intonation /,ıntə'neıʃ(ə)n/ n. **1** modulation of the voice; accent. **2** the act of intoning. **3** accuracy of pitch in playing or singing (has good intonation). **4** the opening phrase of a plainsong melody. □□ **intonational** adj. [med.L intonatio (as INTONE)]

intone /ın'təʊn/ v.tr. **1** recite (prayers etc.) with prolonged sounds, esp. in a monotone. **2** utter with a particular tone. □□ **intoner** n. [med.L intonare (as IN-[2], L tonus TONE)]

in toto /ın 'təʊtəʊ/ adv. completely. [L]

intoxicant /ın'tɒksıkənt/ adj. & n. —adj. intoxicating. —n. an intoxicating substance.

intoxicate /ın'tɒksı,keıt/ v.tr. **1** make drunk. **2** excite or elate beyond self-controe. □□ **intoxication** /-'keıʃ(ə)n/ n. [med.L intoxicare (as IN-[2], toxicare poison f. L toxicum): see TOXIC]

intra- /'ıntrə/ prefix forming adjectives usu. from adjectives, meaning 'on the inside, within' (intramural). [L intra inside]

intracellular /,ıntrə'seljʊlə(r)/ adj. Biol. located or occurring within a cell or cells.

intracranial /,ıntrə'kreınıəl/ adj. within the skull. □□ **intracranially** adv.

intractable /ın'træktəb(ə)l/ adj. **1** hard to control or deal with. **2** difficult, stubborn. □□ **intractability** /-'bılıtı/ n. **intractableness** n. **intractably** adv. [L intractabilis (as IN-[1], TRACTABLE)]

intrados /ın'treıdɒs/ n. the lower or inner curve of an arch. [F (as INTRA-, dos back f. L dorsum)]

intramolecular /,ıntrəmə'lekjʊlə(r)/ adj. within a molecule.

intramural /,ıntrə'mjʊər(ə)l/ adj. **1** situated or done within walls. **2** forming part of normal university or college studies. □□ **intramurally** adv.

intramuscular /,ıntrə'mʌskjʊlə(r)/ adj. in or into a muscle or muscles.

intransigent /ın'trænsıdʒ(ə)nt, -zıdʒ(ə)nt/ adj. & n. —adj. uncompromising, stubborn. —n. an intransigent person. □□ **intransigence** /-dʒ(ə)ns/ n. **intransigency** /-dʒənsı/ n. **intransigently** adv. [F intransigeant f. Sp. los intransigentes

extreme republicans in Cortes, ult. formed as IN-[1] + L transigere transigent- come to an understanding (as TRANS-, agere act)]

intransitive /ın'trænsıtıv, ın'trɑ:n-, -zıtıv/ adj. (of a verb or sense of a verb) that does not take or require a direct object (whether expressed or implied), e.g. look in look at the sky (opp. TRANSITIVE). □□ **intransitively** adv. **intransitivity** /-'tıvıtı/ n. [LL intransitivus (as IN-[1], TRANSITIVE)]

intra-uterine /,ıntrə'ju:tə,raın, -rın/ adj. within the womb.

intravenous /,ıntrə'vi:nəs/ adj. in or into a vein or veins. □□ **intravenously** adv. [INTRA- + L vena vein]

in-tray /'ıntreı/ n. a tray for incoming documents, letters, etc.

intrepid /ın'trepıd/ adj. fearless; very brave. □□ **intrepidity** /-trı'pıdıtı/ n. **intrepidly** adv. [F intrépide or L intrepidus (as IN-[1], trepidus alarmed)]

intricate /'ıntrıkət/ adj. very complicated; perplexingly detailed. □□ **intricacy** /-kəsı/ n. (pl. -ies). **intricately** adv. [ME f. L intricare intricat- (as IN-[2], tricare f. tricae tricks)]

intrigant /'ıntrıgənt/ n. (fem. **intrigante**) an intriguer. [F intriguant f. intriguer: see INTRIGUE]

intrigue v. & n. —v. /ın'tri:g/ (**intrigues, intrigued, intriguing**) **1** intr. (foll. by with) **a** carry on an underhand plot. **b** use secret influence. **2** tr. arouse the curiosity of; fascinate. —n. /ın'tri:g, 'ın-/ **1** an underhand plot or plotting. **2** archaic a secret love affair. □□ **intriguer** /ın'tri:gə(r)/ n. **intriguing** adj. (esp. in sense 2 of v.) **intriguingly** /ın'tri:gıŋ-/ adv. [F intrigue (n.), intriguer (v.) f. It. intrigo, intrigare f. L (as INTRICATE)]

intrinsic /ın'trınzık/ adj. inherent, essential; belonging naturally (intrinsic value). □□ **intrinsically** adv. [ME, = interior, f. F intrinsèque f. LL intrinsecus f. L intrinsecus (adv.) inwardly]

intro /'ıntrəʊ/ n. (pl. -os) colloq. an introduction. [abbr.]

intro- /'ıntrəʊ/ comb. form into (introgression). [L intro to the inside]

introduce /,ıntrə'dju:s/ v.tr. **1** (foll. by to) make (a person or oneself) known by name to another, esp. formally. **2** announce or present to an audience. **3** bring (a custom, idea, etc.) into use. **4** bring (a piece of legislation) before a legislative assembly. **5** (foll. by to) draw the attention or extend the understanding of (a person) to a subject. **6** insert; place in. **7** bring in; usher in; bring forward. **8** begin; occur just before the start of. □□ **introducer** n. **introducible** adj. [ME f. L introducere introduct- (as INTRO-, ducere lead)]

introduction /,ıntrə'dʌkʃ(ə)n/ n. **1** the act or an instance of introducing; the process of being introduced. **2** a formal presentation of one person to another. **3** an explanatory section at the beginning of a book etc. **4** a preliminary section in a piece of music, often thematically different from the main section. **5** an introductory treatise on a subject. **6** a thing introduced. [ME f. OF introduction or L introductio (as INTRODUCE)]

introductory /,ıntrə'dʌktərı/ adj. serving as an introduction; preliminary. [LL introductorius (as INTRODUCTION)]

introit /'ıntrɔıt/ n. a psalm or antiphon sung or said while the priest approaches the altar for the Eucharist. [ME f. OF f. L introitus f. introire introit- enter (as INTRO-, ire go)]

introjection /,ıntrə'dʒekʃ(ə)n/ n. the unconscious incorporation of external ideas into one's mind. [INTRO- after projection]

intromit /,ıntrə'mıt/ v.tr. (**intromitted, intromitting**) **1** archaic (foll. by into) let in, admit. **2** insert. □□ **intromission** /-'mıʃ(ə)n/ n. **intromittent** adj. [L intromittere intromiss- introduce (as INTRO-, mittere send)]

introspection /,ıntrə'spekʃ(ə)n/ n. the examination or observation of one's own mental and emotional processes etc. □□ **introspective** adj. **introspectively** adv. **introspectiveness** n. [L introspicere introspect- look inwards (as INTRO-, specere look)]

introvert n., adj., & v. —n. /'ıntrə,vɜ:t/ **1** Psychol. a person predominantly concerned with his or her own thoughts and feelings rather than with external things. **2** a shy inwardly thoughtful person. —adj. /'ıntrə,vɜ:t/ (also **introverted** /-tıd/) typical or characteristic of an introvert. —v.tr. /ıntrə'vɜ:t/ **1** Psychol. direct (one's thoughts or mind) inwards. **2** Zool. withdraw (an organ etc.) within its own tube or base, like the finger of a glove. □□ **introversion** /-'vɜ:ʃ(ə)n/ n. **introversive** /-'vɜ:sıv/ adj.

b but d dog f few g get h he j yes k cat l leg m man n no p pen r red s sit t top v voice

introverted *adj.* **introvertive** /-ˈvɜːtɪv/ *adj.* [INTRO- + *vert* as in INVERT]

intrude /ɪnˈtruːd/ *v.* (foll. by *on*, *upon*, *into*) **1** *intr.* come uninvited or unwanted; force oneself abruptly on others. **2** *tr.* thrust or force (something unwelcome) on a person. □□ **intrudingly** *adv.* [L *intrudere intrus-* (as IN-², *trudere* thrust)]

intruder /ɪnˈtruːdə(r)/ *n.* a person who intrudes, esp. into a building with criminal intent.

intrusion /ɪnˈtruːʒ(ə)n/ *n.* **1** the act or an instance of intruding. **2** an unwanted interruption etc. **3** *Geol.* an influx of molten rock between or through strata etc. but not reaching the surface. **4** the occupation of a vacant estate etc. to which one has no claim. **5** *Phonet.* the addition of a sound between words or syllables to facilitate pronunciation, e.g. the *r* in *saw a film* (/ˈsɔːrəfɪlm/). [ME f. OF *intrusion* or med.L *intrusio* (as INTRUDE)]

intrusive /ɪnˈtruːsɪv/ *adj.* **1** that intrudes or tends to intrude. **2** characterized by intrusion. □□ **intrusively** *adv.* **intrusiveness** *n.*

intrust var. of ENTRUST.

intubate /ˈɪntjʊˌbeɪt/ *v.tr. Med.* insert a tube into the trachea for ventilation, usu. during anaesthesia. □□ **intubation** /-ˈbeɪʃ(ə)n/ *n.* [IN-² + L *tuba* tube]

intuit /ɪnˈtjuːɪt/ *v.* **1** *tr.* know by intuition. **2** *intr.* receive knowledge by direct perception. □□ **intuitable** *adj.* [L *intueri intuit-* consider (as IN-², *tueri* look)]

intuition /ˌɪntjuːˈɪʃ(ə)n/ *n.* **1** immediate apprehension by the mind without reasoning. **2** immediate apprehension by a sense. **3** immediate insight. □□ **intuitional** *adj.* [LL *intuitio* (as INTUIT)]

intuitionism /ˌɪntjuːˈɪʃəˌnɪz(ə)m/ *n.* (also **intuitionalism**) *Philos.* the theory that the perception of truth is by intuition; the theory that in perception objects are known immediately by intuition; the theory that ethical principles are matters of intuition. □□ **intuitionist** *n.*

intuitive /ɪnˈtjuːɪtɪv/ *adj.* **1** of, characterized by, or possessing intuition. **2** perceived by intuition. □□ **intuitively** *adv.* **intuitiveness** *n.* [med.L *intuitivus* (as INTUIT)]

intuitivism /ɪnˈtjuːɪtɪˌvɪz(ə)m/ *n.* the doctrine that ethical principles can be established by intuition. □□ **intuitivist** *n.*

intumesce /ˌɪntjuːˈmes/ *v.intr.* swell up. □□ **intumescence** *n.* **intumescent** *adj.* [L *intumescere* (as IN-², *tumescere* incept. of *tumēre* swell)]

intussusception /ˌɪntʌsəˈsepʃ(ə)n/ *n.* **1** *Med.* the inversion of one portion of the intestine within another. **2** *Bot.* the deposition of new cellulose particles in a cell wall, to increase the surface area of the cell. [F *intussusception* or mod.L *intussusceptio* f. L *intus* within + *susceptio* f. *suscipere* take up]

intwine var. of ENTWINE.

Inuit /ˈɪnjuːɪt, ˈɪnʊɪt/ *n.* (also **Innuit**) (*pl.* same or **Inuits**) a N. American Eskimo. [Eskimo *inuit* people]

inundate /ˈɪnʌnˌdeɪt/ *v.tr.* (often foll. by *with*) **1** flood. **2** overwhelm (*inundated with enquiries*). □□ **inundation** /-ˈdeɪʃ(ə)n/ *n.* [L *inundare* flow (as IN-², *unda* wave)]

inure /ɪˈnjʊə(r)/ *v.* **1** *tr.* (often in *passive*; foll. by *to*) accustom (a person) to something esp. unpleasant. **2** *intr. Law* come into operation; take effect. □□ **inurement** *n.* [ME f. AF *eneurer* f. phr. *en eure* (both unrecorded) in use or practice, f. *en* in + OF *e(u)vre* work f. L *opera*]

in utero /ɪn ˈjuːtəˌrəʊ/ *adv.* in the womb; before birth. [L]

in vacuo /ɪn ˈvækjʊəʊ/ *adv.* in a vacuum. [L]

invade /ɪnˈveɪd/ *v.tr.* (often *absol.*) **1** enter (a country etc.) under arms to control or subdue it. **2** swarm into. **3** (of a disease) attack (a body etc.). **4** encroach upon (a person's rights, esp. privacy). □□ **invader** *n.* [L *invadere invas-* (as IN-², *vadere* go)]

invaginate /ɪnˈvædʒɪˌneɪt/ *v.tr.* **1** put in a sheath. **2** turn (a tube) inside out. □□ **invagination** /-ˈneɪʃ(ə)n/ *n.* [IN-² + L *vagina* sheath]

invalid[1] *n.* & *v.* —*n.* /ˈɪnvəˌliːd, -lɪd/ **1** a person enfeebled or disabled by illness or injury. **2** (*attrib.*) **a** of or for invalids (*invalid car*; *invalid diet*). **b** being an invalid (*caring for her invalid mother*). —*v.* /ˈɪnvəˌliːd/ (**invalided**, **invaliding**) **1** *tr.* (often foll. by *out* etc.) remove from active service (one who has become an

invalid). **2** *tr.* (usu. in *passive*) disable (a person) by illness. **3** *intr.* become an invalid. □□ **invalidism** *n.* [L *invalidus* weak, infirm (as IN-¹, VALID)]

invalid[2] /ɪnˈvælɪd/ *adj.* not valid, esp. having no legal force. □□ **invalidly** *adv.* [L *invalidus* (as INVALID¹)]

invalidate /ɪnˈvælɪˌdeɪt/ *v.tr.* **1** make (esp. an argument etc.) invalid. **2** remove the validity or force of (a treaty, contract, etc.). □□ **invalidation** /-ˈdeɪʃ(ə)n/ *n.* [med.L *invalidare invalidat-* (as IN-¹, *validus* VALID)]

invalidity /ˌɪnvəˈlɪdɪtɪ/ *n.* **1** lack of validity. **2** bodily infirmity. [F *invalidité* or med.L *invaliditas* (as INVALID¹)]

invaluable /ɪnˈvæljʊəb(ə)l/ *adj.* above valuation; inestimable. □□ **invaluableness** *n.* **invaluably** *adv.*

Invar /ˈɪnvɑː(r)/ *n. propr.* an iron-nickel alloy with a negligible coefficient of expansion, used in the manufacture of clocks and scientific instruments. [abbr. of INVARIABLE]

invariable /ɪnˈveərɪəb(ə)l/ *adj.* **1** unchangeable. **2** always the same. **3** *Math.* constant, fixed. □□ **invariability** /-ˈbɪlɪtɪ/ *n.* **invariableness** *n.* **invariably** *adv.* [F *invariable* or LL *invariabilis* (as IN-¹, VARIABLE)]

invariant /ɪnˈveərɪənt/ *adj.* & *n.* —*adj.* invariable. —*n. Math.* a function which remains unchanged when a specified transformation is applied. □□ **invariance** *n.*

invasion /ɪnˈveɪʒ(ə)n/ *n.* **1** the act of invading or process of being invaded. **2** an entry of a hostile army into a country. □□ **invasive** /-sɪv/ *adj.* [F *invasion* or LL *invasio* (as INVADE)]

invective /ɪnˈvektɪv/ *n.* **1 a** strongly attacking words. **b** the use of these. **2** abusive rhetoric. [ME f. OF f. LL *invectivus* attacking (as INVEIGH)]

inveigh /ɪnˈveɪ/ *v.intr.* (foll. by *against*) speak or write with strong hostility. [L *invehi* go into, assail (as IN-², *vehi* passive of *vehere* *vect-* carry)]

inveigle /ɪnˈveɪg(ə)l, -ˈviːg(ə)l/ *v.tr.* (foll. by *into*, or *to* + infin.) entice; persuade by guile. □□ **inveiglement** *n.* [earlier *enve(u)gle* f. AF *envegler*, OF *aveugler* to blind f. *aveugle* blind prob. f. Rmc *ab oculis* (unrecorded) without eyes]

invent /ɪnˈvent/ *v.tr.* **1** create by thought, devise; originate (a new method, an instrument, etc.). **2** concoct (a false story etc.). □□ **inventable** *adj.* [ME, = discover, f. L *invenire invent-* find, contrive (as IN-², *venire vent-* come)]

invention /ɪnˈvenʃ(ə)n/ *n.* **1** the process of inventing. **2 a** thing invented; a contrivance, esp. one for which a patent is granted. **3 a** fictitious story. **4** inventiveness. **5** *Mus.* a short piece for keyboard, developing a simple idea. [ME f. L *inventio* (as INVENT)]

inventive /ɪnˈventɪv/ *adj.* **1** able or inclined to invent; original in devising. **2** showing ingenuity of devising. □□ **inventively** *adv.* **inventiveness** *n.* [ME f. F *inventif -ive* or med.L *inventivus* (as INVENT)]

inventor /ɪnˈventə(r)/ *n.* (*fem.* **inventress** /-trɪs/) a person who invents, esp. as an occupation.

inventory /ˈɪnvəntərɪ/ *n.* & *v.* —*n.* (*pl.* **-ies**) **1** a complete list of goods in stock, house contents, etc. **2** the goods listed in this. **3** *US* the total of a firm's commercial assets. —*v.tr.* (**-ies**, **-ied**) **1** make an inventory of. **2** enter (goods) in an inventory. [ME f. med.L *inventorium* f. LL *inventarium* (as INVENT)]

Invercargill /ˌɪnvəˈkɑːgɪl/ a city of New Zealand, capital of Southland region, South Island; pop. (1988) 52,200.

Inverness /ˌɪnvəˈnes/ a city of Scotland, in Highland region, situated at the mouth of the River Ness; pop. (1981) 40,000.

inverse /ˈɪnvɜːs, -ˈvɜːs/ *adj.* & *n.* —*adj.* inverted in position, order, or relation. —*n.* **1** the state of being inverted. **2** (often foll. by *of*) a thing that is the opposite or reverse of another. **3** *Math.* an element which, when combined with a given element in an operation, produces the identity element for that operation. □ **inverse proportion** (or **ratio**) a relation between two quantities such that one increases in proportion as the other decreases. **inverse square law** a law by which the intensity of an effect, such as gravitational force, illumination, etc., changes in inverse proportion to the square of the distance from the source. □□ **inversely** *adv.* [L *inversus* past part. of *invertere*: see INVERT]

inversion /ɪnˈvɜːʃ(ə)n/ n. **1** the act of turning upside down or inside out. **2** the reversal of a normal order, position, or relation. **3** the reversal of the order of words, for rhetorical effect. **4** the reversal of the normal variation of air temperature with altitude. **5** the process or result of inverting. **6** the reversal of direction of rotation of a plane of polarized light. **7** homosexuality. □□ **inversive** /-sɪv/ adj. [L inversio (as INVERT)]

invert v. & n. —v.tr. /ɪnˈvɜːt/ **1** turn upside down. **2** reverse the position, order, or relation of. **3** Mus. change the relative position of the notes of (a chord or interval) by placing the lowest note higher, usu. by an octave. **4** subject to inversion. —n. /ˈɪnvɜːt/ **1** a homosexual. **2** an inverted arch, as at the bottom of a sewer. □ **inverted comma** = quotation mark. **inverted snob** a person who likes or takes pride in what a snob might be expected to disapprove of. **invert sugar** a mixture of dextrose and laevulose. □□ **inverter** /ɪnˈvɜːtə(r)/ n. **invertible** /ɪnˈvɜːtɪb(ə)l/ adj. **invertibility** /-ˈbɪlɪtɪ/ n. [L invertere invers- (as IN-², vertere turn)]

invertebrate /ɪnˈvɜːtɪbrət, -ˌbreɪt/ adj. & n. —adj. **1** (of an animal) not having a backbone. **2** lacking firmness of character. —n. an invertebrate animal. [mod.L invertebrata (pl.) (as IN-¹, VERTEBRA)]

invest /ɪnˈvest/ v. **1** tr. (often foll. by in) apply or use (money), esp. for profit. **2** intr. (foll. by in) **a** put money for profit (into stocks etc.). **b** colloq. buy (invested in a new car). **3** tr. **a** (foll. by with) provide, endue, or attribute (a person with qualities, insignia, or rank). **b** (foll. by in) attribute or entrust (qualities or feelings to a person). **4** tr. cover as a garment. **5** tr. lay siege to. □□ **investable** adj. **investible** adj. **investor** n. [ME f. F investir or L investire investit- (as IN-², vestire clothe f. vestis clothing): sense 1 f. It. investire]

investigate /ɪnˈvestɪˌɡeɪt/ v. **1** tr. **a** inquire into; examine; study carefully. **b** make an official inquiry into. **2** intr. make a systematic inquiry or search. □□ **investigator** n. **investigatory** /-ɡətərɪ/ adj. [L investigare investigat- (as IN-², vestigare track)]

investigation /ɪnˌvestɪˈɡeɪʃ(ə)n/ n. **1** the process or an instance of investigating. **2** a formal examination or study.

investigative /ɪnˈvestɪɡətɪv/ adj. seeking or serving to investigate, esp. (of journalism) inquiring intensively into controversial issues.

investiture /ɪnˈvestɪˌtjʊə(r)/ n. **1** the formal investing of a person with honours or rank, esp. a ceremony at which a sovereign confers honours. **2** (often foll. by with) the act of enduing (with attributes). [ME f. med.L investitura (as INVEST)]

investment /ɪnˈvestmənt/ n. **1** the act or process of investing. **2** money invested. **3** property etc. in which money is invested. **4** the act of besieging; a blockade. □ **investment bank** a US bank that fulfils many of the functions of a UK merchant bank. **investment trust** a trust that buys and sells shares in selected companies to make a profit for its members.

inveterate /ɪnˈvetərət/ adj. **1** (of a person) confirmed in an (esp. undesirable) habit etc. (an inveterate gambler). **2 a** (of a habit etc.) long-established. **b** (of an activity, esp. an undesirable one) habitual. □□ **inveteracy** /-rəsɪ/ n. **inveterately** adv. [ME f. L inveterare inveterat- make old (as IN-², vetus veteris old)]

invidious /ɪnˈvɪdɪəs/ adj. (of an action, conduct, attitude, etc.) likely to excite resentment or indignation against the person responsible, esp. by real or seeming injustice (an invidious position; an invidious task). □□ **invidiously** adv. **invidiousness** n. [L invidiosus f. invidia ENVY]

invigilate /ɪnˈvɪdʒɪˌleɪt/ v.intr. Brit. supervise candidates at an examination. □□ **invigilation** /-ˈleɪʃ(ə)n/ n. **invigilator** n. [orig. = keep watch, f. L invigilare invigilat- (as IN-², vigilare watch f. vigil watchful)]

invigorate /ɪnˈvɪɡəˌreɪt/ v.tr. give vigour or strength to. □□ **invigorating** adj. **invigoratingly** adv. **invigoration** /-ˈreɪʃ(ə)n/ n. **invigorative** /-rətɪv/ adj. **invigorator** n. [IN-² + med.L vigorare vigorat- make strong]

invincible /ɪnˈvɪnsɪb(ə)l/ adj. unconquerable; that cannot be defeated. □□ **invincibility** /-ˈbɪlɪtɪ/ n. **invincibleness** n. **invincibly** adv. [ME f. OF f. L invincibilis (as IN-¹, VINCIBLE)]

inviolable /ɪnˈvaɪələb(ə)l/ adj. not to be violated or profaned.

inviolability /-ˈbɪlɪtɪ/ n. **inviolably** adv. [F inviolable or L inviolabilis (as IN-¹, VIOLATE)]

inviolate /ɪnˈvaɪələt/ adj. not violated or profaned. □□ **inviolacy** /-ləsɪ/ n. **inviolately** adv. **inviolateness** n. [ME f. L inviolatus (as IN-¹, violare, violat- treat violently)]

invisible /ɪnˈvɪzɪb(ə)l/ adj. **1** not visible to the eye, either characteristically or because hidden. **2** too small to be seen or noticed. **3** artfully concealed (invisible mending). □ **invisible exports** (or **imports** etc.) items, esp. services, involving payment between countries but not constituting tangible commodities. □□ **invisibility** /-ˈbɪlɪtɪ/ n. **invisibleness** n. **invisibly** adv. [ME f. OF invisible or L invisibilis (as IN-¹, VISIBLE)]

invitation /ˌɪnvɪˈteɪʃ(ə)n/ n. the process of inviting or fact of being invited, esp. to a social occasion.

invite /ɪnˈvaɪt/ v. & n. —v. **1** tr. (often foll. by to, or to + infin.) ask (a person) courteously to come, or to do something (were invited to lunch; invited them to reply). **2** tr. make a formal courteous request for (invited comments). **3** tr. tend to call forth unintentionally (something unwanted). **4 a** tr. attract. **b** intr. be attractive. —n. /ˈɪnvaɪt/ colloq. an invitation. □□ **invitee** /-ˈtiː/ n. **inviter** n. [F inviter or L invitare]

inviting /ɪnˈvaɪtɪŋ/ adj. **1** attractive. **2** enticing, tempting. □□ **invitingly** adv. **invitingness** n.

in vitro /ɪn ˈviːtrəʊ/ adv. Biol. (of processes or reactions) taking place in a test-tube or other laboratory environment (opp. IN VIVO). [L, = in glass]

in vivo /ɪn ˈviːvəʊ/ adv. Biol. (of processes) taking place in a living organism. [L, = in a living thing]

invocation /ˌɪnvəˈkeɪʃ(ə)n/ n. **1** the act or an instance of invoking, esp. in prayer. **2** an appeal to a supernatural being or beings, e.g. the Muses, for psychological or spiritual inspiration. **3** Eccl. the words 'In the name of the Father' etc. used as the preface to a sermon etc. □□ **invocatory** /ɪnˈvɒkətərɪ/ adj. [ME f. OF f. L invocatio -onis (as INVOKE)]

invoice /ˈɪnvɔɪs/ n. & v. —n. a list of goods shipped or sent, or services rendered, with prices and charges; a bill. —v.tr. **1** make an invoice of (goods and services). **2** send an invoice to (a person). [earlier invoyes pl. of invoy = ENVOY²]

invoke /ɪnˈvəʊk/ v.tr. **1** call on (a deity etc.) in prayer or as a witness. **2** appeal to (the law, a person's authority, etc.). **3** summon (a spirit) by charms. **4** ask earnestly for (vengeance, help, etc.). □□ **invocable** adj. **invoker** n. [F invoquer f. L invocare (as IN-², vocare call)]

involucre /ˈɪnvəˌluːkə(r), -ˌljuːkə(r)/ n. **1** a covering or envelope. **2** Anat. a membranous envelope. **3** Bot. a whorl of bracts surrounding an inflorescence. □□ **involucral** /-ˈluːkr(ə)l, -ˈljuːkr(ə)l/ adj. [F involucre or L involucrum (as INVOLVE)]

involuntary /ɪnˈvɒləntərɪ/ adj. **1** done without the exercise of the will; unintentional. **2** (of a limb, muscle, or movement) not under the control of the will. □□ **involuntarily** adv. **involuntariness** n. [LL involuntarius (as IN-¹, VOLUNTARY)]

involute /ˈɪnvəˌluːt, -ˌljuːt/ adj. & n. —adj. **1** involved, intricate. **2** curled spirally. **3** Bot. rolled inwards at the edges. —n. Geom. the locus of a point fixed on a straight line that rolls without sliding on a curve and is in the plane of that curve (cf. EVOLUTE). [L involutus past part. of involvere: see INVOLVE]

involuted /ˈɪnvəˌluːtɪd, -ˌljuːtɪd/ adj. **1** complicated, abstruse. **2** = INVOLUTE adj. 2.

involution /ˌɪnvəˈluːʃ(ə)n, -ˈljuːʃ(ə)n/ n. **1** the process of involving. **2** an entanglement. **3** intricacy. **4** curling inwards. **5** a part that curls upwards. **6** Math. the raising of a quantity to any power. **7** Physiol. the reduction in size of an organ in old age, or when its purpose has been fulfilled (esp. the uterus after childbirth). □□ **involutional** adj. [L involutio (as INVOLVE)]

involve /ɪnˈvɒlv/ v.tr. **1** (often foll. by in) cause (a person or thing) to participate, or share the experience or effect (in a situation, activity, etc.). **2** imply, entail, make necessary. **3** (foll. by in) implicate (a person in a charge, crime, etc.). **4** include or affect in its operations. **5** (as **involved** adj.) **a** (often foll. by in) concerned or interested. **b** complicated in thought or form. [ME f. L involvere involut- (as IN-², volvere roll)]

involvement /ɪnˈvɒlvmənt/ n. **1** (often foll. by *in*, *with*) the act or an instance of involving; the process of being involved. **2** financial embarrassment. **3** a complicated affair or concern.

invulnerable /ɪnˈvʌlnərəb(ə)l/ adj. that cannot be wounded or hurt, physically or mentally. □□ **invulnerability** /-ˈbɪlɪtɪ/ n. **invulnerably** adv. [L *invulnerabilis* (as IN-¹, VULNERABLE)]

inward /ˈɪnwəd/ adj. & adv. —adj. **1** directed toward the inside; going in. **2** situated within. **3** mental, spiritual. —adv. (also **inwards**) **1** (of motion or position) towards the inside. **2** in the mind or soul. [OE *innanweard* (as IN, -WARD)]

inwardly /ˈɪnwədlɪ/ adv. **1** on the inside. **2** in the mind or soul. **3** (of speaking) not aloud; inaudibly. [OE *inweardlīce* (as INWARD)]

inwardness /ˈɪnwədnɪs/ n. **1** inner nature; essence. **2** the condition of being inward. **3** spirituality.

inwards var. of INWARD adv.

inweave /ɪnˈwiːv/ v.tr. (also **enweave**) (past **-wove** /-ˈwəʊv/; past part. **-woven** /-ˈwəʊv(ə)n/) **1** weave (two or more things) together. **2** intermingle.

inwrap var. of ENWRAP.

inwreathe var. of ENWREATHE.

inwrought /ɪnˈrɔːt, attrib. ˈɪnrɔːt/ adj. **1 a** (often foll. by *with*) (of a fabric) decorated (with a pattern). **b** (often foll. by *in*, *on*) (of a pattern) wrought (in or on a fabric). **2** closely blended.

inyala /ɪnˈjɑːlə/ n. (also **nyala** /ˈnjɑːlə/) (pl. same) a large antelope, *Tragelaphus angasi*, native to S. Africa, with curved horns having a single complete turn. [Zulu]

Io /ˈaɪəʊ/ **1** *Gk Mythol.* priestess of Hera, loved by Zeus who, trying to protect her from the jealousy of Hera, turned her into a beautiful heifer, who wandered far and wide, constantly stung by a gadfly. (See IONIAN SEA and BOSPORUS.) **2** *Astron.* a satellite of the planet Jupiter.

IOC abbr. International Olympic Committee.

iodic /aɪˈɒdɪk/ adj. *Chem.* containing iodine in chemical combination (*iodic acid*). □□ **iodate** /ˈaɪədeɪt/ n.

iodide /ˈaɪədaɪd/ n. *Chem.* any compound of iodine with another element or group.

iodinate /aɪˈɒdɪˌneɪt, ˈaɪə-/ v.tr. treat or combine with iodine. □□ **iodination** /-ˈneɪʃ(ə)n/ n.

iodine /ˈaɪəˌdiːn, -ɪn/ n. **1** *Chem.* a non-metallic element of the halogen group, forming black crystals and a violet vapour, resembling chlorine and bromine in its chemical properties. Identified as an element by Gay-Lussac in 1811, iodine has a number of uses in chemistry; potassium iodide is used in photography. As a constituent of thyroid hormones iodine is required in small amounts in the body, and deficiency can lead to goitre. ¶ Symb.: **I**; atomic number 53. **2** a solution of this in alcohol used as a mild antiseptic. [F *iode* f. Gk *iōdēs* violet-like f. *ion* violet + -INE⁴]

iodism /ˈaɪəˌdɪz(ə)m/ n. *Med.* a condition caused by an overdose of iodides.

iodize /ˈaɪəˌdaɪz/ v.tr. (also **-ise**) treat or impregnate with iodine. □□ **iodization** /-ˈzeɪʃ(ə)n/ n.

iodo- /aɪˈəʊdəʊ/ comb. form (usu. **iod-** before a vowel) *Chem.* iodine.

iodoform /aɪˈəʊdəˌfɔːm, -ˈɒdəˌfɔːm/ n. a pale yellow volatile sweet-smelling solid compound of iodine with antiseptic properties. ¶ Chem. formula: CHI₃. [IODINE after *chloroform*]

IOM abbr. Isle of Man.

ion /ˈaɪən/ n. an atom or group of atoms that has lost one or more electrons (= CATION), or gained one or more electrons (= ANION). □ **ion exchange** the exchange of ions of the same charge between a usu. aqueous solution and a solid, used in water-softening etc. **ion exchanger** a substance or equipment for this process. [Gk, neut. pres. part. of *eimi* go]

-ion suffix (usu. as **-sion, -tion, -xion**; see -ATION, -ITION, -UTION) forming nouns denoting: **1** verbal action (*excision*). **2** an instance of this (*a suggestion*). **3** a resulting state or product (*vexation*; *concoction*). [from or after F -*ion* or L -*io* -*ionis*]

Iona /aɪˈəʊnə/ an island in the Inner Hebrides, site of a monastery founded by St Columba *c.*563 which became a centre for Celtic Christian missions to Scotland.

Ionesco /jɒˈneskəʊ/, Eugene (1912–), French dramatist of Romanian birth, who settled permanently in France in 1938. He was a leading exponent of the Theatre of the Absurd which he demonstrated in his first play *La Cantatrice Chauve* (*The Bald Prima Donna*, 1952), and *Le Roi se meurt* (1962). By employing visual imagery, verbal rhythm, and balletic movement he achieves surrealistic effects and presents a disturbing world where grotesque events or objects symbolize mankind's condition.

Ionia /aɪˈəʊnɪə/ the ancient Greek name for the central part of the west coast of Asia Minor. Tribes speaking the Ionic dialect of Greek left the mainland in the 11th c. BC, according to early tradition, settling in the Aegean islands and in the coastal area of Asia Minor, later known as Ionia, which was colonized by the Greeks from about the 8th c. BC. They retained their distinctive dialect, also spoken in Athens, and are noted for their contributions in science, poetry, and architecture. Throughout the eastern Mediterranean 'Yawani' (= Ionians) became the generic word for 'Greek'.

Ionian /aɪˈəʊnɪən/ n. & adj. —n. a native or inhabitant of ancient Ionia. —adj. of or relating to Ionia or the Ionians. □ **Ionian mode** *Mus.* the mode represented by the natural diatonic scale C–C. [L *Ionius* f. Gk *Iōnios*]

Ionian Islands /aɪˈəʊnɪən/ a chain of islands off the western coast of Greece, of which the largest are Corfu and Cephalonia. The islands constitute a region of modern Greece; pop. (1981) 182,650.

Ionian Sea /aɪˈəʊnɪən/ the part of the Mediterranean Sea between western Greece and southern Italy, at the mouth of the Adriatic. According to one ancient Greek tradition it is named after Io (see entry), who crossed it in her wanderings, rather than after the Ionians.

Ionic /aɪˈɒnɪk/ adj. & n. —adj. **1** of the order of Greek architecture characterized by a column with scroll-shapes on either side of the capital. **2** of the ancient Greek dialect used in Ionia. —n. the Ionic dialect. [L *Ionicus* f. Gk *Iōnikos*]

ionic /aɪˈɒnɪk/ adj. of, relating to, or using ions. □□ **ionically** adv.

ionization /ˌaɪənaɪˈzeɪʃ(ə)n/ n. (also **-isation**) the process of producing ions as a result of solvation, heat, radiation, etc. □ **ionization chamber** an instrument for detecting ionizing radiation.

ionize /ˈaɪəˌnaɪz/ v.tr. & intr. (also **-ise**) convert or be converted into an ion or ions. □ **ionizing radiation** a radiation of sufficient energy to cause ionization in the medium through which it passes. □□ **ionizable** adj.

ionizer /ˈaɪəˌnaɪzə(r)/ n. any thing which produces ionization, esp. a device used to improve the quality of the air in a room etc.

ionosphere /aɪˈɒnəˌsfɪə(r)/ n. an ionized region of the atmosphere above the stratosphere, extending to about 1,000 km above the earth's surface and able to reflect radio waves for long-distance transmission round the earth (cf. TROPOSPHERE). □□ **ionospheric** /-ˈsferɪk/ adj.

-ior¹ /ɪə(r)/ suffix forming adjectives of comparison (*senior*; *ulterior*). [L]

-ior² var. of -IOUR.

iota /aɪˈəʊtə/ n. **1** the ninth letter of the Greek alphabet (*I*, *ι*). **2** (usu. with *neg.*) the smallest possible amount. [Gk *iōta*]

IOU /ˌaɪəʊˈjuː/ n. a signed document acknowledging a debt. [= I owe you]

-iour /ɪə(r)/ suffix (also **-ior**) forming nouns (*saviour*; *warrior*). [-I- (as a stem element) + -OUR², -OR¹]

-ious /-ɪəs, -əs/ suffix forming adjectives meaning 'characterized by, full of', often corresponding to nouns in -*ion* (*cautious*; *curious*; *spacious*). [from or after F -*ieux* f. L -*iosus*]

IOW abbr. Isle of Wight.

Iowa /ˈaɪəwə/ a State in the Middle West of the US, acquired as part of the Louisiana Purchase in 1803; pop. (est. 1985) 2,923,400; capital, Des Moines. It became the 29th State of the US in 1846.

IPA abbr. International Phonetic Alphabet (or Association).

aʊ how eɪ day əʊ no eə hair ɪə near ɔɪ boy ʊə poor aɪə fire aʊə sour (*see over for consonants*)

IPCS *abbr.* (in the UK) Institution of Professional Civil Servants.

ipecac /ˈɪpɪˌkæk/ *n. colloq.* ipecacuanha. [abbr.]

ipecacuanha /ˌɪpɪˌkækjʊˈɑːnə/ *n.* the root of a S. American shrub, *Cephaelis ipecacuanha*, used as an emetic and purgative. [Port. f. Tupi-Guarani *ipekaaguéne* emetic creeper]

Iphigenia /ˌɪfɪdʒɪˈnaɪə/ *Gk legend* the daughter of Agamemnon, who was obliged to offer her as a sacrifice to Artemis when the Greek fleet was becalmed at Aulis (on the coast of Greece) on its way to the Trojan War. The goddess snatched her away to Tauris in the Crimea, where she became a priestess until rescued by Orestes.

Ipiros see EPIRUS.

Ipoh /iːˈpəʊ/ a city of Malaysia, capital of the State of Perak since 1937; pop. (1980) 300,700.

ipomoea /ˌɪpəˈmiːə/ *n.* any twining plant of the genus *Ipomoea*, having trumpet-shaped flowers, e.g. the sweet potato and morning glory. [mod.L f. Gk *ips ipos* worm + *homoios* like]

ips *abbr.* (also **i.p.s.**) inches per second.

ipse dixit /ˌɪpsɪ ˈdɪksɪt/ *n.* a dogmatic statement resting merely on the speaker's authority. [L, he himself said it (orig. of Pythagoras)]

ipsilateral /ˌɪpsɪˈlætər(ə)l/ *adj.* belonging to or occurring on the same side of the body. [irreg. f. L *ipse* self + LATERAL]

ipsissima verba /ɪpˌsɪsɪmə ˈvɜːbə/ *n.pl.* the precise words. [L]

ipso facto /ˌɪpsəʊ ˈfæktəʊ/ *adv.* **1** by that very fact or act. **2** thereby. [L]

IQ *abbr.* intelligence quotient.

Iqbal /ˈɪkbæl/, Sir Muhammad (1875–1938), Islamic poet and philosopher, born in the Punjab in India. Writing in both Persian and Urdu he became a leader of Islamic modernism. He emphasized the international character of Islam but eventually concluded that it could find expression, in the modern world, only in the free association of Muslim States. As president of the Muslim League in 1930 he advocated the creation of a separate Muslim State in NW India.

-ique *archaic var.* of -IC.

Iquitos /ɪˈkiːtɒs/ the principal river port and oil exploration centre in the tropical rainforest of eastern Peru, situated on the west bank of the River Amazon; pop. (est. 1988) 247,000.

IR *abbr.* infrared.

Ir *symb. Chem.* the element iridium.

ir- /ɪ(r)/ *prefix* assim. form of IN-¹, IN-² before *r*.

IRA *abbr.* Irish Republican Army.

irade /ɪˈrɑːdɪ/ *n. hist.* a written decree of the Sultan of Turkey. [Turk. f. Arab. *'irāda* will]

Iráklion see HERAKLION.

Iran /ɪˈrɑːn/ a country in the Middle East lying between the Caspian Sea and the Persian Gulf; pop. (est. 1988) 51,923,700; official language, Persian (Farsi); capital, Tehran. Oil is the chief source of revenue, otherwise the country is largely agricultural; the developing industrial output was largely curtailed by the 1979 revolution. (For its early history, see PERSIA.) The country was successively the centre of the Persian, Seleucid, Parthian, and Sassanian empires. Following the Muslim conquest in the 7th c. it was part of various Turkish, Persian, Tartar, and Mongol empires. A coup in 1925 brought the Pahlavi family to the throne, but following the overthrow of the Shah in 1979 Iran became an Islamic fundamentalist State. From 1980 to 1988 Iran was involved in war with her neighbour Iraq (see GULF WAR 1).

Irangate /ɪˈrɑːnɡeɪt/ a US political scandal of 1987, during the presidency of Ronald Reagan, involving the supplying of arms to Iran (and subsequent release of American hostages) and use of the proceeds to supply arms to the anti-Communist Contras in Nicaragua. [IRAN + (WATER)GATE]

Iranian /ɪˈreɪnɪən/ *adj. & n.* —*adj.* **1** of or relating to Iran (formerly Persia). **2** of the Indo-European group of languages including Persian (Farsi), Pashto, Avestan, and Kurdish. —*n.* **1** a native or national of Iran. **2** a person of Iranian descent.

Iraq /ɪˈrɑːk/ a country in the Middle East bordering on the Persian Gulf, traversed by the Tigris and Euphrates Rivers and corresponding roughly to ancient Mesopotamia; pop. (est. 1988) 17,583,450; official language, Arabic; capital, Baghdad. Oil is the principal source of revenue, but agriculture makes a considerable contribution. The Tigris–Euphrates valley was the site of an early civilization (see MESOPOTAMIA). It was conquered by Arabia in the 7th c. and from 1534 formed part of the Ottoman empire, becoming an independent State after the First World War when the Turks were expelled. Iraq was a kingdom (at first under British administration) until a coup in 1958 overthrew the monarchy and a republic was declared. Saddam Hussein came to power as President in 1979. The country was at war with its eastern neighbour Iran in 1980–8, and in August 1990 Iraq invaded Kuwait in an attempt to obtain that country's wealth and oilfields and to secure its own access to the sea-outlet of the Gulf; it was expelled by an international coalition of forces in Jan.–Feb. 1991 (see GULF WAR).

Iraqi /ɪˈrɑːkɪ/ *adj. & n.* —*adj.* of or relating to Iraq. —*n.* (*pl.* **Iraqis**) **1 a** a native or national of Iraq. **b** a person of Iraqi descent. **2** the form of Arabic spoken in Iraq.

irascible /ɪˈræsɪb(ə)l/ *adj.* irritable; hot-tempered. □□ **irascibility** /-ˈbɪlɪtɪ/ *n.* **irascibly** *adv.* [ME f. F f. LL *irascibilis* f. L *irasci* grow angry f. *ira* anger]

irate /aɪˈreɪt/ *adj.* angry, enraged. □□ **irately** *adv.* **irateness** *n.* [L *iratus* f. *ira* anger]

IRBM *abbr.* intermediate-range ballistic missile.

ire /ˈaɪə(r)/ *n. literary* anger. □□ **ireful** *adj.* [ME f. OF f. L *ira*]

Ireland /ˈaɪələnd/ an island of the British Isles, lying west of Great Britain. Four-fifths of it is occupied by the Republic of Ireland (pop. (est. 1988) 3,531,500; official languages, Irish and English; capital Dublin), and the remainder by Northern Ireland. The soil is fertile and the pasturage lush, swept by warm damp winds from the Atlantic; the economy relies heavily on agriculture, especially beef production and dairy farming. Settled by the Celts, the country became divided into independent tribal territories over which the lords of Tara exercised nominal suzerainty. Christianity reached Ireland, probably by the 4th c., to be consolidated by the work of St Patrick, and after the break-up of the Roman Empire the country became for a time a leading cultural centre, with the monasteries fostering learning and missionary work. English invasions began in the 12th c. under Henry II, but the authority that he established was never secure and by the 16th c. was confined to an area round Dublin (the English Pale) until the Tudors succeeded in extending it over the whole of the island. Revolts against English rule, and against the imposition of Protestantism (which met with unexpectedly stubborn resistance), resulted in the 'plantation' of Ireland by English (and later Scottish) families on confiscated land in an attempt to anglicize the country and secure its allegiance; in Ulster particularly the descendants of such settlers retained a distinctive identity. After an unsuccessful rebellion in 1798, union of Britain and Ireland followed in 1801. In spite of genuine efforts towards its success Ireland sank deeper into destitution. A share of Britain's industrial prosperity reached Protestant Ulster, but the rest of the island found its agricultural produce and assets dropping in value, and at the failure of the potato crop (Ireland's staple) in the 1840s thousands died in the famine, thousands more fled abroad. The Home Rule movement, led by Parnell, failed to achieve its aims in the 19th c. and implementation of a bill passed in 1910 was delayed by the outbreak of the First World War. An Act of 1920 divided Ireland into two parts: Southern Ireland, later recognized as an independent State (called the Irish Free State 1921–37, Eire 1937–49, the Republic of Ireland 1949–), and Northern Ireland (see separate entry).

Irenaeus /ˌaɪrɪˈniːəs/, St (*c.*130–*c.*200), the leading Greek theologian of the 2nd c., bishop of Lyons in Gaul from 177, and author of a detailed attack on Gnosticism. Feast day, (in the East) 23 Aug., (in the West) 28 June.

irenic /aɪˈriːnɪk/ *adj.* (also **irenical**, **eirenic**) *literary* aiming or aimed at peace. [Gk *eirēnikos*: see EIRENICON]

irenicon var. of EIRENICON.

Irian Jaya /ˌɪrɪən ˈdʒaɪə/ (also **West Irian**) a province of eastern

Indonesia comprising the western half of the island of New Guinea together with the adjacent small islands; pop. (1980) 1,173,875; capital, Jayapura.

iridaceous /ˌɪrɪˈdeɪʃəs/ *adj. Bot.* of or relating to the family Iridaceae of plants growing from bulbs, corms, or rhizomes, e.g. iris, crocus, and gladiolus. [mod.L *iridaceus* (as IRIS)]

iridescent /ˌɪrɪˈdes(ə)nt/ *adj.* **1** showing rainbow-like luminous or gleaming colours. **2** changing colour with position. □□ **iridescence** *n.* **iridescently** *adv.* [L IRIS + -ESCENT]

iridium /ɪˈrɪdɪəm/ *n. Chem.* a hard white metallic element of the transition series, related to platinum and resembling polished steel. One of the densest metals known, iridium has limited uses in its pure state, but alloyed with platinum it is used in jewellery, electrical contacts, and other situations where hardness and resistance to corrosion are important. It was discovered in 1803. ¶ Symb.: **Ir**; atomic number 77. [mod.L f. L *iris* rainbow (see IRIS), from its highly coloured salts + -IUM]

Iris /ˈaɪərɪs/ *Gk Mythol.* goddess of the rainbow. When thought of in human form she acts as messenger of the gods, presumably because the rainbow seems to touch both earth and sky.

iris /ˈaɪərɪs/ *n.* **1** the flat circular coloured membrane behind the cornea of the eye, with a circular opening (pupil) in the centre. **2** any herbaceous plant of the genus *Iris*, usu. with tuberous roots, sword-shaped leaves, and showy flowers. **3** (in full **iris diaphragm**) an adjustable diaphragm of thin overlapping plates for regulating the size of a central hole esp. for the admission of light to a lens. [ME f. L *iris iridis* f. Gk *iris iridos* rainbow, iris]

Irish /ˈaɪərɪʃ/ *adj. & n.* —*adj.* of or relating to Ireland; of or like its people. —*n.* **1** the Celtic language of Ireland. (See below.) **2** (prec. by *the*; treated as *pl.*) the people of Ireland. □ **Irish bull** = BULL³. **Irish coffee** coffee mixed with a dash of whisky and served with cream on top. **Irish moss** dried carrageen. **Irish stew** a stew of mutton, potato, and onion. **Irish terrier** a rough-haired light reddish-brown breed of terrier. [ME f. OE *Iras* the Irish]

Irish (or Erse) belongs to the Celtic family of languages and is a distinct variety of Gaelic. It was brought to Ireland by Celtic invaders *c.*1000 BC, and down to the end of the 18th c. was spoken by the great majority of the people especially in areas other than the cities. Its earliest attestation is in inscriptions from the 4th c. AD, written in the Ogham script, and there has been a tradition of literature since the 6th c., with a mass of material from the 9th to 19th c. In the 19th c. English gained ground rapidly and Irish is now spoken regularly only in certain areas in the west of Ireland. Since 1922 the Irish government has organized its revival, and it is now taught in all the schools, but despite this active support and the establishment of Irish as an official language there are probably fewer than 60,000 native speakers. It is the first official language of the Irish Republic (the second is English). A few English words are derived from Irish, e.g. *banshee, blarney, galore, leprechaun,* and *Tory.*

Irishman /ˈaɪərɪʃmən/ *n.* (*pl.* **-men**) a man who is Irish by birth or descent.

Irish Republican Army the military arm of Sinn Fein, formed during the struggle for independence from Britain in 1916–21, which continues to attempt to achieve union between the Republic of Ireland and Northern Ireland in the present day. Having maintained a relatively low level of armed activity up until the late 1960s the IRA split in 1969, and the radical minority, known as the Provisional IRA, stepped up the level of violence against military and civilian targets.

Irish Sea the sea separating Ireland from England and Wales.

Irish Sweepstake (also **Irish Sweep**) a sweepstake on the results of certain major horse-races (especially the Derby and the Grand National), authorized since 1930 by the government of the Republic of Ireland in order to benefit Irish hospitals, which receive most of the profits. It is the largest international lottery. Most of its revenue is derived from the US, though the buying and selling of sweepstake tickets is illegal there and they have to be smuggled into the country.

Irishwoman /ˈaɪərɪʃˌwʊmən/ *n.* (*pl.* **-women**) a woman who is Irish by birth or descent.

iritis /aɪˈraɪtɪs/ *n.* inflammation of the iris.

irk /ɜːk/ *v.tr.* (usu. *impers.;* often foll. by *that* + clause) irritate, bore, annoy. [ME: orig. unkn.]

irksome /ˈɜːksəm/ *adj.* tedious, annoying, tiresome. □□ **irksomely** *adv.* **irksomeness** *n.* [ME, = tired etc., f. IRK + -SOME¹]

Irkutsk /ɪəˈkʊtsk/ the chief city of Siberia, situated on the western shore of Lake Baikal in the Russian SFSR; pop. (est. 1987) 609,000.

IRO *abbr.* **1** (in the UK) Inland Revenue Office. **2** International Refugee Organization.

iroko /ɪˈrəʊkəʊ/ *n.* (*pl.* **-os**) **1** either of two African trees, *Chlorophora excelsa* or *C. regia.* **2** the light-coloured hardwood from these trees. [Ibo]

iron /ˈaɪən/ *n., adj., & v.* —*n.* **1** *Chem.* a silver-white ductile metallic element of great strength. (See below.) ¶ Symb.: **Fe**; atomic number 26. **2** this as a type of unyieldingness or a symbol of firmness (*man of iron; will of iron*). **3** a tool or implement made of iron (*branding iron; curling iron*). **4** a household, now usu. electrical, implement with a flat base which is heated to smooth clothes etc. **5** a golf club with an iron or steel sloping face used for lofting the ball. **6** (usu. in *pl.*) a fetter (*clapped in irons*). **7** (usu. in *pl.*) a stirrup. **8** (often in *pl.*) an iron support for a malformed leg. **9** a preparation of iron as a tonic or dietary supplement (*iron tablets*). —*adj.* **1** made of iron. **2** very robust. **3** unyielding, merciless (*iron determination*). —*v.tr.* **1** smooth (clothes etc.) with an iron. **2** furnish or cover with iron. **3** shackle with irons. □ **in irons** handcuffed, chained, etc. **Iron Age** *Archaeol.* see separate entry. **iron-bark** any of various eucalyptus trees with a thick solid bark and hard dense timber. **iron-bound 1** bound with iron. **2** rigorous; hard and fast. **3** (of a coast) rock-bound. **Iron Chancellor** Bismarck. **Iron Cross** the highest German military decoration for bravery. **Iron Curtain** see separate entry. **Iron Duke** the first Duke of Wellington. **iron hand** firmness or inflexibility (cf. *velvet glove*). **iron in the fire** an undertaking, opportunity, or commitment (usu. in *pl.: too many irons in the fire*). **ironing-board** a flat surface usu. on legs and of adjustable height on which clothes etc. are ironed. **Iron Lady** the nickname given by Soviet journalists to the British Prime Minister Margaret Thatcher. **iron lung** a rigid case fitted over a patient's body, used for administering prolonged artificial respiration by means of mechanical pumps. Such an apparatus was first devised in the US in 1929. **iron maiden** *hist.* an instrument of torture consisting of a coffin-shaped box lined with iron spikes. **iron-mould** (US **-mold**) a spot caused by iron-rust or an ink-stain, esp. on fabric. **iron-on** able to be fixed to the surface of a fabric etc. by ironing. **iron out** remove or smooth over (difficulties etc.). **iron pyrites** see PYRITES. **iron ration** a small emergency supply of food. □□ **ironer** *n.* **ironing** *n.* (in sense 1 of *v.*). **ironless** *adj.* **iron-like** *adj.* [OE *īren, īsern* f. Gmc, prob. f. Celt.]

Iron is one of the most abundant elements, widely distributed throughout the earth's crust in the form of ores, which are easily reduced to the metal, found in its free state only in meteorites, and essential to many types of animal life as a constituent of haemoglobin. Silver-white in colour, it is strong and ductile, with magnetic susceptibility, and is the most extensively used of all metals because of its many properties. Iron was known in Egypt *c.*3000 BC and was used in Europe *c.*1000 BC (see IRON AGE). When purified and alloyed with small quantities of other materials it is known as steel.

Cast iron is obtained by smelting from ores. It is silvery-grey when clean, hard, brittle, crystalline in structure, and contains 2–5% of carbon and smaller quantities of sulphur, phosphorus, and silicon. **Pig-iron** is cast iron as first obtained from the smelting furnace, cast in long blocks (pigs) for convenience. **Wrought iron,** which is highly malleable, is obtained by puddling (= stirring) pig-iron when molten, nearly pure but always containing some slag in the form of filaments and thus showing a fibrous structure.

Iron Age the third stage in the classification of prehistoric periods (see PREHISTORY), when weapons and tools were made of iron. The Hittites in Anatolia were working iron by c.1400 BC, but on a small scale and the technique was not fully understood. By the 12th c. BC its use had spread more widely; the Hebrews and Greeks knew it by 1000 BC, but it was not in use on a large scale until two centuries later. The application of the term ends, in Europe, at the Roman period.

ironclad adj. & n. —adj. /ˌaɪənˈklæd/ **1** clad or protected with iron. **2** impregnable; rigorous. —n. /ˈaɪənˌklæd/ hist. a wooden battleship protected by armour plating. As a result of the loss of French and British wooden battleships during the Crimean War, the French government ordered the construction of five armour-plated vessels for use in the Black Sea, and the first entered service in 1859. In 1862, during the American Civil War, the first 'ironclad' battle took place. The design was quickly adopted by most nations until succeeded by steel-framed Dreadnought-type battleships at the beginning of the 20th c.

Iron Curtain a former barrier to the passage of persons and information at the limit of the Soviet sphere of influence. The first 'iron curtain' (in the literal sense) dates from the rebuilding of Drury Lane Theatre in 1794, after its destruction by a fire which started on the stage, and was designed for lowering as a protection. The figurative sense (= an impenetrable barrier) is found from about 25 years later. The first reference to such a barrier in connection with Russia dates from 1920. In 1945 the phrase occurs in its current application, and its use by W. S. Churchill in 1946 fixed it in the language.

Iron Gate (Romanian *Porţile de Fier*, Serbo-Croatian *Gvozdena Vrata*) a gorge through which a section of the River Danube flows, forming part of the boundary between Romania and Yugoslavia. Navigation was improved by means of a ship canal constructed through it in 1896, and a joint Yugoslav–Romanian project completed a dam and hydroelectric power plant in 1972.

ironic /aɪˈrɒnɪk/ adj. (also **ironical**) **1** using or displaying irony. **2** in the nature of irony. □□ **ironically** adv. [F *ironique* or LL *ironicus* f. Gk *eirōnikos* dissembling (as IRONY[1])]

ironist /ˈaɪərənɪst/ n. a person who uses irony. □□ **ironize** v.intr. (also **-ise**). [Gk *eirōn* dissembler + -IST]

ironmaster /ˈaɪənˌmɑːstə(r)/ n. a manufacturer of iron.

ironmonger /ˈaɪənˌmʌŋgə(r)/ n. Brit. a dealer in hardware etc. □□ **ironmongery** n. (pl. **-ies**).

Ironsides /ˈaɪənˌsaɪdz/ n. a man of great bravery, esp. (as pl.) Cromwell's cavalry troopers during the English Civil War, so called by their Royalist opponents in allusion to their hardiness in battle.

ironstone /ˈaɪənstəʊn/ n. **1** any rock containing a substantial proportion of an iron compound. **2** a kind of hard white opaque stoneware.

ironware /ˈaɪənˌweə(r)/ n. articles made of iron, esp. domestic implements.

ironwork /ˈaɪənwɜːk/ n. **1** things made of iron. **2** work in iron.

ironworks /ˈaɪənwɜːks/ n. (as sing. or pl.) a place where iron is smelted or iron goods are made.

irony[1] /ˈaɪərəni/ n. (pl. **-ies**) **1** an expression of meaning, often humorous or sarcastic, by the use of language of a different or opposite tendency. **2** an ill-timed or perverse arrival of an event or circumstance that is in itself desirable. **3** the use of language with one meaning for a privileged audience and another for those addressed or concerned. [L *ironia* f. Gk *eirōneia* simulated ignorance f. *eirōn* dissembler]

irony[2] /ˈaɪəni/ adj. of or like iron.

Iroquoian /ˌɪrəˈkwɔɪən/ n. & adj. —n. **1** a language family of eastern N. America, including Cherokee and Mohawk. **2** a member of the Iroquois Indians. —adj. of or relating to the Iroquois or the Iroquoian language family or one of its members.

Iroquois /ˈɪrəkwɔɪ/ n. & adj. —n. (pl. same) **1 a** an American Indian confederacy of five peoples formerly inhabiting New York State. **b** a member of any of these peoples. (See below.) **2** any of the languages of these peoples. —adj. of or relating to the Iroquois or their languages. [F f. Algonquin]

Iroquois is the collective designation of the League of Five (later Six) Nations of American Indian tribes (i.e. Huron,

Mohawk, Oneida, Seneca, Onondaga, and Cayuga), speaking Iroquoian languages, which joined in a confederacy c.1570 by the efforts of the Huron prophet Deganawida and his disciple Hiawatha. A powerful force in early colonial history, the divisions in the confederacy occasioned by conflicting support of the various contestants in the War of American Independence saw the rapid decline of the Six Nations in the late 18th c., with half the League (i.e. the Cayugas, Mohawks, and Senecas) migrating north to Canada, where they accepted grants of land as allies of the defeated Loyalists and where they continue to live today. Traditional Iroquois society revolved around matrilineal residential and social organization.

irradiant /ɪˈreɪdɪənt/ adj. literary shining brightly. □□ **irradiance** n.

irradiate /ɪˈreɪdɪeɪt/ v.tr. **1** subject to (any form of) radiation. **2** shine upon; light up. **3** throw light on (a subject). □□ **irradiative** /-dɪətɪv/ adj. [L *irradiare irradiat-* (as IN-[2], *radiare* f. *radius* RAY[1])]

irradiation /ɪˌreɪdɪˈeɪʃ(ə)n/ n. **1** the process of irradiating. **2** shining, illumination. **3** the apparent extension of the edges of an illuminated object seen against a dark background. [F *irradiation* or LL *irradiatio* (as IRRADIATE)]

irrational /ɪˈræʃən(ə)l/ adj. **1** illogical; unreasonable. **2** not endowed with reason. **3** Math. (of a root etc.) not rational; not commensurate with the natural numbers (e.g. a non-terminating decimal). □□ **irrationality** /-ˈnælɪtɪ/ n. **irrationalize** v.tr. (also **-ise**). **irrationally** adv. [L *irrationalis* (as IN-[1], RATIONAL)]

Irrawaddy /ˌɪrəˈwɒdɪ/ the principal river of Burma, 2,090 km (1,300 miles) long. It flows in a large delta into the eastern part of the Bay of Bengal.

irreclaimable /ˌɪrɪˈkleɪməb(ə)l/ adj. that cannot be reclaimed or reformed. □□ **irreclaimably** adv.

irreconcilable /ɪˈrekənˌsaɪləb(ə)l/ adj. & n. —adj. **1** implacably hostile. **2** (of ideas etc.) incompatible. —n. **1** an uncompromising opponent of a political measure etc. **2** (usu. in pl.) any of two or more items, ideas, etc., that cannot be made to agree. □□ **irreconcilability** /-ˈbɪlɪtɪ/ n. **irreconcilableness** n. **irreconcilably** adv.

irrecoverable /ˌɪrɪˈkʌvərəb(ə)l/ adj. that cannot be recovered or remedied. □□ **irrecoverably** adv.

irrecusable /ˌɪrɪˈkjuːzəb(ə)l/ adj. that must be accepted. [F *irrecúsable* or LL *irrecusabilis* (as IN-[1], *recusare* refuse)]

irredeemable /ˌɪrɪˈdiːməb(ə)l/ adj. **1** that cannot be redeemed. **2** hopeless, absolute. **3 a** (of a government annuity) not terminable by repayment. **b** (of paper currency) for which the issuing authority does not undertake ever to pay coin. □□ **irredeemability** /-ˈbɪlɪtɪ/ n. **irredeemably** adv.

irredentist /ˌɪrɪˈdentɪst/ n. **1** (**Irredentist**) an Italian nationalist of the late 19th c. advocating the return to Italy of the Italian-speaking districts of the Austro-Hungarian empire. **2** a person holding similar views of other areas. □□ **irredentism** n. [It. *irredentista* f. (*Italia*) *irredenta* unredeemed (Italy)]

irreducible /ˌɪrɪˈdjuːsɪb(ə)l/ adj. **1** that cannot be reduced or simplified. **2** (often foll. by to) that cannot be brought to a desired condition. □□ **irreducibility** /-ˈbɪlɪtɪ/ n. **irreducibly** adv.

irrefragable /ɪˈrefrəgəb(ə)l/ adj. **1** (of a statement, argument, or person) unanswerable, indisputable. **2** (of rules etc.) inviolable. □□ **irrefragably** adv. [LL *irrefragabilis* (as IN-[1], *refragari* oppose)]

irrefrangible /ˌɪrɪˈfrændʒɪb(ə)l/ adj. **1** inviolable. **2** Optics incapable of being refracted.

irrefutable /ɪˈrefjʊtəb(ə)l, ˌɪrɪˈfjuː-/ adj. that cannot be refuted. □□ **irrefutability** /-ˈbɪlɪtɪ/ n. **irrefutably** adv. [LL *irrefutabilis* (as IN-[1], REFUTE)]

irregular /ɪˈregjʊlə(r)/ adj. & n. —adj. **1** not regular; unsymmetrical, uneven; varying in form. **2** (of a surface) uneven. **3** contrary to a rule, moral principle, or custom; abnormal. **4** uneven in duration, order, etc. **5** (of troops) not belonging to the regular army. **6** Gram. (of a verb, noun, etc.) not inflected according to the usual rules. **7** disorderly. **8** (of a flower) having unequal petals etc. —n. (in pl.) irregular troops. □□

irregularity /-ˈlærɪtɪ/ n. (pl. **-ies**). **irregularly** adv. [ME f. OF *irreguler* f. LL *irregularis* (as IN-¹, REGULAR)]

irrelative /ɪˈrelətɪv/ adj. **1** (often foll. by *to*) unconnected, unrelated. **2** having no relations; absolute. **3** irrelevant. □□ **irrelatively** adv.

irrelevant /ɪˈrelɪv(ə)nt/ adj. (often foll. by *to*) not relevant; not applicable (to a matter in hand). □□ **irrelevance** n. **irrelevancy** n. **irrelevantly** adv.

irreligion /ˌɪrɪˈlɪdʒ(ə)n/ n. disregard of or hostility to religion. □□ **irreligionist** n. [F *irréligion* or L *irreligio* (as IN-¹, RELIGION)]

irreligious /ˌɪrɪˈlɪdʒəs/ adj. **1** indifferent or hostile to religion. **2** lacking a religion. □□ **irreligiously** adv. **irreligiousness** n.

irremediable /ˌɪrɪˈmiːdɪəb(ə)l/ adj. that cannot be remedied. □□ **irremediably** adv. [L *irremediabilis* (as IN-¹, REMEDY)]

irremissible /ˌɪrɪˈmɪsɪb(ə)l/ adj. **1** unpardonable. **2** unalterably obligatory. □□ **irremissibly** adv. [ME f. OF *irremissible* or eccl.L *irremissibilis* (as IN-¹, REMISSIBLE)]

irremovable /ˌɪrɪˈmuːvəb(ə)l/ adj. that cannot be removed, esp. from office. □□ **irremovability** /-ˈbɪlɪtɪ/ n. **irremovably** adv.

irreparable /ɪˈrepərəb(ə)l/ adj. (of an injury, loss, etc.) that cannot be rectified or made good. □□ **irreparability** /-ˈbɪlɪtɪ/ n. **irreparableness** n. **irreparably** adv. [ME f. OF f. L *irreparabilis* (as IN-¹, REPARABLE)]

irreplaceable /ˌɪrɪˈpleɪsəb(ə)l/ adj. **1** that cannot be replaced. **2** of which the loss cannot be made good. □□ **irreplaceably** adv.

irrepressible /ˌɪrɪˈpresɪb(ə)l/ adj. that cannot be repressed or restrained. □□ **irrepressibility** /-ˈbɪlɪtɪ/ n. **irrepressibleness** n. **irrepressibly** adv.

irreproachable /ˌɪrɪˈprəʊtʃəb(ə)l/ adj. faultless, blameless. □□ **irreproachability** /-ˈbɪlɪtɪ/ n. **irreproachableness** n. **irreproachably** adv. [F *irréprochable* (as IN-¹, REPROACH)]

irresistible /ˌɪrɪˈzɪstɪb(ə)l/ adj. **1** too strong or convincing to be resisted. **2** delightful; alluring. □□ **irresistibility** /-ˈbɪlɪtɪ/ n. **irresistibleness** n. **irresistibly** adv. [med.L *irresistibilis* (as IN-¹, RESIST)]

irresolute /ɪˈrezəˌluːt, -ˌljuːt/ adj. **1** hesitant, undecided. **2** lacking in resoluteness. □□ **irresolutely** adv. **irresoluteness** n. **irresolution** /-ˈluːʃ(ə)n, -ˈljuːʃ(ə)n/ n.

irresolvable /ˌɪrɪˈzɒlvəb(ə)l/ adj. **1** that cannot be resolved into its components. **2** (of a problem) that cannot be solved.

irrespective /ˌɪrɪˈspektɪv/ adj. (foll. by *of*) not taking into account; regardless of. □□ **irrespectively** adv.

irresponsible /ˌɪrɪˈspɒnsɪb(ə)l/ adj. **1** acting or done without due sense of responsibility. **2** not responsible for one's conduct. □□ **irresponsibility** /-ˈbɪlɪtɪ/ n. **irresponsibly** adv.

irresponsive /ˌɪrɪˈspɒnsɪv/ adj. (often foll. by *to*) not responsive. □□ **irresponsively** adv. **irresponsiveness** n.

irretrievable /ˌɪrɪˈtriːvəb(ə)l/ adj. that cannot be retrieved or restored. □□ **irretrievability** /-ˈbɪlɪtɪ/ n. **irretrievably** adv.

irreverent /ɪˈrevərənt/ adj. lacking reverence. □□ **irreverence** n. **irreverential** /-ˈrenʃ(ə)l/ adj. **irreverently** adv. [L *irreverens* (as IN-¹, REVERENT)]

irreversible /ˌɪrɪˈvɜːsɪb(ə)l/ adj. not reversible or alterable. □□ **irreversibility** /-ˈbɪlɪtɪ/ n. **irreversibly** adv.

irrevocable /ɪˈrevəkəb(ə)l/ adj. **1** unalterable. **2** gone beyond recall. □□ **irrevocability** /-ˈbɪlɪtɪ/ n. **irrevocably** adv. [ME f. L *irrevocabilis* (as IN-¹, REVOKE)]

irrigate /ˈɪrɪˌgeɪt/ v.tr. **1 a** water (land) by means of channels. **b** (of a stream etc.) supply (land) with water. **2** Med. supply (a wound etc.) with a constant flow of liquid. **3** refresh as with moisture. □□ **irrigable** adj. **irrigation** /-ˈgeɪʃ(ə)n/ n. **irrigative** adj. **irrigator** n. [L *irrigare* (as IN-², *rigare* moisten)]

irritable /ˈɪrɪtəb(ə)l/ adj. **1** easily annoyed or angered. **2** (of an organ etc.) very sensitive to contact. **3** Biol. responding actively to physical stimulus. □□ **irritability** /-ˈbɪlɪtɪ/ n. **irritably** adv. [L *irritabilis* (as IRRITATE)]

irritant /ˈɪrɪt(ə)nt/ adj. & n. —adj. causing irritation. —n. an irritant substance. □□ **irritancy** n.

irritate /ˈɪrɪˌteɪt/ v.tr. **1** excite to anger; annoy. **2** stimulate discomfort or pain in (a part of the body). **3** Biol. stimulate (an organ) to action. □□ **irritatedly** adv. **irritating** adj. **irritatingly** adv. **irritation** /-ˈteɪʃ(ə)n/ n. **irritative** /-tətɪv/ adj. **irritator** n. [L *irritare irritat-*]

irrupt /ɪˈrʌpt/ v.intr. (foll. by *into*) enter forcibly or violently. □□ **irruption** /ɪˈrʌpʃ(ə)n/ n. [L *irrumpere irrupt-* (as IN-², *rumpere* break)]

Irving¹ /ˈɜːvɪŋ/, Sir Henry (1838–1905), real name Henry Brodribb, English actor-manager. In 1871 his appearance at the Lyceum Theatre in the melodrama *The Bells* brought him immediate fame, and he was to dominate the London stage during the next 30 years. In 1874 he first played Hamlet, inaugurating his own management of the Lyceum in the same role in 1878. His tenancy (in association with Miss Ellen Terry) is mainly remembered for his productions of Shakespeare, from *The Merchant of Venice* in 1879 to *Cymbeline* in 1896. He was a good manager and his acting, in spite of mannerisms and a not particularly melodious voice, had enormous power.

Irving² /ˈɜːvɪŋ/, Washington (1783–1859), American writer who first came into literary repute with his burlesque *A History of New York* (1809) by 'Diedrich Knickerbocker'. He visited England where he met Sir Walter Scott, who encouraged him to write his celebrated *The Sketch Book* (1820) which contains his best tales, including 'Rip Van Winkle' and 'The Legend of Sleepy Hollow'. He later held diplomatic posts in Spain and London, and on his return to America was enthusiastically received as the first American author to have achieved international fame. His later works include a life of George Washington (1855–9).

Is. abbr. **1 a** Island(s). **b** Isle(s). **2** (also **Isa.**) Isaiah (Old Testament).

is 3rd sing. present of BE.

Isaac /ˈaɪzək/ Hebrew patriarch, son of Abraham and Sarah and father of Jacob and Esau (Gen. 21: 3 etc.).

isagogic /ˌaɪsəˈgɒdʒɪk/ adj. introductory. [L *isagogicus* f. Gk *eisagōgikos* f. *eisagōgē* introduction f. *eis* into + *agōgē* leading f. *agō* lead]

isagogics /ˌaɪsəˈgɒdʒɪks/ n. an introductory study, esp. of the literary and external history of the Bible.

Isaiah /aɪˈzaɪə/ **1** a Hebrew major prophet of Judah in the 8th c. BC, teaching the supremacy of the God of Israel and emphasizing the moral demands upon worshippers. His expectations for the future centred on his belief in the permanence of the Davidic throne, and the 'Messianic' passages in the prophecies ascribed to him were frequently referred by Christian writers to Jesus Christ. **2** a book of the Old Testament ascribed to him but now generally agreed to fall into sections of which chapters 36–66, and portions of the earlier chapters, have no real claim to be his.

isatin /ˈaɪsətɪn/ n. Chem. a red crystalline derivative of indole used in the manufacture of dyes. [L *isatis* woad f. Gk]

ISBN abbr. international standard book number.

ischaemia /ɪˈskiːmɪə/ n. (US **ischemia**) Med. a reduction of the blood supply to part of the body. □□ **ischaemic** adj. [mod.L f. Gk *iskhaimos* f. *iskhō* keep back]

Ischia /ˈɪskɪə/ an island in the Tyrrhenian Sea off the west coast of Italy, about 26 km (16 miles) SW of Naples.

ischium /ˈɪskɪəm/ n. (pl. **ischia** /-kɪə/) the curved bone forming the base of each half of the pelvis. □□ **ischial** adj. [L f. Gk *iskhion* hip-joint: cf. SCIATIC]

-ise¹ suffix var. of -IZE. ¶ See the note at *-ize*.

-ise² /aɪz, iːz/ suffix forming nouns of quality, state, or function (*exercise*; *expertise*; *franchise*; *merchandise*). [from or after F or OF *-ise* f. L *-itia* etc.]

-ise³ suffix var. of -ISH².

isentropic /ˌaɪsenˈtrɒpɪk/ adj. having equal entropy. [ISO- + ENTROPY]

Iseult /ˈiːzuːlt, ɪˈzuːlt/ (in medieval legend) the sister or daughter of the king of Ireland, and wife of King Mark of Cornwall, loved by Tristram; (in another account) the daughter of the king of Brittany, and wife of Tristram.

Isfahan /ˌɪsfəˈhɑːn/ (also **Esfahan, Ispahan**) an industrial city in west central Iran, the country's third-largest city; pop. (1986)

986,750. Abbas I made it his capital city from 1598, and it became one of the largest and most beautiful cities of this period until captured and destroyed by the Afghans in 1722.

-ish[1] /ɪʃ/ *suffix* forming adjectives: **1** from nouns, meaning: **a** having the qualities or characteristics of (*boyish*). **b** of the nationality of (*Danish*). **2** from adjectives, meaning 'somewhat' (*thickish*). **3** *colloq.* denoting an approximate age or time of day (*fortyish*; *six-thirtyish*). [OE *-isc*]

-ish[2] /ɪʃ/ *suffix* (also **-ise** /aɪz/) forming verbs (*vanish*; *advertise*). [from or after F *-iss-* (in extended stems of verbs in *-ir*) f. L *-isc-* incept. suffix]

Isherwood /ˈɪʃəˌwʊd/, Christopher William Bradshaw (1904–86), English novelist. His novels, *Mr. Norris Changes Trains* (1935), about the adventures in the criminal and political underworld of double-agent Arthur Norris, and *Goodbye to Berlin* (1939), about eccentric witty cabaret artist Sally Bowles (dramatized as *I am a Camera*, 1951; as a musical, *Cabaret*, 1968), vividly portray Germany on the eve of Hitler's rise to power and reflect Isherwood's experiences in Berlin during 1929–33. He collaborated with Auden in several plays and with him left for America in 1939, becoming a US citizen in 1946. After settling in Hollywood he developed an interest in Hindu philosophy and Vedanta and translated several Hindu classics, notably the *Bhagavadgita* (1944). His later novels include *Down there on a Visit* (1962) and *Christopher and his Kind* (1976), a frank account of the homosexual affairs of his young manhood.

Ishmael /ˈɪʃmeɪl/ a son of Abraham and Hagar, of whom it was prophesied 'his hand will be against every man, and every man's hand against him' (Gen. 16: 12). —*n.* an outcast, one at war with society. □□ **Ishmaelite** *n.*

Ishtar /ˈɪʃtɑː(r)/ a Babylonian and Assyrian goddess whose name and functions correspond to those of Astarte.

Isidore[1] /ˈɪzɪˌdɔː(r)/ (6th c.) Greek mathematician and engineer, of Miletus in Ionia, co-architect (with Anthemius of Tralles) of Santa Sophia in Constantinople, and author of a fifteenth book of Euclid's *Elements*.

Isidore[2] /ˈɪzɪdɔː(r)/, St (*c.*560–636), archbishop of Seville and Doctor of the Church, an encyclopedic writer whose works became a storehouse of knowledge freely used by innumerable medieval authors. Feast day, 4 April.

isinglass /ˈaɪzɪŋˌglɑːs/ *n.* **1** a kind of gelatin obtained from fish, esp. sturgeon, and used in making jellies, glue, etc. **2** mica. [corrupt. of obs. Du. *huisenblas* sturgeon's bladder, assim. to GLASS]

Isis /ˈaɪsɪs/ *Egyptian Mythol.* a nature-goddess, wife of Osiris and mother of Horus. Her worship spread to Western Asia, Greece, and Rome, where she was identified with many and varied local goddesses, and became one of the major mystery religions, involving enactment of the myth of the death and resurrection of Osiris.

Iskenderun /ɪsˈkendəˌruːn/ a port and naval base of southern Turkey, on the NE coast of the Mediterranean Sea; pop. (1980) 954,900. Formerly named Alexandretta, it lies on or near the site of Alexandria ad Issum, founded by Alexander the Great in 333 BC. The port was an important outlet for goods from Persia, India, and eastern Asia before the development of sea-routes round the Cape of Good Hope and later through the Suez Canal.

Islam /ˈɪzlɑːm, -læm, -ˈlɑːm/ *n.* **1** the religion of the Muslims, a monotheistic faith regarded as revealed through Muhammad as the Prophet of Allah. (See below.) **2** the Muslim world. □□ **Islamic** /ɪzˈlæmɪk/ *adj.* **Islamism** *n.* **Islamist** *n.* **Islamize** *v.tr.* (also **-ise**). **Islamization** /-aɪˈzeɪʃ(ə)n/ *n.* [Arab. *islām* submission (to God) f. *aslama* resign oneself]

The monotheistic religion founded by the Prophet Muhammad in the Arabian Peninsula in the 7th c. AD is now the professed faith of nearly one thousand million people worldwide. To become a Muslim means both to accept and affirm an individual surrender to God, and to live as a member of a social community. The Muslim performs prescribed acts of worship and strives to fulfil good works within the group; the 'Pillars of Islam' include profession of the faith in a prescribed form, observance of ritual prayer (five obligatory prayer sequences each day as well as

non-obligatory prayers), giving alms to the poor, fasting during the month of Ramadan, and performing the pilgrimage to Mecca. These ritual observances, as well as a code governing social behaviour, were given to Muhammad as a series of revelations, codified in the Koran and supplemented by the deeds and discourse of the Prophet (see SUNNA, HADITH). Islam is regarded by its adherents as the last of the revealed religions (following Judaism and Christianity), and Muhammad is seen as the Seal of the Prophets, building upon and perfecting the examples and teachings of Abraham, Moses, and Jesus. The term Islam carries three interrelated significations: the personal individual submission to Allah; the 'world of Islam' as a concrete historical reality comprising a variety of communities which, however, share not only a common religious outlook but also a common fund of cultural legacies; and finally, the concept of an 'ideal Muslim community' as set forth in the Koran and supporting sources.

Islamabad /ɪzˈlɑːməˌbɑːd/ the capital, since 1967, of Pakistan, replacing Karachi; pop. (1981) 201,000.

Islamic Jehad /dʒɪˈhæd, -ˈhɑːd/ a Muslim fundamentalist terrorist association.

island /ˈaɪlənd/ *n.* **1** a piece of land surrounded by water. **2** anything compared to an island, esp. in being surrounded in some way. **3** = *traffic island*. **4 a** a detached or isolated thing. **b** *Physiol.* a detached portion of tissue or group of cells (cf. ISLET). **5** *Naut.* a ship's superstructure, bridge, etc. □ **islands area** any of three administrative areas in Scotland (Orkney, Shetland, Western Isles), each consisting of a group of islands. [OE *īgland* f. *īg* island + LAND: first syll. infl. by ISLE]

islander /ˈaɪləndə(r)/ *n.* a native or inhabitant of an island.

Islands of the Blessed a mythical abode, often located in the west, near where the sun sets, to which, in the belief of many ancient peoples, the souls of the good were conveyed to a life of bliss.

isle /aɪl/ *n. poet.* (and in place-names) an island or peninsula, esp. a small one. [ME *ile* f. OF *ile* f. L *insula*: later ME & OF *isle* after L]

Isle of Man an island in the Irish Sea which is a British Crown possession enjoying home rule, with its own legislature (the Tynwald) and judicial system; pop. (1981) 64,679; capital, Douglas. The island was part of the Norse kingdom of the Hebrides in the Middle Ages, passing into Scottish hands in 1266 for a time, until the English gained control in the early 15th c. Its ancient language, Manx, is still used for ceremonial purposes.

Isle of Wight /waɪt/ an island off the south coast of England, a county since 1974; pop. (1981) 115,400.

islet /ˈaɪlɪt/ *n.* **1** a small island. **2** *Anat.* a portion of tissue structurally distinct from surrounding tissues. **3** an isolated place. □ **islets of Langerhans** *Physiol.* groups of pancreatic cells secreting insulin and glucagon. [OF, dimin. of *isle* ISLE]

ism /ˈɪz(ə)m/ *n. colloq.* usu. *derog.* any distinctive but unspecified doctrine or practice of a kind with a name in *-ism*.

-ism /ˈɪz(ə)m/ *suffix* forming nouns, esp. denoting: **1** an action or its result (*baptism*; *organism*). **2** a system, principle, or ideological movement (*Conservatism*; *jingoism*; *feminism*). **3** a state or quality (*heroism*; *barbarism*). **4** a basis of prejudice or discrimination (*racism*; *sexism*). **5** a peculiarity in language (*Americanism*). **6** a pathological condition (*alcoholism*; *Parkinsonism*). [from or after F *-isme* f. L *-ismus* f. Gk *-ismos* or *-isma* f. *-izō* -IZE]

Ismaili /ɪzˈmaɪlɪ/ *n.* (pl. **Ismailis**) a member of a Shiite Muslim sect that seceded from the main group in the 8th c. over the question of succession to the position of imam. They regarded Ismail, eldest son of the sixth imam, as the seventh and final imam, while the rest of the Shiites supported the second son, Musa al-Kazim. The Ismaili movement (which consisted of several groups rather than one unified body) represented a revolutionary political force in its early stages, and its adherents developed an elaborate esoteric doctrine (diverging considerably from the rest of Islam) concerning the believer's place in the cosmos and the highly structured path to spiritual fulfilment. Initiation into the group's doctrines was a long process to which only a few were admitted, and the organization tended to be that of a very hierarchical secret society. It eventually split into many sub-sects, of which the best known is that headed by the Aga Khan. Today Ismailis are found especially in India, Pakistan, and East Africa, with smaller groups in Syria, Iran, and some other countries.

isn't /ˈɪz(ə)nt/ *contr.* is not.

ISO *abbr.* **1** (in the UK) Imperial Service Order. **2** International Organization for Standardization.

iso- /ˈaɪsəʊ/ *comb. form* **1** equal (*isometric*). **2** *Chem.* isomeric, esp. of a hydrocarbon with a branched chain of carbon atoms (*isobutane*). [Gk *isos* equal]

isobar /ˈaɪsəʊˌbɑː(r)/ *n.* **1** a line on a map connecting positions having the same atmospheric pressure at a given time or on average over a given period. **2** a curve for a physical system at constant pressure. **3** one of two or more isotopes of different elements, with the same atomic weight. □□ **isobaric** /-ˈbærɪk/ *adj.* [Gk *isobarēs* of equal weight (as ISO-, *baros* weight)]

isocheim /ˈaɪsəʊˌkaɪm/ *n.* a line on a map connecting places having the same average temperature in winter. [ISO- + Gk *kheima* winter weather]

isochromatic /ˌaɪsəʊkrəʊˈmætɪk/ *adj.* of the same colour.

isochronous /aɪˈsɒkrənəs/ *adj.* **1** occurring at the same time. **2** occupying equal time. □□ **isochronously** *adv.* [ISO- + Gk *khronos* time]

isoclinal /ˌaɪsəʊˈklaɪn(ə)l/ *adj.* (also **isoclinic** /-ˈklɪnɪk/) **1** *Geol.* (of a fold) in which the two limbs are parallel. **2** corresponding to equal values of magnetic dip. [ISO- + CLINE]

isoclinic var. of ISOCLINAL.

Isocrates /aɪˈsɒkrəˌtiːz/ (436–338 BC) Athenian orator. His written speeches were vehicles for his political ideals, the union of Greeks under the shared hegemony of Athens and Sparta, and later under the championship of Philip II of Macedon; he also advocated a Panhellenic crusade against Persia. His style is elaborate and studied. His influential educational system provided a combination of philosophical and rhetorical instruction.

isodynamic /ˌaɪsəʊdaɪˈnæmɪk/ *adj.* corresponding to equal values of (magnetic) force.

isoenzyme /ˈaɪsəʊˌenzaɪm/ *n.* *Biochem.* one of two or more enzymes with identical function but different structure.

isogeotherm /ˌaɪsəʊˈdʒiːəˌθɜːm/ *n.* a line or surface connecting points in the interior of the earth having the same temperature. □□ **isogeothermal** /-ˈθɜːm(ə)l/ *adj.*

isogloss /ˈaɪsəʊˌglɒs/ *n.* a line on a map marking an area having a distinct linguistic feature.

isogonic /ˌaɪsəʊˈgɒnɪk/ *adj.* corresponding to equal values of magnetic declination.

isohel /ˈaɪsəʊˌhel/ *n.* a line on a map connecting places having the same duration of sunshine. [ISO- + Gk *hēlios* sun]

isohyet /ˌaɪsəʊˈhaɪɪt/ *n.* a line on a map connecting places having the same amount of rainfall in a given period. [ISO- + Gk *huetos* rain]

isolate /ˈaɪsəˌleɪt/ *v.tr.* **1 a** place apart or alone, cut off from society. **b** place (a patient thought to be contagious or infectious) in quarantine. **2 a** identify and separate for attention (*isolated the problem*). **b** *Chem.* separate (a substance) from a mixture. **3** insulate (electrical apparatus). □□ **isolable** /ˈaɪsələb(ə)l/ *adj.* **isolatable** *adj.* **isolator** *n.* [orig. in past part., f. F *isolé* f. It. *isolato* f. LL *insulatus* f. L *insula* island]

isolated /ˈaɪsəˌleɪtɪd/ *adj.* **1** lonely; cut off from society or contact; remote (*feeling isolated; an isolated farmhouse*). **2** untypical, unique (*an isolated example*).

isolating /ˈaɪsəˌleɪtɪŋ/ *adj.* (of a language) having each element as an independent word without inflections.

isolation /ˌaɪsəˈleɪʃ(ə)n/ *n.* the act or an instance of isolating; the state of being isolated or separated. □ **in isolation** considered singly and not relatively. **isolation hospital** (or **ward** etc.) a hospital, ward, etc., for patients with contagious or infectious diseases.

isolationism /ˌaɪsəˈleɪʃəˌnɪz(ə)m/ *n.* the policy of holding aloof from the affairs of other countries or groups esp. in politics. □□ **isolationist** *n.*

isoleucine /ˌaɪsəʊˈluːsiːn/ *n.* *Biochem.* an amino acid that is a

constituent of proteins and an essential nutrient. [G *Isoleucin* (see ISO-, LEUCINE)]

isomer /ˈaɪsəmə(r)/ *n.* **1** *Chem.* one of two or more compounds with the same molecular formula but a different arrangement of atoms and different properties. **2** *Physics* one of two or more atomic nuclei that have the same atomic number and the same mass number but different energy states. □□ **isomeric** /-ˈmerɪk/ *adj.* **isomerism** /aɪˈsɒməˌrɪz(ə)m/ *n.* **isomerize** /aɪˈsɒməˌraɪz/ *v.* (also **-ise**). [G f. Gk *isomerēs* sharing equally (as ISO-, *meros* share)]

isomerous /aɪˈsɒmərəs/ *adj.* *Bot.* (of a flower) having the same number of petals in each whorl. [Gk *isomerēs*: see ISOMER]

isometric /ˌaɪsəʊˈmetrɪk/ *adj.* **1** of equal measure. **2** *Physiol.* (of muscle action) developing tension while the muscle is prevented from contracting. **3** (of a drawing etc.) with the plane of projection at equal angles to the three principal axes of the object shown. **4** *Math.* (of a transformation) without change of shape or size. □□ **isometrically** *adv.* **isometry** /aɪˈsɒmɪtrɪ/ *n.* (in sense 4). [Gk *isometria* equality of measure (as ISO-, -METRY)]

isometrics /ˌaɪsəʊˈmetrɪks/ *n.pl.* a system of physical exercises in which muscles are caused to act against each other or against a fixed object.

isomorph /ˈaɪsəʊˌmɔːf/ *n.* an isomorphic substance or organism. [ISO- + Gk *morphē* form]

isomorphic /ˌaɪsəʊˈmɔːfɪk/ *adj.* (also **isomorphous** /-fəs/) **1** exactly corresponding in form and relations. **2** *Crystallog.* having the same form. □□ **isomorphism** *n.*

-ison /ˈɪs(ə)n/ *suffix* forming nouns, = -ATION (*comparison; garrison; jettison; venison*). [OF *-aison* etc. f. L *-atio* etc.: see -ATION]

isophote /ˈaɪsəʊˌfəʊt/ *n.* a line (imaginary or in a diagram) of equal brightness or illumination. [ISO- + Gk *phōs phōtos* light]

isopleth /ˈaɪsəʊˌpleθ/ *n.* a line on a map connecting places having equal incidence of a meteorological feature. [ISO- + Gk *plēthos* fullness]

isopod /ˈaɪsəʊˌpɒd/ *n.* any crustacean of the order *Isopoda*, including woodlice and slaters, often parasitic and having a flattened body with seven pairs of legs. [F *isopode* f. mod.L *Isopoda* (as ISO-, Gk *pous podos* foot)]

isosceles /aɪˈsɒsɪˌliːz/ *adj.* (of a triangle) having two sides equal. [LL f. Gk *isoskelēs* (as ISO-, *skelos* leg)]

isoseismal /ˌaɪsəʊˈsaɪzm(ə)l/ *adj. & n.* (also **isoseismic** /-mɪk/) —*adj.* having equal strength of earthquake shock. —*n.* a line on a map connecting places having an equal strength of earthquake shock.

isostasy /aɪˈsɒstəsɪ/ *n.* *Geol.* the general state of equilibrium of the earth's crust, with the rise and fall of land relative to sea. □□ **isostatic** /ˌaɪsəʊˈstætɪk/ *adj.* [ISO- + Gk *stasis* station]

isothere /ˈaɪsəʊˌθɪə(r)/ *n.* a line on a map connecting places having the same average temperature in the summer. [ISO- + Gk *theros* summer]

isotherm /ˈaɪsəʊˌθɜːm/ *n.* **1** a line on a map connecting places having the same temperature at a given time or on average over a given period. **2** a curve for changes in a physical system at a constant temperature. □□ **isothermal** /-ˈθɜːm(ə)l/ *adj.* **isothermally** /-ˈθɜːməlɪ/ *adv.* [F *isotherme* (as ISO-, Gk *thermē* heat)]

isotonic /ˌaɪsəʊˈtɒnɪk/ *adj.* **1** having the same osmotic pressure. **2** *Physiol.* (of muscle action) taking place with normal contraction. □□ **isotonically** *adv.* **isotonicity** /-təˈnɪsɪtɪ/ *n.* [Gk *isotonos* (as ISO-, TONE)]

isotope /ˈaɪsəˌtəʊp/ *n.* *Chem.* any of two or more types of atom of the same element that contain equal numbers of protons but different numbers of neutrons in their nuclei, and hence differ in atomic weight but not in chemical properties. The term was coined in 1913 by F. Soddy. Most elements consist of one stable (non-radioactive) isotope; there are also numerous radioactive isotopes, the majority of them artificially created. □□ **isotopic** /-ˈtɒpɪk/ *adj.* **isotopically** /-ˈtɒpɪkəlɪ/ *adv.* **isotopy** /aɪˈsɒtəpɪ/ *n.* [ISO- + Gk *topos* place (i.e. in the periodic table of elements)]

isotropic /ˌaɪsəʊˈtrɒpɪk/ *adj.* having the same physical properties in all directions (opp. ANISOTROPIC). □□ **isotropically** *adv.* **isotropy** /aɪˈsɒtrəpɪ/ *n.* [ISO- + Gk *tropos* turn]

Ispahan see ISFAHAN.

I-spy /ˈaɪˈspaɪ/ n. a game in which players try to identify something observed by one of them, with its initial letter as a clue.

Israel[1] /ˈɪzreɪ(ə)l/ **1** (also **children of Israel**) the Hebrew nation or people traditionally descended from the patriarch Jacob (his alternative name was 'Israel', whose 12 sons became founders of the 12 tribes. **2** the northern kingdom of the Hebrews (c.930–721 BC, in contrast to Judah), whose inhabitants were carried away to captivity in Assyria. The name 'Israel' is first found on the Moabite Stone (c.850 BC) commemorating the successes of the king of Moab against Israel. □□ **Israelite** /ˈɪzrəˌlaɪt/ adj. & n. [Heb. yisrā'ēl he that strives with God; see Gen. 32: 28]

Israel[2] /ˈɪzreɪl/ a country in SW Asia, with the River Jordan forming part of its eastern border and with a coastline on the Mediterranean Sea; pop. (est. 1988) 4,297,400; official language, Hebrew; capital (not recognized as such by the UN), Jerusalem. Much of the country is very fertile, and since 1948 massive irrigation programmes have brought large areas of former desert under cultivation. The 'Holy Land' of Jews and Christians, and with Jerusalem sacred also to Muslims, it contains numerous sites that attract both pilgrims and tourists. Remains of early man were found in caves on Mount Carmel, and the country is rich in archaeological remains of all periods. Although it is the ancient and traditional home of the Jewish people, for most of its history it was controlled by one or other of the powerful nations of each succeeding era (see ISRAEL[1] and PALESTINE), until following the surrender of the British mandate at the end of the Second World War the independent Jewish State of Israel was proclaimed in 1948. Conflict with the surrounding Arab States led to wars in 1948, 1956, 1967, and 1973, and resulted in Israel's expansion to her present boundaries. In the late 1980s an extreme right-wing government, the immigration of thousands of Soviet Jews, the uprising in the occupied territories (see INTIFADA), and (in 1990–1) Palestinian support for Saddam Hussein of Iraq in the Gulf War, produced dangerous tensions. Israel has, however, emerged as one of the strongest military powers in the Middle East, and despite a high inflation rate, the development of the economy has made it the most industrialized country in the region. □□ **Israeli** /ɪzˈreɪlɪ/ adj. & n.

Israfel /ˈɪzrəˌfel/ (in Muslim tradition) the angel of music, who will sound the trumpet on the Day of Judgement.

Issachar /ˈɪsəkə(r)/ **1** Hebrew patriarch, son of Jacob and Leah (Gen. 30: 18). **2** the tribe of Israel traditionally descended from him.

Issigonis /ˌɪsɪˈɡəʊnɪs/, Alec Arnold Constantine (1906–88), British engineer and car designer, of Greek parentage. His most famous designs were the Morris Minor and the Mini motor car, a revolutionary novelty in 1959 and still in production at the time of his death.

ISSN abbr. international standard serial number.

issuant /ˈɪʃuːənt, ˈɪsjuː-/ adj. Heraldry (esp. of a beast with only the upper part shown) rising from the bottom or top of a bearing.

issue /ˈɪʃuː, ˈɪsjuː-/ n. & v. —n. **1 a** a giving out or circulation of shares, notes, stamps, etc. **b** a quantity of coins, supplies, copies of a newspaper or book etc., circulated or put on sale at one time. **c** an item or amount given out or distributed. **d** each of a regular series of a magazine etc. (the May issue). **2 a** an outgoing, an outflow. **b** a way out, an outlet esp. the place of the emergence of a stream etc. **3** a point in question; an important subject of debate or litigation. **4** a result; an outcome; a decision. **5** Law children, progeny (without male issue). **6** archaic a discharge of blood etc. —v. (**issues**, **issued**, **issuing**) **1** intr. (often foll. by out, forth) literary go or come out. **2** tr. **a** send forth; publish; put into circulation. **b** supply, esp. officially or authoritatively (foll. by to, with: issued passports to them; issued them with passports; issued orders to the staff). **3** intr. **a** (often foll. by from) be derived or result. **b** (foll. by in) end, result. **4** intr. (foll. by from) emerge from a condition. □ **at issue 1** under discussion; in dispute. **2** at variance. **issue of fact** (or **law**) a dispute at law when the significance of a fact or facts is denied or when the application of the law is contested. **join** (or **take**) **issue** identify an issue for argument (foll. by with, on). **make an issue of** make a fuss about; turn into a subject of contention. □□ **issuable** adj. **issuance** n.

issueless adj. **issuer** n. [ME f. OF ult. f. L exitus past part. of exire EXIT]

-ist /ɪst/ suffix forming personal nouns (and in some senses related adjectives) denoting: **1** an adherent of a system etc. in -ism: see -ISM 2 (Marxist; fatalist). **2 a** a member of a profession (pathologist). **b** a person concerned with something (tobacconist). **3** a person who uses a thing (violinist; balloonist; motorist). **4** a person who does something expressed by a verb in -ize (plagiarist). **5** a person who subscribes to a prejudice or practises discrimination (racist; sexist). [OF -iste, L -ista f. Gk -istēs]

Istanbul /ˌɪstænˈbʊl/ a port and the former capital (until 1923) of Turkey, situated on the Bosporus and partly in Europe, partly in Asia, to which it is linked by two suspension bridges; pop. (1985) 5,494,900. It was formerly the Roman city of Constantinople, ancient Byzantium; most of its characteristic buildings date from the Ottoman era (1453–1923).

isthmian /ˈɪsmɪən, ˈɪsθ-/ adj. of or relating to an isthmus, esp. (**Isthmian**) to the Isthmus of Corinth in southern Greece.

isthmus /ˈɪsməs, ˈɪsθ-/ n. **1** a narrow piece of land connecting two larger bodies of land. **2** Anat. a narrow part connecting two larger parts. [L f. Gk isthmos]

istle /ˈɪstlɪ/ n. a fibre used for cord, nets, etc., obtained from agave. [Mex. ixtli]

IT abbr. information technology.

It. abbr. Italian.

it[1] /ɪt/ pron. (poss. **its**; pl. **they**) **1** the thing (or occas. the animal or child) previously named or in question (took a stone and threw it). **2** the person in question (Who is it? It is I; is it a boy or a girl?). **3** as the subject of an impersonal verb (it is raining; it is winter; it is Tuesday; it is two miles to Bath). **4** as a substitute for a deferred subject or object (it is intolerable, this delay; it is silly to talk like that; I take it that you agree). **5** as a substitute for a vague object (brazen it out; run for it!). **6** as the antecedent to a relative word (it was an owl I heard). **7** exactly what is needed (absolutely it). **8** the extreme limit of achievement. **9** colloq. sexual intercourse; sex appeal. **10** (in children's games) a player who has to perform a required feat, esp. to catch the others. □ **that's it** colloq. that is: **1** what is required. **2** the difficulty. **3** the end, enough. **this is it** colloq. **1** the expected event is at hand. **2** this is the difficulty. [OE hit neut. of HE]

it[2] /ɪt/ n. colloq. Italian vermouth (gin and it). [abbr.]

i.t.a. abbr. (also **ITA**) initial teaching alphabet.

Itaipu /iːˈtaɪpuː/ a dam on the Paraná River in SW Brazil, one of the world's largest hydroelectric installations, formally opened in 1982.

ital. abbr. italic (type).

Italian /ɪˈtæljən/ n. & adj. —n. **1 a** a native or national of Italy. **b** a person of Italian descent. **2** the official language of Italy, a Romance language which in many ways has remained closer to Latin than have the others of this group. It is spoken by some 60 million people in Italy and Switzerland, and by large numbers of speakers in the US and some in South America. —adj. of or relating to Italy or its people or language. □ **Italian vermouth** a sweet kind of vermouth. [ME f. It. Italiano f. Italia Italy]

Italianate /ɪˈtæljəˌneɪt/ adj. of Italian style or appearance. [It. Italianato]

Italic /ɪˈtælɪk/ adj. of ancient Italy. □ **Italic languages** the Italic branch of the Indo-European family of languages, comprising Latin, Oscan, Umbrian, and the dialects of various mountain tribes of central Italy. The term is more often confined to Oscan and Umbrian, the two chief non-Latin dialects of the group. [L italicus f. Gk italikos Italian]

italic /ɪˈtælɪk/ adj. & n. —adj. Printing **1** of the sloping kind of letters now used esp. for emphasis or distinction and in foreign words. The prototype of this cursive typeface was cut c.1499 for the Venetian printer Aldus Manutius (see entry). It was derived from informal sloped scripts and had numerous tied letters. The typeface was widely copied and less cramped designs superseded the original. Italic was originally used for setting complete texts, but the practice diminished and the use is now more restricted. **2** (of handwriting) compact and pointed like early

Italian handwriting. —*n.* **1** a letter in italic type. **2** this type. [as ITALIC]

italicize /ɪˈtælɪˌsaɪz/ *v.tr.* (also **-ise**) print in italics. □□ **italicization** /-ˈzeɪʃ(ə)n/ *n.*

Italiot /ɪˈtælɪət/ *n. & adj.* —*n.* an inhabitant of the Greek colonies in ancient Italy. —*adj.* of or relating to the Italiots. [Gk *Italiōtēs* f. *Italia* Italy]

Italo- /ˈɪtələʊ/ *comb. form* Italian; Italian and.

Italy /ˈɪtəlɪ/ a country in southern Europe comprising a peninsula that juts south into the Mediterranean Sea, and a number of offshore islands of which the largest are Sicily and Sardinia; pop. (est. 1988) 57,455,350; official language, Italian; capital, Rome. The centre of the Roman Empire, Italy was dominated by the city-states and the papacy in the Middle Ages, but fell under Spanish and Austrian rule in the 16th–17th c. Modern Italy was created by the nationalist movement of the mid-19th c., led by Garibaldi and the kingdom of Sardinia, the monarch of the latter country becoming king of Italy in 1861. Italy entered the First World War on the Allied side in 1915, but after the war the country was taken over by the Fascist dictator Mussolini; participation in support of Germany during the Second World War resulted in defeat and much devastation. A republic was established by popular vote in 1946. The country is divided between the industrialized north and the agricultural south, and by European standards has experienced a considerable degree of political instability in recent decades.

itch /ɪtʃ/ *n. & v.* —*n.* **1** an irritation in the skin. **2** an impatient desire; a hankering. **3** (prec. by *the*) (in general use) scabies. —*v.intr.* **1** feel an irritation in the skin, causing a desire to scratch it. **2** (usu. foll. by *to* + infin.) (of a person) feel a desire to do something (*am itching to tell you the news*). □ **itching palm** avarice. **itch-mite** a parasitic arthropod, *Sarcoptes scabiei*, which burrows under the skin causing scabies. [OE *gycce, gyccan* f. WG]

itchy /ˈɪtʃɪ/ *adj.* (**itchier, itchiest**) having or causing an itch. □ **have itchy feet** *colloq.* **1** be restless. **2** have a strong urge to travel. □□ **itchiness** *n.*

it'd /ˈɪtəd/ *contr. colloq.* **1** it had. **2** it would.

-ite[1] /aɪt/ *suffix* forming nouns meaning 'a person or thing connected with': **1** in names of persons: **a** as natives of a country (*Israelite*). **b** often *derog.* as followers of a movement etc. (*pre-Raphaelite; Trotskyite*). **2** in names of things: **a** fossil organisms (*ammonite*). **b** minerals (*graphite*). **c** constituent parts of a body or organ (*somite*). **d** explosives (*dynamite*). **e** commercial products (*ebonite; vulcanite*). **f** salts of acids having names in *-ous* (*nitrite; sulphite*). [from or after F *-ite* f. L *-ita* f. Gk *-itēs*]

-ite[2] /aɪt, ɪt/ *suffix* **1** forming adjectives (*erudite; favourite*). **2** forming nouns (*appetite*). **3** forming verbs (*expedite; unite*). [from or after L *-itus* past part. of verbs in *-ēre, -ere,* and *-ire*]

item /ˈaɪtəm/ *n. & adv.* —*n.* **1 a** any of a number of enumerated or listed things. **b** an entry in an account. **2** an article, esp. one for sale (*household items*). **3** a separate or distinct piece of news, information, etc. —*adv.* archaic (introducing the mention of each item) likewise, also. [orig. as adv.: L, = in like manner, also]

itemize /ˈaɪtəˌmaɪz/ *v.tr.* (also **-ise**) state or list item by item. □□ **itemization** /-ˈzeɪʃ(ə)n/ *n.* **itemizer** *n.*

iterate /ˈɪtəˌreɪt/ *v.tr.* repeat; state repeatedly. □□ **iteration** /-ˈreɪʃ(ə)n/ *n.* [L *iterare iterat-* f. *iterum* again]

iterative /ˈɪtərətɪv/ *adj. Gram.* = FREQUENTATIVE. □□ **iteratively** *adv.*

Ithaca /ˈɪθəkə/ an island off the western coast of Greece, the legendary home of Odysseus.

ithyphallic /ˌɪθɪˈfælɪk/ *adj. Gk Hist.* **1 a** of the phallus carried in Bacchic festivals. **b** (of a statue etc.) having an erect penis. **2** lewd, licentious. **3** (of a poem or metre) used for Bacchic hymns. [LL *ithyphallicus* f. Gk *ithuphallikos* f. *ithus* straight, *phallos* PHALLUS]

-itic /ˈɪtɪk/ *suffix* forming adjectives and nouns corresponding to nouns in *-ite, -itis,* etc. (*Semitic; arthritic; syphilitic*). [from or after F *-itique* f. L *-iticus* f. Gk *-itikos:* see *-IC*]

itinerant /aɪˈtɪnərənt, ɪ-/ *adj. & n.* —*adj.* travelling from place to place. —*n.* an itinerant person; a tramp. □ **itinerant judge**

(or **minister** etc.) a judge, minister, etc. travelling within a circuit. □□ **itineracy** *n.* **itinerancy** *n.* [LL *itinerari* travel f. L *iter itiner-* journey]

itinerary /aɪˈtɪnərərɪ, ɪ-/ *n. & adj.* —*n.* (pl. **-ies**) **1** a detailed route. **2** a record of travel. **3** a guidebook. —*adj.* of roads or travelling. [LL *itinerarius* (adj.), *-um* (n.) f. L *iter:* see ITINERANT]

itinerate /aɪˈtɪnəˌreɪt, ɪ-/ *v.intr.* travel from place to place or (of a minister etc.) within a circuit. □□ **itineration** /-ˈreɪʃ(ə)n/ *n.* [LL *itinerari:* see ITINERANT]

-ition /ˈɪʃ(ə)n/ *suffix* forming nouns, = -ATION (*admonition; perdition; position*). [from or after F *-ition* or L *-itio -itionis*]

-itious[1] /ˈɪʃəs/ *suffix* forming adjectives corresponding to nouns in *-ition* (*ambitious; suppositious*). [L *-itio* etc. + -OUS]

-itious[2] /ˈɪʃəs/ *suffix* forming adjectives meaning 'related to, having the nature of' (*adventitious; suppositious*). [L *-icius* + -OUS, commonly written with *t* in med.L manuscripts]

-itis /ˈaɪtɪs/ *suffix* forming nouns, esp.: **1** names of inflammatory diseases (*appendicitis; bronchitis*). **2** *colloq.* in extended uses with ref. to conditions compared to diseases (*electionitis*). [Gk *-itis,* forming fem. of adjectives in *-itēs* (with *nosos* 'disease' implied)]

-itive /ˈɪtɪv/ *suffix* forming adjectives, = -ATIVE (*positive; transitive*). [from or after F *-itif -itive* or L *-itivus* f. participial stems in *-it-:* see -IVE]

it'll /ˈɪt(ə)l/ *contr. colloq.* it will; it shall.

ITN *abbr.* (in the UK) Independent Television News.

ITO *abbr.* International Trade Organization.

-itor /ˈɪtə(r)/ *suffix* forming agent nouns, usu. from Latin words (sometimes via French) (*creditor*). See also -OR[1].

-itory /ˈɪtərɪ/ *suffix* forming adjectives meaning 'relating to or involving (a verbal action)' (*inhibitory*). See also -ORY[2]. [L *-itorius*]

-itous /ˈɪtəs/ *suffix* forming adjectives corresponding to nouns in *-ity* (*calamitous; felicitous*). [from or after F *-iteux* f. L *-itosus*]

its /ɪts/ *poss.pron.* of it; of itself (*can see its advantages*).

it's /ɪts/ *contr.* **1** it is. **2** it has.

itself /ɪtˈself/ *pron.* emphatic and refl. form of IT[1]. □ **by itself** apart from its surroundings, automatically, spontaneously. **in itself** viewed in its essential qualities (*not in itself a bad thing*). [OE f. IT[1] + SELF, but often treated as ITS + SELF (cf. *its own self*)]

itsy-bitsy /ˌɪtsɪˈbɪtsɪ/ *adj.* (also **itty-bitty** /ˌɪtɪˈbɪtɪ/) *colloq.* usu. *derog.* tiny, insubstantial, slight. [redupl. of LITTLE, infl. by BIT[1]]

ITU *abbr.* International Telecommunication Union.

ITV *abbr.* (in the UK) Independent Television.

-ity /ˈɪtɪ/ *suffix* forming nouns donating: **1** quality or condition (*authority; humility; purity*). **2** an instance or degree of this (*a monstrosity; humidity*). [from or after F *-ité* f. L *-itas -itatis*]

IU *abbr.* international unit.

IUD *abbr.* **1** intra-uterine (contraceptive) device. **2** intra-uterine death (of the foetus before birth).

-ium /ɪəm/ *suffix* forming nouns denoting esp.: **1** (also **-um**) names of metallic elements (*uranium; tantalum*). **2** a region of the body (*pericardium; hypogastrium*). **3** a biological structure (*mycelium; prothallium*). [from or after L *-ium* f. Gk *-ion*]

IUPAC /ˈjuːpæk/ *abbr.* International Union of Pure and Applied Chemistry.

IV *abbr.* intravenous.

Ivan /ˈaɪv(ə)n/ the name of several rulers of Russia:

Ivan I (*c.*1304–41), grand duke of Muscovy 1328–40. He strengthened and enlarged the duchy, making Moscow the ecclesiastical capital.

Ivan III 'the Great' (1440–1505), grand duke of Muscovy 1462–1505. He consolidated and enlarged his territory, defending it against a Tartar invasion in 1480, and established autocratic government.

Ivan IV 'the Terrible' (1530–84), first tsar of Muscovy 1533–84. Although an energetic and intelligent ruler Ivan was prone to bouts of paranoiac violence, being particularly suspicious of his own nobles, the Boyars. In the early years following the end of the regency in 1547 Ivan carried out some important administrative reforms and pursued a successful expansionist foreign policy, but in later life his rule became disastrously despotic, and he was subject to fits of rage, in one of which he killed his son. Periodic pogroms, most notably those at Novgorod in 1567 and Moscow in 1572, left Russia weak and divided, while most of his foreign conquests were eventually lost to the Poles.

I've /aɪv/ *contr.* I have.

-ive /ɪv/ *suffix* forming adjectives meaning 'tending to, having the nature of', and corresponding nouns (*suggestive*; *corrosive*; *palliative*; *coercive*; *talkative*). □□ **-ively** *suffix* forming adverbs. **-iveness** *suffix* forming nouns. [from or after F *-if -ive* f. L *-ivus*]

Ives /aɪvz/, Charles (1874–1954), American highly original composer, strongly influenced by popular music and the sounds of everyday life and at the same time innovative and forward-looking, developing from the experiments in his father, a town bandmaster, the use of polyrhythm, polytonality, quartertones, note-clusters, and aleatory techniques. In the two pieces for small orchestra *The Unanswered Question* and *Central Park in the Dark* (both 1906) two orchestras, each with its own conductor, play independently, never synchronizing, an effect dating back to his memories of two bands playing different marches in different streets in his home town.

IVF *abbr.* in vitro fertilization.

ivied /ˈaɪvɪd/ *adj.* overgrown with ivy.

ivory /ˈaɪvərɪ/ *n.* (*pl.* **-ies**) **1** a hard creamy-white substance composing the main part of the tusks of an elephant, hippopotamus, walrus, and narwhal. **2** the colour of this. **3** (usu. in *pl.*) **a** an article made of ivory. **b** *sl.* anything made of or resembling ivory, esp. a piano key or a tooth. □ **fossil ivory** ivory from the tusks of a mammoth. **ivory black** black pigment from calcined ivory or bone. **ivory-nut** the seed of a corozo palm, *Phytelephas macrocarpa*, used as a source of vegetable ivory for carving: also called *corozo-nut*. **ivory tower** a state of seclusion or separation from the ordinary world and the harsh realities of life. **vegetable ivory** a hard white material obtained from the endosperm of the ivory-nut. □□ **ivoried** *adj.* [ME f. OF *yvoire* ult. f. L *ebur eboris*]

Ivory Coast a country in West Africa on the Gulf of Guinea, between Liberia and Ghana; pop. (est. 1988) 11,184,850; official language, French; capital, Abidjan. The area was explored by the Portuguese in the late 15th c., and subsequently disputed by traders from various European countries who sought the ivory from which the country takes its name, and slaves. It was made a French protectorate in 1842, and became an autonomous republic within the French Community in 1958 and a fully independent republic outside it in 1960. One of the more developed of African economies, it is noted for its forest resources which make it the leading African exporter of tropical wood.

ivy /ˈaɪvɪ/ *n.* (*pl.* **-ies**) **1** a climbing evergreen shrub, *Hedera helix*, with usu. dark-green shining five-angled leaves. **2** any of various other climbing plants including ground ivy and poison ivy. [OE ifig]

Ivy League a name applied to a group of long-established eastern US universities of high academic and social prestige, including Harvard, Yale, Princeton, and Columbia.

Iwo Jima /ˌiːwəʊ ˈdʒiːmə/ a small volcanic island, the largest of the Volcano Islands in the western Pacific, 1,222 km (760 miles) south of Tokyo. During the Second World War it was the heavily fortified site of a Japanese air base, and its attack and capture in 1944–5 was one of the severest US campaigns. It was returned to Japan in 1968.

IWW *abbr.* Industrial Workers of the World.

ixia /ˈɪksɪə/ *n.* any iridaceous plant of the genus *Ixia* of S. Africa, with large showy flowers. [L f. Gk, a kind of thistle]

Ixion /ˈɪksɪən/ *Gk Mythol.* the Greek Cain, the first to murder one of his kin. He was purified by Zeus, but tried to seduce Hera, and was first deceived with a cloud-image of her (on which he begat the Centaurs) and afterwards was punished by being pinned to a fiery wheel that revolved unceasingly through the underworld.

izard /ˈɪzɑːd/ *n.* a chamois. [F *isard*, of unkn. orig.]

-ize /aɪz/ *suffix* (also **-ise**) forming verbs, meaning: **1** make or become such (*Americanize*; *pulverize*; *realize*). **2** treat in such a way (*monopolize*; *pasteurize*). **3 a** follow a special practice (*economize*). **b** have a specified feeling (*sympathize*). **4** affect with, provide with, or subject to (*oxidize*; *hospitalize*). ¶ The form *-ize* has been in use in English since the 16th c.; it is widely used in American English, but is not an Americanism. The alternative spelling *-ise* (reflecting a French influence) is in common use, esp. in British English, and is obligatory in certain cases: (*a*) where it forms part of a larger word-element, such as *-mise* (= sending) in *compromise*, and *-prise* (= taking) in *surprise*; and (*b*) in verbs corresponding to a noun with *-s-* in the stem, such as *advertise* and *televise*. □□ **-ization** /-ˈzeɪʃ(ə)n/ *suffix* forming nouns. **-izer** *suffix* forming agent nouns. [from or after F *-iser* f. LL *-izare* f. Gk *-izō*]

Izmir /ɪzˈmɪə(r)/ (formerly **Smyrna** /ˈsmɜːnə/) a seaport and naval base in western Turkey, on an inlet of the Aegean Sea; pop. (1985) 1,489,800. It is the third-largest city of Turkey.

izmit /ɪzˈmɪt/ a city of NW Turkey, situated on the Gulf of Izmit, an inlet of the Sea of Marmara; pop. (1985) 236,100.

Iznik /ɪzˈnɪk/ a town of NW Turkey, situated to the south-east of the Sea of Marmara; pop. 14,000. Built on the site of ancient Nicaea, it has been a noted centre for the production of coloured tiles since the 16th c.

J

J¹ /dʒeɪ/ n. (also **j**) (pl. **Js** or **J's**) **1** the tenth letter of the alphabet. **2** (as a Roman numeral) = i in a final position (ij; vj).

J² abbr. (also **J.**) **1** joule(s). **2** Judge. **3** Justice.

jab /dʒæb/ v. & n. —v.tr. (**jabbed, jabbing**) **1 a** poke roughly. **b** stab. **2** (foll. by into) thrust (a thing) hard or abruptly. —n. **1** an abrupt blow with one's fist or a pointed implement. **2** colloq. a hypodermic injection, esp. a vaccination. [orig. Sc. var. of JOB²]

Jabalpur /ˌdʒʌbəlˈpʊə(r)/ an industrial city and military post of central India, in Madhya Pradesh; pop. (1981) 758,000.

jabber /ˈdʒæbə(r)/ v. & n. —v. **1** intr. chatter volubly and incoherently. **2** tr. utter (words) fast and indistinctly. —n. meaningless jabbering; a gabble. [imit.]

jabberwocky /ˈdʒæbəˌwɒki/ n. (pl. **-ies**) a piece of nonsensical writing or speech, esp. for comic effect. [title of a poem in Lewis Carroll's Through the Looking-Glass (1871)]

jabiru /ˈdʒæbɪˌruː/ n. **1** a large stork, Jabiru mycteria, of Central and S. America. **2** a black-necked stork, Xenorhyncus asiaticus, of Asia and Australia. [Tupi-Guarani jabirú]

jaborandi /ˌdʒæbəˈrændi/ n. (pl. **jaborandis**) **1** any shrub of the genus Pilocarpus, of S. America. **2** the dried leaflets of this, having diuretic and diaphoretic properties. [Tupi-Guarani jaburandi]

jabot /ˈʒæbəʊ/ n. an ornamental frill or ruffle of lace etc. on the front of a shirt or blouse. [F, orig. = crop of a bird]

jacana /ˈdʒækənə, -sənə/ n. any of various small tropical wading birds of the family Jacanidae, with elongated toes and hind-claws which enable them to walk on floating leaves etc. [Port. jaçanã f. Tupi-Guarani jasaná]

jacaranda /ˌdʒækəˈrændə/ n. **1** any tropical American tree of the genus Jacaranda, with trumpet-shaped blue flowers. **2** any tropical American tree of the genus Dalbergia, with hard scented wood. [Tupi-Guarani jacarandá]

jacinth /ˈdʒæsɪnθ, ˈdʒeɪ-/ n. a reddish-orange variety of zircon used as a gem. [ME iacynt etc. f. OF iacinte or med.L jacint(h)us f. L hyacinthus HYACINTH]

jack¹ /dʒæk/ n. & v. —n. **1** a device for lifting heavy objects, esp. the axle of a vehicle off the ground while changing a wheel etc. **2** a court-card with a picture of a man, esp. a soldier, page, or knave, etc. **3** a ship's flag, esp. one flown from the bow and showing nationality. **4** a device using a single plug to connect an electrical circuit. **5** a small white ball in bowls, at which the players aim. **6 a** = JACKSTONE. **b** (in pl.) a game of jackstones. **7** (**Jack**) the familiar form of John esp. typifying the common man or the male of a species (I'm all right, Jack). **8** the figure of a man striking the bell on a clock. **9** sl. a detective; a policeman. **10** US sl. money. **11** = LUMBERJACK. **12** = STEEPLEJACK. **13** a device for turning a spit. **14** any of various marine perchlike fish of the family Carangidae, including the amberjack. **15** a device for plucking the string of a harpsichord etc., one being operated by each key. —v.tr. (usu. foll. by up) **1** raise with or as with a jack (in sense 1). **2** colloq. raise e.g. prices. □ **every man jack** each and every person. **Jack Frost** frost personified. **jack in** (or **up**) sl. abandon (an attempt etc.). **jack-in-the-box** a toy figure that springs out of a box when it is opened. **jack-in-office** a self-important minor official. **jack of all trades** a person who can do many different kinds of work. **jack-o'-lantern 1** a will-o'-the-wisp. **2** a lantern made esp. from a hollowed pumpkin with holes for facial features. **jack plane** a medium-sized plane for use in rough joinery. **jack plug** a plug for use with a jack (see sense 4 of n.). **Jack tar** a sailor. **on one's jack** (or **Jack Jones**) sl. alone; on one's own. [ME Iakke, a pet-name for John, erron. assoc. with F Jacques James]

jack² /dʒæk/ n. **1** = BLACKJACK³. **2** hist. a sleeveless padded tunic worn by foot-soldiers. [ME f. OF jaque, of uncert. orig.]

jackal /ˈdʒæk(ə)l/ n. **1** any of various wild doglike mammals of the genus Canis, esp. C. aureus, found in Africa and S. Asia, usu. hunting or scavenging for food in packs. **2** colloq. **a** a person who does preliminary drudgery for another. **b** a person who assists another's immoral behaviour. [Turk. çakal f. Pers. šagāl]

jackanapes /ˈdʒækəˌneɪps/ n. archaic **1** a pert or insolent fellow. **2** a mischievous child. **3** a tame monkey. [earliest as Jack Napes (1450): supposed to refer to the Duke of Suffolk, whose badge was an ape's clog and chain]

jackaroo /ˌdʒækəˈruː/ n. (also **jackeroo**) Austral. colloq. a novice on a sheep-station or cattle-station. [JACK¹ + KANGAROO]

jackass /ˈdʒækæs/ n. **1** a male ass. **2** a stupid person.

jackboot /ˈdʒækbuːt/ n. **1** a large boot reaching above the knee. **2** this as a symbol of fascism or military oppression. □□ **jackbooted** adj.

jackdaw /ˈdʒækdɔː/ n. a small grey-headed crow, Corvus monedula, often frequenting rooftops and nesting in tall buildings, and noted for its inquisitiveness (cf. DAW).

jackeroo var. of JACKAROO.

jacket /ˈdʒækɪt/ n. & v. —n. **1 a** a sleeved short outer garment. **b** a thing worn esp. round the torso for protection or support (life-jacket). **2** a casing or covering, e.g. as insulation round a boiler. **3** = dust-jacket. **4** the skin of a potato, esp. when baked whole. **5** an animal's coat. —v.tr. (**jacketed, jacketing**) cover with a jacket. □ **jacket potato** a baked potato served with the skin on. [ME f. OF ja(c)quet dimin. of jaque JACK²]

jackfish /ˈdʒækfɪʃ/ n. (pl. same) = PIKE¹.

jackfruit /ˈdʒækfruːt/ n. **1** an East Indian tree, Artocarpus heterophyllus, bearing fruit resembling breadfruit. **2** this fruit. [Port. jaca f. Malayalam chakka + FRUIT]

jackhammer /ˈdʒækˌhæmə(r)/ n. US a pneumatic hammer or drill.

jackknife /ˈdʒæknaɪf/ n. & v. —n. (pl. **-knives**) **1** a large clasp-knife. **2** a dive in which the body is first bent at the waist and then straightened. —v.intr. (**-knifed, -knifing**) (of an articulated vehicle) fold against itself in an accidental skidding movement.

jackpot /ˈdʒækpɒt/ n. a large prize or amount of winnings, esp. accumulated in a game or lottery etc. □ **hit the jackpot** colloq. **1** win a large prize. **2** have remarkable luck or success. [JACK¹ n. 2 + POT¹: orig. in a form of poker with two jacks as minimum to open the pool]

jackrabbit /ˈdʒækˌræbɪt/ n. US any of various large prairie hares of the genus Lepus with very long ears and hind legs.

Jack Russell /dʒæk ˈrʌs(ə)l/ n. **1** a terrier of a breed with short legs. **2** this breed.

jacksnipe /ˈdʒæksnaɪp/ n. a small snipe, Lymnocryptes minimus.

Jackson¹ /ˈdʒæks(ə)n/, Andrew (1767–1845), 7th President of the US, 1829–37, known as 'Old Hickory'. After an active early career in which he defeated a British Army at New Orleans (1815), successfully invaded Florida (1818), and waged several campaigns against the Indians, as well as serving as a Congressman, Senator, and State judge and earning a reputation as a duellist, Jackson was elected President in 1829 and initiated the spoils system while generally strengthening presidential powers. He retired in 1837 and lived out his life at his home in Tennessee.

Jackson² /ˈdʒæks(ə)n/, Michael (1958–), American singer and songwriter, who started by performing with his brothers in the Jackson Five and later had a very successful solo career.

Jackson³ Thomas Jonathan ('Stonewall') (1824–63), Confederate general of the American Civil War, who made his mark as a brigade commander at the first battle of Bull Run in 1861 (where a successful defensive stand earned him his nickname). As the trusted deputy of Robert E. Lee he played a crucial part in the Confederate victories in Virginia in the first two years of the war. Jackson died after being mistakenly shot by his own troops at the battle of Chancellorsville.

Jacksonville /ˈdʒæksən,vɪl/ the largest city of Florida, named after President Andrew Jackson; pop. (1982) 556,400.

jackstaff /ˈdʒækstɑːf/ n. Naut. **1** a staff at the bow of a ship for a jack. **2** a staff carrying the flag that is to show above the masthead.

jackstone /ˈdʒækstəʊn/ n. **1** a small piece of metal etc. used with others in tossing-games. Also called JACK¹. **2** (in pl.) **a** a game with a ball and jackstones. **b** the game of jacks.

jackstraw /ˈdʒækstrɔː/ n. a spillikin.

Jack the Ripper a notorious Victorian murderer, never identified, who carried out a series of grisly murders of prostitutes in the East End of London in 1888–9. In each case the body was mutilated in a way that indicated a knowledge of anatomy. The authorities received taunting notes from a person calling himself Jack the Ripper and claiming to be the murderer, but the case remains unsolved.

Jacob /ˈdʒeɪkəb/ a Hebrew partiarch (see ISRAEL¹), the younger of the twin sons of Isaac and Rebecca. He tricked his brother Esau (see entry) out of his birthright. □ **Jacob's ladder** (with ref. to Jacob's dream of a ladder reaching to heaven, as described in Gen. 28: 12) **1** a plant, Polemonium caeruleum, with corymbs of blue or white flowers, and leaves suggesting a ladder. **2** a rope-ladder with wooden rungs. **Jacob's staff** (with ref. to the staffs used by Jacob, as described in Gen. 30: 37–43) **1** a surveyor's iron-shod rod used instead of a tripod. **2** an instrument used for measuring distances and heights. [Heb. ya'aqōb following after, supplanter]

Jacobean /ˌdʒækəˈbiːən/ adj. & n. —adj. **1** of or relating to the reign of James I of England. **2** (of furniture) in the style prevalent then, esp. of the colour of dark oak. —n. a Jacobean person. [mod.L Jacobaeus f. eccl.L Jacobus James f. Gk Iakōbos Jacob]

Jacobin /ˈdʒækəbɪn/ n. **1 a** hist. a member of an extreme political party during the French Revolution. Taking their name from the old Jacobin convent (see sense 2) where they held their first meetings in 1789, the Jacobins were the most radical of the large political groups formed in the wake of the revolution of 1789, advocating complete equality and democracy and willing to undertake extreme actions to realize their goals. **b** any extreme radical. **2** archaic a Dominican friar. **3** (jacobin) a pigeon with reversed feathers on the back of its neck like a cowl. □ **Jacobinic** /-ˈbɪnɪk/ adj. **Jacobinical** /-ˈbɪnɪk(ə)l/ adj. **Jacobinism** n. [orig. in sense 2 by assoc. with the Rue St Jacques in Paris: ME f. F f. med.L Jacobinus f. eccl.L Jacobus]

Jacobite¹ /ˈdʒækəˌbaɪt/ n. a follower of Jacobus Bardaeus (6th-c. Syrian monophysite monk). The Jacobites (not so called until 787) became the national Church of Syria; a small membership still exists. [L Jacobus (see JACOBEAN)]

Jacobite² /ˈdʒækəˌbaɪt/ n. hist. a supporter of the deposed James II, or of his descendants, or of the Stuarts after the Revolution of 1688, in their claim to the British throne. The Jacobites drew most of their support from Catholic clans of the Scottish Highlands, backed by France only when it suited her political convenience. Three serious attempts were launched to regain the throne in 1689–90, 1715, and 1745–6, but support finally collapsed when the clans were suppressed after the battle of Culloden. □ **Jacobitical** /-ˈbɪtɪk(ə)l/ adj. **Jacobitism** n. [L Jacobus James: see JACOBEAN]

Jacobs /ˈdʒeɪkəbz/, William Wymark (1863–1943), English author, remembered especially for his short stories. These fall roughly into two groups: those dealing humorously with the escapades of sailors and of country characters and rogues (as in the 'Claybury' stories), and tales of the macabre, such as the celebrated 'The Monkey's Paw', which was dramatized with great success.

jaconet /ˈdʒækənɪt/ n. a cotton cloth like cambric, esp. a dyed waterproof kind for poulticing etc. [Urdu jagannāthi f. Jagannath (now Puri) in India, its place of origin: see JUGGERNAUT]

Jacquard /ˈdʒækɑːd/ n. **1** an apparatus with perforated cards, fitted to a loom to facilitate the weaving of figured fabrics. **2** (in full **Jacquard loom**) a loom fitted with this. **3** a fabric or article

made with this, with an intricate variegated pattern. [J. M. Jacquard, Fr. inventor d. 1834]

jactitation /ˌdʒæktɪˈteɪʃ(ə)n/ n. **1** Med. **a** the restless tossing of the body in illness. **b** the twitching of a limb or muscle. **2** archaic the offence of falsely claiming to be a person's wife or husband. [med.L jactitatio false declaration f. L jactitare boast, frequent. of jactare throw: sense 1 f. earlier jactation]

Jacuzzi /dʒəˈkuːzɪ/ n. (pl. **Jacuzzis**) propr. a large bath with underwater jets of water to massage the body. [name of the inventor and manufacturers]

jade¹ /dʒeɪd/ n. **1** a hard usu. green stone composed of silicates of calcium and magnesium, or of sodium and aluminium, used for ornaments and implements. **2** the green colour of jade. [F: le jade for l'ejade f. Sp. piedra de ijada stone of the flank, i.e. stone for colic (which it was believed to cure)]

jade² /dʒeɪd/ n. **1** an inferior or worn-out horse. **2** derog. a disreputable woman. [ME: orig. unkn.]

jaded /ˈdʒeɪdɪd/ adj. tired or worn out; surfeited. □□ **jadedly** adv. **jadedness** n.

jadeite /ˈdʒeɪdaɪt/ n. a green, blue, or white sodium aluminium silicate form of jade.

j'adoube /ʒɑːˈduːb/ int. Chess a declaration by a player intending to adjust the placing of a piece without making a move with it. [F, = I adjust]

jaeger /ˈjeɪɡə(r)/ n. (also **yager**) US = SKUA. [G Jäger hunter f. jagen to hunt]

Jaffa /ˈdʒæfə/ n. a large oval thick-skinned variety of orange. [Jaffa in Israel, near where it was first grown]

Jaffna /ˈdʒæfnə/ **1** a district at the northern tip of Sri Lanka, dominated by a Hindu Tamil population; pop. (1981) 830,000. **2** its capital city; pop. (1981) 118,200.

jag¹ /dʒæɡ/ n. & v. —n. a sharp projection of rock etc. —v.tr. (**jagged**, **jagging**) **1** cut or tear unevenly. **2** make indentations in. □□ **jagger** n. [ME, prob. imit.]

jag² /dʒæɡ/ n. sl. **1** a drinking bout; a spree. **2** a period of indulgence in an activity, emotion, etc. [orig. 16th c., = load for one horse: orig. unkn.]

Jagannatha /ˌdʒæɡəˈnɑːθə/ Hinduism the form of Krishna worshipped in Puri, Orissa. In the annual festival held in June or July his image is carried through the streets in a heavy chariot dragged along by devotees; some devotees are said to have thrown themselves under its wheels. [Skr., = lord of the world]

jagged /ˈdʒæɡɪd/ adj. **1** with an unevenly cut or torn edge. **2** deeply indented; with sharp points. □□ **jaggedly** adv. **jaggedness** n.

jaggy /ˈdʒæɡɪ/ adj. (**jaggier**, **jaggiest**) **1** = JAGGED. **2** (also **jaggie**) Sc. prickly.

jaguar /ˈdʒæɡjʊə(r)/ n. a large flesh-eating spotted feline, Panthera onca, of Central and S. America. [Tupi-Guarani jaguara]

jaguarundi /ˌdʒæɡwəˈrʌndɪ/ n. (pl. **jaguarundis**) a long-tailed slender feline, Felis yaguarondi, of Central and S. America. [Tupi-Guarani]

jai alai /ˈhaɪ əˌlaɪ/ n. a game like pelota played with large curved wicker baskets. [Sp. f. Basque jai festival + alai merry]

jail /dʒeɪl/ n. & v. (also **gaol**) —n. **1** a place to which persons are committed by a court for detention. **2** confinement in a jail. —v.tr. put in jail. [ME gayole f. OF jaiole, jeole & ONF gaole f. Rmc dimin. of L cavea CAGE]

jailbird /ˈdʒeɪlbɜːd/ n. (also **gaolbird**) a prisoner or habitual criminal.

jailbreak /ˈdʒeɪlbreɪk/ n. (also **gaolbreak**) an escape from jail.

jailer /ˈdʒeɪlə(r)/ n. (also **gaoler**) a person in charge of a jail or of the prisoners in it.

Jain /dʒaɪn/ n. & adj. —n. an adherent of Jainism. —adj. of or relating to this religion. [Hindi f. Skr. jainas saint, victor f. jīna victorious]

Jainism /ˈdʒaɪnɪz(ə)m/ n. a non-theistic religion founded in India in the 6th c. BC by Vardhamana Mahavira as a reaction against the teachings of orthodox Brahminism. Its central doctrine is non-injury to living creatures. Salvation is attained by perfection of the soul through successive lives (see KARMA).

æ cat ɑ: arm e bed ɜ: her ɪ sit iː see ɒ hot ɔ: saw ʌ run ʊ put uː too ə ago aɪ my

Unlike Buddhism, Jainism survives in India today but never spread outside it. There are two major sects: the white-robed Svetambaras and the naked Digambaras. □□ **Jainist** n.

Jaipur /dʒaɪˈpʊə(r)/ a city of NW India, the capital of Rajasthan; pop. (1981) 1,005,000.

Jakarta see DJAKARTA.

jake /dʒeɪk/ adj. Austral. & NZ sl. all right; satisfactory. [20th c.: orig. uncert.]

Jalalabad /dʒəˈlæləˌbæd/ a city of eastern Afghanistan, situated midway between Kabul and the city of Peshwar in Pakistan; pop. (est. 1984) 61,000.

jalap /ˈdʒæləp/ n. a purgative drug obtained esp. from the tuberous roots of a Mexican climbing plant, *Exogonium purga*. [F f. Sp. *jalapa* f. *Jalapa*, *Xalapa*, city in Mexico, f. Aztec *Xalapan* sand by the water]

Jalisco /hæˈliːskəʊ/ a State of west central Mexico; pop. (est. 1988) 5,198,400; capital, Guadalajara.

jalopy /dʒəˈlɒpɪ/ n. (pl. **-ies**) colloq. a dilapidated old motor vehicle. [20th c.: orig. unkn.]

jalousie /ˈʒæluˌziː/ n. a blind or shutter made of a row of angled slats to keep out rain etc. and control the influx of light. [F (as JEALOUSY)]

Jam. abbr. **1** Jamaica. **2** James (New Testament).

jam¹ /dʒæm/ v. & n. —v.tr. & intr. (**jammed**, **jamming**) **1 a** tr. (usu. foll. by *into*) squeeze or wedge into a space. **b** intr. become wedged. **2 a** tr. cause (machinery or a component) to become wedged or immovable so that it cannot work. **b** intr. become jammed in this way. **3** tr. push or cram together in a compact mass. **4** intr. (foll. by *in*, *on to*) push or crowd (*they jammed on to the bus*). **5** tr. **a** block (a passage, road, etc.) by crowding or obstructing. **b** (foll. by *in*) obstruct the exit of (*we were jammed in*). **6** tr. (usu. foll. by *on*) apply (brakes etc.) forcefully or abruptly. **7** tr. make (a radio transmission) unintelligible by causing interference. **8** colloq. (in jazz etc.) extemporize with other musicians. —n. **1** a squeeze or crush. **2** a crowded mass (*traffic jam*). **3** colloq. an awkward situation or predicament. **4** a stoppage (of a machine etc.) due to jamming. **5** (in full **jam session**) colloq. improvised playing by a group of jazz musicians. □ **jam-packed** colloq. full to capacity. □□ **jammer** n. [imit.]

jam² /dʒæm/ n. & v. —n. **1** a conserve of fruit and sugar boiled to a thick consistency. **2** Brit. colloq. something easy or pleasant (*money for jam*). —v.tr. (**jammed**, **jamming**) **1** spread jam on. **2** make (fruit etc.) into jam. □ **jam tomorrow** a pleasant thing often promised but usu. never forthcoming. [perh. = JAM¹]

Jamaica /dʒəˈmeɪkə/ an island country in the Caribbean Sea south-east of Cuba, a member State of the Commonwealth; pop. (est. 1988) 2,458,100; official language, English; capital, Kingston. The economy is based on both agriculture and industry, in the latter respect particularly upon bauxite and aluminium, but chronic unemployment has continued to cause severe social problems. Discovered by Columbus in 1494, Jamaica remained a Spanish colony until conquered by the British in 1655. British colonial rule was threatened by popular violence in the mid-19th c. which led to the suspension of representative government for two decades, but self-government was granted in 1944, and in 1962 Jamaica became an independent Commonwealth State. □□ **Jamaican** adj. & n.

jamb /dʒæm/ n. Archit. a side post or surface of a doorway, window, or fireplace. [ME f. OF *jambe* ult. f. LL *gamba* hoof]

jambalaya /ˌdʒæmbəˈlaɪə/ n. a dish of rice with shrimps, chicken, etc. [Louisiana F f. mod. Prov. *jambalaia*]

jamboree /ˌdʒæmbəˈriː/ n. **1** a celebration or merrymaking. **2** a large rally of Scouts. [19th c.: orig. unkn.]

James¹ /dʒeɪmz/ the name of seven Stuart kings of Scotland:

James I (1394–1437), son of Robert III, reigned 1406–37. Captured by the English while a child, James remained a captive until he was able to buy his freedom in 1424. He returned to a land riven by nobles' feuds, and managed to restore some measure of royal authority, but only at the cost of making powerful enemies, some of whom eventually murdered him in Perth.

James II (1430–60), son of James I, reigned 1437–60. Coming to the throne as a minor after his father's murder, James II

eventually broke free from the domination of his regents and considerably strengthened the position of the Crown by crushing the Black Douglases, the most powerful noble house in the country. He was killed by the accidental explosion of a cannon at the siege of Roxburgh Castle.

James III (1451–88), son of James II, reigned 1460–88. A weaker man than either his father or grandfather, James III proved increasingly unable to control his nobles who eventually raised an army against him, using his son (the future James IV) as a figurehead. The King was defeated at Sauchieburn near Stirling and killed by an unknown hand while fleeing the field.

James IV (1473–1513), son of James III, reigned 1488–1513. Strongest of the Stuart kings of Scotland, James IV re-established royal power throughout the realm, most notably in the turbulent Highlands. He took an active part in European alliance politics, forging a dynastic link with England through his marriage to the daughter of Henry VII, and revitalizing the traditional pact with France. When England and France went to war in 1513, he supported the latter and invaded England at the head of a large army. He died along with many of his nobles when this army was defeated by the Earl of Surrey at Flodden.

James V (1512–42), son of James IV, reigned 1513–42. Both during his long minority and after his marriage to Mary of Guise, the Scotland of James V was dominated by French interests. The later years of his reign were marred by the return of nobles' discontent, rising Protestant agitation, and trouble with Henry VIII's England. He died young, leaving only an infant daughter.

James VI, VII see JAMES².

James² /dʒeɪmz/ the name of two kings of England and Scotland:

James I (James VI of Scotland, 1566–1625), son of Mary Queen of Scots, king of Scotland 1567–1625 and of England 1603–25. Having survived a long and difficult minority, James had largely succeeded in restoring royal authority in Scotland before inheriting the throne of England on the extinction of the Tudor line. He was a difficult and at times erratic monarch, and although he managed to avoid serious trouble in the deepening constitutional and religious crisis in his new kingdom, his lack of decisiveness and the fecklessness of his declining years, when government was effectively in the hands of his favourite the Duke of Buckingham, left his son Charles I a difficult and potentially explosive legacy.

James II (James VII of Scotland, 1633–1701), younger son of Charles I, reigned 1685–8. James was an accomplished soldier and sailor in the reign of his elder brother Charles II, but lost the support of many of his subjects soon after his accession as a result of his strong Catholic views and his attempts to reassert royal absolutism. Although he put down the rebellion of the Duke of Monmouth in 1685 he was deposed three years later in favour of William and Mary, and failed to regain his throne despite military action in Ireland and Scotland in 1689–90. He died in exile in France, leaving the Jacobite claim to the throne in the hands of his son James, the Old Pretender.

James³ /dʒeɪmz/, Henry (1843–1916), American novelist and critic, younger brother of the philosopher William James. Educated in New York and Europe, he moved to Paris (1875) where he became influenced by Turgenev, Flaubert, Zola, and others; from 1876 he lived in England. His early novels, which deal predominantly with the impact of the older European civilizations on American life, include *Roderick Hudson* (1875) and *Portrait of a Lady* (1881). To this period belong *The Bostonians* (1886), about American society, *What Maisie knew* (1897), concerning English life, and the ghost story *The Turn of the Screw* (1898). International themes are revived in his mature though stylistically obscure works *The Wings of the Dove* (1902), *The Ambassadors* (1903), and *The Golden Bowl* (1904). James was the first important writer in English to give systematic criticism to the art of the novel, and, by his own example, demonstrated the scope of psychological and aesthetic considerations that the form could encompass. His critical essays are collected in *The House of Fiction* (1957).

James⁴ /dʒeɪmz/, Jesse (Woodson) (1847–82), American outlaw, who joined with his brother Frank (1843–1915) and others to form the most notorious band of outlaws in US history, specializing in bank and train robberies.

James⁵ /ˈdʒeɪmz/, Lady Phyllis Dorothy (1920–), English author of detective novels, which include *Shroud for a Nightingale* (1971) and *A Taste for Death* (1986).

James⁶ /ˈdʒeɪmz/, St **1** 'the Great', an Apostle, elder brother of St John, martyred in AD 44. According to an old Spanish tradition his body was translated to Santiago de Compostela. Feast day, 25 July. **2** 'the Less', an Apostle, son of Alphaeus. Feast day, 1 May. **3** a person described as 'the Lord's brother', a leader of the Church at Jerusalem until put to death by the Sanhedrin in AD 62; **Epistle of St James** a book of the New Testament traditionally ascribed to him. □ **St James's Palace** see separate entry.

James⁷ /ˈdʒeɪmz/, William (1842–1910), American philosopher and psychologist. Belonging to a family of Irish Calvinist stock he taught at Harvard where his philosophical work was bound up with an interest in psychology and physiology. Influenced by Peirce, James was a leading exponent of pragmatism. Its central theme is a functional definition of truth as that which we must take account of in order to survive and prosper; truth is what works for us rather than a depiction of some structural relation between ideas and reality. A similar approach to religious and moral beliefs is found in *The Varieties of Religious Experience* (1902) and *The Meaning of Truth* (1909). In psychology he introduced the concept of the 'stream of consciousness', which was influential also in philosophy and in literature. The novelist Henry James was his brother.

James Bay /ˈdʒeɪmz/ a shallow southern arm of Hudson Bay, Canada. The bay was discovered in 1610 by Henry Hudson but was later named after Captain Thomas James who explored the region in 1631.

Jameson Raid /ˈdʒeɪms(ə)n/ an abortive raid made into Boer territory by pro-British extremists led by Dr L. S. Jameson in 1895 in an attempt to incite an uprising among recent, non-Boer immigrants. The raid seriously heightened tension in South Africa and contributed to the eventual outbreak of the Second Boer War.

Jamestown¹ /ˈdʒeɪmstaʊn/ the site of an English colony established in Virginia in 1607 during the reign of James I. Built on a marshy and unhealthy site, the town suffered badly at the hands of fire, disease, and Indians, and was finally abandoned when the colony's capital was moved to Williamsburg at the end of the 17th c.

Jamestown² /ˈdʒeɪmztaʊn/ the capital and chief port of the island of St Helena; pop. 1,500.

jamjar /ˈdʒæmdʒɑː(r)/ n. a glass jar for containing jam.

Jammu and Kashmir /ˈdʒʌmuː, kæʃˈmɪə(r)/ a State in NW India; pop. (1981) 5,981,600; capitals, Srinagar (in summer) and Jammu (in winter). (See KASHMIR.)

jammy /ˈdʒæmɪ/ adj. (**jammier**, **jammiest**) **1** covered with jam. **2** *Brit. colloq.* **a** lucky. **b** profitable.

Jamshid /dʒæmˈʃiːd/ *Persian Mythol.* a legendary early king of Persia, reputed inventor of the arts of medicine, navigation, iron-working, etc. He was king of the peris, condemned to assume human form for boasting of his immortality, and ruled Persia for 700 years.

Jan. *abbr.* January.

Janáček /ˈjænəˌtʃek/, Leoš (1854–1928), Czech composer and conductor, who combined a sense of Czech nationalism with a powerful modernity, expressed not so much by breaking away from traditional forms and harmonic thinking as by the juxtaposition of conflicting elements: romantic melodic writing side by side with stark dissonant passages, lush orchestration offset by harsh widely spaced sonorities. In his operas emotions are portrayed with unflinching clarity, enhanced by their unusual settings.

jane /dʒeɪn/ n. *sl.* a woman (*a plain jane*). [the name *Jane*]

jangle /ˈdʒæŋg(ə)l/ v. & n. —v. **1** *intr.* & *tr.* make, or cause (a bell etc.) to make, a harsh metallic sound. **2** *tr.* irritate (the nerves etc.) by discordant sound or speech etc. —n. a harsh metallic sound. [ME f. OF *jangler*, of uncert. orig.]

Janglish /ˈdʒæŋglɪʃ/ n. = JAPLISH. [Japanese + English]

janissary var. of JANIZARY.

janitor /ˈdʒænɪtə(r)/ n. **1** a doorkeeper. **2** a caretaker of a building. □□ **janitorial** /-ˈtɔːrɪəl/ adj. [L f. *janua* door]

janizary /ˈdʒænɪzərɪ/ n. (also **janissary** /-sərɪ/) (pl. -ies) **1** *hist.* a member of the Turkish infantry forming the Sultan's guard and the main fighting force of the Turkish army from the late 14th to early 19th c. **2** a devoted follower or supporter. [ult. f. Turk. *yeniçeri* f. *yeni* new + *çeri* troops]

jankers /ˈdʒæŋkəz/ n. *Mil. sl.* punishment for defaulters. [20th c.: orig. unkn.]

Jan Mayen /jæn ˈmaɪən/ a barren and virtually uninhabited island in the Arctic Ocean between Greenland and Norway, annexed by Norway in 1929. It was probably first sighted by Henry Hudson in 1607, but is named after a Dutch sea captain, Jan May, who claimed the island for his company and his country.

Jansen /ˈdʒæns(ə)n/, Cornelius (1585–1638), Dutch Roman Catholic theologian, bishop of Ypres in Flanders and founder of Jansenism. Jansen held that the natural human will is perverse and incapable of doing good.

Jansenism /ˈdʒænsənɪzm/ n. a religious movement of the 17th and 18th c., based on the writings of Jansen and characterized by general harshness and moral rigour. Its most famous exponent was Pascal. The movement received papal condemnation and its adherents were persecuted in France (though tolerated in The Netherlands) during most of the 18th c. □□ **Jansenist** n.

Janssens /ˈdʒæns(ə)nz/, Abraham (1575–1632), Flemish painter. He worked at first in the mannerist and later in the classical baroque style; in his *Lamentation* and *Crucifixion* balance and harmony are combined with decorative beauty and detail. The influence of Rubens is apparent in his later works.

January /ˈdʒænjʊərɪ/ n. (pl. -ies) the first month of the year. [ME f. AF *Jenever* f. L *Januarius* (*mensis*) (month) of Janus]

Janus /ˈdʒeɪnəs/ **1** *Rom. Mythol.* an ancient Italian deity, guardian of doorways, gates, and beginnings, and protector of the State in time of war, whose festival was held on 9 Jan. He is usually represented with two faces, one at the front and one at the back of his head, so that he looks both forwards and backwards. **2** *Astron.* a satellite of the planet Saturn, discovered in 1966.

Jap /dʒæp/ n. & adj. *colloq.* often *offens.* = JAPANESE. [abbr.]

Japan /dʒəˈpæn/ a country in eastern Asia, occupying a festoon of islands in the Pacific roughly parallel with the east coast of the Asiatic mainland; pop. (est. 1988) 122,626,000; official language, Japanese; capital, Tokyo. Japan is now the leading economic power in SE Asia and the most highly industrialized country in that region, with a range of manufacturing industries that includes electrical goods, motor vehicles, chemicals, and shipping. According to Japanese tradition, the empire was founded in 660 BC by the emperor Jimmu, a descendant of the sun goddess. After a long period of courtly rule centred on Kyoto, from the 12th c. onwards the country was dominated by succeeding clans of military warriors. With the restoration of direct Imperial rule in 1868 it entered the modernizing process, which was accelerated by wars against China (1894–5) and Russia (1904–5), but Japan did not become a major world power until the 20th c. Its occupation of the Chinese province of Manchuria in 1931 was followed by full-scale invasion of China in 1937. In 1936 an alliance was formed with Germany and later with Italy. After attacking Pearl Harbor (1941) the Japanese invaded Malaya and captured Hong Kong, Manila and Singapore. Their advance was halted by a series of US air and naval victories in 1942–4, and Japan surrendered in 1945 after the dropping of atomic bombs on Hiroshima and Nagasaki; a constitutional monarchy was established in 1947. □ **Sea of Japan** the sea between Japan and the mainland of Asia. [Chinese *Riben* sunrise (*ri* sun, *ben* origin)]

japan /dʒəˈpæn/ n. & v. —n. **1** a hard usu. black varnish, esp. of a kind brought orig. from Japan. **2** work in a Japanese style. —v.tr. (**japanned**, **japanning**) **1** varnish with japan. **2** make black and glossy as with japan.

Japanese /ˌdʒæpəˈniːz/ n. & adj. —n. (pl. same) **1 a** a native or national of Japan. **b** a person of Japanese descent. **2** the official language of Japan, spoken by virtually the whole population of that country. (See below.) —*adj.* of or relating to Japan or its people or language. □ **Japanese cedar** = CRYPTOMERIA. **Japanese print** a colour print from woodblocks. **Japanese quince** = JAPONICA.

Japanese is an agglutinative language. It contains many Chinese loan-words and has no genders, no article, and no number in nouns or verbs. It is written vertically, in a system that is partly ideographic and partly syllabic. The ideographs (known as *kanji*) were adopted from the Chinese in the early centuries of the Christian era and designate the chief meaningful elements of the language. They are supplemented by two groups of syllabic characters (*kana*), known as *hiragana* and *katakana*, for the agglutinative and inflexional endings. Attempts have been made to abolish characters altogether, but this is unsatisfactory since many words look exactly alike when written in Roman letters. There is no definite link between Japanese and any other language, although it may be related to Korean.

jape /dʒeɪp/ *n. & v.* —*n.* a practical joke. —*v.intr.* play a joke. □□ **japery** *n.* [ME: orig. uncert.]

Japheth /'dʒeɪfeθ/ a son of Noah (Gen. 10: 1); traditional ancestor of the peoples living round the Mediterranean. His name is probably to be connected with that of Iapetus, ancestor of the human race in Greek mythology.

Japlish /'dʒæplɪʃ/ *n.* a blend of Japanese and English, used in Japan. [*Japanese* + *English*]

japonica /dʒə'pɒnɪkə/ *n.* any flowering shrub of the genus *Chaenomeles*, esp. *C. speciosa*, with round white, green, or yellow edible fruits and bright red flowers. Also called *Japanese quince*. [mod.L, fem. of *japonicus* Japanese]

Jaques-Dalcroze /ˌʒɑːˈkdælˈkrəʊz/, Émile (1865–1950), Swiss music teacher and composer, the originator of eurhythmics.

jar¹ /dʒɑː(r)/ *n.* **1 a** a container of glass, earthenware, plastic, etc., usu. cylindrical. **b** the contents of this. **2** *Brit. colloq.* a glass of beer. □□ **jarful** *n.* (*pl.* **-fuls**). [F *jarre* f. Arab. *jarra*]

jar² /dʒɑː(r)/ *v. & n.* —*v.* (**jarred, jarring**) **1** *intr.* (often foll. by *on*) (of sound, words, manner, etc.) sound discordant or grating (on the nerves etc.). **2 a** *tr.* (foll. by *against, on*) strike or cause to strike with vibration or a grating sound. **b** *intr.* (of a body affected) vibrate gratingly. **3** *tr.* send a shock through (a part of the body) (*the fall jarred his neck*). **4** *intr.* (often foll. by *with*) (of an opinion, fact, etc.) be at variance; be in conflict or in dispute. —*n.* **1** a jarring sound or sensation. **2** a physical shock or jolt. **3** lack of harmony; disagreement. [16th c.: prob. imit.]

jar³ /dʒɑː(r)/ *n.* □ **on the jar** ajar. [late form of obs. *char* turn: see AJAR¹, CHAR²]

jardinière /ˌʒɑːdɪˈnjeə(r)/ *n.* **1** an ornamental pot or stand for the display of growing plants. **2** a dish of mixed vegetables. [F]

jargon¹ /'dʒɑːɡən/ *n.* **1** words or expressions used by a particular group or profession (*medical jargon*). **2** barbarous or debased language. **3** gibberish. □□ **jargonic** /-'ɡɒnɪk/ *adj.* **jargonistic** /-'nɪstɪk/ *adj.* **jargonize** *v.tr. & intr.* (also **-ise**). [ME f. OF: orig. unkn.]

jargon² /'dʒɑːɡən/ *n.* (also **jargoon** /dʒɑː'ɡuːn/) a translucent, colourless, or smoky variety of zircon. [F f. It. *giargone*, prob. ult. formed as ZIRCON]

jargonelle /ˌdʒɑːɡəˈnel/ *n.* an early-ripening variety of pear. [F, dimin. of JARGON²]

jarl /jɑːl/ *n. hist.* a Norse or Danish chief. [ON, orig. = man of noble birth, rel. to EARL]

jarrah /'dʒærə/ *n.* **1** the Australian mahogany gum-tree, *Eucalyptus marginata*. **2** the durable timber of this. [Aboriginal *djarryl*]

Jarrow /'dʒærəʊ/ a town in north-east England on the Tyne estuary. It was the cultural jewel in the Northumbrian crown until the Viking invasions; the Venerable Bede lived and worked in its monastery. Its name is now associated with the hunger-marches to London that epitomized the despair of the economic depression of the 1930s.

Jarry /'dʒærɪ/, Alfred (1873–1907), French dramatist, remembered chiefly for his satirical farce *Ubu Roi* (*Ubu the King*,

1896). Jarry became a legendary character, adopting Ubu's grotesque absurdities and living a life of dissipation. He is regarded as a precursor of surrealism and the Theatre of the Absurd.

Jas. *abbr.* James (also in New Testament).

jasmine /'dʒæsmɪn, 'dʒæz-/ *n.* (also **jasmin, jessamin** /'dʒesəmɪn/, **jessamine** /'dʒesəmɪn/) any of various ornamental shrubs of the genus *Jasminum* usu. with white or yellow flowers. □ **jasmine tea** a tea perfumed with dried jasmine blossom. [F *jasmin, jessemin* f. Arab. *yās(a)mīn* f. Pers. *yāsamīn*]

Jason /'dʒeɪs(ə)n/ *Gk legend* the son of the king of Iolcos in Thessaly, and leader of the Argonauts in the quest for the Golden Fleece.

jaspé /'dʒæspeɪ/ *adj.* like jasper; randomly coloured (esp. of cotton fabric). [F, past part. of *jasper* marble f. *jaspe* JASPER]

jasper /'dʒæspə(r)/ *n.* an opaque variety of quartz, usu. red, yellow, or brown in colour. [ME f. OF *jasp(r)e* f. L *iaspis* f. Gk, of oriental orig.]

Jassy see IASI.

Jat /dʒɑːt/ *n.* a member of an Indo-Aryan people widely distributed in NW India. [Hindi *jāt*]

Jataka /'dʒɑːtəkə/ *n.* any of the various stories of the former lives of the Buddha found in Buddhist literature. [Skr., f. *jata* born]

jato /'dʒeɪtəʊ/ *n.* (*pl.* **-os**) *Aeron.* **1** jet-assisted take-off. **2** an auxiliary power unit providing extra thrust at take-off. [abbr.]

jaundice /'dʒɔːndɪs/ *n. & v.* —*n.* **1** *Med.* a condition with yellowing of the skin or whites of the eyes, often caused by obstruction of the bile duct or by liver disease. **2** disordered (esp. mental) vision. **3** envy. —*v.tr.* **1** affect with jaundice. **2** (esp. as **jaundiced** *adj.*) affect (a person) with envy, resentment, or jealousy. [ME *iaunes* f. OF *jaunice* yellowness f. *jaune* yellow]

jaunt /dʒɔːnt/ *n. & v.* —*n.* a short excursion for enjoyment. —*v.intr.* take a jaunt. □ **jaunting car** a light two-wheeled horse-drawn vehicle formerly used in Ireland. [16th c.: orig. unkn.]

jaunty /'dʒɔːntɪ/ *adj.* (**jauntier, jauntiest**) **1** cheerful and self-confident. **2** sprightly. □□ **jauntily** *adv.* **jauntiness** *n.* [earlier *jentee* f. F *gentil* GENTLE]

Java /'dʒɑːvə/ a large island of the Malay Archipelago; pop. (1980) 91,269,500 (with Madura). The island was chiefly under Dutch rule from the 17th c. until it was occupied by Japanese troops in 1942; it was formed part of Indonesia since 1950. □ **Java Man** the fossil hominid, whose remains were first found in Java in 1891 (see PITHECANTHROPUS). **Java sparrow** a finch, *Padda oryzivora*.

Javan /'dʒɑːv(ə)n/ *n. & adj.* = JAVANESE.

Javanese /ˌdʒɑːvəˈniːz/ *n. & adj.* (*pl.* same) **1 a** a native of Java in Indonesia. **b** a person of Javanese descent. **2** the language of Java, which belongs to the Malayo-Polynesian group of languages and is spoken by about 45 million people. —*adj.* of or relating to Java, its people, or its language.

javelin /'dʒævəlɪn, -vlɪn/ *n.* **1** a light spear thrown in a competitive sport or as a weapon. **2** the athletic event or sport of throwing the javelin. [F *javeline, javelot* f. Gallo-Roman *gabalottus*]

jaw /dʒɔː/ *n. & v.* —*n.* **1 a** each of the upper and lower bony structures in vertebrates forming the framework of the mouth and containing the teeth. **b** the parts of certain invertebrates used for the ingestion of food. **2 a** (in *pl.*) the mouth with its bones and teeth. **b** the narrow mouth of a valley, channel, etc. **c** the gripping parts of a tool or machine. **d** gripping-power (*jaws of death*). **3** *colloq.* **a** talkativeness; tedious talk (*hold your jaw*). **b** a sermonizing talk; a lecture. —*v. colloq.* **1** *intr.* speak esp. at tedious length. **2** *tr.* **a** persuade by talking. **b** admonish or lecture. □ **jaw-breaker** *colloq.* a word that is very long or hard to pronounce. [ME f. OF *joe* cheek, jaw, of uncert. orig.]

jawbone /'dʒɔːbəʊn/ *n.* **1** each of the two bones forming the lower jaw in most mammals. **2** these two combined into one in other mammals.

jay /dʒeɪ/ *n.* **1 a** a noisy chattering European bird, *Garrulus glandarius*, with vivid pinkish-brown, blue, black, and white plumage. **b** any other bird of the subfamily Garrulinae. **2** a person who chatters impertinently. [ME f. OF f. LL *gaius, gaia*, perh. f. L praenomen *Gaius*: cf. *jackdaw, robin*]

jaywalk /ˈdʒeɪwɔːk/ v.intr. cross or walk in the street or road without regard for traffic. □□ **jaywalker** n.

jazz /dʒæz/ n. & v. —n. **1** a type of 20th-c. music. (See below.) **2** *sl.* pretentious talk or behaviour, nonsensical stuff (*all that jazz*). —v.intr. play or dance to jazz. □ **jazz up** brighten or enliven. □□ **jazzer** n. [20th c.: orig. uncert.]

Jazz was developed in the southern US early in the 20th c., blending West African rhythms with elements from ragtime, brass bands, spirituals, blues, and work-songs. Its characteristic features are improvisation, syncopation, and strong rhythm. In its earliest form—'Dixieland'—jazz was played by small groups. During the 1920s bands became larger, leading to the 'swing' of the 1930s emphasizing pre-arranged orchestrations. 'Be-bop' in the early 1940s marked a return to smaller groups, playing complex melodies with extreme syncopation. Later developments have included modal and atonal experiments, and attempts to fuse jazz with classical or rock music.

jazzman /ˈdʒæzmæn/ n. (pl. **-men**) a jazz-player.

jazzy /ˈdʒæzɪ/ adj. (**jazzier, jazziest**) **1** of or like jazz. **2** vivid, unrestrained, showy. □□ **jazzily** adv. **jazziness** n.

JCB /ˌdʒeɪsiːˈbiː/ n. propr. a type of mechanical excavator with a shovel at the front and a digging arm at the rear. [*J. C. Bamford*, the makers]

JCL abbr. *Computing* job-control language.

JCR abbr. *Brit.* Junior Common (or Combination) Room.

jealous /ˈdʒeləs/ adj. **1** (often foll. by *of*) fiercely protective (of rights etc.). **2** afraid, suspicious, or resentful of rivalry in love or affection. **3** (often foll. by *of*) envious or resentful (of a person or a person's advantages etc.). **4** (of God) intolerant of disloyalty. **5** (of inquiry, supervision, etc.) vigilant. □□ **jealously** adv. [ME f. OF *gelos* f. med.L *zelosus* ZEALOUS]

jealousy /ˈdʒeləsɪ/ n. (pl. **-ies**) **1** a jealous state or feeling. **2** an instance of this. [ME f. OF *gelosie* (as JEALOUS)]

jean /dʒiːn/ n. twilled cotton cloth. [ME, attrib. use of *Jene* f. OF *Janne* f. med.L *Janua* Genoa]

Jeanneret /ˈdʒenəˌreɪ/, Charles Edouard, see LE CORBUSIER.

Jean Paul /ʒɑ̃ː ˈpɔːl/ Johann Paul Friedrich Richter (1763–1825), German Romantic novelist. The humble village surroundings of his childhood are idyllically represented in his works. His best-known novels include *Hesperus* (1795), *Quintus Fixlein* (1796), and *Siebenkäs* (1796), which combine humour and sentiment with mystic idealism.

Jeans /dʒiːnz/, Sir James Hopwood (1877–1946), English physicist, mathematician, and writer on astronomy. He was the first to propose (in 1928) that matter is continuously created throughout the universe.

jeans /dʒiːnz/ n.pl. trousers made of jean or (more usually) denim, for informal wear.

Jedburgh /ˈdʒedbərə/ a town in southern Scotland near the English border, where disputes frequently arose between border peoples, giving its name to **Jedburgh justice**, a summary procedure whereby a person is sentenced first and tried later.

Jeddah /ˈdʒedə/ (also **Jiddah** /ˈdʒɪdə/) a seaport on the Red Sea coast of Saudi Arabia; pop. 561,100.

Jeep /dʒiːp/ n. propr. a small sturdy esp. military motor vehicle with four-wheel drive. [orig. US, f. *GP* = general purposes, infl. by 'Eugene the Jeep', an animal in a comic strip]

jeepers /ˈdʒiːpəz/ int. *US sl.* expressing surprise etc. [corrupt. of *Jesus*]

jeer /dʒɪə(r)/ v. & n. —v. **1** intr. (usu. foll. by *at*) scoff derisively. **2** tr. scoff at; deride. —n. a scoff or taunt. □□ **jeeringly** adv. [16th c.: orig. unkn.]

Jeeves /dʒiːvz/, Reginald. Bertie Wooster's resourceful and omniscient valet in the novels of P. G. Wodehouse.

Jeez /dʒiːz/ int. *sl.* a mild expression of surprise, discovery, etc. (cf. GEE¹). [abbr. of JESUS]

Jefferies /ˈdʒefrɪz/, John Richard (1848–87), English writer with a remarkable power of observing nature and representing it in combination with a strain of poetry and philosophy. He is

probably best known for the boys' book *Bevis* (1882) and his autobiography *The Story of my Heart* (1883).

Jefferson /ˈdʒefəs(ə)n/, Thomas (1743–1826), 3rd President of the US 1801–9. As a delegate to the Continental Congress (1775–6), Jefferson drafted the Declaration of Independence and thereafter played a key role in the American leadership during the War of Independence. After serving in several important government posts he was chosen as President by the House of Representatives after tying with his opponent in electoral votes. Very much a philosopher-statesman in the mould of the Enlightenment, Jefferson advocated decentralization and the restrained use of presidential power. After his retirement he founded the University of Virginia and actively fostered the growth of culture in what was still a relatively young country.

Jefferson City /ˈdʒefəs(ə)n/ the capital of Missouri; pop. (1980) 33,619. It is named after President Thomas Jefferson.

jehad var. of JIHAD.

Jehovah /dʒɪˈhəʊvə/ God, the name of God used in the Old Testament. [med. L *IeHoVa(H)*, erroneously formed f. YHVH (the ineffable name of God) and the vowels of *adonai* (Heb., = my lord) which was substituted for it in reading the Hebrew Bible; cf. YAHWEH]

Jehovah's Witness n. a member of a sect of American origin, the Watch Tower Bible and Tract Society, founded *c.*1879 by Charles Taze Russell (1852–1916) of Pittsburgh, Pennsylvania, denying many of the traditional Christian doctrines and refusing to acknowledge the claims of the State when these conflict with the sect's principles.

Jehovist /dʒəˈhəʊvɪst/ n. = YAHWIST.

Jehu /ˈdʒiːhjuː/ king of Israel (9th c. BC), famous for driving his chariot furiously (2 Kings 9).

jejune /dʒɪˈdʒuːn/ adj. **1** intellectually unsatisfying; shallow. **2** puerile. **3** (of ideas, writings, etc.) meagre, scanty; dry and uninteresting. **4** (of the land) barren, poor. □□ **jejunely** adv. **jejuneness** n. [orig. = fasting, f. L *jejunus*]

jejunum /dʒɪˈdʒuːnəm/ n. *Anat.* the part of the small intestine between the duodenum and ileum. [L, neut. of *jejunus* fasting]

Jekyll and Hyde /ˌdʒekɪl ənd ˈhaɪd/ n. a person in whom two personalities (one good, one evil) alternate. [R. L. Stevenson's story *The Strange Case of Dr Jekyll and Mr Hyde*, in which the respected Dr Jekyll could transform himself by means of a potion into the evil Mr Hyde, in whom was embodied only the evil side of Jekyll]

jell /dʒel/ v.intr. *colloq.* **1 a** set as a jelly. **b** (of ideas etc.) take a definite form. **2** (of two different things) cohere. [back-form. f. JELLY]

jellaba var. of DJELLABA.

Jellicoe /ˈdʒelɪˌkəʊ/ John Rushworth, 1st Earl (1859–1935), British admiral, commander of the Grand Fleet at the battle of Jutland. After the war he was appointed Governor-General of New Zealand (1920–4).

jellify /ˈdʒelɪˌfaɪ/ v.tr. & intr. (**-ies, -ied**) turn into jelly; make or become like jelly. □□ **jellification** /-fɪˈkeɪʃ(ə)n/ n.

jelly /ˈdʒelɪ/ n. & v. —n. (pl. **-ies**) **1 a** a soft stiffish semi-transparent preparation of boiled sugar and fruit-juice or milk etc., often cooled in a mould and eaten as a dessert. **b** a similar preparation of fruit-juice etc. for use as a jam or a condiment (*redcurrant jelly*). **c** a similar preparation derived from meat, bones, etc., and gelatin (*marrowbone jelly*). **2** any substance of a similar consistency. **3** *Brit. sl.* gelignite (cf. GELLY). —v. (**-ies, -ied**) **1** intr. & tr. set or cause to set as a jelly, congeal. **2** tr. set (food) in a jelly (*jellied eels*). □ **jelly baby** *Brit.* a jelly-like sweet in the stylized shape of a baby. **jelly bag** a bag for straining juice for jelly. **jelly bean** a jelly-like sweet in the shape of a bean. □□ **jelly-like** adj. [ME f. OF *gelee* frost, jelly, f. Rmc *gelata* f. L *gelare* freeze f. *gelu* frost]

jellyfish /ˈdʒelɪfɪʃ/ n. (pl. usu. **same**) **1** a marine coelenterate of the class Scyphozoa having an umbrella-shaped jelly-like body and stinging tentacles. **2** *colloq.* a feeble person.

jemmy /ˈdʒemɪ/ n. & v. (US **jimmi** /ˈdʒɪmɪ/) —n. (pl. **-ies** or **jimmis**) a burglar's short crowbar, usu. made in sections.

æ *cat* ɑː *arm* e *bed* ɜː *her* ɪ *sit* iː *see* ɒ *hot* ɔː *saw* ʌ *run* ʊ *put* uː *too* ə *ago* aɪ *my*

—*v.tr.* (**-ies, -ied**) force open with a jemmy. [pet-form of the name *James*]

Jena /ˈjeɪnə/ a university town in central Germany, scene of a battle (1806) in which Napoleon defeated the Prussians; pop. (1986) 107,300.

je ne sais quoi /ʒə nə seɪ ˈkwɑː, dʒə-/ *n.* an indefinable something. [F, = I do not know what]

Jenkins's Ear /ˈdʒeŋkɪnzɪz/, **War of** a war between England and Spain (1739). Robert Jenkins, a British sea captain, appeared before the Commons in 1738 to produce what he claimed was his ear, cut off by the Spanish in the West Indies while carrying out a search of his ship. His story was probably at least partially fabricated, but it caused great popular indignation and precipitated a naval war with Spain (a war already much sought after in many circles) in the following year.

Jenner /ˈdʒenə(r)/, Edward (1749–1823), English physician, the pioneer of vaccination. His home was at Berkeley in Gloucestershire where there was a local belief that dairymaids who had had cowpox did not catch smallpox, which was then a very common epidemic disease in all ranks of society. This led Jenner to the idea of deliberately infecting people with cowpox in order to protect them from the more serious disease, a practice which was eventually accepted throughout the world and led to the extermination of smallpox. In the intervals of medical practice he indulged his keen interest in natural history, and in 1787 wrote a paper on the habits of the cuckoo.

jennet /ˈdʒenɪt/ *n.* a small Spanish horse. [F *genet* f. Sp. *jinete* light horseman f. Arab. *zenāta* Berber tribe famous as horsemen]

jenny /ˈdʒenɪ/ *n.* (*pl.* **-ies**) 1 *hist.* = *spinning-jenny.* 2 a female donkey or ass. 3 a locomotive crane. □ **jenny-wren** a popular name for a female wren. [pet-form of the name *Janet*]

jeopardize /ˈdʒepədaɪz/ *v.tr.* (also **-ise**) endanger; put into jeopardy.

jeopardy /ˈdʒepədɪ/ *n.* 1 danger, esp. of severe harm or loss. 2 *Law* danger resulting from being on trial for a criminal offence. [ME *iuparti* f. OF *ieu parti* divided (i.e. even) game, f. L *jocus* game + *partitus* past part. of *partire* divide f. *pars partis* part]

Jephthah /ˈdʒefθə/ a judge of Israel who sacrificed his daughter in consequence of a vow that if victorious against the Ammonites he would sacrifice the first living thing that met him on his return (Judges 11, 12). A similar rash promise was made by Idomeneus in Greek legend.

Jer. *abbr.* Jeremiah (Old Testament).

jerbil var. of GERBIL.

jerboa /dʒɜːˈbəʊə/ *n.* any small desert rodent of the family Dipodidae with long hind legs and the ability to make large jumps. [mod.L f. Arab. *yarbūʿ* flesh of loins, jerboa]

jeremiad /ˌdʒerɪˈmaɪæd/ *n.* a doleful complaint or lamentation; a list of woes. [F *jérémiade* f. *Jérémie* Jeremiah f. eccl.L *Jeremias*, with ref. to the Lamentations of Jeremiah in the Old Testament]

Jeremiah /ˌdʒerɪˈmaɪə/ 1 a Hebrew major prophet (c.650 –c.585 BC) who saw the fall of Assyria, the conquest of his country by Egypt and then by Babylon, and the destruction of Jerusalem. 2 a book of the Old Testament containing his prophecies. —*n.* a pessimistic person.

Jerez /ˈhereθ/ (also **Jerez de la Frontera**) a town in Andalusia, Spain, centre of the sherry-making industry; pop. (1986) 180,400.

Jericho /ˈdʒerɪˌkəʊ/ an ancient city north of the Dead Sea, now in Israel, occupied from c.9000 BC and one of the oldest continuously inhabited cities in the world. Little remains of the late Bronze Age period, the probable date of its destruction by Joshua recorded in the Old Testament.

jerk[1] /dʒɜːk/ *n. & v.* —*n.* 1 a sharp sudden pull, twist, twitch, start, etc. 2 a spasmodic muscular twitch. 3 (in *pl.*) *Brit. colloq.* exercises (*physical jerks*). 4 *sl.* a fool; a stupid person. —*v.* 1 *intr.* move with a jerk. 2 *tr.* pull, thrust, twist, etc., with a jerk. 3 *tr.* throw with a suddenly arrested motion. 4 *tr. Weight-lifting* raise (a weight) from shoulder-level to above the head. □ **jerk off** *coarse sl.* masturbate. ¶ Usually considered a taboo use. □□ **jerker** *n.* [16th c.: perh. imit.]

jerk[2] /dʒɜːk/ *v.tr.* cure (beef) by cutting it in long slices and drying

it in the sun. [Amer. Sp. *charquear* f. *charqui* f. Quechua *echarqui* dried flesh]

jerkin /ˈdʒɜːkɪn/ *n.* 1 a sleeveless jacket. 2 *hist.* a man's close-fitting jacket, often of leather. [16th c.: orig. unkn.]

jerky /ˈdʒɜːkɪ/ *adj.* (**jerkier, jerkiest**) 1 having sudden abrupt movements. 2 spasmodic. □□ **jerkily** *adv.* **jerkiness** *n.*

jeroboam /ˌdʒerəˈbəʊəm/ *n.* a wine bottle of 4–12 times the ordinary size. [*Jeroboam* a 'mighty man of valour' king of Israel, 10th c. BC (1 Kings 11: 28, 14: 16)]

Jerome[1] /dʒəˈrəʊm/, Jerome Klapka (1859–1927), English novelist and playwright, author of the humorous novel *Three Men in a Boat* (1889) and the play *The Passing of the Third Floor Back* (1908).

Jerome[2] /dʒeˈrəʊm/, St (Latin name *Eusebius Hieronymus; c.*342–420), Doctor of the Church, born in Dalmatia. He was a scholar, traditionalist, and monastic figure, who acted as secretary to Pope Damasus in Rome from 382 to 385, and finally settled at Bethlehem where he ruled a newly-founded monastery and devoted his life to study. His greatest achievement was the translation of most of the Bible from the original Hebrew and Greek into the language of the people of his time (the VULGATE). Since the 13th c. he has often been depicted in art with a red hat, on the supposition that Damasus created him a cardinal; he is also often shown with a lion at his feet. Feast day, 30 Sept.

Jerry /ˈdʒerɪ/ *n.* (*pl.* **-ies**) *Brit. sl.* 1 a German (esp. in military contexts). 2 the Germans collectively. [prob. alt. of *German*]

jerry /ˈdʒerɪ/ *n.* (*pl.* **-ies**) *Brit. sl.* a chamber-pot. [perh. a shortening of JEROBOAM]

jerry-builder /ˈdʒerɪˌbɪldə(r)/ *n.* a builder of unsubstantial houses with poor-quality materials. □□ **jerry-building** *n.* **jerry-built** *adj.*

jerrycan /ˈdʒerɪˌkæn/ *n.* (also **jerrican**) a kind of (orig. German) petrol- or water-can. [JERRY + CAN[2]]

jerrymander var. of GERRYMANDER.

Jersey /ˈdʒɜːzɪ/ the largest of the Channel Islands; pop. (1981) 76,050; capital, St Helier. —*n.* a breed of light-brown dairy cattle that originated in Jersey, producing milk with a high fat content; an animal of this breed. □ **the Jersey Lily** the nickname of Lillie Langtry.

jersey /ˈdʒɜːzɪ/ *n.* (*pl.* **-eys**) 1 a knitted usu. woollen pullover or similar garment. 2 a plain-knitted (orig. woollen) fabric. [JERSEY]

Jerusalem /dʒəˈruːsələm/ the holy city of the Jews, sacred also to Christians and Muslims, lying in the Judaean hills about 30 km (20 miles) from the Jordan River, proclaimed by the State of Israel as its capital; pop. (1987) 482,700. It was a Canaanite stronghold, captured by David (c.1000 BC) who made it the capital of the national State; after the building of the Temple by Solomon it became a religious as well as a political capital. Since then it has shared the troubled history of its area — destroyed by the Babylonians in 586 BC and by the Romans in AD 70, refounded by Hadrian as a gentile city (AD 135) under the name of Aelia Capitolina, destroyed again by the Persians in 614, and fought over by Saracens and Crusaders in the Middle Ages; Suleiman the Magnificent rebuilt its walls (1542). From 1947 the city was divided between the States of Israel and Jordan until the Israelis occupied the whole city in June 1967. Its Christian history begins with the short ministry of Christ, culminating in his crucifixion. For Muslims Jerusalem is the holiest city after Mecca and Medina, containing the Dome of the Rock, one of Islam's most sacred sites. □ **the New Jerusalem** the abode of the blessed in heaven. **New Jerusalem Church** the followers of Swedenborg.

Jerusalem artichoke /dʒəˈruːsələm/ *n.* 1 a species of sunflower, *Helianthus tuberosus*, with edible underground tubers. 2 this tuber used as a vegetable. [corrupt. of It. *girasole* sunflower]

Jespersen /ˈjespəs(ə)n/, Jens Otto Harry (1860–1943), Danish philologist and writer on grammar and linguistics. His great work was *Modern English Grammar* (1909–49).

jess /dʒes/ *n. & v.* —*n.* a short strap of leather, silk, etc., put round the leg of a hawk in falconry. —*v.tr.* put jesses on (a hawk etc.). [ME *ges* f. OF *ges*, *get* ult. f. L *jactus* a throw f. *jacere jact-* to throw]

jessamin (also **jessamine**) var. of JASMINE.

Jesse /ˈdʒesɪ/ the father of David (1 Sam. 16), hence represented as the first in the genealogy of Jesus Christ. □ **Jesse window** a church window showing Christ's descent from Jesse, usually in the form of a **tree of Jesse**, a tree springing from Jesse and ending in Jesus or the Virgin and Holy Child, with the intermediate descendants placed on scrolls of foliage branching out of each other.

jest /dʒest/ n. & v. —n. **1 a** a joke. **b** fun. **2 a** raillery, banter. **b** an object of derision (*a standing jest*). —v.intr. **1** joke; make jests. **2** fool about; play or act triflingly. □ **in jest** in fun. □□ **jestful** adj. [orig. = exploit, f. OF *geste* f. L *gesta* neut. pl. past part. of *gerere* do]

jester /ˈdʒestə(r)/ n. a professional joker or 'fool' at a medieval court etc., traditionally wearing a cap and bells and carrying a 'sceptre'.

Jesu /ˈdʒiːzjuː/ archaic, vocative Jesus.

Jesuit /ˈdʒezjʊɪt/ n. a member of the Society of Jesus, an order of priests founded in 1534 in Paris by Ignatius Loyola, Francis Xavier, and others. The Society became the spearhead of the Counter-Reformation, though originally intended as a missionary order. Its genius is found in Ignatius' *Spiritual Exercises* (see IGNATIUS LOYOLA). The success of the Jesuits as missionaries, teachers, scholars, and spiritual directors—as well as the fear they have inspired—manifests how close they have been to their ideal of a disciplined force, effective in the cause of the Roman Church. [F *jésuite* or mod.L *Jesuita* f. *Jesus*: see JESUS]

Jesuitical /ˌdʒezjʊˈɪtɪk(ə)l/ adj. **1** of or concerning the Jesuits. **2** often *offens.* dissembling or equivocating. The Jesuits were accused by their enemies of using clever but false reasoning, and this suspicion gave rise to an offensive sense of *Jesuitical*. □□ **Jesuitically** adv.

Jesus /ˈdʒiːzəs/ (also **Jesus Christ**) the central figure of the Christian religion. He was a Jew living in Palestine at the beginning of the 1st c. AD, who in about AD 28–30 conducted a mission of preaching and healing (with reported miracles), which is described in the New Testament. He was arrested and put to death by crucifixion. Belief in his resurrection from the dead spread among his followers who saw in this proof that he was the Christ or Messiah, the fulfilment of the hopes of Israel, and indeed of all mankind. Further beliefs arose—about his virgin birth, and that he is the living Son of God, who has the power to grant eternal life to all who believe in him.

JET abbr. Joint European Torus, a machine for conducting experiments in nuclear fusion, established by the EEC at Culham in Oxfordshire as the centre for all such Western European research.

jet[1] /dʒet/ n. & v. —n. **1** a stream of water, steam, gas, flame, etc. shot out esp. from a small opening. **2** a spout or nozzle for emitting water etc. in this way. **3 a** a jet engine. **b** an aircraft powered by one or more jet engines. —v. (**jetted**, **jetting**) **1** intr. spurt out in jets. **2** tr. & intr. colloq. send or travel by jet plane. □ **jet engine** an engine using jet propulsion for forward thrust, an aircraft engine that takes in air and ejects hot compressed air and exhaust gases (see TURBO-JET). **jet-foil** n. a vessel that travels above the surface of the water on struts attached to underwater foils. **jet lag** extreme tiredness and other bodily effects felt after a long flight involving marked differences of local time. **jet-propelled 1** having jet propulsion. **2** (of a person etc.) very fast. **jet propulsion** see separate entry. **jet set** colloq. wealthy people frequently travelling by air, esp. for pleasure. **jet-setter** colloq. a member of the jet set. **jet stream 1** a narrow current of very strong winds encircling the globe several miles above the earth, blowing in an approximately horizontal direction predominantly from west to east. **2** the stream from a jet engine. [earlier as verb (in sense 1): F *jeter* throw ult. f. L *jactare* frequent. of *jacere jact-* throw]

jet[2] /dʒet/ n. **1 a** a hard black variety of lignite capable of being carved and highly polished. **b** (attrib.) made of this. **2** (in full

jet-black) a deep glossy black colour. [ME f. AF *geet*, OF *jaiet* f. L *gagates* f. Gk *gagatēs* f. *Gagai* in Asia Minor]

jeté /ʒeˈteɪ/ n. Ballet a spring or leap with one leg forward and the other stretched backwards. [F, past part. of *jeter* throw: see JET[1]]

jet propulsion n. ejection of a usually high-speed jet of gas (or liquid) as a source of propulsive power, especially for aircraft. Simple examples are the movement of a balloon suddenly released after being inflated, and of the cuttlefish which propels itself by exuding spurts of its 'ink'. The principle of jet propulsion for aircraft was discussed in the 1860s, but its successful application awaited the development of the turbo-jet engine (see TURBO-JET).

jetsam /ˈdʒetsəm/ n. discarded material washed ashore, esp. that thrown overboard to lighten a ship etc. (cf. FLOTSAM). [contr. of JETTISON]

jettison /ˈdʒetɪs(ə)n, -z(ə)n/ v. & n. —v.tr. **1 a** throw (esp. heavy material) overboard to lighten a ship, hot-air balloon, etc. **b** drop (goods) from an aircraft. **2** abandon; get rid of (something no longer wanted). —n. the act of jettisoning. [ME f. AF *getteson*, OF *getaison* f. L *jactatio -onis* f. *jactare* throw: see JET[1]]

jetton /ˈdʒet(ə)n/ n. a counter with a stamped or engraved design esp. for insertion like a coin to operate a machine etc. [F *jeton* f. *jeter* throw, add up accounts: see JET[1]]

jetty /ˈdʒetɪ/ n. (pl. **-ies**) **1** a pier or breakwater constructed to protect or defend a harbour, coast, etc. **2** a landing-pier. [ME f. OF *jetee*, fem. past part. of *jeter* throw: see JET[1]]

jeu d'esprit /ʒɜː deˈspriː/ n. (pl. ***jeux d'esprit*** pronunc. same) a witty or humorous (usu. literary) trifle. [F, = game of the spirit]

jeunesse dorée /ʒɜːˈnes ˈdɔreɪ/ n. = gilded youth (see GILD[1]). [F]

Jew /dʒuː/ n. & v. —n. **1** a person of Hebrew descent or whose religion is Judaism. (See below.) **2** sl. offens. (as a stereotype) a person considered to be parsimonious or to drive a hard bargain in trading. —v.tr. (**jew**) sl. offens. get a financial advantage over. □ **jew's harp** see separate entry. [ME f. OF *giu* f. L *judaeus* f. Gk *ioudaios* ult. f. Heb. *yʰûdî* f. *yʰûdâh* Judah]

European Jews were traditionally the subject of persecution by the Christian majority, partly as a result of religious prejudice but also because of jealousy of Jewish commercial success and because the Jewish community tended to maintain a separate and highly distinct identity. Anti-Semitism was a feature of European life from the Middle Ages, the killing of Jews being a common response to economic or social crisis, and in the modern age anti-Semitism became a central part of many right-wing political philosophies, most notably Nazism. In medieval England, Jews were particularly familiar as money-lenders, their activities being publicly regulated for them by the Crown, whose protégés they were. (In private, Christians also practised money-lending, though forbidden to do so by Canon Law.) Thus the name of Jew came to be associated in the popular mind with usury and any extortionate practices that might be supposed to accompany it, and gained an offensive sense in some contexts.

jewel /ˈdʒuːəl/ n. & v. —n. **1 a** a precious stone. **b** this as used for its hardness as a bearing in watchmaking. **2** a personal ornament containing a jewel or jewels. **3** a precious person or thing. —v.tr. (**jewelled**, **jewelling**; US **jeweled**, **jeweling**) **1** (esp. as **jewelled** adj.) adorn or set with jewels. **2** (in watchmaking) set with jewels. □ **jewel-fish** a scarlet and green tropical cichlid fish, *Hemichromis bimaculatus*. □□ **jewelly** adj. [ME f. AF *juel*, *jeuel*, OF *joel*, of uncert. orig.]

jeweller /ˈdʒuːələ(r)/ n. (US **jeweler**) a maker of or dealer in jewels or jewellery. □ **jeweller's rouge** finely ground rouge for polishing. [ME f. AF *jueler*, OF *juelier* (as JEWEL)]

jewellery /ˈdʒuːəlrɪ/ n. (also **jewelry** /ˈdʒuːəlrɪ/) jewels or other ornamental objects, esp. for personal adornment, regarded collectively. [ME f. OF *juelerie* and f. JEWEL, JEWELLER]

Jewess /ˈdʒuːes/ n. a female Jew.

jewfish /ˈdʒuːfɪʃ/ n. **1** a grouper, *Epinephelus itajara*, of N. American, Atlantic, and Pacific coasts. **2** any of various large Australian fish used as food, esp. the mulloway.

Jewish /ˈdʒuːɪʃ/ adj. **1** of or relating to Jews. **2** of Judaism. □

Jewish calendar a complex ancient calendar in use among Jews. It is a lunar calendar adapted to the solar year, having normally 12 months, but 13 months in leap years which occur 7 times in every cycle of 19 years. The years are reckoned from the Creation (3761 BC); the months are Nisan (normally March–April), Iyar (April–May), Sivan (May–June), Tammuz (June–July), Ab (July–Aug.), Elul (Aug.–Sept.), Tishri (Sept.–Oct.), Cheshvan (Oct.–Nov.), Kislev (Nov.–Dec.), Teveth (Dec.–Jan.), Shebat (Jan.–Feb.), Adar (Feb.–Mar.), 2nd Adar (intercalary month). The ecclesiastical year begins with Nisan and ends with Tishri. □□ **Jewishly** adv. **Jewishness** n.

Jewry /'dʒʊərɪ/ n. (pl. **-ies**) **1** Jews collectively. **2** hist. a Jews' quarter in a town etc. [ME f. AF juerie, OF juierie (as JEW)]

Jew's harp n. a musical instrument consisting of a small U-shaped metal frame held in the teeth while a springy metal clip joining its ends is twanged with a finger. The strip can produce only one note but the harmonics of this note are produced by resonance by altering the shape of the mouth-cavity. The name of the instrument is an ancient one, but no connection with Jews has been established with certainty.

Jezebel /'dʒezəb(ə)l/ (9th c. BC) a Phoenician princess, daughter of Ethbaal king of Sidon and according to ancient tradition great-aunt of the legendary Dido (Elissa), queen of Carthage. She became the wife of Ahab king of Israel (I Kings 16: 31), and was denounced by Elijah for introducing the worship of Baal into Israel; she was killed when Jehu triumphed over Ahab. Puritan England was shocked by the fact that she 'painted her face', a practice which would have caused no surprise to her contemporaries since the use of cosmetics was widespread at that time. — n. a shameless or immoral woman.

Jhelum /'dʒeɪləm/ a river that rises in the Himalayas and flows through the Vale of Kashmir into the province of Punjab in Pakistan, where it meets the Chenab River. It is one of the 'five rivers' that gave Punjab its name. In ancient times it was called the Hydaspes.

Jiangsu /dʒɪæŋ'su:/ (also **Kiangsu**) a province of eastern China; pop. (est. 1986) 62,130,000; capital, Nanjing.

Jiangxi /dʒɪæŋ'ʃi:/ (also **Kiangsi**) a province of SE China; pop. (est. 1986) 35,090,000; capital, Nanchang.

jib¹ /dʒɪb/ n. & v. — n. **1** a triangular staysail from the outer end of the jib-boom to the top of the foremast or from the bowsprit to the masthead. **2** the projecting arm of a crane. — v.tr. & intr. (**jibbed**, **jibbing**) (of a sail etc.) pull or swing round from one side of the ship to the other; gybe. □ **jib-boom** a spar run out from the end of the bowsprit. [17th c.: orig. unkn.]

jib² /dʒɪb/ v.intr. (**jibbed**, **jibbing**) **1 a** (of an animal, esp. a horse) stop and refuse to go on; move backwards or sideways instead of going on. **b** (of a person) refuse to continue. **2** (foll. by at) show aversion to (a person or course of action). □□ **jibber** n. [19th c.: orig. unkn.]

jibba /'dʒɪbə/ n. (also **jibbah**) a long coat worn by Muslim men. [Egypt. var. of Arab. jubba]

jibe¹ var. of GIBE.

jibe² US var. of GYBE.

jibe³ /dʒaɪb/ v.intr. (usu. foll. by with) US colloq. agree; be in accord. [19th c.: orig. unkn.]

Jibuti see DJIBOUTI.

jiff /dʒɪf/ n. (also **jiffy**, pl. **-ies**) colloq. a short time; a moment (in a jiffy; half a jiff). [18th c.: orig. unkn.]

Jiffy bag /'dʒɪfɪ/ n. propr. a type of padded envelope for postal use.

jig /dʒɪg/ n. & v. — n. **1 a** a lively dance with leaping movements. **b** the music for this, usu. in triple time. **2** a device that holds a piece of work and guides the tools operating on it. — v. (**jigged**, **jigging**) **1** intr. dance a jig. **2** tr. & intr. move quickly and jerkily up and down. **3** tr. work on or equip with a jig or jigs. □ **jig about** fidget. [16th c.: orig. unkn.]

jigger¹ /'dʒɪgə(r)/ n. **1** Naut. **a** a small tackle consisting of a double and single block with a rope. **b** a small sail at the stern. **c** a small smack having this. **2** sl. a gadget. **3** Golf an iron club with a narrow face. **4** Billiards colloq. a cue-rest. **5 a** a measure of spirits etc. **b** a small glass holding this. **6** a person or thing that jigs.

jigger² /'dʒɪgə(r)/ n. **1** = CHIGOE. **2** US = CHIGGER 2. [corrupt.]

jiggered /'dʒɪgəd/ adj. colloq. (as a mild oath) confounded (I'll be jiggered). [euphem.]

jiggery-pokery /ˌdʒɪgərɪ'pəʊkərɪ/ n. Brit. colloq. deceitful or dishonest dealing, trickery. [cf. Sc. joukery-pawkery f. jouk dodge, skulk]

jiggle /'dʒɪg(ə)l/ v. (often foll. by about etc.) **1** tr. shake lightly; rock jerkily. **2** intr. fidget. □□ **jiggly** adj. [JIG or JOGGLE¹]

jigsaw /'dʒɪgsɔː/ n. **1 a** (in full **jigsaw puzzle**) a puzzle consisting of a picture on board or wood etc. cut into irregular interlocking pieces to be shuffled and reassembled for amusement. The first jigsaw puzzles (18th c.) were maps, mounted on wood and cut into oddly-shaped pieces. **b** a mental puzzle resolvable by assembling various pieces of information. **2** a machine saw with a fine blade enabling it to cut curved lines in a sheet of wood, metal, etc.

jihad /dʒɪ'hæd, -'hɑːd/ n. (also **jehad**) (in Islam) a holy war. One of the basic duties of a Muslim, prescribed as a religious duty by the Koran and by tradition, is to struggle against external threats to the vigour of the Islamic community and also against personal resistance to the rule of divine law within oneself. [Arab. jihād fight, struggle]

Jilin /dʒiː'lɪn/ (also **Kilin**) a province of NE China; pop. (est. 1986) 23,150,000; capital, Changchun.

jill var. of GILL⁴.

jilt /dʒɪlt/ v. & n. — v.tr. abruptly reject or abandon (a lover etc.). — n. a person (esp. a woman) who jilts a lover. [17th c.: orig. unkn.]

Jim Crow /dʒɪm 'krəʊ/ n. US **1** the policy of segregating and discriminating against Blacks, esp. by laws passed in the southern States of the US in the late 19th c. The policy was not seriously challenged until after the Second World War, by which time racial barriers had been eroded. **2** offens. a Black. **3** an implement for straightening iron bars or bending rails by screw pressure. □□ **Jim Crowism** n. (in sense 1). [from the refrain 'jump Jim Crow' of a plantation song]

jim-jams /'dʒɪmdʒæmz/ n.pl. **1** sl. = delirium tremens. **2** colloq. a fit of depression or nervousness. [fanciful redupl.]

Jimmu /'dʒɪmuː/ the legendary first emperor of Japan (660 BC), descendant of the sun goddess and founder of the imperial dynasty.

jimmy US var. of JEMMY.

jimson /'dʒɪms(ə)n/ n. (in full **jimson weed**) US a highly poisonous tall weed, Datura stramonium, with large trumpet-shaped flowers. [Jamestown in Virginia]

Jinan /dʒiː'næn/ (also **Tsinan**) a city of eastern China, the capital of Shangong province; pop. (est. 1986) 1,430,000.

jingle /'dʒɪŋg(ə)l/ n. & v. — n. **1** a mixed noise as of bells or light metal objects being shaken together. **2 a** a repetition of the same sound in words, esp. as an aid to memory or to attract attention. **b** a short verse of this kind used in advertising etc. — v. **1** intr. & tr. make or cause to make a jingling sound. **2** intr. (of writing) be full of alliterations, rhymes, etc. □□ **jingly** adj. (**jinglier**, **jingliest**). [ME: imit.]

jingo /'dʒɪŋgəʊ/ n. (pl. **-oes**) a supporter of policy favouring war; a blustering patriot. □ **by jingo!** a mild oath. □□ **jingoism** n. **jingoist** n. **jingoistic** /-'ɪstɪk/ adj. [17th c.: orig. a conjuror's word: polit. sense orig. a nickname for a supporter of Disraeli in sending the British fleet into Turkish waters in 1878 to resist the advance of Russia, f. use of by jingo (= by God) in a popular music-hall refrain of 1878 : 'We don't want to fight, yet by Jingo! if we do, We've got the ships, we've got the men, and got the money too'.]

jink /dʒɪŋk/ v. & n. — v. **1** intr. move elusively; dodge. **2** tr. elude by dodging. — n. an act of dodging or eluding. [orig. Sc.: prob. imit. of nimble motion]

Jinnah /'dʒɪnə/, Muhammad Ali (1876–1948), founder of Pakistan. An influential member of the Muslim League (the chief Muslim political party in British India), he led it in its struggle with the Hindu-dominated Indian National Congress, and from 1928 onwards, at conferences on Indian independence, championed the rights of the Muslim minority. After 1935, when self-governing Hindu provinces began to be formed, his fear that Muslims would be excluded from office led him to campaign for a separate Muslim State. When the State of Pakistan was finally set up under the India Independence Act of 1947, he was its first Governor-General.

jinnee /dʒɪˈniː/ n. (also **jinn, djinn** /dʒɪn/) (pl. **jinn** or **djinn**) *Islamic Mythol.* any of the supernatural beings, similar to but distinguished from angels, able to appear in human and animal form, and to help or hinder human beings according to their prescribed rule in the cosmos. [Arab. *jinnī*, pl. *jinn*: cf. GENIE]

jinx /dʒɪŋks/ n. & v. *colloq.* —n. a person or thing that seems to cause bad luck. —v.tr. (often in *passive*) subject (a person) to an unlucky force. [perh. var. of *jynx* wryneck, charm]

jitter /ˈdʒɪtə(r)/ n. & v. *colloq.* —n. (**the jitters**) extreme nervousness. —v.intr. be nervous; act nervously. □□ **jittery** adj. **jitteriness** n. [20th c.: orig. unkn.]

jitterbug /ˈdʒɪtəˌbʌg/ n. & v. —n. **1** a nervous person. **2** hist. **a** a fast popular dance. **b** a person fond of dancing this. —v.intr. (**-bugged, -bugging**) dance the jitterbug.

jiu-jitsu var. of JU-JITSU.

jive /dʒaɪv/ n. & v. —n. **1** a jerky lively style of dance esp. popular in the 1950s. **2** music for this. —v.intr. **1** dance the jive. **2** play jive music. □□ **jiver** n. [20th c.: orig. uncert.]

jizz /dʒɪz/ n. the characteristic impression given by an animal or plant. [20th c.: orig. unkn.]

Jnr. abbr. Junior.

jo /dʒəʊ/ n. (pl. **joes**) *Sc.* a sweetheart or beloved. [var. of JOY]

Joachim /ˈdʒəʊəkɪm/, St, the husband of St Anne and father of the Virgin Mary. He is first mentioned in an apocryphal work of the 2nd c., and then rarely referred to until much later times.

Joan of Arc /dʒəʊn, ɑːk/ St (1412–31), a French peasant girl who became a national heroine. Inspired by 'voices' of St Catherine and St Michael, she led the French armies against the English, relieved Orleans, and stood beside the French king Charles VII at his coronation. Captured by the Burgundians, she was handed over to the English, tried, condemned for heresy, and burnt at the stake in Rouen. She was canonized in 1920. Feast day, 30 May.

Job /dʒəʊb/ **1** a book of the Old Testament, variously dated 5th–2nd c. BC. **2** its hero, a wealthy and prosperous man whose patience and exemplary piety are tried by dire and undeserved misfortunes, and who, in spite of his bitter lamentations, remains finally confident in the goodness and justice of God. □ **Job's comforter** a person who under the guise of comforting aggravates distress (Job 16: 2). **Job's tears** the seeds of a grass, *Coix lacryma-jobi*, used as beads.

job¹ /dʒɒb/ n. & v. —n. **1** a piece of work, esp. one done for hire or profit. **2** a paid position of employment. **3** *colloq.* anything one has to do. **4** *colloq.* a difficult task (*had a job to find them*). **5** a product of work, esp. if well done. **6** *Computing* an item of work regarded separately. **7** *sl.* a crime, esp. a robbery. **8** a transaction in which private advantage prevails over duty or public interest. **9** a state of affairs or set of circumstances (*is a bad job*). —v. (**jobbed, jobbing**) **1** intr. do jobs; do piece-work. **2** a intr. deal in stocks. **b** tr. buy and sell (stocks or goods) as a middleman. **3** **a** intr. turn a position of trust to private advantage. **b** tr. deal corruptly with (a matter). **4** tr. *US sl.* swindle. □ **job-control language** *Computing* a language enabling the user to determine the tasks to be undertaken by the operating system. **job-hunt** *colloq.* seek employment. **job lot** a miscellaneous group of articles, esp. bought together. **jobs for the boys** *colloq.* profitable situations etc. to reward one's supporters. **job-sharing** an arrangement by which a full-time job is done jointly by several part-time employees who share the remuneration. **just the job** *colloq.* exactly what is wanted. **make a job** (or **good job**) **of** do thoroughly or successfully. **on the job** *colloq.* **1** at work; in the course of doing a piece of work. **2** engaged in sexual intercourse. **out of a job** unemployed. [16th c.: orig. unkn.]

job² /dʒɒb/ v. & n. —v. (**jobbed, jobbing**) **1** tr. prod; stab slightly.

2 intr. (foll. by *at*) thrust. —n. a prod or thrust; a jerk at a horse's bit. [ME, app. imit.: cf. JAB]

jobber /ˈdʒɒbə(r)/ n. **1** *Brit.* a principal or wholesaler dealing on the Stock Exchange. ¶ Up to Oct. 1986 permitted to deal only with brokers, not directly with the public. From Oct. 1986 the name has ceased to be in official use (see BROKER 2). **2** *US* **a** a wholesaler. **b** *derog.* a broker (see BROKER 2). **3** a person who jobs. [JOB¹]

jobbery /ˈdʒɒbərɪ/ n. corrupt dealing.

jobbing /ˈdʒɒbɪŋ/ adj. working on separate or occasional jobs (esp. of a computer, gardener, or printer).

jobcentre /ˈdʒɒbˌsentə(r)/ n. *Brit.* any of several government offices displaying information about available jobs.

jobless /ˈdʒɒblɪs/ adj. without a job; unemployed. □□ **joblessness** n.

jobsheet /ˈdʒɒbʃiːt/ n. a sheet for recording details of jobs done.

jobwork /ˈdʒɒbwɜːk/ n. work done and paid for by the job.

Jocasta /dʒəˈkæstə/ *Gk legend* the mother and wife of Oedipus.

Jock /dʒɒk/ n. *sl.* a Scotsman. [Sc. form of the name *Jack* (see JACK¹)]

jock /dʒɒk/ n. *colloq.* a jockey. [abbr.]

jockey /ˈdʒɒkɪ/ n. & v. —n. (pl. **-eys**) a rider in horse-races, esp. a professional one. —v. (**-eys, -eyed**) **1** tr. **a** trick or cheat (a person). **b** outwit. **2** tr. (foll. by *away, out, in,* etc.) draw (a person) by trickery. **3** intr. cheat. □ **jockey cap** a cap with a long peak, as worn by jockeys. **jockey for position** try to gain an advantageous position esp. by skilful manoeuvring or unfair action. □□ **jockeydom** n. **jockeyship** n. [dimin. of JOCK]

Jockey Club a club whose stewards are the central authority for the administration and control of horse-racing in England. It was founded in 1750.

jockstrap /ˈdʒɒkstræp/ n. a support or protection for the male genitals, worn esp. by sportsmen. [sl. *jock* genitals + STRAP]

jocose /dʒəˈkəʊs/ adj. **1** playful in style. **2** fond of joking, jocular. □□ **jocosely** adv. **jocoseness** n. **jocosity** /-ˈkɒsɪtɪ/ n. (pl. **-ies**). [L *jocosus* f. *jocus* jest]

jocular /ˈdʒɒkjʊlə(r)/ adj. **1** merry; fond of joking. **2** of the nature of a joke; humorous. □□ **jocularity** /-ˈlærɪtɪ/ n. (pl. **-ies**). **jocularly** adv. [L *jocularis* f. *joculus* dimin. of *jocus* jest]

jocund /ˈdʒɒkənd/ adj. *literary* merry, cheerful, sprightly. □□ **jocundity** /dʒəˈkʌndɪtɪ/ n. (pl. **-ies**). **jocundly** adv. [ME f. OF f. L *jocundus, jucundus* f. *juvare* delight]

Jodhpur /ˈdʒɒdpʊə(r)/ **1** a city of western India, in Rajasthan State; pop. (1981) 494,000. **2** a former princely State of India, now part of Rajasthan.

jodhpurs /ˈdʒɒdpəz/ n.pl. long breeches for riding etc., close-fitting from the knee to the ankle. [JODHPUR city]

Jodrell Bank /ˈdʒɒdr(ə)l/ the site in Cheshire of the Nuffield Radio Astronomy Laboratory of Manchester University. It has one of the world's largest radio telescopes, with a giant reflector, 76 m (250 ft.) in diameter, that can be tilted in any direction.

Joe Bloggs /dʒəʊ ˈblɒgz/ n. *Brit. colloq.* a hypothetical average man.

Joe Blow /dʒəʊ ˈbləʊ/ n. *US colloq.* = JOE BLOGGS.

Joel /ˈdʒəʊ(ə)l/ **1** a Hebrew minor prophet of the 5th or possibly 9th c. BC. **2** a book of the Old Testament containing his prophecies.

joey /ˈdʒəʊɪ/ n. (pl. **-eys**) *Austral.* **1** a young kangaroo. **2** a young animal. [Aboriginal *joë*]

Joffre /ʒɒfr/, Joseph Jacques Césaire (1852–1931), French military leader during the First World War, commander-in-chief on the western front 1914–16. He was largely responsible for success in the first battle of the Marne (see entry), but took responsibility for French unpreparedness at Verdun, and resigned.

jog /dʒɒg/ v. & n. —v. (**jogged, jogging**) **1** intr. run at a slow pace, esp. as physical exercise. **2** intr. (of a horse) move at a jogtrot. **3** intr. (often foll. by *on, along*) proceed laboriously; trudge. **4** intr. go on one's way. **5** intr. proceed; get through the time (*we must jog on somehow*). **6** intr. move up and down with an unsteady motion. **7** *tr.* nudge (a person), esp. to arouse attention. **8** *tr.* shake with a push or jerk. **9** *tr.* stimulate (a person's or one's own memory). —*n.* **1** a shake, push, or nudge. **2** a slow walk or trot. [ME: app. imit.]

jogger /'dʒɒgə(r)/ *n.* a person who jogs, esp. one who runs for physical exercise.

joggle[1] /'dʒɒg(ə)l/ *v. & n.* —*v.tr. & intr.* shake or move by or as if by repeated jerks. —*n.* **1** a slight shake. **2** the act or action of joggling. [frequent. of JOG]

joggle[2] /'dʒɒg(ə)l/ *n. & v.* —*n.* **1** a joint of two pieces of stone or timber, contrived to prevent their sliding on one another. **2** a notch in one of the two pieces, a projection in the other, or a small piece let in between the two, for this purpose. —*v.tr.* join with a joggle. [perh. f. *jog* = JAG[1]]

Jogjakarta /ˌjɒgjə'kɑːtə/ a city on the island of Java, capital of Indonesia 1945–9; pop. (1980) 398,700.

jogtrot /'dʒɒgtrɒt/ *n.* **1** a slow regular trot. **2** a monotonous progression.

Johannesburg /dʒəʊ'hænɪsˌbɜːg/ a city of Transvaal, the largest city of the Republic of South Africa and the centre of its gold-mining industry; pop. (1985) 1,609,400.

John[1] /dʒɒn/ (1165–1216), son of Henry II, king of England 1199–1216, nicknamed John Lackland because, unlike his elder brothers, he did not receive a large fief from his father. On his accession he was recognized by both England and Normandy, but lost Normandy and other areas of France by 1205. At home, his despotic inclinations caused him to fall foul of both the Church and the barons. His refusal to accept the papal nominee Stephen Langton as Archbishop of Canterbury led to England's being placed under an interdict in 1208, and to his own excommunication. His character, a mixture of brutality, cowardice, and sloth, caused him to be generally hated and despised. The English barons opposed his high-handed methods of raising money and forced him to sign Magna Carta in 1215; when John ignored its provisions civil war broke out, and he died on campaign.

John[2] /dʒɒn/ the name of six kings of Portugal:

John I 'the Great' (1357–1433), reigned 1385–1433. Regent from 1383, John defeated a Castilian attempt to seize the throne, and, after being chosen king, won a final decisive victory over the Castilians at Aljubarrota in 1385 with English help. He established an English alliance, married a daughter of John of Gaunt, and presided over a long period of peace and prosperity notable for his encouragement of voyages of discovery.

John IV 'the Fortunate' (1605–1656), reigned 1640–56. The founder of the Braganza dynasty, he expelled a Spanish usurper and proclaimed himself king in 1640. He defeated the Spanish at Montijo in 1644, drove the Dutch out of Brazil in 1654, and generally restored Portugal's international position.

John[3] /dʒɒn/, Augustus (1878–1961), British painter, born in Wales, who studied at the Slade School in London and began to exhibit at the New English Art Club in 1903. His 'Smiling Woman' (1910), a portrait of his wife, is considered one of his masterpieces. Other portraits include those of Hardy, Shaw, Yeats, Joyce, and Dylan Thomas, indicating the literary and artistic milieu of which he was part. He was a fine draughtsman, and his modified post-impressionist approach lent an individual vitality and colour to his landscapes and drawings which set him apart. John was seen as a notorious rebel, a leader of independent thought in English art.

John[4] /dʒɒn/, Don (c.1545–78) of Austria, Spanish soldier. The illegitimate son of the Emperor Charles V, John led the Christian fleet to victory over the Turks at Lepanto in 1571, but afterwards, as Governor-General of The Netherlands, fell foul of his half-brother Philip II and was deposed.

John[5] /dʒɒn/, Gwen (Gwendolen Mary), (1876–1939), British painter, sister of Augustus John, who took lessons, in Paris, from Whistler. The influence of his grey tonality can be seen in her works, which are largely figures of girls or nuns in interior settings, watercolour genre scenes, and landscapes. From 1904 she worked as Rodin's model, and was his devoted friend and

mistress. After 1898 she lived in France and became a devout Roman Catholic and a recluse.

John[6] /dʒɒn/, St **1** an Apostle (called also St John the Evangelist or St John the Divine), son of a Galilean fisherman and brother of St James. He was credited since very early times (probably erroneously) with the authorship of the fourth Gospel, the Apocalypse, and three epistles of the New Testament. Feast day, 27 Dec. **2** the fourth Gospel. **3** any of the three epistles attributed to St John.

john /dʒɒn/ *n. US sl.* a lavatory. [the name *John*]

John Bull /dʒɒn 'bʊl/ *n.* a personification of England or the typical Englishman, represented as a stout red-faced farmer-like man in a top hat and high boots. It was originally the name of a character representing the English nation in J. Arbuthnot's satire 'Law is a Bottomless Pit' (1712).

John Chrysostom, St, see CHRYSOSTOM.

John Dory /dʒɒn 'dɔːrɪ/ *n.* (*pl.* **-ies**) a European marine fish, *Zeus faber*, with a laterally flattened body and a black spot on each side.

johnny /'dʒɒnɪ/ *n.* (*pl.* **-ies**) *Brit. colloq.* a fellow; a man. □ **johnny-come-lately** *colloq.* a recently arrived person. [familiar form of the name *John*]

John of Damascus, St (c.675–c.749), Greek theologian, a Doctor of the Church, born in Damascus of a rich and influential Christian family. In about 716 he withdrew to a monastery near Jerusalem, where he wrote his most important work 'The Fount of Wisdom', which deals in turn with philosophy, heresy, and the orthodox faith. This last section (*De Fide Orthodoxa*) had immense influence for centuries in the East and the West; it summarizes the teachings of the Greek Fathers of the Church on the principal mysteries of the Christian faith, including the Trinity, the Incarnation, and the Eucharist. He also wrote three important and topical tracts against the iconoclasts. Feast day, 4 Dec. (formerly in the West, 27 March).

John of the Cross, St (1542–91), Spanish mystic and poet, joint founder, with St Teresa, of the 'Discalced' (i.e. reformed) Carmelite order. His extensive treatises on the mystical life include accounts of the purgation and purification of the soul which are regarded as amongst the finest mystical literature. He was declared Doctor of the Church in 1926.

John o'Groats /dʒɒn ə 'grəʊts/ a village on the extreme NE point of the Scottish mainland. It is the reputed site of a house built in the 16th c. by a Dutchman, John Groot. (See LAND'S END.)

John Paul II (Karol Jozef Wojtyla, 1920–), Polish-born cleric, pope 1978– , who has travelled abroad extensively during his papacy.

John Sobieski /səʊ'bjeskɪ/ (1624–96), king of Poland 1674–96. Sobieski was elected king of Poland, as John III, in 1674 after a distinguished early career as a soldier. In 1683 he relieved Vienna when it was besieged by the Turks, thereby becoming the hero of the Christian world, but at home his rule was not particularly distinguished and failed to improve Poland's bad political situation.

Johnson[1] /'dʒɒns(ə)n/, Amy (1903–41), English aviator who established several long-distance records with her solo flights to Australia (1930), Tokyo (1932), and to and from the Cape of Good Hope (1936).

Johnson[2] /'dʒɒns(ə)n/, Andrew (1808–75), 17th President of the US, 1865–9, who became President as a result of Lincoln's assassination in April 1865. His lenient policy towards the Southern States after the American Civil War brought him into bitter conflict with the Republican majority in Congress, and his dismissal of his Secretary of War (1867) gave his enemies an excuse for his impeachment (1868); he was acquitted by a single vote.

Johnson[3] /'dʒɒns(ə)n/, Cornelius (also Jonson Van Ceulen), (1593–1661), portrait painter, born in London of Dutch parents. Probably trained in Holland, from 1619–43 he painted many portraits in England before going to live in Holland. His style is best exemplified by sensitive individual portrait heads. He painted for Charles I and are widely outside court circles.

Johnson[4] /'dʒɒns(ə)n/, Lyndon Baines (1908–73), 36th President of the US, 1963–8, who became President on the assassination of John F. Kennedy and was elected in his own right in 1964. His administration introduced an ambitious programme of social and economic reform, but urban tension increased: Martin Luther King and Malcolm X were assassinated, and there was serious race riots in many cities. The increasing involvement of the US in the Vietnam war overshadowed all domestic reforms and led Johnson on an increasingly unpopular course involving conscription and high casualties; he refused to seek re-election.

Johnson[5] /ˈdʒɒns(ə)n/, Samuel (1709–84), English poet, critic, and lexicographer. He suffered from impaired eyesight, depression, and poverty, and he left Oxford without a degree. After a period as a teacher, and his marriage to Mrs Porter (a widow twice his age), he left for London (1737) and began writing for *The Gentleman's Magazine*. He produced his own journal, *The Rambler* (1750–2), written almost entirely by himself. His best poetic works include *London* (1738) and *The Vanity of Human Wishes* (1749); these and his didactic romance *Rasselas* (1759) showed his strength as a moralist. After nine years of labour he published his *Dictionary* (1755) which earned him an Oxford degree (see DICTIONARY). In 1763 Johnson met his biographer, Boswell, while Burke, Goldsmith, Reynolds, and others, were friends as well as members of his literary club. His finest critical works are his Preface to his edition of Shakespeare (1765), and *The Lives of the English Poets* (1779–81). Johnson's reputation rests partly on Boswell's evocation of his humanity, his brilliant conversation, and his surges of eloquence whose effect was increased by the rollings of his huge form.

Johnsonian /dʒɒnˈsəʊnɪən/ *adj.* **1** of or relating to Samuel Johnson. **2** typical of his style of writing.

John the Baptist, St, a preacher who appeared *c.* AD 27 on the banks of the Jordan, demanding repentance and baptism from his hearers in view of the approach of the Kingdom of God. Among those whom he baptized was Christ. Later, his denunciation of Herod Antipas for his marriage led to his imprisonment and subsequent beheading (Matt. 14: 1–12).

Johor /dʒəˈhɔː(r)/ (also **Johore**) a State of Malaysia, at the southernmost point of mainland Asia, joined to Singapore by a causeway; pop. (1980) 1,638,200; capital, Johor Baharu. From 1914 to 1948 it was a British protectorate.

joie de vivre /ˌʒwɑː də ˈviːvrə/ *n.* a feeling of healthy and exuberant enjoyment of life. [F, = joy of living]

join /dʒɔɪn/ *v. & n.* —*v.* **1** *tr.* (often foll. by *to, together*) put together; fasten, unite (one thing or person to another or several together). **2** *tr.* connect (points) by a line etc. **3** *tr.* become a member of (an association, society, organization, etc.). **4** *tr.* take one's place with or in (a company, group, procession, etc.). **5** *tr.* **a** come into the company of (a person). **b** (foll. by *in*) take part with (others) in an activity etc. (*joined me in condemnation of the outrage*). **c** (foll. by *for*) share the company of for a specified occasion (*may I join you for lunch?*). **6** *intr.* (often foll. by *with, to*) come together; be united. **7** *intr.* (often foll. by *in*) take part with others in an activity etc. **8** *tr.* be or become connected or continuous with (*the Inn joins the Danube at Passau*). —*n.* a point, line, or surface at which two or more things are joined. □ **join battle** begin fighting. **join forces** combine efforts. **join hands 1 a** clasp each other's hands. **b** clasp one's hands together. **2** combine in an action or enterprise. **join up 1** enlist for military service. **2** (often foll. by *with*) unite, connect. □□ **joinable** *adj.* [ME f. OF *joindre* (stem *joign-*) f. L *jungere junct-* join: cf. YOKE]

joinder /ˈdʒɔɪndə(r)/ *n. Law* the act of bringing together. [AF f. OF *joindre* to join]

joiner /ˈdʒɔɪnə(r)/ *n.* **1** a person who makes furniture and light woodwork. **2** *colloq.* a person who readily joins societies etc. □□ **joinery** *n.* (in sense 1). [ME f. AF *joignour*, OF *joigneor* (as JOIN)]

joint /dʒɔɪnt/ *n., adj., & v.* —*n.* **1 a** a place at which two things are joined together. **b** a point at which, or a contrivance by which, two parts of an artificial structure are joined. **2** a structure in an animal body by which two bones are fitted together. **3 a** any of the parts into which an animal carcass is divided for food. **b** any of the parts of which a body is made up. **4** *sl.* a place of meeting for drinking etc. **5** *sl.* a marijuana cigarette. **6** the part of a stem from which a leaf or branch grows. **7** a piece of flexible material forming the hinge of a book-cover. **8** *Geol.* a

fissure in a mass of rock. —*adj.* **1** held or done by, or belonging to, two or more persons etc. in conjunction (*a joint mortgage; joint action*). **2** sharing with another in some action, state, etc. (*joint author; joint favourite*). —*v.tr.* **1** connect by joints. **2** divide (a body or member) at a joint or into joints. **3** fill up the joints of (masonry etc.) with mortar etc.; trim the surface of (a mortar joint). **4** prepare (a board etc.) for being joined to another by planing its edge. □ **joint account** a bank account held by more than one person, each of whom has the right to deposit and withdraw funds. **joint and several** (of a bond etc.) signed by more than one person, of whom each is liable for the whole sum. **joint stock** capital held jointly; a common fund. **joint-stock company** one formed on the basis of a joint stock. **out of joint 1** (of a bone) dislocated. **2** out of order. □□ **jointless** *adj.* **jointly** *adv.* [ME f. OF, past part. of *joindre* JOIN]

jointer /ˈdʒɔɪntə(r)/ *n.* **1 a** a plane for jointing. **b** a tool for jointing or pointing masonry. **2** a worker employed in jointing wires, pipes, etc.

jointress /ˈdʒɔɪntrɪs/ *n.* a widow who holds a jointure. [obs. *jointer* joint possessor]

jointure /ˈdʒɔɪntʃə(r)/ *n. & v.* —*n.* an estate settled on a wife for the period during which she survives her husband. —*v.tr.* provide (a wife) with a jointure. [ME f. OF f. L *junctura* (as JOIN)]

joist /dʒɔɪst/ *n.* each of a series of parallel supporting beams of timber, steel, etc., used in floors, ceilings, etc. □□ **joisted** *adj.* [ME f. OF *giste* ult. f. L *jacēre* lie]

jojoba /həʊˈhəʊbə/ *n.* a plant, *Simmondsia chinensis*, with seeds yielding an oily extract used in cosmetics etc. [Mex. Sp.]

joke /dʒəʊk/ *n. & v.* —*n.* **1 a** a thing said or done to excite laughter. **b** a witticism or jest. **2** a ridiculous thing, person, or circumstance. —*v.* **1** *intr.* make jokes. **2** *tr.* poke fun at; banter. □ **no joke** *colloq.* a serious matter. □□ **jokingly** *adv.* **joky** *adj.* (also **jokey**). **jokily** *adv.* **jokiness** *n.* [17th c. (*joque*), orig. sl.: perh. f. L *jocus* jest]

joker /ˈdʒəʊkə(r)/ *n.* **1** a person who jokes. **2** *sl.* a fellow; a man. **3** a playing-card usu. with a figure of a jester, used in some games esp. as a wild card. **4** *US* a clause unobtrusively inserted in a bill or document and affecting its operation in a way not immediately apparent. **5** an unexpected factor or resource. □ **the joker in the pack** an unpredictable factor or participant.

jolie laide /ˌʒɒli ˈleɪd/ *n.* (pl. *jolies laides* pronunc. same) = BELLE LAIDE. [F f. *jolie* pretty + *laide* ugly]

Joliot /ˈʒɒljəʊ/, Jean-Frédéric (1900–58), French nuclear physicist. He gave up a career in engineering to study radioactivity and in 1925 became Madame Curie's assistant at the Radium Institute. There, he worked with her daughter Irène, whom he married, and took the name Joliot-Curie; their joint discovery of artificial radioactivity earned them the 1935 Nobel Prize for chemistry. This research allowed Sir James Chadwick to discover the neutron when he reviewed their experiments in Cambridge. Shortly before the Second World War Joliot demonstrated that a nuclear chain reaction was possible, and after the war both he and his wife became involved with the development of nuclear energy and the establishment of the French atomic energy commission, but were removed from this government body because of their communism. Irène, like her mother, died of leukaemia.

jollify /ˈdʒɒlɪˌfaɪ/ *v.tr. & intr.* (-**ies**, -**ied**) make or be merry, esp. in drinking. □□ **jollification** /-fɪˈkeɪʃ(ə)n/ *n.*

jollity /ˈdʒɒlɪtɪ/ *n.* (pl. -**ies**) **1** merrymaking; festiveness. **2** (in pl.) festivities. [ME f. OF *joliveté* (as JOLLY[1])]

jolly[1] /ˈdʒɒlɪ/ *adj., adv., v., & n.* —*adj.* (**jollier, jolliest**) **1** cheerful and good-humoured; merry. **2** festive, jovial. **3** slightly drunk. **4** *colloq.* (of a person or thing) very pleasant, delightful (often iron.: *a jolly shame*). —*adv. colloq.* very (*they were jolly unlucky*). —*v.tr.* (-**ies**, -**ied**) **1** (usu. foll. by *along*) *colloq.* coax or humour (a person) in a friendly way. **2** chaff, banter. —*n.* (pl. -**ies**) *colloq.* a party or celebration. □ **Jolly Roger** a pirates' black flag, usu. with the skull and crossbones. □□ **jollily** *adv.* **jolliness** *n.* [ME f. OF *jolif* gay, pretty, perh. f. ON *jól* YULE]

jolly[2] /ˈdʒɒlɪ/ *n.* (pl. -**ies**) (in full **jolly boat**) a clinker-built ship's boat smaller than a cutter. [18th c.: orig. unkn.: perh. rel. to YAWL]

Jolson /ˈdʒəʊls(ə)n/, Al (real name Asa Yoelson, 1886–1950), Russian-born American singer, black-face comedian, and film actor. He made the Gershwin song 'Swanee' his trade mark, and appeared in the first publicly performed sound film *The Jazz Singer* (1927).

jolt /dʒəʊlt, dʒɒlt/ v. & n. —v. **1** *tr.* disturb or shake from the normal position (esp. in a moving vehicle) with a jerk. **2** *tr.* give a mental shock to; perturb. **3** *intr.* (of a vehicle) move along with jerks, as on a rough road. —n. **1** such a jerk. **2** a surprise or shock. □□ **jolty** *adj.* (**joltier, joltiest**). [16th c.: orig. unkn.]

Jomon /ˈdʒəʊmən/ *adj.* of a kind of very early hand-made pottery of Japan, decorated with a characteristic cord-pattern (*jomon*), or the early neolithic or pre-neolithic culture (*c*.3000 BC) characterized by this pottery. [Jap.]

Jon. *abbr.* **1** Jonah (Old Testament). **2** Jonathan.

Jonah /ˈdʒəʊnə/ **1** a Hebrew minor prophet. **2** a book of the Old Testament bearing his name, telling of God's call to him to go to Nineveh and preach repentance, his disobedience and attempted escape by sea, his punishment of being thrown overboard and swallowed by a great fish, his deliverance, and the final success of his mission. —n. a person who is believed to bring bad luck.

Jonathan /ˈdʒɒnəθən/ son of Saul and friend of David, killed at the battle of Mount Gilboa (1 Sam. 13 ff.).

Jones[1] /dʒəʊnz/, Daniel (1881–1967), British linguistics scholar, one of the founders of modern phonetic studies in Britain. He was responsible for describing, and setting out in his *English Pronouncing Dictionary*, the educated speech used in southern England by those influenced by attendance at the great public schools, a style of pronunciation which by the 19th c. had become characteristic of the upper classes throughout the country. He also invented a system of cardinal vowels, making it possible for variations of vowel-sounds to be described by reference to these.

Jones[2] /dʒəʊnz/, Inigo (1573–1652), English architect and stage designer about whose early life little is known. He was greatly impressed by Palladian architecture while on a visit to Italy (*c*.1600). He introduced movable stage scenery and was for many years involved with costume design for court masques. His two best-known architectural works, Queen's House, Greenwich, 1616–35 (an Italian villa design), and the Banqueting House, Whitehall, 1619–21 (an Italian palace design), were built after he became Surveyor to the Crown (1614). His works reflect, in a more subdued form, his debt to Palladio and the High Renaissance, and he was instrumental in introducing this Italian style into England.

Jones[3] /dʒəʊnz/, John Paul (1747–92), American admiral and popular hero, born in Scotland, famous for his exploits round the northern coasts of Britain during the War of American Independence.

Jones[4] /dʒəʊnz/, Robert Tyre ('Bobby') (1902–71), American amateur golfer, probably the greatest player the game has known. In a career spanning only 8 years of serious golf, during which he played only intermittently between studying for degree courses in law, English literature, and engineering, he entered for 27 major championships and won 13 of them, retiring from competitive golf at the end of 1930. He later inaugurated the Masters tournament.

Jong /dʒɒŋ/, Erica Mann (1942–), American poet and novelist. Her novels include *Fanny* (1980), which is a picaresque novel in a pseudo-18th-c. style, and *Parachutes and Kisses* (1984).

jongleur /dʒɔ̃ˈɡlɜː(r)/ n. *hist.* an itinerant minstrel. [F, var. of *jougleur* JUGGLER]

Jönköping /jɜːnˈtʃɜːpɪŋ/ an industrial city of southern Sweden, at the south end of Lake Vättern; pop. (1987) 109,000.

jonquil /ˈdʒɒnkwɪl/ n. a bulbous plant, *Narcissus jonquilla*, with clusters of small fragrant yellow flowers. [mod.L *jonquilla* or F *jonquille* f. Sp. *junquillo* dimin. of *junco*: see JUNCO]

Jonson /ˈdʒɒns(ə)n/, Ben(jamin) (1572/3–1637), English dramatist and poet. His first important play *Every Man in his Humour* (1598) established his 'comedy of humours' whereby each character is dominated by a particular obsession. *Sejanus* (1603) and *Catiline* (1611) are his only tragedies, both on Roman themes. These closely follow classical models, as do his many court masques (with scenery by Inigo Jones) in which he embodied the 'antimasque', as a deliberate foil to the principal masque. His vigorous even savage humour and his originality are best manifested in his greatest comedies *Volpone* (1605/6), *The Alchemist* (1612), and *Bartholomew Fayre* (1614). His prestige and influence remained unrivalled in the 17th c. (he was ranked above Shakespeare). He presided over a literary circle which met at the Mermaid Tavern and his friends included Shakespeare, Bacon, and Donne, and younger writers known as 'the tribe of Ben'. Jonson is buried in Westminster Abbey.

Jordaens /jɔːˈdɑːns/, Jacob (1593–1678), Flemish painter of religious, genre, and mythological subjects, best known for his peasant scenes using a technique of thick impasto. He was influenced by Caravaggio and by Rubens, his contemporary. He was commissioned in 1660, along with Rembrandt and Lievens, to make paintings for the Town Hall in Amsterdam, an indication of his standing.

Jordan /ˈdʒɔːd(ə)n/ **1** a river flowing southward from the Anti-Lebanon mountains through the Sea of Galilee into the Dead Sea. **2** the Hashemite Kingdom of the Jordan, an Arab State east of the River Jordan, bordered by Syria, Israel, Saudi Arabia, and Iraq; pop. (est. 1988) 2,850,500; official language, Arabic; capital, Amman. Romans, Arabs, and Crusaders dominated the area successively until it fell under Turkish rule in the 16th c. In 1916 the land east of the River Jordan was made a British protectorate, the Amirate of Transjordan; this became independent in 1946 and changed its name to the Hashemite Kingdom of Jordan in 1949. During the Arab-Israeli war of 1948–9 the Jordanians overran a large area on the west bank of the river, but were driven from this by Israel in the Six-Day War of 1967. Its natural resources are meagre, and its only outlet to the sea is the port of Aqaba at the NE end of the Red Sea. The most important industries are phosphate mining and tourism. □□ **Jordanian** /-ˈdeɪnɪən/ adj. & n.

jorum /ˈdʒɔːrəm/ n. **1** a large drinking-bowl. **2** its contents, esp. punch. [perh. f. *Joram* (2 Sam. 8: 10)]

Jos. *abbr.* Joseph.

Joseph[1] /ˈdʒəʊsɪf/ Hebrew patriarch, son of Jacob and Rachel, sold by his brothers into captivity in Egypt, where he attained high office (Gen. 30–50).

Joseph[2] /ˈdʒəʊsɪf/, St, a carpenter of Nazareth, husband of the Virgin Mary, to whom she was betrothed at the time of the Annunciation. Feast day, 19 March.

Josephine /ˈdʒəʊzɪfiːn/ (Marie Rose Joséphine Tascher de la Pagerie) (1763–1814), Empress of France. A West Indian by birth, Josephine, who had previously been married to the Viscount de Beauharnais, married Napoleon in 1796. Her failure to give the Emperor the heir he desired led to a breakdown of the marriage, and in 1809 Napoleon divorced her in order to marry the Austrian princess Marie-Louise.

Joseph of Arimathea /ˌærɪməˈθiːə/ a member of the Council at Jerusalem who, after the Crucifixion, asked Pilate for Christ's body, which he buried. The story that he came to England with the Holy Grail and built the first church at Glastonbury is not found before the 13th c.

Josephus /dʒəʊˈsiːfəs/, Flavius (*c*.37–*c*.100), Jewish priest of aristocratic descent, native of Palestine, Pharisee, and Jewish historian. A zealous defender of Jewish religion and culture, he was politically pro-Roman and without sympathy for extreme Jewish nationalism. Captured in 67 during the revolt against the Romans, he saved his life by prophesying that Vespasian would become emperor, and during the siege of Jerusalem acted as interpreter to Titus. He returned with Titus to Rome, received Roman citizenship and a pension, and devoted himself to literary work; his *Jewish War* included an eyewitness account of the events that led to its outbreak.

josh /dʒɒʃ/ n. & v. *sl.* —n. a good-natured or teasing joke. —v. **1** *tr.* tease or banter. **2** *intr.* indulge in ridicule. □□ **josher** n. [19th c.: orig. unkn.]

Josh. *abbr.* Joshua (Old Testament).

Joshua /ˈdʒɒʃʊə/ **1** the Israelite leader (probably 13th c. BC) who succeeded Moses and led his people into the Promised Land. **2** the sixth book of the Old Testament, telling of the conquest of Canaan and its division among the twelve tribes of Israel.

Josquin des Prez see DES PREZ.

joss /dʒɒs/ n. a Chinese idol. □ **joss-house** a Chinese temple. **joss-stick** a stick of fragrant tinder mixed with clay, burnt as incense. [perh. ult. f. Port. *deos* f. L *deus* god]

josser /ˈdʒɒsə(r)/ n. Brit. sl. **1** a fool. **2** a fellow. [JOSS + -ER¹: cf. Austral. sense 'clergyman']

jostle /ˈdʒɒs(ə)l/ v. & n. —v. **1** tr. push against; elbow. **2** tr. (often foll. by *away*, *from*, etc.) push (a person) abruptly or roughly. **3** intr. (foll. by *against*) knock or push, esp. in a crowd. **4** intr. (foll. by *with*) struggle; have a rough exchange. —n. **1** the act or an instance of jostling. **2** a collision. [ME: earlier *justle* f. JOUST + -LE⁴]

jot /dʒɒt/ v. & n. —v.tr. (**jotted**, **jotting**) (usu. foll. by *down*) write briefly or hastily. —n. (usu. with *neg.* expressed or implied) a very small amount (*not one jot*). [earlier as noun: L f. Gk *iōta*: see IOTA]

jotter /ˈdʒɒtə(r)/ n. a small pad or notebook for making notes etc.

jotting /ˈdʒɒtɪŋ/ n. (usu. in *pl.*) a note; something jotted down.

Jötun /ˈjɜːʊtʊn/ n.pl. Scand. Mythol. giants, enemies of the gods.

Jotunheim /ˈjɜːʊtʊnˌhaɪm/ a mountain range in south central Norway. Its highest peak is Glittertind (2,470 m, 8,104 ft.).

Joule /dʒuːl/, James Prescott (1818–89), English physicist from a wealthy brewing family, who experimented in his private laboratory and at the brewery. He was taught privately by Dalton, then an old man, and established that all forms of energy (heat, mechanical, or electrical) were basically the same and interchangeable. This was the basis of what is now called the first law of thermodynamics. He demonstrated this by means of very careful measurements, for instance, of the thermal effects of an electric current caused by the resistance of the wire, now known as Joule's Law. In 1852 he and Thomson, later Lord Kelvin, discovered the fall in temperature when gases expand (the Joule-Thomson effect), which led to the development of the refrigerator and to a new branch of science, cryogenics. The joule (see entry) is named after him.

joule /dʒuːl/ n. the SI unit of work or energy equal to the work done by a force of one newton when its point of application moves one metre in the direction of action of the force, equivalent to a watt-second. ¶ Symb.: **J**. [J. P. JOULE]

jounce /dʒaʊns/ v.tr. & intr. bump, bounce, jolt. [ME: orig. unkn.]

journal /ˈdʒɜːn(ə)l/ n. **1** a newspaper or periodical. **2** a daily record of events. **3** Naut. a logbook. **4** a book in which business transactions are entered, with a statement of the accounts to which each is to be debited and credited. **5** the part of a shaft or axle that rests on bearings. **6** (**the Journals**) Parl. a record of daily proceedings. [ME f. OF *jurnal* f. LL *diurnalis* DIURNAL]

journalese /ˌdʒɜːnəˈliːz/ n. a hackneyed style of language characteristic of some newspaper writing.

journalism /ˈdʒɜːnəˌlɪz(ə)m/ n. the business or practice of writing and producing newspapers.

journalist /ˈdʒɜːnəlɪst/ n. a person employed to write for or edit a newspaper or journal. □□ **journalistic** /-ˈlɪstɪk/ adj. **journalistically** /-ˈlɪstɪkəlɪ/ adv.

journalize /ˈdʒɜːnəˌlaɪz/ v.tr. (also **-ise**) record in a private journal.

journey /ˈdʒɜːnɪ/ n. & v. —n. (pl. **-eys**) **1** an act of going from one place to another, esp. at a long distance. **2** the distance travelled in a specified time (*a day's journey*). **3** the travelling of a vehicle along a route at a stated time. —v.intr. (**-eys**, **-eyed**) make a journey. □□ **journeyer** n. [ME f. OF *jornee* day, day's work or travel, ult. f. L *diurnus* daily]

journeyman /ˈdʒɜːnɪmən/ n. (pl. **-men**) **1** a qualified mechanic or artisan who works for another. **2** derog. **a** a reliable but not outstanding worker. **b** a mere hireling. [JOURNEY in obs. sense 'day's work' + MAN]

joust /dʒaʊst/ n. & v. hist. —n. a combat between two knights on horseback with lances. —v.intr. engage in a joust. □□ **jouster** n. [ME f. OF *juster* bring together ult. f. L *juxta* near]

Jove /dʒəʊv/ n. Rom. Mythol. Jupiter. □ **by Jove!** an exclamation of surprise or approval. [ME f. L *Jovis* genit. of OL *Jovis* used as genit. of JUPITER]

jovial /ˈdʒəʊvɪəl/ adj. **1** merry. **2** convivial. **3** hearty and good-humoured. □□ **joviality** /-ˈælɪtɪ/ n. **jovially** adv. [F f. LL *jovialis* of Jupiter (as JOVE), with ref. to the supposed influence of the planet Jupiter on those born under it]

Jovian /ˈdʒəʊvɪən/ adj. **1** Rom. Mythol. of or like Jupiter. **2** of the planet Jupiter.

jowar /dʒaʊˈwɑː(r)/ n. = DURRA. [Hindi *jawār*]

jowl¹ /dʒaʊl/ n. **1** the jaw or jawbone. **2** the cheek (*cheek by jowl*). □□ **-jowled** adj. (in comb.). [ME *chavel* jaw f. OE *ceafl*]

jowl² /dʒaʊl/ n. **1** the external loose skin on the throat or neck when prominent. **2** the dewlap of oxen, wattle of a bird, etc. □□ **jowly** adj. [ME *cholle* neck f. OE *ceole*]

joy /dʒɔɪ/ n. & v. —n. **1** (often foll. by *at*, *in*) a vivid emotion of pleasure; extreme gladness. **2** a thing that causes joy. **3** Brit. colloq. satisfaction, success (*got no joy*). —v. esp. poet. **1** intr. rejoice. **2** tr. gladden. □ **joy-bells** bells rung on festive occasions. **wish a person joy of** iron. be gladly rid of (what that person has to deal with). □□ **joyless** adj. **joylessly** adv. [ME f. OF *joie* ult. f. L *gaudium* f. *gaudēre* rejoice]

Joyce /dʒɔɪs/, James Augustine Aloysius (1882–1941), Irish novelist and poet. Renouncing Irish Catholicism he left Ireland permanently in 1904 with Nora Barnacle (whom he later married) and thereafter lived in Trieste, Zurich, and Paris. His first important work *Dubliners* (1914; short stories) depicts Dublin as 'the centre of paralysis'. His autobiographical novel *A Portrait of the Artist as a Young Man* (1916) introduced Stephen Dedalus, who reappears in *Ulysses* (1922), his greatest novel. *Ulysses* and his second important work *Finnegan's Wake* (1939) revolutionized the form and structure of the novel and influenced the development of the 'stream of consciousness', while pushing linguistic experiment to the extreme limits of communication.

Joycean /ˈdʒɔɪsɪən/ adj. & n. —adj. of or characteristic of James Joyce or his writings. —n. a specialist in or admirer of Joyce's works.

joyful /ˈdʒɔɪfʊl/ adj. full of, showing, or causing joy. □□ **joyfully** adv. **joyfulness** n.

joyous /ˈdʒɔɪəs/ adj. (of an occasion, circumstance, etc.) characterized by pleasure or joy; joyful. □□ **joyously** adv. **joyousness** n.

joyride /ˈdʒɔɪraɪd/ n. & v. colloq. —n. a ride for pleasure in a motor car, esp. without the owner's permission. —v.intr. (past **-rode** /-rəʊd/; past part. **-ridden** /-rɪd(ə)n/) go for a joyride. □□ **joyrider** n.

joystick /ˈdʒɔɪstɪk/ n. **1** colloq. the control column of an aircraft. **2** a lever that can be moved in several directions to control the movement of an image on a VDU screen.

JP abbr. Justice of the Peace.

Jr. abbr. Junior.

jt. abbr. joint.

Juan Fernandez Islands /hwæn fəˈnændez/ a group of three almost uninhabited islands in the Pacific Ocean 640 km (400 miles) west of Chile. (See Alexander SELKIRK.)

Juba¹ /ˈdʒuːbə/ a river of East Africa, rising in the highlands of central Ethiopia and flowing southwards through Somalia to the Indian Ocean. In 1925 the surrounding territory of Jubaland was transferred from Kenya to Italian Somaliland.

Juba² /ˈdʒuːbə/ the capital of the southern region of Sudan; pop. (1973) 56,737.

jube /dʒuːb/ n. Austral. & NZ = JUJUBE 2. [abbr.]

jubilant /ˈdʒuːbɪlənt/ adj. exultant, rejoicing, joyful. □□ **jubilance** n. **jubilantly** adv. [L *jubilare jubilat-* shout for joy]

jubilate /ˈdʒuːbɪˌleɪt/ v.intr. exult; be joyful. □□ **jubilation** /-ˈleɪʃ(ə)n/ n. [L *jubilare* (as JUBILANT)]

jubilee /ˈdʒuːbɪˌliː/ n. **1** a time or season of rejoicing. **2** an anniversary, esp. the 25th or 50th. **3** *Jewish Hist.* a year of emancipation and restoration, kept every 50 years. **4** *RC Ch.* a period of remission from the penal consequences of sin, granted under certain conditions for a year usu. at intervals of 25 years. **5** exultant joy. [ME f. OF *jubilé* f. LL *jubilaeus* (*annus*) (year) of jubilee ult. f. Heb. *yōbēl*, orig. = ram, ram's-horn trumpet]

Jud. *abbr.* Judith (Apocrypha).

Judaea /dʒuːˈdiːə/ the name in Graeco-Roman times for the southern district of ancient Palestine, west of the Jordan, which was the region occupied by the Jews from 537 BC after their return from the Babylonian Captivity. □□ **Judaean** *adj.*

Judaeo- /dʒuːˈdiːəʊ/ *comb. form* (US **Judeo-**) Jewish; Jewish and. [L *judaeus* Jewish]

Judah /ˈdʒuːdə/ the most powerful of the twelve tribes of Israel. After the reign of Solomon it formed a separate kingdom, with Benjamin, which outlasted that of the northern tribes (see ISRAEL¹).

Judaic /dʒuːˈdeɪɪk/ *adj.* of or characteristic of the Jews or Judaism. [L *Judaicus* f. Gk *Ioudaikos* f. *Ioudaios* JEW]

Judaism /ˈdʒuːdeɪɪz(ə)m/ *n.* **1** the religion of the Jews, with a belief in one God and a basis in Mosaic and rabbinical teachings. (See below.) **2** the Jews collectively. □□ **Judaist** *n.* [ME f. LL *Judaismus* f. Gk *Ioudaïsmos* (as JUDAIC)]

  The Jews were a race called to reject polytheism and worship the one God, the Creator. This monotheism, inherited by both Christianity and Islam, is the heart of the Jewish experience. But it is more than a speculative belief: the decisive events of their history, such as the call of Abraham, the Exodus, the witness of the prophets and the Exile, all draw out its radical moral character of abandonment to God and his often mysterious purposes, with rejection of any human self-reliance.

Judaize /ˈdʒuːdeɪaɪz/ *v.* (also **-ise**) **1** *intr.* follow Jewish customs or rites. **2** *tr.* **a** make Jewish. **b** convert to Judaism. □□ **Judaization** /-ˈzeɪʃ(ə)n/ *n.* [LL *judaizare* f. Gk *ioudaizō* (as JUDAIC)]

Judas /ˈdʒuːdəs/ *n.* **1** a person who betrays a friend. **2** (**judas**) a peep-hole in a door. □ **Judas-tree** a Mediterranean tree, *Cercis siliquastrum*, with purple flowers usu. appearing before the leaves. [JUDAS ISCARIOT]

Judas /ˈdʒuːdəs/ *n.* an infamous traitor. [f. foll.]

Judas Iscariot /ˌdʒuːdəs ɪˈskærɪət/ the Apostle who betrayed Christ to the Jewish authorities—the Gospels leave his motive uncertain. He later committed suicide.

Judas Maccabaeus see MACCABEES.

judder /ˈdʒʌdə(r)/ *v. & n. esp. Brit.* —*v.intr.* **1** (esp. of a mechanism) vibrate noisily or violently. **2** (of a singer's voice) oscillate in intensity. —*n.* an instance of juddering. [imit.: cf. SHUDDER]

Jude /dʒuːd/, St, an Apostle, also called Judas, generally identified with Jude the brother of James (*Jude* 1), martyred in Persia with St Simon. The last epistle of the New Testament is traditionally ascribed to him. Feast day (with St Simon) 28 Oct.

Judeo- US var. of JUDAEO-.

Judg. *abbr.* Judges (Old Testament).

judge /dʒʌdʒ/ *n. & v.* —*n.* **1** a public officer appointed to hear and try causes in a court of justice. **2** a person appointed to decide a dispute or contest. **3 a** a person who decides a question. **b** a person regarded in terms of capacity to decide on the merits of a thing or question (*am no judge of that; a good judge of art*). **4** *Jewish Hist.* a leader having temporary authority in Israel in the period between Joshua and the kings (*c.*13th–11th c. BC). **Judges** the seventh book of the Old Testament, describing the gradual conquest of Canaan under various leaders (*judges*) in an account that is parallel to that of the Book of Joshua and probably gives a truer picture. —*v.* **1** *tr.* **a** try (a cause) in a court of justice. **b** pronounce sentence on (a person). **2** *tr.* form an opinion about; estimate, appraise. **3** *tr.* act as a judge of (a dispute or contest). **4** *tr.* (often foll. by *to* + infin. or *that* + clause) conclude, consider, or suppose. **5** *intr.* **a** form a judgement. **b** act as judge. □ **Judge Advocate General** an officer in supreme control of the courts martial in the armed forces. **Judges' Rules** *Brit.* a set of rules about the mode of questioning of suspects by police. Although the rules have no force in law, if they are not observed a court may decline to admit an accused person's statements in evidence. □□ **judgelike** *adj.* **judgeship** *n.* [ME f. OF *juge* (n.), *juger* (v.) f. L *judex judicis* f. *jus* law + *-dicus* speaking]

judgement /ˈdʒʌdʒmənt/ *n.* (also **judgment**) **1** the critical faculty; discernment (*an error of judgement*). **2** good sense. **3** an opinion or estimate (*in my judgement*). **4** the sentence of a court of justice; a decision by a judge. **5** often *joc.* a misfortune viewed as a deserved recompense (*it is a judgement on you for getting up late*). **6** criticism. □ **against one's better judgement** contrary to what one really feels to be advisable. **judgement by default** see DEFAULT. **Judgement Day** the day on which the Last Judgement is believed to take place. **judgement-seat** a judge's seat; a tribunal. **the Last Judgement** (in some beliefs) the judgement of mankind by God, expected to take place at the end of the world. [ME f. OF *jugement* (as JUDGE)]

judgemental /dʒʌdʒˈment(ə)l/ *adj.* (also **judgmental**) **1** of or concerning or by way of judgement. **2** condemning, critical. □□ **judgementally** *adv.*

judicature /ˈdʒuːdɪkətʃə(r), -ˈdɪkətʃə(r)/ *n.* **1** the administration of justice. **2** a judge's office or term of office. **3** judges collectively. **4** a court of justice. [med.L *judicatura* f. L *judicare* to judge]

judicial /dʒuːˈdɪʃ(ə)l/ *adj.* **1** of, done by, or proper to a court of law. **2** having the function of judgement (*a judicial assembly*). **3** of or proper to a judge. **4** expressing a judgement; critical. **5** impartial. **6** regarded as a divine judgement. □ **judicial factor** *Sc.* an official receiver. **judicial separation** the separation of man and wife by decision of a court. □□ **judicially** *adv.* [ME f. L *judicialis* f. *judicium* judgement f. *judex* JUDGE]

judiciary /dʒuːˈdɪʃɪərɪ/ *n.* (*pl.* **-ies**) the judges of a State collectively. [L *judiciarius* (as JUDICIAL)]

judicious /dʒuːˈdɪʃəs/ *adj.* **1** sensible, prudent. **2** sound in discernment and judgement. □□ **judiciously** *adv.* **judiciousness** *n.* [F *judicieux* f. L *judicium* (as JUDICIAL)]

Judith /ˈdʒuːdɪθ/ a book of the Apocrypha recounting the story of Judith, a rich Israelite widow who saved the town of Bethulia from Nebuchadnezzar's army by captivating the besieging general Holofernes and cutting off his head while he slept.

judo /ˈdʒuːdəʊ/ *n.* a sport of unarmed combat that developed from ju-jitsu primarily in Japan, founded by Dr Jigoro Kano (1860–1938). Its aim is to train the body and cultivate the mind through practice of the methods of attack and defence. □□ **judoist** *n.* [Jap. f. *jū* gentle + *dō* way]

Judy /ˈdʒuːdɪ/ *n.* (*pl.* **-ies**) **1** see PUNCH. **2** (also **judy**) *sl.* a woman. [pet-form of the name *Judith*]

jug /dʒʌg/ *n. & v.* —*n.* **1 a** a deep vessel for holding liquids, with a handle and often with a spout or lip shaped for pouring. **b** the contents of this; a jugful. **2** US a large jar with a narrow mouth. **3** *sl.* prison. **4** (in *pl.*) US *coarse sl.* a woman's breasts. —*v.tr.* (**jugged, jugging**) **1** (usu. as **jugged** *adj.*) stew or boil (a hare or rabbit) in a covered vessel. **2** *sl.* imprison. □□ **jugful** *n.* (*pl.* **-fuls**). [perh. f. *Jug*, pet-form of the name *Joan* etc.]

Jugendstil /ˈjuːɡəntˌʃtiːl/ *n.* the German name for *art nouveau*. [G f. *Jugend* youth + *Stil* style]

Juggernaut /ˈdʒʌɡəˌnɔːt/ = JAGANNATHA.

juggernaut /ˈdʒʌɡəˌnɔːt/ *n.* **1** esp. *Brit.* a large heavy motor vehicle, esp. an articulated lorry. **2** a huge or overwhelming force or object. **3** (**Juggernaut**) an institution or notion to which persons blindly sacrifice themselves or others. [Hindi *Jagannath* f. Skr. *Jagannātha* JAGANNATHA]

juggins /ˈdʒʌɡɪnz/ *n. Brit. sl.* a simpleton. [perh. f. proper name *Juggins* (as JUG): cf. MUGGINS]

juggle /ˈdʒʌɡ(ə)l/ *v. & n.* —*v.* **1** *intr.* (often foll. by *with*) perform feats of dexterity, esp. by tossing objects in the air and catching them, keeping several in the air at the same time. **b** *tr.* perform such feats with. **2** *tr.* continue to deal with (several activities) at once, esp. with ingenuity. **3** *intr.* (foll. by *with*) **a** deceive or cheat. **b** misrepresent (facts). **c** rearrange adroitly. —*n.* **1** a piece of juggling. **2** a fraud. [ME, back-form. f. JUGGLER or f. OF *jogler, jugler* f. L *joculari* jest f. *joculus* dimin. of *jocus* jest]

juggler /ˈdʒʌɡlə(r)/ *n.* **1 a** a person who juggles. **b** a conjuror. **2** a trickster or impostor. □□ **jugglery** *n.* [ME f. OF *jougleur -eor* f. L *joculator -oris* (as JUGGLE)]

Jugoslav var. of YUGOSLAV.

jugular /ˈdʒʌɡjʊlə(r)/ *adj. & n.* —*adj.* **1** of the neck or throat. **2**

(of fish) having ventral fins in front of the pectoral fins. —*n.* = *jugular vein.* □ **jugular vein** any of several large veins of the neck which carry blood from the head. [LL *jugularis* f. L *jugulum* collar-bone, throat, dimin. of *jugum* YOKE]

jugulate /ˈdʒʌgjuːˌleɪt/ *v.tr.* **1** kill by cutting the throat. **2** arrest the course of (a disease etc.) by a powerful remedy. [L *jugulare* f. *jugulum* (as JUGULAR)]

Jugurtha /dʒəˈgɜːθə/ (d. 104 BC) joint ruler of Numidia from 118 BC. His attacks on his royal partners prompted intervention by Rome and led to the outbreak of the Jugurthine War (described by the historian Sallust). He was eventually captured by Marius and executed in Rome.

juice /dʒuːs/ *n.* **1** the liquid part of vegetables or fruits. **2** the fluid part of an animal body or substance, esp. a secretion (*gastric juice*). **3** the essence or spirit of anything. **4** *colloq.* petrol or electricity as a source of power. □□ **juiceless** *adj.* [ME f. OF *jus* f. L *jus* broth, juice]

juicy /ˈdʒuːsɪ/ *adj.* (**juicier, juiciest**) **1** full of juice; succulent. **2** *colloq.* substantial or interesting; racy, scandalous. **3** *colloq.* profitable. □□ **juicily** *adv.* **juiciness** *n.*

ju-jitsu /dʒuːˈdʒɪtsuː/ *n.* (also **jiu-jitsu, ju-jutsu**) a Japanese method of self-defence using throws, punches, kicks, arm-locks, etc. and seeking to utilize the opponent's strength and weight to his or her disadvantage. It began to take on a systematized form in the latter half of the 16th c. and many schools developed, each distinguished by its individual features. It fell into disrepute for various reasons (including its ruthlessness), and the expansion of judo further reduced its popularity. [Jap. *jūjutsu* f. *jū* gentle + *jutsu* skill]

ju-ju /ˈdʒuːdʒuː/ *n.* **1** a charm or fetish of some W. African peoples. **2** a supernatural power attributed to this. [perh. f. F *joujou* toy]

jujube /ˈdʒuːdʒuːb/ *n.* **1 a** any plant of the genus *Zizyphus* bearing edible acidic berry-like fruits. **b** this fruit. **2** a lozenge of gelatin etc. flavoured with or imitating this. [F *jujube* or med.L *jujuba* ult. f. Gk *zizuphon*]

ju-jutsu var. of JU-JITSU.

jukebox /ˈdʒuːkbɒks/ *n.* a machine that automatically plays a selected musical recording when a coin is inserted. [Gullah *juke* disorderly + BOX¹]

Jul. *abbr.* July.

julep /ˈdʒuːlep/ *n.* **1 a** a sweet drink, esp. as a vehicle for medicine. **b** a medicated drink as a mild stimulant etc. **2** *US* iced and flavoured spirits and water (*mint julep*). [ME f. OF f. Arab. *julāb* f. Pers. *gulāb* f. *gul* rose + *āb* water]

Julian¹ /ˈdʒuːlɪən/ *adj.* of or associated with Julius Caesar. □ **Julian calendar** calendar introduced by Julius Caesar in 46 BC and slightly modified under Augustus (see MONTH), in which the ordinary year has 365 days, and every fourth year is a leap year of 366 days (see also GREGORIAN CALENDAR). [L *Julianus* f. *Julius*]

Julian² /ˈdʒuːlɪən/ 'the Apostate' (Flavius Claudius Julianus, 332–63), Roman emperor 360–3, nephew of Constantine. He restored paganism as the State cult in place of Christianity, but this move was reversed after his death on campaign against the Persians. His own religious belief was based on a Neoplatonist monotheism; several of his works (in Greek) survive, including a prose *Hymn to the Sun.*

Julian Alps an Alpine range in NW Yugoslavia and NE Italy, rising to a height of 2,863 m (9,395 ft.) at Triglav which is the highest peak in Yugoslavia.

julienne /ˌdʒuːlɪˈen/ *n. & adj.* —*n.* foodstuff, esp. vegetables, cut into short thin strips. —*adj.* cut into thin strips. [F f. the name *Jules* or *Julien*]

Juliet cap /ˈdʒuːlɪət/ *n.* a small network ornamental cap worn by brides etc. [the heroine of Shakesp. *Romeo & Juliet*]

Julius Caesar /ˌdʒuːlɪəs ˈsiːzə(r)/, Gaius (100–44 BC), Roman general and statesman, of formidable intellect and physical energy. A member of the so-called First Triumvirate of 60 BC with Pompey and Crassus, from 58 to 51 BC he was engaged in the wars which completed the Roman conquest of Gaul, during which he mounted raids on Britain (55 and 54 BC). He was

not popular as a person, but the victories achieved under his leadership assured him of the devotion of his soldiers, as well as enhancing his prestige, so that when disagreement with Pompey led to civil war he was sufficiently confident of his role to cross the River Rubicon (49 BC), defeating Pompey at Pharsalus in the following year. Now the undisputed first man in Rome, he carried through a series of reforms (including that of the calendar), and received extraordinary offices and honours; his monarchical tendencies were cut short by his murder on the Ides (15th) of March 44 BC in a conspiracy led by Brutus and Cassius. He was deified after his death. Of his writings there survive commentaries on the Gallic and Civil Wars, written in a spare style.

July /dʒuːˈlaɪ/ *n.* (pl. **Julys**) the seventh month of the year. [ME f. AF *julie* f. L *Julius* (*mensis* month), named after Julius Caesar, who was born in this month]

jumble /ˈdʒʌmb(ə)l/ *v. & n.* —*v.* **1** *tr.* (often foll. by *up*) confuse; mix up. **2** *intr.* move about in disorder. —*n.* **1** a confused state or heap; a muddle. **2** *Brit.* articles collected for a jumble sale. □ **jumble sale** *Brit.* a sale of miscellaneous usu. second-hand articles, esp. for charity. □□ **jumbly** *adj.* [prob. imit.]

jumbo /ˈdʒʌmbəʊ/ *n. & adj. colloq.* —*n.* (pl. **-os**) **1** a large animal (esp. an elephant), person, or thing. **2** (in full **jumbo jet**) a large airliner with capacity for several hundred passengers. ¶ Usu. applied specifically to the Boeing 747. —*adj.* **1** very large of its kind. **2** extra large (*jumbo packet*). [19th c. (orig. of a person): orig. unkn.: popularized as the name of a zoo elephant sold in 1882]

jumbuck /ˈdʒʌmbʌk/ *n. Austral. colloq.* a sheep. [Aboriginal]

Jumna /ˈdʒʌmnə/ a river of northern India, rising in the Himalayas and flowing into the Ganges below Allahabad.

jump /dʒʌmp/ *v. & n.* —*v.* **1** *intr.* move off the ground or other surface (usu. upward, at least initially) by sudden muscular effort in the legs. **2** *intr.* (often foll. by *up, from, in, out,* etc.) move suddenly or hastily in a specified way (*we jumped into the car*). **3** *intr.* give a sudden bodily movement from shock or excitement etc. **4** *intr.* undergo a rapid change, esp. an advance in status. **5** *intr.* (often foll. by *about*) change or move rapidly from one idea or subject to another. **6 a** *intr.* rise or increase suddenly (*prices jumped*). **b** *tr.* cause to do this. **7** *tr.* **a** pass over (an obstacle, barrier, etc.) by jumping. **b** move or pass over (an intervening thing) to a point beyond. **8** *tr.* skip or pass over (a passage in a book etc.). **9** *tr.* cause (a thing, or an animal, esp. a horse) to jump. **10** *intr.* (foll. by *to, at*) reach a conclusion hastily. **11** *tr.* (of a train) leave (the rails) owing to a fault. **12** *tr.* ignore and pass (a red traffic-light etc.). **13** *tr.* get on or off (a train etc.) quickly, esp. illegally or dangerously. **14** *tr.* pounce on or attack (a person) unexpectedly. **15** *tr.* take summary possession of (a claim allegedly abandoned or forfeit by the former occupant). —*n.* **1** the act or an instance of jumping. **2 a** a sudden bodily movement caused by shock or excitement. **b** (**the jumps**) *colloq.* extreme nervousness or anxiety. **3** an abrupt rise in amount, price, value, status, etc. **4** an obstacle to be jumped, esp. by a horse. **5 a** a sudden transition. **b** a gap in a series, logical sequence, etc. □ **get** (or **have**) **the jump on** *colloq.* get (or have) an advantage over (a person) by prompt action. **jump at** accept eagerly. **jump bail** see BAIL¹. **jump down a person's throat** *colloq.* reprimand or contradict a person fiercely. **jumped-up** *colloq.* upstart; presumptuously arrogant. **jump the gun** see GUN. **jumping-off place** (or **point** etc.) the place or point of starting. **jump-jet** a jet aircraft that can take off and land vertically. **jump-lead** a cable for conveying current from the battery of a motor vehicle to boost (or recharge) another. **jump-off** a deciding round in a showjumping competition. **jump on** *colloq.* attack or criticize severely and without warning. **jump out of one's skin** *colloq.* be extremely startled. **jump the queue 1** push forward out of one's turn. **2** take unfair precedence over others. **jump-rope** *US* a skipping-rope. **jump seat** *US* a folding extra seat in a motor vehicle. **jump ship** (of a seaman) desert. **jump-start** *v.tr.* start (a motor vehicle) by pushing it or with jump-leads. —*n.* the action of jump-starting. **jump suit** a one-piece garment for the whole body, of a kind orig. worn by paratroopers. **jump to it** *colloq.* act promptly and energetically.

one jump ahead one stage further on than a rival etc. **on the jump** *colloq.* on the move; in a hurry. □□ **jumpable** *adj.* [16th c.: prob. imit.]

jumper[1] /'dʒʌmpə(r)/ *n.* **1** a knitted pullover. **2** a loose outer jacket of canvas etc. worn by sailors. **3** *US* a pinafore dress. [prob. f. (17th-c., now dial.) *jump* short coat perh. f. F *jupe* f. Arab. *jubba*]

jumper[2] /'dʒʌmpə(r)/ *n.* **1** a person or animal that jumps. **2** *Electr.* a short wire used to make or break a circuit. **3** a rope made fast to keep a yard, mast, etc., from jumping. **4** a heavy chisel-ended iron bar for drilling blast-holes.

jumping bean /'dʒʌmpɪŋ/ *n.* the seed of a Mexican plant that jumps with the movement of the larva inside.

jumping jack /'dʒʌmpɪŋ/ *n.* **1** a small firework producing repeated explosions. **2** a toy figure of a man, with movable limbs.

jumpy /'dʒʌmpɪ/ *adj.* (**jumpier, jumpiest**) **1** nervous; easily startled. **2** making sudden movements, esp. of nervous excitement. □□ **jumpily** *adv.* **jumpiness** *n.*

Jun. *abbr.* **1** June. **2** Junior.

junco /'dʒʌŋkəʊ/ *n.* (*pl.* **-os** or **-oes**) any small American finch of the genus *Junco*. [Sp. f. L *juncus* rush plant]

junction /'dʒʌŋkʃ(ə)n/ *n.* **1** a point at which two or more things are joined. **2** a place where two or more railway lines or roads meet, unite, or cross. **3** the act or an instance of joining. **4** *Electronics* a region of transition in a semiconductor between regions where conduction is mainly by electrons and regions where it is mainly by holes. □ **junction box** a box containing a junction of electric cables etc. [L *junctio* (as JOIN)]

juncture /'dʒʌŋktʃə(r)/ *n.* **1** a critical convergence of events; a critical point of time (*at this juncture*). **2** a place where things join. **3** an act of joining. [ME f. L *junctura* (as JOIN)]

June /dʒuːn/ *n.* the sixth month of the year. [ME f. OF *juin* f. L *Junius* var. of *Junonius* sacred to Juno]

Juneau /'dʒuːnəʊ/ the capital and a seaport of Alaska; pop. (1980) 19,500. The city developed after the discovery of gold by Joseph Juneau in 1880.

Jung /jʊŋ/, Carl Gustav (1875–1961), Swiss psychologist, collaborator with Freud in the development of the psychoanalytic theory of personality, though he later divorced himself from Freud's viewpoint because of its preoccupation with sexuality as the determinant of personality. Jung originated the concept of two types of personality, introvert and extrovert, and four psychological functions (sensation, intuition, thinking, and feeling), of which one or more are held to predominate in any one person. His most novel proposition, expressed in his major work *The Psychology of the Unconscious* (1912) was the existence of a 'collective unconscious' (see COLLECTIVE), a conception which he combined with a theory of archetypes that he believed were of importance for study of the history and psychology of religion.

Jungfrau /'jʊŋfraʊ/ a mountain in the Swiss Alps, 4,158 m (13,642 ft.) high.

Jungian /'jʊŋɪən/ *adj. & n.* —*adj.* of Carl Jung or his system of analytical psychology. —*n.* a supporter of Jung or of his system.

jungle /'dʒʌŋg(ə)l/ *n.* **1 a** land overgrown with underwood or tangled vegetation, esp. in the tropics. **b** an area of such land. **2** a wild tangled mass. **3** a place of bewildering complexity or confusion, or of a struggle for survival (*blackboard jungle*). □ **jungle fever** a severe form of malaria. **law of the jungle** a state of ruthless competition. □□ **jungled** *adj.* **jungly** *adj.* [Hindi *jangal* f. Skr. *jangala* desert, forest]

junior /'dʒuːnɪə(r)/ *adj. & n.* —*adj.* **1** less advanced in age. **2** (foll. by *to*) inferior in age, standing, or position. **3** the younger (esp. appended to a name for distinction from an older person of the same name). **4** of less or least standing; of the lower or lowest position (*junior partner*). **5** *Brit.* (of a school) having pupils in a younger age-range, usu. 7–11. **6** *US* of the year before the final year at university, high school, etc. —*n.* **1** a junior person. **2** one's inferior in length of service etc. **3** a junior student. **4** a barrister who is not a QC. **5** *US colloq.* a young male child, esp. in relation to his family. □ **junior college** *US* a college offering a two-year course esp. in preparation for completion at senior

college. **junior common** (or **combination**) **room** *Brit.* **1** a room for social use by the junior members of a college. **2** the junior members collectively. **junior lightweight** see LIGHTWEIGHT. **junior middleweight** see MIDDLEWEIGHT. □□ **juniority** /-'ɒrɪtɪ/ *n.* [L, compar. of *juvenis* young]

juniper /'dʒuːnɪpə(r)/ *n.* any evergreen shrub or tree of the genus *Juniperus*, esp. *J. communis* with prickly leaves and dark purple berry-like cones. □ **oil of juniper** oil from juniper cones used in medicine and in flavouring gin etc. [ME f. L *juniperus*]

junk[1] /dʒʌŋk/ *n. & v.* —*n.* **1** discarded articles; rubbish. **2** anything regarded as of little value. **3** *sl.* a narcotic drug, esp. heroin. **4** old cables or ropes cut up for oakum etc. **5** *Brit.* a lump or chunk. **6** *Naut.* hard salt meat. **7** a lump of fibrous tissue in the sperm whale's head, containing spermaceti. —*v.tr.* discard as junk. □ **junk bond** *US Commerce* a bond bearing high interest but judged to be a very risky investment, issued by a company seeking to raise a large amount of capital quickly, e.g. in order to finance a takeover. This derogatory term is applied when there is doubt about the company's ability to pay the interest, as it intended, from income generated by the assets purchased. The practice of issuing such bonds dates from the mid 1970s. **junk food** food with low nutritional value. **junk mail** unsolicited advertising matter sent by post. **junk shop** a shop selling cheap second-hand goods or antiques. [ME: orig. unkn.]

junk[2] /dʒʌŋk/ *n.* a flat-bottomed sailing vessel used in the China seas, with a prominent stem and lugsails. [obs. F *juncque*, Port. *junco*, or Du. *jonk*, f. Jav. *djong*]

junker /'jʊŋkə(r)/ *n. hist.* **1** a young German nobleman. **2** a member of an exclusive (Prussian) aristocratic party. □□ **junkerdom** *n.* [G, earlier *Junkher* f. OHG (as YOUNG, HERR)]

junket /'dʒʌŋkɪt/ *n. & v.* —*n.* **1** a dish of sweetened and flavoured curds, often served with fruit or cream. **2** a feast. **3** a pleasure outing. **4** *US* an official's tour at public expense. —*v.intr.* (**junketed, junketing**) feast, picnic. □□ **junketing** *n.* [ME *jonket* f. OF *jonquette* rush-basket (used to carry junket) f. *jonc* rush f. L *juncus*]

junkie /'dʒʌŋkɪ/ *n. sl.* a drug addict.

Juno /'dʒuːnəʊ/ **1** *Rom. Mythol.* an early and very important Italian goddess, in functions resembling Hera with whom she was anciently identified, and a great goddess of the Roman State. **2** *Astron.* one of the minor planets, discovered in 1804.

Junoesque /ˌdʒuːnəʊ'esk/ *adj.* resembling the goddess Juno in stately beauty.

Junr. *abbr.* Junior.

junta /'dʒʌntə/ *n.* **1 a** a political or military clique or faction taking power after a revolution or *coup d'état.* **b** a secretive group; a cabal. **2** a deliberative or administrative council in Spain or Portugal. [Sp. & Port. f. L *juncta*, fem. past part. (as JOIN)]

Jupiter /'dʒuːpɪtə(r)/ **1** *Rom. Mythol.* originally a sky-god, associated with lightning and the thunderbolt; later, the chief of the gods, giver of victory, identified with Zeus. **2** *Astron.* a planet revolving in orbit between the orbits of Mars and Saturn. It is the largest planet of the solar system, with an equatorial diameter of 143,800 km, a massive atmosphere (its major component is hydrogen) with swirling clouds of ammonia and methane, a thin system of encircling rings, and a retinue of at least thirteen moons. A familiar planet to the ancients, Jupiter appears as one of the brightest objects in the night sky. Seen through a small telescope, coloured bands on its surface are obvious; these we now know to be due to atmospheric circulation, as is the Great Red Spot, a cyclonic weather system in the southern hemisphere extending over 10,000 km which has persisted at least since the beginning of telescopic observations. [OL *Jovis pater* father of the bright heaven]

Jura[1] /'dʒʊərə/ a system of mountain ranges, on the border of France and Switzerland, which has given its name to the Jurassic period when most of its rocks were laid down.

Jura[2] /'dʒʊərə/ an island of the Inner Hebrides, separated from the west coast of Scotland by the Sound of Jura.

jural /'dʒʊər(ə)l/ *adj.* **1** of law. **2** of rights and obligations. [L *jus juris* law, right]

Jurassic /dʒʊəˈræsɪk/ adj. & n. Geol. —adj. of or relating to the second period of the Mesozoic era, following the Triassic and preceding the Cretaceous, lasting from about 213 to 144 million years ago. During this period dinosaurs and other reptiles attained their maximum size and were found on land, in the sea, and in the air. The first birds appeared towards the end of the period. —n. this era or system. [F jurassique f. Jura (Mountains): cf. Triassic]

jurat¹ /ˈdʒʊəræt/ n. Brit. 1 a municipal officer (esp. of the Cinque Ports) holding a position similar to that of an alderman. 2 an honorary judge or magistrate in the Channel Islands. [ME f. med.L juratus past part. of L jurare swear]

jurat² /ˈdʒʊəræt/ n. a statement of the circumstances in which an affidavit was made. [L juratum neut. past part. (as JURAT¹)]

juridical /dʒʊəˈrɪdɪk(ə)l/ n. 1 of judicial proceedings. 2 relating to the law. □□ **juridically** adv. [L juridicus f. jus juris law + -dicus saying f. dicere say]

jurisconsult /ˌdʒʊərɪskənˈsʌlt/ n. a person learned in law; a jurist. [L jurisconsultus f. jus juris law + consultus skilled: see CONSULT]

jurisdiction /ˌdʒʊərɪsˈdɪkʃ(ə)n/ n. 1 (often foll. by over, of) the administration of justice. 2 a legal or other authority. b the extent of this; the territory it extends over. □□ **jurisdictional** adj. [ME f. OF jurediction, juridiction, L jurisdictio f. jus juris law + dictio DICTION]

jurisprudence /ˌdʒʊərɪsˈpruːd(ə)ns/ n. 1 the science or philosophy of law. 2 skill in law. □□ **jurisprudent** adj. & n. **jurisprudential** /-ˈdenʃ(ə)l/ adj. [LL jurisprudentia f. L jus juris law + prudentia knowledge: see PRUDENT]

jurist /ˈdʒʊərɪst/ n. 1 an expert in law. 2 a legal writer. 3 US a lawyer. □□ **juristic** /-ˈrɪstɪk/ adj. **juristical** /-ˈrɪstɪk(ə)l/ adj. [F juriste or med.L jurista f. jus juris law]

juror /ˈdʒʊərə(r)/ n. 1 a member of a jury. 2 a person who takes an oath (cf. NONJUROR). [ME f. AF jurour, OF jureor f. L jurator -oris f. jurare jurat- swear]

jury /ˈdʒʊəri/ n. (pl. -ies) 1 a body of usu. twelve persons sworn to render a verdict on the basis of evidence submitted to them in a court of justice. 2 a body of persons selected to award prizes in a competition. □ **jury-box** the enclosure for the jury in a lawcourt. [ME f. AF & OF juree oath, inquiry, f. jurata fem. past part. of L jurare swear]

juryman /ˈdʒʊərɪmən/ n. (pl. -men) a member of a jury.

jury-rigged /ˈdʒʊərɪrɪgd/ adj. Naut. having temporary makeshift rigging. [perh. ult. f. OF ajurie aid]

jurywoman /ˈdʒʊərɪˌwʊmən/ n. (pl. -women) a woman member of a jury.

Jussieu /ˈʒuːsɪ3ː/, Antoine Laurent de (1748–1836), a member of a French family of botanists whose home was a centre for plant collection and research. From extensive observation he grouped plants into families on the basis of common essential properties, and in Genera Plantarum (1789) developed the system on which modern classification of plants is based.

jussive /ˈdʒʌsɪv/ adj. Gram. expressing a command. [L jubēre juss-command]

just /dʒʌst/ adj. & adv. —adj. 1 acting or done in accordance with what is morally right or fair. 2 (of treatment etc.) deserved (a just reward). 3 (of feelings, opinions, etc.) well-grounded (just resentment). 4 right in amount etc.; proper. —adv. 1 exactly (just what I need). 2 exactly or nearly at this or that moment; a little time ago (I have just seen them). 3 colloq. simply, merely (we were just good friends; it just doesn't make sense). 4 barely; no more than (I just managed it; just a minute). 5 colloq. positively (it is just splendid). 6 quite (not just yet; it is just as well that I checked). 7 colloq. really, indeed (won't I just tell him!). 8 in questions, seeking precise information (just how did you manage?). □ **just about** colloq. almost exactly; almost completely. **just in case** as a precaution. **just now 1** at this moment. 2 a little time ago. **just so 1** exactly arranged (they like everything just so). 2 it is exactly as you say. □□ **justly** adv. **justness** n. [ME f. OF juste f. L justus f. jus right]

justice /ˈdʒʌstɪs/ n. 1 just conduct. 2 fairness. 3 the exercise of authority in the maintenance of right. 4 judicial proceedings (was duly brought to justice; the Court of Justice). 5 a a magistrate. b a judge, esp. (in England) of the Supreme Court of Judicature. □ **do justice to** treat fairly or appropriately; show due appreciation of. **do oneself justice** perform in a manner worthy of one's abilities. **in justice to** out of fairness to. **Justice of the Peace** an unpaid lay magistrate appointed to preserve the peace in a county, town, etc., hear minor cases, grant licences, etc. **Mr** (or **Mrs**) **Justice** Brit. a form of address or reference to a Supreme Court Judge. **with justice** reasonably. □□ **justiceship** n. (in sense 5). [ME f. OF f. L justitia (as JUST)]

justiciable /dʒʌsˈtɪʃ(ə)l/ adj. liable to legal consideration. [OF f. justicier bring to trial f. med.L justitiare (as JUSTICE)]

justiciary /dʒʌsˈtɪʃjərɪ/ n. & adj. —n. (pl. -ies) an administrator of justice. —adj. of the administration of justice. [med.L justitiarius f. L justitia: see JUSTICE]

justifiable /ˈdʒʌstɪˌfaɪəb(ə)l/ adj. that can be justified or defended. □ **justifiable homicide** killing regarded as lawful and without criminal guilt, esp. the execution of a death sentence. □□ **justifiability** /-ˈbɪlɪtɪ/ n. **justifiableness** n. **justifiably** adv. [F f. justifier: see JUSTIFY]

justify /ˈdʒʌstɪˌfaɪ/ v.tr. (-ies, -ied) 1 show the justice or rightness of (a person, act, etc.). 2 demonstrate the correctness of (an assertion etc.). 3 adduce adequate grounds for (conduct, a claim, etc.). 4 a (esp. in passive) (of circumstances) be such as to justify. b vindicate. 5 (as **justified** adj.) just, right (am justified in assuming). 6 Theol. declare (a person) righteous. 7 Printing adjust (a line of type) to fill a space evenly. □□ **justification** /-fɪˈkeɪʃ(ə)n/ n. **justificatory** /-fɪˌkeɪtərɪ/ adj. **justifier** n. [ME f. F justifier f. LL justificare do justice to f. L justus JUST]

Justinian /dʒʌsˈtɪnɪən/ (Flavius Petrus Sabbatius Justinianus, 483–565) Roman emperor from 527. He had a deep sense of the past greatness of the Roman Empire and was determined to restore it, by recovering the lost provinces of the West, by reforming its administrative abuses, and by codifying and rationalizing its legal system, making it his aim to restore religious and political unity. Under his general Belisarius Africa was reconquered from the Vandals (533) and Italy from the Ostrogoths (533–40); in 551 part of Spain was conquered from the Visigoths. His codification of the law produced an authoritative and ordered statement; the insistence that the monarch's will was supreme legitimized the State's control over ecclesiastical affairs which characterized the subsequent history of the Byzantine Church. Justinian carried out an active building programme throughout the Empire, erecting fortresses and churches and restoring aqueducts and other public buildings. His supreme achievement was Santa Sophia at Constantinople.

Justin Martyr /ˈdʒʌstɪn ˈmɑːtə(r)/, St (c.100–165), Christian philosopher and martyr, who taught at Ephesus and then at Rome. His surviving writings are apostolic in purpose. Justin and some of his followers were denounced as Christians, and on refusing to sacrifice to the gods they were scourged and beheaded; the authentic record of their martyrdom survives, based on an official court report. Feast day, 1 June (formerly 14 April in the West).

jut /dʒʌt/ v. & n. —v.intr. (**jutted**, **jutting**) (often foll. by out, forth) protrude, project. —n. a projection; a protruding point. [var. of JET¹]

Jute /dʒuːt/ n. a member of a Low-German tribe that invaded southern England (according to legend under Horsa and Hengist) in the 5th c. and set up a kingdom in Kent. □□ **Jutish** adj. [repr. med.L Jutae, Juti, in OE Eotas, Iotas = Icel. Iótar people of Jutland in Denmark]

jute /dʒuːt/ n. 1 a rough fibre made from the bark of E. Indian plants of the genus Corchorus, used for making twine and rope, and woven into sacking, mats, etc. 2 either of two plants Corchorus capsularis or C. olitorius yielding this fibre. [Bengali jhōṭo f. Skr. jūṭa = jaṭā braid of hair]

Jutland /ˈdʒʌtlənd/ (Danish **Jylland** /ˈjuːlæn/) a peninsula of NW Europe stretching northwards from Germany to form part of Denmark. □ **Battle of Jutland** a major naval battle in which the British Grand Fleet under Admiral Jellicoe and the German High Seas Fleet under Admiral Scheer fought the only full fleet action of the First World War in the North Sea west of Jutland on 31 May 1916. Although the Germans had the better of the early part of the engagement, they eventually escaped from superior British fire-power only as a result of poor British communications and the advent of darkness. Jellicoe was criticized for not winning a decisive victory, but in fact the German fleet never again sought a full-scale engagement, and British control of the North Sea remained unshaken.

Juvenal /ˈdʒuːvən(ə)l/ (Decimus Junius Juvenalis, *c*.60–*c*.130) Roman satirist. His sixteen hexameter satires, written, he says, out of a sense of indignation, present a savage attack on the vice and folly of Roman society. His anger was fuelled by the poverty which made him an unwilling dependent of the rich, and by his bitterness towards the emperor Domitian.

juvenescence /ˌdʒuːvɪˈnes(ə)ns/ *n.* **1** youth. **2** the transition from infancy to youth. □□ **juvenescent** *adj.* [L *juvenescere* reach the age of youth f. *juvenis* young]

juvenile /ˈdʒuːvəˌnaɪl/ *adj. & n.* —*adj.* **1 a** young, youthful. **b** of or for young persons. **2** suited to or characteristic of youth. **3** often *derog.* immature (*behaving in a very juvenile way*). —*n.* **1** a young person. **2** *Commerce* a book intended for young people. **3** an actor playing the part of a youthful person. □ **juvenile court** a court for the trial of children under 17. **juvenile delinquency** offences committed by a person or persons below the age of legal responsibility. **juvenile delinquent** such an offender. □□ **juvenilely** *adv.* **juvenility** /-ˈnɪlɪtɪ/ *n.* [L *juvenilis* f. *juvenis* young]

juvenilia /ˌdʒuːvəˈnɪlɪə/ *n.pl.* works produced by an author or artist in youth. [L, neut. pl. of *juvenilis* (as JUVENILE)]

juxtapose /ˌdʒʌkstəˈpəʊz/ *v.tr.* **1** place (things) side by side. **2** (foll. by *to, with*) place (a thing) beside another. □□ **juxtaposition** /-pəˈzɪʃ(ə)n/ *n.* **juxtapositional** /-pəˈzɪʃən(ə)l/ *adj.* [F *juxtaposer* f. L *juxta* next: see POSE¹]

Jylland see JUTLAND.

Jyväskylä /juːˈvɑːskjʊlə/ a city of central Finland, capital of Keski-Suomi province; pop. (1987) 65,719.

K

K¹ /keɪ/ *n.* (also **k**) (*pl.* **Ks** or **K's**) the eleventh letter of the alphabet.

K² *abbr.* (also **K.**) **1** kelvin(s). **2** King, King's. **3** Köchel (catalogue of Mozart's works). **4** (also **k**) (prec. by a numeral) **a** *Computing* a unit of 1,024 (i.e. 2¹⁰) bytes or bits, or loosely 1,000. **b** 1,000. [sense 4 as abbr. of KILO-]

K³ *symb. Chem.* the element potassium.

k *abbr.* **1** kilo-. **2** knot(s).

K2 /keɪˈtuː/ the second highest peak in the world (8,611 m, 28,250 ft.), in the western Himalayas. Discovered in 1856, it was named K2 because it was the second peak measured in the Karakoram range. It has also been known as Mount Godwin-Austen, after Col. H. H. Godwin-Austen, its first surveyor.

ka /kɑː/ *n.* the ancient Egyptian name for the lasting part of the individual human being or god, which survived (with the soul) after death and could reside in a statue of the dead person.

Kaaba /ˈkɑːəbə/ *n.* (also **Caaba**) a building at Mecca, the Muslim Holy of Holies, containing a sacred black stone. It is a pre-Islamic granite and marble shrine shaped like an irregular cube of about 12 × 10 × 15 metres (40 × 33 × 50 ft.), said to have been constructed by Abraham upon divine command (some say it was built by Adam). It is considered by Muslims as the 'navel' of the earth and indeed as the centre of the cosmos, the point where communications with heaven and the underworld of the spirits is easiest. Now surrounded by the Great Mosque, the Kaaba—or rather its north-west wall—replaced Jerusalem during Muhammad's lifetime as the point which all Muslims face in ritual prayer. The entire cube is covered by a black cloth covering (*kiswa*) around which the *shahāda*, or witness of the faith, is woven in gold. The Egyptian government traditionally provides a new kiswa each year. The Kaaba is the focal point of the first ritual devotions of the pilgrims (see HADJ) who walk round it seven times, touching or kissing the sacred black stone. This is a stone of basalt, originally about 30 cm (12 inches) in diameter, lodged in the eastern corner of the shrine, said to have been conveyed to Abraham by the angel Gabriel and originally white in colour, its present black colour being due to contact with the sin of the pre-Islamic period. It is thought that on Judgement Day the stone will speak as witness to the sins of humanity. [Arab. *Ka'ba* = cube]

kabaddi /kəˈbɑːdɪ/ *n.* a game popular in northern India and Pakistan, played between two teams of 9 boys or young men. It is a traditional team pursuit game, requiring the players to run and hold their breath for a long time. [Tamil]

Kabalega /ˌkæbəˈleɪgə/ a national park in NW Uganda, established in 1952. The Kabalega Falls (formerly called Murchison Falls), a waterfall on the Victoria Nile near Lake Albert, lie within it.

kabbala var. of CABBALA.

kabuki /kəˈbuːkɪ/ *n.* a form of popular traditional Japanese drama with highly stylized song, acted by males only. It originated in narrative dances performed by women in the early 17th c. but by the end of that century was part danced, part acted, and performed by men, who until the 19th c. specialized in male or female roles. Unashamedly commercial, it adopted from other theatre forms. Kabuki actors used their whole bodies to express complex emotions through stylized and exaggerated techniques. The plays were divided mainly into historical plays, domestic dramas, and dance pieces, a programme consisting of scenes or acts from several different plays. The kabuki theatre still flourishes. [Jap. f. *ka* + song, *bu* dance + *ki* art]

Kabul /ˈkɑːbʊl/ the capital of Afghanistan; pop. (est. 1984) 1,179,300.

kachina /kəˈtʃiːnə/ *n.* **1** an American Indian ancestral spirit. **2** (in full **kachina dancer**) a person who represents a kachina in ceremonial dances. □ **kachina doll** a wooden doll representing a kachina. [Hopi, = supernatural]

Kaddish /ˈkædɪʃ/ *n.* **1** a Jewish mourner's prayer. **2** a doxology in the synagogue service. [Aram. *ḳaddîš* holy]

kadi var. of CADI.

Kaffir /ˈkæfə(r)/ *n.* **1** *hist.* **a** a member of the Xhosa-speaking peoples of S. Africa. **b** the language of these peoples. **2** *S.Afr. offens.* any Black African. [Arab. *kāfir* infidel f. *kafara* not believe]

kaffiyeh var. of KEFFIYEH.

Kafir /ˈkæfə(r)/ *n.* a native of the Hindu Kush mountains of NE Afghanistan. [formed as KAFFIR]

Kafka /ˈkæfkə/, Franz (1883–1924), German-speaking Jewish novelist, born in Prague. His short stories, *The Judgement* (1916) and *The Metamorphosis* (1917) were among the few works published in his lifetime. His novels *The Trial* (1925), *The Castle* (1926), and the unfinished *America* (1927) were published posthumously by his friend Max Brod, against Kafka's testamentary directions. Guilt is one of his major themes, and his work is characterized by its lack of scenic description and its portrayal of an enigmatic reality where the individual is seen as lonely, perplexed, and threatened. The term 'Kafkaesque' is used to describe work which employs similar narrative techniques and evokes a similarly uneasy response.

kaftan var. of CAFTAN.

Kagoshima /ˌkægɒˈʃiːmə/ a city and port of Japan, on Kyushu Island; pop. (1987) 525,000. St Francis Xavier landed here in 1549.

kai /kaɪ/ *n. NZ colloq.* food. [Maori]

kail var. of KALE.

kailyard var. of KALEYARD.

Kairouan /ˌkaɪruːˈɑːn/ a Muslim holy city in northern Tunisia; pop. (1984) 72,250.

Kaiser /ˈkaɪzə(r)/, Georg (1878–1945), German dramatist, the prolific and inventive author of some sixty plays, of which *Die Bürger von Calais* (1914) was his masterpiece. *Die Koralle* (1917), *Gas I* (1918), and *Gas II* (1920) make up the so-called *Gas-Trilogie*, a gruesome interpretation of futuristic science which ends with extinction of all life by poisonous gas. These works were leading examples of German expressionist theatre.

kaiser /ˈkaɪzə(r)/ *n. hist.* an emperor, esp. the German Emperor, the Emperor of Austria, or the head of the Holy Roman Empire. □□ **kaisership** *n.* [in mod. Eng. f. G *Kaiser* and Du. *keizer*; in ME f. OE *cāsere* f. Gmc adoption (through Gk *kaisar*) of L *Caesar*: see CAESAR]

kaka /ˈkɑːkɑː/ *n.* (*pl.* **kakas**) a large New Zealand parrot, *Nestor meridionalis*, with olive-brown plumage. [Maori]

kakapo /ˈkɑːkəpəʊ/ *n.* (*pl.* **-os**) an owl-like flightless New Zealand parrot, *Strigops habroptilus*. [Maori, = night kaka]

kakemono /ˌkækɪˈməʊnəʊ/ *n.* (*pl.* **-os**) a vertical Japanese wall-picture, usu. painted or inscribed on paper or silk and mounted on rollers. [Jap. f. *kake-* hang + *mono* thing]

kala-azar /ˌkɑːlɑːˈzɑː(r)/ *n.* a tropical disease caused by the parasitic protozoan *Leishmania donovani*, which is transmitted to man by sandflies. [Assamese f. *kālā* black + *āzār* disease]

Kalahari Desert /ˌkæləˈhɑːrɪ/ a high barren plateau in southern Africa north of the Orange River, mainly in Botswana.

kale /keɪl/ *n.* (also **kail**) **1** a variety of cabbage, esp. one with wrinkled leaves and no compact head. Also called *curly kale*. **2** *US sl.* money. [ME, northern form of COLE]

kaleidoscope /kəˈlaɪdəskəʊp/ *n.* **1** a tube containing mirrors and pieces of coloured glass or paper, whose reflections produce changing patterns when the tube is rotated. **2** a constantly changing group of bright or interesting objects. □□

b *but* d *dog* f *few* g *get* h *he* j *yes* k *cat* l *leg* m *man* n *no* p *pen* r *red* s *sit* t *top* v *voice*

kaleidoscopic /-ˈskɒpɪk/ adj. **kaleidoscopical** /-ˈskɒpɪk(ə)l/ adj. [Gk kalos beautiful + eidos form + -SCOPE]

kalends var. of CALENDS.

Kalevala /ˈkɑːlɪˌvɑːlə/ the Finnish national epic poem, compiled from popular lays of great antiquity transmitted orally until the 19th c., concerned with the myths of Finland and the conflicts of the Finns with the Lapps. [Finnish f. kaleva of a hero + -la home]

kaleyard /ˈkeɪljɑːd/ n. (also **kailyard**) Sc. a kitchen garden. □ **kaleyard school** a group of 19th-c. fiction writers including J. M. Barrie, who described local town life in Scotland in a romantic vein and with much use of the vernacular. [KALE + YARD²]

Kalgoorlie /kælˈɡʊəlɪ/ a gold-mining town at the western end of the Nullarbor Plain in Western Australia; pop. (est. 1987) 11,100.

Kali /ˈkɑːlɪ/ Hinduism the most terrifying goddess, wife of Siva (see PARVATI), often identified with Durga. She is usually depicted as black, naked, old, and hideous, with a necklace of skulls, a belt of severed hands, and a protruding blood-stained tongue. The infamous thugs (see entry) were her devotees. [Skr., = black]

kali /ˈkælɪ, ˈkeɪlɪ/ n. a glasswort, Salsola kali, with fleshy jointed stems, having a high soda content. [Arab. ḳali ALKALI]

Kalidasa /ˌkælɪˈdɑːsə/ (3rd c.) Indian poet and dramatist. Little is known of his life and he is best known for his celebrated drama Sakuntala, the story of King Dushyanta's love and courtship of the maiden Sakuntala, whom he first observed while hunting in the forest.

Kalimantan /ˌkælɪˈmæntæn/ part of the island of Borneo, lying to the south of Sarawak and Sabah and belonging to Indonesia; pop. (1980) 6,723,000.

Kalinin¹ /kəˈliːnɪn/, Mikhail Ivanovich (1875–1946), Communist leader and statesman, head of State in the USSR from 1919 until 1946. He was one of the founders of the Bolsheviks' newspaper Pravda (= Truth).

Kalinin² /kəˈliːnɪn/ an industrial port of the USSR, on the River Volga, called Tver until 1931 and then renamed in honour of President Kalinin; pop. (est. 1987) 447,000.

Kaliningrad /kəˈliːnɪnˌɡræd/ a Baltic seaport of the Russian SFSR, formerly called Königsberg, assigned to the Soviet Union in 1945 and renamed in honour of President Kalinin. The philosopher Immanuel Kant was born here in 1724. Kaliningrad is the home of the Soviet navy's Baltic fleet; its port is ice-free all the year round.

Kalmar /ˈkælmɑː(r)/ a city of SE Sweden, opposite the island of Oland; pop. (1987) 54,900.

kalmia /ˈkælmɪə/ n. a N. American evergreen shrub of the genus Kalmia, esp. K. latifolia, with showy pink flowers. [mod.L f. P. Kalm, Sw. botanist d. 1779]

Kalmuck /ˈkælmʌk/ adj. & n. —adj. of a Buddhist Mongolian people of central Asia who invaded Russia in the 17th–18th c. and settled along the lower Volga. Many migrated to Chinese Turkestan in the 18th c. —n. 1 a member of this people. 2 the Ural-Altaic language of this people. [Russ. kalmyk]

kalong /ˈkɑːlɒŋ/ n. any of various fruit-eating bats of the family Pteropodidae, esp. Pteropus edulis; a flying fox. [Malay]

kalpa /ˈkælpə/ n. Hinduism & Buddhism the period between the beginning and the end of the world considered as the day of Brahma (4,320 million human years). [Skr.]

Kama /ˈkɑːmə/ Hinduism the god of sexual love, usually presented as a beautiful youth with a bow of sugar-cane, a bowstring of bees, and arrows of flowers. [Skr., = love]

Kama Sutra /ˈkɑːmə ˈsuːtrə/ an ancient Sanskrit treatise on the art of love and sexual technique. [Skr., = love-treatise]

Kamchatka /kæmˈtʃætkə/ a peninsula in the north-east of the USSR, separating the Sea of Okhotsk from the Bering Sea. Its chief port is Petropavlovsk-Kamchatskiy.

kame /keɪm/ n. a short ridge of sand and gravel deposited from the water of a melted glacier. [Sc. form of COMB]

Kamerlingh Onnes /ˌkæmələŋ ˈɒnɪs/, Heike (1853–1926),

Dutch physicist who studied cryogenic phenomena. Onnes succeeded in liquefying first oxygen (1906) and then helium (1908). He discovered the phenomenon of superconductivity in 1911 and was awarded the Nobel Prize for physics two years later.

kamikaze /ˌkæmɪˈkɑːzɪ/ n. & adj. —n. hist. 1 a Japanese aircraft loaded with explosives and deliberately crashed by its pilot on its target. 2 the pilot of such an aircraft. —adj. 1 of or relating to a kamikaze. 2 reckless, dangerous, potentially self-destructive. [Jap. f. kami divinity + kaze wind]

Kampala /kæmˈpɑːlə/ the capital of Uganda, on Victoria Nyanza (Lake Victoria); pop. (1980) 458,400.

kampong /ˈkæmpɒŋ/ n. a Malayan enclosure or village. [Malay: cf. COMPOUND²]

Kampuchea /ˌkæmpʊˈtʃɪə/ see CAMBODIA.

Kan. abbr. Kansas.

kana /ˈkɑːnə/ n. any of various Japanese syllabaries. [Jap.]

kanaka /kəˈnækə, -ˈnɑːkə/ n. a South Sea Islander, esp. (formerly) one employed in forced labour in Australia. [Hawaiian, = man]

Kanarese /ˌkænəˈriːz/ adj. & n. —adj. of or relating to Kanara, a district in SW India, or its people or language. —n. (pl. same) 1 a native of Kanara. 2 the language spoken there (now generally and officially called **Kannada**), a member of the Dravidian language group, closely allied to Telugu, with about 22 million speakers. Its alphabet is similar to that of Telugu, developed from the Grantha script.

Kanchenjunga /ˌkæntʃenˈdʒʊŋɡə/ (also **Kinchinjunga** /ˌkɪn-/) a mountain in the Himalayas on the border between Nepal and Sikkim, height 8,586 m (28,168 ft.), the world's third-highest mountain. Its summit is split into five separate peaks, whence its name, which in Tibetan means 'the five treasures of the snows'.

Kandahar /ˌkændəˈhɑː(r)/ the largest city of southern Afghanistan; pop. (est. 1984) 203,000. It was the first capital of Afghanistan when the country became independent in the mid-18th c.

Kandinsky /kænˈdɪnskɪ/, Wassily (1866–1944), Russian painter and theorist, usually considered the initiator of abstraction or non-objectivity in painting. Born in Moscow, he studied law and political economics, but in 1896 settled in Munich to study art. Kandinsky's paintings at first belonged to the mainstream of German expressionism, but by 1910–11 his rich colour and simplified rather crude forms had begun to take on an independent meaning and life of their own. His booklet Concerning the Spiritual in Art (1910) provided the theoretical basis for these experiments. Deeply influenced by the theosophy of Mme Blavatsky and Steiner, he evolved principles of transcendental meaning in colour and form; it is a matter of contention whether Kandinsky in Munich or Delaunay in Paris produced the first non-objective painting. He edited the Blaue Reiter almanac with Franz Marc, and the attention given there to Schoenberg's exactly contemporary principles of atonality in music is worthy of note. In 1914 Kandinsky returned to Russia, where he supported the revolution. Although receiving several State appointments after 1917, he felt obliged to leave Russia when social realism was applied as the official style. Settling in Germany, he was appointed to the staff of the Bauhaus in 1922, and remained there until obliged to leave, for Paris, in 1933. His abstract work of this period adopted a new geometric quality, his ideas being published in his booklet Point and Line to Plane of 1926.

Kandy /ˈkændɪ/ 1 a town in the highlands of central Sri Lanka, containing one of the most sacred Buddhist shrines; pop. (1981) 97,800. 2 a former independent kingdom in Ceylon. The town of Kandy was its capital (1480–1815).

kangaroo /ˌkæŋɡəˈruː/ n. a plant-eating marsupial of the genus Macropus, native to Australia and New Guinea, with a long tail and strongly developed hindquarters enabling it to travel by jumping. □ **kangaroo closure** Brit. Parl. a closure involving the chairperson of a committee selecting some amendments for discussion and excluding others. **kangaroo court** an improperly constituted or illegal court held by strikers etc. **kangaroo mouse** any small rodent of the genus Microdipodops, native to N. America, with long hind legs for hopping. **kangaroo paw**

any plant of the genus *Angiozanthos*, with green and red woolly flowers. **kangaroo-rat** any burrowing rodent of the genus *Dipodomys*, having elongated hind feet. **kangaroo vine** an evergreen climbing plant, *Cissus antarctica*, with tooth-edged leaves. [Aboriginal name]

KaNgwane /ˌkɑːˈŋgwɑːneɪ/ a tribal homeland of the Swazi people in eastern Transvaal; pop. (1985) 389,000.

kanji /ˈkændʒɪ/ n. Japanese writing using Chinese characters. [Jap. f. *kan* Chinese + *ji* character]

Kannada /ˈkænədə/ n. the Kanarese language. [Kanarese *kannaḍa*]

Kano /ˈkɑːnəʊ/ the chief city of northern Nigeria; pop. (1983) 487,100.

kanoon /kəˈnuːn/ n. an instrument like a zither, with fifty to sixty strings. [Pers. or Arab. *ḳānūn*]

Kanpur /kɑːnˈpʊə(r)/ (formerly **Cawnpore** /kɔːnˈpɔː(r)/) a city of India, on the River Ganges in Uttar Pradesh; pop. (1981) 1,688,000. It is famous for a massacre of British soldiers and European families in July 1857, during the Indian Mutiny.

Kans. *abbr.* Kansas.

Kansas /ˈkænsəs/ a State in the Middle West of the US acquired as part of the Louisiana Purchase in 1803; pop. (est. 1985) 2,364,200; capital, Topeka. It became the 34th State of the US in 1861.

Kansas City /ˈkænsəs/ two adjacent cities with the same name situated at the junction of the Missouri and Kansas rivers, one in NE Kansas (1980 pop. 161,150) and the other in NW Missouri (1982 pop. 445,200).

Kansu see GANSU.

Kant /kɑːnt/, Immanuel (1724–1804), German philosopher, who never travelled more than 40 miles from his native town, Königsberg, where he was a professor at the university from 1770 to 1797. His most important book is the *Critique of Pure Reason* (1781, 1787). According to Kant, the world of which we are aware is constructed out of the given material by our ways of classifying it. The human mind can never grasp the ultimate nature of reality, of 'things-in-themselves'; these can neither be confirmed, denied, nor scientifically demonstrated. What it can know are the objects of experience, 'phenomena', which it interprets by imposing upon them its built-in notions of space and time and ordering the sense-data according to its a priori concepts, the twelve 'categories' of thought which he grouped into those of quantity, quality, reason, and modality. His *Critique of Practical Reason* (1788) deals with ethics. Kant held that there is an absolute moral law, the 'categorical imperative' whose motivation is reason and a requirement of consistency ('act as if the principle by which you act were about to be turned into a universal law of nature'). Towards the end of his life in his work *Perpetual Peace* (1795) he advocated a federation of free States, bound by a covenant forbidding war.

Kanto /kænˈtəʊ/ a region of Japan, on the island of Honshu; pop. (1986) 37,156,000; capital, Tokyo.

KANU /ˈkɑːnuː/ *abbr.* Kenya African National Union.

Kaohsiung /ˌkaʊʃɪˈʊŋ/ the largest seaport of Taiwan, situated on the west coast of the island; pop. (1987) 1,300,000.

kaolin /ˈkeɪəlɪn/ n. a fine soft white clay produced by the decomposition of other clays or feldspar, used esp. for making porcelain and in medicines. Also called *china clay*. □□ **kaolinic** /-ˈlɪnɪk/ adj. **kaolinize** v.tr. (also -**ise**). [F f. Chin. *gaoling* the name of a mountain f. *gao* high + *ling* hill]

kaon /ˈkeɪɒn/ n. *Physics* a meson having a mass several times that of a pion. [*ka* repr. the letter *K* (as symbol for the particle) + -ON]

kapellmeister /kəˈpelˌmaɪstə(r)/ n. (pl. same) the conductor of an orchestra, opera, choir, etc., esp. in German contexts. [G f. *Kapelle* court orchestra f. It. *cappella* CHAPEL + *Meister* master]

kapok /ˈkeɪpɒk/ n. a fine fibrous cotton-like substance found surrounding the seeds of a tropical tree, *Ceiba pentandra*, used for stuffing cushions, soft toys, etc. [ult. f. Malay *kāpoq*]

kappa /ˈkæpə/ n. the tenth letter of the Greek alphabet (K, κ). [Gk]

kaput /kæˈpʊt/ *predic.adj. sl.* broken, ruined; done for. [G *kaputt*]

karabiner /ˌkærəˈbiːnə(r)/ n. a coupling link with safety closure, used by mountaineers. [G, lit. 'carbine']

Karachi /kəˈrɑːtʃɪ/ the largest city of Pakistan, capital of Sind province; pop. (1981) 5,103,000. It was the capital of Pakistan 1947–59.

Karadzić /kəˈrɑːʒɪtʃ/, Vuk Stefanović (1787–1864), Serbian author, grammarian, and lexicographer, the 'father' of modern Serbian literature.

Karaite /ˈkeərəˌaɪt/ n. a member of a Jewish sect chiefly in the Crimea etc., founded in the 8th c., rejecting rabbinical tradition and basing its tenets on a literal interpretation of the Scriptures. [Heb. *qerāïm* scripturalists f. *qārā* read]

Karajan /ˈkærəjən/, Herbert von (1908–89), Austrian conductor, associated especially with the Berlin Philharmonic Orchestra, the Vienna State Opera, and the Salzburg Festival. In 1967 he founded the Salzburg Easter Festival of operas.

Karakoram /ˌkærəˈkɔːrəm/ a great chain of mountains lying to the north of the west end of the Himalayas.

karakul /ˈkærəˌkʊl/ n. (also **caracul**) **1** a variety of Asian sheep with a dark curled fleece when young. **2** fur made from or resembling this. Also called *Persian lamb*. [Russ.]

Kara Kum Desert /ˌkærə ˈkuːm/ a desert area in Soviet Turkmenistan, situated between the Aral Sea and the frontier with Iran.

Kara Sea /ˈkɑːrə/ an arm of the Arctic Ocean to the east of the island of Novaya Zemlaya and to the north of the mainland of the USSR.

karat *US var. of* CARAT 2.

karate /kəˈrɑːtɪ/ n. a Japanese system of unarmed combat using the hands and feet as weapons. It involves a training of the mind as well as the body, and seeks to concentrate the body's power at the point of impact. Modern karate is a product of the 20th c., but its roots can be traced back to before the time of Christ, and Okinawa, China, and India have all contributed to its development. [Jap. f. *kara* empty + *te* hand]

Karawanken Alps /ˌkɑːrəˈvæŋken/ a range of the eastern Alps on the frontier between Austria and Yugoslavia. The highest peak is Hochstuhl (2,238 m, 7,341 ft.).

Karbala /ˈkɑːbələ/ a holy city of the Shiite Muslims, in southern Iraq; pop. (est. 1985) 184,600. On this site in AD 680 Husein, grandson of Muhammad, was killed while defending his succession to the khalifate; his tomb is one of the greatest Shiite shrines.

Karelia /kəˈriːlɪə/ a region on the frontier of Finland and the Soviet Union, which formed an independent Finnish State in medieval times and whose folk-tales were the source of the Finnish epic, the *Kalevala*. In the 16th c. Karelia came under Swedish rule and in 1721 it was annexed by Russia. Following Finland's declaration of independence in 1917, part of Karelia became a region of Finland and part an autonomous republic of the Soviet Union. After the Russian-Finnish War of 1939–40 the greater part of Finnish Karelia was ceded to the Soviet Union. □□ **Karelian** adj. & n.

Karen /kəˈren/ n. & adj. —n. **1** any of a group of non-Burmese Mongoloid tribes, most of whom live in east Burma. **2** a member of these tribes. **3** their language, probably of the Sino-Tibetan family. —adj. of or relating to the Karens or their language. [Burmese *ka-reng* wild, dirty, low-caste man]

Kariba /kəˈriːbə/ a town of Zimbabwe, originally built (1957) to house the workers building the Kariba Dam, and settlers; pop. (1982) 12,400. Its name means 'where the waters have been trapped'. □ **Kariba Dam** a concrete arch dam built across the Zambezi River, creating Lake Kariba and serving as a bridge between Zambia and Zimbabwe. **Lake Kariba** the artificial lake on the Zambia-Zimbabwe frontier, created by damming the Zambezi, providing hydroelectric power for a wide area in both countries.

Karl-Marx-Stadt see CHEMNITZ.

Karloff /ˈkɑːlɒf/, Boris (real name William Henry Pratt, 1887–1969), English-born American film actor, whose name is associated chiefly with horror films after his success as the man-made monster in *Frankenstein* (1931).

Karlovy Vary /ˌkɑːləvɪ ˈvɑːrɪ/ (German **Carlsbad** /ˈkɑːlzbæd/) a spa town in western Czechoslovakia, famous since the 14th c. for its alkaline thermal springs; pop. (1984) 59,200.

Karlsruhe /ˈkɑːlzruːə/ an industrial town and port on the Rhine in western Germany; pop. (1987) 268,300.

karma /ˈkɑːmə/ n. *Buddhism* & *Hinduism* **1** the sum of a person's actions in previous states of existence, viewed as deciding his or her fate in future existences. The doctrine reflects the Hindu belief that this life is but one of a chain of successive existences by transmigration, each life's condition being explained by actions in a previous life. **2** destiny. □□ **karmic** *adj.* [Skr., = action, fate]

Karnak /ˈkɑːnæk/ a village in Egypt, site of the northern complex of monuments of ancient Thebes, including the great temple of Amun.

Karnataka /kəˈnɑːtəkə/ a State in southern India, formerly called Mysore; pop. (1981) 37,043,450; capital, Bangalore.

Kärnten see CARINTHIA.

Karoo /kəˈruː/ n. (also **Karroo**) an elevated semi-desert plateau in S. Africa. [Afrik. f. Hottentot *karo* dry]

karpov /ˈkɑːpɒf/, Anatoli (1951–), Soviet chess-player, world champion from 1975 until defeated by Gary Kasparov in 1985.

karri /ˈkærɪ/ n. (pl. **karris**) **1** a tall W. Australian tree, *Eucalyptus diversicolor*, with a hard red wood. **2** the timber from this. [Aboriginal]

Karroo var. of KAROO.

Kars /kɑːs/ a city of NE Turkey, noted for its cheese, woollen textiles, felt, and carpet-weaving; pop. (1985) 70,400. In the 9th–10th c. it was the capital of an independent Armenian principality.

karst /kɑːst/ n. a limestone region with underground drainage and many cavities and passages caused by the dissolution of the rock. [the *Karst*, a limestone region in NW Yugoslavia]

kart n. a miniature wheeled vehicle usually consisting of a tubular frame with a small rear-mounted engine and a seat for the driver. It is used for a motor-racing sport (**karting**), and is an American invention dating from 1956. The first vehicles incorporated surplus 750 cc engines that had been intended to power rotary lawnmowers whose manufacture was abandoned when the mowers proved unreliable. [commercial alteration of *cart*]

karyo- /ˈkærɪəʊ/ *comb. form* Biol. denoting the nucleus of a cell. [Gk *karuon* kernel]

karyokinesis /ˌkærɪəʊkɪˈniːsɪs/ n. *Biol.* the division of a cell nucleus during mitosis. [KARYO- + Gk *kinēsis* movement f. *kineō* move]

karyotype /ˈkærɪətaɪp/ n. the number and structure of the chromosomes in the nucleus of a cell.

kasbah /ˈkæzbɑː/ n. (also **casbah**) **1** the citadel of an Arab city in North Africa. **2** the old crowded part near this, especially in Algiers. [F *casbah* f. Arab. *kas(a)ba* citadel]

Kashmir /kæʃˈmɪə(r)/ a former State on the border of India, since 1947 disputed between India and Pakistan. It was partitioned in 1949, the NW area becoming Azad Kashmir (= Free Kashmir), controlled by Pakistan, and the remainder being incorporated into India as the State of Jammu and Kashmir (see entry). Sporadic fighting continued into the mid-1980s and broke out again in 1990.

Kasparov /ˈkæspərɒf/, Gary (original name Gary Weinstein, 1963), Soviet chess-player, who at the age of 22 became the youngest-ever world champion, defeating Anatoli Karpov in 1985, 1986, and 1987.

Kassite /ˈkæsaɪt/ n. & *adj.* —n. **1** a member of an Elamite people from the Zagros mountains in western Iran, who ruled Babylonia from the 18th to the 12th c. BC until overthrown by Assyria. **2** their language. —*adj.* of the Kassites or their language. [native name]

Kasur /kəˈsʊə(r)/ a city of NE Pakistan, in Punjab province; pop. (1981) 155,000.

katabatic /ˌkætəˈbætɪk/ *adj.* Meteorol. (of wind) caused by air flowing downwards (cf. ANABATIC). [Gk *katabatikos* f. *katabainō* go down]

katabolism var. of CATABOLISM.

katakana /ˌkætəˈkɑːnə/ n. an angular form of Japanese kana. [Jap., = side kana]

Kathiawar /ˌkætɪəˈwɑː(r)/ a peninsula on the west coast of India, in the State of Gujarat.

Kathmandu /ˌkætmænˈduː/ the capital of Nepal, situated in the Himalayas at 1,370 m (*c*.4,500 ft.); pop. (1981) 235,000.

kathode var. of CATHODE.

Katowice /ˌkætəˈviːtseɪ/ a city of southern Poland, the industrial centre of the Upper Silesian coal-mining region; pop. (1985) 363,000.

Kattegat /ˈkætɪˌɡæt/ the sea-channel separating Sweden and Denmark.

katydid /ˈkeɪtɪdɪd/ n. any of various green grasshoppers of the family Tettigoniidae, native to the US. [imit. of the sound it makes]

Kauffmann /ˈkaʊfmæn/, Angelica (1740–1807), Swiss painter who as a young woman travelled widely in Europe. In Rome she was introduced into the neoclassical circle, and in 1764 painted her famous portrait of Winckelmann. In London from 1766, she was a friend of Reynolds and a foundation member of the Royal Academy. Her work was greatly admired, and although she painted large canvases of classical subjects she is best represented in her small-scale decorative panels for ceilings, walls, and furniture, as commissioned by the Adam Brothers for houses they designed. She left England and settled in Rome in 1782, with her second husband Antonio Zucchi, also a decorative painter. She is a rare example of a female artist who achieved professional status in the 18th c.

Kaunda /kɑːˈʊndə/, Kenneth David (1924–), Zambian statesman, the first President of his country after it became an independent republic (1964).

kauri /ˈkaʊrɪ/ n. (pl. **kauris**) a coniferous New Zealand tree, *Agathis australis*, which produces valuable timber and a resin. □ **kauri-gum** this resin. [Maori]

kava /ˈkɑːvə/ n. **1** a Polynesian shrub, *Piper methys*. **2** an intoxicating drink made from the crushed roots of this. [Polynesian]

Kaválla /kəˈvælə/ a port on the Aegean coast of Macedonia in NE Greece; pop. (1981) 56,375. It occupies the site of Neapolis, the port of ancient Philippi.

kawa-kawa /ˈkɑːwəˌkɑːwə/ n. a New Zealand shrub, *Macropiper excelsum*, with aromatic leaves. [Maori]

Kawasaki /ˌkæwəˈsɑːkɪ/ an industrial city on Honshu Island, Japan; pop. (1987) 1,096,000.

Kawthoolay /ˌkɔːθuːˈleɪ/ (also **Kawthulei**) a State of east Burma; pop. (1983) 1,057,500; capital, Pa-an. The Karen people of this State are engaged in armed conflict with the Burmese government in an attempt to gain independence.

kayak /ˈkaɪæk/ n. **1** a light covered-in canoe-type boat consisting of a wooden framework covered with sealskins, in which the paddler sits facing forward and using a double-bladed paddle, used by the Eskimo for fishing. **2** a boat developed from this, used for touring and sport. [Eskimo]

kayo /keɪˈəʊ/ v. & n. colloq. —v.tr. (**-oes, -oed**) knock out; stun by a blow. —n. (pl. **-os**) a knockout. [repr. pronunc. of *KO*]

Kazakhstan /ˌkæzɑːkˈstɑːn/ the Kazakh SSR, the second-largest constituent republic of the USSR, extending from the Caspian Sea east to the Altai mountains and Mongolia; pop. (est. 1987) 16,244,000; capital, Alma-Ata.

Kazan /kəˈzæn, -ˈzænjə/ a city and port of European Russia, on the River Volga, capital of the Tatar SSR; pop. (1983) 1,031,000.

kazoo /kəˈzuː/ n. a toy musical instrument into which the player sings or hums. [19th c., app. with ref. to the sound produced]

KB *abbr.* (in the UK) King's Bench.

KBE *abbr.* (in the UK) Knight Commander of the Order of the British Empire.

KC *abbr.* **1** King's College. **2** King's Counsel.

kc *abbr.* kilocycle(s).

KCB abbr. (in the UK) Knight Commander of the Order of the Bath.

KCMG abbr. (in the UK) Knight Commander of the Order of St Michael and St George.

kc/s abbr. kilocycles per second.

KCVO abbr. (in the UK) Knight Commander of the Royal Victorian Order.

KE abbr. kinetic energy.

kea /ˈkiːə, ˈkeɪə/ n. a parrot, *Nestor notabilis*, of New Zealand, with brownish-green and red plumage. [Maori, imit.]

Kean, Edmund (1787–1833), English actor, with a reputation as the greatest tragic actor of his day. After a wild and uncared-for childhood, from 1814, when he played Shylock in London, his place on the stage was assured. Although less good in any character that called for virtue or sustained nobility, as Macbeth, Shylock, or Iago he was unmatchable. His life was as fierce as much of his playing: he drank to excess, and was often absent from the theatre. His last role was as Othello to his son's Iago; he collapsed during the performance and died a few weeks later.

Keaton /ˈkiːt(ə)n/, Buster (Joseph Francis) (1895–1966), American comic silent-film actor and director, noted for his presentation of emotional restraint which established an essential calm in the midst of the wildest events. In his mastery of screen comedy he is rivalled only by Chaplin.

Keats, /kiːts/ John (1795–1821), English poet who was apprenticed to an apothecary-surgeon but with encouragement from the poet Leigh Hunt turned to literature. His *Poems* (1817) and *Endymion* (1818) received harsh criticism. In 1818 he fell in love with Fanny Brawne, and the following year wrote his greatest poems, including 'Hyperion', 'Ode on a Grecian Urn', 'Ode to Melancholy', and 'Ode to a Nightingale', all published in 1820. By now he was ill with tuberculosis and he died in Rome in the following year. A principal figure of the Romantic movement, Keats was commended by Arnold for his 'intellectual and spiritual passion' for beauty. His *Letters* (1848, 1878) reveal his profoundest thoughts on love, poetry, and the nature of man.

kebab /kɪˈbæb/ n. (usu. in *pl.*) small pieces of meat, vegetables, etc., packed closely and cooked on a skewer. [Urdu f. Arab. *kabāb*]

Keble /ˈkiːb(ə)l/, John (1792–1866), a leader of the Oxford Movement. His assize sermon on *National Apostasy* (1833), preached while he was Professor of Poetry at Oxford, challenged the masses to take stock of their weakening Christian faith, and is usually regarded as the beginning of the movement. The aim of the sermon was political rather than theological, directed at the new idea that the law of the land need not coincide with the Church's teaching. In this it ultimately failed, but the work of his followers was victorious in reviving traditional Catholic teaching, and did much to define and mould the Church of England.

Kebnekaise /ˌkebnəˈkaɪsə/ the highest peak in Sweden, in Norrbotten county, rising to a height of 2,117 m (6,962 ft.).

Kedah /ˈkeda/ a State of Malaysia, in the north-west of the Malay peninsula; pop. (1980) 1,116,100; capital, Alor Setar.

kedge /kedʒ/ v. & n. — v. 1 *tr.* move (a ship) by means of a hawser attached to a small anchor. 2 *intr.* (of a ship) move in this way. — n. (in full **kedge-anchor**) a small anchor for this purpose. [perh. a specific use of obs. *cagge*, dial. *cadge* bind, tie]

kedgeree /ˈkedʒərɪ, -ˈriː/ n. 1 an Indian dish of rice, split pulse, onions, eggs, etc. 2 a European dish of fish, rice, hard-boiled eggs, etc. [Hindi *khichṛī*, Skr. *k'rsara* dish of rice and sesame]

keek /kiːk/ v. & n. Sc. — v.*intr.* peep. — n. a peep. [ME *kike*: cf. MDu., MLG *kīken*]

keel[1] /kiːl/ n. & v. — n. 1 the lengthwise timber or steel structure along the base of a ship, airship, or some aircraft, on which the framework of the whole is built up. 2 *poet.* a ship. 3 a ridge along the breastbone of many birds; a carina. 4 *Bot.* a prow-shaped pair of petals in a corolla etc. — v. 1 (often foll. by *over*) **a** *intr.* turn over or fall down. **b** *tr.* cause to do this. 2 *tr.* & *intr.* turn keel upwards. □□ **keelless** adj. [ME *kele* f. ON *kjölr* f. Gmc]

keel[2] /kiːl/ n. Brit. hist. 1 a flat-bottomed vessel, esp. of the kind formerly used on the River Tyne etc. for loading coal-ships. 2

an amount carried by such a vessel. [ME *kele* f. MLG *kēl*, MDu. *kiel* ship, boat, f. Gmc]

keelhaul /ˈkiːlhɔːl/ v.*tr.* 1 drag (a person) through the water under the keel of a ship as a punishment. 2 scold or rebuke severely.

Keeling Islands see COCOS ISLANDS.

keelson /ˈkiːls(ə)n/ n. (also **kelson** /ˈkels(ə)n/) a line of timber fastening a ship's floor-timbers to its keel. [ME *kelswayn*, perh. f. LG *kielswīn* f. *kiel* KEEL[1] + (prob.) *swīn* SWINE used as the name of a timber]

keen[1] /kiːn/ adj. 1 (of a person, desire, or interest) eager, ardent (*a keen sportsman*). 2 (foll. by *on*) much attracted by; fond of or enthusiastic about. 3 (of the senses) sharp; highly sensitive. 4 intellectually acute. 5 **a** having a sharp edge or point. **b** (of an edge etc.) sharp. 6 (of a sound, light, etc.) penetrating, vivid, strong. 7 (of a wind, frost, etc.) piercingly cold. 8 (of a pain etc.) acute, bitter. 9 Brit. (of a price) competitive. 10 *colloq.* excellent. □□ **keenly** adv. **keenness** n. [OE *cēne* f. Gmc]

keen[2] /kiːn/ n. & v. — n. an Irish funeral song accompanied with wailing. — v. 1 *intr.* utter the keen. 2 *tr.* bewail (a person) in this way. 3 *tr.* utter in a wailing tone. □□ **keener** n. [Ir. *caoine* f. *caoinim* wail]

Keene /kiːn/, Charles Samuel (1823–91), English caricaturist, self-taught and noted for his spontaneity of execution and subtle characterizations. He was associated with the weekly journal *Punch* from 1851.

keep /kiːp/ v. & n. — v. (*past* and *past part.* **kept** /kept/) 1 *tr.* have continuous charge of; retain possession of. 2 *tr.* (foll. by *for*) retain or reserve for a future occasion or time (*will keep it for tomorrow*). 3 *tr.* & *intr.* retain or remain in a specified condition, position, course, etc. (*keep cool; keep off the grass; keep them happy*). 4 *tr.* put or store in a regular place (*knives are kept in this drawer*). 5 *tr.* (foll. by *from*) cause to avoid or abstain from something (*will keep you from going too fast*). 6 *tr.* detain; cause to be late (*what kept you?*). 7 *tr.* **a** observe or pay due regard to (a law, custom, etc.) (*keep one's word*). **b** honour or fulfil (a commitment, undertaking, etc.). **c** respect the commitment implied by (a secret etc.). **d** act fittingly on the occasion of (*keep the sabbath*). 8 *tr.* own and look after (animals) for amusement or profit (*keeps bees*). 9 *tr.* **a** provide for the sustenance of (a person, family, etc.). **b** (foll. by *in*) maintain (a person) with a supply of. 10 *tr.* carry on; manage (a shop, business, etc.). 11 **a** *tr.* maintain (accounts, a diary, etc.) by making the requisite entries. **b** *tr.* maintain (a house) in proper order. 12 *tr.* have (a commodity) regularly on sale (*do you keep buttons?*). 13 *tr.* guard or protect (a person or place, a goal in football, etc.). 14 *tr.* preserve in being; continue to have (*keep order*). 15 *intr.* (foll. by verbal noun) continue or do repeatedly or habitually (*why do you keep saying that?*). 16 *tr.* continue to follow (a way or course). 17 *intr.* **a** (esp. of perishable commodities) remain in good condition. **b** (of news or information etc.) admit of being withheld for a time. 18 *tr.* remain in (one's bed, room, house, etc.). 19 *tr.* retain one's place in (a seat or saddle, one's ground, etc.) against opposition or difficulty. 20 *tr.* maintain (a person) in return for sexual favours (*a kept woman*). — n. 1 maintenance or the essentials for this (esp. food) (*hardly earn your keep*). 2 charge or control (*is in your keep*). 3 *hist.* a tower or stronghold. □ **for keeps** *colloq.* (esp. of something received or won) permanently, indefinitely. **how are you keeping?** how are you? **keep at** persist or cause to persist with. **keep away** (often foll. by *from*) 1 avoid being near. 2 prevent from being near. **keep back** 1 remain or keep at a distance. 2 retard the progress of. 3 conceal; decline to disclose. 4 retain, withhold (*kept back £50*). **keep one's balance** 1 remain stable; avoid falling. 2 retain one's composure. **keep down** 1 hold in subjection. 2 keep low in amount. 3 lie low; stay hidden. 4 manage not to vomit (food eaten). **keep one's feet** manage not to fall. **keep-fit** regular exercises to promote personal fitness and health. **keep one's hair on** see HAIR. **keep one's hand in** see HAND. **keep in** 1 confine or restrain (one's feelings etc.). 2 remain or confine indoors. 3 keep (a fire) burning. **keep in with** remain on good terms with. **keep off** 1 stay or cause to stay away from. 2 ward off; avert. 3 abstain from. 4 avoid (a subject) (*let's keep off religion*). **keep on** 1 continue to do something; do continually (*kept on* *laughing*). **2** continue to use or employ. **3** (foll. by *at*) pester or harass. **keep out 1** keep or remain outside. **2** exclude. **keep state 1** maintain one's dignity. **2** be difficult of access. **keep to 1** adhere to (a course, schedule, etc.). **2** observe (a promise). **3** confine oneself to. **keep to oneself 1** avoid contact with others. **2** refuse to disclose or share. **keep together** remain or keep in harmony. **keep track of** see TRACK[1]. **keep under** hold in subjection. **keep up 1** maintain (progress etc.). **2** prevent (prices, one's spirits, etc.) from sinking. **3** keep in repair, in an efficient or proper state, etc. **4** carry on (a correspondence etc.). **5** prevent (a person) from going to bed, esp. when late. **6** (often foll. by *with*) manage not to fall behind. **keep up with the Joneses** strive to compete socially with one's neighbours. **keep one's word** see WORD. □□ **keepable** *adj.* [OE *cēpan*, of unkn. orig.]

keeper /ˈkiːpə(r)/ *n.* **1** a person who keeps or looks after something or someone. **2** a custodian of a museum, art gallery, forest, etc. **3 a** = GAMEKEEPER. **b** a person in charge of animals in a zoo. **4 a** = *wicket-keeper*. **b** = GOALKEEPER. **5** a fruit etc. that remains in good condition. **6** a bar of soft iron across the poles of a horseshoe magnet to maintain its strength. **7 a** a plain ring to preserve a hole in a pierced ear lobe; a sleeper. **b** a ring worn to guard against the loss of a more valuable one.

keeping /ˈkiːpɪŋ/ *n.* **1** custody, charge (*in safe keeping*). **2** agreement, harmony (esp. *in* or *out of keeping*).

keepsake /ˈkiːpseɪk/ *n.* a thing kept for the sake of or in remembrance of the giver.

keeshond /ˈkeɪshɒnd/ *n.* **1** a dog of a Dutch breed with long thick hair like a large Pomeranian. **2** this breed. [Du.]

kef /kef/ *n.* (also **kif** /kɪf/) **1** a drowsy state induced by marijuana etc. **2** the enjoyment of idleness. **3** a substance smoked to produce kef. [Arab. *kayf* enjoyment, well-being]

Kefallinía see CEPHALONIA.

keffiyeh /keˈfiːjeɪ/ *n.* (also **kaffiyeh**) a Bedouin Arab's kerchief worn as a head-dress. [Arab. *keffiya, kūfiyya*, perh. f. LL *cofea* COIF]

Keflavik /ˈkeflə,viːk/ a fishing-port in SW Iceland; pop. (1987) 7,133. Iceland's international airport is located nearby.

keg /keg/ *n.* a small barrel, usu. of less than 10 gallons or (in the US) 30 gallons. □ **keg beer** beer supplied from a sealed metal container. [ME *cag* f. ON *kaggi*, of unkn. orig.]

keister /ˈkiːstə(r), ˈkaɪstə(r)/ *n. US sl.* **1** the buttocks. **2** a suitcase, satchel, handbag, etc. [orig. unkn.]

Kekulé /ˈkekjʊˌleɪ/, Friedrich August, von Stradonitz (1829–96), German chemist, one of the founders of structural organic chemistry. His training as an architect may have aided him in visualizing the structure of molecules. He concentrated on carbon compounds and in 1858 suggested that carbon was quadrivalent, that is that each carbon atom could combine with four other atoms; furthermore, they could combine with other carbon atoms and form complex chains. However, Kekulé is best known for discovering the ring structure of benzene, which came to him in a waking dream as a chain of six carbon atoms whirling round, like a snake biting its own tail. A new generation of chemists could now assign such structures to other organic compounds.

Kelantan /keˈlænt(ə)n/ a State of Malaysia, in the north of the Malay peninsula; pop. (1980) 893,750; capital, Kota Baharu.

Keller /ˈkelə(r)/, Helen Adams (1880–1968), American author who, although she became blind and deaf before she was two years old, graduated in 1904 and became a prominent social reformer, raising money for the education of handicapped people. Her books include *The Story of My Life* (1902).

Kellogg Pact /ˈkelɒg/ a treaty renouncing war as an instrument of national policy, signed in Paris in 1928 by representatives of 15 nations. [F. B. *Kellogg* (d. 1937), US Secretary of State 1924–9]

Kells /kelz/, **Book of** an illuminated manuscript of the gospels, perhaps made by Irish monks in Iona in the 8th or early 9th c., now kept at Trinity College, Dublin. [*Kells*, town in Co. Meath, Ireland, where formerly kept]

Kelly[1] /ˈkelɪ/, Edward ('Noel') (1855–80), Australian bushranger, leader of a band of desperadoes consisting of himself, his brother Dan, and two confederates. Their exploits, which

included horse and cattle stealing and bank raids, created great public excitement and a legend of their reckless courage, giving rise to the phrase 'as game as Ned Kelly'. Outlawed in NE Victoria in 1878, they came to a dramatic end in 1880 with a shoot-out and the eventual hanging of Ned Kelly.

Kelly[2] /ˈkelɪ/, Grace Patricia (1928–82), American film actress, whose films include *High Noon* (1952) and *The Swan* (1956). She retired from films on her marriage to Prince Rainier III of Monaco in 1956.

keloid /ˈkiːlɔɪd/ *n.* fibrous tissue formed at the site of a scar or injury. [Gk *khēlē* claw + -OID]

kelp /kelp/ *n.* **1** any of several large broad-fronded brown seaweeds esp. of the genus *Laminaria*, suitable for use as manure. **2** the calcined ashes of seaweed formerly used in glass-making and soap manufacture because of their high content of sodium, potassium, and magnesium salts. [ME *culp(e)*, of unkn. orig.]

kelpie /ˈkelpɪ/ *n. Sc.* **1** a water-spirit, usu. in the form of a horse, reputed to delight in the drowning of travellers etc. **2** an Australian sheepdog orig. bred from a Scottish collie. [18th c.: orig. unkn.]

kelson var. of KEELSON.

Kelt var. of CELT.

kelt /kelt/ *n.* a salmon or sea trout after spawning. [ME: orig. unkn.]

kelter var. of KILTER.

Kelvin /ˈkelvɪn/, William Thomson, 1st Baron (1824–1907), British physicist, born in Belfast, who was appointed professor of natural philosophy at Glasgow in 1846 and did not retire until 1895. He worked on a great range of scientific problems. Amongst his greatest successes was his formulation in 1850 of the second law of thermodynamics (according to which heat cannot pass from a hotter to a colder body without work being done, in other words, perpetual motion is an impossibility). He introduced an absolute temperature scale, the unit of which is named the kelvin in his honour. His concept of an electromagnetic field was derived from his own extensive researches into magnetism and electricity and those of Faraday before him, and in turn influenced Maxwell's electromagnetic theory of light, which Kelvin never accepted. He became best known to the general public for his involvement in the laying of the first Atlantic cable, for which he invented the siphon recorder and a sensitive mirror galvanometer. Indeed, he devised many scientific instruments, including electrometers, galvanometers, deep-sea sounding gear, a mariner's compass, and an electric clock. His calculation of the age of the earth in 1862, based on its rate of cooling, was a gross underestimate and was controversial, but showed that physics (or geophysics) could be useful in helping to establish a geological time-scale. He is buried in Westminster Abbey.

kelvin /ˈkelvɪn/ *n.* the SI unit of thermodynamic temperature, the fraction 1/273.16 of the thermodynamic temperature of the triple point of water, adopted in 1954 and 1967 for international use. It is equal in magnitude to the degree celsius. ¶ Abbr.: **K**. □ **Kelvin scale** a scale of temperature with absolute zero as zero. [Lord *Kelvin*, Brit. physicist d. 1907]

Kemal Pasha /ˌkeməl ˈpɑːʃə/ see ATATÜRK.

Kemble[1] /ˈkemb(ə)l/, Frances Anne ('Fanny') (1809–93), English actress, daughter of Charles Kemble. She was a success in both comedy and tragedy. As well as playing a number of Shakespearian roles (including Juliet and Portia) she revived a number of tragic parts formerly associated with her aunt, Mrs Siddons.

Kemble[2] /ˈkemb(ə)l/, John Philip (1757–1823), English actor, brother of Mrs Siddons. He was at his best in heavy dramatic parts, including Wolsey in Shakespeare's *Henry VIII*, Brutus in *Julius Caesar*, and Coriolanus. He was successively manager of Drury Lane and Coven Garden theatres. His younger brothers Stephen (1758–1822) and Charles (1775–1854) were also on the stage.

Kemerovo /ˈkemərəvə/ an industrial city of the Soviet Union, situated to the east of Novosibirsk in central Siberia; pop. (est. 1987) 520,000.

w we z zoo ʃ she ʒ decision θ thin ð this ŋ ring x loch tʃ chip dʒ jar (*see over for vowels*)

kemp /kemp/ n. coarse hair in wool. □□ **kempy** adj. [ME f. ON kampr beard, whisker]

kempt /kempt/ adj. combed; neatly kept. [past part. of (now dial.) kemb COMB v. f. OE cemban f. Gmc]

ken /ken/ n. & v. —n. range of sight or knowledge (it's beyond my ken). —v.tr. (**kenning**; past and past part. **kenned** or **kent**) Sc. & N.Engl. **1** recognize at sight. **2** know. [OE cennan f. Gmc]

kendo /ˈkendəʊ/ n. the Japanese sport of fencing with two-handed bamboo swords. Its origins go back more than 1,500 years, developing from the need for non-lethal practice in the art of swordsmanship which was an essential skill for the samurai of medieval Japan, and changing from training for battle to a sport. [Jap., = sword-way]

Kennedy /ˈkenədɪ/, John Fitzgerald (1917–63), 35th President of the US, 1961–3. A national war hero during the Second World War, Kennedy served successively as Congressman and Senator for Massachusetts between 1947 and 1960 before becoming at 43 the youngest man (and also the first Catholic) to be elected President. Kennedy gained a popular reputation as an advocate of civil rights and as an opponent of Communist Russia (particularly during the Cuban Missile Crisis of 1962), but was assassinated in Dallas, Texas, in November 1963.

kennel /ˈken(ə)l/ n. & v. —n. **1** a small shelter for a dog. **2** (in pl.) a breeding or boarding establishment for dogs. **3** a mean dwelling. —v. (**kennelled, kennelling**; US **kenneled, kenneling**) **1** tr. put into or keep in a kennel. **2** intr. live in or go to a kennel. [ME f. OF chenil f. med.L canile (unrecorded) f. L canis dog]

Kenneth /ˈkenɪθ/ the name of two Scottish kings, Kenneth I MacAlpin (d. c.860), traditional founder of the kingdom of Scotland, and Kenneth II (d. 995).

kenning /ˈkenɪŋ/ n. a compound expression in Old English and Old Norse poetry, e.g. oar-steed = ship. [ME, = 'teaching' etc. f. KEN]

kenosis /kɪˈnəʊsɪs/ n. Theol. the renunciation of the divine nature, at least in part, by Christ in the Incarnation. □□ **kenotic** /-ˈnɒtɪk/ adj. [Gk. kenōsis f. kenoō to empty f. kenos empty]

kenspeckle /ˈkenˌspek(ə)l/ adj. Sc. conspicuous. [kenspeck of Scand. orig.: rel. to KEN]

Kent[1] /kent/ a county of SE England; pop. (1981) 1,484,300; county town, Maidstone.

Kent[2] /kent/, William (1685–1748), English architect, landscape designer, and decorative painter. Assisted by local patrons he travelled to Italy in 1709, where he studied and became a guide and agent for English noblemen on tour. He met Lord Burlington, returned to England with him in 1719, and enjoyed his friendship and patronage for the rest of his life. With Burlington he promoted the development of a neo-Palladian style which reinterpreted the classicism of the 16th-c. architect Andrea Palladio. His major works include Lord Leicester's Holkham Hall, garden designs for Burlington's own Chiswick villa, Rousham, and Stowe. Kent's principles of landscape design broke down the formality of existing taste, opening the way for the innovations of Capability Brown.

kent past and past part. of KEN.

Kentish /ˈkentɪʃ/ adj. of Kent in England. □ **Kentish fire** Brit. a prolonged volley of rhythmic applause or a demonstration of dissent. [OE Centisc f. Cent f. L Cantium]

kentledge /ˈkentlɪdʒ/ n. Naut. pig-iron etc. used as permanent ballast. [F quintelage ballast, with assim. to kentle obs. var. of QUINTAL]

Kentucky /kenˈtʌkɪ/ a State in the central south-eastern US; pop. (est. 1985) 3,660,300; capital, Frankfort. □ **Kentucky Derby** an annual horse-race for 3-year-olds at Louisville, Kentucky, founded in 1875.

Kenya /ˈkenjə/ a country in East Africa, a member State of the Commonwealth, bisected by the equator and with a coastline on the Indian Ocean; pop. (est. 1988) 23,341,600; official language, Swahili (also English); capital, Nairobi. Largely populated by Bantu peoples, Kenya was not exposed to European influence until the arrival of the British in the late 19th c. After the opening up of the interior it became a Crown Colony in 1920

and attracted a large number of white settlers. The demands these made on land caused increasingly severe problems with the native population and resulted in the Mau Mau rebellion of the 1950s. The admission of native Kenyans into government eventually defused the situation and the country was granted independence in 1963, becoming a republic in 1964 and a one-party State in 1982; in 1990 there were demands for a multi-party system. The economy is based on agriculture, the tea crop being particularly important. Kenya is now one of the most stable and prosperous of African nations, wealth being largely concentrated in the temperate agricultural south. Tourism is also important, the main attraction being the wildlife reserves. □□ **Kenyan** adj. & n.

Kenya, Mount the second-highest mountain in Africa, rising to a height of 5,200 m (17,058 ft) in central Kenya, just south of the equator. The country Kenya is named after it.

Kenyatta /kenˈjætə/, Jomo (c.1894–1978), Kenyan statesman. After spending a long period in prison through involvement with the Mau Mau, Kenyatta led his country to independence in 1963 and served as its first President from 1964 until his death.

kepi /ˈkepɪ, ˈkeɪpɪ/ n. (pl. **kepis**) a French military cap with a horizontal peak. [F képi f. Swiss G käppi dimin. of kappe cap]

Kepler /ˈkeplə(r)/, Johannes (1571–1630), German astronomer and court mathematician to Rudolph II of Prague. He studied theology at Tübingen, where he became acquainted with the Copernican system, and fled to Prague after the expulsion of the Protestants, becoming Tycho Brahe's assistant and, later, successor. His studies of the positions of Mars led to the formulation of his first two laws of motion, which recognized the elliptical orbits of the planets about the sun. In 1620, his book Harmonices Mundi expounded the Third Law of planetary dynamics, relating the distances of the planets from the sun to their orbital periods. Although his work accounted concisely and mathematically for the detailed planetary observations of Tycho, and his analysis foreshadowed the general application of the scientific method to astronomy, Kepler remained influenced by the astrological notions of his day, and sought an inner relationship between the planets that would express the 'music of the spheres'. His exposition of the ratios between planetary orbits as just those which would allow the crystal spheres which carried the planets to accommodate the five perfect Platonic solids is but one example of the medieval approach to cosmology which he retained.

kept past and past part. of KEEP.

Kerala /ˈkerələ/ a State in SW India, constituted in 1956; pop. (1981) 25,403,200; capital, Trivandrum. □□ **Keralite** /-laɪt/ adj. & n.

keratin /ˈkerətɪn/ n. a fibrous protein which occurs in hair, feathers, hooves, claws, horns, etc. [Gk keras keratos horn + -IN]

keratinize /ˈkerətɪˌnaɪz/ v.tr. & intr. (also **-ise**) cover or become covered with a deposit of keratin. □□ **keratinization** /-ˈzeɪʃ(ə)n/ n.

keratose /ˈkerəˌtəʊs/ adj. (of sponge) composed of a horny substance. [Gk keras keratos horn + -OSE[1]]

kerb /kɜːb/ n. Brit. a stone edging to a pavement or raised path. □ **kerb-crawler** a person who indulges in kerb-crawling. **kerb-crawling** the practice of driving slowly along the edge of a road, soliciting passers-by. **kerb drill** precautions, esp. looking to right and left, before crossing a road. [var. of CURB]

kerbstone /ˈkɜːbstəʊn/ n. each of a series of stones forming a kerb.

kerchief /ˈkɜːtʃiːf, -tʃɪf/ n. **1** a cloth used to cover the head. **2** poet. a handkerchief. □□ **kerchiefed** adj. [ME curchef f. AF courchef, OF couvrechief f. couvrir COVER + CHIEF head]

kerf /kɜːf/ n. **1** a slit made by cutting, esp. with a saw. **2** the cut end of a felled tree. [OE cyrf f. Gmc (as CARVE)]

kerfuffle /kəˈfʌf(ə)l/ n. esp. Brit. colloq. a fuss or commotion. [Sc. curfuffle f. fuffle to disorder: imit.]

Kerguelen Islands /kɜːˈɡeɪlən/ a group of virtually uninhabited islands in the southern Indian Ocean, comprising the island of Kerguelen and some 300 small islets, forming part of French Southern and Antarctic Territories. They are named after the Breton navigator Yves-Joseph de Kerguélen-Trémarec, who discovered them in 1772.

Kérkira see CORFU.

Kerkrade /ˈkɜːkrɑːdə/ a mining town of The Netherlands, situated on the German border 30 km (19 miles) east of Maastricht; pop. (1987) 53,000. An international music competition is held here every four years.

Kermadec Islands /kɜːˈmædək/ a group of islands in the SW Pacific, north of New Zealand, administered by New Zealand since 1887. The largest of the group is Raoul or Sunday Island.

kermes /ˈkɜːmɪz/ n. **1** the female of a bug, *Kermes ilicis*, with a berry-like appearance. **2** (in full **kermes oak**) an evergreen oak, *Quercus coccifera*, of S. Europe and N. Africa, on which this insect feeds. **3** a red dye made from the dried bodies of these insects. **4** (in full **kermes mineral**) a bright red hydrous trisulphide of antimony. [F *kermès* f. Arab. & Pers. *ḳirmiz*: rel. to CRIMSON]

kermis /ˈkɜːmɪs/ n. **1** a periodical country fair, esp. in The Netherlands. **2** *US* a charity bazaar. [Du., orig. = mass on the anniversary of the dedication of a church, when yearly fair was held: f. *kerk* formed as CHURCH + *mis*, *misse* MASS²]

Kern /kɜːn/, Jerome (1885–1945), American composer of popular melodies and songs, several of which were featured in films, including 'Ol' Man River' (first sung by Paul Robeson) and 'Smoke gets in your Eyes'.

kern¹ /kɜːn/ n. *Printing* the part of a metal type projecting beyond its body or shank. □□ **kerned** adj. [perh. f. F *carne* corner f. OF *charne* f. L *cardo cardinis* hinge]

kern² /kɜːn/ n. (also **kerne**) **1** *hist.* a light-armed Irish foot-soldier. **2** a peasant; a boor. [ME f. Ir. *ceithern*]

kernel /ˈkɜːn(ə)l/ n. **1** a central, softer, usu. edible part within a hard shell of a nut, fruit stone, seed, etc. **2** the whole seed of a cereal. **3** the nucleus or essential part of anything. [OE *cyrnel*, dimin. of CORN¹]

kerosine /ˈkɛrəˌsiːn/ n. (also **kerosene**) esp. *US* a fuel oil suitable for use in jet engines and domestic heating boilers; paraffin oil. [Gk *kēros* wax + -ENE]

Kerouac /ˈkɛruˌæk/, Jack (Jean-Louis Lefris de Kérouac, 1922–69), American novelist and poet, born of French-Canadian parents. He is famous for his semi-autobiographical novel *On the Road* (1957), which describes the Wanderings across America, casual friendships, and affairs of a young writer and his friend and hero.

Kerry /ˈkɛrɪ/ a county of SW Ireland, in the province of Munster; pop. (est. 1986) 123,900; capital, Tralee. —n. (pl. **-ies**) **1** an animal of a breed of small black dairy cattle. **2** this breed. □ **Kerry blue 1** a terrier of a breed with a silky blue-grey coat. **2** this breed.

kersey /ˈkɜːzɪ/ n. (pl. **-eys**) **1** a kind of coarse narrow cloth woven from long wool, usu. ribbed. **2** a variety of this. [ME, prob. f. *Kersey* in Suffolk]

kerseymere /ˈkɜːzɪmɪə(r)/ n. a twilled fine woollen cloth. [alt. of *cassimere*, var. of CASHMERE, assim. to KERSEY]

Kesey /ˈkiːsɪ/, Ken (1935–), American novelist. His best-known novel *One Flew over the Cuckoo's Nest* (1962), which was made into a successful film, is based on his experiences in a mental hospital.

keskidee var. of KISKADEE.

kestrel /ˈkɛstr(ə)l/ n. any small falcon, esp. *Falco tinnunculus*, which hovers whilst searching for its prey. [ME *castrell*, perh. f. F dial. *casserelle*, F *créc(er)elle*, perh. imit. of its cry]

ketch /kɛtʃ/ n. a two-masted fore-and-aft rigged sailing-boat with a mizen-mast stepped forward of the rudder and smaller than its foremast. [ME *catche*, prob. f. CATCH]

ketchup /ˈkɛtʃʌp/ n. (also **catchup** /ˈkætʃʌp/) a spicy sauce made from tomatoes, mushrooms, vinegar, etc., used as a condiment. [Chin. dial. *kōechiap* pickled-fish brine]

ketone /ˈkiːtəʊn/ n. any of a class of organic compounds in which two hydrocarbon groups are linked by a carbonyl group, e.g. propanone (acetone). □ **ketone body** *Biochem.* any of several ketones produced in the body during the metabolism of fats. □□ **ketonic** /kɪˈtɒnɪk/ adj. [G *Keton* alt. of *Aketon* ACETONE]

ketonuria /ˌkiːtəʊˈnjʊərɪə/ n. the excretion of abnormally large amounts of ketone bodies in the urine.

ketosis /kɪˈtəʊsɪs/ n. a condition characterized by raised levels of ketone bodies in the body, associated with fat metabolism and diabetes. □□ **ketotic** /-ˈtɒtɪk/ adj.

Kettering /ˈkɛtərɪŋ/, Charles Franklin (1876–1958), American engineer responsible for many significant developments in automobile engineering, beginning with the electric starter (1912) which opened the way to women drivers. He joined the General Motors Corporation in 1919 and was leader of research there until he retired in 1947. During this time he led the team which discovered tetra-ethyl lead as a powerful antiknock agent and went on to define the 'octane number' method of rating the antiknock properties of fuels. After an unsuccessful attempt to produce air-cooled engines he turned to the development of 2-stroke diesel engines which came into widespread use for railway locomotives and long-distance road coaches. He was also responsible for the development first of synchromesh gearboxes then of fully-automatic transmissions, also of power steering. For the refrigerator division he was involved in the development of a range of safe refrigerants.

kettle /ˈkɛt(ə)l/ n. a vessel, usu. of metal with a lid, spout, and handle, for boiling water in. □ **kettle hole** a depression in the ground in a glaciated area. **a pretty kettle of fish** an awkward state of affairs. □□ **kettleful** n. (pl. **-fuls**). [ME f. ON *ketill* ult. f. L *catillus* dimin. of *catinus* deep food-vessel]

kettledrum /ˈkɛt(ə)lˌdrʌm/ n. a large drum shaped like a bowl with a membrane adjustable for tension (and so pitch) stretched across. □□ **kettledrummer** n.

keV abbr. kilo-electronvolt.

Kevlar /ˈkɛvlə(r)/ n. propr. a synthetic fibre of high tensile strength used esp. as a reinforcing agent in the manufacture of rubber products, e.g. tyres.

Kew Gardens /kjuː/ the Royal Botanic Gardens at Kew near Richmond upon Thames, London. Originally the garden of Kew House, it was developed as a botanic garden by the mother of George III from 1761, with the aid of Sir Joseph Banks, and was presented to the nation in 1841.

kewpie /ˈkjuːpɪ/ n. a small chubby doll with wings and a curl or topknot. [CUPID + -IE]

key¹ /kiː/ n. & v. —n. (pl. **keys**) **1** an instrument, usu. of metal, for moving the bolt of a lock forwards or backwards to lock or unlock. **2** a similar implement for operating a switch in the form of a lock. **3** an instrument for grasping screws, pegs, nuts, etc., esp. one for winding a clock etc. **4** a lever depressed by the finger in playing the organ, piano, flute, concertina, etc. **5** (often in *pl.*) each of several buttons for operating a typewriter, word processor, or computer terminal, etc. **6** what gives or precludes the opportunity for or access to something. **7** (*attrib.*) essential; of vital importance (*the key element in the problem*). **8** a place that by its position gives control of a sea, territory, etc. **9 a** a solution or explanation. **b** a word or system for solving a cipher or code. **c** an explanatory list of symbols used in a map, table, etc. **d** a book of solutions to mathematical problems etc. **e** a literal translation of a book written in a foreign language. **f** the first move in a chess-problem solution. **10** *Mus.* a system of notes definitely related to each other, based on a particular note, and predominating in a piece of music (*a study in the key of C major*). **11** a tone or style of thought or expression. **12** a piece of wood or metal inserted between others to secure them. **13** the part of a first coat of wall plaster that passes between the laths and so secures the rest. **14** the roughness of a surface, helping the adhesion of plaster etc. **15** the samara of a sycamore etc. **16** a mechanical device for making or breaking an electric circuit, e.g. in telegraphy. —v.tr. (**keys, keyed**) **1** (foll. by *in, on,* etc.) fasten with a pin, wedge, bolt, etc. **2** (often foll. by *in*) enter (data) by means of a keyboard. **3** roughen (a surface) to help the adhesion of plaster etc. **4** (foll. by *to*) align or link (one thing to another). **5** regulate the pitch of the strings of (a violin etc.). **6** word (an advertisement in a particular periodical) so that answers to it can be identified (usu. by varying the form of address given). □ **key industry** an industry essential to the carrying on of others, e.g. coal-mining, dyeing. **key map** a map in bare outline, to simplify the use of a full map. **key money** *Brit.* a payment demanded from an incoming tenant for the provision of a key to the premises. **key-ring** a ring for keeping keys on. **key signature** *Mus.* any of several combinations of sharps or flats after the clef at the beginning of each staff indicating the key of a composition. **key up** (often foll. by *to*, or *to* + infin.) make (a person) nervous or tense; excite. □□ **keyer** *n.* **keyless** *adj.* [OE *cǽg*, of unkn. orig.]

key² /kiː/ *n.* a low-lying island or reef, esp. in the W. Indies (cf. CAY). [Sp. *cayo* shoal, reef, infl. by QUAY]

keyboard /ˈkiːbɔːd/ *n.* & *v.* —*n.* a set of keys on a typewriter, computer, piano, etc. —*v.tr.* enter (data) by means of a keyboard. □□ **keyboarder** *n.*

keyhole /ˈkiːhəʊl/ *n.* a hole by which a key is put into a lock.

Keynes /keɪnz/, John Maynard, 1st Baron (1883–1946), English economist, advocate of the planned economy and of the view that full employment is not a natural condition and requires positive intervention by the State, with government spending in excess of revenue by borrowing to finance the resultant deficit. Keynes served as an adviser to the Treasury during both World Wars and represented that department at the Versailles Peace Conference, subsequently becoming one of the most influential critics of the Treaty. He was an outspoken opponent of the orthodox economic policies of the British government during the interwar depression, and his theories influenced Roosevelt's decision to introduce the American 'New Deal'. His most important works include *The Economic Consequences of the Peace* (1919), *A Treatise on Money* (1930), and *The General Theory of Employment, Interest and Money* (1936). □□ **Keynesian** *adj.* & *n.* **Keynesianism** *n.*

keynote /ˈkiːnəʊt/ *n.* **1** a prevailing tone or idea (*the keynote of the whole occasion*). **2** (*attrib.*) intended to set the prevailing tone at a meeting or conference (*keynote address*). **3** *Mus.* the note on which a key is based.

keypad /ˈkiːpæd/ *n.* a miniature keyboard or set of buttons for operating a portable electronic device, telephone, etc.

keypunch /ˈkiːpʌntʃ/ *n.* & *v.* —*n.* a device for transferring data by means of punched holes or notches on a series of cards or paper tape. —*v.tr.* transfer (data) by means of a keypunch. □□ **keypuncher** *n.*

Keys, House of see HOUSE OF KEYS.

keystone /ˈkiːstəʊn/ *n.* **1** the central principle of a system, policy, etc., on which all the rest depends. **2** a central stone at the summit of an arch locking the whole together.

keystroke /ˈkiːstrəʊk/ *n.* a single depression of a key on a keyboard, esp. as a measure of work.

keyway /ˈkiːweɪ/ *n.* a slot for receiving a machined key.

keyword /ˈkiːwɜːd/ *n.* **1** the key to a cipher etc. **2 a** a word of great significance. **b** a significant word used in indexing.

KG *abbr.* (in the UK) Knight of the Order of the Garter.

kg *abbr.* kilogram(s).

KGB /ˌkeɪdʒiːˈbiː/ *n.* the Soviet secret police organization created upon Stalin's death (1953) to take over State security, with responsibility for external espionage, internal counter-intelligence, and internal 'crimes against the State'. Its most famous chairman has been Yuri Andropov (1967–82), who was Soviet leader 1982–4. [Russ., abbr. of *Komitet gosudarstvennoi bezopasnosti* Committee of State Security]

Kgs. *abbr.* Kings (Old Testament).

Khabarovsk /ˌkæbəˈrɒfsk/ **1** a territory of the Russian Soviet republic, in eastern Siberia; pop. (1985) 1,728,000. **2** its capital city; pop. (1983) 560,000.

khaddar /ˈkædə(r)/ *n.* Indian homespun cloth. [Hindi]

khaki /ˈkɑːkɪ/ *adj.* & *n.* —*adj.* dust-coloured; dull brownish-yellow. —*n.* (*pl.* **khakis**) **1** khaki fabric of twilled cotton or wool, used esp. in military dress. **2** the dull brownish-yellow colour of this. [Urdu *k̲āk̲ī* dust-coloured f. *k̲āk* dust]

khalasi /kəˈlæsɪ/ *n.* (*pl.* **khalasis**) a native Indian servant or labourer, esp. one employed as a seaman. [Hind.]

Khalkís see CHALCIS.

Khama /ˈkɑːmə/, Sir Seretse (1921–80), Botswana statesman,

the first President of his country when it became independent in 1966. He was heir to the chieftainship of the ruling tribe in Bechuanaland (now Botswana), but was banished because of opposition to his marriage (1948) to an Englishwoman. Renouncing his chieftainship he returned with his wife in 1956, and formed a political party which won a landslide victory in 1965 in the first elections to be held on the basis of universal suffrage; he held office first as Prime Minister, then as President, until his death. A strong believer in multiracial democracy, he strengthened the economy of Botswana and achieved universal free education.

Khambat, Gulf of see CAMBAY, GULF OF.

khamsin /ˈkæmsɪn/ *n.* (also **hamsin** /ˈhæ-/) an oppressive hot south or south-east wind occurring in Egypt for about 50 days in March, April, and May. [Arab. *k̲amsīn* f. *k̲amsūn* fifty]

khan¹ /kɑːn, kæn/ *n.* **1** a title given to rulers and officials in Central Asia, Afghanistan, etc. **2** *hist.* **a** the supreme ruler of the Turkish, Tartar, and Mongol tribes. **b** the emperor of China in the Middle Ages. □□ **khanate** *n.* [Turki *k̲ān* lord]

khan² /kɑːn, kæn/ *n.* a caravanserai. [Arab. *k̲ān* inn]

Khaniá see CANEA.

Kharg island /kɑːg/ a small island at the head of the Persian Gulf, site of Iran's principal deep-water oil terminal.

Kharkov /ˈkɑːkɒf/ an industrial city of Ukraine, situated to the east of Kiev in the Donets coal basin; pop. (est. 1987) 1,587,000.

Khartoum /kɑːˈtuːm/ the capital of Sudan, situated at the junction of the Blue Nile and the White Nile; pop. (1983) 476,200.

Khedive /kɪˈdiːv/ *n. hist.* the title of the viceroy of Egypt under Turkish rule 1867–1914. □□ **Khedival** *adj.* **Khedivial** *adj.* [F *khédive*, ult. f. Pers. *k̲adīv* prince]

Khios see CHIOS.

Khmer /kmeə(r)/ *n.* **1** a native of the ancient kingdom of Khmer in SE Asia, which reached the peak of its power in the 11th c., ruling over the entire Mekong valley from the capital at Angkor, and was destroyed by Siamese conquests in the 12th and 14th c. **2** the monosyllabic language of this people, belonging to the Mon-Khmer group of the Austro-Asiatic family. The official language of Cambodia, spoken by most of its population (some 6 million people), it is the most important member of the Mon-Khmer group. **3** a native of the Khmer Republic (the official name in 1970–5 of what is now Cambodia). —*adj.* of the Khmers or their language. □ **Khmer Rouge** /ruːʒ/ the Communist guerrilla organization prominent in the wars in the region in the 1960s and 1970s, holding power 1975–9 (see CAMBODIA). [native name]

Khomeini /xɒˈmeɪnɪ/, Ruhollah (1900–89), known as Ayatollah Khomeini, Iranian Shiite Muslim leader who returned to Iran in 1979, after 16 years in exile, and established an overtly Islamic constitution, with strict authoritarian rule, in the revolt against westernization that accompanied the overthrow of the Shah.

Khonsu /ˈkɒnsuː/ *Egyptian Mythol.* a moon god, whose principal cult centre was at Thebes, a member of the Theban triad as the divine son of Amun and Mut. His name means 'he who crosses'.

Khorramshahr /ˌxɔːrəmˈʃɑː(r)/ an oil-port on the Shatt-al-Arab waterway in western Iran, known as Mohammerah until 1924. It was almost totally destroyed during the Iran-Iraq war of 1980–8.

Khrushchev /ˈkrʊʃtʃɒf/, Nikita Sergeevich (1894–1971), Soviet statesman. The first strong leader to emerge in the USSR after the death of Stalin, Khrushchev became leader after succeeding Bulganin as Premier in 1958, having already played a prominent part in the 'de-Stalinization' programme. The most flamboyant of Soviet leaders, Khrushchev exacerbated the poor state of relations with the West and the US in particular, but was eventually forced to back down in the Cuban missile crisis of 1962. He was deposed two years later by Kosygin and Brezhnev.

Khufu /ˈkuːfuː/ (also known as *Cheops*, *c.*2551–2528 BC) a pharaoh of the 4th Dynasty in ancient Egypt, who commissioned the building of the great pyramid at Giza.

Khulna /ˈkuːlnə/ an industrial city of Bangladesh, on the Ganges delta; pop. (1981) 646,350.

Khunerjab Pass /ˈkʌnəˌjɑːb/ a high-altitude pass through the Himalayas, on the Karakoram highway linking China and Pakistan.

Khyber Pass /ˈkaɪbə(r)/ the major mountain pass on the border between northern Pakistan and Afghanistan. The pass was for long of great commercial and strategic importance, the route by which successive invaders entered India, and was garrisoned by the British intermittently between 1839 and 1947.

kHz abbr. kilohertz.

kiang /kɪˈæŋ/ n. a wild Tibetan ass, Equus hemionus kiang, with a thick furry coat. [Tibetan kyang]

Kiangsu see JIANGSU.

kibble¹ /ˈkɪb(ə)l/ v.tr. grind coarsely. [18th c.: orig. unkn.]

kibble² /ˈkɪb(ə)l/ n. Brit. an iron hoisting-bucket used in mines. [G Kübel (cf. OE cyfel) f. med.L cupellus, corn-measure, dimin. of cuppa cup]

kibbutz /kɪˈbʊts/ n. (pl. **kibbutzim** /-ˈtsiːm/) a communal esp. farming settlement in Israel. [mod.Heb. ḳibbūṣ gathering]

kibbutznik /kɪˈbʊtsnɪk/ n. a member of a kibbutz. [Yiddish (as KIBBUTZ)]

kibe /kaɪb/ n. an ulcerated chilblain, esp. on the heel. [ME, prob. f. Welsh cibi]

kibitka /kɪˈbɪtkə/ n. **1** a type of Russian hooded sledge. **2 a** a Tartar's circular tent, covered with felt. **b** a Tartar household. [Russ. f. Tartar kibitz]

kibitz /ˈkɪbɪts/ v.intr. colloq. act as a kibitzer. [Yiddish f. G kiebitzen (as KIBITZER)]

kibitzer /ˈkɪbɪtsə(r), kɪˈbɪtsə(r)/ n. colloq. **1** an onlooker at cards etc., esp. one who offers unwanted advice. **2** a busybody, a meddler. [Yiddish kibitser f. G Kiebitz lapwing, busybody]

kiblah /ˈkɪblə/ n. (also **qibla**) **1** the direction of the Kaaba (the sacred building at Mecca), to which Muslims turn at prayer. **2** = MIHRAB. [Arab. ḳibla that which is opposite]

kibosh /ˈkaɪbɒʃ/ n. (also **kybosh**) sl. nonsense. □ **put the kibosh on** put an end to; finally dispose of. [19th c.: orig. unkn.]

kick¹ /kɪk/ v. & n. —v. **1** tr. strike or propel forcibly with the foot or hoof etc. **2** intr. (usu. foll. by at, against) **a** strike out with the foot. **b** express annoyance at or dislike of (treatment, a proposal, etc.); rebel against. **3** tr. sl. give up (a habit). **4** tr. (often foll. by out etc.) expel or dismiss forcibly. **5** refl. be annoyed with oneself (I'll kick myself if I'm wrong). **6** tr. Football score (a goal) by a kick. **7** intr. Cricket (of a ball) rise sharply from the pitch. —n. **1 a** a blow with the foot or hoof etc. **b** the delivery of such a blow. **2** colloq. **a** a sharp stimulant effect, esp. of alcohol (has some kick in it; a cocktail with a kick in it). **b** (often in pl.) a pleasurable thrill (did it just for kicks; got a kick out of flying). **3** strength, resilience (have no kick left). **4** colloq. a specified temporary interest or enthusiasm (on a jogging kick). **5** the recoil of a gun when discharged. **6** Brit. Football colloq. a player of specified kicking ability (is a good kick). □ **kick about** (or **around**) colloq. **1 a** drift idly from place to place. **b** be unused or unwanted. **2 a** treat roughly or scornfully. **b** discuss (an idea) unsystematically. **kick against the pricks** see PRICK. **kick the bucket** sl. die. **kick-down** a device for changing gear in a motor vehicle by full depression of the accelerator. **kick one's heels** see HEEL. **kick in 1** knock down (a door etc.) by kicking. **2** esp. US sl. contribute (esp. money); pay one's share. **kick in the pants** (or **teeth**) colloq. a humiliating punishment or set-back. **kick off 1 a** Football begin or resume a match. **b** colloq. begin. **2** remove (shoes etc.) by kicking. **kick-off 1** Football the start or resumption of a match. **2** (in **for a kick-off**) colloq. for a start (that's wrong for a kick-off). **kick over the traces** see TRACE². **kick-pleat** a pleat in a narrow skirt to allow freedom of movement. **kick-turn** a standing turn in skiing. **kick up** (or **kick up a fuss, dust,** etc.) create a disturbance; object or register strong disapproval. **kick up one's heels** frolic. **kick a person upstairs** shelve a person by giving him or her promotion or a title. □□ **kickable** adj. **kicker** n. [ME kike, of unkn. orig.]

kick² /kɪk/ n. an indentation in the bottom of a glass bottle. [19th c.: orig. unkn.]

kickback /ˈkɪkbæk/ n. colloq. **1** the force of a recoil. **2** payment for collaboration, esp. collaboration for profit.

kickshaw /ˈkɪkʃɔː/ n. **1** archaic, usu. derog. a fancy dish in cookery. **2** something elegant but insubstantial; a toy or trinket. [F quelque chose something]

kicksorter /ˈkɪkˌsɔːtə(r)/ n. colloq. a device for analysing electrical pulses according to amplitude.

kickstand /ˈkɪkstænd/ n. a rod attached to a bicycle or motor cycle and kicked into a vertical position to support the vehicle when stationary.

kick-start /ˈkɪkstɑːt/ n. & v. —n. (also **kick-starter**) a device to start the engine of a motor cycle etc. by the downward thrust of a pedal. —v.tr. start (a motor cycle etc.) in this way.

kid¹ /kɪd/ n. & v. —n. **1** a young goat. **2** the leather made from its skin. **3** sl. a child or young person. —v.intr. (**kidded, kidding**) (of a goat) give birth. □ **handle with kid gloves** handle in a gentle, delicate, or gingerly manner. **kid brother** (or **sister**) sl. a younger brother or sister. **kid-glove** (attrib.) dainty or delicate. **kids' stuff** sl. something very simple. [ME kide f. ON kith f. Gmc]

kid² /kɪd/ v. (**kidded, kidding**) colloq. **1** tr. & refl. deceive, trick (don't kid yourself; kidded his mother that he was ill). **2** tr. & intr. tease (only kidding). □ **no kidding** (or **kid**) sl. that is the truth. □□ **kidder** n. **kiddingly** adv. [perh. f. KID¹]

kid³ /kɪd/ n. hist. a small wooden tub, esp. a sailor's mess tub for grog or rations. [perh. var. of KIT¹]

Kidd /kɪd/, Captain William (1645–1701), British pirate. Sent to the Indies in 1695 in command of an anti-pirate expedition, Kidd turned pirate himself, but was eventually arrested in New York (where he had gone in hope of getting a pardon) and sent back to London where he was hanged. His supposed buried treasure has become the subject of legend and is still being searched for today.

Kidderminster carpet /ˈkɪdəˌmɪnstə(r)/ n. a carpet made of two cloths of different colours woven together so that the carpet is reversible. [Kidderminster in S. England]

kiddie /ˈkɪdɪ/ n. (also **kiddy**) (pl. **-ies**) sl. = KID¹ n. 3.

kiddle /ˈkɪd(ə)l/ n. **1** a barrier in a river with an opening fitted with nets etc. to catch fish. **2** an arrangement of fishing-nets hung on stakes along the seashore. [ME f. AF kidel, OF quidel, guidel]

kiddo /ˈkɪdəʊ/ n. (pl. **-os**) sl. = KID¹ n. 3.

kiddy var. of KIDDIE.

kidnap /ˈkɪdnæp/ v.tr. (**kidnapped, kidnapping**; US **kidnaped, kidnaping**) **1** carry off (a person etc.) by illegal force or fraud esp. to obtain a ransom. **2** steal (a child). □□ **kidnapper** n. [back-form. f. kidnapper f. KID¹ + nap = NAB]

kidney /ˈkɪdnɪ/ n. (pl. **-eys**) **1** either of a pair of organs in the abdominal cavity of mammals, birds, and reptiles, which remove nitrogenous wastes from the blood and excrete urine. **2** the kidney of a sheep, ox, or pig as food. **3** temperament, nature, kind (a man of that kidney; of the right kidney). □ **kidney bean 1** a dwarf French bean. **2** a scarlet runner bean. **kidney dish** a kidney-shaped dish, esp. one used in surgery. **kidney machine** = artificial kidney. **kidney-shaped** shaped like a kidney, with one side concave and the other convex. **kidney vetch** a herbaceous plant, Anthyllis vulneraria: also called lady's finger. [ME kidnei, pl. kidneiren, app. partly f. ei EGG¹]

kidskin /ˈkɪdskɪn/ n. = KID¹ n. 2.

kiekie /ˈkiːkiː/ n. a New Zealand climbing plant with edible bracts, and leaves which are used for basket-making etc. [Maori]

Kiel /kiːl/ a German naval port and capital of Schleswig-Holstein; pop. (1987) 243,600. □ **Kiel Canal** a canal connecting the North Sea with the Baltic. It runs from Kiel on the Baltic to Brunsbüttel at the mouth of the Elbe, and was opened in 1895.

Kierkegaard /ˈkɪəkəˌɡɑːd/, Søren (1813–55), Danish philosopher, of a wealthy Lutheran family. To the prevailing Hegelian philosophy he opposed his own 'existential' dialectics, pointing out what was involved in the position of man 'existing before God', i.e. relating only to God. His oft-repeated statement 'truth is subjectivity' links truth with the existing subject instead of with its object, and so, in the last resort, makes its communication to other subjects impossible. Kierkegaard drew the theological consequences from this position by denying the possibility of an objective system of doctrinal truths, but his religious works have aroused less interest than his philosophical writings. His influence on contemporary thought has been considerable.

kieselguhr /ˈkiːz(ə)lˌgʊə(r)/ n. diatomaceous earth forming deposits in lakes and ponds and used as a filter, filler, insulator, etc., in various manufacturing processes. [G f. *Kiesel* gravel + dial. *Guhr* earthy deposit]

Kiev /ˈkiːef/ a leading industrial city and cultural centre of the Soviet Union, capital of Ukraine; pop. (est. 1987) 2,554,000.

kif var. of KEF.

Kigali /kɪˈgɑːlɪ/ the capital of Rwanda; pop. (1981) 156,650.

kike /kaɪk/ n. esp. *US sl. offens.* a Jew. [20th c.: orig. uncert.]

Kikládhes see CYCLADES.

Kikuyu /kɪˈkuːjuː/ n. & adj. —n. (*pl.* same or **Kikuyus**) **1** a member of an agricultural Black people, the largest Bantu-speaking group in Kenya. **2** the language of this people. —adj. of or relating to this people or their language. [native name]

Kildare /kɪlˈdeə(r)/ a county of eastern Ireland, in the province of Leinster; pop. (est. 1986) 116,000; capital, Naas.

kilderkin /ˈkɪldəkɪn/ n. **1** a cask for liquids etc., holding 16 or 18 gallons. **2** this measure. [ME, alt. of *kinderkin* f. MDu. *kinde(r)kin*, *kinneken*, dimin. of *kintal* QUINTAL]

Kilimanjaro /ˌkɪlɪmənˈdʒɑːrəʊ/ an extinct volcano in Tanzania. It has twin peaks, the higher of which, Kibo (5,895 m, 19,340 ft.), is the highest mountain in Africa.

Kilkenny /kɪlˈkenɪ/ the county town of Co. Kilkenny, in southern Ireland; pop. (1981) 16,900. □ **Kilkenny cats** cats proverbially said to have fought until only the tails remained.

kill /kɪl/ v. & n. —v.tr. **1 a** deprive of life or vitality; put to death; cause the death of. **b** (*absol.*) cause or bring about death (*must kill to survive*). **2** destroy; put an end to (feelings etc.) (*overwork killed my enthusiasm*). **3** *refl.* (often foll. by pres. part.) **a** overexert oneself (*don't kill yourself lifting them all at once*). **b** laugh heartily. **4** *colloq.* overwhelm (a person) with amusement, delight, etc. (*the things he says really kill me*). **5** switch off (a spotlight, engine, etc.). **6** *colloq.* delete (a line, paragraph, etc.) from a computer file. **7** *colloq.* cause pain or discomfort to (*my feet are killing me*). **8** pass (time, or a specified amount of it) usu. while waiting for a specific event (*had an hour to kill before the interview*). **9** defeat (a bill in Parliament). **10** *colloq.* consume the entire contents of (a bottle of wine etc.). **11 a** *Tennis* etc. hit (the ball) so skilfully that it cannot be returned. **b** stop (the ball) dead. **12** neutralize or render ineffective (taste, sound, colour, etc.) (*thick carpet killed the sound of footsteps*). —n. **1** an act of killing (esp. an animal). **2** an animal or animals killed, esp. by a sportsman. **3** *colloq.* the destruction or disablement of an enemy aircraft, submarine, etc. □ **dressed to kill** dressed showily, alluringly, or impressively. **in at the kill** present at or benefiting from the successful conclusion of an enterprise. **kill off 1** get rid of or destroy completely (esp. a number of persons or things). **2** (of an author) bring about the death of (a fictional character). **kill or cure** (usu. *attrib.*) (of a remedy etc.) drastic, extreme. **kill two birds with one stone** achieve two aims at once. **kill with kindness** spoil (a person) with overindulgence. [ME *cülle*, *kille*, perh. ult. rel. to QUELL]

Killarney /kɪˈlɑːnɪ/ a town in Co. Kerry in the south-west of Ireland, famous for the beauty of the nearby lakes and mountains; pop. (1981) 9,100.

killdeer /ˈkɪldɪə(r)/ n. a large American plover, *Charadrius vociferus*, with a plaintive song. [imit.]

killer /ˈkɪlə(r)/ n. **1 a** a person, animal, or thing that kills. **b** a murderer. **2** *colloq.* **a** an impressive, formidable, or excellent thing (*this one is quite difficult, but the next one is a real killer*). **b** a hilarious joke. **c** a decisive blow (*his brilliant header proved to be the killer*). □ **killer instinct 1** an innate tendency to kill. **2** a ruthless streak. **killer whale** a voracious cetacean, *Orcinus orca*, with a white belly and prominent dorsal fin.

killick /ˈkɪlɪk/ n. **1** a heavy stone used by small craft as an anchor. **2** a small anchor. **3** *Brit. naval sl.* a leading seaman. [17th c.: orig. unkn.]

killifish /ˈkɪlɪfɪʃ/ n. **1** any small fresh- or brackish-water fish of the family Cyprinodontidae, many of which are brightly coloured. **2** a brightly-coloured tropical aquarium fish, *Pterolebias peruensis*. [perh. f. *kill* stream f. Du. *kil* + FISH¹]

killing /ˈkɪlɪŋ/ n. & adj. —n. **1 a** the causing of death. **b** an instance of this. **2** a great (esp. financial) success (*make a killing*). —adj. *colloq.* **1** overwhelmingly funny. **2** exhausting; very strenuous. □ **killing-bottle** a bottle containing poisonous vapour to kill insects collected as specimens. □□ **killingly** adv.

killjoy /ˈkɪldʒɔɪ/ n. a person who throws gloom over or prevents other people's enjoyment.

kiln /kɪln/ n. a furnace or oven for burning, baking, or drying, esp. for calcining lime or firing pottery etc. [OE *cylene* f. L *culina* kitchen]

kiln-dry /ˈkɪlndraɪ/ v.tr. (**-ies**, **-ied**) dry in a kiln.

kilo /ˈkiːləʊ/ n. (*pl.* **-os**) **1** a kilogram. **2** a kilometre. [F: abbr.]

kilo- /ˈkɪləʊ/ comb. form denoting a factor of 1,000 (esp. in metric units). ¶ Abbr.: **k**, or **K** in *Computing*. [F f. Gk *khilioi* thousand]

kilobyte /ˈkɪləˌbaɪt/ n. *Computing* 1,024 (i.e. 2¹⁰) bytes as a measure of memory size.

kilocalorie /ˈkɪləˌkælərɪ/ n. = CALORIE 2.

kilocycle /ˈkɪləˌsaɪk(ə)l/ n. a former measure of frequency, equivalent to 1 kilohertz. ¶ Abbr.: **kc**.

kilogram /ˈkɪləˌgræm/ n. (also **-gramme**) the SI unit of mass, established in 1889 for international use, equivalent to the international prototype, made of platinum–iridium, kept at Sèvres near Paris (approx. 2.205 lb.). ¶ Abbr.: **kg**. [F *kilogramme* (as KILO, GRAM¹)]

kilohertz /ˈkɪləˌhɜːts/ n. a measure of frequency equivalent to 1,000 cycles per second. ¶ Abbr.: **kHz**.

kilojoule /ˈkɪləˌdʒuːl/ n. 1,000 joules, esp. as a measure of the energy value of foods. ¶ Abbr.: **kJ**.

kilolitre /ˈkɪləˌliːtə(r)/ n. (*US* **-liter**) 1,000 litres (equivalent to 220 imperial gallons). ¶ Abbr.: **kl**.

kilometre /ˈkɪləˌmiːtə(r), disp. kɪˈlɒmɪtə(r)/ n. (*US* **kilometer**) a metric unit of measurement equal to 1,000 metres (approx. 0.62 miles). ¶ Abbr.: **km**. □□ **kilometric** /ˌkɪləˈmetrɪk/ adj. [F *kilomètre* (as KILO-, METRE¹)]

kiloton /ˈkɪləˌtʌn/ n. (also **kilotonne**) a unit of explosive power equivalent to 1,000 tons of TNT.

kilovolt /ˈkɪləˌvɒlt/ n. 1,000 volts. ¶ Abbr.: **kV**.

kilowatt /ˈkɪləˌwɒt/ n. 1,000 watts. ¶ Abbr.: **kW**.

kilowatt-hour /ˌkɪləwɒtˈaʊə(r)/ n. a measure of electrical energy equivalent to a power consumption of 1,000 watts for one hour. ¶ Abbr.: **kWh**.

Kilroy /ˈkɪlrɔɪ/ the name of a mythical person, popularized by American servicemen in the Second World War, who left such inscriptions as 'Kilroy was here' on walls etc. all over the world. There are many unverifiable accounts of the origin of the name.

kilt /kɪlt/ n. & v. —n. **1** a skirtlike garment, usu. of pleated tartan cloth and reaching to the knees, as traditionally worn by Highland men. **2** a similar garment worn by women and children. —v.tr. **1** tuck up (skirts) round the body. **2** (esp. as **kilted** adj.) gather in vertical pleats. □□ **kilted** adj. [orig. as verb: ME, of Scand. orig.]

kilter /ˈkɪltə(r)/ n. (also **kelter** /ˈkel-/) good working order (esp. *out of kilter*). [17th c.: orig. unkn.]

kiltie /ˈkɪltɪ/ n. a wearer of a kilt, esp. a kilted Highland soldier.

Kimberley /ˈkɪmbəlɪ/ a city of Cape Province, South Africa, that has been a diamond-mining centre since the early 1970s; pop. (1985) 149,700.

kimberlite /ˈkɪmbəˌlaɪt/ n. *Mineral.* a rare igneous blue-tinged rock sometimes containing diamonds, found in South Africa and Siberia. Also called *blue ground* (see BLUE¹). [KIMBERLEY]

kimono /kɪˈməʊnəʊ/ n. (*pl.* **-os**) **1** a long loose Japanese robe worn with a sash. **2** a European dressing-gown modelled on this. □□ **kimonoed** adj. [Jap.]

kin /kɪn/ n. & adj. —n. one's relatives or family. —predic.adj. (of a person) related (*we are kin; he is kin to me*) (see also AKIN). □ **kith and kin** see KITH. **near of kin** closely related by blood, or in character. **next of kin** see NEXT. ☐☐ **kinless** *adj.* [OE *cynn* f. Gmc]

-kin /kɪn/ *suffix* forming diminutive nouns (*catkin*; *manikin*). [from or after MDu. *-kijn*, *-ken*, OHG *-chin*]

kina /ˈkiːnə/ *n.* the monetary unit of Papua New Guinea. [Papuan]

Kinabalu /ˌkɪnəbəˈluː/ a mountain in the State of Sabah in eastern Malaysia, the highest peak of Borneo and of SE Asia, rising to a height of 4,094 m (13,431 ft.)

kinaesthesia /ˌkɪnəsˈθiːzɪə/ *n.* (*US* **kinesthesia**) a sense of awareness of the position and movement of the voluntary muscles of the body. ☐☐ **kinaesthetic** /-ˈθetɪk/ *adj.* [Gk *kineō* move + *aisthēsis* sensation]

Kinchinjunga see KANCHENJUNGA.

kincob /ˈkɪnkɒb/ *n.* a rich Indian fabric embroidered with gold or silver. [Urdu f. Pers. *kamḵāb* f. *kamḵā* damask]

kind[1] /kaɪnd/ *n.* **1 a** a race or species (*human kind*). **b** a natural group of animals, plants, etc. (*the wolf kind*). **2** class, type, sort, variety (*what kind of job are you looking for?*). ¶ In sense 2, *these* (or *those*) *kind* is often encountered when followed by a plural, as in *I don't like these kind of things*, but *this kind* and *these kinds* are usually preferred. **3** each of the elements of the Eucharist (*communion under* (or *in*) *both kinds*). **4** the manner or fashion natural to a person etc. (*act after their kind*; *true to kind*). ☐ **kind of** *colloq.* to some extent (*felt kind of sorry*; *I kind of expected it*). **a kind of** used to imply looseness, vagueness, exaggeration, etc., in the term used (*a kind of Jane Austen of our times*; *I suppose he's a kind of doctor*). **in kind 1** in the same form, likewise (*was insulted and replied in kind*). **2** (of payment) in goods or labour as opposed to money (*received their wages in kind*). **3** character, quality (*differ in degree but not in kind*). **law of kind** *archaic* nature in general; the natural order. **nothing of the kind 1** not at all like the thing in question. **2** (expressing denial) not at all. **of its kind** within the limitations of its own class (*good of its kind*). **of a kind 1** *derog.* scarcely deserving the name (*a choir of a kind*). **2** similar in some important respect (*they're two of a kind*). **one's own kind** those with whom one has much in common. **something of the kind** something like the thing in question. [OE *cynd(e)*, *gecynd(e)* f. Gmc]

kind[2] /kaɪnd/ *adj.* **1** of a friendly, generous, benevolent, or gentle nature. **2** (usu. foll. by *to*) showing friendliness, affection, or consideration. **3 a** affectionate. **b** *archaic* loving. [OE *gecynde* (as KIND[1]): orig. = 'natural, native']

kinda /ˈkaɪndə/ *colloq.* = *kind of*. [corrupt.]

kindergarten /ˈkɪndəˌɡɑːt(ə)n/ *n.* an establishment for preschool learning. (See FROEBEL.) [G, = children's garden]

kind-hearted /kaɪndˈhɑːtɪd/ *adj.* of a kind disposition. ☐☐ **kind-heartedly** *adv.* **kind-heartedness** *n.*

kindle /ˈkɪnd(ə)l/ *v.* **1** *tr.* light or set on fire (a flame, fire, substance, etc.). **2** *intr.* catch fire, burst into flame. **3** *tr.* arouse or inspire (*kindle enthusiasm for the project*; *kindle jealousy in a rival*). **4** *intr.* (usu. foll. by *to*) respond, react (to a person, an action, etc.) (*kindle to his courage*). **5** *intr.* become animated, glow with passion etc. (*her imagination kindled*). **6** *tr.* & *intr.* make or become bright (*kindle the embers to a glow*). ☐☐ **kindler** *n.* [ME f. ON *kynda*, kindle: cf. ON *kindill* candle, torch]

kindling /ˈkɪndlɪŋ/ *n.* small sticks etc. for lighting fires.

kindly[1] /ˈkaɪndlɪ/ *adv.* **1** in a kind manner (*spoke to the child kindly*). **2** often *iron.* used in a polite request or demand (*kindly acknowledge this letter*; *kindly leave me alone*). ☐ **look kindly upon** regard sympathetically. **take a thing kindly** like or be pleased by it. **take kindly to** be pleased by or endeared to (a person or thing). **thank kindly** thank very much. [OE *gecyndelīce* (as KIND[2])]

kindly[2] /ˈkaɪndlɪ/ *adj.* (**kindlier**, **kindliest**) **1** kind, kind-hearted. **2** (of climate etc.) pleasant, genial. **3** *archaic* native-born (*a kindly Scot*). ☐☐ **kindlily** *adv.* **kindliness** *n.* [OE *gecyndelic* (as KIND[1])]

kindness /ˈkaɪndnɪs/ *n.* **1** the state or quality of being kind. **2** a kind act.

kindred /ˈkɪndrɪd/ *n.* & *adj.* —*n.* **1** one's relations, referred to collectively. **2** a relationship by blood. **3** a resemblance or affinity in character. —*adj.* **1** related by blood or marriage. **2** allied or similar in character (*other kindred symptoms*). ☐ **kindred spirit**

a person whose character and outlook have much in common with one's own. [ME f. KIN + *-red* f. OE *ræden* condition]

kine /kaɪn/ *archaic pl.* of COW[1].

kinematics /ˌkɪnɪˈmætɪks, ˌkaɪ-/ *n.pl.* (usu. treated as *sing.*) the branch of mechanics concerned with the motion of objects without reference to the forces which cause the motion. ☐☐ **kinematic** *adj.* **kinematically** *adv.* [Gk *kinēma -matos* motion f. *kineō* move + -ICS]

kinematograph var. of CINEMATOGRAPH.

kinesics /kɪˈniːsɪks/ *n.pl.* (usu. treated as *sing.*) **1** the study of body movements and gestures which contribute to communication. **2** these movements; body language. [Gk *kinēsis* motion (as KINETIC)]

kinesiology /kɪˌniːsɪˈɒlədʒɪ/ *n.* the study of the mechanics of body movements.

kinesthesia *US* var. of KINAESTHESIA.

kinetic /kɪˈnetɪk, kaɪ-/ *adj.* of or due to motion. ☐ **kinetic art** a form of art that depends on movement for its effect. **kinetic energy** the energy of motion. **kinetic theory** see separate entry. ☐☐ **kinetically** *adv.* [Gk *kinētikos* f. *kineō* move]

kinetics /kɪˈnetɪks, kaɪ-/ *n.pl.* **1** = DYNAMICS 1a. **2** (usu. treated as *sing.*) the branch of physical chemistry concerned with measuring and studying the rates of chemical reactions.

kinetic theory *n.* a theory that attempts to explain many of the observed properties of matter (e.g. heat, the melting of solids, the evaporation of liquids) as due to the continual motion of the discrete particles (atoms and molecules) of which they consist. In solids the particles vibrate about a fixed point; in liquids they 'slide over' one another but remain in close contact; in gases they move freely and independently. According to the kinetic theory the temperature of a solid, liquid, or gas is due to the mean kinetic energy distributed among its particles; evaporation from a liquid is due to the escape of the more rapidly moving molecules. The theory has existed in a rudimentary form from antiquity but it was not until the 19th c. that it acquired its present form, mainly through the investigations of Rudolf Clausius, James Clerk Maxwell, and Ludwig Boltzmann. It has successfully explained and predicted many other physical and chemical properties of matter, and is a powerful and well established instrument of scientific method today.

kinetin /ˈkaɪnɪtɪn/ *n. Biochem.* a synthetic kinin used to stimulate cell division in plants. [as KINETIC + -IN]

kinfolk *US* var. of KINSFOLK.

King[1] /kɪŋ/, Billie Jean (1943–), American tennis-player, winner of the women's singles championship at Wimbledon 1966–8, 1972–3, and 1975.

King[2] /kɪŋ/ Martin Luther (1929–68), Black Baptist minister and American civil rights leader, an outstanding orator, who opposed discrimination against Blacks by organizing nonviolent mass demonstrations. He was awarded the Nobel Peace Prize in 1964, and was assassinated in 1968.

king /kɪŋ/ *n.* & *v.* —*n.* **1** (as a title usu. **King**) a male sovereign, esp. the hereditary ruler of an independent State. **2** a person or thing pre-eminent in a specified field or class (*railway king*). **3** a large (or the largest) kind of plant, animal, etc. (*king penguin*). **4** *Chess* the piece on each side which the opposing side has to checkmate to win. **5** a piece in draughts with extra capacity of moving, made by crowning an ordinary piece that has reached the opponent's baseline. **6** a court-card bearing a representation of a king and usu. ranking next below an ace. **7** (**the King**) (in the UK) the national anthem when there is a male sovereign. **8** (**Kings**) either of two books of the Old Testament recording Jewish history from the accession of Solomon to the destruction of the Temple in 586 BC. —*v.tr.* make (a person) king. ☐ **King Charles spaniel** a spaniel of a small black and tan breed. **king cobra** a large and venomous hooded Indian snake, *Ophiophagus hannah*. **king-crab 1** = *horseshoe crab*. **2** *US* any of various large edible spider crabs. **king-fish** any of various large fish, esp. the opah or mulloway. **king it 1** play or act the king. **2** (usu. foll. by *over*) govern, control. **King James Bible** (or **Version**) = *Authorized Version* (see entry). **King Log, King Stork** rulers going respectively to extremes of *laissez-faire* and active oppression. The allusion is to the fable in which the frogs, dissatisfied with their inert King Log, appealed to Jupiter, who sent them King Stork who gobbled them all up. **King of Arms** *Heraldry* (in the UK) a chief herald (at the College of Arms: Garter, Clarenceux, and Norroy and Ulster; in Scotland: Lyon). **king of beasts** the lion. **king of birds** the eagle. **King of the Castle** a children's game consisting of trying to displace a rival from a mound. **King of Kings 1** God. **2** the title assumed by many eastern kings. **king-post** an upright post from the tie-beam of a roof to the apex of a truss. **King's Bench** see BENCH. **king's bishop, knight,** etc. *Chess* (of pieces which exist in pairs) the piece starting on the king's side of the board. **King's bounty** see BOUNTY. **King's colour** see COLOUR. **King's Counsel** see COUNSEL. **King's English** see ENGLISH. **King's evidence** see EVIDENCE. **king's evil** *hist.* scrofula, formerly held to be curable by the royal touch. **King's Guide** see GUIDE. **King's highway** see HIGHWAY. **king-size** (or **-sized**) larger than normal; very large. **King's Messenger** see MESSENGER. **king's pawn** *Chess* the pawn in front of the king at the beginning of a game. **King's Proctor** see PROCTOR. **king's ransom** a fortune. **King's Scout** see SCOUT[1]. **King's speech** see SPEECH. □□ **kinghood** *n.* **kingless** *adj.* **kinglike** *adj.* **kingly** *adj.* **kingliness** *n.* **kingship** *n.* [OE *cyning, cyng* f. Gmc]

kingbird /ˈkɪŋbɜːd/ *n.* any flycatcher of the genus *Tyrannus*, with olive-grey plumage and long pointed wings.

kingbolt /ˈkɪŋbəʊlt/ *n.* = KINGPIN.

kingcraft /ˈkɪŋkrɑːft/ *n. archaic* the skilful exercise of kingship.

kingcup /ˈkɪŋkʌp/ *n. Brit.* a marsh marigold.

kingdom /ˈkɪŋdəm/ *n.* **1** an organized community headed by a king. **2** the territory subject to a king. **3 a** the spiritual reign attributed to God (*Thy kingdom come*). **b** the sphere of this (*kingdom of heaven*). **4** a domain belonging to a person, animal, etc. **5** a province of nature (*the vegetable kingdom*). **6** a specified mental or emotional province (*kingdom of the heart; kingdom of fantasy*). **7** *Biol.* the highest category in taxonomic classification. □ **come into** (or **to**) **one's kingdom** achieve recognition or supremacy. **kingdom come** *sl.* eternity; the next world. **till kingdom come** *sl.* for ever. □□ **kingdomed** *adj.* [OE *cyningdōm* (as KING)]

kingfisher /ˈkɪŋˌfɪʃə(r)/ *n.* any bird of the family Alcedinidae esp. *Alcedo atthis* with a long sharp beak and brightly coloured plumage, which dives for fish in rivers etc.

King Kong /kɒŋ/ an ape-like monster featured in a film of that name (1933).

kinglet /ˈkɪŋlɪt/ *n.* **1** a petty king. **2** *US* any of various small birds of the family Regulidae, esp. the goldcrest.

kingmaker /ˈkɪŋˌmeɪkə(r)/ *n.* a person who makes kings, leaders, etc., through the exercise of political influence, orig. with ref. to the Earl of Warwick in the reign of Henry VI of England.

kingpin /ˈkɪŋpɪn/ *n.* **1 a** a main or large bolt in a central position. **b** a vertical bolt used as a pivot. **2** an essential person or thing, esp. in a complex system.

Kingsley /ˈkɪŋzlɪ/, Charles (1819–75), English novelist and clergyman, professor of modern history at Cambridge (1860–9). His concern for the injustices suffered by the working classes is expressed in his novels *Yeast* (1850) and *Alton Locke* (1850). His historical novel *Westward Ho!* (1855) and his classic children's book *The Water-Babies* (1863) are characteristically didactic.

Kingston /ˈkɪŋst(ə)n/ the capital and chief port of Jamaica; pop. (1982) 524,600.

Kingston-upon-Hull /ˌkɪŋst(ə)n, ˈhʌl/ the official name of Hull.

Kingstown /ˈkɪŋstaʊn/ the capital of St Vincent; pop. (1987) 28,900.

kinin /ˈkaɪnɪn/ *n.* **1** any of a group of polypeptides present in the blood after tissue damage. **2** any of a group of compounds which promote cell division and inhibit ageing in plants. [Gk *kineō* move + -IN]

kink /kɪŋk/ *n.* & *v.* — *n.* **1 a** a short backward twist in wire or tubing etc. such as may cause an obstruction. **b** a tight wave in human or animal hair. **2** a mental twist or quirk. — *v.intr.* & *tr.*

form or cause to form a kink. [MLG *kinke* (v.) prob. f. Du. *kinken*]

kinkajou /ˈkɪŋkəˌdʒuː/ *n.* a Central and S. American nocturnal fruit-eating mammal, *Potos flavus*, with a prehensile tail and living in trees. [F *quincajou* f. N.Amer. Ind.: cf. Algonquin *kwingwaage* wolverine]

Kinki /ˈkiːnkiː/ a region of Japan, in the south of Honshu island; pop. (1986) 21,932,000; capital, Osaka.

kinky /ˈkɪŋkɪ/ *adj.* (**kinkier, kinkiest**) **1** *colloq.* **a** given to or involving abnormal sexual behaviour. **b** (of clothing etc.) bizarre in a sexually provocative way. **2** strange, eccentric. **3** having kinks or twists. □□ **kinkily** *adv.* **kinkiness** *n.* [KINK + -Y[1]]

kino /ˈkiːnəʊ/ *n.* (*pl.* **-os**) a catechu-like gum produced by various trees and used in medicine and tanning as an astringent. [W. Afr.]

-kins /kɪnz/ *suffix* = -KIN, often with suggestions of endearment (*babykins*).

kinsfolk /ˈkɪnzfəʊk/ *n.pl.* (*US* **kinfolk**) one's relations by blood.

Kinshasa /kɪnˈʃɑːsə/ (formerly *Léopoldville*) the capital of Zaïre, founded in 1881 by the explorer H. M. Stanley; pop. (est. 1984) 2,653,550.

kinship /ˈkɪnʃɪp/ *n.* **1** blood relationship. **2** the sharing of characteristics or origins.

kinsman /ˈkɪnzmən/ *n.* (*pl.* **-men**; *fem.* **kinswoman**, *pl.* **-women**) **1** a blood relation or *disp.* a relation by marriage. **2** a member of one's own tribe or people.

kiosk /ˈkiːɒsk/ *n.* **1** a light open-fronted booth or cubicle from which food, newspapers, tickets, etc. are sold. **2** a telephone box. **3** *Austral.* a building in which refreshments are served in a park, zoo, etc. **4** a light open pavilion in Turkey and Iran. [F *kiosque* f. Turk. *kiūshk* pavilion f. Pers. *guš*]

kip[1] /kɪp/ *n.* & *v. Brit. sl.* — *n.* **1** a sleep or nap. **2** a bed or cheap lodging-house. **3** (also **kip-house** or **-shop**) a brothel. — *v.intr.* (**kipped, kipping**) sleep, take a nap. [cf. Da. *kippe* mean hut]

kip[2] /kɪp/ *n.* the hide of a young or small animal as used for leather. [ME: orig. unkn.]

kip[3] /kɪp/ *n.* (*pl.* same or **kips**) the basic monetary unit of Laos. [Thai]

kip[4] /kɪp/ *n. Austral. sl.* a small piece of wood from which coins are spun in the game of two-up. [perh. f. E dial.: cf. *keper* a flat piece of wood preventing a horse from eating the corn, or Ir. dial. *kippeen* f. Ir. *cipín* a little stick]

Kipling /ˈkɪplɪŋ/, Rudyard (1865–1936), English writer and poet, born in Bombay. His education in England is depicted in his schoolboy tales *Stalky and Co.* (1899). Working as a journalist in India (1882–9) he published poems and short stories, and received celebrity with *Barrack-Room Ballads* (1892). Kipling's output was vast and varied. His fluent versification with its echoes of hymns and ballads, and his use of colloquial speech, in prose and verse, has been variously judged; his belief in duty, responsibility, and personal honour has given his works a powerful moral force. His most durable achievements were his tales for children, notably *The Jungle Book* (1894), *Just So Stories* (1902), and his picaresque novel of India *Kim* (1901). Widely regarded as unofficial poet laureate, in 1907 he became the first English writer to be awarded the Nobel Prize for literature.

kipper /ˈkɪpə(r)/ *n.* & *v.* — *n.* **1** a kippered fish, esp. herring. **2** a male salmon in the spawning season. — *v.tr.* cure (a herring etc.) by splitting open, salting, and drying in the open air or smoke. [ME: orig. uncert.]

kipsie /ˈkɪpsɪ/ *n.* (also **kipsy**) (*pl.* **-ies**) *Austral. sl.* a house, home, lean-to, or shelter. [perh. f. KIP[1]]

kir /kɜː(r)/ *n.* a drink made from dry white wine and crème de cassis. [Canon Felix *Kir* d. 1968, said to have invented the recipe]

kirby-grip /ˈkɜːbɪgrɪp/ *n.* (also **Kirbigrip** *propr.*) a type of sprung hairgrip. [*Kirby*, part of orig. manufacturer's name]

Kirchhoff /ˈkɪrxhɒf/, Gustav Robert (1824–87), German physicist who, working with Bunsen, developed a technique of spectrum analysis and, using this, discovered the elements caesium and rubidium (1860–1). He also worked on electrical circuits and the flow of currents.

Kirghiz /kɪəˈgɪz, ˈkɜːgɪz/ *n.* & *adj.* — *n.* (*pl.* same) **1** a member

b but   d dog   f few   g get   h he   j yes   k cat   l leg   m man   n no   p pen   r red   s sit   t top   v voice

of a Mongol people living in central Asia between the Volga and the Irtysh rivers. **2** the language of this people. —*adj.* of or relating to this people or their language. [Kirghiz]

Kirghizia /kɜːˈgiːzɪə/ the Kirghiz republic, a constituent republic of the USSR, on the Chinese frontier; pop. (est. 1987) 4,143,000; capital, Frunze.

Kiribati /ˈkɪrɪˌbæs/ a small country in the SW Pacific, consisting of groups of islands including the former Gilbert Islands; pop. (est. 1988) 67,600; official languages, English and local dialect; capital, Tarawa. First sighted by the Spaniards in the mid-16th c., the islands were visited by the British in the 18th c. and named after Thomas Gilbert, an English adventurer who arrived there in 1788; they became a favourite centre for the hunting of sperm whales. Britain declared a protectorate over the Gilbert and Ellice Islands in 1892, and they became a colony in 1915. Links with the Ellice Islands (now Tuvalu) ended in 1975, and in 1979 Kiribati became an independent republic within the Commonwealth. The phosphate deposits which were formerly a main source of revenue are almost exhausted, and the principal exports are copra and fish; budgetary assistance is provided by aid from the UK.

Kirin see JILIN.

Kiritimati /ˌkɪrɪtɪˈmɑːtɪ/ the largest atoll in the world, one of the Line Islands of Kiribati in the Pacific Ocean; pop. (1985) 1,737. It is used by Britain as an air base.

kirk /kɜːk/ *n. Sc. & N.Engl.* **1** a church. **2** (**the Kirk** or **the Kirk of Scotland**) the Church of Scotland as distinct from the Church of England or from the Episcopal Church in Scotland. □ **Kirk-session 1** the lowest court in the Church of Scotland. **2** *hist.* the lowest court in other Presbyterian Churches, composed of ministers and elders. [ME f. ON *kirkja* f. OE *cir(i)ce* CHURCH]

Kirkcaldy /kɜːˈkɔːdɪ/ an industrial town of eastern Scotland, on the north shore of the Firth of Forth; pop. (1981) 46,500. It is the birthplace of the economist Adam Smith and the architect Robert Adam.

kirkman /ˈkɜːkmən/ *n.* (*pl.* **-men**) *Sc. & N.Engl.* a member of the Church of Scotland.

Kirkuk /kəˈkʊk/ an industrial city of northern Iraq, centre of the oil industry in that region; pop. (1970) 207,852.

Kirov /ˈkɪərɒf/ an industrial town and port of the USSR, northeast of Gorky, on the Vyatka River; pop. (est. 1987) 421,000.

Kirovabad /ˌkɪərəʊəˈbæd/ a former name of Gandzhe.

kirsch /kɪəʃ/ *n.* (also **kirschwasser** /ˈkɪəʃˌvʌsə(r)/) a brandy distilled from the fermented juice of cherries. [G *Kirsche* cherry, *Wasser* water]

kirtle /ˈkɜːt(ə)l/ *n. archaic* **1** a woman's gown or outer petticoat. **2** a man's tunic or coat. [OE *cyrtel* f. Gmc, ult. perh. f. L *curtus* short]

Kiruna /kɪˈruːnə/ the northernmost town of Sweden, situated at the centre of the Lapland iron-mining region; pop. (1983) 28,600. It is sometimes referred to as 'the world's largest town' because of its extensive administrative district.

Kirundi /kɪˈrʊndɪ/ *n.* a Bantu language, the official language of Burundi.

Kishinev /ˌkɪʃɪˈnjɒf/ the capital of the Moldavian SSR; pop. (est. 1987) 663,000.

kiskadee /ˌkɪskəˈdiː/ *n.* (also **keskidee** /ˌkeskɪˈdiː/) a tyrant flycatcher, *Pitangus sulphuratus*, of Central and S. America with brown and yellow plumage. [imit. of its cry]

kismet /ˈkɪsmet, ˈkɪz-/ *n.* destiny, fate. [Turk. f. Arab. *ḳisma(t)* f. *ḳasama* divide]

kiss /kɪs/ *v. & n.* —*v.* **1** *tr.* touch with the lips, esp. as a sign of love, affection, greeting, or reverence. **2** *tr.* express (greeting or farewell) in this way. **3** *absol.* (of two persons) touch each others' lips in this way. **4** *tr.* (also *absol.*) (of a snooker ball etc. in motion) lightly touch (another ball). —*n.* **1** a touch with the lips in kissing. **2** the slight impact when one snooker ball etc. lightly touches another. **3** a small sweetmeat or piece of confectionery. □ **kiss and tell** recount one's sexual exploits. **kiss a person's arse** *coarse sl.* act obsequiously towards a person. **kiss away**

remove (tears etc.) by kissing. **kiss-curl** a small curl of hair on the forehead, at the nape, or in front of the ear. **kiss the dust** submit abjectly; be overthrown. **kiss goodbye to** *colloq.* accept the loss of. **kiss the ground** prostrate oneself as a token of homage. **kissing cousin** (or **kin** or **kind**) a distant relative (given a formal kiss on occasional meetings). **kissing-gate** *Brit.* a gate hung in a V- or U-shaped enclosure, to let one person through at a time. **kiss of death** an apparently friendly act which causes ruin. **kiss off** *sl.* **1** dismiss, get rid of. **2** go away, die. **kiss of life** mouth-to-mouth resuscitation. **kiss of peace** *Eccl.* a ceremonial kiss, esp. during the Eucharist, as a sign of unity. **kiss the rod** accept chastisement submissively. □□ **kissable** *adj.* [OE *cyssan* f. Gmc]

kisser /ˈkɪsə(r)/ *n.* **1** a person who kisses. **2** (orig. *Boxing*) *sl.* the mouth; the face.

Kissinger /ˈkɪsɪndʒə(r)/, Henry Alfred (1923–), American diplomat, Secretary of State 1973–7. He helped to achieve an improvement of relations (*détente*) with the Soviet Union, a resolution of the Indo-Pakistan war (1971), rapprochement with Communist China (1972), which the US now recognized for the first time, and above all the ending of the Vietnam war (1973), for which he was jointly awarded a Nobel Peace Prize. Later in 1973 he helped to resolve the Arab-Israeli war and restored US diplomatic relations with Egypt, becoming known for his 'shuttle diplomacy' while acting as mediator in the conflict between Israel and Syria (1974).

kissogram /ˈkɪsəˌgræm/ *n.* (also **Kissagram** *propr.*) a novelty telegram or greetings message delivered with a kiss.

kissy /ˈkɪsɪ/ *adj. colloq.* given to kissing (*not the kissy type*).

kist var. of CIST¹.

Kiswahili /ˌkɪswɑːˈhiːlɪ/ *n.* one of the six languages preferred for use in Africa by the Organization for African Unity. [Swahili *ki-* prefix for an abstract or inanimate object]

kit¹ /kɪt/ *n. & v.* —*n.* **1** a set of articles, equipment, or clothing needed for a specific purpose (*first-aid kit; bicycle-repair kit*). **2** the clothing etc. needed for any activity, esp. sport (*football kit*). **3** a set of all the parts needed to assemble an item, e.g. a piece of furniture, a model, etc. **4** *Brit.* a wooden tub. —*v.tr.* (**kitted**, **kitting**) (often foll. by *out*, *up*) equip with the appropriate clothing or tools. [ME f. MDu. *kitte* wooden vessel, of unkn. orig.]

kit² /kɪt/ *n.* **1** a kitten. **2** a young fox, badger, etc. [abbr.]

kit³ /kɪt/ *n. hist.* a small fiddle esp. as used by a dancing-master. [perh. f. L *cithara*; see CITTERN]

Kitakyushu /ˌkiːtəˈkjuːʃuː/ an industrial city of southern Japan, on Kyushu Island; pop. (1987) 1,042,000.

kitbag /ˈkɪtbæg/ *n.* a large, usu. cylindrical bag used for carrying a soldier's, traveller's, or sportsman's equipment.

Kit-Cat Club /ˈkɪtkæt/ a club founded in the early part of the 18th c. by leading Whigs, including (according to Pope) Steele, Addison, Congreve, and Vanbrugh.

kit-cat /ˈkɪtkæt/ *n.* (in full **kit-cat portrait**) a portrait of less than half length, but including one hand; usu. 36 × 28 in. [named after a series of portraits of the members of the *Kit-Cat Club*.

kitchen /ˈkɪtʃɪn, -tʃ(ə)n/ *n.* **1** the room or area where food is prepared and cooked. **2** (*attrib.*) of or belonging to the kitchen (*kitchen knife; kitchen table*). **3** *sl.* the percussion section of an orchestra. □ **everything but the kitchen sink** everything imaginable. **kitchen cabinet** a group of unofficial advisers thought to be unduly influential (orig. those of president Andrew Jackson of the US, *c*.1830). **kitchen garden** a garden where vegetables and sometimes fruit or herbs are grown. **kitchen midden** a prehistoric refuse-heap which marks an ancient settlement, chiefly containing bones, seashells, etc. **kitchen-sink** (in art forms) depicting extreme realism, esp. drabness or sordidness. **kitchen-sink drama** a term applied in the British theatre after John Osborne's *Look Back in Anger* (1956) and Arnold Wesker's plays such as *Roots* (1959) to plays using working-class settings rather than the drawing-rooms of conventional middle-class drama. **kitchen-sink school** a group of British painters who, in the late 1940s and early 1950s, chose drab and sordid themes and aggressive techniques expressive of the postwar mood of dissatisfaction with the current state of affairs. **kitchen tea** *Austral.* & *NZ* a party held before a wedding to which female guests bring items of kitchen equipment as presents. [OE *cycene* f. L *coquere* cook]

Kitchener[1] /ˈkɪtʃɪnə(r)/ a city in SE Ontario, Canada, 88 km (55 miles) west of Toronto; pop. (1986) 150,600; metropolitan area pop. 311,200. Settled by German Mennonites in 1806, it bore several names before being changed from Berlin to Kitchener, in honour of Field Marshal Kitchener, in 1916.

Kitchener[2] /ˈkɪtʃɪnə(r)/, Horatio Herbert, Earl Kitchener of Khartoum (1850–1916), British soldier and statesman who became a national hero following his defeat of the Dervishes at Omdurman and reconquest of the Sudan in 1898. He served as Roberts's chief of staff in the Boer War, and then successively as commander-in-chief, India, and consul-general, Egypt, before being made Secretary of State for War at the outbreak of the First World War. Kitchener was among the first to recognize that the war would be a long one, and was responsible for organizing the large volunteer army which eventually fought the war on the Western Front. As the war progressed, however, he proved unequal to the demands of his post and gradually lost influence, although he kept his Cabinet post until he was drowned when HMS *Hampshire* struck a mine while carrying him on a mission to Russia.

Kitchener bun /ˈkɪtʃɪnə(r)/ *n. Austral.* a cream-filled bun coated with cinnamon and sugar. [after KITCHENER]

kitchenette /ˌkɪtʃɪˈnet, -tʃəˈnet/ *n.* a small kitchen or part of a room fitted as a kitchen.

kitchenware /ˈkɪtʃɪnˌweə(r), ˈkɪtʃ(ə)n-/ *n.* the utensils used in the kitchen.

kite /kaɪt/ *n. & v.* —*n.* **1** a toy consisting of a light framework with thin material stretched over it, flown in the wind at the end of a long string. **2** any of various soaring birds of prey esp. of the genus *Milvus* with long wings and usu. a forked tail. **3** *Brit. sl.* an aeroplane. **4** *sl.* a fraudulent cheque, bill, or receipt. **5** *Geom.* a quadrilateral figure symmetrical about one diagonal. **6** *sl.* a letter or note, esp. one that is illicit or surreptitious. **7** (in *pl.*) the highest sail of a ship, set only in a light wind. **8** *archaic* a dishonest person, a sharper. —*v.* **1** *intr.* soar like a kite. **2** *tr.* (also *absol.*) originate or pass (fraudulent cheques, bills, or receipts). **3** *tr.* (also *absol.*) raise (money by dishonest means) (*kite a loan*). □ **kite balloon** a sausage-shaped captive balloon for military observations. **kite-flying** fraudulent practice. [OE *cȳta*, of unkn. orig.]

Kitemark /ˈkaɪtmɑːk/ *n.* (in the UK) the official kite-shaped mark on goods approved by the British Standards Institution.

kith /kɪθ/ *n.* □ **kith and kin** friends and relations. [OE *cȳthth* f. Gmc]

kitsch /kɪtʃ/ *n.* (often *attrib.*) garish, pretentious, or sentimental art, usu. vulgar and worthless (*kitsch plastic models of the royal family*). □□ **kitschy** *adj.* (**kitschier, kitschiest**). **kitschiness** *n.* [G]

kitten /ˈkɪt(ə)n/ *n. & v.* —*n.* **1** a young cat. **2** a young ferret etc. —*v.intr.* & *tr.* (of a cat etc.) give birth or give birth to. □ **have kittens** *Brit. colloq.* be extremely upset, anxious, or nervous. [ME *kito(u)n, ketoun* f. OF *chitoun, chetoun* dimin. of *chat* CAT]

kittenish /ˈkɪtənɪʃ/ *adj.* **1** like a young cat; playful and lively. **2** flirtatious. □□ **kittenishly** *adv.* **kittenishness** *n.* [KITTEN]

kittiwake /ˈkɪtɪˌweɪk/ *n.* either of two small gulls, *Rissa tridactyla* and *R. brevirostris*, nesting on sea cliffs. [imit. of its cry]

kittle /ˈkɪt(ə)l/ *adj.* (also **kittle-cattle** /ˈkɪt(ə)l ˌkæt(ə)l/) **1** (of a person) capricious, rash, or erratic in behaviour. **2** difficult to deal with. [ME (now Sc. & dial.) *kittle* tickle, prob. f. ON *kitla*]

kitty[1] /ˈkɪtɪ/ *n.* (*pl.* **-ies**) **1** a fund of money for communal use. **2** the pool in some card-games. **3** the jack in bowls. [19th c.: orig. unkn.]

kitty[2] /ˈkɪtɪ/ *n.* (*pl.* **-ies**) a pet-name or a child's name for a kitten or cat.

Kitwe /ˈkiːtweɪ/ the second-largest city of Zambia, situated in the copperbelt mining region; pop. (est. 1987) 449,400.

Kivu /ˈkiːvuː/, **Lake** a lake in central Africa, on the Zaïre-Rwanda frontier.

kiwi /ˈkiːwiː/ *n.* (*pl.* **kiwis**) **1** a flightless New Zealand bird of the genus *Apteryx* with hairlike feathers and a long bill. Also called APTERYX. **2** (**Kiwi**) *colloq.* a New Zealander, esp. a soldier or member of a national sports team. □ **kiwi fruit** (or **berry**) the fruit of a climbing plant, *Actinidia chinensis*, having a thin hairy skin, green flesh, and black seeds: also called *Chinese gooseberry*. [Maori]

kJ *abbr.* kilojoule(s).

KKK *abbr. US* Ku Klux Klan.

kl *abbr.* kilolitre(s).

Klaproth /ˈklæprəʊt/, Martin Heinrich (1743–1817), German chemist, one of the founders of chemical analysis. He discovered the elements zirconium and uranium (actually, the oxide) in 1789, rediscovered and named titanium in 1795, and recognized chromium in 1797, tellurium in 1798, and cerium in 1803. Several of these were also discovered independently by other chemists. A follower of Lavoisier, he helped to introduce the latter's new system of chemistry into Germany.

Klaxon /ˈklæks(ə)n/ *n. propr.* a horn or warning hooter, orig. on a motor vehicle. [name of the manufacturing company]

Klee /kleɪ/, Paul (1879–1940), Swiss painter who trained in Munich, where he settled in 1906. He began as a graphic artist and was influenced by Blake, Goya, Beardsley, Ensor, and Toulouse-Lautrec, and exhibited with Kandinsky, whose interest in music, poetry, and eastern philosophy he shared. In 1920 Klee was appointed to the staff of the Bauhaus and taught there until 1933, when he left Germany for Switzerland. He developed an international reputation as a modernist, after 1920, and it is interesting that seventeen of his works appeared in the Degenerate Art exhibition mounted by the Nazi régime in Munich in 1937.

Kleenex /ˈkliːneks/ *n.* (*pl.* same or **Kleenexes**) orig. *US propr.* an absorbent disposable paper tissue, used esp. as a handkerchief.

Klein bottle /ˈklaɪn/ *n. Math.* a closed surface with only one side, formed by passing the neck of a tube through the side of the tube to join the hole in the base. [F. *Klein*, Ger. mathematician d. 1925]

Klemperer /ˈklempərə(r)/, Otto (1885–1973), German-born conductor and composer, who received early encouragement from Mahler. He left Germany in 1933. At first a champion of new work and opera, he later gained a great reputation as a conductor of the symphonies of German and Austrian composers, notably Beethoven, Brahms, and Mahler.

klepht /kleft/ *n.* **1** a member of the original body of Greeks who refused to submit to the Turks in the 15th c. **2** any of their descendants. **3** a brigand or bandit. [mod. Gk *klephtēs* f. Gk *kleptēs* thief]

kleptomania /ˌkleptəʊˈmeɪnɪə/ *n.* a recurrent urge to steal, usu. without regard for need or profit. □□ **kleptomaniac** /-nɪˌæk/ *n. & adj.* [Gk *kleptēs* thief + -MANIA]

klieg /kliːg/ *n.* (also **klieg light**) a powerful lamp in a film studio etc. [A. T. & J. H. *Kliegl*, Amer. inventors d. 1927, 1959]

klipspringer /ˈklɪpˌsprɪŋə(r)/ *n.* a S. African dwarf antelope, *Oreotragus oreotragus*, which can bound up and down rocky slopes. [Afrik. f. *klip* rock + *springer* jumper]

Klondike /ˈklɒndaɪk/ a river and district in Yukon, Canada. The discovery of gold there in 1896 led to a spectacular gold-rush. —*n.* a source of valuable material.

kloof /kluːf/ *n.* a steep-sided ravine or valley in S. Africa. [Du., = cleft]

Klosters /ˈklɒstəz/ an Alpine winter sports resort near Davos in eastern Switzerland.

kludge /klʌdʒ/ *n.* orig. *US sl.* **1** an ill-assorted collection of poorly matching parts. **2** *Computing* a machine, system, or program that has been badly put together.

klystron /ˈklaɪstrɒn/ *n.* an electron tube that generates or amplifies microwaves by velocity modulation. [Gk *kluzō klus-* wash over]

km *abbr.* kilometre(s).

K-meson /keɪˈmezɒn, -ˈmiːzɒn/ *n.* = KAON. [K (see KAON) + MESON]

kn. *abbr. Naut.* knot(s).

knack /næk/ *n.* **1** an acquired or intuitive faculty of doing a thing adroitly. **2** a trick or habit of action or speech etc. (*has a knack of offending people*). **3** *archaic* an ingenious device (see KNICK-KNACK). [ME, prob. identical with *knack* sharp blow or sound f. LG, ult. imit.]

knacker /'nækə(r)/ *n. & v. Brit.* —*n.* **1** a buyer of useless horses for slaughter. **2** a buyer of old houses, ships, etc. for the materials. —*v.tr. sl.* **1** kill. **2** (esp. as **knackered** *adj.*) exhaust, wear out. [19th c.: orig. unkn.]

knackery /'nækəri/ *n.* (*pl.* **-ies**) a knacker's yard or business.

knag /næg/ *n.* **1** a knot in wood; the base of a branch. **2** a short dead branch. **3** a peg for hanging things on. □□ **knaggy** *adj.* [ME, perh. f. LG *Knagge*]

knap[1] /næp/ *n. chiefly dial.* the crest of a hill or of rising ground. [OE *cnæp(p)*, perh. rel. to ON *knappr* knob]

knap[2] /næp/ *v.tr.* (**knapped**, **knapping**) **1** break (stones for roads or building, flints, or *Austral.* ore) with a hammer. **2** *archaic* knock, rap, snap asunder. □□ **knapper** *n.* [ME, imit.]

knapsack /'næpsæk/ *n.* a soldier's or hiker's bag with shoulder-straps, carried on the back, and usu. made of canvas or weatherproof material. [MLG, prob. f. *knappen* bite + SACK[1]]

knapweed /'næpwiːd/ *n.* any of various plants of the genus *Centaurea*, having thistle-like purple flowers. [ME, orig. *knopweed* f. KNOP + WEED]

knar /nɑː(r)/ *n.* a knot or protuberance in a tree trunk, root, etc. [ME *knarre*, rel. to MLG, M.Du., MHG *knorre* knobbed protuberance]

knave /neɪv/ *n.* **1** a rogue, a scoundrel. **2** = JACK[1] *n.* 2. □□ **knavery** *n.* (*pl.* **-ies**). **knavish** *adj.* **knavishly** *adv.* **knavishness** *n.* [OE *cnafa* boy, servant, f. WG]

knawel /'nɔːəl/ *n.* any low-growing plant of the genus *Scleranthus*. [G *Knauel*]

knead /niːd/ *v.tr.* **1 a** work (a yeast mixture, clay, etc.) into dough, paste, etc. by pummelling. **b** make (bread, pottery, etc.) in this way. **2** blend or weld together (*kneaded them into a unified group*). **3** massage (muscles etc.) as if kneading. □□ **kneadable** *adj.* **kneader** *n.* [OE *cnedan* f. Gmc]

knee /niː/ *n. & v.* —*n.* **1 a** (often *attrib.*) the joint between the thigh and the lower leg in humans. **b** the corresponding joint in other animals. **c** the area around this. **d** the upper surface of the thigh of a sitting person; the lap (*held her on his knee*). **2** the part of a garment covering the knee. **3** anything resembling a knee in shape or position, esp. a piece of wood or iron bent at an angle, a sharp turn in a graph, etc. —*v.tr.* (**knees**, **kneed**, **kneeing**) **1** touch or strike with the knee (*kneed the ball past him*; *kneed him in the groin*). **2** *colloq.* cause (trousers) to bulge at the knee. □ **bend** (or **bow**) **the knee** kneel, esp. in submission. **bring a person to his** or **her knees** reduce a person to submission. **knee-bend** the action of bending the knee, esp. as a physical exercise in which the body is raised and lowered without the use of the hands. **knee-breeches** close-fitting trousers reaching to or just below the knee. **knee-deep 1** (usu. foll. by *in*) **a** immersed up to the knees. **b** deeply involved. **2** so deep as to reach the knees. **knee-high** so high as to reach the knees. **knee-hole** a space for the knees, esp. under a desk. **knee-jerk 1** a sudden involuntary kick caused by a blow on the tendon just below the knee. **2** (*attrib.*) predictable, automatic, stereotyped. **knee-joint 1** = senses 1a, b of *n.* **2** a joint made of two pieces hinged together. **knee-length** reaching to the knees. **knee-pan** the kneecap. **knees-up** *Brit. colloq.* a lively party or gathering. **on** (or **on one's**) **bended knee** (or **knees**) kneeling, esp. in supplication, submission, or worship. [OE *cnēo(w)*]

kneecap /'niːkæp/ *n. & v.* —*n.* **1** the convex bone in front of the knee-joint. **2** a protective covering for the knee. —*v.tr.* (**-capped**, **-capping**) *colloq.* shoot (a person) in the knee or leg as a punishment, esp. for betraying a terrorist group. □□ **kneecapping** *n.*

kneel /niːl/ *v.intr.* (*past* and *past part.* **knelt** /nelt/ or esp. *US* **kneeled**) fall or rest on the knees or a knee. [OE *cnēowlian* (as KNEE)]

kneeler /'niːlə(r)/ *n.* **1** a hassock or cushion used for kneeling, esp. in church. **2** a person who kneels.

knell /nel/ *n. & v.* —*n.* **1** the sound of a bell, esp. when rung solemnly for a death or funeral. **2** an announcement, event, etc., regarded as a solemn warning of disaster. —*v.* **1** *intr.* **a** (of a bell) ring solemnly, esp. for a death or funeral. **b** make a doleful or ominous sound. **2** *tr.* proclaim by or as by a knell (*knelled the death of all their hopes*). □ **ring the knell of** announce or herald the end of. [OE *cnyll*, *cnyllan*: perh. infl. by *bell*]

Kneller /'nelə(r)/, Sir Godfrey (1649–1723), German-born portrait painter who established a prolific workshop in London from 1674. He was a dominant court and society painter, executing commissions for Charles II and James II, and becoming principal painter to William and Mary at their accession. His best work captures the sitter's personality, and is more than a mere visual record. Although Kneller always painted the faces the work of many assistants can often be seen in backgrounds and details. Knighted in 1692 and created a baronet in 1715, he was the most socially eminent and successful English artist of his age.

knelt *past* and *past part.* of KNEEL.

Knesset /'knesɪt/ *n.* the parliament of the State of Israel. [Heb., lit. gathering]

knew *past* of KNOW.

knickerbocker /'nɪkəˌbɒkə(r)/ *n.* **1** (in *pl.*) loose-fitting breeches gathered at the knee or calf. **2** (**Knickerbocker**) **a** a New Yorker. **b** a descendant of the original Dutch settlers in New York. □ **Knickerbocker Glory** ice-cream served with other ingredients in a tall glass. [Diedrich *Knickerbocker*, pretended author of W. Irving's *History of New York* (1809)]

knickers /'nɪkəz/ *n.pl.* **1** *Brit.* a woman's or girl's undergarment covering the body from the waist or hips to the top of the thighs and having leg-holes or separate legs. **2** esp. *US* **a** knickerbockers. **b** a boy's short trousers. **3** (as *int.*) *Brit. sl.* an expression of contempt. [abbr. of KNICKERBOCKER]

knick-knack /'nɪknæk/ *n.* **1** a useless and usu. worthless ornament; a trinket. **2** a small, dainty article of furniture, dress, etc. □□ **knick-knackery** *n.* **knick-knackish** *adj.* [redupl. of *knack* in obs. sense 'trinket']

knife /naɪf/ *n. & v.* —*n.* (*pl.* **knives** /naɪvz/) **1 a** a metal blade used as a cutting tool with usu. one long sharp edge fixed rigidly in a handle or hinged (cf. PENKNIFE). **b** a similar tool used as a weapon. **2** a cutting-blade forming part of a machine. **3** (as **the knife**) a surgical operation or operations. —*v.tr.* **1** cut or stab with a knife. **2** *sl.* bring about the defeat of (a person) by underhand means. □ **at knife-point** threatened with a knife or an ultimatum etc. **before you can say knife** *colloq.* very quickly or suddenly. **get one's knife into** treat maliciously or vindictively, persecute. **knife-board** a board on which knives are cleaned. **knife-edge 1** the edge of a knife. **2** a position of extreme danger or uncertainty. **3** a steel wedge on which a pendulum etc. oscillates. **4** = ARÊTE. **knife-grinder 1** a travelling sharpener of knives etc. **2** a person who grinds knives etc. during their manufacture. **knife-machine** a machine for cleaning knives. **knife-pleat** a narrow flat pleat on a skirt etc., usu. overlapping another. **knife-rest** a metal or glass support for a carving-knife or -fork at table. **knife-throwing** a circus etc. act in which knives are thrown at targets. **night of the long knives** see LONG[1]. **that one could cut with a knife** *colloq.* (of an accent, atmosphere, etc.) very obvious, oppressive, etc. □□ **knifelike** *adj.* **knifer** *n.* [OE *cnif* f. ON *knifr* f. Gmc]

knight /naɪt/ *n. & v.* —*n.* **1** a man awarded a non-hereditary title (*Sir*) by a sovereign in recognition of merit or service. **2** *hist.* **a** a man, usu. noble, raised esp. by a sovereign to honourable military rank after service as a page and squire. **b** a military follower or attendant, esp. of a lady as her champion in a war or tournament. **3** a man devoted to the service of a woman, cause, etc. **4** *Chess* a piece usu. shaped like a horse's head. **5 a** *Rom.Hist.* a member of the class of *equites*, orig. the cavalry of the Roman army. **b** *Gk Hist.* a citizen of the second class in Athens. **6** (in full **knight of the shire**) *hist.* a gentleman representing a shire or county in parliament. —*v.tr.* confer a knighthood on. □ **knight bachelor** (*pl.* **knights bachelor**) a knight not belonging to a special order. **knight commander** see COMMANDER. **knight errant 1** a medieval knight wandering in search of chivalrous adventures. **2** a man of a chivalrous or quixotic nature. **knight-errantry** the practice or conduct of a knight errant. **knight marshal** *hist.* an officer of the royal household with judicial functions. **knight of the road** *colloq.* **1** a highwayman. **2** a commercial traveller. **3** a tramp. **4** a lorry driver or taxi driver. **knight-service** *hist.* the tenure of land by military service. □□ **knighthood** *n.* **knightlike** *adj.* **knightly** *adj. & adv. poet.* **knightliness** *n.* [OE *cniht* boy, youth, hero f. WG]

knightage /ˈnaɪtɪdʒ/ *n.* **1** knights collectively. **2** a list and account of knights.

Knights Hospitallers /hɒsˈpɪt(ə)l(ə)rz/ a military religious order founded as the Knights of the Hospital of St John at Jerusalem in the 11th c. Their headquarters were later at Rhodes (1309–1522), then Malta (1530–1798). Originally protectors of pilgrims, they also undertook the care of the sick and became a powerful and wealthy military force, with foundations in various European countries, and valiant fighters against the Turks. Gradually there was a decline in morals and discipline, and their military power ended when Malta was surrendered to Napoleon (1798). In England their property was sequestered in 1540, and the order remained dormant until revived on a mainly Anglican basis in 1831, and constituted an order of chivalry in 1888. It was responsible for the foundation of the St John Ambulance Association in 1878 and the St John Ambulance Brigade in 1888 (now St John Ambulance).

Knights Templars the 'Poor Knights of Christ and of the Temple of Solomon', a military order founded in 1118 to protect pilgrims from bandits in the Holy Land, where they were given quarters on the site of Solomon's temple in Jerusalem. The order became powerful and wealthy, particularly in the 13th c. Their wealth was deposited in 'temples' in Paris and London and they became trusted bankers. Their arrogance towards rulers, their wealth, and their rivalry with the Knights Hospitallers, led to their downfall. Philip IV of France coveted their wealth and brought false charges of sodomy, blasphemy, and heresy against the order. It was suppressed in 1312, and many of its possessions were given to the Hospitallers. The Inner and Middle Temple in London are on the site of the Templars' English headquarters.

knish /knɪʃ/ *n.* a dumpling of flaky dough filled with cheese etc. and baked or fried. [Yiddish f. Russ.]

knit /nɪt/ *v. & n.* —*v.* (**knitting**; *past* and *past part.* **knitted** or (esp. in senses 2–4) **knit**) **1** *tr.* (also *absol.*) **a** make (a garment, blanket, etc.) by interlocking loops of esp. wool with knitting-needles. **b** make (a garment etc.) with a knitting machine. **c** make (a plain stitch) in knitting (*knit one, purl one*). **2 a** *tr.* contract (the forehead) in vertical wrinkles. **b** *intr.* (of the forehead) contract; frown. **3** *tr. & intr.* (often foll. by *together*) make or become close or compact esp. by common interests etc. (*a close-knit group*). **4** *intr.* (often foll. by *together*) (of parts of a broken bone) become joined; heal. —*n.* knitted material or a knitted garment. □ **knit up 1** make or repair by knitting. **2** conclude, finish, or end. □□ **knitter** *n.* [OE *cnyttan* f. WG: cf. KNOT[1]]

knitting /ˈnɪtɪŋ/ *n.* **1** a garment etc. in the process of being knitted. **2 a** the act of knitting. **b** an instance of this. □ **knitting-machine** a machine used for mechanically knitting garments etc. **knitting-needle** a thin pointed rod of steel, wood, plastic, etc., used esp. in pairs for knitting.

knitwear /ˈnɪtweə(r)/ *n.* knitted garments.

knives *pl.* of KNIFE.

knob /nɒb/ *n. & v.* —*n.* **1 a** a rounded protuberance, esp. at the end or on the surface of a thing. **b** a handle of a door, drawer, etc., shaped like a knob. **c** a knob-shaped attachment for pulling, turning, etc. (*press the knob under the desk*). **2** a small, usu. round, piece (of butter, coal, sugar, etc.). —*v.* (**knobbed**, **knobbing**) **1** *tr.* provide with knobs. **2** *intr.* (usu. foll. by *out*) bulge. □ **with knobs on** *Brit. sl.* that and more (used as a retort to an insult, in emphatic agreement, etc.) (*and the same to you with knobs on*). □□ **knobby** *adj.* **knoblike** *adj.* [ME f. MLG *knobbe* knot, knob, bud: cf. KNOP, NOB[2], NUB]

knobble /ˈnɒb(ə)l/ *n.* a small knob. □□ **knobbly** *adj.* [ME, dimin. of KNOB: cf. Du. & LG *knobbel*]

knobkerrie /ˈnɒbˌkerɪ/ *n.* a short stick with a knobbed head used as a weapon esp. by S. African tribes. [after Afrik. *knopkierie*]

knobstick /ˈnɒbstɪk/ *n.* **1** = KNOBKERRIE. **2** *archaic* = BLACKLEG.

knock /nɒk/ *v. & n.* —*v.* **1 a** *tr.* strike (a hard surface) with an audible sharp blow (*knocked the table three times*). **b** *intr.* strike, esp. a door, to gain admittance (*can you hear someone knocking?*; *knocked at the door*). **2** *tr.* make (a hole, a dent, etc.) by knocking (*knock a hole in the fence*). **3** *tr.* (usu. foll. by *in, out, off*, etc.) drive (a thing, a person, etc.) by striking (*knocked the ball into the hole*; *knocked those ideas out of his head*; *knocked her hand away*). **4** *tr. sl.* criticize. **5** *intr.* **a** (of a motor or other engine) make a thumping or rattling noise esp. as the result of a loose bearing. **b** = PINK[3]. **6** *tr. Brit. sl.* make a strong impression on, astonish. **7** *tr. Brit. coarse sl. offens.* = *knock off 7.* —*n.* **1** an act of knocking. **2** a sharp rap, esp. at a door. **3** an audible sharp blow. **4** the sound of knocking in esp. a motor engine. **5** *Cricket colloq.* an innings. □ **knock about** (or **around**) **1** strike repeatedly; treat roughly (*knocked her about*). **2** lead a wandering adventurous life; wander aimlessly. **3** be present without design or volition (*there's a cup knocking about somewhere*). **4** (usu. foll. by *with*) be associated socially (*knocks about with his brother*). **knock against 1** collide with. **2** come across casually. **knock back 1** *Brit. sl.* eat or drink, esp. quickly. **2** *Brit. sl.* disconcert. **3** *Austral. & NZ colloq.* refuse, rebuff. **knock-back** *n. Austral. & NZ colloq.* a refusal, a rebuff. **knock the bottom out of** see BOTTOM. **knock down 1** strike (esp. a person) to the ground with a blow. **2** demolish. **3** (usu. foll. by *to*) (at an auction) dispose of (an article) to a bidder by a knock with a hammer (*knocked the Picasso down to him for a million*). **4** *colloq.* lower the price of (an article). **5** take (machinery, furniture, etc.) to pieces for transportation. **6** *US sl.* steal. **7** *Austral. & NZ sl.* spend (a pay cheque etc.) freely. **knock-down** *attrib.adj.* **1** (of a blow, misfortune, argument, etc.) overwhelming. **2** *Brit.* (of a price) very low. **3** (of a price at auction) reserve. **4** (of furniture etc.) easily dismantled and reassembled. —*n. Austral. & NZ sl.* an introduction (to a person). **knock for knock agreement** an agreement between insurance companies by which each pays its own policyholder regardless of liability. **knock one's head against** come into collision with (unfavourable facts or conditions). **knocking-shop** *Brit. sl.* a brothel. **knock into a cocked hat** see COCK[1]. **knock into the middle of next week** *colloq.* send (a person) flying, esp. with a blow. **knock into shape** see SHAPE. **knock-kneed** having knock knees. **knock knees** an abnormal condition with the legs curved inwards at the knee. **knock off 1** strike off with a blow. **2** *colloq.* **a** finish work (*knocked off at 5.30*). **b** finish (work) (*knocked off work early*). **3** *colloq.* dispatch (business). **4** *colloq.* rapidly produce (a work of art, verses, etc.). **5** (often foll. by *from*) deduct (a sum) from a price, bill, etc. **6** *sl.* steal. **7** *Brit. coarse sl. offens.* have sexual intercourse with (a woman). **8** *sl.* kill. **knock on** *Rugby Football* drive (a ball) with the hand or arm towards the opponents' goal-line. **knock-on** *n.* an act of knocking on. **knock-on effect** a secondary, indirect, or cumulative effect. **knock on the head 1** stun or kill (a person) by a blow on the head. **2** *colloq.* put an end to (a scheme etc.). **knock on** (or **knock**) **wood** *US* = *touch wood*. **knock out 1** make (a person) unconscious by a blow on the head. **2** knock down (a boxer) for a count of 10, thereby winning the contest. **3** defeat, esp. in a knockout competition. **4** *sl.* astonish. **5** (*refl.*) *colloq.* exhaust (*knocked themselves out swimming*). **6** *colloq.* make or write (a plan etc.) hastily. **7** empty (a tobacco-pipe) by tapping. **8** *Austral., NZ, & US sl.* earn. **knock sideways** *colloq.* disconcert; astonish. **knock spots off** defeat easily. **knock together** put together or assemble hastily or roughly. **knock under** submit. **knock up 1** make or arrange hastily. **2** drive upwards with a blow. **3 a** become exhausted or ill. **b** exhaust or make ill. **4** *Brit.* arouse (a person) by a knock at the door. **5** *Cricket* score (runs) rapidly. **6** esp. *US sl.* make pregnant. **7** practise a ball game before formal play begins. **knock-up** *n.* a practice at tennis etc. **take a** (or **the**) **knock** be hard hit financially or emotionally. [ME f. OE *cnocian*: prob. imit.]

knockabout /ˈnɒkəbaʊt/ *adj. & n.* —*attrib.adj.* **1** (of comedy) boisterous; slapstick. **2** (of clothes) suitable for rough use. **3**

Austral. of a farm or station handyman. —*n.* **1** *Austral.* a farm or station handyman. **2** a knockabout performer or performance.

knocker /ˈnɒkə(r)/ *n.* **1** a metal or wooden instrument hinged to a door for knocking to call attention. **2** a person or thing that knocks. **3** (in *pl.*) *coarse sl.* a woman's breasts. **4** a person who buys or sells door to door. □ **knocker-up** *Brit. hist.* a person employed to rouse early workers by knocking at their doors or windows. **on the knocker 1 a** (buying or selling) from door to door. **b** (obtained) on credit. **2** *Austral. & NZ colloq.* promptly. **up to the knocker** *Brit. sl.* in good condition; to perfection.

knockout /ˈnɒkaʊt/ *n.* **1** the act of making unconscious by a blow. **2** *Boxing* etc. a blow that knocks an opponent out. **3** a competition in which the loser in each round is eliminated (also *attrib.*: *a knockout round*). **4** *colloq.* an outstanding or irresistible person or thing. □ **knockout drops** a drug added to a drink to cause unconsciousness.

knoll¹ /nəʊl/ *n.* a small hill or mound. [OE *cnoll* hilltop, rel. to MDu., MHG *knolle* clod, ON *knollr* hilltop]

knoll² /nəʊl/ *v. & n. archaic* —*v.* **1** *tr. & intr.* = KNELL. **2** *tr.* summon by the sound of a bell. —*n.* = KNELL. [ME, var. of KNELL: perh. imit.]

knop /nɒp/ *n.* **1** a knob, esp. ornamental. **2** an ornamental loop or tuft in yarn. **3** *archaic* a flower-bud. [ME f. MLG, MDu. *knoppe*]

knopkierie /ˈknɒpˌkɪərɪ/ *n. S.Afr.* = KNOBKERRIE. [Afrik.]

Knossos /ˈknɒsɒs/ the principal city of Minoan Crete, near the port of Heraklion. It was occupied from neolithic times until *c.*1200 BC. Excavations by Sir Arthur Evans from 1900 onwards revealed remains of a luxurious and spectacularly decorated complex of buildings which he named the Palace of Minos, with frescoes of landscapes, animal life, and the sport of bull-leaping. In *c.*1450 BC Crete was overrun by the Mycenaeans, but the palace was not finally destroyed until the 14th or early 13th c. BC.

knot¹ /nɒt/ *n. & v.* —*n.* **1 a** an intertwining of a rope, string, tress of hair, etc., with another, itself, or something else to join or fasten together. **b** a set method of tying a knot (*a reef knot*). **c** a ribbon etc. tied as an ornament and worn on a dress etc. **d** a tangle in hair, knitting, etc. **2 a** a unit of a ship's or aircraft's speed equivalent to one nautical mile per hour (see *nautical mile*). **b** a division marked by knots on a log-line, as a measure of speed. **c** *colloq.* a nautical mile. **3** (usu. foll. by *of*) a group or cluster (*a small knot of journalists at the gate*). **4** something forming or maintaining a union; a bond or tie, esp. of wedlock. **5** a hard lump of tissue in an animal or human body. **6 a** a knob or protuberance in a stem, branch, or root. **b** a hard mass formed in a tree trunk at the intersection with a branch. **c** a round cross-grained piece in timber where a branch has been cut through. **d** a node on the stem of a plant. **7** a difficulty; a problem. **8** a central point in a problem or the plot of a story etc. **9** (in full **porter's knot**) *Brit. hist.* a double shoulder-pad and forehead-loop used for carrying loads. —*v.* (**knotted, knotting**) **1** *tr.* tie (a string etc.) in a knot. **2** *tr.* entangle. **3** *tr.* knit (the brows). **4** *tr.* unite closely or intricately (*knotted together in intrigue*). **5 a** *intr.* make knots for fringing. **b** *tr.* make (a fringe) with knots. □ **at a rate of knots** *colloq.* very fast. **get knotted!** *sl.* an expression of disbelief, annoyance, etc. **knot-garden** an intricately designed formal garden. **knot-hole** a hole in a piece of timber where a knot has fallen out (sense 6). **tie in knots** *colloq.* baffle or confuse completely. □□ **knotless** *adj.* **knotter** *n.* **knotting** *n.* (esp. in sense 5 of *v.*). [OE *cnotta* f. WG]

knot² /nɒt/ *n.* a small sandpiper, *Calidris canutus.* [ME: orig. unkn.]

knotgrass /ˈnɒtɡrɑːs/ *n.* **1** a common weed, *Polygonum aviculare,* with creeping stems and small pink flowers. **2** = POLYGONUM. Also called KNOTWEED.

knotty /ˈnɒtɪ/ *adj.* (**knottier, knottiest**) **1** full of knots. **2** hard to explain; puzzling (*a knotty problem*). □□ **knottily** *adv.* **knottiness** *n.*

knotweed /ˈnɒtwiːd/ *n.* = POLYGONUM.

knotwork /ˈnɒtwɜːk/ *n.* ornamental work representing or consisting of intertwined cords.

knout /naʊt, nuːt/ *n. & v.* —*n. hist.* a scourge used in imperial Russia, often causing death. —*v.tr.* flog with a knout. [F f. Russ. *knut* f. Icel. *knútr,* rel. to KNOT¹]

know /nəʊ/ *v. & n.* —*v.* (*past* **knew** /njuː/; *past part.* **known** /nəʊn/) **1** *tr.* (often foll. by *that, how, what,* etc.) **a** have in the mind; have learnt; be able to recall (*knows a lot about cars; knows what to do*). **b** (also *absol.*) be aware of (a fact) (*he knows I am waiting; I think he knows*). **c** have a good command of (a subject or language) (*knew German; knows his tables*). **2** *tr.* be acquainted or friendly with (a person or thing). **3** *tr.* **a** recognize; identify (*I knew him at once; knew him for an American*). **b** (foll. by *to* + infin.) be aware of (a person or thing) as being or doing what is specified (*knew them to be rogues*). **c** (foll. by *from*) be able to distinguish (one from another) (*did not know him from Adam*). **4** *tr.* be subject to (*her joy knew no bounds*). **5** *tr.* have personal experience of (fear etc.). **6** *tr.* (as **known** *adj.*) **a** publicly acknowledged (*a known thief; a known fact*). **b** *Math.* (of a quantity etc.) having a value that can be stated. **7** *intr.* have understanding or knowledge. **8** *tr. archaic* have sexual intercourse with. —*n.* (in phr. **in the know**) *colloq.* well-informed; having special knowledge. □ **all one knows** (or **knows how**) **1** all one can (*did all he knew to stop it*). **2** to the utmost of one's power (*tried all she knew*). **before one knows where one is** with baffling speed. **be not to know 1** have no way of learning (*wasn't to know they'd arrive late*). **2** be not to be told (*she's not to know about the party*). **don't I know it!** *colloq.* an expression of rueful assent. **don't you know** *colloq.* or *joc.* an expression used for emphasis (*such a bore, don't you know*). **for all** (or **aught**) **I know** so far as my knowledge extends. **have been known to** be known to have done (*they have been known to not turn up*). **I knew it!** I was sure that this would happen. **I know what** I have a new idea, suggestion, etc. **know about** have information about. **know-all** *colloq.* a person who seems to know everything. **know best** be or claim to be better informed etc. than others. **know better than** (foll. by *that,* or *to* + infin.) be wise, well-informed, or well-mannered enough to avoid (specified behaviour etc.). **know by name** I have heard the name of. **2** be able to give the name of. **know by sight** recognize the appearance (only) of. **know how** know the way to do something. **know-how** *n.* **1** practical knowledge; technique, expertise. **2** natural skill or invention. **know-it-all** = know-all. **know-nothing 1** an ignorant person. **2** an agnostic. **know of** be aware of; have heard of (*not that I know of*). **know one's own mind** be decisive, not vacillate. **know the ropes** (or **one's stuff**) be fully knowledgeable or experienced. **know a thing or two** be experienced or shrewd. **know what's what** have adequate knowledge of the world, life, etc. **know who's who** be aware of who or what each person is. **not if I know it** only against my will. **not know that . . .** *colloq.* be fairly sure that . . . not (*I don't know that I want to go*). **not know what hit one** be suddenly injured, killed, disconcerted, etc. **not want to know** refuse to take any notice of. **what do you know** (or **know about that**)? *colloq.* an expression of surprise. **you know** *colloq.* **1** an expression implying something generally known or known to the hearer (*you know, the pub on the corner*). **2** an expression used as a gap-filler in conversation. **you know something** (or **what**)? I am going to tell you something. **you-know-what** (or **-who**) a thing or person unspecified but understood. **you never know** nothing in the future is certain. □□ **knowable** *adj.* **knower** *n.* [OE (ge)*cnāwan,* rel. to CAN¹, KEN]

knowing /ˈnəʊɪŋ/ *n. & adj.* —*n.* the state of being aware or informed of any thing. —*adj.* **1** usu. *derog.* cunning; sly. **2** showing knowledge; shrewd. □ **there is no knowing** no one can tell. □□ **knowingness** *n.*

knowingly /ˈnəʊɪŋlɪ/ *adv.* **1** consciously; intentionally (*had never knowingly injured him*). **2** in a knowing manner (*smiled knowingly*).

knowledge /ˈnɒlɪdʒ/ *n.* **1 a** (usu. foll. by *of*) awareness or familiarity gained by experience (of a person, fact, or thing) (*have no knowledge of that*). **b** a person's range of information (*is not within his knowledge*). **2 a** (usu. foll. by *of*) a theoretical or practical understanding of a subject, language, etc. (*has a good knowledge of Greek*). **b** the sum of what is known (*every branch of knowledge*). **3** *Philos.* true, justified belief; certain understanding, as opp. to opinion. **4** = *carnal knowledge.* □ **come to one's knowledge** become known to one. **to my knowledge 1** so far as I know. **2**

as I know for certain. [ME *knaulege*, with earlier *knawlechen* (v.) formed as KNOW + OE -*lǣcan* f. *lāc* as in WEDLOCK]

knowledgeable /ˈnɒlɪdʒəb(ə)l/ *adj.* (also **knowledgable**) well-informed; intelligent. □□ **knowledgeability** /-ˈbɪlɪtɪ/ *n.* **knowledgeableness** *n.* **knowledgeably** *adv.*

known *past part.* of KNOW.

Knox[1] /nɒks/, John (*c.*1505–72), Scottish Protestant reformer. After early involvement in the Scottish Reformation, and more than a decade spent preaching in various parts of Protestant Europe, Knox returned to his homeland in 1559 and played a central part in the overthrow of the French regency and the establishment of a Scottish Protestant State. During the brief reign of the Catholic queen Mary Queen of Scots he was the spokesman of the religious interests opposed to her. A fiery orator, Knox was very much a radical in his own day, but considerably more moderate than many of his 17th-c. successors.

Knox[2] /nɒks/, Ronald Arbuthnott (1888–1957), British Roman Catholic priest whose translation of the Bible from the Vulgate (1945–9) was accepted for use in the Roman Catholic Church. He also wrote detective stories and various works of humour.

Knt. *abbr.* Knight.

knuckle /ˈnʌk(ə)l/ *n. & v.* —*n.* **1** the bone at a finger-joint, esp. that adjoining the hand. **2 a** a projection of the carpal or tarsal joint of a quadruped. **b** a joint of meat consisting of this with the adjoining parts, esp. of bacon or pork. —*v.tr.* strike, press, or rub with the knuckles. □ **go the knuckle** *Austral. sl.* fight, punch. **knuckle-bone 1** bone forming a knuckle. **2** the bone of a sheep or other animal corresponding to or resembling a knuckle. **3** a knuckle of meat. **knuckle-bones 1** animal knuckle-bones used in the game of jacks. **2** the game of jacks. **knuckle down** (often foll. by *to*) **1** apply oneself seriously (to a task etc.). **2** (also **knuckle under**) give in; submit. **knuckle sandwich** *sl.* a punch in the mouth. **rap on** (or **over**) **the knuckles** see RAP[1]. □□ **knuckly** *adj.* [ME *knokel* f. MLG, MDu. *knökel*, dimin. of *knoke* bone]

knuckleduster /ˈnʌk(ə)l,dʌstə(r)/ *n.* a metal guard worn over the knuckles in fighting, esp. to increase the effect of the blows.

knur /nɜː(r)/ *n.* (also **knurr**) **1** a hard excrescence on the trunk of a tree. **2** a hard concretion. [ME *knorre*, var. of KNAR]

knurl /nɜːl/ *n.* a small projecting knob, ridge, etc. □□ **knurled** /nɜːld/ *adj.* [KNUR]

KO *abbr.* **1** knockout. **2** kick-off.

koa /ˈkəʊə/ *n.* **1** a Hawaiian tree, *Acacia koa*, which produces dark red wood. **2** this wood. [Hawaiian]

koala /kəʊˈɑːlə/ *n.* (in full **koala bear**) an Australian bearlike marsupial, *Phascolarctos cinereus*, having thick grey fur and feeding on eucalyptus leaves. [Aboriginal *kūl(l)a*]

koan /ˈkəʊæn/ *n.* a riddle used in Zen Buddhism to demonstrate the inadequacy of logical reasoning. [Jap., = public matter (for thought)]

Kobe /ˈkəʊbeɪ/ a seaport of Japan, on Honshu Island; pop. (1987) 1,413,000.

København see COPENHAGEN.

kobold /ˈkəʊbɒld/ *n. Germanic Mythol.* **1** a familiar spirit; a brownie. **2** an underground spirit in mines etc. [G]

Koch /kɒx/, Robert (1843–1910), German bacteriologist. As a young country doctor he studied an outbreak of anthrax in local cattle, and successfully identified and cultured the bacillus causing this. He devised new and better methods for obtaining pure cultures, and identified first the tuberculosis bacillus (his greatest discovery) and then the organism that causes cholera. He also studied typhoid fever, malaria, and other tropical diseases, and formulated rules as to the conditions which must be satisfied before a disease can be ascribed to a specific micro-organism. The techniques that he devised are the basis of modern methods. Koch was awarded the Nobel Prize for medicine in 1905.

Köchel number /ˈkɜːx(ə)l/ *n. Mus.* a number given to each of Mozart's compositions in the complete catalogue of his works compiled by Köchel and his successors. [L. von *Köchel*, Austrian scientist d. 1877]

KO'd /keɪˈəʊd/ *adj.* knocked out. [abbr.]

Kodály /ˈkəʊdaɪ/, Zoltán (1882–1967), Hungarian composer whose works include operas and orchestral and choral music. He attached equal importance to his work in collecting and publishing folk-songs and his long composing career which spanned 70 years. He heard and was influenced by Debussy's music while in Paris, but his main source of inspiration was his native land, and Bartók described his music as 'the most perfect embodiment of the Hungarian spirit'.

Kodiak /ˈkəʊdɪæk/ *n.* (in full **Kodiak bear**) a large Alaskan brown bear, *Ursus arctos middendorffi.* [Kodiak Island, Alaska]

koel /ˈkəʊəl/ *n.* a dark-coloured cuckoo, *Eudynamys scolopacea.* [Hindi *kóīl* f. Skr. *kokila*]

Koestler /ˈkɜːstlə(r)/, Arthur (1905–83), Hungarian-born essayist and novelist, in his youth a science correspondent. His best-known novel *Darkness at Noon* (1940) exposed the Stalinist purges of the 1930s. In *The Sleepwalkers* (1959) and other late works he questioned some of the common assumptions of science, and left money in his will for research into the paranormal. He and his wife committed suicide together.

Koh-i-noor /ˈkəʊɪ,nʊə(r)/ *n.* an Indian diamond, famous for its size, one of the treasures of Aurangzeb, with a history going back to the 14th c. It became one of the British Crown jewels on the annexation of the Punjab in 1849. [Pers. *kōh-i ñr* mountain of light]

Kohl /kəʊl/, Helmut (1930–), German statesman, Chancellor of the Federal Republic of Germany from 1982, and of a united Germany from October 1990.

kohl /kəʊl/ *n.* a black powder, usu. antimony sulphide or lead sulphide, used as eye make-up esp. in Eastern countries. [Arab. *kuḥl*]

kohlrabi /kəʊlˈrɑːbɪ/ *n.* (*pl.* **kohlrabies**) a variety of cabbage with an edible turnip-like swollen stem. [G f. It. *cavoli rape* (pl.) f. med.L *caulorapa* (as COLE, RAPE[2])]

koine /ˈkɔɪnɪ/ *n.* **1** the common language of the Greeks from the close of the classical period to the Byzantine era. **2** a common language shared by various peoples; a lingua franca. [Gk *koinē* (*dialektos*) common (language)]

kola var. of COLA.

Kola Peninsula /ˈkəʊlə/ a peninsula on the north-west coast of the Soviet Union, separating the White Sea from the Barents Sea. The port of Murmansk lies on its northern coast.

kolinsky /kəˈlɪnskɪ/ *n.* (*pl.* **-ies**) **1** the Siberian mink, *Mustela sibirica*, having a brown coat in winter. **2** the fur of this. [Russ. *kolinskiĭ* f. *Kola* in NW Russia]

kolkhoz /ˈkɒlkɒz, kalkˈhɔːz/ *n.* a collective farm in the USSR. [Russ. f. *kollektivnoe khozyaĭstvo* collective farm]

Köln see COLOGNE.

komitadji (also **komitaji**) var. of COMITADJI.

Komodo /kəˈməʊdəʊ/ a small island of Indonesia, situated between the islands of Sumbawa and Flores.

komodo dragon /kəˈməʊdəʊ/ *n.* (also **komodo lizard**) a large monitor lizard, *Varanus komodoensis.* It is the largest extant species of lizard and is found only on Komodo and a few neighbouring islands.

Kompong Som /ˈkɒmpɒŋ sɒm/ the chief deep-water port of Cambodia, situated on the Gulf of Thailand.

Komsomol /ˈkɒmsə,mɒl/ *n.* **1** an organization for Communist youth in the Soviet Union. **2** a member of this. [Russ. f. *Kommunisticheskiĭ soyuz molodezhi* Communist League of Youth]

Königsberg /ˈkɜːnɪgz,beəg/ a city now called Kaliningrad (see entry), formerly the capital of East Prussia.

Kon-Tiki /kɒnˈtɪkɪ/ the raft made of balsa logs in which the Norwegian anthropologist Thor Heyerdahl (see entry) sailed from the western coast of Peru to the islands of Polynesia in 1947. It was named after an Inca god.

Konya /ˈkɒnjə/ a city on the south-west edge of the central plateau of Turkey; pop. (1985) 438,850. Known in Roman times as Iconium, towards the end of the 11th c. it became the capital of the Seljuk sultans of Rum and was renamed Konya. In the

13th c. it was the home of the Islamic poet and mystic Jalal al-Din Rumi (see entry), founder of the whirling dervishes.

koodoo var. of KUDU.

kook /kuːk/ n. & adj. US sl. —n. a crazy or eccentric person. — adj. crazy; eccentric. [20th c.: prob. f. CUCKOO]

kookaburra /ˈkʊkəˌbʌrə/ n. any Australian kingfisher of the genus Dacelo, esp. D. novaeguineae, which makes a strange laughing cry. Also called laughing jackass. [Aboriginal]

kooky /ˈkuːkɪ/ adj. (kookier, kookiest) sl. crazy. □□ kookily adv. kookiness n.

kop /kɒp/ n. 1 S.Afr. a prominent hill or peak. 2 (Kop) Football a high bank of terracing for standing spectators, esp. supporting the home side. [Afrik. f. Du., = head: cf. COP²]

kopek (also **kopeck**) var. of COPECK.

kopi /ˈkəʊpɪ/ n. Austral. powdered gypsum. [Aboriginal]

koppie /ˈkɒpɪ/ n. (also **kopje**) S.Afr. a small hill. [Afrik. koppie, Du. kopje, dimin. of kop head]

koradji /kəˈrædʒɪ/ n. (pl. **koradjis**) Austral. an Aboriginal medicine man. [Aboriginal]

Koran /kɔːˈrɑːn, kə-/ n. (also **Qur'an** /kə-/), **the** the holy book of Islam, composed of the revelations which came to the Prophet Muhammad during his lifetime, from c.610 to his death in 632. Written in Arabic, the revelations are grouped into 114 units of varying sizes which are known as suras; the first sura is said as part of the ritual prayer. The traditional arrangement of the suras is not chronological but rather according to length, from the longest. The revelations touch upon all aspects of human existence, from the doctrinally focused revelations of Muhammad's early career in Mecca to those concerning social organization and legislation, which were communicated while the Muslim community was based in Medina (622–30). Considered to be the direct and inimitable word of God, which is applicable for all time and in all circumstances to the regulation and religious expression of human society, the Koran is held by Muslims to be untranslatable, although versions or interpretations in many other languages are available. The Koran is regarded as the ultimate exemplar of Arabic linguistic and literary prowess and the supreme and perfect guide to Arabic grammar and stylistics. Its memorization forms the basis of a traditional Islamic elementary education in a 'Koran school'. □□ **Koranic** /-ˈrænɪk, -ˈrɑːnɪk/ adj. [Arab. ḳurʾān recitation f. ḳara'a read]

Korbut /ˈkɔːbət/, Olga (1955–), Soviet gymnast, whose performances (especially at the 1972 Olympic Games) greatly increased the popularity of the sport.

Korda /ˈkɔːdə/, Sir Alexander (1893–1956), real name Sándor Kellner, Hungarian-born film producer and director, who settled in England and in 1932 formed London Film Productions. His extravagant films, which achieved international recognition, included The Private Life of Henry VIII (1933), Rembrandt (1936), both of which he directed himself, Catherine the Great, The Scarlet Pimpernel (both 1934), Sanders of the River, The Ghost Goes West (both 1935), Things to Come, and Elephant Boy (both 1936). By 1939 he had over-extended himself and lost Denham Studios, which he had built, and though he later refloated London Films he never regained his earlier eminence.

Kordofan /ˌkɔːdəˈfɑːn/ a region of central Sudan; pop. (1983) 3,093,300.

Korea /kəˈriːə/ a country in eastern Asia situated on a peninsula between the Sea of Japan and the Yellow Sea, now divided along the 38th parallel into the People's Democratic Republic of Korea (North Korea; pop. (est. 1988) 21,983,800; capital, Pyongyang) and the Republic of Korea (South Korea; pop. (est. 1988) 42,772,950; capital, Seoul); the official language of both countries is Korean. Possessed of a distinct national and cultural identity and ruled from the 14th c. by the Korean Yi Dynasty, Korea has suffered as a result of its position between Chinese and Japanese spheres of influence. Chinese domination was ended by the Sino-Japanese War (1894–5) and after the Russo-Japanese War a decade later the country was finally annexed by Japan in 1910. After the Japanese surrender at the end of the Second World War, the northern half of the country was occupied by the Soviets and the southern half by the Americans.

Separate countries were created in 1948 and two years later the Northern invasion of the South resulted in the Korean War (1950–3). The borders were restored at the end of the war but both countries were some time in recovering from the devastation caused by military operations. Each is now prospering, particularly the South which is now the most rapidly growing industrial nation in the world.

Korean /kəˈriːən/ adj. of Korea or its people or language. —n. 1 a native or national of North or South Korea. 2 the language of North and South Korea, spoken by about 60 million people. Its linguistic affiliations are uncertain although it seems most similar to Japanese. Its vocabulary and orthography has been heavily influenced by Chinese. The Korean alphabet is the only true alphabetical script native to the Far East.

korfball /ˈkɔːfbɔːl/ n. a game like basketball played by two teams consisting of 6 men and 6 women each. [Du. korfbal f. korf basket + bal ball]

Kortrijk /ˈkɔːtraɪk/ (French **Courtrai**) a textile manufacturing city of Belgium, in the province of West Flanders; pop. (1988) 76,314.

Korup /ˈkɒrəp/ a national park in western Cameroon, established in 1961 to protect a large area of tropical rain forest.

Kos see Cos.

Kosciusko[1] /kɒsˈtʃʊʃkəʊ/, Thaddeus (1746–1817), Polish soldier and patriot. A trained soldier, he offered his services to the American rebels during the War of Independence and was made Colonel of Engineers in 1776. He returned to Poland after the war and led the rebellion against foreign rule in 1794. Captured and imprisoned by the Russians (1794–6), he eventually moved to France, where he devoted the rest of his life to the cause of Polish independence.

Kosciusko[2] /kɒsˈtʃʊskəʊ/, **Mount** the highest mountain in Australia, rising to a height of 2,228 m (7,234 ft.) in the Great Dividing Range in New South Wales.

kosher /ˈkəʊʃə(r), ˈkɒʃ-/ adj. & n. —adj. 1 (of food or premises in which food is sold, cooked, or eaten) fulfilling the requirements of Jewish law. 2 colloq. correct; genuine; legitimate. —n. 1 kosher food. 2 a kosher shop. [Heb. kāšēr proper]

Kosovo /ˈkɒsəˌvəʊ/ an autonomous province of Serbia in southern Yugoslavia; pop. (1981) 1,584,400; capital, Pristina. It borders on Albania and the majority of the people are Albanians.

Kossuth /ˈkɒsuːθ/, Lajos (1802–94), Hungarian statesman and patriot. After an early career as an opponent of Hapsburg domination of Hungary, he led the 1848 insurrection and was appointed governor of the country during the brief period of independence. The uprising was crushed in 1849, and he fled into exile where he spent the rest of his life.

Kosygin /kɒˈsiːgɪn/, Alexsei Nikolayevich (1904–80), Soviet statesman. Mayor of Leningrad in 1938–9, he became a Central Committee member in 1939 and went on to hold a series of ministerial posts, mostly concerned with finance and industry. He succeeded Khrushchev as Prime Minister in 1964, but devoted most of his attention to internal economic affairs, being gradually eased out of the leadership by Brezhnev.

Kota Baharu /ˌkəʊtə ˈbɑːruː/ the capital of Kelantan; pop. (1980) 170,600. Its name means 'new fort'.

Kota Kinabalu /ˈkəʊtə ˌkɪnəbəˈluː/ a seaport and capital of Sabah, on the north coast of Borneo; pop. (1980) 56,000. Its name means 'fort of (Mount) Kinabalu'.

Kotka /ˈkɒtkə/ a seaport of SE Finland; pop. (1987) 57,745.

koto /ˈkəʊtəʊ/ n. (pl. **-os**) a Japanese musical instrument with 13 long esp. silk strings. [Jap.]

kotow var. of KOWTOW.

Kotzebue /ˈkɒtsəˌbuːeɪ/, August von (1761–1819), German dramatist whose many sentimental plays were very popular in their day, notably Die deutschen Kleinstädter (1803), and Das Kind der Liebe (1790), adapted as Lovers' Vows and made famous in Jane Austen's Mansfield Park. He was a political informant to Tsar Alexander I and was assassinated by the Germans. His son, Otto von Kotzebue (1787–1846), was a navigator and explorer, discoverer of an inlet of NW Alaska (Kotzebue Sound) now named after him.

koumiss /ˈkuːmɪs/ n. (also **kumiss**, **kumis**) a fermented liquor prepared from esp. mare's milk, used by Asian nomads and medicinally. [Tartar *kumiz*]

kourbash /ˈkʊəbæʃ/ n. (also **kurbash**) a whip, esp. of hippopotamus hide, used as an instrument of punishment in Turkey and Egypt. [Arab. *kurbāj* f. Turk. *kırbāç* whip]

Kourou /kʊˈruː/ the second-largest settlement in French Guiana; pop. (1982) 6,465. A satellite-launching station was established near Kourou in 1967.

kowhai /ˈkəʊwaɪ/ n. any of several trees or shrubs of the genus *Sophora*, esp. *S. microphylla* native to New Zealand, with pendant clusters of yellow flowers. [Maori]

Kowloon /kaʊˈluːn/ a peninsula at the southern tip of mainland Hong Kong, with a population density of 28,500 people per sq. km.

kowtow /kaʊˈtaʊ/ n. & v. (also **kotow** /kaʊˈtaʊ/) —n. hist. the Chinese custom of kneeling and touching the ground with the forehead in worship or submission. —v.intr. **1** hist. perform the kowtow. **2** (usu. foll. by to) act obsequiously. [Chin. *ketou* f. *ke* knock + *tou* head]

KP n. US Mil. colloq. **1** enlisted men detailed to help the cooks. **2** kitchen duty. [abbr. of *kitchen police*]

k.p.h. abbr. kilometres per hour.

Kr symb. Chem. the element krypton.

Kra /krɑː/, **Isthmus of** the narrowest section of the Malay Peninsula, in SW Thailand and southern Burma.

kraal /krɑːl/ n. S.Afr. **1** a village of huts enclosed by a fence. **2** an enclosure for cattle or sheep. [Afrik. f. Port. *curral*, of Hottentot orig.]

Krafft-Ebing /krʌftˈeɪbɪŋ/, Richard von (1840–1902), German physician and psychologist. He is best known for having established the relationship between syphilis and general paralysis, and for his *Psychopathia Sexualis* (1886), a pioneer examination of sexual aberrations.

kraft /krɑːft/ n. (in full **kraft paper**) a kind of strong smooth brown wrapping paper. [G f. Sw., = strength]

krait /kraɪt/ n. any venomous snake of the genus *Bungarus* of E. Asia. [Hindi *karait*]

Krakatoa /ˌkrækəˈtəʊə/ a small volcanic island in Indonesia, lying between Java and Sumatra, scene of a great eruption in 1883.

kraken /ˈkrɑːkən/ n. a large mythical sea-monster said to appear off the coast of Norway. [Norw.]

Kraków see CRACOW.

krans /krɑːns/ n. S.Afr. a precipitous or overhanging wall of rocks. [Afrik. f. Du. *krans* coronet]

Krasnodar /ˈkræsnəˌdɑː(r)/ **1** a territory of the Russian republic, in the north Caucasus; pop. (1985) 4,992,000. **2** its capital city; pop. (1983) 595,000.

Krasnoyarsk /ˌkræsnəˈjɑːsk/ **1** a territory of the Russian republic, in central Siberia; pop. (1985) 3,430,000. **2** its capital city; pop. (1983) 845,000.

Kraut /kraʊt/ n. sl. offens. a German. [shortening of SAUERKRAUT]

Krebs /krebz/, Sir Hans Adolf (1900–81), British biochemist, born in Germany, who (while in Germany) discovered the cycle of reactions by which urea is synthesized by the liver. After moving to Britain in 1933 came his greatest discovery (1937), the **Krebs cycle**, a series of biochemical reactions which constitutes a major part of the process of respiration in most living cells.

Krefeld /ˈkreɪfelt/ an industrial town and port on the Rhine in Germany; pop. (1987) 216,600.

Kreisler /ˈkraɪslə(r)/, Fritz (1875–1962), Austrian-born violinist and composer, who after 1939 lived chiefly in the US, taking American citizenship. A noted interpreter of the standard classics, until 1935 he attributed some of his own compositions to 17th- and 18th-c. composers. He gave the first performance of Elgar's violin concerto (1910), which is dedicated to him.

kremlin /ˈkremlɪn/ n. **1** a citadel within a Russian town, traditionally the centre of administration as well as the last bastion of defence. **2** (**the Kremlin**) **a** the citadel in Moscow. **b** the

USSR Government housed within it. [F, f. Russ. *Kreml'*, of Tartar orig.]

kriegspiel /ˈkriːɡspiːl/ n. **1** a war-game in which blocks representing armies etc. are moved about on maps. **2** a form of chess with an umpire, in which each player has only limited information about the opponent's moves. [G f. *Krieg* war + *Spiel* game]

Kriemhild /ˈkriːmhɪlt/ (in the Nibelungenlied) a Burgundian princess, wife of Siegfried and later of Etzel (Attila), whom she marries in order to be revenged on her brothers for Siegfried's murder.

krill /krɪl/ n. tiny planktonic crustaceans found in the seas around the Antarctic and eaten by baleen whales. [Norw. *kril* tiny fish]

krimmer /ˈkrɪmə(r)/ n. a grey or black fur obtained from the wool of young Crimean lambs. [G f. *Krim* Crimea]

kris /kriːs/ n. (also **crease**, **creese**) a Malay or Indonesian dagger with a wavy blade. [ult. f. Malay *k(i)rīs*]

Krishna[1] /ˈkrɪʃnə/ *Hinduism* one of the most popular gods, the eighth and most important avatar (incarnation) of Vishnu. He is worshipped in several forms: as the child god whose miracles and pranks are extolled in the Puranas; as the divine cowherd whose erotic exploits, especially with his favourite, Radha, have produced both romantic and religious literature; and as the divine charioteer who preaches to Arjuna on the battlefield in the Bhagavadgita. [Skr., = black]

Krishna[2] /ˈkrɪʃnə/ a river that rises in the Western Ghats of India and flows generally eastwards to the Bay of Bengal.

Krishnaism /ˈkrɪʃnəˌɪz(ə)m/ n. *Hinduism* the worship of Krishna as an incarnation of Vishnu.

Kristallnacht /ˈkrɪstəlˌnaxt/ the occasion of concerted violence by Nazis throughout Germany and Austria against Jews and their property on the night of 9–10 Nov. 1938. Its name refers to the broken glass produced by the smashing of shop windows etc. The event marked an escalation of the persecution of Jews in the Third Reich. [G, = night of crystal or of (broken) glass]

Kristiansand /ˌkriːstjənˈsɑːn/ a passenger ferry port on the Skagerrak in southern Norway, founded in 1641 by Christian IV; pop. (1988) 63,500.

Kriti see CRETE.

Krivoy Rog /krɪˈvɔɪ rɒɡ/ an industrial city of Ukraine, at the centre of an iron-ore basin; pop. (est. 1987) 698,000.

kromesky /krəˈmeskɪ/ n. (pl. **-ies**) a croquette of minced meat or fish, rolled in bacon and fried. [app. f. Pol. *kromeczka* small slice]

krona /ˈkrəʊnə/ n. **1** (pl. **kronor** /ˈkrəʊnə(r)/) the chief monetary unit of Sweden. **2** (pl. **kronur** /ˈkrəʊnə(r)/) the chief monetary unit of Iceland. [Sw. & Icel., = CROWN]

krone /ˈkrəʊnə/ n. (pl. **kroner** /ˈkrəʊnə(r)/) the chief monetary unit of Denmark and of Norway. [Da. & Norw., = CROWN]

Kronos /ˈkrɒnəs/ = CRONUS.

Kroo var. of KRU.

Kropotkin /krəˈpɒtkɪn/, Peter Alexeevich, Prince (1842–1921), Russian anarchist. A geographer of some distinction, he carried out important explorations of Siberia, Finland, and Manchuria before devoting his life to political activities, in particular the espousal of anarchism, of which he was one of the most influential exponents. Arrested in 1874, he escaped abroad two years later and only returned to Russia after the Russian Revolution in 1917.

Kru /kruː/ n. & adj. (also **Kroo**) —n. (pl. same) a member of a Black seafaring people on the coast of Liberia. —adj. of or concerning the Kru. [W. Afr.]

Kru Coast /kruː/ a section of the south-east coast of Liberia, north-west of Cape Palmas.

Kruger /ˈkruːɡə(r)/, Stephanus Johannes Paulus, (1825–1904), 'Oom Paul', South African soldier and statesman. Kruger led the Afrikaners to victory in the First Boer War in 1881 and afterwards served as President of the Transvaal from 1883 to 1899. His refusal to allow equal rights to non-Boer immigrants was one of the causes of the Second Boer War, during which Kruger was forced to flee the country. He died in exile in Switzerland in 1904.

Kruger National Park a national park of South Africa, in NE Transvaal. Designated in 1926, the park was originally a game reserve established in 1898 by President Kruger.

krugerrand /ˈkruːgəˌrænd, -ˌrɑːnt/ *n.* a S. African gold coin depicting President Kruger. [KRUGER + RAND¹]

krummhorn /ˈkrʌmhɔːn/ *n.* (also **crumhorn**) a medieval wind instrument with a double reed and a curved end. It had seven finger-holes with three extension keys for low notes. [G f. *krumm* crooked + *Horn* HORN]

Krupp /krʊp/, Alfred (1812–87), German arms manufacturer, who in the 1840s began to manufacture ordnance in the iron-works founded in Essen by his father, and built up the works to be the largest such firm on the Continent of Europe. Under the management of successive members of the family the Krupp Works continued to play a pre-eminent part in German arms production through to the end of the Second World War.

krypton /ˈkrɪptɒn/ *n. Chem.* a rare colourless odourless element of the noble gas group, discovered in 1898 by Sir William Ramsay and M. W. Travers (1872–1961) by distillation of liquid air. It is used in various types of electric lamps and bulbs. Although chemically almost inert, it can be made to combine with fluorine. The metre is defined in terms of a transition of one of its isotopes. ¶ Symb.: **Kr**; atomic number 36. [Gk *krupton* hidden, neut. adj. f. *kruptō* hide]

KS *abbr.* **1** *US* Kansas (in official postal use). **2** *Brit.* King's Scholar.

Kshatriya /ˈkʃætrɪə, ˈkʃɑː-/ *n.* a member of the second of the four great Hindu classes, the warrior or baronial caste. His function is to protect society, to fight in wartime and govern in peacetime. [Skr. f. *kshatra* rule]

K. St. J. *abbr.* Knight of the Order of St John.

KT *abbr.* **1** Knight Templar. **2** (in the UK) Knight of the Order of the Thistle.

Kt. *abbr.* Knight.

kt. *abbr.* knot.

Ku *symb. Chem.* the element kurchatovium.

Kuala Lumpur /ˈkwɑːlə ˈlʊmpʊə(r)/ the capital of the Federation of Malaysia, proclaimed Federal Territory in 1974; pop. (1980) 937,875.

Kuan Yin /kwɑːn/ (in Chinese Buddhism) the goddess of compassion.

Kublai Khan /ˌkuːblaɪ ˈkɑːn/ (1216–94), Mongol emperor of China, grandson of Genghis Khan. With his brother Mangu, then Mongol Khan, Kublai conquered southern China in 1252–9. On Mangu's death in 1259 he was elected Khan himself, completing the pacification of China and adopting the name Yuan for the dynasty. He successfully invaded Korea and Burma, but failed in attacks on Java and Japan. His reign was notable for his policy of religious toleration and for his humane treatment of conquered peoples.

Kuching /ˈkuːtʃɪŋ/ the capital and a port of Sarawak; pop. (1980) 1,307,600.

kudos /ˈkjuːdɒs/ *n. colloq.* glory; renown. [Gk]

kudu /ˈkuːduː/ *n.* (also **koodoo**) either of two African antelopes, *Tragelaphus strepsiceros* or *T. imberbis*, with white stripes and corkscrew-shaped ridged horns. [Xhosa-Kaffir *iqudu*]

kudzu /ˈkʌdzuː/ *n.* (in full **kudzu vine**) a quick-growing climbing plant, *Pueraria thunbergiana*, with reddish-purple flowers. [Jap. *kuzu*]

Kufic /ˈkjuːfɪk/ *n. & adj.* (also **Cufic**) —*n.* an early angular form of the Arabic alphabet found chiefly in decorative inscriptions. —*adj.* of or in this type of script. [*Kufa*, ancient city S. of Baghdad]

Kuibishev /ˈkuːɪbɪˌʃef/ an industrial city of the Soviet Union, situated to the west of the Ural Mountains, on the River Volga; pop. (est. 1987) 1,280,000.

Ku Klux Klan /ˌkuːklʌksˈklæn, ˌkjuː-/ *n.* an American secret society of White people , founded in the southern States in the wake of the Civil War. Although originally intended to defend the southern way of life against northern attempts to change

it, the society rapidly became devoted to keeping the Black population from attaining equality, and adopted terrorism and murder as means to that end. Although the original Klan was outlawed by Congress in 1871, a similar organization exists to this day. □□ **Ku Klux Klansman** *n.* (*pl.* **-men**). [perh. f. Gk *kuklos* circle + CLAN]

kukri /ˈkʊkrɪ/ *n.* (*pl.* **kukris**) a curved knife broadening towards the point, used by Gurkhas. [Hindi *kuk̲r̲ī*]

kulak /ˈkuːlæk/ *n. hist.* a peasant working for personal profit in Soviet Russia. [Russ., = fist, tight-fisted person]

kulan /ˈkuːlən/ *n.* a wild ass of SW Asia, closely related to the kiang. [Tartar]

kultur /kʊlˈtʊə(r)/ *n. esp. derog.* German civilization and culture, seen as racist, authoritarian, and militaristic. [G f. L *cultura* CULTURE]

kulturkampf /kʊlˈtʊəkæmpf/ *n. hist.* the conflict between the German government (headed by Bismarck) and the papacy for the control of schools and Church appointments (1872–87). This attempt to break the authority and influence of the Catholic Church in the new German empire failed in its long-term aims and was to a considerable extent responsible for delaying the integration of traditionally Catholic areas of Germany. [G (as KULTUR, *Kampf* struggle)]

kumara /ˈkuːmərə/ *n.* NZ a sweet potato. [Maori]

kumis (also **kumiss**) var. of KOUMISS.

kümmel /ˈkʊm(ə)l/ *n.* a sweet liqueur flavoured with caraway and cumin seeds. [G (as CUMIN)]

kumquat /ˈkʌmkwɒt/ *n.* (also **cumquat**) **1** an orange-like fruit with a sweet rind and acid pulp, used in preserves. **2** any shrub or small tree of the genus *Fortunella* yielding this. [Cantonese var. of Chin. *kin kü* golden orange]

kung fu /kʊŋ ˈfuː, kʌŋ/ *n.* the Chinese form of karate. [Chin. *gongfu* f. *gong* merit + *fu* master]

Kunlun Shan /ˈkʊnlʊn ʃɑːn/ a range of mountains in western China, on the edge of the Tibetan plateau.

Kunming /kʊnˈmɪŋ/ the capital of Yunnan province in south China; pop. (est. 1986) 1,490,000.

Kuomintang /ˌkwːəʊmɪnˈtæŋ/ *n.* (also **Guomindang**) a nationalist radical party founded in China under Sun Yat-sen in 1912 and led, after his death in 1925, by Chiang Kai-Shek, constituting the government before the Communist Party took power in October 1949, and subsequently forming the central administration of Taiwan. [Chinese, = national people's party]

Kuopio /ˈkwəʊpɪˌəʊ/ **1** a province of central Finland; pop. (1987) 255,705. **2** its capital city; pop. (1987) 78,619.

kurbash var. of KOURBASH.

kurchatovium /ˌkɜːtʃəˈtəʊvɪəm/ *n. Chem.* the Russian name for RUTHERFORDIUM. The preferred name is now *unnilquadium*. ¶ Symb.: **Ku**; atomic number 104. [I. V. *Kurchatov*, Russ. physicist d. 1960]

Kurd /kɜːd/ *n.* a member of a mainly pastoral Aryan Islamic people living in the region known as Kurdistan. After the Gulf War of 1991 most of the Kurds of Iraq, some two million people, harassed by the Iraqi army for their opposition to Saddam Hussein, made their way through the mountains of northern Iraq to seek refuge in the frontier regions of Turkey and Iran; thousands died from cold, hunger, and disease. [Kurdish]

kurdaitcha /kəˈdaɪtʃə/ *n. Austral.* **1** the tribal use of a bone in spells intended to cause sickness or death. **2** a man empowered to point the bone at a victim. [Aboriginal]

Kurdish /ˈkɜːdɪʃ/ *adj. & n.* —*adj.* of or relating to the Kurds or their language. —*n.* the language spoken by some 5 million people in the region of Kurdistan. It belongs to the Indo-Iranian language group and is generally written in an Arabic script.

Kurdistan /ˌkɜːdɪˈstɑːn/ *n.* a region inhabited by the Kurds, covering parts of Turkey, Iraq, Iran, Syria, and the USSR.

Kuria Muria Islands /ˌkʊərɪə ˈmʊərɪə/ a group of five islands in the Arabian Sea, with few inhabitants, belonging to Oman. They were ceded to Britain in 1854 and returned to Oman in 1967.

Kurile Islands /ˈkjʊəriːl/ (also **Kuril Islands** or **Kurils**) a group of 56 islands between the Sea of Okhotsk and the North Pacific Ocean, stretching from the southern tip of the Kamchatka peninsula to the NE corner of the island of Hokkaido. The islands were given to Japan in exchange for the northern part of Sakhalin Island in 1875, but were returned to the Soviet Union in 1945.

Kurosawa /ˌkʊərəˈsɑːwə/, Akira (1910–), Japanese film director, a stylist who bases most of his films on his own ideas. He was introduced to the West by *Rashomon* (1950), and his continuing popularity there is founded on his 'sword-fight' films such as *The Seven Samurai* (1954). He also treats modern themes, mainly of social injustice, including *Living* (1952) and *Red Beard* (1965), and has made adaptations of Dostoevsky (*The Idiot*, 1951), Gorky (*The Lower Depths*, 1957), and Shakespeare (*The Throne of Blood*, 1957, from *Macbeth*).

kurrajong /ˈkʌrəˌdʒɒŋ/ n. (also **currajong**) an Australian tree, *Brachychiton populneum*, which produces a tough bast fibre. [Aboriginal]

kursaal /ˈkʊəzɑːl/ n. **1** a building for the use of visitors at a health resort, esp. at a German spa. **2** a casino. [G f. *Kur* CURE + *Saal* room]

kurta /ˈkɜːtə/ n. (also **kurtha**) a loose shirt or tunic worn by esp. Hindu men and women. [Hind.]

kurtosis /kɜːˈtəʊsɪs/ n. *Statistics* the sharpness of the peak of a frequency-distribution curve. [mod.L f. Gk *kurtōsis* bulging f. *kurtos* convex]

Kusadasi /kuːˈʃædəsɪ/ a resort town on the Aegean coast of western Turkey, south of Izmir; pop. 17,000.

Kutch /kʊtʃ/, **Rann of** a large salt-marsh on the frontier between India and Pakistan. Most of it lies in the State of Gujarat, the remainder in the province of Sind in SE Pakistan.

Kuwait /kuːˈweɪt/ an Arab sheikdom on the NW coast of the Persian Gulf, one of the world's leading oil-producing countries; pop. (est. 1988)1,938,000; official language, Arabic; capital, Kuwait, pop. 400,000. Kuwait was an autonomous sheikdom from the 18th c. It became a British protectorate from 1897, and fully independent again in 1961. In August 1990 it was invaded and occupied by Iraq (see GULF WAR 2). □□ **Kuwaiti** *adj.* & n.

kV *abbr.* kilovolt(s).

Kuznetz Basin /kʊzˈnjets/ (also **Kuznetsk** or **Kuzbas** /kʊzˈbæs/) an industrial region of the Soviet Union, situated in the valley of the Tom River, between Tomsk and Novokuznetsk. The region is rich in iron and coal deposits.

kvass /kvɑːs/ n. a fermented beverage, low in alcohol, made from rye-flour or bread with malt in the Soviet Union. [Russ. *kvas*]

kW *abbr.* kilowatt(s).

KWAC /kwæk/ n. *Computing* etc. keyword and context. [abbr.]

kwacha /ˈkwɑːtʃə/ n. the chief monetary unit of Zambia. [native word, = dawn]

KwaNdebele /ˌkwɑːəndəˈbiːlɪ/ a tribal homeland of the Ndbele people in NE Transvaal, South Africa; pop. (1985) 233,000.

Kwangsi see GUANGXI.

Kwangtung see GUANGDONG.

kwashiorkor /ˌkwɒʃɪˈɔːkɔː(r)/ n. a form of malnutrition caused by a protein deficiency of diet, esp. in young children in the tropics. [native name in Ghana]

KwaZulu /kwɑːˈzuːluː/ a tribal homeland of the Zulu people in South Africa; pop. (1985) 3,737,000. Until 1972 the area was known as Zululand.

Kweichow see GUIZHOU.

Kweilin see GUILIN.

Kweiyang see GUIYANG.

kWh *abbr.* kilowatt-hour(s).

KWIC /kwɪk/ n. *Computing* etc. keyword in context. [abbr.]

KWOC /kwɒk/ n. *Computing* etc. keyword out of context. [abbr.]

KY *abbr.* US Kentucky (in official postal use).

Ky. *abbr.* Kentucky.

kyanite /ˈkaɪəˌnaɪt/ n. a blue crystalline mineral of aluminium silicate. □□ **kyanitic** /-ˈnɪtɪk/ *adj.* [Gk *kuanos* dark blue]

kyanize /ˈkaɪəˌnaɪz/ *v.tr.* (also **-ise**) treat (wood) with a solution of corrosive sublimate to prevent decay. [J. H. *Kyan*, Engl. inventor d. 1850]

kybosh var. of KIBOSH.

Kyd /kɪd/, Thomas (1558–94), English dramatist, a friend of Marlowe. His anonymously published *Spanish Tragedy* (1592) was an exceptionally popular play on the Elizabethan stage, and an early example of revenge tragedy. The only work published under his name was a translation of Robert Garnier's *Cornelia* (1594; reissued as *Pompey the Great*, 1595). Other works attributed to Kyd are *The Tragedye of Solyman and Perseda* (1592) and a lost pre-Shakespearian play on Hamlet.

kyle /kaɪl/ n. (in Scotland) a narrow channel between islands or between an island and the mainland. [Gael. *caol* strait]

kylie /ˈkaɪlɪ/ n. W. *Austral.* a boomerang. [Aboriginal]

kylin /ˈkiːlɪn/ n. a mythical composite animal figured on Chinese and Japanese ceramics. [Chin. *qilin* f. *qi* male + *lin* female]

kyloe /ˈkaɪləʊ/ n. *Brit.* **1** an animal of a breed of small usu. black long-horned highland cattle. **2** this breed. [*Kyloe* in Northumberland]

kymograph /ˈkaɪməˌgrɑːf/ n. an instrument for recording variations in pressure, e.g. in sound waves or in blood within blood-vessels. □□ **kymographic** /-ˈgræfɪk/ *adj.* [Gk *kuma* wave + -GRAPH]

Kyoto /kɪˈəʊtəʊ/ a city of Japan, the imperial capital 794–1868; pop. (1987) 1,469,000.

kyphosis /kaɪˈfəʊsɪs/ n. *Med.* excessive outward curvature of the spine, causing hunching of the back (opp. LORDOSIS). □□ **kyphotic** /-ˈfɒtɪk/ *adj.* [mod.L f. Gk *kuphōsis* f. *kuphos* bent]

Kyrenia /kaɪˈriːnɪə/ a port on the central part of the north coast of Cyprus; pop. (1973) 3,892.

Kyrie /ˈkɪərɪˌeɪ/ (in full **Kyrie eleison** /ɪˈleɪɪˌzɒn, -ˌsɒn, eɪˈleɪ-/) n. **1 a** a short repeated invocation used in the RC and Greek Orthodox Churches, esp. at the beginning of the mass. **b** a response sometimes used in the Anglican Communion Service. **2** a musical setting of the Kyrie. [ME f. med.L f. Gk *Kurie eleēson* Lord, have mercy]

Kyushu /kɪˈuːʃuː/ the most southerly of the four main islands of Japan; pop. (1986) 13,295,000; capital, Fukuoka.

L

L¹ /el/ n. (also **l**) (pl. **Ls** or **L's**) **1** the twelfth letter of the alphabet. **2** (as a Roman numeral) 50. **3** a thing shaped like an L, esp. a joint connecting two pipes at right angles.

L² abbr. (also **L.**) **1** Lake. **2** Brit. learner driver (cf. L-PLATE). **3** Liberal. **4** Licentiate. **5** Biol. Linnaeus. **6** Lire.

l abbr. (also **l.**) **1** left. **2** line. **3** litre(s). **4** length. **5** archaic pound(s) (money).

£ abbr. (preceding a numeral) pound or pounds (of money). [L libra]

LA abbr. **1** Library Association. **2** Los Angeles. **3** US Louisiana (in official postal use).

La symb. Chem. the element lanthanum.

La. abbr. Louisiana.

la var. of LAH.

laager /ˈlɑːgə(r)/ n. & v. —n. **1** esp. S.Afr. a camp or encampment, esp. formed by a circle of wagons. **2** Mil. a park for armoured vehicles. —v. **1** tr. **a** form (vehicles) into a laager. **b** encamp (people) in a laager. **2** intr. encamp. [Afrik. f. Du. leger: see LEAGUER²]

Lab. abbr. **1** Labour. **2** Labrador.

lab /læb/ n. colloq. a laboratory. [abbr.]

Laban /ˈlɑːbən/, Rudolf von (1879–1958), real name R. L. de Varaljan, Hungarian dancer, choreographer, ballet master, and dance theoretician. He was the leader of the Central European school of modern dance, of far greater importance as an intellectual and theoretician than as a choreographer. His greatest contribution was Kinetographie Laban, his system of dance notation, further developed by his pupils. After emigrating to England in 1938 he concentrated on modern educational dance and on research into movement and movement notation in industrial processes.

labarum /ˈlæbərəm/ n. **1** a symbolic banner. **2** Constantine the Great's imperial standard, said to have been devised by him in 312 after a vision, consisting of a spear converted by a transverse bar into a cross and surmounted by a wreath enclosing the Christian monogram of the first two letters (chi rho) of Christos (Gk, = Christ); any of several variants of this. It was an adaptation of the traditional Roman military standard. [LL: orig. unkn.]

labdanum var. of LADANUM.

labefaction /ˌlæbɪˈfækʃ(ə)n/ n. literary a shaking, weakening, or downfall. [L labefacere weaken f. labi fall + facere make]

label /ˈleɪb(ə)l/ n. & v. —n. **1 a** a usu. small piece of paper, card, linen, metal, etc., for attaching to an object and giving its name, information about it, instructions for use, etc. **2** esp. derog. a short classifying phrase or name applied to a person, a work of art, etc. **3 a** a small fabric label sewn into a garment bearing the maker's name. **b** the logo, title, or trademark of esp. a fashion or recording company (brought it out under his own label). **c** the piece of paper in the centre of a gramophone record describing its contents etc. **4** an adhesive stamp on a parcel etc. **5** a word placed before, after, or in the course of a dictionary definition etc. to specify its subject, register, nationality, etc. **6** Archit. a dripstone. **7** Heraldry the mark of an eldest son, consisting of a superimposed horizontal bar with usu. three downward projections. —v.tr. (**labelled**, **labelling**) **1** attach a label to. **2** (usu. foll. by as) assign to a category (labelled them as irresponsible). **3 a** replace (an atom) by an atom of a usu. radioactive isotope as a means of identification. **b** replace an atom in (a molecule) or atoms in the molecules of (a substance). **4** (as **labelled** adj.) made identifiable by the replacement of atoms. □□ **labeller** n. [ME f. OF, = ribbon, prob. f. Gmc (as LAP¹)]

labia pl. of LABIUM.

labial /ˈleɪbɪəl/ adj. & n. —adj. **1 a** of the lips. **b** Zool. of, like, or serving as a lip, a liplike part, or a labium. **2** Dentistry designating the surface of a tooth adjacent to the lips. **3** Phonet. (of a sound) requiring partial or complete closure of the lips (e.g. p, b, f, v, m, w; and vowels in which lips are rounded, e.g. oo in moon). —n. Phonet. a labial sound. □ **labial pipe** Mus. an organ-pipe having lips; a flue-pipe. □□ **labialism** n. **labialize** v.tr. (also **-ise**). **labially** adv. [med.L labialis f. L labia lips]

labiate /ˈleɪbɪət/ n. & adj. —n. any plant of the family Labiatae, including mint and rosemary, having square stems and a corolla or calyx divided into two parts suggesting lips. —adj. **1** Bot. of or relating to the Labiatae. **2** Bot. & Zool. like a lip or labium. [mod.L labiatus (as LABIUM)]

labile /ˈleɪbaɪl, -bɪl/ adj. Chem. (of a compound) unstable; liable to displacement or change esp. if an atom or group is easily replaced by other atoms or groups. □□ **lability** /ləˈbɪlɪtɪ/ n. [ME f. LL labilis f. labi to fall]

labio- /ˈleɪbɪəʊ/ comb. form of the lips. [as LABIUM]

labiodental /ˌleɪbɪəʊˈdent(ə)l/ adj. (of a sound) made with the lips and teeth, e.g. f and v.

labiovelar /ˌleɪbɪəʊˈviːlə(r)/ adj. (of a sound) made with the lips and soft palate, e.g. w.

labium /ˈleɪbɪəm/ n. (pl. **labia** /-bɪə/) **1** (usu. in pl.) Anat. each of the two pairs of skin folds that enclose the vulva. **2** the lower lip in the mouth-parts of an insect or crustacean. **3** a lip, esp. the lower one of a labiate plant's corolla. □ **labia majora** /məˈdʒɔːrə/ the larger outer pair of labia (in sense 1). **labia minora** /mɪˈnɔːrə/ the smaller inner pair of labia (in sense 1). [L, = lip]

labor etc. US & Austral. var. of LABOUR etc.

laboratory /ləˈbɒrətərɪ/ n. (pl. **-ies**) a room or building fitted out for scientific experiments, research, teaching, or the manufacture of drugs and chemicals. [med.L laboratorium f. L laborare LABOUR]

laborious /ləˈbɔːrɪəs/ adj. **1** needing hard work or toil (a laborious task). **2** (esp. of literary style) showing signs of toil; pedestrian; not fluent. □□ **laboriously** adv. **laboriousness** n. [ME f. OF laborieus f. L laboriosus (as LABOUR)]

labour /ˈleɪbə(r)/ n. & v. (US, Austral. **labor**) —n. **1 a** physical or mental work; exertion; toil. **b** such work considered as supplying the needs of a community. **2 a** workers, esp. manual, considered as a class or political force (a dispute between capital and labour). **b** (**Labour**) the Labour Party. **3** the process of childbirth; the period from the start of uterine contractions to delivery (has been in labour for three hours). **4** a particular task, esp. of a difficult nature. —v. **1** intr. work hard; exert oneself. **2** intr. (usu. foll. by for, or to + infin.) strive for a purpose (laboured to fulfil his promise). **3** tr. **a** treat at excessive length; elaborate needlessly (I will not labour the point). **b** (as **laboured** adj.) done with great effort; not spontaneous or fluent. **4** intr. (often foll. by under) suffer under (a disadvantage or delusion) (laboured under universal disapproval). **5** intr. proceed with trouble or difficulty (laboured slowly up the hill). **6** intr. (of a ship) roll or pitch heavily. **7** tr. archaic or poet. till (the ground). □ **labour camp** a prison camp enforcing a regime of hard labour. **Labour Day** May 1 (or in the US and Canada the first Monday in September), celebrated in honour of working people. **Labour Exchange** Brit. colloq. or hist. an employment exchange; a jobcentre. **labour force** the body of workers employed, esp. at a single plant. **labouring man** a labourer. **labour-intensive** (of a form of work) needing a large work force. **labour in vain** make a fruitless effort. **labour-market** the supply of labour with reference to the demand on it. **labour of Hercules** a task needing enormous strength or effort. **labour of love** a task done for pleasure, not reward. **Labour Party** see separate entry. **labour-saving** (of an appliance etc.) designed to reduce or

aʊ how eɪ day əʊ no eə hair ɪə near ɔɪ boy ʊə poor aɪə fire aʊə sour (see over for consonants)

eliminate work. **labour union** US a trade union. **lost labour** fruitless effort. [ME f. OF labo(u)r, labourer f. L labor, -oris, laborare]

labourer /ˈleɪbərə(r)/ n. (US **laborer**) **1** a person doing unskilled, usu. manual, work for wages. **2** a person who labours. [ME f. OF laboureur (as LABOUR)]

Labourite /ˈleɪbəˌraɪt/ n. (also **Laborite**) a member or follower of the Labour Party.

Labour Party 1 a British political party formed to represent the interests of ordinary working people and in its heyday enjoying the support of the industrial working class and those members of the middle and professional classes whose views were socialist or reformist. It had its roots in the trade union movement which, in 1900, combined with the small Independent Labour Party, the Social Democratic Federation, and the Fabian Society to form the Labour Representation Committee, which changed its name to the Labour Party after electoral successes in 1906. After the First World War, Labour was reorganized as a true national party and replaced the Liberals as the country's second major political party. Having formed minority governments in 1924 and 1929–31, the Labour Party entered Churchill's wartime coalition before forming its first majority government under Attlee (1945–51). It subsequently held power in 1964–70 and 1974–9, the emphasis of its policies being on nationalization of industries etc. and on governmental control. **2** any similar political party in other countries.

labra pl. of LABRUM.

Labrador[1] /ˈlæbrəˌdɔː(r)/ **1** (in a broad sense, in full **Labrador-Ungava**) the NE peninsula of Canada, from Hudson Bay to the mouth of the St Lawrence. It has been the subject of much dispute between Newfoundland and Quebec; in 1927 the eastern seaboard was awarded to Newfoundland. **2** (in a restricted sense) the part of the peninsula belonging to Newfoundland, which since 1949 has formed the mainland section of Newfoundland and Labrador province; chief town, Battle Harbour. □ **Labrador Current** a cold ocean current moving southwards from the Arctic Ocean along part of the east coast of North America.

Labrador[2] /ˈlæbrəˌdɔː(r)/ n. (in full **Labrador dog** or **retriever**) **1** a retriever of a breed with a black or golden coat often used as a gun dog or as a guide for a blind person. **2** this breed.

labret /ˈlæbrɪt/ n. a piece of shell, bone, etc., inserted in the lip as an ornament. [LABRUM]

labrum /ˈleɪbrəm/ n. (pl. **labra** /-brə/) the upper lip in the mouth-parts of an insect. [L, = lip: rel. to LABIUM]

La Bruyère /lɑː bruːˈjeə(r)/, Jean de (1645–96), French moralist, who studied law and entered the service of Louis II, 'le Grand Condé'. His famous Caractères, on the model of Theophrastus, are portrait sketches (often of living people with disguised names) exposing the vanity and corruption of human behaviour and giving a vivid satirical picture of Parisian society.

Labuan /ləˈbuːən/ a small island off the north coast of Borneo, forming a Federal Territory of Malaysia; pop. (1980) 12,200; capital Victoria.

laburnum /ləˈbɜːnəm/ n. any small tree of the genus Laburnum with racemes of golden flowers yielding poisonous seeds. Also called golden chain. [L]

labyrinth /ˈlæbərɪnθ/ n. **1** a complicated irregular network of passages or paths etc.; a maze. The term was first used of the building constructed by Daedalus for King Minos of Crete, from which nobody could escape; the Minotaur live therein. **2** an intricate or tangled arrangement. **3** Anat. the complex arrangement of bony and membranous canals and chambers of the inner ear which constitute the organs of hearing and balance. □ **labyrinth fish** = GOURAMI. □□ **labyrinthian** /-ˈrɪnθɪən/ adj. **labyrinthine** /-ˈrɪnθaɪn/ adj. [F labyrinthe or L labyrinthus f. Gk laburinthos]

LAC abbr. Leading Aircraftman.

lac[1] /læk/ n. a resinous substance secreted as a protective covering by the lac insect, and used to make varnish and shellac. □ **lac insect** an Asian scale insect, Laccifer lacca, living in trees. [ult. f. Hind. lākh f. Prakrit lakkha f. Skr. lākṣā]

lac[2] var. of LAKH.

Laccadive Islands /ˈlækədɪv/ see LAKSHADWEEP.

laccolith /ˈlækəlɪθ/ n. Geol. a lens-shaped intrusion of igneous rock which thrusts the overlying strata into a dome. [Gk lakkos reservoir + -LITH]

lace /leɪs/ n. & v. —n. **1** a fine open fabric, esp. of cotton or silk, made by weaving thread in patterns and used esp. to trim blouses, underwear, etc. **2** a cord or leather strip passed through eyelets or hooks on opposite sides of a shoe, corsets, etc., pulled tight and fastened. **3** braid used for trimming esp. dress uniform (gold lace). —v. **1** tr. (usu. foll. by up) **a** fasten or tighten (a shoe, corsets, etc.) with a lace or laces. **b** compress the waist of (a person) with a laced corset. **2** tr. flavour or fortify (coffee, beer, etc.) with a dash of spirits. **3** tr. (usu. foll. by with) **a** streak (a sky etc.) with colour (cheek laced with blood). **b** interlace or embroider (fabric) with thread etc. **4** tr. & (foll. by into) intr. colloq. lash, beat, defeat. **5** tr. (often foll. by through) pass (a shoelace etc.) through. **6** tr. trim with lace. □ **lace-glass** Venetian glass with lacelike designs. **lace-pillow** a cushion placed on the lap and providing support in lacemaking. **lace-up** —n. a shoe fastened with a lace. —attrib.adj. (of a shoe etc.) fastened by a lace or laces. [ME f. OF laz, las, lacier ult. f. L laqueus noose]

La Ceiba /lɑː ˈseɪbə/ a seaport on the Caribbean coast of Honduras; pop. (1986) 63,800.

lacemaker /ˈleɪsˌmeɪkə(r)/ n. a person who makes lace, esp. professionally. □□ **lacemaking** n.

lacerate /ˈlæsəreɪt/ v.tr. **1** mangle or tear (esp. flesh or tissue). **2** distress or cause pain to (the feelings, the heart, etc.). □□ **lacerable** adj. **laceration** /-ˈreɪʃ(ə)n/ n. [L lacerare f. lacer torn]

lacertian /ləˈsɜːtɪən/ n. & adj. (also **lacertilian** /ˌlæsəˈtɪlɪən/, **lacertine** /ˈlæsəˌtaɪn/) —n. any reptile of the suborder Lacertilia, including lizards. —adj. of or relating to the Lacertilia; lizard-like, saurian. [L lacerta lizard]

lacewing /ˈleɪswɪŋ/ n. a neuropterous insect.

lacewood /ˈleɪswʊd/ n. the timber of the plane tree.

laches /ˈlætʃɪz, ˈleɪ-/ n. Law delay in performing a legal duty, asserting a right, claiming a privilege, etc. [ME f. AF laches(se), OF laschesse f. lasche ult. f. L laxus loose]

Lachesis /ˈlækɪsɪs/ Gk Mythol. one of the three Fates (see FATES). [Gk, = getting by lot]

Lachlan /ˈlæklən/ a river of New South Wales, Australia, that rises in the Great Dividing Range and flows north-west then south-west to join the Murrumbidgee River. It is named after Lachlan Macquarie (see MACQUARIE).

lachryma Christi /ˌlækrɪmə ˈkrɪstɪ/ n. any of various wines from the slopes of Mt. Vesuvius. [L, = Christ's tear]

lachrymal /ˈlækrɪm(ə)l/ adj. & n. (also **lacrimal**, **lacrymal**) —adj. **1** literary of or for tears. **2** (usu. as **lacrimal**) Anat. concerned in the secretion of tears (lacrimal canal; lacrimal duct). —n. **1** = lachrymal vase. **2** (in pl.) (usu. as **lacrimals**) the lacrimal organs. □ **lachrymal vase** hist. a phial holding the tears of mourners at a funeral. [ME f. med.L lachrymalis f. L lacrima tear]

lachrymation /ˌlækrɪˈmeɪʃ(ə)n/ n. (also **lacrimation**, **lacrymation**) formal the flow of tears. [L lacrimatio f. lacrimare weep (as LACHRYMAL)]

lachrymator /ˈlækrɪˌmeɪtə(r)/ n. an agent irritating the eyes, causing tears.

lachrymatory /ˈlækrɪmətərɪ/ adj. & n. —adj. formal of or causing tears. —n. (pl. **-ies**) a name applied to phials of a kind found in ancient Roman tombs and thought to be lachrymal vases.

lachrymose /ˈlækrɪˌməʊs/ adj. formal given to weeping; tearful. □□ **lachrymosely** adv. [L lacrimosus f. lacrima tear]

lacing /ˈleɪsɪŋ/ n. **1** lace trimming, esp. on a uniform. **2** a laced fastening on a shoe or corsets. **3** colloq. a beating. **4** a dash of spirits in a beverage. □ **lacing course** a strengthening course built into an arch or wall.

laciniate /ləˈsɪnɪət/ adj. (also **laciniated** /-ˌeɪtɪd/) Bot. & Zool. divided into deep narrow irregular segments; fringed. □□ **laciniation** /-ˈeɪʃ(ə)n/ n. [L lacinia flap of a garment]

lack /læk/ n. & v. —n. (usu. foll. by of) an absence, want, or deficiency (a lack of talent; felt the lack of warmth). —v.tr. be without or deficient in (lacks courage). □ **for lack of** owing to the absence of (*went hungry for lack of money*). **lack for** lack. [ME *lac, lacen,* corresp. to MDu., MLG *lak* deficiency, MDu. *laken* to lack]

lackadaisical /ˌlækəˈdeɪzɪk(ə)l/ *adj.* **1** unenthusiastic; listless; idle. **2** feebly sentimental and affected. □□ **lackadaisically** *adv.* **lackadaisicalness** *n.* [archaic *lackaday, -daisy* (int.): see ALACK]

lacker var. of LACQUER.

lackey /ˈlækɪ/ *n.* & *v.* (also **lacquey**) —*n.* (*pl.* **-eys**) **1** *derog.* **a** a servile political follower. **b** an obsequious parasitical person. **2** **a** a (usu. liveried) footman or manservant. **b** a servant. —*v.tr.* (**-eys, -eyed**) *archaic* behave servilely to; dance attendance on. □ **lackey moth** a moth, *Malacosoma neustria*, developing from a brightly striped caterpillar. [F *laquais,* obs. *alaquais* f. Cat. *alacay* = Sp. ALCALDE]

lacking /ˈlækɪŋ/ *adj.* **1** absent or deficient (*money was lacking; is lacking in determination*). **2** *colloq.* deficient in intellect; mentally subnormal.

lackland /ˈlæklənd/ *n.* & *adj.* —*n.* **1** a person having no land. **2** (**Lackland**) a nickname for King John of England. —*adj.* having no land.

lacklustre /ˈlækˌlʌstə(r)/ *adj.* (*US* **lackluster**) **1** lacking in vitality, force, or conviction. **2** (of the eye) dull.

Laconia /ləˈkəʊnɪə/ an ancient territory of SW Greece, now a department, its ancient capital, Sparta, being still the administrative centre. □□ **Laconian** *adj.* & *n.*

laconic /ləˈkɒnɪk/ *adj.* **1** (of a style of speech or writing) brief; concise; terse. **2** (of a person) laconic in speech etc. □□ **laconically** *adv.* **laconicism** /-ˌsɪz(ə)m/ *n.* [L f. Gk *Lakōnikos* f. *Lakōn* Spartan, the Spartans being known for their terse speech]

laconism /ˈlækəˌnɪz(ə)m/ *n.* **1** brevity of speech. **2** a short pithy saying. [Gk *lakōnismos* f. *lakōnizō* behave like a Spartan: see LACONIC]

lacquer /ˈlækə(r)/ *n.* & *v.* (also **lacker**) —*n.* **1** a sometimes coloured liquid made of shellac dissolved in alcohol, or of synthetic substances, that dries to form a hard protective coating for wood, brass, etc. **2** a chemical substance sprayed on hair to keep it in place. **3** the sap of the lacquer-tree used to varnish wood etc. —*v.tr.* coat with lacquer. □ **lacquer-tree** an E. Asian tree, *Rhus verniciflua,* the sap of which is used as a hard-wearing varnish for wood. □□ **lacquerer** *n.* [obs. F *lacre* sealing-wax, f. unexpl. var. of Port. *laca* LAC[1]]

lacquey var. of LACKEY.

lacrimal var. of LACHRYMAL.

lacrimation var. of LACHRYMATION.

lacrosse /ləˈkrɒs/ *n.* a field game played with a netted stick (a *crosse*) with which a ball is driven or thrown, caught, and carried, and scoring is by goals. It is said that lacrosse was born of the North American Indian, christened by the French, but adopted and raised by the Canadians. The game was played by Indians in southern Canada and parts of the US in the 17th c. or earlier; called *baggataway,* it had a religious significance and was also a means of training tribal warriors. The form of the stick or racket used vaguely resembled a bishop's crozier (Fr. *crosse*). By the mid-19th c. White men were playing the game, and it spread from America and Canada to Britain. [F f. *la* the + CROSSE]

lacrymal var. of LACHRYMAL.

lacrymation var. of LACHRYMATION.

lactase /ˈlækteɪz, -teɪs/ *n. Biochem.* any of a group of enzymes which catalyse the hydrolysis of lactose to glucose and galactose. [F f. *lactose* LACTOSE]

lactate[1] /lækˈteɪt/ *v.intr.* (of mammals) secrete milk. [as LACTATION]

lactate[2] /ˈlækteɪt/ *n. Chem.* any salt or ester of lactic acid.

lactation /lækˈteɪʃ(ə)n/ *n.* **1** the secretion of milk by the mammary glands. **2** the suckling of young. [L *lactare* suckle f. *lac lactis* milk]

lacteal /ˈlæktɪəl/ *adj.* & *n.* —*adj.* **1** of milk. **2** conveying chyle or other milky fluid. —*n.* (in *pl.*) the lymphatic vessels of the small intestine which absorb digested fats. [L *lacteus* f. *lac lactis* milk]

lactescence /lækˈtes(ə)ns/ *n.* **1** a milky form or appearance. **2** a milky juice. [L *lactescere* f. *lactēre* be milky (as LACTIC)]

lactescent /lækˈtes(ə)nt/ *adj.* **1** milky. **2** yielding a milky juice.

lactic /ˈlæktɪk/ *adj. Chem.* of, relating to, or obtained from milk. □ **lactic acid** a clear odourless syrupy carboxylic acid formed in sour milk, and produced in the muscle tissues during strenuous exercise. [L *lac lactis* milk]

lactiferous /lækˈtɪfərəs/ *adj.* yielding milk or milky fluid. [LL *lactifer* (as LACTIC)]

lacto- /ˈlæktəʊ/ *comb. form* milk. [L *lac lactis* milk]

lactobacillus /ˌlæktəʊbəˈsɪləs/ *n.* (*pl.* **-bacilli** /-laɪ/) *Biol.* any Gram-positive rod-shaped bacterium of the genus *Lactobacillus,* producing lactic acid from the fermentation of carbohydrates.

lactometer /lækˈtɒmɪtə(r)/ *n.* an instrument for testing the density of milk.

lactone /ˈlæktəʊn/ *n. Chem.* any of a class of cyclic esters formed by the elimination of water from a hydroxy-carboxylic acid. [G *Lacton*]

lactoprotein /ˌlæktəʊˈprəʊtiːn/ *n.* the albuminous constituent of milk.

lactose /ˈlæktəʊs, -təʊz/ *n. Chem.* a sugar that occurs in milk, and is less sweet than sucrose. [as LACTO-]

lacuna /ləˈkjuːnə/ *n.* (*pl.* **lacunae** /-niː/ or **lacunas**) **1** a hiatus, blank, or gap. **2** a missing portion or empty page, esp. in an ancient MS, book, etc. **3** *Anat.* a cavity or depression, esp. in bone. □□ **lacunal** *adj.* **lacunar** *adj.* **lacunary** *adj.* **lacunose** *adj.* [L, = pool, f. *lacus* LAKE[1]]

lacustrine /ləˈkʌstraɪn/ *adj. formal* **1** of or relating to lakes. **2** living or growing in or beside a lake. [L *lacus* LAKE[1], after *palustris* marshy]

LACW *abbr.* Leading Aircraftwoman.

lacy /ˈleɪsɪ/ *adj* (**lacier, laciest**) of or resembling lace fabric. □□ **lacily** *adv.* **laciness** *n.*

lad /læd/ *n.* **1 a** a boy or youth. **b** a young son. **2** (esp. in *pl.*) *colloq.* a man; a fellow, esp. a workmate, drinking companion, etc. (*he's one of the lads*). **3** *colloq.* a high-spirited fellow; a rogue (*he's a bit of a lad*). **4** *Brit.* a stable-worker (regardless of age). □ **lad's love** = SOUTHERNWOOD. [ME *ladde,* of unkn. orig.]

Ladakh /ləˈdɑːk/ a high-altitude region of eastern Kashmir in NW India. Its chief town is Leh.

ladanum /ˈlædənəm/ *n.* (also **labdanum** /ˈlæbdənəm/) a gum resin from plants of the genus *Cistus,* used in perfumery etc. [L f. Gk *ladanon* f. *lēdon* mastic]

ladder /ˈlædə(r)/ *n.* & *v.* —*n.* **1** a set of horizontal bars of wood or metal fixed between two uprights and used for climbing up or down. **2** *Brit.* a vertical strip of unravelled fabric in a stocking etc. resembling a ladder. **3 a** a hierarchical structure. **b** such a structure as a means of advancement, promotion, etc. —*v. Brit.* **1** *intr.* (of a stocking etc.) develop a ladder. **2** *tr.* cause a ladder in (a stocking etc.). □ **ladder-back** an upright chair with a back resembling a ladder. **ladder-stitch** transverse bars in embroidery. **ladder tournament** a sporting contest with each participant listed and entitled to a higher place by defeating the one above. [OE *hlǣd(d)er,* ult. f. Gmc: cf. LEAN[1]]

laddie /ˈlædɪ/ *n. colloq.* a young boy or lad.

lade /leɪd/ *v.* (*past part.* **laden** /ˈleɪd(ə)n/) **1** *tr.* **a** put cargo on board (a ship). **b** ship (goods) as cargo. **2** *intr.* (of a ship) take on cargo. **3** *tr.* (as **laden** *adj.*) (usu. foll. by *with*) **a** (of a vehicle, donkey, person, tree, table, etc.) heavily loaded. **b** (of the conscience, spirit, etc.) painfully burdened with sin, sorrow, etc. [OE *hladan*]

la-di-da /ˌlɑːdɪˈdɑː/ *adj.* & *n. colloq.* —*adj.* pretentious or snobbish, esp. in manner or speech. —*n.* **1** a la-di-da person. **2** la-di-da speech or manners. [imit. of an affected manner of speech]

ladies *pl.* of LADY.

ladify var. of LADYFY.

Ladin /ləˈdiːn/ *n.* the Rhaeto-Romanic dialect of the Engadine in Switzerland. [Romansh, f. L *latinus* LATIN]

lading /ˈleɪdɪŋ/ *n.* **1** a cargo. **2** the act or process of lading.

Ladino /ləˈdiːnəʊ/ *n.* (*pl.* **-os**) **1** the Spanish dialect of the Sephardic Jews. **2** a mestizo or Spanish-speaking White person in

Central America. [Sp., orig. = Latin, f. L (as LADIN)]

Ladislaus /ˈlædɪsˌlaʊs/ the name of several kings of Hungary:

Ladislaus I (c.1040–95), reigned 1077–95, conquered Croatia and Bosnia and extended Hungarian power into Transylvania, as well as establishing order in his kingdom and advancing the spread of Christianity. He supported Pope Gregory VII in his confrontation with the Emperor Henry VI and was canonized in 1192.

Ladislaus II (1262–90), reigned 1272–90, was killed after two years of civil war following the declaration of a crusade against him by Pope Nicholas IV.

ladle /ˈleɪd(ə)l/ n. & v. —n. **1** a large long-handled spoon with a cup-shaped bowl used for serving esp. soups and gravy. **2** a vessel for transporting molten metal in a foundry. —v.tr. (often foll. by *out*) transfer (liquid) from one receptacle to another. □ **ladle out** distribute, esp. lavishly. □□ **ladleful** n. (pl. **-fuls**). **ladler** n. [OE *hlædel* f. *hladan* LADE]

Ladoga /ˈlɑːdəgə/ the largest European lake, in the USSR, near the Finnish border.

lady /ˈleɪdɪ/ n. (pl. **-ies**) **1 a** a woman regarded as being of superior social status or as having the refined manners associated with this (cf. GENTLEMAN). **b** (**Lady**) a title used by peeresses, female relatives of peers, the wives and widows of knights, etc. **2** (often *attrib.*) a woman; a female person or animal (*ask that lady over there; lady butcher; lady dog*). **3** *colloq.* **a** a wife. **b** a man's girlfriend. **4** a ruling woman (*lady of the house; lady of the manor*). **5** (in *pl.* as a form of address) a female audience or the female part of an audience. **6** *hist.* a woman to whom a man, esp. a knight, is chivalrously devoted; a mistress. □ **find the lady** = *three-card trick*. **the Ladies** (or **Ladies'**) *Brit.* a women's public lavatory. **ladies' chain** a figure in a quadrille etc. **ladies' fingers** = OKRA (cf. *lady's finger*). **Ladies' Gallery** a public gallery in the House of Commons, reserved for women. **ladies' (**or **lady's) man** a man fond of female company; a seducer. **ladies' night** a function at a men's club etc. to which women are invited. **ladies' room** a women's lavatory in a hotel, office, etc. **Lady altar** the altar in a Lady chapel. **Lady Bountiful** a patronizingly generous lady of the manor etc. (a character in Farquhar's *The Beaux' Stratagem*). **Lady chapel** a chapel in a large church or cathedral, usu. to the E. of the high altar, dedicated to the Virgin Mary. **Lady Day** the Feast of the Annunciation, 25 Mar. **lady-fern** a slender fern, *Athyrium filix-femina*. **lady-in-waiting** a lady attending a queen or princess. **lady-killer** a practised and habitual seducer. **lady-love** a man's sweetheart. **Lady Mayoress** the wife of a Lord Mayor. **Lady Muck** *sl. derog.* a socially pretentious woman. **lady of the bedchamber** = *lady-in-waiting*. **lady of easy virtue** a sexually promiscuous woman; a prostitute. **Lady of the Lamp** Florence Nightingale (see entry). **lady's bedstraw** a yellow-flowered herbaceous plant, *Galium verum*. **lady's companion** a roll containing cottons etc. **lady's finger 1** = *kidney vetch*. **2** = LADY-FINGER (cf. *ladies' fingers*). **lady's maid** a lady's personal maidservant. **lady's mantle** any rosaceous plant of the genus *Alchemilla* with yellowish-green clustered flowers. **lady-smock** = *cuckoo flower* 1. **lady's slipper** any orchidaceous plant of the genus *Cypripedium*, with a usu. yellow slipper-shaped lip on its flowers. **lady's tresses** any white-flowered orchid of the genus *Spiranthes*. **Lady Superior** the head of a convent or nunnery in certain orders. **my lady** a form of address used chiefly by servants etc. to holders of the title 'Lady'. **my lady wife** *joc.* my wife. **old lady** *colloq.* **1** a mother. **2** a wife or mistress. **Our Lady** the Virgin Mary. □□ **ladyhood** n. [OE *hlǣfdige* f. *hlāf* LOAF¹ + (unrecorded) *dig-* knead, rel. to DOUGH: in *Lady Day* etc. f. OE genit. *hlǣfdigan* (Our) Lady's]

ladybird /ˈleɪdɪbɜːd/ n. a coleopterous insect of the family Coccinellidae, with wing-covers usu. of a reddish-brown colour with black spots.

ladybug /ˈleɪdɪbʌg/ n. US = LADYBIRD.

ladyfinger /ˈleɪdɪfɪŋgə(r)/ n. US a finger-shaped sponge cake.

ladyfy /ˈleɪdɪfaɪ/ v.tr. (also **ladify**) (**-ies, -ied**) **1** make a lady of. **2** call (a person) 'lady'. **3** (as **ladyfied** adj.) having the manner of a fine lady.

ladylike /ˈleɪdɪˌlaɪk/ adj. **1 a** with the modesty, manners, etc., of a lady. **b** befitting a lady. **2** (of a man) effeminate.

ladyship /ˈleɪdɪʃɪp/ n. *archaic* being a lady. □ **her** (or **your** or **their**) **ladyship** (or **ladyships**) **1** a respectful form of reference or address to a Lady or Ladies. **2** *iron.* a form of reference or address to a woman thought to be giving herself airs.

Ladysmith /ˈleɪdɪˌsmɪθ/ a town in Natal, besieged by Boers 2 Nov. 1899–28 Feb. 1900, relieved by Sir R. H. Buller (d. 1908).

lae /ˈlɑːeɪ/ an industrial seaport and the second-largest city of Papua New Guinea; pop. (1980) 61,600.

laevo- /ˈliːvəʊ/ comb. form (also **levo-**) on or to the left. [L *laevus* left]

laevorotatory /ˌliːvəʊˈrəʊtətərɪ/ adj. (US **levorotatory**) *Chem.* having the property of rotating the plane of a polarized light ray to the left (anti-clockwise facing the oncoming radiation).

laevulose /ˈliːvjʊˌləʊs, -ˌləʊz/ n. (US **levulose**) = FRUCTOSE. [LAEVO- + -ULE + -OSE²]

La Fayette /lɑː faɪˈet/ Marie Joseph Paul Yves Roch Gilbert du Motier, Marquis de (1757–1834), French soldier and liberal statesman. As a young man, La Fayette was one of the leaders of the French expeditionary force which fought alongside the Americans in the second half of the War of Independence. He played a crucial part in the early phase of the French Revolution, commanding the National Guard and advocating moderate policies, but was subsequently forced from the scene by more radical opponents.

La Fontaine /lɑː fɒnˈteɪn/, Jean de (1621–95), French poet, author of *Fables* drawn from oriental, classical, and modern sources. They include such tales as 'The Cicada and the Ant' and 'The Crow and the Fox' which have enjoyed wide popularity. His bawdy verse tales *Contes et Nouvelles* (1664–74) were drawn from Ariosto, Boccaccio, and others; many of them were censured for their immorality and La Fontaine is said to have publicly disavowed them after his religious conversion in 1692.

lag¹ /læg/ v. & n. —v.intr. (**lagged, lagging**) **1** (often foll. by *behind*) fall behind; not keep pace. **2** *US Billiards* make the preliminary strokes that decide which player shall begin. —n. **1** a delay. **2** *Physics* **a** retardation in a current or movement. **b** the amount of this. □ **lag of tide** the interval by which a tide falls behind mean time at the 1st and 3rd quarters of the moon (cf. PRIMING²). □□ **lagger** n. [orig. = hindmost person, hang back: perh. f. a fanciful distortion of LAST¹ in a children's game (*fog, seg, lag,* = 1st, 2nd, last, in dial.)]

lag² /læg/ v. & n. —v.tr. (**lagged, lagging**) enclose or cover in lagging. —n. **1** the non-heat-conducting cover of a boiler etc.; lagging. **2** a piece of this. [prob. f. Scand.: cf. ON *lögg* barrel-rim, rel. to LAY¹]

lag³ /læg/ n. & v. *sl.* —n. (esp. as **old lag**) a habitual convict. —v.tr. (**lagged, lagging**) **1** send to prison. **2** apprehend; arrest. [19th c.: orig. unkn.]

lagan /ˈlægən/ n. goods or wreckage lying on the bed of the sea, sometimes with a marking buoy etc. for later retrieval. [OF, perh. of Scand. orig., f. root of LIE¹, LAY¹]

lager /ˈlɑːgə(r)/ n. a kind of beer, effervescent and light in colour and body. □ **lager lout** *colloq.* a youth who behaves badly as a result of excessive drinking. [G *Lagerbier* beer brewed for keeping f. *Lager* store]

Lagerlöf /ˈlɑːgəˌlɜːf/, Selma (Ottiliana Lovisa) (1858–1940), Swedish writer of fiction, who made her name with *Gösta Berlings Saga* (1891). Romantic in mood, her work was inspired by local legends and traditions. She was awarded the Nobel Prize for literature in 1909, the first woman to win a Nobel Prize in any field.

laggard /ˈlægəd/ n. & adj. —n. a dawdler; a person who lags behind. —adj. dawdling; slow. □□ **laggardly** adj. & adv. **laggardness** n. [LAG¹]

lagging /ˈlægɪŋ/ n. material providing heat insulation for a boiler, pipes, etc. [LAG²]

lagomorph /ˈlægəˌmɔːf/ n. *Zool.* any mammal of the order Lagomorpha, including hares and rabbits. [Gk *lagōs* hare + *morphē* form]

lagoon /lə'gu:n/ n. **1** a stretch of salt water separated from the sea by a low sandbank, coral reef, etc. **2** the enclosed water of an atoll. **3** US, Austral., & NZ a small freshwater lake near a larger lake or river. **4** an artificial pool for the treatment of effluent or to accommodate an overspill from surface drains during heavy rain. [F lagune or It. & Sp. laguna f. L lacuna: see LACUNA]

Lagos /'leɪgɒs/ the capital and chief port of Nigeria; pop. (1983) 1,097,000.

Lagrange /la:'grãʒ/, Joseph Louis, Comte de (1736–1813), mathematician, born in Italy of French parents. He is remembered for his proof that every positive integer can be expressed as a sum of at most four squares and for his study of the solution of algebraic equations which, many years later, provided the inspiration for the founding of the theory of groups and Galois theory. But his greatest and most influential work was the Traité de mécanique analytique (1788) which was the culmination of his extensive work on mechanics and its application to the description of planetary and lunar motion.

lah /la:/ n. (also **la**) Mus. **1** (in tonic sol-fa) the sixth note of a major scale. **2** the note A in the fixed-doh system. [ME f. L labii: see GAMUT]

lahar /'la:ha:(r)/ n. a mud-flow composed mainly of volcanic debris. [Jav.]

Lahore /lə'hɔ:(r)/ the capital of Punjab province and second-largest city of Pakistan; pop. (1981) 2,922,000.

laic /'leɪɪk/ adj. & n. —adj. non-clerical; lay; secular; temporal. —n. formal a lay person; a non-cleric. □□ **laical** adj. **laically** adv. [LL f. Gk laikos f. laos people]

laicity /leɪ'ɪsɪtɪ/ n. the status or influence of the laity.

laicize /'leɪɪsaɪz/ v.tr. (also **-ise**) **1** make (an office etc.) tenable by lay people. **2** subject (a school or institution) to the control of lay people. **3** secularize. □□ **laicization** /-'zeɪʃ(ə)n/ n.

laid past and past part. of LAY¹.

lain past part. of LIE¹.

lair¹ /leə(r)/ n. & v. —n. **1 a** a wild animal's resting-place. **b** a person's hiding-place; a den (tracked him to his lair). **2** a place where domestic animals lie down. **3** Brit. a shed or enclosure for cattle on the way to market. —v. **1** intr. go to or rest in a lair. **2** tr. place (an animal) in a lair. □□ **lairage** n. [OE leger f. Gmc: cf. LIE¹]

lair² /leə(r)/ n. & v. Austral. sl. —n. a youth or man who dresses flashily and shows off. —v.intr. (often foll. by up or dress) behave or dress like a lair. □□ **lairy** adj. [lair back-form. f. lairy, alt. f. LEERY]

laird /'leəd/ n. Sc. a landed proprietor. □□ **lairdship** n. [Sc. form of LORD]

laissez-aller /ˌleseɪ'æleɪ/ n. (also **laisser-aller**) unconstrained freedom; an absence of constraint. [F, = let go]

laissez-faire /ˌleseɪ'feə(r)/ n. (also **laisser-faire**) the theory or practice of governmental abstention from interference in the workings of the market etc. [F, = let act]

laissez-passer /ˌleseɪ'pæseɪ/ n. (also **laisser-passer**) a document allowing the holder to pass; a permit. [F, = let pass]

laity /'leɪɪtɪ/ n. (usu. prec. by the; usu. treated as pl.) **1** lay people, as distinct from the clergy. **2** non-professionals. [ME f. LAY² + -ITY]

lake¹ /leɪk/ n. a large body of water surrounded by land. □ **Lake District** (or **the Lakes**) the region of the English lakes in Cumbria. **lake-dweller** a prehistoric inhabitant of a lake-dwelling. **lake-dwellings** a prehistoric dwelling built on piles driven into the bed or shore of a lake. Such dwellings occur in Switzerland and northern Italy from neolithic to Iron Age periods (4th–1st millennium BC) and in other parts of temperate Europe in the Iron Age (7th–1st c. BC). **Lake Poets** (or **Lake School**) the poets Coleridge, Southey, and Wordsworth, who lived in and were inspired by the Lake District. □□ **lakeless** adj. **lakelet** n. [ME f. OF lac f. L lacus basin, pool, lake]

lake² /leɪk/ n. **1** a reddish colouring orig. made from lac (crimson lake). **2** a complex formed by the action of dye and mordants applied to fabric to fix colour. **3** any insoluble product of a soluble dye and mordant. [var. of LAC¹]

Lakeland /'leɪklənd/ n. = Lake District. □ **Lakeland terrier 1** a terrier of a small stocky breed originating in the Lake District. **2** this breed.

lakeside /'leɪksaɪd/ attrib.adj. beside a lake.

lakh /læk, la:k/ n. (also **lac**) Ind. (usu. foll. by of) a hundred thousand (rupees etc.). [Hind. lākh f. Skr. lakṣa]

Lakshadweep /ˌlækʃæ'dwi:p/ a Union Territory of India, formerly the Laccadive, Minicoy, and Amindivi Islands, off the coast of Malabar; pop. (1981) 40,200; capital, Kavaratti.

Lakshmi /'lʌkʃmɪ/ Hinduism the goddess of prosperity, and consort of Vishnu. She assumes different forms in order to accompany her husband in his incarnations (e.g. Sita, Radha). [Skr., = prosperity]

Lallan /'lælən/ n. & adj. Sc. —n. (now usu. **Lallans**) a Lowland Scots dialect, esp. as a literary language. —adj. of or concerning the Lowlands of Scotland. [var. of LOWLAND]

lallation /læ'leɪʃ(ə)n/ n. **1** the pronunciation of r as l. **2** imperfect speech, esp. that of young children. [L lallare lallat- sing a lullaby]

lallygag /'lælɪgæg/ v.intr. (**lallygagged, lallygagging**) US sl. **1** loiter. **2** cuddle amorously. [20th c.: orig. unkn.]

La Louvière /la: lu:v'leə(r)/ an industrial city of Belgium, in the province of Hainaut; pop. (1988) 76,300.

Lam. abbr. Lamentations (Old Testament).

lam¹ /læm/ v. (**lammed, lamming**) sl. **1** tr. thrash; hit. **2** intr. (foll. by into) hit (a person etc.) hard with a stick etc. [perh. f. Scand.: cf. ON lemja beat so as to LAME]

lam² /læm/ n. □ **on the lam** US sl. in flight, esp. from the police. [20th c.: orig. unkn.]

lama /'la:mə/ n. **1** an honorific applied to a spiritual leader in Tibetan Buddhism, whether a reincarnate lama (e.g. the Dalai Lama; see entry) or one who has earned the title in this life. **2** any Tibetan Buddhist monk. [Tibetan blama (with silent b) superior one]

Lamaism /'la:məɪz(ə)m/ n. a common but (strictly) incorrect term for Tibetan Buddhism. □□ **Lamaist** n.

Lamarck /læ'ma:k/, Jean Baptiste de (1744–1829), French botanist and zoologist who among others anticipated Darwin's concept of organic evolution. He suggested that species could have evolved from each other by small changes in their structure, and the mechanism of this change was that characteristics acquired in order to survive could be passed on to offspring. His theory found little favour in his lifetime (it was criticized notably by Cuvier), and he died in poverty, but the concept of inheritance of acquired characteristics was revived by those who did not accept Darwin's later theory of natural selection as explaining evolution.

Lamartine /ˌla:ma:'ti:n/, Alphonse de (1790–1869), French poet. A diplomat in Italy from 1820, he turned to politics during the Revolution of 1830 and was Foreign Minister during that of 1848. His speeches in the cause of liberty and justice aroused the imagination of his countrymen, and Méditations poétiques (1820) established him as a leading figure of the French Romantic movement. In these plaintive melodious verses, some inspired by his love for the 'Elvire' of many of his poems, he used Nature to reflect the poet's moods, and brought a fresh lyricism to French poetry. His other works include Jocelyn (1836) and La Chute d'un ange (1838), fragments of a projected epic poem, and biographical, historical, political, and travel works.

lamasery /'la:məsrɪ, lə'ma:sərɪ/ n. (pl. **-ies**) a common but strictly incorrect term for a Tibetan Buddhist monastery. [F lamaserie irreg. f. lama LAMA]

Lamb /læm/, Charles (1775–1834), English essayist and critic. He devoted much of his life to caring for his sister Mary, who had killed their mother during one of her recurrent bouts of insanity; together they wrote Tales from Shakespear (1807) for children. His Specimens of English Dramatic Poets (1808) is an anthology of scenes and speeches from Elizabethan and Jacobean dramatists which drew the attention of his contemporaries to that period of drama. Lamb's essays were published in the important periodicals of his day, including his most famous series, The Essays of Elia (1820–3); Lamb adopted the name 'Elia' to save the susceptibilities of his brother John, then a clerk in the South-Sea House (the subject of the first Essay). The semi-autobiographical essays, dealing with mankind at large, are presented with wit and pathos in a literary and archaic style; the character of the narrator, 'a bundle of prejudices' much attracted to the whimsical and eccentric, is maintained throughout the series.

lamb /læm/ n. & v. —n. **1** a young sheep. **2** the flesh of a lamb as food. **3** a mild or gentle person, esp. a young child. —v. **1 a** tr. (in passive) (of a lamb) be born. **b** intr. (of a ewe) give birth to lambs. **2** tr. tend (lambing ewes). □ **The Lamb** (or **The Lamb of God**) a name for Christ (see John 1: 29) (cf. AGNUS DEI). **lamb's fry** lamb's testicles or other offal as food. **lamb's lettuce** a plant, *Valerianella locusta*, used in salad. **lamb's-tails** catkins from the hazel tree. **like a lamb** meekly, obediently. □□ **lamber** n. **lambhood** n. **lambkin** n. **lamblike** adj. [OE *lamb* f. Gmc]

lambaste /læm'beɪst/ v.tr. (also **lambast** /-'bæst/) colloq. **1** thrash; beat. **2** criticize severely. [LAM[1] + BASTE[3]]

lambda /'læmdə/ n. **1** the eleventh letter of the Greek alphabet (*Λ*, *λ*). **2** (as *λ*) the symbol for wavelength. [ME f. Gk *la(m)bda*]

lambent /'læmbənt/ adj. **1** (of a flame or a light) playing on a surface with a soft radiance but without burning. **2** (of the eyes, sky, etc.) softly radiant. **3** (of wit etc.) lightly brilliant. □□ **lambency** n. **lambently** adv. [L *lambere lambent-* lick]

Lambert /'læmbət/, (Leonard) Constant (1905–51), English composer, conductor, and critic, a pupil of Vaughan Williams. While still a student he gained a commission from Diaghilev for the ballet *Romeo and Juliet* (1926), and thereafter took a leading part in the establishment of British ballet, being musical director of Sadler's Wells from 1930 to 1947. His book *Music Ho!* (1934) is an important commentary on the music of that time.

lambert /'læmbət/ n. a former unit of luminance, equal to the emission or reflection of one lumen per square centimetre. [J. H. *Lambert*, Ger. physicist d. 1777]

Lambeth Palace /'læmbəθ/ a palace in the London borough of Lambeth, south of the Thames, that since 1197 has been the residence of the archbishop of Canterbury.

lambrequin /'læmbrɪkɪn, 'læmbə-/ n. **1** US a short piece of drapery hung over the top of a door or a window or draped on a mantelpiece. **2** Heraldry = MANTLING. [F f. Du. (unrecorded) *lamperkin*, dimin. of *lamper* veil]

lambskin /'læmskɪn/ n. a prepared skin from a lamb with the wool on or as leather.

lambswool /'læmzwʊl/ n. (also **lamb's-wool**) soft fine wool from a young sheep used in knitted garments etc.

lame /leɪm/ adj. & v. —adj. **1** disabled, esp. in the foot or leg; limping; unable to walk normally (*lame in his right leg*). **2 a** (of an argument, story, excuse, etc.) unconvincing; unsatisfactory; weak. **b** (of verse etc.) halting. —v.tr. **1** make lame; disable. **2** harm permanently. □ **lame-brain** US colloq. a stupid person. **lame duck 1** a disabled or weak person. **2** a defaulter on the Stock Exchange. **3** a firm etc. in financial difficulties. **4** US an official (esp. the President) in the final period of office, after the election of a successor. □□ **lamely** adv. **lameness** n. **lamish** adj. [OE *lama* f. Gmc]

lamé /'lɑːmeɪ/ n. & adj. —n. a fabric with gold or silver threads interwoven. —adj. (of fabric, a dress, etc.) having such threads. [F]

lamella /lə'melə/ n. (pl. **lamellae** /-liː/) **1** a thin layer, membrane, scale, or platelike tissue or part, esp. in bone tissue. **2** Bot. a membranous fold in a chloroplast. □□ **lamellar** adj. **lamellate** /'læmə,leɪt/ adj. **lamelliform** adj. **lamellose** /-ləʊs/ adj. [L, dimin. of *lamina*: see LAMINA]

lamellibranch /lə'melɪ,bræŋk/ n. any aquatic mollusc having a shell formed of two pieces or valves, e.g. a mussel or oyster. Also called BIVALVE. [LAMELLA + Gk *bragkhia* gills]

lamellicorn /lə'melɪ,kɔːn/ n. & adj. —n. any beetle of the family Lamellicornia, having lamelliform antennae, including the stag beetle, cockchafer, dung-beetle, etc. —adj. having lamelliform antennae. [mod.L *lamellicornis* f. L *lamella* (see LAMELLA) + *cornu* horn]

lament /lə'ment/ n. & v. —n. **1** a passionate expression of grief. **2** a song or poem of mourning or sorrow. —v.tr. (also absol.) **1** express or feel grief for or about; regret (*lamented the loss of his ticket*). **2** (as **lamented** adj.) a conventional expression referring to a recently dead person (*your late lamented father*). □ **lament for** (or **over**) mourn or regret. □□ **lamenter** n. **lamentingly** adv. [L *lamentum*]

lamentable /'læməntəb(ə)l/ adj. **1** (of an event, fate, condition, character, etc.) deplorable; regrettable. **2** archaic mournful. □□ **lamentably** adv. [ME f. OF *lamentable* or L *lamentabilis* (as LAMENT)]

lamentation /,læmən'teɪʃ(ə)n/ n. **1** the act or an instance of lamenting. **2** a lament. □ **Lamentations** (in full **The Lamentations of Jeremiah**) a book of the Old Testament traditionally ascribed to Jeremiah but probably of a later period, telling of the desolation of Judah after the destruction of Jerusalem in 586 BC. [ME f. OF *lamentation* or L *lamentatio* (as LAMENT)]

lamina /'læmɪnə/ n. (pl. **laminae** /-,niː/) a thin plate or scale, e.g. of bone, stratified rock, or vegetable tissue. □□ **laminose** adj. [L]

laminar /'læmɪnə(r)/ adj. **1** consisting of laminae. **2** Physics (of a flow) taking place along constant streamlines, not turbulent.

laminate v., n., & adj. —v. /'læmɪ,neɪt/ **1** tr. beat or roll (metal) into thin plates. **2** tr. overlay with metal plates, a plastic layer, etc. **3** tr. manufacture by placing layer on layer. **4** tr. & intr. split or be split into layers or leaves. —n. /'læmɪnət/ a laminated structure or material, esp. of layers fixed together to form rigid or flexible material. —adj. /'læmɪnət/ in the form of lamina or laminae. □□ **lamination** /-'neɪʃ(ə)n/ n. **laminator** n. [LAMINA + -ATE[2], -ATE[3]]

Lammas /'læməs/ n. (in full **Lammas Day**) the first day of August, formerly observed as an English harvest festival at which loaves made from the first ripe corn were consecrated; in Scotland, one of the quarter days. [OE *hlāfmæsse* (as LOAF[1], MASS[2])]

lammergeyer /'læmə,gaɪə(r)/ n. a large vulture, *Gypaetus barbatus*, with a very large wingspan (often of 3 m) and dark beardlike feathers on either side of its beak. [G *Lämmergeier* f. *Lämmer* lambs + *Geier* vulture]

lamp /læmp/ n. & v. —n. **1** a device for producing a steady light, esp.: **a** an electric bulb, and usu. its holder and shade or cover (*bedside lamp; bicycle lamp*). **b** an oil-lamp. **c** a usu. glass holder for a candle. **d** a gas-jet and mantle. **2** a source of spiritual or intellectual inspiration. **3** poet. the sun, the moon, or a star. **4** a device producing esp. ultraviolet or infrared radiation as a treatment for various complaints. —v. **1** intr. poet. shine. **2** tr. supply with lamps; illuminate. **3** tr. US sl. look at. □ **lamp-chimney** a glass cylinder enclosing and making a draught for an oil-lamp flame. **lamp-holder** a device for supporting a lamp, esp. an electric one. **lamp standard** = LAMPPOST. □□ **lampless** adj. [ME f. OF *lampe* f. LL *lampada* f. accus. of L *lampas* torch f. Gk]

lampblack /'læmpblæk/ n. a pigment made from soot.

lamplight /'læmplaɪt/ n. light given by a lamp or lamps.

lamplighter /'læmp,laɪtə(r)/ n. **1** hist. a person who lights street lamps. **2** US a spill for lighting lamps. □ **like a lamplighter** with great speed.

lampoon /læm'puːn/ n. & v. —n. a satirical attack on a person etc. —v.tr. satirize. □□ **lampooner** n. **lampoonery** n. **lampoonist** n. [F *lampon*, conjectured to be f. *lampons* let us drink f. *lamper* gulp down f. *laper* LAP[3]]

lamppost /'læmppəʊst/ n. a tall post supporting a street-light.

lamprey /'læmprɪ/ n. (pl. **-eys**) any eel-like aquatic vertebrate of the family Petromyzonidae, without scales, paired fins, or jaws, but having a sucker mouth with horny teeth and a rough tongue. [ME f. OF *lampreie* f. med.L *lampreda*: cf. LL *lampetra* perh. f. L *lambere* lick + *petra* stone]

lampshade /'læmpʃeɪd/ n. a translucent cover for a lamp used to soften or direct its light.

Lancashire /'læŋkəʃɪə(r)/ a county of NW England; pop. (1981) 1,385,700; county town, Preston.

b but d dog f few g get h he j yes k cat l leg m man n no p pen r red s sit t top v voice

Lancaster /ˈlæŋkæstə(r)/ **1** a city in Lancashire, formerly its county town; pop. (1981) 44,447. **2** *hist.* the name of the English royal house descended from John of Gaunt, Duke of Lancaster (4th son of Edward III), which ruled England from 1399 (Henry IV) until the death of Henry VI (1471).

Lancastrian /læŋˈkæstrɪən/ *adj. & n. —adj.* **1** of Lancashire or Lancaster. **2** of the family descended from John of Gaunt, Duke of Lancaster, or of the Red Rose party supporting it in the Wars of the Roses (cf. YORKIST). *—n.* **1** a native of Lancashire or Lancaster. **2** a member or adherent of the Lancastrian family.

lance /lɑːns/ *n. & v. —n.* **1 a** a long weapon with a wooden shaft and a pointed steel head, used by a horseman in charging. **b** a similar weapon used for spearing a fish, killing a harpooned whale, etc. **2** a metal pipe supplying oxygen to burn metal. **3** = LANCER. *—v.tr.* **1** *Surgery* prick or cut open with a lancet. **2** pierce with a lance. **3** *poet.* fling; launch. □ **break a lance** (usu. foll. by *for, with*) argue. **lance-bombardier** a rank in the Royal Artillery corresponding to lance-corporal in the infantry. **lance-corporal** the lowest rank of NCO in the Army. **lance-jack** *Brit. sl.* a lance-corporal or lance-bombardier. **lance-sergeant** a corporal acting as sergeant. **lance-snake** = FER DE LANCE. [ME f. OF *lancier* f. L *lancea: lance-corporal* on analogy of obs. *lancepesade* lowest grade of NCO ult. f. It. *lancia spezzata* broken lance]

lancelet /ˈlɑːnslɪt/ *n.* any small non-vertebrate fishlike chordate of the family Branchiostomidae, that burrows in sand. [LANCE *n.* + -LET, with ref. to its thin form]

Lancelot /ˈlɑːnsəlɒt/ (in Arthurian legend) the most famous of Arthur's knights, lover of Queen Guinevere.

lanceolate /ˈlɑːnsɪələt/ *adj.* shaped like a lance-head, tapering to each end. [LL *lanceolatus* f. *lanceola* dimin. of *lancea* lance]

lancer /ˈlɑːnsə(r)/ *n.* **1** *hist.* a soldier of a cavalry regiment armed with lances. **2** (*in pl.*) **a** a quadrille for 8 or 16 pairs. **b** the music for this. [F *lancier* (as LANCE)]

lancet /ˈlɑːnsɪt/ *n.* a small broad two-edged surgical knife with a sharp point. □ **lancet arch** (or **light** or **window**) a narrow arch or window with a pointed head. □□ **lanceted** *adj.* [ME f. OF *lancette* (as LANCE)]

lancewood /ˈlɑːnswʊd/ *n.* a tough elastic wood from a W. Indian tree *Oxandra lanceolata*, used for carriage-shafts, fishing-rods, etc.

Lanchow see LANZHOU.

Lancs. *abbr.* Lancashire.

Land /lʌnt/ *n.* (*pl.* **Länder** /ˈlendə(r)/) a province of Germany or Austria. [G (as LAND)]

land /lænd/ *n. & v. —n.* **1** the solid part of the earth's surface (opp. SEA, WATER, AIR). **2 a** an expanse of country; ground; soil. **b** such land in relation to its use, quality, etc., or (often prec. by *the*) as a basis for agriculture (*building land; this is good land; works on the land*). **3** a country, nation, or State (*land of hope and glory*). **4 a** landed property. **b** (*in pl.*) estates. **5** the space between the rifling-grooves in a gun. **6** *Sc.* a building containing several dwellings. **7** *S.Afr.* ground fenced off for tillage. **8** a strip of plough or pasture land parted from others by drain-furrows. *—v.* **1 a** *tr. & intr.* set or go ashore. **b** *intr.* (often foll. by *at*) disembark (*landed at the harbour*). **2** *tr.* bring (an aircraft, its passengers, etc.) to the ground or the surface of water. **3** *intr.* (of an aircraft, bird, parachutist, etc.) alight on the ground or water. **4** *tr.* bring (a fish) to land. **5** *tr. & intr.* (also *refl.*; often foll. by *up*) *colloq.* bring to, reach, or find oneself in a certain situation, place, or state (*landed himself in jail; landed up in France; landed her in trouble; landed up penniless*). **6** *tr. colloq.* a deal (a person etc.) a blow etc. (*landed him one in the eye*). **b** (foll. by *with*) present (a person) with (a problem, job, etc.). **7** *tr.* set down (a person, cargo, etc.) from a vehicle, ship, etc. **8** *tr. colloq.* win or obtain (a prize, job, etc.) esp. against strong competition. □ **how the land lies** what is the state of affairs. **in the land of the living** *joc.* still alive. **land-agency 1** the stewardship of an estate. **2** an agency for the sale etc. of estates. **land-agent 1** the steward of an estate. **2** an agent for the sale of estates. **land-bank** a bank issuing banknotes on the securities of landed property. **land breeze** a breeze blowing towards the sea from the land, esp. at night. **land-bridge** a neck of land joining two large land masses. **land-crab** a crab, *Cardisoma guanhumi*, that lives in burrows inland and migrates in large numbers to the sea to breed. **land force** (or **forces**) armies, not naval or air forces. **land-form** a natural feature of the earth's surface. **land-girl** *Brit.* a woman doing farm work, esp. in wartime. **land-grabber** an illegal seizer of land, esp. a person who took the land of an evicted Irish tenant. **land-law** (usu. in *pl.*) the law of landed property. **land-line** a means of telecommunication over land. **land-locked** almost or entirely enclosed by land. **land mass** a large area of land. **land-mine 1** an explosive mine laid in or on the ground. **2** a parachute mine. **land of cakes** Scotland. **land office** *US* an office recording dealings in public land. **land-office business** *US* enormous trade. **land of Nod** sleep (with pun on the phr. in Gen. 4:16). **land on one's feet** attain a good position, job, etc., by luck. **land-tax** *hist.* a tax assessed on landed property. **land-tie** a rod, beam, or piece of masonry securing or supporting a wall etc. by connecting it with the ground. **land-wind** a wind blowing seaward from the land. **land yacht** a vehicle with wheels and sails for recreational use on a beach etc. □□ **lander** *n.* **landless** *adj.* **landward** *adj. & adv.* **landwards** *adv.* [OE f. Gmc]

landau /ˈlændɔː/ *n.* a four-wheeled enclosed carriage with a removable front cover and a back cover that can be raised and lowered. [*Landau* near Karlsruhe in Germany, where it was first made]

landaulet /ˌlændɔːˈlet/ *n.* **1** a small landau. **2** *hist.* a car with a folding hood over the rear seats.

landed /ˈlændɪd/ *adj.* **1** owning land (*landed gentry*). **2** consisting of, including, or relating to land (*landed property*).

Länder *pl.* of LAND.

landfall /ˈlændfɔːl/ *n.* the approach to land, esp. for the first time on a sea or air journey.

landfill /ˈlændfɪl/ *n.* **1** waste material etc. used to landscape or reclaim areas of ground. **2** the process of disposing of rubbish in this way.

landgrave /ˈlændɡreɪv/ *n.* (*fem.* **landgravine** /-ɡrəˌviːn/) *hist.* **1** a count having jurisdiction over a territory. **2** the title of certain German princes. □□ **landgraviate** /-ˈɡreɪvɪət/ *n.* [MLG *landgrave*, MHG *lantgrāve* (as LAND, G *Graf* COUNT²)]

landholder /ˈlændˌhəʊldə(r)/ *n.* the proprietor or, esp., the tenant of land.

landing /ˈlændɪŋ/ *n.* **1 a** the act or process of coming to land. **b** an instance of this. **c** (also **landing-place**) a place where ships etc. land. **2 a** a platform between two flights of stairs, or at the top or bottom of a flight. **b** a passage leading to upstairs rooms. □ **landing-craft** any of several types of craft esp. designed for putting troops and equipment ashore. **landing-gear** the undercarriage of an aircraft. **landing-net** for landing a large fish which has been hooked. **landing-stage** a platform, often floating, on which goods and passengers are disembarked. **landing-strip** an airstrip.

landlady /ˈlændˌleɪdɪ/ *n.* (*pl.* **-ies**) **1** a woman who lets land, a building, part of a building, etc., to a tenant. **2** a woman who keeps a public house, boarding-house, or lodgings.

ländler /ˈlendlə(r)/ *n.* **1** an Austrian dance in triple time, a precursor of the waltz. **2** the music for a ländler. [G f. *Landl* Upper Austria]

landloper /ˈlændˌləʊpə(r)/ *n. esp. Sc.* a vagabond. [MDu. *landlooper* (as LAND, *loopen* run, formed as LEAP)]

landlord /ˈlændlɔːd/ *n.* **1** a man who lets land, a building, part of a building, etc., to a tenant. **2** a man who keeps a public house, boarding-house, or lodgings.

landlubber /ˈlændˌlʌbə(r)/ *n.* a person unfamiliar with the sea or sailing.

landmark /ˈlændmɑːk/ *n.* **1 a** a conspicuous object in a district etc. **b** an object marking the boundary of an estate, country, etc. **2** an event, change, etc. marking a stage or turning-point in history etc.

landocracy /lænˈdɒkrəsɪ/ *n.* (*pl.* **-ies**) *joc.* the landed class. □□ **landocrat** /ˈlændəˌkræt/ *n.*

Landor /ˈlændə(r)/, Walter Savage (1775–1864), English writer.

His exotic oriental tale *Gebir: A Poem in seven Books* (1798) won him the admiration and friendship of Southey. During his long residence in Italy he wrote his best-known prose work *Imaginary Conversations of Literary Men and Statesmen* (1824–8). In verse and prose his elaborate and highly polished style shows a clear debt to classical forms and themes.

landowner /ˈlændˌəʊnə(r)/ *n.* an owner of land. □□ **landowning** *adj. & n.*

landrail /ˈlændreɪl/ *n.* = CORNCRAKE.

landscape /ˌlændskeɪp, ˈlæns-/ *n. & v.* —*n.* **1** natural or imaginary scenery, as seen in a broad view. **2** (often *attrib.*) a picture representing this; the genre of landscape painting. **3** (in graphic design etc.) a format in which the width of an illustration etc. is greater than the height (cf. PORTRAIT). —*v.tr.* (also *absol.*) improve (a piece of land) by landscape gardening. □ **landscape gardener** (or **architect**) a person who plans the layout of landscapes, esp. extensive grounds. **landscape gardening** (or **architecture**) the laying out of esp. extensive grounds to resemble natural scenery. **landscape-marble** marble with treelike markings. **landscape-painter** an artist who paints landscapes. □□ **landscapist** *n.* [MDu. *landscap* (as LAND, -SHIP)]

Landseer /ˈlændsɪə(r)/, Sir Edwin (1802–73), English painter and occasional sculptor, known best for his animal subjects. He was Queen Victoria's favourite painter, and engravings of his works spread his popularity far and wide, their often sentimental manner appealing greatly to contemporary taste, and were instrumental in establishing the Victorian liking for Highland hunting genre. As a sculptor he is best known for the bronze lions which he modelled in 1867 for the base of Nelson's Column in Trafalgar Square, London.

Land's End a rocky promontory in Cornwall forming the SW extremity of England. It is approximately 1,400 km (876 miles) by road from John o' Groats.

landslide /ˈlændslaɪd/ *n.* **1** the sliding down of a mass of land from a mountain, cliff, etc. **2** an overwhelming majority for one side in an election.

landslip /ˈlændslɪp/ *n.* = LANDSLIDE 1.

landsman /ˈlændzmən/ *n.* (*pl.* **-men**) a non-sailor.

Landsteiner /ˈlændstaɪnə(r)/, Karl (1868–1943), Austrian physician whose work covered many fields but whose main interest was in immunology. In 1930 he was awarded a Nobel Prize for his work on blood groups; the classification system of the four main groups, which he devised in the first decade of the 20th c., has remained in use and made it possible for blood transfusions to be carried out successfully. Landsteiner was the first to describe the rhesus factor in blood (1940).

lane /leɪn/ *n.* **1** a narrow, often rural, road, street, or path. **2** a division of a road for a stream of traffic (*three-lane highway*). **3** a strip of track or water for a runner, rower, or swimmer in a race. **4** a path or course prescribed for or regularly followed by a ship, aircraft, etc. (*ocean lane*). **5** a gangway between crowds of people, objects, etc. □ **it's a long lane that has no turning** change is inevitable. [OE: orig. unkn.]

Langland /ˈlæŋlənd/, William (*c.*1330–*c.*1386), English poet. Little is known of his life and identity but he was probably in minor orders and possibly lived in the Malvern district and London. He was the author of *Piers Plowman* (*c.*1367–70), the greatest allegorical poem of the Middle English alliterative revival, in the form of a spiritual pilgrimage guided by the Plowman on a journey in search of Truth. The author expresses concretely his concern with the corruption of the Church and the suffering of the poor.

langlauf /ˈlæŋlaʊf/ *n.* cross-country skiing; a cross-country skiing race. [G, = long run]

Langley /ˈlæŋlɪ/, Samuel Pierpoint (1834–1906), American astronomer and aviation pioneer. His work on aerodynamics contributed to the design of early aeroplanes.

langouste /lɑ̃ˈguːst/ *n.* a crawfish or spiny lobster. [F]

langoustine /ˌlɑ̃guːˈstiːn, ˈlɒŋɡʊstiːn/ *n.* = NORWAY LOBSTER. [F]

lang syne /læŋ ˈsaɪn/ *adv. & n.* Sc. —*adv.* in the distant past. —*n.* the old days (cf. AULD LANG SYNE). [= long since]

Langton /ˈlæŋt(ə)n/, Stephen (d. 1228), Archbishop of Canterbury who defended the Church's interests against King John with some success, was intermediary during the negotiations leading to the signing of Magna Carta, and protected the young Henry III against baronial domination. His reputation as perhaps England's greatest medieval archbishop rests mainly on his promotion of the interests of the English Church in the face of conflicting pressures from the papacy and the English throne.

Langtry /ˈlæŋtrɪ/, Lillie (1853–1929), real name Emilie Charlotte le Breton, British actress, born in the island of Jersey and known as the Jersey Lily, noted for her beauty and for being the first woman of high social position to go on the stage. She became an intimate friend of the Prince of Wales, later Edward VII.

language /ˈlæŋgwɪdʒ/ *n.* **1** the method of human communication, either spoken or written, consisting of the use of words in an agreed way. **2** the language of a particular community or country etc. (*speaks several languages*). **3 a** the faculty of speech. **b** a style or the faculty of expression; the use of words, etc. (*his language was poetic; hasn't the language to express it*). **c** (also **bad language**) coarse, crude, or abusive speech (*didn't like his language*). **4** a system of symbols and rules for writing computer programs or algorithms. **5** any method of expression (*the language of mime; sign language*). **6** a professional or specialized vocabulary. **7** literary style. □ **language laboratory** a room equipped with tape recorders etc. for learning a foreign language. **language of flowers** a set of symbolic meanings attached to different flowers. **speak the same language** have a similar outlook, manner of expression, etc. [ME f. OF *langage* ult. f. L *lingua* tongue]

langue de chat /ˌlɑ̃g də ˈʃɑ/ *n.* a very thin finger-shaped crisp biscuit or piece of chocolate. [F, = cat's tongue]

Languedoc /lɑ̃ɡˈdɒk/ a former province of southern France stretching from the Rhône valley to the northern foothills of the Pyrenees. The name now generally refers to the coastal plain lying between the Cévennes Mountains and the Mediterranean. Lower Languedoc has united with the former province of Roussillon to form the modern French region of Languedoc-Roussillon; pop. (1982) 1,926,500; capital, Montpellier. [see LANGUE D'OC]

langue d'oc /lɑ̃g ˈdɒk/ *n.* the form of medieval French spoken south of the Loire, the basis of modern Provençal. [OF, = language of 'oc', i.e. using the word *oc* (f. L *hoc* this) for 'yes', in contrast to *langue d'oïl*, the language spoken north of this region, where *oïl* (f. L *hoc ille*) was used, and which has developed into standard modern French *oui* = yes]

langue d'oïl /lɑ̃g ˈdɔɪl/ *n.* medieval French as spoken north of the Loire, the basis of modern French. [see LANGUE D'OC]

languid /ˈlæŋgwɪd/ *adj.* **1** lacking vigour; idle; inert; apathetic. **2** (of ideas etc.) lacking force; uninteresting. **3** (of trade etc.) slow-moving; sluggish. **4** faint; weak. □□ **languidly** *adv.* **languidness** *n.* [F *languide* or L *languidus* (as LANGUISH)]

languish /ˈlæŋgwɪʃ/ *v.intr.* **1** be or grow feeble; lose or lack vitality. **2** put on a sentimentally tender or languid look. □ **languish for** droop or pine for. **languish under** suffer under (esp. depression, confinement, etc.). □□ **languisher** *n.* **languishingly** *adv.* **languishment** *n.* [ME f. OF *languir*, ult. f. L *languēre*, rel. to LAX]

languor /ˈlæŋgə(r)/ *n.* **1** lack of energy or alertness; inertia; idleness; dullness. **2** faintness; fatigue. **3** a soft or tender mood or effect. **4** an oppressive stillness (of the air etc.). □□ **languorous** *adj.* **languorously** *adv.* [ME f. OF f. L *languor -oris* (as LANGUISH)]

langur /lʌŋˈguːə(r)/ *n.* any of various Asian long-tailed monkeys esp. of the genus *Presbytis*. [Hindi]

laniary /ˈlænɪərɪ/ *adj. & n.* —*adj.* (of a tooth) adapted for tearing; canine. —*n.* (*pl.* **-ies**) a laniary tooth. [L *laniarius* f. *lanius* butcher f. *laniare* to tear]

laniferous /ləˈnɪfərəs/ *adj.* (also **lanigerous** /ləˈnɪdʒərəs/) wool-bearing. [L *lanifer, -ger* f. *lana* wool]

lank /læŋk/ *adj.* **1** (of hair, grass, etc.) long, limp, and straight. **2**

thin and tall. **3** shrunken; spare. □□ **lankly** *adv.* **lankness** *n.* [OE *hlanc* f. Gmc: cf. FLANK, LINK[1]]

lanky /ˈlæŋkɪ/ *adj.* (**lankier**, **lankiest**) (of limbs, a person, etc.) ungracefully thin and long or tall. □□ **lankily** *adv.* **lankiness** *n.*

lanner /ˈlænə(r)/ *n.* a S. European falcon, *Falco biarmicus*, esp. the female. [ME f. OF *lanier* perh. f. OF *lanier* cowardly, orig. = weaver f. L *lanarius* wool-merchant f. *lana* wool]

lanneret /ˈlænərɪt/ *n.* a male lanner, smaller than the female. [ME f. OF *laneret* (as LANNER)]

lanolin /ˈlænəlɪn/ *n.* a fat found naturally on sheep's wool and used purified for cosmetics etc. [G f. L *lana* wool + *oleum* oil]

Lansing /ˈlænsɪŋ/ the capital of Michigan; pop. (1980) 130,414.

lansquenet /ˈlænskənət/ *n.* **1** a card-game of German origin. **2** a German mercenary soldier in the 16th–17th c. [F f. G *Landsknecht* (as LAND, *Knecht* soldier f. OHG *kneht*: see KNIGHT)]

lantana /lænˈteɪnə/ *n.* any evergreen shrub of the genus *Lantana*, with usu. yellow or orange flowers. [mod.L]

Lantau /lænˈdaʊ/ an island of Hong Kong, situated to the west of Hong Kong Island.

lantern /ˈlænt(ə)n/ *n.* **1 a** a lamp with a transparent usu. glass case protecting a candle flame etc. **b** a similar electric etc. lamp. **c** its case. **2 a** a raised structure on a dome, room, etc., glazed to admit light. **b** a similar structure for ventilation etc. **3** the light-chamber of a lighthouse. **4** = *magic lantern.* □ **lantern fish** any marine fish of the family Myctophidae, having small light organs on the head and body. **lantern-fly** (*pl.* **-flies**) any tropical homopterous insect of the family Fulgoridae, formerly thought to be luminous. **lantern-jawed** having lantern jaws. **lantern jaws** long thin jaws and chin, giving a hollow look to the face. **lantern-slide** a slide for projection by a magic lantern etc. (see SLIDE *n.* 5b). **lantern-wheel** a lantern-shaped gearwheel; a trundle. [ME f. OF *lanterne* f. L *lanterna* f. Gk *lamptēr* torch, lamp]

lanthanide /ˈlænθənaɪd/ *n. Chem.* an element of the lanthanide series. □ **lanthanide series** a series of 15 metallic elements from lanthanum to lutetium in the periodic table, having similar chemical properties: also called *rare earths* (see RARE[1]). [G *Lanthanid* (as LANTHANUM)]

lanthanum /ˈlænθənəm/ *n. Chem.* a silvery metallic element of the lanthanide series, first discovered (as the oxide) in 1839. Purified lanthanum metal has few uses, but it is a component of certain alloys, and the oxide is used in the manufacture of specialized types of glass. ¶ Symb.: **La**; atomic number 57. [Gk *lanthanō* escape notice, from having remained undetected in cerium oxide]

lanugo /ləˈnjuːgəʊ/ *n.* fine soft hair, esp. that which covers the body and limbs of a human foetus. [L, = down f. *lana* wool]

lanyard /ˈlænjəd, -jɑːd/ *n.* **1** a cord hanging round the neck or looped round the shoulder, esp. of a Scout or sailor etc., to which a knife, a whistle, etc., may be attached. **2** *Naut.* a short rope or line used for securing, tightening, etc. **3** a cord attached to a breech mechanism for firing a gun. [ME f. OF *laniere*, *lasniere*: assim. to YARD[1]]

Lanzhou /lænˈdʒaʊ/ (also **Lanchow** /lænˈtʃaʊ/) a city of northern China, capital of Gansu province; pop. (est. 1986) 1,350,000.

Laocoon /leɪˈɒkəʊˌɒn/ *Gk legend* a Trojan priest who, with his two sons, was crushed to death by two great sea-serpents as a penalty for warning the Trojans against drawing the wooden horse of the Greeks into Troy. The incident is the subject of one of the most famous examples of ancient sculpture, now in the Vatican Museum. This masterpiece, probably of the Pergamene school (2nd c. BC), in Pliny's time stood in the palace of the emperor Titus in Rome, but later disappeared and was dramatically rediscovered in 1506, when it made a great impression, especially on Michelangelo.

Laodicean /ˌleɪəʊdɪˈsiːən/ *adj. & n.* —*adj.* lukewarm or halfhearted, esp. in religion or politics. —*n.* such a person. [L *Laodicea* in Asia Minor (with ref. to the early Christians there: see Rev. 3:16)]

Laoighis /ˈleɪɪʃ/ (also **Leix**) a county of central Ireland, in the province of Leinster; pop. (est. 1986) 53,270. It was formerly called Queen's County.

Laos /ˈlaːɒs/ a small landlocked country of SE Asia, formerly part of French Indochina; pop. (est. 1988) 3,849,750; official language, Laotian; capital, Vientiane. Laos became independent of France in 1949, but for most of the next 25 years was torn by strife and civil war between the Communist Pathet Lao movement (latterly aided by the North Vietnamese) and government supporters (aided by the US and Thai mercenaries). In 1975 the Pathet Lao achieved total control of the country, the king abdicated, and Laos was proclaimed a People's Democratic Republic. □□ **Laotian** /ˈlaʊʃən, laːˈəʊʃən/ *adj. & n.*

Lao-tzu /ˌlaːəʊˈtsuː/ (also **Laoze**) **1** the legendary founder of Taoism and traditonal author of the Tao-te-Ching, its most sacred scripture. **2** this scripture. [Chinese, = Lao the Master]

lap[1] /læp/ *n.* **1 a** the front of the body from the waist to the knees of a sitting person (*sat on her lap; caught it in his lap*). **b** the clothing, esp. a skirt, covering the lap. **c** the front of a skirt held up to catch or contain something. **2** a hollow among hills. **3 a** hanging flap on a garment, a saddle, etc. □ **in** (or **on**) **a person's lap** as a person's responsibility. **in the lap of the gods** (of an event etc.) open to chance; beyond human control. **in the lap of luxury** in extremely luxurious surroundings. **lap-dog** a small pet dog. **lap robe** *US* a travelling-rug. □□ **lapful** *n.* (*pl.* **-fuls**). [OE *læppa* fold, flap]

lap[2] /læp/ *n. & v.* —*n.* **1 a** one circuit of a racetrack etc. **b** a section of a journey etc. (*finally we were on the last lap*). **2 a** an amount of overlapping or projecting part. **3 a** a layer or sheet (of cotton etc. being made) wound on a roller. **b** a single turn of rope, silk, thread, etc., round a drum or reel. **4** a rotating disk for polishing a gem or metal. —*v.* (**lapped**, **lapping**) **1** *tr.* lead or overtake (a competitor in a race) by one or more laps. **2** *tr.* (often foll. by *about*, *round*) coil, fold, or wrap (a garment etc.) round esp. a person. **3** *tr.* (usu. foll. by *in*) enfold or swathe (a person) in wraps etc. **4** *tr.* (as **lapped** *adj.*) (usu. foll. by *in*) protectively encircled; enfolded caressingly. **5** *tr.* surround (a person) with an influence etc. **6** *intr.* (usu. foll. by *over*) project; overlap. **7** *tr.* cause to overlap. **8** *tr.* polish (a gem etc.) with a lap. □ **half-lap** = *lap joint.* **lap joint** the joining of rails, shafts, etc., by halving the thickness of each at the joint and fitting them together. **lap of honour** a ceremonial circuit of a football pitch, a track, etc., by a winner or winners. **lap-strake** *n.* a clinker-built boat. —*adj.* clinker-built. **lap-weld** *v.tr.* weld with overlapping edges. —*n.* such a weld. [ME, prob. f. LAP[1]]

lap[3] /læp/ *v. & n.* —*v.* (**lapped**, **lapping**) **1** *tr.* **a** (also *absol.*) (usu. of an animal) drink (liquid) with the tongue. **b** (usu. foll. by *up*, *down*) consume (liquid) greedily. **c** (usu. foll. by *up*) consume (gossip, praise, etc.) greedily. **2 a** *tr.* (of water) move or beat upon (a shore) with a rippling sound as of lapping. **b** *intr.* (of waves etc.) move in ripples; make a lapping sound. —*n.* **1 a** the process or an act of lapping. **b** the amount of liquid taken up. **2** the sound of wavelets on a beach. **3** liquid food for dogs. **4** *sl.* **a** a weak beverage. **b** any liquor. [OE *lapian* f. Gmc]

laparoscope /ˈlæpərəˌskəʊp/ *n. Surgery* a fibre optic instrument inserted through the abdominal wall to give a view of the organs in the abdomen. □□ **laparoscopy** /-ˈrɒskəpɪ/ *n.* (*pl.* **-ies**). [Gk *lapara* flank + -SCOPE]

laparotomy /ˌlæpəˈrɒtəmɪ/ *n.* (*pl.* **-ies**) a surgical incision into the abdominal cavity for exploration or diagnosis. [Gk *lapara* flank + -TOMY]

La Paz /laː ˈpæz/ the seat of government of Bolivia; pop. (1985) 992,600.

lapel /ləˈpel/ *n.* the part of a coat, jacket, etc., folded back against the front round the neck opening. □□ **lapelled** *adj.* [LAP[1] + -EL]

lapicide /ˈlæpɪˌsaɪd/ *n.* a person who cuts or engraves on stone. [L *lapicida* irreg. f. *lapis -idis* stone: see -CIDE]

lapidary /ˈlæpɪdərɪ/ *adj. & n.* —*adj.* **1** concerned with stone or stones. **2** engraved upon stone. **3** (of writing style) dignified and concise, suitable for inscriptions. —*n.* (*pl.* **-ies**) a cutter, polisher, or engraver of gems. [ME f. L *lapidarius* f. *lapis -idis* stone]

lapilli /ləˈpɪlaɪ/ *n.pl.* stone fragments ejected from volcanoes. [It. f. L, pl. dimin. of *lapis* stone]

lapis lazuli /ˌlæpɪs ˈlæzjuːlɪ, -ˌlaɪ/ *n.* **1** a blue mineral containing sodium aluminium silicate and sulphur, used as a gemstone. **2** a bright blue pigment formerly made from this. **3** its colour. [ME f. L *lapis* stone + med.L *lazuli* genit. of *lazulum* f. Pers. (as AZURE)]

Lapith /ˈlæpɪθ/ *n.* Gk Mythol. a member of a Thessalian people who fought and defeated the Centaurs.

Laplace /laˈplɑːs/, Pierre Simon, Marquis de (1749–1827), French applied mathematician and theoretical physicist. Like his near-contemporary Lagrange, he devoted his greatest work, the *Traité de mécanique céleste* (1799–1825), to an extensive mathematical analysis of geophysical matters and of planetary and lunar motion. He is known for his innovative work on partial differential equations, for his contributions to probability theory, and for various other mathematical discoveries, but his reputation is mixed: he is also known for his sycophantic relationship to Napoleon Bonaparte and for phrases such as 'il est aisé de voir' which occur frequently but inaccurately in his writings.

Lapland /ˈlæplænd/ the region inhabited by Lapps, the most northerly part of Scandinavia, stretching from the Norwegian coast to the White Sea. □□ **Laplander** *n.*

Lapp *n.* **1** a member of the indigenous population of the extreme north of Scandinavia. **2** their language. (See below.) —*adj.* of or relating to the Lapps or their language. □□ **Lappish** *adj. & n.* [Sw. *Lapp*, perh. orig. a term of contempt; cf. MHG *lappe* simpleton]

Originating in the region of Lake Onega in Russia the Lapps moved westward 10,000 years ago. Although nominally under Swedish and Norwegian control since the Middle Ages, their Christianization was not completed until the 18th c. The Lappish language, of which there are several mutually unintelligible dialects, is related to Finnish. Today the majority of Lapps live in Norway and Sweden with small communities in Finland and the USSR. Traditionally associated with the domestication and herding of reindeer, few Lapps continue the nomadic herding of the animals. Approximately 50 per cent of the Lapps now live in permanent settlements with year-round pasture, and another 40 per cent live on the coasts and derive their livelihood from a combination of fishing, hunting, trapping, and farming. Scandinavian industrialization—particularly hydroelectric schemes, mining, and new roads—has severely disrupted the Lapps' traditional lifestyle.

lappet /ˈlæpɪt/ *n.* **1** a small flap or fold of a garment etc. **2** a hanging or loose piece of flesh, such as a lobe or wattle. □□ **lappeted** *adj.* [LAP¹ + -ET¹]

lapse /læps/ *n. & v.* —*n.* **1** a slight error; a slip of memory etc. **2** a weak or careless decline into an inferior state. **3** (foll. by *of*) an interval or passage of time (*after a lapse of three years*). **4** Law the termination of a right or privilege through disuse or failure to follow appropriate procedures. —*v.intr.* **1** fail to maintain a position or standard. **2** (foll. by *into*) fall back into an inferior or previous state. **3** (of a right or privilege etc.) become invalid because it is not used or claimed or renewed. **4** (as **lapsed** *adj.*) (of a person or thing) that has lapsed. □ **lapse rate** *Meteorol.* the rate at which the temperature falls with increasing altitude. □□ **lapser** *n.* [L *lapsus* f. *labi laps*- glide, slip, fall]

lapstone /ˈlæpstəʊn/ *n.* a shoemaker's stone held in the lap and used to beat leather on.

lapsus calami /ˌlæpsəs ˈkæləˌmaɪ/ *n.* (*pl.* same) a slip of the pen. [L: see LAPSE]

lapsus linguae /ˌlæpsəs ˈlɪŋgwaɪ/ *n.* a slip of the tongue. [L: see LAPSE]

Laptev Sea /ˈlæptef/ an arm of the Arctic Ocean lying to the north of mainland USSR, between the Taimyr peninsula and the New Siberian Islands.

laptop /ˈlæptɒp/ *n.* (*attrib.*) (of a microcomputer) portable and suitable for use while travelling.

lapwing /ˈlæpwɪŋ/ *n.* a plover, *Vanellus vanellus*, with black and white plumage, crested head, and a shrill cry. [OE *hlēapewince* f. *hlēapan* LEAP + WINK: assim. to LAP¹, WING]

larboard /ˈlɑːbəd/ *n. & adj. Naut. archaic* = PORT³. [ME *lade-*, *ladde-*, *lathe-* (perh. = LADE + BOARD): later assim. to *starboard*]

larceny /ˈlɑːsənɪ/ *n.* (*pl.* **-ies**) the theft of personal property. ¶ In 1968 replaced as a statutory crime in English law by *theft*. □□ **larcener** *n.* **larcenist** *n.* **larcenous** *adj.* [OF *larcin* f. L *latrocinium* f. *latro* robber, mercenary f. Gk *latreus*]

larch /lɑːtʃ/ *n.* **1** a deciduous coniferous tree of the genus *Larix*, with bright foliage and producing tough timber. **2** (in full **larchwood**) its wood. [MHG *larche* ult. f. L *larix -icis*]

lard /lɑːd/ *n. & v.* —*n.* the internal fat of the abdomen of pigs, esp. when rendered and clarified for use in cooking and pharmacy. —*v.tr.* **1** insert strips of fat or bacon in (meat etc.) before cooking. **2** (foll. by *with*) embellish (talk or writing) with foreign or technical terms. [ME f. OF *lard* bacon f. L *lardum*, *laridum*, rel. to Gk *larinos* fat]

larder /ˈlɑːdə(r)/ *n.* **1** a room or cupboard for storing food. **2** a wild animal's store of food, esp. for winter. [ME f. OF *lardier* f. med.L *lardarium* (as LARD)]

lardon /ˈlɑːd(ə)n/ *n.* (also **lardoon** /-ˈduːn/) a strip of fat bacon used to lard meat. [ME f. F *lardon* (as LARD)]

lardy /ˈlɑːdɪ/ *adj.* like or with lard. □ **lardy-cake** *Brit.* a cake made with lard, currants, etc.

lares /ˈlɑːriːz/ *n.pl. Rom.Hist.* gods worshipped, together with the penates, by households in ancient Rome. They are probably originally deities of the farm-land. □ **lares and penates** the home. [L]

large /lɑːdʒ/ *adj. & n.* —*adj.* **1** of considerable or relatively great size or extent. **2** of the larger kind (*the large intestine*). **3** of wide range; comprehensive. **4** pursuing an activity on a large scale (*large farmer*). —*n.* (**at large**) **1** at liberty. **2** as a body or whole (*popular with the people at large*). **3** (of a narration etc.) at full length and with all details. **4** without a specific target (*scatters insults at large*). **5** *US* representing a whole area and not merely a part of it (*congressman at large*). □ **in large** on a large scale. **large as life** see LIFE. **large-minded** liberal; not narrow-minded. **larger than life** see LIFE. **large-scale** made or occurring on a large scale or in large amounts. □□ **largeness** *n.* **largish** *adj.* [ME f. OF f. fem. of L *largus* copious]

largely /ˈlɑːdʒlɪ/ *adv.* to a great extent; principally (*is largely due to laziness*).

largesse /lɑːˈʒes/ *n.* (also **largess**) **1** money or gifts freely given, esp. on an occasion of rejoicing, by a person in high position. **2** generosity, beneficence. [ME f. OF *largesse* ult. f. L *largus* copious]

larghetto /lɑːˈgetəʊ/ *adv., adj., & n. Mus.* —*adv. & adj.* in a fairly slow tempo. —*n.* (*pl.* **-os**) a larghetto passage or movement. [It., dimin. of LARGO]

largo /ˈlɑːgəʊ/ *adv., adj., & n. Mus.* —*adv. & adj.* in a slow tempo and dignified in style. —*n.* (*pl.* **-os**) a largo passage or movement. [It., = broad]

lariat /ˈlærɪət/ *n.* **1** a lasso. **2** a tethering-rope, esp. used by cowboys. [Sp. *la reata* f. *reatar* tie again (as RE-, L *aptare* adjust f. *aptus* APT, fit)]

Larissa /ləˈrɪsə/ (Greek **Lárisa**) a city of NE Greece, capital of Thessaly; pop. (1981) 102,000.

lark¹ /lɑːk/ *n.* **1** any small bird of the family Alaudidae with brown plumage, elongated hind claw, and tuneful song, esp. the skylark. **2** any of various similar birds such as the meadow lark. [OE *lāferce*, *læwerce*, of unkn. orig.]

lark² /lɑːk/ *n. & v. colloq.* —*n.* **1** a frolic or spree; an amusing incident; a joke. **2** *Brit.* a type of activity, affair, etc. (*fed up with this digging lark*). —*v.intr.* (foll. by *about*) play tricks; frolic. □□ **larky** *adj.* **larkiness** *n.* [19th c.: orig. uncert.]

Larkin /ˈlɑːkɪn/, Philip Arthur (1922–85), English poet and novelist. His early poems were influenced by Yeats, including those collected in *The North Ship* (1945). Larkin's own poetic voice became distinct in *The Less Deceived* (1955) where the colloquial bravura of poems such as 'Toads' is offset by the half-tones and bitter lyricism of other pieces. *The Whitsun Weddings* (1964) adds a range of melancholy urban and suburban landscapes, and a

b *but* d *dog* f *few* g *get* h *he* j *yes* k *cat* l *leg* m *man* n *no* p *pen* r *red* s *sit* t *top* v *voice*

stoic wit, while many of the poems in *High Windows* (1974) show a preoccupation with death and transience. The adaptation of contemporary speech rhythms and vocabulary to an unobtrusive elegance distinguishes much of his work. His novels include *Jill* (1946) and *A Girl in Winter* (1947).

larkspur /ˈlɑːkspɜː(r)/ *n.* any of various plants of the genus *Consolida*, with a spur-shaped calyx.

larn /lɑːn/ *v. colloq.* or *joc.* **1** *intr.* = LEARN. **2** *tr.* teach (*that'll larn you*). [dial. form of LEARN]

La Rochefoucauld /lɑːˌrɒʃfuːˈkəʊ/, François de Marsillac, Duc de (1613–80), French moralist, active in abortive intrigues against Richelieu and Mazarin, related in his *Mémoires* (1662). His chief work, the *Maximes* (1665), consists of 504 brief reflections, in a highly polished style, analysing the motives of human conduct embodying a cynical philosophy that finds in self-love the prime motive of all action.

Larousse /lɑːˈruːs/, Pierre (1817–75), French lexicographer and encyclopedist, who edited the *Grand Dictionnaire universel du XIXᵉ siècle* (1866–76), which aimed to comprehend every department of human knowledge. In 1852 he founded, with Augustin Boyer, the publishing house of Larousse, which continues to issue the dictionaries and reference works that bear its name.

larrikin /ˈlærɪkɪn/ *n. Austral.* a hooligan. [also Engl. dial.: perh. f. the name *Larry* (pet-form of *Lawrence*) + -KIN]

larrup /ˈlærəp/ *v.tr.* (**larruped**, **larruping**) *colloq.* thrash. [dial.: perh. f. LATHER]

Larry /ˈlærɪ/ *n.* □ **as happy as Larry** *colloq.* extremely happy. [20th c.: orig. uncert.: cf. LARRIKIN]

larva /ˈlɑːvə/ *n.* (*pl.* **larvae** /-viː/) **1** the stage of development of an insect between egg and pupa, e.g. a caterpillar. **2** an immature form of other animals that undergo some metamorphosis, e.g. a tadpole. □□ **larval** *adj.* **larvicide** /ˈlɑːvɪˌsaɪd/ *n.* [L, = ghost, mask]

laryngeal /ləˈrɪndʒɪəl/ *adj.* **1** of or relating to the larynx. **2** *Phonet.* (of a sound) made in the larynx.

laryngitis /ˌlærɪnˈdʒaɪtɪs/ *n.* inflammation of the larynx. □□ **laryngitic** /-ˈdʒɪtɪk/ *adj.*

laryngoscope /ləˈrɪŋɡəˌskəʊp/ *n.* an instrument for examining the larynx, or for inserting a tube through it.

laryngotomy /ˌlærɪŋˈɡɒtəmɪ/ *n.* (*pl.* **-ies**) a surgical incision of the larynx, esp. to provide an air passage when breathing is obstructed.

larynx /ˈlærɪŋks/ *n.* (*pl.* **larynges** /ləˈrɪndʒiːz/) the hollow muscular organ forming an air passage to the lungs and holding the vocal cords in humans and other mammals. [mod.L f. Gk *larugx -ggos*]

lasagne /ləˈsænjə, -ˈsɑːnjə/ *n.* pasta in the form of sheets or wide ribbons, esp. as cooked and served with minced meat and cheese sauce. [It., pl. of *lasagna* f. L *lasanum* cooking-pot]

La Salle /lɑː ˈsɑːl/, Robert Cavalier, Sieur de (1643–87), French explorer. A settler in French Canada, La Salle sailed down the Ohio and Mississippi Rivers to the Gulf of Mexico in 1682, naming the valley of the latter river Louisiana in honour of Louis XIV. He returned to France and was appointed Viceroy of North America, returning in 1684 with a colonizing expedition. This venture went disastrously wrong, landing in Texas by mistake and squandering time and resources in fruitless attempts to get back to the Mississippi. Eventually La Salle's followers, embittered by their wanderings and his harsh discipline, mutinied and killed their leader.

Lascar /ˈlæskə(r)/ *n.* an E. Indian seaman. [ult. f. Urdu & Pers. *laškar* army]

lascivious /ləˈsɪvɪəs/ *adj.* **1** lustful. **2** inciting to or evoking lust. □□ **lasciviously** *adv.* **lasciviousness** *n.* [ME f. LL *lasciviosus* f. L *lascivia* lustfulness f. *lascivus* sportive, wanton]

lase /leɪz/ *v.intr.* **1** function as or in a laser. **2** (of a substance) undergo the physical processes employed in a laser. [back-form. f. LASER]

laser /ˈleɪzə(r)/ *n.* any device is capable of emitting a very intense narrow parallel beam of highly monochromatic and coherent light (or other electromagnetic radiation), either continuously or in pulses, and operates by using light to stimulate the emission of more light of the same wavelength and phase by atoms or molecules that have been excited by some means. The light is reflected back and forth between mirrors, building up into an intense beam. The power and pinpoint accuracy of laser beams finds applications in industry, medicine, and research, e.g. in drilling holes in metal and diamonds, providing standards of straightness in engineering, undertaking surgery on the retina, and in holography. The first laser was built in 1960 in the US by the American physicist T. H. Maiman; the term now includes devices emitting radiation other than light. [light amplification by stimulated emission of radiation: cf. MASER]

laservision /ˈleɪzəˌvɪʒ(ə)n/ *n.* a system for the reproduction of video signals recorded on a disc with a laser. [LASER + VISION, after TELEVISION]

lash /læʃ/ *v. & n.* —*v.* **1** *intr.* make a sudden whiplike movement with a limb or flexible instrument. **2** *tr.* beat with a whip, rope, etc. **3** *intr.* pour or rush with great force. **4** *intr.* (foll. by *at*, *against*) strike violently. **5** *tr.* castigate in words. **6** *tr.* urge on as with a lash. **7** *tr.* (foll. by *down*, *together*, etc.) fasten with a cord, rope, etc. **8** *tr.* (of rain, wind, etc.) beat forcefully upon. —*n.* **1 a** a sharp blow made by a whip, rope, etc. **b** (prec. by *the*) punishment by beating with a whip etc. **2** the flexible end of a whip. **3** (usu. in *pl.*) an eyelash. □ **lash out 1** speak or hit out angrily. **2** spend money extravagantly, be lavish. **lash-up** a makeshift or improvised structure or arrangement. □□ **lasher** *n.* **lashingly** *adv.* (esp. in senses 4–5 of *v.*). **lashless** *adj.* [ME: prob. imit.]

lashing /ˈlæʃɪŋ/ *n.* **1** a beating. **2** cord used for lashing.

lashings /ˈlæʃɪŋz/ *n.pl. Brit. colloq.* (foll. by *of*) plenty; an abundance.

Las Palmas /lɑːs ˈpælmɑːs/ resort in the Canary Islands, on the NW coast of Gran Canaria; pop. (1986) 372,270.

lass /læs/ *n.* esp. *Sc.* & *N.Engl.* or *poet.* a girl or young woman. [ME *lasce* ult. f. ON *laskwa* unmarried (fem.)]

Lassa fever /ˈlæsə/ *n.* an acute virus disease, with fever, of tropical Africa. It was first reported at the village of Lassa in Nigeria in 1969, and has a high mortality rate.

lassie /ˈlæsɪ/ *n. colloq.* = LASS.

lassitude /ˈlæsɪˌtjuːd/ *n.* **1** languor, weariness. **2** disinclination to exert or interest oneself. [F *lassitude* or L *lassitudo* f. *lassus* tired]

lasso /læˈsuː, ˈlæsəʊ/ *n.* & *v.* —*n.* (*pl.* **-os** or **-oes**) a rope with a noose at one end, used esp. in N. America for catching cattle etc. —*v.tr.* (**-oes**, **-oed**) catch with a lasso. □□ **lassoer** *n.* [Sp. *lazo* LACE]

Lassus /ˈlæsʊs/, Orlande de (*c.*1532–94), Flemish composer, who entered the service of Duke Albrecht V in Munich and built up one of the most celebrated centres of music in Europe. One of the great polyphonic masters of the 16th c., he reveals something of the melancholia from which he suffered in later years in music of expressive intensity such as the settings he made of the seven Penitential Psalms.

last¹ /lɑːst/ *adj.*, *adv.*, & *n.* —*adj.* **1** after all others; coming at or belonging to the end. **2 a** most recent; next before a specified time (*last Christmas*; *last week*). **b** preceding; previous in a sequence (*got on at the last station*). **3** only remaining (*the last biscuit*; *our last chance*). **4** (prec. by *the*) least likely or suitable (*the last person I'd want*; *the last thing I'd have expected*). **5** the lowest in rank (*the last place*). —*adv.* **1** after all others (esp. in *comb.*: *last-mentioned*). **2** on the last occasion before the present (*when did you last see him?*). **3** (esp. in enumerating) lastly. —*n.* **1** a person or thing that is last, last-mentioned, most recent, etc. **2** (prec. by *the*) the last mention or sight etc. (*shall never hear the last of it*). **3** the last performance of certain acts (*breathed his last*). **4** (prec. by *the*) **a** the end or last moment. **b** death. □ **at last** (or **at long last**) in the end; after much delay. **last agony** the pangs of death. **last ditch** a place of final desperate defence (often with hyphen) *attrib.*). **Last Judgement** see JUDGEMENT. **last minute** (or **moment**) the time just before an important event (often with hyphen) *attrib.*). **last name** surname. **last post** see POST³. **last rites** sacred rites for a person about to die. **the last**

straw a slight addition to a burden or difficulty that makes it finally unbearable. **Last Supper** see separate entry. **last thing** adv. very late, esp. as a final act before going to bed. **the last word 1** a final or definitive statement (*always has the last word; is the last word on this subject*). **2** (often foll. by *in*) the latest fashion. **on one's last legs** see LEG. **pay one's last respects** see RESPECT. **to** (or **till**) **the last** till the end; esp. till death. [OE *latost* superl.: see LATE]

last² /la:st/ v.intr. **1** remain unexhausted or adequate or alive for a specified or considerable time; suffice (*enough food to last us a week; the battery lasts and lasts*). **2** continue for a specified time (*the journey lasts an hour*). □ **last out** remain adequate or in existence for the whole of a period previously stated or implied. [OE *lǣstan* f. Gmc]

last³ /la:st/ n. a shoemaker's model for shaping or repairing a shoe or boot. □ **stick to one's last** not meddle with what one does not understand. [OE *lǣste* last, *lǣst* boot, *lāst* footprint f. Gmc]

lasting /'la:stɪŋ/ adj. **1** continuing, permanent. **2** durable. □□ **lastingly** adv. **lastingness** n.

lastly /'la:stlɪ/ adv. finally; in the last place.

Last Supper the final meal of Christ with his Apostles on the night before the Crucifixion. Traditionally it has been regarded as the Passover meal, since the Synoptic Gospels appear to put it on the evening when the Passover celebrations began and the paschal lamb was consumed. The Gospel of St John, however, places the Crucifixion itself a few hours before the Passover meal.

Las Vegas /læs 'veɪgəs/ a city of southern Nevada, noted for its casinos and nightclubs; pop. (1980) 164,700.

lat. abbr. latitude.

Latakia /ˌlætə'ki:ə/ a seaport on the coast of Syria, opposite the NE tip of Cyprus; pop. (1981) 196,800. It is famous for its tobacco.

latch /lætʃ/ n. & v. —n. **1** a bar with a catch and lever used as a fastening for a gate etc. **2** a spring-lock preventing a door from being opened from the outside without a key after being shut. —v.tr. & intr. fasten or be fastened with a latch. □ **latch on** (often foll. by *to*) colloq. **1** attach oneself (to). **2** understand. **on the latch** fastened by the latch only, not locked. [prob. f. (now dial.) *latch* (v.) seize f. OE *læccan* f. Gmc]

latchkey /'lætʃki:/ n. (pl. **-eys**) a key of an outer door. □ **latchkey child** a child who is alone at home after school until a parent returns from work.

late /leɪt/ adj. & adv. —adj. **1** after the due or usual time; occurring or done after the proper time (*late for dinner; a late milk delivery*). **2 a** far on in the day or night or in a specified time or period. **b** far on in development. **3** flowering or ripening towards the end of the season (*late strawberries*). **4** (prec. by *the* or *my*, *his*, etc.) no longer alive or having the specified status (*my late husband; the late president*). **5** of recent date (*the late storms*). —adv. **1** after the due or usual time (*arrived late*). **2** far on in time (*this happened later on*). **3** at or till a late hour. **4** at a late stage of development. **5** formerly but not now (*late of the Scillies*). □ **at the latest** as the latest time envisaged (*will have done it by six at the latest*). **late in the day** colloq. at a late stage in the proceedings, esp. too late to be useful. **late Latin** see LATIN. **the latest** the most recent news, fashion, etc. (*have you heard the latest?*). □□ **lateness** n. [OE *læt* (adj.), *late* (adv.) f. Gmc]

latecomer /'leɪtˌkʌmə(r)/ n. a person who arrives late.

lateen /lə'ti:n/ adj. (of a ship) rigged with a lateen sail. □ **lateen sail** a triangular sail on a long yard at an angle of 45° to the mast. [F (*voile*) *latine* Latin (sail), because common in the Mediterranean]

lately /'leɪtlɪ/ adv. not long ago; recently; in recent times. [OE *lætlīce* (as LATE, -LY²)]

La Tène /la: 'ten/ adj. of or relating to the second phase of the European Iron Age, named after the type-site at the east end of Lake Neuchâtel, Switzerland, and dating from the mid-5th c. BC until the Roman conquest. The culture of this period (which follows the Hallstatt) represents the height of early Celtic achievement. It is characterized by hill-forts, developments in agriculture (see CELT), rich and elaborate burials, and artefacts

of excellent craftsmanship and artistic design, ornamented with the very idiosyncratic Celtic style of swinging swelling lines, lively and yet restful.

latent /'leɪt(ə)nt/ adj. **1** concealed, dormant. **2** existing but not developed or manifest. □ **latent heat** Physics the heat required to convert a solid into a liquid or vapour, or a liquid into a vapour, without change of temperature. **latent image** Photog. an image not yet made visible by developing. □□ **latency** n. **latently** adv. [L *latēre* latent- be hidden]

-later /lətə(r)/ comb. form denoting a person who worships a particular thing or person (*idolater*). [Gk: see LATRIA]

lateral /'lætər(ə)l/ adj. & n. —adj. **1** of, at, towards, or from the side or sides. **2** descended from a brother or sister of a person in direct line. —n. a side part etc., esp. a lateral shoot or branch. □ **lateral line** Zool. a visible line along the side of a fish consisting of a series of sense organs acting as vibration receptors. **lateral thinking** a method of solving problems indirectly or by apparently illogical methods. □□ **laterally** adv. [L *lateralis* f. *latus lateris* side]

Lateran /'lætərən/ the site in Rome containing the basilica of St John the Baptist (St John Lateran) which is the cathedral church of Rome, and the Lateran Palace where the popes resided until the 14th c. Five general ecclesiastical councils of the Western Church were held in the basilica (1123, 1139, 1179, 1215, 1512–17). □□ **Lateran treaty** a treaty signed in 1929 in the Lateran Palace, a concordat between the kingdom of Italy and the Holy See, recognizing as fully sovereign and independent a new (papal) State called Vatican City.

laterite /'lætəˌraɪt/ n. a red or yellow ferruginous clay, friable and hardening in air, used for making roads in the tropics. □□ **lateritic** /-'rɪtɪk/ adj. [L *later* brick + -ITE¹]

latex /'leɪteks/ n. (pl. **latexes** or **latices** /-tɪˌsi:z/) **1** a milky fluid of mixed composition found in various plants and trees, esp. the rubber tree, and used for commercial purposes. **2** a synthetic product resembling this. [L, = liquid]

lath /la:θ/ n. & v. —n. (pl. **laths** /la:ðs, la:ðz/) a thin flat strip of wood, esp. each of a series forming a framework or support for plaster etc. —v.tr. attach laths to (a wall or ceiling). □ **lath and plaster** a common material for interior walls and ceilings etc. [OE *lætt*]

lathe /leɪð/ n. a machine for shaping wood, metal, etc., by means of a rotating drive which turns the piece being worked on against changeable cutting tools. [prob. rel. to ODa. *lad* structure, frame, f. ON *hlath*, rel. to *hlatha* LADE]

lather /'la:ðə(r), 'læðə(r)/ n. & v. —n. **1** a froth produced by agitating soap etc. and water. **2** frothy sweat, esp. of a horse. **3** a state of agitation. —v. **1** intr. (of soap etc.) form a lather. **2** tr. cover with lather. **3** intr. (of a horse etc.) develop or become covered with lather. **4** tr. colloq. thrash. □□ **lathery** adj. [OE *lēathor* (n.), *lēthran* (v.)]

lathi /'la:tɪ/ n. (pl. **lathis**) (in India) a long heavy iron-bound bamboo stick used as a weapon, esp. by police. [Hindi *lāṭhī*]

latices pl. of LATEX.

Latimer /'lætɪmə(r)/, Hugh (c.1485–1555), English reformer and martyr, a priest and influential preacher, noted for his homely style, ready wit, extreme Protestant doctrines, and denunciation of social wrongs. When Henry VIII formally broke with the papacy in 1534 Latimer became one of the King's chief advisers, and was made bishop of Worcester in 1535, but opposed Henry's 'Six Articles' aimed at preventing the spread of Reformation doctrines and practices and was obliged to resign his see. Under Edward VI he returned to favour, but on Mary's accession he was imprisoned, refused to accept certain Catholic doctrines, and was burnt at the stake with Ridley at Oxford.

Latin /'lætɪn/ n. & adj. —n. **1** the language of ancient Rome and its empire. (See below.) **2** Rom.Hist. an inhabitant of ancient Latium in Central Italy. —adj. **1** of or in Latin. **2** of the countries or peoples (e.g. France and Spain) using languages developed from Latin. **3** Rom.Hist. of or relating to ancient Latium or its inhabitants. **4** of the Roman Catholic Church. □ **Latin Church** the Western Church. **Latin cross** a plain cross with the lowest arm longer than the other three. □□ **Latinism** n. **Latinist** n. [ME f. OF Latin or L Latinus f. Latium]

Latin is an Indo-European language, inflected and with complex syntax, the ancestor of all the Romance languages. It was originally the dialect of the people of Latium (Latini), a district of Italy lying south of the Apennines and east of the Tiber, and the rise of Rome led to its spread as the official and literary language of the Roman Empire. In the Middle Ages it remained the international medium of communication in western Europe, the language of law, the sciences, and in particular of liturgy; it was the official language of the Roman Catholic Church until the mid-20th c. Latin of the post-classical period is distinguished chronologically as late Latin (c.AD 200–600) and medieval Latin (c.600–1500); silver Latin is the literary language and style of the century following the death of Augustus in AD 14; the term vulgar Latin is applied to popular and provincial forms of Latin, especially those from which the Romance languages developed.

Latin America the parts of Central and South America where Spanish or Portuguese is the main language. □ **Latin American Free Trade Area** an economic grouping of South American countries which in 1981 became the **Latin American Integration Association**. Its headquarters are in Montevideo. □□ **Latin American** adj. & n.

Latinate /ˈlætɪˌneɪt/ adj. having the character of Latin.

Latinize /ˈlætɪˌnaɪz/ v. (also **-ise**) **1** tr. give a Latin or Latinate form to. **2** tr. translate into Latin. **3** tr. make conformable to the ideas, customs, etc., of the ancient Romans, Latin peoples, or Latin Church. **4** intr. use Latin forms, idioms, etc. □□ **Latinization** /-ˈzeɪʃ(ə)n/ n. **Latinizer** n. [LL latinizare (as LATIN)]

latish /ˈleɪtɪʃ/ adj. & adv. fairly late.

latitude /ˈlætɪˌtjuːd/ n. **1** Geog. **a** the angular distance on a meridian north or south of the equator, expressed in degrees and minutes. **b** (usu. in pl.) regions or climes, esp. with reference to temperature (warm latitudes). **2** freedom from narrowness; liberality of interpretation. **3** tolerated variety of action or opinion (was allowed much latitude). **4** Astron. the angular distance of a celestial body or point from the ecliptic. □ **high latitudes** regions near the poles. **low latitudes** regions near the equator. □□ **latitudinal** /-ˈtjuːdɪn(ə)l/ adj. **latitudinally** /-ˈtjuːdɪnəlɪ/ adv. [ME, = breadth, f. L latitudo -dinis f. latus broad]

latitudinarian /ˌlætɪˌtjuːdɪˈneərɪən/ adj. & n. —adj. allowing latitude esp. in religion; showing no preference among varying creeds and forms of worship. The term Latitudinarian was opprobriously applied in the 17th c. to Anglican divines who, while remaining in the Church of England, attached relatively little importance to matters of dogmatic truth, ecclesiastical organization, and liturgical practice, and deprecated quarrels over these, regarding personal piety and morality as of more consequence. —n. a person with a latitudinarian attitude. □□ **latitudinarianism** n. [L latitudo -dinis breadth + -ARIAN]

Latium /ˈleɪʃɪəm/ (Italian **Lazio** /ˈlætsɪˌəʊ/) a region of west central Italy; pop. (1981) 5,001,700; capital, Rome.

Latona /ləˈtəʊnə/ Rom. Mythol. = LETO.

latria /ˈlætrɪə/ n. Theol. supreme worship allowed to God alone. [LL f. Gk latreia worship f. latreuō serve]

latrine /ləˈtriːn/ n. a communal lavatory, esp. in a camp, barracks, etc. [F f. L latrina, shortening of lavatrina f. lavare wash]

-latry /lətrɪ/ comb. form denoting worship (idolatry). [Gk latreia: see LATRIA]

latten /ˈlæt(ə)n/ n. an alloy of copper and zinc, often rolled into sheets, and formerly used for monumental brasses and church articles. [ME latoun f. OF laton, leiton]

latter /ˈlætə(r)/ adj. **1 a** denoting the second-mentioned of two, or disp. the last-mentioned of three or more. **b** (prec. by the; usu. absol.) the second- or last-mentioned person or thing. **2** nearer to the end (the latter part of the year). **3** recent. **4** belonging to the end of a period, of the world, etc. □ **latter-day** modern, newfangled. **Latter-day Saints** the Mormons' name for themselves. [OE lætra, compar. of læt LATE]

latterly /ˈlætəlɪ/ adv. **1** in the latter part of life or of a period. **2** recently.

lattice /ˈlætɪs/ n. **1 a** a structure of crossed laths or bars with spaces between, used as a screen, fence, etc. **b** (in full **lattice-work**) laths arranged in lattice formation. **2** Crystallog. a regular periodic arrangement of atoms, ions, or molecules in a crystalline solid. □ **lattice frame** (or **girder**) a girder or truss made of top and bottom members connected by struts usu. crossing diagonally. **lattice window** a window with small panes set in diagonally crossing strips of lead. □□ **latticed** adj. **latticing** n. [ME f. OF lattis f. latte lath f. WG]

Latvia /ˈlætvɪə/ an area on the shores of the Baltic Sea and the Gulf of Riga, a Baltic province of the Russian Empire after having been under Polish and then Swedish rule. It was proclaimed an independent republic in 1918 but in 1940 was annexed by the USSR as a constituent republic; pop. (est. 1987) 2,647,000; capital, Riga. Growth of a nationalist movement in the 1980s led to demands for independence from Moscow.

Latvian /ˈlætvɪən/ n. & adj. —n. **1 a** a native of Latvia. **b** a person of Latvian descent. **2** the language of Latvia, also called Lettish, spoken by some 1,500,000 people, most closely related to Lithuanian with which it constitutes the Baltic language group. —adj. of or relating to Latvia or its people or language.

Laud /lɔːd/, William (1573–1645), English cleric, Archbishop of Canterbury from 1633. Although Protestant he opposed the prevailing Calvinism and attempted to impose liturgical uniformity on both Roman Catholics and Puritans by restoring pre-Reformation practices, arousing the bitter hostility of both parties. His attempt to impose these reforms in Scotland led to war and his downfall, and he was impeached, imprisoned, and executed for treason in a trial generally agreed to have been without regard for justice. His apparent failure arose from his inability to understand the popular leaning towards Puritanism and the hatred aroused by his violent measures against those who did not share his views on ritual.

laud /lɔːd/ v. & n. —v.tr. praise or extol, esp. in hymns. —n. **1** literary praise; a hymn of praise. **2** (in pl.) the first religious service of the day in the Western (Roman Catholic) Church. In the Book of Common Prayer parts of Lauds and Matins were combined to form the service of Morning Prayer. [ME: (n.) f. OF laude, (v.) f. L laudare, f. L laus laudis praise]

laudable /ˈlɔːdəb(ə)l/ adj. commendable, praiseworthy. □□ **laudably** /-ˈbɪlɪtɪ/ n. **laudably** adv. [ME f. L laudabilis (as LAUD)]

laudanum /ˈlɔːdnəm, ˈlɒd-/ n. a solution containing morphine and prepared from opium, formerly used as a narcotic painkiller. [mod.L, the name given by Paracelsus to a costly medicament, later applied to preparations containing opium: perh. var. of LADANUM]

laudation /lɔːˈdeɪʃ(ə)n/ n. formal praise. [L laudatio -onis (as LAUD)]

laudatory /ˈlɔːdətərɪ/ adj. (also **laudative** /-tɪv/) expressing praise.

laugh /lɑːf/ v. & n. —v. **1** intr. make the spontaneous sounds and movements usual in expressing lively amusement, scorn, derision, etc. **2** tr. express by laughing. **3** tr. bring (a person) into a certain state by laughing (laughed them into agreeing). **4** intr. (foll. by at) ridicule, make fun of (laughed at us for going). **5** intr. (**be laughing**) colloq. be in a fortunate or successful position. **6** intr. esp. poet. make sounds reminiscent of laughing. —n. **1** the sound or act or manner of laughing. **2** colloq. a comical or ridiculous thing. □ **have the last laugh** be ultimately the winner. **laugh in a person's face** show open scorn for a person. **laugh off** get rid of (embarrassment or humiliation) with a jest. **laugh on the other side of one's face** change from enjoyment or amusement to displeasure, shame, apprehension, etc. **laugh out of court** deprive of a hearing by ridicule. **laugh up one's sleeve** be secretly or inwardly amused. □□ **laugher** n. [OE hlæhhan, hliehhan f. Gmc]

laughable /ˈlɑːfəb(ə)l/ adj. ludicrous; highly amusing. □□ **laughably** adv.

laughing /ˈlɑːfɪŋ/ n. & adj. —n. laughter. —adj. in senses of LAUGH v. □ **laughing-gas** nitrous oxide as an anaesthetic, formerly used without oxygen and causing an exhilarating effect when inhaled. **laughing hyena** see HYENA. **laughing jackass** = KOOKABURRA. **laughing-stock** a person or thing open to general ridicule. **no laughing matter** something serious. □□ **laughingly** *adv.*

laughter /ˈlɑːftə(r)/ *n.* the act or sound of laughing. [OE *hleahtor* f. Gmc]

Laughton /ˈlɔːt(ə)n/, Charles (1899–1962), English-born actor, who became an American citizen in 1940. His appearance and approach lent themselves to tyrannical roles such as Henry VIII (1933) and Captain Bligh (1935), and he conveyed with conviction the artist's twenty-five years of physical and mental struggle in *Rembrandt* (1956). He returned to the English stage in roles that included King Lear (1959).

launce /lɑːns, læns/ *n.* a sand eel. [perh. f. LANCE: cf. *garfish*]

Launceston /ˈlɔːnsəst(ə)n/ the second-largest city of Tasmania; pop. (1986) 88,500.

launch¹ /lɔːntʃ/ *v. & n.* —*v.* **1** *tr.* set (a vessel) afloat. **2** *tr.* hurl or send forth (a weapon, rocket, etc.). **3** *tr.* start or set in motion (an enterprise, a person on a course of action, etc.). **4** *tr.* formally introduce (a new product) with publicity etc. **5** *intr.* (often foll. by *out*, *into*, etc.) **a** make a start, esp. on an ambitious enterprise. **b** burst into strong language etc. —*n.* the act or an instance of launching. □ **launch** (or **launching**) **pad** a platform with a supporting structure, from which rockets are launched. [ME f. AF *launcher*, ONF *lancher*, OF *lancier* LANCE *v.*]

launch² /lɔːntʃ/ *n.* **1** a large motor boat, used esp. for pleasure. **2** a man-of-war's largest boat. [Sp. *lancha* pinnace perh. f. Malay *lancharan* f. *lanchār* swift]

launcher /ˈlɔːntʃə(r)/ *n.* a structure or device to hold a rocket during launching.

launder /ˈlɔːndə(r)/ *v. & n.* —*v.tr.* **1** wash and iron (clothes, linen, etc.). **2** *colloq.* transfer (funds) to conceal a dubious or illegal origin. —*n.* a channel for conveying liquids, esp. molten metal. □□ **launderer** *n.* [ME *launder* (n.) washer of linen, contr. of *lavander* f. OF *lavandier* ult. f. L *lavanda* things to be washed, neut. pl. gerundive of *lavare* wash]

launderette /lɔːnˈdret/ *n.* (also **laundrette**) an establishment with coin-operated washing-machines and driers for public use.

laundress /ˈlɔːndrɪs/ *n.* a woman who launders clothes, linen, etc., esp. professionally.

laundry /ˈlɔːndrɪ/ *n.* (pl. **-ies**) **1** an establishment for washing clothes or linen. **2** clothes or linen for laundering or newly laundered. [contr. f. *lavendry* (f. OF *lavanderie*) after LAUNDER]

Laurasia /lɔːˈreɪʒə/ a vast continental area thought to have once existed in the northern hemisphere and to have broken up in Mesozoic or late Palaeozoic times, forming North America, Greenland, Europe, and most of Asia north of the Himalayas. [*Laurentia*, name given to the ancient forerunner of N. America + *Eurasia*]

laureate /ˈlɒrɪət, ˈlɔː-/ *adj. & n.* —*adj.* **1** wreathed with laurel as a mark of honour. **2** consisting of laurel; laurel-like. —*n.* **1** a person who is honoured for outstanding creative or intellectual achievement (*Nobel laureate*). **2** a Poet Laureate. (See below.) □□ **laureateship** *n.* [L *laureatus* f. *laurea* laurel-wreath f. *laurus* laurel]

  In early use the title 'laureate' (implying 'worthy of the Muses' crown') was given generally to eminent poets, and sometimes conferred by certain universities. In modern use it is given to a poet who is appointed to write poems for State occasions and who receives a stipend as an officer of the Royal Household. The first Poet Laureate in the modern sense was Ben Jonson, but the title seems to have been first held by his successor Davenant (appointed in 1638). There is no official evidence for the tradition that Samuel Daniel (1599), or Spenser before him, held the title, though Daniel was often at court in James I's reign and Spenser had received a pension from the Queen. Dryden, Wordsworth, and Tennyson are among later holders of the title, which at present is held by Ted Hughes.

laurel /ˈlɒr(ə)l/ *n. & v.* —*n.* **1** = BAY². **2 a** (in *sing.* or *pl.*) the foliage of the bay-tree used as an emblem of victory or distinction in poetry usu. formed into a wreath or crown. **b** (in *pl.*) honour or distinction. **3** any plant with dark-green glossy leaves like a bay-tree, e.g. cherry-laurel, mountain laurel, spurge laurel. —*v.tr.* (**laurelled**, **laurelling**; *US* **laureled**, **laureling**) wreathe

with laurel. □ **look to one's laurels** beware of losing one's pre-eminence. **rest on one's laurels** be satisfied with what one has done and not seek further success. [ME *lorer* f. OF *lorier* f. Prov. *laurier* f. *laur* f. L *laurus*]

Laurel and Hardy /ˌlɒr(ə)l ˈhɑːdɪ/ Stan Laurel (real name Arthur Stanley Jefferson, born in England, 1890–1965) and Oliver Hardy (1892–1957), American comedians. 'Ollie' played the fat pompous father-figure and Laurel the then irresponsible and destructive child, tearful in a crisis, in a number of films from 1931 onwards.

Laurence /ˈlɒrəns/, St (d. 258), deacon of Rome, and martyr. According to tradition (widely rejected by modern scholars) when asked by the Prefect of Rome to deliver up the treasure of the Church he assembled and presented the poor; he was punished by being roasted on the famous but unhistorical gridiron (he was probably beheaded).

Laurentian Plateau /lɒˈrenʃ(ə)n/ the Canadian Shield (see SHIELD *n.* 2e).

laurustinus /ˌlɒrəˈstaɪnəs/ *n.* an evergreen winter-flowering shrub, *Viburnum tinus*, with dense glossy green leaves and white or pink flowers. [mod.L f. L *laurus* laurel + *tinus* wild laurel]

Lausanne /ləʊˈzæn/ a town of Switzerland, on the north shore of Lake Geneva; pop. (1986) 262,200.

lav /læv/ *n. Brit. colloq.* lavatory. [abbr.]

lava /ˈlɑːvə/ *n.* **1** the molten matter which flows from a volcano. **2** the solid substance which it forms on cooling. [It. f. *lavare* wash f. L]

lavabo /ləˈvɑːbəʊ/ *n.* (pl. **-os**) **1** *RC Ch.* **a** the ritual washing of the celebrant's hands at the offertory of the Mass. **b** a towel or basin used for this. **2** a monastery washing-trough. **3** a washbasin. [L, = I will wash, first word of Psalm 26: 6]

lavage /ˈlævɪdʒ/ *n. Med.* the washing-out of a body cavity, such as the colon or stomach, with water or a medicated solution. [F f. *laver* wash: see LAVE]

lavation /ləˈveɪʃ(ə)n/ *n. formal* washing. [L *lavatio* f. *lavare* wash]

lavatorial /ˌlævəˈtɔːrɪəl/ *adj.* (esp. of humour) relating to lavatories and their use.

lavatory /ˈlævətərɪ/ *n.* (pl. **-ies**) **1** a large receptacle for urine and faeces, usu. with running water and a flush mechanism as a means of disposal. **2** a room or compartment containing one or more of these. □ **lavatory paper** = *toilet paper*. [ME, = washing vessel, f. LL *lavatorium* f. L *lavare lavat-* wash]

lave /leɪv/ *v.tr. literary* **1** wash, bathe. **2** (of water) wash against; flow along. [ME f. OF *laver* f. L *lavare* wash, perh. coalescing with OE *lafian*]

lavender /ˈlævɪndə(r)/ *n. & v.* —*n.* **1 a** any small evergreen shrub of the genus *Lavandula*, with narrow leaves and blue, purple, or pink aromatic flowers. **b** its flowers and stalks dried and used to scent linen, clothes, etc. **2 a** pale blue colour with a trace of red. —*v.tr.* put lavender among (linen etc.). □ **lavender-water** a perfume made from distilled lavender, alcohol, and ambergris. [ME f. AF *lavendre*, ult. f. med.L *lavandula*]

Laver /ˈleɪvə(r)/, Rodney George (1938–), Australian tennis player, the second man (after Don Budge, 1938) to win the four major singles championships in one year (1962) and the first to repeat this (1969).

laver¹ /ˈleɪvə(r), ˈlɑːvə(r)/ *n.* any of various edible seaweeds, esp. *Porphyra umbilicalis*, having sheetlike fronds. □ **laver bread** a Welsh dish of laver which is boiled, dipped in oatmeal, and fried. [L]

laver² /ˈleɪvə(r)/ *n.* **1** *Bibl.* a large brass vessel for Jewish priests' ritual ablutions. **2** *archaic* a washing or fountain basin; a font. [ME *lavo(u)r* f. OF *laveo(i)r* f. LL (as LAVATORY)]

Lavery /ˈleɪvərɪ/, Sir John (1856–1941), British painter, born in Belfast. His early work was influenced by Whistler and the impressionists, and held a promise which was not fulfilled as in later life he succumbed to the facile lures of a society portrait painter.

lavish /ˈlævɪʃ/ *adj. & v.* —*adj.* **1** giving or producing in large quantities; profuse. **2** generous, unstinting. **3** excessive, overabundant. —*v.tr.* (often foll. by *on*) bestow or spend (money, effort, praise, etc.) abundantly. □□ **lavishly** adv. **lavishness** n. [ME f. obs. lavish, lavas (n.) profusion f. OF lavasse deluge of rain f. laver wash]

Lavoisier /laːˈvwaːziˌeɪ/, Antoine Laurent (1743–94), French scientist, regarded as the father of modern chemistry. He followed the family tradition of studying law, but his first love was science which, apart from chemistry, included for him agriculture, geology, and experimental physics. The chemical revolution which he caused was to describe the true nature of combustion, to introduce rigorous methods of analysis, and to develop a new rational chemical nomenclature, published in 1789. He realized in 1774 that it was Priestley's 'dephlogisticated air' that combined with substances during burning, renamed this gas 'oxygen' in 1779, because he thought it a constituent of all acids and, in 1783, suggested that water was made up of the gases of oxygen and hydrogen; but in this he was anticipated by Cavendish. The holder of a number of important public offices, he supplemented his private income by becoming a member of a consortium that gathered the indirect taxes for the government, and it was this position that led to his death by guillotine during the Reign of Terror of the French Revolution.

Law /lɔː/, (Andrew) Bonar (1858–1923), Canadian-born British Conservative statesman, Prime Minister for six months in 1922–3, when he resigned because of ill health.

law /lɔː/ n. **1 a** a rule enacted or customary in a community and recognized as enjoining or prohibiting certain actions and enforced by the imposition of penalties. **b** a body of such rules (the law of the land; forbidden under Scots law). **2** the controlling influence of laws; a state of respect for laws (law and order). **3** laws collectively as a social system or subject of study (was reading law). **4** (with defining word) any of the specific branches or applications of law (commercial law; law of contract). **5** binding force or effect (their word is law). **6** (prec. by the) **a** the legal profession. **b** colloq. the police. **7** the statute and common law (opp. EQUITY). **8** (in pl.) jurisprudence. **9 a** the judicial remedy; litigation. **b** the lawcourts as providing this (go to law). **10** a rule of action or procedure, e.g. in a game, social context, form of art, etc. **11** a regularity in natural occurrences, esp. as formulated or propounded in particular instances (the laws of nature; the law of gravity; Parkinson's law). **12 a** divine commandments as expressed in the Bible or other sources. **b** (**Law of Moses**) the precepts of the Pentateuch. □ **c** (**the Law**) the Pentateuch as distinguished from the other parts of the Old Testament (the Prophets and the Writings). **at** (or **in**) **law** according to the laws. **be a law unto oneself** do what one feels is right; disregard custom. **go to law** take legal action; make use of the lawcourts. **law-abiding** obedient to the laws. **law-abidingness** obedience to the laws. **law agent** (in Scotland) a solicitor. **law centre** Brit. an independent publicly-funded advisory service on legal matters. **Law Lord** a member of the House of Lords qualified to perform its legal work. (See Lords Temporal.) **law of diminishing returns** see DIMINISH. **law of nature** = natural law. **laws of war** the limitations on belligerents' action recognized by civilized nations. **law term** a period appointed for the sitting of lawcourts. **lay down the law** be dogmatic or authoritarian. **take the law into one's own hands** redress a grievance by one's own means, esp. by force. [OE lagu f. ON lag something 'laid down' or fixed, rel. to LAY[1]]

lawbreaker /ˈlɔːˌbreɪkə(r)/ n. a person who breaks the law. □□ **lawbreaking** n. & adj.

lawcourt /ˈlɔːkɔːt/ n. a court of law.

lawful /ˈlɔːfʊl/ adj. conforming with, permitted by, or recognized by law; not illegal or (of a child) illegitimate. □□ **lawfully** adv. **lawfulness** n.

lawgiver /ˈlɔːˌɡɪvə(r)/ n. a person who lays down laws.

lawless /ˈlɔːlɪs/ adj. **1** having no laws or enforcement of them. **2** disregarding laws. **3** unbridled, uncontrolled. □□ **lawlessly** adv. **lawlessness** n.

lawmaker /ˈlɔːˌmeɪkə(r)/ n. a legislator.

lawman /ˈlɔːmæn/ n. (pl. **-men**) US a law-enforcement officer, esp. a sheriff or policeman.

lawn[1] /lɔːn/ n. a piece of grass kept mown and smooth in a garden, park, etc. □ **lawn tennis** a game that was originally a modification of tennis (see entry) played by two persons (singles) or four (doubles) with a soft ball on an outdoor grass or hard court without walls. It became popular in Victorian times as a diversion for the middle classes ('real' tennis was always an aristocratic sport), a perfect game for large gardens and a leisured society. [ME laund glade f. OF launde f. OCelt., rel. to LAND]

lawn[2] /lɔːn/ n. a fine linen or cotton fabric used for clothes. □□ **lawny** adj. [ME, prob. f. Laon in France]

lawnmower /ˈlɔːnˌməʊə(r)/ n. a machine for cutting the grass on a lawn.

Lawrence[1] /ˈlɒrəns/, David Herbert (1885–1930), English novelist, poet, critic, and painter, son of a Nottinghamshire miner and an ex-schoolteacher who encouraged Lawrence to become a teacher. In 1911 he published his first novel, and achieved success with his closely autobiographical Sons and Lovers (1913). In 1912 he eloped with the German wife of a Nottingham professor, subsequently travelling extensively with her: Kangaroo (1923) was written in Australia and The Plumed Serpent (1926) in New Mexico, where he became seriously ill. Lawrence is remembered most for his exploration of marital and sexual relations: The Rainbow (1915) was declared obscene, and Women in Love (1920) was described as an 'analytical study of sexual depravity'. In 1925 he returned to Europe, living mainly in Italy where he finished Lady Chatterley's Lover (1928) not published in Britain in its unexpurgated form until 1960. Its publishers were then prosecuted under the Obscene Publications Act and acquitted after a celebrated trial which influenced writing and publishing thereafter. Lawrence was a moralist and believed that modern man was becoming divorced from his natural feelings. By illuminating areas of human experience not previously explored in fiction he shocked the reading public. His verse, collected in Complete Poems (1957), had the immediacy and personal quality of his prose.

Lawrence[2] /ˈlɒrəns/, Sir Thomas (1769–1830), English painter, self-taught, whose portrait of Queen Charlotte, painted in 1789 and exhibited the following year at the Royal Academy, brought his first success. Many portrait commissions followed, displaying fine draughtsmanship if often with exaggerated surface effects. By 1810, his style now more subdued, he was recognized as the leading portrait painter of his time and was sent by the Prince Regent, in 1818, to paint the portraits of heads of State and military leaders after the allied victory over Napoleon. Lawrence, as well as being a painter and public figure, was a connoisseur, with perhaps the finest collection ever made of old master drawings.

Lawrence[3] /ˈlɒrəns/, Thomas Edward (1888–1935), English soldier and writer, known as 'Lawrence of Arabia', who helped to organize and lead the Arab revolt against the Turks in the Middle East during the second half of the First World War. His guerrilla activities behind Turkish lines drew thousands of enemy soldiers away from the front and contributed to Allenby's eventual victory in Palestine; they are described in his powerful classic Seven Pillars of Wisdom (1926), important as a document of military history and as a revelation of the author's complex personality. After the war Lawrence became disillusioned with his public life. He enlisted in the RAF under a pseudonym ('J. H. Ross') to avoid attention and joined the tank corps as 'T. E. Shaw', later returning to the RAF; this period is reflected in his posthumously-published The Mint. Shortly after retiring he was killed in a motor-cycle accident near his Dorset home. His multiple roles—man of action, poet, ascetic, leader of men—have fascinated the public and his many biographers.

lawrencium /ləˈrensɪəm/ n. Chem. an artificially made transuranic radioactive metallic element, first obtained in 1961 by bombarding californium with boron ions. ¶ Symb.: **Lw**; atomic number 103. [E. O. Lawrence, Amer. physicist d. 1958]

lawsuit /ˈlɔːsuːt, -sjuːt/ n. the process or an instance of making a claim in a lawcourt.

lawyer /ˈlɔːjə(r), ˈlɔːjə(r)/ n. a member of the legal profession, esp. a solicitor. □□ **lawyerly** adj. [ME law(i)er f. LAW]

lax /læks/ adj. **1** lacking care, concern, or firmness. **2** loose, relaxed; not compact. **3** Phonet. pronounced with the vocal muscles relaxed. □□ **laxity** *n.* **laxly** *adv.* **laxness** *n.* [ME, = loose, f. L *laxus*: rel. to SLACK¹]

laxative /ˈlæksətɪv/ *adj. & n.* —*adj.* tending to stimulate or facilitate evacuation of the bowels. —*n.* a laxative medicine. [ME f. OF *laxatif -ive* or LL *laxativus* f. L *laxare* loosen (as LAX)]

lay¹ /leɪ/ *v. & n.* —*v.* (*past* and *past part.* **laid** /leɪd/) **1** *tr.* place on a surface, esp. horizontally or in the proper or specified place. **2** *tr.* put or bring into a certain or the required position or state (*laid his hand on her arm*; *lay a carpet*). **3** *intr. dial.* or *erron.* lie. ¶ This use, incorrect in standard English, is probably partly encouraged by confusion with *lay* as the past of *lie*, as in *the dog lay on the floor* which is correct; *the dog is laying on the floor* is not correct. **4** *tr.* make by laying (*lay the foundations*). **5** *tr.* (often *absol.*) (of a hen bird) produce (an egg). **6** *tr.* **a** cause to subside or lie flat. **b** deal with to remove (a ghost, fear, etc.). **7** *tr.* place or present for consideration (a case, proposal, etc.). **8** *tr.* set down as a basis or starting-point. **9** *tr.* (usu. foll. by *on*) attribute or impute (blame etc.). **10** *tr.* locate (a scene etc.) in a certain place. **11** *tr.* prepare or make ready (a plan or a trap). **12** *tr.* prepare (a table) for a meal. **13** *tr.* place or arrange the material for (a fire). **14** *tr.* put down as a wager; stake. **15** *tr.* (foll. by *with*) coat or strew (a surface). **16** *tr. sl. offens.* have sexual intercourse with (esp. a woman). —*n.* **1** the way, position, or direction in which something lies. **2** *sl. offens.* a partner (esp. female) in sexual intercourse. **3** the direction or amount of twist in rope-strands. □ **in lay** (of a hen) laying eggs regularly. **laid-back** *colloq.* relaxed, unbothered, easygoing. **laid paper** paper with the surface marked in fine ribs. **laid up** confined to bed or the house. **lay about one 1** hit out on all sides. **2** criticize indiscriminately. **lay aside 1** put to one side. **2** cease to practise or consider. **3** save (money etc.) for future needs. **lay at the door of** see DOOR. **lay back** cause to slope back from the vertical. **lay bare** expose, reveal. **lay a charge** make an accusation. **lay claim to** claim as one's own. **lay down 1** put on the ground. **2** relinquish; give up (an office). **3** formulate (a rule or principle). **4** pay or wager (money). **5** begin to construct (a ship or railway). **6** store (wine) in a cellar. **7** set down on paper. **8** sacrifice (one's life). **9** convert (land) into pasture. **10** record (esp. popular music). **lay down the law** see LAW. **lay one's hands on** obtain, acquire, locate. **lay hands on 1** seize or attack. **2** place one's hands on or over, esp. in confirmation, ordination, or spiritual healing. **lay hold of** seize or grasp. **lay in** provide oneself with a stock of. **lay into** *colloq.* punish or scold heavily. **lay it on thick** (or **with a trowel**) *colloq.* flatter or exaggerate grossly. **lay low** overthrow, kill, or humble. **lay off 1** discharge (workers) temporarily because of a shortage of work. **2** *colloq.* desist. **lay-off** *n.* **1** a temporary discharge of workers. **2** a period when this is in force. **lay on 1** provide (a facility, amenity, etc.). **2** impose (a penalty, obligation, etc.). **3** inflict (blows). **4** spread on (paint etc.). **lay on the table** see TABLE. **lay open 1** break the skin of. **2** (foll. by *to*) expose (to criticism etc.). **lay out 1** spread out. **2** expose to view. **3** prepare (a corpse) for burial. **4** *colloq.* knock unconscious. **5** dispose (grounds etc.) according to a plan. **6** expend (money). **7** *refl.* (foll. by *to* + infin.) take pains (to do something) (*laid themselves out to help*). **lay store by** see STORE. **lay to rest** bury in a grave. **lay up 1** store, save. **2** put (a ship etc.) out of service. **lay waste** see WASTE. [OE *lecgan* f. Gmc]

lay² /leɪ/ *adj.* **1 a** non-clerical. **b** not ordained into the clergy. **2 a** not professionally qualified, esp. in law or medicine. **b** of or done by such persons. □ **lay brother** (or **sister**) a person who has taken the vows of a religious order but is not ordained and is employed in ancillary or manual work. **lay reader** a lay person licensed to conduct some religious services. [ME f. OF *lai* f. eccl.L *laicus* f. Gk *laikos* LAIC]

lay³ /leɪ/ *n.* **1** a short lyric or narrative poem meant to be sung. **2** a song. [ME f. OF *lai*, Prov. *lais*, of unkn. orig.]

lay⁴ *past* of LIE¹.

layabout /ˈleɪəˌbaʊt/ *n.* a habitual loafer or idler.

Layamon /ˈlaɪəmən/ (late 12th c.) English poet and priest, author of the verse chronicle, the *Brut*, a history of England from the arrival of the legendary Brutus to Cadwallader (AD 689). One of the earliest major works in Middle English, it introduces for

the first time in English the story of King Arthur, Lear, and other figures prominent in later English literature.

lay-by /ˈleɪbaɪ/ *n.* (*pl.* **lay-bys**) **1** *Brit.* an area at the side of an open road where vehicles may stop. **2** a similar arrangement on a canal or railway. **3** *Austral. & NZ* a system of paying a deposit to secure an article for later purchase.

layer /ˈleɪə(r)/ *n. & v.* —*n.* **1** a thickness of matter, esp. one of several, covering a surface. **2** a person or thing that lays. **3** a hen that lays eggs. **4** a shoot fastened down to take root while attached to the parent plant. —*v.tr.* **1 a** arrange in layers. **b** cut (hair) in layers. **2** propagate (a plant) as a layer. □ **layer-out** a person who prepares a corpse for burial. □□ **layered** *adj.* [ME f. LAY¹ + -ER¹]

layette /leɪˈet/ *n.* a set of clothing, toilet articles, and bedclothes for a newborn child. [F, dimin. of OF *laie* drawer f. MDu. *laege*]

lay figure /leɪ/ *n.* **1** a dummy or jointed figure of a human body used by artists for arranging drapery on etc. **2** an unrealistic character in a novel etc. **3** a person lacking in individuality. [lay f. obs. *layman* f. Du. *leeman* f. obs. *led* joint]

layman /ˈleɪmən/ *n.* (*pl.* **-men**; *fem.* **laywoman**, *pl.* **-women**) **1** any non-ordained member of a Church. **2** a person without professional or specialized knowledge in a particular subject.

La'youn /lɑːˈjuːn/ (Arabic **El Aaiún** /el aɪˈuːn/) the capital of Western Sahara; pop. (1982) 96,800.

layout /ˈleɪaʊt/ *n.* **1** the disposing or arrangement of a site, ground, etc. **2** the way in which plans, printed matter, etc., are arranged or set out. **3** something arranged or set out in a particular way. **4** the make-up of a book, newspaper, etc.

layover /ˈleɪˌəʊvə(r)/ *n.* a period of rest or waiting before a further stage in a journey etc.; a stopover.

layshaft /ˈleɪʃɑːft/ *n.* a second or intermediate transmission shaft in a machine.

lazar /ˈlæzə(r)/ *n. archaic* a poor and diseased person, esp. a leper. [ME f. med.L *lazarus* f. the name in Luke 16: 20]

lazaret /ˌlæzəˈret/ *n.* (also **lazaretto** /-ˈretəʊ/) (*pl.* **lazarets** or **lazarettos**) **1** a hospital for diseased people, esp. lepers. **2** a building or ship for quarantine. **3** the after part of a ship's hold, used for stores. [(F *lazaret*) f. It. *lazzaretto* f. *lazzaro* LAZAR]

laze /leɪz/ *v. & n.* —*v.* **1** *intr.* spend time lazily or idly. **2** *tr.* (often foll. by *away*) pass (time) in this way. —*n.* a spell of lazing. [back-form. f. LAZY]

Lazio see LATIUM.

lazuli /ˈlæzjuːlɪ, -ˌlaɪ/ *n.* = LAPIS LAZULI. [abbr.]

lazy /ˈleɪzɪ/ *adj.* (**lazier**, **laziest**) **1** disinclined to work, doing little work. **2** of or inducing idleness. **3** (of a river) slow-moving. □□ **lazily** *adv.* **laziness** *n.* [earlier *laysie*, *lasie*, *laesy*, perh. f. LG: cf. LG *lasich* idle]

lazybones /ˈleɪzɪˌbəʊnz/ *n.* (*pl.* same) *colloq.* a lazy person.

lb. *abbr.* a pound or pounds (weight). [L *libra*]

l.b. *abbr. Cricket* leg-bye(s), leg-byed.

LBC *abbr.* London Broadcasting Company.

L/Bdr *abbr.* Lance-Bombardier.

l.b.w. *abbr. Cricket* leg before wicket.

l.c. *abbr.* **1** in the passage etc. cited. **2** lower case. **3** letter of credit. [sense 1 f. L *loco citato*]

LCC *abbr. hist.* London County Council.

LCD *abbr.* **1** liquid crystal display. **2** lowest (or least) common denominator.

LCM *abbr.* lowest (or least) common multiple.

L/Cpl *abbr.* Lance-Corporal.

LD *abbr.* lethal dose, usu. with a following numeral indicating the percentage of a group of animals killed by such a dose (LD_{50}).

Ld. *abbr.* Lord.

Ldg. *abbr.* Leading (Seaman etc.).

L-dopa /elˈdəʊpə/ *n.* = LEVODOPA.

LDS *abbr.* Licentiate in Dental Surgery.

-le¹ /(ə)l/ *suffix* forming nouns, esp.: **1** names of appliances or instruments (*handle*; *thimble*). **2** names of animals and plants (*beetle*; *thistle*). ¶ The suffix has ceased to be syllabic in *fowl*, *snail*, *stile*. [ult. from or repr. OE *-el* etc. f. Gmc, with many IE cognates]

-le² /(ə)l/ *suffix* (also **-el**) forming nouns with (or orig. with) diminutive sense, or = -AL (*angle*; *castle*; *mantle*; *syllable*; *novel*; *tunnel*). [ME *-el*, *-elle* f. OF ult. f. L forms *-ellus*, *-ella*, etc.]

-le³ /(ə)l/ *suffix* forming adjectives, often with (or orig. with) the sense 'apt or liable to' (*brittle*; *fickle*; *little*; *nimble*). [ME f. OE *-el* etc. f. Gmc, corresp. to L *-ulus*]

-le⁴ /(ə)l/ *suffix* forming verbs, esp. expressing repeated action or movement or having diminutive sense (*bubble*; *crumple*; *wriggle*). ¶ Examples from OE are *handle*, *nestle*, *startle*, *twinkle*. [OE *-lian* f. Gmc]

LEA *abbr.* (in the UK) Local Education Authority.

lea /liː/ *n. poet.* a piece of meadow or pasture or arable land. [OE *lēa(h)* f. Gmc]

Leach /liːtʃ/, Bernard Howell (1887–1979), British potter, born in Hong Kong, the main influence on 20th-c. ceramics in Britain. After studying in Japan, Peking, and Korea he returned to settle in Britain in 1920 and, with the Japanese potter Shoji Hamada, founded his Pottery at St Ives in Cornwall. He practised and taught for more than fifty years, amalgamating the ideas and methods of traditional Japanese pottery and aspects of English medieval pottery, which he revived.

leach /liːtʃ/ *v.* **1** *tr.* make (a liquid) percolate through some material. **2** *tr.* subject (bark, ore, ash, or soil) to the action of percolating fluid. **3** *tr. & intr.* (foll. by *away*, *out*) remove (soluble matter) or be removed in this way. □□ **leacher** *n.* [prob. repr. OE *leccan* to water, f. WG]

lead¹ /liːd/ *v. & n.* —*v.* (*past* and *past part.* **led** /led/) **1** *tr.* cause to go with one, esp. by guiding or showing the way or by going in front and taking a person's hand or an animal's halter etc. **2** *tr.* **a** direct the actions or opinions of. **b** (often foll. by *to*, or to + *infin.*) guide by persuasion or example or argument (*what led you to that conclusion?*; *was led to think you may be right*). **3** *tr.* (also *absol.*) provide access to; bring to a certain position or destination (*this door leads you into a small room*; *the road leads to Lincoln*; *the path leads uphill*). **4** *tr.* pass or go through (a life etc. of a specified kind) (*led a miserable existence*). **5** *tr.* **a** have the first place in (*lead the dance*; *leads the world in sugar production*). **b** (*absol.*) go first; be ahead in a race or game. **c** (*absol.*) be pre-eminent in some field. **6** *tr.* be in charge of (*leads a team of researchers*). **7** *tr.* **a** direct by example. **b** set (a fashion). **c** be the principal player of (a group of musicians). **8** *tr.* (also *absol.*) begin a round of play at cards by playing (a card) or a card of (a particular suit). **9** *intr.* (foll. by *to*) have as an end or outcome; result in (*what does all this lead to?*). **10** *intr.* (foll. by *with*) *Boxing* make an attack (with a particular blow). **11** **a** *intr.* (foll. by *with*) (of a newspaper) use a particular item as the main story (*led with the Stock Market crash*). **b** *tr.* (of a story) be the main feature of (a newspaper or part of it) (*the royal wedding will lead the front page*). **12** *tr.* (foll. by *through*) make (a liquid, strip of material, etc.) pass through a pulley, channel, etc. —*n.* **1** guidance given by going in front; example. **2 a** a leading place; the leadership (*is in the lead*; *take the lead*). **b** the amount by which a competitor is ahead of the others (*a lead of ten yards*). **3** a clue, esp. an early indication of the resolution of a problem (*is the first real lead in the case*). **4** a strap or cord for leading a dog etc. **5** a conductor (usu. a wire) conveying electric current from a source to an appliance. **6 a** the chief part in a play etc. **b** the person playing this. **7** (in full **lead story**) the item of news given the greatest prominence in a newspaper or magazine. **8 a** the act or right of playing first in a game or round of cards. **b** the card led. **9** the distance advanced by a screw in one turn. **10 a** an artificial watercourse, esp. one leading to a mill. **b** a channel of water in an ice-field. □ **lead astray** see ASTRAY. **lead by the nose** cajole (a person) into compliance. **lead a person a dance** see DANCE. **lead-in 1** an introduction, opening, etc. **2** a wire leading in from outside, esp. from an aerial to a receiver or transmitter. **lead off 1** begin; make a start. **2** *colloq.* lose one's temper. **lead-off** *n.* an action beginning a process. **lead on 1** entice into going further than was intended. **2** mislead or deceive. **lead time** the time between the initiation and completion of a production process. **lead up the garden path** *colloq.* mislead. **lead the way** see WAY. □□ **leadable** *adj.* [OE *lǣdan* f. Gmc]

lead² /led/ *n. & v.* —*n.* **1** *Chem.* a heavy bluish-grey soft ductile

metallic element. (See below.) ¶ Symb.: **Pb**; atomic number 82. **2 a** graphite. It is also called 'black lead'; this name was applied before the composition of the substance was known. **b** a thin length of this for use in a pencil. **3** a lump of lead used in sounding water. **4** (in *pl.*) *Brit.* **a** strips of lead covering a roof. **b** a piece of lead-covered roof. **5** (in *pl.*) *Brit.* lead frames holding the glass of a lattice or stained-glass window. **6** *Printing* a blank space between lines of print (orig. with ref. to the metal strip used to give this space). **7** (*attrib.*) made of lead. —*v.tr.* **1** cover, weight, or frame (a roof or window panes) with lead. **2** *Printing* separate lines of (printed matter) with leads. **3** add a lead compound to (petrol etc.). □ **lead acetate** a white crystalline compound of lead that dissolves in water to form a sweet-tasting solution. **lead-free** (of petrol) without added tetraethyl lead. **lead pencil** a pencil of graphite enclosed in wood. **lead-poisoning** acute or chronic poisoning by absorption of lead into the body. **lead shot** = SHOT¹ 3b. **lead tetraethyl** = TETRAETHYL LEAD. **lead wool** a fibrous form of lead, used for jointing water pipes. □□ **leadless** *adj.* [OE *lēad* f. WG]

Lead was known to the ancient Egyptians and Babylonians, and was used by the Romans for making water-pipes. It is durable, resistant to corrosion, and a poor conductor of electricity; it has been used in roofing, ammunition, damping sound and vibration, storage batteries, cable sheathing, and shielding radioactive material. Lead compounds have been used in crystal glass, as an antiknock agent in petrol, and were formerly used extensively in paints. Lead and its compounds can accumulate in the body as poisons.

leaden /'led(ə)n/ *adj.* **1** of or like lead. **2** heavy, slow, burdensome (*leaden limbs*). **3** inert, depressing (*leaden rule*). **4** lead-coloured (*leaden skies*). □ **leaden seal** a stamped piece of lead holding the ends of a wire used as a fastening. □□ **leadenly** *adv.* **leadenness** *n.* [OE *lēaden* (as LEAD²)]

leader /'liːdə(r)/ *n.* **1 a** a person or thing that leads. **b** a person followed by others. **2 a** the principal player in a music group or of the first violins in an orchestra. **b** *US* a conductor of an orchestra. **3** *Brit.* = *leading article*. **4** a short strip of non-functioning material at each end of a reel of film or recording tape for connection to the spool. **5** (in full **Leader of the House**) *Brit.* a member of the government, in the House of Commons or Lords, officially responsible for initiating business in Parliament. **6** a shoot of a plant at the apex of a stem or of the main branch. **7** (in *pl.*) *Printing* a series of dots or dashes across the page to guide the eye, esp. in tabulated material. **8** the horse placed at the front in a team or pair. □□ **leaderless** *adj.* **leadership** *n.* [OE *lǣdere* (as LEAD¹)]

leading¹ /'liːdɪŋ/ *adj. & n.* —*adj.* chief; most important. —*n.* guidance, leadership. □ **leading aircraftman** the rank above aircraftman in the RAF. **leading article** a newspaper article giving the editorial opinion. **leading counsel** the senior barrister of two or more in a case. **leading edge 1** the foremost edge of an aerofoil, esp. a wing or propeller blade. **2** *Electronics* the part of a pulse in which the amplitude increases (opp. *trailing edge*). **leading lady** the actress playing the principal part. **leading light** a prominent and influential person. **leading man** the actor playing the principal part. **leading note** *Mus.* = SUBTONIC. **leading question** a question that prompts the answer wanted. **leading seaman** the rank next below NCO in the Royal Navy. **leading-strings** (or **-reins**) **1** strings for guiding children learning to walk. **2** oppressive supervision or control. **leading tone** *US Mus.* = *leading note*.

leading² /'ledɪŋ/ *n. Printing* = LEAD² *n.* 6.

leadwort /'ledwɜːt/ *n.* = PLUMBAGO 2.

leaf /liːf/ *n. & v.* —*n.* (*pl.* **leaves** /liːvz/) **1 a** each of several flattened usu. green structures of a plant, usu. on the side of a stem or branch and the main organ of photosynthesis. **b** other similar plant structures, e.g. bracts, sepals, and petals (*floral leaf*). **2 a** foliage regarded collectively. **b** the state of having leaves out (*a tree in leaf*). **3** the leaves of tobacco or tea. **4** a single thickness of paper, esp. in a book with each side forming a page. **5** a very thin sheet of metal, esp. gold or silver. **6 a** the hinged part or flap of a door, shutter, table, etc. **b** an extra section inserted to extend a table. —*v.* **1** *intr.* put forth leaves. **2** *tr.* (foll.

aʊ **how** eɪ **day** əʊ **no** eə **hair** ɪə **near** ɔɪ **boy** ʊə **poor** aɪə **fire** aʊə **sour**   (*see over for consonants*) by *through*) turn over the pages of (a book etc.). □ **leaf-green** the colour of green leaves. **leaf insect** any insect of the family Phylliidae, having a flattened body leaflike in appearance. **leaf-miner** any of various larvae burrowing in leaves, esp. moth caterpillars of the family Gracillariidae. **leaf-monkey** a langur. **leaf-mould** soil consisting chiefly of decayed leaves. **leaf spring** a spring made of strips of metal. **leaf-stalk** a petiole. □□ **leafage** *n.* **leafed** *adj.* (also in *comb.*). **leafless** *adj.* **leaflessness** *n.* **leaflike** *adj.* [OE *lēaf* f. Gmc]

leafhopper /ˈliːfˌhɒpə(r)/ *n.* any homopterous insect of the family Cicadellidae, which sucks the sap of plants and often causes damage and spreads disease.

leaflet /ˈliːflɪt/ *n. & v.* —*n.* **1** a young leaf. **2** *Bot.* any division of a compound leaf. **3** a sheet of (usu. printed) paper (sometimes folded but not stitched) giving information, esp. for free distribution. —*v.tr.* (**leafleted, leafleting**) distribute leaflets to.

leafy /ˈliːfɪ/ *adj.* (**leafier, leafiest**) **1** having many leaves. **2** resembling a leaf. □□ **leafiness** *n.*

league[1] /liːɡ/ *n. & v.* —*n.* **1** a collection of people, countries, groups, etc., combining for a particular purpose, esp. mutual protection or cooperation. **2** an agreement to combine in this way. **3** a group of sports clubs which compete over a period for a championship. **4** a class of contestants. —*v.intr.* (**leagues, leagued, leaguing**) (often foll. by *together*) join in a league. □ **in league** allied, conspiring. **league football** *Austral.* Rugby League or Australian Rules football played in leagues. **league table 1** a listing of competitors as a league, showing their ranking according to performance. **2** any list of ranking order. [F *ligue* or It. *liga*, var. of *lega* f. *legare* bind f. L *ligare*]

league[2] /liːɡ/ *n. archaic* a varying measure of travelling-distance by land, usu. about three miles. [ME, ult. f. LL *leuga, leuca*, of Gaulish orig.]

League of Arab States a regional organization, founded in 1945 with headquarters in Cairo, whose purpose is to ensure cooperation among its member States and protect their independence and sovereignty.

League of Nations an association of self-governing States, dominions, and colonies established in 1919 by the Treaty of Versailles, at the instigation of the US President Woodrow Wilson, 'to promote international co-operation and to achieve international peace and security'. Although the League accomplished much of value in postwar economic reconstruction, it failed in its prime purpose through the refusal of member nations to put international interests before national ones, and was powerless in the face of Italian, German, and Japanese expansionism. By the outbreak of the Second World War the League of Nations was little more than a helpless spectator, and the war itself destroyed it entirely. (See UNITED NATIONS.)

leaguer[1] /ˈliːɡə(r)/ *n.* esp. *US* a member of a league.

leaguer[2] /ˈliːɡə(r)/ *n. & v.* = LAAGER. [Du. *leger* camp, rel. to LAIR[1]]

leak /liːk/ *n. & v.* —*n.* **1 a** a hole in a vessel, pipe, or container etc. caused by wear or damage, through which matter, esp. liquid or gas, passes accidentally in or out. **b** the matter passing in or out through this. **c** the act or an instance of leaking. **2 a** a similar escape of electrical charge. **b** the charge that escapes. **3** the intentional disclosure of secret information. —*v.* **1 a** *intr.* (of liquid, gas, etc.) pass in or out through a leak. **b** *tr.* lose or admit (liquid, gas, etc.) through a leak. **2** *tr.* intentionally disclose (secret information). **3** *intr.* (often foll. by *out*) (of a secret, secret information) become known. □ **have** (or **take**) **a leak** *sl.* urinate. □□ **leaker** *n.* [ME prob. f. LG]

leakage /ˈliːkɪdʒ/ *n.* **1** the action or result of leaking. **2** what leaks in or out. **3** an intentional disclosure of secret information.

Leakey /ˈliːkɪ/, Louis Seymour Bazett (1903–72), British archaeologist and anthropologist, a Kenyan citizen from 1964, noted for his work on human origins in East Africa, where after the Second World War his excavations brought to light the remains of early hominids and their implements at Olduvai Gorge (see entry). His work has been continued by his wife Mary Douglas Leakey (1913–) and his son Richard Erskine Leakey (1944–).

leaky /ˈliːkɪ/ *adj.* (**leakier, leakiest**) **1** having a leak or leaks. **2** given to letting out secrets. □□ **leakiness** *n.*

leal /liːl/ *adj. Sc.* loyal, honest. [ME f. AF *leal*, OF *leel, loial* (as LOYAL)]

Lean /liːn/, Sir David (1908–91), English film director, whose many successful films include *Brief Encounter* (1945), *Great Expectations* (1946), *The Bridge on the River Kwai* (1957), *Lawrence of Arabia* (1962), *Dr Zhivago* (1965), and *A Passage to India* (1985).

lean[1] /liːn/ *v. & n.* —*v.* (*past and past part.* **leaned** /liːnd, lent/ or **leant** /lent/) **1** *intr. & tr.* (often foll. by *across, back, over,* etc.) be or place in a sloping position; incline from the perpendicular. **2** *intr. & tr.* (foll. by *against, on, upon*) rest or cause to rest for support against etc. **3** *intr.* (foll. by *on, upon*) rely on; derive support from. **4** *intr.* (foll. by *to, towards*) be inclined or partial to; have a tendency towards. —*n.* a deviation from the perpendicular; an inclination (*has a decided lean to the right*). □ **lean on** *colloq.* put pressure on (a person) to act in a certain way. **lean over backwards** see BACKWARDS. **lean-to** (*pl.* **-tos**) a building with its roof leaning against a larger building or a wall. [OE *hleonian, hlinian* f. Gmc]

lean[2] /liːn/ *adj. & n.* —*adj.* **1** (of a person or animal) thin; having no superfluous fat. **2** (of meat) containing little fat. **3 a** meagre; of poor quality (*lean crop*). **b** not nourishing (*lean diet*). **4** unremunerative. —*n.* the lean part of meat. □ **lean years** years of scarcity. □□ **leanly** *adv.* **leanness** *n.* [OE *hlæne* f. Gmc]

Leander /lɪˈændə(r)/ **1** *Gk legend* the lover of Hero (see entry). **2** (in full **Leander Club**) the oldest amateur rowing club in the world, founded early in the 19th c. Membership is a mark of distinction in the rowing world, and a large proportion of its members are former Oxford and Cambridge oarsmen.

leaning /ˈliːnɪŋ/ *n.* a tendency or partiality.

leap /liːp/ *v. & n.* —*v.* (*past and past part.* **leaped** /liːpt, lept/ or **leapt** /lept/) **1** *intr.* jump or spring forcefully. **2** *tr.* jump across. **3** *intr.* (of prices etc.) increase dramatically. —*n.* a forceful jump. □ **by leaps and bounds** with startlingly rapid progress. **leap in the dark** a daring step or enterprise whose consequences are unpredictable. **leap to the eye** be immediately apparent. **leap year** a year, occurring once in four, with 366 days (including 29th Feb. as an intercalary day). □□ **leaper** *n.* [OE *hlȳp, hlēapan* f. Gmc: *leap year* prob. refers to the fact that feast-days after Feb. in such a year fall two days later (instead of the normal one day later) than in the previous year]

leap-frog /ˈliːpfrɒɡ/ *n. & v.* —*n.* a game in which players in turn vault with parted legs over another who is bending down. —*v.* (**-frogged, -frogging**) **1** *intr.* (foll. by *over*) perform such a vault. **2** *tr.* vault over in this way. **3** *tr. & intr.* (of two or more people, vehicles, etc.) overtake alternately.

Lear /lɪə(r)/, Edward (1812–88), English artist and poet, the twentieth child of a stockbroker of Danish descent. At the age of 15 he was obliged to earn his own living, and began his artistic career by making tinted drawings of birds; in 1831 he became employed as a draughtsman in the gardens of the Zoological Society. Lear came under the patronage of the Earl of Derby, for whose grandchildren he wrote *A Book of Nonsense* (1845) with his own limericks and illustrations, the first of his series of nonsense verses in which he combines linguistic fantasies and inventiveness with touches of underlying melancholy. His reputation as a water-colourist has risen steadily since his death.

learn /lɜːn/ *v.* (*past and past part.* **learned** /lɜːnt, lɜːnd/ or **learnt** /lɜːnt/) **1** *tr.* gain knowledge of or skill in by study, experience, or being taught. **2** *tr.* (foll. by *to* + infin.) acquire or develop a particular ability (*learn to swim*). **3** *tr.* commit to memory (*will try to learn your names*). **4** *intr.* (foll. by *of*) be informed about. **5** *tr.* (foll. by *that, how,* etc. + clause) become aware of by information or from observation. **6** *intr.* receive instruction; acquire knowledge or skill. **7** *tr. archaic* or *sl.* teach. □ **learn one's lesson** see LESSON. □□ **learnable** *adj.* **learnability** /-nəˈbɪlɪtɪ/ *n.* [OE *leornian* f. Gmc: cf. LORE[1]]

learned /ˈlɜːnɪd/ *adj.* **1** having much knowledge acquired by study. **2** showing or requiring learning (*a learned work*). **3** studied or pursued by learned persons. **4** concerned with the interests of learned persons; scholarly (*a learned journal*). **5** *Brit.* as a courteous description of a lawyer in certain formal contexts (*my learned friend*). □□ **learnedly** *adv.* **learnedness** *n.* [ME f. LEARN in the sense 'teach']

learner /ˈlɜːnə(r)/ n. **1** a person who is learning a subject or skill. **2** (in full **learner driver**) a person who is learning to drive a motor vehicle and has not yet passed a driving test.

learning /ˈlɜːnɪŋ/ n. knowledge acquired by study. [OE *leornung* (as LEARN)]

lease /liːs/ n. & v. —n. an agreement by which the owner of a building or land allows another to use it for a specified time, usu. in return for payment. —v.tr. grant or take on lease. □ **a new lease of** (US **on**) **life** a substantially improved prospect of living, or of use after repair. □□ **leasable** adj. **leaser** n. [ME f. AF *les*, OF *lais*, *leis* f. *lesser*, *laissier* leave f. L *laxare* make loose (*laxus*)]

leaseback /ˈliːsbæk/ n. the leasing of a property back to the vendor.

leasehold /ˈliːshəʊld/ n. & adj. —n. **1** the holding of property by lease. **2** property held by lease. —adj. held by lease. □□ **leaseholder** n.

Lease-Lend n. = LEND-LEASE.

leash /liːʃ/ n. & v. —n. a thong for holding a dog; a dog's lead. —v.tr. **1** put a leash on. **2** restrain. □ **straining at the leash** eager to begin. [ME f. OF *lesse*, *laisse* f. specific use of *laisser* let run on a slack lead: see LEASE]

least /liːst/ adj., n., & adv. —adj. **1** smallest, slightest, most insignificant. **2** (prec. by *the*; esp. with *neg*.) any at all (*it does not make the least difference*). **3** (of a species or variety) very small (*least tern*). —n. the least amount. —adv. in the least degree. □ **at least 1** at all events; anyway; even if there is doubt about a more extended statement. **2** (also **at the least**) not less than. **in the least** (or **the least**) (usu. with *neg*.) in the smallest degree; at all (*not in the least offended*). **least common denominator, multiple** see DENOMINATOR, MULTIPLE. **to say the least** (or **the least of it**) used to imply the moderation of a statement (*that is doubtful to say the least*). [OE *lǣst*, *lǣsest* f. Gmc]

leastways /ˈliːstweɪz/ adv. (also **leastwise** /-waɪz/) dial. or at least, or rather.

leat /liːt/ n. Brit. an open watercourse conducting water to a mill etc. [OE *-gelǣt* (as Y- + root of LET[1])]

leather /ˈleðə(r)/ n. & v. —n. **1 a** material made from the skin of an animal by tanning or a similar process. **b** (*attrib*.) made of leather. **2 a** a piece of leather for polishing with. **3** the leather part or parts of something. **4** sl. a cricket-ball or football. **5** (in pl.) leather clothes, esp. leggings, breeches, or clothes for wearing on a motor cycle. **6** a thong (*stirrup-leather*). —v.tr. **1** cover with leather. **2** polish or wipe with a leather. **3** beat, thrash (orig. with a leather thong). □ **leather-jacket 1** Brit. a crane-fly grub with a tough skin. **2** any of various tough-skinned marine fish of the family Monacanthidae. **leather-neck** Naut. sl. a soldier or (esp. US) a marine (with reference to the leather stock formerly worn by them). [OE *lether* f. Gmc]

leatherback /ˈleðəˌbæk/ n. a large marine turtle, *Dermochelys coriacea*, having a thick leathery carapace.

leathercloth /ˈleðəˌklɒθ/ n. strong fabric coated to resemble leather.

leatherette /ˌleðəˈret/ n. imitation leather.

leathern /ˈleð(ə)n/ n. archaic made of leather.

leathery /ˈleðərɪ/ adj. **1** like leather. **2** (esp. of meat etc.) tough. □□ **leatheriness** n.

leave[1] /liːv/ v. & n. —v. (past and past part. **left** /left/) **1 a** tr. go away from; cease to remain in or on (*left him quite well an hour ago*; *leave the track*; *leave here*). **b** intr. (often foll. by *for*) depart (*we leave tomorrow*; *has just left for London*). **2** tr. cause to or let remain; depart without taking (*has left his gloves*; *left a slimy trail*; *left a bad impression*; *six from seven leaves one*). **3** tr. (also absol.) cease to reside at or attend or belong to or work for (*has left the school*; *I am leaving for another firm*). **4** tr. abandon, forsake, desert. **5** tr. have remaining after one's death (*leaves a wife and two children*). **6** tr. bequeath. **7** tr. (foll. by *to* + infin.) allow (a person or thing) to do something without interference or assistance (*leave the future to take care of itself*). **8** tr. (foll. by *to*) commit or refer to another person (*leave that to me*; *nothing was left to chance*). **9** tr. **a** abstain from consuming or dealing with. **b** (in passive; often foll. by *over*) remain over. **10** tr. **a** deposit or entrust (a thing) to be

attended to, collected, delivered, etc., in one's absence (*left a message with his secretary*). **b** depute (a person) to perform a function in one's absence. **11** tr. allow to remain or cause to be in a specified state or position (*left the door open*; *the performance left them unmoved*; *left nothing that was necessary undone*). **12** tr. pass (an object) so that it is in a specified relative direction (*leave the church on the left*). —n. the position in which a player leaves the balls in billiards, croquet, etc. □ **be left with 1** retain (a feeling etc.). **2** be burdened with (a responsibility etc.). **be well left** be well provided for by a legacy etc. **get left** colloq. be deserted or worsted. **have left** have remaining (*has no friends left*). **leave alone 1** refrain from disturbing, not interfere with. **2** not have dealings with. **leave be** colloq. refrain from disturbing, not interfere with. **leave behind 1** go away without. **2** leave as a consequence or a visible sign of passage. **3** pass. **leave a person cold** (or **cool**) not impress or excite a person. **leave go** colloq. relax one's hold. **leave hold of** cease holding. **leave it at that** colloq. abstain from comment or further action. **leave much** (or **a lot** etc.) **to be desired** be highly unsatisfactory. **leave off 1** come to or make an end. **2** discontinue (*leave off work*; *leave off talking*). **3** cease to wear. **leave out** omit, not include. **leave over** Brit. leave to be considered, settled, or used later. **leave a person to himself** or **herself 1** not attempt to control a person. **2** leave a person solitary. **left at the post** beaten from the start of a race. **left for dead** abandoned as being beyond rescue. **left luggage** Brit. luggage deposited for later retrieval, esp. at a railway station. □□ **leaver** n. [OE *lǣfan* f. Gmc]

leave[2] /liːv/ n. **1** (often foll. by *to* + infin.) permission. **2 a** (in full **leave of absence**) permission to be absent from duty. **b** the period for which this lasts. □ **by** (or **with**) **your leave** often iron. an expression of apology for taking a liberty or making an unwelcome statement. **on leave** legitimately absent from duty. **take one's leave** bid farewell. **take one's leave of** bid farewell to. **take leave of one's senses** see SENSE. **take leave to** venture or presume to. [OE *lēaf* f. WG: cf. LIEF, LOVE]

leaved /liːvd/ adj. **1** having leaves. **2** (in *comb*.) having a leaf or leaves of a specified kind or number (*four-leaved clover*).

leaven /ˈlev(ə)n/ n. & v. —n. **1 a** a substance added to dough to make it ferment and rise, esp. yeast, or fermenting dough reserved for the purpose. **b** (foll. by *of*) a tinge or admixture of a specified quality. —v.tr. **1** ferment (dough) with leaven. **2 a** permeate and transform. **b** (foll. by *with*) modify with a tempering element. □ **the old leaven** traces of the unregenerate state (cf. 1 Cor. 5:6–8). [ME f. OF *levain* f. Gallo-Roman spec. use of L *levamen* relief f. *levare* lift]

leaves pl. of LEAF.

leavings /ˈliːvɪŋz/ n.pl. things left over, esp. as worthless.

Lebanon /ˈlebənən/ a country in SW Asia with a coastline on the Mediterranean Sea; pop. (est. 1988) 2,674,400; official language, Arabic; capital, Beirut. The country was once heavily forested, but little remains of the famous cedars of Lebanon, imported by the pharaohs of ancient Egypt for coffins and for buildings and by Solomon for his temple. Until the mid-1970s the country's main sources of income were based on international trade and commerce, with Beirut the commercial capital of the Middle East. Lebanon has a number of archaeological sites, with Baalbek as its showpiece and Byblos one of the oldest continuously inhabited cities in the world. Part of the Ottoman empire from the 16th c., it became a French mandate after the First World War and achieved independence after the defeat of the Vichy garrison by the Allies during the Second World War. For a generation the Christian community dominated the country, but friction between these and the Muslims, the influx of Palestinian refugees, and repeated Middle Eastern wars, have continually destabilized the country, leading to intermittent (later continuous) civil war and military intervention by her neighbours and making Lebanon one of the most troubled areas in the world. □□ **Lebanese** /-ˈniːz/ adj. & n.

Lebanon Mountains a range of mountains in Lebanon, running parallel to the Mediterranean coast and rising to a height of 3,087 m (10,022 ft.) at Qornet es Saouda. They are separated from the Anti-Lebanon rnage on the Syrian frontier by the Beka'a Valley.

Lebensraum /ˈleɪbənzˌraʊm/ *n.* the territory which a State or nation believes is needed for its natural development. [G, = living-space (orig. with reference to Germany, esp. in the 1930s)]

Leblanc /ləˈblɑ̃/, Nicolas (1742–1806), French surgeon and chemist, who became interested in the large-scale manufacture of soda because of a prize offered by the Académie Royale des Sciences. In 1789 he developed the process that bears his name for making soda ash (sodium carbonate) from sodium chloride (common salt), which made possible the large-scale manufacture of glass, soaps, paper, and other chemicals, but by then it was too late for him to be awarded the prize. The factory he set up with others was confiscated during the French Revolution, the eventual compensation was insufficient to restart the business, and he committed suicide.

Lebowa /ləˈbəʊə/ a tribal homeland of the North Sotho people in South Africa; pop. (1985) 1,842,000.

Lebrun /ləˈbrɜː/, Charles (1619–90), French painter, designer, and decorator, who was influenced by Raphael and especially Poussin and in 1648 was a prominent figure in the foundation of the Académie Royale de Peinture et Sculpture. His importance in the history of French art is twofold. First, in the employ of Louis XIV from 1661, he executed works which reflected the power and splendour of the Sun King's court and established himself as a leading exponent of 17th-c. French classicism; his decorative scenes at Versailles, including painting, furniture, garden sculpture, and tapestry design (in 1663 he was appointed director of the Gobelins factory) must be seen as a highlight in his *œuvre*. Secondly, as director of the Académie from 1663 he turned it into a channel for imposing a codified system of orthodoxy in matters of art, laying the basis of academicism.

Le Carré /lə ˈkæreɪ/, John (pseudonym of David John Moore Cornwell, 1931–), English novelist, who served in the Foreign Service in the early 1960s. His first thriller *Call for the Dead* (1961) introduces mastermind and secret agent George Smiley, who reappears in many of his later books. *The Spy Who Came in from the Cold* (1963), a cold-war thriller inspired by the Berlin wall, brought him immediate fame, and with *The Looking Glass War* (1965), *Tinker, Tailor, Soldier, Spy* (1974), *Smiley's People* (1980), *The Little Drummer Girl* (1983), and many others, he has confirmed his reputation for realistic fictional studies of espionage.

lech /letʃ/ *v. & n. colloq.* —*v.intr.* feel lecherous; behave lustfully. —*n.* **1** a strong desire, esp. sexual. **2** a lecher. [back-form. f. LECHER: (n.) perh. f. *letch* longing]

lecher /ˈletʃə(r)/ *n.* a lecherous man; a debauchee. [ME f. OF *lecheor* etc. f. *lechier* live in debauchery or gluttony f. Frank., rel. to LICK]

lecherous /ˈletʃərəs/ *adj.* lustful, having strong or excessive sexual desire. □□ **lecherously** *adv.* **lecherousness** *n.* [ME f. OF *lecheros* etc. f. *lecheur* LECHER]

lechery /ˈletʃərɪ/ *n.* unrestrained indulgence of sexual desire. [ME f. OF *lecherie* f. *lecheur* LECHER]

lecithin /ˈlesɪθɪn/ *n.* **1** any of a group of phospholipids found naturally in animals, egg-yolk, and some higher plants. **2** a preparation of this used to emulsify foods etc. [Gk *lekithos* egg-yolk + -IN]

Leclanché /ləˈklɑ̃ʃeɪ/, Georges (1839–82), French chemist, inventor of a primary cell (named after him) that has a zinc cathode in contact with zinc chloride, ammonium chloride (solution or paste) as the electrolyte, and a carbon anode in contact with a mixture of manganese dioxide and carbon powder.

Leconte de Lisle /ləˈkɔ̃t də ˈliːl/ Charles-Marie-René (1818–94), French poet, whose inspiration was drawn from Greek, Egyptian, and Nordic mythology, biblical history, exotic eastern scenery, and archaeological beauty. His poetry is marked by a formal perfection and static visual quality, though his choice of subject was often directed by his pessimistic and atheistic view of life.

Le Corbusier /lə kɔːˈbjuːzɪˌeɪ/ (1887–1965), real name Charles-Edouard Jeanneret, French architect of Swiss parentage, who began as a painter of semi-abstract compositions and became a great influence on modern architecture through his designs, buildings, and writings, and his use of steel and raw concrete. He began architectural practice in 1922 with his cousin Pierre Jeanneret, and their early buildings already showed Le Corbusier's genius for subtle manipulation of pure geometrical forms as well as his imaginative application of new technical ideas. Their most important buildings include the Centrosoyons (cooperative) building in Moscow (1928), and the hostel for Swiss students in Paris (1931–3) with Le Corbusier's characteristic use of *pilotis* to raise the building off the ground. His visit to Brazil in 1936 greatly influenced the modern architectural movement in that country. The UN Secretariat building in New York (1951) owes its basic conception and clarity of form to his ideas. He was involved also in the planning of functional cities (e.g. Chandigarh in India).

lectern /ˈlektɜːn, -t(ə)n/ *n.* **1** a stand for holding a book in a church or chapel, esp. for a bible from which lessons are to be read. **2** a similar stand for a lecturer etc. [ME *lettorne* f. OF *let(t)run*, med.L *lectrum* f. *legere lect-* read]

lection /ˈlekʃ(ə)n/ *n.* a reading of a text found in a particular copy or edition. [L *lectio* reading (as LECTERN)]

lectionary /ˈlekʃənərɪ/ *n.* (*pl.* **-ies**) **1** a list of portions of Scripture appointed to be read at divine service. **2** a book containing such portions. [ME f. med.L *lectionarium* (as LECTION)]

lector /ˈlektɔː(r)/ *n.* **1** a reader, esp. of lessons in a church service. **2** (*fem.* **lectrice** /lekˈtriːs/) a lecturer or reader, esp. one employed in a foreign university to give instruction in his or her native language. [L f. *legere lect-* read]

lecture /ˈlektʃə(r)/ *n. & v.* —*n.* **1** a discourse giving information about a subject to a class or other audience. **2** a long serious speech esp. as a scolding or reprimand. —*v.* **1** *intr.* (often foll. by *on*) deliver a lecture or lectures. **2** *tr.* talk seriously or reprovingly to (a person). **3** *tr.* instruct or entertain (a class or other audience) by a lecture. [ME f. OF *lecture* or med.L *lectura* f. L (as LECTOR)]

lecturer /ˈlektʃərə(r)/ *n.* a person who lectures, esp. as a teacher in higher education.

lectureship /ˈlektʃəʃɪp/ *n.* the office of lecturer. ¶ The form *lecturership*, which is strictly more regular, is in official use at Oxford University and elsewhere, but is not widely current.

lecythus /ˈlesɪθəs/ *n.* (*pl.* **lecythi** /-ˌθaɪ/) *Gk Antiq.* a thin narrow-necked vase or flask. [Gk *lēkuthos*]

LED *abbr.* light-emitting diode.

led *past* and *past part.* of LEAD[1].

Leda /ˈliːdə/ *Gk Mythol.* the wife of Tyndareus king of Sparta. She was loved by Zeus who visited her in the form of a swan; among her children were the Dioscuri, Helen, and Clytemnestra.

lederhosen /ˈleɪdəˌhəʊz(ə)n/ *n.pl.* leather shorts as worn by men in Bavaria etc. [G, = leather trousers]

ledge /ledʒ/ *n.* **1** a narrow horizontal surface projecting from a wall etc. **2** a shelflike projection on the side of a rock or mountain. **3** a ridge of rocks, esp. below water. **4** *Mining* a stratum of metal-bearing rock. □□ **ledged** *adj.* **ledgy** *adj.* [perh. f. ME *legge* LAY[1]]

ledger /ˈledʒə(r)/ *n.* **1** a tall narrow book in which a firm's accounts are kept, esp. one which is the principal book of a set and contains debtor-and-creditor accounts. **2** a flat gravestone. **3** a horizontal timber in scaffolding, parallel to the face of the building. □ **ledger line** *Mus.* = LEGER LINE. **ledger-tackle** a kind of fishing tackle in which a lead weight keeps the bait on the bottom. [ME f. senses of Du. *ligger* and *legger* (f. *liggen* LIE[1], *leggen* LAY[1]) & pronunc. of ME *ligge, legge*]

Lee /liː/, Robert Edward (1807–70), American Confederate general, commander of the army of Northern Virginia. Widely acclaimed as the greatest military leader of the American Civil War, Lee led the main Confederate army in the eastern theatre for most of the war. Revered by his own men and respected by his opponents, he did more than any other individual to prolong Confederate resistance against the Union's greater manpower and industrial might.

lee /liː/ *n.* **1** shelter given by a neighbouring object (*under the lee*

æ cat ɑː arm e bed ɜː her ɪ sit iː see ɒ hot ɔː saw ʌ run ʊ put uː too ə ago aɪ my

of). **2** (in full **lee side**) the sheltered side, the side away from the wind (opp. *weather side*). □ **lee-board** a plank frame fixed to the side of a flat-bottomed vessel and let down into the water to diminish leeway. **lee shore** the shore to leeward of a ship. [OE *hlēo* f. Gmc]

leech[1] /liːtʃ/ n. **1** any freshwater or terrestrial annelid worm of the class *Hirudinea* with suckers at both ends, esp. *Hirudo medicinalis*, a bloodsucking parasite of vertebrates formerly much used medicinally. **2** a person who extorts profit from or sponges on others. □ **like a leech** persistently or clingingly present. [OE *lǣce*, assim. to LEECH[2]]

leech[2] /liːtʃ/ n. archaic or joc. a physician; a healer. [OE *lǣce* f. Gmc]

leech[3] /liːtʃ/ n. **1** a perpendicular or sloping side of a square sail. **2** the side of a fore-and-aft sail away from the mast or stay. [ME, perh. rel. to ON *lik*, a nautical term of uncert. meaning]

leechcraft /liːtʃkrɑːft/ n. archaic the art of healing. [OE *lǣcecræft* (as LEECH[2], CRAFT)]

Leeds /liːdz/ an industrial city in West Yorkshire; pop. (1981) 451,800.

leek /liːk/ n. **1** an alliaceous plant, *Allium porrum*, with flat overlapping leaves forming an elongated cylindrical bulb, used as food. **2** this as a Welsh national emblem. [OE *lēac* f. Gmc]

leer[1] /lɪə(r)/ v. & n. —*v.intr.* look slyly or lasciviously or maliciously. —n. a leering look. □□ **leeringly** adv. [perh. f. obs. *leer* cheek f. OE *hlēor*, as though 'to glance over one's cheek']

leer[2] var. of LEHR.

leery /lɪərɪ/ adj. (**leerier**, **leeriest**) sl. **1** knowing, sly. **2** (foll. by *of*) wary. □□ **leeriness** n. [perh. f. obs. *leer* looking askance f. LEER[1] + -Y[1]]

lees /liːz/ n.pl. **1** the sediment of wine etc. (*drink to the lees*). **2** dregs, refuse. [pl. of ME *lie* f. OF *lie* f. med.L *lia* f. Gaulish]

leet[1] /liːt/ n. hist. **1** (in full **Court leet**) a yearly or half-yearly court of record that lords of certain manors might hold. **2** its jurisdiction or district. [ME f. AF *lete* (= AL *leta*), of unkn. orig.]

leet[2] /liːt/ n. Sc. a selected list of candidates for some office. □ **short leet** = *short list*. [ME *lite* etc., prob. f. AF & OF *lit(t)e*, var. of *liste* LIST[1]]

Leeuwenhoek /leɪvən,huːk/, Antoni van (1632–1723), Dutch naturalist. Apprenticed to a Delft cloth-merchant, he developed a lens for scientific purposes from those used to inspect cloth, and was the first to observe bacteria, protozoa, and yeast. He accurately described red blood corpuscles, capillaries, striated muscle fibres, spermatozoa, and the crystalline lens of the eye. Being without Latin he was out of touch with the scientific community and his very original work on micro-organisms became known through the Royal Society's translation and publication of his letters.

leeward /liːwəd, *Naut.* luːəd/ adj., adv., & n. —adj. & adv. on or towards the side sheltered from the wind (opp. WINDWARD). —n. the leeward region, side, or direction (*to leeward; on the leeward of*).

Leeward Islands /liːwəd/ a group of islands in the eastern Caribbean which constitute the northern part of the Lesser Antilles. The largest are Guadeloupe, Antigua, St Kitts, and Montserrat. Their name refers to the fact that they are further from the direction of prevailing winds, which are easterly, than are the Windward Islands.

leewardly /liːwədlɪ/ adj. (of a ship) apt to drift to leeward.

leeway /liːweɪ/ n. **1** the sideways drift of a ship to leeward of the desired course. **2 a** allowable deviation or freedom of action. **b** *US* margin of safety. □ **make up leeway** struggle out of a bad position, recover lost time, etc.

Le Fanu /lefən,juː, lə'fɑːnuː/, Joseph Sheridan (1814–73), Irish novelist who achieved recognition as a writer of stories of mystery, suspense, and the supernatural. His best-known works include, *The House by the Churchyard* (1861), *Uncle Silas* (1864), and the collection of ghost stories *In a Glass Darkly* (1872).

left[1] /left/ adj., adv., & n. (opp. RIGHT). —adj. **1** on or towards the side of the human body which corresponds to the position of

west if one regards oneself as facing north. **2** on or towards the part of an object which is analogous to a person's left side or (with opposite sense) which is nearer to an observer's left hand. **3** (also **Left**) Polit. of the Left. —adv. on or to the left side. —n. **1** the left-hand part or region or direction. **2** Boxing **a** the left hand. **b** a blow with this. **3 a** (often **Left**) Polit. a group or section favouring radical socialism (orig. the more radical section of a continental legislature, seated on the president's left); such radicals collectively. **b** the more advanced or innovative section of any group. **4** the side of a stage which is to the left of a person facing the audience. **5** (esp. in marching) the left foot. **6** the left wing of an army. □ **have two left feet** be clumsy. **left and right** = *right and left*. **left bank** the bank of a river on the left facing downstream. **left bower** see BOWER[3]. **left field** Baseball the part of the outfield to the left of the batter as he or she faces the pitcher. **left hand 1** the hand of the left side. **2** (usu. prec. by *at, on, to*) the region or direction on the left side of a person. **left-hand** adj. **1** on or towards the left side of a person or thing (*left-hand drive*). **2** done with the left hand (*left-hand blow*). **3 a** (of rope) twisted counter-clockwise. **b** (of a screw) = LEFT-HANDED. **left turn** a turn that brings one's front to face as one's left side did before. **left wing 1** the radical or socialist section of a political party. **2** the left side of a football etc. team on the field. **3** the left side of an army. **left-wing** adj. socialist, radical. **left-winger** a person on the left wing. **marry with the left hand** marry morganatically (see LEFT-HANDED). □□ **leftish** adj. [ME *lüft, lift, left*, f. OE, orig. sense 'weak, worthless']

left[2] past and past part. of LEAVE[1].

left-handed /left'hændɪd/ adj. **1** using the left hand by preference as more serviceable than the right. **2** (of a tool etc.) made to be used with the left hand. **3** (of a blow) struck with the left hand. **4 a** turning to the left; towards the left. **b** (of a racecourse) turning anticlockwise. **c** (of a screw) advanced by turning to the left (anticlockwise). **5** awkward, clumsy. **6 a** (of a compliment) ambiguous. **b** of doubtful sincerity or validity. **7** (of a marriage) morganatic (from a German custom by which the bridegroom gave the bride his left hand in such marriages). □□ **left-handedly** adv. **left-handedness** n.

left-hander /left'hændə(r)/ n. **1** a left-handed person. **2** a left-handed blow.

leftie var. of LEFTY.

leftism /leftɪz(ə)m/ n. Polit. the principles or policy of the left. □□ **leftist** n. & adj.

leftmost /leftməʊst/ adj. furthest to the left.

leftovers /left,əʊvəz/ n.pl. items (esp. of food) remaining after the rest has been used.

leftward /leftwəd/ adv. & adj. —adv. (also **leftwards** /-wədz/) towards the left. —adj. going towards or facing the left.

lefty /leftɪ/ n. (also **leftie**) (pl. -**ies**) colloq. **1** Polit. a left-winger. **2** a left-handed person.

leg /leg/ n. & v. —n. **1 a** each of the limbs on which a person or animal walks and stands. **b** the part of this from the hip to the ankle. **2** a leg of an animal or bird as food. **3** an artificial leg (*wooden leg*). **4** a part of a garment covering a leg or part of a leg. **5 a** a support of a chair, table, bed, etc. **b** a long thin support or prop, esp. a pole. **6** Cricket the half of the field (as divided lengthways through the pitch) in which the striker's feet are placed (opp. OFF). **7 a** a section of a journey. **b** a section of a relay race. **c** a stage in a competition. **d** one of two or more games constituting a round. **8** one branch of a forked object. **9** *Naut.* a run made on a single tack. **10** archaic an obeisance made by drawing back one leg and bending it while keeping the front leg straight. —*v.tr.* (**legged**, **legging**) propel (a boat) through a canal tunnel by pushing with one's legs against the tunnel sides. □ **feel** (or **find**) **one's legs** become able to stand or walk. **give a person a leg up** help a person to mount a horse etc. or get over an obstacle or difficulty. **have the legs of** be able to go further than. **have no legs** colloq. (of a golf ball etc.) have not enough momentum to reach the desired point. **keep one's legs** not fall. **leg before wicket** Cricket (of a batsman) out because of illegally obstructing the ball with a part of the body other than the hand. **leg break** Cricket **1** a ball which deviates from the leg side after bouncing. **2** such deviation. **leg-bye** see BYE[1]. **leg-cutter** *Cricket* a fast leg break. **leg-iron** a shackle or fetter for the leg. **leg it** *colloq.* walk or run hard. **leg-of-mutton sail** a triangular mainsail. **leg-of-mutton sleeve** a sleeve which is full and loose on the upper arm but close-fitting on the forearm. **leg-pull** *colloq.* a hoax. **leg-rest** a support for a seated invalid's leg. **leg-room** space for the legs of a seated person. **leg-show** a theatrical performance by scantily-dressed women. **leg slip** *Cricket* a fielder stationed for a ball glancing off the bat to the leg side behind the wicket. **leg spin** *Cricket* a type of spin which causes the ball to deviate from the leg side after bouncing. **leg stump** *Cricket* the stump on the leg side. **leg theory** *Cricket* bowling to leg with fielders massed on that side. **leg trap** *Cricket* a group of fielders near the wicket on the leg side. **leg warmer** either of a pair of tubular knitted garments covering the leg from ankle to thigh. **not have a leg to stand on** be unable to support one's argument by facts or sound reasons. **on one's last legs** near death or the end of one's usefulness etc. **on one's legs 1** (also **on one's hind legs**) standing esp. to make a speech. **2** well enough to walk about. **take to one's legs** run away. □□ **legged** /legd, ˈlegɪd/ *adj.* (also in *comb.*). **legger** *n.* [ME f. ON *leggr* f. Gmc]

legacy /ˈlegəsɪ/ *n.* (*pl.* **-ies**) **1** a gift left in a will. **2** something handed down by a predecessor (*legacy of corruption*). □ **legacy-hunter** a person who pays court to another to secure a legacy. [ME f. OF *legacie* legateship f. med.L *legatia* f. L *legare* bequeath]

legal /ˈliːg(ə)l/ *adj.* **1** of or based on law; concerned with law; falling within the province of law. **2** appointed or required by law. **3** permitted by law, lawful. **4** recognized by law, as distinct from equity. **5** *Theol.* **a** of the Mosaic law. **b** of salvation by works rather than by faith. □ **legal aid** payment from public funds allowed, in cases of need, to help pay for legal advice or proceedings. **legal fiction** an assertion accepted as true (though probably fictitious) to achieve a useful purpose, esp. in legal matters. **legal holiday** *US* a public holiday established by law. **legal proceedings** see PROCEEDING. **legal separation** see SEPARATION. **legal tender** currency that cannot legally be refused in payment of a debt (usu. up to a limited amount for coins not made of gold). □□ **legally** *adv.* [F *légal* or L *legalis* f. *lex legis* law: cf. LEAL, LOYAL]

legalese /ˌliːgəˈliːz/ *n. colloq.* the technical language of legal documents.

legalism /ˈliːgəlɪz(ə)m/ *n.* **1** excessive adherence to law or formula. **2** *Theol.* adherence to the Law rather than to the Gospel, the doctrine of justification by works. □□ **legalist** *n.* **legalistic** /-ˈlɪstɪk/ *adj.* **legalistically** /-ˈlɪstɪkəlɪ/ *adv.*

legality /lɪˈgælɪtɪ, liːˈg-/ *n.* (*pl.* **-ies**) **1** lawfulness. **2** legalism. **3** (in *pl.*) obligations imposed by law. [F *légalité* or med.L *legalitas* (as LEGAL)]

legalize /ˈliːgəlaɪz/ *v.tr.* (also **-ise**) **1** make lawful. **2** bring into harmony with the law. □□ **legalization** /-ˈzeɪʃ(ə)n/ *n.*

legate /ˈlegət/ *n.* **1** a member of the clergy representing the Pope. **2** *Rom.Hist.* **a** a deputy of a general. **b** a governor or deputy governor of a province. **3** *archaic* an ambassador or delegate. □ **legate a latere** /ɑː ˈlætəˌreɪ/ a papal legate of the highest class, with full powers. □□ **legateship** *n.* **legatine** /-tɪn/ *adj.* [OE f. OF *legat* f. L *legatus* past part. of *legare* depute, delegate]

legatee /ˌlegəˈtiː/ *n.* the recipient of a legacy. [as LEGATOR + -EE]

legation /lɪˈgeɪʃ(ə)n/ *n.* **1** a body of deputies. **2 a** the office and staff of a diplomatic minister (esp. when not having ambassadorial rank). **b** the official residence of a diplomatic minister. **3** a legateship. **4** the sending of a legate or deputy. [ME f. OF *legation* or L *legatio* (as LEGATE)]

legato /lɪˈgɑːtəʊ/ *adv., adj., & n. Mus.* —*adv. & adj.* in a smooth flowing manner, without breaks between notes (cf. STACCATO, TENUTO). —*n.* (*pl.* **-os**) **1** a legato passage. **2** legato playing. [It., = bound, past part. of *legare* f. L *ligare* bind]

legator /lɪˈgeɪtə(r)/ *n.* the giver of a legacy. [archaic *legate* bequeath f. L *legare* (as LEGACY)]

legend /ˈledʒ(ə)nd/ *n.* **1 a** a traditional story sometimes popularly regarded as historical but unauthenticated; a myth. **b** such stories collectively. **c** a popular but unfounded belief. **d** *colloq.* a subject of such beliefs (*became a legend in his own lifetime*). **2 a** an inscription, esp. on a coin or medal. **b** *Printing* a caption. **c** wording on a map etc. explaining the symbols used. **3** *hist.* **a** the story of a saint's life. **b** a collection of lives of saints or similar stories. □□ **legendry** *n.* [ME (in sense 3) f. OF *legende* f. med.L *legenda* what is to be read, neut. pl. gerundive of L *legere* read]

legendary /ˈledʒəndərɪ/ *adj.* **1** of or connected with legends. **2** described in a legend. **3** *colloq.* remarkable enough to be a subject of legend. **4** based on a legend. □□ **legendarily** *adv.* [med.L *legendarius* (as LEGEND)]

legerdemain /ˌledʒədəˈmeɪn/ *n.* **1** sleight of hand; conjuring or juggling. **2** trickery, sophistry. [ME f. F *léger de main* light of hand, dextrous]

leger line /ˈledʒə(r)/ *n. Mus.* a short line added for notes above or below the range of a staff. [var. of LEDGER]

legging /ˈlegɪŋ/ *n.* (usu. in *pl.*) a stout protective outer covering for the leg from the knee to the ankle.

leggy /ˈlegɪ/ *adj.* (**leggier, leggiest**) **1 a** long-legged. **b** (of a woman) having attractively long legs. **2** long-stemmed. □□ **legginess** *n.*

Leghorn /ˈleghɔːn/ (Italian **Livorno** /liːˈvɔːnəʊ/) a port in NW Italy, on the Ligurian coast of Tuscany; pop. (1981) 175,700.

leghorn /ˈleghɔːn, lɪˈgɔːn/ *n.* **1 a** fine plaited straw. **b** a hat of this. **2** (**Leghorn**) **a** a bird of a small hardy breed of domestic fowl. **b** this breed. [LEGHORN, from where the straw and fowls were imported]

legible /ˈledʒɪb(ə)l/ *adj.* (of handwriting, print, etc.) clear enough to read; readable. □□ **legibility** /-ˈbɪlɪtɪ/ *n.* **legibly** *adv.* [ME f. LL *legibilis* f. *legere* read]

legion /ˈliːdʒ(ə)n/ *n. & adj.* —*n.* **1** a division of 3,000–6,000 men, including a complement of cavalry, in the ancient Roman army. **2** a large organized body. **3** a vast host, multitude, or number. —*predic.adj.* great in number (*his good works have been legion*). □ **American Legion** (in the US) an association of ex-servicemen formed in 1919. **foreign legion** see separate entry. **Legion of Honour** a French order of distinction founded in 1802. **Royal British Legion** see separate entry. [ME f. OF f. L *legio -onis* f. *legere* choose]

legionary /ˈliːdʒənərɪ/ *adj. & n.* —*adj.* of a legion or legions. —*n.* (*pl.* **-ies**) a member of a legion. [L *legionarius* (as LEGION)]

legioned /ˈliːdʒ(ə)nd/ *adj. poet.* arrayed in legions.

legionella /ˌliːdʒəˈnelə/ *n.* the bacterium *Legionella pneumophila*, which causes legionnaires' disease.

legionnaire /ˌliːdʒəˈneə(r)/ *n.* **1** a member of a foreign legion. **2** a member of the American Legion or the Royal British Legion. □ **legionnaires' disease** a form of bacterial pneumonia first identified after an outbreak at an American Legion meeting in 1976 (cf. LEGIONELLA). [F *légionnaire* (as LEGION)]

legislate /ˈledʒɪsˌleɪt/ *v.intr.* **1** make laws. **2** (foll. by *for*) make provision by law. [back-form. f. LEGISLATION]

legislation /ˌledʒɪsˈleɪʃ(ə)n/ *n.* **1** the process of making laws. **2** laws collectively. [LL *legis latio* f. *lex legis* law + *latio* proposing f. *lat-* past part. stem of *ferre* bring]

legislative /ˈledʒɪslətɪv/ *adj.* of or empowered to make legislation. □□ **legislatively** *adv.*

legislator /ˈledʒɪsˌleɪtə(r)/ *n.* **1** a member of a legislative body. **2** a lawgiver. [L (as LEGISLATION)]

legislature /ˈledʒɪsˌleɪtʃə(r), -lətʃə(r)/ *n.* the legislative body of a State.

legit /lɪˈdʒɪt/ *adj. & n. colloq.* —*adj.* legitimate. —*n.* **1** legitimate drama. **2** an actor in legitimate drama. [abbr.]

legitimate *adj. & v.* —*adj.* /lɪˈdʒɪtɪmət/ **1 a** (of a child) born of parents lawfully married to each other. **b** (of a parent, birth, descent, etc.) with, of, through, etc., a legitimate child. **2** lawful, proper, regular, conforming to the standard type. **3** logically admissible. **4 a** (of a sovereign's title) based on strict hereditary right. **b** (of a sovereign) having a legitimate title. **5** constituting or relating to serious drama (including both comedy and tragedy) as distinct from musical comedy, farce, revue, etc. The term arose in the 18th c. during the struggle of the patent theatres, Covent Garden and Drury Lane, against the illegitimate theatres springing up all over London. It covered plays dependent entirely on acting, with little or no singing, dancing, or spectacle. —*v.tr.* /lɪˈdʒɪtɪˌmeɪt/ **1** make legitimate by decree, enactment, or proof. **2** justify, serve as a justification for. □□ **legitimacy** /-məsɪ/ *n.* **legitimately** /-mətlɪ/ *adv.* **legitimation** /-ˈmeɪʃ(ə)n/ *n.* [med.L *legitimare* f. L *legitimus* lawful f. *lex legis* law]

legitimatize /lɪˈdʒɪtɪməˌtaɪz/ *v.tr.* (also **-ise**) legitimize. □□ **legitimatization** /-ˈzeɪʃ(ə)n/ *n.*

legitimism /lɪˈdʒɪtɪˌmɪz(ə)m/ *n.* adherence to a sovereign or pretender whose claim is based on direct descent (esp. in French and Spanish history). □□ **legitimist** *n.* & *adj.* [F *légitimisme* f. *légitime* LEGITIMATE]

legitimize /lɪˈdʒɪtɪˌmaɪz/ *v.tr.* (also **-ise**) **1** make legitimate. **2** serve as a justification for. □□ **legitimization** /-ˈzeɪʃ(ə)n/ *n.*

legless /ˈleglɪs/ *adj.* **1** having no legs. **2** *sl.* drunk, esp. too drunk to stand.

legman /ˈlegmæn/ *n.* (*pl.* **-men**) a person employed to go about gathering news or running errands etc.

Lego /ˈlegəʊ/ *n. propr.* a construction toy consisting of interlocking plastic building blocks. [Da. *legetøj* toys f. *lege* to play]

legume /ˈlegjuːm/ *n.* **1** the seed pod of a leguminous plant. **2** any seed, pod, or other edible part of a leguminous plant used as food. [F *légume* f. L *legumen -minis* f. *legere* pick, because pickable by hand]

leguminous /lɪˈgjuːmɪnəs/ *adj.* of or like the family Leguminosae, including peas and beans, having seeds in pods and usu. root nodules able to fix nitrogen. [mod.L *leguminosus* (as LEGUME)]

legwork /ˈlegwɜːk/ *n.* work which involves a lot of walking, travelling, or physical activity.

Leh /leɪ/ a town of northern India, in the east of Jammu and Kashmir. It is the chief town of the Himalayan region of Ladakh.

Lehár /ˈleɪhɑː(r)/, Franz (Ferencz) (1870–1948), Hungarian composer, noted especially for his operettas, of which the most famous is *The Merry Widow* (1905).

Le Havre /lə ˈhɑːvr/ a port in NW France, on the English Channel, at the mouth of the Seine; pop. (1982) 254,600.

lehr /lɪə(r)/ *n.* (also **leer**) a furnace used for the annealing of glass. [17th c.: orig. unkn.]

lei[1] /ˈleɪiː, leɪ/ *n.* a Polynesian garland of flowers. [Hawaiian]

lei[2] *pl.* of LEU.

Leibniz /ˈlaɪbnɪts/, Gottfried Wilhelm (1646–1716), German rationalist philosopher. A man of wide-ranging expertise, who served at the court of the Duke of Brunswick-Lüneburg, he worked on the problem of the continuum and the laws of motion, and discovered the infinitesimal calculus independently of Newton, which made his disputes with Newton's followers acrimonious. He believed that the world is fundamentally harmonious and good. In his philosophical writings he argued that it is composed of single units (monads) which are simple yet each in its own way mirrors the whole universe; each is self-contained, but acts in harmony with every other, and they form a continuously ascending series from the lowest (which is next to nothing) to the highest (which is God; though in some places he speaks as though God were outside the series). Their preestablished harmony is ordained by God who, Leibniz argued, never acted except for a reason that required it, and so the world that he had created was the best of all possible worlds (a view satirized in Voltaire's *Candide*). Throughout his life Leibniz was ardently devoted to the cause of international peace.

Leicester /ˈlestə(r)/ *n.* a kind of mild firm cheese, usu. orange-coloured and orig. made in Leicestershire.

Leicestershire /ˈlestəˌʃɪə(r)/ a midland county of England; pop. (1981) 858,700; county town, Leicester.

Leichhardt /ˈlaɪkhɑːt/, Friedrich Wilhelm Ludwig (1813–48), German-born explorer of Australia. Having emigrated to Australia in 1841, Leichhardt began a series of geological surveys of that continent, crossing from Moreton Bay to Port Esslington in 1843–5, but disappearing without trace in the area of the

Cogoon River on another attempt at an east–west crossing in 1848.

Leics. *abbr.* Leicestershire.

Leiden /ˈlaɪd(ə)n/ (formerly **Leyden**) an industrial and university city of The Netherlands, 15 km (9 miles) north-east of the Hague; pop. (1987) 107,900. The university was founded in 1575. The painter Rembrandt was born in this city (1606), and the 'Leyden jar' (see entry) was invented here.

Leif Ericsson see ERICSSON[2].

Leighton /ˈleɪt(ə)n/, Frederic, Lord (1830–96), English painter and sculptor who was the leading exponent of Victorian neo-classicism. He studied painting in Italy, Germany, and Paris, and first gained renown with his work *Cimabue's Madonna carried in procession through the streets of Florence*, exhibited at the Royal Academy in 1855 and bought by Queen Victoria. He was chiefly a painter of large-scale mythological and genre scenes, and he dominated the London art world in his day. Made a baronet, President of the Royal Academy, and, in 1895, a peer, he enjoyed great success, building Leighton House in London, famous for its Arab Hall, decorated with objects collected on trips to the East.

Leinster /ˈlenstə(r)/ a province of the Republic of Ireland; pop. (est. 1986) 1,851,100; capital, Dublin.

Leipzig /ˈlaɪpzɪg/ a city in east central Germany, a centre of the publishing and music trade; pop. (1986) 552,100. An annual fair has been held here since the 12th c.

leishmaniasis /ˌliːʃməˈnaɪəsɪs/ *n.* any of several diseases caused by parasitic protozoans of the genus *Leishmania* transmitted by the bite of sandflies. [W. B. *Leishman*, Brit. physician d. 1926]

leister /ˈliːstə(r)/ *n.* & *v.* —*n.* a pronged salmon-spear. —*v.tr.* pierce with a leister. [ON *ljóstr* f. *ljósta* to strike]

leisure /ˈleʒə(r)/ *n.* **1** free time; time at one's own disposal. **2** enjoyment of free time. **3** (usu. foll. by *for*, or *to* + infin.) opportunity afforded by free time. □ **at leisure 1** not occupied. **2** in an unhurried manner. **at one's leisure** when one has time. □□ **leisureless** *adj.* [ME f. AF *leisour*, OF *leisir* ult. f. L *licēre* be allowed]

leisured /ˈleʒəd/ *adj.* having ample leisure.

leisurely /ˈleʒəlɪ/ *adj.* & *adv.* —*adj.* having leisure; acting or done at leisure; unhurried, relaxed. —*adv.* without hurry. □□ **leisureliness** *n.*

leisurewear /ˈleʒəˌweə(r)/ *n.* informal clothes, especially tracksuits and other sportswear.

leitmotif /ˈlaɪtməʊˌtiːf/ *n.* (also **leitmotiv**) a recurrent theme associated throughout a musical, literary, etc. composition with a particular person, idea, or situation. [G *Leitmotiv* (as LEAD[1], MOTIVE)]

Leitrim /ˈliːtrɪm/ a county of western Ireland, in the province of Connaught; pop. (est. 1986) 27,000; capital, Carrick-on-Shannon.

lek[1] /lek/ *n.* the chief monetary unit of Albania. [Albanian]

lek[2] /lek/ *n.* a patch of ground used by groups of certain birds during the breeding season as a setting for the males' display and their meeting with the females. [perh. f. Sw. *leka* to play]

Lely /ˈliːlɪ/, Sir Peter (1618–80), portrait painter, born in Germany of Dutch parents and trained at Haarlem in The Netherlands before coming to London in 1643, where he had a large practice by 1650. He became principal court painter to Charles II and attained a high social standing, being knighted in 1680. Many works survive, his early portraits imbued with a Dutch solidity. Less fluent than Van Dyck, he was a flattering if repetitious portraitist whose works mirror the external trappings of royal court life, but with little evidence of psychological insight. He consolidated the tradition of society portrait painting.

LEM *abbr.* lunar excursion module.

leman /ˈlemən/ *n.* (*pl.* **lemans**) *archaic* **1** a lover or sweetheart. **2** an illicit lover, esp. a mistress. [ME *leofman* (as LIEF, MAN)]

Le Mans /lə ˈmɑ̃/ an industrial town of NW France; pop. (1982) 191,000. The town has a motor-racing circuit on which a 24-hour endurance race (established in 1923) for GT and sports cars takes place each summer; since 1928 the winner has been the car that travels farthest in the allotted time.

lemma /ˈlemə/ *n.* **1** an assumed or demonstrated proposition used in an argument or proof. **2 a** a heading indicating the subject or argument of a literary composition, a dictionary entry, etc. **b** (*pl.* **lemmata** /-mətə/) a heading indicating the subject or argument of an annotation. **3** a motto appended to a picture etc. [L f. Gk *lēmma -matos* thing assumed, f. the root of *lambanō* take]

lemme /ˈlemɪ/ *colloq.* let me. [corrupt.]

lemming /ˈlemɪŋ/ *n.* any small arctic rodent of the genus *Lemmus*, esp. *L. lemmus* of Norway which is reputed to rush headlong into the sea and drown during migration. [Norw.]

Lemnos /ˈlemnɒs/ (Greek **Límnos** /ˈliːmnɒs/) a Greek island in the north of the Aegean Sea; capital, Kástron.

lemon /ˈlemən/ *n.* **1 a** a pale-yellow thick-skinned oval citrus fruit with acidic juice. **b** a tree of the species *Citrus limon* which produces this fruit. **2** a pale-yellow colour. **3** *colloq.* a person or thing regarded as feeble or unsatisfactory or disappointing. □ **lemon balm** a bushy plant, *Melissa officinalis*, with leaves smelling and tasting of lemon. **lemon curd** (or **cheese**) a conserve made from lemons, butter, eggs, and sugar, with the consistency of cream cheese. **lemon drop** a boiled sweet flavoured with lemon. **lemon geranium** a lemon-scented pelargonium, *Pelargonium crispum*. **lemon grass** any fragrant tropical grass of the genus *Cymbopogon*, yielding an oil smelling of lemon. **lemon squash** *Brit.* a soft drink made from lemons and other ingredients, often sold in concentrated form. **lemon-squeezer** a device for extracting the juice from a lemon. **lemon thyme** a herb, *Thymus citriodorus*, with lemon-scented leaves used for flavouring. **lemon verbena** (or **plant**) a shrub, *Lippia citriodora*, with lemon-scented leaves. □□ **lemony** *adj.* [ME f. OF *limon* f. Arab. *līma*: cf. LIME²]

lemonade /ˌleməˈneɪd/ *n.* **1** an effervescent or still drink made from lemon juice. **2** a synthetic substitute for this.

lemon sole /ˈlemən/ *n.* a flat-fish, *Microstomus kitt*, of the plaice family. [F *limande*]

lemur /ˈliːmə(r)/ *n.* any arboreal primate of the family Lemuridae native to Madagascar, with a pointed snout and long tail. [mod.L f. L *lemures* (pl.) spirits of the dead, from its spectre-like face]

Lena /ˈliːnə/ a river rising west of Lake Baikal, the most easterly of the three great Siberian rivers flowing to the Arctic Ocean, famous for the gold-fields in its basin.

Lenclos /lɑ̃ˈkləʊ/, Anne de (known as Ninon de Lenclos) (1620–1705), a famous French beauty, who retained her physical attractiveness until an advanced age, numbered many of the great Frenchmen of the day among her lovers, and presided over one of the most distinguished literary salons of the age.

lend /lend/ *v.tr.* (*past* and *past part.* **lent** /lent/) **1** (usu. foll. by *to*) grant (to a person) the use of (a thing) on the understanding that it or its equivalent shall be returned. **2** allow the use of (money) at interest. **3** bestow or contribute (something temporary) (*lend assistance*; *lends a certain charm*). □ **lend an ear** (or **one's ears**) listen. **lend a hand** = *give a hand* (see HAND). **lending library** a library from which books may be temporarily taken away with or *Brit.* without direct payment. **lend itself to** (of a thing) be suitable for. **lend oneself to** accommodate oneself to (a policy or purpose). □□ **lendable** *adj.* **lender** *n.* **lending** *n.* [ME, earlier *lēne(n)* f. OE *lǣnan* f. *lǣn* LOAN¹]

Lendl /ˈlend(ə)l/, Ivan (1960–), American tennis-player, born in Czechoslovakia, who won many championships in the 1980s.

Lend-Lease *n.* an arrangement (1941) whereby the US supplied equipment etc. to the UK and her allies in the Second World War, originally as a loan in return for the use of British-owned military bases.

length /leŋθ, leŋkθ/ *n.* **1** measurement or extent from end to end; the greater of two or the greatest of three dimensions of a body. **2** extent in, of, or with regard to, time (*a stay of some length*; *the length of a speech*). **3** the distance a thing extends (*at arm's length*; *ships a cable's length apart*). **4** the length of a horse, boat, etc., as a measure of the lead in a race. **5** a long stretch or extent (*a length of hair*). **6** a degree of thoroughness in action (*went to great lengths*; *prepared to go to any length*). **7** a piece of material of a certain length (*a length of cloth*). **8** *Prosody* the quantity of a vowel or syllable. **9** *Cricket* **a** the distance from the batsman at

which the ball pitches (*the bowler keeps a good length*). **b** the proper amount of this. **10** the extent of a garment in a vertical direction when worn. **11** the full extent of one's body. □ **at length 1** (also **at full** or **great** etc. **length**) in detail, without curtailment. **2** after a long time, at last. [OE *lengthu* f. Gmc (as LONG¹)]

lengthen /ˈleŋθ(ə)n, ˈleŋkθ(ə)n/ *v.* **1** *tr.* & *intr.* make or become longer. **2** *tr.* make (a vowel) long. □□ **lengthener** *n.*

lengthman /ˈleŋθmən/ *n.* (*pl.* **-men**) *Brit.* a person employed to maintain a section of railway or road.

lengthways /ˈleŋθweɪz, ˈleŋkθ-/ *adv.* in a direction parallel with a thing's length.

lengthwise /ˈleŋθwaɪz, ˈleŋkθ-/ *adv.* & *adj.* —*adv.* lengthways. —*adj.* lying or moving lengthways.

lengthy /ˈleŋθɪ, ˈleŋkθɪ/ *adj.* (**lengthier, lengthiest**) **1** of unusual length. **2** (of speech, writing, style, a speaker, etc.) tedious, prolix. □□ **lengthily** *adv.* **lengthiness** *n.*

lenient /ˈliːnɪənt/ *adj.* **1** merciful, tolerant, not disposed to severity. **2** (of punishment etc.) mild. **3** *archaic* emollient. □□ **lenience** *n.* **leniency** *n.* **leniently** *adv.* [L *lenire lenit-* soothe f. *lenis* gentle]

Lenin /ˈlenɪn/, Nicolai, the assumed name of Vladimir Ilyich Ulyanov (1870–1924), Russian revolutionary statesman. A lawyer by training, Lenin was arrested in 1895 for socialist agitation and was subsequently exiled to Siberia. Living in Switzerland from 1900, he became the leader of the Bolshevik party and took a prominent part in socialist organization and propaganda in the years preceding the First World War. He returned to Russia after the overthrow of the Tsar in 1917 and quickly established Bolshevik control over the revolution, emerging as Premier and virtual dictator of the new communist State. He took Russia out of the war and successfully resisted counter-revolutionary forces in the Russian Civil War (1918–21), but was forced to moderate his socio-economic policies to give the country a chance to recover from the dislocation caused by war and revolution. In 1918 he was severely injured by a would-be assassin, and died in 1924 before he had completed the reconstruction of the Marxist State.

Leninakan /ˌlenɪnəˈkɑːn/ a city in the Soviet republic of Armenia; pop. est. 1983) 218,000. The city (called *Alexandropol* until 1924) was destroyed by an earthquake in 1926 and again in 1988.

Leningrad /ˈlenɪnˌɡræd/ a city of the USSR on an inlet of the Gulf of Finland; pop. (est. 1987) 4,948,000. It was founded in 1703 by Peter the Great as his 'Window on the West', under the name St Petersburg, and was the capital of Russia from then until 1918. It was called Petrograd from 1914 until 1924, when it was renamed after Lenin. During the Second World War it was subjected to a 900-day siege which began in 1941.

Leninism /ˈlenɪˌnɪz(ə)m/ *n.* Marxism as interpreted and applied by Lenin. □□ **Leninist** *n.* & *adj.* **Leninite** *n.* & *adj.*

lenition /liːˈnɪʃ(ə)n/ *n.* (in Celtic languages) the process or result of articulating a consonant softly. [L *lenis* soft, after G *Lenierung*]

lenitive /ˈlenɪtɪv/ *adj.* & *n.* —*adj.* *Med.* soothing. —*n.* **1** *Med.* a soothing drug or appliance. **2** a palliative. [ME f. med.L *lenitivus* (as LENIENT)]

lenity /ˈlenɪtɪ/ *n.* (*pl.* **-ies**) *literary* **1** mercifulness, gentleness. **2** an act of mercy. [F *lénité* or L *lenitas* f. *lenis* gentle]

Lennon /ˈlenən/, John (1940–80), English rock musician, a member of the Beatles (see entry).

leno /ˈliːnəʊ/ *n.* (*pl.* **-os**) an open-work fabric with the warp threads twisted in pairs before weaving. [F *linon* f. *lin* flax f. L *linum*]

Le Nôtre /lə ˈnəʊtr/, André (1613–1700), French landscape gardener who from the 1630s was engaged in design of the grounds of many châteaux and town houses. He designed some of the best examples of formal French gardens, including the parks of Vaux-le-Vicomte and Versailles, begun in 1655 and 1662 respectively. These incorporated his ideas on architecturally conceived garden schemes: geometric formality and perfect equilibrium of all the individual elements—sculpture, fountains, parterres, and open spaces. Le Nôtre's gardens became a part of the architecture, an extension of the châteaux themselves. His influence was felt throughout the Continent and in England, where his style was imitated.

lens /lenz/ n. **1** a piece of a transparent substance with one or (usu.) both sides curved for concentrating or dispersing light-rays esp. in optical instruments. **2** a combination of lenses used in photography. **3** Anat. = crystalline lens. **4** Physics a device for focusing or otherwise modifying the direction of movement of light, sound, electrons, etc. □□ **lensed** adj. **lensless** adj. [L lens lentis lentil (from the similarity of shape)]

Lent /lent/ n. **1** Eccl. the period from Ash Wednesday to Holy Saturday, of which the 40 weekdays are devoted to fasting and penitence in commemoration of Christ's fasting in the wilderness. **2** (in pl.) the boat races held at Cambridge in the Lent term. □ **Lent lily** Brit. a daffodil, esp. a wild one. **Lent term** Brit. the term at a university etc. in which Lent falls. [ME f. LENTEN]

lent past and past part. of LEND.

-lent /lənt/ suffix forming adjectives (pestilent; violent) (cf. -ULENT). [L -lentus -ful]

Lenten /'lent(ə)n/ adj. of, in, or appropriate to, Lent. □ **Lenten fare** food without meat. [orig. as noun, = spring, f. OE lencten f. Gmc, rel. to LONG¹, perh. with ref. to lengthening of the day in spring: now regarded as adj. f. LENT + -EN²]

lenticel /'lentɪˌsel/ n. Bot. any of the raised pores in the stems of woody plants that allow gas exchange between the atmosphere and the internal tissues. [mod.L lenticella dimin. of L lens: see LENS]

lenticular /len'tɪkjʊlə(r)/ adj. **1** shaped like a lentil or a biconvex lens. **2** of the lens of the eye. [L lenticularis (as LENTIL)]

lentil /'lentɪl/ n. **1** a leguminous plant, Lens culinaris, yielding edible biconvex seeds. **2** this seed, esp. used as food with the husk removed. [ME f. OF lentille f. L lenticula (as LENS)]

lento /'lentəʊ/ adj. & adv. Mus. —adj. slow. —adv. slowly. [It.]

lentoid /'lentɔɪd/ adj. = LENTICULAR 1. [L lens (see LENS) + -OID]

Leo¹ /'liːəʊ/ **1** a sickle-shaped constellation, traditionally regarded as contained in the figure of a lion. A rich swarm of meteors (the Leonids) is associated with the constellation when dust from the disintegration of a comet of 1866, which had an orbital period of 33 years, collides with the atmosphere three times a century. **2** the fifth sign of the zodiac (the Lion), which the sun enters about 21 July. —n. (pl. -os) a person born when the sun is in this sign. [OE f. L, = LION]

Leo² /'liːəʊ/ the name of 13 popes:

Leo I, St, 'the Great' (d. 461), pope from 440 and Doctor of the Church. His statement of the doctrine of the Incarnation was accepted at the Council of Chalcedon (451). His greatest achievement was the extension and consolidation of the power of the Roman see, claiming jurisdiction in Africa, Spain, and Gaul. He persuaded the Huns to retire beyond the Danube, and secured concessions from the Vandals when they captured Rome.

Leo X (Giovanni de' Medici, 1475–1521) pope from 1513, who excommunicated Luther and bestowed on Henry VIII of England the title of 'Defender of the Faith'.

Leo³ /'liːəʊ/ the name of 6 Byzantine emperors:

Leo I 'the Great', emperor 457–74.

Leo III (c.680–741), emperor 717–41. Known as 'the Isaurian' after the dynasty which he founded, Leo came to prominence as a soldier before overthrowing Theodosius III and seizing the throne. He threw back several Muslim invasions and carried out an extensive series of financial, legal, administrative, and military reforms, but his iconoclastic policies caused severe problems and led to a complete rupture with the papacy.

León /lei'ɒn/ the second-largest city of Nicaragua; pop. (1985) 101,000.

Leonardo da Vinci /ˌliːəˈnɑːdəʊ dɑː ˈvɪntʃɪ/ (1452–1519), Italian painter and designer, a supreme example of a Renaissance genius, born at Vinci in Tuscany, the illegitimate son of a Florentine notary. He devoted his restlessly curious mind and indefatigable mental energy to a variety of theoretical and practical problems, making studies of flowers, clouds, skeletons, etc., from nature, drawing up plans for a type of aircraft (see HELICOPTER) and a submarine, and anticipating many of the

machines and methods of modern mechanical engineering, and though not always able to see things through to a successful practical conclusion emerged as the most divergent thinker of his period. The most tangible examples of his creative energies are his paintings, although it is unlikely that he saw himself as a full-time artist. A period in Milan (1482–99) saw the execution of three of his great works, the Virgin of the Rocks, the Sforza Monument (never completed), and the Last Supper in the refectory of Sta Maria delle Grazie. He painted the Mona Lisa in Florence (c.1504–5), and his last work was St John (c.1515) an even more enigmatic work than the better-known portrait. He died at Cloux (now Clos-Lucé) in France, having left Italy in 1516 at the invitation of Francis I. The nineteen known sketchbooks and notebooks of Leonardo's work reveal his wide range of interests and bear witness to his place as one who helped to usher in the High Renaissance.

Leonid /'liːənɪd/ n. any of the meteors that seem to radiate from the direction of the constellation Leo (see LEO¹). [L leo (see LEO) leonis + -ID³]

Leonine /'liːəˌnaɪn/ adj. & n. —adj. of Pope Leo; made or invented by Pope Leo. —n. (in pl.) leonine verse. □ **Leonine City** the part of Rome round the Vatican fortified by Pope Leo IV (d. 855). **leonine verse 1** medieval Latin verse in hexameter or elegiac metre with internal rhyme. **2** English verse with internal rhyme. [the name Leo (as LEONINE)]

leonine /'liːəˌnaɪn/ adj. **1** like a lion. **2** of or relating to lions. [ME f. OF leonin -ine or L leoninus f. leo leonis lion]

leopard /'lepəd/ n. (fem. **leopardess** /-dɪs/) **1** any large African or South Asian flesh-eating cat, Panthera pardus, with either a black-spotted yellowish-fawn or all black coat. Also called PANTHER. The name 'leopard' was originally given to the animal now called a cheetah (the 'hunting-leopard') which was thought to be a cross between the lion and a 'pard' or panther (formerly supposed to be a more powerful leopard). The animal varies greatly in size and markings. The black form is widely known as the 'black panther'. **2** Heraldry a lion passant guardant as in the arms of England. **3** (attrib.) spotted like a leopard (leopard moth). □ **leopard's bane** any plant of the genus Doronicum, with large yellow daisy-like flowers. [ME f. OF f. LL f. late Gk leopardos (as LION, PARD)]

Leopold I /'liːəˌpəʊld/ (1790–1865), king of Belgium 1831–65. The fourth son of the Duke of Saxe-Coburg-Saalfield, Leopold was an uncle of Queen Victoria. In 1830 he refused the throne of Greece, but a year later accepted that of newly independent Belgium, reigning peacefully thereafter.

Léopoldville /'liːəˌpəʊldvɪl/ the former name (until 1966) of Kinshasa.

leotard /'liːəˌtɑːd/ n. a close-fitting one-piece garment worn by ballet-dancers, acrobats, etc. [J. Léotard, French trapeze artist d. 1870]

Lepanto /ləˈpæntəʊ/ a strait at the entrance to the Gulf of Corinth, scene of a naval battle (1571) in which the fleet of the Holy League (the papacy, Venice, and Spain) under the command of Don John of Austria defeated a large Turkish fleet, ending for the time being the Turkish naval threat in the Mediterranean.

leper /'lepə(r)/ n. **1** a person suffering from leprosy. **2** a person shunned on moral grounds. [ME, prob. attrib. use of leper leprosy f. OF lepre f. L lepra f. Gk, fem. of lepros scaly f. lepos scale]

lepidopterous /ˌlepɪˈdɒptərəs/ adj. of the order Lepidoptera of insects, with four scale-covered wings often brightly coloured, including butterflies and moths. □□ **lepidopteran** adj. & n. **lepidopterist** n. [Gk lepis -idos scale + pteron wing]

leporine /'lepəˌraɪn/ adj. of or like hares. [L leporinus f. lepus -oris hare]

leprechaun /'leprəˌkɔːn/ n. a small mischievous sprite in Irish folklore. [OIr. luchorpán f. lu small + corp body]

leprosy /'leprəsɪ/ n. **1** a contagious bacterial disease that affects the skin, mucous membranes, and nerves, causing disfigurement and deformities. It is caused by the presence of the bacillus Mycobacterium leprae, first demonstrated by the Norwegian Gerhard Hansen (1841–1912; whence its alternative name Hansen's disease) and is now almost entirely a tropical disease, with many millions of sufferers in Africa and Asia. Common in medieval Europe, it was gradually stamped out by strict isolation and improved hygiene. The disease takes two main forms, of which the more acute malignant type is sometimes fatal. To the layman it was always a disease that created both fear and superstition, but modern methods of treatment are effective if applied in the early stages. Among those who have worked heroically among sufferers are the missionary Father Damien (1840–89) and Albert Schweitzer. **2** moral corruption or contagion. [LEPROUS + -Y³]

leprous /ˈleprəs/ adj. **1** suffering from leprosy. **2** like or relating to leprosy. [ME f. OF f. LL leprosus f. lepra: see LEPER]

lepta pl. of LEPTON¹.

Leptis Magna /ˌleptɪs ˈmægnə/ an ancient seaport and trading centre on the Mediterranean coast of Libya, near Homs. Founded by the Phoenicians (perhaps before 600 BC) it was settled from Carthage and became a Roman colony under Trajan. It was one of the three chief cities of Tripolitania; most of its impressive remains date from the reign of Septimius Severus (c.200), a native of the city.

lepto- /ˈleptəʊ/ comb. form small, narrow. [Gk leptos fine, small, thin, delicate]

leptocephalic /ˌleptəsɪˈfælɪk/ adj. (also **leptocephalous** /-ˈsefələs/) narrow-skulled.

leptodactyl /ˌleptəʊˈdæktɪl/ adj. & n. —adj. having long slender toes. —n. a bird having these.

lepton¹ /ˈlept(ə)n/ n. (pl. **lepta** /-tə/) a Greek coin worth one-hundredth of a drachma. [Gk lepton (nomisma coin) neut. of leptos small]

lepton² /ˈleptɒn/ n. (pl. **leptons**) Physics any of a class of elementary particles which do not undergo strong interaction, e.g. an electron, muon, or neutrino. [LEPTO- + -ON]

leptospirosis /ˌleptəspɪˈrəʊsɪs/ n. an infectious disease caused by bacteria of the genus Leptospira, that occurs in rodents, dogs, and other mammals, and can be transmitted to man. [LEPTO- + SPIRO-¹ + -OSIS]

leptotene /ˈleptəˌtiːn/ n. Biol. the first stage of the prophase of meiosis in which each chromosome is apparent as two fine chromatids. [LEPTO- + Gk tainia band]

Lesage /ləˈsɑːʒ/, Alain-René (1668–1747), French novelist and playwright, whose masterpiece is the picaresque novel Gil Blas (1715–35).

lesbian /ˈlezbɪən/ n. & adj. —n. a homosexual woman. —adj. **1** of homosexuality in women. **2** (**Lesbian**) of Lesbos. □□ **lesbianism** n. [L Lesbius f. Gk Lesbios f. LESBOS, home of the reputedly homosexual Sappho]

Lesbos /ˈlezbɒs/ (Greek **Lésvos** /ˈlezvɒs/) the largest of the Greek islands, lying off the western coast of Turkey, whose artistic Golden Age of the late 7th and early 6th c. BC produced the poets Alcaeus and Sappho. The chief town of modern Lesbos is Mytilene.

lese-majesty /liːz ˈmædʒɪstɪ/ n. (also **lèse-majesté** /leɪz ˈmæʒeˌsteɪ/) **1** treason. **2** an insult to a sovereign or ruler. **3** presumptuous conduct. [F lèse-majesté f. L laesa majestas injured sovereignty f. laedere laes- injure + majestas MAJESTY]

lesion /ˈliːʒ(ə)n/ n. **1** damage. **2** injury. **3** Med. a morbid change in the functioning or texture of an organ etc. [ME f. OF f. L laesio -onis f. laedere laes- injure]

Lesotho /ləˈsuːtuː/ a landlocked mountainous country, a member State of the Commonwealth with few natural resources (though diamonds are found), forming an enclave in the republic of South Africa; pop. (est. 1988) 1,666,000; official languages, Sesotho and English; capital, Maseru. The country came under British protection (as Basutoland) in 1868, and became an independent kingdom in 1966, changing its name to Lesotho.

less /les/ adj., adv., n., & prep. —adj. **1** smaller in extent, degree, duration, number, etc. (of less importance; in a less degree). **2** of smaller quantity, not so much (opp. MORE) (find less difficulty; eat less meat). **3** disp. fewer (eat less biscuits). **4** of lower rank etc. (no less a person than; James the Less). —adv. to a smaller extent, in a lower degree. —n. a smaller amount or quantity or number

(cannot take less; for less than £10; is little less than disgraceful). —prep. minus (made £1,000 less tax). □ **in less than no time** joc. very quickly or soon. **much** (or **still**) **less** with even greater force of denial (do not suspect him of negligence, much less of dishonesty). [OE læssa (adj.), læs (adv.), f. Gmc]

-less /lɪs/ suffix forming adjectives and adverbs: **1** from nouns, meaning 'not having, without, free from' (doubtless; powerless). **2** from verbs, meaning 'not affected by or doing the action of the verb' (fathomless; tireless). □□ **-lessly** suffix forming adverbs. **-lessness** suffix forming nouns. [OE -lēas f. lēas devoid of]

lessee /leˈsiː/ n. (often foll. by of) a person who holds a property by lease. □□ **lesseeship** n. [ME f. AF past part., OF lessé (as LEASE)]

lessen /ˈles(ə)n/ v.tr. & intr. make or become less, diminish.

Lesseps /leˈseps/, Ferdinand Marie, Vicomte de (1805–94), French diplomat, best known for his work on the Suez Canal. He spent several years in Egypt in the French consular service, and becoming aware of plans to join the Mediterranean and Red Seas by means of a sea level canal without locks, from 1854 onwards devoted his skills to the project. Digging by Egyptian labourers began in 1859 but was slow until 1863 when machine dredgers were brought into use and enabled the canal to be opened with great ceremony in 1869. Ten years later he became involved in the building of the Panama Canal, but not being an engineer he did not realize the difficulties of this very different enterprise, which involves raising the level of the canal by huge locks to cross the mountainous isthmus. This and the incidence of yellow fever caused abandonment of the project in 1888 and the Panama Canal was not built until 1912, well after de Lesseps' death.

lesser /ˈlesə(r)/ adj. (usu. attrib.) not so great as the other or the rest (the lesser evil; the lesser celandine). [double compar., f. LESS + -ER³]

Lessing¹ /ˈlesɪŋ/, Doris (May) (1919–), English novelist and short-story writer, brought up in Southern Rhodesia (now Zimbabwe). Her most substantial work, the novel sequence Children of Darkness (1952–69), reflects her preoccupation with feminism and left-wing politics.

Lessing² /ˈlesɪŋ/, Gotthold Ephraim (1729–81), German dramatist and critic. His principal dramatic works were the tragedies Emilia Galotti (1772) and Miss Sara Sampson (1755), the first significant domestic tragedy in German, the serious comedy Minna von Barnhelm (1767), and Nathan der Weise (1779), a plea for religious toleration. In his critical works, such as Briefe die neueste Litteratur betreffend (1759–65) and Laokoon (1766), he emancipated German literature from the narrow conventions of the French classical school. Lessing won the admiration of many 19th-c. English writers for his mundane and liberal beliefs and the clarity of his prose.

lesson /ˈles(ə)n/ n. & v. —n. **1 a** an amount of teaching given at one time. **b** the time assigned to this. **2** (in pl.; foll. by in) systematic instruction (gives lessons in dancing; took lessons in French). **3** a thing learnt or to be learnt by a pupil. **4 a** an occurrence, example, rebuke, or punishment, that serves or should serve to warn or encourage (let that be a lesson to you). **b** a thing inculcated by experience or study. **5** a passage from the Bible read aloud during a church service, esp. either of two readings at morning and evening prayer in the Church of England. —v.tr. archaic **1** instruct. **2** admonish, rebuke. □ **learn one's lesson** profit from or bear in mind a particular (usu. unpleasant) experience. **teach a person a lesson** punish a person, esp. as a deterrent. [ME f. OF leçon f. L lectio -onis: see LECTION]

lessor /leˈsɔː(r)/ n. a person who lets a property by lease. [AF f. lesser: see LEASE]

lest /lest/ conj. **1** in order that not, for fear that (lest we forget). **2** that (afraid lest we should be late). [OE thȳ læs the whereby less that, later the læste, ME lest(e)]

Lésvos see LESBOS.

let¹ /let/ v. & n. —v. (**letting**; past and past part. **let**) **1** tr. **a** allow to, not prevent or forbid (we let them go). **b** cause to (let me know; let it be known). **2** tr. (foll. by into) **a** allow to enter. **b** make acquainted with (a secret etc.). **c** inlay in. **3** tr. Brit. grant the use of (rooms, land, etc.) for rent or hire (*was let to the new tenant for a year*). **4** *tr.* allow or cause (liquid or air) to escape (*let blood*). **5** *tr.* award (a contract for work). **6** *aux.* supplying the first and third persons of the imperative in exhortations (*let us pray*), commands (*let it be done at once; let there be light*), assumptions (*let AB be equal to CD*), and permission or challenge (*let him do his worst*). —*n. Brit.* the act or an instance of letting a house, room, etc. (*a long let*). □ **let alone 1** not to mention, far less or more (*hasn't got a television, let alone a video*). **2** = **let be. let be** not interfere with, attend to, or do. **let down 1** lower. **2** fail to support or satisfy, disappoint. **3** lengthen (a garment). **4** deflate (a tyre). **let-down** *n.* a disappointment. **let down gently** avoid humiliating abruptly. **let drop** (or **fall**) **1** drop (esp. a word or hint) intentionally or by accident. **2** (foll. by *on, upon, to*) *Geom.* draw (a perpendicular) from an outside point to a line. **let fly 1** (often foll. by *at*) attack physically or verbally. **2** discharge (a missile). **let go 1** release, set at liberty. **2 a** (often foll. by *of*) lose or relinquish one's hold. **b** lose hold of. **3** cease to think or talk about. **let oneself go 1** give way to enthusiasm, impulse, etc. **2** cease to take trouble, neglect one's appearance or habits. **let in 1** allow to enter (*let the dog in; let in a flood of light; this would let in all sorts of evils*). **2** (usu. foll. by *for*) involve (a person, often oneself) in loss or difficulty. **3** (foll. by *on*) allow (a person) to share privileges, information, etc. **4** inlay (a thing) in another. **let oneself in** enter a building by means of a latchkey. **let loose** release or unchain (a dog, fury, a maniac, etc.). **let me see** see SEE¹. **let off 1 a** fire (a gun). **b** explode (a bomb or firework). **2** allow or cause (steam, liquid, etc.) to escape. **3** allow to alight from a vehicle etc. **4 a** not punish or compel. **b** (foll. by *with*) punish lightly. **5** *Brit.* let (part of a house etc.). **let-off** *n.* being allowed to escape something. **let off steam** see STEAM. **let on** *colloq.* **1** reveal a secret. **2** pretend (*let on that he had succeeded*). **let out 1** allow to go out, esp. through a doorway. **2** release from restraint. **3** (often foll. by *that* + clause) reveal (a secret etc.). **4** make (a garment) looser esp. by adjustment at a seam. **5** put out to rent esp. to several tenants, or to contract. **6** exculpate. **let-out** *n. colloq.* an opportunity to escape. **let rip** see RIP¹. **let slip** see SLIP¹. **let through** allow to pass. **let up** *colloq.* **1** become less intense or severe. **2** relax one's efforts. **let-up** *n. colloq.* **1** a reduction in intensity. **2** a relaxation of effort. **to let** available for rent. [OE *lǣtan* f. Gmc, rel. to LATE]

let² /let/ *n.* & *v.* —*n.* **1** (in lawn tennis, squash, etc.) an obstruction of a ball or a player in certain ways, requiring the ball to be served again. **2** (*archaic* except in **without let or hindrance**) obstruction, hindrance. —*v.tr.* (**letting**; *past* and *past part.* **letted** or **let**) *archaic* hinder, obstruct. [OE *lettan* f. Gmc, rel. to LATE]

-let /lɪt, lət/ *suffix* forming nouns, usu. diminutives (*flatlet, leaflet*) or denoting articles of ornament or dress (*anklet*). [orig. corresp. (in *bracelet, crosslet,* etc.) to F *-ette* added to nouns in *-el*]

lethal /ˈliːθ(ə)l/ *adj.* causing or sufficient to cause death. □ **lethal chamber** a chamber in which animals may be killed painlessly with gas. **lethal dose** the amount of a toxic compound or drug that causes death in humans or animals. □□ **lethality** /lɪˈθælɪtɪ/ *n.* **lethally** *adv.* [L *let(h)alis* f. *letum* death]

lethargy /ˈleθədʒɪ/ *n.* **1** lack of energy or vitality; a torpid, inert, or apathetic state. **2** *Med.* morbid drowsiness or prolonged and unnatural sleep. □□ **lethargic** /lɪˈθɑːdʒɪk/ *adj.* **lethargically** /lɪ ˈθɑːdʒɪkəlɪ/ *adv.* [ME f. OF *litargie* f. LL *lethargia* f. Gk *lēthargia* f. *lēthargos* forgetful f. *lēth-, lanthanomai* forget]

Lethe /ˈliːθiː/ *Gk Mythol.* one of the rivers of the underworld, whose water when drunk made the souls of the dead forget their life on earth. —*n.* forgetfulness of the past. □□ **Lethean** /liːˈθiːən/ *adj.* [L, use of Gk *lēthē* forgetfulness (as LETHARGY)]

Leticia /ləˈtiːsɪə/ a town and river port of Colombia, on the upper reaches of the Amazon; pop. (1985) 19,250.

Leto /ˈliːtəʊ/ *Gk Mythol.* the daughter of a Titan, mother (by Zeus) of Artemis and Apollo.

let's /lets/ *contr.* let us (*let's go now*).

Lett /let/ *n. archaic* = LATVIAN *n.* [G *Lette* f. Lettish *Latvi*]

letter /ˈletə(r)/ *n.* & *v.* —*n.* **1 a** a character representing one or more of the simple or compound sounds used in speech, any of the alphabetic symbols. **b** (in *pl.*) *colloq.* the initials of a degree

etc. after the holder's name. **c** *US* a school or college initial as a mark of proficiency in games etc. **2 a** a written, typed, or printed communication, usu. sent by post or messenger. **b** (in *pl.*) an addressed legal or formal document for any of various purposes. **3** the precise terms of a statement, the strict verbal interpretation (opp. SPIRIT *n.* 6) (*according to the letter of the law*). **4** (in *pl.*) **a** literature. **b** acquaintance with books, erudition. **c** authorship (*the profession of letters*). **5** *Printing* **a** types collectively. **b** a fount of type. —*v. tr.* **1 a** inscribe letters on. **b** impress a title etc. on (a book-cover). **2** classify with letters. □ **letter-bomb** a terrorist explosive device in the form of a postal packet. **letter-box** esp. *Brit.* a box or slot into which letters are posted or delivered. **letter-card** a folded card with a gummed edge for posting as a letter. **letter-heading** = LETTERHEAD. **letter of comfort** an assurance about a debt, short of a legal guarantee, given to a bank by a third party. **letter of credence** see CREDENCE. **letter of credit** see CREDIT. **letter-perfect** *Theatr.* knowing one's part perfectly. **letter-quality** of the quality of printing suitable for a business letter; producing print of this quality. **letters missive** see MISSIVE. **letters of administration** authority to administer the estate of an intestate. **letters of marque** see MARQUE². **letters patent** see PATENT. **letter-writer 1** a person who writes letters. **2** a book giving guidance on writing letters. **man of letters** a scholar or author. **to the letter** with adherence to every detail. □□ **letterer** *n.* **letterless** *adj.* [ME f. OF *lettre* f. L *litera, littera* letter of alphabet, (in *pl.*) epistle, literature]

lettered /ˈletəd/ *adj.* well read or educated.

letterhead /ˈletəˌhed/ *n.* **1** a printed heading on stationery. **2** stationery with this.

lettering /ˈletərɪŋ/ *n.* **1** the process of inscribing letters. **2** letters inscribed.

letterpress /ˈletəˌpres/ *n.* **1 a** the contents of an illustrated book other than the illustrations. **b** printed matter relating to illustrations. **2** printing from raised type, not from lithography or other planographic processes.

Lettic /ˈletɪk/ *adj.* & *n. archaic* —*adj.* **1** = LATVIAN *adj.* **2** of or relating to the Baltic group of languages. —*n.* **1** = LATVIAN *n.* 2.

Lettish /ˈletɪʃ/ *adj.* & *n. archaic* = LATVIAN.

lettuce /ˈletɪs/ *n.* **1** a composite plant, *Lactuca sativa*, with crisp edible leaves used in salads. **2** any of various plants resembling this. [ME *letus(e)*, rel. to OF *laitue* f. L *lactuca* f. *lac lactis* milk, with ref. to its milky juice]

leu /ˈleɪuː/ *n.* (*pl.* **lei** /leɪ/) the basic monetary unit of Romania. [Romanian, = lion]

leucine /ˈluːsiːn/ *n. Biochem.* an amino acid present in protein and essential in the diet of vertebrates. [F f. Gk *leukos* white + -IN]

leuco- /ˈluːkəʊ/ *comb. form* white. [Gk *leukos* white]

leucocyte /ˈluːkəˌsaɪt/ *n.* (also **leukocyte**) **1** a white blood cell. **2** any blood cell that contains a nucleus. □□ **leucocytic** /-ˈsɪtɪk/ *adj.*

leucoma /luːˈkəʊmə/ *n.* a white opacity in the cornea of the eye.

leucorrhoea /ˌluːkəˈriːə/ *n.* a whitish or yellowish discharge of mucus from the vagina.

leucotomy /luːˈkɒtəmɪ/ *n.* (*pl.* **-ies**) the surgical lesions of white nerve fibres within the brain, formerly used in psychosurgery.

leukaemia /luːˈkiːmɪə/ *n.* (*US* **leukemia**) *Med.* any of a group of malignant diseases in which the bone-marrow and other blood-forming organs produce increased numbers of leucocytes. □□ **leukaemic** *adj.* [mod.L f. G *Leukämie* f. Gk *leukos* white + *haima* blood]

leukocyte var. of LEUCOCYTE.

Leuven /ˈlɜːv(ə)n/ (French **Louvain** /ˈluːvæ̃/) a town in Belgium, in the province of Brabant, with a university (founded in 1425) that is the oldest in Belgium; pop. (1988) 84,180.

Lev. *abbr.* Leviticus (Old Testament).

Levalloisean /ˌləvælˈwɑːzɪən/ *adj.* & *n.* —*adj.* of a flint-working technique first employed in the late Acheulian period in western Europe and associated with numerous Mousterian industries throughout the world, named after the type-site of Levallois in northern France, NW of Paris. The technique involves trimming a piece of flint and then striking the required flake from it; the flake produced has one face trimmed and the other plane, and the residual core is tortoise-shaped, domed with one face plane. —*n.* this industry.

Levant /lɪˈvænt/ *n.* (prec. by *the*) the eastern part of the Mediterranean with its islands and neighbouring countries. □ **Levant morocco** high-grade large-grained morocco leather. [F, pres. part. of *lever* rise, used as noun = point of sunrise, east]

levant /lɪˈvænt/ *v.intr. Brit.* abscond or bolt, esp. with betting or gaming losses unpaid. [perh. f. LEVANT]

levanter[1] /lɪˈvæntə(r)/ *n.* **1** a strong easterly Mediterranean wind. **2** (**Levanter**) a native or inhabitant of the Levant in the eastern Mediterranean.

levanter[2] /lɪˈvæntə(r)/ *n.* a person who levants.

Levantine /lɪˈvæntaɪn, ˈlevən-/ *adj. & n.* —*adj.* of or trading to the Levant. —*n.* a native or inhabitant of the Levant.

levator /lɪˈveɪtə(r)/ *n.* a muscle that lifts the structure into which it is inserted. [L, = one who lifts f. *levare* raise]

levee[1] /ˈlevɪ/ *n.* **1** *archaic* or *US* an assembly of visitors or guests, esp. at a formal reception. **2** *hist.* (in the UK) an assembly held by the sovereign or sovereign's representative at which men only were received. **3** *hist.* a reception of visitors on rising from bed. [F *levé* var. of *lever* rising f. *lever* to rise: see LEVY]

levee[2] /ˈlevɪ, lɪˈviː/ *n. US* **1** an embankment against river floods. **2** a natural embankment built up by a river. **3** a landing-place, a quay. [F *levée* fem. past part. of *lever* raise: see LEVY]

level /ˈlev(ə)l/ *n., adj., & v.* —*n.* **1** a horizontal line or plane. **2** a height or value reached, a position on a real or imaginary scale (*eye level; sugar level in the blood; danger level*). **3** a social, moral, or intellectual standard. **4** a plane of rank or authority (*discussions at Cabinet level*). **5 a** an instrument giving a line parallel to the plane of the horizon for testing whether things are horizontal. **b** *Surveying* an instrument for giving a horizontal line of sight. **6** a more or less level surface. **7** a flat tract of land. —*adj.* **1** having a flat and even surface; not bumpy. **2** horizontal; perpendicular to the plumb-line. **3** (often foll. by *with*) **a** on the same horizontal plane as something else. **b** having equality with something else. **c** (of a spoonful etc.) with the contents flat with the brim. **4** even, uniform, equable, or well-balanced in quality, style, temper, judgement, etc. **5** (of a race) having the leading competitors close together. —*v.* (**levelled, levelling**; *US* **leveled, leveling**) **1** *tr.* make level, even, or uniform. **2** *tr.* (often foll. by *to* or *with*) the ground, in the dust) raze or demolish. **3** *tr.* (also *absol.*) aim (a missile or gun). **4** *tr.* (also *absol.*; foll. by *at, against*) direct (an accusation, criticism, or satire). **5** *tr.* abolish (distinctions). **6** *intr.* (usu. foll. by *with*) *sl.* be frank or honest. **7** *tr.* place on the same level. **8** *tr.* (also *absol.*) *Surveying* ascertain differences in the height of (land). □ **do one's level best** *colloq.* do one's utmost; make all possible efforts. **find one's level 1** reach the right social, intellectual, etc. place in relation to others. **2** (of a liquid) reach the same height in receptacles or regions which communicate with each other. **level crossing** *Brit.* a crossing of a railway and a road, or two railways, at the same level. **level down** bring down to a standard. **levelling-screw** a screw for adjusting parts of a machine etc. to an exact level. **level off** make or become level or smooth. **level out** make or become level, remove differences from. **level pegging** *Brit.* equality of scores or achievements. **level up** bring up to a standard. **on the level** *colloq. adv.* honestly, without deception. —*adj.* honest, truthful. **on a level with** in the same horizontal plane as. **2** equal with. □□ **levelly** *adv.* **levelness** *n.* [ME f. OF *livel* ult. f. L *libella* dimin. of *libra* scales, balance]

level-headed /ˌlev(ə)lˈhedɪd/ *adj.* mentally well-balanced, cool, sensible. □□ **level-headedly** *adv.* **level-headedness** *n.*

leveller /ˈlevələ(r)/ *n.* (*US* **leveler**) **1** a person who advocates the abolition of social distinctions. **2** (**Leveller**) *hist.* an extreme radical dissenter in 17th-c. England. **3** a person or thing that levels.

lever /ˈliːvə(r)/ *n. & v.* —*n.* **1** a bar resting on a pivot, used to help lift a heavy or firmly fixed object. **2** *Mech.* a simple machine consisting of a rigid bar pivoted about a fulcrum (fixed point)

which can be acted upon by a force (effort) in order to move a load. It is the simplest, oldest, and most adaptable of mechanisms. **3** a projecting handle moved to operate a mechanism. **4** a means of exerting moral pressure. —*v.* **1** *intr.* use a lever. **2** *tr.* (often foll. by *away, out, up,* etc.) lift, move, or act on with a lever. □ **lever escapement** a mechanism connecting the escape wheel and the balance wheel using two levers. **lever watch** a watch with a lever escapement. [ME f. OF *levier, leveor* f. *lever* raise: see LEVY]

leverage /ˈliːvərɪdʒ/ *n.* **1** the action of a lever; a way of applying a lever. **2** the power of a lever; the mechanical advantage gained by use of a lever. **3** a means of accomplishing a purpose; power, influence. **4** a set or system of levers. **5** *US Commerce* gearing. □ **leveraged buyout** esp. *US* the buyout of a company by its management using outside capital.

leveret /ˈlevərɪt/ *n.* a young hare, esp. one in its first year. [ME f. AF, dimin. of *levre,* OF *lievre* f. L *lepus leporis* hare]

Leverhulme /ˈliːvəˌhjuːm/, William Hesketh Lever, 1st Viscount (1851–1925), English industrialist who, with his brother, started the manufacture of soap from vegetable oil (instead of tallow) under the trade name Sunlight. By 1888 the success of their enterprise enabled them to begin building the factory centre at Port Sunlight in Cheshire, on the River Mersey, with model housing for the workers, for whom they also introduced medical care, pensions, and a form of profit-sharing. In the 20th c. Lever Bros. expanded by mergers and purchase and came to form the basis of the international corporation Unilever.

Le Verrier /lə ˈverjeɪ/, Urbain (1811–77), French mathematician whose analysis of the motions of the planets suggested that an unknown body was perturbing the orbit of Uranus (the same conclusion was reached almost simultaneously by the English mathematician John Couch Adams). Under the prompting of Le Verrier, the German astronomer Galle searched the region of the sky in which the mysterious perturber was predicted to lie, and discovered the planet Neptune on 23 Sept. 1846.

Levi[1] /ˈliːvaɪ/ **1** a Hebrew patriarch, son of Jacob and Leah (Gen. 29: 34). **2** the tribe of Israel traditionally descended from him.

Levi[2] /ˈliːvɪ/, Peter Chad Tigar (1931–   ), English poet, classical scholar, and travel writer, whose poems mingle imagery and themes from classical antiquity, British history, Christianity, and domestic life.

leviable see LEVY.

leviathan /lɪˈvaɪəθ(ə)n/ *n.* **1** *Bibl.* a sea-monster. **2** anything very large or powerful, esp. a ship. **3** an autocratic monarch or State (in allusion to a book by Hobbes, 1651). [ME f. LL f. Heb. *liwyāṯān*]

levigate /ˈlevɪˌgeɪt/ *v.tr.* **1** reduce to a fine smooth powder. **2** make a smooth paste of. □□ **levigation** /-ˈgeɪʃ(ə)n/ *n.* [L *levigare levigat-* f. *levis* smooth]

levin /ˈlevɪn/ *n. archaic* **1** lightning. **2** a flash of lightning. [ME *leven(e),* prob. f. ON]

levirate /ˈliːvɪrət, ˈlev-/ *n.* a custom of the ancient Jews and some other peoples by which a man is obliged to marry his brother's widow. □□ **leviratic** /-ˈrætɪk/ *adj.* **leviratical** /-ˈrætɪk(ə)l/ *adj.* [L *levir* brother-in-law + -ATE[1]]

Levis /ˈliːvaɪz/ *n.pl. propr.* a type of (orig. blue) denim jeans or overalls reinforced with rivets. [*Levi* Strauss, orig. *US* manufacturer in 1860s]

Lévi-Strauss /ˌleɪvɪˈstraʊs/, Claude (1908–   ), French social anthropologist, a leading exponent of structuralism in his analysis of cultural systems. He is noted also for his study of myth.

levitate /ˈlevɪteɪt/ *v.* **1** *intr.* rise and float in the air (esp. with reference to spiritualism). **2** *tr.* cause to do this. □□ **levitation** /-ˈteɪʃ(ə)n/ *n.* **levitator** *n.* [L *levis* light, after GRAVITATE]

Levite /ˈliːvaɪt/ *n.* a member of the Hebrew tribe of Levi, from which priests were drawn until after the Exile, when Levites were allotted only inferior duties in the Temple. [ME f. LL *levita* f. Gk *leuitēs* f. *Leui* f. Heb. *lēwî* Levi]

Levitical /lɪˈvɪtɪk(ə)l/ *adj.* **1** of the Levites or the tribe of Levi. **2** of the Levites' ritual. **3** of Leviticus. [LL *leviticus* f. Gk *leuitikos* (as LEVITE)]

æ cat ɑː arm e bed ɜː her ɪ sit iː see ɒ hot ɔː saw ʌ run ʊ put uː too ə ago aɪ my

Leviticus /lɪˈvɪtɪkəs/ the third book of the Old Testament, containing details of laws and ritual. [L, = (book) of the Levites]

levity /ˈlevɪtɪ/ n. 1 lack of serious thought, frivolity, unbecoming jocularity. 2 inconstancy. 3 undignified behaviour. 4 archaic lightness of weight. [L levitas f. levis light]

levo- US var. of LAEVO-.

levodopa /ˌliːvəˈdəʊpə/ n. laevorotatory dopa (see DOPA).

levulose US var. of LAEVULOSE.

levy /ˈlevɪ/ v. & n. —v.tr. (-ies, -ied) 1 a impose (a rate or toll). b raise (contributions or taxes). c (also absol.) raise (a sum of money) by legal execution or process (the debt was levied on the debtor's goods). d seize (goods) in this way. e extort (levy blackmail). 2 enlist or enrol (troops etc.). 3 (usu. foll. by upon, against) wage, proceed to make (war). —n. (pl. -ies) 1 a the collecting of a contribution, tax, etc., or of property to satisfy a legal judgement. b a contribution, tax, etc., levied. 2 a the act or an instance of enrolling troops etc. b (in pl.) men enrolled. c a body of men enrolled. d the number of men enrolled. □□ **leviable** adj. [ME f. OF levee fem. past part. of lever f. L levare raise f. levis light]

lewd /ljuːd/ adj. 1 lascivious. 2 indecent, obscene. □□ **lewdly** adv. **lewdness** n. [OE lǣwede LAY², of unkn. orig.]

Lewis¹ /ˈluːɪs/ the northern part of the northernmost and largest island (Lewis with Harris) of the Western Isles of Scotland.

Lewis² /ˈluːɪs/, Clive Staples (1898–1963), English literary scholar who taught at Oxford University from 1925 to 1954 and then held a chair of English at Cambridge until 1963. His works include science fiction, and he became celebrated for his books of popular Christian apologetics, including The Screwtape Letters (1942), and his series of fantasies for children about the imaginary country of 'Narnia'.

Lewis³ /ˈluːɪs/, Meriwether (1774–1809), American explorer. Formerly private secretary to President Jefferson, he was named by the President to lead an expedition to explore the newly acquired Louisiana Purchase, and chose William Clark as co-leader. Between 1804 and 1806 the Lewis and Clark Expedition successfully crossed America from St Louis to the mouth of the Columbia River and returned (once again by land). During the last two years of his life (1807–9) Lewis served as Governor of the Louisiana Territory.

Lewis⁴ /ˈluːɪs/, Percy Wyndham (1882–1957), British novelist and painter, a leader of the vorticist movement, who with Ezra Pound edited the journal Blast (1914–15). His satirical novels and polemical works include The Apes of God (1930), The Revenge for Love (1937), and The Human Age (1928–55, unfinished). He expounds his philosophical ideas in Time and the Western World (1927) and in his two autobiographies (1937, 1950). Critical of the increasing mechanization and hollowness of 20th-c. civilization, his savage satirical attacks on his contemporaries (especially the Bloomsbury Group), and his sympathies with Fascism and Hitler, alienated him from the literary world.

Lewis⁵ /ˈluːɪs/, (Harry) Sinclair (1885–1951), American novelist, who became highly successful with Main Street (1920), a social satire on dull small-town Mid-West life. He strengthened his reputation with Babbitt (1922), about a Mid-West house agent who questions conventions in middle-class society, Arrowsmith (1925), describing the career of a bacteriologist, Elmer Gantry (1927), a satiric view of Mid-West religious evangelism, and Dodsworth (1929). He was awarded the Nobel Prize for literature in 1930, the first American writer to achieve this.

lewis /ˈluːɪs/ n. an iron contrivance for gripping heavy blocks of stone or concrete for lifting. [18th c.: orig. unkn.]

Lewis gun /ˈluːɪs/ n. a light machine-gun with a magazine, air cooling, and operation by gas from its own firing. [I. N. Lewis, Amer. soldier d. 1931, its inventor]

lewisite /ˈluːɪˌsaɪt/ n. an irritant gas that produces blisters, developed for use in chemical warfare. [W. L. Lewis, Amer. chemist d. 1943 + -ITE¹]

lex domicilii /ˌleks dɒmɪˈsɪlɪˌaɪ/ n. Law the law of the country in which a person is domiciled. [L]

lexeme /ˈleksiːm/ n. Linguistics a basic lexical unit of a language comprising one or several words, the elements of which do not separately convey the meaning of the whole. [LEXICON + -EME]

lex fori /leks ˈfɔːraɪ/ n. Law the law of the country in which an action is brought. [L]

lexical /ˈleksɪk(ə)l/ adj. 1 of the words of a language. 2 of or as of a lexicon. □□ **lexically** adv. [Gk lexikos, lexikon: see LEXICON]

lexicography /ˌleksɪˈkɒɡrəfɪ/ n. the compiling of dictionaries. □□ **lexicographer** n. **lexicographic** /-kəˈɡræfɪk/ adj. **lexicographical** /-kəˈɡræfɪk(ə)l/ adj. **lexicographically** /-kəˈɡræfɪkəlɪ/ adv.

lexicology /ˌleksɪˈkɒlədʒɪ/ n. the study of the form, history, and meaning of words. □□ **lexicological** /-kəˈlɒdʒɪk(ə)l/ adj. **lexicologically** /-kəˈlɒdʒɪkəlɪ/ adv. **lexicologist** n.

lexicon /ˈleksɪkən/ n. 1 a dictionary, esp. of Greek, Hebrew, Syriac, or Arabic. Until the 19th c. dictionaries of these languages were usually in Latin and entitled lexicon rather than dictionarius. 2 the vocabulary of a person, language, branch of knowledge, etc. [mod.L f. Gk lexikon (biblion book), neut. of lexikos f. lexis word f. legō speak]

lexigraphy /lekˈsɪɡrəfɪ/ n. a system of writing in which each character represents a word. [Gk lexis (see LEXICON) + -GRAPHY]

Lexington /ˈleksɪŋt(ə)n/ a residential town close to Boston, Mass., the scene in 1775 of the first battle in the War of American Independence; pop. (1980) 29,500.

lexis /ˈleksɪs/ n. 1 words, vocabulary. 2 the total stock of words in a language. [Gk: see LEXICON]

lex loci /leks ˈləʊsaɪ/ n. Law the law of the country in which a transaction is performed, a tort is committed, or a property is situated. [L]

lex talionis /ˌleks tælɪˈəʊnɪs/ n. the law of retaliation, whereby a punishment resembles the offence committed, in kind and degree. [L]

ley¹ /leɪ/ n. a field temporarily under grass. □ **ley farming** alternate growing of crops and grass. [ME (orig. adj.), perh. f. OE, rel. to LAY¹, LIE¹]

ley² /liː, leɪ/ n. the supposed straight line of a prehistoric track, usu. between hilltops. [var. of LEA]

Leyden /ˈleɪd(ə)n/ see LEIDEN. □ **Leyden jar** a kind of electrical condenser with a glass jar as a dielectric between sheets of tin foil, invented in 1745 at Leyden University.

Leyte /ˈleɪtɪ/ an island in the central Philippines; pop. (1980) 1,302,650. Tacloban and Ormoc are the chief towns.

LF abbr. low frequency.

LH abbr. Biochem. luteinizing hormone.

l.h. abbr. left hand.

Lhasa /ˈlɑːsə/ the capital of the Autonomous Region of Tibet in SW China, situated in the Himalayas at 3,600 m (c.11,800 ft.); pop. (est. 1986) 310,000. Its inaccessibility and the hostility of the Tibetan Buddhist priests to foreign visitors earned it the title of the Forbidden City. It was the spiritual centre of Lamaism and the seat (until 1959) of the Dalai Lama.

LI abbr. 1 Light Infantry. 2 US Long Island.

Li symb. Chem. the element lithium.

liability /ˌlaɪəˈbɪlɪtɪ/ n. (pl. -ies) 1 the state of being liable. 2 a person or thing that is troublesome as an unwelcome responsibility; a handicap. 3 what a person is liable for, esp. (in pl.) debts or pecuniary obligations.

liable /ˈlaɪəb(ə)l/ predic.adj. 1 legally bound. 2 (foll. by to) subject to (a tax or penalty). 3 (foll. by to + infin.) under an obligation. 4 (foll. by to) exposed or open to (something undesirable). 5 (foll. by to + infin.) disp. apt, likely (it is liable to rain). 6 (foll. by for) answerable. [ME perh. f. AF f. OF lier f. L ligare bind]

liaise /lɪˈeɪz/ v.intr. (foll. by with, between) colloq. establish cooperation, act as a link. [back-form. f. LIAISON]

liaison /lɪˈeɪzɒn/ n. 1 communication or cooperation, esp. between military forces or units. 2 an illicit sexual relationship. 3 the binding or thickening agent of a sauce. 4 the sounding of an ordinarily silent final consonant before a word beginning with a vowel (or a mute h in French). □ **liaison officer** an officer acting as a link between allied forces or units of the same force. [F f. lier bind f. L ligare]

liana /lɪˈɑːnə/ n. (also **liane** /-ˈɑːn/) any of several climbing and twining plants of tropical forests. [F *liane*, *lierne* clematis, of uncert. orig.]

Liaoning /ˌliːaʊˈnɪŋ/ a province of NE China; pop. (est. 1986) 37,260,000; capital, Shenyang.

liar /ˈlaɪə(r)/ n. a person who tells a lie or lies, esp. habitually. □ **liar dice** a game with poker dice in which the result of a throw may be announced falsely. [OE *lēogere* (as LIE², -AR⁴)]

lias /ˈlaɪəs/ n. **1** (**Lias**) *Geol.* the lower strata of the Jurassic system of rocks, consisting of shales and limestones rich in fossils. **2** a blue limestone rock found in SW England. □□ **liassic** /laɪˈæsɪk/ *adj.* (in sense 1). [ME f. OF *liois* hard limestone, prob. f. Gmc]

Lib. *abbr.* Liberal.

lib /lɪb/ n. colloq. liberation (*women's lib*). [abbr.]

libation /laɪˈbeɪʃ(ə)n, lɪ-/ n. **1 a** the pouring out of a drink-offering to a god. **b** such a drink-offering. **2** *joc.* a potation. [ME f. L *libatio* f. *libare* pour as offering]

libber /ˈlɪbə(r)/ n. colloq. an advocate of women's liberation.

libel /ˈlaɪb(ə)l/ n. & v. —n. **1** *Law* **a** a published false statement damaging to a person's reputation (cf. SLANDER). **b** the act of publishing this. **2 a** a false and defamatory written statement. **b** (foll. by *on*) a thing that brings discredit by misrepresentation etc. (*the portrait is a libel on him; the book is a libel on human nature*). **3 a** (in civil and ecclesiastical law) the plaintiff's written declaration. **b** *Sc. Law* a statement of the grounds of a charge. **4** (in full **public libel**) *Law* the publication of a libel that also involves the criminal law. —v.tr. (**libelled**, **libelling**; US **libeled**, **libeling**) **1** defame by libellous statements. **2** accuse falsely and maliciously. **3** *Law* publish a libel against. **4** (in ecclesiastical law) bring a suit against. □ **criminal libel** *Law* a deliberate defamatory statement in a permanent form. □□ **libeller** n. [ME f. OF f. L *libellus* dimin. of *liber* book]

libellous /ˈlaɪbələs/ adj. containing or constituting a libel. □□ **libellously** adv.

liber /ˈlaɪbə(r)/ n. bast. [L, = bark]

liberal /ˈlɪbər(ə)l/ adj. & n. —adj. **1** given freely; ample, abundant. **2** (often foll. by *of*) giving freely, generous, not sparing. **3** open-minded, not prejudiced. **4** not strict or rigorous; (of interpretation) not literal. **5** for general broadening of the mind, not professional or technical (*liberal studies*). **6 a** favouring individual liberty, free trade, and moderate political and social reform. **b** (**Liberal**) of or characteristic of Liberals or a Liberal Party. **7** *Theol.* regarding many traditional beliefs as dispensable, invalidated by modern thought, or liable to change (*liberal Protestant; liberal Judaism*). —n. **1** a person of liberal views. **2** (**Liberal**) a supporter or member of a Liberal Party. □ **liberal arts 1** *US* the arts as distinct from science and technology. **2** *hist.* the medieval trivium and quadrivium. **Liberal Democrat** (in the UK) a member of a party (formerly the *Social and Liberal Democrats*) formed from the Liberal Party and members of the Social Democratic Party. **Liberal Party** see separate entry. □□ **liberalism** n. **liberalist** n. **liberalistic** /-ˈlɪstɪk/ adj. **liberally** adv. **liberalness** n. [ME, orig. = befitting a free man, f. OF f. L *liberalis* f. *liber* free (man)]

liberality /ˌlɪbəˈrælɪtɪ/ n. **1** free giving, munificence. **2** freedom from prejudice, breadth of mind. [ME f. OF *liberalite* or L *liberalitas* (as LIBERAL)]

liberalize /ˈlɪbərəlaɪz/ v.tr. & intr. (also **-ise**) make or become more liberal or less strict. □□ **liberalization** /-ˈzeɪʃ(ə)n/ n. **liberalizer** n.

Liberal Party 1 a political party advocating liberal policies. **2** a British political party which emerged in the 1860s from the old Whig party, encompassing not only former Whigs but also Radicals and former Peelite Conservatives. Dominated by Gladstone until the 1890s, the Liberal Party advocated free trade, political reform, and a restrained foreign policy. With Gladstone's conversion to Home Rule, the party was weakened by the defection of the Unionists and only returned to a position of strength under Campbell-Bannerman and Asquith in the decade before the First World War. Lloyd George's revolt against Asquith's wartime administration fatally weakened the Liberals and after the war they lost their position as one of the two major parties to Labour. The Liberals have not regained their

former eminence. The name was discontinued in official use in 1988, when the party regrouped with others to form the Social and Liberal Democrats (see *Liberal Democrat*).

liberate /ˈlɪbəˌreɪt/ v.tr. **1** (often foll. by *from*) set at liberty, set free. **2** free (a country etc.) from an oppressor or an enemy occupation. **3** (often as **liberated** adj.) free (a person) from rigid social conventions, esp. in sexual behaviour. **4** *sl.* steal. **5** *Chem.* release (esp. a gas) from a state of combination. □□ **liberator** n. [L *liberare liberat-* f. *liber* free]

liberation /ˌlɪbəˈreɪʃ(ə)n/ n. the act or an instance of liberating; the state of being liberated. □ **liberation theology** a theory which interprets liberation from social, political, and economic oppression as an anticipation of ultimate salvation. □□ **liberationist** n. [ME f. L *liberatio* f. *liberare*: see LIBERATE]

Liberia /laɪˈbɪərɪə/ a country in West Africa, bordering on the Atlantic, between the Ivory Coast and Sierra Leone; pop. (est. 1988) 2,463,200; official language, English; capital, Monrovia. Liberia is the oldest republic in the continent of Africa, and the only one never to have known colonial status. Founded in 1822 as a settlement for freed Black slaves from the US, with which country it maintains a traditional friendship, it was proclaimed independent in 1847. The country's rich mineral resources form the basis of its economy, and it is a major producer of iron ore. Civil war in 1989–91 cost thousands of lives and brought famine in its wake. □□ **Liberian** adj. & n. [L *liber* free]

libertarian /ˌlɪbəˈteərɪən/ n. & adj. —n. **1** an advocate of liberty. **2** a believer in free will (opp. NECESSITARIAN). —adj. believing in free will. □□ **libertarianism** n.

libertine /ˈlɪbəˌtiːn, -tɪn, -ˌtaɪn/ n. & adj. —n. **1** a dissolute or licentious person. **2** a free thinker on religion. **3** a person who follows his or her own inclinations. —adj. **1** licentious, dissolute. **2** freethinking. **3** following one's own inclinations. □□ **libertinage** n. **libertinism** n. [L *libertinus* freedman f. *libertus* made free f. *liber* free]

liberty /ˈlɪbətɪ/ n. (pl. **-ies**) **1 a** freedom from captivity, imprisonment, slavery, or despotic control. **b** a personification of this. **2 a** the right or power to do as one pleases. **b** (foll. by *to* + infin.) right, power, opportunity, permission. **c** *Philos.* freedom from control by fate or necessity. **3 a** (usu. in *pl.*) a right, privilege, or immunity, enjoyed by prescription or grant. **b** (in *sing.* or *pl.*) *hist.* an area having such privileges etc., esp. a district controlled by a city though outside its boundary or an area outside a prison where some prisoners might reside. **4** setting aside of rules or convention. □ **at liberty 1** free, not imprisoned (*set at liberty*). **2** (foll. by *to* + infin.) entitled, permitted. **3** available, disengaged. **liberty boat** *Brit. Naut.* a boat carrying liberty men. **liberty bodice** a close-fitting under-bodice. **liberty hall** a place where one may do as one likes. **liberty horse** a horse performing in a circus without a rider. **liberty man** *Brit. Naut.* a sailor with leave to go ashore. **liberty of the subject** the rights of a subject under constitutional rule. **Liberty ship** *hist.* a prefabricated US-built freighter of the war of 1939–45. **take liberties 1** (often foll. by *with*) behave in an unduly familiar manner. **2** (foll. by *with*) deal freely or superficially with rules or facts. **take the liberty** (foll. by *to* + infin., or *of* + verbal noun) presume, venture. [ME f. OF *liberté* f. L *libertas -tatis* f. *liber* free]

Liberty, Statue of a statue on an island at the entrance to New York harbour, a symbol of welcome to immigrants, representing a draped female figure carrying a book of laws in her left hand and holding aloft a torch in her right. Dedicated in 1886, it was the work of the French sculptor F. A. Bartholdi (who used his mother as a model) and was the gift of the French to the American people, commemorating the alliance of France and the US during the War of American Independence and marking its centenary.

Liberty Bell a large bell that is the traditional symbol of US freedom, bearing the legend 'Proclaim liberty throughout all the land unto all the inhabitants thereof (Leviticus 25: 10). Hung in the State House Steeple, Philadelphia, in 1753, it was first rung on 8 July 1776 to celebrate the first public reading of the Declaration of Independence, and cracked irreparably when rung for George Washington's birthday in 1846. it is now housed near Independence Hall, Philadelphia.

libidinous /lɪˈbɪdɪnəs/ adj. lustful. □□ **libidinously** adv. **libidinousness** n. [ME f. L libidinosus f. libido -dinis lust]

libido /lɪˈbiːˌdəʊ, lɪˈbaɪdəʊ/ n. (pl. -os) Psychol. psychic drive or energy, esp. that associated with sexual desire. □□ **libidinal** /lɪˈbɪdɪn(ə)l/ adj. **libidinally** adv. [L: see LIBIDINOUS]

Lib-Lab /lɪbˈlæb, ˈlɪb-/ adj. Brit. hist. Liberal and Labour. [abbr.]

Libra /ˈliːbrə, ˈlɪb-, ˈlaɪb-/ 1 a constellation, traditionally regarded as contained in the figure of scales. 2 the seventh sign of the zodiac (the Balance or Scales), which the sun enters at the autumnal equinox. —n. a person born when the sun is in this sign. □□ **Libran** n. & adj. [ME f. L, orig. = pound weight]

librarian /laɪˈbreərɪən/ n. a person in charge of, or an assistant in, a library. □□ **librarianship** n. [L librarius: see LIBRARY]

library /ˈlaɪbrərɪ/ n. (pl. -ies) 1 a a collection of books etc. for use by the public or by members of a group. b a person's collection of books. 2 a room or building containing a collection of books (for reading or reference rather than for sale). 3 a a similar collection of films, records, computer routines, etc. b the place where these are kept. 4 a series of books issued by a publisher in similar bindings etc., usu. as a set. 5 a public institution charged with the care of a collection of books, films, etc. □ **library edition** a strongly bound edition. **library school** a college or a department in a university or polytechnic teaching librarianship. **library science** the study of librarianship. [ME f. OF librairie f. L libraria (taberna shop), fem. of librarius bookseller's, of books, f. liber libri book]

libration /laɪˈbreɪʃ(ə)n/ n. an apparent oscillation of a heavenly body, esp. the moon, by which the parts near the edge of the disc are alternately in view and out of view. [L libratio f. librare f. libra balance]

libretto /lɪˈbretəʊ/ n. (pl. **libretti** /-tɪ/ or -os) the text of an opera or other long musical vocal work. □□ **librettist** n. [It., dimin. of libro book f. L liber libri]

Libreville /ˈliːbrəˌviːl/ the capital of Gabon; pop. (1983) 350,000.

Librium /ˈlɪbrɪəm/ n. propr. a white crystalline drug used as a tranquillizer.

Libya /ˈlɪbɪə/ a country in North Africa consisting chiefly of desert, with a narrow coastal plain bordering on the Mediterranean Sea; pop. (est. 1988) 3,956,200; official language, Arabic; capital, Tripoli. The country has major deposits of oil, now the main source of revenue. Having formed part of the Roman Empire, Libya was conquered by the Arabs, finally brought under Turkish domination in the 16th c., and annexed by Italy in 1912 and partially colonized. During the Second World War it was the scene of heavy fighting, and, after a brief period of French and British administration, achieved full independence in 1951. After prolonged political disturbances the country has emerged with a radical revolutionary leadership and an economy bolstered by its large oil exports. Relations with neighbouring countries are very difficult.

Libyan /ˈlɪbɪən, ˈlɪbjən/ adj. & n. —adj. 1 of or relating to modern Libya. 2 of ancient N. Africa west of Egypt. 3 of or relating to the Berber group of languages. —n. 1 a a native or national of modern Libya. b a person of Libyan descent. 2 an ancient language of the Berber group.

lice pl. of LOUSE.

licence /ˈlaɪs(ə)ns/ n. (US **license**) 1 a permit from an authority to own or use something (esp. a dog, gun, television set, or vehicle), do something (esp. marry, print something, preach, or drive on a public road), or carry on a trade (esp. in alcoholic liquor). 2 leave, permission (have I your licence to remove the fence?). 3 a liberty of action, esp. when excessive; disregard of law or propriety, abuse of freedom. b licentiousness. 4 a writer's or artist's irregularity in grammar, metre, perspective, etc., or deviation from fact, esp. for effect (poetic licence). 5 a university certificate of competence in a faculty. □ **license plate** US the number plate of a licensed vehicle. [ME f. OF f. L licentia f. licēre be lawful: -se by confusion with LICENSE]

license /ˈlaɪs(ə)ns/ v.tr. (also **licence**) 1 grant a licence to (a person). 2 authorize the use of (premises) for a certain purpose, esp. the sale and consumption of alcoholic liquor. 3 authorize the publication of (a book etc.) or the performance of (a play).

4 archaic allow. □ **licensed victualler** see VICTUALLER. □□ **licensable** adj. **licenser** n. **licensor** n. [ME f. LICENCE: -se on analogy of the verbs PRACTISE, PROPHESY, perh. after ADVISE, where the sound differs from the corresp. noun]

licensee /ˌlaɪsənˈsiː/ n. the holder of a licence, esp. to sell alcoholic liquor.

licentiate /laɪˈsenʃɪət, -ʃət/ n. 1 a holder of a certificate of competence to practise a certain profession, or of a university licence. 2 a licensed preacher not yet having an appointment, esp. in a Presbyterian church. [ME f. med.L licentiatus past part. of licentiare f. L licentia: see LICENCE]

licentious /laɪˈsenʃəs/ adj. 1 immoral in sexual relations. 2 archaic disregarding accepted rules or conventions. □□ **licentiously** adv. **licentiousness** n. [L licentiosus f. licentia: see LICENCE]

lichee var. of LYCHEE.

lichen /ˈlaɪkən, ˈlɪtʃ(ə)n/ n. 1 any plant organism of the group Lichenes, composed of a fungus and an alga in symbiotic association, usu. of green, grey, or yellow tint and growing on and colouring rocks, tree-trunks, roofs, walls, etc. (See below.) 2 any of several types of skin disease in which small round hard lesions occur close together. □□ **lichened** adj. (in sense 1). **lichenology** /-ˈnɒlədʒɪ/ n. (in sense 1). **lichenous** adj. (in sense 2). [L f. Gk leikhēn]

There are encrusting, leaflike, and branching forms of lichen. The alga provides nutrients for the fungus, and the fungus presumably supplies a suitable protective environment. Classification is complicated because many types were named before their symbiotic nature was realized; they are now classified mainly by their fungal component. Lichens are small, slow-growing, very hardy, and are distributed worldwide, often growing on bare rock surfaces and in polar regions where other plants cannot survive, forming an important source of food for browsing animals in tundra regions. Their economic uses include the production of dyes, and they are also used as pollution indicators.

lich-gate /ˈlɪtʃɡeɪt/ n. (also **lych-gate**) a roofed gateway to a churchyard where a coffin awaits the clergyman's arrival. [ME f. OE līc corpse f. Gmc + GATE¹]

licit /ˈlɪsɪt/ adj. not forbidden; lawful. □□ **licitly** adv. [L licitus past part. of licēre be lawful]

lick /lɪk/ v. & n. —v.tr. & intr. 1 tr. pass the tongue over, esp. to taste, moisten, or (of animals) clean. 2 tr. bring into a specified condition or position by licking (licked it all up; licked it clean). 3 a tr. (of a flame, waves, etc.) touch; play lightly over. b intr. move gently or caressingly. 4 colloq. a defeat, excel. b surpass the comprehension of (has got me licked). 5 colloq. thrash. —n. 1 an act of licking with the tongue. 2 = salt-lick. 3 colloq. a fast pace (at a lick; at full lick). 4 colloq. a a small amount, quick treatment with (foll. by of: a lick of paint). b a quick wash. 5 a smart blow with a stick etc. □ **a lick and a promise** colloq. a hasty performance of a task, esp. of washing oneself. **lick a person's boots** (or **shoes**) toady; be servile. **lick into shape** see SHAPE. **lick one's lips** (or **chops**) 1 look forward with relish. 2 show one's satisfaction. **lick one's wounds** be in retirement after defeat. □□ **licker** n. (also in comb.). [OE liccian f. WG]

lickerish /ˈlɪkərɪʃ/ adj. (also **liquorish**) 1 lecherous. 2 a fond of fine food. b greedy, longing. [ME lickerous f. OF lecheros: see LECHER]

lickety-split /ˌlɪkətɪˈsplɪt/ adv. colloq. at full speed; headlong. [prob. f. LICK (cf. at full lick) + SPLIT]

licking /ˈlɪkɪŋ/ n. colloq. 1 a thrashing. 2 a defeat.

lickspittle /ˈlɪkˌspɪt(ə)l/ n. a toady.

licorice var. of LIQUORICE.

lictor /ˈlɪktɔː(r)/ n. (usu. in pl.) Rom.Hist. an officer attending the consul or other magistrate, bearing the fasces, and executing sentence on offenders. [ME f. L, perh. rel. to ligare bind]

lid /lɪd/ n. 1 a hinged or removable cover, esp. for the top of a container. 2 = EYELID. 3 the operculum of a shell or a plant. 4 sl. a hat. □ **put the lid** (or **tin lid**) **on** Brit. colloq. 1 be the culmination of. 2 put a stop to. **take the lid off** colloq. expose (a scandal etc.). □□ **lidded** adj. (also in comb.). **lidless** adj. [OE hlid f. Gmc]

Liddell /ˈlɪd(ə)l/, Eric (1902–45), British athlete, born in China. Although best known as a sprinter, his greatest success was winning the 400 m race in the Paris Olympics of 1924. This achievement was celebrated in the film Chariots of Fire (1981).

Liddell Hart /ˌlɪd(ə)l ˈhɑːt/, Sir Basil Henry (1895–1970), British military historian and theorist. Appalled at the slaughter and exhaustion produced by trench warfare in the First World War, he evolved his 'indirect approach', arguing that strategy should aim to dislocate the enemy's morale and so affect his capacity to fight, and that the tank and the aeroplane provided the means of victory. Ironically, his ideas were less influential in Britain than in Germany, where the idea of strategic penetration by tank divisions was successfully adopted in the Second World War.

Lidingö /ˈliːdɪŋˌgɜː/ an island in the Baltic Sea, forming a residential suburb of Stockholm; pop. (1983) 37,600.

lido /ˈliːdəʊ, ˈlaɪ-/ n. (pl. **-os**) a public open-air swimming-pool or bathing-beach. [It. f. Lido, the name of a bathing-beach near Venice, f. L litus shore]

Lie /liː/, Trygve Halvdan (1896–1968), Norwegian politician, the first Secretary-General of the United Nations (1946–53).

lie¹ /laɪ/ v. & n. —v.intr. (**lying** /ˈlaɪɪŋ/; past **lay** /leɪ/; past part. **lain** /leɪn/) **1** be in or assume a horizontal position on a supporting surface; be at rest on something. **2** (of a thing) rest flat on a surface (snow lay on the ground). **3** (of abstract things) remain undisturbed or undiscussed etc. (let matters lie). **4 a** be kept or remain or be in a specified, esp. concealed, state or place (lie hidden; lie in wait; malice lay behind those words; they lay dying; the books lay unread; the money is lying in the bank). **b** (of abstract things) exist, reside; be in a certain position or relation (foll. by in, with, etc.: the answer lies in education; my sympathies lie with the family). **5 a** be situated or stationed (the village lay to the east; the ships are lying off the coast). **b** (of a road, route, etc.) lead (the road lies over mountains). **c** be spread out to view (the desert lay before us). **6** (of the dead) be buried in a grave. **7** (foll. by with) archaic have sexual intercourse. **8** Law be admissible or sustainable (the objection will not lie). **9** (of a game-bird) not rise. —n. **1 a** the way or direction or position in which a thing lies. **b** Golf the position of a golf ball when about to be struck. **2** the place of cover of an animal or a bird. □ **as far as in me lies** to the best of my power. **let lie** not raise (a controversial matter etc.) for discussion etc. **lie about** (or **around**) be left carelessly out of place. **lie ahead** be going to happen; be in store. **lie back** recline so as to rest. **lie down** assume a lying position; have a short rest. **lie-down** n. a short rest. **lie down under** accept (an insult etc.) without protest. **lie heavy** cause discomfort or anxiety. **lie in 1** remain in bed in the morning. **2** archaic be brought to bed in childbirth. **lie-in** n. a prolonged stay in bed in the morning. **lie in state** (of a deceased great personage) be laid in a public place of honour before burial. **lie low 1** keep quiet or unseen. **2** be discreet about one's intentions. **lie off** Naut. stand some distance from shore or from another ship. **the lie of the land** the current state of affairs. **lie over** be deferred. **lie to** Naut. come almost to a stop facing the wind. **lie up** (of a ship) go into dock or be out of commission. **lie with** (often foll. by to + infin.) be the responsibility of (a person) (it lies with you to answer). **take lying down** (usu. with neg.) accept (defeat, rebuke, etc.) without resistance or protest etc. [OE licgan f. Gmc]

lie² /laɪ/ n. & v. —n. **1** an intentionally false statement (tell a lie; pack of lies). **2** imposture; false belief (live a lie). —v.intr. & tr. (**lies, lied, lying** /ˈlaɪɪŋ/) **1** intr. **a** tell a lie or lies (they lied to me). **b** (of a thing) be deceptive (the camera cannot lie). **2** tr. (usu. refl.; foll. by into, out of) get (oneself) into or out of a situation by lying (lied themselves into trouble; lied my way out of danger). □ **give the lie to** serve to show the falsity of (a supposition etc.). **lie-detector** an instrument for determining whether a person is telling the truth by testing for physiological changes considered to be symptomatic of lying. The first instrument so used was devised by J. A. Larson in Berkeley, California, in 1921. [OE lyge lēogan f. Gmc]

Liebfraumilch /ˈliːbfraʊmɪlk/ n. a light white wine from the Rhine region. [G f. Liebfrau the Virgin Mary, the patroness of the convent where it was first made + Milch milk]

Liebig /ˈliːbɪx/, Baron Justus von (1803–73), German chemist and outstanding teacher. With the German chemist Friedrich Wöhler (1800–82), famous for his synthesis of urea, he discovered in 1831 the 'benzoyl radical' (now known as the benzoyl group), and demonstrated that such radicals were groups of atoms that remained unchanged in many chemical reactions. He applied chemistry to physiology and to agriculture (which inspired the founding of the Rothamsted Agricultural Research Station), stressed the importance of artificial manures (fertilizers), and developed techniques for organic quantitative analysis.

Liechtenstein /ˈlɪktənˌstaɪn/ a small independent principality (created in 1719) in the Rhine valley between Switzerland and Austria; pop. (est. 1988) 27,825; official language, German; capital, Vaduz. □□ **Liechtensteiner** n.

lied /liːd, liːt/ n. (pl. **lieder** /ˈliːdə(r)/) a type of German song, esp. of the Romantic period, usu. for solo voice with piano accompaniment. [G]

lief /liːf/ adv. archaic gladly, willingly. (usu. **had lief, would lief**) [orig. as adj. f. OE lēof dear, pleasant, f. Gmc, rel. to LEAVE², LOVE]

Liège /lɪˈeɪʒ/ (Flemish **Luik** /laɪk/) **1** a province of east Belgium; pop. (1987) 992,000. **2** its capital city; pop. (1987) 200,300.

liege /liːdʒ/ adj. & n. usu. hist. —adj. (of a superior) entitled to receive or (of a vassal) bound to give feudal service or allegiance. —n. **1** (in full **liege lord**) a feudal superior or sovereign. **2** (usu. in pl.) a vassal or subject. [ME f. OF lige, liege f. med.L laeticus, prob. f. Gmc]

liegeman /ˈliːdʒmæn/ n. (pl. **-men**) hist. a sworn vassal; a faithful follower.

lien /ˈliːən/ n. Law a right over another's property to protect a debt charged on that property. [F f. OF loien f. L ligamen bond f. ligare bind]

lierne /lɪˈɜːn/ n. Archit. (in vaulting) a short rib connecting the bosses and intersections of the principal ribs. [ME f. F: see LIANA]

lieu /ljuː/ n. □ **in lieu 1** instead. **2** (foll. by of) in the place of. [ME f. F f. L locus place]

Lieut. abbr. Lieutenant.

lieutenant /lefˈtenənt/ n. **1** a deputy or substitute acting for a superior. **2 a** an army officer next in rank below captain. **b** a naval officer next in rank below lieutenant commander. **3** US a police officer next in rank below captain. □ **lieutenant colonel** (or **commander** or **general**) officers ranking next below colonel, commander, or general. **lieutenant-governor** the acting or deputy governor of a State, province, etc., under a governor or Governor-General. **Lieutenant of the Tower** the acting commandant of the Tower of London. □□ **lieutenancy** n. (pl. **-ies**). [ME f. OF (as LIEU, TENANT)]

life /laɪf/ n. (pl. **lives** /laɪvz/) **1** the condition which distinguishes active animals and plants from inorganic matter, including the capacity for growth, functional activity, and continual change preceding death. **2 a** living things and their activity (insect life; is there life on Mars?). **b** human presence or activity (no sign of life). **3 a** the period during which life lasts, or the period from birth to the present time or from the present time to death (have done it all my life; will regret it all my life; life membership). **b** the duration of a thing's existence or of its ability to function; validity, efficacy, etc. (the battery has a life of two years). **4 a** a person's state of existence as a living individual (sacrificed their lives; took many lives). **b** a living person (many lives were lost). **5 a** an individual's occupation, actions, or fortunes; the manner of one's existence (that would make life easy; start a new life). **b** a particular aspect of this (love-life; private life). **6** the active part of existence; the business and pleasures of the world (travel is the best way to see life). **7** man's earthly or supposed future existence. **8 a** energy, liveliness, animation (full of life; put some life into it!). **b** an animating influence (was the life of the party). **9** the living, esp. nude, form or model (taken from the life). **10** a written account of a person's life; a biography. **11** colloq. a sentence of imprisonment for life (they were all serving life). **12** a chance; a fresh start (cats have nine lives; gave the player three lives). □ **come to life 1** emerge from unconsciousness or inactivity; begin operating. **2** (of an inanimate object) assume an imaginary animation. **for dear** (or **one's**) **life** as if or in order to escape death; as a matter of extreme urgency (*hanging on for dear life; run for your life*). **for life** for the rest of one's life. **for the life of** (foll. by pers. pron.) even if (one's) life depended on it (*cannot for the life of me remember*). **give one's life 1** (foll. by *for*) die; sacrifice oneself. **2** (foll. by *to*) dedicate oneself. **large as life** *colloq.* in person, esp. prominently (*stood there large as life*). **larger than life 1** exaggerated. **2** (of a person) having an exuberant personality. **life-and-death** vitally important; desperate (*a life-and-death struggle*). **life cycle** the series of changes in the life of an organism including reproduction. **life expectancy** the average period that a person at a specified age may expect to live. **life-force** inspiration or a driving force or influence. **life-form** an organism. **life-giving** that sustains life or uplifts and revitalizes. **Life Guards** (in the UK) a regiment of the royal household cavalry. **life history** the story of a person's life, esp. told at tedious length. **life insurance** insurance for a sum to be paid on the death of the insured person. **life-jacket** a buoyant or inflatable jacket for keeping a person afloat in water. **life peer** *Brit.* a peer whose title lapses on death. **life-preserver 1** a short stick with a heavily loaded end. **2** a life-jacket etc. **life-raft** an inflatable or timber etc. raft for use in an emergency instead of a boat. **life-saver** *colloq.* **1** a thing that saves one from serious difficulty. **2** *Austral.* & *NZ* = LIFEGUARD. **life sciences** biology and related subjects. **life sentence 1** a sentence of imprisonment for life. **2** an illness or commitment etc. perceived as a continuing threat to one's freedom. **life-size** (or **-sized**) of the same size as the person or thing represented. **life-support** *adj.* (of equipment) allowing vital functions to continue in an adverse environment or during severe disablement. **life-support machine** *Med.* a ventilator or respirator. **life's-work** a task etc. pursued throughout one's lifetime. **lose one's life** be killed. **a matter of life and death** a matter of vital importance. **not on your life** *colloq.* most certainly not. **save a person's life 1** prevent a person's death. **2** save a person from serious difficulty. **take one's life in one's hands** take a crucial personal risk. **to the life** true to the original. [OE *līf* f. Gmc]

lifebelt /ˈlaɪfbelt/ *n.* a belt of buoyant or inflatable material for keeping a person afloat in water.

lifeblood /ˈlaɪfblʌd/ *n.* **1** the blood, as being necessary to life. **2** the vital factor or influence.

lifeboat /ˈlaɪfbəʊt/ *n.* **1** a specially constructed boat for rescuing those in distress at sea, launched from the land. In 1785 a patent was granted to Lionel Lukin for an 'insubmergible boat'. He converted a flat-bottomed fishing-boat by adding buoyancy chambers at bow and stern, a false keel, and a projecting gunwale to serve as a fender. It was used for rescuing those in danger in the sea off the coast of NE England. **2** a ship's small boat for use in emergency.

lifebuoy /ˈlaɪfbɔɪ/ *n.* a buoyant support (usu. a ring) for keeping a person afloat in water.

lifeguard /ˈlaɪfɡɑːd/ *n.* an expert swimmer employed to rescue bathers from drowning.

lifeless /ˈlaɪflɪs/ *adj.* **1** lacking life; no longer living. **2** unconscious. **3** lacking movement or vitality. □□ **lifelessly** *adv.* **lifelessness** *n.* [OE *līflēas* (as LIFE, -LESS)]

lifelike /ˈlaɪflaɪk/ *adj.* closely resembling the person or thing represented. □□ **lifelikeness** *n.*

lifeline /ˈlaɪflaɪn/ *n.* **1 a** a rope etc. used for life-saving, e.g. that attached to a lifebuoy. **b** a diver's signalling line. **2** a sole means of communication or transport. **3** a fold in the palm of the hand, regarded as significant in palmistry. **4** an emergency telephone counselling service.

lifelong /ˈlaɪflɒŋ/ *adj.* lasting a lifetime.

lifer /ˈlaɪfə(r)/ *n. sl.* a person serving a life sentence.

lifestyle /ˈlaɪfstaɪl/ *n.* the particular way of life of a person or group.

lifetime /ˈlaɪftaɪm/ *n.* **1** the duration of a person's life. **2** the duration of a thing or its usefulness. **3** *colloq.* an exceptionally long time. □ **of a lifetime** such as does not occur more than once in a person's life (*the chance of a lifetime; the journey of a lifetime*).

Liffey /ˈlɪfi/ a river of eastern Ireland, flowing from the Wicklow mountains to Dublin Bay. The city of Dublin is situated at its mouth.

lift /lɪft/ *v.* & *n.* —*v.* **1** *tr.* (often foll. by *up, off, out*, etc.) raise or remove to a higher position. **2** *intr.* go up; be raised; yield to an upward force (*the window will not lift*). **3** *tr.* give an upward direction to (the eyes or face). **4** *tr.* **a** elevate to a higher plane of thought or feeling (*the news lifted their spirits*). **b** make less heavy or dull; add interest to (something esp. artistic). **c** enhance, improve (*lifted their game after half-time*). **5** *intr.* (of a cloud, fog, etc.) rise, disperse. **6** *tr.* remove (a barrier or restriction). **7** *tr.* transport (supplies, troops, etc.) by air. **8** *tr. colloq.* **a** steal. **b** plagiarize (a passage of writing etc.). **9** *Phonet.* **a** *tr.* make louder; raise the pitch of. **b** *intr.* (of the voice) rise. **10** *tr.* dig up (esp. potatoes etc. at harvest). **11** *intr.* (of a floor) swell upwards, bulge. **12** *tr.* hold or have on high (*the church lifts its spire*). **13** *tr.* hit (a cricket-ball) into the air. **14** *tr.* (usu. in *passive*) perform cosmetic surgery on (esp. the face or breasts) to reduce sagging. —*n.* **1** the act of lifting or process of being lifted. **2** a free ride in another person's vehicle (*gave them a lift*). **3 a** *Brit.* a platform or compartment housed in a shaft for raising and lowering persons or things to different floors of a building or different levels of a mine etc. (See below.) **b** a similar apparatus for carrying persons up or down a mountain etc. (see *ski-lift*). **4 a** transport by air (see AIRLIFT *n.*). **b** a quantity of goods transported by air. **5** the upward pressure which air exerts on an aerofoil to counteract the force of gravity. **6** a supporting or elevating influence; a feeling of elation. **7** a layer of leather in the heel of a boot or shoe, esp. to correct shortening of a leg or increase height. **8 a** a rise in the level of the ground. **b** the extent to which water rises in a canal lock. □ **lift down** pick up and bring to a lower position. **lift a finger** (or **hand** etc.) (in *neg.*) make the slightest effort (*didn't lift a finger to help*). **lift off** (of a spacecraft or rocket) rise from the launching pad. **lift-off** *n.* the vertical take-off of a spacecraft or rocket. **lift up one's head** hold one's head high with pride. **lift up one's voice** sing out. □□ **liftable** *adj.* **lifter** *n.* [ME f. ON *lypta* f. Gmc]

Stationary engines were used from the early 19th c. to raise and lower a rope-supported platform bearing miners up and down a mineshaft, replacing the earlier windlass or horse-operated revolving drum which had served the same purpose. The American inventor James Borgardus proposed a steam passenger elevator for the New York World's Fair in 1853. In 1854 E. G. Otis displayed the first efficient elevator with a safety device, and installed one in a New York department store in 1857. The first lift in Europe was built at the Paris Exhibition of 1867; it was operated hydraulically. The electric lift did not come until near the end of the century. Its invention was doubly important for the skyscraper: without it such a building would not have been feasible, and the economic height of the skyscraper is limited by the fact that beyond a certain point so many lifts are required to serve its offices or flats that they occupy too large a proportion of the floor-space.

ligament /ˈlɪɡəmənt/ *n.* **1** *Anat.* **a** a short band of tough flexible fibrous connective tissue linking bones together. **b** any membranous fold keeping an organ in position. **2** *archaic* a bond of union. □□ **ligamental** /-ˈment(ə)l/ *adj.* **ligamentary** /-ˈmentərɪ/ *adj.* **ligamentous** /-ˈmentəs/ *adj.* [ME f. L *ligamentum* bond f. *ligare* bind]

ligand /ˈlɪɡənd/ *n. Chem.* an ion or molecule attached to a metal atom by covalent bonding in which both electrons are supplied by one atom. [L *ligandus* gerundive of *ligare* bind]

ligate /lɪˈɡeɪt/ *v.tr. Surgery* tie up (a bleeding artery etc.). □□ **ligation** *n.* [L *ligare ligat-*]

ligature /ˈlɪɡətʃə(r)/ *n.* & *v.* —*n.* **1** a tie or bandage, esp. in surgery for a bleeding artery etc. **2** *Mus.* a slur; a tie. **3** *Printing* two or more letters joined, e.g. æ. **4** a bond; a thing that unites. **5** the act of tying or binding. —*v.tr.* bind or connect with a ligature. [ME f. LL *ligatura* f. L *ligare ligat-* tie, bind]

liger /ˈlaɪɡə(r)/ *n.* the offspring of a lion and a tigress (cf. TIGON). [portmanteau word f. LION + TIGER]

Ligeti /ˈliːɡetɪ/, György (1923–), Hungarian composer. His early works employ electronic means, but from 1958 he has returned to traditional forces to express his complex and mathematically worked out musical thought. The wit of his *Aventures* (1962), for three singers and seven instrumentalists, was developed into satire in his opera *Le grand Macabre* (1978).

light[1] /laɪt/ *n.*, *v.*, & *adj.* —*n.* **1** the natural agent (visible or other electromagnetic radiation from the sun, a fire, a lamp, etc.) that stimulates sight and makes things visible. (See below.) **2** the medium or condition of the space in which this is present. **3** an appearance of brightness (*saw a distant light*). **4 a** a source of light, e.g. the sun, or a lamp, fire, etc. **b** (in *pl.*) illuminations. **5** (often in *pl.*) a traffic-light (*went through a red light; stop at the lights*). **6 a** the amount or quality of illumination in a place (*bad light stopped play*). **b** one's fair or usual share of this (*you are standing in my light*). **7 a** a flame or spark serving to ignite (*struck a light*). **b** a device producing this (*have you got a light?*). **8** the aspect in which a thing is regarded or considered (*appeared in a new light*). **9 a** mental illumination; elucidation, enlightenment. **b** hope, happiness; a happy outcome. **c** spiritual illumination by divine truth. **10** vivacity, enthusiasm, or inspiration visible in a person's face, esp. in the eyes. **11** (in *pl.*) a person's mental powers or ability (*according to one's lights*). **12** an eminent person (*a leading light*). **13 a** the bright part of a thing; a highlight. **b** the bright parts of a picture etc. esp. suggesting illumination (*light and shade*). **14 a** a window or opening in a wall to let light in. **b** the perpendicular division of a mullioned window. **c** a pane of glass esp. in the side or roof of a greenhouse. **15** (in a crossword etc.) each of the items filling a space and to be deduced from the clues. **16** *Law* the light falling on windows, the obstruction of which by a neighbour is illegal. —*v.* (*past* **lit** /lɪt/; *past part.* **lit** or (*attrib.*) **lighted**) **1** *tr.* & *intr.* set burning or begin to burn; ignite. **2** *tr.* provide with light or lighting. **3** *tr.* show (a person) the way or surroundings with a light. **4** *intr.* (usu. foll. by *up*) (of the face or eyes) brighten with animation. —*adj.* **1** well provided with light; not dark. **2** (of a colour) pale (*light blue; a light-blue ribbon*). □ **bring** (or **come**) **to light** reveal or be revealed. **festival of lights 1** = HANUKKAH. **2** = DIWALI. **in a good** (or **bad**) **light** giving a favourable (or unfavourable) impression. **in the light of** having regard to; drawing information from. **light-bulb** a glass bulb containing an inert gas and a metal filament, providing light when an electric current is passed through. **lighting-up time** the time during or after which vehicles on the road must show the prescribed lights. **light meter** an instrument for measuring the intensity of the light, esp. to show the correct photographic exposure. **light of day 1** daylight, sunlight. **2** general notice; public attention. **light of one's life** usu. *joc.* a much-loved person. **light-pen** (or **-gun**) **1** a penlike or gunlike photosensitive device held to the screen of a computer terminal for passing information on to it. **2** a light-emitting device used for reading bar-codes. **light show** a display of changing coloured lights for entertainment. **light up 1** *colloq.* begin to smoke a cigarette etc. **2** switch on lights or lighting; illuminate a scene. **light-year 1** *Astron.* the distance light travels in one year, nearly 6 million million miles. **2** (in *pl.*) *colloq.* a long distance or great amount. **lit up** *colloq.* drunk. **out like a light** deeply asleep or unconscious. **throw** (or **shed**) **light on** help to explain. □□ **lightish** *adj.* **lightless** *adj.* **lightness** *n.* [OE *lēoht*, *līht*, *līhtan* f. Gmc]

Light is any electromagnetic radiation (see RADIATION) whose wavelengths fall within the range to which the human retina responds. This wavelength range lies between about 400 nanometres (violet light) and 750 nanometres (red light). White light consists of a roughly equal mixture of all visible wavelengths, which can be separated to yield the colours of the spectrum, as was first demonstrated conclusively by Newton. The nature of light has been a subject of dispute since ancient times. The speed of light was shown to be finite in the 17th c., and at about the same time two rival theories of its nature, a corpuscular (particle) theory and a wave theory, were proposed. The former, advocated by Newton, predominated until about 1800, when experiments showed that light could be made to produce interference patterns characteristic of waves. Following the

work of J. C. Maxwell later in the century it became clear that light was a form of electromagnetic radiation. Although the wave theory seemed well established, in the 20th c. it has become apparent that light consists of energy quanta called 'photons' which behave partly like waves and partly like particles. The velocity of light is 299,792 km per second.

light[2] /laɪt/ *adj.*, *adv.*, & *v.* —*adj.* **1** of little weight; not heavy; easy to lift. **2 a** relatively low in weight, amount, density, intensity, etc. (*light arms; light traffic; light metal; light rain; a light breeze*). **b** deficient in weight (*light coin*). **c** (of an isotope etc.) having not more than the usual mass. **3 a** carrying or suitable for small loads (*light aircraft; light railway*). **b** (of a ship) unladen. **c** carrying only light arms, armaments, etc. (*light brigade; light infantry*). **d** (of a locomotive) with no train attached. **4 a** (of food, a meal, etc.) small in amount; easy to digest (*had a light lunch*). **b** (of drink) not heavy on the stomach or strongly alcoholic. **5 a** (of entertainment, music, etc.) intended for amusement, rather than edification; not profound. **b** frivolous, thoughtless, trivial (*a light remark*). **6** (of sleep or a sleeper) easily disturbed. **7** easily borne or done (*light duties*). **8** nimble; quick-moving (*a light step; light of foot; a light rhythm*). **9** (of a building etc.) graceful, elegant, delicate. **10** (of type) not heavy or bold. **11 a** free from sorrow; cheerful (*a light heart*). **b** giddy (*light in the head*). **12** (of soil) not dense; porous. **13** (of pastry, sponge, etc.) fluffy and well-aerated during cooking and with the fat fully absorbed. **14** (of a woman) unchaste or wanton; fickle. —*adv.* **1** in a light manner (*tread light; sleep light*). **2** with a minimum load or minimum luggage (*travel light*). —*v.intr.* (*past* and *past part.* **lit** /lɪt/ or **lighted**) **1** (foll. by *on*, *upon*) come upon or find by chance. **2** *archaic* alight, descend. **b** (foll. by *on*) land on (shore etc.). □ **lighter-than-air** (of an aircraft) weighing less than the air it displaces. **light-fingered** given to stealing. **light flyweight** see FLYWEIGHT. **light-footed** nimble. **light-footedly** nimbly. **light-headed** giddy, frivolous, delirious. **light-headedly** in a light-headed manner. **light-headedness** being light-headed. **light-hearted 1** cheerful. **2** (unduly) casual, thoughtless. **light-heartedly** in a light-hearted manner. **light-heartedness** being light-hearted. **light heavyweight** see HEAVYWEIGHT. **light industry** the manufacture of small or light articles. **light into** *colloq.* attack. **light middleweight** see MIDDLEWEIGHT. **light out** *colloq.* depart. **light touch** delicate or tactful treatment. **light welterweight** see WELTERWEIGHT. **make light of** treat as unimportant. **make light work of** do a thing quickly and easily. □□ **lightish** *adj.* **lightness** *n.* [OE *lēoht*, *līht*, *līhtan* f. Gmc, the verbal sense from the idea of relieving a horse etc. of weight]

lighten[1] /ˈlaɪt(ə)n/ *v.* **1 a** *tr.* & *intr.* make or become lighter in weight. **b** *tr.* reduce the weight or load of. **2** *tr.* bring relief to (the heart, mind, etc.). **3** *tr.* mitigate (a penalty).

lighten[2] /ˈlaɪt(ə)n/ *v.* **1 a** *tr.* shed light on. **b** *tr.* & *intr.* make or grow bright. **2** *intr.* **a** shine brightly; flash. **b** emit lightning (*it is lightening*).

lightening /ˈlaɪtənɪŋ/ *n.* a drop in the level of the womb during the last weeks of pregnancy.

lighter[1] /ˈlaɪtə(r)/ *n.* a device for lighting cigarettes etc.

lighter[2] /ˈlaɪtə(r)/ *n.* a boat, usu. flat-bottomed, for transferring goods from a ship to a wharf or another ship. [ME f. MDu. *lichter* (as LIGHT[2] in the sense 'unload')]

lighterage /ˈlaɪtərɪdʒ/ *n.* **1** the transference of cargo by means of a lighter. **2** a charge made for this.

lighterman /ˈlaɪtəmən/ *n.* (*pl.* **-men**) a person who works on a lighter.

lighthouse /ˈlaɪthaʊs/ *n.* a tower or other structure containing a beacon light to warn or guide ships at sea. One of the earliest was the Pharos off Alexandria, one of the Seven Wonders of the World, which used a fire of burning wood, as did later lighthouses until first oil lamps and then electric lamps came into use, giving greatly increased power. The intensity of the light is increased by the use of mirrors and lenses to concentrate the light into a narrow beam which usually sweeps round in a horizontal circle at a fixed speed. Nowadays lighthouses are equipped also with radio beacons, and each has a characteristic pattern of light or radio signals which enables it to be identified.

lighting /ˈlaɪtɪŋ/ n. **1** equipment in a room or street etc. for producing light. **2** the arrangement or effect of lights.

lightly /ˈlaɪtlɪ/ adv. in a light (esp. frivolous or unserious) manner. □ **get off lightly** escape with little or no punishment. **take lightly** not be serious about (a thing).

lightning /ˈlaɪtnɪŋ/ n. & adj. —n. a flash of bright light produced by an electric discharge between clouds or between clouds and the ground. —attrib.adj. very quick (with lightning speed). □ **lightning-conductor** (or **-rod**) a metal rod or wire fixed to an exposed part of a building or to a mast to divert lightning into the earth or sea. Its invention is associated with the work of Benjamin Franklin. **lightning strike** a strike by workers at short notice, esp. without official union backing. [ME, differentiated from lightening, verbal noun f. LIGHTEN²]

lightproof /ˈlaɪtpruːf/ adj. able to resist the harmful effects of (esp. excessive) light.

lights /laɪts/ n.pl. the lungs of sheep, pigs, bullocks, etc., used as a food esp. for pets. [ME, noun use of LIGHT²: cf. LUNG]

lightship /ˈlaɪtʃɪp/ n. a moored or anchored ship with a beacon light.

lightsome /ˈlaɪtsəm/ adj. gracefully light; nimble; merry. □□ **lightsomely** adv. **lightsomeness** n.

lightweight /ˈlaɪtweɪt/ adj. & n. —adj. **1** (of a person, animal, garment, etc.) of below average weight. **2** of little importance or influence. —n. **1** a lightweight person, animal, or thing. **2 a** a weight in certain sports intermediate between featherweight and welterweight, in the amateur boxing scale 57–60 kg but differing for professionals, wrestlers, and weightlifters. **b** a sportsman of this weight. □ **junior lightweight 1** a weight in professional boxing of 57.1–59 kg. **2** a professional boxer of this weight.

lightwood /ˈlaɪtwʊd/ n. **1** a tree with a light wood. **2** US wood or a tree with wood that burns with a bright flame.

ligneous /ˈlɪɡnɪəs/ adj. **1** (of a plant) woody (opp. HERBACEOUS). **2** of the nature of wood. [L ligneus (as LIGNI-)]

ligni- /ˈlɪɡnɪ/ comb. form wood. [L lignum wood]

lignify /ˈlɪɡnɪˌfaɪ/ v.tr. & intr. (**-ies**, **-ied**) Bot. make or become woody by the deposition of lignin.

lignin /ˈlɪɡnɪn/ n. Bot. a complex organic polymer deposited in the cell-walls of many plants making them rigid and woody. [as LIGNI- + -IN]

lignite /ˈlɪɡnaɪt/ n. a soft brown coal showing traces of plant structure, intermediate between bituminous coal and peat. □□ **lignitic** /-ˈnɪtɪk/ adj. [F (as LIGNI-, -ITE¹)]

lignocaine /ˈlɪɡnəˌkeɪn/ n. Pharm. a local anaesthetic for the gums, mucous membranes, or skin, usu. given by injection. [ligno- (as LIGNI-) for XYLO- + COCA + -INE⁴]

lignum vitae /ˌlɪɡnəm ˈvaɪtɪ, ˈviːtaɪ/ n. = GUAIACUM 2a. [L, = wood of life]

ligroin /ˈlɪɡrəʊɪn/ n. Chem. a volatile hydrocarbon mixture obtained from petroleum and used as a solvent. [20th c.: orig. unkn.]

ligulate /ˈlɪɡjʊlət/ adj. Bot. having strap-shaped florets. [formed as LIGULE + -ATE²]

ligule /ˈlɪɡjuːl/ n. Bot. a narrow projection from the top of a leaf-sheath of a grass. [L ligula strap, spoon f. lingere lick]

Liguria /laɪˈdʒʊərɪə/ **1** a region of northern Italy; pop. (1981) 1,807,900; capital, Genoa. It once formed the republic of Genoa or Ligurian Republic, formed in 1797 after Napoleon's Italian campaign, annexed to France in 1805, and subsequently merged in the kingdom of Italy. **2** the more extensive region inhabited by the ancient Ligurians. [L, f. Ligur (see LIGURIAN adj. 2) f. Gk Ligus]

Ligurian /laɪˈdʒʊərɪən/ adj. & n. —adj. **1** of Liguria or its people or language. **2** of an ancient people (the Ligures) inhabiting NW Italy, Switzerland, and SE Gaul and speaking a pre-Italic Indo-European language. —n. **1** a native or inhabitant of Liguria. **2** the language of the ancient Ligurians. □ **Ligurian Republic** see LIGURIA. **Ligurian Sea** the part of the Mediterranean between Corsica and the NW coast of Italy round Genoa.

ligustrum /lɪˈɡʌstrəm/ n. = PRIVET. [L]

likable var. of LIKEABLE.

like¹ /laɪk/ adj., prep., adv., conj., & n. —adj. (often governing a noun as if a transitive participle such as resembling) (**more like**, **most like**) **1 a** having some or all of the qualities of another or each other or an original; alike (in like manner; as like as two peas; is very like her brother). **b** resembling in some way, such as; in the same class as (good writers like Dickens). **c** (usu. in pairs correlatively) as one is so will the other be (like mother, like daughter). **2** characteristic of (it is not like them to be late). **3** in a suitable state or mood for (doing or having something) (felt like working; felt like a cup of tea). —prep. in the manner of; to the same degree as (drink like a fish; sell like hot cakes; acted like an idiot). —adv. **1** archaic likely (they will come, like enough). **2** archaic in the same manner (foll. by as: sang like as a nightingale). **3** sl. so to speak (did a quick getaway, like; as I said, like, I'm no Shakespeare). **4** colloq. likely, probably (as like as not). —conj. colloq. disp. **1** as (cannot do it like you do). **2** as if (ate like they were starving). —n. **1** a counterpart; an equal; a similar person or thing (shall not see its like again; compare like with like). **2** (prec. by the) a thing or things of the same kind (will never do the like again). □ **and the like** and similar things; et cetera (music, painting, and the like). **be nothing like** (usu. with compl.) be in no way similar or comparable or adequate. **like anything** see ANYTHING. **like** (or **as like**) **as not** probably. **like-minded** having the same tastes, opinions, etc. **like-mindedly** in accordance with the same tastes etc. **like-mindedness** being like-minded. **like so** colloq. like this; in this manner. **the likes of** colloq. a person such as. **more like it** colloq. nearer what is required. [ME līc, līk, shortened form of OE gelīc ALIKE]

like² /laɪk/ v. & n. —v.tr. **1** find agreeable or enjoyable or satisfactory (like reading; like the sea; like to dance). **b** be fond of (a person). **2 a** choose to have; prefer (like my coffee black; do not like such things discussed). **b** wish for or be inclined to (would like a cup of tea; should like to come). **3** (usu. in interrog.; prec. by how) feel about; regard (how would you like it if it happened to you?). —n. (in pl.) the things one likes or prefers. □ **I like that!** iron. as an exclamation expressing affront. **like it or not** colloq. whether it is acceptable or not. [OE līcian f. Gmc]

-like /laɪk/ comb. form forming adjectives from nouns, meaning 'similar to, characteristic of' (doglike; shell-like; tortoise-like). ¶ In formations intended as nonce-words, or not generally current, the hyphen should be used. It may be omitted when the first element is of one syllable, but nouns in -l always require it.

likeable /ˈlaɪkəb(ə)l/ adj. (also **likable**) pleasant; easy to like. □□ **likeableness** n. **likeably** /-blɪ/ adv.

likelihood /ˈlaɪklɪˌhʊd/ n. probability; being likely. □ **in all likelihood** very probably.

likely /ˈlaɪklɪ/ adj. & adv. —adj. **1** probable; such as well might happen or be true (it is not likely that they will come; the most likely place is London; a likely story). **2** (foll. by to + infin.) to be reasonably expected (he is not likely to come now). **3** promising; apparently suitable (this is a likely spot; three likely lads). —adv. probably (is very likely true). □ **as likely as not** probably. **not likely!** colloq. certainly not, I refuse. □□ **likeliness** n. [ME f. ON líkligr (as LIKE¹, -LY¹)]

liken /ˈlaɪkən/ v.tr. (foll. by to) point out the resemblance of (a person or thing to another). [ME f. LIKE¹ + -EN¹]

likeness /ˈlaɪknɪs/ n. **1** (foll. by between, to) resemblance. **2** (foll. by of) a semblance or guise (in the likeness of a ghost). **3** a portrait or representation (is a good likeness). [OE gelīcnes (as LIKE¹, -NESS)]

likewise /ˈlaɪkwaɪz/ adv. **1** also, moreover, too. **2** similarly (do likewise). [for in like wise]

liking /ˈlaɪkɪŋ/ n. **1** what one likes; one's taste (is it to your liking?). **2** (foll. by for) regard or fondness; taste or fancy (had a liking for toffee). [OE līcung (as LIKE², -ING¹)]

lilac /ˈlaɪlək/ n. & adj. —n. **1** any shrub or small tree of the genus Syringa, esp. S. vulgaris with fragrant pale pinkish-violet or white blossoms. **2** a pale pinkish-violet colour. —adj. of this colour. [obs. F f. Sp. f. Arab. līlāk f. Pers. līlak, var. of nīlak bluish f. nīl blue]

liliaceous /ˌlɪlɪˈeɪʃəs/ adj. **1** of or relating to the family Liliaceae of plants with elongated leaves growing from a corm, bulb, or rhizome, e.g. tulip, lily, or onion. **2** lily-like. [LL *liliaceus* f. L *lilium* lily]

Lilienthal /'li:lɪən,tæl/, Otto (1848–96), German pioneer in the design and flying of gliders. Trained as an engineer, he invented a light steam motor and received a medal for his work on marine signals. In his flying experiments he constructed wings connected to a tail, made of osier wands and covered with shirt fabric, fitted them to his shoulders, and took off by running downhill into the wind, hanging from the fabric and landing on his feet at the bottom of the hill. In 1896 he experimented with a small motor to flap the wings. Working with his brother Gustavus he made over 2,000 flights in various gliders, many from a special hill which he built near Berlin, before being killed in a crash. He also studied the science of bird flight and published the results, demonstrating the superiority of a curved over a flat wing.

Lilith /'lɪlɪθ/ a female demon of Jewish folklore, who tries to kill newborn children. In the Talmud she is the first wife of Adam, dispossessed by Eve. [Heb., = night-monster]

Lille /li:l/ an industrial city of NW France, the capital of Nord-Pas-de-Calais region; pop. (1982) 174,000.

Lilliburlero /ˌlɪlɪbə'lɪərəʊ/ the title and part of the refrain of a song ridiculing the Irish, popular at the end of the 17th c. especially among soldiers and supporters of William III during the revolution of 1688. The tune (of unknown origin) first appeared in print in 1686, and was set to satirical verses, with the mock Irish word 'Lilliburlero' as a refrain, in the following year; it has remained a song of the Orange party, set to different words, as 'Protestant Boys'.

lilliputian /ˌlɪlɪ'pju:ʃ(ə)n/ n. & adj. —n. a diminutive person or thing. —adj. diminutive. [*Lilliput* in Swift's *Gulliver's Travels*]

Lilo /'laɪləʊ/ n. (pl. -os) propr. a type of inflatable mattress. [f. *lie low*]

Lilongwe /lɪ'lɒŋweɪ/ the capital of Malawi; pop. (est. 1985) 186,800.

lilt /lɪlt/ n. & v. —n. **1 a** a light springing rhythm or gait. **b** a song or tune marked by this. **2** (of the voice) a characteristic cadence or inflection; a pleasant accent. —v.intr. (esp. as **lilting** adj.) move or speak etc. with a lilt (*a lilting step; a lilting melody*). [ME *lilte, lülte*, of unkn. orig.]

lily /'lɪlɪ/ n. (pl. -ies) **1 a** any bulbous plant of the genus *Lilium* with large trumpet-shaped often spotted flowers on a tall slender stem, e.g. the madonna lily and tiger lily. **b** any of several other plants of the family Liliaceae with similar flowers, e.g. the African lily. **c** the water lily. **2** a person or thing of special whiteness or purity. **3** a heraldic fleur-de-lis. **4** (attrib.) **a** delicately white (*a lily hand*). **b** pallid. □ **lily-livered** cowardly. **lily of the valley** any liliaceous plant of the genus *Convallaria*, with oval leaves in pairs and racemes of white bell-shaped fragrant flowers. **lily-pad** a floating leaf of a water lily. **lily-white 1** as white as a lily. **2** faultless. □□ **lilied** adj. [OE *lilie* f. L *lilium* prob. f. Gk *leirion*]

Lima /'li:mə/ the capital of Peru, founded by Pizarro in 1535; pop. (est. 1988) 417,900.

lima bean /'li:mə/ n. **1** a tropical American bean plant, *Phaseolus limensis*, having large flat white edible seeds. **2** the seed of this plant. [LIMA]

Limassol /'lɪmə,sɒl/ a port on the south coast of Cyprus, on Akrotiri Bay; pop. (1976) 98,700.

limb¹ /lɪm/ n. **1** any of the projecting parts of a person's or animal's body used for contact or movement. **2** a large branch of a tree. **3** a branch of a cross. **4** a spur of a mountain. **5** a clause of a sentence. □ **out on a limb 1** isolated, stranded. **2** at a disadvantage. **tear limb from limb** violently dismember. **with life and limb** (esp. escape) without grave injury. □□ **limbed** adj. (also in comb.). **limbless** adj. [OE *lim* f. Gmc]

limb² /lɪm/ n. **1** Astron. **a** a specified edge of the sun, moon, etc. (*eastern limb; lower limb*). **b** the graduated edge of a quadrant etc. **2** Bot. the broad part of a petal, sepal, or leaf. [F *limbe* or L *limbus* hem, border]

limber¹ /'lɪmbə(r)/ adj. & v. —adj. **1** lithe, agile, nimble. **2**

flexible. —v. (usu. foll. by *up*) **1** tr. make (oneself or a part of the body etc.) supple. **2** intr. warm up in preparation for athletic etc. activity. □□ **limberness** n. [16th c.: orig. uncert.]

limber² /'lɪmbə(r)/ n. & v. —n. the detachable front part of a gun-carriage, consisting of two wheels, axle, pole, and ammunition-box. —v. **1** tr. attach a limber to (a gun etc.). **2** intr. fasten together the two parts of a gun-carriage. [ME *limo(u)r*, app. rel. to med.L *limonarius* f. *limo -onis* shaft]

limbo¹ /'lɪmbəʊ/ n. (pl. -os) **1** (in medieval Christian theology) a region on the border of hell, the supposed abode of pre-Christian righteous persons and of unbaptized infants. **2** an intermediate state or condition of awaiting a decision etc. **3** prison, confinement. **4** a state of neglect or oblivion. [ME f. med.L phr. *in limbo*, f. *limbus*: see LIMB²]

limbo² /'lɪmbəʊ/ n. (pl. -os) a W. Indian dance in which the dancer bends backwards to pass under a horizontal bar which is progressively lowered to a position just above the ground. [a W. Indian word, perh. = LIMBER¹]

Limburg /'lɪmbɜ:g/ a former duchy of Lorraine, divided in 1839 between Belgium and the Netherlands, and now forming: **1** (French **Limbourg** /læbʊəg/) a province of NE Belgium; pop. (1982) 720,766; capital, Hasselt. **2** a province of SE Netherlands; pop. (1988) 1,095,424; capital, Maastricht.

Limburger /'lɪm,bɜ:gə(r)/ n. a soft white cheese with a characteristic strong smell, orig. made in Limburg. [Du. f. LIMBURG in Belgium]

lime¹ /laɪm/ n. & v. —n. **1** (in full **quicklime**) a white caustic alkaline substance (calcium oxide) obtained by heating limestone and used for making mortar or as a fertilizer or bleach etc. **2** = BIRDLIME. —v.tr. **1** treat (wood, skins, land, etc.) with lime. **2** archaic catch (a bird etc.) with birdlime. □ **lime water** an aqueous solution of calcium hydroxide used esp. to detect the presence of carbon dioxide. □□ **limeless** adj. **limy** adj. (**limier, limiest**). [OE *lim* f. Gmc, rel. to LOAM]

lime² /laɪm/ n. **1 a** a round citrus fruit like a lemon but greener, smaller, and more acid. **b** the tree, *Citrus aurantifolia*, bearing this. **2** (in full **lime-juice**) the juice of limes as a drink and formerly esp. as a cure for scurvy. **3** (in full **lime-green**) a pale green colour like a lime. [F f. mod.Prov. *limo*, Sp. *lima* f. Arab. *līma*: cf. LEMON]

lime³ /laɪm/ n. **1** (in full **lime-tree**) any ornamental tree of the genus *Tilia*, esp. *T. europaea* with heart-shaped leaves and fragrant yellow blossom. Also called LINDEN. **2** the wood of this. [alt. of *line* = OE *lind* = LINDEN]

limekiln /'laɪmkɪln/ n. a kiln for heating limestone to produce quicklime.

limelight /'laɪmlaɪt/ n. **1** an intense white light obtained by heating a cylinder of lime in an oxyhydrogen flame, used formerly in theatres. **2** (prec. by *the*) the full glare of publicity; the focus of attention.

limepit /'laɪmpɪt/ n. a pit containing lime for steeping hides to remove hair.

Limerick /'lɪmərɪk/ **1** a county of SW Ireland, in the province of Munster; pop. (1981) 161,661. **2** its capital city, situated on the River Shannon; pop. (est. 1986) 76,550.

limerick /'lɪmərɪk/ n. a humorous (often bawdy) form of five-line stanza with a rhyme-scheme *aabba*. The form was popularized by Edward Lear in the 19th c. [said to be from the chorus 'will you come up to Limerick?' sung between improvised verses at a gathering: f. LIMERICK]

limestone /'laɪmstəʊn/ n. Geol. a sedimentary rock composed mainly of calcium carbonate, used as building material and in the making of cement.

limewash /'laɪmwɒʃ/ n. a mixture of lime and water for coating walls.

Limey /'laɪmɪ/ n. (pl. -eys) US sl. offens. a British person (orig. a sailor) or ship. [LIME², because of the former enforced consumption of lime-juice in the British Navy as a drink to prevent scurvy]

limit /'lɪmɪt/ n. & v. —n. **1** a point, line, or level beyond which something does not or may not extend or pass. **2** (often in pl.)

the boundary of an area. **3** the greatest or smallest amount permissible or possible (*upper limit*; *lower limit*). **4** *Math.* a quantity which a function or sum of a series can be made to approach as closely as desired. —*v.tr.* (**limited, limiting**) **1** set or serve as a limit to. **2** (foll. by *to*) restrict. □ **be the limit** *colloq.* be intolerable or extremely irritating. **off limits** *US* out of bounds. **within limits** moderately; with some degree of freedom. **without limit** with no restriction. □□ **limitable** *adj.* **limitative** /-tətɪv/ *adj.* **limiter** *n.* [ME f. L *limes limitis* boundary, frontier]

limitary /ˈlɪmɪtərɪ/ *adj.* **1** subject to restriction. **2** of, on, or serving as a limit.

limitation /ˌlɪmɪˈteɪʃ(ə)n/ *n.* **1** the act or an instance of limiting; the process of being limited. **2** a condition of limited ability (often in *pl.*: *know one's limitations*). **3** a limiting rule or circumstance (often in *pl.*: *has its limitations*). **4** a legally specified period beyond which an action cannot be brought, or a property right is not to continue. [ME f. L *limitatio* (as LIMIT)]

limited /ˈlɪmɪtɪd/ *adj.* **1** confined within limits. **2** not great in scope or talents (*has limited experience*). **3 a** few, scanty, restricted (*limited accommodation*). **b** restricted to a few examples (*limited edition*). □ **limited** (or **limited liability**) **company** a company whose owners are legally responsible only to a limited amount for its debts. **limited liability** *Brit.* the status of being legally responsible only to a limited amount for debts of a trading company. □□ **limitedly** *adv.* **limitedness** *n.*

limitless /ˈlɪmɪtlɪs/ *adj.* **1** extending or going on indefinitely (*a limitless expanse*). **2** unlimited (*limitless generosity*). □□ **limitlessly** *adv.* **limitlessness** *n.*

limn /lɪm/ *v.tr.* **1** *archaic* paint (esp. a miniature portrait). **2** *hist.* illuminate (manuscripts). □□ **limner** *n.* [obs. *lumine* illuminate f. OF *luminer* f. L *luminare*: see LUMEN]

limnology /lɪmˈnɒlədʒɪ/ *n.* the study of the physical phenomena of lakes and other fresh waters. □□ **limnological** /-nəˈlɒdʒɪk(ə)l/ *adj.* **limnologist** *n.* [Gk *limnē* lake + -LOGY]

Límnos see LEMNOS.

limo /ˈlɪməʊ/ *n.* (*pl.* **-os**) *US colloq.* a limousine. [abbr.]

Limoges /lɪˈməʊʒ/ a city of west central France, capital of Limousin region, famous in the 16th–17th c. for enamel work and later for porcelain; pop. (1982) 144,000.

Limón /lɪˈmɒn/ (also **Puerto Limón** /ˈpwɜːtəʊ/) the chief Caribbean port of Costa Rica; pop. (1984) 52,600.

Limousin /ˌlɪmuːˈsæ̃/ a region and former province of central France; pop. (1982) 737,150; capital, Limoges.

limousine /ˈlɪməˌziːn, ˌlɪməˈziːn, ˈlɪməˌziːn/ *n.* a large luxurious motor car, often with a partition behind the driver. [F, orig. a caped cloak worn in the former French province of LIMOUSIN]

limp[1] /lɪmp/ *v. & n.* —*v.intr.* **1** walk lamely. **2** (of a damaged ship, aircraft, etc.) proceed with difficulty. **3** (of verse) be defective. —*n.* a lame walk. □□ **limper** *n.* **limpingly** *adv.* [rel. to obs. *limphalt* lame, OE *lemp-healt*]

limp[2] /lɪmp/ *adj.* **1** not stiff or firm; easily bent. **2** without energy or will. **3** (of a book) having a soft cover. □□ **limply** *adv.* **limpness** *n.* [18th c.: orig. unkn.: perh. rel. to LIMP[1] in the sense 'hanging loose']

limpet /ˈlɪmpɪt/ *n.* **1** any of various marine gastropod molluscs, esp. the common limpet *Patella vulgata*, with a shallow conical shell and a broad muscular foot that sticks tightly to rocks. **2** a clinging person. □ **limpet mine** a mine designed to be attached to a ship's hull and set to explode after a certain time. [OE *lempedu* f. med.L *lampreda* limpet, LAMPREY]

limpid /ˈlɪmpɪd/ *adj.* **1** (of water, eyes, etc.) clear, transparent. **2** (of writing) clear and easily comprehended. □□ **limpidity** /-ˈpɪdɪtɪ/ *n.* **limpidly** *adv.* **limpidness** *n.* [F *limpide* or L *limpidus*, perh. rel. to LYMPH]

Limpopo /lɪmˈpəʊpəʊ/ a river of SE Africa (1,770 km, 1,100 miles) flowing into the Indian Ocean in Mozambique. For much of its course it forms the northern boundary of the Transvaal with Botswana and Zimbabwe.

Linacre /ˈlɪnəkə(r)/, Thomas (1460?–1524), English physician and classical scholar who has been called the 'restorer of learning' in England. He wrote elementary and advanced textbooks

on Latin grammar, and his students of Greek included Thomas More and probably Erasmus. Linacre's translations into Latin from Galen's Greek works on medicine and philosophy brought about a revival of studies in anatomy, botany, and clinical medicine in Britain. He founded medical lectureships in Oxford and Cambridge, and was instrumental in founding the College of Physicians in London, being its first president.

linage /ˈlaɪnɪdʒ/ *n.* **1** the number of lines in printed or written matter. **2** payment by the line.

linchpin /ˈlɪntʃpɪn/ *n.* **1** a pin passed through an axle-end to keep a wheel in position. **2** a person or thing vital to an enterprise, organization, etc. [ME *linch* f. OE *lynis* + PIN]

Lincoln[1] /ˈlɪŋkən/ the capital of Nebraska, named (in 1867) after Abraham Lincoln; pop. (1980) 171,932.

Lincoln[2] /ˈlɪŋkən/ a city in eastern England, county town of Lincolnshire; pop. (est. 1987) 79,600. □ **Lincoln green** a bright green cloth of a kind orig. made at Lincoln.

Lincoln[3] /ˈlɪŋkən/, Abraham (1809–65), 16th President of the US 1861–5. Having established an early reputation as a lawyer in rural Illinois, Lincoln became a nationally known figure as a result of his unsuccessful campaign for election to the Senate in 1858. His election as Republican President two years later, on a platform held by the Southern States to be antipathetic to their interests, helped precipitate the American Civil War. As a war leader Lincoln eventually managed to unite the Union cause behind the cause of emancipation, largely as a result of his diplomatic ability in handling both his political colleagues and the army, and easily won re-election in 1864. He was assassinated by a Southern fanatic in Ford's Theatre, Washington, in April 1865, shortly after the surrender of the main Confederate army had brought the war to an end.

Lincolnshire /ˈlɪŋkənʃɪə(r)/ an eastern county of England; pop. (1981) 552,000; county town, Lincoln.

Lincoln's Inn /ˈlɪŋkənz/ one of the Inns of Court (see INN). Thomas de Lincoln, king's sergeant in the 14th c., may have been an early landlord.

Lincs. *abbr.* Lincolnshire.

linctus /ˈlɪŋktəs/ *n.* a syrupy medicine, esp. a soothing cough mixture. [L f. *lingere* lick]

Lind /lɪnd/, Jenny (Johanna) (1820–87), Swedish soprano, known as 'the Swedish nightingale', noted for the purity and agility of her voice. She sang in opera, oratorio, and concerts all over Europe and in the US, creating a sensation wherever she appeared. She did much work for charitable causes in England and Sweden.

lindane /ˈlɪndeɪn/ *n.* *Chem.* a colourless crystalline chlorinated derivative of cyclohexane used as an insecticide. [T. van der *Linden*, Du. chemist b. 1884]

Lindbergh /ˈlɪndbɜːɡ/, Charles Augustus (1902–74), American aviator of Swedish descent who made the first solo transatlantic flight, taking 33½ hours, on 20/21 May 1927, from New York to Paris, in a single-engined monoplane *Spirit of St Louis*. A popular figure, almost a folk-hero, he moved to Europe with his wife to escape the publicity ensuing from the kidnapping and murder of his two-year-old son. In the early years of the Second World War he vigorously opposed American involvement.

linden /ˈlɪnd(ə)n/ *n.* a lime-tree. [(orig. adj.) f. OE *lind* lime-tree: cf. LIME[3]]

Lindisfarne /ˈlɪndɪsˌfɑːn/ a small island (since the 11th c. also called *Holy Island*) off the coast of Northumberland, site of a church and monastery founded by St Aidan (635), a missionary centre of the Celtic Church.

Lindsay /ˈlɪn(d)zɪ/ the name of a family of Australian artists who for over half a century played a leading role in Australian art through one or other of its members. These include Sir Lionel Lindsay (1874–1961), art critic, watercolour painter, and graphic artist, who did much to arouse Australian interest in the collection of original prints, and his brother Norman Lindsay (1879–1969), graphic artist, painter, critic, and novelist.

line[1] /laɪn/ *n. & v.* —*n.* **1** a continuous mark or band made on a surface (*drew a line*). **2** use of lines in art, esp. draughtsmanship or engraving (*boldness of line*). **3** a thing resembling such a mark esp. a furrow or wrinkle. **4** *Mus.* **a** each of (usu. five) horizontal marks forming a stave in musical notation. **b** a sequence of notes or tones forming an instrumental or vocal melody. **5 a** a straight or curved continuous extent of length without breadth. **b** the track of a moving point. **6 a** a contour or outline, esp. as a feature of design (*admired the sculpture's clean lines; this year's line is full at the back; the ship's lines*). **b** a facial feature (*the cruel line of his mouth*). **7 a** (on a map or graph) a curve connecting all points having a specified common property. **b** (**the Line**) the Equator. **8 a** a limit or boundary. **b** a mark limiting the area of play, the starting or finishing point in a race, etc. **c** the boundary between a credit and a debit in an account. **9 a** a row of persons or things. **b** a direction as indicated by them (*line of march*). **c** *US* a queue. **10 a** a row of printed or written words. **b** a portion of verse written in one line. **11** (in *pl.*) **a** a piece of poetry. **b** the words of an actor's part. **c** a specified amount of text etc. to be written out as a school punishment. **12** a short letter or note (*drop me a line*). **13** (in *pl.*) = *marriage lines*. **14** a length of cord, rope, wire, etc., usu. serving a specified purpose, esp. a fishing-line or clothes-line. **15 a** a wire or cable for a telephone or telegraph. **b** a connection by means of this (*am trying to get a line*). **16 a** a single track of a railway. **b** one branch or route of a railway system, or the whole system under one management. **17 a** a regular succession of buses, ships, aircraft, etc., plying between certain places. **b** a company conducting this (*shipping line*). **18** a connected series of persons following one another in time (esp. several generations of a family); stock, succession (*a long line of craftsmen; next in line to the throne*). **19 a** a course or manner of procedure, conduct, thought, etc. (*did it along these lines; don't take that line with me*). **b** policy (*the party line*). **c** conformity (*bring them into line*). **20** a direction, course, or channel (*lines of communication*). **21** a department of activity; a province; a branch of business (*not in my line*). **22** a class of commercial goods (*a new line in hats*). **23** *colloq.* a false or exaggerated account or story; a dishonest approach (*gave me a line about missing the bus*). **24 a** a connected series of military fieldworks, defences, etc. (*behind enemy lines*). **b** an arrangement of soldiers or ships side by side; a line of battle (*ship of the line*). **c** (prec. by *the*) regular army regiments (not auxiliary forces or Guards). **25** each of the very narrow horizontal sections forming a television picture. **26** a narrow range of the spectrum that is noticeably brighter or darker than the adjacent parts. **27** the level of the base of most letters in printing and writing. **28** (as a measure) one twelfth of an inch. —*v.* **1** *tr.* mark with lines. **2** *tr.* cover with lines (*a face lined with pain*). **3** *tr. & intr.* position or stand at intervals along (*crowds lined the route*). □ **all along the line** at every point. **bring into line** make conform. **come into line** conform. **end of the line** the point at which further effort is unproductive or one can go no further. **get a line on** *colloq.* learn something about. **in line for** likely to receive. **in the line of** in the course of (esp. duty). **in** (or **out of**) **line with** in (or not in) accordance with. **lay** (or **put**) **it on the line** speak frankly. **line-drawing** a drawing in which images are produced from variations of lines. **line of fire** the expected path of gunfire, a missile, etc. **line of force** *Physics* an imaginary line which represents the strength and direction of a magnetic, gravitational, or electric field at any point. **line of march** the route taken in marching. **line of vision** the straight line along which an observer looks. **line-out** (in Rugby Football) parallel lines of opposing forwards at right angles to the touchline for the throwing in of the ball. **line printer** a machine that prints output from a computer a line at a time rather than character by character. **line up 1** arrange or be arranged in a line or lines. **2** have ready; organize (*had a job lined up*). **line-up** *n.* **1** a line of people for inspection. **2** an arrangement of persons in a team or nations etc. in an alliance. **on the line 1** at risk (*put my reputation on the line*). **2** speaking on the telephone. **3** (of a picture in an exhibition) hung with its centre about level with the spectator's eye. **out of line** not in alignment; discordant. [ME *line, ligne* f. OF *ligne* ult. f. L *linea* f. *linum* flax, & f. OE *līne* rope, series]

line² /laɪn/ *v.tr.* **1 a** cover the inside surface of (a garment, box, etc.) with a layer of usu. different material. **b** serve as a lining for. **2** cover as if with a lining (*shelves lined with books*). **3** *colloq.* fill, esp. plentifully. □ **line one's pocket** (or **purse**) make money, usu. by corrupt means. [ME f. obs. *line* flax, with ref. to the use of linen for linings]

lineage /ˈlɪnɪdʒ/ *n.* lineal descent; ancestry, pedigree. [ME f. OF *linage, lignage* f. Rmc f. L *linea* LINE¹]

lineal /ˈlɪnɪəl/ *adj.* **1** in the direct line of descent or ancestry. **2** linear; of or in lines. □□ **lineally** *adv.* [ME f. OF f. LL *linealis* (as LINE¹)]

lineament /ˈlɪnɪəmənt/ *n.* (usu. in *pl.*) a distinctive feature or characteristic, esp. of the face. [ME f. L *lineamentum* f. *lineare* make straight f. *linea* LINE¹]

linear /ˈlɪnɪə(r)/ *adj.* **1 a** of or in lines; in lines rather than masses (*linear development*). **b** of length (*linear extent*). **2** long and narrow and of uniform breadth. **3** involving one dimension only. □ **linear accelerator** *Physics* an accelerator in which particles travel in straight lines, not in closed orbits. **linear equation** an equation between two variables that gives a straight line when plotted on a graph. **linear motor** a motor producing straight-line (not rotary) motion by means of a magnetic field. □□ **linearity** /-ˈærɪtɪ/ *n.* **linearize** *v.tr.* (also **-ise**). **linearly** *adv.* [L *linearis* f. *linea* LINE¹]

Linear A the earlier of two related forms of writing discovered at Knossos in Crete by Sir Arthur Evans between 1894 and 1901, found on fewer than 400 tablets and stone vases dating from *c.*1700 to 1450 BC and still largely unintelligible. □ **Linear B** the later form, occurring also on the mainland of Greece, found on thousands of tablets dating from *c.*1450 to 1200 BC, shown in 1952 by the British architect and scholar Michael Ventris to be a syllabary imperfectly adapted to the writing of Mycenaean Greek. The scripts are composed of linear signs derived from older hieroglyphic or pictographic script, and were used to record details of palace administration.

lineation /ˌlɪnɪˈeɪʃ(ə)n/ *n.* **1** a marking with or drawing of lines. **2** a division into lines. [ME f. L *lineatio* f. *lineare* make straight]

Line Islands a group of eleven islands in the central Pacific Ocean. Eight of the islands are part of the Republic of Kiribati, the remaining three are uninhabited dependencies of the US.

lineman /ˈlaɪnmən/ *n.* (*pl.* **-men**) **1 a** a person who repairs and maintains telephone or electrical etc. lines. **b** a person who tests the safety of railway lines. **2** *US Football* a player in the line formed before a scrimmage.

linen /ˈlɪnɪn/ *n. & adj.* —*n.* **1 a** cloth woven from flax. **b** a particular kind of this. **2** (*collect.*) articles made or orig. made of linen, calico, etc., as sheets, cloths, shirts, undergarments, etc. —*adj.* made of linen or flax (*linen cloth*). □ **linen basket** a basket for soiled clothes. **wash one's dirty linen in public** be indiscreet about one's domestic quarrels etc. [OE *līnen* f. WG, rel. to obs. *line* flax]

linenfold /ˈlɪnɪnˌfəʊld/ *n.* (often *attrib.*) a carved or moulded ornament representing a fold or scroll of linen (*linenfold panelling*).

liner¹ /ˈlaɪnə(r)/ *n.* a ship or aircraft etc. carrying passengers on a regular line. □ **liner train** a fast goods train with detachable containers on permanently coupled wagons.

liner² /ˈlaɪnə(r)/ *n.* a removable lining.

-liner /ˈlaɪnə(r)/ *comb. form* (prec. by a numeral, usu. *one* or *two*) *colloq.* a spoken passage of a specified number of lines in a play etc. (*a one-liner*).

linesman /ˈlaɪnzmən/ *n.* (*pl.* **-men**) **1** (in games played on a pitch or court) an umpire's or referee's assistant who decides whether a ball falls within the playing area or not. **2** *Brit.* = LINEMAN 1.

ling¹ /lɪŋ/ *n.* a long slender marine fish, *Molva molva*, of N. Europe, used as food. [ME *leng(e)*, prob. f. MDu. rel. to LONG¹]

ling² /lɪŋ/ *n.* any of various heathers, esp. *Calluna vulgaris*. □□ **lingy** *adj.* [ME f. ON *lyng*]

-ling¹ /lɪŋ/ *suffix* **1** denoting a person or thing: **a** connected with (*hireling; sapling*). **b** having the property of being (*weakling; underling*) or undergoing (*starveling*). **2** denoting a diminutive (*duckling*), often derogatory (*lordling*). [OE (as -LE¹ + -ING³): sense 2 f. ON]

-ling[2] /lɪŋ/ *suffix* forming adverbs and adjectives (*darkling; grovelling*) (cf. -LONG). [OE f. Gmc]

linga /ˈlɪŋgə/ *n.* (also **lingam** /ˈlɪŋgæm/) a phallus, esp. as the Hindu symbol of Siva. [Skr. *lingam*, lit. 'mark']

linger /ˈlɪŋgə(r)/ *v.intr.* **1 a** be slow or reluctant to depart. **b** stay about. **-c** (foll. by *over, on,* etc.) dally (*lingered over dinner*; *lingered on what they said*). **2** (esp. of an illness) be protracted. **3** (foll. by *on*) (of a dying person or custom) be slow in dying; drag on feebly. □□ **lingerer** *n.* **lingeringly** *adv.* [ME *lenger*, frequent. of *leng* f. OE *lengan* f. Gmc, rel. to LENGTHEN]

lingerie /ˈlæʒərɪ/ *n.* women's underwear and nightclothes. [F f. *linge* linen]

lingo /ˈlɪŋgəʊ/ *n.* (*pl.* **-os** or **-oes**) *colloq.* **1** a foreign language. **2** the vocabulary of a special subject or group of people. [prob. f. Port. *lingoa* f. L *lingua* tongue]

lingua franca /ˌlɪŋgwə ˈfræŋkə/ *n.* (*pl.* **lingua francas**) **1** a language adopted as a common language between speakers whose native languages are different. **2** a system for mutual understanding. **3** *hist.* a mixture of Italian with French, Greek, Arabic, and Spanish, used in the Levant. [It., = Frankish tongue]

lingual /ˈlɪŋgw(ə)l/ *adj.* **1** of or formed by the tongue. **2** of speech or languages. □□ **lingualize** *v.tr.* (also **-ise**). **lingually** *adv.* [med.L *lingualis* f. L *lingua* tongue, language]

linguiform /ˈlɪŋgwɪˌfɔːm/ *adj. Bot., Zool.,* & *Anat.* tongue-shaped. [L *lingua* tongue + -FORM]

linguist /ˈlɪŋgwɪst/ *n.* a person skilled in languages or linguistics. [L *lingua* language]

linguistic /lɪŋˈgwɪstɪk/ *adj.* of or relating to language or the study of languages. □□ **linguistically** *adv.*

linguistics /lɪŋˈgwɪstɪks/ *n.* the scientific study of languages and their structure. (See below.) □□ **linguistician** /-ˈstɪʃ(ə)n/ *n.* [F *linguistique* or G *Linguistik* (as LINGUIST)]

Concern with language started early. By the 4th c. BC in India there was a flourishing tradition of grammatical analysis of language which must be older than its best-known exponent (Pānini, 4th c. BC), and work on the subject continued thereafter though it did not make any impact on the West until the 19th c. General discussion of a semi-philosophical nature about language started in Greece in the 5th–4th c. BC and grammatical analysis developed soon after, creating a new linguistic terminology and defining a number of categories (e.g. the parts of speech) used to analyse Greek. These were accepted with modifications in Rome and applied to Latin—thus marking the beginning of the Western grammatical tradition which continued in the Middle Ages when the grammar of Priscian was standard for a long period. During the 13th and 14th c. speculative grammar tried to establish parallels between grammatical and metaphysical categories; languages were deemed to diverge because of superficial differences only. The Renaissance saw a great expansion in the number of languages known and analysed and this increase in knowledge was encouraged by the various translations of the Bible prompted by the Reformation. The problem of the connection between linguistic and logical categories, between language and thought, was discussed at length in the 17th and 18th c. in France and elsewhere. The *Grammaire générale et raisonnée* of Port-Royal, which had immense importance, explicitly aimed at recognizing the underlying features common to all languages and showing their link with logical categories. The 19th c. shifted its interests to historical and comparative linguistics, aiming at identifying language families, reconstructing disappeared protolanguages, and tracing the history of languages (see INDO-EUROPEAN). It was argued that linguistic facts could be explained only in historical and not in logical terms and it was assumed that this period had seen the start of 'scientific' linguistics. Most of the concrete results are still valid but similar claims about 'scientificity' have been made more than once in the 20th c. where the emphasis has shifted from historical to descriptive and theoretical linguistics (concerned with spoken and not written language) and where we have seen the rise of structuralism and of generative and transformational grammar.

linguodental /ˌlɪŋgwəʊˈdent(ə)l/ *adj.* (of a sound) made with the tongue and teeth. [L *lingua* tongue + DENTAL]

liniment /ˈlɪnɪmənt/ *n.* an embrocation, usu. made with oil. [LL *linimentum* f. L *linire* smear]

lining /ˈlaɪnɪŋ/ *n.* **1** a layer of material used to line a surface etc. **2** an inside layer or surface etc. (*stomach lining*).

link[1] /lɪŋk/ *n.* & *v.* —*n.* **1** one loop or ring of a chain etc. **2 a** a connecting part, esp. a thing or person that unites or provides continuity; one in a series. **b** a state or means of connection. **3** a means of contact by radio or telephone between two points. **4** a means of travel or transport between two places. **5** = *cuff-link* (see CUFF[1]). **6** a measure equal to one-hundredth of a surveying chain (7.92 inches). —*v.* **1** *tr.* (foll. by *together, to, with*) connect or join (two things or one to another). **2** *tr.* clasp or intertwine (hands or arms). **3** *intr.* (foll. by *on, to, in to*) be joined; attach oneself to (a system, company, etc.). □ **link up** (foll. by *with*) connect or combine. **link-up** *n.* an act or result of linking up. [ME f. ON f. Gmc]

link[2] /lɪŋk/ *n. hist.* a torch of pitch and tow for lighting the way in dark streets. [16th c.: perh. f. med.L *li(n)chinus* wick f. Gk *lukhnos* light]

linkage /ˈlɪŋkɪdʒ/ *n.* **1** a connection. **2** a system of links; a linking or link.

linkman /ˈlɪŋkmæn/ *n.* (*pl.* **-men**) **1** a person providing continuity in a broadcast programme. **2** a player between the forwards and half-backs or strikers and backs in football etc.

Linköping /lɪnˈkɜːpɪŋ/ an industrial town in SE Sweden; pop. (1987) 118,600.

links /lɪŋks/ *n.pl.* **1** (treated as *sing.* or *pl.*) a golf-course, esp. one having undulating ground, coarse grass, etc. **2** *Sc. dial.* level or undulating sandy ground near a seashore, with turf and coarse grass. [pl. of *link* 'rising ground' f. OE *hlinc*]

linn /lɪn/ *n. Sc.* **1 a** a waterfall. **b** a pool below this. **2** a precipice; a ravine. [Gael. *linne*]

Linnaean /lɪˈniːən, lɪˈneɪən/ *adj.* & *n.* —*adj.* of or relating to Linnaeus or his system of binary nomenclature in the classification of plants and animals. —*n.* a follower of Linnaeus. ¶ Spelt *Linnean* in *Linnean Society*.

Linnaeus /lɪˈniːəs/, Carolus (Latinized name of Carl Linné, 1707–78), Swedish naturalist, founder of modern systematic botany and zoology. In the 18th c. there were conflicting systems of classification. Interest in the variety of stamens in flowers led Linnaeus to devise a system of twenty-four classes of plants grouped on this basis, and he became the authority to whom an army of correspondents all over the world sent specimens. He described over 7,000 plants, giving them binomial Latin names—*genus* or group-name, and *species* identifying the plant, often describing its use, appearance, or geographical location. It was a practical classification and the use of Latin made it internationally acceptable; it forms the basis of modern plant nomenclature, although his classification was later superseded by that of Jussieu. His classification of animals was less satisfactory as he paid little attention to internal anatomy. He was an astute observer and his experiments in controlling insect pests with other insects led him to the idea of a 'balance in nature' where there is a continual 'war of all against all'.

linnet /ˈlɪnɪt/ *n.* a finch, *Acanthis cannabina*, with brown and grey plumage. [OF *linette* f. *lin* flax (the bird feeding on flax-seeds)]

lino /ˈlaɪnəʊ/ *n.* (*pl.* **-os**) linoleum. [abbr.]

linocut /ˈlaɪnəʊˌkʌt/ *n.* **1** a design or form carved in relief on a block of linoleum. **2** a print made from this. □□ **linocutting** *n.*

linoleum /lɪˈnəʊlɪəm/ *n.* a material consisting of a canvas backing thickly coated with a preparation of linseed oil and powdered cork etc., used esp. as a floor-covering. □□ **linoleumed** *adj.* [L *linum* flax + *oleum* oil]

Linotype /ˈlaɪnəʊˌtaɪp/ *n. Printing propr.* a composing-machine producing lines of words as single strips of metal, used esp. for newspapers. [= *line o' type*]

linsang /ˈlɪnsæŋ/ *n.* any of various civet-like cats, esp. of the genus *Poiana* of Africa. [Jav.]

linseed /ˈlɪnsiːd/ *n.* the seed of flax. □ **linseed cake** pressed linseed used as cattle-food. **linseed meal** ground linseed. **linseed oil** oil extracted from linseed and used in paint and varnish. [OE *līnsǣd* f. *līn* flax + *sǣd* seed]

linsey-woolsey /ˌlɪnzɪ'wʊlzɪ/ n. a fabric of coarse wool woven on a cotton warp. [ME f. *linsey* coarse linen, prob. f. *Lindsey* in Suffolk + WOOL, with jingling ending]

linstock /'lɪnstɒk/ n. *hist.* a match-holder used to fire cannon. [earlier *lintstock* f. Du. *lontstok* f. *lont* match + *stok* stick, with assim. to LINT]

lint /lɪnt/ n. **1** a fabric, orig. of linen, with a raised nap on one side, used for dressing wounds. **2** fluff. **3** *Sc.* flax. □□ **linty** adj. [ME *lyn(n)et*, perh. f. OF *linette* linseed f. *lin* flax]

lintel /'lɪnt(ə)l/ n. *Archit.* a horizontal supporting piece of timber, stone, etc., across the top of a door or window. □□ **lintelled** adj. (US **linteled**). [ME f. OF *lintel* threshold f. Rmc *limitale* (unrecorded), infl. by LL *liminare* f. L *limen* threshold]

linter /'lɪntə(r)/ n. *US* **1** a machine for removing the short fibres from cotton seeds after ginning. **2** (in *pl.*) these fibres. [LINT + -ER¹]

liny /'laɪnɪ/ adj. (**linier**, **liniest**) marked with lines; wrinkled.

Linz /lɪnts/ the chief industrial city of northern Austria, situated on the River Danube; pop. (1981) 200,000.

lion /'laɪən/ n. **1** (*fem.* **lioness** /-nɪs/) a large flesh-eating cat, *Panthera leo*, of Africa and S. Asia, with a tawny coat and, in the male, a flowing shaggy mane. **2** (**the Lion**) the zodiacal sign or constellation Leo. **3** a brave or celebrated person. **4** the lion as a national emblem of Great Britain or as a representation in heraldry. **5** (**Lions**) the Rugby Union team representing Britain, so called from the symbol on their official tie. □ **lion-heart** a courageous person (esp. as a sobriquet of Richard I of England). **lion-hearted** brave and generous. **Lion of the North** a name given to Gustavus Adolphus, king of Sweden, in recognition of his military exploits. **the lion's share** the largest or best part. □□ **lionhood** n. **lion-like** adj. [ME f. AF *liun* f. L *leo -onis* f. Gk *leōn leontos*]

lionize /'laɪənaɪz/ v.tr. (also **-ise**) treat as a celebrity. □□ **lionization** /-'zeɪʃ(ə)n/ n. **lionizer** n.

lip /lɪp/ n. & v. —n. **1 a** either of the two fleshy parts forming the edges of the mouth-opening. **b** a thing resembling these. **c** = LABIUM. **2** the edge of a cup, vessel, etc., esp. the part shaped for pouring from. **3** *colloq.* impudent talk (*that's enough of your lip!*). —v.tr. (**lipped**, **lipping**) **1 a** touch with the lips; apply the lips to. **b** touch lightly. **2** *Golf* **a** hit a ball just to the edge of (a hole). **b** (of a ball) reach the edge of (a hole) but fail to drop in. □ **bite one's lip** repress an emotion; stifle laughter, a retort, etc. **curl one's lip** express scorn. **hang on a person's lips** listen attentively to a person. **lick one's lips** see LICK. **lip-read** (*past* and *past part.* **-read** /-red/) (esp. of a deaf person) understand (speech) entirely from observing a speaker's lip-movements. **lip-reader** a person who lip-reads. **lip-service** an insincere expression of support etc. **pass a person's lips** be eaten, drunk, spoken, etc. **smack one's lips** part the lips noisily in relish or anticipation, esp. of food. □□ **lipless** adj. **liplike** adj. **lipped** adj. (also in *comb.*). [OE *lippa* f. Gmc]

Lipari Islands /'lɪpərɪ/ a group of seven volcanic islands (the ancient Aeolian Islands) north of Sicily, in Italian possession. The only active volcano is on Stromboli.

lipase /'laɪpeɪz, -peɪs/ n. *Biochem.* an enzyme that catalyses the decomposition of fats. [Gk *lipos* fat + -ASE]

lipid /'lɪpɪd/ n. *Chem.* any of a group of organic compounds that are insoluble in water but soluble in organic solvents, including fatty acids, oils, waxes, and steroids. [F *lipide* (as LIPASE)]

lipidosis /ˌlɪpɪ'dəʊsɪs/ n. (also **lipoidosis** /ˌlɪpɔɪ-/) (pl. **-doses** /-siːz/) any disorder of lipid metabolism in the body tissues.

Lipizzaner var. of LIPPIZANER.

lipography /lɪ'pɒgrəfɪ/ n. the omission of letters or words in writing. [Gk *lip-* stem of *leipō* omit + -GRAPHY]

lipoid /'lɪpɔɪd/ adj. resembling fat.

lipoprotein /ˌlaɪpəʊ'prəʊtiːn/ n. *Biochem.* any of a group of proteins that are combined with fats or other lipids. [Gk *lipos* fat + PROTEIN]

liposome /'laɪpəʊˌsəʊm/ n. *Biochem.* a minute artificial spherical sac usu. of a phospholipid membrane enclosing an aqueous core. [G. *Liposom*: see LIPID]

Lippi¹ /'lɪpɪ/, Filippino (*c.*1457–1504), Italian painter, son of Fra Filippo Lippi (see LIPPI²). Having trained with his father and probably with Botticelli he worked (*c.*1481–3) on scenes from the life of St Peter in the Brancacci Chapel, Florence, a project begun by Masolino and Masaccio. In 1488 he went to Rome to decorate the Carafa Chapel, and his style was greatly influenced by this Roman experience. It could be said that his work borders on the bizarre at times, anticipating mannerist developments. At his best in a painting such as *Vision of St Bernard* (*c.*1486) his sensitivity to Flemish colour influences is seen. Highly regarded in his own lifetime, Filippino's reputation suffered a decline until 20th-c. criticism redefined his *œuvre*.

Lippi² /'lɪpɪ/, Fra Filippo (*c.* 1406–69), Italian early Renaissance Florentine painter. He joined a Carmelite order but left it shortly after executing a fresco *The Relaxation of the Carmelite Rule* (*c.*1432). His love affair with a novice (by whom he had a son; see LIPPI¹) romantically embroidered by Vasari, has given rise to the picture of a worldly Renaissance artist, rebelling against the discipline of the Church, which inspired Browning. Until *c.*1440 Masaccio's influence is clearly detected in Filippo's work, after which his style became less monumental and more decorative. Characteristically he preferred subjects with the Madonna as the central feature, stressing the human aspect of the theme, and his style served as a major source for the 19th-c. Pre-Raphaelites.

Lippizaner /ˌlɪpɪt'sɑːnə(r)/ n. (also **Lippizaner**) **1** a horse of a fine white breed used esp. in displays of dressage. **2** this breed. [G f. *Lippiza* in Yugoslavia, the home of the former Austrian Imperial Stud where such a strain of horses was orig. bred]

lippy /'lɪpɪ/ adj. (**lippier**, **lippiest**) *colloq.* **1** insolent, impertinent. **2** talkative.

lipsalve /'lɪpsælv/ n. **1** a preparation, usu. in stick form, to prevent or relieve sore lips. **2** flattery.

lipstick /'lɪpstɪk/ n. a small stick of cosmetic for colouring the lips.

liquate /lɪ'kweɪt/ v.tr. separate or purify (metals) by liquefying. □□ **liquation** /-'kweɪʃ(ə)n/ n. [L *liquare* melt, rel. to LIQUOR]

liquefy /'lɪkwɪˌfaɪ/ v.tr. & intr. (also **liquify**) (**-ies**, **-ied**) *Chem.* make or become liquid. □□ **liquefacient** /-'feɪʃ(ə)nt/ adj. & n. **liquefaction** /-'fækʃ(ə)n/ n. **liquefactive** /-'fæktɪv/ adj. **liquefiable** adj. **liquefier** n. [F *liquéfier* f. L *liquefacere* f. *liquēre* be liquid]

liquescent /lɪ'kwes(ə)nt/ adj. becoming or apt to become liquid. [L *liquescere* (as LIQUEFY)]

liqueur /lɪ'kjʊə(r)/ n. any of several strong sweet alcoholic spirits, variously flavoured, usu. drunk after a meal. [F, = LIQUOR]

liquid /'lɪkwɪd/ adj. & n. —adj. **1** having a consistency like that of water or oil, flowing freely but of constant volume. **2** having the qualities of water in appearance; translucent (*liquid blue*; *a liquid lustre*). **3** (of a gas, e.g. air, hydrogen) reduced to a liquid state by intense cold. **4** (of sounds) clear and pure; harmonious, fluent. **5** (of assets) easily converted into cash. **6** not fixed; fluid (*liquid opinions*). —n. **1** a liquid substance. **2** *Phonet.* the sound of *l* or *r*. □ **liquid crystal** a turbid liquid with some order in its molecular arrangement. **liquid crystal display** a form of visual display in electronic devices, in which the reflectivity of a matrix of liquid crystals changes as a signal is applied. **liquid measure** a unit for measuring the volume of liquids. **liquid paraffin** *Pharm.* a colourless odourless oily liquid obtained from petroleum and used as a laxative. □□ **liquidly** adv. **liquidness** n. [ME f. L *liquidus* f. *liquēre* be liquid]

liquidambar /ˌlɪkwɪ'dæmbə(r)/ n. **1** any tree of the genus *Liquidambar* yielding a resinous gum. **2** this gum. [mod.L app. f. L *liquidus* (see LIQUID) + med.L *ambar* amber]

liquidate /'lɪkwɪˌdeɪt/ v. **1 a** tr. wind up the affairs of (a company or firm) by ascertaining liabilities and apportioning assets. **b** intr. (of a company) be liquidated. **2** tr. clear or pay off (a debt).

3 *tr.* put an end to or get rid of (esp. by violent means). [med.L *liquidare* make clear (as LIQUID)]

liquidation /ˌlɪkwɪˈdeɪʃ(ə)n/ *n.* the process of liquidating a company etc. □ **go into liquidation** (of a company etc.) be wound up and have its assets apportioned.

liquidator /ˈlɪkwɪˌdeɪtə(r)/ *n.* a person called in to wind up the affairs of a company etc.

liquidity /lɪˈkwɪdɪtɪ/ *n.* (*pl.* **-ies**) **1** the state of being liquid. **2 a** availability of liquid assets. **b** (in *pl.*) liquid assets. [F *liquidité* or med.L *liquiditas* (as LIQUID)]

liquidize /ˈlɪkwɪˌdaɪz/ *v.tr.* (also **-ise**) reduce (esp. food) to a liquid or puréed state.

liquidizer /ˈlɪkwɪˌdaɪzə(r)/ *n.* a machine for liquidizing.

liquify var. of LIQUEFY.

liquor /ˈlɪkə(r)/ *n.* & *v.* —*n.* **1** an alcoholic (esp. distilled) drink. **2** water used in brewing. **3** other liquid, esp. that produced in cooking. **4** *Pharm.* a solution of a specified drug in water. —*v.tr.* **1** dress (leather) with grease or oil. **2** steep (malt etc.) in water. [ME f. OF *lic(o)ur* f. L *liquor -oris* (as LIQUID)]

liquorice /ˈlɪkərɪs, -rɪʃ/ *n.* (also **licorice**) **1** a black root extract used as a sweet and in medicine. **2** the leguminous plant *Glycyrrhiza glabra* from which it is obtained. [ME f. AF *lycorys*, OF *licoresse* f. LL *liquiritia* f. Gk *glukurrhiza* f. *glukus* sweet + *rhiza* root]

liquorish /ˈlɪkərɪʃ/ *adj.* **1** = LICKERISH. **2** fond of or indicating a fondness for liquor. □□ **liquorishly** *adv.* **liquorishness** *n.* [var. of LICKERISH, misapplied]

lira /ˈlɪərə/ *n.* (*pl.* **lire** /ˈlɪəre, ˈlɪərɪ/) **1** the chief monetary unit of Italy. **2** the chief monetary unit of Turkey. [It. f. Prov. *liura* f. L *libra* pound (weight etc.)]

Lisbon /ˈlɪzbən/ (Portuguese **Lisboa** /liːʒˈbʊə/) the capital and chief port of Portugal, at the mouth of the river Tagus; pop. (est. 1984) 807,900.

lisle /laɪl/ *n.* (in full **lisle thread**) a fine smooth cotton thread for stockings etc. [*Lisle*, former spelling of LILLE, where orig. made]

lisp /lɪsp/ *n.* & *v.* —*n.* **1** a speech defect in which *s* is pronounced like *th* in *thick* and *z* is pronounced like *th* in *this*. **2** a rippling of waters; a rustling of leaves. —*v.intr.* & *tr.* speak or utter with a lisp. □□ **lisper** *n.* **lispingly** *adv.* [OE *wlispian* (recorded in *āwlyspian*) f. *wlisp* (adj.) lisping, of uncert. orig.]

lissom /ˈlɪsəm/ *adj.* (also **lissome**) lithe, supple, agile. □□ **lissomly** *adv.* **lissomness** *n.* [ult. f. LITHE + -SOME¹]

list¹ /lɪst/ *n.* & *v.* —*n.* **1** a number of connected items, names, etc., written or printed together usu. consecutively to form a record or aid to memory (*shopping list*). **2** (in *pl.*) **a** palisades enclosing an area for a tournament. **b** the scene of a contest. **3** *Brit.* **a** a selvage or edge of cloth, usu. of different material from the main body. **b** such edges used as a material. —*v.* **1** *tr.* make a list of. **2** *tr.* enter in a list. **3** *tr.* (as **listed** *adj.*) **a** (of securities) approved for dealings on the Stock Exchange. **b** (of a building in the UK) officially designated as being of historical importance and having protection from demolition or major alterations. **4** *tr.* & *intr. archaic* enlist. □ **enter the lists** issue or accept a challenge. **list price** the price of something as shown in a published list. □□ **listable** *adj.* [OE *liste* border, strip f. Gmc]

list² /lɪst/ *v.* & *n.* —*v.intr.* (of a ship etc.) lean over to one side, esp. owing to a leak or shifting cargo (cf. HEEL²). —*n.* the process or an instance of listing. [17th c.: orig. unkn.]

listen /ˈlɪs(ə)n/ *v.intr.* **1 a** make an effort to hear something. **b** attentively hear a person speaking. **2** (foll. by *to*) **a** give attention with the ear (*listened to my story*). **b** take notice of; respond to advice or a request or to the person expressing it. **3** (also **listen out**) (often foll. by *for*) seek to hear or be aware of by waiting alertly. □ **listen in 1** tap a telephonic communication. **2** use a radio receiving set. **listening-post 1 a** a point near an enemy's lines for detecting movements by sound. **b** a station for intercepting electronic communications. **2** a place for the gathering of information from reports etc. [OE *hlysnan* f. WG]

listenable /ˈlɪsənəb(ə)l/ *adj.* easy or pleasant to listen to. □□ **listenability** /-əˈbɪlɪtɪ/ *n.*

listener /ˈlɪsənə(r)/ *n.* **1** a person who listens. **2** a person receiving broadcast radio programmes.

Lister /ˈlɪstə(r)/, Joseph, 1st Baron (1827–1912), English surgeon, inventor of antiseptic techniques in surgery. In 1865 he became acquainted with Pasteur's theory that putrefaction is due to micro-organisms, and realized its significance in connection with sepsis in wounds, a major cause of deaths in patients who had undergone surgery; this was the first application of the theory to human disease. In the same year at Glasgow Royal Infirmary Lister first used carbolic acid dressings as a protective barrier against infection, and later used a carbolic spray in the operating theatre. After about 1883 aseptic rather than antiseptic techniques became popular, though Lister believed in the use of both.

lister /ˈlɪstə(r)/ *n. US* a plough with a double mould-board. [*list* prepare land for a crop + -ER¹]

listeria /lɪˈstɪərɪə/ *n.* any motile rodlike bacterium of the genus *Listeria*, esp. *L. monocytogenes* infecting humans and animals eating contaminated food. [mod.L f. LISTER]

listing /ˈlɪstɪŋ/ *n.* **1** a list or catalogue (see LIST¹ 1). **2** the drawing up of a list. **3** *Brit.* selvage (see LIST¹ *n.* 3).

listless /ˈlɪstlɪs/ *adj.* lacking energy or enthusiasm; disinclined for exertion. □□ **listlessly** *adv.* **listlessness** *n.* [ME f. obs. *list* inclination + -LESS]

Liszt /lɪst/, Franz (Ferenc) (1811–86), Hungarian composer and pianist. A child prodigy, he gave his first recital at the age of 9. Many of his piano works demand great technical skill, as well as expressing the lyrical side of his nature. His orchestral works are equally important and innovative in conception, particularly those inspired by literary sources such as the Faust and Dante Symphonies (1854–7, 1855–6), Liszt's affair with the Countess Marie d'Agoult produced three children, one of whom, Cosima, was to marry Wagner. In 1865 he took minor orders, becoming the Abbé Liszt, and the oratorios *The Legend of St Elizabeth* (1857–62) and *Christus* (1862–7) date from this period. Liszt's championing of Wagner, the forming of a 'New German' school of composers, and above all his own startling originality, were to have far-reaching consequences for the music of the 19th and 20th c.

lit *past* and *past part.* of LIGHT¹, LIGHT².

Li (Tai) Po /liː taɪ ˈpəʊ/ (also **Li Bo**) (701–62), major Chinese poet, a romantic bohemian whose vain attempts to win official position alternated with long periods of wandering. Favourite themes include wine, friendship, and the beauties of nature.

litany /ˈlɪtənɪ/ *n.* (*pl.* **-ies**) **1 a** a series of petitions for use in church services or processions, usu. recited by the clergy and responded to in a recurring formula by the people. **b** (**the Litany**) that contained in the Book of Common Prayer. **2 a** tedious recital (*a litany of woes*). [ME f. OF *letanie* f. eccl.L *litania* f. Gk *litaneia* prayer f. *litē* supplication]

litchi var. of LYCHEE.

-lite /laɪt/ *suffix* forming names of minerals (*rhyolite*; *zeolite*). [F f. Gk *lithos* stone]

liter *US* var. of LITRE.

literacy /ˈlɪtərəsɪ/ *n.* the ability to read and write. [LITERATE + -ACY after *illiteracy*]

literae humaniores /ˌlɪtəraɪ huːˌmænɪˈɔːrez/ *n. Brit.* the name of the school of classics and philosophy at Oxford University. [L, = the more humane studies]

literal /ˈlɪtər(ə)l/ *adj.* & *n.* —*adj.* **1** taking words in their usual or primary sense without metaphor or allegory (*literal interpretation*). **2** following the letter, text, or exact or original words (*literal translation*; *a literal transcript*). **3** (in full **literal-minded**) (of a person) prosaic; matter of fact. **4 a** not exaggerated (*the literal truth*). **b** so called without exaggeration (*a literal extermination*). **5** *colloq. disp.* so called with some exaggeration or using metaphor (*a literal avalanche of mail*). **6** of, in, or expressed by a letter or the letters of the alphabet. **7** *Algebra* not numerical. —*n.* *Printing* a misprint of a letter. □□ **literality** /-ˈrælɪtɪ/ *n.* **literalize** *v.tr.* (also **-ise**). **literally** *adv.* **literalness** *n.* [ME f. OF *literal* or LL *litteralis* f. L *littera* (as LETTER)]

literalism /ˈlɪtərəˌlɪz(ə)m/ *n.* insistence on a literal interpretation; adherence to the letter. □□ **literalist** n. **literalistic** /-ˈlɪstɪk/ adj.

literary /ˈlɪtərərɪ/ adj. **1** of, constituting, or occupied with books or literature or written composition, esp. of the kind valued for quality of form. **2** well informed about literature. **3** (of a word or idiom) used chiefly in literary works or other formal writing. □ **literary executor** SEE EXECUTOR. **literary history** the history of the treatment of a subject in literature. □□ **literarily** adv. **literariness** n. [L litterarius (as LETTER)]

literate /ˈlɪtərət/ adj. & n. —adj. able to read and write. —n. a literate person. □□ **literately** adv. [ME f. L litteratus (as LETTER)]

literati /ˌlɪtəˈrɑːtiː/ n.pl. **1** men of letters. **2** the learned class. [L, pl. of literatus (as LETTER)]

literatim /ˌlɪtəˈrɑːtɪm/ adv. letter for letter; textually, literally. [med.L]

literation /ˌlɪtəˈreɪʃ(ə)n/ n. the representation of sounds etc. by a letter or group of letters. [L litera LETTER]

literature /ˈlɪtərətʃə(r), ˈlɪtrə-/ n. **1** written works, esp. those whose value lies in beauty of language or in emotional effect. **2** the realm of letters. **3** the writings of a country or period. **4** literary production. **5** colloq. printed matter, leaflets, etc. **6** the material in print on a particular subject (there is a considerable literature on geraniums). [ME, = literary culture, f. L litteratura (as LITERATE)]

-lith /lɪθ/ suffix denoting types of stone (laccolith; monolith). [Gk lithos stone]

litharge /ˈlɪθɑːdʒ/ n. a usu. red crystalline form of lead monoxide. [ME f. OF litarge f. L lithargyrus f. Gk litharguros f. lithos stone + arguros silver]

lithe /laɪð/ adj. flexible, supple. □□ **lithely** adv. **litheness** n. **lithesome** adj. [OE līthe f. Gmc]

lithia /ˈlɪθɪə/ n. lithium oxide. □ **lithia water** water containing lithium salts and used against gout. [mod.L, alt. of earlier lithion f. Gk neut. of litheios f. lithos stone, after soda etc.]

lithic /ˈlɪθɪk/ adj. **1** of, like, or made of stone. **2** Med. of a calculus. [Gk lithikos as LITHIA]

lithium /ˈlɪθɪəm/ n. Chem. a soft silver-white element of the alkali-metal group. It is the lightest of these metals. First discovered in 1817, lithium and its compounds now have numerous commercial uses in alloys, lubricating greases, chemical reagents, etc. Lithium carbonate is used in the treatment of manic depression. ¶ Symb.: **Li**; atomic number 3. [LITHIA + -IUM]

litho /ˈlaɪθəʊ/ n. & v. colloq. —n. = LITHOGRAPHY. —v.tr. (-oes, -oed) produce by lithography. [abbr.]

litho- /ˈlɪθəʊ, ˈlaɪθəʊ/ comb. form stone. [Gk lithos stone]

lithograph /ˈlɪθəˌɡrɑːf, ˈlaɪθə-/ n. & v. —n. a lithographic print. —v.tr. **1** print by lithography. **2** write or engrave on stone. [back-form. f. LITHOGRAPHY]

lithography /lɪˈθɒɡrəfɪ/ n. a process of obtaining prints from a stone or metal surface so treated that what is to be printed can be inked but the remaining area rejects ink. (See below.) □□ **lithographer** n. **lithographic** /ˌlɪθəˈɡræfɪk/ adj. **lithographically** /ˌlɪθəˈɡræfɪkəlɪ/ adv. [G Lithographie (as LITHO-, -GRAPHY)]

This planographic printing technique was invented in 1798 by a Bavarian playwright, Aloys Senefelder, while experimenting with methods of duplicating his plays. He first drew images in greasy ink or crayon on a flat piece of local limestone. When the stone was mildly etched with acid, treated with gum arabic, and subsequently moistened with water, it remained uniformly damp in the non-greasy areas. Ink then applied over the whole surface was repelled by the damp areas but retained by the greasy images, from which a replica could be obtained by pressing a piece of paper on to the stone. Nowadays, in place of stones, thin metal printing plates (usually aluminium) carry the image. In the printing press, these are wrapped round a cylinder and damped and inked alternately by rollers. This rotary process considerably speeds the taking of multiple lithographic prints. In offset lithography, the inked image is transferred (or set off) from the printing plate on to an intermediate rubber-covered transfer cylinder before being printed on to the chosen

substrate. Photo litho offset involves the photographic capture and deposition of the image on to a specially sensitized plate, which is then appropriately processed before use on the press. Half-tone screens, which break material up into suitably sized dots, are used when transferring images of varying tonal values from original to plate, via either a camera or a special scanning device.

lithology /lɪˈθɒlədʒɪ/ n. the science of the nature and composition of rocks. □□ **lithological** /-θəˈlɒdʒɪk(ə)l/ adj.

lithophyte /ˈlɪθəˌfaɪt/ n. Bot. a plant that grows on stone.

lithopone /ˈlɪθəˌpəʊn/ n. a white pigment of zinc sulphide, barium sulphate, and zinc oxide. [LITHO- + Gk ponos work]

lithosphere /ˈlɪθəˌsfɪə(r)/ n. **1** the layer including the earth's crust and upper mantle. **2** solid earth (opp. HYDROSPHERE, ATMOSPHERE). □□ **lithospheric** /-ˈsferɪk/ adj.

lithotomy /lɪˈθɒtəmɪ/ n. (pl. **-ies**) the surgical removal of a stone from the urinary tract, esp. the bladder. □□ **lithotomist** n. **lithotomize** v.tr. (also **-ise**). [LL f. Gk lithotomia (as LITHO-, -TOMY)]

lithotripsy /ˈlɪθəˌtrɪpsɪ/ n. (pl. **-ies**) a treatment using ultrasound to shatter a stone in the bladder into small particles that can be passed through the urethra. □□ **lithotripter** n. **lithotriptic** adj. [LITHO- + Gk tripsis rubbing f. tribo rub]

Lithuania /ˌlɪθjuːˈeɪnɪə/ an area between Latvia and Poland, a State of medieval Europe that became a province of the Russian empire in the 18th c. It was declared an independent republic in 1918, but in 1940 was annexed by the USSR as a constituent republic; pop. (est. 1987) 3,641,000; capital Vilnius (Vilna). Growth of a nationalist movement in the 1980s led to demands for independence from Moscow.

Lithuanian /ˌlɪθjuːˈeɪnɪən, ˌlɪθuː-/ n. & adj. —n. **1 a** a native of Lithuania. **b** a person of Lithuanian descent. **2** the language of Lithuania, spoken by some 3 million people, most closely related to Latvian, with which it constitutes the Baltic language group. —adj. of or relating to Lithuania or its people or language.

litigant /ˈlɪtɪɡənt/ n. & adj. —n. a party to a lawsuit. —adj. engaged in a lawsuit. [F (as LITIGATE)]

litigate /ˈlɪtɪˌɡeɪt/ v. **1** intr. go to law; be a party to a lawsuit. **2** tr. contest (a point) in a lawsuit. □□ **litigable** /ˈlɪtɪɡəb(ə)l/ adj. **litigation** /-ˈɡeɪʃ(ə)n/ n. **litigator** n. [L litigare litigat- f. lis litis lawsuit]

litigious /lɪˈtɪdʒəs/ adj. **1** given to litigation; unreasonably fond of going to law. **2** disputable in a lawcourt; offering matter for a lawsuit. **3** of lawsuits. □□ **litigiously** adv. **litigiousness** n. [ME f. OF litigieux or L litigiosus f. litigium litigation: see LITIGATE]

litmus /ˈlɪtməs/ n. a dye obtained from lichens that is red under acid conditions and blue under alkaline conditions. □ **litmus paper** paper stained with litmus to be used as a test for acids or alkalis. [ME f. ONorw. litmosi f. ON litr dye + mosi moss]

litotes /laɪˈtəʊtiːz/ n. ironical understatement, esp. the expressing of an affirmative by the negative of its contrary (e.g. I shan't be sorry for I shall be glad). [LL f. Gk litotēs f. litos plain, meagre]

litre /ˈliːtə(r)/ n. (US **liter**) a metric unit of capacity, formerly defined as the volume of one kilogram of water under standard conditions, now equal to 1 cubic decimetre (about 1.75 pints). □□ **litreage** /ˈliːtərɪdʒ/ n. [F f. litron, an obs. measure of capacity, f. med.L f. Gk litra a Sicilian monetary unit]

Litt.D. abbr. Doctor of Letters. [L Litterarum Doctor]

litter /ˈlɪtə(r)/ n. & v. —n. **1 a** refuse, esp. paper, discarded in an open or public place. **b** odds and ends lying about. **c** (attrib.) for disposing of litter (litter-bin). **2** a state of untidiness, disorderly accumulation of papers etc. **3** the young animals brought forth at a birth. **4** a vehicle containing a couch shut in by curtains and carried on men's shoulders or by beasts of burden. **5** a framework with a couch for transporting the sick and wounded. **6 a** straw, rushes, etc., as bedding. **b** esp. for animals. **b** straw and dung in a farmyard. —v.tr. **1** make (a place) untidy with litter. **2** scatter untidily and leave lying about. **3** give birth to (whelps etc.). **4** (often foll. by down) **a** provide (a horse etc.) with litter as bedding. **b** spread litter or straw on (a floor) or in (a stable). □ **litter-lout** = LITTERBUG. □□ **littery** adj.

(in senses 1, 2 of n.). [ME f. AF litere, OF litiere f. med.L lectaria f. L lectus bed]

littérateur /ˌlɪtərɑːˈtɜː(r)/ n. a literary person. [F]

litterbug /ˈlɪtəˌbʌg/ n. a person who carelessly leaves litter in a public place.

little /ˈlɪt(ə)l/ adj., n., & adv. —adj. (**littler, littlest; less** /les/ or **lesser** /ˈlesə(r)/; **least** /liːst/) 1 small in size, amount, degree, etc.; not great or big: often used to convey affectionate or emotional overtones, or condescension, not implied by small (a friendly little chap; a silly little fool; a nice little car). 2 a short in stature (a little man). b of short distance or duration (will go a little way with you; wait a little while). 3 (prec. by a) a certain though small amount of (give me a little butter). 4 trivial; relatively unimportant (exaggerates every little difficulty). 5 not much; inconsiderable (gained little advantage from it). 6 operating on a small scale (the little shopkeeper). 7 as a distinctive epithet: a of a smaller or the smallest size etc. (little finger). b that is the smaller or smallest of the name (little auk; little grebe). 8 young or younger (a little boy; my little sister). 9 as of a child, evoking tenderness, condescension, amusement, etc. (we know their little ways). 10 mean, paltry, contemptible (you little sneak). —n. 1 not much; only a small amount (got very little out of it; did what little I could). 2 (usu. prec. by a) a a certain but no great amount (knows a little of everything; every little helps). b a short time or distance (after a little). —adv. (**less, least**) 1 to a small extent only (little-known authors; is little more than speculation). 2 not at all; hardly (they little thought). 3 (prec. by a) somewhat (is a little deaf). □ **in little** on a small scale. **the Little Bear** the constellation Ursa Minor. **little by little** by degrees; gradually. **the Little Corporal** a nickname given to Napoleon by the soldiers in his army, with whom he was always very popular. **little end** the smaller end of a connecting-rod, attached to the piston. **Little Englander** hist. a person desiring to restrict the dimensions of the British Empire and Britain's responsibilities. **little finger** the smallest finger, at the outer end of the hand. **little man** esp. joc. (as a form of address) a boy. **Little Masters** English mistranslation of the German word Kleinmeister or 'Masters in Little', which describes a group of 16th-c. Nürnberg engravers, all influenced by Dürer, who worked small-dimension plates with biblical, mythological, and genre scenes. **little ones** young children or animals. **little or nothing** hardly anything. **the little people** fairies. **Little Russian** hist. a Ukrainian. —adj. Ukrainian. **little slam** Bridge the winning of 12 tricks. **little theatre** a small playhouse, esp. one used for experimental productions. **the little woman** colloq. often derog. one's wife. **no little** considerable, a good deal of (took no little trouble over it). **not a little** n. much; a great deal. —adv. extremely (not a little concerned). □□ **littleness** n. [OE lytel f. Gmc]

Little Bighorn /ˈbɪghɔːn/ the site in Montana of the defeat of General George Custer by Sioux Indians on 25 June 1876, popularly known as Custer's Last Stand (see CUSTER).

Little Rock /rɒk/ the capital of Arkansas; pop. (1980) 158,461.

littoral /ˈlɪtər(ə)l/ adj. & n. —adj. of or on the shore of the sea, a lake, etc. —n. a region lying along a shore. [L littoralis f. litus litoris shore]

Littré /ˈliːtreɪ/, Émile (1801–81), French philosopher and lexicographer, author of the Dictionnaire de la langue française (1863–77). He was a follower of Comte, after whose death he became the leading exponent of the positivist philosophy. He also edited and translated the works of Hippocrates (1839–61) and wrote an Histoire de la langue française (1862).

liturgical /lɪˈtɜːdʒɪk(ə)l/ adj. of or related to liturgies or public worship. □□ **liturgically** adv. **liturgist** /ˈlɪtədʒɪst/ n. [med.L f. Gk leitourgikos as LITURGY]

liturgy /ˈlɪtədʒɪ/ n. (pl. **-ies**) 1 a a form of public worship. b a set of formularies for this. c public worship in accordance with a prescribed form. 2 (**the Liturgy**) the Book of Common Prayer. 3 the Communion office of the Orthodox Church. 4 Gk Antiq. a public office or duty performed voluntarily by a rich Athenian. [F liturgie or LL liturgia f. Gk leitourgia public worship f. leitourgos minister f. leit- public + ergon work]

livable var. of LIVEABLE.

live¹ /lɪv/ v. 1 intr. have (esp. animal) life; be or remain alive. 2 intr. (foll. by on) subsist or feed (lives on fruit). 3 intr. (foll. by on, off) depend for subsistence (lives off the family; lives on income from investments). 4 intr. (foll. by on, by) sustain one's position or repute (live on their reputation; lives by his wits). 5 tr. a (with compl.) spend, pass, experience (lived a happy life). b express in one's life (was living a lie). 6 intr. conduct oneself in a specified way (live quietly). 7 intr. arrange one's habits, expenditure, feeding, etc. (live modestly). 8 intr. make or have one's abode. 9 intr. (foll. by in) spend the daytime (the room does not seem to be lived in). 10 intr. (of a person or thing) survive. 11 intr. (of a ship) escape destruction. 12 intr. enjoy life intensely or to the full (you haven't lived till you've drunk champagne). □ **live and let live** condone others' failings so as to be similarly tolerated. **live down** (usu. with neg.) cause (past guilt, embarrassment, etc.) to be forgotten by different conduct over a period of time (you'll never live that down!). **live in** Brit. (of a domestic employee) reside on the premises of one's work. **live-in** attrib.adj. (of a sexual partner) cohabiting. **live it up** colloq. live gaily and extravagantly. **live out** 1 survive (a danger, difficulty, etc.). 2 (of a domestic employee) reside away from one's place of work. **live through** survive; remain alive at the end of. **live to** survive and reach (lived to a great age). **live to oneself** live in isolation. **live together** (esp. of a man and woman not married to each other) share a home and have a sexual relationship. **live up to** honour or fulfil; put into practice (principles etc.). **live with** 1 share a home with. 2 tolerate; find congenial. **long live . . . !** an exclamation of loyalty (to a person etc. specified). [OE libban, lifian, f. Gmc]

live² /laɪv/ adj. 1 (attrib.) that is alive; living. 2 (of a broadcast) heard or seen at the time of its performance, not from a recording. 3 full of power, energy, or importance; not obsolete or exhausted (disarmament is still a live issue). 4 expending or still able to expend energy in various forms, esp.: a (of coals) glowing, burning. b (of a shell) unexploded. c (of a match) unkindled. d (of a wire etc.) connected to a source of electrical power. 5 (of rock) not detached, seeming to form part of the earth's frame. 6 (of a wheel or axle etc. in machinery) moving or imparting motion. □ **live bait** small fish used to entice prey. **live load** the weight of persons or goods in a building or vehicle. **live oak** an American evergreen tree, Quercus virginiana. **live wire** an energetic and forceful person. [apheric form of ALIVE]

liveable /ˈlɪvəb(ə)l/ adj. (also **livable**) 1 (of a house, room, climate, etc.) fit to live in. 2 (of a life) worth living. 3 (of a person) companionable; easy to live with. □□ **liveability** /-ˈbɪlɪtɪ/ n. **liveableness** n.

livelihood /ˈlaɪvlɪhʊd/ n. a means of living; sustenance. [OE līflād f. līf LIFE + lād course (see LOAD): assim. to obs. livelihood liveliness]

livelong¹ /ˈlɪvlɒŋ/ adj. poet. or rhet. in its entire length or apparently so (the livelong day). [ME lefe longe (as LIEF, LONG¹): assim. to LIVE¹]

livelong² /ˈlɪvlɒŋ/ n. an orpine. [LIVE¹ + LONG¹]

lively /ˈlaɪvlɪ/ adj. (**livelier, liveliest**) 1 full of life; vigorous, energetic. 2 brisk (a lively pace). 3 vivid, stimulating (a lively discussion). 4 vivacious, jolly, sociable. 5 joc. exciting, dangerous, difficult (the press is making things lively for them). 6 (of a colour) bright and vivid. 7 lifelike, realistic (a lively description). 8 (of a boat etc.) rising lightly to the waves. □□ **livelily** adv. **liveliness** n. [OE līflic (as LIFE, -LY¹)]

liven /ˈlaɪv(ə)n/ v.tr. & intr. (often foll. by up) colloq. brighten, cheer.

liver¹ /ˈlɪvə(r)/ n. 1 a a large lobed glandular organ in the abdomen of vertebrates, secreting bile. (See below.) b a similar organ in other animals. 2 the flesh of an animal's liver as food. 3 (in full **liver-colour**) a dark reddish-brown. □ **liver chestnut** see CHESTNUT. **liver fluke** either of two types of fluke, esp. Fasciola hepatica, the adults of which live within the liver tissues of vertebrates, and the larvae within snails. **liver of sulphur** a liver-coloured mixture of potassium sulphides etc., used as a lotion in skin disease. **liver salts** Brit. salts to cure dyspepsia or biliousness. **liver sausage** a sausage containing cooked liver etc. □□ **liverless** adj. [OE lifer f. Gmc]

The liver's main function is the chemical processing of the

products of digestion into substances which will be useful to the rest of the body. It makes many of the proteins of blood-plasma, converts glucose into glycogen (which it stores for reconversion into glucose when the body needs it), neutralizes harmful substances absorbed from the intestine, and stores certain minerals, such as iron, and vitamins. Its other major function is the secretion of bile, which is essential for the proper digestion and absorption of fats.

The liver was anciently supposed to be the seat of love and of violent passion generally, whence expressions such as *lily-livered* (= cowardly).

liver² /ˈlɪvə(r)/ n. a person who lives in a specified way (*a clean liver*).

liverish /ˈlɪvərɪʃ/ adj. **1** suffering from a disorder of the liver. **2** peevish, glum. □□ **liverishly** adv. **liverishness** n.

Liverpool¹ /ˈlɪvəˌpuːl/ a city and seaport in NW England, county town of Merseyside; pop. (1981) 544,850. Its port trade developed in the 17th c.; it became an important centre of the slave traffic from Africa to the West Indies and later of the textile industry, importing cotton from America and exporting the textiles produced in Lancashire and Yorkshire. Liverpool's traditional industries of shipbuilding and engineering have declined, but it remains the chief Atlantic port of Europe. It was the birthplace of George Stubbs (1724), A. H. Clough (1819), W. E. Gladstone (1809), and the Beatles (1940s).

Liverpool² /ˈlɪvəˌpuːl/, Robert Banks Jenkinson, 2nd Earl of (1770–1828), British statesman, who reluctantly took office as Prime Minister (1812–27) after the assassination of Spencer Perceval. After the Napoleonic Wars his government took repressive measures to deal with popular discontent (see PETERLOO), opposing both parliamentary reform and Catholic emancipation, but towards the end of his tenure the more liberal influences of people such as Sir Robert Peel led him to support the introduction of some important reforms.

Liverpudlian /ˌlɪvəˈpʌdlɪən/ n. & adj. —n. a native of Liverpool. —adj. of or relating to Liverpool. [joc. f. LIVERPOOL¹ + PUDDLE]

liverwort /ˈlɪvəˌwɜːt/ n. any small leafy or thalloid bryophyte of the class Hepaticae, of which some have liver-shaped parts.

livery¹ /ˈlɪvərɪ/ n. (pl. -ies) **1 a** distinctive clothing worn by a member of a City Company or by a servant. **b** membership of a City livery company. **2** a distinctive guise or marking or outward appearance (*birds in their winter livery*). **3** a distinctive colour scheme in which the vehicles, aircraft, etc., of a particular company or line are painted. **4** US a place where horses can be hired. **5** *hist.* a provision of food or clothing for retainers etc. **6** *Law* **a** the legal delivery of property. **b** a writ allowing this. □ **at livery** (of a horse) kept for the owner and fed and groomed for a fixed charge. **livery company** see separate entry. **livery stable** a stable where horses are kept at livery or let out for hire. □□ **liveried** adj. (esp. in senses 1, 2). [ME f. AF *liverê*, OF *livrée*, fem. past part. of *livrer* DELIVER]

livery² /ˈlɪvərɪ/ adj. **1** of the consistency or colour of liver. **2** *Brit.* (of soil) tenacious. **3** *colloq.* liverish.

livery company n. *Brit.* any of the London City Companies that formerly had a distinctive costume. They are descended from medieval craft guilds. The companies are now largely social and charitable organizations; none are now trading companies, though some still have some involvement with the operation of their original trade; several support public schools (e.g. Merchant Taylors, Haberdashers), and collectively they are involved in various forms of technical education.

liveryman /ˈlɪvərɪmən/ n. (pl. -men) **1** *Brit.* a member of a livery company. **2** a keeper of or attendant in a livery stable.

lives pl. of LIFE.

livestock /ˈlaɪvstɒk/ n. (usu. treated as pl.) animals, esp. on a farm, regarded as an asset.

livid /ˈlɪvɪd/ adj. **1** *colloq.* furiously angry. **2 a** of a bluish leaden colour. **b** discoloured as by a bruise. □□ **lividity** /lɪˈvɪdɪtɪ/ n. **lividly** adv. **lividness** n. [F *livide* or L *lividus* f. *livère* be bluish]

living /ˈlɪvɪŋ/ n. & adj. —n. **1** a livelihood or means of maintenance (*made my living as a journalist; what does she do for a living?*). **2** *Brit. Eccl.* a position as a vicar or rector with an income

or property. —adj. **1** contemporary; now existent (*the greatest living poet*). **2** (of a likeness or image of a person) exact. **3** (of a language) still in vernacular use. **4** (of water) perennially flowing. **5** (of rock etc.) = LIVE² 5. □ **living death** a state of hopeless misery. **living-room** a room for general day use. **within living memory** within the memory of people still living.

Livingstone¹ /ˈlɪvɪŋstən/ see MARAMBA.

Livingstone² /ˈlɪvɪŋstən/, David (1813–73), Scottish missionary and explorer. He first went to Bechuanaland as a missionary in 1841, travelling extensively in the interior, discovering Lake Ngami (1849) and the Zambesi River (1851), before undertaking a great journey from Cape Town to west central Africa (1852–6) on which he discovered Victoria Falls. Welcomed back to Britain in 1855 as a popular hero, Livingstone returned to Africa as consul at Quelimane (1858–64), and made further expeditions into the interior in the Zambesi region, before returning once again to Britain to attempt to expose the Portuguese slave trade. He returned to Africa for the last time in 1866 to lead an expedition into central Africa in search of the source of the Nile. His disappearance became a Victorian *cause célèbre* and he was eventually found in poor health by the explorer Stanley at Ujiji on the eastern shore of Lake Tanganyika in 1871. He died in Africa and his body was brought home and buried in Westminster Abbey.

Livonia /lɪˈvəʊnɪə/ (German **Livland** /ˈlɪvlænd/) a former region on the east coast of the Baltic Sea, north of Lithuania, comprising most of modern Latvia and Estonia (see entries). It was named after the Livs, a Finno-Ugrian people living in part of the coastal region. Conquered and Christianized in the early 13th c. by a crusading order of knights, who ruled it until the late 16th c., it was then divided between Lithuania, Poland, and Sweden, and was ceded to Peter the Great of Russia in 1721.

Livorno see LEGHORN.

Livy /ˈlɪvɪ/ (Titus Livius, 59 BC–AD 17) Roman historian, born at Padua. His history of Rome from its foundation to his own time contained 142 books of which 35 survive (including the earliest history of the war with Hannibal). Livy's genius lay in his power of vivid historical reconstruction as he sought to give Rome a history that in conception and style should be worthy of her imperial rise and greatness. Though falling below modern critical standards in use of sources, and liable to mislead through ignorance of military matters and Roman institutions, he reproduces tradition faithfully. His success was immediate and lasting, and the popularity of his work endured into the Middle Ages, the Renaissance, and beyond.

lixiviate /lɪkˈsɪvɪˌeɪt/ v.tr. separate (a substance) into soluble and insoluble constituents by the percolation of liquid. □□ **lixiviation** /-ˈeɪʃ(ə)n/ n. [L *lixivius* made into lye f. *lix* lye]

lizard /ˈlɪzəd/ n. any reptile of the suborder Lacertilia, having usu. a long body and tail, four legs, movable eyelids, and a rough or scaly hide. [ME f. OF *lesard(e)* f. L *lacertus*]

LJ abbr. (pl. L JJ) (in the UK) Lord Justice.

Ljubljana /luːbˈljɑːnə/ a city in northern Yugoslavia, capital of the republic of Slovenia; pop. (1981) 305,200.

LL abbr. Lord Lieutenant.

ll. abbr. lines.

'll v. (usu. after pronouns) shall, will (*I'll; that'll*). [abbr.]

llama /ˈlɑːmə/ n. **1 a** S. American ruminant, *Lama glama*, kept as a beast of burden and for its soft woolly fleece. **2** the wool from this animal, or cloth made from it. [Sp., prob. f. Quechua]

llanero /ljɑːˈneərəʊ/ n. (pl. -os) an inhabitant of the llanos. [Sp.]

llano /ˈlɑːnəʊ, ˈljɑː-/ n. (pl. -os) a treeless grassy plain or steppe, esp. in S. America. [Sp. f. L *planum* plain]

LL B abbr. Bachelor of Laws. [L *legum baccalaureus*]

LL D abbr. Doctor of Laws. [L *legum doctor*]

LL M abbr. Master of Laws. [L *legum magister*]

Lloyd /lɔɪd/, Marie (1870–1922), real name Matilda Wood, the most famous English music-hall singer of all time, known for her saucy songs and extravagant costumes.

Lloyd George /lɔɪd ˈdʒɔːdʒ/, David, 1st Earl Lloyd George of

Dwyfor (1863–1945), British Liberal statesman who early established a reputation as a radical orator. As Chancellor of the Exchequer (1908–15) under Asquith his social reforms included the introduction of old-age pensions and of national insurance, while his People's Budget (1909), proposing a tax on the value of land, was rejected by the Lords and led to a prolonged political crisis and reform of the House of Lords. He became dissatisfied with Asquith's leadership and overthrew him at the end of 1916. As Prime Minister, Lloyd George proved a good war leader and was re-elected with a large majority after the war. He successfully pressed for a moderate treaty at the Paris peace talks, but at home his administration was threatened by economic problems and trouble in Ireland. He was forced to resign in 1922 after the Conservatives on whom he had depended since his revolt against Asquith withdrew their support, and although he eventually returned to the Liberal Party as leader in 1926, he never held office again.

Lloyd's /lɔɪdz/ an association of underwriters in London (not, as is often supposed, an insurance firm) incorporated by statute in 1871. Its members are private syndicates, elected after close scrutiny of their finances and required to deposit a substantial sum as security against their underwriting activities. It is named after the 17th-c. coffee-house of Edward Lloyd (d. 1713), in which underwriters and merchants congregated. For the benefit of his customers Lloyd built up an unrivalled intelligence system and displayed lists of the latest ship movements. Out of this practice a newspaper, *Lloyd's List*, was started in 1734, giving daily news of the movements etc. of shipping. Originally Lloyd's dealt only in marine insurance, but it now undertakes most other kinds, and its business in marine and aircraft insurance is international. (See also LUTINE.)

Lloyd's Register of Shipping is a separate and independent society which surveys and classifies ships over a certain tonnage, publishing details of these each year on the basis of reports by its surveyors. In the 18th-c. the finest ships were classed as 'A1 at Lloyd's', indicating (by A) that the hull was in first-class condition and (by 1) that the same was true of the fittings; whence 'A1' has passed into the language as a standard of excellence.

Lloyd Webber /lɔɪd ˈwebə(r)/, Andrew (1948–), English composer, whose works include the highly successful musical plays *Evita* (1976), *Cats* (1981), and *The Phantom of the Opera* (1986), and the choral *Requiem Mass* (1985).

LM *abbr.* **1** long metre. **2** lunar module.

lm *abbr.* lumen(s).

ln *abbr.* natural logarithm. [mod.L *logarithmus naturalis*]

lo /ləʊ/ *int. archaic* calling attention to an amazing sight. □ **lo and behold** *joc.* a formula introducing a surprising or unexpected fact. [OE *lā* int. of surprise etc., & ME *lō* = *lōke* LOOK]

loach /ləʊtʃ/ *n.* any small edible freshwater fish of the family Cobitidae. [ME f. OF *loche*, of unkn. orig.]

load /ləʊd/ *n. & v.* —*n.* **1 a** what is carried or is to be carried; a burden. **b** an amount usu. or actually carried (often in *comb.*: *a busload of tourists; a lorry-load of bricks*). **2** a unit of measure or weight of certain substances. **3** a burden or commitment of work, responsibility, care, grief, etc. **4** (in *pl.*; often foll. by *of*) *colloq.* plenty; a lot. **5 a** *Electr.* the amount of power supplied by a generating system at any given time. **b** *Electronics* an impedance or circuit that receives or develops the output of a transistor or other device. **6** the weight or force borne by the supporting part of a structure. **7** a material object or force acting as a weight or clog. **8** the resistance of machinery to motive power. —*v.* **1** *tr.* **a** put a load on or aboard (a person, vehicle, ship, etc.). **b** place (a load or cargo) aboard a ship, on a vehicle, etc. **2** *intr.* (often foll. by *up*) (of a ship, vehicle, or person) take a load aboard, pick up a load. **3** *tr.* (often foll. by *with*) **a** add weight to; be a weight or burden upon. **b** oppress (*a stomach loaded with food*). **4** *tr.* strain the bearing-capacity of (*a table loaded with food*). **5** *tr.* (also **load up**) (foll. by *with*) **a** supply overwhelmingly (*loaded us with work*). **b** assail overwhelmingly (*loaded us with abuse*). **6** *tr.* charge (a firearm) with ammunition. **7** *tr.* insert (the required operating medium) in a device, e.g. film in a camera, magnetic tape in a tape recorder, a program into

a computer, etc. **8** *tr.* add an extra charge to (an insurance premium) in the case of a poorer risk. **9** *tr.* **a** weight with lead. **b** give a bias to (dice, a roulette wheel, etc.) with weights. □ **get a load of** *sl.* listen attentively to; notice. **load-displacement** (or **-draught**) the displacement of a ship when laden. **load line** a Plimsoll line. [OE *lād* way, journey, conveyance, f. Gmc: rel. to LEAD[1], LODE]

loaded /ˈləʊdɪd/ *adj.* **1** bearing or carrying a load. **2** *sl.* **a** wealthy. **b** drunk. **c** *US* drugged. **3** (of dice etc.) weighted or given a bias. **4** (of a question or statement) charged with some hidden or improper implication.

loader /ˈləʊdə(r)/ *n.* **1** a loading-machine. **2** (in *comb.*) a gun, machine, lorry, etc., loaded in a specified way (*breech-loader*). **3** an attendant who loads guns at a shoot. □□ **-loading** *adj.* (in *comb.*) (in sense 2).

loading /ˈləʊdɪŋ/ *n.* **1** *Electr.* the maximum current or power taken by an appliance. **2** an increase in an insurance premium due to a factor increasing the risk involved (see LOAD *v.* 8). **3** *Austral.* an increment added to a basic wage for special skills etc.

loadstar var. of LODESTAR.

loadstone var. of LODESTONE.

loaf[1] /ləʊf/ *n.* (*pl.* **loaves** /ləʊvz/) **1** a portion of baked bread, usu. of a standard size or shape. **2** a quantity of other food formed into a particular shape (*sugar loaf; meat loaf*). **3** *sl.* the head, esp. as a source of common sense (*use your loaf*). □ **loaf sugar** a sugar loaf as a whole or cut into lumps. [OE *hlāf* f. Gmc]

loaf[2] /ləʊf/ *v. & n.* —*v.* **1** *intr.* (often foll. by *about, around*) spend time idly; hang about. **2** *tr.* (foll. by *away*) waste (time) idly (*loafed away the morning*). **3** *intr.* saunter. —*n.* an act or spell of loafing. [prob. a back-form. f. LOAFER]

loafer /ˈləʊfə(r)/ *n.* **1** an idle person. **2** (**Loafer**) *propr.* a leather shoe shaped like a moccasin with a flat heel. [perh. f. G *Landläufer* vagabond]

loam /ləʊm/ *n.* **1** a fertile soil of clay and sand containing decayed vegetable matter. **2** a paste of clay and water with sand, chopped straw, etc., used in making bricks, plastering, etc. □□ **loamy** *adj.* **loaminess** *n.* [OE *lām* f. WG, rel. to LIME[1]]

loan[1] /ləʊn/ *n. & v.* —*n.* **1** something lent, esp. a sum of money to be returned normally with interest. **2** the act of lending or state of being lent. **3** funds acquired by the State, esp. from individuals, and regarded as a debt. **4** a word, custom, etc., adopted by one people from another. —*v.tr.* lend (esp. money). □ **loan shark** *colloq.* a person who lends money at exorbitant rates of interest. **loan-translation** an expression adopted by one language from another in a more or less literally translated form. **on loan** acquired or given as a loan. □□ **loanable** *adj.* **loanee** /ləʊˈniː/ *n.* **loaner** *n.* [ME *lan* f. ON *lán* f. Gmc: cf. LEND]

loan[2] /ləʊn/ *n.* (also **loaning** /ˈləʊnɪŋ/) *Sc.* **1** a lane. **2** an open place where cows are milked. [ME var. of LANE]

loanholder /ˈləʊnˌhəʊldə(r)/ *n.* **1** a person holding securities for a loan. **2** a mortgagee.

loanword /ˈləʊnwɜːd/ *n.* a word adopted, usu. with little modification, from a foreign language.

loath /ləʊθ/ *predic.adj.* (also **loth**) (usu. foll. by *to* + *infin.*) disinclined, reluctant, unwilling (*was loath to admit it*). □ **nothing loath** *adj.* quite willing. [OE *lāth* f. Gmc]

loathe /ləʊð/ *v.tr.* regard with disgust; abominate, detest. □□ **loather** *n.* **loathing** *n.* [OE *lāthian* f. Gmc, rel. to LOATH]

loathsome /ˈləʊðsəm/ *adj.* arousing hatred or disgust; offensive, repulsive. □□ **loathsomely** *adv.* **loathsomeness** *n.* [ME f. *loath* disgust f. LOATHE]

loaves *pl.* of LOAF[1].

lob /lɒb/ *v. & n.* —*v.tr.* (**lobbed, lobbing**) **1** hit or throw (a ball or missile etc.) slowly or in a high arc. **2** send (an opponent) a lobbed ball. —*n.* **1 a** a ball struck in a high arc. **b** a stroke producing this result. **2** *Cricket* a slow underarm ball. [earlier as noun, prob. f. LG or Du.]

Lobachevski /ˌlɒbəˈtʃefskɪ/ Nikolai Ivanovich (1792–1856), Russian mathematician who, at about the same time as Gauss in Germany and János Bolyai in Hungary, discovered non-Euclidean geometry. His work was entirely independent of theirs despite suggestions to the contrary in the song by the American singer Tom Lehrer that has immortalized his name.

lobar /ˈləʊbə(r)/ adj. **1** of the lungs (lobar pneumonia). **2** of, relating to, or affecting a lobe.

lobate /ˈləʊbeɪt/ adj. Biol. having a lobe or lobes. □□ **lobation** /-ˈbeɪʃ(ə)n/ n.

lobby /ˈlɒbɪ/ n. & v. —n. (pl. **-ies**) **1** a porch, ante-room, entrance-hall, or corridor. **2 a** (in the House of Commons) a large hall used esp. for interviews between MPs and members of the public. **b** (also **division lobby**) each of two corridors to which MPs retire to vote. **3 a** a body of persons seeking to influence legislators on behalf of a particular interest (the anti-abortion lobby). **b** an organized attempt by members of the public to influence legislators (a lobby of MPs). **4** (prec. by the) (in the UK) a group of journalists who receive unattributable briefings from the government (lobby correspondent). —v. (**-ies, -ied**) **1** tr. solicit the support of (an influential person). **2** tr. (of members of the public) seek to influence (the members of a legislature). **3** intr. frequent a parliamentary lobby. **4** tr. (foll. by through) get (a bill etc.) through a legislature, by interviews etc. in the lobby. □□ **lobbyer** n. **lobbyism** n. **lobbyist** n. [med.L lobia, lobium LODGE]

lobe /ləʊb/ n. **1** a roundish and flattish projecting or pendulous part, often each of two or more such parts divided by a fissure (lobes of the brain). **2** = ear lobe (see EAR[1]). □□ **lobed** adj. **lobeless** adj. [LL f. Gk lobos lobe, pod]

lobectomy /ləˈbektəmɪ/ n. (pl. **-ies**) Surgery the excision of a lobe of an organ such as the thyroid gland, lung, etc.

lobelia /ləˈbiːlɪə/ n. any plant of the genus Lobelia, with blue, scarlet, white, or purple flowers having a deeply cleft corolla. [M. de Lobel, Flemish botanist in England d. 1616]

Lobito /lʊˈbiːtəʊ/ a seaport on the Atlantic coast of Angola; pop. 60,000. Linked by rail to Zaïre, Zambia, and the Mozambique port of Beira, Lobito is one of the best natural harbours on the west coast of Africa.

lobotomy /ləˈbɒtəmɪ/ n. (pl. **-ies**) Surgery = LEUCOTOMY. [LOBE + -TOMY]

lobscouse /ˈlɒbskaʊs/ n. a sailor's dish of meat stewed with vegetables and ship's biscuit. [18th c.: orig. unkn.: cf. Du. lapskous, Da., Norw., G Lapskaus]

lobster /ˈlɒbstə(r)/ n. & v. —n. **1** any large marine crustacean of the family Nephropidae, with stalked eyes and two pincer-like claws as the first pair of ten limbs. **2** its flesh as food. —v.intr. catch lobsters. □ **lobster-pot** a basket in which lobsters are trapped. **lobster thermidor** /ˈθɜːmɪdɔː(r)/ a mixture of lobster meat, mushrooms, cream, egg yolks, and sherry, cooked in a lobster shell. [OE lopustre, corrupt. of L locusta crustacean, locust: thermidor f. the name of the 11th month of the Fr. revolutionary calendar]

lobule /ˈlɒbjuːl/ n. a small lobe. □□ **lobular** adj. **lobulate** /-lət/ adj. [LOBE]

lobworm /ˈlɒbwɜːm/ n. **1** a large earthworm used as fishing-bait. **2** = LUGWORM. [LOB in obs. sense 'pendulous object']

local /ˈləʊk(ə)l/ adj. & n. —adj. **1** belonging to or existing in a particular place or places. **2** peculiar to or only encountered in a particular place or places. **3** of or belonging to the neighbourhood (the local doctor). **4** of or affecting a part and not the whole, esp. of the body (local pain; a local anaesthetic). **5** in regard to place. —n. a local person or thing, esp.: **1** an inhabitant of a particular place regarded with reference to that place. **2** a local train, bus, etc. **3** (often prec. by the) Brit. colloq. a local public house. **4** a local anaesthetic. **5** US a local branch of a trade union. □ **local authority** Brit. an administrative body in local government. **local Derby** see DERBY. **local government** a system of administration of a county, district, parish, etc., by the elected representatives of those who live there. **Local Group** the cluster of galaxies of which our Galaxy is a member. **local option** (or **veto**) esp. US a system whereby the inhabitants of a district may prohibit the sale of alcoholic liquor there. **local preacher** a Methodist lay person authorized to conduct services in a particular circuit. **local time 1** time measured from the sun's transit over the meridian of a place. **2** the time as reckoned

in a particular place, esp. with reference to an event recorded there. **local train** a train stopping at all the stations on its route. □□ **locally** adv. **localness** n. [ME f. OF f. LL localis f. L locus place]

locale /ləʊˈkɑːl/ n. a scene or locality, esp. with reference to an event or occurrence taking place there. [F local (n.) (as LOCAL), respelt to indicate stress: cf. MORALE]

localism /ˈləʊkəˌlɪz(ə)m/ n. **1** preference for what is local. **2** a local idiom, custom, etc. **3** a attachment to a place. **b** a limitation of ideas etc. resulting from this.

locality /ləʊˈkælɪtɪ/ n. (pl. **-ies**) **1** a district or neighbourhood. **2** the site or scene of something, esp. in relation to its surroundings. **3** the position of a thing; the place where it is. [F localité or LL localitas (as LOCAL)]

localize /ˈləʊkəˌlaɪz/ v.tr. (also **-ise**) **1** restrict or assign to a particular place. **2** invest with the characteristics of a particular place. **3** attach to districts; decentralize. □□ **localizable** adj. **localization** /-ˈzeɪʃ(ə)n/ n.

Locarno /ləˈkɑːnəʊ/ a resort in southern Switzerland, at the north end of Lake Maggiore; pop. (1980) 14,103.

locate /ləʊˈkeɪt/ v. **1** tr. discover the exact place or position of (locate the enemy's camp). **2** tr. establish in a place or in its proper place. **3** tr. state the locality of. **4** tr. (in passive) be situated. **5** intr. (often foll. by in) US take up residence or business (in a place). □□ **locatable** adj. **locator** n. [L locare locat- f. locus place]

location /ləʊˈkeɪʃ(ə)n/ n. **1** a particular place; the place or position in which a person or thing is. **2** the act of locating or process of being located. **3** an actual place or natural setting featured in a film or broadcast, as distinct from a simulation in a studio (filmed entirely on location). **4** S.Afr. an area where Blacks are obliged to live, usu. on the outskirts of a town or city. [L locatio (as LOCATE)]

locative /ˈlɒkətɪv/ n. & adj. Gram. —n. the case of nouns, pronouns, and adjectives, expressing location. —adj. of or in the locative. [formed as LOCATE + -IVE, after vocative]

loc. cit. abbr. in the passage already cited. [L loco citato]

loch /lɒk, lɒx/ n. Sc. **1** a lake. **2** an arm of the sea, esp. when narrow or partially land-locked. [ME f. Gael.]

lochia /ˈlɒkɪə, ˈləʊ-/ n. a discharge from the uterus after childbirth. □□ **lochial** adj. [mod.L f. Gk lokhia neut. pl. of lokhios of childbirth]

Loch Ness monster /nes/ an immense aquatic creature alleged to live in the deep waters of Loch Ness in Highland, Scotland. Reported appearances date from the time of St Columba (6th c.), who, according to a chronicler, saw it about to attack a man in the water and commanded it to go away, whereupon it retreated. The construction of a motor road immediately beside the loch in 1933 produced a flood of alleged sightings.

loci pl. of LOCUS.

loci classici pl. of LOCUS CLASSICUS.

lock[1] /lɒk/ n. & v. —n. **1** a mechanism for fastening a door, lid, etc., with a bolt that requires a key of a particular shape, or a combination of movements (see combination lock), to work it. **2** a confined section of a canal or river where the level can be changed for raising and lowering boats between adjacent sections by the use of gates and sluices. **3 a** the turning of the front wheels of a vehicle to change its direction of motion. **b** (in full **full lock**) the maximum extent of this. **4** an interlocked or jammed state. **5** Wrestling a hold that keeps an opponent's limb fixed. **6** (in full **lock forward**) Rugby Football a player in the second row of a scrum. **7** an appliance to keep a wheel from revolving or slewing. **8** a mechanism for exploding the charge of a gun. **9** = airlock 2. —v. **1 a** tr. fasten with a lock. **b** tr. (foll. by up) shut and secure (esp. a building) by locking. **c** intr. (of a door, window, box, etc.) have the means of being locked. **2** tr. (foll. by up, in, into) enclose (a person or thing) by locking or as if by locking. **3** tr. (often foll. by up, away) store or allocate inaccessibly (capital locked up in land). **4** tr. (foll. by in) hold fast (in sleep or enchantment etc.). **5** tr. (usu. in passive) (of land, hills, etc.) enclose. **6** tr. & intr. make or become rigidly fixed or immovable. **7** intr. & tr. become or cause to become jammed or caught. **8** *tr.* (often in *passive*; foll. by *in*) entangle in an embrace or struggle. **9** *tr.* provide (a canal etc.) with locks. **10** *tr.* (foll. by *up*, *down*) convey (a boat) through a lock. **11** *intr.* go through a lock on a canal etc. □ **lock-keeper** a keeper of a lock on a river or canal. **lock-knit** knitted with an interlocking stitch. **lock-nut** *Mech.* a nut screwed down on another to keep it tight. **lock on** to locate or cause to locate by radar etc. and then track. **lock out** **1** keep (a person) out by locking the door. **2** (of an employer) submit (employees) to a lockout. **lock step** marching with each person as close as possible to the one in front. **lock stitch** see separate entry. **lock, stock, and barrel** the whole of a thing. —*adv.* completely. **under lock and key** securely locked up. □□ **lockable** *adj.* **lockless** *adj.* [OE *loc* f. Gmc]

lock² /lɒk/ *n.* **1 a** a portion of hair that coils or hangs together. **b** (in *pl.*) the hair of the head. **2** a tuft of wool or cotton. □□ **-locked** *adj.* (in *comb.*). [OE *locc* f. Gmc]

lockage /ˈlɒkɪdʒ/ *n.* **1** the amount of rise and fall effected by canal locks. **2** a toll for the use of a lock. **3** the construction or use of locks. **4** locks collectively; the aggregate of locks constructed.

Locke¹ /lɒk/, John (1632–1704), English philosopher, a founder of empiricism and political liberalism. In 1690 he published his *Two Treatises of Government*, designed to combat the theory of the 'divine right of kings' and to justify the Revolution of 1688, finding the origin of the civil State in a contract: the authority of rulers has a human origin, and is limited. His views on the philosophy of politics were influential throughout the following century. Locke's most famous work, *An Essay concerning Human Understanding* (1690), is an attempt to demonstrate what can and cannot be known, in order to guide us to the proper use of our understanding and show us how we should live. Denying that any ideas are innate he argued instead for the central empiricist tenet that all knowledge is derived from sense-experience, and attempted a classification of the sources of various ideas. He concluded that we can know something of the world but not everything, and that we cannot know why things are as they are, that the same was true of morality, and our limited knowledge must be reinforced by faith; in his last major work *The Reasonableness of Christianity* (1695) Locke turned firmly to revelation.

Locke² /lɒk/, Joseph (1805–60), English railway designer who in a lifelong association with Thomas Brassey built lines in England, the west coast line to Scotland, and trunk lines in France. He is honoured on both sides of the Channel as one of the great railway pioneers.

locker /ˈlɒkə(r)/ *n.* **1** a small lockable cupboard or compartment, esp. each of several for public use. **2** *Naut.* a chest or compartment for clothes, stores, ammunition, etc. **3** a person or thing that locks. □ **locker-room** a room containing lockers (in sense 1), esp. in a pavilion or sports centre.

locket /ˈlɒkɪt/ *n.* **1** a small ornamental case holding a portrait, lock of hair, etc., and usu. hung from the neck. **2** a metal plate or band on a scabbard. [OF *locquet* dimin. of *loc* latch, lock, f. WG (as LOCK¹)]

lockfast /ˈlɒkfɑːst/ *adj. Sc.* secured with a lock.

lockjaw /ˈlɒkdʒɔː/ *n.* = TRISMUS. ¶ Not in technical use.

lockout /ˈlɒkaʊt/ *n.* the exclusion of employees by their employer from their place of work until certain terms are agreed to.

locksman /ˈlɒksmən/ *n.* (*pl.* **-men**) a lock-keeper.

locksmith /ˈlɒksmɪθ/ *n.* a maker and mender of locks.

lock stitch *n.* a secure sewing-machine stitch made by locking together two threads or stitches. The needle descends through the fabric, carrying the thread; when it rises the thread forms a loop on the underside of the fabric, a second thread from a shuttle or bobbin is passed through this loop, and the interlocked threads are pulled tight when the fabric is advanced for the next stitch.

lock-up /ˈlɒkʌp/ *n. & adj.* —*n.* **1** a house or room for the temporary detention of prisoners. **2** *Brit.* non-residential premises etc. that can be locked up, esp. a small shop or storehouse. **3 a** the locking up of premises for the night. **b** the time of doing this. **4 a** the unrealizable state of invested capital. **b** an amount of capital locked up. —*attrib.adj. Brit.* that can be locked up (*lock-up shop*).

loco¹ /ˈləʊkəʊ/ *n.* (*pl.* **-os**) *colloq.* a locomotive engine. [abbr.]

loco² /ˈləʊkəʊ/ *adj. & n.* —*adj. sl.* crazy. —*n.* (*pl.* **-oes** or **-os**) (in full **loco-weed**) a poisonous leguminous plant of the US causing brain disease in cattle eating it. [Sp., = insane]

locomotion /ˌləʊkəˈməʊʃ(ə)n/ *n.* **1** motion or the power of motion from one place to another. **2** travel; a means of travelling, esp. an artificial one. [L *loco* ablat. of *locus* place + *motio* MOTION]

locomotive /ˌləʊkəˈməʊtɪv/ *n. & adj.* —*n.* (in full **locomotive engine**) an engine powered by steam, diesel fuel, or electricity, used for pulling trains. *adj.* **1** of or relating to or effecting locomotion (*locomotive power*). **2** having the power of or given to locomotion; not stationary.

locomotor /ˌləʊkəˈməʊtə(r)/ *adj.* of or relating to locomotion. [LOCOMOTION + MOTOR]

loculus /ˈlɒkjʊləs/ *n.* (*pl.* **loculi** /-ˌlaɪ/) *Zool., Anat., & Bot.* each of a number of small separate cavities. □□ **locular** *adj.* [L, dimin. of *locus*: see LOCUS]

locum /ˈləʊkəm/ *n. colloq.* = LOCUM TENENS. [abbr.]

locum tenens /ˌləʊkəm ˈtiːnenz, ˈtenenz/ *n.* (*pl.* **locum tenentes** /ˌləʊkəm tɪˈnentiːz/) a deputy acting esp. for a cleric or doctor. □□ **locum tenency** /ˌləʊkəm ˈtenənsɪ/ *n.* [med.L, one holding a place: see LOCUS, TENANT]

locus /ˈləʊkəs, ˈlɒkəs/ *n.* (*pl.* **loci** /-saɪ, -kaɪ, -kiː/) **1** a position or point, esp. in a text, treatise, etc. **2** *Math.* a curve etc. formed by all the points satisfying a particular equation of the relation between coordinates, or by a point, line, or surface moving according to mathematically defined conditions. **3** *Biol.* the position of a gene, mutation, etc. on a chromosome. [L, = place]

locus classicus /ˌləʊkəs ˈklæsɪkəs, ˌlɒkəs/ *n.* (*pl.* **loci classici** /ˌləʊsaɪ ˈklæsɪˌsaɪ, ˌlɒkiː ˈklæsɪˌkiː/) the best known or most authoritative passage on a subject. [L]

locus standi /ˌləʊkəs ˈstændaɪ, ˌlɒkəs/ *n.* a recognized or identifiable (esp. legal) status.

locust /ˈləʊkəst/ *n.* **1** any of various African and Asian grasshoppers of the family Acrididae, migrating in swarms and destroying vegetation. **2** *US* a cicada. **3** (in full **locust bean**) a carob. **4** (in full **locust tree**) **a** a carob tree. **b** = ACACIA 2. **c** = KOWHAI. □ **locust-bird** (or **-eater**) any of various birds feeding on locusts. [ME f. OF *locuste* f. L *locusta* lobster, locust]

locution /ləˈkjuːʃ(ə)n/ *n.* **1** a word or phrase, esp. considered in regard to style or idiom. **2** style of speech. [ME f. OF *locution* or L *locutio* f. *loqui locut-* speak]

lode /ləʊd/ *n.* a vein of metal ore. [var. of LOAD]

loden /ˈləʊd(ə)n/ *n.* **1** a thick waterproof woollen cloth. **2** the dark green colour in which this is often made. [G]

lodestar /ˈləʊdstɑː(r)/ *n.* (also **loadstar**) **1** a star that a ship etc. is steered by, esp. the pole star. **2 a** a guiding principle. **b** an object of pursuit. [LODE in obs. sense 'way, journey' + STAR]

lodestone /ˈləʊdstəʊn/ *n.* (also **loadstone**) **1** magnetic oxide of iron, magnetite. **2 a** a piece of this used as a magnet. **b** a thing that attracts.

lodge /lɒdʒ/ *n. & v.* —*n.* **1** a small house at the gates of a park or in the grounds of a large house, occupied by a gatekeeper, gardener, etc. **2** any large house or hotel, esp. in a resort. **3** a house occupied in the hunting or shooting season. **4 a** a porter's room or quarters at the gate of a college or other large building. **b** the residence of a head of a college, esp. at Cambridge. **5** the members or the meeting-place of a branch of a society such as the Freemasons. **6** a local branch of a trade union. **7** a beaver's or otter's lair. **8** a N. American Indian's tent or wigwam. —*v.* **1** *tr.* deposit in court or with an official a formal statement of (complaint or information). **2** *tr.* deposit (money etc.) for security. **3** *tr.* bring forward (an objection etc.). **4** *tr.* (foll. by *in*, *with*) place (power etc.) in a person or group. **5** *tr. & intr.* make or become fixed or caught without further movement (*the bullet lodged in his brain*; *the tide lodges mud in the cavities*). **6** *tr.* **a** provide with sleeping quarters. **b** receive as a guest or inmate. **c**

establish as a resident in a house or room or rooms. **7** *intr.* reside or live, esp. as a guest paying for accommodation. **8** *tr.* serve as a habitation for; contain. **9** *tr.* (in *passive*; foll. by *in*) be contained in. **10 a** *tr.* (of wind or rain) flatten (crops). **b** *intr.* (of crops) be flattened in this way. [ME *loge* f. OF *loge* arbour, hut, f. med.L *laubia, lobia* (see LOBBY) f. Gmc]

lodgement /ˈlɒdʒm(ə)nt/ *n.* **1** the act of lodging or process of being lodged. **2** the depositing or a deposit of money. **3** an accumulation of matter intercepted in fall or transit. [F *logement* (as LODGE)]

lodger /ˈlɒdʒə(r)/ *n.* a person receiving accommodation in another's house for payment.

lodging /ˈlɒdʒɪŋ/ *n.* **1** temporary accommodation (*a lodging for the night*). **2** (in *pl.*) a room or rooms (other than in a hotel) rented for lodging in. **3** a dwelling-place. **4** (in *pl.*) the residence of a head of a college at Oxford. □ **lodging-house** a house in which lodgings are let.

lodicule /ˈlɒdɪˌkjuːl/ *n. Bot.* a small green or white scale below the ovary of a grass flower. [L *lodicula* dimin. of *lodix* coverlet]

Lodz /wʊtʃ/ (Polish Łódź) the second-largest city in Poland; pop. (1985) 849,000.

loess /ˈləʊɪs, lɜːs/ *n.* a deposit of fine light-coloured wind-blown dust found esp. in the basins of large rivers and very fertile when irrigated. □□ **loessial** /ləʊˈesɪəl, ˈlɜːsɪəl/ *adj.* [G *Löss* f. Swiss G *lösch* loose f. *lösen* loosen]

loft /lɒft/ *n. & v.* —*n.* **1** the space under the roof of a house, above the ceiling of the top floor; an attic. **2** a room over a stable, esp. for hay and straw. **3** a gallery in a church or hall (*organ-loft*). **4** US an upstairs room. **5** a pigeon-house. **6** *Golf* **a** a backward slope in a club-head. **b** a lofting stroke. —*v.tr.* **1 a** send (a ball etc.) high up. **b** clear (an obstacle) in this way. **2** (esp. as **lofted** *adj.*) give a loft to (a golf club). [OE f. ON *lopt* air, sky, upper room, f. Gmc (as LIFT)]

Lofoten Islands /ləˈfəʊt(ə)n/ an island group in the Norwegian Sea, off the north-west coast of Norway, south-west of the Ver-staalen group.

lofter /ˈlɒftə(r)/ *n.* a golf club for lofting the ball.

lofty /ˈlɒftɪ/ *adj.* (**loftier, loftiest**) **1** *literary* (of things) of imposing height, towering, soaring (*lofty heights*). **2** consciously haughty, aloof, or dignified (*lofty contempt*). **3** exalted or noble; sublime (*lofty ideals*). □□ **loftily** *adv.* **loftiness** *n.* [ME f. LOFT as in *aloft*]

log[1] /lɒg/ *n. & v.* —*n.* **1** an unhewn piece of a felled tree, or a similar rough mass of wood, esp. cut for firewood. **2 a** a float attached to a line wound on a reel for gauging the speed of a ship. **b** any other apparatus for the same purpose. **3** a record of events occurring during and affecting the voyage of a ship or aircraft (including the rate of a ship's progress shown by a log: see sense 2). **4** any systematic record of things done, experienced, etc. **5** = LOGBOOK. —*v.tr.* (**logged, logging**) **1 a** enter (the distance made or other details) in a ship's logbook. **b** enter details about (a person or event) in a logbook. **c** (of a ship) achieve (a certain distance). **2 a** enter (information) in a regular record. **b** attain (a cumulative total of time etc. recorded in this way) (*logged 50 hours on the computer*). **3** cut into logs. □ **like a log 1** in a helpless or stunned state (*fell like a log under the left hook*). **2** without stirring (*slept like a log*). **log cabin** a hut built of logs. **log in** = log on. **log-jam** a crowded mass of logs in a river. **2** a deadlock. **log-line** a line to which a ship's log (see sense 2a of *n.*) is attached. **log on** (or **off**) go through the procedures to begin (or conclude) use of a computer system. [ME: orig. unkn.]

log[2] /lɒg/ *n.* a logarithm (esp. prefixed to a number or algebraic symbol whose logarithm is to be indicated). [abbr.]

-log US var. of -LOGUE.

logan /ˈləʊgən/ *n.* (in full **logan-stone**) a poised heavy stone rocking at a touch. [= *logging* f. dial. *log* to rock + STONE]

loganberry /ˈləʊgənbərɪ/ *n.* (*pl.* **-ies**) **1** a hybrid, *Rubus loganobaccus*, between a blackberry and a raspberry with dull red acid fruits. **2** the fruit of this plant. [J. H. *Logan*, Amer. horticulturalist d. 1928 + BERRY]

logarithm /ˈlɒgəˌrɪð(ə)m/ *n.* **1** any of a series of arithmetic

exponents tabulated to simplify computation by making it possible to use addition and subtraction instead of multiplication and division. (See NAPIER.) **2** the power to which a fixed number or base (see BASE[1] 7) must be raised to produce a given number (*the logarithm of 1000 to base 10 is 3*). ¶ Abbr.: **log**. □ **common logarithm** a logarithm to the base 10. **natural** (or **Napierian**) **logarithm** a logarithm to the base *e* (2.71828.....). ¶ Abbr.: **ln** or **log**$_e$. □□ **logarithmic** /-ˈrɪðmɪk/ *adj.* **logarithmically** /-ˈrɪðmɪkəlɪ/ *adv.* [mod.L *logarithmus* f. Gk *logos* reckoning, ratio + *arithmos* number]

logbook /ˈlɒgbʊk/ *n.* **1** a book containing a detailed record or log. **2** *Brit.* a document recording the registration details of a motor vehicle. ¶ Now officially called *vehicle registration document*.

loge /ləʊʒ/ *n.* a private box or enclosure in a theatre. [F]

log$_e$ /ˈlɒgiː/ *abbr.* natural logarithm.

-loger /lədʒə(r)/ *comb. form* forming nouns, = -LOGIST. [after *astrologer*]

logger /ˈlɒgə(r)/ *n. US* a lumberjack.

loggerhead /ˈlɒgəhed/ *n.* **1** an iron instrument with a ball at the end heated for melting pitch etc. **2** any of various large-headed animals, esp. a turtle (*Caretta caretta*) or shrike (*Lanius ludovicianus*). **3** *archaic* a blockhead or fool. □ **at loggerheads** (often foll. by *with*) disagreeing or disputing. [prob. f. dial. *logger* block of wood for hobbling a horse + HEAD]

loggia /ˈləʊdʒə, ˈlɒ-/ *n.* **1** an open-sided gallery or arcade. **2** an open-sided extension of a house. [It., = LODGE]

logging /ˈlɒgɪŋ/ *n.* the work of cutting and preparing forest timber.

logia *pl.* of LOGION.

logic /ˈlɒdʒɪk/ *n.* **1 a** the science of reasoning, proof, thinking, or inference. (See below.) **b** a particular scheme of or treatise on this. **2 a** a chain of reasoning (*I don't follow your logic*). **b** the correct or incorrect use of reasoning (*your logic is flawed*). **c** ability in reasoning (*argues with great learning and logic*). **d** arguments (*is not governed by logic*). **3 a** the inexorable force or compulsion of a thing (*the logic of events*). **b** the necessary consequence of (an argument, decision, etc.). **4 a** a system or set of principles underlying the arrangements of elements in a computer or electronic device so as to perform a specified task. **b** logical operations collectively. □□ **logician** /ləˈdʒɪʃ(ə)n/ *n.* [ME f. OF *logique* f. LL *logica* f. Gk *logikē* (*tekhnē*) (art) of reason: see LOGOS]

Logic is the systematic study of the patterns of argument, and in particular of those patterns of argument that are valid, i.e. such that if the premises are true then of necessity the conclusion is true. The chief instrument of advance has been the development of symbols which make it possible to abstract from particular premisses and conclusions and consider only the patterns. The process was begun by Aristotle, who gave rules for which syllogisms are valid. Since the 19th c. the formulation of such rules has drawn on the concepts and techniques of mathematics, using symbols to replace ordinary language; the greatest advance was made by Gottlob Frege (1848–1925) who devised a simple method of handling 'all' and 'some'. (Questions can be raised about how far the systems of Frege and Russell preserve what is ordinarily meant by the words they replace with symbols.) In the 20th c. there have come to be two branches. *Philosophical logic* is the study of certain expressions of ordinary language to see how they do work: the goal of seeing which inferences are valid may be forgotten. *Mathematical* or *formal logic*, see MATHEMATICAL.

-logic /ˈlɒdʒɪk/ *comb. form* (also **-logical**) forming adjectives corresponding esp. to nouns in -*logy* (*pathological; theological*). [from or after Gk -*logikos*: see -IC, -ICAL]

logical /ˈlɒdʒɪk(ə)l/ *adj.* **1** of logic or formal argument. **2** not contravening the laws of thought, correctly reasoned. **3** deducible or defensible on the ground of consistency; reasonably to be believed or done. **4** capable of correct reasoning. □ **logical atomism** *Philos.* the theory that all propositions can be analysed into simple independent elements. **logical necessity** the compulsion to believe that of which the opposite is inconceivable. □□ **logicality** /-ˈkælɪtɪ/ *n.* **logically** *adv.* [med.L *logicalis* f. LL *logica* (as LOGIC)]

logical positivism *n.* the theories of the Vienna Circle (influentially expounded by A. J. Ayer in *Language, Truth, and Logic,* 1936) aimed at evolving formal methods, similar to those of the mathematical sciences, for the verification of empirical questions and therefore eliminating metaphysical and other more speculative questions. A statement, they held, has meaning only if its truth or falsity can be tested empirically; logical and mathematical statements are tautologous because they are valid only within their own system; moral and value judgements are subjective and therefore without universal application; metaphysical and religious speculation is logically ill-founded. □□ **logical positivist** one who holds such theories.

logion /ˈlɒɡɪən/ *n.* (*pl.* **logia** /-ɡɪə/) a saying attributed to Christ, esp. one not recorded in the canonical Gospels. [Gk, = oracle f. *logos* word]

-logist /lədʒɪst/ *comb. form* forming nouns denoting a person skilled or involved in a branch of study etc. with a name in *-logy* (*archaeologist; etymologist*).

logistics /ləˈdʒɪstɪks/ *n.pl.* **1** the organization of moving, lodging, and supplying troops and equipment. **2** the detailed organization and implementation of a plan or operation. □□ **logistic** *adj.* **logistical** *adj.* **logistically** *adv.* [F *logistique* f. *loger* lodge]

logo /ˈləʊɡəʊ, ˈlɒɡəʊ/ *n.* (*pl.* **-os**) *colloq.* = LOGOTYPE 2. [abbr.]

logogram /ˈlɒɡəˌɡræm/ *n.* a sign or character representing a word, esp. in shorthand. [Gk *logos* word + -GRAM]

logomachy /ləˈɡɒməkɪ/ *n.* (*pl.* **-ies**) *literary* a dispute about words; controversy turning on merely verbal points. [Gk *logomakhia* f. *logos* word + *makhia* fighting]

logorrhoea /ˌlɒɡəˈrɪə/ *n.* (*US* **logorrhea**) an excessive flow of words esp. in mental illness. [Gk *logos* word + *rhoia* flow]

Logos /ˈlɒɡɒs/ *n.* the Word of God, or Second Person of the Trinity, incarnate in Jesus Christ according to the fourth Gospel. [Gk, = word, reason (*legō* speak)]

logotype /ˈlɒɡəˌtaɪp/ *n.* **1** *Printing* a single piece of type that prints a word or group of separate letters. **2 a** an emblem or device used as the badge of an organization in display material. **b** *Printing* a single piece of type that prints this. [Gk *logos* word + TYPE]

logrolling /ˈlɒɡˌrəʊlɪŋ/ *n.* *US* **1** *colloq.* the practice of exchanging favours, esp. (in politics) of exchanging votes to mutual benefit. **2** a sport in which two contestants stand on a floating log and try to knock each other off. □□ **logroll** *v.intr.* & *tr.* **logroller** *n.* [polit. sense f. phr. *you roll my log and I'll roll yours*]

-logue /lɒɡ/ *comb. form* (*US* **-log**) **1** forming nouns denoting talk (*dialogue*) or compilation (*catalogue*). **2** = -LOGIST (*ideologue*). [from or after F *-logue* f. Gk *-logos, -logon*]

logwood /ˈlɒɡwʊd/ *n.* **1** a W. Indian tree, *Haematoxylon campechianum.* **2** the wood of this, producing a substance used in dyeing.

-logy /lədʒɪ/ *comb. form* forming nouns denoting: **1** (usu. as **-ology**) a subject of study or interest (*archaeology; zoology*). **2** a characteristic of speech or language (*tautology*). **3** discourse (*trilogy*). [F *-logie* or med.L *-logia* f. Gk (as LOGOS)]

Lohengrin /ˈləʊhɪnˌɡrɪn/ *French* & *German legend* the son of Perceval. He was summoned from the temple of the Grail and borne in a swan-boat to Antwerp to defend Elsa of Brabant against Frederick of Telramund, who wished to marry her (against her will). He overcame Frederick and consented to marry Elsa on condition that she did not ask who he was, but Elsa broke this condition and he was carried away again in the swan-boat. This forms the subject of a music drama by Wagner, produced in 1850. A similar tale is told of Helias, the legendary grandfather of Godfrey de Bouillon (leader of the first Crusade).

loin /lɔɪn/ *n.* **1** (in *pl.*) the part of the body on both sides of the spine between the false ribs and the hip-bones. **2** a joint of meat that includes the loin vertebrae. [ME f. OF *loigne* ult. f. L *lumbus*]

loincloth /ˈlɔɪnklɒθ/ *n.* a cloth worn round the loins, esp. as a sole garment.

Loire /lɑˈwɑː(r)/ the longest river of France (1,015 km, 630 miles), flowing from the Massif Central north and west to the Atlantic Ocean at St Nazaire. Principal cities upon it are Orléans, Tours,

and Nantes; the valley is particularly noted for the châteaux that lie along its course.

loiter /ˈlɔɪtə(r)/ *v.* **1** *intr.* hang about; linger idly. **2** *intr.* travel indolently and with long pauses. **3** *tr.* (foll. by *away*) pass (time etc.) in loitering. □ **loiter with intent** hang about in order to commit a felony. □□ **loiterer** *n.* [ME f. MDu. *loteren* wag about]

Loki /ˈləʊkɪ/ *Scand. Mythol.* a spirit of evil and mischief who contrived the death of Balder.

Lola Montez /ˈləʊlə ˈmɒntɪz/ (1818–61), stage name of the actress and adventuress Marie Dolores Eliza Rosanna Gilbert, who, after making a considerable name for herself as a dancer, became the mistress of Ludwig I of Bavaria and all but ruled the country through him until banished as a result of foreign influence.

loll /lɒl/ *v.* **1** *intr.* stand, sit, or recline in a lazy attitude. **2** *intr.* (foll. by *out*) (of the tongue) hang out. **3** *tr.* (foll. by *out*) hang (one's tongue) out. **4** *tr.* let (one's head or limbs) rest lazily on something. □□ **loller** *n.* [ME: prob. imit.]

Lolland /ˈlɒlɑːn/ a Danish island in the Baltic Sea to the south of Zealand and west of Falster. Its name means 'low land'.

Lollard /ˈlɒləd/ *n.* any of the followers of the 14th-c. religious reformer John Wyclif or those who held opinions similar to his on the necessity for the Church to aid men to live a life of evangelical poverty and imitate Christ. The name itself was a term of contempt, derived from a Dutch word meaning 'mumbler'. Official attitudes to the Lollards varied considerably, but they were generally held to be heretics and often severely persecuted. Their ideas influenced the thought of John Huss, who in turn influenced Martin Luther. □□ **Lollardism** *n.* [MDu. *lollaerd* f. *lollen* mumble]

lollipop /ˈlɒlɪˌpɒp/ *n.* a large usu. flat rounded boiled sweet on a small stick. □ **lollipop man** (or **lady** or **woman**) *Brit. colloq.* an official using a circular sign on a stick to stop traffic for children to cross the road, esp. near a school. [perh. f. dial. *lolly* tongue + POP¹]

lollop /ˈlɒləp/ *v.intr.* (**lolloped**, **lolloping**) *colloq.* **1** flop about. **2** move or proceed in a lounging or ungainly way. [prob. f. LOLL, assoc. with TROLLOP]

lolly /ˈlɒlɪ/ *n.* (*pl.* **-ies**) **1** *colloq.* **a** a lollipop. **b** *Austral.* a sweet. **c** *Brit.* = *ice lolly.* **2** *Brit. sl.* money. [abbr. of LOLLIPOP]

Lombard /ˈlɒmbɑːd/ *n.* & *adj.* —*n.* **1** a member of a Germanic people from the lower Elbe who invaded Italy in 568 and founded a kingdom (overthrown by Charlemagne in 774) in the valley of the Po. **2** a native of Lombardy. **3** the dialect of Lombardy. —*adj.* of or relating to the Lombards or Lombardy. □□ **Lombardic** /-ˈbɑːdɪk/ *adj.* [ME f. OF *lombard* or MDu. *lombaerd,* f. It. *lombardo* f. med.L *Longobardus* f. L *Langobardus* f. Gmc]

Lombard Street a street in the City of London formerly occupied by Lombard bankers and still containing many of the chief London banks.

Lombardy /ˈlɒmbədɪ/ (Italian **Lombardia**) a region of central northern Italy, lying mainly between the Alps and the River Po, which became part of the kingdom of Italy in 1859; pop. (1981) 8,891,650. Milan is its principal city. □ **Lombardy poplar** a variety of poplar with an especially tall slender form.

Lombok /ˈlɒmbɒk/ an island of the Lesser Sundas, Indonesia, situated between Bali and Sumbawa.

Lomé /ˈləʊmeɪ/ the capital and chief port of Togo; pop. (1983) 366,500. □ **Lomé Convention** a trade agreement of 1975, reached in Lomé, between the EEC and 46 African, Caribbean, and Pacific Ocean States, for technical cooperation and development aid. A second agreement was signed in 1979 by a larger group.

loment /ˈləʊmənt/ *n. Bot.* a kind of pod that breaks up when mature into one-seeded joints. □□ **lomentaceous** /-ˈteɪʃ(ə)s/ *adj.* [L *lomentum* bean-meal (orig. cosmetic) f. *lavare* wash]

Lomond /ˈləʊmənd/, **Loch** the largest freshwater lake in Scotland, divided between Strathclyde and Central regions.

London¹ /ˈlʌnd(ə)n/ the capital of the United Kingdom, a port on the River Thames and a commercial, business, and cultural centre; pop. (1981) 6,696,000. Settled by the Romans as a port and trading centre (*Londinium*), London has flourished since the Middle Ages. After the plague of 1665 and the fire of 1666 much of it was rebuilt under the direction of Sir Christopher Wren. Air raids in the Second World War obliterated whole areas of streets and damaged most public buildings; post-war reconstruction has added tower blocks of geometrical aspect to the landscape. □ **London clay** a geological formation in the lower division of the Eocene in SE England. **London plane** a hybrid plane-tree resistant to smoke and therefore often planted in streets. **London pride** a pink-flowered saxifrage, *Saxifraga* × *urbium*. □□ **Londoner** *n*.

London[2] /ˈlʌnd(ə)n/ an industrial city of Canada, situated to the north of Lake Erie in SE Ontario; pop. (1986) 269,100; metropolitan area pop. 342,300.

London[3] /ˈlʌnd(ə)n/, John ('Jack') Griffith (1876–1916), American novelist. He grew up in poverty, scratching a living in various legal and illegal ways and taking part in the Klondike gold rush of 1897—experiences which provided the material for his works and made him a socialist. His most famous novel is *The Call of the Wild* (1903).

Londonderry /ˈlʌndənˌderɪ/ **1** a county of Northern Ireland. **2** its county town, reputedly founded by St Columba in 546. The town was named 'Derry' [f. Gael., = oak grove], a name still retained in the titles of certain organizations etc., until 1613 when it was given to the City of London as part of the area to be colonized, and was renamed Londonderry. In 1689 it was besieged by James II for 105 days before being relieved.

lone /ləʊn/ *attrib.adj.* **1** (of a person) solitary; without a companion or supporter. **2** (of a place) unfrequented, uninhabited, lonely. **3** *literary* feeling or causing to feel lonely. □ **lone hand 1** a hand played or a player playing against the rest at quadrille and euchre. **2** a person or action without allies. **lone wolf** a person who prefers to act alone. [ME, f. ALONE]

lonely /ˈləʊnlɪ/ *adj.* (**lonelier, loneliest**) **1** solitary, companionless, isolated. **2** (of a place) unfrequented. **3** sad because without friends or company. □ **lonely heart** a lonely person (in sense 3). □□ **loneliness** *n*.

loner /ˈləʊnə(r)/ *n.* a person or animal that prefers to associate with others.

lonesome /ˈləʊnsəm/ *adj.* **1** solitary, lonely. **2** feeling lonely or forlorn. **3** causing such a feeling. □ **by** (or **on**) **one's lonesome** all alone. □□ **lonesomely** *adv.* **lonesomeness** *n*.

long[1] /lɒŋ/ *adj., n., & adv.* —*adj.* (**longer** /ˈlɒŋgə(r)/; **longest** /ˈlɒŋgɪst/) **1** measuring much from end to end in space or time; not soon traversed or finished (*a long line; a long journey; a long time ago*). **2** (following a measurement) in length or duration (*2 metres long; the vacation is two months long*). **3** relatively great in extent or duration (*a long meeting*). **4 a** consisting of a large number of items (*a long list*). **b** seemingly more than the stated amount; tedious, lengthy (*ten long miles; tired after a long day*). **5** of elongated shape. **6 a** lasting or reaching far back or forward in time (*a long friendship*). **b** (of a person's memory) retaining things for a long time. **7** far-reaching; acting at a distance; involving a great interval or difference. **8** *Phonet.* & *Prosody* (of a vowel or syllable: **a** having the greater of the two recognized durations. **b** stressed. **c** (of a vowel in English) having the pronunciation shown in the name of the letter (as in *pile* and *cute* which have a long *i* and *u*, as distinct from *pill* and *cut*) (cf. SHORT *adj.* 6). **9** (of odds or a chance) reflecting or representing a low level of probability. **10** *Stock Exch.* **a** (of stocks) bought in large quantities in advance, with the expectation of a rise in price. **b** (of a broker etc.) buying etc. on this basis. **11** (of a bill of exchange) maturing at a distant date. **12** (of a cold drink) large and refreshing. **13** *colloq.* (of a person) tall. **14** (foll. by *on*) *colloq.* well supplied with. —*n.* **1** a long interval or period (*shall not be away for long; it will not take long*). **2** *Phonet.* **a** a long syllable or vowel. **b** a mark indicating that a vowel is long. **3 a** long-dated stock. **b** a person who buys this. —*adv.* (**longer** /ˈlɒŋgə(r)/; **longest** /ˈlɒŋgɪst/) **1** by or for a long time (*long before; long ago; long live the king!*). **2** (following nouns of duration) throughout a specified time (*all day long*). **3** (in *compar.*; with *neg.*) after an implied point of time (*shall not wait any longer*). □ **as** (or **so**) **long as 1** during the whole time that. **2** provided that; only if. **at**

long last see LAST[1]. **before long** fairly soon (*shall see you before long*). **be long** (often foll. by *pres. part.* or *in* + verbal noun) take a long time; be slow (*was long finding it out; the chance was long in coming; I shan't be long*). **by a long chalk** see CHALK. **in the long run 1** over a long period. **2** eventually; finally. **long ago** in the distant past. **long-ago** *adj.* that is in the distant past. **the long and the short of it 1** all that can or need be said. **2** the eventual outcome. **long-case clock** a grandfather clock. **long-chain** (of a molecule) containing a chain of many carbon atoms. **long-dated** (of securities) not due for early payment or redemption. **long-day** (of a plant) needing a long daily period of light to cause flowering. **long-distance 1** (of a telephone call, public transport, etc.) between distant places. **2** (of a weather forecast) long-range. **long division** division of numbers with details of the calculations written down. **long dozen** thirteen. **long-drawn** (or **-drawn-out**) prolonged, esp. unduly. **long face** a dismal or disappointed expression. **long-faced** with a long face. **long field** *Cricket* **1** = *long off*. **2** = *long on*. **3** the part of the field behind the bowler. **long figure** (or **price**) a heavy cost. **long haul 1** the transport of goods or passengers over a long distance. **2** a prolonged effort or task. **long-headed** shrewd, far-seeing, sagacious. **long-headedness** being long-headed. **long hop** a short-pitched easily hit ball in cricket. **long house** (in Britain) an old type of dwelling built to house family and animals under the same roof. (See also LONGHOUSE.) **long hundredweight** see HUNDREDWEIGHT. **long in the tooth** rather old (orig. of horses, from the recession of the gums with age). **long johns** *colloq.* underpants with full-length legs. **long jump** an athletic contest of jumping as far as possible along the ground in one leap. **long leg** *Cricket* **1** a fielder far behind the batsman on the leg side. **2** this position. **long-legged** speedy. **long-life** (of consumable goods) treated to preserve freshness. **long-lived** having a long life; durable. **long measure** a measure of length (metres, miles, etc.). **long metre** a hymn stanza of four lines with eight syllables each. **2** a quatrain of iambic tetrameters with alternate lines rhyming. **long off** (or **on**) *Cricket* **1** a fielder far behind the bowler and towards the off (or on) side. **2** this position. **Long Parliament** see separate entry. **long-player** a long-playing record. **long-playing** (of a gramophone record) playing for about 20–30 minutes on each side. **long-range 1** (of a missile etc.) having a long range. **2** of or relating to a period of time far into the future. **long-running** continuing for a long time. **long ship** *hist.* a long narrow warship with many rowers. Such ships were used by Scandinavian maritime peoples until the mid-18th c. **long shot 1** a wild guess or venture. **2** a bet at long odds. **3** *Cinematog.* a shot including objects at a distance. **long sight** the ability to see clearly only what is comparatively distant. **long-sleeved** with sleeves reaching to the wrist. **long-standing** that has long existed; not recent. **long-suffering** bearing provocation patiently. **long-sufferingly** in a long-suffering manner. **long suit 1** many cards of one suit in a hand (esp. more than 3 or 4 in a hand of 13). **2** a thing at which one excels. **long-term** occurring in or relating to a long period of time (*long-term plans*). **long-time** that has been such for a long time. **long ton** see TON[1]. **long tongue** loquacity. **long vacation** *Brit.* the summer vacation of lawcourts and universities. **long waist** a low or deep waist of a dress or body. **long wave** a radio wave of frequency less than 300 kHz. **night of the long knives 1** a treacherous massacre, as (according to legend) the Britons by Hengist in 472, or of Ernst Roehm and his associates by Hitler on 29–30 June 1934. **2** a similar ruthless or decisive action. **not by a long shot** by no means. □□ **longish** *adj.* [OE *long, lang*]

long[2] /lɒŋ/ *v.intr.* (foll. by *for* or *to* + infin.) have a strong wish or desire for. [OE *langian* seem long to]

long. *abbr.* longitude.

-long /lɒŋ/ *comb. form* forming adjectives and adverbs: **1** for the duration of (*lifelong*). **2** = -LING[2] (*headlong*).

Long Beach a resort city in California, situated to the south of Los Angeles; pop. (1982) 371,400. In 1967 the ocean liner *Queen Mary* was brought to Long Beach and converted into a hotel and tourist attraction.

longboard /ˈlɒŋbɔːd/ *n.* US a type of surfboard.

b but d dog f few g get h he j yes k cat l leg m man n no p pen r red s sit t top v voice

longboat /ˈlɒŋbəʊt/ *n.* a sailing ship's largest boat.

longbow /ˈlɒŋbəʊ/ *n.* a bow drawn by hand and shooting a long feathered arrow.

longe var. of LUNGE².

longeron /ˈlɒndʒərən/ *n.* a longitudinal member of a plane's fuselage. [F, = girder]

longevity /lɒnˈdʒevɪtɪ/ *n.* long life. [LL *longaevitas* f. L *longus* long + *aevum* age]

Longfellow /ˈlɒŋfeləʊ/, Henry Wadsworth (1807–82), American poet, who was professor of modern languages at Harvard (1836–54) having travelled extensively in Europe. His first wife died in Holland and his prose romance *Hyperion* (1839) is a product of his bereavement into which are woven philosophical discourses, poems, and legends. His *Ballads and other Poems* (1841) contains such well-known pieces as 'The Wreck of the Hesperus' and 'The Village Blacksmith'. Longfellow's popularity increased with subsequent volumes, including *Evangeline* (1849) set in Acadia (now Nova Scotia) with fine evocations of 'the forest primeval' and his best-known work, *The Song of Hiawatha* (1855), a narrative poem reproducing American Indian stories; its metre and novel subject-matter attracted many parodies and imitations.

Longford /ˈlɒŋfəd/ **1** a county of central Ireland, in the province of Leinster; pop. (est. 1986) 31,500. **2** its capital city; pop. (1981) 6,548.

longhair /ˈlɒŋheə(r)/ *n.* a person characterized by the associations of long hair, esp. a hippie or intellectual.

longhand /ˈlɒŋhænd/ *n.* ordinary handwriting (as opposed to shorthand or typing or printing).

longhorn /ˈlɒŋhɔːn/ *n.* **1** one of a breed of cattle with long horns. **2** any beetle of the family Cerambycidae with long antennae.

longhouse /ˈlɒŋhaʊs/ *n.* **1 a** *hist.* the traditional communal dwelling of the Iroquois and other Indians in North America. **b** a building on an Iroquois reservation, used as a church and meeting hall. **2** a large communal village house in parts of Malaysia and Indonesia. (See also *long house*.)

longicorn /ˈlɒndʒɪˌkɔːn/ *n.* a longhorn beetle. [mod.L *longicornis* f. L *longus* long + *cornu* horn]

longing /ˈlɒŋɪŋ/ *n.* & *adj.* —*n.* a feeling of intense desire. —*adj.* having or showing this feeling. □□ **longingly** *adv.*

Longinus /lɒnˈdʒaɪnəs/ the name given to the author of a Greek literary treatise *On the Sublime* (probably of the 1st c. AD), a critical analysis of what constituted literary greatness, showing concern with the moral function of literature and impatience with pedantry. The period of its greatest influence extends from Boileau's French translation (1674) to the early 19th c.

Long Island an island of New York State, separated from mainland Connecticut by **Long Island Sound**, an arm of the Atlantic Ocean.

longitude /ˈlɒŋgɪˌtjuːd, ˈlɒndʒ-/ *n.* **1** *Geog.* the angular distance east or west from a standard meridian such as Greenwich to the meridian of any place. ¶ Symb.: λ. **2** *Astron.* the angular distance of a celestial body north or south of the ecliptic measured along a great circle through the body and the poles of the ecliptic. [ME f. L *longitudo -dinis* f. *longus* long]

longitudinal /ˌlɒŋgɪˈtjuːdɪn(ə)l, ˌlɒndʒ-/ *adj.* **1** of or in length. **2** running lengthwise. **3** of longitude. □ **longitudinal wave** a wave vibrating in the direction of propagation. □□ **longitudinally** *adv.*

Long March the epic withdrawal of the Chinese Communists from SE to NW China in 1934–5, over a distance of 9,600 km (6,000 miles). By 1934 the nationalist Kuomintang had almost destroyed the Communist rural base (the Jiangxi Soviet, formed in 1931), and a force of 100,000 evacuated the area. Led by Mao Tse-tung from 1935, it travelled through mountainous terrain cut by several major rivers, and in October some 6,000 survivors reached Yan'an. Other groups arrived later, in all about 20,000 surviving the journey.

Long Parliament the Parliament which sat from Nov. 1640 to March 1653, was restored for a short time in 1659, and finally voted its own dissolution in 1660. It was summoned by Charles I and sat through the English Civil War and on into the interregnum which followed.

longshore /ˈlɒŋʃɔː(r)/ *adj.* **1** existing on or frequenting the shore. **2** directed along the shore. [*along shore*]

longshoreman /ˈlɒŋʃɔːmən/ *n.* (*pl.* **-men**) *US* a docker.

long-sighted /lɒŋˈsaɪtɪd, ˈlɒŋ-/ *adj.* **1** having long sight. **2** having imagination or foresight. □□ **long-sightedly** *adv.* **long-sightedness** *n.*

longstop /ˈlɒŋstɒp/ *n.* **1** *Cricket* **a** a position directly behind the wicket-keeper. **b** a fielder in this position. **2** a last resort.

longueur /lɔ̃ˈgɜː(r)/ *n.* **1** a tedious passage in a book etc. **2** a tedious stretch of time. [F, = length]

longways /ˈlɒŋweɪz/ *adv.* (also **longwise** /ˈlɒŋwaɪz/) = LENGTHWAYS.

long-winded /lɒŋˈwɪndɪd/ *adj.* **1** (of speech or writing) tediously lengthy. **2** able to run a long distance without rest. □□ **long-windedly** *adv.* **long-windedness** *n.*

lonicera /ləˈnɪsərə/ *n.* **1** a dense evergreen shrub, *Lonicera nitidum*, much used as hedging. **2** = HONEYSUCKLE. [A. *Lonicerus*, Ger. botanist d. 1586]

loo¹ /luː/ *n. Brit. colloq.* a lavatory. [20th c.: orig. uncert.]

loo² /luː/ *n.* **1** a round card-game with penalties paid to the pool. **2** this penalty. □ **loo table** a kind of circular table. [abbr. of obs. *lanterloo* f. F *lanturlu*, refrain of a song]

loof var. of LUFF.

loofah /ˈluːfə/ *n.* (also **luffa** /ˈlʌfə/) **1** a climbing gourdlike plant, *Luffa cylindrica*, native to Asia, producing edible marrow-like fruits. **2** the dried fibrous vascular system of this fruit used as a sponge. [Egypt. Arab. *lūfa*, the plant]

look /lʊk/ *v., n.,* & *int.* —*v.* **1 a** *intr.* (often foll. by *at*) use one's sight; turn one's eyes in some direction. **b** *tr.* turn one's eyes on; contemplate or examine (*looked me in the eyes*). **2** *intr.* **a** make a visual or mental search (*I'll look in the morning*). **b** (foll. by *at*) consider, examine (*we must look at the facts*). **3** *intr.* (foll. by *for*) **a** search for. **b** hope or be on the watch for. **c** expect. **4** *intr.* inquire (*when one looks deeper*). **5** *intr.* have a specified appearance; seem (*look a fool*; *look foolish*). **6** *intr.* (foll. by *to*) **a** consider; take care of; be careful about (*look to the future*). **b** rely on (a person or thing) (*you can look to me for support*). **c** expect; count on; aim at. **7** *intr.* (foll. by *into*) investigate or examine. **8** *tr.* (foll. by *what, where, etc.* + *clause*) ascertain or observe by sight (*look where we are*). **9** *intr.* (of a thing) face or be turned, or have or afford an outlook, in a specified direction. **10** *tr.* express, threaten, or show (an emotion etc.) by one's looks. **11** *intr.* (foll. by *that* + *clause*) take care; make sure. **12** *intr.* (foll. by *to* + *infin.*) expect (*am looking to finish this today*). —*n.* **1** an act of looking; the directing of the eyes to look at a thing or person; a glance (*a scornful look*). **2** (in *sing.* or *pl.*) the appearance of a face; a person's expression or personal aspect. **3** the (esp. characteristic) appearance of a thing (*the place has a European look*). —*int.* (also **look here!**) calling attention, expressing a protest, etc. □ **look after 1** attend to; take care of. **2** follow with the eye. **3** seek for. **look one's age** appear to be as old as one really is. **look-alike** a person or thing closely resembling another (*a Prince Charles look-alike*). **look alive** (or **lively**) *colloq.* be brisk and alert. **look as if** suggest by appearance the belief that (*it looks as if he's gone*). **look back 1** (foll. by *on, upon, to*) turn one's thoughts to (something past). **2** (usu. with *neg.*) cease to progress (*since then we have never looked back*). **3** *Brit.* make a further visit later. **look before you leap** avoid precipitate action. **look daggers** see DAGGER. **look down on** (or **upon** or **look down one's nose at**) regard with contempt or a feeling of superiority. **look for trouble** see TROUBLE. **look forward to** await (an expected event) eagerly or with specified feelings. **look in** make a short visit or call. **look-in** *n. colloq.* **1** an informal call or visit. **2** a chance of participation or success (*never gets a look-in*). **look a person in the eye** (or **eyes** or **face**) look directly and unashamedly at him or her. **look like 1** have the appearance of. **2** *Brit.* seem to be (*they look like winning*). **3** threaten or promise (*it looks like rain*). **4** indicate the presence of (*it looks like woodworm*). **look on 1** (often foll. by *as*) regard (*looks on you as a friend*; *looked on them with disfavour*). **2** be a spectator; avoid participation. **look oneself** appear in good health (esp. after illness etc.). **look out 1** direct one's sight or put one's head out of a window etc. **2** (often foll.

by *for*) be vigilant or prepared. **3** (foll. by *on*, *over*, etc.) have or afford a specified outlook. **4** search for and produce (*shall look one out for you*). **look over 1** inspect or survey (*looked over the house*). **2** examine (a document etc.) esp. cursorily (*shall look it over*). **look round 1** look in every or another direction. **2** examine the objects of interest in a place (*you must come and look round sometime*). **3** examine the possibilities etc. with a view to deciding on a course of action. **look-see** *colloq.* a survey or inspection. **look sharp** act promptly; make haste (orig. = keep strict watch). **look small** see SMALL. **look through 1** examine the contents of, esp. cursorily. **2** penetrate (a pretence or pretender) with insight. **3** ignore by pretending not to see (*I waved, but you just looked through me*). **look up 1** search for (esp. information in a book). **2** *colloq.* go to visit (a person) (*had intended to look them up*). **3** raise one's eyes (*looked up when I went in*). **4** improve, esp. in price, prosperity, or well-being (*things are looking up all round*). **look a person up and down** scrutinize a person keenly or contemptuously. **look up to** respect or venerate. **not like the look of** find alarming or suspicious. □□ **-looking** *adj.* (in *comb.*). [OE *lōcian* f. WG]

looker /ˈlʊkə(r)/ *n.* **1** a person having a specified appearance (*a good-looker*). **2** *colloq.* an attractive woman. □ **looker-on** a person who is a mere spectator.

looking-glass /ˈlʊkɪŋˌglɑːs/ *n.* a mirror for looking at oneself.

lookout /ˈlʊkaʊt/ *n.* **1** a watch or looking out (*on the lookout for bargains*). **2 a** a post of observation. **b** a person or party or boat stationed to keep watch. **3** a view over a landscape. **4** a prospect of luck (*it's a bad lookout for them*). **5** *colloq.* a person's own concern.

loom[1] /luːm/ *n.* an apparatus for weaving yarn or thread into fabric. The craft of weaving is an ancient one, and hand-operated looms are still in use as a craft or cottage industry. A horizontal loom is pictured on a pottery dish, dating from *c.*4400 BC, found at al-Badari in Egypt; the vertical loom dates from the time of the 18th Dynasty (*c.*1567–1320 BC). Similar devices were known in many other early civilizations. The power-loom was invented by Cartwright (1785), and modern looms are power-driven using either a flying shuttle, which is given sufficient impulse to carry it across the warp, or air or water jets to blow the weft thread across the warp. [ME *lōme* f. OE *gelōma* tool]

loom[2] /luːm/ *v. & n.* —*v.intr.* (often foll. by *up*) **1** come into sight dimly, esp. as a vague and often magnified or threatening shape. **2** (of an event or prospect) be ominously close. —*n.* a vague often exaggerated first appearance of land at sea etc. [prob. f. LG or Du.: cf. E Fris. *lōmen* move slowly, MHG *lüemen* be weary]

loon /luːn/ *n.* **1** US any aquatic diving bird of the family Gaviidae, with a long slender body and a sharp bill; a diver. **2** *colloq.* a crazy person (cf. LOONY). [alt. f. *loom* f. ON *lómr*]

loony /ˈluːnɪ/ *n. & adj. sl.* —*n.* (*pl.* **-ies**) a mad or silly person; a lunatic. —*adj.* (**loonier**, **looniest**) crazy, silly. □ **loony-bin** *sl.* a mental home or hospital. □□ **looniness** *n.* [abbr. of LUNATIC]

loop /luːp/ *n. & v.* —*n.* **1 a** a figure produced by a curve, or a doubled thread etc., that crosses itself. **b** anything forming this figure. **2** a similarly shaped attachment or ornament formed of cord or thread etc. and fastened at the crossing. **3** a ring or curved piece of material as a handle etc. **4** a contraceptive coil. **5** (in full **loop-line**) a railway or telegraph line that diverges from a main line and joins it again. **6** a manoeuvre in which an aeroplane describes a vertical loop. **7** *Skating* a manoeuvre describing a curve that crosses itself, made on a single edge. **8** *Electr.* a complete circuit for a current. **9** an endless strip of tape or film allowing continuous repetition. **10** *Computing* a programmed sequence of instructions that is repeated until or while a particular condition is satisfied. —*v.* **1** *tr.* form (thread etc.) into a loop or loops. **2** *tr.* enclose with or as with a loop. **3** *tr.* (often foll. by *up*, *back*, *together*) fasten or join with a loop or loops. **4** *intr.* a form a loop. **b** move in looplike patterns. **5** *intr.* (also **loop the loop**) *Aeron.* perform an aerobatic loop. [ME: orig. unkn.]

looper /ˈluːpə(r)/ *n.* **1** a caterpillar of the geometer moth which progresses by arching itself into loops. **2** a device for making loops.

loophole /ˈluːphəʊl/ *n. & v.* —*n.* **1** a means of evading a rule

etc. without infringing the letter of it. **2** a narrow vertical slit in a wall for shooting or looking through or to admit light or air. —*v.tr.* make loopholes in (a wall etc.). [ME *loop* in the same sense + HOLE]

loopy /ˈluːpɪ/ *adj.* (**loopier**, **loopiest**) **1** *sl.* crazy. **2** having many loops.

loose /luːs/ *adj., n., & v.* —*adj.* **1 a** not or no longer held by bonds or restraint. **b** (of an animal) not confined or tethered etc. **2** detached or detachable from its place (*has come loose*). **3** not held together or contained or fixed. **4** not specially fastened or packaged (*loose papers; had her hair loose*). **5** hanging partly free (*a loose end*). **6** slack, relaxed; not tense or tight. **7** not compact or dense (*loose soil*). **8** (of language, concepts, etc.) inexact; conveying only the general sense. **9** (preceding an agent noun) doing the expressed action in a loose or careless manner (*a loose thinker*). **10** morally lax; dissolute (*loose living*). **11** (of the tongue) likely to speak indiscreetly. **12** (of the bowels) tending to diarrhoea. **13** *Sport* **a** (of a ball) in play but not in any player's possession. **b** (of play etc.) with the players not close together. **14** *Cricket* **a** (of bowling) inaccurately pitched. **b** (of fielding) careless or bungling. **15** (in *comb.*) loosely (*loose-flowing; loose-fitting*). —*n.* **1** a state of freedom or unrestrainedness. **2** loose play in football (*in the loose*). **3** free expression. —*v.tr.* **1** release; set free; free from constraint. **2** untie or undo (something that constrains). **3** detach from moorings. **4** relax (*loosed my hold on it*). **5** discharge (a gun or arrow etc.). □ **at a loose end** (US **at loose ends**) (of a person) unoccupied, esp. temporarily. **loose box** a compartment for a horse, in a stable or vehicle, in which it can move about. **loose change** money as coins in the pocket etc. for casual use. **loose cover** *Brit.* a removable cover for a chair or sofa etc. **loose-leaf** *adj.* (of a notebook, manual, etc.) with each leaf separate and removable. —*n.* a loose-leaf notebook etc. **loose-limbed** having supple limbs. **loose order** an arrangement of soldiers etc. with wide intervals. **on the loose 1** escaped from captivity. **2** having a free enjoyable time. □□ **loosely** *adv.* **looseness** *n.* **loosish** *adj.* [ME *lōs* f. ON *lauss* f. Gmc]

loosen /ˈluːs(ə)n/ *v.* **1** *tr. & intr.* make or become less tight or compact or firm. **2** *tr.* make (a regime etc.) less severe. **3** *tr.* release (the bowels) from constipation. **4** *tr.* relieve (a cough) from dryness. □ **loosen a person's tongue** make a person talk freely. **loosen up** = *limber up* (see LIMBER[1]). □□ **loosener** *n.*

loosestrife /ˈluːsstraɪf/ *n.* **1** any marsh plant of the genus *Lysimachia*, esp. the golden or yellow loosestrife, *L. vulgaris*. **2** any plant of the genus *Lythrum*, esp. the purple loosestrife *L. salicaria*, with racemes of star-shaped purple flowers. [LOOSE + STRIFE, taking the Gk name *lusimakhion* (f. *Lusimakhos*, its discoverer) as if directly f. *luō* undo + *makhē* battle]

loot /luːt/ *n. & v.* —*n.* **1** goods taken from an enemy; spoil. **2** booty; illicit gains made by an official. **3** *sl.* money. —*v.tr.* **1** rob (premises) or steal (goods) left unprotected, esp. after riots or other violent events. **2** plunder or sack (a city, building, etc.). **3** carry off as booty. □□ **looter** *n.* [Hindi *lūṭ*]

lop[1] /lɒp/ *v. & n.* —*v.* (**lopped**, **lopping**) **1** *tr.* **a** (often foll. by *off*, *away*) cut or remove (a part or parts) from a whole, esp. branches from a tree. **b** remove branches from (a tree). **2** *tr.* (often foll. by *off*, *away*) remove (items) as superfluous. **3** *intr.* (foll. by *at*) make lopping strokes on (a tree etc.). —*n.* parts lopped off, esp. branches and twigs of trees. □ **lop and top** (or **crop**) the trimmings of a tree. □□ **lopper** *n.* [ME f. OE *loppian* (unrecorded): cf. obs. *lip* to prune]

lop[2] /lɒp/ *v.* (**lopped**, **lopping**) **1** *intr. & tr.* hang limply. **2** *intr.* (foll. by *about*) slouch, dawdle; hang about. **3** *intr.* move with short bounds. **4** *tr.* (of an animal) let (the ears) hang. □ **lop-ears** drooping ears. **lop-eared** (of an animal) having drooping ears. □□ **loppy** *adj.* [rel. to LOB]

lope /ləʊp/ *v. & n.* —*v.intr.* (esp. of animals) run with a long bounding stride. —*n.* a long bounding stride. [ME, var. of Sc. *loup* f. ON *hlaupa* LEAP]

lopho- /ˈlɒfəʊ, ˈlɒfəʊ/ *comb. form Zool.* crested. [Gk *lophos* crest]

lophobranch /ˈlɒfəˌbræŋk, ˈlɒf-/ *adj.* (of a fish) having the gills arranged in tufts. [LOPHO- + BRANCHIA]

lophodont /ˈlɒfəˌdɒnt, ˈlɒf-/ *n. & adj.* —*adj.* having transverse

meditation with the feet resting on the thighs. [L f. Gk *lōtos*, of Semitic orig.]

Louangphrabang see LUANG PRABANG.

louche /luːʃ/ *adj.* disreputable, shifty. [F, = squinting]

loud /laʊd/ *adj.* & *adv.* —*adj.* **1 a** strongly audible, esp. noisily or oppressively so. **b** able or liable to produce loud sounds (*a loud engine*). **c** clamorous, insistent (*loud complaints*). **2** (of colours, design, etc.) gaudy, obtrusive. **3** (of behaviour) aggressive and noisy. —*adv.* in a loud manner. □ **loud hailer** an electronic device for amplifying the sound of the voice so that it can be heard at a distance. **loud-mouth** *colloq.* a loud-mouthed person. **loud-mouthed** *colloq.* noisily self-assertive; vociferous. **out loud 1** aloud. **2** loudly (*laughed out loud*). □□**louden** *v.tr.* & *intr.* **loudish** *adj.* **loudly** *adv.* **loudness** *n.* [OE *hlūd* f. WG]

loudspeaker /laʊdˈspiːkə(r)/ *n.* an apparatus that converts electrical impulses into sound, esp. music and voice.

lough /lɒk, lɒx/ *n.* Ir. = LOCH. [Ir. *loch* LOCH, assim. to the related obs. ME form *lough*]

Louis[1] /ˈluːɪ/ the name of 18 kings of France:

Louis IX (1214–70), son of Louis VIII, reigned 1226–70, canonized as St Louis. Renowned for his honesty and pure character, Louis far exceeded the normal medieval moral standards of kingship, displaying such fairness (although not weakness) in his exercise of power as to be recognized in many ways as the arbiter of Europe. His reign was dominated by his two crusades to the Holy Land, neither of which proved successful: the first (1248–50) ended in disaster with his capture by the Egyptians, the second (1270) in his own death from plague at Carthage.

Louis XI (1423–83), son of Charles VII, reigned 1461–83. Frequently known as the 'Spider King' because of his frequent recourse to intrigue, Louis completed the work of his father in rebuilding France as a modern European power. His reign was dominated by his struggle with Charles the Rash, Duke of Burgundy, a struggle which ended with Charles's death in battle against the Swiss in 1477 and the French absorption of much of Burgundy's former territory along their border.

Louis XIV (1638–1715), son of Louis XIII, reigned 1643–1715. The reign of Louis XIV represented the high point of the Bourbon dynasty and of French power in Europe. Its magnificence earned him the name of the 'Sun King', but his brand of absolutism was to leave severe troubles for his less powerful successors, while his almost constant wars of expansion united Europe against him, and, despite the reforms of Colbert, gravely weakened France's financial position. The Treaty of Utrecht, which ended the War of the Spanish Succession, was symbolic of the ultimate failure of Louis' attempt at European hegemony, preventing as it did the union of the French and Spanish crowns.

Louis XVI (1754–93), grandson and successor of Louis XV, reigned 1774–93. A well-intentioned but weak monarch, Louis was unable to prevent political discontent in France leading to revolution. When the French Revolution broke out, the King persistently misinterpreted the situation and took refuge in a series of half measures which proved disastrous to his cause. Eventually, with the revolution becoming progressively more extreme and with foreign invaders massing on the borders, the monarchy was abolished and Louis was executed.

Louis[2] /ˈluːɪ/ the name of two kings of Hungary:

Louis I 'the Great' (1326–82), king of Hungary 1342–82 and of Poland 1370–82. He fought two successful wars against Venice (1357–8, 1378–81), and the rulers of Serbia, Walachia, Moldavia, and Bulgaria became his vassals. Under his rule Hungary became a powerful State, though Poland was troubled by revolts.

Louis[3] /ˈluːɪ/, Joe (real name Joseph Louis Barrow, 1914–81), American boxer, known as the 'Brown Bomber', heavyweight champion of the world 1937–49.

louis /ˈluːɪ/ *n.* (*pl.* same /ˈluːɪz/) *hist.* (in full **louis d'or** /-ˈdɔː(r)/) a former French gold coin worth about 20 francs. [LOUIS, the name of kings of France]

Louisiana /luːˌiːzɪˈænə/ a State in the south-western US, bordering on the Gulf of Mexico; pop. (est. 1985) 4,206,100; capital, Baton Rouge. The territory was claimed by France in 1682 and named in honour of Louis XIV. It was sold by the French republic to the US in 1803, becoming the 18th State in 1812 □ **Louisiana purchase** territory sold by France to the US in 1803, comprising the western part of the Mississippi valley. The area had been explored by France, ceded to Spain in 1762, and returned to France in 1800.

Louis Philippe /ˌluːɪ fɪˈliːp/ (1773–1850), king of France 1830–48. As the Duc d'Orléans, Louis Philippe participated in the early, liberal phase of the French Revolution, but later went into exile abroad, building up a considerable fortune in England. Returning to France after the restoration of the Bourbons, he became the focus for liberal discontent, and after the overthrow of Charles X in 1830 was made king. His bourgeois-style regime was popular at first, and presided over a period of commercial growth, but it was gradually undermined by radical discontent and overthrown in a brief uprising in 1848, with Louis retiring once more to exile in England.

Louisville /ˈluːˌivɪl/ an industrial city in NW Kentucky; pop. (1982) 293,500. The annual Kentucky Derby (see entry) takes place on the Churchill Downs racetrack here.

lounge /laʊndʒ/ *v.* & *n.* —*v.intr.* **1** recline comfortably and casually; loll. **2** stand or move about idly. —*n.* **1** a place for lounging, esp.: **a** a public room (e.g. in a hotel). **b** a place in an airport etc. with seats for waiting passengers. **c** a sitting-room in a house. **2** a spell of lounging. □ **lounge bar** *Brit.* a more comfortable room for drinking in a public house. **lounge lizard** *colloq.* an idler in fashionable society. **lounge suit** *Brit.* a man's formal suit for ordinary day wear. [perh. f. obs. *lungis* lout]

lounger /ˈlaʊndʒə(r)/ *n.* **1** a person who lounges. **2** a piece of furniture for relaxing on. **3** a casual garment for wearing when relaxing.

loupe /luːp/ *n.* a small magnifying glass used by jewellers etc. [F]

lour /ˈlaʊə(r)/ *v.* & *n.* (also **lower**) —*v.intr.* **1** frown; look sullen. **2** (of the sky etc.) look dark and threatening. —*n.* **1** a scowl. **2** a gloomy look (of the sky etc.). □□ **louringly** *adv.* **loury** *adj.* [ME *loure*, of unkn. orig.]

Lourdes /lʊəd/ a town in SW France where in 1858 a peasant girl, Bernadette Soubirous, claimed to have had visions of the Virgin Mary. At the same time a spring appeared, and miraculous healings were reported. It is now a major centre of pilgrimage.

Lourenço Marques /ləˈrensəʊ mɑːk/ the former name (until 1976) of Maputo.

louse /laʊs/ *n.* & *v.* —*n.* **1** (*pl.* **lice** /laɪs/) **a** a parasitic insect, *Pediculus humanus*, infesting the human hair and skin and transmitting various diseases. **b** any insect of the order Anoplura or Mallophaga parasitic on mammals, birds, fish, or plants. **2** *sl.* (*pl.* **louses**) a contemptible or unpleasant person. —*v.tr.* remove lice from. □ **louse up** *sl.* make a mess of. [OE *lūs*, pl. *lȳs*]

lousewort /ˈlaʊswɜːt/ *n.* any plant of the genus *Pedicularis* with purple-pink flowers found in marshes and wet places.

lousy /ˈlaʊzɪ/ *adj.* (**lousier, lousiest**) **1** infested with lice. **2** *colloq.* very bad; disgusting (also as a term of general disparagement). **3** *colloq.* (often foll. by *with*) well supplied; teeming (with). □□ **lousily** *adv.* **lousiness** *n.*

lout /laʊt/ *n.* a rough, crude, or ill-mannered person (usu. a man). □□ **loutish** *adj.* **loutishly** *adv.* **loutishness** *n.* [perh. f. archaic *lout* to bow]

Louth /laʊθ/ a county of Ireland, in the province of Leinster; pop. (est. 1986) 97,700; capital, Dundalk.

Louvain see LEUVEN.

Louvre /luːvr/ the national museum and art gallery of France, in Paris, housed in the former royal palace, on the site of an earlier fortress and arsenal, built by Francis I (d. 1547) and later extended. When the court moved to Versailles in 1678 its conversion into a museum was begun. It was Francis I who set the pattern for royal collecting and patronage which persisted until the Revolution, and the royal collections, greatly increased by Louis XIV, formed the nucleus of the national collection which is an epitome of French history and culture.

louvre /ˈluːvə(r)/ *n.* (also **louver**) **1** each of a set of overlapping slats designed to admit air and some light and exclude rain. **2**

a domed structure on a roof with side openings for ventilation etc. □ **louvre-boards** the slats or boards making up a louvre. □□ **louvred** adj. [ME f. OF lover, lovier skylight, prob. f. Gmc]

lovable /ˈlʌvəb(ə)l/ adj. (also **loveable**) inspiring or deserving love or affection. □□ **lovability** /-ˈbɪlɪtɪ/ n. **lovableness** n. **lovably** adv.

lovage /ˈlʌvɪdʒ/ n. **1** a S. European herb, Levisticum officinale, used for flavouring etc. **2** a white-flowered umbelliferous plant, Ligusticum scoticum. [ME loveache alt. f. OF levesche f. LL levisticum f. L ligusticum neut. of ligusticus Ligurian]

lovat /ˈlʌvət/ n. (also attrib.) a muted green colour found esp. in tweed and woollen garments. [Lovat in Scotland]

love /lʌv/ n. & v. —n. **1** an intense feeling of deep affection or fondness for a person or thing; great liking. **2** sexual passion. **3** sexual relations. **4 a** a beloved one; a sweetheart (often as a form of address). **b** Brit. colloq. a form of address regardless of affection. **5** colloq. a person of whom one is fond. **6** affectionate greetings (give him my love). **7** (often **Love**) a representation of Cupid. **8** (in some games) no score; nil. —v.tr. **1** (also absol.) feel love or deep fondness for. **2** delight in; admire; greatly cherish. **3** colloq. like very much (loves books). **4** (foll. by verbal noun, or to + infin.) be inclined, esp. as a habit; greatly enjoy; find pleasure in (children love dressing up; loves to find fault). □ **fall in love** (often foll. by with) develop a great (esp. sexual) love (for). **for love** for pleasure not profit. **for the love of** for the sake of. **in love** (often foll. by with) deeply enamoured (of). **love affair** a romantic or sexual relationship between two people in love. **love-apple** archaic a tomato. **love-bird** any of various African and Madagascan parrots, esp. Agapornis personata. **love-child** an illegitimate child. **love-feast 1** a meal affirming brotherly love among early Christians. **2** a religious service of Methodists, etc., imitating this. **love game** a game in which the loser makes no score. **love-hate relationship** an intensely emotional relationship in which one or each party has ambivalent feelings of love and hate for the other. **love-in-a-mist** a blue-flowered garden plant, Nigella damascena, with many delicate green bracts. **love-letter** a letter expressing feelings of sexual love. **love-lies-bleeding** a garden plant, Amaranthus caudatus, with drooping spikes of purple-red blooms. **love-match** a marriage made for love's sake. **love-nest** a place of intimate lovemaking. **love-seat** an armchair or small sofa for two. **make love** (often foll. by to) **1** have sexual intercourse (with). **2** archaic pay amorous attention (to). **not for love or money** colloq. not in any circumstances. **out of love** no longer in love. □□ **loveworthy** adj. [OE lufu f. Gmc]

loveable var. of LOVABLE.

Lovelace /ˈlʌvleɪs/, Richard (1618–57/8), English Cavalier poet. In 1642 he was committed to prison, where he probably wrote the song 'To Althea from Prison'. He rejoined Charles I in 1645 and was again imprisoned in 1648; during this time he prepared his Lucasta which includes some of his best lyrics. Lovelace died in poverty, having spent his fortune in the Royalist cause.

loveless /ˈlʌvlɪs/ adj. without love; unloving or unloved or both. □□ **lovelessly** adv. **lovelessness** n.

Lovell /ˈlʌv(ə)l/, Sir (Alfred Charles) Bernard (1913–), English physicist and astronomer, a pioneer of radio astronomy, founder and director of Jodrell Bank observatory.

lovelock /ˈlʌvlɒk/ n. a curl or lock of hair worn on the temple or forehead.

lovelorn /ˈlʌvlɔːn/ adj. pining from unrequited love.

lovely /ˈlʌvlɪ/ adj. & n. —adj. (**lovelier, loveliest**) **1** exquisitely beautiful. **2** colloq. pleasing, delightful. —n. (pl. **-ies**) colloq. a pretty woman. □ **lovely and** colloq. delightfully (lovely and warm). □□ **lovelily** adv. **loveliness** n. [OE luflic (as LOVE)]

lovemaking /ˈlʌvˌmeɪkɪŋ/ n. **1** amorous sexual activity, esp. sexual intercourse. **2** archaic courtship.

lover /ˈlʌvə(r)/ n. **1** a person in love with another. **2** a person with whom another is having sexual relations. **3** (in pl.) a couple in love or having sexual relations. **4** a person who likes or enjoys something specified (a music lover; a lover of words). □□ **loverless** adj.

lovesick /ˈlʌvsɪk/ adj. languishing with romantic love. □□ **lovesickness** n.

lovesome /ˈlʌvsəm/ adj. literary lovely, lovable.

lovey /ˈlʌvɪ/ n. (pl. **-eys**) colloq. love, sweetheart (esp. as a form of address).

lovey-dovey /ˌlʌvɪˈdʌvɪ/ adj. fondly affectionate, esp. unduly sentimental.

loving /ˈlʌvɪŋ/ adj. & n. —adj. feeling or showing love; affectionate. —n. affection; active love. □ **loving-cup** a two-handled drinking-cup passed round at banquets. **loving-kindness** tenderness and consideration. □□ **lovingly** adv. **lovingness** n. [OE lufiende (as LOVE)]

low[1] /ləʊ/ adj., n., & adv. —adj. **1** of less than average height; not high or tall or reaching far up (a low wall). **2 a** situated close to ground or sea level etc.; not elevated in position (low altitude). **b** (of the sun) near the horizon. **c** (of latitude) near the equator. **3** of or in humble rank or position (of low birth). **4** of small or less than normal amount or extent or intensity (low price; low temperature; low in calories). **5** small or reduced in quantity (stocks are low). **6** coming below the normal level (a dress with a low neck). **7 a** dejected; lacking vigour (feeling low; in low spirits). **b** poorly nourished; indicative of poor nutrition. **8** (of a sound) not shrill or loud or high-pitched. **9** not exalted or sublime; commonplace. **10** unfavourable (a low opinion). **11** abject, mean, vulgar (low cunning; low slang). **12** (in compar.) situated on less high land or to the south. **13** (of a geographical period) earlier. —n. **1** a low or the lowest level or number (the dollar has reached a new low). **2** an area of low pressure. —adv. **1** in or to a low position or state. **2** in a low tone (speak low). **3** (of a sound) at or to a low pitch. □ **low-born** of humble birth. **Low Church** the section of the Church of England which gives a relatively unimportant or 'low' place to the claims of the episcopate, priesthood, and sacraments, and approximates to Protestant Nonconformists in its beliefs. Originally used of the Latitudinarians, the term has been applied, since the time of the Oxford Movement, to Evangelicals. **low-class** of low quality or social class. **low comedy** that in which the subject and the treatment border on farce. **low-cut** (of a dress etc.) made with a low neckline. **low-down** adj. abject, mean, dishonourable. —n. colloq. (usu. foll. by on) the relevant information (about). **lowest common denominator, multiple** see DENOMINATOR, MULTIPLE. **low frequency** (in radio) 30–300 kilohertz. **low gear** see GEAR. **Low German** see GERMAN. **low-grade** of low quality or strength. **low-key** lacking intensity or prominence; restrained. **Low Latin** medieval and later forms of Latin. **low-level** Computing (of a programming language) close in form to machine language. **low-loader** a lorry with a low floor and no sides, for heavy loads. **low-lying** at low altitude (above sea level etc.). **low mass** see MASS[2]. **low-pitched 1** (of a sound) low. **2** (of a roof) having only a slight slope. **low pressure 1** little demand for activity or exertion. **2** an atmospheric condition with pressure below average. **low profile** avoidance of attention or publicity. **low-profile** adj. (of a motor-vehicle tyre) having a greater width than usual in relation to height. **low relief** see RELIEF 6a. **low-rise** (of a building) having few storeys. **low season** the period of fewest visitors at a resort etc. **low-spirited** dejected, dispirited. **low-spiritedness** dejection, depression. **low spirits** dejection, depression. **Low Sunday** the Sunday after Easter. **low tide** the time or level of the tide at its ebb. **low water** the tide at its lowest. **low-water mark 1** the level reached at low water. **2** a minimum recorded level or value etc. **Low Week** the week beginning with Low Sunday. □□ **lowish** adj. **lowness** n. [ME lāh f. ON lágr f. Gmc]

low[2] /ləʊ/ n. & v. —n. a sound made by cattle; a moo. —v.intr. utter this sound. [OE hlōwan f. Gmc]

lowboy /ˈləʊbɔɪ/ n. US a low chest or table with drawers and short legs.

lowbrow /ˈləʊbraʊ/ adj. & n. —adj. not highly intellectual or cultured. —n. a lowbrow person. □□ **lowbrowed** adj.

Low Countries the district now forming The Netherlands, Belgium, and Luxembourg.

Lowell[1] /ˈləʊəl/, Amy Lawrence (1874–1925), American poet.

After producing her first volume of relatively conventional poetry she took up imagism and visited England in 1913 and 1914 where she met Pound (who adopted the expression 'Amygism') and other imagists. Her subsequent volumes show her increasing allegiance to the movement and her experiments in 'polyphonic prose', including *Men, Women and Ghosts* (1916; which contains 'Patterns'); her love of New England is expressed in 'Lilacs' and 'Purple Grackles' (in *What's O'Clock*, 1925).

Lowell[2] /'ləʊəl/, James Russell (1819–91), American poet and critic. His works include volumes of verse, the satirical *Biglow Papers* (1848 and 1867; prose and verse), memorial odes after the Civil War, and various volumes of essays including *Among my Books* (1870) and *My Study Window* (1871).

Lowell[3] /'ləʊəl/, Robert Traill Spence (1917–77), American poet, born in Boston of distinguished New England ancestry. In 1940 he married novelist Jean Stafford (he subsequently married writers Elizabeth Hardwick, 1949, and Caroline Blackwood, 1973) and became a fanatical convert to Roman Catholicism. His first volume *Land of Unlikeness* (1944) betrays the conflict of Catholicism and his Boston ancestry. During the Second World War he was imprisoned as, in effect, a conscientious objector. Subsequent volumes include *Life Studies* (1959) and *For the Union Dead* (1964), and he reached the height of his public fame during his opposition to the Vietnam war and support of Senator McCarthy, as recorded in *Notebook 1967–1968* (1968). He suffered recurring bouts of manic disorder and alcoholism and his confessional volume of poems *The Dolphin* (1973) caused a scandal with its revelations of marital anguish. A legendary figure in his lifetime, he was an ironic intellectual whose ambiguous complex imagery satisfied the demands of contemporary criticism.

lower[1] /'ləʊə(r)/ *adj. & adv.* —*adj.* (*compar.* of LOW[1]). **1** less high in position or status. **2 a** situated below another part (*lower lip*; *lower atmosphere*). **b** (of a geological or archaeological period) earlier. (Cf. UPPER.) **3 a** situated on less high land (*Lower Egypt*). **b** situated to the South (*Lower California*). **4** (of a mammal, plant, etc.) evolved to only a slight degree (e.g. a platypus or fungus). —*adv.* in or to a lower position, status, etc. □ **lower case** see CASE[2]. **lower class** working-class people and their families. **lower-class** *adj.* of the lower class. **lower deck 1** the deck of a ship situated immediately over the hold. **2** the petty officers and men of a ship collectively. **Lower House** the larger and usu. elected body in a legislature, esp. the House of Commons. **lower regions** (or **world**) hell; the realm of the dead. □□ **lowermost** *adj.*

lower[2] /'ləʊə(r)/ *v.* **1** *tr.* let or haul down. **2** *tr. & intr.* make or become lower. **3** *tr.* reduce the height or pitch or elevation of (*lower your voice*; *lower one's eyes*). **4** *tr.* degrade. **5** *tr. & intr.* diminish.

lower[3] var. of LOUR.

lowland /'ləʊlənd/ *n. & adj.* —*n.* **1** (usu. in *pl.*) low-lying country. **2** (**Lowland**) (usu. in *pl.*) the region of Scotland lying south and east of the Highlands. —*adj.* of or in lowland or the Scottish Lowlands. □□ **lowlander** *n.* (also **Lowlander**).

lowlight /'ləʊlaɪt/ *n.* **1** a monotonous or dull period; a feature of little prominence (*one of the lowlights of the evening*). **2** (usu. in *pl.*) a dark tint in the hair produced by dyeing. [after HIGHLIGHT]

lowly /'ləʊlɪ/ *adj.* (**lowlier**, **lowliest**) **1** humble in feeling, behaviour, or status. **2** modest, unpretentious. **3** (of an organism) evolved to only a slight degree. □□ **lowlily** *adv.* **lowliness** *n.*

low-minded /ləʊ'maɪndɪd/ *adj.* vulgar or ignoble in mind or character. □□ **low-mindedness** *n.*

Lowry[1] /'laʊrɪ/, (Clarence) Malcolm (1909–57), English novelist, who went to sea on leaving school, travelling to the Far East, and based his first novel *Ultramarine* (1933) on his experiences. His masterpiece is *Under the Volcano* (1947), an account of tensions in Mexico in the 1930s, where he had settled. Lowry was a chronic alcoholic, as are many of his characters.

Lowry[2] /'laʊrɪ/, Lawrence Stephen (1887–1976), English artist. He spent most of his life in Salford, near Manchester, which became the characteristic industrial landscape of his pictures. Deliberately adopting a childlike manner of visualization, he painted small matchstick figures set against the iron and brick expanse of the town, to provide a wry perspective on life in the industrial North, combining penetration and compassion, revealing the alienation of the lonely and mankind's inconsequence against the juggernaut of industrialism.

lox[1] /lɒks/ *n.* liquid oxygen. [abbr.]

lox[2] /lɒks/ *n.* US smoked salmon. [Yiddish *laks*]

loyal /'lɔɪəl/ *adj.* **1** (often foll. by *to*) true or faithful (to duty, love, or obligation). **2** steadfast in allegiance; devoted to the legitimate sovereign or government of one's country. **3** showing loyalty. □ **loyal toast** a toast to the sovereign. □□ **loyally** *adv.* [F f. OF *loial* etc. f. L *legalis* LEGAL]

loyalist /'lɔɪəlɪst/ *n.* **1** a person who remains loyal to the legitimate sovereign etc., esp. in the face of rebellion or usurpation. **2** (**Loyalist**) a supporter of Parliamentary union between Great Britain and Northern Ireland. □□ **loyalism** *n.*

loyalty /'lɔɪəltɪ/ *n.* (*pl.* **-ies**) **1** the state of being loyal. **2** (often in *pl.*) a feeling or application of loyalty.

Loyalty Islands a group of islands in the SW Pacific forming part of the French overseas territory of New Caledonia; pop. (1983) 15,500. The group includes the three main islands of Maré, Lifou, and Uvéa in addition to a large number of small islets.

lozenge /'lɒzɪndʒ/ *n.* **1** a rhombus or diamond figure. **2** a small sweet or medicinal tablet, orig. lozenge-shaped, for dissolving in the mouth. **3** a lozenge-shaped pane in a window. **4** *Heraldry* a lozenge-shaped device. **5** the lozenge-shaped facet of a cut gem. □□ **lozenged** *adj.* (in sense 4). **lozengy** *adj.* [ME f. OF *losenge*, ult. of Gaulish or Iberian orig.]

LP *abbr.* **1** long-playing (gramophone record). **2** low pressure.

LPG *abbr.* liquefied petroleum gas.

L-plate /'elpleɪt/ *n. Brit.* a sign bearing the letter L, attached to the front and rear of a motor vehicle to indicate that it is being driven by a learner.

LPO *abbr.* London Philharmonic Orchestra.

LSD *abbr.* lysergic acid diethylamide.

l.s.d. /ˌeles'diː/ *n.* (also **£.s.d.**) *Brit.* **1** pounds, shillings, and pence (in former British currency). **2** money, riches. [L *librae, solidi, denarii*]

LSE *abbr.* London School of Economics.

LSO *abbr.* London Symphony Orchestra.

Lt. *abbr.* **1** Lieutenant. **2** light.

LTA *abbr.* Lawn Tennis Association.

Ltd. *abbr.* Limited.

Lu *symb. Chem.* the element lutetium.

Lualaba /ˌluːə'lɑːbə/ a river that rises in SE Zaïre and flows northwards for about 640 km (400 miles) before joining with the Luapula to form the Zaïre River.

Luanda /luː'ændə/ the capital of Angola; pop. (1988) 1,800,000.

Luang Prabang /luːˌæŋ prə'bæŋ/ (also **Louangphrabang**) a town in the west of Laos, on the Mekong River; pop. (est. 1984) 44,000. It was the capital of a kingdom of the same name from 1707 until the reorganization of 1946–7, when Vientiane became the administrative capital and Luang Prabang remained the royal residence and Buddhist religious centre of Laos.

lubber /'lʌbə(r)/ *n.* a big clumsy fellow; a lout. □ **lubber line** *Naut.* a line marked on a compass, showing the ship's forward direction. □□ **lubberlike** *adj.* **lubberly** *adj. & adv.* [ME, perh. f. OF *lobeor* swindler, parasite f. *lober* deceive]

Lübeck /'luːbek/ a port on the Baltic coast of Germany; pop. (1987) 209,200.

Lublin /'lʊblɪn/ a manufacturing city in eastern Poland; pop. (1985) 324,000.

lubra /'luːbrə/ *n. Austral.* sometimes *derog.* an Aboriginal woman. [F *loubra* f. Tasmanian]

lubricant /'luːbrɪkənt/ *n. & adj.* —*n.* a substance used to reduce friction. —*adj.* lubricating.

lubricate /'luːbrɪkeɪt/ *v.tr.* **1** reduce friction in (machinery etc.) by applying oil or grease etc. **2** make slippery or smooth with oil or grease. □□ **lubrication** /-ˈkeɪʃ(ə)n/ *n.* **lubricative** /-kətɪv/ *adj.* **lubricator** *n.* [L *lubricare lubricat-* f. *lubricus* slippery]

lubricious /luːˈbrɪʃəs/ *adj.* (also **lubricous** /ˈluːbrɪkəs/) **1** slippery, smooth, oily. **2** lewd, prurient, evasive. □□ **lubricity** *n.* [L *lubricus* slippery]

Lubumbashi /ˌluːbʊmˈbæʃɪ/ a city in SE Zaïre, formerly called Elisabethville, capital of the Shaba copper-mining region; pop. (1984) 543,300.

Lucan[1] /ˈluːkən/ *adj.* of or relating to St Luke. [eccl.L *Lucas* f. Gk *Loukas* Luke]

Lucan[2] /ˈluːkən/ (Marcus Annaeus Lucanus, 39–65) Roman poet of Spanish origin, nephew of the younger Seneca. At first an intimate of Nero, he was forced to commit suicide after joining a conspiracy against the emperor. His major work, a hexameter epic in ten books *The Civil War* (also known as the *Pharsalia*), deals with the civil war between Julius Caesar and Pompey; his republican and Stoic ideals find expression in the depiction of Cato; a rhetorical and hyperbolical manner is the vehicle for the extravagant horrors of the subject-matter.

Lucas van Leyden /ˌluːkəs væn ˈlaɪd(ə)n/ (1494–1533), Dutch painter of portraits and religious works who was also an outstanding graphic artist, influenced by Dürer. Early technical masterpieces include *Muhammad and the Monk*, an engraving of 1508 done when he was only 14 years old, and *Ecce Homo* (1510). Perspective was less important to him than the genre anecdote, as seen in his painting *Chess Players* (c.1508). He died at an early age, contemporary historians placing him at the forefront of 16th-c. Dutch art, although he was untouched by the Renaissance and did not exercise much influence over many artists, Rembrandt standing as an exception.

luce /luːs/ *n.* a pike (fish), esp. when full-grown. [ME f. OF *lus, luis* f. LL *lucius*]

lucent /ˈluːs(ə)nt/ *adj. literary* **1** shining, luminous. **2** translucent. □□ **lucency** *n.* **lucently** *adv.* [L *lucēre* shine (as LUX)]

Lucerne /luːˈsɜːn/ (German **Luzern**) a resort on the western shore of Lake Lucerne, in central Switzerland; pop. (1986) 160,600.

lucerne /luːˈsɜːn/ *n.* (also **lucern**) *Brit.* = ALFALFA. [F *luzerne* f. mod. Prov. *luzerno* glow-worm, with ref. to its shiny seeds]

lucid /ˈluːsɪd/ *adj.* **1** expressing or expressed clearly; easy to understand. **2** of or denoting intervals of sanity between periods of insanity or dementia. **3** *Bot.* with a smooth shining surface. **4** *poet.* bright. □□ **lucidity** /-ˈsɪdɪtɪ/ *n.* **lucidly** *adv.* **lucidness** *n.* [L *lucidus* (perh. through F *lucide* or It. *lucido*) f. *lucēre* shine (as LUX)]

Lucifer /ˈluːsɪfə(r)/ *n.* **1** Satan, the Devil, whose fall from heaven Jerome and other early Christian writers thought was alluded to in Isaiah 14: 12 (where the word *Lucifer* (L, = light-bringing) is an epithet of the king of Babylon). **2** *poet.* the morning star (the planet Venus). **3** (**lucifer**) *archaic* a friction match. [OE f. L, = light-bringing, morning-star (as LUX, *-fer* f. *ferre* bring)]

luck /lʌk/ *n.* **1** chance regarded as the bringer of good or bad fortune. **2** circumstances of life (beneficial or not) brought by this. **3** good fortune; success due to chance (*in luck; out of luck*). □ **for luck** to bring good fortune. **good luck 1** good fortune. **2** an omen of this. **hard luck** worse fortune than one deserves. **no such luck** *colloq.* unfortunately not. **try one's luck** make a venture. **with luck** if all goes well. **worse luck** *colloq.* unfortunately. [ME f. LG *luk* f. MLG *geluke*]

luckily /ˈlʌkɪlɪ/ *adv.* **1** (qualifying a whole sentence or clause) fortunately (*luckily there was enough food*). **2** in a lucky or fortunate manner.

luckless /ˈlʌklɪs/ *adj.* having no luck; unfortunate. □□ **lucklessly** *adv.* **lucklessness** *n.*

Lucknow /ˈlʌknaʊ/ the capital of Uttar Pradesh in India; pop. (1981) 1,007,000. The city was besieged twice by native insurgents during the Indian Mutiny in 1857.

lucky /ˈlʌkɪ/ *adj.* (**luckier, luckiest**) **1** having or resulting from good luck, esp. as distinct from skill or design or merit. **2** bringing good luck (*a lucky mascot*). **3** fortunate, appropriate (*a lucky guess*). □ **lucky dip** *Brit.* a tub containing different articles

concealed in wrapping or bran etc., and chosen at random by participants. □□ **luckiness** *n.*

lucrative /ˈluːkrətɪv/ *adj.* profitable, yielding financial gain. □□ **lucratively** *adv.* **lucrativeness** *n.* [ME f. L *lucrativus* f. *lucrari* to gain]

lucre /ˈluːkə(r)/ *n. derog.* financial profit or gain. □ **filthy lucre** see FILTHY. [ME f. F *lucre* or L *lucrum*]

Lucretia /luːˈkriːʃjə/ *Rom. legend* the wife of Tarquinius Collatinus. She was raped by a son of Tarquin the Proud and took her own life; this led to the expulsion of the Tarquins from Rome by a rebellion under Brutus.

Lucretius /luːˈkriːʃəs/ (Titus Lucretius Carus, c.94–c.55 BC) Roman didactic poet, of whose life little is known (the story that he committed suicide after being driven mad by a love-potion is probably apocryphal). His hexameter poem *On the Nature of Things* is an exposition of the atomist physics of the Epicureans; a thoroughgoing materialism is directed to the evangelical goal of giving men peace of mind by showing that their fear of the gods and of death is baseless; despite an apparently unpromising subject, the combination of philosophical zeal and poetic sublimity is unequalled in Latin.

lucubrate /ˈluːkjʊˌbreɪt/ *v.intr. literary* **1** write or study, esp. by night. **2** express one's meditations in writing. □□ **lucubrator** *n.* [L *lucubrare lucubrat-* work by lamplight (as LUX)]

lucubration /ˌluːkjʊˈbreɪʃ(ə)n/ *n. literary* **1** nocturnal study or meditation. **2** (usu. in *pl.*) literary writings, esp. of a pedantic or elaborate character. [L *lucubratio* (as LUCUBRATE)]

Lucullan /luːˈkʌlən, lʊ-/ *adj.* profusely luxurious. [L. Licinius *Lucullus*, Roman general of 1st c. BC famous for his lavish banquets]

lud /lʌd/ *n. Brit.* □ **m'lud** (or **my lud**) a form of address to a judge in a court of law. [corrupt. of LORD]

Lüda /luːˈdɑː/ a city and port in Liaoning province in NE China, comprising the cities and ports of Lüshun and Dalian (whence its name; pop. (est. 1986) 1,630,000. Lüshun was known as Port Arthur while the area was leased to the Russians (1898–1905), who made this ice-free port the headquarters of their Pacific fleet.

Luddite /ˈlʌdaɪt/ *n. & adj.* —*n.* **1** *hist.* a member of the bands of English craftsmen who, when their jobs were threatened by the progressive introduction of machinery into their trades in the early 19th c., attempted to reverse the trend towards mechanization by wrecking the offending machines. Although the Luddites were never well organized, they were taken very seriously by the government of the day which was haunted by the spectre of a popular uprising. **2** a person opposed to increased industrialization or new technology. —*adj.* of the Luddites or their beliefs. □□ **Luddism** *n.* **Ludditism** *n.* [perh. f. Ned *Lud*, an insane person said to have destroyed two stocking-frames c.1779]

Ludendorff /ˈluːdənˌdɔːf/, Erich (1865–1937), German general during the First World War. With Hindenburg, he directed the war effort until the final offensive failed (Sept. 1918). He later joined the Nazi party.

ludicrous /ˈluːdɪkrəs/ *adj.* absurd or ridiculous; laughable. □□ **ludicrously** *adv.* **ludicrousness** *n.* [L *ludicrus* prob. f. *ludicrum* stage play]

ludo /ˈluːdəʊ/ *n. Brit.* a simple board game in which counters are moved round according to the throw of dice. [L, = I play]

Ludwig /ˈlʊdvɪɡ/ the name of three kings of Bavaria:

Ludwig I (1786–1868), reigned 1825–48. In the early years of his reign Ludwig pursued relatively moderate reform policies, but after the 1830 liberal disturbances across Europe he inclined more and more towards reactionary catholicism. His domination by the dancer Lola Montez led to increasing unrest against his rule, and after a series of radical protests in 1847–8 he was forced to abdicate in favour of his son Maximilian.

Ludwig II (1845–86), reigned 1864–86. Ludwig II sided with the losing Austrians in the Austro-Prussian War of 1866, but afterwards came increasingly under Prussian influence and eventually joined the new German Empire, having obtained special legislative concessions for his country. A patron of the arts, and a friend of Wagner, in the last years of his reign he became a recluse and concentrated on building a series of elaborate castles at ruinous expense. He was declared insane and deposed in 1886 and drowned himself in Lake Starnberg almost immediately afterwards.

lues /ˈluːiːz/ n. (in full **lues venerea** /vɪˈnɪərɪə/) syphilis. ▫▫ **luetic** /luːˈetɪk/ adj. [L]

luff /lʌf/ n. & v. (also **loof** /luːf/) Naut. —n. **1** the edge of the fore-and-aft sail next to the mast or stay. **2** Brit. the broadest part of the ship's bow where the sides begin to curve in. —v.tr. (also absol.) **1** steer (a ship) nearer the wind. **2** turn (the helm) so as to achieve this. **3** obstruct (an opponent in yacht-racing) by sailing closer to the wind. **4** raise or lower (the jib of a crane or derrick). [ME lo(o)f f. OF lof, prob. f. LG]

luffa var. of LOOFAH.

Luftwaffe /ˈlʊftˌvæfə/ n. hist. the German Air Force before and during the Second World War. [G f. Luft air + Waffe weapon]

lug[1] /lʌg/ v. & n. —v. (**lugged, lugging**) **1** tr. **a** drag or tug (a heavy object) with effort or violence. **b** (usu. foll. by round, about) carry (something heavy) around with one. **2** tr. (usu. foll. by in, into) introduce (a subject etc.) irrelevantly. **3** tr. (usu. foll. by along, to) force (a person) to join in an activity. **4** intr. (usu. foll. by at) pull hard. —n. **1** a hard or rough pull. **2** (in pl.) US affectation (put on lugs). [ME, prob. f. Scand.: cf. Sw. lugga pull a person's hair f. lugg forelock]

lug[2] /lʌg/ n. **1** Sc. or colloq. an ear. **2** a projection on an object by which it may be carried, fixed in place, etc. **3** esp. US sl. a lout; a sponger; a stupid person. [prob. of Scand. orig.: cf. LUG[1]]

lug[3] /lʌg/ n. = LUGWORM. [17th c.: orig. unkn.]

lug[4] /lʌg/ n. = LUGSAIL. [abbr.]

Lugano /luːˈgɑːnəʊ/ a resort in southern Switzerland, on the north shore of Lake Lugano (which extends into Italy); pop. (1980) 27,800.

luge /luːʒ/ n. & v. —n. a light toboggan for one or two people, ridden in the sitting position. —v.intr. ride on a luge. [Swiss F]

Luger /ˈluːgə(r)/ n. a type of German automatic pistol. [G. Luger, German firearms expert d. 1922]

luggage /ˈlʌgɪdʒ/ n. suitcases, bags, etc. to hold a traveller's belongings. ▫ **luggage-van** Brit. a railway carriage for travellers' luggage. [LUG[1] + -AGE]

lugger /ˈlʌgə(r)/ n. a small ship carrying two or three masts with a lugsail on each. [LUGSAIL + -ER[1]]

lughole /ˈlʌghəʊl, ˈlʌgəʊl/ n. sl. the ear orifice. [LUG[2] + HOLE]

lugsail /ˈlʌgseɪl, -s(ə)l/ n. Naut. a quadrilateral sail which is bent on and hoisted from a yard. [prob. f. LUG[2]]

lugubrious /luːˈguːbrɪəs, lʊ-/ adj. doleful, mournful, dismal. ▫▫ **lugubriously** adv. **lugubriousness** n. [L lugubris f. lugēre mourn]

lugworm /ˈlʌgwɜːm/ n. any polychaete worm of the genus Arenicola, living in muddy sand and leaving characteristic worm-casts on lower shores, and often used as bait by fishermen. [LUG[3]]

Luik see LIÈGE.

Luke /luːk/, St **1** an Apostle, physician, possibly the son of a Greek freedman of Rome, closely associated with St Paul, and traditionally the author of the third Gospel and the Acts of the Apostles. Feast day, 18 Oct. **2** the third Gospel. ▫ **St Luke's summer** Brit. a period of fine weather expected about 18 Oct.

lukewarm /luːkˈwɔːm, ˈluːk-/ adj. **1** moderately warm; tepid. **2** unenthusiastic, indifferent. ▫▫ **lukewarmly** adv. **lukewarmness** n. [ME f. (now dial.) luke, lew f. OE]

lull /lʌl/ v. & n. —v. **1** tr. soothe or send to sleep gently. **2** tr. (usu. foll. by into) deceive (a person) into confidence (lulled into a false sense of security). **3** tr. allay (suspicions etc.) usu. by deception. **4** intr. (of noise, a storm, etc.) abate or fall quiet. —n. a temporary quiet period in a storm or in any activity. [ME, imit. of sounds used to quieten a child]

lullaby /ˈlʌləbaɪ/ n. & v. —n. (pl. -ies) **1** a soothing song to send a child to sleep. **2** the music for this. —v.tr. (-ies, -ied) sing to sleep. [as LULL + -by as in BYE-BYE[2]]

Lully /ˈluːlɪ/, Jean-Baptiste (1632–87), composer who was born in Florence but lived in France from the age of 14, changing his name and his nationality in 1661. He entered the service of the young Louis XIV as a dancer and soon became one of the most powerful figures at court. He created and drummed into superb shape a small orchestra of string players known as the Petits Violons, and in 1672 bought the privilege to establish a Royal Academy of Music together with the right of veto on any work which involved singing throughout. Lully's own operas mark the beginning of the French operatic tradition; many were not only popular in his own lifetime—the inevitable result of his monopoly—but also continued to hold the stage in France for nearly a century after their composition. They reveal his skill as an orchestrator and his sensitivity to French declamation. He died from gangrene as the result of striking his foot with the long staff he used for beating time on the floor.

lulu /ˈluːluː/ n. sl. a remarkable or excellent person or thing. [19th c., perh. f. Lulu, pet form of Louise]

lumbago /lʌmˈbeɪgəʊ/ n. rheumatic pain in the muscles of the lower back. [L f. lumbus loin]

lumbar /ˈlʌmbə(r)/ adj. Anat. relating to the loin, esp. the lower back area. ▫ **lumbar puncture** the withdrawal of spinal fluid from the lower back with a hollow needle, usu. for diagnosis. [med.L lumbaris f. L lumbus loin]

lumber[1] /ˈlʌmbə(r)/ v.intr. (usu. foll. by along, past, by, etc.) move in a slow clumsy noisy way. ▫▫ **lumbering** adj. [ME lomere, perh. imit.]

lumber[2] /ˈlʌmbə(r)/ n. & v. —n. **1** disused articles of furniture etc. inconveniently taking up space. **2** useless or cumbersome objects. **3** US partly prepared timber. —v. **1** tr. **a** (usu. foll. by with) leave (a person etc.) with something unwanted or unpleasant (always lumbering me with the cleaning). **b** (as **lumbered** adj.) in an unwanted or inconvenient situation (afraid of being lumbered). **2** tr. (usu. foll. by together) heap or group together carelessly. **3** tr. (usu. foll. by up) obstruct. **4** intr. cut and prepare forest timber for transport. ▫ **lumber-jacket** a jacket, usu. of warm checked material, of the kind worn by lumberjacks. **lumber-room** a room where disused or cumbrous things are kept. ▫▫ **lumberer** n. (in sense 4 of v.). **lumbering** n. (in sense 4 of v.). [perh. f. LUMBER[1]: later assoc. with obs. lumber pawnbroker's shop]

lumberjack /ˈlʌmbədʒæk/ n. (also **lumberman** pl. **-men**) esp. US one who fells, prepares, or conveys lumber.

lumbersome /ˈlʌmbəsəm/ adj. unwieldy, awkward.

lumbrical muscle /ˈlʌmbrɪk(ə)l/ n. any of the muscles flexing the fingers or toes. [mod.L lumbricalis f. L lumbricus earthworm, with ref. to its shape]

lumen /ˈluːmen/ n. **1** Physics the SI unit of luminous flux, equal to the amount of light emitted per second in a unit solid angle of one steradian from a uniform source of one candela. ¶ Abbr.: **lm. 2** Anat. (pl. **lumina** /-mɪnə/) a cavity within a tube, cell, etc. ▫▫ **luminal** /ˈluːmɪn(ə)l/ adj. [L lumen luminis a light, an opening]

Lumière /ˈljuːmɪˌeə(r)/, Auguste (1862–1954) and Louis (1864–1948), French inventors and pioneers of cinema. Their Cinématographe, initially a camera and projector in one, was patented in 1895 and gave its first public performance later in the same year.

Luminal /ˈluːmɪn(ə)l/ n. propr. phenobarbitone. [as LUMEN + -al as in veronal]

luminance /ˈluːmɪnəns/ n. Physics the intensity of light emitted from a surface per unit area in a given direction. [L luminare illuminate (as LUMEN)]

luminary /ˈluːmɪnərɪ/ n. (pl. **-ies**) **1** literary a natural light-giving body, esp. the sun or moon. **2** a person as a source of intellectual light or moral inspiration. **3** a prominent member of a group or gathering (a host of show-business luminaries). [ME f. OF luminarie or LL luminarium f. L LUMEN]

luminescence /ˌluːmɪˈnes(ə)ns/ n. the emission of light by a substance other than as a result of incandescence. ▫▫ **luminescent** adj. [as LUMEN + -ESCENCE (see -ESCENT)]

luminiferous /ˌluːmɪˈnɪfərəs, ˌljuː-/ adj. producing or transmitting light.

luminous /ˈluːmɪnəs, ˈljuː-/ adj. **1** full of or shedding light;

radiant, bright, shining. **2** phosphorescent, visible in darkness (*luminous paint*). **3** (esp. of a writer or a writer's work) throwing light on a subject. **4** of visible radiation (*luminous intensity*). □□ **luminosity** /-'nɒsɪtɪ/ *n*. **luminously** *adj*. **luminousness** *n*. [ME f. OF *lumineux* or L *luminosus*]

lumme /'lʌmɪ/ *int. Brit. sl.* an expression of surprise or interest. [= (*Lord*) *love me*]

lummox /'lʌməks/ *n. US colloq.* a clumsy or stupid person. [19th c. in US & dial.: orig. unkn.]

lump[1] /lʌmp/ *n. & v.* —*n.* **1** a compact shapeless or unshapely mass. **2** *sl.* a quantity or heap. **3** a tumour, swelling, or bruise. **4** a heavy, dull, or ungainly person. **5** (prec. by *the*) *Brit.* casual workers in the building and other trades who are paid in lump sums. —*v.* **1** *tr.* (usu. foll. by *together, with, in with, under*, etc.) mass together or group indiscriminately. **2** *tr.* carry or throw carelessly (*lumping crates round the yard*). **3** *intr.* become lumpy. **4** *intr.* (usu. foll. by *along*) proceed heavily or awkwardly. **5** *intr.* (usu. foll. by *down*) sit down heavily. □ **in the lump** taking things as a whole; in a general manner. **lump in the throat** a feeling of pressure there, caused by emotion. **lump sugar** sugar shaped into lumps or cubes. **lump sum 1** a sum covering a number of items. **2** money paid down at once (opp. INSTALMENT). □□ **lumper** *n*. (in sense 2 of *v*.). [ME, perh. of Scand. orig.]

lump[2] /lʌmp/ *v.tr. colloq.* endure or suffer (a situation) ungraciously. □ **like it or lump it** put up with something whether one likes it or not. [imit.: cf. *dump, grump*, etc.]

lumpectomy /lʌm'pektəmɪ/ *n.* (*pl.* -**ies**) the surgical removal of a usu. cancerous lump from the breast.

lumpenproletariat /'lʌmpən,prəʊlɪ,teərɪət/ *n.* (esp. in Marxist terminology) the unorganized and unpolitical lower orders of society, not interested in revolutionary advancement. □□ **lumpen** *adj*. [G f. *Lumpen* rag, rogue: see PROLETARIAT]

lumpfish /'lʌmpfɪʃ/ *n.* (*pl.* -**fishes** or -**fish**) a spiny-finned fish, *Cyclopterus lumpus*, of the N. Atlantic with modified pelvic fins for clinging to objects. [MLG *lumpen*, MDu. *lumpe* (perh. = LUMP[1]) + FISH[1]]

lumpish /'lʌmpɪʃ/ *adj.* **1** heavy and clumsy. **2** stupid, lethargic. □□ **lumpishly** *adv*. **lumpishness** *n*.

lumpsucker /'lʌmp,sʌkə(r)/ *n.* = LUMPFISH.

lumpy /'lʌmpɪ/ *adj.* (**lumpier, lumpiest**) **1** full of or covered with lumps. **2** (of water) cut up by the wind into small waves. □□ **lumpily** *adv*. **lumpiness** *n*.

lunacy /'lu:nəsɪ/ *n.* (*pl.* -**ies**) **1** insanity (orig. of the intermittent kind attributed to changes of the moon); the state of being a lunatic. **2** *Law* such mental unsoundness as interferes with civil rights or transactions. **3** great folly or eccentricity; a foolish act.

luna moth /'lu:nə/ *n.* a N. American moth, *Actias luna*, with crescent-shaped spots on its pale green wings. [L *luna*, = moon (from its markings)]

lunar /'lu:nə(r), 'lju:-/ *adj.* **1** of, relating to, or determined by the moon. **2** concerned with travel to the moon and related research. **3** (of light, glory, etc.) pale, feeble. **4** crescent-shaped, lunate. **5** of or containing silver (from alchemists' use of *luna* (= moon) for 'silver'). □ **lunar caustic** silver nitrate, esp. in stick form. **lunar cycle** = METONIC CYCLE. **lunar distance** the angular distance of the moon from the sun, a planet, or a star, used in finding longitude at sea. **lunar module** a small craft used for travelling between the moon's surface and a spacecraft in orbit around the moon. **lunar month 1** the period of the moon's revolution, esp. the interval between new moons of about 29½ days. **2** (in general use) a period of four weeks. **lunar nodes** the points at which the moon's orbit cuts the ecliptic. **lunar observation** the finding of longitude by lunar distance. **lunar orbit 1** the orbit of the moon round the earth. **2** an orbit round the moon. **lunar year** a period of 12 lunar months. [L *lunaris* f. *luna* moon]

lunate /'lu:neɪt, 'lju:-/ *adj. & n.* —*adj.* crescent-shaped. —*n.* a crescent-shaped prehistoric implement etc. □ **lunate bone** a crescent-shaped bone in the wrist. [L *lunatus* f. *luna* moon]

lunatic /'lu:nətɪk/ *n. & adj.* —*n.* **1** an insane person. **2** someone foolish or eccentric. —*adj.* mad, foolish. □ **lunatic asylum** *hist.* a mental home or mental hospital. **lunatic fringe** an extreme

or eccentric minority group. [ME f. OF *lunatique* f. LL *lunaticus* f. L *luna* moon]

lunation /lu:'neɪʃ(ə)n, lju:-/ *n.* the interval between new moons, about 29½ days. [ME f. med.L *lunatio* (as LUNATIC)]

lunch /lʌntʃ/ *n. & v.* —*n.* **1** the meal eaten in the middle of the day. **2** a light meal eaten at any time. —*v.* **1** *intr.* eat one's lunch. **2** *tr.* provide lunch for. □ **lunch-box** a container for a packed meal. **lunch-hour** (or -**time**) a break from work, when lunch is eaten. □□ **luncher** *n*. [LUNCHEON]

luncheon /'lʌntʃ(ə)n/ *n. formal* lunch. □ **luncheon meat** a usu. tinned block of ground meat ready to cut and eat. **luncheon voucher** *Brit.* a voucher or ticket issued to employees as part of their pay, exchangeable for food at many restaurants and shops. [17th c.: orig. unkn.]

luncheonette /,lʌntʃə'net/ *n.* orig. *US* a small restaurant or snack bar serving light lunches.

Lund /lʊnd/ a city in SW Sweden, with a university founded in 1666; pop. (1987) 84,300.

lune /lu:n/ *n. Geom.* a crescent-shaped figure formed on a sphere or plane by two arcs intersecting at two points. [F f. L *luna* moon]

lunette /lu:'net/ *n.* **1** an arched aperture in a domed ceiling to admit light. **2** a crescent-shaped or semicircular space or alcove which contains a painting, statue, etc. **3** a watch-glass of flattened shape. **4** a ring through which a hook is placed to attach a vehicle to the vehicle towing it. **5** a temporary fortification with two faces forming a salient angle, and two flanks. **6** *RC Ch.* a holder for the consecrated host in a monstrance. [F, dimin. of *lune* (see LUNE)]

lung /lʌŋ/ *n.* either of the pair of respiratory organs which bring air into contact with the blood in humans and many other vertebrates. □ **lung-power** the power of one's voice. □□ **lunged** *adj.* **lungful** *n.* (*pl.* -**fuls**). **lungless** *adj.* [OE *lungen* f. Gmc, rel. to LIGHT[2]]

lunge[1] /lʌndʒ/ *n. & v.* —*n.* **1** a sudden movement forward. **2** a thrust with a sword etc., esp. the basic attacking move in fencing. **3** a movement forward by bending the front leg at the knee while keeping the back leg straight. —*v.* **1** *intr.* make a lunge. **2** *intr.* (usu. foll. by *at, out*) deliver a blow from the shoulder in boxing. **3** *tr.* drive (a weapon etc.) violently in some direction. [earlier *allonge* f. F *allonger* lengthen f. *à* to + *long* LONG[1]]

lunge[2] /lʌndʒ, lju:-/ *n. & v.* (also **longe**) —*n.* **1** a long rope on which a horse is held and made to move in a circle round its trainer. **2** a circular exercise-ground for training horses. —*v.tr.* exercise (a horse) with or in a lunge. [F *longe, allonge* (as LUNGE[1])]

lungfish /'lʌŋfɪʃ/ *n.* any freshwater fish of the order Dipnoi, having gills and a modified swim bladder used as lungs, and able to aestivate to survive drought.

lungi /'lʊŋgiː/ *n.* (*pl.* **lungis**) a length of cotton cloth, usu. worn as a loincloth in India, or as a skirt in Burma (now Myanmar) where it is the national dress for both sexes. [Urdu]

lungwort /'lʌŋwɜːt/ *n.* **1** any herbaceous plant of the genus *Pulmonaria*, esp. *P. officinalis* with white-spotted leaves likened to a diseased lung. **2** a lichen, *Lobaria pulmonaria*, used as a remedy for lung disease.

lunisolar /,lu:nɪ'səʊlə(r)/ *adj.* of or concerning the sun and moon. □ **lunisolar period** a period of 532 years between the repetitions of both solar and lunar cycles. **lunisolar year** a year with divisions regulated by changes of the moon and an average length made to agree with the solar year. [L *luna* moon + *sol* sun]

lunula /'lu:njʊlə/ *n.* (*pl.* **lunulae** /-,li:/) **1** a crescent-shaped mark, esp. the white area at the base of the fingernail. **2** a crescent-shaped Bronze-Age ornament. [L, dimin. of *luna* moon]

lupin /'lu:pɪn/ *n.* (also **lupine** /-pɪn/) **1** any plant of the genus *Lupinus*, with long tapering spikes of blue, purple, pink, white, or yellow flowers. **2** (in *pl.*) seeds of the lupin. [ME f. L *lupinus*]

lupine /'lu:paɪn/ *adj.* of or like a wolf or wolves. [L *lupinus* f. *lupus* wolf]

lupus /'lu:pəs/ *n.* any of various ulcerous skin diseases, esp. tuberculosis of the skin. □ **lupus vulgaris** /vʌl'geərɪs/ tuberculosis with dark red patches on the skin, usu. due to direct inoculation of the tuberculosis bacillus into the skin. □□ **lupoid** *adj.* **lupous** *adj.* [L, = wolf]

lur /lʊə(r)/ *n.* (also **lure** /ljʊə(r)/) a bronze S-shaped trumpet of prehistoric times, still used in Scandinavia to call cattle. [Da. & Norw.]

lurch[1] /lɜ:tʃ/ *n. & v.* —*n.* a stagger, a sudden unsteady movement or leaning. —*v.intr.* stagger, move suddenly and unsteadily. [orig. Naut., *lee-lurch* alt. of *lee-latch* drifting to leeward]

lurch[2] /lɜ:tʃ/ *n.* □ **leave in the lurch** desert (a friend etc.) in difficulties. [orig. = a severe defeat in a game, f. F *lourche* (also the game itself, like backgammon)]

lurcher /ˈlɜ:tʃə(r)/ *n.* **1** *Brit.* a cross-bred dog, usu. a retriever, collie, or sheepdog crossed with a greyhound, used esp. for hunting and by poachers for retrieving game. **2** *archaic* a petty thief, swindler, or spy. [f. obs. *lurch* (v.) var. of LURK]

lure[1] /ljʊə(r), lʊə(r)/ *v. & n.* —*v.tr.* **1** (usu. foll. by *away*, *into*) entice (a person, an animal, etc.) usu. with some form of bait. **2** attract back again or recall (a person, animal, etc.) with the promise of a reward. —*n.* **1** a thing used to entice. **2** (usu. foll. by *of*) the attractive or compelling qualities (of a pursuit etc.). **3** a falconer's apparatus for recalling a hawk, consisting of a bunch of feathers attached to a thong, within which the hawk finds food while being trained. □□ **luring** *adj.* **luringly** *adv.* [ME f. OE *luere* f. Gmc]

lure[2] var. of LUR.

Lurex /ˈljʊəreks/ *n. propr.* **1** a type of yarn which incorporates a glittering metallic thread. **2** fabric made from this yarn.

lurid /ˈljʊərɪd, ˈlʊə-/ *adj.* **1** vivid or glowing in colour (*lurid orange*). **2** of an unnatural glare (*lurid nocturnal brilliance*). **3** sensational, horrifying, or terrible (*lurid details*). **4** showy, gaudy (*paperbacks with lurid covers*). **5** ghastly, wan (*lurid complexion*). **6** *Bot.* of a dingy yellowish brown. □ **cast a lurid light on** explain or reveal (facts or character) in a horrific, sensational, or shocking way. □□ **luridly** *adv.* **luridness** *n.* [L *luridus* f. *luror* wan or yellow colour]

lurk /lɜ:k/ *v. & n.* —*v.intr.* **1** linger furtively or unobtrusively. **2 a** lie in ambush. **b** (usu. foll. by *in*, *under*, *about*, etc.) hide, esp. for sinister purposes. **3** (as **lurking** *adj.*) latent, semi-conscious (*a lurking suspicion*). —*n.* *Austral. sl.* a dodge, racket, or scheme; a method of profitable business. □□ **lurker** *n.* [ME perh. f. LOUR with frequent. -*k* as in TALK]

Lusaka /luːˈsɑːkə/ the capital of Zambia; pop. (est. 1987) 819,000.

luscious /ˈlʌʃəs/ *adj.* **1 a** richly sweet in taste or smell. **b** *colloq.* delicious. **2** (of literary style, music, etc.) over-rich in sound, imagery, or voluptuous suggestion. **3** voluptuously attractive. □□ **lusciously** *adv.* **lusciousness** *n.* [ME perh. alt. of obs. *licious* f. DELICIOUS]

lush[1] /lʌʃ/ *adj.* **1** (of vegetation, esp. grass) luxuriant and succulent. **2** luxurious. □□ **lushly** *adv.* **lushness** *n.* [ME, perh. var. of obs. *lash* soft, f. OF *lasche* lax (see LACHES): assoc. with LUSCIOUS]

lush[2] /lʌʃ/ *n. & v.* esp. *US sl.* —*n.* **1** alcohol, liquor. **2** an alcoholic, a drunkard. —*v.* **1** *tr. & intr.* drink (alcohol). **2** *tr.* ply with alcohol. [18th c.: perh. joc. use of LUSH[1]]

Lüshun /luːˈʃuːn/ see LÜDA.

Lusitania[1] /ˌluːsɪˈteɪnɪə/ an ancient province of Hispania, almost identical with modern Portugal.

Lusitania[2] /ˌluːsɪˈteɪnɪə/ a Cunard liner which was sunk by a German submarine in the Atlantic in May 1915 with the loss of over 1,000 lives. The anti-German feeling that this event generated in the US was a factor in bringing that country into the First World War.

lust /lʌst/ *n. & v.* —*n.* **1** strong sexual desire. **2 a** (usu. foll. by *for*, *of*) a passionate desire for (*a lust for power*). **b** (usu. foll. by *of*) a passionate enjoyment of (*the lust of battle*). **3** (usu. in *pl.*) a sensuous appetite regarded as sinful (*the lusts of the flesh*). —*v.intr.* (usu. foll. by *after*, *for*) have a strong or excessive (esp. sexual) desire. □□ **lustful** *adj.* **lustfully** *adv.* **lustfulness** *n.* [OE f. Gmc]

luster *US* var. of LUSTRE[1].

lustra *pl.* of LUSTRUM.

lustral /ˈlʌstr(ə)l/ *adj.* relating to or used in ceremonial purification. [L *lustralis* (as LUSTRUM)]

lustrate /ˈlʌstreɪt/ *v.tr.* purify by expiatory sacrifice, ceremonial washing, or other such rite. □□ **lustration** /-ˈstreɪʃ(ə)n/ *n.* [L *lustrare* (as LUSTRUM)]

lustre[1] /ˈlʌstə(r)/ *n. & v.* (*US* **luster**) —*n.* **1** gloss, brilliance, or sheen. **2** a shining or reflective surface. **3 a** a thin metallic coating giving an iridescent glaze to ceramics. **b** = LUSTREWARE. **4** a radiance or attractiveness; splendour, glory, distinction (of achievements etc.) (*add lustre to; shed lustre on*). **5 a** a prismatic glass pendant on a chandelier etc. **b** a cut-glass chandelier or candelabrum. **6 a** *Brit.* a thin dress-material with a cotton warp, woollen weft, and a glossy surface. **b** any fabric with a sheen or gloss. —*v.tr.* put lustre on (pottery, a cloth, etc.). □□ **lustreless** *adj.* (*US* **lusterless**). **lustrous** *adj.* **lustrously** *adv.* **lustrousness** *n.* [F f. It. *lustro* f. *lustrare* f. L *lustrare* illuminate]

lustre[2] /ˈlʌstə(r)/ *n.* (*US* **luster**) = LUSTRUM. [ME, Anglicized f. LUSTRUM]

lustreware /ˈlʌstəˌweə(r)/ *n.* (*US* **lusterware**) ceramics with an iridescent glaze. [LUSTRE[1]]

lustrum /ˈlʌstrəm/ *n.* (*pl.* **lustra** /-strə/ or **lustrums**) a period of five years. [L, an orig. purificatory sacrifice after a quinquennial census]

lusty /ˈlʌstɪ/ *adj.* (**lustier**, **lustiest**) **1** healthy and strong. **2** vigorous or lively. □□ **lustily** *adv.* **lustiness** *n.* [ME f. LUST + -Y[1]]

lusus /ˈljuːsəs, ˈluː-/ *n.* (in full **lusus naturae** /nəˈtjʊəriː, -ˈtʊəraɪ/) a freak of nature. [L]

lutanist var. of LUTENIST.

lute[1] /luːt, ljuːt/ *n.* a plucked stringed instrument with frets and a round body, resembling a halved pear. In Europe it was one of the most important solo instruments from the 16th to the 18th c., and with the 20th-c. revival of interest in music of this period it has regained something of its former popularity. The lute was brought to Spain by the Moors at least as early as the 11th c., at that time having no frets and being plucked by a plectrum rather than the fingers. The word is also used to describe the many different plucked instruments of Asia and eastern Europe which have a bowl-shaped body: a form of 'long lute' (with neck longer than the body) was known in Mesopotamia in the 2nd millennium BC, while a short-necked instrument was played in Greece from *c.*800 BC. [ME f. F *lut*, *leüt*, prob. f. Prov. *laüt* f. Arab. *al-'ūd*]

lute[2] /luːt, ljuːt/ *n. & v.* —*n.* **1** clay or cement used to stop a hole, make a joint airtight, coat a crucible, protect a graft, etc. **2** a rubber seal for a jar etc. —*v.tr.* apply lute to. [ME f. OF *lut* f. L *lutum* mud, clay]

lutecium var. of LUTETIUM.

lutein /ˈluːtɪ-ɪn, ˈljuː-/ *n. Chem.* a pigment of a deep yellow colour found in egg-yolk etc. [L *luteum* yolk of egg, neut. of *luteus* yellow]

luteinizing hormone /ˈluːtəˌnaɪzɪŋ/ *n. Biochem.* a hormone secreted by the anterior pituitary gland that in females stimulates ovulation and in males stimulates the synthesis of androgen. ¶ Abbr.: **LH.** [LUTEIN]

lutenist /ˈluːtənɪst/ *n.* (also **lutanist**) a lute-player. [med.L *lutanista* f. *lutana* LUTE[1]]

luteo- /ˈluːtɪəʊ, ˈljuː-/ *comb. form* orange-coloured. [as LUTEOUS + -o-]

luteofulvous /ˌluːtɪəʊˈfʌlvəs, ˌljuː-/ *adj.* orange-tawny.

luteous /ˈluːtɪəs, ˈljuː-/ *adj.* of a deep orange yellow or greenish yellow. [L *luteus* f. *lutum* WELD[2]]

lutestring /ˈluːtstrɪŋ, ˈljuː-/ *n. archaic* a glossy silk fabric. [app. f. *lustring* f. F *lustrine* or It. *lustrino* f. *lustro* LUSTRE[1]]

lutetium /luːˈtiːʃəm, ljuː-/ *n.* (also **lutecium**) *Chem.* a silvery metallic element of the lanthanide series. ¶ Symb.: **Lu.** [F *lutecium* f. L *Lutetia* the ancient name of Paris]

Luther /ˈluːθə(r)/, Martin (1483–1546), German Protestant theologian, founder of the German Reformation. His religious ideas brought political consequences which influenced European history for centuries. In 1505 he became an Augustinian friar, and later taught at the newly founded university of Wittenberg, latterly as professor of Scripture. His study of the Bible, the influence of Augustine and late medieval German mysticism, and his own experience of the religious life led him to see an analogy between the religion of his day and the Judaism St Paul had relinquished, and the Pauline doctrine of justification by faith became for Luther the touchstone of reform. Public controversy, sparked off by his *95 Theses* (1517), led quickly to a break between Luther and the Church. Justification by faith alone implied for him the freedom of the Christian to dispense with a priestly system mediating between people and God. Marriage of the clergy, restoration of the chalice to the laity, the translation of the Scriptures, all pointed to the equality of men before God, though, as Luther's opposition to the Peasants' Revolt (1524–6) revealed, this had no political consequences. Through his German Bible and hymns, Luther's influence on German religion and on the German language has been enormous.

Lutheran /ˈluːθərən, ˈljuː-/ *n. & adj.* —*n.* **1** a follower of Martin Luther. **2** a member of the Lutheran Church. —*adj.* of or characterized by the theology of Martin Luther. □ **Lutheran Church** the Church accepting the Augsburg Confession of 1530, with justification by faith alone as a cardinal doctrine. □□ **Lutheranism** *n.* **Lutheranize** *v.tr. & intr.* (also **-ise**).

Lutine Bell /ˈluːtiːn/ the bell of HMS *Lutine*, which sank in 1799. The ship was carrying a large amount of coin and bullion, and the loss fell on the underwriters, who were members of Lloyd's of London. When the bell was recovered during salvage operations it was taken to Lloyd's, where it now hangs. It is rung (and business is halted) whenever there is an important announcement to be made to the underwriters. It was formerly rung once if a ship had sunk and twice for good news. [F, fem. of *lutin* spirit, imp]

luting /ˈluːtɪŋ/ *n.* = LUTE² *n.*

Lutyens¹ /ˈlʌtjənz/, (Agnes) Elizabeth (1906–83), English composer, daughter of Sir Edwin Lutyens. She was one of the first English composers to use the 12-note system. Her works include operas, orchestral and choral works, and chamber music; she has written nearly 200 scores for films and radio, and incidental music for plays.

Lutyens² /ˈlʌtjənz/, Sir Edwin Landseer (1869–1944), English architect who dominated design in the early 1900s. He established his reputation designing country houses, moving from a romantic red-brick style to Palladian-influenced formal designs. His immense output included the British Embassy, Washington (1926), and, most importantly, his work in designing the Indian capital, New Delhi (1915–30), where his mature public style is dramatically demonstrated.

lutz /lʊts/ *n.* a jump in ice-skating in which the skater takes off from the outside back edge of one skate and lands, after a complete rotation in the air, on the outside back edge of the opposite skate. [prob. f. Gustave *Lussi* b. 1898, who invented it]

lux /lʌks/ *n.* (*pl.* same) *Physics* the SI unit of illumination, equivalent to one lumen per square metre. ¶ Abbr.: **lx**. [L *lux lucis* light]

luxe /lʊks, lʌks/ *n.* luxury (cf. DE LUXE). [F f. L *luxus*]

Luxembourg /ˈlʌksəmˌbɜːɡ/ a country in western Europe, situated between Belgium, Germany, and France; pop. (est. 1988) 366,200; official language, French; capital, Luxembourg, seat of the European Court of Justice and the Secretariat of the parliament of the EEC; pop. (1987) 76,640. The country is rich in iron ore and its economic prosperity is based chiefly on its large iron and steel industries. Becoming a Hapsburg possession in the 15th c., Luxembourg was Spanish until 1713 and then Austrian until annexed by France in 1795. As a result of the Treaty of Vienna in 1815 it became a grand duchy, though in 1839 it lost its western province to Belgium. Occupied by Germany during both World Wars, Luxembourg formed a customs union with Belgium in 1922 which was extended in 1948 into the Benelux Customs Union which included The Netherlands. □□ **Luxembourger** *n.*

Luxor /ˈlʌksɔː(r)/ a city of Egypt, site of the southern complex of monuments of ancient Thebes; pop. (est. 1986) 147,900. [Arab. *al-uqṣur* the castles]

luxuriant /lʌɡˈzjʊərɪənt, lʌkˈsj-, lʌɡˈʒʊə-/ *adj.* **1** (of vegetation etc.) lush, profuse in growth. **2** prolific, exuberant, rank (*luxuriant imagination*). **3** (of literary or artistic style) florid, richly ornate. □□ **luxuriance** *n.* **luxuriantly** *adv.* [L *luxuriare* grow rank f. *luxuria* LUXURY]

luxuriate /lʌɡˈzjʊərɪˌeɪt, lʌkˈsj-, lʌɡˈʒʊə-/ *v.intr.* **1** (foll. by *in*) take self-indulgent delight in, enjoy in a luxurious manner. **2** take one's ease, relax in comfort.

luxurious /lʌɡˈzjʊərɪəs, lʌkˈsj-, lʌɡˈʒʊə-/ *adj.* **1** supplied with luxuries. **2** extremely comfortable. **3** fond of luxury, self-indulgent, voluptuous. □□ **luxuriously** *adv.* **luxuriousness** *n.* [ME f. OF *luxurios* f. L *luxuriosus* (as LUXURY)]

luxury /ˈlʌkʃərɪ/ *n.* (*pl.* **-ies**) **1** choice or costly surroundings, possessions, food, etc.; luxuriousness (*a life of luxury*). **2** something desirable for comfort or enjoyment, but not indispensable. **3** (*attrib.*) providing great comfort, expensive (*a luxury flat; a luxury holiday*). [ME f. OF *luxurie, luxure* f. L *luxuria* f. *luxus* abundance]

Luzon /luːˈzɒn/ the largest island of the Philippines, containing its capital (Manila).

LV *abbr. Brit.* luncheon voucher.

Lvov /ləˈvɒf/ an industrial city in Ukraine, near the Polish frontier; pop. (est. 1987) 767,000.

Lw *symb. Chem.* the element lawrencium.

LWM *abbr.* low-water mark.

lx *abbr.* lux.

LXX *abbr.* Septuagint. [Latin numeral, = 70]

-ly¹ /lɪ/ *suffix* forming adjectives esp. from nouns, meaning: **1** having the qualities of (*princely; manly*). **2** recurring at intervals of (*daily; hourly*). [from or after OE *-lic* f. Gmc, rel. to LIKE¹]

-ly² /lɪ/ *suffix* forming adverbs from adjectives, denoting esp. manner or degree (*boldly; happily; miserably; deservedly; amusingly*). [from or after OE *-lice* f. Gmc (as -LY¹)]

lycanthrope /ˈlaɪkənˌθrəʊp/ *n.* **1** a werewolf. **2** an insane person who believes that he or she is an animal, esp. a wolf. [mod.L *lycanthropus* f. Gk (as LYCANTHROPY)]

lycanthropy /laɪˈkænθrəpɪ/ *n.* **1** the mythical transformation of a person into a wolf (see also WEREWOLF). **2** a form of madness involving the delusion of being a wolf, with changed appetites, voice, etc. [mod.L *lycanthropia* f. Gk *lukanthrōpia* f. *lukos* wolf + *anthrōpos* man]

lycée /ˈliːseɪ/ *n.* (*pl.* **lycées**) a State secondary school in France. [F f. L (as LYCEUM)]

Lyceum /laɪˈsiːəm/ *n.* **1 a** the garden at Athens in which Aristotle taught philosophy. **b** Aristotelian philosophy and its followers. **2** (**lyceum**) *US hist.* a literary institution, lecture-hall, or teaching-place. [L f. Gk *Lukeion* neut. of *Lukeios* epithet of Apollo (from whose neighbouring temple the Lyceum was named)]

lychee /ˈlaɪtʃɪ, ˈlɪ-/ *n.* (also **litchi, lichee**) **1** a sweet fleshy fruit with a thin spiny skin. **2** the tree, *Nephelium litchi*, orig. from China, bearing this. [Chin. *lizhi*]

lych-gate var. of LICH-GATE.

lychnis /ˈlɪknɪs/ *n.* any herbaceous plant of the genus *Lychnis*, including ragged robin. [L f. Gk *lukhnis* a red flower f. *lukhnos* lamp]

Lycia /ˈlɪsɪə/ the ancient name for the region of SW Asia Minor between Caria and Pamphylia. □□ **Lycian** *adj. & n.*

lycopod /ˈlaɪkəˌpɒd/ *n.* any of various club-mosses, esp. of the genus *Lycopodium*. [Anglicized form of LYCOPODIUM]

lycopodium /ˌlaɪkəˈpəʊdɪəm/ *n.* **1** = LYCOPOD. **2 a** fine powder of spores from this, used as an absorbent in surgery, and in making fireworks etc. [mod.L f. Gk *lukos* wolf + *pous podos* foot]

Lycra /ˈlaɪkrə/ *n. propr.* an elastic polyurethane fibre or fabric used esp. for close-fitting sports clothing.

Lycurgus /laɪˈkɜːɡəs/ the reputed founder of the constitution of ancient Sparta, probably of about the end of the 9th c. BC.

Lydgate /ˈlɪdɡeɪt/, John (?1370–1449), English poet, a prolific writer of verse often in a Chaucerian vein. His longer works include the *Troy Book* (1412–20), telling the 'noble storye' of Troy, written at the request of Prince Henry (later Henry V), *The Siege of Thebes* (1420–2) and *The Fall of Princes* (1431–8). He enjoyed great popularity up to the 17th c. but later critics have found his work dull and prolix.

Lydia /ˈlɪdɪə/ the ancient name for the region of western Asia Minor south of Mysia and north of Caria. It was a powerful kingdom c.700–c.546 BC, and by the time of its last king (Croesus) had considerably extended its territory. Lydia was probably the first realm to use coined money.

Lydian /ˈlɪdɪən/ adj. & n. —n. **1** a native or inhabitant of ancient Lydia. **2** the language of this people. —adj. of or relating to the people of Lydia or their language. □ **Lydian mode** Mus. the mode represented by the natural diatonic scale F–F. [L Lydius f. Gk Ludios of Lydia]

lye /laɪ/ n. **1** water that has been made alkaline by lixiviation of vegetable ashes. **2** any strong alkaline solution, esp. of potassium hydroxide used for washing or cleansing. [OE lēag f. Gmc: cf. LATHER]

Lyell /ˈlaɪəl/, Sir Charles (1797–1875), Scottish geologist whose textbook Principles of Geology (1830–3) influenced a generation of geologists. He held that the earth's features were shaped over a long period of time by natural processes, and not during short periodic tremendous upheavals as proposed by the 'catastrophist' school of thought. In this he revived the theories of James Hutton, but his influence on geological opinion was much greater. His views cleared the way for Darwin's theory of evolution which Lyell, after some hesitation, accepted.

lying[1] /ˈlaɪɪŋ/ pres. part. of LIE[1]. —n. a place to lie (a dry lying).

lying[2] /ˈlaɪɪŋ/ pres. part. of LIE[2]. —adj. deceitful, false. □□ **lyingly** adv.

lyke-wake /ˈlaɪkweɪk/ n. Brit. a night-watch over a dead body. [perh. f. ON: cf. LICH(-GATE), WAKE[1]]

Lyly /ˈlɪlɪ/, John (?1554–1606), English poet and dramatist. His most popular works in Elizabethan times were his prose romances Euphues: The Anatomy of Wit (1578) and Euphues and his England (1580), written in a characteristically elaborate style where ornament takes priority over sense; their peculiar style became known as 'Euphuism'. His plays, all written for performance by boy actors to courtly audiences, are now admired for their flexible use of dramatic prose and their grace and wit.

lymph /lɪmf/ n. **1** Physiol. a colourless fluid containing white blood cells, drained from the tissues and conveyed through the body in the lymphatic system. **2** this fluid used as a vaccine. **3** exudation from a sore etc. **4** poet. pure water. □ **lymph gland** (or **node**) a small mass of tissue in the lymphatic system where lymph is purified and lymphocytes are formed. □□ **lymphoid** adj. **lymphous** adj. [F lymphe or L lympha, limpa water]

lymphatic /lɪmˈfætɪk/ adj. & n. —adj. **1** of or secreting or conveying lymph (lymphatic gland). **2** (of a person) pale, flabby, or sluggish. —n. a veinlike vessel conveying lymph. □ **lymphatic system** a network of vessels conveying lymph. [orig. = frenzied, f. L lymphaticus mad f. Gk numpholēptos seized by nymphs: now assoc. with LYMPH (on the analogy of spermatic etc.)]

lymphocyte /ˈlɪmfəˌsaɪt/ n. a form of leucocyte occurring in the blood, in lymph, etc. □□ **lymphocytic** /-ˈsɪtɪk/ adj.

lymphoma /lɪmˈfəʊmə/ n. (pl. **lymphomata** /-mətə/) any malignant tumour of the lymph nodes, excluding leukaemia.

lyncean /lɪnˈsiːən/ adj. lynx-eyed, keen-sighted. [L lynceus f. Gk lugkeios f. lugx LYNX]

lynch /lɪntʃ/ v.tr. (of a body of people) put (a person) to death for an alleged offence without a legal trial. □ **lynch law** the procedure of a self-constituted illegal court that punishes or executes. □□ **lyncher** n. **lynching** n. [Lynch's law, after Capt. W. Lynch, judge in Virginia c.1780]

lynchet /ˈlɪntʃɪt/ n. (in the UK) a ridge or ledge formed by ancient ploughing on a slope. [linch f. OE hlinc: cf. LINKS]

lynchpin var. of LINCHPIN.

lynx /lɪŋks/ n. **1** a medium-sized cat, Felis lynx, with short tail, spotted fur, and tufted ear-tips. **2** its fur. □ **lynx-eyed** keen-sighted. □□ **lynxlike** adj. [ME f. L f. Gk lugx]

Lyon /ˈlaɪən/ n. (in full **Lord Lyon** or **Lyon King of Arms**) the chief herald of Scotland. □ **Lyon Court** the court over which he presides. [archaic form. of LION: named f. the lion on the royal shield]

Lyons /ˈliːɔ̃/ (French **Lyon**) a city in SE France, situated at the confluence of the Rhône and Saône rivers, capital of the Rhône-Alpes region; pop. (1982) 418,500.

lyophilic /ˌlaɪəˈfɪlɪk/ adj. (of a colloid) readily dispersed by a solvent. [Gk luō loosen, dissolve + Gk philos loving]

lyophilize /laɪˈɒfɪˌlaɪz/ v.tr. (also **-ise**) freeze-dry.

lyophobic /ˌlaɪəˈfəʊbɪk/ adj. (of a colloid) not lyophilic. [Gk luō loosen, dissolve + -PHOBIC (see -PHOBIA)]

Lyra /ˈlaɪrə/ a northern constellation, the Lyre, whose brightest star, Vega, dominates the heavens in summer and is the fifth-brightest star visible.

lyrate /ˈlaɪərət/ adj. Biol. lyre-shaped.

lyre /ˈlaɪə(r)/ n. a plucked stringed instrumented in which strings are fixed to a crossbar supported by two arms. It was one of the most important instruments of ancient Greece (Homer describes Achilles playing the lyre when the embassy from Agamemnon visited him in his tent) but is widespread now only in eastern Africa. □ **lyre-bird** any Australian bird of the family Menuridae, the male of which has a lyre-shaped tail display. **lyre-flower** a bleeding heart. [ME f. OF lire f. L lyra f. Gk lura]

lyric /ˈlɪrɪk/ adj. & n. —adj. **1** (of poetry) expressing the writer's emotions, usu. briefly and in stanzas or recognized forms. **2** (of a poet) writing in this manner. **3** of or for the lyre. **4** meant to be sung, fit to be expressed in song, songlike (lyric drama; lyric opera). —n. **1** a lyric poem or verse. **2** (in pl.) lyric verses. **3** (usu. in pl.) the words of a song. [F lyrique or L lyricus f. Gk lurikos (as LYRE)]

lyrical /ˈlɪrɪk(ə)l/ adj. **1** = LYRIC. **2** resembling, couched in, or using language appropriate to, lyric poetry. **3** colloq. highly enthusiastic (wax lyrical about). □□ **lyrically** adv. **lyricalness** n.

lyricism /ˈlɪrɪˌsɪz(ə)m/ n. **1** the character or quality of being lyric or lyrical. **2** a lyrical expression. **3** high-flown sentiments.

lyricist /ˈlɪrɪsɪst/ n. a person who writes the words to a song.

lyrist n. **1** /ˈlaɪərɪst/ a person who plays the lyre. **2** /ˈlɪrɪst/ a lyric poet. [L lyrista f. Gk luristēs f. lura lyre]

Lysander /laɪˈsændə(r)/ (d. 395 BC) Spartan general and statesman, who was instrumental in the final defeat of Athens in the Peloponnesian War. He destroyed the Athenian navy at Aegospotami in 405 BC, and conducted the subsequent blockade of the Piraeus.

lyse /laɪs/ v.tr. & intr. bring about or undergo lysis. [back-form. f. LYSIS]

Lysenko /lɪˈsɛŋkəʊ/, Trofim Denisovich (1898–1976), Soviet biologist and geneticist, an adherent of Lamarck's theory of evolution by inheritance of acquired characteristics. Since Lysenko's ideas harmonized with Marxist ideology he was favoured by Stalin, and dominated Soviet genetics until 1948. Many false claims resulted during this unfortunate phase, notably that wheat grown in cold climates would 'vernalize' or become adapted genetically to resist low temperatures.

lysergic acid /laɪˈsɜːdʒɪk/ n. a crystalline acid extracted from ergot or prepared synthetically. □ **lysergic acid diethylamide** /ˌdaɪəˈθaɪləˌmaɪd/ a powerful hallucinogenic drug. ¶ Abbr.: LSD. [hydrolysis + ergot + -IC]

lysin /ˈlaɪsɪn/ n. a protein in the blood able to cause lysis. [G Lysine]

lysine /ˈlaɪsiːn/ n. Biochem. an amino acid present in protein and essential in the diet of vertebrates. [G Lysin, ult. f. LYSIS]

Lysippus /laɪˈsɪpəs/ (4th c. BC) Greek sculptor of Sicyon, official portraitist and favourite court sculptor of Alexander the Great. There are no works extant which are indisputably attributed to him but clear literary evidence survives, especially through Pliny, of his great influence on contemporaries and later artists. Although he also worked in marble, his bronze athletes, especially the Apoxyomenos (athlete cleaning himself, c.320–315 BC, of which a Roman copy exists) are his best-known works and support the tradition that he introduced a new scheme of proportions for the human body. He can be seen as the last great sculptor in the 4th-c. tradition, his innovations maturing in the works of Hellenistic sculptors.

lysis /ˈlaɪsɪs/ n. (pl. **lyses** /-siːz/) the disintegration of a cell. [L f. Gk lusis loosening f. luō loosen]

w we z zoo ʃ she ʒ decision θ thin ð this ŋ ring x loch tʃ chip dʒ jar (see over for vowels)

-lysis /lɪsɪs/ *comb. form* forming nouns denoting disintegration or decomposition (*electrolysis; haemolysis*).

Lysol /ˈlaɪsɒl/ *n. propr.* a mixture of cresols and soft soap, used as a disinfectant. [LYSIS + -OL²]

lysosome /ˈlaɪsəˌsəʊm/ *n.* a cytoplasmic organelle in eukaryotic cells containing degradative enzymes enclosed in a membrane. [LYSIS + -SOME³]

lysozyme /ˈlaɪsəˌzaɪm/ *n. Biochem.* an enzyme found in tears and egg-white which catalyses the destruction of cell walls of certain bacteria. [LYSIS + ENZYME]

lytic /ˈlɪtɪk/ *adj.* of, relating to, or causing lysis.

-lytic /ˈlɪtɪk/ *comb. form* forming adjectives corresponding to nouns in *-lysis*. [Gk *lutikos* (as LYSIS)]

Lytton /ˈlɪt(ə)n/, Edward George Earle, 1st Baron Lytton of Knebworth (1803–73), British novelist and politician, son of General Bulwer, added his mother's name of Lytton when he inherited her estate, Knebworth, in 1843. Educated at Cambridge, he embarked on a political career (first as Liberal, later as Tory MP), and financed his extravagant life-style by a prolific and versatile literary output which spanned the many changes in 19th-c. fiction from his first success *Pelham* (1828), which presents an archetypal wit and dandy as hero, to his immensely successful but now little-read historical romances, such as *The Last Days of Pompeii* (1834). Of his plays *Money* (1840) has been successfully revived.

M

M¹ /em/ n. (pl. **Ms** or **M's**) **1** the thirteenth letter of the alphabet. **2** (as a Roman numeral) 1,000.

M² abbr. (also **M.**) **1** Master. **2** (in titles) Member of. **3** Monsieur. **4** (in the UK in road designations) motorway. **5** mega-. **6** Chem. molar.

m abbr. (also **m.**) **1 a** masculine. **b** male. **2** married. **3** Cricket maiden (over). **4** mile(s). **5** metre(s). **6** million(s). **7** minute(s). **8** Currency mark(s). **9** mare. **10** milli-.

m' adj. = MY (m'lud).

'm n. colloq. madam (in yes'm etc.).

MA abbr. **1** Master of Arts. **2** US Massachusetts (in official postal use).

ma /mɑː/ n. colloq. mother. [abbr. of MAMMA¹]

ma'am /mæm, mɑːm, məm/ n. madam (used esp. in addressing royalty). [contr.]

Maas see MEUSE.

Maastricht /ˈmɑːstrɪxt/ an industrial city of the Netherlands, capital of the province of Limburg, situated on the River Maas near the Belgian frontier; pop. (1987) 115,782.

Maat /mɑːt/ Egyptian Mythol. the goddess of truth, justice, and cosmic order, daughter of Ra. She was the feather (this as a hieroglyphic sign means 'true' or 'just') against which the heart of the deceased was weighed in the balance at the judgement of the dead. She is depicted as a young and beautiful woman, standing or seated, with a feather on her head.

Mabinogion /ˌmæbɪˈnəʊɡɪən/ a collection of Welsh prose tales of the 11th–13th c., dealing with Celtic legends and mythology. [Welsh Mabinogi instruction for young bards]

Mabuse /məˈbjuːz/ (c.1478–1533/6), Flemish painter thus called because of his birthplace, Maubeuge (his real name was Jan Gossaert). Nothing is known of his early life and training, but soon after 1507 he entered the permanent service of Philip of Burgundy. He travelled in Italy where the art of the High Renaissance made a lasting impression on him and he became one of the first artists to disseminate the Italian style in the Netherlands. His works are largely nudes, studies of the Virgin and Child, and commissioned portraits.

Mac /mæk/ n. colloq. **1** a Scotsman. **2** US man (esp. as a form of address). [Mac- as a patronymic prefix in many Scottish and Irish surnames]

mac /mæk/ n. (also **mack**) Brit. colloq. mackintosh. [abbr.]

macabre /məˈkɑːbr/ adj. grim, gruesome. [ME f. OF macabré perh. f. Macabé a Maccabee, with ref. to a miracle play showing the slaughter of the Maccabees]

macadam /məˈkædəm/ n. **1** material for road-making with successive layers of compacted broken stone. **2** = TARMACADAM. □□ **macadamize** v.tr. (also **-ise**). [J. L. McAdam, Brit. surveyor d. 1836, who advocated using this material]

macadamia /ˌmækəˈdeɪmɪə/ n. any Australian evergreen tree of the genus Macadamia, esp. M. ternifolia, bearing edible nutlike seeds. [J. Macadam, Austral. chemist d. 1865]

macaque /məˈkæk/ n. any monkey of the genus Macaca, including the rhesus monkey and Barbary ape, having prominent cheek pouches and usu. a long tail. [F f. Port. macaco f. Fiot makaku some monkeys f. kaku monkey]

macaroni /ˌmækəˈrəʊnɪ/ n. **1** a tubular variety of pasta. **2** (pl. **macaronies**) hist. an 18th-c. British dandy affecting Continental fashions. [It. maccaroni f. late Gk makaria food made from barley]

macaronic /ˌmækəˈrɒnɪk/ n. & adj. —n. (in pl.) burlesque verses containing Latin (or other foreign) words and vernacular words with Latin etc. terminations. —adj. (of verse) of this kind. [mod.L macaronicus f. obs. It. macaronico, joc. formed as MACARONI]

macaroon /ˌmækəˈruːn/ n. a small light cake or biscuit made with white of egg, sugar, and ground almonds or coconut. [F macaron f. It. (as MACARONI)]

MacArthur /məˈkɑːθə(r)/, Douglas (1880–1964), American general who commanded US (later Allied) forces in the SW Pacific during the Second World War. He was in charge of the ceremony at which Japan surrendered, and administered that country during the Allied occupation that followed. In 1950–1 he was commander of military forces in Korea.

Macassar /məˈkæsə(r)/ see UJUNG PADANG. —n. (in full **Macassar oil**) a kind of oil formerly used as a dressing for the hair. Its ingredients were said to come from Macassar.

Macau /məˈkaʊ/ **1** a peninsula in SE China, on the west side of the Pearl River estuary, opposite Hong Kong, forming (with the nearby islands of Taipa and Colôane) an overseas province of Portugal. **2** its capital, a free port and tourist centre which occupies most of the peninsula; pop. (est. 1988) 432,200. Macau is the oldest European settlement in the Far East. Visited by Vasco da Gama in 1497, it was developed by the Portuguese as a trading post, and has been administered as a province by Portugal since 1887.

Macaulay¹ /məˈkɔːlɪ/, Dame (Emilie) Rose (1881–1958), English novelist, much acclaimed in the 1920s for her light satirical novels. Her witty scholarly accounts of her travels in the Mediterranean, written in later life, are also noteworthy.

Macaulay² /məˈkɔːlɪ/, Thomas Babington, 1st Baron (1800–59), English historian, essayist, and philanthropist. As a civil servant in India he established an English system of education there, and devised a new criminal code, before returning to Britain and devoting himself to literature and politics. Among his best-known works were the Lays of Ancient Rome (1842), but his greatest achievement was his detailed History of England (1849–61) from the accession of James II to the death of William III, written with compelling narrative force and lucidity (with a distinct Whig bias) which did much to establish history as the discipline it is today.

macaw /məˈkɔː/ n. any long-tailed brightly coloured parrot of the genus Ara or Anodorhynchus, native to S. and Central America. [Port. macao, of unkn. orig.]

Macbeth /məkˈbeθ/ (c.1005–57), king of Scotland 1040–57, the subject of one of Shakespeare's tragedies. A far more effective ruler than the play suggests, Macbeth came to the throne after murdering Duncan I, but was himself killed 17 years later by Malcolm III.

Macc. abbr. Maccabees (Apocrypha).

Maccabees /ˈmækəbiːz/ **1** a Jewish family which was mainly instrumental in freeing Judaea from the oppression of the Syrian king, Antiochus Epiphanes, and thus stemming the threatened destruction of Judaism by the advance of Hellenism. The revolt was begun in 168 BC by Mattathias, then an aged priest, and the struggle was carried on by his five sons, three of whom (Judas, Jonathan, and Simon) led the Jews in their struggle. **2** four books of Jewish history and theology, of which the first two (whose hero is Judas Maccabaeus) are included in the Apocrypha. □□ **Maccabean** /-ˈbiːən/ adj. [L Maccabaeus f. Gk, epithet of Judas, perh. f. Heb. maqāb hammer]

McCarthy /məˈkɑːθɪ/, Mary Therese (1912–), American novelist and critic. Her novels include The Groves of Academe (1952), which describes the political persecutions of McCarthyism (see entry); The Group (1963), a study of the lives and careers of eight college girls; Birds of America (1971), deploring the effects of growing tourism; and Cannibals and Missionaries (1980), dealing with a hijacking in Holland. She has also published volumes of essays and criticism, short stories, and descriptive profiles of two Italian cities in Venice Observed (1956) and The Stones of Florence (1959). She was married to and divorced from the essayist and critic Edmund Wilson.

aʊ how eɪ day əʊ no eə hair ɪə near ɔɪ boy ʊə poor aɪə fire aʊə sour (see over for consonants)

McCarthyism /mə'ka:θɪˌɪz(ə)m/ n. anti-Communist persecution, verging on public hysteria, prevalent in the US in the decade following the Second World War. Under the leadership of Senator J. R. McCarthy (d. 1957) this witch-hunt for people suspected of Communist beliefs, and their removal especially from government departments, resulted in the ruin of many careers and a nationwide suspicion of Communism which is still apparent in the US.

McCartney /ˌmə'ka:tnɪ/, (James) Paul (1942–), English songwriter and pop musician, a member of the Beatles (see entry).

McCoy /mə'kɔɪ/ n. colloq. □ **the** (or **the real**) **McCoy** the real thing; the genuine article. [19th c.: orig. uncert.]

MacDiarmid /mək'dɜ:mɪd/, Hugh (pseudonym of Christopher Murray Grieve, 1892–1978), Scottish poet, nationalist, and Marxist. In 1922, influenced by James Joyce's Ulysses, he began to write lyrics in a synthetic Scots that drew on various dialects, fortifying the oral idiom with archaisms, and produced his materpiece A Drunk Man Looks at the Thistle (1926). In the 1930s he wrote political poetry, including First Hymn to Lenin (1931).

Macdonald[1] /mək'dɒnəld/, Flora (1722–90), a popular Jacobite heroine who aided Charles Edward Stuart's escape from Scotland, after his defeat at Culloden in 1746, by smuggling him over to the Isle of Skye in a small boat under the eyes of government forces.

MacDonald[2] /mək'dɒnəld/, James Ramsay (1866–1937), British statesman. Leader of the Parliamentary Labour Party before the First World War, he resigned because of his pacifist views. Resuming leadership of the party in 1922, he led the short-lived Labour government of 1924 and was elected Prime Minister again in 1929, but without an overall majority. Faced with economic crisis, and weakened by splits in his own party, he formed a National Government with some Conservatives and Liberals, an act for which he was expelled from the Labour Party. MacDonald remained Prime Minister until succeeded by Baldwin in 1935.

MacDonnell Ranges /mək'dɒn(ə)l/ a series of mountain ranges extending westwards from Alice Springs in Northern Territory, Australia. The highest peak is Mt Liebig which rises to a height of 1,524 m (4,948 ft.). Explored in 1860 by John McDouall Stuart, they were named after Sir Richard Macdonnell who was governor of South Australia at that time.

mace[1] /meɪs/ n. **1** a staff of office, esp. the symbol of the Speaker's authority in the House of Commons. **2** hist. a heavy club usu. having a metal head and spikes. **3** a stick used in the game of bagatelle. **4** = mace-bearer. □ **mace-bearer** an official who carries a mace on ceremonial occasions. [ME f. OF mace, masse f. Rmc mattea (unrecorded) club]

mace[2] /meɪs/ n. the dried outer covering of the nutmeg, used as a spice. [ME macis (taken as pl.) f. OF macis f. L macir a red spicy bark]

macédoine /'mæsɪˌdwa:n/ n. mixed vegetables or fruit, esp. cut up small or in jelly. [F, = Macedonia, with ref. to the mixture of peoples there]

Macedon /'mæsɪd(ə)n/ ancient Macedonia.

Macedonia /ˌmæsɪ'dəʊnɪə/ **1** an ancient country (now lying within northern Greece and SE Yugoslavia) at the NE end of the Greek peninsula, including the coastal plain around Salonika and the mountain ranges behind. It was the seat of a kingdom which under Philip II and Alexander the Great became a world power. **2** a region in the north-east of modern Greece, stretching from Mount Athos to the Yugoslav frontier; pop. (1981) 2,121,950; capital, Salonica. **3** a constituent republic of Yugoslavia; pop. (1981) 1,909,100; capital, Skopje. □□ **Macedonian** adj. & n.

macer /'meɪsə(r)/ n. a mace-bearer, esp. Sc. an official keeping order in a lawcourt. [ME f. OF massier f. masse: see MACE[1]]

macerate /'mæsəˌreɪt/ v. **1** tr. & intr. make or become soft by soaking. **2** intr. waste away by fasting. □□ **maceration** /-'reɪʃ(ə)n/ n. **macerator** n. [L macerare macerat-]

Macgillicuddy's Reeks /məˈgɪlɪˌkʌdɪ ri:ks/ a range of hills in County Kerry in SW Ireland.

Mach /ma:k, mæk/, Ernst (1838–1916), Austrian physicist and philosopher of science. His belief that all knowledge of the world comes from sensations, and that science should be solely concerned with observables, inspired the logical positivist philosophers of the Vienna Circle in the 1920s, and also scientists such as Einstein in the formulation of his theory of relativity, and the 'Copenhagen school' of quantum mechanics. In commemoration of his work on aerodynamics, his name has been preserved in the Mach number —n. (in full **Mach number**) the ratio of the speed of a body to the speed of sound in the surrounding medium. □ **Mach one** (or **two** etc.) the speed (or twice the speed) of sound.

machete /mə'tʃetɪ, mə'ʃetɪ/ n. (also **matchet** /'mætʃɪt/) a broad heavy knife used in Central America and the W. Indies as an implement and weapon. [Sp. f. macho hammer f. LL marcus]

Machiavelli /ˌmækɪə'velɪ/, Niccolo di Bernardo dei (1469–1527), Florentine statesman and political philosopher. After holding high office he was exiled by the Medicis on suspicion of conspiracy, but was subsequently restored to some degree of favour. He produced an important study of the art of war and a series of works on political philosophy, but his best-known work was The Prince (1513), a treatise on statecraft directed to the attainment of a united Italy by means that included cruelty and bad faith. Selected maxims from it were translated into French, and attacked by the French Huguenot Gentillet, and it was from an English translation of this treatise that the Elizabethans derived their knowledge of, and hostility to, Machiavelli.

machiavellian /ˌmækɪə'velɪən/ adj. elaborately cunning; scheming, unscrupulous. □□ **machiavellianism** n. [MACHIAVELLI]

machicolate /mə'tʃɪkəˌleɪt/ v.tr. (usu. as **machicolated** adj.) furnish (a parapet etc.) with openings between supporting corbels for dropping stones etc. on attackers. □□ **machicolation** /-'leɪʃ(ə)n/ n. [OF machicoler, ult. f. Prov. machacol f. macar crush + col neck]

machinable /mə'ʃi:nəb(ə)l/ adj. capable of being cut by machine tools. □□ **machinability** /-'bɪlɪtɪ/ n.

machinate /'mækɪˌneɪt, 'mæʃ-/ v.intr. lay plots; intrigue. □□ **machination** /-'neɪʃ(ə)n/ n. **machinator** n. [L machinari contrive (as MACHINE)]

machine /mə'ʃi:n/ n. & v. —n. **1** an apparatus using or applying mechanical power, having several parts each with a definite function and together performing certain kinds of work. **2** a particular kind of machine, esp. a vehicle, a piece of electrical or electronic apparatus, etc. **3** an instrument that transmits a force or directs its application. **4** the controlling system of an organization etc. (the party machine). **5** a person who acts mechanically and with apparent lack of emotion. —v.tr. make or operate on with a machine (esp. in sewing or printing). □ **machine code** (or **language**) a computer language that a particular computer can respond to directly. **machine-readable** in a form that a computer can process. **machine tool** a mechanically operated tool for working on metal, wood, or plastics. **machine-tooled** **1** shaped by a machine tool. **2** (of artistic presentation etc.) precise, slick, esp. excessively so. [F f. L machina f. Gk makhana Doric form of mēkhanē f. mēkhos contrivance]

machine-gun /mə'ʃi:ngʌn/ n. & v. —n. an automatic gun giving continuous fire. (See below.) —v.tr. (**-gunned**, **-gunning**) shoot at with a machine-gun. □□ **machine-gunner** n.

The first mechanically operated (hand-cranked) 'revolving battery gun' was the invention of a London lawyer, James Puckle, and was patented in 1718. It was actually produced, but its flintlock mechanism was unreliable. Other notable inventors include R. J. Gatling (1862), B. B. Hotchkiss (1877), I. N. Lewis, and J. M. Browning; the first satisfactory fully automatic weapon was that of H. S. Maxim (1884). The machine-gun dominated the battlefields in the First World War and continued in use in the Second.

machinery /mə'ʃi:nərɪ/ n. (pl. **-ies**) **1** machines collectively. **2** the components of a machine; a mechanism. **3** (foll. by of) an organized system. **4** (foll. by for) the means devised or available (the machinery for decision-making).

machinist /mə'ʃi:nɪst/ n. **1** a person who operates a machine, esp. a sewing-machine or a machine tool. **2** a person who makes machinery.

machismo /mə'ʃɪzməʊ, -'kɪzməʊ/ n. exaggeratedly assertive manliness; a show of masculinity. [Sp. f. *macho* MALE f. L *masculus*]

Machmeter /'mɑːkˌmiːtə(r), 'mæk-/ n. an instrument indicating air speed in the form of a Mach number.

macho /'mætʃəʊ/ adj. & n. —adj. showily manly or virile. —n. (pl. **-os**) **1** a macho man. **2** = MACHISMO. [MACHISMO]

machtpolitik /'mɑːxtpɒlɪˌtiːk/ n. power politics. [G]

Machu Picchu /ˌmɑːtʃuː 'pɪktʃuː/ a fortified Inca town in Peru, which the invading Spaniards never found. Perhaps not an important fortress, it is dramatically perched on a steep-sided ridge. The town contains a palace, a temple to the sun, and extensive cultivation terraces. Discovered in 1911, it was named after the mountain that rises above it.

macintosh var. of MACKINTOSH.

mack var. of MAC.

Mackay /mə'kaɪ/ a port in NE Australia, on the coast of Queensland; pop. (est. 1987) 50,000.

Mackenzie[1] /mə'kenzɪ/, Sir Alexander (1764–1820), Scottish explorer of Canada. Mackenzie entered the service of the North West Fur Company in 1779, undertaking explorations all over NW Canada. He discovered the Mackenzie River in 1789 and in 1793 became the first white man to reach the Pacific Ocean by land along a northern route.

Mackenzie[2] /mə'kenzɪ/, Sir (Edward Montague) Compton (1883–1972), English novelist and author of essays, memoirs, and poems. One of his best-known works is the semi-autobiographical *Sinister Street* (1913–14), a novel about growing up. In later life his works were in a lighter vein and include the humorous novel *Whisky Galore* (1947, filmed 1949), a story (based on an actual event) of the foundering of a whisky-laden ship near the shore of an island and the subsequent abstraction of its cargo by the local population.

Mackenzie[3] /mə'kenzɪ/, William Lyon (1795–1861), Canadian revolutionary. Unhappy with the pace of reform in the colony of Upper Canada, Mackenzie, a radical journalist, led a short-lived rebellion in 1837, unsuccessfully attempting to set up a new government in Toronto.

Mackenzie River /mə'kenzɪ/ the longest river of Canada, 1,700 km (1,060 miles) long, flowing NE from the Great Slave Lake to the Beaufort Sea, a section of the Arctic Ocean. It is named after Sir Alexander Mackenzie (see entry).

mackerel /'mækr(ə)l/ n. (pl. same or **mackerels**) a N. Atlantic marine fish, *Scomber scombrus*, with a greenish-blue body, used for food. □ **mackerel shark** a porbeagle. **mackerel sky** a sky dappled with rows of small white fleecy clouds, like the pattern on a mackerel's back. [ME f. AF *makerel*, OF *maquerel*]

McKinlay /mə'kɪnlɪ/, John (1819–72), Scottish-born explorer. Having emigrated to New South Wales in 1836, McKinlay was appointed by the South Australia government in 1861 to lead an expedition to search for the missing explorers Burke and Wills. Although he found only traces of part of the Burke and Wills party, he carried out valuable exploratory work in the interior and got his entire party back safely despite tremendous hardships. On another expedition into the interior in 1865, it was once again his skill as a leader which saved the group when faced with extraordinarily unfavourable climatic conditions.

McKinley /mə'kɪnlɪ/, William (1843–1901), 25th President of the US, 1897–1901. He supported US expansion into the Pacific, fighting the Spanish-American War (see entry) and accepting the consequent acquisitions of Puerto-Rico, Guam, and the Philippines, as well as annexing Hawaii.

McKinley /mə'kɪnlɪ/, **Mount** a peak in Alaska, the highest in North America, rising to a height of 6,194 m (20,110 ft.). It is named after President William McKinley.

Mackintosh /'mækɪntɒʃ/, Charles Rennie (1868–1928), Scottish architect and designer, a leading exponent of art nouveau and precursor of several of the more advanced trends in 20th-c. architecture, where he pioneered the new conception of the role of function. His influence was very great abroad, especially in Austria and Germany, but less so in Britain. His fame rests to a large extent on his Glasgow School of Art and the four Glasgow tearooms, designed with all their furniture and equipment.

mackintosh /'mækɪnˌtɒʃ/ n. (also **macintosh**) **1** *Brit.* a waterproof coat or cloak. **2** cloth waterproofed with rubber. [C. *Macintosh*, Sc. inventor d. 1843, who orig. patented the cloth]

mackle /'mæk(ə)l/ n. a blurred impression in printing. [F *macule* f. L *macula* blemish: see MACULA]

macle /'mæk(ə)l/ n. **1** a twin crystal. **2** a dark spot in a mineral. [F f. L (as MACKLE)]

Maclean /mə'kleɪn/, Alistair (1924–87), Scottish author of numerous thrillers, many of which were made into successful films, including *The Guns of Navarone* (1957), and *Where Eagles Dare* (1967).

Maclean /mə'kleɪn/, Donald Duart (1913–), British Foreign Office official and Soviet spy, who fled to the USSR with Guy Burgess in 1951 after being warned by Kim Philby (see entry) that he was under suspicion and about to be interrogated.

McLuhan /mə'kluːən/, (Herbert) Marshall (1911–80), Canadian communications scholar, who made major contributions to the understanding of the role of the media and technology in society. He became famous in the 1960s for his statements that the world had become 'a global village' in its electronic interdependence, and that 'the Medium is the Message', because 'it is the medium that shapes and controls the scale and form of human association and action'.

Macmillan /mək'mɪlən/, Maurice Harold, 1st Earl of Stockton (1894–1987), British Conservative statesman, Prime Minister 1957–63. His ministries saw a period of relative affluence, the limitation of Commonwealth immigration into the UK, and acceptance of the need for independence of African States, but Britain was prevented by de Gaulle's veto from entering the European Economic Community (1963). Macmillan's government was weakened by public concern about an alleged Soviet espionage plot involving his Secretary of State for War, John Profumo.

McNaughten rules /mək'nɔːt(ə)n/ n.pl. (also **M'Naghten rules**) *Brit.* rules governing the decision as to the criminal responsibility of an insane person. [*McNaughten* or *McNaughtan*, name of a 19th-c. accused person]

MacNeice /mək'niːs/, (Frederick) Louis (1907–63), British poet, born in Belfast, educated in England, a contemporary of Auden (with whom he collaborated in *Letters from Iceland*, 1937) at Oxford, where he published his first volume of poems in 1929. MacNeice used many classic verse forms but his distinctive contribution was his deployment of assonance, internal rhythms, and ballad-like repetitions absorbed from the Irish background of his youth. He was an outstanding writer of documentaries and parable plays for radio, notably *The Dark Tower* (1947). Although overshadowed by Auden in the 1930s and 1940s, his reputation revived with the publication of his *Collected Poems* (1960).

Macquarie /mə'kwærɪ/, Lachlan (1762–1824), Australian governor of the convict settlement of New South Wales 1810–21, the last to hold virtually autocratic power. In his view the colony was a settlement for convicts, where free settlers had little place and where convicts should be treated with every encouragement.

macramé /mə'krɑːmɪ/ n. **1** the art of knotting cord or string in patterns to make decorative articles. **2** articles made in this way. [Turk. *makrama* bedspread f. Arab. *miḳrama*]

macro /'mækrəʊ/ n. (also **macro-instruction**) *Computing* a series of abbreviated instructions expanded automatically when required.

macro- /'mækrəʊ/ comb. form **1** long. **2** large, large-scale. [Gk *makro-* f. *makros* long, large]

macrobiotic /ˌmækrəʊbaɪ'ɒtɪk/ adj. & n. —adj. relating to or following a diet (associated esp. with Zen Buddhism) intended to prolong life, comprising pure vegetable foods, brown rice, etc. —n. (in pl.; treated as sing.) the use or theory of such a dietary system.

macrocarpa /ˌmækrəʊ'kɑːpə/ n. an evergreen tree, *Cupressus* *macrocarpa*, often cultivated for hedges or wind-breaks. [mod.L f. Gk MACRO- + *karpos* fruit]

macrocephalic /ˌmækrəʊsɪˈfælɪk/ *adj.* (also **macrocephalous** /-ˈsefələs/) having a long or large head. □□ **macrocephaly** /-ˈsefəlɪ/ *n.*

macrocosm /ˈmækrəʊˌkɒz(ə)m/ *n.* 1 the universe. 2 the whole of a complex structure. □□ **macrocosmic** /-ˈkɒzmɪk/ *adj.* **macrocosmically** /-ˈkɒzmɪkəlɪ/ *adv.*

macroeconomics /ˌmækrəʊˌiːkəˈnɒmɪks/ *n.* the study of large-scale or general economic factors, e.g. national productivity. □□ **macroeconomic** *adj.*

macromolecule /ˌmækrəʊˈmɒlɪˌkjuːl/ *n. Chem.* a molecule containing a very large number of atoms. □□ **macromolecular** /-məˈlekjʊlə(r)/ *adj.*

macron /ˈmækrɒn/ *n.* a written or printed mark (ˉ) over a long or stressed vowel. [Gk *makron* neut. of *makros* large]

macrophage /ˈmækrəʊˌfeɪdʒ/ *n.* a large phagocytic white blood cell usu. occurring at points of infection.

macrophotography /ˌmækrəʊfəˈtɒgrəfɪ/ *n.* photography producing photographs larger than life.

macropod /ˈmækrəʊˌpɒd/ *n.* any plant-eating mammal of the family Macropodidae native to Australia and New Guinea, including kangaroos and wallabies. [MACRO- + Gk *pous podos* foot]

macroscopic /ˌmækrəʊˈskɒpɪk/ *adj.* 1 visible to the naked eye. 2 regarded in terms of large units. □□ **macroscopically** *adv.*

macula /ˈmækjʊlə/ *n.* (*pl.* **maculae** /-ˌliː/) 1 a dark spot, esp. a permanent one, in the skin. 2 (in full **macula lutea** /ˈluːtɪə/) the region of greatest visual acuity in the retina. □□ **macular** *adj.* **maculation** /-ˈleɪʃ(ə)n/ *n.* [L, = spot, mesh]

mad /mæd/ *adj. & v.* —*adj.* (**madder, maddest**) 1 insane; having a disordered mind. 2 (of a person, conduct, or an idea) wildly foolish. 3 (often foll. by *about, on*) wildly excited or infatuated (*mad about football; is chess-mad*). 4 *colloq.* angry. 5 (of an animal) rabid. 6 wildly light-hearted. —*v.* (**madded, madding**) 1 *tr. US* make angry. 2 *intr. archaic* be mad; act madly (*the madding crowd*). □ **like mad** *colloq.* with great energy, intensity, or enthusiasm. **mad cow disease** see BSE. **mad keen** *colloq.* extremely eager. □□ **madness** *n.* [OE *gemǣded* part. form f. *gemād* mad]

Madagascar /ˌmædəˈɡæskə(r)/ an island country in the Indian Ocean, off the east coast of Africa; pop. (est. 1988) 11,073,400; official languages, Malagasy and French; capital, Antananarivo. The island's geological history is puzzling, and many of its plants and animals are not found elsewhere. The people are of mixed Polynesian, Arab, and Black origin, and the economy is mainly agricultural. The fourth-largest island in the world, Madagascar was heavily influenced by Arab settlers before the Portuguese discovery in 1500. The island, despite rival French and British attempts at domination, remained independent until finally colonized by the French in 1896. It regained its independence as the Malagasy Republic in 1960, changing its name back to Madagascar in 1975.

madam /ˈmædəm/ *n.* 1 a polite or respectful form of address or mode of reference to a woman. 2 *Brit. colloq.* a conceited or precocious girl or young woman. 3 a woman brothel-keeper. [ME f. OF *ma dame* my lady]

Madame /məˈdɑːm, ˈmædəm/ *n.* 1 (*pl.* **Mesdames** /meɪˈdɑːm, -ˈdæm/) a title or form of address used of or to a French-speaking woman, corresponding to Mrs or madam. 2 (**madame**) = MADAM 1. [F (as MADAM)]

madcap /ˈmædkæp/ *adj. & n.* —*adj.* 1 wildly impulsive. 2 undertaken without forethought. —*n.* a wildly impulsive person.

madden /ˈmæd(ə)n/ *v.* 1 *tr. & intr.* make or become mad. 2 *tr.* irritate intensely. □□ **maddening** *adj.* **maddeningly** *adv.*

madder /ˈmædə(r)/ *n.* 1 a herbaceous plant, *Rubia tinctorum*, with yellowish flowers. 2 a red dye obtained from the root of the madder, or its synthetic substitute. [OE *mædere*]

made /meɪd/ 1 *past* and *past part.* of MAKE. 2 *adj.* (usu. in *comb.*) **a** (of a person or thing) built or formed (*well-made; strongly-made*). **b** successful (*a self-made man*). □ **have it made** *colloq.* be sure of

success. **made for** ideally suited to. **made of** consisting of. **made of money** *colloq.* very rich.

Madeira[1] /məˈdɪərə/ the largest of a group of islands (**the Madeiras**) in the Atlantic Ocean off NW Africa which are in Portuguese possession but partially autonomous; pop. (est. 1986) 269,500; capital, Funchal. [Port., = timber (f. L *materia* matter), from its thick woods]

Madeira[2] /məˈdɪərə/ a river of NW Brazil which rises on the Bolivian border and flows about 1,450 km (900 miles) to meet the Amazon east of Manaus. It is navigable to large ocean-going vessels as far as Pôrto Velho.

Madeira[3] /məˈdɪərə/ *n.* 1 a fortified white wine from the island of Madeira. 2 (in full **Madeira cake**) a kind of rich sponge cake.

madeleine /ˈmædəˌleɪn/ *n.* a small fancy sponge cake. [F]

Mademoiselle /ˌmædəmwəˈzel/ *n.* (*pl.* **Mesdemoiselles** /ˌmeɪdm-/) 1 a title or form of address used of or to an unmarried French-speaking woman, corresponding to Miss or madam. 2 (**mademoiselle**) **a** a young Frenchwoman. **b** a French governess. [F f. *ma* my + *demoiselle* DAMSEL]

madhouse /ˈmædhaʊs/ *n.* 1 *archaic* or *colloq.* a mental home or hospital. 2 *colloq.* a scene of extreme confusion or uproar.

Madhya Pradesh /ˌmɑːdɪə prəˈdeʃ/ a State in central India, formed in 1956; pop. (1981) 52,131,700; capital, Bhopal.

Madison[1] /ˈmædɪs(ə)n/ the capital of Wisconsin; pop. (1980) 170,616. It is named after President James Madison.

Madison[2] /ˈmædɪs(ə)n/, James (1751–1836), 4th President of the US, 1809–17, who had taken a leading part in drawing up the US constitution (1787) and proposed the Bill of Rights (1791).

madly /ˈmædlɪ/ *adv.* 1 in a mad manner. 2 *colloq.* **a** passionately. **b** extremely.

madman /ˈmædmən/ *n.* (*pl.* **-men**) a man who is mad.

Madonna /məˈdɒnə/ *n. Eccl.* 1 (prec. by *the*) a name for the Virgin Mary. 2 (usu. **madonna**) a picture or statue of the Madonna. □ **madonna lily** the white *Lilium candidum*, as shown in many pictures of the Madonna. [It. f. *ma* = *mia* my + *donna* lady f. L *domina*]

Madras /məˈdrɑːs, -æs/ 1 a seaport on the east coast of India, capital of Tamil Nadu; pop. (1981) 4,277,000. 2 the former name (until 1968) of Tamil Nadu.

madras /məˈdræs/ *n.* a strong cotton fabric with coloured or white stripes, checks, etc. [MADRAS]

madrepore /ˈmædrɪˌpɔː(r)/ *n.* 1 any perforated coral of the genus *Madrepora*. 2 the animal producing this. □□ **madreporic** /-ˈpɒrɪk/ *adj.* [F *madrépore* or mod.L *madrepora* f. It. *madrepora* f. *madre* mother + *poro* PORE[1]]

Madrid /məˈdrɪd/ the capital (since 1561) of Spain, situated on a high plateau almost exactly in the centre of the country; pop. (1986) 3,123,700.

madrigal /ˈmædrɪɡ(ə)l/ *n.* 1 a part-song for several voices, usu. arranged in elaborate counterpoint and without instrumental accompaniment. (See below.) 2 a short love poem. □□ **madrigalian** /-ˈɡeɪlɪən/ *adj.* **madrigalesque** /-ɡəˈlesk/ *adj.* **madrigalist** *n.* [It. *madrigale* f. med.L *matricalis* mother (church), formed as MATRIX]

The term was used in the 14th c. for a genre of Italian song for two or three voices, often comprising two or three stanzas, each of three lines. Today, however, the term is usually thought of in connection with 16th- and early 17th-c. song, a multi-voiced composition but with no fixed form, following the vagaries of the verse and frequently dwelling on particular descriptive or emotive words or phrases. The 20th c. has seen a considerable revival of madrigal singing in Britain and America.

Madura /məˈdʊərə/ an island of Indonesia, off the NE coast of Java. Its chief town is Pamekasan.

Madurai /ˌmɑːdʊˈraɪ/ a city in Tamil Nadu in southern India; pop. (1981) 904,000.

madwoman /ˈmædˌwʊmən/ *n.* (*pl.* **-women**) a woman who is mad.

Maecenas /maɪˈsiːnəs/, Gaius (c.70–8 BC), a wealthy Roman of Etruscan origin who was a close friend and adviser of Augustus but shunned official position, and was renowned for his luxurious habits. Himself a writer, he was an important patron and friend of poets (an occupation for which his name is a byword), among whom were Virgil, Propertius, and Horace.

maelstrom /ˈmeɪlstrəm/ n. **1** a great whirlpool. **2** a state of confusion. [early mod. Du. f. *malen* grind, whirl + *stroom* STREAM]

maenad /ˈmiːnæd/ n. **1** a bacchante. **2** a frenzied woman. □□ **maenadic** /-ˈnædɪk/ adj. [L *Maenas Maenad*- f. Gk *Mainas -ados* f. *mainomai* rave]

maestoso /maɪˈstəʊzəʊ/ adj., adv., & n. Mus. —adj. & adv. to be performed majestically. —n. (pl. -**os**) a piece of music to be performed in this way. [It.]

maestro /ˈmaɪstrəʊ/ n. (pl. **maestri** /-strɪ/ or -**os**) (often as a respectful form of address) **1** a distinguished musician, esp. a conductor or performer. **2** a great performer in any sphere, esp. artistic. [It., = master]

Maeterlinck /ˈmeɪtəlɪŋk/, Maurice (1862–1949), Belgian poet, dramatist, and essayist. He became a leading figure in the symbolist movement with his play *La Princesse Maleine* (1889) and is now chiefly remembered for his *Pelléas et Mélisande* (1892), the source of Debussy's opera of that name (1902), and for the fairy play *L'Oiseau bleu* (*The Blue-bird*, 1909). He drew on traditions of fairy-tale and romance, and the characteristic tone of much of his drama is doom-laden mystery and timeless melancholy. He was awarded the Nobel Prize for literature in 1911.

Mae West /meɪ ˈwest/ n. an inflatable life-jacket. [the professional name of an American actress, (see WEST²) noted for her large bust]

Mafeking /ˈmæfɪkɪŋ/ a South African town (since 1980 Mafikeng, now in Bophuthatswana) in which a small British force under the command of Baden-Powell was besieged by the Boers for 215 days in 1899–1900. Although the town was of little strategic significance, its successful defence, at a time when the Boer War was going very badly for the British, excited great interest, while its relief was hailed almost with a national sense of jubilation.

Mafia /ˈmæfɪə, ˈmɑː-/ n. **1** a secret organization, opposed to legal authority and engaged in crime, that originated in Sicily in the 13th c. and later spread to North and South America, at first among Italian immigrants. Calling itself 'Cosa Nostra' [It., = our affair], it became an integral part of the sophisticated and ruthless organized crime that developed in the US. **2** (**mafia**) a group regarded as exerting a hidden sinister influence. [It. dial. (Sicilian), = bragging]

Mafikeng see MAFEKING.

Mafioso /ˌmæfɪˈəʊsəʊ, ˌmɑː-/ n. (pl. **Mafiosi** /-sɪ/) a member of the Mafia. [It. (as MAFIA)]

mag /mæg/ n. colloq. a magazine (periodical). [abbr.]

mag. abbr. **1** magnesium. **2** magneto. **3** magnetic.

Magadi /məˈɡɑːdɪ/, Lake a lake in the Great Rift Valley, in southern Kenya, whose bed consists chiefly of solid or semi-solid soda.

magazine /ˌmæɡəˈziːn/ n. **1** a periodical publication containing articles, stories, etc., usu. with photographs, illustrations, etc. **2** a chamber for holding a supply of cartridges to be fed automatically to the breech of a gun. **3** a similar device feeding a camera, slide projector, etc. **4** a store for arms, ammunition, and provisions for use in war. **5** a store for explosives. [F *magasin* f. It. *magazzino* f. Arab. *makāzin* pl. of *makzan* storehouse f. *kazana* store up]

magdalen /ˈmæɡdəlɪn/ n. **1** a reformed prostitute. **2** a home for reformed prostitutes. [Mary *Magdalene* of Magdala in Galilee (Luke 8:2), identified (prob. wrongly) with the sinner of Luke 7: 37: f. eccl.L *Magdalena* f. Gk *Magdalēnē*]

Magdalena /ˌmæɡdəˈleɪnə/ the principal river of Colombia, linking the Andean highlands with the coastal lowlands. Flowing northwards for a distance of about 1,610 km (1,000 miles), it meets the Caribbean Sea near Barranquilla.

Magdalenian /ˌmæɡdəˈliːnɪən/ adj. & n. Archaeol. —adj. of the latest palaeolithic industry of Europe, named after the type-site at La Madeleine in the Dordogne region of France and dated to c.15,000–11,000 BC. It is characterized by a range of bone and horn tools, including elaborate bone harpoons; cave art reached a zenith during this period (see ALTAMIRA). —n. this industry. [F *Magdalénien* of *La Madeleine*]

Magdeburg /ˈmæɡdɪˌbɜːɡ/ an industrial city of Germany, the capital of Saxony-Anhalt, situated on the River Elbe and linked to the Rhine and Ruhr by the Mitteland Canal; pop. (est. 1990) 290,000. □ **Magdeburg hemispheres** a pair of copper hemispheres joined to form a hollow globe from which the air could be extracted, after which they were practically inseparable, devised by a German physicist, Otto von Guericke (1602–86), to demonstrate the effect of air pressure.

mage /meɪdʒ/ n. archaic **1** a magician. **2** a wise and learned person. [ME, Anglicized f. MAGUS]

Magellan¹ /məˈɡelən/, Ferdinand (c.1480–1521), Portuguese explorer. On Portuguese service in the East Indies in 1511–12 he explored the Spice Islands, but in 1517 offered his services to Spain to undertake a voyage to the same islands by the western route. Leaving Spain with five vessels in 1519, Magellan reached South America and wintered at Port St Julien before rounding the continent through the strait which now bears his name. In 1521 he discovered the Philippines, but soon after was killed in a native war on Cebu. The survivors of this disaster escaped to the Moluccas and sailed back to Spain round Africa, with the one remaining vessel, thereby completing the first circumnavigation of the globe.

Magellan² /məˈɡelən/, **Strait of** a passage through the islands of Tierra del Fuego at the southern tip of South America, connecting the Atlantic and Pacific Oceans. It is named after Ferdinand Magellan, who discovered it in Oct. 1520.

Magellanic clouds /ˌmædʒəˈlænɪk/ two diffuse luminous regions of the southern sky, now known to be galaxies of irregular shape, containing millions of stars, that are nearest to the Galaxy. [MAGELLAN¹]

magenta /məˈdʒentə/ n. & adj. —n. **1** a brilliant mauvish-crimson shade. **2** an aniline dye of this colour; fuchsine. —adj. of or coloured with magenta. [*Magenta* in N. Italy, town near which the Austrians were defeated by the French under Napoleon III in 1859, shortly before the dye was discovered]

Maggiore /ˌmædʒɪˈɔːreɪ/, **Lake** the second-largest of the lakes of north Italy, extending into southern Switzerland.

maggot /ˈmæɡət/ n. **1** a larva, esp. of the cheese-fly or bluebottle. **2** a whimsical fancy. □□ **maggoty** adj. [ME perh. alt. f. *maddock*, earlier *mathek* f. ON *mathkr*: cf. MAWKISH]

Maghrib /ˈmæɡrɪb/ (also **Maghreb**) a region of North and NW Africa between the Atlantic Ocean and Egypt, comprising the coastal plain and Atlas Mountains of Morocco, together with Algeria, Tunisia, and sometimes also Tripolitania, forming a well-defined zone bounded by sea or desert. It formerly included Moorish Spain (see BARBARY). [Arab., = west]

magi pl. of MAGUS.

magian /ˈmeɪdʒɪən/ adj. & n. —adj. of the magi or Magi. —n. **1** a magus or Magus. **2** a magician. □□ **magianism** n. [L *magus*: see MAGUS]

magic /ˈmædʒɪk/ n., adj., & v. —n. **1 a** the supposed art of influencing the course of events by the occult control of nature or of the spirits. **b** witchcraft. **2** conjuring tricks. **3** an inexplicable or remarkable influence producing surprising results. **4** an enchanting quality or phenomenon. —adj. **1** of or resulting from magic. **2** producing surprising results. **3** colloq. wonderful, exciting. —v.tr. (**magicked, magicking**) change or create by magic, or apparently so. □ **like magic** very rapidly. **magic away** cause to disappear as if by magic. **magic carpet** a mythical carpet able to transport a person on it to any desired place. **magic eye 1** a photoelectric device used in equipment for detection, measurement, etc. **2** a small cathode-ray tube used to indicate the correct tuning of a radio receiver. **magic lantern** a simple form of image-projector using slides. **magic mushroom** a mushroom producing psilocybin. **magic realism** see separate entry. **magic square** a square divided into smaller squares each containing a number such that the sums of all vertical, horizontal, or diagonal rows are equal. [ME f. OF *magique* f. L *magicus* adj., LL *magica* n., f. Gk *magikos* (as MAGUS)]

magical /ˈmædʒɪk(ə)l/ *adj.* **1** of or relating to magic. **2** resembling magic; produced as if by magic. **3** wonderful, enchanting. □□ **magically** *adv.*

magician /məˈdʒɪʃ(ə)n/ *n.* **1** a person skilled in or practising magic. **2** a conjuror. **3** a person with exceptional skill. [ME f. OF *magicien* f. LL *magica* (as MAGIC)]

magic realism *n.* a style of art and literature that uses realistic techniques and detail in portraying imaginative themes or fantasy. The term was originally used to describe the work of a group of German artists in the 1920s, and later to that of American artists such as Charles Sheeles (1883–1965) and Edward Hopper (1882–1967) and to the writings of such Latin American authors as J. L. Borges. Elements of 'magic realism' have been noted in the writings of Günter Grass, J. R. Fowles, and other Europeans. In the 1970s the style was adopted by a number of younger writers of fiction, including Emma Tennant (1938–), Angela Carter (1940–), and Salman Rushdie; in their novels and stories recognizably realistic and everyday elements combine with dream, fairy story, or mythology, often in a pattern of refraction or recurrence.

magilp var. of MEGILP.

Maginot Line /ˈmæʒɪˌnəʊ/ the line of defensive fortifications built along France's NE frontier from Switzerland to Luxembourg, completed in 1936, in which the French placed excessive confidence. Partly because of objections from the Belgians, who were afraid they would be left in an exposed situation, the line was not extended along the Franco-Belgian frontier to the coast. Consequently, although the defences proved impregnable to frontal assault, the line could be outflanked, and this happened when the Germans invaded France in the spring of 1940. It is named after the French Minister of War André Maginot (1877–1932).

magisterial /ˌmædʒɪˈstɪərɪəl/ *adj.* **1** imperious. **2** invested with authority. **3** of or conducted by a magistrate. **4** (of a work, opinion, etc.) highly authoritative. □□ **magisterially** *adv.* [med.L *magisterialis* f. LL *magisterius* f. L *magister* MASTER]

magisterium /ˌmædʒɪˈstɪərɪəm/ *n.* RC Ch. the official teaching of a bishop or pope. [L = the office of a master (as MAGISTERIAL)]

magistracy /ˈmædʒɪstrəsɪ/ *n.* (pl. **-ies**) **1** the office or authority of a magistrate. **2** magistrates collectively.

magistral /məˈdʒɪstr(ə)l/ *adj.* **1** of a master or masters. **2** Pharm. (of a remedy etc.) devised and made up for a particular case (cf. OFFICINAL). [F *magistral* or L *magistralis* f. *magister* MASTER]

magistrate /ˈmædʒɪstrət, -ˌstreɪt/ *n.* **1** a civil officer administering the law. **2** an official conducting a court for minor cases and preliminary hearings (*magistrates' court*). □□ **magistrateship** *n.* **magistrature** /-trəˌtjʊə(r)/ *n.* [ME f. L *magistratus* (as MAGISTRAL)]

Maglemosian /ˌmæɡləˈməʊzɪən/ *adj. & n.* —*adj.* of the first mesolithic industries in northern Europe, named after the type-site Maglemose, a bog (Danish *magle mose* great moss or bog) at Mullerup in Denmark, and dated to *c.*8300–6500 BC. The people were fishers and fowlers, hunting game and gathering natural crops (hazel nuts were relished), but not cultivating crops deliberately nor domesticating animals (except for dogs of a wolfish type). —*n.* this industry.

maglev /ˈmæɡlev/ *n.* (usu. *attrib.*) magnetic levitation, a system in which trains glide above the track in a magnetic field. [abbr.]

magma /ˈmæɡmə/ *n.* (pl. **magmata** /-mətə/ or **magmas**) **1** fluid or semifluid material from which igneous rock is formed by cooling. **2** a crude pasty mixture of mineral or organic matter. □□ **magmatic** /-ˈmætɪk/ *adj.* [ME, = a solid residue f. L f. Gk *magma -atos* f. the root of *massō* knead]

Magna Carta /ˌmæɡnə ˈkɑːtə/ *n.* (also **Magna Charta**) **1** the political charter which King John was forced to sign by his rebellious barons at Runnymede in 1215. The barons, discontented with John's high-handedness, were led by Archbishop Langton to frame a charter which effectively redefined the limits of royal power. Although the charter was often violated by medieval kings, it eventually came to be seen as the seminal document of English constitutional practice. Among its chief provisions were that no freeman should be imprisoned or banished except by the law of the land, and that supplies should not be exacted without the consent of the Common Council of the realm. **2** any similar document of rights. [med.L, = great charter]

magnanimous /mæɡˈnænɪməs/ *adj.* nobly generous; not petty in feelings or conduct. □□ **magnanimity** /ˌmæɡnəˈnɪmɪtɪ/ *n.* **magnanimously** *adv.* [L *magnanimus* f. *magnus* great + *animus* soul]

magnate /ˈmæɡneɪt, -nɪt/ *n.* a wealthy and influential person, esp. in business (*shipping magnate; financial magnate*). [ME f. LL *magnas -atis* f. L *magnus* great]

magnesia /mæɡˈniːʒə, -ʃə, -zjə/ *n.* **1** Chem. magnesium oxide. **2** (in general use) hydrated magnesium carbonate, a white powder used as an antacid and laxative. □□ **magnesian** *adj.* [ME f. med.L f. Gk *Magnēsia* (*lithos*) (stone) of Magnesia in Asia Minor, orig. referring to loadstone]

magnesite /ˈmæɡnɪˌsaɪt/ *n.* a white or grey mineral form of magnesium carbonate.

magnesium /mæɡˈniːzɪəm/ *n.* Chem. a silvery metallic element occurring naturally in magnesite and dolomite. It is a common element in the earth's crust and in the sea. Because of its low density magnesium is used to make strong light alloys in the aerospace industry and for certain consumer goods. It is also used in flash bulbs and pyrotechnics, as it burns in air with a brilliant white flame. Magnesium compounds have various uses, including as important reagents in organic chemistry; magnesium hydroxide is a commonly used antacid and laxative. Magnesium is necessary to life, and in particular forms part of the chlorophyll molecule. ¶ Symb.: **Mg**; atomic number 12. □ **magnesium flare** (or **light**) a blinding white light produced by burning magnesium wire.

magnet /ˈmæɡnɪt/ *n.* **1** a piece of iron, steel, alloy, ore, etc., usu. in the form of a bar or horseshoe, having properties of attracting or repelling iron and of pointing approximately north and south when freely suspended. **2** a lodestone. **3** a person or thing that attracts. [ME f. L *magnes magnetis* f. Gk *magnēs = Magnēs -ētos* (*lithos*) (stone) of Magnesia: cf. MAGNESIA]

magnetic /mæɡˈnetɪk/ *adj.* **1 a** having the properties of a magnet. **b** producing, produced by, or acting by magnetism. **2** capable of being attracted by or acquiring the properties of a magnet. **3** very attractive or alluring (*a magnetic personality*). □ **magnetic compass** = COMPASS 1. **magnetic disk** see DISC. **magnetic equator** an imaginary line, near the equator, on which a magnetic needle has no dip. **magnetic field** see FIELD. **magnetic inclination** = DIP *n.* 8. **magnetic mine** a submarine mine detonated by the proximity of a magnetized body such as that of a ship. **magnetic moment** the property of a magnet that interacts with an applied field to give a mechanical moment. **magnetic needle** a piece of magnetized steel used as an indicator on the dial of a compass and in magnetic and electrical apparatus, esp. in telegraphy. **magnetic north** the point indicated by the north end of a compass needle. **magnetic pole 1** each of the points near the extremities of the axis of rotation of the earth or another body where a magnetic needle dips vertically. **2** each of the regions of an artificial or natural magnet, from which the magnetic forces appear to originate. **magnetic storm** a disturbance of the earth's magnetic field caused by charged particles from the sun etc. **magnetic tape** a tape coated with magnetic material for recording sound or pictures or for the storage of information. □□ **magnetically** *adv.* [LL *magneticus* (as MAGNET)]

magnetism /ˈmæɡnɪˌtɪz(ə)m/ *n.* **1 a** a magnetic phenomena and their study. **b** the property of producing these phenomena. (See below, and also FIELD.) **2** attraction; personal charm. [mod.L *magnetismus* (as MAGNET)]

The phenomenon of magnetism has been known since ancient times. It derived its name in antiquity from an iron ore found near Magnesia in Asia Minor, which had the power to attract iron and other pieces of ore, and also to induce a similar power of attraction in iron. The constant direction of a freely suspended magnetic needle (i.e. a magnetic compass) was first discovered in China and was apparently introduced to Europe in the 12th c. William Gilbert in *De Magnete* (1600) established that the Earth is a great magnet, and raised magnetism to the status of an exact experimental science; before this the mysterious attractive power of a magnet, which was able to pass through wood and stone, had placed magnetism firmly in the sphere of natural magic.

It was Ampère who first suggested that the powers of a magnet are due to the combined effect of tiny electric currents circulating in its atoms. In 1820 Oersted demonstrated that a wire carrying an electric current gave rise to a magnetic field, and in 1831 the converse of this effect, in which a moving magnet induces a current in a wire, was demonstrated by Faraday. It is now generally accepted that all magnetism, including that of the Earth, is due to circulating electric currents. In magnetic materials the magnetism is produced by electrons orbiting within the atoms. In most substances the magnetic effects of different electrons cancel each other out, but in some, such as iron, a net magnetic field can be induced. The magnetism of the Earth itself is thought to be caused by the circulation of molten iron and nickel in the core.

The earliest uses of magnets were as compasses, but nowadays magnetism and especially electromagnetic phenomena have many applications, being fundamental to the operation of electric generators and motors, loudspeakers, lifting magnets, transformers, etc.

magnetite /ˈmægnɪˌtaɪt/ n. magnetic iron oxide. [G *Magnetit* (as MAGNET)]

magnetize /ˈmægnɪˌtaɪz/ v.tr. (also -ise) 1 give magnetic properties to. 2 make into a magnet. 3 attract as or like a magnet. □□ **magnetizable** adj. **magnetization** /-ˈzeɪʃ(ə)n/ n. **magnetizer** n.

magneto /mægˈniːtəʊ/ n. (pl. -os) an electric generator using permanent magnets and producing high voltage, esp. for the ignition of an internal-combustion engine. [abbr. of MAGNETO-ELECTRIC]

magneto- /mægˈniːtəʊ/ comb. form indicating a magnet or magnetism. [Gk *magnēs*: see MAGNET]

magneto-electric /mægˌniːtəʊɪˈlektrɪk/ adj. (of an electric generator) using permanent magnets. □□ **magneto-electricity** /-ˈtrɪsɪtɪ/ n.

magnetograph /mægˈniːtəˌɡrɑːf/ n. an instrument for recording measurements of magnetic quantities.

magnetometer /ˌmægnɪˈtɒmɪtə(r)/ n. an instrument measuring magnetic forces, esp. the earth's magnetism. □□ **magnetometry** n.

magnetomotive /mægˌniːtəʊˈməʊtɪv/ adj. (of a force) being the sum of the magnetizing forces along a circuit.

magneton /ˈmægnɪˌtɒn/ n. a unit of magnetic moment in atomic and nuclear physics. [F *magnéton* (as MAGNETIC)]

magnetosphere /mægˈniːtəˌsfɪə(r)/ n. the region surrounding a planet, star, etc. in which its magnetic field is effective.

magnetron /ˈmægnɪˌtrɒn/ n. an electron tube for amplifying or generating microwaves, with the flow of electrons controlled by an external magnetic field. [MAGNET + -TRON]

Magnificat /mægˈnɪfɪˌkæt/ n. 1 a canticle, the song of praise (so called from the first word of the Latin text) in Luke 1:46–55 sung when the Virgin Mary was greeted by her cousin Elizabeth as the mother of the Lord. Some scholars have argued that Luke attributed it originally to Elizabeth and not to Mary. 2 (**magnificat**) a song of praise. [L. = magnifies (i.e. extols)]

magnification /ˌmægnɪfɪˈkeɪʃ(ə)n/ n. 1 the act or an instance of magnifying; the process of being magnified. 2 the amount or degree of magnification. 3 the apparent enlargement of an object by a lens.

magnificent /mægˈnɪfɪs(ə)nt/ adj. 1 splendid, stately. 2 sumptuously constructed or adorned. 3 splendidly lavish. 4 colloq. fine, excellent. □□ **magnificence** n. **magnificently** adv. [F magnificent or L magnificus f. magnus great]

magnifico /mægˈnɪfɪˌkəʊ/ n. (pl. -oes) a magnate or grandee. [It., = MAGNIFICENT: orig. with ref. to Venice]

magnify /ˈmægnɪˌfaɪ/ v.tr. (-ies, -ied) 1 make (a thing) appear larger than it is, as with a lens. 2 exaggerate. 3 intensify. 4

archaic extol, glorify. □ **magnifying glass** a lens used to produce an enlarged image. □□ **magnifiable** adj. **magnifier** n. [ME f. OF magnifier or L magnificare (as MAGNIFICENT)]

magniloquent /mægˈnɪləkwənt/ adj. 1 grand or grandiose in speech. 2 boastful. □□ **magniloquence** n. **magniloquently** adv. [L magniloquus f. magnus great + -loquus -speaking]

magnitude /ˈmægnɪˌtjuːd/ n. 1 largeness. 2 size. 3 importance. 4 a measure of the relative brightness of stars and other celestial objects, based originally on a scale devised in the 2nd c. BC by Hipparchus (who classified the brightest stars as of the first magnitude, less bright as second, and so on in six classes), but now quantified by a mathematical formula involving the logarithm of the measured energy, and with the scale extended beyond the range of discrimination of unaided vision. □ **absolute magnitude** the magnitude that a star would seem to have if at a distance of 10 parsecs or 32.6 light-years. **apparent magnitude** a star's magnitude as seen from the Earth. **of the first magnitude** very important. [ME f. L magnitudo f. magnus great]

magnolia /mægˈnəʊlɪə/ n. 1 any tree or shrub of the genus *Magnolia*, cultivated for its dark-green foliage and large waxlike flowers in spring. 2 a pale creamy-pink colour. [mod.L f. P. *Magnol*, Fr. botanist d. 1715]

magnox /ˈmægnɒks/ n. any of various magnesium-based alloys used to enclose uranium fuel elements in a nuclear reactor. [magnesium no oxidation]

magnum /ˈmægnəm/ n. (pl. **magnums**) 1 a wine bottle of about twice the standard size. 2 a a cartridge or shell that is especially powerful or large. b (often attrib.) a cartridge or gun adapted so as to be more powerful than its calibre suggests. [L, neut. of magnus great]

magnum opus /ˌmægnəm ˈəʊpəs/ n. 1 a great and usu. large work of art, literature, etc. 2 the most important work of an artist, writer, etc. [L, = great work: see OPUS]

Magog see GOG AND MAGOG.

magpie /ˈmægpaɪ/ n. 1 a European and American crow, *Pica pica*, with a long pointed tail and black and white plumage, reputed to collect objects. 2 any of various birds with plumage like a magpie, esp. *Gymnorhina tibicen* of Australia. 3 an idle chatterer. 4 a person who collects things indiscriminately. 5 a the division of a circular target next to the outer one. b a rifle shot which strikes this. [Mag, abbr. of Margaret + PIE²]

Magritte /maːˈɡriːt/, René François Ghislain (1898–1967), Belgian painter, a leading figure in the surrealist movement. His works display startling juxtapositions of the ordinary, the strange, and the erotic. He had a repertory of obsessive images which appear in ordinary but incongruous surroundings, e.g. enormous rocks which float in the air and fishes with human legs. He also made surrealist analogues of a number of famous paintings.

maguey /ˈmæɡweɪ/ n. an agave plant, esp. one yielding pulque. [Sp. f. Haitian]

magus /ˈmeɪɡəs/ n. (pl. **magi** /ˈmeɪdʒaɪ/) 1 a member of a priestly caste of ancient Persia. 2 a sorcerer. 3 (**the Magi**) the 'wise men' from the East who brought gifts to the infant Christ (Matt. 2: 1–12). The gospel does not mention their number (the later tradition that there were three probably arose from the three gifts of gold, frankincense, and myrrh). The tradition that they were kings appears first in Tertullian (2nd c.); their names, Caspar, Melchior, and Balthasar, are first mentioned in the 6th c. In the Middle Ages they were venerated as saints, and what are claimed to be their relics lie in Cologne cathedral. [ME f. L f. Gk magos f. OPers. magus]

Magyar /ˈmægjɑː(r)/ n. & adj. —n. 1 a member of a Ural-Altaic people now predominant in Hungary. 2 the language of this people. —adj. of or relating to this people or language. [native name]

Mahabad /ˌmɑːhɒˈbɑːd/ a city in NW Iran, near the Iraqi border, with a chiefly Kurdish population; pop. (1986) 63,000. Occupied by Soviet troops in 1941, Mahabad became the centre of a short-lived Soviet-supported Kurdish republic, which was overthrown by the Iranians in 1946.

Mahabharata /ˌmɑːhəˈbɑːrətə/ n. one of the two great Sanskrit epics of the Hindus (the other is the Ramayana) that evolved over centuries to reach its present form c. AD 400. Containing almost 100,000 stanzas, it is probably the longest single poem in the world. The main story describes the civil war waged between the five Pandava brothers and their hundred step-brothers at Kuruksetra near modern Delhi, and there is much legendary, philosophical, and religious material; the numerous interpolated episodes include the Bhagavadgita. [Skr., = the great epic of the Bharata dynasty]

maharaja /ˌmɑːhəˈrɑːdʒə/ n. (also **maharajah**) hist. a title of some Indian princes. [Hindi mahārājā f. mahā great + RAJA]

maharanee /ˌmɑːhəˈrɑːnɪ/ n. (also **maharani**) hist. a maharaja's wife or widow. [Hindi mahārānī f. mahā great + RANEE]

Maharashtra /ˌmɑːhəˈræʃtrə/ a State in Western India bordering on the Arabian Sea, formed in 1960 from the SE part of the former Bombay State; pop. (1981) 62,693,900; capital, Bombay. □□ **Maharashtrian** adj. & n.

maharishi /ˌmɑːhəˈrɪʃɪ/ n. a great Hindu sage or spiritual leader. [Hindi f. mahā great + RISHI]

mahatma /məˈhætmə/ n. **1 a** (in India etc.) a person regarded with reverence. **b** a sage. **2** each of a class of persons in India and Tibet supposed by some to have preternatural powers. [Skr. mahātman f. mahā great + ātman soul]

Mahaweli /ˌmæhɑːˈweɪlɪ, məˈhævəlɪ/ the largest river of Sri Lanka. Rising in the central highlands, it flows 330 km (206 miles) to meet the Bay of Bengal near Trincomalee.

Mahayana /ˌmɑːhəˈjɑːnə/ n. the more general form of Buddhism (see HINAYANA). It survived in India until the Muslim era and also spread to Central Asia, China, Japan, Java, and Sumatra. The stress of the ancient schools (e.g. Theravada) on personal enlightenment is superseded by the ideal of the bod-hisattva who postpones his own salvation for the love of others. [Skr. f. mahā great + yāna vehicle]

Mahdi /ˈmɑːdɪ/ n. (pl. **Mahdis**) (in Islam) a spiritual and tem-poral leader who will be sent by divine command to prepare human society for the end of earthly time through perfectly just government. Not part of orthodox doctrine, this concept was introduced into popular Islam through Sufi channels influ-enced by Christian doctrine. For Shiites, the title refers to the twelfth imam. The title has been claimed by various individuals who sought to establish popular movements of resistance; the most widely known of these was the Sudanese Muhammad Ahmad, who proclaimed himself Mahdi in 1881 in the Sudan and led his followers in resisting Egyptian rule in 1884–5. □□ **Mahdism** n. **Mahdist** n. [Arab. mahdī he who is guided right, past part. of hadā guide]

Mahfouz /mɑːˈfuːz/, Naguib (1911–), Egyptian writer, the first writer in Arabic to win a Nobel Prize for literature (1988). His novels include his masterpiece the Cairo Trilogy (mid-1950s), which monitors the stages of Egyptian nationalism up to the revolution of 1952, and Miramar (1967), an attack on Nasser's subsequent policies; his short stories of the late 1960s examine the aftermath of the 1967 war with Israel.

mah-jong /mɑːˈdʒɒŋ/ n. (also **mah-jongg**) an old Chinese game resembling certain card-games, introduced into Europe and America in the early 1920s, played usually by four persons using 136 or 144 pieces called tiles. [Chin. dial. ma-tsiang, lit. sparrows]

Mahler /ˈmɑːlə(r)/, Gustav (1860–1911), Austrian composer, conductor, and pianist. His name is especially remembered in connection with the Viennese Opera, where he was Director 1897–1907, setting standards still scarcely surpassed; he was forced to leave by the anti-Semitic faction, despite his con-version to the Roman Catholic faith. Mahler was a master of the large-scale form, notably in his symphonies and orchestral songs. For many years his works were regarded with fanatical admiration by a handful of disciples and equally fanatical scorn by a larger number of musicians, but in the 1950s there was a fervent revival of interest. The unconventional form of the symphonies, complex and subtle polyphony, contrasts of irony, pathos, simplicity, and psychological insight, all appealed to later 20th-c. composers and audiences.

mahlstick var. of MAULSTICK.

mahogany /məˈhɒɡənɪ/ n. (pl. **-ies**) **1 a** a reddish-brown wood used for furniture. **b** the colour of this. **2** any tropical tree of the genus Swietenia, esp. S. mahogoni, yielding this wood. [17th c.: orig. unkn.]

mahonia /məˈhəʊnɪə/ n. any evergreen shrub of the genus Mahonia, with yellow bell-shaped or globular flowers. [F mahonne, Sp. mahona, It. maona, Turk. māwuna]

Mahore /məˈhɔː(r)/ (French **Mayotte** /mæˈjɒt/) an island to the east of the Comoros in the Indian Ocean; pop. (1985) 57,350; capital, Dzaoudzi. When the Comoros elected to become inde-pendent in 1974, Mayotte decided to remain an overseas ter-ritory of France. In 1976 the island became a Territorial Collectivity of France.

mahout /məˈhaʊt/ n. (in India etc.) an elephant-driver or -keeper. [Hindi mahāut f. Skr. mahāmātra high official, lit. 'great in measure']

Mahratta var. of MARATHA.

Mahratti var. of MARATHI.

mahseer /ˈmɑːsɪə(r)/ n. either of two freshwater Indian fish, Barbus putitora or B. tor, used as food. [Hindi mahāsir]

Maia /ˈmaɪə/ **1** Gk Mythol. the daughter of Atlas and mother of Hermes [Gk, = mother, nurse]. **2** Rom. Mythol. a goddess associated (for unknown reasons) with Vulcan and also (by con-fusion with 1 above) with Mercury. She was worshipped on 1 May and 15 May; that month is named after her. [perh. f. L root mag- growth, increase]

maid /meɪd/ n. **1** a female domestic servant. **2** archaic or poet. a girl or young woman. □ **maid of honour 1** an unmarried lady attending a queen or princess. **2** a kind of small custard tart. **3** esp. US a principal bridesmaid. □□ **maidish** adj. [ME, abbr. of MAIDEN]

maidan /maɪˈdɑːn/ n. Anglo-Ind. **1** an open space in or near a town. **2** a parade-ground. [Urdu f. Arab. maydān]

maiden /ˈmeɪd(ə)n/ n. **1 a** archaic or poet. a girl; a young unmar-ried woman. **b** (attrib.) unmarried (maiden aunt). **2** Cricket = maiden over. **3** (attrib.) (of a female animal) unmated. **4** (often attrib.) **a** a horse that has never won a race. **b** a race open only to such horses. **5** (attrib.) being or involving the first attempt or occurrence (maiden speech; maiden voyage). □ **maiden name** a wife's surname before marriage. **maiden over** Cricket an over in which no runs are scored off the bat. □□ **maidenhood** n. **maidenish** adj. **maidenlike** adj. **maidenly** adj. [OE mægden, dimin. f. mægeth f. Gmc]

maidenhair /ˈmeɪd(ə)nˌheə(r)/ n. (in full **maidenhair fern**) a fern of the genus Adiantum, esp. A. capillus-veneris, with fine hairlike stalks and delicate fronds. □ **maidenhair tree** = GINKGO.

maidenhead /ˈmeɪd(ə)nˌhed/ n. **1** virginity. **2** the hymen.

maidservant /ˈmeɪdˌsɜːv(ə)nt/ n. a female domestic servant.

maieutic /meɪˈuːtɪk/ adj. (of the Socratic mode of enquiry) serv-ing to bring a person's latent ideas into clear consciousness. [Gk maieutikos f. maieuomai act as a midwife f. maia midwife]

maigre /ˈmeɪɡr(ə)/ adj. RC Ch. **1** (of a day) on which abstinence from meat is ordered. **2** (of food) suitable for eating on maigre days. [F, lit. lean: cf. MEAGRE]

Maigret /ˈmeɪɡreɪ/ a detective-superintendent in the crime stories of Georges Simenon.

mail¹ /meɪl/ n. & v. —n. **1 a** letters and parcels etc. conveyed by post. **b** the postal system. **c** one complete delivery or col-lection of mail. **d** one delivery of letters to one place, esp. to a business on one occasion. **2** a vehicle carrying mail. **3** hist. a bag of letters for conveyance by post. —v.tr. esp. US send (a letter etc.) by post. □ **mail-boat** a boat carrying mail. **mail carrier** US a postman or postwoman. **mail cart** Brit. hist. **1** a cart for carrying mail by road. **2** a light vehicle for carrying children. **mail coach** a railway coach or hist. stagecoach used for carrying mail. **mail drop** US a receptacle for mail. **mailing list** a list of people to whom advertising matter, information, etc., is to be posted. **mail order** an order for goods sent by post. **mail-order firm** a firm doing business by post. **mail train** a train carrying mail. [ME f. OF male wallet f. WG]

mail² /meɪl/ n. & v. —n. **1** armour made of rings, chains, or plates, joined together flexibly. **2** the protective shell, scales, etc., of an animal. —v.tr. clothe with or as if with mail. □ **coat of mail** a jacket covered with mail or composed of mail. **mailed fist** physical force. □□ **mailed** adj. [ME f. OF maille f. L macula spot, mesh]

mailable /ˈmeɪləb(ə)l/ adj. acceptable for conveyance by post.

mailbag /ˈmeɪlbæg/ n. a large sack or bag for carrying mail.

mailbox /ˈmeɪlbɒks/ n. US a letter-box.

Mailer /ˈmeɪlə(r)/, Norman (1923–), American novelist and essayist, whose naturalistic first novel The Naked and the Dead (1948) was based on his army experiences in the Pacific during the Second World War. Much of his work is of a more unorthodox genre, combining journalism, autobiography, political commentary, and fictional passages in a wide range of styles. His works include an ambitious novel, Ancient Evenings (1983), set in ancient Egypt.

maillot /mæˈjəʊ/ n. **1** tights for dancing, gymnastics, etc. **2** a woman's one-piece bathing-suit. **3** a jersey. [F]

mailman /ˈmeɪlmən/ n. (pl. **-men**) US a postman.

mailshot /ˈmeɪlʃɒt/ n. a dispatch of mail, usu. consisting of advertising and promotional material, to a large number of addresses at one time.

maim /meɪm/ v.tr. **1** cripple, disable, mutilate. **2** harm, impair (emotionally maimed by neglect). [ME maime etc. f. OF mahaignier etc., of unkn. orig.]

Maimonides /maɪˈmɒnɪˌdiːz/ Moses ben Maimon (1135–1204), Spanish-Jewish philosopher and Rabbinic scholar, known to Jewish writers as 'Rambam'. He wrote in Hebrew and Arabic, and was much influenced by Aristotelian philosophy; his work had great influence on medieval Christian thought.

main¹ /meɪn/ adj. & n. —adj. **1** chief in size, importance, extent, etc.; principal (the main part; the main point). **2** exerted to the full (by main force). —n. **1** a principal channel, duct, etc., for water, sewage, etc. (water main). **2** (usu. in pl.; prec. by the) **a** the central distribution network for electricity, gas, water, etc. **b** a domestic electricity supply as distinct from batteries. **3** archaic or poet. **a** the ocean or oceans (the Spanish Main). **b** the mainland. □ **in the main** for the most part. **main brace** Naut. the brace attached to the main yard. **the main chance** one's own interests. **main course 1** the chief course of a meal. **2** Naut. the mainsail. **main deck** Naut. **1** the deck below the spar-deck in a man-of-war. **2** the upper deck between the poop and the forecastle in a merchantman. **main line 1** a chief railway line. **2** sl. a principal vein, esp. as a site for a drug injection (cf. MAINLINE). **3** US a chief road or street. **main stem** US colloq. = main street. **main street** the principal street of a town. **Main Street** US materialistic philosophy (after Sinclair Lewis's novel, 1920). **main yard** Naut. the yard on which the mainsail is extended. **with might and main** with all one's force. [ME, partly f. ON megenn, megn (adj.), partly f. OE mægen- f. Gmc: (n.) orig. = physical force]

main² /meɪn/ n. **1** (in the game of hazard) a number (5, 6, 7, 8, or 9) called by a player before dice are thrown. **2** a match between fighting-cocks. [16th c.: prob. orig. main chance: see MAIN¹]

Maine /meɪn/ a north-eastern State of the US, on the Atlantic coast; pop. (est. 1985) 1,125,000; capital, Augusta. Visited by Cabot in 1498 and colonized from England in the 17th–18th c., it became the 23rd State of the US in 1820.

mainframe /ˈmeɪnfreɪm/ n. **1** the central processing unit and primary memory of a computer. **2** (often attrib.) a large computer system.

Mainland /ˈmeɪnlənd/ **1** the largest island in Orkney. **2** the largest island in Shetland.

mainland /ˈmeɪnlənd/ n. a large continuous extent of land, excluding neighbouring islands etc. □□ **mainlander** n.

mainline /ˈmeɪnlaɪn/ v. sl. **1** intr. take drugs intravenously. **2** tr. inject (drugs) intravenously. □□ **mainliner** n.

mainly /ˈmeɪnlɪ/ adv. for the most part; chiefly.

mainmast /ˈmeɪnmɑːst/ n. Naut. the principal mast of a ship.

mainplane /ˈmeɪnpleɪn/ n. the principal supporting surface of an aircraft (cf. TAILPLANE).

mainsail /ˈmeɪnseɪl, -s(ə)l/ n. Naut. **1** (in a square-rigged vessel) the lowest sail on the mainmast. **2** (in a fore-and-aft rigged vessel) a sail set on the after part of the mainmast.

mainspring /ˈmeɪnsprɪŋ/ n. **1** the principal spring of a mechanical watch, clock, etc. **2** a chief motive power; incentive.

mainstay /ˈmeɪnsteɪ/ n. **1** a chief support (has been his mainstay since his trouble). **2** Naut. a stay from the maintop to the foot of the foremast.

mainstream /ˈmeɪnstriːm/ n. **1** (often attrib.) the prevailing trend in opinion, fashion, etc. **2** a type of jazz based on the 1930s swing style and consisting esp. of solo improvisation on chord sequences. **3** the principal current of a river.

maintain /meɪnˈteɪn/ v.tr. **1** cause to continue; keep up, preserve (a state of affairs, an activity, etc.) (maintained friendly relations). **2** (often foll. by in; often refl.) support (life, a condition, etc.) by work, nourishment, expenditure, etc. (maintained him in comfort; maintained themselves by fishing). **3** (often foll. by that + clause) assert (an opinion, statement, etc.) as true (maintained that she was the best; his story was true, he maintained). **4** preserve or provide for the preservation of (a building, machine, road, etc.) in good repair. **5** give aid to (a cause, party, etc.). **6** provide means for (a garrison etc. to be equipped). □ **maintained school** Brit. a school supported from public funds. □□ **maintainable** adj. **maintainability** /-ˈbɪlɪtɪ/ n. [ME f. OF maintenir ult. f. L manu tenēre hold in the hand]

maintainer /meɪnˈteɪnə(r)/ n. **1** a person or thing that maintains. **2** (also **maintainor**) Law hist. a person guilty of maintenance (see MAINTENANCE 3).

maintenance /ˈmeɪntənəns/ n. **1** the process of maintaining or being maintained. **2 a** the provision of the means to support life, esp. by work etc. **b** (also **separate maintenance**) a husband's or wife's provision for a spouse after separation or divorce; alimony. **3** Law hist. the offence of aiding a party in litigation without lawful cause. [ME f. OF f. maintenir: see MAINTAIN]

Maintenon /ˈmæ̃tə̃nɔ̃/, Françoise d'Aubigné, Marquise de (1635–1719), mistress and later second wife of the French king Louis XIV. Devoutly religious and already a middle-aged widow, Madame de Maintenon came to Louis' attention while looking after his children by his previous mistress, Madame de Montespan. After his own wife's death in 1683, Louis married de Maintenon morganatically, and in the last years of his reign she turned him increasingly towards piety.

maintop /ˈmeɪntɒp/ n. Naut. a platform above the head of the lower mainmast.

maintopmast /meɪnˈtɒpməst/ n. Naut. a mast above the head of the lower mainmast.

maiolica /məˈjɒlɪkə/ n. Italian earthenware of the Renaissance period with coloured ornamentation on white enamel. (See also MAJOLICA.) [It. f. former name of Majorca, ships of which brought Spanish wares to Italy]

maisonette /ˌmeɪzəˈnet/ n. (also **maisonnette**) **1** a part of a house, block of flats, etc., forming separate living accommodation, usu. on two floors and having a separate entrance. **2** a small house. [F maisonnette dimin. of maison house]

maître d'hôtel /ˌmetrə dəʊˈtel, ˌmeɪt-/ n. **1** the manager, head steward, etc., of a hotel. **2** a head waiter. [F, = master of (the) house]

maize /meɪz/ n. **1** a cereal plant, Zea mays, native to N. America, yielding large grains set in rows on a cob. **2** the cobs or grains of this (see CORN¹). [F maïs or Sp. maiz, of Carib orig.]

Maj. abbr. Major.

majestic /məˈdʒestɪk/ adj. showing majesty; stately and dignified; grand, imposing. □□ **majestically** adv.

majesty /ˈmædʒɪstɪ/ n. (pl. **-ies**) **1** impressive stateliness, dignity, or authority, esp. of bearing, language, the law, etc. **2 a** royal power. **b** (**Majesty**) part of several titles given to a sovereign or a sovereign's wife or widow or used in addressing them (Your Majesty; Her Majesty the Queen Mother). **3** a picture of God or Christ enthroned within an aureole. □ **Her** (or **His**) **Majesty's** part of the title of several State institutions (Her

Majesty's Stationery Office). [ME f. OF *majesté* f. L *majestas -tatis* (as MAJOR)]

Majlis /ˈmædʒlɪs/ *n. Polit.* the parliament of various N. African or Middle Eastern countries, esp. Iran. [Pers., = assembly]

majolica /məˈjɒlɪkə, məˈdʒɒl-/ *n.* (also **maiolica** /məˈjɒl-/) **1** a 19th-c. trade name for earthenware with coloured decoration on an opaque white glaze. **2** = MAIOLICA. [alt. f. MAIOLICA]

Major /ˈmeɪdʒ(ə)r/, John (1943–), British Conservative statesman, Prime Minister 1990– , the youngest to hold this office in the 20th c.

major /ˈmeɪdʒə(r)/ *adj., n., & v.* —*adj.* **1** important, large, serious, significant (*a major road; a major war; the major consideration must be their health*). **2** (of an operation) serious or life-threatening. **3** *Mus.* **a** (of a scale) having intervals of a semitone between the third and fourth, and seventh and eighth degrees. **b** (of an interval) greater by a semitone than a minor interval (*major third*). **c** (of a key) based on a major scale, tending to produce a bright or joyful effect (*D major*). **4** of full age. **5** *Brit.* (appended to a surname, esp. in public schools) the elder of two brothers or the first to enter the school (*Smith major*). **6** *Logic* **a** (of a term) occurring in the predicate or conclusion of a syllogism. **b** (of a premiss) containing a major term. —*n.* **1** *Mil.* **a** an army officer next below lieutenant-colonel and above captain. **b** an officer in charge of a section of band instruments (*drum major; pipe major*). **2** a person of full age. **3** *US* **a** a student's special subject or course. **b** a student specializing in a specified subject (*a philosophy major*). **4** *Logic* a major term or premiss. —*v.intr.* (foll. by *in*) *US* study or qualify in a subject (*majored in theology*). □ **major axis** the axis of a conic, passing through its foci. **major-general** an officer next below a lieutenant-general. **major league** *US* a league of major importance in baseball etc. **major part** (often foll. by *of*) the majority. **major piece** *Chess* a rook or queen. **major planet** Jupiter, Saturn, Uranus, or Neptune. **major prophet** see PROPHET. **major suit** *Bridge* spades or hearts. □□ **majorship** *n.* [ME f. L, compar. of *magnus* great]

Majorca /məˈjɔːkə/ (Spanish **Mallorca** /mælˈjɔːkə/ the largest of the Balearic Islands; pop. (1981) 561,200; capital, Palma.

major-domo /ˌmeɪdʒəˈdəʊməʊ/ *n.* (pl. **-os**) **1** the chief official of an Italian or Spanish princely household. **2** a house-steward; a butler. [orig. *mayordome* f. Sp. *mayordomo*, It. *maggiordomo* f. med.L *major domus* highest official of the household (as MAJOR, DOME)]

majorette /ˌmeɪdʒəˈret/ *n.* = *drum majorette*. [abbr.]

majority /məˈdʒɒrɪtɪ/ *n.* (pl. **-ies**) **1** (usu. foll. by *of*) the greater number or part. ¶ Strictly used only with countable nouns, e.g. *a majority of people*, and not with mass nouns, e.g. *a majority of the work*. **2** *Polit.* **a** the number by which the votes cast for one party, candidate, etc. exceed those of the next in rank (*won by a majority of 151*). **b** a party etc. receiving the greater number of votes. **3** full legal age (*attained his majority*). **4** the rank of major. □ **the great majority 1** much the greater number. **2** *euphem.* the dead (*has joined the great majority*). **in the majority** esp. *Polit.* belonging to or constituting a majority party etc. **majority rule** the principle that the greater number should exercise greater power. **majority verdict** a verdict given by more than half of the jury, but not unanimous. [F *majorité* f. med.L *majoritas -tatis* (as MAJOR)]

majuscule /ˈmædʒəˌskjuːl/ *n. & adj.* —*n. Palaeog.* **1** a large letter, whether capital or uncial. **2** large lettering. —*adj.* of, written in, or concerning majuscules. □□ **majuscular** /məˈdʒʌskjʊlə(r)/ *adj.* [F f. L *majuscula* (*littera* letter), dimin. of MAJOR]

Makarios III /məˈkærɪɒs/ (Mikhail Khristodolou Mouskos, 1913–77), Greek Cypriot archbishop and statesman, primate and archbishop of the Greek Orthodox Church in Cyprus from 1950, who combined Church leadership with a vigorous political role. He reorganized the movement for enosis (union of Cyprus with Greece) and was exiled (1956–9) by the British for allegedly supporting the EOKA terrorist campaign against the British and Turks. After Cyprus became independent (1959) he was elected as its first President, and although forced briefly into exile by a Greek military coup (1974) continued in office until his death.

Makassar /məˈkæsə(r)/ (also **Makasar** or **Macassar**) a seaport in Indonesia, since 1973 called Ujung Padang. □ **Makassar Strait** a stretch of water separating Borneo and Sulawesi and linking the Sulawesi Sea in the north with the Java Sea in the south.

make /meɪk/ *v. & n.* —*v.* (*past* and *past part.* **made** /meɪd/) **1** *tr.* construct; create; form from parts or other substances (*made a table; made it out of cardboard; made him a sweater*). **2** *tr.* (foll. by *to* + infin.) cause or compel (a person etc.) to do something (*make him repeat it; was made to confess*). **3** *tr.* **a** cause to exist; create; bring about (*made a noise; made an enemy*). **b** cause to become or seem (*made an exhibition of myself; made him angry*). **c** appoint; designate (*made him a Cardinal*). **4** *tr.* compose; prepare; draw up (*made her will; made a film about Japan*). **5** *tr.* constitute; amount to (*makes a difference; 2 and 2 make 4; this makes the tenth time*). **6** *tr.* **a** undertake or agree to (an aim or purpose) (*made a promise; make an effort*). **b** execute or perform (a bodily movement, a speech, etc.) (*made a face; made a bow*). **7** *tr.* gain, acquire, procure (money, a profit, etc.) (*made £20,000 on the deal*). **8** *tr.* prepare (tea, coffee, a dish, etc.) for consumption (*made egg and chips*). **9** *tr.* **a** arrange bedclothes tidily on (a bed) ready for use. **b** arrange and light materials for (a fire). **10** *intr.* **a** proceed (*made towards the river*). **b** (foll. by *to* + infin.) begin an action (*he made to go*). **11** *tr. colloq.* **a** arrive at (a place) or in time for (a train etc.) (*made the border before dark; made the six o'clock train*). **b** manage to attend; manage to attend on (a certain day) or at (a certain time) (*couldn't make the meeting last week; can make any day except Friday*). **c** achieve a place in (*made the first eleven; made the six o'clock news*). **d** *US* achieve the rank of (*made colonel in three years*). **12** *tr.* establish or enact (a distinction, rule, law, etc.). **13** *tr.* consider to be; estimate as (*what do you make the time?; do you make that a 1 or a 7?*). **14** *tr.* secure the success or advancement of (*his mother made him; it made my day*). **15** *tr.* accomplish (a distance, speed, score, etc.) (*made 60 m.p.h. on the motorway*). **16** *tr.* **a** become by development or training (*made a great leader*). **b** serve as (*a log makes a useful seat*). **17** *tr.* (usu. foll. by *out*) represent as; cause to appear as (*makes him out a liar*). **18** *tr.* form in the mind; feel (*I make no judgement*). **19** *tr.* (foll. by *it* + compl.) **a** determine, establish, or choose (*let's make it Tuesday; made it my business to know*). **b** bring to (a chosen value etc.) (*decided to make it a dozen*). **20** *tr. sl.* have sexual relations with. **21** *tr. Cards* **a** win (a trick). **b** play (a card) to advantage. **c** win the number of tricks that fulfils (a contract). **d** shuffle (a pack of cards) for dealing. **22** *tr. Cricket* score (runs). **23** *tr. Electr.* complete or close (a circuit) (opp. BREAK). **24** *intr.* (of the tide) begin to flow or ebb. —*n.* **1** (esp. of a product) a type, origin, brand, etc. of manufacture (*different make of car; our own make*). **2** a kind of mental, moral, or physical structure or composition. **3** an act of shuffling cards. **4** *Electr.* an the making of contact. **b** the position in which this is made. □ **be made for** be ideally suited to. **be made of** consist of (*cake made of marzipan*). **have it made** *colloq.* be sure of success. **made dish** a dish prepared from several separate foods. **made man** a man who has attained success. **made of money** *colloq.* very rich. **made road** a properly surfaced road of tarmac, concrete, etc. **made to measure** (of a suit etc.) made to a specific customer's measurements. **made to order** see ORDER. **make after** *archaic* pursue. **make against** be unfavourable to. **make as if** (or **though**) (foll. by *to* + infin. or conditional) act as if the specified circumstances applied (*made as if to leave; made as if he would hit me; made as if I had not noticed*). **make away** (or **off**) depart hastily. **make away with 1** get rid of; kill. **2** squander. **make-believe** (or **-belief**) **1** pretence. **2** pretended. **make believe** pretend. **make conversation** talk politely. **make a day** (or **night** etc.) **of it** devote a whole day (or night etc.) to an activity. **make do 1** manage with the limited or inadequate means available. **2** (foll. by *with*) manage with (something) as an inferior substitute. **make an example of** punish as a warning to others. **make a fool of** see FOOL¹. **make for 1** tend to result in (happiness etc.). **2** proceed towards (a place). **3** assault; attack. **4** confirm (an opinion). **make friends** (often foll. by *with*) become friendly. **make fun of** see FUN. **make good** see GOOD. **make a habit of** see HABIT. **make a hash of** see HASH¹. **make hay** see HAY¹. **make head or tail of** see HEAD. **make a House** *Polit.* secure the

b *but* d *dog* f *few* g *get* h *he* j *yes* k *cat* l *leg* m *man* n *no* p *pen* r *red* s *sit* t *top* v *voice*

presence of enough members for a quorum or support in the House of Commons. **make it** *colloq.* **1** succeed in reaching, esp. in time. **2** be successful. **3** (usu. foll. by *with*) *sl.* have sexual intercourse (with). **make it up 1** be reconciled, esp. after a quarrel. **2** fill in a deficit. **make it up to** remedy negligence, an injury, etc. to (a person). **make light of** see LIGHT². **make love** see LOVE. **make a meal of** see MEAL¹. **make merry** see MERRY. **make money** acquire wealth or an income. **make the most of** see MOST. **make much** (or **little** or **the best**) **of 1** derive much (or little etc.) advantage from. **2** give much (or little etc.) attention, importance, etc., to. **make a name for oneself** see NAME. **make no bones about** see BONE. **make nothing of 1** do without hesitation. **2** treat as a trifle. **3** be unable to understand, use, or deal with. **make of 1** construct from. **2** conclude to be the meaning or character of (*can you make anything of it?*). **make off** = *make away.* **make off with** carry away; steal. **make oneself scarce** see SCARCE. **make or break** (or **mar**) cause the success or ruin of. **make out 1 a** distinguish by sight or hearing. **b** decipher (handwriting etc.). **2** understand (*can't make him out*). **3** assert; pretend (*made out he liked it*). **4** *colloq.* make progress; fare (*how did you make out?*). **5** (usu. foll. by *to, in favour of*) draw up; write out (*made out a cheque to her*). **6** prove or try to prove (*how do you make that out?*). **make over 1** transfer the possession of (a thing) to a person. **2** refashion (a garment etc.). **make a point of** see POINT. **make sail** *Naut.* **1** spread a sail or sails. **2** start a voyage. **make shift** see SHIFT. **make so bold as to** see BOLD. **make time 1** (usu. foll. by *for* or *to* + infin.) find an occasion when time is available. **2** (usu. foll. by *with*) esp. *US sl.* make sexual advances (to a person). **make-up 1** cosmetics for the face etc., either generally or to create an actor's appearance or disguise. **2** the appearance of the face etc. when cosmetics have been applied (*his make-up was not convincing*). **3** *Printing* the making up of a type. **4** *Printing* the type made up. **5** a person's character, temperament, etc. **6** the composition or constitution (of a thing). **make up 1** serve or act to overcome (a deficiency). **2** complete (an amount, a party, etc.). **3** compensate. **4** be reconciled. **5** put together; compound; prepare (*made up the medicine*). **6** sew (parts of a garment etc.) together. **7** get (a sum of money, a company, etc.) together. **8** concoct (a story). **9** (of parts) compose (a whole). **10 a** apply cosmetics. **b** apply cosmetics to. **11** settle (a dispute). **12** prepare (a bed) for use with fresh sheets etc. **13** *Printing* arrange (type) in pages. **14** compile (a list, an account, a document, etc.). **15** arrange (a marriage etc.). **make up one's mind** decide, resolve. **make up to** curry favour with; court. **make water 1** urinate. **2** (of a ship) take in water. **make way 1** (often foll. by *for*) allow room for others to proceed. **2** achieve progress. **make one's way** proceed. **make with** *US colloq.* supply; perform; proceed with (*made with the feet and left in a hurry*). **on the make** *colloq.* **1** intent on gain. **2** looking for sexual partners. **self-made man** etc. a man etc. who has succeeded by his own efforts. □□ **makable** *adj.* [OE *macian* f. WG: rel. to MATCH¹]

maker /ˈmeɪkə(r)/ *n.* **1** (often in *comb.*) a person or thing that makes. **2** (**our, the,** etc. **Maker**) God. **3** *archaic* a poet.

makeshift /ˈmeɪkʃɪft/ *adj.* & *n.* —*adj.* temporary; serving for the time being (*a makeshift arrangement*). —*n.* a temporary substitute or device.

makeweight /ˈmeɪkweɪt/ *n.* **1** a small quantity or thing added to make up the full weight. **2** an unimportant extra person. **3** an unimportant point added to make an argument seem stronger.

Makgadikgadi Pans /ˌmæɡəˈdiːɡədɪ/ an extensive area of salt-pans in central Botswana. In prehistoric times it formed a large lake.

making /ˈmeɪkɪŋ/ *n.* **1** in senses of MAKE *v.* **2** (in *pl.*) **a** earnings; profit. **b** (foll. by *of*) essential qualities or ingredients (*has the makings of a general; we have the makings of a meal*). **c** *US* & *Austral. colloq.* paper and tobacco for rolling a cigarette. □ **be the making of** ensure the success or favourable development of. **in the making** in the course of being made or formed. [OE *macung* (as MAKE)]

mako¹ /ˈmɑːkəʊ/ *n.* (*pl.* **-os**) a blue shark, *Isurus oxyrinchus*. [Maori]

mako² /ˈmɑːkəʊ/ *n.* (*pl.* **-os**) a small New Zealand tree, *Aristotelia serrata*, with clusters of dark-red berries and large racemes of pink flowers. Also called WINEBERRY. [Maori]

Mal. *abbr.* Malachi (Old Testament).

mal- /mæl/ *comb. form* **1 a** bad, badly (*malpractice*; *maltreat*). **b** faulty, faultily (*malfunction*). **2** not (*maladroit*). [F *mal* badly f. L *male*]

Malabar /ˈmæləbɑː(r)/ *hist.* a coastal district of SW India. □ **Malabar Christians** a group of Christians of SW India, tracing their origin to St Thomas, who according to their tradition landed in these parts. **Malabar Coast** the southern part of the west coast of India, including the coastal region of Karnataka and most of the State of Kerala.

Malabo /məˈlɑːbəʊ/ the capital of Equatorial Guinea; pop. (est. 1986) 10,000.

malabsorption /ˌmæləbˈsɔːpʃ(ə)n/ *n.* imperfect absorption of food material by the small intestine.

Malacca /məˈlækə/ see MELAKA. □ **Strait of Malacca** the channel between the Malaysia peninsula and the Indonesian island of Sumatra, an important sea-passage linking the Indian Ocean to the South China Sea. The port of Singapore lies on this strait.

malacca /məˈlækə/ *n.* (in full **malacca cane**) a rich-brown cane from the stem of the palm-tree *Calamus scipionum*, used for walking-sticks etc. [MALACCA]

Malachi /ˈmæləkaɪ/ the last book of the Old Testament in the English versions, belonging to a period before Ezra and Nehemiah. (Malachi is probably not a personal name.) [Heb. *mālāki* my messenger]

malachite /ˈmæləkaɪt/ *n.* a bright-green mineral of hydrous copper carbonate, taking a high polish and used for ornament. [OF *melochite* f. L *molochites* f. Gk *molokhitis* f. *molokhē* = *malakhē* mallow]

malaco- /ˈmæləkəʊ/ *comb. form* soft. [Gk *malakos* soft]

malacology /ˌmæləˈkɒlədʒɪ/ *n.* the study of molluscs.

malacostracan /ˌmæləˈkɒstrəkən/ *n.* & *adj.* —*n.* any crustacean of the class Malacostraca, including crabs, shrimps, lobsters, and krill. —*adj.* of or relating to this class. [MALACO- + Gk *ostrakon* shell]

maladaptive /ˌmæləˈdæptɪv/ *adj.* (of an individual, species, etc.) failing to adjust adequately to the environment, and undergoing emotional, behavioural, physical, or mental repercussions. □□ **maladaptation** /ˌmælædæpˈteɪʃ(ə)n/ *n.*

maladjusted /ˌmæləˈdʒʌstɪd/ *adj.* **1** not correctly adjusted. **2** (of a person) unable to adapt to or cope with the demands of a social environment. □□ **maladjustment** *n.*

maladminister /ˌmælədˈmɪnɪstə(r)/ *v.tr.* manage or administer inefficiently, badly, or dishonestly. □□ **maladministration** /-ˈstreɪʃ(ə)n/ *n.*

maladroit /ˌmæləˈdrɔɪt, ˈmæl-/ *adj.* clumsy; bungling. □□ **maladroitly** *adv.* **maladroitness** *n.* [F (as MAL-, ADROIT)]

malady /ˈmælədɪ/ *n.* (*pl.* **-ies**) **1** an ailment; a disease. **2** a morbid or depraved condition; something requiring a remedy. [ME f. OF *maladie* f. *malade* sick ult. f. L *male* ill + *habitus* past part. of *habēre* have]

mala fide /ˌmeɪlə ˈfaɪdɪ/ *adj.* & *adv.* —*adj.* acting or done in bad faith. —*adv.* in bad faith. [L]

Malaga /ˈmæləɡə/ a seaport on the Andalusian coast of southern Spain. —*n.* a sweet fortified wine from Málaga.

Malagasy /ˌmæləˈɡæsɪ/ *adj.* & *n.* —*adj.* of or relating to Madagascar or its people or language. —*n.* **1** a native or national of Madagascar. **2** the official language of Madagascar, spoken by its 7 million inhabitants. It is a Malayo-Polynesian language, related to Malay, although the other languages of this group are spoken thousands of miles to the east. [orig. *Malegass, Madegass* f. MADAGASCAR]

malagueña /ˌmæləˈɡenjə/ *n.* **1** a Spanish dance resembling the fandango. **2** a piece of music for or in the style of a fandango. [Sp. (as MALAGA)]

malaise /məˈleɪz/ *n.* **1** a nonspecific bodily discomfort not associated with the development of a disease. **2** a feeling of uneasiness. [F f. OF *mal* bad + *aise* EASE]

Malamud /'mæləməd/, Bernard (1914–86), American novelist and writer of short stories. He is best known for his novel *The Fixer* (1967), the story of a Jewish handyman or 'fixer' in Tsarist Russia just before the First World War, who is falsely accused of murder and turned into a scapegoat for anti-Semitic feeling.

malamute /'mælə,mju:t/ *n.* (also **malemute**) an Eskimo dog. [name of an Alaskan Eskimo tribe]

malanders var. of MALLENDERS.

malapert /'mælə,pɜ:t/ *adj. & n. archaic* —*adj.* impudent; saucy. —*n.* an impudent or saucy person. [ME f. OF (as MAL-, *apert* = *espert* EXPERT)]

malapropism /'mæləprɒ,pɪz(ə)m/ *n.* (also **malaprop** /'mælə,prɒp/) the use of a word in mistake for one sounding similar, to comic effect, e.g. *allegory* for *alligator*. [Mrs *Malaprop* (f. MALAPROPOS) in Sheridan's *The Rivals* (1775)]

malapropos /ˌmælæprə'pəʊ/ *adv., adj., & n.* —*adv.* inopportunely; inappropriately. —*adj.* inopportune; inappropriate. —*n.* something inappropriately said, done, etc. [F *mal à propos* f. *mal* ill: see APROPOS]

malar /'meɪlə(r)/ *adj. & n.* —*adj.* of the cheek. —*n.* a bone of the cheek. [mod.L *malaris* f. L *mala* jaw]

Mälaren /'mela:r(ə)n/ a lake in SE Sweden, extending inland from the Baltic Sea. The city of Stockholm is situated at its outlet.

malaria /mə'leərɪə/ *n.* **1** an intermittent and remittent fever caused by a protozoan parasite of the genus *Plasmodium*, transmitted from infected persons by the bite of a female *Anopheles* mosquito after developing in the body of this insect. One type of malaria causes fever and sweating to occur every third day, another every fourth day, while malignant malaria causes a nearly continuous fever and is associated with dangerous complications and death. Anti-malarial drugs used in treating the disease are usually successful (the earliest known was quinine), and preventive drugs can be taken, but the best means of prevention is to attack the mosquitoes not only with insecticides but by draining the swamps and stagnant waters where they breed. Some mosquitoes have proved able to survive the insecticides used, however, and the disease is still a problem. □□ **malarial** *adj.* **malarian** *adj.* **malarious** *adj.* [It. *mal'aria* bad air, the unwholesome condition of the atmosphere which results from the exhalations of marshy districts, to which the disease was formerly attributed]

malarkey /mə'lɑ:kɪ/ *n. colloq.* humbug; nonsense. [20th c.: orig. unkn.]

malathion /ˌmælə'θaɪən/ *n.* an insecticide containing phosphorus, with low toxicity to plants. [diethyl *maleate* + *thio-* acid + -ON]

Malawi /mə'lɑ:wɪ/ a country of south central Africa, landlocked and almost totally dependent upon Mozambique for access to the sea; pop. (est. 1988) 7,679,400; official language, English; capital, Lilongwe. The Great Rift Valley runs through the country from north to south. Much of the eastern border is formed by Lake Malawi (= NYASA), the third-largest lake in Africa, with a length of *c.*580 km (360 miles). Malawi is the former Nyasaland, a British protectorate from 1891 (following Livingstone's exploration), and from 1953 to 1963 a part of the Federation of Rhodesia and Nyasaland; it became an independent State within the Commonwealth under President Hastings Banda in 1964, and a republic in 1966. □□ **Malawian** *adj. & n.*

Malay /mə'leɪ/ *n. & adj.* —*n.* **1 a** a member of a people predominating in Malaysia and Indonesia. **b** a person of Malay descent. **2** the language of this people, the official language of Malaysia. It belongs to the Malayo-Polynesian language group and is spoken mainly in Malaysia, where it is the mother tongue of about half the population (6 million people). Meaning is shown by the order and grouping of words, not by inflexions. It is virtually the same language as Indonesian. From the 14th c. Malay was written in Arabic script but in the 19th c. the British constructed a Roman-based alphabet which is in general use today. —*adj.* of or relating to this people or language. □□ **Malayan** *n. & adj.* [Malay *malāyu*]

Malayalam /ˌmælə'jɑːləm/ *n.* the Dravidian language of the State of Kerala in S. India. [native]

Malay Archipelago a very large group of islands, including Sumatra, Java, Borneo, the Philippines, and New Guinea, lying SE of Asia and north and NE of Australia.

Malayo- /mə'leɪjəʊ/ *comb. form* Malayan and (*Malayo-Chinese*). [MALAY]

Malayo-Polynesian *adj.* of a family of languages (also called *Austronesian*) extending from Madagascar in the west to the Pacific in the east. They are spoken by some 140 million people of whom all but one million speak a language of the Indonesian group, such as Indonesian, Tagalog, or Malagasy. The other groups are Micronesian, Melanesian, and Polynesian.

Malaysia /mə'leɪʒə/ a country in SE Asia, a federation composed of East Malaysia (the northern part of Borneo, including Sarawak and Sabah) and West Malaysia (the Malayan Peninsula south of Thailand), separated from each other by 650 km (400 miles) of the South China Sea; pop. (est. 1988) 16,398,300; official language, Malay; capital, Kuala Lumpur. West Malaysia is the world's leading producer of rubber and leading exporter of tin, while East Malaysia, although considerably less developed, is an important exporter of oil. The area was opened up by the Portuguese and Dutch in the 16th and 17th c., but was under British influence from the early 19th c. It federated as an independent State of the Commonwealth in 1963 despite opposition from its neighbours Indonesia and the Philippines. □□ **Malaysian** *adj. & n.*

Malcolm /'mælkəm/ the name of four kings of Scotland:
Malcolm III (*c.*1031–93), also called Malcolm Canmore, son of Duncan I, reigned 1058–93, killer of Macbeth. One of the monarchs most responsible for welding Scotland into an organized kingdom, Malcolm spent a large part of his reign involved in intermittent border warfare with the new Norman regime in England, eventually being killed in battle near Alnwick. His wife Margaret (see entry) was later canonized.
Malcolm IV (1141–65), grandson of David I, reigned 1153–65, popularly known as 'the Maiden'. The reign of this youthful and sickly king witnessed a progressive loss of power to Henry II of England.

Malcolm X /ˌmælkəm 'eks/ (born Malcolm Little, 1925–65), American militant Black leader, who rejected the cooperation with White liberals that had marked the civil rights movement and after conversion to Islam in 1946 joined the Black Muslims. In 1964 he broke away from this movement and preached a brotherhood between Black and White. There was active hostility between his followers and the Black Muslims, and he was assassinated in the following year.

malcontent /'mælkən,tent/ *n. & adj.* —*n.* a discontented person; a rebel. —*adj.* discontented or rebellious. [F (as MAL-, CONTENT[1])]

mal de mer /ˌmæl də 'meə(r)/ *n.* seasickness. [F, = sickness of (the) sea]

Maldives /'mɔːldaɪvz/ a country consisting of a chain of coral islands in the Indian Ocean SW of Sri Lanka; pop. (est. 1988) 203,200; official language, a form of Sinhalese; capital, Male. The islands were a British protectorate from 1887 until they became independent under the rule of a sultan in 1965 and then a republic in 1968, with a limited form of membership of the Commonwealth since 1982. □□ **Maldivian** /-'dɪvɪən/ *adj. & n.*

Male /'mɑːleɪ/ the capital of the Maldives; pop. (1985) 46,330.

male /meɪl/ *adj. & n.* —*adj.* **1** of the sex that can beget offspring by fertilization or insemination (*male child; male dog*). **2** of men or male animals, plants, etc.; masculine (*the male sex; a male-voice choir*). **3 a** (of plants or their parts) containing only fertilizing organs. **b** (of plants) thought of as male because of colour, shape, etc. **4** (of parts of machinery etc.) designed to enter or fill the corresponding female part (*a male screw*). —*n.* a male person or animal. □ **male chauvinist** a man who is prejudiced against women or regards women as inferior. **male fern** a common lowland fern, *Dryopteris filixmas*. **male menopause** a crisis of potency, confidence, etc., supposed to afflict men in middle life. □□ **maleness** n. [ME f. OF ma(s)le, f. L masculus f. mas a male]

malediction /ˌmælɪˈdɪkʃ(ə)n/ n. **1** a curse. **2** the utterance of a curse. □□ **maledictive** adj. **maledictory** adj. [ME f. L maledictio f. maledicere speak evil of f. male ill + dicere dict- speak]

malefactor /ˈmælɪˌfæktə(r)/ n. a criminal; an evil-doer. □□ **malefaction** /-ˈfækʃ(ə)n/ n. [ME f. L f. malefacere malefact- f. male ill + facere do]

malefic /məˈlefɪk/ adj. literary (of magical arts etc.) harmful; baleful. [L maleficus f. male ill]

maleficent /məˈlefɪs(ə)nt/ adj. literary **1** (often foll. by to) hurtful. **2** criminal. □□ **maleficence** n. [maleficence formed as MALEFIC after malevolence]

maleic acid /məˈleɪɪk/ n. a colourless crystalline organic acid used in making synthetic resins. [F maléique (as MALIC ACID)]

malemute var. of MALAMUTE.

malevolent /məˈlevələnt/ adj. wishing evil to others. □□ **malevolence** n. **malevolently** adv. [OF malivolent or f. L malevolens f. male ill + volens willing, part. of velle]

malfeasance /mælˈfiːz(ə)ns/ n. Law evil-doing. □□ **malfeasant** n. & adj. [AF malfaisance f. OF malfaisant (as MAL-, faisant part. of faire do f. L facere): cf. MISFEASANCE]

malformation /ˌmælfɔːˈmeɪʃ(ə)n/ n. faulty formation. □□ **malformed** /-ˈfɔːmd/ adj.

malfunction /mælˈfʌŋkʃ(ə)n/ n. & v. —n. a failure to function in a normal or satisfactory manner. —v.intr. fail to function normally or satisfactorily.

Malherbe /mæˈlerb/ François de (1555–1628), French poet, court poet from 1605 until his death. An architect of classicism in poetic form and grammar, he sternly criticized essays of emotion and ornamentation and the use of Latin and dialectal forms. His teaching was mainly oral or circulated in commentaries, and his own poems, painstakingly written and eloquent, were lacking in inspiration.

Mali /ˈmɑːlɪ/ an inland country in West Africa, south of Algeria; pop. (1987) 7,620,225; official language, French; capital, Bamako. The north of the country is desert and most of the population, who depend on livestock for their living, are to be found pursuing a semi-nomadic existence in the south. Colonized by the French in the late 19th c. (and known as Soudan), Mali became a partner with Senegal in the Federation of Mali in 1959 and achieved full independence a year later. Initially a republic, since 1974 Mali has been a one-party State; 1990–1 saw a year of civil unrest in support of a pro-democracy movement. □□ **Malian** adj. & n.

mali /ˈmɑːlɪ/ n. (pl. **malis**) Ind. a member of the gardener caste; a gardener. [Hindi]

malic acid /ˈmælɪk/ n. an organic acid found in unripe apples and other fruits. [F malique f. L malum apple]

malice /ˈmælɪs/ n. **1 a** the intention to do evil. **b** a desire to tease, esp. cruelly. **2** Law wrongful intention, esp. as increasing the guilt of certain offences. □ **malice aforethought** (or **prepense**) Law the intention to commit a crime, esp. murder. [ME f. OF f. L malitia f. malus bad]

malicious /məˈlɪʃəs/ adj. characterized by malice; intending or intended to do harm. □□ **maliciously** adv. **maliciousness** n. [OF malicius f. L malitiosus (as MALICE)]

malign /məˈlaɪn/ adj. & v. —adj. **1** (of a thing) injurious. **2** (of a disease) malignant. **3** malevolent. —v. tr. speak ill of; slander. □□ **maligner** n. **malignity** /məˈlɪɡnɪtɪ/ n. (pl. **-ies**). **malignly** adv. [ME f. OF malin maligne, malignier f. LL malignare contrive maliciously f. L malignus f. malus bad: cf. BENIGN]

malignant /məˈlɪɡnənt/ adj. **1 a** (of a disease) very virulent or infectious (malignant cholera). **b** (of a tumour) tending to invade normal tissue and recur after removal; cancerous. **2** harmful; feeling or showing intense ill will. □ **malignant pustule** a form of anthrax. □□ **malignancy** n. (pl. **-ies**). **malignantly** adv. [LL malignare (as MALIGN)]

Malines see MECHELEN.

malinger /məˈlɪŋɡə(r)/ v.intr. exaggerate or feign illness in order to escape duty, work, etc. □□ **malingerer** n. [back-form. f.

malingerer app. f. F malingre, perh. formed as MAL- + haingre weak]

Malin Head /ˈmælɪn/ a point on the coast of Co. Donegal, the northernmost point of Ireland.

Malinowski /ˌmælɪˈnɒfskɪ/, Bronislaw Kaspar (1884–1942), Polish anthropologist, who initiated the technique of what came to be known as 'participant observation'—living for an extended period among the people he was studying (those of the Trobriand Islands, now part of Papua New Guinea), and participating in their activities, while gathering information.

mall /mæl, mɔːl/ n. **1** a sheltered walk or promenade. **2** an enclosed shopping precinct. **3** hist. **a** = PALL-MALL. **b** an alley used for this. [var. of MAUL: applied to The Mall in London (orig. a pall-mall alley)]

mallard /ˈmælɑːd/ n. (pl. same or **mallards**) **1** a wild duck or drake, Anas platyrhynchos, of the northern hemisphere. **2** the flesh of the mallard. [ME f. OF prob. f. maslart (unrecorded, as MALE)]

Mallarmé /ˌmælɑːˈmeɪ/, Stéphane (1842–98), French poet, a leading symbolist and more recently a hero of structuralism. His best-known poems are 'Herodiade' (c.1871) and 'L'après-midi d'un faun' (1876). His pursuit of perfection led him to use elaborate symbols and metaphors, and to experiment with rhythm and syntax by transposing words and omitting grammatical elements. These tendencies culminated in 'Un coup de dès jamais n'abolira le hasard' (1897), which makes revolutionary use of typographical possibilities to suggest a musical score, and to render the 'prismatic subdivisions of the idea'.

malleable /ˈmælɪəb(ə)l/ adj. **1** (of metal etc.) able to be hammered or pressed permanently out of shape without breaking or cracking. **2** adaptable; pliable, flexible. □□ **malleability** /-ˈbɪlɪtɪ/ n. **malleably** adv. [ME f. OF f. med.L malleabilis f. L malleare to hammer f. malleus hammer]

mallee /ˈmælɪ/ n. Austral. **1** any of several types of eucalyptus, esp. Eucalyptus dumosa, that flourish in arid areas. **2** a scrub formed by mallee. □ **mallee-bird** (or **-fowl** or **-hen**) a megapode, Leipoa ocellata, resembling a turkey. [Aboriginal]

mallei pl. of MALLEUS.

mallemuck var. of MOLLYMAWK.

mallenders /ˈmæləndəz/ n.pl. (also **malanders**) a dry scabby eruption behind a horse's knee. [ME f. OF malandre (sing.) f. L malandria (pl.) neck-pustules]

malleolus /məˈliːələs/ n. (pl. **malleoli** /-ˌlaɪ/) Anat. a bone with the shape of a hammer-head, esp. each of those forming a projection on either side of the ankle. [L, dimin. of malleus hammer]

mallet /ˈmælɪt/ n. **1** a hammer, usu. of wood. **2** a long-handled wooden hammer for striking a croquet or polo ball. [ME f. OF maillet f. mailler to hammer f. mail hammer f. L malleus]

malleus /ˈmælɪəs/ n. (pl. **mallei** /-lɪˌaɪ/) Anat. a small bone in the middle ear transmitting the vibrations of the tympanum to the incus. [L, = hammer]

Mallorca see MAJORCA.

mallow /ˈmæləʊ/ n. **1** any plant of the genus Malva, esp. M. sylvestris, with hairy stems and leaves and pink or purple flowers. **2** any of several other plants of the family Malvaceae, including marsh mallow and tree mallow. [OE meal(u)we f. L malva]

malm /mɑːm/ n. **1** a soft chalky rock. **2** a loamy soil produced by the disintegration of this rock. **3** a fine-quality brick made originally from malm, marl, or a similar chalky clay. [OE mealm- (in compounds) f. Gmc]

Malmö /ˈmælmɜː/ a fortified port in SW Sweden, situated on the Øresund opposite Copenhagen; pop. (1987) 230,800.

malmsey /ˈmɑːmzɪ/ n. a strong sweet wine orig. from Greece, now chiefly from Madeira. [ME f. MDu., MLG malmesie, -eye, f. Monemvasia in S. Greece: cf. MALVOISIE]

malnourished /mælˈnʌrɪʃt/ adj. suffering from malnutrition. □□ **malnourishment** n.

malnourishment /mælˈnʌrɪʃmənt/ n. = MALNUTRITION.

malnutrition /ˌmælnjuːˈtrɪʃ(ə)n/ n. a dietary condition resulting from the absence of some foods or essential elements necessary for health; insufficient nutrition.

malodorous /mælˈəʊdərəs/ adj. evil-smelling.

Malory /ˈmælərɪ/, Sir Thomas (d. 1471), English writer. Although his exact identity is uncertain, he is identified by his modern editor, Vinaver, as Sir Thomas Malory of Newbold Revel, Warwickshire, who after 1450 was charged with crimes of violence, theft, and rape. His major work, Le Morte D'Arthur (printed 1483), is a prose translation of a collection of the legends of King Arthur, skilfully selected from French and other sources. Malory wrote this in prison and it was one of the earliest works to be printed by Caxton.

Malpighi /mælˈpiːgɪ/, Marcello (?1628–94), Italian microscopist. Seeking a mechanical interpretation of animal bodies he looked for and found visible structures underlying physiological functions. He saw the alveoli and capillaries in the lungs and demonstrated the pathway of blood from arteries to veins (confirming Harvey's theory of circulation); he saw the fibres and red cells of clotted blood, and investigated the structures of the kidney and skin. His interest in fine structure led him to embryology as the means by which the machine of the body was put together. He also studied the anatomy of the silkworm, discovered the breathing system of animals, and extended the search for structure into an examination of plant cells. A layer of developing cells in skin tissue (Malpighian layer) and a cluster of capillaries in the kidney are named after him.

Malplaquet /ˌmælplæˈkeɪ/ a village in northern France, scene of a victory (1709) of allied British and Austrian troops over the French (see MARLBOROUGH).

malpractice /mælˈpræktɪs/ n. 1 improper or negligent professional treatment, esp. by a medical practitioner. 2 a criminal wrongdoing; misconduct. b an instance of this.

malt /mɔːlt, mɒlt/ n. & v. —n. 1 barley or other grain that is steeped, germinated, and dried, esp. for brewing or distilling and vinegar-making. 2 colloq. malt whisky; malt liquor. —v. 1 tr. convert (grain) into malt. 2 intr. (of seeds) become malt when germination is checked by drought. □ **malted milk** 1 a hot drink made from dried milk and a malt preparation. 2 the powdered mixture from which this is made. **malt-house** a building used for preparing and storing malt. **malt liquor** alcoholic liquor made from malt by fermentation, not distillation, e.g. beer, stout. **malt whisky** whisky made from malted barley. [OE m(e)alt f. Gmc, rel. to MELT]

Malta /ˈmɔːltə, ˈmɒ-/ an island country in the central Mediterranean, a member State of the Commonwealth, lying about 100 km (60 miles) south of Sicily; pop. (est. 1988) 369,240; official languages, Maltese and English; capital, Valletta. The island was held in turn by Phoenicians, Greeks, Carthaginians, and Arabs, and in 1090 was conquered by Roger of Normandy. Given to the Knights of St John (see KNIGHTS HOSPITALLER; these are also called the Knights of Malta) by the Emperor Charles V in 1530, Malta successfully withstood a long siege by Turkish invaders and remained headquarters for the Order until captured by the French in 1798. It was annexed by Britain in 1814 and subsequently became an important naval base. During the Second World War the island was awarded the George Cross for its endurance under heavy air attack between 1940 and 1942. Independence was granted in 1964, but since that time, despite income from tourism, the economy has experienced considerable difficulties because of the decline of the naval base.

Maltese /mɔːlˈtiːz, mɒl-/ n. & adj. —n. 1 (pl. same) **a** a native or national of Malta. **b** a person of Maltese descent. 2 the language of Malta. —adj. of or relating to Malta or its people or language. □ **Maltese cross** a cross with arms of equal length broadening from the centre, often indented at the ends. **Maltese dog** (or **terrier**) a small breed of spaniel or terrier.

maltha /ˈmælθə/ n. a cement made of pitch and wax or other ingredients. [L f. Gk]

Malthus /ˈmælθəs/, Thomas Robert (1766–1834), English clergyman, a pioneer of the science of political economy. Malthus propounded the theory, very controversial at the time, that the rapidly growing population would soon increase beyond the capacity to feed it and that controls on population were therefore necessary to prevent catastrophe. □□ **Malthusian** /-ˈθjuːzɪən/ adj.

malting /ˈmɔːltɪŋ, ˈmɒl-/ n. 1 the process or an instance of brewing or distilling with malt. 2 = malt-house.

maltose /ˈmɔːltəʊz/ n. Chem. a sugar produced by the hydrolysis of starch under the action of the enzymes in malt, saliva, etc. [F (as MALT)]

maltreat /mælˈtriːt/ v.tr. ill-treat. □□ **maltreater** n. **maltreatment** n. [F maltraiter (as MAL-, TREAT)]

maltster /ˈmɔːltstə(r), ˈmɒl-/ n. a person who makes malt.

malty /ˈmɔːltɪ, ˈmɒl-/ adj. (**maltier**, **maltiest**) of, containing, or resembling malt. □□ **maltiness** n.

Maluku see MOLUCCA ISLANDS.

malvaceous /mælˈveɪʃəs/ adj. Bot. of or relating to the genus Malva or the family Malvaceae, which includes mallow. [L malvaceus f. malva MALLOW]

malversation /ˌmælvəˈseɪʃ(ə)n/ n. formal 1 corrupt behaviour in a position of trust. 2 (often foll. by of) corrupt administration (of public money etc.). [F f. malverser f. L male badly + versari behave]

Malvinas /mælˈviːnəs/, **Islas** the name by which the Falkland Islands are known in Argentina.

malvoisie /ˌmælvwəˈziː/ n. = MALMSEY. [ME f. OF malvesie f. F form of Monemvasia: see MALMSEY]

mam /mæm/ n. colloq. mother. [formed as MAMA]

mama /ˈmæmə, məˈmɑː/ n. colloq. (esp. as a child's term) = MAMMA.

mamba /ˈmæmbə/ n. any venomous African snake of the genus Dendroaspis, esp. the green mamba (D. angusticeps) or black mamba (D. polylepis). [Zulu imamba]

mambo /ˈmæmbəʊ/ n. & v. —n. (pl. -os) 1 a Latin American dance like the rumba. 2 the music for this. —v.intr. (-oes, -oed) perform the mambo. [Amer. Sp. prob. f. Haitian]

mamelon /ˈmæmələn/ n. a small rounded hillock. [F, = nipple f. mamelle breast f. L MAMILLA]

Mameluke /ˈmæməˌluːk/ n. & adj. —n. hist. a member of a body of Turkoman warriors who were originally brought to Egypt as slaves to act as a bodyguard for the caliphs and sultans, and themselves became powerful, ruling as sultans from 1250 until the Ottoman Turks conquered Egypt in 1517, and locally as governors under a Turkish viceroy. Napoleon defeated them in 1798, and the surviving Mamelukes were massacred by Muhammad Ali in 1811. —adj. of the Mamelukes. [F mameluk, ult. f. Arab. mamlūk slave f. malaka possess]

mamilla /məˈmɪlə/ n. (US **mammilla**) (pl. **mamillae** /-liː/) 1 the nipple of a woman's breast. 2 a nipple-shaped organ etc. □□ **mamillary** /ˈmæmɪlərɪ/ adj. **mamillate** /ˈmæmɪˌleɪt/ adj. [L, dimin. of MAMMA²]

mamma¹ /ˈmæmə/ n. (also **momma** /ˈmɒmə/) colloq. (esp. as a child's term) mother. [imit. of child's ma, ma]

mamma² /ˈmæmə/ n. (pl. **mammae** /-miː/) 1 a milk-secreting organ of female mammals. 2 a corresponding non-secretory structure in male mammals. □□ **mammiform** adj. [OE f. L]

mammal /ˈmæm(ə)l/ n. any vertebrate of the class Mammalia, characterized by secretion of milk by the female to feed the young. Mammals evolved from reptiles about 200 million years ago but remained relatively small and inconspicuous until the dinosaurs died out at the end of the Cretaceous period, when they evolved rapidly and became the dominant land vertebrates. There are about 4,000 living species, of which nearly half are rodents and almost another quarter are bats. They are a very diverse group in terms of size, appearance, and behaviour. Mammals display a number of distinctive features which help to account for their success as a group. Along with birds they are warm-blooded, and so can remain active at night or in cold climates; a covering of hair and a layer of fat beneath the skin help to conserve their body heat. Mammals differ from reptiles in the position of their limbs, which are held more vertically beneath the body, making for more efficient locomotion, and in their teeth, which have evolved into a number of different types as an adaptation to particular diets. The mammalian brain is also relatively larger than that of other vertebrate groups, permitting more complex and adaptable behaviour. The three major subgroups of mammals are monotremes (egg-laying mammals, represented only by the platypus and echidnas), marsupials, and placental mammals, which include most of the familiar types: primates (including man), carnivores (such as dogs, cats, and bears), hoofed mammals, rodents, bats, whales, etc. □□ **mammalian** /-ˈmeɪlɪən/ *adj.* & *n.* **mammalogy** /-ˈmælədʒɪ/ *n.* [mod.L *mammalia* neut. pl. of L *mammalis* (as MAMMA²)]

mammaliferous /ˌmæməˈlɪfərəs/ *adj. Geol.* containing mammalian remains.

mammary /ˈmæmərɪ/ *adj.* of the human female breasts or milk-secreting organs of other mammals. □ **mammary gland** the milk-producing gland of female mammals. [MAMMA² + -ARY¹]

mammee /mæˈmiː/ *n.* a tropical American tree, *Mammea americana*, with large red-rinded yellow-pulped fruit. [Sp. *mamei* f. Haitian]

mammilla US var. of MAMILLA.

mammography /mæˈmɒgrəfɪ/ *n. Med.* an X-ray technique of diagnosing and locating abnormalities (esp. tumours) of the breasts. [MAMMA² + -GRAPHY]

Mammon /ˈmæmən/ *n.* **1** wealth regarded as a god or as an evil influence. **2** the worldly rich. 'Mammon' was the Aramaic word for 'riches' (*māmōn*) used in the Greek text of the New Testament in Matt. 6: 24 and Luke 16: 9–13, and retained in the Vulgate. It was taken by medieval writers as the name of the devil of covetousness, and this use was revived by Milton in *Paradise Lost*. □□ **Mammonish** *adj.* **Mammonism** *n.* **Mammonist** *n.* **Mammonite** *n.* [ME f. LL *Mam(m)ona* f. Gk *mamōnas* f. Aram.]

mammoth /ˈmæməθ/ *n.* & *adj.* —*n.* any large extinct elephant of the genus *Mammuthus*, with a hairy coat and curved tusks. —*adj.* huge. [Russ. *mamo(n)t*]

mammy /ˈmæmɪ/ *n.* (*pl.* **-ies**) **1** a child's word for mother. **2** US a Black nursemaid or nanny in charge of White children. [formed as MAMMA¹]

Man. *abbr.* Manitoba.

man /mæn/ *n.* & *v.* —*n.* (*pl.* **men** /men/) **1** an adult human male, esp. as distinct from a woman or boy. **2 a** a creature of the genus *Homo* (see entry), distinguished from other animals by superior mental development, power of articulate speech, and upright stance; a human being; a person (*no man is perfect*). **b** human beings in general; the human race (*man is mortal*). **3** a person showing characteristics associated with males (*she's more of a man than he is*). **4 a** a worker; an employee (*the manager spoke to the men*). **b** a manservant or valet. **c** *hist.* a vassal. **5 a** (usu. in *pl.*) soldiers, sailors, etc., esp. non-officers (*was in command of 200 men*). **b** an individual, usu. male, person (*fought to the last man*). **c** (usu. prec. by *the*, or *poss. pron.*) a person regarded as suitable or appropriate in some way; a person fulfilling requirements (*I'm your man*; *not the man for the job*). **6 a** a husband (*man and wife*). **b** *colloq.* a boyfriend or lover. **7 a** a human being of a specified historical period or character (*Renaissance man*). **b** a type of prehistoric man named after the place where the remains were found (*Peking man*; *Piltdown man*). **8** any one of a set of pieces used in playing chess, draughts, etc. **9** (as second element in *comb.*) a man of a specified nationality, profession, skill, etc. (*Dutchman*; *clergyman*; *horseman*; *gentleman*). **10 a** an expression of impatience etc. used in addressing a male (*nonsense, man!*). **b** *colloq.* a general mode of address among hippies etc. (*blew my mind, man!*). **11** (prec. by *a*) a person; one (*what can a man do?*). **12** a person pursued; an opponent etc. (*the police have so far not caught their man*). **13** (**the Man**) US *sl.* **a** the police. **b** *Black sl.* White people. **14** (in *comb.*) a ship of a specified type (*merchantman*; *Indiaman*). —*v.tr.* (**manned**, **manning**) **1** supply (a ship, fort, factory, etc.) with a person or people for work or defence. **2** work or service or defend (a specified piece of equipment, a fortification, etc.) (*man the pumps*). **3** *Naut.* place men at (a part of a ship). **4** fill (a post or office). **5** (usu. *refl.*) fortify the spirits or courage of (*manned herself for the task*). □ **as one man** in unison; in agreement. **be a man** be courageous; not show fear. **be one's own man 1** be free to act; be independent. **2**

be in full possession of one's faculties etc. **man about town** a fashionable man of leisure. **man and boy** from childhood. **man-at-arms** (*pl.* **men-at-arms**) *archaic* a soldier, esp. when heavily armed and mounted. **man Friday** see FRIDAY. **man-hour** (or **day** etc.) an hour (or day etc.) regarded in terms of the amount of work that could be done by one person within this period. **Man in the Iron Mask** see separate entry. **man in the moon** the semblance of a face seen on the surface of a full moon. **man in** (US **on**) **the street** an ordinary average person, as distinct from an expert. **man-made** (esp. of a textile fibre) made by man, artificial, synthetic. **man of God 1** a clergyman. **2** a male saint. **man of honour** a man whose word can be trusted. **man of the house** the male head of a household. **man of letters** a scholar; an author. **man of the moment** a man of importance at a particular time. **man of straw 1** an insubstantial person; an imaginary person set up as an opponent. **2** a stuffed effigy. **3** a person undertaking a financial commitment without adequate means. **4** a sham argument set up to be defeated. **man-of-war** (*pl.* **men-of-war**) an armed ship, esp. of a specified country. **man of the world** see WORLD. **man-size** (or **-sized**) **1** of the size of a man; very large. **2** big enough for a man. **man to man** with candour; honestly. **men's** (or **men's room**) a usu. public lavatory for men. **my** (or **my good**) **man** a patronizing mode of address to a man. **separate** (or **sort out**) **the men from the boys** *colloq.* find those who are truly virile, competent, etc. **to a man** all without exception. □□ **manless** *adj.* [OE *man(n)*, pl. *menn*, *mannian*, f. Gmc]

mana /ˈmɑːnə/ *n.* **1** power; authority; prestige. **2** supernatural or magical power. [Maori]

manacle /ˈmænək(ə)l/ *n.* & *v.* —*n.* (usu. in *pl.*) **1** a fetter or shackle for the hand; a handcuff. **2** a restraint. —*v.tr.* fetter with manacles. [ME f. OF *manicle* handcuff f. L *manicula* dimin. of *manus* hand]

manage /ˈmænɪdʒ/ *v.* & *n.* —*v.* **1** *tr.* organize; regulate; be in charge of (a business, household, team, a person's career, etc.). **2** *tr.* (often foll. by *to* + infin.) succeed in achieving; contrive (*managed to arrive on time*; *managed a smile*; *managed to ruin the day*). **3** *intr.* **a** (often foll. by *with*) succeed in one's aim, esp. against heavy odds (*managed with one assistant*). **b** meet one's needs with limited resources etc. (*just about manages on a pension*). **4** *tr.* gain influence with or maintain control over (a person etc.) (*cannot manage their teenage son*). **5** *tr.* (also *absol.*; often prec. by *can*, *be able to*) make use of; succeed in (*couldn't manage another bite*; *can you manage by yourself?*). **b** be free to attend on (a certain day) or at (a certain time) (*can you manage Thursday?*). **6** *tr.* handle or wield (a tool, weapon, etc.). **7** *tr.* take or have charge or control of (an animal or animals, esp. cattle). —*n. archaic* **1** a the training of a horse. **b** the trained movements of a horse. **2** a riding-school (cf. MANÈGE). [It. *maneggiare, maneggio* ult. f. L *manus* hand]

manageable /ˈmænɪdʒəb(ə)l/ *adj.* able to be easily managed, controlled, or accomplished etc. □□ **manageability** /-ˈbɪlɪtɪ/ *n.* **manageableness** *n.* **manageably** *adv.*

management /ˈmænɪdʒmənt/ *n.* **1** the process or an instance of managing or being managed. **2 a** the professional administration of business concerns, public undertakings, etc. **b** the people engaged in this. **c** (prec. by *the*) a governing body; a board of directors or the people in charge of running a business, regarded collectively. **3** (usu. foll. by *of*) *Med.* the technique of treating a disease etc. **4** trickery; deceit.

manager /ˈmænɪdʒə(r)/ *n.* **1** a person controlling or administering a business or part of a business. **2** a person controlling the affairs, training, etc. of a person or team in sports, entertainment, etc. **3** *Brit. Parl.* a member of either House of Parliament appointed with others for some duty in which both Houses are concerned. **4** a person regarded in terms of skill in household or financial or other management (*a good manager*). □□ **managerial** /ˌmænɪˈdʒɪərɪəl/ *adj.* **managerially** /-ˈdʒɪərɪəlɪ/ *adv.* **managership** *n.*

manageress /ˌmænɪdʒəˈres/ *n.* a woman manager, esp. of a shop, hotel, theatre, etc.

managing /ˈmænɪdʒɪŋ/ *adj.* **1** (in *comb.*) having executive control or authority (*managing director*). **2** (*attrib.*) fond of controlling affairs etc. **3** *archaic* economical.

Managua /məˈnɑːgwə/ the capital of Nicaragua; pop. (1985) 682,100. The city was almost completely destroyed by an earthquake in 1972.

manakin /ˈmænəkɪn/ *n.* any small bird of the family Pipridae of Central and S. America, the males of which are often brightly coloured. [var. of MANIKIN]

Manama /məˈnɑːmə/ the capital of Bahrain; pop. (1988) 151,000.

mañana /mænˈjɑːnə/ *adv.* & *n.* —*adv.* in the indefinite future (esp. to indicate procrastination). —*n.* an indefinite future time. [Sp., = tomorrow]

Manasseh /məˈnæsɪ, -sə/ **1** a Hebrew patriarch, son of Joseph (Gen. 48: 19). **2** the tribe of Israel traditionally descended from him.

Manasses see PRAYER OF MANASSES.

manatee /ˌmænəˈtiː/ *n.* any large aquatic plant-eating mammal of the genus *Trichechus*, with paddle-like forelimbs, no hind limbs, and a powerful tail. [Sp. *manati* f. Carib *manattoui*]

Manaus /məˈnaʊs/ a city in NW Brazil, capital of Amazonas and principal commercial centre of the upper Amazon region; pop. (1980) 611,750.

Manawatu /ˌmænəˈwɑːtuː/ **1** a river of North Island, New Zealand, flowing into Cook Strait. **2** an administrative region of North Island; pop. (1986) 115,500; chief town, Palmerston North.

Manchester /ˈmæntʃestə(r)/ an industrial city in NW England; pop. (1981) 448,700.

manchineel /ˌmæntʃɪˈniːl/ *n.* a W. Indian tree, *Hippomane mancinella*, with a poisonous and caustic milky sap and acrid apple-like fruit. [F *mancenille* f. Sp. *manzanilla* dimin. of *manzana* apple]

Manchu /mænˈtʃuː/ *n.* & *adj.* —*n.* **1** a member of a Tartar people who conquered China and founded the Ch'ing dynasty (1644–1912). **2** their language, which belongs to the Tungusic group in the Altaic family of languages. At one time it was an official language of China, but it is now spoken only in parts of northern Manchuria. —*adj.* of or relating to the Manchu people or their language. [Manchu, = pure]

Manchuria /mænˈtʃʊərɪə/ a region forming the NE portion of China. In 1932 it was declared an independent State by Japan and renamed *Manchukuo*; it was restored to China in 1945.

manciple /ˈmænsɪp(ə)l/ *n.* an officer who buys provisions for a college, an Inn of Court, etc. [ME f. AF & OF f. L *mancipium* purchase f. *manceps* buyer f. *manus* hand + *capere* take]

Mancunian /mænˈkjuːnɪən/ *n.* & *adj.* —*n.* a native of Manchester. —*adj.* of or relating to Manchester. [L *Mancunium* Roman settlement on site of Manchester]

-mancy /mænsɪ/ *comb. form* forming nouns meaning 'divination by' (*geomancy*; *necromancy*). ☐☐ **-mantic** *comb. form* forming adjectives. [OF *-mancie* f. LL *-mantia* f. Gk *manteia* divination]

Mandaean /mænˈdiːən/ *n.* & *adj.* —*n.* **1** a member of a Gnostic sect (see SABAEAN), surviving in Iraq, who revere John the Baptist. **2** the Aramaic dialect in which their books are written. — *adj.* of or concerning the Mandaeans or their language. [Aram. *mandaiia* Gnostics f. *manda* knowledge]

mandala /ˈmændələ/ *n.* **1** a symbolic circular figure representing the universe in various religions. **2** *Psychol.* such a symbol in a dream, representing the dreamer's search for completeness and self-unity. [Skr. *máṇḍala* disc]

Mandalay /ˌmændəˈleɪ/ a port on the Irrawaddy River in central Burma; pop. (1983) 532,985. Founded in 1857, it was the capital of the Burmese kingdom 1857–85. It is an important Buddhist religious centre.

mandamus /mænˈdeɪməs/ *n. Law* a judicial writ issued as a command to an inferior court, or ordering a person to perform a public or statutory duty. [L, = we command]

mandarin¹ /ˈmændərɪn/ *n.* **1** (**Mandarin**) the most widely spoken form of Chinese and the official language of China. **2** *hist.* a Chinese official in any of nine grades of the pre-Communist civil service. **3 a** a party leader; a bureaucrat. **b** a

powerful member of the establishment. **4 a** a nodding Chinese figure, usu. of porcelain. **b** porcelain etc. decorated with Chinese figures in mandarin dress. ☐ **mandarin collar** a small close-fitting upright collar. **mandarin duck** a small Chinese duck, *Aix galericulata*, noted for its bright plumage. **mandarin sleeve** a wide loose sleeve. ☐☐ **mandarinate** *n.* [Port. *mandarim* f. Malay f. Hindi *mantrī* f. Skr. *mantrin* counsellor]

mandarin² /ˈmændərɪn/ *n.* (also **mandarine** /-ˌriːn/) (in full **mandarin orange**) **1** a small flattish deep-coloured orange with a loose skin. **2** the tree, *Citrus reticulata*, yielding this. Also called TANGERINE. [F *mandarine* (perh. as MANDARIN¹, with ref. to the official's yellow robes)]

mandatary /ˈmændətərɪ/ *n.* (*pl.* **-ies**) esp. *hist.* a person or State receiving a mandate. [LL *mandatarius* (as MANDATE)]

mandate /ˈmændeɪt/ *n.* & *v.* —*n.* **1** an official command or instruction by an authority. **2** support for a policy or course of action, regarded by a victorious party, candidate, etc., as derived from the wishes of the people in an election. **3** a commission to act for another. **4** *Law* a commission by which a party is entrusted to perform a service, often gratuitously and with indemnity against loss by that party. **5** *hist.* a commission from the League of Nations to a member State to administer a territory. **6** a papal decree or decision. —*v.tr.* **1** instruct (a delegate) to act or vote in a certain way. **2** (usu. foll. by *to*) *hist.* commit (a territory etc.) to a mandatary. ☐☐ **mandator** *n.* [L *mandatum*, neut. past part. of *mandare* command f. *manus* hand + *dare* give: sense 2 of n. after F *mandat*]

mandatory /ˈmændətərɪ/ *adj.* & *n.* —*adj.* **1** of or conveying a command. **2** compulsory. —*n.* (*pl.* **-ies**) = MANDATARY. ☐☐ **mandatorily** *adv.* [LL *mandatorius* f. L (as MANDATE)]

Mandela /mænˈdelə/, Nelson Rolihlahla (1918–), Black South African lawyer, a leader of the African National Congress (see entry). Arrested in 1962, he was sentenced to life imprisonment in 1964 and remained in custody until 1989. His authority as a moderate leader of Black South Africans did not diminish, though his absence from the political scene enabled a more militant generation of leaders to emerge; his second wife, Winnie Nomzamo Mandela (1934–), continued to be politically active. After his release Mandela resumed his leadership of the ANC, campaigning for a free, multiracial, and democratic society.

Mandeville /ˈmændəvɪl/, Sir John, the reputed author of a 14th-c. book of travels and travellers' tales which takes the reader to Turkey, Tartary, Persia, Egypt, and India. Written in French and much translated, it was actually compiled by an unknown hand from the works of several writers.

mandible /ˈmændɪb(ə)l/ *n.* **1** the jaw, esp. the lower jaw in mammals and fishes. **2** the upper or lower part of a bird's beak. **3** either half of the crushing organ in an arthropod's mouth-parts. ☐☐ **mandibular** /-ˈdɪbjʊlə(r)/ *adj.* **mandibulate** /-ˈdɪbjʊlət/ *adj.* [ME f. OF *mandible* or LL *mandibula* f. *mandere* chew]

mandolin /ˌmændəˈlɪn/ *n.* (also **mandoline**) a plucked stringed instrument of the lute family with metal strings tuned in pairs and a characteristic tremolo when sustaining long notes. It is played chiefly in folk music. ☐☐ **mandolinist** *n.* [F *mandoline* f. It. *mandolino* dimin. of MANDOLA]

mandorla /mænˈdɔːlə/ *n.* = VESICA 2. [It., = almond]

mandragora /mænˈdrægərə/ *n. hist.* the mandrake, esp. as a type of narcotic (Shakesp. *Othello* III. iii. 334). [OE f. med.L f. L f. Gk *mandragoras*]

mandrake /ˈmændreɪk/ *n.* a poisonous plant, *Mandragora officinarum*, with white or purple flowers and large yellow fruit, having emetic and narcotic properties and possessing a root once thought to resemble the human form and to shriek when plucked. [ME *mandrag(g)e*, prob. f. MDu. *mandrag(r)e* f. med.L (as MANDRAGORA): assoc. with MAN + *drake* dragon (cf. DRAKE¹)]

mandrel /ˈmændr(ə)l/ *n.* **1 a** a shaft in a lathe to which work is fixed while being turned. **b** a cylindrical rod round which metal or other material is forged or shaped. **2** *Brit.* a miner's pick. [16th c.: orig. unkn.]

mandrill /ˈmændrɪl/ *n.* a large W. African baboon, *Papio sphinx*, the adult of which has a brilliantly coloured face and blue-coloured buttocks. [prob. f. MAN + DRILL³]

manducate /ˈmændjʊˌkeɪt/ v.tr. literary chew; eat. □□ **manduction** /-ˈkeɪʃ(ə)n/ n. **manducatory** /-kətərɪ, -ˈkeɪtərɪ/ adj. [L manducare manducat- chew f. manduco guzzler f. mandere chew]

mane /meɪn/ n. 1 long hair growing in a line on the neck of a horse, lion, etc. 2 colloq. a person's long hair. □□ **maned** adj. (also in comb.). **maneless** adj. [OE manu f. Gmc]

manège /mæˈneɪʒ/ n. (also **manege**) 1 a riding-school. 2 the movements of a trained horse. 3 horsemanship. [F manège f. It. (as MANAGE)]

Manes /ˈmeɪniːz/ (c.216–c.276) the Persian founder of Manichaeism (see entry).

manes /ˈmɑːneɪz, ˈmeɪniːz/ n.pl. 1 the deified souls of dead ancestors. 2 (as sing.) the revered ghost of a dead person. [ME f. L]

Manet /ˈmæneɪ/, Édouard (1832–83), French painter, sometimes called the 'father of modern art'. He was greatly admired by the young impressionists from whom, however, he stood somewhat aloof, seeking (with indifferent success) recognition from the official Salon. Manet was essentially a realist: his aim was 'to paint spontaneously what one sees', and the indignation which his paintings aroused can be explained by their challenge to the Old Masters through the introduction of contemporary reality into themes which had become hallowed and innocuous by the unreality conferred on them when they appeared in mythological and historical paintings. His abandonment of half-tones and shadings in favour of a bold use of pure colour added to the effect of frankness and lack of sentimentality. Among his works are some of the most familiar pictures in the world—The Picnic (Déjeuner sur l'herbe, 1863), created a scandal which led to the closing of the exhibition in which it appeared; Olympia (1865), also caused a scandal although Baudelaire and Zola came forward in his support; and A Bar at the Folies-Bergère (1882), his last great work. Afflicted by a wasting disease of the nervous system he resorted to small pictures of flowers when he no longer had strength for larger themes and canvases.

Manetho /mæˈneθəʊ/ (3rd c. BC) an Egyptian priest who in c.280 BC wrote a history of Egypt from mythical times to 323 BC. He arbitrarily divided the succession of rulers known to him into 31 dynasties, an arrangement which it is still convenient to use.

maneuver US var. of MANOEUVRE.

manful /ˈmænfʊl/ adj. brave; resolute. □□ **manfully** adv. **manfulness** n.

mangabey /ˈmæŋɡəˌbeɪ/ n. any small long-tailed W. African monkey of the genus Cercocebus. [Mangabey, a region of Madagascar]

manganese /ˈmæŋɡəˌniːz/ n. 1 Chem. a grey brittle metallic transition element , first isolated in 1774. The presence of manganese is essential to the process of steel manufacture, and special steels high in manganese are produced for heavy-duty work. The element is also required in small amounts by plants and many animals. ¶ Symb.: **Mn**; atomic number 25. 2 (in full **manganese oxide**) the black mineral oxide of this used in the manufacture of glass. □□ **manganic** /-ˈɡænɪk/ adj. **manganous** /ˈmæŋɡənəs/ adj. [F manganèse f. It. manganese, alt. f. MAGNESIA]

mange /meɪndʒ/ n. a skin disease in hairy and woolly animals, caused by an arachnid parasite and occasionally communicated to man. [ME mangie, maniewe f. OF manjue, mangeue itch f. mangier manju- eat f. L manducare chew]

mangel /ˈmæŋɡ(ə)l/ n. (also **mangold** /ˈmæŋɡ(ə)ld/) (in full **mangel-wurzel**, **mangold-wurzel** /-ˈwɜːz(ə)l/) a large kind of beet, Beta vulgaris, used as cattle food. [G Mangoldwurzel f. Mangold beet + Wurzel root]

manger /ˈmeɪndʒə(r)/ n. a long open box or trough in a stable etc., for horses or cattle to eat from. [ME f. OF mangeoire, mangeure ult. f. L (as MANDUCATE)]

mange-tout /ˈmɑ̃ʒtuː, -ˈtuː/ n. the sugar-pea. [F, = eat-all]

mangle¹ /ˈmæŋɡ(ə)l/ n. & v. esp. Brit. hist. —n. a machine having two or more cylinders usu. turned by a handle, between which wet clothes etc. are squeezed and pressed. —v.tr. press (clothes etc.) in a mangle. [Du. mangel(stok) f. mangelen to mangle, ult. f. Gk magganon + stok staff, STOCK]

mangle² /ˈmæŋɡ(ə)l/ v.tr. 1 hack, cut about, or mutilate by blows etc. 2 spoil (a quotation, text, etc.) by misquoting, mispronouncing, etc. 3 cut roughly so as to disfigure. □□ **mangler** n. [AF ma(ha)ngler, app. frequent. of mahaignier MAIM]

mango /ˈmæŋɡəʊ/ n. (pl. **-oes** or **-os**) 1 a fleshy yellowish-red fruit, eaten ripe or used green for pickles etc. 2 the Indian evergreen tree, Mangifera indica, bearing this. [Port. manga f. Malay mangā f. Tamil mānkāy f. mān mango-tree + kāy fruit]

mangold (also **mangold-wurzel**) var. of MANGEL.

mangonel /ˈmæŋɡən(ə)l/ n. Mil. hist. a military engine for throwing stones etc. [ME f. OF mangonel(le), f. med.L manganellus dimin. of LL manganum f. Gk magganon]

mangosteen /ˈmæŋɡəˌstiːn/ n. 1 a white juicy-pulped fruit with a thick reddish-brown rind. 2 the E. Indian tree, Garcinia mangostana, bearing this. [Malay manggustan]

mangrove /ˈmæŋɡrəʊv/ n. any tropical tree or shrub of the genus Rhizophora, growing in shore-mud with many tangled roots above ground. [17th c.: orig. uncert.: assim. to GROVE]

mangy /ˈmeɪndʒɪ/ adj. (**mangier**, **mangiest**) 1 (esp. of a domestic animal) having mange. 2 squalid; shabby. □□ **mangily** adv. **manginess** n.

manhandle /ˈmænˌhænd(ə)l/ v.tr. 1 move (heavy objects) by human effort. 2 colloq. handle (a person) roughly.

Manhattan /mænˈhæt(ə)n/ an island at the mouth of the Hudson River, which was the site of the original Dutch settlement of New Amsterdam, later the city of New York. It is now a borough containing the commercial and cultural centre of the city.

manhattan /mænˈhæt(ə)n/ n. a cocktail made of vermouth, whisky, etc. [MANHATTAN]

Manhattan Project the code name for an American project set up in 1942 to develop an atomic bomb.

manhole /ˈmænhəʊl/ n. a covered opening in a floor, pavement, sewer, etc. for workmen to gain access.

manhood /ˈmænhʊd/ n. 1 the state of being a man rather than a child or woman. 2 a manliness; courage. b a man's sexual potency. 3 the men of a country etc. 4 the state of being human.

manhunt /ˈmænhʌnt/ n. an organized search for a person, esp. a criminal.

mania /ˈmeɪnɪə/ n. 1 Psychol. mental illness marked by periods of great excitement and violence. 2 (often foll. by for) excessive enthusiasm; an obsession (has a mania for jogging). [ME f. LL f. Gk, = madness f. mainomai be mad, rel. to MIND]

-mania /ˈmeɪnɪə/ comb. form 1 Psychol. denoting a special type of mental abnormality or obsession (megalomania; nymphomania). 2 denoting extreme enthusiasm or admiration (bibliomania; Anglomania).

maniac /ˈmeɪnɪˌæk/ n. & adj. —n. 1 colloq. a person exhibiting extreme symptoms of wild behaviour etc.; a madman. 2 colloq. an obsessive enthusiast. 3 Psychol. archaic a person suffering from mania. —adj. of or behaving like a maniac. □□ **maniacal** /məˈnaɪək(ə)l/ adj. **maniacally** /məˈnaɪəkəlɪ/ adv. [LL maniacus f. late Gk maniakos (as MANIA)]

-maniac /ˈmeɪnɪæk/ comb. form forming adjectives and nouns meaning 'affected with -mania' or 'a person affected with -mania' (nymphomaniac).

manic /ˈmænɪk/ adj. of or affected by mania. □ **manic-depressive** Psychol. adj. affected by or relating to a mental disorder with alternating periods of elation and depression. —n. a person having such a disorder. □□ **manically** adv.

Manicaland /məˈniːkəˌlænd/ a gold-mining province of eastern Zimbabwe; pop. (1982) 1,099,200; capital, Mutare (formerly Umtali).

Manichee /ˈmænɪkɪ/ n. 1 an adherent of a religious system with Christian, Gnostic, and pagan elements, founded in Persia in the 3rd c. by Manes (c.216–c.276) and spread widely in the Roman Empire and in Asia, surviving in Chinese Turkestan until the 13th c. The system was based on a supposed primeval conflict between light and darkness, teaching that matter is evil but within each person's brain is imprisoned a particle of the divine 'light' which can be released by the practice of religion, and that Christ, Buddha, the Prophets, and Manes had been sent to help in this task. Severe asceticism was practised within the sect, with the 'elect' living a more rigorous life than the 'hearers' who supported them. **2** *Philos.* a dualist (see DUALISM). □□ **Manichean** /-ˈkiːən/ *adj.* & *n.* (also **Manichaean**). **Manicheism** /-ˈkiːɪz(ə)m/ *n.* (also **Manichaeism**). [LL *Manichaeus* f. late Gk *Manikhaios*, f. MANES or *Manichaeus*]

manicure /ˈmænɪˌkjʊə(r)/ *n.* & *v.* —*n.* **1** a usu. professional cosmetic treatment of the hands and fingernails. **2** = MANICURIST. —*v.tr.* apply a manicure to (the hands or a person). [F f. L *manus* hand + *cura* care]

manicurist /ˈmænɪˌkjʊərɪst/ *n.* a person who manicures hands and fingernails professionally.

manifest[1] /ˈmænɪˌfest/ *adj.* & *v.* —*adj.* clear or obvious to the eye or mind (*his distress was manifest*). —*v.* **1** *tr.* display or show (a quality, feeling, etc.) by one's acts etc. **2** *tr.* show plainly to the eye or mind. **3** *tr.* be evidence of; prove. **4** *refl.* (of a thing) reveal itself. **5** *intr.* (of a ghost) appear. □□ **manifestation** /-ˈsteɪʃ(ə)n/ *n.* **manifestative** /-ˈfestətɪv/ *adj.* **manifestly** *adv.* [ME f. OF *manifeste* (adj.), *manifester* (v.) or L *manifestus, manifestare* f. *manus* hand + *festus* (unrecorded) struck]

manifest[2] /ˈmænɪˌfest/ *n.* & *v.* —*n.* **1** a cargo-list for the use of customs officers. **2** a list of passengers in an aircraft or of trucks etc. in a goods train. —*v.tr.* record (names, cargo, etc.) in a manifest. [It. *manifesto*: see MANIFESTO]

manifesto /ˌmænɪˈfestəʊ/ *n.* (*pl.* **-os**) a public declaration of policy and aims esp. issued before an election by a political party, candidate, government, etc. [It. f. *manifestare* f. L (as MANIFEST[1])]

manifold /ˈmænɪˌfəʊld/ *adj.* & *n.* —*adj.* *literary* **1** many and various (*manifold vexations*). **2** having various forms, parts, applications, etc. **3** performing several functions at once. —*n.* **1** a thing with many different forms, parts, applications, etc. **2** *Mech.* a pipe or chamber branching into several openings. □□ **manifoldly** *adv.* **manifoldness** *n.* [OE *manigfeald* (as MANY, -FOLD)]

manikin /ˈmænɪkɪn/ *n.* (also **mannikin**) **1** a little man; a dwarf. **2** an artist's lay figure. **3** an anatomical model of the body. **4** (usu. **mannikin**) any small finchlike bird of the genus *Lonchura*, native to Africa and Australasia. [Du. *manneken*, dimin. of *man* MAN]

Manila /məˈnɪlə/ the capital and chief port of the Philippines; pop. (1980) 1,630,500 (city); 5,925,900 (metropolitan area). —*n.* (also **Manilla**) **1** a cigar or cheroot made in Manila. **2** (in full **Manila hemp**) the strong fibre of a Philippine tree, *Musa textilis*, used for rope etc. **3** (also **manila**) a strong brown paper made from Manila hemp or other material and used for wrapping paper, envelopes, etc.

manilla /məˈnɪlə/ *n.* a metal bracelet used by African tribes as a medium of exchange. [Sp., prob. dimin. of *mano* hand f. L *manus*]

manille /məˈnɪl/ *n.* the second best trump or honour in ombre or quadrille. [F f. Sp. *malilla* dimin. of *mala* bad f. L *malus*]

Man in the Iron Mask a mysterious prisoner in the Bastille and other prisons in 17th-c. France. According to Dumas' novel of the same name, the man was the twin brother of Louis XIV, his face concealed by a mask so as to prevent his recognition, and a threat to Louis' position on the throne. Various other theories as to the identity of the prisoner (who almost certainly did exist) have been advanced, but it is now considered most likely that he was an Italian agent, Count Matthioli, who had seriously annoyed the king.

manioc /ˈmænɪˌɒk/ *n.* **1** cassava. **2** the flour made from it. [Tupi *mandioca*]

maniple /ˈmænɪp(ə)l/ *n.* **1** *Rom.Hist.* a subdivision of a legion, containing 120 or 60 men. **2** a Eucharistic vestment consisting of a strip hanging from the left arm. [OF *maniple* or L *manipulus* handful, troop f. *manus* hand]

manipulate /məˈnɪpjʊˌleɪt/ *v.tr.* **1** handle, treat, or use, esp. skilfully (a tool, question, material, etc.). **2** manage (a person,

situation, etc.) to one's own advantage, esp. unfairly or unscrupulously. **3** manually examine and treat (a part of the body). **4** *Computing* alter, edit, or move (text, data, etc.). **5** stimulate (the genitals). □□ **manipulable** /-ləb(ə)l/ *adj.* **manipulability** /-ləˈbɪlɪtɪ/ *n.* **manipulatable** *adj.* **manipulation** /-ˈleɪʃ(ə)n/ *n.* **manipulator** *n.* **manipulatory** /-ˈlətərɪ/ *adj.* [back-form. f. *manipulation* f. F *manipulation* f. mod.L *manipulatio* (as MANIPLE), after F *manipuler*]

manipulative /məˈnɪpjʊlətɪv/ *adj.* **1** characterized by unscrupulous exploitation of a situation, person, etc., for one's own ends. **2** of or concerning manipulation. □□ **manipulatively** *adv.* **manipulativeness** *n.*

Manipur /ˌmænɪˈpʊə(r)/ a State of India, east of Assam; pop. (1981) 1,433,700; capital, Imphal. □□ **Manipuri** *adj.* & *n.*

Manit. *abbr.* Manitoba.

Manitoba /ˌmænɪˈtəʊbə/ a province of central Canada (from 1870) with a coastline on Hudson Bay. The area was ceded to Canada by the Hudson's Bay Company in 1869; pop. (1986) 1,071,200; capital, Winnipeg.

manitou /ˈmænɪˌtuː/ *n.* *Amer. Ind.* **1** a good or evil spirit as an object of reverence. **2** something regarded as having supernatural power. [Algonquin *manito, -tu* he has surpassed]

mankind *n.* **1** /mænˈkaɪnd/ the human species. **2** /ˈmænkaɪnd/ male people, as distinct from female.

manky /ˈmæŋkɪ/ *adj.* (**mankier, mankiest**) *colloq.* **1** bad, inferior, defective. **2** dirty. [obs. *mank* mutilated, defective]

manlike /ˈmænlaɪk/ *adj.* **1** having the qualities of a man. **2** (of a woman) mannish. **3** (of an animal, shape, etc.) resembling a human being.

manly /ˈmænlɪ/ *adj.* (**manlier, manliest**) **1** having qualities regarded as admirable in a man, such as courage, frankness, etc. **2** (of a woman) mannish. **3** (of things, qualities, etc.) befitting a man. □□ **manliness** *n.*

Mann /mæn/, Thomas (1875–1955), German novelist and essayist who combined elegance and lucidity of style with acute analytical powers. He achieved literary fame with his first novel *Buddenbrooks* (1901), which describes the decline of a merchant family and has strongly autobiographical features. The role and character of the artist in relation to society is a constant theme in his works, and is linked with the problem of Nazism in *Dr Faustus* (1947), in which a composer epitomizes the degeneration of 20th-c. Germany, exposing Nietzsche and Wagner as its sponsors. Originally a man of somewhat conservative sympathies, he caused surprise by quickly lending his public support to the Weimar Republic. When Hitler came to power Mann was forced into exile, and became a US citizen in 1936. He was awarded the Nobel Prize for literature in 1929.

manna /ˈmænə/ *n.* **1** the substance miraculously supplied as food to the Israelites in the wilderness (Exod. 16). **2** an unexpected benefit (esp. *manna from heaven*). **3** spiritual nourishment, esp. the Eucharist. **4** the sweet dried juice from the manna-ash and other plants, used as a mild laxative. □ **manna-ash** an ash tree native to S. Europe, *Fraxinus ornus*. [OE f. LL f. Gk f. Aram. *mannā* f. Heb. *mān*, explained as = *mān hū*? what is it?, but prob. = Arab. *mann* exudation of common tamarisk (*Tamarix gallica*)]

Mannar /mæˈnɑː(r)/ **1** an island off the NW coast of Sri Lanka, linked to India by the chain of coral islands known as Adam's Bridge. **2** a town on this island; pop. (1981) 14,000.

manned /mænd/ *adj.* (of an aircraft, spacecraft, etc.) having a human crew. [past part. of MAN]

mannequin /ˈmænɪkɪn/ *n.* **1** a model employed by a dressmaker etc. to show clothes to customers. **2** a window dummy. [F, = MANIKIN]

manner /ˈmænə(r)/ *n.* **1** a way a thing is done or happens (*always dresses in that manner*). **2** (in *pl.*) **a** social behaviour (*it is bad manners to stare*). **b** polite or well-bred behaviour (*he has no manners*). **c** modes of life; conditions of society. **3** a person's outward bearing, way of speaking, etc. (*has an imperious manner*). **4 a** a style in literature, art, etc. (*in the manner of Rembrandt*). **b** = MANNERISM 2a. **5** *archaic* a kind or sort (*what manner of man is he?*). □ **all manner of** many different kinds of. **comedy of manners** satirical portrayal of social behaviour, esp. of the upper classes.

in a manner of speaking in some sense; to some extent; so to speak. **manner of means** see MEANS. **to the manner born 1** *colloq.* naturally at ease in a specified job, situation, etc. **2** destined by birth to follow a custom or way of life (Shakesp. *Hamlet* I. iv. 17). □□ **mannerless** *adj.* (in sense 2b of *n.*). [ME f. AF *manere*, OF *maniere* ult. f. L *manuarius* of the hand (*manus*)]

mannered /'mænəd/ *adj.* **1** (in *comb.*) behaving in a specified way (*ill-mannered; well-mannered*). **2** (of a style, artist, writer, etc.) showing idiosyncratic mannerisms. **3** (of a person) eccentrically affected in behaviour.

mannerism /'mænəˌrɪz(ə)m/ *n.* **1** a habitual gesture or way of speaking etc.; an idiosyncrasy. **2 a** excessive addiction to a distinctive style in art or literature. **b** a stylistic trick. **3** a style of Italian art preceding the Baroque, characterized by extreme elegance. (See below.) □□ **mannerist** *n.* **manneristic** /-'rɪstɪk/ *adj.* **manneristical** /-'rɪstɪk(ə)l/ *adj.* **manneristically** /-'rɪstɪkəlɪ/ *adv.* [MANNER]

Although the terms *mannerist* and *mannered* are sometimes applied to any art that is excessively refined and affected, *mannerism* is usually reserved for a definable phase of Italian art from c.1530 to 1590, the period after the High Renaissance. The term derives from the Italian word *maniera*, which in the 16th c. had a particular currency as meaning anything (in art or behaviour) that was especially stylish or graceful. It was a quality sought and admired by painters; only in the 17th c. was the term applied negatively, as defining a highly artificial and overwrought (and therefore degenerate) style, and this prejudice was inherited and legitimized in the 19th c. by the first generation of professional art historians. Mannerist art is characterized by a sense of extreme elegance and grace and is often highly imaginative; in stylistic terms it relies on fine drawing and rich, acid, often artificial colour, with a strong sense of movement and contrast. In their use of perspective mannerist painters often sought a self-conscious virtuosity and deliberately played visual tricks. Pontormo, Vasari, and the later Michelangelo (particularly for his *Last Judgement* 1536–41) are among the typical exponents of the mannerist sensibility. The term is sometimes applied to architecture, notably to the buildings of Giulio Romano near Mantua (from 1526) and to Michelangelo's Laurentian Library at Florence (1524–34), where both deliberately infringed the rules of humanist architecture, and created un-classical combinations of classical elements.

mannerly /'mænəlɪ/ *adj. & adv.* —*adj.* well-mannered; polite. —*adv.* politely. □□ **mannerliness** *n.*

Mannheim /'mænhaɪm/ an industrial port on the Rhine in SW Germany; pop. (1987) 294,600.

mannikin var. of MANIKIN.

mannish /'mænɪʃ/ *adj.* **1** usu. *derog.* (of a woman) masculine in appearance or manner. **2** characteristic of a man. □□ **mannishly** *adv.* **mannishness** *n.* [OE *mennisc* f. (and assim. to) MAN]

Mano /'mɑːnəʊ/ a river of West Africa, rising in Liberia and forming for part of its length the boundary between Liberia and Sierra Leone.

manoeuvre /mə'nuːvə(r)/ *n. & v.* (US **maneuver**) —*n.* **1** a planned and controlled movement or series of moves. **2** (in *pl.*) a large-scale exercise of troops, warships, etc. **3 a** an often deceptive planned or controlled action designed to gain an objective. **b** a skilful plan. —*v.* **1** *intr. & tr.* perform or cause to perform a manoeuvre (*manoeuvred the car into the space*). **2** *intr. & tr.* perform or cause (troops etc.) to perform military manoeuvres. **3 a** *tr.* (usu. foll. by *into, out, away*) force, drive, or manipulate (a person, thing, etc.) by scheming or adroitness. **b** *intr.* use artifice. □□ **manoeuvrable** *adj.* **manoeuvrability** /-vrə'bɪlɪtɪ/ *n.* **manoeuvrer** *n.* [F *manœuvre, manœuvrer* f. med.L *manuoperare* f. L *manus* hand + *operari* to work]

manometer /mə'nɒmɪtə(r)/ *n.* a pressure gauge for gases and liquids. □□ **manometric** /ˌmænə'metrɪk/ *adj.* [F *manomètre* f. Gk *manos* thin]

ma non troppo see TROPPO[1].

Mano Pools /'mɑːnəʊ/ a national park in Zimbabwe, established in 1963 in the Zambezi valley, north-east of Lake Kariba.

manor /'mænə(r)/ *n.* **1** (also **manor-house**) **a** a large country house with lands. **b** the house of the lord of the manor. **2** *Brit.* **a** a unit of land consisting of a lord's demesne and lands rented to tenants etc. **b** *hist.* a feudal lordship over lands. **3** *Brit. colloq.* the district covered by a police station. □□ **manorial** /mə'nɔːrɪəl/ *adj.* [ME f. AF *maner*, OF *maneir*, f. L *manēre* remain]

manpower /'mænˌpaʊə(r)/ *n.* **1** the power generated by a man working. **2** the number of people available for work, service, etc.

manqué /'mɒŋkeɪ/ *adj.* (placed after noun) that might have been but is not; unfulfilled (*a comic actor manqué*). [F, past part. of *manquer* lack]

Man Ray see RAY[2].

Mans, Le see LE MANS.

mansard /'mænsɑːd/ *n.* a roof which has four sloping sides, each of which becomes steeper halfway down. The style was popularized by François Mansart (see entry) but had been in existence earlier, e.g. in part of the roof of the Louvre dating from the mid-16th c. [F *mansarde* f. MANSART]

Mansart /mɑ̃'sɑːr/, François (1598–1666), French classical architect. His first major work was the rebuilding of part of the château of Blois, which incorporated the type of roof now named after him (see MANSARD). Other buildings include a number of town houses in Paris, the château of Maisons (1642–6), and the church of Val-de-Grâce (1645), but his uncompromising disposition and obstinate refusal to keep to any final plan for a building led to his being deprived of this and other commissions. His great-nephew by marriage, Jules Hardouin-Mansart (1646–1708), became architect to Louis XIV and from 1678 was in charge of building at Versailles.

manse /mæns/ *n.* the house of a minister, esp. a Scottish Presbyterian. □ **son** (or **daughter**) **of the manse** the child of a Presbyterian etc. minister. [ME f. med.L *mansus, -sa, -sum*, house f. *manēre mans-* remain]

manservant /'mænˌsɜːv(ə)nt/ *n.* (*pl.* **menservants**) a male servant.

Mansfield /'mænsfiːld/, Katherine (Kathleen Mansfield Beauchamp, 1888–1923), New Zealand-born short-story writer. Her stories, influenced by Chekhov, are marked by intensity and poetic feeling and often pathos or irony.

-manship /mənʃɪp/ *suffix* forming nouns denoting skill in a subject or activity (*craftsmanship; gamesmanship*).

mansion /'mænʃ(ə)n/ *n.* **1** a large house. **2** (usu. in *pl.*) *Brit.* a large building divided into flats. □ **mansion-house** *Brit.* the house of a lord mayor or a landed proprietor. **the Mansion House** the official residence of the Lord Mayor in the city of London, built in 1737–53. [ME f. OF f. L *mansio -onis* a staying (as MANSE)]

manslaughter /'mænˌslɔːtə(r)/ *n.* **1** the killing of a human being. **2** *Law* the unlawful killing of a human being without malice aforethought.

mansuetude /'mænswɪˌtjuːd/ *n.* *archaic* meekness, docility, gentleness. [ME f. OF *mansuetude* or L *mansuetudo* f. *mansuetus* gentle, tame f. *manus* hand + *suetus* accustomed]

manta /'mæntə/ *n.* any large ray of the family Mobulidae, esp. *Manta birostris*, having winglike pectoral fins and a whiplike tail. [Amer. Sp., = large blanket]

Mantegna /mæn'tenjə/, Andrea (1431–1506), Italian painter and engraver, noted especially for his frescos, and for oil-paintings which include the *Triumph of Caesar*, bought by Charles I in 1627 and now at Hampton Court. His frescos for the bridal chamber of the ruling family at Mantua, where he was court painter, show portraits of the family arrayed as narrative pictures round the walls in an illusionist style that makes their events seem to be happening in and outside the room, and a ceiling where the centre appears to be open to the sky. Mantegna had a considerable influence on Giovanni Bellini, who was his brother-in-law.

mantel /'mænt(ə)l/ *n.* **1** = MANTELPIECE 1. **2** = MANTELSHELF. [var. of MANTLE]

mantelet /'mæntəlɪt/ *n.* (also **mantlet** /'mæntlɪt/) **1** *hist.* a woman's short loose sleeveless mantle. **2** a bulletproof screen for gunners. [ME f. OF, dimin. of *mantel* MANTLE]

mantelpiece /ˈmænt(ə)lˌpiːs/ n. **1** a structure of wood, marble, etc. above and around a fireplace. **2** = MANTELSHELF.

mantelshelf /ˈmænt(ə)lˌʃelf/ n. a shelf above a fireplace.

mantic /ˈmæntɪk/ adj. formal of or concerning divination or prophecy. [Gk *mantikos* f. *mantis* prophet]

mantid /ˈmæntɪd/ n. = MANTIS.

mantilla /mænˈtɪlə/ n. a lace scarf worn by Spanish women over the hair and shoulders. [Sp., dimin. of *manta* MANTLE]

mantis /ˈmæntɪs/ n. (pl. same or **mantises**) any insect of the family Mantidae, feeding on other insects etc. □ **praying mantis** a mantis, *Mantis religiosa*, that holds its forelegs in a position suggestive of hands folded in prayer, while waiting to pounce on its prey. [Gk, = prophet]

mantissa /mænˈtɪsə/ n. the part of a logarithm after the decimal point. [L, = makeweight]

mantle /ˈmænt(ə)l/ n. & v. —n. **1** a loose sleeveless cloak, esp. of a woman. **2** a covering (*a mantle of snow*). **3** a spiritual influence or authority (see 2 Kings 2: 13). **4** a fragile lacelike tube fixed round a gas-jet to give an incandescent light. **5** an outer fold of skin enclosing a mollusc's viscera. **6** a bird's back, scapulars, and wing-coverts, esp. if of a distinctive colour. **7** the region between the crust and the core of the earth. —v. **1** tr. clothe in or as if in a mantle; cover, conceal, envelop. **2** intr. **a** (of the blood) suffuse the cheeks. **b** (of the face) glow with a blush. **3** intr. (of a liquid) become covered with a coating or scum. [ME f. OF f. L *mantellum* cloak]

mantlet var. of MANTELET.

mantling /ˈmæntlɪŋ/ n. Heraldry **1** ornamental drapery etc. behind and around a shield. **2** a representation of this. [MANTLE + ING¹]

mantra /ˈmæntrə/ n. **1** a sacred syllable, word, or phrase (especially in Buddhism and Hinduism) believed to possess supernatural powers. A personal mantra is given by the guru at initiation and used as an object of meditation. **2** a Vedic hymn. [Skr., = instrument of thought f. *man* think]

mantrap /ˈmæntræp/ n. a trap for catching poachers, trespassers, etc.

mantua /ˈmæntjʊə/ n. hist. a woman's loose gown of the 17th–18th c. [corrupt. of *manteau* (F, as MANTLE) after *Mantua* in Italy]

Manu /ˈmɑːnʊ/ the archetypal first man of Hindu mythology, survivor of the great flood, and father of the human race, and legendary author of the most famous codes of Hindu religious law, the *Manusmriti* (*The Laws of Manu*) composed in Sanskrit and dating in its present form from the 1st c. BC. [Skr., = man (*man* think)]

manual /ˈmænjʊəl/ adj. & n. —adj. **1** of or done with the hands (*manual labour*). **2** (of a machine etc.) worked by hand, not automatically. —n. **1 a** a book of instructions, esp. for operating a machine or learning a subject; a handbook (*a computer manual*). **b** any small book. **2** an organ keyboard played with the hands not the feet. **3** Mil. an exercise in handling a rifle etc. **4** hist. a book of the forms to be used by priests in the administration of the Sacraments. □ **manual alphabet** sign language. □□ **manually** adv. [ME f. OF *manuel*, f. (and later assim. to) L *manualis* f. *manus* hand]

manufactory /ˌmænjʊˈfæktərɪ/ n. (pl. **-ies**) archaic = FACTORY. [MANUFACTURE, after *factory*]

manufacture /ˌmænjʊˈfæktʃə(r)/ n. & v. —n. **1 a** the making of articles esp. in a factory etc. **b** a branch of an industry (*woollen manufacture*). **2** esp. derog. the merely mechanical production of literature, art, etc. —v.tr. **1** make (articles), esp. on an industrial scale. **2** invent or fabricate (evidence, a story, etc.). **3** esp. derog. make or produce (literature, art, etc.) in a mechanical way. □□ **manufacturable** adj. **manufacturability** /-tʃərəˈbɪlɪtɪ/ n. **manufacturer** n. [F f. It. *manifattura* & L *manufactum* made by hand]

manuka /ˈmæˈnuːkə, ˈmɑːnəkə/ n. Austral. & NZ a small tree, *Leptospermum scoparium*, with aromatic leaves and hard timber. [Maori]

manumit /ˌmænjʊˈmɪt/ v.tr. (**manumitted**, **manumitting**) hist. set (a slave) free. □□ **manumission** /-ˈmɪʃ(ə)n/ n. [ME f. L *manumittere manumiss-* f. *manus* hand + *emittere* send forth]

manure /məˈnjʊə(r)/ n. & v. —n. **1** animal dung, esp. of horses, used for fertilizing land. **2** any compost or artificial fertilizer. —v.tr. (also absol.) apply manure to (land etc.). □□ **manurial** adj. [ME f. AF *mainoverer* = OF *manouvrer* MANOEUVRE]

manuscript /ˈmænjʊskrɪpt/ n. & adj. —n. **1** a book, document, etc. written by hand. **2** an author's handwritten or typed text, submitted for publication. **3** handwritten form (*produced in manuscript*). —adj. written by hand. [med.L *manuscriptus* f. *manu* by hand + *scriptus* past part. of *scribere* write]

Manx /mæŋks/ adj. & n. —adj. of or relating to the Isle of Man or its people or language. —n. **1** the Celtic language of the Isle of Man, a dialect of Gaelic. There are no native speakers alive now but it is still in use for ceremonial purposes. **2** (prec. by *the*; treated as pl.) the Manx people. □ **Manx cat** a tailless cat. [ON f. OIr. *Manu* Isle of Man]

Manxman /ˈmæŋksmən/ n. (pl. **-men**; fem. **Manxwoman**, pl. **-women**) a native of the Isle of Man.

many /ˈmenɪ/ adj. & n. —adj. (**more** /mɔː(r)/; **most** /məʊst/) great in number; numerous (*many times; many people; many a person; his reasons were many*). —n. (as pl.) **1** a large number (*many like skiing; many went*). **2** (prec. by *the*) the multitude of esp. working people. □ **as many** the same number of (*six mistakes in as many lines*). **as many again** the same number additionally (*sixty here and as many again there*). **be too** (or **one too**) **many for** outwit, baffle. **a good** (or **great**) **many** a large ,number. **many-sided** having many sides, aspects, interests, capabilities, etc. **many-sidedness** n. the fact or state of being many-sided. **many's the time** often (*many's the time we saw it*). **many a time** many times. [OE *manig*, ult. f. Gmc]

manzanilla /ˌmænzəˈnɪlə/ n. a pale very dry Spanish sherry. [Sp., lit. 'camomile']

manzanita /ˌmænzəˈniːtə/ n. any of several evergreen shrubs of the genus *Arctostaphylos*, esp. *A. manzanita*, native to California. [Sp., dimin. of *manzana* apple]

Manzoni /mænˈtsəʊnɪ/, Alessandro (1785–1873), Italian novelist, dramatist, and poet, author of the greatest of Italian historical novels *I promessi sposi* (*The Betrothed*, 1825–42). The novel (which had immense patriotic appeal) is set in Lombardy in 1628–31, during the period of Spanish administration, and is remarkable for its powerful characterization of historical figures and ordinary people and for its coherent reconstruction of events.

Maoism /ˈmaʊɪz(ə)m/ n. the Communist doctrines of Mao Zedong. □□ **Maoist** n. & adj.

Maori /ˈmaʊrɪ/ n. & adj. —n. (pl. same or **Maoris**) **1** a member of the brown aboriginal people of New Zealand. Having arrived there first as part of a wave of migration from Tahiti, probably in the 9th c., by 1200 they had established settlements in various parts of the islands. The Maoris now number about 280,000. **2** their Polynesian language, spoken by about 100,000 persons in New Zealand. —adj. of or relating to the Maori or their language. □ **Maori Wars** wars fought intermittently in 1845–8 and 1860–72 between Maoris and the colonial government of New Zealand over the enforced sale of Maori lands to Europeans (see WAITANGI). [native name]

Mao Zedong /maʊ dziːˈdʊŋ/ (also **Mao Tse-tung** /tsiːˈtʊŋ/, 1893–1976) Chinese statesman, whose leadership of the Long March (see entry) established him as the effective leader of the Communist party. Mao was successful in organizing and uniting peasant forces, to whom he gave central importance, and eventually defeated both the occupying Japanese and rival Chinese nationalist forces to form, in 1949, the Chinese People's Republic of which he became President. He resigned as Head of State in 1959 but retained his position as chairman of the Communist Party.

map /mæp/ n. & v. —n. **1 a** a usu. flat representation of the earth's surface, or part of it, showing physical features, cities, etc. (cf. GLOBE). **b** a diagrammatic representation of a route etc. (*drew a map of the journey*). **2** a two-dimensional representation of the stars, the heavens, etc., or of the surface of a planet, the moon, etc. **3** a diagram showing the arrangement or components of a thing. **4** *sl.* the face. —*v.tr.* (**mapped, mapping**) **1** represent (a country etc.) on a map. **2** *Math.* associate each element of (a set) with one element of another set. □ **map out** arrange in detail; plan (a course of conduct etc.). **off the map** *colloq.* **1** of no account; obsolete. **2** very distant. **on the map** *colloq.* prominent, important. **wipe off the map** *colloq.* obliterate. □□ **mapless** *adj.* **mappable** *adj.* **mapper** *n.* [L *mappa* napkin: in med.L *mappa (mundi)* map (of the world)]

maple /ˈmeɪp(ə)l/ *n.* **1** any tree or shrub of the genus *Acer* grown for shade, ornament, wood, or its sugar. **2** the wood of the maple. □ **maple-leaf** the leaf of the maple, used as an emblem of Canada. **maple sugar** a sugar produced by evaporating the sap of the sugar maple etc. **maple syrup** a syrup produced from the sap of the sugar maple etc. [ME *mapul* etc. f. OE *mapeltrēow, mapulder*]

Maputo /məˈpuːtəʊ/ the capital and chief port of Mozambique; pop. (est. 1986) 882,800.

maquette /məˈket/ *n.* **1** a sculptor's small preliminary model in wax, clay, etc. **2** a preliminary sketch. [F f. It. *machietta* dimin. of *macchia* spot]

maquillage /ˌmækiːˈjɑːʒ/ *n.* **1** make-up; cosmetics. **2** the application of make-up. [F f. *maquiller* make up f. OF *masquiller* stain]

Maquis /mæˈkiː/ *n.* **1** the French resistance movement during the German occupation (1940–5). **2** a member of this. [F, = brushwood, f. Corsican It. *macchia* thicket (traditionally used as a refuge by fugitives)]

Mar. *abbr.* March.

mar /mɑː(r)/ *v.tr.* (**marred, marring**) **1** ruin. **2** impair the perfection of; spoil; disfigure. [OE *merran* hinder]

marabou /ˈmærəˌbuː/ *n.* (also **marabout**) **1** a large W. African stork, *Leptoptilos crumeniferus*. **2** a tuft of down from the wing or tail of the marabou used as a trimming for hats etc. [F f. Arab. *murābiṭ* holy man (see MARABOUT), the stork being regarded as holy]

marabout /ˈmærəˌbuːt/ *n.* **1** a Muslim hermit or monk, esp. in N. Africa. **2** a shrine marking a marabout's burial-place. [F f. Port. *marabuto* f. Arab. *murābiṭ* holy man f. *ribāṭ* frontier station, where he acquired merit by combat against the infidel]

maraca /məˈrækə/ *n.* a hollow clublike gourd or gourd-shaped container filled with beans or beads etc. and usu. shaken in pairs as a percussion instrument in Latin American music. [Port. *maracá*, prob. f. Tupi]

Maracaibo /ˌmærəˈkaɪbəʊ/ **1** the largest lake in South America, a large inlet of the Caribbean Sea in NW Venezuela, developed since 1918 as one of the greatest oil-producing regions of the world. **2** a city on the NW shore at the outlet of the lake, the second-largest seaport of Venezuela; pop. (1981) 890,500.

Maramba /məˈræmbə/ the capital of Southern province in Zambia, situated about 5 km (3 miles) from the River Zambezi and the Victoria Falls; pop. (est. 1987) 94,600. Formerly called Livingstone in honour of the explorer, it was the capital of Northern Rhodesia 1911–35.

Marañón /ˌmærænˈjəʊn/ a river of Peru that rises in the Andes and forms one of the principal headwaters of the Amazon.

maraschino /ˌmærəˈskiːnəʊ/ *n.* (pl. **-os**) a strong sweet liqueur made from a small black Dalmatian cherry. □ **maraschino cherry** a cherry preserved in maraschino and used to decorate cocktails etc. [It. f. *marasca* small black cherry, for *amarasca* f. *amaro* bitter f. L *amarus*]

marasmus /məˈræzməs/ *n.* a wasting away of the body. □□ **marasmic** *adj.* [mod.L f. Gk *marasmos* f. *marainō* wither]

Marat /ˈmærɑː/, Jean Paul (1743–93), French revolutionary. A doctor by training, Marat made a reputation for himself during the early days of the French Revolution as one of the most virulent critics of the moderate Girondins. His murder in his bath by a Royalist fanatic, Charlotte Corday, was used as a pretext by Robespierre and the Jacobins to purge their Girondin rivals.

Maratha /məˈrɑːtə, -ˈrætə/ *n.* (also **Mahratta**) a member of a warrior people native to the modern Indian State of Maharashtra. [Hindi *Marhaṭṭa* f. Skr. *Māhārāshṭra* great kingdom]

Marathi /məˈrɑːtɪ, -ˈrætɪ/ *n.* (also **Mahratti**) the language of the Marathas. [MARATHA]

marathon /ˈmærəθ(ə)n/ *n.* **1** a long-distance running race over roads, usu. of 26 miles 385 yards (42.195 km). (See below.) **2** a long-lasting or difficult task, operation, etc. (often *attrib.*: *a marathon shopping expedition*). □□ **marathoner** *n.*

The marathon is a principal event of modern Olympic Games (from 1896 onwards); similar races, open to applicants, are run through the streets in certain cities, e.g. in Boston (annually from 1897) and London (from 1891). It is named after the Marathon in Greece, scene of an Athenian victory over an invading Persian army in 490 BC. Herodotus records that Pheidippides (see entry) ran from Athens to Sparta to secure aid before the battle, but the race instituted in 1896 was based on a later and less sound tradition that a messenger ran from Marathon to Athens with news of the victory and fell dead on arrival.

maraud /məˈrɔːd/ *v.* **1** *intr.* **a** make a plundering raid. **b** pilfer systematically; plunder. **2** *tr.* plunder (a place). □□ **marauder** *n.* [F *marauder* f. *maraud* rogue]

marble /ˈmɑːb(ə)l/ *n. & v.* —*n.* **1** limestone in a metamorphic crystalline (or granular) state, and capable of taking a polish, used in sculpture and architecture. **2** (often *attrib.*). **a** anything made of marble (*a marble clock*). **b** anything resembling marble in hardness, coldness, durability, etc. (*her features were marble*). **3 a** a small ball of marble, glass, clay, etc., used as a toy. **b** (in *pl.*; treated as *sing.*) a game using these. **4** (in *pl.*) *sl.* one's mental faculties (*he's lost his marbles*). **5** (in *pl.*) a collection of sculptures (*Elgin Marbles*). —*v.tr.* **1** (esp. as **marbled** *adj.*) stain or colour (paper, the edges of a book, soap, etc.) to look like variegated marble. **2** (as **marbled** *adj.*) (of meat) streaked with alternating layers of lean and fat. □ **marble cake** a cake with a mottled appearance, made of light and dark sponge. □□ **marbly** *adj.* [ME f. OF *marbre*, *marble*, f. L *marmor* f. Gk *marmaros* shining stone]

Marble Arch an arch with three gateways erected in 1827 in front of Buckingham Palace, and moved in 1851 to its present site at the NE corner of Hyde Park.

marbling /ˈmɑːblɪŋ/ *n.* **1** colouring or marking like marble. **2** streaks of fat in lean meat.

marc /mɑːk/ *n.* **1** the refuse of pressed grapes etc. **2** a brandy made from this. [F f. *marcher* tread, MARCH[1]]

Marcan /ˈmɑːkən/ *adj.* of or relating to St Mark. [L *Marcus* Mark]

marcasite /ˈmɑːkəˌsaɪt/ *n.* **1** a yellowish crystalline iron sulphide mineral. **2** these bronze-yellow crystals used in jewellery. [ME f. med.L *marcasita*, f. Arab. *marḳaṣīṭā* f. Pers.]

marcato /mɑːˈkɑːtəʊ/ *adv. & adj. Mus.* played with emphasis. [It., = marked]

marcel /mɑːˈsel/ *n. & v.* —*n.* (in full **marcel wave**) a deep wave in the hair. —*v.tr.* (**marcelled, marcelling**) wave (hair) with a deep wave. [*Marcel* Grateau, Paris hairdresser d. 1936, who invented the method]

marcescent /mɑːˈses(ə)nt/ *adj.* (of part of a plant) withering but not falling. □□ **marcescence** *n.* [L *marcescere* incept. of *marcēre* wither]

March /mɑːtʃ/ *n.* the third month of the year. □ **March hare** a hare in the breeding season (March), characterized by excessive leaping, strange behaviour, etc. (*mad as a March hare*). [ME f. OF *march(e)*, dial. var. of *marz, mars*, f. L *Martius (mensis)* (month) of Mars, several of whose festivals were held in this month; it was orig. the first month of year and the months September–December were counted from here.]

march[1] /mɑːtʃ/ *v. & n.* —*v.* **1** *intr.* (usu. foll. by *away, off, out,* etc.) walk in a military manner with a regular measured tread. **2** *tr.* (often foll. by *away, on, off,* etc.) cause to march or walk (*marched the army to Moscow; marched him out of the room*). **3** *intr.* **a** walk or proceed steadily, esp. across country. **b** (of events etc.) continue unrelentingly (*time marches on*). **4** *intr.* take part in a protest march. —*n.* **1 a** the act or an instance of marching. **b** the uniform step of troops etc. (*a slow march*). **2** a long difficult walk. **3** a procession as a protest or demonstration. **4** (usu. foll.

by *of*) progress or continuity (*the march of events*). **5 a** a piece of music composed to accompany a march. **b** a composition of similar character and form. □ **marching order** *Mil.* equipment or a formation for marching. **marching orders 1** *Mil.* the direction for troops to depart for war etc. **2** a dismissal (*gave him his marching orders*). **march on 1** advance towards (a military objective). **2** proceed. **march past** *n.* the marching of troops past a saluting-point at a review. —*v.intr.* (of troops) carry out a march past. **on the march 1** marching. **2** in steady progress. □□ **marcher** *n.* [F *marche* (n.), *marcher* (v.), f. LL *marcus* hammer]

march² /maːtʃ/ *n. & v.* —*n. hist.* **1** (usu. in *pl.*) a boundary, a frontier (esp. of the borderland between England and Scotland or Wales). **2** a tract of often disputed land between two countries. —*v.intr.* (foll. by *upon, with*) (of a country, an estate, etc.) have a common frontier with, border on. [ME f. OF *marche, marchir* ult. f. Gmc: cf. MARK¹]

Marche /ˈmaːkeɪ/ (English **the Marches**) a region of east central Italy, between the Apennines and the Adriatic Sea; pop. (1981) 1,414,400; capital, Ancona. [= MARCH²]

marcher /ˈmaːtʃə(r)/ *n.* an inhabitant of a march or border district.

marchioness /ˌmaːʃəˈnes, ˈmaː-/ *n.* **1** the wife or widow of a marquess. **2** a woman holding the rank of marquess in her own right (cf. MARQUISE). [med.L *marchionissa* f. *marchio -onis* captain of the marches (as MARCH²)]

marchpane /ˈmaːtʃpeɪn/ *archaic* var. of MARZIPAN.

Marciano /maːsɪˈaːnəʊ/, Rocky (real name Rocco Francis Marchegiano, 1923–69), American boxer, world heavyweight champion from 1952 until he retired, undefeated, in 1956.

Marconi /maːˈkəʊnɪ/, Guglielmo (1874–1937), Italian electrical engineer, generally regarded as the father of radio. His achievement lay in appreciating the potential of earlier work by Heinrich Hertz on electric waves and of Oliver Lodge's coherer for their detection. Marconi demonstrated radio transmission over a distance of a mile at Bologna in 1895, and by 1901 he was able to transmit a signal across the Atlantic from Poldhu in Cornwall to St John's in Newfoundland. By 1912 he could produce a continuously oscillating wave, essential for transmission of sounds other than Morse code, and went on to develop short-wave transmission over long distances. Shipowners and navies were enthusiastic, and among the first customers were Lloyd's of London. In 1909 he was awarded the Nobel Prize for physics. Marconi had great business ability and set up companies (which flourished) to exploit his work.

Marco Polo /ˌmaːkəʊ ˈpəʊləʊ/ (*c*.1254–*c*.1324), Venetian traveller. Between 1271 and 1275 he accompanied his father and uncle on a journey east from Acre into central Asia, eventually reaching China and the court of Kublai Khan. Polo entered the Mongol diplomatic service, travelling widely in the empire for a decade and a half before returning home (1292–5) via Sumatra, India, and Persia. Captured by the Genoese in 1298, he dictated the story of his travels to a fellow inmate during a year of imprisonment. His book was widely read in subsequent years, adding considerable impetus to the European quest to discover the riches of the East.

Marcus Aurelius see AURELIUS.

Mar del Plata /maː del ˈplaːtə/ a popular resort and fishing centre on the Atlantic coast of central Argentina; pop. (1980) 407,000.

Mardi Gras /ˌmaːdɪ ˈɡraː/ *n.* **1 a** Shrove Tuesday in some Catholic countries. **b** merrymaking on this day. **2** the last day of a carnival etc. **3** *Austral.* a carnival or fair at any time. [F, = fat Tuesday]

Marduk /ˈmaːdʊk/ *Babylonian Mythol.* the chief god of Babylon, also called Bel (= Lord), who became lord of the gods of heaven and earth after conquering Tiamat, the monster of primeval chaos.

mardy /ˈmaːdɪ/ *adj. dial.* sulky, whining, spoilt. [dial. *mard* spoilt, alt. of *marred* f. MAR]

mare¹ /meə(r)/ *n.* **1** the female of any equine animal, esp. the horse. **2** *sl. derog.* a woman. □ **mare's nest** an illusory discovery. **mare's tail 1** a tall slender marsh plant, *Hippuris vulgaris*. **2** (in

pl.) long straight streaks of cirrus cloud. [ME f. OE *mearh* horse f. Gmc: cf. MARSHAL]

mare² /ˈmaːreɪ/ *n.* (*pl.* **maria** /ˈmaːrɪə/ or **mares**) **1** (in full **mare clausum** /ˈklaʊsʊm/) *Law* the sea under the jurisdiction of a particular country. **2** (in full **mare liberum** /ˈliːbərʊm/) *Law* the sea open to all nations. **3 a** any of a number of large dark flat areas on the surface of the moon, once thought to be seas. **b** a similar area on Mars. [L, = sea]

maremma /məˈremə/ *n.* (*pl.* **maremme** /-mɪ/) low marshy unhealthy land near a seashore. [It. f. L *maritima* (as MARITIME)]

Marengo /məˈreŋɡəʊ/ a village near Turin, scene of a decisive French victory of Napoleon's campaign in Italy in 1800. After military reverses had all but destroyed French power in Italy, Napoleon crossed the Alps to defeat and capture an Austrian army, returning Italy to French possession.

Margaret /ˈmaːɡərɪt/, St (*c*.1046–93), Scottish queen, wife of Malcolm III. She exerted a strong influence over royal policy during her husband's reign, and was canonized for her reform of the Scottish Church.

margarine /ˌmaːdʒəˈriːn, ˌmaːɡə-, ˈmaː-/ *n.* a butter-substitute made from vegetable oils or animal fats with milk etc. The world's first substitute food, it was first developed in France in the mid-19th c. [F, misapplication of a chem. term, f. *margarique* f. Gk *margaron* pearl]

Margarita /ˌmaːɡəˈriːtə/ an island resort and free port of Venezuela, in the Caribbean Sea.

margay /ˈmaːɡeɪ/ *n.* a small wild S. American cat, *Felis wiedii*. [F f. Tupi *mbaracaia*]

marge¹ /maːdʒ/ *n. Brit. colloq.* margarine. [abbr.]

marge² /maːdʒ/ *n. poet.* a margin or edge. [F f. L *margo* (as MARGIN)]

margin /ˈmaːdʒɪn/ *n. & v.* —*n.* **1** the edge or border of a surface. **2 a** the blank border on each side of the print on a page etc. **b** a line ruled esp. on exercise paper, marking off a margin. **3** an amount (of time, money, etc.) by which a thing exceeds, falls short, etc. (*won by a narrow margin; a margin of profit*). **4** the lower limit of possibility, success, etc. (*his effort fell below the margin*). **5** *Austral.* an increment to a basic wage, paid for skill. **6** a sum deposited with a stockbroker to cover the risk of loss on a transaction on account. —*v.tr.* (**margined, margining**) provide with a margin or marginal notes. □ **margin of error** a usu. small difference allowed for miscalculation, change of circumstances, etc. **margin release** a device on a typewriter allowing a word to be typed beyond the margin normally set. [ME f. L *margo -ginis*]

marginal /ˈmaːdʒɪn(ə)l/ *adj.* **1 a** of or written in a margin. **b** having marginal notes. **2 a** of or at the edge; not central. **b** not significant or decisive (*the work is of merely marginal interest*). **3** *Brit.* (of a parliamentary seat or constituency) having a small majority at risk in an election. **4** close to the limit, esp. of profitability. **5** (of the sea) adjacent to the shore of a State. **6** (of land) difficult to cultivate; unprofitable. **7** barely adequate; unprovided for. □ **marginal cost** the cost added by making one extra copy etc. □□ **marginality** /-ˈnælɪtɪ/ *n.* **marginally** *adv.* [med.L *marginalis* (as MARGIN)]

marginalia /ˌmaːdʒɪˈneɪlɪə/ *n.pl.* marginal notes. [med.L, neut. pl. of *marginalis*]

marginalize /ˈmaːdʒɪnəˌlaɪz/ *v.tr.* (also **-ise**) make or treat as insignificant. □□ **marginalization** /-ˈzeɪʃ(ə)n/ *n.*

marginate *v. & adj.* —*v.tr.* /ˈmaːdʒɪˌneɪt/ **1** = MARGINALIZE. **2** provide with a margin or border. —*adj.* /ˈmaːdʒɪnət/ *Biol.* having a distinct margin or border. □□ **margination** /-ˈneɪʃ(ə)n/ *n.*

margrave /ˈmaːɡreɪv/ *n. hist.* the hereditary title of some princes of the Holy Roman Empire (orig. of a military governor of a border province). □□ **margravate** /ˈmaːɡrəvət/ *n.* [MDu. *markgrave* border count (as MARK¹, *grave* COUNT² f. OLG *grève*)]

margravine /ˈmaːɡrəˌviːn/ *n. hist.* the wife of a margrave. [Du. *markgravin* (as MARGRAVE)]

marguerite /ˌmaːɡəˈriːt/ *n.* an ox-eye daisy. [F f. L *margarita* f. Gk *margarītēs* f. *margaron* pearl]

Mari /ˈmaːrɪ/ an ancient city on the west bank of the Euphrates, in Syria. Its strategic position commanding major trade routes ensured rapid growth, and by *c.*2500 BC it was thriving, influenced by Sumerian culture. Its period of greatest importance and individuality was from the late 19th–mid 18th c. BC, when it was a kingdom with hegemony over the middle Euphrates valley. The vast palace of the last king, Zimrilim, famous in its day, has yielded an archive of 25,000 tablets, inscribed in cuneiform, which are the principal source for the history of northern Syria and Mesopotamia at that time. The city was sacked by Hammurabi of Babylon in 1759 BC.

maria *pl.* of MARE².

mariage de convenance /ˌmærɪˌɑːʒ də ˌkɔ̃vəˈnɑ̃s/ *n.* = marriage of convenience. [F]

Marian /ˈmeərɪən/ *adj.* RC Ch. of or relating to the Virgin Mary (*Marian vespers*). [L *Maria* Mary]

Mariana Islands /ˌmærɪˈɑːnə/ (also **Marianas**) a group of islands in the NW Pacific, visited by Magellan in 1521 and named Las Marianas in 1668 in honour of Maria Anna (Mariana), widow of Philip IV of Spain. They comprise Guam (see entry) and the islands and atolls of the Northern Marianas. In 1947 the whole group became part of the Trust Territory of the Pacific Islands, administered by the US; in 1975 the islanders of the Northern Marianas voted to establish a commonwealth (self-governing since 1978) in union with the US. The ocean trench **Mariana Trench**) to the south-east of the islands is the greatest known ocean depth (11,033 m, 36,198 ft.).

Maria Theresa /məˌraɪə (-ˌriːə) təˈriːsə (-ˈreɪzə)/ (1717–80) Archduchess of Austria, queen of Hungary and Bohemia 1740–80. The daughter of the Emperor Charles VI, Maria Theresa married the future Emperor Francis I in 1736 and succeeded to the Hapsburg dominions in 1740 by virtue of the Pragmatic Sanction. Her accession was the occasion of the War of the Austrian Succession (1740–8) in which Silesia was lost to Frederick the Great of Prussia. She strengthened and reformed Austria-Hungary, but once again suffered at the hands of the Prussians in the Seven Years War (1756–63). After the death of Francis I in 1765 she ruled, until her death, in conjunction with her son, the Emperor Joseph II.

Marie Antoinette /ˈmɑːrɪ ˌætwɑːˈnet/ (1755–93), queen of France. An Austrian princess, Marie Antoinette married the future Louis XVI of France in 1770, becoming queen four years later. Her lack of formal education minimized her ability to participate in State affairs, while her reckless spending severely strained royal finances and won her widespread unpopularity. Like her husband she was eventually imprisoned during the French Revolution, and was finally executed in October 1793.

marigold /ˈmærɪˌɡəʊld/ *n.* any plant of the genus *Calendula* or *Tagetes*, with golden or bright yellow flowers. [ME f. *Mary* (prob. the Virgin) + dial. *gold*, OE *golde*, prob. rel. to GOLD]

marijuana /ˌmærɪˈhwɑːnə/ *n.* (also **marihuana**) 1 the dried leaves, flowering tops, and stems of the hemp, used as a hallucinogenic drug usu. smoked in cigarettes. 2 the plant yielding these (cf. HEMP). [Amer. Sp.]

marimba /məˈrɪmbə/ *n.* 1 a xylophone played by natives of Africa and Central America. 2 a modern orchestral instrument derived from this. [Congo]

marina /məˈriːnə/ *n.* a specially designed harbour with moorings for pleasure-yachts etc. [It. & Sp. fem. adj. f. *marino* f. L (as MARINE)]

marinade /ˌmærɪˈneɪd, ˈmæ-/ *n. & v.* — *n.* 1 a mixture of wine, vinegar, oil, spices, etc., in which meat, fish, etc., is soaked before cooking. 2 meat, fish, etc., soaked in this liquid. — *v.tr.* soak (meat, fish, etc.) in a marinade. [F f. Sp. *marinada* f. *marinar* pickle in brine f. *marino* (as MARINE)]

marinate /ˈmærɪˌneɪt/ *v.tr.* = MARINADE. □□ **marination** /-ˈneɪʃ(ə)n/ *n.* [It. *marinare* or F *mariner* (as MARINE)]

marine /məˈriːn/ *adj. & n.* — *adj.* 1 of, found in, or produced by the sea. 2 **a** of or relating to shipping or naval matters (*marine insurance*). **b** for use at sea. — *n.* 1 a country's shipping, fleet, or navy (*mercantile marine*; *merchant marine*). 2 a member of a body of troops trained to serve on land or sea. In Britain, the Corps of the Royal Marines (see entry), first formed in 1664, is part of

the Royal Navy. The US Marine Corps was formed in 1775. 3 a picture of a scene at sea. □ **marine stores** new or old ships' material etc. sold as merchandise. **marine trumpet** a large single-stringed viol with a trumpet-like tone. **tell that to the marines** (or **horse marines**) *colloq.* an expression of disbelief. [ME f. OF *marin marine* f. L *marinus* f. *mare* sea]

Mariner /ˈmærɪnə(r)/ a series of US planetary probes (1962–77). Mariners 1 and 8 suffered launch failure, 2 and 5 made close-up observations of Venus, 3 failed to achieve its intended trajectory, 4, 6, 7, and 9 were successful probes to Mars, 10 visited Venus and Mercury, 11 and 12 were renamed Voyager 1 and 2.

mariner /ˈmærɪnə(r)/ *n.* a seaman. □ **mariner's compass** a compass showing magnetic or true north and the bearings from it. [ME f. AF *mariner*, OF *marinier* f. med.L *marinarius* f. L (as MARINE)]

Marinetti /ˌmærɪˈneti/, Filippo Tommaso (1876–1944), Italian dramatist, poet, and novelist. He launched the futurist movement in his Manifesto, published in *Le Figaro* (1909), which exalted the machine age, glorified war, and demanded revolution and innovation in the arts. In his poems he abandoned syntax and grammar, and pioneered visual poetry; in the theatre he destroyed the barriers between stage and audience, staged unrelated actions simultaneously, and initiated the 'synthetic' play. He has profoundly influenced 20th-c. culture but his reputation has been compromised by his support for Fascism.

Mariolatry /ˌmeərɪˈɒlətrɪ/ *n. derog.* idolatrous worship of the Virgin Mary. [L *Maria* Mary + -LATRY, after *idolatry*]

marionette /ˌmærɪəˈnet/ *n.* a puppet worked by strings. [F *marionnette* f. *Marion* dimin. of *Marie* Mary]

Marist /ˈmɑːrɪst/ *n.* a member of the Roman Catholic Society of Mary. [F *Mariste* f. *Marie* Mary]

marital /ˈmærɪt(ə)l/ *adj.* 1 of marriage or the relations between husband and wife. 2 of or relating to a husband. □□ **maritally** *adv.* [L *maritalis* f. *maritus* husband]

maritime /ˈmærɪˌtaɪm/ *adj.* 1 connected with the sea or seafaring (*maritime insurance*). 2 living or found near the sea. [L *maritimus* f. *mare* sea]

Maritime Provinces (also **Maritimes**) the Canadian Provinces of New Brunswick, Nova Scotia, Prince Edward Island, and sometimes Newfoundland, with coastlines on the Gulf of St Lawrence or the Atlantic.

Maritsa /məˈrɪtsə/ a river that rises in the Rila Mountains of Bulgaria and empties into the Aegean Sea. It forms the frontier between Bulgaria and Greece for a small part of its length and that between Greece and Turkey for about 185 km (115 miles). In Greece it is called the Hebros, in Turkish the Meric.

Mariupol /ˌmærɪˈuːpɒl/ an industrial port of the Soviet Union, on the Azov Sea; pop. (est. 1987) 529,000. Between 1948 and 1989 it was named Zhdanov after Andrei Zhdanov, the defender of Leningrad.

Marius /ˈmærɪəs/, Gaius (*c.*157–86 BC), Roman general and politician. A 'new man' (i.e. not of the old aristocracy), his political power was based on popular and military support. Consul for the first time in 107 BC, he established his dominance by victories over Jugurtha and invading Germanic tribes, and reformed the Roman army. Subsequently in and out of power, he was expelled from Italy by Sulla, only to return and take Rome by force in 87 BC. He died in the following year.

marjoram /ˈmɑːdʒərəm/ *n.* either of two aromatic herbs, *Origanum vulgare* (**wild marjoram**) or *Majorana hortensis* (**sweet marjoram**), the fresh or dried leaves of which are used as a flavouring in cookery. [ME & OF *majorane* f. med.L *majorana*, of unkn. orig.]

Mark /mɑːk/, St 1 an Apostle, companion of St Peter and St Paul, traditional author of the second Gospel. Feast day, 25 April. 2 the second Gospel (the earliest in date).

mark¹ /mɑːk/ *n. & v.* — *n.* 1 a trace, sign, stain, scar, etc., on a surface, face, page, etc. 2 (esp. in *comb.*) **a** a written or printed symbol (*exclamation mark*; *question mark*). **b** a numerical or alphabetical award denoting excellence, conduct, proficiency, etc. (*got a good mark for effort*; *gave him a black mark*; *gained 46 marks out of 50*). 3 (usu. foll. by *of*) a sign or indication of quality, character, feeling, etc. (*took off his hat as a mark of respect*). **4 a** a sign, seal, etc., used for distinction or identification. **b** a cross etc. made in place of a signature by an illiterate person. **5 a** a target, object, goal, etc. (*missed the mark with his first play*). **b** a standard for attainment (*his work falls below the mark*). **6** a line etc. indicating a position; a marker. **7** (usu. **Mark**) (followed by a numeral) a particular design, model, etc., of a car, aircraft, etc. (*this is the Mark 2 model*). **8** a runner's starting-point in a race. **9** *Naut.* a piece of material etc. used to indicate a position on a sounding-line. **10 a** *Rugby Football* a heel-mark on the ground made by a player who has caught the ball direct from a kick, knock-on, or throw-forward by an opponent. **b** *Austral. Rules* the catching before it reaches the ground of a ball kicked at least ten metres; the spot from which the subsequent kick is taken. **11** *sl.* the intended victim of a swindler etc. **12** *Boxing* the pit of the stomach. **13** *hist.* a tract of land held in common by a Teutonic or medieval German village community. —*v.tr.* **1 a** make a mark on (a thing or person), esp. by writing, cutting, scraping, etc. **b** put a distinguishing or identifying mark, initials, name, etc., on (clothes etc.) (*marked the tree with their initials*). **2 a** allot marks to; correct (a student's work etc.). **b** record (the points gained in games etc.). **3** attach a price to (goods etc.) (*marked the doll at 50p*). **4** (often foll. by *by*) show or manifest (displeasure etc.) (*marked his anger by leaving early*). **5** notice or observe (*she marked his agitation*). **6 a** characterize or be a feature of (*the day was marked by storms*). **b** acknowledge, recognize, celebrate (*marked the occasion with a toast*). **7** name or indicate (a place on a map, the length of a syllable, etc.) by a sign or mark. **8** characterize (a person or a thing) as (*marked them as weak*). **9 a** *Brit.* keep close to so as to prevent the free movement of (an opponent in sport). **b** *Austral. Rules* catch (the ball). **10** (as **marked** *adj.*) having natural marks (*is marked with silver spots*). **11** (of a graduated instrument) show, register (so many degrees etc.). **12** *US & Austral.* castrate (a lamb). □ **one's mark** *colloq.* **1** what one prefers. **2** an opponent, object, etc., of one's own size, calibre, etc. (*the little one's more my mark*). **beside** (or **off** or **wide of**) **the mark 1** not to the point; irrelevant. **2** not accurate. **make one's mark** attain distinction. **mark down 1** mark (goods etc.) at a lower price. **2** make a written note of. **3** choose (a person) as one's victim. **mark-down** *n.* a reduction in price. **mark off** (often foll. by *from*) separate (one thing from another) by a boundary etc. (*marked off the subjects for discussion*). **mark of mouth** a depression in a horse's incisor indicating age. **mark out 1** plan (a course of action etc.). **2** destine (*marked out for success*). **3** trace out boundaries, a course, etc. **mark time 1** *Mil.* march on the spot, without moving forward. **2** act routinely; go through the motions. **3** await an opportunity to advance. **mark up 1** mark (goods etc.) at a higher price. **2** mark or correct (text etc.) for typesetting or alteration. **mark-up** *n.* **1** the amount added to the cost price of goods to cover overhead charges, profit, etc. **2** the corrections made in marking up text. **mark you** please note (*without obligation, mark you*). **off the mark 1** having made a start. **2** = *beside the mark*. **of mark** noteworthy. **on the mark** ready to start. **on your mark** (or **marks**) (as an instruction) get ready to start (esp. a race). **up to the mark** reaching the usual or normal standard, esp. of health. [OE *me(a)rc* (n.), *mearcian* (v.), f. Gmc]

mark² /maːk/ *n.* **1 a** = DEUTSCHMARK. **b** *hist.* **2** *hist.* **a** a denomination of weight for gold and silver. **b** English money of account. [OE *marc*, prob. rel. to med.L *marca, marcus*]

Mark Antony see ANTONY².

marked /maːkt/ *adj.* **1** having a visible mark. **2** clearly noticeable; evident (*a marked difference*). **3** (of playing-cards) having distinctive marks on their backs to assist cheating. □ **marked man 1** a person whose conduct is watched with suspicion or hostility. **2** a person destined to succeed. □□ **markedly** /-kɪdlɪ/ *adv.* **markedness** /-kɪdnɪs/ *n.* [OE (past part. of MARK¹)]

marker /ˈmaːkə(r)/ *n.* **1** a stone, post, etc., used to mark a position, place reached, etc. **2** a person or thing that marks. **3** a felt-tipped pen with a broad tip. **4** a person who records a score, esp. in billiards. **5** a flare etc. used to direct a pilot to a target. **6** a bookmark. **7** *US sl.* a promissory note; an IOU.

market /ˈmaːkɪt/ *n. & v.* —*n.* **1 a** the gathering of people for the purchase and sale of provisions, livestock, etc., esp. with a number of different vendors. **b** the time of this. **2** an open space or covered building used for this. **3** (often foll. by *for*) a demand for a commodity or service (*goods find a ready market*). **4** a place or group providing such a demand. **5** conditions as regards, or opportunity for, buying or selling. **6** the rate of purchase and sale, market value (*the market fell*). **7** (prec. by *the*) the trade in a specified commodity (*the corn market*). **8** (**the Market**) *Brit.* the European Economic Community. —*v.* (**marketed, marketing**) **1** *tr.* sell. **2** *tr.* offer for sale. **3** *intr.* buy or sell goods in a market. □ **be in the market for** wish to buy. **be on** (or **come into**) **the market** be offered for sale. **make a market** *Stock Exch.* induce active dealing in a stock or shares. **market cross** a structure erected in a market-place, orig. a stone cross, later an arcaded building. **market-day** a day on which a market is regularly held, usu. weekly. **market garden** a place where vegetables and fruit are grown for the market etc. **market gardener** a person who owns or is employed in a market garden. **market maker** *Brit.* a member of the Stock Exchange granted certain privileges and trading to prescribed regulations. **market-place 1** an open space where a market is held in a town. **2** the scene of actual dealings. **market price** the price in current dealings. **market research** the study of consumers' needs and preferences. **market town** *Brit.* a town where a market is held. **market value** value as a saleable thing (opp. *book value*). **put on the market** offer for sale. □□ **marketer** *n.* **marketing** *n.* [ME ult. f. L *mercatus* f. *mercari* buy: see MERCHANT]

marketable /ˈmaːkɪtəb(ə)l/ *adj.* able or fit to be sold. □□ **marketability** /-ˈbɪlɪtɪ/ *n.*

marketeer /ˌmaːkɪˈtɪə(r)/ *n.* **1** a supporter of the EEC and British membership of it. **2** a marketer.

markhor /ˈmaːkɔː(r)/ *n.* a large spiral-horned wild goat, *Capra falconeri*, of N. India. [Pers. *mār-k̲wār* f. *mār* serpent + *k̲wār* -eating]

marking /ˈmaːkɪŋ/ *n.* (usu. in *pl.*) **1** an identification mark, esp. a symbol on an aircraft. **2** the colouring of an animal's fur, feathers, skin, etc. □ **marking-ink** indelible ink for marking linen etc.

Markova /maːˈkəʊvə/, Dame Alicia (real name Lilian Alicia Marks 1910–), English dancer. With the Ballet Rambert and Vic–Wells Ballet she danced the ballerina roles in the first English productions of the classics and created many roles in Ashton's early ballets such as *Façade* (1931). She formed groups with Dolin in 1935, 1945, and 1949, the last becoming the London Festival Ballet in 1950, with Markova prima ballerina until 1952.

Marks /maːks/, Simon, 1st Baron (1888–1964), English retailer and business innovator. He was the son of Michael Marks (d. 1907), a Polish refugee, whose stall in Leeds market (Marks Penny Bazaar) was the nucleus of the company created in 1926 as Marks & Spencer, a chain of retail stores selling clothes, food, and household goods under the brand name 'St Michael'.

marksman /ˈmaːksmən/ *n.* (*pl.* **-men**) a person skilled in shooting, esp. with a pistol or rifle. □□ **marksmanship** *n.*

marl¹ /maːl/ *n. & v.* —*n.* soil consisting of clay and lime, with fertilizing properties. —*v.tr.* apply marl to (the ground). □□ **marly** *adj.* [ME f. OF *marle* f. med.L *margila* f. L *marga*]

marl² /maːl/ *n.* **1** a mottled yarn of differently coloured threads. **2** the fabric made from this. [shortening of *marbled*: see MARBLE]

Marlborough¹ /ˈmɔːlbərə/ an administrative region of South Island, New Zealand; pop. (1986) 38,255; chief town, Blenheim.

Marlborough² /ˈmɔːlbərə/, John Churchill, 1st Duke of (1650–1722), English soldier. After an eventful early military career, which saw him play a leading role in the suppression of the Monmouth rebellion and in the accession of William III, Marlborough was appointed commander of British and Austrian troops in the War of Spanish Succession and won a reputation as one of Britain's greatest military commanders as a result of a series of victories over the French armies of Louis XIV, most notably Blenheim (1704), Ramillies (1706), Oudenarde (1708), and Malplaquet (1709), which spelt the end of Louis' attempts to dominate Europe. Dismissed from all his posts by Queen

Anne in 1711, largely as a result of personal antagonisms, he was restored by George I in 1714 but retired four years later after a stroke.

marlin /ˈmɑːlɪn/ n. US any of various large long-nosed marine fish of the family Istophoridae, esp. the blue marlin Makaira nigricans. [MARLINSPIKE, with ref. to its pointed snout]

marline /ˈmɑːlɪn/ n. Naut. a thin line of two strands. □ **marline-spike** = MARLINSPIKE. [ME f. Du. marlijn f. marren bind + lijn LINE¹]

marlinspike /ˈmɑːlɪnˌspaɪk/ n. Naut. a pointed iron tool used to separate strands of rope or wire. [orig. app. marling-spike f. marl fasten with marline (f. Du. marlen frequent. of MDu. marren bind) + -ING¹ + SPIKE¹]

marlite /ˈmɑːlaɪt/ n. a kind of marl that is not reduced to powder by the action of the air.

Marlowe /ˈmɑːləʊ/, Christopher (1564–93), English dramatist and poet. Born in the same year as Shakespeare, he was the son of a Canterbury shoemaker and was educated at Cambridge University. As a dramatist he came to fame with Tamburlaine the Great (1587/8), which shows a new vitality and strength in the use of blank verse which he developed in his other major plays, including Doctor Faustus (c.1590), Edward II (1592), and The Jew of Malta (1592). His finest poem is the unfinished Hero and Leander (1598; completed by George Chapman). Marlowe had many admirers including Jonson, who praised his 'mighty line', and he profoundly influenced Shakespeare's early historical plays. Marlowe held and propagated atheist opinions, and probably became involved in political intrigues. He was killed in obscure circumstances after a brawl in a Deptford tavern.

marmalade /ˈmɑːməˌleɪd/ n. a preserve of citrus fruit, usu. bitter oranges, made like jam. □ **marmalade cat** a cat with orange fur. [F marmelade f. Port. marmelada quince jam f. marmelo quince f. L melimelum f. Gk melimēlon f. meli honey + mēlon apple]

Marmara /ˈmɑːmərə/, **Sea of** a small inland sea in Turkey connected by the Bosporus to the Black Sea and by the Dardanelles to the Aegean.

Marmite /ˈmɑːmaɪt/ n. **1** Brit. propr. a preparation made from yeast extract and vegetable extract, used in sandwiches and for flavouring. **2 (marmite)** /also mɑːˈmiːt/ an earthenware cooking vessel. [F, = cooking-pot]

marmoreal /mɑːˈmɔːrɪəl/ adj. poet. of or like marble. □□ **marmoreally** adv. [L marmoreus (as MARBLE)]

marmoset /ˈmɑːməˌzet/ n. any of several small tropical American monkeys of the family Callitricidae, having a long bushy tail. [OF marmouset grotesque image, of unkn. orig.]

marmot /ˈmɑːmət/ n. any burrowing rodent of the genus Marmota, with a heavy-set body and short bushy tail. [F marmotte prob. f. Romansh murmont f. L murem (nominative mus) montis mountain mouse]

Marne /mɑːn/ a river of east central France, which rises in the Langres Plateau and flows 525 km (328 miles) to join the Seine near Paris. Its valley was the scene of heavy fighting in two important battles during the First World War. The first battle (6–12 Sept. 1914) halted and repelled the German advance on Paris; the second (15–18 July, followed by a counter-attack) ended the final German offensive.

marocain /ˈmærəˌkeɪn/ n. a dress-fabric of ribbed crêpe. [F, = Moroccan f. Maroc Morocco]

Maronite /ˈmærəˌnaɪt/ n. a member of a Christian sect of Syrian origin, living chiefly in Lebanon. They claim to have been founded by St Maro, a friend of Chrysostom (d. 407), but it seems certain that their origin does not go back beyond the 7th c. Since 1181 they have been in communion with the Roman Catholic Church. [med.L Maronita f. Maro]

maroon¹ /məˈruːn/ adj. & n. —adj. brownish-crimson. —n. **1** this colour. **2** an explosive device giving a loud report. [F marron chestnut f. It. marrone f. med.Gk maraon]

maroon² /məˈruːn/ v. & n. —v.tr. **1** leave (a person) isolated in a desolate place (esp. an island). **2** (of a person or a natural phenomenon) cause (a person) to be unable to leave a place. —n. **1** a person descended from a group of fugitive slaves in

the remoter parts of Surinam and the W. Indies. **2** a marooned person. [F marron f. Sp. cimarrón wild f. cima peak]

marque¹ /mɑːk/ n. a make of motor car, as distinct from a specific model (the Jaguar marque). [F, = MARK¹]

marque² /mɑːk/ n. hist. □ **letters of marque** (or **marque and reprisal**) **1** a licence to fit out an armed vessel and employ it in the capture of an enemy's merchant shipping. **2** (in sing.) a ship carrying such a licence. [ME f. F f. Prov. marca f. marcar seize as a pledge]

marquee /mɑːˈkiː/ n. **1** a large tent used for social or commercial functions. **2** US a canopy over the entrance to a large building. [MARQUISE, taken as pl. & assim. to -EE]

Marquesas Islands /mɑːˈkeɪsəs/ a group of volcanic islands in the South Pacific, forming part of the overseas territory of French Polynesia; pop. 6,550. The island of Nuku Hiva was the home of Herman Melville, author of Moby Dick.

marquess /ˈmɑːkwɪs/ n. a British nobleman ranking between a duke and an earl (cf. MARQUIS). The title was introduced into the peerage of England at the end of the 14th c. and into that of Scotland in the late 15th c.; it had been in use earlier in various European countries. □□ **marquessate** /-sət/ n. [var. of MARQUIS]

marquetry /ˈmɑːkɪtrɪ/ n. (also **marqueterie**) inlaid work in wood, ivory, etc. [F marqueterie f. marqueter variegate f. MARQUE¹]

Marquette /mɑːˈket/, Jacques (1637–75), French Jesuit missionary and explorer. He came to North America in 1666, and played a prominent part in the attempt to Christianize the North American Indians, especially during his mission among the Ottawa tribe. In 1673 he accompanied Louis Jolliet on a voyage down the Wisconsin and Mississippi Rivers as far as the mouth of the Arkansas and then back to Lake Michigan via the Illinois River.

marquis /ˈmɑːkwɪs/ n. a foreign nobleman ranking between a duke and a count (cf. MARQUESS). □□ **marquisate** /-sət/ n. [ME f. OF marchis f. Rmc (as MARCH², -ESE)]

marquise /mɑːˈkiːz/ n. **1 a** the wife or widow of a marquis. **b** a woman holding the rank of marquis in her own right (cf. MARCHIONESS). **2** a finger-ring set with an oval pointed cluster of gems. **3** archaic = MARQUEE. [F, fem. of MARQUIS]

marquisette /ˌmɑːkɪˈzet/ n. a fine light cotton, rayon, or silk fabric for net curtains etc. [F, dimin. of MARQUISE]

Marrakesh /ˌmærəˈkeʃ/ a town in the foothills of the Atlas Mountains, one of the four imperial cities of Morocco; pop. (1982) 439,700.

marram /ˈmærəm/ n. a shore grass, Ammophila arenaria, that binds sand with its tough rhizomes. [ON marálmr f. marr sea + hálmr HAULM]

marriage /ˈmærɪdʒ/ n. **1** the legal union of a man and a woman in order to live together and often to have children. **2** an act or ceremony establishing this union. **3** one particular union of this kind (by a previous marriage). **4** an intimate union (the marriage of true minds). **5** Cards the union of a king and queen of the same suit. □ **by marriage** as a result of a marriage (related by marriage). **in marriage** as husband or wife (give in marriage; take in marriage). **marriage bureau** an establishment arranging introductions between persons wishing to marry. **marriage certificate** a certificate certifying the completion of a marriage ceremony. **marriage guidance** counselling of couples who have problems in married life. **marriage licence** a licence to marry. **marriage lines** Brit. a marriage certificate. **marriage of convenience** a marriage concluded to achieve some practical purpose, esp. financial or political. **marriage settlement** an arrangement securing property between spouses. [ME f. OF mariage f. marier MARRY¹]

marriageable /ˈmærɪdʒəb(ə)l/ adj. **1** fit for marriage, esp. old or rich enough to marry. **2** (of age) fit for marriage. □□ **marriageability** /-ˈbɪlɪtɪ/ n.

married /ˈmærɪd/ adj. & n. —adj. **1** united in marriage. **2** of or relating to marriage (married name; married life). —n. (usu. in pl.) a married person (young marrieds).

marron glacé /ˌmærɒn ˈglɑːseɪ/ n. (pl. **marrons glacés**

pronunc. same) a chestnut preserved in and coated with sugar. [F, = iced chestnut: cf. GLACÉ]

marrow /'mærəʊ/ *n.* **1** (in full **vegetable marrow**) **a** a large usu. white-fleshed edible gourd used as food. **b** the plant, *Cucurbita pepo*, yielding this. **2** a soft fatty substance in the cavities of bones, often taken as typifying vitality. **3** the essential part. □ **to the marrow** right through. □□ **marrowless** *adj.* **marrowy** *adj.* [OE *mearg, mærg* f. Gmc]

marrowbone /'mærəʊˌbəʊn/ *n.* a bone containing edible marrow.

marrowfat /'mærəʊˌfæt/ *n.* a kind of large pea.

marry[1] /'mæri/ *v.* (**-ies, -ied**) **1** *tr.* **a** take as one's wife or husband in marriage. **b** (often foll. by *to*) (of a priest etc.) join (persons) in marriage. **c** (of a parent or guardian) give (a son, daughter, etc.) in marriage. **2** *intr.* **a** enter into marriage. **b** (foll. by *into*) become a member of (a family) by marriage. **3** *tr.* **a** unite intimately. **b** correlate (things) as a pair. **c** *Naut.* splice (rope-ends) together without increasing their girth. □ **marry off** find a wife or husband for. [ME f. OF *marier* f. L *maritare* f. *maritus* husband]

marry[2] /'mæri/ *int. archaic* expressing surprise, asseveration, indignation, etc. [ME, = (the Virgin) *Mary*]

Marryat /'mæriət/, Captain Frederick (1792–1848), English novelist, who resigned his commission in the Navy in 1830 and wrote many novels. Successful among these were his sea-stories, *Peter Simple* (1834), *Mr Midshipman Easy* (1836), and *Masterman Ready* (1841). His works for children include the popular historical story *The Children of the New Forest* (1847).

marrying /'mæriɪŋ/ *adj.* likely or inclined to marry (*not a marrying man*).

Mars /mɑːz/ **1** *Rom. Mythol.* next to Jupiter, the chief ancient Italian god. He is usually considered a war-god and equated with Ares, but has agricultural functions also. **2** *Astron.* the fourth planet in order of distance from the sun, with an orbit lying between that of the earth and Jupiter, a rocky body 6,796 km in diameter. Its characteristic red colour, clearly visible to the naked eye, arises from the iron-rich minerals covering its surface. A tenuous atmosphere of carbon dioxide is dense enough to whip up periodic dust storms which can cover the entire planet, and causes erosion of surface features over long periods. Sinuous channels on the surface, resembling river beds on Earth, and extinct volcanoes hint at vigorous past geological activity, perhaps associated with flows of liquid water, of which none remains. The polar caps are of frozen carbon dioxide, but may contain some water ice. Investigations by space probes show no evidence for the 'canals' reported by the American astronomer Percival Lowell in the early 20th c., nor is there any evidence for life on the planet. There are two small satellites, Phobos and Deimos.

Marsala /mɑː'sɑːlə/ *n.* a dark sweet fortified dessert wine. [*Marsala* in Sicily, where orig. made]

Marseillaise /ˌmɑːseɪ'jeɪz, ˌmɑːsə'leɪz/ *n.* the national anthem of France, composed by a young engineer officer, Rouget de Lisle, in 1792, on the declaration of war against Austria, and first sung in Paris by Marseilles patriots. [F, fem. adj. f. *Marseille* Marseilles]

Marseilles /mɑː'seɪ, -'seɪlz/ (French **Marseille**) a French seaport on the Mediterranean coast, on the site of an ancient Greek colony (*Massilia*); pop. (1982) 1,110,511.

Marsh /mɑːʃ/, Dame Ngaio Edith (1899–1982), New Zealand writer of detective fiction, whose works include *Vintage Murder* (1937), *Surfeit of Lampreys* (1941), and *Final Curtain* (1947).

marsh /mɑːʃ/ *n.* **1** low land flooded in wet weather and usu. watery at all times. **2** (*attrib.*) of or inhabiting marshland. □ **marsh fever** malaria. **marsh gas** methane. **marsh-harrier** a European harrier, *Circus aeruginosus* (see HARRIER[3]). **marsh mallow** a shrubby herbaceous plant, *Althaea officinalis*, the roots of which were formerly used to make marshmallow. **marsh marigold** a golden-flowered ranunculaceous plant, *Caltha palustris*, growing in moist meadows etc.: also called KINGCUP. **marsh tit** a grey tit, *Parus palustris*, inhabiting marshland.

marsh trefoil the buckbean. □□ **marshy** *adj.* (**marshier, marshiest**). **marshiness** *n.* [OE *mer(i)sc* f. WG]

marshal /'mɑːʃ(ə)l/ *n. & v.* —*n.* **1** (**Marshal**) **a** a high-ranking officer in the armed forces (*Air Marshal; Field Marshal; Marshal of France*). **b** a high-ranking officer of state (*Earl Marshal*). **2** an officer arranging ceremonies, controlling procedure at races, etc. **3** *US* the head of a police or fire department. **4** (in full **judge's marshal**) *Brit.* an official accompanying a judge on circuit, with secretarial and social duties. —*v.* (**marshalled, marshalling**; *US* **marshaled, marshaling**) **1** *tr.* arrange (soldiers, facts, one's thoughts, etc.) in due order. **2** *tr.* (often foll. by *into, to*) conduct (a person) ceremoniously. **3** *tr. Heraldry* combine (coats of arms). **4** *intr.* take up positions in due arrangement. □ **marshalling yard** a railway yard in which goods trains etc. are assembled. **Marshal of the Royal Air Force** an officer of the highest rank in the Royal Air Force. □□ **marshaller** *n.* **marshalship** *n.* [ME f. OF *mareschal* f. LL *mariscalcus* f. Gmc, lit. 'horse-servant']

Marshall /'mɑːʃ(ə)l/, George Catlett (1880–1959), US Secretary of State 1947–9 who in 1947 initiated a plan (the European Recovery Program or **Marshall Plan**) to supply certain Western European countries with financial assistance (**Marshall Aid**) to further their recovery after the Second World War. Marshall Aid ended in 1952.

Marshall Islands /'mɑːʃ(ə)l/ a group of islands in the NW Pacific, administered by the US as part of the Pacific Islands Trust Territory from 1947 until 1986, when they became a republic in free association with the US; pop. (1988) 40,600.

marshland /'mɑːʃlənd/ *n.* land consisting of marshes.

marshmallow /mɑːʃ'mæləʊ/ *n.* a soft sweet made of sugar, albumen, gelatin, etc.

Marston Moor /'mɑːst(ə)n/ a moor about 11 km (7 miles) west of York, site of the largest battle (1644) of the English Civil War, in which the combined Royalist armies of Prince Rupert and the Duke of Newcastle were defeated by the English and Scottish Parliamentary armies. The defeat destroyed Royalist power in the north of England and fatally weakened Charles I's cause.

marsupial /mɑː'suːpɪəl/ *n. & adj.* —*n.* any mammal of the order Marsupialia, which includes the kangaroo and opossum. The young, which are born in a very undeveloped state, are nourished and complete their development attached to the teats of the milk-secreting glands, on the mother's abdomen; the external pouch or *marsupium*, from which the order takes its name, is found in many species but is not a universal feature. Apart from the American opossums, present-day marsupials, of which there are under 200 species, are confined to Australasia. —*adj.* **1** of or belonging to this order. **2** of or like a pouch (*marsupial muscle*). [mod.L *marsupialis* f. L *marsupium* f. Gk *marsupion* pouch, dimin. of *marsipos* purse]

Marsyas /'mɑːsɪəs/ *Gk Mythol.* a satyr who took to flute-playing. He challenged Apollo to a musical contest and was flayed alive when he lost.

mart /mɑːt/ *n.* **1** a trade centre. **2** an auction-room. **3 a** a market. **b** a market-place. [ME f. obs. Du. *mart*, var. of *markt* MARKET]

Martaban /ˌmɑːtə'bɑːn/, **Gulf of** an inlet of the Andaman Sea, on the coast of Burma.

martagon /'mɑːtəgən/ *n.* a lily, *Lilium martagon*, with small purple turban-like flowers. [F f. Turk. *martagān* a form of turban]

Martello /mɑː'teləʊ/ *n.* (*pl.* **-os**) (also **Martello tower**) any of the small circular forts erected along the coasts of Britain during the Napoleonic Wars to repel expected French landings. They have massive walls and flat roofs on which guns were mounted. [alt. f. Cape *Mortella* in Corsica, where such a tower offered a stubborn resistance to the British in 1794]

marten /'mɑːtɪn/ *n.* any weasel-like carnivore of the genus *Martes*, having valuable fur. [ME f. MDu. *martren* f. OF (*peau*) *martrine* marten (fur) f. *martre* f. WG]

martensite /'mɑːtɪnˌzaɪt/ *n.* the chief constituent of hardened steel. [A. *Martens*, German metallurgist d. 1914 + -ITE[1]]

Martha /'mɑːθə/ the sister of Lazarus and Mary and friend of Jesus Christ (Luke 10: 40). Her name is used allusively for one much concerned with domestic affairs; in Christian allegory she symbolizes the active life and her sister the contemplative life.

Martial /ˈmɑːʃ(ə)l/ (Marcus Valerius Martialis, c.40–c.104) Roman epigrammatist, originally from Spain. His fifteen books of epigrams, in a variety of metres, reflect all facets of Roman life. He specialized in the witty surprise-ending, and is the chief ancient model for modern epigrammatists.

martial /ˈmɑːʃ(ə)l/ adj. **1** of or appropriate to warfare. **2** warlike, brave; fond of fighting. □ **martial arts** fighting sports such as judo and karate. **martial law** military government, involving the suspension of ordinary law. □□ **martially** adv. [ME f. OF martial or L martialis of the Roman god Mars: see MARS]

Martian /ˈmɑːʃ(ə)n/ adj. & n. —adj. of the planet Mars. —n. a hypothetical inhabitant of Mars. [ME f. OF martien or L Martianus f. Mars: see MARS]

Martin, /ˈmɑːtɪn/, St (d. 397), a patron saint of France. While serving in the Roman army he gave half his cloak to a beggar at Amiens and received a vision of Christ, after which he was baptized. He joined Hilary at Poitiers and founded the first monastery in Gaul. Becoming bishop of Tours c.372, he pioneered the evangelization of the rural areas. Feast day, 11 Nov. □ **St Martin's summer** Brit. a period of fine mild weather occurring about this date.

martin /ˈmɑːtɪn/ n. any of several swallows of the family Hirundinidae, esp. the house-martin and sand-martin. [prob. f. St Martin: see MARTINMAS]

martinet /ˌmɑːtɪˈnet/ n. a strict (esp. military or naval) disciplinarian. □□ **martinettish** adj. (also **martinetish**). [J. Martinet, 17th-c. French drill-master]

martingale /ˈmɑːtɪŋˌɡeɪl/ n. **1** a strap, or set of straps, fastened at one end to the noseband of a horse and at the other end to the girth, to prevent rearing etc. **2** Naut. a rope for holding down the jib-boom. **3** a gambling system of continually doubling the stakes in the hope of an eventual win that must yield a net profit. [F, of uncert. orig.]

Martini[1] /mɑːˈtiːnɪ/ n. **1** propr. a type of vermouth. **2** a cocktail made of gin and French vermouth, and sometimes orange bitters etc. [Martini & Rossi, Italian firm selling vermouth]

Martini[2] /mɑːˈtiːnɪ/, Simone (c.1284–1344), Italian painter, whose work reflects a sense of sumptuous Byzantine colour combined with the strong outline and elegant gesture of the French Gothic manner. To him is attributed the first equestrian portrait in European art—the fresco of an Italian commander on the wall of the Palazzo Pubblico, Siena, opposite his earlier Maestà (1315). The Annunciation (1333) represents the epitome of Simone's lyrical and decorative contribution to the new Gothic taste. His fame spread, and he painted for the papal court at Avignon from c.1340.

Martinique /ˌmɑːtɪˈniːk/ a French West Indian island, one of the Lesser Antilles; pop. (1982) 328,566; capital, Fort de France. Its former capital, St Pierre, was completely destroyed by an eruption of Mont Pelée in 1902.

Martinmas /ˈmɑːtɪnməs/ n. St Martin's day, 11 Nov. It was formerly the usual time in England for hiring servants and for slaughtering cattle to be salted for the winter. [St MARTIN + MASS[2]]

martlet /ˈmɑːtlɪt/ n. **1** Heraldry an imaginary footless bird borne as a charge. **2** archaic **a** a swift. **b** a house-martin. [F martelet alt. f. martinet dimin. f. MARTIN]

martyr /ˈmɑːtə(r)/ n. & v. —n. **1 a** a person who is put to death for refusing to renounce a faith or belief. **b** a person who suffers for adhering to a principle, cause, etc. **2** (foll. by to) a constant sufferer from (an ailment). —v.tr. **1** put to death as a martyr. **2** torment. □ **make a martyr of oneself** accept or pretend to accept unnecessary discomfort etc. [OE martir f. eccl.L martyr f. Gk martur, martus -uros witness]

martyrdom /ˈmɑːtədəm/ n. **1** the sufferings and death of a martyr. **2** torment. [OE martyrdōm (as MARTYR, -DOM)]

martyrize /ˈmɑːtəˌraɪz/ v.tr. & refl. (also **-ise**) make a martyr of. □□ **martyrization** /-ˈzeɪʃ(ə)n/ n.

martyrology /ˌmɑːtəˈrɒlədʒɪ/ n. (pl. **-ies**) **1** a list or register of martyrs. **2** the history of martyrs. □□ **martyrological**

/-rəˈlɒdʒɪk(ə)l/ adj. **martyrologist** n. [med.L martyrologium f. eccl.Gk marturologion (as MARTYR, logos account)]

martyry /ˈmɑːtərɪ/ n. (pl. **-ies**) a shrine or church erected in honour of a martyr. [ME f. med.L martyrium f. Gk marturion martyrdom (as MARTYR)]

Maruts /ˈmɑːrʊts/ n.pl. Hinduism the sons of Rudra, hence also called the Rudras. In the Rig-Veda they are the storm gods, Indra's henchmen.

marvel /ˈmɑːv(ə)l/ n. & v. —n. **1** a wonderful thing. **2** (foll. by of) a wonderful example of (a quality). —v.intr. (**marvelled**, **marvelling**; US **marveled**, **marveling**) literary **1** (foll. by at, or that + clause) feel surprise or wonder. **2** (foll. by how, why, etc. + clause) wonder. □ **marvel of Peru** a showy garden plant, Mirabilis jalapa, with flowers opening in the afternoon. □□ **marveller** n. [ME f. OF merveille, merveiller f. LL mirabilia neut. pl. of L mirabilis f. mirari wonder at: see MIRACLE]

Marvell /ˈmɑːv(ə)l/, Andrew (1621–78), English poet and politician. He was employed as tutor in the households of Lord Fairfax and Cromwell (who is honoured in several of his poems), and in 1657 became assistant to Milton who was a secretary to Cromwell's government. As an MP (1659–78) Marvell wrote pamphlets and verse satires that attacked Charles II and his ministers, particularly for corruption at court and in Parliament. In his lifetime he was almost unknown as a lyric poet, although famed as patriot, satirist, and foe to tyranny; today his oblique and enigmatic treatment of conventional poetic materials has intrigued the modern mind and set him high among the metaphysical poets.

marvellous /ˈmɑːvələs/ adj. (US **marvelous**) **1** astonishing. **2** excellent. **3** extremely improbable. □□ **marvellously** adv. **marvellousness** n. [ME f. OF merveillos f. merveille: see MARVEL]

Marx /mɑːks/, Karl Heinrich (1818–83), German political philosopher and economist. Born of Jewish parents, he studied in Bonn and in Berlin, where he joined the radical followers of Hegel. His rebellious political outlook made a university career impossible and he turned to journalism, living variously in Paris and Brussels until in 1849 he was exiled to England, where his friend and collaborator Engels was already settled. Their pamphlet the Communist Manifesto, still the classic exposition of communism, had been published in 1848; it detailed a programme for socialist revolution to be led by workers of the more industrially advanced States, and appeared at a time when factory workers were suffering the worst results of the Industrial Revolution. In London Marx spent much of his time reading in the British Museum, enlarging the theory of this pamphlet into a series of books, the most important being the three-volume Das Kapital, of which the first volume appeared in 1867 and the remainder after his death. At no time did he concern himself greatly with the practical problems of how the socialist society should be run; his interest was in the revolution itself. He was also a leading figure in the founding of the First International. The prophet of communism, Marx became famous after his death as movements all over the world looked to his writings for the ultimate truth on matters of economics, politics, and philosophy, and the influence of his theories on the socialist movements of modern times has been greater than that of any other man.

Marx Brothers /mɑːks/ an American family of film comedians, consisting of Chico (Leonard, 1891–1961), and his brothers Harpo (Adolph, later Arthur, 1893–1964), Groucho (Julius Henry, 1895–1977), and Zeppo (Herbert, 1900–79), whose films include Horse Feathers (1932), Duck Soup (1933), and A Night at the Opera (1935), all embodying their typically anarchic humour.

Marxism /ˈmɑːksɪz(ə)m/ n. the political and economic theories of Karl Marx, especially that, as labour is basic to wealth, historical development, following scientific laws determined by dialectical materialism, must lead to the violent overthrow of the capitalist class and the taking over of the means of production by the proletariat. Events would then progress towards the ideal of a classless society, but the initial transition could not be effected without violent revolution. □ **Marxism-Leninism** Marxism as developed by Lenin. □□ **Marxist** n. & adj. **Marxist-Leninist** n. & adj.

Mary[1] /ˈmeərɪ/ (in the Bible) **1** the Blessed Virgin Mary, mother of Jesus Christ, daughter of Joachim and Anne, betrothed to Joseph at the time of the Annunciation. **2** Mary Magdalene (= of Magdala), a follower of Christ, commonly identified with the 'sinner' of Luke 7: 37. Feast day, 22 July.

Mary[2] /ˈmeərɪ/ the name of two queens of England:

Mary I (1516–58), daughter of Henry VIII, reigned 1553–8. Having regained the throne after the brief attempt to install Lady Jane Grey in her place, Mary attempted to reverse the country's turn towards Protestantism, which had begun to gain momentum during the short reign of her brother Edward VI. She married Philip II of Spain, and after putting down several revolts, began the series of religious persecutions which earned her the name of 'Bloody Mary'. Mary died childless, however, and the accession of her Protestant sister Elizabeth I guaranteed that England would not revert permanently to Catholicism.

Mary II (1662–94), daughter of James II, reigned 1689–94. Although her father James II was converted to Catholicism, Mary remained a Protestant, and was invited to replace him on the throne after his deposition in 1689. She insisted that her Dutch husband William of Orange be crowned along with her (see WILLIAM III) and afterwards left most of the business of the kingdom to him, although she frequently had to act as sole head of State because of her husband's absence on campaign on the Continent.

Mary Celeste /ˌmeərɪ sɪˈlest/ an American brig that set sail from New York for Genoa and was found in the North Atlantic in December 1872 in perfect condition but abandoned and without her boats. The fate of the crew was never discovered, and the abandonment of the ship remains one of the great mysteries of the sea.

Maryland /ˈmeərɪˌlænd/ a State on the Atlantic coast of the US; pop. (est. 1985) 4,217,000; capital, Annapolis. Colonized from England in the 17th c. and named after Queen Henrietta Maria, wife of Charles I, it was one of the original 13 States of the US (1788).

Mary, Queen of Scots (1542–87), daughter of James V, queen of Scotland 1542–67. Mary was sent to France as an infant, and married briefly to Francis II, but after his premature death returned to Scotland in 1561 to resume personal rule. A devout Catholic, she proved unequal to the task of controlling her Protestant lords led by her half-brother the Earl of Moray. Her position was made even more difficult by two disastrous marriages to Lord Darnley and the Earl of Bothwell, and after the defeat of her supporters she fled to eventual imprisonment in England in 1567. There she became the centre of several Catholic plots against Elizabeth I, and, after the discovery of one of these, was beheaded.

Mary Rose a heavily armed ship of 600 tons, built for Henry VIII and named in honour of his sister Mary Tudor. For some years from 1512 onwards the ship took part in Henry's wars with the French, always as the flagship of the Lord High Admiral, and when going out to engage the French fleet off Portsmouth in July 1545 she was swamped and quickly sank with the loss of nearly all her company. The hull was discovered by skin-divers in 1968, and raised in 1982.

marzipan /ˈmɑːzɪˌpæn, -ˈpæn/ n. & v. —n. **1** a paste of ground almonds, sugar, etc., made up into small cakes etc., or used to coat large cakes. **2** a piece of marzipan. —v.tr. (**marzipanned**, **marzipanning**) cover with or as with marzipan. [G f. It. marzapane]

Masaccio /mæˈsætʃɪˌəʊ/, Tommaso Giovanni di Mone (1401–28), Italian early Renaissance painter, who worked in Florence until a move to Rome in the last year of his short life. He is noted for two important innovations: the central-perspective system, which he learnt from Brunelleschi and used most notably in his fresco of the Trinity, and the use of light to define the construction of the body and its draperies and (in his later works) to unify a whole composition.

Masada /məˈsɑːdə/ a fortress on a steep rocky hill west of the Dead Sea, site of a palace and fortifications built by Herod the Great, but best known as the Jewish stronghold in the Zealots' revolt of AD 66–73. In AD 73 the defenders committed mass suicide rather than surrender to the Romans who had finally breached the citadel after a siege of nearly two years.

Masai /ˈmɑːsaɪ/ n. & adj. —n. (pl. same or **Masais**) **1** a member of a pastoral people of mixed Hamitic stock, inhabiting some of the best grazing lands in Kenya and Tanzania, whose life and livelihood revolve round their cattle-herds. Their contempt for the agriculture practised by their neighbours is well known. The Masai are traditionally credited with fierce raiding of neighbouring tribes, undertaken to protect their herds and prove prowess, not for food. **2** the Nilotic language of the Masai. —adj. of or relating to the Masai or their language. [Bantu]

Masaryk /ˈmæsərɪk/, Tomáš Garrigue (1850–1937), Czechoslovak statesman, who worked with Beneš for his country's independence and became its first President (1918–35) on achieving this. He is regarded as the founder of modern Czechoslovakia as a western-style democracy.

Masbate /mæsˈbɑːtɪ/ **1** an island in the central Philippines; pop. (1980) 584,500. **2** its chief town.

Mascagni /mæsˈkænjiː/, Pietro (1863–1945), Italian composer and conductor, whose compositions include operas and choral works. The abundant success of his opera *Cavalleria Rusticana* (1890) overshadowed all his other operas.

mascara /mæˈskɑːrə/ n. a cosmetic for darkening the eyelashes. [It. *mascara, maschera* MASK]

Mascarene Islands /ˌmæskəˈriːn/ (also **Mascarenes**) a group of islands in the Indian Ocean, including Réunion, Mauritius, and Rodrigues, named after the 16th-c. Portuguese navigator, Mascarenhas.

mascle /ˈmæsk(ə)l/ n. *Heraldry* a lozenge voided, with a central lozenge-shaped aperture. [ME f. AF f. AL *ma(s)cula* f. L MACULA]

mascon /ˈmæskɒn/ n. *Astron.* a concentration of dense matter below the moon's surface, producing a gravitational pull. [*mass concentration*]

mascot /ˈmæskɒt/ n. a person, animal, or thing that is supposed to bring good luck. [F *mascotte* f. mod. Prov. *mascotto* fem. dimin. of *masco* witch]

masculine /ˈmæskjʊlɪn, ˈmɑːs-/ adj. & n. —adj. **1** of or characteristic of men. **2** manly, vigorous. **3** (of a woman) having qualities considered appropriate to a man. **4** *Gram.* of or denoting the gender proper to men's names. —n. *Gram.* the masculine gender; a masculine word. □□ **masculinely** adv. **masculineness** n. **masculinity** /-ˈlɪnɪtɪ/ n. [ME f. OF *masculin -ine* f. L *masculinus* (as MALE)]

Masefield /ˈmeɪsfiːld/, John Edward (1878–1967), English poet. His fascination for the sea is reflected in his first published book *Salt-Water Ballads* (which contained 'I must go down to the sea again'; 1902). His works include the verse narratives, *The Daffodil Fields* (1913), *The Everlasting Mercy* (1911), *Reynard the Fox* (1919), several novels, and the classic children's story *The Midnight Folk* (1927). He was appointed Poet Laureate in 1930.

maser /ˈmeɪzə(r)/ n. a device using the stimulated emission of radiation by excited atoms to amplify or generate coherent monochromatic electromagnetic radiation in the microwave range (cf. LASER). [microwave amplification by the stimulated emission of radiation]

Maseru /ˌmæsəˈruː/ the capital of Lesotho; pop. (1986) 109,400.

mash /mæʃ/ n. & v. —n. **1** a soft mixture. **2** a mixture of boiled grain, bran, etc., given warm to horses etc. **3** *Brit. colloq.* mashed potatoes (*sausage and mash*). **4** a mixture of malt and hot water used to form wort for brewing. **5** a soft pulp made by crushing, mixing with water, etc. —v.tr. **1** reduce (potatoes etc.) to a uniform mass by crushing. **2** crush or pound to a pulp. **3** mix (malt) with hot water to form wort. □□ **masher** n. [OE *māsc* f. WG, perh. rel. to MIX]

Mashhad /mæʃˈhæd/ the second-largest city in Iran, in the north-east of the country, a centre of Shiite pilgrimage; pop. (1986) 1,463,500.

mashie /ˈmæʃɪ/ n. *Golf* an iron formerly used for lofting or for medium distances. [perh. f. F *massue* club]

Mashona var. of SHONA.

Mashonaland /məˈʃəʊnəˌlænd/ *hist.* a province of Southern

Rhodesia, occupied by the Mashona Bantu people. The area is now divided into the three provinces of Mashonaland East, West, and Central in northern Zimbabwe.

mask /mɑːsk/ n. & v. —n. **1** a covering for all or part of the face: **a** worn as a disguise, or to appear grotesque and amuse or terrify. **b** made of wire, gauze, etc., and worn for protection (e.g. by a fencer) or by a surgeon to prevent infection of a patient. **c** worn to conceal the face at balls etc. and usu. made of velvet or silk. **2** a respirator used to filter inhaled air or to supply gas for inhalation. **3** a likeness of a person's face, esp. one made by taking a mould from the face (*death-mask*). **4** a disguise or pretence (*throw off the mask*). **5** a hollow model of a human head worn by ancient Greek and Roman actors. **6** *Photog.* a screen used to exclude part of an image. **7** the face or head of an animal, esp. a fox. **8** = *face-pack*. **9** *archaic* a masked person. —v.tr. **1** cover (the face etc.) with a mask. **2** disguise or conceal (a taste, one's feelings, etc.). **3** protect from a process. **4** *Mil.* **a** conceal (a battery etc.) from the enemy's view. **b** hinder (an army etc.) from action by observing with adequate force. **c** hinder (a friendly force) by standing in its line of fire. □ **masking tape** adhesive tape used in painting to cover areas on which paint is not wanted. □□ **masker** n. [F *masque* f. It. *maschera* f. Arab. *maskara* buffoon f. *sakira* to ridicule]

masked /mɑːskt/ adj. wearing or disguised with a mask. □ **masked ball** a ball at which masks are worn.

maskinonge /ˈmæskɪˌnɒndʒ, -ˈnɒndʒɪ/ n. a large N. American pike, *Esox masquinongy*, esp. in the Great Lakes. [ult. f. Ojibwa, = great fish]

masochism /ˈmæsəˌkɪz(ə)m/ n. **1** a form of (esp. sexual) perversion characterized by gratification derived from one's own pain or humiliation (cf. SADISM). **2** colloq. the enjoyment of what appears to be painful or tiresome. □□ **masochist** n. **masochistic** /-ˈkɪstɪk/ adj. **masochistically** /-ˈkɪstɪkəlɪ/ adv. [L. von Sacher-*Masoch*, Austrian novelist d. 1895, who described cases of it]

Mason /ˈmeɪs(ə)n/, Alfred Edward Woodley (1865–1948), English novelist, author of adventure stories (including *The Four Feathers*, 1902), historical novels (including *Musk and Amber*, 1942), detective novels featuring Inspector Hanaud of the Sûreté, and several plays.

mason /ˈmeɪs(ə)n/ n. & v. —n. **1** a person who builds with stone. **2** (**Mason**) a Freemason. —v.tr. build or strengthen with masonry. □ **mason's mark** a device carved on stone by the mason who dressed it. [ME f. OF *masson*, *maçonner*, ONF *machun*, prob. ult. f. Gmc]

Mason–Dixon line /ˌmeɪs(ə)nˈdɪks(ə)n/ n. (also **Mason and Dixon line**) the boundary line between Pennsylvania and Maryland as laid out in 1763–7 by the English surveyors Charles Mason and Jeremiah Dixon. The term was later applied to the entire southern boundary of Pennsylvania, and regarded as the border between North and South in the US. In the years before the American Civil War it formed the northern boundary of the slave-owning States.

Masonic /məˈsɒnɪk/ adj. of or relating to Freemasons.

masonry /ˈmeɪsənrɪ/ n. **1 a** the work of a mason. **b** stonework. **2** (**Masonry**) Freemasonry. [ME f. OF *maçonerie* (as MASON)]

Masorah /ˈmæsərə/ n. (also **Massorah**) a body of traditional information and comment on the text of the Hebrew Bible. (See MASORETE.) [Heb. *māsōreṯ*, perh. = bond (of the covenant), later = tradition]

Masorete /ˈmæsəˌriːt/ n. (also **Massorete**) any of the Jewish scholars who, between the 6th and 10th c. AD, established a recognized text of the Old Testament (the **Masoretic text**), providing marginal notes and commentaries in order to preserve this from accretion or alteration. They also introduced vowel points and accents to indicate how the words should be pronounced, at a time when Hebrew was ceasing to be a spoken language. □□ **Masoretic** /-ˈretɪk/ adj. [F *Massoret* & mod.L *Massoreta*, orig. a misuse of Heb. (see MASORAH), assim. to -ETE]

masque /mɑːsk/ n. **1** an amateur dramatic and musical entertainment especially in the 16th–17th c., with scenery and elaborate costumes, originally in dumb show but later with metrical dialogue. **2** a dramatic composition for this. The masque derived from a primitive folk ritual featuring the arrival of guests, usually in disguise, bearing gifts to a king or nobleman, who with his household then joined the visitors in a ceremonial dance. The presentation of the gifts soon became an excuse for flowery flattering speeches, while the wearing of outlandish or beautiful costumes and masks led to miming and dancing. The Civil War put an end to the masque, which was never revived. (Milton's *Comus*, though sometimes described as a masque, is strictly a pastoral drama.) □□ **masquer** n. [var. of MASK]

masquerade /ˌmɑːskəˈreɪd, ˌmæs-/ n. & v. —n. **1** a false show or pretence. **2** a masked ball. —v.intr. (often foll. by *as*) appear in disguise, assume a false appearance. □□ **masquerader** n. [F *mascarade* f. Sp. *mascarada* f. *máscara* mask]

Mass. abbr. Massachusetts.

mass[1] /mæs/ n., v., & adj. —n. **1** a coherent body of matter of indefinite shape. **2** a dense aggregation of objects (*a mass of fibres*). **3** (in sing. or pl.; foll. by *of*) a large number or amount. **4** (usu. foll. by *of*) an unbroken expanse (of colour etc.). **5** (foll. by *of*) covered or abounding in (*was a mass of cuts and bruises*). **6** a main portion (of a painting etc.) as perceived by the eye. **7** (prec. by *the*) **a** the majority. **b** (in pl.) the ordinary people. **8** *Physics* the quantity of matter a body contains, measured in terms of resistance to acceleration by a force (i.e., its inertia; see below). **9** (attrib.) relating to, done by, or affecting large numbers of people or things; large-scale (*mass audience*; *mass action*; *mass murder*). —v.tr. & intr. **1** assemble into a mass or as one body (*massed bands*). **2** *Mil.* (with ref. to troops) concentrate or be concentrated. □ **centre of mass** a point representing the mean position of matter in a body or system. **in the mass** in the aggregate. **law of mass action** the principle that the rate of a chemical reaction is proportional to the masses of the reacting substances. **mass defect** the difference between the mass of an isotope and its mass number. **mass energy** a body's ability to do work according to its mass. **mass media** = MEDIA[1] 2. **mass noun** *Gram.* a noun that is not countable and cannot be used with the indefinite article or in the plural (e.g. *bread*). **mass number** the total number of protons and neutrons in a nucleus. **mass observation** *Brit.* the study and recording of the social habits and opinions of ordinary people. **mass-produce** produce by mass production. **mass production** the production of large quantities of a standardized article by a standardized mechanical process. **mass spectrograph** a mass spectrometer in which the particles are detected photographically. **mass spectrometer** an apparatus separating atoms and molecules according to mass by passage in ionic form through electric and magnetic fields, and detecting them photographically or electrically (originally applied specifically to apparatus with electrical detection). It has become an indispensable tool in nuclear physics, analytical chemistry, and (more recently) organic chemistry. **mass spectrum** the distribution of ions shown by the use of a mass spectrograph or mass spectrometer. □□ **massless** adj. [ME f. OF *masse*, *masser* f. L *massa* f. Gk *maza* barley-cake: perh. rel. to *massō* knead]

The earliest scientific concept of mass was formulated in the Middle Ages as a refinement of the vernacular meaning of mass as an aggregation of matter of any kind or shape. In keeping with this older tradition Newton defined mass informally as quantity of matter; subsequently he found it necessary to introduce a more precise conception of mass, and based his new definition on 'inertia', a property possessed by all bodies in all circumstances, the innate resistance which is called into play while any body is being set in motion. For Newton all bodies with the same inertia have the same mass. He also demonstrated that all bodies with the same weight have the same inertia and, therefore, the same mass. The modern scientific concept of mass is an uneasy fusion of the various meanings given to it by Newton. It is regarded as one of the most obscure and abstract and also as one of the most important concepts of physics.

Einstein in his special theory of relativity showed that mass increases with velocity; further, he suggested that the total energy content of every body was measured by the equation $E = mc^2$ (where E is energy, m is mass, and c is the speed of light), and that mass can be converted into energy—a great deal of energy, since c^2 is a very large number. The equation suggests that the release of energy which accompanies even a small loss of mass is enormous. This has been borne out fully by nuclear science; the atomic bomb and nuclear energy depend upon this equation. Einstein's general theory of relativity also provides a rationale for the identity of inertial and gravitational mass, a phenomenon which in Newtonian physics was an unexplained coincidence.

mass² /mæs, mɑːs/ n. (often **Mass**) **1** the Eucharist, esp. in the Roman Catholic Church. **2** a celebration of this. **3** the liturgy used in the mass. **4** a musical setting of parts of this. □ **high mass** mass with incense, music, and usu. the assistance of a deacon and subdeacon. **low mass** mass with no music and a minimum of ceremony. [OE mæsse f. eccl.L missa f. L mittere miss- dismiss, perh. f. the concluding dismissal Ite, missa est Go, it is the dismissal]

Massachusetts /ˌmæsəˈtʃuːsɪts/ a State in the north-eastern US, bordering on the Atlantic; pop. (est. 1985) 5,737,000; capital, Boston. The Pilgrim Fathers landed there in 1620 and founded a Puritan colony. It was one of the original 13 States of the US (1788).

massacre /ˈmæsəkə(r)/ n. & v. —n. **1** a general slaughter (of persons, occasionally of animals). **2** an utter defeat or destruction. —v.tr. **1** make a massacre of. **2** murder (esp. a large number of people) cruelly or violently. [OF, of unkn. orig.]

massage /ˈmæsɑːʒ, -sɑːdʒ/ n. & v. —n. **1** the rubbing, kneading, etc., of muscles and joints of the body with the hands, to stimulate their action, cure strains, etc. **2** an instance of this. —v.tr. **1** apply massage to. **2** manipulate (statistics) to give an acceptable result. □ **massage parlour 1** an establishment providing massage. **2** euphem. a brothel. □□ **massager** n. [F f. masser treat with massage, perh. f. Port. amassar knead, f. massa dough: see MASS¹]

massasauga /ˌmæsəˈsɔːgə/ n. a small N. American rattlesnake, Sistrurus catenatus. [irreg. f. Missisauga River, Ontario]

Massawa /məˈsɑːwə/ the chief port of Ethiopia, in Eritrea, on the Red Sea; pop. 27,500.

massé /ˈmæseɪ/ n. Billiards a stroke made with the cue held nearly vertical. [F, past part. of masser make such a stroke (as MACE¹)]

masseter /mæˈsiːtə(r)/ n. either of two chewing-muscles which run from the temporal bone to the lower jaw. [Gk masētēr f. masaomai chew]

masseur /mæˈsɜː(r)/ n. (fem. **masseuse** /mæˈsɜːz/) a person who provides massage professionally. [F f. masser: see MASSAGE]

massicot /ˈmæsɪkɒt/ n. yellow lead monoxide, used as a pigment. [F, perh. rel. to It. marzacotto unguent prob. f. Arab. mashaḳūnyā]

massif /ˈmæsiːf, mæˈsiːf/ n. a compact group of mountain heights. [F massif used as noun: see MASSIVE]

Massif Central /mæˌsiːf sãˈtrɑːl/ a mountainous plateau in south central France. Covering almost one-sixth of the country, the Massif rises to a height of 1,887 m (6,188 ft.) at Puy de Nancy in the Auvergne Mountains. The south-eastern edge of the plateau is bounded by the Cévennes range.

Massine /mæˈsiːn/ Léonide Fedorovich (1895–1979), Russian-American dancer, choreographer, ballet master, and teacher. As dancer he was most successful in character roles, and as choreographer he was important for his contributions to the comedy genre and as the originator of the symphonic ballet. His many symphonic ballets include Les Présages (Tchaikovsky's Fifth, 1934) and Seventh Symphony (Beethoven, 1938).

Massinger /ˈmæsɪndʒə(r)/, Philip (1583–1640), English dramatist, who collaborated with John Fletcher, and became principal dramatist of the leading theatrical company, the King's Men. His writings include tragedies and tragicomedies, but his most enduring plays are his social comedies A New Way to Pay Old Debts (1625/6) and The City Madam (1632), which show a contempt for the arrogance of an effete aristocracy.

massive /ˈmæsɪv/ adj. **1** large and heavy or solid. **2** (of the

features, head, etc.) relatively large; of solid build. **3** exceptionally large (took a massive overdose). **4** substantial, impressive (a massive reputation). **5** Mineral. not visibly crystalline. **6** Geol. without structural divisions. □□ **massively** adv. **massiveness** n. [ME f. F massif -ive f. OF massiz ult. f. L massa MASS¹]

Masson /ˈmæsɔ̃/, André (1896–1987), French painter, sculptor, engraver, stage designer, and writer, one of the leading figures of surrealism. He was severely wounded in the First World War and deeply scarred emotionally; themes of violence, psychic pain, and eroticism are common in his work.

Massorah var. of MASORAH.

Massorete var. of MASORETE.

mast¹ /mɑːst/ n. & v. —n. **1** a long upright post of timber, iron, etc., set up on a ship's keel, esp. to support sails. **2** a post or lattice-work upright for supporting a radio or television aerial. **3** a flag-pole (half-mast). **4** (in full **mooring-mast**) a strong steel tower to the top of which an airship can be moored. —v.tr. furnish (a ship) with masts. □ **before the mast** serving as an ordinary seaman (quartered in the forecastle). □□ **masted** adj. (also in comb.). **master** n. (also in comb.). [OE mæst f. WG]

mast² /mɑːst/ n. the fruit of the beech, oak, chestnut, and other forest-trees, esp. as food for pigs. [OE mæst f. WG, prob. rel. to MEAT]

mastaba /ˈmæstəbə/ n. **1** an ancient Egyptian tomb, rectangular in shape with sloping sides and a flat roof, standing to a height of 5–6 metres. Such structures were the private tombs of the Old Kingdom period; a great number were found in necropolises, grouped around the royal tomb (e.g. at Saqqara). The interior is composed of two parts: an underground burial chamber, and rooms above it (at ground level) to store offerings etc. **2** a bench, usu. of stone, attached to a house in Islamic countries. [Arab. maṣṭabah bench]

mastectomy /mæsˈtektəmɪ/ n. (pl. **-ies**) Surgery the amputation of a breast. [Gk mastos breast + -ECTOMY]

master /ˈmɑːstə(r)/ n., adj., & v. —n. **1 a** a person having control of persons or things. **b** an employer. **c** a male head of a household (master of the house). **d** the owner of a dog, horse, etc. **e** the owner of a slave. **f** Naut. the captain of a merchant ship. **g** Hunting the person in control of a pack of hounds etc. **2** a male teacher or tutor, esp. a schoolmaster. **3 a** the head of a college, school, etc. **b** the presiding officer of a livery company, Masonic lodge, etc. **4** a person who or gets the upper hand (we shall see which of us is master). **5** a person skilled in a particular trade and able to teach others (often attrib.: master carpenter). **6** a holder of a university degree orig. giving authority to teach in the university (Master of Arts; Master of Science). **7 a** a revered teacher in philosophy etc. **b** (the Master) Christ. **8** a great artist. **9** Chess etc. a player of proved ability at international level. **10** an original version (e.g. of a film or gramophone record) from which a series of copies can be made. **11** (**Master**) a title prefixed to the name of a boy not old enough to be called Mr (Master T. Jones; Master Tom). **b** archaic a title for a man of high rank, learning, etc. **12** (in England and Wales) an official of the Supreme Court. **13** a machine or device directly controlling another (cf. SLAVE). **14** (**Master**) a courtesy title of the eldest son of a Scottish viscount or baron (the Master of Falkland). —adj. **1** commanding, superior (a master spirit). **2** main, principal (master bedroom). **3** controlling others (master plan). —v.tr. **1** overcome, defeat. **2** reduce to subjection. **3** acquire complete knowledge of (a subject) or facility in using (an instrument etc.). **4** rule as a master. □ **be master of 1** have at one's disposal. **2** know how to control. **be one's own master** be independent or free to do as one wishes. **make oneself master of** acquire a thorough knowledge of or facility in using. **Master Aircrew** an RAF rank equivalent to warrant-officer. **master-at-arms** (pl. **masters-at-arms**) the chief police officer on a man-of-war or a merchant ship. **master-class** a class given by a person of distinguished skill, esp. in music. **master-hand 1** a person having commanding power or great skill. **2** the action of such a person. **master-key** a key that opens several locks, each of which also has its own key. **master mariner 1** the captain of a merchant ship. **2** a seaman certified competent to be captain. **master mason 1** a skilled mason, or one in business on his or

b but d dog f few g get h he j yes k cat l leg m man n no p pen r red s sit t top v voice

her own account. **2** a fully qualified Freemason, who has passed the third degree. **Master of Ceremonies** see CEREMONY. **Master of the Rolls** (in England and Wales) a judge who presides over the Court of Appeal and was formerly in charge of the Public Record Office. **master-stroke** an outstandingly skilful act of policy etc. **master-switch** a switch controlling the supply of electricity etc. to an entire system. **master touch** a masterly manner of dealing with something. **master-work** a masterpiece. □□ **masterdom** *n.* **masterhood** *n.* **masterless** *adj.* [OE *mægester* (later also f. OF *maistre*) f. L *magister*, prob. rel. to *magis* more]

masterful /ˈmɑːstəˌfʊl/ *adj.* **1** imperious, domineering. **2** masterly. ¶ Normally used of a person, whereas *masterly* is used of achievements, abilities, etc. □□ **masterfully** *adv.* **masterfulness** *n.*

masterly /ˈmɑːstəlɪ/ *adj.* worthy of a master; very skilful (*a masterly piece of work*). □□ **masterliness** *n.*

mastermind /ˈmɑːstəˌmaɪnd/ *n. & v.* —*n.* **1 a** a person with an outstanding intellect. **b** such an intellect. **2** the person directing an intricate operation. —*v.tr.* plan and direct (a scheme or enterprise).

masterpiece /ˈmɑːstəˌpiːs/ *n.* **1** an outstanding piece of artistry or workmanship. **2** a person's best work.

mastership /ˈmɑːstəʃɪp/ *n.* **1** the position or function of a master, esp. a schoolmaster. **2** dominion, control.

mastersinger /ˈmɑːstəˌsɪŋə(r)/ *n.* = MEISTERSINGER.

Masters Tournament a prestigious golf competition in which golfers (chiefly professionals) compete only by invitation on the basis of their past achievements. It has been held annually since 1934 at Augusta, Georgia, in the US, and was instituted by the US golfer Bobby Jones.

mastery /ˈmɑːstərɪ/ *n.* **1** dominion, sway. **2** masterly skill. **3** (often foll. by *of*) comprehensive knowledge or use of a subject or instrument. **4** (prec. by *the*) the upper hand. [ME f. OF *maistrie* (as MASTER)]

masthead /ˈmɑːsthed/ *n. & v.* —*n.* **1** the highest part of a ship's mast, esp. that of a lower mast as a place of observation or punishment. **2** the title of a newspaper etc. at the head of the front or editorial page. —*v.tr.* **1** send (a sailor) to the masthead. **2** raise (a sail) to its position on the mast.

mastic /ˈmæstɪk/ *n.* **1** a gum or resin exuded from the bark of the mastic tree, used in making varnish. **2** (in full **mastic tree**) the evergreen tree, *Pistacia lentiscus*, yielding this. **3** a waterproof filler and sealant used in building. **4** a liquor flavoured with mastic gum. [ME f. OF f. LL *mastichum* f. L *mastiche* f. Gk *mastikhē*, perh. f. *mastikhaō* (see MASTICATE) with ref. to its use as chewing-gum]

masticate /ˈmæstɪˌkeɪt/ *v.tr.* grind or chew (food) with one's teeth. □□ **mastication** /-ˈkeɪʃ(ə)n/ *n.* **masticator** *n.* **masticatory** *adj.* [LL *masticare masticat-* f. Gk *mastikhaō* gnash the teeth]

mastiff /ˈmæstɪf, ˈmɑːs-/ *n.* **1** a dog of a large strong breed with drooping ears and pendulous lips. **2** this breed of dog. [ME ult. f. OF *mastin* ult. f. L *mansuetus* tame; see MANSUETUDE]

mastitis /mæˈstaɪtɪs/ *n.* an inflammation of the mammary gland (the breast or udder). [Gk *mastos* breast + -ITIS]

mastodon /ˈmæstəˌdɒn/ *n.* a large extinct mammal of the genus *Mammut*, resembling the elephant but having nipple-shaped tubercles on the crowns of its molar teeth. □□ **mastodontic** /-ˈdɒntɪk/ *adj.* [mod.L f. Gk *mastos* breast + *odous odontos* tooth]

mastoid /ˈmæstɔɪd/ *adj. & n.* —*adj.* shaped like a woman's breast. —*n.* **1** = *mastoid process.* **2** *colloq.* mastoiditis. □ **mastoid process** a conical prominence on the temporal bone behind the ear, to which muscles are attached. [F *mastoïde* or mod.L *mastoides* f. Gk *mastoeidēs* f. *mastos* breast]

mastoiditis /ˌmæstɔɪˈdaɪtɪs/ *n.* inflammation of the mastoid process.

masturbate /ˈmæstəˌbeɪt/ *v.intr. & tr.* arouse oneself sexually or cause (another person) to be aroused by manual stimulation of the genitals. □□ **masturbation** /-ˈbeɪʃ(ə)n/ *n.* **masturbator** *n.* **masturbatory** *adj.* [L *masturbari masturbat-*]

mat[1] /mæt/ *n. & v.* —*n.* **1** a piece of coarse material for wiping shoes on, esp. a doormat. **2** a piece of cork, rubber, plastic, etc., to protect a surface from the heat or moisture of an object placed on it. **3** a piece of resilient material for landing on in gymnastics, wrestling, etc. **4** a piece of coarse fabric of plaited rushes, straw, etc., for lying on, packing furniture, etc. **5** a small rug. —*v.* (**matted, matting**) **1 a** *tr.* (esp. as **matted** *adj.*) entangle in a thick mass (*matted hair*). **b** *intr.* become matted. **2** *tr.* cover or furnish with mats. □ **on the mat** *sl.* being reprimanded (orig. in the army, on the orderly-room mat before the commanding officer). [OE *m(e)att(e)* f. WG f. LL *matta*]

mat[2] var. of MATT.

mat[3] /mæt/ *n.* = MATRIX 1. [abbr.]

Matabele /ˌmætəˈbiːlɪ/ *n.* (*pl.* same) a member of a people of Zulu stock living in Zimbabwe. [Ndebele, native name]

Matabeleland /ˌmætəˈbiːlɪˌlænd/ *hist.* a province of Southern Rhodesia lying between the Limpopo and Zambezi rivers and occupied by the Matabele people. It is now divided into the two provinces of Matabeleland North and South, in southern Zimbabwe.

matador /ˈmætəˌdɔː(r)/ *n.* **1** a bullfighter whose task is to kill the bull. **2** a principal card in ombre, quadrille, etc. **3** a domino game in which the piece played must make a total of seven. [Sp. f. *matar* kill f. Pers. *māt* dead]

Mata Hari /ˌmɑːtə ˈhɑːrɪ/ (real name Margaretha Geertruida Zelle, 1876–1917) Dutch courtesan and secret agent. She became a professional dancer in Paris in 1905 and probably worked for both French and German intelligence services before being executed by the French in 1917. [Malay *mata* eye + *hari* day]

match[1] /mætʃ/ *n. & v.* —*n.* **1** a contest or game of skill etc. in which persons or teams compete against each other. **2 a** a person able to contend with another as an equal (*meet one's match*; *be more than a match for*). **b** a person equal to another in some quality (*we shall never see his match*). **c** a person or thing exactly like or corresponding to another. **3** a marriage. **4** a person viewed in regard to his or her eligibility for marriage, esp. as to rank or fortune (*an excellent match*). —*v.* **1 a** *tr.* be equal to or harmonious with; correspond to in some essential respect (*the curtains match the wallpaper*). **b** *intr.* (often foll. by *with*) correspond; harmonize (*his socks do not match*; *does the ribbon match with your hat?*). **2** *tr.* (foll. by *against*, *with*) place (a person etc.) in conflict, contest, or competition with (another). **3** *tr.* find material etc. that matches (another) (*can you match this silk?*). **4** *tr.* find (a person or thing) suitable for another (*matching unemployed workers with vacant posts*). **5** *tr.* prove to be a match for. **6** *tr.* Electronics produce or have an adjustment of (circuits) such that maximum power is transmitted between them. **7** *tr.* (usu. foll. by *with*) *archaic* join (a person) with another in marriage. □ **make a match** bring about a marriage. **match play** *Golf* play in which the score is reckoned by counting the holes won by each side (cf. *stroke play*). **match point 1** *Tennis* etc. **a** the state of a game when one side needs only one more point to win the match. **b** this point. **2** *Bridge* a unit of scoring in matches and tournaments. **to match** corresponding in some essential respect with what has been mentioned (*yellow dress with gloves to match*). **well-matched** fit to contend with each other, live together, etc., on equal terms. □□ **matchable** *adj.* [OE *gemæcca* mate, companion, f. Gmc]

match[2] /mætʃ/ *n.* **1** a short thin piece of wood, wax, etc., tipped with a composition that can be ignited by friction. **2** a piece of wick, cord, etc., designed to burn at a uniform rate, for firing a cannon etc. [ME f. OF *mesche*, *meiche*, perh. f. L *myxa* lamp-nozzle]

matchboard /ˈmætʃbɔːd/ *n.* a board with a tongue cut along one edge and a groove along another, so as to fit with similar boards.

matchbox /ˈmætʃbɒks/ *n.* a box for holding matches.

matchet var. of MACHETE.

matchless /ˈmætʃlɪs/ *adj.* without an equal, incomparable. □□ **matchlessly** *adv.*

matchlock /ˈmætʃlɒk/ *n. hist.* **1** an old type of gun with a lock in which a match was placed for igniting the powder. **2** such a lock.

matchmaker /'mætʃˌmeɪkə(r)/ n. a person fond of scheming to bring about marriages. □□ **matchmaking** n.

matchstick /'mætʃstɪk/ n. the stem of a match.

matchwood /'mætʃwʊd/ n. 1 wood suitable for matches. 2 minute splinters. □ **make matchwood of** smash utterly.

mate¹ /meɪt/ n. & v. —n. 1 a friend or fellow worker. 2 colloq. a general form of address, esp. to another man. 3 a each of a pair, esp. of birds. b colloq. a partner in marriage. c (in comb.) a fellow member or joint occupant of (team-mate; room-mate). 4 Naut. an officer on a merchant ship subordinate to the master. 5 an assistant to a skilled worker (plumber's mate). —v. (often foll. by with) 1 a tr. bring (animals or birds) together for breeding. b intr. (of animals or birds) come together for breeding. 2 a tr. join (persons) in marriage. b intr. (of persons) be joined in marriage. 3 intr. Mech. fit well. □□ **mateless** adj. [ME f. MLG mate f. gemate messmate f. WG, rel. to MEAT]

mate² /meɪt/ n. & v.tr. Chess = CHECKMATE. □ **fool's mate** a series of moves in which the first player is mated at the second player's second move. **scholar's mate** a series of moves in which the second player is mated at the first player's fourth move. [ME f. F mat(er): see CHECKMATE]

maté /'mæteɪ/ n. 1 an infusion of the leaves of a S. American shrub, Ilex paraguayensis. 2 this shrub, or its leaves. 3 a vessel in which these leaves are infused. [Sp. mate f. Quechua mati]

matelot /'mætləʊ/ n. (also **matlow, matlo**) Brit. sl. a sailor. [F matelot]

matelote /'mætəˌləʊt/ n. a dish of fish etc. with a sauce of wine and onions. [F (as MATELOT)]

mater /'meɪtə(r)/ n. Brit. sl. mother. ¶ Now only in jocular or affected use. [L]

materfamilias /ˌmeɪtəfəˈmɪlɪˌæs/ n. the woman head of a family or household (cf. PATERFAMILIAS). [L f. mater mother + familia FAMILY]

material /məˈtɪərɪəl/ n. & adj. —n. 1 the matter from which a thing is made. 2 cloth, fabric. 3 (in pl.) things needed for an activity (building materials; cleaning materials; writing materials). 4 a person or thing of a specified kind or suitable for a purpose (officer material). 5 (in sing. or pl.) information etc. to be used in writing a book etc. (experimental material; materials for a biography). 6 (in sing. or pl., often foll. by of) the elements or constituent parts of a substance. —adj. 1 of matter; corporeal. 2 concerned with bodily comfort etc. (material well-being). 3 (of conduct, points of view, etc.) not spiritual. 4 (often foll. by to) important, essential, relevant (at the material time). 5 concerned with the matter, not the form, of reasoning. □□ **materiality** /-ɪˈælɪtɪ/ n. [ME f. OF materiel, -al, f. LL materialis f. L (as MATTER)]

materialism /məˈtɪərɪəˌlɪz(ə)m/ n. 1 a tendency to prefer material possessions and physical comfort to spiritual values. 2 Philos. a the opinion that nothing exists but matter and its movements and modifications. b the doctrine that consciousness and will are wholly due to material agency. 3 Art a tendency to lay stress on the material aspect of objects. □□ **materialist** n. **materialistic** /-ˈlɪstɪk/ adj. **materialistically** /-ˈlɪstɪkəlɪ/ adv.

materialize /məˈtɪərɪəˌlaɪz/ v. (also **-ise**) 1 intr. become actual fact. 2 a tr. cause (a spirit) to appear in bodily form. b intr. (of a spirit) appear in this way. 3 intr. colloq. appear or be present when expected. 4 tr. represent or express in material form. 5 tr. make materialistic. □□ **materialization** /-ˈzeɪʃ(ə)n/ n.

materially /məˈtɪərɪəlɪ/ adv. 1 substantially, considerably. 2 in respect of matter.

materia medica /məˈtɪərɪə ˈmedɪkə/ n. 1 the remedial substances used in the practice of medicine. 2 the study of the origin and properties of these substances. [mod.L, transl. Gk hulē iatrikē healing material]

matériel /məˌtɪərɪˈel/ n. available means, esp. materials and equipment in warfare (opp. PERSONNEL). [F (as MATERIAL)]

maternal /məˈtɜːn(ə)l/ adj. 1 of or like a mother. 2 motherly. 3 related through the mother (maternal uncle). 4 of the mother in pregnancy and childbirth. □□ **maternalism** n. **maternalistic** /-ˈlɪstɪk/ adj. **maternally** adv. [ME f. OF maternel or L maternus f. mater mother]

maternity /məˈtɜːnɪtɪ/ n. 1 motherhood. 2 motherliness. 3 (attrib.) a for women during and just after childbirth (maternity hospital; maternity leave). b suitable for a pregnant woman (maternity dress; maternity wear). [F maternité f. med.L maternitas -tatis f. L maternus f. mater mother]

mateship /'meɪtʃɪp/ n. Austral. companionship, fellowship.

matey /'meɪtɪ/ adj. & n. (also **maty**) —adj. (**matier, matiest**) (often foll. by with) sociable; familiar and friendly. —n. Brit. (pl. **-eys**) colloq. (usu. as a form of address) mate, companion. □□ **mateyness** n. (also **matiness**). **matily** adv.

math /mæθ/ n. US colloq. mathematics (cf. MATHS). [abbr.]

mathematical /ˌmæθɪˈmætɪk(ə)l/ adj. 1 of or relating to mathematics. 2 (of a proof etc.) rigorously precise. □ **mathematical induction** = INDUCTION 3b. **mathematical logic** the part of mathematics concerned with the study of formal languages, formal reasoning, the nature of mathematical proof, provability of mathematical statements, computability, and other aspects of the foundations of mathematics. Its roots lie in Boole's mid-19th-c. algebraic description of logic. Its growth was enormously stimulated by Principia Mathematica (1910–13) in which A. N. Whitehead and Bertrand Russell attempted to express all of mathematics in formal logical terms, and by Gödel's incompleteness theorem (1931) which, by showing that no such enterprise could ever succeed, has led to investigation of the boundary between what is possible in mathematics and what is not. **mathematical tables** tables of logarithms and trigonometric values etc. □□ **mathematically** adv. [F mathématique or L mathematicus f. Gk mathēmatikos f. mathēma -matos science f. manthanō learn]

mathematics /ˌmæθɪˈmætɪks/ n.pl. 1 (also treated as sing.) the body of knowledge and reasoning about numbers, spatial forms, logic, and relationships between them, and applications to measurement and prediction in science and other areas. The main parts of pure mathematics are algebra (including arithmetic), analysis, geometry (including topology), logic. Applied mathematics includes classical mechanics, continuum mechanics (hydrodynamics, elasticity, etc.), quantum mechanics, relativity theory, statistics, and many other newer areas of application to computing, economics, biological sciences, etc. 2 (as pl.) the use of mathematics in calculation etc. □□ **mathematician** /-məˈtɪʃ(ə)n/ n. [prob. f. F mathématiques pl. f. L mathematica f. Gk mathēmatika: see MATHEMATICAL]

maths /mæθs/ n. Brit. colloq. mathematics (cf. MATH). [abbr.]

Matilda¹ /məˈtɪldə/ (1102–67), queen of England for a few months in 1135, widowed wife of the Emperor Henry V (d.1125), and the only legitimate child of Henry I of England. (See STEPHEN¹.)

Matilda² /məˈtɪldə/ n. Austral. sl. a bushman's bundle; a swag. □ **waltz** (or **walk**) **Matilda** carry a swag. [the name Matilda]

matinée /'mætɪˌneɪ/ n. (US **matinee**) an afternoon performance in the theatre, cinema, etc. □ **matinée coat** (or **jacket**) a baby's short coat. **matinée idol** a handsome actor admired chiefly by women. [F, = what occupies a morning f. matin morning (as MATINS)]

matins /'mætɪnz/ n. (also **mattins**) (as sing or pl.) 1 a a service of morning prayer in the Church of England. b the office of one of the canonical hours of prayer, properly a night office, but also recited with lauds at daybreak or on the previous evening. 2 (also **matin**) poet. the morning song of birds. [ME f. OF matines f. eccl.L matutinas, accus. fem. pl. adj. f. L matutinus of the morning f. Matuta dawn-goddess]

Matisse /mæˈtiːs/, Henri Emile Benoît (1869–1954), French painter who first studied law, which he abandoned after 1890. Matisse was influenced by the impressionists and by Gauguin and Cézanne, colour and simplified design playing an increasingly important role in his art. About 1904 he was experimenting with a free neo-impressionist technique, but by then he was associated with Derain and Vlaminck and was already regarded as a leader of the fauve group, notorious for their crude compositions and arbitrary use of colour. His Bonheur de vivre, exhibited in 1906, heralded a new more personal style—a sense of rhythmic decorative pattern (with a clear debt to the aesthetics of art nouveau) imposed on a flat ground. The imagery of Arcadia, of nude figures frolicking in a Golden Age, was to become a lifelong obsession. He continued to develop throughout his life a style based on simple reductive line on a field of rich, saturated colour, and has exerted a powerful influence on 20th-c. art. Matisse also made prints and sculpture, and produced ballet designs for Diaghilev and Massine.

matlo (also **matlow**) var. of MATELOT.

Matmata /mæt'mɑ:tə/ a town in SE Tunisia, in the Matmata hills, south of Gabès. In this region for many centuries the people have lived in underground dwellings hacked from the tufa.

Mato Grosso /ˌmætəʊ 'ɡrɒsəʊ/ an area of SW Brazil (its Portuguese name means 'dense forest'), now divided into two States: Mato Grosso, pop. (est. 1987) 1,580,900, capital, Cuiabá, and Mato Grosso do Sul, pop. (est. 1987) 1,673,500; capital, Campo Grande.

matrass /'mætrəs/ n. hist. a long-necked glass vessel with a round or oval body, used for distilling etc. [F matras, of uncert. orig.]

matriarch /'meɪtrɪˌɑ:k/ n. a woman who is the head of a family or tribe. □□ **matriarchal** /-'ɑ:k(ə)l/ adj. [L mater mother, on the false analogy of PATRIARCH]

matriarchy /'meɪtrɪˌɑ:kɪ/ n. (pl. **-ies**) a form of social organization in which the mother is the head of the family and descent is reckoned through the female line.

matric /mə'trɪk/ n. Brit. colloq. matriculation. [abbr.]

matrices pl. of MATRIX.

matricide /'meɪtrɪˌsaɪd/ n. **1** the killing of one's mother. **2** a person who does this. □□ **matricidal** adj. [L matricida, matricidium f. mater matris mother]

matriculate /mə'trɪkjʊˌleɪt/ v. **1** intr. be enrolled at a college or university. **2** tr. admit (a student) to membership of a college or university. □□ **matriculatory** adj. [med.L matriculare matriculat- enrol f. LL matricula register, dimin. of L MATRIX]

matriculation /məˌtrɪkjʊ'leɪʃ(ə)n/ n. **1** the act or an instance of matriculating. **2** an examination to qualify for this.

matrilineal /ˌmætrɪ'lɪnɪəl/ adj. of or based on kinship with the mother or the female line. □□ **matrilineally** adv. [L mater matris mother + LINEAL]

matrilocal /ˌmætrɪ'ləʊk(ə)l/ adj. of or denoting a custom in marriage where the husband goes to live with the wife's community. [L mater matris mother + LOCAL]

matrimony /'mætrɪmənɪ/ n. (pl. **-ies**) **1** the rite of marriage. **2** the state of being married. **3 a** a card-game. **b** the combination of king and queen of trumps in some card-games. □□ **matrimonial** /-'məʊnɪəl/ adj. **matrimonially** adv. [ME f. AF matrimonie, OF matremoi(g)ne f. L matrimonium f. mater matris mother]

matrix /'meɪtrɪks/ n. (pl. **matrices** /-ˌsiːz/ or **matrixes**) **1** a mould in which a thing is cast or shaped, such as a gramophone record, printing type, etc. **2 a** an environment or substance in which a thing is developed. **b** a womb. **3** a mass of fine-grained rock in which gems, fossils, etc., are embedded. **4** Math. a rectangular array of elements in rows and columns that is treated as a single element. **5** Biol. the substance between cells or in which structures are embedded. **6** Computing a gridlike array of interconnected circuit elements. □ **matrix printer** = dot matrix printer (see DOT¹). [L, = breeding-female, womb, register f. mater matris mother]

matron /'meɪtrən/ n. **1** a married woman, esp. a dignified and sober one. **2** a woman managing the domestic arrangements of a school etc. **3** Brit. a woman in charge of the nursing in a hospital. ¶ Now usu. called senior nursing officer. □ **matron of honour** a married woman attending the bride at a wedding. □□ **matronhood** n. [ME f. OF matrone f. L matrona f. mater matris mother]

matronly /'meɪtrənlɪ/ adj. like or characteristic of a matron, esp. in respect of staidness or portliness.

Matsuyama /ˌmætsʊ'jɑ:mə/ the capital and largest city of Shikoku island, Japan; pop. (1987) 430,000.

Matt. abbr. Matthew (esp. in the New Testament).

matt /mæt/ adj., n., & v. (also **mat**) —adj. (of a colour, surface, etc.) dull, without lustre. —n. **1** a border of dull gold round a framed picture. **2** (in full **matt paint**) paint formulated to give a dull flat finish (cf. GLOSS¹). **3** the appearance of unburnished gold. —v.tr. (**matted, matting**) **1** make (gilding etc.) dull. **2** frost (glass). [F mat, mater, identical with mat MATE²]

matte¹ /mæt/ n. an impure product of the smelting of sulphide ores, esp. those of copper or nickel. [F]

matte² /mæt/ n. Cinematog. a mask to obscure part of an image and allow another image to be superimposed, giving a combined effect. [F]

matter /'mætə(r)/ n. & v. —n. **1 a** a physical substance in general, as distinct from mind and spirit. **b** that which occupies space and possesses rest mass, including atoms, their major constituents, and substances made of atoms, but not light and other electromagnetic radiation. (See below) **2** a particular substance (colouring matter). **3** (prec. by the; often foll. by with) the thing that is amiss (what is the matter?; there is something the matter with him). **4** material for thought or expression. **5 a** the substance of a book, speech, etc., as distinct from its manner or form. **b** Logic the particular content of a proposition, as distinct from its form. **6** a thing or things of a specified kind (printed matter; reading matter). **7** an affair or situation being considered, esp. in a specified way (a serious matter; the matter of your concern; the matter of your overdraft). **8** Physiol. **a** any substance in or discharged from the body (faecal matter; grey matter). **b** pus. **9** (foll. by of, for) what is or may be a good reason for (complaint, regret, etc.). **10** Printing the body of a printed work, as type or as printed sheets. —v.intr. **1** (often foll. by to) be of importance; have significance (it does not matter to me when it happened). **2** secrete or discharge pus. □ **as a matter of fact** in reality (esp. to correct a falsehood or misunderstanding). **for that matter** (or **for the matter of that**) **1** as far as that is concerned. **2** and indeed also. **in the matter of** as regards. **a matter of 1** approximately (for a matter of 40 years). **2** a thing that relates to, depends on, or is determined by (a matter of habit; only a matter of time before they agree). **a matter of course** see COURSE. **a matter of fact 1** what belongs to the sphere of fact as distinct from opinion etc. **2** Law the part of a judicial inquiry concerned with the truth of alleged facts (see also MATTER-OF-FACT). **a matter of form** a mere routine. **a matter of law** Law the part of a judicial inquiry concerned with the interpretation of the law. **a matter of record** see RECORD. **no matter 1** (foll. by when, how, etc.) regardless of (will do it no matter what the consequences). **2** it is of no importance. **what is the matter with** surely there is no objection to. **what matter?** that need not worry us. [ME f. AF mater(i)e, OF matiere f. L materia timber, substance, subject of discourse]

Until the 19th c., Western scientific thought regarded all bodies as forms of matter or as matter united to spirit. With the advent of Faraday's concept of electric and magnetic fields, and the discovery that light is a form of electromagnetic radiation, a new fundamental distinction gained prominence in physics, that between matter and field. Matter is distinguished from light, radio waves, X-rays, electric and magnetic fields, and gravitational fields. Most material bodies are composed of protons, neutrons, and electrons. Matter may be partly or wholly transformed into kinetic energy and electromagnetic radiation; such transformations account for nuclear energy and for nuclear explosions.

Matterhorn /'mætəˌhɔ:n/ a spectacular Alpine peak on the Swiss–Italian border, rising to 4,477 m (14,688 ft.).

matter-of-fact /ˌmætərə'fækt/ adj. (see also MATTER). **1** unimaginative, prosaic. **2** unemotional. □□ **matter-of-factly** adv. **matter-of-factness** n.

Matthew /'mæθjuː/, St **1** an Apostle, a tax-gatherer from Capernaum in Galilee, traditionally but erroneously supposed to be the author of the first Gospel. Feast day, 21 Sept. **2** the first Gospel, written after AD 70 and based largely on that of St Mark.

Matthew Paris /ˌmæθju 'pærɪs/ (c.1199–1259) English chronicler, a Benedictine monk at St Albans. His Chronica Majora, a history of the world from the Creation to 1259, is a valuable source for contemporary events, notable for its trenchant criticism of ecclesiastical abuses.

Matthews /ˈmæθjuːz/, Sir Stanley (1915–), English Association football player who played for England 54 times. His career in first-class football lasted until he was 50.

Matthias /məˈθaɪəs/, St (1st c. AD), an Apostle, chosen by lot after the Ascension to take the place left by Judas Iscariot, who had betrayed Christ and subsequently committed suicide. Feast day, traditionally 24 (25) Feb. in the West, but since 1969 14 May in the Roman Church, 9 Aug. in the East.

matting /ˈmætɪŋ/ n. **1** fabric of hemp, bast, grass, etc., for mats (*coconut matting*). **2** in senses of MAT¹ v.

mattins var. of MATINS.

mattock /ˈmætək/ n. an agricultural tool shaped like a pickaxe, with an adze and a chisel edge as the ends of the head. [OE *mattuc*, of unkn. orig.]

mattoid /ˈmætɔɪd/ n. a person of erratic mind, a mixture of genius and fool. [It. *mattoide* f. *matto* insane]

mattress /ˈmætrɪs/ n. a fabric case stuffed with soft, firm, or springy material, or a similar case filled with air or water, used on or as a bed. [ME f. OF *materas* f. It. *materasso* f. Arab. *almaṭraḥ* the place, the cushion f. *ṭaraḥa* throw]

maturate /ˈmætjʊˌreɪt/ v.intr. Med. (of a boil etc.) come to maturation. [L *maturatus* (as MATURE v.)]

maturation /ˌmætjʊˈreɪʃ(ə)n/ n. **1 a** the act or an instance of maturing; the state of being matured. **b** the ripening of fruit. **2** Med. **a** the formation of purulent matter. **b** the causing of this. □□ **maturative** /məˈtjʊərətɪv/ adj. [ME f. F *maturation* or med.L *maturatio* f. L (as MATURE v.)]

mature /məˈtjʊə(r)/ adj. & v. —adj. (**maturer, maturest**) **1** with fully developed powers of body and mind, adult. **2** complete in natural development, ripe. **3** (of thought, intentions, etc.) duly careful and adequate. **4** (of a bill etc.) due for payment. —v. **1** tr. & intr. develop fully. **b** tr. & intr. ripen. **c** intr. come to maturity. **2** tr. perfect (a plan etc.). **3** intr. (of a bill etc.) become due for payment. □ **mature student** an adult student who is older than most students. □□ **maturely** adv. **matureness** n. **maturity** n. [ME f. L *maturus* timely, early]

matutinal /ˌmætjuːˈtaɪn(ə)l, məˈtjuːtɪn(ə)l/ adj. **1** of or occurring in the morning. **2** early. [LL *matutinalis* f. L *matutinus*: see MATINS]

maty var. of MATEY.

matzo /ˈmɑːtsəʊ/ n. (pl. **-os** or **matzoth** /-əʊt/) **1** a wafer of unleavened bread for the Passover. **2** such bread collectively. [Yiddish f. Heb. *maṣṣāh*]

Maud /mɔːd/ = Matilda (see entry).

maud /mɔːd/ n. **1** a Scots shepherd's grey striped plaid. **2** a travelling-rug like this. [18th c.: orig. unkn.]

maudlin /ˈmɔːdlɪn/ adj. & n. —adj. weakly or tearfully sentimental, esp. in a tearful and effusive stage of drunkenness. —n. weak or mawkish sentiment. [ME f. OF *Madeleine* f. eccl.L *Magdalena* MAGDALEN, with ref. to pictures of Mary Magdalen weeping]

Maugham /mɔːm/, William Somerset (1874–1965), English novelist and dramatist. His first novel *Lisa of Lambeth* (1897) was followed by many others, including *Of Human Bondage* (1915), *Cakes and Ale* (1930), and *The Razor's Edge* (1944). Among his successful plays are *The Circle* (1921) and *East of Suez* (1922). Maugham's wide travels provided exotic settings for many of his stories; he made his home on the French Riviera in 1926. He was a cynical observer of human frailties, and although his novels remain popular, he states in his autobiography (*The Summing Up*, 1938) that he stood 'in the very front row of the second-raters', a judgement that most critics have endorsed.

maul /mɔːl/ v. & n. —v.tr. **1** beat and bruise. **2** handle roughly or carelessly. **3** damage by criticism. —n. **1** *Rugby Football* a loose scrum with the ball off the ground. **2** a brawl. **3** a special heavy hammer, commonly of wood, esp. for driving piles. □□ **mauler** n. [ME f. OF *mail* f. L *malleus* hammer]

maulstick /ˈmɔːlstɪk/ n. (also **mahlstick**) a light stick with a padded leather ball at one end, held by a painter in one hand to support the other hand. [Du. *maalstok* f. *malen* to paint + *stok* stick]

Mau Mau /maʊ maʊ/ an African secret society, an underground anti-British terrorist movement functioning within the Kikuyu tribe in Kenya in the 1950s, vehicle of native discontent with colonial rule. As the result of a well-organized counter-insurgency campaign the British were eventually able to subdue the terrorists, and went on to institute widespread political and social reforms, eventually leading to Kenyan independence in 1963.

maunder /ˈmɔːndə(r)/ v.intr. **1** talk in a dreamy or rambling manner. **2** move or act listlessly or idly. [perh. f. obs. *maunder* beggar, to beg]

Maundy /ˈmɔːndɪ/ n. the ceremony of washing the feet of a number of poor people, performed by royal or other eminent persons, or by ecclesiastics, on the Thursday before Easter, and commonly followed by the distribution of clothing, food, or money. It was instituted in commemoration of Christ's washing the Apostles' feet at the Last Supper (John 13). In Britain (except in the RC Church) the distribution of Maundy money (see below) is all that remains of this ceremony. From the time of Henry IV the number of recipients has corresponded to the number of years in the sovereign's age, and the value in pence of the amount received by each now corresponds similarly. □ **Maundy money** specially minted silver coins distributed by the sovereign to the poor on Maundy Thursday. The first were issued in 1662. **Maundy Thursday** the Thursday before Easter, celebrated in memory of the Last Supper. [ME f. OF *mandé* f. L *mandatum* MANDATE, commandment (see John 13: 34)]

Maupassant /ˈmoʊpæˌsɑ̃/, Guy de (1850–93), French short-story writer and novelist, a disciple of Flaubert and one of the naturalist writers of Zola's circle. He contributed 'Boule de Suif' to their *Les Soirées de Médan* (1880) and became an immediate celebrity. In his brief creative life he wrote about 300 short stories and six novels, portraying a wide range of society and embracing themes of war, mystery, hallucination, and horror, written in a simple direct narrative style. His best-known novels are *Une Vie* (1883), *Bel-Ami* (1885), and *Pierre et Jean* (1888). He suffered from syphilis which resulted in a mental disorder, and spent the last 18 months of his life in an asylum.

Mauretania /ˌmɒrɪˈteɪnɪə/ the ancient name for the land of the Moors (Latin *Mauri*) in North Africa, reaching from the Atlantic to Numidia, formed into two Roman provinces by the emperor Claudius. It is now part of Morocco and Algeria. □□ **Mauretanian** adj. & n.

Mauriac /ˈmɔːrɪˌæk/, François (1885–1970), French novelist, dramatist, and critic, whose works include *Thérèse Desqueyroux* (1927), *Le Noeud de vipères* (1932), and the drama *Asmodée* (1938). His stories, usually set in the country round Bordeaux, show the conflict between prosperous bourgeois convention, religion, and human frailty. He was awarded the Nobel Prize for literature in 1952.

Mauritania /ˌmɒrɪˈteɪnɪə/ a country in West Africa with a coastline on the Atlantic Ocean; pop. (est. 1988) 1,919,000; official language, French; capital, Nouakchott. The country, which is mainly desert in the north but more fertile in the south, supports a largely pastoral economy. A French protectorate from 1902 and a colony from 1920, Mauritania achieved full independence in 1961. □□ **Mauritanian** adj. & n.

Mauritius /məˈrɪʃəs/ an island country in the Indian Ocean, about 850 km (550 miles) east of Madagascar; pop. (est. 1988) 1,100,000; official language, English; capital, Port Louis. Discovered by the Portuguese in the early 16th c., Mauritius was held by the Dutch (who named it in honour of Prince Maurice) from 1598 to 1710 and then by the French until 1810, when it was ceded to Britain; after 158 years as a Crown colony it became independent as a member of the Commonwealth in 1968. The economy is largely dependent on sugar, and overpopulation and severe unemployment cause continuing social problems. □□ **Mauritian** adj. & n.

Maurya /ˈmaʊrɪə/ **1** a dynasty of ancient India (321– c.184 BC) founded by Chandragupta Maurya, who introduced a centralized government and script and developed a highway network which led to Mauryan control of most of the Indian subcontinent. **2** a member of this dynasty. The oldest extant Indian art originated in this era, which was a period of lively contact between India, the Middle East, and the Mediterranean. □□ **Mauryan** adj.

mausoleum /ˌmɔːsəˈliːəm/ n. a large magnificent tomb. The term was originally applied to the marble tomb at Halicarnassus in Caria (one of the Seven Wonders of the World) ordered for himself by Mausolus king of Caria (d. 353 BC) and erected by his queen Artemisia. It has been variously reconstructed but appears to have consisted of a colonnade (enclosing the sarcophagus) above which rose a pyramid-like structure; fragments of the sculptures which adorned it are in the British Museum. [L f. Gk Mausōleion f. Mausōlos Mausolus]

mauve /məʊv/ adj. & n. —adj. pale purple. —n. **1** this colour. **2** a bright but delicate pale purple dye from coal-tar aniline. □□ **mauvish** adj. [F, lit. = mallow, f. L malva]

maven /ˈmeɪv(ə)n/ n. US colloq. an expert or connoisseur. [Heb. mēbīn]

maverick /ˈmævərɪk/ n. **1** US an unbranded calf or yearling. **2** an unorthodox or independent-minded person. [S. A. Maverick, Texas engineer and rancher d. 1870, who did not brand his cattle]

mavis /ˈmeɪvɪs/ n. poet. or dial. a song thrush. [ME f. OF mauvis, of uncert. orig.]

maw /mɔː/ n. **1 a** the stomach of an animal. **b** the jaws or throat of a voracious animal. **2** colloq. the stomach of a greedy person. [OE maga f. Gmc]

mawkish /ˈmɔːkɪʃ/ adj. **1** sentimental in a feeble or sickly way. **2** having a faint sickly flavour. □□ **mawkishly** adv. **mawkishness** n. [obs. mawk maggot f. ON mathkr f. Gmc]

max. abbr. maximum.

maxi /ˈmæksɪ/ n. (pl. **maxis**) colloq. a maxi-coat, -skirt, etc. [abbr.]

maxi- /ˈmæksɪ/ comb. form very large or long (maxi-coat). [abbr. of MAXIMUM: cf. MINI-]

maxilla /mækˈsɪlə/ n. (pl. **maxillae** /-liː/) **1** the jaw or jawbone, esp. the upper jaw in most vertebrates. **2** the mouth-part of many arthropods used in chewing. □□ **maxillary** adj. [L, = jaw]

Maxim /ˈmæksɪm/, Sir Hiram Stevens (1840–1916), versatile American engineer, who emigrated to England in 1882 and took British nationality in 1900. His most famous invention was the machine-gun that bears his name, which he had designed by 1884 and subsquently manufactured. It was the first fully automatic water-cooled gun, firing 10 shots a second from a 250-round cartridge belt; it reached its full potential only after the development of suitable explosives, in which his estranged brother, Hudson Maxim, played a prominent part. Adopted as a standard weapon by the British Army in 1889, and by major powers throughout the world, it was used with devastating effect in the First World War and marked an important change in battle technique.

maxim /ˈmæksɪm/ n. a general truth or rule of conduct expressed in a sentence. [ME f. F maxime or med.L maxima (propositio), fem. adj. (as MAXIMUM)]

maxima pl. of MAXIMUM.

maximal /ˈmæksɪm(ə)l/ adj. being or relating to a maximum; the greatest possible in size, duration, etc. □□ **maximally** adv.

maximalist /ˈmæksɪməlɪst/ n. a person who rejects compromise and expects a full response to (esp. political) demands. [MAXIMAL, after Russ. maksimalist]

Maximilian /ˌmæksɪˈmɪlɪən/ Ferdinand Maximilian Joseph (1832–67), emperor of Mexico. Brother of the Austro-Hungarian emperor Franz Joseph and Archduke of Austria, Maximilian was established as emperor of Mexico under French auspices in 1864. In 1866, however, Napoleon III was forced to withdraw his support as a result of American pressure, and Maximilian was confronted by a popular uprising led by Juárez. His forces proved unable to resist the rebels on their own and in 1867 he was captured and shot.

maximize /ˈmæksɪˌmaɪz/ v.tr. (also **-ise**) increase or enhance to the utmost. □□ **maximization** /-ˈzeɪʃ(ə)n/ n. **maximizer** n. [L maximus: see MAXIMUM]

maximum /ˈmæksɪməm/ n. & adj. —n. (pl. **maxima** /-mə/) the highest possible or attainable amount. —adj. that is a maximum. [mod.L, neut. of L maximus, superl. of magnus great]

Maxwell /ˈmækswel/, James Clerk (1831–79), Scottish physicist whose electromagnetic theory became the chief inspiration for modern theoretical physics. He became the first Cavendish professor of physics at Cambridge in 1871, where he designed the new laboratory named after Henry Cavendish, whose unpublished papers on electricity he edited. He contributed to thermodynamics, the kinetic theory of gases (he showed the importance of the statistical approach), colour vision (he demonstrated one of the earliest colour photographs in 1861), and to the theory of Saturn's rings, but his greatest achievement was to extend the ideas of Faraday and Kelvin into his field equations of electromagnetism; these not only unified electricity and magnetism, but also identified the electromagnetic nature of light and predicted the existence of other electromagnetic radiation, verified later experimentally by Hertz.

maxwell /ˈmækswel/ n. a unit of magnetic flux in the c.g.s. system, equal to that induced through one square centimetre by a perpendicular magnetic field of one gauss. [J. C. MAXWELL]

May /meɪ/ n. **1** the fifth month of the year. **2** (**may**) the hawthorn or its blossom. **3** poet. bloom, prime. □ **may-apple** an American herbaceous plant, Podophyllum peltatum, bearing a yellow egg-shaped fruit in May. **May-bug** a cockchafer. **May Day** 1 May esp. as a festival (orig. associated with spring fertility rites) with dancing, or (since 1889) as an international holiday in honour of workers. **May queen** a girl chosen to preside over celebrations on May Day. **Queen of the May** = May queen. [ME f. OF mai f. L Maius (mensis) (month) of the goddess Maia (see entry), who was worshipped in this month]

may /meɪ/ v.aux. (3rd sing. present **may**; past **might** /maɪt/) **1** (often foll. by well for emphasis) expressing possibility (it may be true; I may have been wrong; you may well lose your way). **2** expressing permission (you may not go; may I come in?). ¶ Both can and may are used to express permission; in more formal contexts may is usual since can also denotes capability (can I move? = am I physically able to move?; may I move? = am I allowed to move?). **3** expressing a wish (may he live to regret it). **4** expressing uncertainty or irony in questions (who may you be?; who are you, may I ask?). **5** in purpose clauses and after wish, fear, etc. (take such measures as may avert disaster; hope he may succeed). □ **be that as it may** (or that is as may be) that may or may not be so (implying that there are other factors) (be that as it may, I still want to go). [OE mæg f. Gmc, rel. to MAIN[1], MIGHT[2]]

Maya /ˈmɑːjə/ n & adj. —n. **1** (pl. same or **Mayas**) a member of an American Indian people of Yucatan and Central America who still maintain aspects of their ancient culture. (See below.) **2** their language, which is still spoken in various forms by several million people. —adj. of the Maya or their language. □□ **Mayan** adj. & n. [native name]
  The Maya civilization developed over an extensive area and reached its peak in the 4th–8th c., a period distinguished by a spectacular flowering of art and learning, contrasting with primitive agriculture in an area surrounded by primeval forests. Remains include stone temples built on pyramids and ornamented with sculptures; the distinctive art style of this period is highly ornamented and detailed. Among the most striking of the Maya achievements are a system of pictorial writing (still largely undeciphered) and a calendar system, more accurate than the Julian, that was still in use at the time of the Spanish conquest in the 16th c.

maya /ˈmɑːjə/ n. **1** Hinduism illusion, magic, the supernatural power wielded by gods and demons. **2** Hinduism & Buddhism **a** the power by which the universe becomes manifest. **b** the material world, regarded as unreal, presented by this power. [Skr. māyā(mā create)]

maybe /ˈmeɪbiː/ adv. perhaps, possibly. [ME f. it may be]

mayday /ˈmeɪdeɪ/ n. an international radio distress-signal used esp. by ships and aircraft. [repr. pronunc. of F m'aidez help me]

mayest /ˈmeɪɪst/ *archaic* = MAYST.

Mayflower /ˈmeɪflaʊə(r)/ the ship in which, in 1620, the Pilgrim Fathers sailed from Plymouth to establish the first permanent colony in New England. It arrived at Cape Cod (Mass.) on 21 Nov., after a voyage of 66 days.

mayflower /ˈmeɪˌflaʊə(r)/ *n.* any of various flowers that bloom in May, esp. the trailing arbutus, *Epigaea repens.*

mayfly /ˈmeɪflaɪ/ *n.* (*pl.* -**flies**) **1** any insect of the order Ephemeroptera, living briefly in spring in the adult stage. **2** an imitation mayfly used by anglers.

mayhap /meɪˈhæp, ˈmeɪ-/ *adv. archaic* perhaps, possibly. [ME f. *it may hap*]

mayhem /ˈmeɪhem/ *n.* **1** violent or damaging action. **2** *hist.* the crime of maiming a person so as to render him or her partly or wholly defenceless. [AF *mahem*, OF *mayhem* (as MAIM)]

maying /ˈmeɪɪŋ/ *n. & adj.* participation in May Day festivities. [ME f. MAY]

mayn't /ˈmeɪənt/ *contr.* may not.

Mayo /ˈmeɪəʊ/ a county of western Ireland, in the province of Connaught; pop. (est. 1986) 115,000; capital, Castlebar.

mayonnaise /ˌmeɪəˈneɪz/ *n.* **1** a thick creamy dressing made of egg-yolks, oil, vinegar, etc. **2** a (usu. specified) dish dressed with this (*chicken mayonnaise*). [F, perh. f. *mahonnais -aise* of Port *Mahon* on Minorca]

mayor /meə(r)/ *n.* **1** the head of the municipal corporation of a city or borough. **2** (in England, Wales, and N. Ireland) the head of a district council with the status of a borough. □□ **mayoral** *adj.* **mayorship** *n.* [ME f. OF *maire* f. L (as MAJOR)]

mayoralty /ˈmeərəltɪ/ *n.* (*pl.* -**ies**) **1** the office of mayor. **2** a mayor's period of office. [ME f. OF *mairalté* (as MAYOR)]

mayoress /ˈmeərɪs/ *n.* **1** a woman holding the office of mayor. **2** the wife of a mayor. **3** a woman fulfilling the ceremonial duties of a mayor's wife.

Mayotte see MAHORE.

maypole /ˈmeɪpəʊl/ *n.* a pole painted and decked with flowers and ribbons, for dancing round on May Day.

mayst /meɪst/ *archaic* 2nd *sing. present* of MAY.

mayweed /ˈmeɪwiːd/ *n.* the stinking camomile, *Anthemis cotula.* [earlier *maidwede* f. obs. *maithe(n)* f. OE *magothe*, *mægtha* + WEED]

mazard /ˈmæzəd/ *n.* (also **mazzard**) **1** the wild sweet cherry, *Prunus avium*, of Europe. **2** *archaic* a head or face. [alt. of MAZER]

Mazar-e-Sharif /mæˌzɑːriːʃəˈriːf/ the largest city in northern Afghanistan; pop. (est. 1984) 118,000.

Mazarin /ˈmæzəˌræ̃/, Jules (1602–61), Italian-born French statesman. He became the Italian papal legate in Paris in 1634 and was made a cardinal in 1641. In 1642 he succeeded Richelieu as chief minister of France, which he governed during the minority of Louis XIV, imposing an administration which aroused such opposition as to provoke the civil wars of the Fronde, 1648–53. □ **Mazarin Bible** see GUTENBERG.

mazarine /ˌmæzəˈriːn/ *n. & adj.* a rich deep blue. [17th c., perh. f. the name of Cardinal *Mazarin*, French statesman d. 1661, or Duchesse de *Mazarin*, French noblewoman d. 1699]

Mazdaism /ˈmæzdəɪz(ə)m/ *n.* Zoroastrianism, worship of Ahura Mazda. [Avestan *mazda*, the good principle in ancient Persian theology]

maze /meɪz/ *n. & v.* —*n.* **1** a network of paths and hedges designed as a puzzle for those who try to penetrate it. **2** a complex network of paths or passages; a labyrinth. **3** confusion, a confused mass, etc. —*v.tr.* (esp. as **mazed** *adj.*) bewilder, confuse. □□ **mazy** *adj.* (**mazier, maziest**). [ME, orig. as *mased* (adj.): rel. to AMAZE]

mazer /ˈmeɪzə(r)/ *n. hist.* a hardwood drinking-bowl, usu. silver-mounted. [ME f. OF *masere* f. Gmc]

mazurka /məˈzɜːkə/ *n.* **1** a usu. lively Polish dance in triple time. **2** the music for this. [F *mazurka* or G *Masurka*, f. Pol. *mazurka* woman of the province *Mazovia*]

mazzard var. of MAZARD.

Mazzini /mætˈsiːniː/, Giuseppe (1805–72), Italian nationalist and revolutionary, the militant leader of the Risorgimento movement for a united Italian republic.

MB *abbr.* **1** Bachelor of Medicine. **2** *Computing* megabyte. [sense 1 f. L *Medicinae Baccalaureus*]

MBA *abbr.* Master of Business Administration.

Mbabane /ˌəmbɑːˈbɑːnɪ/ the capital of Swaziland; pop. (1986) 38,300.

MBE *abbr.* Member of the Order of the British Empire.

MC *abbr.* **1** Master of Ceremonies. **2** (in the UK) Military Cross. **3** (in the US) Member of Congress.

Mc *abbr.* megacycle(s).

MCC *abbr.* Marylebone Cricket Club, founded in 1787, with its headquarters at Lord's Cricket Ground. It held the tacitly accepted power to maintain, and if necessary amend, the laws of cricket, until government of the game became the official responsibility of the newly created Cricket Council in 1969.

McCarthyism, McCoy see at MACC-.

M.Ch. *abbr.* (also **M.Chir.**) Master of Surgery. [L *Magister Chirurgiae*]

mCi *abbr.* millicurie(s).

McNaughten see at MACN-.

M.Com. *abbr.* Master of Commerce.

MCP *abbr. colloq.* male chauvinist pig.

MCR *abbr. Brit.* Middle Common Room.

Mc/s *abbr.* megacycles per second.

MD *abbr.* **1** Doctor of Medicine. **2** Managing Director. **3** *US* Maryland (in official postal use). **4** mentally deficient. [sense 1 f. L *Medicinae Doctor*]

Md *symb. Chem.* the element mendelevium.

Md. *abbr.* Maryland.

MDMA *abbr.* methylenedioxymethamphetamine, an amphetamine-based drug that causes euphoric and hallucinatory effects, originally produced as an appetite suppressant (see ECSTASY 3).

MDT *abbr. US* Mountain Daylight Time.

ME *abbr.* **1** *US* Maine (in official postal use). **2** myalgic encephalomyelitis, an obscure disease with symptoms like those of influenza and prolonged periods of tiredness and depression.

Me. *abbr.* **1** Maine. **2** *Maître* (title of a French advocate).

me[1] /miː, mɪ/ *pron.* **1** objective case of I[2] (*he saw me*). **2** *colloq.* = I[2] (*it's me all right; is taller than me*). **3** *US colloq.* myself, to or for myself (*I got me a gun*). **4** *colloq.* used in exclamations (*ah me!; dear me!; silly me!*). □ **me and mine** me and my relatives. [OE *me*, *mē* accus. & dative of I[2] f. Gmc]

me[2] /miː/ *n.* (also **mi**) *Mus.* **1** (in tonic sol-fa) the third note of a major scale. **2** the note E in the fixed-doh system. [ME f. L *mira*: see GAMUT]

mea culpa /ˌmiːə ˈkʌlpə, ˌmeɪə ˈkʊlpə/ *n. & int.* —*n.* an acknowledgement of one's fault or error. —*int.* expressing such an acknowledgement. [L, = by my fault]

Mead /miːd/, Margaret (1901–78), American anthropologist and social psychologist, whose works reached popular as well as professional audiences. She worked in Samoa and the New Guinea area and wrote a number of specialized studies of primitive cultures, but was also concerned to relate her findings to current American life and its problems. Her writings raised important questions about social standards and human values, recognizing their importance in determining behaviour but stressing their impermanence as well as their imperfection. One of her best-known books was *Male and Female* (1949), an examination of traditional male–female relationships.

mead[1] /miːd/ *n.* an alcoholic drink of fermented honey and water. [OE *me(o)du* f. Gmc]

mead[2] /miːd/ *n. poet.* or *archaic* = MEADOW. [OE *mæd* f. Gmc, rel. to MOW[1]]

meadow /ˈmedəʊ/ *n.* **1** a piece of grassland, esp. one used for hay. **2** a piece of low well-watered ground, esp. near a river. □ **meadow brown** a common brown butterfly, *Maniola jurtina.* **meadow-grass** a perennial creeping grass, *Poa pratensis.* **meadow lark** *US* any songbird of the genus *Sturnella*, esp. the yellow-breasted *S. magna* of N. America. **meadow pipit** a common pipit, *Anthus pratensis*, native to Europe, Asia, and Africa. **meadow rue** any ranunculaceous plant of the genus *Thalictrum*, esp. *T. flavum* with small yellow flowers. **meadow saffron** a perennial plant, *Colchicum autumnale*, abundant in meadows, with lilac flowers: also called *autumn crocus*. □□ **meadowy** *adj.* [OE *mǣdwe*, oblique case of *mǣd*: see MEAD²]

meadowsweet /ˈmedəʊˌswiːt/ *n.* **1** a rosaceous plant, *Filipendula ulmaria*, common in meadows and damp places, with creamy-white fragrant flowers. **2** any of several rosaceous plants of the genus *Spiraea*, native to N. America.

meagre /ˈmiːgə(r)/ *adj.* (*US* **meager**) **1** lacking in amount or quality (*a meagre salary*). **2** (of literary composition, ideas, etc.) lacking fullness, unsatisfying. **3** (of a person or animal) lean, thin. □□ **meagrely** *adv.* **meagreness** *n.* [ME f. AF *megre*, OF *maigre* f. L *macer*]

meal¹ /miːl/ *n.* **1** an occasion when food is eaten. **2** the food eaten on one occasion. □ **make a meal of 1** treat (a task etc.) too laboriously or fussily. **2** consume as a meal. **meals on wheels** *Brit.* a service by which meals are delivered to old people, invalids, etc. **meal-ticket 1** a ticket entitling one to a meal, esp. at a specified place with reduced cost. **2** a person or thing that is a source of food or income. [OE *mǣl* mark, fixed time, meal f. Gmc]

meal² /miːl/ *n.* **1** the edible part of any grain or pulse (usu. other than wheat) ground to powder. **2** *Sc.* oatmeal. **3** *US* maize flour. **4** any powdery substance made by grinding. □ **meal-beetle** an insect, *Tenebrio molitor*, infesting granaries etc. **meal-worm** the larva of the meal-beetle. [OE *melu* f. Gmc]

mealie /ˈmiːlɪ/ *n.* (also **mielie**) *S.Afr.* **1** (usu. in *pl.*) maize. **2** a corn-cob. [Afrik. *mielie* f. Port. *milho* maize, millet f. L *milium*]

mealtime /ˈmiːltaɪm/ *n.* any of the usual times of eating.

mealy /ˈmiːlɪ/ *adj.* (**mealier, mealiest**) **1 a** of or like meal; soft and powdery. **b** containing meal. **2** (of a complexion) pale. **3** (of a horse) spotty. **4** (in full **mealy-mouthed**) not outspoken; afraid to use plain expressions. □ **mealy bug** any insect of the genus *Pseudococcus*, infesting vines etc., whose body is covered with white powder. □□ **mealiness** *n.*

mean¹ /miːn/ *v.tr.* (*past* and *past part.* **meant** /ment/) **1 a** (often foll. by *to* + infin.) have as one's purpose or intention; have in mind (*they really mean mischief; I didn't mean to break it*). **b** (foll. by *by*) have as a motive in explanation (*what do you mean by that?*). **2** (often in *passive*) design or destine for a purpose (*meant it to be used; mean it for a stopgap; is meant to be a gift*). **3** intend to convey or indicate or refer to (a particular thing or notion) (*I mean we cannot go; I mean Richmond in Surrey*). **4** entail, involve (*it means catching the early train*). **5** (often foll. by *that* + clause) portend, signify (*this means trouble; your refusal means that we must look elsewhere*). **6** (of a word) have as its explanation in the same language or its equivalent in another language. **7** (foll. by *to*) be of some specified importance to (a person), esp. as a source of benefit or object of affection etc. (*that means a lot to me*). □ **mean business** be in earnest. **mean it** not be joking or exaggerating. **mean to say** really admit (usu. in *interrog.*: *do you mean to say you have lost it?*). **mean well** (often foll. by *to*, *towards*, *by*) have good intentions. [OE *mǣnan* f. WG, rel. to MIND]

mean² /miːn/ *adj.* **1** niggardly; not generous or liberal. **2** (of an action) ignoble, small-minded. **3** (of a person's capacity, understanding, etc.) inferior, poor. **4** (of housing) not imposing in appearance; shabby. **5 a** malicious, ill-tempered. **b** *US* vicious or aggressive in behaviour. **6** *colloq.* skilful, formidable (*is a mean fighter*). **7** *colloq.* ashamed (*feel mean*). □ **no mean** a very good (*that is no mean achievement*). **mean White** = *poor White*. □□ **meanly** *adv.* **meanness** *n.* [OE *mǣne*, *gemǣne* f. Gmc]

mean³ /miːn/ *n.* & *adj.* —*n.* **1** a condition, quality, virtue, or course of action equally removed from two opposite (usu. unsatisfactory) extremes. **2** *Math.* **a** the term or one of the terms midway between the first and last terms of an arithmetical or geometrical etc. progression (*2 and 8 have the arithmetic mean 5 and the geometric mean 4*). **b** the quotient of the sum of several quantities and their number, the average. —*adj.* **1** (of a quantity) equally far from two extremes. **2** calculated as a mean. □

mean free path the average distance travelled by a gas molecule etc. between collisions. **mean sea level** the sea level halfway between the mean levels of high and low water. **mean sun** an imaginary sun moving in the celestial equator at the mean rate of the real sun, used in calculating solar time. **mean time** the time based on the movement of the mean sun. [ME f. AF *meen* f. OF *meien*, *moien* f. L *medianus* MEDIAN]

meander /mɪˈændə(r)/ *v.* & *n.* —*v.intr.* **1** wander at random. **2** (of a stream) wind about. —*n.* **1** (in *pl.*) **a** the sinuous windings of a river. **b** winding paths. **2** a circuitous journey. **3** an ornamental pattern of lines winding in and out; a fret. [L *maeander* f. Gk *Maiandros*, the name of a winding river (now the Menderes) in western Turkey]

meandrine /mɪˈændrɪn/ *adj.* full of windings (esp. of corals of the genus *Meandrina*, with a surface like a human brain). [MEANDER + -INE¹]

meanie /ˈmiːnɪ/ *n.* (also **meany**) (*pl.* **-ies**) *colloq.* a mean, niggardly, or small-minded person.

meaning /ˈmiːnɪŋ/ *n.* & *adj.* —*n.* **1** what is meant by a word, action, idea, etc. **2** significance. **3** importance. —*adj.* expressive, significant (*a meaning glance*). □□ **meaningly** *adv.*

meaningful /ˈmiːnɪŋfʊl/ *adj.* **1** full of meaning; significant. **2** *Logic* able to be interpreted. □□ **meaningfully** *adv.* **meaningfulness** *n.*

meaningless /ˈmiːnɪŋlɪs/ *adj.* having no meaning or significance. □□ **meaninglessly** *adv.* **meaninglessness** *n.*

means /miːnz/ *n.pl.* **1** (often treated as *sing.*) that by which a result is brought about (*a means of quick travel*). **2 a** money resources (*live beyond one's means*). **b** wealth (*a man of means*). □ **by all means** (or **all manner of means**) **1** certainly. **2** in every possible way. **3** at any cost. **by means of** by the agency or instrumentality of (a thing or action). **by no means** (or **no manner of means**) not at all; certainly not. **means test** an official inquiry to establish need before financial assistance from public funds is given. [*pl.* of MEAN³]

meant *past* and *past part.* of MEAN¹.

meantime /ˈmiːntaɪm/ *adv.* & *n.* —*adv.* = MEANWHILE. ¶ Less usual than *meanwhile*. —*n.* the intervening period (esp. *in the meantime*). [MEAN³ + TIME]

meanwhile /ˈmiːnwaɪl/ *adv.* & *n.* —*adv.* **1** in the intervening period of time. **2** at the same time. —*n.* the intervening period (esp. *in the meanwhile*). [MEAN³ + WHILE]

meany var. of MEANIE.

measles /ˈmiːz(ə)lz/ *n.pl.* (also treated as *sing.*) **1 a** an acute infectious viral disease marked by red spots on the skin. **b** the spots of measles. **2** a tapeworm disease of pigs. [ME *masele(s)* prob. f. MLG *masele*, MDu. *masel* pustule (cf. Du. *mazelen* measles), OHG *masala*: change of form prob. due to assim. to ME *meser* leper]

measly /ˈmiːzlɪ/ *adj.* (**measlier, measliest**) **1** *colloq.* inferior, contemptible, worthless. **2** of or affected with measles. **3** (of pork) infested with tapeworms. [MEASLES + -Y¹]

measurable /ˈmeʒərəb(ə)l/ *adj.* that can be measured. □ **within a measurable distance of** getting near (something undesirable). □□ **measurability** /-ˈbɪlɪtɪ/ *n.* **measurably** *adv.* [ME f. OF *mesurable* f. LL *mensurabilis* f. *mensurare* (as MEASURE)]

measure /ˈmeʒə(r)/ *n.* & *v.* —*n.* **1** a size or quantity found by measuring. **2** a system of measuring (*liquid measure; linear measure*). **3** a rod or tape etc. for measuring. **4** a vessel of standard capacity for transferring or determining fixed quantities of liquids etc. (*a pint measure*). **5 a** the degree, extent, or amount of a thing. **b** (foll. by *of*) some degree of (*there was a measure of wit in her remark*). **6** a unit of capacity, e.g. a bushel (*20 measures of wheat*). **7** a factor by which a person or thing is reckoned or evaluated (*their success is a measure of their determination*). **8** (usu. in *pl.*) suitable action to achieve some end (*took measures to ensure a good profit*). **9** a legislative enactment. **10** a quantity contained in another an exact number of times. **11** a prescribed extent or quantity. **12** *Printing* the width of a page or column of type. **13 a** poetical rhythm; metre. **b** a metrical group of a dactyl or two iambuses, trochees, spondees, etc. **14** *US Mus.* a bar or the time-content of a bar. **15** *archaic* a dance. **16** a mineral stratum (*coal measures*). —*v.* **1** *tr.* ascertain the extent or quantity of (a thing) by comparison with a fixed unit or with an object of known size. **2** *intr.* be of a specified size (*it measures six inches*). **3** *tr.* ascertain the size and proportion of (a person) for clothes. **4** *tr.* estimate (a quality, person's character, etc.) by some standard or rule. **5** *tr.* (often foll. by *off*) mark (a line etc. of a given length). **6** *tr.* (foll. by *out*) deal or distribute (a thing) in measured quantities. **7** *tr.* (foll. by *with, against*) bring (oneself or one's strength etc.) into competition with. **8** *tr. poet.* traverse (a distance). □ **beyond measure** excessively. **for good measure** as something beyond the minimum; as a finishing touch. **in a** (or **some**) **measure** partly. **made to measure** *Brit.* (of clothes) made from measurements taken. **measure up 1 a** determine the size etc. of by measurement. **b** take comprehensive measurements. **2** (often foll. by *to*) have the necessary qualifications (for). **measuring-jug** (or **-cup**) a jug or cup marked to measure its contents. **measuring-tape** a tape marked to measure length. **measuring-worm** the caterpillar of the geometer moth. [ME f. OF *mesure* f. L *mensura* f. *metiri mens-* measure]

measured /ˈmeʒəd/ *adj.* **1** rhythmical; regular in movement (*a measured tread*). **2** (of language) carefully considered. □□ **measuredly** *adv.*

measureless /ˈmeʒələs/ *adj.* not measurable; infinite. □□ **measurelessly** *adv.*

measurement /ˈmeʒəmənt/ *n.* **1** the act or an instance of measuring. **2** an amount determined by measuring. **3** (in *pl.*) detailed dimensions.

meat /miːt/ *n.* **1** the flesh of animals (esp. mammals) as food. **2** (foll. by *of*) the essence or chief part of. **3** *US* the edible part of fruits, nuts, eggs, shellfish, etc. **4** *archaic* **a** food of any kind. **b** a meal. □ **meat and drink** a source of great pleasure. **meat-axe** a butcher's cleaver. **meat-fly** (*pl.* **-flies**) a fly that breeds in meat. **meat loaf** minced or chopped meat moulded into the shape of a loaf and baked. **meat safe** a cupboard for storing meat, usu. of wire gauze etc. □□ **meatless** *adj.* [OE *mete* food f. Gmc]

meatball /ˈmiːtbɔːl/ *n.* minced meat compressed into a small round ball.

Meath /miːθ/ a county of eastern Ireland, in the province of Leinster; pop. (est. 1986) 103,750; capital, Trim.

meatus /mɪˈeɪtəs/ *n.* (*pl.* same or **meatuses**) *Anat.* a channel or passage in the body or its opening. [L, = passage f. *meare* flow, run]

meaty /ˈmiːtɪ/ *adj.* (**meatier, meatiest**) **1** full of meat; fleshy. **2** of or like meat. **3** full of substance. □□ **meatily** *adv.* **meatiness** *n.*

Mecca /ˈmekə/ the holiest city of the Islamic faith, an oasis town located in the Hijaz region which lies on the Red Sea coast of the Arabian peninsula, now in Saudi Arabia; pop. 366,800. A trading centre in pre-Islamic times, it was in Mecca that the Prophet Muhammad was born and brought up, and it was with local people here that he shared his first revelations. Expelled from the city for his 'disruptive' preaching, he returned to Mecca eight years later as the head of a non-tribally based religious community and made it his capital until his death two years later in AD 632. The centre of Islamic ritual (see KAABA, HADJ) and site of the Great Mosque, Mecca receives thousands of visitors each year at the time of the annual pilgrimage. —*n.* **1** a place one aspires to visit. **2** the birthplace of a faith, policy, pursuit, etc.

mechanic /mɪˈkænɪk/ *n.* a skilled worker, esp. one who makes or uses or repairs machinery. [ME (orig. as *adj.*) f. OF *mecanique* or L *mechanicus* f. Gk *mēkhanikos* (as MACHINE)]

mechanical /mɪˈkænɪk(ə)l/ *adj.* **1** of or relating to machines or mechanisms. **2** working or produced by machinery. **3** (of a person or action) like a machine; automatic; lacking originality. **4 a** (of an agency, principle, etc.) belonging to mechanics. **b** (of a theory etc.) explaining phenomena by the assumption of mechanical action. **5** of or relating to mechanics as a science. □ **mechanical advantage** the ratio of exerted to applied force in a machine. **mechanical drawing** a scale drawing of machinery etc. done with precision instruments. **mechanical**

engineer a person skilled in the branch of engineering dealing with the design, construction, and repair of machines. **mechanical equivalent of heat** the conversion factor between heat energy and mechanical energy. □□ **mechanicalism** *n.* (in sense 4). **mechanically** *adv.* **mechanicalness** *n.* [ME f. L *mechanicus* (as MECHANIC)]

mechanician /ˌmekəˈnɪʃ(ə)n/ *n.* a person skilled in constructing machinery.

mechanics /mɪˈkænɪks/ *n.pl.* (usu. treated as *sing.*) **1** the branch of applied mathematics dealing with motion and tendencies to motion. **2** the science of machinery. **3** the method of construction or routine operation of a thing.

mechanism /ˈmekəˌnɪz(ə)m/ *n.* **1** the structure or adaptation of parts of a machine. **2** a system of mutually adapted parts working together in or as in a machine. **3** the mode of operation of a process. **4** *Art* mechanical execution; technique. **5** *Philos.* the doctrine that all natural phenomena, including life, allow mechanical explanation by physics and chemistry. [mod.L *mechanismus* f. Gk (as MACHINE)]

mechanist /ˈmekənɪst/ *n.* **1** a mechanician. **2** an expert in mechanics. **3** *Philos.* a person who holds the doctrine of mechanism. □□ **mechanistic** /-ˈnɪstɪk/ *adj.* **mechanistically** /-ˈnɪstɪkəlɪ/ *adv.*

mechanize /ˈmekəˌnaɪz/ *v.tr.* (also **-ise**) **1** give a mechanical character to. **2** introduce machines in. **3** *Mil.* equip with tanks, armoured cars, etc. (orig. as a substitute for horse-drawn vehicles and cavalry). □□ **mechanization** /-ˈzeɪʃ(ə)n/ *n.* **mechanizer** *n.*

mechano- /ˈmekənəʊ/ *comb. form* mechanical. [Gk *mēkhano-* f. *mēkhanē* machine]

mechanoreceptor /ˌmekənəʊrɪˈseptə(r)/ *n.* *Biol.* a sensory receptor that responds to mechanical stimuli such as touch or sound.

mechatronics /ˌmekəˈtrɒnɪks/ *n.* the science of the combination of electronics and mechanics in developing new manufacturing techniques. [*mechanics* + *electronics*]

Mechelen /ˈmexələn/ (French **Malines** /mæˈliːn/) a city in northern Belgium, 25 km (15 miles) north of Brussels; pop. (1988) 476,000. It is the metropolitan see of Belgium and has a 12th–14th c. cathedral containing Van Dyck's *Crucifixion*. Mechlin lace (see entry) is named after it.

Mechlin /ˈmeklɪn/ *n.* (in full **Mechlin lace**) lace made at Mechlin (now Mechelen or Malines) in Belgium.

Mecklenburg /ˈmeklənˌbɜːg/ a former State and region of Germany, now (with West Pomerania) a 'Land' (State), on the Baltic coastal plain; pop. (est. 1990) 2,100,000; capital, Schwerin.

M.Econ. *abbr.* Master of Economics.

meconium /mɪˈkəʊnɪəm/ *n.* *Med.* a dark substance forming the first faeces of a newborn infant. [L, lit. poppy-juice, f. Gk *mēkōnion* f. *mēkōn* poppy]

mecu /ˈmeɪkjuː, ˈmiː-/ *n.* one million ecus. [M *abbr.* (= million) + ECU]

Med /med/ *n. colloq.* the Mediterranean Sea. [abbr.]

med. *abbr.* medium.

M.Ed. *abbr.* Master of Education.

medal /ˈmed(ə)l/ *n.* a piece of metal, usu. in the form of a disc, struck or cast with an inscription or device to commemorate an event etc., or awarded as a distinction to a soldier, scholar, athlete, etc., for services rendered, for proficiency, etc. □ **medal play** *Golf* = stroke play. □□ **medalled** *adj.* **medallic** /mɪˈdælɪk/ *adj.* [F *médaille* f. It. *medaglia* ult. f. L *metallum* METAL]

medallion /mɪˈdæljən/ *n.* **1** a large medal. **2** a thing shaped like this, e.g. a decorative panel or tablet, portrait, etc. [F *médaillon* f. It. *medaglione* augment. of *medaglia* (as MEDAL)]

medallist /ˈmedəlɪst/ *n.* (*US* **medalist**) **1** a recipient of a (specified) medal (*gold medallist*). **2** an engraver or designer of medals.

Medan /məˈdɑːn/ a city in Indonesia, on the Deli River in NE Sumatra, capital of North Sumatra province; pop. (1980) 1,378,950.

Medawar /ˈmedəwə(r)/, Sir Peter Brian (1915–87), English immunologist, who in 1960 shared a Nobel Prize for his studies of the biology of tissue transplantation. His early work showed that rejection of grafts was the result of an immune mechanism; his subsequent discovery of 'acquired' tolerance of grafts encouraged the early attempts at human organ transplantation.

meddle /ˈmed(ə)l/ v.intr. (often foll. by *with*, *in*) interfere in or busy oneself unduly with others' concerns. □□ **meddler** n. [ME f. OF *medler*, var. of *mesler* ult. f. L *miscēre* mix]

meddlesome /ˈmedəlsəm/ adj. fond of meddling; interfering. □□ **meddlesomely** adv. **meddlesomeness** n.

Mede /miːd/ n. a member of an ancient Indo-European people whose homeland, Media, lay south-west of the Caspian Sea. In the 7th–6th c. BC they were masters of an empire that included most of modern Iran and extended to Cappadocia and Syria; it passed into Persian control after the defeat of King Astyages by Cyrus in 549 BC. □□ **Median** adj. [ME f. L *Medi* (pl.) f. Gk *Mēdoi*]

Medea /mɪˈdiːə/ Gk legend a sorceress, daughter of Aeetes king of Colchis. She helped Jason to obtain the Golden Fleece, and married him, but was deserted in Corinth and avenged herself by killing their two children. [Gk, = cunning]

Medellín /ˌmedeɪˈiːn/ the second-largest city in Colombia; pop. (1985) 1,468,000. As a major centre of Colombia's notorious drug trade, Medellín gained the reputation of being the city with the highest murder rate in the world.

Media /ˈmiːdɪə/ the country of the Medes.

media[1] /ˈmiːdɪə/ n.pl. **1** pl. of MEDIUM. **2** (usu. prec. by *the*) the main means of mass communication (esp. newspapers and broadcasting) regarded collectively. ¶ Use as a mass noun with a singular verb is common (e.g. *the media is on our side*), but is generally disfavoured (cf. AGENDA, DATA). □ **media event** an event primarily intended to attract publicity.

media[2] /ˈmiːdɪə/ n. (pl. **mediae** /-dɪˌiː/) **1** Phonet. a voiced stop, e.g. g, b, d. **2** Anat. a middle layer of the wall of an artery or other vessel. [L, fem. of *medius* middle]

mediaeval var. of MEDIEVAL.

medial /ˈmiːdɪəl/ adj. **1** situated in the middle. **2** of average size. □□ **medially** adv. [LL *medialis* f. L *medius* middle]

median /ˈmiːdɪən/ adj. & n. —adj. situated in the middle. —n. **1** Anat. a median artery, vein, nerve, etc. **2** Geom. a straight line drawn from any vertex of a triangle to the middle of the opposite side. **3** Math. the middle value of a series of values arranged in order of size. □□ **medianly** adv. [F *médiane* or L *medianus* (as MEDIAL)]

mediant /ˈmiːdɪənt/ n. Mus. the third note of a diatonic scale of any key. [F *médiante* f. It. *mediante* part. of obs. *mediare* come between, f. L (as MEDIATE)]

mediastinum /ˌmiːdɪəˈstiːnəm/ n. (pl. **mediastina** /-nə/) Anat. a membranous middle septum, esp. between the lungs. □□ **mediastinal** adj. [mod.L f. med.L *mediastinus* medial, after L *mediastinus* drudge f. *medius* middle]

mediate v. & adj. —v. /ˈmiːdɪˌeɪt/ **1** intr. (often foll. by *between*) intervene (between parties in a dispute) to produce agreement or reconciliation. **2** tr. be the medium for bringing about (a result) or for conveying (a gift etc.). **3** tr. form a connecting link between. —adj. /ˈmiːdɪət/ **1** connected not directly but through some other person or thing. **2** involving an intermediate agency. □□ **mediately** /-ətlɪ/ adv. **mediation** /-ˈeɪʃ(ə)n/ n. **mediator** /ˈmiːdɪˌeɪtə(r)/ n. **mediatory** /ˈmiːdɪətərɪ/ adj. [LL *mediare mediat-* f. L *medius* middle]

medic[1] /ˈmedɪk/ n. colloq. a medical practitioner or student. [L *medicus* physician f. *medēri* heal]

medic[2] var. of MEDICK.

medicable /ˈmedɪkəb(ə)l/ adj. admitting of remedial treatment. [L *medicabilis* (as MEDICATE)]

Medicaid /ˈmedɪˌkeɪd/ n. (in the US) a Federal system of health insurance for those requiring financial assistance. (See MEDICARE.) [MEDICAL + AID]

medical /ˈmedɪk(ə)l/ adj. & n. —adj. **1** of or relating to the science of medicine in general. **2** of or relating to conditions requiring medical and not surgical treatment (*medical ward*). —n. colloq. a medical examination. □ **medical certificate** a certificate of fitness or unfitness to work etc. **medical exam-**

ination an examination to determine a person's physical fitness. **medical jurisprudence** the law relating to medicine. **medical officer** Brit. a person in charge of the health services of a local authority or other organization. **medical practitioner** a physician or surgeon. □□ **medically** adv. [F *médical* or med.L *medicalis* f. L *medicus*: see MEDIC[1]]

medicament /mɪˈdɪkəmənt, ˈmedɪkəmənt/ n. a substance used for medical treatment. [F *médicament* or L *medicamentum* (as MEDICATE)]

Medicare /ˈmedɪˌkeə(r)/ n. (in the US) a Federal system of health insurance for persons aged 65 and over, introduced in 1965 by President Johnson in a series of reforms which also included Medicaid. [MEDICAL + CARE]

medicate /ˈmedɪˌkeɪt/ v.tr. **1** treat medically. **2** impregnate with a medicinal substance. □□ **medicative** /ˈmedɪkətɪv/ adj. [L *medicari medicat-* administer remedies to f. *medicus*: see MEDIC[1]]

medication /ˌmedɪˈkeɪʃ(ə)n/ n. **1** a substance used for medical treatment. **2** treatment using drugs.

Medicean /ˌmedɪˈsiːən/ adj. of the Medici family, rulers of Florence in the 15th c. [mod.L *Mediceus* f. It. *Medici*]

Medici /ˈmedɪtʃɪ/ an Italian family which dominated Florence in the 15th c., particularly during the lifetimes of Cosimo (1389–1464) and Lorenzo (frequently called 'the Magnificent') (1449–92). In the following century the family rose to become grand dukes of Tuscany, while four members of it reached the papacy (Leo X, d. 1521; Clement VII, d. 1534; Pius IV, d. 1565; Leo XI, pope in 1605) and two others were married to kings of France (Catherine to Henry II, Marie to Henry IV).

medicinal /mɪˈdɪsɪn(ə)l/ adj. & n. —adj. (of a substance) having healing properties. —n. a medicinal substance. □□ **medicinally** adv. [ME f. OF f. L *medicinalis* (as MEDICINE)]

medicine /ˈmedsɪn, -dɪsɪn/ n. **1** the science or practice of the diagnosis, treatment, and prevention of disease, esp. as distinct from surgical methods. (See below.) **2** any drug or preparation used for the treatment or prevention of disease, esp. one taken by mouth. **3** a spell, charm, or fetish which is thought to cure afflictions. □ **a dose** (or **taste**) **of one's own medicine** treatment such as one is accustomed to giving others. **medicine ball** a stuffed leather ball thrown and caught for exercise. **medicine chest** a box containing medicines etc. **medicine man** a person believed to have magical powers of healing, esp. among N. American Indians. **take one's medicine** submit to something disagreeable. [ME f. OF *medecine* f. L *medicina* f. *medicus*: see MEDIC[1]]

Although medicine was practised in ancient Egypt and Mesopotamia, and was studied at Cnidos in Asia Minor in the 7th c. BC, it is the Greek physician Hippocrates (5th c. BC) who is regarded as the 'father of medicine', with his careful recording and comparison of actual clinical cases and discarding of ancient superstitions and theories. Greek physicians were famous, and Galen (2nd c. AD) dominated medical knowledge for nearly 1,500 years. The modern study of anatomy dates from the publication of Vesalius' account of human anatomy in 1543, while William Harvey's discovery of blood circulation was the major advance in physiology in the 17th c. The invention of the microscope made it possible for the Dutchman Anton van Leeuwenhoek to investigate the previously invisible world of micro-organisms. In the 1860s Pasteur made his first investigations which led to the germ theory of disease. This and the discovery of anaesthetics and antiseptics brought about a transformation in medicine, while a host of scientific discoveries (including X-rays) accompanied and succeeded them. The growth of organic chemistry and the work of the German bacteriologist Paul Ehrlich made possible the science of chemotherapy, and antibiotics came into general use during the Second World War (see PENICILLIN). Many virus diseases can be prevented or controlled by inoculation (see JENNER). Improvements in general standards of living, hygiene, and nutrition have all but eliminated many diseases that were formerly common, but increased stress, and longevity itself, have brought their own problems.

Medicine Hat an agricultural centre in SE Alberta, Canada; pop. (1986) 42,300.

medick /ˈmiːdɪk/ n. (also **medic**) any leguminous plant of the genus *Medicago*, esp. alfalfa. [ME f. L *medica* f. Gk *Mēdikē poa* Median grass]

medico /ˈmedɪkəʊ/ n. (pl. **-os**) *colloq.* a medical practitioner or student. [It. f. L (as MEDIC¹)]

medico- /ˈmedɪkəʊ/ *comb. form* medical; medical and (*medicolegal*). [L *medicus* (as MEDIC¹)]

medieval /ˌmedɪˈiːv(ə)l/ adj. (also **mediaeval**) **1** of, or in the style of, the Middle Ages. **2** *colloq.* old-fashioned, archaic. □ **medieval history** the history of the 5th–15th c. **medieval Latin** Latin of about AD 600–1500. □□ **medievalism** n. **medievalist** n. **medievalize** v.tr. & intr. (also **-ise**). **medievally** adv. [mod.L *medium aevum* f. L *medius* middle + *aevum* age]

Medina /meˈdiːnə/ an oasis city in Saudi Arabia, approximately 320 km (200 miles) north of Mecca; pop. 198,200. Considered the second-holiest city of Islam (after Mecca), it was the destination of the Prophet Muhammad's infant Muslim community when they left Mecca in AD 622. He had been invited to Yathrib—as the oasis town was then known—by its populace to assume the role of arbiter in an ongoing conflict between two tribal groups. In Yathrib/Medina the community grew and was consolidated around the home of the Prophet, which is considered the first mosque (*masjid*) in the history of Islam and the model for later structures meant for worship and communal gatherings. The community was based there until the city of Mecca capitulated to Muhammad in AD 630. Muhammad is buried in Medina (its name means 'the city'), and it is customary for the pilgrim to visit the Prophet's tomb following the series of ritual events constituting the formal pilgrimage (hadj) to Mecca.

mediocre /ˌmiːdɪˈəʊkə(r)/ adj. **1** of middling quality, neither good nor bad. **2** second-rate. [F *médiocre* or f. L *mediocris* of middle height or degree f. *medius* middle + *ocris* rugged mountain]

mediocrity /ˌmiːdɪˈɒkrɪtɪ/ n. (pl. **-ies**) **1** the state of being mediocre. **2** a mediocre person or thing.

meditate /ˈmedɪˌteɪt/ v. **1** intr. **a** exercise the mind in (esp. religious) contemplation. **b** (usu. foll. by *on*, *upon*) focus on a subject in this manner. **2** tr. plan mentally; design. □□ **meditation** /-ˈteɪʃ(ə)n/ n. **meditator** n. [L *meditari* contemplate]

meditative /ˈmedɪtətɪv/ adj. **1** inclined to meditate. **2** indicative of meditation. □□ **meditatively** adv. **meditativeness** n.

Mediterranean /ˌmedɪtəˈreɪnɪən/ adj. & n. —adj. **1** of or characteristic of the Mediterranean Sea or the countries in and round it. **2** of or belonging to an extremely artificial sub-racial grouping of people who, as a population, are short (average height *c.*163 cm, 5 ft. 4 in.) with dark skin, hair, and eyes, and dolichocephalic. —n. a native of a country bordering on the Mediterranean. □ **Mediterranean climate** a climate characterized by hot dry summers and warm wet winters. **Mediterranean Sea** an almost land-locked sea between southern Europe and Africa, connected with the Atlantic Ocean by the Strait of Gibraltar and with the Red Sea by the Suez Canal. [L *mediterraneus* inland f. *medius* middle + *terra* land]

medium /ˈmiːdɪəm/ n. & adj. —n. (pl. **media** or **mediums**) **1** the middle quality, degree, etc. between extremes (*find a happy medium*). **2** the means by which something is communicated (*the medium of sound; the medium of television*). **3** the intervening substance through which impressions are conveyed to the senses etc. (*light passing from one medium into another*). **4** *Biol.* the physical environment or conditions of growth, storage, or transport of a living organism (*the shape of a fish is ideal for its fluid medium; growing mould on the surface of a medium*). **5** an agency or means of doing something (*the medium through which money is raised*). **6** the material or form used by an artist, composer, etc. (*language as an artistic medium*). **7** the liquid (e.g. oil or gel) with which pigments are mixed for use in painting. **8** (pl. **mediums**) a person claiming to be in contact with the spirits of the dead and to communicate between the dead and the living. —adj. **1** between two qualities, degrees, etc. **2** average; moderate (*of medium height*). □ **medium bowler** *Cricket* a bowler who bowls at a medium pace. **medium dry** (of sherry, wine, etc.) having a flavour intermediate between dry and sweet. **medium frequency** a radio frequency between 300 kHz and 3 MHz.

medium of circulation something that serves as an instrument of commercial transactions, e.g. coin. **medium-range** (of an aircraft, missile, etc.) able to travel a medium distance. **medium wave** a radio wave of medium frequency. □□ **mediumism** n. (in sense 8 of n.). **mediumistic** /-ˈmɪstɪk/ adj. (in sense 8 of n.). **mediumship** n. (in sense 8 of n.). [L, = middle, neut. of *medius*]

medlar /ˈmedlə(r)/ n. **1** a rosaceous tree, *Mespilus germanica*, bearing small brown apple-like fruits. **2** the fruit of this tree which is eaten when decayed. [ME f. OF *medler* f. L *mespila* f. Gk *mespilē*, *-on*]

medley /ˈmedlɪ/ n., adj., & v. —n. (pl. **-eys**) **1** a varied mixture; a miscellany. **2** a collection of musical items from one work or various sources arranged as a continuous whole. —adj. *archaic* mixed; motley. —v.tr. (**-eys**, **-eyed**) *archaic* make a medley of; intermix. □ **medley relay** a relay race between teams in which each member runs a different distance, swims a different stroke, etc. [ME f. OF *medlee* var. of *meslee* f. Rmc (as MEDDLE)]

Medoc /meɪˈdɒk, ˈmedɒk/ n. a fine red claret from the Médoc region of SW France, between the Bay of Biscay and the estuary of the Gironde River.

medulla /mɪˈdʌlə/ n. **1** the inner region of certain organs or tissues usu. when it is distinguishable from the outer region or cortex, as in hair or a kidney. **2** the myelin layer of certain nerve fibres. **3** the soft internal tissue of plants. □ **medulla oblongata** /ˌɒblɒŋˈɡɑːtə/ the continuation of the spinal cord within the skull, forming the lowest part of the brain stem. □□ **medullary** adj. [L, = pith, marrow, prob. rel. to *medius* middle]

Medusa /mɪˈdjuːsə/ *Gk Mythol.* one of the Gorgons,·the only mortal one, slain by Perseus, who cut off her head.

medusa /mɪˈdjuːsə/ n. (pl. **medusae** /-siː/ or **medusas**) **1** a jellyfish. **2** a free-swimming form of any coelenterate, having tentacles round the edge of a usu. umbrella-shaped jelly-like body, e.g. a jellyfish. □□ **medusan** adj. [L f. Gk *Medousa*, MEDUSA]

meed /miːd/ n. *literary* or *archaic* **1** reward. **2** merited portion (of praise etc.). [OE *mēd* f. WG, rel. to Goth. *mizdō*, Gk *misthos* reward]

meek /miːk/ adj. **1** humble and submissive; suffering injury etc. tamely. **2** piously gentle in nature. □□ **meekly** adv. **meekness** n. [ME *me(o)c* f. ON *mjúkr* soft, gentle]

meerkat /ˈmɪəkæt/ n. the suricate. [Du., = sea-cat]

meerschaum /ˈmɪəʃəm/ n. **1** a soft white form of hydrated magnesium silicate, chiefly found in Turkey, which resembles clay. **2** a tobacco-pipe with the bowl made from this. [G, = sea-foam f. *Meer* sea + *Schaum* foam, transl. Pers. *kef-i-daryā*, with ref. to its frothiness]

Meerut /ˈmɪərət/ a city in Uttar Pradesh in northern India; pop. (1981) 538,000. The Indian Mutiny broke out here in May 1857.

meet¹ /miːt/ v. & n. —v. (past and past part. **met** /met/) **1 a** tr. encounter (a person or persons) by accident or design; come face to face with. **b** intr. (of two or more people) come into each other's company by accident or design (*decided to meet on the bridge*). **2** tr. go to a place to be present at the arrival of (a person, train, etc.). **3 a** tr. (of a moving object, line, feature of landscape, etc.) come together or into contact with (*where the road meets the flyover*). **b** intr. come together or into contact (*where the sea and the sky meet*). **4 a** tr. make the acquaintance of (*delighted to meet you*). **b** intr. (of two or more people) make each other's acquaintance. **5** intr. & tr. come together or come into contact with for the purposes of conference, business, worship, etc. (*the committee meets every week; the union met management yesterday*). **6** tr. **a** (of a person or a group) deal with or answer (a demand, objection, etc.) (*met the original proposal with hostility*). **b** satisfy or conform with (proposals, deadlines, a person, etc.) (*agreed to meet the new terms; did my best to meet them on that point*). **7** tr. pay (a bill etc.); provide the funds required by (a cheque etc.) (*meet the cost of the move*). **8** tr. & (foll. by *with*) intr. experience, encounter, or receive (success, disaster, a difficulty, etc.) (*met their death; met with many problems*). **9** tr. oppose in battle, contest, or confrontation. **10** intr. (of clothes, curtains, etc.) join or fasten correctly (*my jacket won't meet*). —n. **1** the assembly of riders and hounds for a hunt. **2** the assembly of competitors for various sporting activities, esp. athletics. □ **make ends meet** see END. **meet the case** be adequate. **meet the eye** (or **the ear**) be visible (or audible). **meet a person's eye** check if another person is watching and look into his or her eyes in return. **meet a person half way** make a compromise, respond in a friendly way to the advances of another person. **meet up** colloq. happen to meet. **meet with** 1 see sense 8 of v. 2 receive (a reaction) (met with the committee's approval). 3 esp. US = sense 1a of v. **more in it than meets the eye** hidden qualities or complications. □□ **meeter** n. [OE mētan f. Gmc: cf. MOOT]

meet² /miːt/ adj. archaic suitable, fit, proper. □□ **meetly** adv. **meetness** n. [ME (i)mete repr. OE gemǣte f. Gmc, rel. to METE¹]

meeting /ˈmiːtɪŋ/ n. 1 in senses of MEET¹. 2 an assembly of people, esp. the members of a society, committee, etc., for discussion or entertainment. 3 = race meeting. 4 an assembly (esp. of Quakers) for worship. 5 the persons assembled (address the meeting). □ **meeting-house** a place of worship, esp. of Quakers etc.

mega- /ˈmegə/ comb. form 1 large. 2 denoting a factor of one million (10⁶) in the metric system of measurement. ¶ Abbr.: **M**. [Gk f. megas great]

megabuck /ˈmegəˌbʌk/ n. US colloq. a million dollars.

megabyte /ˈmegəˌbaɪt/ n. Computing 1,048,576 (i.e. 2²⁰) bytes as a measure of data capacity, or loosely 1,000,000. ¶ Abbr.: **MB**.

megadeath /ˈmegəˌdeθ/ n. the death of one million people (esp. as a unit in estimating the casualties of war).

Megaera /mɪˈgaɪrə/ Gk Mythol. one of the Furies. [Gk, perh. = she who bewitches]

megahertz /ˈmegəˌhɜːts/ n. one million hertz, esp. as a measure of frequency of radio transmissions. ¶ Abbr.: **MHz**.

megalith /ˈmegəlɪθ/ n. Archaeol. a large stone, esp. one placed upright as a monument or part of one. [MEGA- + Gk lithos stone]

megalithic /ˌmegəˈlɪθɪk/ adj. Archaeol. made of or marked by the use of large stones.

megalo- /ˈmegələʊ/ comb. form great (megalomania). [Gk f. megas megal- great]

megalomania /ˌmegələˈmeɪnɪə/ n. 1 a mental disorder producing delusions of grandeur. 2 a passion for grandiose schemes. □□ **megalomaniac** adj. & n. **megalomaniacal** /-məˈnaɪək(ə)l/ adj. **megalomanic** /-ˈmænɪk/ adj.

megalopolis /ˌmegəˈlɒpəlɪs/ n. 1 a great city or its way of life. 2 an urban complex consisting of a city and its environs. □□ **megalopolitan** /-ləˈpɒlɪt(ə)n/ adj. & n. [MEGA- + Gk polis city]

megalosaurus /ˌmegələˈsɔːrəs/ n. a large flesh-eating dinosaur of the genus Megalosaurus, with stout hind legs and small forelimbs. [MEGALO- + Gk sauros lizard]

megaphone /ˈmegəˌfəʊn/ n. a large funnel-shaped device for amplifying the sound of the voice.

megapode /ˈmegəˌpəʊd/ n. (also **megapod** /-ˌpɒd/) any bird of the family Megapodidae, native to Australasia, that builds a mound of debris for the incubation of its eggs, e.g. a mallee fowl. [mod.L Megapodius (genus-name) formed as MEGA- + Gk pous podos foot]

megaron /ˈmegəˌrɒn/ n. the central hall of a large Mycenaean house. [Gk, = hall]

megaspore /ˈmegəˌspɔː(r)/ n. the larger of the two kinds of spores produced by some ferns (cf. MICROSPORE).

megastar /ˈmegəˌstɑː(r)/ n. a very famous person, esp. in the world of entertainment.

megaton /ˈmegəˌtʌn/ n. (also **megatonne**) a unit of explosive power equal to one million tons of TNT.

megavolt /ˈmegəˌvəʊlt/ n. one million volts, esp. as a unit of electromotive force. ¶ Abbr.: **MV**.

megawatt /ˈmegəˌwɒt/ n. one million watts, esp. as a measure of electrical power as generated by power stations. ¶ Abbr.: **MW**.

Megger /ˈmegə(r)/ n. Electr. propr. an instrument for measuring electrical insulation resistance. [cf. MEGOHM]

Meghalaya /ˌmegəˈleɪə/ a State of India, created in 1970 from parts of Assam; pop. (1981) 1,327,824; capital, Shillong.

megilp /məˈgɪlp/ n. (also **magilp**) a mixture of mastic resin and

linseed oil, added to oil paints, much used in the 19th c. [18th c.: orig. unkn.]

megohm /ˈmegəʊm/ n. Electr. one million ohms. [MEGA- + OHM]

megrim¹ /ˈmiːgrɪm/ n. 1 archaic migraine. 2 a whim, a fancy. 3 (in pl.) **a** depression; low spirits. **b** staggers, vertigo in horses etc. [ME mygrane f. OF MIGRAINE]

megrim² /ˈmegrɪm/ n. any deep-water flat-fish of the family Lepidorhombus, esp. L. whiffiagonis. Also called sail-fluke. [19th c.: orig. unkn.]

meiosis /maɪˈəʊsɪs/ n. 1 Biol. a type of cell division that results in daughter cells with half the chromosome number of the parent cell (cf. MITOSIS). 2 = LITOTES. □□ **meiotic** /-ˈɒtɪk/ adj. **meiotically** /-ˈɒtɪkəlɪ/ adv. [mod.L f. Gk meiōsis f. meioō lessen f. meiōn less]

Meir /meɪˈɪə(r)/, Golda (born Goldie Mabovich, 1898–1978), Israeli stateswoman, born in the Ukraine, who was involved in negotiations over the founding of the State of Israel and was its Prime Minister from 1969 to 1974.

Meissen /ˈmaɪs(ə)n/ n. a city in Germany, near Dresden, where the earliest European porcelain factory was established in 1710 by Frederick Augustus, Elector of Saxony. — n. hard-paste porcelain made at Meissen. In Britain it is often called Dresden china.

Meistersinger /ˈmaɪstəˌsɪŋə(r)/ n. (pl. same) a member of one of the guilds of German lyric poets and musicians. These guilds, usually of burghers and respected master craftsmen, began to be organized from 1311 and continued to flourish until the 17th c. Their technique was elaborate and they were subject to rigid regulations, depicted in Wagner's opera Die Meistersinger von Nürnberg (1868). They represented a middle- and lower-class continuation of the aristocratic minnesinger of preceding centuries. [G f. Meister MASTER + Singer SINGER (see SING)]

Mekele /mɪˈkeɪlɪ/ the capital of Tigray region in northern Ethiopia; pop. (est. 1984) 62,000.

Meknès /mekˈnes/ a city in northern Morocco, one of the country's four imperial cities; pop. (1982) 319,800.

Mekong /miːˈkɒŋ/ the major river of SE Asia, rising in Tibet and flowing south-east and south for 4,180 km (2,600 miles). For part of its course it forms the Burma/Laos and Thailand/Laos border before continuing south across Cambodia and Vietnam to its extensive delta on the South China Sea.

Melaka /məˈlækə/ (formerly **Malacca**) 1 a State in SW Malaysia, on the west coast of the Strait of Malacca; pop. (1980) 464,750. 2 its capital and chief port, founded c.1400 and an important trading centre since the 15th c.; pop. (1980) 88,073.

melamine /ˈmeləˌmiːn/ n. 1 a white crystalline compound that can be copolymerized with methanal to give thermosetting resins. 2 (in full **melamine resin**) a plastic made from melamine and used esp. for laminated coatings. [melam (arbitrary) + AMINE]

melancholia /ˌmelənˈkəʊlɪə/ n. a mental illness marked by depression and ill-founded fears. [LL: see MELANCHOLY]

melancholy /ˈmelənkəlɪ/ n. & adj. —n. (pl. -ies) 1 a pensive sadness. 2 **a** mental depression. **b** a habitual or constitutional tendency to this. 3 hist. one of the four humours; black bile (see HUMOUR n. 5). —adj. (of a person) sad, gloomy; (of a thing) saddening, depressing; (of words, a tune, etc.) expressing sadness. □□ **melancholic** /-ˈkɒlɪk/ adj. **melancholically** /-ˈkɒlɪkəlɪ/ adv. [ME f. OF melancolie f. LL melancholia f. Gk melagkholia f. melas melanos black + kholē bile]

Melanchthon /məˈlæŋkθɒn/, Philipp (1497–1560), German Protestant reformer (real name Schwarzerd) who in 1521 succeeded Luther as leader of the Reformation movement in Germany. Professor of Greek at Wittenberg, he helped to systematize Luther's teachings and produced the first ordered exposition of Reformation doctrine. His attitude to Christianity was humanistic, and he cared for learning as such, writing textbooks that were used for several generations in upper schools and universities.

Melanesia /ˌmeləˈniːʃə/ an island-group in the SW Pacific containing the Bismarck Archipelago, the Solomon Islands, Santa Cruz, Vanuatu, New Caledonia, Fiji, and the intervening islands.

□□ **Melanesian** *adj.* & *n.* [Gk *melas* black (from the colour of the predominant native people), *nēsos* island]

mélange /meɪˈlãʒ/ *n.* a mixture, a medley. [F f. *mêler* mix (as MEDDLE)]

melanin /ˈmelənɪn/ *n.* a dark-brown to black pigment occurring in the hair, skin, and iris of the eye, that is responsible for tanning of the skin when exposed to sunlight. [Gk *melas melanos* black + -IN]

melanism /ˈmeləˌnɪz(ə)m/ *n.* an unusual darkening of body tissues caused by excessive production of melanin.

melanoma /ˌmeləˈnəʊmə/ *n.* a malignant tumour of melanin-forming cells, usu. in the skin. [MELANIN + -OMA]

melanosis /ˌmeləˈnəʊsɪs/ *n.* **1** = MELANISM. **2** a disorder in the body's production of melanin. □□ **melanotic** /-ˈnɒtɪk/ *adj.* [mod.L f. Gk (as MELANIN)]

Melba /ˈmelbə/, Dame Nellie (real name Helen Porter Mitchell, 1861–1931), Australian soprano singer, born near Melbourne, from which city she took her professional name. □ **do a Melba** *Austral. sl.* **1** return from retirement. **2** make several farewell appearances. **Melba sauce** a sauce made from puréed raspberries thickened with icing sugar. **Melba toast** very thin crisp toast. **peach Melba** (F *pêche Melba*) a dish of ice-cream and peaches with liqueur or sauce. It was invented by the French chef Escoffier in 1893 in honour of the singer Dame Nellie Melba when she was staying at the Savoy Hotel in London.

Melbourne[1] /ˈmelbən, -bɔːn/ the capital of Victoria and second-largest city in Australia; pop. (1986) 2,942,000.

Melbourne[2] /ˈmelbən, -bɔːn/, William Lamb, 2nd Viscount (1779–1848), British statesman. During his early parliamentary career Melbourne was a supporter of the moderate policies of Canning. He became Home Secretary in Lord Grey's administration in 1830 and succeeded Grey as Prime Minister in 1834. Out of office briefly in 1834–5, Melbourne then went on to serve as Prime Minister until 1841, pursuing a moderate reform policy despite troubles with Chartist and anti-Corn Laws agitation.

Melchior /ˈmelkɪɔː(r)/ the traditional name of one of the Magi, represented as a king of Nubia.

Melchizedek /melˈtʃɪzɪˌdek/ king of Salem (which is doubtfully identified with Jerusalem) and priest of the most high God, to whom Abraham paid tithes (Gen. 14: 18). He is sometimes quoted as the type of self-originating power, with reference to Heb. 7: 3–4.

meld[1] /meld/ *v.* & *n.* —*v.tr.* (also *absol.*) (in rummy, canasta, etc.) lay down or declare (one's cards) in order to score points. —*n.* a completed set or run of cards in any of these games. [G *melden* announce]

meld[2] /meld/ *v.tr.* & *intr. orig. US* merge, blend, combine. [perh. f. MELT + WELD[1]]

Meleager[1] /ˌmeliˈeɪgə(r)/ *Gk Mythol.* a hero at whose birth the Fates declared that he would die when a brand then on the fire was consumed. His mother Althaea seized the brand and kept it, but threw it into the fire when he quarrelled with and killed her brothers in a hunting expedition, whereupon he died.

Meleager[2] /ˌmeliˈeɪgə(r)/ (*c.*140–*c.*70 BC) Greek poet who lived at Tyre and on the island of Cos, author of many epigrams and of short poems on love and death.

mêlée /ˈmeleɪ/ *n.* (*US* **melee**) **1** a confused fight, skirmish, or scuffle. **2** a muddle. [F (as MEDLEY)]

melic /ˈmelɪk/ *adj.* (of a poem, esp. a Gk lyric) meant to be sung. [L *melicus* f. Gk *melikos* f. *melos* song]

Melilla /meˈliljə/ a Spanish enclave on the Mediterranean coast of Morocco; pop. (1981) 53,600 (with Ceuta).

meliorate /ˈmiːlɪəˌreɪt/ *v.tr.* & *intr. literary* improve (cf. AMELIORATE). □□ **melioration** /-ˈreɪʃ(ə)n/ *n.* **meliorative** /-rətɪv/ *adj.* [LL *meliorare* (as MELIORISM)]

meliorism /ˈmiːlɪəˌrɪz(ə)m/ *n.* a doctrine that the world may be made better by human effort. □□ **meliorist** *n.* [L *melior* better + -ISM]

melisma /mɪˈlɪzmə/ *n.* (*pl.* **melismata** /-mətə/ or **melismas**) *Mus.* a group of notes sung to one syllable of text. □□ **melismatic** /-ˈmætɪk/ *adj.* [Gk]

melliferous /mɪˈlɪfərəs/ *adj.* yielding or producing honey. [L *mellifer* f. *mel* honey]

mellifluous /mɪˈlɪfluəs/ *adj.* (of a voice or words) pleasing, musical, flowing. □□ **mellifluence** *n.* **mellifluent** *adj.* **mellifluously** *adv.* **mellifluousness** *n.* [ME f. OF *melliflue* or LL *mellifluus* f. *mel* honey + *fluere* flow]

Mellon /ˈmelən/, Andrew William (1855–1937), American financier and philanthropist, Secretary of the Treasury 1921–32. He donated his considerable art collection, together with funds, to establish the US National Gallery of Art (1937).

mellow /ˈmeləʊ/ *adj.* & *v.* —*adj.* **1** (of sound, colour, light) soft and rich, free from harshness. **2** (of character) softened or matured by age or experience. **3** genial, jovial. **4** partly intoxicated. **5** (of fruit) soft, sweet, and juicy. **6** (of wine) well-matured, smooth. **7** (of earth) rich, loamy. —*v.tr.* & *intr.* make or become mellow. □□ **mellowly** *adv.* **mellowness** *n.* [ME, perh. f. attrib. use of OE *melu, melw-* MEAL[2]]

melodeon /mɪˈləʊdɪən/ *n.* (also **melodion**) **1** a small organ popular in the 19th c., similar to the harmonium. **2** a small German accordion, played esp. by folk musicians. [MELODY + HARMONIUM with Graecized ending]

melodic /mɪˈlɒdɪk/ *adj.* **1** of or relating to melody. **2** having or producing melody. □ **melodic minor** a scale with the sixth and seventh degrees raised when ascending and lowered when descending. □□ **melodically** *adv.* [F *mélodique* f. LL *melodicus* f. Gk *melōidikos* (as MELODY)]

melodious /mɪˈləʊdɪəs/ *adj.* **1** of, producing, or having melody. **2** sweet-sounding. □□ **melodiously** *adv.* **melodiousness** *n.* [ME f. OF *melodieus* (as MELODY)]

melodist /ˈmelədɪst/ *n.* **1** a composer of melodies. **2** a singer.

melodize /ˈmeləˌdaɪz/ *v.* (also **-ise**) **1** *intr.* make a melody or melodies; make sweet music. **2** *tr.* make melodious. □□ **melodizer** *n.*

melodrama /ˈmeləˌdrɑːmə/ *n.* **1** a sensational dramatic piece with crude appeals to the emotions and usu. a happy ending. **2** the genre of drama of this type. (See below.) **3** language, behaviour, or an occurrence suggestive of this. **4** *hist.* a play with songs interspersed and with orchestral music accompanying the action. □□ **melodramatic** /-drəˈmætɪk/ *adj.* **melodramatically** /-drəˈmætɪkəlɪ/ *adv.* **melodramatist** /-ˈdræmətɪst/ *n.* **melodramatize** /-ˈdræməˌtaɪz/ *v.tr.* (also **-ise**). [earlier *melodrame* f. F *mélodrame* f. Gk *melos* music + F *drame* DRAMA]

This type of play was popular all over Europe in the 19th c. The term derives from the use of incidental music in spoken dramas in Germany and from the French *mélodrame*, a dumb show accompanied by music; its application to Gothic tales of horror and mystery, vice, and virtue triumphant stems from the early works of Goethe and Schiller. The music gradually became less important and the setting less Gothic, and in England there were domestic melodramas, melodramas based on real-life or legendary crimes (as the anonymous *Maria Marten* in the 1830s), and dramatizations of popular novels (Mrs Henry Wood's *East Lynne*, 1861). Melodrama died out early in the 20th c.

melodramatics /ˌmelədrəˈmætɪks/ *n.pl.* melodramatic behaviour, action, or writing.

melody /ˈmelədɪ/ *n.* (*pl.* **-ies**) **1** an arrangement of single notes in a musically expressive succession. **2** the principal part in harmonized music. **3** a musical arrangement of words. **4** sweet music, tunefulness. [ME f. OF *melodie* f. LL *melodia* f. Gk *melōidia* f. *melos* song]

melon /ˈmelən/ *n.* **1** the sweet fruit of various gourds. **2** the gourd producing this (*honeydew melon*; *water melon*). □ **cut the melon 1** decide a question. **2** share abundant profits among a number of people. [ME f. OF f. LL *melo -onis* abbr. of L *melopepo* f. Gk *mēlopepōn* f. *mēlon* apple + *pepōn* gourd f. *pepōn* ripe]

Melpomene /melˈpɒmɪnɪ/ *Gk* & *Rom. Mythol.* the Muse of tragedy. [Gk, = singer]

melt /melt/ *v.* & *n.* —*v.* **1** *intr.* become liquefied by heat. **2** *tr.* change to a liquid condition by heat. **3** *tr.* (as **molten** *adj.*) (usu. of materials that require a great deal of heat to melt them) liquefied by heat (*molten lava; molten lead*). **4 a** *intr.* & *tr.* dissolve. **b** *intr.* (of food) be easily dissolved in the mouth. **5** *intr.* **a** (of a person, feelings, the heart, etc.) be softened as a result of pity, love, etc. **b** dissolve into tears. **6** *tr.* soften (a person, feelings, the heart, etc.) (*a look to melt a heart of stone*). **7** *intr.* (usu. foll. by *into*) change or merge imperceptibly into another form or state (*night melted into dawn*). **8** *intr.* (often foll. by *away*) (of a person) leave or disappear unobtrusively (*melted into the background; melted away into the crowd*). **9** *intr.* (usu. as **melting** *adj.* (of sound) be soft and liquid (*melting chords*). **10** *intr. colloq.* (of a person) suffer extreme heat (*I'm melting in this thick jumper*). —*n.* **1** liquid metal etc. **2** an amount melted at any one time. **3** the process or an instance of melting. □ **melt away** disappear or make disappear by liquefaction. **melt down 1** melt (esp. metal articles) in order to reuse the raw material. **2** become liquid and lose structure (cf. MELTDOWN). **melting-point** the temperature at which any given solid will melt. **melting-pot 1** a pot in which metals etc. are melted and mixed. **2** a place where races, theories, etc. are mixed, or an imaginary pool where ideas are mixed together. **melt water** water formed by the melting of snow and ice, esp. from a glacier. □□ **meltable** *adj.* & *n.* **melter** *n.* **meltingly** *adv.* [OE *meltan, mieltan* f. Gmc, rel. to MALT]

meltdown /ˈmeltdaʊn/ *n.* the melting of (and consequent damage to) a structure, esp. the overheated core of a nuclear reactor.

melton /ˈmelt(ə)n/ *n.* cloth with a close-cut nap, used for overcoats etc. [*Melton Mowbray* in central England]

Melville /ˈmelvɪl/, Herman (1819–91), American novelist and poet. In 1839 he took to the sea as a cabin boy, and a voyage (1841) on a whaler to the South Seas provided the basis for his masterpiece *Moby-Dick* (1851), a dramatic celebration of man's defiance of a demonic God whose agent is the symbolic white whale Moby-Dick; this brilliant work was noted by some critics but few readers. His successful fictional travel narrative *Typee* (1846) and its sequel *Omoo* (1847) were followed by others, all based on his experiences in the South Seas, but his novel *Pierre* (1852) was a critical failure. *The Confidence-Man* (1857) was his last novel and his great creative period perished from public neglect. In addition to his stringent sombre tales and the novella *Billy Budd* (1924, the basis of Benjamin Britten's opera) he was a powerful poet, a satirist, romantic allegorist, and analyst of national character. It was not until the 1920s that he was rediscovered by literary scholars.

member /ˈmembə(r)/ *n.* **1** a person belonging to a society, team, etc. **2** (**Member**) a person formally elected to take part in the proceedings of certain organizations (*Member of Parliament; Member of Congress*). **3** (also *attrib.*) a part or branch of a political body (*member State; a member of the EEC*). **4** a constituent portion of a complex structure. **5** a part of a sentence, equation, group of figures, mathematical set, etc. **6 a** any part or organ of the body, esp. a limb. **b** = PENIS. **7** used in the title awarded to a person admitted to (usu. the lowest grade of) certain honours (*Member of the British Empire*). □□ **membered** *adj.* (also in *comb.*). **memberless** *adj.* [ME f. OF *membre* f. L *membrum* limb]

membership /ˈmembəʃɪp/ *n.* **1** being a member. **2** the number of members. **3** the body of members.

membrane /ˈmembreɪn/ *n.* **1** any pliable sheetlike structure acting as a boundary, lining, or partition in an organism. **2** a thin pliable sheet or skin of various kinds. □□ **membranaceous** /ˌmembrəˈneɪʃəs/ *adj.* **membraneous** /memˈbreɪnɪəs/ *adj.* **membranous** /ˈmembrənəs/ *adj.* [L *membrana* skin of body, parchment (as MEMBER)]

membrum virile /ˌmembrəm vɪˈraɪlɪ/ *n. archaic* the penis. [L, = male member]

memento /mɪˈmentəʊ/ *n.* (*pl.* **-oes** or **-os**) an object kept as a reminder or a souvenir of a person or an event. [L, imper. of *meminisse* remember]

memento mori /mɪˌmentəʊ ˈmɔːrɪ, -raɪ/ *n.* a warning or reminder of death (e.g. a skull). [L, = remember you must die]

Memnon /ˈmemnɒn/ *Gk legend* an Ethiopian king who went to Troy to help Priam, his uncle, and was killed. The 'colossi of Memnon', statues (supposed to represent him) near Thebes in Egypt, whose stones, before the restoration of the statues, were said to sing at dawn, are inscribed with the name of Amenophis III.

memo /ˈmeməʊ/ *n.* (*pl.* **-os**) *colloq.* memorandum. [abbr.]

memoir /ˈmemwɑː(r)/ *n.* **1** a historical account or biography written from personal knowledge or special sources. **2** (in *pl.*) an autobiography or a written account of one's memory of certain events or people. **3 a** an essay on a learned subject specially studied by the writer. **b** (in *pl.*) the proceedings or transactions of a learned society (*Memoirs of the American Mathematical Society*). □□ **memoirist** *n.* [F *mémoire* (masc.), special use of *mémoire* (fem.) MEMORY]

memorabilia /ˌmemərəˈbɪlɪə/ *n.pl.* **1** souvenirs of memorable events. **2** *archaic* memorable or noteworthy things. [L, neut. pl. (as MEMORABLE)]

memorable /ˈmemərəb(ə)l/ *adj.* **1** worth remembering, not to be forgotten. **2** easily remembered. □□ **memorability** /-ˈbɪlɪtɪ/ *n.* **memorableness** *n.* **memorably** *adv.* [ME f. F *mémorable* or L *memorabilis* f. *memorare* bring to mind f. *memor* mindful]

memorandum /ˌmeməˈrændəm/ *n.* (*pl.* **memoranda** /-də/ or **memorandums**) **1** a note or record made for future use. **2** an informal written message, esp. in business, diplomacy, etc. **3** *Law* a document recording the terms of a contract or other legal details. [ME f. L neut. sing. gerundive of *memorare*: see MEMORABLE]

memorial /mɪˈmɔːrɪəl/ *n.* & *adj.* —*n.* **1** an object, institution, or custom established in memory of a person or event (*the Albert Memorial*). **2** (often in *pl.*) *hist.* a statement of facts as the basis of a petition etc.; a record; an informal diplomatic paper. —*adj.* intending to commemorate a person or thing (*memorial service*). □ **Memorial Day** *US* a day on which those who died on active service are remembered, usu. the last Monday in May. □□ **memorialist** *n.* [ME f. OF *memorial* or L *memorialis* (as MEMORY)]

memorialize /mɪˈmɔːrɪəlaɪz/ *v.tr.* (also **-ise**) **1** commemorate. **2** address a memorial to (a person or body).

memoria technica /mɪˌmɔːrɪə ˈteknɪkə/ *n.* a system or contrivance used to assist the memory. [mod.L, = artificial memory]

memorize /ˈmeməraɪz/ *v.tr.* (also **-ise**) commit to memory. □□ **memorizable** *adj.* **memorization** /-ˈzeɪʃ(ə)n/ *n.* **memorizer** *n.*

memory /ˈmemərɪ/ *n.* (*pl.* **-ies**) **1** the faculty by which things are recalled to or kept in the mind. **2 a** this faculty in an individual (*my memory is beginning to fail*). **b** one's store of things remembered (*buried deep in my memory*). **3** a recollection or remembrance (*the memory of better times*). **4** the storage capacity of a computer or other electronic machinery. **5** the remembrance of a person or thing (*his mother's memory haunted him*). **6 a** the reputation of a dead person (*his memory lives on*). **b** in formulaic phrases used of a dead sovereign etc. (*of blessed memory*). **7** the length of time over which the memory or memories of any given person or group extends (*within living memory; within the memory of anyone still working here*). **8** the act of remembering (*a deed worthy of memory*). □ **commit to memory** learn (a thing) so as to be able to recall it. **from memory** without verification in books etc. **in memory of** to keep alive the remembrance of. **memory bank** (or **board**) the memory device of a computer etc. **memory lane** (usu. prec. by *down, along*) an imaginary and sentimental journey into the past. **memory mapping** *Computing* the allocation of peripheral devices to appear located within the main memory of a computer. [ME f. OF *memorie, memoire* f. L *memoria* f. *memor* mindful, remembering, rel. to MOURN]

Memphis[1] /ˈmemfɪs/ an ancient city of Egypt, about 15 km (nearly 10 miles) south of Cairo. It was the capital of Egypt from early dynastic times, and is said to have been founded by Menes, the first ruler of a united Egypt (*c.*3000 BC); it remained one of the principal cities even after the pharaohs of the 18th Dynasty made Thebes their capital (*c.*1550 BC). The monuments of Giza and Saqqara form part of its extensive necropolis.

Memphis[2] /ˈmemfɪs/ a river port on the Mississippi in the extreme south-west of Tennessee; pop. (1982) 645,800. Founded in 1819, it is named after the ancient Egyptian city because of its location on the river. The city is known as the home of the blues, a form of music associated especially with the Black composer W. C. Handy (1873–1958). The civil rights leader Martin Luther King was assassinated here in 1968. The singer Elvis Presley was brought up in Memphis, and his mansion, Graceland, where he is buried, is much visited by his admirers.

memsahib /ˈmemˌsɑːɪb, -sɑːb/ n. Anglo-Ind. hist. a European married woman in India, as spoken of or to by Indians. [MAˈAM + SAHIB]

men pl. of MAN.

menace /ˈmenɪs/ n. & v. —n. 1 a threat. 2 a dangerous or obnoxious thing or person. 3 joc. a pest, a nuisance. —v.tr. & intr. threaten, esp. in a malignant or hostile manner. □□ **menacer** n. **menacingly** adv. [ME ult. f. L minax -acis threatening f. minari threaten]

ménage /meɪˈnɑːʒ/ n. the members of a household. [OF manaige ult. f. L (as MANSION)]

ménage à trois /meɪˌnɑːʒ ɑː ˈtrwɑː/ n. an arrangement in which three people live together, usu. a married couple and the lover of one of them. [F, = household of three (as MÉNAGE)]

menagerie /mɪˈnædʒərɪ/ n. 1 a collection of wild animals in captivity for exhibition etc. 2 the place where these are housed. [F ménagerie (as MÉNAGE)]

Menai Strait /ˈmenaɪ/ the channel separating Anglesey from NW Wales.

Menander /məˈnændə(r)/ (342/1–293/89 BC) the leading writer of comedy in the Hellenistic period, of great influence and popularity in antiquity, but whose works survive only as fragments in papyrus finds. His plays, set in contemporary Greece, deal with domestic situations, with recurring features such as foundling children, kidnapped daughters, and scheming slaves; a love-interest is constant. His verse stays close to colloquial speech and his characters are lifelike; in antiquity he was praised for representing life.

menaquinone /ˌmenəˈkwɪnəʊn/ n. one of the K vitamins, produced by bacteria found in the large intestine, essential for the blood-clotting process. Also called vitamin K_2. [chem. deriv. of methylnaphthoquinone]

menarche /meˈnɑːkɪ/ n. the onset of first menstruation. [mod.L formed as MENO- + Gk arkhē beginning]

Mencius /ˈmensɪəs/ (Latinization of Chinese Meng-tzu or Mengzi Meng the Master) 1 a Chinese philosopher of the 4th c. BC. 2 one of the four great texts of Confucianism published in AD 1190, containing his teachings. The central doctrine is that human nature tends towards the good as water tends to flow downhill.

Mencken /ˈmeŋkən/, Henry Louis (1880–1956), American journalist and literary critic, who boldly attacked the political and literary Establishment and upheld the iconoclasm of writers as diverse as G. B. Shaw, Ibsen, Nietzsche, Zola, and Mark Twain. He strongly opposed European 'patronage' of America, and in his book The American Language (1919) defended the developing vigour and versatility of colloquial American usage.

mend /mend/ v. & n. —v. 1 tr. restore to a sound condition; repair (a broken article, a damaged road, torn clothes, etc.). 2 intr. regain health. 3 tr. improve (mend matters). 4 tr. add fuel to (a fire). —n. a darn or repair in material etc. (a mend in my shirt). □ **mend one's fences** make peace with a person. **mend one's manners** improve one's behaviour. **mend or end** improve or abolish. **mend one's pace** go faster; alter one's pace to another's. **mend one's ways** reform, improve one's habits. **on the mend** improving in health or condition. □□ **mendable** adj. **mender** n. [ME f. AF mender f. amender AMEND]

mendacious /menˈdeɪʃəs/ adj. lying, untruthful. □□ **mendaciously** adv. **mendacity** /-ˈdæsɪtɪ/ n. (pl. **-ies**). [L mendax -dacis perh. f. mendum fault]

Mendel /ˈmend(ə)l/, Gregor Johann (1822–84), Moravian monk, the 'father of genetics'. From his experiments with peas he argued (1855–6) that hybrids of plants showing different characters produced second-generation offspring in which parental characters were inherited in precise ratios. Hybrids exhibit the dominant parental character and produce offspring in which the parental characters re-emerge unchanged. The importance of Mendel's work lies in the fact that he recognized that it is not the characters themselves which are inherited, but the predisposing factors underlying them. After the rediscovery of his ratios in 1900, Mendelism was often thought, wrongly, to be the antithesis of the Darwinian theory of natural selection; in fact, Mendel had demonstrated the primary source of variability in plants and animals, on which natural selection could then operate.

Mendeleev /ˌmendeˈleɪef/, Dmitri Ivanovich (1834–1907), Russian chemist who developed the periodic table in which he classified chemical elements according to their atomic weights in groups with similar properties. This allowed him to systematize much of the existing chemical information, pinpoint elements with incorrectly assigned atomic weights, and also predict the existence of several new elements. His study of gases and liquids led him to the concept of critical temperature, independently of Thomas Andrews (1813–85). The artificial element mendelevium was named after him in 1955.

mendelevium /ˌmendəˈliːvɪəm/ n. Chem. an artificially made transuranic radioactive metallic element, first obtained in 1955 by bombarding einsteinium with helium atoms. ¶ Symb.: **Md**; atomic number 101. [D. I. MENDELEEV]

Mendelian /menˈdiːlɪən/ adj. of Mendel's theory of heredity by genes.

Mendelism /ˈmendəlɪz(ə)m/ n. that part of genetics concerned with the manner in which hereditary factors (genes) and the characteristics they control are inherited during the course of sexual reproduction. The main principles were first outlined by Mendel, although they have been modified by later discoveries.

Mendelssohn /ˈmendəls(ə)n/, (Jakob Ludwig) Felix (1809–47), German composer, born of a Jewish banking family which adopted the Christian faith after moving to Berlin in 1811. He was a child prodigy; his 13 string symphonies, composed 1821–3, reveal a firm grasp of counterpoint and mastery of the classical style, and his overture to A Midsummer Night's Dream was composed at the age of 17. Pianist, organist, and conductor, he combined his musical accomplishments with wide literary knowledge and was a good painter; his love of landscape provides the inspiration for the descriptive Fingal's Cave (1830) and the Fourth (Italian) Symphony (1832). The poetic elegance of his work has caused it to be regarded as superficial because of its lack of impassioned features, and its popularity during his lifetime was followed (from the 1860s) by a severe reaction, but the pendulum has swung again and the craftsmanship, restraint, poetry, and melodic freshness of his compositions are now highly valued.

mendicant /ˈmendɪkənt/ adj. & n. —adj. 1 begging. 2 (of a friar) living solely on alms. —n. 1 a beggar. 2 a mendicant friar. □□ **mendicancy** n. **mendicity** /-ˈdɪsɪtɪ/ n. [L mendicare beg f. mendicus beggar f. mendum fault]

mending /ˈmendɪŋ/ n. 1 the action of a person who mends. 2 things, esp. clothes, to be mended.

Mendoza[1] /menˈdəʊsə/ 1 a province of western Argentina. 2 its capital city, situated at the centre of South America's best-known wine-producing region; pop. (1980) 118,000.

Mendoza[2] /menˈdəʊsə/, Antonio de (1490–1552), a member of an aristocratic Spanish family, appointed as the first viceroy of New Spain (Mexico). He served in that important position from 1535 to 1550 and provided the new colony with resolute leadership; much of his system endured until the 19th c. He improved relations between Spaniards and Indians, and fostered economic development (especially in mining) and educational opportunities for both the Spanish and the Indian populations. In 1551 he became viceroy of Peru, but served there for only a year before his death.

Menelaus /ˌmenɪˈleɪəs/ Gk legend king of Sparta, brother of Agamemnon and husband of Helen who was stolen from him by Paris, an event which provoked the Trojan War. They were reunited after the fall of Troy.

menfolk /ˈmenfəʊk/ n.pl. 1 men in general. 2 the men of one's family.

Meng-tzu /meŋˈtsuː/ see MENCIUS.

menhaden /men'heɪd(ə)n/ n. any large herring-like fish of the genus *Brevoortia*, of the E. coast of N. America, yielding valuable oil and used for manure. [Algonquian: cf. Narragansett *munnawhatteaûg*]

menhir /'menhɪə(r)/ n. *Archaeol.* a tall upright usu. prehistoric monumental stone. [Breton *men* stone + *hir* long]

menial /'miːnɪəl/ adj. & n. —adj. **1** (esp. of unskilled domestic work) degrading, servile. **2** usu. *derog.* (of a servant) domestic. —n. **1** a menial servant. **2** a servile person. □□ **menially** adv. [ME f. OF *meinee* household]

meningitis /ˌmenɪn'dʒaɪtɪs/ n. an inflammation of the meninges due to infection by viruses or bacteria. □□ **meningitic** /-'dʒɪtɪk/ adj.

meninx /'miːnɪŋks/ n. (pl. **meninges** /mɪ'nɪndʒiː/) (usu. in pl.) any of the three membranes that line the skull and vertebral canal and enclose the brain and spinal cord (dura mater, arachnoid, pia mater). □□ **meningeal** /mɪ'nɪndʒɪəl/ adj. [mod.L f. Gk *mēnigx -iggos* membrane]

meniscus /mɪ'nɪskəs/ n. (pl. **menisci** /-saɪ/) **1** *Physics* the curved upper surface of a liquid in a tube, usually concave upwards when the walls are wetted and convex when they are dry, because of the effects of surface tension. **2** a lens that is convex on one side and concave on the other. **3** *Math.* a crescent-shaped figure. □□ **meniscoid** adj. [mod.L f. Gk *mēniskos* crescent, dimin. of *mēnē* moon]

Mennonite /'menəˌnaɪt/ n. a member of a Protestant sect originating in Friesland in the 16th c., maintaining principles similar to those of the Anabaptists, being opposed to infant baptism, the taking of oaths, military service, and the holding of civic offices. In the following centuries many emigrated, first to other European countries and to Russia, later to North and South America, in search of political freedom. [*Menno* Simons, its early leader, d. 1561]

meno- /'menəʊ/ comb. form menstruation. [Gk *mēn mēnos* month]

menology /mɪ'nɒlədʒɪ/ n. (pl. **-ies**) a calendar, esp. that of the Greek Church, with biographies of the saints. [mod.L *menologium* f. eccl.Gk *mēnologion* f. *mēn* month + *logos* account]

menopause /'menəˌpɔːz/ n. **1** the ceasing of menstruation. **2** the period in a woman's life (usu. between 45 and 50) when this occurs (see also *male menopause*). □□ **menopausal** /-'pɔːz(ə)l/ adj. [mod.L *menopausis* (as MENO-, PAUSE)]

menorah /mɪ'nɔːrə/ n. **1** a holy candelabrum having seven branches, used in the ancient temple in Jerusalem, originally that made by the craftsman Bezalel and placed in the sanctuary of the Tabernacle (Exod. 37: 17 ff). It has long been a symbol of Judaism; the menorah framed by two olive branches is the emblem of the State of Israel. **2** a candelabrum having any number of branches, used in modern synagogues. [Heb., = candlestick]

Menorca see MINORCA.

menorrhagia /ˌmenə'reɪdʒɪə/ n. abnormally heavy bleeding at menstruation. [MENO- + stem of Gk *rhēgnumi* burst]

menorrhoea /ˌmenə'rɪə/ n. ordinary flow of blood at menstruation. [MENO- + Gk *rhoia* f. *rheō* flow]

menses /'mensiːz/ n.pl. **1** blood and other materials discharged from the uterus at menstruation. **2** the time of menstruation. [L, pl. of *mensis* month]

Menshevik /'menʃəvɪk/ n. a member of a minority faction of the Russian Socialist Party who opposed the Bolshevik policies of non-cooperation with other opponents of the Tsarist regime and violent revolutionary action by a small political élite. The Mensheviks, along with the other revolutionary groups, were completely defeated by the Bolsheviks in the power struggle following the successful overthrow of the Tsar in 1917. [Russ. *Men'shevik* a member of the minority (*men'she* less; cf. BOLSHEVIK]

mens rea /menz 'riːə/ n. criminal intent; the knowledge of wrongdoing. [L, = guilty mind]

menstrual /'menstrʊəl/ adj. of or relating to the menses or menstruation. □ **menstrual cycle** the process of ovulation and menstruation in female primates. [ME f. L *menstrualis* f. *mensis* month]

menstruate /'menstrʊˌeɪt/ v.intr. undergo menstruation. [LL *menstruare menstruat-* (as MENSTRUAL)]

menstruation /ˌmenstrʊ'eɪʃ(ə)n/ n. the process of discharging blood and other materials from the uterus in sexually mature non-pregnant women at intervals of about one lunar month until the menopause.

menstruous /'menstrʊəs/ adj. **1** of or relating to the menses. **2** menstruating. [ME f. OF *menstrueus* or LL *menstruosus* (as MENSTRUAL)]

menstruum /'menstrʊəm/ n. (pl. **menstrua** /-strʊə/) a solvent. [ME f. L, neut. of *menstruus* monthly f. *mensis* month f. the alchemical parallel between transmutation into gold and the supposed action of menses on the ovum]

mensurable /'mensjʊrəb(ə)l/ adj. **1** measurable, having fixed limits. **2** *Mus.* = MENSURAL 2. [F *mensurable* or LL *mensurabilis* f. *mensurare* to measure f. L *mensura* MEASURE]

mensural /'mensjʊr(ə)l/ adj. **1** of or involving measure. **2** *Mus.* of or involving a fixed rhythm or notes of definite duration (cf. PLAINSONG). [L *mensuralis* f. *mensura* MEASURE]

mensuration /ˌmensjʊə'reɪʃ(ə)n/ n. **1** measuring. **2** *Math.* the measuring of geometric magnitudes such as the lengths of lines, areas of surfaces, and volumes of solids. [LL *mensuratio* (as MENSURABLE)]

menswear /'menzweə(r)/ n. clothes for men.

-ment /mənt/ suffix **1** forming nouns expressing the means or result of the action of a verb (*abridgement*; *embankment*). **2** forming nouns from adjectives (*merriment*; *oddment*). [from or after F f. L *-mentum*]

mental /'ment(ə)l/ adj. & n. —adj. **1** of or in the mind. **2** done by the mind. **3** *colloq.* **a** insane. **b** crazy, wild, eccentric (*is mental about pop music*). —n. *colloq.* a mental patient. □ **mental age** the degree of a person's mental development expressed as an age at which the same degree is attained by an average person. **mental arithmetic** arithmetic performed in the mind. **mental asylum** (or **home** or **hospital** or **institution**) an establishment for the care of mental patients. **mental cruelty** the infliction of suffering on another's mind, esp. *Law* as grounds for divorce. **mental defective** esp. *US* a person with impaired mental abilities. **mental deficiency** imperfect mental development leading to abnormally low intelligence. **mental illness** a disorder of the mind. **mental nurse** a nurse dealing with mentally ill patients. **mental patient** a sufferer from mental illness. **mental reservation** a qualification tacitly added in making a statement etc. □□ **mentally** adv. [ME f. OF *mental* or LL *mentalis* f. L *mens -ntis* mind]

mentalism /'mentəˌlɪz(ə)m/ n. **1** *Philos.* the theory that physical and psychological phenomena are ultimately only explicable in terms of a creative and interpretative mind. **2** *Psychol.* the primitive tendency to personify in spirit form the forces of nature, or endow inert objects with the quality of 'soul'. □□ **mentalist** n. **mentalistic** /-'lɪstɪk/ adj.

mentality /men'tælɪtɪ/ n. (pl. **-ies**) **1** mental character or disposition. **2** kind or degree of intelligence. **3** what is in or of the mind.

mentation /men'teɪʃ(ə)n/ n. **1** mental action. **2** state of mind. [L *mens -ntis* mind]

menthol /'menθɒl/ n. a mint-tasting organic alcohol found in oil of peppermint etc., used as a flavouring and to relieve local pain. [G f. L *mentha* MINT¹]

mentholated /'menθəˌleɪtɪd/ adj. treated with or containing menthol.

mention /'menʃ(ə)n/ v. & n. —v.tr. **1** refer to briefly. **2** specify by name. **3** reveal or disclose (*do not mention this to anyone*). **4** (in dispatches) award (a person) a minor honour for meritorious, usu. gallant, military service. —n. **1** a reference, esp. by name, to a person or thing. **2** (in dispatches) a military honour awarded for outstanding conduct. □ **don't mention it** said in polite dismissal of an apology or thanks. **make mention** (or **no mention**) **of** refer (or not refer) to. **not to mention** introducing a fact or thing of secondary or (as a rhetorical device) of primary importance. □□ **mentionable** adj. [OF f. L *mentio -onis* f. the root of *mens* mind]

mentor /ˈmentɔ:(r)/ n. an experienced and trusted adviser. [F f. L f. Gk Mentōr adviser of the young Telemachus, son of Odysseus, in Homer's *Odyssey* and Fénelon's *Télémaque*]

menu /ˈmenju:/ n. **1 a** a list of dishes available in a restaurant etc. **b** a list of items to be served at a meal. **2** *Computing* a list of options showing the commands or facilities available. □ **menu-driven** (of a program or computer) used by making selections from menus. [F, = detailed list, f. L *minutus* MINUTE²]

Menuhin /ˈmenuɪn/, Sir Yehudi (1916–), American-born violinist, whose performing career began as a child prodigy in 1924. In 1932 he recorded Elgar's violin concerto, conducted by the composer; Bartók wrote a solo violin sonata for him (1942). In recitals Menuhin was frequently partnered by his sister Hephzibah (1921–81, pianist). From 1959 to 1969, having settled in England, he was Director of the Bath Festival, and conducted many concerts with his own chamber orchestra. He founded a School of Music, named after him, now at Stoke d'Abernon, Surrey, in 1963.

Menzies /ˈmenzɪz/, Sir Robert Gordon (1894–1978), Australian statesman, a conservative and avowed anti-communist, Australia's longest-serving prime minister (1939–41 and 1949–66).

meow var. of MIAOW.

MEP abbr. Member of the European Parliament.

mepacrine /ˈmepəkrɪn/ n. *Brit.* quinacrine. [*methyl* + *paludism* (malaria) + *acridine*]

Mephistopheles /ˌmefɪˈstɒfɪˌli:z/ an evil spirit to whom Faust, in the German legend, sold his soul. —n. a fiendish person. □□ **Mephistophelean** /-ˈli:ən/ adj. **Mephistophelian** /-ˈfi:lɪən/ adj. [G (16th c.), of unkn. orig.]

mephitis /mɪˈfaɪtɪs/ n. **1** a noxious emanation, esp. from the earth. **2** a foul-smelling or poisonous stench. □□ **mephitic** /-ˈfɪtɪk/ adj. [L]

-mer /mə(r)/ comb. form denoting a substance of a specified class, esp. a polymer (*dimer*; *isomer*; *tautomer*). [Gk *meros* part, share]

meranti /məˈrænti/ n. a white, red, or yellow hardwood timber from any of various Malayan trees of the genus *Shorea*. [Malay]

mercantile /ˈmɜ:kənˌtaɪl/ adj. **1** of trade, trading. **2** commercial. **3** mercenary, fond of bargaining. □ **mercantile marine** shipping employed in commerce not war. [F f. It. f. *mercante* MERCHANT]

mercantilism /ˈmɜ:kəntɪˌlɪz(ə)m/ n. an old economic theory that money is the only form of wealth. The theory was prevalent between 1500 and 1800, mainly in England and France. It held that exports created wealth for a nation, imports diminished it, and that gold and silver bullion should be accumulated by a country and not exported; imports of manufactured goods should be restricted. The implication of this theory is that trade benefits one country at the expense of another; it became discredited when Adam Smith and others showed that it can benefit both sides. □□ **mercantilist** n.

mercaptan /məˈkæpt(ə)n/ n. = THIOL. [mod.L *mercurium captans* capturing mercury]

Mercator /mɜ:ˈkeɪtə(r)/, Gerardus (Latinized name of Gerhard Kremer, 1512–94), Flemish-born geographer, inventor of a system of map-projection in which the globe is projected on to a cylinder and the meridians of longitude are at right angles to the parallels of latitude, which all have the same length as the equator. His world map of 1569 shows a navigable north-west passage between Asia and America, and a large southern continent. This was immediately influential, whereas his more enduring projection (named after him) was not adopted for many years.

mercenary /ˈmɜ:sɪnərɪ/ adj. & n. —adj. primarily concerned with money or other reward (*mercenary motives*). —n. (pl. -ies) a hired soldier in foreign service. □□ **mercenariness** n. [ME f. L *mercenarius* f. *merces -edis* reward]

mercer /ˈmɜ:sə(r)/ n. *Brit.* a dealer in textile fabrics, esp. silk and other costly materials. □□ **mercery** n. (pl. -ies). [ME f. AF *mercer*, OF *mercier* ult. f. L *merx mercis* goods]

mercerize /ˈmɜ:səˌraɪz/ v.tr. (also -ise) treat (cotton fabric or thread) under tension with caustic alkali to give greater strength and impart lustre. [J. *Mercer*, alleged inventor of the process d. 1866]

merchandise /ˈmɜ:tʃənˌdaɪz/ n. & v. —n. goods for sale. —v. **1** intr. trade, traffic. **2** tr. trade or traffic in. **3** tr. **a** put on the market, promote the sale of (goods etc.). **b** advertise, publicize (an idea or person). □□ **merchandisable** adj. **merchandiser** n. [ME f. OF *marchandise* f. *marchand*: see MERCHANT]

merchant /ˈmɜ:tʃ(ə)nt/ n. **1** a wholesale trader, esp. with foreign countries. **2** esp. *US* & *Sc.* a retail trader. **3** *colloq.* usu. *derog.* a person showing a partiality for a specified activity or practice (*speed merchant*). □ **merchant bank** esp. *Brit.* a bank dealing in commercial loans and finance. **merchant banker** a member of a merchant bank. **merchant marine** *US* = *merchant navy*. **merchant navy** a nation's commercial shipping. **merchant prince** a wealthy merchant. **merchant ship** = MERCHANTMAN. [ME f. OF *marchand*, *marchant* ult. f. L *mercari* trade f. *merx mercis* merchandise]

merchantable /ˈmɜ:tʃəntəb(ə)l/ adj. saleable, marketable. [ME f. *merchant* (v.) f. OF *marchander* f. *marchand*: see MERCHANT]

merchantman /ˈmɜ:tʃəntmən/ n. (pl. -men) a ship conveying merchandise.

Mercia /ˈmɜ:ʃə/ a kingdom that was founded in central England by the invading Angles in the 6th c. and became powerful under Offa in the second half of the 8th c. Its borders fluctuated considerably as a result of the endemic warfare of the period, and by the end of the 9th c. it had lost its separate identity. The name has been revived in 'West Mercia Authority', an area of police administration covering the counties of Hereford and Worcester, and Shropshire. □□ **Mercian** adj. & n. [L f. OE, = people of the marches (i.e. borders, with ref. to the border with Wales)]

merciful /ˈmɜ:sɪˌfʊl/ adj. having or showing or feeling mercy. □□ **mercifulness** n.

mercifully /ˈmɜ:sɪˌfʊlɪ/ adv. **1** in a merciful manner. **2** (qualifying a whole sentence) fortunately (*mercifully, the sun came out*).

merciless /ˈmɜ:sɪləs/ adj. **1** pitiless. **2** showing no mercy. □□ **mercilessly** adv. **mercilessness** n.

mercurial /mɜ:ˈkjʊərɪəl/ adj. & n. —adj. **1** (of a person) sprightly, ready-witted, volatile. **2** of or containing mercury. **3** (**Mercurial**) of the planet Mercury. —n. a drug containing mercury. □□ **mercurialism** n. **mercuriality** /-ˈælɪtɪ/ n. **mercurially** adv. [ME f. OF *mercuriel* or L *mercurialis* (as MERCURY)]

Mercury /ˈmɜ:kjʊrɪ/ **1** *Rom. Mythol.* the god of eloquence, skill, trading, and thieving, the messenger of the gods, early identified with Hermes. **2** *Astron.* the innermost planet of the solar system. Somewhat larger than the moon (its diameter is 4,878 km), it was discovered by the Mariner 10 space probe to have a heavily cratered surface. Early theories that its rotation period was the same as its orbital period, so that it always kept the same face turned towards the sun, are now known to be incorrect, but its 'day' of 58.65 days is precisely two-thirds the length of its 87.97-day 'year' because of the influence of tidal forces from the nearby sun, and daytime temperatures average 170 °C. There is no atmosphere, nor has the planet any satellites. [L *merx mercis* merchandise]

mercury /ˈmɜ:kjʊrɪ/ n. **1** *Chem.* a silvery-white heavy metallic element, liquid at room temperatures. Known to the ancient world, it has long been used in medicines and ointments, although recently its use has declined as its toxicity has become recognized. Its main use is now in batteries, switches, lamps, and other electrical equipment. It is also used in thermometers and barometers, and in alloys (amalgams) with other metals. It can occur in the uncombined state in nature, but its main source is the sulphide, cinnabar. Pollution of seas and lakes by mercury and its compounds has become a serious problem in recent years, although efforts are now being made to control it. ¶ Symb.: **Hg**; atomic number 80. **2** any plant of the genus *Mercurialis*, esp. *M. perenne*. □ **mercury vapour lamp** a lamp in which light is produced by an electric discharge through mercury vapour. □□ **mercuric** /-ˈkjʊərɪk/ adj. **mercurous** adj. [ME f. L *Mercurius* MERCURY]

mercy /'mɜːsɪ/ n. & int. —n. (pl. **-ies**) **1** compassion or forbearance shown to enemies or offenders in one's power. **2** the quality of compassion. **3** an act of mercy. **4** (attrib.) administered or performed out of mercy or pity for a suffering person (mercy killing). **5** something to be thankful for (small mercies). —int. expressing surprise or fear. □ **at the mercy of 1** wholly in the power of. **2** liable to danger or harm from. **have mercy on** (or **upon**) show mercy to. **mercy flight** the transporting by air of an injured or sick person from a remote area to a hospital. [ME f. OF merci f. L merces -edis reward, in LL pity, thanks]

mere¹ /mɪə(r)/ attrib.adj. (**merest**) that is solely or no more or better than what is specified (a mere boy; no mere theory). □ **mere right** Law a right in theory. □□ **merely** adv. [ME f. AF meer, OF mier f. L merus unmixed]

mere² /mɪə(r)/ n. archaic or poet. a lake or pond. [OE f. Gmc]

mere³ /'merɪ/ n. a Maori war-club, esp. one made of greenstone. [Maori]

Meredith /'merədɪθ/, George (1828–1909), English novelist and poet. His finest volume of verse, Modern Love (1862), describes the disillusionment of married love; Meredith's first marriage, to Mary Ellen Nichols (daughter of T. L. Peacock), had not been happy, and she deserted him in 1857. During 1861–2 he lodged for a time with Swinburne and Rossetti in Chelsea. His reputation rests on his novels which began with The Ordeal of Richard Feverel (1859); more successful were Evan Harrington (1861), largely autobiographical, the celebrated The Egoist (1879), and Diana of the Crossways (1885). He received much praise for his narrative skill and his intense psychological exploration, but the elliptic character of his prose has tended to obscure his genius.

meretricious /ˌmerɪ'trɪʃəs/ adj. **1** (of decorations, literary style, etc.) showily but falsely attractive. **2** of or befitting a prostitute. □□ **meretriciously** adv. **meretriciousness** n. [L meretricius f. meretrix -tricis prostitute f. merēri be hired]

merganser /mɜː'gænsə(r)/ n. any of various diving fish-eating northern ducks of the genus Mergus, with a long narrow serrated hooked bill. Also called SAWBILL. [mod.L f. L mergus diver f. mergere dive + anser goose]

merge /mɜːdʒ/ v. **1** tr. & intr. (often foll. by with) **a** combine or be combined. **b** join or blend gradually. **2** intr. & tr. (foll. by in) lose or cause to lose character and identity in (something else). **3** tr. (foll. by in) embody (a title or estate) in (a larger one). □□ **mergence** n. [L mergere mers- dip, plunge, partly through legal AF merger]

merger /'mɜːdʒə(r)/ n. **1** the combining of two commercial companies etc. into one. **2** a merging, esp. of one estate in another. **3** Law the absorbing of a minor offence in a greater one. [AF (as MERGE)]

Mérida /'meɪriːðə/ a city in SE Mexico, the capital of Yucatán State; pop. (1980) 424,500.

meridian /mə'rɪdɪən/ n. & adj. —n. **1** a circle passing through the celestial poles and zenith of any place on the earth's surface. **2 a** a circle of constant longitude, passing through a given place and the terrestrial poles. **b** the corresponding line on a map. **3** archaic the point at which a sun or star attains its highest altitude. **4** prime; full splendour. —adj. **1** of noon. **2** of the period of greatest splendour, vigour, etc. [ME f. OF meridien or L meridianus (adj.) f. meridies midday f. medius middle + dies day]

meridional /mə'rɪdɪən(ə)l/ adj. & n. —adj. **1** of or in the south (esp. of Europe). **2** of or relating to a meridian. —n. an inhabitant of the south (esp. of France). [ME f. OF f. LL meridionalis irreg. f. L meridies: see MERIDIAN]

meringue /mə'ræŋ/ n. **1** a confection of sugar, the white of eggs, etc., baked crisp. **2** a small cake or shell of this, usu. decorated or filled with whipped cream etc. [F, of unkn. orig.]

merino /mə'riːnəʊ/ n. (pl. **-os**) **1** (in full **merino sheep**) a variety of sheep with long fine wool. **2** a soft woollen or wool-and-cotton material like cashmere, orig. of merino wool. **3** a fine woollen yarn. [Sp., of uncert. orig.]

meristem /'merɪˌstem/ n. Bot. a plant tissue consisting of actively dividing cells forming new tissue. □□ **meristematic**

/-stə'mætɪk/ adj. [Gk meristos divisible f. merizō divide f. meros part, after xylem]

merit /'merɪt/ n. & v. —n. **1** the quality of deserving well. **2** excellence, worth. **3** (usu. in pl.) **a** a thing that entitles one to reward or gratitude. **b** esp. Law intrinsic rights and wrongs (the merits of a case). **4** Theol. good deeds as entitling to a future reward. —v.tr. (**merited, meriting**) deserve or be worthy of (reward, punishment, consideration, etc.). □ **make a merit of** regard or represent (one's own conduct) as praiseworthy. **on its merits** with regard only to its intrinsic worth. **Order of Merit** Brit. an order founded in 1902, for distinguished achievement. [ME f. OF merite f. L meritum price, value, = past part. of merēri earn, deserve]

meritocracy /ˌmerɪ'tɒkrəsɪ/ n. (pl. **-ies**) **1** government by persons selected competitively according to merit. **2** a group of persons selected in this way. **3** a society governed by meritocracy.

meritorious /ˌmerɪ'tɔːrɪəs/ adj. **1** (of a person or act) having merit; deserving reward, praise, or gratitude. **2** deserving commendation for thoroughness etc. □□ **meritoriously** adv. **meritoriousness** n. [ME f. L meritorius f. merēri merit- earn]

merle /mɜːl/ n. Sc. or archaic a blackbird. [ME f. F f. L merula]

Merlin /'mɜːlɪn/ (in Arthurian legend) a magician who aided and supported King Arthur. Geoffrey of Monmouth (12th c.) identifies him with a boy (Ambrosius), without mortal sire, who, according to Nennius in his Historia Britonum (c.796), interpreted an omen for the British king Vortigern.

merlin /'mɜːlɪn/ n. a small European or N. American falcon, Falco columbarius, that hunts small birds. [ME f. AF merilun f. OF esmerillon augment. f. esmeril f. Frank.]

merlon /'mɜːlɒn/ n. the solid part of an embattled parapet between two embrasures. [F f. It. merlone f. merlo battlement]

mermaid /'mɜːmeɪd/ n. a legendary sea-creature with a woman's head and trunk and a fish's tail. The mermaid legend involves the concept of an ideal but fatal love, embodied in a hauntingly beautiful, mysterious, and unattainable feminine being; its persistence is not surprising. For centuries there were reports of sightings in many parts of the world until in the 18th c. scepticism set in. In Victorian times stuffed mermaids of regulation design, usually constructed by enterprising Japanese fishermen from the trunk of a monkey and the skin of a fish, were exhibited at fairs. Ancient Babylonian and Semitic mythologies include fish-deities (the male seems earlier than the female), and the Tritons were the mermen of Greek (or rather, pre-Greek) mythology, but all these are a long way from the beautiful mermaid who beguiles sailors to their destruction. If a real animal is sought as the basis of the tradition credit usually goes to the manatee and the dugong, because of the pectoral position of the breasts and the horizontally flattened tail, or (in colder latitudes) to one of the seal family, but to be mistaken for a human form these would have to be seen at a considerable distance. [ME f. MERE² in obs. sense 'sea' + MAID]

merman /'mɜːmæn/ n. (pl. **-men**) the male equivalent of a mermaid.

mero- /'merəʊ/ comb. form partly, partial. [Gk meros part]

Meroe /'merəʊɪ/ an ancient city on the River Nile, in Sudan. It was the capital of the ancient kingdom of Cush from c.590 BC until it fell to the invading Aksumites in the early 4th c. AD.

-merous /mərəs/ comb. form esp. Bot. having so many parts (dimerous; 5-merous). [Gk (as MERO-)]

Merovingian /ˌmerəʊ'vɪndʒɪən/ adj. & n. —adj. of or relating to the Frankish dynasty founded by Clovis and reigning in Gaul and Germany c.500–750. These rulers were overthrown after feuding had weakened royal authority, to be replaced by the Carolingians —n. a member of this dynasty. [F mérovingien f. med.L Merovingi f. L Meroveus name of the reputed founder]

merriment /'merɪmənt/ n. **1** exuberant enjoyment; being merry. **2** mirth, fun.

merry /'merɪ/ adj. (**merrier, merriest**) **1 a** joyous. **b** full of laughter or gaiety. **2** Brit. colloq. slightly drunk. □ **make merry 1** be festive; enjoy oneself. **2** (foll. by over) make fun of. **merry andrew** a mountebank's assistant; a clown or buffoon.

merry thought esp. *Brit.* the wishbone of a bird. **play merry hell with** see HELL. □□ **merrily** *adv.* **merriness** *n.* [OE *myrige* f. Gmc]

merry-go-round /ˈmerɪɡəʊˌraʊnd/ *n.* **1** a revolving machine with wooden horses or cars for riding on at a fair etc. **2** a cycle of bustling activities.

merrymaking /ˈmerɪˌmeɪkɪŋ/ *n.* festivity, fun. □□ **merrymaker** *n.*

Mersa Matruh /ˌmɜːsə məˈtruː/ a town on the Mediterranean coast of Egypt, 250 km (156 miles) west of Alexandria.

Mersey /ˈmɜːzɪ/ a river of NE England, rising in the Peak district and flowing into the Irish Sea near Liverpool.

Merseyside /ˈmɜːzɪˌsaɪd/ a metropolitan county of NW England; pop. (1981) 1,521,900; county town, Liverpool.

mesa /ˈmeɪsə/ *n.* US an isolated flat-topped hill with steep sides, found in landscapes with horizontal strata. [Sp., lit. table, f. L *mensa*]

mésalliance /meɪˈzælɪˌɑ̃s/ *n.* a marriage with a person of a lower social position. [F (as MIS-², ALLIANCE)]

mescal /ˈmeskæl/ *n.* **1 a** maguey. **b** liquor obtained from this. **2** a peyote cactus. □ **mescal buttons** disc-shaped dried tops from the peyote cactus, eaten or chewed as an intoxicant. [Sp. *mezcal* f. Nahuatl *mexcalli*]

mescaline /ˈmeskəˌliːn/ *n.* (also **mescalin** /-lɪn/) a hallucinogenic alkaloid present in mescal buttons.

Mesdames *pl.* of MADAME.

Mesdemoiselles *pl.* of MADEMOISELLE.

mesembryanthemum /mɪˌzembrɪˈænθɪməm/ *n.* any of various succulent plants of the genus *Mesembryanthemum* of S. Africa, having daisy-like flowers in a wide range of bright colours that open fully in sunlight. [mod.L f. Gk *mesembria* noon + *anthemon* flower]

mesencephalon /ˌmesenˈsefəˌlɒn/ *n.* the part of the brain developing from the middle of the primitive or embryonic brain. Also called MIDBRAIN. [Gk *mesos* middle + *encephalon* brain: see ENCEPHALIC]

mesentery /ˈmesəntərɪ/ *n.* (*pl.* **-ies**) a double layer of peritoneum attaching the stomach, small intestine, pancreas, spleen, and other abdominal organs to the posterior wall of the abdomen. □□ **mesenteric** /-ˈterɪk/ *adj.* **mesenteritis** /-ˈraɪtɪs/ *n.* [med.L *mesenterium* f. Gk *mesenterion* (as MESO-, *enteron* intestine)]

mesh /meʃ/ *n.* & *v.* —*n.* **1** a network fabric or structure. **2** each of the open spaces or interstices between the strands of a net or sieve etc. **3** (in *pl.*) a network. **b** a snare. **4** (in *pl.*) *Physiol.* an interlaced structure. —*v.* **1** *intr.* (often foll. by *with*) (of the teeth of a wheel) be engaged (with others). **2** *intr.* be harmonious. **3** *tr.* catch in a net. □ **in mesh** (of the teeth of wheels) engaged. [earlier *meish* etc. f. MDu. *maesche* f. Gmc]

mesial /ˈmiːzɪəl/ *adj.* *Anat.* of, in, or directed towards the middle line of a body. □□ **mesially** *adv.* [irreg. f. Gk *mesos* middle]

mesmerism /ˈmezməˌrɪz(ə)m/ *n.* **1** *Psychol.* **a** a hypnotic state produced in a person by another's influence over the will and nervous system. **b** a doctrine concerning this. **c** an influence producing this. **2** fascination. □□ **mesmeric** /mezˈmerɪk/ *adj.* **mesmerically** /-ˈmerɪkəlɪ/ *adv.* **mesmerist** *n.* [F. A. Mesmer, Austrian physician d. 1815]

mesmerize /ˈmezməˌraɪz/ *v.tr.* (also **-ise**) **1** *Psychol.* hypnotize; exercise mesmerism on. **2** fascinate, spellbind. □□ **mesmerization** /-ˈzeɪʃ(ə)n/ *n.* **mesmerizer** *n.* **mesmerizingly** *adv.*

mesne /miːn/ *adj.* *Law* intermediate. □ **mesne lord** *hist.* a lord holding an estate from a superior feudal lord. **mesne process** proceedings in a suit intervening between a primary and final process. **mesne profits** profits received from an estate by a tenant between two dates. [ME f. law F, var. of AF *meen*, MEAN³: cf. DEMESNE]

meso- /ˈmesəʊ, ˈmez-/ *comb. form* middle, intermediate. [Gk *mesos* middle]

Meso-America the central region of America, from northern Mexico to Nicaragua, especially as a region of American-Indian cultures before the arrival of the Spaniards. □□ **Meso-American** *adj.* & *n.*

mesoblast /ˈmesəʊˌblæst/ *n.* *Biol.* the middle germ-layer of an embryo.

mesoderm /ˈmesəʊˌdɜːm/ *n.* *Biol.* = MESOBLAST. [MESO- + Gk *derma* skin]

mesolithic /ˌmezəʊˈlɪθɪk/ *adj.* & *n.* *Archaeol.* —*adj.* of the transitional period between the palaeolithic and neolithic, especially in Europe, where it falls between the end of the last glacial period (mid-9th millennium BC) and the beginnings of agriculture (see NEOLITHIC). The period is characterized by the use of microliths and the first domestication of any animal (the dog) —*n.* this period. [MESO- + Gk *lithos* stone]

Mesolóngion see MISSOLONGHI.

mesomorph /ˈmesəʊˌmɔːf/ *n.* a person with a compact and muscular build of body (cf. ECTOMORPH, ENDOMORPH). □□ **mesomorphic** /-ˈmɔːfɪk/ *adj.* [MESO- + Gk *morphē* form]

meson /ˈmezɒn, ˈmiːzɒn/ *n.* *Physics* any of a class of elementary particles believed to participate in the forces that hold nucleons together in the atomic nucleus. □□ **mesic** /ˈmezɪk, ˈmiːz-/ *adj.* **mesonic** /mɪˈzɒnɪk/ *adj.* [earlier *mesotron*: cf. MESO-, -ON]

mesopause /ˈmesəʊˌpɔːz/ *n.* the boundary between the mesosphere and the thermosphere, where the temperature stops decreasing with height and starts to increase.

mesophyll /ˈmesəʊˌfɪl/ *n.* the inner tissue of a leaf. [MESO- + Gk *phullon* leaf]

mesophyte /ˈmesəʊˌfaɪt/ *n.* a plant needing only a moderate amount of water.

Mesopotamia /ˌmesəpəˈteɪmɪə/ a region of SW Asia lying between the rivers Tigris and Euphrates. Its alluvial plains were the site of the ancient civilizations of Sumer, Babylon, and Assyria, and now lies within Iraq. □□ **Mesopotamian** *adj.* & *n.* [Gk, f. *mesos* middle, *potamos* river]

mesosphere /ˈmesəʊˌsfɪə(r)/ *n.* the region of the atmosphere extending from the top of the stratosphere to an altitude of about 80 km (50 miles).

Mesozoic /ˌmesəʊˈzəʊɪk/ *adj.* & *n.* *Geol.* —*adj.* of or relating to the geological era between the Palaeozoic and Cenozoic, comprising the Triassic, Jurassic, and Cretaceous periods, and lasting from about 248 to 65 million years ago. It was a time of abundant vegetation and saw the dominance of the reptiles, although by its close they were being rapidly replaced by the mammals. —*n.* this era [MESO- + Gk *zōion* animal]

mesquite /ˈmeskiːt/ *n.* (also **mesquit**) any N. American leguminous tree of the genus *Prosopis*, esp. *P. juliflora*. □ **mesquite bean** a pod from the mesquite, used as fodder. [Mex. Sp. *mezquite*]

mess /mes/ *n.* & *v.* —*n.* **1** a dirty or untidy state of things (*the room is a mess*). **2** a state of confusion, embarrassment, or trouble. **3** something causing a mess, e.g. spilt liquid etc. **4** a domestic animal's excreta. **5 a** a company of persons who take meals together, esp. in the armed forces. **b** a place where such meals or recreation take place communally. **c** a meal taken there. **6** *derog.* a disagreeable concoction or medley. **7** a liquid or mixed food for hounds etc. **8** a portion of liquid or pulpy food. —*v.* **1** *tr.* (often foll. by *up*) **a** make a mess of; dirty. **b** muddle; make into a state of confusion. **2** *intr.* (foll. by *with*) interfere with. **3** *intr.* take one's meals. **4** *intr. colloq.* defecate. □ **make a mess of** bungle (an undertaking). **mess about** (or **around**) **1** act desultorily. **2** *colloq.* make things awkward for; cause arbitrary inconvenience to (a person). **mess-hall** a military dining area. **mess-jacket** a short close-fitting coat worn at the mess. **mess kit** a soldier's cooking and eating utensils. **mess of pottage** a material comfort etc. for which something higher is sacrificed (Gen. 25: 29–34). **mess tin** a small container as part of a mess kit. [ME f. OF *mes* portion of food f. LL *missus* course at dinner, past part. of *mittere* send]

message /ˈmesɪdʒ/ *n.* & *v.* —*n.* **1** an oral or written communication sent by one person to another. **2** an inspired or significant communication from a prophet, writer, or preacher. **3** a mission or errand. **4** (in *pl.*) *Sc.* & *N.Engl.* things bought;

shopping. —v.tr. **1** send as a message. **2** transmit (a plan etc.) by signalling etc. □ **get the message** *colloq.* understand what is meant. **message stick** *Austral.* a stick carved with significant marks, carried as identification by Aboriginal messengers. [ME f. OF ult. f. L *mittere miss-* send]

Messalina /ˌmesəˈliːnə/ (also **Messallina**) **1** Valeria Messalina (c. AD 22–48), wife of the Roman emperor Claudius, her second cousin. She was notorious in Rome for her promiscuity, to which Claudius alone was blind, and for the murders she instigated in court intrigues. **2** Statilia Messalina (1st c.), third wife of Nero (AD 66). After Nero's death she maintained a brilliant position and is said to have been noted for her eloquence and literary culture as well as her beauty.

Messeigneurs *pl.* of MONSEIGNEUR.

messenger /ˈmesɪndʒə(r)/ *n.* **1** a person who carries a message. **2** a person employed to carry messages. □ **King's** (or **Queen's**) **Messenger** a courier in the diplomatic service. **messenger RNA** a form of RNA carrying genetic information from DNA to a ribosome. ¶ Abbr.: **mRNA**. [ME & OF *messager* (as MESSAGE): *-n-* as in *harbinger, passenger*, etc.]

Messiah /mɪˈsaɪə/ *n.* **1 a** the expected deliverer and ruler of the Jewish people, whose coming was prophesied in the Old Testament. **b** Christ, regarded by Christians as this. **2** a liberator or would-be liberator of an oppressed people or country. □□ **Messiahship** *n.* [ME f. OF *Messie* ult. f. Heb. *māšīaḥ* anointed]

Messianic /ˌmesɪˈænɪk/ *adj.* **1** of the Messiah. **2** inspired by hope or belief in a Messiah. □□ **Messianism** /mɪˈsaɪəˌnɪz(ə)m/ *n.* [F *messianique* (as MESSIAH) after *rabbinique* rabbinical]

Messieurs *pl.* of MONSIEUR.

Messina /meˈsiːnə/ a city and harbour of NE Sicily; pop. (1981) 260,200. It is situated on the **Strait of Messina** which separates Sicily from mainland Italy.

messmate /ˈmesmeɪt/ *n.* a person with whom one regularly takes meals, esp. in the armed forces.

Messrs /ˈmesəz/ *pl.* of MR. [abbr. of MESSIEURS]

messuage /ˈmeswɪdʒ/ *n. Law* a dwelling-house with outbuildings and land assigned to its use. [ME f. AF: perh. an alternative form of *mesnage* dwelling]

messy /ˈmesɪ/ *adj.* (**messier**, **messiest**) **1** untidy or dirty. **2** causing or accompanied by a mess. **3** difficult to deal with; full of awkward complications. □□ **messily** *adv.* **messiness** *n.*

mestizo /meˈstiːzəʊ/ *n.* (*pl.* **-os**; *fem.* **mestiza** /-zə/, *pl.* **-as**) a Spaniard or Portuguese of mixed race, esp. the offspring of a Spaniard and an American Indian. [Sp. ult. f. L *mixtus* past part. of *miscēre* mix]

met[1] *past* and *past part.* of MEET[1].

met[2] /met/ *adj. colloq.* **1** meteorological. **2** metropolitan. **3** (**the Met**) **a** (in full **the Met Office**) (in the UK) the Meteorological Office. **b** the Metropolitan Police in London. **c** the Metropolitan Opera House in New York. [abbr.]

meta- /ˈmetə/ *comb. form* (usu. **met-** before a vowel or *h*) **1** denoting change of position or condition (*metabolism*). **2** denoting position: **a** behind. **b** after or beyond (*metaphysics*; *metacarpus*). **c** of a higher or second-order kind (*metalanguage*). **3** *Chem.* **a** relating to two carbon atoms separated by one other in a benzene ring. **b** relating to a compound formed by dehydration (*metaphosphate*). [Gk *meta-, met-, meth-* f. *meta* with, after]

metabolism /mɪˈtæbəˌlɪz(ə)m/ *n.* the sum total of the organized chemical reactions taking place in a living cell, tissue, or organism in order to maintain life. It consists of *anabolism* (or **constructive metabolism**), the building up of tissue etc. by the construction of the proteins, carbohydrates, and fats from which it is made, and *catabolism* (or **destructive metabolism**), the chemical breakdown of complex substances and the consequent production of energy and waste matter. □□ **metabolic** /ˌmetəˈbɒlɪk/ *adj.* **metabolically** /ˌmetəˈbɒlɪkəlɪ/ *adv.* [Gk *metabolē* change (as META-, *bolē* f. *ballō* throw)]

metabolite /mɪˈtæbəˌlaɪt/ *n. Physiol.* a substance formed in or necessary for metabolism.

metabolize /mɪˈtæbəˌlaɪz/ *v.tr.* & *intr.* (also **-ise**) process or be processed by metabolism. □□ **metabolizable** *adj.*

metacarpus /ˌmetəˈkɑːpəs/ *n.* (*pl.* **metacarpi** /-paɪ/) **1** the set of five bones of the hand that connects the wrist to the fingers. **2** this part of the hand. □□ **metacarpal** *adj.* [mod.L f. Gk *metakarpon* (as META-, CARPUS)]

metacentre /ˈmetəˌsentə(r)/ *n.* (*US* **metacenter**) the point of intersection between a line (vertical in equilibrium) through the centre of gravity of a floating body and a vertical line through the centre of pressure after a slight angular displacement, which must be above the centre of gravity to ensure stability. □□ **metacentric** /-ˈsentrɪk/ *adj.* [F *métacentre* (as META-, CENTRE)]

metage /ˈmiːtɪdʒ/ *n.* **1** the official measuring of a load of coal etc. **2** the duty paid for this. [METE[1] + -AGE]

metagenesis /ˌmetəˈdʒenɪsɪs/ *n.* the alternation of generations between sexual and asexual reproduction. □□ **metagenetic** /-dʒɪˈnetɪk/ *adj.* [mod.L (as META-, GENESIS)]

metal /ˈmet(ə)l/ *n., adj.,* & *v.* —*n.* **1 a** any of a class of chemical elements which in general can take the form of opaque solids having a characteristic lustre. (See below.) **b** an alloy of any of these. **2** material used for making glass, in a molten state. **3** *Heraldry* gold or silver as tincture. **4** (in *pl.*) the rails of a railway line. **5** = *road-metal* (see ROAD[1]). —*adj.* made of metal. —*v.tr.* (**metalled, metalling;** *US* **metaled, metaling**) **1** provide or fit with metal. **2** *Brit.* make or mend (a road) with road-metal. □ **metal detector** an electronic device giving a signal when it locates metal. **metal fatigue** fatigue (see FATIGUE *n.* 2) in metal. [ME f. OF *metal* or L *metallum* f. Gk *metallon* mine]

Metals have traditionally been defined as substances which exhibit some or all of the following properties: high density, malleability, ductility, fusibility, strength, hardness, opacity, a characteristic lustre, and an ability to conduct heat and electricity. Because no single combination of these properties applies to all metals but to no other substances, a strict definition of a metal in terms of such properties is not possible. This is partly because many new elements with varying properties have been discovered in recent centuries and classified among the metals. In the ancient world only seven metallic elements were known—gold, silver, copper, iron, lead, tin, and mercury. The modern theory of metals circumvents the problem of definition by describing as a metal any substance in which each atom 'loses' one or more orbiting electrons, which are then able to move freely throughout the metal. This so-called 'sea' of mobile electrons can be shown to account for most of the properties of metals listed above. By this definition about three-quarters of the known elements (of which there are more than 100) are metals when uncombined, although many are too reactive to exist in a stable state in air.

metalanguage /ˈmetəˌlæŋgwɪdʒ/ *n.* **1** a form of language used to discuss a language. **2** a system of propositions about propositions.

metallic /mɪˈtælɪk/ *adj.* **1** of, consisting of, or characteristic of metal or metals. **2** sounding sharp and ringing, like struck metal. **3** having the sheen or lustre of metals. □□ **metallically** *adv.* [L *metallicus* f. Gk *metallikos* (as METAL)]

metalliferous /ˌmetəˈlɪfərəs/ *adj.* bearing or producing metal. [L *metallifer* (as METAL, -FEROUS)]

metallize /ˈmetəˌlaɪz/ *v.tr.* (also **-ise**; *US* **metalize**) **1** render metallic. **2** coat with a thin layer of metal. □□ **metallization** /-ˈzeɪʃ(ə)n/ *n.*

metallography /ˌmetəˈlɒgrəfɪ/ *n.* the descriptive science of the structure and properties of metals. □□ **metallographic** /ˌmetæləˈgræfɪk/ *adj.* **metallographical** /ˌmetæləˈgræfɪk(ə)l/ *adj.* **metallographically** /ˌmetæləˈgræfɪkəlɪ/ *adv.*

metalloid /ˈmetəˌlɔɪd/ *adj.* & *n.* —*adj.* having the form or appearance of a metal. —*n.* any element intermediate in properties between metals and non-metals, e.g. boron, silicon, and germanium.

metallurgy /mɪˈtælədʒɪ, ˈmetəˌlɜːdʒɪ/ *n.* the science concerned with the production, purification, and properties of metals and their application. □□ **metallurgic** /ˌmetəˈlɜːdʒɪk/ *adj.* **metallurgical** /ˌmetəˈlɜːdʒɪk(ə)l/ *adj.* **metallurgically** /ˌmetəˈlɜː-*

dʒɪkəlɪ/ *adv.* **metallurgist** *n.* [Gk *metallon* metal + *-ourgia* working]

metalwork /ˈmet(ə)lwɜːk/ *n.* **1** the art of working in metal. **2** metal objects collectively. □□ **metalworker** *n.*

metamere /ˈmetəˌmɪər/ *n. Zool.* each of several similar segments, that contain the same internal structures, of an animal body. [META- + Gk *meros* part]

metameric /ˌmetəˈmerɪk/ *adj.* **1** *Chem.* having the same proportional composition and molecular weight, but different functional groups and chemical properties. **2** *Zool.* of or relating to metameres. □□ **metamer** /ˈmetəmə(r)/ *n.* **metamerism** /meˈtæməˌrɪz(ə)m/ *n.*

metamorphic /ˌmetəˈmɔːfɪk/ *adj.* **1** of or marked by metamorphosis. **2** *Geol.* (of rock) that has undergone transformation by natural agencies such as heat and pressure (cf. IGNEOUS, SEDIMENTARY), as in the transformation of limestone into marble. The term does not include alterations caused by weathering or consolidation of sediments. □□ **metamorphism** *n.* [META- + Gk *morphē* form]

metamorphose /ˌmetəˈmɔːfəʊz/ *v.tr.* **1** change in form. **2** (foll. by *to, into*) **a** turn (into a new form). **b** change the nature of. [F *métamorphoser* f. *métamorphose* METAMORPHOSIS]

metamorphosis /ˌmetəˈmɔːfəsɪs, ˌmetəməˈfəʊsɪs/ *n.* (*pl.* **metamorphoses** /-ˌsiːz/) **1** a change of form (by natural or supernatural means). **2** a changed form. **3** a change of character, conditions, etc. **4** *Zool.* the transformation between an immature form and an adult form, e.g. from a pupa to an insect, or from a tadpole to a frog. [L f. Gk *metamorphōsis* f. *metamorphoō* transform (as META-, *morphoō* f. *morphē* form)]

metaphase /ˈmetəˌfeɪz/ *n. Biol.* the stage of meiotic or mitotic cell division when the chromosomes become attached to the spindle fibres.

metaphor /ˈmetəˌfɔː(r)/ *n.* **1** the application of a name or descriptive term or phrase to an object or action to which it is imaginatively but not literally applicable (e.g. *a glaring error*). **2** an instance of this. □□ **metaphoric** /-ˈfɒrɪk/ *adj.* **metaphorical** /-ˈfɒrɪk(ə)l/ *adj.* **metaphorically** /-ˈfɒrɪkəlɪ/ *adv.* [F *métaphore* or L *metaphora* f. Gk *metaphora* f. *metapherō* transfer]

metaphrase /ˈmetəˌfreɪz/ *n. & v.* —*n.* literal translation. —*v.tr.* put into other words. □□ **metaphrastic** /-ˈfræstɪk/ *adj.* [mod.L *metaphrasis* f. Gk *metaphrasis* f. *metaphrazō* translate]

metaphysic /ˌmetəˈfɪzɪk/ *n.* a system of metaphysics.

metaphysical /ˌmetəˈfɪzɪk(ə)l/ *adj. & n.* —*adj.* **1** of or relating to metaphysics. **2** based on abstract general reasoning. **3** excessively subtle or theoretical. **4** incorporeal; supernatural. **5** visionary. —*n.* (**the Metaphysicals**) the metaphysical poets. □ **metaphysical poets** a classification of 17th-c. poets, addicted to fanciful conceits and far-fetched imagery, generally taken to include John Donne (regarded as the founder of the 'school'), George Herbert, Richard Crashaw, Henry Vaughan, Andrew Marvell, and Thomas Traherne. The term is misleading since none of these poets is seriously interested in metaphysics and, further, they have little in common. Their reputation dwindled after the Restoration with the new taste for clarity and the impatience with figurative language. Their dramatic revival was delayed until after the First World War; the revaluation of metaphysical poetry was a major feature of the rewriting of English literary history in the first half of the 20th c. □□ **metaphysically** *adv.*

metaphysics /ˌmetəˈfɪzɪks/ *n.pl.* (usu. treated as *sing.*) **1** the branch of speculative inquiry that deals with such concepts as being, knowing, substance, cause, identity, time, space, etc. It discusses, for example, whether there are only minds and their states (*idealism*) or only physical things (*materialism*), or both mental properties and physical things, each distinct from the other. **2** the philosophy of mind. **3** *colloq.* abstract or subtle talk; mere theory. □□ **metaphysician** /-ˈzɪʃ(ə)n/ *n.* **metaphysicize** /-ˈfɪzɪˌsaɪz/ *v.intr.* [ME *metaphysic* f. OF *metaphysique* f. med.L *metaphysica* ult. f. Gk *ta meta ta phusika* the things after the Physics, the title applied, at least from the 1st c. AD, to the 13 books of Aristotle dealing with questions of ontology. The title doubtless originally referred to the position which these books occupied

in the received arrangement of Aristotle's writings, being placed after (*meta*) the *Physics* (i.e. treatises on natural science), but it was from an early period used as a name for the branch of study treated in these books and hence came to be misinterpreted as meaning 'the science of things transcending what is physical or natural'.]

metaplasia /ˌmetəˈpleɪzɪə/ *n. Physiol.* an abnormal change in the nature of a tissue. □□ **metaplastic** /-ˈplæstɪk/ *adj.* [mod.L f. G *Metaplase* f. Gk *metaplasis* (as META-, *plasis* f. *plassō* to mould)]

metapsychology /ˌmetəsaɪˈkɒlədʒɪ/ *n.* the study of the nature and functions of the mind beyond what can be studied experimentally. □□ **metapsychological** /-kəˈlɒdʒɪk(ə)l/ *adj.*

metastable /ˌmetəˈsteɪb(ə)l/ *adj.* **1** (of a state of equilibrium) stable only under small disturbances. **2** passing to another state so slowly as to seem stable. □□ **metastability** /-stəˈbɪlɪtɪ/ *n.*

metastasis /meˈtæstəsɪs/ *n.* (*pl.* **metastases** /-ˌsiːz/) *Physiol.* **1** the transference of a bodily function, disease, etc., from one part or organ to another. **2** the transformation of chemical compounds into others in the process of assimilation by an organism. □□ **metastasize** *v.intr.* (also **-ise**). **metastatic** /ˌmetəˈstætɪk/ *adj.* [LL f. Gk f. *methistēmi* change]

metatarsus /ˌmetəˈtɑːsəs/ *n.* (*pl.* **metatarsi** /-saɪ/) **1** the part of the foot between the ankle and the toes. **2** the set of bones in this. □□ **metatarsal** *adj.* [mod.L (as META-, TARSUS)]

metatherian /ˌmetəˈθɪərɪən/ *n. & adj.* —*n.* any mammal of the infraclass Metatheria, comprising the marsupials and including kangaroos and koalas. —*adj.* of or relating to this infraclass. [META- + Gk *thēr* wild beast]

metathesis /mɪˈtæθɪsɪs/ *n.* (*pl.* **metatheses** /-ˌsiːz/) **1** *Gram.* the transposition of sounds or letters in a word. **2** *Chem.* the interchange of atoms or groups of atoms between two molecules. **3** an instance of either of these. □□ **metathetic** /ˌmetəˈθetɪk/ *adj.* **metathetical** /ˌmetəˈθetɪk(ə)l/ *adj.* [LL f. Gk *metatithēmi* transpose]

metazoan /ˌmetəˈzəʊən/ *n. & adj. Zool.* —*n.* any animal of the subkingdom Metazoa, having multicellular and differentiated tissues. —*adj.* of or relating to the Metazoans. [*Metazoa* f. Gk META- + *zōia* pl. of *zōion* animal]

mete[1] /miːt/ *v.tr.* **1** (usu. foll. by *out*) *literary* apportion or allot (a punishment or reward). **2** *poet.* or *Bibl.* measure. □ **mete-wand** (or **-yard**) a standard of estimation. [OE *metan* f. Gmc., rel. to MEET[1]]

mete[2] /miːt/ *n.* a boundary or boundary stone. [ME f. OF f. L *meta* boundary, goal]

metempsychosis /ˌmetempsaɪˈkəʊsɪs/ *n.* (*pl.* **-psychoses** /-ˌsiːz/) **1** the supposed transmigration of the soul of a human being or animal at death into a new body of the same or a different species. **2** an instance of this. □□ **metempsychosist** *n.* [LL f. Gk *metempsukhōsis* (as META-, EN-[2], *psukhē* soul)]

meteor /ˈmiːtɪə(r)/ *n.* **1** a small body of matter from outer space that becomes incandescent as a result of friction with the air as it passes through the earth's atmosphere. **2** a streak of light emanating from a meteor. □ **meteor shower** a group of meteors appearing to come from one point in the sky. [ME f. mod.L *meteorum* f. Gk *meteōron* neut. of *meteōros* lofty, (as META-, *aeirō* raise)]

Meteora /ˌmetɪˈɔːrə/ a region of eastern Greece, in Thessaly, noted for its monasteries which are precariously perched on curious rock formations that rise out of the Pinós Plain.

meteoric /ˌmiːtɪˈɒrɪk/ *adj.* **1 a** of or relating to the atmosphere. **b** dependent on atmospheric conditions. **2** of meteors. **3** rapid like a meteor; dazzling, transient (*meteoric rise to fame*). □ **meteoric stone** a meteorite. □□ **meteorically** *adv.*

meteorite /ˈmiːtɪəˌraɪt/ *n.* a fallen meteor, or fragment of natural rock or metal from outer space, of sufficient size to survive a fiery passage through the atmosphere and reach the surface of the earth. Rarely more than a few pounds in weight, some have been of much greater mass, their impact leaving a crater, of which perhaps the most famous is Meteor Crater, Flagstaff, Arizona. □□ **meteoritic** /-ˈrɪtɪk/ *adj.*

meteorograph /ˈmiːtɪərəˌɡrɑːf/ *n.* an apparatus that records several meteorological phenomena at the same time. [F *météorographe* (as METEOR, -GRAPH)]

meteoroid /ˈmiːtɪəˌrɔɪd/ n. any small body moving in the solar system that becomes visible as it passes through the earth's atmosphere as a meteor. □□ **meteoroidal** /-ˈrɔɪd(ə)l/ adj.

Meteorological Office (in the UK) a government department providing weather forecasts etc. Its headquarters are in Bracknell, Berks.

meteorology /ˌmiːtɪəˈrɒlədʒɪ/ n. **1** the study of the processes and phenomena of the atmosphere, esp. as a means of forecasting the weather. **2** the atmospheric character of a region. □□ **meteorological** /-rəˈlɒdʒɪk(ə)l/ adj. **meteorologically** /-rəˈlɒdʒɪkəlɪ/ adv. **meteorologist** n. [Gk *meteōrologia* (as METEOR)]

meter[1] /ˈmiːtə(r)/ n. & v. —n. **1** a person or thing that measures, esp. an instrument for recording a quantity of gas, electricity, etc. supplied, present, or needed. **2** = *parking-meter* (see PARK). —v.tr. measure by means of a meter. [ME f. METE[1] + -ER[1]]

meter[2] US var. of METRE[1].

meter[3] US var. of METRE[2].

-meter /mɪtə(r), miːtə(r)/ comb. form **1** forming nouns denoting measuring instruments (*barometer*). **2** *Prosody* forming nouns denoting lines of poetry with a specified number of measures (*pentameter*).

methadone /ˈmeθəˌdəʊn/ n. a potent narcotic analgesic drug used to relieve severe pain, as a linctus to suppress coughs, and as a substitute for morphine or heroin. [6-di*methyl*amino-4, 4-di*phenyl*-3-hept*anone*]

methamphetamine /ˌmeθæmˈfetəmɪn, -ˌmiːn/ n. an amphetamine derivative with quicker and longer action, used as a stimulant. [METHYL + AMPHETAMINE]

methanal /ˈmeθəˌnæl/ n. Chem. = FORMALDEHYDE. [METHANE + ALDEHYDE]

methane /ˈmeθeɪn, ˈmiːθeɪn/ n. Chem. a colourless odourless inflammable gaseous hydrocarbon, the simplest in the alkane series, and the main constituent of natural gas. ¶ Chem. formula: CH_4. [METHYL + -ANE[2]]

methanoic acid /ˌmeθəˈnəʊɪk/ n. Chem. = FORMIC ACID. [METHANE + -IC]

methanol /ˈmeθəˌnɒl/ n. Chem. a colourless volatile inflammable liquid, used as a solvent. ¶ Chem. formula: CH_3OH. Also called *methyl alcohol*. [METHANE + ALCOHOL]

methinks /mɪˈθɪŋks/ v.intr. (past **methought** /mɪˈθɔːt/) archaic it seems to me. [OE *mē thyncth* f. *mē* dative of ME[1] + *thyncth* 3rd sing. of *thyncan* seem, THINK]

methionine /meˈθaɪəˌniːn/ n. Biochem. an amino acid containing sulphur and an important constituent of proteins. [METHYL + Gk *theion* sulphur]

metho /ˈmeθəʊ/ n. (pl. **-os**) Austral. sl. **1** methylated spirit. **2** a person addicted to drinking methylated spirit. [abbr.]

method /ˈmeθəd/ n. **1** a special form of procedure esp. in any branch of mental activity. **2** orderliness; regular habits. **3** the orderly arrangement of ideas. **4** a scheme of classification. **5** *Theatr.* a theory and practice of acting in which the actor seeks to achieve a true interpretation of a part by mentally identifying with the character he or she is playing. Based on the system evolved by Stanislavsky, it came into prominence in the US in the 1930s and was most successful in the work of modern American playwrights such as Tennessee Williams. □ **method in one's madness** sense in what appears to be foolish or strange behaviour. [F *méthode* or L *methodus* f. Gk *methodos* pursuit of knowledge (as META-, *hodos* way)]

methodical /mɪˈθɒdɪk(ə)l/ adj. (also **methodic**) characterized by method or order. □□ **methodically** adv. [LL *methodicus* f. Gk *methodikos* (as METHOD)]

Methodist /ˈmeθədɪst/ n. **1** a member of any of several Protestant religious bodies (now united) originating in an 18th-c. evangelistic movement which grew out of a religious society (nicknamed the 'Holy Club') established within the Church of England (from which it formally separated in 1791) by John and Charles Wesley at Oxford. Its theology is Arminian, and its ordained ministry usually presbyterian; its governing body is

the Conference, composed of ministers and laymen. How the term 'Methodist' came to be applied to the Wesleys' followers is uncertain. **2** (**methodist**) a person who follows or advocates a particular method or system of procedure. □□ **Methodism** n. **Methodistic** /-ˈdɪstɪk/ adj. **Methodistical** /-ˈdɪstɪk(ə)l/ adj. [mod.L *methodista* (as METHOD)]

Methodius /mɪˈθəʊdɪəs/, St (c.815–85), brother of St Cyril (see CYRIL[2]).

methodize /ˈmeθəˌdaɪz/ v.tr. (also **-ise**) **1** reduce to order. **2** arrange in an orderly manner. □□ **methodizer** n.

methodology /ˌmeθəˈdɒlədʒɪ/ n. (pl. **-ies**) **1** the science of method. **2** a body of methods used in a particular branch of activity. □□ **methodological** /-dəˈlɒdʒɪk(ə)l/ adj. **methodologically** /-dəˈlɒdʒɪkəlɪ/ adv. **methodologist** n. [mod.L *methodologia* or F *méthodologie* (as METHOD)]

methought past of METHINKS.

meths /meθs/ n. Brit. colloq. methylated spirit. [abbr.]

Methuselah /mɪˈθjuːzələ/ a patriarch, grandfather of Noah, said (Gen. 5: 27) to have lived 969 years. —n. **1** a very old person or thing. **2** (**methuselah**) a wine bottle of about eight times the standard size.

methyl /ˈmeθɪl, ˈmiːθaɪl/ n. Chem. the univalent hydrocarbon radical CH_3, present in many organic compounds. □ **methyl alcohol** = METHANOL. **methyl benzene** = TOLUENE. □□ **methylic** /mɪˈθɪlɪk/ adj. [G *Methyl* or F *méthyle*, back-form. f. G *Methylen*, F *méthylène*: see METHYLENE]

methylate /ˈmeθɪˌleɪt/ v.tr. **1** mix or impregnate with methanol. **2** introduce a methyl group into (a molecule or compound). □ **methylated spirit** (or **spirits**) alcohol impregnated with methanol to make it unfit for drinking and exempt from duty. □□ **methylation** /-ˈleɪʃ(ə)n/ n.

methylene /ˈmeθɪˌliːn/ n. Chem. the highly reactive divalent group of atoms CH_2. [F *méthylène* f. Gk *methu* wine + *hulē* wood + -ENE]

metic /ˈmetɪk/ n. Gk Antiq. an alien living in a Greek city with some privileges of citizenship. [irreg. f. Gk *metoikos* (as META-, *oikos* dwelling)]

meticulous /məˈtɪkjʊləs/ adj. **1** giving great or excessive attention to details. **2** very careful and precise. □□ **meticulously** adv. **meticulousness** n. [L *meticulosus* f. *metus* fear]

métier /ˈmetjeɪ/ n. **1** one's trade, profession, or department of activity. **2** one's forte. [F ult. f. L *ministerium* service]

metis /meɪˈtiːs/ n. (pl. **metis**; fem. **metisse**, pl. **metisses**) a person of mixed race, esp. the offspring of a White person and an American Indian in Canada. [F *métis*, OF *mestis* f. Rmc, rel. to MESTIZO]

metol /ˈmetɒl/ n. a white soluble powder used as a photographic developer. [G, arbitrary name]

Metonic cycle /mɪˈtɒnɪk/ n. a period of 19 years (235 lunar months), after the lapse of which the new and full moons return to the same day of the year. It was the basis of the ancient Greek calendar and is still used for calculating movable feasts such as Easter. [Gk *Metōn*, Athenian astronomer (5th c. BC)]

metonym /ˈmetənɪm/ n. a word used in metonymy. [back-form. f. METONYMY, after *synonym*]

metonymy /mɪˈtɒnɪmɪ/ n. the substitution of the name of an attribute or adjunct for that of the thing meant (e.g. *Crown* for *king*, *the turf* for *horse-racing*). □□ **metonymic** /ˌmetəˈnɪmɪk/ adj. **metonymical** /ˌmetəˈnɪmɪk(ə)l/ adj. [LL *metonymia* f. Gk *metōnumia* (as META-, *onoma, onuma* name)]

metope /ˈmetəʊp/ n. Archit. a square space between triglyphs in a Doric frieze. [L *metopa* f. Gk *metopē* (as META-, *opē* hole for a beam-end)]

metre[1] /ˈmiːtə(r)/ n. (US **meter**) a metric unit and the base SI unit of linear measure, equal to about 39.4 inches, defined in 1983 as the length of the path travelled by light in a vacuum during a time interval of 1/299 792 458 of a second. When the metric system (see entry) was standardized careful measurements were made of the polar quadrant of the earth through Paris, and the metre was originally defined as one ten millionth

part of this arc. To overcome the impracticability of the definition the French Academy of Sciences used a platinum bar whose
length was equal to the theoretical length, and this (despite an
imperfection in its calculation) was used for the next 90 years.
In 1889 the International Metre was redefined as the distance
between two lines engraved on an alloy bar, and this held until
1960 when the metre was defined in terms of the wavelength
of the krypton-86 atom; it was redefined again in 1983. □
metre-kilogram-second denoting a system of measure using
the metre, kilogram, and second as the basic units of length,
mass, and time. ¶ Abbr.: **mks**. □□ **metreage** /ˈmiːtərɪdʒ/ n. [F
mètre f. Gk *metron* measure]

metre[2] /ˈmiːtə(r)/ n. (*US* **meter**) **1 a** any form of poetic rhythm,
determined by the number and length of feet in a line. **b** a
metrical group or measure. **2** the basic pulse and rhythm of a
piece of music. [OF *metre* f. L *metrum* f. Gk *metron* MEASURE]

metric /ˈmetrɪk/ adj. of or based on the metre. □ **metric system**
see separate entry. **metric ton** (or **tonne**) 1,000 kilograms (2205
lb.). [F *métrique* (as METRE[1])]

-metric /ˈmetrɪk/ comb. form (also **-metrical** /-k(ə)l/) forming
adjectives corresponding to nouns in *-meter* and *-metry* (*thermometric*; *geometric*). □□ **-metrically** comb. form forming adverbs.
[from or after F *métrique* f. L (as METRICAL)]

metrical /ˈmetrɪk(ə)l/ adj. **1** of, relating to, or composed in
metre (*metrical psalms*). **2** of or involving measurement (*metrical
geometry*). □□ **metrically** adv. [ME f. L *metricus* f. Gk *metrikos* (as
METRE[2])]

metricate /ˈmetrɪˌkeɪt/ v.intr. & tr. change or adapt to a metric
system of measurement. □□ **metrication** /-ˈkeɪʃ(ə)n/ n.
metricize /-ˌsaɪz/ v.tr. (also **-ise**).

metric system n. a decimal measuring-system with the
metre, litre, and gram as the units of length, capacity, and
weight or mass. It is the culmination of a long endeavour to
devise a system which is exact, convenient, based on reliable
natural units, and employs a rational notation. The system, first
proposed by Gabriel Mouton of Lyons in 1670, was based on two
natural units—the second, which is a sexagesimal fraction of
the day, and the metre, which is intended to be a decimal
fraction of a meridional quadrant of the earth's surface. It was
standardized in France under the Republican government in
the 1790s and its use was made compulsory there in 1801;
decimal measures based on the metre were introduced for areas
and volumes. Napoleon's conquests facilitated the spread of the
system to many European countries; it is still not adopted for
general use in the US. The most recent development of the
metric system is the International System of Units (see entry).

metritis /mɪˈtraɪtɪs/ n. inflammation of the womb. [Gk *mētra*
womb + -ITIS]

metro /ˈmetrəʊ/ n. (pl. **-os**) an underground railway system in
a city, esp. Paris. [F *métro*, abbr. of *métropolitain* METROPOLITAN]

metrology /mɪˈtrɒlədʒɪ/ n. the scientific study of measurement.
□□ **metrologic** /ˌmetrəˈlɒdʒɪk/ adj. **metrological**
/ˌmetrəˈlɒdʒɪk(ə)l/ adj. [Gk *metron* measure + -LOGY]

metronome /ˈmetrəˌnəʊm/ n. Mus. an instrument marking
time at a selected rate by giving a regular tick. □□ **metronomic**
/-ˈnɒmɪk/ adj. [Gk *metron* measure + *nomos* law]

metronymic /ˌmetrəˈnɪmɪk/ adj. & n. —adj. (of a name) derived
from the name of a mother or female ancestor. —n. a metronymic name. [Gk *mētēr mētros* mother, after *patronymic*]

metropolis /mɪˈtrɒpəlɪs/ n. **1** the chief city of a country; a
capital city. **2** the metropolitan bishop's see. **3** a centre of activity.
[LL f. Gk *mētropolis* parent State f. *mētēr mētros* mother + *polis*
city]

metropolitan /ˌmetrəˈpɒlɪt(ə)n/ adj. & n. —adj. **1** of or relating
to a metropolis, esp. as distinct from its environs (*metropolitan
New York*). **2** belonging to, forming or forming part of, a mother
country as distinct from its colonies etc. (*metropolitan France*). **3**
of an ecclesiastical metropolis. —n. **1** (in full **metropolitan
bishop**) a bishop having authority over the bishops of a
province, in the Western Church equivalent to archbishop, in
the Orthodox Church ranking above archbishop and below patriarch. **2** an inhabitant of a metropolis. □ **metropolitan county**

each of the six conurbations (other than Greater London) established in England by the local government reorganization of
1974, with functions analogous to those of counties. In 1986
their councils were abolished, leaving the districts within the
areas to carry out most of these functions. **metropolitan
magistrate** *Brit.* a paid professional magistrate in London (cf.
stipendiary magistrate). □□ **metropolitanate** n. (in sense 1 of n.).
metropolitanism n. [ME f. LL *metropolitanus* f. Gk *mētropolitēs*
(as METROPOLIS)]

Metropolitan Museum of Art an important museum of
art and archaeology, in New York, founded in 1870.

metrorrhagia /ˌmiːtrəʊˈreɪdʒɪə/ n. abnormal bleeding from
the womb. [mod.L f. Gk *mētra* womb + *-rrhage* as HAEMORRHAGE]

-metry /mɪtrɪ/ comb. form forming nouns denoting procedures
and systems corresponding to instruments in *-meter* (*calorimetry*;
thermometry). [after *geometry* etc. f. Gk *-metria* f. *-metrēs* measurer]

Metternich /ˈmetənɪx/, Prince Clemens Wenzel Lothar
Metternich-Winneburg (1773–1859), Austrian statesman. He
was one of the organizers of the Congress of Vienna in 1814–
15 which devised the settlement of Europe after the Napoleonic
Wars, and thereafter he presided over the maintenance of order
and stability in Europe, espousing a particularly reactionary
brand of conservatism, until forced to resign by the Vienna mob
during the revolutionary disturbances of 1848.

mettle /ˈmet(ə)l/ n. **1** the quality of a person's disposition or
temperament (*a chance to show your mettle*). **2** natural ardour. **3**
spirit, courage. □ **on one's mettle** incited to do one's best. □□
mettled adj. (also in comb.). **mettlesome** adj. [var. of METAL n.]

Metz /mets/ an industrial city in NE France, on the Moselle
River; pop. (1982) 118,500.

meu /mjuː/ n. (also **mew**) = BALDMONEY. [irreg. f. L *meum* f. Gk
mēon]

meunière /mɜːˈnjeə(r)/ adj. (esp. of fish) cooked or served in
lightly browned butter with lemon juice and parsley (*sole meunière*). [F (*à la*) *meunière* (in the manner of) a miller's wife]

Meuse /mɜːz/ (Dutch **Maas** /mɑːs/) a river of NE France, Belgium,
and the Netherlands, flowing into the North Sea.

MeV abbr. mega-electronvolt(s).

Mevlana /mevˈlɑːnə/ see RUMI.

mew[1] /mjuː/ v. & n. —v.intr. (of a cat, gull, etc.) utter its characteristic cry. —n. this sound, esp. of a cat. [ME: imit.]

mew[2] /mjuː/ n. a gull, esp. the common gull, *Larus canus*. [OE
mǣw f. Gmc]

mew[3] /mjuː/ n. & v. —n. a cage for hawks, esp. while moulting.
—v.tr. **1** put (a hawk) in a cage. **2** (often foll. by *up*) shut up;
confine. [ME f. OF *mue* f. *muer* moult f. L *mutare* change]

mew[4] var. of MEU.

mewl /mjuːl/ v.intr. (also **mule**) **1** cry feebly; whimper. **2** mew
like a cat. [imit.: cf. MIAUL]

mews /mjuːz/ n. Brit. a set of stabling round an open yard or
along a lane, now often converted into dwellings. [pl. (now used
as sing.) of MEW[3], orig. of the royal stables on the site of hawks'
mews at Charing Cross in London]

Mexicali /ˌmeksɪˈkɑːlɪ/ the capital of Baja California in NW
Mexico; pop. (1980) 510,550.

Mexico /ˈmeksɪˌkəʊ/ a country in Central America with extensive coastlines on the Atlantic and Pacific Oceans, bordered by
the US to the north; pop. (est. 1988) 83,527,550; official language,
Spanish; capital, Mexico City. Agriculture is heavily dependent
on irrigation. Mexico is now a major oil-producing country and
recent industrialization, centred upon these oil resources, has
revolutionized its economy, but the country has massive international debts. The Aztecs are said to have fulfilled an ancient
prophecy when they saw an eagle perched on a cactus eating a
snake; on this site they founded a city, and the symbol of the
eagle, snake, and cactus is the national emblem of Mexico. The
centre of Aztec and Mayan civilization, Mexico was conquered
and colonized by the Spanish in the early 16th c., remaining
under Spanish rule until independence was achieved in 1821; a
republic was established three years later. Texas rebelled and
broke away in 1836, while all the remaining territory north of

the Rio Grande was lost to the US in the Mexican War of 1846–8. Half a century of political instability, including a brief French occupation and imperial rule by Maximilian (1864–7) ended with the establishment of Diaz as president in the 1870s, but civil war broke out again in 1910–20, leading to partial reform of the political organization. Mexico is now a one-party State. □□ **Mexican** adj. & n. [Mextili, Aztec war-god]

Mexico City the capital of Mexico and most populous city in the world; pop. (1980) 12,932,100. It suffered a severe earthquake in 1985.

Meyerbeer /ˈmaɪəbɪə(r)/, Giacomo (Jakob) (1791–1864), German-Jewish composer, who settled in Paris. His collaboration with the librettist Augustin Scribe resulted in the grand operas Robert le Diable (1831), Les Huguenots (1836), and Le Prophète (1849), which placed him firmly as the leading opera composer in France. He gave Wagner financial and other help in getting his early operas performed, and had some influence on his orchestration, but in later years Wagner attacked him in a pamphlet Judaism in Music. Revivals of Meyerbeer's operas have revealed virtues which were his alone.

mezereon /mɪˈzɪərɪən/ n. a small European and Asian shrub, Daphne mezereum, with fragrant purplish red flowers and red berries. [med.L f. Arab. māzaryūn]

mezuzah /meˈzuːzə/ n. (pl. **mezuzoth** /-zəʊθ/) a parchment inscribed with religious texts and attached in a case to the doorpost of a Jewish house as a sign of faith. [Heb. mᵉzûzāh doorpost]

mezzanine /ˈmetsəˌniːn, ˈmez-/ n. 1 a low storey between two others (usu. between the ground and first floors). 2 Brit. Theatr. **a** a floor or space beneath the stage. **b** US a dress circle. [F f. It. mezzanino dimin. of mezzano middle f. L medianus MEDIAN]

mezza voce /ˌmetsə ˈvəʊtʃeɪ/ adv. Mus. with less than the full strength of the voice or sound. [It., = half voice]

mezzo /ˈmetsəʊ/ adv. & n. Mus. —adv. half, moderately. —n. (in full **mezzo-soprano**) (pl. **-os**) 1 **a** a female singing-voice between soprano and contralto. **b** a singer with this voice. 2 a part written for mezzo-soprano. □ **mezzo forte** fairly loud. **mezzo piano** fairly soft. [It., f. L medius middle]

Mezzogiorno /ˌmetsəʊˈdʒɔːnəʊ/ the economically undeveloped largely agricultural regions of southern Italy. Its Italian name, which means 'midday', refers to the intensity of the sun there in the middle of the day.

mezzo-rilievo /ˈmetsəʊrɪˈljeɪvəʊ/ n. a raised surface in the form of half-relief, in which the figures project half their true proportions. [It., = half-relief]

mezzotint /ˈmetsəʊtɪnt/ n. & v. —n. 1 a method of printing or engraving starting with a uniformly roughened plate, on which the areas left rough give shaded parts and the areas scraped smooth give light. This technique was much used in the 17th, 18th, and early 19th c. for the reproduction of paintings. It was invented by Ludwig von Siegen of Utrecht c.1640, and introduced to England by Prince Rupert (nephew of Charles I) who demonstrated it to Evelyn, who publicized it in his Sculptura (1662). 2 a print produced by this process. —v.tr. engrave in mezzotint. □□ **mezzotinter** n. [It. mezzotinto f. mezzo half + tinto tint]

MF abbr. medium frequency.

mf abbr. mezzo forte.

MFH abbr. Brit. Master of Foxhounds.

MG abbr. 1 machine-gun. 2 Morris Garages (as a make of car).

Mg symb. Chem. the element magnesium.

mg abbr. milligram(s).

MGB n. the Ministry of State Security in the USSR (see MVD). [Russ. abbr.]

Mgr. abbr. 1 Manager. 2 Monseigneur. 3 Monsignor.

mho /məʊ/ n. (pl. **-os**) Electr. the reciprocal of an ohm, a former unit of conductance. [OHM reversed]

MHR abbr. (in the US and Australia) Member of the House of Representatives.

MHz abbr. megahertz.

MI abbr. 1 US Michigan (in official postal use). 2 Brit. hist. Military Intelligence.

mi var. of ME².

mi. abbr. US mile(s).

M.I.5, M.I.6 (in the UK) sections of Military Intelligence which (until 1964) dealt with matters of State security. The names are still in popular use referring to the Security Service and the Secret Intelligence Service (SIS) in Britain. M.I.5, founded in 1909, covered internal security and counter-intelligence on British territory. M.I.6, formed in 1912, operated mainly overseas but with headquarters in London.

Miami /maɪˈæmi/ a city and port on the east coast of Florida; pop. (1982) 382,700. It is an important financial and trading centre, and its subtropical climate and miles of beaches make this and the resort island of Miami Beach, separated from the mainland by Biscayne Bay, a year-round holiday resort.

miaow /mɪˈaʊ/ n. & v. (also **meow**) —n. the characteristic cry of a cat. —v.intr. make this cry. [imit.]

miasma /mɪˈæzmə, maɪ-/ n. (pl. **miasmata** /-mətə/ or **miasmas**) archaic an infectious or noxious vapour. □□ **miasmal** adj. **miasmatic** /-ˈmætɪk/ adj. **miasmic** adj. **miasmically** adv. [Gk, = defilement, f. miainō pollute]

miaul /mɪˈɔːl/ v.intr. cry like a cat; mew. [F miauler: imit.]

Mic. abbr. Micah (Old Testament).

mica /ˈmaɪkə/ n. any of a group of silicate minerals with a layered structure, esp. muscovite. □ **mica-schist** (or **slate**) a fissile rock containing quartz and mica. □□ **micaceous** /-ˈkeɪʃəs/ adj. [L, = crumb]

Micah /ˈmaɪkə/ 1 a Hebrew minor prophet. 2 a book of the Old Testament bearing his name, foretelling the destruction of Samaria and of Jerusalem.

Micawber /mɪˈkɔːbə(r)/ n. a person who is perpetually hoping that something good will turn up while making no positive effort. □□ **Micawberish** adj. **Micawberism** n. [character in Dickens's novel David Copperfield, for whom the model was Dickens's father]

mice pl. of MOUSE.

micelle /mɪˈsel, maɪˈsel/ n. Chem. an aggregate of molecules in a colloidal solution, as occurs e.g. when soap dissolves in water. [mod.L micella dimin. of L mica crumb]

Mich. abbr. 1 Michaelmas. 2 Michigan.

Michael /ˈmaɪk(ə)l/, St, one of the archangels, usually represented slaying a dragon (see Rev. 12: 7). Feast day, 29 Sept. (Michaelmas Day).

Michaelmas /ˈmɪkəlməs/ n. the feast of St Michael, 29 September. □ **Michaelmas daisy** an autumn-flowering aster. **Michaelmas term** Brit. the university and law term beginning near Michaelmas. [OE sancte Micheles mæsse Saint Michael's mass: see MASS²]

Michelangelo Buonarroti /ˌmaɪkəlˈændʒəˌləʊ ˌbəʊnəˈrɒti/ (1475–1564), Italian sculptor, painter, architect, and poet. Essentially self-taught, he was apprenticed to Ghirlandaio and enjoyed the patronage of Lorenzo de Medici. In Rome (1496–1501) he carved the two statues which established his fame—the Bacchus and the Pietà; the latter is his only signed work, tragically expressive, beautiful, and harmonious. The years 1501–5 in Florence mark a great creative period epitomized by his marble David, which embodies civic virtue and Herculean heroism. In Rome again from 1505 his greatest works were executed under papal patronage. The decoration of the Sistine ceiling (1508–12) marks a peak in his œuvre and assured him a place as a leader in the High Renaissance. In 1536–41 he painted the Last Judgement on the east wall of the Sistine Chapel, its elongated forms predicting the mannerist movement. His architectural achievements included the directing, from 1546, of rebuilding at St Peter's and designing its great dome. His poetry, first published by his grandnephew in 1623, offers an insight into Michelangelo the man, as he explores his faith, art, and the notion of love.

He embodied the perfect multi-talented Renaissance man. An exponent of Neoplatonic ideals, he was fêted by popes, enjoying success and power in his own time, and he represented a new status of artist, no longer a mere craftsman as in medieval times. He was the epitome of 'the artist as genius', and his influence on later artists has been profound.

Michelozzo /ˌmiːkeˈlɒtsəʊ/ di Bartolommeo (1396–1472), Florentine architect and sculptor, who was in partnership with Ghiberti (from c.1420) and then Donatello (1423–38), and led a revival of interest in Roman architecture. He was the favourite architect of Cosimo de Medici for whom he built, amongst other works, the Medici Palace (1444–c.1459). One of the most important palace designs of the quattrocento, it constantly influenced later architecture in Florence.

Michelson /ˈmɪtʃəlsən/, Albert Abraham (1852–1931), American physicist who specialized in precision measurement in experimental physics, for which he became in 1907 the first American to be awarded a Nobel Prize. He performed a number of accurate determinations of the velocity of light, begun in 1878, but his crucial experiment, which demonstrated that the hypothetical 'ether' (postulated as the medium through which light and other electromagnetic waves travelled) did not exist, was first performed in 1881, and again in 1887 with the chemist Morley using improved apparatus. The Michelson–Morley result contradicted Newtonian physics and was eventually resolved in 1905 by Einstein's special theory of relativity. In 1920 Michelson used similar apparatus for determining the diameter of the star Betelgeuse.

Michigan /ˈmɪʃɪgən/ a State in the north-western US, with its northern boundary formed by Lakes Huron and Superior; pop. (est. 1985) 9,262,000; capital, Lansing. Explored by the French in the 17th c., it was ceded to Britain in 1763 and acquired by the US in 1783, becoming the 26th State in 1837. □□ **Lake Michigan** one of the five Great Lakes of North America and the only one wholly within the US. The cities of Chicago and Milwaukee are on its shores.

Michoacán /ˌmiːtʃwaˈkɑːn/ a State of western Mexico; pop. (est. 1988) 3,377,700; capital, Morelia.

mick /mɪk/ n. sl. offens. **1** an Irishman. **2** a Roman Catholic. [pet-form of the name *Michael*]

mickey /ˈmɪkɪ/ n. (also **micky**) □ **take the mickey** (often foll. by *out of*) sl. tease, mock, ridicule. [20th c.: orig. uncert.]

Mickey Finn /ˌmɪkɪ ˈfɪn/ n. sl. **1** a strong alcoholic drink, esp. adulterated with a narcotic or laxative. **2** the adulterant itself. [20th c.: orig. uncert.]

Mickey Mouse /ˌmɪkɪ ˈmaʊs/ a Disney cartoon character, who first appeared as Mortimer Mouse in 1927, becoming Mickey in 1928. For the next decade he remained one of the staple figures of Disney's growing reputation. Disney himself always spoke the sound track for Mickey's voice.

mickle /ˈmɪk(ə)l/ adj. & n. (also **muckle** /ˈmʌk(ə)l/) archaic or Sc. —adj. much, great. —n. a large amount. □ **many a little makes a mickle** (orig. erron. **many a mickle makes a muckle**) many small amounts accumulate to make a large amount. [ME f. ON *mikell* f. Gmc]

Mick the Miller /mɪk, ˈmɪlə(r)/ racing greyhound who won many races from 1928 to 1931 and later starred in the film *Wild Boy* (1935).

micky var. of MICKEY.

micro /ˈmaɪkrəʊ/ n. (pl. **-os**) colloq. **1** = MICROCOMPUTER. **2** = MICROPROCESSOR.

micro- /ˈmaɪkrəʊ/ comb. form **1** small (*microchip*). **2** denoting a factor of one millionth (10⁻⁶) (*microgram*). ¶ Symb.: μ. [Gk *mikro-* f. *mikros* small]

microanalysis /ˌmaɪkrəʊəˈnælɪsɪs/ n. the quantitative analysis of chemical compounds using a sample of a few milligrams.

microbe /ˈmaɪkrəʊb/ n. a minute living being; a micro-organism (esp. bacteria causing disease and fermentation). □□ **microbial** /-ˈkrəʊbɪəl/ adj. **microbic** /-ˈkrəʊbɪk/ adj. [F f. Gk *mikros* small + *bios* life]

microbiology /ˌmaɪkrəʊbaɪˈɒlədʒɪ/ n. the scientific study of micro-organisms, e.g. bacteria, viruses, and fungi. □□ **microbiological** /-ˌbaɪəˈlɒdʒɪk(ə)l/ adj. **microbiologically** /-ˌbaɪəˈlɒdʒɪkəlɪ/ adv. **microbiologist** n.

microburst /ˈmaɪkrəʊˌbɜːst/ n. a particularly violent wind shear, esp. during a thunderstorm.

microcephaly /ˌmaɪkrəʊˈsefəlɪ/ n. an abnormal smallness of the head in relation to the rest of the body. □□ **microcephalic** /-sɪˈfælɪk/ adj. & n. **microcephalous** /-ˈsefələs/ adj.

microchip /ˈmaɪkrəʊtʃɪp/ n. a small piece of semiconductor (usu. silicon) used to carry electronic circuits.

microcircuit /ˈmaɪkrəʊˌsɜːkɪt/ n. an integrated circuit on a microchip. □□ **microcircuitry** n.

microclimate /ˈmaɪkrəʊˌklaɪmɪt/ n. the climate of a small local area, e.g. inside a greenhouse. □□ **microclimatic** /-ˈmætɪk/ adj. **microclimatically** /-ˈmætɪkəlɪ/ adv.

microcode /ˈmaɪkrəʊˌkəʊd/ n. **1** = MICROINSTRUCTION. **2** = MICROPROGRAM.

microcomputer /ˈmaɪkrəʊkəmˌpjuːtə(r)/ n. a small computer that contains a microprocessor as its central processor.

microcopy /ˈmaɪkrəʊˌkɒpɪ/ n. & v. —n. (pl. **-ies**) a copy of printed matter that has been reduced by microphotography. —v.tr. (**-ies, -ied**) make a microcopy of.

microcosm /ˈmaɪkrəˌkɒz(ə)m/ n. **1** (often foll. by *of*) a miniature representation. **2** mankind viewed as the epitome of the universe. **3** any community or complex unity viewed in this way. □□ **microcosmic** /-ˈkɒzmɪk/ adj. **microcosmically** /-ˈkɒzmɪkəlɪ/ adv. [ME f. F *microcosme* or med.L *microcosmus* f. Gk *mikros kosmos* little world]

microdot /ˈmaɪkrəʊˌdɒt/ n. a microphotograph of a document etc. reduced to the size of a dot.

micro-economics /ˌmaɪkrəʊˌiːkəˈnɒmɪks/ n. the branch of economics dealing with individual commodities, producers, etc.

micro-electronics /ˌmaɪkrəʊɪlekˈtrɒnɪks/ n. the design, manufacture, and use of microchips and microcircuits.

microfiche /ˈmaɪkrəʊˌfiːʃ/ n. (pl. same or **microfiches**) a flat rectangular piece of film bearing microphotographs of the pages of a printed text or document.

microfilm /ˈmaɪkrəʊfɪlm/ n. & v. —n. a length of film bearing microphotographs of documents etc. —v.tr. photograph (a document etc.) on microfilm.

microfloppy /ˈmaɪkrəʊˌflɒpɪ/ n. (pl. **-ies**) (in full **microfloppy disk**) Computing a floppy disk with a diameter of less than 5¼ inches (usu. 3½ inches).

microform /ˈmaɪkrəʊfɔːm/ n. microphotographic reproduction on film or paper of a manuscript etc.

microgram /ˈmaɪkrəʊˌgræm/ n. one-millionth of a gram.

micrograph /ˈmaɪkrəʊˌɡrɑːf/ n. a photograph taken by means of a microscope.

microgroove /ˈmaɪkrəʊˌɡruːv/ n. a very narrow groove on a long-playing gramophone record.

microinstruction /ˌmaɪkrəʊɪnˈstrʌkʃ(ə)n/ n. a machine-code instruction that effects a basic operation in a computer system.

microlight /ˈmaɪkrəʊˌlaɪt/ n. a kind of motorized hang-glider.

microlith /ˈmaɪkrəʊlɪθ/ n. Archaeol. a minute worked flint, usually mounted on a piece of bone, wood, or horn as part of a composite tool, characteristic especially of mesolithic industries in Europe. □□ **microlithic** /-ˈlɪθɪk/ adj.

micromesh /ˈmaɪkrəʊˌmeʃ/ n. (often attrib.) material, esp. nylon, consisting of a very fine mesh.

micrometer /maɪˈkrɒmɪtə(r)/ n. a gauge for accurately measuring small distances, thicknesses, etc. □□ **micrometry** n.

micrometre /ˈmaɪkrəʊˌmiːtə(r)/ n. one-millionth of a metre.

microminiaturization /ˌmaɪkrəʊˌmɪnɪtʃərəˈzeɪʃ(ə)n/ n. (also **-isation**) the manufacture of very small electronic devices by using integrated circuits.

micron /ˈmaɪkrɒn/ n. one-millionth of a metre. [Gk *mikron* neut. of *mikros* small: cf. MICRO-]

Micronesia /ˌmaɪkrəʊˈniːʒə/ **1** part of the western Pacific Ocean including the Mariana, Caroline, and Marshall Islands and Kiribati (see entries). **2** (in full **Federated States of Micronesia**) the island States of Yap, Kosrae, Truk, and Pohnpei, administered by the US as part of the Pacific Islands Trust Territory from 1947 until 1986, when they entered into free association

with the US as an independent State; pop. (1988) 86,100. □□
Micronesian adj. & n. [MICRO- + Gk nēsos island]

micro-organism /ˌmaɪkrəʊˈɔːɡəˌnɪz(ə)m/ n. any of various microscopic organisms, including algae, bacteria, fungi, protozoa, and viruses.

microphone /ˈmaɪkrəˌfəʊn/ n. an instrument for converting sound waves into electrical energy variations which may be reconverted into sound after transmission by wire or radio or after recording. □□ **microphonic** /-ˈfɒnɪk/ adj.

microphotograph /ˌmaɪkrəʊˈfəʊtəˌɡrɑːf/ n. a photograph reduced to a very small size.

microphyte /ˈmaɪkrəʊˌfaɪt/ n. a microscopic plant.

microprocessor /ˌmaɪkrəʊˈprəʊsesə(r)/ n. an integrated circuit that contains all the functions of a central processing unit of a computer.

microprogram /ˌmaɪkrəʊˈprəʊɡræm/ n. a microinstruction program that controls the functions of a central processing unit of a computer.

micropyle /ˈmaɪkrəʊˌpaɪl/ n. Bot. a small opening in the surface of an ovule, through which pollen passes. [MICRO- + Gk pulē gate]

microscope /ˈmaɪkrəˌskəʊp/ n. an instrument magnifying small objects by means of a lens or lenses so as to reveal details invisible to the naked eye. So-called 'simple microscopes' of one lens (such as those used by Leeuwenhoek, or the modern magnifying glass) were used as early as the 15th c. for examining insects. The compound microscope, which first appeared at the beginning of the 17th c., consists of at least two lenses, mounted in a tube: an 'objective' lens, placed near the specimen, which produces an enlarged image of it, and an eyepiece lens which magnifies this image. Compound microscopes thus permit much greater magnification, but the early instruments also produced distortions of colour or shape in the image, and these problems were fully overcome only in the 19th c. The wave nature of light itself sets a limit to the power of the light microscope to discriminate between points which are closer together than the wavelength of light; beyond this limit an electron microscope (see entry) has to be employed. [mod.L microscopium (as MICRO-, -SCOPE)]

microscopic /ˌmaɪkrəˈskɒpɪk/ adj. 1 so small as to be visible only with a microscope. 2 extremely small. 3 regarded in terms of small units. 4 of the microscope. □□ **microscopical** adj. (in sense 4). **microscopically** adv.

microscopy /maɪˈkrɒskəpɪ/ n. the use of the microscope. □□ **microscopist** n.

microsecond /ˈmaɪkrəʊˌsekənd/ n. one-millionth of a second.

Microsoft /ˈmaɪkrəʊˌsɒft/ n. propr. an operating system for microcomputers. [the name of the developing company]

microsome /ˈmaɪkrəʊˌsəʊm/ n. Biol. a small particle of organelle fragments obtained by centrifugation of homogenized cells. [MICRO- + -SOME³]

microspore /ˈmaɪkrəʊˌspɔː(r)/ n. the smaller of the two kinds of spore produced by some ferns.

microstructure /ˈmaɪkrəʊˌstrʌktʃə(r)/ n. (in a metal or other material) the arrangement of crystals etc. which can be made visible and examined with a microscope.

microsurgery /ˈmaɪkrəʊˌsɜːdʒərɪ/ n. intricate surgery performed using microscopes, enabling the tissue to be operated on with miniaturized precision instruments. □□ **microsurgical** /-ˈsɜːdʒɪk(ə)l/ adj.

microswitch /ˈmaɪkrəʊswɪtʃ/ n. a switch that can be operated rapidly by a small movement.

microtome /ˈmaɪkrəʊˌtəʊm/ n. an instrument for cutting extremely thin sections of material for examination under a microscope. [MICRO- + -TOME]

microtone /ˈmaɪkrəʊˌtəʊn/ n. Mus. an interval smaller than a semitone.

microtubule /ˌmaɪkrəʊˈtjuːbjuːl/ n. Biol. a minute protein filament occurring in cytoplasm and involved in forming the spindles during cell division etc.

microwave /ˈmaɪkrəʊˌweɪv/ n. 1 an electromagnetic wave with a wavelength in the range 0.001–0.3m. Microwaves have wavelengths which are shorter than those of normal radio-waves (whence their name) but longer than those of infrared radiation. They are used in radar, in communications, and in microwave ovens where the moisture present in food selectively absorbs the microwaves, converts the energy into heat, and cooks the food quickly. Microwave heating is also used in various industrial processes. 2 (in full **microwave oven**) an oven that uses microwaves (see sense 1).

micrurgy /ˈmaɪkrəˌdʒɪ/ n. the manipulation of individual cells etc. under a microscope. [MICRO- + Gk -ourgia work]

micturition /ˌmɪktjʊəˈrɪʃ(ə)n/ n. formal urination. [L micturire micturit-, desiderative f. mingere mict- urinate]

mid¹ /mɪd/ attrib.adj. 1 (usu. in comb.) that is the middle of (in mid-air; from mid-June to mid-July). 2 that is in the middle; medium, half. 3 Phonet. (of a vowel) pronounced with the tongue neither high nor low. [OE midd (recorded only in oblique cases), rel. to L medius, Gk mesos]

mid² /mɪd/ prep. poet. = AMID. [abbr. f. AMID]

Midas /ˈmaɪdəs/ Gk legend a king of Phrygia, of whom several stories are told, the most famous being the following. (1) He was given by Dionysus the power of turning everything he touched into gold. Unable to eat or drink, he prayed to be relieved of the gift and was instructed to wash in the river Pactolus, which since then has had golden sands. (2) He declared Pan a better flute-player than Apollo, who thereupon bestowed ass's ears upon him. Midas tried to hide them but his barber whispered the secret to some reeds, which repeat it whenever they rustle in the wind □ **Midas touch** the ability to turn one's activities to financial advantage.

midbrain /ˈmɪdbreɪn/ n. the part of the brain developing from the middle of the primitive or embryonic brain.

midday /ˈmɪddeɪ/ n. the middle of the day; noon. [OE middæg (as MID¹, DAY)]

midden /ˈmɪd(ə)n/ n. 1 a dunghill. 2 a refuse heap near a dwelling. 3 = kitchen midden. [ME myddyng, of Scand. orig.: cf. Da. mødding muck heap]

middle /ˈmɪd(ə)l/ adj., n., & v. —attrib.adj. 1 at an equal distance from the extremities of a thing. 2 (of a member of a group) so placed as to have the same number of members on each side. 3 intermediate in rank, quality, etc. 4 average (of middle height). 5 (of a language) of the period between the old and modern forms. 6 Gram. designating the voice of (esp. Greek) verbs that expresses reciprocal or reflexive action. —n. 1 (often foll. by of) the middle point or position or part. 2 a person's waist. 3 Gram. the middle form or voice of a verb. 4 = middle term. —v.tr. 1 place in the middle. 2 Football return (the ball) from the wing to the midfield. 3 Cricket strike (the ball) with the middle of the bat. 4 Naut. fold in the middle. □ **in the middle of** (often foll. by verbal noun) in the process of; during. **middle age** the period between youth and old age, about 45 to 60. **middle-aged** in middle age. **the Middle Ages** the period of European history from the fall of the Roman Empire in the West (5th c.) to the fall of Constantinople (1453), or more narrowly from the end of the Dark Ages (c.1000) to 1453. **middle-age** (or **-aged**) **spread** the increased bodily girth often associated with middle age. **Middle America 1** Mexico and Central America. **2** the middle class in the US, esp. as a conservative political force. **middle C** Mus. the C near the middle of the piano keyboard, the note between the treble and bass staves, at about 260 Hz. **middle class** the class of society between the upper and the lower, including professional and business workers and their families. **middle-class** adj. of the middle class. **middle common room** Brit. a common room for the use of graduate members of a college who are not Fellows. **middle course** a compromise between two extremes. **middle distance 1** (in a painted or actual landscape) the part between the foreground and the background. **2** Athletics a race distance intermediate between that of a sprint and a long-distance race, now usually 400, 800, or 1500 metres. **middle ear** the cavity of the central part of the ear behind the drum. **the Middle East** the area covered by countries between the Near and Far East, esp. from Egypt to Iran inclusive. **Middle Eastern** of or in the Middle East. **Middle English** the English language from c.1150 to 1500. (See ENGLISH.) **middle finger** the finger next to the forefinger. **middle game** the central phase of a chess game, when strategies are developed. **Middle Kingdom** a period of ancient Egyptian history (c.2040–1640 BC). (See EGYPT.) **middle name 1** a person's name placed after the first name and before the surname. **2** a person's most characteristic quality (*sobriety is my middle name*). **middle-of-the-road** (of a person, course of action, etc.) moderate; avoiding extremes. **middle passage** the sea journey between W. Africa and the W. Indies (with ref. to the slave trade). **middle school** *Brit.* a school for children from about 9 to 13 years old. **middle-sized** of medium size. **Middle Temple** one of the two Inns of Court on the site of the Temple in London (cf. *Inner Temple*). **middle term** *Logic* the term common to both premisses of a syllogism. **middle watch** the watch from midnight to 4 a.m. **middle way 1** = *middle course*. **2** the eightfold path of Buddhism between indulgence and asceticism. **Middle West** that part of the US occupying the northern half of the Mississippi River basin, including the States of Ohio, Indiana, Illinois, Michigan, Wisconsin, Iowa, and Minnesota. [OE *middel* f. Gmc]

middlebrow /ˈmɪd(ə)lˌbraʊ/ *adj. & n. colloq.* —*adj.* claiming to be or regarded as only moderately intellectual. —*n.* a middlebrow person.

middleman /ˈmɪd(ə)lˌmæn/ *n.* (*pl.* **-men**) **1** any of the traders who handle a commodity between its producer and its consumer. **2** an intermediary.

Middlesbrough /ˈmɪdəlzbrə/ the county town of Cleveland; pop. (1981) 150,400. It was the birthplace of Captain James Cook (1728–79).

Middleton /ˈmɪdəlt(ə)n/, Thomas (1580–1627), English dramatist, who wrote and collaborated on many masques and pageants for city ceremonies, and rollicking comedies of London life. His anti-Catholic anti-Spanish satire *A Game at Chesse* (1624) caused him and his players to be summoned before the Privy Council. He is remembered for his two tragedies, *The Changeling* (in collaboration with William Rowley, 1622) and *Women Beware Women* (1620/7).

middleweight /ˈmɪd(ə)lˌweɪt/ *n.* **1** a weight in certain sports intermediate between welterweight and light heavyweight, in the amateur boxing scale 71–5 kg but differing for professionals, wrestlers, and weightlifters. **2** a sportsman of this weight. □ **junior middleweight 1** a weight in professional boxing of 66.7–69.8 kg. **2** a professional boxer of this weight. **light middleweight 1** a weight in amateur boxing of 67–71 kg. **2** an amateur boxer of this weight.

middling /ˈmɪdlɪŋ/ *adj., n., & adv.* —*adj.* **1 a** moderately good (*esp. fair to middling*). **b** *colloq.* (of a person's health) fairly well. **c** second-rate. **2** (of goods) of the second of three grades. —*n.* (in *pl.*) middling goods, esp. flour of medium fineness. —*adv.* fairly or moderately (*middling good*). □□ **middlingly** *adv.* [ME, of Sc. orig.: prob. f. MID¹ + -LING²]

Middx. *abbr.* Middlesex.

middy¹ /ˈmɪdɪ/ *n.* (*pl.* **-ies**) **1** *colloq.* a midshipman. **2** (in full **middy blouse**) a woman's or child's loose blouse with a collar like that worn by sailors.

middy² /ˈmɪdɪ/ *n.* (*pl.* **-ies**) *Austral. sl.* a measure of beer of varying size. [20th c.: orig. unkn.]

Mideast /ˈmɪdiːst/ *n. US* = *Middle East.*

midfield /ˈmɪdfiːld/ *n. Football* the central part of the pitch, away from the goals. □□ **midfielder** *n.*

Midgard /ˈmɪdgɑːd/ *Scand. Mythol.* the region, encircled by the sea, in which men live, the earth. □ **Midgard serpent** a monstrous serpent, the offspring of Loki, thrown by Odin into the sea, where, with its tail in its mouth, it encircled the earth.

midge /mɪdʒ/ *n.* **1** *colloq.* **a** a gnatlike insect. **b** a small person. **2 a** any dipterous non-biting insect of the family *Chironomidae*. **b** any similar insect of the family *Ceratopogonidae* with piercing mouthparts for sucking blood or eating smaller insects. [OE *mycg(e)* f. Gmc]

midget /ˈmɪdʒɪt/ *n.* **1** an extremely small person or thing. **2** (*attrib.*) very small. [MIDGE + -ET¹]

Mid Glamorgan /ɡləˈmɔːgən/ a county of South Wales; pop. (1981) 541,100.

midgut /ˈmɪdgʌt/ *n.* the middle part of the alimentary canal, including the small intestine.

midi /ˈmɪdɪ/ *n.* (*pl.* **midis**) a garment of medium length, usu. reaching to mid-calf. [MID¹ after MINI]

midibus /ˈmɪdɪˌbʌs/ *n.* a bus seating up to about 25 passengers.

midinette /ˌmɪdɪˈnet/ *n.* a Parisian shop-girl, esp. a milliner's assistant. [F f. *midi* midday + *dînette* light dinner]

midiron /ˈmɪdˌaɪən/ *n. Golf* an iron giving medium lift.

midland /ˈmɪdlənd/ *n. & adj.* —*n.* **1** (**the Midlands**) the inland counties of central England. **2** the middle part of a country. —*adj.* **1** of or in the midland or Midlands. **2** Mediterranean. □□ **midlander** *n.*

mid-life /ˈmɪdlaɪf/ *n.* middle age. □ **mid-life crisis** an emotional crisis of self-confidence that can occur in early middle age.

midline /ˈmɪdlaɪn/ *n.* a median line, or plane of bilateral symmetry.

midmost /ˈmɪdməʊst/ *adj. & adv.* in the very middle.

midnight /ˈmɪdnaɪt/ *n.* **1** the middle of the night; 12 o'clock at night. **2** intense darkness. □ **midnight blue** a very dark blue. **midnight sun** the sun visible at midnight during the summer in polar regions. [OE *midniht* (as MID¹, NIGHT)]

mid-off /mɪdˈɒf/ *n. Cricket* the position of the fielder near the bowler on the off side.

mid-on /mɪdˈɒn/ *n. Cricket* the position of the fielder near the bowler on the on side.

Midrash /ˈmɪdræʃ/ *n.* (*pl.* **Midrashim** /-ˈʃɪm/) an ancient Jewish commentary on part of the Hebrew scriptures, attached to the Biblical text. The earliest Midrashim come from the 2nd c. AD, although much of their content is older. [Bibl. Heb. *miḏrāš* commentary]

midrib /ˈmɪdrɪb/ *n.* the central rib of a leaf.

midriff /ˈmɪdrɪf/ *n.* **1 a** the region of the front of the body between the thorax and abdomen. **b** the diaphragm. **2** a garment or part of a garment covering the abdomen. [OE *midhrif* (as MID¹, *hrif* belly)]

midship /ˈmɪdʃɪp/ *n.* the middle part of a ship or boat.

midshipman /ˈmɪdʃɪpmən/ *n.* (*pl.* **-men**) **1** *Brit.* a naval officer of rank between naval cadet and sub-lieutenant. **2** *US* a naval cadet.

midships /ˈmɪdʃɪps/ *adv.* = AMIDSHIPS.

midst /mɪdst/ *prep. & n.* —*prep. poet.* amidst. —*n.* middle (now only in phrases as below). □ **in the midst of** among; in the middle of. **in our** (or **your** or **their**) **midst** among us (or you or them). [ME *middest*, *middes* f. *in middes*, *in middan* (as IN, MID¹)]

midsummer /mɪdˈsʌmə(r), ˈmɪd-/ *n.* the period of or near the summer solstice, about 21 June. □ **Midsummer** (or **Midsummer's**) **Day** 24 June. **midsummer madness** extreme folly. [OE *midsumor* (as MID¹, SUMMER)]

midtown /ˈmɪdtaʊn/ *n. US* the central part of a city between the downtown and uptown areas.

midway /ˈmɪdweɪ/ *adv.* in or towards the middle of the distance between two points.

Midwest /mɪdˈwest/ *n.* = *Middle West.*

midwicket /mɪdˈwɪkɪt/ *n. Cricket* the position of a fielder on the leg side opposite the middle of the pitch.

midwife /ˈmɪdwaɪf/ *n.* (*pl.* **-wives** /-waɪvz/) a person (usu. a woman) trained to assist women in childbirth. □□ **midwifery** /-ˌwɪfrɪ/ *n.* [ME, prob. f. obs. prep. *mid* with + WIFE woman, in the sense of 'one who is with the mother']

midwinter /mɪdˈwɪntə(r)/ *n.* the period of or near the winter solstice, about 22 Dec. [OE (as MID¹, WINTER)]

mielie var. of MEALIE.

mien /miːn/ *n. literary* a person's look or bearing, as showing character or mood. [prob. f. obs. *demean* f. DEMEAN², assim. to F *mine* expression]

Mies van der Rohe /ˌmiːz væn də ˈrəʊ/, Ludwig (1886–1969), German-born architect who succeeded Gropius as director of the

Bauhaus (1930–3). His buildings, devoid of ornament, depend on subtlety of proportion and mechanical precision of finish. In the 1920s he produced pioneer projects for skyscrapers, and designed the German pavilion at the 1929 Barcelona exhibition, now regarded as the classic example of pure geometrical architecture. He also pioneered in furniture design, including the first tubular metal cantilevered chair (1927). In 1937 he emigrated to the US. Among his most important works there is the high-rise Seagram Building, New York (1958).

miff /mɪf/ v. & n. colloq. —v.tr. (usu. in passive) put out of humour; offend. —n. **1** a petty quarrel. **2** a huff. [perh. imit.: cf. G muff, exclam. of disgust]

might[1] /maɪt/ past of MAY, used esp.: **1** in reported speech, expressing possibility (said he might come) or permission (asked if I might leave) (cf. MAY 1, 2). **2** (foll. by perfect infin.) expressing a possibility based on a condition not fulfilled (if you'd looked you might have found it; but for the radio we might not have known). **3** (foll. by present infin. or perfect infin.) expressing complaint that an obligation or expectation is not or has not been fulfilled (he might offer to help; they might have asked; you might have known they wouldn't come). **4** expressing a request (you might call in at the butcher's). **5** colloq. **a** = MAY 1 (it might be true). **b** (in tentative questions) = MAY 2 (might I have the pleasure of this dance?). **c** = MAY 4 (who might you be?). □ **might as well** expressing that it is probably at least as desirable to do a thing as not to do it (finished the work and decided they might as well go to lunch; won't win but might as well try). **might-have-been** colloq. **1** a past possibility that no longer applies. **2** a person who could have been more eminent.

might[2] /maɪt/ n. **1** great bodily or mental strength. **2** power to enforce one's will (usu. in contrast with right). □ **with all one's might** to the utmost of one's power. **with might and main** see MAIN[1]. [OE miht, mieht f. Gmc, rel. to MAY]

mightn't /ˈmaɪt(ə)nt/ contr. might not.

mighty /ˈmaɪtɪ/ adj. & adv. —adj. (**mightier**, **mightiest**) **1** powerful or strong, in body, mind, or influence. **2** massive, bulky. **3** colloq. great, considerable. —adv. colloq. very (a mighty difficult task). □□ **mightily** adv. **mightiness** n. [OE mihtig (as MIGHT[2])]

mignonette /ˌmɪnjəˈnet/ n. **1 a** any of various plants of the genus Reseda, esp. R. odorata, with fragrant grey-green flowers. **b** the colour of these. **2** a light fine narrow pillow-lace. [F mignonnette dimin. of mignon small]

migraine /ˈmiːɡreɪn, ˈmaɪ-/ n. a recurrent throbbing headache that usually affects one side of the head, often accompanied by nausea and disturbance of vision. □□ **migrainous** adj. [F f. LL hemicrania f. Gk hēmikrania (as HEMI-, CRANIUM): orig. of a headache confined to one side of the head]

migrant /ˈmaɪɡrənt/ adj. & n. —adj. that migrates. —n. a migrant person or animal, esp. a bird.

migrate /maɪˈɡreɪt/ v.intr. **1** (of people) move from one place of abode to another, esp. in a different country. **2** (of a bird or fish) change its area of habitation with the seasons. **3** move under natural forces. □□ **migration** /-ˈɡreɪʃ(ə)n/ n. **migrational** /-ˈɡreɪʃ(ə)l/ adj. **migrator** n. **migratory** adj. [L migrare migrat-]

Mihailovich /mɪˈhaɪləˌvɪtʃ/, Draza (1893–1946), Yugoslav partisan leader, who organized royalist supporters during the German occupation of Czechoslovakia in the Second World War. Their relations with the Communist partisans were uneasy, and they were reported to be collaborating with the Germans against Tito. Allied support went to Tito, and after the war Mihailovich was tried and shot for collaboration and war crimes.

mihrab /ˈmiːraːb/ n. a niche or slab in a mosque, used to show the direction of Mecca. [Arab. miḥrāb praying-place]

mikado /mɪˈkaːdəʊ/ n. (pl. -os) hist. the emperor of Japan. [Jap. f. mi august + kado door]

Mike /maɪk/ n. sl. □ **for the love of Mike** an exclamation of entreaty or dismay. [abbr. of the name Michael]

mike[1] /maɪk/ n. colloq. a microphone. [abbr.]

mike[2] /maɪk/ v. & n. Brit. sl. —v.intr. shirk work; idle. —n. an act of shirking. [19th c.: orig. unkn.]

Míkonos see MYKONOS.

mil /mɪl/ n. one-thousandth of an inch, as a unit of measure for the diameter of wire etc. [L millesimum thousandth f. mille thousand]

milady /mɪˈleɪdɪ/ n. (pl. -ies) **1** an English noblewoman or great lady. **2** a form used in speaking of or to such a person. [F f. E my lady: cf. MILORD]

milage var. of MILEAGE.

Milan /mɪˈlæn/ (Italian **Milano** /mɪˈlaːnəʊ/) an industrial city in NW Italy, capital of Lombardy region; pop. (1981) 1,604,800.

Milanese /ˌmɪləˈniːz/ adj. & n. —adj. of or relating to Milan. —n. (pl. same) a native of Milan. □ **Milanese silk** a finely woven silk or rayon.

milch /mɪltʃ/ adj. (of a domestic mammal) giving or kept for milk. □ **milch cow** a source of easy profit, esp. a person. [ME m(i)elche repr. OE mielce (unrecorded) f. Gmc: see MILK]

mild /maɪld/ adj. **1** (esp. of a person) gentle and conciliatory. **2** (of a rule, punishment, illness, feeling, etc.) moderate; not severe. **3** (of the weather, esp. in winter) moderately warm. **4 a** (of food, tobacco, etc.) not sharp or strong in taste etc. **b** Brit. (of beer) not strongly flavoured with hops (cf. BITTER). **5** (of medicine) operating gently. **6** tame, feeble; lacking energy or vivacity. □ **mild steel** steel containing a small percentage of carbon, strong and tough but not readily tempered. □□ **milden** v.tr. & intr. **mildish** adj. **mildness** n. [OE milde f. Gmc]

mildew /ˈmɪldjuː/ n. & v. —n. **1** a destructive growth of minute fungi on plants. **2** a similar growth on paper, leather, etc. exposed to damp. —v.tr. & intr. taint or be tainted with mildew. □□ **mildewy** adj. [OE mildēaw f. Gmc]

mildly /ˈmaɪldlɪ/ adv. in a mild fashion. □ **to put it mildly** as an understatement (implying the reality is more extreme).

mile /maɪl/ n. **1** (also **statute mile**) a unit of linear measure equal to 1,760 yards (approx. 1.609 kilometres). It was originally the Roman measure of 1,000 paces. Its length as a unit used in Britain etc. has varied considerably at different periods and in different localities, chiefly owing to the influence of the agricultural system of measures with which it was brought into relation (see FURLONG). The nautical mile, used in navigation, is a unit of 2,025 yds. (1.852 km). **2** (in pl.) colloq. a great distance or amount (miles better; beat them by miles). **4** a race extending over a mile. [OE mīl ult. f. L mil(l)ia pl. of mille thousand]

mileage /ˈmaɪlɪdʒ/ n. (also **milage**) **1 a** a number of miles travelled, used, etc. **b** the number of miles travelled by a vehicle per unit of fuel. **2** travelling expenses (per mile). **3** colloq. benefit, profit, advantage.

milepost /ˈmaɪlpəʊst/ n. a post one mile from the finishing-post of a race etc.

miler /ˈmaɪlə(r)/ n. colloq. a person or horse qualified or trained specially to run a mile.

milestone /ˈmaɪlstəʊn/ n. **1** a stone set up beside a road to mark a distance in miles. **2** a significant event or stage in a life, history, project, etc.

Miletus /maɪˈliːtəs/ an ancient Greek city in SW Asia Minor, a sea-power and founder of colonies (especially in the 7th–6th c. BC) until its defeat by the Persians in 494 BC. It is associated with the philosophers Thales, Anaximander, and Anaximenes. By the 6th c. AD its harbours had become silted up by the alluvial deposits of the Menderes River (see MEANDER).

milfoil /ˈmɪlfɔɪl/ n. the common yarrow, Achillea millefolium, with small white flowers and finely divided leaves. [ME f. OF f. L millefolium f. mille thousand + folium leaf, after Gk muriophullon]

Milhaud /ˈmiːjəʊ/, Darius (1892–1974), French composer and pianist, who travelled in Brazil before becoming a member of the Paris group of composers known as 'Les Six'. He composed the music to Cocteau's Le Boeuf sur le toit (1919), and his experience of Latin-American music bore fruit in the piano work Saudades do Brasil (1920–1), while a taste for jazz after a visit to the US found expression in the ballet La Création du monde (1923).

miliary /ˈmɪlɪərɪ/ adj. **1** like a millet-seed in size or form. **2** (of a disease) having as a symptom a rash with lesions resembling millet-seed. [L miliarius f. milium millet]

milieu /mɪˈljɜː, ˈmiːljɜː/ n. (pl. **milieux** or **milieus** /-ljɜːz/) one's environment or social surroundings. [F f. mi MID[1] + lieu place]

Militant /ˈmɪlɪt(ə)nt/ n. Brit. **1** one who sympathizes with the views expressed in the Trotskyist newspaper *Militant*, set up in 1964. (In the US, *The Militant* had been the name of the official organ of American Trotskyists.) **2** a supporter of the Militant Tendency. □ **Militant Tendency** a Trotskyist political organization, originally compromising the supporters of the weekly newspaper *Militant* and dedicated to upholding Trotskyist principles within the Labour Party, from which they were later excluded.

militant /ˈmɪlɪt(ə)nt/ adj. & n. —adj. **1** combative; aggressively active esp. in support of a (usu. political) cause. **2** engaged in warfare. —n. a militant person, esp. a political activist. □□ **militancy** n. **militantly** adv. [ME f. OF f. L (as MILITATE)]

militarism /ˈmɪlɪtəˌrɪz(ə)m/ n. **1** the spirit or tendencies of a professional soldier. **2** undue prevalence of the military spirit or ideals. □□ **militaristic** /-ˈrɪstɪk/ adj. **militaristically** /-ˈrɪstɪkəlɪ/ adv. [F *militarisme* (as MILITARY)]

militarist /ˈmɪlɪtərɪst/ n. **1** a person dominated by militaristic ideas. **2** a student of military science.

militarize /ˈmɪlɪtəˌraɪz/ v.tr. (also **-ise**) **1** equip with military resources. **2** make military or warlike. **3** imbue with militarism. □□ **militarization** /-ˈzeɪʃ(ə)n/ n.

military /ˈmɪlɪtərɪ/ adj. & n. —adj. of, relating to, or characteristic of soldiers or armed forces. —n. (as sing. or pl.; prec. by *the*) members of the armed forces, as distinct from civilians and the police. □ **military honours** marks of respect paid by troops at the burial of a soldier, to royalty, etc. **military police** a corps responsible for police and disciplinary duties in the army. **military policeman** a member of the military police. □□ **militarily** adv. **militariness** n. [F *militaire* or L *militaris* f. *miles militis* soldier]

militate /ˈmɪlɪˌteɪt/ v.intr. (usu. foll. by *against*) (of facts or evidence) have force or effect (*what you say militates against our opinion*). ¶ Often confused with *mitigate*. [L *militare militat-* f. *miles militis* soldier]

militia /mɪˈlɪʃə/ n. a military force, esp. one raised from the civil population and supplementing a regular army in an emergency. [L, = military service f. *miles militis* soldier]

militiaman /mɪˈlɪʃəmən/ n. (pl. **-men**) a member of a militia.

milk /mɪlk/ n. & v. —n. **1** an opaque white fluid secreted by female mammals for the nourishment of their young. **2** the milk of cows, goats, or sheep as food. **3** the milklike juice of plants, e.g. in the coconut. **4** a milklike preparation of herbs, drugs, etc. —v.tr. **1** draw milk from (a cow, ewe, goat, etc.). **2 a** exploit (a person) esp. financially. **b** get all possible advantage from (a situation). **3** extract sap, venom, etc. from. **4** sl. tap (telegraph or telephone wires etc.). □ **cry over spilt milk** lament an irremediable loss or error. **in milk** secreting milk. **milk and honey** abundant means of prosperity. **milk and water** a feeble or insipid or mawkish discourse or sentiment. **milk bar** a snack bar selling milk drinks and other refreshments. **milk chocolate** chocolate for eating, made with milk. **milk float** Brit. a small usu. electric vehicle used in delivering milk. **milk-leg** a painful swelling, esp. of the legs, after childbirth. **milk-loaf** a loaf of bread made with milk. **milk of human kindness** kindness regarded as natural to humanity. **Milk of Magnesia** Brit. propr. a white suspension of magnesium hydroxide usu. in water as an antacid or laxative. **milk of sulphur** the amorphous powder of sulphur formed by precipitation. **milk-powder** milk dehydrated by evaporation. **milk pudding** a pudding of rice, sago, tapioca, etc., baked with milk in a dish. **milk round 1** a fixed route on which milk is delivered regularly. **2** a regular trip or tour involving calls at several places. **milk run** a routine expedition or service journey. **milk shake** a drink of milk, flavouring, etc., mixed by shaking or whisking. **milk sugar** lactose. **milk tooth** a temporary tooth in young mammals. **milk-vetch** any leguminous yellow-flowered plant of the genus *Astragalus*. **milk-white** white like milk. □□ **milker** n. [OE *milc, milcian* f. Gmc]

milkmaid /ˈmɪlkmeɪd/ n. a girl or woman who milks cows or works in a dairy.

milkman /ˈmɪlkmən/ n. (pl. **-men**) a person who sells or delivers milk.

milksop /ˈmɪlksɒp/ n. a spiritless man or youth.

milkweed /ˈmɪlkwiːd/ n. any of various wild plants with milky juice.

milkwort /ˈmɪlkwɜːt/ n. any plant of the genus *Polygala*, formerly supposed to increase women's milk.

milky /ˈmɪlkɪ/ adj. (**milkier, milkiest**) **1** of, like, or mixed with milk. **2** (of a gem or liquid) cloudy; not clear. **3** effeminate; weakly amiable. □□ **milkiness** n.

Milky Way a faint band of light crossing the sky, clearly visible on dark moonless nights and discovered by Galileo to be made up of vast numbers of faint stars. It is the plane of our Galaxy in which most stars are located, and telescopic observations in the constellation of Sagittarius, looking towards the galactic centre, show 'clouds' of millions of stars, hosts of nebulae, and a great richness of other celestial phenomena.

Mill /mɪl/, John Stuart (1806–73), English philosopher and economist, strongly influenced by Bentham, who was a friend of his father. His chief concern was to oppose justification that depends on appeal to intuition, authority, custom, or revelation, and his most thoroughgoing defence of this view was in his *System of Logic* (1843), in which he argued that even knowledge of deductive inferences and mathematical truths was empirical. Mill is best known for his political and moral works. In *Utilitarianism* (1861) he developed Bentham's theory, refining it to deal with criticism, and considering explicitly the relation between utilitarianism and justice; his work has become the classic statement of the view. In *On Liberty* (1859) he argued for the importance of individuality, and claimed that self-protection was the only proper reason for interfering with another's freedom. In other works he argued for representative democracy, criticized the contemporary treatment of married women, claimed that an end to economic growth was desirable as well as inevitable, and advocated the replacement of a divisive socioeconomic class structure by a system of worker ownership.

mill¹ /mɪl/ n. & v. —n. **1 a** a building fitted with a mechanical apparatus for grinding corn. **b** such an apparatus. **2** an apparatus for grinding any solid substance to powder or pulp (*peppermill*). **3 a** a building fitted with machinery for manufacturing processes etc. (*cotton-mill*). **b** such machinery. **4 a** a boxing-match. **b** a fist fight. —v. **1** tr. grind (corn), produce (flour), or hull (seeds) in a mill. **2** tr. produce regular ribbed markings on the edge of (a coin). **3** tr. cut or shape (metal) with a rotating tool. **4** intr. (often foll. by *about, around*) (of people or animals) move in an aimless manner, esp. in a confused mass. **5** tr. thicken (cloth etc.) by fulling. **6** tr. beat (chocolate etc.) to froth. **7** tr. sl. beat, strike, fight. □ **go** (or **put**) **through the mill** undergo (or cause to undergo) intensive work or training etc. **mill-dam** a dam put across a stream to make it usable by a mill. **mill-hand** a worker in a mill or factory. **mill-race** a current of water that drives a mill-wheel. **mill-wheel** a wheel used to drive a water-mill. □□ **millable** adj. [OE *mylen* ult. f. LL *molinum* f. L *mola* grindstone, mill f. *molere* grind]

mill² /mɪl/ n. US one-thousandth of a dollar as money of account. [L *millesimum* thousandth: cf. CENT]

Millais /ˈmɪleɪ/, Sir John Everett (1829–96), English painter. A prodigious youthful talent saw him studying at the Royal Academy at the age of eleven. There he met Holman Hunt and, with Rossetti, formed the Pre-Raphaelite Brotherhood in 1848. His early work in that style (e.g. *Christ in the House of His Parents*, 1850) was totally uncompromising in its adherence to a pure vision of nature with vivid colouring, harsh outline, and unidealized figures, and brought the wrath of the critical establishment on his head until defended by Ruskin, whose former wife he married in 1855. However, with growing success he gradually slipped away from the moral and aesthetic rigour of the Pre-Raphaelites to become the archetypal mid-Victorian artist, producing beautifully painted portraits, landscapes, and sentimental genre pictures that cemented his fame (e.g. *Bubbles*, 1886).

millboard /ˈmɪlbɔːd/ n. stout pasteboard for bookbinding etc.

millefeuille /miːlˈfɜːj/ n. a rich confection of puff pastry split and filled with jam, cream, etc. [F, = thousand-leaf]

millenarian /ˌmɪlɪˈneərɪən/ adj. & n. —adj. **1** of or related to the millennium. **2** believing in the millennium. —n. a person who believes in the millennium. [as MILLENARY]

millenary /mɪˈlenərɪ/ n. & adj. —n. (pl. -ies) **1** a period of 1,000 years. **2** the festival of the 1,000th anniversary of a person or thing. **3** a person who believes in the millennium. —adj. of or relating to a millenary. [LL *millenarius* consisting of a thousand f. *milleni* distrib. of *mille* thousand]

millennium /mɪˈlenɪəm/ n. (pl. **millenniums** or **millennia** /-nɪə/) **1** a period of 1,000 years, esp. that of Christ's prophesied reign in person on earth (Rev. 20: 1–5). **2** a period of good government, great happiness, and prosperity. □□ **millennial** adj. **millennialist** n. & adj. [mod.L f. L *mille* thousand after BIENNIUM]

millepede var. of MILLIPEDE.

millepore /ˈmɪlɪˌpɔː(r)/ n. a reef-building coral of the order Milleporina, with polyps protruding through pores in the calcareous exoskeleton. [F *millépore* or mod.L *millepora* f. L *mille* thousand + *porus* PORE¹]

Miller¹ /ˈmɪlə(r)/, (Alton) Glenn (1904–44), American jazz trombonist and band leader, noted for the orchestra which he formed in 1938. He composed the popular songs 'Moonlight Serenade' and 'In the Mood'. A mystery surrounds his death: the aircraft in which he was travelling disappeared while on a routine flight from England to France.

Miller² /ˈmɪlə(r)/, Arthur (1915–), American playwright. His tragedy *Death of a Salesman* (1949) was a powerful indictment of American values. *The Crucible* (1953) was based on the Salem witch trials of 1692. He was married to Marilyn Monroe from 1955 to 1961.

miller /ˈmɪlə(r)/ n. **1** the proprietor or tenant of a corn-mill. **2** a person who works or owns a mill. □ **miller's thumb** a small spiny freshwater fish, *Cottus gobio*: also called BULLHEAD. [ME *mylnere*, prob. f. MLG, MDu. *molner*, *mulner*, OS *mulineri* f. LL *molinarius* f. *molina* MILL¹, assim. to MILL¹]

millesimal /mɪˈlesɪm(ə)l/ adj. & n. —adj. **1** thousandth. **2** of or belonging to a thousandth. **3** of or dealing with thousandths. —n. a thousandth part. □□ **millesimally** adv. [L *millesimus* f. *mille* thousand]

millet /ˈmɪlɪt/ n. **1** any of various cereal plants, esp. *Panicum miliaceum*, bearing a large crop of small nutritious seeds. **2** the seed of this. □ **millet-grass** a tall woodland grass, *Milium effusum*. [ME f. F, dimin. of *mil* f. L *milium*]

milli- /ˈmɪlɪ/ comb. form a thousand, esp. denoting a factor of one thousandth. ¶ Abbr.: **m**. [L *mille* thousand]

milliammeter /ˌmɪlɪˈæmɪtə(r)/ n. an instrument for measuring electrical current in milliamperes.

milliampere /ˌmɪlɪˈæmpeə(r)/ n. one thousandth of an ampere, a measure for small electrical currents.

milliard /ˈmɪljəd, -jɑːd/ n. Brit. one thousand million. ¶ Now largely superseded by *billion*. [F f. *mille* thousand]

millibar /ˈmɪlɪˌbɑː(r)/ n. one-thousandth of a bar, the cgs unit of atmospheric pressure equivalent to 100 pascals.

milligram /ˈmɪlɪˌgræm/ n. one-thousandth of a gram.

millilitre /ˈmɪlɪˌliːtə(r)/ n. one-thousandth of a litre (0.002 pint).

millimetre /ˈmɪlɪˌmiːtə(r)/ n. one-thousandth of a metre (0.039 in.).

milliner /ˈmɪlɪnə(r)/ n. a person who makes or sells women's hats. □□ **millinery** n. [orig. = vendor of goods from *Milan*]

million /ˈmɪljən/ n. & adj. —n. (pl. same or (in sense 2) **millions**) (in sing. prec. by *a* or *one*) **1** a thousand thousand. **2** (in pl.) colloq. a very large number (*millions of years*). **3** (prec. by *the*) the bulk of the population. **4 a** Brit. a million pounds. **b** US a million dollars. —adj. that amount to a million. □ **gone a million** Austral. sl. completely defeated. □□ **millionfold** adj. & adv. **millionth** adj. & n. [ME f. OF, prob. f. It. *millione* f. *mille* thousand + *-one* augment. suffix]

millionaire /ˌmɪljəˈneə(r)/ n. (fem. **millionairess** /-rɪs/) **1** a person whose assets are worth at least one million pounds, dollars, etc. **2** a person of great wealth. [F *millionnaire* (as MILLION)]

millipede /ˈmɪlɪˌpiːd/ n. (also **millepede**) any arthropod of the class Diplopoda, having a long segmented body with two pairs of legs on each segment. [L *millepeda* wood-louse f. *mille* thousand + *pes pedis* foot]

millisecond /ˈmɪlɪˌsekənd/ n. one-thousandth of a second.

millpond /ˈmɪlpɒnd/ n. a pool of water retained by a mill-dam for the operation of a mill. □ **like a millpond** (of a stretch of water) very calm.

Mills /mɪlz/, Sir John (1908–), English actor, who appeared in roles of quiet heroism in *This Happy Breed* (1944) and other war films and in *Scott of the Antarctic* (1948). He appeared later in character roles, winning an Oscar for his portrayal of a village idiot in *Ryan's Daughter* (1971).

Mills bomb /mɪlz/ n. an oval hand-grenade. [invented by Sir W. *Mills* d. 1932]

millstone /ˈmɪlstəʊn/ n. **1** each of two circular stones used for grinding corn. **2** a heavy burden or responsibility (cf. Matt. 18:6).

millwright /ˈmɪlraɪt/ n. a person who designs or builds mills.

milometer /maɪˈlɒmɪtə(r)/ n. an instrument for measuring the number of miles travelled by a vehicle.

milord /mɪˈlɔːd/ n. hist. an Englishman travelling in Europe in aristocratic style. [F f. E *my lord*: cf. MILADY]

Milos /ˈmaɪlɒs, ˈmiː-/ a Greek island in the Cyclades, where a Hellenistic marble statue of Aphrodite was found in 1820 (see VENUS OF MILO).

milt /mɪlt/ n. **1** the spleen in mammals. **2** an analogous organ in other vertebrates. **3** a sperm-filled reproductive gland of a male fish. [OE *milt(e)* f. Gmc, perh. rel. to MELT]

milter /ˈmɪltə(r)/ n. a male fish in spawning-time.

Milton /ˈmɪlt(ə)n/, John (1608–74), English Puritan poet. A London scrivener's son, he attended St Paul's School and Christ's, Cambridge, dedicating himself, as a youth, to the stern chaste life he deemed needful for poetry, and writing three early masterpieces: the 'Nativity Ode', *Comus* (a masque), and 'Lycidas', an elegy for a drowned friend. He became politically active during the Civil War, publishing a renowned plea for a free press (*Areopagitica*, 1644), and, after his unhappy first marriage (1642), several pioneering tracts urging legalization of divorce. As Secretary of State for Foreign Tongues to Cromwell's government he produced propaganda defending Charles I's execution, and the unremitting work destroyed his sight. His three major poems, all completed after he had gone blind (1652), have biblical subjects: *Paradise Lost* (1667, revised 1674), an epic on the fall of man; *Paradise Regained*, on Christ's temptations, and (published with it in 1671) *Samson Agonistes*, in Greek tragic form.

Milwaukee /mɪlˈwɔːkiː/ an industrial port and city in SE Wisconsin, on Lake Michigan; pop. (1982) 631,500. Brewing is one of its major industries.

mimbar /ˈmɪmbɑː(r)/ n. (also **minbar** /ˈmɪn-/) a stepped platform for preaching in a mosque. [Arab. *minbar*]

mime /maɪm/ n. & v. —n. **1** the theatrical technique of suggesting action, character, etc. by gesture and expression without using words. **2** a theatrical performance using this technique. **3** Gk & Rom. Antiq. a simple farcical drama including mimicry. **4** (also **mime artist**) a practitioner of mime. —v. **1** tr. (also absol.) convey (an idea or emotion) by gesture without words. **2** intr. (often foll. by *to*) (of singers etc.) mouth the words of a song etc. along with a soundtrack (*mime to a record*). □□ **mimer** n. [L *mimus* f. Gk *mimos*]

mimeograph /ˈmɪmɪəˌɡrɑːf/ n. & v. —n. **1** (often attrib.) a duplicating machine which produces copies from a stencil. **2** a copy produced in this way. —v.tr. reproduce (text or diagrams) by this process. [irreg. f. Gk *mimeomai* imitate: see -GRAPH]

mimesis /mɪˈmiːsɪs, maɪ-/ n. Biol. a close external resemblance of an animal to another that is distasteful or harmful to predators of the first. [Gk *mimēsis* imitation]

mimetic /mɪˈmetɪk/ *adj.* **1** relating to or habitually practising imitation or mimicry. **2** *Biol.* of or exhibiting mimesis. ☐☐ **mimetically** *adv.* [Gk *mimētikos* imitation (as MIMESIS)]

mimic /ˈmɪmɪk/ *v., n., & adj.* —*v.tr.* (**mimicked, mimicking**) **1** imitate (a person, gesture, etc.) esp. to entertain or ridicule. **2** copy minutely or servilely. **3** (of a thing) resemble closely. —*n.* a person skilled in imitation. —*adj.* having an aptitude for mimicry; imitating; imitative, esp. for amusement. ☐☐ **mimicker** *n.* [L *mimicus* f. Gk *mimikos* (as MIME)]

mimicry /ˈmɪmɪkrɪ/ *n.* (*pl.* **-ies**) **1** the act or art of mimicking. **2** a thing that mimics another. **3** *Zool.* mimesis.

miminy-piminy /ˌmɪmɪnɪ ˈpɪmɪnɪ/ *adj.* overrefined, finical (cf. NIMINY-PIMINY & NAMBY-PAMBY). [imit.]

mimosa /mɪˈməʊzə/ *n.* **1** any leguminous shrub of the genus *Mimosa*, esp. *M. pudica*, having globular usu. yellow flowers and sensitive leaflets which droop when touched. **2** any of various acacia plants with showy yellow flowers. [mod.L, app. f. L (as MIME, because the leaves imitate animals in their sensitivity) + *-osa* fem. suffix]

mimulus /ˈmɪmjʊləs/ *n.* any flowering plant of the genus *Mimulus*, including musk and the monkey flower. [mod.L, app. dimin. of L (as MIME, perh. with ref. to its masklike flowers)]

Min /mɪn/ *n.* any of the Chinese languages or dialects spoken in the Fukien province in SE China. [Chin.]

Min. *abbr.* **1** Minister. **2** Ministry.

min. *abbr.* **1** minute(s). **2** minimum. **3** minim (fluid measure).

mina var. of MYNA.

Minaean /mɪˈniːən/ *n. & adj.* —*n.* **1** a member of a Semitic-speaking people who established a kingdom in southern Arabia *c.*400 BC, absorbed into the Sabaean kingdom by the late 1st c. BC. **2** their language. —*adj.* of the Sabaeans or their language. [L *Minaeus* f. Arab. *Maʿīn*]

minaret /ˌmɪnəˈret/ *n.* a slender turret connected with a mosque and having a balcony from which the muezzin calls at hours of prayer. ☐☐ **minareted** *adj.* [F *minaret* or Sp. *minarete* f. Turk. *minare* f. Arab. *manār*(a) lighthouse, minaret f. *nār* fire, light]

Minas Gerais /ˌmiːnæs ʒeˈraɪs/ a State of SE Brazil, a major source of iron ore, gold, and diamonds; pop. (est. 1987) 15,099,700; capital, Belo Horizonte.

minatory /ˈmɪnətərɪ/ *adj.* threatening, menacing. [LL *minatorius* f. *minari minat-* threaten]

minbar var. of MIMBAR.

mince /mɪns/ *v. & n.* —*v.* **1** *tr.* cut up or grind (esp. meat) into very small pieces. **2** *tr.* (usu. with *neg.*) restrain (one's words etc.) within the bounds of politeness. **3** *intr.* (usu. as **mincing** *adj.*) speak or walk with an affected delicacy. —*n.* esp. *Brit.* minced meat. ☐ **mince matters** (usu. with *neg.*) use polite expressions etc. **mince pie** a usu. small round pie containing mincemeat. ☐☐ **mincer** *n.* **mincingly** *adv.* (in sense 3 of *v.*). [ME f. OF *mincier* ult. f. L (as MINUTIA)]

mincemeat /ˈmɪnsmiːt/ *n.* a mixture of currants, raisins, sugar, apples, candied peel, spices, and often suet. ☐ **make mincemeat of** utterly defeat (a person, argument, etc.).

mind /maɪnd/ *n. & v.* —*n.* **1 a** the seat of consciousness, thought, volition, and feeling. **b** attention, concentration (*my mind keeps wandering*). **2** the intellect; intellectual powers. **3** remembrance, memory (*it went out of my mind; I can't call it to mind*). **4** one's opinion (*we're of the same mind*). **5** a way of thinking or feeling (*shocking to the Victorian mind*). **6** the focus of one's thoughts or desires (*put one's mind to it*). **7** the state of normal mental functioning (*lose one's mind; in one's right mind*). **8** a person as embodying mental faculties (*a great mind*). —*v.tr.* **1** (usu. with *neg.* or *interrog.*) object to (*do you mind if I smoke?; I don't mind your being late*). **2 a** remember; take care to (*mind you come on time*). **b** (often foll. by *out*) take care; be careful. **3** have charge of temporarily (*mind the house while I'm away*). **4** apply oneself to, concern oneself with (business, affairs, etc.) (*I try to mind my own business*). **5** give heed to; notice (*mind the step; don't mind the expense; mind how you go*). **6** *US & Ir.* be obedient to (*mind what your mother says*). ☐ **be in two minds** be undecided. **cast one's mind back** think back; recall an earlier time. **come into a person's mind** be

remembered. **come to mind** (of a thought, idea, etc.) suggest itself. **don't mind me** *iron.* do as you please. **do you mind!** *iron.* an expression of annoyance. **give a person a piece of one's mind** scold or reproach a person. **have a good** (or **great** or **half a**) **mind to** (often as a threat, usu. unfulfilled) feel tempted to (*I've a good mind to report you*). **have** (it) **in mind** intend. **have a mind of one's own** be capable of independent opinion. **have on one's mind** be troubled by the thought of. **in one's mind's eye** in one's imagination or mental view. **mind-bending** *colloq.* (esp. of a psychedelic drug) influencing or altering one's state of mind. **mind-blowing** *sl.* **1** confusing, shattering. **2** (esp. of drugs etc.) inducing hallucinations. **mind-boggling** *colloq.* overwhelming, startling. **mind out for** guard against, avoid. **mind over matter** the power of the mind asserted over the physical universe. **mind one's Ps & Qs** be careful in one's behaviour. **mind-read** discern the thoughts of (another person). **mind-reader** a person capable of mind-reading. **mind-set** habits of mind formed by earlier events. **mind the shop** have charge of affairs temporarily. **mind you** an expression used to qualify a previous statement (*I found it quite quickly; mind you, it wasn't easy*). **mind your back** (or **backs**) *colloq.* an expression to indicate that a person wants to get past. **never mind 1** an expression used to comfort or console. **2** (also **never you mind**) an expression used to evade a question. **open** (or **close**) **one's mind to** be receptive (or unreceptive) to (changes, new ideas, etc.). **put a person in mind of** remind a person of. **put** (or **set**) **a person's mind at rest** reassure a person. **put a person or thing out of one's mind** deliberately forget. **read a person's mind** discern a person's thoughts. **to my mind** in my opinion. [ME *mynd* f. OE *gemynd* f. Gmt]

Mindanao /ˌmɪndəˈnaʊ/ the second-largest island of the Philippines; pop. (est. 1988) 13,432,400; chief city, Davao.

minded /ˈmaɪndɪd/ *adj.* **1** (in *comb.*) **a** inclined to think in some specified way (*mathematically minded; fair-minded*). **b** having a specified kind of mind (*high-minded*). **c** interested in or enthusiastic about a specified thing (*car-minded*). **2** (usu. foll. by *to* + *infin.*) disposed or inclined (to an action).

minder /ˈmaɪndə(r)/ *n.* **1 a** a person whose job it is to attend to a person or thing. **b** (in *comb.*) (*child-minder; machine-minder*). **2** *sl.* **a** a bodyguard, esp. a person employed to protect a criminal. **b** a thief's assistant.

mindful /ˈmaɪndfʊl/ *adj.* (often foll. by *of*) taking heed or care; being conscious. ☐☐ **mindfully** *adv.* **mindfulness** *n.*

mindless /ˈmaɪndlɪs/ *adj.* **1** lacking intelligence; stupid. **2** not requiring thought or skill (*totally mindless work*). **3** (usu. foll. by *of*) heedless of (advice etc.). ☐☐ **mindlessly** *adv.* **mindlessness** *n.*

Mindoro /mɪnˈdɔːrəʊ/ an island in the north-west central Philippines; pop. (1980) 1,031,450.

mine[1] /maɪn/ *poss.pron.* **1** the one or ones belonging to or associated with me (*it is mine; mine are over there*). **2** (*attrib.* before a vowel) *archaic* = MY (*mine eyes have seen; mine host*). ☐ **of mine** of or belonging to me (*a friend of mine*). [OE *mīn* f. Gmc]

mine[2] /maɪn/ *n. & v.* —*n.* **1** an excavation in the earth for extracting metal, coal, salt, etc. **2** an abundant source (of information etc.). **3** a receptacle filled with explosive and placed in the ground or in the water for destroying enemy personnel, ships, etc. **4 a** a subterranean gallery in which explosive is placed to blow up fortifications. **b** *hist.* a subterranean passage under the wall of a besieged fortress. —*v.tr.* **1** obtain (metal, coal, etc.) from a mine. **2** (also *absol.*, often foll. by *for*) dig in (the earth etc.) for ore etc. **3 a** dig or burrow in (usu. the earth). **b** make (a hole, passage, etc.) underground. **4** lay explosive mines under or in. **5** = UNDERMINE. ☐ **mine-detector** an instrument for detecting the presence of mines. ☐☐ **mining** *n.* [ME f. OF *mine*, *miner*, perh. f. Celt.]

minefield /ˈmaɪnfiːld/ *n.* **1** an area planted with explosive mines. **2** a subject or situation presenting unseen hazards.

minelayer /ˈmaɪnˌleɪə(r)/ *n.* a ship or aircraft for laying mines.

miner /ˈmaɪnə(r)/ *n.* **1** a person who works in a mine. **2** any burrowing insect or grub. ☐ **miner's right** *Austral.* a licence to dig for gold etc. on private or public land. [ME f. OF *minĕor*, *minour* (as MINE²)]

mineral /'mɪnər(ə)l/ *n. & adj.* —*n.* **1** any of the species into which natural inorganic substances are classified, having a definite chemical composition and usually a characteristic crystalline structure. A rock may be made up of one type or several types of mineral. **2** a substance obtained by mining. **3** (often in *pl.*) *Brit.* an artificial mineral water or other effervescent drink. —*adj.* **1** of or containing a mineral or minerals. **2** obtained by mining. □ **mineral oil** see OIL. **mineral water 1** water found in nature with some dissolved salts present. **2** an artificial imitation of this, esp. soda water. **3** any effervescent non-alcoholic drink. **mineral wax** a fossil resin, esp. ozocerite. **mineral wool** a wool-like substance made from inorganic material, used for packing etc. [ME f. OF *mineral* or med.L *mineralis* f. *minera* ore f. OF *miniere* mine]

mineralize /'mɪnərəˌlaɪz/ *v.* (also **-ise**) **1** *v.tr. & intr.* change wholly or partly into a mineral. **2** *v.tr.* impregnate (water etc.) with a mineral substance.

mineralogy /ˌmɪnəˈrælədʒɪ/ *n.* the scientific study of minerals. □□ **mineralogical** /-rəˈlɒdʒɪk(ə)l/ *adj.* **mineralogist** *n.*

Minerva /mɪˈnɜːvə/ *Rom. Mythol.* the goddess of handicrafts, widely worshipped and regularly identified with Athene, which led to her being regarded also as the goddess of war.

minestrone /ˌmɪnɪˈstrəʊnɪ/ *n.* a soup containing vegetables and pasta, beans, or rice. [It.]

minesweeper /'maɪnˌswiːpə(r)/ *n.* a ship for clearing away floating and submarine mines.

minever var. of MINIVER.

mineworker /'maɪnˌwɜːkə(r)/ *n.* a person who works in a mine, esp. a coalmine.

Ming /mɪŋ/ the name of the Chinese dynasty founded in 1368 by Chu Yuan-chang after the collapse of Mongol authority in China, and ruling until succeeded by the Manchus in 1644 (see CH'ING). It was a period of expansion and exploration, with lasting contact established in the 16th c. between China and Europe, and a culturally productive period in which the arts flourished. The capital was established at Peking in 1421. —*n.* Chinese porcelain of this period.

mingle /'mɪŋg(ə)l/ *v.tr. & intr.* mix, blend. □ **mingle their** etc. **tears** *literary* weep together. **mingle with** go about among. □□ **mingler** *n.* [ME *mengel* f. obs. *meng* f. OE *mengan*, rel. to AMONG]

mingy /'mɪndʒɪ/ *adj.* (**mingier, mingiest**) *Brit. colloq.* mean, stingy. □□ **mingily** *adv.* [perh. f. MEAN² and STINGY]

Minho /'miːnjəʊ/ (Spanish **Miño**) a river which rises in NW Spain and flows south to the Portuguese frontier which it follows before meeting the Atlantic north of Viana do Castelo.

mini /'mɪnɪ/ *n.* (*pl.* **minis**) **1** *colloq.* a miniskirt, minidress, etc. **2** (**Mini**) *propr.* a make of small car. [abbr.]

mini- /'mɪnɪ/ *comb. form* miniature; very small or minor of its kind (*minibus; mini-budget*). [abbr. of MINIATURE]

miniature /'mɪnɪtʃə(r)/ *adj., n., & v.* —*adj.* **1** much smaller than normal. **2** represented on a small scale. —*n.* **1** any object reduced in size. **2** a small-scale minutely finished portrait. **3** this branch of painting (*portrait in miniature*). **4** a picture or decorated letters in an illuminated manuscript. —*v.tr.* represent on a smaller scale. □ **in miniature** on a small scale. **miniature camera** a camera producing small negatives. □□ **miniaturist** *n.* (in senses 2 and 3 of *n.*). [It. *miniatura* f. med.L *miniatura* f. L *miniare* rubricate, illuminate f. L *minium* red lead, vermilion]

miniaturize /'mɪnɪtʃəˌraɪz/ *v.tr.* (also **-ise**) produce in a smaller version; make small. □□ **miniaturization** /-ˈzeɪʃ(ə)n/ *n.*

minibus /'mɪnɪˌbʌs/ *n.* a small bus for about twelve passengers.

minicab /'mɪnɪˌkæb/ *n. Brit.* a car used as a taxi, but not licensed to ply for hire.

minicomputer /'mɪnɪkəmˌpjuːtə(r)/ *n.* a computer of medium power, more than a microcomputer but less than a mainframe.

minikin /'mɪnɪkɪn/ *adj. & n.* —*adj.* **1** diminutive. **2** affected, mincing. —*n.* a diminutive creature. [obs. Du. *minneken* f. *minne* love + *-ken, -kijn* -KIN]

minim /'mɪnɪm/ *n.* **1** *Mus.* a note having the time value of two crotchets or half a semibreve and represented by a hollow ring with a stem. Also called *half-note*. **2** one-sixtieth of a fluid drachm, about a drop. **3** an object or portion of the smallest size or importance. **4** a single down-stroke of the pen. [ME f. L *minimus* smallest]

minima *pl.* of MINIMUM.

minimal /'mɪnɪm(ə)l/ *adj.* **1** very minute or slight. **2** being or related to a minimum. **3** the least possible in size, duration, etc. **4** *Art* etc. characterized by the use of simple or primary forms or structures etc., often geometric or massive (*huge minimal forms in a few colours*). This trend in painting, and more especially sculpture, arose during the 1950s. It is associated particularly with the US, and its impersonality is seen as a reaction against the emotiveness of abstract expressionism. □□ **minimalism** *n.* (in sense 4). **minimally** *adv.* (in senses 1–3). [L *minimus* smallest]

minimalist /'mɪnɪməlɪst/ *n.* **1** (also *attrib.*) a person advocating small or moderate reform in politics (opp. MAXIMALIST). **2** = MENSHEVIK. **3** a person who advocates or practises minimal art. □□ **minimalism** *n.*

minimax /'mɪnɪˌmæks/ *n.* **1** *Math.* the lowest of a set of maximum values. **2** (usu. *attrib.*) **a** a strategy that minimizes the greatest risk to a participant in a game etc. **b** the theory that in a game with two players, a player's smallest possible maximum loss is equal to the same player's greatest possible minimum gain. [MINIMUM + MAXIMUM]

minimize /'mɪnɪˌmaɪz/ *v.* (also **-ise**) **1** *tr.* reduce to, or estimate at, the smallest possible amount or degree. **2** *tr.* estimate or represent at less than the true value or importance. **3** *intr.* attain a minimum value. □□ **minimization** /-ˈzeɪʃ(ə)n/ *n.* **minimizer** *n.*

minimum /'mɪnɪməm/ *n. & adj.* (*pl.* **minima** /-mə/) —*n.* the least possible or attainable amount (*reduced to a minimum*). —*adj.* that is a minimum. □ **minimum lending rate** the announced minimum percentage at which a central bank will discount bills (cf. *base rate* (see BASE¹)). ¶ Abolished in the UK in 1981. **minimum wage** the lowest wage permitted by law or special agreement. [L, neut. of *minimus* least]

minion /'mɪnjən/ *n. derog.* **1** a servile agent; a slave. **2** a favourite servant, animal, etc. **3** a favourite of a sovereign etc. [F *mignon*, OF *mignot*, of Gaulish orig.]

minipill /'mɪnɪpɪl/ *n.* a contraceptive pill containing a progestogen only (not oestrogen).

miniseries /'mɪnɪˌsɪərɪz/ *n.* a short series of television programmes on a common theme.

miniskirt /'mɪnɪˌskɜːt/ *n.* a very short skirt.

minister /'mɪnɪstə(r)/ *n. & v.* —*n.* **1** a head of a government department. **2** (in full **minister of religion**) a member of the clergy, esp. in the Presbyterian and Nonconformist Churches. **3** a diplomatic agent, usu. ranking below an ambassador. **4** (usu. foll. by *of*) a person employed in the execution of (a purpose, will, etc.) (*a minister of justice*). **5** (in full **minister general**) the superior of some religious orders. —*v.* **1** *intr.* (usu. foll. by *to*) render aid or service (to a person, cause, etc.). **2** *tr.* (usu. foll. by *with*) *archaic* furnish, supply, etc. □ **ministering angel** a kind-hearted person, esp. a woman, who nurses or comforts others (with ref. to Mark 1: 13). **Minister of the Crown** *Brit. Parl.* a member of the Cabinet. **Minister of State** a government minister, in the UK usu. regarded as holding a rank below that of Head of Department. **Minister without Portfolio** a government minister who has Cabinet status, but is not in charge of a specific Department of State. □□ **ministrable** *adj.* [ME f. OF *ministre* f. L *minister* servant f. *minus* less]

ministerial /ˌmɪnɪˈstɪərɪəl/ *adj.* **1** of a minister of religion or a minister's office. **2** instrumental or subsidiary in achieving a purpose (*ministerial in bringing about a settlement*). **3 a** of a government minister. **b** siding with the Ministry against the Opposition. □□ **ministerialist** *n.* (in sense 3b). **ministerially** *adv.* [F *ministériel* or LL *ministerialis* f. L (as MINISTRY)]

ministration /ˌmɪnɪˈstreɪʃ(ə)n/ *n.* **1** (usu. in *pl.*) aid or service (*the kind ministrations of his neighbours*). **2** ministering, esp. in religious matters. **3** (usu. foll. by *of*) the supplying (of help,

justice, etc.). □□ **ministrant** /'mɪnɪstrənt/ *adj. & n.*
ministrative /'mɪnɪstrətɪv/ *adj.* [ME f. OF *ministration* or L *ministratio* (as MINISTER)]

ministry /'mɪnɪstrɪ/ *n.* (*pl.* **-ies**) **1 a** a government department headed by a minister. **b** the building which it occupies (*the Ministry of Defence*). **2 a** (*prec. by the*) the vocation or profession of a religious minister (*called to the ministry*). **b** the office of a religious minister, priest, etc. **c** the period of tenure of this. **3** (*prec. by the*) the body of ministers of a government or of a religion. **4** a period of government under one Prime Minister. **5** ministering, ministration. [ME f. L *ministerium* (as MINISTER)]

miniver /'mɪnɪvə(r)/ *n.* (also **minever**) plain white fur used in ceremonial costume. [ME f. AF *menuver*, OF *menu vair* (as MENU, VAIR)]

mink /mɪŋk/ *n.* **1** either of two small semi-aquatic stoatlike animals of the genus *Mustela*, *M. vison* of N. America and *M. introela* of Europe. **2** the thick brown fur of these. **3** a coat made of this. [cf. Sw. *mänk, menk*]

minke /'mɪŋkə/ *n.* a small baleen whale, *Balaenoptera acutorostrata*, with a pointed snout. [prob. f. *Meincke*, the name of a Norw. whaler]

Minn. *abbr.* Minnesota.

Minneapolis /ˌmɪnɪˈæpəlɪs/ an industrial city and port at the head of navigation on the Mississippi River in SE Minnesota; pop. (1982) 369,200.

minnesinger /'mɪnɪˌsɪŋə(r)/ *n.* (*pl.* same) any of the aristocratic German poet-musicians of the 12th–14th c., the German equivalent of troubadours. [G, = love-singer (*minne* love, from the courtly love that was their chief theme)]

Minnesota /ˌmɪnɪˈsəʊtə/ a State in the north central US on the Canadian border; pop. (est. 1985) 4,076,000; capital, St Paul. Part of it was ceded to Britain by the French in 1763 and acquired by the US in 1783, the remainder forming part of the Louisiana Purchase (1803).

minnow /'mɪnəʊ/ *n.* any of various small freshwater fish of the carp family, esp. *Phoxinus phoxinus*. [late ME *menow*, perh. repr. OE *mynwe* (unrecorded), *myne*: infl. by ME *menuse, menise* f. OF *menuise*, ult. rel. to MINUTIA]

Miño see MINHO.

Minoan /mɪˈnəʊən/ *adj. & n. Archaeol.* —*adj.* of or relating to the Bronze Age civilization centred on Crete (*c.*3000–1100 BC) or its people or language. (See below.) —*n.* **1** an inhabitant of Minoan Crete or the Minoan world. **2** the language or scripts associated with the Minoans. [named after MINOS, to whom the palace excavated at Knossos was attributed]

  This civilization, the earliest on European soil, was first revealed by the excavations of Sir Arthur Evans, who gave it its name, from 1900 onwards after Crete became independent of Turkish rule. It had reached its zenith by the beginning of the late Bronze Age, extending over the islands of the south Aegean while its wares were exported to Cyprus, Syria, and Egypt. Urban centres were constructed, dominated by palaces at Knossos, Mallia, Phaistos, and Zakro. Divided into two periods by an earthquake destruction *c.*1700 BC, the Minoan civilization, noted particularly for its Linear A script and distinctive palatial art and architecture, greatly influenced the Mycenaeans, whose presence in Crete is attested from the 16th c. BC and who succeeded the Minoans in control of the Aegean *c.*1400 BC; the precise dating of successive phases and of the collapse of Minoan civilization is highly controversial.

minor /'maɪnə(r)/ *adj., n., & v.* —*adj.* **1** lesser or comparatively small in size or importance (*minor poet; minor operation*). **2** *Mus.* **a** (of a scale) having intervals of a semitone between the second and third, fifth and sixth, and seventh and eighth degrees. **b** (of an interval) less by a semitone than a major interval. **c** (of a key) based on a minor scale, tending to produce a melancholy effect. **3** *Brit.* (in schools) indicating the younger of two children from the same family or the second to enter the school (usu. put after the name). **4** *Logic* **a** (of a term) occurring as the subject of the conclusion of a categorical syllogism. **b** (of a premiss) containing the minor term in a categorical syllogism. —*n.* **1** a person under the legal age limit or majority (*no unaccompanied minors*).

2 *Mus.* a minor key etc. **3** *US* a student's subsidiary subject or course (cf. MAJOR). **4** *Logic* a minor term or premiss. —*v.intr.* (foll. by *in*) *US* (of a student) undertake study in (a subject) as a subsidiary to a main subject. □ **in a minor key** (of novels, events, people's lives, etc.) understated, uneventful. **minor axis** *Geom.* (of a conic) the axis perpendicular to the major axis. **minor canon** a cleric who is not a member of the chapter, who assists in daily cathedral services. **minor league** *US* (in baseball, football, etc.) a league of professional clubs other than the major leagues. **minor orders** see ORDER. **minor piece** *Chess* a bishop or a knight. **minor planets** (also called *asteroids*) the small rocky bodies (less than a few kilometres across) orbiting the sun. Mostly found in a broad belt between the orbits of Mars and Jupiter, some are found closer to the sun, and may pass within a few million kilometres of Earth. Many satellites of the planets are thought to be captured asteroids. **minor prophet** see PROPHET. **minor suit** *Bridge* diamonds or clubs. [L, = smaller, less, rel. to *minuere* lessen]

Minorca /mɪˈnɔːkə/ (Spanish **Menorca**) the most easterly and second-largest of the Balearic Islands; pop. (1981) 58,700. The capital and chief port, Mahon, was intermittently under British rule from 1708–82.

Minorite /'maɪnəˌraɪt/ *n.* a Franciscan friar, so called because the Franciscans regarded themselves as of humbler rank than members of other orders. [MINOR]

minority /maɪˈnɒrɪtɪ/ *n.* (*pl.* **-ies**) **1** (often foll. by *of*) a smaller number or part, esp. within a political party or structure. **2** the number of votes cast for this (*a minority of two*). **3** the state of having less than half the votes or of being supported by less than half of the body of opinion (*in the minority*). **4** a relatively small group of people differing from others in the society of which they are a part in race, religion, language, political persuasion, etc. **5** (*attrib.*) relating to or done by the minority (*minority interests*). **6 a** the state of being under full legal age. **b** the period of this. [F *minorité* or med.L *minoritas* f. L *minor*: see MINOR]

Minos /'maɪnɒs/ a legendary king of Crete. The traditions concerning him preserve faint reminiscences of the might of the civilization now called Minoan. In Attic tradition his wife was Pasiphaë, and he was a cruel tyrant who every year exacted a tribute of Athenian youths and maidens to be devoured by the Minotaur. □ **Palace of Minos** a building (excavated and reconstructed by Sir Arthur Evans) identified with the largest Minoan palace of Knossos, which yielded local coins portraying the labyrinth as the city's symbol and a Linear B religious tablet which, when eventually deciphered, was found to refer to the 'lady of the labyrinth'.

Minotaur /'maɪnəˌtɔː(r)/ *n. Gk Mythol.* the creature half-man, half-bull, offspring of Pasiphaë and a bull with which she fell in love, confined in Crete in a labyrinth made by Daedalus and fed on human flesh. It was eventually slain by Theseus. [ME f. OF f. L *Minotaurus* f. Gk *Minōtauros* f. MINOS + *tauros* bull]

Minsk /mɪnsk/ an industrial city of the USSR, capital of the Byelorussian republic; pop. (est. 1987) 1,543,000.

minster /'mɪnstə(r)/ *n.* **1** a large or important church (*York Minster*). **2** the church of a monastery. [OE *mynster* f. eccl.L *monasterium* f. Gk *monastērion* MONASTERY]

minstrel /'mɪnstr(ə)l/ *n.* **1** a medieval singer or musician, esp. singing or reciting poetry. **2** *hist.* a person who entertained patrons with singing, buffoonery, etc. **3** (usu. in *pl.*) a member of a band of public entertainers with blackened faces etc., performing songs and music ostensibly of Negro origin. [ME f. OF *menestral* entertainer, servant, f. Prov. *menest(ai)ral* officer, employee, musician, f. LL *ministerialis* official, officer: see MINISTERIAL]

minstrelsy /'mɪnstr(ə)lsɪ/ *n.* (*pl.* **-ies**) **1** the minstrel's art. **2** a body of minstrels. **3** minstrel poetry. [ME f. OF *menestralsie* (as MINSTREL)]

mint¹ /mɪnt/ *n.* **1** any aromatic plant of the genus *Mentha*. **2** a peppermint sweet or lozenge. □ **mint julep** *US* a sweet iced alcoholic drink of bourbon flavoured with mint. **mint sauce** chopped mint in vinegar and sugar, usu. eaten with lamb. □□ **minty** *adj.* (**mintier, mintiest**). [OE *minte* ult. f. L *ment(h)a* f. Gk *minthē*]

mint² /mɪnt/ n. & v. —n. **1** a place where money is coined, usu. under State authority. (See ROYAL MINT.) **2** a vast sum of money (making a mint). **3** a source of invention etc. (a mint of ideas). —v.tr. **1** make (coin) by stamping metal. **2** invent, coin (a word, phrase, etc.). □ **in mint condition** (or **state**) freshly minted; (of books etc.) as new. **mint-mark** a mark on a coin to indicate the mint at which it was struck. **mint-master** the superintendent of coinage at a mint. **mint par** (in full **mint parity**) **1** the ratio between the gold equivalents of currency in two countries. **2** their rate of exchange based on this. □□ **mintage** n. [OE mynet f. WG f. L moneta MONEY]

Minton /ˈmɪnt(ə)n/ n. a kind of pottery made at Stoke-on-Trent, Staffs., by Thomas Minton (1766–1836) and his successors.

minuend /ˈmɪnjʊˌend/ n. Math. a quantity or number from which another is to be subtracted. [L minuendus gerundive of minuere diminish]

minuet /ˌmɪnjʊˈet/ n. & v. —n. **1** a slow stately dance for two in triple time. **2** Mus. the music for this, or music in the same rhythm and style, often as a movement in a suite, sonata, or symphony. —v.intr. (**minueted**, **minueting**) dance a minuet. [F menuet, orig. adj. = fine, delicate, dimin. of menu: see MENU]

minus /ˈmaɪnəs/ prep., adj., & n. —prep. **1** with the subtraction of (7 minus 4 equals 3). ¶ Symb.: -. **2** (of temperature) below zero (minus 2°). **3** colloq. lacking; deprived of (returned minus their dog). —adj. **1** Math. negative. **2** Electronics having a negative charge. —n. **1** = minus sign. **2** Math. a negative quantity. **3** a disadvantage. □ **minus sign** the symbol -, indicating subtraction or a negative value. [L, neut. of minor less]

minuscule /ˈmɪnəˌskjuːl/ n. & adj. —n. **1** Palaeog. a kind of cursive script developed in the 7th c. **2** a lower-case letter. —adj. **1** lower-case. **2** colloq. extremely small or unimportant. □□ **minuscular** /mɪˈnʌskjʊlə(r)/ adj. [F f. L minuscula (littera letter) dimin. of minor: see MINOR]

minute¹ /ˈmɪnɪt/ n. & v. —n. **1** the sixtieth part of an hour. **2** a distance covered in one minute (twenty minutes from the station). **3 a** a moment; an instant; a point of time (expecting her any minute; the train leaves in a minute). **b** (prec. by the) colloq. the present time (what are you doing at the minute?). **c** (foll. by clause) as soon as (call me the minute you get back). **4** the sixtieth part of an angular degree. **5** (in pl.) a brief summary of the proceedings at a meeting. **6** an official memorandum authorizing or recommending a course of action. —v.tr. **1** record (proceedings) in the minutes. **2** send the minutes to (a person). □ **just** (or **wait**) **a minute 1** a request to wait for a short time. **2** as a prelude to a query or objection. **minute-gun** a gun fired at intervals of a minute at funerals etc. **minute-hand** the hand on a watch or clock which indicates minutes. **minute steak** a thin slice of steak to be cooked quickly. **up to the minute** completely up to date. [ME f. OF f. LL minuta (n.), f. fem. of minutus MINUTE²: senses 1 & 4 of noun f. med.L pars minuta prima first minute part (cf. SECOND²): senses 5 & 6 perh. f. med.L minuta scriptura draft in small writing]

minute² /maɪˈnjuːt/ adj. (**minutest**) **1** very small. **2** trifling, petty. **3** (of an inquiry, inquirer, etc.) accurate, detailed, precise. □□ **minutely** adv. **minuteness** n. [ME f. L minutus past part. of minuere lessen]

Minuteman /ˈmɪnɪtˌmæn/ n. (pl. **-men**) US **1** a political watchdog or activist. **2** a type of three-stage intercontinental ballistic missile. **3** hist. an American militiaman of the revolutionary period (ready to march at a minute's notice).

minutia /maɪˈnjuːʃɪə, mɪ-/ n. (pl. **-iae** /-ʃɪˌiː/) (usu. in pl.) a precise, trivial, or minor detail. [L, = smallness, in pl. trifles f. minutus: see MINUTE²]

minx /mɪŋks/ n. a pert, sly, or playful girl. □□ **minxish** adj. **minxishly** adv. [16th c.: orig. unkn.]

Miocene /ˈmaɪəˌsiːn/ adj. & n. Geol. —adj. of or relating to the fourth epoch of the Tertiary period, following the Oligocene and preceding the Pliocene, lasting from about 24.6 to 5.1 million years ago. It was a period of great earth movements during which the Alps and Himalayas were being formed. —n. this epoch or system. [irreg. f. Gk meiōn less + kainos new]

miosis /maɪˈəʊsɪs/ n. (also **myosis**) excessive constriction of the pupil of the eye. □□ **miotic** /maɪˈɒtɪk/ adj. [Gk muō shut the eyes + -OSIS]

Miquelon see ST PIERRE AND MIQUELON.

Mirabeau /ˈmiːrəˌbəʊ/, Honoré Gabriel Riqueti, Comte de (1749–91), French revolutionary. A long-time opponent of the Bourbon regime, Mirabeau rose to prominence in the early days of the French Revolution when he rose to the leadership of the Third Estate in the Estates General, trying to find a moderate solution to the crisis by pressing for a form of constitutional monarchy. He died before the Revolution entered its extremist phase and was later accused, unfairly, of being a royal agent.

mirabelle /ˌmɪrəˈbel/ n. **1 a** a European variety of plum-tree, Prunus insititia, bearing small round yellow fruit. **b** a fruit from this tree. **2** a liqueur distilled from this fruit. [F]

miracle /ˈmɪrək(ə)l/ n. **1** an extraordinary event attributed to some supernatural agency. **2 a** any remarkable occurrence. **b** a remarkable development in some specified area (an economic miracle; the German miracle). **3** (usu. foll. by of) a remarkable or outstanding specimen (the plan was a miracle of ingenuity). □ **miracle drug** a drug which represents a breakthrough in medical science. **miracle play** see MYSTERY PLAY. [ME f. OF f. L miraculum object of wonder f. mirari wonder f. mirus wonderful]

miraculous /mɪˈrækjʊləs/ adj. **1** of the nature of a miracle. **2** supernatural. **3** remarkable, surprising. □□ **miraculously** adv. **miraculousness** n. [F miraculeux or med.L miraculosus f. L (as MIRACLE)]

mirador /ˌmɪrəˈdɔː(r)/ n. a turret or tower etc. attached to a building, and commanding an excellent view. [Sp. f. mirar to look]

mirage /ˈmɪrɑːʒ/ n. **1** an optical illusion caused by atmospheric conditions, esp. the appearance of a sheet of water in a desert or on a hot road from the reflection of light. **2** an illusory thing. [F f. se mirer be reflected, f. L mirare look at]

MIRAS /ˈmaɪræs/ abbr. (also **Miras**) mortgage interest relief at source.

mire /ˈmaɪə(r)/ n. & v. —n. **1** a stretch of swampy or boggy ground. **2** mud, dirt. —v. **1** tr. & intr. plunge or sink in a mire. **2** tr. involve in difficulties. □ **in the mire** in difficulties. [ME f. ON mýrr f. Gmc, rel. to MOSS]

mirepoix /mɪəˈpwɑː/ n. sautéd chopped vegetables, used in sauces etc. [F, f. Duc de Mirepoix, Fr. general d. 1757]

mirk var. of MURK.

mirky var. of MURKY.

Miró /mɪˈrəʊ/, Joan (1893–1983), Spanish painter, from c.1923 among the most prominent of the surrealists. Many of his pictures contain enlarged amoebic forms in rhythmically balanced composition.

mirror /ˈmɪrə(r)/ n. & v. —n. **1** a polished surface, usu. of amalgam-coated glass or metal, which reflects an image; a looking-glass. **2** anything regarded as giving an accurate reflection or description of something else. —v.tr. reflect as in a mirror. □ **mirror carp** a breed of carp with large shiny scales. **mirror finish** a reflective surface. **mirror image** an identical image, but with the structure reversed, as in a mirror. **mirror symmetry** symmetry as of an object and its reflection. **mirror writing** backwards writing, like ordinary writing reflected in a mirror. [ME f. OF mirour ult. f. L mirare look at]

mirth /mɜːθ/ n. merriment, laughter. □□ **mirthful** adj. **mirthfully** adv. **mirthfulness** n. **mirthless** adj. **mirthlessly** adv. **mirthlessness** n. [OE myrgth (as MERRY)]

MIRV abbr. multiple independently-targeted re-entry vehicle (a type of missile).

mis-¹ /mɪs/ prefix added to verbs and verbal derivatives: meaning 'amiss', 'badly', 'wrongly', 'unfavourably' (mislead; misshapen; mistrust). [OE f. Gmc]

mis-² /mɪs/ prefix occurring in a few words adopted from French meaning 'badly', 'wrongly', 'amiss', 'ill-', or having a negative force (misadventure; mischief). [OF mes- ult. f. L minus (see MINUS): assim. to MIS-1]

misaddress /ˌmɪsəˈdres/ v.tr. **1** address (a letter etc.) wrongly. **2** address (a person) wrongly, esp. impertinently.

misadventure /ˌmɪsədˈventʃə(r)/ n. **1** Law an accident without concomitant crime or negligence (death by misadventure). **2** bad luck. **3** a misfortune. [ME f. OF mesaventure f. mesavenir turn out badly (as MIS-², ADVENT: cf. ADVENTURE)]

misalign /ˌmɪsəˈlaɪn/ v.tr. give the wrong alignment to. □□ **misalignment** n.

misalliance /ˌmɪsəˈlaɪəns/ n. an unsuitable alliance, esp. an unsuitable marriage. □□ **misally** v.tr. (-ies, -ied). [MIS-¹ + ALLIANCE, after MÉSALLIANCE]

misanthrope /ˈmɪzənˌθrəʊp, ˈmɪs-/ n. (also **misanthropist** /mɪˈzænθrəpɪst/) **1** a person who hates mankind. **2** a person who avoids human society. □□ **misanthropic** /-ˈθrɒpɪk/ adj. **misanthropical** /-ˈθrɒpɪk(ə)l/ adj. **misanthropically** /-ˈθrɒpɪkəlɪ/ adv. **misanthropy** /mɪˈzænθrəpɪ/ n. **misanthropize** /mɪˈzænθrəˌpaɪz/ v.intr. (also -ise). [F f. Gk misanthrōpos f. misos hatred + anthrōpos man]

misapply /ˌmɪsəˈplaɪ/ v.tr. (-ies, -ied) apply (esp. funds) wrongly. □□ **misapplication** /mɪsˌæplɪˈkeɪʃ(ə)n/ n.

misapprehend /ˌmɪsæprɪˈhend/ v.tr. misunderstand (words, a person). □□ **misapprehension** /-ˈhenʃ(ə)n/ n. **misapprehensive** adj.

misappropriate /ˌmɪsəˈprəʊprɪˌeɪt/ v.tr. apply (usu. another's money) to one's own use, or to a wrong use. □□ **misappropriation** /-prɪˈeɪʃ(ə)n/ n.

misbegotten /ˌmɪsbɪˈɡɒt(ə)n/ adj. **1** illegitimate, bastard. **2** contemptible, disreputable.

misbehave /ˌmɪsbɪˈheɪv/ v.intr. & refl. (of a person or machine) behave badly. □□ **misbehaver** n. **misbehaviour** n.

misbelief /ˌmɪsbɪˈliːf/ n. **1** wrong or unorthodox religious belief. **2** a false opinion or notion.

misc. abbr. miscellaneous.

miscalculate /ˌmɪsˈkælkjʊˌleɪt/ v.tr. (also absol.) calculate (amounts, results, etc.) wrongly. □□ **miscalculation** /-ˈleɪʃ(ə)n/ n.

miscall /mɪsˈkɔːl/ v.tr. **1** call by a wrong or inappropriate name. **2** archaic or dial. call (a person) names.

miscarriage /ˈmɪsˌkærɪdʒ, mɪsˈkærɪdʒ/ n. **1** a spontaneous abortion, esp. before the 28th week of pregnancy. **2** Brit. the failure (of a plan, letter, etc.) to reach completion or its destination. □ **miscarriage of justice** any failure of the judicial system to attain the ends of justice. [MISCARRY, after CARRIAGE]

miscarry /mɪsˈkærɪ/ v.intr. (-ies, -ied) **1** (of a woman) have a miscarriage. **2** Brit. (of a letter etc.) fail to reach its destination. **3** (of a business, plan, etc.) fail, be unsuccessful.

miscast /mɪsˈkɑːst/ v.tr. (past and past part. **-cast**) allot an unsuitable part to (an actor).

miscegenation /ˌmɪsɪdʒɪˈneɪʃ(ə)n/ n. the interbreeding of races, esp. of Whites and non-Whites. [irreg. f. L miscēre mix + genus race]

miscellanea /ˌmɪsəˈleɪnɪə/ n.pl. **1** a literary miscellany. **2** a collection of miscellaneous items. [L neut. pl. (as MISCELLANEOUS)]

miscellaneous /ˌmɪsəˈleɪnɪəs/ adj. **1** of mixed composition or character. **2** (foll. by pl. noun) of various kinds. **3** (of a person) many-sided. □□ **miscellaneously** adv. **miscellaneousness** n. [L miscellaneus f. miscellus mixed f. miscēre mix]

miscellany /mɪˈseləni/ n. (pl. **-ies**) **1** a mixture, a medley. **2** a book containing a collection of stories etc., or various literary compositions. □□ **miscellanist** n. [F miscellanées (fem. pl.) or L MISCELLANEA]

mischance /mɪsˈtʃɑːns/ n. **1** bad luck. **2** an instance of this. [ME f. OF mesch(e)ance f. mescheoir (as MIS-², CHANCE)]

mischief /ˈmɪstʃɪf/ n. **1** conduct which is troublesome, but not malicious, esp. in children. **2** pranks, scrapes (get into mischief; keep out of mischief). **3** playful malice, archness, satire (eyes full of mischief). **4** harm or injury caused by a person or thing. **5** a person or thing responsible for harm or annoyance (that loose connection is the mischief). **6** (prec. by the) the annoying part or aspect (the mischief of it is that etc.). □ **do a person a mischief** wound or kill a person. **get up to** (or **make**) **mischief** create discord. **mischief-maker** one who encourages discord, esp. by

gossip etc. [ME f. OF meschief f. meschever (as MIS-², chever come to an end f. chef head: see CHIEF)]

mischievous /ˈmɪstʃɪvəs/ adj. **1** (of a person) disposed to mischief. **2** (of conduct) playfully malicious. **3** (of a thing) having harmful effects. □□ **mischievously** adv. **mischievousness** n. [ME f. AF meschevous f. meschever: see MISCHIEF]

misch metal /mɪʃ/ n. an alloy of lanthanide metals, usu. added to iron to improve its malleability. [G mischen mix + Metall metal]

miscible /ˈmɪsɪb(ə)l/ adj. (often foll. by with) capable of being mixed. □□ **miscibility** /-ˈbɪlɪtɪ/ n. [med.L miscibilis f. L miscēre mix]

misconceive /ˌmɪskənˈsiːv/ v. **1** intr. (often foll. by of) have a wrong idea or conception. **2** tr. (as **misconceived** adj.) badly planned, organized, etc. **3** tr. misunderstand (a word, person, etc.). □□ **misconceiver** n. **misconception** /-ˈsepʃ(ə)n/ n.

misconduct n. & v. —n. /mɪsˈkɒndʌkt/ **1** improper or unprofessional behaviour. **2** bad management. —v. /ˌmɪskənˈdʌkt/ **1** refl. misbehave. **2** tr. mismanage.

misconstrue /ˌmɪskənˈstruː/ v.tr. (**-construes**, **-construed**, **-construing**) **1** interpret (a word, action, etc.) wrongly. **2** mistake the meaning of (a person). □□ **misconstruction** /-ˈstrʌkʃ(ə)n/ n.

miscopy /mɪsˈkɒpɪ/ v.tr. (**-ies**, **-ied**) copy (text etc.) incorrectly.

miscount /mɪsˈkaʊnt/ v. & n. —v.tr. (also absol.) count wrongly. —n. a wrong count.

miscreant /ˈmɪskrɪənt/ n. & adj. —n. **1** a vile wretch, a villain. **2** archaic a heretic. —adj. **1** depraved, villainous. **2** archaic heretical. [ME f. OF mescreant (as MIS-², creant part. of croire f. L credere believe)]

miscue /mɪsˈkjuː/ n. & v. —n. (in snooker etc.) the failure to strike the ball properly with the cue. —v.intr. (**-cues**, **-cued**, **-cueing** or **-cuing**) make a miscue.

misdate /mɪsˈdeɪt/ v.tr. date (an event, a letter, etc.) wrongly.

misdeal /mɪsˈdiːl/ v. & n. —v.tr. (also absol.) (past and past part. **-dealt** /-ˈdelt/) make a mistake in dealing (cards). —n. **1** a mistake in dealing cards. **2** a misdealt hand.

misdeed /mɪsˈdiːd/ n. an evil deed, a wrongdoing; a crime. [OE misdǣd (as MIS-¹, DEED)]

misdemeanant /ˌmɪsdɪˈmiːnənt/ n. a person convicted of a misdemeanour or guilty of misconduct. [archaic misdemean misbehave]

misdemeanour /ˌmɪsdɪˈmiːnə(r)/ n. (US **misdemeanor**) **1** an offence, a misdeed. **2** Law an indictable offence, (in the UK formerly) less heinous than a felony.

misdiagnose /ˌmɪsˈdaɪəɡˌnəʊz/ v.tr. diagnose incorrectly. □□ **misdiagnosis** /-ˈnəʊsɪs/ n.

misdial /mɪsˈdaɪəl/ v.tr. (also absol.) (**-dialled**, **-dialling**; US **-dialed**, **-dialing**) dial (a telephone number etc.) incorrectly.

misdirect /ˌmɪsdaɪˈrekt, -dɪˈrekt/ v.tr. **1** direct (a person, letter, blow, etc.) wrongly. **2** (of a judge) instruct (the jury) wrongly. □□ **misdirection** n.

misdoing /mɪsˈduːɪŋ/ n. a misdeed.

misdoubt /mɪsˈdaʊt/ v.tr. **1** have doubts or misgivings about the truth or existence of. **2** be suspicious about; suspect that.

miseducation /mɪsˌedjʊˈkeɪʃ(ə)n/ n. wrong or faulty education. □□ **miseducate** /-ˈedjʊˌkeɪt/ v.tr.

mise en scène /ˌmiːz ɑ̃ ˈsen/ n. **1** Theatr. the scenery and properties of a play. **2** the setting or surroundings of an event. [F]

misemploy /ˌmɪsɪmˈplɔɪ/ v.tr. employ or use wrongly or improperly. □□ **misemployment** n.

miser /ˈmaɪzə(r)/ n. **1** a person who hoards wealth and lives miserably. **2** an avaricious person. [L = wretched]

miserable /ˈmɪzərəb(ə)l/ adj. **1** wretchedly unhappy or uncomfortable (felt miserable; a miserable hovel). **2** contemptible, mean. **3** causing wretchedness or discomfort (miserable weather). **4** Sc., Austral., & NZ stingy, mean. □□ **miserableness** n. **miserably** adv. [ME f. F misérable f. L miserabilis pitiable f. miserari to pity f. miser wretched]

misère /mɪˈzeə(r)/ n. Cards (in solo whist etc.) a declaration undertaking to win no tricks. [F, = poverty, MISERY]

miserere /ˌmɪzəˈreərɪ, -ˈrɪərɪ/ n. **1** a cry for mercy. **2** = MISERICORD 1. [ME f. L, imper. of *miserēri* have mercy (as MISER); first word of Ps. 51 in Latin]

misericord /mɪˈzerɪˌkɔːd/ n. **1** a shelving projection on the under side of a hinged seat in a choir stall serving (when the seat is turned up) to help support a person standing. **2** an apartment in a monastery in which some relaxations of discipline are permitted. **3** a dagger for dealing the death stroke. [ME f. OF *misericorde* f. L *misericordia* f. *misericors* compassionate f. stem of *miserēri* pity + *cor cordis* heart]

miserly /ˈmaɪzəlɪ/ adj. like a miser, niggardly. □□ **miserliness** n. [MISER]

misery /ˈmɪzərɪ/ n. (pl. **-ies**) **1** a wretched state of mind, or of outward circumstances. **2** a thing causing this. **3** colloq. a constantly depressed or discontented person. **4** = MISÈRE. □ **put out of its** etc. **misery 1** release (a person, animal, etc.) from suffering or suspense. **2** kill (an animal in pain). [ME f. OF *misere* or L *miseria* (as MISER)]

misfeasance /mɪsˈfiːz(ə)ns/ n. Law a transgression, esp. the wrongful exercise of lawful authority. [ME f. OF *mesfaisance* f. *mesfaire* misdo (as MIS-², *faire* do f. L *facere*): cf. MALFEASANCE]

misfield /mɪsˈfiːld/ v. & n. —v.tr. (also absol.) (in cricket, baseball, etc.) field (the ball) badly. —n. an instance of this.

misfire /mɪsˈfaɪə(r)/ v. & n. —v.intr. **1** (of a gun, motor engine, etc.) fail to go off or start or function regularly. **2** (of an action etc.) fail to have the intended effect. —n. a failure of function or intention.

misfit /ˈmɪsfɪt/ n. **1** a person unsuited to a particular kind of environment, occupation, etc. **2** a garment etc. that does not fit. □ **misfit stream** Geog. a stream not corresponding in size to its valley.

misfortune /mɪsˈfɔːtʃuːn, -tjuːn/ n. **1** bad luck. **2** an instance of this.

misgive /mɪsˈgɪv/ v.tr. (past **-gave** /-ˈgeɪv/; past part. **-given** /-ˈgɪv(ə)n/) (often foll. by about, that) (of a person's mind, heart, etc.) fill (a person) with suspicion or foreboding.

misgiving /mɪsˈgɪvɪŋ/ n. (usu. in pl.) a feeling of mistrust or apprehension.

misgovern /mɪsˈgʌv(ə)n/ v.tr. govern (a State etc.) badly. □□ **misgovernment** n.

misguide /mɪsˈgaɪd/ v.tr. **1** (as **misguided** adj.) mistaken in thought or action. **2** mislead, misdirect. □□ **misguidance** n. **misguidedly** adv. **misguidedness** n.

mishandle /mɪsˈhænd(ə)l/ v.tr. **1** deal with incorrectly or ineffectively. **2** handle (a person or thing) roughly or rudely; ill-treat.

mishap /ˈmɪshæp/ n. an unlucky accident.

mishear /mɪsˈhɪə(r)/ v.tr. (past and past part. **-heard** /-ˈhɜːd/) hear incorrectly or imperfectly.

mishit v. & n. —v.tr. /mɪsˈhɪt/ (**-hitting**; past and past part. **-hit**) hit (a ball etc.) faultily. —n. /ˈmɪshɪt/ a faulty or bad hit.

mishmash /ˈmɪʃmæʃ/ n. a confused mixture. [ME, reduplication of MASH]

Mishnah /ˈmɪʃnə/ n. an authoritative collection of exegetical material embodying the oral tradition of Jewish law. Written in Hebrew and traditionally attributed to Rabbi Judah ha-Nasi (c. AD 200), it forms the first part of the Talmud, with an influence on Judaism second only to that of the Scriptures. □□ **Mishnaic** /-ˈneɪɪk/ adj. [Heb. *mišnāh* (teaching by) repetition]

misidentify /ˌmɪsaɪˈdentɪˌfaɪ/ v.tr. (**-ies, -ied**) identify erroneously. □□ **misidentification** /-fɪˈkeɪʃ(ə)n/ n.

misinform /ˌmɪsɪnˈfɔːm/ v.tr. give wrong information to, mislead. □□ **misinformation** /-fəˈmeɪʃ(ə)n/ n.

misinterpret /ˌmɪsɪnˈtɜːprɪt/ v.tr. (**-interpreted, -interpreting**) **1** interpret wrongly. **2** draw a wrong inference from. □□ **misinterpretation** /-ˈteɪʃ(ə)n/ n. **misinterpreter** n.

misjudge /mɪsˈdʒʌdʒ/ v.tr. (also absol.) **1** judge wrongly. **2** have a wrong opinion of. □□ **misjudgement** n. (also **misjudgment**).

miskey /mɪsˈkiː/ v.tr. (**-keys, -keyed**) key (data) wrongly.

miskick v. & n. —v.tr. /mɪsˈkɪk/ (also absol.) kick (a ball etc.) badly or wrongly. —n. /ˈmɪskɪk/ an instance of this.

Miskito /mɪsˈkiːtəʊ/ adj. & n. (also **Mosquito**) (pl. **-os**) —adj. of or relating to an American Indian people living on the Caribbean coast of Nicaragua and Honduras. —n. **1** a member of this people. **2** their language. [*Misquito*, a section of the east coast of Nicaragua]

Miskolc /ˈmiːʃkɒlts/ the second-largest city in Hungary, an industrial city 145 km (90 miles) north-east of Budapest; pop. (1988) 210,000.

mislay /mɪsˈleɪ/ v.tr. (past and past part. **-laid** /-leɪd/) **1** unintentionally put (a thing) where it cannot readily be found. **2** euphem. lose.

mislead /mɪsˈliːd/ v.tr. (past and past part. **-led** /-ˈled/) **1** cause (a person) to go wrong, in conduct, belief, etc. **2** lead astray or in the wrong direction. □□ **misleader** n.

misleading /mɪsˈliːdɪŋ/ adj. causing to err or go astray; imprecise, confusing. □□ **misleadingly** adv. **misleadingness** n.

mislike /mɪsˈlaɪk/ v.tr. & n. archaic dislike. [OE *mislīcian* (as MIS-¹, LIKE²)]

mismanage /mɪsˈmænɪdʒ/ v.tr. manage badly or wrongly. □□ **mismanagement** n.

mismarriage /mɪsˈmærɪdʒ/ n. an unsuitable marriage or alliance. [MIS-¹ + MARRIAGE]

mismatch v. & n. —v.tr. /mɪsˈmætʃ/ match unsuitably or incorrectly, esp. in marriage. —n. /ˈmɪsmætʃ/ a bad match.

mismated /mɪsˈmeɪtɪd/ adj. **1** (of people) not suited to each other, esp. in marriage. **2** (of objects) not matching.

mismeasure /mɪsˈmeʒə(r)/ v.tr. measure or estimate incorrectly. □□ **mismeasurement** n.

misname /mɪsˈneɪm/ v.tr. = MISCALL.

misnomer /mɪsˈnəʊmə(r)/ n. **1** a name or term used wrongly. **2** the wrong use of a name or term. [ME f. AF f. OF *mesnom(m)er* (as MIS-², *nommer* name f. L *nominare* formed as NOMINATE)]

misogamy /mɪˈsɒgəmɪ/ n. the hatred of marriage. □□ **misogamist** n. [Gk *misos* hatred + *gamos* marriage]

misogyny /mɪˈsɒdʒɪnɪ/ n. the hatred of women. □□ **misogynist** n. **misogynous** adj. [Gk *misos* hatred + *gunē* woman]

mispickel /ˈmɪsˌpɪk(ə)l/ n. Mineral. arsenical pyrites. [G]

misplace /mɪsˈpleɪs/ v.tr. **1** put in the wrong place. **2** bestow (affections, confidence, etc.) on an inappropriate object. **3** time (words, actions, etc.) badly. □□ **misplacement** n.

misplay /mɪsˈpleɪ/ v. & n. —v.tr. play (a ball, card, etc.) in a wrong or ineffective manner. —n. an instance of this.

misprint n. & v. /ˈmɪsprɪnt/ a mistake in printing. —v.tr. /mɪsˈprɪnt/ print wrongly.

misprision¹ /mɪsˈprɪʒ(ə)n/ n. Law **1** (in full **misprision of a felony** or **of treason**) the deliberate concealment of one's knowledge of a crime, treason, etc. **2** a wrong action or omission. [ME f. AF *mesprisioun* f. OF *mesprison* error f. *mesprendre* to mistake (as MIS-², *prendre* take)]

misprision² /mɪsˈprɪʒ(ə)n/ n. **1** a misreading, misunderstanding, etc. **2** (usu. foll. by of) a failure to appreciate the value of a thing. **3** archaic contempt. [MISPRIZE after MISPRISION¹]

misprize /mɪsˈpraɪz/ v.tr. literary despise, scorn; fail to appreciate. [ME f. OF *mesprisier* (as MIS-¹, PRIZE¹)]

mispronounce /ˌmɪsprəˈnaʊns/ v.tr. pronounce (a word etc.) wrongly. □□ **mispronunciation** /-nʌnsɪˈeɪʃ(ə)n/ n.

misquote /mɪsˈkwəʊt/ v.tr. quote wrongly. □□ **misquotation** /-ˈteɪʃ(ə)n/ n.

misread /mɪsˈriːd/ v.tr. (past and past part. **-read** /-ˈred/) read or interpret (text, a situation, etc.) wrongly.

misremember /ˌmɪsrɪˈmembə(r)/ v.tr. remember imperfectly or incorrectly.

misreport /ˌmɪsrɪˈpɔːt/ v. & n. —v.tr. give a false or incorrect report of. —n. a false or incorrect report.

misrepresent /ˌmɪsreprɪˈzent/ v.tr. represent wrongly; give a false or misleading account or idea of. □□ **misrepresentation** /-ˈteɪʃ(ə)n/ n. **misrepresentative** adj.

misrule /mɪsˈruːl/ *n.* & *v.* —*n.* bad government; disorder. —*v.tr.* govern badly.

Miss. *abbr.* Mississippi.

miss¹ /mɪs/ *v.* & *n.* —*v.* **1** *tr.* (also *absol.*) fail to hit, reach, find, catch, etc. (an object or goal). **2** *tr.* fail to catch (a bus, train, etc.). **3** *tr.* fail to experience, see, or attend (an occurrence or event). **4** *tr.* fail to meet (a person); fail to keep (an appointment). **5** *tr.* fail to seize (an opportunity etc.) (*I missed my chance*). **6** *tr.* fail to hear or understand (*I'm sorry, I missed what you said*). **7** *tr.* **a** regret the loss or absence of (a person or thing) (*did you miss me while I was away?*). **b** notice the loss or absence of (an object) (*bound to miss the key if it isn't there*). **8** *tr.* avoid (*go early to miss the traffic*). **9** *tr.* = *miss out* 1. **10** *intr.* (of an engine etc.) fail, misfire. —*n.* **1 a** failure to hit, reach, attain, connect, etc. **2** *colloq.* = MISCARRIAGE 1. □ **be missing** not have (see also MISSING *adj.*). **give** (**a thing**) **a miss** avoid, leave alone (*gave the party a miss*). **miss the boat** (or **bus**) lose an opportunity. **miss fire** (of a gun) fail to go off or hit the mark (cf. MISFIRE). **a miss is as good as a mile** the fact of failure or escape is not affected by the narrowness of the margin. **miss out 1** omit, leave out (*missed out my name from the list*). **2** (usu. foll. by *on*) *colloq.* fail to get or experience (*always misses out on the good times*). **not miss much** be alert. **not miss a trick** never fail to seize an opportunity, advantage, etc. □□ **missable** *adj.* [OE *missan* f. Gmc]

miss² /mɪs/ *n.* **1** a girl or unmarried woman. **2** (**Miss**) **a** the title of an unmarried woman or girl, or of a married woman retaining her maiden name for professional purposes. **b** the title of a beauty queen (*Miss World*). **3** usu. *derog.* or *joc.* a girl, esp. a schoolgirl, with implications of silliness etc. **4** the title used to address a female schoolteacher, shop assistant, etc. □□ **missish** *adj.* (in sense 3). [abbr. of MISTRESS]

missal /ˈmɪs(ə)l/ *n.* RC Ch. **1** a book containing the texts used in the service of the Mass throughout the year. As a liturgical book, the missal appeared from about the 10th c., combining in one book the devotions that had previously appeared in several. **2** a book of prayers, esp. an illuminated one. [ME f. med.L *missale* neut. of eccl.L *missalis* of the mass f. *missa* MASS²]

missel-thrush var. of MISTLE-THRUSH.

misshape /mɪsˈʃeɪp/ *v.tr.* give a bad shape or form to; distort.

misshapen /mɪsˈʃeɪpən/ *adj.* ill-shaped, deformed, distorted. □□ **misshapenly** *adv.* **misshapenness** *n.*

missile /ˈmɪsaɪl/ *n.* **1** an object or weapon suitable for throwing at a target or for discharge from a machine. **2** a weapon, esp. a nuclear weapon, directed by remote control or automatically. □□ **missilery** /-lrɪ/ *n.* [L *missilis* f. *mittere miss-* send]

missing /ˈmɪsɪŋ/ *adj.* **1** not in its place; lost. **2** (of a person) not yet traced or confirmed as alive but not known to be dead. **3** not present.

missing link *n.* **1** a thing lacking to complete a series. **2** a hypothetical creature called upon to bridge the gap between humans and their evolutionary non-human ancestors. The rise of Darwinian evolutionary theory during mid- to late 19th-c. Victorian England questioned biblical authority on mankind's temporal and physical integrity. During this time it was becoming apparent that modern man may have been the result of evolutionary change from some as yet unidentified extinct species. This unknown predecessor was expected to exhibit both ape-like and human physical attributes, for it was popularly, though wrongly, thought that modern man somehow evolved from the extant higher primates, while professionally the belief was that mankind and the higher primates shared a common ancestor. The 'common ancestor or early human' searched for by the scientifically minded, and the hybrid ape-men demanded by popular thought, gave rise to the concept of a 'missing link'. This concept is now defunct for it is known that the evolution of the genus *Homo* (man) has occurred over at least 2 million years: a time that has seen the rise and decline of a series of tool-using hominids of which several evolved no further and have hence become extinct. It is now clear that there is no single 'missing link' to be found in our past but rather a complicated collection of often concurrently existing men or man-like creatures from whom we are derived.

mission /ˈmɪʃ(ə)n/ *n.* **1 a** a particular task or goal assigned to a person or group. **b** a journey undertaken as part of this. **c** a person's vocation (*mission in life*). **2** a military or scientific operation or expedition for a particular purpose. **3** a body of persons sent, esp. to a foreign country, to conduct negotiations etc. **4 a** a body sent to propagate a religious faith. **b** a field of missionary activity. **c** a missionary post or organization. **d** a place of worship attached to a mission. **5** a particular course or period of preaching, services, etc., undertaken by a parish or community. [F *mission* or L *missio* f. *mittere miss-* send]

missionary /ˈmɪʃənərɪ/ *adj.* & *n.* —*adj.* of, concerned with, or characteristic of, religious missions. —*n.* (*pl.* **-ies**) a person doing missionary work. □ **missionary position** *colloq.* a position for sexual intercourse with the woman lying on her back and the man lying on top and facing her. [mod.L *missionarius* f. L (as MISSION)]

missioner /ˈmɪʃənə(r)/ *n.* **1** a missionary. **2** a person in charge of a religious mission.

missis /ˈmɪsɪz/ *n.* (also **missus** /-səz/) *sl.* or *joc.* **1** a form of address to a woman. **2** a wife. □ **the missis** my or your wife. [corrupt. of MISTRESS: cf. MRS]

Mississippi /ˌmɪsɪˈsɪpɪ/ **1** the greatest river of North America, rising near the Canadian border in Minnesota and flowing south to a delta on the Gulf of Mexico. With its chief tributary, the Missouri, it is 5,970 km (3,710 miles) long; it provided a route for early explorers into North America. **2** a State of the US lying east of the lower Mississippi River; pop. (est. 1985) 2,520,700; capital, Jackson. A French colony in the 18th c., it was ceded to Britain in 1763 and to the US in 1783, becoming the 20th State in 1817.

missive /ˈmɪsɪv/ *n.* **1** *joc.* a letter, esp. a long and serious one. **2** an official letter. **letter** (or **letters**) **missive** a letter from a sovereign to a dean and chapter nominating a person to be elected bishop. [ME f. med.L *missivus* f. L (as MISSION)]

Missolonghi /ˌmɪsəˈlɒŋgɪ/ (Greek **Mesolóngion**) a city in western Greece, on the north shore of the Gulf of Patras; pop. (1981) 10,150. The poet Byron died here in 1824 during a Turkish siege.

Missouri /mɪˈzʊərɪ/ **1** one of the main tributaries of the Mississippi, rising in the Rocky Mountains in Montana and flowing into it from the west. **2** a State of the US lying west of the Mississippi River, acquired as part of the Louisiana Purchase (1803) and becoming the 24th State of the US in 1821; pop. (est. 1985) 4,916,800; capital, Jefferson City.

misspell /mɪsˈspel/ *v.tr.* (*past* and *past part.* **-spelt** or **-spelled**) spell wrongly.

misspelling /mɪsˈspelɪŋ/ *n.* a wrong spelling.

misspend /mɪsˈspend/ *v.tr.* (*past* and *past part.* **-spent** /-ˈspent/) (esp. as **misspent** *adj.*) spend amiss or wastefully.

misstate /mɪsˈsteɪt/ *v.tr.* state wrongly or inaccurately.

misstatement /mɪsˈsteɪtmənt/ *n.* a wrong or inaccurate statement.

misstep /mɪsˈstep/ *n.* **1** a wrong step or action. **2** a *faux pas*.

missus var. of MISSIS.

missy /ˈmɪsɪ/ *n.* (*pl.* **-ies**) an affectionate or derogatory form of address to a young girl.

mist /mɪst/ *n.* & *v.* —*n.* **1 a** water vapour near the ground in minute droplets limiting visibility. **b** condensed vapour settling on a surface and obscuring glass etc. **2** dimness or blurring of the sight caused by tears etc. **3** a cloud of particles resembling mist. —*v.tr.* & *intr.* (usu. foll. by *up, over*) cover or become covered with mist or as with mist. □□ **mistful** *adj.* **mistlike** *adj.* [OE f. Gmc]

mistake /mɪˈsteɪk/ *n.* & *v.* —*n.* **1** an incorrect idea or opinion; a thing incorrectly done or thought. **2** an error of judgement. —*v.tr.* (*past* **mistook** /-ˈstʊk/; *past part.* **mistaken** /-ˈsteɪkən/) **1** misunderstand the meaning or intention of (a person, a statement, etc.). **2** (foll. by *for*) wrongly take or identify (*mistook me for you*). **3** choose wrongly (*mistake one's vocation*). □ **and** (or **make**) **no mistake** *colloq.* undoubtedly. **by mistake** accidentally; in error. **there is no mistaking** one is sure to recognize (a person or thing). □□ **mistakable** *adj.* **mistakably** *adv.* [ME f. ON *mistaka* (as MIS-¹, TAKE)]

mistaken /mɪˈsteɪkən/ adj. **1** wrong in opinion or judgement. **2** based on or resulting from this (*mistaken loyalty*; *mistaken identity*). □□ **mistakenly** adv. **mistakenness** n.

misteach /mɪsˈtiːtʃ/ v.tr. (*past* and *past part.* **-taught** /-ˈtɔːt/) teach wrongly or incorrectly.

mister /ˈmɪstə(r)/ n. **1** a man without a title of nobility etc. (*a mere mister*). **2** sl. or joc. a form of address to a man. [weakened form of MASTER in unstressed use before a name: cf. MR]

mistigris /ˈmɪstɪɡrɪs/ n. *Cards* **1** a blank card used as a wild card in a form of draw poker. **2** this game. [F *mistigri* jack of clubs]

mistime /mɪsˈtaɪm/ v.tr. say or do at the wrong time. [OE *mistīmian* (as MIS-¹, TIME)]

mistitle /mɪsˈtaɪt(ə)l/ v.tr. give the wrong title or name to.

mistle thrush /ˈmɪs(ə)l/ n. (also **missel thrush**) a large thrush, *Turdus viscivorus*, with a spotted breast, that feeds on mistletoe berries. [OE *mistel* basil, mistletoe, of unkn. orig.]

mistletoe /ˈmɪs(ə)lˌtəʊ/ n. **1** a parasitic plant, *Viscum album*, growing on apple and other trees and bearing white glutinous berries in winter. **2** a similar plant, *Phoradendron flavescens*, native to N. America. [OE *misteltān* (as MISTLE (THRUSH), *tān* twig)]

mistook *past* of MISTAKE.

mistral /ˈmɪstrɑːl, mɪˈstrɑːl/ n. a cold northerly wind that blows down the Rhône valley and S. France into the Mediterranean. [F & Prov. f. L (as MAGISTRAL)]

mistranslate /ˌmɪstrænzˈleɪt, ˌmɪstrɑː-, -sˈleɪt/ v.tr. translate incorrectly. □□ **mistranslation** n.

mistreat /mɪsˈtriːt/ v.tr. treat badly. □□ **mistreatment** n.

mistress /ˈmɪstrɪs/ n. **1** a female head of a household. **2 a** a woman in authority over others. **b** the female owner of a pet. **3** a woman with power to control etc. (often foll. by *of*: *mistress of the situation*). **4** *Brit.* **a** a female teacher (*music mistress*). **b** a female head of a college etc. **5 a** a woman (other than his wife) with whom a married man has a (usu. prolonged) sexual relationship. **b** *archaic* or *poet.* a woman loved and courted by a man. **6** *archaic* or *dial.* (as a title) = MRS. □ **Mistress of the Robes** a lady in charge of the Queen's wardrobe. [ME f. OF *maistresse* f. *maistre* MASTER]

mistrial /mɪsˈtraɪəl/ n. **1** a trial rendered invalid through some error in the proceedings. **2** *US* a trial in which the jury cannot agree on a verdict.

mistrust /mɪsˈtrʌst/ v. & n. —v.tr. **1** be suspicious of. **2** feel no confidence in (a person, oneself, one's powers, etc.). —n. **1** suspicion. **2** lack of confidence.

mistrustful /mɪsˈtrʌstfʊl/ adj. **1** (foll. by *of*) suspicious. **2** lacking confidence or trust. □□ **mistrustfully** adv. **mistrustfulness** n.

misty /ˈmɪstɪ/ adj. (**mistier, mistiest**) **1** of or covered with mist. **2** indistinct or dim in outline. **3** obscure, vague (*a misty idea*). □□ **mistily** adv. **mistiness** n. [OE *mistig* (as MIST)]

mistype /mɪsˈtaɪp/ v.tr. type wrongly. [MIS-¹ + TYPE]

misunderstand /ˌmɪsʌndəˈstænd/ v.tr. (*past* and *past part.* **-understood** /-ˈstʊd/) **1** fail to understand correctly. **2** (usu. as **misunderstood** adj.) misinterpret the words or actions of (a person).

misunderstanding /ˌmɪsʌndəˈstændɪŋ/ n. **1** a failure to understand correctly. **2** a slight disagreement or quarrel.

misusage /mɪsˈjuːsɪdʒ/ n. **1** wrong or improper usage. **2** ill-treatment.

misuse v. & n. —v.tr. /mɪsˈjuːz/ **1** use wrongly; apply to the wrong purpose. **2** ill-treat. —n. /mɪsˈjuːs/ wrong or improper use or application. □□ **misuser** n.

MIT abbr. Massachusetts Institute of Technology.

Mitanni /mɪˈtænɪ/ a political and geographic term of unknown derivation, first encountered in Egyptian inscriptions dating to Tuthmosis I (c.1520 BC) in reference to a Late Bronze Age hegemony of north Mesopotamian and Syrian States composed of a predominantly Hurrian-speaking populace and ruled by a succession of Indo-European kings. —n.pl. the people of Mitanni. □□ **Mitannian** adj. & n. [orig. unkn.]

Mitchell¹ /ˈmɪtʃ(ə)l/, Margaret (1900–49), American author of the best-selling novel *Gone with the Wind* (1936), set in Georgia

at the time of the American Civil War. The equally popular film was released in 1939.

Mitchell² /ˈmɪtʃ(ə)l/, Reginald Joseph (1895–1937), English aeronautical engineer who designed many successful aircraft for the Schneider Trophy contest in the 1920s and a range of flying boats and amphibious aircraft. His last design was the Spitfire fighter aircraft much used in the Second World War.

mite¹ /maɪt/ n. any small arachnid of the order Acari, having four pairs of legs when adult. □□ **mity** adj. [OE *mīte* f. Gmc]

mite² /maɪt/ n. & adv. —n. **1** *hist.* a Flemish copper coin of small value. **2** any small monetary unit. **3** a small object or person, esp. a child. **4** a modest contribution; the best one can do (*offered my mite of comfort*). —adv. (usu. prec. by *a*) *colloq.* somewhat (*is a mite shy*). [ME f. MLG, MDu. *mīte* f. Gmc: prob. the same as MITE¹]

miter *US* var. of MITRE.

Mitford /ˈmɪtfəd/, Nancy Freeman (1904–73), English writer, daughter of Lord Redesdale who appears in many of her novels (which include *The Pursuit of Love*, 1945, and *Love in a Cold Climate*, 1949) as the eccentric 'Uncle Matthew'. Her book *Noblesse Oblige* (1956) popularized the terms 'U' and 'Non-U' (see the entries) coined by A. S. C. Ross to categorize speech and behaviour.

Mithras /ˈmɪθræs/ *Pers. Mythol.* a god of light, truth, and the plighted word, whose titles include 'Saviour from Death', 'Victorious', and 'Warrior'. These partly explain his attraction for the Roman world, its army, merchants, and those hoping for immortality, and made his worship the principal rival of Christianity in the first three centuries AD. But how, when, and where the god of Persian Zoroastrianism evolved into the Roman god, slayer of the mystic bull and worshipped with secret rites and initiations in a mystery-cult, is an unsolved problem. □□ **Mithraic** /-ˈθreɪɪk/ adj. **Mithraism** /ˈmɪθreɪˌɪz(ə)m/ n. **Mithraist** n. [L *Mithras* f. Gk *Mithras* f. OPers. *Mithra* f. Skr. *Mitra*]

Mithridates /ˌmɪθrɪˈdeɪtiːz/ king of Pontus 120–63 BC. His expansionist policies led to a war with Rome (88–85 BC), in which he occupied most of Asia Minor and much of Greece, until driven back by the Roman general Sulla. Two further wars followed; he was finally defeated by Lucullus and Pompey, and fled to the Crimea. In cunning, courage, and organizing ability Mithridates was Rome's stoutest oriental antagonist, but he failed in the arts of a strategist and could not keep the loyalty of his subordinates. His portraits show that he copied Alexander in personal appearance.

mithridatize /mɪˈθrɪdəˌtaɪz/ v.tr. (also **-ise**) render proof against a poison by administering gradually increasing doses of it. □□ **mithridatic** /-ˈdætɪk/ adj. **mithridatism** /-dəˌtɪz(ə)m/ n. [f. *mithridate* a supposed universal antidote attributed to MITHRIDATES]

mitigate /ˈmɪtɪˌɡeɪt/ v.tr. make milder or less intense or severe; moderate (*your offer certainly mitigated their hostility*). ¶ Often confused with *militate*. □ **mitigating circumstances** *Law* circumstances permitting greater leniency. □□ **mitigable** adj. **mitigation** /-ˈɡeɪʃ(ə)n/ n. **mitigator** n. **mitigatory** adj. [ME f. L *mitigare mitigat-* f. *mitis* mild]

Mitilíni see MYTILENE.

Mitla /ˈmiːtlə/ an ancient city in central Oaxaca in southern Mexico, probably established as a burial site by the Zapotecs from some centuries before the Christian era until the Mixtec expansion overran it c. AD 1000. Its Nahuatl name means 'place of the dead'.

mitochondrion /ˌmaɪtəˈkɒndrɪən/ n. (pl. **mitochondria** /-drɪə/) *Biol.* an organelle found in most eukaryotic cells, containing enzymes for respiration and energy production. [mod.L f. Gk *mitos* thread + *khondrion* dimin. of *khondros* granule]

mitosis /mɪˈtəʊsɪs, maɪ-/ n. *Biol.* a type of cell division that results in two daughter cells each having the same number and kind of chromosomes as the parent nucleus (cf. MEIOSIS). □□ **mitotic** /-ˈtɒtɪk/ adj. [mod.L f. Gk *mitos* thread]

mitral /ˈmaɪtr(ə)l/ adj. of or like a mitre. □ **mitral valve** a two-cusped valve between the left atrium and the left ventricle of the heart. [mod.L *mitralis* f. L *mitra* girdle]

mitre /ˈmaɪtə(r)/ n. & v. (*US* **miter**) —n. **1** a head-dress forming part of the insignia of a bishop in the Western Church, and worn also by abbots and other ecclesiastics as a mark of exceptional dignity. In its modern form it is a tall cap, deeply cleft at the top, the outline of the front and back having the shape of a pointed arch. **2** the joint of two pieces of wood or other material at an angle of 90°, such that the line of junction bisects this angle. **3** a diagonal join of two pieces of fabric that meet at a corner, made by folding. —*v.* **1** *tr.* bestow the mitre on. **2** *tr.* & *intr.* join with a mitre. □ **mitre-block** (or **board** or **box**) a guide for a saw in cutting mitre-joints. **mitre-wheels** a pair of bevelled cog-wheels with teeth set at 45° and axes at right angles. □□ **mitred** *adj.* [ME f. OF f. L *mitra* f. Gk *mitra* girdle, turban]

mitt /mɪt/ *n.* **1** = MITTEN 1. **2** a glove leaving the fingers and thumb-tip exposed. **3** *sl.* a hand or fist. **4** a baseball glove for catching the ball. [abbr. of MITTEN]

mitten /'mɪt(ə)n/ *n.* **1** a glove with two sections, one for the thumb and the other for all four fingers. **2** *sl.* (in *pl.*) boxing gloves. □□ **mittened** *adj.* [ME f. OF *mitaine* ult. f. L *medietas* half: see MOIETY]

Mitterrand /'miːteˌrã/, François Maurice Marie (1916–), French socialist statesman, President of France 1981– . A leader of the French resistance movement during the Second World War, he served in each of the short-lived governments under the Fourth Republic. Having built a coalition between French parties of the Left he was ultimately successful in being elected to the presidency. Early measures to raise basic wages, increase social benefits, and nationalize key industries were followed by economic crisis and a reversal of some policies.

mittimus /'mɪtɪməs/ *n.* a warrant committing a person to prison. [ME f. L, = we send]

Mitty /'mɪtɪ/, Walter. The hero of a story (by James Thurber) who indulged in extravagant daydreams of his own triumphs.

mitzvah /'mɪtsvɑː/ *n.* (*pl.* **mitzvoth** /-vɒt/) *Judaism* **1** a precept or commandment. **2** a good deed done from religious duty. [Heb. *miṣwāh* commandment]

mix /mɪks/ *v.* & *n.* —*v.* **1** *tr.* combine or put together (two or more substances or things) so that the constituents of each are diffused among those of the other(s). **2** *tr.* prepare (a compound, cocktail, etc.) by combining the ingredients. **3** *tr.* combine an activity etc. with another simultaneously (*mix business and pleasure*). **4** *intr.* **a** join, be mixed, or combine, esp. readily (*oil and water will not mix*). **b** be compatible. **c** be sociable (*must learn to mix*). **5** *intr.* **a** (foll. by *with*) (of a person) be harmonious or sociable with; have regular dealings with. **b** (foll. by *in*) participate in. **6** *tr.* drink different kinds of (alcoholic liquor) in close succession. —*n.* **1 a** the act or an instance of mixing; a mixture. **b** the proportion of materials etc. in a mixture. **2** *colloq.* a group of persons of different types (*social mix*). **3** the ingredients prepared commercially for making a cake etc. or for a process such as making concrete. **4** the merging of film pictures or sound. □ **be mixed up in** (or **with**) be involved in or with (esp. something undesirable). **mix in** be harmonious or sociable. **mix it** *colloq.* start fighting. **mix up 1** mix thoroughly. **2** confuse; mistake the identity of. **mix-up** *n.* a confusion, misunderstanding, or mistake. □□ **mixable** *adj.* [back-form. f. MIXED (taken as past part.)]

mixed /mɪkst/ *adj.* **1** of diverse qualities or elements. **2** containing persons from various backgrounds etc. **3** for or involving persons of both sexes (*a mixed school; mixed bathing*). □ **mixed bag** (or **bunch**) a diverse assortment of things or persons. **mixed blessing** a thing having advantages and disadvantages. **mixed crystal** one formed from more than one substance. **mixed doubles** *Tennis* a doubles game with a man and a woman as partners on each side. **mixed economy** an economic system combining private and State enterprise. **mixed farming** farming of both crops and livestock. **mixed feelings** a mixture of pleasure and dismay about something. **mixed grill** a dish of various grilled meats and vegetables etc. **mixed marriage** a marriage between persons of different races or religions. **mixed metaphor** a combination of inconsistent metaphors (e.g. *this tower of strength will forge ahead*). **mixed number** an integer and a proper fraction. **mixed-up** *colloq.* mentally or emotionally

confused; socially ill-adjusted. □□ **mixedness** /-ɪdnɪs/ *n.* [ME *mixt* f. OF *mixte* f. L *mixtus* past part. of *miscēre* mix]

mixer /'mɪksə(r)/ *n.* **1** a device for mixing foods etc. or for processing other materials. **2** a person who manages socially in a specified way (*a good mixer*). **3** a (usu. soft) drink to be mixed with another. **4** *Broadcasting & Cinematog.* **a** a device for merging input signals to produce a combined output in the form of sound or pictures. **b** a person who operates this. □ **mixer tap** a tap through which mixed hot and cold water is drawn by means of separate controls.

Mixtec /'mɪkstek/ *n.* & *adj.* —*n.* **1** (*pl.* same or **-s**) a member of a people of southern Mexico who were outstanding craftsmen in pottery and metallurgy. In the 15th c. they were conquered by the Aztecs. **2** their language. —*adj.* of the Mixtec or their language. [Sp.]

mixture /'mɪkstʃə(r)/ *n.* **1** the process of mixing or being mixed. **2** the result of mixing; something mixed; a combination. **3** *Chem.* the product of the random distribution of one substance through another without any chemical reaction taking place between the components, as distinct from a chemical compound. **4** ingredients mixed together to produce a substance, esp. a medicine (*cough mixture*). **5** a person regarded as a combination of qualities and attributes. **6** gas or vaporized petrol or oil mixed with air, forming an explosive charge in an internal-combustion engine. □ **the mixture as before** the same treatment repeated. [ME f. F *mixture* or L *mixtura* (as MIXED)]

mizen /'mɪz(ə)n/ *n.* (also **mizzen**) *Naut.* (in full **mizen-sail**) the lowest fore-and-aft sail of a fully rigged ship's mizen-mast. □ **mizen-mast** the mast next aft of the mainmast. **mizen yard** that on which the mizen is extended. [ME f. F *misaine* f. It. *mezzana* mizen-sail, fem. of *mezzano* middle: see MEZZANINE]

Mizoram /mɪ'zɔːrəm/ a State of NE India; pop. (1981) 487,800; capital, Aizawl. Separated from Assam in 1972, it was administered as a Union Territory of India until 1986 when it achieved Statehood.

mizzle¹ /'mɪz(ə)l/ *n.* & *v.intr.* drizzle. □□ **mizzly** *adj.* [ME, prob. f. LG *miseln*: cf. MDu. *miezelen*]

mizzle² /'mɪz(ə)l/ *v.intr. Brit. sl.* run away; decamp. [18th c.: orig. unkn.]

Mk. *abbr.* **1** the German mark. **2** Mark (esp. in the New Testament).

mks *abbr.* metre-kilogram-second.

Mkt. *abbr.* Market.

ml *abbr.* **1** millilitre(s). **2** mile(s).

MLA *abbr.* **1** Member of the Legislative Assembly. **2** Modern Language Association (of America).

MLC *abbr.* Member of the Legislative Council.

MLD *abbr.* minimum lethal dose.

MLF *abbr.* multilateral nuclear force.

M.Litt. *abbr.* Master of Letters. [L *Magister Litterarum*]

Mlle *abbr.* (*pl.* **Mlles**) *Mademoiselle.*

MLR *abbr.* minimum lending rate.

MM *abbr.* **1** *Messieurs.* **2** (in the UK) Military Medal. **3** Maelzel's metronome.

mm *abbr.* millimetre(s).

Mmabatho /məˈbɑːtəʊ/ the capital of Bophuthatswana in South Africa; pop. 28,000.

Mme *abbr.* (*pl.* **Mmes**) *Madame.*

m.m.f. *abbr.* magnetomotive force.

M.Mus. *abbr.* Master of Music.

MN *abbr.* **1** *Brit.* Merchant Navy. **2** *US* Minnesota (in official postal use).

Mn *symb. Chem.* the element manganese.

M'Naghten rules var. of MCNAUGHTEN RULES (see at MACN-).

mnemonic /nɪ'mɒnɪk/ *adj.* & *n.* —*adj.* of or designed to aid the memory. —*n.* a mnemonic device. □□ **mnemonically** *adv.* **mnemonist** /'niːmənɪst/ *n.* [med.L *mnemonicus* f. Gk *mnēmonikos* f. *mnēmōn* mindful]

mnemonics /nɪ'mɒnɪks/ *n.pl.* (usu. treated as *sing.*) **1** the art of improving memory. **2** a system for this.

Mnemosyne /niːˈmɒzɪnɪ/ Gk Mythol. the mother of the Muses. [Gk mnēmosunē memory]

MO abbr. **1** Medical Officer. **2** money order. **3** US Missouri (in official postal use).

Mo symb. Chem. the element molybdenum.

Mo. abbr. Missouri.

mo /məʊ/ n. (pl. **mos**) colloq. a moment (wait a mo). [abbr.]

mo. abbr. US month.

moa /ˈməʊə/ n. (pl. **moas**) any extinct flightless New Zealand bird of the family Dinornithidae, resembling the ostrich. [Maori]

Moabite /ˈməʊəˌbaɪt/ adj. & n. —adj. of Moab, an ancient region by the Dead Sea, or its people. —n. a member of a Semitic people traditionally descended from Lot, living in Moab. □ **Moabite Stone** a monument erected by Mesha, king of Moab, c.850 BC which describes (in an early form of the Hebrew language) the campaign between Moab and Israel (2 Kings 3), and furnishes an early example of an inscription in the Phoenician alphabet. It is now in the Louvre.

moan /məʊn/ n. & v. —n. **1** a long murmur expressing physical or mental suffering. **2** a low plaintive sound of wind etc. **3** a complaint; a grievance. —v. **1** intr. make a moan or moans. **2** intr. colloq. complain or grumble. **3** tr. **a** utter with moans. **b** lament. □□ **moaner** n. **moanful** adj. **moaningly** adv. [ME f. OE mān (unrecorded) f. Gmc]

moat /məʊt/ n. & v. —n. a deep defensive ditch round a castle, town, etc., usu. filled with water. —v.tr. surround with or as with a moat. [ME mot(e) f. OF mote, motte mound]

mob /mɒb/ n. & v. —n. **1** a disorderly crowd; a rabble. **2** (prec. by the) usu. derog. the populace. **3** colloq. a gang; an associated group of persons. **4** Austral. a flock or herd. —v.tr. & intr. (**mobbed, mobbing**) **1** tr. **a** crowd round in order to attack or admire. **b** (of a mob) attack. **c** US crowd into (a building). **2** intr. assemble in a mob. □ **mob law** (or **rule**) law or rule imposed and enforced by a mob. □□ **mobber** n. & adj. [abbr. of mobile, short for L mobile vulgus excitable crowd: see MOBILE]

mob-cap /ˈmɒbkæp/ n. hist. a woman's large indoor cap covering all the hair, worn in the 18th and early 19th c. [obs. (18th-c.) mob, orig. = slut + CAP]

mobile /ˈməʊbaɪl/ adj. & n. —adj. **1** movable; not fixed; free or able to move or flow easily. **2** (of the face etc.) readily changing its expression. **3** (of a shop, library, etc.) accommodated in a vehicle so as to serve various places. **4** (of a person) able to change his or her social status. —n. a decorative structure that may be hung so as to turn freely. □ **mobile home** a large caravan permanently parked and used as a residence. **mobile sculpture** a sculpture having moving parts. □□ **mobility** /məˈbɪlɪtɪ/ n. [ME f. F f. L mobilis f. movēre move]

mobilize /ˈməʊbɪˌlaɪz/ v. (also **-ise**) **1** tr. organize for service or action (esp. troops in time of war). **b** intr. be organized in this way. **2** tr. render movable; bring into circulation. □□ **mobilizable** adj. **mobilization** /-ˈzeɪʃ(ə)n/ n. **mobilizer** n. [F mobiliser (as MOBILE)]

Möbius strip /ˈmɜːbɪəs/ n. Math. a one-sided surface formed by joining the ends of a rectangle after twisting one end through 180°. [A. F. Möbius, Ger. mathematician d. 1868]

mobocracy /mɒˈbɒkrəsɪ/ n. (pl. **-ies**) colloq. **1** rule by a mob. **2** a ruling mob.

mobster /ˈmɒbstə(r)/ n. sl. a gangster.

Mobutu Sese Seko /məˈbuːtuː ˌseɪsɪ ˈseɪkəʊ/ (original name Joseph-Désiré Mobutu, 1930–), African statesman, President of Zaïre from 1965, after seizing power in a military coup. He has remained in power though his regime has persistently been shaken by violent opposition, including rebel invasions from neighbouring Angola in 1977–8. □ **Lake Mobutu Sese Seko** see Lake ALBERT.

moccasin /ˈmɒkəsɪn/ n. **1** a type of soft leather slipper or shoe with combined sole and heel, as orig. worn by N. American Indians. **2** (in full **water moccasin**) US a poisonous American snake of the genus Agkistrodon piscivorus. [Amer. Ind. mockasin, makisin]

mocha /ˈmɒkə/ n. **1** a coffee of fine quality. **2** a beverage or flavouring made with this, often with chocolate added. **3** a soft kind of sheepskin. [Mocha, a port on the Red Sea, from where the coffee first came]

Mochica /məˈtʃiːkə/ n. (pl. same) **1** a member of a pre-Inca people living on the coast of Peru AD 100–800, with a highly developed agricultural system, depending on artificial irrigation, and no cities but concentrated ceremonial complexes where the ruling dynasty and administrators lived. **2** their language. [Sp., f. an Indian word; cf. Moche, site and valley on NW coast of Peru]

mock /mɒk/ v., adj., & n. —v. **1 a** tr. ridicule; scoff at. **b** intr. (foll. by at) act with scorn or contempt for. **2** tr. mimic contemptuously. **3** tr. jeer, defy, or delude contemptuously. —attrib.adj. sham, imitation (esp. without intention to deceive); pretended (a mock battle; mock cream). —n. **1** a thing deserving scorn. **2** (in pl.) colloq. mock examinations. □ **make mock** (or **a mock**) **of** ridicule. **mock-heroic** adj. (of a literary style) burlesquing a heroic style. —n. such a style. **mock moon** paraselene. **mock orange** a white-flowered heavy-scented shrub, Philadelphus coronarius. **mock sun** parhelion. **mock turtle soup** soup made from a calf's head etc. to resemble turtle soup. **mock-up** an experimental model or replica of a proposed structure etc. □□ **mockable** adj. **mockingly** adv. [ME mokke, mocque f. OF mo(c)quer deride f. Rmc]

mocker /ˈmɒkə(r)/ n. a person who mocks. □ **put the mockers on** sl. **1** bring bad luck to. **2** put a stop to.

mockery /ˈmɒkərɪ/ n. (pl. **-ies**) **1 a** derision, ridicule. **b** a subject or occasion of this. **2** (often foll. by of) a counterfeit or absurdly inadequate representation. **3** a ludicrously or insultingly futile action etc. [ME f. OF moquerie (as MOCK)]

mockingbird /ˈmɒkɪŋˌbɜːd/ n. a bird that mimics the notes of other birds, esp. the American songbird Mimus polyglottos.

MOD abbr. (in the UK) Ministry of Defence.

mod[1] /mɒd/ adj. & n. colloq. —adj. modern, esp. in style of dress. —n. Brit. a young person (esp. in the 1960s) of a group aiming at sophistication and smart modern dress. □ **mod cons** modern conveniences. [abbr.]

mod[2] /mɒd/ prep. Math. = MODULO. [abbr.]

mod[3] /mɒd/ n. a Highland Gaelic meeting for music and poetry. [Gael. mōd]

modal /ˈməʊd(ə)l/ adj. **1** of or relating to mode or form as opposed to substance. **2** Gram. **a** of or denoting the mood of a verb. **b** (of an auxiliary verb, e.g. would) used to express the mood of another verb. **c** (of a particle) denoting manner. **3** Statistics of or relating to a mode; occurring most frequently in a sample or population. **4** Mus. denoting a style of music using a particular mode. **5** Logic (of a proposition) in which the predicate is affirmed of the subject with some qualification, or which involves the affirmation of possibility, impossibility, necessity, or contingency. □□ **modally** adv. [med.L modalis f. L (as MODE)]

modality /məˈdælɪtɪ/ n. (pl. **-ies**) **1** the state of being modal. **2** (in sing. or pl.) a prescribed method of procedure. [med.L modalitas (as MODAL)]

mode /məʊd/ n. **1** a way or manner in which a thing is done; a method of procedure. **2** a prevailing fashion or custom. **3** Computing a way of operating or using a system (print mode). **4** Statistics the value that occurs most frequently in a given set of data. **5** Mus. **a** each of the scale systems that result when the white notes of the piano are played consecutively over an octave (Lydian mode). **b** each of the two main modern scale systems, the major and minor (minor mode). **6** Logic **a** the character of a modal proposition. **b** = MOOD[2]. **7** Physics any of the distinct kinds or patterns of vibration of an oscillating system. **8** US Gram. = MOOD[2]. [F mode and L modus measure]

model /ˈmɒd(ə)l/ n. & v. —n. **1** a representation in three dimensions of an existing person or thing or of a proposed structure, esp. on a smaller scale (often attrib.: a model train). **2** a simplified (often mathematical) description of a system etc., to assist calculations and predictions. **3** a figure in clay, wax, etc., to be reproduced in another material. **4** a particular design or style of a structure or commodity, esp. of a car. **5 a** an exemplary person or thing (*a model of self-discipline*). **b** (*attrib.*) ideal, exemplary (*a model student*). **6** a person employed to pose for an artist or photographer or to display clothes etc. by wearing them. **7** a garment etc. by a well-known designer, or a copy of this. —*v.* (**modelled, modelling**; *US* **modeled, modeling**) **1** *tr.* **a** fashion or shape (a figure) in clay, wax, etc. **b** (foll. by *after, on*, etc.) form (a thing in imitation of). **2 a** *intr.* act or pose as a model. **b** *tr.* (of a person acting as a model) display (a garment). **3** *tr.* devise a (usu. mathematical) model of (a phenomenon, system, etc.). **4** *tr. Painting* cause to appear three-dimensional. □ **the (New) Model** the plan for the reorganization of the Parliamentary army, passed by the House of Commons in 1644–5. **Model Parliament** that of Nov. 1295, summoned by Edward I to obtain financial aid for his wars and so called in the 19th c. because it was more representative than any previous parliament—but the pattern did not survive. □□ **modeller** *n.* [F *modelle* f. It. *modello* ult. f. L *modulus*: see MODULUS]

modem /ˈməʊdem/ *n.* a combined device for modulation and demodulation, e.g. between a computer and a telephone line. [*modulator* + *demodulator*]

moderate *adj., n.,* & *v.* —*adj.* /ˈmɒdərət/ **1** avoiding extremes; temperate in conduct or expression. **2** fairly or tolerably large or good. **3** (of the wind) of medium strength. **4** (of prices) fairly low. —*n.* /ˈmɒdərət/ a person who holds moderate views, esp. in politics. —*v.* /ˈmɒdəˌreɪt/ **1** *tr.* & *intr.* make or become less violent, intense, rigorous, etc. **2** *tr.* (also *absol.*) act as a moderator of or to. **3** *tr. Physics* retard (neutrons) with a moderator. □□ **moderately** /-rətlɪ/ *adv.* **moderateness** /-rətnəs/ *n.* **moderatism** /ˈmɒdərəˌtɪz(ə)m/ *n.* [ME f. L *moderatus* past part. of *moderare* reduce, control: rel. to MODEST]

moderation /ˌmɒdəˈreɪʃ(ə)n/ *n.* **1** the process or an instance of moderating. **2** the quality of being moderate. **3** *Physics* the retardation of neutrons by a moderator (see MODERATOR 5). **4** (in *pl.*) (**Moderations**) the first public examination in some faculties for the Oxford BA degree. □ **in moderation** in a moderate manner or degree. [ME f. OF f. L *moderatio -onis* (as MODERATE)]

moderato /ˌmɒdəˈrɑːtəʊ/ *adj., adv.,* & *n. Mus.* —*adj.* & *adv.* performed at a moderate pace. —*n.* (*pl.* -**os**) a piece of music to be performed in this way. [It. (as MODERATE)]

moderator /ˈmɒdəˌreɪtə(r)/ *n.* **1** an arbitrator or mediator. **2** a presiding officer. **3** *Eccl.* a Presbyterian minister presiding over an ecclesiastical body. **4** an examiner for Moderations. **5** *Physics* a substance used in a nuclear reactor to retard neutrons. □□ **moderatorship** *n.* [ME f. L (as MODERATE)]

modern /ˈmɒd(ə)n/ *adj.* & *n.* —*adj.* **1** of the present and recent times. **2** in current fashion; not antiquated. —*n.* (usu. in *pl.*) a person living in modern times. □ **modern dance** see BALLET. **modern English** English from about 1500 onwards. (See ENGLISH.) **modern history** history from the end of the Middle Ages to the present day. □□ **modernity** /-ˈdɜːnɪtɪ/ *n.* **modernly** *adv.* **modernness** *n.* [F *moderne* or LL *modernus* f. L *modo* just now]

modernism /ˈmɒdəˌnɪz(ə)m/ *n.* **1 a** modern ideas or methods. **b** the tendency of religious belief to harmonize with modern ideas, esp. a movement in the Roman Catholic Church in the late 19th c., officially condemned by Pope Pius X in 1907. **2** a modern term or expression. □□ **modernist** *n.* **modernistic** /-ˈnɪstɪk/ *adj.* **modernistically** /-ˈnɪstɪkəlɪ/ *adv.*

modernize /ˈmɒdəˌnaɪz/ *v.* (also -**ise**) **1** *tr.* make modern; adapt to modern needs or habits. **2** *intr.* adopt modern ways or views. □□ **modernization** /-ˈzeɪʃ(ə)n/ *n.* **modernizer** *n.*

modest /ˈmɒdɪst/ *adj.* **1** having or expressing a humble or moderate estimate of one's own merits or achievements. **2** diffident, bashful, retiring. **3** decorous in manner and conduct. **4** moderate or restrained in amount, extent, severity, etc.; not excessive or exaggerated (*a modest sum*). **5** (of a thing) unpretentious in appearance etc. □□ **modestly** *adv.* [F *modeste* f. L *modestus* keeping due measure]

modesty /ˈmɒdɪstɪ/ *n.* the quality of being modest.

modicum /ˈmɒdɪkəm/ *n.* (foll. by *of*) a small quantity. [L, = short distance or time, neut. of *modicus* moderate f. *modus* measure]

modification /ˌmɒdɪfɪˈkeɪʃ(ə)n/ *n.* **1** the act or an instance of modifying or being modified. **2** a change made. [F or f. L *modificatio* (as MODIFY)]

modifier /ˈmɒdɪˌfaɪə(r)/ *n.* **1** a person or thing that modifies. **2** *Gram.* a word, esp. an adjective or noun used attributively, that qualifies the sense of another word (e.g. *good* and *family* in *a good family house*).

modify /ˈmɒdɪˌfaɪ/ *v.tr.* (-**ies**, -**ied**) **1** make less severe or extreme; tone down (*modify one's demands*). **2** make partial changes in; make different. **3** *Gram.* qualify or expand the sense of (a word etc.). **4** *Phonet.* change (a vowel) by umlaut. **5** *Chem.* change or replace all the substituent radicals of a polymer, thereby changing its physical properties such as solubility etc. (*modified starch*). □□ **modifiable** *adj.* **modificatory** /-fɪˌkeɪtərɪ/ *adj.* [ME f. OF *modifier* f. L *modificare* (as MODE)]

Modigliani /ˌmɒdɪlˈjɑːnɪ/, Amedeo (1884–1920), Italian painter and sculptor who settled in Paris in 1906. He worked chiefly as a painter of female nudes, in which a somewhat mannered stylization of form was coupled with strong linear qualities and a knowing use of colour, often compared with the style of Botticelli. His friendship with the sculptor Brancusi (d. 1957) saw the production of some assured sculpture reliant on tribal art for its directness and visual power.

modillion /məˈdɪljən/ *n. Archit.* a projecting bracket under the corona of a cornice in the Corinthian and other orders. [F *modillon* f. It. *modiglione* ult. f. L *mutulus* mutule]

modish /ˈməʊdɪʃ/ *adj.* fashionable. □□ **modishly** *adv.* **modishness** *n.*

modiste /mɒˈdiːst/ *n.* a milliner; a dressmaker. [F (as MODE)]

Mods /mɒdz/ *n.pl. colloq.* Moderations (see MODERATION 4). [abbr.]

modular /ˈmɒdjʊlə(r)/ *adj.* of or consisting of modules or moduli. □□ **modularity** /-ˈlærɪtɪ/ *n.* [mod.L *modularis* f. L *modulus*: see MODULUS]

modulate /ˈmɒdjʊˌleɪt/ *v.* **1** *tr.* **a** regulate or adjust. **b** moderate. **2** *tr.* adjust or vary the tone or pitch of (the speaking voice). **3** *tr.* alter the amplitude or frequency of (a wave) by a wave of a lower frequency to convey a signal. **4** *intr.* & *tr. Mus.* (often foll. by *from, to*) change or cause to change from one key to another. □□ **modulation** /-ˈleɪʃ(ə)n/ *n.* **modulator** *n.* [L *modulari modulat-* to measure f. *modus* measure]

module /ˈmɒdjuːl/ *n.* **1** a standardized part or independent unit used in construction, esp. of furniture, a building, or an electronic system. **2** an independent self-contained unit of a spacecraft (*lunar module*). **3** a unit or period of training or education. **4 a** a standard or unit of measurement. **b** *Archit.* a unit of length for expressing proportions, e.g. the semidiameter of a column at the base. [F *module* or L *modulus*: see MODULUS]

modulo /ˈmɒdjʊˌləʊ/ *prep.* & *adj. Math.* using, or with respect to, a modulus (see MODULUS 2). [L, ablat. of MODULUS]

modulus /ˈmɒdjʊləs/ *n.* (*pl.* **moduli** /-ˌlaɪ/) *Math.* **1 a** the magnitude of a real number without regard to its sign. **b** the positive square root of the sum of the squares of the real and imaginary parts of a complex number. **2** a constant factor or ratio. **3** (in number theory) a number used as a divisor for considering numbers in sets giving the same remainder when divided by it. **4** a constant indicating the relation between a physical effect and the force producing it. [L, = measure, dimin. of *modus*]

modus operandi /ˌməʊdəs ˌɒpəˈrændiː/ *n.* (*pl.* **modi operandi** /ˌməʊdiː/) **1** the particular way in which a person performs a task or action. **2** the way a thing operates. [L, = way of operating: see MODE]

modus vivendi /ˌməʊdəs vɪˈvendiː/ *n.* (*pl.* **modi vivendi** /ˌməʊdiː/) **1** a way of living or coping. **2 a** an arrangement whereby those in dispute can carry on pending a settlement. **b** an arrangement between people who agree to differ. [L, = way of living: see MODE]

Moeskroen see MOUSCRON.

mofette /məˈfet/ *n.* **1** a fumerole. **2** an exhalation of vapour from this. [F *mofette* or Neapolitan It. *mofetta*]

mog /mɒg/ *n.* (also **moggie** /ˈmɒgɪ/) *Brit. sl.* a cat. [20th c.: of dial. orig.]

Mogadishu /ˌmɒgəˈdiʃu:/ the capital of Somalia; pop. (est. 1988) 1,000,000.

Mogadon /ˈmɒgəˌdɒn/ n. propr. a hypnotic drug used to treat insomnia.

mogul /ˈməʊg(ə)l/ n. **1** colloq. an important or influential person. **2 (Mogul)** hist. **a** = MUGHAL. **b** (often **the Great Mogul**) any of the emperors of Delhi in the 16th–19th c. [Pers. muḡul: see MUGHAL]

MOH abbr. Medical Officer of Health.

Mohács /məʊˈhɑːtʃ/ a river port and town on the Danube in southern Hungary; pop. (est. 1984) 21,000. It was the site of a battle in 1526, when the Hungarians were defeated by a Turkish force under Suleiman I, and Hungary became part of the Ottoman empire; in 1687 a battle was fought nearby during the campaign that swept the Turks out of Hungary.

mohair /ˈməʊheə(r)/ n. **1** the hair of the angora goat. **2** a yarn or fabric from this, either pure or mixed with wool or cotton. [ult. f. Arab. muḵayyar, lit. choice, select]

Mohammed var. of MUHAMMAD.

Mohawk /ˈməʊhɔːk/ n. **1 a** a member of a tribe of North American Indians. (See IROQUOIS.) **b** the language of this tribe. **2** Skating a step from either edge of the skate to the same edge on the other foot in the opposite direction. [native name]

Mohenjo-Daro /məˌhendʒəʊˈdɑːrəʊ/ an ancient city of the Indus Valley civilization (see entry), in SE Pakistan.

Mohican /məʊˈhiːkən/ n. & adj. —n. a member of a warlike tribe of North American Indians, of Algonquian stock, formerly occupying the western parts of Connecticut and Massachusetts. —adj. **1** of or relating to this people. **2** (of a hairstyle) resembling that of the Mohicans, with the head shaved except for a strip of hair from the middle of the forehead to the back of the neck, often worn in long spikes. [native name]

moho /ˈməʊhəʊ/ n. (pl. **-os**) Geol. (in full **Mohorovičić discontinuity** /ˌməʊhəˈrəʊvɪˌtʃɪtʃ/) the boundary surface between the earth's crust and its mantle, where there is a change in the seismological properties of the rocks. It is believed to exist at a depth of about 10–12 km under the ocean beds and 40–50 km under the continents. [A. Mohorovičić, Yugoslav seismologist d. 1936]

Moholy-Nagy /ˌməʊhɔɪˈnɒdʒ/, Láslò (1895–1946), Hungarian-born painter, sculptor, experimental artist, and writer. He was an inventive artist in the constructivist school, pioneering in the artistic uses of light, movement, photography, film, and plastic materials. From 1923 to 1929 he taught at the Bauhaus with Gropius, and was an influential teacher both there and in the US, where he lived from 1937.

Mohs /məʊz/, Friedrich (1773–1839), German mineralogist who developed a classification of minerals based on physical appearance rather than on chemical properties, but is now chiefly remembered for his classification of the hardness of minerals (Mohs' scale) described in 1812, and consisting of ten reference minerals of increasing hardness, from talc (hardness 1) to diamond (hardness 10). The reference minerals are talc 1, gypsum 2, calcite 3, fluorspar 4, apatite 5, orthoclase 6, quartz 7, topaz 8, corundum 9, diamond 10. Each can scratch the softer minerals, and be scratched only by the harder minerals, within this scale.

moidore /ˈmɔɪdɔː(r)/ n. hist. a Portuguese gold coin, current in England in the 18th c. [Port. moeda d'ouro money of gold]

moiety /ˈmɔɪətɪ/ n. (pl. **-ies**) Law or literary **1** a half. **2** each of the two parts into which a thing is divided. [ME f. OF moité, moitié f. L medietas -tatis middle f. medius (adj.) middle]

moil /mɔɪl/ v. & n. archaic —v.intr. drudge (esp. toil and moil). —n. drudgery. [ME f. OF moillier moisten, paddle in mud, ult. f. L mollis soft]

moire /mwɑː(r)/ n. (in full **moire antique**) watered fabric, orig. mohair, now usu. silk. [F (earlier mouaire) f. MOHAIR]

moiré /ˈmwɑːreɪ/ adj. & n. —adj. **1** (of silk) watered. **2** (of metal) having a patterned appearance like watered silk. —n. **1** this patterned appearance. **2** = MOIRE. [F, past part. of moirer (as MOIRE)]

Moissan /ˈmwɑːsɑ̃/, Ferdinand Frédéric Henri (1852–1907), French chemist and influential teacher of inorganic chemistry, who in 1886 succeeded in isolating the very reactive element fluorine, and who invented in 1892 an electric arc furnace that bears his name, in which he claimed to have synthesized diamonds. This is now in doubt, but the very high temperatures achieved in his furnace made it possible to reduce some uncommon metals from their ores. He was awarded the Nobel Prize for chemistry in 1906.

moist /mɔɪst/ adj. **1 a** slightly wet; damp. **b** (of the season etc.) rainy. **2** (of a disease) marked by a discharge of matter etc. □□ **moistly** adv. **moistness** n. [ME f. OF moiste, ult. from or rel. to L mucidus (see MUCUS) and musteus fresh (see MUST²)]

moisten /ˈmɔɪs(ə)n/ v.tr. & intr. make or become moist.

moisture /ˈmɔɪstʃə(r)/ n. water or other liquid diffused in a small quantity as vapour, or within a solid, or condensed on a surface. □□ **moistureless** adj. [ME f. OF moistour (as MOIST)]

moisturize /ˈmɔɪstʃəˌraɪz/ v.tr. (also **-ise**) make less dry (esp. the skin by use of a cosmetic). □□ **moisturizer** n.

Mojave Desert /məʊˈhɑːvɪ/ a desert in southern California.

moke /məʊk/ n. sl. **1** Brit. a donkey. **2** Austral. a very poor horse. [19th c.: orig. unkn.]

moksa /ˈmɒksə/ n. Hinduism & Jainism. **1** release from the chain of births impelled by the law of karma. **2** the bliss attained by this liberation (cf. NIRVANA). [Skr. mokṣa]

mol /məʊl/ abbr. = MOLE⁴.

molal /ˈməʊl(ə)l/ adj. Chem. (of a solution) containing one mole of solute per kilogram of solvent. □□ **molality** /məˈlælɪtɪ/ n. [MOLE⁴ + -AL]

molar¹ /ˈməʊlə(r)/ adj. & n. —adj. (usu. of a mammal's back teeth) serving to grind. —n. a molar tooth. [L molaris f. mola millstone]

molar² /ˈməʊlə(r)/ adj. **1** of or relating to mass. **2** acting on or by means of large masses or units. [L moles mass]

molar³ /ˈməʊlə(r)/ adj. Chem. **1** of a mass of substance usu. per mole (molar latent heat). **2** (of a solution) containing one mole of solute per litre of solvent. □□ **molarity** /məˈlærɪtɪ/ n. [MOLE⁴ + -AR¹]

molasses /məˈlæsɪz/ n.pl. (treated as sing.) **1** uncrystallized syrup extracted from raw sugar during refining. **2** US treacle. [Port. melaço f. LL mellaceum MUST² f. mel honey]

mold US var. of MOULD¹, MOULD², MOULD³.

Moldavia /mɒlˈdeɪvɪə/ **1** a former Danubian principality from which, together with Wallachia, the kingdom of Romania was formed in 1859. **2** the Moldavian republic, a constituent republic of the USSR, formed from territory ceded by Romania in 1940; pop. (est. 1987) 4,185,000; capital, Kishinev. □□ **Moldavian** adj. & n.

molder US var. of MOULDER.

molding US var. of MOULDING.

moldy US var. of MOULDY.

mole¹ /məʊl/ n. **1** any small burrowing insect-eating mammal of the family Talpidae, esp. Talpa europaea, with dark velvety fur and very small eyes. **2** colloq. **a** a spy established deep within an organization and usu. dormant for a long period while attaining a position of trust. **b** a betrayer of confidential information. [ME molle, prob. f. MDu. moll(e), mol, MLG mol, mul]

mole² /məʊl/ n. a small often slightly raised dark blemish on the skin caused by a high concentration of melanin. [OE māl f. Gmc]

mole³ /məʊl/ n. **1** a massive structure serving as a pier, breakwater, or causeway. **2** an artificial harbour. [F môle f. L moles mass]

mole⁴ /məʊl/ n. Chem. the SI unit of amount of substance equal to the quantity containing as many elementary units as there are atoms in 0.012 kg of carbon-12. The elementary entities must be specified and may be atoms, molecules, ions, electrons, other particles, or specified groups of such particles. The unit was established in 1971 for international use. [G Mol f. Molekül MOLECULE]

mole⁵ /məʊl/ n. Med. an abnormal mass of tissue in the uterus. [F môle f. L mola millstone]

molecular /məˈlekjʊlə(r)/ adj. of, relating to, or consisting of molecules. □ **molecular biology** the study of the structure and function of large molecules associated with living organisms. **molecular sieve** a crystalline substance with pores of molecular dimensions which permit the entry of certain molecules but are impervious to others. **molecular weight** = relative molecular mass. □□ **molecularity** /-ˈlærɪtɪ/ n. **molecularly** adv.

molecule /ˈmɒlɪˌkjuːl/ n. 1 Chem. the smallest fundamental unit (usu. a group of atoms) of a chemical compound that can take part in a chemical reaction. 2 (in general use) a small particle. [F molécule f. mod.L molecula dimin. of L moles mass]

molehill /ˈməʊlhɪl/ n. a small mound thrown up by a mole in burrowing. □ **make a mountain out of a molehill** exaggerate the importance of a minor difficulty.

moleskin /ˈməʊlskɪn/ n. 1 the skin of a mole used as fur. 2 a a kind of cotton fustian with its surface shaved before dyeing. b (in pl.) clothes, esp. trousers, made of this.

molest /məˈlest/ v.tr. 1 annoy or pester (a person) in a hostile or injurious way. 2 attack or interfere with (a person), esp. sexually. □□ **molestation** /ˌmɒleˈsteɪʃ(ə)n, ˌməʊl-/ n. **molester** n. [OF molester or L molestare annoy f. molestus troublesome]

Molière /ˈmɒlieə(r)/ the name assumed by Jean-Baptiste Poquelin (1622–73), French comic dramatist. He began his career as groom-upholsterer to the king, but soon turned to the stage, became an actor, and founded a dramatic company for which he composed comedies and farces. His real genius is first shown in Les Précieuses ridicules (1659), in which, abandoning imitations of Plautus and Terence, he introduced the ridicule of actual French society, with its various types of folly, oddity, pedantry, or vice, as the subject of French comedy. Among his most famous plays, showing a profound understanding of the incongruities of human nature, are Le Tartuffe (1664), Don Juan (1665), Le Misanthrope (1666), L'Avare (1669), Le Bourgeois Gentilhomme (1670), and Le Malade imaginaire (1673). He was the creator of French classical comedy, with a genius for reconciling the comic and the intellectual.

moline /məˈlaɪn/ adj. Heraldry (of a cross) having each extremity broadened and curved back. [prob. f. AF moliné f. molin MILL¹, because of the resemblance to the iron support of a millstone]

Molise /mɒˈliːzɪ/ a region of eastern Italy, on the Adriatic coast; pop. (1981) 328,400; capital, Campobasso.

moll /mɒl/ n. sl. 1 a gangster's female companion. 2 a prostitute. [pet-form of the name Mary]

mollify /ˈmɒlɪˌfaɪ/ v.tr. (-ies, -ied) 1 appease, pacify. 2 reduce the severity of; soften. □□ **mollification** /-fɪˈkeɪʃ(ə)n/ n. **mollifier** n. [ME f. F mollifier or L mollificare f. mollis soft]

mollusc /ˈmɒləsk/ n. (US **mollusk**) any invertebrate of the phylum Mollusca, with a soft body and usu. a hard shell, including limpets, snails, cuttlefish, oysters, mussels, etc. □□ **molluscan** /məˈlʌskən/ adj. **molluscoid** /məˈlʌskɔɪd/ adj. **molluscous** /məˈlʌskəs/ adj. [mod.L mollusca neut. pl. of L molluscus f. mollis soft]

mollycoddle /ˈmɒlɪˌkɒd(ə)l/ v. & n. —v.tr. coddle, pamper. —n. an effeminate man or boy; a milksop. [formed as MOLL + CODDLE]

mollymawk /ˈmɒlɪmɔːk/ n. (also **mallemuck** /ˈmælɪˌmʌk/) any of various small kinds of albatross or similar birds. [Du. mallemok f. mal foolish + mok gull]

Moloch /ˈməʊlɒk/ n. 1 a a Canaanite god to whose image children were sacrificed as burnt offerings (Lev. 18: 21, 2 kings 23:10). b a tyrannical object of sacrifices. 2 (**moloch**) the spiny slow-moving grotesque Australian reptile, Moloch horridus. [LL f. Gk Molokh f. Heb. mōlek]

Molotov /ˈmɒlətɒf/, Vyacheslav Mikhailovich (1890–1986), Soviet statesman, an early member of the Bolsheviks and one of the most important members of the Stalinist party. Prime Minister from 1930 to 1941, he took over responsibility for foreign affairs in 1939, negotiating the Nazi–Soviet Pact and remaining Foreign Secretary throughout the Second World War. He returned to the Foreign Ministry in 1953 after Stalin's death but quarrelled with Khruschev and was expelled from his party posts in 1956. □ **Molotov cocktail** a homemade incendiary device for throwing, usu. consisting of a bottle or other breakable container holding inflammable liquid and with a means of ignition.

molt US var. of MOULT.

molten /ˈməʊlt(ə)n/ adj. melted, esp. made liquid by heat. [past part. of MELT]

molto /ˈmɒltəʊ/ adv. Mus. very (molto sostenuto; allegro molto). [It. f. L multus much]

Molucca Islands /məˈlʌkə/ (also **Moluccas** or **Maluku** /məˈluːkuː/) a group of islands of Indonesia, SE of the Philippines, formerly called the Spice Islands; pop. (1980) 1,411,000; capital, Amboina.

moly /ˈməʊlɪ/ n. (pl. -ies) 1 an alliaceous plant, Allium moly, with small yellow flowers. 2 a mythical herb with white flowers and black roots, endowed with magic properties. [L f. Gk mōlu]

molybdenite /məˈlɪbdɪˌnaɪt/ n. molybdenum disulphide as an ore.

molybdenum /məˈlɪbdɪnəm/ n. Chem. a silver-white brittle metallic transition element occurring naturally in molybdenite, first isolated in 1782. The pure metal is used where resistance to very high temperatures is required, but its main use is as a component in special steels and other alloys, where it imparts strength at high temperatures and resistance to corrosion. ¶ Symb.: **Mo**; atomic number 42. [mod.L, earlier molybdena, orig. = molybdenite, lead ore: L molybdaena f. Gk molubdaina plummet f. molubdos lead]

mom /mɒm/ n. US colloq. mother. [abbr. of MOMMA]

Mombasa /mɒmˈbæsə/ a seaport and industrial city of SE Kenya, on the Indian Ocean; pop. 341,100.

moment /ˈməʊmənt/ n. 1 a very brief portion of time; an instant. 2 a short period of time (wait a moment) (see also MINUTE¹). 3 an exact or particular point of time (at last the moment arrived; I came the moment you called). 4 importance (of no great moment). 5 Physics & Mech. etc. a the turning effect produced by a force acting at a distance on an object. b this effect expressed as the product of the force and the distance from its line of action to a point. □ **at the moment** at this time; now. **in a moment** 1 very soon. 2 instantly. **man** (or **woman** etc.) **of the moment** the one of importance at the time in question. **moment of inertia** Physics the quantity by which the angular acceleration of a body must be multiplied to give corresponding torque. **moment of truth** a time of crisis or test (orig. the final sword-thrust in a bullfight). **not for a** (or **one**) **moment** never; not at all. **this moment** immediately; at once (come here this moment). [ME f. OF f. L momentum: see MOMENTUM]

momenta pl. of MOMENTUM.

momentarily /ˈməʊməntərɪlɪ, -ˈterɪlɪ, -trɪlɪ/ adv. 1 for a moment. 2 US a at any moment. b instantly.

momentary /ˈməʊməntərɪ, -trɪ/ adj. 1 lasting only a moment. 2 short-lived; transitory. □□ **momentariness** n. [L momentarius (as MOMENT)]

momently /ˈməʊməntlɪ/ adv. literary 1 from moment to moment. 2 every moment. 3 for a moment.

momentous /məˈmentəs/ adj. having great importance. □□ **momentously** adv. **momentousness** n.

momentum /məˈmentəm/ n. (pl. **momenta** /-tə/) 1 Physics the quantity of motion of a moving body, measured as a product of its mass and velocity. 2 the impetus gained by movement. 3 strength or continuity derived from an initial effort. [L f. movimentum f. movēre move]

momma /ˈmɒmə/ n. var. of MAMMA¹.

Mommsen /ˈmɒms(ə)n/, Theodor (1817–1903), German historian. His most celebrated works are his History of Rome (1854–6, 1885), and his treatises on Roman constitutional law (1871–88) and on criminal law (1899); he was also editor of the monumental Corpus Inscriptionum Latinarum (1863–) for the Berlin Academy. Mommsen took an active part in politics and was a keen critic of Bismarck. He was awarded the Nobel Prize for literature in 1902.

mommy /'mɒmɪ/ n. (pl. **-ies**) esp. US = MUMMY[1].

Mon /məʊn/ n. & adj. —n. (pl. **Mon** or **Mons**) **1** a member of a people of Indo-Chinese origin, now inhabiting eastern Burma and western Thailand but having their ancient capital at Pegu in southern Burma. **2** their language (see MON-KHMER). —adj. of this people or their language. [native name]

Mon. abbr. Monday.

Monaco /'mɒnə,kəʊ/ a principality in southern Europe on the Mediterranean coast, an enclave within French territory near the Italian frontier; pop. (est. 1988) 28,900; official language, French; capital, Monaco (pop. 1,443). Ruled by the Genoese from medieval times, and by the Grimaldi family from 1297, Monaco was under French occupation from 1793 to 1814 and then was a Sardinian protectorate until 1861. It became a constitutional monarchy in 1911, although the constitution was briefly suspended in 1959–62. The smallest sovereign State in the world apart from the Vatican, Monaco is almost entirely dependent on the tourist trade with over a million visitors a year, and maintains a customs union with France. □□ **Monacan** adj. & n.

monad /'mɒnæd, 'məʊ-/ n. **1** the number one; a unit. **2** Philos. any ultimate unit of being (e.g. a soul, an atom, a person, God), esp. in the philosophy of Leibniz. **3** Biol. a simple organism, e.g. one assumed as the first in the genealogy of living beings. □□ **monadic** /mə'nædɪk/ adj. **monadism** n. (in sense 2). [F monade or LL monas monad- f. Gk monas -ados unit f. monos alone]

monadelphous /,mɒnə'delfəs/ adj. Bot. **1** (of stamens) having filaments united into one bundle. **2** (of a plant) with such stamens. [Gk monos one + adelphos brother]

monadnock /mə'nædnɒk/ n. a steep-sided isolated hill resistant to erosion and rising above a plain. [Mount Monadnock in New Hampshire, US]

Monaghan /'mɒnəhən/ **1** a county in the north of the Irish Republic, in the province of Ulster; pop. (est. 1986) 52,300. **2** its capital city; pop. (1981) 6,275.

Mona Lisa /,məʊnə 'liːzə/ a painting (now in the Louvre) executed 1503–6 by Leonardo da Vinci and known also as La Gioconda, the sitter being the wife of Francesco di Bartolommeo del Giocondo di Zandi. Her enigmatic smile has become the most famous image in the world, whether inspiring reverence (e.g. Walter Pater's prose poem in his Renaissance) or ridicule (e.g. Marcel Duchamp's Dada gesture of adding a moustache).

monandry /mə'nændrɪ/ n. **1** the custom of having only one husband at a time. **2** Bot. the state of having a single stamen. □□ **monandrous** adj. [MONO- after polyandry]

monarch /'mɒnək/ n. **1** a sovereign with the title of king, queen, emperor, empress, or the equivalent. **2** a supreme ruler. **3** a powerful or pre-eminent person. **4** a large orange and black butterfly, Danaus plexippus. □□ **monarchal** /mə'nɑːk(ə)l/ adj. **monarchic** /mə'nɑːkɪk/ adj. **monarchical** /mə'nɑːkɪk(ə)l/ adj. **monarchically** /mə'nɑːkɪkəlɪ/ adv. [ME f. F monarque or LL monarcha f. Gk monarkhēs, -os, f. monos alone + arkhō to rule]

monarchism /'mɒnə,kɪz(ə)m/ n. the advocacy of or the principles of monarchy. □□ **monarchist** n. [F monarchisme (as MONARCHY)]

monarchy /'mɒnəkɪ/ n. (pl. **-ies**) **1** a form of government with a monarch at the head. **2** a State with this. □□ **monarchial** /mɒ'nɑːkɪəl/ adj. [ME f. OF monarchie f. LL monarchia f. Gk monarkhia the rule of one (as MONARCH)]

Monash /'mɒnæʃ/, Sir John (1865–1931), Australian army commander in the First World War. He accompanied his brigade to Gallipoli, and after the evacuation from there he served with distinction in France, where he became recognized as one of the ablest corps commanders.

monastery /'mɒnəstərɪ, -strɪ/ n. (pl. **-ies**) the residence of a religious community, esp. of monks living in seclusion. [ME f. eccl.L monasterium f. eccl.Gk monastērion f. monazō live alone f. monos alone]

monastic /mə'næstɪk/ adj. & n. —adj. **1** of or relating to monasteries or the religious communities living in them. **2** resembling these or their way of life; solitary and celibate. —n. a monk or other follower of a monastic rule. □□ **monastically**

adv. **monasticism** /-,sɪz(ə)m/ n. **monasticize** /-,saɪz/ v.tr. (also **-ise**). [F monastique or LL monasticus f. Gk monastikos (as MONASTERY)]

Monastir /,mɒnə'stɪə(r)/ a resort town on the coast of Tunisia, with an international airport.

monatomic /,mɒnə'tɒmɪk/ adj. Chem. **1** (esp. of a molecule) consisting of one atom. **2** having one replaceable atom or radical.

monaural /mɒ'nɔːr(ə)l/ adj. **1** = MONOPHONIC. **2** of or involving one ear. □□ **monaurally** adv. [MONO- + AURAL]

monazite /'mɒnə,zaɪt/ n. a phosphate mineral containing rare-earth elements and thorium. [G Monazit f. Gk monazō live alone (because of its rarity)]

Mönchengladbach /,mʊnxən'glædbæx/ a city in NW Germany, near Dusseldorf; pop. (1987) 255,100. It is the NATO headquarters for northern Europe.

Monck /mʌŋk/, George (1608–70), English general, created 1st Duke of Albemarle. Although initially a royalist in the Civil War, he became a supporter of Cromwell and campaigned rapidly in Scotland, subduing that country by the end of 1651, and fought at sea in the Dutch war of 1652–4. Excluded from influence in the subsequent military government, however, he and his troops advanced on London, and Monck was instrumental in restoring the monarchy (1660).

mondaine /mɔ̃'den/ adj. & n. —adj. **1** of the fashionable world. **2** worldly. —n. a worldly or fashionable woman. [F, fem. of mondain: see MUNDANE]

Monday /'mʌndeɪ, -dɪ/ n. & adv. —n. the second day of the week, following Sunday. —adv. colloq. **1** on Monday. **2** (**Mondays**) on Mondays; each Monday. [OE mōnandæg day of the moon, transl. LL lunae dies]

Mondrian /'mɒndrɪ,ɑːn/, Piet (Pieter Cornelis Mondriaan, 1872–1944), Dutch painter. A founder of the periodical De Stijl in 1917, he became the main exponent of a new kind of geometrical abstract painting which he named neo-plasticism. The basic elements that he used were straight lines meeting at right angles, and a limited number of primary colours. He influenced the art and taste of the 1930s, including contemporary fashion in commercial and advertisement design.

Monégasque /,mɒneɪ'gæsk/ adj. & n. = MONACAN.

Monel /'məʊn(ə)l/ n. (in full **Monel metal**) propr. a nickel-copper alloy with high tensile strength and resisting corrosion. [A. Monell, US businessman d. 1921]

monetarism /'mʌnɪtə,rɪz(ə)m/ n. the theory or practice of controlling the supply of money as the chief method of stabilizing the economy. This economic theory is based on the belief that the supply of money is the crucial determinant of the level of demand, which argues that strict government control of the money supply is necessary to prevent high inflation, and is opposed to the Keynesian idea that the money supply is largely unimportant in determining demand. Its principal exponent was the American economist Milton Friedman, who held that governments lack the political will to control inflation by cutting government spending, since this move will increase unemployment.

monetarist /'mʌnɪtərɪst/ n. & adj. —n. an advocate of monetarism. —adj. in accordance with the principles of monetarism.

monetary /'mʌnɪtərɪ/ adj. **1** of the currency in use. **2** of or consisting of money. □□ **monetarily** adv. [F monétaire or LL monetarius f. L (as MONEY)]

monetize /'mʌnɪ,taɪz/ v.tr. (also **-ise**) **1** give a fixed value as currency. **2** put (a metal) into circulation as money. □□ **monetization** /-'zeɪʃ(ə)n/ n. [F monétiser f. L (as MONEY)]

money /'mʌnɪ/ n. **1 a** a current medium of exchange in the form of coins and banknotes. **b** a particular form of this (silver money). **2** (pl. **-eys** or **-ies**) (in pl.) sums of money. **3 a** wealth; property viewed as convertible into money. **b** wealth as giving power or influence (money speaks). **c** a rich person or family (has married into money). **4 a** money as a resource (time is money). **b** profit, remuneration (in it for the money). □ **for my money** in my opinion or judgement; for my preference (is too aggressive for *my money*). **have money to burn** see BURN¹. **in the money** *colloq.* having or winning a lot of money. **money box** a box for saving money dropped through a slit. **money-changer** a person whose business it is to change money, esp. at an official rate. **money for jam** (or **old rope**) *colloq.* profit for little or no trouble. **money-grubber** *colloq.* a person greedily intent on amassing money. **money-grubbing** *n.* this practice. —*adj.* given to this. **money market** *Stock Exch.* trade in short-term stocks, loans, etc. **money of account** see ACCOUNT. **money order** an order for payment of a specified sum, issued by a bank or Post Office. **money spider** a small household spider supposed to bring financial luck. **money-spinner** a thing that brings in a profit. **money's-worth** good value for one's money. **put money into** invest in. □□ **moneyless** *adj.* [ME f. OF *moneie* f. L *moneta* mint, money, orig. a title of Juno, in whose temple at Rome money was minted]

moneybags /ˈmʌnɪˌbægz/ *n.pl.* (treated as *sing.*) *colloq.* usu. *derog.* a wealthy person.

moneyed /ˈmʌnɪd/ *adj.* **1** having much money; wealthy. **2** consisting of money (*moneyed assistance*).

moneylender /ˈmʌnɪˌlendə(r)/ *n.* a person who lends money, esp. as a business, at interest. □□ **moneylending** *n.* & *adj.*

moneymaker /ˈmʌnɪˌmeɪkə(r)/ *n.* **1** a person who earns much money. **2** a thing, idea, etc., that produces much money. □□ **moneymaking** *n.* & *adj.*

moneywort /ˈmʌnɪˌwɜːt/ *n.* a trailing evergreen plant, *Lysimachia nummularia*, with round glossy leaves and yellow flowers.

monger /ˈmʌŋgə(r)/ *n.* (usu. in *comb.*) **1** a dealer or trader (*fishmonger; ironmonger*). **2** usu. *derog.* a person who promotes or deals in something specified (*warmonger; scaremonger*). [OE *mangere* f. *mangian* to traffic f. Gmc, ult. f. L *mango* dealer]

Mongol /ˈmɒŋg(ə)l/ *adj.* & *n.* —*adj.* **1** of or relating to the Asian people now inhabiting Mongolia. **2** resembling this people, esp. in appearance. **3** (**mongol**) often *offens.* suffering from Down's syndrome. —*n.* **1** a Mongolian. **2** (**mongol**) often *offens.* a person suffering from Down's syndrome. [native name: perh. f. *mong* brave]

Mongolia /mɒŋˈgəʊlɪə/ a large and sparsely populated country of eastern Asia, bordered by the USSR and China; pop. (est. 1988) 2,067,600; official language, Mongolian; capital, Ulan Bator. The economy is predominantly pastoral and the bulk of the international trade is with the Soviet Union. The centre of the medieval Mongol empire, Mongolia subsequently became a Chinese province, achieving *de facto* independence in 1911. In 1924 it became a Communist State after the Soviet model, and has since gravitated towards the USSR. Free elections were held in 1990, but outside the towns few people know the principles of the new parties.

Mongolian /mɒŋˈgəʊlɪən/ *adj.* & *n.* —*adj.* of Mongolia or its people or language. —*n.* **1** a native or inhabitant of Mongolia. **2** a member of a racial division of mankind (see below). **3** the language of Mongolia, spoken by some 1,500,000 people, chief among a number of related languages and dialects which together form the Mongolian group in the Altaic language family.

Mongolians form one of the major racial divisions of mankind defined by Blumenbach. They occupy three distinct geographical areas: eastern Asia, SE Asia, and the Arctic region of North America, and are characterized by dark eyes, very dark coarse straight hair, pale ivory to dark skin, scant facial and body hair, and the epicanthic skin-fold.

mongolism /ˈmɒŋgəˌlɪz(ə)m/ *n.* = DOWN'S SYNDROME. ¶ The term *Down's syndrome* is now much preferred in medical circles. [MONGOL + -ISM, because its physical characteristics were thought to be reminiscent of Mongolians]

Mongoloid /ˈmɒŋgəˌlɔɪd/ *adj.* & *n.* —*adj.* **1** characteristic of the Mongolians, esp. in having a broad flat yellowish face. **2** (**mongoloid**) often *offens.* having the characteristic symptoms of Down's syndrome. —*n.* a Mongoloid or mongoloid person.

mongoose /ˈmɒŋguːs/ *n.* (*pl.* **mongooses**) any of various small flesh-eating civet-like mammals of the family Viverridae, esp. of the genus *Herpestes*. [Marathi *mangūs*]

mongrel /ˈmʌŋgr(ə)l, ˈmɒŋ-/ *n.* & *adj.* —*n.* **1** a dog of no definable type or breed. **2** any other animal or plant resulting from the crossing of different breeds or types. **3** *derog.* a person of mixed race. —*adj.* of mixed origin, nature, or character. □□ **mongrelism** *n.* **mongrelize** *v.tr.* (also **-ise**). **mongrelization** /-ˈzeɪʃ(ə)n/ *n.* **mongrelly** *adj.* [earlier *meng-, mang-* f. Gmc: prob. rel. to MINGLE]

'mongst *poet.* var. of AMONGST. [see AMONG]

monial /ˈməʊnɪəl/ *n.* a mullion. [ME f. OF *moinel* middle f. *moien* MEAN³]

Monica /ˈmɒnɪkə/, St (*c.*331–87), the mother of St Augustine of Hippo. Feast day, 24 Aug.

monicker var. of MONIKER.

monies see MONEY 2.

moniker /ˈmɒnɪkə(r)/ *n.* (also **monicker**, **monniker**) *sl.* a name. [19th c.: orig. unkn.]

moniliform /məˈnɪlɪˌfɔːm/ *adj.* with a form suggesting a string of beads. [F *moniliforme* or mod.L *moniliformis* f. L *monile* necklace]

monism /ˈmɒnɪz(ə)m, ˈməʊn-/ *n.* **1** any theory denying the duality of matter and mind. **2** the doctrine that only one ultimate principle or being exists (opp. DUALISM and PLURALISM). □□ **monist** *n.* **monistic** /-ˈnɪstɪk/ *adj.* [mod.L *monismus* f. Gk *monos* single]

monition /məˈnɪʃ(ə)n/ *n.* **1** (foll. by *of*) *literary* a warning (of danger). **2** *Eccl.* a formal notice from a bishop or ecclesiastical court admonishing a person not to commit an offence. [ME f. OF f. L *monitio -onis* (as MONITOR)]

monitor /ˈmɒnɪt(ə)r/ *n.* & *v.* —*n.* **1** any of various persons or devices for checking or warning about a situation, operation, etc. **2** a school pupil with disciplinary or other special duties. **3 a** a television receiver used in a studio to select or verify the picture being broadcast. **b** = *visual display unit.* **4** a person who listens to and reports on foreign broadcasts etc. **5** a detector of radioactive contamination. **6** *Zool.* any tropical lizard of the genus *Varanus*, supposed to give warning of the approach of crocodiles. **7** a heavily armed shallow-draught warship. —*v.tr.* **1** act as a monitor of. **2** maintain regular surveillance over. **3** regulate the strength of (a recorded or transmitted signal). □□ **monitorial** /-ˈtɔːrɪəl/ *adj.* **monitorship** *n.* [L f. *monēre* monit- warn]

monitory /ˈmɒnɪtərɪ/ *adj.* & *n.* —*adj.* *literary* giving or serving as a warning. —*n.* (*pl.* **-ies**) *Eccl.* a letter of admonition from the pope or a bishop. [L *monitorius* (as MONITION)]

monk /mʌŋk/ *n.* a member of a religious community of men living under certain vows esp. of poverty, chastity, and obedience. □□ **monkish** *adj.* [OE *munuc* ult. f. Gk *monakhos* solitary f. *monos* alone]

monkey /ˈmʌŋkɪ/ *n.* & *v.* —*n.* (*pl.* **-eys**) **1** any of various New World and Old World primates esp. of the families Cebidae (including capuchins), Callitrichidae (including marmosets and tamarins), and Cercopithecidae (including baboons and apes). **2** a mischievous person, esp. a child (*young monkey*). **3** *sl.* **a** *Brit.* £500. **b** *US* $500. **4** (in full **monkey engine**) a machine hammer for pile-driving etc. —*v.* (**-eys, -eyed**) **1** *tr.* mimic or mock. **2** *intr.* (often foll. by *with*) tamper or play mischievous tricks. **3** *intr.* (foll. by *around, about*) fool around. □ **have a monkey on one's back** *sl.* be a drug addict. **make a monkey of** humiliate by making appear ridiculous. **monkey bread** the baobab tree or its fruit. **monkey business** *colloq.* mischief. **monkey flower** a mimulus, esp. *Mimulus cardinalis*, with bright yellow flowers. **monkey-jacket** a short close-fitting jacket worn by sailors etc. or at a mess. **monkey-nut** a peanut. **monkey-puzzle** a coniferous tree, *Araucaria araucana*, native to Chile, with downward-pointing branches and small close-set leaves. **monkey-suit** *colloq.* evening dress. **monkey tricks** *colloq.* mischief. **monkey wrench** a wrench with an adjustable jaw. □□ **monkeyish** *adj.* [16th c.: orig. unkn. (perh. LG)]

monkeyshine /ˈmʌŋkɪˌʃaɪn/ *n.* (usu. in *pl.*) *US colloq.* = *monkey tricks.*

monkfish /ˈmʌŋkfɪʃ/ *n.* **1** an angler-fish, esp. *Lophius piscatorius*, often used as food. **2** a large cartilaginous fish, *Squatina squatina*, with a flattened body and large pectoral fins. Also called *angel-shark*.

Mon-Khmer /məʊn'kmeə(r)/ *adj.* of a group of Indo-Chinese languages of which the most important are Mon (spoken in eastern Burma and western Thailand) and Khmer (=CAMBODIAN). Mon is now a relatively minor language but in the 13th c. it was extremely influential throughout Burma.

monkshood /'mʌŋkshʊd/ *n. Bot.* a poisonous garden plant *Aconitum napellus*, with hood-shaped blue or purple flowers.

monniker var. of MONIKER.

mono /'mɒnəʊ/ *adj. & n. colloq.* —*adj.* monophonic. —*n.* (*pl.* -os) a monophonic record, reproduction, etc. [abbr.]

mono- /'mɒnəʊ/ *comb. form* (usu. **mon-** before a vowel) **1** one, alone, single. **2** *Chem.* (forming names of compounds) containing one atom or group of a specified kind. [Gk f. *monos* alone]

monoacid /ˌmɒnəʊ'æsɪd/ *adj. Chem.* (of a base) having one replaceable hydroxide ion.

monobasic /ˌmɒnəʊ'beɪsɪk/ *adj. Chem.* (of an acid) having one replaceable hydrogen atom.

monocarpic /ˌmɒnəʊ'kɑːpɪk/ *adj.* (also **monocarpous** /-'kɑːpəs/) *Bot.* bearing fruit only once. [MONO- + Gk *karpos* fruit]

monocausal /ˌmɒnəʊ'kɔːz(ə)l/ *adj.* in terms of a sole cause.

monocephalous /ˌmɒnəʊ'sefələs/ *adj. Bot.* having only one head.

monochord /'mɒnəˌkɔːd/ *n. Mus.* an instrument with a single string and a movable bridge, used esp. to determine intervals. [ME f. OF *monocorde* f. LL *monochordon* f. Gk *monokhordon* (as MONO-, CHORD¹)]

monochromatic /ˌmɒnəkrə'mætɪk/ *adj.* **1** *Physics* (of light or other radiation) of a single wavelength or frequency. **2** containing only one colour. □□ **monochromatically** *adv.*

monochromatism /ˌmɒnəʊ'krəʊmətɪz(ə)m/ *n.* complete colour-blindness in which all colours appear as shades of one colour.

monochrome /'mɒnəˌkrəʊm/ *n. & adj.* —*n.* a photograph or picture done in one colour or different tones of this, or in black and white only. —*adj.* having or using only one colour or in black and white only. □□ **monochromic** /-'krəʊmɪk/ *adj.* [ult. f. Gk *monokhrōmatos* (as MONO-, *khrōmatos* f. *khrōma* colour)]

monocle /'mɒnək(ə)l/ *n.* a single eyeglass. □□ **monocled** *adj.* [F, orig. adj. f. LL *monoculus* one-eyed (as MONO-, *oculus* eye)]

monocline /'mɒnəʊˌklaɪn/ *n. Geol.* a bend in rock strata that are otherwise uniformly dipping or horizontal. □□ **monoclinal** /-'klaɪn(ə)l/ *adj.* [MONO- + Gk *klinō* lean, dip]

monoclinic /ˌmɒnəʊ'klɪnɪk/ *adj.* (of a crystal) having one axial intersection oblique. [MONO- + Gk *klinō* lean, slope]

monoclonal /ˌmɒnəʊ'kləʊn(ə)l/ *adj.* forming a single clone; derived from a single individual or cell. □ **monoclonal antibodies** antibodies produced artificially by a single clone and consisting of identical antibody molecules.

monocoque /'mɒnəˌkɒk/ *n. Aeron.* an aircraft or vehicle structure in which the chassis is integral with the body. [F (as MONO-, *coque* shell)]

monocot /'mɒnəʊˌkɒt/ *n.* = MONOCOTYLEDON. [abbr.]

monocotyledon /ˌmɒnəˌkɒtɪ'liːd(ə)n/ *n. Bot.* any flowering plant with a single cotyledon. □□ **monocotyledonous** *adj.*

monocracy /mə'nɒkrəsɪ/ *n.* (*pl.* -ies) government by one person only. □□ **monocratic** /-'krætɪk/ *adj.*

monocular /mə'nɒkjʊlə(r)/ *adj.* with or for one eye. □□ **monocularly** *adj.* [LL *monoculus* having one eye]

monoculture /'mɒnəʊˌkʌltʃə(r)/ *n.* the cultivation of a single crop.

monocycle /'mɒnəˌsaɪk(ə)l/ *n.* = UNICYCLE.

monocyte /'mɒnəˌsaɪt/ *n. Biol.* a large type of leucocyte.

monodactylous /ˌmɒnə'dæktɪləs/ *adj.* having one finger, toe, or claw.

monodrama /'mɒnəʊˌdrɑːmə/ *n.* a dramatic piece for one performer.

monody /'mɒnədɪ/ *n.* (*pl.* -ies) **1** an ode sung by a single actor in a Greek tragedy. **2** a poem lamenting a person's death. **3**

Mus. a composition with only one melodic line. □□ **monodic** /mə'nɒdɪk/ *adj.* **monodist** *n.* [LL *monodia* f. Gk *monōidia* f. *monōidos* singing alone (as MONO-, ODE)]

monoecious /mə'niːʃəs/ *adj.* **1** *Bot.* with unisexual male and female organs on the same plant. **2** *Zool.* hermaphrodite. [mod.L *Monoecia* the class of such plants (Linnaeus) f. Gk *monos* single + *oikos* house]

monofilament /'mɒnəʊˌfɪləmənt/ *n.* **1** a single strand of manmade fibre. **2** a type of fishing line using this.

monogamy /mə'nɒgəmɪ/ *n.* **1** the practice or state of being married to one person at a time. **2** *Zool.* the habit of having only one mate at a time. □□ **monogamist** *n.* **monogamous** *adj.* **monogamously** *adv.* [F *monogamie* f. eccl.L f. Gk *monogamia* (as MONO-, *gamos* marriage)]

monogenesis /ˌmɒnəʊ'dʒenɪsɪs/ *n.* (also **monogeny** /mə'nɒdʒɪnɪ/) **1** the theory of the development of all beings from a single cell. **2** the theory that mankind descended from one pair of ancestors. □□ **monogenetic** /-dʒɪ'netɪk/ *adj.*

monoglot /'mɒnəˌglɒt/ *adj. & n.* —*adj.* using only one language. —*n.* a monoglot person.

monogram /'mɒnəˌgræm/ *n.* two or more letters, esp. a person's initials, interwoven as a device. □□ **monogrammatic** /-grə'mætɪk/ *adj.* **monogrammed** *adj.* [F *monogramme* f. LL *monogramma* f. Gk (as MONO-, -GRAM)]

monograph /'mɒnəˌgrɑːf/ *n. & v.* —*n.* a separate treatise on a single subject or an aspect of it. —*v.tr.* write a monograph on. □□ **monographer** /mə'nɒgrəfə(r)/ *n.* **monographist** /mə'nɒgrəfɪst/ *n.* **monographic** /ˌmɒnə'græfɪk/ *adj.* [earlier *monography* f. mod.L *monographia* f. *monographus* writer on a single genus or species (as MONO-, -GRAPH, -GRAPHY)]

monogynous /mə'nɒdʒɪnəs/ *adj. Bot.* having only one pistil.

monogyny /mə'nɒdʒɪnɪ/ *n.* the custom of having only one wife at a time.

monohull /'mɒnəʊˌhʌl/ *n.* a boat with a single hull.

monohybrid /ˌmɒnəʊ'haɪbrɪd/ *n.* a hybrid with respect to only one allele.

monohydric /ˌmɒnəʊ'haɪdrɪk/ *adj. Chem.* containing one hydroxyl group.

monokini /ˌmɒnəʊ'kiːnɪ/ *n.* a woman's one-piece beachgarment equivalent to the lower half of a bikini. [MONO- + BIKINI, by false assoc. with BI-]

monolayer /'mɒnəʊˌleɪə(r)/ *n. Chem.* a layer only one molecule in thickness.

monolingual /ˌmɒnəʊ'lɪŋgw(ə)l/ *adj.* speaking or using only one language.

monolith /'mɒnəlɪθ/ *n.* **1** a single block of stone, esp. shaped into a pillar or monument. **2** a person or thing like a monolith in being massive, immovable, or solidly uniform. **3** a large block of concrete. □□ **monolithic** /-'lɪθɪk/ *adj.* [F *monolithe* f. Gk *monolithos* (as MONO-, *lithos* stone)]

monologue /'mɒnəˌlɒg/ *n.* **1 a** a scene in a drama in which a person speaks alone. **b** a dramatic composition for one performer. **2** a long speech by one person in a conversation etc. □□ **monologic** /-'lɒdʒɪk/ *adj.* **monological** /-'lɒdʒɪk(ə)l/ *adj.* **monologist** /mə'nɒlədʒɪst/ *n.* (also **-loguist**). **monologize** /mə'nɒlədʒaɪz/ *v.intr.* (also **-ise**). [F f. Gk *monologos* speaking alone (as MONO-, -LOGUE)]

monomania /ˌmɒnə'meɪnɪə/ *n.* obsession of the mind by one idea or interest. □□ **monomaniac** *n. & adj.* **monomaniacal** /-mə'naɪək(ə)l/ *adj.* [F *monomanie* (as MONO-, -MANIA)]

monomark /'mɒnəʊˌmɑːk/ *n. Brit.* a combination of letters, with or without figures, registered as an identification mark for goods, articles, addresses, etc.

monomer /'mɒnəmə(r)/ *n. Chem.* **1** a unit in a dimer, trimer, or polymer. **2** a molecule or compound that can be polymerized. □□ **monomeric** /-'merɪk/ *adj.*

monomial /mə'nəʊmɪəl/ *adj. & n. Math.* —*adj.* (of an algebraic expression) consisting of one term. —*n.* a monomial expression. [MONO- after *binomial*]

monomolecular /ˌmɒnəʊmə'lekjʊlə(r)/ *adj. Chem.* (of a layer) only one molecule in thickness.

monomorphic /ˌmɒnəˈmɔːfɪk/ adj. (also **monomorphous** /-ˈmɔːfəs/) Biochem. not changing form during development. □□ **monomorphism** n.

mononucleosis /ˌmɒnəʊˌnjuːklɪˈəʊsɪs/ n. an abnormally high proportion of monocytes in the blood, esp. = glandular fever. [MONO- + NUCLEO- + -OSIS]

monopetalous /ˌmɒnəˈpetələs/ adj. Bot. having the corolla in one piece, or the petals united into a tube.

monophonic /ˌmɒnəˈfɒnɪk/ adj. 1 (of sound-reproduction) using only one channel of transmission (cf. STEREOPHONIC). 2 Mus. homophonic. □□ **monophonically** adv. [MONO- + Gk phōnē sound]

monophthong /ˈmɒnəfˌθɒŋ/ n. Phonet. a single vowel sound. □□ **monophthongal** /-ˈθɒŋg(ə)l/ adj. [Gk monophthoggos (as MONO-, phthoggos sound)]

Monophysite /məˈnɒfɪˌzaɪt, ˈmɒnəʊ-/ n. a person who holds that there was in the person of Christ only a single nature, part divine and part human, the human element being totally subordinate to the divine. Its followers became a distinct body after the Council of Chalcedon (451) had defined the orthodox doctrine that there were two natures in Christ, separate and unconfused. Despite attempts at reconciliation by the Byzantine emperors, who saw the unity of the empire threatened, the break became final in the 6th c., and the Coptic and several other Eastern Churches have remained Monophysite. [eccl.L monophysita f. eccl.Gk monophusitēs (as MONO-, phusis nature)]

monoplane /ˈmɒnəˌpleɪn/ n. an aeroplane with one set of wings (cf. BIPLANE).

monopolist /məˈnɒpəlɪst/ n. a person who has or advocates a monopoly. □□ **monopolistic** /-ˈlɪstɪk/ adj.

monopolize /məˈnɒpəˌlaɪz/ v.tr. (also **-ise**) 1 obtain exclusive possession or control of (a trade or commodity etc.). 2 dominate or prevent others from sharing in (a conversation, person's attention, etc.). □□ **monopolization** /-ˈzeɪʃ(ə)n/ n. **monopolizer** n.

Monopoly /məˈnɒpəˌlɪ/ n. propr. a game (invented by Charles Darrow c. 1935) in which players use imitation money to engage in simulated financial dealings. □ **Monopoly money** money that is not 'real'; valueless currency.

monopoly /məˈnɒpəlɪ/ n. (pl. **-ies**) 1 a the exclusive possession or control of the trade in a commodity or service. b this conferred as a privilege by the State. 2 a a commodity or service that is subject to a monopoly. b a company etc. that possesses a monopoly. 3 (foll. by of, US on) exclusive possession, control, or exercise. [L monopolium f. Gk monopōlion (as MONO-, pōleō sell)]

monorail /ˈmɒnəʊˌreɪl/ n. a railway in which the track consists of a single rail, usu. elevated with the train units suspended from it.

monosaccharide /ˌmɒnəʊˈsækəˌraɪd/ n. Chem. a sugar that cannot be hydrolysed to give a simpler sugar, e.g. glucose.

monosodium glutamate /ˌmɒnəʊˈsəʊdɪəm ˈgluːtəˌmeɪt/ n. Chem. a sodium salt of glutamic acid used to flavour food (cf. GLUTAMATE).

monospermous /ˌmɒnəˈspɜːməs/ adj. Bot. having one seed. [MONO- + Gk sperma seed]

monostichous /məˈnɒstɪkəs/ adj. Bot. & Zool. arranged in or consisting of one layer or row. [MONO- + Gk stikhos row]

monosyllabic /ˌmɒnəsɪˈlæbɪk/ adj. 1 (of a word) having one syllable. 2 (of a person or statement) using or expressed in monosyllables. □□ **monosyllabically** adv.

monosyllable /ˈmɒnəˌsɪləb(ə)l/ n. a word of one syllable. □ **in monosyllables** in simple direct words.

monotheism /ˈmɒnəˌθiːɪz(ə)m/ n. the doctrine that there is only one God. □□ **monotheist** n. **monotheistic** /-ˈɪstɪk/ adj. **monotheistically** /-ˈɪstɪkəlɪ/ adv. [MONO- + Gk theos god]

Monothelite /məˈnɒθəˌlaɪt/ n. a person who holds that there was in the person of Christ only one will. The theory (condemned as heresy in 681) was put forward as an attempt to reconcile the orthodox and Monophysite doctrines, but it led only to fresh controversy. [eccl. L monothelita f. eccl. Gk monothelētēs (as MONO-, thelēma will)]

monotint /ˈmɒnəʊtɪnt/ n. = MONOCHROME.

monotone /ˈmɒnəˌtəʊn/ n. & adj. —n. 1 a sound or utterance continuing or repeated on one note without change of pitch. 2 sameness of style in writing. —adj. without change of pitch. [mod.L monotonus f. late Gk monotonos (as MONO-, TONE)]

monotonic /ˌmɒnəˈtɒnɪk/ adj. 1 uttered in a monotone. 2 Math. (of a function or quantity) varying in such a way that it either never decreases or never increases. □□ **monotonically** adv.

monotonous /məˈnɒtənəs/ adj. 1 lacking in variety; tedious through sameness. 2 (of a sound or utterance) without variation in tone or pitch. □□ **monotonize** v.tr. (also **-ise**). **monotonously** adv. **monotonousness** n.

monotony /məˈnɒtənɪ/ n. 1 the state of being monotonous. 2 dull or tedious routine.

monotreme /ˈmɒnəˌtriːm/ n. any mammal of the order Monotremata, native to Australia and New Guinea, including the duckbill and spiny anteater, laying large yolky eggs through a common opening for urine, faeces, etc. [MONO- + Gk trēma -matos hole]

monotype /ˈmɒnəˌtaɪp/ n. 1 (**Monotype**) Printing propr. a typesetting machine that casts and sets up types in individual characters. 2 an impression on paper made from an inked design painted on glass or metal.

monotypic /ˌmɒnəˈtɪpɪk/ adj. having only one type or representative.

monovalent /ˌmɒnəˈveɪlənt/ adj. Chem. having a valency of one; univalent. □□ **monovalence** n. **monovalency** n.

monoxide /məˈnɒksaɪd/ n. Chem. an oxide containing one oxygen atom (carbon monoxide). [MONO- + OXIDE]

Monroe[1] /mənˈrəʊ/, James (1758–1831), 5th President of the US (1817–25), and formulator of the **Monroe Doctrine**, that interference by any European State in the affairs of Spanish-American republics would be regarded as an act unfriendly to the US, and that the American continents were no longer open to European colonial settlement.

Monroe[2] /mənˈrəʊ/, Marilyn (Norma Jean Mortenson, later Baker, 1926–62), American film actress. In the 1940s she became a photographic model and a forces' pin-up, subsequently appearing in comedy films (e.g. Gentlemen Prefer Blondes, 1953) in which she was promoted as a sex symbol. Later she starred in more serious films, the last of which (The Misfits, 1961) was written for her by her third husband, Arthur Miller. Her private life was much publicized; after bouts of depression she died from an overdose of barbiturates.

Monrovia /mɒnˈrəʊvɪə/ the capital of Liberia; pop. (1984) 425,000.

Mons /mɒnz/ (Flemish **Bergen** /ˈbeəxən/) a town in Belgium (pop., 1988, 89,515), site of the first British battle on the Continent in the First World War in August 1914. The Germans were repulsed with heavy losses by accurate British rifle fire.

Monseigneur /ˌmɒnsenˈjɜː(r)/ n. (pl. **Messeigneurs** /ˌmesenˈjɜː(r)/) a title given to an eminent French person, esp. a prince, cardinal, archbishop, or bishop. [F f. mon my + seigneur lord]

Monsieur /məˈsjɜː(r)/ n. (pl. **Messieurs** /meˈsjɜː(r)/) 1 the title or form of address used of or to a French-speaking man, corresponding to Mr or sir. 2 a Frenchman. [F f. mon my + sieur lord]

Monsignor /mɒnˈsiːnjə(r), -njɔː(r)/ n. (pl. **Monsignori** /-ˈnjɔːrɪ/) the title of various Roman Catholic prelates, officers of the papal court, etc. [It., after MONSEIGNEUR: see SIGNOR]

monsoon /mɒnˈsuːn/ n. 1 a wind in S. Asia, esp. in the Indian Ocean, blowing from the south-west in summer (**wet monsoon**) and the north-east in winter (**dry monsoon**). 2 a rainy season accompanying a wet monsoon. 3 any other wind with periodic alternations. □□ **monsoonal** adj. [obs. Du. monssoen f. Port. monção f. Arab. mawsim fixed season f. wasama to mark]

mons pubis /mɒnz ˈpjuːbɪs/ n. a rounded mass of fatty tissue lying over the joint of a man's pubic bones. [L, = mount of the pubes]

monster /ˈmɒnstə(r)/ n. 1 an imaginary creature, usu. large and frightening, compounded of incongruous elements. 2 an inhumanly cruel or wicked person. **3** a misshapen animal or plant. **4** a large hideous animal or thing (e.g. a building). **5** (*attrib.*) huge; extremely large of its kind. [ME f. OF *monstre* f. L *monstrum* portent, monster f. *monēre* warn]

monstera /mɒnˈstɪərə/ *n.* any climbing plant of the genus *Monstera*, including Swiss cheese plant. [mod.L, perh. f. L *monstrum* monster (from the odd appearance of its leaves)]

monstrance /ˈmɒnstrəns/ *n.* RC Ch. a vessel in which the Host is exposed for veneration. [ME, = demonstration, f. med.L *monstrantia* f. L *monstrare* show]

monstrosity /mɒnˈstrɒsɪtɪ/ *n.* (*pl.* **-ies**) **1** a huge or outrageous thing. **2** monstrousness. **3** = MONSTER 3. [LL *monstrositas* (as MONSTROUS)]

monstrous /ˈmɒnstrəs/ *adj.* **1** like a monster; abnormally formed. **2** huge. **3 a** outrageously wrong or absurd. **b** atrocious. □□ **monstrously** *adv.* **monstrousness** *n.* [ME f. OF *monstreux* or L *monstrosus* (as MONSTER)]

mons Veneris /mɒnz ˈvenərɪs/ *n.* a rounded mass of fatty tissue on a woman's abdomen above the vulva. [L, = mount of Venus]

Mont. *abbr.* Montana.

montage /mɒnˈtɑːʒ/ *n.* **1** (in cinematography) **a** a combination of images in quick succession to compress background information or provide atmosphere **b** a system of editing in which the narrative is modified or interrupted to include images that are not necessarily related to the dramatic development. The technique was used notably by Eisenstein. **2 a** the technique of producing a new composite whole from fragments of pictures, words, music, etc. **b** a composition produced in this way. [F f. *monter* MOUNT¹]

Montagna /mɒnˈtɑːnjə/, Bartolommeo Cincani (1450–1523), Italian painter. Probably trained in Venice, he settled in Vicenza and helped establish it as a centre of art. His *Madonna and Child* is a good example of his work, with its strong unaffected composition and muted tonality.

Montaigne /mɒnˈteɪn/, Michel Eyquem de (1533–92), French writer, generally regarded as the inventor of the modern 'essay'. His famous *Essais* (1580–95), vividly translated into English by John Florio (d. 1625), became the subject of philosophical expansion in the 17th c. They reveal the author as a man of insatiable intellectual curiosity, kindly and sagacious, condemning pedantry and lying, but tolerant of an easy morality.

Montana¹ /mɒnˈtænə/ a State of the US on the Canadian border east of the Rocky Mountains; pop. (est. 1985) 786,700; capital, Helena. It formed part of the Louisiana Purchase in 1803 and became the 41st State of the US in 1889.

Montana² /mɒnˈteɪnə/, Joseph C. (1956–), American football player, who joined the San Francisco 49ers as quarterback in 1980 and was instrumental in the team's winning three Super Bowls in the 1980s. His nickname was 'Cool Joe'.

montane /ˈmɒnteɪn/ *adj.* of or inhabiting mountainous country. [L *montanus* (as MOUNT², -ANE¹)]

Montanist /ˈmɒntənɪst/ *n.* a member of a heretical Christian movement, founded in Phrygia in the 2nd c., which reacted against the growing secularism of the Church, desired a stricter adhesion to the principles of primitive Christianity, and prepared for the earthly kingdom of Christ. □□ **Montanism** *n.* [*Montanus* its founder]

Mont Blanc /mɔ̃ ˈblɑ̃/ a peak in the Alps on the border of France and Italy, the highest mountain in Europe (4,180 m, 15,781 ft.).

montbretia /mɒnˈbriːʃə/ *n.* a hybrid plant of the genus *Crocosmia*, with bright orange-yellow trumpet-shaped flowers. [mod.L f. A. F. E. Coquebert de *Montbret*, Fr. botanist d. 1801]

Montcalm /mɒnˈkɑːm/, Louis Joseph de Montcalm-Gozon, Marquis de (1712–59), French soldier, who defended Quebec against Wolfe and was mortally wounded in the battle which followed the scaling of the Heights of Abraham.

monte /ˈmɒntɪ/ *n.* Cards **1** a Spanish game of chance, played with 45 cards. **2** (in full **three-card monte**) a game of Mexican origin played with three cards, similar to three-card trick. [Sp., = mountain, heap of cards]

Monte Albán /ˌmɒnteɪ ɑːlˈbɑːn/ an ancient city in Oaxaca in southern Mexico, occupied from *c.* 900 BC. It was a Zapotec centre from *c.* 1st c. BC until *c.* 900, after which it was occupied by the Mixtecs until the Spanish conquest (16th c.).

Monte Carlo /ˌmɒntɪ ˈkaːləʊ/ one of the three communes of the principality of Monaco, famous as a gambling resort and as the terminus of a car rally; pop. (1985) 12,000. □ **Monte Carlo method.** *Statistics* a method of using the random sampling of numbers in order to estimate the solution to a numerical problem.

Monte Cassino /ˈmɒntɪ kəˈsiːnəʊ/ a hill midway between Rome and Naples; site of the principal monastery of the Benedictines, founded by St Benedict *c.*529. In 1944, during the Second World War, Allied forces advancing towards Rome were halted by German defensive positions to which Monte Cassino was the key; they succeeded in capturing the site only after four months of bitter fighting. The monastery, previously demolished and rebuilt several times, was almost totally destroyed, but has since been restored.

Montego Bay /mɒnˈteɪgəʊ/ a free port and tourist resort on the north coast of Jamaica; pop. (1982) 70,265.

Montenegro /ˌmɒntɪˈniːgrəʊ/ a constituent republic of Yugoslavia; pop. (1981) 584,300; capital, Titograd.

Monterrey /ˌmɒntɪˈreɪ/ an industrial city in NE Mexico, capital of Nueva León State; pop. (1980) 1,916,500.

Montespan /ˈmõtesˌpã/, Françoise-Athénaïs de Rochechouart, Marquise de (1641–1707), mistress of Louis XIV. A great beauty with a notorious temper, de Montespan dominated the king for more than a decade (1667–79), giving him many illegitimate children. Very unpopular at court, she was the subject of repeated plots aimed at supplanting her with a more amenable woman.

Montessori /ˌmɒntɪˈsɔːrɪ/, Maria (1870–1952), Italian educationist. Her success with mentally retarded children led her, in 1907, to apply similar methods to younger children of normal intelligence. The Montessori system, which became worldwide in the 1910s and 1920s, emphasizes free but guided play with apparatus designed to encourage sense perception and mental interest, with less rigid discipline than was formerly common.

Monteverdi /ˌmɒntɪˈveədɪ/, Claudio (1567–1643), Italian composer of sacred and secular music, whose place in the history of Renaissance music can be compared to Shakespeare's in literature. He transformed every genre in which he worked by imaginative use of available styles rather than by revolutionary means. His madrigals cover a period of forty years, and he introduced instrumental accompaniments and chromatic modulations. His *Orfeo* (1607) is the earliest opera to enjoy widespread popularity, while the operas he composed for the newly opened public opera houses in Venice portray clearly defined characters rather than the customary symbolic figures. Above all, the melodic genius and fertility of his music and its harmonic adventurousness are what make it so attractive and 'contemporary' in the 20th c.

Montevideo /ˌmɒntɪvɪˈdeɪəʊ/ the capital and chief port of Uruguay, on the Río de la Plata; pop. (1985) 1,247,900.

Montez /ˈmɒntez/, Lola (original name Marie Dolores Gilbert, 1818–61), Irish-born dancer of great beauty, notorious for her liaison with Ludwig I (see entry) of Bavaria.

Montezuma /ˌmɒntɪˈzuːmə/ (1466–1520), the last ruler of the Aztec empire in Mexico. Defeated by the Spanish conquistadors under Cortés, Montezuma was imprisoned, but subsequently killed while trying to pacify some of his former subjects who had risen against his captors.

Montfort /ˈmɒntfət/, Simon de (1208–65), Earl of Leicester, leader of baronial opposition to Henry III. His campaign against royal encroachment on the privileges gained through Magna Carta, and his use of a parliament which included not only barons, knights, and ecclesiastics but two citizens from every borough in England, established him as one of the earliest exponents of limitations on the authority of the throne. After his defeat and capture of Henry at Lewes in 1264 he enjoyed a brief period as effective ruler of England, but was defeated and killed by reorganized royal forces under Henry's son (later Edward I) at Evesham in 1265.

Montgolfier /mɒnˈɡɒlfɪˌeɪ, -əˈ(r)/, Joseph (1740–1810) and Jacques Étienne (1745–99), French paper-manufacturers and balloonists, the first to arouse scientific and popular interest in ballooning. They began experiments in 1782 and built a large globe of linen and paper, lit a fire on the ground, and let the hot air float up into the globe through its open base so as to lift it. With this they successfully lifted a sheep, goat, and duck on 19 Sept. 1782; manned ascents followed in 1783. Joseph was the only brother to fly, once, in the largest ever hot-air balloon *La Flesselle* (19 Jan. 1784).

Montgomery[1] /mɒntˈɡʌmərɪ, -ˈɡɒmərɪ/ the capital of Alabama; pop. (1980) 177,857.

Montgomery[2] /mɒntˈɡʌmərɪ, -ˈɡɒmərɪ/, Bernard Law, Viscount Montgomery of Alamein (1887–1976), British soldier, who rose to prominence with his appointment to command the Eighth Army in the Western Desert in mid-1942, where his victory at El Alamein proved the decisive battle in the campaign to secure Egypt (and the Suez Canal), and later commanded British forces in the invasion of German-occupied France in 1944. By no means the most brilliant of generals, Montgomery achieved results by concentrating on meticulous planning and attention to logistics, and did much to sustain the spirit of the British Army by an intensive public relations campaign.

month /mʌnθ/ n. 1 (in full **calendar month**) a each of usu. twelve periods into which a year is divided. b a period of time between the same dates in successive calendar months. (See below.) 2 a period of 28 days or of four weeks. 3 = *lunar month*. □ **month of Sundays** a very long period. [OE *mōnath* f. Gmc, rel. to MOON]

The primitive calendar month of ancient nations began on the day of a new moon (or the day after, and thus coincided (except for fractions of a day) with the lunar month. Among many peoples, however, it was from a very early period found desirable that the calendar year should contain an integral number of the smaller periods used in ordinary reckoning, and the lunar months were superseded by a series of twelve periods each having a fixed number of days. In the Julian calendar the months in leap year had alternately 31 and 30 days while in other years February had only 29 instead of 30. Under Augustus this symmetrical arrangement was broken up by the transference of one day from February to August, and one from September and November to October and December respectively, producing the system now in use.

The names of the months date back to Roman times, and some are named after ancient Roman gods and goddesses. (See the individual entries for the names of the months.)

monthly /ˈmʌnθlɪ/ adj., adv., & n. —adj. done, produced, or occurring once a month. —adv. once a month; from month to month. —n. (pl. **-ies**) 1 a monthly periodical. 2 (in pl.) colloq. a menstrual period.

monticule /ˈmɒntɪˌkjuːl/ n. 1 a small hill. 2 a small mound caused by a volcanic eruption. [F f. LL *monticulus* dimin. of *mons* MOUNT[2]]

Montmartre /mɔ̃ˈmɑːtr/ a district in Paris much frequented by artists at the beginning of the 19th c. when it was a village separated from Paris. Many of its buildings have artistic associations, e.g. the Moulin de la Galette painted by Renoir, the Bateau-Lavoir occupied successively by Renoir, van Dongen, and Picasso, and the various houses associated with Utrillo.

Montpelier /mɒntˈpeljə(r)/ the capital of Vermont; pop. (1980) 8,241.

Montpellier /mɔ̃ˈpeljeɪ/ a city of southern France, near the Mediterranean coast; pop. (1982) 201,067. It was the home of a school of medicine, world-famous in medieval times; a university was founded here in 1220.

Montreal /ˌmɒntrɪˈɔːl/ a port on the St Lawrence and the largest city in Canada; pop. (1986) 1,015,400; metropolitan area pop. 2,921,350.

Montreux /mɔ̃ˈtrɜː/ a resort town in Switzerland, at the east end of Lake Geneva; pop. (1980) 19,700. An annual television festival (first held in 1961) takes place here every spring.

Montrose /mɒnˈtrəʊz/, James Graham, Marquis of (1612–50). Although one of the leaders of early Scottish resistance to Charles I, Montrose supported the king when his country entered the English Civil War and, commanding a small army of Irish and Scottish irregulars, inflicted a dramatic series of defeats on the stronger Covenanter forces in the north in 1644–5 before being defeated at Philiphaugh while trying to bring his men south to aid the failing Royalist cause in England. After several years in exile, he returned to Scotland in an ill-fated bid to restore the new king Charles II.

Mont St Michel /mɔ̃ sæ miːˈʃel/ an islet off the coast of Normandy, a rocky peak crowned by a medieval Benedictine abbey-fortress.

Montserrat /ˌmɒntsəˈræt/ one of the Leeward Islands in the West Indies; pop. (est. 1988) 12,000; official language, English; capital, Plymouth. Visited by Columbus in 1493 and named after a monastery in Spain, it was colonized by Irish settlers in 1632 and is now a British dependency.

monument /ˈmɒnjʊmənt/ n. 1 anything enduring that serves to commemorate or make celebrated, esp. a structure or building. 2 a stone or other structure placed over a grave or in a church etc. in memory of the dead. 3 an ancient building or site etc. that has survived or been preserved because of its historical importance. 4 (foll. by *of*, *to*) a typical or outstanding example (*a monument of indiscretion*). 5 a written record. □ **the Monument** a Doric column 60.6 m (202 ft.) high in the City of London, designed by Robert Hooke and Sir Christopher Wren (1671–7) to commemorate the Great Fire of 1666, which broke out in Pudding Lane nearby. [ME f. F f. L *monumentum* f. *monēre* remind]

monumental /ˌmɒnjʊˈment(ə)l/ adj. 1 a extremely great; stupendous (*a monumental achievement*). b (of a literary work) massive and permanent. 2 of or serving as a monument. □ **monumental mason** a maker of tombstones etc. □□ **monumentality** /-ˈtælɪtɪ/ n. **monumentally** adv.

monumentalize /ˌmɒnjʊˈmentəˌlaɪz/ v.tr. (also **-ise**) record or commemorate by or as by a monument.

-mony /mənɪ/ suffix forming nouns esp. denoting an abstract state or quality (*acrimony*; *testimony*). [L *-monia*, *-monium*, rel. to -MENT]

moo /muː/ v. & n. —v.intr. (**moos**, **mooed**) make the characteristic vocal sound of cattle; = LOW[2]. —n. (pl. **moos**) this sound. □ **moo-cow** a childish name for a cow. [imit.]

mooch /muːtʃ/ v. colloq. 1 intr. loiter or saunter desultorily. 2 tr. esp. US a steal. b beg. □□ **moocher** n. [ME, prob. f. OF *muchier* hide, skulk]

mood[1] /muːd/ n. 1 a state of mind or feeling. 2 (in pl.) fits of melancholy or bad temper. 3 (attrib.) inducing a particular mood (*mood music*). □ **in the** (or **no**) **mood** (foll. by *for*, or *to* + infin.) inclined (or disinclined) (*was in no mood to agree*). [OE *mōd* mind, thought, f. Gmc]

mood[2] /muːd/ n. 1 *Gram.* a a form or set of forms of a verb serving to indicate whether it is to express fact, command, wish, etc. (*subjunctive mood*). b the distinction of meaning expressed by different moods. 2 *Logic* any of the classes into which each of the figures of a valid categorical syllogism is subdivided. [var. of MODE, assoc. with MOOD[1]]

moody /ˈmuːdɪ/ adj. & n. —adj. (**moodier**, **moodiest**) given to changes of mood; gloomy, sullen. —n. colloq. a bad mood; a tantrum. □□ **moodily** adv. **moodiness** n. [OE *mōdig* brave (as MOOD[1])]

Moog /muːɡ/ n. (in full **Moog synthesizer**) propr. an electronic instrument with a keyboard, for producing a wide variety of musical sounds: see SYNTHESIZER. [R. A. *Moog*, Amer. engineer b. 1934, who invented it]

moolah /ˈmuːlə/ n. sl. money. [20th c.: orig. unkn.]

moolvi /ˈmuːlvɪ/ n. (also **moolvie**) 1 a Muslim doctor of the law. 2 a learned person or teacher (esp. as a term of respect among Muslims in India). [Urdu *mulvī* f. Arab. *mawlawīy* judicial: cf. MULLAH]

Moon /muːn/, Sun Myung (1920–), Korean religious leader, who in 1954 founded the Holy Spirit Association for the Unification of World Christianity, which became known as the Unification Church (see entry).

moon /muːn/ n. & v. —n. **1 a** the natural satellite of the earth, orbiting it monthly, illuminated by the sun and reflecting some light to the earth. (See below.) **b** this regarded in terms of its waxing and waning in a particular month (*new moon*). **c** the moon when visible (*there is no moon tonight*). **2** a satellite of any planet. **3** (prec. by *the*) something desirable but unattainable (*promised them the moon*). **4** *poet.* a month. —v. **1** *intr.* (often foll. by *about, around,* etc.) move or look listlessly. **2** *tr.* (foll. by *away*) spend (time) in a listless manner. **3** *intr.* (foll. by *over*) act aimlessly or inattentively from infatuation for (a person). □ **moon boot** a thickly-padded boot designed for low temperatures. **moon-faced** having a round face. **over the moon** extremely happy or delighted. □□ **moonless** adj. [OE *mōna* f. Gmc, rel. to MONTH]

The moon orbits Earth at a mean distance of some 400,000 km, and was familiar to our earliest ancestors as the source of night-time illumination. The bright and dark features which outline the face of 'the Man in the Moon' are seen through a telescope to be highland and lowland regions, the former heavily pockmarked by craters due to the impact of millions of meteorites when the solar system was still young. The moon has now been visited by the Apollo astronauts, and the samples of rock and dust which they collected are being analysed to determine the nature and history of our airless companion.

moonbeam /ˈmuːnbiːm/ n. a ray of moonlight.

mooncalf /ˈmuːnkɑːf/ n. a born fool.

moonfish /ˈmuːnfɪʃ/ n. = OPAH.

Moonie /ˈmuːnɪ/ n. sl. a member of the Unification Church. [Sun Myung MOON, its founder]

moonlight /ˈmuːnlaɪt/ n. & v. —n. **1** the light of the moon. **2** (*attrib.*) lighted by the moon. —v.intr. (**-lighted**) *colloq.* have two paid occupations, esp. one by day and one by night. □ **moonlight flit** a hurried departure by night, esp. to avoid paying a debt. □□ **moonlighter** n.

moonlit /ˈmuːnlɪt/ adj. lighted by the moon.

moonquake /ˈmuːnkweɪk/ n. a tremor of the moon's surface.

moonrise /ˈmuːnraɪz/ n. **1** the rising of the moon. **2** the time of this.

moonscape /ˈmuːnskeɪp/ n. **1** the surface or landscape of the moon. **2** an area resembling this; a wasteland.

moonset /ˈmuːnset/ n. **1** the setting of the moon. **2** the time of this.

moonshee /ˈmuːnʃiː/ n. (also *munshi*) a secretary or language-teacher in India. [Urdu *munshī* f. Arab. *munšī* 'writer']

moonshine /ˈmuːnʃaɪn/ n. **1** foolish or unrealistic talk or ideas. **2** *sl.* illicitly distilled or smuggled alcoholic liquor.

moonshiner /ˈmuːnˌʃaɪnə(r)/ n. US sl. an illicit distiller or smuggler of alcoholic liquor.

moonshot /ˈmuːnʃɒt/ n. the launching of a spacecraft to the moon.

moonstone /ˈmuːnstəʊn/ n. feldspar of pearly appearance.

moonstruck /ˈmuːnstrʌk/ adj. mentally deranged.

moony /ˈmuːnɪ/ adj. (**moonier, mooniest**) **1** listless; stupidly dreamy. **2** of or like the moon.

Moor /mʊə(r), mɔː(r)/ n. a member of a Muslim people of mixed Berber and Arab descent, inhabiting NW Africa. [ME f. OF *More* f. L *Maurus* f. Gk *Mauros* inhabitant of Mauretania (see entry)]

moor[1] /mʊə(r), mɔː(r)/ n. **1** a tract of open uncultivated upland, esp. when covered with heather. **2** a tract of ground preserved for shooting. **3** US a fen. □□ **moorish** adj. **moory** adj. [OE *mōr* waste land, marsh, mountain, f. Gmc]

moor[2] /mʊə(r), mɔː(r)/ v. **1** *tr.* make fast (a boat, buoy, etc.) by attaching a cable etc. to a fixed object. **2** *intr.* (of a boat) be moored. □□ **moorage** n. [ME *more*, prob. f. LG or MLG *mōren*]

moorcock /ˈmʊəkɒk, ˈmɔː-/ n. a male moorfowl.

Moore[1] /mʊə(r)/, Francis (1657–?1715), physician, astrologer, and schoolmaster, who in 1699 published an almanac containing weather predictions in order to promote the sale of his pills, and in 1700 one with astrological observations. There are now several almanacs called 'Old Moore', and predictions range far beyond the weather.

Moore[2] /mʊə(r)/, George (1852–1933), Anglo-Irish novelist, who studied painting in Paris and there became influenced by the naturalist techniques of Zola and the Goncourts, evident in his novels *A Mummer's Wife* (1885), set in the Potteries, and *Esther Waters* (1894), which defied Victorian conventions by exploring the problems facing the servant classes. He became involved in the Irish literary revival and collaborated in the planning of the Irish National Theatre. His autobiographical *Confessions of a Young Man* (1888) shows Moore as the champion of aestheticism and French impressionist painting.

Moore[3] /ˈmʊə(r)/, Henry (1898–1986), English sculptor and draughtsman. One of the most important 20th-c. sculptors, his eminence is due to his pioneering and sustained exploration of the suggestive area lying between figuration and abstraction, such ambiguity giving sculpture an enriched potential for expressive communication, particularly in exploiting the human body/landscape analogy. His discovery of African and pre-Columbian art in the 1920s led him to reject modelling for direct carving in stone and wood, working the material sympathetically and allowing natural qualities of grain and texture to influence form. His development of pierced and, later, broken form allowed the fullest interaction between sculpture and environment (e.g. *Reclining Figure* 1938), and much of his work is seen at its best in the open air. His work as a war artist (1940–2) emphasized the human aspect of his art, as in his drawings of sleeping air-raid victims.

Moore[4] /mʊə(r)/, Sir John (1761–1809), British general during the Napoleonic Wars, developer of special light-infantry training within the British army. Moore led an expeditionary force into French-held Spain in 1800 and, confronted by a much larger French army under Marshal Soult, conducted a successful 250-mile retreat in mid-winter, then won a brilliant victory over his pursuers while covering the embarkation of his army at Corunna, being mortally wounded in the process. His burial was the subject of a famous poem by the Irish poet Charles Wolfe.

Moore[5] /mʊə(r)/, Thomas (1779–1852), Irish musician and writer, a friend of Lord Byron. Moore was a skilful writer of patriotic and nostalgic songs, which he set to Irish tunes, mainly of the 18th century; his most famous songs include 'The Harp that once through Tara's Halls', 'The Minstrel Boy', and 'The Last Rose of Summer'. He also wrote satirical works, and won great popular success with his Oriental romance *Lalla Rookh* (1817).

moorfowl /ˈmʊəfaʊl, ˈmɔː-/ n. a red grouse.

moorhen /ˈmʊəhen, ˈmɔː-/ n. **1** a small aquatic bird, *Gallinula chloropus*, with long legs and a short red-yellow bill. **2** a female moorfowl.

mooring /ˈmʊərɪŋ, ˈmɔːrɪŋ/ n. **1 a** a fixed object to which a boat, buoy, etc., is moored. **b** (often in *pl.*) a place where a boat etc. is moored. **2** (in *pl.*) a set of permanent anchors and chains laid down for ships to be moored to.

Moorish /ˈmʊərɪʃ, ˈmɔːrɪʃ/ adj. of or relating to the Moors. □ **Moorish idol** a brightly-coloured Pacific fish of the genus *Zanclus*.

moorland /ˈmʊələnd, ˈmɔː-/ n. an extensive area of moor.

moose /muːs/ n. (*pl.* same) a N. American deer; an elk. [Narragansett *moos*]

Moose Jaw an industrial town in south central Saskatchewan, Canada; pop. (1986) 35,000.

moot /muːt/ adj., v., & n. —adj. (orig. the noun used *attrib.*) **1** debatable, undecided (*a moot point*). **2** US *Law* having no practical significance. —v.tr. raise (a question) for discussion. —n. **1** *hist.* an assembly. **2** *Law* a discussion of a hypothetical case as an academic exercise. [OE *mōt*, and *mōtian* converse, f. Gmc, rel. to MEET[1]]

mop[1] /mɒp/ n. & v. —n. **1** a wad or bundle of cotton or synthetic material fastened to the end of a stick, for cleaning floors etc. **2** a similarly-shaped large or small implement for various purposes. **3** anything resembling a mop, esp. a thick mass of hair. **4** an act of mopping or being mopped (*gave it a mop*). —v.tr.

(**mopped**, **mopping**) **1** wipe or clean with or as with a mop. **2 a** wipe tears or sweat etc. from (one's face or brow etc.). **b** wipe away (tears etc.). □ **mop up 1** wipe up with or as with a mop. **2** *colloq.* absorb (profits etc.). **3** dispatch; make an end of. **4** *Mil.* **a** complete the occupation of (a district etc.) by capturing or killing enemy troops left there. **b** capture or kill (stragglers). □□ **moppy** *adj.* [ME *mappe*, perh. ult. rel. to L *mappa* napkin]

mop[2] /mɒp/ *n. Brit. hist.* an autumn fair or gathering at which farm-hands and servants were formerly hired. [perh. = *mop-fair*, at which a mop was carried by a maidservant seeking employment]

mope /məʊp/ *v. & n.* —*v.intr.* be gloomily depressed or listless; behave sulkily. —*n.* **1** a person who mopes. **2** (**the mopes**) low spirits. □□ **moper** *n.* **mopy** *adj.* (**mopier, mopiest**). **mopily** *adv.* **mopiness** *n.* [16th c.: prob. rel. to *mope*, *mopp(e)* fool]

moped /ˈməʊped/ *n.* a motorized bicycle with an engine capacity below 50 cc. [Sw. (as MOTOR, PEDAL[1])]

mophead /ˈmɒphed/ *n.* a person with thick matted hair.

mopoke /ˈməʊpəʊk/ *n.* (also **morepork** /ˈmɔːpɔːk/) **1** a boobook. **2** an Australian nocturnal insect-eating bird, *Podargus strigoides*. Also called FROGMOUTH. [imit. of the bird's cry]

moppet /ˈmɒpɪt/ *n. colloq.* (esp. as a term of endearment) a baby or small child. [obs. *moppe* baby, doll]

Mopti /ˈmɒptɪ/ a city in central Mali, at the junction of the Niger and Bani rivers; pop. (est.) 53,900.

moquette /mɒˈket/ *n.* a thick pile or looped material used for carpets and upholstery. [F, perh. f. obs. It. *mocaiardo* mohair]

mor /mɔː(r)/ *n.* humus formed under acid conditions. [Da.]

moraine /məˈreɪn/ *n.* an area covered by rocks and debris carried down and deposited by a glacier. □□ **morainal** *adj.* **morainic** *adj.* [F f. It. dial. *morena* f. F dial. *mor(re)* snout f. Rmc]

moral /ˈmɒr(ə)l/ *adj. & n.* —*adj.* **1 a** concerned with goodness or badness of human character or behaviour, or with the distinction between right and wrong. **b** concerned with accepted rules and standards of human behaviour. **2 a** conforming to accepted standards of general conduct. **b** capable of moral action (*man is a moral agent*). **3** (of rights or duties etc.) founded on moral law. **4 a** concerned with morals or ethics (*moral philosophy*). **b** (of a literary work etc.) dealing with moral conduct. **5** concerned with or leading to a psychological effect associated with confidence in a right action (*moral courage; moral support; moral victory*). —*n.* **1 a** a moral lesson (esp. at the end) of a fable, story, event, etc. **b** a moral maxim or principle. **2** (in *pl.*) moral behaviour, e.g. in sexual conduct. □ **moral certainty** probability so great as to allow no reasonable doubt. **moral law** the conditions to be satisfied by any right course of action. **moral majority** the majority of people, regarded as favouring firm moral standards (orig. *Moral Majority*, name of a right-wing US movement). **moral philosophy** the branch of philosophy concerned with ethics. **moral pressure** persuasion by appealing to a person's moral sense. **Moral Re-Armament 1** = OXFORD GROUP. **2** the beliefs of this organization, esp. as applied to international relations. **moral science** systematic knowledge as applied to morals. **moral sense** the ability to distinguish right and wrong. □□ **morally** *adv.* [ME f. L *moralis* f. *mos moris* custom, pl. *mores* morals]

morale /məˈrɑːl/ *n.* the mental attitude or bearing of a person or group, esp. as regards confidence, discipline, etc. [F *moral* respelt to preserve the pronunciation]

moralism /ˈmɒrəlɪz(ə)m/ *n.* **1** a natural system of morality. **2** religion regarded as moral practice.

moralist /ˈmɒrəlɪst/ *n.* **1** a person who practises or teaches morality. **2** a person who follows a natural system of ethics. □□ **moralistic** /-ˈlɪstɪk/ *adj.* **moralistically** /-ˈlɪstɪkəlɪ/ *adv.*

morality /məˈrælɪtɪ/ *n.* (*pl.* -**ies**) **1** the degree of conformity of an idea, practice, etc., to moral principles. **2** right moral conduct. **3** a lesson in morals. **4** the science of morals. **5** a particular system of morals (*commercial morality*). **6** (in *pl.*) moral principles; points of ethics. **7** (in full **morality play**) any of the medieval allegorical dramas, teaching a moral lesson, in which the main characters are personified human qualities. They belong mainly to the 15th c. Among the most celebrated English examples are

Everyman; Ane Satire of the Thrie Estaitis by Sir David Lyndsay; *Magnificence* by Skelton; *King John* by John Bale; *Mankind; The Castle of Perseverance*. [ME f. OF *moralité* or LL *moralitas* f. L (as MORAL)]

moralize /ˈmɒrəlaɪz/ *v.* (also **-ise**) **1** *intr.* (often foll. by *on*) indulge in moral reflection or talk. **2** *tr.* interpret morally; point the moral of. **3** *tr.* make moral or more moral. □□ **moralization** /-ˈzeɪʃ(ə)n/ *n.* **moralizer** *n.* **moralizingly** *adv.* [F *moraliser* or med.L *moralizare* f. L (as MORAL)]

Morar /ˈmɒrə(r)/, **Loch** a loch in western Scotland, the deepest loch in the country (310 m, 1,017 ft.).

morass /məˈræs/ *n.* **1** an entanglement; a disordered situation, esp. one impeding progress. **2** *literary* a bog or marsh. [Du. *moeras* (assim. to *moer* MOOR[1]) f. MDu. *marasch* f. OF *marais* marsh f. med.L *mariscus*]

moratorium /ˌmɒrəˈtɔːrɪəm/ *n.* (*pl.* **moratoriums** or **moratoria** /-rɪə/) **1** (often foll. by *on*) a temporary prohibition or suspension (of an activity). **2 a** a legal authorization to debtors to postpone payment. **b** the period of this postponement. [mod.L, neut. of LL *moratorius* delaying f. L *morari morat-* to delay f. *mora* delay]

Moravian /məˈreɪvɪən/ *n. & adj.* —*n.* **1** a native of Moravia, now a region of Czechoslovakia round the River Morava. **2** a member of a Protestant sect founded in Saxony in 1722 by emigrants from Moravia, holding views derived from the Hussites and a simple unworldly form of Christianity with the Bible as the only source of faith. —*adj.* of, relating to, or characteristic of Moravia or its people.

moray /mɒˈreɪ/ *n.* any tropical eel-like fish of the family Muraenidae, esp. *Muraena helena* found in Mediterranean waters. [Port. *moreia* f. L f. Gk *muraina*]

Moray Firth /ˈmʌrɪ/ a deep inlet of the North Sea on the NE coast of Scotland. The city of Inverness is near its head.

morbid /ˈmɔːbɪd/ *adj.* **1 a** (of the mind, ideas, etc.) unwholesome, sickly. **b** given to morbid feelings. **2** *colloq.* melancholy. **3** *Med.* of the nature of or indicative of disease. □ **morbid anatomy** the anatomy of diseased organs, tissues, etc. □□ **morbidity** /-ˈbɪdɪtɪ/ *n.* **morbidly** *adv.* **morbidness** *n.* [L *morbidus* f. *morbus* disease]

morbific /mɔːˈbɪfɪk/ *adj.* causing disease. [F *morbifique* or mod.L *morbificus* f. L *morbus* disease]

morbilli /mɔːˈbɪlɪ/ *n.pl.* **1** measles. **2** the spots characteristic of measles. [L, pl. of *morbillus* pustule f. *morbus* disease]

mordant /ˈmɔːd(ə)nt/ *adj. & n.* —*adj.* **1** (of sarcasm etc.) caustic, biting. **2** pungent, smarting. **3** corrosive or cleansing. **4** (of a substance) serving to fix colouring-matter or gold leaf on another substance. —*n.* a mordant substance (in senses 3, 4 of *adj.*). □□ **mordancy** *n.* **mordantly** *adv.* [ME f. F, part. of *mordre* bite f. L *mordēre*]

mordent /ˈmɔːd(ə)nt/ *n. Mus.* **1** an ornament consisting of one rapid alternation of a written note with the note immediately below it. **2** a pralltriller. [G f. It. *mordente* part. of *mordēre* bite]

More /mɔː(r)/, **Sir Thomas** (1478–1535), Lord Chancellor of England 1529–32, a deeply religious, learned, and ascetic man, whose house in Chelsea was a centre of intellectual life. His most famous work, *Utopia*, describes an ideal community living (without private property) according to natural law and practising a natural religion, and contains satiric side-thrusts at contemporary abuses. From the time of the accession of Henry VIII (1509) More held a series of public offices, but the turning-point in his fortunes came when he opposed the king's divorce from Catherine of Aragon. He was forced to resign office and lived in retirement until 1534, when he refused to take the oath on the Act of Succession and was imprisoned. In 1535 he was accused of high treason on the ground of his opposition to the Act of Supremacy which confirmed Henry as supreme head of the Church of England, and was beheaded. It would, however, be a mistake to assume that he died in defence of papal power and authority. He was canonized in 1935. Feast day, 22 June.

more /mɔː(r)/ *adj., n., & adv.* —*adj.* **1** existing in a greater or additional quantity, amount, or degree (*more problems than last time; bring some more water*). **2** greater in degree (*more's the pity; the more fool you*). —*n.* a greater quantity, number, or amount (*more than three people; more to it than meets the eye*). —*adv.* **1** in a greater degree (*do it more carefully*). **2** to a greater extent (*people like to walk more these days*). **3** forming the comparative of adjectives and adverbs, esp. those of more than one syllable (*more absurd; more easily*). **4** again (*once more; never more*). **5** moreover. □ **more and more** in an increasing degree. **more like it** see LIKE[1]. **more of** to a greater extent (*more of a poet than a musician*). **more or less 1** in a greater or less degree. **2** approximately; as an estimate. **more so** of the same kind to a greater degree. [OE *māra* f. Gmc]

moreen /mɒˈriːn/ *n.* a strong ribbed woollen or cotton material for curtains etc. [perh. fanciful f. MOIRE]

moreish /ˈmɔːrɪʃ/ *adj.* (also **morish**) *colloq.* pleasant to eat, causing a desire for more.

morel[1] /məˈrel/ *n.* an edible fungus, *Morchella esculenta*, with ridged mushroom caps. [F *morille* f. Du. *morilje*]

morel[2] /məˈrel/ *n.* nightshade. [ME f. OF *morele* fem. of *morel* dark brown ult. f. L *Maurus* MOOR]

morello /məˈreləʊ/ *n.* (*pl.* **-os**) a sour kind of dark cherry. [It. *morello* blackish f. med.L *morellus* f. L (as MOREL[1])]

Morelos /məˈreɪlɒs/ a State of central Mexico; pop. (est. 1988) 1,258,500; capital, Cuernavaca.

moreover /mɔːˈrəʊvə(r)/ *adj.* (introducing or accompanying a new statement) further, besides.

morepork var. of MOPOKE.

mores /ˈmɔːreɪz, -riːz/ *n.pl.* customs or conventions regarded as essential to or characteristic of a community. [L, pl. of *mos* custom]

Moresco var. of MORISCO.

Moresque /mɒˈresk/ *adj.* (of art or architecture) Moorish in style or design. [F f. It. *moresco* f. *Moro* MOOR]

Morgan[1] /ˈmɔːgən/, John Pierpont (1837–1913), American financier, industrialist, and philanthropist, one of the leading art collectors of his day. His main collecting activities were in manuscripts and rare books, and after his death his son, also called John Pierpont Morgan (1867–1943), endowed the Pierpont Morgan Library in New York as a research institute and museum in memory of his father.

Morgan[2] /ˈmɔːgən/, Thomas Hunt (1866–1945), American zoologist, best known for showing the mechanism in the animal cell responsible for the genetics of inheritance. Morgan's studies with the rapidly reproducing fruit fly Drosophila showed that the genetic information was carried by genes arranged along the length of the chromosomes. Though this work was not widely accepted initially, he was awarded a Nobel Prize in 1933.

morganatic /ˌmɔːgəˈnætɪk/ *adj.* **1** (of a marriage) between a person of high rank and another of lower rank, the spouse and children having no claim to the possessions or title of the person of higher rank. **2** (of a wife) married in this way. □□ **morganatically** *adv.* [F *morganatique* or G *morganatisch* f. med.L *matrimonium ad morganaticam* 'marriage with a morning gift', the husband's gift to the wife after consummation being his only obligation in such a marriage]

Morgan le Fay /ˌmɔːgən lə ˈfeɪ/ (in Arthurian legend) 'Morgan the Fairy', a magician, sister of King Arthur. (See FATA MORGANA.)

morgue /mɔːg/ *n.* **1** a mortuary. **2** (in a newspaper office) a room or file of miscellaneous information, esp. for future obituaries. [F, orig. the name of a Paris mortuary]

moribund /ˈmɒrɪˌbʌnd/ *adj.* **1** at the point of death. **2** lacking vitality. □□ **moribundity** /-ˈbʌndɪtɪ/ *n.* [L *moribundus* f. *mori* die]

Morisco /məˈrɪskəʊ/ *n.* & *adj.* (also **Moresco** /-ˈreskəʊ/) —*n.* (*pl.* **-os** or **-oes**) **1** a Moor, esp. in Spain. (See below.) **2** a morris dance. —*adj.* Moorish. [Sp. *morisco* little Moor f. *Moro* MOOR]
The term 'Morisco' is applied especially to the Moors in Spain (or their descendants) who accepted Christian baptism. When the Christians reconquered Muslim Spain in the 11th–15th c. the Islamic religion and customs were at first tolerated (see MUDÉJAR), but after the fall of Granada in 1492 Islam was officially prohibited and Muslims were forced to become Christians or go into exile. Many who remained practised their own religion in private, in spite of persecution, but their political loyalty

was suspect and in 1609 they were expelled, mainly to Africa. [Sp. *morisco* little Moor f. *Moro* MOOR]

morish var. of MOREISH.

Morisot /ˌmɒriːˈsəʊ/, Berthe (1841–95), French impressionist painter, who specialized in gentle domestic scenes and marine painting. Fragonard was her grandfather, she was a pupil of Corot, and she influenced and was influenced by Édouard Manet, for whom she often posed. She married Manet's brother in 1874.

Morland /ˈmɔːlənd/, George (1763–1804), English genre painter. Although indebted to Dutch 17th-c. painters, such as Teniers, his pictures of taverns, cottages, and farmyards were local in inspiration (e.g. *Inside a Stable*, 1791, and *Outside the Ale-House Door*, 1792) and helped to create that fictitious rural England so popular in the 18th and 19th c. His art achieved wide popularity through the engravings of W. and J. Ward.

Morley /ˈmɔːlɪ/, Edward Williams (1838–1923), American chemist who specialized in accurate quantitative measurements such as those of the combining weights of hydrogen and oxygen, but who is best remembered for his collaboration with Michelson (see entry) in their experiment in 1887 to determine the speed of light.

Mormon /ˈmɔːmən/ *n.* a member of the Church of Jesus Christ of Latter-Day Saints, a millenary religion founded in New York (1830) by Joseph Smith (1805–44), who claimed to have discovered, through divine revelation, the 'Book of Mormon', which he translated, relating the history of a group of Hebrews who migrated to America *c.*600 BC; this work is accepted by Mormons as Scripture along with the Bible. A further revelation led him to institute polygamy, a practice which brought the Mormons into conflict with the Federal Government and was abandoned in 1890. Smith was succeeded as leader by Brigham Young (1801–77), who moved the Mormon headquarters to Salt Lake City, Utah, in 1847. Mormon teaching is strongly adventist; the movement has no professional clergy, self-help is emphasized, and tithing and missionary work are demanded from its members. □□ **Mormonism** *n.*

morn /mɔːn/ *n. poet.* morning. [OE *morgen* f. Gmc]

mornay /ˈmɔːneɪ/ *n.* a cheese-flavoured white sauce. [20th c.: orig. uncert.]

morning /ˈmɔːnɪŋ/ *n.* & *int.* —*n.* **1** the early part of the day, esp. from sunrise to noon (*this morning; during the morning; morning coffee*). **2** this time spent in a particular way (*had a busy morning*). **3** sunrise, daybreak. **4** a time compared with the morning, esp. the early part of one's life etc. —*int.* = *good morning* (see GOOD *adj.* 14). □ **in the morning 1** during or in the course of the morning. **2** *colloq.* tomorrow. **morning after** *colloq.* a hangover. **morning-after pill** a contraceptive pill effective when taken some hours after intercourse. **morning coat** a coat with tails, and with the front cut away below the waist. **morning dress** a man's morning coat and striped trousers. **morning glory** any of various twining plants of the genus *Ipomoea*, with trumpet-shaped flowers. **morning-room** a sitting-room for the morning. **morning sickness** nausea felt in the morning in pregnancy. **morning star** a planet or bright star, usu. Venus, seen in the east before sunrise. **morning watch** *Naut.* the 4–8 a.m. watch. [ME *mor(we)ning* f. *morwen* MORN + -ING[1] after *evening*]

Moro /ˈmɔːrəʊ/ *n.* (*pl.* **-os**) a Muslim living in the Philippines. [Sp.; = MOOR]

Morocco /məˈrɒkəʊ/ a country in the NW corner of Africa, with coastlines on the Mediterranean Sea and Atlantic Ocean; pop. (est. 1988) 24,976,200; official language, Arabic; capital, Rabat. The economy is sustained by a well-developed mining industry, the country being one of the leading exporters of phosphates, but agriculture remains the main occupation of its inhabitants. Tourism is also important. Conquered by the Arabs in the 7th c., Morocco was penetrated by the Portuguese in the 15th c. and later fell under French and Spanish influence, each country establishing protectorates in the early 20th c. It became a fully fledged independent State after the withdrawal of the colonial powers in 1956. □□ **Moroccan** *adj.* & *n.*

morocco /məˈrɒkəʊ/ *n.* (*pl.* **-os**) **1** a fine flexible leather made (orig. in Morocco) from goatskins tanned with sumac, used esp. in bookbinding and shoemaking. **2** an imitation of this in grained calf etc.

moron /ˈmɔːrɒn/ n. **1** colloq. a very stupid or foolish person. **2** an adult with a mental age of about 8–12. □□ **moronic** /məˈrɒnɪk/ adj. **moronically** /məˈrɒnɪkəlɪ/ adv. **moronism** n. [Gk mōron, neut. of mōros foolish]

Moroni /məˈrəʊnɪ/ the capital of the Comoros Islands, on the island of Grand Comore; pop. (1980) 20,100.

morose /məˈrəʊs/ adj. sullen and ill-tempered. □□ **morosely** adv. **moroseness** n. [L morosus peevish etc. f. mos moris manner]

morph /mɔːf/ n. = ALLOMORPH. [back-form.]

morpheme /ˈmɔːfiːm/ n. Linguistics **1** a morphological element considered in respect of its functional relations in a linguistic system. **2** a meaningful morphological unit of a language that cannot be further divided (e.g. in, come, -ing, forming incoming). □□ **morphemic** /-ˈfiːmɪk/ adj. **morphemically** /-ˈfiːmɪkəlɪ/ adv. [F morphème f. Gk morphē form, after PHONEME]

morphemics /mɔːˈfiːmɪks/ n.pl. (usu. treated as sing.) Linguistics the study of word structure.

Morpheus /ˈmɔːfiəs/ Rom. Mythol. the son of Somnus (god of sleep) and sender of dreams of human forms.

morphia /ˈmɔːfiə/ n. (in general use) = MORPHINE.

morphine /ˈmɔːfiːn/ n. an analgesic and narcotic drug obtained from opium and used medicinally to relieve pain. □□ **morphinism** /-fɪˌnɪz(ə)m/ n. [G Morphin & mod.L morphia f. MORPHEUS]

morphogenesis /ˌmɔːfəˈdʒenɪsɪs/ n. Biol. the development of form in organisms. □□ **morphogenetic** /-dʒɪˈnetɪk/ adj. **morphogenic** adj. [mod.L f. Gk morphē form + GENESIS]

morphology /mɔːˈfɒlədʒɪ/ n. the study of the forms of things, esp.: **1** Biol. the study of the forms of organisms. **2** Philol. **a** the study of the forms of words. **b** the system of forms in a language. □□ **morphological** /ˌmɔːfəˈlɒdʒɪk(ə)l/ adj. **morphologically** /-fəˈlɒdʒɪkəlɪ/ adv. **morphologist** n. [Gk morphē form + -LOGY]

Morris¹ /ˈmɒrɪs/, William (1834–96), English writer, artist, and designer. Distressed by the poverty of mass-produced design, he championed a return to an ideal of beauty through utility and simplicity. The establishment of his firm, Morris and Co., in 1861 allowed the realization of his essentially medieval aesthetic, recreating a hand industry in a machine age, with craftsmen producing stained glass, wall-paper, tapestry, furniture, and fabrics for the home. The founding of the Kelmscott Press in 1890 influenced English book design. His reformist doctrines were of vital importance to the English Arts and Crafts movement (see entry). Ironically, despite a link with the socialist revival of the 1880s, Morris's greatest success was in the decoration of the homes of the wealthy. □ **Morris chair** a type of plain easy chair with an adjustable back.

morris dance /ˈmɒrɪs/ n. a vigorous folk-dance of ancient date, by groups of men in fancy costume, characteristic of rural England. There are many styles, traditionally associated with different localities, and dress etc. varies: some use handkerchiefs and bells, others sticks. Such dances are referred to in the 14th c. but are probably much earlier, dating back to pre-Christian pagan rituals. By the end of the 19th c. they were dying out and were saved from almost certain extinction by the efforts of Cecil Sharp. □□ **morris dancer** n. **morris dancing** n. [morys, var. of MOORISH (dance)]

morrow /ˈmɒrəʊ/ n. (usu. prec. by the) literary **1** the following day. **2** the time following an event. [ME morwe, moru (as MORN)]

Morse¹ /mɔːs/, Samuel Finley Breese (1791–1872), American painter, noted for his portraits, and a pioneer in the use of the electric telegraph. He conceived the idea for this device in 1832, had the first working model ready a few years later, and extended its range and capabilities in 1837 by means of electromagnetic relays, helped considerably by the physicist Joseph Henry (1797–1878). In England, however, he had been anticipated by Wheatstone. The US Congress gave financial support in 1843 for an experimental line from Washington, DC, to Baltimore, over which Morse sent the famous message 'What hath

God wrought' on 24 May 1844, using his system of signals (the Morse code; see MORSE²).

Morse² /mɔːs/ n. & v. —n. (in full **Morse code**) an alphabet or code in which letters are represented by combinations of long and short light or sound signals. Invented by S. F. B. Morse (see entry) it was adopted internationally in wireless or radio-telegraphy when this superseded wire telegraphy. —v.tr. & intr. signal by Morse code.

morsel /ˈmɔːs(ə)l/ n. a mouthful; a small piece (esp. of food). [ME f. OF, dimin. of mors a bite f. mordēre mors- to bite]

mort /mɔːt/ n. Hunting a note sounded when the quarry is killed. [ME f. OF f. L mors mortis death]

mortadella /ˌmɔːtəˈdelə/ n. (pl. **mortadelle** /-ˈdele/) a large spiced pork sausage. [It. dimin., irreg. f. L murtatum seasoned with myrtle berries]

mortal /ˈmɔːt(ə)l/ adj. & n. —adj. **1** (of a living being, esp. a human) subject to death. **2** (often foll. by to) causing death; fatal. **3** (of a battle) fought to the death. **4** associated with death (mortal agony). **5** (of an enemy) implacable. **6** (of pain, fear, an affront, etc.) intense, very serious. **7** colloq. **a** very great (in a mortal hurry). **b** long and tedious (for two mortal hours). **8** colloq. conceivable, imaginable (every mortal thing; of no mortal use). —n. **1** a mortal being, esp. a human. **2** joc. a person described in some specified way (a thirsty mortal). □ **mortal sin** Theol. a grave sin that is regarded as depriving the soul of divine grace. □□ **mortally** adv. [ME f. OF mortal, mortel or L mortalis f. mors mortis death]

mortality /mɔːˈtælɪtɪ/ n. (pl. **-ies**) **1** the state of being subject to death. **2** loss of life on a large scale. **3 a** the number of deaths in a given period etc. **b** (in full **mortality rate**) a death rate. [ME f. OF mortalité f. L mortalitas -tatis (AS MORTAL)]

mortar /ˈmɔːtə(r)/ n. & v. —n. **1** a mixture of lime with cement, sand, and water, used in building to bond bricks or stones. **2** a short large-bore cannon for firing shells at high angles. **3** a contrivance for firing a lifeline or firework. **4** a vessel made of hard material, in which ingredients are pounded with a pestle. —v.tr. **1** plaster or join with mortar. **2** attack or bombard with mortar shells. □□ **mortarless** adj. (in sense 1). **mortary** adj. (in sense 1). [ME f. AF morter, OF mortier f. L mortarium: partly from LG]

mortarboard /ˈmɔːtəˌbɔːd/ n. **1** an academic cap with a stiff flat square top. **2** a flat board with a handle on the under-surface, for holding mortar in bricklaying etc.

mortgage /ˈmɔːgɪdʒ/ n. & v. —n. **1 a** a conveyance of property by a debtor to a creditor as security for a debt (esp. one incurred by the purchase of the property), on the condition that it shall be returned on payment of the debt within a certain period. **b** a deed effecting this. **2 a** a debt secured by a mortgage. **b** a loan resulting in such a debt. —v.tr. **1** convey (a property) by mortgage. **2** (often foll. by to) pledge (oneself, one's powers, etc.). □ **mortgage rate** the rate of interest charged by a mortgagee. □□ **mortgageable** adj. [ME f. OF, = dead pledge f. mort f. L mortuus dead + gage GAGE¹]

mortgagee /ˌmɔːgɪˈdʒiː/ n. the creditor in a mortgage, usu. a bank or building society.

mortgager /ˈmɔːgɪdʒə(r)/ n. (also **mortgagor** /-ˈdʒɔː(r)/) the debtor in a mortgage.

mortice var. of MORTISE.

mortician /mɔːˈtɪʃ(ə)n/ n. US an undertaker; a manager of funerals. [L mors mortis death + -ICIAN]

mortify /ˈmɔːtɪˌfaɪ/ v. (**-ies**, **-ied**) **1** tr. **a** cause (a person) to feel shamed or humiliated. **b** wound (a person's feelings). **2** tr. bring (the body, the flesh, the passions, etc.) into subjection by self-denial or discipline. **3** intr. (of flesh) be affected by gangrene or necrosis. □□ **mortification** /-fɪˈkeɪʃ(ə)n/ n. **mortifying** adj. **mortifyingly** adv. [ME f. OF mortifier f. eccl.L mortificare kill, subdue f. mors mortis death]

mortise /ˈmɔːtɪs/ n. & v. (also **mortice**) —n. a hole in a framework designed to receive the end of another part, esp. a tenon. —v.tr. **1** join securely, esp. by mortise and tenon. **2** cut a mortise in. □ **mortise lock** a lock recessed into a mortise in the frame of a door or window etc. [ME f. OF mortoise f. Arab. murtazz fixed in]

mortmain /'mɔːtmeɪn/ n. Law 1 the status of lands or tenements held inalienably by an ecclesiastical or other corporation. 2 the land or tenements themselves. [ME f. AF, OF mortemain f. med.L mortua manus dead hand, prob. in allusion to impersonal ownership]

Morton[1] /'mɔːt(ə)n/, 'Jelly Roll' (1885–1941), American jazz pianist, composer, and band-leader. He was one of the principal links between ragtime and jazz proper, and formed his own band, the Red Hot Peppers, to make some classic jazz recordings.

Morton[2] /'mɔːt(ə)n/, John (c.1420–1500), English statesman, who rose to become Henry VII's chief adviser, being appointed Archbishop of Canterbury in 1486 and Chancellor a year later. He is generally associated with the Crown's stringent taxation policies, which gained great unpopularity for the regime in general and Morton in particular. □ **Morton's fork** the argument he used in demanding gifts for the royal treasury: that if a man lived handsomely he was obviously rich, and if simply that economy must have made him so and he could afford a donation.

mortuary /'mɔːtjʊərɪ/ n. & adj. —n. (pl. -ies) a room or building in which dead bodies may be kept until burial or cremation. —adj. of or concerning death or burial. [ME f. AF mortuarie f. med.L mortuarium f. L mortuarius f. mortuus dead]

morula /'mɔːrʊlə/ n. (pl. **morulae** /-ˌliː/) a fully segmented ovum from which a blastula is formed. [mod.L, dimin. of L morum mulberry]

morwong /'mɔːwɒŋ/ n. any of various fish of the family Cheilodactylidae, native to Australasia, used as food. [Aboriginal]

Mosaic /məʊˈzeɪɪk/ adj. of or associated with Moses (in the Hebrew Bible). □ **Mosaic Law** the laws attributed to Moses and listed in the Pentateuch. [F mosaïque or mod.L Mosaicus f. Moses f. Heb. Mōšeh]

mosaic /məʊˈzeɪɪk/ n. & v. —n. 1 a a picture or pattern produced by an arrangement of small variously coloured pieces of glass or stone etc. b work of this kind as an art form. (See below.) 2 a diversified thing. 3 an arrangement of photosensitive elements in a television camera. 4 Biol. a chimera. 5 (in full **mosaic disease**) a virus disease causing leaf-mottling in plants, esp. tobacco, maize, and sugar cane. 6 (attrib.) a of or like a mosaic. b diversified. —v.tr. (**mosaicked, mosaicking**) 1 adorn with mosaics. 2 combine into or as into a mosaic. □ **mosaic gold** 1 tin disulphide. 2 an alloy of copper and zinc used in cheap jewellery etc. □□ **mosaicist** /-ɪsɪst/ n. [ME f. F mosaïque f. It. mosaico f. med.L mosaicus, musaicus f. Gk mous(e)ion mosaic work f. mousa MUSE[1]]

The first extensive use of mosaic was by the Romans, and a crucial technical advance was their invention of a durable and waterproof cement in which the fragments were fixed. Well-preserved examples survive from all parts of the Roman world, a testimony of their durability. The classical Roman mosaic tradition was continued in the Christian period, and survived longest and most splendidly in the Byzantine world, fine examples ranging from the Emperor Justinian's sequences at Ravenna (6th c.) to Hosios Loukas in mainland Greece (11th c.), and the mosaic cycles of Norman Sicily (12th c.) and St Mark's in Venice (13th c.), which deliberately sought to emulate the splendours of the Byzantine court. In the West, from the 13th c. the stylized mosaic technique was superseded by the new naturalistic possibilities of fresco painting. It is a seldom-used art form now, but examples of more modern mosaics include those by Watts and Stevens in St Paul's Cathedral (1863–92). Israel and some countries of South America provide examples of contemporary work.

mosasaurus /ˌmɒsəˈsɔːrəs/ n. any large extinct marine reptile of the genus Mosasaurus, with a long slender body and flipper-like limbs. [mod.L f. Mosa river Meuse (near which it was first discovered) + Gk sauros lizard]

moschatel /ˌmɒskəˈtel/ n. a small plant, Adoxa moschatellina, with pale-green flowers and a musky smell. [F moscatelle f. It. moscatella f. moscato musk]

Moscow /'mɒskəʊ/ the capital of the USSR, on the central Russian plain; pop. (est. 1987) 8,815,000. Moscow is first heard of in 1147; at that time it was a typical Russian village, built on the high right bank of the Moskva River. It soon became the centre of the increasingly powerful Muscovite princes, one of whom in 1380 succeeded in defeating the Tartar overlords of the Russians, and in the 16th c., when Ivan the Terrible proclaimed himself Tsar of all the Russias, Moscow became the capital of the new empire, its central position giving it supreme military and economic value. Though Peter the Great moved his capital to St Petersburg (now Leningrad) in 1712, Moscow remained the heart of Russia, and was the target for the main attacks by Napoleon in 1812 and Hitler in 1941. Three-quarters of the city was destroyed by fire during Napoleon's occupation, but by the mid-19th c. Moscow had become a large and growing industrial city, and after the revolution of 1917 was made the capital of the USSR. Its centre is the Kremlin.

Moseley /'məʊzlɪ/, Henry Gwyn Jeffreys (1887–1915), English physicist who, while working under Rutherford, discovered that there existed a relationship between the atomic numbers of elements and the wavelengths of their emitted X-rays. Thus he demonstrated experimentally the connection between nuclear charge and atomic number, that the element's chemical properties were determined by this number, and that there were only 92 naturally-occurring elements. His short life ended tragically when he was killed in the Gallipoli campaign in the First World War.

moselle /məʊˈzel/ n. a light medium-dry white wine produced in the valley of the river Moselle in Germany.

Moses[1] /'məʊzɪz/ a Hebrew patriarch who, according to the Pentateuch, was born in Egypt and led the Jews away from their bondage there, across the desert. During the journey he was inspired by God on Mount Sinai to write down the Ten Commandments on tablets of stone (Exod. 20); he died in Moab, within sight of the Promised Land.

Moses[2] /'məʊzɪz/, Anna Mary Robertson (known as 'Grandma Moses') (1860–1961), the most famous of American naïve painters, who took up painting seriously only in the 1930s. She produced more than a thousand pictures, her favourite subjects being scenes of the farm life she had known in her younger days. Her works achieved widespread popularity for their brightly coloured freshness and charm.

mosey /'məʊzɪ/ v.intr. (-eys, -eyed) (often foll. by along) sl. walk in a leisurely or aimless manner. [19th c.: orig. unkn.]

moshav /məʊˈʃɑːv/ n. (pl. **moshavim**) a cooperative association of Israeli smallholders. [Heb. mošāḇ, lit. 'dwelling']

Moslem var. of MUSLIM.

Mosley /'məʊzlɪ/, Sir Oswald Ernald (1896–1980), English Fascist leader. One of the brightest young politicians of his day, Mosley sat successively as a Conservative, Independent, and Labour MP before founding the British Union of Fascists in 1932, a political party which failed to find the mass support enjoyed by its European cousins. He was imprisoned for most of the Second World War and made an unsuccessful attempt to form a new right-wing party in Britain after its end.

mosque /mɒsk/ n. a Muslim place of worship. The earliest mosques grew out of the needs of the community and its rituals, and during the first century of the faith a dominant form of mosque architecture developed: a courtyard, forming a place for communal gathering; a covered area used for worship, on the side facing Mecca, frequently domed, with its mihrab or niche oriented towards the Kaaba and showing the direction of prayer; sometimes a space for princes (the maqsura); and a fountain for ablutions, obligatory before prayer. Representations of the human form are forbidden, and decoration is by geometric designs and Arabic calligraphy (e.g. of verses from the Koran). [F mosquée f. It. moschea f. Arab. masjid]

Mosquito /məˈskiːtəʊ/ var. of MISKITO. □ **Mosquito Coast** a sparsely populated strip of swamp, lagoon, and tropical forest along the Caribbean coast of Nicaragua and Honduras, occupied by the Miskito Indians after whom it is named. The British maintained a protectorate over the area intermittently from the 17th c. until the mid-19th c., granting authority to a series of kings.

mosquito /mɒsˈkiːtəʊ/ n. (pl. -oes) any of various slender biting insects, esp. of the genus *Culex*, *Anopheles*, or *Aedes*, the female of which punctures the skin of humans and other animals with a long proboscis to suck their blood and transmits diseases such as filariasis and malaria. □ **mosquito-boat** *US* a motor torpedo-boat. **mosquito-net** a net to keep off mosquitoes. [Sp. & Port., dimin. of *mosca* f. L *musca* fly]

Moss /mɒs/, Stirling (1929–), English motor-racing driver who was especially successful in the 1950s, winning various Grand Prix and other competitions, though the drivers' world championship always eluded him.

moss /mɒs/ *n. & v.* —*n.* **1** any small cryptogamous plant of the class Musci, growing in dense clusters on the surface of the ground, in bogs, on trees, stones, etc. Such plants bear structures resembling roots, stems, and leaves but, unlike higher plants, have no specialized vascular (conducting) tissue. **2** *Sc. & N.Engl.* a bog, esp. a peatbog. —*v.tr.* cover with moss. □ **moss agate** agate with mosslike dendritic markings. **moss-grown** overgrown with moss. **moss-hag** *Sc.* broken ground from which peat has been taken. **moss-stitch** alternate plain and purl in knitting. □□ **mosslike** *adj.* [OE *mos* bog, moss f. Gmc]

Mossad /mɒˈsæd/ **1** the principal secret intelligence service of the State of Israel. Its full title means Supreme Institution for Intelligence and Special Assignments. **2** an earlier organization (Institution for the Second Immigration) formed in 1937 for the purpose of bringing Jews from Europe to Palestine. [Heb. *mosad* institution]

Mossel Bay /ˈmɒs(ə)l/ a seaport and resort in Cape Province in South Africa.

mosso /ˈmɒsəʊ/ *adv. Mus.* with animation or speed. [It., past part. of *muovere* move]

mosstrooper /ˈmɒsˌtruːpə(r)/ *n.* a freebooter of the Scottish Border in the 17th c.

mossy /ˈmɒsɪ/ *adj.* (**mossier, mossiest**) **1** covered in or resembling moss. **2** *US sl.* antiquated, old-fashioned. □□ **mossiness** *n.*

most /məʊst/ *adj., n., & adv.* —*adj.* **1** existing in the greatest quantity or degree (*you have made most mistakes; see who can make the most noise*). **2** the majority of; nearly all of (*most people think so*). —*n.* **1** the greatest quantity or number (*this is the most I can do*). **2** (**the most**) *sl.* the best of all. **3** the majority (*most of them are missing*). —*adv.* **1** in the highest degree (*this is most interesting; what most annoys me*). **2** forming the superlative of adjectives and adverbs, esp. those of more than one syllable (*most certain; most easily*). **3** *US colloq.* almost. □ **at most** no more or better than (*this is at most a makeshift*). **at the most 1** as the greatest amount. **2** not more than. **for the most part 1** as regards the greater part. **2** usually. **make the most of 1** employ to the best advantage. **2** represent at its best or worst. **Most Honourable** a title given to marquises and to members of the Privy Council and the Order of the Bath. **Most Reverend** a title given to archbishops and to Roman Catholic bishops. [OE *māst* f. Gmc]

-most /məʊst/ *suffix* forming superlative adjectives and adverbs from prepositions and other words indicating relative position (*foremost; uttermost*). [OE *-mest* f. Gmc]

mostly /ˈməʊstlɪ/ *adv.* **1** as regards the greater part. **2** usually.

Mosul /ˈməʊsʊl/ the third-largest city in Iraq, situated in the north-west of the country on the right bank of the Tigris, opposite the ruins of Nineveh; pop. (est. 1985) 570,900. It formerly produced fine cotton goods, and gives its name to 'muslin'.

MOT *abbr.* **1** (in the UK) Ministry of Transport. **2** (in full **MOT test**) a compulsory annual test of motor vehicles of more than a specified age.

mot /məʊ/ *n.* (pl. **mots** *pronunc.* same) a witty saying. □ **mot juste** /ˈʒuːst/ (pl. **mots justes** *pronunc.* same) the most appropriate expression. [F, = word, ult. f. L *muttum* uttered sound f. *muttire* murmur]

mote /məʊt/ *n.* a speck of dust. [OE *mot*, corresp. to Du. *mot* dust, sawdust, of unkn. orig.]

motel /məʊˈtel/ *n.* a roadside hotel providing accommodation for motorists and parking for their vehicles. [portmanteau word f. MOTOR + HOTEL]

motet /məʊˈtet/ *n. Mus.* a short usu. unaccompanied sacred choral composition. [ME f. OF, dimin. of *mot*: see MOT]

moth /mɒθ/ *n.* **1** any usu. nocturnal insect of the order Lepidoptera excluding butterflies, having a stout body and without clubbed antennae. **2** any small lepidopterous insect of the family Tineidae breeding in cloth etc., on which its larva feeds. □ **moth-eaten 1** damaged or destroyed by moths. **2** antiquated, time-worn. [OE *moththe*]

mothball /ˈmɒθbɔːl/ *n. & v.* —*n.* a ball of naphthalene etc. placed in stored clothes to keep away moths. —*v.tr.* **1** place in mothballs. **2** leave unused. □ **in mothballs** stored unused for a considerable time.

mother /ˈmʌðə(r)/ *n. & v.* —*n.* **1 a** a woman in relation to a child or children to whom she has given birth. **b** (in full **adoptive mother**) a woman who has continuous care of a child, esp. by adoption. **2** any female animal in relation to its offspring. **3** a quality or condition etc. that gives rise to another (*necessity is the mother of invention*). **4** (in full **Mother Superior**) the head of a female religious community. **5** *archaic* (esp. as a form of address) an elderly woman. **6** (*attrib.*) **a** designating an institution etc. regarded as having maternal authority (*Mother Church; mother earth*). **b** designating the main ship, spacecraft, etc., in a convoy or mission (*the mother craft*). —*v.tr.* **1** give birth to; be the mother of. **2** protect as a mother. **3** give rise to; be the source of. **4** acknowledge or profess oneself the mother of. □ **Mother Carey's chicken** = *storm petrel* **1**. **mother country** a country in relation to its colonies. **mother-figure** an older woman who is regarded as a source of nurture, support, etc. **mother goddess** see separate entry. **Mother Goose rhyme** *US* a nursery rhyme. **mother-in-law** (pl. **mothers-in-law**) the mother of one's husband or wife. **mother-in-law's' tongue** a plant, *Sansevieria trifasciata*, with long erect pointed leaves. **mother-lode** *Mining* the main vein of a system. **mother-naked** stark naked. **mother-of-pearl** a smooth iridescent substance forming the inner layer of the shell of some molluscs. **Mother's Day 1** *Brit.* = MOTHERING SUNDAY. **2** *US* an equivalent day on the second Sunday in May. **mother's ruin** *colloq.* gin. **mother's son** *colloq.* a man (*every mother's son of you*). **mother tongue 1** one's native language. **2** a language from which others have evolved. **mother wit** native wit; common sense. □□ **motherhood** *n.* **motherless** *adj.* **motherlessness** *n.* **motherlike** *adj. & adv.* [OE *mōdor* f. Gmc]

mothercraft /ˈmʌðəˌkrɑːft/ *n.* skill in or knowledge of looking after children as a mother.

mother goddess *n.* a mother-figure deity (also called the Great Mother), goddess of the entire complex of birth and growth, commonly a central figure of early nature-cults where maintenance of fertility was of prime importance in the religion. Such a figure is found in pantheons all over the world; Isis, Astarte, Cybele, and Demeter were traditional mother goddesses in the eastern Mediterranean. The term is often applied to prehistoric female figurines with exaggerated sexual parts, but though these are associated with fertility they do not necessarily represent a female deity.

Mothering Sunday /ˈmʌðərɪŋ/ *n. Brit.* the fourth Sunday in Lent, traditionally a day for honouring mothers with gifts.

motherland /ˈmʌðəˌlænd/ *n.* one's native country.

motherly /ˈmʌðəlɪ/ *adj.* **1** like or characteristic of a mother in affection, care, etc. **2** of or relating to a mother. □□ **motherliness** *n.* [OE *mōdorlic* (as MOTHER)]

mothproof /ˈmɒθpruːf/ *adj. & v.* —*adj.* (of clothes) treated so as to repel moths. —*v.tr.* treat (clothes) in this way.

mothy /ˈmɒθɪ/ *adj.* (**mothier, mothiest**) infested with moths.

motif /məʊˈtiːf/ *n.* **1** a distinctive feature or dominant idea in artistic or literary composition. **2** *Mus.* = FIGURE *n.* 10. **3** an ornament of lace etc. sewn separately on a garment. **4** an ornament on a vehicle identifying the maker, model, etc. [F (as MOTIVE)]

motile /ˈməʊtaɪl/ *adj. Zool. & Bot.* capable of motion. □□ **motility** /-ˈtɪlɪtɪ/ *n.* [L *motus* motion (as MOVE)]

motion /ˈməʊʃ(ə)n/ *n. & v.* —*n.* **1** the act or process of moving or of changing position. **2** a particular manner of moving the body in walking etc. **3** a change of posture. **4** a gesture. **5** a formal proposal put to a committee, legislature, etc. **6** *Law* an application for a rule or order of court. **7 a** an evacuation of the bowels. **b** (in *sing.* or *pl.*) faeces. **8** a piece of moving mechanism. —*v.* (often foll. by *to* + infin.) **1** *tr.* direct (a person) by a sign or gesture. **2** *intr.* (often foll. by *to* a person) make a gesture directing (*motioned to me to leave*). □ **go through the motions 1** make a pretence; do something perfunctorily or superficially. **2** simulate an action by gestures. **in motion** moving; not at rest. **motion picture** (often (with hyphen) *attrib.*) a film (see FILM *n.* 3) with the illusion of movement. **put** (or **set**) **in motion** set going or working. □□ **motional** *adj.* **motionless** *adj.* [ME f. OF f. L *motio -onis* (as MOVE)]

motivate /ˈməʊtɪˌveɪt/ *v.tr.* **1** supply a motive to; be the motive of. **2** cause (a person) to act in a particular way. **3** stimulate the interest of (a person in an activity). □□ **motivation** /-ˈveɪʃ(ə)n/ *n.* **motivational** /-ˈveɪʃən(ə)l/ *adj.* **motivationally** /-ˈveɪʃənəlɪ/ *adv.*

motive /ˈməʊtɪv/ *n., adj.,* & *v.* —*n.* **1** a factor or circumstance that induces a person to act in a particular way. **2** = MOTIF. —*adj.* **1** tending to initiate movement. **2** concerned with movement. —*v.tr.* = MOTIVATE. □ **motive power** a moving or impelling power, esp. a source of energy used to drive machinery. □□ **motiveless** *adj.* **motivelessly** *adv.* **motivelessness** *n.* **motivity** /-ˈtɪvɪtɪ/ *n.* [ME f. OF *motif* (adj. & n.) f. LL *motivus* (adj.) (as MOVE)]

motley /ˈmɒtlɪ/ *adj.* & *n.* —*adj.* (**motlier, motliest**) **1** diversified in colour. **2** of varied character (*a motley crew*). —*n.* **1** an incongruous mixture. **2** *hist.* the particoloured costume of a jester. □ **wear motley** play the fool. [ME *mottelay,* perh. ult. rel. to MOTE]

moto-cross /ˈməʊtəʊˌkrɒs/ *n.* (also called *scrambling*) a form of motor-cycle racing held on a closed circuit consisting of a variety of cross-country terrain and natural obstacles. The sport was developed in southern England in the 1920s. [MOTOR + CROSS-]

moto perpetuo /ˌməʊtəʊ pəˈpetjʊəʊ/ *n. Mus.* a usu. fast-moving instrumental composition consisting mainly of notes of equal value. [It., = perpetual motion]

motor /ˈməʊtə(r)/ *n.* & *v.* —*n.* **1** a thing that imparts motion. **2** a machine (esp. one using electricity or internal combustion) supplying motive power for a vehicle etc. or for some other device with moving parts. **3** *Brit.* = motor car. **4** (*attrib.*) **a** giving, imparting, or producing motion. **b** driven by a motor (*motor-mower*). **c** of or for motor vehicles. **d** *Anat.* relating to muscular movement or the nerves activating it. —*v.intr.* & *tr. Brit.* go or convey in a motor vehicle. □ **motor area** the part of the frontal lobe of the brain associated with the initiation of muscular action. **motor bicycle** a motor cycle or moped. **motor bike** *colloq.* = motor cycle. **motor boat** a motor-driven boat. **motor car, motor cycle** see separate entries. **motor mouth** *US sl.* a person who talks incessantly and trivially. **motor nerve** a nerve carrying impulses from the brain or spinal cord to a muscle. **motor scooter** see SCOOTER. **motor vehicle** a road vehicle powered by an internal-combustion engine. □□ **motorial** /məʊˈtɔːrɪəl/ *adj.* (in sense 4a of *n.*). **motory** *adj.* (in sense 4a of *n.*). [L, = mover (as MOVE)]

motorable /ˈməʊtərəb(ə)l/ *adj.* (of a road) that can be used by motor vehicles.

motorcade /ˈməʊtəˌkeɪd/ *n.* a procession of motor vehicles. [MOTOR, after *cavalcade*]

motor car *n. Brit.* (now usu. *car*) a short-bodied motor-driven vehicle that can carry a driver and usually passengers. Attempts to devise mechanical propulsion began in the 18th c., and the first self-propelled road vehicle—which represented one of the most important advances in the history of transport—was a steam-driven carriage designed and built in France by Joseph Cugnot in 1769; other pioneers included Trevithick of Cornwall. In Britain development clashed with the interests of the promoters of the new railway lines, who used their considerable capital and influence to secure a law (1865) which effectively killed it, requiring every power-driven vehicle on the roads to have a man walking 100 yards in front with a red flag by day and a red lantern by night; the provisions of this law were not abolished until 1896. On the Continent, however, progress was being made with the internal-combustion engine, which Daimler fitted to a cycle and Benz to a three-wheeled vehicle

(1885) that carried two passengers. Early cars were very small two-seat carts, with no roofs, poor springs, and wooden- or wire-spoked wheels. Motorists had to cope with flint roads and discarded nails from horseshoes, and to carry spare tyres etc., for there were no garages to serve them; petrol was obtainable from chemists' shops.

The motor car became significant in its social effects when it began to be built in large numbers by low-cost mass-production methods (see Henry FORD). It is now ubiquitous in industrialized countries and both town and country are planned to accommodate it. Its future is threatened by the increasing cost and future scarcity of the highly specific types of oil fuel on which it relies; introduction of an electrically powered car awaits the design of a suitable battery.

motor cycle *n.* a two-wheeled motor-driven road vehicle, now without pedal propulsion. A cycle powered by a steam engine was patented in France in 1868, and a charcoal-fired steam-powered motor cycle was built by S. H. Roper in the US in 1869. The first practical machine was built in 1885 by Daimler, who fitted an internal-combustion engine into a wooden cycle frame, but it was some years before sustained efforts were made towards its improvement. From this was developed the motor car, but the motor cycle continued as a distinct vehicle, being lighter, cheaper, and more stable on rough ground. After the Second World War it lost sales to the scooter, developed in Italy, and the moped, mostly a French development, but the motor cycle proper was given a new lease of life when Japan entered the market with a large range of models and quickly became the world's largest supplier. □□ **motor cyclist** *n.*

motorist /ˈməʊtərɪst/ *n.* the driver of a motor car.

motorize /ˈməʊtəˌraɪz/ *v.tr.* (also **-ise**) **1** equip (troops etc.) with motor transport. **2** provide with a motor for propulsion etc. □□ **motorization** /-ˈzeɪʃ(ə)n/ *n.*

motorman /ˈməʊtəˌmæn/ *n.* (*pl.* **-men**) the driver of an underground train, tram, etc.

motorway /ˈməʊtəˌweɪ/ *n. Brit.* a main road with separate carriageways and limited access, specially constructed and controlled for fast motor traffic.

Motown /ˈməʊtaʊn/ the nickname (shortening of *Motor Town*) of Detroit, noted since *c.* 1900 for its vehicle-manufacturing industries. —*n.* music with rhythm and blues elements, associated with Detroit and esp. with the first Black-owned record company which was founded in Detroit and took the name 'Motown'. Its style was prominent in pop music of the 1960s.

motte /mɒt/ *n.* a mound forming the site of an ancient castle, camp, etc., found in Britain and parts of northern France, dating from the Norman period onwards. [ME f. OF *mote* (as MOAT)]

mottle /ˈmɒt(ə)l/ *v.* & *n.* —*v.tr.* (esp. as **mottled** *adj.*) mark with spots or smears of colour. —*n.* **1** an irregular arrangement of spots or patches of colour. **2** any of these spots or patches. [prob. back-form. f. MOTLEY]

motto /ˈmɒtəʊ/ *n.* (*pl.* **-oes**) **1** a maxim adopted as a rule of conduct. **2** a phrase or sentence accompanying a coat of arms or crest. **3** a sentence inscribed on some object and expressing an appropriate sentiment. **4** verses etc. in a paper cracker. **5** a quotation prefixed to a book or chapter. **6** *Mus.* a recurrent phrase having some symbolical significance. [It. (as MOT)]

moue /muː/ *n.* = POUT[1] *n.* [F]

moufflon /ˈmuːflɒn/ *n.* (also **mouflon**) a wild mountain sheep, *Ovis musimon,* of S. Europe. [F *mouflon* f. It. *muflone* f. Rmc]

mouillé /ˈmuːjeɪ/ *adj. Phonet.* (of a consonant) palatalized. [F, = wetted]

moujik var. of MUZHIK.

Moulay Idriss /ˌmuːleɪ ˈɪdrɪs/ a Muslim holy town near Meknès in northern Morocco, the burial place of Moulay Idriss I (8th c.), father of the founder of the city of Fez.

mould[1] /məʊld/ *n.* & *v.* (US **mold**) —*n.* **1** a hollow container into which molten metal etc. is poured or soft material is pressed to harden into a required shape. **2 a** a metal or earthenware vessel used to give shape to puddings etc. **b** a pudding etc. made in this way. **3** a form or shape, esp. of an animal body. **4** *Archit.* a moulding or group of mouldings. **5** a frame or template for producing mouldings. **6** character or disposition (*in heroic mould*). —*v.tr.* **1** make (an object) in a required shape or from certain ingredients (*was moulded out of clay*). **2** give a shape to. **3** influence the formation or development of (*consultation helps to mould policies*). **4** (esp. of clothing) fit closely to (*the gloves moulded his hands*). □□ **mouldable** *adj.* **moulder** *n.* [ME mold(e), app. f. OF *modle* f. L *modulus*: see MODULUS]

mould² /məʊld/ *n.* (*US* **mold**) a woolly or furry growth of minute fungi occurring esp. in moist warm conditions. [ME prob. f. obs. *mould* adj.; past part. of *moul* grow mouldy f. ON *mygla*]

mould³ /məʊld/ *n.* (*US* **mold**) **1** loose earth. **2** the upper soil of cultivated land, esp. when rich in organic matter. □ **mould-board** the board in a plough that turns over the furrow-slice. [OE *molde* f. Gmc., rel. to MEAL²]

moulder /ˈməʊldə(r)/ *v.intr.* (*US* **molder**) **1** decay to dust. **2** (foll. by *away*) rot or crumble. **3** deteriorate. [perh. f. MOULD³, but cf. Norw. dial. *muldra* crumble]

moulding /ˈməʊldɪŋ/ *n.* (*US* **molding**) **1 a** an ornamentally shaped outline as an architectural feature, esp. in a cornice. **b** a strip of material in wood or stone etc. for use as moulding. **2** similar material in wood or plastic etc. used for other decorative purposes, e.g. in picture-framing.

mouldy /ˈməʊldɪ/ *adj.* (*US* **moldy**) (**-ier, -iest**) **1** covered with mould. **2** stale; out of date. **3** *colloq.* (as a general term of disparagement) dull, miserable, boring. □□ **mouldiness** *n.*

moulin /ˈmuːlæ̃/ *n.* a nearly vertical shaft in a glacier, formed by surface water percolating through a crack in the ice. [F, lit. = mill]

Moulin Rouge /ˌmuːlæ̃ ˈruːʒ/ a cabaret in Montmartre, Paris, a favourite resort of poets and artists around the turn of the century. Toulouse-Lautrec immortalized its dancers in his posters.

Moulmein /muːlˈmeɪn/ a seaport in SE Burma; pop. (1983) 220,000.

moult /məʊlt/ *v.* & *n.* (*US* **molt**) —*v.* **1** *intr.* shed feathers, hair, a shell, etc., in the process of renewing plumage, a coat, etc. **2** *tr.* (of an animal) shed (feathers, hair, etc.). —*n.* the act or an instance of moulting (*is in moult once a year*). □□ **moulter** *n.* [ME *moute* f. OE *mutian* (unrecorded) f. L *mutare* change: -*l-* after *fault* etc.]

mound¹ /maʊnd/ *n.* & *v.* —*n.* **1** a raised mass of earth, stones, or other compacted material. **2** a heap or pile. **3** a hillock. —*v.tr.* **1** heap up in a mound or mounds. **2** enclose with mounds. [16th c. (orig. = hedge or fence): orig. unkn.]

mound² /maʊnd/ *n. Heraldry* a ball of gold etc. representing the earth, and usu. surmounting a crown. [ME f. OF *monde* f. L *mundus* world]

mount¹ /maʊnt/ *v.* & *n.* —*v.* **1** *tr.* ascend or climb (a hill, stairs, etc.). **2** *tr.* **a** get up on (an animal, esp. a horse) to ride it. **b** set (a person) on horseback. **c** provide (a person) with a horse. **d** (as **mounted** *adj.*) serving on horseback (*mounted police*). **3** *tr.* go up or climb on to (a raised surface). **4** *intr.* **a** move upwards. **b** (often foll. by *up*) increase, accumulate. **c** (of a feeling) become stronger or more intense (*excitement was mounting*). **d** (of the blood) rise into the cheeks. **5** *tr.* (esp. of a male animal) get on to (a female) to copulate. **6** *tr.* (often foll. by *on*) place (an object) on an elevated support. **7** *tr.* **a** set in or attach to a backing, setting, or other support. **b** attach (a picture etc.) to a mount or frame. **c** fix (an object for viewing) on a microscope slide. **8** *tr.* **a** arrange (a play, exhibition, etc.) or present for public view or display. **b** take action to initiate (a programme, campaign, etc.). **9** *tr.* prepare (specimens) for preservation. **10** *tr.* **a** bring into readiness for operation. **b** raise (guns) into position on a fixed mounting. **11** *intr.* rise to a higher level of rank, power, etc. —*n.* **1** a backing, setting, or other support on which a picture etc. is set for display. **2** the margin surrounding a picture or photograph. **3 a** a horse available for riding. **b** an opportunity to ride a horse, esp. as a jockey. **4** = *stamp-hinge* (see HINGE). □ **mount guard** (often foll. by *over*) perform the duty of guarding; take up sentry duty. □□ **mountable** *adj.* **mounter** *n.* [ME f. OF *munter, monter* ult. f. L (as MOUNT²)]

mount² /maʊnt/ *n. archaic* (except before a name): mountain,

hill (*Mount Everest, Mount of Olives*, etc.; see EVEREST, OLIVE, etc.). [ME f. OE *munt* & OF *mont* f. L *mons montis* mountain]

mountain /ˈmaʊntɪn/ *n.* **1** a large natural elevation of the earth's surface rising abruptly from the surrounding level; a large or high and steep hill. **2** a large heap or pile; a huge quantity (*a mountain of work*). **3** a large surplus stock of a commodity (*butter mountain*). □ **make a mountain out of a molehill** see MOLEHILL. **mountain ash 1** a tree, *Sorbus aucuparia*, with delicate pinnate leaves and scarlet berries: also called ROWAN. **2** any of several Australian eucalypts. **mountain bicycle** (or **bike**) a type of pedal cycle with large wheels, thick tyres, straight handlebars, and a large range of gears, suitable for use on steep rugged terrain. **mountain chain** a connected series of mountains. **mountain goat** a white goatlike animal, *Oreamnos americanus*, of the Rocky Mountains etc. **mountain laurel** a N. American shrub, *Kalmia latifolia*. **mountain lion** a puma. **mountain panther** = OUNCE². **mountain range** a line of mountains connected by high ground. **mountain sickness** a sickness caused by the rarefaction of the air at great heights. **Mountain Time** *US* the standard time of parts of Canada and the US in or near the Rocky Mountains. **move mountains 1** achieve spectacular results. **2** make every possible effort. □□ **mountainy** *adj.* [ME f. OF *montaigne* ult. f. L (as MOUNT²)]

mountaineer /ˌmaʊntɪˈnɪə(r)/ *n.* & *v.* —*n.* **1** a person skilled in mountain-climbing. **2** a person living in an area of high mountains. —*v.intr.* climb mountains as a sport. (See below.) □□ **mountaineering** *n.*

From time immemorial people living in mountainous countries have crossed mountain passes in order to get to one valley from another, and in Europe a thousand years ago a few established routes, such as that over the Great St Bernard pass, were in regular use by pilgrims and other travellers. In the 14th c. a few isolated climbs were made by inquiring naturalists to study flowers or rocks, and by the 16th c. some adventurous people were wandering among the Alps for pleasure. In the 18th c. a number of the higher Alpine peaks were climbed for the first time. It was the British who first organized mountaineering as a sport, and in the decade 1855-65 made many first ascents of peaks and crossings of high passes in the Alps before turning their attention to more distant ranges in South America, New Zealand, and Africa, and in the Himalayas. The introduction of artificial aids such as pitons and fixed ropes aroused much controversy. Attempts to conquer the world's highest mountain, Mount Everest, began in 1920 but were unsuccessful until the British expedition led by Sir John Hunt culminated in the ascent to the summit by Sir Edmund Hillary and Sherpa Tenzing Norgay in 1953.

mountainous /ˈmaʊntɪnəs/ *adj.* **1** (of a region) having many mountains. **2** huge.

mountainside /ˈmaʊntɪnˌsaɪd/ *n.* the slope of a mountain below the summit.

Mountbatten /maʊntˈbæt(ə)n/, Louis, 1st Earl Mountbatten of Burma (1900-79), British sailor, soldier, and statesman. A great-grandson of Queen Victoria, Mountbatten served in the Royal Navy before rising to become supreme Allied commander in SE Asia in 1943-5. The qualities of tact and diplomacy that he displayed in this difficult job stood him in good stead when as Viceroy and then Governor-General he oversaw the independence of India and Pakistan in 1947-8. He later went on to become First Sea Lord; he was murdered by the IRA in Ireland while in retirement.

mountebank /ˈmaʊntɪˌbæŋk/ *n.* **1** a swindler; a charlatan. **2** a clown. **3** *hist.* an itinerant quack appealing to an audience from a platform. □□ **mountebankery** *n.* [It. *montambanco* = *monta in banco* climb on bench: see MOUNT¹, BENCH]

Mountie /ˈmaʊntɪ/ *n. colloq.* a member of the Royal Canadian Mounted Police.

mounting /ˈmaʊntɪŋ/ *n.* **1** = MOUNT¹ *n.* 1. **2** in senses of MOUNT¹ *v.* □ **mounting-block** a block of stone placed to help a rider mount a horse.

Mount Isa /ˈaɪzə/ a lead- and silver-mining town in Queensland, Australia; pop. (est. 1987) 24,200.

Mount Vernon /ˈvɜːnən/ the home of George Washington

from 1747 until his death in 1799, on a site overlooking the Potomac River, in NE Virginia, about 24 km (15 miles) from Washington, DC.

mourn /mɔːn/ v. **1** tr. & (foll. by *for*) intr. feel or show deep sorrow or regret for (a dead person, a lost thing, a past event, etc.). **2** intr. show conventional signs of grief for a period after a person's death. [OE *murnan*]

mourner /ˈmɔːnə(r)/ n. **1** a person who mourns, esp. at a funeral. **2** a person hired to attend a funeral.

mournful /ˈmɔːnfʊl/ adj. **1** doleful, sad, sorrowing. **2** expressing or suggestive of mourning. □□ **mournfully** adv. **mournfulness** n.

mourning /ˈmɔːnɪŋ/ n. **1** the expression of deep sorrow, esp. for a dead person, by the wearing of solemn dress. **2** the clothes worn in mourning. □ **in mourning** assuming the signs of mourning, esp. in dress. **mourning-band** a band of black crape etc. round a person's sleeve or hat as a token of mourning. **mourning dove** an American dove with a plaintive note, *Zenaida macroura*. **mourning-paper** notepaper with a black edge. **mourning-ring** a ring worn as a memorial of a deceased person.

mousaka var. of MOUSSAKA.

Mousalla see MUSALA.

mouse /maʊs/ n. & v. —n. (pl. **mice** /maɪs/) **1 a** any of various small rodents of the family Muridae, esp. of the genus *Mus*. **b** any of several similar rodents such as a small shrew or vole. **2** a timid or feeble person. **3** *Computing* a small hand-held device which controls the cursor on a VDU screen. **4** *sl.* a black eye. —v.intr. /also maʊz/ **1** (esp. of a cat, owl, etc.) hunt for or catch mice. **2** (foll. by *about*) search industriously; prowl about as if searching. □ **mouse-coloured 1** dark-grey with a yellow tinge. **2** nondescript light brown. **mouse deer** a chevrotain. **mouse hare** a pika. □□ **mouselike** adj. & adv. **mouser** n. [OE *mūs*, pl. *mȳs* f. Gmc]

mousetrap /ˈmaʊstræp/ n. **1** a sprung trap with bait for catching and usu. killing mice. **2** (often *attrib.*) cheese of poor quality.

moussaka /muːˈsɑːkə, ˌmuːsəˈkɑː/ n. (also **mousaka**) a Greek dish of minced meat, aubergine, etc. with a cheese sauce. [mod. Gk or Turk.]

mousse /muːs/ n. **1 a** a dessert of whipped cream, eggs, etc., usu. flavoured with fruit or chocolate. **b** a meat or fish purée made with whipped cream etc. **2** a preparation applied to the hair enabling it to be styled more easily. [F, = moss, froth]

mousseline /ˈmuːsliːn/ n. **1** a muslin-like fabric of silk etc. **2** a sauce of seasoned or sweet eggs and cream. [F: see MUSLIN]

moustache /məˈstɑːʃ/ n. (US **mustache**) **1** hair left to grow on a man's upper lip. **2** a similar growth round the mouth of some animals. □ **moustache cup** a cup with a partial cover to protect the moustache when drinking. □□ **moustached** adj. [F f. It. *mostaccio* f. Gk *mustax -akos*]

Mousterian /muːˈstɪərɪən/ adj. & n. —adj. *Archaeol.* of or relating to the flint industries of the middle palaeolithic period, named after the type-site, the Moustier cave in the Dordogne region of France, and dated to *c*.70,000–30,000 BC. They are attributed to the Neanderthal peoples living in Europe and around the Mediterranean. —n. such an industry.

mousy /ˈmaʊsi/ adj. (**mousier**, **mousiest**) **1** of or like a mouse. **2** (of a person) shy or timid; ineffectual. **3** = mouse-coloured. □□ **mousily** adv. **mousiness** n.

mouth n. & v. —n. /maʊθ/ (pl. **mouths** /maʊðz/) **1 a** an external opening in the head, through which most animals admit food and emit communicative sounds. **b** (in humans and some animals) the cavity behind it containing the means of biting and chewing and the vocal organs. **2 a** the opening of a container such as a bag or sack. **b** the opening of a cave, volcano, etc. **c** the open end of a woodwind or brass instrument. **d** the muzzle of a gun. **3** the place where a river enters the sea. **4** *colloq.* **a** talkativeness. **b** impudent talk; cheek. **5** an individual regarded as needing sustenance (*an extra mouth to feed*). **6** a horse's readiness to feel and obey the pressure of the bit. —v. /maʊð/ **1** tr. & intr. utter or speak solemnly or with affectations; rant, declaim (*mouthing platitudes*). **2** tr. utter very distinctly. **3** intr. **a** move the

lips silently. **b** grimace. **4** tr. take (food) in the mouth. **5** tr. touch with the mouth. **6** tr. train the mouth of (a horse). □ **give mouth** (of a dog) bark, bay. **keep one's mouth shut** *colloq.* not reveal a secret. **mouth-organ** = HARMONICA. **mouth-to-mouth** (of resuscitation) in which a person breathes into a subject's lungs through the mouth. **mouth-watering 1** (of food etc.) having a delicious smell or appearance. **2** tempting, alluring. **put words into a person's mouth** represent a person as having said something in a particular way. **take the words out of a person's mouth** say what another was about to say. □□ **mouthed** (also in *comb.*). **mouther** /ˈmaʊðə(r)/ n. **mouthless** /ˈmaʊθlɪs/ adj. [OE *mūth* f. Gmc]

mouthful /ˈmaʊθfʊl/ n. (pl. **-fuls**) **1** a quantity, esp. of food, that fills the mouth. **2** a small quantity. **3** a long or complicated word or phrase. **4** *US colloq.* something important said.

mouthpiece /ˈmaʊθpiːs/ n. **1 a** the part of a musical instrument placed between or against the lips. **b** the part of a telephone for speaking into. **c** the part of a tobacco-pipe placed between the lips. **2 a** a person who speaks for another or others. **b** *colloq.* a lawyer. **3** a part attached as an outlet.

mouthwash /ˈmaʊθwɒʃ/ n. **1** a liquid antiseptic etc. for rinsing the mouth or gargling. **2** *colloq.* nonsense.

mouthy /ˈmaʊði/ adj. (**mouthier**, **mouthiest**) **1** ranting, railing. **2** bombastic.

movable /ˈmuːvəb(ə)l/ adj. & n. (also **moveable**) —adj. **1** that can be moved. **2** *Law* (of property) of the nature of a chattel, as distinct from land or buildings. **3** (of a feast or festival) variable in date from year to year. —n. **1** an article of furniture that may be removed from a house, as distinct from a fixture. **2** (in pl.) personal property. □ **movable-doh** *Mus.* applied to a system of sight-singing in which doh is the keynote of any major scale (cf. *fixed-doh*). □□ **movability** /-ˈbɪlɪtɪ/ n. **movableness** n. **movably** adv. [ME f. OF (as MOVE)]

move /muːv/ v. & n. —v. **1** intr. & tr. change one's position or posture, or cause to do this. **2** tr. & intr. put or keep in motion; rouse, stir. **3** intr. make a move in a board-game. **b** tr. change the position of (a piece) in a board-game. **4** intr. (often foll. by *about*, *away*, etc.) go or pass from place to place. **5** intr. take action, esp. promptly (*moved to reduce unemployment*). **6** intr. make progress (*the project is moving fast*). **7** intr. **a** change one's place of residence. **b** (of a business etc.) change to new premises (also *tr.*: *move house*; *move offices*). **8** intr. (foll. by *in*) live or be socially active in (a specified place or group etc.) (*moves in the best circles*). **9** tr. affect (a person) with (usu. tender or sympathetic) emotion. **10** tr. **a** (foll. by *in*) stimulate (laughter, anger, etc., in a person). **b** (foll. by *to*) provoke (a person to laughter etc.). **11** tr. (foll. by *to*, or *to* + infin.) prompt or incline (a person to a feeling or action). **12 a** tr. cause (the bowels) to be evacuated. **b** intr. (of the bowels) be evacuated. **13** tr. (often foll. by *that* + clause) propose in a meeting, deliberative assembly, etc. **14** intr. (foll. by *for*) make a formal request or application. **15** intr. (of merchandise) be sold. —n. **1** the act or an instance of moving. **2** a change of house, business premises, etc. **3** a step taken to secure some action or effect; an initiative. **4 a** the changing of the position of a piece in a board-game. **b** a player's turn to do this. □ **get a move on** *colloq.* **1** hurry up. **2** make a start. **make a move** take action. **move along** (or *on*) change to a new position, esp. to avoid crowding, getting in the way, etc. **move heaven and earth** see HEAVEN. **move in 1** take possession of a new house. **2** get into a position of influence, interference, etc. **3** get into a position of readiness or proximity (for an offensive action etc.). **move mountains** see MOUNTAIN. **move out 1** leave one's home; change one's place of residence. **2** leave a position, job, etc. **move over** (or *up*) adjust one's position to make room for another. **on the move 1** progressing. **2** moving about. [ME f. AF *mover*, OF *moveir* f. L *movēre* mot-]

moveable var. of MOVABLE.

movement /ˈmuːvmənt/ n. **1** the act or an instance of moving or being moved. **2 a** the moving parts of a mechanism (e.g. a clock or watch). **b** a particular group of these. **3 a** a body of persons with a common object (*the peace movement*). **b** a campaign undertaken by such a body. **4** (usu. in *pl.*) a person's activities and whereabouts, esp. at a particular time. **5** *Mus.* a principal division of a longer musical work, self-sufficient in terms of key, tempo, structure, etc. **6** the progressive development of a poem, story, etc. **7** motion of the bowels. **8 a** an activity in a market for some commodity. **b** a rise or fall in price. **9** a mental impulse. **10** a development of position by a military force or unit. [ME f. OF f. med.L *movimentum* (as MOVE)]

mover /ˈmuːvə(r)/ *n.* **1** a person or thing that moves. **2** a person who moves a proposition. **3** *US* a remover of furniture. **4** the author of a fruitful idea.

movie /ˈmuːvɪ/ *n.* esp. *US colloq.* **1** a motion-picture film. **2** (in full **movie-house**) a cinema.

moving /ˈmuːvɪŋ/ *adj.* **1** that moves or causes to move. **2** affecting with emotion. □ **moving pavement** a structure like a conveyor belt for pedestrians. **moving picture** a continuous picture of events obtained by projecting a sequence of photographs taken at very short intervals. **moving staircase** an escalator. □□ **movingly** *adv.* (in sense 2).

mow[1] /məʊ/ *v.tr.* (*past part.* **mowed** or **mown**) **1** cut down (grass, hay, etc.) with a scythe or machine. **2** cut down the produce of (a field) or the grass etc. of (a lawn) by mowing. □ **mow down** kill or destroy randomly or in great numbers. □□ **mowable** *adj.* **mower** *n.* [OE *māwan* f. Gmc, rel. to MEAD[2]]

mow[2] /məʊ/ *n. US or dial.* **1** a stack of hay, corn, etc. **2** a place in a barn where hay etc. is heaped. [OE *mūga*]

moxa /ˈmɒksə/ *n.* a downy substance from the dried leaves of *Artemisia moxa* etc., burnt on the skin in oriental medicine as a counterirritant. [Jap. *mogusa* f. *moe kusa* burning herb]

Mozambique /ˌməʊzæmˈbiːk/ a country on the east coast of Africa, bordered by the Republic of South Africa in the south and west; pop. (est. 1988) 14,947,550; official language, Portuguese; capital, Maputo. The country is largely agricultural, and in relation to its area the export trade is very small. Discovered by Vasco da Gama, Mozambique was colonized by the Portuguese in the early 16th c. and did not gain full independence as a republic until 1975. It has been troubled by the guerrilla activity rife in southern Africa for many years. □□ **Mozambican** *adj.* & *n.*

Mozart /ˈməʊtsɑːt/, Wolfgang Amadeus (1756–91), Austrian composer, born at Salzburg, typically Austrian in that in him a basically Teutonic nature was Italianized. A child prodigy as harpsichordist and composer, he was taken by his father on tours of western Europe and Italy, but most of his mature years were spent at Salzburg and, latterly, Vienna. His flow of unsurpassable Italianate melodic invention and seemingly effortless command of German technique are displayed in more than forty symphonies, nearly thirty piano concertos, and a vast quantity of orchestral and other instrumental music. This kind of symbiosis is still more obvious in his operas, in the greatest of which comedy is always liable to become serious, and even tragic in *Don Giovanni* (1787). In *The Magic Flute* (1791) extremes of profundity and buffoonery are juxtaposed with no sense of incongruity. The most straightforwardly comic is probably *The Marriage of Figaro* (1786). Mozart's subtle creation of character in terms of music is comparable with Shakespeare's in terms of poetry.

mozzarella /ˌmɒtsəˈrelə/ *n.* an Italian curd cheese orig. of buffalo milk. [It.]

MP *abbr.* **1** Member of Parliament. **2 a** military police. **b** military policeman.

mp *abbr.* mezzo piano.

m.p. *abbr.* melting-point.

m.p.g. *abbr.* miles per gallon.

m.p.h. *abbr.* miles per hour.

M.Phil. *abbr.* Master of Philosophy.

MPS *abbr.* Member of the Pharmaceutical Society.

MR *abbr.* Master of the Rolls.

Mr /ˈmɪstə(r)/ *n.* (*pl.* **Messrs**) **1** the title of a man without a higher title (*Mr Jones*). **2** a title prefixed to a designation of office etc. (*Mr President*; *Mr Speaker*). □ **Mr Right** *joc.* a woman's destined husband. [abbr. of MISTER]

MRA *abbr.* Moral Re-Armament.

MRBM *abbr.* medium-range ballistic missile.

MRC *abbr.* (in the UK) Medical Research Council.

MRCA *abbr.* multi-role combat aircraft.

mRNA *abbr. Biol.* messenger RNA.

Mrs /ˈmɪsɪz/ *n.* (*pl.* same or **Mesdames**) the title of a married woman without a higher title (*Mrs Jones*). [abbr. of MISTRESS: cf. MISSIS]

MS *abbr.* **1** manuscript. **2** Master of Science. **3** Master of Surgery. **4** *US* Mississippi (in official postal use). **5** *US* motor ship. **6** multiple sclerosis.

Ms /mɪz, məz/ *n.* the title of a woman without a higher title, used regardless of marital status. [combination of MRS, MISS[2]]

MSC *abbr.* (in the UK) Manpower Services Commission.

M.Sc. *abbr.* Master of Science.

MS-DOS /ˌemesˈdɒs/ *abbr. Computing* Microsoft disk operating system.

MSF *abbr.* (in the UK) Manufacturing, Science, and Finance (Union).

Msgr. *abbr. US* **1** Monseigneur. **2** Monsignor.

MSS /emˈesɪz/ *abbr.* manuscripts.

MST *abbr.* (in Canada and the US) Mountain Standard Time.

MT *abbr.* **1** mechanical transport. **2** *US* Montana (in official postal use).

Mt. *abbr.* Mount.

MTB *abbr.* motor torpedo-boat.

M.Tech. *abbr.* Master of Technology.

mu /mjuː/ *n.* **1** the twelfth Greek letter (M, μ). **2** (μ, as a symbol) = MICRO- 2. □ **mu-meson** = MUON. [Gk]

much /mʌtʃ/ *adj.*, *n.*, & *adv.* —*adj.* **1** existing or occurring in a great quantity (*much trouble*; *not much rain*; *too much noise*). **2** (prec. by *as*, *how*, *that*, etc.) with relative rather than distinctive sense (*I don't know how much money you want*). —*n.* **1** a great quantity (*much of that is true*). **2** (prec. by *as*, *how*, *that*, etc.) with relative rather than distinctive sense (*we do not need that much*). **3** (usu. in *neg.*) a noteworthy or outstanding example (*not much to look at*; *not much of a party*). —*adv.* **1 a** in a great degree (*much to my surprise*; *is much the same*). **b** (qualifying a verb or past participle) greatly (*they much regret the mistake*; *I was much annoyed*). ¶ *Much* implies a strong verbal element in the participle, whereas *very* implies a strong adjectival element: compare the second example above with *I was very annoyed*. **c** qualifying a comparative or superlative adjective (*much better*; *much the most likely*). **2** for a large part of one's time (*is much away from home*). □ **as much** the extent or quantity just specified; the idea just mentioned (*I thought as much*; *as much as that?*). **a bit much** *colloq.* somewhat excessive or immoderate. **make much of** see MAKE. **much as** even though (*cannot come*, *much as I would like to*). **much less** see LESS. **much obliged** see OBLIGE. **not much** *colloq.* **1** *iron.* very much. **2** certainly not. **not much in it** see IN. **too much** *colloq.* an intolerable situation etc. (*that really is too much*). **too much for 1** more than a match for. **2** beyond what is endurable by. □□ **muchly** *adv. joc.* [ME f. *muchel* MICKLE: for loss of *el* cf. BAD, WENCH]

Mucha /ˈmuːkə/, Alphonse (1860–1939), Czech painter and designer, noted for his luxuriously flowing poster designs, which rank among the most distinctive products of the art nouveau style. They often feature beautiful women, and some of the best known were made in Paris in the 1890s for the actress Sarah Bernhardt, for whom he also designed sets, costumes, and jewellery.

Muchinga Mountains /muːˈtʃɪŋɡə/ a range of mountains in eastern Zambia.

muchness /ˈmʌtʃnɪs/ *n.* greatness in quantity or degree. □ **much of a muchness** very nearly the same or alike.

mucilage /ˈmjuːsɪlɪdʒ/ *n.* **1** a viscous substance obtained from plant seeds etc. by maceration. **2** *US* a solution of gum. □□ **mucilaginous** /-ˈlædʒɪnəs/ *adj.* [ME f. F f. LL *mucilago -ginis* musty juice (MUCUS)]

muck /mʌk/ *n.* & *v.* —*n.* **1** farmyard manure. **2** *colloq.* dirt or filth; anything disgusting. **3** *colloq.* an untidy state; a mess. —*v.tr.* **1** (usu. foll. by *up*) *Brit. colloq.* bungle (a job). **2** (foll. by *out*) remove muck from. **3** make dirty. **4** manure with muck. □ **make a muck of** *colloq.* bungle. **muck about** (or **around**) *Brit. colloq.* **1** potter or fool about. **2** (foll. by *with*) fool or interfere with. **muck in** *Brit.* (often foll. by *with*) share tasks etc. equally. **muck sweat** *Brit. colloq.* a profuse sweat. [ME *muk* prob. f. Scand.: cf. ON *myki* dung, rel. to MEEK]

mucker /ˈmʌkə(r)/ *n. sl.* **1** a friend or companion. **2** *US* a rough or coarse person. **3** *Brit.* a heavy fall. □□ **muckerish** *adj.* (in senses 1 and 2). [prob. f. *muck in*: see MUCK]

muckle var. of MICKLE.

muckrake /ˈmʌkreɪk/ *v.intr.* search out and reveal scandal, esp. among famous people. □□ **muckraker** *n.* **muckraking** *n.*

mucky /ˈmʌkɪ/ *adj.* (**muckier, muckiest**) **1** covered with muck. **2** dirty. □□ **muckiness** *n.*

muco- /ˈmjuːkəʊ/ *comb. form Biochem.* mucus, mucous.

mucopolysaccharide /ˌmjuːkəʊˌpɒlɪˈsækəˌraɪd/ *n. Biochem.* any of a group of polysaccharides whose molecules contain sugar residues and are often found as components of connective tissue.

mucosa /mjuːˈkəʊsə/ *n.* (*pl.* **mucosae** /-siː/) a mucous membrane. [mod.L, fem. of *mucosus*: see MUCOUS]

mucous /ˈmjuːkəs/ *adj.* of or covered with mucus. □ **mucous membrane** a mucus-secreting epithelial tissue lining many body cavities and tubular organs. □□ **mucosity** /-ˈkɒsɪtɪ/ *n.* [L *mucosus* (as MUCUS)]

mucro /ˈmjuːkrəʊ/ *n.* (*pl.* **mucrones** /-ˈkrəʊniːz/) *Bot.* & *Zool.* a sharp-pointed part or organ. □□ **mucronate** /-krənət/ *adj.* [L *mucro -onis* sharp point]

mucus /ˈmjuːkəs/ *n.* **1** a slimy substance secreted by a mucous membrane. **2** a gummy substance found in all plants. **3** a slimy substance exuded by some animals, esp. fishes. [L]

mud /mʌd/ *n.* **1** wet soft earthy matter. **2** hard ground from the drying of an area of this. **3** what is worthless or polluting. □ **as clear as mud** *colloq.* not at all clear. **fling** (or **sling** or **throw**) **mud** speak disparagingly or slanderously. **here's mud in your eye!** *colloq.* a drinking-toast. **mud-bath 1** a bath in the mud of mineral springs, esp. to relieve rheumatism etc. **2** a muddy scene or occasion. **mud-brick** a brick made from baked mud. **mud-flat** a stretch of muddy land left uncovered at low tide. **mud pack** a cosmetic paste applied thickly to the face. **mud pie** mud made into a pie shape by a child. **mud puppy** *US* a large nocturnal salamander, *Necturus maculosus*, of eastern US. **mud skipper** any of various gobies of the family Periophthalmidae, able to leave the water and leap on the mud. **mud-slinger** *colloq.* one given to making abusive or disparaging remarks. **mud-slinging** *colloq.* abuse, disparagement. **mud volcano** a volcano discharging mud. **one's name is mud** one is unpopular or in disgrace. [ME *mode, mudde,* prob. f. MLG *mudde,* MHG *mot* bog]

muddle /ˈmʌd(ə)l/ *v.* & *n.* —*v.* **1** *tr.* (often foll. by *up, together*) bring into disorder. **2** *tr.* bewilder, confuse. **3** *tr.* mismanage (an affair). **4** *tr. US* crush and mix (the ingredients for a drink). **5** *intr.* (often foll. by *with*) busy oneself in a confused and ineffective way. —*n.* **1** disorder. **2** a muddled condition. □ **make a muddle of 1** bring into disorder. **2** bungle. **muddle along** (or **on**) progress in a haphazard way. **muddle-headed** stupid, confused. **muddle-headedness** stupidity; a confused state. **muddle through** succeed by perseverance rather than skill or efficiency. **muddle up** confuse (two or more things). □□ **muddler** *n.* **muddlingly** *adv.* [perh. f. MDu. *moddelen,* frequent. of *modden* dabble in mud (as MUD)]

muddy /ˈmʌdɪ/ *adj.* & *v.* —*adj.* (**muddier, muddiest**) **1** like mud. **2** covered in or full of mud. **3** (of liquid) turbid. **4** mentally confused. **5** obscure. **6** (of light) dull. **7** (of colour) impure. —*v.tr.* (**-ies, -ied**) make muddy. □□ **muddily** *adv.* **muddiness** *n.*

Mudéjar /muːˈðeɪhɑː(r)/ *n.* & *adj.* —*n.* (*pl.* **Mudéjares**) **1** any of the Muslims who were allowed to retain their laws and religion in return for their loyalty to a Christian king after the Christian reconquest of the Spanish peninsula from the Moors (11th–15th c.). After 1492 they were treated with less toleration, dubbed Moriscos (see entry), and forced to accept the Christian faith or leave the country. **2** a style of architecture and decorative art of the 12th–15th c., combining Islamic and Gothic elements, produced by the Mudéjares. The architecture is characterized especially by the use of the horseshoe arch and the vault; examples can be seen in the churches and palaces of Toledo, Córdoba, Seville, and Valencia. —*adj.* of the Mudéjares or their art and architecture. [Sp. f. Arab. *mudajjan* permitted to remain]

mudfish /ˈmʌdfɪʃ/ *n.* any fish that burrows in mud, esp. the bowfin.

mudflap /ˈmʌdflæp/ *n.* a flap hanging behind the wheel of a vehicle, to catch mud and stones etc. thrown up from the road.

mudguard /ˈmʌdɡɑːd/ *n.* a curved strip or cover over a wheel of a bicycle or motor cycle to reduce the amount of mud etc. thrown up from the road.

mudlark /ˈmʌdlɑːk/ *n.* **1** *hist.* a destitute child searching in river mud for objects of value. **2** *hist.* a street urchin.

mudstone /ˈmʌdstəʊn/ *n.* a dark clay rock.

muesli /ˈmuːzlɪ, ˈmjuː-/ *n.* a breakfast food of crushed cereals, dried fruits, nuts, etc., eaten with milk. [Swiss G]

muezzin /muːˈezɪn/ *n.* a Muslim crier who proclaims the hours of prayer usu. from a minaret. [Arab. *mu'addin* part. of *'addana* proclaim]

muff¹ /mʌf/ *n.* a fur or other covering, usu. in the form of a tube with an opening at each end for the hands to be inserted for warmth. [Du. *mof,* MDu. *moffel, muffel* f. med.L *muff(u)la,* of unkn. orig.]

muff² /mʌf/ *v.* & *n.* —*v.tr.* **1** bungle; deal clumsily with. **2** fail to catch or receive (a ball etc.). **3** blunder in (a theatrical part etc.). —*n.* **1** a person who is awkward or stupid, orig. in some athletic sport. **2** a failure, esp. to catch a ball at cricket etc. □□ **muffish** *adj.* [19th c.: orig. unkn.]

muffin /ˈmʌfɪn/ *n.* **1** *Brit.* a light flat round spongy cake, eaten toasted and buttered. **2** *US* a similar round cake made from batter or dough. □ **muffin-man** *Brit.* (formerly) a seller of muffins in the street. [18th c.: orig. unkn.]

muffle¹ /ˈmʌf(ə)l/ *v.* & *n.* —*v.tr.* **1** (often foll. by *up*) wrap or cover for warmth. **2** cover or wrap up (a source of sound) to reduce its loudness. **3** (usu. as **muffled** *adj.*) stifle (an utterance, e.g. a curse). **4** prevent from speaking. —*n.* **1** a receptacle in a furnace where substances may be heated without contact with combustion products. **2** a similar chamber in a kiln for baking painted pottery. [ME: (n.) f. OF *moufle* thick glove; (v.) perh. f. OF *enmoufler* f. *moufle*]

muffle² /ˈmʌf(ə)l/ *n.* the thick part of the upper lip and nose of ruminants and rodents. [F *mufle,* of unkn. orig.]

muffler /ˈmʌflə(r)/ *n.* **1** a wrap or scarf worn for warmth. **2** any of various devices used to deaden sound in musical instruments. **3** *US* the silencer of a motor vehicle.

mufti¹ /ˈmʌftɪ/ *n.* a Muslim legal expert empowered to give rulings on religious matters. [Arab. *muftī,* part. of *'aftā* decide a point of law]

mufti² /ˈmʌftɪ/ *n.* plain clothes worn by a person who also wears (esp. military) uniform (*in mufti*). [19th c.: perh. f. MUFTI¹]

mug¹ /mʌɡ/ *n.* & *v.* —*n.* **1 a** a drinking-vessel, usu. cylindrical and with a handle and used without a saucer. **b** its contents. **2** *sl.* the face or mouth of a person. **3** *Brit. sl.* **a** a simpleton. **b** a gullible person. **4** *US sl.* a hoodlum or thug. —*v.* (**mugged, mugging**) **1** *tr.* rob (a person) with violence esp. in a public place. **2** *tr.* thrash. **3** *tr.* strangle. **4** *intr. sl.* make faces, esp. before an audience, a camera, etc. □ **a mug's game** *Brit. colloq.* a foolish or unprofitable activity. **mug shot** *sl.* a photograph of a face, esp. for official purposes. □□ **mugger** *n.* (esp. in sense 1 of *v.*). **mugful** *n.* (*pl.* **-fuls**). **mugging** *n.* (in sense 1 of *v.*). [prob. f. Scand.: sense 2 of *n.* prob. f. the representation of faces on mugs, and sense 3 prob. from this]

mug² /mʌɡ/ *v.tr.* (**mugged, mugging**) *Brit.* (usu. foll. by *up*) *sl.* learn (a subject) by concentrated study. [19th c.: orig. unkn.]

Mugabe /mʊˈɡɑːbɪ/, Robert Gabriel (1924–), African statesman, first prime minister (1980) of Zimbabwe upon its independence, executive President from December 1987.

mugger[1] see MUG[1].

mugger[2] /ˈmʌgə(r)/ n. a broad-nosed Indian crocodile, *Crocodylus palustris*, venerated by many Hindus. [Hindi *magar*]

muggins /ˈmʌgɪnz/ n. (pl. same or **mugginses**) **1** colloq. **a** a simpleton. **b** a person who is easily outwitted (often with allusion to oneself: *so muggins had to pay*). **2** a card-game like snap. [perh. the surname *Muggins*, with allusion to MUG[1]]

muggy /ˈmʌgɪ/ adj. (**muggier, muggiest**) (of the weather, a day, etc.) oppressively damp and warm; humid. □□ **mugginess** n. [dial. *mug* mist, drizzle f. ON *mugga*]

Mughal /ˈmuːgɑːl/ n. **1** a Mongolian. **2** a member of a Mongolian (Muslim) dynasty in India whose empire was consolidated, after the conquests of Tamerlane, by his descendant Babur (reigned *c.*1525–30) and greatly extended by Akbar. Gradually broken up by wars and revolts, and faced by European commerical expansion, the Mughal empire did not finally disappear until after the Indian Mutiny (1857). (Cf. MOGUL 2 b.) [Pers. *mug̲ūl* MONGOL]

mugwort /ˈmʌgwɜːt/ n. any of various plants of the genus *Artemisia*, esp. *A. vulgaris*, with silver-grey aromatic foliage. [OE *mucgwyrt* (as MIDGE, WORT)]

mugwump /ˈmʌgwʌmp/ n. US **1** a great man; a boss. **2** a person who holds aloof, esp. from party politics. [Algonquin *mugquomp* great chief]

Muhammad /məˈhæmɪd/ (*c.*570–632) the founder of the Islamic faith and community. Born in Mecca to poor parents of noble lineage, as a young man he entered commerce, then through his marriage to the wealthy widow Khadīja gained some prominence in the business community as he assumed direction of his wife's commercial ventures. In 610 he received the first of a series of revelations (see KORAN) which shaped his message to the Muslim community and became the doctrinal and legislative basis of Islam. In the face of opposition from the merchants of Mecca—resistance based not only on the alien idea of a monotheistic doctrine in place of devotion to the traditional Arabian deities but also on social and economic concerns, for Muhammad's vision of social organization ran counter to that of a tribally based society—he and his small group of supporters were forced to flee north to Medina in 622. After consolidation of the community there, he led his followers into a series of battles which resulted in the capitulation of Mecca in 630. Muhammad died two years later, having successfully united tribal factions of the Hijāz into a force which would expand the frontiers of Islam. He was buried in Medina; a visit to his tomb is a traditional sequel to the requisite pilgrimage to Mecca. Muslims consider Muhammad to be 'seal of the Prophets', the final messenger sent by God to warn mankind against the consequences of rebelliousness against the divinely ordered way.

Muhammad Ali /məˌhæmɪd ˈɑːlɪ/ (1769–1849), Albanian commander in the Ottoman army, who by 1811 had overthrown the Mamelukes (see entry). Although technically the viceroy of the Ottoman sultan, he was effectively an independent ruler and reorganized the administration, agriculture, commerce, industry, education, and the army, employing chiefly French advisers, making Egypt the leading power in the eastern Mediterranean. In 1841 the Ottoman sultan agreed that his family should be hereditary rulers (pashas) of Egypt, and the dynasty survived until 1952.

Muhammadan /məˈhæməd(ə)n/ n. & adj. (also **Mohammedan**) = MUSLIM. ¶ A term not used or favoured by Muslims, and often regarded as *offens*. □□ **Muhammadanism** n. [MUHAMMAD]

Muir /mjʊə(r)/, Edwin (1887–1959), Scottish poet, whose collections of poems include *The Labyrinth* (1949). His poetry is traditional in form, and much of his imagery is rooted in the landscapes of his native Orkney. During the 1930s his translations of Kafka, done in collaboration with his wife, established Kafka's reputation in Britain.

mujahidin /ˌmuːdʒɑːhɪˈdiːn/ n.pl. (also **mujahedin, -deen**) guerrilla fighters in Islamic countries, esp. supporting Muslim fundamentalism. [Pers. & Arab. *mujāhidīn* pl. of *mujāhid* one who fights a JIHAD]

Mujibur Rahman /ˈmʊdʒɪbə(r) ˈrɑːmən/ (1920–75), Bangladeshi statesman (known as Sheikh Mujib), leader of the East Pakistan secessionist movement and head of the new State's first government (1972). In 1975 he became its first President, and when his attempts to establish a parliamentary democracy failed he assumed dictatorial powers. He and his family were murdered in a military coup.

Mukalla /mʊˈkælə/ a port of Yemen, on the Gulf of Aden.

Mukden see SHENYANG.

mulatto /mjuːˈlætəʊ/ n. & adj. —n. (pl. **-os** or **-oes**) a person of mixed White and Black parentage. —adj. of the colour of mulattos; tawny. [Sp. *mulato* young mule, *mulatto*, irreg. f. *mulo* MULE[1]]

mulberry /ˈmʌlbərɪ/ n. (pl. **-ies**) **1** any deciduous tree of the genus *Morus*, grown originally for feeding silkworms, and now for its fruit and ornamental qualities. **2** its dark-red or white berry. **3** a dark-red or purple colour. [ME *mol-, mool-, mulberry*, dissim. f. *murberie* f. OE *mōrberie*, f. L *morum*: see BERRY]

mulch /mʌltʃ, mʌlʃ/ n. & v. —n. a mixture of wet straw, leaves, etc., spread around or over a plant to enrich or insulate the soil. —v.tr. treat with mulch. [prob. use as noun of *mulsh* soft: cf. dial. *melsh* mild f. OE *melsc*]

mulct /mʌlkt/ v. & n. —v.tr. **1** extract money from by fine or taxation. **2** (often foll. by *of*) deprive by fraudulent means; swindle. **b** obtain by swindling. —n. a fine. [earlier *mult(e)* f. L *multa, mulcta*: (v.) through F *mulcter* & L *mulctare*]

mule[1] /mjuːl/ n. **1** the offspring (usu. sterile) of a male donkey and a female horse, or (in general use) of a female donkey and a male horse (cf. HINNY[1]), used as a beast of burden and proverbial for its stubbornness. **2** a stupid or obstinate person. **3** (often *attrib.*) a hybrid and usu. sterile plant or animal (*mule canary*). **4** (in full **spinning mule**) a kind of spinning-machine producing yarn on spindles, invented in 1779 by Samuel Crompton (d. 1827), so called because it was a cross between Arkwright's 'water frame' and Hargreaves' spinning jenny. It was an improvement upon both, producing yarn of higher quality at greater speed. [ME f. OF *mul(e)* f. L *mulus mula*]

mule[2] /mjuːl/ n. a light shoe or slipper without a back. [F]

mule[3] var. of MEWL.

muleteer /ˌmjuːlɪˈtɪə(r)/ n. a mule-driver. [F *muletier* f. *mulet* dimin. of OF *mul* MULE[1]]

mulga /ˈmʌlgə/ n. Austral. **1** a small spreading tree, *Acacia aneura*. **2** the wood of this tree. **3** scrub or bush. **4** colloq. the outback. [Aboriginal]

Mulhouse /mʊˈluːz/ an industrial city in NE France; pop. (1982) 113,800.

muliebrity /ˌmjuːlɪˈebrɪtɪ/ n. literary **1** womanhood. **2** the normal characteristics of a woman. **3** softness, effeminacy. [LL *muliebritas* f. L *mulier* woman]

mulish /ˈmjuːlɪʃ/ adj. **1** like a mule. **2** stubborn. □□ **mulishly** adv. **mulishness** n.

mull[1] /mʌl/ v.tr. & intr. (often foll. by *over*) ponder or consider. [perh. f. *mull* grind to powder, ME *mul* dust f. MDu.]

mull[2] /mʌl/ v.tr. warm (wine or beer) with added sugar, spices, etc. [17th c.: orig. unkn.]

mull[3] /mʌl/ n. Sc. a promontory. [ME: cf. Gael. *maol*, Icel. *múli*]

mull[4] /mʌl/ n. humus formed under non-acid conditions. [G f. Da. *muld*]

mull[5] /mʌl/ n. a thin soft plain muslin. [abbr. of *mulmull* f. Hindi *malmal*]

mullah /ˈmʌlə/ n. a Muslim learned in Islamic theology and sacred law. [Pers., Turk., Urdu *mullā* f. Arab. *mawlā*]

mullein /ˈmʌlɪn/ n. any herbaceous plant of the genus *Verbascum*, with woolly leaves and yellow flowers. [ME f. OF *moleine* f. Gaulish]

Müller[1] /ˈmʊlə(r)/, Friedrich Max (1823–1900), German philologist, who came to England in 1846 and became a British subject. He was commissioned by the East India Company to produce an edition of the Sanskrit *Rigveda*, and this was published in 1849–73. He also devoted much attention to comparative mythology and the study of religions.

Müller[2] /ˈmʌlə(r)/, Hermann Joseph (1890–1967), American geneticist, who discovered that X-rays can induce changes in genetic material, and recognized the danger of X-radiation to living things. He was awarded a Nobel Prize in 1946.

Müller[3] /ˈmʊlə(r)/, Johannes Peter (1801–58), German anatomist and biologist, a pioneer of comparative and microscopical methods in biology, regarded as one of the most distinguished scientists of 19th-c. Germany.

Müller[4] /ˈmʊlə(r)/, Paul Hermann (1899–1965), Swiss chemist, who synthesized DDT (1939) and discovered its insecticidal properties. He was awarded the 1948 Nobel Prize for medicine.

muller /ˈmʌlə(r)/ n. a stone or other heavy weight used for grinding material on a slab. [ME, perh. f. AF *moldre* grind]

mullet /ˈmʌlɪt/ n. any fish of the family Mullidae (**red mullet**) or Mugilidae (**grey mullet**), usu. with a thick body and a large blunt-nosed head, commonly used as food. [ME f. OF *mulet* dimin. of L *mullus* red mullet f. Gk *mollos*]

mulligatawny /ˌmʌlɪgəˈtɔːnɪ/ n. a highly seasoned soup orig. from India. [Tamil *milagutannir* pepper-water]

mullion /ˈmʌljən/ n. (also **munnion** /ˈmʌn-/) a vertical bar dividing the lights in a window (cf. TRANSOM). □□ **mullioned** adj. [prob. an altered form of MONIAL]

mullock /ˈmʌlək/ n. **1** Austral. or dial. refuse, rubbish. **2** Austral. **a** rock containing no gold. **b** refuse from which gold has been extracted. **3** Austral. ridicule. [ME dimin. of *mul* dust, rubbish, f. MDu.]

mulloway /ˈmʌləˌweɪ/ n. Austral. a large marine fish, *Sciaena antarctica*, used as food. [19th c.: orig. unkn.]

Mulroney /mʌlˈruːnɪ/, (Martin) Brian (1939–), Canadian Conservative statesman, Prime Minister of Canada 1984–

Multan /mʊlˈtɑːn/ a commercial city in Punjab province, Pakistan; pop. (1981) 730,000.

multangular /mʌlˈtæŋjʊlə(r)/ adj. having many angles. [med.L *multangularis* (as MULTI-, ANGULAR)]

multi- /ˈmʌltɪ/ comb. form many; more than one. [L f. *multus* much, many]

multi-access /ˌmʌltɪˈækses/ n. (often attrib.) the simultaneous connection to a computer of a number of terminals.

multiaxial /ˌmʌltɪˈæksɪəl/ adj. of or involving several axes.

multicellular /ˌmʌltɪˈseljʊlə(r)/ adj. Biol. having many cells.

multichannel /ˌmʌltɪˈtʃæn(ə)l/ adj. employing or possessing many communication or television channels.

multicolour /ˈmʌltɪˌkʌlə(r)/ adj. (also **multicoloured**) of many colours.

multicultural /ˌmʌltɪˈkʌltʃər(ə)l/ adj. of or relating to or constituting several cultural or ethnic groups within a society. □□ **multiculturally** adv.

multidimensional /ˌmʌltɪdaɪˈmenʃən(ə)l/ adj. of or involving more than three dimensions. □□ **multidimensionality** /-ˈnælɪtɪ/ n. **multidimensionally** adv.

multidirectional /ˌmʌltɪdaɪˈrekʃən(ə)l/ adj. of, involving, or operating in several directions.

multifaceted /ˌmʌltɪˈfæsɪtɪd/ adj. having several facets.

multifarious /ˌmʌltɪˈfeərɪəs/ adj. **1** (foll. by pl. noun) many and various. **2** having great variety. □□ **multifariously** adv. **multifariousness** n. [L *multifarius*]

multifid /ˈmʌltɪfɪd/ adj. Bot. & Zool. divided into many parts. [L *multifidus* (as MULTI-, *fid-* stem of *findere* cleave)]

multifoil /ˈmʌltɪˌfɔɪl/ n. Archit. an ornament consisting of more than five foils.

multiform /ˈmʌltɪˌfɔːm/ n. (usu. attrib.) **1** having many forms. **2** of many kinds. □□ **multiformity** /-ˈfɔːmɪtɪ/ n.

multifunctional /ˌmʌltɪˈfʌŋkʃən(ə)l/ adj. having or fulfilling several functions.

multigrade /ˈmʌltɪˌgreɪd/ n. (usu. attrib.) an engine oil etc. meeting the requirements of several standard grades.

multilateral /ˌmʌltɪˈlætər(ə)l/ adj. **1 a** (of an agreement, treaty, conference, etc.) in which three or more parties participate. **b** performed by more than one party (*multilateral disarmament*). **2** having many sides. □□ **multilaterally** adv.

multilingual /ˌmʌltɪˈlɪŋgw(ə)l/ adj. in or using several languages. □□ **multilingually** adv.

multimillion /ˈmʌltɪˌmɪljən/ attrib.adj. costing or involving several million (pounds, dollars, etc.) (*multimillion dollar fraud*).

multimillionaire /ˌmʌltɪˌmɪljəˈneə(r)/ n. a person with a fortune of several millions.

multinational /ˌmʌltɪˈnæʃən(ə)l/ adj. & n. —adj. **1** (of a business organization) operating in several countries. **2** relating to or including several nationalities or ethnic groups. —n. a multinational company. □□ **multinationally** adv.

multinomial /ˌmʌltɪˈnəʊmɪəl/ adj. & n. Math. = POLYNOMIAL. [MULTI-, after *binomial*]

multiparous /mʌlˈtɪpərəs/ adj. **1** bringing forth many young at a birth. **2** having borne more than one child. [MULTI- + -PAROUS]

multipartite /ˌmʌltɪˈpɑːtaɪt/ adj. divided into many parts.

multiphase /ˈmʌltɪˌfeɪz/ n. Electr. = POLYPHASE.

multiple /ˈmʌltɪp(ə)l/ adj. & n. —adj. **1** having several or many parts, elements, or individual components. **2** (foll. by pl. noun) many and various. **3** Bot. (of fruit) collective. —n. **1** a number that may be divided by another a certain number of times without a remainder (*56 is a multiple of 7*). **2** a multiple shop or store. □ **least** (or **lowest**) **common multiple** the least quantity that is a multiple of two or more given quantities. **multiple-choice** (of a question in an examination) accompanied by several possible answers from which the correct one has to be chosen. **multiple personality** Psychol. the apparent existence of two or more distinct personalities in one individual. **multiple sclerosis** see SCLEROSIS. **multiple shop** (or **store**) Brit. a shop or store with branches in several places. **multiple standard** see STANDARD. **multiple star** several stars so close as to seem one, esp. when forming a connected system. □□ **multiply** adv. [F f. LL *multiplus* f. L (as MULTIPLEX)]

multiplex /ˈmʌltɪˌpleks/ adj. & v. —adj. **1** manifold; of many elements. **2** involving simultaneous transmission of several messages along a single channel of communication. —v.tr. incorporate into a multiplex signal or system. □□ **multiplexer** n. (also **multiplexor**). [L (as MULTI-, *-plex -plicis* -fold)]

multipliable /ˈmʌltɪˌplaɪəb(ə)l/ adj. that can be multiplied.

multiplicable /ˈmʌltɪˌplɪkəb(ə)l/ adj. = MULTIPLIABLE. [OF *multiplicable* or med.L *multiplicabilis* f. L (as MULTIPLY)]

multiplicand /ˌmʌltɪplɪˈkænd/ n. a quantity to be multiplied by a multiplier. [med.L *multiplicandus* gerundive of L *multiplicare* (as MULTIPLY)]

multiplication /ˌmʌltɪplɪˈkeɪʃ(ə)n/ n. **1** the arithmetical process of multiplying. **2** the act or an instance of multiplying. □ **multiplication sign** the sign (×) to indicate that one quantity is to be multiplied by another, as in $2 \times 3 = 6$. **multiplication table** a list of multiples of a particular number, usu. from 1 to 12. □□ **multiplicative** /-ˈplɪkətɪv/ adj. [ME f. OF *multiplication* or L *multiplicatio* (as MULTIPLY)]

multiplicity /ˌmʌltɪˈplɪsɪtɪ/ n. (pl. **-ies**) **1** manifold variety. **2** (foll. by *of*) a great number. [LL *multiplicitas* (as MULTIPLEX)]

multiplier /ˈmʌltɪˌplaɪə(r)/ n. **1** a quantity by which a given number is multiplied. **2** Econ. a factor by which an increment of income exceeds the resulting increment of saving or investment. **3** Electr. an instrument for increasing by repetition the intensity of a current, force, etc.

multiply /ˈmʌltɪˌplaɪ/ v. (**-ies, -ied**) **1** tr. (also absol.) obtain from (a number) another that is a specified number of times its value (*multiply 6 by 4 and you get 24*). **2** intr. increase in number esp. by procreation. **3** tr. produce a large number of (instances etc.). **4** tr. **a** breed (animals). **b** propagate (plants). [ME f. OF *multiplier* f. L *multiplicare* (as MULTIPLEX)]

multipolar /ˌmʌltɪˈpəʊlə(r)/ adj. having many poles (see POLE[2]).

multiprocessing /ˌmʌltɪˈprəʊsesɪŋ/ n. Computing processing by a number of processors sharing a common memory and common peripherals.

multiprogramming /ˌmʌltɪˈprəʊɡræmɪŋ/ n. Computing the execution of two or more independent programs concurrently.

multi-purpose /ˌmʌltɪˈpɜːpəs/ n. (attrib.) having several purposes.

multiracial /ˌmʌltɪˈreɪʃ(ə)l/ adj. relating to or made up of many human races. □□ **multiracially** adv.

multi-role /ˌmʌltɪˈrəʊl/ n. (attrib.) having several roles or functions.

multi-stage /ˈmʌltɪˌsteɪdʒ/ n. (attrib.) (of a rocket etc.) having several stages of operation.

multi-storey /ˌmʌltɪˈstɔːrɪ/ n. (attrib.) (of a building) having several (esp. similarly designed) storeys.

multitude /ˈmʌltɪˌtjuːd/ n. 1 (often foll. by of) a great number. 2 a large gathering of people; a crowd. 3 (**the multitude**) the common people. 4 the state of being numerous. [ME f. OF f. L multitudo -dinis f. multus many]

multitudinous /ˌmʌltɪˈtjuːdɪnəs/ adj. 1 very numerous. 2 consisting of many individuals or elements. 3 (of an ocean etc.) vast. □□ **multitudinously** adv. **multitudinousness** n. [L (as MULTITUDE)]

multi-user /ˌmʌltɪˈjuːzə(r)/ n. (attrib.) (of a computer system) having a number of simultaneous users (cf. MULTI-ACCESS).

multivalent /ˌmʌltɪˈveɪlənt/ adj. Chem. 1 having a valency of more than two. 2 having a variable valency. □□ **multivalency** n.

multivalve /ˈmʌltɪˌvælv/ n. (attrib.) (of a shell etc.) having several valves.

multiversity /ˌmʌltɪˈvɜːsɪtɪ/ n. (pl. **-ies**) a large university with many different departments. [MULTI- + UNIVERSITY]

multivocal /mʌlˈtɪvək(ə)l/ adj. having many meanings.

multi-way /ˈmʌltɪˌweɪ/ n. (attrib.) having several paths of communication etc.

mum[1] /mʌm/ n. Brit. colloq. mother. [abbr. of MUMMY[1]]

mum[2] /mʌm/ adj. colloq. silent (keep mum). □ **mum's the word** say nothing. [ME: imit. of closed lips]

mum[3] /mʌm/ v.intr. (**mummed**, **mumming**) act in a traditional masked mime. [cf. MUM[2] and MLG mummen]

mumble /ˈmʌmb(ə)l/ v. & n. —v. 1 intr. & tr. speak or utter indistinctly. 2 tr. bite or chew with or as with toothless gums. —n. an indistinct utterance. □□ **mumbler** n. **mumblingly** adv. [ME momele, as MUM[2]: cf. LG mummelen]

mumbo-jumbo /ˌmʌmbəʊˈdʒʌmbəʊ/ n. (pl. **-jumbos**) 1 meaningless or ignorant ritual. 2 language or action intended to mystify or confuse. 3 an object of senseless veneration. [Mumbo Jumbo, a supposed African idol]

mummer /ˈmʌmə(r)/ n. 1 an actor in a traditional mime. 2 archaic or derog. an actor in the theatre. □ **mummers' play** the best-known type of English folk-play, which appears to derive from the folk festivals of primitive agricultural communities. The central theme is the death and resurrection of one of the characters, an obvious re-enactment in human terms of the earth awakening from the death of winter. Texts show a remarkable similarity. The play is first mentioned towards the end of the 18th c. and flourished until the mid-19th c.; it can still be seen in a few English villages. [ME f. OF momeur f. momer MUM[3]]

mummery /ˈmʌmərɪ/ n. (pl. **-ies**) 1 ridiculous (esp. religious) ceremonial. 2 a performance by mummers. [OF momerie (as MUMMER)]

mummify /ˈmʌmɪˌfaɪ/ v.tr. (**-ies**, **-ied**) 1 embalm and preserve (a body) in the form of a mummy (see MUMMY[2]). 2 (usu. as **mummified** adj.) shrivel or dry up (tissues etc.). □□ **mummification** /-fɪˈkeɪʃ(ə)n/ n.

mummy[1] /ˈmʌmɪ/ n. (pl. **-ies**) Brit. colloq. mother. [imit. of a child's pronunc.: cf. MAMMA[1]]

mummy[2] /ˈmʌmɪ/ n. (pl. **-ies**) 1 a body of a human being or animal embalmed for burial, esp. in ancient Egypt. (See below.) 2 a dried-up body. 3 a pulpy mass (beat it to a mummy). 4 a rich brown pigment. [F momie f. med.L mumia f. Arab. mūmiyā f. Pers. mūm wax]

The concept of mummification was based on the belief that the preservation of the body was necessary so that the soul and the ka might meet it again and live with it. The practice developed in the predynastic period with the change from simple desert burials, which had dehydrated and preserved the body naturally, to burial in coffins. Mummification procedures evolved, reaching a peak by the late New Kingdom. The essential steps were removing the viscera, dehydrating the body with natron, treating it with resin, bandaging, and decorating it. The ceremonial aspects were considered crucial, and the procedure could take 70 days.

mumps /mʌmps/ n.pl. 1 (treated as sing.) a contagious and infectious viral disease with swelling of the parotid salivary glands in the face. 2 a fit of sulks. □□ **mumpish** adj. (in sense 2). [archaic mump be sullen]

Munch /mʊŋk/, Edvard (1863–1944), Norwegian painter and engraver, one of the chief sources of German expressionism. His subjects had an intense emotionalism, and he explored the use of violent colour and linear distortion to express anxiety, fear, love, and hatred; among his most famous works is The Cry (1895).

munch /mʌntʃ/ v.tr. eat steadily with a marked action of the jaws. [ME, imit.: cf. CRUNCH]

Munchausen /ˈmʌnˈtʃaʊz(ə)n/, Baron. The hero of a book of fantastic travellers' tales (1785) written in English by a German, Rudolph Erich Raspe. The original Freiherr von Münchhausen is said to have lived in 1720–97, to have served in the Russian army against the Turks, and to have related extravagant tales of his prowess. □ **Munchausen's syndrome** a condition in which a person repeatedly pretends to have a dramatic or severe illness in order to obtain hospital treatment.

München see MUNICH.

Munda /ˈmuːndə/ n. & adj. —n. 1 a member of an ancient people surviving in present times as primitive tribes living in NE India. 2 the group of languages which includes their dialects. —adj. of the Mundas or their languages. [native name]

mundane /mʌnˈdeɪn/ adj. 1 dull, routine. 2 of this world; worldly. □□ **mundanely** adv. **mundaneness** n. **mundanity** /-ˈdænɪtɪ/ n. (pl. **-ies**). [ME f. OF mondain f. LL mundanus f. L mundus world]

mung /mʌŋ/ n. (in full **mung bean**) a leguminous plant, Phaseolus aureus, native to India and used as food. [Hindi mūng]

mungo /ˈmʌŋɡəʊ/ n. (pl. **-os**) the short fibres recovered from heavily felted material. [19th c.: orig. uncert.]

Munich /ˈmjuːnɪk/ (German **München** /ˈmʊnxən/) a city in SW Germany, capital of Bavaria; pop. (1987) 1,274,700. □ **Munich Pact** or **Agreement** an agreement between Britain, France, Germany, and Italy, signed at Munich on 29 Sept. 1938, under which part of Czechoslovakia was ceded to Germany. It is remembered as an act of appeasement.

municipal /mjuːˈnɪsɪp(ə)l/ adj. of or concerning a municipality or its self-government. □□ **municipalize** v.tr. (also **-ise**). **municipalization** /-ˈzeɪʃ(ə)n/ n. **municipally** adv. [L municipalis f. municipium free city f. municeps -cipis citizen with privileges f. munia civic offices + capere take]

municipality /mjuːˌnɪsɪˈpælɪtɪ/ n. (pl. **-ies**) 1 a town or district having local government. 2 the governing body of this area. [F municipalité f. municipal (as MUNICIPAL)]

munificent /mjuːˈnɪfɪs(ə)nt/ adj. (of a giver or a gift) splendidly generous, bountiful. □□ **munificence** n. **munificently** adv. [L munificent-, var. stem of munificus f. munus gift]

muniment /ˈmjuːnɪmənt/ n. (usu. in pl.) 1 a document kept as evidence of rights or privileges etc. 2 an archive. [ME f. OF f. L munimentum defence, in med.L title-deed f. munire munit- fortify]

munition /mjuːˈnɪʃ(ə)n/ n. & v. —n. (usu. in pl.) military weapons, ammunition, equipment, and stores. —v.tr. supply with munitions. [F f. L munitio -onis fortification (as MUNIMENT)]

munitioner /mjuːˈnɪʃənə(r)/ n. a person who makes or supplies munitions.

munnion var. of MULLION.

Munro /mʌnˈrəʊ/, H. H. see SAKI.

munshi var. of MOONSHEE.

Munster[1] /'mʌnstə(r)/ a southern province of the Republic of Ireland; pop. (est. 1986) 1,019,700.

Münster[2] /'mʊnstə(r)/ a city in NW Germany; pop. (1987) 267,600. It was formerly the capital of Westphalia; the Treaty of Westphalia, ending the Thirty Years War, was signed simultaneously here and at Osnabrück in 1648.

munt /mʊnt/ n. S.Afr. sl. offens. a Black African. [Bantu umuntu person]

muntjac /'mʌntdʒæk/ n. (also **muntjak**) any small deer of the genus Muntiacus native to SE Asia, the male having tusks and small antlers. [Sundanese minchek]

Muntz metal /mʌnts/ n. an alloy (60% copper, 40% zinc) used for sheathing ships etc. [G. F. Muntz, Engl. manufacturer d. 1857]

muon /'mju:ɒn/ n. Physics an unstable elementary particle like an electron, but with a much greater mass. [μ (MU), as the symbol for it]

murage /'mjʊərɪdʒ/ n. hist. a tax levied for building or repairing the walls of a town. [ME f. OF, in med.L muragium f. OF mur f. L murus wall]

mural /'mjʊər(ə)l/ n. & adj. —n. a painting executed directly on a wall. —adj. 1 of or like a wall. 2 on a wall. □ **mural crown** Rom. Antiq. a crown or garland given to the soldier who was first to scale the wall of a besieged town. □□ **muralist** n. [F f. L muralis f. murus wall]

Murat /mjʊə'ra:/, Joachim (c.1767–1815), French general, king of Naples 1808–14. One of the most flamboyant of Napoleon's marshals, Murat made his name as a cavalry commander, but like several of his colleagues was not always equal to the challenge of independent command. Having deserted Napoleon in 1814, he returned to his cause in 1815, but was defeated and eventually captured and shot.

Murchison Falls /'mɜ:tʃɪs(ə)n/ 1 the former name of the Kabalega Falls (see KABALEGA). 2 the former name of a waterfall, now known as Kapachira Falls, on the Shire River in southern Malawi.

Murcia /'mɜ:ʃə, Sp. 'mʊəθɪə/ 1 an autonomous region in SE Spain; pop. (1986) 1,014,300. 2 its capital city; pop. (1981) 288,631.

murder /'mɜ:də(r)/ n. & v. —n. 1 the unlawful premeditated killing of a human being by another (cf. MANSLAUGHTER). 2 colloq. an unpleasant, troublesome, or dangerous state of affairs (it was murder here on Saturday). —v.tr. 1 kill (a human being) unlawfully, esp. wickedly or inhumanly. 2 Law kill (a human being) with a premeditated motive. 3 colloq. utterly defeat or spoil by a bad performance, mispronunciation etc. (murdered the soliloquy in the second act). □ **cry blue murder** sl. make an extravagant outcry. **get away with murder** colloq. do whatever one wishes and escape punishment. **murder will out** murder cannot remain undetected. □□ **murderer** n. **murderess** n. [OE morthor & OF murdre f. Gmc]

murderous /'mɜ:dərəs/ adj. (of a person, weapon, action, etc.) capable of, intending, or involving murder or great harm. □□ **murderously** adv. **murderousness** n.

Murdoch[1] /'mɜ:dɒk/, Dame Iris Jean (1919–), English novelist, born in Dublin of Anglo-Irish parents, and educated at Oxford where she subsequently lectured in philosophy. Her first novel Under the Net (1954) was followed by many other successful works portraying sophisticated sexual relationships. Her plots have an operatic quality combining comic, macabre, and bizarre incidents, showing an acute observation of 20th-c. middle-class life and a great ingenuity.

Murdoch[2] /'mɜ:dɒk/, (Keith) Rupert (1931–), Australian-born newspaper publisher and entrepreneur, whose company owns major newspapers also in Britain and the US, together with film and television companies and a UK publishing firm.

mure /mjʊə(r)/ v.tr. archaic 1 immure. 2 (foll. by up) wall up or shut up in an enclosed space. [ME f. OF murer f. mur: see MURAGE]

murex /'mjʊərəks/ n. (pl. **murices** /-rɪˌsiːz/ or **murexes**) any gastropod mollusc of the genus Murex, yielding a purple dye. [L]

Murillo /mjʊə'rɪləʊ/, Bartolomé Esteban (1617–82), Spanish painter. Born in Seville, his early work's dramatic chiaroscuro shows an indebtedness to Zurbarán. His mature subject-matter incorporated two basic themes: genre scenes of sentimentalized urchins and peasants and devotional pictures of delicate colour and ethereal form—his 'estilo vaporoso' (e.g. Immaculate Conception). In 1660 he became first director of the Seville Academy. His reputation and influence stood high throughout the 18th c. but fell sharply because of the mannered vapidity of his imitators.

murine /'mjʊəˌraɪn/ adj. of or like a mouse or mice. [L murinus f. mus muris mouse]

murk /mɜ:k/ n. & adj. (also **mirk**) —n. 1 darkness, poor visibility. 2 air obscured by fog etc. —adj. archaic (of night, day, place, etc.) = MURKY. [prob. f. Scand.: cf. ON myrkr]

murky /'mɜ:kɪ/ adj. (also **mirky**) (**-ier**, **-iest**) 1 dark, gloomy. 2 (of darkness) thick, dirty. 3 suspiciously obscure (murky past). □□ **murkily** adv. **murkiness** n.

Murmansk /mʊə'mænsk/ a port of the Soviet Union on the Kola Bay, an inlet of the Barents Sea; pop. (est. 1987) 432,000. Murmansk is the largest city north of the Arctic Circle; its port is ice-free throughout the year.

murmur /'mɜ:mə(r)/ n. & v. —n. 1 a subdued continuous sound, as made by waves, a brook, etc. 2 a softly spoken or nearly inarticulate utterance. 3 Med. a recurring sound heard in the auscultation of the heart and usu. indicating abnormality. 4 a subdued expression of discontent. —v. 1 intr. make a subdued continuous sound. 2 tr. utter (words) in a low voice. 3 intr. (usu. foll. by at, against) complain in low tones, grumble. □□ **murmurer** n. **murmuringly** adv. **murmurous** adj. [ME f. OF murmurer f. L murmurare: cf. Gk mormurō (of water) roar, Skr. marmaras noisy]

murphy /'mɜ:fɪ/ n. (pl. **-ies**) sl. a potato. [Ir. surname]

Murphy's Law /'mɜ:fɪz/ n. joc. any of various maxims about the apparent perverseness of things (roughly, 'anything that can go wrong will go wrong'). [Irish surname; orig. of phrase uncertain]

murrain /'mʌrɪn/ n. 1 an infectious disease of cattle, carried by parasites. 2 archaic a plague, esp. the potato blight during the Irish famine in the mid-19th c. [ME f. AF moryn, OF morine f. morir f. L mori die]

Murray[1] /'mʌrɪ/ the principal river of Australia, rising in New South Wales and flowing 2,590 km (1,610 miles) westward to the Indian Ocean.

Murray[2] /'mʌrɪ/, (George) Gilbert Aimé (1886–1957), British classical scholar, born in Australia, Regius Professor of Greek at Oxford 1908–36, noted for his ability to make the ancient world sensitively real to his contemporaries. His translations of the plays of Euripides, by romanticizing the originals, appealed to a wide public. Always an eloquent champion of liberal causes, including women's rights, he devoted his energies after 1918 to the furtherance of peace, and as chairman of the League of Nations Union (1922–38) he struggled without much hope to save Europe from war.

Murray[3] /'mʌrɪ/, Sir James Augustus Henry (1837–1915), Scottish-born lexicographer, chief editor of the largest of all dictionaries, the Oxford English Dictionary (1884–1928; originally entitled A New English Dictionary on Historical Principles). The original plan of a four-volume work, to be completed in ten years (i.e. by 1889), was defeated by the complexities of the English language and its development over nine centuries, and nine years' editing produced only the first volume of a work that was to consist ultimately of twelve. In spite of the drain on its resources the University of Oxford recognized that the project was already a national asset: new instalments were eagerly awaited by scholars around the world, and the parts already issued were becoming the final authority on the English language. Murray did not live to see the Dictionary completed; he died after finishing a section of the letter T, two years short of his 80th birthday.

murrey /'mʌrɪ/ n. & adj. archaic —n. the colour of a mulberry; a deep red or purple. —adj. of this colour. [ME f. OF moré f. med.L moratus f. morum mulberry]

murther /'mɜ:ðə(r)/ archaic var. of MURDER.

Mururoa /ˌmʊərʊˈrəʊə/ a remote atoll in the Tuamotu archipelago, French Polynesia, used as a nuclear testing site between 1966 and 1974.

Musala /muːˈsɑːlə/ (also **Mousalla**) the highest peak in Bulgaria, rising to a height of 2,925 m (9,596 ft.) in the Rila Mountains.

Mus.B. abbr. (also **Mus. Bac.**) Bachelor of Music. [L Musicae Baccalaureus]

muscadel var. of MUSCATEL.

Muscadet /ˈmʌskəˌdeɪ/ n. **1** a white wine from the Loire region of France. **2** a variety of grape from which the wine is made. [Muscadet variety of grape]

muscadine /ˈmʌskədɪn, -ˌdaɪn/ n. a variety of grape with a musk flavour, used chiefly in wine-making. [perh. Engl. form f. Prov. MUSCAT]

muscarine /ˈmʌskərɪn/ n. a poisonous alkaloid from the fungus Amanita muscaria. [L muscarius f. musca fly]

Muscat /ˈmʌskæt/ the capital of Oman; pop. (est. 1975) 250,000.

muscat /ˈmʌskət/ n. **1** a sweet fortified white wine made from muscadines. **2** a muscadine. [F f. Prov. muscat muscade (adj.) f. musc MUSK]

muscatel /ˌmʌskəˈtel/ n. (also **muscadel** /-ˈdel/) **1** = MUSCAT. **2** a raisin from a muscadine grape. [ME f. OF f. Prov. dimin. of muscat: see MUSCAT]

muscle /ˈmʌs(ə)l/ n. & v. —n. **1** a fibrous tissue with the ability to contract, producing movement in or maintaining the position of an animal body. (See below.) **2** the part of an animal body that is composed of muscles. **3** physical power or strength. —v.intr. (usu. foll. by in) colloq. force oneself on others; intrude by forceful means. □ **muscle-bound** with muscles stiff and inelastic through excessive exercise or training. **muscle-man** a man with highly developed muscles, esp. one employed as an intimidator. **not move a muscle** be completely motionless. □□ **muscled** adj. (usu. in comb.). **muscleless** adj. **muscly** adj. [F f. L musculus dimin. of mus mouse, from the fancied mouselike form of some muscles]

In all animals except the protozoa and most of the sponges certain cells function as muscle-cells. These cells are very small, but when grouped may form conspicuous columns, bands, or sheets of muscle. Muscular tissue makes movement and stance possible; it converts chemical into mechanical energy, and its chemical reactions produce most of the heat which keeps mammals' and birds' temperature above that of their surroundings. In vertebrates there are three main types of muscle tissue. Skeletal muscles are under voluntary control (at least in humans); they are attached to bones by tendons and move the joints. Cardiac muscle, found only in the heart, is not under direct voluntary control; it is notable for its ability to contract spontaneously and rhythmically (see HEART). Smooth or visceral muscle, which is also controlled involuntarily, is found chiefly in the walls of hollow organs such as the stomach and intestines. Under the microscope voluntary muscle has a striped appearance, while involuntary or smooth muscle shows no stripes. In invertebrates distinctions between different types of muscle tissue are less clear.

muscology /mʌsˈkɒlədʒɪ/ n. the study of mosses. □□ **muscologist** n. [mod.L muscologia f. L muscus moss]

muscovado /ˌmʌskəˈvɑːdəʊ/ n. (pl. **-os**) an unrefined sugar made from the juice of sugar cane by evaporation and draining off the molasses. [Sp. mascabado (sugar) of the lowest quality]

Muscovite /ˈmʌskəˌvaɪt/ n. & adj. —n. **1** a native or citizen of Moscow. **2** archaic a Russian. —adj. **1** of or relating to Moscow. **2** archaic of or relating to Russia. [mod.L Muscovita f. Muscovia = MUSCOVY]

muscovite /ˈmʌskəˌvaɪt/ n. a silver-grey form of mica with a sheetlike crystalline structure that is used in the manufacture of electrical equipment etc. [obs. MUSCOVY glass (in the same sense) + -ITE¹]

Muscovy /ˈmʌskəvɪ/ **1** a principality in west central Russia, founded by Daniel, son of Alexander Nevski, in the late 13th c. Muscovy gradually expanded, despite repeated Tartar depredations, uniting with the neighbouring principality of Vladimir

to form the nucleus of the modern Russian State. **2** (archaic) Russia. □ **Muscovy duck** a tropical American duck, Cairina moschata, with a slight smell of musk (and no connection with Russia). [obs. F Muscovie f. mod.L Moscovia f. Russ. Moskva Moscow]

muscular /ˈmʌskjʊlə(r)/ adj. **1** of or affecting the muscles. **2** having well-developed muscles. □ **muscular Christianity** a Christian life of cheerful physical activity as described in the writings of Charles Kingsley. **muscular dystrophy** see DYSTROPHY. **muscular rheumatism** = MYALGIA. **muscular stomach** see STOMACH. □□ **muscularity** /-ˈlærɪtɪ/ n. **muscularly** adv. [earlier musculous (as MUSCLE)]

musculature /ˈmʌskjʊlətʃə(r)/ n. the muscular system of a body or organ. [F f. L (as MUSCLE)]

Mus.D. abbr. (also **Mus. Doc.**) Doctor of Music. [L Musicae Doctor]

muse¹ /mjuːz/ n. **1** Gk & Rom. Mythol. any of the goddesses who presided over the arts and sciences. They were the daughters of Zeus and Mnemosyne, traditionally nine in number (Calliope, Clio, Euterpe, Terpsichore, Erato, Melpomene, Thalia, Polyhymnia, and Urania), though their functions and names vary considerably in different sources. **2** (usu. prec. by the) **a** a poet's inspiring goddess. **b** a poet's genius. [ME f. OF muse or L musa f. Gk mousa]

muse² /mjuːz/ v. & n. literary —v. **1** intr. **a** (usu. foll. by on, upon) ponder, reflect. **b** (usu. foll. by on) gaze meditatively (on a scene etc.). **2** tr. say meditatively. —n. archaic a fit of abstraction. [ME f. OF muser to waste time f. Rmc perh. f. med.L musum muzzle]

musette /mjuːˈzet/ n. **1 a** a kind of small bagpipe with bellows, common in the French court in the 17th–18th c. **b** a tune imitating the sound of this. **2** a small oboe-like double-reed instrument in 19th-c. France. **3** a popular dance in the courts of Louis XIV and XV, a rustic form of the gavotte. Its name derives from the music's bagpipe-like bass drone. **4** US a small knapsack. [ME f. OF, dimin. of muse bagpipe]

museum /mjuːˈzɪəm/ n. a building used for storing and exhibiting objects of historical, scientific, or cultural interest. □ **museum piece 1** a specimen of art etc. fit for a museum. **2** derog. an old-fashioned or quaint person or object. □□ **museology** /-ˈɒlədʒɪ/ n. [L f. Gk mouseion seat of the Muses: see MUSE¹]

mush¹ /mʌʃ/ n. **1** soft pulp. **2** feeble sentimentality. **3** US maize porridge. □□ **mushy** adj. (**mushier**, **mushiest**). **mushily** adv. **mushiness** n. [app. var. of MASH]

mush² /mʌʃ/ v. & n. US —v.intr. **1** (in imper.) used as a command to dogs pulling a sledge to urge them forward. **2** go on a journey across snow with a dog-sledge. —n. a journey across snow with a dog-sledge. [prob. corrupt. f. F marchons imper. of marcher advance]

mushroom /ˈmʌʃrʊm, -ruːm/ n. & v. —n. **1** the usu. edible spore-producing body of various fungi, esp. Agaricus campestris, with a stem and domed cap, proverbial for its rapid growth. **2** the pinkish-brown colour of this. **3** any item resembling a mushroom in shape (darning mushroom). **4** (usu. attrib.) something that appears or develops suddenly or is ephemeral; an upstart. —v.intr. **1** appear or develop rapidly. **2** expand and flatten like a mushroom cap. **3** gather mushrooms. □ **mushroom cloud** a cloud suggesting the shape of a mushroom, esp. from a nuclear explosion. **mushroom growth 1** a sudden development or expansion. **2** anything undergoing this. □□ **mushroomy** adj. [ME f. OF mousseron f. LL mussirio -onis]

music /ˈmjuːzɪk/ n. **1** the art of combining vocal or instrumental sounds (or both) to produce beauty of form, harmony, and expression of emotion. **2** the sounds so produced. **3** musical compositions. **4** the written or printed score of a musical composition. **5** certain pleasant sounds, e.g. birdsong, the sound of a stream, etc. □ **music box** US = musical box. **music centre** equipment combining radio, record-player, tape recorder, etc. **music drama** Wagnerian-type opera without formal arias etc. and governed by dramatic considerations. **music-hall** see separate entry. **music of the spheres** see SPHERE. **music-paper** paper printed with staves for writing music. **music stand** a rest or frame on which sheet music or a score is supported. **music stool** a stool for a pianist, usu. with adjustable height. **music theatre** in late 20th-c. music, the combination of elements from music and drama in new forms distinct from traditional opera, esp. as designed for small groups of performers. **music to one's ears** something seeming very pleasant to hear. [ME f. OF *musique* f. L *musica* f. Gk *mousikē* (*tekhnē* art) of the Muses (*mousa* Muse: see MUSE[1])]

musical /ˈmjuːzɪk(ə)l/ *adj.* & *n.* —*adj.* **1** of or relating to music. **2** (of sounds, a voice, etc.) melodious, harmonious. **3** fond of or skilled in music (*the musical one of the family*). **4** set to or accompanied by music. —*n.* a musical film or comedy. (See below and MUSICAL COMEDY.) □ **musical box** *Brit.* a mechanical instrument playing a tune by causing a toothed cylinder to strike a comblike metal plate within a box. **musical bumps** a game similar to musical chairs, with players sitting on the floor and the one left standing eliminated. **musical chairs 1** a party game in which the players compete in successive rounds for a decreasing number of chairs. **2** a series of changes or political manoeuvring etc. after the manner of the game. **musical comedy** see separate entry. **musical film** a film in which music is an important feature. **musical glasses** an instrument in which notes are produced by rubbing graduated glass bowls or tubes. **musical saw** a bent saw played with a violin bow. □□ **musicality** /-ˈkælɪtɪ/ *n.* **musicalize** *v.tr.* (also **-ise**). **musically** *adv.* **musicalness** *n.* [ME f. OF f. med.L *musicalis* f. L *musica*: see MUSIC]
The musical as a genre includes both stage and film productions. It developed from musical comedy, having a musical score, often elaborate choreography, and a stronger plot or more serious theme than its predecessors. Notable examples include Lerner and Loewe's *My Fair Lady* (1956), Bernstein's *West Side Story* (1957), Bart's *Oliver!* (1960), and Lloyd Webber's *The Phantom of the Opera* (1986); religious and political topics were introduced in his *Jesus Christ Superstar* (1970) and *Evita* (1978). A further innovation has been the use of a theme rather than a plot, with unconventional music and staging, as in Sondheim's *Company* (1970) and Hamlisch and Kleban's *A Chorus Line* (1975).

musical comedy *n.* an entertainment in which a story is told by a combination of spoken dialogue and songs. Originally the plot was very slight, but with the importation of more serious themes, the word 'comedy' was dropped and the genre became known simply as the 'musical'. Musical comedy dates from the end of the 19th c. and reached its peak in the US in the work of such composers as Jerome Kern, Irving Berlin, Cole Porter, George Gershwin, and Richard Rodgers.

musicale /ˌmjuːzɪˈkɑːl/ *n. US* a musical party. [F fem. adj. (as MUSICAL)]

music-hall *n.* a type of entertainment, or a place for performing this, which flourished in Britain during the second half of the 19th and early 20th c. Originally a simple stage in a hall furnished with tables, chairs, and a bar, the whole presided over by a chairman, it developed into an elaborate two- or three-tier auditorium with a fully equipped stage behind a proscenium arch. The 'turns' on a normal evening's bill—sometimes as many as 25—ranged from acrobats and jugglers to comedians and singers. In its heyday music-hall was the entertainment most loved by working people, but it was killed by the advent of the cinema, radio, and above all television.

musician /mjuːˈzɪʃ(ə)n/ *n.* a person who plays a musical instrument, esp. professionally, or is otherwise musically gifted. □□ **musicianly** *adj.* **musicianship** *n.* [ME f. OF *musicien* f. *musique* (as MUSIC, -ICIAN)]

musicology /ˌmjuːzɪˈkɒlədʒɪ/ *n.* the study of music other than that directed to proficiency in performance or composition. □□ **musicologist** *n.* **musicological** /-kəˈlɒdʒɪk(ə)l/ *adj.* [F *musicologie* or MUSIC + -LOGY]

musique concrète /mjuːˌziːk kɔ̃ˈkret/ *n.* = concrete music. [F]

musk /mʌsk/ *n.* **1** a strong-smelling reddish-brown substance produced by a gland in the male musk deer and used as an ingredient in perfumes. **2** the plant, *Mimulus moschatus*, with pale-green ovate leaves and yellow flowers (orig. with a smell of musk which is no longer perceptible in modern varieties). □ **musk deer** any small Asian deer of the genus *Moschus*, having no antlers and in the male having long protruding canine teeth.

musk duck the Australian duck *Biziura lobata*, having a musky smell. **musk melon** the common yellow or green melon, *Cucumis melo*, usu. with a raised network of markings on the skin. **musk ox** a large goat-antelope, *Ovibos moschatus*, native to N. America, with a thick shaggy coat and small curved horns. **musk-rose** a rambling rose, *Rosa moschata*, with large white flowers smelling of musk. **musk thistle** a nodding thistle, *Carduus nutans*, whose flowers have a musky fragrance. **musk-tree** (or **-wood**) an Australian tree, *Olearia argophylla*, with a musky smell. □□ **musky** *adj.* (**muskier**, **muskiest**). **muskiness** *n.* [ME f. LL *muscus* f. Pers. *mušk*, perh. f. Skr. *muṣka* scrotum (from the shape of the musk deer's gland)]

muskeg /ˈmʌskeg/ *n.* a level swamp or bog in Canada. [Cree]

muskellunge /ˈmʌskəˌlʌndʒ/ *n.* = MASKINONGE. [Algonquian]

musket /ˈmʌskɪt/ *n. hist.* an infantryman's (esp. smooth-bored) light gun, often supported on the shoulder. □ **musket-shot 1** a shot fired from a musket. **2** the range of this shot. [F *mousquet* f. It. *moschetto* crossbow bolt f. *mosca* fly]

musketeer /ˌmʌskɪˈtɪə(r)/ *n. hist.* a soldier armed with a musket.

musketry /ˈmʌskɪtrɪ/ *n.* **1** muskets, or soldiers armed with muskets, referred to collectively. **2** the knowledge of handling muskets.

Muskogean /ˌmʌskəˈgɪən, -ˈkəʊgɪən/ *n.* & *adj.* —*n.* a family of American Indian languages in south-eastern North America. —*adj.* of this family. [*Muskogee* its speakers, perh. of Algonquian origin]

muskrat /ˈmʌskræt/ *n.* **1** a large aquatic rodent, *Ondatra zibethica*, native to N. America, having a musky smell. Also called MUSQUASH. **2** the fur of this.

Muslim /ˈmʊzlɪm, ˈmʌ-/ *n.* & *adj.* (also **Moslem** /ˈmɒzləm/) —*n.* a follower of the Islamic religion. —*adj.* of or relating to Muslims or their religion. [Arab. *muslim*, part. of *aslama*: see ISLAM]

muslin /ˈmʌzlɪn/ *n.* **1** a fine delicately woven cotton fabric. **2** *US* a cotton cloth in plain weave. □□ **muslined** *adj.* [F *mousseline* f. It. *mussolina* f. *Mussolo* MOSUL, where it was made]

musmon /ˈmʌzmən/ *n. Zool.* = MOUFFLON. [L *musimo* f. Gk *mousmōn*]

muso /ˈmjuːzəʊ/ *n.* (*pl.* **-os**) *sl.* a musician, esp. a professional. [abbr.]

musquash /ˈmʌskwɒʃ/ *n.* = MUSKRAT. [Algonquian]

muss /mʌs/ *v.* & *n. US colloq.* —*v.tr.* (often foll. by *up*) disarrange; throw into disorder. —*n.* a state of confusion; untidiness, mess. □□ **mussy** *adj.* (app. var. of MESS)

mussel /ˈmʌs(ə)l/ *n.* **1** any bivalve mollusc of the genus *Mytilus*, living in sea water and often used for food. **2** any similar freshwater mollusc of the genus *Margaritifer* or *Anodonta*, forming pearls. [ME f. OE *mus(c)le* & MLG *mussel*, ult. rel. to L *musculus* (as MUSCLE)]

Mussolini /ˌmʊsəˈliːnɪ/, Benito (1883–1945), Italian dictator, founder and leader of the Italian Fascist Party. He began his political life as a Marxist, calling Marx his 'father and teacher' and 'the magnificent philosopher of working-class violence', and though he broke with Marxism because it was unpatriotic his ideology contained socialist elements right to the end. Mussolini gained power in 1922 and quickly organized his government along dictatorial lines. Although he achieved a certain degree of success with domestic reforms, his aggressive foreign policy led first to the conquest of Ethiopia in 1935–6 and then Italy's entry into the Second World War on Germany's side in 1940. He was captured and executed by Italian Communist partisans in April 1945, a few weeks before the end of the war.

Mussorgsky /məˈsɔːgskɪ/, Modest (1839–81), Russian composer. He trained for the army but resigned his commission to study music in St Petersburg, where he later became a member of the group of composers known as 'The Five', or 'The Mighty Handful'. Most of his best-known works are vocal, his interest in speech rhythms combining with a natural lyricism in his songs. After his death many of his works were completed and altered by Rimsky-Korsakov and others, but recently there has been a tendency to return to Mussorgsky's original scoring, particularly in his monumental opera *Boris Godunov* (1868–74).

Mussulman /ˈmʌsəlmən/ n. & adj. archaic —n. (pl. **-mans** or **-men**) a Muslim. —adj. of or concerning Muslims. [Pers. musulmān orig. adj. f. muslim (as MUSLIM)]

must[1] /mʌst/ v. & n. —v.aux. (3rd sing. present **must**; past **had to** or in indirect speech **must**) (foll. by infin., or absol.) **1 a** be obliged to (you must go to school; must we leave now?; said he must go; I must away). **b** the negative (i.e. lack of obligation) is expressed by not have to or need not; must not denotes positive forbidding, as in you must not smoke. **b** in ironic questions (must you slam the door?). **2** be certain to (we must win in the end; you must be her sister; he must be mad; they must have left by now; seemed as if the roof must blow off). **3** ought to (we must see what can be done; it must be said that). **4** expressing insistence (I must ask you to leave). **5** (foll. by not + infin.) **a** not be permitted to, be forbidden to (you must not smoke). **b** ought not; need not (you mustn't think he's angry; you must not worry). **c** expressing insistence that something should not be done (they must not be told). **6** (as past or historic present) expressing the perversity of destiny (what must I do but break my leg). —n. colloq. a thing that cannot or should not be overlooked or missed (if you go to London St Paul's is a must). □ **I must say** often iron. I cannot refrain from saying (I must say he made a good attempt; a fine way to behave, I must say). **must needs** see NEEDS. [OE mōste past of mōt may]

must[2] /mʌst/ n. grape-juice before fermentation is complete. [OE f. L mustum neut. of mustus new]

must[3] /mʌst/ n. mustiness, mould. [back-form. f. MUSTY]

must[4] /mʌst/ adj. & n. (also **musth**) —adj. (of a male elephant or camel) in a state of frenzy. —n. this state. [Urdu f. Pers. mast intoxicated]

mustache US var. of MOUSTACHE.

mustachio /məˈstɑːʃɪəʊ/ n. (pl. **-os**) (often in pl.) archaic a moustache. □□ **mustachioed** adj. [Sp. mostacho & It. mostaccio (as MOUSTACHE)]

mustang /ˈmʌstæŋ/ n. a small wild horse native to Mexico and California. □ **mustang grape** a grape from the wild vine Vitis candicans, of the southern US, used for making wine. [Sp. mestengo f. mesta company of graziers, & Sp. mostrenco]

mustard /ˈmʌstəd/ n. **1 a** any of various plants of the genus Brassica with slender pods and yellow flowers, esp. B. nigra. **b** any of various plants of the genus Sinapis, esp. S. alba, eaten at the seedling stage, often with cress. **2** the seeds of these which are crushed, made into a paste, and used as a spicy condiment. **3** the brownish-yellow colour of this condiment. **4** sl. a thing which adds piquancy or zest. □ **mustard gas** a colourless oily liquid, whose vapour is a powerful irritant and vesicant. **mustard plaster** a poultice made with mustard. **mustard seed 1** the seed of the mustard plant. **2** a small thing capable of great development (Matt. 13: 31). [ME f. OF mo(u)starde: orig. the condiment as prepared with MUST[2]]

muster /ˈmʌstə(r)/ v. & n. —v. **1** tr. collect (orig. soldiers) for inspection, to check numbers, etc. **2** tr. & intr. collect, gather together. **3** tr. Austral. round up (livestock). —n. **1** the assembly of persons for inspection. **2** an assembly, a collection. **3** Austral. a rounding up of livestock. **4** Austral. sl. attendance (at a meeting, etc.) (had a good muster). □ **muster-book** a book for registering military personnel. **muster in** US enrol (recruits). **muster out** US discharge (soldiers etc.). **muster-roll** an official list of officers and men in a regiment or ship's company. **muster up** collect or summon (courage, strength, etc.). **pass muster** be accepted as adequate. □□ **musterer** n. (in sense 3 of n. & v.). [ME f. OF mo(u)stre ult. f. L monstrare show]

musth var. of MUST[4].

Mustique /muˈstiːk/ a small island in the northern Grenadines, in the Caribbean Sea to the south of St Vincent.

mustn't /ˈmʌs(ə)nt/ contr. must not.

musty /ˈmʌstɪ/ adj. (**mustier, mustiest**) **1** mouldy. **2** of a mouldy or stale smell or taste. **3** stale, antiquated (musty old books). □□ **mustily** adv. **mustiness** n. [perh. alt. f. moisty (MOIST) by assoc. with MUST[2]]

Mut /mʊt/ Egyptian Mythol. a goddess who was the wife of Amun and mother of Khonsu. She is represented as a woman wearing a kind of cap, in the form of a vulture, beneath the double crown; her name means 'the mother', and the vulture hieroglyph which stands for it also means 'mother'.

mutable /ˈmjuːtəb(ə)l/ adj. literary **1** liable to change. **2** fickle. □□ **mutability** /-ˈbɪlɪtɪ/ n. [L mutabilis f. mutare change]

mutagen /ˈmjuːtədʒ(ə)n/ n. an agent promoting mutation, e.g. radiation. □□ **mutagenic** /-ˈdʒenɪk/ adj. **mutagenesis** /-ˈdʒenɪsɪs/ n. [MUTATION + -GEN]

mutant /ˈmjuːt(ə)nt/ adj. & n. —adj. resulting from mutation. —n. a mutant form. [L mutant- part. f. mutare change]

mutate /mjuːˈteɪt/ v.intr. & tr. undergo or cause to undergo mutation. [back-form. f. MUTATION]

mutation /mjuːˈteɪʃ(ə)n/ n. **1** the process or an instance of change or alteration. **2** a genetic change which, when transmitted to offspring, gives rise to heritable variations. **3** a mutant. **4 a** an umlaut. **b** (in a Celtic language) a change of a consonant etc. determined by a preceding word. □□ **mutational** adj. **mutationally** adv. [ME f. L mutatio f. mutare change]

mutatis mutandis /muːˌtɑːtɪs muːˈtændɪs, mjuː-, -iːs/ adv. (in comparing cases) making the necessary alterations. [L]

mutch /mʌtʃ/ n. dial. a woman's or child's linen cap. [ME f. MDu. mutse MHG mütze f. med.L almucia AMICE]

mute /mjuːt/ adj., n., & v. —adj. **1** silent, refraining from or temporarily bereft of speech. **2** not emitting articulate sound. **3** (of a person or animal) dumb. **4** not expressed in speech (mute protest). **5 a** (of a letter) not pronounced. **b** (of a consonant) plosive. **6** (of hounds) not giving tongue. —n. **1** a dumb person (a deaf mute). **2** Mus. **a** a clamp for damping the resonance of the strings of a violin etc. **b** a pad or cone for damping the sound of a wind instrument. **3** an unsounded consonant. **4** an actor whose part is in a dumb show. **5** a dumb servant in oriental countries. **6** a hired mourner. —v.tr. **1** deaden, muffle, or soften the sound of (a thing, esp. a musical instrument). **2 a** tone down, make less intense. **b** (as **muted** adj.) (of colours etc.) subdued (a muted green). □ **mute button** a device on a telephone etc. to temporarily prevent the caller from hearing what is being said at the receiver's end. **mute swan** the common white swan. □□ **mutely** adv. **muteness** n. [ME f. OF muet, dimin. of mu f. L mutus, assim. to L]

mutilate /ˈmjuːtɪˌleɪt/ v.tr. **1 a** deprive (a person or animal) of a limb or organ. **b** destroy the use of (a limb or organ). **2** render (a book etc.) imperfect by excision or some act of destruction. □□ **mutilation** /-ˈleɪʃ(ə)n/ n. **mutilative** /-lətɪv/ adj. **mutilator** n. [L mutilare f. mutilus maimed]

mutineer /ˌmjuːtɪˈnɪə(r)/ n. a person who mutinies. [F mutinier f. mutin rebellious f. muete movement ult. f. L movēre move]

mutinous /ˈmjuːtɪnəs/ adj. rebellious; tending to mutiny. □□ **mutinously** adv. [obs. mutine rebellion f. F mutin: see MUTINEER]

mutiny /ˈmjuːtɪnɪ/ n. & v. —n. (pl. **-ies**) an open revolt against constituted authority, esp. by soldiers or sailors against their officers. —v.intr. (**-ies, -ied**) (often foll. by against) revolt; engage in mutiny. [obs. mutine (as MUTINOUS)]

mutism /ˈmjuːtɪz(ə)m/ n. muteness; silence; dumbness. [F mutisme f. L (as MUTE)]

muton /ˈmjuːtɒn/ n. Biol. the smallest element of genetic material capable of giving rise to a mutant individual.

mutt /mʌt/ n. **1** sl. an ignorant, stupid, or blundering person. **2** derog. a dog. [abbr. of mutton-head]

mutter /ˈmʌtə(r)/ v. & n. —v. **1** intr. speak low in a barely audible manner. **2** intr. (often foll. by against, at) murmur or grumble about. **3** tr. utter (words etc.) in a low tone. **4** tr. say in secret. —n. **1** muttered words or sounds. **2** muttering. □□ **mutterer** n. **mutteringly** adv. [ME, rel. to MUTE]

mutton /ˈmʌt(ə)n/ n. **1** the flesh of sheep used for food. **2** joc. a sheep. □ **mutton-bird** Austral. **1** any bird of the genus Puffinus, esp. the short-tailed shearwater, P. tenuirostris. **2** any of various petrels. **mutton chop 1** a piece of mutton, usu. the rib and half vertebra to which it is attached. **2** (in full **mutton chop whisker**) a side whisker shaped like this. **mutton dressed as lamb** colloq. a usu. middle-aged or elderly woman dressed or made up to appear younger. **mutton-head** colloq. a dull, stupid, person. **mutton-headed** *colloq.* dull, stupid. □□ **muttony** *adj.* [ME f. OF *moton* f. med.L *multo -onis* prob. f. Gaulish]

mutual /ˈmjuːtʃʊəl, -tjʊəl/ *adj.* **1** (of feelings, actions, etc.) experienced or done by each of two or more parties with reference to the other or others (*mutual affection*). **2** *colloq. disp.* common to two or more persons (*a mutual friend; a mutual interest*). **3** standing in (a specified) relation to each other (*mutual well-wishers; mutual beneficiaries*). □ **mutual fund** US a unit trust. **mutual inductance** the property of an electric circuit that causes an electromotive force to be generated in it by change in the current flowing through a magnetically linked circuit. **mutual induction** the production of an electromotive force between adjacent circuits that are magnetically linked. **mutual insurance** insurance in which some or all of the profits are divided among the policyholders. □□ **mutuality** /-ˈælɪtɪ/ *n.* **mutually** *adv.* [ME f. OF *mutuel* f. L *mutuus* mutual, borrowed, rel. to *mutare* change]

mutualism /ˈmjuːtʃʊəˌlɪz(ə)m, ˈmjuːtjʊ-/ *n.* **1** the doctrine that mutual dependence is necessary to social well-being. **2** mutually beneficial symbiosis. □□ **mutualist** *n.* & *adj.* **mutualistic** /-ˈlɪstɪk/ *adj.* **mutualistically** /-ˈlɪstɪkəlɪ/ *adv.*

mutuel /ˈmjuːtjʊəl/ *n.* esp. *US* a totalizator; a pari-mutuel. [abbr. of PARI-MUTUEL]

mutule /ˈmjuːtjuːl/ *n. Archit.* a block derived from the ends of wooden beams projecting under a Doric cornice. [F f. L *mutulus*]

muu-muu /ˈmuːmuː/ *n.* a woman's loose brightly-coloured dress. [Hawaiian]

Muzak /ˈmjuːzæk/ *n.* **1** *propr.* a system of music transmission for playing in public places. **2** (**muzak**) recorded light background music. [alt. f. MUSIC]

muzhik /ˈmuːʒɪk/ *n.* (also **moujik**) *hist.* a Russian peasant. [Russ. *muzhik*]

Muzzafarabad /mʊˌzəfərəˈbɑːd/ the capital of Azad Kashmir (see KASHMIR).

muzzle /ˈmʌz(ə)l/ *n.* & *v.* —*n.* **1** the projecting part of an animal's face, including the nose and mouth. **2** a guard, usu. made of straps or wire, fitted over an animal's nose and mouth to stop it biting or feeding. **3** the open end of a firearm. —*v.tr.* **1** put a muzzle on (an animal etc.). **2** impose silence upon. **3** *Naut.* take in (a sail). □ **muzzle-loader** a gun that is loaded through the muzzle. **muzzle velocity** the velocity with which a projectile leaves the muzzle of a gun. □□ **muzzler** *n.* [ME f. OF *musel* ult. f. med.L *musum*: cf. MUSE²]

muzzy /ˈmʌzɪ/ *adj.* (**muzzier, muzziest**) **1 a** mentally hazy; dull, spiritless. **b** stupid from drinking alcohol. **2** blurred, indistinct. □□ **muzzily** *adv.* **muzziness** *n.* [18th c.: orig. unkn.]

MV *abbr.* **1** motor vessel. **2** muzzle velocity. **3** megavolt(s).

MVD /ˌemviːˈdiː/ *n.* the secret police of the USSR which, together with the MGB (Ministry of State Security), replaced the NKVD in 1946. On Stalin's death (1953) the MVD and MGB were merged under his supporter Lavrenti Beria (see entry) and remained in charge of internal security, but its responsibilities were gradually downgraded in favour of the KGB. [Russ. abbr., = Ministry of Internal Affairs]

MVO *abbr.* (in the UK) Member of the Royal Victorian Order.

MW *abbr.* **1** megawatt(s). **2** medium wave.

mW *abbr.* milliwatt(s).

Mx. *abbr.* **1** maxwell(s). **2** Middlesex (a former county in England).

MY *abbr.* motor yacht.

my /maɪ/ *poss.pron.* (*attrib.*) **1** of or belonging to me or myself (*my house; my own business*). **2** as a form of address in affectionate, sympathetic, jocular, or patronizing contexts (*my dear boy*). **3** in various expressions of surprise (*my God!; oh my!*). **4** *Brit. colloq.* indicating the speaker's husband, wife, child, etc. (*my Johnny's ill again*). □ **my Lady** (or **Lord**) the form of address to certain titled persons. [ME *mī*, reduced f. *mīn* MINE¹]

my- *comb. form* var. of MYO-.

myalgia /maɪˈældʒə/ *n.* a pain in a muscle or group of muscles. □□ **myalgic** *adj.* [mod.L f. Gk *mus* muscle]

myalism /ˈmaɪəˌlɪz(ə)m/ *n.* a kind of sorcery akin to obeah, practised esp. in the W. Indies. [*myal*, prob. of W.Afr. orig.]

myall /ˈmaɪɔːl/ *n.* **1 a** any tree of the genus *Acacia*, esp. *A. pendula*, native to Australia. **b** the hard scented wood of this, used for fences and tobacco-pipes. **2** an Aboriginal living in a traditional way. [Aboriginal *maiäl*]

Myanmar /ˌmiːænˈmɑː(r)/ the official name (since 1989) of Burma.

myasthenia /ˌmaɪəsˈθiːnɪə/ *n.* a condition causing abnormal weakness of certain muscles. [mod.L f. Gk *mus* muscle: cf. ASTHENIA]

mycelium /maɪˈsiːlɪəm/ *n.* (*pl.* **mycelia** /-lɪə/) the vegetative part of a fungus, consisting of microscopic threadlike hyphae. □□ **mycelial** *adj.* [mod.L f. Gk *mukēs* mushroom, after EPITHELIUM]

Mycenae /maɪˈsiːniː/ a city of ancient Greece, situated in the NE Peloponnese a few kilometres from the sea, dominating various land and sea routes, famous in Greek legend as the home of Agamemnon. Its greatest era was the period from *c.*1400 to 1200 BC, during which were constructed the massive walls of Cyclopaean masonry (including the 'Lion Gate', *c.*1250 BC) and the palace on the summit of the hill.

Mycenaean /ˌmaɪsɪˈniːən/ *adj.* & *n.* —*adj. Archaeol.* of or relating to the late Bronze Age civilization in Greece (*c.*1580–1100 BC), depicted in the Homeric poems and represented by finds at Mycenae and other ancient cities of the Peloponnese. (See below.) —*n.* an inhabitant of Mycenae or the Mycenaean world. [L *Mycenaeus*]

The Mycenaeans inherited control of the Aegean after the collapse of the Minoan civilization *c.*1400 BC. Their cities, such as those of Mycenae, Tiryns, and Pylos, were well populated and prosperous, with fortified citadels enclosing impressive palaces. Artefacts of ivory, gold, and inlaid bronze, of advanced technique and exquisite workmanship, are found in tombs that must have been those of royalty. The language they used was a form of Greek, and transactions were recorded in the script known as Linear B (see entry). Trade with other Mediterranean countries flourished, and Mycenaean products are found from southern Italy to Palestine and Syria. The end of Mycenaean power coincided with a period of general upheaval and migrations at the end of the Bronze Age in the Mediterranean.

-mycin /ˈmaɪsɪn/ *comb. form* used to form the names of antibiotic compounds derived from fungi. [Gk *mukēs* fungus + -IN]

mycology /maɪˈkɒlədʒɪ/ *n.* **1** the study of fungi. **2** the fungi of a particular region. □□ **mycological** /-kəˈlɒdʒɪk(ə)l/ *adj.* **mycologically** /-kəˈlɒdʒɪkəlɪ/ *adv.* **mycologist** *n.* [Gk *mukēs* mushroom + -LOGY]

mycorrhiza /ˌmaɪkəˈraɪzə/ *n.* (*pl.* **mycorrhizae** /-ziː/) a symbiotic association of a fungus and the roots of a plant. □□ **mycorrhizal** *adj.* [mod.L f. Gk *mukēs* mushroom + *rhiza* root]

mycosis /maɪˈkəʊsɪs/ *n.* any disease caused by a fungus, e.g. ringworm. □□ **mycotic** /-ˈkɒtɪk/ *adj.* [Gk *mukēs* mushroom + -OSIS]

mycotoxin /ˌmaɪkəˈtɒksɪn/ *n.* any toxic substance produced by a fungus.

mycotrophy /maɪˈkɒtrəfɪ/ *n.* the condition of a plant which has mycorrhizae and is perhaps helped to assimilate nutrients as a result. □□ **mycotrophic** *adj.* [G *Mykotrophie* f. Gk *mukēs* mushroom + *trophē* nourishment]

mydriasis /mɪˈdraɪəsɪs/ *n.* excessive dilation of the pupil of the eye. [L f. Gk *mudriasis*]

myelin /ˈmaɪɪlɪn/ *n.* a white substance which forms a sheath around certain nerve-fibres. □□ **myelination** /-ˈneɪʃ(ə)n/ *n.* [Gk *muelos* marrow + -IN]

myelitis /maɪɪˈlaɪtɪs/ *n.* inflammation of the spinal cord. [mod.L f. Gk *muelos* marrow]

myeloid /ˈmaɪɪlɔɪd/ *adj.* of or relating to bone marrow or the spinal cord. [Gk *muelos* marrow]

myeloma /ˌmaɪɪˈləʊmə/ *n.* (*pl.* **myelomas** or **myelomata** /-mətə/) a malignant tumour of the bone marrow. [mod.L, as MYELITIS + -OMA]

Mykonos /'mɪkə,nɒs/ (Greek **Míkonos** /'miːkə,nɒs/) a Greek island of the Cyclades in the Aegean Sea.

mylodon /'maɪləd(ə)n/ n. an extinct gigantic ground sloth of the genus *Mylodon*, with cylindrical teeth and found in deposits formed during the ice age of the Pleistocene epoch in South America. [mod.L f. Gk *mulē* mill, molar + *odous odontos* tooth]

Mymenshingh /ˌmaɪmən'sɪŋ/ a port on the Brahmaputra River in central Bangladesh; pop. (1981) 190,900.

myna /'maɪnə/ n. (also **mynah, mina**) any of various SE Asian starlings, esp. *Gracula religiosa* able to mimic the human voice. [Hindi *mainā*]

myo- /'maɪəʊ/ *comb. form* (also **my-** before a vowel) muscle. [Gk *mus muos* muscle]

myocardium /ˌmaɪəʊ'kaːdɪəm/ n. (pl. **myocardia** /-dɪə/) the muscular tissue of the heart. □□ **myocardiac** adj. **myocardial** adj. [MYO- + Gk *kardia* heart]

myofibril /ˌmaɪəʊ'faɪbrɪl/ n. any of the elongated contractile threads found in striated muscle cells.

myogenic /ˌmaɪə'dʒenɪk/ adj. originating in muscle tissue.

myoglobin /ˌmaɪəʊ'gləʊbɪn/ n. an oxygen-carrying protein containing iron and found in muscle cells.

myology /maɪ'ɒlədʒɪ/ n. the study of the structure and function of muscles.

myope /'maɪəʊp/ n. a short-sighted person. [F f. LL *myops* f. Gk *muōps* f. *muō* shut + *ōps* eye]

myopia /maɪ'əʊpɪə/ n. **1** short-sightedness. **2** lack of imagination or intellectual insight. □□ **myopic** /-'ɒpɪk/ adj. **myopically** /-'ɒpɪkəlɪ/ adv. [mod.L (as MYOPE)]

myosis var. of MIOSIS.

myosotis /ˌmaɪə'səʊtɪs/ n. (also **myosote** /'maɪə,səʊt/) any plant of the genus *Myosotis* with blue, pink, or white flowers, esp. a forget-me-not. [L f. Gk *muosōtis* f. *mus muos* mouse + *ous ōtos* ear]

myotonia /ˌmaɪə'təʊnɪə/ n. the inability to relax voluntary muscle after vigorous effort. □□ **myotonic** /-'tɒnɪk/ adj. [MYO- + Gk *tonos* tone]

myriad /'mɪrɪəd/ n. & adj. *literary* —n. **1** an indefinitely great number. **2** ten thousand. —adj. of an indefinitely great number. [LL *mirias miriad-* f. Gk *murias -ados* f. *murioi* 10,000]

myriapod /'mɪrɪə,pɒd/ n. & adj. —n. any land-living arthropod of the group Myriapoda, with numerous leg-bearing segments, e.g. centipedes and millipedes. —adj. of or relating to this group. [mod.L *Myriapoda* (as MYRIAD, Gk *pous podos* foot)]

myrmidon /'mɜːmɪd(ə)n/ n. **1** a hired ruffian. **2** a base servant. [L *Myrmidones* (pl.) f. Gk *Murmidones*, warlike Thessalian people who went with Achilles to Troy]

myrobalan /maɪ'rɒbələn/ n. **1** (in full **myrobalan plum**) = cherry plum. **2** (in full **myrobalan nut**) the fruit of an Asian tree, *Terminalia chebula*, used in medicines, for tanning leather, and to produce inks and dyes. [F *myrobolan* or L *myrobalanum* f. Gk *murobalanos* f. *muron* unguent + *balanos* acorn]

Myron /'maɪrən/ (mid-5th c. BC) Greek sculptor. Only two certain copies of his work survive, the most important being the 'Discobolus' (discus-thrower) demonstrating his interest in symmetry and the drama of a physical endeavour, a preoccupation of this phase of early classical sculpture.

myrrh[1] /mɜː(r)/ n. a gum resin from several trees of the genus *Commiphora* used, esp. in the Near East, in perfumery, medicine, incense, etc. □□ **myrrhic** adj. **myrrhy** adj. [OE *myrra, myrre* f. L *myrr(h)a* f. Gk *murra*, of Semitic orig.]

myrrh[2] /mɜː(r)/ n. = sweet cicely. [L *myrris* f. Gk *murris*]

myrtaceous /mɜː'teɪʃ(ə)s/ adj. of or relating to the plant family Myrtaceae, including myrtles.

myrtle /'mɜːt(ə)l/ n. **1** an evergreen shrub of the genus *Myrtus* with aromatic foliage and white flowers, esp. *M. communis*, bearing purple-black ovoid berries. **2** US = PERIWINKLE[1]. [ME f. med.L *myrtilla, -us* dimin. of L *myrta, myrtus* f. Gk *murtos*]

myself /maɪ'self/ pron. **1** emphat. form of I[2] or ME[1] (*I saw it myself*; *I like to do it myself*). **2** refl. form of ME[1] (*I was angry with myself*; *able to dress myself*; *as bad as myself*). **3** in my normal state of body and mind (*I'm not myself today*). **4** poet. = I[2]. □ **by myself** see *by*

oneself. **I myself** I for my part (*I myself am doubtful*). [ME[1] + SELF: *my-* partly after *herself* with *her* regarded as poss. pron.]

Mysia /'mɪsɪə/ the ancient name for the region of NW Asia Minor south of the Hellespont and the Sea of Marmara. □□ **Mysian** adj. & n.

Mysore /maɪ'sɔː(r)/ see KARNATAKA.

mysterious /mɪ'stɪərɪəs/ adj. **1** full of or wrapped in mystery. **2** (of a person) delighting in mystery. □□ **mysteriously** adv. **mysteriousness** n. [F *mystérieux* f. *mystère* f. OF (as MYSTERY[1])]

mystery[1] /'mɪstərɪ/ n. (pl. **-ies**) **1** a secret, hidden, or inexplicable matter (*the reason remains a mystery*). **2** secrecy or obscurity (*wrapped in mystery*). **3** (attrib.) secret, undisclosed (*mystery guest*). **4** the practice of making a secret of (esp. unimportant) things (*engaged in mystery and intrigue*). **5** (in full **mystery story**) a fictional work dealing with a puzzling event, esp. a crime (*a well-known mystery writer*). **6 a** a religious truth divinely revealed, esp. one beyond human reason. **b** *RC Ch.* a decade of the rosary. **7** (in *pl.*) **a** the secret religious rites of the ancient Greeks, Romans, etc. (See below.) **b** *archaic* the Eucharist. □ **make a mystery of** treat as an impressive secret. **mystery play** see separate entry. **mystery tour** (or **trip**) a pleasure excursion to an unspecified destination. [ME f. OF *mistere* or L *mysterium* f. Gk *mustērion*, rel. to MYSTIC]

The 'mysteries' or 'mystery religions' were secret forms of worship, in contradistinction to the very public nature of most Greek and Roman religious observances, and were available only to people who had been specially initiated. They involved ritual purification, secret rites, and probably an enactment of the myth of Demeter and Persephone; initiates were promised a happy existence in another world after death. The Eleusinian mysteries, celebrated at Eleusis, 22 km (14 miles) north-west of Athens, were the most famous, and attracted visitors from the whole of Greece.

mystery[2] /'mɪstərɪ/ n. (pl. **-ies**) *archaic* a handicraft or trade, esp. as referred to in indentures etc. (*art and mystery*). [ME f. med.L *misterium* contr. of *ministerium* MINISTRY, assoc. with MYSTERY[1]]

mystery play n. any of the vernacular religious dramas of the Middle Ages. Some writers have drawn a distinction between 'mystery plays' (dealing with Gospel events only) and 'miracle plays' (based on stories of the saints), but this is not generally observed in English where originally 'miracle' was used for both kinds of play, though a parallel distinction between *mystère* and *miracle* exists in French. A further confusion arises because the plays were often acted by the trade guilds (these were also religious fraternities) which were called 'mysteries' from the old use of this term to mean 'occupation'. Early religious dramas were performed in churches, often on feast days (which were also public holidays), especially Corpus Christi, Christmas, Easter, and Whitsun. They became increasingly secular and were moved outdoors, performed on temporary stages or on wagons which were trundled along an established route, stopping at fixed points where the audience awaited them. Individual dramas merged into a cycle of plays, and the four great English collections are known by the names of the towns where they are said to have been performed—York, Chester, Coventry, and Wakefield (also called Towneley, from the owners of the manuscript).

mystic /'mɪstɪk/ n. & adj. —n. a person who seeks by contemplation and self-surrender to obtain unity or identity with or absorption into the Deity or the ultimate reality, or who believes in the spiritual apprehension of truths that are beyond the understanding. Mysticism is a widespread experience in Christianity and in many non-Christian religions, e.g. Buddhism, Taoism, Hinduism, and Islam. —adj. **1** mysterious and awe-inspiring. **2** spiritually allegorical or symbolic. **3** occult, esoteric. **4** of hidden meaning. □□ **mysticism** /-,sɪz(ə)m/ n. [ME f. OF *mystique* or L *mysticus* f. Gk *mustikos* f. *mustēs* initiated person f. *muō* close the eyes or lips, initiate]

mystical /'mɪstɪk(ə)l/ adj. of mystics or mysticism. □□ **mystically** adv.

mystify /'mɪstɪ,faɪ/ v.tr. (**-ies, -ied**) **1** bewilder, confuse. **2** hoax, take advantage of the credulity of. **3** wrap up in mystery. □□

mystification /-fɪˈkeɪʃ(ə)n/ n. [F mystifier (irreg. formed as MYSTIC or MYSTERY¹)]

mystique /mɪˈstiːk/ n. **1** an atmosphere of mystery and veneration attending some activity or person. **2** any skill or technique impressive or mystifying to the layman. [F f. OF (as MYSTIC)]

myth /mɪθ/ n. **1** a traditional narrative usu. involving supernatural or imaginary persons and embodying popular ideas on natural or social phenomena etc. **2** such narratives collectively. **3** a widely held but false notion. **4** a fictitious person, thing, or idea. **5** an allegory (the Platonic myth). □□ **mythic** adj. **mythical** adj. **mythically** adv. [mod.L mythus f. LL mythos f. Gk muthos]

mythi pl. of MYTHUS.

mythicize /ˈmɪθɪˌsaɪz/ v.tr. (also **-ise**) treat (a story etc.) as a myth; interpret mythically. □□ **mythicism** /-ˌsɪz(ə)m/ n. **mythicist** /-sɪst/ n.

mytho- /ˈmɪθəʊ/ comb. form myth.

mythogenesis /ˌmɪθəʊˈdʒenɪsɪs/ n. the production of myths.

mythographer /mɪˈθɒɡrəfə(r)/ n. a compiler of myths.

mythography /mɪˈθɒɡrəfɪ/ n. the representation of myths in plastic art.

mythology /mɪˈθɒlədʒɪ/ n. (pl. **-ies**) **1** a body of myths (Greek mythology). **2** the study of myths. □□ **mythologer** n. **mythologic** /-θəˈlɒdʒɪk/ adj. **mythological** /-θəˈlɒdʒɪk(ə)l/ adj. **mythologically** /-θəˈlɒdʒɪkəlɪ/ adv. **mythologist** n.

mythologize v.tr. & intr. (also **-ise**). **mythologizer** n. [ME f. F mythologie or LL mythologia f. Gk muthologia (as MYTHO-, -LOGY)]

mythomania /ˌmɪθəʊˈmeɪnɪə/ n. an abnormal tendency to exaggerate or tell lies. □□ **mythomaniac** /-ˌɪæk/ n. & adj.

mythopoeia /ˌmɪθəʊˈpiːə/ n. the making of myths. □□ **mythopoeic** adj. (also **mythopoetic** /-pəʊˈetɪk/).

mythus /ˈmɪθəs/ n. (pl. **mythi** /-θaɪ/) literary a myth. [mod.L: see MYTH]

Mytilene /ˌmɪtɪˈliːnɪ/ (Greek **Mitilíni**) the chief town of the island of Lesbos in the Aegean Sea.

myxo- /ˈmɪksəʊ/ comb. form (also **myx-** before a vowel) mucus. [Gk muxa mucus]

myxoedema /ˌmɪksəˈdiːmə/ n. (US **myxedema**) a syndrome caused by hypothyroidism, resulting in thickening of the skin, weight gain, mental dullness, loss of energy, and sensitivity to cold.

myxoma /mɪkˈsəʊmə/ n. (pl. **myxomas** or **myxomata** /-mətə/) a benign tumour of mucous or gelatinous tissue. □□ **myxomatous** /-ˈsɒmətəs/ adj. [mod.L (as MYXO-, -OMA)]

myxomatosis /ˌmɪksəməˈtəʊsɪs/ n. an infectious usu. fatal viral disease in rabbits, causing swelling of the mucous membranes.

myxomycete /ˌmɪksəʊmaɪˈsiːt/ n. any of a group of small acellular organisms inhabiting damp areas.

myxovirus /ˈmɪksəʊˌvaɪərəs/ n. any of a group of viruses including the influenza virus.

N

N¹ /en/ *n.* (also **n**) (*pl.* **Ns** or **N's**) **1** the fourteenth letter of the alphabet. **2** *Printing* en. **3** *Math.* an indefinite number. □ **to the nth** (or **nth degree**) **1** *Math.* to any required power. **2** to any extent; to the utmost.

N² *abbr.* (also **N.**) **1** North; Northern. **2** newton(s). **3** *Chess* knight. **4** New. **5** nuclear.

N³ *symb. Chem.* the element nitrogen.

n *abbr.* (also **n.**) **1** name. **2** nano-. **3** neuter. **4** noon. **5** note. **6** noun.

'n *conj.* (also **'n'**) *colloq.* and. [abbr.]

-n¹ *suffix* see -EN².

-n² *suffix* see -EN³.

Na *symb. Chem.* the element sodium.

na /nɑ/ *adv. Sc.* (in *comb.*) usu. with an auxiliary verb) = NOT (*I canna do it; they didna go*).

n/a *abbr.* **1** not applicable. **2** not available.

NAAFI /'næfɪ/ *abbr. Brit.* **1** Navy, Army, and Air Force Institutes. **2** a canteen for servicemen run by the NAAFI.

nab /næb/ *v.tr.* (**nabbed, nabbing**) *sl.* **1** arrest; catch in wrongdoing. **2** seize, grab. [17th c., also *napp*, as in KIDNAP: orig. unkn.]

Nabataean /ˌnæbə'tiːən/ *n. & adj.* —*n.* **1** a member of an ancient Arabian people. (See below.) **2** their language, a form of Aramaic strongly influenced by Arabic. —*adj.* of the Nabataeans or their language. [L *Nabataeus*, Gk *Nabataios* (*Nebatu* native name of country)]

The Nabataeans seem originally to have been a nomadic Arab tribe. They formed an independent State 312–63 BC, prospering from control of the transit trade, conveying South Arabian goods to the Mediterranean, which converged at their capital Petra (now in Jordan). Their culture reflects Babylonian, Arab, Greek, and Roman influence in its speech, religion, art, and architecture. From AD 63 they became allies and vassals of Rome, and in AD 106 Trajan transformed their kingdom into the Roman province of Arabia.

Nabeul /næ'bɜːl/ a resort city in NE Tunisia, on the Cape Bon peninsula; pop. (1984) 39,500.

nabi /'nɑːbɪ/ *n.* a member of a group of late 19th-c. French post-impressionists. Paul Sérusier, a follower of Gauguin, and Maurice Denis stressed the rejection of naturalism for a pictorial reality that dealt with ideas and mystic perceptions. Paul Ranson, K.-X. Roussel, Pierre Bonnard, Édouard Vuillard, and Félix Vallotton were all members of the group, working variously in painting, book illustration, posters, and other media. The flat areas of emphatic colour that typify their work owe a stylistic debt to Gauguin and Japanese prints. [Heb. *nābhi* prophet]

Nablus /'næbləs/ a town in the Israeli-occupied West Bank area, 66 km (41 miles) north of Jerusalem; pop. (est. 1984) 80,000. It is close to the site of the Canaanite city of Shechem, important in ancient times because of its position in the centre of an east-west mountain pass across Samaria.

nabob /'neɪbɒb/ *n.* **1** *hist.* a Muslim official or governor under the Mogul empire. **2** (formerly) a conspicuously wealthy person, esp. one returned from India with a fortune. [Port. *nababo* or Sp. *nabab*, f. Urdu (as NAWAB)]

Nabokov /nə'bəʊkɒf, 'næbəˌkɒf/, Vladimir Vladimorovich (1899–1977), Russian novelist and poet. He left Russia for Germany in 1919, studied at Trinity College, Cambridge (1919–23), lived in Berlin (1923–37), in Paris (1937–40), and in 1940 moved to the US where he became professor of poetry at Cornell University. The outstanding success of his novel *Lolita* (1955) enabled him to devote himself entirely to writing. From 1959 he lived in Montreux. He was a stylist with great narrative and descriptive skill combined with an unusual linguistic inventiveness in both Russian and English; his critical work *Lectures on English Literature* (1980) shows his admiration for Dickens, Stevenson, and Joyce.

Nacala /nə'kɑːlə/ a deep-water port on the NE coast of Mozambique, linked by rail with landlocked Malawi.

nacarat /'nækəˌræt/ *n.* a bright orange-red colour. [F, perh. f. Sp. & Port. *nacardo* (*nacar* NACRE)]

nacelle /nə'sel/ *n.* **1** the outer casing of the engine of an aircraft. **2** the car of an airship. [F, f. LL *navicella* dimin. of L *navis* ship]

nacho /'nætʃəʊ/ *n.* (*pl.* **-os**) (usu. in *pl.*) a tortilla chip, usu. topped with melted cheese and spices etc. [20th c.: orig. uncert.]

NACODS /'neɪkɒdz/ *abbr.* (in the UK) National Association of Colliery Overmen, Deputies, and Shotfirers.

nacre /'neɪkə(r)/ *n.* mother-of-pearl from any shelled mollusc. □□ **nacred** *adj.* **nacreous** /'neɪkrɪəs/ *adj.* **nacrous** /-krəs/ *adj.* [F]

Nader /'neɪdə(r)/, Ralph (1934–), American reformer, a law graduate, who initiated a campaign on behalf of public safety that gave impetus to the consumer-protection movement of the 1960s onwards. His book *Unsafe at Any Speed* (1965), an investigation into the safety of automobiles, was a controversial best-seller and, in spite of bitter opposition from the industrial giants, led to federal legislation concerning safety standards. Nader was credited with being the moving force behind legislation in a number of other fields, including radiation hazards, food packaging, and the use of cyclamates and of DDT.

nadir /'neɪdɪə(r), 'næd-/ *n.* **1** the part of the celestial sphere directly below an observer (opp. ZENITH). **2** the lowest point in one's fortunes; a time of deep despair. [ME f. OF f. Arab. *naẓīr* (*as-samt*) opposite (to the zenith)]

naevus /'niːvəs/ *n.* (*US* **nevus**) (*pl.* **naevi** /-vaɪ/) **1** a birthmark in the form of a raised red patch on the skin. **2** = MOLE². □□ **naevoid** *adj.* [L]

naff¹ /næf/ *v.intr. sl.* **1** (in *imper.*, foll. by *off*) go away. **2** (as **naffing** *adj.*) used as an intensive to express annoyance etc. [prob. euphem. for FUCK: cf. EFF]

naff² /næf/ *adj. sl.* **1** unfashionable; socially awkward. **2** worthless, rubbishy. [20th c.: orig. unkn.]

Naffy /'næfɪ/ *n. sl.* = NAAFI. [phonet. sp.]

nag¹ /næg/ *v. & n.* —*v.* (**nagged, nagging**) **1 a** *tr.* annoy or irritate (a person) with persistent fault-finding or continuous urging. **b** *intr.* (often foll. by *at*) find fault, complain, or urge, esp. persistently. **2** *intr.* (of a pain) ache dully but persistently. **3 a** *tr.* worry or preoccupy (a person, the mind, etc.) (*his mistake nagged him*). **b** *intr.* (often foll. by *at*) worry or gnaw. —*n.* a persistently nagging person. □□ **nagger** *n.* **naggingly** *adv.* [of dial., perh. Scand. or LG, orig.: cf. Norw. & Sw. *nagga* gnaw, irritate, LG (*g*)*naggen* provoke]

nag² /næg/ *n.* **1** *colloq.* a horse. **2** a small riding-horse or pony. [ME: orig. unkn.]

Naga /'nɑːgə/ *n.* **1** a member of a group of tribes living in or near the Naga Hills of Burma and in NE India. **2** their language, a member of the Tibetan language group. [as NAGA]

naga /'nɑːgə/ *n. Hinduism* a member of a race of semi-divine creatures, half-snake half-human. [Skr., = serpent]

Nagaland /'nɑːgəˌlænd/ a State in NE India; pop. (1981) 773,300; capital, Kohima.

Nagar Haveli see DADRA AND NAGAR HAVELI.

Nagasaki /ˌnægə'sɑːkɪ/ Japanese city, target of the second atomic bomb attack, on 9 Aug. 1945 (see HIROSHIMA); pop. (1987) 447,000.

Nagorno-Karabakh /nə'gɔːnəʊˌkærə'bæx/ an autonomous region of the Soviet republic of Azerbaijan in the southern foothills of the Caucasus; pop. (est. 1987) 180,000; capital, Stepanakert. The desire of the largely Armenian population to be separated from Muslim Azerbaijan and united with the Soviet republic of Armenia has given rise to ethnic conflict.

Nagoya /nə'gɔɪə/ the capital of Chubu region on Honshu Island, Japan; pop. (1987) 2,091,000.

Nagpur /'nɑːgpʊə(r)/ a city in central India, in Maharashtra State; pop. (1981) 1,298,000.

Nagy /'nɒdʒ/, Imre (1896–1958), Hungarian Communist statesman, Prime Minister 1953–5. He became popular because of his policy of liberalization, and when restored to power in 1956 appointed non-Communists to his coalition, announced Hungary's withdrawal from the Warsaw Pact, and sought a neutral status for his country. This was unacceptable to the USSR (and to some Hungarians), whose forces attacked Budapest and overcame resistance. Nagy and some of his followers were handed over to the new Hungarian regime, which executed them in secret.

Nah. abbr. Nahum (Old Testament).

Nahuatl /nɑː'wɑːt(ə)l, 'nɑː-/ n. & adj. —n. 1 a member of a group of peoples native to S. Mexico and Central America, including the Aztecs. 2 the language of these people. —adj. of or concerning the Nahuatl peoples or language. □□ **Nahuatlan** adj. [Sp. f. Nahuatl]

Nahum /'neɪhəm/ 1 a Hebrew minor prophet. 2 a book of the Old Testament containing his prophecy of the fall of Nineveh (early 7th c. BC).

naiad /'naɪæd/ n. (pl. **naiads** or **-des** /-ˌdiːz/) 1 Mythol. a water-nymph. 2 the larva of a dragonfly etc. 3 any aquatic plant of the genus Najas, with narrow leaves and small flowers. [L Naias Naïad- f. Gk Naias -ados f. naō flow]

nail /neɪl/ n. & v. —n. 1 a small usu. sharpened metal spike with a broadened flat head, driven in with a hammer to join things together or to serve as a peg, protection (cf. HOBNAIL), or decoration. 2 **a** a horny covering on the upper surface of the tip of the human finger or toe. **b** a claw or talon. **c** a hard growth on the upper mandible of some soft-billed birds. 3 hist. a measure of cloth length (equal to 2¼ inches). —v.tr. 1 fasten with a nail or nails (nailed it to the beam; nailed the planks together). 2 fix or keep (a person, attention, etc.) fixed. 3 **a** secure, catch, or get hold of (a person or thing). **b** expose or discover (a lie or a liar). □ **hard as nails** 1 callous; unfeeling. 2 in good physical condition. **nail-biting** causing severe anxiety or tension. **nail-brush** a small brush for cleaning the nails. **nail one's colours to the mast** persist; refuse to give in. **nail down** 1 bind (a person) to a promise etc. 2 define precisely. 3 fasten (a thing) with nails. **nail enamel** US = nail polish. **nail-file** a roughened metal or emery strip used for smoothing the nails. **nail-head** Archit. an ornament like the head of a nail. **nail in a person's coffin** something thought to increase the risk of death. **nail polish** a varnish applied to the nails to colour them or make them shiny. **nail-punch** (or **-set**) a tool for sinking the head of a nail below a surface. **nail-scissors** small curved scissors for trimming the nails. **nail up** 1 close (a door etc.) with nails. 2 fix (a thing) at a height with nails. **nail varnish** Brit. = nail polish. **on the nail** (esp. of payment) without delay (cash on the nail). □□ **nailed** adj. (also in comb.). **nailless** adj. [OE nægel, næglan f. Gmc]

nailer /'neɪlə(r)/ n. a nail-maker. □□ **nailery** n.

nainsook /'neɪnsʊk/ n. a fine soft cotton fabric, orig. Indian. [Hindi nainsukh f. nain eye + sukh pleasure]

Naipaul /'naɪpɔːl/, Vidiadhar Surajprasad (1932–), West Indian novelist, now living in England. His early works are comedies of manners, set in Trinidad, as is his novel A House for Mr Biswas (1961), but later his work became more overtly political and pessimistic. The Mimic Men (1967) and In a Free State (1971) explore problems of nationality and identity; Guerrillas (1975) describes political and sexual violence in the Caribbean; A Bend in the River (1979) is a horrifying portrait of emergent Africa. He has also written travel books, including An Area of Darkness (1964), a controversial and critical account of India. His brother Shiva Naipaul (1945–85) was also a novelist.

naira /'naɪrə/ n. the chief monetary unit of Nigeria. [contr. of NIGERIA]

Nairobi /naɪ'rəʊbɪ/ the capital of Kenya, situated at 1,680 m (c.5,500 ft.); pop. (1985) 1,100,000.

naïve /nɑː'iːv, naɪ'iːv/ adj. (also **naive**) 1 artless; innocent; unaffected. 2 foolishly credulous; simple. □□ **naïvely** adv. **naïveness** n. [F, fem. of naif f. L nativus NATIVE]

naïvety /nɑː'iːvtɪ, naɪ-/ n. (also **naivety**, **naïveté** /nɑː'iːvteɪ/) (pl. **-ies** or **naïvetés**) 1 the state or quality of being naïve. 2 a naïve action. [F naïveté (as NAIVE)]

Najaf /'nædʒæf/ a holy city of the Shiite Muslims, in southern Iraq; pop. (est. 1985) 242,600.

naked /'neɪkɪd/ adj. 1 without clothes; nude. 2 plain; undisguised; exposed (the naked truth; his naked soul). 3 (of a light, flame, etc.) unprotected from the wind etc.; unshaded. 4 defenceless. 5 without addition, comment, support, evidence, etc. (his naked word; naked assertion). 6 **a** (of landscape) barren; treeless. **b** (of rock) exposed; without soil etc. 7 (of a sword etc.) unsheathed. 8 (usu. foll. by of) devoid; without. 9 without leaves, hairs, scales, shell, etc. 10 (of a room, wall, etc.) without decoration, furnishings, etc.; empty, plain. □ **naked boys** (or **lady** or **ladies**) the meadow saffron, which flowers while leafless: also called autumn crocus. **the naked eye** unassisted vision, e.g. without a telescope, microscope, etc. □□ **nakedly** adv. **nakedness** n. [OE nacod f. Gmc]

naker /'neɪkə(r)/ n. hist. a kettledrum. [ME f. OF nacre nacaire f. Arab. naḳḳāra drum]

Nakhichevan /ˌnɑːxɪtʃə'vɑːn/ 1 a predominantly Muslim autonomous republic of the Soviet Union, situated on the frontiers of Turkey and Iran and forming part of the republic of Azerbaijan, from which it is separated by a narrow strip of Armenia; pop. (est. 1987) 278,000. In 1990 it was the first Soviet territory to declare unilateral independence since the 1917 revolution. 2 its capital city, an ancient settlement perhaps dating from c. 1500 BC, believed in Armenian tradition to have been founded by Noah.

Nakhon Sawan /nɑːˌkɒn sə'wɑːn/ a port at the junction of the Ping and Nan rivers in central Thailand; pop. (1980) 1,059,900.

Nakuru /næ'kuːruː/ an industrial city in western Kenya; pop. 92,850. Nearby is Lake Nakuru which is famous for its spectacular flocks of flamingos.

NALGO /'nælgəʊ/ abbr. (in the UK) National and Local Government Officers' Association.

Nam /næm/ colloq. Vietnam. [abbr.]

Namaqualand /nə'mɑːkwəˌlænd/ the homeland of the Nama people of SW Namibia and South Africa. Little Namaqualand lies immediately to the south of the Orange River in the Cape Province of South Africa, while Great Namaqualand lies to the north of the river in Namibia.

namby-pamby /ˌnæmbɪ'pæmbɪ/ adj. & n. —adj. 1 lacking vigour or drive; weak. 2 insipidly pretty or sentimental. —n. (pl. **-ies**) 1 a namby-pamby person. 2 namby-pamby talk. [fanciful formulation on name of Ambrose Philips, Engl. pastoral writer d. 1749]

name /neɪm/ n. & v. —n. 1 **a** the word by which an individual person, animal, place, or thing is known, spoken of, etc. (mentioned him by name; her name is Joanna). **b** all who go under one name; a family, clan, or people in terms of its name (the Scottish name). 2 **a** a usu. abusive term used of a person etc. (called him names). **b** a word denoting an object or esp. a class of objects, ideas, etc. (what is the name of that kind of vase?; that sort of behaviour has no name). 3 a famous person (many great names were there). 4 a reputation, esp. a good one (has a name for honesty; their name is guarantee enough). 5 something existing only nominally (opp. FACT, REALITY). 6 (attrib.) widely known (a name brand of shampoo). —v.tr. 1 give a usu. specified name to (named the dog Spot). 2 call (a person or thing) by the right name (named the man in the photograph). 3 mention; specify; cite (named his requirements). 4 nominate, appoint, etc. (was named the new chairman). 5 specify as something desired (named it as her dearest wish). 6 Brit. Parl. (of the Speaker) mention (an MP) as disobedient to the chair. □ **by name** called (Tom by name). **have to one's name** possess. **in all but name** virtually. **in name** (or **name only**) as a mere formality; hardly at all (is the leader in name only). **in a person's**

name = *in the name of*. **in the name of** calling to witness; invoking (*in the name of goodness*). **in one's own name** independently; without authority. **make a name for oneself** become famous. **name after** (*US* **for**) call (a person) by the name of (a specified person) (*named him after his uncle Roger*). **name-calling** abusive language. **name-child** (usu. foll. by *of*) one named after another person. **name-day 1** the feast-day of a saint after whom a person is named. **2** *Brit.* = *ticket-day*. **name the day** arrange a date (esp. of a woman fixing the date for her wedding). **name-drop** (**-dropped, -dropping**) indulge in name-dropping. **name-dropper** a person who name-drops. **name-dropping** the familiar mention of famous people as a form of boasting. **name names** mention specific names, esp. in accusation. **name of the game** *colloq.* the purpose or essence of an action etc. **name-part** the title role in a play etc. **name-plate** a plate or panel bearing the name of an occupant of a room etc. **name-tape** a tape fixed to a garment etc. and bearing the name of the owner. **of** (or **by**) **the name of** called. **put one's name down for 1** apply for. **2** promise to subscribe (a sum). **what's in a name?** names are arbitrary labels. **you name it** *colloq.* no matter what; whatever you like. □□ **nameable** *adj*. [OE *nama, noma*, (*ge*)*namian* f. Gmc, rel. to L *nomen*, Gk *onoma*]

nameless /ˈneɪmlɪs/ *adj*. **1** having no name or name-inscription. **2** inexpressible; indefinable (*a nameless sensation*). **3** unnamed; anonymous, esp. deliberately (*our informant, who shall be nameless*). **4** too loathsome or horrific to be named (*nameless vices*). **5** obscure; inglorious. **6** illegitimate. □□ **namelessly** *adv*. **namelessness** *n*.

namely /ˈneɪmlɪ/ *adv*. that is to say; in other words.

Namen see NAMUR.

namesake /ˈneɪmseɪk/ *n*. a person or thing having the same name as another (*was her aunt's namesake*). [prob. f. phr. *for the name's sake*]

Namibia /nəˈmɪbɪə/ a country in SW Africa, between Angola and Cape Province; pop. (est. 1988) 1,301,600; official languages, Afrikaans and English; capital, Windhoek. Namibia is an arid country, with few perennial streams and with large tracts of desert along the coast and in the east. As South West Africa, from 1884 it was a German protectorate, but in 1919 was mandated to South Africa by the League of Nations. Despite increasing international insistence, after 1946, that this mandate had ended, South Africa had continued to administer the country for many years. It finally became independent in March 1990 after free elections had been held towards the end of 1989. □□ **Namibian** *adj*. & *n*. [*Namib* desert on western coast of southern Africa]

namma var. of GNAMMA.

Namur /nəˈmʊə(r)/ (Flemish **Namen** /ˈnɑːmən/) **1** a province in central Belgium; pop. (1987) 415,326. The province was the scene of the last great German offensive in the Ardennes in 1945. **2** its capital city, at the junction of the Meuse and Sambre rivers; pop. (1988) 103,100.

nan /næn/ *n*. (also **nana, nanna** /ˈnænə/) *Brit. colloq.* grandmother. [childish pronunc.]

nana /ˈnɑːnə/ *n. sl.* a silly person; a fool. [perh. f. BANANA]

Nanaimo /næˈnaɪmoʊ/ a port of British Columbia, Canada, on the east coast of Vancouver Island; pop. (1986) 50,900.

Nanak /ˈnɑːnək/ (1469–1539) the Indian founder of Sikhism (see entry), known as Guru Nanak. He was of Hindu family, living in a Muslim-owned village in the part of Punjab which is now in Pakistan, and is believed by Sikhs to have been born to be God's messenger and in a state of enlightenment at his birth. He travelled widely, seeking neither to unite the Hindu and Muslim faiths nor to create a new religion, but preaching that spiritual liberation could be achieved, this teachings are contained in a number of hymns which form part of the Adi Granth.

Nanchang /nænˈtʃæŋ/ the capital of Jiangxi province in SE China; pop. (est. 1986) 1,120,000.

Nancy /ˈnɑːsɪ/ the capital of Lorraine in NE France; pop. (1982) 99,300.

nancy /ˈnænsɪ/ *n*. & *adj*. (also **nance** /næns/) *sl*. —*n*. (*pl*. **-ies**) (in full **nancy boy**) an effeminate man, esp. a homosexual. —*adj*. effeminate. [pet-form of the name *Ann*]

Nandi /ˈnændɪ/ *Hinduism* the bull of Siva, which is his vehicle and symbolizes fertility. [Skr., = the happy one]

Nanjing /nænˈdʒɪŋ/ (also **Nanking** /nænˈkɪŋ/) a city of eastern China, on the Yangtze River, that has served at times as the country's capital and is now the capital of Jiansu province; pop. (est. 1986) 2,250,000.

nankeen /nænˈkiːn, næn-/ *n*. **1** a yellowish cotton cloth. **2** a yellowish buff colour. **3** (in *pl*.) trousers of nankeen. [*Nankin(g)* in China, where orig. made]

nanna var. of NAN.

nanny /ˈnænɪ/ *n*. & *v*. —*n*. (*pl*. **-ies**) **1 a** a child's nurse. **b** an unduly protective person, institution, etc. (*the nanny State*). **2** = NAN. **3** (in full **nanny-goat**) a female goat. —*v.tr*. (**-ies, -ied**) be unduly protective towards. [formed as NANCY]

nano- /ˈnænəʊ, ˈneɪnəʊ/ *comb. form* denoting a factor of 10^{-9} (*nanosecond*). [L f. Gk *nanos* dwarf]

nanometre /ˈnænəʊˌmiːt(ə)r/ *n*. one thousand-millionth of a metre.

nanosecond /ˈnænəʊˌsekənd/ *n*. one thousand-millionth of a second.

Nansen /ˈnæns(ə)n/, Fridtjof (1861–1930), Norwegian polar explorer and statesman. In 1888 he led the first expedition to cross the Greenland ice-fields. His most famous Arctic adventure, however, began in 1893 when he sailed his tiny vessel the *Fram* north of Siberia, intending to reach the North Pole by allowing the ship to become frozen in the ice and letting the current carry it towards Greenland. It drifted as far north as 84° 4′ and in 1895 Nansen and one companion left here and made for the Pole on foot, reaching a latitude of 86° 14′, the highest then achieved. In 1922 Nansen was awarded the Nobel Peace Prize for organizing relief work after the First World War among prisoners of war, refugees, and victims of the Russian famine.

Nantes /nãt/ a city of western France, on the River Loire, capital of Pays de la Loire region; pop. (1982) 247,200. □□ **Edict of Nantes** the edict of Henry IV of France (1598) granting toleration to Protestants, revoked by Louis XIV (1685).

naos /ˈneɪɒs/ *n*. (*pl*. **naoi** /ˈneɪɔɪ/) *Gk Hist.* the inner part of a temple. [Gk, = temple]

nap[1] /næp/ *v*. & *n*. —*v.intr*. (**napped, napping**) sleep lightly or briefly. —*n*. a short sleep or doze, esp. by day (*took a nap*). □ **catch a person napping 1** find a person asleep or off guard. **2** detect in negligence or error. [OE *hnappian*, rel. to OHG (*h*)*naffezan* to slumber]

nap[2] /næp/ *n*. & *v*. —*n*. **1** the raised pile on textiles, esp. velvet. **2** a soft downy surface. **3** *Austral. colloq*. blankets, bedding, swag. —*v.tr*. (**napped, napping**) raise a nap on (cloth). □□ **napless** *adj*. [ME *noppe* f. MDu., MLG *noppe* nap, *noppen* trim nap from]

nap[3] /næp/ *n*. & *v*. —*n*. **1 a** a form of whist in which players declare the number of tricks they expect to take, up to five. **b** a call of five in this game. **2 a** the betting of all one's money on one horse etc. **b** a tipster's choice for this. —*v.tr*. (**napped, napping**) name (a horse etc.) as a probable winner. □ **go nap 1** attempt to take all five tricks in nap. **2** risk everything in one attempt. **3** win all the matches etc. in a series. **nap hand** a good winning position worth risking in a venture. **not go nap on** *Austral. colloq.* not be too keen on; not care much for. [abbr. of orig. name of game NAPOLEON]

napa var. of NAPPA.

napalm /ˈneɪpɑːm/ *n*. & *v*. —*n*. **1** a thickening agent produced from naphthenic acid, other fatty acids, and aluminium. **2** a jellied petrol made from this, used in incendiary bombs. —*v.tr*. attack with napalm bombs. [NAPHTHENIC + *palmitic acid* in coconut oil]

nape /neɪp/ *n*. the back of the neck. [ME: orig. unkn.]

napery /ˈneɪpərɪ/ *n*. *Sc*. or *archaic* household linen, esp. table linen. [ME f. OF *naperie* f. *nape* (as NAPKIN)]

Naphtali /ˈnæftəlɪ/ **1** a Hebrew patriarch, son of Jacob and Bilhah (Gen. 30: 7–8). **2** the tribe of Israel traditionally descended from him.

b **but** d **dog** f **few** g **get** h **he** j **yes** k **cat** l **leg** m **man** n **no** p **pen** r **red** s **sit** t **top** v **voice**

naphtha /ˈnæfθə/ n. an inflammable oil obtained by the dry distillation of organic substances such as coal, shale, or petroleum. [L f. Gk, = inflammable volatile liquid issuing from the earth, of Oriental origin]

naphthalene /ˈnæfθəˌliːn/ n. a white crystalline aromatic substance produced by the distillation of coal tar and used in mothballs and the manufacture of dyes etc. □□ **naphthalic** /-ˈθælɪk/ adj. [NAPHTHA + -ENE]

naphthene /ˈnæfθiːn/ n. any of a group of cycloalkanes. [NAPHTHA + -ENE]

naphthenic /næfˈθiːnɪk/ adj. of a naphthene or its radical. □ **naphthenic acid** any carboxylic acid resulting from the refining of petroleum.

Napier[1] /ˈneɪpɪə(r)/ a seaport on Hawke's Bay, North Island, New Zealand; pop. (1988) 107,500.

Napier[2] /ˈneɪpɪə(r)/, John (1550–1617), Scottish landowner, famous as the inventor (simultaneously with, but completely independently of, the German Joost Bürgi) of logarithms. His tables, modified and republished by Henry Briggs, had an immediate and lasting influence on mathematics. □ **Napier's bones** slips of bone etc. marked with digits and formerly used to facilitate the operations of multiplication and division, according to a method devised by Napier. □□ **Napierian** /neɪˈpɪərɪən/ adj.

napkin /ˈnæpkɪn/ n. **1** (in full **table napkin**) a square piece of linen, paper, etc. used for wiping the lips, fingers, etc. at meals, or serving fish etc. on; a serviette. **2** Brit. a baby's nappy. **3** a small towel. □ **napkin-ring** a ring used to hold (and distinguish) a person's table napkin when not in use. [ME f. OF nappe f. L mappa (MAP)]

Naples /ˈneɪpəlz/ (Italian **Napoli** /ˈnæpəlɪ/) a city and port on the west coast of Italy south of Rome; pop. (1981) 1,212,400. It was formerly the capital of the Kingdom of Naples and Sicily (see SICILY). [L Neapolis f. Gk f. neos new + polis city]

Napoleon /nəˈpəʊlɪən/ the name of three rulers of France:
Napoleon I (Napoléon Bonaparte, 1769–1821), emperor 1804–14. Having risen to power in the service of Revolutionary France, Napoleon became successively First Consul and Emperor, and, after a series of dramatic military victories, including Austerlitz (1805), Jena (1806), and Wagram (1809), established a French empire stretching from Spain to Poland. He also made his brother Joseph (1768–1844) king of Naples 1806–8 and of Spain 1808–13, and his younger brother Louis (1778–1846) king of Holland 1806–10. British seapower, however, frustrated his plans to invade England, and resulted in the destruction of the French fleet at Trafalgar; then, after the disastrous failure of his attack on Russia in 1812, his conquests were gradually lost to a coalition of all his major opponents. Forced into exile in 1814, he returned briefly to power a year later, but after his defeat at Waterloo he was once again exiled, this time to the island of St Helena, where he died.
Napoleon III (Charles Louis Napoléon Bonaparte, 1808–73), emperor 1852–70. A nephew of Napoleon I, Napoleon III came to power in a coup launched in the confused situation prevailing after the 1848 revolution. Modelling his regime very much upon that of his uncle, he embarked on an aggressive foreign policy, including intervention in Mexico, participation in the Crimean War, and war against Austria in Italy. At home, however, his position became uncertain, and after his defeat at Sedan in the Franco-Prussian War he abdicated and went into exile in England.

napoleon /nəˈpəʊlɪən/ n. **1** hist. a gold twenty-franc piece minted in the reign of Napoleon I. **2** hist. a 19th-c. high boot. **3** = NAP[3]. **4** US = MILLEFEUILLE. □ **double napoleon** hist. a forty-franc piece. [F napoléon f. Napoléon NAPOLEON]

Napoleonic Wars /nəˌpəʊlɪˈɒnɪk/ a series of campaigns (1800–15) of French armies under Napoleon I against Austria, Russia, Great Britain, Portugal, Prussia, and other European powers.

nappa /ˈnæpə/ n. (also **napa**) a soft leather made by a special process from the skin of sheep or goats. [Napa in California]

nappe /næp/ n. Geol. a sheet of rock that has moved sideways over neighbouring strata, usu. as a result of overthrust. [F nappe tablecloth]

napper /ˈnæpə(r)/ n. Brit. sl. the head. [18th c.: orig. uncert.]

nappy /ˈnæpɪ/ n. (pl. **-ies**) Brit. a piece of towelling or other absorbent material wrapped round a baby to absorb or retain urine and faeces. □ **nappy rash** inflammation of a baby's skin, caused by prolonged contact with a damp nappy. [abbr. of NAPKIN]

Nara /ˈnɑːrə/ a city on Honshu Island, Japan; pop. (1987) 334,000. It was the first capital of Japan, 710–84.

narceine /ˈnɑːsɪˌiːn/ n. a narcotic alkaloid obtained from opium. [F narcéine f. Gk narkē numbness]

narcissism /ˈnɑːsɪˌsɪz(ə)m, nɑːˈsɪs-/ n. Psychol. excessive or erotic interest in oneself, one's physical features, etc. □□ **narcissist** n. **narcissistic** /-ˈsɪstɪk/ adj. **narcissistically** /-ˈsɪstɪkəlɪ/ adv. [NARCISSUS]

Narcissus /nɑːˈsɪsəs/ Gk Mythol. a beautiful youth who, falling in love with his own reflection in a spring, pined away and was changed into the flower that bears his name. (See also ECHO.)

narcissus /nɑːˈsɪsəs/ n. (pl. **narcissi** /-saɪ/ or **narcissuses**) any bulbous plant of the genus Narcissus, esp. N. poeticus bearing a heavily scented single flower with an undivided corona edged with crimson and yellow. [L f. Gk narkissos (= NARCISSUS), perh. f. narkē numbness, with ref. to its narcotic effects]

narcolepsy /ˈnɑːkəˌlepsɪ/ n. Med. a disease with fits of sleepiness and drowsiness. □□ **narcoleptic** /-ˈleptɪk/ adj. & n. [Gk narkoō make numb, after EPILEPSY]

narcosis /nɑːˈkəʊsɪs/ n. **1** Med. the working or effects of soporific narcotics. **2** a state of insensibility. [Gk narkōsis f. narkoō make numb]

narcotic /nɑːˈkɒtɪk/ adj. & n. —adj. **1** (of a substance) inducing drowsiness, sleep, stupor, or insensibility. **2** (of a drug) affecting the mind. **3** of or involving narcosis. **4** soporific. —n. a narcotic substance, drug, or influence. □□ **narcotically** adv. **narcotism** /ˈnɑːkəˌtɪz(ə)m/ n. **narcotize** /ˈnɑːkəˌtaɪz/ v.tr. (also **-ise**). **narcotization** /ˌnɑːkətaɪˈzeɪʃ(ə)n/ n. [ME f. OF narcotique or med.L f. Gk narkōtikos (as NARCOSIS)]

nard /nɑːd/ n. **1** any of various plants yielding an aromatic balsam used by the ancients. **2** = SPIKENARD. [ME f. L nardus f. Gk nardos f. Semitic word]

nardoo /nɑːˈduː/ n. **1** a clover-like plant, Marsilea drummondii, native to Australia. **2** a food made from the spores of this plant. [Aboriginal]

nares /ˈneəriːz/ n.pl. Anat. the nostrils. □□ **narial** adj. [pl. of L naris]

narghile /ˈnɑːgɪlɪ/ n. an oriental tobacco-pipe with the smoke drawn through water; a hookah. [Pers. nārgīleh (nārgīl coconut)]

nark /nɑːk/ n. & v. Brit. sl. —n. **1** a police informer or decoy. **2** Austral. an annoying person or thing. —v.tr. (usu. in passive) annoy; infuriate (was narked by their attitude). □ **nark it!** stop that! [Romany nāk nose]

narky /ˈnɑːkɪ/ adj. (**narkier, narkiest**) sl. bad-tempered, irritable. [NARK]

Narmada /ˈnɑːmʌdə/ a river of central India, sacred to Hindus, that rises in Madhya Pradesh and flows westwards to the Gulf of Cambay.

Narragansett /ˌnærəˈgænsət/ n. & adj. —n. **1** a member of an American Indian people originally living in New England. **2** their Algonquian language. —adj. of this people or their language. [Algonquian, = people of the small point (of land)]

narrate /nəˈreɪt/ v.tr. (also absol.) **1** give a continuous story or account of. **2** provide a spoken commentary or accompaniment for (a film etc.). □□ **narratable** adj. **narration** /nəˈreɪʃ(ə)n/ n. [L narrare narrat-]

narrative /ˈnærətɪv/ n. & adj. —n. **1** a spoken or written account of connected events in order of happening. **2** the practice or art of narration. —adj. in the form of, or concerned with, narration (narrative verse). □□ **narratively** adv. [F narratif -ive f. LL narrativus (as NARRATE)]

narrator /nəˈreɪtə(r)/ n. **1** an actor, announcer, etc. who delivers a commentary in a film, broadcast, etc. **2** a person who narrates. [L (as NARRATE)]

narrow /ˈnærəʊ/ adj., n., & v. —adj. (**narrower, narrowest**) **1**

a of small width in proportion to length; lacking breadth. **b** confined or confining; constricted (*within narrow bounds*). **2** of limited scope; restricted (*in the narrowest sense*). **3** with little margin (*a narrow escape*). **4** searching; precise; exact (*a narrow examination*). **5** = NARROW-MINDED. **6** (of a vowel) tense. **7** of small size. —*n.* **1** (usu. in *pl.*) the narrow part of a strait, river, sound, etc. **2** a narrow pass or street. —*v.* **1** *intr.* become narrow; diminish; contract; lessen. **2** *tr.* make narrow; constrict; restrict. □ **narrow boat** *Brit.* a canal boat, esp. one less than 7 ft. (2.1 metres) wide. **narrow circumstances** poverty. **narrow cloth** cloth less than 52 inches wide. **narrow gauge** a railway track that has a smaller gauge than the standard one. **narrow seas** the English Channel and the Irish Sea. **narrow squeak 1** a narrow escape. **2** a success barely attained. □□ **narrowish** *adj.* **narrowly** *adv.* **narrowness** *n.* [OE *nearu nearw-* f. Gmc]

narrow-minded /ˌnærəʊˈmaɪndɪd/ *adj.* rigid or restricted in one's views, intolerant, prejudiced, illiberal. □□ **narrow-mindedly** *adv.* **narrow-mindedness** *n.*

narthex /ˈnɑːθeks/ *n.* **1** a railed-off antechamber or porch etc. at the western entrance of some early Christian churches, used by catechumens, penitents, etc. **2** a similar antechamber in a modern church. [L f. Gk *narthēx* giant fennel, stick, casket, narthex]

Narvik /ˈnɑːvɪk/ an ice-free port on the NW coast of Norway opposite the Lofoten Islands, linked by rail to the iron-ore mines of northern Sweden; pop. (1980) 19,300.

narwhal /ˈnɑːw(ə)l/ *n.* an Arctic white whale, *Monodon monoceros*, the male of which has a long straight spirally fluted tusk developed from one of its teeth. Also called BELUGA. [Du. *narwal* f. Da. *narhval* f. *hval* whale: cf. ON *náhvalr* (perh. f. *nár* corpse, with ref. to its skin-colour)]

nary /ˈneərɪ/ *adj. colloq.* or *dial.* not a; no (*nary a one*). [f. *ne'er a*]

NAS *abbr. Brit.* Noise Abatement Society.

NASA /ˈnæsə/ *abbr.* (also **Nasa**) National Aeronautics and Space Administration, a body (set up in 1958) responsible for organizing research in extraterrestrial space conducted by the US.

nasal /ˈneɪz(ə)l/ *adj. & n.* —*adj.* **1** of, for, or relating to the nose. **2** *Phonet.* (of a letter or a sound) pronounced with the breath passing through the nose, e.g. *m, n, ng,* or French *en, un,* etc. **3** (of the voice or speech) having an intonation caused by breathing through the nose. —*n.* **1** *Phonet.* a nasal letter or sound. **2** *hist.* a nose-piece on a helmet. □□ **nasality** /-ˈzælɪtɪ/ *n.* **nasalize** *v.intr.* & *tr.* (also **-ise**). **nasalization** /-ˈzeɪʃ(ə)n/ *n.* **nasally** *adv.* [F *nasal* or med.L *nasalis* f. L *nasus* nose]

nascent /ˈnæs(ə)nt, ˈneɪs-/ *adj.* **1** in the act of being born. **2** just beginning to be; not yet mature. **3** *Chem.* just being formed and therefore unusually reactive (*nascent hydrogen*). □□ **nascency** /ˈnæsənsɪ/ *n.* [L *nasci nascent-* be born]

naseberry /ˈneɪzbərɪ/ *n.* (*pl.* **-ies**) a sapodilla. [Sp. & Port. *néspera* medlar f. L (see MEDLAR): assim. to BERRY]

Naseby /ˈneɪzbɪ/ a village in Northamptonshire, scene of the last major battle (1645) of the main phase of the English Civil War, in which the last Royalist army in England, commanded by Prince Rupert and the King himself, was comprehensively defeated by the larger and better organized New Model Army under Fairfax and Oliver Cromwell. Following the destruction of his army Charles I's cause collapsed completely; the monarchy was never so powerful again.

Nash[1] /næʃ/, John (1752–1835), English architect, designer of the terraces near Regent's Park, London, and also of Regent Street (the buildings have since been replaced) and other parts of London.

Nash[2] /næʃ/, Ogden (1902–71), American writer of sophisticated doggerel verse, renowned for his puns, epigrams, wildly asymmetrical lines, and other verbal eccentricities, with witty observations on social and domestic life.

Nash[3] /næʃ/, Paul (1889–1946), English painter, print-maker, and designer. His first mature paintings date from his experience as a war artist in the First World War, with scenes of devastation recorded in a modernist fashion. In the 1920s he became known as a designer, particularly in book illustration. In 1933 he founded 'Unit One'—a cross-section of avant-garde

tendencies in British art. It was surrealism, however, that liberated his imagination in the 1930s, resulting in a number of enigmatic and haunting pictures based on dream-experience or provocative landscape motifs, e.g. *Pillar and Moon*. As a war artist in the Second World War he recorded the Battle of Britain in pictures—e.g. *Totes Meer*—that transmogrified the conflict into another reality.

Nash[4] /næʃ/, Richard, 'Beau Nash' (1674–1762), English gambler and fashion-setter. An accomplished gamester, Nash established Bath as the centre of fashionable society and dictated fashion and etiquette in the early Georgian age.

Nashe /næʃ/, Thomas (1567–1601), English pamphleteer and dramatist, who made fervent attacks on Puritanism in satirical works such as the pamphlet *Pierce Pennilesse* (1592). His best-known work *The Unfortunate Traveller* (1594) is an exuberant medley of picaresque narrative and pseudo-historical fantasy. His dramatic works include *Summer's Last Will and Testament* (1600), and *The Isle of Dogs* (1897, with Ben Jonson) which attacked so many current abuses that he and others were imprisoned for seditious and slanderous language.

Nashville /ˈnæʃvɪl/ the capital of Tennessee; pop. (1982) 455,250. The city is noted for its music industry and is the site of Opryland USA (a family entertainment complex) and the Country Music Hall of Fame.

naso- /ˈneɪzəʊ/ *comb. form* nose. [L *nasus* nose]

naso-frontal /ˌneɪzəʊˈfrʌnt(ə)l/ *adj.* of or relating to the nose and forehead.

Nassau /ˈnæsɔː/ the capital of the Bahamas; pop. (1980) 135,437.

Nasser /ˈnɑːsə(r)/, Gamal Abdel (1918–70), Egyptian statesman. After leading a military coup to depose King Farouk in 1952, Nasser became President of the new Republic of Egypt in 1956 after an election at which voting was compulsory and he was the only candidate. His nationalization of the Suez Canal brought war with Britain, France, and Israel in 1956, while as effectively leader of the Arab world, seeking to advance the cause of Arab unity, he was largely responsible for the escalation of tension leading to the Arab–Israeli War of 1967. With massive Soviet aid he launched a programme of domestic modernization, including the building of the high dam at Aswan. □ **Lake Nasser** a lake in southern Egypt created by the building of the two dams at Aswan.

nastic /ˈnæstɪk/ *adj. Bot.* (of the movement of plant parts) not determined by an external stimulus. [Gk *nastos* squeezed together f. *nassō* to press]

nasturtium /nəˈstɜːʃəm/ *n.* **1** (in general use) a trailing plant, *Tropaeolum majus*, with rounded edible leaves and bright orange, yellow, or red flowers. **2** any cruciferous plant of the genus *Nasturtium*, including watercress. [L]

nasty /ˈnɑːstɪ/ *adj.* (**nastier, nastiest**) **1 a** highly unpleasant (*a nasty experience*). **b** annoying; objectionable (*the car has a nasty habit of breaking down*). **2** difficult to negotiate; dangerous, serious (*a nasty fence; a nasty question; a nasty illness*). **3** (of a person or animal) ill-natured, ill-tempered, spiteful; violent, offensive (*nasty to his mother; turns nasty when he's drunk*). **4** (of the weather) foul, wet, stormy. **5 a** disgustingly dirty, filthy. **b** unpalatable; disagreeable (*nasty smell*). **c** (of a wound) septic. **6 a** obscene. **b** delighting in obscenity. □ **a nasty bit** (or **piece**) **of work** *colloq.* an unpleasant or contemptible person. **a nasty one 1** a rebuff; a snub. **2** an awkward question. **3** a disabling blow etc. □□ **nastily** *adv.* **nastiness** *n.* [ME: orig. unkn.]

NAS/UWT *abbr.* (in the UK) National Association of Schoolmasters and Union of Women Teachers.

Nat. *abbr.* **1** National. **2** Nationalist. **3** Natural.

Natal /nəˈtæl/ the eastern coastal province of the Republic of South Africa; pop. (1985) 2,145,000; capital, Pietermaritzburg. It was first settled by a few British traders in 1823, then by Boers in 1838, when it became a Boer republic. Annexed by the British in 1845, it acquired internal self-government in 1893; from 1910 it was a province of the Union of South Africa. [named *Terra Natalis* (L, = land of the day of birth) by Vasco da Gama because he sighted the entrance to what is now Durban harbour on Christmas Day, 1497]

æ cat ɑː arm e bed ɜː her ɪ sit iː see ɒ hot ɔː saw ʌ run ʊ put uː too ə ago aɪ my

natal /ˈneɪt(ə)l/ adj. of or from one's birth. [ME f. L natalis (as NATION)]

natality /nəˈtælɪtɪ/ n. (pl. **-ies**) birth rate. [F natalité (as NATAL)]

natation /nəˈteɪʃ(ə)n/ n. formal or literary the act or art of swimming. [L natatio f. natare swim]

natatorial /ˌneɪtəˈtɔːrɪəl, ˌnæ-/ adj. (also **natatory** /ˈneɪtətərɪ, nəˈteɪtərɪ/) formal **1** swimming. **2** of or concerning swimming. [LL natatorius f. L natator swimmer (as NATATION)]

natatorium /ˌneɪtəˈtɔːrɪəm/ n. US a swimming-pool, esp. indoors. [LL neut. of natatorius (see NATATORIAL)]

natch /nætʃ/ adv. colloq. = NATURALLY. [abbr.]

nates /ˈneɪtiːz/ n.pl. Anat. the buttocks. [L]

NATFHE abbr. (in the UK) National Association of Teachers in Further and Higher Education.

nathless /ˈneɪθlɪs/ adv. (also **natheless**) archaic nevertheless. [ME f. OE nā not (f. ne not + ā ever) + THE + læs LESS]

nation /ˈneɪʃ(ə)n/ n. **1** a community of people of mainly common descent, history, language, etc., forming a State or inhabiting a territory. **2** a tribe or confederation of tribes of N. American Indians. □ **law of nations** Law international law. □□ **nationhood** n. [ME f. OF f. L natio -onis f. nasci nat- be born]

national /ˈnæʃ(ə)n(ə)l/ adj. & n. —adj. **1** of or common to a nation or the nation. **2** peculiar to or characteristic of a particular nation. —n. **1** a citizen of a specified country, usu. entitled to hold that country's passport (French nationals). **2** a fellow countryman. **3** (**the National**) = Grand National. □ **national anthem** a song adopted by a nation, expressive of its identity etc. and intended to inspire patriotism. **National Assembly 1** an elected house of legislature in various countries. **2** hist. the elected legislature in France 1789–91. **National Assistance** hist. **1** (in Britain) the former official name for supplementary benefits under National Insurance. **2** such benefits. **national bank** US a bank chartered under the federal government. **national convention** US a convention of a major political party, nominating candidates for the presidency etc. **national debt** the money owed by a State because of loans to it and secured against the national income. The permanent national debt in Britain was first established as a result of borrowing to finance the wars against Louis XIV of France at the end of the 17th c., and has been managed by the Bank of England since 1750. **national football** Austral. Australian Rules football. **National Front** an extreme right-wing British political party, formed in 1967 by a merger of the British National Party with the League of Empire Loyalists, holding extreme reactionary views on immigration etc. **national grid** Brit. **1** the network of high-voltage electric power lines between major power stations. **2** the metric system of geographical coordinates used in maps of the British Isles. **National Guard** (in the US) the primary reserve force partly maintained by the States but available for federal use. **National Health** (or **Health Service**) (in the UK) a system of national medical care paid for mainly by taxation and started in 1948. **national income** the total money earned within a nation. **National Insurance** (in the UK) the system of compulsory payments by employed persons (supplemented by employers) to provide State assistance in sickness, unemployment, retirement, etc. **national park** an area of natural beauty protected by the State for the use of the general public. **national service** Brit. hist. service in the army etc. under conscription. **National Socialism** hist. (more commonly known as Nazism; see NAZI) the doctrines of nationalism, racial purity, etc., adopted by the Nazis. **National Socialist** hist. a member of the fascist party implementing National Socialism in Germany, 1933–45. □□ **nationally** adv. [F (as NATION)]

National Gallery a gallery in Trafalgar Square, London, holding one of the chief national collections of pictures. The collection began in 1824 when Parliament voted money for the purchase of 38 pictures from the J. J. Angerstein collection. The present building, built in 1833–7 and at first shared with the Royal Academy, was opened in 1838.

nationalism /ˈnæʃənəˌlɪz(ə)m/ n. **1 a** patriotic feeling, principles, etc. **b** an extreme form of this; chauvinism. **2** a policy of national independence. □□ **nationalist** n. & adj. **nationalistic** /-ˈlɪstɪk/ adj. **nationalistically** /-ˈlɪstɪkəlɪ/ adv.

nationality /ˌnæʃəˈnælɪtɪ/ n. (pl. **-ies**) **1 a** the status of belonging to a particular nation (what is your nationality?; has British nationality). **b** a nation (people of all nationalities). **2** the condition of being national; distinctive national qualities. **3** an ethnic group forming a part of one or more political nations. **4** existence as a nation; nationhood. **5** patriotic sentiment.

nationalize /ˈnæʃənəˌlaɪz/ v.tr. (also **-ise**) **1** take over (railways, coal-mines, the steel industry, land, etc.) from private ownership on behalf of the State. **2 a** make national. **b** make into a nation. **3** naturalize (a foreigner). □□ **nationalization** /-ˈzeɪʃ(ə)n/ n. **nationalizer** n. [F nationaliser (as NATIONAL)]

National Trust a trust for the preservation of places of historic interest or natural beauty. That in England, Wales, and Northern Ireland was founded in 1893, incorporated in 1907, and supported by endowment and private subscription. The National Trust for Scotland is a Scottish institution (founded in 1931) with similar aims.

nationwide /ˈneɪʃ(ə)nˌwaɪd/ adj. extending over the whole nation.

native /ˈneɪtɪv/ n. & adj. —n. **1 a** (usu. foll. by of) a person born in a specified place, or whose parents are domiciled in that place at the time of the birth (a native of Bristol). **b** a local inhabitant. **2** often offens. **a** a member of a non-White indigenous people, as regarded by the colonial settlers. **b** S.Afr. a Black person. **3** (usu. foll. by of) an indigenous animal or plant. **4** an oyster reared in British waters, esp. in artificial beds (a Whitstable native). **5** Austral. a White person born in Australia. —adj. **1** (usu. foll. by to) belonging to a person or thing by nature; inherent; innate (spoke with the facility native to him). **2** of one's birth or birthplace (native dress; native country). **3** belonging to one by right of birth. **4** (usu. foll. by to) belonging to a specified place (the anteater is native to S. America). **5 a** (esp. of a non-European) indigenous; born in a place. **b** of the natives of a place (native customs). **6** unadorned; simple; artless. **7** Geol. (of metal etc.) found in a pure or uncombined state. **8** Austral. & NZ resembling an animal or plant familiar elsewhere (native rabbit). □ **go native** (of a settler) adopt the local way of life, esp. in a non-European country. **native bear** Austral. & NZ = KOALA. **native rock** rock in its original place. □□ **natively** adv. **nativeness** n. [ME (earlier as adj.) f. OF natif -ive or L nativus f. nasci nat- be born]

nativism /ˈneɪtɪˌvɪz(ə)m/ n. Philos. the doctrine of innate ideas. □□ **nativist** n.

nativity /nəˈtɪvɪtɪ/ n. (pl. **-ies**) **1** (esp. **the Nativity**) **a** the birth of Christ. **b** the festival of Christ's birth; Christmas. **2** a picture of the Nativity. **3** birth. **4** the horoscope at a person's birth. **5 a** the birth of the Virgin Mary or St John the Baptist. **b** the festival of the nativity of the Virgin (8 Sept.) or St John (24 June). □ **nativity play** a play usu. performed by children at Christmas dealing with the birth of Christ. [ME f. OF nativité f. LL nativitas -tatis f. L (as NATIVE)]

NATO /ˈneɪtəʊ/ abbr. (also **Nato**) North Atlantic Treaty Organization, an association of European and North American States, formed in 1949 for the defence of Europe and the North Atlantic against the perceived threat of Soviet aggression. Under strong influence from its most powerful member, the US, it now includes all the major non-neutral Western powers.

Natron /ˈneɪtrən/, **Lake** a lake in northern Tanzania, with large deposits of soda.

natron /ˈneɪtrən/ n. a mineral form of hydrated sodium salts found in dried lake beds. [F f. Sp. natrón f. Arab. naṭrūn f. Gk nitron NITRE]

NATSOPA /nætˈsəʊpə/ abbr. (in the UK) National Society of Operative Printers, Graphical and Media Personnel (orig. Printers and Assistants).

natter /ˈnætə(r)/ v. & n. colloq. —v.intr. **1** chatter idly. **2** grumble; talk fretfully. —n. **1** aimless chatter. **2** grumbling talk. □□ **natterer** n. [orig. Sc., imit.]

natterjack /ˈnætəˌdʒæk/ n. a toad, Bufo calamita, with a bright yellow stripe down its back, and moving by running not hopping. [perh. f. NATTER, from its loud croak, + JACK¹]

nattier blue /'nætɪə(r)/ n. a soft shade of blue. [much used by J. M. Nattier, Fr. painter d. 1766]

natty /'næti/ adj. (**nattier**, **nattiest**) colloq. **1 a** smartly or neatly dressed, dapper. **b** spruce; trim; smart (a natty blouse). **2** deft. □□ **nattily** adv. **nattiness** n. [orig. sl., perh. rel. to NEAT¹]

Natufian /na:'tu:fiən/ adj. & n. —adj. of a late mesolithic industry of Palestine, which provides evidence for the first settled villages and is characterized by the use of microliths and of bone for implements. It is named after the type-site, a cave at Wadi an-Natuf, 27 km (17 miles) north of Jerusalem. —n. this industry.

natural /'nætʃər(ə)l/ adj. & n. —adj. **1 a** existing in or caused by nature; not artificial (natural landscape). **b** uncultivated; wild (existing in its natural state). **2** in the course of nature; not exceptional or miraculous (died of natural causes; a natural occurrence). **3** (of human nature etc.) not surprising; to be expected (natural for her to be upset). **4 a** (of a person or a person's behaviour) unaffected, easy, spontaneous. **b** (foll. by to) spontaneous, easy (friendliness is natural to him). **5 a** (of qualities etc.) inherent; innate (a natural talent for music). **b** (of a person) having such qualities (a natural linguist). **6** not disguised or altered (as by make-up etc.). **7** lifelike; as if in nature (the portrait looked very natural). **8** likely by its or their nature to be such (natural enemies; the natural antithesis). **9** having a physical existence as opposed to what is spiritual, intellectual, etc. (the natural world). **10 a** related by nature, out of wedlock, esp. in a specified manner (her natural son). **b** illegitimate (a natural child). **11** based on the innate moral sense; instinctive (natural justice). **12** Mus. **a** (of a note) not sharpened or flattened (B natural). **b** (of a scale) not containing any sharps or flats. **13** not enlightened or communicated by revelation (the natural man). —n. **1** colloq. (usu. foll. by for) a person or thing naturally suitable, adept, expert, etc. (a natural for the championship). **2** archaic a person mentally deficient from birth. **3** Mus. **a** a sign (♮) denoting a return to natural pitch after a sharp or a flat. **b** a natural note. **c** a white key on a piano. **4 a** Cards a hand making 21 in the first deal in pontoon. **b** a throw of 7 or 11 at craps. **5** a pale fawn colour. □ **natural-born** having a character or position by birth. **natural childbirth** Med. childbirth with minimal medical or technological intervention. **natural classification** a scientific classification according to natural features. **natural death** death by age or disease, not by accident, poison, violence, etc. **natural food** food without preservatives etc. **natural gas** an inflammable mainly methane gas found in the earth's crust, not manufactured. **natural historian** a writer or expert on natural history. **natural history** **1** the study of animals or plants esp. as set forth for popular use. **2** an aggregate of the facts concerning the flora and fauna etc. of a particular place or class (a natural history of the Isle of Wight). **natural key** (or **scale**) Mus. a key or scale having no sharps or flats, i.e. C major and A minor. **natural language** a language that has developed naturally. **natural law** **1** Philos. unchanging moral principles common to all people by virtue of their nature as human beings. **2** a correct statement of an invariable sequence between specified conditions and a specified phenomenon. **3** the laws of nature; regularity in nature (where they saw chance, we see natural law). **natural life** the duration of one's life on earth. **natural logarithm** see LOGARITHM. **natural magic** magic involving the supposed invocation of impersonal spirits. **natural note** Mus. a note that is neither sharp nor flat. **natural numbers** the integers 1, 2, 3, etc. **natural philosopher** archaic a physicist. **natural philosophy** archaic physics. **natural religion** a religion based on reason (opp. revealed religion); deism. **natural resources** materials or conditions occurring in nature and capable of economic exploitation. **natural science** the sciences used in the study of the physical world, e.g. physics, chemistry, geology, biology, botany. **natural selection** see separate entry. **natural theology** the knowledge of God as gained by the light of natural reason. **natural uranium** unenriched uranium. **natural virtues** Philos. justice, prudence, temperance, fortitude. **natural year** the time taken by one revolution of the earth round the sun, 365 days 5 hours 48 minutes. □□ **naturalness** n. [ME f. OF naturel f. L naturalis (as NATURE)]

naturalism /'nætʃərə,lɪz(ə)m/ n. **1** the theory or practice in art and literature of representing nature, character, etc. realistically and in great detail. (See below.) **2 a** Philos. a theory of the world that excludes the supernatural or spiritual. **b** any moral or religious system based on this theory. **3** action based on natural instincts. **4** indifference to conventions. [NATURAL, in Philos. after F naturalisme]

In its simplest usage naturalism means the representation of form as found in nature, with avoidance of stylized or conceptual forms; in this sense the art of classical Greece is naturalistic (in contrast to Egyptian art), and that of the Italian Renaissance is a revival of naturalism; a work of art is conceived as a mirror for natural beauty. As applied to a particular school of painting the term was first used of the 17th-c. followers of Caravaggio, with reference to their doctrine of copying nature faithfully whether it seems to us ugly or beautiful. It was later applied specifically to an artistic and literary movement of the 19th c., influenced by Darwin's evolutionary theories, Comte's scientific ideas applied to the study of society, and the historian Taine's deterministic approach. It is characterized by a refusal to idealize experience and by the persuasion that human life is strictly subject to natural laws. The new naturalism can be detected in minutely detailed and closely observed painting (its influence is apparent in the works of Van Gogh and the Barbizon painters), and in the rise of the naturalist novel, Zola's Le Roman expérimental (1880) being regarded as the manifesto of the movement. Among the dramatists influenced by naturalism are Henry Becque, Hauptmann, Strindberg, Ibsen, Chekhov, and Dreiser.

naturalist /'nætʃərəlɪst/ n. & adj. —n. **1** an expert in natural history. **2** a person who believes in or practises naturalism. —adj. = NATURALISTIC.

naturalistic /,nætʃərə'lɪstɪk/ adj. **1** imitating nature closely; lifelike. **2** of or according to naturalism. **3** of natural history. □□ **naturalistically** adv.

naturalize /'nætʃərə,laɪz/ v. (also **-ise**) **1** tr. admit (a foreigner) to the citizenship of a country. **2** tr. introduce (an animal, plant, etc.) into another region so that it flourishes in the wild. **3** tr. adopt (a foreign word, custom, etc.). **4** intr. become naturalized. **5** tr. Philos. exclude from the miraculous; explain naturalistically. **6** tr. free from conventions; make natural. **7** tr. cause to appear natural. **8** intr. study natural history. □□ **naturalization** /-'zeɪʃ(ə)n/ n. [F naturaliser (as NATURAL)]

naturally /'nætʃərəli/ adv. **1** in a natural manner. **2** as a natural result. **3** (qualifying a whole sentence) as might be expected; of course.

natural selection n. the process favouring the survival of those organisms that are best adapted to their environment. The way that this operates can be seen in the survival and numerical predominance of darker-coloured moths in industrially polluted areas of Britain, where they are less visible against dark tree-trunks than are the lighter-coloured species, of which a considerable number are eaten by predators. (See EVOLUTION.)

nature /'neɪtʃə(r)/ n. **1** a thing's or person's innate or essential qualities or character (not in their nature to be cruel; is the nature of iron to rust). **2** (often **Nature**) **a** the physical power causing all the phenomena of the material world (Nature is the best physician). **b** these phenomena, including plants, animals, landscape, etc. (nature gives him comfort). **3** a kind, sort, or class (things of this nature). **4** = human nature. **5 a** a specified element of human character (the rational nature; our animal nature). **b** a person of a specified character (even strong natures quail). **6 a** an uncultivated or wild area, condition, community, etc. **b** the countryside, esp. when picturesque. **7** inherent impulses determining character or action. **8** heredity as an influence on or determinant of personality (opp. NURTURE). **9** a living thing's vital functions or needs (such a diet will not support nature). □ **against nature** unnatural; immoral. **against** (or **contrary to**) **nature** miraculous; miraculously. **back to nature** returning to a pre-civilized or natural state. **by nature** innately. **from nature** Art using natural objects as models. **human nature** general human characteristics, feelings, etc. **in nature 1** actually existing. **2**

anywhere; at all. **in** (or **of**) **the nature of** characteristically resembling or belonging to the class of (*the answer was in the nature of an excuse*). **in a state of nature 1** in an uncivilized or uncultivated state. **2** totally naked. **3** in an unregenerate state. **law of nature** = *natural law* 2. **nature cure** = NATUROPATHY. **nature-printing** a method of producing a print of leaves etc. by pressing them on a prepared plate. **nature reserve** a tract of land managed so as to preserve its flora, fauna, physical features, etc. **nature study** the practical study of plant and animal life etc. as a school subject. **nature trail** a signposted path through the countryside designed to draw attention to natural phenomena. [ME f. OF f. L *natura* f. *nasci nat-* be born]

natured /ˈneɪtʃəd/ *adj.* (in comb.) having a specified disposition (*good-natured*; *ill-natured*).

naturism /ˈneɪtʃəˌrɪz(ə)m/ *n.* **1** nudism. **2** naturalism in regard to religion. **3** the worship of natural objects. □□ **naturist** *n.*

naturopathy /ˌneɪtʃəˈrɒpəθɪ/ *n.* **1** the treatment of disease etc. without drugs, usu. involving diet, exercise, massage, etc. **2** this regimen used preventively. □□ **naturopath** /ˈneɪtʃərəˌpæθ/ *n.* **naturopathic** /ˌneɪtʃərəˈpæθɪk/ *adj.*

naught /nɔːt/ *n.* & *adj.* — *n.* **1** *archaic* or *literary* nothing, nought. **2** US = NOUGHT. — *adj.* (usu. *predic.*) *archaic* or *literary* worthless; useless. □ **bring to naught** ruin; baffle. **come to naught** be ruined or baffled. **set at naught** disregard; despise. [OE *nāwiht*, -*wuht* f. *nā* (see NO²) + *wiht* WIGHT]

naughty /ˈnɔːtɪ/ *adj.* (**naughtier, naughtiest**) **1** (esp. of children) disobedient; badly behaved. **2** *colloq. joc.* indecent. **3** *archaic* wicked. □□ **naughtily** *adv.* **naughtiness** *n.* [ME f. NAUGHT + -Y¹]

nauplius /ˈnɔːplɪəs/ *n.* (*pl.* **nauplii** /-plɪˌaɪ/) the first larval stage of some crustaceans. [L, = a kind of shellfish, or f. Gk *Nauplios* son of Poseidon]

Nauru /naʊˈruː/ a small but relatively rich country that is an island in the SW Pacific, lying near the Equator; pop. (est. 1988) 8,900; official language, English. Discovered by the British in 1798, it was annexed by Germany in 1888, and became a British mandate after the First World War. Since 1968 it has been an independent republic with a limited form of membership of the Commonwealth. Its economy is heavily dependent upon the mining of phosphates, of which it has the world's richest deposits. □□ **Nauruan** *adj.* & *n.*

nausea /ˈnɔːzɪə, -sɪə/ *n.* **1** a feeling of sickness with an inclination to vomit. **2** loathing; revulsion. [L f. Gk *nausia* f. *naus* ship]

nauseate /ˈnɔːzɪˌeɪt, -sɪˌeɪt/ *v.* **1** *tr.* affect with nausea (*was nauseated by the smell*). **2** *intr.* (usu. foll. by *at*) loathe food, an occupation, etc.; feel sick. □□ **nauseating** *adj.* **nauseatingly** *adv.* [L *nauseare* (as NAUSEA)]

nauseous /ˈnɔːzɪəs, -sɪəs/ *adj.* **1** causing nausea. **2** offensive to the taste or smell. **3** disgusting; loathsome. □□ **nauseously** *adv.* **nauseousness** *n.* [L *nauseosus* (as NAUSEA)]

nautch /nɔːtʃ/ *n.* a performance of professional Indian dancing-girls. □ **nautch-girl** a professional Indian dancing-girl. [Urdu (Hindi) *nāch* f. Prakrit *nachcha* f. Skr. *nṛtja* dancing]

nautical /ˈnɔːtɪk(ə)l/ *adj.* of or concerning sailors or navigation; naval; maritime. □ **nautical almanac** a yearbook containing astronomical and tidal information for navigators etc. **nautical mile** a unit of approx. 2,025 yards (1,852 metres): also called *sea mile*. □□ **nautically** *adv.* [F *nautique* or f. L *nauticus* f. Gk *nautikos* f. *nautēs* sailor f. *naus* ship]

Nautilus /ˈnɔːtɪləs/ the first nuclear-powered submarine, launched in 1954. This US Navy vessel, capable of prolonged submersion, made a historic journey (1–5 Aug. 1958) from Alaska to the Greenland Sea, pasing under the thick polar ice-cap of the North Pole.

nautilus /ˈnɔːtɪləs/ *n.* (*pl.* **nautiluses** or **nautili** /-ˌlaɪ/) **1** any cephalopod of the genus *Nautilus* with a light brittle spiral shell, esp. (**pearly nautilus**) one having a chambered shell with nacreous septa. **2** (in full **paper nautilus**) any small floating octopus of the genus *Argonauta*, of which the female has a very thin shell and webbed sail-like arms. [L f. Gk *nautilos*, lit. sailor (as NAUTICAL)]

Navajo /ˈnævəˌhəʊ/ *n.* (also **Navaho**) (*pl.* **-os**) **1** a member of an American Indian people native to New Mexico and Arizona. **2** the language of this people. [Sp., = pueblo]

naval /ˈneɪv(ə)l/ *adj.* **1** of, in, for, etc. the navy or a navy. **2** of or concerning ships (*a naval battle*). □ **naval academy** a college for training naval officers. **naval architect** a designer of ships. **naval architecture** the designing of ships. **naval officer** an officer in a navy. **naval stores** all materials used in shipping. □□ **navally** *adv.* [L *navalis* f. *navis* ship]

navarin /ˈnævəˌræ̃/ *n.* a casserole of mutton or lamb with vegetables. [F]

Navarino /ˌnævəˈriːnəʊ/, **battle of** a decisive naval battle in the Greek struggle for independence of the Ottoman empire, fought in 1827 in the Bay of Navarinou off Pylos in the Peloponnese, in which Britain, Russia, and France sent a combined fleet which destroyed the Egyptian and Turkish fleet.

Navarre /nəˈvɑː(r)/ **1** a former Franco-Spanish kingdom in the Pyrenees area. Navarre achieved independence in the 10th c. under Sancho III, but during the Middle Ages fell at various times under French or Spanish domination. The southern part of the country was conquered by Ferdinand V in 1512 while the northern part passed to France in 1589 through inheritance by Henry IV. **2** (Spanish **Navarra**) an autonomous region of northern Spain; pop. (1986) 512,700; capital Pamplona.

nave¹ /neɪv/ *n.* the central part of a church, usu. from the west door to the chancel and excluding the side aisles. [med.L *navis* f. L *navis* ship]

nave² /neɪv/ *n.* the hub of a wheel. [OE *nafu, nafa* f. Gmc, rel. to NAVEL]

navel /ˈneɪv(ə)l/ *n.* **1** a depression in the centre of the belly caused by the detachment of the umbilical cord. **2** a central point. □ **navel orange** a large seedless orange with a navel-like formation at the top. [OE *nafela* f. Gmc, rel. to NAVE²]

navelwort /ˈneɪvəlˌwɜːt/ *n.* a pennywort.

navicular /nəˈvɪkjʊlə(r)/ *adj.* & *n.* — *adj.* boat-shaped. — *n.* (in full **navicular bone**) a boat-shaped bone in the foot or hand. □ **navicular disease** an inflammatory disease of the navicular bone in horses, causing lameness. [F *naviculaire* or LL *navicularis* f. L *navicula* dimin. of *navis* ship]

navigable /ˈnævɪɡəb(ə)l/ *adj.* **1** (of a river, the sea, etc.) affording a passage for ships. **2** (of a ship etc.) seaworthy (*in navigable condition*). **3** (of a balloon, airship, etc.) steerable. □□ **navigability** /-ˈbɪlɪtɪ/ *n.* [F *navigable* or L *navigabilis* (as NAVIGATE)]

navigate /ˈnævɪˌɡeɪt/ *v.* **1** *tr.* manage or direct the course of (a ship, aircraft, etc.). **2** *tr.* **a** sail on (a sea, river, etc.). **b** travel or fly through (the air). **3** *intr.* (of a passenger in a vehicle) assist the driver by map-reading etc. **4** *intr.* sail a ship; sail in a ship. **5** *tr.* (often *refl.*) *colloq.* steer (oneself, a course, etc.) through a crowd etc. [L *navigare* f. *navis* ship + *agere* drive]

navigation /ˌnævɪˈɡeɪʃ(ə)n/ *n.* **1** the act or process of navigating. **2** any of several methods of determining or planning a ship's or aircraft's position and course by geometry, astronomy, etc. (See below.) **3** a voyage. □ **inland navigation** communication by canals and rivers. **navigation light** a light on a ship or aircraft at night, indicating its position and direction. **navigation satellite**, an artificial satellite whose orbit is accurately known and made available, so that signals from it may be used for navigational purposes. □□ **navigational** *adj.* [F or f. L *navigatio* (as NAVIGATE)]

In ancient times navigation depended upon observation of landmarks and the positions of the stars. Navigational instruments included the compass, introduced in the 12th–13th c. (see COMPASS), the astrolabe, and the quadrant. The problem of determining longitude was not solved until the 18th c., with the development of an accurate marine chronometer and the sextant. The 20th c. has seen the introduction of radio signals, with the use of radar and of navigation satellites for both sea and air navigation.

navigator /ˈnævɪˌɡeɪtə(r)/ *n.* **1** a person skilled or engaged in navigation. **2** an explorer by sea. [L (as NAVIGATE)]

Navratilova /ˌnævrətɪˈləʊvə/, **Martina** (1956–), American tennis-player, born in Czechoslovakia. She won many championships in the 1980s, and in 1990 won the women's singles championship at Wimbledon for the ninth time, setting a new record.

navvy /ˈnævɪ/ n. & v. Brit. —n. (pl. **-ies**) a labourer employed in building or excavating roads, canals, etc. —v.intr. (**-ies**, **-ied**) work as a navvy. [abbr. of NAVIGATOR]

navy /ˈneɪvɪ/ n. (pl. **-ies**) **1** (often **the Navy**) **a** the whole body of a State's ships of war, including crews, maintenance systems, etc. (See below.) **b** the officers and men of a navy. **2** (in full **navy blue**) a dark-blue colour as used in naval uniform. **3** poet. a fleet of ships. □ **Navy Department** US the government department in charge of the navy. **Navy List** Brit. an official list containing the names of all naval officers etc. **navy yard** US a government shipyard with civilian labour. [ME, = fleet f. OF *navie* ship, fleet f. Rmc & pop.L *navia* ship f. L *navis*]

Creation of the basis of a naval force in England is usually credited to Alfred the Great (9th c.), who sought to defend his land against the marauding Norsemen. In medieval times England's navy was generally provided by the Cinque Ports, but the Tudor monarchs Henry VIII and Elizabeth I began to establish a regular government-controlled force. Reforms and expansion in the 17th c. built the Royal Navy into the most powerful in the world, a position it retained until the Second World War.

nawab /nəˈwɑːb, -ˈwɔːb/ n. **1** the title of a distinguished Muslim in Pakistan. **2** hist. the title of a governor or nobleman in India. [Urdu *nawwāb* pl. f. Arab. *nā'ib* deputy: cf. NABOB]

Naxos /ˈnæksəs/ the largest of the Greek islands of the Cyclades in the south Aegean.

nay /neɪ/ adv. & n. —adv. **1** or rather; and even; and more than that (*impressive, nay, magnificent*). **2** archaic = NO² adv. 1. —n. **1** the word 'nay'. **2** a negative vote (*counted 16 nays*). [ME f. ON *nei* f. *ne* not + *ei* AYE²]

Nayarit /ˌnaɪəˈriːt/ a State of western Mexico; pop. (est. 1988) 846,300; capital, Tepic.

naysay /ˈneɪseɪ/ v. (3rd sing. present **-says**; past and past part. **-said**) esp. US **1** intr. utter a denial or refusal. **2** tr. refuse or contradict. □□ **naysayer** n.

Nazarene /ˌnæzəˈriːn, ˈnæ-/ n. & adj. —n. **1 a** (prec. by *the*) Christ. **b** (esp. in Jewish or Muslim use) a Christian. **2** a native or inhabitant of Nazareth. **3** a member of an early Jewish-Christian sect. The name was given by 4th-c. writes to groups of Christians of Jewish race in Syria, who continued to obey much of the Jewish Law although they were otherwise orthodox Christians. They used a version of the Gospel in Aramaic. **4** a member of a group of German painters called the Brotherhood of St Luke, founded in 1809, who aspired to revive religious painting by a return to the art and working practices of medieval Germany and early Renaissance Italy. From 1810 they lived and worked in the disused monastery of San Isidoro, Rome; their style was marked by strong outlines and pure colour reminiscent of quattrocento art. The most important participants were Cornelius, Overbeck, Pforr, and Schadow. —adj. of or concerning Nazareth, the Nazarenes, etc. [ME f. LL *Nazarenus* f. Gk *Nazarēnos* f. *Nazaret* Nazareth]

Nazareth /ˈnæzərəθ/ a town of lower Galilee, now in Israel, first mentioned in the Gospels, where Mary and Joseph lived and Christ spent his youth.

Nazarite /ˈnæzəˌraɪt/ n. (more correctly **Nazirite**) any of the Israelites specially consecrated to the service of God who were under vows to abstain from wine, let their hair grow, and avoid the defilement of contact with a dead body (Num. 6). [LL *Nazaraeus* f. Heb. *nāzīr* f. *nāzar* to separate or consecrate oneself]

Nazca Lines /ˈnæzkə/ a group of huge drawings of animals, abstract designs, and straight lines on the coastal plain north of Nazca in southern Peru, made by cleaning and aligning the surface stones to expose the underlying sand. They belong to a pre-Inca culture of that region, and their purpose is uncertain; some hold the designs to represent a vast calendar or astronomical information. Virtually indecipherable at ground level, the lines are clearly visible from the air; they have been preserved by the extreme dryness of the region.

Nazi /ˈnɑːtsɪ, ˈnɑːzɪ/ n. & adj. —n. (pl. **Nazis**) **1** hist. a member of the National Socialist (Workers') Party in Germany, led by Adolf Hitler. (See below.) **2** derog. a person holding extreme racist or authoritarian views or behaving brutally. **3** a person belonging to any organization similar to the Nazis. —adj. of or concerning the Nazis, Nazism, etc. □□ **Nazidom** n. **Nazify** /-ˌfaɪ/ v.tr. (**-ies**, **-ied**). **Naziism** /-iˌɪz(ə)m/ n. **Nazism** /ˈnɑːtsɪz(ə)m/ n. [repr. pronunc. of *Nati-* in G *Nationalsozialist*]

The National Socialist (Workers') Party was formed in Munich soon after the First World War to espouse a right-wing brand of nationalist authoritarianism. It was dominated from its early days by Hitler who forced his own ideas upon it, most notably anti-Semitism, a belief in the racial superiority of Aryan Germans, a determination to overthrow the Treaty of Versailles, and a pervasive ethos of leader-worship. The initial popularity of Nazism (as witnessed by an increase in party membership from 176,000 in 1929 to 2,000,000 in early 1933) was due to Hitler's charismatic appeal and to the dreadful conditions prevalent in Germany during the Depression. After his election as Chancellor in January 1933, Hitler built up a Nazi dictatorship in which the party effectively controlled the State at all levels. The Nazi Party collapsed at the end of the Second World War and was formally outlawed by the new West German constitution.

Nazirite var. of NAZARITE.

NB abbr. **1** US Nebraska (in official postal use). **2** New Brunswick. **3** no ball. **4** Scotland (North Britain). **5** nota bene.

Nb symb. Chem. the element niobium.

NBC abbr. (in the US) National Broadcasting Company.

n.b.g. abbr. no bloody good.

N. by E. abbr. North by East.

N. by W. abbr. North by West.

NC abbr. North Carolina (also in official postal use).

NCB abbr. hist. (in the UK) National Coal Board. ¶ Since 1987 officially called *British Coal*.

NCO abbr. non-commissioned officer.

NCU abbr. (in the UK) National Communications Union.

ND abbr. US North Dakota (in official postal use).

Nd symb. Chem. the element neodymium.

n.d. abbr. no date.

-nd¹ suffix forming nouns (*fiend; friend*). [OE *-ond*, orig. part. ending]

-nd² suffix see -AND, -END.

N.Dak. abbr. North Dakota.

Ndebele /ˌəndəˈbiːlɪ/ n. (pl. same) **1** a member of a Zulu people branches of which are found in Zimbabwe (where they are better known as the Matabele) and in the Transvaal. **2** the language of this people. [native name]

N'Djamena /ˌəndʒæˈmeɪnə/ (formerly, until 1973, **Fort Lamy** /læˈmiː/) the capital of Chad; pop. (est. 1984) 402,000.

Ndola /ənˈdəʊlə/ the capital of the Copperbelt mining province of central Zambia; pop. (est. 1987) 418,100.

NE abbr. **1** north-east. **2** north-eastern.

Ne symb. Chem. the element neon.

né /neɪ/ adj. born (indicating a man's previous name) (*Lord Beaconsfield, né Benjamin Disraeli*). [F, past part. of *naître* be born: cf. NÉE]

Neagh /neɪ/, **Lough** a lake in Northern Ireland, the largest lake in the British Isles.

Neanderthal man /nɪˈændəˌtɑːl/ the first fossil hominid to be identified as such, and the best known, named after remains found in the Neanderthal valley in western Germany in 1856. *Homo* (*sapiens*) *neanderthalensis* is found throughout Europe and the Near East, and also the remainder of the Old World in variant forms, during the late Middle and Upper Pleistocene *c*.80,000–*c*.30,000 years ago. Within western Europe his remains are associated with the middle palaeolithic Mousterian stone-tool industries that disappeared with the arrival of Cro-Magnon man (fully modern man). Neanderthal man developed from *Homo erectus*, though the widespread distribution of intermediate forms hinders an attempt to resolve any single geographical locality as the origin of the development. The fate of the Neanderthal populations is equally hard to discern: they

æ cat ɑː arm e bed ɜː her ɪ sit iː see ɒ hot ɔː saw ʌ run ʊ put uː too ə ago aɪ my

either became assimilated into the encroaching fully modern populations or died out in the time-honoured evolutionary manner. Neanderthal man was a fully erect biped of stocky build, with a long low skull, prominent brow ridges and occiputs, and a jutting face. The popular impression of him as a stooping brute is incorrect and derives from the original poor reconstruction of the first find from the Neanderthal valley; it has also been suggested that this individual suffered from a vitamin D deficiency (rickets) and/or syphilis.

neap /niːp/ n. & v. —n. (in full **neap tide**) a tide just after the first and third quarters of the moon when there is least difference between high and low water. —v. **1** intr. (of a tide) tend towards or reach the highest point of a neap tide. **2** tr. (in passive) (of a ship) be kept aground, in harbour, etc., by a neap tide. [OE *nēpflōd* (cf. FLOOD), of unkn. orig.]

Neapolitan /nɪəˈpɒlɪt(ə)n/ n. & adj. —n. a native or citizen of Naples in Italy. —adj. of or relating to Naples. □ **Neapolitan ice-cream** ice-cream made in layers of different colours. **Neapolitan violet** a sweet-scented double viola. [ME f. L *Neapolitanus* f. L *Neapolis* NAPLES]

near /nɪə(r)/ adv., prep., adj., & v. —adv. **1** (often foll. by *to*) to or at a short distance in space or time; close by (*the time drew near; dropped near to them*). **2** closely (*as near as one can guess*). **3** archaic almost, nearly (*very near died*). **4** archaic parsimoniously; meanly (*lives very near*). —prep. (compar. & superl. also used) **1** to or at a short distance (in space, time, condition, or resemblance) from (*stood near the back; occurs nearer the end; the sun is near setting*). **2** (in comb.) **a** that is almost (*near-hysterical; a near-Communist*). **b** intended as a substitute for; resembling (*near-beer*). —adj. **1** (usu. predic.) close at hand; close to, in place or time (*the man nearest you; in the near future*). **2 a** closely related (*a near relation*). **b** intimate (*a near friend*). **3** (of a part of a vehicle, animal, or road) left (*the near fore leg; near side front wheel* (orig. of the side from which one mounted)) (opp. OFF). **4** close; narrow (*a near escape; a near guess*). **5** (of a road or way) direct. **6** niggardly, mean. —v. **1** tr. approach; draw near to (*neared the harbour*). **2** intr. draw near (*could distinguish them as they neared*). □ **come** (or **go**) **near** (foll. by verbal noun, or *to* + verbal noun) be on the point of, almost succeed in (*came near to falling*). **go near** (foll. by *to* + infin.) narrowly fail. **near at hand 1** within easy reach. **2** in the immediate future. **the Near East** the region comprising the countries of the eastern Mediterranean, sometimes also including those of the Balkan peninsula, SW Asia, or North Africa. **Near Eastern** of the Near East. **near go** colloq. a narrow escape. **near the knuckle** colloq. verging on the indecent. **near miss 1** (of a bomb etc.) close to the target. **2** a situation in which a collision is narrowly avoided. **3** (of an attempt) almost but not quite successful. **near sight** esp. US = short sight. **near thing** a narrow escape. **near upon** archaic not far in time from. □□ **nearish** adj. **nearness** n. [ME f. ON *nær*, orig. compar. of *ná* = OE *nēah* NIGH]

nearby adj. & adv. —adj. /ˈnɪəbaɪ/ situated in a near position (*a nearby hotel*). —adv. /nɪəˈbaɪ/ close; not far away.

Nearctic /nɪˈɑːktɪk/ adj. of or relating to the Arctic and the temperate parts of N. America as a zoogeographical region. [NEO- + ARCTIC]

nearly /ˈnɪəlɪ/ adv. **1** almost (*we are nearly there*). **2** closely (*they are nearly related*). □ **not nearly** nothing like; far from (*not nearly enough*).

nearside /ˈnɪəsaɪd/ n. (often attrib.) esp. Brit. the left side of a vehicle, animal, etc. (cf. OFFSIDE n.).

near-sighted /nɪəˈsaɪtɪd/ adj. esp. US = short-sighted. □□ **near-sightedly** adv. **near-sightedness** n.

neat[1] /niːt/ adj. **1** tidy and methodical. **2** elegantly simple in form etc.; well-proportioned. **3** (of language, style, etc.) brief, clear, and pointed; epigrammatic. **4 a** cleverly executed (*a neat piece of work*). **b** deft; dextrous. **5** (of esp. alcoholic liquor) undiluted. **6** US sl. (as a general term of approval) good, pleasing, excellent. □□ **neatly** adv. **neatness** n. [F net f. L nitidus shining f. nitēre shine]

neat[2] /niːt/ n. archaic **1** a bovine animal. **2** (as pl.) cattle. □ **neat's-foot oil** oil made from boiled cow-heel and used to dress leather. [OE nēat f. Gmc]

neaten /ˈniːt(ə)n/ v.tr. make neat.

neath /niːθ/ prep. poet. beneath. [BENEATH]

NEB abbr. **1** (in the UK) National Enterprise Board. **2** New English Bible.

Neb. abbr. Nebraska.

neb /neb/ n. Sc. & N.Engl. **1** a beak or bill. **2** a nose; a snout. **3** a tip, spout, or point. [OE nebb ult. f. Gmc: cf. NIB]

nebbish /ˈnebɪʃ/ n. & adj. colloq. —n. a submissive or timid person. —adj. submissive; timid. [Yiddish nebach poor thing!]

Nebr. abbr. Nebraska.

Nebraska /nɪˈbræskə/ a State in the central US; pop. (est. 1985) 1,570,000; capital, Lincoln. Acquired as part of the Louisiana Purchase in 1803, it became the 37th State of the US in 1867.

Nebuchadnezzar /ˌnebjʊkədˈnezə(r)/ king of Babylon 605–562 BC, who rebuilt the city with massive fortification walls, a huge temple, and a ziggurat, and extended his rule over ancient Palestine and neighbouring countries. In 586 BC he captured and destroyed Jerusalem and deported its leaders. —n. a wine bottle of about 20 times the standard size.

nebula /ˈnebjʊlə/ n. (pl. **nebulae** /-ˌliː/ or **nebulas**) **1** Astron. a cloud of gas or dust situated within the interstellar space of a galaxy (usually our own) and appearing as either a bright or a dark cloud according to whether or not there are stars present to make it luminous. Some distant galaxies were formerly known as spiral or extragalactic nebulae. The term was originally applied to any indistinct cloud-like patch revealed by a telescope. **2** Med. a clouded spot on the cornea causing defective vision. [L, = mist]

nebular /ˈnebjʊlə(r)/ adj. of or relating to a nebula or nebulae. □ **nebular theory** (or **hypothesis**) the theory that the solar and stellar systems were developed from a primeval nebula.

nebulous /ˈnebjʊləs/ adj. **1** cloudlike. **2 a** formless, clouded. **b** hazy, indistinct, vague (*put forward a few nebulous ideas*). **3** Astron. of or like a nebula or nebulae. □ **nebulous star** a small cluster of indistinct stars, or a star in a luminous haze. □□ **nebulosity** /-ˈlɒsɪtɪ/ n. **nebulously** adv. **nebulousness** n. [ME f. F nébuleux or L nebulosus (as NEBULA)]

nebuly /ˈnebjʊlɪ/ adj. Heraldry wavy in form; cloudlike. [F nébulé f. med.L nebulatus f. L NEBULA]

necessarian /ˌnesɪˈseərɪən/ n. & adj. = NECESSITARIAN. □□ **necessarianism** n.

necessarily /ˈnesəsərɪlɪ, -ˈserɪlɪ/ adv. as a necessary result; inevitably.

necessary /ˈnesəsərɪ/ adj. & n. —adj. **1** requiring to be done, achieved, etc.; requisite, essential (*it is necessary to work; lacks the necessary documents*). **2** determined, existing, or happening by natural laws, predestination, etc., not by free will; inevitable (*a necessary evil*). **3** Philos. (of a concept or a mental process) inevitably resulting from or produced by the nature of things etc., so that the contrary is impossible. **4** Philos. (of an agent) having no independent volition. —n. (pl. **-ies**) (usu. in pl.) any of the basic requirements of life, such as food, warmth, etc. □ **the necessary** colloq. **1** money. **2** an action, item, etc., needed for a purpose (*they will do the necessary*). [ME f. OF necessaire f. L necessarius f. necesse needful]

necessitarian /nɪˌsesɪˈteərɪən/ n. & adj. Philos. —n. a person who holds that all action is predetermined and free will is impossible. —adj. of or concerning such a person or theory (opp. LIBERTARIAN). □□ **necessitarianism** n.

necessitate /nɪˈsesɪteɪt/ v.tr. **1** make necessary (esp. as a result) (*will necessitate some sacrifice*). **2** US (usu. foll. by *to* + infin.) force or compel (a person) to do something. [med.L necessitare compel (as NECESSITY)]

necessitous /nɪˈsesɪtəs/ adj. poor; needy. [F nécessiteux or f. NECESSITY + -OUS]

necessity /nɪˈsesɪtɪ/ n. (pl. **-ies**) **1 a** an indispensable thing; a necessary (*central heating is a necessity*). **b** (usu. foll. by *of*) indispensability (*the necessity of a warm overcoat*). **2** a state of things or circumstances enforcing a certain course (*there was a necessity to hurry*). **3** imperative need (*necessity is the mother of invention*). **4** want; poverty; hardship (*stole because of necessity*). **5**

constraint or compulsion regarded as a natural law governing all human action. □ **of necessity** unavoidably. [ME f. OF *nécessité* f. L *necessitas -tatis* f. *necesse* needful]

Nechtansmere /ˈnektənzˌmɪə(r)/ the site (near Forfar in Tayside, Scotland) of a battle in 685 in which the Northumbrians were decisively defeated by the Picts. Their expansion northward was permanently thwarted, and they were forced to withdraw south of the Firth of Forth.

neck /nek/ n. & v. —n. **1 a** the part of the body connecting the head to the shoulders. **b** the part of a shirt, dress, etc. round or close to the neck. **2 a** something resembling a neck, such as the narrow part of a cavity or vessel, a passage, channel, pass, isthmus, etc. **b** the narrow part of a bottle near the mouth. **3** the part of a violin etc. bearing the finger-board. **4** the length of a horse's head and neck as a measure of its lead in a race. **5** the flesh of an animal's neck (*neck of lamb*). **6** *Geol.* solidified lava or igneous rock in an old volcano crater or pipe. **7** *Archit.* the lower part of a capital. **8** *sl.* impudence (*you've got a neck, asking that*). —v. **1** *intr.* & *tr. colloq.* kiss and caress amorously. **2 a** *tr.* form a narrowed part in. **b** *intr.* form a narrowed part. □ **get it in the neck** *colloq.* **1** receive a severe reprimand or punishment. **2** suffer a fatal or severe blow. **neck and neck** running level in a race etc. **neck of the woods** *colloq.* a usu. remote locality. **neck or nothing** risking everything on success. **up to one's neck** (often foll. by *in*) *colloq.* very deeply involved; very busy. □□ **necked** *adj.* (also in *comb.*). **necker** *n.* (in sense 1 of *v.*). **neckless** *adj.* [OE *hnecca* ult. f. Gmc]

neckband /ˈnekbænd/ n. a strip of material round the neck of a garment.

neckcloth /ˈnekklɒθ/ n. *hist.* a cravat.

Necker /ˈnekə(r)/, Jacques (1732–1804), Swiss banker, director-general of French finances 1777–81. He made social and administrative reforms, but aroused the hostility of a leading minister and of Queen Marie Antoinette, and was forced to resign. In 1788, when France was on the verge of bankruptcy, he was recalled to office and proposed a programme of reform, but again aroused the hostility of the Court. News of his dismissal on 11 July 1789 angered the people and, with other rumours, led to the attack on the Bastille. He was reinstated on 20 July but again proved ineffectual and resigned a year later.

neckerchief /ˈnekətʃɪf/ n. a square of cloth worn round the neck.

necking /ˈnekɪŋ/ n. *Archit.* = NECK *n.* 7.

necklace /ˈnekləs, -lɪs/ n. & v. —n. **1** a chain or string of beads, precious stones, links, etc., worn as an ornament round the neck. **2** *S.Afr.* a tyre soaked or filled with petrol, placed round a victim's neck, and set alight. —v.tr. *S.Afr.* kill with a 'necklace'.

necklet /ˈneklɪt/ n. **1** = NECKLACE *n.* 1. **2** a strip of fur worn round the neck.

neckline /ˈneklaɪn/ n. the edge or shape of the opening of a garment at the neck (*a square neckline*).

necktie /ˈnektaɪ/ n. esp. *US* = TIE *n.* 2. □ **necktie party** *sl.* a lynching or hanging.

neckwear /ˈnekweə(r)/ n. collars, ties, etc.

necro- /ˈnekrəʊ/ *comb. form* corpse. [from or after Gk *nekro-* f. *nekros* corpse]

necrobiosis /ˌnekrəʊbaɪˈəʊsɪs/ n. decay in the tissues of the body, esp. swelling of the collagen bundles in the dermis. □□ **necrobiotic** /-ˈɒtɪk/ *adj.*

necrolatry /neˈkrɒlətrɪ/ n. worship of, or excessive reverence towards, the dead.

necrology /neˈkrɒlədʒɪ/ n. (pl. **-ies**) **1** a list of recently dead people. **2** an obituary notice. □□ **necrological** /-rəˈlɒdʒɪk(ə)l/ *adj.*

necromancy /ˈnekrəʊˌmænsɪ/ n. **1** the prediction of the future by the supposed communication with the dead. **2** witchcraft. □□ **necromancer** *n.* **necromantic** /-ˈmæntɪk/ *adj.* [ME f. OF *nigromancie* f. med.L *nigromantia* changed (by assoc. with L *niger nigri* black) f. LL *necromantia* f. Gk *nekromanteia* (as NECRO-, -MANCY)]

necrophilia /ˌnekrəˈfɪlɪə/ n. (also **necrophily** /nɪˈkrɒfɪlɪ/) a morbid and esp. erotic attraction to corpses. □□ **necrophil** /ˈnek-/

n. **necrophile** /ˈnekrəˌfaɪl/ n. **necrophiliac** /-ˈfɪlɪˌæk/ n. **necrophilic** *adj.* **necrophilism** /-ˈkrɒfɪˌlɪz(ə)m/ n. **necrophilist** /-ˈkrɒfɪlɪst/ n. [NECRO- + Gk *-philia* loving]

necrophobia /ˌnekrəˈfəʊbɪə/ n. an abnormal fear of death or dead bodies.

necropolis /neˈkrɒpəlɪs/ n. an ancient cemetery or burial place.

necropsy /ˈneˌkrɒpsɪ/ n. (also **necroscopy** /-ˈkrɒskəpɪ/) (pl. **-ies**) = AUTOPSY 1. [NECRO- after AUTOPSY, or + -SCOPY]

necrosis /neˈkrəʊsɪs/ n. *Med.* & *Physiol.* the death of tissue caused by disease or injury, esp. as one of the symptoms of gangrene or pulmonary tuberculosis. □□ **necrose** /-ˈkrəʊs/ *v.intr.* **necrotic** /-ˈkrɒtɪk/ *adj.* **necrotize** /ˈnekrəˌtaɪz/ *v.intr.* (also **-ise**). [mod.L f. Gk *nekrōsis* (as NECRO-, -OSIS)]

nectar /ˈnektə(r)/ n. **1** a sugary substance produced by plants and made into honey by bees. **2** (in Greek and Roman mythology) the drink of the gods. **3** a drink compared to this. □□ **nectarean** /-ˈteərɪən/ *adj.* **nectareous** /-ˈteərɪəs/ *adj.* **nectariferous** /-ˈrɪfərəs/ *adj.* **nectarous** *adj.* [L f. Gk *nektar*]

nectarine /ˈnektərɪn, -ˌriːn/ n. **1** a variety of peach with a thin brightly-coloured smooth skin and firm flesh. **2** the tree bearing this. [orig. as adj., = nectar-like, f. NECTAR + -INE[4]]

nectary /ˈnektərɪ/ n. (pl. **-ies**) the nectar-secreting organ of a flower or plant. [mod.L *nectarium* (as NECTAR)]

NEDC *abbr.* (in the UK) National Economic Development Council.

neddy /ˈnedɪ/ n. (pl. **-ies**) *colloq.* **1** a donkey. **2** (**Neddy**) = NEDC. [dimin. of *Ned*, pet-form of the name *Edward*]

née /neɪ/ adj. (*US* **nee**) (used in adding a married woman's maiden name after her surname) born (*Mrs Ann Smith, née Jones*). [F, fem. past part. of *naître* be born]

need /niːd/ v. & n. —v. **1** *tr.* stand in want of; require (*needs a new coat*). **2** *tr.* (foll. by *to* + infin.; *3rd sing. present neg. or interrog.* **need** without *to*) be under the necessity or obligation (*it needs to be done carefully; he need not come; need you ask?*). **3** *intr. archaic* be necessary. —n. **1 a** a want or requirement (*my needs are few; the need for greater freedom*). **b** a thing wanted (*my greatest need is a car*). **2** circumstances requiring some course of action; necessity (*there is no need to worry; if need arise*). **3** destitution; poverty. **4** a crisis; an emergency (*failed them in their need*). □ **at need** in time of need. **had need** *archaic* ought to (*had need remember*). **have need of** require; want. **have need to** require to (*has need to be warned*). **in need** requiring help. **in need of** requiring. **need not have** did not need to (but did). [OE *nēodian, nēd* f. Gmc]

needful /ˈniːdfʊl/ adj. **1** requisite; necessary; indispensable. **2** (prec. by *the*) **a** what is necessary. **b** *colloq.* money or action needed for a purpose. □□ **needfully** *adv.* **needfulness** *n.*

needle /ˈniːd(ə)l/ n. & v. —n. **1 a** a very thin small piece of smooth steel etc. pointed at one end and with a slit (eye) for thread at the other, used in sewing. **b** a larger plastic, wooden, etc. slender stick without an eye, used in knitting. **c** a slender hooked stick used in crochet. **2** a pointer on a dial (see *magnetic needle*). **3** any of several small thin pointed instruments, esp.: **a** a surgical instrument for stitching. **b** the end of a hypodermic syringe. **c** = STYLUS. **d** an etching tool. **e** a steel pin exploding the cartridge of a breech-loading gun. **4 a** an obelisk (*Cleopatra's Needle*). **b** a pointed rock or peak. **5** the leaf of a fir or pine tree. **6** a beam used as a temporary support during underpinning. **7** *Brit. sl.* a fit of bad temper or nervousness (*got the needle while waiting*). —v.tr. **1** *colloq.* incite or irritate; provoke (*the silence needled him*). **2** sew, pierce, or operate on with a needle. □ **needle game** (or **match** etc.) *Brit.* a contest that is very close or arouses personal grudges. **needle in a haystack** something almost impossible to find because it is concealed by so many other things etc. **needle-lace** lace made with needles not bobbins. **needle-point 1** a very sharp point. **2** = *needle-lace*. **3** = GROS OR PETIT POINT. **needle's eye** (or **eye of a needle**) the least possible aperture, esp. with ref. to Matt. 19: 24. **needle time** an agreed maximum allowance of time for broadcasting music from records. **needle valve** a valve closed by a thin tapering part. [OE *nǣdl* f. Gmc]

needlecord /ˈniːd(ə)lˌkɔːd/ n. a fine-ribbed corduroy fabric.

needlecraft /ˈniːd(ə)lˌkrɑːft/ n. skill in needlework.

needlefish /'niːd(ə)lfɪʃ/ n. a garfish.

needleful /'niːd(ə)lˌfʊl/ n. (pl. **-fuls**) the length of thread etc. put into a needle at one time.

Needles /'niːdəlz/, **the** a group of rocks in the sea off the south coast of England, near the Isle of Wight.

needless /'niːdlɪs/ adj. **1** unnecessary. **2** uncalled for; gratuitous. □ **needless to say** of course; it goes without saying. □□ **needlessly** adv. **needlessness** n.

needlewoman /'niːd(ə)lˌwʊmən/ n. (pl. **-women**) **1** a seamstress. **2** a woman or girl with specified sewing skill (a good needlewoman).

needlework /'niːd(ə)lˌwɜːk/ n. sewing or embroidery.

needs /niːdz/ adv. archaic (usu. prec. or foll. by must) of necessity (must needs decide). [OE nēdes (as NEED, -S³)]

needy /'niːdɪ/ adj. (**needier, neediest**) **1** (of a person) poor; destitute. **2** (of circumstances) characterized by poverty. □□ **neediness** n.

neep /niːp/ n. Sc. & N.Engl. a turnip. [OE næp f. L napus]

ne'er /neə(r)/ adv. poet. = NEVER. □ **ne'er-do-well** n. a good-for-nothing person. —adj. good-for-nothing. [ME contr. of NEVER]

nefarious /nɪ'feəriəs/ adj. wicked; iniquitous. □□ **nefariously** adv. **nefariousness** n. [L nefarius f. nefas wrong f. ne- not + fas divine law]

Nefertiti /ˌnefə'tiːtɪ/ the chief wife of Akhenaten, possibly co-ruler towards the end of his reign. She fully supported her husband's religious reforms and is invariably represented beside him, with their daughters, on reliefs from Tell el-Amarna. Best known from the painted limestone bust of her (now in Berlin), she merited her name which means 'the beautiful (one) is come' (which did not, however, allude to her own beauty).

neg. abbr. negative.

negate /nɪ'geɪt/ v.tr. **1** nullify; invalidate. **2** imply, involve, or assert the non-existence of. **3** be the negation of. □□ **negator** n. [L negare negat- deny]

negation /nɪ'geɪʃ(ə)n/ n. **1** the absence or opposite of something actual or positive. **2 a** the act of denying. **b** an instance of this. **3** (usu. foll. by of) a refusal, contradiction, or denial. **4** a negative statement or doctrine. **5** a negative or unreal thing; a nonentity. **6** Logic the assertion that a certain proposition is false. □□ **negatory** /'negətɔːrɪ/ adj. [F negation or L negatio (as NEGATE)]

negative /'negətɪv/ adj., n. & v. —adj. **1** expressing or implying denial, prohibition, or refusal (a negative vote; a negative answer). **2** (of a person or attitude): **a** lacking positive attributes; apathetic; pessimistic. **b** opposing or resisting; uncooperative. **3** marked by the absence of qualities (a negative reaction; a negative result from the test). **4** of the opposite nature to a thing regarded as positive (debt is negative capital). **5** Algebra (of a quantity) less than zero, to be subtracted from others or from zero (opp. POSITIVE). **6** Electr. **a** of the kind of charge carried by electrons (opp. POSITIVE). **b** containing or producing such a charge. —n. **1** a negative statement, reply, or word (hard to prove a negative). **2** Photog. **a** an image with black and white reversed or colours replaced by complementary ones, from which positive pictures are obtained. **b** a developed film or plate bearing such an image. **3** a negative quality; an absence of something. **4** (prec. by the) a position opposing the affirmative. **5** Logic = NEGATION 6. —v.tr. **1** refuse to accept or countenance; veto; reject. **2** disprove (an inference or hypothesis). **3** contradict (a statement). **4** neutralize (an effect). □ **in the negative** with negative effect; so as to reject a proposal etc.; no (the answer was in the negative). **negative evidence** (or **instance**) evidence of the non-occurrence of something. **negative feedback 1** the return of part of an output signal to the input, tending to decrease the amplification etc. **2** feedback that tends to diminish or counteract the process giving rise to it. **negative geotropism** see GEOTROPISM. **negative income tax** an amount credited as allowance to a taxed income, and paid as benefit when it exceeds debited tax. **negative pole** the south-seeking pole of a magnet. **negative proposition** Logic = NEGATION 6. **negative quantity** joc. nothing. **negative sign** a symbol (−) indicating subtraction or a value less than zero. **negative virtue** abstention from vice. □□ **negatively** adv.

negativeness n. **negativity** /-'tɪvɪtɪ/ n. [ME f. OF negatif -ive or LL negativus (as NEGATE)]

negativism /'negətɪˌvɪz(ə)m/ n. **1** a negative position or attitude; extreme scepticism, criticism, etc. **2** denial of accepted beliefs. □□ **negativist** n. **negativistic** /-'vɪstɪk/ adj.

Negev /'negev/ a triangular semi-desert region of southern Israel between Beersheba and the Gulf of Aqaba.

neglect /nɪ'glekt/ v. & n. —v.tr. **1** fail to care for or to do; be remiss about (neglected their duty; neglected his children). **2** (foll. by verbal noun, or to + infin.) fail; overlook or forget the need to (neglected to inform them; neglected telling them). **3** not pay attention to; disregard (neglected the obvious warning). —n. **1** lack of caring; negligence (the house suffered from neglect). **2 a** the act of neglecting. **b** the state of being neglected (the house fell into neglect). **3** (usu. foll. by of) disregard. □□ **neglectful** adj. **neglectfully** adv. **neglectfulness** n. [L neglegere neglect- f. neg- not + legere choose, pick up]

negligée /'neglɪˌʒeɪ/ n. (also **negligee, négligé**) **1** (usu. **negligee**) a woman's dressing-gown of thin fabric. **2** unceremonious or informal attire. [F, past part. of négliger NEGLECT]

negligence /'neglɪdʒ(ə)ns/ n. **1 a** a lack of proper care and attention; carelessness. **b** an act of carelessness. **2** Law = contributory negligence. **3** Art freedom from restraint or artificiality. □□ **negligent** adj. **negligently** adv. [ME f. OF negligence or L negligentia f. negligere = neglegere: see NEGLECT]

negligible /'neglɪdʒɪb(ə)l/ adj. not worth considering; insignificant. □ **negligible quantity** a person etc. that need not be considered. □□ **negligibility** /-'bɪlɪtɪ/ n. **negligibly** adv. [obs. F f. négliger NEGLECT]

Negombo /nɪ'gɒmbəʊ/ a seaport on the west coast of Sri Lanka; pop. (1981) 60,700.

negotiable /nɪ'gəʊʃəb(ə)l/ adj. **1** open to discussion or modification. **2** able to be negotiated. □□ **negotiability** /-'bɪlɪtɪ/ n.

negotiate /nɪ'gəʊʃɪˌeɪt/ v. **1** intr. (usu. foll. by with) confer with others in order to reach a compromise or agreement. **2** tr. arrange (an affair) or bring about (a result) by negotiating (negotiated a settlement). **3** tr. find a way over, through, etc. (an obstacle, difficulty, fence, etc.). **4** tr. **a** transfer (a cheque etc.) to another for a consideration. **b** convert (a cheque etc.) into cash or notes. **c** get or give value for (a cheque etc.) in money. □□ **negotiant** /-ʃɪənt/ n. **negotiation** /-ʃɪ'eɪʃ(ə)n, -sɪ'eɪʃ(ə)n/ n. **negotiator** n. [L negotiari f. negotium business f. neg- not + otium leisure]

Negress /'niːgrɪs/ n. a female Negro.

Negrillo /nɪ'grɪləʊ/ n. (pl. **-os**) a member of a very small Negroid people native to Central and southern Africa. [Sp., dimin. of NEGRO]

Negri Sembilan /ˌnəˌgriː səm'biːlən/ a State of Malaysia, on the Malay Peninsula; pop. (1980) 573,600; capital, Seremban.

Negrito /nɪ'griːtəʊ/ n. (pl. **-os**) a member of a small Negroid people native to the Malayo-Polynesian region. (See PYGMY.) [as NEGRILLO]

Negritude /'niːgrɪˌtjuːd/ n. **1** the quality or state of being a Negro. **2** the affirmation or consciousness of the value of Negro culture. [F négritude NIGRITUDE]

Negro¹ /'niːgrəʊ/ n. & adj. —n. (pl. **-oes**) a member of the black- or dark-skinned group of human populations that exist or originated in Africa south of the Sahara. Their physical attributes include (though with wide variations) woolly hair, thick lips, a broad short nose, projecting jaws, and legs that are long relative to the torso. ¶ Now often considered offens.; the term Black is usually preferred. —adj. **1** of or concerning Negroes. **2** (as **negro**) Zool. black or dark (negro ant). □ **Negro spiritual** a religious song derived from the musical traditions of Black people in the southern US. [Sp. & Port., f. L niger nigri black]

Negro² /'neɪgrəʊ/, **Rio** a major river of South America which rises as the Guainia in eastern Colombia and flows about 2,255 km (1,400 miles) through NW Brazil before joining the Amazon near Manaus.

Negroid /'niːgrɔɪd/ adj. & n. —adj. **1** (of features etc.) characterizing a member of the Negro race, esp. in having dark skin, tightly curled hair, and a broad flattish nose. **2** of or concerning Negroes. —n. a Negro. [NEGRO]

Negros /'neɪgrɒs/ the fourth-largest island of the Philippines; pop. (1980) 2,749,700; chief city, Bacolod.

Negus /'niːgəs/ n. hist. the title of the ruler of Ethiopia. [Amh. n'gus king]

negus /'niːgəs/ n. hist. a hot drink of port, sugar, lemon, and spice. [Col. F. Negus d. 1732, its inventor]

Neh. abbr. Nehemiah (Old Testament).

Nehemiah /ˌniːə'maɪə/ 1 a Jewish leader who (c.444 BC) supervised the rebuilding of the walls of Jerusalem and (c.432 BC) introduced moral and religious reforms. His work was continued by Ezra. 2 a book of the Old Testament telling of this rebuilding and of the reforms.

Nehru /'neəruː/, Pandit Jawaharlal (1889–1964), Indian statesman. An early associate of Gandhi, Nehru was among the early leaders of the Indian National Congress, eventually playing a major part in the negotiations preceding independence. He then served as the first Prime Minister of independent India from 1947 until his death. Two years later his daughter, Mrs Indira Gandhi (see entry), became Prime Minister.

neigh /neɪ/ n. & v. —n. 1 the high whinnying sound of a horse. 2 any similar sound, e.g. a laugh. —v. 1 intr. make such a sound. 2 tr. say, cry, etc. with such a sound. [OE hnǣgan, of imit. orig.]

neighbour /'neɪbə(r)/ n. & v. (US **neighbor**) —n. 1 a person living next door to or near or nearest another (my next-door neighbour; his nearest neighbour is 12 miles away; they are neighbours). 2 a a person regarded as having the duties or claims of friendliness, consideration, etc., of a neighbour. b a fellow human being, esp. as having claims on friendship. 3 a person or thing near or next to another (my neighbour at dinner). 4 (attrib.) neighbouring. —v. 1 tr. border on; adjoin. 2 intr. (often foll. by on, upon) border; adjoin. □□ **neighbouring** adj. **neighbourless** adj. **neighbourship** n. [OE nēahgebūr (as NIGH: gebūr, cf. BOOR)]

neighbourhood /'neɪbəˌhʊd/ n. (US **neighborhood**) 1 a a district, esp. one forming a community within a town or city. b the people of a district; one's neighbours. 2 neighbourly feeling or conduct. □ **in the neighbourhood of** roughly; about (paid in the neighbourhood of £100). **neighbourhood watch** systematic local vigilance by householders to discourage crime, esp. against property.

neighbourly /'neɪbəlɪ/ adj. (US **neighborly**) characteristic of a good neighbour; friendly; kind. □□ **neighbourliness** n.

Neill /niːl/, Alexander Sutherland (1883–1973), Scottish-born teacher and educationist. Disillusioned with conventional educational practice, in 1924 he set up the progressive school, Summershill (first at Lyme Regis in Dorset, later at Leiston in Suffolk), for which he became famous, arousing both admiration and hostility.

neither /'naɪðə(r), 'niːð-/ adj., pron., adv., & conj. —adj. & pron. (foll. by sing. verb) 1 not the one nor the other (of two things); not either (neither of the accusations is true; neither of them knows; neither wish was granted; neither went to the fair). 2 disp. none of any number of specified things. —adv. 1 not either; not on the one hand (foll. by nor; introducing the first of two or more things in the negative: neither knowing nor caring; would neither come in nor go out; neither the teachers nor the parents nor the children). 2 not either; also not (if you do not, neither shall I). 3 (with neg.) disp. either (I don't know that neither). —conj. archaic nor yet; nor (I know not, neither can I guess). [ME naither, neither f. OE nowther contr. of nōhwæther (as NO², WHETHER): assim. to EITHER]

Nejd /nedʒd/ the central region of Saudi Arabia, consisting chiefly of desert.

nek /nek/ n. S.Afr. = COL 1. [Du., = NECK]

nekton /'nekt(ə)n/ n. Zool. any aquatic animal able to swim and move independently. [G f. Gk nēkton neut. of nēktos swimming f. nēkhō swim]

nelly /'nelɪ/ n. (pl. **-ies**) a silly or effeminate person. □ **not on your nelly** Brit. sl. certainly not. [perh. f. the name Nelly: idiom f. rhyming sl. Nelly Duff = puff = breath: cf. not on your life]

Nelson[1] /'nels(ə)n/ a port on the north coast of South Island, New Zealand; pop. (1988) 45,200.

Nelson[2] /'nels(ə)n/, Horatio, Viscount Nelson, Duke of Bronté

(1758–1805), British admiral whose victories at sea during the early years of the Napoleonic Wars assured British naval supremacy and made him a national hero, though his affair with Emma, Lady Hamilton, caused great scandal. While still a captain he played a crucial part in the victory over the Spanish at Cape St Vincent in 1797; in the following year he destroyed the French fleet in the Mediterranean at Aboukir Bay, and in 1801 at Copenhagen disobeyed his superior's order to withdraw and won a total victory over the Danes. His final and most famous victory, over the combined fleets of France and Spain at Trafalgar in 1805, effectively ended Napoleon's challenge to British sea power and saved Britain from invasion, although Nelson himself was mortally wounded in the course of the battle.

nelson /'nels(ə)n/ n. a wrestling-hold in which one arm is passed under the opponent's arm from behind and the hand is applied to the neck (**half nelson**), or both arms and hands are applied (**full nelson**). [app. f. the name Nelson]

nelumbo /nɪ'lʌmbəʊ/ n. (pl. **-os**) any water lily of the genus Nelumbo, native to India and China, bearing small pink flowers. Also called LOTUS. [mod.L f. Sinh. neḷum(bu)]

nematocyst /nɪ'mætəsɪst, 'nemə-/ n. a specialized cell in a jellyfish etc. containing a coiled thread that can be projected as a sting. [as NEMATODE + CYST]

nematode /'nemətəʊd/ n. any parasitic or free-living worm of the phylum Nematoda, with a slender unsegmented cylindrical shape. Also called ROUNDWORM. [Gk nēma -matos thread + -ODE[1]]

Nembutal /'nembjuːˌtɑːl/ n. propr. a sodium salt of pentobarbitone, used as a sedative and anticonvulsant. [Na (= sodium) + 5-ethyl-5-(1-methylbutyl) barbiturate + -AL]

nem. con. abbr. with no one dissenting. [L nemine contradicente]

nemertean /nɪ'mɜːtɪən/ n. & adj. (also **nemertine** /-taɪn/) —n. any marine ribbon worm of the phylum Nemertea, often very long and brightly coloured, found in tangled knots in coastal waters of Europe and the Mediterranean. —adj. of or relating to this class. [mod.L Nemertes f. Gk Nēmertēs name of a sea nymph]

nemesia /nɪ'miːʒə/ n. any S. African plant of the genus Nemesia, cultivated for its variously coloured and irregular flowers. [mod.L f. Gk nemesion, the name of a similar plant]

Nemesis /'nemɪsɪs/ Gk Mythol. a goddess, usually the personification of retribution or righteous indignation, especially that of the gods at human wrongdoing. It is puzzling, however, that she is also a deity of the type of Artemis, pursued amorously by Zeus and taking various non-human forms to evade him. [Gk, = retribution (f. nemō give what is due)]

nemesis /'nemɪsɪs/ n. (pl. **nemeses** /-ˌsiːz/) 1 retributive justice. 2 a a downfall caused by this. b an agent of such a downfall. [as NEMESIS]

Nennius /'nenɪəs/ (c.800) Welsh writer, the author or reviser of the Historia Britonum, a collection of notes from several sources on the history and geography of Britain. It is chiefly interesting for the account it purports to give of the historical Arthur.

neo- /'niːəʊ/ comb. form 1 new, modern. 2 a new or revived form of. [Gk f. neos new]

neoclassical /ˌniːəʊ'klæsɪk(ə)l/ adj. (also **neoclassic** /-sɪk/) of or relating to a revival of a classical style or treatment in art, literature, music, etc. In art, the term refers to an aesthetic movement and artistic style which originated in Rome in the mid-18th c. and spread rapidly over Europe and North America, combining a reaction against the excesses of the late baroque and rococo with a new interest in the antique. It was stimulated by discoveries at Herculaneum and Pompeii, the publication of illustrations of archaeological and architectural remains, and the writings of the German art historian Winckelmann, who praised the calm simplicity and noble grandeur of antique art. In music, the term refers to a trend which developed in the 1920s when several composers, especially Stravinsky and Hindemith, wrote works in 17th- and 18th-c. forms and styles as a reaction against the elaborate orchestration of the late 19th-c. Romantics. □□ **neoclassicism** /-ˌsɪz(ə)m/ n. **neoclassicist** /-sɪst/ n.

neocolonialism /ˌniːəʊkə'ləʊnɪəˌlɪz(ə)m/ n. the use of

economic, political, or other pressures to control or influence other countries, esp. former dependencies. □□ **neocolonialist** *n.* & *adj.*

neodymium /ˌniːəˈdɪmɪəm/ *n. Chem.* a silver-grey naturally-occurring metallic element of the lanthanide series, discovered in 1885. The metal is used in certain alloys; its compounds are used in ceramics and for colouring glass. ¶ Symb.: **Nd**; atomic number 60. [NEO- + DIDYMIUM]

neo-impressionism *n.* a movement in French painting. The term was coined by the critic Félix Fénéon in 1886 on seeing pointillist works by Seurat, Signac, and Pissarro at the last impressionist exhibition. The neo-impressionists saw themselves as refining and improving upon impressionist style by introducing greater compositional structure to painting and rationalizing impressionist colour technique. They adhered to classical principles of pictorial composition in pictures that are made up of small dots of pure unmixed colour in an attempt to give greater luminosity. □□ **neo-impressionist** *adj.* & *n.*

neolithic /ˌniːəˈlɪθɪk/ *adj.* & *n. Archaeol.* —*adj.* of or relating to the later part of the Stone Age, when ground or polished stone weapons and implements prevailed. —*n.* this period, which saw the introduction of agriculture and the domestication of animals, sometimes called the 'Neolithic Revolution', turning mankind from being dependent on nature to controlling it at least partially and indirectly. The change led to the establishment of settled communities, accumulation of food and wealth, and heavier growth of population. In the Old World, agriculture began in the Near East by the 8th millenium BC and had spread to northern Europe by the 4th millennium BC. [NEO- + Gk *lithos* stone]

neologism /niːˈɒlədʒɪz(ə)m/ *n.* **1** a new word or expression. **2** the coining or use of new words. □□ **neologist** *n.* **neologize** /-ˌdʒaɪz/ *v.intr.* (also **-ise**). [F *néologisme* (as NEO-, -LOGY, -ISM)]

neomycin /ˌniːəʊˈmaɪsɪn/ *n.* an antibiotic related to streptomycin.

neon /ˈniːɒn/ *n. Chem.* an inert gaseous element occurring in traces in the atmosphere, discovered in 1898. Obtained by the distillation of liquid air, neon is mainly used in fluorescent lamps and advertising signs as it emits a reddish-orange glow when electricity is passed through it in a sealed low-pressure tube. It has no known chemical compounds.¶ Symb.: **Ne**; atomic number 10. [Gk, neut. of *neos* new]

neonate /ˈniːəˌneɪt/ *n.* a newborn child. □□ **neonatal** /-ˈneɪt(ə)l/ *adj.* [mod.L *neonatus* (as NEO-, L *nasci nat-* be born)]

neophyte /ˈniːəˌfaɪt/ *n.* **1** a new convert, esp. to a religious faith. **2** *RC Ch.* **a** a novice of a religious order. **b** a newly ordained priest. **3** a beginner; a novice. [eccl.L *neophytus* f. NT Gk *neophutos* newly planted (as NEO- *phuton* plant)]

neoplasm /ˈniːəʊˌplæz(ə)m/ *n.* a new and abnormal growth of tissue in some part of the body, esp. a tumour. □□ **neoplastic** /-ˈplæstɪk/ *adj.* [NEO- + Gk *plasma* formation: see PLASMA]

neo-plasticism /ˌniːəʊˈplæstɪˌsɪz(ə)m/ *n.* a movement or style in art originated by the Dutch painter Piet Mondrian, characterized by the use of primary colours and abstract forms.

Neoplatonism /ˌniːəʊˈpleɪtəˌnɪz(ə)m/ *n.* the revived Platonism—really a synthesis of elements from the philosophies of Plato, Pythagoras, Aristotle, and the Stoics, with overtones of Oriental mysticism—which was the dominant philosophy of the pagan world from the mid-3rd c. AD down to the closing of the pagan schools by Justinian in 529, and strongly influenced medieval and Renaissance thought. Its abiding shape was given to it by Plotinus, whose central doctrine postulates a hierarchy of being, at the summit of which is the transcendent One, immaterial and indescribable. The human soul aspires to knowledge of this One through ascetic virtue and sustained contemplation, and in doing so rises above the imperfection and multiplicity of the material world; a philosophical and religious system developed by the followers of Plotinus in the third c., combining Platonic thought with oriental mysticism. □□ **Neoplatonic** /-pləˈtɒnɪk/ *adj.* **Neoplatonist** *n.*

neoprene /ˈniːəʊˌpriːn/ *n.* a synthetic rubber-like polymer. [NEO- + *chloroprene* etc. (perh. f. PROPYL + -ENE)]

Neoptolemus /ˌniːəpˈtɒlɪməs/ *Gk legend* the son of Achilles. [Gk, = young warrior]

neoteny /nɪˈɒtɪnɪ/ *n.* the retention of juvenile features in the adult form of some animals, e.g. an axolotl. □□ **neotenic** /-ˈtenɪk/ *adj.* **neotenous** *adj.* [G *Neotenie* (as NEO- + Gk *teinō* extend)]

neoteric /ˌniːəˈterɪk/ *adj. literary* recent; newfangled; modern. [LL *neotericus* f. Gk *neōterikos* (*neōteros* compar. of *neos* new)]

neotropical /ˌniːəʊˈtrɒpɪk(ə)l/ *adj.* of or relating to tropical and S. America as a biogeographical region.

Nepal /nəˈpɔːl/ a country in southern Asia, bordered by China (Tibet) to the north and India to the south, dominated by the Himalayas including Mount Everest; pop. (est. 1988) 18,252,000; official language, Nepali; capital, Kathmandu. A remote landlocked and mountainous country, Nepal has a very poor transportation and communications system and few regular contacts with the outside world. The country was conquered by the Gurkhas in the 18th c. and despite defeats by the British in the early 19th c. has maintained its independence, supplying contingents of soldiers to fight in British armies up to the present day. Gautama Buddha was born in Nepal. Democratic elections were held in 1990 after 18 years as an absolute monarchy.

Nepalese /ˌnepəˈliːz/ *adj.* & *n.* (*pl.* same) = NEPALI.

Nepali /nɪˈpɔːlɪ/ *n.* & *adj.* —*n.* (*pl.* same or **Nepalis**) **1 a** a native or national of Nepal. **b** a person of Nepali descent. **2** the official language of Nepal, spoken also in parts of NE India. It belongs to the Indic branch of the Indo-European family of languages. —*adj.* of or relating to Nepal or its language or people.

nepenthe /nɪˈpenθɪ/ *n.* = NEPENTHES 1. [var. of NEPENTHES, after It. *nepente*]

nepenthes /nɪˈpenθiːz/ *n.* **1** *poet.* a drug causing forgetfulness of grief. **2** any pitcher-plant of the genus *Nepenthes*. [L f. Gk *nēpenthes* (*pharmakon* drug), neut. of *nēpenthēs* f. *nē-* not + *penthos* grief]

nephew /ˈnevjuː, ˈnef-/ *n.* a son of one's brother or sister, or of one's brother-in-law or sister-in-law. [ME f. OF *neveu* f. L *nepos nepotis* grandson, nephew]

nephology /nɪˈfɒlədʒɪ/ *n.* the study of clouds. [Gk *nephos* cloud + -LOGY]

nephrite /ˈnefraɪt/ *n.* a green, yellow, or white calcium magnesium silicate form of jade. [G *Nephrit* f. Gk *nephros* kidney, with ref. to its supposed efficacy in treating kidney disease]

nephritic /nɪˈfrɪtɪk/ *adj.* **1** of or in the kidneys; renal. **2** of or relating to nephritis. [LL *nephriticus* f. Gk *nephritikos* (as NEPHRITIS)]

nephritis /nɪˈfraɪtɪs/ *n.* inflammation of the kidneys. Also called *Bright's disease*. [LL f. Gk *nephros* kidney]

nephro- /ˈnefrəʊ/ *comb. form* (usu. **nephr-** before a vowel) kidney. [Gk f. *nephros* kidney]

Nepia /ˈniːpɪə/, George (1905–86), New Zealand rugby football player.

ne plus ultra /ˌneɪ plʊs ˈʊltrɑː/ *n.* **1** the furthest attainable point. **2** the culmination, acme, or perfection. [L, = not further beyond, the supposed inscription on the Pillars of Hercules (the Strait of Gibraltar) prohibiting passage by ships]

nepotism /ˈnepəˌtɪz(ə)m/ *n.* favouritism shown to relatives in conferring offices or privileges. □□ **nepotist** *n.* **nepotistic** /-ˈtɪstɪk/ *adj.* [F *népotisme* f. It. *nepotismo* f. *nepote* NEPHEW: orig. with ref. to popes with illegitimate sons euphemistically called nephews]

Neptune /ˈneptjuːn/ **1** *Rom. Mythol.* the god of water (not of the sea, though his identification with Poseidon extended his cult in this aspect). **2** *Astron.* the third-largest of the planets, most distant of the giant planets of the solar system, orbiting the sun at a distance of almost four and a half thousand million km. It was discovered in 1846 by J. G. Galle, working at the Berlin Observatory and using the calculations of Le Verrier (similar predictions had been made by the English mathematician John Couch Adams). Little is known of this world (49,500 km in diameter) save that it possesses a dense cold atmosphere of hydrogen and helium, probably lying on top of a mantle of icy materials which surround a dense solid core. The surface temperature is probably less than 60° above absolute zero. There are two named moons, Triton and Nereid, and six others.

Neptunian /nepˈtjuːnɪən/ adj. **1** Geol. produced by the action of water; maintaining that the action of water played a principal part in the formation of certain rocks (see NEPTUNIST). **2** of the planet Neptune.

Neptunist /ˈneptjuːnɪst/ n. a person (esp. in the 18th c.) maintaining the Neptunian theory of the origin of certain rocks (opp. Plutonist or Vulcanist).

neptunium /nepˈtjuːnɪəm/ n. Chem. a radioactive transuranic metallic element, first obtained in 1940 by irradiating uranium with neutrons and since discovered in trace amounts in nature. ¶ Symb.: Np; atomic number 93. [NEPTUNE, as the next planet beyond Uranus, + -IUM]

NERC abbr. (in the UK) Natural Environment Research Council.

nerd /nɜːd/ n. (also **nurd**) esp. US sl. a foolish, feeble, or uninteresting person. □□ **nerdy** adj. [20th c.: orig. uncert.]

nereid /ˈnɪərɪɪd/ n. Gk Mythol. any of the sea-nymphs, daughters of Nereus. They include Thetis, mother of Achilles. [L Nereïs Nereïd- f. Gk Nēreïs -idos daughter of Nereus]

Nereus /ˈnɪərɪəs/ Gk Mythol. an old sea-god who had the power, like Proteus, of assuming various forms.

nerine /nɪˈraɪnɪ/ n. any S. African plant of the genus Nerine, bearing flowers with usu. six narrow strap-shaped petals, often crimped and twisted. [mod.L f. the L name of a water-nymph]

Nero /ˈnɪərəʊ/ (Nero Claudius Caesar, 15–68) Roman emperor 54–68, the adopted successor of Claudius. His reign started promisingly, but after procuring the murder of his mother Agrippina in 59, he became increasingly capricious and repressive. Executions of leading Romans on charges of treason led to conspiracies against him and more executions; his unpopularity was increased by a fire which destroyed half of Rome in 64 and during which he was rumoured to have recited his own poem on the fall of Troy. A wave of uprisings in 68 led to his flight from Rome and to suicide. A lover of things Greek, he was an extravagant practitioner and patron of the arts.

neroli /ˈnɪərəlɪ/ n. (in full **neroli oil**) an essential oil from the flowers of the Seville orange, used in perfumery. [F néroli f. It. neroli, perh. f. the name of an Italian princess]

Nerva /ˈnɜːvə/, Marcus Cocceius (30–98), Roman emperor 96–8. Appointed emperor by the Senate after the murder of Domitian, he returned to a liberal and constitutional form of rule after the autocracy of his predecessor.

nervate /ˈnɜːveɪt/ adj. (of a leaf) having veins. □□ **nervation** /-ˈveɪʃ(ə)n/ n. [NERVE + -ATE²]

nerve /nɜːv/ n. & v. —n. **1 a** a fibre or bundle of fibres that transmits impulses of sensation or motion between the brain or spinal cord and other parts of the body. **b** the material constituting these. **2 a** coolness in danger; bravery; assurance. **b** colloq. impudence, audacity (they've got a nerve). **3** (in pl.) **a** the bodily state in regard to physical sensitiveness and the interaction between the brain and other parts. **b** a state of heightened nervousness or sensitivity; a condition of mental or physical stress (need to calm my nerves). **4** a rib of a leaf, esp. the midrib. **5** poet. archaic a sinew or tendon. —v.tr. **1** (usu. refl.) brace (oneself) to face danger, suffering, etc. **2** give strength, vigour, or courage to. □ **get on a person's nerves** irritate or annoy a person. **have nerves of iron** (or **steel**) (of a person etc.) be not easily upset or frightened. **nerve-cell** an elongated branched cell transmitting impulses in nerve tissue. **nerve-centre 1** a group of closely connected nerve cells associated in performing some function. **2** the centre of control of an organization etc. **nerve gas** a poisonous gas affecting the nervous system. **nerve-racking** stressful, frightening; straining the nerves. □□ **nerved** adj. (also in comb.). [ME, = sinew, f. L nervus, rel. to Gk neuron]

nerveless /ˈnɜːvlɪs/ adj. **1** inert, lacking vigour or spirit. **2** confident; not nervous. **3** (of style) diffuse. **4** Bot. & Entomol. without nervures. **5** Anat. & Zool. without nerves. □□ **nervelessly** adv. **nervelessness** n.

Nervi /ˈnɜːvɪ/, Pier Luigi (1891–1979), Italian architectural engineer, regarded as one of Europe's most innovative designers of the 20th c. He is known for his mastery of new technology and materials, especially reinforced concrete, which he used with effect in his Giovanni Berta stadium in Florence (1929–32). His Exhibition Hall at Turin (1948–9) incorporated his theories on 'strength through form', with an enormous lightweight roof, similar to his earlier military hangar designs (from 1935). In 1952 he was appointed one of the architects to collaborate on the design of the UNESCO building in Paris. His major architectural projects of the 1950s include Naples Railway Station (1954) and the Pirelli skyscraper in Milan of 1958; his later works include San Francisco Cathedral.

nervine /ˈnɜːvaɪn/ adj. & n. —adj. relieving nerve-disorders. —n. a nervine drug. [F nervin (as NERVE)]

nervo- /ˈnɜːvəʊ/ comb. form (also **nerv-** before a vowel) a nerve or the nerves.

nervous /ˈnɜːvəs/ adj. **1** having delicate or disordered nerves. **2** timid or anxious. **3 a** excitable; highly strung; easily agitated. **b** resulting from this temperament (nervous tension; a nervous headache). **4** affecting or acting on the nerves. **5** (foll. by of + verbal noun) reluctant, afraid (am nervous of meeting them). □ **nervous breakdown** a period of mental illness, usu. resulting from severe depression or anxiety. **nervous system** see separate entry. **nervous wreck** colloq. a person suffering from mental stress, exhaustion, etc. □□ **nervously** adv. **nervousness** n. [ME f. L nervosus (as NERVE)]

nervous system n. the nerves and nerve-centres as a whole, allowing an animal to coordinate its response to its environment, and (in some) to initiate behaviour. □ **autonomic nervous system** (in man and other vertebrates) that controlling or influencing involuntary functions (e.g. heartbeat, digestive processes). **central nervous system** the brain and spinal cord of vertebrates; an equivalent concentration of nerve cells in invertebrates. **peripheral nervous system** (in vertebrates) that consisting of the cranial nerves (supplying the face and head), spinal nerves (distributed to the limb and trunk muscles and skin), and the autonomic nervous system.

nervure /ˈnɜːvjʊə(r)/ n. **1** each of the hollow tubes that form the framework of an insect's wing; a venule. **2** the principal vein of a leaf. [F nerf nerve]

nervy /ˈnɜːvɪ/ adj. (**nervier**, **nerviest**) **1** nervous; easily excited or disturbed. **2** US bold, impudent. **3** archaic sinewy, strong. □□ **nervily** adv. **nerviness** n.

Nesbit /ˈnezbɪt/, Edith (1858–1924), English writer, best remembered for her humorous imaginative stories for children, such as The Treasure Seekers (1899) and The Wouldbegoods (1901). Other titles with a lasting appeal include The Phoenix and the Carpet (1904) and The Railway Children (1906). She and her first husband, Hubert Bland, were founder members of the Fabian Society.

nescient /ˈnesɪənt/ adj. literary (foll. by of) lacking knowledge; ignorant. □□ **nescience** n. [LL nescientia f. L nescire not know f. ne- not + scire know]

ness /nes/ n. a headland or promontory. [OE næs, rel. to OE nasu NOSE]

-ness /nɪs/ suffix forming nouns from adjectives, and occas. other words, expressing: **1** state or condition, or an instance of this (bitterness; conceitedness; happiness; a kindness). **2** something in a certain state (wilderness). [OE -nes, -ness f. Gmc]

nest /nest/ n. & v. —n. **1** a structure or place where a bird lays eggs and shelters its young. **2** an animal's or insect's breeding-place or lair. **3** a snug or secluded retreat or shelter. **4** (often foll. by of) a place fostering something undesirable (a nest of vice). **5** a brood or swarm. **6** a group or set of similar objects, often of different sizes and fitting together for storage (a nest of tables). —v. **1** intr. use or build a nest. **2** intr. take wild birds' nests or eggs. **3** intr. (of objects) fit together or one inside another. **4** tr. (usu. as **nested** adj.) establish in or as in a nest. □ **nest egg 1** a sum of money saved for the future. **2** a real or artificial egg left in a nest to induce hens to lay eggs there. □□ **nestful** n. (pl. **-fuls**). **nesting** n. (in sense 2 of v.). **nestlike** adj. [OE nest]

nestle /ˈnes(ə)l/ v. **1** intr. (often foll. by down, in, etc.) settle oneself comfortably. **2** *intr.* press oneself against another in affection etc. **3** *tr.* (foll. by *in*, *into*, etc.) press (a head or shoulder etc.) affectionately or snugly. **4** *intr.* lie half hidden or embedded. [OE *nestlian* (as NEST)]

nestling /ˈneslɪŋ, ˈnest-/ *n.* a bird that is too young to leave its nest.

Nestor /ˈnestə(r)/ *Gk legend* a king of Pylos in the Peloponnese, who in old age led his subjects to the Trojan War, where his wisdom and eloquence were proverbial.

Nestorianism /nesˈtɔːrɪəˌnɪz(ə)m/ *n.* the doctrine that there were two separate persons, one human and one divine, in the incarnate Christ, as opposed to the orthodox teaching that there was a single person, both God and man. The theory takes its name from Nestorius, patriarch of Constantinople from 428. What he actually taught, and how far it was heretical, is now disputed, but a violent controversy developed over the use of the term *theotokos* (Gk, = bearer of God) as an epithet of the Virgin Mary, and Nestorius was deposed and banished. His supporters in Syria and Persia gradually constituted themselves into a separate Nestorian Church, which became active in missionary work in India, Arabia, and China before suffering drastic losses in the Mongol invasions of Persia in the 14th c.

net[1] /net/ *n. & v.* —*n.* **1** an open-meshed fabric of cord, rope, fibre, etc. **2** a piece of net used esp. to restrain, contain, or delimit, or to catch fish or other animals. **3** a structure with net to enclose an area of ground, esp. in sport. **4 a** a structure with net used in various games, esp. forming the goal in football, netball, etc., and dividing the court in tennis etc. **b** (often in *pl.*) a practice-ground in cricket, surrounded by nets. **5** a system or procedure for catching or entrapping a person or persons. **6** = NETWORK. —*v.* (**netted**, **netting**) **1** *tr.* **a** cover, confine, or catch with a net. **b** procure as with a net. **2** *tr.* hit (a ball) into the net, esp. of a goal. **3** *intr.* make netting. **4** *tr.* make (a purse, hammock, etc.) by knotting etc. threads together to form a net. **5** *tr.* fish with nets, or set nets, in (a river). **6** *tr.* (usu. as **netted** *adj.*) mark with a netlike pattern; reticulate. □□ **netful** *n.* (*pl.* **-fuls**). [OE *net, nett*]

net[2] /net/ *adj. & v.* (also **nett**) —*adj.* **1** (esp. of money) remaining after all necessary deductions, or free from deductions. **2** (of a price) to be paid in full; not reducible. **3** (of a weight) excluding that of the packaging or container etc. **4** (of an effect, result, etc.) ultimate, effective. —*v.tr.* (**netted**, **netting**) gain or yield (a sum) as net profit. □ **net book agreement** an agreement, set up in 1899, between booksellers and publishers, by which booksellers will not offer books to the public at a price below that marked on the book's cover. Exceptions include school textbooks, books that are remaindered at a reduced price, and books offered in a national book sale. **net profit** the effective profit; the actual gain after working expenses have been paid. **net ton** see TON[1]. [F *net* NEAT[1]]

netball /ˈnetbɔːl/ *n.* a seven-a-side game in which a ball has to be thrown so as to fall through an elevated horizontal ring from which a net hangs. It was introduced into England from the US in 1895 as the indoor version of basketball, and is played almost entirely by girls and women, and mainly in English-speaking countries.

nether /ˈneðə(r)/ *adj. archaic* = LOWER[1]. □ **nether regions** (or **world**) hell; the underworld. □□ **nethermost** *adj.* [OE *nithera* etc. f. Gmc]

Netherlands /ˈneðələndz/, **The** (Dutch **Nederland**). **1** a country (often called Holland) in western Europe bordering on the North Sea, with Belgium on its southern frontier; pop. (est. 1988) 14,716,100; official language, Dutch; capital, Amsterdam; seat of government, The Hague. **2** *hist.* the Low Countries, the area now occupied by Holland, Belgium, Luxembourg, and small parts of France and Germany. □□ **Netherlander** *n.* **Netherlandish** *adj.* [Du. (as NETHER, LAND)]
The area was occupied by Celts and Frisians who came under Roman rule from the 1st c. BC until the 4th c. AD, and was then overrun by German tribes with the Franks establishing an ascendancy (5th–8th c.). During the Middle Ages it was divided between numerous principalities. Part of the Hapsburg empire

in the 16th c., the northern (Dutch) part revolted against Spanish attempts to crush the Protestant faith and won independence in a series of wars lasting into the 17th c., becoming a Protestant republic; meanwhile the southern part passed to the Spanish Hapsburgs and then in 1713 to the Austrian Hapsburgs. Prior to wars with England and France the country enjoyed great prosperity and became a centre of art and scholarship as well as a leading maritime power, building up a vast commercial empire in the East Indies, South Africa, and Brazil, but in the 18th c. sharply declined as a European power. In 1814 north and south were united under a monarchy, but the south revolted in 1830 and became an independent kingdom, Belgium, in 1839; Luxembourg gained its independence in 1867. The Netherlands managed to maintain its neutrality in the First World War but was occupied by the Germans in the Second. The postwar period has seen the country turn away from its traditional dependence on agriculture to emerge as an industrial power.

Netherlands Antilles two groups of Dutch islands in the West Indies. One group comprises the islands of Bonaire and Curaçao which lie 60 km (37 miles) north of the Venezuelan coast. The more northerly group, which includes the islands of St Eustatius, St Martin, and Saba is situated at the northern end of the Lesser Antilles; capital; Willemstad; pop. (1988) 182,700. The islands were settled by the Dutch between 1634 and 1648 and later, with Aruba, formed part of the Dutch West Indies (1828) and Netherland Antilles (1845). In 1954 the islands were granted self-government and in 1986 Aruba separated from the group in advance of becoming an independent State.

netsuke /ˈnetsʊkɪ/ *n.* (*pl.* same or **netsukes**) (in Japan) a carved button-like ornament, esp. of ivory or wood, formerly worn to suspend articles from a girdle. [Jap.]

nett var. of NET[2].

netting /ˈnetɪŋ/ *n.* **1** netted fabric. **2** a piece of this.

nettle /ˈnet(ə)l/ *n. & v.* —*n.* **1** any plant of the genus *Urtica*, esp. *U. dioica*, with jagged leaves covered with stinging hairs. **2** any of various plants resembling this. —*v.tr.* **1** irritate, provoke, annoy. **2** sting with nettles. □ **nettle-rash** a skin eruption like nettle stings. [OE *netle, netele*]

network /ˈnetwɜːk/ *n. & v.* —*n.* **1** an arrangement of intersecting horizontal and vertical lines, like the structure of a net. **2** a complex system of railways, roads, canals, etc. **3** a group of people who exchange information, contacts, and experience for professional or social purposes. **4** a chain of interconnected computers, machines, or operations. **5** a system of connected electrical conductors. **6** a group of broadcasting stations connected for a simultaneous broadcast of a programme. —*v.* **1** *tr.* broadcast on a network. **2** *intr.* establish a network. **3** *tr.* link (machines, esp. computers) to operate interactively. **4** *intr.* be a member of a network (see sense 3 of *n.*).

networker /ˈnetˌwɜːkə(r)/ *n.* **1** *Computing* a member of an organization or computer network who operates from home or from an external office. **2** a member of a professional or social network.

Neuchatel /ˌnɜːʃæˈtel/, **Lake** the largest lake lying wholly within Switzerland, situated at the foot of the Jura Mountains in western Switzerland.

Neumann /ˈnɔɪmən/, John von (1903–57), Hungarian-born mathematician who migrated to the US in 1930. His fundamental contributions ranged over the whole of mathematics, from the purest parts of logic and set theory to the most practical areas of application in economics, computer design, aerodynamics, meteorology, and astrophysics. His analysis (1927–32) of the mathematics of quantum mechanics supplied that infant theory with the necessary environment in which to grow and founded a vigorous new area of mathematical research (algebras of operators in Hilbert space). He established the mathematical theory of games (see GAME THEORY) and, with Oskar Morgenstern, exhibited its applications to economics and policy-making. But perhaps his most influential contributions were his work at Los Alamos on the harnessing of nuclear energy both for military and for peacetime uses, and his work on the design and use of high-speed electronic computing machines, the immediate forerunners of the ubiquitous computers that have so enormously changed our world.

neume /njuːm/ n. (also **neum**) Mus. a sign in plainsong indicating a note or group of notes to be sung to a syllable. [ME f. OF neume f. med.L neu(p)ma f. Gk pneuma breath]

neural /ˈnjʊər(ə)l/ adj. of or relating to a nerve or the central nervous system. □□ **neurally** adv. [Gk neuron nerve]

neuralgia /njʊəˈrældʒə/ n. an intense intermittent pain along the course of a nerve, esp. in the head or face. □□ **neuralgic** adj. [as NEURAL + -ALGIA]

neurasthenia /ˌnjʊərəsˈθiːnɪə/ n. a general term for fatigue, anxiety, listlessness, etc. (not in medical use). □□ **neurasthenic** /-ˈθenɪk/ adj. & n. [Gk neuron nerve + ASTHENIA]

neuritis /njʊəˈraɪtɪs/ n. inflammation of a nerve or nerves. □□ **neuritic** /-ˈrɪtɪk/ adj. [formed as NEURO- + -ITIS]

neuro- /ˈnjʊərəʊ/ comb. form a nerve or the nerves. [Gk neuron nerve]

neurogenesis /ˌnjʊərəʊˈdʒenɪsɪs/ n. the growth and development of nervous tissue.

neurogenic /ˌnjʊərəʊˈdʒenɪk/ adj. caused by or arising in nervous tissue.

neuroglia /njʊəˈrɒglɪə/ n. the connective tissue supporting the central nervous system. [NEURO- + Gk glia glue]

neurohormone /ˌnjʊərəʊˈhɔːməʊn/ n. a hormone produced by nerve-cells and secreted into the circulation.

neurology /njʊəˈrɒlədʒɪ/ n. the scientific study of nerve systems. □□ **neurological** /-rəˈlɒdʒɪk(ə)l/ adj. **neurologically** /-rəˈlɒdʒɪkəlɪ/ adv. **neurologist** n. [mod.L neurologia f. mod. Gk (as NEURO-, -LOGY)]

neuroma /njʊəˈrəʊmə/ n. (pl. **neuromas** or **neuromata** /-mətə/) a tumour on a nerve or in nerve-tissue. [Gk neuron nerve + -OMA]

neuromuscular /ˌnjʊərəʊˈmʌskjʊlə(r)/ adj. of or relating to nerves and muscles.

neuron /ˈnjʊərɒn/ n. (also **neurone** /-rəʊn/) a specialized cell transmitting nerve impulses; a nerve-cell. □□ **neuronal** /-ˈrəʊn(ə)l/ adj. **neuronic** /-ˈrɒnɪk/ adj. [Gk neuron nerve]

neuropath /ˈnjʊərəʊˌpæθ/ n. a person affected by nervous disease, or with an abnormally sensitive nervous system. □□ **neuropathic** /-ˈpæθɪk/ adj. **neuropathy** /-ˈrɒpəθɪ/ n.

neuropathology /ˌnjʊərəʊpəˈθɒlədʒɪ/ n. the pathology of the nervous system. □□ **neuropathologist** n.

neurophysiology /ˌnjʊərəʊˌfɪzɪˈɒlədʒɪ/ n. the physiology of the nervous system. □□ **neurophysiological** /-zɪəˈlɒdʒɪk(ə)l/ adj. **neurophysiologist** n.

neuropteran /njʊəˈrɒptərən/ n. any insect of the order Neuroptera, including lacewings, having four finely-veined membranous leaflike wings. □□ **neuropterous** adj. [NEURO- + Gk pteron wing]

neurosis /njʊəˈrəʊsɪs/ n. (pl. **neuroses** /-siːz/) a mental illness characterized by irrational or depressive thought or behaviour, caused by a disorder of the nervous system usu. without organic change. [mod.L (as NEURO-, -OSIS)]

neurosurgery /ˌnjʊərəʊˈsɜːdʒərɪ/ n. surgery performed on the nervous system, esp. the brain and spinal cord. □□ **neurosurgeon** n. **neurosurgical** adj.

neurotic /njʊəˈrɒtɪk/ adj. & n. —adj. 1 caused by or relating to neurosis. 2 (of a person) suffering from neurosis. 3 colloq. abnormally sensitive or obsessive. —n. a neurotic person. □□ **neurotically** adv. **neuroticism** /-ˌsɪz(ə)m/ n.

neurotomy /njʊəˈrɒtəmɪ/ n. (pl. **-ies**) the operation of cutting a nerve, esp. to produce sensory loss.

neurotransmitter /ˈnjʊərəʊtrænsˌmɪtə(r)/ n. Biochem. a chemical substance released from a nerve fibre that effects the transfer of an impulse to another nerve or muscle.

Neusiedler See /ˈnɔɪziːdlə(r) zeɪ/ (Hungarian **Fertö Tó** /ˈfɜː tuː təʊ/) a shallow steppe lake straddling the frontier between eastern Austria and NW Hungary.

neuter /ˈnjuːtə(r)/ adj., n., & v. —adj. 1 Gram. (of a noun etc.) neither masculine nor feminine. 2 (of a plant) having neither pistils nor stamen. 3 (of an insect) sexually undeveloped. —n. 1 Gram. a neuter gender or word. 2 a a non-fertile insect, esp. a worker bee or ant. b a castrated animal. —v.tr. castrate or spay. [ME f. OF neutre or L neuter neither f. ne- not + uter either]

neutral /ˈnjuːtr(ə)l/ adj. & n. —adj. 1 not helping or supporting either of two opposing sides, esp. States at war or in dispute; impartial. 2 belonging to a neutral party, State, etc. (neutral ships). 3 indistinct, vague, indeterminate. 4 (of a gear) in which the engine is disconnected from the driven parts. 5 (of colours) not strong or positive; grey or beige. 6 Chem. neither acid nor alkaline. 7 Electr. neither positive nor negative. 8 Biol. sexually undeveloped; asexual. —n. 1 a a neutral State or person. b a subject of a neutral State. 2 a neutral gear. □□ **neutrally** adv. [ME f. obs. F neutral or L neutralis of neuter gender (as NEUTER)]

neutralism /ˈnjuːtrəˌlɪz(ə)m/ n. a policy of political neutrality. □□ **neutralist** n.

neutralize /ˈnjuːtrəˌlaɪz/ v.tr. (also **-ise**) 1 make neutral. 2 counterbalance; render ineffective by an opposite force or effect. 3 exempt or exclude (a place) from the sphere of hostilities. □□ **neutralization** /-ˈzeɪʃ(ə)n/ n. **neutralizer** n. [F neutraliser f. med.L neutralizare (as NEUTRAL)]

neutrino /njuːˈtriːnəʊ/ n. (pl. **-os**) any of a group of stable elementary particles with zero electric charge and probably zero mass, which travel at the speed of light. [It., dimin. of neutro neutral (as NEUTER)]

neutron /ˈnjuːtrɒn/ n. an elementary particle of about the same mass as a proton but without an electric charge, present in all atomic nuclei except those of ordinary hydrogen. (See below.) □ **neutron bomb** a bomb producing neutrons and little blast, causing damage to life but little destruction to property. **neutron star** a hypothetical object of very small radius (typically 30 km), thought to form after a supernova explosion near the end of the life cycle of a massive star, when the original atomic material of the star has been compressed to such high densities that neutrons form from electrically charged particles. [NEUTRAL + -ON]

Intense research into the structure and properties of atomic nuclei led to the discovery of the neutron (the term was suggested by Rutherford) in 1932. Although neutrons have no resultant electric charge they behave like tiny magnets, which suggests that they have an internal electrical structure. Free neutrons are unstable, with a half-life of approximately 1,000 seconds. Because they are electrically neutral, a beam of neutrons can easily penetrate the nucleus of an atom, rendering it unstable and inducing radioactive fission. Neutrons are particularly important in nuclear reactors where a controlled flux of slow neutrons, produced in the reaction itself, also maintains that reaction.

Nev. abbr. Nevada.

Nevada /nɪˈvɑːdə/ a State of the western US; pop. (est. 1985) 800,500; capital, Carson City. Acquired from Mexico in 1848, it became the 36th State of the US in 1864.

névé /ˈneveɪ/ n. an expanse of granular snow not yet compressed into ice at the head of a glacier. [Swiss F, = glacier, ult. f. L nix nivis snow]

never /ˈnevə(r)/ adv. 1 a at no time; on no occasion; not ever (have never been to Paris; never saw them again). b colloq. as an emphatic negative (I never heard you come in). 2 not at all (never fear). 3 colloq. (expressing surprise) surely not (you never left the key in the lock!). □ **never-never** (often prec. by the) Brit. colloq. hire purchase. **never-never land** an imaginary utopian place. **never a one** none. **never say die** see DIE¹. **well I never!** expressing great surprise. [OE næfre f. ne not + æfre EVER]

nevermore /ˌnevəˈmɔː(r)/ adv. at no future time.

Never-Never Austral. the far interior of Australia; the remote outback; esp. (**Never-Never Land** or **Country**) a region of Northern Territory south-east of Darwin. The reason calling the area by this name is disputed. The chief settlement is Katherine.

nevertheless /ˌnevəðəˈles/ adv. in spite of that; notwithstanding; all the same.

Nevis /ˈniːvɪs/ one of the Leeward Islands, forming part of the

State of St Kitts and Nevis; pop. approx. 9,300; capital, Charlestown.

Nevsky /ˈnevskɪ/, Alexander (1220–63), Russian soldier prince, famous for his victories over the invading Swedes in 1240 on the River Neva (from which he got his name) and the Teutonic Knights two years later on the ice of Lake Peipus.

nevus US var. of NAEVUS.

new /njuː/ adj. & adv. —adj. **1 a** of recent origin or arrival. **b** made, invented, discovered, acquired, or experienced recently or now for the first time (a new star; has many new ideas). **2** in original condition; not worn or used. **3 a** renewed or reformed (a new life; the new order). **b** reinvigorated (felt like a new person). **4** different from a recent previous one (has a new job). **5** in addition to others already existing (have you been to the new supermarket?). **6** (often foll. by to) unfamiliar or strange (a new sensation; the idea was new to me). **7** (often foll. by at) (of a person) inexperienced, unaccustomed (to doing something) (am new at this business). **8** (usu. prec. by the) often derog. **a** later, modern. **b** newfangled. **c** given to new or modern ideas (the new man). **d** recently affected by social change (the new rich). **9** (often prec. by the) advanced in method or theory (the new formula). **10** (in place-names) discovered or founded later than and named after (New York; New Zealand). —adv. (usu. in comb.) **1** newly, recently (new-found; new-baked). **2** anew, afresh. □ **new birth** Theol. spiritual regeneration. **new broom** see BROOM. **New Commonwealth** see COMMONWEALTH. **new deal** new arrangements or conditions, esp. when better than the earlier ones. (See also NEW DEAL.) **New Kingdom** a period of ancient Egyptian history (see EGYPT). **new-laid** (of an egg) freshly laid. **new look** a new or revised appearance or presentation, esp. of something familiar. **the new mathematics** (or **maths**) a system of teaching mathematics to children, with emphasis on investigation by them and on set theory. **New Model Army** see MODEL. **new moon 1** the moon when first seen as a crescent after conjunction with the sun. **2** the time of its appearance. **a new one** (often foll. by on) colloq. an account or idea not previously encountered (by a person). **new potatoes** the earliest potatoes of a new crop. **new star** a nova. **new style** dating reckoned by the reformed or Gregorian Calendar. **New Testament** see separate entry. **new town** Brit. a town established as a completely new settlement with government sponsorship. **new wave 1** = NOUVELLE VAGUE. **2** a style of rock music popular in the 1970s. **New World** North and South America regarded collectively in relation to Europe. The term was first applied to the Americas (also to other areas, e.g. Australia) after the early voyages of European explorers. (Cf. old world.) **new year 1** the calendar year just begun or about to begin. **2** the first few days of a year. **New Year's Day** 1 January. **New Year's Eve** 31 December. □□ **newish** adj. **newness** n. [OE nīwe f. Gmc]

Newark /ˈnjuːək/ an industrial city of New Jersey, on the Passaic River; pop. (1982) 320,500.

newborn /njuːˈbɔːn, ˈnjuːbɔːn/ adj. **1** (of a child etc.) recently born. **2** spiritually reborn; regenerated.

New Britain an island of Papua New Guinea, lying between the islands of New Guinea and New Ireland; pop. (1980) 219,100; capital, Rabaul.

New Brunswick /ˈbrʌnzwɪk/ a maritime province (from 1867) of SE Canada, settled by the French and ceded to Britain in 1713; pop. (1986) 710,400; capital, Fredericton.

New Caledonia an island in the SW Pacific Ocean, since 1946 forming, with its dependencies, a French Overseas Territory; pop. (est. 1988) 151,000; capital, Nouméa. It was inhabited for at least 3,000 years before the arrival of Captain James Cook (1774), who named the main island after the Roman name for Scotland. The French annexed the island in 1853, and after the discovery of nickel there (1863) it assumed some economic importance for France. There has been a growing movement for independence.

Newcastle[1] /ˈnjuːkɑːs(ə)l/ an industrial port on the coast of New South Wales, Australia; pop. (1986) 429,300.

Newcastle[2] /ˈnjuːˌkɑːs(ə)l/, Thomas Pelham-Holles, 1st Duke of (1693–1768), British statesman, Prime Minister 1754–6 and (in coalition with the elder Pitt until 1761) 1757–62.

Newcastle upon Tyne a city on the River Tyne in NE England; pop. (1981) 203,600.

Newcomen /ˈnjuːkʌmən/, Thomas (1663–1729), English metalworker, inventor of the first practical steam engine, which is named after him. The engine was a steam-operated pump; its design infringed the patent held by Thomas Savery, and was later greatly improved by James Watt.

newcomer /ˈnjuːˌkʌmə(r)/ n. **1** a person who has recently arrived. **2** a beginner in some activity.

New Deal the economic measures introduced by Franklin D. Roosevelt as President of the US in 1933 to counteract the effects of the Great Depression which had gravely affected the American economy. The New Deal depended largely on a massive public works programme, complemented by the large-scale granting of loans, and succeeded in reducing unemployment by between 7 and 10 million.

newel /ˈnjuːəl/ n. **1** the supporting central post of winding stairs. **2** the top or bottom supporting post of a stair-rail. [ME f. OF noel, nouel, knob f. med.L nodellus dimin. of L nodus knot]

New England the part of the US comprising the States of Maine, New Hampshire, Vermont, Massachusetts, Rhode Island, and Connecticut. The name was given to it by the English explorer John Smith in 1614.

newfangled /njuːˈfæŋɡ(ə)ld/ adj. derog. different from what one is used to; objectionably new. [ME newfangle (now dial.) liking what is new f. newe NEW adv. + -fangel f. OE fangol (unrecorded) inclined to take]

New Forest an area of heath and woodland in south Hampshire, reserved as Crown property since 1079, originally (by William I) as a royal hunting area. William II was killed by an arrow when hunting there in 1100.

Newfoundland /ˈnjuːfəndlənd, -ˈfaʊndlənd/ a large island at the mouth of the St Lawrence River. It was discovered in 1497 by John Cabot, and founded as an English colony by Sir Humphrey Gilbert; in 1949 it was united with Labrador (as Newfoundland and Labrador) as a province of Canada; pop. (1986) 568,300; capital, St John's. —n. (in full **Newfoundland dog**) **1** a dog of a very large breed with a thick coarse coat. **2** this breed. □□ **Newfoundlander** n.

Newgate /ˈnjuːɡeɪt/ a former London prison, originally the gatehouse of the main west gate to the city, first used as a prison in the early Middle Ages and rebuilt and enlarged with funds left to the city by Richard Whittington. Its unsanitary conditions became notorious in the 18th c. before the building was burnt down in the anti-Catholic riots of 1780. A new edifice was erected on the same spot soon after but was demolished in 1902 to make way for the Central Criminal Court. The Newgate Calendar (or Malefactors' Bloody Register) was published c.1774 and dealt with notorious crimes from 1700 to that date; later series were issued c.1826.

New Hampshire a State in the north-eastern US, bordering on the Atlantic; pop. (est. 1985) 920,600; capital, Concord. It was settled from England in the 17th c. and was one of the original 13 States of the US.

New Hebrides see VANUATU.

Ne Win /neɪ ˈwɪn/ (1911–), Burmese general and statesman, chief of staff to Aung San's Burma National Army from 1943, prime minister 1958–60, and head of State from 1962, following the success of the military coup which he led. His military dictatorship restructured the political system of Burma, establishing a one-party State; although he stepped down from the presidency in 1981, and nominally retired altogether in 1988, his influence remained considerable.

New Ireland an island of Papua New Guinea, lying to the north of New Britain; pop. (1980) 65,650; capital, Kavieng.

New Jersey a State of the US, bordering on the Atlantic; pop. (est. 1985) 7,365,000; capital, Trenton. Colonized by Dutch settlers and ceded to Britain in 1664, it became one of the original 13 States of the US.

Newlands /ˈnjuːləndz/, John Alexander Reina (1837–98), English industrial chemist who proposed a periodic table shortly before Mendeleev, based on his 'law of octaves'. He observed that if elements were arranged in order of atomic weight, similar chemical properties appeared in every eighth element, a pattern he likened to the musical scale. The significance of his idea was not understood until Mendeleev's periodic table of chemical classification, based on his periodic law, had been accepted.

newly /ˈnjuːlɪ/ adv. **1** recently (a friend newly arrived; a newly-discovered country). **2** afresh, anew (newly painted). **3** in a new or different manner (newly arranged). □ **newly-wed** a recently married person.

Newman[1] /ˈnjuːmən/, Barnett (1905–70), American painter, one of the originators (c.1948) of colour field painting, in which pictorial incident within the painting is replaced by an overall effect orientated to the canvas edge. The characteristic look of his paintings was of large rectangular bands of uniformly saturated pigment dividing the canvas into two or more coloured areas. A dramatic move away from the dynamic gestural painting of abstract expressionism, his art had a profound influence in the 1950s.

Newman[2] /ˈnjuːmən/, John Henry (1801–91), a leader of the Oxford Movement, and later cardinal. He wrote twenty-four of the Tracts for the Times, initially defending Anglicanism, but from 1839 he came increasingly to doubt the Anglican claims, and in 1845 was received into the Roman Catholic Church. His works include Apologia pro vita sua (1864), written in answer to Charles Kingsley, and his poem The Dream of Gerontius (1865), depicting the soul's journey to God.

Newman[3] /ˈnjuːmən/, Paul (1925–), American film actor, director, and producer. His characteristic role was as the cool and witty hero, with an ironic detachment masking a certain idealism, in films that include Hud (1963), Butch Cassidy and the Sundance Kid (1969), and The Sting (1973).

Newmarket /ˈnjuːˌmɑːkɪt/ a town in Suffolk, noted as a horse-racing centre; pop. (1981) 16,129. —n. a gambling card-game in which players seek to play cards that match those on the table.

New Mexico a State in the south-western US; pop. (est. 1985) 1,303,300; capital, Santa Fé. Obtained from Mexico in 1848 and 1854, it became the 47th State of the US in 1912.

New Orleans /ɔːˈlɪənz/ an industrial port of Louisiana, on the Gulf of Mexico; pop. (1982) 564,600. The city is noted for its annual Mardi Gras celebrations and for its association with the origins of jazz (see entry).

New Plymouth a seaport on the west coast of North Island, New Zealand; pop. (1988) 47,800.

Newry /ˈnjuːrɪ/ a port in County Down, in the south-east of Northern Ireland; pop. (1981) 19,400.

news /njuːz/ n.pl. (usu. treated as sing.) **1** information about important or interesting recent events, esp. when published or broadcast. **2** (prec. by the) a broadcast report of news. **3** newly received or noteworthy information. **4** (foll. by to) colloq. information not previously known (to a person) (that's news to me). □ **news agency** an organization that collects and distributes news items. **news bulletin** a collection of items of news, esp. for broadcasting. **news conference** a press conference. **news-gatherer** n. a person who researches news items esp. for broadcast or publication. **news-gathering** this process. **news room** a room in a newspaper or broadcasting office where news is processed. **news-sheet** a simple form of newspaper; a newsletter. **news-stand** a stall for the sale of newspapers. **news-vendor** a newspaper-seller. □□ **newsless** adj. [ME, pl. of NEW after OF noveles or med.L nova neut. pl. of novus new]

newsagent /ˈnjuːzˌeɪdʒ(ə)nt/ n. Brit. a seller of or shop selling newspapers and usu. related items, e.g. stationery.

newsboy /ˈnjuːzbɔɪ/ n. a boy who sells or delivers newspapers.

newsbrief /ˈnjuːzbriːf/ n. a short item of news, esp. on television; a newsflash.

newscast /ˈnjuːzkɑːst/ n. a radio or television broadcast of news reports.

newscaster /ˈnjuːzˌkɑːstə(r)/ n. = NEWSREADER.

newsdealer /ˈnjuːzˌdiːlə(r)/ n. US = NEWSAGENT.

newsflash /ˈnjuːzflæʃ/ n. a single item of important news broadcast separately and often interrupting other programmes.

newsgirl /ˈnjuːzɡɜːl/ n. a girl who sells or delivers newspapers.

newsletter /ˈnjuːzˌletə(r)/ n. an informal printed report issued periodically to the members of a society, business, organization, etc.

newsman /ˈnjuːzmæn/ n. (pl. **-men**) a newspaper reporter; a journalist.

newsmonger /ˈnjuːzˌmʌŋɡə(r)/ n. a gossip.

New South Wales a State in SE Australia, first colonized from Britain in 1788 and federated with the other States of Australia in 1901; pop. (1986) 5,570,000; capital, Sydney.

newspaper /ˈnjuːzˌpeɪpə(r)/ n. **1** a printed publication (usu. daily or weekly) containing news, advertisements, correspondence, etc. (See below.) **2** the sheets of paper forming this (wrapped in newspaper).

Daily publication of news dates back to ancient Rome where, in 59 BC, the practice began of writing public announcements about social and political matters (the Acta Diurna, = daily gazette) on a large whitened board in the city centre. For centuries news was circulated to important persons by letters. Handwritten news-sheets circulated reports of current events, and the invention of printing enabled more to be circulated at lower cost. The first regular public newspapers appeared in Europe in the mid-17th c., and the first English daily paper, the Daily Courant, in 1702; they were subject to various kinds of control. In England, government censorship was not ended until 1695, and reporting of Parliamentary debates was forbidden until 1772. The papers were often corrupt (bribes were used to control their comments on public figures) and prosecutions for libel were freely made by the royal family, government, and Church authorities who were the recipients of published criticism. A tax on newspapers, instituted in 1712, continued under various forms for nearly 150 years. During the 18th c., however, increasing revenue from advertisements (see ADVERTISE) encouraged editors to resist bribes, and reporting became more independent. During the 19th c. improvements in printing technology, and the setting up of international news agencies, together with the spread of literacy (which newspapers aided) all contributed to the general expansion of newspapers, and from the 1890s a more popular approach, offering amusing or sensational items of news, was introduced from America (see NORTHCLIFFE). In the 20th c. many newspapers have merged into large groups and a number of the less successful papers have ceased to be published. Introduction of computer technology has transformed established methods of production.

newspaperman /ˈnjuːzˌpeɪpəˌmæn/ n. (pl. **-men**) a journalist.

Newspeak /ˈnjuːzspiːk/ n. ambiguous euphemistic language used esp. in political propaganda. [an artificial official language in George Orwell's Nineteen Eighty-Four (1949)]

newsprint /ˈnjuːzprɪnt/ n. a type of low-quality paper on which newspapers are printed.

newsreader /ˈnjuːzˌriːdə(r)/ n. a person who reads out broadcast news bulletins.

newsreel /ˈnjuːzriːl/ n. a short cinema film of recent events. The regular issue of newsreels in the conventional sense—several short items grouped together—was begun in 1908. During the 1930s they appeared once or twice a week in Britain and America and lasted about 15 minutes, forming a familiar part of cinema programmes. Newsreels played an important role in the Second World War, but after the war the greater topicality of television caused them to be dropped.

newsworthy /ˈnjuːzˌwɜːðɪ/ adj. topical; noteworthy as news. □□ **newsworthiness** n.

newsy /ˈnjuːzɪ/ adj. (**newsier**, **newsiest**) colloq. full of news.

newt /njuːt/ n. any of various small amphibians, esp. of the genus Triturus, having a well-developed tail. [ME f. ewt, with n from an (cf. NICKNAME): var. of evet EFT]

New Territories that part of the territory of Hong Kong lying to the north of the Kowloon peninsula and including the islands of Lantau, Tsing Yi, and Lamma. Under the 1898 Convention of Peking the New Territories (comprising 92 per cent of the land area of Hong Kong) were leased to Britain by China for a period of 99 years. (See HONG KONG.)

b but d dog f few g get h he j yes k cat l leg m man n no p pen r red s sit t top v voice

New Testament the 27 books of the Bible recording the life and teaching of Christ and some of his earliest followers, written originally in Greek. At an early date the Church came to regard some of its own writings, especially those held to be of Apostolic origin, as of equal authority and inspiration to those received from Judaism. The canon of the New Testament, based on the four Gospels and the Epistles of St Paul, came into existence largely without definition. It was probably formally fixed at Rome in 382 when the Christian Old Testament (based on the Septuagint) was also defined.

Newton /'nju:t(ə)n/, Sir Isaac (1642–1727), English mathematician and physicist, the greatest single influence on theoretical physics until Einstein. His most productive period, which he called his *annus mirabilis* (1666–7), was when Cambridge University, where he had taken his bachelor's degree in 1665, was closed because of the plague. Retreating to his parents' home in Lincolnshire he laid the foundations of his future successes in mathematics, optics, dynamics (mechanics), and astronomy. He discovered the binomial theorem, and made contributions to algebra, geometry, and the theory of infinite series, all somewhat overshadowed by his most famous contribution to mathematics—the differential calculus (his 'method of fluxions') for finding rates of change of varying quantities, and his discovery of its relationship with what is now called integration (then 'quadrature'), the problem of finding the area of a figure circumscribed by curved boundaries. A bitter quarrel with the philosopher Leibniz ensued, as to which of them had discovered calculus first. His optical experiments, begun in 1666, led to his discovery that white light is made up of a mixture of coloured rays. In his major treatise, *Philosophiae Naturalis Principia Mathematica*, he gave a mathematical description of the laws of mechanics and gravitation, and applied this theory to explain planetary and lunar motion. For most purposes Newtonian mechanics has survived even the 20th-c. introduction of relativity theory and quantum mechanics (to both of which theories it stands as a first, but very good, approximation) as a mathematical description of terrestrial and cosmological phenomena. In 1699 Newton was appointed Master of the Mint, and was responsible for an urgently needed reform of the coinage. He entered Parliament as MP for Cambridge University in 1701, and in 1703 was elected President of the Royal Society, whose reputation he greatly increased over the following twenty-four years. Newton interested himself also in alchemy, astrology, and theology, and attempted a biblical chronology. He disliked criticism, and was involved in several bitter controversies with fellow scientists. The newton (see entry) is named in his honour. He is buried in Westminster Abbey.

newton /'nju:t(ə)n/ *n. Physics* the SI unit of force that, acting on a mass of one kilogram, increases its velocity by one metre per second every second along the direction that it acts. ¶ Abbr.: **N.** [Sir Isaac NEWTON]

Newtonian /nju:'təʊnɪən/ *adj.* of or devised by Isaac Newton. □ **Newtonian mechanics** the system of mechanics which relies on Newton's laws of motion concerning the relations between forces acting and motions occurring. **Newtonian telescope** a reflecting telescope with a small secondary mirror at 45° to the main beam of light to reflect it into a magnifying eyepiece.

New York 1 a State of the US, bordering on the Atlantic, one of the original 13 States of the Union (1788); pop. (est. 1985) 17,558,200; capital, Albany. **2** the richest and most populous city of the US (pop. (1984) 7,165,000), and its greatest port, containing the financial centre Wall Street, industries of every kind, two universities, and an opera house, art galleries and museums that are world famous, and the headquarters of the United Nations. The Hudson River and Manhattan Island were discovered in 1609, and in 1629 Dutch colonists purchased Manhattan from the Indians for 24 dollars' worth of trinkets, establishing a settlement there which they called New Amsterdam. In 1664 the English naval officer who received the Dutch surrender renamed it in honour of the Duke of York (later James II), who was at that time Lord High Admiral of England. In 1789 George Washington took his oath as first President of the US in New York. Because of the island's small area and the

firm foundations afforded by its rock, Manhattan has been built upwards, with skyscrapers that give its characteristic skyline.

New Zealand /'zi:lənd/ a country in the South Pacific, a member State of the Commonwealth, about 1,900 km (1,200 miles) east of Australia, consisting of two major islands (North and South Islands) separated by Cook Strait, and several smaller islands; pop. (est. 1988) 3,343,300; capital, Wellington. The discoverers and first colonists of the country were Polynesians (see MAORI). It was sighted by the Dutch navigator Tasman in 1642, and named after The Netherlands province of Zeeland. The islands were circumnavigated by Cook in 1769–70, and came under British sovereignty in 1840; colonization led to a series of wars with the native Maoris in the 1860s and 1870s. Full dominion status was granted in 1907, and independence in 1931. In recent years there has been a huge increase in Polynesian immigrants. The economy is heavily agricultural, with meat, wool, and dairy products forming the principal exports; there has been a boom in horticulture and an increase in small manufacturing industries. The country has reserves of coal and iron ore, and natural gas is also found. Tourism is an expanding industry. □□ **New Zealander** *n.*

next /nekst/ *adj., adv., n.,* & *prep.* —*adj.* **1** (often foll. by *to*) being or positioned or living nearest (*in the next house; the chair next to the fire*). **2** the nearest in order of time; the first or soonest encountered or considered (*next Friday; ask the next person you see*). —*adv.* **1** (often foll. by *to*) in the nearest place or degree (*put it next to mine; came next to last*). **2** on the first or soonest occasion (*when we next meet*). —*n.* the next person or thing. —*prep. colloq.* next to. □ **next-best** the next in order of preference. **next door** see DOOR. **next of kin** the closest living relative or relatives. **next** to almost (*next to nothing left*). **the next world** see WORLD. [OE *nēhsta* superl. (as NIGH)]

nexus /'neksəs/ *n.* (*pl.* same) **1** a connected group or series. **2** a bond; a connection. [L f. *nectere nex-* bind]

Ney /neɪ/, Michel (1768–1815), French marshal, one of Napoleon's leading generals, known for his personal courage as 'the bravest of the brave'. He commanded the French cavalry at Waterloo, and after Napoleon's defeat and final overthrow was executed by the Bourbons despite attempts by Wellington and other allied leaders to intervene on his behalf.

NF *abbr.* (in the UK) National Front.

Nfld *abbr.* (also **NF**) Newfoundland.

NFU *abbr.* (in the UK) National Farmers' Union.

n.g. *abbr.* no good.

NGA *abbr.* (in the UK) National Graphical Association.

ngaio /'naɪəʊ/ *n.* (*pl.* **-os**) a small New Zealand tree, *Myoporum laetum*, with edible fruit and light white timber. [Maori]

Ngamiland /ŋ'gɑ:mɪˌlænd/ a district of NW Botswana that includes the Okavango marshes and Lake Ngami.

Ngata /'ŋɑ:tə/, Sir Apirana Turupa (1874–1950), New Zealand Maori leader and politician, who as Minister for Native Affairs devoted much time to Maori resettlement on the land. Believing firmly in the continuing individuality of the Maori people, he sought to preserve the characteristic elements of their life and culture, including tribal customs and folklore, and emphasized pride in Maori traditions and history.

NGO *abbr.* non-governmental organization.

Ngorongoro Crater /ŋɡəʊrənˈɡəʊrəʊ/ a huge extinct volcanic crater in NE Tanzania, designated a conservation area in 1959 to protect the wildlife that is abundant within it. The area includes the Olduvai Gorge (see entry).

NH *abbr. US* New Hampshire (also in official postal use).

NHI *abbr.* (in the UK) National Health Insurance.

NHS *abbr.* (in the UK) National Health Service.

Nhulunbuy /ˌnjuːlənˈbaɪ/ a bauxite-mining centre on the Gove Peninsula of Arnhem Land in Northern Territory, Australia; pop. (1986) 3,800.

NI *abbr.* **1** (in the UK) National Insurance. **2** Northern Ireland.

Ni *symb. Chem.* the element nickel.

niacin /'naɪəsɪn/ *n.* = NICOTINIC ACID. [*nicotinic acid* + -IN]

Niagara /naɪˈægərə/ a river forming the US–Canada border between Lakes Erie and Ontario, famous for its spectacular waterfalls which are over 45 m (150 ft.) high. The falls are a major source of hydroelectric power.

Niamey /ˈnjɑːmeɪ/ the capital of Niger; pop. (1983) 399,100.

nib /nɪb/ *n. & v.* —*n.* **1** the point of a pen, which touches the writing surface. **2** (in *pl.*) shelled and crushed coffee or cocoa beans. **3** the point of a tool etc. —*v.* (**nibbed, nibbing**) **1** *tr.* provide with a nib. **2** *tr.* mend the nib of. **3** *tr. & intr.* nibble. [prob. f. MDu. *nib* or MLG *nibbe*, var. of *nebbe* NEB]

nibble /ˈnɪb(ə)l/ *v. & n.* —*v.* **1** *tr. &* (foll. by *at*) *intr.* **a** take small bites at. **b** eat in small amounts. **c** bite at gently or cautiously or playfully. **2** *intr.* (foll. by *at*) show cautious interest in. —*n.* **1** an instance of nibbling. **2** a very small amount of food. **3** *Computing* half a byte, i.e. 4 bits. □□ **nibbler** *n.* [prob. of LG or Du. orig.: cf. LG *nibbeln* gnaw]

Nibelung /ˈniːbəˌlʊŋ/ *Germanic Mythol.* **1** a member of a Scandinavian race of dwarfs, owners of a hoard of gold and magic treasures, who were ruled by Nibelung, king of Nibelheim (land of mist). **2** (in the Nibelungenlied) any of the supporters of Siegfried, the subsequent possessor of the hoard; any of the Burgundians who stole it from him.

Nibelungenlied /ˈniːbəˌlʊŋənˌliːd/ a 13th-c. Germanic poem, embodying a story found in the Edda, telling of the life and death of Siegfried, a prince of The Netherlands, and of its avenging by his wife Kriemhild, a Burgundian princess. There have been many adaptations of the story, including Wagner's epic music drama *Der Ring des Nibelungen* (1852–74). [NIBELUNG + G *lied* song]

niblick /ˈnɪblɪk/ *n. Golf* an iron with a large round heavy head, used esp. for playing out of bunkers. [19th c.: orig. unkn.]

nibs /nɪbz/ *n.* □ **his nibs** *joc. colloq.* a mock title used with reference to an important or self-important person. [19th c.: orig. unkn. (cf. earlier *nabs*)]

Nicaea /naɪˈsiːə/ an ancient city in Asia Minor, on the site of modern Iznik, important in Roman and Byzantine times. It was the sit of two ecumenical councils of the Church. The first, in 325, condemned Arianism and produced a creed (see NICENE CREED). The second, in 787, condemned the iconoclasts.

Nicaragua[1] /ˌnɪkəˈrægjʊə/ the largest country in Central America, with a coastline on both the Atlantic and the Pacific Ocean; pop. (est. 1988) 3,407,200; official language, Spanish; capital, Managua. Columbus sighted the eastern coast in 1502, and the country was colonized by the Spaniards in the early 16th c. It broke away in 1821, and after brief membership of the Central American Federation became an independent republic in 1838. Since then its history has been scarred by border disputes and internal disturbances, the last witnessing the successful overthrow of the dictator Anastasio Somoza in 1979, followed by a counter-revolutionary campaign against the new left-wing Sandinista regime. In the 1990 election Daniel Ortega and the Sandinistas were defeated, and Nicaragua had a democratically elected government. The country's economy, frequently disrupted by war, is overwhelmingly agricultural. □□ **Nicaraguan** *adj. & n.*

Nicaragua[2], **Lake** a lake near the west coast of Nicaragua. With an area of 8,026 sq. km (3,100 sq. miles) it is the largest lake in Central America.

Nice /niːs/ a resort city on the French Riviera; pop. (1982) 338,500.

nice /naɪs/ *adj.* **1** pleasant, agreeable, satisfactory. **2** (of a person) kind, good-natured. **3** *iron.* bad or awkward (*a nice mess you've made*). **4 a** fine or subtle (*a nice distinction*). **b** requiring careful thought or attention (*a nice problem*). **5** fastidious; delicately sensitive. **6** punctilious, scrupulous (*were not too nice about their methods*). **7** (foll. by an *adj.*, often with *and*) satisfactory or adequate in terms of the quality described (*a nice long time; nice and warm*). □ **nice work** a task well done. □□ **nicely** *adv.* **niceness** *n.* **nicish** *adj.* (also **niceish**). [ME, = stupid, wanton f. OF, = silly, simple f. L *nescius* ignorant (as *nescience*: see NESCIENT)]

Nicene Creed /naɪˈsiːn, ˈnaɪ-/ *n.* a formal statement of Christian belief that appears in the Thirty-nine Articles, based on that adopted at the first Council of Nicaea in 325. [*Nicene* ME f. LL *Nicenus* of Nicaea]

nicety /ˈnaɪsɪtɪ/ *n.* (*pl.* **-ies**) **1** a subtle distinction or detail. **2** precision, accuracy. **3** intricate or subtle quality (*a point of great nicety*). **4** (in *pl.*) **a** minutiae; fine details. **b** refinements, trimmings. □ **to a nicety** with exactness. [ME f. OF *niceté* (as NICE)]

niche /nɪtʃ, niːʃ/ *n. & v.* —*n.* **1** a shallow recess, esp. in a wall to contain a statue etc. **2** a comfortable or suitable position in life or employment. **3** an appropriate combination of conditions for a species to thrive. —*v.tr.* (often as **niched** *adj.*) **1** place in a niche. **2** ensconce (esp. oneself) in a recess or corner. [F f. *nicher* make a nest, ult. f. L *nidus* nest]

Nicholas[1] /ˈnɪkələs/ the name of two emperors of Russia:

Nicholas I (1796–1855), brother of Alexander I, reigned 1825–55. A far harsher character than his predecessor Alexander, Nicholas pursued rigidly conservative policies, maintaining serfdom and building up a large secret police which proved more than a match for radical reformers. He was largely concerned with keeping the peace in Europe, but his expansionist policies in the Near East finally brought war with Britain and France in the Crimea.

Nicholas II (1868–1918), son of Alexander III, reigned 1894–1917. Reactionary and ineffective, Nicholas proved incapable of coping with the dangerous political legacy left him by his father and tended to fall too easily under the sway of favourites such as Rasputin who, like the Tsar, failed to perceive the need for reform. After the disastrous war with Japan (1904–5) Russia was racked by unrest, but the programme of reforms initiated thereafter (including the creation of the Duma) did no more than paper over the cracks, and the Tsarist regime disintegrated altogether under the strain of fresh military disasters during the First World War. Nicholas was forced to abdicate after the Russian Revolution in 1917 and was murdered along with his family by the Bolsheviks a year later.

Nicholas[2] /ˈnɪkələs/, St (4th c.), bishop of Myra in Lycia and patron saint of children, sailors, and Russia. Little is known of his life but he was the subject of many legends, and immensely popular in the West following the translation of his supposed remains to Bari in SE Italy (1087). The cult of Santa Claus (a corruption of his name) arose in North America from the Dutch custom of giving gifts to children on his feast-day (6 Dec.), a practice now usually transferred to Christmas.

Nicholson /ˈnɪkəls(ə)n/, Ben (1894–1982), English painter and maker of painted reliefs, one of the most distinguished pioneers of abstract art in Britain, noted especially for his still lifes. From 1932 to 1951 he was married to Barbara Hepworth.

Nichrome /ˈnaɪkrəʊm/ *n. propr.* a group of nickel-chromium alloys used for making wire in heating elements etc. [NICKEL + CHROME]

Nick /nɪk/ *n.* □ **Old Nick** the Devil. [prob. f. a pet-form of the name *Nicholas*]

nick[1] /nɪk/ *n. & v.* —*n.* **1** a small cut or notch. **2** *Brit. sl.* **a** a prison. **b** a police station. **3** (prec. by *in* with *adj.*) *Brit. colloq.* condition (*in reasonable nick*). **4** the junction between the floor and walls in a squash court. —*v.tr.* **1** make a nick or nicks in. **2** *Brit. sl.* **a** steal. **b** arrest, catch. □ **in the nick of time** only just in time; just at the right moment. [ME: orig. uncert.]

nick[2] /nɪk/ *v.intr. Austral. sl.* (foll. by *off, in,* etc.) move quickly or furtively. [19th c.: orig. uncert. (cf. NIP[1] 4)]

nickel /ˈnɪk(ə)l/ *n. & v.* —*n.* **1** *Chem.* a malleable ductile silver-white metallic transition element. (See below.). ¶ Symb.: **Ni**; atomic number 28. **2** *colloq.* a US five-cent coin. —*v.tr.* (**nickelled, nickelling**; US **nickeled, nickeling**) coat with nickel. □ **nickel brass** an alloy of copper, zinc, and a small amount of nickel. **nickel-plated** coated with nickel by plating. **nickel silver** = *German silver*. **nickel steel** a type of stainless steel with chromium and nickel. □□ **nickelic** *adj.* **nickelous** *adj.* [abbr. of G *Kupfernickel* copper-coloured ore, from which nickel was first obtained, f. *Kupfer* copper + *Nickel* demon, with ref. to the ore's failure to yield copper]

Nickel, first isolated in 1751, is widely used in alloys (especially with iron, where it imparts strength and resistance to corrosion) and in coinage. The unalloyed metal is used to form a protective and decorative coat on other metals, and as a catalyst in the hydrogenation of oils to form fats, notably in the manufacture of margarine.

nickelodeon /ˌnɪkəˈləʊdɪən/ n. US colloq. a jukebox. [NICKEL + MELODEON]

nicker /ˈnɪkə(r)/ n. (pl. same) Brit. sl. a pound (in money). [20th c.: orig. unkn.]

nick-nack var. of KNICK-KNACK.

nickname /ˈnɪkneɪm/ n. & v. —n. a familiar or humorous name given to a person or thing instead of or as well as the real name. —v.tr. 1 give a nickname to. 2 call (a person or thing) by a nickname. [ME f. eke-name, with n from an (cf. NEWT): eke = addition, f. OE ēaca (as EKE)]

Nicobar Islands see ANDAMAN AND NICOBAR ISLANDS.

nicol /ˈnɪk(ə)l/ n. (in full **nicol prism**) a device for producing plane-polarized light, consisting of two pieces of cut calcite cemented together with Canada balsam. [W. Nicol, Sc. physicist d. 1851, its inventor]

Nicosia /ˌnɪkəˈsiːə/ the capital of Cyprus, divided since 1974 into Greek and Turkish sectors; pop. (est. 1982) 161,000.

nicotine /ˈnɪkəˌtiːn/ n. a colourless poisonous alkaloid present in tobacco. □□ **nicotinism** n. **nicotinize** v.tr. (also -ise). [F f. mod.L nicotiana (herba) tobacco-plant, f. J. Nicot, Fr. diplomat & introducer of tobacco into France in the 16th c.]

nicotinic acid /ˌnɪkəˈtɪnɪk/ n. a vitamin of the B complex, found in milk, liver, and yeast, a deficiency of which causes pellagra. Also called NIACIN.

nictitate /ˈnɪktɪˌteɪt/ v.intr. close and open the eyes; blink or wink. □ **nictitating membrane** a clear membrane forming a third eyelid in amphibians, birds, and some other animals, that can be drawn across the eye to give protection without loss of vision. □□ **nictitation** /-ˈteɪʃ(ə)n/ n. [med.L nictitare frequent. of L nictare blink]

nide /naɪd/ n. (Brit. **nye** /naɪ/) a brood of pheasants. [F nid or L nidus: see NIDUS]

nidificate /ˈnɪdɪfɪˌkeɪt/ v.intr. = NIDIFY.

nidify /ˈnɪdɪˌfaɪ/ v.intr. (-ies, -ied) (of a bird) build a nest. □□ **nidification** /-fɪˈkeɪʃ(ə)n/ n. [L nidificare f. NIDUS nest]

nidus /ˈnaɪdəs/ n. (pl. **nidi** /-daɪ/ or **niduses**) 1 a place in which an insect etc. deposits its eggs, or in which spores or seeds develop. 2 a place in which something is nurtured or developed. [L, rel. to NEST]

niece /niːs/ n. a daughter of one's brother or sister, or of one's brother-in-law or sister-in-law. [ME f. OF ult. f. L neptis granddaughter]

niello /nɪˈeləʊ/ n. (pl. **nielli** /-liː/ or **-os**) 1 a black composition of sulphur with silver, lead, or copper, for filling engraved lines in silver or other metal. 2 a such ornamental work. b an object decorated with this. □□ **nielloed** adj. [It. f. L nigellus dimin. of niger black]

nielsbohrium /niːlzˈbɔːrɪəm/ n. the Russian name for the element of atomic number 105, a short-lived artificially produced radioactive transuranic element (cf. HAHNIUM). The preferred name for it is now unnilpentium. [Niels BOHR]

Niemeyer /ˈniːmaɪə(r)/, Oscar (1907–), Brazilian architect, who was one of the team which produced designs for the UN headquarters in New York, and whose supreme achievement was his designing of the main public buildings of Brasilia (1950–60) within the master plan drawn up by Lúcio Costa.

Nietzsche /ˈniːtʃə/, Friedrich Wilhelm (1844–1900), German philosopher and writer of Polish descent, an admirer and sometime friend of Wagner. He was briefly a professor at Basle but spent most of his life writing in isolation, frustrated at lack of recognition; in 1889 his lack of mental balance developed into permanent insanity. Roused by Darwin he argued forcefully that since human life has no meaning bestowed upon it supernaturally it must create meaning; this theme appears in his novel Thus Spake Zarathustra (1883), where he speaks of the 'death of God'. The principal features of his doctrine are contempt for

Christianity with its compassion for the weak, and exaltation of the 'will to dominate' and of the 'superman', unscrupulous and pitiless, superior to ordinary morality, who tramples on the feeble and will replace the Christian ideal. He divided mankind into a small dominant 'master-class' and a large dominated 'herd'—a thesis which became part of the Nazi culture after Nietzsche's death. His writings are often obscure and open to different interpretations.

niff /nɪf/ n. & v. Brit. colloq. —n. a smell, esp. an unpleasant one. —v.intr. smell, stink. □□ **niffy** adj. (**niffier, niffiest**). [orig. dial.]

nifty /ˈnɪftɪ/ adj. (**niftier, niftiest**) colloq. 1 clever, adroit. 2 smart, stylish. □□ **niftily** adv. **niftiness** n. [19th c.: orig. uncert.]

Niger[1] /ˈnaɪdʒə(r)/ a river of West Africa, flowing in a curve from the NE frontier of Sierra Leone to the Gulf of Guinea, length 4,100 km (2,550 miles). [L, = black]

Niger[2] /niːˈʒeə(r)/ a landlocked country of West Africa, lying mainly in the Sahara, taking its name from the river that flows through the SW part of its territory, and bounded by Mali, Algeria, and Libya on its west and north, by Burkina, Nigeria, and Chad on its south and east; pop. (est. 1988) 7,213,900; official language, French; capital, Niamey. A French colony (part of French West Africa) from 1922, it became an autonomous republic within the French Community in 1958 and fully independent in 1960. Ground-nuts are a main export and the country's uranium deposits are being exploited.

Niger-Congo a group of languages, the largest in Africa, named after the rivers Niger and Congo. It includes the languages spoken by most of the indigenous peoples of western, central, and southern Africa: the important Bantu group, the Mande group (West Africa), the Voltaic group (Burkina), and the Kwa group (Nigeria) which includes Yoruba and Ibo.

Nigeria /naɪˈdʒɪərɪə/ a country on the west coast of Africa, a member State of the Commonwealth, bordered by the River Niger to the north; pop. (est. 1988) 111,903,500; official language, English; capital, Lagos. The country was the site of highly developed kingdoms in the Middle Ages, and the coast was explored by the Portuguese in the 15th c. The area of the Niger delta came gradually under British influence in the 18th and 19th c., particularly during the period between the annexation of Lagos in 1861 and the unification of the protectorates of Southern and Northern Nigeria into a single colony in 1914. Independence came in 1960 and the State became a republic in 1963, but since that time it has been troubled by political instability, particularly a civil war with the breakaway eastern area of Biafra (1967–70). The discovery of oil in the 1960s and 1970s resulted in a dramatic expansion of the economy and a shift away from the traditional industries of farming, fishing, and forestry. Nigeria has emerged as one of the world's major exporters of oil, which now accounts for over 90 per cent of its export earnings and makes its economy vulnerable to changes in the world prices of oil. □□ **Nigerian** adj. & n.

niggard /ˈnɪgəd/ n. & adj. —n. a mean or stingy person. —adj. archaic = NIGGARDLY. [ME, alt. f. earlier (obs.) nigon, prob. of Scand. orig.: cf. NIGGLE]

niggardly /ˈnɪgədlɪ/ adj. & adv. —adj. 1 stingy, parsimonious. 2 meagre, scanty. —adv. in a stingy or meagre manner. □□ **niggardliness** n.

nigger /ˈnɪgə(r)/ n. offens. 1 a Black person. 2 a dark-skinned person. □ **a nigger in the woodpile** a hidden cause of trouble or inconvenience. [earlier neger f. F nègre f. Sp. negro NEGRO]

niggle /ˈnɪg(ə)l/ v. & n. —v. 1 intr. be over-attentive to details. 2 intr. find fault in a petty way. 3 tr. colloq. irritate; nag pettily. —n. a trifling complaint or criticism; a worry or annoyance. [app. of Scand. orig.: cf. Norw. nigla]

niggling /ˈnɪglɪŋ/ adj. 1 troublesome or irritating in a petty way. 2 trifling or petty. □□ **nigglingly** adv.

nigh /naɪ/ adv., prep., & adj. archaic or dial. near. [OE nēh, nēah]

night /naɪt/ n. 1 the period of darkness between one day and the next; the time from sunset to sunrise. 2 nightfall (shall not reach home before night). 3 the darkness of night (as black as night). 4 a night or evening appointed for some activity, or spent or regarded in a certain way (last night of the Proms; a great night out).

aʊ how eɪ day əʊ no eə hair ɪə near ɔɪ boy ʊə poor aɪə fire aʊə sour (see over for consonants)

□ **night-blindness** = NYCTALOPIA. **night fighter** an aeroplane used for interception at night. **night-hawk 1** a nocturnal prowler, esp. a thief. **2** a nightjar. **night-life** entertainment available at night in a town. **night-light** a dim light kept on in a bedroom at night. **night-long** throughout the night. **night nurse** a nurse on duty during the night. **night of the long knives** see LONG¹. **night-owl** *colloq.* a person active at night. **night safe** a safe with access from the outer wall of a bank for the deposit of money etc. when the bank is closed. **night school** an institution providing evening classes for those working by day. **night shift** a shift of workers employed during the night. **night-soil** the contents of cesspools etc. removed at night, esp. for use as manure. **night-time** the time of darkness. **night-watchman 1** a person whose job is to keep watch by night. **2** *Cricket* an inferior batsman sent in when a wicket falls near the close of a day's play. □□ **nightless** *adj.* [OE *neaht, niht* f. Gmc]

nightbird /ˈnaɪtbɜːd/ *n.* a person who habitually goes about at night.

nightcap /ˈnaɪtkæp/ *n.* **1** *hist.* a cap worn in bed. **2** a hot or alcoholic drink taken at bedtime.

nightclothes /ˈnaɪtkləʊðz/ *n.* clothes worn in bed.

nightclub /ˈnaɪtklʌb/ *n.* a club that is open at night and provides refreshment and entertainment.

nightdress /ˈnaɪtdres/ *n.* a woman's or child's loose garment worn in bed.

nightfall /ˈnaɪtfɔːl/ *n.* the onset of night; the end of daylight.

nightgown /ˈnaɪtɡaʊn/ *n.* **1** = NIGHTDRESS. **2** *hist.* a dressing-gown.

nightie /ˈnaɪtɪ/ *n. colloq.* a nightdress. [abbr.]

Nightingale /ˈnaɪtɪŋˌɡeɪl/, Florence (1820–1910), English nurse and medical reformer who became famous during the Crimean War for her attempts to publicize and improve the state of the army's medical arrangements. She took a party of nurses to the unhealthy and dangerous army hospital at Scutari, where she became known as the 'Lady of the Lamp' for her nightly rounds, and devoted the rest of her life to attempts to improve public health and hospital care.

nightingale /ˈnaɪtɪŋˌɡeɪl/ *n.* any small reddish-brown bird of the genus *Luscinia,* esp. *L. megarhynchos,* of which the male sings melodiously, esp. at night. [OE *nihtegala* (whence obs. *nightgale*) f. Gmc: for -n- cf. FARTHINGALE]

nightjar /ˈnaɪtdʒɑː(r)/ *n.* any nocturnal bird of the family Caprimulgidae, having a characteristic harsh cry.

nightly /ˈnaɪtlɪ/ *adj. & adv.* —*adj.* **1** happening, done, or existing in the night. **2** recurring every night. —*adv.* every night. [OE *nihtlic* (as NIGHT)]

nightmare /ˈnaɪtmeə(r)/ *n.* **1** a frightening or unpleasant dream. **2** *colloq.* a terrifying or very unpleasant experience or situation. **3** a haunting or obsessive fear. □□ **nightmarish** *adj.* **nightmarishly** *adv.* [an evil spirit (incubus) once thought to lie on and suffocate sleepers: OE *mære* incubus]

nightshade /ˈnaɪtʃeɪd/ *n.* any of various poisonous plants, esp. of the genus *Solanum,* including *S. nigrum* (**black nightshade**) with black berries, and *S. dulcamara* (**woody nightshade**) with red berries. □ **deadly nightshade** = BELLADONNA. [OE *nihtscada* app. formed as NIGHT + SHADE, prob. with ref. to its poisonous properties]

nightshirt /ˈnaɪtʃɜːt/ *n.* a long shirt worn in bed.

nightspot /ˈnaɪtspɒt/ *n.* a nightclub.

nightstick /ˈnaɪtstɪk/ *n.* US a policeman's truncheon.

nigrescent /nɪˈgres(ə)nt/ *adj.* blackish. □□ **nigrescence** *n.* [L *nigrescere* grow black f. *niger nigri* black]

nigritude /ˈnɪɡrɪˌtjuːd/ *n.* blackness. [L *nigritudo* (as NIGRESCENT)]

nihilism /ˈnaɪɪˌlɪz(ə)m, ˈnaɪhɪˌlɪz(ə)m/ *n.* **1** negative doctrines or the rejection of all religious and moral principles, often involving a general sense of despair coupled with the belief that life is devoid of meaning. **2** *Philos.* an extreme form of scepticism maintaining that nothing in our world has a real existence. **3** the doctrine of a Russian extreme-revolutionary party in the 19th–20th c. finding nothing to approve of in the established order or social and political institutions. □□ **nihilist** *n.* **nihilistic** /-ˈlɪstɪk/ *adj.* [L *nihil* nothing]

nihility /naɪˈhɪlɪtɪ/ *n.* (*pl.* **-ies**) **1** non-existence, nothingness. **2** a mere nothing; a trifle. [med.L *nihilitas* (as NIHILISM)]

nihil obstat /ˌnaɪhɪl ˈɒbstæt/ *n.* **1** *RC Ch.* a certificate that a book is not open to objection on doctrinal or moral grounds. **2** an authorization or official approval. [L, = nothing hinders]

Nijinsky /nɪˈʒɪnskɪ/, Vaslav Fomich (1890–1950), Russian dancer and choreographer. As a dancer he had exceptional technical virtuosity and instinctive dramatic gifts. Diaghilev made him the star of his Paris seasons and later his touring ensemble, and he was idolized for his performances in the classics and Fokine's ballets, including *Spectre de la Rose* (1911). Diaghilev encouraged him to attempt choreography; the outcome was Debussy's *L'Après-midi d'un faune* (1912) and *Jeux,* and Stravinsky's *Le Sacre du printemps* (1913), which foreshadowed many developments of later avant-garde choreography. Nijinsky's career declined after his separation from Diaghilev, and was brought to a premature end by *dementia praecox.*

Nijmegen /ˈnaɪmeɪɡən/ an industrial town in The Netherlands, on the River Waal, 20 km (12 miles) south of Arnhem; pop. (1987) 145,816.

-nik /nɪk/ *suffix* forming nouns denoting a person associated with a specified thing or quality (*beatnik; refusenik*). [Russ. (as SPUTNIK) and Yiddish]

Nike /ˈnaɪkɪ/ *Gk Mythol.* the goddess of victory. [Gk *nikē* victory]

Nikkei index /ˈniːkeɪ/ *n.* a figure indicating the relative price of a representative set of shares on the Tokyo Stock Exchange, calculated since 1974 by Japan's principal financial daily newspaper. The index was originally calculated (from 1949) by the Tokyo Stock Exchange itself. [abbr. Jap. *Nihon Kezai Shimbun* Japanese Economic Journal]

Niklaus /ˈnɪklaʊs/, Jack William (1940–), American golfer, winner of a record number of tournaments.

nil /nɪl/ *n.* nothing; no number or amount (esp. as a score in games). [L, = *nihil* nothing]

Nile¹ /naɪl/ a river which flows from east central Africa 6,695 km (4,160 miles) northwards through Egypt to the Mediterranean Sea. Seasonal flooding in Egypt has been controlled by the construction of a dam at Aswan which also provides hydroelectric power. □ **Blue Nile** the easterly of the Nile's two main branches, flowing from the Ethiopian Highlands to a confluence with the White Nile at Khartoum. **White Nile** the westerly and longer branch.

Nile² /naɪl/ *n. & adj.* (in full **Nile-blue, Nile-green**) pale greenish blue or green.

nilgai /ˈnɪlɡaɪ/ *n.* a large short-horned Indian antelope, *Boselaphus tragocamelus.* [Hindi *nīlgāī* f. *nīl* blue + *gāī* cow]

Nilotic /naɪˈlɒtɪk/ *adj.* **1** of or relating to the Nile or the Nile region of Africa or its inhabitants. **2** of or relating to a group of languages spoken in Egypt and the Sudan, and further south in Kenya and Tanzania. The western group includes Luo (Kenya), Dinka (Sudan), and Lango (Uganda); the eastern group includes Masai (Kenya and Tanzania) and Turkana (Kenya). [L *Niloticus* f. Gk *Neilōtikos* f. *Neilos* Nile]

nim /nɪm/ *n.* a game in which two players must alternately take one or more objects from one of several heaps and seek either to avoid taking or to take the last remaining object. [20th c.: perh. f. archaic *nim* take (as NIMBLE), or G *nimm* imper. of *nehmen* take]

nimble /ˈnɪmb(ə)l/ *adj.* (**nimbler, nimblest**) **1** quick and light in movement or action; agile. **2** (of the mind) quick to comprehend; clever, versatile. □□ **nimbleness** *n.* **nimbly** *adv.* [OE *næmel* quick to seize f. *niman* take f. Gmc, with -b- as in THIMBLE]

nimbostratus /ˌnɪmbəʊˈstreɪtəs, -ˈstrɑːtəs/ *n.* (*pl.* **nimbostrati** /-taɪ/) *Meteorol.* a low dark-grey layer of cloud. [mod.L, f. NIMBUS + STRATUS]

nimbus /ˈnɪmbəs/ *n.* (*pl.* **nimbi** /-baɪ/ or **nimbuses**) **1 a** a bright cloud or halo investing a deity or person or thing. **b** the halo of a saint etc. **2** *Meteorol.* a rain-cloud. □□ **nimbused** *adj.* [L, = cloud, aureole]

b but   d dog   f few   g get   h he   j yes   k cat   l leg   m man   n no   p pen   r red   s sit   t top   v voice

Nîmes /niːm/ a city in southern France, with many well-preserved Roman remains; pop. (1982) 129,900.

niminy-piminy /ˌnɪmɪnɪˈpɪmɪnɪ/ adj. feeble, affected; lacking in vigour. [cf. MIMINY-PIMINY, NAMBY-PAMBY]

Nimrod /ˈnɪmrɒd/ the great-grandson of Noah, traditional founder of the Babylonian dynasty, noted as a mighty hunter (Gen. 10: 8–9). [Heb. Nimrōd valiant].

Nimrud /ˈnɪmrʊd/ the modern name of ancient Kalhu (Calah of Genesis), situated on the eastern bank of the Tigris south of Nineveh. It was inaugurated as the Assyrian capital in 879 BC by Ashurnasirpal II (883–859 BC) which was later supplanted by Khorsabad with the accession of Sargon II (722–705 BC), and finally destroyed by the Medes in 612 BC. British excavations under Henry A. Layard and later Sir Max Mallowan uncovered palaces of the Assyrian kings with monumental sculptured reliefs, carved ivory furniture inlays, and metalwork.

nincompoop /ˈnɪŋkəmˌpuːp/ n. a simpleton; a fool. [17th c.: orig. unkn.]

nine /naɪn/ n. & adj. —n. 1 one more than eight, or one less than ten; the sum of five units and four units. 2 a symbol for this (9, ix, IX). 3 a size etc. denoted by nine. 4 a set or team of nine individuals. 5 the time of nine o'clock (is it nine yet?). 6 a card with nine pips. 7 (the Nine) the nine muses. —adj. that amount to nine. □ dressed up to the nines dressed very elaborately. nine days' wonder a person or thing that is briefly famous. nine times out of ten nearly always. nine to five a designation of typical office hours. [OE nigon f. Gmc]

ninefold /ˈnaɪnfəʊld/ adj. & adv. 1 nine times as much or as many. 2 consisting of nine parts.

ninepin /ˈnaɪnpɪn/ n. 1 (in pl.; usu. treated as sing.) a game in which nine pins are set up at the end of an alley and bowled at in an attempt to knock them down. 2 a pin used in this game.

nineteen /naɪnˈtiːn/ n. & adj. —n. 1 one more than eighteen, nine more than ten. 2 the symbol for this (19, xix, XIX). 3 a size etc. denoted by nineteen. —adj. that amount to nineteen. □ talk nineteen to the dozen see DOZEN. □□ nineteenth adj. & n. [OE nigontyne]

ninety /ˈnaɪntɪ/ n. & adj. —n. (pl. -ies) 1 the product of nine and ten. 2 a symbol for this (90, xc, XC). 3 (in pl.) the numbers from 90 to 99, esp. the years of a century or of a person's life. —adj. that amount to ninety. □ ninety-first, -second, etc. the ordinal numbers between ninetieth and a hundredth. ninety-one, -two, etc. the cardinal numbers between ninety and a hundred. □□ ninetieth adj. & n. ninetyfold adj. & adv. [OE nigontig]

Nineveh /ˈnɪnɪvə/ the capital of Assyria from the reign of Sennacherib (704–681 BC) until its sack by a coalition of Babylonians and Medes in 612 BC, located east of the Tigris opposite Mosul. First excavated by the French and later by the British, Nineveh is noted for its monumental Neo-Assyrian palace, library, and statuary as well as for its crucial sequence of prehistoric pottery.

Ningxia /ˈnɪŋʃɪɑː/ (also **Ningsia**) an autonomous region of northern China; pop., (est. 1986) 4,240,000; capital, Yinchuan.

Ninian /ˈnɪnɪən/, St (c.360–c.432), Scottish missionary. According to Bede he founded a church at Whithorn in Wigtownshire and from there evangelized the 'southern Picts'.

ninja /ˈnɪndʒə/ n. a person skilled in ninjutsu. [Jap.]

ninjutsu /nɪnˈdʒʊtsuː/ n. one of the Japanese martial arts, characterized by stealthy movement and camouflage. [Jap.]

ninny /ˈnɪnɪ/ n. (pl. -ies) a foolish or simple-minded person. [perh. f. innocent]

ninon /ˈniːnɔ̃/ n. a lightweight silk dress fabric. [F]

ninth /naɪnθ/ n. & adj. —n. 1 the position in a sequence corresponding to the number 9 in the sequence 1–9. 2 something occupying this position. 3 each of nine equal parts of a thing. 4 Mus. a an interval or chord spanning nine consecutive notes in the diatonic scale (e.g. C to D an octave higher). b a note separated from another by this interval. —adj. that is the ninth. □□ ninthly adv.

Niobe /ˈnaɪəbɪ/ Gk Mythol. the daughter of Tantalus, and mother of a large family. Apollo and Artemis, enraged because she boasted herself superior to their mother Leto, slew her children. Niobe herself was turned into a stone, and her tears into streams that trickled from it. The figure carved on a mountain east of Manisa in Turkey, formerly identified as that seen by Pausanias and others, is now thought to be a fertility goddess and of Hittite workmanship, and the identification has been transferred to a natural formation resembling a weeping woman, found near the town of Manisa.

niobium /naɪˈəʊbɪəm/ n. Chem. a rare grey-blue metallic transition element, used in a number of alloys. First discovered in 1801, it is normally found in ores containing tantalum, which has similar chemical properties.¶ Symb.: Nb; atomic number 41. Also called COLUMBIUM. □□ niobic adj. niobous adj. [Niobe daughter of Tantalus: so called because first found in TANTALITE]

Nip /nɪp/ n. sl. offens. a Japanese person. [abbr. of NIPPONESE]

nip[1] /nɪp/ v. & n. —v. (nipped, nipping) 1 tr. pinch, squeeze, or bite sharply. 2 tr. (often foll. by off) remove by pinching etc. 3 tr. (of the cold, frost, etc.) cause pain or harm to. 4 intr. (foll. by in, out, etc.) Brit. colloq. go nimbly or quickly. 5 tr. US sl. steal, snatch. —n. 1 a a pinch, a sharp squeeze. b a bite. 2 a biting cold. b a check to vegetation caused by this. □ nip and tuck US neck and neck. nip in the bud suppress or destroy (esp. an idea) at an early stage. □□ nipping adj. [ME, prob. of LG or Du. orig.]

nip[2] /nɪp/ n. & v. —n. a small quantity of spirits. —v.intr. (nipped, nipping) drink spirits. [prob. abbr. of nipperkin small measure: cf. LG, Du. nippen to sip]

nipa /ˈniːpə/ n. 1 an E. Indian palm-tree, Nipa fruticans, with a creeping trunk and large feathery leaves. 2 an alcoholic drink made from its sap. [Sp. & Port. f. Malay nīpah]

nipper /ˈnɪpə(r)/ n. 1 a person or thing that nips. 2 the claw of a crab, lobster, etc. 3 Brit. colloq. a young child. 4 (in pl.) any tool for gripping or cutting, e.g. forceps or pincers.

nipple /ˈnɪp(ə)l/ n. 1 a small projection in which the mammary ducts of either sex of mammals terminate and from which in females milk is secreted for the young. 2 the teat of a feeding-bottle. 3 a device like a nipple in function, e.g. the tip of a grease-gun. 4 a nipple-like protuberance. 5 US a short section of pipe with a screw-thread at each end for coupling. [16th c., also neble, nible, perh. dimin. f. neb]

nipplewort /ˈnɪp(ə)lˌwɜːt/ n. a yellow-flowered weed, Lapsana communis.

Nipponese /ˌnɪpəˈniːz/ n. & adj. —n. (pl. same) a Japanese person. —adj. Japanese. [Jap. Nippon Japan, lit. 'land of the rising sun']

nippy /ˈnɪpɪ/ adj. (nippier, nippiest) colloq. 1 quick, nimble, active. 2 chilly, cold. □□ nippily adv. [NIP¹ + -Y¹]

NIREX /ˈnaɪreks/ abbr. (in the UK) Nuclear Industry Radioactive Waste Executive.

nirvana /nɜːˈvɑːnə, nɪə-/ n. the final goal of Buddhism, a transcendent state in which there is neither suffering, desire, nor sense of self (atman), with release from the effects of karma. [Skr. nirvāṇa extinction (i.e. the extinction of illusion, since suffering, desire, and self are all illusions)] f. nirvā be extinguished f. nis out + vā- to blow]

nisei /niːˈseɪ/ n. US an American whose parents were immigrants from Japan. [Jap., lit. 'second generation']

nisi /ˈnaɪsaɪ/ adj. Law that takes effect only on certain conditions (decree nisi). [L, = 'unless']

Nissen hut /ˈnɪs(ə)n/ n. a tunnel-shaped hut of corrugated iron with a cement floor. [P. N. Nissen, British engineer d. 1930, its inventor]

nit[1] /nɪt/ n. 1 the egg or young form of a louse or other parasitic insect esp. of human head-lice or body-lice. 2 Brit. sl. a stupid person. □ nit-pick colloq. indulge in nit-picking. nit-picker colloq. a person who nit-picks. nit-picking n. & adj. colloq. fault-finding in a petty manner. [OE hnitu f. WG]

nit[2] /nɪt/ int. Austral. sl. used as a warning that someone is approaching. □ keep nit keep watch; act as guard. [19th c.: orig. unkn.: cf. NIX³]

niter US var. of NITRE.

nitinol /ˈnɪtɪˌnɒl/ n. an alloy of nickel and titanium. [Ni + Ti + Naval Ordnance Laboratory, Maryland, US]

nitrate n. & v. —n. /ˈnaɪtreɪt/ **1** any salt or ester of nitric acid. **2** potassium or sodium nitrate when used as a fertilizer. —v.tr. /naɪˈtreɪt/ Chem. treat, combine, or impregnate with nitric acid. □□ **nitration** /-ˈtreɪʃ(ə)n/ n. [F as NITRE, -ATE¹)]

nitre /ˈnaɪtə(r)/ n. (US **niter**) saltpetre, potassium nitrate. [ME f. OF f. L nitrum f. Gk nitron, of Semitic orig.]

nitric /ˈnaɪtrɪk/ adj. of or containing nitrogen, esp. in the quinquevalent state. □ **nitric acid** a colourless corrosive poisonous liquid. ¶ Chem. formula: HNO₃. **nitric oxide** a colourless gas. ¶ Chem. formula: NO. [F nitrique (as NITRE)]

nitride /ˈnaɪtraɪd/ n. Chem. a binary compound of nitrogen with a more electropositive element. [NITRE + -IDE]

nitrify /ˈnaɪtrɪˌfaɪ/ v.tr. (-**ies**, -**ied**) **1** impregnate with nitrogen. **2** convert (nitrogen, usu. in the form of ammonia) into nitrites or nitrates. □□ **nitrifiable** adj. **nitrification** /-fɪˈkeɪʃ(ə)n/ n. [F nitrifier (as NITRE)]

nitrile /ˈnaɪtraɪl/ n. Chem. an organic compound consisting of an alkyl radical bound to a cyanide radical.

nitrite /ˈnaɪtraɪt/ n. any salt or ester of nitrous acid.

nitro- /ˈnaɪtrəʊ/ comb. form **1** of or containing nitric acid, nitre, or nitrogen. **2** made with or by use of any of these. **3** of or containing the monovalent -NO₂ group (the nitro groups in TNT). [Gk (as NITRE)]

nitrobenzene /ˌnaɪtrəʊˈbenziːn/ n. a yellow oily liquid made by the nitration of benzene and used to make aniline etc.

nitrocellulose /ˌnaɪtrəʊˈseljʊˌləʊz, -ˌləʊs/ n. a highly flammable material made by treating cellulose with concentrated nitric acid, used in the manufacture of explosives and celluloid.

nitrogen /ˈnaɪtrədʒ(ə)n/ n. Chem. a colourless tasteless odourless gaseous element that forms four-fifths of the atmosphere by volume. Pure nitrogen is obtained mainly by distillation of liquefied air. It is a comparatively unreactive element, and is used in situations where an inert atmosphere is needed. Liquid nitrogen is used as a coolant. Nitrogen is essential to life, being a major constituent of proteins and other biological molecules. It forms a range of compounds including nitric acid, ammonia, and nitrogenous fertilizers. ¶ Symb.: N; atomic number 7. □ **nitrogen cycle** see separate entry. **nitrogen fixation** a chemical process in which atmospheric nitrogen is assimilated into organic compounds in living organisms and hence into the nitrogen cycle. □□ **nitrogenous** /-ˈtrɒdʒɪnəs/ adj. [F nitrogène (as NITRO-, -GEN)]

nitrogen cycle n. the cycle of processes in which nitrogen is absorbed from and replaced in the atmosphere. Nitrogen exists in a free state in the air; it is converted to ammonia and thence into compounds mainly by the action of certain bacteria. These compounds are deposited in the soil, from which they are assimilated by plants which are eaten by animals, and returned to the atmosphere when these organic substances decay.

nitroglycerine /ˌnaɪtrəʊˈglɪsərɪn/ n. (also **nitroglycerin**) an explosive yellow liquid made by reacting glycerol with a mixture of concentrated sulphuric and nitric acids.

nitrous /ˈnaɪtrəs/ adj. of, like, or impregnated with nitrogen, esp. in the tervalent state. □ **nitrous acid** a weak acid existing only in solution and in the gas phase. ¶ Chem. formula: HNO₂. **nitrous oxide** a colourless gas used as an anaesthetic (= laughing-gas) and as an aerosol propellant. ¶ Chem. formula: N₂O. [L nitrosus (as NITRE), partly through F nitreux]

nitty-gritty /ˌnɪtɪˈgrɪtɪ/ n. sl. the realities or practical details of a matter. [20th c.: orig. uncert.]

nitwit /ˈnɪtwɪt/ n. colloq. a stupid person. □□ **nitwittery** /-ˈwɪtərɪ/ n. [perh. f. NIT¹ + WIT¹]

nitwitted /ˈnɪtwɪtɪd/ adj. stupid. □□ **nitwittedness** /-ˈwɪtɪdnɪs/ n.

Niue /ˈnjuːeɪ/ the largest coral island in the world, situated to the east of the islands of Tonga; pop. (1986) 2,500. Annexed by New Zealand in 1901, the island achieved self-government in free association with New Zealand in 1974.

Nivernais /ˌniːvəˈneɪ/ a former duchy and province of central France. Its capital was the city of Nevers.

nix¹ /nɪks/ n. & v. sl. —n. **1** nothing. **2** a denial or refusal. —v.tr. **1** cancel. **2** reject. [G, colloq. var. of nichts nothing]

nix² /nɪks/ n. (fem. **nixie** /ˈnɪksɪ/) a water-elf. [G (fem. Nixe)]

nix³ /nɪks/ int. Brit. sl. giving warning to confederates etc. that a person in authority is approaching. [19th c.: perh. = NIX¹]

Nixon /ˈnɪks(ə)n/, Richard Milhous (1913–), 37th President of the US, 1969–74. As Vice-President under Eisenhower (1953–60) he had earned a reputation for skilful diplomacy and in his first term achieved many successes, especially in foreign affairs, but his second term was marred by the scandal of Watergate (see entry) and he became the first President to resign from office.

Nizhny Novgorod /ˌnɪʒnɪ ˈnɒvgərɒd/ the former name (until 1932) of Gorky.

NJ abbr. US New Jersey (also in official postal use).

Nkruma /nˈkruːmə/, Kwame (1909–72), the first leader of Ghana after it achieved independence in 1957. Nkruma became one of the most influential African statesmen as a result of his flamboyant style of politics, but his corrupt dictatorial methods seriously damaged his country's economy and eventually led to his overthrow in 1966.

NKVD /ˌenkeɪviːˈdiː/ n. the Soviet secret police agency responsible from 1934 for internal security and the labour prison camps, having absorbed the functions of the former Ogpu (see entry). Mainly concerned with political offenders, it was notably used for Stalin's purges, and merged with the MVD in 1946. After Beria's fall in 1953 it was placed under the KGB (see entry). [Russ. abbr., = People's Commissariat of Internal Affairs]

NM abbr. US New Mexico (in official postal use).

n.m. abbr. nautical mile.

N.Mex. abbr. New Mexico.

NMR abbr. (also **nmr**) nuclear magnetic resonance.

NNE abbr. north-north-east.

NNW abbr. north-north-west.

No¹ symb. Chem. the element nobelium.

No² var. of NOH.

No. abbr. **1** number. **2** US North. [sense 1 f. L numero, ablat. of numerus number]

no¹ /nəʊ/ adj. **1** not any (there is no excuse; no circumstances could justify it; no two of them are alike). **2** not a, quite other than (is no fool; is no part of my plan; caused no slight inconvenience). **3** hardly any (is no distance; did it in no time). **4** used elliptically as a slogan, notice, etc., to forbid, reject, or deplore the thing specified (no parking; no surrender). □ **by no means** see MEANS. **no-account** unimportant, worthless. **no-ball** Cricket n. an unlawfully delivered ball (counting one to the batting side if not otherwise scored from). —v.tr. pronounce (a bowler) to have bowled a no-ball. **no-claim** (or **-claims**) **bonus** a reduction of the insurance premium charged when the insured has not made a claim under the insurance during an agreed preceding period. **no date** (of a book etc.) not bearing a date of publication etc. **no dice** see DICE. **no doubt** see DOUBT. **no end** see END. **no entry** (of a notice) prohibiting vehicles or persons from entering a road or place. **no-fault** US (of insurance) valid regardless of the allocation of blame for an accident etc. **no fear** see FEAR. **no-frills** lacking ornament or embellishment. **no go** impossible, hopeless. **no-go area** an area forbidden to unauthorized people. **no good** see GOOD. **no-good** see GOOD. **no-hitter** US Baseball a game in which a team does not get a player to first base. **no-hoper** Austral. sl. a useless person. **no joke** see JOKE. **no joy** see JOY n. 3. **no little** see LITTLE. **no man** no person, nobody. **no man's land 1** Mil. the space between two opposing armies. **2** an area not assigned to any owner. **3** an area not clearly belonging to any one subject etc. **no-no** colloq. a thing not possible or acceptable. **no-nonsense** serious, without flippancy. **no place** US nowhere. **no-show** a person who has reserved a seat etc. but neither uses it nor cancels the reservation. **no side** Rugby Football **1** the end of a game. **2** the referee's announcement of this. **no small** see SMALL. **no sweat** colloq. no bother, no trouble. **no thoroughfare** an indication that passage along a street, path, etc., is blocked or prohibited. **no time** see TIME. **no trumps** (or **trump**) Bridge a declaration

æ cat ɑː arm e bed ɜː her ɪ sit iː see ɒ hot ɔː saw ʌ run ʊ put uː too ə ago aɪ my

or bid involving playing without a trump suit. **no-trumper** *Bridge* a hand on which a no-trump bid can suitably be, or has been, made. **no way** *colloq.* **1** it is impossible. **2** I will not agree etc. **no whit** see WHIT. **no-win** of or designating a situation in which success is impossible. **no wonder** see WONDER. . . . **or no** . . . regardless of the . . . (*rain or no rain, I shall go out*). **there is no** . . . **ing** it is impossible to . . . (*there is no accounting for tastes; there was no mistaking what he meant*). [ME f. *nān, nōn* NONE[1], orig. only before consonants]

no² /nəʊ/ *adv.* & *n.* —*adv.* **1** equivalent to a negative sentence: the answer to your question is negative, your request or command will not be complied with, the statement made or course of action intended or conclusion arrived at is not correct or satisfactory, the negative statement made is correct. **2** (foll. by *compar.*) by no amount; not at all (*no better than before*). **3** *Sc.* not (*will ye no come back again?*). —*n.* (*pl.* **noes**) **1** an utterance of the word *no*. **2** a denial or refusal. **3** a negative vote. □ **is no more** has died or ceased to exist. **no better than she should be** morally suspect; sexually promiscuous. **no can do** *colloq.* I am unable to do it. **the noes have it** the negative voters are in the majority. **no less** (often foll. by *than*) **1** as much (*gave me £50, no less; gave me no less than £50; is no less than a scandal; a no less fatal victory*). **2** as important (*no less a person than the President*). **3** *disp.* no fewer (*no less than ten people have told me*). **no longer** not now or henceforth as formerly. **no more** *n.* nothing further (*have no more to say; want no more of it*). —*adj.* not any more (*no more wine?*). —*adv.* **1** no longer. **2** never again. **3** to no greater extent (*is no more a lord than I am; could no more do it than fly in the air*). **4** just as little, neither (*you did not come, and no more did he*). **no, no** an emphatic equivalent of a negative sentence (cf. sense 1 of *adv.*). **no-see-em** (or **-um**) *US* a small bloodsucking insect, esp. a midge of the family *Ceratopogonidae*. **no sooner** . . . **than** see SOON. **not take no for an answer** persist in spite of refusals. **or no** or not (*pleasant or no, it is true*). **whether or no 1** in either case. **2** (as an indirect question) which of a case and its negative (*tell me whether or no*). [OE *nō, nā* f. *ne* not + *ō, ā* ever]

n.o. *abbr. Cricket* not out.

Noah /ˈnəʊə/ a Hebrew patriarch represented as tenth in descent from Adam. According to the story in Genesis he made the ark which saved his family and specimens of every animal from the flood sent by God to destroy the world, and his sons Ham, Shem, and Japheth were regarded as ancestors of all the races of mankind (Gen. 5–10). The tradition of a great flood in very early times is found also in other countries (see DEUCALION and GIL-GAMESH). □ **Noah's ark 1 a** the ship in which (according to the Bible) Noah, his family, and the animals were saved. **b** an imitation of this as a child's toy. **2** a large or cumbrous or old-fashioned trunk or vehicle. **3** a small bivalve mollusc, *Arca tetragona*, with a boat-shaped shell.

nob¹ /nɒb/ *n. Brit. sl.* a person of wealth or high social position. [orig. Sc. *knabb, nab*; 18th c., of unkn. orig.]

nob² /nɒb/ *n. sl.* the head. □ **his nob** *Cribbage* a score of one point for holding the jack of the same suit as a card turned up by the dealer. [perh. var. of KNOB]

nobble /ˈnɒb(ə)l/ *v.tr. Brit. sl.* **1** tamper with (a racehorse) to prevent its winning. **2** get hold of (money etc.) dishonestly. **3** catch (a criminal). **4** secure the support of or weaken (a person) esp. by underhand means. **5** seize, grab. [prob. = dial. *knobble, knubble* knock, beat, f. KNOB]

nobbler /ˈnɒblə(r)/ *n. Austral. sl.* a glass or drink of liquor. [19th c.: orig. unkn.]

Nobelist /nəʊˈbelɪst/ *n. US* a winner of a Nobel prize.

nobelium /nəʊˈbiːlɪəm/ *n. Chem.* a radioactive transuranic metallic element, first obtained in 1958 by bombarding curium with carbon ions. ¶ Symb.: **No**; atomic number 102. [*Nobel* (see NOBEL PRIZE) + -IUM]

Nobel Prize /ˈnəʊbel, -ˈbel/ any of the (orig. five) prizes awarded annually to the person or persons adjudged by Swedish learned societies to have done the most significant recent work in physics, chemistry, medicine, and literature, and to the person who is adjudged by the Norwegian parliament to have rendered the greatest service to the cause of peace. They were established by

the will of Alfred Bernhard Nobel (1833–96), Swedish chemist, engineer, and inventor of dynamite and other high explosives, and are traditionally awarded on 10 Dec., the anniversary of his death. A Nobel Prize for economic sciences was added in 1969, financed by the Swedish National Bank.

nobiliary /nəˈbɪljərɪ/ *adj.* of the nobility. □ **nobiliary particle** a preposition forming part of a title of nobility (e.g. French *de*, German *von*). [F *nobiliaire* (as NOBLE)]

nobility /nəʊˈbɪlɪtɪ/ *n.* (*pl.* **-ies**) **1** nobleness of character, mind, birth, or rank. **2** (prec. by *a, the*) a class of nobles, an aristocracy. [ME f. OF *nobilité* or L *nobilitas* (as NOBLE)]

noble /ˈnəʊb(ə)l/ *adj.* & *n.* —*adj.* (**nobler, noblest**) **1** belonging by rank, title, or birth to the aristocracy. **2** of excellent character; having lofty ideals; free from pettiness and meanness, magnanimous. **3** of imposing appearance, splendid, magnificent, stately. **4** excellent, admirable (*noble horse; noble cellar*). —*n.* **1** a nobleman or noblewoman. **2** *hist.* a former English gold coin first issued in 1351. □ **noble gas** any of the 6 chemically similar gaseous elements helium, neon, argon, krypton, xenon, and radon. They are very unreactive and were formerly believed never to combine with other elements, but a few compounds of krypton, xenon, and radon have now been prepared. **noble metal** a metal (e.g. gold, silver, or platinum) that resists chemical action, does not corrode or tarnish in air or water, and is not easily attacked by acids. **noble savage** primitive man idealized as in Romantic literature. **the noble science** boxing. □□ **nobleness** *n.* **nobly** *adv.* [ME f. OF f. L (g)*nobilis*, rel. to KNOW]

nobleman /ˈnəʊb(ə)lmən/ *n.* (*pl.* **-men**) a man of noble rank or birth, a peer.

noblesse /nəʊˈbles/ *n.* the class of nobles (esp. of a foreign country). □ **noblesse oblige** /ɒˈbliːʒ/ privilege entails responsibility. [ME = nobility, f. OF (as NOBLE)]

noblewoman /ˈnəʊb(ə)l,wʊmən/ *n.* (*pl.* **-women**) a woman of noble rank or birth, a peeress.

nobody /ˈnəʊbədɪ/ *pron.* & *n.* —*pron.* no person. —*n.* (*pl.* **-ies**) a person of no importance, authority, or position. □ **like nobody's business** see BUSINESS. **nobody's fool** see FOOL. [ME f. NO¹ + BODY (= person)]

nock /nɒk/ *n.* & *v.* —*n.* **1** a notch at either end of a bow for holding the string. **2 a** a notch at the butt-end of an arrow for receiving the bowstring. **b** a notched piece of horn serving this purpose. —*v.tr.* set (an arrow) on the string. [ME, perh. = *nock* forward upper corner of some sails, f. MDu. *nocke*]

noctambulist /nɒkˈtæmbjʊlɪst/ *n.* a sleepwalker. □□ **noctambulism** *n.* [L *nox noctis* night + *ambulare* walk]

noctule /ˈnɒktjuːl/ *n.* a large W. European bat, *Nyctalus noctula*. [F f. It. *nottola* bat]

nocturn /ˈnɒktɜːn/ *n. RC Ch.* a part of matins orig. said at night. [ME f. OF *nocturne* or eccl.L *nocturnum* neut. of L *nocturnus*: see NOCTURNAL]

nocturnal /nɒkˈtɜːn(ə)l/ *adj.* of or in the night; done or active by night. □ **nocturnal emission** involuntary emission of semen during sleep. □□ **nocturnally** *adv.* [LL *nocturnalis* f. L *nocturnus* of the night f. *nox noctis* night]

nocturne /ˈnɒktɜːn/ *n.* **1** *Mus.* a short composition of a romantic nature, usu. for piano. **2** a picture of a night scene. [F (as NOCTURN)]

nocuous /ˈnɒkjʊəs/ *adj. literary* noxious, harmful. [L *nocuus* f. *nocēre* hurt]

nod /nɒd/ *v.* & *n.* —*v.* (**nodded, nodding**) **1** *intr.* incline one's head slightly and briefly in greeting, assent, or command. **2** *intr.* let one's head fall forward in drowsiness; be drowsy. **3** *tr.* incline (one's head). **4** *tr.* signify (assent etc.) by a nod. **5** *intr.* (of flowers, plumes, etc.) bend downwards and sway, or move up and down. **6** *intr.* make a mistake due to a momentary lack of alertness or attention. **7** *intr.* (of a building etc.) incline from the perpendicular (*nodding to its fall*). —*n.* a nodding of the head. □ **get the nod** *US* be chosen or approved. **nodding acquaintance** (usu. foll. by *with*) a very slight acquaintance with a person or subject. **nod off** *colloq.* fall asleep. **nod through** *colloq.* **1** I approve on the nod. **2** *Brit. Parl.* formally count (a Member of Parliament) as if having voted when unable to do so. **on the nod** *colloq.* **1**

with merely formal assent and no discussion. **2** on credit. □□ **noddingly** adv. [ME nodde, of unkn. orig.]

noddle[1] /'nɒd(ə)l/ n. colloq. the head. [ME nodle, of unkn. orig.]

noddle[2] /'nɒd(ə)l/ v.tr. nod or wag (one's head). [NOD + -LE⁴]

Noddy /'nɒdɪ/ a character in the writings of Enid Blyton, a toy figure of a boy whose head is so fixed that he has to nod when he speaks.

noddy /'nɒdɪ/ n. (pl. **-ies**) **1** a simpleton. **2** any of various tropical sea birds of the genus Anous, resembling terns. [prob. f. obs. noddy foolish, which is perh. f. NOD]

node /nəʊd/ n. **1** Bot. **a** the part of a plant stem from which one or more leaves emerge. **b** a knob on a root or branch. **2** Anat. a natural swelling or bulge in an organ or part of the body. **3** Astron. either of two points at which a planet's orbit intersects the plane of the ecliptic or the celestial equator. **4** Physics a point of minimum disturbance in a standing wave system. **5** Electr. a point of zero current or voltage. **6** Math. **a** a point at which a curve intersects itself. **b** a vertex in a graph. **7** a component in a computer network. □□ **nodal** adj. **nodical** adj. (in sense 3). [L nodus knot]

nodi pl. of NODUS.

nodose /nə'dəʊs/ adj. knotty, knotted. □□ **nodosity** /-'dɒsɪtɪ/ n. [L nodosus (as NODE)]

nodule /'nɒdjuːl/ n. **1** a small rounded lump of anything, e.g. flint in chalk, carbon in cast iron, or a mineral on the seabed. **2** a small swelling or aggregation of cells, e.g. a small tumour, node, or ganglion, or a swelling on a root of a legume containing bacteria. □□ **nodular** adj. **nodulated** adj. **nodulation** /-'leɪʃ(ə)n/ n. **nodulose** adj. **nodulous** adj. [L nodulus dimin. of nodus: see NODUS]

nodus /'nəʊdəs/ n. (pl. **nodi** /-daɪ/) a knotty point, a difficulty, a complication in the plot of a story etc. [L, = knot]

Noel /nəʊ'el/ n. Christmas (esp. as a refrain in carols). [F f. L (as NATAL)]

Noether /'nɜːtə(r)/, Emmy (1882–1935), German mathematician whose uncanny ability to distil the essentials from an algebraic situation and generalize to exactly the right level led her to simplify and greatly extend the work of her predecessors, particularly Hilbert and Dedekind, on rings and their ideals. Her colleagues were more aware than she was of her lack of status in what was then a man's world: Hilbert's argument to a meeting of the Göttingen faculty in 1915, that this was a university and not a bathing establishment, was unsuccessful, and her position there remained insecure and unsalaried until terminated by the anti-Semitic laws of 1933. Nevertheless, through her lectures, seminars, and conversations she exercised an enormous influence and inaugurated the modern period in algebraic geometry and abstract algebra.

noetic /nəʊ'etɪk, nəʊ'iːtɪk/ adj. & n. —adj. **1** of the intellect. **2** purely intellectual or abstract. **3** given to intellectual speculation. —n. (in sing. or pl.) the science of the intellect. [Gk noētikos f. noētos intellectual f. noeō apprehend]

nog[1] /nɒg/ n. & v. —n. **1** a small block or peg of wood. **2** a snag or stump on a tree. **3** nogging. —v.tr. (**nogged, nogging**) **1** secure with nogs. **2** build in the form of nogging. [17th c.: orig. unkn.]

nog[2] /nɒg/ n. **1** Brit. a strong beer brewed in East Anglia. **2** an egg-flip. [17th c.: orig. unkn.]

noggin /'nɒgɪn/ n. **1** a small mug. **2** a small measure, usu. ¼ pint, of spirits. **3** sl. the head. [17th c.: orig. unkn.]

nogging /'nɒgɪŋ/ n. brickwork or timber braces in a timber frame. [NOG¹ + -ING¹]

Noh /nəʊ/ n. (also **No**) a form of traditional Japanese drama, evolved from Shinto rites and dating from the 14th to the 15th c. It flourished in the 17th–19th c. and has since been revived. The plays were short, and five made up a complete programme. The general tone was noble, the language honorific and sonorous, and the subject-matter taken mainly from Japan's classical literature. The players were all male, the chorus playing a passive narrative role and even chanting the lines of the principal characters while the latter executed certain dances. About two hundred Noh plays are extant; they are comparable in various respects with early Greek drama. [Jap. nō]

nohow /'nəʊhaʊ/ adv. **1** US in no way; by no means. **2** dial. out of order; out of sorts.

noil /nɔɪl/ n. (in sing. or pl.) short wool-combings. [perh. f. OF noel f. med.L nodellus dimin. of L nodus knot]

noise /nɔɪz/ n. & v. —n. **1** a sound, esp. a loud or unpleasant or undesired one. **2** a series of loud sounds, esp. shouts; a confused sound of voices and movements. **3** irregular fluctuations accompanying a transmitted signal but not relevant to it. **4** (in pl.) conventional remarks, or speechlike sounds without actual words (made sympathetic noises). —v. **1** tr. (usu. in passive) make public; spread abroad (a person's fame or a fact). **2** intr. archaic make much noise. □ **make a noise 1** (usu. foll. by about) talk or complain much. **2** be much talked of; attain notoriety. **noise-maker** a device for making a loud noise at a festivity etc. **noise pollution** harmful or annoying noise. **noises off** sounds made off stage to be heard by the audience of a play. [ME f. OF, = outcry, disturbance, f. L nausea: see NAUSEA]

noiseless /'nɔɪzlɪs/ adj. **1** silent. **2** making no avoidable noise. □□ **noiselessly** adv. **noiselessness** n.

noisette /nwɑː'zet/ n. a small round piece of meat etc. [F, dimin. of noix nut]

noisome /'nɔɪsəm/ adj. literary **1** harmful, noxious. **2** evil-smelling. **3** objectionable, offensive. □□ **noisomeness** n. [ME f. obs. noy f. ANNOY]

noisy /'nɔɪzɪ/ adj. (**noisier, noisiest**) **1** full of or attended with noise. **2** making or given to making much noise. **3** clamorous, turbulent. **4** (of a colour, garment, etc.) loud, conspicuous. □□ **noisily** adv. **noisiness** n.

Nolan /'nəʊlən/, Sir Sidney (1917–), Australian painter, internationally known for his paintings of events from Australian history around which legends have gathered, beginning with his Ned Kelly paintings (1946). His interpretations are often whimsical and at times humorous.

nolens volens /ˌnəʊlenz 'vəʊlenz/ adv. literary willy-nilly, perforce. [L participles, = unwilling, willing]

nolle prosequi /ˌnɒlɪ 'prɒsɪˌkwaɪ/ n. Law **1** the relinquishment by a plaintiff or prosecutor of all or part of a suit. **2** the entry of this on record. [L, = refuse to pursue]

nom. abbr. nominal.

nomad /'nəʊmæd/ n. & adj. —n. **1** a member of a tribe roaming from place to place for pasture. **2** a wanderer. —adj. **1** living as a nomad. **2** wandering. □□ **nomadic** /-'mædɪk/ adj. **nomadically** /-'mædɪkəlɪ/ adv. **nomadism** n. **nomadize** v.intr. (also **-ise**). [F nomade f. L nomas nomad- f. Gk nomas -ados f. nemō to pasture]

nombril /'nɒmbrɪl/ n. Heraldry the point halfway between fess point and the base of the shield. [F, = navel]

nom de guerre /ˌnɒm də 'geə(r)/ n. (pl. **noms de guerre** pronunc. same) an assumed name under which a person fights, plays, writes, etc. [F, = war-name]

nom de plume /ˌnɒm də 'pluːm/ n. (pl. **noms de plume** pronunc. same) an assumed name under which a person writes. [formed in E of F words, = pen-name, after NOM DE GUERRE]

nomen /'nəʊmen/ n. an ancient Roman's second name, indicating the gens, as in Marcus Tullius Cicero. [L, = name]

nomenclature /nəʊ'menklətʃə(r), 'nəʊmən ˌkleɪtʃə(r)/ n. **1** a person's or community's system of names for things. **2** the terminology of a science etc. **3** systematic naming. **4** a catalogue or register. □□ **nomenclative** adj. **nomenclatural** /-'klætʃər(ə)l/ adj. [F f. L nomenclatura f. nomen + calare call]

nominal /'nɒmɪn(ə)l/ adj. **1** existing in name only; not real or actual (nominal and real prices; nominal ruler). **2** (of a sum of money, rent, etc.) virtually nothing; much below the actual value of a thing. **3** of or in names (nominal and essential distinctions). **4** consisting of or giving the names (nominal list of officers). **5** of or as or like a noun. □ **nominal definition** a statement of all that is connoted in the name of a concept. **nominal value** the face value (of a coin, shares, etc.). □□ **nominally** adv. [ME f. F nominal or L nominalis f. nomen -inis name]

nominalism /ˈnɒmɪnəˌlɪz(ə)m/ n. Philos. the doctrine that universals or general ideas are mere names (opp. REALISM). □□ **nominalist** n. **nominalistic** /-ˈlɪstɪk/ adj. [F nominalisme (as NOMINAL)]

nominalize /ˈnɒmɪnəˌlaɪz/ v.tr. (also **-ise**) form a noun from (a verb, adjective, etc.), e.g. output, truth, from put out, true. □□ **nominalization** /-ˈzeɪʃ(ə)n/ n.

nominate /ˈnɒmɪˌneɪt/ v.tr. **1** propose (a candidate) for election. **2** appoint to an office (a board of six nominated and six elected members). **3** name or appoint (a date or place). **4** mention by name. **5** call by the name of, designate. □□ **nominator** n. [L nominare nominat- (as NOMINAL)]

nomination /ˌnɒmɪˈneɪʃ(ə)n/ n. **1** the act or an instance of nominating; the state of being nominated. **2** the right of nominating for an appointment (have a nomination at your disposal). [ME f. OF nomination or L nominatio (as NOMINATE)]

nominative /ˈnɒmɪnətɪv/ n. & adj. —n. Gram. **1** the case of nouns, pronouns, and adjectives, expressing the subject of a verb. **2** a word in this case. —adj. **1** Gram. of or in this case. **2** /-neɪtɪv/ of, or appointed by, nomination (as distinct from election). □□ **nominatival** /-ˈtaɪv(ə)l/ adj. [ME f. OF nominatif -ive or L nominativus (as NOMINATE), transl. Gk onomastikē (ptōsis case)]

nominee /ˌnɒmɪˈniː/ n. **1** a person who is nominated for an office or as the recipient of a grant etc. **2** Commerce a person (not necessarily the owner) in whose name a stock etc. is registered. [NOMINATE]

nomogram /ˈnɒməˌɡræm, ˈnəʊm-/ n. (also **nomograph** /-ˌɡrɑːf/) a graphical presentation of relations between quantities whereby the value of one may be found by simple geometrical construction (e.g. drawing a straight line) from those of others. □□ **nomographic** /-ˈɡræfɪk/ adj. **nomographically** /-ˈɡræfɪkəlɪ/ adv. **nomography** /nəˈmɒɡrəfɪ/ n. [Gk nomo- f. nomos law + -GRAM]

nomothetic /ˌnɒməˈθetɪk, ˌnəʊm-/ adj. **1** stating (esp. scientific) laws. **2** legislative. [obs. nomothete legislator f. Gk nomothetēs]

-nomy /nəmɪ/ comb. form denoting an area of knowledge or the laws governing it (aeronomy; economy).

non- /nɒn/ prefix giving the negative sense of words with which it is combined, esp.: **1** not doing or having or involved with (non-attendance; non-payment; non-productive). **2 a** not of the kind or class described (non-alcoholic; non-member; non-event). **b** forming terms used adjectivally (non-union; non-party). **3** a lack of (non-access). **4** (with adverbs) not in the way described (non-aggressively). **5** forming adjectives from verbs, meaning 'that does not' or 'that is not meant to (or to be)' (non-skid; non-iron). **6** used to form a neutral negative sense when a form in in- or un- has a special sense or (usu. unfavourable) connotation (non-controversial; non-effective; non-human). ¶ The number of words that can be formed with this prefix is unlimited; consequently only a selection, considered the most current or semantically noteworthy, can be given here. [from or after ME no(u)n- f. AF noun-, OF non-, nom- f. L non not]

nona- /ˈnɒnə/ comb. form nine. [L f. nonus ninth]

non-abstainer /ˌnɒnəbˈsteɪnə(r)/ n. a person who does not abstain (esp. from alcohol).

non-acceptance /ˌnɒnəkˈsept(ə)ns/ n. a lack of acceptance.

non-access /nɒnˈækses/ n. a lack of access.

non-addictive /ˌnɒnəˈdɪktɪv/ adj. (of a drug, habit, etc.) not causing addiction.

nonage /ˈnəʊnɪdʒ, ˈnɒn-/ n. **1** hist. the state of being under full legal age, minority. **2** a period of immaturity. [ME f. AF nounage, OF nonage (as NON-, AGE)]

nonagenarian /ˌnəʊnədʒɪˈneərɪən, ˌnɒn-/ n. & adj. —n. a person from 90 to 99 years old. —adj. of this age. [L nonagenarius f. nonageni distributive of nonaginta ninety]

non-aggression /ˌnɒnəˈɡreʃ(ə)n/ n. lack of or restraint from aggression (often attrib.: non-aggression pact).

nonagon /ˈnɒnəɡən/ n. a plane figure with nine sides and angles. [L nonus ninth, after HEXAGON]

non-alcoholic /ˌnɒnælkəˈhɒlɪk/ adj. & n. (of a drink etc.) not containing alcohol.

non-aligned /ˌnɒnəˈlaɪnd/ adj. (of States etc.) not aligned with another (esp. major) power. □□ **non-alignment** n.

non-allergic /ˌnɒnəˈlɜːdʒɪk/ adj. not causing allergy; not allergic.

non-ambiguous /ˌnɒnæmˈbɪɡjʊəs/ adj. not ambiguous. ¶ Neutral in sense: see NON- 6, UNAMBIGUOUS.

non-appearance /ˌnɒnəˈpɪərəns/ n. failure to appear or be present.

non-art /nɒnˈɑːt/ n. something that avoids the normal forms of art.

nonary /ˈnəʊnərɪ/ adj. & n. —adj. Math. (of a scale of notation) having nine as its base. —n. (pl. **-ies**) a group of nine. [L nonus ninth]

non-Aryan /nɒnˈeɪrɪən/ adj. & n. —adj. (of a person or language) not Aryan or of Aryan descent. —n. a non-Aryan person.

non-attached /ˌnɒnəˈtætʃd/ adj. that is not attached. ¶ Neutral in sense: see NON- 6, UNATTACHED.

non-attendance /ˌnɒnəˈtend(ə)ns/ n. failure to attend.

non-attributable /ˌnɒnəˈtrɪbjʊtəb(ə)l/ adj. that cannot or may not be attributed to a particular source etc. □□ **non-attributably** adv.

non-availability /ˌnɒnəˌveɪləˈbɪlɪtɪ/ n. a state of not being available.

non-believer /ˌnɒnbɪˈliːvə(r)/ n. a person who does not believe or has no (esp. religious) faith.

non-belligerency /ˌnɒnbəˈlɪdʒərənsɪ/ n. a lack of belligerency.

non-belligerent /ˌnɒnbəˈlɪdʒərənt/ adj. & n. —adj. not engaged in hostilities. —n. a non-belligerent nation, State, etc.

non-biological /ˌnɒnbaɪəˈlɒdʒɪk(ə)l/ adj. not concerned with biology or living organisms.

non-Black /nɒnˈblæk/ adj. & n. —adj. **1** (of a person) not Black. **2** of or relating to non-Black people. —n. a non-Black person.

non-breakable /nɒnˈbreɪkəb(ə)l/ adj. not breakable.

non-capital /nɒnˈkæpɪt(ə)l/ adj. (of an offence) not punishable by death.

non-Catholic /nɒnˈkæθəlɪk, -ˈkæθlɪk/ adj. & n. —adj. not Roman Catholic. —n. a non-Catholic person.

nonce /nɒns/ n. □ **for the nonce** for the time being; for the present occasion. **nonce-word** a word coined for one occasion. [ME for than anes (unrecorded) = for the one, altered by wrong division (cf. NEWT)]

nonchalant /ˈnɒnʃələnt/ adj. calm and casual, unmoved, unexcited, indifferent. □□ **nonchalance** n. **nonchalantly** adv. [F, part. of nonchaloir f. chaloir be concerned]

non-Christian /nɒnˈkrɪstjən, -ˈkrɪstʃ(ə)n/ adj. & n. —adj. not Christian. —n. a non-Christian person.

non-citizen /nɒnˈsɪtɪz(ə)n/ n. a person who is not a citizen (of a particular State, town, etc.).

non-classified /nɒnˈklæsɪfaɪd/ adj. (esp. of information) that is not classified. ¶ Neutral in sense: see NON- 6, UNCLASSIFIED.

non-clerical /nɒnˈklerɪk(ə)l/ adj. not doing or involving clerical work.

non-collegiate /nɒnkəˈliːdʒət/ adj. **1** not attached to a college. **2** not having colleges.

non-com /ˈnɒnkɒm/ n. colloq. a non-commissioned officer. [abbr.]

non-combatant /nɒnˈkɒmbət(ə)nt/ n. a person not fighting in a war, esp. a civilian, army chaplain, etc.

non-commissioned /ˌnɒnkəˈmɪʃ(ə)nd/ adj. Mil. (of an officer) not holding a commission.

noncommittal /ˌnɒnkəˈmɪt(ə)l/ adj. avoiding commitment to a definite opinion or course of action. □□ **noncommittally** adv.

non-communicant /ˌnɒnkəˈmjuːnɪkənt/ n. a person who is not a communicant (esp. in the religious sense).

non-communicating /ˌnɒnkəˈmjuːnɪˌkeɪtɪŋ/ adj. that does not communicate.

non-communist /nɒnˈkɒmjʊnɪst/ adj. & n. (also **non-Communist** with ref. to a particular party) —adj. not advocating or practising communism. —n. a non-communist person.

non-compliance /ˌnɒnkəmˈplaɪəns/ n. failure to comply; a lack of compliance.

non compos mentis /ˌnɒn kɒmpɒs ˈmentɪs/ adj. (also *non compos*) not in one's right mind. [L, = not having control of one's mind]

non-conductor /ˌnɒnkənˈdʌktə(r)/ n. a substance that does not conduct heat or electricity. □□ **non-conducting** adj.

non-confidential /ˌnɒnkɒnfɪˈdenʃ(ə)l/ adj. not confidential. □□ **non-confidentially** adv.

nonconformist /ˌnɒnkənˈfɔːmɪst/ n. 1 a person who does not conform to the doctrine or discipline of an established Church, esp. (**Nonconformist**) a member of a (usu. Protestant) sect dissenting from the Anglican Church. 2 a person who does not conform to a prevailing principle. □□ **nonconformism** n. **Nonconformism** n.

nonconformity /ˌnɒnkənˈfɔːmɪtɪ/ n. 1 a nonconformists as a body, esp. (**Nonconformity**) Protestants dissenting from the Anglican Church. b the principles or practice of nonconformists, esp. (**Nonconformity**) Protestant dissent. 2 (usu. foll. by to) failure to conform to a rule etc. 3 lack of correspondence between things.

non-contagious /ˌnɒnkənˈteɪdʒəs/ adj. not contagious.

non-content /ˈnɒnkənˌtent/ n. Brit. a negative voter in the House of Lords.

non-contentious /ˌnɒnkənˈtenʃəs/ adj. not contentious.

non-contributory /ˌnɒnkənˈtrɪbjʊtərɪ/ adj. not contributing or (esp. of a pension scheme) involving contributions.

non-controversial /ˌnɒnkɒntrəˈvɜːʃ(ə)l/ adj. not controversial. ¶ Neutral in sense: see NON- 6, UNCONTROVERSIAL.

non-cooperation /ˌnɒnkəʊˌɒpəˈreɪʃ(ə)n/ n. failure to cooperate; a lack of cooperation.

non-delivery /ˌnɒndɪˈlɪvərɪ/ n. failure to deliver.

non-denominational /ˌnɒndɪˌnɒmɪˈneɪʃən(ə)l/ adj. not restricted as regards religious denomination.

nondescript /ˈnɒndɪskrɪpt/ adj. & n. —adj. lacking distinctive characteristics, not easily classified, neither one thing nor another. —n. a nondescript person or thing. □□ **nondescriptly** adv. **nondescriptness** n. [NON- + descript described f. L descriptus (as DESCRIBE)]

non-destructive /ˌnɒndɪˈstrʌktɪv/ adj. that does not involve destruction or damage.

non-drinker /nɒnˈdrɪŋkə(r)/ n. a person who does not drink alcoholic liquor.

non-driver /nɒnˈdraɪvə(r)/ n. a person who does not drive a motor vehicle.

none[1] /nʌn/ pron., adj., & adv. —pron. 1 (foll. by of) a not any of (none of this concerns me; none of them have found it; none of your impudence!). b not any one of (none of them has come). ¶ The verb following none in this sense can be singular or plural according to the sense. 2 a no persons (none but fools have ever believed it). b no person (none can tell). —adj. (usu. with a preceding noun implied) 1 no; not any (you have money and I have none; would rather have a bad reputation than none at all). 2 not to be counted in a specified class (his understanding is none of the clearest; if a linguist is wanted, I am none). —adv. (foll. by the + compar., or so, too) by no amount; not at all (am none the wiser; are none too fond of him). □ **none the less** nevertheless. **none other** (usu. foll. by than) no other person. **none-so-pretty** London Pride. [OE nān f. ne not + ān ONE]

none[2] /nəʊn/ n. (also in pl.) 1 the office of the fifth of the canonical hours of prayer, orig. said at the ninth hour (3 p.m.). 2 this hour. [F f. L nona fem. sing. of nonus ninth: cf. NOON]

non-earning /nɒnˈɜːnɪŋ/ adj. not earning (esp. a regular wage or salary).

non-effective /ˌnɒnɪˈfektɪv/ adj. that does not have an effect. ¶ Neutral in sense: see NON- 6, INEFFECTIVE.

non-ego /nɒnˈiːgəʊ/ n. Philos. all that is not the conscious self.

nonentity /nɒˈnentɪtɪ/ n. (pl. **-ies**) 1 a person or thing of no

importance. 2 a non-existence. b a non-existent thing, a figment. [med.L nonentitas non-existence]

nones /nəʊnz/ n.pl. in the ancient Roman calendar, the ninth day before the ides by inclusive reckoning, i.e. the 7th day of March, May, July, October, the 5th of other months. [OF nones f. L nonae fem. pl. of nonus ninth]

non-essential /ˌnɒnɪˈsenʃ(ə)l/ adj. not essential. ¶ Neutral in sense: see NON- 6, INESSENTIAL.

nonesuch var. of NONSUCH.

nonet /nəʊˈnet/ n. 1 Mus. a a composition for nine voices or instruments. b the performers of such a piece. 2 a group of nine. [It. nonetto f. nono ninth f. L nonus]

nonetheless var. of none the less.

non-Euclidean /ˌnɒnjuːˈklɪdɪən/ adj. denying or going beyond Euclidean principles in geometry.

non-European /ˌnɒnjʊərəˈpɪən/ adj. & n. —adj. not European. —n. a non-European person.

non-event /ˌnɒnɪˈvent/ n. an unimportant or anticlimactic occurrence.

non-existent /ˌnɒnɪgˈzɪst(ə)nt/ adj. not existing. □□ **non-existence** n.

non-explosive /ˌnɒnɪkˈspləʊsɪv/ adj. (of a substance) that does not explode.

non-fattening /nɒnˈfætənɪŋ/ adj. (of food) that does not fatten.

nonfeasance /nɒnˈfiːz(ə)ns/ n. failure to perform an act required by law. [NON-: see MISFEASANCE]

non-ferrous /nɒnˈferəs/ adj. (of a metal) other than iron or steel.

non-fiction /nɒnˈfɪkʃ(ə)n/ n. literary work other than fiction, including biography and reference books. □□ **non-fictional** adj.

non-flam /nɒnˈflæm/ adj. = NON-FLAMMABLE.

non-flammable /nɒnˈflæməb(ə)l/ adj. not inflammable.

non-fulfilment /ˌnɒnfʊlˈfɪlmənt/ n. failure to fulfil (an obligation).

non-functional /nɒnˈfʌŋkʃən(ə)l/ adj. not having a function.

nong /nɒŋ/ n. Austral. sl. a foolish or stupid person. [20th c.: orig. unkn.]

non-governmental /ˌnɒngʌvən̩ˈment(ə)l/ adj. not belonging to or associated with a government.

non-human /nɒnˈhjuːmən/ adj. & n. —adj. (of a being) not human. —n. a non-human being. ¶ Neutral in sense: see NON-6, INHUMAN, UNHUMAN.

non-infectious /ˌnɒnɪnˈfekʃəs/ adj. (of a disease) not infectious.

non-inflected /ˌnɒnɪnˈflektɪd/ adj. (of a language) not having inflections.

non-interference /ˌnɒnɪntəˈfɪərəns/ n. a lack of interference.

non-intervention /ˌnɒnɪntəˈvenʃ(ə)n/ n. the principle or practice of not becoming involved in others' affairs, esp. by one State in regard to another.

non-intoxicating /ˌnɒnɪnˈtɒksɪˌkeɪtɪŋ/ adj. (of drink) not causing intoxication.

non-iron /nɒnˈaɪən/ adj. (of a fabric) that needs no ironing.

nonjoinder /nɒnˈdʒɔɪndə(r)/ n. Law the failure of a partner etc. to become a party to a suit.

nonjuror /nɒnˈdʒʊərə(r)/ n. a person who refuses to take an oath, esp. hist. a member of the clergy refusing to take the oath of allegiance to William and Mary in 1689. □□ **nonjuring** adj.

non-jury /nɒnˈdʒʊərɪ/ adj. (of a trial) without a jury.

non-linear /nɒnˈlɪnɪə(r)/ adj. not linear, esp. with regard to dimension.

non-literary /nɒnˈlɪtərərɪ/ adj. (of writing, a text, etc.) not literary in character.

non-logical /nɒnˈlɒdʒɪk(ə)l/ adj. not involving logic. ¶ Neutral in sense: see NON- 6, ILLOGICAL. □□ **non-logically** adv.

non-magnetic /ˌnɒnmægˈnetɪk/ adj. (of a substance) not magnetic.

non-member /nɒnˈmembə(r)/ n. a person who is not a

member (of a particular association, club, etc.). □□ **non-membership** n.

non-metal /nɒn'met(ə)l/ adj. not made of metal. □□ **non-metallic** /-mɪ'tælɪk/ adj.

non-militant /nɒn'mɪlɪt(ə)nt/ adj. not militant.

non-military /nɒn'mɪlɪtərɪ/ adj. not military; not involving armed forces, civilian.

non-ministerial /ˌnɒnmɪnɪ'stɪərɪəl/ adj. not ministerial (esp. in political senses).

non-moral /nɒn'mɒr(ə)l/ adj. not concerned with morality. ¶ Neutral in sense: see NON- 6, AMORAL, IMMORAL. □□ **non-morally** adv.

non-natural /nɒn'næt∫ər(ə)l/ adj. not involving natural means or processes. ¶ Neutral in sense: see NON- 6, UNNATURAL.

non-negotiable /ˌnɒnnɪ'gəʊ∫əb(ə)l/ adj. that cannot be negotiated (esp. in financial senses).

non-net /nɒn'net/ adj. (of a book) not subject to a minimum selling price.

non-nuclear /nɒn'nju:klɪə(r)/ adj. 1 not involving nuclei or nuclear energy. 2 (of a State etc.) not having nuclear weapons.

non-observance /ˌnɒnəb'zɜ:v(ə)ns/ n. failure to observe (esp. an agreement, requirement, etc.).

non-operational /ˌnɒnɒpə'reɪ∫ən(ə)l/ adj. 1 that does not operate. 2 out of order.

non-organic /ˌnɒnɔ:'gænɪk/ adj. not organic. ¶ Neutral in sense: see NON- 6, INORGANIC.

nonpareil /'nɒnpər(ə)l, ˌnɒnpə'reɪl/ adj. & n. —adj. unrivalled or unique. —n. such a person or thing. [F f. pareil equal f. pop.L pariculus dimin. of L par]

non-participating /ˌnɒnpɑ:'tɪsɪˌpeɪtɪŋ/ adj. not taking part.

non-partisan /ˌnɒnpɑ:tɪ'zæn/ adj. not partisan.

non-party /nɒn'pɑ:tɪ/ adj. independent of political parties.

non-payment /nɒn'peɪmənt/ n. failure to pay; a lack of payment.

non-person /'nɒn,pɜ:s(ə)n/ n. a person regarded as non-existent or insignificant (cf. UNPERSON).

non-personal /nɒn'pɜ:sən(ə)l/ adj. not personal. ¶ Neutral in sense: see NON- 6, IMPERSONAL.

non-physical /nɒn'fɪzɪk(ə)l/ adj. not physical. □□ **non-physically** adv.

non placet /nɒn 'pleɪset/ n. a negative vote in a Church or university assembly. [L, = it does not please]

non-playing /nɒn'pleɪɪŋ/ adj. that does not play or take part (in a game etc.).

nonplus /nɒn'plʌs/ v. & n. —v.tr. (**nonplussed, nonplussing**) completely perplex. —n. a state of perplexity, a standstill (at a nonplus; reduce to a nonplus). [L non plus not more]

non-poisonous /nɒn'pɔɪzənəs/ adj. (of a substance) not poisonous.

non-political /ˌnɒnpə'lɪtɪk(ə)l/ adj. not political; not involved in politics.

non-porous /nɒn'pɔ:rəs/ adj. (of a substance) not porous.

non possumus /nɒn 'pɒsjʊməs/ n. a statement of inability to act in a matter. [L, = we cannot]

non-productive /ˌnɒnprə'dʌktɪv/ adj. not productive. ¶ Neutral in sense: see NON- 6, UNPRODUCTIVE. □□ **non-productively** adv.

non-professional /ˌnɒnprə'fe∫ən(ə)l/ adj. not professional (esp. in status). ¶ Neutral in sense: see NON- 6, UNPROFESSIONAL.

non-profit /nɒn'prɒfɪt/ adj. not involving or making a profit.

non-profit-making /nɒn'prɒfɪt,meɪkɪŋ/ adj. (of an enterprise) not conducted primarily to make a profit.

non-proliferation /ˌnɒnprə,lɪfə'reɪ∫(ə)n/ n. the prevention of an increase in something, esp. possession of nuclear weapons.

non-racial /nɒn'reɪ∫(ə)l/ adj. not involving race or racial factors.

non-reader /nɒn'ri:də(r)/ n. a person who cannot read.

non-resident /nɒn'rezɪd(ə)nt/ adj. & n. —adj. 1 not residing in a particular place, esp. (of a member of the clergy) not residing where his or her duties require. 2 not requiring the

holder to reside at the place of work. —n. a non-resident person, esp. a person using some of the facilities of a hotel. □□ **non-residence** n. **non-residential** /-'den∫(ə)l/ adj.

non-resistance /ˌnɒnrɪ'zɪst(ə)ns/ n. failure to resist; a lack of resistance.

non-returnable /ˌnɒnrɪ'tɜ:nəb(ə)l/ adj. that may or need or will not be returned.

non-rigid /nɒn'rɪdʒɪd/ adj. (esp. of materials) not rigid.

non-scientific /nɒn,saɪən'tɪfɪk/ adj. not involving science or scientific methods. ¶ Neutral in sense: see NON- 6, UNSCIENTIFIC. □□ **non-scientist** /-'saɪəntɪst/ n.

non-sectarian /ˌnɒnsek'teərɪən/ adj. not sectarian.

nonsense /'nɒns(ə)ns/ n. 1 a (often as int.) absurd or meaningless words or ideas; foolish or extravagant conduct. b an instance of this. 2 a scheme, arrangement, etc., that one disapproves of. 3 (often attrib.) a form of literature meant to amuse by absurdity (nonsense verse). □□ **nonsensical** /-'sensɪk(ə)l/ adj. **nonsensicality** /nɒn,sensɪ'kælɪtɪ/ n. (pl. **-ies**). **nonsensically** /-'sensɪkəlɪ/ adv.

non sequitur /nɒn 'sekwɪtə(r)/ n. a conclusion that does not logically follow from the premisses. [L, = it does not follow]

non-sexual /nɒn'seksjʊəl, -'∫ʊəl/ adj. not based on or involving sex. □□ **non-sexually** adv.

non-skid /nɒn'skɪd/ adj. 1 that does not skid. 2 that inhibits skidding.

non-slip /nɒn'slɪp/ adj. 1 that does not slip. 2 that inhibits slipping.

non-smoker /nɒn'sməʊkə(r)/ n. 1 a person who does not smoke. 2 a train compartment etc. in which smoking is forbidden. □□ **non-smoking** adj. & n.

non-soluble /nɒn'sɒljʊb(ə)l/ adj. (esp. of a substance) not soluble. ¶ Neutral in sense: see NON- 6, INSOLUBLE.

non-specialist /nɒn'spe∫əlɪst/ n. a person who is not a specialist (in a particular subject).

non-specific /ˌnɒnspɪ'sɪfɪk/ adj. that cannot be specified.

non-standard /nɒn'stændəd/ adj. not standard.

non-starter /nɒn'stɑ:tə(r)/ n. 1 a person or animal that does not start in a race. 2 colloq. a person or thing that is unlikely to succeed or be effective.

non-stick /nɒn'stɪk/ adj. 1 that does not stick. 2 that does not allow things to stick to it.

non-stop /nɒn'stɒp/ adj., adv., & n. —adj. 1 (of a train etc.) not stopping at intermediate places. 2 (of a journey, performance, etc.) done without a stop or intermission. —adv. without stopping or pausing. —n. a non-stop train etc.

non-subscriber /ˌnɒnsəb'skraɪbə(r)/ n. a person who is not a subscriber.

nonsuch /'nʌnsʌt∫/ n. (also **nonesuch**) 1 a person or thing that is unrivalled, a paragon. 2 a leguminous plant, Medicago lupulina, with black pods. [NONE¹ + SUCH, usu. now assim. to NON-]

nonsuit /nɒn'sju:t, -'su:t/ n. & v. Law —n. the stoppage of a suit by the judge when the plaintiff fails to make out a legal case or to bring sufficient evidence. —v.tr. subject (a plaintiff) to a nonsuit. [ME f. AF no(u)nsuit]

non-swimmer /nɒn'swɪmə(r)/ n. a person who cannot swim.

non-technical /nɒn'teknɪk(ə)l/ adj. 1 not technical. 2 without technical knowledge.

non-toxic /nɒn'tɒksɪk/ adj. not toxic.

non-transferable /ˌnɒntræns'fɜ:rəb(ə)l/ adj. that may not be transferred.

non-U /nɒn'ju:/ adj. colloq. not characteristic of the upper class. (See MITFORD.) [NON- + U²]

non-uniform /nɒn'ju:nɪˌfɔ:m/ adj. not uniform.

non-union /nɒn'ju:nɪən/ adj. 1 not belonging to a trade union. 2 not done or produced by members of a trade union.

non-usage /nɒn'ju:zɪdʒ, -'ju:sɪdʒ/ n. failure to use.

non-use /nɒn'ju:s/ n. failure to use.

non-user /nɒn'ju:zə(r)/ n. Law the failure to use a right, by which it may be lost. [AF nonuser (unrecorded) (as NON-, USER)]

non-verbal /nɒn'vɜ:b(ə)l/ adj. not involving words or speech. □□ **non-verbally** adv.

aʊ how eɪ day əʊ no eə hair ɪə near ɔɪ boy ʊə poor aɪə fire aʊə sour (see over for consonants)

non-vintage /nɒnˈvɪntɪdʒ/ adj. (of wine etc.) not vintage.

non-violence /nɒnˈvaɪələns/ n. the avoidance of violence, esp. as a principle. □□ **non-violent** adj.

non-volatile /nɒnˈvɒləˌtaɪl/ adj. (esp. of a substance) not volatile.

non-voting /nɒnˈvəʊtɪŋ/ adj. not having or using a vote. □□ **non-voter** n.

non-White /nɒnˈwaɪt/ adj. & n. —adj. 1 (of a person) not White. 2 of or relating to non-White people. —n. a non-White person.

non-word /ˈnɒnwɜːd/ n. an unrecorded or unused word.

noodle¹ /ˈnuːd(ə)l/ n. a strip or ring of pasta. [G Nudel]

noodle² /ˈnuːd(ə)l/ n. 1 a simpleton. 2 sl. the head. [18th c.: orig. unkn.]

nook /nʊk/ n. a corner or recess; a secluded place. [ME nok(e) corner, of unkn. orig.]

nooky /ˈnʊkɪ/ n. (also **nookie**) sl. sexual intercourse. [20th c.: perh. f. NOOK]

noon /nuːn/ n. 1 twelve o'clock in the day, midday. 2 the culminating point. [OE nōn f. L nona (hora) ninth hour: orig. = 3 p.m. (cf. NONE²)]

noonday /ˈnuːndeɪ/ n. midday.

no one /ˈnəʊ wʌn/ n. no person; nobody.

noontide /ˈnuːntaɪd/ n. (also **noontime** /-taɪm/) midday.

noose /nuːs/ n. & v. —n. 1 a loop with a running knot, tightening as the rope or wire is pulled, esp. in a snare, lasso, or hangman's halter. 2 a snare or bond. 3 joc. the marriage tie. —v.tr. 1 catch with or enclose in a noose, ensnare. 2 a make a noose on (a cord). b (often foll. by round) arrange (a cord) in a noose. □ **put one's head in a noose** bring about one's own downfall. [ME nose, perh. f. OF no(u)s f. L nodus knot]

nopal /ˈnəʊp(ə)l/ n. any American cactus of the genus Nopalea, esp. N. cochinellifera grown in plantations for breeding cochineal. [F & Sp. f. Nahuatl nopalli cactus]

nope /nəʊp/ adv. colloq. = NO² adv. 1. [NO²]

nor /nɔː(r), nə(r)/ conj. 1 and not; and not either (neither one thing nor the other; not a man nor a child was to be seen; I said I had not seen it, nor had I; all that is true, nor must we forget ...; can neither read nor write). 2 and no more; neither ('I cannot go'—'Nor can I'). □ **nor ... nor** ... poet. or archaic neither ... nor ... [ME, contr. f. obs. nother f. OE nawther, nāhwæther (as NO², WHETHER)]

nor' /nɔː(r)/ n. & adj. & adv. (esp. in compounds) = NORTH (nor'ward; nor'wester). [abbr.]

noradrenalin /ˌnɔːrəˈdrenəlɪn/ n. (also **noradrenaline**) a hormone released by the adrenal medulla and by sympathetic nerve endings as a neurotransmitter. [normal + ADRENALIN]

Nordic /ˈnɔːdɪk/ adj. & n. —adj. 1 of or relating to an extremely artificial sub-racial grouping of people who, as a population, are tall, with fair colouring, and dolichocephalic. 2 of or relating to Scandinavia or Finland. 3 (of skiing) with cross-country work and jumping. —n. a Nordic person, esp. a native of Scandinavia or Finland. [F nordique f. nord north]

Nordkyn /ˈnɔːkən/ a promontory in NE Norway, to the east of North Cape, considered to be the northernmost point of Europe.

Norfolk /ˈnɔːfək/ a county of eastern England; pop. (1981) 710,400; county town, Norwich. □ **Norfolk jacket** n. a man's loose belted jacket, with box pleats.

Norfolk Island /ˈnɔːfək/ an island in the Pacific Ocean to the east of Australia and the north of New Zealand, administered as an external territory of Australia; pop. (1986) 1,977. Occupied from 1788 to 1814 as a penal colony, the island was settled by the descendants of the mutineers from the Bounty in 1856.

nork /nɔːk/ n. (usu. in pl.) Austral. sl. a woman's breast. [20th c.: orig. uncert.]

norland /ˈnɔːlənd/ n. Brit. a northern region. [contr. of NORTHLAND]

norm /nɔːm/ n. 1 a standard or pattern or type. 2 a standard quantity to be produced or amount of work to be done. 3 customary behaviour etc. [L norma carpenter's square]

normal /ˈnɔːm(ə)l/ adj. & n. —adj. 1 conforming to a standard; regular, usual, typical. 2 free from mental or emotional disorder.

3 Geom. (of a line) at right angles, perpendicular. 4 Chem. (of a solution) containing one gram-equivalent of solute per litre. —n. 1 a the normal value of a temperature etc., esp. blood-heat. b the usual state, level, etc. 2 Geom. a line at right angles. □ **normal distribution** Statistics a function that represents the distribution of many random variables as a symmetrical bell-shaped graph. **normal school** (in the US, France, etc.) a school or college for training teachers. □□ **normalcy** n. esp. US. **normality** /-ˈmælɪtɪ/ n. [F normal or L normalis (as NORM)]

normalize /ˈnɔːməˌlaɪz/ v. (also **-ise**) 1 tr. make normal. 2 intr. become normal. 3 tr. cause to conform. □□ **normalization** /-ˈzeɪʃ(ə)n/ n. **normalizer** n.

normally /ˈnɔːməlɪ/ adv. 1 in a normal manner. 2 usually.

Norman /ˈnɔːmən/ n. & adj. —n. 1 a native or inhabitant of Normandy. 2 a descendant of the people of mixed Scandinavian and Frankish origin established there in early medieval times. They were the dominant military power in western Europe in the 11th c., conquering England in 1066 and setting up Norman kingdoms as far afield as Sicily, Greece, and the Holy Land. 3 Norman French. 4 Archit. the style of Romanesque architecture developed by the Normans and employed in England after the Conquest, with rounded arches and heavy pillars. 5 any of the English kings from William I to Stephen. —adj. 1 of or relating to the Normans. 2 of or relating to the Norman style of architecture. □ **Norman Conquest** see CONQUEST. **Norman English** English as spoken or influenced by the Normans. **Norman French** French as spoken by the Normans or (after 1066) in English lawcourts. □□ **Normanesque** /-ˈnesk/ adj. **Normanism** n. **Normanize** v.tr. & intr. (also **-ise**). [OF Normans pl. of Normant f. ON Northmathr (as NORTH, MAN)]

Normandy /ˈnɔːməndɪ/ 1 a former province of NW France with its coastline on the English Channel, now divided into the two regions of Upper Normandy (Haute-Normandie) and Lower Normandy (Basse-Normandie). It was given by Charles III of France to Rollo, first Duke of Normandy, in 912, and was contested between France and Britain throughout the Middle Ages until finally conquered by France in the mid-15th c. 2 the name of the royal house including William I and II, Henry I, and Stephen, which ruled England from 1066 until 1154.

normative /ˈnɔːmətɪv/ adj. of or establishing a norm. □□ **normatively** adv. **normativeness** n. [F normatif -ive f. L norma (see NORM)]

Norn /nɔːn/ n. Scand. Mythol. the personification of fate or destiny, usually in the form of a virgin goddess (Urd, Urdar, Verdandi, Skuld). [ON: orig. unkn.]

Norrköping /ˈnɔːkəpɪŋ/ an industrial seaport on an inlet of the Baltic Sea in SE Sweden; pop. (1987) 119,000.

Norroy /ˈnɒrɔɪ/ n. (in full **Norroy and Ulster**) Heraldry (in the UK) the title given to the third King of Arms, with jurisdiction north of the Trent and (since 1943) in N. Ireland (cf. CLARENCEUX, King of Arms). [ME f. AF norroi (unrecorded) f. OF nord north, roi king]

Norse /nɔːs/ n. & adj. —n. 1 a the Norwegian language. b the Scandinavian language-group. 2 (prec. by the; treated as pl.) a the Norwegians. b the Vikings. —adj. of ancient Scandinavia, esp. Norway. □ **Old Norse** the Germanic language of Norway and its colonies, or of Scandinavia, down to the 14th c. It is the ancestor of the Scandinavian languages and is most clearly preserved in the saga literature of Iceland. □□ **Norseman** n. (pl. **-men**). [Du. noor(d)sch f. noord north]

North /nɔːθ/, Frederick, Lord (1732–92), British Whig statesman, Prime Minister 1770–82. He was popular as a peacetime premier and in the early years of the War of American Independence (which he had sought to avoid), but increasing frustration at failures in America, and opposition propaganda suggesting that his ministry was being sustained in power by excessive Crown patronage and influence, brought his resignation in 1782.

north /nɔːθ/ n., adj., & adv. —n. 1 a the point of the horizon 90° anticlockwise from east. b the compass point corresponding to this. c the direction in which this lies. 2 (usu. **the North**) a the part of the world or a country or a town lying to the north, esp. = *north country* or *Northern States*. **b** the Arctic. **c** the industrialized nations. **3** (**North**) *Bridge* a player occupying the position designated 'north'. —*adj*. **1** towards, at, near, or facing north. **2** coming from the north (*north wind*). —*adv*. **1** towards, at, or near the north. **2** (foll. by *of*) further north than. □ **north and south** lengthwise along a line from north to south. **North Atlantic Drift** see GULF STREAM. **north by east** (or **west**) between north and north-north-east (or north-north-west). **north country** the northern part of England (north of the Humber). **North-countryman** (*pl.* **-men**) a native of the north country. **north light** light from the north, esp. as desired by painters and in factory design. **north pole** see POLE². **to the north** (often foll. by *of*) in a northerly direction. [OE f. Gmc]

North America the northern half of the American land mass, connected to South America by the Isthmus of Panama, bordered by the Atlantic Ocean to the east and the Pacific Ocean to the west. (See AMERICA.) The southern part of the continent was colonized by the Spanish in the 16th c., while the eastern coast was opened up by the British and French in the 17th c., rivalry between the two ending in British victory during the Seven Years War. The American colonies won their independence in the War of American Independence (1775–83), while Canada was granted its own constitution in 1867. The 19th c. saw the gradual development of the western half of the continent, the emergence of Mexico as an independent State, and the growth of the United States as a world power. The US has progressively dominated the continent, both economically and politically, Canada having a very small population relative to its size and Mexico sharing, albeit to a much lesser extent, the problems of its Central American neighbours to the south. □□ **North American** *adj.* & *n*.

Northamptonshire /nɔːˈθæmptənʃə(r)/ an east midland county of England; pop. (1981) 532,500; county town, Northampton.

Northants /nɔːˈθænts/ *abbr.* Northamptonshire.

North Atlantic Treaty Organization see NATO.

northbound /ˈnɔːθbaʊnd/ *adj.* travelling or leading northwards.

North Cape (Norwegian **Nordkapp** /ˈnɔːkæp/) a promontory on Magerøya Island, off the north coast of Norway. Situated on the edge of the Barents Sea, North Cape is the northernmost point of the world accessible by car.

North Carolina /ˌkærəˈlaɪnə/ a State of the US on the Atlantic coast, settled by the English and named after Charles I; pop. (est. 1985) 5,881,000; capital, Raleigh. It was one of the original 13 States of the US (1788).

Northcliffe /ˈnɔːθklɪf/, Alfred Charles William Harmsworth, Viscount (1865–1922), British newspaper proprietor. With his younger brother Harold (later Lord Rothermere), Northcliffe built up a large newspaper empire in the years preceding the First World War, including *The Times*, the *Daily Mail*, and the *Daily Mirror*. During the war he used his press empire to exercise a strong if at times erratic influence over British war policy and in 1918 was given control of overseas propaganda.

North Dakota /dəˈkəʊtə/ a State in the north central US, bordering on Canada; pop. (est. 1985) 652,700; capital, Bismarck. Acquired partly by the Louisiana Purchase in 1803 and partly from Britain by treaty in 1818, it became the 39th State of the US in 1889.

north-east *n.* **1** the point of the horizon midway between north and east. **2** the compass point corresponding to this. **3** the direction in which this lies. **4** (usu. **the North-East**) the part of a country or town lying to the north-east. —*adj.* of, towards, or coming from the north-east. —*adv.* towards, at, or near the north-east. □ **North-east Passage** a passage for ships along the northern coast of Europe and Asia, formerly thought of as a possible route to the East. □□ **north-easterly** *adj.* & *adv.* **north-eastern** *adj.*

northeaster /nɔːˈθiːstə(r)/ *n.* a north-east wind.

norther /ˈnɔːθə(r)/ *n.* US a strong cold north wind blowing in autumn and winter over Texas, Florida, and the Gulf of Mexico.

northerly /ˈnɔːðəlɪ/ *adj., adv.,* & *n.* —*adj.* & *adv.* **1** in a northern

position or direction. **2** (of wind) blowing from the north. —*n.* (*pl.* **-ies**) (usu. in *pl.*) a wind blowing from the north.

northern /ˈnɔːð(ə)n/ *adj.* **1** of or in the north; inhabiting the north. **2** lying or directed towards the north. □ **Northern Cross** the constellation Cygnus. **Northern hemisphere** the half of the earth north of the equator. **northern lights** the aurora borealis. **Northern States** the States in the north of the US. □□ **northernmost** *adj.* [OE *northerne* (as NORTH, -ERN)]

Northern Circars /sɜːˈkɑːz/ a name formerly used of the coastal region of eastern India between the Krishna River and Orissa, now in Andhra Pradesh.

northerner /ˈnɔːðənə(r)/ *n.* a native or inhabitant of the north.

Northern Ireland a unit of the UK comprising the six north-eastern counties of Ireland, established in 1920 when these withdrew from the newly constituted Irish Free State (see IRELAND); pop. (est. 1987) 1,575,200. At first a self-governing province with its parliament meeting at Stormont Castle in Belfast, it was dominated by the Ulster Unionist party, opposed by an increasing Roman Catholic minority favouring union with the Irish Republic. Discrimination against the latter group in local government, employment, and housing led to violent conflicts and (from 1969) the presence of British army units to keep the peace. Continuing terrorist activities resulted in the suspension of the Stormont assembly and imposition of direct rule from Westminster. Attempts to organize an agreed and permanent system of government have so far met with failure.

Northern Rhodesia see ZAMBIA.

Northern Territory a territory in central north Australia, the administration of which was taken over from South Australia by the Commonwealth of Australia in 1911; it became self-governing within the Commonwealth in 1978; pop. (1986) 156,700; capital, Darwin.

northing /ˈnɔːθɪŋ/ *n. Naut.* the distance travelled or measured northward.

Northland /ˈnɔːθlənd/ *n. poet.* the northern lands; the northern part of a country. [OE (as NORTH, LAND)]

Northman /ˈnɔːθmən/ *n.* (*pl.* **-men**) a native of Scandinavia, esp. of Norway. [OE]

north-north-east *n., adj.,* & *adv.* midway between north and north-east.

north-north-west *n., adj.,* & *adv.* midway between north and north-west.

North Rhine-Westphalia (German **Nordrhein-Westfalen** /nɔːtˌraɪnvestˈfɑːlən/) a 'Land' (State) of Germany; pop. (1987) 16,672,000; capital, Düsseldorf.

North Sea that part of the Atlantic Ocean between the mainland of Europe and the east coast of Britain. Since 1960 it has become important for the exploitation of oil and gas deposits under the sea-bed.

North Star the pole star (see POLARIS).

Northumb. *abbr.* Northumberland.

Northumberland /nɔːˈθʌmbələnd/ a county in the extreme north-east of England; pop. (1981) 299,400; county town, Morpeth.

Northumbria /nɔːˈθʌmbrɪə/ an ancient Anglo-Saxon kingdom extending from the Humber to the Forth. The name has been revived in 'Northumbria Authority', an area of police administration in NE England. □□ **Northumbrian** *adj.* & *n.* [obs. *Northumber*, persons living beyond the Humber, f. OE *Northhymbre*]

northward /ˈnɔːθwəd/ *adj., adv.,* & *n.* —*adj.* & *adv.* (also **northwards**) towards the north. —*n.* a northward direction or region.

north-west *n.* **1** the point of the horizon midway between north and west. **2** the compass point corresponding to this. **3** the direction in which this lies. **4** (usu. **the North-West**) the part of a country or town lying to the north-west. —*adj.* of, towards, or coming from the north-west. —*adv.* towards, at, or near the north-west. □ **North-west Passage** a passage for ships along the northern coast of North America, formerly thought of as a possible route from the Atlantic to the Pacific and sought by Sebastian Cabot and others. □□ **north-westerly** adj. & adv. **north-western** adj.

northwester /nɔːˈθwestə(r)/ n. a north-west wind.

North-west Frontier Province a province of NW Pakistan; pop. (1981) 11,061,000; capital, Peshawar.

Northwest Territories the part of Canada lying north of the 60th parallel, administered by the Hudson's Bay Company from 1670 and transferred by Britain to Canada in 1870; pop. (1986) 52,200.

Northwest Territory a region of the US lying between the Mississippi and Ohio Rivers and the Great Lakes, acquired in 1783 after the War of American Independence.

North Yorkshire a county of NE England; pop. (1981) 676,500; county town, Northallerton.

Norway /ˈnɔːweɪ/ a country (its name means 'north way') occupying the northern and western part of the Scandinavian peninsula; pop. (est. 1988) 4,190,750; official language, Norwegian; capital, Oslo. An independent if often divided kingdom in Viking and early medieval times, Norway was united with Denmark and Sweden by the Union of Kolmar in 1397, and after the latter's departure in 1523, was reduced to little more than a Danish territory. Ceded to Sweden in 1814, it finally regained its independence in 1905, only to lose it for the period of the Nazi occupation of 1940–5. With a small population confined to a mountainous coastal strip, Norway is heavily dependent on foreign trade, although the opening up of the North Sea oil fields has recently benefited the economy greatly. □ **Norway lobster** a small European lobster, *Nephrops norvegicus*. **Norway rat** the common brown rat, *Rattus norvegicus*.

Norwegian /nɔːˈwiːdʒ(ə)n/ n. & adj. —n. **1 a** a native or national of Norway. **b** a person of Norwegian descent. **2** the official language of Norway, spoken by its 4 million inhabitants, which belongs to the Scandinavian language group. During the Middle Ages Danish gradually replaced Norwegian as the language of the upper classes in Norway, the peasants continuing to speak Norwegian, and there are still two separate forms of the modern language, *Bokmål* or *Riksmål*, the more widely used (also called Dano-Norwegian), a modified form of the Danish language used in Norway after its separation from Denmark (1814) following four centuries of union, and *Nynorsk* (= new Norwegian, formerly called *Landsmål*), a literary form devised by the Norwegian philologist Ivar Aasen (d. 1896) from the country dialects most closely descended from Old Norse, and considered to be a purer form of the language than Bokmål. —adj. of or relating to Norway or its people or language. [med.L *Norvegia* f. ON *Norvegr* (as NORTH, WAY), assim. to *Norway*]

nor'-wester /nɔːˈwestə(r)/ n. **1** a northwester. **2** a glass of strong liquor. **3** an oilskin hat, a sou'wester. [contr.]

Norwich /ˈnɒrɪdʒ, -ɪtʃ/ the county town of Norfolk; pop. (1981) 122,900.

Nos. abbr. numbers. [cf. No.]

nose /nəʊz/ n. & v. —n. **1** an organ above the mouth on the face or head of a human or animal, containing nostrils and used for smelling and breathing. **2 a** the sense of smell (*dogs have a good nose*). **b** the ability to detect a particular thing (*a nose for scandal*). **3** the odour or perfume of wine, tea, tobacco, hay, etc. **4** the open end or nozzle of a tube, pipe, pair of bellows, retort, etc. **5 a** the front end or projecting part of a thing, e.g. of a car or aircraft. **b** = NOSING. **6** sl. an informer of the police. —v. **1** tr. (often foll. by *out*) **a** perceive the smell of, discover by smell. **b** detect. **2** tr. thrust or rub one's nose against or into, esp. in order to smell. **3** intr. (usu. foll. by *about*, *around*, etc.) pry or search. **4 a** intr. make one's way cautiously forward. **b** tr. make (one's or its way). □ **as plain as the nose on your face** easily seen. **by a nose** by a very narrow margin (*won the race by a nose*). **count noses** count those present, one's supporters, etc.; decide a question by mere numbers. **cut off one's nose to spite one's face** disadvantage oneself in the course of trying to disadvantage another. **get up a person's nose** sl. annoy a person. **keep one's nose clean** sl. stay out of trouble, behave properly. **keep one's nose to the grindstone** see GRINDSTONE. **nose-cone** the cone-shaped nose of a rocket etc. **nose-flute** a

musical instrument blown with the nose in Fiji etc. **nose leaf** a fleshy part on the nostrils of some bats, used for echo location. **nose-monkey** the proboscis monkey. **nose-piece 1** = NOSE-BAND. **2** the part of a helmet etc. protecting the nose. **3** the part of a microscope to which the object-glass is attached. **nose-rag** sl. a pocket handkerchief. **nose-to-tail** (of vehicles) moving or stationary one close behind another, esp. in heavy traffic. **nose-wheel** a landing-wheel under the nose of an aircraft. **on the nose 1** US sl. precisely. **2** Austral. sl. annoying. **put a person's nose out of joint** colloq. embarrass, disconcert, frustrate, or supplant a person. **rub a person's nose in it** see RUB. **see no further than one's nose** be short-sighted, esp. in foreseeing the consequences of one's actions etc. **speak through one's nose** pronounce words with a nasal twang. **turn up one's nose** (usu. foll. by *at*) colloq. show disdain. **under a person's nose** colloq. right before a person (esp. of defiant or unnoticed actions). **with one's nose in the air** haughtily. □□ **nosed** adj. (also in comb.). **noseless** adj. [OE *nosu*]

nosebag /ˈnəʊzbæg/ n. a bag containing fodder, hung on a horse's head.

noseband /ˈnəʊzbænd/ n. the lower band of a bridle, passing over the horse's nose.

nosebleed /ˈnəʊzbliːd/ n. an instance of bleeding from the nose.

nosedive /ˈnəʊzdaɪv/ n. & v. —n. **1** a steep downward plunge by an aeroplane. **2** a sudden plunge or drop. —v.intr. make a nosedive.

nosegay /ˈnəʊzɡeɪ/ n. a bunch of flowers, esp. a sweet-scented posy. [NOSE + GAY in obs. use = ornament]

nosepipe /ˈnəʊzpaɪp/ n. a piece of piping used as a nozzle.

nosering /ˈnəʊzrɪŋ/ n. a ring fixed in the nose of an animal (esp. a bull) for leading it, or of a person for ornament.

nosey var. of NOSY.

nosh /nɒʃ/ v. & n. sl. —v.tr. & intr. **1** eat or drink. **2** US eat between meals. —n. **1** food or drink. **2** US a snack. □ **nosh-up** Brit. a large meal. [Yiddish]

noshery /ˈnɒʃərɪ/ n. (pl. **-ies**) sl. a restaurant or snack bar.

nosing /ˈnəʊzɪŋ/ n. a rounded edge of a step, moulding, etc., or a metal shield for it.

nosography /nəˈsɒɡrəfɪ/ n. the systematic description of diseases. [Gk *nosos* disease + -GRAPHY]

nosology /nəˈsɒlədʒɪ/ n. the branch of medical science dealing with the classification of diseases. □□ **nosological** /ˌnɒsəˈlɒdʒɪk(ə)l/ adj. [Gk *nosos* disease + -LOGY]

nostalgia /nɒˈstældʒɪə, -dʒə/ n. **1** (often foll. by *for*) sentimental yearning for a period of the past. **2** regretful or wistful memory of an earlier time. **3** severe homesickness. □□ **nostalgic** adj. **nostalgically** adv. [mod.L f. Gk *nostos* return home]

nostoc /ˈnɒstɒk/ n. any gelatinous blue-green unicellular alga of the genus *Nostoc*, that can fix nitrogen from the atmosphere. [name invented by Paracelsus]

Nostradamus /ˌnɒstrəˈdɑːməs/ the Latinized name of Michel de Nostredame (1503–66), Provençal astrologer whose extensive prophecies, decidedly apocalyptic in tone, were given extensive credence in the mid-16th c. at the French court, where he was for a time personal physician to Charles IX.

nostril /ˈnɒstrɪl/ n. either of two external openings of the nasal cavity in vertebrates that admit air to the lungs and smells to the olfactory nerves. □□ **nostrilled** adj. (also in comb.). [OE *nosthyrl*, *nosterl* f. *nosu* NOSE + *thyr(e)l* hole; cf. THRILL]

nostrum /ˈnɒstrəm/ n. **1** a quack remedy, a patent medicine, esp. one prepared by the person recommending it. **2** a pet scheme, esp. for political or social reform. [L, neut. of *noster* our, used in sense 'of our own make']

nosy /ˈnəʊzɪ/ adj. & n. (also **nosey**) —adj. (**nosier**, **nosiest**) **1** colloq. inquisitive, prying. **2** having a large nose. **3** having a distinctive (good or bad) smell. —n. (pl. **-ies**) a person with a large nose. □ **Nosy Parker** esp. Brit. colloq. a busybody. □□ **nosily** adv. **nosiness** n.

not /nɒt/ adv. expressing negation, esp.: **1** (also **n't** joined to a preceding verb) following an auxiliary verb or *be* or (in a question) the subject of such a verb (*I cannot say; she isn't there; didn't* *you tell me?; am I not right?; aren't we smart?*). ¶ Use with other verbs is now *archaic* (*I know not; fear not*), except with participles and infinitives (*not knowing, I cannot say; we asked them not to come*). **2** used elliptically for a negative sentence or verb or phrase (*Is she coming?—I hope not; Do you want it?—Certainly not!*). **3** used to express the negative of other words (*not a single one was left; Are they pleased?—Not they; he is not my cousin, but my nephew*). □ **not at all** (in polite reply to thanks) there is no need for thanks. **not but what** *archaic* **1** all the same; nevertheless (*I cannot do it; not but what a stronger man might*). **2** not such . . . or so . . . that . . . not (*not such a fool but what he can see it*). **not half** see HALF. **not least** with considerable importance, notably. **not much** see MUCH. **not quite 1** almost (*am not quite there*). **2** noticeably not (*not quite proper*). **not that** (foll. by clause) it is not to be inferred that (*if he said so—not that he ever did—he lied*). **not a thing** nothing at all. **not very** see VERY. [ME contr. of NOUGHT]

nota bene /ˌnəʊtə ˈbeneɪ/ *v.tr.* (as *imper.*) observe what follows, take notice (usu. drawing attention to a following qualification of what has preceded). [L, = note well]

notability /ˌnəʊtəˈbɪlɪtɪ/ *n.* (*pl.* -ies) **1** the state of being notable (*names of no historical notability*). **2** a prominent person. [ME f. OF *notabilité* or LL *notabilitas* (as NOTABLE)]

notable /ˈnəʊtəb(ə)l/ *adj. & n.* —*adj.* worthy of note; striking, remarkable, eminent. —*n.* an eminent person. □□ **notableness** *n.* **notably** *adv.* [ME f. OF f. L *notabilis* (as NOTE)]

notarize /ˈnəʊtəˌraɪz/ *v.tr.* (also **-ise**) *US* certify (a document) as a notary.

notary /ˈnəʊtərɪ/ *n.* (*pl.* -ies) (in full **notary public**) a person authorized to perform certain legal formalities, esp. to draw up or certify contracts, deeds, etc. □□ **notarial** /nəʊˈteərɪəl/ *adj.* **notarially** /nəʊˈteərɪəlɪ/ *adv.* [ME f. L *notarius* secretary (as NOTE)]

notate /nəʊˈteɪt/ *v.tr.* write in notation. [back-form. f. NOTATION]

notation /nəʊˈteɪʃ(ə)n/ *n.* **1 a** the representation of numbers, quantities, pitch and duration etc. of musical notes, etc. by symbols. **b** any set of such symbols. **2 a** a set of symbols used to represent chess moves, dance steps, etc. **3** *US* a note or annotation. **b** a record. **4** = *scale of notation* (see SCALE³). □□ **notational** *adj.* [F *notation* or L *notatio* (as NOTE)]

notch /nɒtʃ/ *n. & v.* —*n.* **1** a V-shaped indentation on an edge or surface. **2** a nick made on a stick etc. in order to keep count. **3** *colloq.* a step or degree (*move up a notch*). **4** *US* a deep gorge. —*v.tr.* **1** make notches in. **2** (foll. by *up*) record or score with or as with notches. **3** secure or insert by notches. □□ **notched** *adj.* **notcher** *n.* **notchy** *adj.* (**notchier, notchiest**). [AF *noche* perh. f. a verbal form *nocher* (unrecorded), of uncert. orig.]

note /nəʊt/ *n. & v.* —*n.* **1** a brief record of facts, topics, thoughts, etc., as an aid to memory, for use in writing, public speaking, etc. (often in *pl.*: *make notes; spoke without notes*). **2** an observation, usu. unwritten, of experiences etc. (*compare notes*). **3** a short or informal letter. **4** a formal diplomatic or parliamentary communication. **5** a short annotation or additional explanation in a book etc.; a footnote. **6 a** *Brit.* = BANKNOTE (*a five-pound note*). **b** a written promise or notice of payment of various kinds. **7 a** notice, attention (*worthy of note*). **b** distinction, eminence (*a person of note*). **8 a** a written sign representing the pitch and duration of a musical sound. **b** a single tone of definite pitch made by a musical instrument, the human voice, etc. **c** a key of a piano etc. **9 a** a bird's song or call. **b** a single tone in this. **10** a quality or tone of speaking, expressing mood or attitude etc. (*sound a note of warning; ended on a note of optimism*). **11** a characteristic; a distinguishing feature. —*v.tr.* **1** observe, notice; give or draw attention to. **2** (often foll. by *down*) record as a thing to be remembered or observed. **3** (in *passive*; often foll. by *for*) be famous or well known (for a quality, activity, etc.) (*were noted for their generosity*). □ **hit** (or **strike**) **the right note** speak or act in exactly the right manner. **of note** important, distinguished (*a person of note*). **take note** (often foll. by *of*) observe; pay attention (to). □□ **noted** *adj.* (in sense 3 of *v.*). **noteless** *adj.* [ME f. OF *note* (n.), *noter* (v.) f. L *nota* mark]

notebook /ˈnəʊtbʊk/ *n.* a small book for making or taking notes.

notecase /ˈnəʊtkeɪs/ *n.* a wallet for holding banknotes.

notelet /ˈnəʊtlɪt/ *n.* a small folded sheet of paper, usu. with a decorative design, for an informal letter.

notepaper /ˈnəʊtˌpeɪpə(r)/ *n.* paper for writing letters.

noteworthy /ˈnəʊtˌwɜːðɪ/ *adj.* worthy of attention; remarkable. □□ **noteworthiness** *n.*

nothing /ˈnʌθɪŋ/ *n. & adv.* —*n.* **1** not anything (*nothing has been done; have nothing to do*). **2** no thing (often foll. by *compl.*: *I see nothing that I want; can find nothing useful*). **3 a** a person or thing of no importance or concern; a trivial event or remark (*was nothing to me; the little nothings of life*). **b** (*attrib.*) *colloq.* of no value; indeterminate (*a nothing sort of day*). **4** non-existence; what does not exist. **5** (in calculations) no amount; nought (*a third of nothing is nothing*). —*adv.* **1** not at all, in no way (*helps us nothing; is nothing like enough*). **2** *US colloq.* not at all (*Is he ill?—Ill nothing, he's dead.*). □ **be nothing to 1** not concern. **2** not compare with. **be** (or **have**) **nothing to do with 1** have no connection with. **2** not be involved or associated with. **for nothing 1** at no cost; without payment. **2** to no purpose. **have nothing on 1** be naked. **2** have no engagements. **no nothing** *colloq.* (concluding a list of negatives) nothing at all. **nothing doing** *colloq.* **1 a** there is no prospect of success or agreement. **b** I refuse. **2** nothing is happening. **nothing** (or **nothing else**) **for it** (often foll. by *but to* + infin.) no alternative (*nothing for it but to pay up*). **nothing** (or **not much**) **in it** (or **to it**) untrue or unimportant. **2** simple to do. **3** no (or little) advantage to be seen in one possibility over another. **nothing less than** at least (*nothing less than a disaster*). **think nothing of it** do not apologize or feel bound to show gratitude. [OE *nān thing* (as NO¹, THING)]

nothingness /ˈnʌθɪŋnɪs/ *n.* **1** non-existence; the non-existent. **2** worthlessness, triviality, insignificance.

notice /ˈnəʊtɪs/ *n. & v.* —*n.* **1** attention, observation (*it escaped my notice*). **2** a displayed sheet etc. bearing an announcement or other information. **3 a** an intimation or warning, esp. a formal one to allow preparations to be made (*give notice; at a moment's notice*). **b** (often foll. by *to* + infin.) a formal announcement or declaration of intention to end an agreement or leave employment at a specified time (*hand in one's notice; notice to quit*). **4** a short published review or comment about a new play, book, etc. —*v.tr.* **1** (often foll. by *that, how*, etc. + clause) perceive, observe; take notice of. **2** remark upon; speak of. □ **at short** (or **a moment's**) **notice** with little warning. **notice-board** *Brit.* a board for displaying notices. **take notice** (or **no notice**) show signs (or no signs) of interest. **take notice of 1** observe; pay attention to. **2** act upon. **under notice** served with a formal notice. [ME f. OF f. L *notitia* being known f. *notus* past part. of *noscere* know]

noticeable /ˈnəʊtɪsəb(ə)l/ *adj.* **1** easily seen or noticed; perceptible. **2** noteworthy. □□ **noticeably** *adv.*

notifiable /ˈnəʊtɪˌfaɪəb(ə)l/ *adj.* (of a disease) that must be notified to the health authorities.

notify /ˈnəʊtɪˌfaɪ/ *v.tr.* (**-ies, -ied**) **1** (often foll. by *of*, or *that* + clause) inform or give notice to (a person). **2** make known; announce or report (a thing). □□ **notification** /-fɪˈkeɪʃ(ə)n/ *n.* [ME f. OF *notifier* f. L *notificare* f. *notus* known: see NOTICE]

notion /ˈnəʊʃ(ə)n/ *n.* **1 a** a concept or idea; a conception (*it was an absurd notion*). **b** an opinion (*has the notion that people are honest*). **c** a vague view or understanding (*have no notion what you mean*). **2** an inclination, impulse, or intention (*has no notion of conforming*). **3** (in *pl.*) small, useful articles, esp. haberdashery. [L *notio* idea f. *notus* past part. of *noscere* know]

notional /ˈnəʊʃən(ə)l/ *adj.* **1 a** hypothetical, imaginary. **b** (of knowledge etc.) speculative; not based on experiment etc. **2** *Gram.* (of a verb) conveying its own meaning, not auxiliary. □□ **notionally** *adv.* [obs. F *notional* or med.L *notionalis* (as NOTION)]

notochord /ˈnəʊtəˌkɔːd/ *n.* a cartilaginous skeletal rod supporting the body in all embryo and some adult chordate animals. [Gk *nōton* back + CHORD²]

notorious /nəʊˈtɔːrɪəs/ *adj.* well known, esp. unfavourably (*a notorious criminal; notorious for its climate*). □□ **notoriety** /-təˈraɪətɪ/ *n.* **notoriously** *adv.* [med.L *notorius* f. L *notus* (as NOTION)]

notornis /nə'tɔːnɪs/ n. a rare flightless New Zealand bird, *Porphyrio mantelli*, with a large bill and brightly coloured plumage. Also called TAKAHE. [Gk *notos* south + *ornis* bird]

Notre-Dame /ˌnɒtrə'daːm/ the gothic cathedral church of Paris, dedicated to the Virgin Mary, on the Île de la Cité (an island in the Seine), begun in 1163 and effectively finished by 1250. It is especially noted for its innovatory flying buttresses, sculptured façade, and great rose windows with 13th-c. stained glass. [F, = our lady]

Nottinghamshire /'nɒtɪŋəmˌʃɪə(r)/ a midland county of England; pop. (1981) 994,200; county town, Nottingham.

Notts. /nɒts/ *abbr.* Nottinghamshire.

notwithstanding /ˌnɒtwɪθ'stændɪŋ, -wɪð'stændɪŋ/ *prep., adv., & conj.* —*prep.* in spite of; without prevention by (*notwithstanding your objections*; *this fact notwithstanding*). —*adv.* nevertheless; all the same. —*conj.* (usu. foll. by *that* + clause) although. [ME, orig. absol. part. f. NOT + WITHSTAND + -ING²]

Nouadhibou /ˌnwædɪ'buː/ the principal port of Mauritania; pop. 22,000. Formerly known as Port Étienne, Nouadhibou is linked by rail to the iron-ore mines of Zouérate on the western edge of the Sahara.

Nouakchott /'nwækʃɒt/ the capital of Mauritania; pop. (est. 1985) 500,000.

nougat /'nuːɡaː/ n. a sweet made from sugar or honey, nuts, and egg-white. [F f. Prov. *nogat* f. *noga* nut]

nought /nɔːt/ n. **1** the digit 0; a cipher. **2** *poet.* or *archaic* (in certain phrases) nothing (cf. NAUGHT). □ **noughts and crosses** a paper-and-pencil game with a square grid of nine squares, in which players seek to complete a row of three noughts or three crosses entered alternately. [OE *nōwiht* f. *ne* not + *ōwiht* var. of *āwiht* AUGHT¹]

Nouméa /nuː'meɪə/ the capital (formerly called *Port de France*) of New Caledonia; pop. (1983) 60,100.

noun /naʊn/ n. *Gram.* a word (other than a pronoun) or group of words used to name or identify any of a class of persons, places, or things (**common noun**), or a particular one of these (**proper noun**). □□ **nounal** *adj.* [ME f. AF f. L *nomen* name]

nourish /'nʌrɪʃ/ v.tr. **1 a** sustain with food. **b** enrich; promote the development of (the soil etc.). **c** provide with intellectual or emotional sustenance or enrichment. **2** foster or cherish (a feeling etc.). □□ **nourisher** n. [ME f. OF *norir* f. L *nutrire*]

nourishing /'nʌrɪʃɪŋ/ adj. (esp. of food) containing much nourishment; sustaining. □□ **nourishingly** adv.

nourishment /'nʌrɪʃmənt/ n. sustenance, food.

nous /naʊs/ n. **1** *colloq.* common sense; gumption. **2** *Philos.* the mind or intellect. [Gk]

nouveau riche /ˌnuːvəʊ 'riːʃ/ n. (pl. **nouveaux riches** pronunc. same) a person who has recently acquired (usu. ostentatious) wealth. [F, = new rich]

nouvelle cuisine /ˌnuːvel kwɪ'ziːn/ n. a modern style of cookery avoiding heaviness and emphasizing presentation. [F, = new cookery]

nouvelle vague /ˌnuːvel 'vaːɡ/ n. a new trend, esp. in French film-making of the early 1960s. [F, fem. of *nouveau* new + *vague* wave]

Nov. *abbr.* November.

nova /'nəʊvə/ n. (pl. **novae** /-viː/ or **novas**) a star showing a sudden large increase of brightness and then subsiding. The so-called 'new stars' of early astronomers, these are actually old stars which undergo a dramatic outburst, increasing in brightness by a factor of many thousands and returning to their original state over the space of a few months. They are classed as a type of cataclysmic variable, where material falling from a companion star to the surface of a white dwarf collects for several thousand years, increasing in density and temperature until it suddenly undergoes a runaway thermonuclear reaction, blasting much of the accumulated material back into space. Novae are often visible at peak brightness in small telescopes, and may sometimes become bright enough to be visible to the naked eye. [L, fem. of *novus* new, because orig. thought to be a new star]

Nova Lisboa see HUAMBO.

Nova Scotia /ˌnəʊvə 'skəʊʃə/ a province of SE Canada, comprising a peninsula projecting into the Atlantic and the adjoining Cape Breton island; pop. (1986) 873,200; capital, Halifax. Settled by the French in the early 18th c. (see ACADIA) it changed hands several times between the French and English until ceded to Britain in 1713, becoming a province of Canada in 1867. □□ **Nova Scotian** *adj. & n.*

Novaya Zemlya /'nəʊvəjə ˌzemlɪ'aː/ two large uninhabited islands in the Arctic Ocean to the north of the Taimyr Peninsula, USSR.

novel¹ /'nɒv(ə)l/ n. **1** a fictitious prose story of book length. **2** (prec. by *the*) this type of literature. [It. *novella* (*storia* story) fem. of *novello* new f. L *novellus* f. *novus*]

novel² /'nɒv(ə)l/ adj. of a new kind or nature; strange; previously unknown. □□ **novelly** adv. [ME f. OF f. L *novellus* f. *novus* new]

novelese /ˌnɒvə'liːz/ n. *derog.* a style characteristic of inferior novels.

novelette /ˌnɒvə'let/ n. **1 a** a short novel. **b** *Brit. derog.* a light romantic novel. **2** *Mus.* a piano piece in free form with several themes.

novelettish /ˌnɒvə'letɪʃ/ adj. *derog.* in the style of a light romantic novel; sentimental.

novelist /'nɒvəlɪst/ n. a writer of novels. □□ **novelistic** /-'lɪstɪk/ adj.

novelize /'nɒvəlaɪz/ v.tr. (also **-ise**) make into a novel. □□ **novelization** /-'zeɪʃ(ə)n/ n.

novella /nə'velə/ n. (pl. **novellas**) a short novel or narrative story; a tale. [It.: see NOVEL¹]

Novello /nə'veləʊ/, Ivor (real name David Ivor Davies, 1893–1951), Welsh born composer, actor, and playwright. In 1914 he wrote 'Keep the Home Fires Burning', which became one of the most popular songs of the First World War. Later he wrote, composed, and acted in the series of operettas that include *Glamorous Night* (1935), *The Dancing Years* (1939), and *King's Rhapsody* (1942).

novelty /'nɒvəltɪ/ n. & adj. —n. (pl. **-ies**) **1 a** newness; new character. **b** originality. **2** a new or unusual thing or occurrence. **3** a small toy or decoration etc. of novel design. **4** (*attrib.*) having novelty (*novelty toys*). [ME f. OF *novelté* (as NOVEL²)]

November /nə'vembə(r)/ n. the eleventh month of the year. [ME f. OF *novembre* f. L *November* f. *novem* nine (orig. the ninth month of the Roman year)]

novena /nə'viːnə/ n. *RC Ch.* a devotion consisting of special prayers or services on nine successive days. [med.L f. L *novem* nine]

Noverre /nɒ've(r)/, Jean-Georges (1727–1810), French dancer, choreographer, ballet master, and dance theorist, a great reformer who stressed the dramatic mission of the ballet.

novice /'nɒvɪs/ n. **1 a** a probationary member of a religious order, before the taking of vows. **b** a new convert. **2** a beginner; an inexperienced person. **3** an animal that has not won a major prize in a competition. [ME f. OF f. L *novicius* f. *novus* new]

noviciate /nə'vɪʃɪət/ n. (also **novitiate**) **1** the period of being a novice. **2** a religious novice. **3** novices' quarters. [F *noviciat* or med.L *noviciatus* (as NOVICE)]

Novi Sad /ˌnɒvɪ 'saːt/ an industrial city of Yugoslavia, capital of the autonomous province of Vojvodina; pop. (1981) 257,700.

Novocaine /'nəʊvəˌkeɪn/ n. (also **novocaine**) *propr.* a local anaesthetic derived from benzoic acid. [L *novus* new + COCAINE]

Novokuznetsk /ˌnɒvəkuz'netsk/ an industrial city of the Soviet Union in the Kuznetz Basin in central Siberia; pop. (est. 1987) 589,000.

Novosibirsk /ˌnɒvəsɪ'bɪəsk/ a city of the Soviet Union, to the west of the Kuznetz Basin, on the Riber Ob; pop. (est. 1987) 1,423,000.

now /naʊ/ adv., conj., & n. —adv. **1** at the present or mentioned time. **2** immediately (*I must go now*). **3** by this or that time (*it was now clear*). **4** under the present circumstances (*I cannot now agree*). **5** on this further occasion (*what do you want now?*). **6** in the immediate past (*just now*). **7** (esp. in a narrative or discourse) then, next (*the police now arrived*; *now to consider the next point*). **8**

(without reference to time, giving various tones to a sentence) surely, I insist, I wonder, etc. (*now what do you mean by that?; oh come now!*). —*conj.* (often foll. by *that* + clause) as a consequence of the fact (*now that I am older; now you mention it*). —*n.* this time; the present (*should be there by now; has happened before now*). □ **as of now** from or at this time. **for now** until a later time (*goodbye for now*). **now and again** (or **then**) from time to time; intermittently. **now or never** an expression of urgency. [OE *nū*]

nowadays /'naʊəˌdeɪz/ *adv.* & *n.* —*adv.* at the present time or age; in these times. —*n.* the present time.

noway /'nəʊweɪ/ *adv.* = NOWISE; (see *no way*).

Nowel (also **Nowell**) *archaic var.* of NOEL.

nowhere /'nəʊweə(r)/ *adv.* & *pron.* —*adv.* in or to no place. —*pron.* no place. □ **be** (or **come in**) **nowhere** be unplaced in a race or competition. **come from nowhere** be suddenly evident or successful. **get nowhere** make or cause to make no progress. **in the middle of nowhere** *colloq.* remote from urban life. **nowhere near** not nearly. [OE *nāhwǣr* (as NO[1], WHERE)]

nowise /'nəʊwaɪz/ *adv.* in no manner; not at all.

nowt /naʊt/ *n. colloq.* or *dial.* nothing. (var. of NOUGHT)

noxious /'nɒkʃəs/ *adj.* harmful, unwholesome. □□ **noxiously** *adv.* **noxiousness** *n.* [f. L *noxius* f. *noxa* harm]

noyau /'nwɑːjəʊ/ *n.* (*pl.* **noyaux** /-jəʊz/) a liqueur of brandy flavoured with fruit-kernels. [F, = kernel, ult. f. L *nux nucis* nut]

nozzle /'nɒz(ə)l/ *n.* a spout on a hose etc. from which a jet issues. [NOSE + -LE[2]]

NP *abbr.* Notary Public.

Np *symb. Chem.* the element neptunium.

n.p. *abbr.* **1** new paragraph. **2** no place of publication.

NPA *abbr.* (in the UK) Newspaper Publishers' Association.

NPL *abbr.* (in the UK) National Physical Laboratory.

nr. *abbr.* near.

NS *abbr.* **1** new style. **2** new series. **3** Nova Scotia.

NSB *abbr.* (in the UK) National Savings Bank.

NSC *abbr.* (in the US) National Security Council.

NSF *abbr.* (in the US) National Science Foundation.

NSPCC *abbr.* (in the UK) National Society for the Prevention of Cruelty to Children.

NSW *abbr.* New South Wales.

NT *abbr.* **1** New Testament. **2** Northern Territory (of Australia). **3** no trumps.

n't /ənt/ *adv.* (in *comb.*) = NOT (usu. with *is, are, have, must*, and the auxiliary verbs *can, do, should, would; isn't; mustn't*) (see also CAN'T, DON'T, WON'T). [contr.]

Nth. *abbr.* North.

nth see N[1].

NTP *abbr.* normal temperature and pressure.

nu /njuː/ *n.* the thirteenth letter of the Greek alphabet (*N, ν*). [Gk]

nuance /'njuːɑ̃s/ *n.* & *v.* —*n.* a subtle difference in or shade of meaning, feeling, colour, etc. —*v.tr.* give a nuance or nuances to. [F f. *nuer* to shade, ult. f. L *nubes* cloud]

nub /nʌb/ *n.* **1** the point or gist (of a matter or story). **2** a small lump, esp. of coal. **3** a stub; a small residue. □□ **nubby** *adj.* [app. var. of *knub*, f. MLG *knubbe, knobbe* KNOB]

nubble /'nʌb(ə)l/ *n.* a small knob or lump. □□ **nubbly** *adj.* [dimin. of NUB]

Nubia /'njuːbɪə/ a region of southern Egypt and northern Sudan which includes the Nile valley between Aswan and Khartoum and the Nubian Desert to the east. Nubia fell under ancient Egyptian rule from the time of the Middle Kingdom, soon after 2000 BC, and from about the 15th c. BC was ruled by an Egyptian viceroy. The country was Egyptianized, and trade (especially in gold) flourished. By the 8th c. BC, however, as Egypt's centralized control disintegrated, a Nubian kingdom emerged, and for a brief period extended its power over Egypt. Much of Nubia is now drowned by the waters of Lake Nasser, formed by the building of the two dams at Aswan. Nubians constitute an ethnic minority group in Egypt. □□ **Nubian** *adj.* & *n.*

nubile /'njuːbaɪl/ *adj.* (of a woman) marriageable or sexually attractive. □□ **nubility** /-'bɪlɪtɪ/ [L *nubilis* f. *nubere* become the wife of]

nuchal /'njuːk(ə)l/ *adj.* of or relating to the nape of the neck. [*nucha* nape f. med.L *nucha* medulla oblongata f. Arab. *nuḵaʿ* spinal marrow]

nuci- /njuːsɪ/ *comb. form* nut. [L *nux nucis* nut]

nuciferous /njuː'sɪfərəs/ *adj. Bot.* bearing nuts.

nucivorous /njuː'sɪvərəs/ *adj.* nut-eating.

nuclear /'njuːklɪə(r)/ *adj.* **1** of, relating to, or constituting a nucleus. **2** using nuclear energy (*nuclear reactor*). **3** having nuclear weapons. □ **nuclear bomb** a bomb involving the release of energy by nuclear fission or fusion or both. **nuclear disarmament** the renunciation of nuclear weapons. **nuclear energy** energy obtained by nuclear fission or fusion. **nuclear family** a couple and their children, regarded as a basic social unit. **nuclear fission** see separate entry. **nuclear force** a strong attractive force between nucleons in the atomic nucleus that holds the nucleus together. **nuclear-free** free from nuclear weapons, power, etc. **nuclear fuel** a substance that will sustain a fission chain reaction so that it can be used as a source of nuclear energy. **nuclear fusion** see separate entry. **nuclear magnetic resonance** the absorption of electromagnetic radiation by a nucleus having a magnetic moment when in an external magnetic field, used mainly as an analytical technique and in body imaging for diagnosis. ¶ Abbr.: NMR, nmr. **nuclear physics** the physics of atomic nuclei and their interactions, esp. in the generation of nuclear energy. **nuclear power 1** electric or motive power generated by a nuclear reactor. **2** a country that has nuclear weapons. **nuclear reactor** see separate entry. **nuclear umbrella** supposed protection afforded by an alliance with a country possessing nuclear weapons. **nuclear warfare** warfare in which nuclear weapons are used. **nuclear waste** any radioactive waste material from the reprocessing of spent nuclear fuel. **nuclear winter** obstruction of sunlight as a potential result of nuclear warfare, characterized by extreme cold temperatures and other effects catastrophic to animal and vegetable life, caused by an atmospheric layer of smoke and dust particles blocking the sun's rays. [NUCLEUS + -AR[1]]

nuclear fission *n.* the splitting of an atomic nucleus into smaller nuclei of roughly equal size, with consequent release of energy, discovered in 1938 by two German chemists, Otto Hahn and F. Strassmann. It can occur either spontaneously or after the impact of another particle. The principal elements capable of undergoing fission are plutonium, uranium, and thorium.

nuclear fusion *n.* the union of atomic nuclei to form heavier nuclei. For the lighter elements this process results in an enormous release of energy, but it can occur only at very high temperatures. The sun's energy arises mainly from the conversion of its hydrogen into helium by fusion. This is also the principle behind the hydrogen bomb, the necessary high temperatures being created by an initial atomic explosion. Research continues into harnessing fusion so that it can be used in power stations, the major obstacle being how to contain the reacting substances, whose temperatures can rise to millions of degrees Celsius.

nuclear reactor *n.* an assembly of fissile and other materials (e.g. moderators) in which a controlled chain reaction can take place, the peaceful application of the chain reaction that was first used in the atom bomb. The heat obtained when a reactor is in operation is continually carried away to where it can be used in a boiler to generate electrical power. Some reactors are involved in the production of radioactive material for medical and other purposes. The first atom 'pile' or reactor was built by the physicist Enrico Fermi at the University of Chicago in 1942.

nuclease /'njuːklɪˌeɪz/ *n.* an enzyme that catalyses the breakdown of nucleic acids.

nucleate /'njuːklɪˌeɪt/ *adj.* & *v.* —*adj.* having a nucleus. —*v.intr.* & *tr.* form or form into a nucleus. □□ **nucleation** /-'eɪʃ(ə)n/ *n.* [LL *nucleare nucleat-* form a kernel (as NUCLEUS)]

nuclei *pl.* of NUCLEUS.

nucleic acid /njuː'kliːɪk, -'kleɪɪk/ *n.* either of two complex organic molecules (DNA and RNA), consisting of many nucleotides linked in a long chain, and present in all living cells.

nucleo- /ˈnjuːklɪəʊ/ *comb. form* nucleus; nucleic acid (*nucleo-protein*).

nucleolus /njuːˈkliːələs, -klɪˈəʊləs/ *n.* (*pl.* **nucleoli** /-laɪ/) a small dense spherical structure within a non-dividing nucleus. □□ **nucleolar** *adj.* [LL, dimin. of L *nucleus*: see NUCLEUS]

nucleon /ˈnjuːklɪˌɒn/ *n.* Physics a proton or neutron.

nucleonics /ˌnjuːklɪˈɒnɪks/ *n.pl.* (treated as *sing.*) the branch of science and technology concerned with atomic nuclei and nucleons, esp. the exploitation of nuclear power. □□ **nucleonic** *adj.* [NUCLEAR, after *electronics*]

nucleoprotein /ˌnjuːklɪəʊˈprəʊtiːn/ *n.* a complex of nucleic acid and protein.

nucleoside /ˈnjuːklɪəˌsaɪd/ *n.* Biochem. an organic compound consisting of a purine or pyrimidine base linked to a sugar, e.g. adenosine.

nucleotide /ˈnjuːklɪəˌtaɪd/ *n.* Biochem. an organic compound consisting of a nucleoside linked to a phosphate group.

nucleus /ˈnjuːklɪəs/ *n.* (*pl.* **nuclei** /-lɪˌaɪ/) **1 a** the central part or thing round which others are collected. **b** the kernel of an aggregate or mass. **2** an initial part meant to receive additions. **3** Astron. the solid part of a comet's head. **4** Physics the positively charged central core of an atom that contains most of its mass. (See below.) **5** Biol. a large dense organelle of eukaryotic cells, containing the genetic material. **6** a discrete mass of grey matter in the central nervous system. [L, = kernel, inner part, dimin. of *nux nucis* nut]

Ernest Rutherford in 1911 and afterwards established that the positive charge and most of the mass of each atom is concentrated in a volume which is about 1/10,000 of the diameter of the atom as a whole. He called this dense core the atomic 'nucleus' in 1912; its diameter is approximately 10^{-13} cm. Subsequent research established that the nucleus consists of protons and neutrons only, bound together by very powerful forces which do not extend significantly beyond the nucleus itself. The nucleus can vibrate, rotate, and alter its shape, properties which can be recognized through energy changes and by means of various other phenomena.

nuclide /ˈnjuːklaɪd/ *n.* Physics a certain type of atom characterized by the number of protons and neutrons in its nucleus. □□ **nuclidic** /njuːˈklɪdɪk/ *adj.* [NUCLEUS + Gk *eidos* form]

nude /njuːd/ *adj. & n.* —*adj.* naked, bare, unclothed. —*n.* **1** a painting, sculpture, photograph, etc. of a nude human figure; such a figure. **2** a nude person. **3** (prec. by *the*) **a** an unclothed state. **b** the representation of an undraped human figure as a genre in art. □ **nude contract** Law = bare contract. [L *nudus*]

nudge /nʌdʒ/ *v. & n.* —*v.tr.* **1** prod gently with the elbow to attract attention. **2** push gently or gradually. **3** give a gentle reminder or encouragement to (a person). —*n.* the act or an instance of nudging; a gentle push. □□ **nudger** *n.* [17th c.: orig. unkn.: cf. Norw. dial. *nugga*, *nyggja* to push, rub]

nudist /ˈnjuːdɪst/ *n.* a person who advocates or practises going unclothed. □□ **nudism** *n.*

nudity /ˈnjuːdɪtɪ/ *n.* the state of being nude; nakedness.

Nuer /ˈnuːə(r)/ *n. & adj.* —*n.* (*pl.* **Nuer**) **1** a member of an African people living in south-eastern Sudan. **2** the language of this people. —*adj.* of the Nuer or their language. [native name]

Nuevo León /ˌnweɪvəʊ leɪˈɒn/ a State of NE Mexico; pop. (est. 1988) 3,146,200; capital, Monterrey.

Nuffield /ˈnʌfiːld/, William Richard Morris, 1st Viscount (1877–1963), the most influential British motor manufacturer, a good engineer and a good businessman. Working in Oxford, he started (like most early car-makers) by building bicycles. He made his first car in 1913 and afterwards introduced automobile mass-manufacture to Britain in his Oxford factory. In later life he devoted his considerable fortune to philanthropic purposes, and the University of Oxford in particular has benefited greatly, both in the provision of hospital buildings and in the endowment of chairs of medicine and surgery; his name is also preserved in Nuffield College which he endowed for the study of social sciences.

nugatory /ˈnjuːgətərɪ/ *adj.* **1** futile, trifling, worthless. **2** inoperative; not valid. [L *nugatorius* f. *nugari* to trifle f. *nugae* jests]

nugget /ˈnʌgɪt/ *n.* **1 a** a lump of gold, platinum, etc., as found in the earth. **b** a lump of anything compared to this. **2** something valuable for its size (often abstract in sense: *a little nugget of information*). [app. f. dial. *nug* lump etc.]

nuisance /ˈnjuːs(ə)ns/ *n.* **1** a person, thing, or circumstance causing trouble or annoyance. **2** anything harmful or offensive to the community or a member of it and for which a legal remedy exists. □ **nuisance value** an advantage resulting from the capacity to harass or frustrate. [ME f. OF, = hurt, f. *nuire* *nuis-* f. L *nocēre* to hurt]

NUJ *abbr.* (in the UK) National Union of Journalists.

nuke /njuːk/ *n. & v. colloq.* —*n.* a nuclear weapon. —*v.tr.* bomb or destroy with nuclear weapons. [abbr.]

Nuku'alofa /ˌnuːkuːəˈlɒfə/ the capital of Tonga, situated on the island of Tongatapu; pop. (1986) 28,900.

null /nʌl/ *adj. & n.* —*adj.* **1** (esp. **null and void**) invalid; not binding. **2** non-existent; amounting to nothing. **3** having or associated with the value zero. **4** Computing **a** empty; having no elements (*null list*). **b** all the elements of which are zeros (*null matrix*). **5** without character or expression. —*n.* a dummy letter in a cipher. □ **null character** Computing a character denoting nothing, usu. represented by a zero. **null hypothesis** a hypothesis suggesting that the difference between statistical samples does not imply a difference between populations. **null instrument** an instrument used by adjustment to give a reading of zero. **null link** Computing a reference incorporated into the last item in a list to indicate there are no further items in the list. [F *nul nulle* or L *nullus* none f. *ne* not + *ullus* any]

nullah /ˈnʌlə/ *n.* Anglo-Ind. a dry river-bed or ravine. [Hindi *nālā*]

nulla-nulla /ˈnʌləˌnʌlə/ *n.* (also **nulla**) Austral. a hardwood club used by Aborigines. [Aboriginal]

Nullarbor Plain /ˈnʌləˌbɔː(r)/ a vast plain in SW Australia stretching inland from the Great Australian Bight. [L *nullus arbor* no tree]

nullify /ˈnʌlɪˌfaɪ/ *v.tr.* (**-ies, -ied**) make null; neutralize, invalidate, cancel. □□ **nullification** /-fɪˈkeɪʃ(ə)n/ *n.* **nullifier** *n.*

nullipara /nʌˈlɪpərə/ *n.* a woman who has never borne a child. □□ **nulliparous** *adj.* [mod.L f. L *nullus* none + *para* fem. of *-parus* f. *parere* bear children]

nullipore /ˈnʌlɪˌpɔː(r)/ *n.* any of various seaweeds able to secrete lime. [L *nullus* none + PORE¹]

nullity /ˈnʌlɪtɪ/ *n.* (*pl.* **-ies**) **1** Law **a** being null; invalidity, esp. of marriage. **b** an act, document, etc., that is null. **2 a** nothingness. **b** a mere nothing; a nonentity. [F *nullité* or med.L *nullitas* f. L *nullus* none]

NUM *abbr.* (in the UK) National Union of Mineworkers.

Num. *abbr.* Numbers (Old Testament).

Numa Pompilius /ˌnjuːmə pɒmˈpɪlɪəs/ the legendary second king of Rome, successor to Romulus, revered by the ancient Romans as the founder of nearly all their religious institutions.

numb /nʌm/ *adj. & v.* —*adj.* (often foll. by *with*) deprived of feeling or the power of motion (*numb with cold*). —*v.tr.* **1** make numb. **2** stupefy, paralyse. □□ **numb-fish** = electric ray. □□ **numbly** *adv.* **numbness** *n.* [ME *nome(n)* past part. of *nim* take: for *-b* cf. THUMB]

numbat /ˈnʌmbæt/ *n.* a small Australian marsupial, *Myrmecobius fasciatus*, with a bushy tail and black and white striped back. [Aboriginal]

number /ˈnʌmbə(r)/ *n. & v.* —*n.* **1 a** an arithmetical value representing a particular quantity and used in counting and making calculations. (See below.) **b** a word, symbol, or figure representing this; a numeral. **c** an arithmetical value showing position in a series esp. for identification, reference, etc. (*registration number*). **2** (often foll. by *of*) the total count or aggregate (*the number of accidents has decreased; twenty in number*). **3 a** the study of the behaviour of numbers; numerical reckoning (*the laws of number*). **b** (in *pl.*) arithmetic (*not good at numbers*). **4 a** (in *sing.* or *pl.*) a quantity or amount; a total; a count (*a large number of people; only in small numbers*). **b** (in *pl.*) numerical preponderance (*force of numbers*; *there is safety in numbers*). **5 a** a person or thing having a place in a series, esp. a single issue of a magazine, an item in a programme, etc. **b** a song, dance, musical item, etc. **6** company, collection, group (*among our number*). **7** *Gram.* **a** the classification of words by their singular or plural forms. **b** a particular such form. **8** *colloq.* a person or thing regarded familiarly or affectionately (usu. qualified in some way: *an attractive little number*). **9** (**Numbers**) the fourth book of the Old Testament, relating the experiences of the Israelites under Moses during their wanderings in the desert. The English title is explained by its two records of a census; its Hebrew title means 'in the wilderness'. —*v.tr.* **1** include (*I number you among my friends*). **2** assign a number or numbers to. **3** have or amount to (a specified number). **4 a** count. **b** include. □ **by numbers** following simple instructions (as if) identified by numbers. **one's days are numbered** one does not have long to live. **have a person's number** *colloq.* understand a person's real motives, character, etc. **have a person's number on it** (of a bomb, bullet, etc.) be destined to hit a specified person. **number cruncher** *Computing & Math. sl.* a machine capable of complex calculations etc. **number crunching** the act or process of making these calculations. **one's number is up** *colloq.* one is finished or doomed to die. **a number of** some, several. ¶ Use with a plural verb is now standard: *a number of problems remain*. **number one** *n. colloq.* oneself (*always takes care of number one*). —*adj.* most important (*the number one priority*). **number-plate** a plate on a vehicle displaying its registration number. **numbers game 1** usu. *derog.* action involving only arithmetical work. **2** *US* a lottery based on the occurrence of unpredictable numbers in the results of races etc. **Number Ten** 10 Downing Street, the official London home of the British Prime Minister. **number two** a second in command. **without number** innumerable. [ME f. OF *nombre* (n.), *nombrer* (v.) f. L *numerus*, *numerare*]

Numbers are mathematical abstractions originally (and still mainly) used for counting and measurement. Natural numbers, also known as positive integers, are the numbers 1, 2, 3, ... (sometimes 0 is also included) used in counting. Integers are natural numbers, 0, and their negatives -1, -2, -3, ... Rational numbers are the fractions p/q (where p and q are integers and q is not 0). Real numbers are the numbers used in measurement; they are limits of sequences of rational numbers; usually described by decimal expansions that go on for ever. Complex numbers are numbers of the form $a + bi$ in which a and b are real numbers and i is an imagined square root of -1. Note the hierarchy: all natural numbers are integers, all integers are rational numbers, all rational numbers are real numbers, all real numbers are complex numbers. Algebraic numbers are those (complex numbers) that are roots of polynomial equations with integer coefficients; transcendental numbers are the complex numbers that are not algebraic. Transfinite numbers are the cardinal and ordinal numbers assigned to infinite sets in Cantor's set theory.

numberless /ˈnʌmbəlɪs/ *adj.* innumerable.

numbles /ˈnʌmb(ə)lz/ *n.pl. Brit. archaic* a deer's entrails. [ME f. OF *numbles*, *nombles* loin etc., f. L *lumbulus* dimin. of *lumbus* loin: cf. UMBLES]

numbskull var. of NUMSKULL.

numdah /ˈnʌmdɑː/ *n.* an embroidered felt rug from India etc. [Urdu *namdā* f. Pers. *namad* carpet]

numen /ˈnjuːmen/ *n.* (*pl.* **numina** /-mɪnə/) a presiding deity or spirit. [L *numen* -*minis*]

numerable /ˈnjuːmərəb(ə)l/ *adj.* that can be counted. □□ **numerably** *adv.* [L *numerabilis* f. *numerare* NUMBER v.]

numeral /ˈnjuːmər(ə)l/ *n. & adj.* —*n.* a word, figure, or group of figures denoting a number. —*adj.* of or denoting a number. [LL *numeralis* f. L (as NUMBER)]

numerate /ˈnjuːmərət/ *adj.* acquainted with the basic principles of mathematics. □□ **numeracy** *n.* [L *numerus* number + -ATE² after *literate*]

numeration /ˌnjuːməˈreɪʃ(ə)n/ *n.* **1 a** a method or process of numbering or computing. **b** calculation. **2** the expression in words of a number written in figures. [ME f. L *numeratio* payment, in LL numbering (as NUMBER)]

numerator /ˈnjuːməˌreɪtə(r)/ *n.* **1** the number above the line in a vulgar fraction showing how many of the parts indicated by the denominator are taken (e.g. 2 in $\frac{2}{3}$). **2** a person or device that numbers. [F *numérateur* or LL *numerator* (as NUMBER)]

numerical /njuːˈmerɪk(ə)l/ *adj.* (also **numeric**) of or relating to a number or numbers (*numerical superiority*). □ **numerical analysis** the branch of mathematics that deals with the development and use of numerical methods for solving problems. □□ **numerically** *adv.* [med.L *numericus* (as NUMBER)]

numerology /ˌnjuːməˈrɒlədʒɪ/ *n.* (*pl.* **-ies**) the study of the supposed occult significance of numbers. □□ **numerological** /-rəˈlɒdʒɪk(ə)l/ *adj.* **numerologist** *n.* [L *numerus* number + -LOGY]

numerous /ˈnjuːmərəs/ *adj.* **1** (with *pl.*) great in number (*received numerous gifts*). **2** consisting of many (*a numerous family*). □□ **numerously** *adv.* **numerousness** *n.* [L *numerosus* (as NUMBER)]

Numidia /njuːˈmɪdɪə/ an ancient kingdom (later a Roman province) in North Africa, east of Mauretania and west of Carthage, now part of Algeria. □□ **Numidian** *adj. & n.*

numina *pl.* of NUMEN.

numinous /ˈnjuːmɪnəs/ *adj.* **1** indicating the presence of a divinity. **2** spiritual. **3** awe-inspiring. [L *numen*: see NUMEN]

numismatic /ˌnjuːmɪzˈmætɪk/ *adj.* of or relating to coins or medals. □□ **numismatically** *adv.* [F *numismatique* f. L *numisma* f. Gk *nomisma* -*atos* current coin f. *nomizō* use currently]

numismatics /ˌnjuːmɪzˈmætɪks/ *n.pl.* (usu. treated as *sing.*) the study of coins or medals. □□ **numismatist** /-ˈmɪzmətɪst/ *n.*

numismatology /njuːˌmɪzməˈtɒlədʒɪ/ *n.* = NUMISMATICS.

nummulite /ˈnʌmjʊˌlaɪt/ *n.* a disc-shaped fossil shell of a foraminiferous protozoan found in Tertiary strata. [L *nummulus* dimin. of *nummus* coin]

numnah /ˈnʌmnə/ *n.* a saddle-cloth or pad placed under a saddle. [Urdu *namdā*: see NUMDAH]

numskull /ˈnʌmskʌl/ *n.* (also **numbskull**) a stupid or foolish person. [NUMB + SKULL]

nun /nʌn/ *n.* a member of a community of women living apart under religious vows. □□ **nunhood** *n.* **nunlike** *adj.* **nunnish** *adj.* [ME f. OE *nunne* and OF *nonne* f. eccl.L *nonna* fem. of *nonnus* monk, orig. a title given to an elderly person]

nunatak /ˈnʌnəˌtæk/ *n.* an isolated peak of rock projecting above a surface of land ice or snow e.g. in Greenland. [Eskimo]

nun-buoy /ˈnʌnbɔɪ/ *n.* a buoy circular in the middle and tapering to each end. [obs. *nun* child's top + BUOY]

Nunc Dimittis /nʌŋk ˈdɪmɪtɪs/ the canticle beginning thus (L, = 'Lord, now let (your servant) depart'), the first words of the Song of Simeon (Luke 2: 29).

nunciature /ˈnʌnʃəˌtjʊə(r)/ *n. RC Ch.* the office or tenure of a nuncio. [It. *nunziatura* (as NUNCIO)]

nuncio /ˈnʌnʃɪəʊ, -sɪəʊ/ *n.* (*pl.* **-os**) *RC Ch.* a papal ambassador. [It. f. L *nuntius* messenger]

nuncupate /ˈnʌŋkjuˌpeɪt/ *v.tr.* declare (a will or testament) orally, not in writing. □□ **nuncupation** /-ˈpeɪʃ(ə)n/ *n.* **nuncupative** /-pətɪv/ *adj.* [L *nuncupare* nuncupat- name]

nunnery /ˈnʌnərɪ/ *n.* (*pl.* **-ies**) a religious house of nuns; a convent.

NUPE /ˈnjuːpɪ/ *abbr.* (in the UK) National Union of Public Employees.

nuptial /ˈnʌpʃ(ə)l/ *adj. & n.* —*adj.* of or relating to marriage or weddings. —*n.* (usu. in *pl.*) a wedding. [F *nuptial* or L *nuptialis* f. *nuptiae* wedding f. *nubere* nupt- wed]

NUR *abbr.* (in the UK) National Union of Railwaymen. ¶ See RMT.

nurd var. of NERD.

Nuremberg /ˈnjʊərəmˌbɜːg/ (German **Nürnberg** /ˈnʊənˌbeəg/) a city of Bavaria in Germany; pop. (1987) 467,400. It was a leading cultural centre in the 15th and 16th centuries, and was the home of Albrecht Durer and Hans Sachs. Nazi party congresses were held here in the 1930s, as were the trials of war criminals at the end of the Second World War. After the war it was carefully reconstructed, as its cobbled streets and timbered houses had been reduced to rubble by Allied bombing.

Nureyev /ˈnjʊərɪˌef, njʊˈreɪef/, Rudolf (1939–), Russian ballet-dancer, who defected to the West in 1961. A dancer of dazzling virtuosity and vigorous but controlled expressiveness, he has taken the leading roles of the classical and standard modern repertory and created others, particularly in a noted partnership with Margot Fonteyn. He has also choreographed and staged a number of works.

nurse /nɜːs/ n. & v. —n. **1** a person trained to assist doctors in caring for the sick or infirm. **2** a person employed or trained to take charge of young children. **3** archaic = wet-nurse. **4** Forestry a tree planted as a shelter to others. **5** Zool. a sexually imperfect bee, ant, etc., caring for a young brood; a worker. —v. **1 a** intr. work as a nurse. **b** tr. attend to (a sick person). **c** tr. give medical attention to (an illness or injury). **2** tr. & intr. feed or be fed at the breast. **3** tr. (in passive; foll. by in) be brought up in (a specified condition) (nursed in poverty). **4** tr. hold or treat carefully or caressingly (sat nursing my feet). **5** tr. **a** foster; promote the development of (the arts, plants, etc.). **b** harbour or nurture (a grievance, hatred, etc.). **c** pay special attention to (nursed the voters). **6** tr. Billiards keep (the balls) together for a series of cannons. [reduced f. ME and OF norice, nurice f. LL nutricia fem. of L nutricius f. nutrix -icis f. nutrire NOURISH]

nurseling var. of NURSLING.

nursemaid /ˈnɜːsmeɪd/ n. **1** a woman in charge of a child or children. **2** a person who watches over or guides another carefully.

nursery /ˈnɜːsərɪ/ n. (pl. -ies) **1 a** a room or place equipped for young children. **b** = day nursery. **2** a place where plants, trees, etc., are reared for sale or transplantation. **3** any sphere or place in or by which qualities or types of people are fostered or bred. **4** Billiards **a** grouped balls (see NURSE v. 6). **b** (in full **nursery cannon**) a cannon on three close balls. □ **nursery nurse** a person trained to take charge of babies and young children. **nursery rhyme** a simple traditional song or story in rhyme for children. **nursery school** a school for children between the ages of three and five. **nursery slopes** Skiing gentle slopes suitable for beginners. **nursery stakes** a race for two-year-old horses.

nurseryman /ˈnɜːsərɪmən/ n. (pl. -men) an owner of or worker in a plant nursery.

nursing /ˈnɜːsɪŋ/ n. **1** the practice or profession of caring for the sick as a nurse. **2** (attrib.) concerned with or suitable for nursing the sick or elderly etc. (nursing home; nursing sister). □ **nursing officer** a senior nurse (see senior nursing officer).

nursling /ˈnɜːslɪŋ/ n. (also **nurseling**) an infant that is being suckled.

nurture /ˈnɜːtʃə(r)/ n. & v. —n. **1** the process of bringing up or training (esp. children); fostering care. **2** nourishment. **3** sociological factors as an influence on or determinant of personality (opp. NATURE). —v.tr. **1** bring up; rear. **2** nourish. □□ **nurturer** n. [ME f. OF nour(e)ture (as NOURISH)]

NUS abbr. **1** (in the UK) National Union of Seamen. ¶ See RMT. **2** (in the UK) National Union of Students.

NUT abbr. (in the UK) National Union of Teachers.

Nut /nʊt/ Egyptian Mythol. the sky-goddess, thought to swallow the sun at night and give birth to it in the morning. She is usually depicted as a naked woman, with her body arched above the earth which she touches with her feet and hands.

nut /nʌt/ n. & v. —n. **1 a** a fruit consisting of a hard or tough shell around an edible kernel. **b** this kernel. **2** a pod containing hard seeds. **3** a small usu. square or hexagonal flat piece of metal or other material with a threaded hole through it for screwing on the end of a bolt to secure it. **4** sl. a person's head. **5** sl. **a** a crazy or eccentric person. **b** an obsessive enthusiast or devotee (a health-food nut). **6** a small lump of coal, butter, etc. **7 a** a device fitted to the bow of a violin for adjusting its tension. **b** the fixed ridge on the neck of a stringed instrument over which the strings pass. **8** (in pl.) coarse sl. the testicles. —v.intr. (**nutted**, **nutting**) seek or gather nuts (go nutting). □ **do one's nut** sl. be extremely angry or agitated. **for nuts** colloq. even tolerably well (cannot sing for nuts). **nut cutlet** a cutlet-shaped portion of meat-substitute, made from nuts etc. **nut-house**

sl. a mental home or hospital. **nut-oil** an oil obtained from hazelnuts and walnuts and used in paints and varnishes. **nuts and bolts** colloq. the practical details. **nut-tree** any tree bearing nuts, esp. a hazel. **off one's nut** sl. crazy. □□ **nutlike** adj. [OE hnutu f. Gmc]

nutant /ˈnjuːt(ə)nt/ adj. Bot. nodding, drooping. [L nutare nod]

nutation /njuːˈteɪʃ(ə)n/ n. **1** the act or an instance of nodding. **2** Astron. a periodic oscillation of the earth's poles. **3** oscillation of a spinning top. **4** the spiral movement of a plant organ during growth. [L nutatio (as NUTANT)]

nutcase /ˈnʌtkeɪs/ n. sl. a crazy or foolish person.

nutcracker /ˈnʌtˌkrækə(r)/ n. (usu. in pl.) a device for cracking nuts. □ **Nutcracker man** a nickname for the fossil hominid Australopithecus boisei, especially the specimen discovered at Olduvai, Tanzania, in 1959. Similar remains, including the characteristic large premolar teeth, have also been found in South Africa.

nutgall /ˈnʌtgɔːl/ n. a gall found on dyer's oak, used as a dyestuff.

nuthatch /ˈnʌthætʃ/ n. any small bird of the family Sittidae, climbing up and down tree-trunks and feeding on nuts, insects, etc. [NUT + hatch rel. to HATCH²]

nutlet /ˈnʌtlɪt/ n. a small nut or nutlike fruit.

nutmeg /ˈnʌtmeg/ n. **1** an evergreen E. Indian tree, Myristica fragrans, yielding a hard aromatic spheroidal seed. **2** the seed of this used as a spice and in medicine. □ **nutmeg-apple** the fruit of this tree, yielding mace and nutmeg. [ME: partial transl. of OF nois mug(u)ede ult. f. L nux nut + LL muscus MUSK]

nutria /ˈnjuːtrɪə/ n. the skin or fur of a coypu. [Sp., = otter]

nutrient /ˈnjuːtrɪənt/ n. & adj. —n. any substance that provides essential nourishment for the maintenance of life. —adj. serving as or providing nourishment. [L nutrire nourish]

nutriment /ˈnjuːtrɪmənt/ n. **1** nourishing food. **2** an intellectual or artistic etc. nourishment or stimulus. □□ **nutrimental** /-ˈment(ə)l/ adj. [L nutrimentum (as NUTRIENT)]

nutrition /njuːˈtrɪʃ(ə)n/ n. **1 a** the process of providing or receiving nourishing substances. **b** food, nourishment. **2** the study of nutrients and nutrition. □□ **nutritional** adj. [F nutrition or LL nutritio (as NUTRIENT)]

nutritionist /njuːˈtrɪʃənɪst/ n. a person who studies or is an expert on the processes of human nourishment.

nutritious /njuːˈtrɪʃəs/ adj. efficient as food; nourishing. □□ **nutritiously** adv. **nutritiousness** n. [L nutritius (as NURSE)]

nutritive /ˈnjuːtrɪtɪv/ adj. & n. —adj. **1** of or concerned in nutrition. **2** serving as nutritious food. —n. a nutritious article of food. [ME f. F nutritif -ive f. med.L nutritivus (as NUTRIENT)]

nuts /nʌts/ adj. & int. —adj. sl. crazy, mad, eccentric. —int. sl. an expression of contempt or derision (nuts to you). □ **be nuts about** (or **on**) colloq. be enthusiastic about or very fond of.

nutshell /ˈnʌtʃel/ n. the hard exterior covering of a nut. □ **in a nutshell** in a few words.

nutter /ˈnʌtə(r)/ n. Brit. sl. a crazy or eccentric person.

nutty /ˈnʌtɪ/ adj. (**nuttier**, **nuttiest**) **1 a** full of nuts. **b** tasting like nuts. **2** sl. = NUTS adj. □□ **nuttiness** n.

Nuuk see GODTHÅB.

nux vomica /nʌks ˈvɒmɪkə/ n. **1** an E. Indian tree, Strychnos nux-vomica, yielding a poisonous fruit. **2** the seeds of this tree, containing strychnine. [med.L f. L nux nut + vomicus f. vomere vomit]

nuzzle /ˈnʌz(ə)l/ v. **1** tr. prod or rub gently with the nose. **2** intr. (foll. by into, against, up to) press the nose gently. **3** tr. (also refl.) nestle; lie snug. [ME f. NOSE + -LE⁴]

NV abbr. US Nevada (in official postal use).

NW abbr. **1** north-west. **2** north-western.

NY abbr. US New York (also in official postal use).

nyala var. of INYALA.

Nyasa /naɪˈæsə/ (name means 'lake') (also called **Lake Malawi**) a lake in the south-east of central Africa, the third largest lake of Africa. It lies within Malawi and Mozambique and borders on Tanzania.

b but d dog f few g get h he j yes k cat l leg m man n no p pen r red s sit t top v voice

Nyasaland /naɪˈæsəˌlænd/ the former name of Malawi until it gained independence in 1966.

NYC *abbr.* New York City.

nyctalopia /ˌnɪktəˈləʊpɪə/ *n.* the inability to see in dim light or at night. Also called *night-blindness*. [LL f. Gk *nuktalōps* f. *nux nuktos* night + *alaos* blind + *ōps* eye]

nyctitropic /ˌnɪktɪˈtrəʊpɪk/ *adj. Bot.* (of plant movements) occurring at night and caused by changes in light and temperature. [Gk *nukti-* comb. form of *nux nuktos* night + *tropos* turn]

nye var. of NIDE.

Nyerere /njeˈreərɪ/, Julius Kambarage (1922–), African statesman who became the first premier of Tanganyika following its independence in 1961 and President a year later. In 1964 he successfully negotiated a union with Zanzibar and remained President of the new State of Tanzania until his retirement in 1985.

nylghau /ˈnɪlɡɔː/ *n.* = NILGAI. [Hind. f. Pers. *nīlgāw* f. *nīl* blue + *gāw* cow]

nylon /ˈnaɪlɒn/ *n.* **1** any of various synthetic polyamide fibres having a protein-like structure, with tough, lightweight, elastic properties, used in industry and for textiles etc. (See below.) **2** a nylon fabric. **3** (in *pl.*) stockings made of nylon. [invented word, suggested by *cotton* and *rayon*; there is no evidence to support the derivations frequently given for this word in popular sources]
  Nylon was devised by the American chemist W. H. Carothers, of the du Pont chemical company; its production was announced in 1938. Unlike natural fibres it is resistant to destruction by bacteria, fungus, insects, or rodents, and is widely used for textile fabrics and in industry.

nymph /nɪmf/ *n.* **1** any of various mythological semi-divine spirits regarded as maidens and associated with aspects of nature, esp. rivers and woods. **2** *poet.* a beautiful young woman. **3 a** an immature form of some insects. **b** a young dragonfly or damselfly. □□ **nymphal** *adj.* **nymphean** /-ˈfiːən/ *adj.* **nymphlike** *adj.* [ME f. OF *nimphe* f. L *nympha* f. Gk *numphē*]

nymphae /ˈnɪmfiː/ *n.pl. Anat.* the labia minora. [L, pl. of *nympha*: see NYMPH]

nymphet /ˈnɪmfet, -ˈfet/ *n.* **1** a young nymph. **2** *colloq.* a sexually attractive young woman.

nympho /ˈnɪmfəʊ/ *n.* (*pl.* **-os**) *colloq.* a nymphomaniac. [abbr.]

nympholepsy /ˈnɪmfəˌlepsɪ/ *n.* ecstasy or frenzy caused by desire of the unattainable. [NYMPHOLEPT after *epilepsy*]

nympholept /ˈnɪmfəˌlept/ *n.* a person inspired by violent enthusiasm esp. for an ideal. □□ **nympholeptic** /-ˈleptɪk/ *adj.* [Gk *numpholēptos* caught by nymphs (as NYMPH, *lambanō* take)]

nymphomania /ˌnɪmfəˈmeɪnɪə/ *n.* excessive sexual desire in women. □□ **nymphomaniac** *n.* & *adj.* [mod.L (as NYMPH, -MANIA)]

Nyslott see SAVONLINNA.

nystagmus /nɪˈstæɡməs/ *n.* rapid involuntary movements of the eyes. □□ **nystagmic** *adj.* [Gk *nustagmos* nodding f. *nustazō* nod]

NZ *abbr.* New Zealand.

O

O¹ /əʊ/ n. (also **o**) (pl. **Os** or **O's**) **1** the fifteenth letter of the alphabet. **2** (**o**) nought, zero (in a sequence of numerals esp. when spoken). **3** a human blood type of the ABO system.

O² abbr. (also **O.**) Old.

O³ symb. Chem. the element oxygen.

O⁴ /əʊ/ int. **1** var. of OH¹. **2** prefixed to a name in the vocative (O God). [ME, natural excl.]

O' /əʊ, ə/ prefix of Irish patronymic names (O'Connor). [Ir. ó, ua, descendant]

o' /ə/ prep. of, on (esp. in phrases: o'clock; will-o'-the-wisp). [abbr.]

-o /əʊ/ suffix forming usu. sl. or colloq. variants or derivatives (beano; wino). [perh. OH¹ as joc. suffix]

-o- /əʊ/ suffix the terminal vowel of combining forms (spectro-; chemico-; Franco-). ¶ Often elided before a vowel, as in neuralgia. [orig. Gk]

oaf /əʊf/ n. (pl. **oafs**) **1** an awkward lout. **2** a stupid person. □□ **oafish** adj. **oafishly** adv. **oafishness** n. [orig. = elf's child, var. of obs. auf f. ON álfr elf]

oak /əʊk/ n. **1** any tree or shrub of the genus Quercus usu. having lobed leaves and bearing acorns. **2** the durable wood of this tree, used esp. for furniture and in building. **3** (attrib.) made of oak (oak table). **4** a heavy outer door of a set of university college rooms. **5** (**the Oaks**) (treated as sing.) an annual race for three-year-old fillies run at Epsom in Surrey, England, over the same course as the Derby and three days after it. It was first run in 1779, and is named after the 12th Earl of Derby's shooting-box, 'The Oaks'. □ **oak-apple** (or **-gall**) an apple-like gall containing larvae of certain wasps, found on oak trees. **Oak-apple Day** 29 May, the day of Charles II's restoration in 1660, on which oak-apples or oak-leaves were worn in memory of the royal-oak incident (see ROYAL). □□ **oaken** adj. [OE āc f. Gmc]

Oakland /ˈəʊklənd/ an industrial port on the east side of San Francisco Bay in western California; pop. (1982) 344,650.

Oakley /ˈəʊklɪ/, Annie (full name Phoebe Anne Oakley Mozee, 1860–1926), American markswoman. She married Frank E. Butler, a vaudeville marksman, and in 1885 they joined Buffalo Bill's Wild West Show, of which she became a star attraction for the next 17 years. The musical Annie Get Your Gun (1948), with music by Irving Berlin, was based on her life.

oakum /ˈəʊkəm/ n. a loose fibre obtained by picking old rope to pieces and used esp. in caulking. [OE ǣcumbe, ācumbe, lit. 'off-combings']

O. & M. abbr. organization and methods.

OAP abbr. Brit. old-age pensioner.

OAPEC abbr. Organization of Arab Petroleum Exporting Countries.

oar /ɔ:(r)/ n. **1** a pole with a blade used for rowing or steering a boat by leverage against the water. **2** a rower. □ **put one's oar in** interfere, meddle. **rest** (US **lay**) **on one's oars** relax one's efforts. □□ **oared** adj. (also in comb.). **oarless** adj. [OE ār f. Gmc, perh. rel. to Gk eretmos oar]

oarfish /ˈɔ:fɪʃ/ n. a ribbonfish, Regalecus glesne.

oarlock /ˈɔ:lɒk/ n. US a rowlock.

oarsman /ˈɔ:zmən/ n. (pl. **-men**) fem. **oarswoman**, pl. **-women**) a rower. □□ **oarsmanship** n.

oarweed /ˈɔ:wi:d/ n. (also **oreweed**) any large marine alga esp. of the genus Laminaria, often growing along shores.

OAS abbr. **1** Organization of American States. **2** on active service.

oasis /əʊˈeɪsɪs/ n. (pl. **oases** /-si:z/) **1** a fertile spot in a desert, where water is found. **2** an area or period of calm in the midst of turbulence. [LL f. Gk, app. of Egypt. orig.]

oast /əʊst/ n. a kiln for drying hops. □ **oast-house** a building containing this. [OE āst f. Gmc]

oat /əʊt/ n. **1 a** a cereal plant, Avena sativa, cultivated in cool climates. **b** (in pl.) the grain yielded by this, used as food. **2** any other cereal of the genus Avena, esp. the wild oat, A. fatua. **3** poet. the oat-stem used as a musical pipe by shepherds etc., usu. in pastoral or bucolic poetry. **4** (in pl.) sl. sexual gratification. □ **feel one's oats** colloq. **1** be lively. **2** US feel self-important. **oat-grass** any of various grasses, esp. of the genus Arrhenatherum. **off one's oats** colloq. not hungry. **sow one's oats** (or **wild oats**) indulge in youthful excess or promiscuity. □□ **oaten** adj. [OE āte, pl. ātan, of unkn. orig.]

oatcake /ˈəʊtkeɪk/ n. a thin unleavened biscuit-like food made of oatmeal, common in Scotland and N. England.

Oates /əʊts/, Titus (1649–1705), Protestant clergyman, fabricator of the Popish Plot (see entry), which he 'discovered' while serving as chaplain to the Protestant servants of the Catholic Duke of Norfolk. He was condemned and imprisoned for perjury, but subsequently released and granted a pension.

oath /əʊθ/ n. (pl. **oaths** /əʊðz/) **1** a solemn declaration or undertaking (often naming God) as to the truth of something or as a commitment to future action. **2** a statement or promise contained in an oath (oath of allegiance). **3** a profane or blasphemous utterance; a curse. □ **on** (or **under**) **oath** having sworn a solemn oath. **take** (or **swear**) **an oath** make such a declaration or undertaking. [OE āth f. Gmc]

oatmeal /ˈəʊtmi:l/ n. **1** meal made from ground oats used esp. in porridge and oatcakes. **2** a greyish-fawn colour flecked with brown.

OAU abbr. Organization of African Unity.

Oaxaca /wəˈhɑ:kə/ a State of southern Mexico; pop. (est. 1988) 2,650,200; capital, Oaxaca de Juárez.

OB abbr. Brit. outside broadcast.

Ob /ɒb/ the principal river of the west Siberian lowlands and one of the largest rivers in the Soviet Union. Rising in the Altai Mountains, it flows generally north and west for 5,410 km (3,481 miles) before entering the Ob Bay, an inlet of the Kara Sea, a part of the Arctic Ocean.

ob. abbr. he or she died. [L obiit]

ob- /ɒb/ prefix (also **oc-** before c, **of-** before f, **op-** before p) occurring mainly in words of Latin origin, meaning: **1** exposure, openness (object; obverse). **2** meeting or facing (occasion; obvious). **3** direction (oblong; offer). **4** opposition, hostility, or resistance (obstreperous; opponent; obstinate). **5** hindrance, blocking, or concealment (obese; obstacle; occult). **6** finality or completeness (obsolete; occupy). **7** (in modern technical words) inversely; in a direction or manner contrary to the usual (obconical; obovate). [L f. ob towards, against, in the way of]

Obad. abbr. Obadiah (Old Testament).

Obadiah /ˌəʊbəˈdaɪə/ n. **1** a Hebrew minor prophet. **2** the shortest book of the Old Testament, bearing his name.

obbligato /ˌɒblɪˈgɑ:təʊ/ n. (pl. **-os**) Mus. an accompaniment, usu. special and unusual in effect, forming an integral part of a composition (with violin obbligato). [It., = obligatory, f. L obligatus past part. (as OBLIGE)]

obconical /ɒbˈkɒnɪk(ə)l/ adj. (also **obconic**) in the form of an inverted cone.

obcordate /ɒbˈkɔ:deɪt/ adj. Biol. in the shape of a heart and attached at the pointed end.

obdurate /ˈɒbdjʊrət/ adj. **1** stubborn. **2** hardened against persuasion or influence. □□ **obduracy** n. **obdurately** adv. **obdurateness** n. [ME f. L obduratus past part. of obdurare (as OB-, durare harden f. durus hard)]

OBE abbr. (in the UK) Officer of the Order of the British Empire.

obeah /ˈəʊbɪə/ n. (also **obi** /ˈəʊbɪ/) a kind of sorcery practised esp. in the West Indies. [W. Afr.]

æ cat ɑ: arm e bed ɜ: her ɪ sit i: see ɒ hot ɔ: saw ʌ run ʊ put u: too ə ago aɪ my

obeche /əʊˈbiːtʃɪ/ n. **1** a West African tree, *Triplochiton scleroxylon*. **2** the light-coloured timber from this. [Nigerian name]

obedience /əʊˈbiːdɪəns/ n. **1** obeying as an act or practice or quality. **2** submission to another's rule or authority. **3** compliance with a law or command. **4** *Eccl.* **a** compliance with a monastic rule. **b** a sphere of authority (*the Roman obedience*). □ **in obedience to** actuated by or in accordance with. [ME f. OF f. L *obedientia* (as OBEY)]

obedient /əʊˈbiːdɪənt/ adj. **1** obeying or ready to obey. **2** (often foll. by *to*) submissive to another's will; dutiful (*obedient to the law*). □□ **obediently** adv. [ME f. OF f. L *obediens -entis* (as OBEY)]

obeisance /əʊˈbeɪs(ə)ns/ n. **1** a bow, curtsey, or other respectful or submissive gesture (*make an obeisance*). **2** homage, submission, deference (*pay obeisance*). □□ **obeisant** adj. **obeisantly** adv. [ME f. OF *obeissance* (as OBEY)]

obeli pl. of OBELUS.

obelisk /ˈɒbəlɪsk/ n. **1 a** a tapering usu. four-sided stone pillar set up as a monument or landmark etc. **b** a mountain, tree, etc., of similar shape. **2** = OBELUS. [L *obeliscus* f. Gk *obeliskos* dimin. of *obelos* SPIT²]

obelize /ˈɒbəˌlaɪz/ v.tr. (also **-ise**) mark with an obelus as spurious etc. [Gk *obelizō* f. *obelos*: see OBELISK]

obelus /ˈɒbələs/ n. (pl. **obeli** /-ˌlaɪ/) **1** a dagger-shaped reference mark in printed matter. **2** a mark (− or ÷) used in ancient manuscripts to mark a word or passage, esp. as spurious. [L f. Gk *obelos* SPIT²]

Oberammergau /ˌəʊbəˈræməˌɡaʊ/ a village in the Bavarian Alps of SW Germany, site of the most famous of the few surviving Passion plays. It has been performed every tenth year (with few exceptions) from 1634 as a result of a vow made during an epidemic of plague, and remains entirely amateur, the villagers dividing the parts among themselves and being responsible also for the production, music, costumes, and scenery.

obese /əʊˈbiːs/ adj. very fat; corpulent. □□ **obeseness** n. **obesity** n. [L *obesus* (as OB-, *edere* eat)]

obey /əʊˈbeɪ/ v. **1** tr. **a** carry out the command of (*you will obey me*). **b** carry out (a command) (*obey orders*). **2** intr. do what one is told to do. **3** tr. be actuated by (a force or impulse). □□ **obeyer** n. [ME f. OF *obeir* f. L *obedire* (as OB-, *audire* hear)]

obfuscate /ˈɒbfʌˌskeɪt/ v.tr. **1** obscure or confuse (a mind, topic, etc.). **2** stupefy, bewilder. □□ **obfuscation** /-ˈkeɪʃ(ə)n/ n. **obfuscatory** adj. [LL *obfuscare* (as OB-, *fuscus* dark)]

obi¹ var. of OBEAH.

obi² /ˈəʊbɪ/ n. (pl. **obis**) a broad sash worn with a Japanese kimono. [Jap. *obi* belt]

obit /ˈɒbɪt, ˈəʊbɪt/ n. *colloq.* an obituary. [abbr.]

obiter dictum /ˌɒbɪtə ˈdɪktəm/ n. (pl. **obiter dicta** /-tə/) **1** a judge's expression of opinion uttered in court or giving judgement, but not essential to the decision and therefore without binding authority. **2** an incidental remark. [L f. *obiter* by the way + *dictum* a thing said]

obituary /əˈbɪtjʊərɪ/ n. (pl. **-ies**) **1** a notice of a death or deaths esp. in a newspaper. **2** an account of the life of a deceased person. **3** (*attrib.*) of or serving as an obituary. □□ **obituarial** /-tjʊˈeərɪəl/ adj. **obituarist** n. [med.L *obituarius* f. L *obitus* death f. *obire obit-* die (as OB-, *ire* go)]

object n. & v. —n. /ˈɒbdʒɪkt/ **1** a material thing that can be seen or touched. **2** (foll. by *of*) a person or thing to which action or feeling is directed (*the object of attention; the object of our study*). **3** a thing sought or aimed at; a purpose. **4** *Gram.* a noun or its equivalent governed by an active transitive verb or by a preposition. **5** *Philos.* a thing external to the thinking mind or subject. **6** *derog.* a person or thing of esp. a pathetic or ridiculous appearance. **7** *Computing* a package of information and a description of its manipulation. —v. /əbˈdʒekt/ **1** intr. (often foll. by *to*, *against*) express or feel opposition, disapproval, or reluctance; protest (*I object to being treated like this; objecting against government policies*). **2** tr. (foll. by *that* + clause) state as an objection (*objected that they were kept waiting*). **3** tr. (foll. by *to*, *against*, or *that* + clause) adduce (a quality or fact) as contrary or damaging (to a

case). □ **no object** not forming an important or restricting factor (*money no object*). **object-ball** *Billiards* etc. that at which a player aims the cue-ball. **object-glass** the lens in a telescope etc. nearest to the object observed. **object language 1** a language described by means of another language (see METALANGUAGE). **2** *Computing* a language into which a program is translated by means of a compiler or assembler. **object-lesson** a striking practical example of some principle. **object of the exercise** the main point of an activity. □□ **objectless** /ˈɒbdʒɪktlɪs/ adj. **objector** /əbˈdʒektə(r)/ n. [ME f. med.L *objectum* thing presented to the mind, past part. of L *objicere* (as OB-, *jacere ject-* throw)]

objectify /ɒbˈdʒektɪˌfaɪ/ v.tr. (**-ies**, **-ied**) **1** make objective; embody. **2** present as an object of perception. □□ **objectification** /-fɪˈkeɪʃ(ə)n/ n.

objection /əbˈdʒekʃ(ə)n/ n. **1** an expression or feeling of opposition or disapproval. **2** the act of objecting. **3** an adverse reason or statement. [ME f. OF *objection* or LL *objectio* (as OBJECT)]

objectionable /əbˈdʒekʃ(ə)nəb(ə)l/ adj. **1** open to objection. **2** unpleasant, offensive. □□ **objectionableness** n. **objectionably** /-blɪ/ adv.

objective /əbˈdʒektɪv/ adj. & n. —adj. **1** external to the mind; actually existing; real. **2** (of a person, writing, art, etc.) dealing with outward things or exhibiting facts uncoloured by feelings or opinions; not subjective. **3** *Gram.* (of a case or word) constructed as or appropriate to the object of a transitive verb or preposition (cf. ACCUSATIVE). **4** aimed at (*objective point*). **5** (of symptoms) observed by another and not only felt by the patient. —n. **1** something sought or aimed at; an objective point. **2** *Gram.* the objective case. **3** = object-glass. □□ **objectival** /ˌɒbdʒekˈtaɪv(ə)l/ adj. **objectively** adv. **objectiveness** n. **objectivity** /ˌɒbdʒekˈtɪvɪtɪ/ n. **objectivize** /əbˈdʒektɪˌvaɪz/ v.tr. (also **-ise**). **objectivization** /əbˌdʒektɪvaɪˈzeɪʃ(ə)n/ n. [med.L *objectivus* (as OBJECT)]

objectivism /əbˈdʒektɪˌvɪz(ə)m/ n. **1** the tendency to lay stress on what is objective. **2** *Philos.* the belief that certain things (esp. moral truths) exist apart from human knowledge or perception of them. □□ **objectivist** n. **objectivistic** /-ˈvɪstɪk/ adj.

objet d'art /ˌɒbʒeɪ ˈdɑː/ n. (pl. **objets d'art** pronunc. same) a small decorative object. [F, lit. 'object of art']

objurgate /ˈɒbdʒəˌɡeɪt/ v.tr. *literary* chide or scold. □□ **objurgation** /-ˈɡeɪʃ(ə)n/ n. **objurgatory** /ɒbˈdʒɜːɡətərɪ/ adj. [L *objurgare objurgat-* (as OB-, *jurgare* quarrel f. *jurgium* strife)]

oblanceolate /ɒbˈlɑːnsɪələt/ adj. *Bot.* (esp. of leaves) lanceolate with the more pointed end at the base.

oblate¹ /ˈɒbleɪt/ n. a person dedicated to a monastic or religious life or work. [F f. med.L *oblatus* f. *offere oblat-* offer (as OB-, *ferre* bring)]

oblate² /ˈɒbleɪt/ adj. *Geom.* (of a spheroid) flattened at the poles (cf. PROLATE). [mod.L *oblatus* (as OBLATE¹)]

oblation /əʊˈbleɪʃ(ə)n/ n. *Relig.* **1** a thing offered to a divine being. **2** the presentation of bread and wine to God in the Eucharist. □□ **oblational** adj. **oblatory** /ˈɒblətərɪ/ adj. [ME f. OF *oblation* or LL *oblatio* (as OBLATE¹)]

obligate v. & adj. —v.tr. /ˈɒblɪˌɡeɪt/ **1** (usu. in *passive*; foll. by *to* + infin.) bind (a person) legally or morally. **2** *US* commit (assets) as security. —adj. /ˈɒblɪɡət/ *Biol.* that has to be as described (*obligate parasite*). □□ **obligator** n. [L *obligare obligat-* (as OBLIGE)]

obligation /ˌɒblɪˈɡeɪʃ(ə)n/ n. **1** the constraining power of a law, precept, duty, contract, etc. **2** a duty; a burdensome task. **3** a binding agreement, esp. one enforceable under legal penalty; a written contract or bond. **4 a** a service or benefit (*repay an obligation*). **b** indebtedness for this (*be under an obligation*). □ **day of obligation** *Eccl.* a day on which all are required to attend Mass or Communion. **of obligation** obligatory. □□ **obligational** adj. [ME f. OF f. L *obligatio -onis* (as OBLIGE)]

obligatory /əˈblɪɡətərɪ/ adj. **1** legally or morally binding. **2** compulsory and not merely permissive. **3** constituting an obligation. □□ **obligatorily** adv. [ME f. LL *obligatorius* (as OBLIGE)]

oblige /əˈblaɪdʒ/ v. **1** tr. (foll. by *to* + infin.) constrain, compel. **2** tr. be binding on. **3** tr. **a** make indebted by conferring a favour. **b** (foll. by *with*, or *by* + verbal noun) gratify (*oblige me by leaving*). **c** perform a service for (often *absol.*: *will you oblige?*). **4** tr. (in *passive*; foll. by *to*) be indebted (*am obliged to you for your help*). **5** *intr. colloq.* (foll. by *with*) make a contribution of a specified kind (*Doris obliged with a song*). **6** *tr. archaic* or *Law* (foll. by *to*, or *to* + infin.) bind by oath, promise, contract, etc. □ **much obliged** an expression of thanks. □□ **obliger** *n*. [ME f. OF *obliger* f. L *obligare* (as OB-, *ligare* bind)]

obligee /ˌɒblɪˈdʒiː/ *n. Law* a person to whom another is bound by contract or other legal procedure (cf. OBLIGOR).

obliging /əˈblaɪdʒɪŋ/ *adj.* courteous, accommodating; ready to do a service or kindness. □□ **obligingly** *adv.* **obligingness** *n*.

obligor /ˌɒblɪˈɡɔː(r)/ *n. Law* a person who is bound to another by contract or other legal procedure (cf. OBLIGEE).

oblique /əˈbliːk/ *adj., n., & v.* —*adj.* **1 a** slanting; declining from the vertical or horizontal. **b** diverging from a straight line or course. **2** not going straight to the point; roundabout, indirect. **3** *Geom.* **a** (of a line, plane figure, or surface) inclined at other than a right angle. **b** (of an angle) acute or obtuse. **c** (of a cone, cylinder, etc.) with an axis not perpendicular to the plane of its base. **4** *Anat.* neither parallel nor perpendicular to the long axis of a body or limb. **5** *Bot.* (of a leaf) with unequal sides. **6** *Gram.* denoting any case other than the nominative or vocative. —*n.* **1** an oblique stroke (/). **2** an oblique muscle. —*v.intr.* (**obliques, obliqued, obliquing**) esp. *Mil.* advance obliquely. □ **oblique oration** (or **speech**) = *reported speech* (see REPORT). **oblique sphere** see SPHERE. □□ **obliquely** *adv.* **obliqueness** *n*. **obliquity** /əˈblɪkwɪtɪ/ *n*. [ME f. F f. L *obliquus*]

obliterate /əˈblɪtəˌreɪt/ *v.tr.* **1 a** blot out; efface, erase, destroy. **b** leave no clear traces of. **2** deface (a postage stamp etc.) to prevent further use. □□ **obliteration** /-ˈreɪʃ(ə)n/ *n*. **obliterative** /-rətɪv/ *adj.* **obliterator** *n*. [L *obliterare* (as OB-, *litera* LETTER)]

oblivion /əˈblɪvɪən/ *n*. **1 a** the state of having or being forgotten. **b** disregard; an unregarded state. **2** an amnesty or pardon. □ **fall into oblivion** be forgotten or disused. [ME f. OF f. L *oblivio -onis* f. *oblivisci* forget]

oblivious /əˈblɪvɪəs/ *adj.* **1** (often foll. by *of*) forgetful, unmindful. **2** (foll. by *to*, *of*) unaware or unconscious of. □□ **obliviously** *adv.* **obliviousness** *n*. [ME f. L *obliviosus* (as OBLIVION)]

oblong /ˈɒblɒŋ/ *adj. & n.* —*adj.* **1** deviating from a square form by having one long axis, esp. rectangular with adjacent sides unequal. **2** greater in breadth than in height. —*n.* an oblong figure or object. [ME f. L *oblongus* longish (as OB-, *longus* long)]

obloquy /ˈɒbləkwɪ/ *n*. **1** the state of being generally ill spoken of. **2** abuse, detraction. [ME f. LL *obloquium* contradiction f. L *obloqui* deny (as OB-, *loqui* speak)]

obnoxious /əbˈnɒkʃəs/ *adj.* offensive, objectionable, disliked. □□ **obnoxiously** *adv.* **obnoxiousness** *n*. [orig. = vulnerable (to harm), f. L *obnoxiosus* or *obnoxius* (as OB-, *noxa* harm: assoc. with NOXIOUS)]

oboe /ˈəʊbəʊ/ *n*. **1 a** a woodwind double-reed instrument of treble pitch and plaintive incisive tone, with a range of over two-and-a-half octaves, developed in France in the 17th c. **b** its player. **2** an organ stop with a quality resembling an oboe. □ **oboe d'amore** /dæˈmɔːreɪ/ an oboe with a pear-shaped bell and mellow tone, pitched a minor third below a normal oboe, commonly used in baroque music. □□ **oboist** /ˈəʊbəʊɪst/ *n*. [It. *oboe* or F *hautbois* f. *haut* high + *bois* wood: *d'amore* = of love]

obol /ˈɒb(ə)l/ *n*. an ancient Greek coin, equal to one-sixth of a drachma. [L *obolus* f. Gk *obolos*, var. of *obelos* OBELUS]

Obote /əˈbəʊtɪ/, Apollo Milton (1924–), Ugandan statesman, the first Prime Minister of his country on its independence (1962). He held office until 1966 and then assumed full power as President. Overthrown by Idi Amin in 1971, he returned from exile to resume the presidency in 1980, but failed either to restore the economy or stop corruption and tribal violence, and was again overthrown in 1985.

obovate /ɒbˈəʊveɪt/ *adj. Biol.* (of a leaf) ovate with the narrower end at the base.

obscene /əbˈsiːn/ *adj.* **1** offensively or repulsively indecent, esp. by offending accepted sexual morality. **2** *colloq.* highly offensive or repugnant (*an obscene accumulation of wealth*). **3** *Brit. Law* (of a publication) tending to deprave or corrupt. □□ **obscenely** *adv.*

obsceneness *n*. [F *obscène* or L *obsc(a)enus* ill-omened, abominable]

obscenity /əbˈsenɪtɪ/ *n*. (*pl.* **-ies**) **1** the state or quality of being obscene. **2** an obscene action, word, etc. [L *obscaenitas* (as OBSCENE)]

obscurantism /ˌɒbskjʊəˈræntɪz(ə)m/ *n*. opposition to knowledge and enlightenment. □□ **obscurant** /əbˈskjʊərənt/ *n*. **obscurantist** *n*. [*obscurant* f. G f. L *obscurans* f. *obscurare*: see OBSCURE]

obscure /əbˈskjʊə(r)/ *adj. & v.* —*adj.* **1** not clearly expressed or easily understood. **2** unexplained, doubtful. **3** dark, dim. **4** indistinct; not clear. **5** hidden; remote from observation. **6 a** unnoticed. **b** (of a person) undistinguished, hardly known. **7** (of a colour) dingy, dull, indefinite. —*v.tr.* **1** make obscure, dark, indistinct, or unintelligible. **2** dim the glory of; outshine. **3** conceal from sight. □ **obscure vowel** = *indeterminate vowel*. □□ **obscuration** /-ˈreɪʃ(ə)n/ *n*. **obscurely** *adv.* [ME f. OF *obscur* f. L *obscurus* dark]

obscurity /əbˈskjʊərɪtɪ/ *n*. (*pl.* **-ies**) **1** the state of being obscure. **2** an obscure person or thing. [F *obscurité* f. L *obscuritas* (as OBSCURE)]

obsecration /ˌɒbsɪˈkreɪʃ(ə)n/ *n*. earnest entreaty. [ME f. L *obsecratio* f. *obsecrare* entreat (as OB-, *sacrare* f. *sacer sacri* sacred)]

obsequies /ˈɒbsɪkwɪz/ *n.pl.* **1** funeral rites. **2** a funeral. □□ **obsequial** /əbˈsiːkwɪəl/ *adj.* [ME, pl. of obs. *obsequy* f. AF *obsequie*, OF *obseque* f. med.L *obsequiae* f. L *exsequiae* funeral rites (see EXEQUIES): assoc. with *obsequium* (see OBSEQUIOUS)]

obsequious /əbˈsiːkwɪəs/ *adj.* servilely obedient or attentive. □□ **obsequiously** *adv.* **obsequiousness** *n*. [ME f. L *obsequiosus* f. *obsequium* compliance (as OB-, *sequi* follow)]

observance /əbˈzɜːv(ə)ns/ *n*. **1** the act or process of keeping or performing a law, duty, custom, ritual, etc. **2** an act of a religious or ceremonial character; a customary rite. **3** the rule of a religious order. **4** *archaic* respect, deference. [ME f. OF f. L *observantia* (as OBSERVE)]

observant /əbˈzɜːv(ə)nt/ *adj. & n.* —*adj.* **1** acute or diligent in taking notice. **2** attentive in esp. religious observances (*observant few*). —*n.* (**Observant**) a member of the branch of the Franciscan order that observes the strict rule. □□ **observantly** *adv.* [F (as OBSERVE)]

observation /ˌɒbzəˈveɪʃ(ə)n/ *n*. **1** the act or an instance of noticing; the condition of being noticed. **2** perception; the faculty of taking notice. **3** a remark or statement, esp. one that is of the nature of a comment. **4 a** the accurate watching and noting of phenomena as they occur in nature with regard to cause and effect or mutual relations. **b** the noting of the symptoms of a patient, the behaviour of a suspect, etc. **5** the taking of the sun's or another heavenly body's altitude to find a latitude or longitude. **6** *Mil.* the watching of a fortress or hostile position or movements. □ **observation car** esp. *US* a carriage in a train built so as to afford good views. **observation post** *Mil.* a post for watching the effect of artillery fire etc. **under observation** being watched. □□ **observational** *adj.* **observationally** *adv.* [ME f. L *observatio* (as OBSERVE)]

observatory /əbˈzɜːvətɔrɪ/ *n*. (*pl.* **-ies**) a room or building equipped for the observation of natural, esp. astronomical or meteorological, phenomena. [mod.L *observatorium* f. L *observare* (as OBSERVE)]

observe /əbˈzɜːv/ *v*. **1** *tr.* (often foll. by *that*, *how* + clause) perceive, note; take notice of; become conscious of. **2** *tr.* watch carefully. **3** *tr.* **a** follow or adhere to (a law, command, method, principle, etc.). **b** keep or adhere to (an appointed time). **c** maintain (silence). **d** duly perform (a rite). **e** celebrate (an anniversary). **4** *tr.* examine and note (phenomena) without the aid of experiment. **5** *tr.* (often foll. by *that* + clause) say, esp. by way of comment. **6** *intr.* (foll. by *on*) make a remark or remarks about. □□ **observable** *adj.* **observably** *adv.* [ME f. OF *observer* f. L *observare* watch (as OB-, *servare* keep)]

observer /əbˈzɜːvə(r)/ *n*. **1** a person who observes. **2** an interested spectator. **3** a person who attends a conference etc. to note the proceedings but does not participate. **4 a** a person trained to notice and identify aircraft. **b** a person carried in an aeroplane to note the enemy's position etc.

obsess /əb'ses/ v.tr. (often in *passive*) preoccupy, haunt; fill the mind of (a person) continually. □□ **obsessive** adj. & n. **obsessively** adv. **obsessiveness** n. [L *obsidēre obsess-* (as OB-, *sedēre* sit)]

obsession /əb'seʃ(ə)n/ n. **1** the act of obsessing or the state of being obsessed. **2** a persistent idea or thought dominating a person's mind. **3** a condition in which such ideas are present. □□ **obsessional** adj. **obsessionalism** n. **obsessionally** adv. [L *obsessio* (as OBSESS)]

obsidian /əb'sɪdɪən/ n. a dark glassy volcanic rock formed from hardened lava. [L *obsidianus*, error for *obsianus* f. *Obsius*, the name (in Pliny) of the discoverer of a similar stone]

obsolescent /ˌɒbsə'les(ə)nt/ adj. becoming obsolete; going out of use or date. □□ **obsolescence** n. [L *obsolescere obsolescent-* (as OB-, *solēre* be accustomed)]

obsolete /'ɒbsəˌliːt/ adj. **1** disused, discarded, antiquated. **2** Biol. less developed than formerly or than in a cognate species; rudimentary. □□ **obsoletely** adv. **obsoleteness** n. **obsoletism** n. [L *obsoletus* past part. (as OBSOLESCENT)]

obstacle /'ɒbstək(ə)l/ n. a person or thing that obstructs progress. □ **obstacle-race** a race in which various obstacles have to be negotiated. [ME f. OF f. L *obstaculum* f. *obstare* impede (as OB-, *stare* stand)]

obstetric /əb'stetrɪk/ adj. (also **obstetrical**) of or relating to childbirth and associated processes. □□ **obstetrically** adv. **obstetrician** /-stə'trɪʃ(ə)n/ n. [mod.L *obstetricus* for L *obstetricius* f. *obstetrix* midwife f. *obstare* be present (as OB-, *stare* stand)]

obstetrics /əb'stetrɪks/ n.pl. (treated as *sing.*) the branch of medicine and surgery concerned with childbirth and midwifery.

obstinate /'ɒbstɪnət/ adj. **1** stubborn, intractable. **2** firmly adhering to one's chosen course of action or opinion despite dissuasion. **3** inflexible, self-willed. **4** unyielding; not readily responding to treatment etc. □□ **obstinacy** n. **obstinately** adv. [ME f. L *obstinatus* past part. of *obstinare* persist (as OB-, *stare* stand)]

obstreperous /əb'strepərəs/ adj. **1** turbulent, unruly; noisily resisting control. **2** noisy, vociferous. □□ **obstreperously** adv. **obstreperousness** n. [L *obstreperus* f. *obstrepere* (as OB-, *strepere* make a noise)]

obstruct /əb'strʌkt/ v.tr. **1** block up; make hard or impossible to pass. **2** prevent or retard the progress of; impede. □□ **obstructor** n. [L *obstruere obstruct-* (as OB-, *struere* build)]

obstruction /əb'strʌkʃ(ə)n/ n. **1** the act or an instance of blocking; the state of being blocked. **2** the act of making or the state of becoming more or less impassable. **3** an obstacle or blockage. **4** the retarding of progress by deliberate delays, esp. of Parliamentary business. **5** *Sport* the act of unlawfully obstructing another player. **6** *Med.* a blockage in a bodily passage, esp. in an intestine. □□ **obstructionism** n. (in sense 4). **obstructionist** n. (in sense 4). [L *obstructio* (as OBSTRUCT)]

obstructive /əb'strʌktɪv/ adj. & n. —adj. causing or intended to cause an obstruction. —n. an obstructive person or thing. □□ **obstructively** adv. **obstructiveness** n.

obtain /əb'teɪn/ v. **1** tr. acquire, secure; have granted to one. **2** intr. be prevalent or established or in vogue. □□ **obtainable** adj. **obtainability** /-'bɪlɪtɪ/ n. **obtainer** n. **obtainment** n. **obtention** /əb'tenʃ(ə)n/ n. [ME f. OF *obtenir* f. L *obtinēre obtent-* keep (as OB-, *tenēre* hold)]

obtrude /əb'truːd/ v. **1** intr. be or become obtrusive. **2** tr. (often foll. by *on, upon*) thrust forward (oneself, one's opinion, etc.) importunately. □□ **obtruder** n. **obtrusion** /-'truːʒ(ə)n/ n. [L *obtrudere obtrus-* (as OB-, *trudere* push)]

obtrusive /əb'truːsɪv/ adj. **1** unpleasantly or unduly noticeable. **2** obtruding oneself. □□ **obtrusively** adv. **obtrusiveness** n. [as OBTRUDE]

obtund /əb'tʌnd/ v.tr. blunt or deaden (a sense or faculty). [ME f. L *obtundere obtus-* (as OB-, *tundere* beat)]

obtuse /əb'tjuːs/ adj. **1** dull-witted; slow to understand. **2** of blunt form; not sharp-pointed or sharp-edged. **3** (of an angle)

more than 90° and less than 180°. **4** (of pain or the senses) dull; not acute. □□ **obtusely** adv. **obtuseness** n. **obtusity** n. [L *obtusus* past part. (as OBTUND)]

obverse /'ɒbvɜːs/ n. & adj. —n. **1 a** the side of a coin or medal etc. bearing the head or principal design. **b** this design (cf. REVERSE). **2** the front or proper or top side of a thing. **3** the counterpart of a fact or truth. —adj. **1** *Biol.* narrower at the base or point of attachment than at the apex or top (see OB- 7). **2** answering as the counterpart to something else. □□ **obversely** adv. [L *obversus* past part. (as OBVERT)]

obvert /əb'vɜːt/ v.tr. *Logic* alter (a proposition) so as to infer another proposition with a contradictory predicate, e.g. *no men are immortal to all men are mortal*. □□ **obversion** n. [L *obvertere obvers-* (as OB-, *vertere* turn)]

obviate /'ɒbvɪˌeɪt/ v.tr. get round or do away with (a need, inconvenience, etc.). □□ **obviation** /-'eɪʃ(ə)n/ n. [LL *obviare* oppose (as OB-, *via* way)]

obvious /'ɒbvɪəs/ adj. easily seen or recognized or understood; palpable, indubitable. □□ **obviously** adv. **obviousness** n. [L *obvius* f. *ob viam* in the way]

OC abbr. Officer Commanding.

oc- /ɒk/ prefix assim. form of OB- before *c*.

ocarina /ˌɒkə'riːnə/ n. a small egg-shaped ceramic (usu. terracotta) or metal wind instrument with holes for the fingers. Invented *c.*1860, it was used mainly as a toy and sometimes nicknamed 'sweet potato' (as in the once-popular song *Sweet Potato Piper*). [It. f. *oca* goose (from its shape)]

OCAS abbr. Organization of Central American States.

O'Casey /əu'keɪsɪ/, Sean (1880–1964), Irish playwright, born in Dublin of poor Protestant parents. He spent 9 years from 1903 as a railway labourer and developed an enthusiasm for the theatre through amateur dramatics. His three tragicomedies, *The Shadow of a Gunman* (1923), *Juno and the Paycock* (1924), and *The Plough and the Stars* (1926), deal realistically with the dangers of Irish patriotism, with tenement life, self-deception, and survival. He settled in England permanently in 1926. *The Silver Tassie* (1928) introduced the symbolic expressionist techniques which he developed in later works.

Occam's razor /ˌɒkəmz/ n. the principle attributed to the English philosopher William of Occam (see entry) that the fewest possible assumptions should be made in explaining a thing.

occasion /ə'keɪʒ(ə)n/ n. & v. —n. **1 a** a special or noteworthy event or happening (*dressed for the occasion*). **b** the time or occurrence of this (*on the occasion of their marriage*). **2** (often foll. by *for*, or *to* + infin.) a reason, ground, or justification (*there is no occasion to be angry*). **3** a juncture suitable for doing something; an opportunity. **4** an immediate but subordinate or incidental cause (*the assassination was the occasion of the war*). —v.tr. **1** be the occasion or cause of; bring about esp. incidentally. **2** (foll. by *to* + infin.) cause (a person or thing to do something). □ **on occasion** now and then; when the need arises. **rise to the occasion** produce the necessary will, energy, ability, etc., in unusually demanding circumstances. **take occasion** (foll. by *to* + infin.) make use of the opportunity. [ME f. OF *occasion* or L *occasio* juncture, reason, f. *occidere occas-* go down (as OB-, *cadere* fall)]

occasional /ə'keɪʒ(ə)n(ə)l/ adj. **1** happening irregularly and infrequently. **2** made or meant for, or associated with, a special occasion. **3** acting on a special occasion. □ **occasional cause** a secondary cause; an occasion (see OCCASION n. 4). **occasional table** a small table for irregular and varied use. □□ **occasionality** /-'nælɪtɪ/ n. **occasionally** adv.

Occident /'ɒksɪd(ə)nt/ n. *poet.* or *rhet.* **1** (prec. by *the*) the West. **2** western Europe. **3** Europe, America, or both, as distinct from the Orient. **4** European in contrast to Oriental civilization. [ME f. OF f. L *occidens -entis* setting, sunset, west (as OCCASION)]

occidental /ˌɒksɪ'dent(ə)l/ adj. & n. —adj. **1** of the Occident. **2** western. **3** of Western nations. —n. (**Occidental**) a native of the Occident. □□ **occidentalism** n. **occidentalist** n. **occidentalize** v.tr. (also **-ise**). **occidentally** adv. [ME f. OF *occidental* or L *occidentalis* (as OCCIDENT)]

occipito- /ɒkˈsɪpɪtəʊ/ *comb. form* the back of the head. [as OCCIPUT]

occiput /ˈɒksɪˌpʌt/ *n.* the back of the head. □□ **occipital** /-ˈsɪpɪt(ə)l/ *adj.* [ME f. L *occiput* (as OB-, *caput* head)]

Occitan /ˈɒksɪt(ə)n/ *n.* (also *attrib.*) the Provençal language. □□ **Occitanian** /-ˈteɪnɪən/ *n.* & *adj.* [F: cf. LANGUE D'OC]

occlude /əˈkluːd/ *v.tr.* **1** stop up or close (pores or an orifice). **2** *Chem.* absorb and retain (gases or impurities). □ **occluded front** *Meteorol.* a front resulting from occlusion. [L *occludere occlus-* (as OB-, *claudere* shut)]

occlusion /əˈkluːʒ(ə)n/ *n.* **1** the act or process of occluding. **2** *Meteorol.* a phenomenon in which the cold front of a depression overtakes the warm front, causing upward displacement of warm air between them. **3** *Dentistry* the position of the teeth when the jaws are closed. **4** the blockage or closing of a hollow organ etc. (*coronary occlusion*). **5** *Phonet.* the momentary closure of the vocal passage. □□ **occlusive** *adj.*

occult *adj.* & *v.* —*adj.* /ˈɒkʌlt, ˈɒkʌlt/ **1** involving the supernatural; mystical, magical. **2** kept secret; esoteric. **3** recondite, mysterious; beyond the range of ordinary knowledge. **4** *Med.* not obvious on inspection. —*v.tr.* /ˈɒkʌlt/ *Astron.* (of a concealing body much greater in size than the concealed body) hide from view by passing in front; conceal by being in front. □ **the occult** occult phenomena generally. **occulting light** a lighthouse light that is cut off at regular intervals. □□ **occultation** /-ˈteɪʃ(ə)n/ *n.* **occultism** *n.* **occultist** *n.* **occultly** *adv.* **occultness** *n.* [L *occulere occult-* (as OB-, *celare* hide)]

occupant /ˈɒkjʊpənt/ *n.* **1** a person who occupies, resides in, or is in a place etc. (*both occupants of the car were unhurt*). **2** a person holding property, esp. land, in actual possession. **3** a person who establishes a title by taking possession of something previously without an established owner. □□ **occupancy** *n.* (*pl.* **-ies**). [F *occupant* or L *occupans -antis* (as OCCUPY)]

occupation /ˌɒkjʊˈpeɪʃ(ə)n/ *n.* **1** what occupies one; a means of passing one's time. **2** a person's temporary or regular employment; a business, calling, or pursuit. **3** the act of occupying or state of being occupied. **4 a** the act of taking or holding possession of (a country, district, etc.) by military force. **b** the state or time of this. **5** tenure, occupancy. **6** (*attrib.*) for the sole use of the occupiers of the land concerned (*occupation road*). [ME f. AF *ocupacioun*, OF *occupation* f. L *occupatio -onis* (as OCCUPY)]

occupational /ˌɒkjʊˈpeɪʃən(ə)l/ *adj.* **1** of or in the nature of an occupation or occupations. **2** (of a disease, hazard, etc.) rendered more likely by one's occupation. □ **occupational therapy** mental or physical activity designed to assist recovery from disease or injury.

occupier /ˈɒkjʊˌpaɪə(r)/ *n. Brit.* a person residing in a property as its owner or tenant.

occupy /ˈɒkjʊˌpaɪ/ *v.tr.* (**-ies, -ied**) **1** reside in; be the tenant of. **2** take up or fill (space or time or a place). **3** hold (a position or office). **4** take military possession of (a country, region, town, strategic position). **5** place oneself in (a building etc.) forcibly or without authority. **6** (usu. in *passive*; often foll. by *in, with*) keep busy or engaged. [ME f. OF *occuper* f. L *occupare* seize (as OB-, *capere* take)]

occur /əˈkɜː(r)/ *v.intr.* (**occurred, occurring**) **1** come into being as an event or process at or during some time; happen. **2** exist or be encountered in some place or conditions. **3** (foll. by *to*; usu. foll. by *that* + clause) come into the mind of, esp. as an unexpected or casual thought (*it occurred to me that you were right*). [L *occurrere* go to meet, present itself (as OB-, *currere* run)]

occurrence /əˈkʌrəns/ *n.* **1** the act or an instance of occurring. **2** an incident or event. □ **of frequent occurrence** often occurring. [*occurrent* that occurs f. F f. L *occurrens -entis* (as OCCUR)]

ocean /ˈəʊʃ(ə)n/ *n.* **1 a** a large expanse of sea, esp. each of the main areas called the Atlantic, Pacific, Indian, Arctic, and Southern (or Antarctic) Oceans. **b** these regarded cumulatively as the body of water surrounding the land of the globe. **2** (usu. prec. by *the*) the sea. **3** (often in *pl.*) a very large expanse or quantity of anything (*oceans of time*). □ **ocean-going** (of a ship) able to cross oceans. **ocean tramp** a merchant ship, esp. a steamer, running on no regular line or route. □□ **oceanward** *adv.* (also **-wards**). [ME f. OF *occean* f. L *oceanus* f. Gk *ōkeanos* stream encircling the earth's disc, Atlantic]

oceanarium /ˌəʊʃəˈneərɪəm/ *n.* (*pl.* **oceanariums** or **-ria** /-rɪə/) a large seawater aquarium for keeping sea animals. [OCEAN + -ARIUM, after *aquarium*]

Oceania /ˌəʊsɪˈɑːnɪə/ the islands of the Pacific and adjacent seas. □□ **Oceanian** *adj.* & *n.* [mod.L f. F *Océanie* f. L (as OCEAN)]

oceanic /ˌəʊʃɪˈænɪk, ˌəʊsɪ-/ *adj.* **1** of, like, or near the ocean. **2** (of a climate) governed by the ocean. **3** of the part of the ocean distant from the continents. **4** (**Oceanic**) of Oceania.

Oceanid /əʊˈsiːənɪd/ *n.* (*pl.* **Oceanids** or **-ides** /ˌəʊsɪˈænɪˌdiːz/) *Gk Mythol.* an ocean nymph. [Gk *ōkeanis -idos* daughter of OCEANUS]

oceanography /ˌəʊʃəˈnɒɡrəfɪ/ *n.* the study of the oceans. □□ **oceanographer** *n.* **oceanographic** /-nəˈɡræfɪk/ *adj.* **oceanographical** /-nəˈɡræfɪk(ə)l/ *adj.*

Oceanus /ˌəʊsɪˈeɪnəs/ *Gk Mythol.* the son of Uranus and Gaia, and father of the ocean nymphs (Oceanids) and river gods. He is the personification of the river encircling the whole world.

ocellus /ɒˈseləs/ *n.* (*pl.* **ocelli** /-laɪ/) **1** each of the simple, as opposed to compound, eyes of insects etc. **2** a spot of colour surrounded by a ring of a different colour on the wing of a butterfly etc. □□ **ocellar** *adj.* **ocellate** /ˈɒsɪlət/ *adj.* **ocellated** /ˈɒsɪˌleɪtɪd/ *adj.* [L, dimin. of *oculus* eye]

ocelot /ˈɒsɪˌlɒt/ *n.* **1** a medium-sized cat, *Felis pardalis*, native to S. and Central America, having a deep yellow or orange coat with black striped and spotted markings. **2** its fur. [F, abbr. by Buffon f. Nahuatl *tlalocelotl* jaguar of the field, and applied to a different animal]

och /ɒx/ *int. Sc.* & *Ir.* expressing surprise or regret. [Gael. & Ir.]

oche /ˈɒkɪ/ *n.* (also **hockey** /ˈɒkɪ, ˈhɒkɪ/) *Darts* the line behind which the players stand when throwing. [20th c.: orig. uncert. (perh. connected with OF *ochen* cut a deep notch in)]

ocher *US* var. of OCHRE.

ochlocracy /ɒkˈlɒkrəsɪ/ *n.* (*pl.* **-ies**) mob rule. □□ **ochlocrat** /ˈɒkləˌkræt/ *n.* **ochlocratic** /ˌɒkləˈkrætɪk/ *adj.* [F *ochlocratie* f. Gk *okhlokratia* f. *okhlos* mob]

ochone /ɒˈxəʊn/ *int.* (also **ohone**) *Sc.* & *Ir.* expressing regret or lament. [Gael. & Ir. *ochóin*]

ochre /ˈəʊkə(r)/ *n.* (*US* **ocher**) **1** a mineral of clay and ferric oxide, used as a pigment varying from light yellow to brown or red. **2** a pale brownish yellow. □□ **ochreish** *adj.* **ochreous** /ˈəʊkrɪəs/ *adj.* **ochrous** /ˈəʊkrəs/ *adj.* **ochry** /ˈəʊkrɪ/ *adj.* [ME f. OF *ocre* f. L *ochra* f. Gk *ōkhra* yellow ochre]

-ock /ək/ *suffix* forming nouns orig. with diminutive sense (*hillock; bullock*). [from or after OE *-uc, -oc*]

ocker /ˈɒkə(r)/ *n. Austral. sl.* a boorish or aggressive Australian (esp. as a stereotype). [20th c.: orig. uncert.]

o'clock /əˈklɒk/ *adv.* of the clock (used to specify the hour) (*6 o'clock*).

O'Connell /əʊˈkɒn(ə)l/, Daniel (1775–1847), Irish nationalist leader and social reformer, whose election to Parliament in 1828 forced the British government to grant Catholic emancipation in order to enable him to take his seat in the House of Commons, for which Roman Catholics were previously ineligible. In the 1840s his campaign for the repeal of union with Britain by constitutional methods was unsuccessful, and he lost the support of many nationalists and radicals.

OCR *abbr.* optical character recognition.

Oct. *abbr.* October.

oct. *abbr.* octavo.

oct- /ɒkt/ *comb. form* assim. form of OCTA-, OCTO- before a vowel.

octa- /ˈɒktə/ *comb. form* (also **oct-** before a vowel) eight. [Gk *okta-* f. *oktō* eight]

octad /ˈɒktæd/ *n.* a group of eight. [LL *octas octad-* f. Gk *oktas -ados* f. *oktō* eight]

octagon /ˈɒktəɡən/ *n.* **1** a plane figure with eight sides and angles. **2** an object or building with this cross-section. □□ **octagonal** /-ˈtæɡən(ə)l/ *adj.* **octagonally** /-ˈtæɡənəlɪ/ *adv.* [L *octagonos* f. Gk *octagōnos* (as OCTA-, -GON)]

octahedron /ˌɒktəˈhiːdrən, -ˈhedrən/ *n.* (*pl.* **octahedrons** or

octahedra /-drə/) **1** a solid figure contained by eight (esp. triangular) plane faces. **2** a body, esp. a crystal, in the form of a regular octahedron. □ **regular octahedron** an octahedron contained by equal and equilateral triangles. □□ **octahedral** adj. [Gk oktaedron (as OCTA-, -HEDRON)]

octal /ˈɒkt(ə)l/ adj. reckoning or proceeding by eights (octal scale).

octamerous /ɒkˈtæmərəs/ adj. **1** esp. Bot. having eight parts. **2** Zool. having organs arranged in eights.

octane /ˈɒkteɪn/ n. a colourless inflammable hydrocarbon of the alkane series. ¶ Chem. formula: C_8H_{18}. □ **high-octane** (of fuel used in internal-combustion engines) having good antiknock properties, not detonating readily during the power stroke. **octane number** (or **rating**) a figure indicating the antiknock properties of a fuel. [OCT- + -ANE]

octant /ˈɒkt(ə)nt/ n. **1** an arc of a circle equal to one eighth of the circumference. **2** such an arc with two radii, forming an area equal to one eighth of the circle. **3** each of eight parts into which three planes intersecting (esp. at right angles) at a point divide the space or the solid body round it. **4** Astron. a point in a body's apparent course 45° distant from a given point, esp. a point at which the moon is 45° from conjunction or opposition with the sun. **5** an instrument in the form of a graduated eighth of a circle, used in astronomy and navigation. [L octans octanthalf-quadrant f. octo eight]

octaroon var. of OCTOROON.

octastyle /ˈɒktəˌstaɪl/ adj. & n. —adj. having eight columns at the end or in front. —n. an octastyle portico or building. [L octastylus f. Gk oktastulos (as OCTA- + stulos pillar)]

octavalent /ˌɒktəˈveɪlənt/ adj. Chem. having a valency of eight. [OCTA- + VALENCE[1]]

octave /ˈɒktɪv/ n. **1** Mus. **a** a series of eight notes occupying the interval between (and including) two notes, one having twice or half the frequency of vibration of the other. **b** this interval. **c** each of the two notes at the extremes of this interval. **d** these two notes sounding together. **2** a group or stanza of eight lines; an octet. **3 a** the seventh day after a festival. **b** a period of eight days including a festival and its octave. **4** a group of eight. **5** the last of eight parrying positions in fencing. **6** Brit. a wine-cask holding an eighth of a pipe. □ **law of octaves** that formulated (1863–6) by J. A. R. Newlands, who noted that the chemical elements, when arranged in order of their atomic weights, exhibited a recurring regularity of properties after each series of 8 elements, an anticipation of the periodic law. [ME f. OF f. L octava dies eighth day (reckoned inclusively)]

Octavian /ɒkˈteɪvɪən/ the name (Gaius Julius Caesar Octavianus) taken by Gaius Octavius on his recognition in 43 BC as the adopted son of Julius Caesar, and by which he was known until his assumption of the title Augustus in 27 BC.

octavo /ɒkˈteɪvəʊ, ɒkˈtɑːvəʊ/ n. (pl. **-os**) **1** a size of book or page given by folding a standard sheet three times to form a quire of eight leaves. **2** a book or sheet of this size. ¶ Abbr.: **8vo**. [L in octavo in an eighth f. octavus eighth]

octennial /ɒkˈtenɪəl/ adj. **1** lasting eight years. **2** occurring every eight years. [LL octennium period of eight years (as OCT-, annus year)]

octet /ɒkˈtet/ n. (also **octette**) **1** Mus. **a** a composition for eight voices or instruments. **b** the performers of such a piece. **2** a group of eight. **3** the first eight lines of a sonnet. **4** Chem. a stable group of eight electrons. [It. ottetto or G Oktett: assim. to OCT-, DUET, QUARTET]

octo- /ˈɒktəʊ/ comb. form (also **oct-** before a vowel) eight. [L octo or Gk oktō eight]

October /ɒkˈtəʊbə(r)/ n. the tenth month of the year. □ **October Revolution** a revolutionary movement in Russia in 1917 (see REVOLUTION 1). **October War** the Yom Kippur war. [OE f. L (as OCTO-): cf. DECEMBER, SEPTEMBER]

Octobrist /ɒkˈtəʊbrɪst/ n. hist. a member of the moderate party in the Russian Duma, supporting the Imperial Constitutional Manifesto of 30 Oct. 1905. [OCTOBER, after Russ. oktyabrist]

octocentenary /ˌɒktəʊsenˈtiːnərɪ/ n. & adj. —n. (pl. **-ies**) **1** an eight-hundredth anniversary. **2** a celebration of this. —adj. of or relating to an octocentenary.

octodecimo /ˌɒktəʊˈdesɪˌməʊ/ n. (pl. **-os**) **1** a size of book or page given by folding a standard sheet into eighteen leaves. **2** a book or sheet of this size. [in octodecimo f. L octodecimus eighteenth]

octogenarian /ˌɒktəʊdʒɪˈneərɪən/ n. & adj. —n. a person from 80 to 89 years old. —adj. of this age. [L octogenarius f. octogeni distributive of octoginta eighty]

octopod /ˈɒktəˌpɒd/ n. any cephalopod of the order Octopoda, with eight arms usu. having suckers, and a round saclike body, including octopuses. [Gk oktōpous -podos f. oktō eight + pous foot]

octopus /ˈɒktəpəs/ n. (pl. **-es**) **1** any cephalopod of the genus Octopus having eight suckered arms, a soft saclike body, and strong beaklike jaws. **2** an organized and usu. harmful ramified power or influence. [Gk oktōpous: see OCTOPOD]

octoroon /ˌɒktəˈruːn/ n. (also **octaroon**) the offspring of a quadroon and a White, a person of one-eighth Negro blood. [OCTO- after QUADROON]

octosyllabic /ˌɒktəʊsɪˈlæbɪk/ adj. & n. —adj. having eight syllables. —n. an octosyllabic verse. [LL octosyllabus (as OCTO-, SYLLABLE)]

octosyllable /ˌɒktəˈsɪləb(ə)l/ n. & adj. —n. an octosyllabic verse or word. —adj. = OCTOSYLLABIC.

octroi /ˈɒktrwɑː/ n. **1** a duty levied in some European countries on goods entering a town. **2 a** the place where this is levied. **b** the officials by whom it is levied. [F f. octroyer grant, f. med.L auctorizare: see AUTHORIZE]

octuple /ˈɒktjʊp(ə)l/ adj., n., & v. —adj. eightfold. —n. an eightfold amount. —v.tr. & intr. multiply by eight. [F octuple or L octuplus (adj.) f. octo eight: cf. DOUBLE]

ocular /ˈɒkjʊlə(r)/ adj. & n. —adj. of or connected with the eyes or sight; visual. —n. the eyepiece of an optical instrument. □ **ocular spectrum** see SPECTRUM. □□ **ocularly** adv. [F oculaire f. LL ocularis f. L oculus eye]

ocularist /ˈɒkjʊlərɪst/ n. a maker of artificial eyes. [F oculariste (as OCULAR)]

oculate /ˈɒkjʊlət/ adj. = OCELLATE (see OCELLUS). [L oculatus f. oculus eye]

oculist /ˈɒkjʊlɪst/ n. a person who specializes in the medical treatment of eye disorders or defects. □□ **oculistic** /-ˈlɪstɪk/ adj. [F oculiste f. L oculus eye]

oculo- /ˈɒkjʊləʊ/ comb. form eye (oculo-nasal). [L oculus eye]

OD[1] abbr. ordnance datum.

OD[2] /əʊˈdiː/ n. & v. esp. US sl. —n. an overdose, esp. of a narcotic drug. —v.intr. (**OD's, OD'd, OD'ing**) take an overdose. [abbr.]

od[1] /ɒd/ n. a hypothetical power once thought to pervade nature and account for various scientific phenomena. [arbitrary term coined in G by Baron von Reichenbach, Ger. scientist d. 1869]

od[2] /ɒd/ n. (as int. or in oaths) archaic = GOD. [corruption]

o.d. abbr. outer diameter.

odal var. of UDAL.

odalisque /ˈəʊdəlɪsk/ n. hist. an Eastern female slave or concubine, esp. in the Turkish Sultan's seraglio. [F f. Turk. odalik f. oda chamber + lik function]

odd /ɒd/ adj. & n. —adj. **1** extraordinary, strange, queer, remarkable, eccentric. **2** casual, occasional, unconnected (odd jobs; odd moments). **3** not normally noticed or considered; unpredictable (in some odd corner; picks up odd bargains). **4** additional; beside the reckoning (earned the odd pound). **5 a** (of numbers such as 3 and 5) not integrally divisible by two. **b** (of things or persons numbered consecutively) bearing such a number (no parking on odd dates). **6** left over when the rest have been distributed or divided into pairs (have got an odd sock). **7** detached from a set or series (a few odd volumes). **8** (appended to a number, sum, weight, etc.) somewhat more than (forty odd; forty-odd people). **9** by which a round number, given sum, etc., is exceeded (we have 102—what shall we do with the odd 2?). —n. Golf a handicap of one stroke at each hole. □ **odd job** a casual isolated piece of work. **odd job man** (or **odd jobber**) Brit. a person who does odd jobs. **odd man out 1** a person or thing differing from all the others in a group in some respect. **2** a method of selecting one of three or more persons e.g. by tossing a coin. □□ **oddish** adj. **oddly** adv.

oddness n. [ME f. ON *odda-* in *odda-mathr* third man, odd man, f. *oddi* angle]

oddball /ˈɒdbɔːl/ n. colloq. **1** an odd or eccentric person. **2** (attrib.) strange, bizarre.

Oddfellow /ˈɒdfeləʊ/ n. a member of a fraternity similar to the Freemasons.

oddity /ˈɒdɪtɪ/ n. (pl. **-ies**) **1** a strange person, thing, or occurrence. **2** a peculiar trait. **3** the state of being odd.

oddment /ˈɒdmənt/ n. **1** an odd article; something left over. **2** (in pl.) miscellaneous articles. **3** Brit. Printing matter other than the main text.

odds /ɒdz/ n.pl. **1** the ratio between the amounts staked by the parties to a bet, based on the expected probability either way. **2** the chances or balance of probability in favour of or against some result (the odds are against it; the odds are that it will rain). **3** the balance of advantage (the odds are in your favour; won against all the odds). **4** an equalizing allowance to a weaker competitor. **5** a difference giving an advantage (it makes no odds). □ **at odds** (often foll. by with) in conflict or at variance. **by all odds** certainly. **lay** (or **give**) **odds** offer a bet with odds favourable to the other better. **odds and ends** miscellaneous articles or remnants. **odds-on** a state when success is more likely than failure, esp. as indicated by the betting odds. **over the odds** above a generally agreed price etc. **take odds** offer a bet with odds unfavourable to the other better. **what's the odds?** colloq. what does it matter? [app. pl. of ODD n.: cf. NEWS]

ode /əʊd/ n. **1** a rhymed (rarely unrhymed) lyric, often in the form of an address, generally dignified or exalted in subject, feeling, and style, but sometimes (in earlier use) simple and familiar (though less so than a song). **2** hist. a poem meant to be sung. [F f. LL *oda* f. Gk *ōidē* Attic form of *aoidē* song f. *aeidō* sing]

-ode[1] /əʊd/ suffix forming nouns meaning 'thing of the nature of' (*geode*; *trematode*). [Gk *-ōdēs* adj. ending]

-ode[2] /əʊd/ comb. form Electr. forming names of electrodes, or devices having them (*cathode*; *diode*). [Gk *hodos* way]

Odense /ˈəʊdənsə/ a port on the island of Fünen (Fyn), Denmark; pop. (1988) 174,000. It is the birthplace of Hans Andersen.

Oder /ˈəʊdə(r)/ (Czech and Polish **Odra** /ˈɒdrə/) a river of central Europe. Rising in the mountains of Czechoslovakia, it flows 907 km (567 miles) north through western Poland to meet the River Neisse where it forms the border between Poland and Germany before emptying into the Baltic Sea. This frontier, known as the Oder-Neisse Line, was adopted at the Potsdam Conference in 1945.

Odessa /əʊˈdesə/ a Ukrainian city and seaport on the NW coast of the Black Sea; pop. (est. 1987) 1,141,000.

Odets /əʊˈdets/, Clifford (1906–63), American dramatist. He was a founder member in 1931 of the Group Theatre, which followed the naturalistic methods of the Moscow Art Theatre, and his reputation was made when it performed his play *Waiting for Lefty* (1935), about a taxi-drivers' strike. This was followed by two other dramas of social conflict, *Till the Day I Die* and *Awake and Sing!* (both 1935). Later works include *The Big Knife* (1948), an attack on the corruptions of Hollywood.

odeum /ˈəʊdɪəm/ n. (pl. **odeums** or **odea** /-dɪə/) a building for musical performances, esp. among the ancient Greeks and Romans. [F *odéum* or L *odeum* f. Gk *ōideion* (as ODE)]

Odin /ˈəʊdɪn/ Scand. Mythol. the supreme god and creator, god of victory and the dead, represented as an old one-eyed man of great wisdom. Wednesday is named after him.

odious /ˈəʊdɪəs/ adj. hateful, repulsive. □□ **odiously** adv. **odiousness** n. [ME f. OF *odieus* f. L *odiosus* (as ODIUM)]

odium /ˈəʊdɪəm/ n. a general or widespread dislike or reprobation incurred by a person or associated with an action. [L, = hatred f. *odi* to hate]

odometer /əʊˈdɒmɪtə(r)/ n. (also **hodometer** /hɒ-/) an instrument for measuring the distance travelled by a wheeled vehicle. □□ **odometry** n. [F *odomètre* f. Gk *hodos* way: see -METER]

odonto- /əʊˈdɒntəʊ/ comb. form tooth. [Gk *odous odont-* tooth]

odontoglossum /əʊˌdɒntəˈglɒsəm/ n. any of various orchids

bearing flowers with jagged edges like tooth-marks. [ODONTO- + Gk *glōssa* tongue]

odontoid /əʊˈdɒntɔɪd/ adj. toothlike. □ **odontoid process** a projection from the second cervical vertebra. [Gk *odontoeidēs* (as ODONTO- + Gk *eidos* form)]

odontology /ˌəʊdɒnˈtɒlədʒɪ/ n. the scientific study of the structure and diseases of teeth. □□ **odontological** /-təˈlɒdʒɪk(ə)l/ adj. **odontologist** n.

odor US var. of ODOUR.

odoriferous /ˌəʊdəˈrɪfərəs/ adj. diffusing a scent, esp. an agreeable one; fragrant. □□ **odoriferously** adv. [ME f. L *odorifer* (as ODOUR)]

odorous /ˈəʊdərəs/ adj. **1** having a scent. **2** = ODORIFEROUS. □□ **odorously** adv. [L *odorus* fragrant (as ODOUR)]

odour /ˈəʊdə(r)/ n. (US **odor**) **1** the property of a substance that has an effect on the nasal sense of smell. **2** a lasting quality or trace attaching to something (an odour of intolerance). **3** regard, repute (in bad odour). □□ **odourless** adj. (in sense 1). [ME f. AF *odour*, OF *odor* f. L *odor -oris* smell, scent]

Odysseus /əˈdɪsjəs/ Gk legend king of Ithaca, called Ulysses by the Romans, renowned for cunning. He survived the Trojan War but Poseidon kept him from home for ten years while his wife Penelope waited. (See ODYSSEY.)

Odyssey /ˈɒdɪsɪ/ a Greek hexameter epic poem in 24 books traditionally ascribed to Homer. It tells of the travels of the ever-resourceful Odysseus during his years of wandering after the sack of Troy, and of his eventual return home to Ithaca and his slaying of the evil suitors of his faithful wife Penelope. His adventures include amorous liaisons with Calypso and the witch Circe, hospitality at the court of the pleasure-loving Phaeacians, the evocation of the famous dead from the underworld, and encounters with a number of fabulous monsters, including the Cyclops Polyphemus and Scylla and Charybdis. —**odyssey** n. (pl. **-eys**) a series of wanderings; a long adventurous journey. □□ **Odyssean** adj. [L *Odyssea* f. Gk *Odusseia*]

OECD abbr. Organization for Economic Cooperation and Development.

OED abbr. Oxford English Dictionary.

oedema /ɪˈdiːmə/ n. (US **edema**) a condition characterized by an excess of watery fluid collecting in the cavities or tissues of the body. Also called DROPSY. □□ **oedematose** adj. **oedematous** adj. [LL f. Gk *oidēma -atos* f. *oideō* swell]

Oedipus /ˈiːdɪpəs/ Gk legend the son of Laius king of Thebes, and Jocasta. He unwittingly killed his father and married Jocasta, and when the facts were discovered went mad and put out his own eyes, while Jocasta hanged herself. [Gk = swollen foot, from the story that Laius ran a spike through the infant's feet before leaving it to die]

Oedipus complex /ˈiːdɪpəs/ n. Psychol. (according to Freud etc.) the complex of emotions aroused in a young (esp. male) child by a subconscious sexual desire for the parent of the opposite sex and wish to exclude the parent of the same sex. □□ **Oedipal** adj.

oenology /iːˈnɒlədʒɪ/ n. (US **enology**) the study of wines. □□ **oenological** /ˌiːnəˈlɒdʒɪk(ə)l/ adj. **oenologist** n. [Gk *oinos* wine]

Oenone /iːˈnəʊnɪ/ Gk legend a nymph of Mount Ida and lover of Paris, who deserted her for Helen.

oenophile /ˈiːnəfaɪl/ n. a connoisseur of wines. □□ **oenophilist** /iːˈnɒfɪlɪst/ n. [as OENOLOGY]

o'er /ˈəʊə(r)/ adv. & prep. poet. = OVER. [contr.]

Oersted /ˈɜːsted/, Hans Christian (1777–1851), Danish physicist, who in 1820 discovered that an electric current has a magnetic effect. He noticed the deflection of a compass needle placed near a wire carrying a current. The unit of magnetic field strength named after him (the *oersted*) is replaced in the SI system by the ampere per metre.

oesophagus /iːˈsɒfəgəs/ n. (US **esophagus**) (pl. **oesophagi** /-dʒaɪ/ or **-guses**) the part of the alimentary canal from the mouth to the stomach; the gullet. □□ **oesophageal** /iːˌsɒfəˈdʒiːəl, ˌiːsəˈfædʒɪəl/ adj. [ME f. Gk *oisophagos*]

b **but** d **dog** f **few** g **get** h **he** j **yes** k **cat** l **leg** m **man** n **no** p **pen** r **red** s **sit** t **top** v **voice**

oestrogen /ˈiːstrədʒ(ə)n/ n. (US **estrogen**) **1** any of various steroid hormones developing and maintaining female characteristics of the body. **2** this hormone produced artificially for use in oral contraceptives etc. □□ **oestrogenic** /-ˈdʒenɪk/ adj. **oestrogenically** /-ˈdʒenɪkəlɪ/ adv. [OESTRUS + -GEN]

oestrus /ˈiːstrəs/ n. (also **oestrum**, US **estrus**, **estrum**) a recurring period of sexual receptivity in many female mammals; heat. □□ **oestrous** adj. [Gk oistros gadfly, frenzy]

œuvre /ˈɜːvr/ n. the works of an author, painter, composer, etc., esp. regarded collectively. [F, = work, f. L opera]

of /ɒv, əv/ prep. connecting a noun (often a verbal noun) or pronoun with a preceding noun, adjective, adverb, or verb, expressing a wide range of relations broadly describable as follows: **1** origin, cause, or authorship (paintings of Turner; people of Rome; died of malnutrition). **2** the material or substance constituting or identifying a thing (a house of cards; was built of bricks). **3** belonging, connection, or possession (a thing of the past; articles of clothing; the head of the business; the tip of the iceberg). **4** identity or close relation (the city of Rome; a pound of apples; a fool of a man). **5** removal, separation, or privation (north of the city; got rid of them; robbed us of £1000). **6** reference, direction, or respect (beware of the dog; suspected of lying; very good of you; short of money; the selling of goods). **7** objective relation (love of music; in search of peace). **8** partition, classification, or inclusion (no more of that; part of the story; a friend of mine; this sort of book; some of us will stay). **9** description, quality, or condition (the hour of prayer; a person of tact; a girl of ten; on the point of leaving). **10** US time in relation to the following hour (a quarter of three). □ **be of** possess intrinsically; give rise to (is of great interest). **of all** designating the (nominally) least likely or expected example (you of all people!). **of all the nerve** (or **cheek** etc.) an exclamation of indignation at a person's impudence etc. **of an evening** (or **morning** etc.) colloq. **1** on most evenings (or mornings etc.). **2** at some time in the evenings (or mornings etc.). **of late** recently. **of old** formerly; long ago. [OE, unaccented form of æf, f. Gmc]

of- /ɒf/ prefix assim. form of OB- before f.

ofay /ˈəʊfeɪ/ n. US sl. offens. a White person (esp. used by Blacks). [20th c.: prob. of Afr. orig.]

Off. abbr. **1** Office. **2** Officer.

off /ɒf/ adv., prep., adj., & n. —adv. **1** away; at or to a distance (drove off; is three miles off). **2** out of position; not on or touching or attached; loose, separate, gone (has come off; take your coat off). **3** so as to be rid of (sleep it off). **4** so as to break continuity or continuance; discontinued, stopped (turn off the radio; take a day off; the game is off). **5** not available as a choice, e.g. on a menu (chips are off). **6** to the end; entirely; so as to be clear (clear off; finish off; pay off). **7** situated as regards money, supplies, etc. (is badly off; is not very well off). **8** off-stage (noises off). **9** (of food etc.) beginning to decay. **10** (with preceding numeral) denoting a quantity produced or made at one time (esp. one-off). —prep. **1 a** from; away or down or up from (fell off the chair; took something off the price; jumped off the edge). **b** not on (was already off the pitch). **2 a** (temporarily) relieved of or abstaining from (off duty; am off my diet). **b** not attracted by for the time being (off their food; off smoking). **c** not achieving or doing one's best in (off form; off one's game). **3** using as a source or means of support (live off the land). **4** leading from; not far from (a street off the Strand). **5** at a short distance to sea from (sank off Cape Horn). —adj. **1** far, further (the off side of the wall). **2** (of a part of a vehicle, animal, or road) right (the off front wheel). **3** Cricket designating the half of the field (as divided lengthways through the pitch) to which the striker's feet are pointed. —n. **1** Cricket the off side. **2** the start of a race. □ **a bit off** Brit. colloq. **1** rather annoying or unfair. **2** somewhat unwell (am feeling a bit off). **off and on** intermittently; now and then. **off-centre** not quite coinciding with a central position. **the off chance** see CHANCE. **off colour 1** not in good health. **2** US somewhat indecent. **off the cuff** see CUFF¹. **off-day** a day when one is not at one's best. **off-drive** Cricket drive (the ball) to the off side. **off one's feet** see FOOT. **off form** see FORM. **off guard** see GUARD. **off one's hands** see HAND. **off one's head** see HEAD. **off-key 1** out of tune. **2** not quite suitable or fitting. **off-licence** Brit. **1** a shop selling alcoholic drink for consumption elsewhere. **2** a licence for this. **off limits** see LIMIT.

off-line Computing (of a computer terminal or process) not directly controlled by or connected to a central processor. **off of** sl. disp. = OFF prep. (picked it off of the floor). **off-peak** used or for use at times other than those of greatest demand. **off the peg** see PEG. **off-piste** (of skiing) away from prepared ski runs. **off the point** adj. irrelevant. —adv. irrelevantly. **off-putting** Brit. disconcerting; repellent. **off the record** see RECORD. **off-road** attrib.adj. **1** away from the road, on rough terrain. **2** (of a vehicle etc.) designed for rough terrain or for cross-country driving. **off-season** a time when business etc. is slack. **off-stage** adj. & adv. not on the stage and so not visible or audible to the audience. **off-street** (esp. of parking vehicles) other than on a street. **off-time** a time when business etc. is slack. **off-the-wall** sl. crazy, absurd, outlandish. **off-white** white with a grey or yellowish tinge. [orig. var. of OF, to distinguish the sense]

Offa /ˈɒfə/ (d. 796) king of Mercia 757–96. □ **Offa's Dyke** a series of earthworks running from near the mouth of the Wye to near the mouth of the Dee, built or repaired by Offa to mark the boundary established by his wars with the Welsh.

offal /ˈɒf(ə)l/ n. **1** the less valuable edible parts of a carcass, esp. the entrails and internal organs. **2** refuse or waste stuff. **3** carrion; putrid flesh. [ME f. MDu. afval f. af OFF + vallen FALL]

Offaly /ˈɒfəlɪ/ a county of Ireland, in the province of Leinster; pop. (est. 1986) 59,800; capital, Tullamore.

offbeat adj. & n. —adj. /ˈɒfbiːt, ɒfˈbiːt/ **1** not coinciding with the beat. **2** eccentric, unconventional. —n. /ˈɒfbiːt/ any of the unaccented beats in a bar.

offcut /ˈɒfkʌt/ n. a remnant of timber, paper, etc., after cutting.

Offenbach /ˈɒfənˌbɑːx/, Jacques (1819–80), German-born French composer, Jacob Eberst, who adopted the name of the German town in which his father lived. He began composing operettas in 1853, writing no fewer than ninety in the next quarter-century. His two-act opera Orphée aux enfers (Orpheus in the Underworld) was produced in 1858, and by the 1860s his fame as a witty and satirical composer was widespread. Later he turned away from the frivolous style, which was less to the taste of the Parisian public than it had been before the war of 1870–1, and composed Les Contes d'Hoffmann (Tales of Hoffmann), based on three stories by the German writer E. T. A. Hoffmann; it was not produced until after his death.

offence /əˈfens/ n. (US **offense**) **1** an illegal act; a transgression or misdemeanour. **2** a wounding of the feelings; resentment or umbrage (no offence was meant). **3** the act of attacking or taking the offensive; aggressive action. □ **give offence** cause hurt feelings. **take offence** suffer hurt feelings. □□ **offenceless** adj. [orig. = stumbling, stumbling-block: ME & OF offens f. L offensus annoyance, and ME & F offense f. L offensa a striking against, hurt, displeasure, both f. offendere (as OB-, fendere fens- strike)]

offend /əˈfend/ v. **1** tr. cause offence to or resentment in; wound the feelings of. **2** tr. displease or anger. **3** intr. (often foll. by against) do wrong; transgress. □□ **offendedly** adv. **offender** n. **offending** adj. [ME f. OF offendre f. L (as OFFENCE)]

offense US var. of OFFENCE.

offensive /əˈfensɪv/ adj. & n. —adj. **1** giving or meant or likely to give offence; insulting (offensive language). **2** disgusting, foul-smelling, nauseous, repulsive. **3 a** aggressive, attacking. **b** (of a weapon) meant for use in attack. —n. **1** an aggressive action or attitude (take the offensive). **2** an attack, an offensive campaign or stroke. **3** aggressive or forceful action in pursuit of a cause (a peace offensive). □□ **offensively** adv. **offensiveness** n. [F offensif -ive or med.L offensivus (as OFFENCE)]

offer /ˈɒfə(r)/ v. & n. —v. **1** tr. present for acceptance or refusal or consideration (offered me a drink; was offered a lift; offer one's services; offer no apology). **2** intr. (foll. by to + infin.) express readiness or show intention (offered to take the children). **3** tr. provide; give an opportunity for. **4** tr. make available for sale. **5** tr. (of a thing) present to one's attention or consideration (each day offers new opportunities). **6** tr. present (a sacrifice, prayer, etc.) to a deity. **7** intr. present itself; occur (as opportunity offers). **8** tr. give an opportunity for (battle) to an enemy. **9** tr. attempt, or try to show (violence, resistance, etc.). —n. **1** an expression of readiness to do or give if desired, or to buy or sell (for a certain amount). **2** an amount offered. **3** a proposal (esp. of marriage). **4** a bid. □ **on offer** for sale at a certain (esp. reduced) price. □□ **offerer** *n.* **offeror** *n.* [OE *offrian* in religious sense, f. L *offerre* (as OB-, *ferre* bring)]

offering /ˈɒfərɪŋ/ *n.* **1** a contribution, esp. of money, to a Church. **2** a thing offered as a religious sacrifice or token of devotion. **3** anything, esp. money, contributed or offered.

offertory /ˈɒfətərɪ, -trɪ/ *n.* (*pl.* **-ies**) **1** *Eccl.* **a** the offering of the bread and wine at the Eucharist. **b** an anthem accompanying this. **2 a** the collection of money at a religious service. **b** the money collected. [ME f. eccl.L *offertorium* offering f. LL *offert-* for L *oblat-* past part. stem of *offerre* OFFER]

offhand *adj.* & *adv.* —*adj.* /ɒfˈhænd, ˈɒfhænd/ curt or casual in manner. —*adv.* /ɒfˈhænd/ **1** in an offhand manner. **2** without preparation or premeditation. □□ **offhanded** *adj.* **offhandedly** *adv.* **offhandedness** *n.*

office /ˈɒfɪs/ *n.* **1** a room or building used as a place of business, esp. for clerical or administrative work. **2** a room or department or building for a particular kind of business (*ticket office*; *post office*). **3** the local centre of a large business (*our London office*). **4** *US* the consulting-room of a professional person. **5** a position with duties attached to it; a place of authority or trust or service, esp. of a public nature. **6** tenure of an official position, esp. that of a minister of State or of the party forming the Government (*hold office*; *out of office for 13 years*). **7** (**Office**) the quarters or staff or collective authority of a Government department etc. (*Foreign Office*). **8** a duty attaching to one's position; a task or function. **9** (usu. in *pl.*) a piece of kindness or attention; a service (esp. *through the good offices of*). **10** *Eccl.* **a** an authorized form of worship (*Office for the Dead*). **b** (in full **divine office**) the daily service of the Roman Catholic breviary (*say the office*). **11** a ceremonial duty. **12** (in *pl.*) *Brit.* the parts of a house devoted to household work, storage, etc. **13** *sl.* a hint or signal. □ **the last offices** rites due to the dead. **office-bearer** an official or officer. **office block** a large building designed to contain business offices. **office boy** (or **girl**) a young man (or woman) employed to do minor jobs in a business office. **office hours** the hours during which business is normally conducted. **office of arms** the College of Arms, or a similar body in another country. **office-worker** an employee in a business office. [ME f. OF f. L *officium* performance of a task (in med.L also office, divine service), f. *opus* work + *facere* fic- do]

officer /ˈɒfɪsə(r)/ *n.* & *v.* —*n.* **1** a person holding a position of authority or trust, esp. one with a commission in the armed services, in the mercantile marine, or on a passenger ship. **2** a policeman or policewoman. **3** a holder of a post in a society (e.g. the president or secretary). **4** a holder of a public, civil, or ecclesiastical office; a sovereign's minister; an appointed or elected functionary (usu. with a qualifying word: *medical officer*; *probation officer*; *returning officer*). **5** a bailiff (*the sheriff's officer*). **6** a member of the grade below commander in the Order of the British Empire etc. —*v.tr.* **1** provide with officers. **2** act as the commander of. □ **officer of arms** a herald or pursuivant. [ME f. AF *officer*, OF *officier* f. med.L *officiarius* f. L *officium*: see OFFICE]

official /əˈfɪʃ(ə)l/ *adj.* & *n.* —*adj.* **1** of or relating to an office (see OFFICE *n.* 5, 6) or its tenure or duties. **2** characteristic of officials and bureaucracy. **3** emanating from or attributable to a person in office; properly authorized. **4** holding office; employed in a public capacity. **5** *Med.* according to the pharmacopoeia, officinal. —*n.* **1** a person holding office or engaged in official duties. **2** (in full **official principal**) the presiding officer or judge of an archbishop's, bishop's, or esp. archdeacon's court. □ **official birthday** *Brit.* a day in June chosen for the observance of the sovereign's birthday. **official secrets** confidential information involving national security. □□ **officialdom** *n.* **officialism** *n.* **officially** *adv.* [ME (as noun) f. OF f. L *officialis* (as OFFICE)]

officialese /əˌfɪʃəˈliːz/ *n. derog.* the formal precise language characteristic of official documents.

officiant /əˈfɪʃɪənt/ *n.* a person who officiates at a religious ceremony.

officiate /əˈfɪʃɪˌeɪt/ *v.intr.* **1** act in an official capacity, esp. on a particular occasion. **2** perform a divine service or ceremony. □□

officiation *n.* **officiator** *n.* [med.L *officiare* perform a divine service (*officium*): see OFFICE]

officinal /ˌɒfɪˈsiːn(ə)l, əˈfɪsɪn(ə)l/ *adj.* **1 a** (of a medicine) kept ready for immediate dispensing. **b** made from the pharmacopoeia recipe (cf. MAGISTRAL). **c** (of a name) adopted in the pharmacopoeia. **2** (of a herb or drug) used in medicine. □□ **officinally** *adv.* [med.L *officinalis* f. L *officina* workshop]

officious /əˈfɪʃəs/ *adj.* **1** asserting one's authority aggressively; domineering. **2** intrusive or excessively enthusiastic in offering help etc.; meddlesome. **3** *Diplomacy* informal, unofficial. □□ **officiously** *adv.* **officiousness** *n.* [L *officiosus* obliging f. *officium*: see OFFICE]

offing /ˈɒfɪŋ/ *n.* the more distant part of the sea in view. □ **in the offing** not far away; likely to appear or happen soon. [perh. f. OFF + -ING¹]

offish /ˈɒfɪʃ/ *adj. colloq.* inclined to be aloof. □□ **offishly** *adv.* **offishness** *n.* [OFF: cf. *uppish*]

offload /ˈɒfləʊd, ɒfˈləʊd/ *v.tr.* get rid of (esp. something unpleasant) by giving it to someone else.

off-price /ˈɒfpraɪs/ *adj.* *US* involving merchandise sold at a lower price than that recommended by the manufacturer.

offprint /ˈɒfprɪnt/ *n.* a printed copy of an article etc. originally forming part of a larger publication.

offscreen /ˈɒfskriːn/ *adj.* & *adv.* —*adj.* not appearing on a cinema, television, or VDU screen. —*adv.* **1** without use of a screen. **2** outside the view presented by a cinema-film scene.

offset *n.* & *v.* —*n.* /ˈɒfset/ **1** a side-shoot from a plant serving for propagation. **2** an offshoot or scion. **3** a compensation; a consideration or amount diminishing or neutralizing the effect of a contrary one. **4** *Archit.* a sloping ledge in a wall etc. where the thickness of the part above is diminished. **5** a mountain-spur. **6** a bend in a pipe etc. to carry it past an obstacle. **7** (often *attrib.*) a method of printing in which ink is transferred from a plate or stone to a uniform rubber surface and from there to paper etc. (*offset litho*). **8** *Surveying* a short distance measured perpendicularly from the main line of measurement. —*v.tr.* /ˈɒfset, ɒfˈset/ (**-setting**; *past* and *past part.* **-set**) **1** counterbalance, compensate. **2** place out of line. **3** print by the offset process.

offshoot /ˈɒfʃuːt/ *n.* **1** a side-shoot or branch. **2** something derivative.

offshore /ˈɒfʃɔː(r)/ *adj.* **1** situated at sea some distance from the shore. **2** (of the wind) blowing seawards. **3** (of goods, funds, etc.) made or registered abroad.

offside *adj.* & *n.* —*adj.* /ɒfˈsaɪd/ *Sport* (of a player in a field game) in a position, usu. ahead of the ball, that is not allowed if it affects play. —*n.* /ˈɒfsaɪd/ (often *attrib.*) esp. *Brit.* the right side of a vehicle, animal, etc. (cf. NEARSIDE).

offsider /ɒfˈsaɪdə(r)/ *n.* *Austral. colloq.* a partner, assistant, or deputy.

offspring /ˈɒfsprɪŋ/ *n.* (*pl.* same) **1** a person's child or children or descendant(s). **2** an animal's young or descendant(s). **3** a result. [OE *ofspring* f. OF from + *springan* SPRING *v.*]

oft /ɒft/ *adv. archaic* or *literary* often (usu. in *comb.*: *oft-recurring*). □ **oft-times** *adv.* [OE]

often /ˈɒf(ə)n, ˈɒft(ə)n/ *adv.* (**oftener**, **oftenest**) **1 a** frequently; many times. **b** at short intervals. **2** in many instances. □ **as often as not** in roughly half the instances. [ME: extended f. OFT, prob. after *selden* = SELDOM]

Ogaden /ˌɒɡəˈden, ˈɒɡə-/ a desert region in SE Ethiopia, largely inhabited by Somali nomads. Successive governments of neighbouring Somalia have laid claim to this territory which they call Western Somalia.

ogam var. of OGHAM.

ogdoad /ˈɒɡdəʊˌæd/ *n.* a group of eight. [LL *ogdoas ogdoad-* f. Gk *ogdoas -ados* f. *ogdoos* eighth f. *oktō* eight]

ogee /ˈəʊdʒiː, -ˈdʒiː/ *adj.* & *n.* *Archit.* —*adj.* showing in section a double continuous S-shaped curve. —*n.* an S-shaped line or moulding. □ **ogee arch** an arch with two ogee curves meeting at the apex. □□ **ogee'd** *adj.* [app. f. OGIVE, as being the usu. moulding in groin-ribs]

ogham /ˈɒɡəm/ *n.* (also **ogam**) **1** an ancient British and Irish alphabet of twenty characters, probably invented in the 4th c. AD, formed by parallel strokes on either side of or across a continuous line. **2** an inscription in this alphabet. **3** each of its characters. [OIr. *ogam*, referred to *Ogma*, its supposed inventor]

ogive /ˈəʊdʒaɪv, -ˈdʒaɪv/ n. **1** a pointed or Gothic arch. **2** one of the diagonal groins or ribs of a vault. **3** an S-shaped line. **4** *Statistics* a cumulative frequency graph. □□ **ogival** *adj.* [ME f. F, of unkn. orig.]

ogle /ˈəʊg(ə)l/ v. & n. —v. **1** tr. eye amorously or lecherously. **2** intr. look amorously. —n. an amorous or lecherous look. □□ **ogler** n. [prob. LG or Du.: cf. LG *oegeln*, frequent. of *oegen* look at]

OGPU /ˈɒgpuː/ n. (also **Ogpu**) a security police agency established in 1922 as GPU and renamed after the formation of the USSR (1923). It existed to suppress counter-revolution, uncover political dissidents, and (after 1928) to enforce the collectivization of farming. The agency had its own army and a vast network of spies. It was absorbed into the NKVD in 1934. [Russ. abbr., = United State Political Directorate]

ogre /ˈəʊgə(r)/ n. (fem. **ogress** /-grɪs/) **1** a man-eating giant in folklore etc. **2** a terrifying person. □□ **ogreish** *adj.* (also **ogrish**). [F, first used by Perrault in 1697, of unkn. orig.]

OH abbr. US Ohio (in official postal use).

oh[1] /əʊ/ int. (also **O**) expressing surprise, pain, entreaty, etc. (*oh, what a mess; oh for a holiday*). □ **oh boy** expressing surprise, excitement, etc. **oh well** expressing resignation. [var. of O⁴]

oh[2] /əʊ/ n. = O¹ 2.

o.h.c. abbr. overhead camshaft.

O'Higgins /əʊˈhɪgɪnz/, Bernardo (c. 1778–1842), Chilean revolutionary leader, son of a Spanish officer of Irish origin. He put himself at the head of the independence movement in Chile and, with the help of San Martín, liberator of Argentina, led the army which triumphed over Spanish forces in 1817 and won independence for his country. For the next six years he was supreme director of Chile, but then fell from power and was obliged to live in exile in Peru for the remainder of his life.

Ohio /əʊˈhaɪəʊ/ a State in the north-eastern US, bordering on Lake Erie; pop. (est. 1985) 10,797,600; capital, Columbus. Acquired by Britain from France in 1763 and by the US in 1783, it became the 17th State of the US in 1803.

Ohm /əʊm/, Georg Simon (1789–1854), German physicist who discovered the law, named after him, that the electric current flowing through a wire is directly proportional to the potential difference (voltage) and inversely proportional to the resistance. The ohm (see entry) is named in his honour.

ohm /əʊm/ n. *Electr.* the SI unit of resistance, transmitting a current of one ampere when subjected to a potential difference of one volt. ¶ Symb.: Ω. □□ **ohmage** n. [G. S. OHM]

ohmmeter /ˈəʊmˌmiːtə(r)/ n. an instrument for measuring electrical resistance.

OHMS abbr. on Her (or His) Majesty's Service.

Ohm's law /əʊmz/ n. *Electr.* a law stating that current is proportional to voltage and inversely proportional to resistance.

oho /əʊˈhəʊ/ int. expressing surprise or exultation. [ME f. O⁴ + HO]

ohone var. of OCHONE.

Ohrid /ˈɒxrɪd/, Lake a lake on the frontier between Yugoslavia and Albania.

o.h.v. abbr. overhead valve.

oi /ɔɪ/ int. calling attention or expressing alarm etc. [var. of HOY¹]

-oid /ɔɪd/ suffix forming adjectives and nouns, denoting form or resemblance (*asteroid; rhomboid; thyroid*). □□ **-oidal** suffix forming adjectives. **-oidally** suffix forming adverbs. [mod.L *-oides* f. Gk *-oeidēs* f. *eidos* form]

oidium /əʊˈɪdɪəm/ n. (pl. **oidia** /-dɪə/) spores formed by the breaking up of fungal hyphae into cells. [mod.L f. Gk *ōion* egg + *-idion* dimin. suffix]

oil /ɔɪl/ n. & v. —n. **1** any of various thick, viscous, usu. inflammable liquids insoluble in water but soluble in organic solvents. (See below.) **2** US petroleum. **3** (in comb.) using oil as fuel (*oil-heater*). **4 a** (usu. in pl.) = oil-paint. **b** colloq. a picture painted in

oil-paints. **5** (in pl.) = OILSKIN. —v. **1** tr. apply oil to; lubricate. **2** tr. impregnate or treat with oil (*oiled silk*). **3** tr. & intr. supply with or take on oil as fuel. **4** tr. & intr. make (butter, grease, etc.) into or (of butter etc.) become an oily liquid. □ **oil-bird** a guacharo. **oil drum** a metal drum used for transporting oil. **oiled silk** silk made waterproof with oil. **oil engine** an engine driven by the explosion of vaporized oil mixed with air. **oil-fired** using oil as fuel. **oil a person's hand** (or **palm**) bribe a person. **oil-lamp** a lamp using oil as fuel. **oil-meal** ground oilcake. **oil of vitriol** see VITRIOL. **oil-paint** (or **-colour**) a mix of ground colour pigment and oil. **oil-painting 1** the art of painting in oil-paints (Vasari attributes its invention to Jan van Eyck at the beginning of the 15th c.). **2** a picture painted in oil-paints. **oil-palm** either of two trees, *Elaeis guineensis* of W. Africa, or *E. oleifera* of the US, from which palm oil is extracted. **oil-pan** an engine sump. **oil-paper** a paper made transparent or waterproof by soaking in oil. **oil-press** an apparatus for pressing oil from seeds etc. **oil rig** a structure with equipment for drilling an oil well. **oil-sand** a stratum of porous rock yielding petroleum. **oil-seed** any of various seeds from cultivated crops yielding oil, e.g. rape, peanut, or cotton. **oil-shale** a fine-grained rock from which oil can be extracted. **oil-slick** a smooth patch of oil, esp. one on the sea. **oil-tanker** a ship designed to carry oil in bulk. **oil one's tongue** say flattering or glib things. **oil well** a well from which mineral oil is drawn. **oil the wheels** help make things go smoothly. **well oiled** colloq. very drunk. □□ **oilless** adj. [ME oli, oile f. AF, ONF olie = OF oile etc. f. L oleum (olive) oil f. olea olive]

Oils are classified thus: (i) non-volatile *fatty* or *fixed oils* of animal or vegetable origin, used as varnishes, lubricants, illuminants, soap constituents, etc., chemically identical with fats, (ii) *essential* or *volatile oils*, chiefly of vegetable origin, giving plants etc. their scent, used in medicine and perfumery, and (iii) *mineral oils*, consisting mainly of hydrocarbons, thought to be the remains of tiny living organisms deposited millions of years ago and now found trapped in underground reservoirs, detectable by seismic surveys and by drilling. The modern mineral oil industry dates from 1859, when a well was bored at Titusville in Pennsylvania. (This was not the first strike; oil had been found in Ohio in 1841 during drilling for salt.) Petroleum oils are the main source of energy in developed countries for heating and transport, and are used as the basis of a whole range of chemicals, particularly plastics.

oilcake /ˈɔɪlkeɪk/ n. a mass of compressed linseed etc. left after oil has been extracted, used as fodder or manure.

oilcan /ˈɔɪlkæn/ n. a can containing oil, esp. one with a long nozzle for oiling machinery.

oilcloth /ˈɔɪlklɒθ/ n. **1** a fabric waterproofed with oil. **2** an oilskin. **3** a canvas coated with linseed or other oil and used to cover a table or floor.

oiler /ˈɔɪlə(r)/ n. **1** an oilcan for oiling machinery. **2** an oil-tanker. **3** US **a** an oil well. **b** (in pl.) oilskin.

oilfield /ˈɔɪlfiːld/ n. an area yielding mineral oil.

oilman /ˈɔɪlmən/ n. (pl. **-men**) a person who deals in oil.

oilskin /ˈɔɪlskɪn/ n. **1** cloth waterproofed with oil. **2 a** a garment made of this. **b** (in pl.) a suit made of this.

oilstone /ˈɔɪlstəʊn/ n. a fine-grained flat stone used with oil for sharpening flat tools, e.g. chisels, planes, etc. (cf. WHETSTONE).

oily /ˈɔɪli/ adj. (**oilier**, **oiliest**) **1** of, like, or containing much oil. **2** covered or soaked with oil. **3** (of a manner etc.) fawning, insinuating, unctuous. □□ **oilily** adv. **oiliness** n.

oink /ɔɪŋk/ v.intr. (of a pig) make its characteristic grunt. [imit.]

ointment /ˈɔɪntmənt/ n. a smooth greasy healing or cosmetic preparation for the skin. [ME oignement, ointment, f. OF oignement ult. f. L (as UNGUENT): oint- after obs. oint anoint f. OF, past part. of oindre ANOINT]

Oireachtas /ˈɪərəxˌθæs/ n. the legislature of the Irish Republic, consisting of the President, Dáil, and Seanad. [Ir.]

Oisin /ˈəʊʃiːn/ see OSSIAN.

Ojibwa /əʊˈdʒɪbweɪ/ n. & adj. —n. **1** a member of an Algonquian people of North American Indians inhabiting the lands round Lake Superior and (more recently) certain adjacent areas. **2** their language. —*adj.* of this people or their language. [native name, f. root meaning 'puckered', with ref. to their moccasins]

OK[1] /əʊˈkeɪ/ *adj., adv., n., & v.* (also **okay**) *colloq.* —*adj.* (often as *int.* expressing agreement or acquiescence) all right; satisfactory. —*adv.* well, satisfactorily (*that worked out OK*). —*n.* (*pl.* **OKs**) approval, sanction. —*v.tr.* (**OK's, OK'd, OK'ing**) give an OK to; approve, sanction. [orig. US: prob. abbr. of *orl* (or *oll*) *korrect*, joc. form of 'all correct', and first used in 1839; it was used as a slogan for a candidate from Old Kinderhook in the American election of 1840; other suggestions about its origin are without acceptable foundation]

OK[2] *abbr.* US Oklahoma (in official postal use).

okapi /əʊˈkɑːpɪ/ *n.* (*pl.* same or **okapis**) a ruminant mammal, *Okapia johnstoni*, native to N. and NE Zaïre, with a head resembling that of a giraffe and a body resembling that of a zebra, having a dark chestnut coat and transverse stripes on the hindquarters and upper legs only. It was discovered in 1900. [Central Afr. native name]

Okara /əʊˈkɑːrə/ a commercial city in Punjab province, NE Pakistan; pop. (1981) 154,000.

Okavango /ˌəʊkəˈvæŋgəʊ/ a river of SW Africa rising in central Angola and flowing 1,600 km (1,000 miles) across NE Namibia into Botswana, where it drains into the extensive Okavango marshes of Ngamiland.

okay var. of OK[1].

okey-dokey /ˌəʊkɪˈdəʊkɪ/ *adj. & adv.* (also **okey-doke** /-ˈdəʊk/) *sl.* = OK[1]. [redupl.]

Okhotsk /əʊˈxɒtsk/, **Sea of** an inlet of the North Pacific Ocean off the east coast of mainland USSR, bounded to the east by the Kamchatka Peninsula and to the south-east by the Kuril Islands which stretch in a long line from Kamchatka to the north-east corner of the Japanese island of Hokkaido.

Okinawa /ˌɒkɪˈnɑːwə/ **1** a region of Japan, in the southern Ryuku islands; pop. (1986) 1,190,000; capital, Naha. **2** the largest of these islands. It was captured from the Japanese in the Second World War by a US assault in April–June 1945. With its bases commanding the approaches to Japan it was a key objective, defended by the Japanese almost to the last man, with kamikaze air attacks inflicting substantial damage on US ships. After the war it was retained under US administration until 1972.

Okla. *abbr.* Oklahoma.

Oklahoma /ˌəʊkləˈhəʊmə/ a State of the US lying west of Arkansas, acquired as part of the Louisiana Purchase in 1803; pop. (est. 1985) 3,025,500; capital, Oklahoma City. In 1834–89 it was declared Indian territory in which Europeans were forbidden to settle. It became the 46th State of the US in 1907.

okra /ˈəʊkrə, ˈɒkrə/ *n.* **1** a malvaceous African plant, *Abelmoschus esculentus*, yielding long ridged seed-pods. **2** the seed-pods eaten as a vegetable and used to thicken soups and stews. Also called GUMBO, *ladies' fingers.* [W.Afr. native name]

-ol[1] /ɒl/ *suffix Chem.* the termination of *alcohol*, used in names of alcohols or analogous compounds (*methanol*; *phenol*).

-ol[2] /ɒl/ *comb. form* = -OLE. [L *oleum* oil]

Olaf /ˈəʊlæf/ the name of five kings of Norway:

    Olaf I Tryggvason (969–1000), reigned 995–1000. According to legend he was brought up in Russia, being converted to Christianity and carrying out extensive Viking raids before returning to Norway to be accepted as king. He jumped overboard and disappeared after his fleet was defeated by the combined forces of Denmark and Sweden at the battle of Svöld, but his exploits as a warrior and his popularity as sovereign made him a national legend.

    Olaf II Haraldsson (c.995–1030), reigned 1016–30. Notable for his attempts to spread Christianity in his kingdom, Olaf was forced into exile by a rebellion in 1028 and killed in battle at Stiklestad while attempting to return. He was canonized in 1164 and became the patron saint of Norway.

    Olaf V (1903–91), reigned 1957–91, succeeding his father King Haakon VII.

Öland /ˈɜːlænd/ a narrow island in the Baltic Sea, off the SE coast of Sweden.

old /əʊld/ *adj.* (**older, oldest**) (cf. ELDER, ELDEST). **1 a** advanced in age; far on in the natural period of existence. **b** not young or near its beginning. **2** made long ago. **3** long in use. **4** worn or dilapidated or shabby from the passage of time. **5** having the characteristics (experience, feebleness, etc.) of age (*the child has an old face*). **6** practised, inveterate (*an old offender; old in crime*). **7** belonging only or chiefly to the past; lingering on; former (*old times; haunted by old memories*). **8** dating from far back; long established or known; ancient, primeval (*old as the hills; old friends; an old family*). **9** (appended to a period of time) of age (*is four years old; a four-year-old boy; a four-year-old*). **10** (of language) as used in former or earliest times. **11** *colloq.* as a term of affection or casual reference (*good old Charlie; old shipmate*). **12** the former or first of two or more similar things (*our old house; wants his old job back*). □ **old age** the later part of normal life. **old-age pension** (introduced in Britain by Lloyd George in 1908) = *retirement pension*. **old-age pensioner** a person receiving this. **Old Bill** *Brit. sl.* the police. **old bird** a wary person. **old boy 1** a former male pupil of a school. **2** *colloq.* **a** an elderly man. **b** an affectionate form of address to a boy or man. **old boy network** *Brit. colloq.* preferment in employment of those from a similar social background, esp. fellow ex-pupils of public schools. **the old country** the native country of colonists etc. **Old English** see ENGLISH. **old-fashioned** in or according to a fashion or tastes no longer current; antiquated. **Old French** the French language of the period before *c.*1400. **old fustic** see FUSTIC. **old girl 1** a former female pupil of a school. **2** *colloq.* **a** an elderly woman. **b** an affectionate term of address to a girl or woman. **Old Glory** *US* the Stars and Stripes, the US national flag. **old gold** a dull brownish-gold colour. **Old Guard** the French Imperial Guard created by Napoleon I in 1804. **old guard** the original or past or conservative members of a group. **old hand** a person with much experience. **old hat** *colloq.* something tediously familiar or out of date. **Old High German** High German (see GERMAN) up to *c.*1200. **Old Hickory** *US* the nickname of Andrew Jackson (President of the US 1829–37), from his toughness of character. **Old Kingdom** a period of ancient Egyptian history (see EGYPT). **old lady** *colloq.* one's mother or wife. **old lag** see LAG[3]. **Old Lady of Threadneedle Street** the nickname of the Bank of England, which stands in this street (see THREADNEEDLE STREET). The term dates from the late 18th c. **old maid 1** *derog.* an elderly unmarried woman. **2** a prim and fussy person. **3** a card-game in which players try not to be left with an unpaired queen. **old-maidish** like an old maid. **old man** *colloq.* **1** one's husband or father. **2** one's employer or other person in authority over one. **3** an affectionate form of address to a boy or man. **old man's beard** a wild clematis, *Clematis vitalba*, with grey fluffy hairs round the seeds: also called *traveller's joy* (see TRAVELLER). **old master 1** a great artist of former times, esp. of the 13th–17th c. in Europe. **2** a painting by such a painter. **old moon** the moon in its last quarter, before the new moon. **Old Nick** *colloq.* the Devil. **Old Norse** see NORSE. **an old one** a familiar joke. **Old Pals Act** *Brit.* the principle that friends should always help one another. **Old Pretender** see PRETENDER. **old retainer** see RETAINER 3b. **old school 1** traditional attitudes. **2** people having such attitudes. **old school tie** *Brit.* **1** a necktie with a characteristic pattern worn by the pupils of a particular (usu. public) school. **2** the principle of excessive loyalty to traditional values. **old soldier** an experienced person, esp. in an arduous activity. **old stager** an experienced person, an old hand. **old style** of a date reckoned by the Julian calendar. **Old Testament** see separate entry. **old-time** belonging to former times. **old-timer** *US* a person with long experience or standing. **old wives' tale** a foolish or unscientific tradition or belief. **old woman** *colloq.* **1** one's wife or mother. **2** a fussy or timid man. **old-womanish** fussy and timid. **Old World** Europe, Asia, and Africa, the part known by the ancients to exist (cf. *New World*). **old-world** belonging to or associated with old times. **old year** the year just ended or about to end. □□ **oldish** *adj.* **oldness** *n.* [OE *ald* f. WG]

Old Bailey the Central Criminal Court, formerly standing in an ancient bailey of London city wall. The present court, trying offences committed in the City and the Greater London area, and certain other offences, was built in 1903–6 on the site of Newgate Prison.

Old Contemptibles the veterans of the British Expeditionary Force sent to France in 1914, so named because of a German reference to the contemptible little army facing them.

Old Dominion a name adopted by the colony of Virginia after it had been raised to the status of Dominion by Charles II for its prompt recognition of him after his restoration to the throne in 1660.

olden /'əʊld(ə)n/ *adj. archaic* of old; of a former age (esp. *in olden times*).

oldie /'əʊldɪ/ *n. colloq.* an old person or thing.

oldster /'əʊldstə(r)/ *n.* an old person. [OLD + -STER, after *youngster*]

Old Testament the first 39 books of the Bible, the Jewish scriptures containing an account of the creation, the origin of mankind, God's covenant with the Jews, and their early history. Most of the books were written in Hebrew, some in Aramaic. They were classified by the Jews into three groups: the Law (i.e. the Pentateuch), the Prophets (Joshua, Judges, 1 & 2 Samuel, 1 & 2 Kings, Isaiah, Jeremiah, Ezekiel, and the twelve Minor Prophets), and the 'Writings', comprising the remaining books; the canon of the Jewish scriptures was probably settled by about AD 100.

Olduvai Gorge /'ɒldʊˌvaɪ/ a gorge 48 km (30 miles) long and up to 90 metres (300 ft.) deep, in northern Tanzania, in which the exposed strata contain numerous fossils spanning the full range of the Pleistocene period. Most importantly, the Gorge has provided the longest sequence of hominid presence and activity yet discovered anywhere in the world, with fossils, stone-tool industries, and other evidence of hominid activities that date from *c.*2.1–1.7 million years ago for the oldest dated deposits to *c.*22,000 years ago for the most recent fossil-bearing deposits. The hominids found at individual sites within the Gorge include *Australopithecus boisei* (the *Zinjanthropus* fossils), *Homo habilis*, and *Homo erectus.*

Old Vic the popular name of a London theatre, opened in 1818 as the Royal Coburg and renamed the Royal Victoria Theatre in honour of Princess (later Queen) Victoria in 1833. Its standards declined and it suffered various vicissitudes until under the management of Lilian Baylis from 1912 it gained an enduring reputation for its Shakespearian productions.

-ole /əʊl/ *comb. form* forming names of esp. heterocyclic compounds (*indole*). [L *oleum* oil]

oleaceous /ˌəʊlɪ'eɪʃəs/ *adj.* of the plant family Oleaceae, including olive and jasmine. [mod.L *Oleaceae* f. L *olea* olive-tree]

oleaginous /ˌəʊlɪ'ædʒɪnəs/ *adj.* **1** having the properties of or producing oil. **2** oily, greasy. **3** obsequious, ingratiating. [F *oléagineux* f. L *oleaginus* f. *oleum* oil]

oleander /ˌəʊlɪ'ændə(r)/ *n.* an evergreen poisonous shrub, *Nerium oleander*, native to the Mediterranean and bearing clusters of white, pink, or red flowers. [med.L]

oleaster /ˌəʊlɪ'æstə(r)/ *n.* any of various trees of the genus *Elaeagnus*, often thorny and with evergreen leathery foliage, esp. *E. angustifolia* bearing olive-shaped yellowish fruits. Also called *Russian olive.* [ME f. L f. *olea* olive-tree: see -ASTER]

olecranon /əʊ'lekrəˌnɒn, ˌəʊlɪ'kreɪnən/ *n.* a bony prominence on the upper end of the ulna at the elbow. [Gk *ōle(no)kranon* f. *ōlenē* elbow + *kranion* head]

olefin /'əʊlɪfɪn/ *n.* (also **olefine**) *Chem.* = ALKENE. [F *oléfiant* oil-forming (with ref. to oily ethylene dichloride)]

oleic acid /əʊ'liːɪk/ *n.* an unsaturated fatty acid present in many fats and soaps. □□ **oleate** /'əʊlɪət/ *n.* [L *oleum* oil]

oleiferous /ˌəʊlɪ'ɪfərəs/ *adj.* yielding oil. [L *oleum* oil + -FEROUS]

oleo- /'əʊlɪəʊ/ *comb. form* oil. [L *oleum* oil]

oleograph /'əʊlɪəˌgrɑːf/ *n.* a print made to resemble an oil-painting.

oleomargarine /ˌəʊlɪəʊˌmɑː'dʒɑːriːn, -'mɑːdʒərɪn, -ˌmɑːgə'riːn/ *n.* **1** a fatty substance extracted from beef fat and often used in margarine. **2** *US* a margarine made from vegetable oils.

oleometer /ˌəʊlɪ'ɒmɪtə(r)/ *n.* an instrument for determining the density and purity of oils.

oleo-resin /ˌəʊlɪəʊ'rezɪn/ *n.* a natural or artificial mixture of essential oils and a resin, e.g. balsam.

oleum /'əʊlɪəm/ *n.* concentrated sulphuric acid containing excess sulphur trioxide in solution forming a dense corrosive liquid. [L, = oil]

O level /əʊ/ *n. Brit. hist.* = ordinary level. [abbr.]

olfaction /ɒl'fækʃ(ə)n/ *n.* the act or capacity of smelling; the sense of smell. □□ **olfactive** *adj.* [L *olfactus* a smell f. *olēre* to smell + *facere fact-* make]

olfactory /ɒl'fæktərɪ/ *adj.* of or relating to the sense of smell (*olfactory nerves*). [L *olfactare* frequent. of *olfacere* (as OLFACTION)]

olibanum /ɒ'lɪbənəm/ *n.* an aromatic gum resin from any tree of the genus *Boswellia*, used as incense. [ME f. med.L f. LL *libanus* f. Gk *libanos* frankincense, of Semitic orig.]

oligarch /'ɒlɪˌgɑːk/ *n.* a member of an oligarchy. [Gk *oligarkhēs* f. *oligoi* few + *arkhō* to rule]

oligarchy /'ɒlɪˌgɑːkɪ/ *n.* (*pl.* -**ies**) **1** government by a small group of people. **2** a State governed in this way. **3** the members of such a government. □□ **oligarchic** /-'gɑːkɪk/ *adj.* **oligarchical** /-'gɑːkɪk(ə)l/ *adj.* **oligarchically** /-'gɑːkɪkəlɪ/ *adv.* [F *oligarchie* or med.L *oligarchia* f. Gk *oligarkhia* (as OLIGARCH)]

oligo- /'ɒlɪgəʊ/ *comb. form* few, slight. [Gk *oligos* small, *oligoi* few]

Oligocene /'ɒlɪgəˌsiːn/ *adj. & n. Geol.* —*adj.* of or relating to the third epoch of the Tertiary period, following the Eocene and preceding the Miocene, lasting from about 38 to 24.6 million years ago. It was a time of falling world temperatures. —*n.* this epoch or system. [as OLIGO- + Gk *kainos* new]

oligopoly /ˌɒlɪ'gɒpəlɪ/ *n.* (*pl.* -**ies**) a state of limited competition between a small number of producers or sellers. □□ **oligopolist** *n.* **oligopolistic** /-'lɪstɪk/ *adj.* [OLIGO-, after MONOPOLY]

oligosaccharide /ˌɒlɪgəʊ'sækəˌraɪd/ *n.* any carbohydrate whose molecules are composed of a relatively small number of monosaccharide units.

oligotrophic /ˌɒlɪgəʊ'trɒfɪk/ *adj.* (of a lake etc.) relatively poor in plant nutrients. □□ **oligotrophy** /ˌɒlɪ'gɒtrəfɪ/ *n.*

olio /'əʊlɪəʊ/ *n.* (*pl.* -**os**) **1** a mixed dish; a stew of various meats and vegetables. **2** a hotchpotch or miscellany. [Sp. *olla* stew f. L *olla* cooking-pot]

olivaceous /ˌɒlɪ'veɪʃəs/ *adj.* olive-green; of a dusky yellowish green.

olivary /'ɒlɪvərɪ/ *adj. Anat.* olive-shaped; oval. [L *olivarius* (as OLIVE)]

olive /'ɒlɪv/ *n. & adj.* —*n.* **1** (in full **olive tree**) any evergreen tree of the genus *Olea*, having dark-green lance-shaped leathery leaves with silvery undersides, esp. *O. europaea* of the Mediterranean, and *O. africana* native to S. Africa. **2** the small oval fruit of this, having a hard stone and bitter flesh, green when unripe and bluish-black when ripe. **3** (in full **olive-green**) the greyish-green colour of an unripe olive. **4** the wood of the olive tree. **5** *Anat.* each of a pair of olive-shaped swellings in the medulla oblongata. **6 a** any olive-shaped gastropod of the genus *Oliva.* **b** the shell of this. **7** a slice of beef or veal made into a roll with stuffing inside and stewed. —*adj.* **1** coloured like an unripe olive. **2** (of the complexion) yellowish-brown, sallow. □ **olive branch 1** the branch of an olive tree as a symbol of peace. **2** a gesture of reconciliation or friendship. **olive crown** a garland of olive leaves as a sign of victory. **olive drab** the dull olive colour of US army uniforms. **olive oil** an oil extracted from olives used esp. in cookery. [ME f. OF f. L *oliva* f. Gk *elaia* f. *elaion* oil]

Oliver /'ɒlɪvə(r)/ see ROLAND.

Olives /'ɒlɪvz/, **Mount of** the highest point in the range of hills to the east of Jerusalem.

Olivier /ə'lɪvɪˌeɪ/, Laurence Kerr, Baron (1907–89), English actor and director, famous as a Shakespearian actor and producer and with a considerable career in the cinema since 1929. He was director of the National Theatre for ten years from 1963. His films include *Wuthering Heights* (1939), *Rebecca* (1940), and *The*

Prince and the Showgirl (1957), but his main contribution to cinema was in Shakespeare adaptations. He produced, co-directed, and starred in *Henry V* (1944), and directed and starred in *Hamlet* (1948) and *Richard III* (1955). The Olivier Theatre, part of the National Theatre, is named in his honour.

olivine /ˈɒlɪˌviːn/ n. *Mineral.* a naturally occurring form of magnesium-iron silicate, usu. olive-green and found in igneous rocks.

olla podrida /ˌɒlə pəˈdriːdə/ n. = OLIO. [Sp., lit. 'rotten pot' (as OLIO + L *putridus*: cf. PUTRID)]

olm /ɒlm/ n. a blind cave-dwelling salamander, *Proteus anguinus*, native to SE Europe, usu. transparent but turning brown in light and having external gills. [G]

Olmec /ˈɒlmek/ n. (pl. same) **1** a member of a prehistoric people inhabiting the coast of Veracruz and western Tabasco on the Gulf of Mexico c.1200–100 BC, who established what was probably the first developed civilization of Mesoamerica. They are noted for their sculptures, especially the massive stone-hewn heads with realistic features and round helmets, and small jade carvings featuring a jaguar. **2** a member of a native American people living in the highlands of Mexico or migrating to the Gulf coast during the 12th c. [Nahuatl, = people of the rubber(-tree) country]

Olmos /ˈɒlmɒs/ a small town on the eastern edge of the Sechura Desert in northern Peru, which gave its name to a major irrigation project initiated in 1926 for the purpose of increasing cotton and sugar production in the arid lowlands of this region.

-ology /ˈɒlədʒɪ/ comb. form see -LOGY.

Olomouc /ˌɒlɒˈmaʊts/ an industrial city on the Morava River in central Czechoslovakia; pop. (1986) 106,000.

oloroso /ˌɒləˈrəʊsəʊ/ n. (pl. -os) a heavy dark medium-sweet sherry. [Sp., lit. 'fragrant']

Olympia[1] /əˈlɪmpɪə/ the site (in the western Peloponnese) of the chief sanctuary of Zeus in ancient Greece, the venue of the pan-Hellenic Olympic Games, after which the site is named.

Olympia[2] /əˈlɪmpɪə/ the capital of Washington State; pop. (1980) 27,447.

Olympiad /əˈlɪmpɪˌæd/ n. **1 a** a period of four years between Olympic games, used by the ancient Greeks in dating events. **b** a four-yearly celebration of the ancient Olympic Games. **2** a celebration of the modern Olympic Games. **3** a regular international contest in chess etc. [ME f. F *Olympiade* f. L *Olympias Olympiad-* f. Gk *Olumpias Olumpiad-* f. *Olumpios*: see OLYMPIAN, OLYMPIC]

Olympian /əˈlɪmpɪən/ adj. & n. —adj. **1 a** of or associated with Mount Olympus. **b** celestial, godlike. **2** (of manners etc.) magnificent, condescending, superior. **3 a** of or relating to ancient Olympia in Greece. **b** = OLYMPIC. —n. **1** any of the pantheon of twelve gods regarded as living on Olympus. **2** a person of great attainments or of superhuman calm and detachment. [L *Olympus* or *Olympia*: see OLYMPIC]

Olympic /əˈlɪmpɪk/ adj. & n. —adj. of ancient Olympia or the Olympic games. —n. (**the Olympics**) the Olympic games. [L *Olympicus* f. Gk *Olumpikos* of Olympus or Olympia (the latter being named from the games in honour of Zeus of OLYMPUS)]

Olympic Games a festival of sport held at Olympia (traditionally from 776 BC, every fourth year) by the ancient Greeks, with athletic, musical, and literary competitions, in honour of Olympian Zeus, until abolished by the emperor Theodosius in AD 393, after Greece had lost its independence. A modern revival of this, an international athletic and sports meeting, has been held at various centres every four years since 1896 (except during the two World Wars). The initiative for this revival came from the French aristocrat Baron de Coubertin, troubled by the growing commercialism of 19th-c. sport, as an amateur championship for the world's sportsmen.

Olympus /əˈlɪmpəs/, **Mount** a lofty mountain in NE Greece at the east end of the range dividing Thessaly from Macedonia. In Greek mythology it was the home of the gods and the court of Zeus. [pre-Greek wd, = mountain]

OM abbr. (in the UK) Order of Merit.

om (esp. in Buddhism and Hinduism) a mystic syllable, considered the most sacred mantra. It appears at the beginning and end of most Sanskrit recitations, prayers, and texts. [Skr., a universal affirmation]

-oma /ˈəʊmə/ n. forming nouns denoting tumours and other abnormal growths (*carcinoma*). [mod.L f. Gk *-ōma* suffix denoting the result of verbal action]

Omagh /əʊˈmɑː/ the county town of Tyrone, Northern Ireland; pop. (1981) 14,600.

Omaha /ˈəʊməˌhɑː/ a city in eastern Nebraska, on the Missouri River; pop. (1982) 328,550.

Oman /əʊˈmɑːn/ a country in SW Asia at the eastern corner of the Arabian Peninsula; pop. (est. 1988) 1,265,400; official language, Arabic; capital, Muscat. An independent sultanate, known as Muscat and Oman until 1970, Oman fell increasingly under British influence in the mid-19th c., becoming a protectorate in 1891, and despite the general British withdrawal from the area in the postwar years, the sultanate still retains links with the UK. The discovery of oil in 1964 revolutionized the Oman economy, bringing wealth out of all proportion to its size and small population. □ **Gulf of Oman** an inlet of the Arabian Sea, connected by the Strait of Hormuz to the Persian Gulf. □□ **Omani** adj. & n.

Omar I /ˈəʊmɑː(r)/ (c.581–644) Muslim caliph, 634–44. An early opponent of Muhammad, Omar was converted to Islam in 617 and after becoming Caliph in 634 began an extensive series of conquests, adding Syria, Palestine, and Egypt to the Muslim empire before being assassinated by a Persian slave at Medina.

Omar Khayyám /ˌəʊmɑː kaɪˈɑːm/ (d. 1123) Persian poet, mathematician, and astronomer. He is remembered for his *rubais* (quatrains) containing his meditations on the mysteries of existence, translated and adapted by Edward Fitzgerald in *The Rubaiyat of Omar Khayyám* (1859) into a cynical yet poetic sequence, sceptical of divine providence and concentrating on the pleasures of the fleeting moment. The felicitously phrased aphorisms are frequently quoted, particularly the counsel to drink and make merry while life lasts.

omasum /əʊˈmeɪsəm/ n. (pl. **omasa** /-sə/) the third stomach of a ruminant. [L, = bullock's tripe]

ombre /ˈɒmbə(r)/ n. a card-game for three, popular in Europe in the 17th–18th c. [Sp. *hombre* man, with ref. to one player seeking to win the pool]

ombré /ˈɔ̃breɪ/ adj. (of a fabric etc.) having gradual shading of colour from light to dark. [F, past part. of *ombrer* to shadow (as UMBER)]

ombro- /ˈɒmbrəʊ/ comb. form rain. [Gk *ombros* rain-shower]

ombudsman /ˈɒmbʊdzmən/ n. (pl. **-men**) an official appointed to investigate complaints by individuals against maladministration esp. by public authorities; spec. in the UK, the Parliamentary Commissioner for Administration (corresp. to Swedish *justitieombudsmannen*). In Sweden, an *ombudsman* is a deputy of a group, particularly a trade union or a business concern, appointed to handle the legal affairs of the group and protect its interests generally. The office of *justitieombudsmannen* was instituted in Sweden in 1809. The office of ombudsman was introduced in Finland in 1919, in Denmark in 1954, and in Norway in 1962; in the UK the first one took office in 1967. [Sw., = legal representative]

Omdurman /ˈɒmdɜːmən/ the capital of the Mahdist State of Sudan following the British recapture of Khartoum in 1885, scene of Kitchener's decisive victory over the Mahdi's successor, the Khalifa, in 1898, which marked the end of the Dervish uprising.

-ome /əʊm/ suffix forming nouns denoting objects or parts of a specified nature (*rhizome*; *trichome*). [var. of -OMA]

omega /ˈəʊmɪgə/ n. **1** the last (24th) letter of the Greek alphabet (Ω, ω). **2** the last of a series; the final development. [Gk, *ō mega* = great O]

omelette /ˈɒmlɪt/ n. (also **omelet**) a dish of beaten eggs cooked in a frying-pan and served plain or with a savoury or sweet filling. [F *omelette*, obs. *amelette* by metathesis f. *alumette* var. of *alumelle* f. *lemele* knife-blade f. L *lamella*: see LAMELLA]

omen /ˈəʊmən, -men/ n. & v. —n. **1** an occurrence or object regarded as portending good or evil. **2** prophetic significance (of good omen). —v.tr. (usu. in passive) portend; foreshow. □□ **omened** adj. (also in comb.). [L omen ominis]

omentum /əʊˈmentəm/ n. (pl. **omenta** /-tə/) a fold of peritoneum connecting the stomach with other abdominal organs. □□ **omental** adj. [L]

omertà /ˌəʊmeəˈtɑː/ n. a code of silence, esp. as practised by the Mafia. [It., = conspiracy of silence]

omicron /əˈmaɪkrən/ n. the fifteenth letter of the Greek alphabet (O, o). [Gk, o mikron = small o]

ominous /ˈɒmɪnəs/ adj. **1** threatening; indicating disaster or difficulty. **2** of evil omen; inauspicious. **3** giving or being an omen. □□ **ominously** adv. **ominousness** n. [L ominosus (as OMEN)]

omission /əˈmɪʃ(ə)n/ n. **1** the act or an instance of omitting or being omitted. **2** something that has been omitted or overlooked. □□ **omissive** adj. [ME f. OF omission or LL omissio (as OMIT)]

omit /əˈmɪt/ v.tr. (**omitted**, **omitting**) **1** leave out; not insert or include. **2** leave undone. **3** (foll. by verbal noun or to + infin.) fail or neglect (omitted saying anything; omitted to say). □□ **omissible** adj. [ME f. L omittere omiss- (as OB-, mittere send)]

ommatidium /ˌɒməˈtɪdɪəm/ n. (pl. **ommatidia** /-dɪə/) a structural element in the compound eye of an insect. [mod.L f. Gk ommatidion dimin. of omma ommat- eye]

omni- /ˈɒmnɪ/ comb. form **1** all; of all things. **2** in all ways or places. [L f. omnis all]

omnibus /ˈɒmnɪbəs/ n. & adj. —n. **1** formal = BUS. **2** a volume containing several novels etc. previously published separately. —adj. **1** serving several purposes at once. **2** comprising several items. [F f. L (dative pl. of omnis), = for all]

omnicompetent /ˌɒmnɪˈkɒmpɪt(ə)nt/ adj. **1** able to deal with all matters. **2** having jurisdiction in all cases. □□ **omnicompetence** n.

omnidirectional /ˌɒmnɪdɪˈrekʃən(ə)l/ adj. (of an aerial etc.) receiving or transmitting in all directions.

omnifarious /ˌɒmnɪˈfeərɪəs/ adj. of all sorts or varieties. [LL omnifarius (as OMNI-): cf. MULTIFARIOUS]

omnipotent /ɒmˈnɪpət(ə)nt/ adj. **1** having great or absolute power. **2** having great influence. □□ **omnipotence** n. **omnipotently** adv. [ME f. OF f. L omnipotens (as OMNI-, POTENT¹)]

omnipresent /ˌɒmnɪˈprez(ə)nt/ adj. **1** present everywhere at the same time. **2** widely or constantly encountered. □□ **omnipresence** n. [med.L omnipraesens (as OMNI-, PRESENT¹)]

omniscient /ɒmˈnɪsɪənt, -ʃɪənt/ adj. knowing everything or much. □□ **omniscience** n. **omnisciently** adv. [med.L omnisciens -entis (as OMNI-, scire know)]

omnium gatherum /ˌɒmnɪəm ˈgæðərəm/ n. colloq. a miscellany or strange mixture. [mock L f. L omnium of all + GATHER]

omnivorous /ɒmˈnɪvərəs/ adj. **1** feeding on many kinds of food, esp. on both plants and flesh. **2** making use of everything available. □□ **omnivore** /ˈɒmnɪvɔː(r)/ n. **omnivorously** adv. **omnivorousness** n. [L omnivorus (as OMNI-, -VOROUS)]

omphalo- /ˈɒmfələʊ/ comb. form navel. [Gk (as OMPHALOS)]

omphalos /ˈɒmfəˌlɒs/ n. Gk Antiq. **1** a conical stone (esp. that at Delphi) representing the navel of the earth. **2** a boss on a shield. **3** a centre or hub. [Gk, = navel, boss, hub]

Omsk /ɒmsk/ a city of the Soviet Union on the Irtysh River in central Siberia; pop. (est. 1987) 1,134,000.

on /ɒn/ prep., adv., adj., & n. —prep. **1** (so as to be) supported by or attached to or covering or enclosing (sat on a chair; stuck on the wall; rings on her fingers; leaned on his elbow). **2** carried with; about the person of (have you a pen on you?). **3** (of time) exactly at; during; contemporaneously with (on 29 May; on the hour; on schedule; working on Tuesday). **4** immediately after or before (I saw them on my return). **5** as a result of (on further examination I found this). **6** (so as to be) having membership etc. of or residence at or in (she is on the board of directors; lives on the continent). **7** supported financially by (lives on £50 a week; lives on his wits). **8** close to; just by (a house on the sea; lives on the main road). **9** in the direction of; against. **10** so as to threaten; touching or striking (advanced on him; pulled a knife on me; a punch on the nose). **11** having as an axis or pivot (turned on his heels). **12** having as a basis or motive (works on a ratchet; arrested on suspicion). **13** having as a standard, confirmation, or guarantee (had it on good authority; did it on purpose; I promise on my word). **14** concerning or about (writes on frogs). **15** using or engaged with (is on the pill; here on business). **16** so as to affect (walked out on her). **17** at the expense of (the drinks are on me; the joke is on him). **18** added to (disaster on disaster; ten pence on a pint of beer). **19** in a specified manner or style (often foll. by the + adj. or noun: on the cheap; on the run). —adv. **1** (so as to be) covering or in contact with something, esp. of clothes (put your boots on). **2** in the appropriate direction; towards something (look on). **3** further forward; in an advanced position or state (time is getting on; it happened later on). **4** with continued movement or action (went plodding on; keeps on complaining). **5** in operation or activity (the light is on; the chase was on). **6** due to take place as planned (is the party still on?). **7** colloq. **a** (of a person) willing to participate or approve, or make a bet. **b** (of an idea, proposal, etc.) practicable or acceptable (that's just not on). **8** being shown or performed (a good film on tonight). **9** (of an actor) on stage. **10** (of an employee) on duty. **11** forward (head on). —adj. Cricket designating the part of the field on the striker's side and in front of the wicket. —n. Cricket the on side. □ **be on about** refer to or discuss esp. tediously or persistently (what are they on about?). **be on at** colloq. nag or grumble at. **be on to 1** realize the significance or intentions of. **2** get in touch with (esp. by telephone). **on and off** intermittently; now and then. **on and on** continually; at tedious length. **on-line** Computing (of equipment or a process) directly controlled by or connected to a central processor. **on-off 1** (of a switch) having two positions, 'on' and 'off'. **2** = on and off. **on-stage** adj. & adv. on the stage; visible to the audience. **on-street** (with ref. to parking vehicles) at the side of a street. **on time** punctual, punctually. **on to** to a position or state on or in contact with (cf. ONTO). [OE on, an f. Gmc]

-on /ɒn/ suffix Physics, Biochem., & Chem. forming nouns denoting: **1** elementary particles (meson; neutron). **2** quanta (photon). **3** molecular units (codon). **4** substances (interferon; parathion). [ION, orig. in electron]

onager /ˈɒnəgə(r)/ n. **1** a wild ass, esp. Equus hemionus of Central Asia. **2** hist. an ancient military engine for throwing rocks. [ME f. L f. Gk onagros f. onos ass + agrios wild]

onanism /ˈəʊnəˌnɪz(ə)m/ n. **1** masturbation. **2** coitus interruptus. □□ **onanist** n. **onanistic** /-ˈnɪstɪk/ adj. [F onanisme or mod.L onanismus f. Onan (Gen. 38:9)]

Onassis /əˈnæsɪs/, Aristotle Socrates (1906–75), Greek shipping magnate and international businessman, born at Smyrna (Izmir) in Turkey. He was also the founder of the Greek national airline Olympic Airways.

ONC abbr. (in the UK) Ordinary National Certificate.

once /wʌns/ adv., conj., & n. —adv. **1** on one occasion or for one time only (did not once say please; have read it once). **2** at some point or period in the past (could once play chess). **3** ever or at all (if you once forget it). **4** multiplied by one; by one degree. —conj. as soon as (once they have gone we can relax). —n. one time or occasion (just the once). □ **all at once 1** without warning; suddenly. **2** all together. **at once 1** immediately. **2** simultaneously. **for once** on this (or that) occasion, even if at no other. **once again** (or **more**) another time. **once and for all** (or **once for all**) (done) in a final or conclusive manner, esp. so as to end hesitation or uncertainty. **once** (or **every once**) **in a while** from time to time; occasionally. **once or twice** a few times. **once-over** colloq. a rapid preliminary inspection or piece of work. **once upon a time** at some vague time in the past. [ME ānes, ōnes, genit. of ONE]

oncer /ˈwʌnsə(r)/ n. **1** Brit. hist. sl. a one-pound note. **2** colloq. a thing that occurs only once. **3** Austral. colloq. an election of an MP likely to serve only one term.

onco- /ˈɒŋkəʊ/ comb. form Med. tumour. [Gk ogkos mass]

oncogene /ˈɒŋkəˌdʒiːn/ n. a gene which can transform a cell into a tumour cell. □□ **oncogenic** /-ˈdʒenɪk/ adj. **oncogenous** /-ˈkɒdʒɪnəs/ adj.

oncology /ɒŋˈkɒlədʒɪ/ n. Med. the study of tumours.

oncoming /ˈɒnˌkʌmɪŋ/ adj. & n. —adj. approaching from the front. —n. an approach or onset.

oncost /ˈɒnkɒst/ n. Brit. an overhead expense.

OND abbr. (in the UK) Ordinary National Diploma.

on dit /ɔ̃ ˈdiː/ n. (pl. **on dits** pronunc. same) a piece of gossip or hearsay. [F, = they say]

one /wʌn/ adj., n., & pron. —adj. **1** single and integral in number. **2** (with a noun implied) a single person or thing of the kind expressed or implied (one of the best; a nasty one). **3 a** particular but undefined, esp. as contrasted with another (that is one view; one thing after another). **b** colloq. (as an emphatic) a noteworthy example of (that is one difficult question). **4** only such (the one man who can do it). **5** forming a unity (one and undivided). **6** identical; the same (of one opinion). —n. **1 a** the lowest cardinal number. **b** a thing numbered with it. **2** unity; a unit (one is half of two; came in ones and twos). **3** a single thing or person or example (often referring to a noun previously expressed or implied: the big dog and the small one). **4** colloq. an alcoholic drink (have a quick one; have one on me). **5** a story or joke (the one about the frog). —pron. **1** a person of a specified kind (loved ones; like one possessed). **2** any person, as representing people in general (one is bound to lose in the end). **3** I, me (one would like to help). ¶ Often regarded as an affectation. □ **all one** (often foll. by to) a matter of indifference. **at one** in agreement. **for one** being one, even if the only one (I for one do not believe it). **for one thing** as a single consideration, ignoring others. **one another** each the other or others (as a formula of reciprocity: love one another). **one-armed bandit** colloq. a fruit machine worked by a long handle at the side. **one by one** singly, successively. **one day 1** on an unspecified day. **2** at some unspecified future date. **one-horse 1** using a single horse. **2** colloq. small, poorly equipped. **one-liner** colloq. a single brief sentence, often witty or apposite. **one-man** involving, done, or operated by only one man. **one-night stand 1** a single performance of a play etc. in a place. **2** colloq. a sexual liaison lasting only one night. **one-off** colloq. made or done as the only one; not repeated. **one or two** see OR¹. **one-piece** (of a bathing-suit etc.) made as a single garment. **one-sided 1** favouring one side in a dispute; unfair, partial. **2** having or occurring on one side only. **3** larger or more developed on one side. **one-sidedly** in a one-sided manner. **one-sidedness** the act or state of being one-sided. **one-time** former. **one-to-one** with one member of one group corresponding to one of another. **one-track mind** a mind preoccupied with one subject. **one-two** colloq. **1** Boxing the delivery of two punches in quick succession. **2** Football etc. a series of reciprocal passes between two advancing players. **one-up** colloq. having a particular advantage. **one-upmanship** colloq. the art of maintaining a psychological advantage. **one-way** allowing movement or travel in one direction only. [OE ān f. Gmc]

-one /əʊn/ suffix Chem. forming nouns denoting various compounds, esp. ketones (acetone). [Gk -ōnē fem. patronymic]

onefold /ˈwʌnfəʊld/ adj. consisting of only one member or element; simple.

Onega /əˈniːgə/ the second-largest European lake, in the USSR, on the Finnish border.

Oneida Community /əʊˈnaɪdə/ a radical religious community, founded in New York State in 1848. Originally embracing primitive Christian beliefs, communal economic practices, and polygamous marital practices, the Oneida Community proved a considerable economic success, and, although it gradually gave up its radical social and economic ideas, has continued to flourish since becoming a joint-stock company (1881), carrying on various industries, especially the manufacture of silver plate, as a commercial venture. [name of N. Amer. Indian tribe orig. inhabiting New York State]

O'Neill /əʊˈniːl/, Eugene Gladstone (1888–1953), American playwright. His first full-length play Beyond the Horizon (1920) won a Pulitzer Prize, and was followed by Anna Christie (1921) and many other plays, some of which powerfully and poetically criticized contemporary materialistic values. He adapted the theme of the Oresteia to the aftermath of the American Civil War in his

trilogy Mourning Becomes Electra (1931). His most important later plays were The Iceman Cometh (1946), a tragedy about a collection of bar-room derelicts, and his masterpiece Long Day's Journey into Night (1956), a semi-autobiographical tragedy portraying mutually destructive inter-family relationships. O'Neill was awarded the Nobel Prize for literature in 1936.

oneiric /əˈnaɪrɪk/ adj. of or relating to dreams or dreaming. [Gk oneiros dream]

oneiro- /əˈnaɪrəʊ/ comb. form dream. [Gk oneiros dream]

oneiromancy /əˈnaɪrəˌmænsɪ/ n. the interpretation of dreams.

oneness /ˈwʌnnɪs/ n. **1** the fact or state of being one; singleness. **2** uniqueness. **3** agreement; unity of opinion. **4** identity, sameness.

oner /ˈwʌnə(r)/ n. Brit. sl. **1** one pound (of money). **2** a remarkable person or thing.

onerous /ˈɒnərəs, ˈəʊn-/ adj. **1** burdensome; causing or requiring trouble. **2** Law involving heavy obligations. □□ **onerously** adv. **onerousness** n. [ME f. OF onereus f. L onerosus f. onus oneris burden]

oneself /wʌnˈself/ pron. the reflexive and (in apposition) emphatic form of one (kill oneself; one has to do it oneself).

onestep /ˈwʌnstep/ n. a vigorous kind of foxtrot in duple time.

onflow /ˈɒnfləʊ/ n. an onward flow.

onglaze /ˈɒngleɪz/ adj. (of painting etc.) done on a glazed surface.

ongoing /ˈɒnˌgəʊɪŋ/ adj. **1** continuing to exist or be operative etc. **2** that is or are in progress (ongoing discussions). □□ **ongoingness** n.

onion /ˈʌnjən/ n. **1** a liliaceous plant, Allium cepa, having a short stem and bearing greenish-white flowers. **2** the swollen bulb of this with many concentric skins used in cooking, pickling, etc. □ **know one's onions** be fully knowledgeable or experienced. **onion dome** a bulbous dome on a church, palace, etc. **onion-skin 1** the brown outermost skin or any outer skin of an onion. **2** thin smooth translucent paper. □□ **oniony** adj. [ME f. AF union, OF oignon ult. f. L unio -onis]

onlooker /ˈɒnˌlʊkə(r)/ n. a non-participating observer; a spectator. □□ **onlooking** adj.

only /ˈəʊnlɪ/ adv., adj., & conj. —adv. **1** solely, merely, exclusively; and no one or nothing more besides (I only want to sit down; will only make matters worse; needed six only; is only a child). **2** no longer ago than (saw them only yesterday). **3** not until (arrives only on Tuesday). **4** with no better result than (hurried home only to find her gone). ¶ In informal English only is usually placed between the subject and verb regardless of what it refers to (e.g. I only want to talk to you); in more formal English it is often placed more exactly, esp. to avoid ambiguity (e.g. I want to talk only to you). In speech, intonation usually serves to clarify the sense. —attrib.adj. **1** existing alone of its or their kind (their only son). **2** best or alone worth knowing (the only place to eat). —conj. colloq. **1** except that; but for the fact that (I would go, only I feel ill). **2** but then (as an extra consideration) (he always makes promises, only he never keeps them). □ **only-begotten** literary begotten as the only child. **only too** extremely (is only too willing). [OE ānlic, ǣnlic, ME onliche (as ONE, -LY²)]

o.n.o. abbr. Brit. or near offer.

onomastic /ˌɒnəˈmæstɪk/ adj. relating to names or nomenclature. [Gk onomastikos f. onoma name]

onomastics /ˌɒnəˈmæstɪks/ n.pl. (treated as sing.) the study of the origin and formation of (esp. personal) proper names.

onomatopoeia /ˌɒnəˌmætəˈpiːə/ n. **1** the formation of a word from a sound associated with what is named (e.g. cuckoo, sizzle). **2** the use of such words. □□ **onomatopoeic** adj. **onomatopoeically** adv. [LL f. Gk onomatopoiia word-making f. onoma -matos name + poieō make]

onrush /ˈɒnrʌʃ/ n. an onward rush.

onscreen /ˈɒnskriːn/ adj. & adv. —adj. appearing on a cinema, television, or VDU screen. —adv. **1** on or by means of a screen. **2** within the view presented by a cinema-film scene.

onset /ˈɒnset/ n. **1** an attack. **2** a beginning, esp. an energetic or determined one.

onshore /ˈɒnʃɔː(r)/ adj. **1** on the shore. **2** (of the wind) blowing from the sea towards the land.

onside /'ɒnsaɪd, ɒn'saɪd/ *adj.* (of a player in a field game) in a lawful position; not offside.

onslaught /'ɒnslɔːt/ *n.* a fierce attack. [earlier *anslaight* f. MDu. *aenslag* f. *aen* on + *slag* blow, with assim. to obs. *slaught* slaughter]

Ont. *abbr.* Ontario.

-ont /ɒnt/ *comb. form Biol.* denoting an individual of a specified type (*symbiont*). [Gk *ōn ont-* being]

Ontario /ɒn'teərɪˌəʊ/ a province of south-east Canada (from 1867), settled by the French and English in the 17th c. and ceded to Britain in 1763; pop. (1986) 9,113,500; capital, Toronto. □ **Lake Ontario** the smallest and most easterly of the Great Lakes, lying between the province and New York State.

onto /'ɒntu:/ *prep. disp.* to a position or state on or in contact with (cf. *on to*). ¶ The form *onto* is still not fully accepted in the way that *into* is, although it is in wide use. It is however useful in distinguishing sense as between *we drove on to the beach* (i.e. in that direction) and *we drove onto the beach* (i.e. in contact with it).

ontogenesis /ˌɒntə'dʒenɪsɪs/ *n.* the origin and development of an individual (cf. PHYLOGENESIS). □□ **ontogenetic** /-dʒɪ'netɪk/ *adj.* **ontogenetically** /-dʒɪ'netɪkəlɪ/ *adv.* [formed as ONTOGENY + Gk *genesis* birth]

ontogeny /ɒn'tɒdʒənɪ/ *n.* = ONTOGENESIS. □□ **ontogenic** /-tə'dʒenɪk/ *adj.* **ontogenically** /-tə'dʒenɪkəlɪ/ *adv.* [Gk *ōn ont-* being, pres. part. of *eimi* be + -GENY]

ontology /ɒn'tɒlədʒɪ/ *n.* the branch of metaphysics dealing with the nature of being. □□ **ontological** /-tə'lɒdʒɪk(ə)l/ *adj.* **ontologically** /-tə'lɒdʒɪkəlɪ/ *adv.* **ontologist** *n.* [mod.L *ontologia* f. Gk *ōn ont-* being + -LOGY]

onus /'əʊnəs/ *n.* (*pl.* **onuses**) a burden, duty, or responsibility. [L]

onward /'ɒnwəd/ *adv.* & *adj.* —*adv.* (also **onwards**) **1** further on. **2** towards the front. **3** with advancing motion. —*adj.* directed onwards.

onyx /'ɒnɪks/ *n.* a semiprecious variety of agate with different colours in layers. □ **onyx marble** banded calcite etc. used as a decorative material. [ME f. OF *oniche, onix* f. L f. Gk *onux* fingernail, onyx]

oo- /'əʊə/ *comb. form* (US **oö-**) *Biol.* egg, ovum. [Gk *ōion* egg]

oocyte /'əʊəˌsaɪt/ *n.* an immature ovum in an ovary.

oodles /'uːd(ə)lz/ *n.pl. colloq.* a very great amount. [19th-c. US: orig. unkn.]

oof /uːf/ *n. sl.* money, cash. [Yiddish *ooftisch,* G *auf dem Tische* on the table (of money in gambling)]

oofy /'uːfɪ/ *adj. sl.* rich, wealthy. □□ **oofiness** *n.*

oogamous /əʊ'ɒgəməs/ *adj.* reproducing by the union of mobile male and immobile female cells. □□ **oogamy** *n.*

oogenesis /ˌəʊə'dʒenɪsɪs/ *n.* the production or development of an ovum.

ooh /uː/ *int.* expressing surprise, delight, pain, etc. [natural exclam.]

oolite /'əʊəˌlaɪt/ *n.* **1** a sedimentary rock, usu. limestone, consisting of rounded grains made up of concentric layers. **2** = OOLITH. □□ **oolitic** /-'lɪtɪk/ *adj.* [F *oölithe* (as OO-, -LITE)]

oolith /'əʊəlɪθ/ *n.* any of the rounded grains making up oolite.

oology /əʊ'ɒlədʒɪ/ *n.* the study or collecting of birds' eggs. □□ **oological** /ˌəʊə'lɒdʒɪk(ə)l/ *adj.* **oologist** *n.*

oolong /'uːlɒŋ/ *n.* a dark kind of cured China tea. [Chin. *wulong* black dragon]

oomiak var. of UMIAK.

oompah /'ʊmpɑː/ *n. colloq.* the rhythmical sound of deep-toned brass instruments in a band. [imit.]

oomph /ʊmf/ *n. sl.* **1** energy, enthusiasm. **2** attractiveness, esp. sexual appeal. [20th c.: orig. uncert.]

-oon /uːn/ *suffix* forming nouns, orig. from French words in stressed *-on* (*balloon; buffoon*). ¶ Replaced by *-on* in recent borrowings and those with unstressed *-on* (*baron*). [L *-o -onis,* sometimes via It. *-one*]

oops /uːps, ʊps/ *int. colloq.* expressing surprise or apology, esp. on making an obvious mistake. [natural exclam.]

oosperm /'əʊəˌspɜːm/ *n.* a fertilized ovum.

Oostende see OSTEND.

ooze¹ /uːz/ *v.* & *n.* —*v.* **1** *intr.* (of fluid) pass slowly through the pores of a body. **2** *intr.* trickle or leak slowly out. **3** *intr.* (of a substance) exude moisture. **4** *tr.* exude or exhibit (a feeling) liberally (*oozed sympathy*). —*n.* **1** a sluggish flow or exudation. **2** an infusion of oak-bark or other vegetable matter, used in tanning. □□ **oozy** *adj.* **oozily** *adv.* **ooziness** *n.* [orig. as noun (sense 2), f. OE *wōs* juice, sap]

ooze² /uːz/ *n.* **1** a deposit of wet mud or slime, esp. at the bottom of a river, lake, or estuary. **2** a bog or marsh; soft muddy ground. □□ **oozy** *adj.* [OE *wāse*]

OP *abbr.* **1** *RC Ch.* Order of Preachers (Dominican). **2** observation post. **3** opposite prompt.

op /ɒp/ *n. colloq.* operation (in surgical and military senses).

op. /ɒp/ *abbr.* **1** *Mus.* opus. **2** operator.

op- /ɒp/ *prefix* assim. form of OB- before *p*.

o.p. *abbr.* **1** out of print. **2** overproof.

opacify /əʊ'pæsɪˌfaɪ/ *v.tr.* & *intr.* (**-ies, -ied**) make or become opaque. □□ **opacifier** *n.*

opacity /ə'pæsɪtɪ/ *n.* **1** the state of being opaque. **2** obscurity of meaning. **3** obtuseness of understanding. [F *opacité* f. L *opacitas -tatis* (as OPAQUE)]

opah /'əʊpə/ *n.* a large rare deep-sea fish, *Lampris guttatus,* usu. having a silver-blue back with white spots and crimson fins. Also called MOONFISH. [W. Afr. name]

opal /'əʊp(ə)l/ *n.* a quartzlike form of hydrated silica, usu. white or colourless and sometimes showing changing colours, often used as a gemstone. □ **opal glass** a semi-translucent white glass. [F *opale* or L *opalus* prob. ult. f. Skr. *upalas* precious stone]

opalescent /ˌəʊpə'les(ə)nt/ *adj.* showing changing colours like an opal. □□ **opalesce** *v.intr.* **opalescence** *n.*

opaline /'əʊpəˌlaɪn/ *adj.* & *n.* —*adj.* opal-like, opalescent, iridescent. —*n.* opal glass.

opaque /əʊ'peɪk/ *adj.* & *n.* —*adj.* (**opaquer, opaquest**) **1** not transmitting light. **2** impenetrable to sight. **3** obscure; not lucid. **4** obtuse, dull-witted. —*n.* **1** an opaque thing or substance. **2** a substance for producing opaque areas on negatives. □□ **opaquely** *adv.* **opaqueness** *n.* [ME *opak* f. L *opacus:* spelling now assim. to F]

op art /ɒp/ *n. colloq.* = OPTICAL ART. [abbr.]

op. cit. *abbr.* in the work already quoted. [L *opere citato*]

OPEC /'əʊpek/ *abbr.* Organization of Petroleum Exporting Countries.

open /'əʊpən/ *adj., v.,* & *n.* —*adj.* **1** not closed or locked or blocked up; allowing entrance or passage or access. **2 a** (of a room, field, or other area) having its door or gate in a position allowing access, or part of its confining boundary removed. **b** (of a container) not fastened or sealed; in a position or with the lid etc. in a position allowing access to the inside part. **3** unenclosed, unconfined, unobstructed (*the open road; open views*). **4 a** uncovered, bare, exposed (*open drain; open wound*). **b** *Sport* (of a goal mouth or other object of attack) unprotected, vulnerable. **5** undisguised, public, manifest; not exclusive or limited (*open scandal; open hostilities*). **6** expanded, unfolded, or spread out (*had the map open on the table*). **7** (of a fabric) not close; with gaps or intervals. **8 a** (of a person) frank and communicative. **b** (of the mind) accessible to new ideas; unprejudiced or undecided. **9 a** (of an exhibition, shop, etc.) accessible to visitors or customers; ready for business. **b** (of a meeting) admitting all, not restricted to members etc. **10 a** (of a race, competition, scholarship, etc.) unrestricted as to who may compete. **b** (of a champion, scholar, etc.) having won such a contest. **11** (of government) conducted in an informative manner receptive to enquiry, criticism, etc., from the public. **12** (foll. by *to*) **a** willing to receive (*is open to offers*). **b** (of a choice, offer, or opportunity) still available (*there are three courses open to us*). **c** likely to suffer from or be affected by (*open to abuse*). **13 a** (of the mouth) with lips apart, esp. in surprise or incomprehension. **b** (of the ears or eyes) eagerly attentive. **14** *Mus.* **a** (of a string) allowed to vibrate along its whole length. **b** (of a pipe) unstopped at each end. **c** (of a note) sounded from an open string or pipe. **15** (of an electrical circuit) having a break in the conducting path. **16** (of the bowels) not constipated. **17** (of a return ticket) not restricted as to day of travel. **18** (of a cheque) not crossed. **19** (of a boat) without a deck. **20** (of a river or harbour) free of ice. **21** (of the weather or winter) free of frost. **22** *Phonet.* **a** (of a vowel) produced with a relatively wide opening of the mouth. **b** (of a syllable) ending in a vowel. **23** (of a town, city, etc.) not defended even if attacked. —*v.* **1** *tr.* & *intr.* make or become open or more open. **2 a** *tr.* change from a closed or fastened position so as to allow access (*opened the door; opened the box*). **b** *intr.* (of a door, lid, etc.) have its position changed to allow access (*the door opened slowly*). **3** *tr.* remove the sealing or fastening element of (a container) to get access to the contents (*opened the envelope*). **4** *intr.* (foll. by *into, on to*, etc.) (of a door, room, etc.) afford access as specified (*opened on to a large garden*). **5 a** *tr.* start or establish or set going (a business, activity, etc.). **b** *intr.* be initiated; make a start (*the session opens tomorrow; the story opens with a murder*). **c** *tr.* (of a counsel in a lawcourt) make a preliminary statement in (a case) before calling witnesses. **6** *tr.* **a** spread out or unfold (a map, newspaper, etc.). **b** (often *absol.*) refer to the contents of (a book). **7** *intr.* (often foll. by *with*) (of a person) begin speaking, writing, etc. (*he opened with a warning*). **8** *intr.* (of a prospect) come into view; be revealed. **9** *tr.* reveal or communicate (one's feelings, intentions, etc.). **10** *tr.* make (one's mind, heart, etc.) more sympathetic or enlightened. **11** *tr.* ceremonially declare (a building etc.) to be completed and in use. **12** *tr.* break up (ground) with a plough etc. **13** *tr.* cause evacuation of (the bowels). **14** *Naut.* **a** *tr.* get a view of by change of position. **b** *intr.* come into full view. —*n.* **1** (prec. by *the*) **a** open space or country or air. **b** public notice or view; general attention (esp. *into the open*). **2** an open championship, competition, or scholarship. □ **be open with** speak frankly to. **keep open house** see HOUSE. **open air** (usu. prec. by *the*) a free or unenclosed space outdoors. **open-air** (*attrib.*) out of doors. **open-and-shut** (of an argument, case, etc.) straightforward and conclusive. **open-armed** cordial; warmly receptive. **open book** a person who is easily understood. **open day** a day when the public may visit a place normally closed to them. **open door** free admission of foreign trade and immigrants. **open-door** *adj.* open, accessible, public. **open the door to** see DOOR. **open-ended** having no predetermined limit or boundary. **open a person's eyes** see EYE. **open-eyed 1** with the eyes open. **2** alert, watchful. **open-faced** having a frank or ingenuous expression. **open-handed** generous. **open-handedly** generously. **open-handedness** generosity. **open-hearted** frank and kindly. **open-heartedness** an open-hearted quality. **open-hearth process** see separate entry. **open-heart surgery** surgery with the heart exposed and the blood made to bypass it. **open house** welcome or hospitality for all visitors. **open ice** ice through which navigation is possible. **open letter** a letter, esp. of protest, addressed to an individual and published in a newspaper or journal. **open market** an unrestricted market with free competition of buyers and sellers. **open-minded** accessible to new ideas; unprejudiced. **open-mindedly** in an open-minded manner. **open-mindedness** the quality of being open-minded. **open-mouthed** with the mouth open, esp. in surprise. **open out 1** unfold; spread out. **2** develop, expand. **3** become communicative. **4** accelerate. **open-plan** (usu. *attrib.*) (of a house, office, etc.) having large undivided rooms. **open prison** a prison with the minimum of physical restraints on prisoners. **open question** a matter on which differences of opinion are legitimate. **open-reel** (of a tape recorder) having reels of tape requiring individual threading, as distinct from a cassette. **open sandwich** a sandwich without a top slice of bread. **open sea** an expanse of sea away from land. **open season** the season when restrictions on the killing of game etc. are lifted. **open secret** a supposed secret that is known to many people. **open sesame** see SESAME. **open shop 1** a business etc. where employees do not have to be members of a trade union (opp. *closed shop*). **2** this system. **open society** a society with wide dissemination of information and freedom of belief. **open up 1** unlock (premises).

2 make accessible. **3** reveal; bring to notice. **4** accelerate esp. a motor vehicle. **5** begin shooting or sounding. **open verdict** a verdict affirming that a crime has been committed but not specifying the criminal or (in case of violent death) the cause. **with open arms** see ARM[1]. □□ **openable** *adj.* **openness** *n.* [OE *open*]

opencast /ˈəʊpənˌkɑːst/ *adj.* *Brit.* (of a mine or mining) with removal of the surface layers and working from above, not from shafts.

opener /ˈəʊpənə(r), ˈəʊpnə(r)/ *n.* **1** a device for opening tins, bottles, etc. **2** *colloq.* the first item on a programme etc. **3** *Cricket* an opening batsman. □ **for openers** *colloq.* to start with.

open-hearth process *n.* a process for making steel, in which scrap iron or steel, limestone, and molten or cold pig-iron are melted together using a shallow reverberatory furnace. First operated *c.*1860, the process was producing most of the world's steel until *c.*1955. Although slower than the Bessemer process it is under closer control and can melt scrap and cold iron, which the Bessemer process cannot. (See STEEL.)

opening /ˈəʊpənɪŋ, ˈəʊpnɪŋ/ *n.* & *adj.* —*n.* **1** an aperture or gap, esp. allowing access. **2** a favourable situation or opportunity. **3** a beginning; an initial part. **4** *Chess* a recognized sequence of moves at the beginning of a game. **5** a counsel's preliminary statement of a case in a lawcourt. —*adj.* initial, first. □ **opening-time** *Brit.* the time at which public houses may legally open for custom.

openly /ˈəʊpənlɪ/ *adv.* **1** frankly, honestly. **2** publicly; without concealment. [OE *openlīce* (as OPEN, -LY[2])]

Open University a university (founded in Britain in 1969) with no formal requirements for entry to its first-degree courses, and providing instruction by a combination of television, radio, and correspondence courses and by audiovisual centres.

openwork /ˈəʊpənˌwɜːk/ *n.* a pattern with intervening spaces in metal, leather, lace, etc.

opera[1] /ˈɒpərə, ˈɒprə/ *n.* **1 a** a dramatic work in one or more acts, set to music for singers (usu. in costume) and instrumentalists. **b** this as a genre. (See below.) **2** a building for the performance of opera. □ **opera-glasses** small binoculars for use at the opera or theatre. **opera-hat** a man's tall collapsible hat. **opera-house** a theatre for the performance of opera. [It. f. L, = labour, work]

Opera was born in Italy in the 16th c. Although there had previously been stage works involving music, the creation of a dramatic work to be sung throughout was a new concept, derived from theories of the nature of the music of the ancient Greeks and put into practice by a group of intellectuals based in Florence. The earliest operas involved the talents of the composers Jacopo Peri (*Dafne*, 1598, now lost, and *Euridice*, 1600, including some settings by his rival Caccini) and Giulio Caccini (*Euridice*, 1600–2, the first published opera), and the poet Ottavio Rinuccini; better known today are the operas of Claudio Monteverdi. The first public opera house, the Teatro San Cassiano, was opened in Venice in 1637, and since then opera has become celebrated, and among those with a puritan streak notorious, for the extravagance of its plots, the range of its emotional power, the huge sums of money needed to attract star singers (and the volatile temperament of its prima donnas), and the irresistible and inexhaustible attraction it holds for its lovers.

opera[2] *pl.* of OPUS.

operable /ˈɒpərəb(ə)l/ *adj.* **1** that can be operated. **2** suitable for treatment by surgical operation. □□ **operability** /-ˈbɪlɪtɪ/ *n.* [LL *operabilis* f. L (as OPERATE)]

opera buffa /ˌɒpərə ˈbuːfə/ *n.* (esp. Italian) comic opera, esp. with characters drawn from everyday life. [It.]

opéra comique /ˌɒpeˌrɑ kɒˈmiːk/ *n.* (esp. French) opera on a light-hearted theme, with spoken dialogue. [F]

operand /ˈɒpəˌrænd/ *n.* *Math.* the quantity etc. on which an operation is to be done. [L *operandum* neut. gerundive of *operari*: see OPERATE]

opera seria /ˌɒpərə ˈsɪərɪə/ *n.* (esp. 18th-c. Italian) opera on a serious, usu. classical or mythological theme. [It.]

operate /ˈɒpəˌreɪt/ v. **1** tr. manage, work, control; put or keep in a functional state. **2** intr. be in action; function. **3** intr. produce an effect; exercise influence (the tax operates to our disadvantage). **4** intr. (often foll. by on) **a** perform a surgical operation. **b** conduct a military or naval action. **c** be active in business etc., esp. dealing in stocks and shares. **5** intr. (foll. by on) influence or affect (feelings etc.). **6** tr. bring about; accomplish. □ **operating system** the basic software that enables the running of a computer program. **operating theatre** (or **room**) a room for surgical operations. [L operari to work f. opus operis work]

operatic /ˌɒpəˈrætɪk/ adj. **1** of or relating to opera. **2** resembling or characteristic of opera. □□ **operatically** adv. [irreg. f. OPERA[1], after dramatic]

operatics /ˌɒpəˈrætɪks/ n.pl. the production and performance of operas.

operation /ˌɒpəˈreɪʃ(ə)n/ n. **1 a** the action or process or method of working or operating. **b** the state of being active or functioning (not yet in operation). **c** the scope or range of effectiveness of a thing's activity. **2** an active process; a discharge of a function (the operation of breathing). **3** a piece of work, esp. one in a series (often in pl.: begin operations). **4** an act of surgery performed on a patient. **5 a** a strategic movement of troops, ships, etc. for military action. **b** preceding a code-name (Operation Overlord). **6** a financial transaction. **7** Math. the subjection of a number or quantity or function to a process affecting its value or form, e.g. multiplication, differentiation. □ **operations research** = operational research. [ME f. OF f. L operatio -onis (as OPERATE)]

operational /ˌɒpəˈreɪʃən(ə)l/ adj. **1 a** of or used for operations. **b** engaged or involved in operations. **2** able or ready to function. □ **operational research** the application of scientific principles to business management, providing a quantitative basis for complex decisions. □□ **operationally** adv.

operative /ˈɒpərətɪv/ adj. & n. —adj. **1** in operation; having effect. **2** having the principal relevance ('may' is the operative word). **3** of or by surgery. **4** Law expressing an intent to perform a transaction. —n. **1** a worker, esp. a skilled one. **2** US a private detective. □□ **operatively** adv. **operativeness** n. [LL operativus f. L (as OPERATE)]

operator /ˈɒpəˌreɪtə(r)/ n. **1** a person operating a machine etc., esp. making connections of lines in a telephone exchange. **2** a person operating or engaging in business. **3** colloq. a person acting in a specified way (a smooth operator). **4** Math. a symbol or function denoting an operation (e.g. ×, +). [LL f. L operari (as OPERATE)]

operculum /əˈpɜːkjʊləm, əʊˈp-/ n. (pl. **opercula** /-lə/) **1** Zool. **a** a flaplike structure covering the gills in a fish. **b** a platelike structure closing the aperture of a gastropod mollusc's shell when the organism is retracted. **c** any of various other parts covering or closing an aperture, such as a flap over the nostrils in some birds. **2** Bot. a lidlike structure of the spore-containing capsule of mosses. □□ **opercular** adj. **operculate** /-lət/ adj. **operculi-** comb. form. [L f. operire cover]

operetta /ˌɒpəˈretə/ n. **1** a one-act or short opera. **2** a light opera. [It., dimin. of opera: see OPERA]

ophicleide /ˈɒfɪˌklaɪd/ n. **1** an obsolete usu. bass brass wind instrument developed from the serpent. **2** a powerful organ reed-stop. [F ophicléide f. Gk ophis serpent + kleis kleidos key]

ophidian /əʊˈfɪdɪən/ n. & adj. —n. any reptile of the suborder Serpentes (formerly Ophidia), including snakes. —adj. **1** of or relating to this group. **2** snakelike. [mod.L Ophidia f. Gk ophis snake]

ophio- /ˈɒfɪəʊ/ comb. form snake. [Gk ophis snake]

Ophir /ˈəʊfə(r)/ (in the Old Testament) an unidentified region, perhaps in SE Arabia, famous for its fine gold and precious stones.

ophthalmia /ɒfˈθælmɪə/ n. an inflammation of the eye, esp. conjunctivitis. [LL f. Gk f. ophthalmos eye]

ophthalmic /ɒfˈθælmɪk/ adj. of or relating to the eye and its diseases. □ **ophthalmic optician** an optician qualified to prescribe as well as dispense spectacles and contact lenses. [L ophthalmicus f. Gk ophthalmikos (as OPHTHALMIA)]

ophthalmo- /ɒfˈθælməʊ/ comb. form Optics denoting the eye. [Gk ophthalmos eye]

ophthalmology /ˌɒfθælˈmɒlədʒɪ/ n. the scientific study of the eye. □□ **ophthalmological** /-məˈlɒdʒɪk(ə)l/ adj. **ophthalmologist** n.

ophthalmoscope /ɒfˈθælməˌskəʊp/ n. an instrument for inspecting the retina and other parts of the eye. □□ **ophthalmoscopic** /-ˈskɒpɪk/ adj.

-opia /ˈəʊpɪə/ comb. form denoting a visual disorder (myopia). [Gk f. ōps eye]

opiate adj., n., & v. —adj. /ˈəʊpɪət/ **1** containing opium. **2** narcotic, soporific. —n. /ˈəʊpɪət/ **1** a drug containing opium, usu. to ease pain or induce sleep. **2** a thing which soothes or stupefies. —v.tr. /ˈəʊpɪˌeɪt/ **1** mix with opium. **2** stupefy. [med.L opiatus, -um, opiare f. L opium: see OPIUM]

Opie /ˈəʊpɪ/, John (1761–1807), English painter. A carpenter's son, he was promoted on his arrival in London (1781) as the 'Cornish wonder'—a self-taught genius—and was made a Royal Academician in 1787. His portraiture (e.g. Mary Wollstonecraft) brought him wealth and reputation, while his history painting, especially for Boydell's Shakespeare Gallery, was both popular and influential.

opine /əʊˈpaɪn/ v.tr. (often foll. by that + clause) hold or express as an opinion. [L opinari think, believe]

opinion /əˈpɪnjən/ n. **1** a belief or assessment based on grounds short of proof. **2** a view held as probable. **3** (often foll. by on) what one thinks about a particular topic or question (my opinion on capital punishment). **4 a** a formal statement of professional advice (will get a second opinion). **b** Law a formal statement of reasons for a judgement given. **5** an estimation (had a low opinion of it). □ **be of the opinion that** believe or maintain that. **in one's opinion** according to one's view or belief. **a matter of opinion** a disputable point. **opinion poll** = GALLUP POLL. **public opinion** views generally prevalent, esp. on moral questions. [ME f. OF f. L opinio -onis (as OPINE)]

opinionated /əˈpɪnjəˌneɪtɪd/ adj. conceitedly assertive or dogmatic in one's opinions. □□ **opinionatedly** adv. **opinionatedness** n. [obs. opinionate in the same sense f. OPINION]

opium /ˈəʊpɪəm/ n. **1** a reddish-brown heavy-scented addictive drug prepared from the juice of the opium poppy, used in medicine as an analgesic and narcotic. **2** anything regarded as soothing or stupefying. □ **opium den** a haunt of opium-smokers. **opium poppy** a poppy, Papaver somniferum, native to Europe and E. Asia, with white, red, pink, or purple flowers. [ME f. L f. Gk opion poppy-juice f. opos juice]

Opium War the war between Britain and China (1839–42) and later (1856–60) Britain and France against China, following China's attempt to prohibit the (illegal) importation of opium from British India into China, and Chinese restrictions on foreign trade. Defeat of the Chinese resulted in the ceding of Hong Kong to Britain and the opening of five 'treaty ports' to traders.

opopanax /əʊˈpɒpəˌnæks/ n. **1 a** an umbelliferous plant, Opopanax chironium, with yellow flowers. **b** a resinous gum obtained from the roots of this plant and used in perfume. **2** = sponge tree. [ME f. L f. Gk f. opos juice + panax formed as PANACEA]

Oporto /əʊˈpɔːtəʊ/ (Portuguese **Porto**) the principal city of northern Portugal, on the River Douro; pop. (est. 1984) 327,350.

opossum /əˈpɒsəm/ n. **1 a** any mainly tree-living marsupial of the family Didelphidae, native to America, having a prehensile tail and hind feet with an opposable thumb. **b** (in full **water opossum**) an opossum, Chironectes minimus, suited to an aquatic habitat and having webbed hind feet. Also called YAPOK. **2** Austral. & NZ = POSSUM 2. [Virginian Ind. āpassūm]

opp. abbr. opposite.

Oppenheimer /ˈɒpənˌhaɪmə(r)/, Julius Robert (1904–67), American theoretical physicist who, as director of the laboratory at Los Alamos in New Mexico, US, led the team which designed and built the first atomic bomb during the Second World War. After the war he opposed development of the hydrogen bomb and—like a number of intellectuals of his day—fell foul of the Senate committee investigating alleged un-American activities.

His security clearance was withdrawn in 1953 and his advisory activities stopped; with the passing of the McCarthy era his public standing was restored.

oppo /ˈɒpəʊ/ n. (pl. **-os**) Brit. colloq. a colleague or friend. [*opposite number*]

opponent /əˈpəʊnənt/ n. & adj. —n. a person who opposes or belongs to an opposing side. —adj. opposing, contrary, opposed. □ **opponent muscle** a muscle enabling the thumb to be placed front to front against a finger of the same hand. □□ **opponency** n. [L *opponere opponent-* (as OB-, *ponere* place)]

opportune /ˈɒpəˌtjuːn/ adj. **1** (of a time) well-chosen or especially favourable or appropriate (*an opportune moment*). **2** (of an action or event) well-timed; done or occurring at a favourable or useful time. □□ **opportunely** adv. **opportuneness** n. [ME f. OF *opportun -une* f. L *opportunus* (as OB-, *portus* harbour), orig. of the wind driving towards the harbour]

opportunism /ˌɒpəˈtjuːnɪz(ə)m, ˈɒpə-/ n. **1** the adaptation of policy or judgement to circumstances or opportunity, esp. regardless of principle. **2** the seizing of opportunities when they occur. □□ **opportunist** n. **opportunistic** /-ˈnɪstɪk/ adj. **opportunistically** /-ˈnɪstɪkəlɪ/ adv. [OPPORTUNE after It. *opportunismo* and F *opportunisme* in political senses]

opportunity /ˌɒpəˈtjuːnɪtɪ/ n. (pl. **-ies**) **1** a good chance; a favourable occasion. **2** a chance or opening offered by circumstances. **3** good fortune. □ **opportunity knocks** an opportunity occurs. [ME f. OF *opportunité* f. L *opportunitas -tatis* (as OPPORTUNE)]

opposable /əˈpəʊzəb(ə)l/ adj. **1** able to be opposed. **2** Zool. (of the thumb in primates) capable of facing and touching the other digits on the same hand.

oppose /əˈpəʊz/ v.tr. (often absol.) **1** set oneself against; resist, argue against. **2** be hostile to. **3** take part in a game, sport, etc., against (another competitor or team). **4** (foll. by *to*) place in opposition or contrast. □ **as opposed to** in contrast with. □□ **opposer** n. [ME f. OF *opposer* f. L *opponere*: see OPPONENT]

opposite /ˈɒpəzɪt/ adj., n., adv., & prep. adj. **1** (often foll. by *to*) having a position on the other or further side, facing or back to back. **2** (often foll. by *to*, *from*) **a** of a contrary kind; diametrically different. **b** being the other of a contrasted pair. **3** (of angles) between opposite sides of the intersection of two lines. **4** Bot. (of leaves etc.) placed at the same height on the opposite sides of the stem, or placed straight in front of another organ. —n. an opposite thing or person or term. —adv. **1** in an opposite position (*the tree stands opposite*). **2** (of a leading theatrical etc. part) in a complementary role to (another performer). —prep. in a position opposite to (*opposite the house is a tree*). □ **opposite number** a person holding an equivalent position in another group or organization. **opposite prompt** the side of a theatre stage usually to an actor's right. **the opposite sex** women in relation to men or vice versa. □□ **oppositely** adv. **oppositeness** n. [ME f. OF f. L *oppositus* past part. of *opponere*: see OPPONENT]

opposition /ˌɒpəˈzɪʃ(ə)n/ n. **1** resistance, antagonism. **2** the state of being hostile or in conflict or disagreement. **3** contrast or antithesis. **4 a** a group or party of opponents or competitors. **b** (**the Opposition**) Brit. the principal parliamentary party opposed to that in office. **5** the act of opposing or placing opposite. **6 a** diametrically opposite position. **b** Astrol. & Astron. the position of two heavenly bodies when their longitude differs by 180°, as seen from the earth. □□ **oppositional** adj. [ME f. OF f. L *oppositio* (as OB-, POSITION)]

oppress /əˈpres/ v.tr. **1** keep in subservience by coercion. **2** govern or treat harshly or with cruel injustice. **3** weigh down (with cares or unhappiness). □□ **oppressor** n. [ME f. OF *oppresser* f. med.L *oppressare* (as OB-, PRESS¹)]

oppression /əˈpreʃ(ə)n/ n. **1** the act or an instance of oppressing; the state of being oppressed. **2** prolonged harsh or cruel treatment or control. **3** mental distress. [OF f. L *oppressio* (as OPPRESS)]

oppressive /əˈpresɪv/ adj. **1** oppressing; harsh or cruel. **2** difficult to endure. **3** (of weather) close and sultry. □□ **oppressively** adv. **oppressiveness** n. [F *oppressif -ive* f. med.L *oppressivus* (as OPPRESS)]

opprobrious /əˈprəʊbrɪəs/ adj. (of language) severely scornful; abusive. □□ **opprobriously** adv. [ME f. LL *opprobriosus* (as OPPROBRIUM)]

opprobrium /əˈprəʊbrɪəm/ n. **1** disgrace or bad reputation attaching to some act or conduct. **2** a cause of this. [L f. *opprobrum* (as OB-, *probrum* disgraceful act)]

oppugn /əˈpjuːn/ v.tr. literary call into question; controvert. □□ **oppugner** n. [ME f. L *oppugnare* attack, besiege (as OB-, L *pugnare* fight)]

oppugnant /əˈpʌgnənt/ adj. formal attacking; opposing. □□ **oppugnance** n. **oppugnancy** n. **oppugnation** /-ˈneɪʃ(ə)n/ n.

opsimath /ˈɒpsɪˌmæθ/ n. literary a person who learns only late in life. □□ **opsimathy** /-ˈsɪməθɪ/ n. [Gk *opsimathēs* f. *opse* late + *math-* learn]

opsonin /ˈɒpsənɪn/ n. an antibody which assists the action of phagocytes. □□ **opsonic** /ɒpˈsɒnɪk/ adj. [Gk *opsōnion* victuals + -IN]

opt /ɒpt/ v.intr. (usu. foll. by *for*, *between*) exercise an option; make a choice. □ **opt out** (often foll. by *of*) choose not to participate (*opted out of the race*). [F *opter* f. L *optare* choose, wish]

optant /ˈɒpt(ə)nt/ n. **1** a person who may choose one of two nationalities. **2** a person who chooses or has chosen.

optative /ɒpˈteɪtɪv, ˈɒptətɪv/ adj. & n. Gram. —adj. expressing a wish. —n. the optative mood. □ **optative mood** a set of verb-forms expressing a wish etc., distinct esp. in Sanskrit and Greek. □□ **optatively** adv. [F *optatif -ive* f. LL *optativus* (as OPT)]

optic /ˈɒptɪk/ adj. & n. —adj. of or relating to the eye or vision (*optic nerve*). —n. **1** a lens etc. in an optical instrument. **2** archaic or joc. the eye. **3** (**Optic**) Brit. propr. a device fastened to the neck of a bottle for measuring out spirits etc. □ **optic angle** the angle formed by notional lines from the extremities of an object to the eye, or by lines from the eyes to a given point. **optic axis 1** a line passing through the centre of curvature of a lens or spherical mirror and parallel to the axis of symmetry. **2** the direction in a doubly refracting crystal for which no double refraction occurs. **optic lobe** the dorsal lobe in the brain from which the optic nerve arises. [F *optique* or med.L *opticus* f. Gk *optikos* f. *optos* seen]

optical /ˈɒptɪk(ə)l/ adj. **1** of sight; visual. **2 a** of or concerning sight or light in relation to each other. **b** belonging to optics. **3** (esp. of a lens) constructed to assist sight or on the principles of optics. □ **optical activity** Chem. the property of rotating the plane of polarization of plane-polarized light. **optical art** see separate entry. **optical brightener** any fluorescent substance used to produce a whitening effect on laundry. **optical character recognition** the identification of printed characters using photoelectric devices. **optical disc** see DISC. **optical fibre** thin glass fibre through which light can be transmitted. **optical glass** a very pure kind of glass used for lenses etc. **optical illusion 1** a thing having an appearance so resembling something else as to deceive the eye. **2** an instance of mental misapprehension caused by this. **optical microscope** a microscope using the direct perception of light (cf. *electron microscope*). □□ **optically** adv.

optical art n. a form of abstract art and visual decoration, developed in the 1960s, in which optical effects are used to provide illusions of movement in the patterns produced, or designs in which conflicting patterns emerge and overlap. Bridget Riley and Victor Vasarely are its most famous exponents.

optician /ɒpˈtɪʃ(ə)n/ n. **1** a maker or seller of optical instruments, esp. spectacles and contact lenses. **2** a person trained in the detection and correction of poor eyesight (see OPTOMETRIST). [F *opticien* f. med.L *optica* (as OPTIC)]

optics /ˈɒptɪks/ n.pl. (treated as *sing.*) the scientific study of sight and the behaviour of light, or of other radiation or particles (*electron optics*).

optima pl. of OPTIMUM.

optimal /ˈɒptɪm(ə)l/ adj. best or most favourable, esp. under a particular set of circumstances. □□ **optimally** adv. [L *optimus* best]

optimism /ˈɒptɪˌmɪz(ə)m/ n. **1** an inclination to hopefulness and confidence (opp. PESSIMISM). **2** Philos. **a** the doctrine, esp. as set forth by Leibniz, that this world is the best of all possible worlds. **b** the theory that good must ultimately prevail over evil in the universe. □□ **optimist** *n.* **optimistic** /-'mɪstɪk/ *adj.* **optimistically** /-'mɪstɪkəlɪ/ *adv.* [F *optimisme* f. L OPTIMUM]

optimize /'ɒptɪˌmaɪz/ *v.* (also **-ise**) **1** *tr.* make the best or most effective use of (a situation, an opportunity, etc.). **2** *intr.* be an optimist. □□ **optimization** /-'zeɪʃ(ə)n/ *n.* [L *optimus* best]

optimum /'ɒptɪməm/ *n.* & *adj.* —*n.* (*pl.* **optima** /-mə/ or **optimums**) **1 a** the most favourable conditions (for growth, reproduction, etc.). **b** the best or most favourable situation. **2** the best possible compromise between opposing tendencies. —*adj.* = OPTIMAL. [L, neut. (as n.) of *optimus* best]

option /'ɒpʃ(ə)n/ *n.* **1 a** the act or an instance of choosing; a choice. **b** a thing that is or may be chosen (*those are the options*). **2** the liberty of choosing; freedom of choice. **3** *Stock Exch.* etc. the right, obtained by payment, to buy, sell, etc. specified stocks etc. at a specified price within a set time. □ **have no option but to** must. **keep** (or **leave**) **one's options open** not commit oneself. [F or f. L *optio*, stem of *optare* choose]

optional /'ɒpʃən(ə)l/ *adj.* being an option only; not obligatory. □□ **optionality** /-'nælɪtɪ/ *n.* **optionally** *adv.*

optometer /ɒp'tɒmɪtə(r)/ *n.* an instrument for testing the refractive power and visual range of the eye. □□ **optometric** /ˌɒptə'metrɪk/ *adj.* **optometry** *n.* [Gk *optos* seen + -METER]

optometrist /ɒp'tɒmɪtrɪst/ *n.* esp. *US* **1** a person who practises optometry. **2** = *ophthalmic optician.*

optophone /'ɒptəˌfəʊn/ *n.* an instrument converting light into sound, and so enabling the blind to read print etc. by ear. [Gk *optos* seen + -PHONE]

opulent /'ɒpjʊlənt/ *adj.* **1** ostentatiously rich; wealthy. **2** luxurious (*opulent surroundings*). **3** abundant; profuse. □□ **opulence** *n.* **opulently** *adv.* [L *opulens, opulent-* f. *opes* wealth]

opuntia /əʊ'pʌnʃɪə/ *n.* any cactus of the genus *Opuntia*, with jointed cylindrical or elliptical stems and barbed bristles. Also called *prickly pear.* [L plant-name f. *Opus -untis* in Locris in ancient Greece]

opus /'əʊpəs, 'ɒp-/ *n.* (*pl.* **opuses** or **opera** /'ɒpərə/) **1** *Mus.* **a** a separate musical composition or set of compositions of any kind. **b** (also **op.**) used before a number given to a composer's work, usu. indicating the order of publication (*Beethoven, op. 15*). **2** any artistic work (cf. MAGNUM OPUS). □ **opus Dei** /'deɪɪ/ *Eccl.* **1** liturgical worship regarded as man's primary duty to God. **2** (**Opus Dei**) a Roman Catholic organization of laymen and priests founded in Spain in 1928 with the aim of re-establishing Christian values in society. [L, = work]

opuscule /ə'pʌskjuːl/ *n.* (also **opusculum** /ə'pʌskjʊləm/) (*pl.* **opuscules** or **opuscula** /-lə/) a minor (esp. musical or literary) work. [F f. L *opusculum* dimin. of OPUS]

OR *abbr.* **1** operational research. **2** *US* Oregon (in official postal use). **3** other ranks.

or¹ /ɔː(r), ə(r)/ *conj.* **1 a** introducing the second of two alternatives (*white or black*). **b** introducing all but the first, or only the last, of any number of alternatives (*white or grey or black; white, grey, or black*). **2** (often prec. by *either*) introducing the only remaining possibility or choice given (*take it or leave it; either come in or go out*). **3** (prec. by *whether*) introducing the second part of an indirect question or conditional clause (*ask him whether he was there or not; must go whether I like or dislike it*). **4** introducing a synonym or explanation of a preceding word etc. (*suffered from vertigo or giddiness*). **5** introducing a significant afterthought (*he must know—or is he bluffing?*). **6** = *or else* (*run or you'll be late*). **7** *poet.* each of two; either (*or in the heart or in the head*). □ **not A or B** not A, and also not B. **one or two** (or **two or three** etc.) *colloq.* a few. **or else 1** otherwise (*do it now, or else you will have to do it tomorrow*). **2** *colloq.* expressing a warning or threat (*hand over the money or else*). **or rather** introducing a rephrasing or qualification of a preceding statement etc. (*he was there, or rather I heard that he was*). **or so** (after a quantity or a number) or thereabouts (*send me ten or so*). [reduced form of obs. *other* conj. (which superseded OE *oththe* or), of uncert. orig.]

or² /ɔː(r)/ *n.* & *adj. Heraldry* —*n.* a gold or yellow colour. —*adj.* (usu. following noun) gold or yellow (*a crescent or*). [F f. L *aurum* gold]

-or¹ /ə(r)/ *suffix* forming nouns denoting a person or thing performing the action of a verb, or an agent more generally (*actor; escalator; tailor*) (see also -ATOR, -ITOR). [L *-or, -ator,* etc., sometimes via AF *-eour,* OF *-ëor, -ëur*]

-or² /ə(r)/ *suffix* forming nouns denoting state or condition (*error; horror*). [L *-or -oris,* sometimes via (or after) OF *-or, -ur*]

-or³ /ə(r)/ *suffix* forming adjectives with comparative sense (*major; senior*). [AF *-our* f. L *-or*]

-or⁴ /ə(r)/ *suffix US* = -OUR¹.

orache /'ɒrɪtʃ/ *n.* (also **orach**) an edible plant, *Atriplex hortensis,* with red, yellow, or green leaves sometimes used as a substitute for spinach or sorrel. Also called SALTBUSH. [ME *arage* f. AF *arasche* f. L *atriplex* f. Gk *atraphaxus*]

oracle /'ɒrək(ə)l/ *n.* **1 a** a place at which advice or prophecy was sought from the gods in classical antiquity. **b** the usu. ambiguous or obscure response given at an oracle. **c** a prophet or prophetess at an oracle. **2 a** a person or thing regarded as an infallible guide to future action etc. **b** a saying etc. regarded as infallible guidance. **3** divine inspiration or revelation. **4** (**Oracle**) *Brit. propr.* a teletext service provided by Independent Television. [ME f. OF f. L *oraculum* f. *orare* speak]

oracular /ə'rækjʊlə(r)/ *adj.* **1** of or concerning an oracle or oracles. **2** (esp. of advice etc.) mysterious or ambiguous. **3** prophetic. □□ **oracularity** /-'lærɪtɪ/ *n.* **oracularly** *adv.* [L (as ORACLE)]

oracy /'ɔːrəsɪ/ *n.* the ability to express oneself fluently in speech. [L *os oris* mouth, after *literacy*]

Oradea /ɒ'rɑːdɪə/ an industrial city in Western Romania; pop. (1985) 208,500.

oral /'ɔːr(ə)l/ *adj.* & *n.* —*adj.* **1** by word of mouth; spoken; not written (*the oral tradition*). **2** done or taken by the mouth (*oral contraceptive*). **3** of the mouth. **4** *Psychol.* of or concerning an early supposed stage of infant emotional and sexual development, in which the mouth is of central interest. —*n. colloq.* a spoken examination, test, etc. □ **oral sex** sexual activity in which the genitals of one partner are stimulated by the mouth of the other. **oral society** a society that has not reached the stage of literacy. □□ **orally** *adv.* [LL *oralis* f. L *os oris* mouth]

Oran /ɔː'rɑːn/ (Arabic **Wahran** /wɑː'rɑːn/) a seaport on the Mediterranean coast of Algeria; pop. (1983) 663,500.

Orange¹ /ɒ'rɑ̃ʒ/ a town and principality on the Rhône, which in the 16th c. passed to the House of Nassau, later rulers of the Netherlands. □ **House of Orange** /'ɒrɪndʒ/ the Dutch royal house. **William of Orange** William III. [L *Arausio* name of the town]

Orange² /'ɒrɪndʒ/ *adj.* of the extreme Protestants in Ireland, especially in Ulster, in reference to the secret political Association of Orangemen formed in 1795 for the defence of Protestantism and maintenance of Protestant ascendancy in Ireland. It was probably named from the wearing of orange badges etc. as a symbol of adherence to William III, of the House of Orange, who defeated the Catholic James II at the battle of the Boyne in 1690. □□ **Orangeism** *n.*

orange /'ɒrɪndʒ/ *n.* & *adj.* —*n.* **1 a** a large roundish juicy citrus fruit with a bright reddish-yellow tough rind. **b** any of various trees or shrubs of the genus *Citrus,* esp. *C. sinensis* or *C. aurantium,* bearing fragrant white flowers and yielding this fruit. **2** a fruit or plant resembling this. **3 a** the reddish-yellow colour of an orange. **b** orange pigment. —*adj.* orange-coloured; reddish-yellow. □ **orange blossom** the flowers of the orange tree, traditionally worn by the bride at a wedding. **orange flower water** a solution of neroli in water. **orange peel 1** the skin of an orange. **2** a rough surface resembling this. **orange pekoe** tea made from very small leaves. **orange squash** *Brit.* a soft drink made from oranges and other ingredients, often sold in concentrated form. **orange-stick** a thin stick, pointed at one end and usu. of orange wood, for manicuring the fingernails. **orange-wood** the wood of the orange tree. [ME f. OF *orenge,* ult. f. Arab. *nāranj* f. Pers. *nārang*]

orangeade /ˌɒrɪndʒ'eɪd/ *n.* a usu. fizzy non-alcoholic drink flavoured with orange.

Orange Free State /ˈɒrɪndʒ/ an inland province of the Republic of South Africa; pop. (1985) 1,776,900; capital, Bloemfontein. First settled by Boers trekking from Cape Colony (1836–8), it was annexed by Britain in 1848 but restored in 1854 to the Boers, who established the Orange Free State Republic. It was re-annexed by Britain in 1900, as the Orange River Colony, was given internal self-government in 1907, and became a province of the Union of South Africa in 1910, as the Orange Free State. [*House of* ORANGE¹]

Orangeman /ˈɒrɪndʒmən/ n. (pl. **-men**) see ORANGE².

Orange River the longest river in South Africa, flowing westward for 1,859 km (1,155 miles) into the Atlantic across almost the whole breadth of the continent.

orangery /ˈɒrɪndʒərɪ/ n. (pl. **-ies**) a place, esp. a special structure, where orange-trees are cultivated.

orang-utan /ɔːˌræŋuːˈtæn/ n. (also **orang-outang** /-uːˈtæŋ/) a large red long-haired tree-living ape, *Pongo pygmaeus*, native to Borneo and Sumatra, with characteristic long arms and hooked hands and feet. [Malay *ōrang ūtan* wild man]

Oranjestad /ɒˈrænjəˌstɑːt/ the capital of the Dutch island of Aruba in the West Indies; pop. (1981) 20,000.

orate /ɔːˈreɪt/ v.intr. esp. joc. or derog. make a speech or speak, esp. pompously or at length. [back-form. f. ORATION]

oration /ɔːˈreɪʃ(ə)n, ə-/ n. 1 a formal speech, discourse, etc., esp. when ceremonial. 2 Gram. a way of speaking; language. [ME f. L *oratio* discourse, prayer f. *orare* speak, pray]

orator /ˈɒrətə(r)/ n. 1 a a person making a speech. b an eloquent public speaker. 2 (in full **public orator**) an official speaking for a university on ceremonial occasions. ☐☐ **oratorial** /-ˈtɔːrɪəl/ adj. [ME f. AF *oratour*, OF *orateur* f. L *orator* -*oris* speaker, pleader (as ORATION)]

oratorio /ˌɒrəˈtɔːrɪəʊ/ n. (pl. **-os**) a semi-dramatic work for orchestra and voices esp. on a sacred theme, performed without costume, scenery, or action. The first oratorios proper were composed in the early 17th c. ☐☐ **oratorial** adj. [It. f. eccl.L *oratorium*, orig. of musical services at church of Oratory of St Philip Neri in Rome]

oratory /ˈɒrətərɪ/ n. (pl. **-ies**) 1 the art or practice of formal speaking, esp. in public. 2 exaggerated, eloquent, or highly coloured language. 3 a small chapel, esp. for private worship. 4 (**Oratory**) RC Ch. a a religious society of priests without vows founded in Rome in 1564 and providing plain preaching and popular services. b a branch of this in England etc. ☐☐ **oratorian** /-ˈtɔːrɪən/ adj. & n. **oratorical** /-ˈtɒrɪk(ə)l/ adj. [senses 1 and 2 f. L *ars oratoria* art of speaking; senses 3 and 4 ME f. AF *oratorie*, OF *oratoire* f. eccl.L *oratorium*: both f. L *oratorius* f. *orare* pray, speak]

orb /ɔːb/ n. & v. —n. 1 a globe surmounted by a cross esp. carried by a sovereign at a coronation. 2 a sphere; a globe. 3 *poet.* a heavenly body. 4 *poet.* an eyeball; an eye. —v. 1 tr. enclose in (an orb); encircle. 2 intr. form or gather into an orb. [L *orbis* ring]

orbicular /ɔːˈbɪkjʊlə(r)/ adj. formal 1 circular and flat; disc-shaped; ring-shaped. 2 spherical; globular; rounded. 3 forming a complete whole. ☐☐ **orbicularity** /-ˈlærɪtɪ/ n. **orbicularly** adv. [ME f. LL *orbicularis* f. L *orbiculus* dimin. of *orbis* ring]

orbiculate /ɔːˈbɪkjʊlət/ adj. Bot. (of a leaf etc.) almost circular.

orbit /ˈɔːbɪt/ n. & v. —n. 1 a the curved, usu. closed course of a planet, satellite, etc. b (prec. by *in*, *into*, *out of*, etc.) the state of motion in an orbit. c one complete passage around an orbited body. 2 the path of an electron round an atomic nucleus. 3 a range or sphere of action. 4 a the eye socket. b the skin around the eye of a bird or insect. —v. (**orbited**, **orbiting**) 1 intr. a (of a satellite etc.) go round in orbit. b fly in a circle. 2 tr. move in orbit round. 3 tr. put into orbit. ☐☐ **orbiter** n. [L *orbita* course, track (in med.L eye-cavity): fem. of *orbitus* circular f. *orbis* ring]

orbital /ˈɔːbɪt(ə)l/ adj. & n. —adj. 1 Anat., Astron., & Physics of an orbit or orbits. 2 (of a road) passing round the outside of a town. —n. Physics a state or function representing the possible motion of an electron round an atomic nucleus. ☐ **orbital sander** a sander having a circular and not oscillating motion.

orca /ˈɔːkə/ n. 1 any of various whales, esp. the killer whale. 2

any other large sea-animal or monster. [F *orque* or L *orca* a kind of whale]

Orcadian /ɔːˈkeɪdɪən/ adj. & n. —adj. of or relating to the Orkney Islands. —n. a native of the Orkney Islands. [L *Orcades* Orkney Islands]

Orcagna /ɔːˈkɑːnjə/ the nickname (= archangel) of Andrea di Cione (active c.1308–68), Florentine painter, sculptor, and architect occupying a key position between Giotto and Fra Angelico. His painting represents a return to a hieratic brightly coloured style fusing Gothic and Byzantine elements, in opposition to Giotto's naturalism, and may have been a product of new devotional attitudes in the aftermath of the Black Death (1348). His sculpture follows Andrea Pisano in style (e.g. the tabernacle reliefs on Or San Michele, Florence, 1359). As an architect he worked on the cathedrals of Orvieto and Florence. He had two brothers: Nardo (fl. c.1343–66) and Jacopo di Cione (fl. 1365–98) who worked in a similar style.

orch. abbr. 1 orchestrated by. 2 orchestra.

orchard /ˈɔːtʃəd/ n. a piece of enclosed land with fruit-trees. ☐☐ **orchardist** n. [OE *ortgeard* f. L *hortus* garden + YARD²]

orcharding /ˈɔːtʃədɪŋ/ n. the cultivation of fruit-trees.

orchardman /ˈɔːtʃədmən/ n. (pl. **-men**) a fruit-grower.

orchestra /ˈɔːkɪstrə/ n. 1 a usu. large group of instrumentalists, esp. combining strings, woodwinds, brass, and percussion (*symphony orchestra*). (See below.) 2 a (in full **orchestra pit**) the part of a theatre, opera house, etc., where the orchestra plays, usu. in front of the stage and on a lower level. b US the stalls in a theatre. 3 the semicircular space in front of an ancient Greek theatre-stage where the chorus danced and sang. ☐ **orchestra stalls** the front of the stalls. ☐☐ **orchestral** /-ˈkestr(ə)l/ adj. **orchestrally** /-ˈkestrəlɪ/ adv. [L f. Gk *orkhēstra* f. *orkheomai* to dance (see sense 3)]

In its modern definition the orchestra dates from the 18th c. when the forces required for orchestral music settled into four main categories with standard members: woodwind (flutes, clarinets, oboes, bassoons), brass (horns, trumpets, trombones, tubas), percussion (drums, with many optional extras), and strings (first and second violins, violas, cellos, double basses). The 19th c. saw a great increase in the number and variety of instruments in the orchestra, but in the 20th c. a return has frequently been made to smaller, chamber groups.

orchestrate /ˈɔːkɪˌstreɪt/ v.tr. 1 arrange, score, or compose for orchestral performance. 2 combine, arrange, or build up (elements of a situation etc.) for maximum effect. ☐☐ **orchestration** /-ˈstreɪʃ(ə)n/ n. **orchestrator** n.

orchid /ˈɔːkɪd/ n. 1 any usu. epiphytic plant of the family Orchidaceae, bearing flowers in fantastic shapes and brilliant colours, usu. having one petal larger than the others and variously spurred, lobed, pouched, etc. 2 a flower of any of these plants. ☐☐ **orchidaceous** /-ˈdeɪʃəs/ adj. **orchidist** n. **orchidology** /-ˈdɒlədʒɪ/ n. [mod.L *Orchid(ace)ae* irreg. f. L *orchis*: see ORCHIS]

orchil /ˈɔːtʃɪl/ n. (also **orchilla** /ɔːˈtʃɪlə/, **archil** /ˈɑːtʃɪl/) 1 a red or violet dye from lichen, esp. from *Roccella tinctoria*, often used in litmus. 2 the tropical lichen yielding this. [ME f. OF *orcheil* etc. perh. ult. f. L *herba urceolaris* a plant for polishing glass pitchers]

orchis /ˈɔːkɪs/ n. 1 any orchid of the genus *Orchis*, with a tuberous root and an erect fleshy stem having a spike of usu. purple or red flowers. 2 any of various wild orchids. [L f. Gk *orkhis*, orig. = testicle (with ref. to the shape of its tuber)]

orchitis /ɔːˈkaɪtɪs/ n. inflammation of the testicles. [mod.L f. Gk *orkhis* testicle]

orcin /ˈɔːsɪn/ n. (also **orcinol** /ˈɔːsɪˌnɒl/) a crystalline substance, becoming red in air, extracted from any of several lichens and used to make dyes. [mod.L *orcina* f. It. *orcello* orchil]

Orczy /ˈɔːkzɪ/, Baroness Emmusca (1865–1947), Hungarian-born British novelist whose best-known novel is *The Scarlet Pimpernel* (1905), telling of the adventures of an English nobleman smuggling aristocrats out of France during the French Revolution.

ord. abbr. ordinary.

ordain /ɔːˈdeɪn/ v.tr. 1 confer holy orders on; appoint to the

Christian ministry (*ordained him priest; was ordained in 1970*). **2 a** (often foll. by *that* + clause) decree (*ordained that he should go*). **b** (of God, fate, etc.) destine; appoint (*has ordained us to die*). □□ **ordainer** *n*. **ordainment** *n*. [ME f. AF *ordeiner*, OF *ordein-* stressed stem of *ordener* f. L *ordinare* f. *ordo -inis* order]

ordeal /ɔːˈdiːl/ *n*. **1** a painful or horrific experience; a severe trial. **2** *hist*. an ancient esp. Germanic test of guilt or innocence by subjection of the accused to severe pain or torture, survival of which was taken as divine proof of innocence. □ **ordeal tree** the tanghin. [OE *ordǣl*, *ordēl* f. Gmc: cf. DEAL[1]]

order /ˈɔːdə(r)/ *n*. & *v*. —*n*. **1 a** the condition in which every part, unit, etc. is in its right place; tidiness (*restored some semblance of order*). **b** a usu. specified sequence, succession, etc. (*alphabetical order; the order of events*). **2** (in *sing*. or *pl*.) an authoritative command, direction, instruction, etc. (*only obeying orders; gave orders for it to be done; the judge made an order*). **3** a state of peaceful harmony under a constituted authority (*order was restored; law and order*). **4** (esp. in *pl*.) a social class, rank, etc., constituting a distinct group in society (*the lower orders; the order of baronets*). **5** a kind; a sort (*talents of a high order*). **6 a** a usu. written direction to a manufacturer, tradesman, waiter, etc. to supply something. **b** the quantity of goods etc. supplied. **7** the constitution or nature of the world, society, etc. (*the moral order; the order of things*). **8** *Biol*. a taxonomic rank below a class and above a family. **9** (esp. **Order**) a fraternity of monks and friars, or formerly of knights, bound by a common rule of life (*the Franciscan order; the order of Templars*). **10 a** any of the grades of the Christian ministry. **b** (in *pl*.) the status of a member of the clergy (*Anglican orders*). **11 a** any of the styles of ancient architecture distinguished by the type of column used. The principal classical orders are the Doric, Ionic, Corinthian, Tuscan, and Composite, the first three being Greek in origin and the others Roman. The simplicity or elaborateness of each influenced the overall look of the building, and their differing proportional relations determined those of the whole edifice. **b** any style or mode of architecture subject to uniform established proportions. **12** (esp. **Order**) **a** a company of distinguished people instituted esp. by a sovereign to which appointments are made as an honour or reward (*Order of the Garter; Order of Merit*). **b** the insignia worn by members of an order. **13** *Math*. **a** a degree of complexity of a differential equation (*equation of the first order*). **b** the order of the highest derivative in the equation. **14** *Math*. **a** the size of a matrix. **b** the number of elements of a finite group. **15** *Eccl*. the stated form of divine service (*the order of confirmation*). **16** the principles of procedure, decorum, etc., accepted by a meeting, legislative assembly, etc. or enforced by its president. **17** *Mil*. **a** a style of dress and equipment (*review order*). **b** (prec. by *the*) the position of a company etc. with arms ordered (see *order arms*). **18 a** Masonic or similar fraternity. **19** any of the nine grades of angelic beings (seraphim, cherubim, thrones, dominations, principalities, powers, virtues, archangels, angels). **20** a pass admitting the bearer to a theatre, museum, private house, etc. free or cheap or as a privilege. —*v.tr*. **1** (usu. foll. by *to* + infin., or *that* + clause) command; bid; prescribe (*ordered him to go; ordered that they should be sent*). **2** command or direct (a person) to a specified destination (*was ordered to Singapore; ordered them home*). **3** direct a manufacturer, waiter, tradesman, etc. to supply (*ordered a new suit; ordered dinner*). **4** put in order; regulate (*ordered her affairs*). **5** (of God, fate, etc.) ordain (*fate ordered it otherwise*). **6** *US* command (a thing) done or (a person) dealt with (*ordered it settled; ordered him expelled*). □ **by order** according to the proper authority. **holy orders** the status of a member of the clergy, esp. the grades of bishop, priest, and deacon. **in bad** (or **good** etc.) **order** not working (or working properly etc.). **in order 1** one after another according to some principle. **2** ready or fit for use. **3** according to the rules (of procedure at a meeting etc.). **in order that** with the intention; so that. **in order to** with the purpose of doing; with a view to. **keep order** enforce orderly behaviour. **made to order 1** made according to individual requirements, measurements, etc. (opp. *ready-made*). **2** exactly what is wanted. **minor orders** *RC Ch. hist*. the grades of members of the clergy below that of deacon. **not in order** not working properly. **of** (or **in** or **on**) **the order of 1** approximately.

2 having the order of magnitude specified by (*of the order of one in a million*). **on order** (of goods etc.) ordered but not yet received. **order about 1** dominate; command officiously. **2** send hither and thither. **order arms** *Mil*. hold a rifle with its butt on the ground close to one's right side. **order book 1** a book in which a tradesman enters orders. **2** the level of incoming orders. **order-form** a printed form in which details are entered by a customer. **Order in Council** *Brit*. a sovereign's order on an administrative matter given by the advice of the Privy Council. **Order of the Bath** (or **Garter** or **Merit**) each of several honours conferred by the sovereign for services etc. to the State. **order of the day 1** the prevailing state of things. **2** a principal topic of action or a procedure decided upon. **3** business set down for treatment; a programme. **order of magnitude** a class in a system of classification determined by size, usu. by powers of 10. **Order! Order!** *Parl*. a call for silence or calm, esp. by the Speaker of the House of Commons. **order-paper** esp. *Parl*. a written or printed order of the day; an agenda. **order to view** a house-agent's request for a client to be allowed to inspect premises. **out of order 1** not working properly. **2** not according to the rules (of a meeting, organization, etc.). **take orders 1** accept commissions. **2** accept and carry out commands. **3** (also **take holy orders**) be ordained. □□ **orderer** *n*. [ME f. OF *ordre* f. L *ordo ordinis* row, array, degree, command, etc.]

orderly /ˈɔːdəlɪ/ *adj*. & *n*. —*adj*. **1** methodically arranged; regular. **2** obedient to discipline; well-behaved; not unruly. **3** *Mil*. **a** of or concerned with orders. **b** charged with the conveyance or execution of orders. —*n*. (*pl*. **-ies**) **1** an esp. male cleaner in a hospital. **2** a soldier who carries orders for an officer etc. □ **orderly book** *Brit. Mil*. a regimental or company book for entering orders. **orderly officer** *Brit. Mil*. the officer of the day. **orderly room** *Brit. Mil*. a room in a barracks used for company business. □□ **orderliness** *n*.

ordinal /ˈɔːdɪn(ə)l/ *n*. & *adj*. —*n*. **1** (in full **ordinal number**) a number defining a thing's position in a series, e.g. 'first', 'second', 'third', etc. (cf. CARDINAL). **2** *Eccl*. a service-book, esp. one with the forms of service used at ordinations. —*adj*. **1 a** of or relating to an ordinal number. **b** defining a thing's position in a series etc. **2** *Biol*. of or concerning an order (see ORDER *n*. 8). [ME f. LL *ordinalis* & med.L *ordinale* neut. f. L (as ORDER)]

ordinance /ˈɔːdɪnəns/ *n*. **1** an authoritative order; a decree. **2** an enactment by a local authority. **3** a religious rite. **4** *archaic* = ORDONNANCE. [ME f. OF *ordenance* f. med.L *ordinantia* f. L *ordinare*: see ORDAIN]

ordinand /ˈɔːdɪnænd/ *n*. *Eccl*. a candidate for ordination. [L *ordinandus*, gerundive of *ordinare* ORDAIN]

ordinary /ˈɔːdɪnərɪ/ *adj*. & *n*. —*adj*. **1 a** regular, normal, customary, usual (*in the ordinary course of events*). **b** boring; commonplace (*an ordinary little man*). **2** *Brit. Law* (esp. of a judge) having immediate or *ex officio* jurisdiction, not deputed. —*n*. (*pl*. **-ies**) **1** *Brit. Law* a person, esp. a judge, having immediate or *ex officio* jurisdiction. **2** (**the Ordinary**) **a** an archbishop in a province. **b** a bishop in a diocese. **3** (usu. **Ordinary**) *RC Ch*. **a** those parts of a service, esp. the mass, which do not vary from day to day. **b** a rule or book laying down the order of divine service. **4** *Heraldry* a charge of the earliest, simplest, and commonest kind (esp. chief, pale, bend, fess, bar, chevron, cross, saltire). **5** (**Ordinary**) (also **Lord Ordinary**) any of the judges of the Court of Session in Scotland, constituting the Outer House. **6** an ungeared bicycle of an early type, with a large front wheel and small rear wheel, so called for some years after the introduction of the 'safety' type (see BICYCLE). **7** *Brit. hist*. **a** a public meal provided at a fixed time and price at an inn etc. **b** an establishment providing this. **8** *US* a tavern. □ **in ordinary** *Brit*. by permanent appointment (esp. to the royal household) (*physician in ordinary*). **in the ordinary way** if the circumstances are or were not exceptional. **ordinary level** *Brit. hist*. the lowest of the three levels of the GCE examination. **ordinary scale** = *decimal scale*. **ordinary seaman** a sailor of the lowest rank, that below able-bodied seaman. **ordinary shares** *Brit*. shares entitling holders to a dividend from net profits (cf. *preference shares*). **out of the ordinary** unusual. □□ **ordinarily** *adv*. **ordinariness** *n*. [ME f. L *ordinarius* orderly (as ORDER)]

ordinate /ˈɔːdɪnɪt/ *n. Math.* a straight line from any point drawn parallel to one coordinate axis and meeting the other, usually a coordinate measured parallel to the vertical (cf. ABSCISSA). [L *linea ordinata applicata* line applied parallel f. *ordinare*: see ORDAIN]

ordination /ˌɔːdɪˈneɪʃ(ə)n/ *n.* **1 a** the act of conferring holy orders esp. on a priest or deacon. **b** the admission of a priest etc. to church ministry. **2** the arrangement of things etc. in ranks; classification. **3** the act of decreeing or ordaining. [ME f. OF *ordination* or L *ordinatio* (as ORDAIN)]

ordnance /ˈɔːdnəns/ *n.* **1** mounted guns; cannon. **2** a branch of government service dealing esp. with military stores and materials. □ **ordnance datum** *Brit.* mean sea level as defined for Ordnance Survey. **Ordnance map** *Brit.* a map produced by Ordnance Survey. **Ordnance Survey** *Brit.* (in the UK) an official survey organization, orig. under the Master of the Ordnance, preparing large-scale detailed maps of the whole country. [ME var. of ORDINANCE]

ordonnance /ˈɔːdənəns/ *n.* the systematic arrangement esp. of literary or architectural work. [F f. OF *ordenance*: see ORDINANCE]

Ordovician /ˌɔːdəˈvɪsɪən, ˌɔːdəʊˈvɪʃɪən/ *adj. & n. Geol.* —*adj.* of or relating to the second period of the Palaeozoic era, following the Cambrian and preceding the Silurian, lasting from about 505 to 438 million years ago. It saw both the diversification of many invertebrate groups and the appearance of the first vertebrates (jawless fish). —*n.* this period or system. [L *Ordovices* ancient British tribe in N. Wales]

ordure /ˈɔːdjʊə(r)/ *n.* **1** excrement; dung. **2** obscenity; filth; foul language. [ME f. OF f. *ord* foul f. L *horridus*: see HORRID]

Ore. *abbr.* Oregon.

ore /ɔː(r)/ *n.* a naturally occurring solid material from which metal or other valuable minerals may be extracted. [OE *ōra* unwrought metal, *ār* bronze, rel. to L *aes* crude metal, bronze]

öre /ˈʊərə/ *n.* (also **øre**) a Scandinavian monetary unit equal to one-hundredth of a krona or krone. [Swedish]

oread /ˈɔːrɪˌæd/ *n. Gk & Rom. Mythol.* a mountain nymph. [ME f. L *oreas -ados* f. Gk *oreias* f. *oros* mountain]

Örebro /ˈɜːrəˌbruː/ an industrial city in south central Sweden; pop. (1987) 119,000.

orectic /əˈrektɪk/ *adj. Philos. & Med.* of or concerning desire or appetite. [Gk *orektikos* f. *oregō* stretch out]

Oreg. *abbr.* Oregon.

oregano /ˌɒrɪˈɡɑːnəʊ/ *n.* the dried leaves of wild marjoram used as a culinary herb (cf. MARJORAM). [Sp., = ORIGANUM]

Oregon /ˈɒrɪɡən/ a State of the US, on the Pacific coast, occupied jointly by British and Americans until 1846, when it was ceded to the US; pop. (est. 1985) 2,633,150; capital, Salem. It became the 33rd State of the US in 1859. □ **Oregon Trail** the route from the Missouri across Oregon, some 3,000 km (2,000 miles) in length followed by settlers moving west, especially in the 1840s.

Ore Mountains /ɔː(r)/ (German **Erzgebirge** /ˈɜːtsɡəˌbɪrɡə/) a range of mountains on the frontier between Germany and Czechoslovakia.

Orenburg /ˈɒrənˌbɜː(r)/ a city of the Soviet Union in the south-western foothills of the Ural Mountains; pop. (est. 1987) 537,000.

oreography var. of OROGRAPHY.

Orestes /ɒˈrestiːz/ *Gk legend* the son of Agamemnon and Clytemnestra. He killed his mother and her lover Aegisthus to avenge the murder of Agamemnon.

Øresund /ˈɜːrəˌsʊnd/ (English **the Sound**) a narrow channel between Sweden and the Danish island of Zealand.

oreweed var. of OARWEED.

orfe /ɔːf/ *n.* a golden-coloured ide. [G & F: cf. L *orphus* f. Gk *orphos* sea-perch]

organ /ˈɔːɡən/ *n.* **1 a** a usu. large musical instrument having pipes supplied with air from bellows, sounded by keys, and distributed into sets or stops which form partial organs, each with a separate keyboard (*choir organ*; *pedal organ*). (See below.) **b** a smaller instrument without pipes, producing similar sounds electronically. **c** a smaller keyboard wind instrument with metal reeds; a harmonium. **d** = *barrel-organ*. **2 a** a usu. self-contained part of an organism having a special vital function (*vocal organs*; *digestive organs*). **b** esp. *joc.* the penis. **3** a medium of communication, esp. a newspaper, sectarian periodical, etc. **4** *archaic* a professionally trained singing voice. **5** *Phrenol. archaic* a region of the brain held to be the seat of a particular faculty. □ **organ-blower** a person or mechanism working the bellows of an organ. **organ-grinder** the player of a barrel-organ. **organ-loft** a gallery in a church or concert-room for an organ. **organ of Corti** see CORTI. **organ-pipe** any of the pipes on an organ. **organ-screen** an ornamental screen usu. between the choir and the nave of a church, cathedral, etc., on which the organ is placed. **organ-stop 1** a set of pipes of a similar tone in an organ. **2** the handle of the mechanism that brings it into action. [ME f. OE *organa* & OF *organe*, f. L *organum* f. Gk *organon* tool]

The organ has been associated with the church for nearly a millennium, but its invention *c.*246 BC is attributed to Ktesibios, an engineer based in Alexandria. His instrument used water to pump the bellows and a row of reed pipes for making the sound. Roman interest in the organ was attested in 1931 when an instrument built in AD 228 was excavated at Aquincum in Hungary, but its importance in the West stems from a gift of one from Emperor Constantine V to Pepin, king of the Franks, in 757. In the mid-10th c. a huge organ belonging to Winchester Cathedral apparently required no fewer than 70 strong men to work the 26 bellows. Among celebrated organ builders are 'Father' Smith (c.1630–1708), who built instruments for the Banqueting House in Whitehall, Westminster Abbey, and Durham Cathedral, and Aristide Cavaillé-Coll (1811–98), who revolutionized the tonal design, incorporating a rich variety of orchestral stops.

organdie /ˈɔːɡəndɪ, -ˈɡændɪ/ *n.* (*US* **organdy**) (*pl.* **-ies**) a fine translucent cotton muslin, usu. stiffened. [F *organdi*, of unkn. orig.]

organelle /ˌɔːɡəˈnel/ *n. Biol.* any of various organized or specialized structures which form part of a cell. [mod.L *organella* dimin.; see ORGAN, -LE]

organic /ɔːˈɡænɪk/ *adj.* **1 a** *Physiol.* of or relating to a bodily organ or organs. **b** *Med.* (of a disease) affecting the structure of an organ. **2** (of a plant or animal) having organs or an organized physical structure. **3** *Agriculture* produced or involving production without the use of chemical fertilizers, pesticides, etc. (*organic crop*; *organic farming*). **4** *Chem.* (of a compound etc.) containing carbon (opp. INORGANIC). **5 a** structural, inherent. **b** constitutional, fundamental. **6** organized, systematic, coordinated (*an organic whole*). □ **organic chemistry** the chemistry of carbon compounds. **organic law** a law stating the formal constitution of a country. □□ **organically** *adv.* [F *organique* f. L *organicus* f. Gk *organikos* (as ORGAN)]

organism /ˈɔːɡəˌnɪz(ə)m/ *n.* **1** a living individual consisting of a single cell or of a group of interdependent parts sharing the life processes. **2 a** an individual live plant or animal. **b** the material structure of this. **3** a whole with interdependent parts compared to a living being. [F *organisme* (as ORGANIZE)]

organist /ˈɔːɡənɪst/ *n.* the player of an organ.

organization /ˌɔːɡənaɪˈzeɪʃ(ə)n/ *n.* (also **-isation**) **1** the act or an instance of organizing; the state of being organized. **2** an organized body, esp. a business, government department, charity, etc. **3** systematic arrangement; tidiness. □ **organization man** a man who subordinates his individuality and his personal life to the organization he serves. □□ **organizational** *adj.* **organizationally** *adv.*

Organization for Economic Cooperation and Development an organization formed in 1961 (replacing the Organization for European Economic Cooperation) to assist the economy of its member nations and to promote world trade. Its members include the industrialized countries of Western Europe together with Australia, Japan, New Zealand, and the US. Its headquarters are in Paris.

Organization of African Unity an association of African States founded in 1963 for mutual cooperation and the elimination of colonialism in Africa. It is based in Addis Ababa.

b *but* d *dog* f *few* g *get* h *he* j *yes* k *cat* l *leg* m *man* n *no* p *pen* r *red* s *sit* t *top* v *voice*

Organization of American States an association of American countries. Originally founded in 1890 for largely commercial purposes, it adopted its present name and charter in 1948. Its aims are to work for peace and prosperity in the region and to uphold the sovereignty of member nations. Its headquarters are in Washington, DC.

Organization of Arab Petroleum Exporting Countries an association of Arab countries, founded in 1968, to promote economic cooperation and safeguard its members' interests and to ensure the supply of oil to consumer markets. It is based in Kuwait.

Organization of Central American States an association founded in 1951 (a new charter being negotiated in 1962) for economic and political cooperation. Its members (Guatemala, Honduras, El Salvador, and Costa Rica) succeeded in establishing the Central American Common Market in 1960, but cooperated in little else.

Organization of the Petroleum Exporting Countries an association of the thirteen major oil-producing countries, founded in 1960 to coordinate policies. Its headquarters are in Vienna.

organize /'ɔːgəˌnaɪz/ v.tr. (also **-ise**) **1 a** give an orderly structure to, systematize. **b** bring the affairs of (another person or oneself) into order; make arrangements for (a person). **2 a** arrange for or initiate (a scheme etc.). **b** provide; take responsibility for (*organized some sandwiches*). **3** (often *absol.*) **a** enrol (new members) in a trade union, political party, etc. **b** form (a trade union or other political group). **4 a** form (different elements) into an organic whole. **b** form (an organic whole). **5** (esp. as **organized** *adj.*) make organic; make into a living being or tissue. □□ **organizable** *adj.* **organizer** *n.* [ME f. OF *organiser* f. med.L *organizare* f. L (as ORGAN)]

organo- /'ɔːgənəʊ/ *comb. form* **1** esp. *Biol.* organ. **2** *Chem.* organic. [Gk (as ORGAN)]

organoleptic /ˌɔːgənəʊ'leptɪk/ *adj.* affecting the organs of sense. [ORGANO- + Gk *lēptikos* disposed to take f. *lambanō* take]

organometallic /ɔːˌgænəʊmɪ'tælɪk/ *adj.* (of a compound) organic and containing a metal.

organon /'ɔːgəˌnɒn/ *n.* (also **organum** /'ɔːgənəm/) an instrument of thought, esp. a means of reasoning or a system of logic. [Gk *organon* & L *organum* (as ORGAN): *Organon* was the title of Aristotle's logical writings, and *Novum* (new) *Organum* that of Bacon's]

organotherapy /ˌɔːgənəʊ'θerəpɪ/ *n.* the treatment of disease with extracts of organs.

organza /ɔː'gænzə/ *n.* a thin stiff transparent silk or synthetic dress fabric. [prob. f. *Lorganza* (US trade name)]

organzine /'ɔːgənˌziːn, -'gænziːn/ *n.* a silk thread in which the main twist is in a contrary direction to that of the strands. [F *organsin* f. It. *organzino*, of unkn. orig.]

orgasm /'ɔːgæz(ə)m/ *n.* & v. —*n.* **1 a** the climax of sexual excitement, esp. during sexual intercourse. **b** an instance of this. **2** violent excitement; rage. —*v.intr.* experience a sexual orgasm. □□ **orgasmic** /-'gæzmɪk/ *adj.* **orgasmically** /-'gæzmɪkəlɪ/ *adv.* **orgastic** /-'gæstɪk/ *adj.* **orgastically** /-'gæstɪkəlɪ/ *adv.* [F *orgasme* or mod.L f. Gk *orgasmos* f. *orgaō* swell, be excited]

orgeat /'ɔːdʒɪˌæt, -ˈʒɑː/ *n.* a cooling drink made from barley or almonds and orange-flower water. [F f. Prov. *orjat* f. *ordi* barley f. L *hordeum*]

orgiastic /ˌɔːdʒɪ'æstɪk/ *adj.* of or resembling an orgy. □□ **orgiastically** *adv.* [Gk *orgiastikos* f. *orgiastēs* agent-noun f. *orgiazō* hold an orgy]

orgulous /'ɔːgjʊləs/ *adj.* *archaic* haughty; splendid. [ME f. OF *orguillus* f. *orguill* pride f. Frank.]

orgy /'ɔːdʒɪ/ *n.* (pl. **-ies**) **1** a wild drunken festivity at which indiscriminate sexual activity takes place. **2** excessive indulgence in an activity. **3** (usu. in pl.) *Gk & Rom. Hist.* secret rites used in the worship of esp. Bacchus, celebrated with dancing, drunkenness, singing, etc. [orig. pl., f. F *orgies* f. L *orgia* f. Gk *orgia* secret rites]

oribi /'ɒrɪbɪ/ *n.* (pl. same or **oribis**) a small S. African grazing antelope, *Ourebia ourebi*, having a reddish fawn back and white underparts. [prob. Khoisan]

oriel /'ɔːrɪəl/ *n.* **1** a large polygonal recess built out usu. from an upper storey and supported from the ground or on corbels. **2** (in full **oriel window**) **a** any of the windows in an oriel. **b** the projecting window of an upper storey. [ME f. OF *oriol* gallery, of unkn. orig.]

orient /'ɔːrɪənt/ *n., adj.,* & v. —*n.* **1** (**the Orient**) **a** *poet.* the east. **b** the countries E. of the Mediterranean, esp. E. Asia. **2** an orient pearl. —*adj.* **1** *poet.* oriental. **2** (of precious stones and esp. the finest pearls coming orig. from the East) lustrous; sparkling; precious. **3** *archaic* **a** radiant. **b** (of the sun, daylight, etc.) rising. —v. /'ɔːrɪˌent, 'ɒr-/ **1** *tr.* **a** place or exactly determine the position of with the aid of a compass; settle or find the bearings of. **b** (often foll. by *towards*) bring (oneself, different elements, etc.) into a clearly understood position or relationship; direct. **2** *tr.* **a** place or build (a church, building, etc.) facing towards the East. **b** bury (a person) with the feet towards the East. **3** *intr.* turn eastward or in a specified direction. □ **Orient Express** the name of a train which ran (from 1883 to 1961) between Paris and Istanbul and other Balkan cities, via Vienna, and of its successors. **orient oneself** determine how one stands in relation to one's surroundings. [ME f. OF *orient, orienter* f. L *oriens -entis* rising, sunrise, east, f. *oriri* rise]

oriental /ˌɔːrɪ'ent(ə)l, ˌɒr-/ *adj.* & *n.* —*adj.* **1** (often **Oriental**) **a** of or characteristic of Eastern civilization etc. **b** of or concerning the East, esp. E. Asia. **2** (of a pearl etc.) orient. —*n.* (esp. **Oriental**) a native of the Orient. □□ **orientalism** *n.* **orientalist** *n.* **orientalize** v.intr. & *tr.* (also **-ise**). **orientally** *adv.* [ME f. OF *oriental* or L *orientalis* (as ORIENT)]

orientate /'ɒrɪenˌteɪt, 'ɔːr-/ v.tr. & *intr.* = ORIENT v. [prob. backform. f. ORIENTATION]

orientation /ˌɒrɪen'teɪʃ(ə)n, ˌɔːr-/ *n.* **1** the act or an instance of orienting; the state of being oriented. **2 a** a relative position. **b** a person's attitude or adjustment in relation to circumstances, esp. politically or psychologically. **3** an introduction to a subject or situation; a briefing. **4** the faculty by which birds etc. find their way home from a distance. □ **orientation course** esp. *US* a course giving information to newcomers to a university etc. □□ **orientational** *adj.* [app. f. ORIENT]

orienteering /ˌɔːrɪen'tɪərɪŋ, ˌɒr-/ *n.* a competitive sport in which runners cross open country with a map, compass, etc. Although 'chart and compass' races were held in the sports meetings of British army units in the early 20th c., orienteering is generally recognized as being of Scandinavian origin, first introduced as a sport for young people in Sweden in 1918. □□ **orienteer** *n.* & v.intr. [Sw. *orientering*]

orifice /'ɒrɪfɪs/ *n.* an opening, esp. the mouth of a cavity, a bodily aperture, etc. [F f. LL *orificium* f. *os oris* mouth + *facere* make]

oriflamme /'ɒrɪˌflæm/ *n.* **1** *hist.* the sacred scarlet silk banner of St Denis given to early French kings by the abbot of St Denis on setting out for war. **2** a standard, a principle, or an ideal as a rallying-point in a struggle. **3** a bright conspicuous object, colour, etc. [ME f. OF f. L *aurum* gold + *flamma* flame]

origami /ˌɒrɪ'gɑːmɪ/ *n.* the Japanese art of folding paper into decorative shapes and figures. [Jap. f. *ori* fold + *kami* paper]

origan /'ɒrɪgən/ *n.* (also **origanum** /ə'rɪgənəm/) any plant of the genus *Origanum*, esp. wild marjoram (see MARJORAM). [(ME f. OF *origan*) f. L *origanum* f. Gk *origanon*]

Origen /'ɒrɪdʒ(ə)n/ (*c*.185–*c*.254) Alexandrian biblical scholar and theologian. Of his numerous works the most famous was the *Hexapla*, an edition of the Old Testament with six or more parallel versions. He recognized literal, moral, and allegorical interpretations of Scripture, preferring the last. Many of his writings have perished and most of the others survive only in fragments or in Latin translations, partly because of later condemnations of his teaching and partly because of the exorbitant length and diffusiveness of his work.

origin /'ɒrɪdʒɪn/ *n.* **1** a beginning or starting-point; a derivation; a source (*a word of Latin origin*). **2** (often in pl.) a person's ancestry (*what are his origins?*). **3** *Anat.* **a** a place at which a muscle is firmly attached. **b** a place where a nerve or blood vessel begins or branches from a main nerve or blood vessel. **4** *Math.* a fixed point from which coordinates are measured. [F *origine* or f. L *origo -ginis* f. *oriri* rise]

original /ə'rɪdʒɪn(ə)l/ *adj. & n.* —*adj.* **1** existing from the beginning; innate. **2** novel; inventive; creative (*has an original mind*). **3** serving as a pattern; not derivative or imitative; firsthand (*in the original Greek; has an original Rembrandt*). —*n.* **1** an original model, pattern, picture, etc. from which another is copied or translated (*kept the copy and destroyed the original*). **2** an eccentric or unusual person. **3 a** a garment specially designed for a fashion collection. **b** a copy of such a garment made to order. □ **original instrument** a musical instrument, or a copy of one, dating from the time the music played on it was composed. **original print** a print made directly from an artist's own woodcut, etching, etc., and printed under the artist's supervision. **original sin** (in Christian theology) the innate depravity held to be common to all human beings in consequence of the Fall. Medieval theologians were particularly occupied with its nature and transmission, but from the 18th c. onwards the influence of rationalism and natural science has attenuated the dogma, which has been given up almost completely by Liberal Protestantism and Modernism. □□ **originally** *adv.* [ME f. OF *original* or L *originalis* (as ORIGIN)]

originality /ə,rɪdʒɪ'nælɪtɪ/ *n.* (*pl.* **-ies**) **1** the power of creating or thinking creatively. **2** newness or freshness (*this vase has originality*). **3** an original act, thing, trait, etc.

originate /ə'rɪdʒɪ,neɪt/ *v.* **1** *tr.* cause to begin; initiate. **2** *intr.* (usu. foll. by *from, in, with*) have as an origin; begin. □□ **origination** /-'neɪʃ(ə)n/ *n.* **originative** /-nətɪv/ *adj.* **originator** *n.* [med. L *originare* (as ORIGIN)]

orinasal /,ɔːrɪ'neɪz(ə)l/ *adj.* (esp. of French nasalized vowels) sounded with both the mouth and the nose. [L *os oris* mouth + NASAL]

o-ring /'əʊrɪŋ/ *n.* a gasket in the form of a ring with a circular cross-section.

Orinoco /,ɒrɪ'nəʊkəʊ/ a river in the north of South America, 2,060 km (1,280 miles) long, flowing from the Guiana Highlands through Venezuela to the Atlantic Ocean.

oriole /'ɔːrɪəʊl/ *n.* **1** any Old World bird of the genus *Oriolus*, many of which have brightly coloured plumage (see *golden oriole*). **2** any New World bird of the genus *Icterus*, with similar coloration. [med.L *oriolus* f. OF *oriol* f. L *aureolus* dimin. of *aureus* golden f. *aurum* gold]

Orion /ə'raɪən/ **1** *Gk legend* a giant and hunter, said to have been changed into a constellation at his death. The association of his name with the constellation occurs in Homer, making it an unprecedentedly early star-myth. **2** *Astron.* a conspicuous constellation containing many bright stars including **Orion's belt** three stars in a short line. **Orion's hound** Sirius.

orison /'ɒrɪz(ə)n/ *n.* (usu. in *pl.*) *archaic* a prayer. [ME f. AF *ureison*, OF *oreison* f. L (as ORATION)]

Orissa /ə'rɪsə/ a State in eastern India; pop. (1981) 26,272,050; capital, Bhubaneswar.

-orium /'ɔːrɪəm/ *suffix* forming nouns denoting a place for a particular function (*auditorium*; *crematorium*). [L. neut. of adjectives in *-orius*: see -ORY¹]

Oriya /ə'riːə/ *adj. & n.* —*adj.* **1** of Odra, an ancient region of India corresponding to the State of Orissa. **2** of Orissa (which takes its name from Odra). —*n.* **1** a native of Odra. **2** the Indo-European language of Odra/Orissa, which is descended from Sanskrit and closely related to Bengali, spoken by some 20 million people. [Hindi, f. *Odra*]

Orkney Islands /'ɔːknɪ/ (also **Orkneys**) a group of islands off the NE tip of Scotland, colonized by the Vikings in the 9th c. and ruled by Norway and Denmark until they came into Scottish possession (together with Shetland) in 1472 as security against the unpaid dowry of Margaret of Denmark after her marriage to James III. They constitute an islands area (Orkney) of Scotland; pop. (1981) 19,300; chief town, Kirkwall.

orle /'ɔːl/ *n. Heraldry* a narrow band or border of charges near the edge of a shield. [F *o(u)rle* f. *ourler* to hem, ult. f. L *ora* edge]

Orleans /ɔː'liːənz/ (French **Orléans**) a French city on the River Loire, scene of Joan of Arc's first victory over the English during the Hundred Years War; pop. (1982) 105,600.

Orlon /'ɔːlɒn/ *n. propr.* a man-made fibre and fabric for textiles and knitwear. [invented word, after NYLON]

orlop /'ɔːlɒp/ *n.* the lowest deck of a ship with three or more decks. [ME f. MDu. *overloop* covering f. *overloopen* run over (as OVER-, LEAP)]

Ormazd /'ɔːməzd/ see AHURA MAZDA.

ormer /'ɔːmə(r)/ *n.* an edible univalve mollusc, *Haliotis tuberculata*, having a flattened shell with a series of holes of increasing size along the outer margin. Also called *sea-ear*. [Channel Islands F f. F *ormier* f. L *auris maris* ear of sea]

ormolu /'ɔːmə,luː/ *n.* **1** (often *attrib.*) **a** a gilded bronze or gold-coloured alloy of copper, zinc, and tin used to decorate furniture, make ornaments, etc. **b** articles made of or decorated with these. **2** showy trash. [F *or moulu* powdered gold (for use in gilding)]

Ormuz /'ɔːmʊz/ var. of HORMUZ.

ornament /'ɔːnəmənt/ *n. & v.* —*n.* **1 a** a thing used or serving to adorn, esp. a small trinket, vase, figure, etc. (*a mantelpiece crowded with ornaments; her only ornament was a brooch*). **b** a quality or person conferring adornment, grace, or honour (*an ornament to her profession*). **2** decoration added to embellish esp. a building (*a tower rich in ornament*). **3** (in *pl.*) *Mus.* embellishments and decorations made to a melody. **4** (usu. in *pl.*) the accessories of worship, e.g. the altar, chalice, sacred vessels, etc. —*v.tr.* /'ɔːnə,ment/ adorn; beautify. □□ **ornamentation** /-men'teɪʃ(ə)n/ *n.* [ME f. AF *urnement*, OF *o(u)rnement* f. L *ornamentum* equipment f. *ornare* adorn]

ornamental /,ɔːnə'ment(ə)l/ *adj. & n.* —*adj.* serving as an ornament; decorative. —*n.* a thing considered to be ornamental, esp. a cultivated plant. □□ **ornamentalism** *n.* **ornamentalist** *n.* **ornamentally** *adv.*

ornate /ɔː'neɪt/ *adj.* **1** elaborately or highly decorated. **2** (of literary style) convoluted; flowery. □□ **ornately** *adv.* **ornateness** *n.* [ME f. L *ornatus* past part. of *ornare* adorn]

ornery /'ɔːnərɪ/ *adj. US colloq.* **1** cantankerous; unpleasant. **2** of poor quality. □□ **orneriness** *n.* [var. of ORDINARY]

ornithic /ɔː'nɪθɪk/ *adj.* of or relating to birds. [Gk *ornithikos* birdlike (as ORNITHO-)]

ornitho- /'ɔːnɪθəʊ/ *comb. form* bird. [Gk f. *ornis ornithos* bird]

ornithology /,ɔːnɪ'θɒlədʒɪ/ *n.* the scientific study of birds. □□ **ornithological** /-θə'lɒdʒɪk(ə)l/ *adj.* **ornithologically** /-θə'lɒdʒɪkəlɪ/ *adv.* **ornithologist** *n.* [mod.L *ornithologia* f. Gk *ornithologos* treating of birds (as ORNITHO-, -LOGY)]

ornithorhynchus /,ɔːnɪθəʊ'rɪŋkəs/ *n.* = PLATYPUS. [ORNITHO- + Gk *rhugkhos* bill]

oro- /'ɔːrəʊ/ *comb. form* mountain. [Gk *oros* mountain]

orogeny /ɒ'rɒdʒɪnɪ/ *n.* (also **orogenesis** /,ɒrəʊ'dʒenɪsɪs/) the process of the formation of mountains. □□ **orogenetic** /,ɒrəʊdʒɪ'netɪk/ *adj.* **orogenic** /,ɒrə'dʒenɪk/ *adj.*

orography /ɒ'rɒgrəfɪ, ɔː-/ *n.* (also **oreography** /,ɒrɪ'ɒgrəfɪ/) the branch of physical geography dealing with mountains. □□ **orographic** /-rə'græfɪk/ *adj.* **orographical** /-'græfɪk(ə)l/ *adj.*

Orontes /ə'rɒntiːz/ a river of SW Asia, rising near Baalbek in Lebanon and flowing through western and northern Syria before turning west and south-west through southern Turkey into the Mediterranean Sea. It is an important source of water for irrigation, especially in Syria.

orotund /'ɒrə,tʌnd, 'ɔːr-/ *adj.* **1** (of the voice or phrasing) full, round; imposing. **2** (of writing, style, expression, etc.) pompous; pretentious. [L *ore rotundo* with rounded mouth]

orphan /'ɔːf(ə)n/ *n. & v.* —*n.* (often *attrib.*) **1** a child bereaved of a parent or usu. both parents. **2** a person bereft of previous protection, advantages, etc. —*v.tr.* bereave (a child) of its parents or a parent. □□ **orphanhood** *n.* **orphanize** *v.tr.* (also **-ise**). [ME f. LL *orphanus* f. Gk *orphanos* bereaved]

orphanage /'ɔːfənɪdʒ/ *n.* **1** a usu. residential institution for the care and education of orphans. **2** orphanhood.

Orphean /ɔːˈfiːən/ adj. like the music of Orpheus; melodious; entrancing. [L Orpheus (adj.) f. Gk Orpheios f. Orpheus]

Orpheus /ˈɔːfjəs/ either a real person, founder of Orphism, or purely mythical. He appears in ancient Greek literature and art as a singer who, with his lyre, sang and played so wonderfully that wild beasts were spellbound by his music. He visited the underworld and persuaded its lord to release his wife Euridice from the dead, but lost her because he failed to obey the condition that he must not look back at her until they had reached the world of the living.

Orphic /ˈɔːfɪk/ adj. 1 of or concerning Orpheus or Orphism (sense 1); oracular; mysterious. 2 = ORPHEAN. [L Orphicus f. Gk Orphikos f. Orpheus]

Orphism /ˈɔːfɪz(ə)m/ n. 1 a mystic religion of ancient Greece, originating in the 7th or 6th c. BC and based in poems (now lost) attributed to Orpheus, emphasizing the mixture of good (or divine) and evil in human nature and the necessity that individuals should rid themselves of the evil part by ritual and moral purification throughout a series of reincarnations. It sank to the level of a superstition in the 5th c., though the profound thoughts which underlay it were perceived by Pindar and Plato; its high ideas were mixed up with crude myths, and misused by base priests and charlatans. 2 a short-lived art movement (c.1912) within cubism, pioneered by a group of French painters calling themselves La Section d'Or (Golden Section), which emphasized the lyrical use of colour in pure abstract designs rather than the austere intellectual cubism of Picasso, Braque, and Gris.

orphrey /ˈɔːfrɪ/ n. (pl. -eys) an ornamental stripe or border or separate piece of ornamental needlework, esp. on ecclesiastical vestments. [ME orfreis (taken as pl.) (gold) embroidery f. OF f. med.L aurifrisium etc. f. L aurum gold + Phrygius Phrygian, also 'embroidered']

orpiment /ˈɔːpɪmənt/ n. 1 a mineral form of arsenic trisulphide, formerly used as a dye and artist's pigment. Also called yellow arsenic. 2 (in full red orpiment) = REALGAR. [ME f. OF f. L auripigmentum f. aurum gold + pigmentum pigment]

orpine /ˈɔːpɪn/ n. (also orpin) a succulent herbaceous purple-flowered plant, Sedum telephium. Also called LIVELONG². [ME f. OF orpine, prob. alt. of ORPIMENT, orig. of a yellow-flowered species of the same genus]

orra /ˈɒrə/ adj. Sc. 1 not matched; odd. 2 occasional; extra. [18th c.: orig. unkn.]

orrery /ˈɒrərɪ/ n. (pl. -ies) a clockwork model of the solar system. [named after the fourth Earl of Orrery, for whom one was made]

orris /ˈɒrɪs/ n. 1 any plant of the genus Iris, esp. I. florentina. 2 = ORRISROOT. □ **orris-powder** powdered orrisroot. [16th c.: app. an unexpl. alt. of IRIS]

orrisroot /ˈɒrɪsˌruːt/ n. the fragrant rootstock of the orris, used in perfumery and formerly in medicine.

ortanique /ˈɔːtəˌniːk/ n. a citrus fruit produced by crossing an orange and a tangerine. [orange + tangerine + unique]

ortho- /ˈɔːθəʊ/ comb. form 1 a straight, rectangular, upright. b right, correct. 2 Chem. a relating to two adjacent carbon atoms in a benzene ring. b relating to acids and salts (e.g. orthophosphates) giving meta- compounds on removal of water. [Gk orthos straight]

orthocephalic /ˌɔːθəʊsɪˈfælɪk/ adj. having a head with a medium ratio of breadth to height.

orthochromatic /ˌɔːθəʊkrəʊˈmætɪk/ adj. giving fairly correct relative intensity to colours in photography by being sensitive to all except red.

orthoclase /ˈɔːθəʊˌkleɪs/ n. a common alkali feldspar usu. occurring as variously coloured crystals, used in ceramics and glass-making. [ORTHO- + Gk klasis breaking]

orthodontics /ˌɔːθəˈdɒntɪks/ n.pl. (treated as sing.) (also **orthodontia** /-ˈdɒntɪə/) the treatment of irregularities in the teeth and jaws. □□ **orthodontic** adj. **orthodontist** n. [ORTHO- + Gk odous odont- tooth]

orthodox /ˈɔːθəˌdɒks/ adj. 1 a holding correct or currently accepted opinions, esp. on religious doctrine, morals, etc. b not independent-minded; unoriginal; unheretical. 2 (of religious doctrine, standards of morality, etc.) generally accepted as right or true; authoritatively established; conventional. 3 (also **Orthodox**) (of Judaism) strictly keeping to traditional doctrine and ritual. □□ **orthodoxly** adv. [eccl.L orthodoxus f. Gk orthodoxos f. doxa opinion]

Orthodox Church the Eastern or Greek Church, having the Patriarch of Constantinople as its head, and the national Churches of Russia, Romania, etc. in communion with it. Separation from the Western Church came in the 4th c., originally through cultural and political factors, focused from the 5th c. onwards on differences of doctrine and ritual, and took formal effect in 1054 when the Pope and the Patriarch of Constantinople excommunicated each other. In the latter part of the 20th c. the Orthodox Churches have taken an active part in the ecumenical movement; the mutual excommunications of 1054 were abolished in 1965.

orthodoxy /ˈɔːθəˌdɒksɪ/ n. (pl. -ies) 1 the state of being orthodox. 2 a the orthodox practice of Judaism. b the body of orthodox Jews. 3 esp. Relig. an authorized or generally accepted theory, doctrine, etc. [LL orthodoxia f. late Gk orthodoxia sound doctrine (as ORTHODOX)]

orthoepy /ˈɔːθəʊˌɪpɪ, ɔːˈθəʊɪpɪ/ n. the scientific study of the correct pronunciation of words. □□ **orthoepic** /-ˈepɪk/ adj. **orthoepist** n. [Gk orthoepeia correct speech (as ORTHO-, epos word)]

orthogenesis /ˌɔːθəʊˈdʒɛnɪsɪs/ n. a theory of evolution which proposes that variations follow a defined direction and are not merely sporadic and fortuitous. □□ **orthogenetic** /-dʒɪˈnetɪk/ adj. **orthogenetically** /-dʒɪˈnetɪkəlɪ/ adv.

orthognathous /ɔːˈθɒɡnəθəs/ adj. (of mammals, including man) having a jaw which does not project forwards and a facial angle approaching a right angle. [ORTHO- + Gk gnathos jaw]

orthogonal /ɔːˈθɒɡən(ə)l/ adj. of or involving right angles. [F f. orthogone (as ORTHO-, -GON)]

orthography /ɔːˈθɒɡrəfɪ/ n. (pl. -ies) 1 a correct or conventional spelling. b spelling with reference to its correctness (dreadful orthography). c the study or science of spelling. 2 a perspective projection used in maps and elevations in which the projection lines are parallel. b a map etc. so projected. □□ **orthographer** n. **orthographic** /-ˈɡræfɪk/ adj. **orthographical** /-ˈɡræfɪk(ə)l/ adj. **orthographically** /-ˈɡræfɪkəlɪ/ adv. [ME f. OF ortografie f. L orthographia f. Gk orthographia (as ORTHO-, -GRAPHY)]

orthopaedics /ˌɔːθəˈpiːdɪks/ n.pl. (treated as sing.) (US **-pedics**) the branch of medicine dealing with the correction of deformities of bones or muscles, orig. in children. □□ **orthopaedic** adj. **orthopaedist** n. [F orthopédie (as ORTHO-, pédie f. Gk paideia rearing of children)]

orthopteran /ɔːˈθɒptərən/ n. any insect of the order Orthoptera, with straight narrow forewings, and hind legs modified for jumping etc., including grasshoppers and crickets. □□ **orthopterous** adj. [ORTHO- + Gk pteros wing]

orthoptic /ɔːˈθɒptɪk/ adj. relating to the correct or normal use of the eyes. □□ **orthoptist** n. [ORTHO- + Gk optikos of sight: see OPTIC]

orthoptics /ɔːˈθɒptɪks/ n. Med. the study or treatment of irregularities of the eyes, esp. with reference to the eye-muscles.

orthorhombic /ˌɔːθəʊˈrɒmbɪk/ adj. Crystallog. (of a crystal) characterized by three mutually perpendicular axes which are unequal in length, as in topaz and talc.

orthotone /ˈɔːθəˌtəʊn/ adj. & n. —adj. (of a word) having an independent stress pattern, not enclitic nor proclitic. —n. a word of this kind.

ortolan /ˈɔːtələn/ n. (in full **ortolan bunting**) Zool. a small European bird, Emberiza hortulana, eaten as a delicacy. [F f. Prov., lit. gardener, f. L hortulanus f. hortulus dimin. of hortus garden]

Orton /ˈɔːt(ə)n/, John Kingsley ('Joe') (1933–67), English playwright, author of bizarre black comedies which include Entertaining Mr Sloane (1964), Loot (1965), and the posthumously performed What the Butler Saw (1969). Orton, a homosexual, was murdered by his lover, who then committed suicide.

Oruro /əˈrʊərəʊ/ the chief mining city of western Bolivia; pop. (1985) 178,400.

Orvieto /ɔːvɪˈeɪtəʊ/ a wine-producing area in Umbria in Italy.

Orwell /ˈɔːwel/, George (pseudonym of Eric Arthur Blair, 1903–50), English novelist and essayist with socialist preoccupations, an acute observer of social deprivation and injustice. Born in Bengal, he served with the Indian Imperial Police in Burma (1922–7), and his experiences are reflected in his first novel *Burmese Days* (1934). He resigned to escape from imperialism and 'man's dominion over man', returning to Europe to live in poverty as described in *Down and Out in Paris and London* (1933). Subsequent works include *The Road to Wigan Pier* (1937), an impassioned documentary of unemployment and proletarian life. In the Spanish Civil War he fought on the side of the Republicans and returned, demoralized and with a throat injury that permanently impeded his speech, to criticize Communist beliefs in *Homage to Catalonia* (1939) and the satire *Animal Farm* (1945). *Nineteen Eighty-four* (1949) is a nightmare view of a future totalitarian State; Orwell wrote it in an isolated house on the island of Jura in the Hebrides, financially secure with the royalties from *Animal Farm* but knowing that his life was drawing to its close because of the tuberculosis from which he shortly died.

Orwellian /ɔːˈwelɪən/ *adj.* of or characteristic of the writings of George Orwell, esp. with reference to the totalitarian development of the State as depicted in *1984* and *Animal Farm*.

-ory[1] /ərɪ/ *suffix* forming nouns denoting a place for a particular function (*dormitory*; *refectory*). □□ **-orial** /ˈɔːrɪəl/ *suffix* forming adjectives. [L *-oria, -orium*, sometimes via ONF and AF *-orie*, OF *-oire*]

-ory[2] /ərɪ/ *suffix* forming adjectives (and occasionally nouns) relating to or involving a verbal action (*accessory*; *compulsory*; *directory*). [L *-orius*, sometimes via AF *-ori(e)*, OF *-oir(e)*]

oryx /ˈɒrɪks/ *n.* any large straight-horned antelope of the genus *Oryx*, native to Africa and Arabia. [ME f. L f. Gk *orux* stonemason's pickaxe, f. its pointed horns]

OS *abbr.* **1** old style. **2** ordinary seaman. **3** (in the UK) Ordnance Survey. **4** outsize. **5** out of stock.

Os *symb. Chem.* the element osmium.

Osage orange /ˈəʊseɪdʒ/ *n.* **1** a hardy thorny tree, *Maclura pomifera*, of the US, bearing inedible wrinkled orange-like fruit. **2** the durable orange-coloured timber from this. [name of a N. American Indian tribe]

Osaka /əʊˈsɑːkə/ a port and commercial city of Japan, capital of Kinki region on Honshu Island; pop. (1987) 2,546,00.

Osborne /ˈɒzbɔːn/, John James (1929–　），English dramatist. His first play *Look back in Anger* (1956) startled contemporary taste with the vehemence of its tirades against middle-class values, and earned him the cachet 'angry young man'. Later plays include *The Entertainer* (1957) and *Luther* (1961).

Oscan /ˈɒskən/ *n.* & *adj.* —*n.* the ancient language of Campania in Italy, related to Latin and surviving only in inscriptions in an alphabet derived from Etruscan. —*adj.* relating to or written in Oscan. [L *Oscus*]

Oscar /ˈɒskə(r)/ *n.* any of several gold statuettes awarded annually by the Academy of Motion Picture Arts and Sciences (Hollywood, US) for excellence in film acting, directing, etc. Such 'Academy awards' have been made annually since 1928. [man's given name; the statuette is said to have reminded Margaret Herrick, then librarian of the Academy and later its Executive Director, of her Uncle Oscar (i.e. Oscar Pierce, American wheat and fruit grower)]

oscillate /ˈɒsɪˌleɪt/ *v.* **1** *intr.* & *tr.* **a** swing to and fro like a pendulum. **b** move to and fro between points. **2** *intr.* vacillate; vary between extremes of opinion, action, etc. **3** *intr. Physics* move with periodic regularity. **4** *intr. Electr.* (of a current) undergo high-frequency alternations as across a spark-gap or in a valve-transmitter circuit. **5** *intr.* (of a radio receiver) radiate electromagnetic waves owing to faulty operation. □□ **oscillation** /-ˈleɪʃ(ə)n/ *n.* **oscillator** *n.* **oscillatory** /ɒˈsɪlətərɪ, ˈɒsɪˌleɪtərɪ/ *adj.* [L *oscillare oscillat-* swing]

oscillo- /əˈsɪləʊ/ *comb. form* oscillation, esp. of electric current.

oscillogram /əˈsɪləˌɡræm/ *n.* a record obtained from an oscillograph.

oscillograph /əˈsɪləˌɡrɑːf/ *n.* a device for recording oscillations. □□ **oscillographic** /-ˈɡræfɪk/ *adj.* **oscillography** /-ˈlɒɡrəfɪ/ *n.*

oscilloscope /əˈsɪləˌskəʊp/ *n.* a device for viewing oscillations by a display on the screen of a cathode-ray tube. □□ **oscilloscopic** /-ˈskɒpɪk/ *adj.*

oscine /ˈɒsɪn/ *adj.* (also **oscinine** /ˈɒsɪˌniːn/) of or relating to the suborder Oscines of passerine birds including many of the songbirds. [L *oscen -cinis* songbird (as OB-, *canere* sing)]

oscitation /ˌɒsɪˈteɪʃ(ə)n/ *n. formal* **1** yawning; drowsiness. **2** inattention; negligence. [L *oscitatio* f. *oscitare* gape f. *os* mouth + *citare* move]

oscula *pl.* of OSCULUM.

oscular /ˈɒskjʊlə(r)/ *adj.* **1** of or relating to the mouth. **2** of or relating to kissing. [L *osculum* mouth, kiss, dimin. of *os* mouth]

osculate /ˈɒskjʊˌleɪt/ *v.* **1** *tr. Math.* (of a curve or surface) have contact of at least the second order with; have two branches with a common tangent, with each branch extending in both directions of the tangent. **2** *v.intr.* & *tr. joc.* kiss. **3** *intr. Biol.* (of a species etc.) be related through an intermediate species; have common characteristics with another or with each other. □□ **osculant** *adj.* **osculation** /-ˈleɪʃ(ə)n/ *n.* **osculatory** /ˈɒskjʊlətərɪ/ *adj.* [L *osculari* kiss (as OSCULAR)]

osculum /ˈɒskjʊləm/ *n.* (*pl.* **oscula** /-lə/) a mouthlike aperture, esp. of a sponge. [L: see OSCULAR]

-ose[1] /əʊs/ *suffix* forming adjectives denoting possession of a quality (*grandiose*; *verbose*). □□ **-osely** *suffix* forming adverbs. **-oseness** *suffix* forming nouns (cf. -OSITY). [from or after L *-osus*]

-ose[2] /əʊs/ *suffix Chem.* forming names of carbohydrates (*cellulose*; *sucrose*). [after GLUCOSE]

osier /ˈəʊzɪə(r)/ *n.* **1** any of various willows, esp. *Salix viminalis*, with long flexible shoots used in basketwork. **2** a shoot of a willow. □ **osier-bed** a place where osiers are grown. [ME f. OF: cf. med.L *auseria* osier-bed]

Osiris /əˈsaɪrɪs/ *Egyptian Mythol.* a divinity originally connected with fertility, known chiefly through the legend (made famous by Plutarch) of his death (at the hands of his brother Seth) and subsequent restoration to a new life as ruler of the afterlife. In the Old Kingdom he was identified with the deceased pharaoh, but eventually all the dead could claim the title 'the Osiris'.

-osis /əʊsɪs/ *suffix* (*pl.* **-oses** /əʊsiːz/) denoting a process or condition (*apotheosis*; *metamorphosis*), esp. a pathological state (*acidosis*; *neurosis*; *thrombosis*). [L f. Gk *-ōsis* suffix of verbal nouns]

-osity /ˈɒsɪtɪ/ *suffix* forming nouns from adjectives in *-ose* (see -OSE[1]) and *-ous* (*verbosity*; *curiosity*). [F *-osité* or L *-ositas -ositatis*: cf. -ITY]

Osler /ˈəʊzlə(r)/, Sir William (1849–1919), Canadian-born physician and classical scholar, professor of medicine at McGill, Pennsylvania, Johns Hopkins, and Oxford University, whose *Principles and Practice of Medicine* (1892) became the chosen clinical textbook for English-speaking medical students. At Johns Hopkins he instituted a model teaching unit in which clinical observation was combined with laboratory research, but, in spite of the often extravagant homage subsequently paid to Osler's memory, medical education in the US and elsewhere has followed a different model in which medical teachers are rarely engaged in medical practice.

Ösling /ˈɜːslɪŋ/ a region of the Ardennes Forest in the north of Luxembourg.

Oslo /ˈɒzləʊ/ the capital and chief port of Norway; pop. (est. 1988) 453,700.

Osman /ˈɒzmən/ (1259–1326) Turkish conqueror, founder of the Ottoman or Osmanli dynasty. After succeeding his father as leader of the Seljuk Turks in 1288 Osman reigned as sultan, conquering NW Asia Minor, and assumed the title of Emir in 1299.

Osmanli /ɒzˈmænlɪ, ɒs-/ *adj.* & *n.* = OTTOMAN. [Turk. f. *Osman* f. Arab. *'uṯmān* (see OTTOMAN) + *-li* adj. suffix]

osmic /ˈɒzmɪk/ *adj.* of or relating to odours or the sense of smell. □□ **osmically** *adv.* [Gk *osmē* smell, odour]

osmium /ˈɒzmɪəm/ *n. Chem.* a hard bluish-white transition element. It is thought to be the densest non-radioactive element, and was first isolated in 1804. Its main use is in alloys with platinum and related metals, where it contributes hardness; an alloy with iridium is used in fountain-pen nibs. Osmium tetroxide is commonly used for staining tissues in electron microscopy. ¶ Symb.: **Os**; atomic number 76. [Gk *osmē* smell (from the pungent smell of its tetroxide)]

osmosis /ɒzˈməʊsɪs/ n. **1** *Biochem.* the passage of a solvent from a less concentrated into a more concentrated solution through a semipermeable membrane, permeable to the solvent but not to the solute. It occurs partly because of interactions between the solute molecules and the solvent, and partly because the presence of the solute reduces the number of molecules of solvent per unit area on one side of the partition. The process continues until the pressure of the more concentrated solution exceeds that of the less concentrated; this pressure difference is known as the osmotic pressure. Osmosis was first studied by Jean Nollet (1700–70). It is now recognized as a very important mechanism in plant and animal physiology, playing a vital role in the passage of water into and out of living cells. It also has applications in the desalination of water. **2** any process by which something is acquired by absorption. □□ **osmotic** /-ˈmɒtɪk/ adj. **osmotically** /-ˈmɒtɪkəlɪ/ adv. [orig. *osmose*, after F f. Gk *ōsmos* push]

osmund /ˈɒzmənd/ n. (also **osmunda** /-də/) any fern of the genus *Osmunda*, esp. the royal fern, having large divided fronds. [ME f. AF, of uncert. orig.]

Osnabrück /ˈɒznəˌbrʊk/ a textile-manufacturing city in NW Germany; pop. (1987) 153,800.

osprey /ˈɒspreɪ, -prɪ/ n. (pl. **-eys**) **1** a large bird of prey, *Pandion haliaetus*, with a brown back and white markings, feeding on fish. Also called *fish-hawk*. **2** a plume on a woman's hat. [ME f. OF *ospres* app. ult. f. L *ossifraga* osprey f. *os* bone + *frangere* break]

Ossa[1] /ˈɒsə/ a lofty mountain in Thessaly, Greece, south of Olympus. (See PELION.)

Ossa[2] /ˈɒsə/, **Mount** the highest mountain on the island of Tasmania, rising to a height of 1,617 m (5,305 ft.).

ossein /ˈɒsɪɪn/ n. the collagen of bones. [L *osseus* (as OSSEOUS)]

osseous /ˈɒsɪəs/ adj. **1** consisting of bone. **2** having a bony skeleton. **3** ossified. [L *osseus* f. *os ossis* bone]

Ossian /ˈɒʃɪən, ˈɒsɪən/ anglicized form of Oisín, a legendary Irish warrior and bard, whose name became well known internationally in 1760–3 when the Scottish poet James Macpherson published what was later discovered to be his own verse as an alleged translation of 3rd-c. Gaelic tales.

ossicle /ˈɒsɪk(ə)l/ n. **1** *Anat.* any small bone, esp. of the middle ear. **2** a small piece of bonelike substance. [L *ossiculum* dimin. (as OSSEOUS)]

Ossie var. of AUSSIE.

ossify /ˈɒsɪˌfaɪ/ v.tr. & intr. (**-ies, -ied**) **1** turn into bone; harden. **2** make or become rigid, callous, or unprogressive. □□ **ossific** /ɒˈsɪfɪk/ adj. **ossification** /-fɪˈkeɪʃ(ə)n/ n. [F *ossifier* f. L *os ossis* bone]

osso bucco /ˌɒsəʊ ˈbʊkəʊ/ n. shin of veal containing marrowbone stewed in wine with vegetables. [It., = marrowbone]

ossuary /ˈɒsjʊərɪ/ n. (pl. **-ies**) **1** a receptacle for the bones of the dead; a charnel-house; a bone-urn. **2** a cave in which ancient bones are found. [LL *ossuarium* irreg. f. *os ossis* bone]

Ostade /ɒˈstɑːdə/, Adriaen van (1610–85), Dutch painter and engraver. Trained at Haarlem, possibly in Frans Hals's studio, his early work depicts lively scenes of peasants carousing or brawling in crowded taverns or barns, but he is known principally for his genre scenes. His brother and pupil, Isaak (1621–49), painted for only a decade but produced genre pictures—usually outdoor peasant scenes—that hint at a great talent cut short by his early death.

osteitis /ˌɒstɪˈaɪtɪs/ n. inflammation of the substance of a bone. [Gk *osteon* bone + -ITIS]

Ostend /ɒˈstend/ (Flemish **Oostende** /əʊˈstendə/, French **Ostende** /ɒˈstãd/) a seaport and resort on the coast of Belgium, with ferry links to Dover.

ostensible /ɒˈstensɪb(ə)l/ adj. concealing the real; professed (*his ostensible function was that of interpreter*). □□ **ostensibly** adv. [F f.

med.L *ostensibilis* f. L *ostendere ostens-* stretch out to view (as OB-, *tendere* stretch)]

ostensive /ɒˈstensɪv/ adj. **1** directly demonstrative. **2** (of a definition) indicating by direct demonstration that which is signified by a term. □□ **ostensively** adv. **ostensiveness** n. [LL *ostensivus* (as OSTENSIBLE)]

ostensory /ɒˈstensərɪ/ n. (pl. **-ies**) *RC Ch.* a receptacle for displaying the host to the congregation; a monstrance. [med.L *ostensorium* (as OSTENSIBLE)]

ostentation /ˌɒstenˈteɪʃ(ə)n/ n. **1** a pretentious and vulgar display esp. of wealth and luxury. **2** the attempt or intention to attract notice; showing off. □□ **ostentatious** adj. **ostentatiously** adv. [ME f. OF f. L *ostentatio -onis* f. *ostentare* frequent. of *ostendere*: see OSTENSIBLE]

osteo- /ˈɒstɪəʊ/ comb. form bone. [Gk *osteon*]

osteoarthritis /ˌɒstɪəʊɑːˈθraɪtɪs/ n. a degenerative disease of joint cartilage, esp. in the elderly. □□ **osteoarthritic** /-ˈθrɪtɪk/ adj.

osteogenesis /ˌɒstɪəʊˈdʒenɪsɪs/ n. the formation of bone. □□ **osteogenetic** /-dʒɪˈnetɪk/ adj.

osteology /ˌɒstɪˈɒlədʒɪ/ n. the study of the structure and function of the skeleton and bony structures. □□ **osteological** /-əˈlɒdʒɪk(ə)l/ adj. **osteologically** /-əˈlɒdʒɪkəlɪ/ adv. **osteologist** n.

osteomalacia /ˌɒstɪəʊməˈleɪʃɪə/ n. softening of the bones, often through a deficiency of vitamin D and calcium. □□ **osteomalacic** /-ˈlæsɪk/ adj. [mod.L (as OSTEO-, Gk *malakos* soft)]

osteomyelitis /ˌɒstɪəʊmaɪˈlaɪtɪs/ n. inflammation of the bone or of bone marrow, usu. due to infection.

osteopathy /ˌɒstɪˈɒpəθɪ/ n. the treatment of disease through the manipulation of bones (especially the spine) and muscles (their displacement or deformity being the supposed cause of problems). The system was founded by an American doctor, A. T. Still, who, after failing to persuade various medical schools to accept his ideas, established a new school in Missouri in 1892 to put them into practice. □□ **osteopath** /ˈɒstɪəˌpæθ/ n. **osteopathic** /ˌɒstɪəˈpæθɪk/ adj.

osteoporosis /ˌɒstɪəʊpəˈrəʊsɪs/ n. a condition of brittle and fragile bones caused by loss of bony tissue, esp. as a result of hormonal changes, or deficiency of calcium or vitamin D. [OSTEO- + Gk *poros* passage, pore]

Österreich see AUSTRIA.

Ostia /ˈɒstɪə/ the ancient city and harbour of Latium, said to be the first colony founded by Rome. It was buried, and its ruins were preserved, by the gradual silting up of the River Tiber.

ostinato /ˌɒstɪˈnɑːtəʊ/ n. (pl. **-os**) (often *attrib.*) *Mus.* a persistent phrase or rhythm repeated through all or part of a piece. [It., = OBSTINATE]

ostler /ˈɒslə(r)/ n. *Brit. hist.* a stableman at an inn. [f. earlier HOSTLER, *hosteler* f. AF *hostiler*, OF *(h)ostelier* (as HOSTEL)]

Ostmark /ˈɒstmɑːk/ n. *hist.* the chief monetary unit of former East Germany. [G, = east mark: see MARK[2]]

Ostpolitik /ˈɒstpɒlɪˌtiːk/ n. the foreign policy of many western European countries with reference to the Communist bloc. The term was used in the Federal Republic of Germany (West Germany) to describe the opening of relations with the Eastern bloc in the 1960s—a reversal of West Germany's refusal to recognize the legitimacy of the German Democratic Republic (East Germany). The policy was pursued with particular vigour by Willy Brandt (see entry). [G f. *Ost* east + *Politik* politics]

ostracize /ˈɒstrəˌsaɪz/ v.tr. (also **-ise**) **1** exclude (a person) from a society, favour, common privileges, etc.; refuse to associate with. **2** (esp. in ancient Athens) banish (a powerful or unpopular citizen) for five or ten years by popular vote. □□ **ostracism** /-ˌsɪz(ə)m/ n. [Gk *ostrakizō* f. *ostrakon* shell, potsherd (used to write a name on in voting)]

Ostrava /ˈɒstrəvə/ an industrial city in the Moravian lowlands of central Czechoslovakia; pop. (1986) 328,000.

ostrich /ˈɒstrɪtʃ/ n. **1** a large African swift-running flightless bird, *Struthio camelus*, with long legs and two toes on each foot. **2** a person who refuses to accept facts (from the notion that ostriches bury their heads in the sand when pursued, believing that they cannot then be seen). □ **ostrich-farm** a place that breeds ostriches for their feathers. **ostrich-plume** a feather or bunch of feathers of an ostrich. [ME f. OF *ostric*(h)*e* f. L *avis* bird + LL *struthio* f. Gk *strouthiōn* ostrich f. *strouthos* sparrow, ostrich]

Ostrogoth /ˈɒstrəˌgɒθ/ *n. hist.* a member of the Eastern branch of the Goths, who conquered Italy in the 5th–6th c. □□ **Ostrogothic** /-ˈgɒθɪk/ *adj.* [LL *Ostrogothi* (pl.) f. Gmc *austro-* (unrecorded) east + LL *Gothi* Goths: see GOTH]

Oswald /ˈɒzw(ə)ld/, St (d. 992), early English churchman. A Benedictine monk who rose first to become Bishop of Worcester and then Archbishop of York, St Oswald, along with St Dunstan, was responsible for the revival of the Church and of learning in 10th-c. England.

OT *abbr.* Old Testament.

-ot[1] /ət/ *suffix* forming nouns, orig. diminutives (*ballot; chariot; parrot*). [F]

-ot[2] /ət/ *suffix* forming nouns denoting persons (*patriot*), e.g. natives of a place (*Cypriot*). [F *-ote*, L *-ota*, Gk *-ōtēs*]

OTC *abbr.* (in the UK) Officers' Training Corps.

other /ˈʌðə(r)/ *adj., n. or pron., & adv.* —*adj.* **1** not the same as one or some already mentioned or implied; separate in identity or distinct in kind (*other people; use other means; I assure you, my reason is quite other*). **2 a** further; additional (*a few other examples*). **b** alternative of two (*open your other eye*) (cf. *every other*). **3** (prec. by *the*) that remains after all except the one or ones in question have been considered, eliminated, etc. (*must be in the other pocket; where are the other two?; the other three men left*). **4** (foll. by *than*) apart from; excepting (*any person other than you*). —*n. or pron.* (orig. an ellipt. use of the adj., now with pl. in *-s*) **1** an additional, different, or extra person, thing, example, etc. (*one or other of us will be there; some others have come*) (see also ANOTHER, each other). **2** (in pl.; prec. by *the*) the ones remaining (*where are the others?*). —*adv.* (usu. foll. by *than*) disp. otherwise (*cannot react other than angrily*). ¶ In this sense *otherwise* is standard except in less formal use. □ **no other** *archaic* nothing else (*I can do no other*). **of all others** out of the many possible or likely (*on this night of all others*). **on the other hand** see HAND. **the other day** (or **night** or **week** etc.) a few days etc. ago (*heard from him the other day*). **other-directed** governed by external circumstances and trends. **other half** *colloq.* one's wife or husband. **the other place** *Brit. joc.* Oxford University as regarded by Cambridge, and vice versa. **other ranks** soldiers other than commissioned officers. **the other thing** esp. *joc.* an unexpressed alternative (*if you don't like it, do the other thing*). **other things being equal** if conditions are or were alike in all but the point in question. **the other woman** a married man's mistress. **the other world** see WORLD. **someone** (or **something** or **somehow** etc.) **or other** some unspecified person, thing, manner, etc. [OE *ōther* f. Gmc]

otherness /ˈʌðənɪs/ *n.* **1** the state of being different; diversity. **2** a thing or existence other than the thing mentioned and the thinking subject.

otherwhere /ˈʌðəˌweə(r)/ *adv. archaic* or *poet.* elsewhere.

otherwise /ˈʌðəˌwaɪz/ *adv. & adj.* —*adv.* **1** else; or else; in the circumstances other than those considered etc. (*bring your umbrella, otherwise you will get wet*). **2** in other respects (*he is untidy, but otherwise very suitable*). **3** (often foll. by *than*) in a different way (*could not have acted otherwise; cannot react otherwise than angrily*). **4** as an alternative (*otherwise known as Jack*). —*adj.* **1** (*predic.*) in a different state (*the matter is quite otherwise*). **2** *archaic* that would otherwise exist (*their otherwise dullness*). □ **and** (or **or**) **otherwise** the negation or opposite of a specified thing) (*the merits or otherwise of the Bill; experiences pleasant and otherwise*). [OE *on ōthre wisan* (as OTHER, WISE[2])]

other-worldly /ˌʌðəˈwɜːldlɪ/ *adj.* **1** unworldly; impractical. **2** concerned with life after death etc. □□ **other-worldliness** *n.*

Othman /ˈɒθmən/ *var.* of OSMAN.

Otho /ˈəʊθəʊ/, Marcus Salvius (32–69), acclaimed Roman emperor on 15 Jan. 69 after he had procured the death of Galba in a conspiracy of the Praetorian Guard. The legions of the Rhine, however, had already chosen Vitellius and Otho committed suicide on 16 Apr. after they had defeated his own troops.

otic /ˈəʊtɪk/ *adj.* of or relating to the ear. [Gk *ōtikos* f. *ous ōtos* ear]

-otic /ˈɒtɪk/ *suffix* forming adjectives and nouns corresponding to nouns in *-osis*, meaning 'affected with or producing or resembling a condition in *-osis*' or 'a person affected with this' (*narcotic; neurotic; osmotic*). □□ **-otically** *suffix* forming adverbs. [from or after F *-otique* f. L f. Gk *-ōtikos* adj. suffix]

otiose /ˈəʊʃɪəʊs, ˈəʊt-, -əʊz/ *adj.* **1** serving no practical purpose; not required; functionless. **2** *archaic* indolent; futile. □□ **otiosely** *adv.* **otioseness** *n.* [L *otiosus* f. *otium* leisure]

Otis /ˈəʊtɪs/, Elisha Graves (1811–61), American inventor and manufacturer, who produced the first efficient elevator with a safety device (see LIFT). In 1852, while working in a bedstead factory in New York, he devised a mechanical hoist for carrying machinery to the upper floors, with a device to prevent it from falling even if the lifting cable broke.

otitis /ə'taɪtɪs/ *n.* inflammation of the ear. [mod.L (as OTO-)]

oto- /ˈəʊtəʊ/ *comb. form* ear. [Gk *ōto-* f. *ous ōtos* ear]

otolaryngology /ˌəʊtəˌlærɪnˈgɒlədʒɪ/ *n.* the study of diseases of the ear and throat. □□ **otolaryngological** /-gəˈlɒdʒɪk(ə)l/ *adj.* **otolaryngologist** *n.*

otolith /ˈəʊtəlɪθ/ *n.* any of the small particles of calcium carbonate in the inner ear. □□ **otolithic** /-ˈlɪθɪk/ *adj.*

otology /əʊˈtɒlədʒɪ/ *n.* the study of the anatomy and diseases of the ear. □□ **otological** /-təˈlɒdʒɪk(ə)l/ *adj.* **otologist** *n.*

Otomi /ˌəʊtəˈmiː/ *n.* (pl. same) **1** a member of an Indian people inhabiting parts of central Mexico. **2** their language. [Sp. f. Nahuatl]

otorhinolaryngology /ˌəʊtəˌraɪnəʊˌlærɪnˈgɒlədʒɪ/ *n.* the study of diseases of the ear, nose, and throat.

otoscope /ˈəʊtəˌskəʊp/ *n.* an apparatus for examining the eardrum and the passage leading to it from the ear. □□ **otoscopic** /-ˈskɒpɪk/ *adj.*

Otranto /ɒˈtræntəʊ/, **Strait of** a channel linking the Adriatic Sea with the Ionian Sea and separating the 'heel' of Italy from Albania.

ottava rima /ɒˌtɑːvə ˈriːmə/ *n.* a stanza of eight lines of 10 or 11 syllables, rhyming *abababcc*. [It., lit. eighth rhyme]

Ottawa /ˈɒtəwə/ the federal capital of Canada, on the Ottawa River (a tributary of the St Lawrence) and the Rideau Canal; pop. (1986) 300,760. Founded in 1827, the city received its present name in 1854 and was chosen as capital (of the United Provinces of Canada) by Queen Victoria in 1858.

otter /ˈɒtə(r)/ *n.* **1 a** any of several aquatic fish-eating mammals of the family Mustelidae, esp. of the genus *Lutra*, having strong claws and webbed feet. **b** its fur or pelt. **2** = *sea otter*. **3** a piece of board used to carry fishing-bait in water. **4** a type of paravane, esp. as used on non-naval craft. □ **otter-board** a device for keeping the mouth of a trawl-net open. **otter-dog** (or **-hound**) a dog of a breed used in otter-hunting. [OE *otr, ot*(*t*)*or* f. Gmc]

Otto /ˈɒtəʊ/, Nikolaus August (1832–91), German engineer who has given his name to the four-stroke cycle on which most internal-combustion engines work. This consists of an induction stroke during which a mixture of fuel and air is drawn in; a compression stroke, at the end of which the mixture is ignited by a spark; an expansion stroke during which hot gases force the piston up; an exhaust stroke when the cylinder contents are ejected to the atmosphere. Otto's patent of 1876 was invalidated ten years later when it was found that Beau de Rochas had described the successful cycle earlier, so enabling other manufacturers to adopt it.

otto *var.* of ATTAR.

Otto I /ˈɒtəʊ/ 'the Great' (912–73), German ruler. Succeeding his father Henry I as king of the Germans in 936, Otto carried out a policy of eastward expansion from his Saxon homeland and defeated the invading Hungarians in 955. He was crowned Holy Roman Emperor in 962 and began to establish a strong imperial presence in Italy to rival that of the papacy.

Ottoman /ˈɒtəmən/ *adj. & n.* —*adj. hist.* **1** of or concerning the dynasty of Osman or Othman I, the branch of the Turks to which he belonged, or the empire ruled by his descendants (see OTTOMAN EMPIRE). **2** Turkish. —*n.* (*pl.* **Ottomans**) an Ottoman person; a Turk. □ **the Ottoman Porte** see PORTE. [F f. Arab. *'uṭmānī* adj. of Othman (*'uṭmān*)]

ottoman /ˈɒtəmən/ n. (pl. **ottomans**) **1 a** an upholstered seat, usu. square and without a back or arms, sometimes a box with a padded top. **b** a footstool of similar design. **2** a heavy silken fabric with a mixture of cotton or wool. [F *ottomane* fem. (as OTTOMAN)]

Ottoman empire the Turkish empire, established in northern Anatolia by Osman or Othman at the end of the 13th c. and expanded by his successors to include all of Asia Minor and much of SE Europe. Ottoman power received a severe check with the invasion of Tamerlane in 1401, but expansion resumed several decades later, resulting in the capture of Constantinople in 1453. The empire reached its zenith under Suleiman in the mid-16th c., dominating the eastern Mediterranean and threatening central Europe, but thereafter it began to decline. Still powerful in the 17th c., it had, by the 19th c., become the 'sick man of Europe', eventually collapsing in the early 20th c.

Otway /ˈɒtweɪ/, Thomas (1652–85), English playwright. After failing as an actor he wrote for the stage and achieved success with his second play *Don Carlos* (1676), a tragedy in rhymed verse. He had a burning passion for the actress Mrs Elizabeth Barry who acted in his two great blank verse tragedies, *The Orphan* (1680) and *Venice Preserved* (1682), probably the finest tragedies of the period. He also wrote several comedies and poems.

OU abbr. Brit. **1** Open University. **2** Oxford University.

Ouagadougou /ˌwɑːɡəˈduːɡuː/ the capital of Burkina; pop. (1985) 442,223.

oubliette /ˌuːblɪˈet/ n. a secret dungeon with access only through a trapdoor. [F f. *oublier* forget]

ouch /aʊtʃ/ int. expressing pain or annoyance. [imit.: cf. G *autsch*]

Oudenarde /ˈuːdənɑːd/ (Flemish **Oudenaarde**, French **Audenarde** /ˌəʊdəˈnɑːr/) a town in eastern Flanders in Belgium, scene of a victory (1708) of allied British and Austrian troops under Marlborough and Prince Eugene over the French.

Oudh /aʊd/ a region of northern India, now part of Ultar Pradesh. Formerly an independent kingdom until it fell under Muslim rule in the 11th c. and later acquired a measure of independence in the early 18th c.; annexation by Britain (1856) was one of the causes of the Indian Mutiny in 1857.

ought[1] /ɔːt/ v.aux. (usu. foll. by *to* + infin.; present and past indicated by the following infin.) **1** expressing duty or rightness (*we ought to love our neighbours*). **2** expressing shortcoming (*it ought to have been done long ago*). **3** expressing advisability or prudence (*you ought to go for your own good*). **4** expressing esp. strong probability (*he ought to be there by now*). □ **ought not** the negative form of *ought* (*he ought not to have stolen it*). [OE *āhte*, past of *āgan* OWE]

ought[2] /ɔːt/ n. (also **aught**) colloq. a figure denoting nothing; nought. [perh. f. *an ought* for a NOUGHT; cf. ADDER]

ought[3] var. of AUGHT[1].

oughtn't /ˈɔːt(ə)nt/ contr. ought not.

Ouida /ˈwiːdə/ (pseudonym of Marie Louise de la Ramée 1839–1908) English novelist, who lived a lavish life mostly in Italy and wrote 45 novels, often set in a fashionable world far removed from reality. These include *Under Two Flags* (1867), *Folle-Farine* (1871), and *Two Little Wooden Shoes* (1874). She suffered frequent ridicule for her extravagantly portrayed heroes, miracles of strengh, courage, and beauty, but her faults were redeemed by her vigorous narrative.

Ouija /ˈwiːdʒə/ n. (in full **Ouija board**) propr. a board having letters or signs at its rim to which a planchette, movable pointer, or upturned glass points in answer to questions from attenders at a seance etc. [F *oui* yes + G *ja* yes]

Oulu /ˈaʊluː/ (Swedish **Uleåborg** /ˈuːliˌɔːˌbɔː(r)/) **1** a province in central Finland; pop. (1987) 433,715. **2** its capital city, a port on the Gulf of Bothnia; pop. (1987) 98,582.

ounce[1] /aʊns/ n. **1 a** a unit of weight of one-sixteenth of a pound avoirdupois (approx. 28 grams). ¶ Abbr.: **oz. b** a unit of one-twelfth of a pound troy or apothecaries' measure, equal to 480 grains (approx. 31 grams). **2** a small quantity. □ **fluid ounce** Brit. **1** a unit of capacity equal to one-twentieth of a pint (approx. 0.028 litre). **2** US a unit of capacity equal to one-sixteenth of a

pint (approx. 0.034 litre). [ME & OF *unce* f. L *uncia* twelfth part of pound or foot: cf. INCH[1]]

ounce[2] /aʊns/ n. an Asian wild cat, *Panthera uncia*, with leopard-like markings on a cream-coloured coat. Also called *mountain panther, snow leopard*. [ME f. OF *once* (earlier *lonce*) = It. *lonza* ult. f. L *lynx*: see LYNX]

OUP abbr. Oxford University Press.

our /ˈaʊə(r)/ poss.pron. (attrib.) **1** of or belonging to us or ourselves (*our house; our own business*). **2** of or belonging to all people (*our children's future*). **3** (esp. as **Our**) of Us the king or queen, emperor or empress, etc. (*given under Our seal*). **4** of us, the editorial staff of a newspaper etc. (*a foolish adventure in our view*). **5** Brit. colloq. indicating a relative, acquaintance, or colleague of the speaker (*our Barry works there*). □ **Our Father 1** the Lord's Prayer. **2** God. **Our Lady** the Virgin Mary. **Our Lord 1** Jesus Christ. **2** God. **Our Saviour** Jesus Christ. [OE *ūre* orig. genit. pl. of 1st pers. pron. = of us, later treated as possessive adj.]

-our[1] /ə(r)/ suffix var. of -OR[2] surviving in some nouns (*ardour; colour; valour*).

-our[2] /ə(r)/ suffix var. of -OR[1] (*saviour*).

ours /ˈaʊəz/ poss.pron. the one or ones belonging to or associated with us (*it is ours; ours are over there*). □ **of ours** of or belonging to us (*a friend of ours*).

ourself /aʊəˈself/ pron. archaic a word formerly used instead of *myself* by a sovereign, newspaper editorial staff, etc. (cf. OUR 3, 4).

ourselves /aʊəˈselvz/ pron. **1 a** emphat. form of WE or US (*we ourselves did it; made it ourselves; for our friends and ourselves*). **b** refl. form of US (*are pleased with ourselves*). **2** in our normal state of body or mind (*not quite ourselves today*). □ **be ourselves** act in our normal unconstrained manner. **by ourselves** see *by oneself*.

-ous /əs/ suffix **1** forming adjectives meaning 'abounding in, characterized by, of the nature of' (*envious; glorious; mountainous; poisonous*). **2** Chem. denoting a state of lower valence than the corresponding word in *-ic* (*ferrous*). □□ **-ously** suffix forming adverbs. **-ousness** suffix forming nouns. [from or after AF *-ous*, OF *-eus*, f. L *-osus*]

ousel var. of OUZEL.

oust /aʊst/ v.tr. **1** (usu. foll. by *from*) drive out or expel, esp. by forcing oneself into the place of. **2** (usu. foll. by *of*) Law put (a person) out of possession; deprive. [AF *ouster*, OF *oster* take away, f. L *obstare* oppose, hinder (as OB-, *stare* stand)]

ouster /ˈaʊstə(r)/ n. **1** ejection as a result of physical action, judicial process, or political upheaval. **2** esp. US dismissal, expulsion.

out /aʊt/ adv., prep., n., adj., int., & v. —adv. **1** away from or not in or at a place etc. (*keep him out; get out of here; my son is out in Canada*). **2** (forming part of phrasal verbs) **a** indicating dispersal away from a centre etc. (*hire out; share out; board out*). **b** indicating coming or bringing into the open for public attention etc. (*call out; send out; shine out; stand out*). **c** indicating a need for attentiveness (*watch out; look out; listen out*). **3** not in one's house, office, etc. (*went out for a walk*). **4** to or at an end; completely (*tired out; die out; out of bananas; fight it out; typed it out*). **5** (of a fire, candle, etc.) not burning. **6** in error (*was 3% out in my calculations*). **7** colloq. unconscious (*she was out for five minutes*). **8 a** (of a tooth) extracted. **b** (of a joint, bone, etc.) dislocated (*put his shoulder out*). **9** (of a party, politician, etc.) not in office. **10** (of a jury) considering its verdict in secrecy. **11** (of workers) on strike. **12** (of a secret) revealed. **13** (of a flower) blooming, open. **14** (of a book) published. **15** (of a star) visible after dark. **16** unfashionable (*turn-ups are out*). **17** (of a batsman, batter, etc.) no longer taking part as such, having been caught, stumped, etc. **18** not worth considering; rejected (*that idea is out*). **19** colloq. (prec. by superl.) known to exist (*the best game out*). **20** (of a stain, mark, etc.) not visible, removed (*painted out the sign*). **21** (of time) not spent working (*took five minutes out*). **22** (of a rash, bruise, etc.) visible. **23** (of the tide) at the lowest point. **24** Boxing unable to rise from the floor (*out for the count*). **25** archaic (of a young upper-class woman) introduced into society. **26** (in a radio conversation etc.) transmission ends (*over and out*). —prep. **1** out of (*looked out the window*). **2** archaic outside; beyond the limits of. —n. **1** colloq. a way of escape; an excuse. **2 (the outs)** the political party out of office. —*adj.* **1** (of a match) played away. **2** (of an island) away from the mainland. —*int.* a peremptory dismissal, reproach, etc. (*out, you scoundrel!*). —*v.* **1** *tr.* **a** put out. **b** *colloq.* eject forcibly. **2** *intr.* come or go out; emerge (*murder will out*). **3** *tr. Boxing* knock out. □ **at outs** at variance or enmity. **not out** *Cricket* (of a side or a batsman) not having been caught, bowled, etc. **out and about** (of a person, esp. after an illness) engaging in normal activity. **out and away** by far. **out and out 1** thorough; surpassing. **2** thoroughly; surpassingly. **out at elbows** see ELBOW. **out for** having one's interest or effort directed to; intent on. **out of 1** from within (*came out of the house*). **2** not within (*I was never out of England*). **3** from among (*nine people out of ten; must choose out of these*). **4** beyond the range of (*is out of reach*). **5** without or so as to be without (*was swindled out of his money; out of breath; out of sugar*). **6** from (*get money out of him*). **7** owing to; because of (*asked out of curiosity*). **8** by the use of (material) (*what did you make it out of?*). **9** at a specified distance from (a town, port, etc.) (*seven miles out of Liverpool*). **10** beyond (*something out of the ordinary*). **11** *Racing* (of an animal, esp. a horse) born of. **out of bounds** see BOUND². **out of date** see DATE¹. **out of doors** see DOOR. **out of drawing** see DRAWING. **out of hand** see HAND. **out of it** not included; forlorn. **out of order** see ORDER. **out of pocket** see POCKET. **out of the question** see QUESTION. **out of sorts** see SORT. **out of temper** see TEMPER. **out of this world** see WORLD. **out of the way** see WAY. **out to** keenly striving to do. **out to lunch** *colloq.* crazy, mad. **out with** an exhortation to expel or dismiss (an unwanted person). **out with it** say what you are thinking. [OE *ūt*, OHG *ūz*, rel. to Skr. *ud*-]

out- /aʊt/ *prefix* added to verbs and nouns, meaning: **1** so as to surpass or exceed (*outdo; outnumber*). **2** external, separate (*outline; outhouse; outdoors*). **3** out of; away from; outward (*outspread; outgrowth*).

out-act /aʊtˈækt/ *v.tr.* surpass in acting or performing.

outage /ˈaʊtɪdʒ/ *n.* a period of time during which a power-supply etc. is not operating.

out-and-outer /ˌaʊtəndˈaʊtə(r)/ *n. sl.* **1** a thorough or supreme person or thing. **2** an extremist.

outback /ˈaʊtbæk/ *n. esp. Austral.* the remote and usu. uninhabited inland districts. □□ **outbacker** *n.*

outbalance /aʊtˈbæləns/ *v.tr.* **1** count as more important than. **2** outweigh.

outbid /aʊtˈbɪd/ *v.tr.* (**-bidding**; *past* and *past part.* **-bid**) **1** bid higher than (another person) at an auction. **2** surpass in exaggeration etc.

outblaze /aʊtˈbleɪz/ *v.* **1** *intr.* blaze out or outwards. **2** *tr.* blaze more brightly than.

outboard /ˈaʊtbɔːd/ *adj., adv., & n.* —*adj.* **1** (of a motor) portable and attachable to the outside of the stern of a boat. **2** (of a boat) having an outboard motor. —*adj. & adv.* on, towards, or near the outside of esp. a ship, an aircraft, etc. —*n.* **1** an outboard engine. **2** a boat with an outboard engine.

outbound /ˈaʊtbaʊnd/ *adj.* outward bound.

outbrave /aʊtˈbreɪv/ *v.tr.* **1** outdo in bravery. **2** face defiantly.

outbreak /ˈaʊtbreɪk/ *n.* **1** a usu. sudden eruption of anger, war, disease, rebellion, etc. **2** an outcrop.

outbreeding /ˈaʊtˌbriːdɪŋ/ *n.* the theory or practice of breeding from animals not closely related. □□ **outbreed** *v.intr. & tr.* (*past and past part.* **-bred**).

outbuilding /ˈaʊtˌbɪldɪŋ/ *n.* a detached shed, barn, garage, etc. within the grounds of a main building; an outhouse.

outburst /ˈaʊtbɜːst/ *n.* **1** an explosion of anger etc., expressed in words. **2** an act or instance of bursting out. **3** an outcrop.

outcast /ˈaʊtkɑːst/ *n. & adj.* —*n.* **1** a person cast out from or rejected by his or her home, country, society, etc. **2** a tramp or vagabond. —*adj.* rejected; homeless; friendless.

outcaste *n. & v.* —*n.* /ˈaʊtkɑːst/ (also *attrib.*) **1** a person who has no caste, esp. in Hindu society. **2** a person who has lost his or her caste. —*v.tr.* /-ˈkɑːst/ cause (a person) to lose his or her caste.

outclass /aʊtˈklɑːs/ *v.tr.* **1** belong to a higher class than. **2** defeat easily.

outcome /ˈaʊtkʌm/ *n.* a result; a visible effect.

outcrop /ˈaʊtkrɒp/ *n. & v.* —*n.* **1 a** the emergence of a stratum, vein, or rock, at the surface. **b** a stratum etc. emerging. **2** a noticeable manifestation or occurrence. —*v.intr.* (**-cropped**, **-cropping**) appear as an outcrop; crop out.

outcry /ˈaʊtkraɪ/ *n.* (*pl.* **-ies**) **1** the act or an instance of crying out. **2** an uproar. **3** a noisy or prolonged public protest.

outdance /aʊtˈdɑːns/ *v.tr.* surpass in dancing.

outdare /aʊtˈdeə(r)/ *v.tr.* **1** outdo in daring. **2** overcome by daring.

outdated /aʊtˈdeɪtɪd/ *adj.* out of date; obsolete.

outdistance /aʊtˈdɪst(ə)ns/ *v.tr.* leave (a competitor) behind completely.

outdo /aʊtˈduː/ *v.tr.* (*3rd sing. present* **-does**; *past* **-did**; *past part.* **-done**) exceed or excel in doing or performance; surpass.

outdoor /ˈaʊtdɔː(r)/ *adj.* done, existing, or used out of doors.

outdoors /aʊtˈdɔːz/ *adv. & n.* —*adv.* in or into the open air; out of doors. —*n.* the world outside buildings; the open air.

outer /ˈaʊtə(r)/ *adj. & n.* —*adj.* **1** outside; external (*pierced the outer layer*). **2** farther from the centre or inside; relatively far out. **3** objective or physical, not subjective or psychical. —*n.* **1 a** the division of a target furthest from the bull's-eye. **b** a shot that strikes this. **2** an outer garment or part of one. **3** *Austral. sl.* the part of a racecourse outside the enclosure. **4** an outer container for transport or display. □ **the outer bar** see BAR¹. **outer garments** clothes worn over other clothes or outdoors. **Outer House** *Sc. Law* the hall where judges of the Court of Session sit singly. **outer man** (or **woman**) personal appearance; dress. **outer planet** a planet with an orbit outside the earth's. **outer space** the universe beyond the earth's atmosphere. **the outer world** people outside one's own circle. [ME f. OUT, replacing UTTER¹]

outermost /ˈaʊtəˌməʊst/ *adj.* furthest from the inside; the most far out.

outerwear /ˈaʊtəˌweə(r)/ *n.* = **outer garments**.

outface /aʊtˈfeɪs/ *v.tr.* disconcert or defeat by staring or by a display of confidence.

outfall /ˈaʊtfɔːl/ *n.* the mouth of a river, drain, etc., where it empties into the sea etc.

outfield /ˈaʊtfiːld/ *n.* **1** the outer part of a cricket or baseball field. **2** outlying land. □□ **outfielder** *n.*

outfight /aʊtˈfaɪt/ *v.tr.* fight better than; beat in a fight.

outfit /ˈaʊtfɪt/ *n. & v.* —*n.* **1** a set of clothes worn or esp. designed to be worn together. **2** a complete set of equipment etc. for a specific purpose. **3** *colloq.* a group of people regarded as a unit, organization, etc.; a team. —*v.tr.* (also *refl.*) (**-fitted**, **-fitting**) provide with an outfit, esp. of clothes.

outfitter /ˈaʊtˌfɪtə(r)/ *n.* a supplier of equipment, esp. of men's clothing; a haberdasher.

outflank /aʊtˈflæŋk/ *v.tr.* **1 a** extend one's flank beyond that of (an enemy). **b** outmanoeuvre (an enemy) in this way. **2** get the better of; confound (an opponent).

outflow /ˈaʊtfləʊ/ *n.* **1** an outward flow. **2** the amount that flows out.

outfly /aʊtˈflaɪ/ *v.tr.* (**-flies**; *past* **-flew**; *past part.* **-flown**) **1** surpass in flying. **2** fly faster or farther than.

outfox /aʊtˈfɒks/ *v.tr. colloq.* outwit.

outgeneral /aʊtˈdʒenər(ə)l/ *v.tr.* (**-generalled**, **-generalling**; US **-generaled**, **-generaling**) **1** outdo in generalship. **2** get the better of by superior strategy or tactics.

outgo /aʊtˈgəʊ/ *v. & n.* —*v.tr.* (*3rd sing. present* **-goes**; *past* **-went**; *past part.* **-gone**) *archaic* go faster than; surpass. —*n.* /ˈaʊtgəʊ/ (*pl.* **-goes**) expenditure of money, effort, etc.

outgoing /ˈaʊtˌgəʊɪŋ/ *adj. & n.* —*adj.* **1** friendly; sociable; extrovert. **2** retiring from office. **3** going out or away. —*n.* **1** (in *pl.*) expenditure. **2** the act or an instance of going out.

outgrow /aʊtˈgrəʊ/ *v.tr.* (*past* **-grew**; *past part.* **-grown**) **1** grow too big for (one's clothes). **2** leave behind (a childish habit, taste, ailment, etc.) as one matures. **3** grow faster or taller than (a person, plant, etc.). □ **outgrow one's strength** become lanky and weak through too rapid growth.

outgrowth /ˈaʊtɡrəʊθ/ n. **1** something that grows out. **2** an offshoot; a natural product. **3** the process of growing out.

outguess /aʊtˈɡes/ v.tr. guess correctly what is intended by (another person).

outgun /aʊtˈɡʌn/ v.tr. (**-gunned**, **-gunning**) **1** surpass in military or other power or strength. **2** shoot better than.

outhouse /ˈaʊthaʊs/ n. **1** a building, esp. a shed, lean-to, barn, etc. built next to or in the grounds of a house. **2** US an outdoor lavatory.

outing /ˈaʊtɪŋ/ n. **1** a short holiday away from home, esp. of one day or part of a day; a pleasure-trip, an excursion. **2** any brief journey from home. **3** an appearance in an outdoor match, race, etc. [OUT v. = put out, go out + -ING¹]

outjockey /aʊtˈdʒɒkɪ/ v.tr. (**-eys**, **-eyed**) outwit by adroitness or trickery.

outjump /aʊtˈdʒʌmp/ v.tr. surpass in jumping.

outlander /ˈaʊtˌlændə(r)/ n. a foreigner, alien, or stranger.

outlandish /aʊtˈlændɪʃ/ adj. **1** looking or sounding foreign. **2** bizarre, strange, unfamiliar. □□ **outlandishly** adv. **outlandishness** n. [OE ūtlendisc f. ūtland foreign country f. OUT + LAND]

outlast /aʊtˈlɑːst/ v.tr. last longer than (a person, thing, or duration) (*outlasted its usefulness*).

outlaw /ˈaʊtlɔː/ n. & v. —n. **1** a fugitive from the law. **2** hist. a person deprived of the protection of the law. —v.tr. **1** declare (a person) an outlaw. **2** make illegal; proscribe (a practice etc.). □ **outlaw strike** an unofficial strike. □□ **outlawry** n. [OE ūtlaga, ūtlagian f. ON ūtlagi f. ūtlagr outlawed, rel. to OUT, LAW]

outlay /ˈaʊtleɪ/ n. what is spent on something.

outlet /ˈaʊtlet, -lɪt/ n. **1** a means of exit or escape. **2** (usu. foll. by *for*) a means of expression (of a talent, emotion, etc.) (*find an outlet for tension*). **3** an agency, distributor, or market for goods (*a new retail outlet in China*). **4** US a power point. [ME f. OUT- + LET¹]

outlier /ˈaʊtˌlaɪə(r)/ n. **1** (also *attrib.*) an outlying part or member. **2** Geol. a younger rock formation isolated in older rocks. **3** Statistics a result differing greatly from others in the same sample.

outline /ˈaʊtlaɪn/ n. & v. —n. **1** a rough draft of a diagram, plan, proposal, etc. **2 a** a précis of a proposed novel, article, etc. **b** a verbal description of essential parts only; a summary. **3** a sketch containing only contour lines. **4** (in *sing.* or *pl.*) **a** lines enclosing or indicating an object (*the outline of a shape under the blankets*). **b** a contour. **c** an external boundary. **5** (in *pl.*) the main features or general principles (*the outlines of a plan*). **6** the representation of a word in shorthand. —v.tr. **1** draw or describe in outline. **2** mark the outline of. □ **in outline** sketched or represented as an outline.

outlive /aʊtˈlɪv/ v.tr. **1** live longer than (another person). **2** live beyond (a specified date or time). **3** live through (an experience).

outlook /ˈaʊtlʊk/ n. **1** the prospect for the future (*the outlook is bleak*). **2** one's mental attitude or point of view (*narrow in their outlook*). **3** what is seen on looking out.

outlying /ˈaʊtˌlaɪɪŋ/ adj. situated far from a centre; remote.

outmanoeuvre /ˌaʊtməˈnuːvə(r)/ v.tr. (US **-maneuver**) **1** use skill and cunning to secure an advantage over (a person). **2** outdo in manoeuvring.

outmatch /aʊtˈmætʃ/ v.tr. be more than a match for (an opponent etc.); surpass.

outmeasure /aʊtˈmeʒə(r)/ v.tr. exceed in quantity or extent.

outmoded /aʊtˈməʊdɪd/ adj. **1** no longer in fashion. **2** obsolete. □□ **outmodedly** adv. **outmodedness** n.

outmost /ˈaʊtməʊst/ adj. **1** outermost, furthest. **2** uttermost. [ME, var. of utmost UTMOST]

outnumber /aʊtˈnʌmbə(r)/ v.tr. exceed in number.

outpace /aʊtˈpeɪs/ v.tr. **1** go faster than. **2** outdo in a contest.

out-patient /ˈaʊtˌpeɪʃ(ə)nt/ n. a hospital patient who is resident at home but attends regular appointments in hospital.

outperform /ˌaʊtpəˈfɔːm/ v.tr. **1** perform better than. **2** surpass in a specified field or activity. □□ **outperformance** n.

outplacement /ˈaʊtˌpleɪsmənt/ n. the act or process of finding new employment for esp. executive workers who have been dismissed or made redundant.

outplay /aʊtˈpleɪ/ v.tr. surpass in playing; play better than.

outpoint /aʊtˈpɔɪnt/ v.tr. (in various sports, esp. boxing) score more points than.

outport /ˈaʊtpɔːt/ n. **1** a subsidiary port. **2** Can. a small remote fishing village.

outpost /ˈaʊtpəʊst/ n. **1** a detachment set at a distance from the main body of an army, esp. to prevent surprise. **2** a distant branch or settlement. **3** the furthest territory of an (esp. the British) empire.

outpouring /ˈaʊtˌpɔːrɪŋ/ n. **1** (usu. in *pl.*) a copious spoken or written expression of emotion. **2** what is poured out.

output /ˈaʊtpʊt/ n. & v. —n. **1** the product of a process, esp. of manufacture, or of mental or artistic work. **2** the quantity or amount of this. **3** the printout, results, etc. supplied by a computer. **4** the power etc. delivered by an apparatus. **5** a place where energy, information, etc. leaves a system. —v.tr. (**-putting**; *past* and *past part.* **-put** or **-putted**) **1** put or send out. **2** (of a computer) supply (results etc.).

outrage /ˈaʊtreɪdʒ/ n. & v. —n. **1** an extreme or shocking violation of others' rights, sentiments, etc. **2** a gross offence or indignity. **3** fierce anger or resentment (*a feeling of outrage*). —v.tr. **1** subject to outrage. **2** injure, insult, etc. flagrantly. **3** shock and anger. [ME f. OF outrage f. outrer exceed f. outre f. L ultra beyond]

outrageous /aʊtˈreɪdʒəs/ adj. **1** immoderate. **2** shocking. **3** grossly cruel. **4** immoral, offensive. □□ **outrageously** adv. **outrageousness** n. [ME f. OF outrageus (as OUTRAGE)]

outran past of OUTRUN.

outrange /aʊtˈreɪndʒ/ v.tr. (of a gun or its user) have a longer range than.

outrank /aʊtˈræŋk/ v.tr. **1** be superior in rank to. **2** take priority over.

outré /ˈuːtreɪ/ adj. **1** outside the bounds of what is usual or proper. **2** eccentric or indecorous. [F, past part. of outrer: see OUTRAGE]

outreach v. & n. —v.tr. /aʊtˈriːtʃ/ **1** reach further than. **2** surpass. **3** poet. stretch out (one's arms etc.). —n. /ˈaʊtriːtʃ/ **1 a** any organization's involvement with or influence in the community, esp. in the context of social welfare. **b** the extent of this. **2** the extent or length of reaching out (*an outreach of 38 metres*).

out-relief /ˈaʊtrɪˌliːf/ n. Brit. hist. assistance given to very poor people not living in a workhouse etc.; outdoor relief.

outride /aʊtˈraɪd/ v.tr. (*past* **-rode**; *past part.* **-ridden**) **1** ride better, faster, or further than. **2** (of a ship) come safely through (a storm etc.).

outrider /ˈaʊtˌraɪdə(r)/ n. **1** a mounted attendant riding ahead of, or with, a carriage etc. **2** a motor cyclist acting as a guard in a similar manner. **3** US a herdsman keeping cattle within bounds. □□ **outriding** n.

outrigged /ˈaʊtrɪɡd/ adj. (of a boat etc.) having outriggers.

outrigger /ˈaʊtˌrɪɡə(r)/ n. **1** a beam, spar, or framework, rigged out and projecting from or over a ship's side for various purposes. **2** a similar projecting beam etc. in a building. **3** a log etc. fixed parallel to a canoe to stabilize it. **4 a** an extension of the splinter-bar of a carriage etc. to enable another horse to be harnessed outside the shafts. **b** a horse harnessed in this way. **5 a** an iron bracket bearing a rowlock attached horizontally to a boat's side to increase the leverage of the oar. **b** a boat fitted with these. [OUT- + RIG¹: perh. partly after obs. (Naut.) outligger]

outright adv. & adj. —adv. /aʊtˈraɪt/ **1** altogether, entirely (*proved outright*). **2** not gradually, nor by degrees, nor by instalments (*bought it outright*). **3** without reservation, openly (*denied the charge outright*). —adj. /ˈaʊtraɪt/ **1** downright, direct, complete (*their resentment turned to outright anger*). **2** undisputed, clear (*the outright winner*). □□ **outrightness** n.

outrival /aʊtˈraɪv(ə)l/ v.tr. (**-rivalled, -rivalling**; US **-rivaled, -rivaling**) outdo as a rival.

outrode past of OUTRIDE.

outrun v. & n. —v.tr. /aʊtˈrʌn/ (**-running**; past **-ran**; past part. **-run**) **1 a** run faster or farther than. **b** escape from. **2** go beyond (a specified point or limit). —n. /ˈaʊtrʌn/ Austral. a sheep-run distant from its homestead.

outrush /ˈaʊtrʌʃ/ n. **1** a rushing out. **2** a violent overflow.

outsail /aʊtˈseɪl/ v.tr. sail better or faster than.

outsat past and past part. of OUTSIT.

outsell /aʊtˈsel/ v.tr. (past and past part. **-sold**) **1** sell more than. **2** be sold in greater quantities than.

outset /ˈaʊtset/ n. the start, beginning. □ **at** (or **from**) **the outset** from the beginning.

outshine /aʊtˈʃaɪn/ v.tr. (past and past part. **-shone**) shine brighter than; surpass in ability, excellence, etc.

outshoot /aʊtˈʃuːt/ v.tr. (past and past part. **-shot**) **1** shoot better or further than (another person). **2** esp. US score more goals, points, etc. than (another player or team).

outside n., adj., adv., & prep. —n. /aʊtˈsaɪd, ˈaʊtsaɪd/ **1** the external side or surface; the outer parts (painted blue on the outside). **2** the external appearance; the outward aspect of a building etc. **3** (of a path) the side away from the wall or next to the road. **4** (also attrib.) all that is without; the world as distinct from the thinking subject (learn about the outside world; viewed from the outside the problem is simple). **5** a position on the outer side (the gate opens from the outside). **6** colloq. the highest computation (it is a mile at the outside). **7** an outside player in football etc. **8** (in pl.) the outer sheets of a ream of paper. —adj. /ˈaʊtsaɪd/ **1** of or on or nearer the outside; outer. **2 a** not of or belonging to some circle or institution (outside help; outside work). **b** (of a broker) not a member of the Stock Exchange. **3** (of a chance etc.) remote; very unlikely. **4** (of an estimate etc.) the greatest or highest possible (the outside price). **5** (of a player in football etc.) positioned nearest to the edge of the field. —adv. /aʊtˈsaɪd/ **1** on or to the outside. **2** in or to the open air. **3** not within or enclosed or included. **4** sl. not in prison. —prep. /aʊtˈsaɪd/ (also disp. foll. by of) **1** not in; to or at the exterior of (meet me outside the post office). **2** external to, not included in, beyond the limits of (outside the law). □ **at the outside** (of an estimate etc.) at the most. **get outside of** sl. eat or drink. **outside and in** outside and inside. **outside broadcast** Brit. a broadcast made on location and not in a studio. **outside edge** (on an ice-skate) each of the edges facing outwards when both feet are together. **outside in** = inside out. **outside interest** a hobby; an interest not connected with one's work or normal way of life. **outside seat** a seat nearer the end of a row. **outside track** the outside lane of a sports track etc. which is longer because of the curve.

outsider /aʊtˈsaɪdə(r)/ n. **1 a** a non-member of some circle, party, profession, etc. **b** an uninitiated person, a layman. **2** a person without special knowledge, breeding, etc., or not fit to mix with good society. **3** a competitor, applicant, etc. thought to have little chance of success.

outsit /aʊtˈsɪt/ v.tr. (**-sitting**; past and past part. **-sat**) sit longer than (another person or thing).

outsize /ˈaʊtsaɪz/ adj. & n. —adj. **1** unusually large. **2** (of garments etc.) of an exceptionally large size. —n. an exceptionally large person or thing, esp. a garment. □□ **outsizeness** n.

outskirts /ˈaʊtskɜːts/ n.pl. the outer border or fringe of a town, district, subject, etc.

outsmart /aʊtˈsmaːt/ v.tr. colloq. outwit, be cleverer than.

outsold past and past part. of OUTSELL.

outspan /ˈaʊtspæn/ v. & n. S.Afr. —v. (**-spanned, -spanning**) **1** tr. (also absol.) unharness (animals) from a cart, plough, etc. **2** intr. break a wagon journey. —n. a place for grazing or encampment. [S.Afr. Du. uitspannen unyoke]

outspend /aʊtˈspend/ v.tr. (past and past part. **-spent**) spend more than (one's resources or another person).

outspoken /aʊtˈspəʊkən/ adj. given to or involving plain speaking; frank in stating one's opinions. □□ **outspokenly** adv. **outspokenness** n.

outspread adj. & v. —adj. /aʊtˈspred, ˈaʊtspred/ spread out; fully extended or expanded. —v.tr. & intr. /aʊtˈspred/ (past and past part. **-spread**) spread out; expand.

outstanding /aʊtˈstændɪŋ/ adj. **1 a** conspicuous, eminent, esp. because of excellence. **b** (usu. foll. by at, in) remarkable in (a specified field). **2** (esp. of a debt) not yet settled (£200 still outstanding). □□ **outstandingly** adv.

outstare /aʊtˈsteə(r)/ v.tr. **1** outdo in staring. **2** abash by staring.

outstation /ˈaʊtˌsteɪʃ(ə)n/ n. **1** a branch of an organization, enterprise, or business in a remote area or at a considerable distance from headquarters. **2** esp. Austral. & NZ part of a farming estate separate from the main estate.

outstay /aʊtˈsteɪ/ v.tr. **1** stay beyond the limit of (one's welcome, invitation, etc.). **2** stay or endure longer than (another person etc.).

outstep /aʊtˈstep/ v.tr. (**-stepped, -stepping**) step outside or beyond.

outstretch /ˈaʊtstretʃ, aʊtˈstretʃ/ v.tr. **1** (usu. as **outstretched** adj.) reach out or stretch out (esp. one's hands or arms). **2** reach or stretch further than.

outstrip /aʊtˈstrɪp/ v.tr. (**-stripped, -stripping**) **1** pass in running etc. **2** surpass in competition or relative progress or ability.

out-swinger /ˈaʊtˌswɪŋə(r)/ n. a ball that swings away from the batsman.

out-take /ˈaʊtteɪk/ n. a length of film or tape rejected in editing.

out-talk /aʊtˈtɔːk/ v.tr. outdo or overcome in talking.

out-think /aʊtˈθɪŋk/ v.tr. (past and past part. **-thought**) outwit; outdo in thinking.

out-thrust adj., v., & n. —adj. /ˈaʊtθrʌst/ extended; projected (ran forward with out-thrust arms). —v.tr. /aʊtˈθrʌst/ (past and past part. **-thrust**) thrust out. —n. /ˈaʊtθrʌst/ **1** the act or an instance of thrusting forcibly outward. **2** the act or an instance of becoming prominent or noticeable.

out-top /aʊtˈtɒp/ v.tr. (**-topped, -topping**) surmount, surpass in height, extent, etc.

out-tray /ˈaʊttreɪ/ n. a tray for outgoing documents, letters, etc.

out-turn /ˈaʊttɜːn/ n. **1** the quantity produced. **2** the result of a process or sequence of events.

outvalue /aʊtˈvæljuː/ v.tr. (**-values, -valued, -valuing**) be of greater value than.

outvote /aʊtˈvəʊt/ v.tr. defeat by a majority of votes.

outwalk /aʊtˈwɔːk/ v.tr. **1** outdo in walking. **2** walk beyond.

outward /ˈaʊtwəd/ adj., adv., & n. —adj. **1** situated on or directed towards the outside. **2** going out (on the outward voyage). **3** bodily, external, apparent, superficial (in all outward respects). **4** archaic outer (the outward man). —adv. (also **outwards**) in an outward direction; towards the outside. —n. the outward appearance of something; the exterior. □ **outward bound 1** (of a ship, passenger, etc.) going away from home. **2** (**Outward Bound**) (in the UK) a movement to provide adventure training, naval training, and other outdoor activities for young people. **outward form** appearance. **outward things** the world around us. **to outward seeming** apparently. □□ **outwardly** adv. [OE ūtweard (as OUT, -WARD)]

outwardness /ˈaʊtwədnɪs/ n. **1** external existence; objectivity. **2** an interest or belief in outward things, objective-mindedness.

outwards var. of OUTWARD adv.

outwash /ˈaʊtwɒʃ/ n. the material carried from a glacier by melt water and deposited beyond the moraine.

outwatch /aʊtˈwɒtʃ/ v.tr. **1** watch more than or longer than. **2** archaic keep awake beyond the end of (night etc.).

outwear v. & n. —v.tr. /aʊtˈweə(r)/ (past **-wore**; past part. **-worn**) **1** exhaust; wear out; wear away. **2** live or last beyond the duration of. **3** (as **outworn** adj.) out of date, obsolete. —n. /ˈaʊtweə(r)/ outer clothing.

outweigh /aʊtˈweɪ/ v.tr. exceed in weight, value, importance, or influence.

outwent past of OUTGO.

outwit /aʊtˈwɪt/ v.tr. (**-witted**, **-witting**) be too clever or crafty for; deceive by greater ingenuity.

outwith /aʊtˈwɪθ/ prep. Sc. outside, beyond.

outwore past of OUTWEAR.

outwork /ˈaʊtwɜːk/ n. **1** an advanced or detached part of a fortification. **2** work done outside the shop or factory which supplies it. □□ **outworker** n. (in sense 2).

outworn past part. of OUTWEAR.

ouzel /ˈuːz(ə)l/ n. (also **ousel**) **1** = ring ouzel (see RING¹). **2** = water ouzel. **3** archaic a blackbird. [OE ōsle blackbird, of unkn. orig.]

ouzo /ˈuːzəʊ/ n. (pl. **-os**) a Greek aniseed-flavoured spirit. [mod.Gk]

ova pl. of OVUM.

oval /ˈəʊv(ə)l/ adj. & n. —adj. **1** egg-shaped, ellipsoidal. **2** having the outline of an egg, elliptical. —n. **1** an egg-shaped or elliptical closed curve. **2** any object with an oval outline. **3** Austral. a ground for Australian Rules football. □ **Oval Office** the office of the US President in the White House. □□ **ovality** /-ˈvælɪtɪ/ n. **ovally** adv. **ovalness** n. [med.L ovalis (as OVUM)]

Ovamboland /əʊˈvæmbəʊˌlænd/ the homeland of the Ovambo people of northern Namibia.

ovary /ˈəʊvərɪ/ n. (pl. **-ies**) **1** each of the female reproductive organs in which ova are produced. **2** the hollow base of the carpel of a flower, containing one or more ovules. □□ **ovarian** /əˈveərɪən/ adj. **ovariectomy** /-rɪˈektəmɪ/ n. (pl. **-ies**) (in sense 1). **ovariotomy** /-rɪˈɒtəmɪ/ n. (pl. **-ies**) (in sense 1). **ovaritis** /-ˈraɪtɪs/ n. (in sense 1). [mod.L ovarium (as OVUM)]

ovate /ˈəʊveɪt/ adj. Biol. egg-shaped as a solid or in outline; oval. [L ovatus (as OVUM)]

ovation /əʊˈveɪʃ(ə)n/ n. **1** an enthusiastic reception, esp. spontaneous and sustained applause. **2** Rom. Antiq. a lesser form of triumph. □ **standing ovation** prolonged applause during which the crowd or audience rise to their feet. □□ **ovational** adj. [L ovatio f. ovare exult]

oven /ˈʌv(ə)n/ n. **1** an enclosed compartment of brick, stone, or metal for cooking food. **2** a chamber for heating or drying. **3** a small furnace or kiln used in chemistry, metallurgy, etc. □ **oven-ready** (of food) prepared before sale so as to be ready for immediate cooking in the oven. [OE ofen f. Gmc]

ovenbird /ˈʌv(ə)nˌbɜːd/ n. any Central or S. American bird of the family Furnariidae, many of which make domed nests.

ovenproof /ˈʌv(ə)nˌpruːf/ adj. suitable for use in an oven; heat-resistant.

ovenware /ˈʌv(ə)nˌweə(r)/ n. dishes that can be used for cooking food in the oven.

over /ˈəʊvə(r)/ adv., prep., n., & adj. —adv. expressing movement or position or state above or beyond something stated or implied: **1** outward and downward from a brink or from any erect position (knocked the man over). **2** so as to cover or touch a whole surface (paint it over). **3** so as to produce a fold, or reverse a position; with the effect of being upside down. **4 a** across a street or other space (decided to cross over; came over from America). **b** for a visit etc. (invited them over last night). **5** with transference or change from one hand or part to another (went over to the enemy; swapped them over). **6** with motion above something; so as to pass across something (climb over; fly over; boil over). **7** from beginning to end with repetition or detailed concentration (think it over; did it six times over). **8** in excess; more than is right or required (left over). **9** for or until a later time (hold it over). **10** at an end; settled (the crisis is over; all is over between us). **11** (in full **over to you**) (as int.) (in radio conversations etc.) said to indicate that it is the other person's turn to speak. **12** (as int.) Cricket an umpire's call to change ends. —prep. **1** above, in, or to a position higher than; upon. **2** out and down from; down from the edge of (fell over the cliff). **3** so as to cover (a hat over his eyes). **4** above and across; so as to clear (flew over the North Pole; a bridge over the Thames). **5** concerning; engaged with; as a result of; while

occupied with (laughed over a good joke; fell asleep over the newspaper). **6 a** in superiority of; superior to; in charge of (a victory over the enemy; reign over three kingdoms). **b** in preference to. **7** divided by. **8 a** throughout; covering the extent of (travelled over most of Africa; a blush spread over his face). **b** so as to deal with completely (went over the plans). **9 a** for the duration of (stay over Saturday night). **b** at any point during the course of (I'll do it over the weekend). **10** beyond; more than (bids of over £50; are you over 18?). **11** transmitted by (heard it over the radio). **12** in comparison with (gained 20% over last year). **13** having recovered from (am now over my cold; will get over it in time). —n. Cricket **1** a sequence of balls (now usu. six), bowled from one end of the pitch. **2** play resulting from this (a maiden over). —adj. (see also OVER-). **1** upper, outer. **2** superior. **3** extra. □ **begin** (or **start** etc.) **over** US begin again. **get it over with** do or undergo something unpleasant etc. so as to be rid of it. **give over** (usu. as int.) colloq. stop talking. **not over** not very; not at all (not over friendly). **over again** once again, again from the beginning. **over against** in an opposite situation to; adjacent to, in contrast with. **over-age** over a certain age limit. **over all** taken as a whole. **over and above** in addition to; not to mention (£100 over and above the asking price). **over and over** so that the same thing or the same point comes up again and again (said it over and over; rolled it over and over). **over the fence** Austral. & NZ sl. unreasonable; unfair; indecent. **over one's head** see HEAD. **over the hill** see HILL. **over the moon** see MOON. **over-the-top** colloq. (esp. of behaviour, dress, etc.) outrageous, excessive. **over the way** (in a street etc.) facing or opposite. [OE ofer f. Gmc]

over- /ˈəʊvə(r)/ prefix added to verbs, nouns, adjectives, and adverbs, meaning: **1** excessively; to an unwanted degree (overheat; overdue). **2** upper, outer, extra (overcoat; overtime). **3** 'over' in various senses (overhang; overshadow). **4** completely, utterly (overawe; overjoyed).

over-abundant /ˌəʊvərəˈbʌnd(ə)nt/ adj. in excessive quantity. □□ **over-abound** /-ˈbaʊnd/ v.intr. **over-abundance** n. **over-abundantly** adv.

overachieve /ˌəʊvərəˈtʃiːv/ v. **1** intr. do more than might be expected (esp. scholastically). **2** tr. achieve more than (an expected goal or objective etc.). □□ **overachievement** n. **overachiever** n.

overact /ˌəʊvərˈækt/ v.tr. & intr. act in an exaggerated manner.

over-active /ˌəʊvərˈæktɪv/ adj. excessively active. □□ **over-activity** /-ˈtɪvɪtɪ/ n.

overage /ˈəʊvərɪdʒ/ n. a surplus or excess, esp. an amount greater than estimated.

overall adj., adv., & n. —adj. /ˈəʊvərɔːl/ **1** from end to end (overall length). **2** total, inclusive of all (overall cost). —adv. /ˌəʊvərˈɔːl/ in all parts; taken as a whole (overall, the performance was excellent). —n. /ˈəʊvərɔːl/ **1** Brit. an outer garment worn to keep out dirt, wet, etc. **2** (in pl.) protective trousers, dungarees, or a combination suit, worn by workmen etc. **3** Brit. close-fitting trousers worn as part of army uniform. □□ **overalled** /ˈəʊvərɔːld/ adj.

overambitious /ˌəʊvəræmˈbɪʃəs/ adj. excessively ambitious. □□ **overambition** n. **overambitiously** adv.

over-anxious /ˌəʊvərˈæŋkʃəs/ adj. excessively anxious. □□ **over-anxiety** /-æŋˈzaɪɪtɪ/ n. **over-anxiously** adv.

overarch /ˌəʊvərˈɑːtʃ/ v.tr. form an arch over. □□ **overarching** adj.

overarm /ˈəʊvərˌɑːm/ adj. & adv. **1** Cricket & Tennis etc. with the hand above the shoulder (bowl it overarm; an overarm service). **2** Swimming with one or both arms lifted out of the water during a stroke.

overate past of OVEREAT.

overawe /ˌəʊvərˈɔː/ v.tr. **1** restrain by awe. **2** keep in awe.

overbalance /ˌəʊvəˈbæləns/ v. & n. —v. **1** tr. cause (a person or thing) to lose its balance and fall. **2** intr. fall over, capsize. **3** tr. outweigh. —n. **1** an excess. **2** the amount of this.

overbear /ˌəʊvəˈbeə(r)/ v.tr. (past **-bore**; past part. **-borne**) **1** (as **overbearing** adj.) **a** domineering, masterful. **b** overpowering. **2** bear down; upset by weight, force, or emotional pressure. **3**

put down or repress by power or authority. **4** surpass in importance etc., outweigh. □□ **overbearingly** adv. **overbearingness** n.

overbid v. & n. —v. /ˌəʊvəˈbɪd/ (**-bidding**; past and past part. **-bid**) **1** tr. make a higher bid than. **2** tr. (also absol.) Bridge **a** bid more on (one's hand) than warranted. **b** overcall. —n. /ˈəʊvəbɪd/ a bid that is higher than another, or higher than is justified. □□ **overbidder** n.

overblouse /ˈəʊvəˌblaʊz/ n. a garment like a blouse, but worn without tucking it into a skirt or trousers.

overblown /ˌəʊvəˈbləʊn/ adj. **1** excessively inflated or pretentious. **2** (of a flower or a woman's beauty etc.) past its prime.

overboard /ˈəʊvəˌbɔːd/ adv. from on a ship into the water (fall overboard). □ **go overboard 1** be highly enthusiastic. **2** behave immoderately; go too far. **throw overboard** abandon, discard.

overbold /ˌəʊvəˈbəʊld/ adj. excessively bold.

overbook /ˌəʊvəˈbʊk/ v.tr. (also absol.) make too many bookings for (an aircraft, hotel, etc.).

overboot /ˈəʊvəˌbuːt/ n. a boot worn over another boot or shoe.

overbore past of OVERBEAR.

overborne past part. of OVERBEAR.

overbought past and past part. of OVERBUY.

overbrim /ˌəʊvəˈbrɪm/ v. (**-brimmed, -brimming**) **1** tr. flow over the brim of. **2** intr. (of a vessel or liquid) overflow at the brim.

overbuild /ˌəʊvəˈbɪld/ v.tr. (past and past part. **-built**) **1** build over or upon. **2** place too many buildings on (land etc.).

overburden /ˌəʊvəˈbɜːd(ə)n/ v. & n. —v.tr. burden (a person, thing, etc.) to excess. —n. **1** rock etc. that must be removed prior to mining the mineral deposit beneath it. **2** an excessive burden. □□ **overburdensome** adj.

Overbury /ˈəʊvəbəri/, Sir Thomas (1581–1613), English poet and courtier, remembered for his 'Characters', on the model of those of Theophrastus. He was sent to the Tower on the pretext of his refusal of a diplomatic post, where he was poisoned to death by the agents of Lady Essex whose marriage to her patron Robert Carr (afterwards Earl of Somerset) he had opposed. The subsequent prosecution of the conspirators was conducted by Francis Bacon. The whole business is a historical mystery.

overbusy /ˌəʊvəˈbɪzi/ adj. excessively busy.

overbuy /ˌəʊvəˈbaɪ/ v.tr. & intr. (past and past part. **-bought**) buy (a commodity etc.) in excess of immediate need.

overcall v. & n. —v.tr. /ˌəʊvəˈkɔːl/ (also absol.) Bridge **1** make a higher bid than (a previous bid or opponent). **2** Brit. = OVERBID v. 2a. —n. /ˈəʊvəˌkɔːl/ an act or instance of overcalling.

overcame past of OVERCOME.

overcapacity /ˌəʊvəkəˈpæsɪti/ n. a state of saturation or an excess of productive capacity.

overcapitalize /ˌəʊvəˈkæpɪtəˌlaɪz/ v.tr. (also **-ise**) fix or estimate the capital of (a company etc.) too high.

overcareful /ˌəʊvəˈkeəfʊl/ adj. excessively careful. □□ **overcarefully** adv.

overcast adj., v., & n. —adj. /ˈəʊvəˌkɑːst/ **1** (of the sky, weather, etc.) covered with cloud; dull and gloomy. **2** (in sewing) edged with stitching to prevent fraying. —v.tr. /ˌəʊvəˈkɑːst/ (past and past part. **-cast**) **1** cover (the sky etc.) with clouds or darkness. **2** stitch over (a raw edge etc.) to prevent fraying. —n. /ˈəʊvəˌkɑːst/ a cloud covering part of the sky.

overcautious /ˌəʊvəˈkɔːʃəs/ adj. excessively cautious. □□ **overcaution** n. **overcautiously** adv. **overcautiousness** n.

overcharge /ˌəʊvəˈtʃɑːdʒ/ v. & n. —v.tr. **1 a** charge too high a price to (a person) or for (a thing). **b** charge (a specified sum) beyond the right price. **2** put too much charge into (a battery, gun, etc.). **3** put exaggerated or excessive detail into (a description, picture, etc.). —n. an excessive charge (of explosive, money, etc.).

overcheck /ˈəʊvəˌtʃek/ n. **1** a combination of two different-sized check patterns. **2** a cloth with this pattern.

overcloud /ˌəʊvəˈklaʊd/ v.tr. **1** cover with cloud. **2** mar, spoil,

or dim, esp. as the result of anxiety etc. (overclouded by uncertainties). **3** make obscure.

overcoat /ˈəʊvəˌkəʊt/ n. **1** a heavy coat, esp. one worn over indoor clothes for warmth outdoors in cold weather. **2** a protective coat of paint etc.

overcome /ˌəʊvəˈkʌm/ v. (past **-came**; past part. **-come**) **1** tr. prevail over, master, conquer. **2** tr. (as **overcome** adj.) **a** exhausted, made helpless. **b** (usu. foll. by with, by) affected by (emotion etc.). **3** intr. be victorious. [OE ofercuman (as OVER-, COME)]

overcompensate /ˌəʊvəˈkɒmpenˌseɪt/ v. **1** tr. (usu. foll. by for) compensate excessively for (something). **2** intr. Psychol. strive for power etc. in an exaggerated way, esp. to make allowance or amends for a real or fancied grievance, defect, handicap, etc. □□ **overcompensation** /-penˈseɪʃ(ə)n/ n. **overcompensatory** /-ˈseɪtəri/ adj.

overconfident /ˌəʊvəˈkɒnfɪd(ə)nt/ adj. excessively confident. □□ **overconfidence** n. **overconfidently** adv.

overcook /ˌəʊvəˈkʊk/ v.tr. cook too much or for too long. □□ **overcooked** adj.

overcritical /ˌəʊvəˈkrɪtɪk(ə)l/ adj. excessively critical; quick to find fault.

overcrop /ˌəʊvəˈkrɒp/ v.tr. (**-cropped, -cropping**) exhaust (the land) by the continuous growing of crops.

overcrowd /ˌəʊvəˈkraʊd/ v.tr. fill (a space, object, etc.) beyond what is usual or comfortable. □□ **overcrowding** n.

over-curious /ˌəʊvəˈkjʊərɪəs/ adj. excessively curious. □□ **over-curiosity** /ˌəʊvəkjʊərɪˈɒsɪti/ n. **over-curiously** adv.

over-delicate /ˌəʊvəˈdelɪkət/ adj. excessively delicate. □□ **over-delicacy** n.

overdevelop /ˌəʊvədɪˈveləp/ v.tr. (**-developed, -developing**) **1** develop too much. **2** Photog. treat with developer for too long.

overdo /ˌəʊvəˈduː/ v.tr. (3rd sing. present **-does**; past **-did**; past part. **-done**) **1** carry to excess, go too far, exaggerate (I think you overdid the sarcasm). **2** (esp. as **overdone** adj.) overcook. □ **overdo it** (or **things**) exhaust oneself. [OE oferdōn (as OVER-, DO¹)]

overdose /ˈəʊvəˌdəʊs/ n. & v. —n. an excessive dose (of a drug etc.). —v.tr. give an excessive dose of (a drug etc.) or to (a person). □□ **overdosage** /ˌəʊvəˈdəʊsɪdʒ/ n.

overdraft /ˈəʊvəˌdrɑːft/ n. **1** a deficit in a bank account caused by drawing more money than is credited to it. **2** the amount of this.

overdraw /ˌəʊvəˈdrɔː/ v. (past **-drew**; past part. **-drawn**) **1** tr. **a** draw a sum of money in excess of the amount credited to (one's bank account). **b** (as **overdrawn** adj.) having overdrawn one's account. **2** intr. overdraw one's account. **3** tr. exaggerate in describing or depicting. □□ **overdrawer** n. (in senses 1 & 2).

overdress v. & n. —v. /ˌəʊvəˈdres/ **1** tr. dress with too much display or formality. **2** intr. overdress oneself. —n. /ˈəʊvəˌdres/ a dress worn over another dress or a blouse etc.

overdrink /ˌəʊvəˈdrɪŋk/ v.intr. & refl. (past **-drank**; past part. **-drunk**) drink too much.

overdrive /ˈəʊvəˌdraɪv/ n. **1 a** a mechanism in a motor vehicle providing a gear ratio higher than that of the usual gear. **b** an additional speed-increasing gear. **2** (usu. prec. by in, into) a state of high or excessive activity.

overdub v. & n. —v.tr. /ˌəʊvəˈdʌb/ (**-dubbed, -dubbing**) (also absol.) impose (additional sounds) on an existing recording. —n. /ˈəʊvəˌdʌb/ the act or an instance of overdubbing.

overdue /ˌəʊvəˈdjuː/ adj. **1** past the time when due or ready. **2** not yet paid, arrived, born, etc., though after the expected time. **3** (of a library book etc.) retained longer than the period allowed.

overeager /ˌəʊvərˈiːgə(r)/ adj. excessively eager. □□ **overeagerly** adv. **overeagerness** n.

overeat /ˌəʊvərˈiːt/ v.intr. & refl. (past **-ate**; past part. **-eaten**) eat too much.

overelaborate /ˌəʊvərɪˈlæbərət/ adj. excessively elaborate. □□ **overelaborately** adv.

over-emotional /ˌəʊvərɪˈməʊʃən(ə)l/ adj. excessively emotional. □□ **over-emotionally** adv.

overemphasis /ˌəʊvər'emfəsɪs/ n. excessive emphasis. □□ **overemphasize** /-fəˌsaɪz/ v.tr. & intr. (also **-ise**).

overenthusiasm /ˌəʊvərɪn'θjuːzɪˌæz(ə)m, -ˈθuːzɪˌæz(ə)m/ n. excessive enthusiasm. □□ **overenthusiastic** /-ˈæstɪk/ adj. **overenthusiastically** /-ˈæstɪkəli/ adv.

overestimate v. & n. —v.tr. /ˌəʊvər'estɪˌmeɪt/ (also absol.) form too high an estimate of (a person, ability, cost, etc.). —n. /-mət/ too high an estimate. □□ **overestimation** /-ˈmeɪʃ(ə)n/ n.

overexcite /ˌəʊvərɪk'saɪt/ v.tr. excite excessively. □□ **overexcitement** n.

over-exercise /ˌəʊvər'eksəˌsaɪz/ v. & n. —v. 1 tr. use or exert (a part of the body, one's authority, etc.) too much. 2 intr. take too much exercise; overexert oneself. —n. excessive exercise.

overexert /ˌəʊvərɪg'zɜːt/ v.tr. & refl. exert too much. □□ **overexertion** /-ɪg'zɜːʃ(ə)n/ n.

overexpose /ˌəʊvərɪk'spəʊz/ v.tr. (also absol.) 1 expose too much, esp. to the public eye. 2 Photog. expose (film) for too long a time. □□ **overexposure** n.

overextend /ˌəʊvərɪk'stend/ v.tr. 1 extend (a thing) too far. 2 (also refl.) take on (oneself) or impose on (another person) an excessive burden of work.

overfall /'əʊvəˌfɔːl/ n. 1 a turbulent stretch of sea etc. caused by a strong current or tide over a submarine ridge, or by a meeting of currents. 2 a place provided on a dam, weir, etc. for the overflow of surplus water.

overfamiliar /ˌəʊvəfə'mɪlɪə(r)/ adj. excessively familiar.

overfatigue /ˌəʊvəfə'tiːg/ n. excessive fatigue.

overfeed /ˌəʊvə'fiːd/ v.tr. (past and past part. **-fed**) feed excessively.

overfill /ˌəʊvə'fɪl/ v.tr. & intr. fill to excess or to overflowing.

overfine /ˌəʊvə'faɪn/ adj. excessively fine; too precise.

overfish /ˌəʊvə'fɪʃ/ v.tr. deplete (a stream etc.) by too much fishing.

overflow v. & n. —v. /ˌəʊvə'fləʊ/ 1 tr. **a** flow over (the brim, limits, etc.). **b** flow over the brim or limits of. 2 intr. **a** (of a receptacle etc.) be so full that the contents overflow it (until the cup was overflowing). **b** (of contents) overflow a container. 3 tr. (of a crowd etc.) extend beyond the limits of (a room etc.). 4 tr. flood (a surface or area). 5 intr. (foll. by with) be full of. 6 intr. (of kindness, a harvest, etc.) be very abundant. —n. /'əʊvəˌfləʊ/ (also attrib.) 1 what overflows or is superfluous (mop up the overflow; put the overflow audience in another room). 2 an instance of overflowing (overflow occurs when both systems are run together). 3 (esp. in a bath or sink) an outlet for excess water etc. 4 Computing the generation of a number having more digits than the assigned location. □ **overflow meeting** a meeting for those who cannot be accommodated at the main gathering. [OE oferflōwan (as OVER-, FLOW)]

overfly /ˌəʊvə'flaɪ/ v.tr. (**-flies**; past **-flew**; past part. **-flown**) fly over or beyond (a place or territory). □□ **overflight** /'əʊvəˌflaɪt/ n.

overfold /'əʊvəˌfəʊld/ n. a series of strata folded so that the middle part is upside down.

overfond /ˌəʊvə'fɒnd/ adj. (often foll. by of) having too great an affection or liking (for a person or thing) (overfond of chocolate; an overfond parent). □□ **overfondly** adv. **overfondness** n.

overfulfil /ˌəʊvəfʊl'fɪl/ v.tr. (US **-fulfill**) (**-fulfilled**, **-fulfilling**) fulfil (a plan, quota, etc.) beyond expectation or before the appointed time. □□ **overfulfilment** n.

overfull /ˌəʊvə'fʊl/ adj. filled excessively or to overflowing.

overgeneralize /ˌəʊvə'dʒenərəˌlaɪz/ v. (also **-ise**) 1 intr. draw general conclusions from inadequate data etc. 2 intr. argue more widely than is justified by the available evidence, by circumstances, etc. 3 tr. draw an over-general conclusion from (data, circumstances, etc.). □□ **overgeneralization** /-ˈzeɪʃ(ə)n/ n.

overgenerous /ˌəʊvə'dʒenərəs/ adj. excessively generous. □□ **overgenerously** adv.

overglaze /'əʊvəˌgleɪz/ n. & adj. —n. 1 a second glaze applied to ceramic ware. 2 decoration on a glazed surface. —adj. (of painting etc.) done on a glazed surface.

overground /'əʊvəˌgraʊnd/ adj. 1 raised above the ground. 2 not underground.

overgrow /ˌəʊvə'grəʊ/ v.tr. (past **-grew**; past part. **-grown**) 1 (as **overgrown** adj. /ˌəʊvə'grəʊn, 'əʊvəˌgrəʊn/) **a** abnormally large (a great overgrown child). **b** wild; grown over with vegetation (an overgrown pond). 2 grow over, overspread, esp. so as to choke (nettles have overgrown the pathway). 3 grow too big for (one's strength etc.). □□ **overgrowth** n.

overhand /'əʊvəˌhænd/ adj. & adv. 1 (in cricket, tennis, baseball, etc.) thrown or played with the hand above the shoulder. 2 Swimming = OVERARM. 3 **a** with the palm of the hand downward or inward. **b** with the hand above the object held. □ **overhand knot** a simple knot made by forming a loop and passing the free end through it.

overhang v. & n. —v. /ˌəʊvə'hæŋ/ (past and past part. **-hung**) 1 tr. & intr. project or hang over. 2 tr. menace, preoccupy, threaten. —n. /'əʊvəˌhæŋ/ 1 the overhanging part of a structure or rock-formation. 2 the amount by which this projects.

overhaste /ˌəʊvə'heɪst/ n. excessive haste. □□ **overhasty** adj. **overhastily** adv.

overhaul v. & n. —v.tr. /ˌəʊvə'hɔːl/ 1 **a** take to pieces in order to examine. **b** examine the condition of (and repair if necessary). 2 overtake. —n. /'əʊvəˌhɔːl/ a thorough examination, with repairs if necessary. [orig. Naut., = release (rope-tackle) by slackening]

overhead adv., adj., & n. —adv. /ˌəʊvə'hed/ 1 above one's head. 2 in the sky or in the storey above. —adj. /'əʊvəhed/ 1 (of a driving mechanism etc.) above the object driven. 2 (of expenses) arising from general running costs, as distinct from particular business transactions. —n. /'əʊvəˌhed/ (in pl. or US in sing.) overhead expenses.

overhear /ˌəʊvə'hɪə(r)/ v.tr. (past and past part. **-heard**) (also absol.) hear as an eavesdropper or as an unperceived or unintentional listener.

overheat /ˌəʊvə'hiːt/ v. 1 tr. & intr. make or become too hot; heat to excess. 2 tr. (as **overheated** adj.) too passionate about a matter.

Overijssel /ˌəʊvər'aɪs(ə)l/ a province of the east central Netherlands, north of the Ijssel River; pop. (1988) 1,010,000; capital, Zwolle.

overindulge /ˌəʊvərɪn'dʌldʒ/ v.tr. & intr. indulge to excess. □□ **overindulgence** n. **overindulgent** adj.

overinsure /ˌəʊvərɪn'ʃʊə(r)/ v.tr. insure (property etc.) for more than its real value; insure excessively. □□ **overinsurance** n.

overissue /ˌəʊvər'ɪʃuː:, -'ɪsjuː/ v. & n. —v.tr. (**-issues**, **-issued**, **-issuing**) issue (notes, shares, etc.) beyond the authorized amount, or the ability to pay. —n. the notes, shares, etc., or the amount so issued.

overjoyed /ˌəʊvə'dʒɔɪd/ adj. (often foll. by at, to hear, etc.) filled with great joy.

overkill n. & v. —n. /'əʊvəkɪl/ 1 the amount by which destruction or the capacity for destruction exceeds what is necessary for victory or annihilation. 2 excess; excessive behaviour. —v.tr. & intr. /'əʊvəkɪl, ˌəʊvə'kɪl/ kill or destroy to a greater extent than necessary.

overladen /ˌəʊvə'leɪd(ə)n/ adj. bearing or carrying too large a load.

overlaid past and past part. of OVERLAY[1].

overlain past part. of OVERLIE.

overland /'əʊvəˌlænd/ adj., adv., & v. —adj. & adv. /also ˌəʊvə'lænd/ 1 by land. 2 not by sea. —v. Austral. 1 tr. drive (livestock) overland. 2 intr. go a long distance overland.

overlander /'əʊvəˌlændə(r)/ n. Austral. 1 a person who drives livestock overland (orig. one who drove stock from New South Wales to the Colony of South Australia). 2 sl. a tramp, a sundowner.

overlap v. & n. —v. /ˌəʊvə'læp/ (**-lapped**, **-lapping**) 1 tr. (of part of an object) partly cover (another object). 2 tr. cover and extend beyond. 3 intr. (of two things) partly coincide; not be completely separate (where psychology and philosophy overlap). —n. /'əʊvəˌlæp/ 1 an instance of overlapping. 2 the amount of this.

over-large /ˌəʊvəˈlɑːdʒ/ *adj.* too large.

overlay[1] *v. & n.* —*v.tr.* /ˌəʊvəˈleɪ/ (*past and past part.* **-laid**) **1** lay over. **2** (foll. by *with*) cover the surface of (a thing) with (a coating etc.). **3** overlie. —*n.* /ˈəʊvəˌleɪ/ **1** a thing laid over another. **2** (in printing, mapreading, etc.) a transparent sheet to be superimposed on another sheet. **3** *Computing* **a** the process of transferring a block of data etc. to replace what is already stored. **b** a section so transferred. **4** a coverlet, small tablecloth, etc.

overlay[2] *past of* OVERLIE.

overleaf /ˌəʊvəˈliːf/ *adv.* on the other side of the leaf (of a book) (*see the diagram overleaf*).

overleap /ˌəʊvəˈliːp/ *v.tr.* (*past and past part.* **-leaped** or **-leapt**) **1** leap over, surmount. **2** omit, ignore. [OE *oferhlēapan* (as OVER, LEAP)]

overlie /ˌəʊvəˈlaɪ/ *v.tr.* (**-lying**; *past* **-lay**; *past part.* **-lain**) **1** lie on top of. **2** smother (a child etc.) by lying on top.

overload *v. & n.* —*v.tr.* /ˌəʊvəˈləʊd/ load excessively; force (a person, thing, etc.) beyond normal or reasonable capacity. —*n.* /ˈəʊvəˌləʊd/ an excessive quantity; a demand etc. which surpasses capability or capacity.

over-long /ˌəʊvəˈlɒŋ/ *adj. & adv.* too or excessively long.

overlook *v. & n.* —*v.tr.* /ˌəʊvəˈlʊk/ **1** fail to notice; ignore, condone (an offence etc.). **2** have a view from above, be higher than. **3** supervise, oversee. **4** bewitch with the evil eye. —*n.* /ˈəʊvəˌlʊk/ *US* a commanding position or view. □□ **overlooker** /ˈəʊvəˌlʊkə(r)/ *n.*

overlord /ˈəʊvəlɔːd/ *n.* a supreme lord. □□ **overlordship** *n.*

overly /ˈəʊvəlɪ/ *adv.* esp. *US & Sc.* excessively; too.

overlying *pres. part.* of OVERLIE.

overman *v. & n.* —*v.tr.* /ˌəʊvəˈmæn/ (**-manned**, **-manning**) provide with too large a crew, staff, etc. —*n.* /ˈəʊvəˌmæn/ (*pl.* **-men**) **1** an overseer in a colliery. **2** *Philos.* = SUPERMAN.

overmantel /ˈəʊvəˌmænt(ə)l/ *n.* ornamental shelves etc. over a mantelpiece.

over-many /ˌəʊvəˈmenɪ/ *adj.* too many; an excessive number.

overmaster /ˌəʊvəˈmɑːstə(r)/ *v.tr.* master completely, conquer. □□ **overmastering** *adj.* **overmastery** *n.*

overmatch /ˌəʊvəˈmætʃ/ *v.tr.* be more than a match for; defeat by superior strength etc.

overmeasure /ˈəʊvəˌmeʒə(r)/ *n.* an amount beyond what is proper or sufficient.

over-much /ˌəʊvəˈmʌtʃ/ *adv. & adj.* —*adv.* to too great an extent; excessively. —*adj.* excessive; superabundant.

over-nice /ˌəʊvəˈnaɪs/ *adj.* excessively fussy, punctilious, particular, etc. □□ **over-niceness** *n.* **over-nicety** *n.*

overnight /ˌəʊvəˈnaɪt/ *adv. & adj.* —*adv.* **1** for the duration of a night (*stay overnight*). **2** during the course of a night. **3** suddenly, immediately (*the situation changed overnight*). —*adj.* **1** for use overnight (*an overnight bag*). **2** done etc. overnight (*an overnight stop*).

overnighter /ˌəʊvəˈnaɪtə(r)/ *n.* **1** a person who stops at a place overnight. **2** an overnight bag.

overpaid *past and past part.* of OVERPAY.

overparted /ˌəʊvəˈpɑːtɪd/ *adj. Theatr.* having too demanding a part to play; cast beyond one's ability.

over-particular /ˌəʊvəpəˈtɪkjʊlə(r)/ *adj.* excessively particular or fussy.

overpass *n. & v.* —*n.* /ˈəʊvəˌpɑːs/ a road or railway line that passes over another by means of a bridge. —*v.tr.* /ˌəʊvəˈpɑːs/ **1** pass over or across or beyond. **2** get to the end of; surmount. **3** (as **overpassed** or **overpast**) that has gone by, past.

overpay /ˌəʊvəˈpeɪ/ *v.tr.* (*past and past part.* **-paid**) recompense (a person, service, etc.) too highly. □□ **overpayment** *n.*

overpitch /ˌəʊvəˈpɪtʃ/ *v.tr.* **1** *Cricket* bowl (a ball) so that it pitches or would pitch too near the stumps. **2** exaggerate.

overplay /ˌəʊvəˈpleɪ/ *v.tr.* play (a part) to excess; give undue importance to; overemphasize. □ **overplay one's hand** **1** be unduly optimistic about one's capabilities. **2** spoil a good case by exaggerating its value.

overplus /ˈəʊvəˌplʌs/ *n.* a surplus, a superabundance. [ME. partial transl. of AF *surplus* or med.L *su(pe)rplus*]

overpopulated /ˌəʊvəˈpɒpjʊˌleɪtɪd/ *adj.* having too large a population. □□ **overpopulation** /-ˈleɪʃ(ə)n/ *n.*

overpower /ˌəʊvəˈpaʊə(r)/ *v.tr.* **1** reduce to submission, subdue. **2** make (a thing) ineffective or imperceptible by greater intensity. **3** (of heat, emotion, etc.) be too intense for, overwhelm. □□ **overpowering** *adj.* **overpoweringly** *adv.*

overprice /ˌəʊvəˈpraɪs/ *v.tr.* price (a thing) too highly.

overprint *v. & n.* —*v.tr.* /ˌəʊvəˈprɪnt/ **1** print further matter on (a surface already printed, esp. a postage stamp). **2** print (further matter) in this way. **3** *Photog.* print (a positive) darker than was intended. **4** (also *absol.*) print too many copies of (a work). —*n.* /ˈəʊvəˌprɪnt/ **1** the words etc. overprinted. **2** an overprinted postage stamp.

overproduce /ˌəʊvəprəˈdjuːs/ *tr.* (*usu. absol.*) **1** produce more of (a commodity) than is wanted. **2** produce to an excessive degree. □□ **overproduction** *n.*

overproof /ˈəʊvəˌpruːf/ *adj.* containing more alcohol than proof spirit does.

overqualified /ˌəʊvəˈkwɒlɪˌfaɪd/ *adj.* too highly qualified (esp. for a particular job etc.).

overran *past of* OVERRUN.

overrate /ˌəʊvəˈreɪt/ *v.tr.* assess too highly.

overreach /ˌəʊvəˈriːtʃ/ *v.tr.* circumvent, outwit; get the better of by cunning or artifice. □ **overreach oneself 1** strain oneself by reaching too far. **2** defeat one's object by going too far.

overreact /ˌəʊvərɪˈækt/ *v.intr.* respond more forcibly etc. than is justified. □□ **overreaction** *n.*

overrefine /ˌəʊvərɪˈfaɪn/ *v.tr.* (also *absol.*) **1** refine too much. **2** make too subtle distinctions in (an argument etc.).

override *v. & n.* —*v.tr.* /ˌəʊvəˈraɪd/ (*past* **-rode**; *past part.* **-ridden**) **1** have or claim precedence or superiority over (*an overriding consideration*). **2 a** intervene and make ineffective. **b** interrupt the action of (an automatic device) esp. to take manual control. **3 a** trample down or underfoot. **b** supersede arrogantly. **4** extend over, esp. (of a part of a fractured bone) overlap (another part). **5** ride over (enemy country). **6** exhaust (a horse etc.) by hard riding. —*n.* /ˈəʊvəˌraɪd/ **1** the action or process of suspending an automatic function. **2** a device for this.

overrider /ˈəʊvəˌraɪdə(r)/ *n. Brit.* each of a pair of projecting pieces on the bumper of a car.

overripe /ˌəʊvəˈraɪp/ *adj.* (esp. of fruit etc.) past its best; excessively ripe; full-blown.

overrode *past of* OVERRIDE.

overruff *v. & n.* —*v.tr.* /ˌəʊvəˈrʌf/ (also *absol.*) overtrump. —*n.* /ˈəʊvəˌrʌf/ an instance of this.

overrule /ˌəʊvəˈruːl/ *v.tr.* **1** set aside (a decision, argument, proposal, etc.) by exercising a superior authority. **2** annul a decision by or reject a proposal of (a person) in this way.

overrun *v. & n.* —*v.tr.* /ˌəʊvəˈrʌn/ (**-running**; *past* **-ran**; *past part.* **-run**) **1** (of vermin, weeds, etc.) swarm or spread over. **2** conquer or ravage (territory) by force. **3** (of time, expenditure, production, etc.) exceed (a fixed limit). **4** *Printing* carry over (a word etc.) to the next line or page. **5** *Mech.* rotate faster than. **6** flood (land). —*n.* /ˈəʊvəˌrʌn/ **1** an instance of overrunning. **2** the amount of this. **3** the movement of a vehicle at a speed greater than is imparted by the engine. [OE *oferyrnan* (as OVER-, RUN)]

oversailing /ˌəʊvəˈseɪlɪŋ/ *adj.* (of a part of a building) projecting beyond what is below. [OVER + F *saillir* SALLY[1]]

oversaw *past of* OVERSEE.

overscrupulous /ˌəʊvəˈskruːpjʊləs/ *adj.* excessively scrupulous or particular.

overseas *adv. & adj.* —*adv.* /ˌəʊvəˈsiːz/ (also **oversea**) abroad (*was sent overseas for training; came back from overseas*). —*adj.* /ˈəʊvəˌsiːz/ (also **oversea**) **1** foreign; across or beyond the sea. **2** of or connected with movement or transport over the sea (*overseas postage rates*).

oversee /ˌəʊvəˈsiː/ *v.tr.* (**-sees**; *past* **-saw**; *past part.* **-seen**) officially supervise (workers, work, etc.). [OE *ofersēon* look at from above (as OVER-, SEE[1])]

overseer /ˈəʊvəˌsiːə(r)/ n. a person who supervises others, esp. workers. □ **overseer of the poor** Brit. hist. a parish official who administered funds to the poor. [OVERSEE]

oversell /ˌəʊvəˈsel/ v.tr. (past and past part. **-sold**) (also absol.) **1** sell more of (a commodity etc.) than one can deliver. **2** exaggerate the merits of.

over-sensitive /ˌəʊvəˈsensɪtɪv/ adj. excessively sensitive; easily hurt by, or too quick to react to, outside influences. □□ **over-sensitiveness** n. **over-sensitivity** /-ˈtɪvɪtɪ/ n.

overset /ˌəʊvəˈset/ v.tr. (**-setting**; past and past part. **-set**) **1** overturn, upset. **2** Printing set up (type) in excess of the available space.

oversew /ˈəʊvəˌsəʊ/ v.tr. (past part. **-sewn** or **-sewed**) **1** sew (two edges) with every stitch passing over the join. **2** join the sections of (a book) by a stitch of this type.

oversexed /ˌəʊvəˈsekst/ adj. having unusually strong sexual desires.

overshadow /ˌəʊvəˈʃædəʊ/ v.tr. **1** appear much more prominent or important than. **2** cast into the shade; shelter from the sun. [OE ofersceadwian (as OVER-, SHADOW)]

overshoe /ˈəʊvəˌʃuː/ n. a shoe of rubber, felt, etc., worn over another as protection from wet, cold, etc.

overshoot v. & n. —v.tr. /ˌəʊvəˈʃuːt/ (past and past part. **-shot**) **1** pass or send beyond (a target or limit). **2** (of an aircraft) fly beyond or taxi too far along (the runway) when landing or taking off. —n. /ˈəʊvəˌʃuːt/ **1** the act of overshooting. **2** the amount of this. □ **overshoot the mark** go beyond what is intended or proper; go too far. **overshot wheel** a waterwheel operated by the weight of water falling into buckets attached to its periphery.

overside /ˌəʊvəˈsaɪd/ adv. over the side of a ship (into a smaller boat, or into the sea).

oversight /ˈəʊvəˌsaɪt/ n. **1** a failure to notice something. **2** an inadvertent mistake. **3** supervision.

oversimplify /ˌəʊvəˈsɪmplɪˌfaɪ/ v.tr. (**-ies**, **-ied**) (also absol.) distort (a problem etc.) by stating it in too simple terms. □□ **oversimplification** /-fɪˈkeɪʃ(ə)n/ n.

oversize /ˈəʊvəˌsaɪz/ adj. (also **-sized** /-ˌsaɪzd/) of more than the usual size.

overskirt /ˈəʊvəˌskɜːt/ n. an outer or second skirt.

overslaugh /ˈəʊvəˌslɔː/ n. & v. —n. Brit. Mil. the passing over of one's turn of duty. —v.tr. **1** Brit. Mil. pass over (one's duty) in consideration of another duty that takes precedence. **2** US pass over in favour of another. **3** US omit to consider. [Du. overslag (n.) f. overslaan omit (as OVER, slaan strike)]

oversleep /ˌəʊvəˈsliːp/ v.intr. & refl. (past and past part. **-slept**) **1** continue sleeping beyond the intended time of waking. **2** sleep too long.

oversleeve /ˈəʊvəˌsliːv/ n. a protective sleeve covering an ordinary sleeve.

oversold past and past part. of OVERSELL.

oversolicitous /ˌəʊvəsəˈlɪsɪtəs/ adj. excessively worried, anxious, eager, etc. □□ **oversolicitude** n.

oversoul /ˈəʊvəˌsəʊl/ n. God as a spirit animating the universe and including all human souls.

overspecialize /ˌəʊvəˈspeʃəˌlaɪz/ v.intr. (also **-ise**) concentrate too much on one aspect or area. □□ **overspecialization** /-ˈzeɪʃ(ə)n/ n.

overspend /ˌəʊvəˈspend/ v. (past and past part. **-spent**) **1** intr. & refl. spend too much. **2** tr. spend more than (a specified amount).

overspill /ˈəʊvəˌspɪl/ n. **1** what is spilt over or overflows. **2** the surplus population leaving a country or city to live elsewhere.

overspread /ˌəʊvəˈspred/ v.tr. (past and past part. **-spread**) **1** become spread or diffused over. **2** cover or occupy the surface of. **3** (as **overspread** adj.) (usu. foll. by with) covered (high mountains overspread with trees). [OE ofersprædan (as OVER-, SPREAD)]

overstaff /ˌəʊvəˈstɑːf/ v.tr. provide with too large a staff.

overstate /ˌəʊvəˈsteɪt/ v.tr. **1** state (esp. a case or argument) too strongly. **2** exaggerate. □□ **overstatement** n.

overstay /ˌəʊvəˈsteɪ/ v.tr. stay longer than (one's welcome, a time limit, etc.).

oversteer /ˌəʊvəˈstɪə(r)/ v. & n. —v.intr. (of a motor vehicle) have a tendency to turn more sharply than was intended. —n. this tendency.

overstep /ˌəʊvəˈstep/ v.tr. (**-stepped**, **-stepping**) **1** pass beyond (a boundary or mark). **2** violate (certain standards of behaviour etc.).

overstock /ˌəʊvəˈstɒk/ v.tr. stock excessively.

overstrain /ˌəʊvəˈstreɪn/ v.tr. strain too much.

overstress /ˌəʊvəˈstres/ v. & n. —v.tr. stress too much. —n. an excessive degree of stress.

overstretch /ˌəʊvəˈstretʃ/ v.tr. **1** stretch too much. **2** (esp. as **overstretched** adj.) make excessive demands on (resources, a person, etc.).

overstrung adj. **1** /ˌəʊvəˈstrʌŋ/ (of a person, disposition, etc.) intensely strained, highly strung. **2** /ˈəʊvəˌstrʌŋ/ (of a piano) with strings in sets crossing each other obliquely.

overstudy /ˌəʊvəˈstʌdɪ/ v.tr. (**-ies**, **-ied**) **1** study beyond what is necessary or desirable. **2** (as **overstudied** adj.) excessively deliberate; affected.

overstuff /ˌəʊvəˈstʌf/ v.tr. **1** stuff more than is necessary. **2** (as **overstuffed** adj.) (of furniture) made soft and comfortable by thick upholstery.

oversubscribe /ˌəʊvəsəbˈskraɪb/ v.tr. (usu. as **oversubscribed** adj.) subscribe for more than the amount available of (a commodity offered for sale etc.) (the offer was oversubscribed).

oversubtle /ˌəʊvəˈsʌt(ə)l/ adj. excessively subtle; not plain or clear.

oversupply /ˌəʊvəsəˈplaɪ/ v. & n. —v.tr. (**-ies**, **-ied**) supply with too much. —n. an excessive supply.

oversusceptible /ˌəʊvəsəˈseptɪb(ə)l/ adj. too susceptible or vulnerable.

overt /əʊˈvɜːt, ˈəʊvɜːt/ adj. unconcealed; done openly. □□ **overtly** adv. **overtness** n. [ME f. OF past part. of ovrir open f. L aperire]

overtake /ˌəʊvəˈteɪk/ v.tr. (past **-took**; past part. **-taken**) **1** (also absol.) catch up with and pass in the same direction. **2** (of a storm, misfortune, etc.) come suddenly or unexpectedly upon. **3** become level with and exceed (a compared value etc.).

overtask /ˌəʊvəˈtɑːsk/ v.tr. **1** give too heavy a task to. **2** be too heavy a task for.

overtax /ˌəʊvəˈtæks/ v.tr. **1** make excessive demands on (a person's strength etc.). **2** tax too heavily.

overthrow v. & n. —v.tr. /ˌəʊvəˈθrəʊ/ (past **-threw**; past part. **-thrown**) **1** remove forcibly from power. **2** put an end to (an institution etc.). **3** conquer, overcome. **4** knock down, upset. —n. /ˈəʊvəˌθrəʊ/ **1** a defeat or downfall. **2** Cricket **a** a fielder's return of the ball, not stopped near the wicket and so allowing further runs. **b** such a run. **3** Archit. a panel of decorated wrought-iron work in an arch or gateway.

overthrust /ˈəʊvəˌθrʌst/ n. Geol. the thrust of esp. lower strata on one side of a fault over those on the other side.

overtime /ˈəʊvəˌtaɪm/ n. & adv. —n. **1** the time during which a person works at a job in addition to the regular hours. **2** payment for this. **3** US Sport = extra time. —adv. in addition to regular hours.

overtire /ˌəʊvəˈtaɪə(r)/ v.tr. & refl. exhaust or wear out (esp. an invalid etc.).

overtone /ˈəʊvəˌtəʊn/ n. **1** Mus. any of the tones above the lowest in a harmonic series. **2** a subtle or elusive quality or implication (sinister overtones). [OVER- + TONE, after G Oberton]

overtop /ˌəʊvəˈtɒp/ v.tr. (**-topped**, **-topping**) **1** be or become higher than. **2** surpass.

overtrain /ˌəʊvəˈtreɪn/ v.tr. & intr. subject to or undergo too much (esp. athletic) training with a consequent loss of proficiency.

overtrick /ˈəʊvəˌtrɪk/ n. Bridge a trick taken in excess of one's contract.

overtrump /ˌəʊvəˈtrʌmp/ v.tr. (also absol.) play a higher trump than (another player).

---

aʊ how eɪ day əʊ no eə hair ɪə near ɔɪ boy ʊə poor aɪə fire aʊə sour (see over for consonants)

overture /ˈəʊvətjʊə(r)/ n. **1** an orchestral piece opening an opera etc. **2** a one-movement composition in this style. **3** (usu. in pl.) **a** an opening of negotiations. **b** a formal proposal or offer (esp. *make overtures to*). **4** the beginning of a poem etc. [ME f. OF f. L *apertura* APERTURE]

overturn v. & n. —v. /ˌəʊvəˈtɜːn/ **1** tr. cause to fall down or over; upset. **2** tr. reverse; subvert; abolish; invalidate. **3** intr. fall down; fall over. —n. /ˈəʊvətɜːn/ a subversion, an act of upsetting.

overuse v. & n. —v.tr. /ˌəʊvəˈjuːz/ use too much. —n. /ˌəʊvəˈjuːs/ excessive use.

overvalue /ˌəʊvəˈvæljuː/ v.tr. (**-values**, **-valued**, **-valuing**) value too highly; have too high an opinion of.

overview /ˈəʊvəˌvjuː/ n. a general survey.

overweening /ˌəʊvəˈwiːnɪŋ/ adj. arrogant, presumptuous, conceited, self-confident. □□ **overweeningly** adv. **overweeningness** n.

overweight adj., n., & v. —adj. /ˌəʊvəˈweɪt/ beyond an allowed or suitable weight. —n. /ˈəʊvəˌweɪt/ excessive or extra weight; preponderance. —v.tr. /ˌəʊvəˈweɪt/ (usu. foll. by *with*) load unduly.

overwhelm /ˌəʊvəˈwelm/ v.tr. **1** overpower with emotion. **2** (usu. foll. by *with*) overpower with an excess of business etc. **3** bring to sudden ruin or destruction; crush. **4** bury or drown beneath a huge mass, submerge utterly.

overwhelming /ˌəʊvəˈwelmɪŋ/ adj. irresistible by force of numbers, influence, amount, etc. □□ **overwhelmingly** adv. **overwhelmingness** n.

overwind v. & n. —v.tr. /ˌəʊvəˈwaɪnd/ (past and past part. **-wound**) wind (a mechanism, esp. a watch) beyond the proper stopping point. —n. /ˈəʊvəˌwaɪnd/ an instance of this.

overwinter /ˌəʊvəˈwɪntə(r)/ v. **1** intr. (usu. foll. by *at*, *in*) spend the winter. **2** intr. (of insects, fungi, etc.) live through the winter. **3** tr. keep (animals, plants, etc.) alive through the winter.

overwork /ˌəʊvəˈwɜːk/ v. & n. —v. **1** intr. work too hard. **2** tr. cause (another person) to work too hard. **3** tr. weary or exhaust with too much work. **4** tr. make excessive use of. —n. excessive work.

overwound past and past part. of OVERWIND.

overwrite /ˌəʊvəˈraɪt/ v. (past **-wrote**; past part. **-written**) **1** tr. write on top of (other writing). **2** tr. Computing destroy (data) in (a file etc.) by entering new data. **3** intr. (esp. as **overwritten** adj.) write too elaborately or too ornately. **4** intr. & refl. write too much; exhaust oneself by writing. **5** tr. write too much about. **6** intr. (esp. as **overwriting** n.) in shipping insurance, accept more risk than the premium income limits allow.

overwrought /ˌəʊvəˈrɔːt/ adj. **1** overexcited, nervous, distraught. **2** overdone; too elaborate.

overzealous /ˌəʊvəˈzeləs/ adj. too zealous in one's attitude, behaviour, etc.; excessively enthusiastic. □□ **overzeal** /-ˈziːl/ n.

ovi-¹ /ˈəʊvɪ/ comb. form egg, ovum. [L *ovum* egg]

ovi-² /ˈəʊvɪ/ comb. form sheep. [L *ovis* sheep]

ovibovine /ˌəʊvɪˈbəʊvaɪn/ adj. & n. Zool. —adj. having characteristics intermediate between a sheep and an ox. —n. such an animal, e.g. a musk-ox.

Ovid /ˈɒvɪd/ (Publius Ovidius Naso, 43 BC–c.AD 17) the youngest and most productive of the great Roman poets who wrote under Augustus. His wit and fluency are most clearly seen in his elegiac poems on love: the *Amores* (Loves), three books of personal love-poems, the *Heroides* (Heroines), imaginary letters from legendary heroines to their absent lovers, the *Ars Amatoria* (Art of Love) and the *Remedia Amoris* (Remedies for Love), mock-didactic poems on the art of falling in and out of love. The *Metamorphoses* is a hexameter epic, a kaleidoscopic retelling of Greek and Roman myths arranged in roughly chronological order. His irreverent attitudes offended Augustus, and in AD 8, possibly after a scandal involving the latter's daughter Julia, he was exiled to Tomis (modern Constanza) on the Black Sea, from where he continued to write elegiac poems describing his plight and unsuccessfully seeking pardon.

oviduct /ˈəʊvɪˌdʌkt/ n. the tube through which an ovum passes from the ovary. □□ **oviducal** /-ˈdjuːk(ə)l/ adj. **oviductal** /-ˈdʌkt(ə)l/ adj.

Oviedo /ˌɒvɪˈeɪdəʊ/ a city of NW Spain, capital of Asturias region; pop. (1986) 190,650.

oviform /ˈəʊvɪfɔːm/ adj. egg-shaped.

ovine /ˈəʊvaɪn/ adj. of or like sheep. [LL *ovinus* f. L *ovis* sheep]

oviparous /əʊˈvɪpərəs/ adj. Zool. producing young by means of eggs expelled from the body before they are hatched (cf. VIVIPAROUS). □□ **oviparity** /-ˈpærɪtɪ/ n. **oviparously** adv.

oviposit /ˌəʊvɪˈpɒzɪt/ v.intr. (**oviposited**, **ovipositing**) lay an egg or eggs, esp. with an ovipositor. □□ **oviposition** /-pəˈzɪʃ(ə)n/ n. [OVI-¹ + L *ponere posit-* to place]

ovipositor /ˌəʊvɪˈpɒzɪtə(r)/ n. a pointed tubular organ with which a female insect deposits her eggs. [mod.L f. OVI-¹ + L *positor* f. *ponere posit-* to place]

ovoid /ˈəʊvɔɪd/ adj. & n. —adj. **1** (of a solid or of a surface) egg-shaped. **2** oval, with one end more pointed than the other. —n. an ovoid body or surface. [F *ovoïde* f. mod.L *ovoides* (as OVUM)]

ovolo /ˈəʊvələʊ/ n. (pl. **ovoli** /-liː/) Archit. a rounded convex moulding. [It. dimin. of *ovo* egg f. L OVUM]

ovotestis /ˌəʊvəˈtestɪs/ n. (pl. **-testes** /-tiːz/) Zool. an organ producing both ova and spermatozoa. [OVUM + TESTIS]

ovoviviparous /ˌəʊvəʊvɪˈvɪpərəs/ adj. Zool. producing young by means of eggs hatched within the body (cf. OVIPAROUS, VIVIPAROUS). □□ **ovoviviparity** /-ˈpærɪtɪ/ n. [OVUM + VIVIPAROUS]

ovulate /ˈɒvjʊˌleɪt/ v.intr. produce ova or ovules, or discharge them from the ovary. □□ **ovulation** /-ˈleɪʃ(ə)n/ n. **ovulatory** adj. [mod.L *ovulum* (as OVULE)]

ovule /ˈəʊvjuːl/ n. the part of the ovary of seed plants that contains the germ cell; an unfertilized seed. □□ **ovular** adj. [F f. mod.L *ovulum*, dimin. of OVUM]

ovum /ˈəʊvəm/ n. (pl. **ova** /ˈəʊvə/) **1** a mature reproductive cell of female animals, produced by the ovary. **2** the egg cell of plants. [L, = egg]

ow /aʊ/ int. expressing sudden pain. [natural exclam.]

owe /əʊ/ v.tr. **1 a** be under obligation (to a person etc.) to pay or repay (money etc.) (*we owe you five pounds*; *owe more than I can pay*). **b** (absol., usu. foll. by *for*) be in debt (*still owe for my car*). **2** (often foll. by *to*) render (gratitude etc., a person honour, gratitude, etc.) (*owe grateful thanks to*). **3** (usu. foll. by *to*) be indebted to a person or thing for (*we owe to Newton the principle of gravitation*). □ **owe a person a grudge** cherish resentment against a person. **owe it to oneself** (often foll. by *to* + infin.) need (to do) something to protect one's own interests. [OE *āgan* (see OUGHT¹) f. Gmc]

Owen¹ /ˈəʊɪn/, Robert (1771–1858), British socialist and philanthropist. A pioneer socialist thinker, Owen attempted to put his ideas into action in the New Lanark cotton mills and in a series of cooperative communities. Although these ideas did not always work well in practice, they had an important long-term effect on the development of British socialist thought and on the practice of industrial relations.

Owen² /ˈəʊɪn/, Wilfrid (1893–1918), English poet of the First World War. He was invalided out of the army in 1917 and in hospital met Siegfried Sassoon who encouraged him to speak out against the war; on returning to the trenches he found his own voice as a poet. Only five of his poems appeared in his lifetime and his reputation has grown since Sassoon's edition of his poems in 1920 and Edmund Blunden's in 1931; among the most famous are 'Strange Meeting' and 'Anthem for Doomed Youth'. Owen adopted technical experiments using assonantal rhyme to produce bleak realism and indignation at the horrors of war and pity for its victims—of whom he became one, killed in action in the last hours of the war.

Owen Glendower /ˌəʊɪn glenˈdaʊə(r)/ see GLENDOWER.

Owens /ˈəʊɪnz/, James Cleveland (Jesse) (1913–80), American athlete of track and field events, who in 1935 equalled or broke six world records in 45 minutes, and in 1936 won four gold medals at the Olympic Games in Berlin, equalling or breaking twelve Olympic records.

owing /ˈəʊɪŋ/ predic.adj. **1** owed; yet to be paid (*the balance owing*).

---

b *but* d *dog* f *few* g *get* h *he* j *yes* k *cat* l *leg* m *man* n *no* p *pen* r *red* s *sit* t *top* v *voice*

2 (foll. by *to*) **a** caused by; attributable to (*the cancellation was owing to ill health*). **b** (as *prep.*) because of (*trains are delayed owing to bad weather*).

owl /aʊl/ *n.* **1** any nocturnal bird of prey of the order Strigiformes, with large eyes and a hooked beak, including barn owls, tawny owls, etc. **2** *colloq.* a person compared to an owl, esp. in looking solemn or wise. □ **owl-light** dusk, twilight. **owl-monkey** (*pl.* **-eys**) a douroucouli. □□ **owlery** *n.* (*pl.* **-ies**). **owlish** *adj.* **owlishly** *adv.* **owlishness** *n.* (in sense 2). **owl-like** *adj.* [OE *ūle* f. Gmc]

owlet /ˈaʊlɪt/ *n.* a small or young owl.

own /əʊn/ *adj. & v.* —*adj.* (prec. by possessive) **1 a** belonging to oneself or itself; not another's (*saw it with my own eyes*). **b** individual, peculiar, particular (*a charm all of its own*). **2** used to emphasize identity rather than possession (*cooks his own meals*). **3** (*absol.*) **a** private property (*is it your own?*). **b** kindred (*among my own*). —*v.* **1** *tr.* have as property; possess. **2 a** *tr.* confess; admit as valid, true, etc. (*own their faults; owns he did not know*). **b** *intr.* (foll. by *to*) confess to (*owned to a prejudice*). **3** *tr.* acknowledge paternity, authorship, or possession of. □ **come into one's own 1** receive one's due. **2** achieve recognition. **get one's own back** (often foll. by *on*) *colloq.* get revenge. **hold one's own** maintain one's position; not be defeated or lose strength. **of one's own** belonging to oneself alone. **on one's own 1** alone. **2** independently, without help. **own brand** (often *attrib.*) goods manufactured specially for a retailer and bearing the retailer's name. **own goal 1** a goal scored (usu. by mistake) against the scorer's own side. **2** an act or initiative that has the unintended effect of harming one's own interests. **own up** (often foll. by *to*) confess frankly. □□ **-owned** *adj.* (in *comb.*). [OE *āgen, āgnian*: see OWE]

owner /ˈəʊnə(r)/ *n.* **1** a person who owns something. **2** *sl.* the captain of a ship. **3** *owner-occupier* a person who owns the house etc. he or she lives in. □□ **ownerless** *adj.* **ownership** *n.*

owt /aʊt/ *n.* *colloq.* or *dial.* anything. [var. of AUGHT[1]]

ox /ɒks/ *n.* (*pl.* **oxen** /ˈɒks(ə)n/) **1** any bovine animal, esp. a large usu. horned domesticated ruminant used for draught, for supplying milk, and for eating as meat. **2** a castrated male of a domesticated species of cattle, *Bos taurus*. □ **ox-fence** a strong fence for keeping in cattle, consisting of railings, a hedge, and often a ditch. **ox-pecker** any African bird of the genus *Buphagus*, feeding on skin parasites living on animals. [OE *oxa* f. Gmc]

ox- var. of OXY-[2].

oxalic acid /ɒkˈsælɪk/ *n.* *Chem.* a very poisonous and sour acid found in sorrel and rhubarb leaves. ¶ *Chem.* formula: (COOH)₂. □□ **oxalate** /ˈɒksəˌleɪt/ *n.* [F *oxalique* f. L *oxalis* f. Gk *oxalis* wood sorrel]

oxalis /ˈɒksəlɪs/ *n.* any plant of the genus *Oxalis*, with trifoliate leaves and white or pink flowers. [L f. Gk f. *oxus* sour]

oxbow /ˈɒksbəʊ/ *n.* **1** a U-shaped collar of an ox-yoke. **2 a** a loop formed by a horseshoe bend in a river. **b** a lake formed when the river cuts across the narrow end of the loop.

Oxbridge /ˈɒksbrɪdʒ/ *n.* *Brit.* **1** (also *attrib.*) Oxford and Cambridge universities regarded together, esp. in contrast to newer institutions. **2** (often *attrib.*) the characteristics of these universities. [portmanteau word f. Ox(ford) + (Cam)bridge]

oxen *pl.* of OX.

oxer /ˈɒksə(r)/ *n.* an ox-fence.

ox-eye /ˈɒksaɪ/ *n.* a plant with a flower like the eye of an ox. □ **ox-eye daisy** *n.* a daisy, *Leucanthemum vulgare*, having flowers with white petals and a yellow centre: also called *white ox-eye*. □□ **ox-eyed** *adj.*

Oxf. *abbr.* Oxford.

Oxfam /ˈɒksfæm/ *abbr.* Oxford Committee for Famine Relief.

Oxford /ˈɒksfəd/ a midland city on the River Thames, the seat of a major English university organized as a federation of colleges; pop. (1981) 99,200. A university (*studium generale*) was organized there soon after 1167, perhaps as a result of a migration of students from Paris. The first colleges were founded in the 13th c.—University (1249), Balliol (1263), and Merton (1264)—and Oxford rose to equal status with the great European

medieval universities, numbering among its scholars the philosopher and scientist Roger Bacon, and Sir Thomas More; Erasmus lectured there. A centre of royalism during the 17th c., Oxford declined during the 18th c. but was revived in the 1800s, particularly as a result of a renaissance in religious thought. The University includes the Bodleian Library (see entry). The first women's college, Lady Margaret Hall, was founded in 1878. In 1988–9 there were 10,005 undergraduates in residence (6,004 men, 4001 women) and 3,613 postgraduates (2,410 men, 203 women). □ **Oxford bags** wide baggy trousers. **Oxford blue** dark blue, sometimes with a purple tinge. **Oxford English Dictionary** see MURRAY[3]. **Oxford Group** a religious movement founded at Oxford in 1921, with discussion of personal problems by groups.

Oxford Movement a movement (1833–45), centred at Oxford and led by Keble, Newman, and Pusey, which aimed at restoring traditional Catholic teaching within the Church of England; its principles were set out in the *Tracts for the Times*. The Movement emphasized ceremonial, set up the first Anglican religious communities, and contributed to social work and scholarship. At first it met with much hostility, but its concern for a higher standard of worship has ultimately influenced most groups within the Church of England and even many Nonconformists.

Oxfordshire /ˈɒksfədˌʃɪə(r)/ a SE midland county of England; pop. (1981) 542,700; county town, Oxford.

oxherd /ˈɒkshɜːd/ *n.* a cowherd.

oxhide /ˈɒkshaɪd/ *n.* **1** the hide of an ox. **2** leather made from this.

oxidant /ˈɒksɪd(ə)nt/ *n.* an oxidizing agent. □□ **oxidation** /-ˈdeɪʃ(ə)n/ *n.* **oxidational** /-ˈdeɪʃən(ə)l/ *adj.* **oxidative** /-ˌdeɪtɪv/ *adj.* [F, part. of *oxider* (as OXIDE)]

oxide /ˈɒksaɪd/ *n.* a binary compound of oxygen. [F f. *oxygène* OXYGEN + *-ide* after *acide* ACID]

oxidize /ˈɒksɪˌdaɪz/ *v.* (also **-ise**) **1** *intr. & tr.* combine or cause to combine with oxygen. **2** *tr. & intr.* cover (metal) or (of metal) become covered with a coating of oxide; make or become rusty. **3** *intr. & tr.* undergo or cause to undergo a loss of electrons. □ **oxidized silver** the popular name for silver covered with a dark coat of silver sulphide. **oxidizing agent** *Chem.* a substance that brings about oxidation by being reduced and gaining electrons. □□ **oxidizable** *adj.* **oxidization** /-ˈzeɪʃ(ə)n/ *n.* **oxidizer** *n.*

oxlip /ˈɒkslɪp/ *n.* **1** a woodland primula, *Primula elatior*. **2** (in general use) a natural hybrid between a primrose and a cowslip.

Oxon. /ˈɒks(ə)n/ *abbr.* **1** Oxfordshire. **2** of Oxford University or the diocese of Oxford. [abbr. of med.L *Oxoniensis* f. *Oxonia*: see OXONIAN]

Oxonian /ɒkˈsəʊnɪən/ *adj. & n.* —*adj.* of or relating to Oxford or Oxford University. —*n.* **1** a member of Oxford University. **2** a native or inhabitant of Oxford. [*Oxonia* Latinized name of *Ox(en)ford*]

oxtail /ˈɒksteɪl/ *n.* the tail of an ox, often used in making soup.

oxter /ˈɒkstə(r)/ *n.* *Sc. & N.Engl.* the armpit. [OE *ōhsta, ōxta*]

oxtongue /ˈɒkstʌŋ/ *n.* **1** the tongue of an ox, esp. cooked as food. **2** any composite plant of the genus *Picris*, with bright yellow flowers.

oxy-[1] /ˈɒksɪ/ *comb. form* denoting sharpness (*oxytone*). [Gk *oxu-* f. *oxus* sharp]

oxy-[2] /ˈɒksɪ/ *comb. form* (also **ox-** /ɒks/) *Chem.* oxygen (*oxyacetylene*). [abbr.]

oxyacetylene /ˌɒksɪəˈsetɪˌliːn/ *adj.* of or using a mixture of oxygen and acetylene, esp. in cutting or welding metals (*oxyacetylene burner*).

oxyacid /ˈɒksɪˌæsɪd/ *n.* *Chem.* an acid containing oxygen.

oxygen /ˈɒksɪdʒ(ə)n/ *n.* *Chem.* a colourless tasteless odourless gaseous element, essential to plant and animal life. (See below.) ¶ Symb.: **O**; atomic number 8. □ **oxygen mask** a mask placed over the nose and mouth to supply oxygen for breathing. **oxygen tent** a tentlike enclosure supplying a patient with air rich in oxygen. □□ **oxygenous** /ɒkˈsɪdʒɪnəs/ *adj.* [F *oxygène* acidifying principle (as OXY- 2): it was at first held to be the essential principle in the formation of acids]

Oxygen was discovered in 1774 by Joseph Priestley (see entry). It forms about 20 per cent of the earth's atmosphere by volume. Many rocks are formed chiefly of oxygen compounds, and it is the most abundant element in the earth's crust. It exists in two forms: atmospheric oxygen, which consists of diatomic molecules, and ozone (see entry). Oxygen is essential to plant and animal life. It is a constituent of most of the compounds found in living organisms, and the processes of respiration and combustion involve its ability to combine readily with other elements. Water is a compound of hydrogen and oxygen. Industrially, pure oxygen is obtained by distillation of liquefied air; it is used in the steel-making and chemical industries, and in medicine.

oxygenate /ˈɒksɪdʒəˌneɪt, ɒkˈsɪ-/ v.tr. **1** supply, treat, or mix with oxygen; oxidize. **2** charge (blood) with oxygen by respiration. □□ **oxygenation** /-ˈneɪʃ(ə)n/ n. [F oxygéner (as OXYGEN)]

oxygenator /ˈɒksɪdʒəˌneɪtə(r)/ n. an apparatus for oxygenating the blood.

oxygenize /ˈɒksɪdʒəˌnaɪz, ɒkˈsɪ-/ (also **-ise**) v.tr. = OXYGENATE.

oxyhaemoglobin /ˌɒksɪˌhiːməˈɡləʊbɪn/ n. Biochem. a bright red complex formed when haemoglobin combines with oxygen.

oxymoron /ˌɒksɪˈmɔːrɒn/ n. rhet. a figure of speech in which apparently contradictory terms appear in conjunction (e.g. faith unfaithful kept him falsely true). [Gk oxumōron neut. of oxumōros pointedly foolish f. oxus sharp + mōros foolish]

oxytocin /ˌɒksɪˈtəʊsɪn/ n. **1** a hormone released by the pituitary gland that causes increased contraction of the womb during labour and stimulates the ejection of milk into the ducts of the breasts. **2** a synthetic form of this used to induce labour etc. [oxytocic accelerating parturition f. Gk oxutokia sudden delivery (as OXY-[1], tokos childbirth)]

oxytone /ˈɒksɪˌtəʊn/ adj. & n. —adj. (esp. in ancient Greek) having an acute accent on the last syllable. —n. a word of this kind. [Gk oxutonos (as OXY-[1], tonos tone)]

oyer and terminer /ˌɔɪə(r) ənd ˈtɜːmɪnə(r)/ n. hist. a commission issued to judges on a circuit to hold courts. [ME f. AF oyer et terminer f. L audire hear + et and + terminare determine]

oyez /əʊˈjes, -ˈjez/ int. (also **oyes**) uttered, usu. three times, by a public crier or a court officer to command silence and attention. [ME f. AF, OF oiez, oyez, imper. pl. of oïr hear f. L audire]

oyster /ˈɔɪstə(r)/ n. **1** any of various bivalve molluscs of the family Ostreidae or Aviculidae, esp. an edible kind, Ostrea edulis, of European waters. **2** an oyster-shaped morsel of meat in a fowl's back. **3** something regarded as containing all that one desires (the world is my oyster). **4** (in full **oyster-white**) a white colour with a grey tinge. □ **oyster-bank** (or **-bed**) a part of the sea-bottom where oysters breed or are bred. **oyster-catcher** any usu. coastal wading bird of the genus Haematopus, with a strong orange-coloured bill, feeding on shellfish. **oyster-farm** an area of the seabed used for breeding oysters. **oyster-plant** **1** = SALSIFY. **2** a blue-flowered plant, Mertensia maritima, growing on beaches. [ME & OF oistre f. L ostrea, ostreum f. Gk ostreon]

Oz /ɒz/ n. Austral. sl. Australia. [abbr.]

oz. abbr. ounce(s). [It. f. onza ounce]

Ozark Mountains /ˈəʊzɑːk/ (also **Ozarks**) a plateau dissected by rivers, valleys, and streams, lying between the Missouri and Arkansas rivers and within Missouri, Arkansas, Oklahoma, Kansas, and Illinois.

ozocerite /əʊˈzəʊkəˌraɪt/ n. (also **ozokerite**) a waxlike fossil paraffin used for candles, insulation, etc. [G Ozokerit f. Gk ozō smell + kēros wax]

ozone /ˈəʊzəʊn/ n. **1** Chem. a colourless unstable gas with a pungent odour and powerful oxidizing properties, used for bleaching etc. It can be formed by passing an electrical discharge through oxygen, and is present in the air after a thunderstorm. The greatest concentration of ozone is in the upper atmosphere, where it forms as a result of the interaction of oxygen and ultraviolet rays from the sun (the ozone layer; see below). ¶ Chem. formula: O_3. **2** colloq. **a** invigorating air at the seaside etc. **b** exhilarating influence. □ **ozone-friendly** (of manufactured articles) containing chemicals that are not destructive to the ozone layer. **ozone layer** a layer of ozone in the stratosphere that absorbs most of the sun's ultraviolet radiation. □□ **ozonic** /əʊˈzɒnɪk/ adj. **ozonize** v.tr. (also **-ise**). **ozonization** /-ˈzeɪʃ(ə)n/ n. **ozonizer** n. [G Ozon f. Gk, neut. pres. part. of ozō smell]

Ozzie var. of AUSSIE.

P

P¹ /piː/ n. (also **p**) (pl. **Ps** or **P's**) the sixteenth letter of the alphabet.

P² abbr. (also **P.**) **1** (on road signs) parking. **2** Chess pawn. **3** Physics poise (unit). **4** (also Ⓡ) proprietary.

P³ symb. Chem. the element phosphorus.

p abbr. (also **p.**) **1** Brit. penny, pence. **2** page. **3** pico-. **4** piano (softly).

PA abbr. **1** personal assistant. **2** public address (esp. PA system). **3** Press Association. **4** US Pennsylvania (in official postal use).

Pa symb. Chem. the element protactinium.

pa /paː/ n. colloq. father. [abbr. of PAPA]

p.a. abbr. per annum.

Paarl /paːl/ a town in the south-west of Cape Province, South Africa, at the centre of a famous wine-producing region.

pabulum /ˈpæbjʊləm/ n. food, esp. for the mind (mental pabulum). [L f. pascere feed]

PABX abbr. Brit. private automatic branch exchange.

PAC abbr. Pan-African Congress.

paca /ˈpækə/ n. any tailless rodent of the genus Cuniculus, esp. the spotted cavy of S. and Central America. [Sp. & Port., f. Tupi]

pace¹ /peɪs/ n. & v. —n. **1 a** a single step in walking or running. **b** the distance covered in this (about 75 cm or 30 in.). **c** the distance between two successive stationary positions of the same foot in walking. **2** speed in walking or running. **3** Theatr. & Mus. speed or tempo in theatrical or musical performance (played with great pace). **4** a rate of progression. **5 a** a manner of walking or running; a gait. **b** any of various gaits, esp. of a trained horse etc. (rode at an ambling pace). —v. **1** intr. **a** walk (esp. repeatedly or methodically) with a slow or regular pace (pacing up and down). **b** (of a horse) = AMBLE. **2** tr. traverse by pacing. **3** tr. set the pace for (a rider, runner, etc.). **4** tr. (foll. by out) measure (a distance) by pacing. □ **keep pace** (often foll. by with) advance at an equal rate (as). **pace bowler** Cricket a bowler who delivers the ball at high speed without spin. **pace-setter 1** a leader. **2** = PACEMAKER 1. **put a person through his** (or **her**) **paces** test a person's qualities in action etc. **set the pace** determine the speed, esp. by leading. **stand** (or **stay**) **the pace** be able to keep up with others. □□ **-paced** adj. **pacer** n. [ME f. OF pas f. L passus f. pandere pass- stretch]

pace² /ˈpɑːtʃeɪ, ˈpeɪsɪ/ prep. (in stating a contrary opinion) with due deference to (the person named). [L, ablat. of pax peace]

pacemaker /ˈpeɪsˌmeɪkə(r)/ n. **1** a competitor who sets the pace in a race. **2** a natural or artificial device for stimulating the heart muscle and determining the rate of its contractions.

pacha var. of PASHA.

pachinko /pəˈtʃɪŋkəʊ/ n. a Japanese form of pinball. [Jap.]

pachisi /pəˈtʃiːzɪ/ n. a four-handed Indian board-game with six cowries used like dice. [Hindi, = of 25 (the highest throw)]

pachyderm /ˈpækɪˌdɜːm/ n. any thick-skinned mammal, esp. an elephant or rhinoceros. □□ **pachydermatous** /-ˈdɜːmətəs/ adj. [F pachyderme f. Gk pakhudermos f. pakhus thick + derma -matos skin]

pacific /pəˈsɪfɪk/ adj. & n. —adj. **1** characterized by or tending to peace; tranquil. **2** (**Pacific**) of or adjoining the Pacific Ocean. —n. (**the Pacific**) the Pacific Ocean. □ **Pacific Ocean** the world's largest ocean, covering one-third of the earth's surface (181,300,000 sq. km, 70 million sq. miles), separating Asia and Australia from North and South America and extending from Antarctica in the south to the Bering Strait (which links it to the Arctic Ocean) in the north. It was named by its first European navigator, Magellan, because he experienced calm weather there. **Pacific Time** the standard time used in the Pacific region of Canada and the US. □□ **pacifically** adv. [F pacifique or L pacificus f. pax pacis peace]

pacification /ˌpæsɪfɪˈkeɪʃ(ə)n/ n. the act of pacifying or the process of being pacified. □□ **pacificatory** /pəˈsɪfɪkətərɪ/ adj. [F f. L pacificatio -onis (as PACIFY)]

pacifier /ˈpæsɪˌfaɪə(r)/ n. **1** a person or thing that pacifies. **2** US a baby's dummy.

pacifism /ˈpæsɪˌfɪz(ə)m/ n. the belief that war and violence are morally unjustified and that all disputes can be settled by peaceful means. □□ **pacifist** n. & adj. [F pacifisme f. pacifier PACIFY]

pacify /ˈpæsɪˌfaɪ/ v.tr. (**-ies, -ied**) **1** appease (a person, anger, etc.). **2** bring (a country etc.) to a state of peace. [ME f. OF pacifier or L pacificare (as PACIFIC)]

pack¹ /pæk/ n. & v. —n. **1 a** a collection of things wrapped up or tied together for carrying. **b** = BACKPACK. **2** a set of items packaged for use or disposal together. **3** usu. derog. a lot or set (of similar things or persons) (a pack of lies; a pack of thieves). **4** Brit. a set of playing cards. **5 a** a group of hounds esp. for foxhunting. **b** a group of wild animals, esp. wolves, hunting together. **6** an organized group of Cub Scouts or Brownies. **7** Rugby Football a team's forwards. **8 a** a medicinal or cosmetic substance applied to the skin; = face-pack. **b** a hot or cold pad of absorbent material for treating a wound etc. **9** = pack ice. **10** a quantity of fish, fruit, etc., packed in a season etc. **11** Med. **a** the wrapping of a body or part of a body in a wet sheet etc. **b** a sheet etc. used for this. —v. **1** tr. (often foll. by up) **a** fill (a suitcase, bag, etc.) with clothes and other items. **b** put (things) together in a bag or suitcase, esp. for travelling. **2** intr. & tr. come or put closely together; crowd or cram (packed a lot into a few hours; passengers packed like sardines). **3** tr. (in passive; often foll. by with) be filled (with); contain extensively (the restaurant was packed; the book is packed with information). **4** tr. fill (a hall, theatre, etc.) with an audience etc. **5** tr. cover (a thing) with something pressed tightly round. **6** intr. be suitable for packing. **7** tr. colloq. **a** carry (a gun etc.). **b** be capable of delivering (a punch) with skill or force. **8** intr. (of animals or Rugby forwards) form a pack. □ **pack-animal** an animal for carrying packs. **pack-drill** a military punishment of marching up and down carrying full equipment. **packed lunch** a lunch carried in a bag, box, etc., esp. to work, school, etc. **packed out** colloq. full, crowded. **pack ice** an area of large crowded pieces of floating ice in the sea. **pack it in** (or **up**) colloq. end or stop it. **pack off** send (a person) away, esp. abruptly or promptly. **pack-rat** US a large hoarding rodent. **pack-saddle** a saddle adapted for supporting packs. **pack up** colloq. **1** (esp. of a machine) stop functioning; break down. **2** retire from an activity, contest, etc. **send packing** colloq. dismiss (a person) summarily. □□ **packable** adj. [ME f. MDu., MLG pak, pakken, of unkn. orig.]

pack² /pæk/ v.tr. select (a jury etc.) or fill (a meeting) so as to secure a decision in one's favour. [prob. f. obs. verb pact f. PACT]

package /ˈpækɪdʒ/ n. & v. —n. **1 a** a bundle of things packed. **b** a parcel, box, etc., in which things are packed. **2** (in full **package deal**) a set of proposals or items offered or agreed to as a whole. **3** Computing a piece of software suitable for various applications rather than one which is custom-built. **4** colloq. = package holiday. —v.tr. make up into or enclose in a package. □ **package holiday** (or **tour** etc.) a holiday or tour etc. with all arrangements made at an inclusive price. □□ **packager** n. [PACK¹ + -AGE]

packaging /ˈpækɪdʒɪŋ/ n. **1** a wrapping or container for goods. **2** the process of packing goods.

packer /ˈpækə(r)/ n. a person or thing that packs, esp. a dealer who prepares and packs food for transportation and sale.

packet /ˈpækɪt/ n. **1** a small package. **2** colloq. a large sum of money won, lost, or spent. **3** (in full **packet-boat**) hist. a mail-boat or passenger ship. [PACK¹ + -ET¹]

packhorse /ˈpækhɔːs/ n. a horse for carrying loads.

packing /ˈpækɪŋ/ n. 1 the act or process of packing. 2 material used as padding to pack esp. fragile articles. 3 material used to seal a join or assist in lubricating an axle. □ **packing-case** a case (usu. wooden) or framework for packing goods in.

packthread /ˈpækθred/ n. stout thread for sewing or tying up packs.

pact /pækt/ n. an agreement or a treaty. [ME f. OF pact(e) f. L pactum, neut. past part. of pacisci agree]

pad¹ /pæd/ n. & v. —n. 1 a piece of soft material used to reduce friction or jarring, fill out hollows, hold or absorb liquid, etc. 2 a number of sheets of blank paper fastened together at one edge, for writing or drawing on. 3 = ink-pad. 4 the fleshy underpart of an animal's foot or of a human finger. 5 a guard for the leg and ankle in sports. 6 a flat surface for helicopter take-off or rocket-launching. 7 colloq. a lodging, esp. a bedsitter or flat. 8 the floating leaf of a water lily. —v.tr. (**padded, padding**) 1 provide with a pad or padding; stuff. 2 (foll. by out) lengthen or fill out (a book etc.) with unnecessary material. □ **padded cell** a room with padded walls in a mental hospital. [prob. of LG or Du. orig.]

pad² /pæd/ v. & n. —v. (**padded, padding**) 1 intr. walk with a soft dull steady step. 2 a tr. tramp along (a road etc.) on foot. b intr. travel on foot. —n. the sound of soft steady steps. [LG padden tread, pad PATH]

Padang /pæˈdæŋ/ a seaport of Indonesia, capital of West Sumatra province; pop. (1980) 480,900.

padding /ˈpædɪŋ/ n. soft material used to pad or stuff with.

paddle¹ /ˈpæd(ə)l/ n. & v. —n. 1 a short broad-bladed oar used without a rowlock. 2 a paddle-shaped instrument. 3 Zool. a fin or flipper. 4 each of the boards fitted round the circumference of a paddle-wheel or mill-wheel. 5 the action or a spell of paddling. —v. 1 intr. & tr. move on water or propel a boat by means of paddles. 2 intr. & tr. row gently. 3 tr. esp. US colloq. spank. □ **paddle-boat** (or **-steamer** etc.) a boat, steamer, etc., propelled by a paddle-wheel. **paddle-wheel** a wheel for propelling a ship, with boards round the circumference so as to press backwards against the water. □□ **paddler** n. [15th c.: orig. unkn.]

paddle² /ˈpæd(ə)l/ v. & n. —v.intr. walk barefoot or dabble the feet or hands in shallow water. —n. the action or a spell of paddling. □□ **paddler** n. [prob. of LG or Du. orig.: cf. LG paddeln tramp about]

paddock /ˈpædək/ n. 1 a small field, esp. for keeping horses in. 2 a turf enclosure adjoining a racecourse where horses or cars are assembled before a race. 3 Austral. & NZ a field; a plot of land. [app. var. of (now dial.) parrock (OE pearruc: see PARK]

Paddy /ˈpædɪ/ n. (pl. **-ies**) colloq. often offens. an Irishman. [pet-form of the Irish name Padraig (= Patrick)]

paddy¹ /ˈpædɪ/ n. (pl. **-ies**) 1 (in full **paddy-field**) a field where rice is grown. 2 rice before threshing or in the husk. [Malay pādī]

paddy² /ˈpædɪ/ n. (pl. **-ies**) Brit. colloq. a rage; a fit of temper. [PADDY]

pademelon /ˈpædɪˌmelən/ n. any small wallaby of the genus Thylogale, inhabiting the coastal scrub of Australia. [corrupt. of an Aboriginal name]

Paderewski /ˌpɑːdəˈrefskɪ/, Ignacy Jan (1860–1941), Polish pianist, composer, and statesman. He became one of the most famous international pianists and also received acclaim for his compositions, which include a piano concerto, a symphony, and the opera Manru (1901). Always a fervent nationalist, he became the first prime minister of an independent Poland (1919) but resigned after only 10 months in office and resumed his musical career.

padlock /ˈpædlɒk/ n. & v. —n. a detachable lock hanging by a pivoted hook on the object fastened. —v.tr. secure with a padlock. [ME f. LOCK¹: first element unexpl.]

Padma /ˈpædmə/ a river of southern Bangladesh, formed by the meeting of the Ganges and Brahmaputra near Rajbari.

padouk /pəˈduːk/ n. 1 any timber tree of the genus Pterocarpus, esp. P. indicus. 2 the wood of this tree, resembling rosewood. [Burmese]

padre /ˈpɑːdrɪ, -dreɪ/ n. a chaplain in any of the armed services. [It., Sp., & Port., = father, priest, f. L pater patris father]

padsaw /ˈpædsɔː/ n. a saw with a narrow blade, for cutting curves.

Padua /ˈpædjuːə/ (Italian **Padova** /ˈpædəvə/) a city in NE Italy; pop. (1981) 234,700. It was the birthplace of the Roman historian Livy and the artist Mantegna; Dante lived in Padua, and St Antony of Padua is buried there. Galileo taught at its university (founded in 1222).

paean /ˈpiːən/ n. (US **pean**) a song of praise or triumph. [L f. Doric Gk paian hymn of thanksgiving to Apollo (under the name of Paian)]

paederast var. of PEDERAST.

paederasty var. of PEDERASTY.

paediatrics /ˌpiːdɪˈætrɪks/ n.pl. (treated as sing.) (US **pediatrics**) the branch of medicine dealing with children and their diseases. □□ **paediatric** adj. **paediatrician** /-əˈtrɪʃ(ə)n/ n. [PAEDO- + Gk iatros physician]

paedo- /ˈpiːdəʊ/ comb. form (US **pedo-**) child. [Gk pais paid- child]

paedophile /ˈpiːdəˌfaɪl/ n. (US **pedophile**) a person who displays paedophilia.

paedophilia /ˌpiːdəˈfɪlɪə/ n. (US **pedophilia**) sexual desire directed towards children.

paella /paɪˈelə, pɑː-/ n. a Spanish dish of rice, saffron, chicken, seafood, etc., cooked and served in a large shallow pan. [Catalan f. OF paele f. L patella pan]

paeon /ˈpiːən/ n. a metrical foot of one long syllable and three short syllables in any order. □□ **paeonic** /piːˈɒnɪk/ adj. [L f. Gk paiōn, the Attic form of paian PAEAN]

paeony var. of PEONY.

pagan /ˈpeɪɡən/ n. & adj. —n. a person not subscribing to any of the main religions of the world, esp. formerly regarded by Christians as unenlightened or heathen. —adj. 1 a of or relating to or associated with pagans. b irreligious. 2 identifying divinity or spirituality in nature; pantheistic. □□ **paganish** adj. **paganism** n. **paganize** v.tr. & intr. (also **-ise**). [ME f. L paganus villager, rustic f. pagus country district: in Christian L = civilian, heathen]

Paganini /ˌpæɡəˈniːnɪ/, Niccolò (1782–1840), Italian violinist and composer, who lived an extraordinary life as a travelling violinist. He possessed a brilliant technical skill, a personal magnetism, and a mephistophelean appearance that mesmerized his audiences (particularly the female members) and led some critics to speak of diabolical powers. He did not confine his skills to playing the violin but took up the guitar during a love affair in the 1830s; he also commissioned Berlioz to write a viola concerto for him (which, however, he never played), and his own compositions for the violin bear witness to his prowess.

Page /peɪdʒ/, Sir Frederick Handley (1885–1962), English aircraft designer, founder of Handley Page Ltd. (1909), the first British aircraft manufacturing company. He was responsible for the design and construction of many famous aircraft including Handley Page bombers of the First World War, Hannibal airliners, Hampden and Halifax bombers of the Second World War, and many postwar aircraft. In 1919 he formed Handley Page Transport Ltd., operating London–Paris and London–Brussels–Switzerland flights until 1924. He was also famous for his design of the slotted aerofoil.

page¹ /peɪdʒ/ n. & v. —n. 1 a a leaf of a book, periodical, etc. b each side of this. c what is written or printed on this. 2 a an episode that might fill a page in written history etc.; a record. b a memorable event. —v.tr. paginate. [F f. L pagina f. pangere fasten]

page² /peɪdʒ/ n. & v. —n. 1 a boy or man, usu. in livery, employed to run errands, attend to a door, etc. 2 a boy employed as a personal attendant of a person of rank, a bride, etc. 3 hist. a boy in training for knighthood and attached to a knight's service. —v.tr. 1 (in hotels, airports, etc.) summon by making an announcement or by sending a messenger. 2 summon by means of a pager. □ **page-boy 1** = PAGE² n. 2. 2 a woman's hairstyle with the hair reaching to the shoulder and rolled under at the ends. [ME f. OF, perh. f. It. *paggio* f. Gk *paidion*, dimin. of *pais paidos* boy]

pageant /ˈpædʒ(ə)nt/ n. **1 a** a brilliant spectacle, esp. an elaborate parade. **b** a spectacular procession, or play performed in the open, illustrating historical events. **c** a tableau etc. on a fixed stage or moving vehicle. **2** an empty or specious show. [ME *pagyn*, of unkn. orig.]

pageantry /ˈpædʒəntrɪ/ n. (pl. **-ies**) **1** elaborate or sumptuous show or display. **2** an instance of this.

pager /ˈpeɪdʒə(r)/ n. a radio device with a bleeper, activated from a central point to alert the person wearing it.

paginal /ˈpædʒɪn(ə)l/ adj. **1** of pages (of books etc.). **2** corresponding page for page. □□ **paginary** adj. [LL *paginalis* (as PAGE[1])]

paginate /ˈpædʒɪˌneɪt/ v.tr. assign numbers to (the pages of a book etc.). □□ **pagination** /-ˈneɪʃ(ə)n/ n. [F *paginer* f. L *pagina* PAGE[1]]

pagoda /pəˈɡəʊdə/ n. **1** a Hindu or Buddhist temple or sacred building, esp. a many-tiered tower, in India and the Far East. **2** an ornamental imitation of this. □ **pagoda-tree** any of various trees, esp. *Sophora japonica*, resembling a pagoda in shape. [Port. *pagode*, prob. ult. f. Pers. *butkada* idol temple]

pah /pɑː/ int. expressing disgust or contempt. [natural utterance]

Pahang /pəˈhæŋ/ a State of Malaysia, on the Malay Peninsula; pop. (1980) 798,800; capital, Kuantan.

Pahlavi /ˈpɑːləvɪ/ n. (also **Pehlevi** /ˈpeɪləvɪ/) the language of Persia spoken from the 3rd c. BC until the 10th c. AD, the official language of the Sassanian empire. It was closely related to Avestan and was written in a version of the Aramaic script. □ **Pahlavi dynasty** the Iranian dynasty founded by Reza Khan (1878–1944), an army officer who became shah of Iran 1925–41. He was succeeded by his son, who was overthrown in 1979 (see IRAN). [Pers. *pahlawī* f. *pahlav* f. *parthava* Parthia]

paid past and past part. of PAY[1].

pail /peɪl/ n. **1** a bucket. **2** an amount contained in this. □□ **pailful** n. (pl. **-fuls**). [OE *pægel* gill (cf. MDu. *pegel* gauge), assoc. with OF *paelle*: see PAELLA]

Pailin /ˈpeɪlɪn/ a ruby-mining town in western Cambodia, close to the frontier with Thailand.

paillasse var. of PALLIASSE.

paillette /pælˈjet, paɪˈjet/ n. **1** a piece of bright metal used in enamel painting. **2** a spangle. [F, dimin. of *paille* f. L *palea* straw, chaff]

pain /peɪn/ n. & v. —n. **1 a** the range of unpleasant bodily sensations produced by illness or by harmful physical contact etc. **b** a particular kind or instance of this (often in pl.: *suffering from stomach pains*). **2** mental suffering or distress. **3** (in pl.) careful effort; trouble taken (*take pains; got nothing for my pains*). **4** (also **pain in the neck**) colloq. a troublesome person or thing; a nuisance. —v.tr. **1** cause pain to. **2** (as **pained** adj.) expressing pain (*a pained expression*). □ **in pain** suffering pain. **on** (or **under**) **pain of** with (death etc.) as the penalty. [ME f. OF *peine* f. L *poena* penalty]

Paine /peɪn/, Thomas (1737–1809), English writer and political theorist, who lost his job as an excise officer in 1774 after agitating for higher wages in the service and went to America, where he became involved in the political controversies which led to independence. His pamphlet *Common Sense* (1776) influenced the American Declaration of Independence and provided the arguments to justify it. He returned to England, and in 1791–2 he published *The Rights of Man* in support of republicanism, a reply to Burke's *Reflections on the Revolution in France*. His radical views alarmed the British government and he fled to France. There he supported the Revolution but opposed the execution of Louis XVI. He was imprisoned for a year, and narrowly escaped the guillotine. While in prison he completed *The Age of Reason*, a provocative attack on Christianity. In 1802 he returned to America.

Paine Towers /ˈpaɪneɪ/ a group of spectacular granite peaks in southern Chile, rising to a height of 2,668 m (8,755 ft.).

painful /ˈpeɪnfʊl/ adj. **1** causing bodily or mental pain or distress. **2** (esp. of part of the body) suffering pain. **3** causing trouble or difficulty; laborious (*a painful climb*). □□ **painfully** adv. **painfulness** n.

painkiller /ˈpeɪnˌkɪlə(r)/ n. a medicine or drug for alleviating pain. □□ **painkilling** adj.

painless /ˈpeɪnlɪs/ adj. not causing or suffering pain. □□ **painlessly** adv. **painlessness** n.

painstaking /ˈpeɪnzˌteɪkɪŋ/ adj. careful, industrious, thorough. □□ **painstakingly** adv. **painstakingness** n.

paint /peɪnt/ n. & v. —n. **1 a** a colouring matter, esp. in liquid form for imparting colour to a surface. **b** this as a dried film or coating (*the paint peeled off*). **2** joc. or archaic cosmetic make-up, esp. rouge or nail varnish. —v.tr. **1 a** cover the surface of (a wall, object, etc.) with paint. **b** apply paint of a specified colour to (*paint the door green*). **2** depict (an object, scene, etc.) with paint; produce (a picture) by painting. **3** describe vividly as if by painting (*painted a gloomy picture of the future*). **4** joc. or archaic **a** apply liquid or cosmetic to (the face, skin, etc.). **b** apply (a liquid to the skin etc.). □ **painted lady** an orange-red butterfly, esp. *Cynthia cardui*, with black and white spots. **paint out** efface with paint. **paint shop** the part of a factory where goods are painted, esp. by spraying. **paint-stick** a stick of water-soluble paint used like a crayon. **paint the town red** colloq. enjoy oneself flamboyantly. □□ **paintable** adj. [ME f. *peint* past part. of OF *peindre* f. L *pingere* *pict-* paint]

paintbox /ˈpeɪntbɒks/ n. a box holding dry paints for painting pictures.

paintbrush /ˈpeɪntbrʌʃ/ n. a brush for applying paint.

painter[1] /ˈpeɪntə(r)/ n. a person who paints, esp. an artist or decorator. [ME f. OF *peintour* ult. f. L *pictor* (as PAINT)]

painter[2] /ˈpeɪntə(r)/ n. a rope attached to the bow of a boat for tying it to a quay etc. [ME, prob. f. OF *penteur* rope from a masthead: cf. G *Pentertakel* f. *pentern* fish the anchor]

painterly /ˈpeɪntəlɪ/ adj. **1 a** using paint well; artistic. **b** characteristic of a painter or paintings. **2** (of a painting) lacking clearly defined outlines.

painting /ˈpeɪntɪŋ/ n. **1** the process or art of using paint. **2** a painted picture.

paintwork /ˈpeɪntwɜːk/ n. **1** a painted surface or area in a building etc. **2** the work of painting.

painty /ˈpeɪntɪ/ adj. (**paintier**, **paintiest**) **1** of or covered in paint. **2** (of a picture etc.) overcharged with paint.

pair /peə(r)/ n. & v. —n. **1** a set of two persons or things used together or regarded as a unit (*a pair of gloves; a pair of eyes*). **2** an article (e.g. scissors, trousers, or pyjamas) consisting of two joined or corresponding parts not used separately. **3 a** an engaged or married couple. **b** a mated couple of animals. **4** two horses harnessed side by side (*a coach and pair*). **5** the second member of a pair in relation to the first (*cannot find its pair*). **6** two playing cards of the same denomination. **7** Parl. either or both of two MPs etc. on opposite sides absenting themselves from voting by mutual arrangement. —v.tr. & intr. **1** (often foll. by *off*) arrange or be arranged in couples. **2 a** join or be joined in marriage. **b** (of animals) mate. **3** Parl. form a pair. □ **in pairs** in twos. **pair production** Physics the conversion of a radiation quantum into an electron and a positron. **pair royal** a set of three cards of the same denomination. [ME f. OF *paire* f. L *paria* neut. pl. of *par* equal]

paisa /ˈpaɪzə/ n. (pl. **paise** /-zeɪ/ or -zə/) a coin and monetary unit of India, Pakistan, Nepal, and Bangladesh, equal to one-hundredth of a rupee or taka. [Hindi]

Paisley /ˈpeɪzlɪ/ a town in Strathclyde region in central Scotland; pop. (1981) 84,800. —n. (often attrib.) **1** a distinctive detailed pattern of curved feather-shaped figures. **2** a soft woollen garment having this pattern.

pajamas US var. of PYJAMAS.

pakeha /ˈpɑːkɪˌhɑː/ n. NZ a White person as opposed to a Maori. [Maori]

Paki /ˈpækɪ/ n. (pl. **Pakis**) Brit. sl. offens. a Pakistani, esp. an immigrant in Britain. [abbr.]

w we z zoo ʃ she ʒ decision θ thin ð this ŋ ring x loch tʃ chip dʒ jar (see over for vowels)

Pakistan /ˌpɑːkɪˈstɑːn, ˌpæk-/ a country in southern Asia, bordered by Afghanistan to the north and India to the east; pop. (est. 1988) 107,467,450; official language, Urdu; capital, Islamabad. Part of the Indian subcontinent, Pakistan was created as a separate country, comprising the territory to the NE and NW of India in which the population was predominantly Muslim, following the British withdrawal in 1947. East Pakistan became the independent State of Bangladesh in 1972 after war between India and Pakistan in December 1971; Pakistan withdrew from the Commonwealth as a protest against the decision of Britain, Australia, and New Zealand to recognize Bangladesh, but rejoined in 1989. Pakistan's history since independence has been characterized by border disputes with India over Kashmir, the involvement of the army in politics, and recently by the threat to its northern frontier caused by the war in Afghanistan. The economy is predominantly agricultural, wheat, cotton, and rice being the principal crops. □□ **Pakistani** adj. & n. [Punjab, Afghan Frontier, Kashmir, Baluchistan, lands where Muslims predominated]

pakora /pəˈkɔːrə/ n. a piece of cauliflower, carrot, or other vegetable, coated in seasoned batter and deep-fried. [Hind.]

Pakse /ˈpækseɪ/ a town in southern Laos, on the Mekong River; pop. 44,800.

pal /pæl/ n. & v. —n. colloq. a friend, mate, or comrade. —v.intr. (**palled, palling**) (usu. foll. by up) associate; form a friendship. [Romany = brother, mate, ult. f. Skr. bhrātr BROTHER]

palace /ˈpælɪs/ n. **1** the official residence of a sovereign, president, archbishop, or bishop. **2** a splendid mansion; a spacious building. □ **palace revolution** (or **coup**) the (usu. non-violent) overthrow of a sovereign, government, etc. at the hands of senior officials. [ME f. OF palais f. L Palatium Palatine (hill) in Rome where the house of the emperor was situated]

Palace of Westminster see WESTMINSTER.

paladin /ˈpælədɪn/ n. hist. **1** any of the twelve peers of Charlemagne's court, of whom the Count Palatine was the chief. **2** a knight errant; a champion. [F paladin f. It. paladino f. L palatinus: see PALATINE¹]

Palaearctic /ˌpælɪˈɑːktɪk/ adj. Zool. of the Arctic and temperate parts of the old world. [PALAEO- + ARCTIC]

palaeo- /ˈpælɪəʊ, ˈpeɪlɪəʊ/ comb. form (US **paleo-**) ancient, old; of ancient (esp. prehistoric) times. [Gk palaios ancient]

palaeobotany /ˌpælɪəʊˈbɒtənɪ/ n. the study of fossil plants.

Palaeocene /ˈpælɪəˌsiːn/ adj. & n. (US **Paleocene**) Geol. —adj. of or relating to the earliest epoch of the Tertiary period, following the Cretaceous period and preceding the Eocene epoch, lasting from about 65 to 54.9 million years ago. The sudden diversification of the mammals is a notable feature of the epoch. —n. this epoch or system. [PALAEO- + Gk kainos new]

palaeoclimatology /ˌpælɪəʊˌklaɪməˈtɒlədʒɪ, ˌpeɪlɪəʊ-/ n. (US **paleoclimatology**) the study of the climate in geologically past times.

palaeogeography /ˌpælɪəʊdʒɪˈɒgrəfɪ, ˌpeɪlɪəʊ-/ n. (US **paleogeography**) the study of the geographical features at periods in the geological past.

palaeography /ˌpælɪˈɒgrəfɪ/ n. (US **paleography**) the study of writing and documents from the past. □□ **palaeographer** n. **palaeographic** /-əˈgræfɪk/ adj. **palaeographical** /-əˈgræfɪk(ə)l/ adj. **palaeographically** /-əˈgræfɪkəlɪ/ adv. [F paléographie f. mod.L palaeographia (as PALAEO-, -GRAPHY)]

palaeolithic /ˌpælɪəʊˈlɪθɪk/ adj. & n. (US **paleolithic**) —adj. Archaeol. of or relating to the earlier part of the Stone Age, when primitive stone implements were used. —n. this period, which extends from the first appearance of artefacts, some 2.5 million years ago, to the end of the last ice age c.10,000 BC. It has been divided into the lower palaeolithic, with the earliest forms of mankind and the presence of hand-axe industries, ending c.80,000 BC, middle palaeolithic (or Mousterian), the era of Neanderthal man, ending c.33,000 BC, and upper palaeolithic, which saw the development of Homo sapiens. [PALAEO- + Gk lithos stone]

palaeomagnetism /ˌpælɪəʊˈmægnɪˌtɪz(ə)m/ n. (US **paleomagnetism**) the study of the magnetism remaining in rocks.

palaeontology /ˌpælɪɒnˈtɒlədʒɪ, ˌpeɪlɪ-/ n. (US **paleontology**) the study of life in the geological past. □□ **palaeontological** /-təˈlɒdʒɪkəl/ adj. **palaeontologist** n. [PALAEO- + Gk onta neut. pl. of ōn being, part. of eimi be + -LOGY]

Palaeozoic /ˌpælɪəʊˈzəʊɪk/ adj. & n. (also **Paleozoic**) Geol. —adj. of or relating to the geological era between the Precambrian and the Mesozoic. The era comprises the Cambrian, Ordovician, Silurian, Devonian, Carboniferous, and Permian periods. It lasted from about 590 to 248 million years ago, beginning with the first appearance of fossils bearing hard shells and ending with the rise to dominance of the reptiles. —n. this era (cf. CENOZOIC, MESOZOIC). [PALAEO- + Gk zōē life, zōos living]

palaestra /pəˈliːstrə, -ˈlaɪstrə/ n. (also **palestra** /-ˈlestrə/) Gk & Rom. Antiq. a wrestling-school or gymnasium. [ME f. L palaestra f. Gk palaistra f. palaiō wrestle]

palais /ˈpæleɪ/ n. colloq. a public hall for dancing. [F palais (de danse) (dancing) hall]

palanquin /ˌpælənˈkiːn/ n. (also **palankeen**) (in India and the East) a covered litter for one passenger. [Port. palanquim: cf. Hindi pālkī f. Skr. palyanka bed, couch]

palatable /ˈpælətəb(ə)l/ adj. **1** pleasant to taste. **2** (of an idea, suggestion, etc.) acceptable, satisfactory. □□ **palatability** /-ˈbɪlɪtɪ/ n. **palatableness** n. **palatably** adv.

palatal /ˈpælət(ə)l/ adj. & n. —adj. **1** of the palate. **2** (of a sound) made by placing the surface of the tongue against the hard palate (e.g. y in yes). —n. a palatal sound. □□ **palatalize** v.tr. (also **-ise**). **palatalization** /-ˈzeɪʃ(ə)n/ n. **palatally** adv. [F (as PALATE)]

palate /ˈpælət/ n. **1** a structure closing the upper part of the mouth cavity in vertebrates. **2** the sense of taste. **3** æ mental taste or inclination; liking. [ME f. L palatum]

palatial /pəˈleɪʃ(ə)l/ adj. (of a building) like a palace, esp. spacious and splendid. □□ **palatially** adv. [L (as PALACE)]

palatinate /pəˈlætɪˌneɪt/ n. territory under the jurisdiction of a Count Palatine.

palatine¹ /ˈpæləˌtaɪn/ adj. (also **Palatine**) hist. **1** (of an official or feudal lord) having local authority that elsewhere belongs only to a sovereign (Count Palatine). **2** (of a territory) subject to this authority. □ **Count Palatine** (in the later Roman Empire) a count (comes) attached to the imperial palace and having supreme judicial authority in certain causes; (under the German emperors) a count having supreme jurisdiction in his fief; (in English history) an **Earl Palatine**, the proprietor of a County Palatine, now applied to the earldom of Chester and duchy of Lancaster, dignities which are attached to the Crown. **County Palatine** (in England) a county of which the earl formerly had royal privileges, with exclusive jurisdiction (now Cheshire and Lancashire, formerly also Durham, Pembroke, Ely, etc.). [ME f. F palatin -ine f. L palatinus of the PALACE]

palatine² /ˈpæləˌtaɪn/ adj. & n. —adj. of or connected with the palate. —n. (in full **palatine bone**) each of two bones forming the hard palate. [F palatin -ine (as PALATE)]

Palau /pəˈlaʊ/ (also **Belau** /bəˈlaʊ/) a group of islands in the western Pacific Ocean, part of the US Trust Territory of the Pacific Islands from 1947 and internally self-governing since 1980; pop. (est. 1988) 14,100; capital, Koror.

palaver /pəˈlɑːvə(r)/ n. & v. —n. **1** fuss and bother, esp. prolonged and tedious. **2** profuse or idle talk. **3** cajolery. **4** colloq. an affair or business. **5** esp. hist. a parley between African or other natives and traders. —v. **1** intr. talk profusely. **2** tr. flatter, wheedle. [Port. palavra word f. L (as PARABLE)]

Palawan /pəˈlɑːwən/ a long narrow island in the western Philippines, separating the Sulu Sea from the South China Sea; pop. (1980) 371,800.

pale¹ /peɪl/ adj. & v. —adj. **1** (of a person or complexion) of a whitish or ashen appearance. **2 a** (of a colour) faint; not dark or deep. **b** faintly coloured. **3** of faint lustre; dim. —v. **1** intr. & tr. grow or make pale. **2** intr. (often foll. by before, beside) become feeble in comparison (with). □□ **palely** adv. **paleness** n. **palish** adj. [ME f. OF pale, palir f. L pallidus f. pallēre be pale]

pale² /peɪl/ n. **1** a pointed piece of wood for fencing etc.; a stake. **2** a boundary. **3** an enclosed area, often surrounded by a palisade or ditch. **4** Heraldry a vertical stripe in the middle of a shield. □

beyond the pale outside the bounds of acceptable behaviour.

the English Pale *hist.* **1** the small area round Calais, the only part of France remaining in English hands after the Hundred Years War until its loss in 1558. **2** (also **the Pale**) that part of Ireland over which England exercised jurisdiction, varying in extent at different times from the reign of Henry II until the full conquest of Ireland under Elizabeth I. **in pale** *Heraldry* arranged vertically. [ME f. OF *pal* f. L *palus* stake]

palea /ˈpeɪlɪə/ *n.* (*pl.* **paleae** /-lɪˌiː/) *Bot.* a chafflike bract, esp. in a flower of grasses. [L, = chaff]

paled /peɪld/ *adj.* having palings.

paleface /ˈpeɪlfeɪs/ *n.* a name supposedly used by the N. American Indians for the White man.

Palembang /paːˈlembaːŋ, ˌpaːləmˈbaːŋ/ a deepwater port of Indonesia, capital of South Sumatra province; pop. (1980) 787,200.

Palenque /pəˈleŋkeɪ/ a Mayan city of *c.*300–900 in southern Mexico. Its ancient name is lost and it is named after a neighbouring village.

paleo- *comb. form* US var. of PALAEO-.

Paleocene US var. of PALAEOCENE.

Paleozoic US var. of PALAEOZOIC.

Palermo /pəˈlɜːməʊ/ the capital of Sicily, a seaport on the north coast of the island; pop. (1981) 701,800.

Palestine /ˈpælɪˌstaɪn/ a territory in SW Asia on the eastern coast of the Mediterranean Sea, which in biblical times comprised the kingdom of Isreal and Judah (see ISRAEL[1]). There have been many changes in the frontiers in the course of history. The land was controlled at various times by the Egyptian, Assyrian, Persian, and Roman empires before being conquered by the Arabs in AD 634. It remained in Muslim hands, except for a brief hiatus during the Crusades (1098–1197), until the First World War, being part of the Ottoman empire from 1516 to 1917, when Turkish and German forces were defeated by the British at Megiddo. The name 'Palestine' was revived as an official political title for the land west of the Jordan mandated to Britain in 1920. Jewish immigration, encouraged by the Balfour Declaration of 1917, became quite heavy, and Palestine ceased to exist as a political entity in 1948 when the State of Israel was established. The name continues to be used, however, to describe a geographical entity, particularly in the context of Arab aims for the resettlement of people who left the area when the State of Israel was established, or in subsequent struggles. □□ **Palestinian** /ˌpælɪˈstɪnɪən/ *adj.* & *n.* [Gk *Palaistinē* (used in early Christian writing), L (*Syria*) *Palaestina* (name of Roman province), f. *Philistia* land of the Philistines]

Palestine Liberation Organization a politico-military body formed in 1964 to unite various Palestinian Arab groups. From 1967 it was dominated by the Al Fatah group led by Yasser Arafat, and was soon active in guerrilla activities against Israel. The activities of radical factions of the movement caused trouble with the host country Jordan, and following a brief civil war in 1970 it moved to Lebanon and Syria. In 1974 the organization was recognized by the Arab nations as the representative of all Palestinians and in 1976 was invited to take part in a UN debate. The Israeli invasion of Lebanon in 1982 disorganized its military power and caused serious strains within its political superstructure. Having regrouped, at first in Libya, it eventually (in 1986) transferred its headquarters to Baghdad. From 1986 Jordan ceased to recognize it as representative of the Palestinians living in Israeli-occupied territories.

palestra var. of PALAESTRA.

Palestrina /ˌpæleˈstriːnə/, Giovanni Pierluigi da (1525/6–1594), Italian composer, who took his name from his birthplace, a small hill town near Rome. He composed several madrigals but is known for his sacred music, and his flowing style came to represent the lost purity of Roman Catholic music for worship in the years after instruments were admitted into church services.

palette /ˈpælɪt/ *n.* **1** a thin board or slab or other surface, usu. with a hole for the thumb, on which an artist lays and mixes colours. **2** the range of colours used by an artist. □

palette-knife 1 a thin steel blade with a handle for mixing colours or applying or removing paint. **2** a kitchen knife with a long blunt round-ended flexible blade. [F, dimin. of *pale* shovel f. L *pala* spade]

palfrey /ˈpɔːlfrɪ/ *n.* (*pl.* **-eys**) *archaic* a horse for ordinary riding, esp. for women. [ME f. OF *palefrei* f. med.L *palefredus*, LL *paraveredus* f. Gk *para* beside, extra, + L *veredus* light horse, of Gaulish orig.]

Pali /ˈpaːlɪ/ *n.* an Indic language, closely related to Sanskrit, in which the sacred texts of Theravada Buddhism are written. It was spoken in northern India in the 5th–2nd c. BC. As the language of a large part of the Buddhist scriptures it was brought to Sri Lanka and Burma, and, though not spoken there, became the vehicle of a large literature of commentaries and chronicles. [Skr. *pāli-bhāsā* f. *pāli* canon + *bhāsā* language]

palimony /ˈpælɪmənɪ/ *n.* esp. US colloq. an allowance made by one member of an unmarried couple to the other after separation. [PAL + ALIMONY]

palimpsest /ˈpælɪmpˌsest/ *n.* **1** a piece of writing-material or manuscript on which the original writing has been effaced to make room for other writing. **2** a monumental brass turned and re-engraved on the reverse side. [L *palimpsestus* f. Gk *palimpsēstos* f. *palin* again + *psēstos* rubbed smooth]

palindrome /ˈpælɪnˌdrəʊm/ *n.* a word or phrase that reads the same backwards as forwards (e.g. *rotator*, *nurses run*). □□ **palindromic** /-ˈdrɒmɪk/ *adj.* **palindromist** *n.* [Gk *palindromos* running back again f. *palin* again + *drom-* run]

paling /ˈpeɪlɪŋ/ *n.* **1** a fence of pales. **2** a pale.

palingenesis /ˌpælɪnˈdʒenɪsɪs/ *n. Biol.* the exact reproduction of ancestral characteristics in ontogenesis. □□ **palingenetic** /-dʒəˈnetɪk/ *adj.* [Gk *palin* again + *genesis* birth, GENESIS]

palinode /ˈpælɪˌnəʊd/ *n.* **1** a poem in which the writer retracts a view or sentiment expressed in a former poem. **2** a recantation. [F *palinode* or LL *palinodia* f. Gk *palinōidia* f. *palin* again + *ōidē* song]

palisade /ˌpælɪˈseɪd/ *n.* & *v.* —*n.* **1 a** a fence of pales or iron railings. **b** a strong pointed wooden stake used in a close row for defence. **2** US (in *pl.*) a line of high cliffs. —*v.tr.* enclose or provide with a palisade. □ **palisade layer** *Bot.* a layer of elongated cells below the epidermis. [F *palissade* f. Prov. *palissada* f. *palissa* paling ult. f. L *palus* stake]

Palisades /ˌpælɪˈseɪdz/ a district of New Jersey, west of the Hudson River, dominated by a long ridge of basalt.

Palissy /ˈpælɪsɪ/, Bernard (*c.*1510–90), French master potter, who enjoyed court patronage and became famous for his richly coloured ware ornamented in relief with snakes, lizards, frogs, fish, foliage, etc., cast from the life, for which he was given the title 'inventor of the king's rustic pottery'. Wares of this type continued to be produced regionally in France for some two centuries after his death.

Palk Strait /pɒlk/ a channel separating Sri Lanka from the southern tip of India, north of Adam's Bridge.

pall[1] /pɔːl/ *n.* **1** a cloth spread over a coffin, hearse, or tomb. **2** a shoulder-band with pendants, worn as an ecclesiastical vestment and sign of authority. **3** a dark covering (*a pall of darkness*; *a pall of smoke*). **4** *Heraldry* a Y-shaped bearing charged with crosses representing the front of an ecclesiastical pall. [OE *pæll*, f. L *pallium* cloak]

pall[2] /pɔːl/ *v.* **1** *intr.* (often foll. by *on*) become uninteresting (to). **2** *tr.* satiate, cloy. [ME, f. APPAL]

palladia *pl.* of PALLADIUM[2].

Palladian /pəˈleɪdɪən/ *adj. Archit.* in the neoclassical style of Palladio. The term is applied to a phase of English architecture from *c.*1715, when a revival of interest in the ideas and designs of Palladio and his English follower, Inigo Jones, led to a reaction against the baroque. □□ **Palladianism** *n.*

Palladio /pəˈlaːdɪˌəʊ/, Andrea (1508–80), Italian architect, born in Padua, who was one of the most important architect/theorists of 16th-c. Italy. He went to Rome in 1540–1 and published a guide to the antiquities of that city, and this interest in classical harmony of proportion permeates all his own works. Among his architectural designs were villas for use as summer residences, their façades often having the appearance of an antique temple. His palace designs often show classical influence and he executed much distinctive work on Venetian churches. He published a philosophical and visual analysis of his work, *I Quattro Libri dell'Architettura* (1570), which was very influential and was the main source of inspiration for the English Palladian movement.

palladium[1] /pə'leɪdɪəm/ *n. Chem.* a white ductile metallic element chemically related to platinum. First isolated in 1803, palladium is important as a catalyst, and the metal and its alloys are used in electrical contacts, precision instruments, and jewellery. ¶ Symb.: **Pd**; atomic number 46. [mod.L f. *Pallas*, an asteroid discovered (1803) just before the element, + -IUM; cf. CERIUM]

palladium[2] /pə'leɪdɪəm/ *n.* (*pl.* **palladia** /-dɪə/) a safeguard or source of protection. [ME f. L f. Gk *palladion* image of Pallas (Athene), a protecting deity]

Pallas /'pæləs/ *Gk Mythol.* one of the names (of unknown meaning) of Athene.

pallbearer /'pɔːlˌbeərə(r)/ *n.* a person helping to carry or officially escorting a coffin at a funeral.

pallet[1] /'pælɪt/ *n.* 1 a straw mattress. 2 a mean or makeshift bed. [ME *pailet, paillet* f. AF *paillete* straw f. OF *paille* f. L *palea*]

pallet[2] /'pælɪt/ *n.* 1 a flat wooden blade with a handle, used in ceramics to shape clay. 2 = PALETTE. 3 a portable platform for transporting and storing loads. 4 a projection transmitting motion from an escapement to a pendulum etc. 5 a projection on a machine-part, serving to change the mode of motion of a wheel. □□ **palletize** *v.tr.* (also **-ise**) (in sense 3). [F *palette*: see PALETTE]

pallia *pl.* of PALLIUM.

palliasse /'pælɪˌæs/ *n.* (also **paillasse**) a straw mattress. [F *paillasse* f. It. *pagliaccio* ult. f. L *palea* straw]

palliate /'pælɪˌeɪt/ *v.tr.* 1 alleviate (disease) without curing it. 2 excuse, extenuate. □□ **palliation** /-'eɪʃ(ə)n/ *n.* **palliator** *n.* [LL *palliare* to cloak f. *pallium* cloak]

palliative /'pælɪətɪv/ *n. & adj.* —*n.* anything used to alleviate pain, anxiety, etc. —*adj.* serving to alleviate. □□ **palliatively** *adv.* [F *palliatif -ive* or med.L *palliativus* (as PALLIATE)]

pallid /'pælɪd/ *adj.* pale, esp. from illness. □□ **pallidity** /-'lɪdɪtɪ/ *n.* **pallidly** *adv.* **pallidness** *n.* [L *pallidus* PALE[1]]

pallium /'pælɪəm/ *n.* (*pl.* **palliums** or **pallia** /-lɪə/) 1 an ecclesiastical pall, esp. that sent by the Pope to an archbishop as a symbol of authority. 2 *hist.* a man's large rectangular cloak esp. as worn in antiquity. 3 *Zool.* the mantle of a mollusc or brachiopod. [L]

pall-mall /pæl'mæl, pel'mel/ *n. hist.* a 16th- and 17th-c. game in which a boxwood ball was driven with a mallet through an iron ring suspended at the end of a long alley. The street Pall Mall in London was on the site of a pall-mall alley, whence its name. [obs. F *pallemaille* f. It. *pallamaglio* f. *palla* ball + *maglio* mallet]

pallor /'pælə(r)/ *n.* paleness. [L f. *pallēre* be pale]

pally /'pælɪ/ *adj.* (**pallier, palliest**) *colloq.* like a pal; friendly.

palm[1] /pɑːm/ *n.* 1 any usu. tropical tree of the family Palmae, with no branches and a mass of large pinnate or fan-shaped leaves at the top. 2 the leaf of this tree as a symbol of victory. 3 **a** supreme excellence. **b** a prize for this. 4 a branch of various trees used instead of a palm in non-tropical countries, esp. in celebrating Palm Sunday. □ **palm oil** oil from the fruit of any of various palms. **Palm Sunday** the Sunday before Easter, on which Christ's entry into Jerusalem is celebrated by processions in which branches of palms are carried. **palm wine** an alcoholic drink made from fermented palm sap. □□ **palmaceous** /pæl'meɪʃəs/ *adj.* [OE *palm(a)* f. Gmc f. L *palma* PALM[2], its leaf being likened to a spread hand]

palm[2] /pɑːm/ *n. & v.* —*n.* 1 the inner surface of the hand between the wrist and fingers. 2 the part of a glove that covers this. 3 the palmate part of an antler. —*v.tr.* conceal in the hand. □ **in the palm of one's hand** under one's control or influence.

palm off 1 (often foll. by *on*) **a** impose or thrust fraudulently (on a person). **b** cause a person to accept unwillingly or unknowingly (*palmed my old typewriter off on him*). 2 (often foll. by *with*) cause (a person) to accept unwillingly or unknowingly (*palmed him off with my old typewriter*). □□ **palmar** /'pælmə(r)/ *adj.* **palmed** *adj.* **palmful** *n.* (*pl.* **-fuls**). [ME *paume* f. OF *paume* f. L *palma*: later assim. to L]

Palma /'pælmə/ (in full **Palma de Mallorca**) an industrial port, resort, and capital of the Balearic Islands, chief town of the island of Majorca; pop. (1986) 321,100.

palmate /'pælmeɪt/ *adj.* 1 shaped like an open hand. 2 having lobes etc. like spread fingers. [L *palmatus* (as PALM[2])]

palmer /'pɑːmə(r)/ *n.* 1 *hist.* **a** a pilgrim returning from the Holy Land with a palm branch or leaf. **b** an itinerant monk under a vow of poverty. 2 a hairy artificial fly used in angling. 3 (in full **palmer-worm**) a destructive hairy caterpillar of a European moth, *Euproctis chrysorrhoea*. [ME f. AF *palmer*, OF *palmier* f. med.L *palmarius* pilgrim]

Palmerston /'pɑːməst(ə)n/, Henry John Temple, 3rd Viscount (1784–1865), British statesman. Foreign Secretary between 1830 and 1841, and again from 1846 to 1851, Palmerston actively pursued liberal policies in all spheres of British influence, supporting Belgian independence, sustaining Turkey against Russian expansionism, and declaring the Opium War against China. As Prime Minister (1855–8 and 1859–65) Palmerston was the dominant political figure of the mid-19th c., overseeing the successful conclusion of the Crimean War, the suppression of the Indian Mutiny, and the maintenance of neutrality during the American Civil War.

Palmerston North /'pɑːməst(ə)n/ a city on North island, New Zealand; pop. (1988) 67,700.

palmette /pæl'met/ *n. Archaeol.* an ornament of radiating petals like a palm-leaf. [F, dimin. of *palme* PALM[1]]

palmetto /pæl'metəʊ/ *n.* (*pl.* **-os**) a small palm tree, e.g. any of various fan palms of the genus *Sabal* or *Chamaerops*. [Sp. *palmito*, dimin. of *palma* PALM[1], assim. to It. words in *-etto*]

palmiped /'pælmɪˌped/ *adj. & n.* (also **palmipede** /-ˌpiːd/) — *adj.* web-footed. —*n.* a web-footed bird. [L *palmipes -pedis* (as PALM[2], *pes pedis* foot)]

palmistry /'pɑːmɪstrɪ/ *n.* the pseudo-science of divination by the lines and swellings of the hand. It can be traced back to ancient China and flourished in classical Greece and medieval Christendom. The parts of the hand were held to correspond to various parts of the body, traits of personality, and to the heavenly bodies. There was a close link between palmistry and astrology, both claiming the ability to predict the future; one practitioner is said to have foretold the election of Pope Leo X by reading his palm. Palmistry enjoyed a considerable vogue in Renaissance Europe, often associated with physiognomy and other forms of divination; English writers in this field drew heavily on the Continental tradition. Simple cheap guides brought the basic rules to a vast audience. Palmistry was always a controversial subject: while practitioners claimed support from Scripture, other contemporaries denounced it as diabolic, and it was condemned by papal bulls in 1586 and 1631. After a long decline it enjoyed a certain revival in the 19th c., linked to the renewed interest in physiognomy. □□ **palmist** *n.* [ME (orig. *palmestry*) f. PALM[2]: second element unexpl.]

Palm Springs a fashionable desert oasis and resort city in SE California; pop. (1980) 32,350.

palmy /'pɑːmɪ/ *adj.* (**palmier, palmiest**) 1 of or like or abounding in palms. 2 triumphant, flourishing (*palmy days*).

Palmyra /pæl'maɪrə/ the Greek name for the Semitic *Tadmor* (= city of palms), an oasis settlement in the Syrian desert, known from the 1st c. BC first as an independent State and then, after AD 18, as a Roman dependency which flourished between the 1st–3rd c. AD, supplanting Petra as the leading caravan city on the east–west trade route. Built mainly during the 1st c. AD on the model of a Roman city, Palmyra briefly regained its independence in the 260s as the capital of the dynasts Oele-anthus, Vaballath, and Queen Zenobia who dominated Syria-Palestine as far as Egypt before being defeated by Aurelian who destroyed Palmyra in 273.

palmyra /pælˈmaɪərə/ n. an Asian palm, *Borassus flabellifer*, with fan-shaped leaves used for matting etc. [Port. *palmeira* palm-tree, assim. to PALMYRA]

Palomar /ˈpæləˌmɑː(r)/, **Mount** a mountain peak in southern California, rising to a height of 1,867 m (6,126 ft.), on which is located an astronomical observatory having a 5-metre (200-inch) reflector. Its Mexican name means 'place of the pigeons'.

palomino /ˌpæləˈmiːnəʊ/ n. (pl. **-os**) a golden or cream-coloured horse with a light-coloured mane and tail, orig. bred in the south-western US. [Amer. Sp. f. Sp. *palomino* young pigeon f. *paloma* dove f. L *palumba*]

paloverde /ˌpæləʊˈvɜːdɪ/ n. any yellow-flowered thorny tree of the genus *Cercidium* in Arizona etc. [Amer. Sp., = green tree]

palp /pælp/ n. (also **palpus** /ˈpælpəs/) (pl. **palps** or **palpi** /-paɪ/) a segmented sense-organ at the mouth of an arthropod; a feeler. □□ **palpal** adj. [L *palpus* f. *palpare* feel]

palpable /ˈpælpəb(ə)l/ adj. **1** that can be touched or felt. **2** readily perceived by the senses or mind. □□ **palpability** /-ˈbɪlɪtɪ/ n. **palpably** adv. [ME f. LL *palpabilis* (as PALPATE)]

palpate /pælˈpeɪt/ v.tr. examine (esp. medically) by touch. □□ **palpation** /-ˈpeɪʃ(ə)n/ n. [L *palpare palpat-* touch gently]

palpebral /ˈpælpɪbr(ə)l/ adj. of or relating to the eyelids. [LL *palpebralis* f. L *palpebra* eyelid]

palpitate /ˈpælpɪˌteɪt/ v.intr. **1** pulsate, throb. **2** tremble. □□ **palpitant** adj. [L *palpitare* frequent. of *palpare* touch gently]

palpitation /ˌpælpɪˈteɪʃ(ə)n/ n. **1** throbbing, trembling. **2** (often in pl.) increased activity of the heart due to exertion, agitation, or disease. [L *palpitatio* (as PALPITATE)]

palpus var. of PALP.

palsgrave /ˈpɔːlzgreɪv/ n. a Count Palatine. [Du. *paltsgrave* f. *palts* palatinate + *grave* count]

palstave /ˈpɔːlsteɪv/ n. Archaeol. a type of chisel made of bronze etc. shaped to fit into a split handle. [Da. *paalstav* f. ON *pálstavr* f. *páll* hoe (cf. L *palus* stake) + *stafr* STAFF¹]

palsy /ˈpɔːlzɪ/ n. & v. —n. (pl. **-ies**) **1** paralysis, esp. with involuntary tremors. **2 a** a condition of utter helplessness. **b** a cause of this. —v.tr. (**-ies, -ied**) **1** affect with palsy. **2** render helpless. [ME *pa(r)lesi* f. OF *paralisie* ult. f. L *paralysis*: see PARALYSIS]

palter /ˈpɔːltə(r), ˈpɒl-/ v.intr. **1** haggle or equivocate. **2** trifle. □□ **palterer** n. [16th c.: orig. unkn.]

paltry /ˈpɔːltrɪ, ˈpɒl-/ adj. (**paltrier, paltriest**) worthless, contemptible, trifling. □□ **paltriness** n. [16th c.: f. *paltry* trash app. f. *palt, pelt* rubbish + -RY (cf. *trumpery*): cf. LG *paltrig* ragged]

paludal /pəˈljuːd(ə)l, ˈpæl-/ adj. **1** of a marsh. **2** malarial. □□ **paludism** n. (in sense 2). [L *palus -udis* marsh + -AL]

paly /ˈpeɪlɪ/ adj. Heraldry divided into equal vertical shapes. [OF *palé* f. *pal* PALE²]

palynology /ˌpælɪˈnɒlədʒɪ/ n. the study of pollen, spores, etc., for rock-dating and the study of past environments. □□ **palynological** /-nəˈlɒdʒɪk(ə)l/ adj. **palynologist** n. [Gk *palunō* sprinkle + -LOGY]

Pamirs /pəˈmɪəz/ a mountain system of central Asia, partly in the USSR and extending into China and Afghanistan.

pampas /ˈpæmpəs/ n.pl. large treeless plains in S. America. □ **pampas-grass** a tall grass, *Cortaderia selloana*, from S. America, with silky flowering plumes. [Sp. f. Quechua *pampa* plain]

pamper /ˈpæmpə(r)/ v.tr. **1** overindulge (a person, taste, etc.), cosset. **2** spoil (a person) with luxury. □□ **pamperer** n. [ME, prob. of LG or Du. orig.]

pampero /pæmˈpeərəʊ/ n. (pl. **-os**) a strong cold SW wind in S. America, blowing from the Andes to the Atlantic. [Sp. (as PAMPAS)]

pamphlet /ˈpæmflɪt/ n. & v. —n. a small, usu. unbound booklet or leaflet containing information or a short treatise. —v.tr. (**pamphleted, pamphleting**) distribute pamphlets to. [ME f.

Pamphilet, the familiar name of the 12th-c. Latin love poem *Pamphilus seu de Amore*]

pamphleteer /ˌpæmflɪˈtɪə(r)/ n. & v. —n. a writer of (esp. political) pamphlets. —v.intr. write pamphlets.

Pamphylia /pæmˈfɪlɪə/ the ancient name for the southern coastal region of Asia Minor, between Lycia and Cilicia. □□ **Pamphylian** adj. & n.

Pamplona /pæmˈpləʊnə/ the capital of the former kingdom and modern region of Navarre in nothern Spain; pop. (1986) 183,700. The city is noted for its fiesta of San Fermin in July, celebrated with the running of bulls through the city streets.

Pamporovo /ˌpæmpəˈrəʊvəʊ/ a skiing resort in the Rhodope Mountains of southern Bulgaria.

Pan /pæn/ Gk Mythol. a god of flocks and herds, native to Arcadia, thought of as loving mountains, caves, and lonely places, and as musical (his instrument being the pan-pipes), capable of causing 'panic' terror like that of a frightened and stampeding herd. He is represented with the horns, ears, and legs of a goat on a man's body. [Gk, prob. = the feeder (i.e. herdsman); the ancients regularly associated his name with Gk *pas* or *pan* = all, interpreting this as implying a 'universal' god, but this has nothing to do with his native worship or any normal developments of it]

pan¹ /pæn/ n. & v. —n. **1 a** a vessel of metal, earthenware, or plastic, usu. broad and shallow, used for cooking and other domestic purposes. **b** the contents of this. **2** a panlike vessel in which substances are heated etc. **3** any similar shallow container such as the bowl of a pair of scales or that used for washing gravel etc. to separate gold. **4** Brit. the bowl of a lavatory. **5** part of the lock that held the priming in old guns. **6** a hollow in the ground (*salt-pan*). **7** a hard substratum of soil. **8** US sl. the face. —v. (**panned, panning**) **1** tr. colloq. criticize severely. **2 a** tr. (foll. by *off, out*) wash (gold-bearing gravel) in a pan. **b** intr. search for gold by panning gravel. **c** intr. (foll. by *out*) (of gravel) yield gold. □ **pan out** (of an action etc.) turn out in a specified way. □□ **panful** n. (pl. **-fuls**). **panlike** adj. [OE *panne*, perh. ult. f. L *patina* dish]

pan² /pæn/ v. & n. —v. (**panned, panning**) **1** tr. swing (a cine-camera) horizontally to give a panoramic effect or to follow a moving object. **2** intr. (of a cine-camera) be moved in this way. —n. a panning movement. [abbr. of PANORAMA]

pan³ /pɑːn/ n. Bot. **1** a leaf of the betel. **2** this enclosing lime and areca-nut parings, chewed in India etc. [Hindi f. Skr. *parna* feather, leaf]

pan- /pæn/ comb. form **1** all; the whole of. **2** relating to the whole or all the parts of a continent, racial group, religion, etc. (*pan-American; pan-African; pan-Hellenic; pan-Anglican*). [Gk f. *pan* neut. of *pas* all]

panacea /ˌpænəˈsiːə/ n. a universal remedy. □□ **panacean** adj. [L f. Gk *panakeia* f. *panakēs* all-healing (as PAN-, *akos* remedy)]

panache /pəˈnæʃ/ n. **1** assertiveness or flamboyant confidence of style or manner. **2** hist. a tuft or plume of feathers, esp. as a head-dress or on a helmet. [F f. It. *pennacchio* f. LL *pinnaculum* dimin. of *pinna* feather]

panada /pəˈnɑːdə/ n. **1** a thick paste of flour etc. **2** bread boiled to a pulp and flavoured. [Sp. ult. f. L *panis* bread]

Pan-African Congress a South African political movement, formed in 1959, that was a militant offshoot of the African National Congress (see entry). It was outlawed in 1960.

Panaji /pæˈnɑːdʒɪ/ a city in western India, capital of the State of Goa; pop. (1981) 76,800.

Panama /ˌpænəˈmɑː/ a country in Central America, situated on the isthmus which connects North and South America; pop. (est. 1988) 2,323,600; official language, Spanish; capital, Panama City. Colonized by Spain in the early 16th c., Panama was freed from imperial control in 1821 and briefly joined the Federation of Grand Colombia before becoming a Colombian province. It gained full independence in 1903, although the construction of the Panama Canal and the leasing of the zone around it to the US until 1977 split the country in two. The economy is largely agricultural, although shipping registration and newly discovered copper deposits also provide important sources of income. □□ **Panamanian** /-ˈmeɪnɪən/ adj. & n.

panama /ˈpænəˌmɑː/ n. a hat of strawlike material made from the leaves of a pine-tree. [*Panama* in Central America]

Panama Canal a canal about 81 km (51 miles) long, across the isthmus of Panama, connecting the Atlantic and Pacific Oceans. It was begun by Ferdinand de Lesseps in 1882, abandoned through bankruptcy in 1889, and built by the US in 1904–14 in territory (the *Panama Canal Zone*) that was ceded in perpetuity from the Republic of Panama; by a treaty of 1977 this territory reverted to Panamanian jurisdiction. Control of the Canal itself remains with the US until 1999, after which it will be ceded to Panama.

Panama City the capital of Panama; pop. (1980) 386,400.

panatella /ˌpænəˈtelə/ n. a long thin cigar. [Amer. Sp. *panatela*, = long thin biscuit f. It. *panatella* dimin. of *panata* (as PANADA)]

Panay /pæˈnaɪ/ an island in the central Philippines; pop. (1980) 2,595,300; chief city, Iloilo.

pancake /ˈpænkeɪk, ˈpæŋ-/ n. & v. —n. **1** a thin flat cake of batter usu. fried and turned in a pan and rolled up with a filling. **2** a flat cake of make-up etc. —v. **1** intr. make a pancake landing. **2** tr. cause (an aircraft) to pancake. □ **flat as a pancake** completely flat. **Pancake Day** Shrove Tuesday (on which pancakes are traditionally eaten). **pancake landing** an emergency landing by an aircraft with its undercarriage still retracted, in which the pilot attempts to keep the aircraft in a horizontal position throughout. [ME f. PAN¹ + CAKE]

panchayat /pʌnˈtʃaɪət/ n. a village council in India. [Hindi f. Skr. *pancha* five]

Panchen Lama /ˈpæntʃ(ə)n ˌlɑːmə/ n. a Tibetan lama ranking next after the Dalai lama. [Tibetan *panchen* great learned one]

panchromatic /ˌpænkrəʊˈmætɪk/ adj. Photog. (of a film etc.) sensitive to all visible colours of the spectrum.

pancreas /ˈpæŋkrɪəs/ n. a gland near the stomach supplying the duodenum with digestive fluid and secreting insulin into the blood. □□ **pancreatic** /-ˈætɪk/ adj. **pancreatitis** /-ˈtaɪtɪs/ n. [mod.L f. Gk *pagkreas* (as PAN-, *kreas* -atos flesh)]

pancreatin /ˈpæŋkrɪətɪn/ n. a digestive extract containing pancreatic enzymes, prepared from animal pancreases.

panda /ˈpændə/ n. **1** (also **giant panda**) a large bearlike mammal, *Ailuropoda melanoleuca*, native to limited mountainous forested areas in China and Tibet, having characteristic black and white markings. First described by the French missionary Armand David (d. 1900) in 1869, it was known as the parti-coloured bear until its zoological relationship to the red panda (see sense 2) was established in 1901. **2** (also **red panda**) a Himalayan racoon-like mammal, *Ailurus fulgens*, with reddish-brown fur and a long bushy tail. □ **panda car** Brit. a police patrol car (orig. white with black stripes on the doors). [Nepali name]

pandect /ˈpændekt/ n. (usu. in pl.) **1** a complete body of laws. **2** hist. a compendium in 50 books of the Roman civil law made by order of Justinian in the 6th c. [F *pandecte* or L *pandecta pandectes* f. Gk *pandektēs* all-receiver (as PAN-, *dektēs* f. *dekhomai* receive)]

pandemic /pænˈdemɪk/ adj. & n. —adj. (of a disease) prevalent over a whole country or the world. —n. a pandemic disease. [Gk *pandēmos* (as PAN-, *dēmos* people)]

pandemonium /ˌpændɪˈməʊnɪəm/ n. **1** uproar; utter confusion. **2** a scene of this. [mod.L (place of all demons in Milton's *Paradise Lost*) f. PAN- + Gk *daimōn* DEMON]

pander /ˈpændə(r)/ v. & n. —v.intr. (foll. by to) gratify or indulge a person, a desire or weakness, etc. —n. **1** a go-between in illicit love affairs; a procurer. **2** a person who encourages coarse desires. [*Pandare*, a character who acted as go-between for the lovers in Boccaccio and in Chaucer's *Troilus and Criseyde*, f. L *Pandarus* f. Gk *Pandaros*]

pandit var. of PUNDIT 1.

P. & O. abbr. Peninsular and Oriental Shipping Company (or Line).

Pandora /pænˈdɔːrə/ Gk Mythol. in Hesiod's tale, Zeus punished mankind in general by creating woman to their confusion. The first woman was called Pandora, because she had 'all gifts' from the gods (she is probably, in reality, an earth-goddess, the All-giver). Prometheus' simple brother, Epimetheus (= After-thinker) married her despite his brother's warnings, and she let out all the evils from the store-jar where they were kept; hope alone remained to assuage the lot of mankind. The tale is a piece of satire against women (compare the part played by Eve in the Hebrew myth). □ **Pandora's box** a process that once activated will generate many unmanageable problems. [Gk *Pandōra* all-gifted (as PAN-, *dōron* gift)]

p. & p. abbr. Brit. postage and packing.

pane /peɪn/ n. **1** a single sheet of glass in a window or door. **2** a rectangular division of a chequered pattern etc. [ME f. OF *pan* f. L *pannus* piece of cloth]

panegyric /ˌpænɪˈdʒɪrɪk/ n. a laudatory discourse; a eulogy. □□ **panegyrical** adj. [F *panégyrique* f. L *panegyricus* f. Gk *panēgurikos* of public assembly (as PAN-, *ēguris* = *agora* assembly)]

panegyrize /ˈpænɪdʒɪˌraɪz/ v.tr. (also **-ise**) speak or write in praise of; eulogize. □□ **panegyrist** /-ˈdʒɪrɪst/ n. [Gk *panēgurizō* (as PANEGYRIC)]

panel /ˈpæn(ə)l/ n. & v. —n. **1 a** a distinct, usu. rectangular, section of a surface (e.g. of a wall, door, or vehicle). **b** a control panel (see CONTROL n. 5). **c** = *instrument panel*. **2** a strip of material as part of a garment. **3** a group of people forming a team in a broadcast game, discussion, etc. **4** Brit. hist. a list of medical practitioners registered in a district as accepting patients under the National Insurance Act. **5 a** a list of available jurors; a jury. **b** Sc. a person or persons accused of a crime. —v.tr. (**panelled, panelling**; US **paneled, paneling**) **1** fit or provide with panels. **2** cover or decorate with panels. □ **panel-beater** one whose job is to beat out the metal panels of motor vehicles. **panel game** a broadcast quiz etc. played by a panel. **panel heating** the heating of rooms by panels in the wall etc. containing the sources of heat. **panel pin** a thin nail with a very small head. **panel saw** a saw with small teeth for cutting thin wood for panels. **panel truck** US a small enclosed delivery truck. [ME & OF = piece of cloth, ult. f. L *pannus*: see PANE]

panelling /ˈpænəlɪŋ/ n. (US **paneling**) **1** panelled work. **2** wood for making panels.

panellist /ˈpænəlɪst/ n. (US **panelist**) a member of a panel (esp. in broadcasting).

pang /pæŋ/ n. (often in pl.) a sudden sharp pain or painful emotion. [16th c.: var. of earlier *prange* pinching f. Gmc]

panga /ˈpæŋɡə/ n. a bladed African tool like a machete. [native name in E. Africa]

Pangaea /pænˈdʒɪə/ a vast continental area or supercontinent comprising all the continental crust of the earth which is postulated to have existed in late Palaeozoic or Mesozoic times before breaking up into Gondwanaland and Laurasia. [PAN- + Gk *gaia* land, earth]

pangolin /pæŋˈɡəʊlɪn/ n. any scaly anteater of the genus *Manis*, native to Asia and Africa, having a small head with elongated snout and tongue, and a tapering tail. [Malay *peng-gōling* roller (from its habit of rolling itself up)]

panhandle /ˈpænˌhænd(ə)l/ n. & v. US —n. a narrow strip of territory extending from one State into another. —v.tr. & intr. colloq. beg for money in the street. □□ **panhandler** n.

panic¹ /ˈpænɪk/ n. & v. —n. **1 a** a sudden uncontrollable fear or alarm. **b** (attrib.) characterized or caused by panic (*panic buying*). **2** infectious apprehension or fright esp. in commercial dealings. —v.tr. & intr. (**panicked, panicking**) (often foll. by into) affect or be affected with panic (*was panicked into buying*). □ **panic button** a button for summoning help in an emergency. **panic-monger** a person who fosters a panic. **panic stations** a state of emergency. **panic-stricken** (or **-struck**) affected with panic; very apprehensive. □□ **panicky** adj. [F *panique* f. mod.L *panicus* f. Gk *panikos* f. Pan a rural god causing terror]

panic² /ˈpænɪk/ n. any grass of the genus *Panicum*, including millet and other cereals. [OE f. L *panicum* f. *panus* thread on bobbin, millet-ear f. Gk *pēnos* web]

panicle /ˈpænɪk(ə)l/ n. Bot. a loose branching cluster of flowers, as in oats. □□ **panicled** adj. [L paniculum dimin. of panus thread]

Panini /ˈpɑːnɪnɪ/ (c. 400 BC), Indian grammarian, author of a treatise on Sanskrit in which he outlined rules for the derivation of grammatical forms.

panjandrum /pænˈdʒændrəm/ n. 1 a mock title for an important person. 2 a pompous or pretentious official etc. [app. invented in nonsense verse by S. Foote 1755]

Panjshir /ˈpænʃɪə(r)/ a range of mountains in the Hindu Kush in eastern Afghanistan, situated to the north of Kabul.

Pankhurst /ˈpæŋkhɜːst/, Mrs Emmeline (1858–1928), British suffragette leader. A convinced feminist, she founded the Women's Social and Political Union in 1903 and was more responsible than anyone else for keeping the suffragette cause in the public eye and eventually winning the vote for women, although her militant activities frequently resulted in terms of imprisonment.

Panmunjom /ˌpænmʊnˈdʒɒm/ a village in the demilitarized zone between North and South Korea where the armistice bringing to an end the Korean War was signed on 27 July 1953.

panne /pæn/ n. (in full **panne velvet**) a velvet-like fabric of silk or rayon with a flattened pile. [F]

pannier /ˈpænɪə(r)/ n. 1 a basket, esp. one of a pair carried by a beast of burden. 2 each of a pair of bags or boxes on either side of the rear wheel of a bicycle or motor cycle. 3 hist. **a** part of a skirt looped up round the hips. **b** a frame supporting this. [ME f. OF panier f. L panarium bread-basket f. panis bread]

pannikin /ˈpænɪkɪn/ n. Brit. 1 a small metal drinking-cup. 2 the contents of this. [PAN¹ + -KIN, after cannikin]

panoply /ˈpænəplɪ/ n. (pl. **-ies**) 1 a complete or splendid array. 2 a complete suit of armour. □□ **panoplied** adj. [F panoplie or mod.L panoplia full armour f. Gk (as PAN-, oplia f. hopla arms)]

panoptic /pænˈɒptɪk/ adj. showing or seeing the whole at one view. [Gk panoptos seen by all, panoptēs all-seeing]

panorama /ˌpænəˈrɑːmə/ n. 1 an unbroken view of a surrounding region. 2 a complete survey or presentation of a subject, sequence of events, etc. 3 a picture or photograph containing a wide view. 4 a continuous passing scene. □□ **panoramic** /-ˈræmɪk/ adj. **panoramically** /-ˈræmɪkəlɪ/ adv. [PAN- + Gk horama view f. horaō see]

pan-pipes /ˈpænpaɪps/ n.pl. a musical instrument orig. associated with the Greek rural god Pan, made from three or more tubes of different lengths joined in a row (or in some areas of a block of wood with tubes drilled down into it) with mouthpieces in line, and sounded by blowing across the top. It is known to have been used in neolithic times, though probably not in the West until about the 6th c. BC. Our name for it derives from the legend in which the god Pan was frustrated in his pursuit of the nymph Syrinx by her transformation into a reed which Pan cut into pieces and then, relenting, kissed, his breath causing the broken reed to sound.

pansy /ˈpænzɪ/ n. (pl. **-ies**) 1 any garden plant of the genus Viola, with flowers of various rich colours. 2 colloq. derog. **a** an effeminate man. **b** a male homosexual. [F pensée thought, pansy f. penser think f. L pensare frequent. of pendere pens- weigh]

pant /pænt/ v. & n. —v. 1 intr. breathe with short quick breaths. 2 tr. (often foll. by out) utter breathlessly. 3 intr. (often foll. by for) yearn or crave. 4 intr. (of the heart etc.) throb violently. —n. 1 a panting breath. 2 a throb. □□ **pantingly** adv. [ME f. OF pantaisier ult. f. Gk phantasioō cause to imagine (as FANTASY)]

pantalets /ˌpæntəˈlets/ n.pl. (also **pantalettes**) hist. 1 long underpants worn by women and girls in the 19th c., with a frill at the bottom of each leg. 2 women's cycling trousers. [dimin. of PANTALOON]

Pantaloon /ˌpæntəˈluːn/ a Venetian character in Italian comedy represented as a foolish old man wearing pantaloons, spectacles, and slippers. [Pantalone It. perh. f. San Pantalone, favourite Venetian saint in former times]

pantaloons /ˌpæntəˈluːnz/ n.pl. 1 hist. men's close-fitting breeches fastened below the calf or at the foot. 2 esp. US trousers. [F pantalon f. It. pantalone PANTALOON]

Pantanal /ˌpæntəˈnæl/ a vast region of tropical swamp-forest lying in the upper reaches of the Paraguay River in SW Brazil.

pantechnicon /pænˈteknɪkən/ n. Brit. a large van for transporting furniture. [PAN- + TECHNIC orig. as the name of a bazaar and then a furniture warehouse]

Panthalassa /ˌpænθəˈlæsə/ a universal sea or single ocean, such as would have surrounded Pangoea. [PAN- + Gk thalassa sea]

pantheism /ˈpænθɪˌɪz(ə)m/ n. 1 the belief that God is identifiable with the forces of nature and with natural substances. 2 worship that admits or tolerates all gods. □□ **pantheist** n. **pantheistic** /-ˈɪstɪk/ adj. **pantheistical** /-ˈɪstɪk(ə)l/ adj. **pantheistically** /-ˈɪstɪkəlɪ/ adv. [PAN- + Gk theos god]

pantheon /ˈpænθɪən/ n. 1 a temple dedicated to all the gods, esp. (**Pantheon**) the circular one still standing in Rome, erected in the early 2nd c. AD probably on the site of an earlier one built by Agrippa. 2 the deities of a people collectively. 3 (**Pantheon**) a building in which the illustrious dead are buried or have memorials, esp. (**Panthéon**) the former church of St Geneviève in Paris (which in some respects resembles the Pantheon in Rome). [ME f. L f. Gk pantheion (as PAN-, theion holy f. theos god)]

panther /ˈpænθə(r)/ n. 1 a leopard, esp. with black fur. 2 US a puma. [ME f. OF pantere f. L panthera f. Gk panthēr]

pantie-girdle /ˈpæntɪˌɡɜːd(ə)l/ n. a woman's girdle with a crotch shaped like pants.

panties /ˈpæntɪz/ n.pl. colloq. short-legged or legless underpants worn by women and girls. [dimin. of PANTS]

pantihose /ˈpæntɪˌhəʊz/ n. (US **panty hose**) (usu. treated as pl.) women's tights. [PANTIES + HOSE]

pantile /ˈpæntaɪl/ n. a roof-tile curved to form an S-shaped section, fitted to overlap. [PAN¹ + TILE]

panto /ˈpæntəʊ/ n. (pl. **-os**) Brit. colloq. = PANTOMIME 1. [abbr.]

panto- /ˈpæntəʊ/ comb. form all, universal. [Gk pas pantos all]

pantograph /ˈpæntəˌɡrɑːf/ n. 1 Art & Painting an instrument for copying a plan or drawing etc. on a different scale by a system of jointed rods. 2 a jointed framework conveying a current to an electric vehicle from overhead wires. □□ **pantographic** /-ˈgræfɪk/ adj. [PANTO- + Gk -graphos writing]

pantomime /ˈpæntəˌmaɪm/ n. 1 Brit. a theatrical entertainment based on a fairy tale, with music, topical jokes, etc., usu. produced about Christmas. (See below.) 2 the use of gestures and facial expression to convey meaning, esp. in drama and dance. 3 colloq. an absurd or outrageous piece of behaviour. □□ **pantomimic** /-ˈmɪmɪk/ adj. [F pantomime or L pantomimus f. Gk pantomimos (as PANTO-, MIME)]

In ancient Rome the Latin pantomimus denoted a player who represented in dumb show the different characters in a short scene based on classical history or mythology. In England it became the name by which the harlequinade (see entry) was known. By the 20th c. the form of this had changed. The entertainment (still known as pantomime), primarily for children and associated with Christmas, is now based on the dramatization of a fairy-tale or nursery story, and includes (as well as the traditional transformation scene) songs and topical jokes, buffoonery and slapstick, and standard characters such as a pantomime 'dame' played by a man, a principal boy played by a woman, and a pantomime animal (e.g. a horse, cat, goose) played by actors dressed in a comic costume, with some regional variations. Although less popular than formerly, pantomimes remain a feature of the English Christmas season.

pantothenic acid /ˌpæntəˈθenɪk/ n. a vitamin of the B complex, found in rice, bran, and many other foods, and essential for the oxidation of fats and carbohydrates. [Gk pantothen from every side]

pantry /ˈpæntrɪ/ n. (pl. **-ies**) 1 a small room or cupboard in which crockery, cutlery, table linen, etc., are kept. 2 a larder. [ME f. AF panetrie, OF paneterie f. panetier baker ult. f. LL panarius bread-seller f. L panis bread]

pantryman /ˈpæntrɪmən/ n. (pl. **-men**) a butler or a butler's assistant.

pants /pænts/ n.pl. 1 Brit. underpants or knickers. 2 US trousers or slacks. □ **bore** (or **scare** etc.) **the pants off** *colloq.* bore, scare, etc., to an intolerable degree. **pants** (or **pant**) **suit** *esp. US* a trouser suit. **with one's pants down** *colloq.* in an embarrassingly unprepared state. [abbr. of PANTALOONS]

panty hose *US* var. of PANTIHOSE.

panzer /ˈpæntsə(r), ˈpænz-/ *n.* **1** (in *pl.*) armoured troops. **2** (*attrib.*) heavily armoured (*panzer division*). [G, = coat of mail]

Paolo Veronese see VERONESE.

pap[1] /pæp/ *n.* **1 a** soft or semi-liquid food for infants or invalids. **b** a mash or pulp. **2** light or trivial reading matter; nonsense. □□ **pappy** *adj.* [ME prob. f. MLG, MDu. *pappe*, prob. ult. f. L *pappare* eat]

pap[2] /pæp/ *n. archaic* or *dial.* the nipple of a breast. [ME, of Scand. orig.: ult. imit. of sucking]

papa /pəˈpɑː/ *n. archaic* father (esp. as a child's word). [F f. LL f. Gk *papas*]

papabile /pəˈpɑːbɪˌleɪ/ *adj.* suitable for high office. [It., = suitable to be pope, f. L *papa* pope]

papacy /ˈpeɪpəsɪ/ *n.* (*pl.* **-ies**) **1** a pope's office or tenure. **2** the papal system. [ME f. med.L *papatia* f. *papa* pope]

papain /pəˈpeɪɪn/ *n.* an enzyme obtained from unripe pawpaws, used to tenderize meat and as a food supplement to aid digestion. [PAPAYA + -IN]

papal /ˈpeɪp(ə)l/ *adj.* of or relating to a pope or to the papacy. □□ **papally** *adv.* [ME f. OF f. med.L *papalis* f. eccl.L *papa* POPE[1]]

Papal States the territory held by the Church in central Italy, based originally on the 8th-c. Donation of Pepin, which promised Frankish conquests of former Lombard lands to the pope. The Church's holdings were greatly extended by Innocent III in the early 13th c. and reconquered by Julius II 300 years later. At their greatest extent the Papal States included Romagna, Ferrara, Ravenna, and much of Tuscany. The States were incorporated in Italy in 1860, as was Rome itself ten years later.

paparazzo /ˌpæpəˈrɑːtsəʊ/ *n.* (*pl.* **paparazzi** /-tsɪ/) a freelance photographer who pursues celebrities to get photographs of them. [It.]

papaverous /pəˈpeɪvərəs/ *adj.* like or related to the poppy. □□ **papaveraceous** /-ˈreɪʃəs/ *adj.* [L *papaver* poppy]

papaw var. of PAWPAW.

papaya /pəˈpaɪə/ *n.* = PAWPAW 1. [earlier form of PAWPAW]

Papeete /ˌpɑːpɪˈeɪtɪ, -ˈiːtɪ/ the capital of French Polynesia, situated on the NW coast of Tahiti; pop. 78,800.

paper /ˈpeɪpə(r)/ *n. & v.* —*n.* **1** a material manufactured in thin sheets from the pulp of wood or other fibrous substances, used for writing or drawing or printing on, or as wrapping material etc. (See below.) **2** (*attrib.*) **a** made of or using paper. **b** flimsy like paper. **3** = NEWSPAPER. **4 a** a document printed on paper. **b** (in *pl.*) documents attesting identity or credentials. **c** (in *pl.*) documents belonging to a person or relating to a matter. **5** *Commerce* **a** negotiable documents, e.g. bills of exchange. **b** (*attrib.*) recorded on paper though not existing (*paper profits*). **6 a** a set of questions to be answered at one session in an examination. **b** the written answers to these. **7** = WALLPAPER. **8** an essay or dissertation, esp. one read to a learned society or published in a learned journal. **9** a piece of paper, esp. as a wrapper etc. **10** *Theatr. sl.* free tickets or the people admitted by them (*the house is full of paper*). —*v.tr.* **1** apply paper to, esp. decorate (a wall etc.) with wallpaper. **2** (foll. by *over*) **a** cover (a hole or blemish) with paper. **b** disguise or try to hide (a fault etc.). **3** *Theatr. sl.* fill (a theatre) by giving free passes. □ **on paper 1** in writing. **2** in theory; to judge from written or printed evidence. **paper-boy** (or **-girl**) a boy or girl who delivers or sells newspapers. **paper-chase** a cross-country run in which the runners follow a trail marked by torn-up paper. **paper-clip** a clip of bent wire or of plastic for holding several sheets of paper together. **paper-hanger** a person who decorates with wallpaper, esp. professionally. **paper-knife** a blunt knife for opening letters etc. **paper-mill** a mill in which paper is made. **paper money** money in the form of banknotes. **paper mulberry** a small Asiatic tree, *Broussonetia papyrifera*, of the mulberry family, whose bark is used for making paper and cloth.

paper nautilus see NAUTILUS 2. **paper round 1** a job of regularly delivering newspapers. **2** a route taken doing this. **paper tape** *Computing* tape made of paper, esp. that on which data or instructions are represented by means of holes punched in it, for conveying to a processor etc. **paper tiger** an apparently threatening, but ineffectual, person or thing. □□ **paperer** *n.* **paperless** *adj.* [ME f. AF *papir*, = OF *papier* f. L *papyrus*: see PAPYRUS]

The essence of paper-making is the compact interlacing of natural fibres. It originated in China about 2,000 years ago, when the fibres used were bamboo, rags, and old fishing-nets. In the 8th c. the Arabs learnt the process from Chinese prisoners captured in war; they used mostly flax as fibre. Knowledge of it spread to Baghdad by the 8th c. (the time of Haroun al-Raschid of *Arabian Nights* fame), and thence to Egypt and Morocco. The Moors brought it to Spain in the 12th c. and it spread northwards in Europe, reaching England (where paper had been used since the early 14th c.) in the 15th c. Rags were the main source of fibre until the 19th c., when wood fibres came into use and are now the main constituent, though rags, straw, esparto grass, and waste paper are important ingredients for mixing with wood fibres. The fibres are pulped, and this pulp is washed, bleached, and dried before passing to a paper mill, where it is dissolved in water and beaten to a uniform consistency, often with additives such as size, dye, or filler. A thin stream is made to flow on to a wire mesh belt which allows water to drain away, leaving a felt of sufficient strength to pass between heated rollers which compress and dry the paper. Special papers are coated with, for example, white clay to give an especially smooth surface for fine printing of illustrations.

paperback /ˈpeɪpəˌbæk/ *adj. & n.* —*adj.* (of a book) bound in stiff paper not boards. —*n.* a paperback book.

paperweight /ˈpeɪpəˌweɪt/ *n.* a small heavy object for keeping loose papers in place.

paperwork /ˈpeɪpəˌwɜːk/ *n.* routine clerical or administrative work.

papery /ˈpeɪpərɪ/ *adj.* like paper in thinness or texture.

Paphlagonia /ˌpæfləˈgəʊnɪə/ the ancient name for the region of northern Asia Minor lying along the Black Sea between Bithynia and Pontus. □□ **Paphlagonian** *adj. & n.*

papier mâché /ˌpæpjeɪ ˈmæʃeɪ/ *n.* paper pulp used for moulding into boxes, trays, etc. [F, = chewed paper]

papilionaceous /pəˌpɪljəˈneɪʃəs/ *adj.* (of a plant) with a corolla like a butterfly. [mod.L *papilionaceus* f. L *papilio -onis* butterfly]

papilla /pəˈpɪlə/ *n.* (*pl.* **papillae** /-liː/) **1** a small nipple-like protuberance in a part or organ of the body. **2** *Bot.* A small fleshy projection on a plant. □□ **papillary** *adj.* **papillate** /ˈpæpɪˌleɪt/ *adj.* **papillose** /ˈpæpɪˌləʊs/ *adj.* [L, = nipple, dimin. of *papula*: see PAPULA]

papilloma /ˌpæpɪˈləʊmə/ *n.* (*pl.* **papillomas** or **papillomata** /-mətə/) a wartlike usu. benign tumour.

papillon /pəˈpɪljən/ *n.* **1** a toy dog of a breed with ears suggesting the form of a butterfly. **2** this breed. [F, = butterfly, f. L *papilio -onis*]

papist /ˈpeɪpɪst/ *n. & adj. often derog.* —*n.* **1** a Roman Catholic. **2** *hist.* an advocate of papal supremacy. —*adj.* of or relating to Roman Catholics. □□ **papistic** /pəˈpɪstɪk/ *adj.* **papistical** /pəˈpɪstɪk(ə)l/ *adj.* **papistry** *n.* [F *papiste* or mod.L *papista* f. eccl.L *papa* POPE[1]]

papoose /pəˈpuːs/ *n.* a N. American Indian young child. [Algonquin]

pappus /ˈpæpəs/ *n.* (*pl.* **pappi** /-paɪ/) a group of hairs on the fruit of thistles, dandelions, etc. □□ **pappose** *adj.* [L f. Gk *pappos*]

paprika /ˈpæprɪkə, pəˈpriːkə/ *n.* **1** *Bot.* a red pepper. **2** a condiment made from it. [Magyar]

pap test /pæp/ *n.* a test done by a cervical smear. [abbr. of G. N. *Papanicolaou*, US scientist d. 1962]

Papua New Guinea /ˈpæpʊə, ˈgɪnɪ/ a country in the Pacific off the NE coast of Australia; pop. (est. 1988) 3,649,500; official language, English; capital, Port Moresby. Papua was discovered in 1526–7 by a Portuguese navigator, who gave it its name (a Malayan word, = woolly-haired). Papua New Guinea was formed from the administrative union, in 1949, of Papua (SE New Guinea with adjacent islands), an Australian Territory since 1906, and the Trust Territory of New Guinea (NE Guinea), an Australian trusteeship since 1921. In 1975 the combined territories became an independent State within the Commonwealth. It is a country of 700 different languages. □□ **Papua New Guinean** adj. & n.

papula /ˈpæpjʊlə/ n. (also **papule** /-pjuːl/) (pl. **papulae** /-liː/) **1** a pimple. **2** a small fleshy projection on a plant. □□ **papular** adj. **papulose** adj. **papulous** adj. [L]

papyrology /ˌpæpɪˈrɒlədʒɪ/ n. the study of ancient papyri. □□ **papyrological** /-rəˈlɒdʒɪk(ə)l/ adj. **papyrologist** n.

papyrus /pəˈpaɪərəs/ n. (pl. **papyri** /-raɪ/) **1** an aquatic plant, Cyperus papyrus, with dark green stems topped with fluffy inflorescences. **2 a** a writing-material prepared in ancient Egypt from the pithy stem of this. (See below.) **b** a document written on this. [ME f. L papyrus f. Gk papuros]

Sheets of papyrus were a major export of ancient Egypt. Production and marketing of this as a writing-material was a royal monopoly, and the secret of its preparation was jealously guarded. Pliny the Elder describes the process of cutting tissue-thin strips of the stem of the plant and laying them across each other, but his account is defective. After the introduction of papermaking, the production of papyrus in Egypt rapidly declined and then ceased altogether, and the papyrus plant itself disappeared from the country until recently re-introduced.

par¹ /pɑː(r)/ n. **1** the average or normal amount, degree, condition, etc. (feel below par; be up to par). **2** equality; an equal status or footing (on a par with). **3** Golf the number of strokes a first-class player should normally require for a hole or course. **4** Stock Exch. the face value of stocks and shares etc. (at par). **5** (in full **par of exchange**) the recognized value of one country's currency in terms of another's. □ **above** (or **below**) **par** Stock Exch. at a premium (or discount). **at par** Stock Exch. at face value. **par for the course** colloq. what is normal or expected in any given circumstances. [L (adj. & n.) = equal, equality]

par² /pɑː(r)/ n. Brit. esp. Journalism colloq. paragraph. [abbr.]

par. abbr. (also **para.**) paragraph.

par- /pər, pær, pɑː/ prefix var. of PARA-¹ before a vowel or h; (paraldehyde; parody; parhelion).

Para see BELEM.

para /ˈpærə/ n. colloq. **1** a paratrooper. **2** a paragraph. [abbr.]

para-¹ /ˈpærə/ prefix (also **par-**) **1** beside (paramilitary). **2** beyond (paranormal). **3** Chem. **a** modification of (paraldehyde). **b** relating to diametrically opposite carbon atoms in a benzene ring (paradichlorobenzene). [from or after Gk para- f. para beside, past, beyond]

para-² /ˈpærə/ comb. form protect, ward off (parachute; parasol). [F f. It. f. L parare defend]

parabiosis /ˌpærəbaɪˈəʊsɪs/ n. Biol. the natural or artificial joining of two individuals. □□ **parabiotic** /-ˈɒtɪk/ adj. [mod.L, formed as PARA-¹ + Gk biōsis mode of life f. bios life]

parable /ˈpærəb(ə)l/ n. **1** a narrative of imagined events used to illustrate a moral or spiritual lesson. **2** an allegory. [ME f. OF parabole f. LL sense 'allegory, discourse' of L parabola comparison]

parabola /pəˈræbələ/ n. an open plane curve formed by the intersection of a cone with a plane parallel to its side, resembling the path of a projectile under the action of gravity. [mod.L f. Gk parabolē placing side by side, comparison (as PARA-¹, bolē f. ballō)]

parabolic /ˌpærəˈbɒlɪk/ adj. **1** of or expressed in a parable. **2** of or like a parabola. □□ **parabolically** adv. [LL parabolicus f. Gk parabolikos (as PARABOLA)]

parabolical /ˌpærəˈbɒlɪk(ə)l/ adj. = PARABOLIC 1.

paraboloid /pəˈræbəˌlɔɪd/ n. **1** (in full **paraboloid of revolution**) a solid generated by the rotation of a parabola about its axis of symmetry. **2** a solid having two or more non-parallel parabolic cross-sections. □□ **paraboloidal** adj.

Paracel Islands /ˌpærəˈsel/ (also **Paracels**) a group of about 130 small barren coral islands and reefs in the South China Sea to the south-east of the Chinese island of Hainan. The islands,

which lie close to deposits of oil, are claimed by both China and Vietnam.

Paracelsus /ˌpærəˈselsəs/ (real name Theophrastus Phillipus Aureolus Bombastus von Hohenheim, c.1493–1541), Swiss physician, of an iconoclastic and violent temper, who developed a totally new approach to medicine and philosophy. He lectured in German rather than the accepted Latin, and condemned all current academic medical teaching not based on observation and experience. He introduced chemical remedies to replace traditional herbal ones and turned alchemy away from its limited aims of discovering the philosopher's stone and the elixir of life and gave it a wider perspective. Paracelsus had a new concept of disease: he saw illness as coming from a specific external cause rather than being caused by an imbalance of the humours in the body. This modernity was countered by his overall occultist perspective in which the cosmos and man were interconnected by spiritual forces, and the powers of the stars could send down the seeds of disease. His study of a disease of miners was one of the first accounts of an occupational disease. His influence was greatest in the hundred years after his death, when most of his writings were published.

paracetamol /ˌpærəˈsetəˌmɒl, -ˈsiːtəˌmɒl/ n. **1** a drug used to relieve pain and reduce fever. **2** a tablet of this. [para-acetylaminophenol]

parachronism /pəˈrækrəˌnɪz(ə)m/ n. an error in chronology, esp. by assigning too late a date. [PARA-¹ + Gk khronos time, perh. after anachronism]

parachute /ˈpærəˌʃuːt/ n. & v. —n. **1** a rectangular or umbrella-shaped apparatus allowing a person or heavy object attached to it to descend slowly from a height, esp. from an aircraft, or to retard motion in other ways. (See below.) **2** (attrib.) dropped or to be dropped by parachute (parachute troops; parachute flare). —v.tr. & intr. convey or descend by parachute. [F (as PARA-², CHUTE¹)]

The principle of the parachute had, like many principles, been noted by Leonardo da Vinci. The first man to demonstrate it in action was L. S. Lenormand of France in 1783, jumping from a high tower. A few years later French balloonists made successful descents, and in the 19th c. hot-air balloons were used by parachutists who jumped for public entertainment. In the 20th c. parachuting has become a sophisticated sport.

parachutist /ˈpærəˌʃuːtɪst/ n. **1** a person who uses a parachute. **2** (in pl.) parachute troops.

Paraclete /ˈpærəˌkliːt/ n. the Holy Spirit as advocate or counsellor (John 14:16, 26, etc.). [ME f. OF paraclet f. LL paracletus f. Gk paraklētos called in aid (as PARA-¹, klētos f. kaleō call)]

parade /pəˈreɪd/ n. & v. —n. **1 a** a formal or ceremonial muster of troops for inspection. **b** = parade-ground. **2** a public procession. **3** ostentatious display (made a parade of their wealth). **4** a public square, promenade, or row of shops. —v. **1** intr. assemble for parade. **2 a** tr. march through (streets etc.) in procession. **b** intr. march ceremonially. **3** tr. display ostentatiously. □ **on parade 1** taking part in a parade. **2** on display. **parade-ground** a place for the muster of troops. □□ **parader** n. [F, = show, f. Sp. parada and It. parata ult. f. L parare prepare, furnish]

paradiddle /ˈpærəˌdɪd(ə)l/ n. a drum roll with alternate beating of sticks. [imit.]

paradigm /ˈpærəˌdaɪm/ n. an example or pattern, esp. a representative set of the inflections of a noun, verb, etc. □□ **paradigmatic** /-dɪgˈmætɪk/ adj. **paradigmatically** /-dɪgˈmætɪkəlɪ/ adv. [LL paradigma f. Gk paradeigma f. paradeiknumi show side by side (as PARA-¹, deiknumi show)]

paradise /ˈpærəˌdaɪs/ n. **1** (in some religions) heaven as the ultimate abode of the just. **2** a place or state of complete happiness. **3** (in full **earthly paradise**) the abode of Adam and Eve in the biblical account of the Creation; the garden of Eden. □□ **paradisaical** /-dɪˈseɪɪk(ə)l/ adj. **paradisal** /ˈpærəˌdaɪs(ə)l/ adj. **paradisiacal** /-dɪˈsaɪək(ə)l/ adj. **paradisiacal** /-ˈdɪsɪk(ə)l/ adj. [ME f. OF paradis f. LL paradisus f. Gk paradeisos f. Avestan pairidaēza park]

parados /ˈpærəˌdɒs, -ˌdəʊ/ n. an elevation of earth behind a fortified place as a protection against attack from the rear, esp.

a mound along the back of a trench. [F (as PARA-², *dos* back f. L *dorsum*)]

paradox /ˈpærəˌdɒks/ *n.* **1 a** a seemingly absurd or contradictory statement, even if actually well-founded. **b** a self-contradictory or essentially absurd statement. **2** a person or thing conflicting with a preconceived notion of what is reasonable or possible. **3** a paradoxical quality or character. [orig. = a statement contrary to accepted opinion, f. LL *paradoxum* f. Gk *paradoxon* neut. adj. (as PARA-¹, *doxa* opinion)]

paradoxical /ˌpærəˈdɒksɪk(ə)l/ *adj.* **1** of or like or involving paradox. **2** fond of paradox. □□ **paradoxically** *adv.*

paraffin /ˈpærəfɪn/ *n.* **1** an inflammable waxy or oily substance obtained by distillation from petroleum or shale, used in liquid form (also **paraffin oil**) esp. as a fuel. **2** *Chem.* = ALKANE. □ **paraffin wax** paraffin in its solid form. [G (1830) f. L *parum* little + *affinis* related, from the small affinity it has for other substances]

paragoge /ˌpærəˈɡoʊdʒɪ/ *n.* the addition of a letter or syllable to a word in some contexts or as a language develops (e.g. *t* in *peasant*). □□ **paragogic** /-ˈɡɒdʒɪk/ *adj.* [LL f. Gk *paragōgē* derivation (as PARA-¹, *agōgē* f. *agō* lead)]

paragon /ˈpærəɡən/ *n.* **1 a** a model of excellence. **b** a supremely excellent person or thing. **2** (foll. by *of*) a model (of virtue etc.). **3** a perfect diamond of 100 carats or more. [obs. F f. It. *paragone* touchstone, f. med.Gk *parakonē* whetstone]

paragraph /ˈpærəˌɡrɑːf/ *n. & v.* —*n.* **1** a distinct section of a piece of writing, beginning on a new usu. indented line. **2** a symbol (usu. ¶) used to mark a new paragraph, and also as a reference mark. **3** a short item in a newspaper, usu. of only one paragraph. —*v.tr.* arrange (a piece of writing) in paragraphs. □□ **paragraphic** /-ˈɡræfɪk/ *adj.* [F *paragraphe* or med.L *paragraphus* f. Gk *paragraphos* short stroke marking a break in sense (as PARA-¹, *graphō* write)]

Paraguay /ˈpærəˌɡwaɪ/ an inland country in South America, situated between Argentina, Bolivia, and Brazil; pop. (est. 1988) 4,010,000; official language, Spanish; capital, Asunción. Once part of the Spanish viceroyalties of Peru and La Plata, Paraguay achieved its independence in 1811, but was devastated, losing over half of its population, in the megalomaniac dictator Solano Lopez's war against Brazil, Argentina, and Uruguay in 1865–70. It gained land to the west as a result of the Chaco War with Bolivia in 1932–5, but the country has remained backward and agricultural with a low standard of living and an uncertain political system. □□ **Paraguayan** *adj. & n.*

parakeet /ˈpærəˌkiːt/ *n.* (US also **parrakeet**) any of various small usu. long-tailed parrots. [OF *paroquet*, It. *parrocchetto*, Sp. *periquito*, perh. ult. f. dimin. of *Pierre* etc. Peter: cf. PARROT]

paralanguage /ˈpærəˌlæŋɡwɪdʒ/ *n.* elements or factors in communication that are ancillary to language proper, e.g. intonation and gesture.

paraldehyde /pəˈrældɪˌhaɪd/ *n.* a cyclic polymer of acetaldehyde, used as a narcotic and sedative. [PARA-¹ + ALDEHYDE]

paralegal /ˌpærəˈliːɡ(ə)l/ *adj. & n.* esp. *US* —*adj.* of or relating to auxiliary aspects of the law. —*n.* a person trained in subsidiary legal matters. [PARA-¹ + LEGAL]

paralipomena /ˌpærəlɪˈpɒmɪnə/ *n.pl.* (also **-leipomena** /-laɪˈpɒmɪnə/) **1** things omitted from a work and added as a supplement. **2** *Bibl.* the books of Chronicles in the Old Testament, containing particulars omitted from Kings. [ME f. eccl.L f. Gk *paraleipomena* f. *paraleipō* omit (as PARA-¹, *leipō* leave)]

paralipsis /ˌpærəˈlɪpsɪs/ *n.* (also **-leipsis** /-ˈlaɪpsɪs/) (*pl.* **-ses** /-siːz/) *Rhet.* **1** the device of giving emphasis by professing to say little or nothing of a subject, as in *not to mention their unpaid debts of several millions.* **2** an instance of this. [LL f. Gk *paraleipsis* passing over (as PARA-¹, *leipsis* f. *leipō* leave)]

parallax /ˈpærəˌlæks/ *n.* **1** the apparent difference in the position or direction of an object caused when the observer's position is changed. **2** the angular amount of this. □□ **parallactic** /-ˈlæktɪk/ *adj.* [F *parallaxe* f. mod.L *parallaxis* f. Gk *parallaxis* change f. *parallassō* to alternate (as PARA-¹, *allassō* exchange f. *allos* other)]

parallel /ˈpærəˌlel/ *adj., n., & v.* —*adj.* **1 a** (of lines or planes) side by side and having the same distance continuously between

them. **b** (foll. by *to, with*) (of a line or plane) having this relation (to another). **2** (of circumstances etc.) precisely similar, analogous, or corresponding. **3 a** (of processes etc.) occurring or performed simultaneously. **b** *Computing* involving the simultaneous performance of operations. —*n.* **1** a person or thing precisely analogous or equal to another. **2** a comparison (*drew a parallel between the two situations*). **3** (in full **parallel of latitude**) *Geog.* **a** each of the imaginary parallel circles of constant latitude on the earth's surface. **b** a corresponding line on a map (*the 49th parallel*). **4** *Printing* two parallel lines (‖) as a reference mark. —*v.tr.* (**paralleled, paralleling**) **1** be parallel to; correspond to. **2** represent as similar; compare. **3** adduce as a parallel instance. □ **in parallel** (of electric circuits) arranged so as to join at common points at each end. **parallel bars** a pair of parallel rails on posts for gymnastics. □□ **parallelism** *n.* [F *parallèle* f. L *parallelus* f. Gk *parallēlos* (as PARA-¹, *allēlos* one another)]

parallelepiped /ˌpærəleˈlepɪˌped, -lɪˈpaɪpɪd/ *n.* *Geom.* a solid body of which each face is a parallelogram. [Gk *parallēlepipedon* (as PARALLEL, *epipedon* plane surface)]

parallelogram /ˌpærəˈlelaˌɡræm/ *n.* *Geom.* a four-sided plane rectilinear figure with opposite sides parallel. □ **parallelogram of forces 1** a parallelogram illustrating the theorem that if two forces acting at a point are represented in magnitude and direction by two sides of a parallelogram meeting at that point, their resultant is represented by the diagonal drawn from that point. **2** this theorem. [F *parallélogramme* f. LL *parallelogrammum* f. Gk *parallēlogrammon* (as PARALLEL, *grammē* line)]

paralogism /pəˈrælədʒɪz(ə)m/ *n.* *Logic* **1** a fallacy. **2** illogical reasoning (esp. of which the reasoner is unconscious). □□ **paralogist** *n.* **paralogize** *v.intr.* (also **-ise**). [F *paralogisme* f. LL *paralogismus* f. Gk *paralogismos* f. *paralogizomai* reason falsely f. *paralogos* contrary to reason (as PARA-¹, *logos* reason)]

paralyse /ˈpærəˌlaɪz/ *v.tr.* (*US* **paralyze**) **1** affect with paralysis. **2** render powerless; cripple. □□ **paralysation** /-ˈzeɪʃ(ə)n/ *n.* **paralysingly** *adv.* [F *paralyser* f. *paralysie*: cf. PALSY]

paralysis /pəˈrælɪsɪs/ *n.* (*pl.* **paralyses** /-ˌsiːz/) **1** a nervous condition with impairment or loss of esp. the motor function of the nerves. **2** a state of utter powerlessness. [L f. Gk *paralusis* f. *paraluō* disable (as PARA-¹, *luō* loosen)]

paralytic /ˌpærəˈlɪtɪk/ *adj. & n.* —*adj.* **1** affected by paralysis. **2** *sl.* very drunk. —*n.* a person affected by paralysis. □□ **paralytically** *adv.* [ME f. OF *paralytique* f. L *paralyticus* f. Gk *paralutikos* (as PARALYSIS)]

paramagnetic /ˌpærəmæɡˈnetɪk/ *adj.* (of a body or substance) tending to become weakly magnetized so as to lie parallel to a magnetic field force. □□ **paramagnetism** /-ˈmæɡnɪˌtɪz(ə)m/ *n.*

Paramaribo /ˌpærəˈmærɪboʊ/ the capital of Suriname; pop. (1980) 192,800; urban district pop. 67,900.

paramatta var. of PARRAMATTA.

paramecium /ˌpærəˈmiːsɪəm/ *n.* (also **paramoecium**) any freshwater protozoan of the genus *Paramecium*, of a characteristic slipper-like shape covered with cilia. [mod.L f. Gk *paramēkēs* oval (as PARA-¹, *mēkos* length)]

paramedic /ˌpærəˈmedɪk/ *n.* a paramedical worker. [abbr.]

paramedical /ˌpærəˈmedɪk(ə)l/ *adj.* (of services etc.) supplementing and supporting medical work.

parameter /pəˈræmɪtə(r)/ *n.* **1** *Math.* a quantity constant in the case considered but varying in different cases. **2 a** an (esp. measurable or quantifiable) characteristic or feature. **b** (loosely) a constant element or factor, esp. serving as a limit or boundary. □□ **parametric** /ˌpærəˈmetrɪk/ *adj.* **parametrize** *v.tr.* (also **-ise**). [mod.L f. Gk *para* beside + *metron* measure]

paramilitary /ˌpærəˈmɪlɪtərɪ/ *adj.* (of forces) ancillary to and similarly organized to military forces.

paramnesia /ˌpærəmˈniːzɪə/ *n.* *Psychol.* = DÉJÀ VU. [PARA-¹ + AMNESIA]

paramo /ˈpærəˌmoʊ/ *n.* (*pl.* **-os**) a high treeless plateau in tropical S. America. [Sp. & Port. f. L *paramus*]

paramoecium var. of PARAMECIUM.

paramount /ˈpærəˌmaʊnt/ *adj.* **1** supreme; requiring first consideration; pre-eminent (*of paramount importance*). **2** in supreme authority. □□ **paramountcy** n. **paramountly** adv. [AF para-mont f. OF par by + amont above: cf. AMOUNT]

paramour /'pærə,mʊə(r)/ n. archaic or derog. an illicit lover of a married person. [ME f. OF par amour by love]

Paraná /,pærə'nɑː/ a river of South America, rising in SE Brazil and flowing about 3,300 km (2,060 miles) southwards before meeting the River Plate estuary in Argentina. For part of its length it follows the SE frontier of Paraguay.

parang /'pæræŋ/ n. a large heavy Malayan knife used for clear-ing vegetation etc. [Malay]

paranoia /,pærə'nɔɪə/ n. **1** a mental disorder esp. characterized by delusions of persecution and self-importance. **2** an abnormal tendency to suspect and mistrust others. □□ **paranoiac** adj. & n. **paranoiacally** adv. **paranoic** /-'nəʊɪk, -'nɔɪk/ adj. **paranoically** /-'nəʊɪkəlɪ, -'nɔɪkəlɪ/ adv. **paranoid** /'pærə,nɔɪd/ adj. & n. [mod.L f. Gk f. paranoos distracted (as PARA-¹, noos mind)]

paranormal /,pærə'nɔː(ə)l/ adj. beyond the scope of normal objective investigation or explanation. □□ **paranormally** adv.

parapet /'pærəpɪt/ n. **1** a low wall at the edge of a roof, balcony, etc., or along the sides of a bridge. **2** a defence of earth or stone to conceal and protect troops. □□ **parapeted** adj. [F parapet or It. parapetto breast-high wall (as PARA-², petto breast f. L pectus)]

paraph /'pærəf/ n. a flourish after a signature, orig. as a pre-caution against forgery. [ME f. F paraphe f. med.L paraphus for paragraphus PARAGRAPH]

paraphernalia /,pærəfə'neɪlɪə/ n.pl. (also treated as sing.) mis-cellaneous belongings, items of equipment, accessories, etc. [orig. = property owned by a married woman, f. med.L para-phernalia f. LL parapherna f. Gk parapherna personal articles which a woman could keep after marriage, as opp. to her dowry which went to her husband (as PARA-¹, pherna f. phernē dower)]

paraphrase /'pærə,freɪz/ n. & v. —n. a free rendering or rewording of a passage. —v.tr. express the meaning of (a pas-sage) in other words. □□ **paraphrastic** /-'fræstɪk/ adj. [F para-phrase or L paraphrasis f. Gk paraphrasis f. paraphrazō (as PARA-¹ phrazō tell)]

paraplegia /,pærə'pliːdʒə/ n. paralysis of the legs and part or the whole of the trunk. □□ **paraplegic** adj. & n. [mod.L f. Gk paraplēgia f. paraplēssō (as PARA-¹, plēssō strike)]

parapsychology /,pærəsaɪ'kɒlədʒɪ/ n. the study of mental phe-nomena outside the sphere of ordinary psychology (hypnosis, telepathy, etc.). □□ **parapsychological** /-,saɪkə'lɒdʒɪk(ə)l/ adj. **parapsychologist** n.

paraquat /'pærə,kwɒt/ n. a quick-acting herbicide, becoming inactive on contact with the soil. [PARA-¹ + QUATERNARY (from the position of the bond between the two parts of the molecule relative to quaternary nitrogen atom)]

parascending /'pærə,sendɪŋ/ n. a sport in which participants wearing open parachutes are towed behind a vehicle or motor boat to gain height before release for a conventional descent, usu. towards a predetermined target. □□ **parascender** n.

paraselene /,pærəsɪ'liːnɪ/ n. (pl. **paraselenae** /-niː/) a bright spot, esp. an image of the moon, on a lunar halo. Also called mock moon. [mod.L (as PARA-¹, Gk selēnē moon)]

parasite /'pærə,saɪt/ n. **1** an organism living in or on another and benefiting at the expense of the other. **2** a person who lives off or exploits another or others. **3** Philol. an inorganic sound or letter developing from an adjacent one. □□ **parasitic** /-'sɪtɪk/ adj. **parasitical** /-'sɪtɪk(ə)l/ adj. **parasitically** /-'sɪtɪkəlɪ/ adv. **parasiticide** /-'sɪtɪ,saɪd/ n. **parasitism** n. **parasitology** /-'tɒlədʒɪ/ n. **parasitologist** /-'tɒlədʒɪst/ n. [L parasitus f. Gk para-sitos one who eats at another's table (as PARA-¹, sitos food)]

parasitize /'pærəsɪ,taɪz/ v.tr. (also **-ise**) infest as a parasite. □□ **parasitization** /-'zeɪʃ(ə)n/ n.

parasol /'pærə,sɒl/ n. a light umbrella used to give shade from the sun. [F f. It. parasole (as PARA-², sole sun f. L sol)]

parasympathetic /,pærə,sɪmpə'θetɪk/ adj. Anat. relating to the part of the nervous system that consists of nerves leaving the lower end of the spinal cord and connecting with those in or near the viscera (cf. SYMPATHETIC 9). [PARA-¹ + SYMPATHETIC, because some of these nerves run alongside sympathetic nerves]

parasynthesis /,pærə'sɪnθɪsɪs/ n. Philol. a derivation from a compound, e.g. black-eyed from black eye(s) + -ed. □□ **parasynthetic** /-'θetɪk/ adj. [Gk parasunthesis (as PARA-¹, SYNTHESIS)]

parataxis /,pærə'tæksɪs/ n. Gram. the placing of clauses etc. one after another, without words to indicate coordination or subordination, e.g. Tell me, how are you? □□ **paratactic** /-'tæktɪk/ adj. **paratactically** /-'tæktɪkəlɪ/ adv. [Gk parataxis (as PARA-¹, taxis arrangement f. tassō arrange)]

parathion /,pærə'θaɪən/ n. a highly toxic agricultural insect-icide. [PARA-¹ + THIO- + -ON]

parathyroid /,pærə'θaɪrɔɪd/ n. & adj. Anat. —n. a gland next to the thyroid, secreting a hormone that regulates calcium levels in the body. —adj. of or associated with this gland.

paratroop /'pærə,truːp/ n. (attrib.) of or consisting of paratroops (paratroop regiment).

paratrooper /'pærə,truːpə(r)/ n. a member of a body of paratroops.

paratroops /'pærə,truːps/ n.pl. troops equipped to be dropped by parachute from aircraft. [contr. of PARACHUTE + TROOP]

paratyphoid /,pærə'taɪfɔɪd/ n. & adj. —n. a fever resembling typhoid but caused by various different though related bacteria. —adj. of, relating to, or caused by this fever.

paravane /'pærə,veɪn/ n. a torpedo-shaped device towed at a depth regulated by its vanes or planes to cut the moorings of submerged mines.

par avion /,pɑːr æ'vjɔ̃/ adv. by airmail. [F, = by aeroplane]

parboil /'pɑːbɔɪl/ v.tr. partly cook by boiling. [ME f. OF par-bo(u)illir f. LL perbullire boil thoroughly (as PER-, bullire boil: con-fused with PART)]

parbuckle /'pɑː,bʌk(ə)l/ n. & v. —n. a rope arranged like a sling, for raising or lowering casks and cylindrical objects. —v.tr. raise or lower with this. [earlier parbunkle, of unkn. orig.: assoc. with BUCKLE]

parcel /'pɑːs(ə)l/ n. & v. —n. **1 a** goods etc. wrapped up in a single package. **b** a bundle of things wrapped up, usu. in paper. **2** a piece of land, esp. as part of an estate. **3** a quantity dealt with in one commercial transaction. **4** archaic part. —v.tr. (**parcelled, parcelling**; US **parceled, parceling**) **1** (foll. by up) wrap as a parcel. **2** (foll. by out) divide into portions. **3** cover (rope) with strips of canvas. □ **parcel post** the branch of the postal service dealing with parcels. [ME f. OF parcelle ult. f. L particula (as PART)]

parch /pɑːtʃ/ v. **1** tr. & intr. make or become hot and dry. **2** tr. roast (peas, corn, etc.) slightly. [ME perch, parche, of unkn. orig.]

parched /pɑːtʃt/ adj. **1** hot and dry; dried out with heat. **2** colloq. thirsty.

parchment /'pɑːtʃmənt/ n. **1 a** an animal skin, esp. that of a sheep or goat, prepared as a writing or painting surface. **b** a manuscript written on this. **2** (in full **vegetable parchment**) high-grade paper made to resemble parchment. [ME f. OF parchemin, ult. a blend of LL pergamina writing material from Pergamum (in Asia Minor) with Parthica pellis Parthian skin (leather)]

parclose /'pɑː,kləʊz/ n. a screen or railing in a church, sep-arating a side chapel. [ME f. OF parclos -ose past part. of parclore enclose]

pard /pɑːd/ n. archaic or poet. a leopard. [ME f. OF f. L pardus f. Gk pardos]

pardalote /'pɑːdə,ləʊt/ n. any small brightly-coloured Aus-tralian bird of the genus Pardalotus, with spotted plumage. Also called diamond-bird. [mod.L Pardalotus f. Gk pardalōtos spotted like a leopard (as PARD)]

pardner /'pɑːdnə(r)/ n. US colloq. a partner or comrade. [corrupt.]

pardon /'pɑːd(ə)n/ n., v., & int. —n. **1** the act of excusing or forgiving an offence, error, etc. **2** (in full **free pardon**) a remis-sion of the legal consequences of a crime or conviction. **3** RC Ch. an indulgence. —v.tr. **1** release from the consequences of an offence, error, etc. **2** forgive or excuse a person for (an offence etc.). **3** make (esp. courteous) allowances for; excuse. —int. (also **pardon me** or **I beg your pardon**) **1** a formula of apology

or disagreement. **2** a request to repeat something said. □□
pardonable adj. **pardonably** adv. [ME f. OF pardun, pardoner f.
med.L perdonare concede, remit (as PER-, donare give)]

pardoner /ˈpɑːdənə(r)/ n. hist. a person licensed to sell papal
pardons or indulgences. [ME f. AF (as PARDON)]

pare /peə(r)/ v.tr. **1 a** trim or shave (esp. fruit and vegetables) by
cutting away the surface or edge. **b** (often foll. by off, away) cut
off (the surface or edge). **2** (often foll. by away, down) diminish
little by little. □□ **parer** n. [ME f. OF parer adorn, peel (fruit), f.
L parare prepare]

paregoric /ˌpærɪˈɡɒrɪk/ n. (in full **paregoric elixir**) hist. a cam-
phorated tincture of opium used to reduce pain. [LL paregoricus
f. Gk parēgorikos soothing (as PARA-¹, -agoros speaking f. agora
assembly)]

pareira /pəˈreərə/ n. a drug from the root of a Brazilian shrub,
Chondrodendron tomentosum, used as a muscle relaxant in surgery
etc. [Port. parreira vine trained against a wall]

parenchyma /pəˈreŋkɪmə/ n. **1** Anat. the functional part of an
organ as distinguished from the connective and supporting
tissue. **2** Bot. the cellular material, usu. soft and succulent, found
esp. in the softer parts of leaves, pulp of fruits, bark and pith of
stems, etc. □□ **parenchymal** adj. **parenchymatous** /-ˈkɪmətəs/
adj. [Gk paregkhuma something poured in besides (as PARA-¹,
egkhuma infusion f. egkheō pour in)]

parent /ˈpeərənt/ n. & v. —n. **1** a person who has begotten or
borne offspring; a father or mother. **2** a person who has adopted
a child. **3** a forefather. **4** an animal or plant from which others
are derived. **5** a source or origin. **6** an initiating organization
or enterprise. —v.tr. (also absol.) be a parent of. □ **parent
company** a company of which other companies are
subsidiaries. **parent–teacher association** a local organization
of parents and teachers for promoting closer relations and
improving educational facilities at a school. □□ **parental**
/pəˈrent(ə)l/ adj. **parentally** /pəˈrentəlɪ/ adv. **parenthood** n. [ME
f. OF f. L parens parentis f. parere bring forth]

parentage /ˈpeərəntɪdʒ/ n. lineage; descent from or through
parents (their parentage is unknown). [ME f. OF (as PARENT)]

parenteral /pəˈrentər(ə)l/ adj. Med. administered or occurring
elsewhere than in the alimentary canal. □□ **parenterally** adv.
[PARA-¹ + Gk enteron intestine]

parenthesis /pəˈrenθəsɪs/ n. (pl. **parentheses** /-ˌsiːz/) **1 a** a word,
clause, or sentence inserted as an explanation or afterthought
into a passage which is grammatically complete without it, and
usu. marked off by brackets or dashes or commas. **b** (in pl.) a
pair of round brackets () used for this. **2** an interlude or interval.
□ **in parenthesis** as a parenthesis or afterthought. [LL f. Gk
parenthesis f. parentithēmi put in beside]

parenthesize /pəˈrenθəˌsaɪz/ v.tr. (also **-ise**) **1** (also absol.) insert
as a parenthesis. **2** put into brackets or similar punctuation.

parenthetic /ˌpærənˈθetɪk/ adj. **1** of or by way of a parenthesis.
2 interposed. □□ **parenthetical** adj. **parenthetically** adv. [PAR-
ENTHESIS after synthesis, synthetic, etc.]

parenting /ˈpeərəntɪŋ/ n. the occupation or concerns of parents.

parergon /pəˈrɜːɡən/ n. (pl. **parerga** /-ɡə/) **1** work subsidiary to
one's main employment. **2** an ornamental accessory. [L f. Gk
parergon (as PARA-¹, ergon work)]

paresis /pəˈriːsɪs, ˈpærɪsɪs/ n. (pl. **pareses** /-siːz/) Med. partial
paralysis. □□ **paretic** /-ˈretɪk/ adj. [mod.L f. Gk f. pariēmi let go
(as PARA-¹, hiēmi let go)]

par excellence /ˌpɑːr eksəˈlɑ̃s/ adv. as having special excellence;
being the supreme example of its kind (the short story par excellence). [F, = by excellence]

parfait /ˈpɑːfeɪ/ n. **1** a rich iced pudding of whipped cream, eggs,
etc. **2** layers of ice-cream, meringue, etc., served in a tall glass.
[F parfait PERFECT adj.]

pargana /pəˈɡʌnə/ n. (also **pergunnah, pergana**) (in India) a
group of villages or a subdivision of a district. [Urdu pargana
district]

parget /ˈpɑːdʒɪt/ v. & n. —v.tr. (**pargeted, pargeting**) **1** plaster
(a wall etc.) esp. with an ornamental pattern. **2** roughcast.
—n. **1** plaster applied in this way; ornamental plasterwork. **2**

roughcast. [ME f. OF pargeter, parjeter f. par all over + jeter throw]

parhelion /pɑːˈhiːlɪən/ n. (pl. **parhelia** /-lɪə/) a bright spot on
the solar halo. Also called mock sun, sun-dog. □□ **parheliacal**
/-hɪˈlaɪək(ə)l/ adj. **parhelic** adj. [L parelion f. Gk (as PARA-¹, hēlios
sun)]

pariah /pəˈraɪə, ˈpærɪə/ n. **1** a social outcast. **2** hist. a member
of a low caste or of no caste in S. India. □ **pariah-dog** =
PYE-DOG. [Tamil paṟaiyar pl. of paṟaiyan hereditary drummer f.
paṟai drum]

Parian /ˈpeərɪən/ adj. of the Greek island of Paros in the Aegean
Sea, famous since the 6th c. BC for its fine-textured white marble,
much used by sculptors.

parietal /pəˈraɪət(ə)l/ adj. **1** Anat. of the wall of the body or any
of its cavities. **2** Bot. of the wall of a hollow structure etc. **3** US
relating to residence within a college. □ **parietal bone** either
of a pair of bones forming the central part of the sides and top
of the skull. [F pariétal or LL parietalis f. L paries -etis wall]

pari-mutuel /ˌpɑːriːˈmjuːtjuːˌel/ n. **1** a form of betting in which
those backing the first three places divide the losers' stakes (less
the operator's commission). **2** a totalizator. [F, = mutual stake]

paring /ˈpeərɪŋ/ n. a strip or piece cut off.

pari passu /ˌpɑːrɪ ˈpæsuː, ˌpærɪ/ adv. **1** with equal speed. **2**
simultaneously and equally. [L]

Paris¹ /ˈpærɪs/ the capital and political, commercial, and cultural centre of France, situated on the River Seine; pop. (est.
1982) 2,188,918. It developed as a Roman town (Lutetia) and
became firmly established as a capital after 987, when Hugo
Capet became king of France. □ **Paris green** a poisonous chemical used as a pigment and insecticide.

Paris² /ˈpærɪs/ Gk legend the son of Priam and Hecuba, he was
known also as Alexander. Appointed by the gods to adjudge the
prize of beauty among the three goddesses Hera, Athene, and
Aphrodite, he awarded it to Aphrodite, who promised him the
fairest woman in the world — Helen, wife of Menelaus king of
Sparta. He abducted Helen, thus bringing about the Trojan War
in which he was killed. The 'Judgement of Paris' is a favourite
theme in art from the mid-7th c. BC onwards. Its story is essentially a folk-tale of choice (between kingship, warlike prowess,
and love, offered by the goddesses respectively) comparable to
the Hebrew story of Solomon's choice (between wisdom, long
life, riches, and destruction of enemies) told in 1 Kings 3: 5 ff.

Paris³ /ˈpærɪs/, Matthew (d. 1259), English historian, a monk at
the Benedictine monastery of St Albans where he became chief
chronicler. From 1235 to 1259 he continued the compilation of
the Chronica Maiora, his greatest work, which he expanded to
include accounts of events in foreign countries as well as
England, from the Creation to 1259. It surpasses any other
English chronicle for the vigour and brightness of its narrative.

parish /ˈpærɪʃ/ n. **1** an area having its own church and clergy.
2 (in full **civil parish**) a district constituted for purposes of
local government. (See below.) **3** the inhabitants of a parish. **4**
US a county in Louisiana. □ **parish clerk** an official performing
various duties concerned with the church. **parish council** Brit.
the administrative body in a civil parish. **parish pump** (often
attrib.) a symbol of a parochial or restricted outlook. **parish
register** a book recording christenings, marriages, and burials,
at a parish church. [ME paroche, parosse f. OF paroche, paroisse f.
eccl.L parochia, paroechia f. Gk paroikia sojourning f. paroikos (as
PARA-¹, -oikos -dwelling f. oikeō dwell)]

From the 17th c. parishes and churchwardens were entrusted
with local administration, chiefly relating to Poor Law and highways. Urban parishes were abolished as a unit of local government in 1933, but rural parishes have continued even after
the local government reorganization of 1974; their responsibilities now include recreational facilities, allotments, cemeteries, etc.

parishioner /pəˈrɪʃənə(r)/ n. an inhabitant of a parish. [obs.
parishen f. ME f. OF parossien, formed as PARISH]

Parisian /pəˈrɪzɪən/ adj. & n. —adj. of or relating to Paris in
France. —n. **1** a native or inhabitant of Paris. **2** the kind of
French spoken in Paris. [F parisien]

parison /ˈpærɪs(ə)n/ n. a rounded mass of glass formed by rolling immediately after taking it from the furnace. [F *paraison* f. *parer* prepare f. L *parare*]

parity[1] /'pærɪtɪ/ *n.* **1** equality or equal status, esp. as regards status or pay. **2** parallelism or analogy (*parity of reasoning*). **3** equivalence of one currency with another; being at par. **4** (of a number) the fact of being even or odd. **5** *Physics* (of a quantity) the fact of changing its sign or remaining unaltered under a given transformation of coordinates etc. [F *parité* or LL *paritas* (as PAR[1])]

parity[2] /'pærɪtɪ/ *n. Med.* **1** the fact or condition of having borne children. **2** the number of children previously borne. [formed as -PAROUS + -ITY]

Park /pɑːk/, Mungo (1771–1806), Scottish explorer. A surgeon in the mercantile marine, Park undertook a series of explorations in West Africa in 1795–6, sailing up the River Gambia, crossing Senegal and navigating the River Niger before being captured by a local Arab chief. He escaped from captivity four months later and returned to Britain after a year and a half in the interior. Bored with his medical practice in Scotland, Park returned to the Niger in 1805 but was drowned during a fight with Africans a year later.

park /pɑːk/ *n. & v.* —*n.* **1** a large public garden in a town, for recreation. **2** a large enclosed piece of ground, usu. with woodland and pasture, attached to a country house etc. **3 a** a large area of land kept in its natural state for public recreational use. **b** a large enclosed area of land used to accommodate wild animals in captivity (*wildlife park*). **4** an area for motor vehicles etc. to be left in (*car park*). **5** the gear position or function in automatic transmission in which the gears are locked, preventing the vehicle's movement. **6** an area devoted to a specified purpose (*industrial park*). **7 a** *US* a sports ground. **b** (usu. prec. by *the*) a football pitch. —*v.tr.* **1** (also *absol.*) leave (a vehicle) usu. temporarily, in a car park, by the side of the road, etc. **2** *colloq.* deposit and leave, usu. temporarily. □ **parking-light** a small light at the side of a vehicle, for use when the vehicle is parked at night. **parking-lot** *US* an outdoor area for parking vehicles. **parking-meter** a coin-operated meter which receives fees for vehicles parked in the street and indicates the time available. **parking-ticket** a notice, usu. attached to a vehicle, of a penalty imposed for parking illegally. **park oneself** *colloq.* sit down. [ME f. OF *parc* f. med.L *parricus* of Gmc orig., rel. to *pearruc*: see PADDOCK]

parka /'pɑːkə/ *n.* **1** a skin jacket with hood, worn by Eskimos. **2** a similar windproof fabric garment worn by mountaineers etc. [Aleutian]

Parker[1] /'pɑːkə(r)/, Charlie (Christopher) (1920–55), American jazz saxophonist. In New York he played with some of the great names of jazz, including Thelonious Monk and Dizzy Gillespie, and became one of the key figures of the 'bebop' movement, making some classic recordings with Miles Davis in 1945.

Parker[2] /'pɑːkə(r)/, Dorothy Rothschild (1893–1967), American humorous writer and drama critic, noted for her viperish wit.

parkin /'pɑːkɪn/ *n. Brit.* a cake or biscuit made with oatmeal, ginger, and treacle or molasses. [perh. f. the name *Parkin*, dimin. of *Peter*]

Parkinsonism /'pɑːkɪnsənɪz(ə)m/ *n.* = PARKINSON'S DISEASE.

Parkinson's disease /'pɑːkɪns(ə)nz/ *n.* a progressive disease of the nervous system with tremor, muscular rigidity, and emaciation. Also called PARKINSONISM. [J. *Parkinson*, Engl. surgeon d. 1824]

Parkinson's law /'pɑːkɪns(ə)nz/ *n.* the notion that work expands so as to fill the time available for its completion. [C. N. *Parkinson*, Engl. writer b. 1909]

parkland /'pɑːklænd/ *n.* open grassland with clumps of trees etc.

parkway /'pɑːkweɪ/ *n.* **1** *US* an open landscaped highway. **2** *Brit.* a railway station with extensive parking facilities.

parky /'pɑːkɪ/ *adj.* (**parkier**, **parkiest**) *Brit. colloq.* chilly. [19th c.: orig. unkn.]

Parl. *abbr. Brit.* **1** Parliament. **2** Parliamentary.

parlance /'pɑːləns/ *n.* a particular way of speaking, esp. as regards choice of words, idiom, etc. [OF f. *parler* speak, ult. f. L *parabola* (see PARABLE): in LL = 'speech']

parlay /'pɑːleɪ/ *v. & n. US* —*v.tr.* **1** use (money won on a bet) as a further stake. **2** increase in value by or as if by parlaying. —*n.* **1** an act of parlaying. **2** a bet made by parlaying. [F *paroli* f. It. f. *paro* like f. L *par* equal]

parley /'pɑːlɪ/ *n. & v.* —*n.* (*pl.* **-eys**) a conference for debating points in a dispute, esp. a discussion of terms for an armistice etc. —*v.intr.* (**-leys**, **-leyed**) (often foll. by *with*) hold a parley. [perh. f. OF *parlee*, fem. past part. of *parler* speak: see PARLANCE]

parliament /'pɑːləmənt/ *n.* **1** (**Parliament**) **a** (in the UK) the highest legislature, consisting of the Sovereign, the House of Lords, and the House of Commons. (See below.) **b** the members of this legislature for a particular period, esp. between one dissolution and the next. **2** a similar legislature in other nations and States. [ME f. OF *parlement* speaking (as PARLANCE)]

The British Parliament now consists of a council forming, with the Sovereign, the supreme legislature of the United Kingdom, consisting of the House of Lords (Spiritual and Temporal) and the House of Commons (elected representatives of towns etc.). It emerged in medieval times as the assembly of the king and his Lords, meeting irregularly, summoned and dismissed by the king, to discuss judicial and other matters of general importance, especially finances. To these assemblies, since the establishment of the idea that taxation required consent, from the 13th c. knights and burgesses who represented their shires and boroughs were occasionally summoned. The practice developed of the 'Commons' assembly meeting separately from the 'Lords', but it remained for a long time in the shadow of the latter, not gaining its own meeting chamber until the 16th c. and not having free speech, regular meetings, and control over taxation established as rights until the Glorious Revolution in the late 17th c. After the passing of the first Reform Act (1832) the traditional influence of the landed aristocracy began to decline, and the Parliament Act of 1911 reduced the power of the House of Lords to simple delay of legislation. A further Act in 1949 reduced the period of delay and ended it completely for financial legislation; the House of Commons is now unequivocally the more powerful and important body. The building in which Parliament meets was designed by Sir Charles Barry and erected after the destruction by fire of the Palace of Westminster, its meeting-place, in 1834.

parliamentarian /ˌpɑːləmənˈteərɪən/ *n. & adj.* —*n.* **1** a member of a parliament, esp. one well-versed in its procedures. **2** *hist.* an adherent of Parliament in the English Civil War of the 17th c. —*adj.* = PARLIAMENTARY.

parliamentary /ˌpɑːləˈmentərɪ/ *adj.* **1** of or relating to a parliament. **2** enacted or established by a parliament. **3** (of language) admissible in a parliament; polite. □ **Parliamentary Commissioner for Administration** the official name of the ombudsman in the UK. **parliamentary private secretary** a member of parliament assisting a government minister.

parlour /'pɑːlə(r)/ *n.* (*US* **parlor**) **1** a sitting-room in a private house. **2** a room in a hotel, convent, etc., for the private use of residents. **3** esp. *US* a shop providing specified goods or services (*beauty parlour*; *ice-cream parlour*). **4** a room or building equipped for milking cows. **5** (*attrib.*) *derog.* denoting support for political views by those who do not try to practise them (*parlour socialist*). □ **parlour game** an indoor game, esp. a word game. **parlour-maid** *hist.* a maid who waits at table. [ME f. AF *parlur*, OF *parleor*, *parleur*: see PARLANCE]

parlous /'pɑːləs/ *adj. & adv. archaic* or *joc.* —*adj.* **1** dangerous or difficult. **2** hard to deal with. —*adv.* extremely. □□ **parlously** *adv.* **parlousness** *n.* [ME, = PERILOUS]

Parma /'pɑːmə/ a city and province (formerly a duchy) of north Italy. □ **Parma violet** a variety of sweet violet with heavy scent and lavender-coloured flowers often crystallized for food decoration.

Parmenides /pɑːˈmenɪˌdiːz/ (early 5th c. BC) Greek philosopher from Elea in southern Italy. By a vigorous analysis, set out in a hexameter poem, of the term 'to be' he deduced that what is must be one, eternal, perfect, and indivisible, and that the plurality of objects in the common-sense world have no real being and cannot be the object of true knowledge.

Parmesan /ˌpɑːmɪˈzæn, ˈpɑː-/ n. a kind of hard dry cheese made orig. at Parma and used esp. in grated form. [F f. It. *parmegiano* of Parma in Italy]

Parmigianino /ˌpɑːmɪdʒəˈniːnəʊ/ Girolano Francesco Maria Mazzola (1503–40), Italian painter from Lombardy, sometimes called Parmigiano. A follower of Correggio, his etiolated and graceful figure style ranks as one of the highest points of refinement of mannerism. His work includes religious and mythological paintings and frescoes, portraiture, and some of the earliest known Italian etchings.

Parnassian /pɑːˈnæsɪən/ adj. & n. —adj. **1** of Parnassus. **2** poetic. **3** of or relating to a group of French poets in the late 19th c., emphasizing strictness of form, named from the anthology *Le Parnasse contemporain* (1866). —n. a member of this group.

Parnassus /pɑːˈnæsəs/ a mountain of central Greece, which rises above Delphi. In antiquity it was a sacred mountain, associated with Apollo and the Muses and hence a symbol of poetry.

Parnell /pɑːˈnel/, Charles Stewart (1846–91), Irish Nationalist leader. Elected to Parliament in 1875, Parnell became leader of the supporters of Home Rule for Ireland, and, through his mastery of parliamentary tactics, was successful in gaining great public exposure for Irish grievances. His political influence increased greatly after the 1885 elections, which left the Irish Nationalists the balance of power, and he supported Gladstone following the latter's acceptance of Home Rule. In 1890, however, involvement in a divorce case ruined Parnell's career and he died in obscurity a year later.

parochial /pəˈrəʊkɪəl/ adj. **1** of or concerning a parish. **2** (of affairs, views, etc.) merely local, narrow or restricted in scope. □□ **parochialism** n. **parochiality** /-ˈælɪtɪ/ n. **parochially** adv. [ME f. AF *parochiel*, OF *parochial* f. eccl.L *parochialis* (as PARISH)]

parody /ˈpærədɪ/ n. & v. —n. (pl. **-ies**) **1** a humorous exaggerated imitation of an author, literary work, style, etc. **2** a feeble imitation; a travesty. —v.tr. (**-ies, -ied**) **1** compose a parody of. **2** mimic humorously. □□ **parodic** /pəˈrɒdɪk/ adj. **parodist** n. [LL *parodia* or Gk *parōidia* burlesque poem (as PARA-¹, *ōidē* ode)]

parol /pəˈrəʊl/ adj. & n. Law —adj. **1** given orally. **2** (of a document) not given under seal. —n. an oral declaration. [OF *parole* (as PAROLE)]

parole /pəˈrəʊl/ n. & v. —n. **1 a** the release of a prisoner temporarily for a special purpose or completely before the expiry of a sentence, on the promise of good behaviour. **b** such a promise. **2** a word of honour. —v.tr. put (a prisoner) on parole. □ **on parole** released on the terms of parole. □□ **parolee** /-ˈliː/ n. [F, = word: see PARLANCE]

paronomasia /ˌpærənəˈmeɪzɪə/ n. a play on words; a pun. [L f. Gk *paronomasia* (as PARA-¹, *onomasia* naming f. *onomazō* to name f. *onoma* a name)]

paronym /ˈpærənɪm/ n. **1** a word cognate with another. **2** a word formed from a foreign word. □□ **paronymous** /pəˈrɒnɪməs/ adj. [Gk *parōnumon*, neut. of *parōnumos* (as PARA-¹, *onuma* name)]

Paros /ˈpeərɒs/ a Greek island of the Cyclades in the south Aegean, noted for its marble (see PARIAN).

parotid /pəˈrɒtɪd/ adj. & n. —adj. situated near the ear. —n. (in full **parotid gland**) a salivary gland in front of the ear. □ **parotid duct** a duct opening from the parotid gland into the mouth. [F *parotide* or L *parotis* parotid- f. Gk *parōtis -idos* (as PARA-¹, *ous ōtos* ear)]

parotitis /ˌpærəˈtaɪtɪs/ n. **1** inflammation of the parotid gland. **2** mumps. [PAROTID + -ITIS]

-parous /pərəs/ comb. form bearing offspring of a specified number or kind (*multiparous*; *viviparous*). [L *-parus* -bearing f. *parere* bring forth]

Parousia /pəˈruːzɪə/ n. Theol. the supposed second coming of Christ. [Gk, = presence, coming]

paroxysm /ˈpærəkˌsɪz(ə)m/ n. **1** (often foll. by *of*) a sudden attack or outburst (of rage, laughter, etc.). **2** a fit of disease. □□

paroxysmal /-ˈsɪzm(ə)l/ adj. [F *paroxysme* f. med.L *paroxysmus* f. Gk *paroxusmos* f. *paroxunō* exasperate (as PARA-¹, *oxunō* sharpen f. *oxus* sharp)]

paroxytone /pəˈrɒksɪˌtəʊn/ adj. & n. —adj. (esp. in ancient Greek) having an acute accent on the last syllable but one. —n. a word of this kind. [mod.L f. Gk *paroxutonos* (as PARA-¹, OXYTONE)]

parpen /ˈpɑːpən/ n. a stone passing through a wall from side to side, with two smooth vertical faces. [ME f. OF *parpain*, prob. ult. f. L *per* through + *pannus* piece of cloth, in Rmc 'piece of wall']

parquet /ˈpɑːkɪ, -keɪ/ n. & v. —n. **1** a flooring of wooden blocks arranged in a pattern. **2** US the stalls of a theatre. —v.tr. (**parqueted** /-keɪd/; **parqueting** /-keɪɪŋ/) furnish (a room) with a parquet floor. [F, = small compartment, floor, dimin. of *parc* PARK]

parquetry /ˈpɑːkɪtrɪ/ n. the use of wooden blocks to make floors or inlay for furniture.

Parr /pɑː(r)/, Catherine (1512–48), sixth wife of Henry VIII. Having married the king in 1543 she nursed him through his last years, successfully avoiding the worst effects of his erratic bouts of temper.

parr /pɑː(r)/ n. a young salmon with blue-grey finger-like markings on its sides, younger than a smolt. [18th c.: orig. unkn.]

parrakeet US var. of PARAKEET.

parramatta /ˌpærəˈmætə/ n. (also **paramatta**) a light dress fabric of wool and silk or cotton. [*Parramatta* in New South Wales, Australia]

parricide /ˈpærɪˌsaɪd/ n. **1** the killing of a near relative, esp. of a parent. **2** an act of parricide. **3** a person who commits parricide. □□ **parricidal** /-ˈsaɪd(ə)l/ adj. [F *parricide* or L *parricida* (= sense 3), *parricidium* (= sense 1), of uncert. orig., assoc. in L with *pater* father and *parens* parent]

parrot /ˈpærət/ n. & v. —n. **1** any of various mainly tropical birds of the order Psittaciformes, with a short hooked bill, often having vivid plumage and able to mimic the human voice. **2** a person who mechanically repeats the words or actions of another. —v.tr. (**parroted, parroting**) repeat mechanically. □ **parrot-fashion** (learning or repeating) mechanically without understanding. **parrot-fish** any fish of the genus *Scarus*, with a mouth like a parrot's bill and forming a protective mucous cocoon against predators. [prob. f. obs. or dial. F *perrot* parrot, dimin. of *Pierre* Peter: cf. PARAKEET]

Parry /ˈpærɪ/, Sir (Charles) Hubert (Hastings) (1848–1918), director of the Royal College of Music from 1894 until his death, and Professor of Music at Oxford University 1900–8. His literary interests informed his vocal music to inspire such fine works as the cantata *Blest Pair of Sirens* (1887) and the six motets called *Songs of Farewell*, written in 1916 during the First World War. His setting of William Blake's *Jerusalem* (1916) has achieved the status of a national song.

parry /ˈpærɪ/ v. & n. —v.tr. (**-ies, -ied**) **1** avert or ward off (a weapon or attack), esp. with a countermove. **2** deal skilfully with (an awkward question etc.). —n. (pl. **-ies**) an act of parrying. [prob. repr. F *parez* imper. of *parer* f. It. *parare* ward off]

parse /pɑːz/ v.tr. **1** describe (a word in context) grammatically, stating its inflection, relation to the sentence, etc. **2** resolve (a sentence) into its component parts and describe them grammatically. □□ **parser** n. esp. Computing [perh. f. ME *pars* parts of speech f. OF *pars*, pl. of *part* PART, infl. by L *pars* part]

parsec /ˈpɑːsek/ n. a unit of stellar distance, equal to about 3.25 light years (3.08 × 10¹⁶ metres), the distance at which the mean radius of the earth's orbit subtends an angle of one second of arc. [PARALLAX + SECOND²]

Parsee /ˈpɑːsiː/ n. **1** an adherent of Zoroastrianism. **2** a descendant of the Persians who fled to India from Muslim persecution in the 7th–8th c. **3** = PAHLAVI. □□ **Parseeism** n. [Pers. *pārsī* Persian f. *pārs* Persia]

Parsifal /ˈpɑːsɪf(ə)l/ var. of PERCEVAL.

parsimony /ˈpɑːsɪmənɪ/ n. **1** carefulness in the use of money or other resources. **2** meanness, stinginess. □ **law of**

parsimony the assertion that no more causes or forces should be assumed than are necessary to account for the facts. □□ **parsimonious** /-ˈməʊnɪəs/ *adj.* **parsimoniously** /-ˈməʊnɪəslɪ/ *adv.* **parsimoniousness** /-ˈməʊnɪəsnɪs/ *n.* [ME f. L *parsimonia, parcimonia* f. *parcere* pars- spare]

parsley /ˈpɑːslɪ/ *n.* a biennial herb, *Petroselinum crispum*, with white flowers and crinkly aromatic leaves, used for seasoning and garnishing food. □ **parsley fern** a fern, *Cryptogramma crispa*, with leaves like parsley. **parsley-piert** a dwarf annual herb, *Aphanes arvensis*. [ME *percil, per(e)sil* f. OF *peresil*, and OE *petersilie* ult. f. L *petroselinum* f. Gk *petroselinon; parsley-piert* prob. corrupt. of F *perce-pierre* pierce stone]

parsnip /ˈpɑːsnɪp/ *n.* **1** a biennial umbelliferous plant, *Pastinaca sativa*, with yellow flowers and a large pale-yellow tapering root. **2** this root eaten as a vegetable. [ME *pas(se)nep* (with assim. to *nep* turnip) f. OF *pasnaie* f. L *pastinaca*]

parson /ˈpɑːs(ə)n/ *n.* **1** a rector. **2** a vicar or any beneficed member of the clergy. **3** *colloq.* any (esp. Protestant) member of the clergy. □ **parson's nose** the piece of fatty flesh at the rump of a fowl. □□ **parsonical** /-ˈsɒnɪk(ə)l/ *adj.* [ME *person(e), parson* f. OF *persone* f. L *persona* PERSON (in med.L *rector*)]

parsonage /ˈpɑːsənɪdʒ/ *n.* a church house provided for a parson.

part /pɑːt/ *n., v., & adv.* —*n.* **1** some but not all of a thing or number of things. **2** an essential member or constituent of anything (*part of the family; a large part of the job*). **3** a component of a machine etc. (*spare parts; needs a new part*). **4 a** a portion of a human or animal body. **b** (in *pl.*) = *private parts*. **5** a division of a book, broadcast serial, etc., esp. as much as is issued or broadcast at one time. **6** each of several equal portions of a whole (*the recipe has 3 parts sugar to 2 parts flour*). **7 a** a portion allotted; a share. **b** a person's share in an action or enterprise (*will have no part in it*). **c** one's duty (*was not my part to interfere*). **8 a** a character assigned to an actor on stage. **b** the words spoken by an actor on stage. **c** a copy of these. **9** *Mus.* a melody or other constituent of harmony assigned to a particular voice or instrument. **10** each of the sides in an agreement or dispute. **11** (in *pl.*) a region or district (*am not from these parts*). **12** (in *pl.*) abilities (*a man of many parts*). **13** *US* = PARTING 2. —*v.* **1** *tr. & intr.* divide or separate into parts (*the crowd parted to let them through*). **2** *intr.* **a** leave one another's company (*they parted the best of friends*). **b** (foll. by *from*) say goodbye to. **3** *tr.* cause to separate (*they fought hard and had to be parted*). **4** *intr.* (foll. by *with*) give up possession of; hand over. **5** *tr.* separate (the hair of the head on either side of the parting) with a comb. —*adv.* to some extent; partly (*is part iron and part wood; a lie that is part truth*). □ **for the most part** see MOST. **for one's part** as far as one is concerned. **in part** (or **parts**) to some extent; partly. **look the part** appear suitable for a role. **on the part of** on the behalf or initiative of (*no objection on my part*). **part and parcel** (usu. foll. by *of*) an essential part. **part company** see COMPANY. **part-exchange** *n.* a transaction in which goods are given as part of the payment for other goods, with the balance in money. —*v.tr.* give (goods) in such a transaction. **part of speech** *n.* each of the categories to which words are assigned in accordance with their grammatical and semantic functions (in English esp. noun, pronoun, adjective, adverb, verb, preposition, conjunction, and interjection). **part-song** a song with three or more voice-parts, often without accompaniment, and harmonic rather than contrapuntal in character. **part time** less than the full time required by an activity. **part-time** *adj.* occupying or using only part of one's working time. **part-timer** a person employed in part-time work. **part-work** *Brit.* a publication appearing in several parts over a period of time. **play a part 1** be significant or contributory. **2** act deceitfully. **3** perform a theatrical role. **take in good part** see GOOD. **take part** (often foll. by *in*) assist or have a share (in). **take the part of** support; back up. **three parts** three quarters. [ME f. OF f. L *pars partis* (n.), *partire, partiri* (v.)]

partake /pɑːˈteɪk/ *v.intr.* (*past* **partook** /-ˈtʊk/; *past part.* **partaken** /-ˈteɪkən/) **1** (foll. by *of, in*) take a share or part. **2** (foll. by *of*) eat or drink some or *colloq.* all (of a thing). **3** (foll. by *of*) have some (of a quality etc.) (*their manner partook of insolence*). □□ **partakable** *adj.* **partaker** *n.* [16th c.: back-form. f. *partaker, partaking* = part-taker etc.]

parterre /pɑːˈteə(r)/ *n.* **1** a level space in a garden occupied by flower-beds arranged formally. **2** *US* the ground floor of a theatre auditorium, esp. the pit overhung by balconies. [F, = *par terre* on the ground]

parthenogenesis /ˌpɑːθɪnəʊˈdʒenɪsɪs/ *n. Biol.* reproduction by a male gamete without fertilization, esp. as a normal process in invertebrates and lower plants. □□ **parthenogenetic** /-dʒɪˈnetɪk/ *adj.* **parthenogenetically** /-dʒɪˈnetɪkəlɪ/ *adv.* [mod.L f. Gk *parthenos* virgin + *genesis* as GENESIS]

Parthenon /ˈpɑːθɪnən/ the temple of Athene Parthenos (= the maiden), built on the Acropolis at Athens in 447–432 BC by Pericles to honour the city's patron goddess and to commemorate the recent Greek victory over the Persians. Designed by the architects Ictinus and Callicrates with sculptures by Phidias, including a colossal gold and ivory statue of Athene (known from descriptive accounts) and the 'Elgin marbles' now in the British Museum, the Parthenon was partly financed by tribute from the league of Greek States led by Athens, and housed the treasuries of Athens and the league.

Parthian /ˈpɑːθɪən/ *adj. & n.* —*adj.* of the ancient Asian kingdom of Parthia or its people, whose homeland lay SE of the Caspian Sea. From *c.*250 BC–*c.*AD 230 they ruled an empire stretching from the Euphrates to the Indus, with Ecbatana as its capital. Their culture contained a mixture of Greek and Iranian elements. The Parthians were superb horsemen, original and competent in warfare. —*n.* a native of Parthia. □ **Parthian shot** a telling remark reserved for the moment of departure, so called from the trick used by Parthians of shooting arrows while in real or pretended flight.

partial /ˈpɑːʃ(ə)l/ *adj. & n.* —*adj.* **1** not complete; forming only part (*a partial success*). **2** biased, unfair. **3** (foll. by *to*) having a liking for. —*n. Mus.* any of the constituents of a musical sound. □ **partial eclipse** an eclipse in which only part of the luminary is covered or darkened. **partial verdict** a verdict finding a person guilty of part of a charge. □□ **partially** *adv.* **partialness** *n.* [ME f. OF *parcial* f. LL *partialis* (as PART)]

partiality /ˌpɑːʃɪˈælɪtɪ/ *n.* **1** bias, favouritism. **2** (foll. by *for*) fondness. [ME f. OF *parcialité* f. med.L *partialitas* (as PARTIAL)]

participant /pɑːˈtɪsɪpənt/ *n.* a participator.

participate /pɑːˈtɪsɪˌpeɪt/ *v.intr.* **1** (foll. by *in*) take a part or share (in). **2** *literary* or *formal* (foll. by *of*) have a certain quality (*the speech participated of wit*). □□ **participation** /-ˈpeɪʃ(ə)n/ *n.* **participator** *n.* **participatory** *adj.* [L *participare* f. *particeps -cipis* taking part, formed as PART + -*cip-* = *cap-* stem of *capere* take]

participle /ˈpɑːtɪˌsɪp(ə)l/ *n. Gram.* a word formed from a verb (e.g. *going, gone, being, been*) and used in compound verb-forms (e.g. *is going, has been*) or as an adjective (e.g. *working woman, burnt toast*). □□ **participial** /-ˈsɪpɪəl/ *adj.* **participially** /-ˈsɪpɪəlɪ/ *adv.* [ME f. OF, by-form of *participe* f. L *participium* (as PARTICIPATE)]

particle /ˈpɑːtɪk(ə)l/ *n.* **1** a minute portion of matter. **2** the least possible amount (*not a particle of sense*). **3** *Gram.* **a** a minor part of speech, esp. a short undeclinable one. **b** a common prefix or suffix such as *in-, -ness*. [ME f. L *particula* (as PART)]

particoloured /ˈpɑːtɪˌkʌləd/ *adj.* partly of one colour, partly of another or others. [PARTY² + COLOURED]

particular /pəˈtɪkjʊlə(r)/ *adj. & n.* —*adj.* **1** relating to or considered as one thing or person as distinct from others; individual (*in this particular instance*). **2** more than is usual; special, noteworthy (*took particular trouble*). **3** scrupulously exact; fastidious. **4** detailed (*a full and particular account*). **5** *Logic* (of a proposition) in which something is asserted of some but not all of a class (opp. UNIVERSAL). —*n.* **1** a detail; an item. **2** (in *pl.*) points of information; a detailed account. □ **in particular** especially, specifically. [ME f. OF *particuler* f. L *particularis* (as PARTICLE)]

particularism /pəˈtɪkjʊləˌrɪz(ə)m/ *n.* **1** exclusive devotion to one party, sect, etc. **2** the principle of leaving political independence to each State in an empire or federation. **3** the theological doctrine of individual election or redemption. □□ **particularist** *n.* [F *particularisme*, mod.L *particularismus*, and G *Partikularismus* (as PARTICULAR)]

particularity /pəˌtɪkjʊˈlærɪtɪ/ n. **1** the quality of being individual or particular. **2** fullness or minuteness of detail in a description.

particularize /pəˈtɪkjʊləˌraɪz/ v.tr. (also **-ise**) tr. (also absol.) **1** name specially or one by one. **2** specify (items). □□ **particularization** /-ˈzeɪʃ(ə)n/ n. [F particulariser (as PARTICULAR)]

particularly /pəˈtɪkjʊləlɪ/ adv. **1** especially, very. **2** specifically (they particularly asked for you). **3** in a particular or fastidious manner.

particulate /pəˈtɪkjʊˌleɪt, -lət/ adj. & n. —adj. in the form of separate particles. —n. matter in this form. [L particula PARTICLE]

parting /ˈpɑːtɪŋ/ n. **1** a leave-taking or departure (often attrib.: parting words). **2** Brit. the dividing line of combed hair. **3** a division; an act of separating. □ **parting shot** = PARTHIAN SHOT.

parti pris /ˌpɑːtɪ ˈpriː/ n. & adj. —n. a preconceived view; a bias. —adj. prejudiced, biased. [F, = side taken]

partisan /ˈpɑːtɪˌzæn, -ˈzæn/ n. & adj. (also **partizan**) **1** a strong, esp. unreasoning, supporter of a party, cause, etc. **2** Mil. a guerrilla in wartime. —adj. **1** of or characteristic of partisans. **2** loyal to a particular cause; biased. □□ **partisanship** n. [F f. It. dial. partigiano etc. f. parte PART]

partita /pɑːˈtiːtə/ n. (pl. **partite** /-teɪ/) Mus. **1** a suite. **2** an air with variations. [It., fem. past part. of partire divide, formed as PART]

partite /ˈpɑːtaɪt/ adj. **1** divided (esp. in comb.: tripartite). **2** Bot. & Zool. divided to or nearly to the base. [L partitus past part. of partiri PART v.]

partition /pɑːˈtɪʃ(ə)n/ n. & v. —n. **1** division into parts, esp. Polit. of a country with separate areas of government. **2** a structure dividing a space into two parts, esp. a light interior wall. —v.tr. **1** divide into parts. **2** (foll. by off) separate (part of a room etc.) with a partition. □□ **partitioned** adj. **partitioner** n. **partitionist** n. [ME f. OF f. L partitio -onis (as PARTITE)]

partitive /ˈpɑːtɪtɪv/ adj. & n. Gram. —adj. (of a word, form, etc.) denoting part of a collective group or quantity. —n. a partitive word (e.g. some, any) or form. □ **partitive genitive** a genitive used to indicate a whole divided into or regarded in parts, expressed in English by of as in most of us. □□ **partitively** adv. [F partitif -ive or med.L partitivus (as PARTITE)]

partizan var. of PARTISAN.

partly /ˈpɑːtlɪ/ adv. **1** with respect to a part or parts. **2** to some extent.

partner /ˈpɑːtnə(r)/ n. & v. —n. **1** a person who shares or takes part with another or others, esp. in a business firm with shared risks and profits. **2** a companion in dancing. **3** a player (esp. one of two) on the same side in a game. **4** either member of a married couple, or of an unmarried couple living together. —v.tr. **1** be the partner of. **2** associate as partners. □□ **partnerless** adj. [ME, alt. of parcener joint heir, after PART]

partnership /ˈpɑːtnəʃɪp/ n. **1** the state of being a partner or partners. **2** a joint business. **3** a pair or group of partners.

partook past of PARTAKE.

partridge /ˈpɑːtrɪdʒ/ n. (pl. same or **partridges**) **1** any game-bird of the genus Perdix, esp. P. perdix of Europe and Asia. **2** any other of various similar birds of the family Phasianidae, including the snow partridge. [ME partrich etc. f. OF perdriz etc. f. L perdix -dicis: for -dge cf. CABBAGE]

parturient /pɑːˈtjʊərɪənt/ adj. about to give birth. [L parturire be in labour, incept. f. parere part- bring forth]

parturition /ˌpɑːtjʊˈrɪʃ(ə)n/ n. formal the act of bringing forth young; childbirth. [LL parturitio (as PARTURIENT)]

party¹ /ˈpɑːtɪ/ n. & v. —n. (pl. **-ies**) **1** a social gathering, usu. of invited guests. **2** a body of persons engaged in an activity or travelling together (fishing party; search party). **3** a group of people united in a cause, opinion, etc., esp. a political group organized on a national basis. **4** a person or persons forming one side in an agreement or dispute. **5** (foll. by to) Law an accessory (to an action). **6** colloq. a person. —v.tr. & intr. (**-ies, -ied**) entertain at or attend a party. □ **party line 1** the policy adopted by a political party. **2** a telephone line shared by two or more subscribers.

party-wall a wall common to two adjoining buildings or rooms. [ME f. OF partie ult. f. L partire: see PART]

party² /ˈpɑːtɪ/ adj. Heraldry divided into parts of different colours. [ME f. OF parti f. L (as PARTY¹)]

Parvati /ˈpɑːvətɪ/ Hinduism a benevolent goddess, wife of Siva, mother of Ganesha and Skanda. She is often identified with Uma, Sati, Devi, and Sakti, and in her malevolent aspect with Durga and Kali. [Skr., = daughter of the mountain]

parvenu /ˈpɑːvəˌnuː/ n. & adj. —n. (fem. **parvenue**) **1** a person of obscure origin who has gained wealth or position. **2** an upstart. —adj. **1** associated with or characteristic of such a person. **2** upstart. [F, past part. of parvenir arrive f. L pervenire (as PER-, venire come)]

parvis /ˈpɑːvɪs/ n. (also **parvise**) **1** an enclosed area in front of a cathedral, church, etc. **2** a room over a church porch. [ME f. OF parvis ult. f. LL paradisus PARADISE, a court in front of St Peter's, Rome]

pas /pɑː/ n. (pl. same) a step in dancing, esp. in classical ballet. □ **pas de chat** /də ˈʃɑː/ a leap in which each foot in turn is raised to the opposite knee. **pas de deux** /də ˈdɜː/ a dance for two persons. **pas glissé** see GLISSÉ. **pas seul** /ˈsɜːl/ a solo dance. [F, = step]

Pascal¹ /pæˈskɑːl/ n. a computer language used esp. in training, named after Blaise Pascal.

Pascal² /pæsˈkɑːl/, Blaise (1623–62), French mathematician, physicist, and religious philosopher. A mathematical child prodigy, before the age of 16 he had proved one of the most important theorems in the projective geometry of conics, and at 19 constructed an arithmetic calculating machine to assist his father in his accounting. It was the first mechanical calculator to be offered for sale, of which seven still exist. From barometric experiments he concluded that air has weight; he confirmed the view that the vacuum could exist; while from his hydrostatic experiments he derived 'Pascal's principle' that the pressure of a fluid at rest is transmitted equally in all directions. He founded the theory of probabilities in 1654 when corresponding with Fermat, and also developed a forerunner of integral calculus. After a spiritual experience in 1654 he entered a Jansenist convent, where he wrote two classics of French devotional thought, his Lettres Provinciales (1656–7), directed against the casuistry of the Jesuits, and his posthumously published Pensées (1670), directed principally against free-thinkers. The pascal (see entry) and a computer language (PASCAL¹) are named in his honour.

pascal /ˈpæsk(ə)l/ n. the SI unit of pressure, equal to one newton per square metre. [B. PASCAL]

paschal /ˈpæsk(ə)l/ adj. **1** of or relating to the Jewish Passover. **2** of or relating to Easter. □ **paschal lamb 1** a lamb sacrificed at Passover. **2** Christ. [ME f. OF pascal f. eccl.L paschalis f. pascha f. Gk paskha f. Aram. pasḥa, rel. to Heb. pesaḥ PASSOVER]

pash /pæʃ/ n. sl. a brief infatuation. [abbr. of PASSION]

pasha /ˈpɑːʃə/ n. (also **pacha**) hist. the title (placed after the name) of a Turkish officer of high rank, e.g. a military commander, the governor of a province, etc. [Turk. paşa, prob. = başa f. baş head, chief]

pashm /ˈpæʃəm/ n. the under-fur of some Tibetan animals, esp. that of goats as used for Cashmere shawls.

Pashto /ˈpʌʃtəʊ/ n. & adj. —n. the Iranian language of the Pathans, the official language of Afghanistan, spoken by some 10 million people there and another 6 million in NW Pakistan. It is an Indo-Iranian language and, like Persian, is written in a form of the Arabic script. —adj. of or in this language. [Pashto]

Pašić /ˈpæʃiːtʃ/, Nikola (1845–1926), Serbian statesman, a founder of Yugoslavia. He was twice Premier of the newly formed kingdom (1921–4, 1924–6) in which Serbs were united with Croats and Slovenes.

Pasiphaë /pəˈsɪfəˌiː/ Gk legend the wife of Minos and mother of the Minotaur.

paso doble /ˌpæsəʊ ˈdəʊbleɪ/ n. **1** a ballroom dance based on a Latin American style of marching. **2** this style of marching. [Sp., = double step]

pasque-flower /ˈpæskˌflaʊə(r)/ n. a ranunculaceous plant, *Pulsatilla vulgaris*, with bell-shaped purple flowers and fernlike foliage. Also called ANEMONE. [earlier *passe-flower* f. F *passe-fleur*: assim. to *pasque* = obs. *pasch* (as PASCHAL), Easter]

pasquinade /ˌpæskwɪˈneɪd/ n. a lampoon or satire, orig. one displayed in a public place. [It. *pasquinata* f. *Pasquino*, a statue in Rome on which abusive Latin verses were annually posted]

pass[1] /pɑːs/ v. & n. —v. (*past part.* **passed**) (see also PAST). **1** *intr.* (often foll. by *along, by, down, on,* etc.) move onward; proceed, esp. past some point of reference (*saw the procession passing*). **2** *tr.* **a** go past; leave (a thing etc.) on one side or behind in proceeding. **b** overtake, esp. in a vehicle. **c** go across (a frontier, mountain range, etc.). **3** *intr.* & *tr.* be transferred or cause to be transferred from one person or place to another (*pass the butter*; *the title passes to his son*). **4** *tr.* surpass; be too great for (*it passes my comprehension*). **5** *intr.* get through; effect a passage. **6** *intr.* **a** be accepted as adequate; go uncensured (*let the matter pass*). **b** (foll. by *as, for*) be accepted or currently known as. **c** *US* (of a person with some Black ancestry) be accepted as White. **7** *tr.* move; cause to go (*passed her hand over her face*; *passed a rope round it*). **8 a** *intr.* (of a candidate in an examination) be successful. **b** *tr.* be successful in (an examination). **c** *tr.* (of an examiner) judge the performance of (a candidate) to be satisfactory. **9 a** *tr.* (of a bill) be examined and approved by (a parliamentary body or process). **b** *tr.* cause or allow (a bill) to proceed to further legislative processes. **c** *intr.* (of a bill or proposal) be approved. **10** *intr.* **a** occur, elapse (*the remark passed unnoticed*; *time passes slowly*). **b** happen; be done or said (*heard what passed between them*). **11 a** *intr.* circulate; be current. **b** *tr.* put into circulation (*was passing forged cheques*). **12** *tr.* spend or use up (a certain time or period) (*passed the afternoon reading*). **13** *tr.* (also *absol.*) (in field games) send (the ball) to another player of one's own side. **14** *intr.* forgo one's turn or chance in a game etc. **15** *intr.* (foll. by *to, into*) change from one form (to another). **16** *intr.* come to an end. **17** *tr.* discharge from the body as or with excreta. **18** *tr.* (foll. by *on, upon*) **a** utter (criticism) about. **b** pronounce (a judicial sentence) on. **19** *intr.* (often foll. by *on, upon*) adjudicate. **20** *tr.* not declare or pay (a dividend). **21** *tr.* cause (troops etc.) to go by esp. ceremonially. —n. **1** an act or instance of passing. **2 a** success in an examination. **b** *Brit.* the status of a university degree without honours. **3** written permission to pass into or out of a place, or to be absent from quarters. **4 a** a ticket or permit giving free entry or access etc. **b** = *free pass*. **5** (in field games) a transference of the ball to another player on the same side. **6** a thrust in fencing. **7** a juggling trick. **8** an act of passing the hands over anything, as in conjuring or hypnotism. **9** a critical position (*has come to a fine pass*). □ **in passing 1** by the way. **2** in the course of speech, conversation, etc. **make a pass at** *colloq.* make amorous or sexual advances to. **pass away 1** *euphem.* die. **2** cease to exist; come to an end. **pass by 1** go past. **2** disregard, omit. **passed pawn** *Chess* a pawn that has advanced beyond the pawns on the other side. **pass one's eye over** read (a document etc.) cursorily. **pass muster** see MUSTER. **pass off 1** (of feelings etc.) disappear gradually. **2** (of proceedings) be carried through (in a specified way). **3** (foll. by *as*) misrepresent (a person or thing) as something else. **4** evade or lightly dismiss (an awkward remark etc.). **pass on 1** proceed on one's way. **2** *euphem.* die. **3** transmit to the next person in a series. **pass out 1** become unconscious. **2** *Brit. Mil.* complete one's training as a cadet. **3** distribute. **pass over 1** omit, ignore, or disregard. **2** ignore the claims of (a person) to promotion or advancement. **3** *euphem.* die. **pass round 1** distribute. **2** send or give to each of a number in turn. **pass through** experience. **pass the time of day** see TIME. **pass up** *colloq.* refuse or neglect (an opportunity etc.). **pass water** urinate. □□ **passer** n. [ME f. OF *passer* ult. f. L *passus* PACE[1]]

pass[2] /pɑːs/ n. **1** a narrow passage through mountains. **2** a navigable channel, esp. at the mouth of a river. □ **sell the pass** betray a cause. [ME, var. of PACE[1], infl. by F *pas* and by PASS[1]]

passable /ˈpɑːsəb(ə)l/ adj. **1** barely satisfactory; just adequate. **2** (of a road, pass, etc.) that can be passed. □□ **passableness** n. **passably** adv. [ME f. OF (as PASS[1])]

passacaglia /ˌpæsəˈkɑːlɪə/ n. *Mus.* an instrumental piece usu.

with a ground bass. [It. f. Sp. *pasacalle* f. *pasar* pass + *calle* street: orig. often played in the streets]

passage[1] /ˈpæsɪdʒ/ n. **1** the process or means of passing; transit. **2** = PASSAGEWAY. **3** the liberty or right to pass through. **4 a** the right of conveyance as a passenger by sea or air. **b** a journey by sea or air. **5** a transition from one state to another. **6 a** a short extract from a book etc. **b** a section of a piece of music. **7** the passing of a bill etc. into law. **8** (in *pl.*) an interchange of words etc. **9** *Anat.* a duct etc. in the body. □ **passage of** (or **at**) **arms** a fight or dispute. **work one's passage** earn a right (orig. of passage) by working for it. [ME f. OF (as PASS[1])]

passage[2] /ˈpæsɪdʒ/ v. **1** *intr.* (of a horse or rider) move sideways, by the pressure of the rein on the horse's neck and of the rider's leg on the opposite side. **2** *tr.* make (a horse) do this. [F *passager*, earlier *passéger* f. It. *passeggiare* to walk, pace f. *passeggio* walk f. L *passus* PACE[1]]

passageway /ˈpæsɪdʒˌweɪ/ n. a narrow way for passing along, esp. with walls on either side; a corridor.

passant /ˈpæs(ə)nt/ adj. *Heraldry* (of an animal) walking and looking to the dexter side, with three paws on the ground and the right forepaw raised. [ME f. OF, part. of *passer* PASS[1]]

passband /ˈpɑːsbænd/ n. a frequency band within which signals are transmitted by a filter without attenuation.

passbook /ˈpɑːsbʊk/ n. a book issued by a bank or building society etc. to an account-holder recording sums deposited and withdrawn.

Passchendaele /ˈpæʃ(ə)nˌdeɪl/ a Belgian village marking the furthest point of the British advance during the Ypres offensive of 1917. Eight weeks of heavy rain had made conditions for the exhausted armies almost impossible. Here (as on the Somme) there was heavy loss of life, tolerated only in the fervent patriotism of the time.

passé /ˈpæseɪ/ adj. (*fem.* **passée**) **1** behind the times; out of date. **2** past its prime. [F, past part. of *passer* PASS[1]]

passementerie /ˈpæsməntrɪ/ n. a trimming of gold or silver lace, braid, beads, etc. [F f. *passement* gold lace etc. f. *passer* PASS[1]]

passenger /ˈpæsɪndʒə(r)/ n. **1** a traveller in or on a public or private conveyance (other than the driver, pilot, crew, etc.). **2** *colloq.* a member of a team, crew, etc., who does no effective work. **3** (*attrib.*) for the use of passengers (*passenger seat*). □ **passenger-mile** one mile travelled by one passenger, as a unit of traffic. **passenger-pigeon** an extinct wild pigeon of N. America, capable of long flight. [ME f. OF *passager* f. OF *passager* (adj.) passing (as PASSAGE[1]): -n- as in *messenger* etc.]

passe-partout /ˌpæspɑːˈtuː, ˌpɑːs-/ n. **1** a master-key. **2** a picture-frame (esp. for mounted photographs) consisting of two pieces of glass stuck together at the edges with adhesive tape. **3** adhesive tape or paper used for this. [F, = passes everywhere]

passer-by /ˌpɑːsəˈbaɪ/ n. (*pl.* **passers-by**) a person who goes past, esp. by chance.

passerine /ˈpæsəˌriːn/ n. & adj. —n. any perching bird of the order Passeriformes, having feet with three toes pointing forward and one pointing backwards, including sparrows and most land birds. —adj. **1** of or relating to this order. **2** of the size of a sparrow. [L *passer* sparrow]

passible /ˈpæsɪb(ə)l/ adj. *Theol.* capable of feeling or suffering. □□ **passibility** /-ˈbɪlɪtɪ/ n. [ME f. OF *passible* or LL *passibilis* f. L *pati pass-* suffer]

passim /ˈpæsɪm/ adv. (of allusions or references in a published work) to be found at various places throughout the text. [L f. *passus* scattered f. *pandere* spread]

passing /ˈpɑːsɪŋ/ adj. & n. —adj. **1** in senses of PASS v. **2** transient, fleeting (*a passing glance*). **3** cursory, incidental (*a passing reference*). —n. **1** in senses of PASS v. **2** *euphem.* the death of a person (*mourned his passing*). □ **passing note** *Mus.* a note not belonging to the harmony but interposed to secure a smooth transition. **passing shot** *Tennis* a shot aiming the ball beyond and out of reach of the other player. □□ **passingly** adv.

passion /ˈpæʃ(ə)n/ n. **1** strong barely controllable emotion. **2** an outburst of anger (*flew into a passion*). **3** intense sexual love. **4 a** strong enthusiasm (*has a passion for football*). **b** an object arousing this. **5** (**the Passion**) **a** *Relig.* the suffering of Christ during his last days. **b** a narrative of this from the Gospels. **c** a musical setting of any of these narratives. □ **passion-flower** any climbing plant of the genus *Passiflora*, with a flower that was supposed to suggest the crown of thorns and other things associated with the Passion of Christ. **passion-fruit** the edible fruit of some species of passion-flower, esp. *Passiflora edulis*: also called GRANADILLA. **passion-play** see separate entry. **Passion Sunday** the fifth Sunday in Lent. **Passion Week 1** the week between Passion Sunday and Palm Sunday. **2** = *Holy Week*. □□ **passionless** *adj.* [ME f. OF f. LL *passio -onis* f. L *pati pass-* suffer]

passional /ˈpæʃən(ə)l/ *adj. & n.* —*adj.* *literary* of or marked by passion. —*n.* a book of the sufferings of saints and martyrs.

passionate /ˈpæʃənət/ *adj.* **1** dominated by or easily moved to strong feeling, esp. love or anger. **2** showing or caused by passion. □□ **passionately** *adv.* **passionateness** *n.* [ME f. med.L *passionatus* (as PASSION)]

passion-play *n.* a medieval religious drama in the vernacular dealing with the events of Christ's Passion from the Last Supper to the Crucifixion. The establishment of the feast of Corpus Christi in 1313 gave a great impetus to the enactment of passion-plays throughout Europe, but most of them died out during the 15th c. The best-known of the few that survive is that given at Oberammergau (see entry).

Passiontide /ˈpæʃ(ə)nˌtaɪd/ *n.* the last two weeks of Lent.

passivate /ˈpæsɪˌveɪt/ *v.tr.* make (esp. metal) passive (see PASSIVE). □□ **passivation** /-ˈveɪʃ(ə)n/ *n.*

passive /ˈpæsɪv/ *adj.* **1** suffering action; acted upon. **2** offering no opposition; submissive. **3 a** not active; inert. **b** (of a metal) abnormally unreactive. **4** *Gram.* designating the voice in which the subject undergoes the action of the verb (e.g. in *they were killed*). **5** (of a debt) incurring no interest payment. □ **passive obedience 1** surrender to another's will without cooperation. **2** compliance with commands irrespective of their nature. **passive resistance** a non-violent refusal to cooperate. One of the most successful campaigns was that led by Gandhi against British rule in India. His example was an inspiration for the Civil Rights movements in the US from the 1950s, but similar methods have failed in less liberal regimes. **passive smoking** the involuntary inhaling, esp. by a non-smoker, of smoke from others' cigarettes etc. □□ **passively** *adv.* **passiveness** *n.* **passivity** /-ˈsɪvɪtɪ/ *n.* [ME f. OF *passif -ive* or L *passivus* (as PASSION)]

passkey /ˈpɑːskiː/ *n.* **1** a private key to a gate etc. for special purposes. **2** a master-key.

passmark /ˈpɑːsmɑːk/ *n.* the minimum mark needed to pass an examination.

Passover /ˈpɑːsˌəʊvə(r)/ *n.* **1** (Heb. *Pesach*) the Jewish festival celebrated each spring, held from 14 to 21 Nisan and commemorating the liberation of the Israelites from slavery in Egypt (see EXODUS). It may have been originally an agricultural feast. **2** = *paschal lamb*. [*pass over* = pass without touching, with ref. to the exemption of the Israelites from the death of the first-born (Exod. 12)]

passport /ˈpɑːspɔːt/ *n.* **1** an official document issued by a government certifying the holder's identity and citizenship, and entitling the holder to travel under its protection to and from foreign countries. **2** (foll. by *to*) a thing that ensures admission or attainment (*a passport to success*). [F *passeport* (as PASS¹, PORT¹)]

password /ˈpɑːswɜːd/ *n.* a selected word or phrase securing recognition, admission, etc., when used by those to whom it is disclosed.

past /pɑːst/ *adj., n., prep., & adv.* —*adj.* **1** gone by in time and no longer existing (*in past years; the time is past*). **2** recently completed or gone by (*the past month; for some time past*). **3** relating to a former time (*past president*). **4** *Gram.* expressing a past action or state. —*n.* **1** (prec. by *the*) **a** past time. **b** what has happened in past time (*cannot undo the past*). **2** a person's past life or career, esp. if discreditable (*a man with a past*). **3** a past tense or form. —*prep.* **1** beyond in time or place (*is past two o'clock; ran past the house*). **2** beyond the range, duration, or compass of (*past belief; past endurance*). —*adv.* so as to pass by (*hurried past*). □ **not put it past a person** believe it possible of a person. **past it** *colloq.*

incompetent or unusable through age. **past master 1** a person who is especially adept or expert in an activity, subject, etc. **2** a person who has been a master in a guild, Freemason's lodge, etc. **past perfect** = PLUPERFECT. [past part. of PASS¹ v.]

pasta /ˈpæstə/ *n.* **1** a dried flour paste used in various shapes in cooking (e.g. lasagne, spaghetti). **2** a cooked dish made from this. [It., = PASTE]

paste /peɪst/ *n. & v.* —*n.* **1** any moist fairly stiff mixture, esp. of powder and liquid. **2** a dough of flour with fat, water, etc., used in baking. **3** an adhesive of flour, water, etc., esp. for sticking paper and other light materials. **4** an easily spread preparation of ground meat, fish, etc. (*anchovy paste*). **5** a hard vitreous composition used in making imitation gems. **6** a mixture of clay, water, etc., used in making ceramic ware, esp. a mixture of low plasticity used in making porcelain. —*v.tr.* **1** fasten or coat with paste. **2** *sl.* **a** beat or thrash. **b** bomb or bombard heavily. □ **paste-up** a document prepared for copying etc. by combining and pasting various sections on a backing. □□ **pasting** *n.* (esp. in sense 2 of v.). [ME f. OF f. LL *pasta* small square medicinal lozenge f. Gk *pastē* f. *pastos* sprinkled]

pasteboard /ˈpeɪstbɔːd/ *n.* **1** a sheet of stiff material made by pasting together sheets of paper. **2** (*attrib.*) **a** flimsy, unsubstantial. **b** fake.

pastel /ˈpæst(ə)l/ *n.* **1** a crayon consisting of powdered pigments bound with a gum solution. **2** a work of art in pastel. **3** a light and subdued shade of a colour. □□ **pastelist** *n.* **pastellist** *n.* [F *pastel* or It. *pastello*, dimin. of *pasta* PASTE]

pastern /ˈpæst(ə)n/ *n.* **1** the part of a horse's foot between the fetlock and the hoof. **2** a corresponding part in other animals. [ME *pastron* f. OF *pasturon* f. *pasture* hobble ult. f. L *pastorius* of a shepherd: see PASTOR]

Pasternak /ˈpæstəˌnæk/, Boris Leonidovich (1890–1960), Russian poet and novelist. Born into a cultured Jewish family he studied music, which he abandoned for poetry, and philosophy; his third volume of poems *My Sister, Life* (1922) established his reputation. In the 1930s his position became increasingly difficult and he began his 'long silent duel' with Stalin; after 1933 none of his works could be published in Russia. During this time he made important translations of Goethe's *Faust*, of many of Shakespeare's plays, and of other English writers. His greatest work, *Doctor Zhivago* (1957) was internationally successful but has never been published in the USSR; the work witnessed the experience of the Russian intelligentsia before, during, and after the Revolution and the heroine, Lara, was based on Olga Ivinskaya (Pasternak's companion of his later years) who was subsequently imprisoned. Pasternak was awarded the Nobel Prize for literature in 1958, but declined it after a vehement political campaign against him.

Pasteur /pæsˈtɜː(r)/, Louis (1822–95), French chemist and bacteriologist. His early work laid the basis for a new approach to chemical structures and composition, but he became a French hero and is popularly remembered for his 'germ theory': Pasteur argued that each fermentation process could be traced to a specific living micro-organism. By sterilization or 'pasteurization' a product, such as milk or wine, could be preserved; from this he developed an interest in diseases. Although not as original as once suggested, Pasteur worked on problems of immediate economic and industrial application. He isolated bacilli attacking silkworms and found methods both of detecting diseased stock and of preventing the disease from spreading; this saved the silk industry of France and other countries. He then turned to the fatal cattle disease of anthrax and the problem of chicken cholera; in both areas he was able to isolate the bacillus responsible and cultivate attenuated forms which he then used to inoculate healthy animals. His last triumph was to make a successful vaccine against rabies.

pasteurize /ˈpɑːstjəˌraɪz, -tʃəˌraɪz, ˈpæst-/ *v.tr.* (also **-ise**) subject (milk etc.) to the process of partial sterilization by heating. □□ **pasteurization** /-ˈzeɪʃ(ə)n/ *n.* **pasteurizer** *n.* [L. PASTEUR]

pasticcio /pæsˈtɪtʃəʊ/ *n.* (*pl.* **-os**) = PASTICHE. [It.: see PASTICHE]

pastiche /pæˈstiːʃ/ *n.* **1** a medley, esp. a picture or a musical composition, made up from or imitating various sources. **2** a literary or other work of art composed in the style of a well-known author. [F f. It. *pasticcio* ult. f. LL *pasta* PASTE]

pastille /'pæstɪl/ n. **1** a small sweet or lozenge. **2** a small roll of aromatic paste burnt as a fumigator etc. □ **pastille-burner** an ornamental ceramic container in which an aromatic pastille may be burnt. [F f. L *pastillus* little loaf, lozenge f. *panis* loaf]

pastime /'pɑːstaɪm/ n. **1** a pleasant recreation or hobby. **2** a sport or game. [PASS¹ + TIME]

pastis /'pæstɪs/ n. an aniseed-flavoured aperitif. [F]

pastor /'pɑːstə(r)/ n. **1** a minister in charge of a church or a congregation. **2** a person exercising spiritual guidance. **3** a pink starling, *Sturnus roseus*. □□ **pastorship** n. [ME f. AF & OF *pastour* f. L *pastor -oris* shepherd f. *pascere* past- feed, graze]

pastoral /'pɑːstər(ə)l/ adj. & n. —adj. **1** of, relating to, or associated with shepherds or flocks and herds. **2** (of land) used for pasture. **3** (of a poem, picture, etc.) portraying country life, usu. in a romantic or idealized form. **4** of or appropriate to a pastor. —n. **1** a pastoral poem, play, picture, etc. **2** a letter from a pastor (esp. a bishop) to the clergy or people. □ **pastoral staff** a bishop's crosier. **pastoral theology** that considering spiritual truth in relation to spiritual needs. □□ **pastoralism** n. **pastorality** /-'rælɪtɪ/ n. **pastorally** adv. [ME f. L *pastoralis* (as PASTOR)]

pastorale /ˌpæstə'rɑːl, -lɪ/ n. (pl. **pastorales** or **pastorali** /-liː/) **1** a slow instrumental composition in compound time, usu. with drone notes in the bass. **2** a simple musical play with a rural subject. [It. (as PASTORAL)]

pastoralist /'pɑːstərəlɪst/ n. Austral. a farmer of sheep or cattle.

pastorate /'pɑːstərət/ n. **1** the office or tenure of a pastor. **2** a body of pastors.

pastrami /pæ'strɑːmɪ/ n. seasoned smoked beef. [Yiddish]

pastry /'peɪstrɪ/ n. (pl. **-ies**) **1** a dough of flour, fat, and water baked and used as a base and covering for pies etc. **2 a** food, esp. cake, made wholly or partly of this. **b** a piece or item of this food. □ **pastry-cook** a cook who specializes in pastry, esp. for public sale. [PASTE after OF *pastaierie*]

pasturage /'pɑːstʃərɪdʒ/ n. **1** land for pasture. **2** the process of pasturing cattle etc. [OF (as PASTURE)]

pasture /'pɑːstjə(r)/ n. & v. —n. **1** land covered with grass etc. suitable for grazing animals, esp. cattle or sheep. **2** herbage for animals. —v. **1** tr. put (animals) to graze in a pasture. **2** intr. & tr. (of animals) graze. [ME f. OF f. LL *pastura* (as PASTOR)]

pasty¹ /'pæstɪ/ n. (pl. **-ies**) a pastry case with a sweet or savoury filling, baked without a dish to shape it. [ME f. OF *pasté* ult. f. LL *pasta* PASTE]

pasty² /'peɪstɪ/ adj. (**pastier, pastiest**) **1** of or like or covered with paste. **2** unhealthily pale (esp. in complexion) (*pasty-faced*). □□ **pastily** adv. **pastiness** n.

Pat /pæt/ n. a nickname for an Irishman. [abbr. of the name *Patrick*]

Pat. abbr. Patent.

pat¹ /pæt/ v. & n. —v. (**patted, patting**) **1** tr. strike gently with the hand or a flat surface. **2** tr. flatten or mould by patting. **3** tr. strike gently with the inner surface of the hand, esp. as a sign of affection, sympathy, or congratulation. **4** intr. (foll. by *on*, *upon*) beat lightly. —n. **1** a light stroke or tap, esp. with the hand in affection etc. **2** the sound made by this. **3** a small mass (esp. of butter) formed by patting. □ **pat-a-cake** a child's game with the patting of hands (the first words of a nursery rhyme). **pat on the back** a gesture of approval or congratulation. **pat a person on the back** congratulate a person. [ME, prob. imit.]

pat² /pæt/ adj. & adv. —adj. **1** known thoroughly and ready for any occasion. **2** apposite or opportune, esp. unconvincingly so (*gave a pat answer*). —adv. **1** in a pat manner. **2** appositely, opportunely. □ **have off pat** know or have memorized perfectly. **stand pat** esp. US **1** stick stubbornly to one's opinion or decision. **2** Poker retain one's hand as dealt; not draw other cards. □□ **patly** adv. **patness** n. [16th c.: rel. to PAT¹]

pat³ /pæt/ n. □ **on one's pat** Austral. sl. on one's own. [*Pat Malone*, rhyming slang for *own*]

patagium /ˌpætə'dʒaɪəm/ n. (pl. **patagia** /-'dʒaɪə/) Zool. **1** the

wing-membrane of a bat or similar animal. **2** a scale covering the wing-joint in moths and butterflies. [med.L use of L *patagium* f. Gk *patageion* gold edging]

Patagonia /ˌpætə'gəʊnɪə/ the southernmost region of South America, chiefly a dry barren plateau in southern Argentina and Chile between the Andes and the Atlantic. □□ **Patagonian** adj. & n. [obs. *Patagon* member of a tribe of South American Indians alleged by 17th–18th c. travellers to be the tallest known people]

patball /'pætbɔːl/ n. **1** a simple game of ball played between two players. **2** derog. lawn tennis.

patch /pætʃ/ n. & v. —n. **1** a piece of material or metal etc. used to mend a hole or as reinforcement. **2** a pad worn to protect an injured eye. **3** a dressing etc. put over a wound. **4** a large or irregular distinguishable area on a surface. **5** colloq. a period of time in terms of its characteristic quality (*went through a bad patch*). **6** a piece of ground. **7** colloq. an area assigned to or patrolled by an authorized person, esp. a police officer. **8** a number of plants growing in one place (*brier patch*). **9** a scrap or remnant. **10** a temporary electrical connection. **11** hist. a small disc etc. of black silk attached to the face, worn esp. by women in the 17th–18th c. for adornment. **12** Mil. a piece of cloth on a uniform as the badge of a unit. —v.tr. **1** (often foll. by *up*) repair with a patch or patches; put a patch or patches on. **2** (of material) serve as a patch to. **3** (often foll. by *up*) put together, esp. hastily or in a makeshift way. **4** (foll. by *up*) settle (a quarrel etc.) esp. hastily or temporarily. □ **not a patch on** colloq. greatly inferior to. **patch cord** an insulated lead with a plug at each end, for use with a patchboard. **patch panel** = PATCHBOARD. **patch pocket** one made of a piece of cloth sewn on a garment. **patch test** a test for allergy by applying to the skin patches containing allergenic substances. □□ **patcher** n. [ME *pacche, patche*, perh. var. of *peche* f. OF *pieche* dial. var. of *piece* PIECE]

patchboard /'pætʃbɔːd/ n. a board with electrical sockets linked to enable changeable permutations of connection.

patchouli /pə'tʃuːlɪ, 'pætʃʊlɪ/ n. **1** a strongly scented E. Indian plant, *Pogostemon cablin*. **2** the perfume obtained from this. [a native name in Madras]

patchwork /'pætʃwɜːk/ n. **1** needlework using small pieces of cloth with different designs, forming a pattern. **2** a thing composed of various small pieces or fragments.

patchy /'pætʃɪ/ adj. (**patchier, patchiest**) **1** uneven in quality. **2** having or existing in patches. □□ **patchily** adv. **patchiness** n.

pate /peɪt/ n. archaic or colloq. the head, esp. representing the seat of intellect. [ME: orig. unkn.]

pâte /pɑːt/ n. the paste of which porcelain is made. [F, = PASTE]

pâté /'pæteɪ/ n. a rich paste or spread of mashed and spiced meat or fish etc. □ **pâté de foie gras** /də fwɑː 'ɡrɑː/ a paste of fatted goose liver. [F f. OF *pasté* (as PASTY¹)]

patella /pə'telə/ n. (pl. **patellae** /-liː/) the kneecap. □□ **patellar** adj. **patellate** /-lət/ adj. [L, dimin. of *patina*: see PATEN]

paten /'pæt(ə)n/ n. **1** a shallow dish used for the bread at the Eucharist. **2** a thin circular plate of metal. [ME ult. f. OF *patene* or L *patena, patina* shallow dish f. Gk *patanē* a plate]

patent /'peɪt(ə)nt, 'pæt-/ n., adj., & v. —n. **1** a government authority to an individual or organization conferring a right or title, esp. the sole right to make or use or sell some invention. (See below.) **2** a document granting this authority (for an invention or process protected by it. —adj. **1** /'peɪt(ə)nt/ obvious, plain. **2** conferred or protected by patent. **3 a** made and marketed under a patent; proprietary. **b** to which one has a proprietary claim. **4** esp. as might be patented; ingenious, well-contrived. **5** (of an opening etc.) allowing free passage. —v.tr. obtain a patent for (an invention). □ **letters patent** an open document from a sovereign or government conferring a patent or other right. **patent leather** leather with a glossy varnished surface. **patent medicine** medicine made and marketed under a patent and available without prescription. **patent office** an office from which patents are issued. **Patent Roll** (in the UK) a list of patents issued in a year. **patent theatre** a theatre established by royal patent, (in London) the theatres of Covent Garden and Drury Lane, whose patents were granted by Charles

II in 1662. □□ **patency** n. **patentable** adj. **patently** /ˈpeɪtəntlɪ/ adv. (in sense 1 of adj.). [ME f. OF patent and L patēre lie open]

Patents for inventions seem to have been introduced in Italy in the 15th c. and spread to other European States. In England, Elizabeth I and James I granted monopolies to favourites by means of literae patentes ('letters patent'), open letters addressed to all to whom they might come, relating not only to new inventions etc. but also to known commodities. General dissatisfaction with this system led to the passing of the Statute of Monopolies (1623), which declared such grants void but allowed future patents to confer exclusive rights on an inventor for a period of 14 years. The granting of patents in the UK is now regulated by statute, and patents are issued by and under the seal of the Patent Office.

patentee /ˌpeɪtənˈtiː/ n. **1** a person who takes out or holds a patent. **2** a person for the time being entitled to the benefit of a patent.

patentor /ˈpeɪtəntə(r)/ n. a person or body that grants a patent.

Pater /ˈpeɪtə(r)/, Walter Horatio (1839–94), English essayist and critic, greatly influenced by the Pre-Raphaelites. Among his friends were Swinburne and Rossetti. He came to fame with *Studies in the History of the Renaissance* (1873) which included his essays on the then neglected Botticelli, and on Leonardo da Vinci with its celebrated evocation of the Mona Lisa. Though attacked by some as unscholarly and morbid the work had a profound influence on undergraduates of the time and on the aesthetic movement. His other major works include *Marius the Epicurean* (1885), a fictional biography set in the Rome of Marcus Aurelius, which develops his ideas on 'art for art's sake', and *Appreciations: with an Essay on Style* (1889) which established his position as a critic and a master of English prose.

pater /ˈpeɪtə(r)/ n. Brit. colloq. father. ¶ Now only in jocular or affected use. [L]

paterfamilias /ˌpeɪtəfəˈmɪlɪˌæs/ n. the male head of a family or household. [L, = father of the family]

paternal /pəˈtɜːn(ə)l/ adj. **1** of or like or appropriate to a father. **2** fatherly. **3** related through the father. **4** (of a government etc.) limiting freedom and responsibility by well-meant regulations. □□ **paternally** adv. [LL paternalis f. L paternus f. pater father]

paternalism /pəˈtɜːnəˌlɪz(ə)m/ n. the policy of governing in a paternal way, or behaving paternally to one's associates or subordinates. □□ **paternalist** n. **paternalistic** /-ˈlɪstɪk/ adj. **paternalistically** /-ˈlɪstɪkəlɪ/ adv.

paternity /pəˈtɜːnɪtɪ/ n. **1** fatherhood. **2** one's paternal origin. **3** the source or authorship of a thing. □ **paternity test** a blood test to determine whether a man may be or cannot be the father of a particular child. [ME f. OF paternité or LL paternitas]

paternoster /ˌpætəˈnɒstə(r)/ n. **1 a** the Lord's Prayer, esp. in Latin. **b** a rosary bead indicating that this is to be said. **2** a lift consisting of a series of linked doorless compartments moving continuously on a circular belt. [OE f. L pater noster our father]

path /pɑːθ/ n. (pl. **paths** /pɑːðz/) **1** a way or track laid down for walking or made by continual treading. **2** the line along which a person or thing moves (flight path). **3** a course of action or conduct. **4** a sequence of movements or operations taken by a system. □□ **pathless** adj. [OE pæth f. WG]

-path /pæθ/ comb. form forming nouns denoting: **1** a practitioner of curative treatment (homoeopath; osteopath). **2** a person who suffers from a disease (psychopath). [back-form. f. -PATHY, or f. Gk -pathēs -sufferer (as PATHOS)]

Pathan /pəˈtɑːn/ n. a member of a Pashto-speaking people inhabiting NW Pakistan and SE Afghanistan. [Hindi]

Pathé /ˈpæθeɪ/, Charles (1863–1957), French pioneer in the film industry, who initiated the system of leasing (rather than selling) copies of films. In the early years of the 20th c. he and his brothers built up a company which dominated the manufacture of stock and equipment and the production, distribution, and exhibition of films until disrupted by the outbreak of the First World War and the growing challenge of American companies, which obliged them to sell or liquidate their concerns.

pathetic /pəˈθetɪk/ adj. **1** arousing pity or sadness or contempt. **2** Brit. colloq. miserably inadequate. **3** archaic of the emotions. □

pathetic fallacy the attribution of human feelings and responses to inanimate things, esp. in art and literature. □□ **pathetically** adv. [F pathétique f. LL patheticus f. Gk pathētikos (as PATHOS)]

pathfinder /ˈpɑːθˌfaɪndə(r)/ n. **1** a person who explores new territory, investigates a new subject, etc. **2** an aircraft or its pilot sent ahead to locate and mark the target area for bombing.

patho- /ˈpæθəʊ/ comb. form disease. [Gk pathos suffering: see PATHOS]

pathogen /ˈpæθədʒ(ə)n/ n. an agent causing disease. □□ **pathogenic** /-ˈdʒenɪk/ adj. **pathogenous** /-ˈθɒdʒənəs/ adj. [PATHO- + -GEN]

pathogenesis /ˌpæθəˈdʒenɪsɪs/ n. (also **pathogeny** /pəˈθɒdʒənɪ/) the manner of development of a disease. □□ **pathogenetic** /-dʒɪˈnetɪk/ adj.

pathological /ˌpæθəˈlɒdʒɪk(ə)l/ adj. **1** of pathology. **2** of or caused by a physical or mental disorder (a pathological fear of spiders). □□ **pathologically** adv.

pathology /pəˈθɒlədʒɪ/ n. **1** the science of bodily diseases. **2** the symptoms of a disease. □□ **pathologist** n. [F pathologie or mod.L pathologia (as PATHO-, -LOGY)]

pathos /ˈpeɪθɒs/ n. a quality in speech, writing, events, etc., that excites pity or sadness. [Gk pathos suffering, rel. to paskhō suffer, penthos grief]

pathway /ˈpɑːθweɪ/ n. **1** a path or its course. **2** Biochem. etc. a sequence of reactions undergone in a living organism.

-pathy /pəθɪ/ comb. form forming nouns denoting: **1** curative treatment (allopathy; homoeopathy). **2** feeling (telepathy). [Gk patheia suffering]

patience /ˈpeɪʃ(ə)ns/ n. **1** calm endurance of hardship, provocation, pain, delay, etc. **2** tolerant perseverance or forbearance. **3** the capacity for calm self-possessed waiting. **4** esp. Brit. a game for one player in which cards taken in random order have to be arranged in certain groups or sequences. □ **have no patience with 1** be unable to tolerate. **2** be irritated by. [ME f. OF f. L patientia (as PATIENT)]

patient /ˈpeɪʃ(ə)nt/ adj. & n. —adj. having or showing patience. —n. a person receiving or registered to receive medical treatment. □□ **patiently** adv. [ME f. OF f. L patiens -entis pres. part. of pati suffer]

patina /ˈpætɪnə/ n. (pl. **patinas**) **1** a film, usu. green, formed on the surface of old bronze. **2** a similar film on other surfaces. **3** a gloss produced by age on woodwork. □□ **patinated** /-ˌneɪtɪd/ adj. **patination** /-ˈneɪʃ(ə)n/ n. [It. f. L patina dish]

patio /ˈpætɪəʊ/ n. (pl. **-os**) **1** a paved usu. roofless area adjoining and belonging to a house. **2** an inner court open to the sky in a Spanish or Spanish-American house. [Sp.]

patisserie /pəˈtiːsərɪ/ n. **1** a shop where pastries are made and sold. **2** pastries collectively. [F pâtisserie f. med.L pasticium pastry f. pasta PASTE]

Patmore /ˈpætmɔː(r)/, Coventry Kersey Dighton (1823–96), English poet, author of the long and popular sequence of poems *The Angel in the House* (1854–63) in praise of married love. His friends included Tennyson, Ruskin, and Robert Browning, and his work was admired by the Pre-Raphaelites. After his conversion to Roman Catholicism he wrote a number of meditations on religious subjects and formed friendships with other Catholic writers.

Patmos /ˈpætmɒs/ a Greek island in the Aegean Sea, where, according to legend, St John lived in exile and saw the visions of the Apocalypse.

Patna /ˈpætnə/ the capital of the State of Bihar in India; pop. (1981) 916,000. □ **Patna rice** long-grained rice, orig. that of Patna, now also grown elsewhere, esp. in the US.

patois /ˈpætwɑː/ n. (pl. same /-wɑːz/) the dialect of the common people in a region, differing fundamentally from the literary language. [F, = rough speech, perh. f. OF patoier treat roughly f. patte paw]

Paton /ˈpeɪt(ə)n/, Alan Stewart (1903–88), South African writer and Liberal politician. His most famous work is the novel *Cry, the Beloved Country* (1948), a sensitive and unsentimental study of the workings of the apartheid system, and a moving plea for racial understanding and cooperation.

Patras /ˈpætrəs/ (Greek **Pátrai** /ˈpætraɪ/) an industrial port in the NW Peloponnese, on the Gulf of Patras; pop. (1981) 154,600.

patrial /ˈpeɪtrɪəl/ adj. & n. Brit. hist. —adj. having the right to live in the UK through the British birth of a parent or a grandparent. —n. a person with this right. □□ **patriality** /-ˈælɪtɪ/ n. [obs. F patrial or med.L patrialis f. L patria fatherland f. pater father]

patriarch /ˈpeɪtrɪˌɑːk/ n. **1** the male head of a family or tribe. **2** (often in pl.) Bibl. any of those regarded as fathers of the human race, esp. the sons of Jacob, or Abraham, Isaac, and Jacob, and their forefathers. **3** Eccl. **a** the title of a chief bishop, esp. those presiding over the Churches of Antioch, Alexandria, Constantinople, and (formerly) Rome; now also the title of the heads of certain autocephalous Orthodox Churches. **b** (in the Roman Catholic Church) a bishop ranking next above primates and metropolitans, and immediately below the pope. **c** the head of a Uniate community. **4 a** the founder of an order, science, etc. **b** a venerable old man. **c** the oldest member of a group. □□ **patriarchal** /-ˈɑːk(ə)l/ adj. **patriarchally** /-ˈɑːkəlɪ/ adv. [ME f. OF patriarche f. eccl.L patriarcha f. Gk patriarkhēs f. patria family f. patēr father + -arkhēs -ruler]

patriarchate /ˈpeɪtrɪˌɑːkət/ n. **1** the office, see, or residence of an ecclesiastical patriarch. **2** the rank of a tribal patriarch. [med.L patriarchatus (as PATRIARCH)]

patriarchy /ˈpeɪtrɪˌɑːkɪ/ n. (pl. **-ies**) a system of society, government, etc., ruled by a man and with descent through the male line. □□ **patriarchism** n. [med.L patriarchia f. Gk patriarkhia (as PATRIARCH)]

patrician /pəˈtrɪʃ(ə)n/ n. & adj. —n. **1** hist. a member of the ancient Roman nobility (cf. PLEBEIAN). **2** hist. a nobleman in some Italian republics. **3** an aristocrat. —adj. **1** noble, aristocratic. **2** hist. of the ancient Roman nobility. [ME f. OF patricien f. L patricius having a noble father f. pater patris father]

patriciate /pəˈtrɪʃɪət/ n. **1** a patrician order; an aristocracy. **2** the rank of patrician. [L patriciatus (as PATRICIAN)]

patricide /ˈpætrɪˌsaɪd/ n. = PARRICIDE (esp. with reference to the killing of one's father). □□ **patricidal** /-ˈsaɪd(ə)l/ adj. [LL patricida, patricidium, alt. of L parricida, parricidium (see PARRICIDE) after pater father]

Patrick /ˈpætrɪk/, St (5th c.), apostle and patron saint of Ireland. His Confessions (spiritual autobiography) are the chief source for the events of his life; early accounts by others are confused and full of the miraculous. Of Romano-British parentage, he was captured at the age of 16 by raiders and carried off to Ireland as a slave; there he experienced a religious conversion. Escaping after six years, probably to Gaul, he was ordained and returned to Ireland c.432. The details of his mission are uncertain but he travelled about the country, did much to convert the pagan west, organized the scattered Christian communities which he found in the north, and founded the archiepiscopal see of Armagh c.444. Favourite legends include his expulsion of snakes from Ireland. Feast day, 17 March.

patrilineal /ˌpætrɪˈlɪnɪəl/ adj. of or relating to, or based on kinship with, the father or descent through the male line. [L pater patris father + LINEAL]

patrimony /ˈpætrɪmənɪ/ n. (pl. **-ies**) **1** property inherited from one's father or ancestor. **2** a heritage. **3** the endowment of a church etc. □□ **patrimonial** /-ˈməʊnɪəl/ adj. [ME patrimoigne f. OF patrimoine f. L patrimonium f. pater patris father]

patriot /ˈpeɪtrɪət, ˈpæt-/ n. a person who is devoted to and ready to support or defend his or her country. □□ **patriotic** /-ˈɒtɪk/ adj. **patriotically** /-ˈɒtɪklɪ/ adv. **patriotism** n. [F patriote f. LL patriota f. Gk patriōtēs f. patrios of one's fathers f. patēr patros father]

patristic /pəˈtrɪstɪk/ adj. of the early Christian writers (the Church Fathers) or their work. □□ **patristics** n.pl. (usu. treated as sing.). [G patristisch f. L pater patris father]

patrol /pəˈtrəʊl/ n. & v. —n. **1** the act of walking or travelling around an area, esp. at regular intervals, in order to protect or supervise it. **2** one or more persons or vehicles assigned to be sent

out on patrol, esp. a detachment of guards, police, etc. **3 a** a detachment of troops sent out to reconnoitre. **b** such reconnaissance. **4** a routine operational voyage of a ship or aircraft. **5** a routine monitoring of astronomical or other phenomena. **6** Brit. an official controlling traffic where children cross the road. **7** a unit of six to eight Scouts or Guides. —v. (**patrolled**, **patrolling**) **1** tr. carry out a patrol of. **2** intr. act as a patrol. □ **patrol car** a police car used in patrolling roads and streets. **patrol wagon** esp. US a police van for transporting prisoners. □□ **patroller** n. [F patrouiller paddle in mud f. patte paw: (n.) f. G Patrolle f. F patrouille]

patrolman /pəˈtrəʊlmən/ n. (pl. **-men**) US a policeman of the lowest rank.

patrology /pəˈtrɒlədʒɪ/ n. (pl. **-ies**) **1** the study of the Fathers of the Church. **2** a collection of such writings. □□ **patrological** /ˌpætrəˈlɒdʒɪk(ə)l/ adj. **patrologist** n. [Gk patēr patros father]

patron /ˈpeɪtrən/ n. (fem. **patroness**) **1** a person who gives financial or other support to a person, cause, work of art, etc., esp. one who buys works of art. **2** a usu. regular customer of a shop etc. **3** Rom. Antiq. **a** the former owner of a freed slave. **b** the protector of a client. **4** Brit. a person who has the right of presenting a member of the clergy to a benefice. □ **patron saint** the protecting or guiding saint of a person, place, etc. [ME f. OF f. L patronus protector of clients, defender f. pater patris father]

patronage /ˈpætrənɪdʒ/ n. **1** the support, promotion, or encouragement given by a patron. **2** a patronizing or condescending manner. **3** Rom. Antiq. the rights and duties or position of a patron. **4** Brit. the right of presenting a member of the clergy to a benefice etc. **5** a customer's support for a shop etc. [ME f. OF (as PATRON)]

patronal /ˈpætrən(ə)l, ˈpeɪt-, pəˈtrəʊn(ə)l/ adj. of or relating to a patron saint (the patronal festival). [F patronal or LL patronalis (as PATRON)]

patronize /ˈpætrəˌnaɪz/ v.tr. (also **-ise**) **1** treat condescendingly. **2** act as a patron towards (a person, cause, artist, etc.); support; encourage. **3** frequent (a shop etc.) as a customer. □□ **patronization** /-ˈzeɪʃ(ə)n/ n. **patronizer** n. **patronizing** adj. **patronizingly** adv. [obs. F patroniser or med.L patronizare (as PATRON)]

patronymic /ˌpætrəˈnɪmɪk/ n. & adj. —n. a name derived from the name of a father or ancestor, e.g. Johnson, O'Brien, Ivanovich. —adj. (of a name) so derived. [LL patronymicus f. Gk patrōnumikos f. patrōnumos f. patēr patros father + onuma, onoma name]

patroon /pəˈtruːn/ n. US hist. a landowner with manorial privileges under the Dutch governments of New York and New Jersey. [Du., = PATRON]

patsy /ˈpætsɪ/ n. (pl. **-ies**) esp. US sl. a person who is deceived, ridiculed, tricked, etc. [20th c.: orig. unkn.]

Pattaya /pæˈtaɪə/ a beach resort in Thailand, situated to the south-east of Bangkok.

pattée /ˈpæteɪ, -tɪ/ adj. (of a cross) having almost triangular arms becoming very broad at the ends so as to form a square. [F f. patte paw]

patten /ˈpæt(ə)n/ n. hist. a shoe or clog with a raised sole or set on an iron ring, for walking in mud etc. [ME f. OF patin f. patte paw]

patter[1] /ˈpætə(r)/ v. & n. —v. **1** intr. make a rapid succession of taps, as of rain on a window-pane. **2** intr. run with quick short steps. **3** tr. cause (water etc.) to patter. —n. a rapid succession of taps, short light steps, etc. [PAT[1]]

patter[2] /ˈpætə(r)/ n. & v. —n. **1 a** the rapid speech used by a comedian or introduced into a song. **b** the words of a comic song. **2** the words used by a person selling or promoting a product; a sales pitch. **3** the special language or jargon of a profession, class, etc. —v. **1** tr. repeat (prayers etc.) in a rapid mechanical way. **2** intr. talk glibly or mechanically. [ME f. pater = PATERNOSTER]

pattern /ˈpæt(ə)n/ n. & v. —n. **1** a repeated decorative design on wallpaper, cloth, a carpet, etc. **2** a regular or logical form, order, or arrangement of parts (behaviour pattern; the pattern of one's daily life). **3** a model or design, e.g. of a garment, from which copies can be made. **4** an example of excellence; an ideal; a model (*a pattern of elegance*). **5** a wooden or metal figure from which a mould is made for a casting. **6** a sample (of cloth, wallpaper, etc.). **7** the marks made by shots, bombs, etc. on a target or target area. **8** a random combination of shapes or colours. —*v.tr.* **1** (usu. foll. by *after, on*) model (a thing) on a design etc. **2** decorate with a pattern. □ **pattern bombing** bombing over a large area, not on a single target. [ME *patron* (see PATRON): differentiated in sense and spelling since the 16th–17th c.]

patty /ˈpætɪ/ *n.* (*pl.* **-ies**) **1** a little pie or pastry. **2** US a small flat cake of minced meat etc. [F *pâté* PASTY¹]

pattypan /ˈpætɪˌpæn/ *n.* a pan for baking a patty.

patulous /ˈpætjʊləs/ *adj.* **1** (of branches etc.) spreading. **2** *formal* open; expanded. □□ **patulously** *adv.* **patulousness** *n.* [L *patulus* f. *patēre* be open]

paua /ˈpaʊə/ *n.* **1** a large edible New Zealand shellfish of the genus *Haliotis*. **2** its ornamental shell. **3** a fish-hook made from this. [Maori]

paucity /ˈpɔːsɪtɪ/ *n.* smallness of number or quantity. [ME f. OF *paucité* or f. L *paucitas* f. *paucus* few]

Pauillac /paʊˈjɑːk/ a commune in the Médoc district of SW France, noted for its wines.

Paul¹ /pɔːl/, St (1st c. AD), a Jew (also called Saul) of Tarsus, with the status of a Roman citizen. He was brought up as a Pharisee and at first opposed the followers of Christ, assisting at the martyrdom of St Stephen. On a mission to Damascus he was converted to Christianity after a vision, and became the 'Apostle of the Gentiles' and the first great Christian missionary and theologian. His missionary journeys are described in the Acts of the Apostles, and the letters to the Churches written by or attributed to him form part of the New Testament. He was martyred at Rome *c.*AD 64. Feast day, 29 June.

Paul² /pɔːl/ the name of six popes:

Paul III Alessandro Farnese, 1468–1549, pope from 1534. A zealous Church reformer and patron of the arts, he commissioned Michelangelo to paint the fresco of the *Last Judgement* for the Sistine Chapel and to design the dome of St Peter's, confirmed the constitution of the Jesuits, established the Inquisition in Rome as a Church department, and initiated the ecumenical Council of Trent. It was he who excommunicated Henry VIII of England.

Pauli /ˈpaʊlɪ/, Wolfgang (1900–58), Austrian-born physicist, best remembered for his 'exclusion principle', postulated in 1925, according to which at most two electrons could occupy each energy level or orbital around the atomic nucleus, but only if they had opposite spin. This made it easier to understand the structure of the atom and the chemical properties of the elements. The principle was later extended to a whole class of subatomic particles, the fermions, which includes the electron. In 1931 he proposed the existence of a new subatomic particle, the neutrino, later discovered by Fermi. He was awarded the 1945 Nobel Prize for physics.

Pauline /ˈpɔːlaɪn/ *adj.* of or relating to St Paul (*the Pauline epistles*). [ME f. med.L *Paulinus* f. L *Paulus* Paul]

Pauling /ˈpɔːlɪŋ/, Linus Carl (1901–   ), American chemist, particularly renowned for his study of molecular structure and chemical bonding, especially of living tissue such as the complex protein molecule, for which he received the 1954 Nobel Prize for chemistry. After the Second World War he became increasingly involved with the peace movement and attempts to ban nuclear weapons, for which he was awarded the Nobel Peace Prize in 1962 and thus (like Madame Curie) achieved the rare distinction of receiving two Nobel Prizes.

Paul Jones /pɔːl ˈdʒəʊnz/ *n.* a ballroom dance during which the dancers change partners after circling in concentric rings of men and women. [the name of John *Paul Jones* (d. 1792), Scottish-born naval officer noted for his victories for the Americas during the War of Independence]

Paul Pry /pɔːl ˈpraɪ/ *n.* an inquisitive person. [character in US song (1820)]

paulownia /pɔːˈləʊnɪə/ *n.* any Chinese tree of the genus *Paulownia*, with fragrant purple flowers. [Anna *Paulovna*, Russian princess d. 1865]

paunch /pɔːntʃ/ *n.* & *v.* —*n.* **1** the belly or stomach, esp. when protruding. **2** a ruminant's first stomach; the rumen. **3** *Naut.* a thick strong mat. —*v.tr.* disembowel (an animal). □□ **paunchy** *adj.* (**paunchier, paunchiest**). **paunchiness** *n.* [ME f. AF *pa(u)nche*, ONF *panche* ult. f. L *pantex panticis* bowels]

pauper /ˈpɔːpə(r)/ *n.* **1** a person without means; a beggar. **2** *hist.* a recipient of poor-law relief. **3** *Law* a person who may sue in *forma pauperis*. □□ **pauperdom** /-dəm/ *n.* **pauperism** /-ˌrɪz(ə)m/ *n.* **pauperize** *v.tr.* (also **-ise**). **pauperization** /-ˈzeɪʃ(ə)n/ *n.* [L, = poor]

Pausanias /pɔːˈseɪnɪˌæs/ (2nd c.) Greek traveller and geographer. His *Description of Greece* (in ten books) is a guide to the topography and antiquities of Greece, and is still an invaluable source of information.

pause /pɔːz/ *n.* & *v.* —*n.* **1** an interval of inaction, esp. when due to hesitation; a temporary stop. **2** a break in speaking or reading; a silence. **3** *Mus.* a mark (⌒) over a note or rest that is to be lengthened by an unspecified amount. —*v.intr.* **1** make a pause; wait. **2** (usu. foll. by *upon*) linger over (a word etc.). □ **give pause to** cause (a person) to hesitate. [ME f. OF *pause* or L *pausa* f. Gk *pausis* f. *pauō* stop]

pavage /ˈpeɪvɪdʒ/ *n.* **1** paving. **2** a tax or toll towards the paving of streets. [ME f. OF f. *paver* PAVE]

pavane /pəˈvɑːn/ *n.* (also **pavan** /ˈpæv(ə)n/) *hist.* **1** a stately dance in elaborate clothing. **2** the music for this. [F *pavane* f. Sp. *pavana*, perh. f. *pavon* peacock]

Pavarotti /ˌpævəˈrɒtɪ/, Luciano (1935–   ), Italian operatic tenor. He made his début as Rudolfo in Puccini's *La Bohème* in 1961 and achieved rapid success in this and a number of other leading roles, including that of the Duke in *Rigoletto* and Radamès in *Aida*.

pave /peɪv/ *v.tr.* **1 a** cover (a street, floor, etc.) with paving etc. **b** cover or strew (a floor etc.) with anything (*paved with flowers*). **2** prepare (*paved the way for her arrival*). □ **paving-stone** a large flat usu. rectangular piece of stone etc. for paving. □□ **paver** *n.* **paving** *n.* **pavior** /ˈpeɪvjə(r)/ *n.* (also **paviour**). [ME f. OF *paver*, back-form. (as PAVEMENT)]

pavé /ˈpæveɪ/ *n.* **1** a paved street, road, or path. **2** a setting of jewels placed closely together. [F, past part. of *paver*: see PAVE]

pavement /ˈpeɪvmənt/ *n.* **1** *Brit.* a paved path for pedestrians at the side of and a little higher than a road. **2** the covering of a street, floor, etc., made of tiles, wooden blocks, asphalt, and esp. of rectangular stones. **3** *US* a roadway. **4** *Zool.* a pavement-like formation of close-set teeth, scales, etc. □ **pavement artist 1** *Brit.* an artist who draws on paving-stones with coloured chalks, hoping to be given money by passers-by. **2** *US* an artist who displays paintings for sale on a pavement. [ME f. OF f. L *pavimentum* f. *pavire* beat, ram]

pavilion /pəˈvɪljən/ *n.* & *v.* —*n.* **1** *Brit.* a building at a cricket or other sports ground used for changing, refreshments, etc. **2** a summerhouse or other decorative building in a garden. **3** a tent, esp. a large one with crenellated decorations at a show, fair, etc. **4** a building used for entertainments. **5** a temporary stand at an exhibition. **6** a detached building at a hospital. **7** a usu. highly decorated subdivision of a building. **8** the part of a cut gemstone below the girdle. —*v.tr.* enclose in or provide with a pavilion. [ME f. OF *pavillon* f. L *papilio -onis* butterfly, tent]

pavior, paviour see PAVE.

Pavlov /ˈpævlɒf/, Ivan Petrovich (1849–1936), Russian physiologist who was awarded a Nobel Prize in 1904 for his work on digestion, but is best known for his later studies on the conditioned reflex. He showed by experiment with dogs how the secretion of saliva can be stimulated not only by food but also by the sound of a bell which has been paired repeatedly with the presentation of food, and comes to elicit salivation when presented alone. Pavlov then applied his findings to show the importance of such reflexes in human and animal behaviour. His experiments form the basis for much current research in the field of conditioning.

Pavlova /ˈpævləvə, -ˈləʊvə/ Anna Pavlovna (1881–1931), Russian dancer. By 1906 she had danced all the traditional ballerina roles and in 1907 she created Fokine's *Dying Swan*, her most famous solo dance. In 1908 she began to tour abroad, making her New York and London débuts in 1910, settling in England where she assembled her own company, and embarking on numerous tours which made her a pioneer of classical ballet all over the world. She had a unique lightness, grace, poetry, and spirituality, and became a household name; her aesthetic principles were strictly conservative.

pavlova /pævˈləʊvə/ n. a meringue cake with cream and fruit. [A. PAVLOVA]

Pavlovian /pævˈləʊvɪən/ adj. of or relating to I. P. Pavlov, or his work, esp. on conditioned reflexes.

pavonine /ˈpævəˌnaɪn/ adj. of or like a peacock. [L *pavoninus* f. *pavo -onis* peacock]

paw /pɔː/ n. & v. —n. 1 a foot of an animal having claws or nails. 2 *colloq.* a person's hand. —v. 1 *tr.* strike or scrape with a paw or foot. 2 *intr.* scrape the ground with a paw or hoof. 3 *tr. colloq.* fondle awkwardly or indecently. [ME *pawe, powe* f. OF *poue* etc. ult. f. Frank.]

pawky /ˈpɔːkɪ/ adj. (**pawkier, pawkiest**) *Sc. & dial.* 1 drily humorous. 2 shrewd. □□ **pawkily** adv. **pawkiness** n. [Sc. & N.Engl. dial. *pawk* trick, of unkn. orig.]

pawl /pɔːl/ n. & v. —n. 1 a lever with a catch for the teeth of a wheel or bar. 2 *Naut.* a short bar used to lock a capstan, windlass, etc., to prevent it from recoiling. —v.tr. secure (a capstan etc.) with a pawl. [perh. f. LG & Du. *pal*, rel. to *pal* fixed]

pawn[1] /pɔːn/ n. 1 *Chess* a piece of the smallest size and value. 2 a person used by others for their own purposes. [ME f. AF *poun*, OF *peon* f. med.L *pedo -onis* foot-soldier f. L *pes pedis* foot: cf. PEON]

pawn[2] /pɔːn/ v. & n. —v.tr. 1 deposit (an object), esp. with a pawnbroker, as security for money lent. 2 pledge or wager (one's life, honour, word, etc.). —n. 1 an object left as security for money etc. lent. 2 anything or any person left with another as security etc. □ **in** (or **at**) **pawn** (of an object etc.) held as security. [ME f. OF *pan, pand, pant*, pledge, security f. WG]

pawnbroker /ˈpɔːnˌbrəʊkə(r)/ n. a person who lends money at interest on the security of personal property pawned. Such a practice existed in China more than 2,000 years ago, but in Europe it dates from the Middle Ages. It was introduced into England by the Lombards in the 13th c. □□ **pawnbroking** n.

pawnshop /ˈpɔːnʃɒp/ n. a shop where pawnbroking is conducted.

pawpaw /ˈpɔːpɔː/ n. (also **papaw** /pəˈpɔː/, **papaya** /pəˈpaɪə/) **1 a** an elongated melon-shaped fruit with edible orange flesh and small black seeds. **b** a tropical tree, *Carica papaya*, bearing this and producing a milky sap from which papain is obtained. **2** *US* a N. American tree, *Asimina triloba*, with purple flowers and edible fruit. [earlier *papay(a)* f. Sp. & Port. *papaya*, of Carib orig.]

PAX abbr. private automatic (telephone) exchange.

pax /pæks/ n. 1 the kiss of peace. 2 (as *int.*) *Brit. sl.* a call for a truce (used esp. by schoolchildren). [ME f. L, = peace]

Paxton /ˈpækst(ə)n/, Sir Joseph (1801–65), one of the great Victorians. He became head gardener to the Duke of Devonshire at Chatsworth when only 23, and designed a series of greenhouses, using iron and glass, predecessors of the Crystal Palace for which he is chiefly remembered. He also designed parks and conventional country houses.

pay[1] /peɪ/ v. & n. —v.tr. (past and past part. **paid** /peɪd/) 1 (also *absol.*) give (a person etc.) what is due for services done, goods received, debts incurred, etc. (*paid him in full; I assure you I have paid*). **2 a** give (a usu. specified amount) for work done, a debt, a ransom, etc. (*they pay £5 an hour*). **b** (foll. by *to*) hand over the amount of (a debt, wages, recompense, etc.) to (*paid the money to the assistant*). **3 a** give, bestow, or express (attention, respect, a compliment, etc.) (*paid them no heed*). **b** make (a visit, a call, etc.) (*paid a visit to their uncle*). **4** (also *absol.*) (of a business, undertaking, attitude, etc.) be profitable or advantageous to (a person etc.). **5** reward or punish (*can never pay you for what you have done for us; I shall pay you for that*). **6** (usu. as **paid** adj.) recompense (work, time, etc.) (*paid holiday*). **7** (usu. foll. by *out, away*) let out

(a rope) by slackening it. —n. wages; payment. □ **in the pay of** employed by. **paid holidays** an agreed holiday period for which wages are paid as normal. **paid-up member** (esp. of a trade-union member) a person who has paid the subscriptions in full. **pay-as-you-earn** *Brit.* the deduction of income tax from wages at source. **pay-bed** a hospital bed for private patients. **pay-claim** a demand for an increase in pay, esp. by a trade union. **pay-day** a day on which payment, esp. of wages, is made or expected to be made. **pay dearly** (usu. foll. by *for*) 1 obtain at a high cost, great effort, etc. 2 suffer for a wrongdoing etc. **pay dirt** (or **gravel**) *US* 1 *Mineral.* ground worth working for ore. 2 a financially promising situation. **pay envelope** *US* = *pay-packet*. **pay for** 1 hand over the price of. 2 bear the cost of. 3 suffer or be punished for (a fault etc.). **pay in** pay (money) into a bank account. **paying guest** a boarder. **pay its** (or **one's**) **way** cover costs; not be indebted. **pay one's last respects** show respect towards a dead person by attending the funeral. **pay off** 1 dismiss (workers) with a final payment. 2 *colloq.* yield good results; succeed. 3 pay (a debt) in full. 4 (of a ship) turn to leeward through the movement of the helm. **pay-off** n. *sl.* 1 an act of payment. 2 a climax. 3 a final reckoning. **pay out** (or **back**) punish or be revenged on. **pay-packet** *Brit.* a packet or envelope containing an employee's wages. **pay phone** a coin-box telephone. **pay the piper and call the tune** pay for, and therefore have control over, a proceeding. **pay one's respects** make a polite visit. **pay station** *US* = *pay phone*. **pay through the nose** *colloq.* pay much more than a fair price. **pay up** pay the full amount, or the full amount of. **put paid to** *colloq.* 1 deal effectively with (a person). 2 terminate (hopes etc.). □□ **payer** n. [ME f. OF *paie, payer* f. L *pacare* appease f. *pax pacis* peace]

pay[2] /peɪ/ v.tr. (past and past part. **payed**) *Naut.* smear (a ship) with pitch, tar, etc. as a defence against wet. [OF *peier* f. L *picare* f. *pix picis* PITCH[2]]

payable /ˈpeɪəb(ə)l/ adj. 1 that must be paid; due (*payable in April*). 2 that may be paid. 3 (of a mine etc.) profitable.

payback /ˈpeɪbæk/ n. 1 a financial return; a reward. 2 the profit from an investment etc., esp. one equal to the initial outlay. □ **payback period** the length of time required for an investment to pay for itself in terms of profits or savings.

PAYE abbr. *Brit.* pay-as-you-earn.

payee /peɪˈiː/ n. a person to whom money is paid or is to be paid.

payload /ˈpeɪləʊd/ n. 1 the part of an aircraft's load from which revenue is derived. **2 a** the explosive warhead carried by an aircraft or rocket. **b** the instruments etc. carried by a spaceship.

paymaster /ˈpeɪˌmɑːstə(r)/ n. 1 an official who pays troops, workmen, etc. 2 a person, organization, etc., to whom another owes duty or loyalty because of payment given. 3 (in full **Paymaster General**) *Brit.* the minister at the head of the Treasury department responsible for payments.

payment /ˈpeɪmənt/ n. 1 the act or an instance of paying. 2 an amount paid. 3 reward, recompense. [ME f. OF *paiement* (as PAY[1])]

paynim /ˈpeɪnɪm/ n. *archaic* 1 a pagan. 2 a non-Christian, esp. a Muslim. [ME f. OF *pai(e)nime* f. eccl.L *paganismus* heathenism (as PAGAN)]

payola /peɪˈəʊlə/ n. esp. *US* 1 a bribe offered in return for unofficial promotion of a product etc. in the media. 2 the practice of such bribery. [PAY[1] + -*ola* as in *Victrola*, make of gramophone]

payroll /ˈpeɪrəʊl/ n. a list of employees receiving regular pay.

paysage /peɪˈzɑːʒ/ n. 1 a rural scene; a landscape. 2 landscape painting. □□ ***paysagist*** /ˈpeɪzɑːdʒɪst/ n. [F f. *pays* country: see PEASANT]

Paz /pæz/, Octavio (1914–), Mexican poet and writer, who lived in England, France, and the US as well as in his own country and was Mexico's ambassador to India from 1962 to 1968. His *Collected Poems* (in Spanish and English) were published in 1988.

Pb symb. *Chem.* the element lead. [L *plumbum*]

PBX abbr. private branch exchange (private telephone switchboard).

PC *abbr.* **1** (in the UK) police constable. **2** (in the UK) Privy Counsellor. **3** personal computer.

p.c. *abbr.* **1** per cent. **2** postcard.

PCB *abbr.* **1** *Computing* printed circuit board. **2** *Chem.* polychlorinated biphenyl, any of several toxic aromatic compounds containing two benzene molecules in which hydrogens have been replaced by chlorine atoms, formed as waste in industrial processes.

PCM *abbr.* pulse code modulation.

pct. *abbr. US* per cent.

PD *abbr. US* Police Department.

Pd *symb. Chem.* the element palladium.

pd. *abbr.* paid.

p.d.q. *abbr. colloq.* pretty damn quick.

PDT *abbr. US* Pacific Daylight Time.

PE *abbr.* physical education.

p/e *abbr.* price/earnings (ratio).

pea /piː/ *n.* **1 a** a hardy climbing plant, *Pisum sativum*, with seeds growing in pods and used for food. **b** its seed. **2** any of several similar plants (*sweet pea; chick-pea*). □ **pea-brain** *colloq.* a stupid or dim-witted person. **pea-green** bright green. **pea-souper** *Brit. colloq.* a thick yellowish fog. [back-form. f. PEASE (taken as pl.: cf. CHERRY)]

peace /piːs/ *n.* **1 a** quiet; tranquillity (*needs peace to work well*). **b** mental calm; serenity (*peace of mind*). **2 a** (often *attrib.*) freedom from or the cessation of war (*peace talks*). **b** (esp. **Peace**) a treaty of peace between two States etc. at war. **3** freedom from civil disorder. **4** *Eccl.* a ritual liturgical greeting. □ **at peace 1** in a state of friendliness. **2** serene. **3** *euphem.* dead. **hold one's peace** keep silence. **keep the peace** prevent, or refrain from, strife. **make one's peace** (often foll. by *with*) re-establish friendly relations. **make peace** bring about peace; reconcile. **the peace** (or **the queen's peace**) peace existing within a realm; civil order. **Peace Corps** *US* an organization sending young people to work as volunteers in developing countries. **peace dividend** money saved by the reduction of expenditure on weapons and defence after the relaxation of tension between Western and Soviet bloc countries in 1990. **peace-offering 1** a propitiatory or conciliatory gift. **2** *Bibl.* an offering presented as a thanksgiving to God. **peace-pipe** a tobacco-pipe as a token of peace among US Indians. [ME f. AF *pes*, OF *pais* f. L *pax pacis*]

peaceable /ˈpiːsəb(ə)l/ *adj.* **1** disposed to peace; unwarlike. **2** free from disturbance; peaceful. □□ **peaceableness** *n.* **peaceably** *adv.* [ME f. OF *peisible, plaisible* f. LL *placibilis* pleasing f. L *placēre* please]

peaceful /ˈpiːsfʊl/ *adj.* **1** characterized by peace; tranquil. **2** not violating or infringing peace (*peaceful coexistence*). **3** belonging to a state of peace. □□ **peacefully** *adv.* **peacefulness** *n.*

peacemaker /ˈpiːsˌmeɪkə(r)/ *n.* a person who brings about peace. □□ **peacemaking** *n.* & *adj.*

peacetime /ˈpiːstaɪm/ *n.* a period when a country is not at war.

peach[1] /piːtʃ/ *n.* **1 a** a round juicy stone-fruit with downy cream or yellow skin flushed with red. **b** the tree, *Prunus persica*, bearing it. **2** the yellowish-pink colour of a peach. **3** *colloq.* **a** a person or thing of superlative quality. **b** an attractive young woman. □ **peach-bloom** an oriental porcelain-glaze of reddish pink, usu. with green markings. **peach-blow 1** a delicate purplish-pink colour. **2** = *peach-bloom.* **peaches and cream** (of a complexion) creamy skin with downy pink cheeks. **peach Melba** see MELBA. □□ **peachy** *adj.* (**peachier, peachiest**). **peachiness** *n.* [ME f. OF *peche, pesche,* f. med.L *persica* f. L *persicum* (*malum*), lit. Persian apple]

peach[2] /piːtʃ/ *v.* **1** *intr.* (usu. foll. by *against, on*) *colloq.* turn informer; inform. **2** *tr. archaic* inform against. [ME f. *appeach* f. AF *enpecher,* OF *empechier* IMPEACH]

pea-chick /ˈpiːtʃɪk/ *n.* a young peafowl. [formed as PEACOCK + CHICK[1]]

Peacock /ˈpiːkɒk/, Thomas Love (1785–1866), English novelist and poet. His satirical romances, which include *Headlong Hall* (1816), *Nightmare Abbey* (1818), *Crotchet Castle* (1831), and *Gryll Grange* (1860–1), survey the contemporary cultural scene from a radical viewpoint, often in convivial argument between strange characters (some based on real people, including his friend Shelley) at dinner in a country house; the plots are slender and are diversified by clever songs. Peacock's sceptical attitude to the fashionable cult of the arts is apparent in his critical work *The Four Ages of Poetry* (1820), to which Shelley replied in *A Defence of Poetry* (1821).

peacock /ˈpiːkɒk/ *n.* **1** a male peafowl, having brilliant plumage and a tail (with eyelike markings) that can be expanded erect in display like a fan. **2** an ostentatious strutting person. □ **peacock blue** the lustrous greenish blue of a peacock's neck. **peacock butterfly** a butterfly, *Inachis io*, with eyelike markings on its wings. [ME *pecock* f. OE *pēa* f. L *pavo* + COCK[1]]

peafowl /ˈpiːfaʊl/ *n.* **1** a peacock or peahen. **2** a pheasant of the genus *Pavo.*

peahen /ˈpiːhen/ *n.* a female peafowl.

pea-jacket /ˈpiːˌdʒækɪt/ *n.* a sailor's short double-breasted overcoat of coarse woollen cloth. [prob. f. Du. *pijjakker* f. *pij* coat of coarse cloth + *jekker* jacket: assim. to JACKET]

peak[1] /piːk/ *n.* & *v.* —*n.* **1** a projecting usu. pointed part, esp.: **a** the pointed top of a mountain. **b** a mountain with a peak. **c** a stiff brim at the front of a cap. **d** a pointed beard. **e** the narrow part of a ship's hold at the bow or stern (*forepeak; after-peak*). **f** *Naut.* the upper outer corner of a sail extended by a gaff. **2 a** the highest point in a curve (*on the peak of the wave*). **b** the time of greatest success (in a career etc.). **c** the highest point on a graph etc. —*v.intr.* reach the highest value, quality, etc. (*output peaked in September*). □ **Peak District** an area in Derbyshire where there are many peaks. **peak hour** the time of the most intense traffic etc. **peak-load** the maximum of electric power demand etc. □□ **peaked** *adj.* **peaky** *adj.* **peakiness** *n.* [prob. back-form. f. *peaked* var. of dial. *picked* pointed (PICK[2])]

peak[2] /piːk/ *v.intr.* **1** waste away. **2** (as **peaked** *adj.*) sharp-featured; pinched. [16th c.: orig. unkn.]

Peake /piːk/, Mervyn Laurence (1911–68), British novelist, poet, and artist, who illustrated a number of his own works. He is remembered most for the trilogy *Titus Groan* (1946), *Gormenghast* (1950), and *Titus Alone* (1959), a novel of Gothic fantasy.

peaky /ˈpiːkɪ/ *adj.* (**peakier, peakiest**) **1** sickly; puny. **2** white-faced.

peal[1] /piːl/ *n.* & *v.* —*n.* **1 a** the loud ringing of a bell or bells, esp. a series of changes. **b** a set of bells. **2** a loud repeated sound, esp. of thunder, laughter, etc. —*v.* **1** *intr.* sound forth in a peal. **2** *tr.* utter sonorously. **3** *tr.* ring (bells) in peals. [ME *pele* f. *apele* APPEAL]

peal[2] /piːl/ *n.* a salmon grilse. [16th c.: orig. unkn.]

pean[1] /piːn/ *n. Heraldry* fur represented as sable spotted with or. [16th c.: orig. unkn.]

pean[2] *US* var. of PAEAN.

peanut /ˈpiːnʌt/ *n.* **1** a leguminous plant, *Arachis hypogaea*, bearing pods that ripen underground and contain seeds used as food and yielding oil. **2** the seed of this plant. **3** (in *pl.*) *colloq.* a paltry or trivial thing or amount, esp. of money. □ **peanut butter** a paste of ground roasted peanuts.

pear /peə(r)/ *n.* **1** a yellowish or brownish-green fleshy fruit, tapering towards the stalk. **2** any of various trees of the genus *Pyrus* bearing it, esp. *P. communis.* □ **pear-drop** a small sweet with the shape of a pear. [OE *pere, peru* ult. f. L *pirum*]

pearl[1] /pɜːl/ *n.* & *v.* —*n.* **1 a** (often *attrib.*) a usu. white or bluish-grey hard mass formed within the shell of a pearl-oyster or other bivalve mollusc, highly prized as a gem for its lustre (*pearl necklace*). **b** an imitation of this. **c** (in *pl.*) a necklace of pearls. **d** = *mother-of-pearl* (cf. *seed-pearl*). **2** a precious thing; the finest example. **3** anything resembling a pearl, e.g. a dewdrop, tear, etc. —*v.* **1** *tr. poet.* **a** sprinkle with pearly drops. **b** make pearly in colour etc. **2** *tr.* reduce (barley etc.) to small rounded grains. **3** *intr.* fish for pearl-oysters. **4** *intr. poet.* form pearl-like drops. □ **cast pearls before swine** offer a treasure to a person unable to appreciate it. **pearl ash** commercial potassium carbonate. **pearl barley** barley reduced to small round grains by grinding. **pearl bulb** a translucent electric light bulb. **pearl button** a button made of mother-of-pearl or an imitation of it.

pearl-diver a person who dives for pearl-oysters. **pearl millet** a tall cereal, *Pennisetum typhoides*. **pearl onion** a very small onion used in pickles. **pearl-oyster** any of various marine bivalve molluscs of the genus *Pinctada*, bearing pearls. □□ **pearler** *n.* [ME f. OF *perle* prob. f. L *perna* leg (applied to leg-of-mutton-shaped bivalve)]

pearl² /pɜːl/ *n. Brit.* = PICOT. [var. of PURL¹]

pearled /pɜːld/ *adj.* **1** adorned with pearls. **2** formed into pearl-like drops or grains. **3** pearl-coloured.

pearlescent /pɜːˈles(ə)nt/ *adj.* having or producing the appearance of mother-of-pearl.

Pearl Harbor a harbour on the island of Oahu, one of the Hawaiian islands, site of a major American naval base, where a surprise attack on 7 Dec. 1941, delivered (without a declaration of war) by Japanese carrier-borne aircraft, inflicted heavy damage and brought the US into the Second World War. [tr. Hawaiian *Wai Momi*, lit. = pearl waters]

pearlite var. of PERLITE.

pearlized /ˈpɜːlaɪzd/ *adj.* treated so as to resemble mother-of-pearl.

Pearl River a river of southern China, forming part of the delta of the Xi River. Flowing through the city of Canton (Guangzhou), it widens into a bay that forms an inlet of the South China Sea between Hong Kong and Macau.

pearlware /ˈpɜːlweə(r)/ *n.* a fine white glazed earthenware.

pearlwort /ˈpɜːlwɜːt/ *n. Bot.* any small herbaceous plant of the genus *Sagina*, inhabiting rocky and sandy areas.

pearly /ˈpɜːlɪ/ *adj. & n.* —*adj.* (**pearlier, pearliest**) **1** resembling a pearl; lustrous. **2** containing pearls or mother-of-pearl. **3** adorned with pearls. —*n.* (*pl.* **-ies**) (in *pl.*) *Brit.* **1** pearly kings and queens. **2** a pearly king's or queen's clothes or pearl buttons. □ **Pearly Gates** *colloq.* the gates of Heaven. **pearly king** (or **queen**) *Brit.* a London costermonger (or his wife) wearing clothes covered with pearl buttons. **pearly nautilus** see NAUTILUS. □□ **pearliness** *n.*

pearmain /ˈpeəmeɪn, ˈpɜː-/ *n.* a variety of apple with firm white flesh. [ME, = warden pear, f. OF *parmain, permain*, prob. ult. f. L *parmensis* of Parma in Italy]

peart /pɜːt/ *adj. US* lively; cheerful. [var. of PERT]

Peary /ˈpɪərɪ/, Robert Edwin (1856–1920), US explorer, generally credited with leading the first expedition to reach the North Pole (1909).

Peary Land /ˈpɪərɪ/ a mountainous region on the Arctic coast of northern Greenland. It is named after Robert E. Peary, who explored it in 1892 and 1900.

peasant /ˈpez(ə)nt/ *n.* **1** esp. *colloq.* a countryman or countrywoman; a rustic. **2 a** a worker on the land, esp. a labourer or smallholder. **b** *hist.* a member of an agricultural class dependent on subsistence farming. **3** *derog.* a lout; a boorish person. □□ **peasantry** *n.* (*pl.* **-ies**). **peasanty** *adj.* [ME f. AF *paisant*, OF *paisent*, earlier *paisenc* f. *païs* country ult. f. L *pagus* canton]

Peasants' Revolt an uprising in England (1381) when widespread unrest, caused by poor economic conditions and repressive legislation, culminated in revolt among the peasant and artisan classes, particularly in Kent and Essex. The rebels marched on London, occupying the city and executing unpopular ministers, but after the death of their leader, Wat Tyler, they were persuaded to disperse after the young king Richard II had granted some of their demands. Afterwards the government went back on its promises and rapidly re-established control.

pease /piːz/ *n.pl. archaic* peas. □ **pease-pudding** boiled split peas (served esp. with boiled ham). [OE *pise* pea, pl. *pisan*, f. LL *pisa* f. L *pisum* f. Gk *pison*: cf. PEA]

peashooter /ˈpiːˌʃuːtə(r)/ *n.* a small tube for blowing dried peas through as a toy.

peat /piːt/ *n.* **1** vegetable matter decomposed in water and partly carbonized, used for fuel, in horticulture, etc. **2** a cut piece of this. □□ **peaty** *adj.* [ME f. AL *peta*, perh. f. Celt.: cf. PIECE]

peatbog /ˈpiːtbɒg/ *n.* a bog composed of peat.

peatmoss /ˈpiːtmɒs/ *n.* **1** a peatbog. **2** any of various mosses of the genus *Sphagnum*, which grow in damp conditions and form peat as they decay.

peau-de-soie /ˌpəʊdəˈswɑː/ *n.* a smooth finely-ribbed satiny fabric of silk or rayon. [F, = skin of silk]

pebble /ˈpeb(ə)l/ *n.* **1** a small smooth stone worn by the action of water. **2 a** a type of colourless transparent rock-crystal used for spectacles. **b** a lens of this. **c** (*attrib.*) *colloq.* (of a spectacle-lens) very thick and convex. **3** an agate or other gem, esp. when found as a pebble in a stream etc. □ **not the only pebble on the beach** (esp. of a person) easily replaced. **pebble-dash** mortar with pebbles in it used as a coating for external walls. □□ **pebbly** *adj.* [OE *papel-stān* pebble-stone, *pyppelrīpig* pebble-stream, of unkn. orig.]

p.e.c. *abbr.* photoelectric cell.

pecan /ˈpiːkən/ *n.* **1** a pinkish-brown smooth nut with an edible kernel. **2** a hickory, *Carya illinoensis*, of the southern US, producing this. [earlier *paccan*, of Algonquian orig.]

peccable /ˈpekəb(ə)l/ *adj. formal* liable to sin. □□ **peccability** /-ˈbɪlɪtɪ/ *n.* [F, f. med.L *peccabilis* f. *peccare* sin]

peccadillo /ˌpekəˈdɪləʊ/ *n.* (*pl.* **-oes** or **-os**) a trifling offence; a venial sin. [Sp. *pecadillo*, dimin. of *pecado* sin f. L (as PECCANT)]

peccant /ˈpekənt/ *adj. formal* **1** sinning. **2** inducing disease; morbid. □□ **peccancy** *n.* [F *peccant* or L *peccare* sin]

peccary /ˈpekərɪ/ *n.* (*pl.* **-ies**) any American wild pig of the family Tayassuidae, esp. *Tayassu tajacu* and *T. pecari*. [Carib *pakira*]

peccavi /peˈkɑːvɪ/ *int. & n.* —*int.* expressing guilt. —*n.* (*pl.* **peccavis**) a confession of guilt. [L, = I have sinned]

pêche Melba /peʃ ˈmelbə/ *n.* = peach Melba (see MELBA). [F]

peck¹ /pek/ *v. & n.* —*v.tr.* **1** strike or bite (something) with a beak. **2** kiss (esp. a person's cheek) hastily or perfunctorily. **3 a** make (a hole) by pecking. **b** (foll. by *out, off*) remove or pluck out by pecking. **4** *colloq.* (also *absol.*) eat (food) listlessly; nibble at. **5** mark with short strokes. **6** (usu. foll. by *up, down*) break up with pick etc. —*n.* **1 a** a stroke or bite with a beak. **b** a mark made by this. **2** a hasty or perfunctory kiss. **3** *sl.* food. □ **peck at 1** eat (food) listlessly; nibble. **2** carp at; nag. **3** strike (a thing) repeatedly with a beak. **pecking** (or **peck**) **order** a social hierarchy, orig. as observed among hens. [ME prob. f. MLG *pekken*, of unkn. orig.]

peck² /pek/ *n.* **1** a measure of capacity for dry goods, equal to 2 gallons or 8 quarts. **2** a vessel used to contain this amount. □ **a peck of** a large number or amount of (troubles, dirt, etc.). [ME f. AF *pek*, of unkn. orig.]

pecker /ˈpekə(r)/ *n.* **1** a bird that pecks (*woodpecker*). **2** *US coarse sl.* the penis. □ **keep your pecker up** *Brit. colloq.* remain cheerful.

peckish /ˈpekɪʃ/ *adj. colloq.* **1** hungry. **2** *US* irritable.

pecorino /ˌpekəˈriːnəʊ/ *n.* (*pl.* **-os**) an Italian cheese made from ewes' milk. [It. f. *pecorino* (adj.) of ewes f. *pecora* sheep]

Pécs /peɪtʃ/ an industrial city in SW Hungary, at the centre of a noted wine-producing region; pop. (1988) 182,000.

pecten /ˈpektɪn/ *n.* (*pl.* **pectens** or **pectines** /-tɪˌniːz/) *Zool.* **1** a comblike structure of various kinds in animal bodies. **2** any bivalve mollusc of the genus *Pecten*. Also called SCALLOP. □□ **pectinate** /-nət/ *adj.* **pectinated** /-ˌneɪtɪd/ *adj.* **pectination** /-ˈneɪʃ(ə)n/ *n.* (all in sense 1). [L *pecten pectinis* comb]

pectin /ˈpektɪn/ *n. Biochem.* any of various soluble gelatinous polysaccharides found in ripe fruits etc. and used as a setting agent in jams and jellies. □□ **pectic** *adj.* [Gk *pēktos* congealed f. *pēgnumi* make solid]

pectoral /ˈpektər(ə)l/ *adj. & n.* —*adj.* **1** of or relating to the breast or chest; thoracic (*pectoral fin; pectoral muscle*). **2** worn on the chest (*pectoral cross*). —*n.* **1** (esp. in *pl.*) a pectoral muscle. **2** a pectoral fin. **3** an ornamental breastplate esp. of a Jewish high priest. [ME f. OF f. L *pectorale* (n.), *pectoralis* (adj.) f. *pectus pectoris* breast, chest]

pectose /ˈpektəʊs/ *n. Biochem.* an insoluble polysaccharide derivative found in unripe fruits and converted into pectin by ripening, heating, etc. [*pectic* (see PECTIN) + -OSE²]

peculate /ˈpekjʊˌleɪt/ *v.tr. & intr.* embezzle (money). □□ **peculation** /-ˈleɪʃ(ə)n/ *n.* **peculator** *n.* [L *peculari* rel. to *peculium*: see PECULIAR]

peculiar /pɪˈkjuːlɪə(r)/ adj. & n. —adj. **1** strange; odd; unusual (a peculiar flavour; is a little peculiar). **2 a** (usu. foll. by to) belonging exclusively (a fashion peculiar to the time). **b** belonging to the individual (in their own peculiar way). **3** particular; special (a point of peculiar interest). —n. **1** a peculiar property, privilege, etc. **2** a parish or church exempt from the jurisdiction of the diocese in which it lies. [ME f. L peculiaris of private property f. peculium f. pecu cattle]

peculiarity /pɪˌkjuːlɪˈærɪtɪ/ n. (pl. -ies) **1 a** idiosyncrasy; unusualness; oddity. **b** an instance of this. **2** a characteristic or habit (meanness is his peculiarity). **3** the state of being peculiar.

peculiarly /pɪˈkjuːlɪəlɪ/ adv. **1** more than usually; especially (peculiarly annoying). **2** oddly. **3** as regards oneself alone; individually (does not affect him peculiarly).

pecuniary /pɪˈkjuːnɪərɪ/ adj. **1** of, concerning, or consisting of, money (pecuniary aid; pecuniary considerations). **2** (of an offence) entailing a money penalty or fine. □□ **pecuniarily** adv. [L pecuniarius f. pecunia money f. pecu cattle]

pedagogue /ˈpedəˌɡɒɡ/ n. archaic or derog. a schoolmaster; a teacher. □□ **pedagogic** /-ˈɡɒɡɪk, -ˈɡɒdʒɪk/ adj. **pedagogical** /-ˈɡɒɡɪk(ə)l, -ˈɡɒdʒɪk(ə)l/ adj. **pedagogically** /-ˈɡɒɡɪkəlɪ, -ˈɡɒdʒɪkəlɪ/ adv. **pedagogism** n. (also **pedagoguism**). [ME f. L paedagogus f. Gk paidagōgos f. pais paidos boy + agōgos guide]

pedagogy /ˈpedəˌɡɒdʒɪ, -ˌɡɒɡɪ/ n. the science of teaching. □□ **pedagogics** /-ˈɡɒdʒɪks, -ˈɡəʊdʒɪks/ n. [F pédagogie f. Gk paidagōgia (as PEDAGOGUE)]

pedal¹ /ˈped(ə)l/ n. & v. —n. **1** any of several types of foot-operated levers or controls for mechanisms, esp.: **a** either of a pair of levers for transmitting power to a bicycle or tricycle wheel etc. **b** any of the foot-operated controls in a motor vehicle. **c** any of the foot-operated keys of an organ used for playing notes, or for drawing out several stops at once etc. **d** each of the foot-levers on a piano etc. for making the tone fuller or softer. **e** each of the foot-levers on a harp for altering the pitch of the strings. **2** a note sustained in one part, usu. the bass, through successive harmonies, some of which are independent of it. —v. (**pedalled, pedalling**; US **pedaled, pedaling**) **1** intr. operate a cycle, organ, etc. by using the pedals. **2** tr. work (a bicycle etc.) with the pedals. □ **pedal cycle** a bicycle. [F pédale f. It. pedale f. L (as PEDAL²)]

pedal² /ˈped(ə)l, ˈpiːd(ə)l/ adj. Zool. of the foot or feet (esp. of a mollusc). [L pedalis f. pes pedis foot]

pedalo /ˈpedəˌləʊ/ n. (pl. -os) a pedal-operated pleasure-boat.

pedant /ˈped(ə)nt/ n. **1** a person who insists on strict adherence to formal rules or literal meaning at the expense of a wider view. **2** a person who rates academic learning or technical knowledge above everything. **3** a person who is obsessed by a theory; a doctrinaire. □□ **pedantic** /pɪˈdæntɪk/ adj. **pedantically** /pɪˈdæntɪkəlɪ/ adv. **pedantize** v.intr. & tr. (also -ise). **pedantry** n. (pl. -ies). [F pédant f. It. pedante: app. formed as PEDAGOGUE]

pedate /ˈpedeɪt/ adj. **1** Zool. having feet. **2** Bot. (of a leaf) having divisions like toes or a bird's claws. [L pedatus f. pes pedis foot]

peddle /ˈped(ə)l/ v. **1** tr. **a** sell (goods), esp. in small quantities, as a pedlar. **b** advocate or promote (ideas, a philosophy, a way of life, etc.). **2** tr. sell (drugs) illegally. **3** intr. engage in selling, esp. as a pedlar. [back-form. f. PEDLAR]

peddler /ˈpedlə(r)/ n. **1** a person who sells drugs illegally. **2** US var. of PEDLAR.

pederast /ˈpedəˌræst/ n. (also **paederast**) a man who performs pederasty.

pederasty /ˈpedəˌræstɪ/ n. (also **paederasty**) anal intercourse between a man and a boy. [mod.L paederastia f. Gk paiderastia f. pais paidos boy + erastēs lover]

pedestal /ˈpedɪst(ə)l/ n. & v. —n. **1** a base supporting a column or pillar. **2** the stone etc. base of a statue etc. **3** either of the two supports of a knee-hole desk or table, usu. containing drawers. —v.tr. (**pedestalled, pedestalling**; US **pedestaled, pedestaling**) set or support on a pedestal. □ **pedestal table** a table with a single central support. **put** (or **set**) **on a pedestal** regard as highly admirable, important, etc.; venerate. [F piédestal f. It. piedestallo f. piè foot f. L pes pedis + di of + stallo STALL¹]

pedestrian /pɪˈdestrɪən/ n. & adj. —n. **1** (often attrib.) a person who is walking, esp. in a town (pedestrian crossing). **2** a person who walks competitively. —adj. prosaic; dull; uninspired. □ **pedestrian crossing** Brit. a specified part of a road where pedestrians have right of way to cross. **pedestrian precinct** an area of a town restricted to pedestrians. □□ **pedestrianism** n. **pedestrianize** v.tr. & intr. (also -ise). **pedestrianization** /-ˈzeɪʃ(ə)n/ n. [F pédestre or L pedester -tris]

pediatrics US var. of PAEDIATRICS.

pedicab /ˈpedɪˌkæb/ n. a pedal-operated rickshaw.

pedicel /ˈpedɪs(ə)l/ n. (also **pedicle** /ˈpedɪk(ə)l/) **1** a small (esp. subordinate) stalklike structure in a plant or animal (cf. PEDUNCLE). **2** Surgery part of a graft left temporarily attached to its original site. □□ **pedicellate** /-səˌleɪt/ adj. **pediculate** /pɪˈdɪkjʊlət/ adj. [mod.L pedicellus & L pediculus dimin. of pes pedis foot]

pedicular /pɪˈdɪkjʊlə(r)/ adj. (also **pediculous** /-ləs/) infested with lice. □□ **pediculosis** /-ˈləʊsɪs/ n. [L pedicularis, -losus f. pediculus louse]

pedicure /ˈpedɪˌkjʊə(r)/ n. & v. —n. **1** the care or treatment of the feet, esp. of the toenails. **2** a person practising this, esp. professionally. —v.tr. treat (the feet) by removing corns etc. [F pédicure f. L pes pedis foot + curare: see CURE]

pedigree /ˈpedɪˌɡriː/ n. **1** (often attrib.) a recorded line of descent of a person or esp. a pure-bred domestic or pet animal. **2** the derivation of a word. **3** a genealogical table. **4** colloq. the 'life history' of a person, thing, idea, etc. □□ **pedigreed** adj. [ME pedegru etc. f. AF f. OF pie de grue (unrecorded) crane's foot, a mark denoting succession in pedigrees]

pediment /ˈpedɪmənt/ n. **1 a** the triangular front part of a building in Grecian style, surmounting esp. a portico of columns. **b** a similar part of a building in Roman or Renaissance style. **2** Geol. a broad flattish rock surface at the foot of a mountain slope. □□ **pedimental** /-ˈment(ə)l/ adj. **pedimented** adj. [earlier pedament, periment, perh. corrupt. of PYRAMID]

pedlar /ˈpedlə(r)/ n. (US **peddler**) **1** a travelling seller of small items esp. carried in a pack etc. **2** (usu. foll. by of) a retailer of gossip etc. □□ **pedlary** n. [ME pedlere alt. of pedder f. ped pannier, of unkn. orig.]

pedo- comb. form US var. of PAEDO-.

pedology /pɪˈdɒlədʒɪ/ n. the scientific study of soil, esp. its formation, nature, and classification. □□ **pedological** /ˌpedəˈlɒdʒɪk(ə)l/ adj. **pedologist** n. [Russ. pedologiya f. Gk pedon ground]

pedometer /pɪˈdɒmɪtə(r)/ n. an instrument for estimating the distance travelled on foot by recording the number of steps taken. [F pédomètre f. L pes pedis foot]

peduncle /pɪˈdʌŋk(ə)l/ n. **1** Bot. the stalk of a flower, fruit, or cluster, esp. a main stalk bearing a solitary flower or subordinate stalks (cf. PEDICEL). **2** Zool. a stalklike projection in an animal body. □□ **peduncular** /-kjʊlə(r)/ adj. **pedunculate** /-kjʊlət/ adj. [mod.L pedunculus f. L pes pedis foot: see -UNCLE]

pee /piː/ v. & n. colloq. —v. (**pees, peed**) **1** intr. urinate. **2** tr. pass (urine, blood, etc.) from the bladder. —n. **1** urination. **2** urine. [initial letter of PISS]

peek /piːk/ v. & n. —v.intr. (usu. foll. by in, out, at) look quickly or slyly; peep. —n. a quick or sly look. [ME pike, pyke, of unkn. orig.]

peekaboo /ˈpiːkəˌbuː/ adj. & n. —adj. **1** (of a garment etc.) transparent or having a pattern of small holes. **2** (of a hairstyle) concealing one eye with a fringe or wave. —n. US = BO-PEEP. [PEEK + BOO]

Peel /piːl/, Sir Robert (1788–1850), British statesman. Peel proved an outstanding Home Secretary (1822–7 and 1828–30), establishing the Metropolitan Police and carrying through a wide-ranging series of legal and penal reforms. As leader of the Conservatives, his Tamworth Manifesto (1834) established his belief in reform where necessary, and although his first term as Prime Minister lasted only a few months (1834–5), his second term (1841–6) proved a model of good government. His repeal of the Corn Laws in 1846, however, split the Conservative Party and forced his resignation. In the last years of his career, he and

æ cat ɑ: arm e bed ɜ: her ɪ sit iː see ɒ hot ɔ: saw ʌ run ʊ put uː too ə ago aɪ my

his remaining followers generally supported the Whig policies of free trade. Peel himself died in 1850 after a riding accident.

peel[1] /piːl/ v. & n. —v. **1** tr. **a** strip the skin, rind, bark, wrapping, etc. from (a fruit, vegetable, tree, etc.). **b** (usu. foll. by *off*) strip (skin, peel, wrapping, etc.) from a fruit etc. **2** intr. **a** (of a tree, an animal's or person's body, a painted surface, etc.) become bare of bark, skin, paint, etc. **b** (often foll. by *off*) (of bark, a person's skin, paint, etc.) flake off. **3** intr. (often foll. by *off*) colloq. (of a person) strip for exercise etc. **4** tr. *Croquet* send (another player's ball) through the hoops. —n. the outer covering of a fruit, vegetable, prawn, etc.; rind. □ **peel off 1** veer away and detach oneself from a group of marchers, a formation of aircraft, etc. **2** colloq. strip off one's clothes. □□ **peeler** n. (in sense 1 of v.). [earlier *pill*, *pele* (orig. = plunder) f. ME *pilien* etc. f. OE *pilian* (unrecorded) f. L *pilare* f. *pilus* hair]

peel[2] /piːl/ n. a shovel, esp. a baker's shovel for bringing loaves etc. into or out of an oven. [ME & OF *pele* f. L *pala*, rel. to *pangere* fix]

peel[3] /piːl/ n. (also **pele**) *hist.* a small square tower built in the 16th c. in the border counties of England and Scotland for defence against raids. [ME *pel* stake, palisade, f. AF & OF *pel* f. L *palus* stake: cf. PALE[2]]

peeler /ˈpiːlə(r)/ n. *Brit. archaic sl.* or *dial.* a policeman. [Sir Robert PEEL]

peeling /ˈpiːlɪŋ/ n. a strip of the outer skin of a vegetable, fruit, etc. (*potato peelings*).

Peelite /ˈpiːlaɪt/ n. *hist.* a Conservative supporting Sir Robert Peel, esp. with reference to the repeal of the Corn Laws (1846).

peen /piːn/ n. & v. —n. the wedge-shaped or thin or curved end of a hammer-head (opp. FACE n. 5a). —v.tr. **1** hammer with a peen. **2** treat (sheet metal) with a stream of metal shot in order to shape it. [17th c.: also *pane*, app. f. F *panne* f. Du. *pen* f. L *pinna* point]

Peenemünde /ˌpeɪnəˈmʊndə/ a village in NE Germany, on the Baltic coast, that was the chief site of German rocket research and testing during the Second World War.

peep[1] /piːp/ v. & n. —v.intr. **1** (usu. foll. by *at*, *in*, *out*, *into*) look through a narrow opening; look furtively. **2** (usu. foll. by *out*) (of daylight, a flower beginning to bloom, etc.) come slowly into view; emerge. **b** (of a quality etc.) show itself unconsciously. —n. **1** a furtive or peering glance. **2** the first appearance (*at peep of day*). □ **peep-bo** = BO-PEEP. **peep-hole** a small hole that may be looked through. **peeping Tom** a furtive voyeur (from the name of a Coventry tailor said to have peeped at Lady Godiva when she rode naked through Coventry). **peep-of-day boys** a Protestant organization in Ireland (1784–95) searching opponents' houses at daybreak for arms. **peep-sight** the aperture backsight of some rifles. **peep-toe** (or **-toed**) (of a shoe) leaving the toes partly bare. [ME: cf. PEEK, PEER[1]]

peep[2] /piːp/ v. & n. —v.intr. make a shrill feeble sound as of young birds, mice, etc.; squeak; chirp. —n. such a sound. [imit.: cf. CHEEP]

peeper /ˈpiːpə(r)/ n. **1** a person who peeps. **2** colloq. an eye. **3** *US sl.* a private detective.

peep-show n. a device, usually in the form of a box, with a small eyepiece, inside which are arranged the receding elements of a perspective view. Originally a scientific toy for the educated rich, in the latter part of the 17th c. it became a public entertainment, a fairground sideshow, and a children's plaything. Peep-shows have vanished from contemporary life, though some of the children's peep-shows have been preserved.

peepul /ˈpiːp(ə)l/ n. (also **pipal**) = BO-TREE. [Hindi *pīpal* f. Skr. *pippala*]

peer[1] /pɪə(r)/ v.intr. **1** (usu. foll. by *into*, *at*, etc.) look keenly or with difficulty (*peered into the fog*). **2** appear; peep out. **3** *archaic* come into view. [var. of *pire*, LG *pīren*; perh. partly f. APPEAR]

peer[2] /pɪə(r)/ n. & v. —n. **1 a** (*fem.* **peeress**) a member of one of the degrees of the nobility in Britain, i.e. a duke, marquis, earl, viscount, or baron. (See below.) **b** a noble of any country. **2** a person who is equal in ability, standing, rank, or value; a contemporary (*tried by a jury of his peers*). —v.intr. & tr. (usu. foll. by *with*) rank or cause to rank equally. □ **peer group** a group

of people of the same age, status, interests, etc. **peer of the realm** (or **the United Kingdom**) any of the class of peers whose adult members may all sit in the House of Lords. □□ **peerless** adj. [ME f. AF & OF *pe(e)r*, *perer* f. LL *pariare* f. L *par* equal]

Of the British peers, earls and barons were the earliest to appear; dukes were created from 1337, marquises from the end of the 14th c., and viscounts from 1440. The main privilege of peers nowadays is to sit and vote in the House of Lords; they are debarred from election to the House of Commons.

peerage /ˈpɪərɪdʒ/ n. **1** peers as a class; the nobility. **2** the rank of peer or peeress (*was given a life peerage*). **3** a book containing a list of peers with their genealogy etc.

peeve /piːv/ v. & n. *colloq.* —v.tr. (usu. as **peeved** adj.) annoy; vex; irritate. —n. **1** a cause of annoyance. **2** vexation. [back-form. f. PEEVISH]

peevish /ˈpiːvɪʃ/ adj. querulous; irritable. □□ **peevishly** adv. **peevishness** n. [ME, = foolish, mad, spiteful, etc., of unkn. orig.]

peewit /ˈpiːwɪt/ n. (also **pewit**) **1** a lapwing. **2** its cry. [imit.]

peg /peg/ n. & v. —n. **1 a** a usu. cylindrical pin or bolt of wood or metal, often tapered at one end, and used for holding esp. two things together. **b** such a peg attached to a wall etc. and used for hanging garments etc. on. **c** a peg driven into the ground and attached to a rope for holding up a tent. **d** a bung for stoppering a cask etc. **e** each of several pegs used to tighten or loosen the strings of a violin etc. **f** a small peg, matchstick, etc. stuck into holes in a board for calculating the scores at cribbage. **2** *Brit.* = *clothes-peg*. **3** *Brit.* a measure of spirits or wine. —v.tr. (**pegged**, **pegging**) **1** (usu. foll. by *down*, *in*, *out*, etc.) fix (a thing) with a peg. **2** *Econ.* **a** stabilize (prices, wages, exchange rates, etc.). **b** prevent the price of (stock etc.) from falling or rising by freely buying or selling at a given price. **3** mark (the score) with pegs on a cribbage-board. □ **off the peg** (of clothes) ready-made. **peg away** (often foll. by *at*) work consistently and esp. for a long period. **peg down** restrict (a person etc.) to rules, a commitment, etc. **peg-leg 1** an artificial leg. **2** a person with an artificial leg. **peg on** = *peg away*. **peg out 1** *sl.* die. **2** score the winning point at cribbage. **3** *Croquet* hit the peg with the ball as the final stroke in a game. **4** mark the boundaries of (land etc.). **a peg to hang an idea** etc. **on** a suitable occasion or pretext etc. for it. **a round** (or **square**) **peg in a square** (or **round**) **hole** a misfit. **take a person down a peg or two** humble a person. [ME, prob. of LG or Du. orig.: cf. MDu. *pegge*, Du. dial. *peg*, LG *pigge*]

Pegasus /ˈpeɡəsəs/ **1** *Gk Mythol.* a winged horse sprung from the blood of Medusa when Perseus cut off her head. He became the favourite of the Muses, and carried the thunderbolt of Zeus. His legend probably goes back to pre-Greek Asia Minor. In ancient sources he has no connection with poets beyond the fact that he created the spring Hippocrene; in Roman times he became a symbol of immortality. **2** *Astron.* a northern constellation, figured as a winged horse, containing three stars of moderate brightness forming with one star of Andromeda a large square (the 'square of Pegasus').

pegboard /ˈpeɡbɔːd/ n. a board having a regular pattern of small holes for pegs, used for commercial displays, games, etc.

pegmatite /ˈpeɡmətaɪt/ n. a coarsely crystalline type of granite. [Gk *pēgma -atos* thing joined together f. *pēgnumi* fasten]

pegtop /ˈpeɡtɒp/ n. a pear-shaped spinning-top with a metal pin or peg forming the point, spun by the rapid uncoiling of a string wound round it.

Pegu /peˈɡuː/ a city and port of southern Burma, probably founded as capital of the Mon kingdom in 825 and a centre of Buddhist culture; pop. (1983) 150,400.

Pehlevi var. of PAHLAVI.

PEI abbr. Prince Edward Island.

peignoir /ˈpeɪnwɑː(r)/ n. a woman's loose dressing-gown. [F f. *peigner* to comb]

Peirce /ˈpɪəs/, Charles Sandars (1839–1914), American philosopher, one of the founders of American pragmatism. He held that the aim of philosophical inquiry was to secure stability in beliefs, and that the fixation of beliefs should be based on the method of science. On his conception of scientific method, a theory is to be assessed according to its practical consequences; accordingly connections between beliefs and the actions that result from them were crucial to his view of philosophy. His theory of meaning is suggestive of the verification demanded by the logical positivists, but unlike some other pragmatists he insisted on the difference between true and merely useful beliefs. He also worked extensively in formal logic, arriving independently at some of the conclusions first reached by Frege.

pejorative /prɪˈdʒɒrətɪv, ˈpiːˈdʒɔ-/ adj. & n. —adj. (of a word, an expression, etc.) depreciatory. —n. a depreciatory word. □□ **pejoratively** adv. [F péjoratif -ive f. LL pejorare make worse (pejor)]

pekan /ˈpekən/ n. a N. American flesh-eating mammal, *Martes pennanti*, valued for its fur. [Can.F f. Abnaki *pékané*]

peke /piːk/ n. colloq. a Pekingese dog. [abbr.]

Peking /piːkɪŋ/ (now transliterated as **Beijing**) the capital of China; pop. (1982) 9,230,687. The city developed from Kublai Khan's capital built in the late 13th c. and was the capital of China, except for brief periods, from 1421. At its centre lies the 'Forbidden City', a walled area containing a number of buildings including the imperial palaces of the emperors of China (1421–1911), entry to which was forbidden to all except the imperial family and servants. [Chinese, = northern capital]

Pekingese /ˌpiːkɪˈniːz/ n. & adj. (also **Pekinese**) —n. (pl. same) **1 a** a lap-dog of a short-legged breed with long hair and a snub nose, originally brought to Europe from the Summer Palace at Peking in 1860. **b** this breed. **2** a citizen of Peking (Beijing) in China. **3** the form of the Chinese language used in Peking. —adj. of or concerning Peking or its language or citizens.

Peking man a fossil hominid (*Homo erectus pekinensis*) first described from remains found in 1926 in caves near the village of Choukoutien near Peking and at that time assigned to a new species (*Sinanthropus pekinensis*). All the fossils found before the Second World War, except for two teeth, were lost during the war (casts of the originals survive), but the excavations that were resumed in 1949 have since produced large quantities of cranial fossils and abundant evidence of the activities of these hominids, including the use of controlled fire and the manufacture and use of stone tools. The cave deposits in which the fossils were found have been dated to c.500,000 years ago for the oldest and c.230,000 years ago for more recent levels (the middle Pleistocene period).

pekoe /ˈpiːkəʊ/ n. a superior kind of black tea. [Chin. dial. *pek-ho* f. *pek* white + *ho* down, leaves being picked young with down on them]

pelage /ˈpelɪdʒ/ n. the fur, hair, wool, etc. of a mammal. [F f. *poil* hair]

pelagian /prɪˈleɪdʒɪən/ adj. & n. —adj. inhabiting the open sea. —n. an inhabitant of the open sea. [L *pelagius* f. Gk *pelagios* of the sea (*pelagos*)]

pelagic /prɪˈlædʒɪk/ adj. **1** of or performed on the open sea (*pelagic whaling*). **2** (of marine life) belonging to the upper layers of the open sea. [L *pelagicus* f. Gk *pelagikos* (as PELAGIAN)]

Pelagius /pəˈleɪdʒɪəs/ (died c.420) the Latinized name of a British (or perhaps Irish) lay monk and theologian who denied the doctrine of original sin and maintained that the human will is capable of good without the help of divine grace. He went to Rome c.400; his doctrines were opposed by St Augustine of Hippo and condemned as heresy. □□ **Pelagian** adj. & n. **Pelagianism** n.

pelargonium /ˌpelɑːˈɡəʊnɪəm/ n. any plant of the genus *Pelargonium*, with red, pink, or white flowers and fragrant leaves. Also called GERANIUM. [mod.L f. Gk *pelargos* stork: cf. GERANIUM]

Pelasgian /prɪˈlæzɡɪən/ n. & adj. —n. a member of an ancient people inhabiting the coasts and islands of the eastern Mediterranean, especially the Aegean Sea, before the arrival of Greek-speaking peoples in the Bronze Age. —adj. of the Pelasgians. [L *Pelasgius* f. Gk *Pelasgios*]

Pelé /ˈpeleɪ/ (real name Edson Arantes do Nascimento, 1940–), Brazilian footballer, the greatest inside forward of his time, who became internationally famous when he played for Brazil at the age of 17, when his country won the World Cup (1958).

pele var. of PEEL³.

Peleus /ˈpiːlɪəs/ Gk Mythol. a king of Phthia in Thessaly, who is the subject of a number of legends. He was given as wife the sea-nymph Thetis; their child was Achilles.

pelf /pelf/ n. derog. or joc. money; wealth. [ME f. ONF f. OF *pelfre*, *peufre* spoils, of unkn. orig.: cf. PILFER]

Pelham /ˈpeləm/, Henry (1696–1754), British statesman, Prime Minister 1743–54 after having held various offices in Walpole's Cabinet, 1721–42. During his period in power he reduced the national debt and in 1748 introduced a period of peace and prosperity by bringing the War of the Austrian Succession (1740–8) to an end. His ministry also introduced legislation adopting the Gregorian calendar. His death in office is often regarded as a major factor in producing the political instability of the 1760s.

pelham /ˈpeləm/ n. a horse's bit combining a curb and a snaffle. [the surname *Pelham*]

pelican /ˈpelɪkən/ n. any large gregarious waterfowl of the family Pelecanidae with a large bill and a pouch in the throat for storing fish. □ **pelican crossing** (in the UK) a pedestrian crossing with traffic lights operated by pedestrians. [OE *pellican* & OF *pelican* f. LL *pelicanus* f. Gk *pelekan* prob. f. *pelekus* axe, with ref. to its bill]

Pelion /ˈpiːlɪən/ a wooded mountain near the coast of SE Thessaly, Greece, the home of the centaurs in Greek mythology. The Giants were said to have piled Olympus on Ossa (another Thessalian mountain) and Ossa on Pelion in their attempt to reach heaven and destroy the gods.

pelisse /prɪˈliːs/ n. hist. **1** a woman's cloak with armholes or sleeves, reaching to the ankles. **2** a fur-lined cloak, esp. as part of a hussar's uniform. [F f. med.L *pellicia (vestis)* (garment) of fur f. *pellis* skin]

pelite /ˈpiːlaɪt/ n. a rock composed of claylike sediment. [Gk *pēlos* clay, mud]

pellagra /prɪˈlæɡrə, -ˈleɪɡrə/ n. a disease caused by deficiency of nicotinic acid, characterized by cracking of the skin and often resulting in insanity. □□ **pellagrous** adj. [It. f. *pelle* skin, after PODAGRA]

pellet /ˈpelɪt/ n. & v. —n. **1** a small compressed ball of paper, bread, etc. **2** a pill. **3 a** a small mass of bones, feathers, etc. regurgitated by a bird of prey. **b** a small hard piece of animal, usu. rodent, excreta. **4 a** a piece of small shot. **b** an imitation bullet for a toy gun. —v.tr. (**pelleted**, **pelleting**) **1** make into a pellet or pellets. **2** hit with (esp. paper) pellets. □□ **pelletize** v.tr. (also -ise). [ME f. OF *pelote* f. L *pila* ball]

pellicle /ˈpelɪk(ə)l/ n. a thin skin, membrane, or film. □□ **pellicular** /-ˈlɪkjʊlə(r)/ adj. [F *pellicule* f. L *pellicula*, dimin. of *pellis* skin]

pellitory /ˈpelɪtərɪ/ n. any of several wild plants, esp.: **1** (in full **pellitory of Spain**) a composite plant, *Anacyclus pyrethrum*, with a pungent-flavoured root, used as a local irritant etc. **2** (in full **pellitory of the wall**) a low bushy plant, *Parietaria judaica*, with greenish flowers growing on or at the foot of walls. [(sense 1) alt. f. ME f. OF *peletre, peretre* f. L *pyrethrum* f. Gk *purethron* feverfew: (sense 2) ult. f. OF *paritaire* f. LL *parietaria* f. L *paries -etis* wall]

pell-mell /pelˈmel/ adv., adj., & n. —adv. **1** headlong, recklessly (*rushed pell-mell out of the room*). **2** in disorder or confusion (*stuffed the papers together pell-mell*). —adj. confused, tumultous. —n. confusion; a mixture. [F *pêle-mêle*, OF *pesle mesle, mesle pesle*, etc., redupl. of *mesle* f. *mesler* mix]

pellucid /prɪˈluːsɪd, -ˈljuːsɪd/ adj. **1** (of water, light, etc.) transparent, clear. **2** (of style, speech, etc.) not confused; clear. **3** mentally clear. □□ **pellucidity** /-ˈsɪdɪtɪ/ n. **pellucidly** adv. [L *pellucidus* f. *perlucēre* (as PER-, *lucēre* shine)]

Pelmanism /ˈpelmənɪz(ə)m/ n. **1** a system of memory-training orig. devised by the Pelman Institute. **2** a card-game based on this. □□ **Pelmanize** v.tr. (also -ise).

pelmet /ˈpelmɪt/ n. a narrow border of cloth, wood, etc. above esp. a window, concealing the curtain rail. [prob. f. F PALMETTE]

Peloponnese /ˈpeləpəˌniːs/ (Greek **Pelopónnisos** /ˌpeləˈpɒnɪˌsɒs/) the mountainous southern peninsula of Greece, connected to the mainland by the Isthmus of Corinth; pop. (1981) 1,012,500. Its Greek name means 'island of Pelops'.

Peloponnesian War /ˌpeləpəˈniːʃ(ə)n/ the war of 431–404 BC fought against Athens by Sparta and her allies, hostile to the Athenian empire. It ended in the total defeat of Athens and the transfer, for a brief period, of the leadership of Greece to Sparta.

Pelops /ˈpiːlɒps/ *Gk Mythol.* son of Tantalus, brother of Niobe, and father of Atreus. (See TANTALUS.)

pelorus /pɪˈlɔːrəs/ n. a sighting device like a ship's compass for taking bearings. [perh. f. *Pelorus*, reputed name of Hannibal's pilot]

pelota /pɪˈlɒtə, pɪˈləʊtə/ n. a Basque or Spanish game played in a walled court with a ball and a basket-like structure fitted over the hand. It was originally played with the bare hand, a glove, or a short bat; the basket-glove (*chistera*) was adopted in about 1860. [Sp., = ball, augment. of *pella* f. L *pila*]

pelt¹ /pelt/ v. & n. —v. 1 tr. (usu. foll. by *with*) **a** hurl many small missiles at. **b** strike repeatedly with missiles. **c** assail (a person etc.) with insults, abuse, etc. 2 intr. (usu. foll. by *down*) (of rain etc.) fall quickly and torrentially. 3 intr. run fast. 4 intr. (often foll. by *at*) fire repeatedly. —n. the act or an instance of pelting. □ **at full pelt** as fast as possible. [16th c.: orig. unkn.]

pelt² /pelt/ n. 1 the undressed skin of a fur-bearing mammal. 2 the skin of a sheep, goat, etc. with short wool, or stripped ready for tanning. 3 *joc.* the human skin. □□ **peltry** n. [ME f. obs. *pellet* skin, dimin. of *pel* f. AF *pell*, OF *pel*, or back-form. f. *peltry*, AF *pelterie*, OF *peleterie* f. *peletier* furrier, ult. f. L *pellis* skin]

pelta /ˈpeltə/ n. (*pl.* **peltae** /-tiː/) 1 a small light shield used by the ancient Greeks, Romans, etc. 2 *Bot.* a shieldlike structure. □□ **peltate** adj. [L f. Gk *peltē*]

pelvic /ˈpelvɪk/ adj. of or relating to the pelvis. □ **pelvic girdle** the bony or cartilaginous structure in vertebrates to which the posterior limbs are attached.

pelvis /ˈpelvɪs/ n. (*pl.* **pelvises** or **pelves** /-viːz/) 1 a basin-shaped cavity at the lower end of the torso of most vertebrates, formed from the innominate bone with the sacrum and other vertebrae. 2 the basin-like cavity of the kidney. [L, = basin]

Pemba /ˈpembə/ 1 a seaport in NE Mozambique; pop. (1980) 41,200. 2 an island off the east coast of Tanzania; pop. (est. 1985) 256,950.

Pembs. abbr. Pembrokeshire (a former county in Wales).

pemmican /ˈpemɪkən/ n. 1 a cake of dried pounded meat mixed with melted fat, orig. made by N. American Indians. 2 beef so treated and flavoured with currants etc. for use by Arctic travellers etc. [Cree *pimecan* f. *pime* fat]

pemphigus /ˈpemfɪgəs/ n. Med. the formation of watery blisters or eruptions on the skin. □□ **pemphigoid** adj. **pemphigous** adj. [mod.L f. Gk *pemphix -igos* bubble]

PEN abbr. International Association of Poets, Playwrights, Editors, Essayists, and Novelists.

Pen. abbr. Peninsula.

pen¹ /pen/ n. & v. —n. 1 an instrument for writing or drawing with ink, orig. consisting of a shaft with a sharpened quill or metal nib, now more widely applied. 2 **a** (usu. prec. by *the*) the occupation of writing. **b** a style of writing. 3 *Zool.* the internal feather-shaped cartilaginous shell of certain cuttlefish, esp. squid. —v.tr. (**penned**, **penning**) 1 write. 2 compose and write. □ **pen and ink** n. 1 the instruments of writing. 2 writing. **pen-and-ink** adj. drawn or written with ink. **pen-feather** a quill-feather of a bird's wing. **pen-friend** a friend communicated with by letter only. **pen-light** a small electric torch shaped like a fountain-pen. **pen-name** a literary pseudonym. **pen-pal** colloq. = *pen-friend*. **pen-pusher** colloq. derog. a clerical worker. **pen-pushing** colloq. derog. clerical work. **put pen to paper** begin writing. [ME f. OF *penne* f. L *penna* feather]

pen² /pen/ n. & v. —n. 1 a small enclosure for cows, sheep, poultry, etc. 2 a place of confinement. 3 an enclosure for sheltering submarines. 4 a Jamaican farm or plantation. —v.tr. (**penned**, **penning**) (often foll. by *in*, *up*) enclose or shut in a pen. [OE *penn*, of unkn. orig.]

pen³ /pen/ n. a female swan. [16th c.: orig. unkn.]

pen⁴ /pen/ n. US sl. = PENITENTIARY n. 1. [abbr.]

penal /ˈpiːn(ə)l/ adj. 1 **a** of or concerning punishment or its infliction (*penal laws; a penal sentence; a penal colony*). **b** (of an offence) punishable, esp. by law. 2 extremely severe (*penal taxation*). □ **penal servitude** hist. imprisonment with compulsory labour. □□ **penally** adv. [ME f. OF *penal* or L *poenalis* f. *poena* PAIN]

penalize /ˈpiːnəˌlaɪz/ v.tr. (also **-ise**) 1 subject (a person) to a penalty or comparative disadvantage. 2 make or declare (an action) penal. □□ **penalization** /-ˈzeɪʃ(ə)n/ n.

penalty /ˈpenəltɪ/ n. (*pl.* **-ies**) 1 **a** a punishment, esp. a fine, for a breach of law, contract, etc. **b** a fine paid. 2 a disadvantage, loss, etc., esp. as a result of one's own actions (*paid the penalty for his carelessness*). 3 **a** a disadvantage imposed on a competitor or side in a game etc. for a breach of the rules etc. **b** (attrib.) awarded against a side incurring a penalty (*penalty kick; penalty goal*). 4 *Bridge* etc. points gained by opponents when a contract is not fulfilled. □ **penalty area** *Football* the ground in front of the goal in which a foul by defenders involves the award of a penalty kick. **penalty box** *Ice Hockey* an area reserved for penalized players and some officials. **the penalty of** a disadvantage resulting from (a quality etc.). **penalty rate** *Austral.* an increased rate of pay for overtime. **under** (or on) **penalty of** under the threat of (dismissal etc.). [AF *penalte* (unrecorded), F *pénalité* f. med.L *penalitas* (as PENAL)]

penance /ˈpenəns/ n. & v. —n. 1 an act of self-punishment as reparation for guilt. 2 **a** (in the RC and Orthodox Church) a sacrament including confession of and absolution for a sin. **b** a penalty imposed esp. by a priest, or undertaken voluntarily, for a sin. —v.tr. impose a penance on. □ **do penance** perform a penance. [ME f. OF f. L *paenitentia* (as PENITENT)]

Penang /pɪˈnæŋ/ (also **Pinang**) 1 an island off the coast of the Malay peninsula. 2 a State of Malaysia consisting of this island and a coastal strip on the mainland; pop. (1980) 954,600; capital, George Town (on Penang island).

penannular /penˈænjʊlə(r)/ adj. almost ringlike. [L *paene* almost + ANNULAR]

penates /pɪˈnɑːtiːz, -teɪz/ n.pl. Rom. Hist. the household gods, esp. of the storeroom, worshipped in close conjunction with Vesta and the lares (see entry) by households in ancient Rome. [L f. *penus* provision of food]

pence pl. of PENNY.

penchant /ˈpɑ̃ʃɑ̃/ n. an inclination or liking (*has a penchant for old films*). [F, pres. part. of *pencher* incline]

pencil /ˈpensɪl/ n. & v. —n. 1 (often attrib.) **a** an instrument for writing or drawing, usu. consisting of a thin rod of graphite etc. enclosed in a wooden cylinder (*a pencil sketch*). **b** a similar instrument with a metal or plastic cover and retractable lead. **c** a cosmetic in pencil form. 2 (attrib.) resembling a pencil in shape (*pencil skirt*). 3 *Optics* a set of rays meeting at a point. 4 *Geom.* a figure formed by a set of straight lines meeting at a point. 5 a draughtsman's art or style. —v.tr. (**pencilled**, **pencilling**; US **penciled**, **penciling**) 1 tint or mark with or as if with a pencil. 2 (usu. foll. by *in*) **a** write, esp. tentatively or provisionally (*have pencilled in the 29th for our meeting*). **b** (esp. as **pencilled** adj.) fill (an area) with soft pencil strokes (*pencilled in her eyebrows*). □ **pencil-case** a container for pencils etc. **pencil-sharpener** a device for sharpening a pencil by rotating it against a cutting edge. □□ **penciller** n. [ME f. OF *pincel* ult. f. L *penicillum* paintbrush, dimin. of *peniculus* brush, dimin. of *penis* tail]

pendant /ˈpend(ə)nt/ n. (also **pendent**) 1 a hanging jewel etc., esp. one attached to a necklace, bracelet, etc. 2 a light fitting, ornament, etc., hanging from a ceiling. 3 *Naut.* **a** a short rope hanging from the head of a mast etc., used for attaching tackles. **b** = PENNANT 1. 4 the shank and ring of a pocket-watch by which it is suspended. 5 /ˈpend(ə)nt, ˈpɑ̃dɑ̃/ (usu. foll. by *to*) a match, companion, parallel, complement, etc. [ME f. OF f. *pendre* hang f. L *pendere*]

pendent /ˈpend(ə)nt/ adj. (also **pendant**) 1 **a** hanging. **b** overhanging. 2 undecided; pending. 3 *Gram.* (esp. of a sentence) incomplete; not having a finite verb (*pendent nominative*). □□ **pendency** *n*. [ME (as PENDANT)]

pendente lite /penˌdentɪ ˈlaɪtɪ/ *adv. Law* during the progress of a suit. [L]

pendentive /penˈdentɪv/ *n. Archit.* a curved triangle of vaulting formed by the intersection of a dome with its supporting arches. [F *pendentif -ive* (adj.) (as PENDANT)]

Penderecki /ˌpendəˈretskɪ, Krzysztof (1933–), Polish composer. His music frequently uses unorthodox means for effect, including sounds drawn from extra-musical sources and note-clusters, and his best-known works have religious themes. In 1960 he composed a *Threnody to the Victims of Hiroshima*.

pending /ˈpendɪŋ/ *adj. & prep.* —*predic.adj.* **1** awaiting decision or settlement, undecided (*a settlement was pending*). **2** about to come into existence (*patent pending*). —*prep.* **1** during (*pending these negotiations*). **2** until (*pending his return*). □ **pending-tray** a tray for documents, letters, etc., awaiting attention. [after F *pendant* (see PENDENT)]

pendragon /penˈdrægən/ *n. hist.* an ancient British or Welsh prince (often as a title). (See UTHER PENDRAGON.) [Welsh, = chief war-leader, f. *pen* head + *dragon* standard]

penduline /ˈpendjʊˌlaɪn/ *adj.* **1** (of a nest) suspended. **2** (of a bird) of a kind that builds such a nest. [F (as PENDULOUS)]

pendulous /ˈpendjʊləs/ *adj.* **1** (of ears, breasts, flowers, bird's nests, etc.) hanging down; drooping and esp. swinging. **2** oscillating. □□ **pendulously** *adv.* [L *pendulus* f. *pendēre* hang]

pendulum /ˈpendjʊləm/ *n.* **1** a weight suspended so as to swing freely, or oscillate. **2** an instrument consisting of a rod with a weight or 'bob' at the end, so suspended as to swing to and fro by the action of gravity and used for various mechanical etc. purposes, especially as an essential part of a clock, serving (by the evenness of its vibrations) to regulate and control the movement of the works so as to maintain a constant rate of going and enable it to keep regular time. The principle of the pendulum was discovered by Galileo in the 16th c. □ **swing of the pendulum** the tendency of public opinion to oscillate between extremes, esp. between political parties. [L neut. adj. (as PENDULOUS)]

Penelope /pɪˈneləpɪ/ *Gk legend* the wife of Odysseus. When her husband did not return after the fall of Troy she was pressed to marry one of her numerous suitors, but put them off for a while by saying that she would marry only when she had finished the piece of weaving on which she was engaged, and every night unravelling the work she had done during the day.

peneplain /ˈpiːnɪˌpleɪn/ *n. Geol.* a fairly flat area of land produced by erosion. [L *paene* almost + PLAIN¹]

penetralia /ˌpenɪˈtreɪlɪə/ *n.pl.* **1** innermost shrines or recesses. **2** secret or hidden parts; mysteries. [L, neut. pl. of *penetralis* interior (as PENETRATE)]

penetrate /ˈpenɪˌtreɪt/ *v.* **1** *tr.* **a** find access into or through, esp. forcibly. **b** (usu. foll. by *with*) imbue (a person or thing) with; permeate. **2** *tr.* see into, find out, or discern (a person's mind, the truth, a meaning, etc.). **3** *tr.* see through (darkness, fog, etc.) (*could not penetrate the gloom*). **4** *intr.* be absorbed by the mind (*my hint did not penetrate*). **5** *tr.* (as **penetrating** *adj.*) **a** having or suggesting sensitivity or insight (*a penetrating remark*). **b** (of a voice etc.) easily heard through or above other sounds; piercing. **6** *tr.* (of a man) put the penis into the vagina of (a woman). **7** *intr.* (usu. foll. by *into, through, to*) make a way. □□ **penetrable** /-trəb(ə)l/ *adj.* **penetrability** /-trəˈbɪlɪtɪ/ *n.* **penetrant** *adj. & n.* **penetratingly** *adv.* **penetration** /-ˈtreɪʃ(ə)n/ *n.* **penetrative** /-trətɪv/ *adj.* **penetrator** *n.* [L *penetrare* place or enter within f. *penitus* interior]

penguin /ˈpeŋgwɪn/ *n.* any flightless sea bird of the family Spheniscidae of the southern hemisphere, with black upper-parts and white under-parts, and wings developed into scaly flippers for swimming underwater. [16th c., orig. = great auk: orig. unkn.]

penholder /ˈpenˌhəʊldə(r)/ *n.* the esp. wooden shaft of a pen with a metal nib.

penicillate /ˈpenɪsɪlət, -ˌsɪlɪt/ *adj. Biol.* **1** having or forming a

small tuft or tufts. **2** marked with streaks as of a pencil or brush. [L *penicillum*: see PENCIL]

penicillin /ˌpenɪˈsɪlɪn/ *n.* any of various antibiotics produced naturally by moulds of the genus *Penicillium*, or synthetically, and able to prevent the growth of certain disease-causing bacteria. It was the first antibiotic to be used therapeutically, during the Second World War. (See FLOREY.) [mod.L *Penicillium* genus name f. L *penicillum*: see PENCIL]

penile /ˈpiːnaɪl/ *adj.* of or concerning the penis. [mod.L *penilis*]

penillion *pl.* of PENNILL.

peninsula /pɪˈnɪnsjʊlə/ *n.* a piece of land almost surrounded by water or projecting far into a sea or lake etc. □□ **peninsular** *adj.* [L *paeninsula* f. *paene* almost + *insula* island]

Peninsular War the campaign waged on the Spanish peninsula between the French and the British, the latter assisted by Spanish and Portuguese allies, from 1808 to 1814 during the Napoleonic Wars. Although an early British expedition (commanded in the later stages by Sir John Moore) was forced to evacuate the peninsula in 1809 after its Spanish allies had been defeated, a second expedition, led by Wellington, finally drove the French back over the Pyrenees in early 1814 after a long and bloody campaign in which the advantage swung from one side to the other several times.

penis /ˈpiːnɪs/ *n.* (*pl.* **penises** or **penes** /-niːz/) **1** the male organ of copulation and (in mammals) urination. **2** the male copulatory organ in lower vertebrates. [L, = tail, penis]

penitent /ˈpenɪt(ə)nt/ *adj. & n.* —*adj.* regretting and wishing to atone for sins etc.; repentant. —*n.* **1** a repentant sinner. **2** a person doing penance under the direction of a confessor. **3** (in *pl.*) various RC orders associated for mutual discipline etc. □□ **penitence** *n.* **penitently** *adv.* [ME f. OF f. L *paenitens* f. *paenitēre* repent]

penitential /ˌpenɪˈtenʃ(ə)l/ *adj.* of or concerning penitence or penance. □ **penitential psalms** seven psalms (6, 32, 38, 51, 102, 130, 143) expressing penitence. □□ **penitentially** *adv.* [OF *penitencial* f. LL *paenitentialis* f. *paenitentia* penitence (as PENITENT)]

penitentiary /ˌpenɪˈtenʃərɪ/ *n. & adj.* —*n.* (*pl.* **-ies**) **1** *US* a reformatory prison. **2** an office in the papal court deciding questions of penance, dispensations, etc. —*adj.* **1** of or concerning penance. **2** of or concerning reformatory treatment. **3** *US* (of an offence) making a culprit liable to a prison sentence. □ **Grand Penitentiary** a cardinal presiding over the penitentiary. [ME f. med.L *paenitentiarius* (adj. & n.) (as PENITENT)]

penknife /ˈpennaɪf/ *n.* a small folding knife, esp. for carrying in a pocket.

penman /ˈpenmən/ *n.* (*pl.* **-men**) **1** a person who writes by hand with a specified skill (*a good penman*). **2** an author. □□ **penmanship** *n.*

Penn /pen/, William (1644–1718), Quaker and founder of Pennsylvania, eldest son of Admiral Sir William Penn who captured Jamaica from the Dutch (1655). Sent down from Oxford University in 1661 for refusing to conform with the restored Anglicanism, he was imprisoned in the Tower for writing in defence of Quaker practices. Acquitted in 1670, he became increasingly interested in the foundation of a colony in America which would ensure freedom of conscience for Quakers and others; this he achieved when in 1682 Charles II granted him a charter to a large tract of land in North America, for which he drew up a constitution permitting all forms of worship compatible with monotheism and religious liberty.

Penn. *abbr.* (also **Penna.**) Pennsylvania.

pennant /ˈpenənt/ *n.* **1** *Naut.* a tapering flag, esp. that flown at the masthead of a vessel in commission. **2** = PENDANT 3a. **3** = PENNON. **4** *US* a flag denoting a sports championship etc. [blend of PENDANT and PENNON]

penniless /ˈpenɪlɪs/ *adj.* having no money; destitute. □□ **pennilessly** *adv.* **pennilessness** *n.*

pennill /ˈpenɪl/ *n.* (*pl.* **penillion** /peˈnɪljən/) (usu. in *pl.*) an improvised stanza sung to a harp accompaniment at an eisteddfod etc. [Welsh f. *penn* head]

Pennines /ˈpenaɪnz/ *n.pl.* (also **Pennine Chain**) a range of hills in northern England extending northwards from the Peak District in Derbyshire to the Scottish border, described as the 'Backbone of England'.

pennon /'penən/ n. **1** a long narrow flag, triangular or swallow-tailed, esp. as the military ensign of lancer regiments. **2** *Naut.* a long pointed streamer on a ship. **3** a flag. □□ **pennoned** adj. [ME f. OF f. L *penna* feather]

penn'orth var. of PENNYWORTH.

Pennsylvania /ˌpensɪl'veɪnɪə/ a State of the north-eastern US, founded by William Penn and named after his father, Admiral Sir William Penn; pop. (est. 1985) 11,864,700; capital, Harrisburg. It was one of the original 13 States of the US (1787). □ **Pennsylvania Dutch 1** a dialect of High German spoken by descendants of 17th–18th-c. German and Swiss immigrants to Pennsylvania etc. **2** (as *pl.*) these settlers or their descendants.

Pennsylvanian /ˌpensɪl'veɪnɪən/ n. & adj. —n. **1** a native or inhabitant of Pennsylvania. **2** (prec. by *the*) esp. *US Geol.* the upper Carboniferous period or system. —adj. **1** of or relating to Pennsylvania. **2** esp. *US Geol.* of or relating to the upper Carboniferous period or system.

penny /'penɪ/ n. (*pl.* for separate coins **-ies**, for a sum of money **pence** /pens/) **1** a British coin and monetary unit equal to one-hundredth of a pound. ¶ Abbr.: **p. 2** *hist.* a former British bronze coin and monetary unit equal to one-two-hundred-and-fortieth of a pound. ¶ Abbr.: **d.** (See below.) **3** *US colloq.* a one-cent coin. **4** *Bibl.* a denarius. □ **in for a penny, in for a pound** an exhortation to total commitment to an undertaking. **like a bad penny** continually returning when unwanted. **pennies from heaven** unexpected benefits. **penny black** the first adhesive postage stamp (1840, value one penny), printed in black. **penny cress** *Bot.* a plant, *Thlaspi arvense*, with flat round pods. **penny dreadful** *Brit.* a cheap sensational comic or story-book. **the penny drops** *colloq.* one begins to understand at last. **penny farthing** *Brit.* an early type of bicycle with one large and one small wheel. (See BICYCLE.) **a penny for your thoughts** a request to a thoughtful person to confide in the speaker. **penny-in-the-slot** (of a machine) activated by a coin pushed into a slot. **penny-pincher** a niggardly person. **penny-pinching** n. meanness. —adj. mean. **penny post** *hist.* the system of carrying letters at a standard charge of one penny each instead of at varying rates according to distance, especially that established in the UK in 1840 at the instigation of Sir Rowland Hill, who invented (amongst other things) an adhesive stamp. **penny whistle** a tin pipe with six holes giving different notes. **penny wise** too careful in saving small amounts. **penny wise and pound foolish** mean in small expenditures but wasteful of large amounts. **a pretty penny** a large sum of money. **two a penny** almost worthless though easily obtained. [OE *penig, penning* f. Gmc, perh. rel. to PAWN²]
The coining of silver pennies for general circulation in Britain ceased with the reign of Charles II; a small number have since been regularly coined as Maundy money. Copper pennies began to be coined in 1797, and the term 'copper' for 'penny' has remained in use long after this ceased to be the material used.

-penny /pənɪ/ comb. form *Brit.* forming attributive adjectives meaning 'costing . . . pence' (esp. in pre-decimal currency) (*fivepenny*).

pennyroyal /ˌpenɪ'rɔɪəl/ n. **1** a creeping mint, *Mentha pulegium*, cultivated for its supposed medicinal properties. **2** *US* an aromatic plant, *Hedeoma pulegioides*. [app. f. earlier *puliol(e) ryall* f. AF *puliol*, OF *pouliol* ult. f. L *pulegium* + real ROYAL]

pennyweight /'penɪˌweɪt/ n. a unit of weight, 24 grains or one-twentieth of an ounce troy.

pennywort /'penɪˌwɜːt/ n. any of several wild plants with rounded leaves, esp.: **1** (**wall pennywort**) *Umbilicus rupestris*, growing in crevices. **2** (**marsh** or **water pennywort**) *Hydrocotyle vulgaris*, growing in marshy places. [ME, f. PENNY + WORT]

pennyworth /'penɪˌwɜːθ/ n. (also **penn'orth** /'penəθ/) **1** as much as can be bought for a penny. **2** a bargain of a specified kind (*a bad pennyworth*). □ **not a pennyworth** not the least bit.

penology /piː'nɒlədʒɪ/ n. the study of the punishment of crime and of prison management. □□ **penological** /-nə'lɒdʒɪk(ə)l/ adj. **penologist** n. [L *poena* penalty + -LOGY]

pensée /pɑ̃'seɪ/ n. a thought or reflection put into literary form; an aphorism. [F]

pensile /'pensaɪl/ adj. **1** hanging down; pendulous. **2** (of a bird etc.) building a pensile nest. [L *pensilis* f. *pendēre pens-* hang]

pension¹ /'penʃ(ə)n/ n. & v. —n. **1 a** a regular payment made by a government to people above a specified age, to widows, or to the disabled. **b** similar payments made by an employer etc. on the retirement of an employee. **2 a** a pension paid to a scientist, artist, etc. for services to the state, or to fund work. **b** any pension paid esp. by a government on charitable grounds. —v.tr. **1** grant a pension to. **2** bribe with a pension. □ **pension off 1** dismiss with a pension. **2** cease to employ or use. □□ **pensionless** adj. [ME f. OF f. L *pensio -onis* payment f. *pendere pens-* pay]

pension² /pɑ̃'sjɔ̃/ n. a European, esp. French, boarding-house providing full or half board at a fixed rate. □ **en pension** /ɔ̃/ as a boarder. [F: see PENSION¹]

pensionable /'penʃənəb(ə)l/ adj. **1** entitled to a pension. **2** (of a service, job, etc.) entitling an employee to a pension. □□ **pensionability** /-'bɪlɪtɪ/ n.

pensionary /'penʃənərɪ/ adj. & n. —adj. of or concerning a pension. —n. (*pl.* **-ies**) **1** a pensioner. **2** a creature; a hireling. □ **Grand Pensionary** *hist.* the first minister of Holland and Zealand (1619–1794). [med.L *pensionarius* (as PENSION¹)]

pensioner /'penʃənə(r)/ n. a recipient of a pension, esp. the retirement pension. [ME f. AF *pensionner*, OF *pensionnier* (as PENSION¹)]

pensive /'pensɪv/ adj. **1** deep in thought. **2** sorrowfully thoughtful. □□ **pensively** adv. **pensiveness** n. [ME f. OF *pensif, -ive* f. *penser* think f. L *pensare* frequent. of *pendere pens-* weigh]

penstemon var. of PENTSTEMON.

penstock /'penstɒk/ n. **1** a sluice; a floodgate. **2** *US* a channel for conveying water to a water-wheel. [PEN² in sense 'mill-dam' + STOCK]

pent /pent/ adj. (often foll. by *in, up*) closely confined; shut in (*pent up feelings*). [past part. of *pend* var. of PEN² v.]

penta- /'pentə/ comb. form **1** five. **2** *Chem.* (forming the names of compounds) containing five atoms or groups of a specified kind (*pentachloride; pentoxide*). [Gk f. *pente* five]

pentachord /'pentəˌkɔːd/ n. **1** a musical instrument with five strings. **2** a series of five musical notes.

pentacle /'pentək(ə)l/ n. a figure used as a symbol, esp. in magic, e.g. a pentagram. [med.L *pentaculum* (as PENTA-)]

pentad /'pentæd/ n. **1** the number five. **2** a group of five. [Gk *pentas -ados* f. *pente* five]

pentadactyl /ˌpentə'dæktɪl/ adj. *Zool.* having five toes or fingers.

Pentagon /'pentəgən/ n., **the** the headquarters of the US Department of Defense, near Washington, DC. Built in 1941–3 in the form of five concentric pentagons, it covers 13.8 hectares (34 acres) and is one of the world's largest office buildings. The name is used allusively for the US military leadership.

pentagon /'pentəgən/ n. a plane figure with five sides and angles. □□ **pentagonal** /-'tægən(ə)l/ adj. [F *pentagone* or f. LL *pentagonus* f. Gk *pentagōnon* (as PENTA-, -GON)]

pentagram /'pentəˌgræm/ n. a five-pointed star formed by extending the sides of a pentagon both ways until they intersect, formerly used as a mystic symbol. [Gk *pentagrammon* (as PENTA-, -GRAM)]

pentagynous /pen'tædʒɪnəs/ adj. *Bot.* having five pistils.

pentahedron /ˌpentə'hiːdrən/ n. a solid figure with five faces. □□ **pentahedral** adj.

pentamerous /pen'tæmərəs/ adj. **1** *Bot.* having five parts in a flower-whorl. **2** *Zool.* having five joints or parts.

pentameter /pen'tæmɪtə(r)/ n. **1** a verse of five feet, e.g. English iambic verse of ten syllables. **2** a form of Gk or Latin dactylic verse composed of two halves each of two feet and a long syllable, used in elegiac verse. [L f. Gk *pentametros* (as PENTA-, -METER)]

pentandrous /pen'tændrəs/ adj. *Bot.* having five stamens.

pentane /'penteɪn/ n. Chem. a hydrocarbon of the alkane series. ¶ Chem. formula: C_5H_{12}. [Gk pente five + ALKANE]

pentangle /'penˌtæŋg(ə)l/ n. = PENTAGRAM. [ME perh. f. med.L pentaculum PENTACLE, assim. to L angulus ANGLE]

pentanoic acid /ˌpentəˈnəʊɪk/ n. Chem. a colourless liquid carboxylic acid used in making perfumes. [PENTANE]

pentaprism /'pentəˌprɪz(ə)m/ n. a five-sided prism with two silvered surfaces used in a viewfinder to obtain a constant deviation of all rays of light through 90°.

Pentateuch /'pentəˌtjuːk/ n. the first five books of the Old Testament, traditionally ascribed to Moses but now held by scholars to have been compiled from documents dating from 9th to 5th c. BC incorporating material from oral traditions of varying dates. □□ **pentateuchal** /-'tjuːk(ə)l/ adj. [eccl.L pentateuchus f. eccl.Gk pentateukhos (as PENTA-, teukhos implement, book)]

pentathlon /pen'tæθlən/ n. an athletic contest in which each competitor takes part in the five different events which it comprises. It was a feature of the Olympic Games in ancient Greece. The modern men's pentathlon consists of fencing, shooting, swimming, riding, and cross-country running; the women's pentathlon consists of sprinting, hurdling, long jump, high jump, and putting the shot. □□ **pentathlete** /-'tæθliːt/ n. [Gk f. pente five + athlon contest]

pentatonic /ˌpentəˈtɒnɪk/ adj. Mus. 1 consisting of five notes. 2 relating to such a scale.

pentavalent /ˌpentəˈveɪlənt/ adj. Chem. having a valency of five; quinquevalent.

Pentecost /'pentɪˌkɒst/ n. 1 a Whit Sunday. b a festival celebrating the descent of the Holy Spirit on Whit Sunday. 2 a the Jewish harvest festival, on the fiftieth day after the second day of Passover (Lev. 23: 15–16). b a synagogue ceremony on the anniversary of the giving of the Law on Mount Sinai. [OE pentecosten & OF pentecoste, f. eccl.L pentecoste f. Gk pentēkostē (hēmera) fiftieth (day)]

Pentecostal /ˌpentɪˈkɒst(ə)l/ adj. & n. —adj. (also **pentecostal**) 1 of or relating to Pentecost. 2 of or designating Christian sects and individuals who emphasize the gifts of the Holy Spirit, are often fundamentalist in outlook, and express religious feelings by clapping, shouting, dancing, etc. (See below.) —n. a Pentecostalist. □□ **Pentecostalism** n. **Pentecostalist** adj. & n.
   The Pentecostal religious movement began in the early 20th c. among believers seeking the same experience and gifts as those recorded in Acts 2: 1–4 at Pentecost. Emphasis is on the corporate element in worship (often involving great spontaneity) and speaking in 'tongues' (often generally unintelligible utterances, arising from the intensity of emotion and religious experience), with prophecy, healing, and exorcism. Manifestations of this nature, occurring in revivalist meetings at Los Angeles in 1906, were the first to attract worldwide attention.

Penthesilea /ˌpenθesɪˈliːə/ Gk legend the queen of the Amazons, who came to the help of Troy after the death of Hector and was slain by Achilles.

penthouse /'penthaʊs/ n. 1 a house or flat on the roof or the top floor of a tall building. 2 a sloping roof, esp. of an outhouse built on to another building. 3 an awning, a canopy. [ME pentis f. OF apentis, -dis, f. med.L appendicium, in LL = appendage, f. L (as APPEND): infl. by HOUSE]

pentimento /ˌpentɪˈmentəʊ/ n. (pl. **pentimenti** /-tiː/) the phenomenon of earlier painting showing through a layer or layers of paint on a canvas. [It., = repentance]

pentobarbitone /ˌpentəˈbɑːbɪˌtəʊn/ n. (US **pentobarbital** /-ˌtæl/) a narcotic and sedative barbiturate drug formerly used to relieve insomnia. [PENTA-, BARBITONE, BARBITAL]

pentode /'pentəʊd/ n. a thermionic valve having five electrodes. [Gk pente five + hodos way]

pentose /'pentəʊz/ n. Biochem. any monosaccharide containing five carbon atoms, including ribose. [PENTA- + -OSE²]

pent-roof /'pentruːf/ n. a roof sloping in one direction only. [PENTHOUSE + ROOF]

pentstemon /pent'stiːmən, 'pentstəmən/ n. (also **penstemon**

/pen'stiːmən/) any American herbaceous plant of the genus Penstemon, with showy flowers and five stamens, one of which is sterile. [mod.L, irreg. f. PENTA- + Gk stēmōn warp, used for 'stamen']

pentyl /'pentɪl/ n. = AMYL. [PENTANE + -YL]

penult /pɪ'nʌlt, 'piːnʌlt/ n. & adj. —n. the last but one (esp. syllable). —adj. last but one. [abbr. of L paenultimus (see PENULTIMATE) or of PENULTIMATE]

penultimate /pɪ'nʌltɪmət/ adj. & n. —adj. last but one. —n. 1 the last but one. 2 the last syllable but one. [L paenultimus f. paene almost + ultimus last, after ultimate]

penumbra /pɪ'nʌmbrə/ n. (pl. **penumbrae** /-briː/ or **penumbras**) 1 a the partly shaded region around the shadow of an opaque body, esp. that around the total shadow of the moon or earth in an eclipse. b the less dark outer part of a sunspot. 2 a partial shadow. □□ **penumbral** adj. [mod.L f. L paene almost + UMBRA shadow]

penurious /pɪ'njʊərɪəs/ adj. 1 poor; destitute. 2 stingy; grudging. 3 scanty. □□ **penuriously** adv. **penuriousness** n. [med.L penuriosus (as PENURY)]

penury /'penjʊrɪ/ n. (pl. **-ies**) 1 destitution; poverty. 2 a lack; scarcity. [ME f. L penuria, perh. rel. to paene almost]

Penza /'pjenzə/ a city in the Soviet Union situated on the River Sura, a tributary of the Volga; pop. (est. 1987) 540,000.

peon /'piːən/ n. 1 a a Spanish American day labourer or farmworker. b a poor or destitute South American. 2 /'piːən, pjuːn/ an Indian office messenger, attendant, or orderly. 3 a bullfighter's assistant. 4 hist. a worker held in servitude in the southern US. □□ **peonage** n. [Port. peão & Sp. peon f. med.L pedo -onis walker f. L pes pedis foot: cf. PAWN¹]

peony /'piːənɪ/ n. (also **paeony**) (pl. **-ies**) any herbaceous plant of the genus Paeonia, with large globular red, pink, or white flowers, often double in cultivated varieties. [OE peonie f. L paeonia f. Gk paiōnia f. Paiōn, physician of the gods]

people /'piːp(ə)l/ n. & v. —n. 1 (usu. as pl.) a persons composing a community, tribe, race, nation, etc. (the English people; a warlike people; the peoples of the Commonwealth). b a group of persons of a usu. specified kind (the chosen people; these people here; right-thinking people). 2 (prec. by the; treated as pl.) a the mass of people in a country etc. not having special rank or position. b these considered as an electorate (the people will reject it). 3 parents or other relatives (my people are French). 4 a subjects, armed followers, a retinue, etc. b a congregation of a parish priest etc. 5 persons in general (people do not like rudeness). —v.tr. (usu. foll. by with) 1 fill with people, animals, etc.; populate. 2 (esp. as **peopled** adj.) inhabit; occupy; fill (thickly peopled). □ **people's democracy** a political system, esp. in E. Europe, with power regarded as invested in the people. **Peoples of the Sea** see SEA PEOPLES. [ME f. AF poeple, people, OF pople, peuple, f. L populus]

People's Liberation Army the armed forces of the People's Republic of China, including all its land, sea, and air forces. The PLA traces its origins to an unsuccessful uprising by Communist-led troops against pro-Nationalist forces at Nanchang in Kiangsi Province on 1 August 1927, and this date is celebrated annually as its anniversary.

PEP abbr. Brit. 1 Political and Economic Planning. 2 Personal Equity Plan.

pep /pep/ n. & v. colloq. —n. vigour; go; spirit. —v.tr. (**pepped**, **pepping**) (usu. foll. by up) fill with vigour. □ **pep pill** a pill containing a stimulant drug. **pep talk** a usu. short talk intended to enthuse, encourage, etc. [abbr. of PEPPER]

peperino /ˌpepəˈriːnəʊ/ n. a light porous (esp. brown) volcanic rock formed of small grains of sand, cinders, etc. [It. f. pepere pepper]

peperoni var. of PEPPERONI.

peplum /'pepləm/ n. 1 a short flounce etc. at waist level, esp. of a blouse or jacket over a skirt. 2 Gk Antiq. a woman's outer garment. [L f. Gk peplos]

pepo /'piːpəʊ/ n. (pl. **-os**) any fleshy fruit of the melon or cucumber type, with numerous seeds and surrounded by a hard skin. [L, = pumpkin, f. Gk pepōn abbr. of pepōn sikuos ripe gourd]

b but   d dog   f few   g get   h he   j yes   k cat   l leg   m man   n no   p pen   r red   s sit   t top   v voice

pepper /ˈpepə(r)/ n. & v. —n. **1 a** a hot aromatic condiment from the dried berries of certain plants used whole or ground. **b** any climbing vine of the genus *Piper*, esp. *P. nigrum*, yielding these berries. **2** anything hot or pungent. **3 a** any plant of the genus *Capsicum*, esp. *C. annuum*. **b** the fruit of this used esp. as a vegetable or salad ingredient. **4** = CAYENNE. —v.tr. **1** sprinkle or treat with or as if with pepper. **2 a** pelt with missiles. **b** hurl abuse etc. at. **3** punish severely. □ **black pepper** the unripe ground or whole berries of *Piper nigrum* as a condiment. **green pepper** the unripe fruit of *Capsicum annuum*. **pepper-mill** a device for grinding pepper by hand. **pepper-pot 1** a small container with a perforated lid for sprinkling pepper. **2** a W. Indian dish of meat etc. stewed with cayenne pepper. **3** *colloq.* a Jamaican. **red** (or **yellow**) **pepper** the ripe fruit of *Capsicum annuum*. **sweet pepper** a pepper with a relatively mild taste. **white pepper** the ripe or husked ground or whole berries of *Piper nigrum* as a condiment. [OE *piper*, *pipor* f. L *piper* f. Gk *peperi* f. Skr. *pippalī*- berry, peppercorn]

pepperbox /ˈpepəˌbɒks/ n. = *pepper-pot*.

peppercorn /ˈpepəˌkɔːn/ n. **1** the dried berry of *Piper nigrum* as a condiment. **2** (in full **peppercorn rent**) a nominal rent.

peppermint /ˈpepəmɪnt/ n. **1 a** a mint plant, *Mentha piperita*, grown for the strong-flavoured oil obtained from its leaves. **b** the oil from this. **2** a sweet flavoured with peppermint. **3** *Austral.* any of various eucalyptuses yielding oil with a similar flavour. □□ **pepperminty** adj.

pepperoni /ˌpepəˈrəʊni/ n. (also **peperoni**) beef and pork sausage seasoned with pepper. [It. *peperone* chilli]

pepperwort /ˈpepəˌwɜːt/ n. any cruciferous plant of the genus *Lepidium*, esp. garden cress.

peppery /ˈpepəri/ adj. **1** of, like, or containing much, pepper. **2** hot-tempered. **3** pungent; stinging. □□ **pepperiness** n.

peppy /ˈpepi/ adj. (**peppier, peppiest**) *colloq.* vigorous, energetic, bouncy. □□ **peppily** adv. **peppiness** n.

pepsin /ˈpepsɪn/ n. an enzyme contained in the gastric juice, which hydrolyses proteins. [G f. Gk *pepsis* digestion]

peptic /ˈpeptɪk/ adj. concerning or promoting digestion. □ **peptic glands** glands secreting gastric juice. **peptic ulcer** an ulcer in the stomach or duodenum. [Gk *peptikos* able to digest (as PEPTONE)]

peptide /ˈpeptaɪd/ n. *Biochem.* any of a group of organic compounds consisting of two or more amino acids bonded in sequence. Some are important as hormones, others as antibiotics. Polypeptides are the constituents of proteins. [G *Peptid*, back-form. (as POLYPEPTIDE)]

peptone /ˈpeptəʊn/ n. a protein fragment formed by hydrolysis in the process of digestion. □□ **peptonize** /-təˌnaɪz/ v.tr. (also **-ise**). [G *Pepton* f. Gk *peptos*, neut. *pepton* cooked]

Pepys /piːps/, Samuel (1633–1703), English diarist. He became secretary of the Admiralty in 1672 but was deprived of his post in 1679 and committed to the Tower for his alleged complicity in the Popish Plot, being reappointed in 1684. Pepys is remembered for his *Diary* which remains an important document of contemporary life and manners, seen through the author's own experiences as Admiralty official and observer of court life, written with engaging sincerity and humanity. The *Diary* remained in cipher until 1825 when it was deciphered by John Smith.

per /pɜː(r)/ prep. **1** for each; for every (*two sweets per child; five miles per hour*). **2** by means of; by; through (*per post; per rail*). **3** (in full **as per**) in accordance with (*as per instructions*). **4** *Heraldry* in the direction of. □ **as per usual** *colloq.* as usual. [L]

per- /pɜː(r), pə(r)/ *prefix* **1** forming verbs, nouns, and adjectives meaning: **a** through; all over (*perforate; perforation; pervade*). **b** completely; very (*perfervid; perturb*). **c** to destruction; to the bad (*pervert; perdition*). **2** *Chem.* having the maximum of some element in combination, esp.: **a** in the names of binary compounds in *-ide* (*peroxide*). **b** in the names of oxides, acids, etc. in *-ic* (*perchloric; permanganic*). **c** in the names of salts of these acids (*perchlorate; permanganate*). [L *per-* (as PER)]

peradventure /ˌpərədˈventʃə(r), ˌper-/ adv. & n. archaic or joc. —adv. perhaps. —n. uncertainty; chance; conjecture; doubt (esp. *beyond* or *without peradventure*). [ME f. OF *per* or *par auenture* by chance (as PER, ADVENTURE)]

Perak /ˈpeərə, peˈræk/ a State of Malaysia, on the west side of the Malay Peninsula, a major tin-mining centre; pop. (1980) 1,743,650; capital, Ipoh.

perambulate /pəˈræmbjʊˌleɪt/ v. **1** tr. walk through, over, or about (streets, the country, etc.). **2** intr. walk from place to place. **3** tr. **a** travel through and inspect (territory). **b** formally establish the boundaries of (a parish etc.) by walking round them. □□ **perambulation** /-ˈleɪʃ(ə)n/ n. **perambulatory** adj. [L *perambulare perambulat-* (as PER-, *ambulare* walk)]

perambulator /pəˈræmbjʊˌleɪtə(r)/ n. *Brit. formal* = PRAM. [PERAMBULATE]

per annum /pər ˈænəm/ adv. for each year. [L]

percale /pəˈkeɪl/ n. a closely woven cotton fabric like calico. [F, of uncert. orig.]

per capita /pə ˈkæpɪtə/ adv. & adj. (also **per caput** /ˈkæpʊt/) for each person. [L, = by heads]

perceive /pəˈsiːv/ v.tr. **1** apprehend, esp. through the sight; observe. **2** (usu. foll. by *that, how*, etc. + clause) apprehend with the mind; understand. **3** regard mentally in a specified manner (*perceives the universe as infinite*). □□ **perceivable** adj. **perceiver** n. [ME f. OF *perçoivre*, f. L *percipere* (as PER-, *capere* take)]

per cent /pə ˈsent/ adv. & n. (US **percent**) —adv. in every hundred. —n. **1** percentage. **2** one part in every hundred (*half a per cent*). **3** (in pl.) *Brit.* public securities yielding interest of so much per cent (*three per cents*).

percentage /pəˈsentɪdʒ/ n. **1** a rate or proportion per cent. **2** a proportion. **3** *colloq.* personal benefit or advantage.

percentile /pəˈsentaɪl/ n. *Statistics* one of 99 values of a variable dividing a population into 100 equal groups as regards the value of that variable.

percept /ˈpɜːsept/ n. *Philos.* **1** an object of perception. **2** a mental concept resulting from perceiving, esp. by sight. [L *perceptum* perceived (thing), neut. past part. of *percipere* PERCEIVE, after *concept*]

perceptible /pəˈseptɪb(ə)l/ adj. capable of being perceived by the senses or intellect. □□ **perceptibility** /-ˈbɪlɪti/ n. **perceptibly** adv. [OF *perceptible* or LL *perceptibilis* f. L (as PERCEIVE)]

perception /pəˈsepʃ(ə)n/ n. **1 a** the faculty of perceiving. **b** an instance of this. **2** (often foll. by *of*) **a** the intuitive recognition of a truth, aesthetic quality, etc. **b** an instance of this (*a sudden perception of the true position*). **3** *Philos.* the ability of the mind to refer sensory information to an external object as its cause. □□ **perceptional** adj. **perceptual** /pəˈseptjʊəl/ adj. **perceptually** /pəˈseptjʊəli/ adv. [ME f. L *perceptio* (as PERCEIVE)]

perceptive /pəˈseptɪv/ adj. **1** capable of perceiving. **2** sensitive; discerning; observant (*a perceptive remark*). □□ **perceptively** adv. **perceptiveness** n. **perceptivity** /-ˈtɪvɪti/ n. [med.L *perceptivus* (as PERCEIVE)]

Perceval[1] /ˈpɜːsɪv(ə)l/, Sir. A legendary figure of great antiquity, found in French, German, and English poetry from the late 12th c. onwards. He is the hero of a number of legends, some of which are associated with the Holy Grail. (See CHRÉTIEN DE TROYES.)

Perceval[2] /ˈpɜːsɪv(ə)l/, Spencer (1762–1812), British Conservative statesman, Prime Minister 1809–12, who was shot dead in the lobby of the House of Commons by a deranged bankrupt with a grievance against the government.

perch[1] /pɜːtʃ/ n. & v. —n. **1** a usu. horizontal bar, branch, etc. used by a bird to rest on. **2** a usu. high or precarious place for a person or thing to rest on. **3** a measure of length, esp. for land, of 5½ yards (see GUNTER; cf. ROD, POLE). —v.intr. & tr. (usu. foll. by *on*) settle or rest, or cause to settle or rest on or as if on a perch etc. (*the bird perched on a branch; a town perched on a hill*). □ **knock a person off his perch 1** vanquish, destroy. **2** make less confident or secure. **square perch** 30¼ sq. yards. [ME f. OF *perche, percher* f. L *pertica* pole]

perch[2] /pɜːtʃ/ n. (pl. same or **perches**) any spiny-finned freshwater edible fish of the genus *Perca*, esp. *P. fluviatilis* of Europe. [ME f. OF *perche* f. L *perca* f. Gk *perkē*]

perchance /pə'tʃɑːns/ adv. archaic or poet. **1** by chance. **2** possibly; maybe. [ME f. AF par chance f. par by, CHANCE]

percher /'pɜːtʃə(r)/ n. any bird with feet adapted for perching; a passerine.

percheron /'peəʃə,rɔ̃/ n. a powerful breed of cart-horse. [F, orig. bred in le Perche, a district of N. France]

perchlorate /pə'klɔːreɪt/ n. Chem. a salt or ester of perchloric acid.

perchloric acid /pə'klɔːrɪk/ n. Chem. a strong liquid acid containing heptavalent chlorine. [PER- + CHLORINE]

percipient /pə'sɪpɪənt/ adj. & n. —adj. **1** able to perceive; conscious. **2** discerning; observant. —n. a person who perceives, esp. something outside the range of the senses. □□ **percipience** n. **percipiently** adv. [L (as PERCEIVE)]

percolate /'pɜːkə,leɪt/ v. **1** intr. (often foll. by through) **a** (of liquid etc.) filter or ooze gradually (esp. through a porous surface). **b** (of an idea etc.) permeate gradually. **2** tr. prepare (coffee) by repeatedly passing boiling water through ground beans. **3** tr. ooze through; permeate. **4** tr. strain (a liquid, powder, etc.) through a fine mesh etc. □□ **percolation** /-'leɪʃ(ə)n/ n. [L percolare (as PER-, colare strain f. colum strainer)]

percolator /'pɜːkə,leɪtə(r)/ n. a machine for making coffee by circulating boiling water through ground beans.

per contra /pɜː 'kɒntrə/ adv. on the opposite side (of an account, assessment, etc.); on the contrary. [It.]

percuss /pə'kʌs/ v.tr. Med. tap (a part of the body) gently with a finger or an instrument as part of a diagnosis. [L percutere percuss- strike (as PER-, cutere = quatere shake)]

percussion /pə'kʌʃ(ə)n/ n. **1** Mus. **a** (often attrib.) the playing of music by striking instruments with sticks etc. (a percussion band). **b** the section of such instruments in an orchestra (asked the percussion to stay behind). (See below.) **2** Med. the act or an instance of percussing. **3** the forcible striking of one esp. solid body against another. □ **percussion cap** a small amount of explosive powder contained in metal or paper and exploded by striking, used esp. in toy guns and formerly in some firearms. □□ **percussionist** n. **percussively** adj. **percussively** adv. **percussiveness** n. [F percussion or L percussio (as PERCUSS)]

In an orchestra the standard percussion instruments are the drums and cymbals, but there is a long list of possible extras which includes the glockenspiel, xylophone, triangle, gongs and bells of various kinds, castanets, rattles, and tambourine, thunder and wind machines, and such 'instruments' as a typewriter or a gun. Percussion instruments fall into two categories: those tunable to a definite pitch, and those of indefinite pitch, used for their quality of sound rather than to provide any specific note or notes.

percutaneous /,pɜːkjʊ'teɪnɪəs/ adj. esp. Med. made or done through the skin. [L per cutem through the skin]

Percy /'pɜːsɪ/, Sir Henry, 'Hotspur' (1364–1403), English soldier. Son of the First Earl of Northumberland, he was one of the most eminent English soldiers of the day and was eventually killed at the battle of Shrewsbury during his father's revolt against Henry IV.

per diem /pə 'diːem, 'daɪem/ adv., adj. & n. —adv. & adj. for each day. —n. an allowance or payment for each day. [L]

perdition /pə'dɪʃ(ə)n/ n. eternal death; damnation. [ME f. OF perdiciun or eccl.L perditio f. L perdere destroy (as PER-, dere dit- = dare give)]

perdurable /pə'djʊərəb(ə)l/ adj. formal permanent; eternal; durable. □□ **perdurability** /-'bɪlɪtɪ/ n. **perdurably** adv. [ME f. OF f. LL perdurabilis (as PER-, DURABLE)]

père /peə(r)/ n. (added to a surname to distinguish a father from a son) the father, senior (cf. FILS). [F, = father]

Père David's deer /,peə 'deɪvɪdz/ n. a large slender-antlered deer, Elaphurus davidianus. [after Father A. David, Fr. missionary d. 1900]

peregrinate /'perɪgrɪ,neɪt/ v.intr. archaic or joc. travel; journey, esp. extensively or at leisure. □□ **peregrination** /-'neɪʃ(ə)n/ n. **peregrinator** n. [L peregrinari (as PEREGRINE)]

peregrine /'perɪgrɪn/ n. & adj. —n. (in full **peregrine falcon**)

a kind of falcon much used for hawking. [L peregrinus f. peregre abroad f. per through + ager field]

Perelman /'per(ə)lmən/, Sidney Joseph (1904–79), American humorous writer of short stories and sketches, most of which appeared in the New Yorker. He also worked in Hollywood as a scriptwriter, notably on some of the Marx Brothers films.

peremptory /pə'remptərɪ, 'perɪm-/ adj. **1** (of a statement or command) admitting no denial or refusal. **2** (of a person, a person's manner, etc.) dogmatic; imperious; dictatorial. **3** Law not open to appeal or challenge; final. **4** absolutely fixed; essential. □ **peremptory challenge** Law a defendant's objection to a proposed juror, made without needing to give a reason. □□ **peremptorily** adv. **peremptoriness** n. [AF peremptorie, OF peremptoire f. L peremptorius deadly, decisive, f. perimere perempt-destroy, cut off (as PER-, emere take, buy)]

perennial /pə'renɪəl/ adj. & n. —adj. **1** lasting through a year or several years. **2** (of a plant) lasting several years (cf. ANNUAL). **3** lasting a long time or for ever. **4** (of a stream) flowing through all seasons of the year. —n. a perennial plant (a herbaceous perennial). □□ **perenniality** /-'ælɪtɪ/ n. **perennially** adv. [L perennis (as PER-, annus year)]

perestroika /,pere'strɔɪkə/ n. the policy or practice of restructuring or reforming, esp. of the economic and political system of the Soviet Union since 1985. [Russ. perestroĭka = restructuring]

Pérez de Cuellar /,peres deɪ 'kweljɑː(r)/, Javier (1920–), Peruvian diplomat, Secretary-General of the United Nations 1982–.

perfect /'pɜːfɪkt/ adj., v., & n. —adj. **1** complete; not deficient. **2** faultless (a perfect diamond). **3** very satisfactory (a perfect evening). **4** exact; precise (a perfect circle). **5** entire; unqualified (a perfect stranger). **6** Math. (of a number) equal to the sum of its divisors. **7** Gram. (of a tense) denoting a completed action or event in the past, formed in English with have or has and the past participle, as in they have eaten. **8** Mus. (of pitch) absolute. **9** Bot. **a** (of a flower) having all four types of whorl. **b** (of a fungus) in the stage where the sexual spores are formed. **10** (often foll. by in) thoroughly trained or skilled (is perfect in geometry). —v.tr. /pə'fekt/ **1** make perfect; improve. **2** carry through; complete. **3** complete (a sheet) by printing the other side. —n. Gram. the perfect tense. □ **perfect binding** a form of bookbinding in which the leaves are attached to the spine by gluing rather than sewing. **perfect interval** Mus. a fourth or fifth as it would occur in a major or minor scale starting on the lower note of the interval, or octave. **perfect pitch** = absolute pitch 1. □□ **perfecter** n. **perfectible** /pə'fektɪb(ə)l/ adj. **perfectibility** /pə,fektɪ'bɪlɪtɪ/ n. **perfectness** n. [ME and OF parfit, perfet f. L perfectus past part. of perficere complete (as PER-, facere do)]

perfecta /pə'fektə/ n. US a form of betting in which the first two places in a race must be predicted in the correct order. [Amer. Sp. quiniela perfecta perfect quinella]

perfection /pə'fekʃ(ə)n/ n. **1** the act or process of making perfect. **2** the state of being perfect; faultlessness, excellence. **3** a perfect person, thing, or example. **4** an accomplishment. **5** full development; completion. □ **to perfection** exactly; completely. [ME f. OF f. L perfectio -onis (as PERFECT)]

perfectionism /pə'fekʃə,nɪz(ə)m/ n. **1** the uncompromising pursuit of excellence. **2** Philos. the belief that religious or moral perfection is attainable. □□ **perfectionist** n. & adj. [PERFECT]

perfective /pə'fektɪv/ adj. & n. Gram. —adj. (of an aspect of a verb etc.) expressing the completion of an action (opp. IMPERFECTIVE). —n. the perfective aspect or form of a verb. [med.L perfectivus (as PERFECT)]

perfectly /'pɜːfɪktlɪ/ adv. **1** completely; absolutely (I understand you perfectly). **2** quite, completely (is perfectly capable of doing it). **3** in a perfect way.

perfecto /pə'fektəʊ/ n. (pl. **-os**) orig. US a large thick cigar pointed at each end. [Sp., = perfect]

perfervid /pə'fɜːvɪd/ adj. literary very fervid. □□ **perfervidly** adv. **perfervidness** n. [mod.L perfervidus (as PER-, FERVID)]

perfidy /'pɜːfɪdɪ/ n. breach of faith; treachery. □□ **perfidious** /-'fɪdɪəs/ adj. **perfidiously** /-'fɪdɪəslɪ/ adv. [L perfidia f. perfidus treacherous (as PER-, fidus f. fides faith)]

perfoliate /pəˈfəʊlɪət/ *adj.* (of a plant) having the stalk apparently passing through the leaf. [mod.L *perfoliatus* (as PER-, FOLIATE)]

perforate *v. & adj.* —*v.* /ˈpɜːfəˌreɪt/ **1** *tr.* make a hole or holes through; pierce. **2** *tr.* make a row of small holes in (paper etc.) so that a part may be torn off easily. **3** *tr.* make an opening into; pass into or extend through. **4** *intr.* (usu. foll. by *into, through*, etc.) penetrate. —*adj.* /ˈpɜːfərət/ perforated. □□ **perforation** /-ˈreɪʃ(ə)n/ *n.* **perforative** /ˈpɜːfərətɪv/ *adj.* **perforator** /ˈpɜːfəˌreɪtə(r)/ *n.* [L *perforare* (as PER-, *forare* pierce)]

perforce /pəˈfɔːs/ *adv.* archaic unavoidably; necessarily. [ME f. OF *par force* by FORCE[1]]

perform /pəˈfɔːm/ *v.* **1** *tr.* (also *absol.*) carry into effect; be the agent of; do (a command, promise, task, etc.). **2** *tr.* (also *absol.*) go through, execute (a public function, play, piece of music, etc.). **3** *intr.* act in a play; play music, sing, etc. (*likes performing*). **4** *intr.* (of a trained animal) execute tricks etc. at a public show. □□ **performable** *adj.* **performability** /-ˈbɪlɪtɪ/ *n.* **performatory** *adj. & n.* (*pl.* **-ies**). **performer** *n.* **performing** *adj.* [ME f. AF *parfourmer* f. OF *parfournir* (assim. to *forme* FORM) f. *par* PER- + *fournir* FURNISH]

performance /pəˈfɔːməns/ *n.* **1** (usu. foll. by *of*) **a** the act or process of performing or carrying out. **b** the execution or fulfilment (of a duty etc.). **2** a staging or production (of a drama, piece of music, etc.) (*the afternoon performance*). **3** a person's achievement under test conditions etc. (*put up a good performance*). **4** *colloq.* a fuss; a scene; a public exhibition (*made such a performance about leaving*). **5 a** the capabilities of a machine, esp. a car or aircraft. **b** (*attrib.*) of high capability (*a performance car*).

performative /pəˈfɔːmətɪv/ *adj. & n.* —*adj.* **1** of or relating to performance. **2** denoting an utterance that effects an action by being spoken or written (e.g. *I bet, I apologize*). —*n.* a performative utterance.

performing arts /pəˈfɔːmɪŋ/ *n.pl.* the arts, such as drama, music, and dance, that require performance for their realization.

perfume /ˈpɜːfjuːm/ *n. & v.* —*n.* **1** a sweet smell. **2** fluid containing the essence of flowers etc.; scent. —*v.tr.* /also pəˈfjuːm/ (usu. as **perfumed** *adj.*) impart a sweet scent to; impregnate with a sweet smell. □□ **perfumy** *adj.* [F *parfum, parfumer* f. obs. It. *parfumare, perfumare* (as PER-, *fumare* smoke, FUME): orig. of smoke from a burning substance]

perfumer /pəˈfjuːmə(r)/ *n.* a maker or seller of perfumes. □□ **perfumery** *n.* (*pl.* **-ies**).

perfunctory /pəˈfʌŋktərɪ/ *adj.* **1** done merely for the sake of getting through a duty. **2** superficial; mechanical. □□ **perfunctorily** *adv.* **perfunctoriness** *n.* [LL *perfunctorius* careless f. L *perfungi perfunct-* (as PER-, *fungi* perform)]

perfuse /pəˈfjuːz/ *v.tr.* **1** (often foll. by *with*) **a** besprinkle (with water etc.). **b** cover or suffuse (with radiance etc.). **2** pour or diffuse (water etc.) through or over. **3** *Med.* cause a fluid to pass through (an organ etc.). □□ **perfusion** /-ˈ3(ə)n/ *n.* **perfusive** /-sɪv/ *adj.* [L *perfundere perfus-* (as PER-, *fundere* pour)]

Pergamum /ˈpɜːɡəməm/ (now Bergama in Turkey) the dynastic capital of the Attalid kings (3rd–2nd c. BC), situated on a rocky hill near the western coast of Asia Minor, one of the greatest and most beautiful of the Hellenistic cities. With its palace, famous school of sculpture, library second only to that of Alexandria, and kings who were philosophers at least in their spare time, Pergamum was a cultural even more than a political and commercial centre. □□ **Pergamene** /-miːn/ *adj. & n.*

pergana var. of PARGANA.

pergola /ˈpɜːɡələ/ *n.* an arbour or covered walk, formed of growing plants trained over trellis-work. [It. f. L *pergula* projecting roof f. *pergere* proceed]

pergunnah var. of PARGANA.

perhaps /pəˈhæps/ *adv.* **1** it may be; possibly (*perhaps it is lost*). **2** introducing a polite request (*perhaps you would open the window?*). [PER + HAP]

peri /ˈpɪərɪ/ *n.* (*pl.* **peris**) **1** (in Persian mythology) a fairy; a good (*orig.* evil) genius. **2** a beautiful or graceful being. [Pers. *parī*]

peri- /ˈperɪ/ *prefix* **1** round, about. **2** *Astron.* the point nearest to (*perigee; perihelion*). [Gk *peri* around, about]

perianth /ˈperɪˌænθ/ *n.* the outer part of a flower. [F *périanthe* f. mod.L *perianthium* (as PERI- + Gk *anthos* flower)]

periapt /ˈperɪˌæpt/ *n.* a thing worn as a charm; an amulet. [F *périapte* f. Gk *periapton* f. *haptō* fasten]

pericardium /ˌperɪˈkɑːdɪəm/ *n.* (*pl.* **pericardia** /-dɪə/) the membranous sac enclosing the heart. □□ **pericardiac** /-dɪˌæk/ *adj.* **pericardial** *adj.* **pericarditis** /-ˈdaɪtɪs/ *n.* [mod.L f. Gk *perikardion* (as PERI- + *kardia* heart)]

pericarp /ˈperɪˌkɑːp/ *n.* the part of a fruit formed from the wall of the ripened ovary. [F *péricarpe* f. Gk *perikarpion* pod, shell (as PERI-, *karpos* fruit)]

perichondrium /ˌperɪˈkɒndrɪəm/ *n.* the membrane enveloping cartilage tissue (except at the joints). [PERI- + Gk *khondros* cartilage]

periclase /ˈperɪˌkleɪs/ *n.* a pale mineral consisting of magnesia. [mod.L *periclasia*, erron. f. Gk *peri* exceedingly + *klasis* breaking, from its perfect cleavage]

Pericles /ˈperɪˌkliːz/ (*c.*495–429 BC) Athenian statesman and general. The most influential politician in mid-5th c. Athens, he promoted an imperialist policy and masterminded Athenian strategy in the Peloponnesian War. He was building commissioner for the Parthenon and other buildings, a great orator, and a friend of leading philosophers, writers, and artists, including Anaxagoras, Sophocles, and Phidias. His name is inseparably attached to the greatest age of Athens.

periclinal /ˌperɪˈklaɪn(ə)l/ *adj.* *Geol.* (of a mound etc.) sloping down in all directions from a central point. [Gk *periklinēs* sloping on all sides (as PERI-, CLINE)]

pericope /pəˈrɪkəpɪ/ *n.* a short passage or paragraph, esp. a portion of Scripture read in public worship. [LL f. Gk *perikopē* (as PERI-, *kopē* cutting f. *koptō* cut)]

pericranium /ˌperɪˈkreɪnɪəm/ *n.* the membrane enveloping the skull. [mod.L f. Gk (as PERI-, *kranion* skull)]

peridot /ˈperɪˌdɒt/ *n.* a green variety of olivine, used esp. as a semiprecious stone. [ME f. OF *peritot*, of unkn. orig.]

perigee /ˈperɪˌdʒiː/ *n.* the point in a celestial body's orbit where it is nearest the earth (opp. APOGEE). □□ **perigean** /ˌperɪˈdʒiːən/ *adj.* [F *périgée* f. mod.L f. Gk *perigeion* round the earth (as PERI-, *gē* earth)]

periglacial /ˌperɪˈɡleɪʃ(ə)l, -sɪəl/ *adj.* of or relating to a region adjoining a glacier.

Périgord /ˌperɪˈɡɔːr/ a district (a former province) in SW France.

perigynous /pəˈrɪdʒɪnəs/ *adj.* (of stamens) situated around the pistil or ovary. [mod.L *perigynus* (as PERI-, -GYNOUS)]

perihelion /ˌperɪˈhiːlɪən/ *n.* (*pl.* **perihelia** /-lɪə/) the point of closest approach to the sun by an orbiting planet or satellite. Such a position can generally be calculated by the laws of classical mechanics, but the systematic change in the perihelion position of Mercury could be explained only by Einstein's general theory of relativity, for which it constituted an important test. [Graecized f. mod.L *perihelium* (as PERI-, Gk *hēlios* sun)]

peril /ˈperɪl/ *n. & v.* —*n.* serious and immediate danger. —*v.tr.* (**perilled, perilling;** US **periled, periling**) threaten; endanger. □ **at one's peril** at one's own risk. **in peril of** with great risk to (*in peril of your life*). **peril point** US *Econ.* a critical threshold or limit. [ME f. OF f. L *peric(u)lum*]

perilous /ˈperɪləs/ *adj.* **1** full of risk; dangerous; hazardous. **2** exposed to imminent risk of destruction etc. □□ **perilously** *adv.* **perilousness** *n.* [ME f. OF *perillous* f. L *periculosus* f. *periculum*: see PERIL]

perilune /ˈperɪˌluːn, -ˌljuːn/ *n.* the point in a body's lunar orbit where it is closest to the moon (opp. APOLUNE). [PERI- + L *luna* moon, after *perigee*]

perilymph /ˈperɪlɪmf/ *n.* the fluid in the labyrinth of the ear.

perimeter /pəˈrɪmɪtə(r)/ *n.* **1 a** the circumference or outline of a closed figure. **b** the length of this. **2 a** the outer boundary of an enclosed area. **b** a defended boundary. **3** an instrument for measuring a field of vision. □□ **perimetric** /ˌperɪˈmetrɪk/ *adj.* [F *périmètre* or f. L *perimetrus* f. Gk *perimetros* (as PERI-, *metros* f. *metron* measure)]

perinatal /ˌperɪˈneɪt(ə)l/ *adj.* of or relating to the time immediately before and after birth.

perineum /ˌperɪˈniːəm/ *n.* the region of the body between the anus and the scrotum or vulva. □□ **perineal** *adj.* [LL f. Gk *perinaion*]

period /ˈpɪərɪəd/ *n. & adj.* —*n.* **1** a length or portion of time (*showers and bright periods*). **2** a distinct portion of history, a person's life, etc. (*the Georgian period; Picasso's Blue Period*). **3** *Geol.* a time forming part of a geological era (*the Quaternary period*). **4 a** an interval between recurrences of an astronomical or other phenomenon. **b** the time taken by a planet to rotate about its axis. **5** the time allowed for a lesson in school. **6** an occurrence of menstruation. **7 a** a complete sentence, esp. one consisting of several clauses. **b** (in *pl.*) rhetorical language. **8** esp. *US* **a** = *full stop* (see FULL[1]). **b** used at the end of a sentence etc. to indicate finality, absoluteness, etc. (*we want the best, period*). **9 a** a set of figures marked off in a large number to assist in reading. **b** a set of figures repeated in a recurring decimal. **c** the smallest interval over which a function takes the same value. **10** *Chem.* a sequence of elements between two noble gases forming a row in the periodic table. —*adj.* belonging to or characteristic of some past period (*period furniture*). □ **of the period** of the era under discussion (*the custom of the period*). **period piece** an object or work whose main interest lies in its historical etc. associations. [ME f. OF *periode* f. L *periodus* f. Gk *periodos* (as PERI-, *odos* = *hodos* way)]

periodate /pəˈraɪədeɪt/ *n. Chem.* a salt or ester of periodic acid.

periodic /ˌpɪərɪˈɒdɪk/ *adj.* **1** appearing or occurring at regular intervals. **2** of or concerning the period of a celestial body (*periodic motion*). **3** (of diction etc.) expressed in periods (see PERIOD *n.* 7a). □ **periodic decimal** *Math.* a set of figures repeated in a recurring decimal. **periodic function** *Math.* a function returning to the same value at regular intervals. **periodic table** an arrangement of elements in order of increasing atomic number which also brings together those whose atoms have a similar pattern of orbiting electrons. Chemically related elements consequently tend to appear in the same column or row of the table. The earliest form of the table was devised by Mendeleev. □□ **periodicity** /-rɪəˈdɪsɪtɪ/ *n.* [F *périodique* or L *periodicus* f. Gk *periodikos* (as PERIOD)]

periodic acid /ˌpɜːraɪˈɒdɪk/ *n. Chem.* a hygroscopic solid acid containing heptavalent iodine. [PER- + IODINE]

periodical /ˌpɪərɪˈɒdɪk(ə)l/ *n. & adj.* —*n.* a newspaper, magazine, etc. issued at regular intervals, usu. monthly or weekly. —*adj.* **1** published at regular intervals. **2** periodic, occasional. □□ **periodically** *adv.*

periodization /ˌpɪərɪədaɪˈzeɪʃ(ə)n/ *n.* the division of history into periods.

periodontics /ˌperɪəˈdɒntɪks/ *n.pl.* (treated as *sing.*) the branch of dentistry concerned with the structures surrounding and supporting the teeth. □□ **periodontal** *adj.* **periodontist** *n.* [PERI- + Gk *odous odont-* tooth]

periodontology /ˌperɪədɒnˈtɒlədʒɪ/ *n.* = PERIODONTICS.

periosteum /ˌperɪˈɒstɪəm/ *n.* (*pl.* **periostea** /-tɪə/) a membrane enveloping the bones where no cartilage is present. □□ **periosteal** *adj.* **periostitis** /-ˈstaɪtɪs/ *n.* [mod.L f. Gk *periosteon* (as PERI-, *osteon* bone)]

peripatetic /ˌperɪpəˈtetɪk/ *adj. & n.* —*adj.* **1** (of a teacher) working in more than one school or college etc. **2** going from place to place; itinerant. **3** (**Peripatetic**) Aristotelian (from Aristotle's habit of walking in the Lyceum whilst teaching). —*n.* a peripatetic person, esp. a teacher. □□ **peripatetically** *adv.* **peripateticism** /-ˌsɪz(ə)m/ *n.* [ME f. OF *peripatetique* or L *peripateticus* f. Gk *peripatētikos* f. *peripateō* (as PERI-, *pateō* walk)]

peripeteia /ˌperɪpɪˈtaɪə, -ˈtiːə/ *n.* a sudden change of fortune in a drama or in life. [Gk (as PERI-, *pet-* f. *piptō* fall)]

peripheral /pəˈrɪfər(ə)l/ *adj. & n.* —*adj.* **1** of minor importance; marginal. **2** of the periphery; on the fringe. **3** *Anat.* near the surface of the body, with special reference to the circulation and nervous system. **4** (of equipment) used with a computer

etc. but not an integral part of it. —*n.* a peripheral device or piece of equipment. □ **peripheral nervous system** see NERVOUS SYSTEM. □□ **peripherally** *adv.*

periphery /pəˈrɪfərɪ/ *n.* (*pl.* **-ies**) **1** the boundary of an area or surface. **2** an outer or surrounding region (*built on the periphery of the old town*). [LL *peripheria* f. Gk *periphereia* circumference (as PERI-, *phereia* f. *phero* bear)]

periphrasis /pəˈrɪfrəsɪs/ *n.* (*pl.* **periphrases** /-ˌsiːz/) **1** a roundabout way of speaking; circumlocution. **2** a roundabout phrase. [L f. Gk f. *periphrazō* (as PERI-, *phrazō* declare)]

periphrastic /ˌperɪˈfræstɪk/ *adj. Gram.* **1** of or involving periphrasis. **2** (of a case, tense, etc.) formed by combination of words rather than by inflection (e.g. *did go*, *of the people* rather than *went*, *the people's*). □□ **periphrastically** *adv.* [Gk *periphrastikos* (as PERIPHRASIS)]

peripteral /pəˈrɪptər(ə)l/ *adj.* (of a temple) surrounded by a single row of columns. [Gk *peripteron* (as PERI-, Gk *pteron* wing)]

periscope /ˈperɪˌskəʊp/ *n.* an apparatus with a tube and mirrors or prisms, by which an observer in a trench, submerged submarine, or at the rear of a crowd etc., can see things otherwise out of sight.

periscopic /ˌperɪˈskɒpɪk/ *adj.* of a periscope. □ **periscopic lens** a lens allowing distinct vision over a wide angle. □□ **periscopically** *adv.*

perish /ˈperɪʃ/ *v.* **1** *intr.* be destroyed; suffer death or ruin. **2 a** *intr.* (esp. of rubber, a rubber object, etc.) lose its normal qualities; deteriorate, rot. **b** *tr.* cause to rot or deteriorate. **3** *tr.* (in *passive*) suffer from cold or exposure (*we were perished standing outside*). □ **perish the thought** an exclamation of horror against an unwelcome idea. □□ **perishless** *adj.* [ME f. OF *perir* f. L *perire* pass away (as PER-, *ire* go)]

perishable /ˈperɪʃəb(ə)l/ *adj. & n.* —*adj.* liable to perish; subject to decay. —*n.* a thing, esp. a foodstuff, subject to speedy decay. □□ **perishability** /-ˈbɪlɪtɪ/ *n.* **perishableness** *n.*

perisher /ˈperɪʃə(r)/ *n. Brit. sl.* an annoying person.

perishing /ˈperɪʃɪŋ/ *adj. & adv. colloq.* —*adj.* **1** confounded. **2** freezing cold, extremely chilly. —*adv.* confoundedly. □□ **perishingly** *adv.*

perisperm /ˈperɪˌspɜːm/ *n.* a mass of nutritive material outside the embryo-sac in some seeds. [PERI- + Gk *sperma* seed]

peristalsis /ˌperɪˈstælsɪs/ *n.* an involuntary muscular wavelike movement by which the contents of the alimentary canal etc. are propelled along. □□ **peristaltic** *adj.* **peristaltically** *adv.* [mod.L f. Gk *peristellō* wrap around (as PERI-, *stellō* place)]

peristome /ˈperɪˌstəʊm/ *n.* **1** *Bot.* a fringe of small teeth around the mouth of a capsule in mosses and certain fungi. **2** *Zool.* the parts surrounding the mouth of various invertebrates. [mod.L *peristoma* f. PERI- + Gk *stoma* mouth]

peristyle /ˈperɪˌstaɪl/ *n.* a row of columns surrounding a temple, court, cloister, etc.; a space surrounded by columns. [F *péristyle* f. L *peristylum* f. Gk *peristulon* (as PERI-, *stulos* pillar)]

peritoneum /ˌperɪtəˈniːəm/ *n.* (*pl.* **peritoneums** or **peritonea** /-ˈniːə/) the double serous membrane lining the cavity of the abdomen. □□ **peritoneal** *adj.* [LL f. Gk *peritonaion* (as PERI-, *tonaion* f. *-tonos* stretched)]

peritonitis /ˌperɪtəˈnaɪtɪs/ *n.* an inflammatory disease of the peritoneum.

periwig /ˈperɪwɪg/ *n. esp. hist.* a wig. □□ **periwigged** *adj.* [alt. of PERUKE, with *-wi-* for F *-u-* sound]

periwinkle[1] /ˈperɪˌwɪŋk(ə)l/ *n.* **1** any plant of the genus *Vinca*, esp. an evergreen trailing plant with blue or white flowers. **2** a tropical shrub, *Catharanthus roseus*, native to Madagascar. [ME f. AF *pervenke*, OF *pervenche* f. LL *pervinca*, assim. to PERIWINKLE[2]]

periwinkle[2] /ˈperɪˌwɪŋk(ə)l/ *n.* = WINKLE. [16th c.: orig. unkn.]

perjure /ˈpɜːdʒə(r)/ *v.refl. Law* **1** wilfully tell an untruth when on oath. **2** (as **perjured** *adj.*) guilty of or involving perjury. □□ **perjurer** *n.* [ME f. OF *parjurer* f. L *perjurare* (as PER-, *jurare* swear)]

perjury /ˈpɜːdʒərɪ/ *n.* (*pl.* **-ies**) *Law* **1** a breach of an oath, esp. the act of wilfully telling an untruth when on oath. **2** the practice of this. □□ **perjurious** /-ˈdʒʊərɪəs/ *adj.* [ME f. AF *perjurie* f. OF *parjurie* f. L *perjurium* (as PERJURE)]

perk¹ /pɜːk/ v. & adj. —v.tr. raise (one's head etc.) briskly. — adj. perky; pert. □ **perk up 1** recover confidence, courage, life, or zest. **2** restore confidence or courage or liveliness in (esp. another person). **3** smarten up. [ME, perh. f. var. of PERCH¹]

perk² /pɜːk/ n. Brit. colloq. a perquisite. [abbr.]

perk³ /pɜːk/ v. colloq. **1** intr. (of coffee) percolate, make a bubbling sound in the percolator. **2** tr. percolate (coffee). [abbr. of PERCOLATE]

Perkin /ˈpɜːkɪn/, Sir William Henry (1838–1907), English chemist who prepared the first synthetic dyestuff, mauve, made from aniline. The discovery was made almost by accident, at the age of 18, when he was trying to synthesize the important drug quinine.

perky /ˈpɜːkɪ/ adj. (**perkier, perkiest**) **1** self-assertive; saucy; pert. **2** lively; cheerful. □□ **perkily** adv. **perkiness** n.

Perlis /ˈpɜːlɪs/ the smallest State of Malaysia, the most northerly of those on the Malay Peninsula; pop. (1980) 148,300; capital, Kangar.

perlite /ˈpɜːlaɪt/ n. (also **pearlite**) a glassy type of vermiculite, expandable to a solid form by heating, used for insulation etc. [F f. perle pearl]

Perm /pɜːm/ an industrial city of the soviet Union in the western foothills of the Ural Mountains; pop. (est. 1987) 1,075,000.

perm¹ /pɜːm/ n. & v. —n. a permanent wave. —v.tr. give a permanent wave to (a person or a person's hair). [abbr.]

perm² /pɜːm/ n. & v. colloq. —n. a permutation. —v.tr. make a permutation of. [abbr.]

permafrost /ˈpɜːməˌfrɒst/ n. subsoil which remains below freezing-point throughout the year, as in polar regions. [PERMANENT + FROST]

permalloy /ˈpɜːməˌlɔɪ/ n. an alloy of nickel and iron that is easily magnetized and demagnetized. [PERMEABLE + ALLOY]

permanent /ˈpɜːmənənt/ adj. lasting, or intended to last or function, indefinitely (opp. TEMPORARY). □ **permanent magnet** a magnet retaining its magnetic properties without continued excitation. **Permanent Secretary** (or **Under-secretary** etc.) Brit. a senior grade in the Civil Service, often a permanent adviser to a minister. **permanent set 1** the irreversible deformation of a substance after being subjected to stress. **2** the amount of this. **permanent tooth** a tooth succeeding a milk tooth in a mammal, and lasting most of the mammal's life. **permanent wave** an artificial wave in the hair, intended to last for some time. **permanent way** Brit. the finished roadbed of a railway. □□ **permanence** n. **permanency** n. **permanentize** v.tr. (also **-ise**). **permanently** adv. [ME f. OF permanent or L permanēre (as PER-, manēre remain)]

permanganate /pɜːˈmæŋgəˌneɪt, -nət/ n. Chem. any salt of permanganic acid, esp. potassium permanganate.

permanganic acid /ˌpɜːmæŋˈgænɪk/ n. Chem. an acid containing heptavalent manganese. [PER- + MANGANIC: see MANGANESE]

permeability /ˌpɜːmɪəˈbɪlɪtɪ/ n. **1** the state or quality of being permeable. **2** a quantity measuring the influence of a substance on the magnetic flux in the region it occupies.

permeable /ˈpɜːmɪəb(ə)l/ adj. capable of being permeated. [L permeabilis (as PERMEATE)]

permeate /ˈpɜːmɪˌeɪt/ v. **1** tr. penetrate throughout; pervade; saturate. **2** intr. (usu. foll. by through, among, etc.) diffuse itself. □□ **permeance** n. **permeant** adj. **permeation** /-ˈeɪʃ(ə)n/ n. **permeator** n. [L permeare permeat- (as PER-, meare pass, go)]

Permian /ˈpɜːmɪən/ adj. & n. Geol. —adj. of or relating to the final period of the Palaeozoic era, following the Carboniferous and preceding the Triassic, lasting from about 286 to 248 million years ago. The climate was hot and dry in many parts of the world during this period, which also saw the extinction of many marine animals, including trilobites, and the proliferation of reptiles. —n. this period or system. [Perm in Russia]

per mille /pɜː ˈmɪlɪ/ adv. (also **per mil** /mɪl/) in every thousand. [L]

permissible /pəˈmɪsɪb(ə)l/ adj. allowable. □□ **permissibility** /-ˈbɪlɪtɪ/ n. **permissibly** adv. [ME f. F or f. med.L permissibilis (as PERMIT)]

permission /pəˈmɪʃ(ə)n/ n. (often foll. by to + infin.) consent; authorization. [ME f. OF or f. L permissio (as PERMIT)]

permissive /pəˈmɪsɪv/ adj. **1** tolerant; liberal, esp. in sexual matters (the permissive society). **2** giving permission. □ **permissive legislation** legislation giving powers but not enjoining their use. □□ **permissively** adv. **permissiveness** n. [ME f. OF (-if -ive) or med.L permissivus (as PERMIT)]

permit v. & n. —v. /pəˈmɪt/ (**permitted, permitting**) **1** tr. give permission or consent to; authorize (permit me to say). **2 a** tr. allow; give an opportunity to (permit the traffic to flow again). **b** intr. give an opportunity (circumstances permitting). **3** intr. (foll. by of) admit; allow for. —n. /ˈpɜːmɪt/ **1 a** a document giving permission to act in a specified way (was granted a work permit). **b** a document etc. which allows entry into a specified zone. **2** formal permission. □□ **permittee** /ˌpɜːmɪˈtiː/ n. **permitter** n. [L permittere (as PER-, mittere miss- let go)]

permittivity /ˌpɜːmɪˈtɪvɪtɪ/ n. Electr. a quantity measuring the ability of a substance to store electrical energy in an electric field.

permutate /ˈpɜːmjuːˌteɪt/ v.tr. change the order or arrangement of. [as PERMUTE, or back-form. f. PERMUTATION]

permutation /ˌpɜːmjʊˈteɪʃ(ə)n/ n. **1 a** an ordered arrangement or grouping of a set of numbers, items, etc. **b** any one of the range of possible groupings. **2** any combination or selection of a specified number of things from a larger group, esp. Brit. matches in a football pool. □□ **permutational** adj. [ME f. OF or f. L permutatio (as PERMUTE)]

permute /pəˈmjuːt/ v.tr. alter the sequence or arrangement of. [ME f. L permutare (as PER-, mutare change)]

Permutit /ˈpɜːmjʊtɪt/ n. propr. an artificial zeolite used as an ion exchanger esp. for the softening of water. [G f. L permutare to exchange]

Pernambuco see RECIFE.

pernicious /pəˈnɪʃəs/ adj. destructive; ruinous; fatal. □ **pernicious anaemia** see ANAEMIA. □□ **perniciously** adv. **perniciousness** n. [L perniciosus f. pernicies ruin f. nex necis death]

pernickety /pəˈnɪkɪtɪ/ adj. colloq. **1** fastidious. **2** precise or over-precise. **3** ticklish, requiring tact or careful handling. [19th-c. Sc.: orig. unkn.]

pernoctate /pəˈnɒkteɪt/ v.intr. formal pass or spend the night. □□ **pernoctation** /-ˈteɪʃ(ə)n/ n. [LL pernoctatio f. L pernoctare pernoctat- (as PER-, noctare f. nox noctis night)]

Perón /peˈrɒn/, Juan Domingo (1895–1974), Argentinian statesman. A career army officer, Perón was a member of the military junta which seized power in Argentina in 1943. He was elected President in 1946 and re-elected in 1951, deriving much of his own popularity from the charismatic appeal of his wife Eva ('Evita'). Following her death in 1952, his popularity declined sharply, particularly after he came into conflict with the Catholic Church, and in 1955 he was forced into exile. Following a resurgence by the Peronist party in the early 1970s, Perón returned to power in October 1973, only to die less than a year later. His second wife succeeded him as leader but was overthrown by the army in March 1976. □□ **Peronist** adj. & n.

peroneal /ˌperəˈniːəl/ adj. Anat. relating to or near the fibula. [mod.L peronaeus peroneal muscle f. perone fibula f. Gk peronē pin, fibula]

perorate /ˈperəˌreɪt/ v.intr. **1** sum up and conclude a speech. **2** speak at length. [L perorare perorat- (as PER-, orare speak)]

peroration /ˌperəˈreɪʃ(ə)n/ n. the concluding part of a speech, forcefully summing up what has been said.

peroxidase /pəˈrɒksɪˌdeɪz, -ˌdeɪs/ n. Biochem. any of a class of enzymes found esp. in plants, which catalyze the oxidation of a substrate by hydrogen peroxide.

peroxide /pəˈrɒksaɪd/ n. & v. —n. Chem. **1 a** = hydrogen peroxide. **b** (often attrib.) a solution of hydrogen peroxide used to bleach the hair or as an antiseptic. **2** a compound of oxygen with another element containing the greatest possible proportion of oxygen. **3** any salt or ester of hydrogen peroxide. —v.tr. bleach (the hair) with peroxide. [PER- + OXIDE]

perpendicular /ˌpɜːpənˈdɪkjʊlə(r)/ *adj. & n.* —*adj.* **1 a** at right angles to the plane of the horizon. **b** (usu. foll. by *to*) *Geom.* at right angles (to a given line, plane, or surface). **2** upright, vertical. **3** (of a slope etc.) very steep. **4** (**Perpendicular**) *Archit.* of the third stage of English Gothic (late 14th–16th c.) with vertical tracery in large windows. **5** *joc.* in a standing position. —*n.* **1** a perpendicular line. **2** a plumb-rule or a similar instrument. **3** (prec. by *the*) a perpendicular line or direction (*is out of the perpendicular*). □□ **perpendicularity** /-ˈlærɪtɪ/ *n.* **perpendicularly** *adv.* [ME f. L *perpendicularis* f. *perpendiculum* plumb-line f. PER- + *pendēre* hang]

perpetrate /ˈpɜːpɪˌtreɪt/ *v.tr.* commit or perform (a crime, blunder, or anything outrageous). □□ **perpetration** /-ˈtreɪʃ(ə)n/ *n.* **perpetrator** *n.* [L *perpetrare perpetrat-* (as PER-, *patrare* effect)]

perpetual /pəˈpetjʊəl/ *adj.* **1** eternal; lasting for ever or indefinitely. **2** continuous, uninterrupted. **3** *colloq.* frequent, much repeated (*perpetual interruptions*). **4** permanent during life (*perpetual secretary*). □ **perpetual calendar** a calendar which can be adjusted to show any combination of day, month, and year. **perpetual check** *Chess* the position of play when a draw is obtained by repeated checking of the king. **perpetual motion** the motion of a hypothetical machine which once set in motion would run for ever unless subject to an external force or to wear. □□ **perpetualism** *n.* **perpetually** *adv.* [ME f. OF *perpetuel* f. L *perpetualis* f. *perpetuus* f. *perpes -etis* continuous]

perpetuate /pəˈpetjʊˌeɪt/ *v.tr.* **1** make perpetual. **2** preserve from oblivion. □□ **perpetuance** *n.* **perpetuation** /-ˈeɪʃ(ə)n/ *n.* **perpetuator** *n.* [L *perpetuare* (as PERPETUAL)]

perpetuity /ˌpɜːpɪˈtjuːɪtɪ/ *n.* (*pl.* -ies) **1** the state or quality of being perpetual. **2** a perpetual annuity. **3** a perpetual possession or position. □ **in** (or **to** or **for**) **perpetuity** for ever. [ME f. OF *perpetuité* f. L *perpetuitas -tatis* (as PERPETUAL)]

perpetuum mobile /pɜːˌpetjuːəm ˈməʊbɪlɪ/ *n.* **1** = *perpetual motion.* **2** *Mus.* = MOTO PERPETUO. [L *perpetuus* continuous + *mobilis* movable, after PRIMUM MOBILE]

Perpignan /ˌpɜːpiːnˈjã/ a city of southern France, in the NE foothills of the Pyrenees; pop. (1982) 113,650.

perplex /pəˈpleks/ *v.tr.* **1** puzzle, bewilder, or disconcert (a person, a person's mind, etc.). **2** complicate or confuse (a matter). **3** (as **perplexed** *adj.*) *archaic* entangled, intertwined. □□ **perplexedly** /-ɪdlɪ/ *adv.* **perplexingly** *adv.* [back-form. f. *perplexed* f. obs. *perplex* (adj.) f. OF *perplexe* or L *perplexus* (as PER-, *plexus* past part. of *plectere* plait)]

perplexity /pəˈpleksɪtɪ/ *n.* (*pl.* -ies) **1** bewilderment; the state of being perplexed. **2** a thing which perplexes. **3** *archaic* an entangled state. [ME f. OF *perplexité* or LL *perplexitas* (as PERPLEX)]

per pro. /pɜː ˈprəʊ/ *abbr.* through the agency of (used in signatures). ¶ The correct sequence is A *per pro.* B, where B is signing on behalf of A. [L *per procurationem*]

perquisite /ˈpɜːkwɪzɪt/ *n.* **1** an extra profit or allowance additional to a main income etc. **2** a customary extra right or privilege. **3** an incidental benefit attached to employment etc. **4** a thing which has served its primary use and to which a subordinate or servant has a customary right. [ME f. med.L *perquisitum* f. L *perquirere* search diligently for (as PER-, *quaerere* seek)]

Perrault /peˈrəʊ/, Charles (1628–1703), French poet and critic, a member of the *Académie française* from 1671. He is remembered for his fairy tales, translated into English as 'Mother Goose Tales' by Robert Samber in 1729, containing among others, 'Sleeping Beauty', 'Little Red Riding Hood', 'Puss in Boots', and 'Cinderella'.

Perrier /ˈperɪˌeɪ/ *n. propr.* an effervescent natural mineral water. [the name of a spring at Vergèze, France, its source]

perron /ˈperən/ *n.* an exterior staircase leading up to a main entrance to a church or other (usu. large) building. [ME f. OF ult. f. L *petra* stone]

Perry /ˈperɪ/, Frederick John (1909–), English lawn tennis and table tennis player, a brilliant match player who won a number of titles. His record of winning the men's singles championship at Wimbledon in three successive years (1934–6) was unequalled until the success of Bjorn Borg (1976–80).

perry /ˈperɪ/ *n.* (*pl.* -ies) *Brit.* a drink like cider, made from the fermented juice of pears. [ME *pereye* etc. f. OF *peré*, ult. f. L *pirum* pear]

per se /pɜː ˈseɪ/ *adv.* by or in itself; intrinsically. [L]

persecute /ˈpɜːsɪˌkjuːt/ *v.tr.* **1** subject (a person etc.) to hostility or ill-treatment, esp. on the grounds of political or religious belief. **2** harass; worry. **3** (often foll. by *with*) bombard (a person) with questions etc. □□ **persecutor** *n.* **persecutory** *adj.* [ME f. OF *persecuter* back-form. f. *persecuteur* persecutor f. LL *persecutor* f. L *persequi* (as PER-, *sequi secut-* follow, pursue)]

persecution /ˌpɜːsɪˈkjuːʃ(ə)n/ *n.* the act or an instance of persecuting; the state of being persecuted. □ **persecution complex** (or **mania**) an irrational obsessive fear that others are scheming against one.

Persephone /pɜːˈsefənɪ/ *Gk Mythol.* a pre-Greek goddess later identified with the virgin daughter (Kore) of the corn-goddess Demeter, with whom she was often worshipped. She was carried off by Pluto and made queen of the underworld. Demeter, vainly seeking her, refused to let the earth bring forth its fruits until her daughter was restored to her, but Persephone had eaten some pomegranate-seeds in the other world and so could not return entirely but was obliged to spend some part of every year underground. Her story symbolizes the life and growth of corn.

Persepolis /pəˈsepəlɪs/ an ancient Persian city, ceremonial capital of the Achaemenids, founded by Darius I and almost completed by his successors, Xerxes and Artaxerxes, before its destruction and looting by Alexander the Great in 330 BC. Impressive remains of functional and ceremonial buildings adorned by sculptured friezes and cuneiform inscriptions in Old Persian were rediscovered in the 16th c. and first excavated in the 1930s.

Perseus /ˈpɜːsjəs/ **1** *Gk Mythol.* the son of Zeus and Danae. He cut off the head of the gorgon Medusa and gave it to Athene, rescued and married Andromeda, and became king of Tiryns in Greece. **2** *Astron.* a northern constellation between Cassiopeia and Taurus, including part of the Milky Way.

perseverance /ˌpɜːsɪˈvɪərəns/ *n.* **1** the steadfast pursuit of an objective. **2** (often foll. by *in*) constant persistence (in a belief etc.). [ME f. OF f. L *perseverantia* (as PERSEVERE)]

perseverate /pəˈsevəˌreɪt/ *v.intr.* **1** continue action etc. for an unusually or excessively long time. **2** *Psychol.* tend to prolong or repeat a response after the original stimulus has ceased. □□ **perseveration** /-ˈreɪʃ(ə)n/ *n.* [L *perseverare* (as PERSEVERE)]

persevere /ˌpɜːsɪˈvɪə(r)/ *v.intr.* (often foll. by *in, at, with*) continue steadfastly or determinedly; persist. [ME f. OF *perseverer* f. L *perseverare* persist f. *perseverus* very strict (as PER-, *severus* severe)]

Persia /ˈpɜːʃə/ the ancient and now the alternative name of Iran. It was the site of an ancient kingdom that in the 6th c. BC formed an empire by Cyrus' conquests of Media, Lydia, and Babylonia; at its greatest the empire included all western Asia, Egypt, and parts of eastern Europe, until overthrown by Alexander the Great (331 BC). (See IRAN).

Persian /ˈpɜːʃ(ə)n/ *n. & adj.* —*n.* **1 a** a native or inhabitant of ancient or modern Persia (now Iran). **b** a person of Persian descent. **2** the language of ancient Persia or modern Iran. ¶ With modern reference the preferred terms are *Iranian* and *Farsi*. (See below.) **3** (in full **Persian cat**) **a** a cat of a breed with long silky hair and a thick tail. **b** this breed. —*adj.* of or relating to Persia or its people or language. □ **Persian carpet** (or **rug**) a carpet or rug of a traditional pattern made in Persia. **Persian lamb** the silky tightly curled fur of a young karakul, used in clothing. [ME f. OF *persien* f. med.L]

The Persian language, spoken by over 25 million people in Iran and Afghanistan, belongs to the Indo-Iranian language group. It is attested from the 6th c. BC when Old Persian was the language of the Persian Empire, which at one time spread from the Mediterranean to India. Old Persian was written in cuneiform, but in the 2nd c. BC the Persians created their own alphabet (Pahlavi), which remained in use until the Islamic conquest in the 7th c.; since then Persian or Farsi has been written in the Arabic script.

Persian Gulf (also called the **Arabian Gulf**) an arm of the

Arabian Sea, to which it is connected by the Strait of Hormuz and the Gulf of Oman, separating the Arabian peninsula from mainland Asia.

Persian Wars the wars fought between Greece and Persia in the 5th c. BC, in which the Persians sought to extend their territory over the Greek world. They began in 490 BC when Darius sent an expedition to punish the Greeks for having supported the Ionian cities in their unsuccessful revolt (499–494 BC) against Persian rule; the Persians were defeated by a small force of Athenians at Marathon (see entry). Ten years later his son Xerxes attempted an invasion with a land and sea force, crossing the Hellespont with a bridge of boats. He won a land-battle at Thermopylae and devastated Attica, but Persian forces were defeated on land at Plataea and in a sea-battle at Salamis (479 BC), and retreated. Intermittent war continued in various areas until peace was signed in 449 BC. As a result of the wars the Greeks in general became increasingly conscious of their own nationality, and the city-state of Athens gained enormously in pride and self-confidence.

persiennes /ˌpɜːsɪˈenz/ n.pl. window shutters, or outside blinds, with louvres. [F, fem. pl. of obs. persien Persian]

persiflage /ˈpɜːsɪˌflɑːʒ/ n. light raillery, banter. [F persifler banter, formed as PER- + siffler whistle]

persimmon /pɜːˈsɪmən/ n. 1 any usu. tropical evergreen tree of the genus Diospyros bearing edible tomato-like fruits. 2 the fruit of this. [corrupt. of an Algonquian word]

persist /pəˈsɪst/ v.intr. 1 (often foll. by in) continue firmly or obstinately (in an opinion or a course of action) esp. despite obstacles, remonstrance, etc. 2 (of an institution, custom, phenomenon, etc.) continue in existence; survive. [L persistere (as PER-, sistere stand)]

persistent /pəˈsɪst(ə)nt/ adj. 1 continuing obstinately; persisting. 2 enduring. 3 constantly repeated (persistent nagging). 4 Biol. (of horns, leaves, etc.) remaining instead of falling off in the normal manner. □□ **persistence** n. **persistency** n. **persistently** adv.

person /ˈpɜːs(ə)n/ n. 1 an individual human being (a cheerful and forthright person). 2 the living body of a human being (hidden about your person). 3 Gram. any of three classes of personal pronouns, verb-forms, etc.: the person speaking (**first person**); the person spoken to (**second person**); the person spoken of (**third person**). 4 (in comb.) used to replace -man in offices open to either sex (salesperson). 5 (in Christianity) God as Father, Son, or Holy Ghost (three persons in one God). 6 euphem. the genitals (expose one's person). 7 a character in a play or story. □ **in one's own person** oneself; as oneself. **in person** physically present. **person-to-person** 1 between individuals. 2 (of a phone call) booked through the operator to a specified person. [ME f. OF persone f. L persona actor's mask, character in a play, human being]

persona /pɜːˈsəʊnə/ n. (pl. **personae** /-niː/) 1 an aspect of the personality as shown to or perceived by others (opp. ANIMA). 2 Literary criticism an author's assumed character in his or her writing. □ **persona grata** /ˈɡrɑːtə/ a person, esp. a diplomat, acceptable to certain others. **persona non grata** /nɒn, nəʊn ˈɡrɑːtə/ a person not acceptable. [L (as PERSON)]

personable /ˈpɜːsənəb(ə)l/ adj. pleasing in appearance and behaviour. □□ **personableness** n. **personably** adv.

personage /ˈpɜːsənɪdʒ/ n. 1 a person, esp. of rank or importance. 2 a character in a play etc. [ME f. PERSON + -AGE, infl. by med.L personagium effigy & F personnage]

personal /ˈpɜːsən(ə)l/ adj. 1 one's own; individual; private. 2 done or made in person (made a personal appearance; my personal attention). 3 directed to or concerning an individual (a personal letter). 4 referring (esp. in a hostile way) to an individual's private life or concerns (making personal remarks; no need to be personal). 5 of the body and clothing (personal hygiene; personal appearance). 6 existing as a person, not as an abstraction or thing (a personal God). 7 Gram. of or denoting one of the three persons (personal pronoun). □ **personal column** the part of a newspaper devoted to private advertisements or messages. **personal computer** a computer designed for use by a single individual, esp. in an office or business environment. **personal equation** 1 the allowance for an individual person's time of reaction in making observations, esp. in astronomy. 2 a bias or prejudice. **personal equity plan** a scheme for limited personal investment in shares, unit trusts, etc. **personal identification number** a number allocated to an individual, serving as a password esp. for a cash dispenser, computer, etc. **personal pronoun** a pronoun replacing the subject, object, etc., of a clause etc., e.g. I, we, you, them, us. **personal property** (or **estate**) Law all one's property except land and those interests in land that pass to one's heirs (cf. REAL¹ adj. 3). **personal service** individual service given to a customer. **personal stereo** a small portable audio cassette player, often with radio, or compact disc player, used with lightweight headphones. **personal touch** a way of treating a matter characteristic of or designed for an individual. [ME f. OF f. L personalis (as PERSON)]

personality /ˌpɜːsəˈnælɪtɪ/ n. (pl. **-ies**) 1 the distinctive character or qualities of a person, often as distinct from others (an attractive personality). 2 a famous person; a celebrity (a TV personality). 3 a person who stands out from others by virtue of his or her character (is a real personality). 4 personal existence or identity; the condition of being a person. 5 (usu. in pl.) personal remarks. □ **have personality** have a lively character or noteworthy qualities. **personality cult** the extreme adulation of an individual. [ME f. OF personalité f. LL personalitas -tatis (as PERSONAL)]

personalize /ˈpɜːsənəˌlaɪz/ v.tr. (also **-ise**) 1 make personal, esp. by marking with one's name etc. 2 personify. □□ **personalization** /-ˈzeɪʃ(ə)n/ n.

personally /ˈpɜːsənəlɪ/ adv. 1 in person (see to it personally). 2 for one's own part (speaking personally). 3 as a person (a God existing personally). 4 in a personal manner (took the criticism personally).

personalty /ˈpɜːsənltɪ/ n. (pl. **-ies**) Law one's personal property or estate (opp. REALTY). [AF personalté (as PERSONAL)]

personate /ˈpɜːsəˌneɪt/ v.tr. 1 play the part of (a character in a drama etc.; another type of person). 2 pretend to be (another person), esp. for fraudulent purposes; impersonate. □□ **personation** /-ˈneɪʃ(ə)n/ n. **personator** n. [LL personare personat- (as PERSON)]

personhood /ˈpɜːsənˌhʊd/ n. the quality or condition of being an individual person.

personification /pəˌsɒnɪfɪˈkeɪʃ(ə)n/ n. 1 the act of personifying. 2 (foll. by of) a person or thing viewed as a striking example of (a quality etc.) (the personification of ugliness).

personify /pəˈsɒnɪˌfaɪ/ v.tr. (**-ies**, **-ied**) 1 attribute a personal nature to (an abstraction or thing). 2 symbolize (a quality etc.) by a figure in human form. 3 (usu. as **personified** adj.) embody (a quality) in one's own person; exemplify typically (has always been kindness personified). □□ **personifier** n. [F personnifier (as PERSON)]

personnel /ˌpɜːsəˈnel/ n. a body of employees, persons involved in a public undertaking, armed forces, etc. □ **personnel carrier** an armoured vehicle for transporting troops etc. **personnel department** etc. the part of an organization concerned with the appointment, training, and welfare of employees. [F, orig. adj. = personal]

perspective /pəˈspektɪv/ n. & adj. —n. 1 a the art of drawing solid objects on a two-dimensional surface so as to give the right impression of relative positions, size, etc. (See below.) b a picture drawn in this way. 2 the apparent relation between visible objects as to position, distance, etc. 3 a mental view of the relative importance of things (keep the right perspective). 4 a geographical or imaginary prospect. —adj. of or in perspective. □ **in perspective** 1 drawn or viewed according to the rules of perspective. 2 correctly regarded in terms of relative importance. □□ **perspectival** /-ˈtaɪv(ə)l/ adj. **perspectively** adv. [ME f. med.L perspectiva (ars art) f. perspicere perspect- (as PER-, specere spect- look)]

Brunelleschi (early 15th c.) is generally acknowledged to have been the originator of the first demonstration of scientific perspective. Shortly afterwards his fellow architect Alberti devised a perspective construction for the special use of painters, described in his treatise On Painting (1436).

aʊ how eɪ day əʊ no eə hair ɪə near ɔɪ boy ʊə poor aɪə fire aʊə sour (see over for consonants)

Perspex /ˈpɜːspeks/ n. propr. a tough light transparent acrylic thermoplastic used instead of glass. [L perspicere look through (as PER-, specere look)]

perspicacious /ˌpɜːspɪˈkeɪʃəs/ adj. having mental penetration or discernment. □□ **perspicaciously** adv. **perspicaciousness** n. **perspicacity** /-ˈkæsɪtɪ/ n. [L perspicax -acis (as PERSPEX)]

perspicuous /pəˈspɪkjʊəs/ adj. 1 easily understood; clearly expressed. 2 (of a person) expressing things clearly. □□ **perspicuity** /-ˈkjuːɪtɪ/ n. **perspicuously** adv. **perspicuousness** n. [ME, = transparent f. L perspicuus (as PERSPECTIVE)]

perspiration /ˌpɜːspɪˈreɪʃ(ə)n/ n. 1 = SWEAT. 2 sweating. □□ **perspiratory** /-ˈspɪrətərɪ/ adj. [F (as PERSPIRE)]

perspire /pəˈspaɪə(r)/ v. 1 intr. sweat or exude perspiration, esp. as the result of heat, exercise, anxiety, etc. 2 tr. sweat or exude (fluid etc.). [F perspirer f. L perspirare (as PER-, spirare breathe)]

persuade /pəˈsweɪd/ v.tr. & refl. 1 (often foll. by of, or that + clause) cause (another person or oneself) to believe; convince (persuaded them that it would be helpful; tried to persuade me of its value). 2 a (often foll. by to + infin.) induce (another person or oneself) (persuaded us to join them; managed to persuade them at last). b (foll. by away from, down to, etc.) lure, attract, entice, etc. (persuaded them away from the pub). □□ **persuadable** adj. **persuadability** /-dəˈbɪlɪtɪ/ n. **persuasible** adj. [L persuadēre (as PER-, suadēre suas- advise)]

persuader /pəˈsweɪdə(r)/ n. 1 a person who persuades. 2 sl. a gun or other weapon.

persuasion /pəˈsweɪʒ(ə)n/ n. 1 persuading (yielded to persuasion). 2 persuasiveness (use all your persuasion). 3 a belief or conviction (my private persuasion). 4 a religious belief, or the group or sect holding it (of a different persuasion). 5 colloq. any group or party (the male persuasion). [ME f. L persuasio (as PERSUADE)]

persuasive /pəˈsweɪsɪv/ adj. able to persuade. □□ **persuasively** adv. **persuasiveness** n. [F persuasif -ive or med.L persuasivus (as PERSUADE)]

PERT abbr. programme evaluation and review technique.

pert /pɜːt/ adj. 1 saucy or impudent, esp. in speech or conduct. 2 (of clothes etc.) neat and suggestive of jauntiness. 3 = PEART. □□ **pertly** adv. **pertness** n. [ME f. OF apert f. L apertus past part. of aperire open & f. OF aspert f. L expertus EXPERT]

pertain /pəˈteɪn/ v.intr. 1 (foll. by to) a relate or have reference to. b belong to as a part or appendage or accessory. 2 (usu. foll. by to) be appropriate to. [ME f. OF partenir f. L pertinēre (as PER-, tenēre hold)]

Perth[1] /pɜːθ/ the capital of the State of Western Australia, on the estuary of the River Swan; pop. (1986) 1,025,300 (including the port of Fremantle).

Perth[2] /pɜːθ/ a royal burgh at the head of the Tay estuary in eastern Scotland; pop. (1981) 43,000.

pertinacious /ˌpɜːtɪˈneɪʃəs/ adj. stubborn; persistent; obstinate (in a course of action etc.). □□ **pertinaciously** adv. **pertinaciousness** n. **pertinacity** /-ˈnæsɪtɪ/ n. [L pertinax (as PER-, tenax tenacious)]

pertinent /ˈpɜːtɪnənt/ adj. 1 (often foll. by to) relevant to the matter in hand; apposite. 2 to the point. □□ **pertinence** n. **pertinency** n. **pertinently** adv. [ME f. OF pertinent or L pertinēre (as PERTAIN)]

perturb /pəˈtɜːb/ v.tr. 1 throw into confusion or disorder. 2 disturb mentally; agitate. 3 Physics & Math. subject (a physical system, or a set of equations, or its solution) to a perturbation. □□ **perturbable** adj. **perturbative** /pəˈtɜːbətɪv, ˈpɜːtəˌbeɪtɪv/ adj. **perturbingly** adv. [ME f. OF pertourber f. L (as PER-, turbare disturb)]

perturbation /ˌpɜːtəˈbeɪʃ(ə)n/ n. 1 the act or an instance of perturbing; the state of being perturbed. 2 a cause of disturbance or agitation. 3 Physics a slight alteration of a physical system, e.g. of the electrons in an atom, caused by a secondary influence. 4 Astron. a minor deviation in the course of a celestial body, caused by the attraction of a neighbouring body.

pertussis /pəˈtʌsɪs/ n. whooping cough. [mod.L f. PER- + L tussis cough]

Peru /pəˈruː/ a country in South America on the Pacific coast,

traversed throughout its length by the Andes; pop. (est. 1988) 21,255,900; official languages, Spanish and Quechua; capital, Lima. Agriculture is important, and cattle, sheep, llamas, and alpacas are bred in the mountain districts. Fish-meal is exported, and mineral exports include lead, zinc, copper, iron ore, and silver. The centre of the Inca empire, Peru was conquered by the Spanish conquistador Pizarro in 1532 and remained under Spanish control for nearly three centuries until liberated by Bolivar and San Martín in 1820–4; a democratic republic was then established. It lost territory in the south to Chile in the War of the Pacific (1879–83) and had border disputes with Colombia and Ecuador to the north in the 1930s and 1940s. Although beset by communication difficulties due to the mountainous terrain, Peru's mining industry has given it one of the most stable of South American economies.

peruke /pəˈruːk/ n. hist. a wig. [F perruque f. It. perrucca parrucca, of unkn. orig.]

peruse /pəˈruːz/ v.tr. 1 (also absol.) read or study, esp. thoroughly or carefully. 2 examine (a person's face etc.) carefully. □□ **perusal** n. **peruser** n. [ME, orig. = use up, prob. f. AL f. Rmc (as PER-, USE)]

Peruvian /pəˈruːvɪən/ n. & adj. —n. 1 a native or national of Peru. 2 a person of Peruvian descent. —adj. of or relating to Peru. □ **Peruvian bark** the bark of the cinchona tree. [mod.L Peruvia Peru]

perv /pɜːv/ n. & v. (also **perve**) sl. —n. 1 a sexual pervert. 2 Austral. an erotic gaze. —v.intr. 1 act like a sexual pervert. 2 (foll. by at, on) Austral. gaze with erotic interest. [abbr.]

pervade /pəˈveɪd/ v.tr. 1 spread throughout, permeate. 2 (of influences etc.) become widespread among or in. 3 be rife among or through. □□ **pervasion** /-ʒ(ə)n/ n. [L pervadere (as PER-, vadere vas- go)]

pervasive /pəˈveɪsɪv/ adj. 1 pervading. 2 able to pervade. □□ **pervasively** adv. **pervasiveness** n.

perve var. of PERV.

perverse /pəˈvɜːs/ adj. 1 (of a person or action) deliberately or stubbornly departing from what is reasonable or required. 2 persistent in error. 3 wayward; intractable; peevish. 4 perverted; wicked. 5 (of a verdict etc.) against the weight of evidence or the judge's direction. □□ **perversely** adv. **perverseness** n. **perversity** n. (pl. -ies). [ME f. OF pervers perverse f. L perversus (as PERVERT)]

perversion /pəˈvɜːʃ(ə)n/ n. 1 an act of perverting; the state of being perverted. 2 a perverted form of an act or thing. 3 a a preference for an abnormal form of sexual activity. b such an activity. [ME f. L perversio (as PERVERT)]

pervert v. & n. —v.tr. /pəˈvɜːt/ 1 turn (a person or thing) aside from its proper use or nature. 2 misapply or misconstrue (words etc.). 3 lead astray (a person, a person's mind, etc.) from right opinion or conduct, or esp. religious belief. 4 (as **perverted** adj.) showing perversion. —n. /ˈpɜːvɜːt/ 1 a perverted person. 2 a person showing sexual perversion. □□ **perversive** /pəˈvɜːsɪv/ adj. **pervertedly** /pəˈvɜːtɪdlɪ/ adv. **perverter** /-ˈvɜːtə(r)/ n. [ME f. OF pervertir or f. L pervertere (as PER-, vertere vers- turn): cf. CONVERT]

pervious /ˈpɜːvɪəs/ adj. 1 permeable. 2 (usu. foll. by to) a affording passage. b accessible (to reason etc.). □□ **perviousness** n. [L pervius (as PER-, vius f. via way)]

Pesach /ˈpeɪsɑːx/ n. the Passover festival. [Heb. Pesaḥ]

peseta /pəˈseɪtə/ n. the chief monetary unit of Spain, orig. a silver coin. [Sp., dimin. of pesa weight f. L pensa pl. of pensum: see POISE[1]]

Peshawar /pəˈʃɑːwə(r)/ the capital of North-west Frontier Province, Pakistan; pop. (1981), 555,000.

Peshitta /pəˈʃiːtə/ n. the official ancient Syriac version of the Bible in Syriac-speaking Christian lands from the early 5th c. [Syriac, = simple, plain]

pesky /ˈpeskɪ/ adj. (**peskier, peskiest**) esp. US colloq. troublesome; confounded; annoying. □□ **peskily** adv. **peskiness** n. [18th c.: perh. f. PEST]

peso /ˈpeɪsəʊ/ n. (pl. **-os**) 1 the chief monetary unit of several Latin American countries and of the Philippines. 2 a note or coin worth one peso. [Sp., = weight, f. L pensum: see POISE[1]]

pessary /ˈpesərɪ/ n. (pl. **-ies**) Med. **1** a device worn in the vagina to support the uterus or as a contraceptive. **2** a vaginal suppository. [ME f. LL *pessarium, pessulum* f. *pessum, pessus* f. Gk *pessos* oval stone]

pessimism /ˈpesɪˌmɪz(ə)m/ n. **1** a tendency to take the worst view or expect the worst outcome. **2** *Philos.* a belief that this world is as bad as it could be or that all things tend to evil (opp. OPTIMISM). □□ **pessimist** n. **pessimistic** /-ˈmɪstɪk/ adj. **pessimistically** /-ˈmɪstɪkəlɪ/ adv. [L *pessimus* worst, after OPTIMISM]

pest /pest/ n. **1** a troublesome or annoying person or thing; a nuisance. **2** a destructive animal, esp. an insect which attacks crops, livestock, etc. **3** *archaic* a pestilence; a plague. □ **pest-house** *hist.* a hospital for sufferers from the plague etc. [F *peste* or L *pestis* plague]

Pestalozzi /ˌpestəˈlɒtsɪ/, Johann Heinrich (1746–1827), Swiss educational reformer, a pioneer of primary education for the masses and especially for destitute children. Greatly influenced by Rousseau's *Émile* (see ROUSSEAU²), he believed that education should develop and train all a child's faculties, should allow for individual differences and pace of development, and that moral education and family life were of great importance. His attempts to put his ideas into practice ended in failure but his theories and methods were influential in the development of elementary education. His work is commemorated in the Pestalozzi International Children's Villages, the first of which was established at Trogen in Switzerland, in 1946, for war orphans.

pester /ˈpestə(r)/ v.tr. trouble or annoy, esp. with frequent or persistent requests. □□ **pesterer** n. [prob. f. *impester* f. F *empestrer* encumber: infl. by PEST]

pesticide /ˈpestɪˌsaɪd/ n. a substance used for destroying insects or other organisms harmful to cultivated plants or to animals. □□ **pesticidal** /-ˈsaɪd(ə)l/ adj.

pestiferous /peˈstɪfərəs/ adj. **1** noxious; pestilent. **2** harmful; pernicious; bearing moral contagion. [L *pestifer, -ferus* (as PEST)]

pestilence /ˈpestɪləns/ n. a fatal epidemic disease, esp. bubonic plague. [ME f. OF f. L *pestilentia* (as PESTILENT)]

pestilent /ˈpestɪlənt/ adj. **1** destructive to life, deadly. **2** harmful or morally destructive. **3** *colloq.* troublesome; annoying. □□ **pestilently** adv. [L *pestilens, pestilentus* f. *pestis* plague]

pestilential /ˌpestɪˈlenʃ(ə)l/ adj. **1** of or relating to pestilence. **2** dangerous; troublesome; pestilent. □□ **pestilentially** adv. [ME f. med.L *pestilentialis* f. L *pestilentia* (as PESTILENT)]

pestle /ˈpes(ə)l/ n. & v. —n. **1** a club-shaped instrument for pounding substances in a mortar. **2** an appliance for pounding etc. —v. **1** tr. pound with a pestle or in a similar manner. **2** intr. use a pestle. [ME f. OF *pestel* f. L *pistillum* f. *pinsare pist-* to pound]

pestology /peˈstɒlədʒɪ/ n. the scientific study of pests (esp. harmful insects) and of methods of dealing with them. □□ **pestological** /-stəˈlɒdʒɪk(ə)l/ adj. **pestologist** n.

Pet. abbr. Peter (New Testament).

pet¹ /pet/ n., adj., & v. —n. **1** a domestic or tamed animal kept for pleasure or companionship. **2** a darling, a favourite (often as a term of endearment). —attrib.adj. **1** kept as a pet (*pet lamb*). **2** of or for pet animals (*pet food*). **3** often *joc.* favourite or particular (*pet aversion*). **4** expressing fondness or familiarity (*pet name*). —v.tr. (**petted, petting**) **1** treat as a pet. **2** (also *absol.*) fondle, esp. erotically. □□ **petter** n. [16th-c. Sc. & N.Engl. dial.: orig. unkn.]

pet² /pet/ n. a feeling of petty resentment or ill-humour (esp. *be in a pet*). [16th c.: orig. unkn.]

peta- /ˈpetə/ comb. form denoting a factor of 10^{15}. [perh. f. PENTA-]

Pétain /peˈtæ̃/, Henri Philippe (1856–1951), French general and head of State. He served with distinction in the First World War, halting the German advance at Verdun (1916) and becoming commander-in-chief of French forces in 1917. Later he entered politics. In the Second World War, with France on the verge of defeat (1940), as Premier he concluded an armistice with Nazi Germany which surrendered three-fifths of France to German control. He established an authoritarian government at Vichy, soon dominated by pro-German collaborators. In 1945 Pétain

received a death sentence for collaboration, but this was commuted to life imprisonment.

petal /ˈpet(ə)l/ n. each of the parts of the corolla of a flower. □□ **petaline** /-ˌlaɪn, -lɪn/ adj. **petalled** adj. (also in *comb.*). **petal-like** adj. **petaloid** adj. [mod.L *petalum*, in LL metal plate f. Gk *petalon* leaf f. *petalos* outspread]

petard /pɪˈtɑːd/ n. *hist.* **1** a small bomb used to blast down a door etc. **2** a kind of firework or cracker. □ **hoist with one's own petard** affected oneself by one's schemes against others. [F *pétard* f. *péter* break wind]

petasus /ˈpetəsəs/ n. **1** an ancient Greek hat with a low crown and broad brim, esp. (in Greek mythology) as worn by Hermes. **2** the winged hat of Hermes. [L f. Gk *petasos*]

petaurist /pəˈtɔːrɪst/ n. any flying squirrel of the genus *Petaurista*, native to E. Asia. [Gk *petauristēs* performer on a springboard (*petauron*)]

Pete /piːt/ n. □ **for Pete's sake** see SAKE¹. [abbr. of the name Peter]

petechia /pɪˈtiːkɪə/ n. (pl. **petechiae** /-kɪˌiː/) Med. a small red or purple spot as a result of bleeding into the skin. □□ **petechial** adj. [mod.L f. It. *petecchia* a freckle or spot on one's face]

Peter /ˈpiːtə(r)/, St (died c.AD 67), an Apostle, originally called Simon, prominent among the disciples, a man of action, ardent and impetuous. The tradition connecting him with Rome is early; in Roman Catholic belief he was the founder and first bishop of the Church there. He was martyred, probably in Rome; in popular belief he is represented as the keeper of the door of heaven, whence his attribute of a set of keys. Feast day, 29 June. □ **Epistle of St Peter** either of the two epistles in the New Testament ascribed to St Peter. **Peter's Pence 1** *hist.* an annual tribute of a penny from every householder having land of a certain value, paid to the papal see at Rome from Anglo-Saxon times (c.787) until discontinued by statute in 1534 after Henry VIII's break with Rome. **2** *RCCh.* (since 1860) a voluntary payment to the papal treasury. [Gk f. *petros* stone]

Peter I /ˈpiːtə(r)/ 'the Great' (1672–1725), emperor of Russia 1682–1725. After a troubled minority during which he was denied effective power by his half-sister Sofia, Peter finally established his authority in 1689–94 and began a policy of expansion to the south and north-west. He reformed his armed forces along Western lines and engaged in a long war with Charles XII of Sweden, a war from which Russia, after severe initial setbacks, finally emerged victorious. On the domestic front, Peter's reign was characterized by a systematic attempt to reform Russian government and administration similarly, and although he faced considerable internal opposition, and was engaged in almost constant warfare along his borders, he succeeded in transforming Russia into a modern European power which would henceforth play a significant part in international affairs in central Europe.

peter¹ /ˈpiːtə(r)/ v. & n. —v.intr. **1** (foll. by *out*) (orig. of a vein of ore etc.) diminish, come to an end. **2** *Bridge* play an echo. —n. *Bridge* an echo. [19th c.: orig. unkn.]

peter² /ˈpiːtə(r)/ n. *sl.* **1** a prison cell. **2** a safe. [perh. f. the name Peter]

Peterloo /ˌpiːtəˈluː/ an event of 16 Aug. 1819, an attack by Manchester Yeomanry against a large but peaceable crowd. Sent to arrest the speaker at a rally of supporters of political reform in St Peter's Field, Manchester, the local yeomanry lost their heads and charged the crowd. In the resulting fracas, named Peterloo in ironical reference to the Battle of Waterloo, 11 civilians were killed and more than 500 injured.

peterman /ˈpiːtəmən/ n. (pl. **-men**) *sl.* a safe-breaker.

Peter Pan /ˌpiːtə ˈpæn/ the hero of J. M. Barrie's play of the same name (1904), a boy who never grew up. —n. a person who retains youthful features, or who is immature.

Peter Principle /ˈpiːtə/ n. *joc.* the principle that members of a hierarchy are promoted until they reach the level at which they are no longer competent. [L. J. *Peter*, its propounder, b. 1919]

petersham /ˈpiːtəʃəm/ n. thick corded silk ribbon used for stiffening in dressmaking etc. [Lord *Petersham*, Engl. army officer d. 1851]

Peter the Hermit (c.1050–1115) French monk, one of the most eloquent preachers of the First Crusade, who set out for the Holy Land in 1096 with an enthusiastic band of peasants, most of whom were massacred by the Turks. After his death he became the hero of many legends.

pethidine /ˈpeθɪˌdiːn/ n. a synthetic soluble analgesic used esp. in childbirth. [perh. f. PIPERIDINE (from which the drug is derived) + ETHYL]

petiole /ˈpetɪˌəʊl/ n. the slender stalk joining a leaf to a stem. □□ **petiolar** adj. **petiolate** /-lət/ adj. [F pétiole f. L petiolus little foot, stalk]

Petipa /pe'tiːpə/, Marius (1818–1910), French dancer, choreographer, and ballet master, who became principal dancer in St Petersburg in 1847 and first ballet master in 1862. He choreographed about 50 ballets for the Imperial Theatres in St Petersburg and Moscow, collaborating closely with Tchaikovsky on the *Nutcracker*, and was responsible for leading the Tsarist ballet to its magnificent climax. His noble classicism and consciousness of form were once considered old-fashioned, but were vindicated by Diaghilev's production of *The Sleeping Princess* in 1921; his œuvre is now considered one of the greatest achievements in the history of ballet.

petit /ˈpetɪ/ adj. esp. Law petty; small; of lesser importance. □ **petit jury** = petty jury. [ME f. OF, = small, f. Rmc, perh. imit. of child's speech]

petit bourgeois /ˌpetɪ ˈbʊəʒwaː, ˌpətɪ/ n. (pl. **petits bourgeois** pronunc. same) a member of the lower middle classes. [F]

petite /pə'tiːt/ adj. (of a woman) of small and dainty build. □ **petite bourgeoisie** /ˌbʊəʒwaːˈziː/ the lower middle classes. [F, fem. of PETIT]

petit four /ˌpetɪ ˈfɔː(r), ˌpətɪ/ n. (pl. **petits fours** /ˈfɔːz/) a very small fancy cake or biscuit. [F, = little oven]

petition /pɪˈtɪʃ(ə)n/ n. & v. —n. **1** a supplication or request. **2** a formal written request, esp. one signed by many people, appealing to authority in some cause. **3** Law an application to a court for a writ etc. —v. **1** tr. make or address a petition to (*petition your MP*). **2** intr. (often foll. by *for*, *to*) appeal earnestly or humbly. □ **Petition of Right 1** hist. a parliamentary declaration of rights and liberties of the people assented to by Charles I in 1628. **2** Law a common-law remedy against the crown for the recovery of property. □□ **petitionable** adj. **petitionary** adj. **petitioner** n. [ME f. OF f. L petitio -onis]

petitio principii /pɪˌtɪʃɪəʊ prɪnˈkɪpɪˌaɪ/ n. a logical fallacy in which a conclusion is taken for granted in the premiss; begging the question. [L, = assuming a principle: see PETITION]

petit-maître /ˌpətɪ'meɪtr/ n. a dandy or coxcomb. [F, = little master]

petit mal /ˌpetɪ 'mæl, ˌpətɪ/ n. a mild form of epilepsy with only momentary loss of consciousness (cf. GRAND MAL). [F, = little sickness]

petit point /ˌpetɪ 'pwæ̃, ˌpətɪ 'pɔɪnt/ n. **1** embroidery on canvas using small stitches. **2** tent-stitch. [F, = little point]

petits pois /ˌpetɪ 'pwaː, ˌpətɪ/ n.pl. small green peas. [F]

Petra /ˈpetrə/ an ancient city in southern Jordan, that was the capital of the Nabataeans by 312 BC. After AD 105 it ceased to be the administrative centre but remained the religious metropolis of Arabia. Petra lies in a hollow surrounded by mountains; the only access is by narrow gorges. The ruins of the city itself, though extensive, are not impressive, but the rock-hewn temples and tombs in the surrounding hills are magnificent ('a rose-red city, half as old as Time'); the site was rediscovered in 1812 by the Swiss traveller Burckhardt.

Petrarch /ˈpetraːk/ Francesco Petrarca, (1304–74), Italian poet, who has been called the father of modern poetry. His verse, especially his love-poems to the idealized woman he calls Laura, made him a national celebrity; he was crowned poet laureate in Rome in 1341. He was also important as a leader, with his friend Boccaccio, in the rediscovery of classical antiquity, rejecting medieval scholasticism and insisting on the continuity between pagan and Christian culture.

Petrarchan /pɪˈtraːkən/ adj. denoting a sonnet of the kind used by Petrarch, with an octave rhyming abbaabba, and a sestet usu. rhyming cdcdcd or cdecde.

petrel /ˈpetr(ə)l/ n. any of various sea birds of the family Procellariidae or Hydrobatidae, usu. flying far from land. [17th c. (also *pitteral*), of uncert. orig.: later assoc. with St Peter (Matt. 14: 30)]

Petri dish /ˈpetrɪ, 'piːt-/ n. a shallow covered dish used for the culture of bacteria etc. [J. R. Petri, Ger. bacteriologist d. 1921]

Petrie /ˈpiːtrɪ/, Sir William Matthew Flinders (1853–1942), English Egyptologist who introduced scientific field archaeology to Egypt and laid the foundations of all modern studies of ancient Egypt with his technique of 'artefact analysis' and his system of 'sequence dating'—comparative dating on typological grounds—which he devised and presented in the publications of his excavations in Egypt and Palestine.

petrifaction /ˌpetrɪˈfækʃ(ə)n/ n. **1** the process of fossilization whereby organic matter is turned into a stony substance. **2** a petrified substance or mass. **3** a state of extreme fear or terror. [PETRIFY after *stupefaction*]

petrify /ˈpetrɪˌfaɪ/ v. (**-ies**, **-ied**) **1** tr. paralyse with fear, astonishment, etc. **2** tr. change (organic matter) into a stony substance. **3** intr. become like stone. **4** tr. deprive (the mind, a doctrine, etc.) of vitality; deaden. [F pétrifier f. med.L petrificare f. L petra rock f. Gk]

petro- /ˈpetrəʊ/ comb. form **1** rock. **2** petroleum (*petrochemistry*). [Gk petros stone or petra rock]

petrochemical /ˌpetrəʊˈkemɪk(ə)l/ n. & adj. —n. a substance industrially obtained from petroleum or natural gas. —adj. of or relating to petrochemistry or petrochemicals.

petrochemistry /ˌpetrəʊˈkemɪstrɪ/ n. **1** the chemistry of rocks. **2** the chemistry of petroleum.

petrodollar /ˈpetrəʊˌdɒlə(r)/ n. a notional unit of currency earned by a petroleum-exporting country.

petroglyph /ˈpetrəʊglɪf/ n. a rock-carving, esp. a prehistoric one. [PETRO- + Gk glyphē carving]

petrography /pe'trɒgrəfɪ/ n. the scientific description of the composition and formation of rocks. □□ **petrographer** n. **petrographic** /-'græfɪk/ adj. **petrographical** /-'græfɪk(ə)l/ adj.

petrol /ˈpetr(ə)l/ n. Brit. **1** refined petroleum used as a fuel in motor vehicles, aircraft, etc. **2** (attrib.) concerned with the supply of petrol (*petrol pump*; *petrol station*). □ **petrol bomb** a simple bomb made of a petrol-filled bottle and a wick. [F pétrole f. med.L petroleum: see PETROLEUM]

petrolatum /ˌpetrə'leɪtəm/ n. US petroleum jelly. [mod.L f. PETROL + -atum]

petroleum /pɪˈtrəʊlɪəm/ n. a hydrocarbon oil found in the upper strata of the earth, refined for use as a fuel for heating and in internal-combustion engines, for lighting, dry-cleaning, etc. □ **petroleum ether** a volatile liquid distilled from petroleum, consisting of a mixture of hydrocarbons. **petroleum jelly** a translucent solid mixture of hydrocarbons used as a lubricant, ointment, etc. [med.L f. L petra rock f. Gk + L oleum oil]

petrolic /pɪˈtrɒlɪk/ adj. of or relating to petrol or petroleum.

petrology /pɪˈtrɒlədʒɪ/ n. the study of the origin, structure, composition, etc., of rocks. □□ **petrologic** /ˌpetrə'lɒdʒɪk/ adj. **petrological** /ˌpetrə'lɒdʒɪk(ə)l/ adj. **petrologist** n.

Petronius /pɪˈtrəʊnɪəs/ (1st c. AD) Roman writer, author of the *Satyricon*, a satirical novel of which only fragments survive. Its most complete episode tells of the tastelessly extravagant banquet of the *nouveau-riche* Trimalchio. The author is probably identical with the Petronius who was 'arbiter elegantiae' (= master of taste) at Nero's court, who committed suicide in AD 66.

Petropavlovsk-Kamchatski /ˈpetrəpævˌlɒfskkæm-ˌtʃætskɪ/ a Soviet port and naval base on the east coast of the Kamchatka peninsula in eastern Siberia; pop. (1985) 252,000.

petrous /ˈpetrəs/ adj. **1** Anat. denoting the hard part of the temporal bone protecting the inner ear. **2** Geol. of, like, or relating to rock. [L petrosus f. L petra rock f. Gk]

petticoat /ˈpetɪˌkəʊt/ n. **1** a woman's or girl's skirted undergarment hanging from the waist or shoulders. **2** sl. **a** a woman or girl. **b** (in *pl.*) the female sex. **3** (*attrib.*) often *derog.* feminine; associated with women (*petticoat pedantry*). □□ **petticoated** *adj.* **petticoatless** *adj.* [ME f. *petty coat*]

pettifog /ˈpetɪˌfog/ *v.intr.* (**pettifogged, pettifogging**) **1** practise legal deception or trickery. **2** quibble or wrangle about petty points. [back-form. f. PETTIFOGGER]

pettifogger /ˈpetɪˌfogə(r)/ *n.* **1** a rascally lawyer; an inferior legal practitioner. **2** a petty practitioner in any activity. □□ **pettifoggery** *n.* **pettifogging** *adj.* [PETTY + *fogger* underhand dealer, prob. f. *Fugger* family of merchants in Augsburg in the 15th–16th c.]

pettish /ˈpetɪʃ/ *adj.* peevish, petulant; easily put out. □□ **pettishly** *adv.* **pettishness** *n.* [PET² + -ISH¹]

petty /ˈpetɪ/ *adj.* (**pettier, pettiest**) **1** unimportant; trivial. **2** mean, small-minded; contemptible. **3** minor; inferior; on a small scale (*petty princes*). **4** *Law* (of a crime) of lesser importance (*petty sessions*) (cf. COMMON, GRAND). □ **petty bourgeois** = PETIT BOURGEOIS. **petty bourgeoisie** = *petite bourgeoisie*. **petty cash** money from or for small items of receipt or expenditure. **petty jury** a jury of 12 persons who try the final issue of fact in civil or criminal cases and pronounce a verdict. **petty officer** a naval NCO. **petty treason** see TREASON. □□ **pettily** *adv.* **pettiness** *n.* [ME *pety*, var. of PETIT]

petulant /ˈpetjʊlənt/ *adj.* peevishly impatient or irritable. □□ **petulance** *n.* **petulantly** *adv.* [F *pétulant* f. L *petulans -antis* f. *petere* seek]

petunia /pɪˈtjuːnɪə/ *n.* **1** any plant of the genus *Petunia* with white, purple, red, etc., funnel-shaped flowers. **2** a dark violet or purple colour. [mod.L f. F *petun* f. Guarani *petŷ* tobacco]

petuntse /pɪˈtʊntsɪ, -ˈtʌnts/ *n.* a white variable feldspathic mineral used for making porcelain. [Chin. *baidunzi* f. *bai* white + *dun* stone + suffix -*zi*]

pew /pjuː/ *n. & v.* —*n.* **1** (in a church) a long bench with a back; an enclosed compartment. **2** *Brit. colloq.* a seat (esp. *take a pew*). —*v.tr.* furnish with pews. □□ **pewage** *n.* **pewless** *adj.* [ME *pywe*, *puwe* f. OF *puye* balcony f. L *podia* pl. of PODIUM]

pewit var. of PEEWIT.

pewter /ˈpjuːtə(r)/ *n.* **1** a grey alloy of tin with lead, copper, or antimony or various other metals. **2** utensils made of this. **3** *sl.* a tankard etc. as a prize. □□ **pewterer** *n.* [ME f. OF *peutre, peualtre* f. Rmc, of unkn. orig.]

peyote /peɪˈəʊtɪ/ *n.* **1** any Mexican cactus of the genus *Lophophora*, esp. *L. williamsii* having no spines and button-like tops when dried. **2** a hallucinogenic drug containing mescaline prepared from this. [Amer. Sp. f. Nahuatl *peyotl*]

Pf. *abbr.* pfennig.

Pfc. *abbr.* *US* Private First Class.

pfennig /ˈpfenɪg, ˈfenɪg/ *n.* a small German coin, worth one-hundredth of a mark. [G, rel. to PENNY]

PG *abbr.* **1** (of films) classified as suitable for children subject to parental guidance. **2** paying guest.

PGA *abbr.* Professional Golfers' Association.

pH /piːˈeɪtʃ/ *n.* *Chem.* a logarithm of the reciprocal of the hydrogen-ion concentration in moles per litre of a solution, giving a measure of its acidity or alkalinity. [G, f. *Potenz* power + H (symbol for hydrogen)]

Phaedra /ˈfiːdrə/ *Gk legend* the wife of Theseus. She conceived a passion for her stepson Hippolytus, who rejected her, whereupon she hanged herself, leaving behind a letter which accused him. Theseus would not believe his son's protestations of innocence and banished him.

Phaethon /ˈfeɪəθɒn/ *Gk Mythol.* the son of Helios the sun-god. He asked to drive his father's solar chariot for a day, but could not control the immortal horses and the chariot plunged too near the earth until Zeus, to save the earth from destruction, killed Phaethon with a thunderbolt.

phaeton /ˈfeɪt(ə)n/ *n.* **1** a light open four-wheeled carriage, usu. drawn by a pair of horses. **2** *US* a touring-car. [F *phaéton* f. L *Phaethon* f. Gk *Phaethōn*, PHAETHON]

phage /feɪdʒ, fɑːʒ/ *n.* = BACTERIOPHAGE. [abbr.]

phagocyte /ˈfægəˌsaɪt/ *n.* a type of cell capable of engulfing and absorbing foreign matter, esp. a leucocyte ingesting bacteria in the body. □□ **phagocytic** /-ˈsɪtɪk/ *adj.* [Gk *phag-* eat + -CYTE]

phagocytosis /ˌfægəsaɪˈtəʊsɪs/ *n.* the ingestion of bacteria etc. by phagocytes. □□ **phagocytize** /ˈfægə-/ *v.tr.* (also **-ise**). **phagocytose** /ˈfægə-/ *v.tr.*

-phagous /fəgəs/ *comb. form* that eats (as specified) (*ichthyophagous*). [L -*phagus* f. Gk -*phagos* f. *phagein* eat]

-phagy /fədʒɪ/ *comb. form* the eating of (specified food) (*ichthyophagy*). [Gk -*phagia* (as -PHAGOUS)]

phalange /ˈfælændʒ/ *n.* **1** *Anat.* = PHALANX 4. **2** (**Phalange**) a right-wing activist Maronite party in Lebanon (cf. FALANGE). [F f. L *phalanx*: see PHALANX]

phalangeal /fəˈlændʒɪəl/ *adj.* *Anat.* of or relating to a phalanx.

phalanger /fəˈlændʒə(r)/ *n.* any of various marsupials of the family Phalangeridae, including cuscuses and possums. [F f. Gk *phalaggion* spider's web, f. the webbed toes of its hind feet]

phalanx /ˈfælæŋks/ *n.* (pl. **phalanxes** or **phalanges** /ˈfælænˌdʒiːz/) **1** *Gk Antiq.* a line of battle, esp. a body of Macedonian infantry drawn up in close order. **2** a set of people etc. forming a compact mass, or banded for a common purpose. **3** a bone of the finger or toe. **4** *Bot.* a bundle of stamens united by filaments. [L f. Gk *phalagx -ggos*]

phalarope /ˈfæləˌrəʊp/ *n.* any small wading or swimming bird of the subfamily Phalaropodidae, with a straight bill and lobed feet. [F f. mod.L *Phalaropus*, irreg. f. Gk *phalaris* coot + *pous podos* foot]

phalli pl. of PHALLUS.

phallic /ˈfælɪk/ *adj.* **1** of, relating to, or resembling a phallus. **2** *Psychol.* denoting the stage of male sexual development characterized by preoccupation with the genitals. □□ **phallically** *adv.* [F *phallique* & Gk *phallikos* (as PHALLUS)]

phallocentric /ˌfæləʊˈsentrɪk/ *adj.* centred on the phallus or on male attitudes. □□ **phallocentricity** /-ˈtrɪsɪtɪ/ *n.* **phallocentrism** /-trɪz(ə)m/ *n.*

phallus /ˈfæləs/ *n.* (pl. **phalli** /-laɪ/ or **phalluses**) **1** the (esp. erect) penis. **2** an image of this as a symbol of generative power in nature. □□ **phallicism** /-lɪˌsɪz(ə)m/ *n.* **phallism** *n.* [LL f. Gk *phallos*]

phanariot /fəˈnærɪət/ *n.* *hist.* a member of a class of Greek officials in Constantinople under the Ottoman Empire. [mod.Gk *phanariōtēs* f. *Phanar* the part of the city where they lived f. Gk *phanarion* lighthouse (on the Golden Horn)]

phanerogam /ˈfænərəˌgæm/ *n.* *Bot.* a plant that has stamens and pistils, a flowering plant (cf. CRYPTOGAM). □□ **phanerogamic** /-ˈgæmɪk/ *adj.* **phanerogamous** /-ˈrɒgəməs/ *adj.* [F *phanérogame* f. Gk *phaneros* visible + *gamos* marriage]

phantasize var. of FANTASIZE.

phantasm /ˈfæntæz(ə)m/ *n.* **1** an illusion, a phantom. **2** (usu. foll. by *of*) an illusory likeness. **3** a supposed vision of an absent (living or dead) person. □□ **phantasmal** /-ˈtæzm(ə)l/ *adj.* **phantasmic** /-ˈtæzmɪk/ *adj.* [ME f. OF *fantasme* f. L f. Gk *phantasma* f. *phantazō* make visible f. *phainō* show]

phantasmagoria /ˌfæntæzməˈgɔːrɪə/ *n.* **1** a shifting series of real or imaginary figures as seen in a dream. **2** an optical device for rapidly varying the size of images on a screen. □□ **phantasmagoric** /-ˈgɒrɪk/ *adj.* **phantasmagorical** /-ˈgɒrɪk(ə)l/ *adj.* [prob. f. F *fantasmagorie* (as PHANTASM + fanciful ending)]

phantast var. of FANTAST.

phantasy var. of FANTASY.

phantom /ˈfæntəm/ *n. & adj.* —*n.* **1** a ghost; an apparition; a spectre. **2** a form without substance or reality; a mental illusion. **3** *Med.* a model of the whole or part of the body used to practise or demonstrate operative or therapeutic methods. —*adj.* merely apparent; illusory. □ **phantom circuit** an arrangement of telegraph or other electrical wires equivalent to an extra circuit. **phantom limb** a continuing sensation of the presence of a limb which has been amputated. **phantom pregnancy** *Med.* the symptoms of pregnancy in a person not actually pregnant. [ME f. OF *fantosme* ult. f. Gk *phantasma* (as PHANTASM)]

Pharaoh /ˈfeərəʊ/ *n.* **1** the ruler of ancient Egypt. **2** the title of this ruler. □ **Pharaoh's serpent** an indoor firework burning and uncoiling in serpentine form. □□ **Pharaonic** /ˌfeəreɪˈɒnɪk/ adj. [OE f. eccl.L Pharao f. Gk Pharaō f. Heb. parʿōh f. Egypt. prʿo great house]

Pharisee /ˈfærɪˌsiː/ n. **1** a member of an ancient Jewish sect. (See below.) **2** a self-righteous person; a hypocrite. □□ **Pharisaic** /ˌfærɪˈseɪɪk/ adj. **Pharisaical** /ˌfærɪˈseɪɪk(ə)l/ adj. **Pharisaism** /ˈfærɪseɪˌɪz(ə)m/ n. [OE fariseus & OF pharise f. eccl.L pharisaeus f. Gk Pharisaios f. Aram. pʾrīšayyā pl. f. Heb. pārûš separated]

   The Pharisees are mentioned only by Josephus and in the New Testament, where they are held to have pretensions to superior sanctity. Unlike the Sadducees, who tried to apply Mosaic law strictly, the Pharisees allowed some interpretation, and although in the Gospels they are represented as the chief opponents of Christ they seem to have been less hostile than the Sadducees to the nascent Church, with whom they shared belief in the resurrection.

pharmaceutical /ˌfɑːməˈsjuːtɪk(ə)l/ adj. **1** of or engaged in pharmacy. **2** of the use or sale of medicinal drugs. □□ **pharmaceutically** adv. **pharmaceutics** n. [LL pharmaceuticus f. Gk pharmakeutikos f. pharmakeutēs druggist f. pharmakon drug]

pharmacist /ˈfɑːməsɪst/ n. a person qualified to prepare and dispense drugs.

pharmacognosy /ˌfɑːməˈkɒɡnəsɪ/ n. the science of drugs, esp. relating to medicinal products in their natural or unprepared state. [Gk pharmakon drug + gnōsis knowledge]

pharmacology /ˌfɑːməˈkɒlədʒɪ/ n. the science of the action of drugs on the body. □□ **pharmacological** /-kəˈlɒdʒɪk(ə)l/ adj. **pharmacologically** /-kəˈlɒdʒɪkəlɪ/ adv. **pharmacologist** n. [mod.L pharmacologia f. Gk pharmakon drug]

pharmacopoeia /ˌfɑːməkəˈpiːə/ n. **1** a book, esp. one officially published, containing a list of drugs with directions for use. **2** a stock of drugs. □□ **pharmacopoeial** adj. [mod.L f. Gk pharmakopoiia f. pharmakopoios drug-maker (as PHARMACOLOGY + -poios making)]

pharmacy /ˈfɑːməsɪ/ n. (pl. **-ies**) **1** the preparation and the (esp. medicinal) dispensing of drugs. **2** a pharmacist's shop, a dispensary. [ME f. OF farmacie f. med.L pharmacia f. Gk pharmakeia practice of the druggist f. pharmakeus f. pharmakon drug]

Pharos /ˈfeərɒs/ a lighthouse, one of the earliest known, erected by Ptolemy II c.280 BC on the island of Pharos, off the coast of Alexandria. Often considered one of the Seven Wonders of the World, it is said to have been over 130 m (440 ft.) high and to have been visible from 67 km (42 miles) away. It was finally destroyed in 1375.

pharos /ˈfeərɒs/ n. a lighthouse or a beacon to guide sailors. [L f. Gk Pharos PHAROS]

pharyngo- /fəˈrɪŋɡəʊ/ comb. form denoting the pharynx.

pharyngotomy /ˌfærɪŋˈɡɒtəmɪ/ n. (pl. **-ies**) an incision into the pharynx.

pharynx /ˈfærɪŋks/ n. (pl. **pharynges** /-rɪnˌdʒiːz/) a cavity, with enclosing muscles and mucous membrane, behind the nose and mouth, and connecting them to the oesophagus. □□ **pharyngal** /-ˈrɪŋɡ(ə)l/ adj. **pharyngeal** /-ˈdʒiːəl/ adj. **pharyngitis** /-ˈdʒaɪtɪs/ n. [mod.L f. Gk pharugx -ggos]

phase /feɪz/ n. & v. —n. **1** a distinct period or stage in a process of change or development. **2** each of the aspects of the moon or a planet, according to the amount of its illumination, esp. the new moon, the first quarter, the last quarter, and the full moon. **3** Physics a stage in a periodically recurring sequence, esp. of alternating electric currents or light vibrations. **4** a difficult or unhappy period, esp. in adolescence. **5** a genetic or seasonal variety of an animal's coloration etc. **6** Chem. a distinct and homogeneous form of matter separated by its surface from other forms. —v.tr. carry out (a programme etc.) in phases or stages. □ **in phase** having the same phase at the same time. **out of phase** not in phase. **phase in** (or out) bring gradually into (or out of) use. **phase rule** Chem. a rule relating numbers of phases, constituents, and degrees of freedom. **three-phase** (of an electric generator, motor, etc.) designed to supply or use simultaneously three separate alternating currents of the same voltage, but with phases differing by a third of a period. □□

phasic adj. [F phase & f. earlier phasis f. Gk phasis appearance f. phainō phan- show]

phatic /ˈfætɪk/ adj. (of speech etc.) used to convey general sociability rather than to communicate a specific meaning, e.g. 'nice morning, isn't it?' [Gk phatos spoken f. phēmi phan- speak]

Ph.D. abbr. Doctor of Philosophy. [L philosophiae doctor]

pheasant /ˈfez(ə)nt/ n. any of several long-tailed game-birds of the family Phasianidae, orig. from Asia. □□ **pheasantry** n. (pl. **-ies**). [ME f. AF fesaunt f. OF faisan f. L phasianus f. Gk phasianos (bird) of the river Phasis in Asia Minor]

Pheidippides /faɪˈdɪpɪˌdiːz/ the Athenian herald who was sent to Sparta to ask for aid when the Persians were known to have landed at Marathon in 490 BC. He is said to have covered the 250 km (150 miles) in two days on foot.

phenacetin /fɪˈnæsɪtɪn/ n. an acetyl derivative of phenol used to treat fever etc. [PHENO- + ACETYL + -IN]

pheno- /ˈfiːnəʊ/ comb. form **1** Chem. derived from benzene (phenol; phenyl). **2** showing (phenocryst). [Gk phainō shine (with ref. to substances used for illumination), show]

phenobarbitone /ˌfiːnəʊˈbɑːbɪˌtəʊn/ n. (US **phenobarbital** /-t(ə)l/) a narcotic and sedative barbiturate drug used esp. to treat epilepsy.

phenocryst /ˈfiːnəkrɪst/ n. a large or conspicuous crystal in porphyritic rock. [F phénocryste (as PHENO-, CRYSTAL)]

phenol /ˈfiːnɒl/ n. Chem. **1** the monohydroxyl derivative of benzene used in dilute form as an antiseptic and disinfectant. Also called CARBOLIC. ¶ Chem. formula: C_6H_5OH. **2** any hydroxyl derivative of an aromatic hydrocarbon. □□ **phenolic** /fɪˈnɒlɪk/ adj. [F phénole f. phène benzene (formed as PHENO-)]

phenolphthalein /ˌfiːnɒlˈθeɪliːn/ n. Chem. a white crystalline solid used in solution as an acid-base indicator and medicinally as a laxative. [PHENOL + phthal f. NAPHTHALENE + -IN]

phenomena pl. of PHENOMENON.

phenomenal /fɪˈnɒmɪn(ə)l/ adj. **1** of the nature of a phenomenon. **2** extraordinary, remarkable, prodigious. **3** perceptible by, or perceptible only to, the senses. □□ **phenomenalize** v.tr. (also **-ise**). **phenomenally** adv.

phenomenalism /fɪˈnɒmɪnəˌlɪz(ə)m/ n. Philos. **1** the doctrine that human knowledge is confined to the appearances presented to the senses. **2** the doctrine that appearances are the foundation of all our knowledge. □□ **phenomenalist** n. **phenomenalistic** /-ˈlɪstɪk/ adj.

phenomenology /fɪˌnɒmɪˈnɒlədʒɪ/ n. Philos. **1** the science of phenomena as distinct from that of being (ontology). **2** the philosophical movement that concentrates on the study of consciousness and its immediate objects. (See HUSSERL.) □□ **phenomenological** /-nəˈlɒdʒɪk(ə)l/ adj. **phenomenologically** /-nəˈlɒdʒɪkəlɪ/ adv.

phenomenon /fɪˈnɒmɪnən/ n. (pl. **phenomena** /-nə/) **1** a fact or occurrence that appears or is perceived, esp. one of which the cause is in question. **2** a remarkable person or thing. **3** Philos. the object of a person's perception; what the senses or the mind notice. [LL f. Gk phainomenon neut. pres. part. of phainomai appear f. phainō show]

phenotype /ˈfiːnəˌtaɪp/ n. Biol. a set of observable characteristics of an individual or group as determined by its genotype and environment. □□ **phenotypic** /-ˈtɪpɪk/ adj. **phenotypical** /-ˈtɪpɪk(ə)l/ adj. **phenotypically** /-ˈtɪpɪkəlɪ/ adv. [G Phaenotypus (as PHENO-, TYPE)]

phenyl /ˈfiːnaɪl, -nɪl/ n. Chem. the univalent radical formed from benzene by the removal of a hydrogen atom. [PHENO- + -YL]

phenylalanine /ˌfiːnaɪˈlæləˌniːn/ n. Biochem. an amino acid widely distributed in plant proteins and essential in the human diet. [PHENYL + ALANINE]

phenylketonuria /ˌfiːnaɪlˌkiːtəˈnjʊərɪə/ n. an inherited inability to metabolize phenylalanine, ultimately leading to mental deficiency if untreated. [PHENYL + KETONE + -URIA]

pheromone /ˈferəˌməʊn/ n. a chemical substance secreted and released by an animal for detection and response by another usu. of the same species. □□ **pheromonal** /-ˈməʊn(ə)l/ adj. [Gk pherō convey + HORMONE]

---

b but   d dog   f few   g get   h he   j yes   k cat   l leg   m man   n no   p pen   r red   s sit   t top   v voice

phew /fju:/ int. an expression of impatience, discomfort, relief, astonishment, or disgust. [imit. of puffing]

phi /faɪ/ n. the twenty-first letter of the Greek alphabet (Φ, φ). [Gk]

phial /ˈfaɪəl/ n. a small glass bottle, esp. for liquid medicine. [ME f. OF *fiole* f. L *phiola phiala* f. Gk *phialē*, a broad flat vessel: cf. VIAL]

Phi Beta Kappa /faɪ biːtə ˈkæpə/ **1** the oldest American college fraternity, an honorary society to which distinguished undergraduate (and occasionally graduate) scholars may be elected, named from the initial letters of its Greek motto, = 'philosophy the guide to life'. **2** a member of this society.

Phidias /ˈfɪdɪæs, ˈfaɪ-/ (5th c. BC) Athenian sculptor. His two greatest works, both executed in gold and ivory, were colossal statues of Zeus at Olympia and of Athene Parthenos for the Parthenon in Athens. He was appointed in 447 BC by the statesman Pericles to plan and supervise public building on the Acropolis and transformed Pericles' ideal of the grandeur of Athens into a reality, but both fell foul of political envy and Phidias was sent to trial in 432 BC accused of misappropriating gold and ivory. His career seems to have terminated then but he remains the most innovative highly individual artist of his time, and his sculptures can be seen as epitomizing the pinnacle of achievement in Greek art.

Phil. abbr. **1** Philadelphia. **2** Philharmonic. **3** Philippians (New Testament). **4** Philosophy.

phil- comb. form var. of PHILO-.

-phil comb. form var. of -PHILE.

philabeg var. of FILIBEG.

Philadelphia /ˌfɪləˈdelfɪə/ the chief city of Pennsylvania, founded by William Penn and other Quakers; pop. (1982) 1,665,382. [Gk *philadelphia* brotherly love]

philadelphus /ˌfɪləˈdelfəs/ n. any highly-scented deciduous flowering shrub of the genus *Philadelphus*, esp. the mock orange. [mod.L f. Gk *philadelphon*]

philander /fɪˈlændə(r)/ v.intr. (often foll. by *with*) flirt or have casual affairs with women; womanize. □□ **philanderer** n. [*philander* (n.) used in Gk literature as the proper name of a lover, f. Gk *philandros* fond of men f. *anēr* male person: see PHIL-]

philanthrope /ˈfɪlənˌθrəʊp/ n. = PHILANTHROPIST (see PHILANTHROPY). [Gk *philanthrōpos* (as PHIL-, *anthrōpos* human being)]

philanthropic /ˌfɪlənˈθrɒpɪk/ adj. loving one's fellow men; benevolent. □□ **philanthropically** adv. [F *philanthropique* (as PHILANTHROPE)]

philanthropy /fɪˈlænθrəpɪ/ n. **1** a love of mankind. **2** practical benevolence, esp. charity on a large scale. □□ **philanthropism** n. **philanthropist** n. **philanthropize** v.tr. & intr. (also **-ise**). [LL *philanthropia* f. Gk *philanthrōpia* (as PHILANTHROPE)]

philately /fɪˈlætəlɪ/ n. the collection and study of postage stamps. □□ **philatelic** /ˌfɪləˈtelɪk/ adj. **philatelically** /ˌfɪləˈtelɪkəlɪ/ adv. **philatelist** n. [F *philatélie* f. Gk *ateleia* exemption from payment f. a- not + *telos* toll, tax. When a letter was 'carriage-free', or carriage prepaid by the sender, it was formerly stamped with the word *free*; the fact is now indicated by its bearing a postage stamp or a frank]

Philby /ˈfɪlbɪ/, Harold Adrian Russell ('Kim') (1912–88), British intelligence officer and Soviet spy, who defected to the USSR in 1963 after supplying that country with quantities of secret information for more than twenty years. He became a Soviet citizen and was given high rank in the KGB.

-phile /faɪl/ comb. form (also **-phil** /fɪl/) forming nouns and adjectives denoting fondness for what is specified (*bibliophile*; *Francophile*). [Gk *philos* dear, loving]

Philem. abbr. Philemon (New Testament).

Philemon¹ /fɪˈliːmən/ Gk Mythol. a good old countryman who lived with his wife Baucis in Phrygia, and offered hospitality to Zeus and Hermes who had come to earth, without revealing their identities, to test people's piety. Philemon and Baucis were subsequently saved from a flood which covered the district.

Philemon² /fɪˈliːmən/ **Epistle to Philemon** a book of the New Testament, an epistle of St Paul to a well-to-do Christian living probably at Colossae in Phrygia.

philharmonic /ˌfɪlhɑːˈmɒnɪk/ adj. **1** fond of music. **2** used characteristically in the names of orchestras, choirs, etc. (*Royal Philharmonic Orchestra*). [F *philharmonique* f. It. *filarmonico* (as PHIL-, HARMONIC)]

philhellene /ˈfɪlheˌliːn, -ˈheliːn/ n. (often attrib.) **1** a lover of Greece and Greek culture. **2** hist. a supporter of the cause of Greek independence. □□ **philhellenic** /-ˈliːnɪk/ adj. **philhellenism** /-ˈhelɪˌnɪz(ə)m/ n. **philhellenist** /-ˈhelɪnɪst/ n. [Gk *philellēn* (as PHIL-, HELLENE)]

-philia /ˈfɪlɪə/ comb. form **1** denoting (esp. abnormal) fondness or love for what is specified (*necrophilia*). **2** denoting undue inclination (*haemophilia*). □□ **-philiac** /-lɪˌæk/ comb. form forming nouns and adjectives. **-philic** comb. form forming adjectives. **-philous** comb. form forming adjectives. [Gk f. *philos* loving]

Philip¹ /ˈfɪlɪp/, St **1** an Apostle, commemorated with St James the Less on 1 May. **2** 'the Evangelist', one of seven deacons appointed to superintend the secular business of the Church at Jerusalem (Acts 6: 5–6).

Philip² /ˈfɪlɪp/ the name of five kings of Macedonia:

Philip II (*c*.382–336 BC), reigned 359–336 BC, father of Alexander the Great. He unified Macedonia and fostered its economic growth, and introduced the phalanx formation in the army. His victory over Athens and Thebes at the battle of Chaeronea in 338 BC established his hegemony over Greece. He was assassinated as he was about to lead an expedition against Persia.

Philip V (238–179 BC), reigned 221–179 BC. A brilliant soldier, his aggressive policies led to a series of confrontations with the Romans, who forced a peace settlement on him after defeating him at Cynoscephalae in Thessaly in 197 BC.

Philip³ /ˈfɪlɪp/ (French *Philippe*) the name of several kings of France:

Philip II 'Philip Augustus' (1165–1223), son of Louis VII, reigned 1180–1223. His reign was marked by the most dramatic expansion of Capetian influence for several centuries. Having first come to terms with his own nobility, Philip proceeded to attack the English Plantagenet empire in France, getting the better, by a mixture of force and diplomacy, of Henry II, Richard I, and John, and occupying Normandy, Anjou, and Poitou. At the end of his reign, as a result of the Albigensian Crusade, Philip also succeeded in adding fresh territories in the south to his kingdom.

Philip IV 'the Fair' (1268–1314), son of Philip III, reigned 1285–1314. Philip IV continued the Capetian policy of extending French dominions, engaging in wars of expansion with England and Flanders. His reign, however, was dominated by his struggle with the papacy, during which he was excommunicated by Boniface VIII before establishing French domination over the Holy See, and by his persecution of the Knights Templar, for financial reasons, which ended with the dissolution of the order, the execution of its leaders, and the seizure of its property by the Crown.

Philip VI of Valois (1293–1350), cousin of Charles IV, reigned 1328–50. The founder of the Valois dynasty, Philip came to the throne under the Salic Law when the posthumous child of his cousin Charles IV, to whom he had been declared regent, proved to be a girl. His claim was disputed by the English king Edward III, who could trace a claim through the female line, and war between the two countries, which was to develop into the Hundred Years War, ensued. Philip got much the worse of the early engagements of the war, losing the battle of Crécy in 1346 with heavy casualties to his army.

Philip⁴ /ˈfɪlɪp/ (Spanish *Felipe*) the name of several kings of Spain:

Philip I (1478–1506), son of Maximilian I of Austria, reigned 1504–6. Philip became Duke of Burgundy in 1482 and married Juana of Castile, daughter of Ferdinand and Isabella, ten years later. After Isabella's death in 1504 he ruled Castile jointly with his wife, but did not actually return to Spain until 1506. He died three months later, possibly poisoned, but he had established the Hapsburgs as the ruling dynasty in his new country.

Philip II (1527–98), reigned 1556–98. The son of Charles V, who abdicated in his favour in 1556, Philip married four times, his second wife (1554) being Mary I of England. His reign was entirely dominated by an anti-Protestant crusade which exhausted the Spanish economy and led to the country's rapid decline in the 17th c. Philip failed to suppress the revolt in the Netherlands (1567–79) and although he conquered Portugal in 1580–1, his war against England (1587–9) also proved a failure, an attempted Spanish invasion being thwarted by the defeat of the Armada in 1588.

Philip V (1683–1746), grandson of Louis XIV, reigned 1700–24, 1724–46. First Bourbon king of Spain, Philip's selection as successor to Charles II led to the War of the Spanish Succession (1701–14). Formally recognized as king by the Treaty of Utrecht, Philip abdicated in favour of his son Louis in 1724 but returned to the throne following Louis' death eight months later.

Philippi /ˈfɪlɪpaɪ/ an ancient city in eastern Macedonia, the scene in 42 BC of the two battles in which Antony and Octavian defeated Brutus and Cassius.

Philippians /fɪˈlɪpɪənz/ **Epistle to the Philippians** a book of the New Testament, an epistle of St Paul to the Church at Philippi in Macedonia.

philippic /fɪˈlɪpɪk/ n. a bitter verbal attack or denunciation. [L *philippicus* f. Gk *philippikos* the name of Demosthenes' speeches against Philip II of Macedon and Cicero's against Mark Antony]

Philippine /ˈfɪlɪpiːn/ adj. of or relating to the Philippine Islands or their people; Filipino. [PHILIP⁴ II of Spain]

Philippines /ˈfɪlɪpiːnz/ a country in SE Asia consisting of a chain of over 7,000 islands of the Malay Archipelago, the chief of which are Luzon in the north and Mindanao in the south, all separated from the Asian mainland by the South China Sea; pop. (est. 1988) 63,199,300; official languages Pilipino and English; capital, Manila. The Portuguese navigator Magellan visited the islands in 1521 and was killed there. Conquered by Spain in 1565, and named 'Filipinas' after the king's son, the islands were ceded to the US following the Spanish-American War in 1898. Occupied by the Japanese between 1941 and 1944, the Philippines achieved full independence as a republic in 1946; it has continued to maintain close links with the US. Most of the area remains backward and agricultural, with the exception of the major population centre on Luzon.

Philistine /ˈfɪlɪˌstaɪn/ n. & adj. —n. **1** a member of a non-Semitic people opposing the Israelites in ancient Palestine.(See below.) —adj. of the Philistines. [ME f. F *Philistin* or LL *Philistinus* f. Gk *Philistinos* = *Palaistinos* f. Heb. *p'lišti*]

The Philistines ('Peleset' of Egyptian inscriptions from the time of Rameses III, c.1190 BC), from whom the country of Palestine took its name, were one of the Sea Peoples who, according to the Bible, came from Caphtor/Crete and settled the southern coastal plain of Canaan in the 12th c. BC. Governed by a league of five city-states (Gaza, Ashkelon, Ashdod, Gath, and Ekron), they gained control of the land and sea routes and acquired a monopoly of metal technology. After repeated conflicts with the Israelites they were defeated by David c.1000 BC and subsequently declined into obscurity after losing control of the sea trade to the Phoenicians.

philistine /ˈfɪlɪstaɪn/ n. & adj. —n. a person who is hostile or indifferent to culture, or whose interests are material or commonplace. —adj. having such characteristics. □□ **philistinism** /-stɪnɪz(ə)m/ n. [PHILISTINE]

Phillips /ˈfɪlɪps/ n. (usu. attrib.) propr. denoting a screw with a cross-shaped slot for turning, or a corresponding screwdriver. [name of the original US manufacturer]

phillumenist /fɪˈljuːmənɪst, fɪˈluː-/ n. a collector of matchbox labels. □□ **phillumeny** n. [PHIL- + L *lumen* light]

Philly /ˈfɪlɪ/ n. US sl. Philadelphia. [abbr.]

Philo /ˈfaɪləʊ/ (c.20 BC–c. AD 50), Jewish philosopher of Alexandria, author of numerous works (written in Greek). His most influential achievement was his development of the allegorical interpretation of Scripture, which enabled him to discover much of Greek philosophy in the Old Testament.

philo- /ˈfɪləʊ/ comb. form (also **phil-** before a vowel or h) denoting a liking for what is specified.

philodendron /ˌfɪləʊˈdendrən/ n. (pl. **philodendrons** or **philodendra** /-drə/) any tropical American climbing plant of

the genus *Philodendron*, with bright foliage. [PHILO- + Gk *dendron* tree]

philogynist /fɪˈlɒdʒɪnɪst/ n. a person who likes or admires women. [PHILO- + Gk *gunē* woman]

philology /fɪˈlɒlədʒɪ/ n. **1** the science of language, esp. in its historical and comparative aspects. **2** the love of learning and literature. □□ **philologian** /-ləˈləʊdʒ(ə)n/ n. **philologist** n. **philological** /-ləˈlɒdʒɪk(ə)l/ adj. **philologically** /-ləˈlɒdʒɪkəlɪ/ adv. **philologize** v.intr. (also **-ise**). [F *philologie* f. L *philologia* love of learning f. Gk (as PHILO-, -LOGY)]

Philomel /ˈfɪləmel/ (also **Philomela** /ˌfɪləˈmiːlə/) Gk Mythol. the daughter of a legendary king of Athens. She was turned into a swallow and her sister Procne into a nightingale (or, in Latin versions, into a nightingale and Procne into a swallow). —n. poet. the nightingale. [earlier *philomene* f. med.L *philomena* f. L *philomela* nightingale f. Gk *philomēla*]

philoprogenitive /ˌfɪləʊprəʊˈdʒenɪtɪv/ adj. **1** prolific. **2** loving one's offspring.

philosopher /fɪˈlɒsəfə(r)/ n. **1** a person engaged or learned in philosophy or a branch of it. **2** a person who lives by philosophy. **3** a person who shows philosophic calmness in trying circumstances. □ **philosophers'** (or **philosopher's**) **stone** the supreme object of alchemy, a substance supposed to change other metals into gold or silver. [ME f. AF *philosofre* var. of OF, *philosophe* f. L *philosophus* f. Gk *philosophos* (as PHILO-, *sophos* wise)]

philosophical /ˌfɪləˈsɒfɪk(ə)l/ adj. (also **philosophic**) **1** of or according to philosophy. **2** skilled in or devoted to philosophy or learning; learned (*philosophical society*). **3** wise; serene; temperate. **4** calm in adverse circumstances. □□ **philosophically** adv. [LL *philosophicus* f. L *philosophia* (as PHILOSOPHY)]

philosophize /fɪˈlɒsəˌfaɪz/ v. (also **-ise**) **1** intr. reason like a philosopher. **2** intr. moralize. **3** intr. speculate; theorize. **4** tr. render philosophic. □□ **philosophizer** n. [app. f. F *philosopher*]

philosophy /fɪˈlɒsəfɪ/ n. (pl. **-ies**) **1** the use of reason and argument in seeking truth and knowledge of reality, esp. of the causes and nature of things and of the principles governing existence, the material universe, perception of physical phenomena, and human behaviour. **2 a** a particular system or set of beliefs reached by this. **b** a personal rule of life. **3** advanced learning in general (*doctor of philosophy*). **4** serenity; calmness; conduct governed by a particular philosophy. [ME f. OF *filosofie* f. L *philosophia* wisdom f. Gk (as PHILO-, *sophos* wise)]

philtre /ˈfɪltə(r)/ n. (US **philter**) a drink supposed to excite sexual love in the drinker. [F *philtre* f. L *philtrum* f. Gk *philtron* f. *phileō* to love]

-phily /ˈfɪlɪ/ comb. form = -PHILIA.

phimosis /faɪˈməʊsɪs/ n. a constriction of the foreskin, making it difficult to retract. □□ **phimotic** /-ˈmɒtɪk/ adj. [mod.L f. Gk, = muzzling]

phiz /fɪz/ n. (also **phizog** /ˈfɪzɒg/) Brit. colloq. **1** the face. **2** the expression on a face. [abbr. of *phiznomy* = PHYSIOGNOMY]

phlebitis /flɪˈbaɪtɪs/ n. inflammation of the walls of a vein. □□ **phlebitic** /-ˈbɪtɪk/ adj. [mod.L f. Gk f. *phleps phlebos* vein]

phlebotomy /flɪˈbɒtəmɪ/ n. **1** the surgical opening or puncture of a vein. **2** esp. hist. blood-letting as a medical treatment. □□ **phlebotomist** n. **phlebotomize** v.tr. (also **-ise**). [ME f. OF *flebothomi* f. LL *phlebotomia* f. Gk f. *phleps phlebos* vein + -TOMY]

phlegm /flem/ n. **1** the thick viscous substance secreted by the mucous membranes of the respiratory passages, discharged by coughing. **2 a** coolness and calmness of disposition. **b** sluggishness or apathy (supposed to result from too much phlegm (see sense 3) in the constitution). **3** archaic phlegm regarded as one of the four bodily humours. □□ **phlegmy** adj. [ME & OF *fleume* f. LL *phlegma* f. Gk *phlegma -atos* inflammation f. *phlegō* burn]

phlegmatic /fleɡˈmætɪk/ adj. stolidly calm; unexcitable, unemotional. □□ **phlegmatically** adv.

phloem /ˈfləʊem/ n. Bot. the tissue conducting food material in plants (cf. XYLEM). [Gk *phloos* bark]

phlogiston /fləˈdʒɪst(ə)n, -ˈɡɪst(ə)n/ n. a substance formerly supposed to exist in all combustible bodies, and to be released in

æ cat ɑː arm e bed ɜː her ɪ sit iː see ɒ hot ɔː saw ʌ run ʊ put uː too ə ago aɪ my

combustion. [mod.L f. Gk *phlogizō* set on fire f. *phlox phlogos* flame]

phlox /flɒks/ *n.* any cultivated plant of the genus *Phlox*, with scented clusters of esp. white, blue, and red flowers. [L f. Gk *phlox*, the name of a plant (lit. flame)]

Phnom Penh /nɒm ˈpen/ the capital of Cambodia; pop. (est. 1983) 500,000.

-phobe /fəʊb/ *comb. form* forming nouns and adjectives denoting fear or dislike of what is specified (*xenophobe*). [F f. L *-phobus* f. Gk *-phobos* f. *phobos* fear]

phobia /ˈfəʊbɪə/ *n.* an abnormal or morbid fear or aversion. □□ **phobic** *adj.* & *n.* [-PHOBIA used as a separate word]

-phobia /ˈfəʊbɪə/ *comb. form* forming abstract nouns denoting fear or aversion of what is specified (*agoraphobia*; *xenophobia*). □□ **-phobic** *comb. form* forming adjectives. [L f. Gk]

Phoebe /ˈfiːbɪ/ *Gk Mythol.* a Titaness, daughter of Uranus (Heaven) and Gaia (Earth). She became the mother of Leto and thus the grandmother of Apollo and Artemis. In the later Greek writers her name was often used for Selene (Moon). [Gk *Phoibē* bright one]

phoebe /ˈfiːbɪ/ *n.* any American flycatcher of the genus *Sayornis*. [imit.: infl. by the name]

Phoebus /ˈfiːbəs/ *Gk Mythol.* an epithet of Apollo, sometimes identified with the sun. [Gk *Phoibos* bright one]

Phoenician /fəˈnɪʃ(ə)n, fəˈniː-/ *n.* & *adj.* —*n.* a member of a Semitic people of ancient Phoenicia in S. Syria or of its colonies. (See below.) —*adj.* of or relating to Phoenicia or its people or colonies. [ME f. OF *phenicien* f. L *Phoenicia* f. L *Phoenice* f. Gk *Phoinikē* Phoenicia]

   The Phoenicians were a Semitic-speaking people of unknown origin but culturally descended from the Canaanites in the 2nd millennium BC, who occupied the coastal plain of modern Lebanon and Syria in the early 1st millennium BC and derived their prosperity from trade and manufacturing industries in textiles, glass, metalware, carved ivory, wood, and jewellery. Their trading contacts extended throughout Asia, and reached westwards as far as Africa (where they founded Carthage), Spain, and possibly Britain. The Phoenicians continued to thrive under Assyrian and then Persian suzerainty until 332 BC when the capital, Tyre, was sacked and the country incorporated in the Greek world by Alexander the Great. The Phoenician alphabet was borrowed by the Greeks and thence passed down into Western cultural tradition.

Phoenix /ˈfiːnɪks/ the capital and largest city of Arizona; pop. (1982) 824,200.

phoenix /ˈfiːnɪks/ *n.* **1** a mythical bird, the only one of its kind, that after living for five or six centuries in the Arabian desert, burnt itself on a funeral pyre and rose from the ashes with renewed youth to live through another cycle. **2** a unique person or thing. [OE & OF *fenix* f. L *phoenix* f. Gk *phoinix* Phoenician, purple, phoenix]

Phoenix Islands a group of eight islands forming part of the Republic of Kiribati in the SW Pacific.

pholas /ˈfəʊləs/ *n.* a piddock, esp. of the genus *Pholas*. [mod.L f. Gk *phōlas* that lurks in a hole (*phōleos*)]

phon /fɒn/ *n.* a unit of the perceived loudness of sounds. [Gk *phōnē* sound]

phonate /ˈfəʊneɪt/ *v.intr.* utter a vocal sound. □□ **phonation** /ˈneɪʃ(ə)n/ *n.* **phonatory** /ˈfəʊnətərɪ/ *adj.* [Gk *phōnē* voice]

phone[1] /fəʊn/ *n.* & *v.tr.* & *intr. colloq.* = TELEPHONE. □ **phone book** = telephone directory. **phone-in** *n.* a broadcast programme during which the listeners or viewers telephone the studio etc. and participate. [abbr.]

phone[2] /fəʊn/ *n.* a simple vowel or consonant sound. [formed as PHONEME]

-phone /fəʊn/ *comb. form* forming nouns and adjectives meaning: **1** an instrument using or connected with sound (*telephone*; *xylophone*). **2** a person who uses a specified language (*anglophone*). [Gk *phōnē* voice, sound]

phonecard /ˈfəʊnkɑːd/ *n.* a card containing prepaid units for use with a Cardphone.

phoneme /ˈfəʊniːm/ *n.* any of the units of sound in a specified language that distinguish one word from another (e.g. *p*, *b*, *d*, *t* as in pad, pat, bad, bat, in English). □□ **phonemic** /-ˈniːmɪk/ *adj.* **phonemics** /-ˈniːmɪks/ *n.* [F *phonème* f. Gk *phōnēma* sound, speech f. *phōneō* speak]

phonetic /fəˈnetɪk/ *adj.* **1** representing vocal sounds. **2** (of a system of spelling etc.) having a direct correspondence between symbols and sounds. **3** of or relating to phonetics. □□ **phonetically** *adv.* **phoneticism** /-ˌsɪz(ə)m/ *n.* **phoneticist** /-sɪst/ *n.* **phoneticize** /-ˌsaɪz/ *v.tr.* (also **-ise**). [mod.L *phoneticus* f. Gk *phōnētikos* f. *phōneō* speak]

phonetics /fəˈnetɪks/ *n.pl.* (usu. treated as *sing.*) **1** vocal sounds and their classification. **2** the study of these. □□ **phonetician** /ˌfəʊnɪˈtɪʃ(ə)n/ *n.*

phonetist /ˈfəʊnɪtɪst/ *n.* **1** a person skilled in phonetics. **2** an advocate of phonetic spelling.

phoney /ˈfəʊnɪ/ *adj.* & *n.* (also **phony**) *colloq.* —*adj.* (**phonier**, **phoniest**) **1** sham; counterfeit. **2** fictitious; fraudulent. —*n.* (*pl.* **-eys** or **-ies**) a phoney person or thing. □□ **phonily** *adv.* **phoniness** *n.* [20th c.: orig. unkn.]

phonic /ˈfɒnɪk, ˈfəʊ-/ *adj.* & *n.* —*adj.* of sound; acoustic; of vocal sounds. —*n.* (in *pl.*) a method of teaching reading based on sounds. □□ **phonically** *adv.* [Gk *phōnē* voice]

phono- /ˈfəʊnəʊ/ *comb. form* denoting sound. [Gk *phōnē* voice, sound]

phonogram /ˈfəʊnəˌgræm/ *n.* a symbol representing a spoken sound.

phonograph /ˈfəʊnəˌgrɑːf/ *n.* **1** *Brit.* an early form of gramophone using cylinders and able to record as well as reproduce sound. **2** *US* a gramophone.

phonography /fəˈnɒgrəfɪ/ *n.* **1** writing in esp. shorthand symbols, corresponding to the sounds of speech. **2** the recording of sounds by phonograph. □□ **phonographic** /ˌfəʊnəˈgræfɪk/ *adj.*

phonology /fəˈnɒlədʒɪ/ *n.* the study of sounds in a language. □□ **phonological** /ˌfəʊnəˈlɒdʒɪk(ə)l, ˌfɒn-/ *adj.* **phonologically** /ˌfəʊnəˈlɒdʒɪkəlɪ, ˌfɒn-/ *adv.* **phonologist** *n.*

phonon /ˈfəʊnɒn/ *n.* *Physics* a quantum of sound or elastic vibrations. [Gk *phōnē* sound, after PHOTON]

phony var. of PHONEY.

phooey /ˈfuːɪ/ *int.* an expression of disgust or disbelief. [imit.]

-phore /fɔː(r)/ *comb. form* forming nouns meaning 'bearer' (*ctenophore*; *semaphore*). □□ **-phorous** /fərəs/ *comb. form* forming adjectives. [mod.L f. Gk *-phoros -phoron* bearing, bearer f. *pherō* bear]

phoresy /fɒˈriːsɪ, ˈfɒrəsɪ/ *n.* *Biol.* an association in which one organism is carried by another, without being a parasite. □□ **phoretic** /fɒˈretɪk/ *adj.* [F *phorésie* f. Gk *phorēsis* being carried]

phormium /ˈfɔːmɪəm/ *n.* **1** a liliaceous plant, *Phormium tenax*, yielding a leaf-fibre that is used commercially. **2** New Zealand flax. [mod.L f. Gk *phormion* a species of plant]

phosgene /ˈfɒzdʒiːn/ *n.* a colourless poisonous gas (carbonyl chloride), formerly used in warfare. ¶ Chem. formula: $COCl_2$. [Gk *phōs* light + -GEN, with ref. to its orig. production by the action of sunlight on chlorine and carbon monoxide]

phosphatase /ˈfɒsfəˌteɪz, -teɪs/ *n.* *Biochem.* any enzyme that catalyses the synthesis or hydrolysis of an organic phosphate.

phosphate /ˈfɒsfeɪt/ *n.* **1** any salt or ester of phosphoric acid, esp. used as a fertilizer. **2** an effervescent drink containing a small amount of phosphate. □□ **phosphatic** /-ˈfætɪk/ *adj.* [F f. *phosphore* PHOSPHORUS]

phosphene /ˈfɒsfiːn/ *n.* the sensation of rings of light produced by pressure on the eyeball due to irritation of the retina. [irreg. f. Gk *phōs* light + *phainō* show]

phosphide /ˈfɒsfaɪd/ *n.* *Chem.* a binary compound of phosphorus with another element or group.

phosphine /ˈfɒsfiːn/ *n.* *Chem.* a colourless ill-smelling gas, phosphorus trihydride. ¶ Chem. formula: PH_3. □□ **phosphinic** /-ˈfɪnɪk/ *adj.* [PHOSPHO- + -INE[4], after *amine*]

phosphite /ˈfɒsfaɪt/ *n.* *Chem.* any salt or ester of phosphorous acid. [F (as PHOSPHO-)]

phospho- /ˈfɒsfəʊ/ *comb. form* denoting phosphorus. [abbr.]

phospholipid /ˌfɒsfəˈlɪpɪd/ n. Biochem. any lipid consisting of a phosphate group and one or more fatty acids.

phosphor /ˈfɒsfə(r)/ n. 1 = PHOSPHORUS. 2 a synthetic fluorescent or phosphorescent substance esp. used in cathode-ray tubes. □ **phosphor bronze** a tough hard bronze alloy containing a small amount of phosphorus, used esp. for bearings. [G f. L phosphorus PHOSPHORUS]

phosphorate /ˈfɒsfəˌreɪt/ v.tr. combine or impregnate with phosphorus.

phosphorescence /ˌfɒsfəˈres(ə)ns/ n. 1 radiation similar to fluorescence but detectable after excitation ceases. 2 the emission of light without combustion or perceptible heat. □□ **phosphoresce** v.intr. **phosphorescent** adj.

phosphorite /ˈfɒsfəˌraɪt/ n. a non-crystalline form of apatite.

phosphorus /ˈfɒsfərəs/ n. Chem. a non-metallic element occurring naturally in various phosphate rocks and existing in allotropic forms which can be grouped together in three major categories: white phosphorus, red phosphorus, and black phosphorus. Of these, white phosphorus is the most reactive. Usually yellowish because of impurities, it is waxy, poisonous, and luminous in the dark. It was first isolated in the 17th c.; its discovery led to attempts to obtain instant flame, and eventually to the invention of matches. Phosphorus is essential to life, and a major use of phosphorus compounds is as fertilizers. Other uses are as insecticides and poison gases. ¶ Symb.: **P**; atomic number 15. □□ **phosphoric** /-ˈfɒrɪk/ adj. **phosphorous** adj. [L, = morning star, f. Gk phōsphoros f. phōs light + -phoros -bringing]

phosphorylate /fɒsˈfɒrɪˌleɪt/ v.tr. Chem. introduce a phosphate group into (an organic molecule etc.). □□ **phosphorylation** /-ˈleɪʃ(ə)n/ n.

phossy jaw /ˈfɒsɪ/ n. colloq. hist. gangrene of the jawbone caused by phosphorus poisoning. [abbr.]

phot /fɒt, fəʊt/ n. a unit of illumination equal to one lumen per square centimetre. [Gk phōs phōtos light]

photic /ˈfəʊtɪk/ adj. 1 of or relating to light. 2 (of ocean layers) reached by sunlight.

photism /ˈfəʊtɪz(ə)m/ n. a hallucinatory sensation or vision of light. [Gk phōtismos f. phōtizō shine f. phōs phōtos light]

Photius /ˈfəʊtɪəs/ (c.820–?897) Byzantine scholar and patriarch of Constantinople. His most important work is the Library (Bibliotheca), a critical account of 280 earlier prose works and an invaluable source of information about many works now lost.

photo /ˈfəʊtəʊ/ n. & v. —n. (pl. -os) = PHOTOGRAPH n. —v.tr. (-oes, -oed) = PHOTOGRAPH v. □ **photo-call** an occasion on which theatrical performers, famous personalities, etc., pose for photographers by arrangement. **photo finish** a close finish of a race or contest, esp. one where the winner is only distinguishable on a photograph. [abbr.]

photo- /ˈfəʊtəʊ/ comb. form denoting: 1 light (photosensitive). 2 photography (photocomposition). [Gk phōs phōtos light, or as abbr. of PHOTOGRAPH]

photobiology /ˌfəʊtəʊbaɪˈɒlədʒɪ/ n. the study of the effects of light on living organisms.

photocell /ˈfəʊtəʊˌsel/ n. = photoelectric cell.

photochemistry /ˌfəʊtəʊˈkemɪstrɪ/ n. the study of the chemical effects of light. □□ **photochemical** adj.

photocomposition /ˌfəʊtəʊˌkɒmpəˈzɪʃ(ə)n/ n. = FILMSETTING.

photoconductivity /ˌfəʊtəʊˌkɒndʌkˈtɪvɪtɪ/ n. conductivity due to the action of light. □□ **photoconductive** /-kənˈdʌktɪv/ adj. **photoconductor** /-kənˈdʌktə(r)/ n.

photocopier /ˈfəʊtəʊˌkɒpɪə(r)/ n. a machine for producing photocopies.

photocopy /ˈfəʊtəʊˌkɒpɪ/ n. & v. —n. (pl. -ies) a photographic copy of printed or written material produced by a process involving the action of light on a specially prepared surface. —v.tr. (-ies, -ied) make a photocopy of. □□ **photocopiable** adj.

photodiode /ˌfəʊtəʊˈdaɪəʊd/ n. a semiconductor diode responding electrically to illumination.

photoelectric /ˌfəʊtəʊɪˈlektrɪk/ adj. marked by or using emissions of electrons from substances exposed to light. □

photoelectric cell a device using this effect to generate current. □□ **photoelectricity** /-ˈtrɪsɪtɪ/ n.

photoelectron /ˌfəʊtəʊɪˈlektrɒn/ n. an electron emitted from an atom by interaction with a photon, esp. one emitted from a solid surface by the action of light.

photoemission /ˌfəʊtəʊɪˈmɪʃ(ə)n/ n. the emission of electrons from a surface by the action of light incident on it. □□ **photoemitter** n.

photofit /ˈfəʊtəʊfɪt/ n. a reconstructed picture of a person (esp. one sought by the police) made from composite photographs of facial features (cf. IDENTIKIT).

photogenic /ˌfəʊtəʊˈdʒenɪk, -ˈdʒiːnɪk/ adj. 1 (esp. of a person) having an appearance that looks pleasing in photographs. 2 Biol. producing or emitting light. □□ **photogenically** adv.

photogram /ˈfəʊtəʊˌgræm/ n. 1 a picture produced with photographic materials but without a camera. 2 archaic a photograph.

photogrammetry /ˌfəʊtəʊˈgræmɪtrɪ/ n. the use of photography for surveying. □□ **photogrammetrist** n.

photograph /ˈfəʊtəʊˌɡrɑːf/ n. & v. —n. a picture taken by means of the chemical action of light or other radiation on sensitive film. (See PHOTOGRAPHY.) —v.tr. (also absol.) take a photograph of (a person etc.). □□ **photographable** adj. **photographer** /fəˈtɒɡrəfə(r)/ n. **photographic** /-ˈgræfɪk/ adj. **photographically** /-ˈgræfɪkəlɪ/ adv.

photography /fəˈtɒɡrəfɪ/ n. the taking and processing of photographs.

The world's first photograph was taken in 1826 by a Frenchman, J. N. Niepce, who (by an exposure lasting several hours) produced a picture of barn-roofs, the view from his window, on a pewter plate, using a substance that hardened under the influence of light. The next landmark in photographic history was the daguerrotype (see entry), first shown to the public in 1838–9—a single and unique image with fine detail in the definition. This was followed by the invention of a negative process, devised by an English amateur scientist, W. H. Fox Talbot, by which an unlimited number of prints could be produced; subsequent developments consisted mainly of improvements of his work. The introduction in 1856 of flexible film instead of a glass plate made it possible for cameras to be not only smaller and lighter but simpler and cheaper (see CAMERA). Colour photography developed from the experiments of Clerk Maxwell in 1861.

Photography has become important in science and industry, in aerial reconnaissance, and in medicine. Interest in it as an art form is as old as the process itself. Photographic societies were soon formed and techniques were explored at first with the idea of giving to the medium the manipulative latitude of painting, then (by c.1890) for their own sake. New freedoms in the other arts, and especially in painting, were paralleled in photography as surrealists experimented with dark-room tricks, and Max Ernst and others produced photomontages, until realism again became popular in the 1930s. An immense range of photographic materials, equipment, and skills now makes photography as versatile a medium as painting.

photogravure /ˌfəʊtəʊɡrəˈvjʊə(r)/ n. 1 an image produced from a photographic negative transferred to a metal plate and etched in. 2 this process. [F (as PHOTO-, gravure engraving)]

photojournalism /ˌfəʊtəʊˈdʒɜːnəˌlɪz(ə)m/ n. the art or practice of relating news by photographs, with or without an accompanying text, esp. in magazines etc. □□ **photojournalist** n.

photolithography /ˌfəʊtəʊlɪˈθɒɡrəfɪ/ n. (also **photolitho** /-ˈlaɪθəʊ/) lithography using plates made photographically. □□ **photolithographer** n. **photolithographic** /-θəˈgræfɪk/ adj. **photolithographically** /-θəˈgræfɪkəlɪ/ adv.

photolysis /fəʊˈtɒlɪsɪs/ n. decomposition or dissociation of molecules by the action of light. □□ **photolyse** /ˈfəʊtəʊˌlaɪz/ v.tr. & intr. **photolytic** /-təˈlɪtɪk/ adj.

photometer /fəʊˈtɒmɪtə(r)/ n. an instrument for measuring light. □□ **photometric** /ˌfəʊtəʊˈmetrɪk/ adj. **photometry** /-ˈtɒmɪtrɪ/ n.

photomicrograph /ˌfəʊtəʊˈmaɪkrəˌgrɑːf/ n. a photograph of an image produced by a microscope. □□ **photomicrography** /-ˈkrɒgrəfi/ n.

photomontage /ˌfəʊtəʊmɒnˈtɑːʒ/ n. **1** the technique of producing a montage (see MONTAGE 2) using photographs. **2** a composite picture produced in this way.

photon /ˈfəʊtɒn/ n. a quantum of electromagnetic radiation energy, proportional to the frequency of radiation. [Gk *phōs phōtos* light, after *electron*]

photo-offset /ˌfəʊtəʊˈɒfset/ n. offset printing with plates made photographically.

photoperiod /ˌfəʊtəʊˈpɪərɪəd/ n. the period of daily illumination which an organism receives. □□ **photoperiodic** /-ɪˈɒdɪk/ adj.

photoperiodism /ˌfəʊtəʊˈpɪərɪəˌdɪz(ə)m/ n. the response of an organism to changes in the lengths of the daily periods of light.

photophobia /ˌfəʊtəʊˈfəʊbɪə/ n. an abnormal fear of or aversion to light. □□ **photophobic** adj.

photorealism /ˌfəʊtəʊˈriːəlɪz(ə)m/ n. detailed and unidealized representation in art, characteristically of the banal, vulgar, or sordid aspects of life.

photoreceptor /ˌfəʊtəʊrɪˈseptə(r)/ n. any living structure that responds to incident light.

photosensitive /ˌfəʊtəʊˈsensɪtɪv/ adj. reacting chemically, electrically, etc., to light. □□ **photosensitivity** /-ˈtɪvɪtɪ/ n.

photosetting /ˈfəʊtəʊˌsetɪŋ/ n. = FILMSETTING. □□ **photoset** v.tr. (past and past part. **-set**). **photosetter** n.

photosphere /ˈfəʊtəʊˌsfɪə(r)/ n. the luminous envelope of a star from which its light and heat radiate. □□ **photospheric** /-ˈsferɪk/ adj.

Photostat /ˈfəʊtəʊˌstæt/ n. & v. —n. propr. **1** a type of machine for making photocopies. **2** a copy made by this means. —v.tr. (**photostat**) (**-statted**, **-statting**) make a Photostat of. □□ **photostatic** /-ˈstætɪk/ adj.

photosynthesis /ˌfəʊtəʊˈsɪnθɪsɪs/ n. the process in which the energy of sunlight is used by organisms, esp. green plants to synthesize carbohydrates from carbon dioxide and water. □□ **photosynthesize** v.tr. & intr. (also **-ise**). **photosynthetic** /-ˈθetɪk/ adj. **photosynthetically** /-ˈθetɪkəlɪ/ adv.

phototransistor /ˌfəʊtəʊtrænˈzɪstə(r), -trɑːnˈzɪstə(r), -ˈsɪstə(r)/ n. a transistor that responds to incident light by generating and amplifying an electric current.

phototropism /ˌfəʊtəʊˈtrəʊpɪz(ə)m, fəˈtɒtrəˌpɪz(ə)m/ n. the tendency of a plant etc. to bend or turn towards or away from a source of light. □□ **phototropic** /-ˈtrɒpɪk/ adj.

photovoltaic /ˌfəʊtəʊvɒlˈteɪk/ adj. relating to the production of electric current at the junction of two substances exposed to light.

phrasal /ˈfreɪz(ə)l/ adj. Gram. consisting of a phrase. □ **phrasal verb** an idiomatic phrase consisting of a verb and an adverb (e.g. *break down*) or a verb and a preposition (e.g. *see to*).

phrase /freɪz/ n. & v. —n. **1** a group of words forming a conceptual unit, but not a sentence. **2** an idiomatic or short pithy expression. **3** a manner or mode of expression (*a nice turn of phrase*). **4** Mus. a group of notes forming a distinct unit within a larger phrase. —v.tr. **1** express in words (*phrased the reply badly*). **2** (esp. when reading aloud or speaking) divide (sentences etc.) into units so as to convey the meaning of the whole. **3** Mus. divide (music) into phrases etc. in performance. □ **phrase book** a book for tourists etc. listing useful expressions with their equivalent in a foreign language. □□ **phrasing** n. [earlier *phrasis* f. L f. Gk f. *phrazō* declare, tell]

phraseogram /ˈfreɪzɪəˌgræm/ n. a written symbol representing a phrase, esp. in shorthand.

phraseology /ˌfreɪzɪˈɒlədʒɪ/ n. (pl. **-ies**) **1** a choice or arrangement of words. **2** a mode of expression. □□ **phraseological** /-zɪəˈlɒdʒɪk(ə)l/ adj. [mod.L *phraseologia* f. Gk *phraseōn* genit. pl. of *phrasis* PHRASE]

phreatic /frɪˈætɪk/ adj. Geol. **1** (of water) situated underground in the zone of saturation; ground water. **2** (of a volcanic eruption or explosion) caused by the heating and expansion of underground water. [Gk *phrear phreatos* well]

phrenetic /frɪˈnetɪk/ adj. **1** frantic. **2** fanatic. □□ **phrenetically** adv. [ME, var. of FRENETIC]

phrenic /ˈfrenɪk/ adj. Anat. of or relating to the diaphragm. [F *phrénique* f. Gk *phrēn phrenos* diaphragm, mind]

phrenology /frɪˈnɒlədʒɪ/ n. hist. the study of the shape and size of the cranium as a supposed indication of character and mental faculties. □□ **phrenological** /-nəˈlɒdʒɪk(ə)l/ adj. **phrenologist** n.

Phrygia /ˈfrɪdʒɪə/ the ancient name for an area of the central plateau and western Asia Minor, south of Bithynia. Its inhabitants were immigrants from Thrace, who established a kingdom centred at Gordion, west of present-day Ankara, that reached the peak of its power in the 8th c. BC under Midas and was overthrown by the Cimmerians c.680 BC. After its absorption by the powerful kingdom of Lydia in the 6th c. BC Phrygia was never independent again.

Phrygian /ˈfrɪdʒɪən/ n. & adj. —n. **1** a native or inhabitant of ancient Phrygia. **2** the language of this people. —adj. of or relating to Phrygia or its people or language. □ **Phrygian bonnet** (or **cap**) an ancient conical cap with the top bent forwards, now identified with the cap of liberty. **Phrygian mode** Mus. the mode represented by the natural diatonic scale E–E.

phthalic acid /ˈfθælɪk/ n. Chem. one of three isomeric dicarboxylic acids derived from benzene. □□ **phthalate** /-leɪt/ n. [abbr. of NAPHTHALIC: see NAPHTHALENE]

phthisis /ˈfθaɪsɪs, ˈθaɪ-/ n. any progressive wasting disease, esp. pulmonary tuberculosis. □□ **phthisic** adj. **phthisical** adj. [L f. Gk f. *phthinō* to decay]

Phuket /puːˈket/ **1** the largest island of Thailand, situated at the head of the Strait of Malacca off the west coast of the Malay Peninsula. **2** a port at the south end of this island, a major resort centre and outlet to the Indian Ocean.

phut /fʌt/ n. a dull abrupt sound as of an impact or explosion. □ **go phut** colloq. (esp. of a scheme or plan) collapse, break down. [perh. f. Hindi *phaṭnā* to burst]

phycology /faɪˈkɒlədʒɪ/ n. the study of algae. □□ **phycological** /-kəˈlɒdʒɪk(ə)l/ adj. **phycologist** n. [Gk *phukos* seaweed + -LOGY]

phycomycete /ˌfaɪkəʊˈmaɪsiːt/ n. any of various fungi which typically form non-septate mycelium. [Gk *phukos* seaweed + pl. of Gk *mukēs* mushroom]

phyla pl. of PHYLUM.

phylactery /fɪˈlæktərɪ/ n. (pl. **-ies**) **1** a small leather box containing Hebrew texts on vellum, worn by Jewish men at morning prayer as a reminder to keep the law. **2** an amulet; a charm. **3** a usu. ostentatious religious observance. **4** a fringe; a border. [ME f. OF f. LL *phylacterium* f. Gk *phulaktērion* amulet f. *phulassō* guard]

phyletic /faɪˈletɪk/ adj. Biol. of or relating to the development of a species or other group. [Gk *phuletikos* f. *phuletēs* tribesman f. *phulē* tribe]

phyllo- /ˈfɪləʊ/ comb. form leaf. [Gk *phullo-* f. *phullon* leaf]

phyllode /ˈfɪləʊd/ n. a flattened leaf-stalk resembling a leaf. [mod.L *phyllodium* f. Gk *phullōdēs* leaflike (as PHYLLO-)]

phyllophagous /fɪˈlɒfəgəs/ adj. feeding on leaves.

phylloquinone /ˌfaɪləʊˈkwɪnəʊn/ n. one of the K vitamins, found in cabbage, spinach, and other leafy green vegetables, and essential for the blood clotting process. Also called vitamin K_1.

phyllostome /ˈfɪləʊstəʊm/ n. any bat of the family Phyllostomatidae having a nose leaf. [PHYLLO- + Gk *stoma* mouth]

phyllotaxis /ˌfɪləʊˈtæksɪs/ n. (also **phyllotaxy** /-ˈtæksɪ/) the arrangement of leaves on an axis or stem. □□ **phyllotactic** adj.

phylloxera /ˌfɪlɒkˈsɪərə, fɪˈlɒksərə/ n. any plant-louse of the genus *Phylloxera*, esp. of a species attacking vines. [mod.L f. Gk *phullon* leaf + *xēros* dry]

phylo- /ˈfaɪləʊ/ comb. form Biol. denoting a race or tribe. [Gk *phulon*, *phulē*]

phylogenesis /ˌfaɪləʊˈdʒenəsɪs/ n. (also **phylogeny** /faɪˈlɒdʒənɪ/) **1** the evolutionary development of an organism or groups of organisms. **2** a history of this. ▫▫ **phylogenetic** /-dʒɪ'netɪk/ *adj.* **phylogenic** /-'dʒenɪk/ *adj.*

phylum /'faɪləm/ *n.* (*pl.* **phyla** /-lə/) *Biol.* a taxonomic rank below kingdom comprising a class or classes and subordinate taxa. [mod.L f. Gk *phulon* race]

physalis /faɪ'sælɪs/ *n.* any plant of the genus *Physalis*, bearing fruit surrounded by lantern-like calyxes (see *Chinese lantern* 2). [Gk *physallis* bladder, with ref. to the inflated calyx]

physic /'fɪzɪk/ *n.* & *v.* esp. *archaic.* —*n.* **1** a medicine (*a dose of physic*). **2** the art of healing. **3** the medical profession. —*v.tr.* (**physicked, physicking**) dose with physic. ▫ **physic garden** a garden for cultivating medicinal herbs etc. [ME f. OF *fisique* medicine f. L *physica* f. Gk *phusikē* (*epistēmē*) (knowledge) of nature]

physical /'fɪzɪk(ə)l/ *adj.* & *n.* —*adj.* **1** of or concerning the body (*physical exercise; physical education*). **2** of matter; material (*both mental and physical force*). **3 a** of, or according to, the laws of nature (*a physical impossibility*). **b** belonging to physics (*physical science*). —*n.* (in full **physical examination**) a medical examination to determine physical fitness. ▫ **physical chemistry** the application of physics to the study of chemical behaviour. **physical geography** geography dealing with natural features. **physical jerks** *colloq.* physical exercises. **physical science** the sciences used in the study of inanimate natural objects, e.g. physics, chemistry, astronomy, etc. **physical training** exercises promoting bodily fitness and strength. ▫▫ **physicality** /-'kælɪtɪ/ *n.* **physically** *adv.* **physicalness** *n.* [ME f. med.L *physicalis* f. L *physica* (as PHYSIC)]

physician /fɪ'zɪʃ(ə)n/ *n.* **1 a** a person legally qualified to practise medicine and surgery. **b** a specialist in medical diagnosis and treatment. **c** any medical practitioner. **2** a healer (*work is the best physician*). [ME f. OF *fisicien* (as PHYSIC)]

physicist /'fɪzɪsɪst/ *n.* a person skilled or qualified in physics.

physico- *comb. form* **1** physical (and). **2** of physics (and). [Gk *phusikos* (as PHYSIC)]

physico-chemical /ˌfɪzɪkəʊ'kemɪk(ə)l/ *adj.* relating to physics and chemistry or to physical chemistry.

physics /'fɪzɪks/ *n.* the science dealing with the properties and interactions of matter and energy. (See below.) [pl. of *physic* physical (thing), after L *physica*, Gk *phusika* natural things f. *phusis* nature]

The subject-matter of physics has undergone marked changes throughout the centuries. For Aristotle it included the study of all natural phenomena, but excluded quantitative subjects such as mechanics, music, and optics which were regarded as dealing with artefacts. By the 17th c. astronomy, mechanics, and optics were being treated mathematically, but a qualitative experimental physics remained, dealing especially with so-called 'imponderable fluids' such as heat, electricity, and magnetism. During the 18th c. physics concentrated increasingly on the more fundamental and general properties of matter, other phenomena being dealt with under the disciplines of chemistry, biology, etc. Mathematics was applied to all branches of physics during the 19th c. and by 1900 the structure of 'classical physics', describing the properties of matter on the macroscopic scale and at relatively low velocities, was largely complete. Since that time, however, the theories of modern physics, and in particular relativity, quantum theory, and the physics of atomic and subatomic particles, have transformed our overall understanding of the universe.

physio /'fɪzɪəʊ/ *n.* (*pl.* **-os**) *colloq.* a physiotherapist. [abbr.]

physio- /'fɪzɪəʊ/ *comb. form* nature; what is natural. [Gk *phusis* nature]

physiocracy /ˌfɪzɪ'ɒkrəsɪ/ *n.* (*pl.* **-ies**) *hist.* **1** government according to the natural order, esp. as advocated by some 18th-c. economists. **2** a society based on this. ▫▫ **physiocrat** /'fɪzɪəʊˌkræt/ *n.* **physiocratic** /-ɪə'krætɪk/ *adj.* [F *physiocratie* (as PHYSIO-, -CRACY)]

physiognomy /ˌfɪzɪ'ɒnəmɪ/ *n.* (*pl.* **-ies**) **1 a** the cast or form of a person's features, expression, body, etc. **b** the art of supposedly judging character from facial characteristics etc. **2** the external features of a landscape etc. **3** a characteristic, esp. moral, aspect.

▫▫ **physiognomic** /-zɪə'nɒmɪk/ *adj.* **physiognomical** /-zɪə'nɒmɪk(ə)l/ *adj.* **physiognomically** /-zɪə'nɒmɪkəlɪ/ *adv.* **physiognomist** *n.* [ME *fisnomie* etc. f. OF *phisonomie* f. med.L *phisonomia* f. Gk *phusiognōmonia* judging of a man's nature (by his features) (as PHYSIO-, *gnōmōn* judge)]

physiography /ˌfɪzɪ'ɒɡrəfɪ/ *n.* the description of nature, of natural phenomena, or of a class of objects; physical geography. ▫▫ **physiographer** *n.* **physiographic** /-zɪə'ɡræfɪk/ *adj.* **physiographical** /-zɪə'ɡræfɪk(ə)l/ *adj.* **physiographically** /-zɪə'ɡræfɪkəlɪ/ *adv.* [F *physiographie* (as PHYSIO-, -GRAPHY)]

physiological /ˌfɪzɪə'lɒdʒɪk(ə)l/ *adj.* (also **physiologic**) of or concerning physiology. ▫ **physiological salt solution** a saline solution having a concentration about equal to that of body fluids. ▫▫ **physiologically** *adv.*

physiology /ˌfɪzɪ'ɒlədʒɪ/ *n.* **1** the science of the functions of living organisms and their parts. **2** these functions. ▫▫ **physiologist** *n.* [F *physiologie* or L *physiologia* f. Gk *phusiologia* (as PHYSIO-, -LOGY)]

physiotherapy /ˌfɪzɪəʊ'θerəpɪ/ *n.* the treatment of disease, injury, deformity, etc., by physical methods including manipulation, massage, infrared heat treatment, remedial exercise, etc., not by drugs. ▫▫ **physiotherapist** *n.*

physique /fɪ'ziːk/ *n.* the bodily structure, development, and organization of an individual (*an undernourished physique*). [F, orig. adj. (as PHYSIC)]

-phyte /faɪt/ *comb. form* forming nouns denoting a vegetable or plantlike organism (*saprophyte; zoophyte*). ▫▫ **-phytic** /'fɪtɪk/ *comb. form* forming adjectives. [Gk *phuton* plant f. *phuō* come into being]

phyto- /'faɪtəʊ/ *comb. form* denoting a plant.

phytochemistry /ˌfaɪtəʊ'kemɪstrɪ/ *n.* the chemistry of plant products. ▫▫ **phytochemical** *adj.* **phytochemist** *n.*

phytochrome /'faɪtəʊˌkrəʊm/ *n. Biochem.* a blue-green pigment found in many plants, and regulating various developmental processes according to the nature and timing of the light it absorbs. [PHYTO- + Gk *khrōma* colour]

phytogenesis /ˌfaɪtəʊ'dʒenɪsɪs/ *n.* (also **phytogeny** /-'tɒdʒɪnɪ/) the science of the origin or evolution of plants.

phytogeography /ˌfaɪtəʊdʒɪ'ɒɡrəfɪ/ *n.* the geographical distribution of plants.

phytopathology /ˌfaɪtəʊpə'θɒlədʒɪ/ *n.* the study of plant diseases.

phytophagous /faɪ'tɒfəɡəs/ *adj.* feeding on plants.

phytoplankton /ˌfaɪtəʊ'plæŋkt(ə)n/ *n.* plankton consisting of plants.

phytotomy /faɪ'tɒtəmɪ/ *n.* the dissection of plants.

phytotoxic /ˌfaɪtəʊ'tɒksɪk/ *adj.* poisonous to plants.

phytotoxin /ˌfaɪtəʊ'tɒksɪn/ *n.* **1** any toxin derived from a plant. **2** a substance poisonous or injurious to plants, esp. one produced by a parasite.

pi¹ /paɪ/ *n.* **1** the sixteenth letter of the Greek alphabet (Π, π). **2** (as π) the symbol of the ratio of the circumference of a circle to its diameter (approx. 3.14159). ▫ **pi-meson** = PION. [Gk: sense 2 f. Gk *periphereia* circumference]

pi² /paɪ/ *adj. Brit. sl.* pious. ▫ **pi jaw** a long moralizing lecture or reprimand. [abbr.]

pi³ *US* var. of PIE³.

piacular /paɪ'ækjʊlə(r)/ *adj. formal* **1** expiatory. **2** needing expiation. [L *piacularis* f. *piaculum* expiation f. *piare* appease]

Piaf /pjɑːf/, Edith (real name Edith Giovanna Gassion, 1915–63), French music-hall and cabaret singer and songwriter, whose songs include 'La vie en rose'. Her name is taken from a colloquial French word (*piaf*) meaning 'sparrow', referring to her small size.

piaffe /pɪ'æf/ *v.intr.* (of a horse etc.) move as in a trot, but slower. [F *piaffer* to strut]

piaffer /pɪ'æfə(r)/ *n.* the action of piaffing.

Piaget /pɪ'æʒeɪ/, Jean (1897–1980), Swiss psychologist whose work has provided the single biggest impact on the study of the development of thought processes. His central thesis is that

æ cat ɑː arm e bed ɜː her ɪ sit iː see ɒ hot ɔː saw ʌ run ʊ put uː too ə ago aɪ my

children initially lack intellectual and logical abilities, which they acquire through experience and interaction with the world around them, proceeding through a series of fixed stages of cognitive development, each being a prerequisite for the next.

pia mater /ˌpaɪə ˈmeɪtə(r)/ n. Anat. the delicate innermost membrane enveloping the brain and spinal cord (see MENINX). [med.L, = tender mother, transl. of Arab. al-'umm al-raḳīḳa: cf. DURA MATER]

piani pl. of PIANO².

pianism /ˈpiːəˌnɪz(ə)m/ n. 1 the art or technique of piano-playing. 2 the skill or style of a composer of piano music. □□ **pianistic** /-ˈnɪstɪk/ adj. **pianistically** /-ˈnɪstɪklɪ/ adv.

pianissimo /ˌpiːəˈnɪsɪˌməʊ/ adj., adv., & n. Mus. —adj. performed very softly. —adv. very softly. —n. (pl. -os or **pianissimi** /-mɪ/) a passage to be performed very softly. [It., superl. of PIANO²]

pianist /ˈpiːənɪst/ n. the player of a piano. [F pianiste (as PIANO¹)]

piano¹ /pɪˈænəʊ/ n. (pl. -os) a large musical instrument played by pressing down keys on a keyboard and causing hammers to strike metal strings, the vibration from which is stopped by dampers when the keys are released. (See below.) □ **piano-accordion** an accordion with the melody played on a small vertical keyboard like that of a piano. **piano organ** a mechanical piano constructed like a barrel-organ. **piano-player** 1 a pianist. 2 a contrivance for playing a piano automatically. **piano roll** a roll of paper with perforations, used in a Pianola to reproduce music by allowing air to pass through the holes to depress the keys. [It., abbr. of PIANOFORTE]
The pianoforte (commonly called 'piano') was developed in Italy in the early 18th c. and so called because it was designed to produce both soft (piano) and loud (forte) notes. It superseded the clavichord and harpsichord, having a louder tone than the former and a greater expressive range than the latter. Two instruments survive by Bartolomeo Cristofori, who has some claim to be the inventor of the piano, dating from 1720 and 1726 respectively. Today the most common forms are the grand piano (ranging in size from 'baby grand' to 'concert grand') and the upright, with strings running perpendicularly rather than horizontally, but the earliest models were of harpsichord shape; in the mid-18th c. the square piano was the principal domestic instrument.

piano² /ˈpjɑːnəʊ/ adj., adv., & n. —adj. 1 Mus. performed softly. 2 subdued. —adv. 1 Mus. softly. 2 in a subdued manner. —n. (pl. -os or **piani** /-nɪ/) Mus. a piano passage. [It. f. L planus flat, (of sound) soft]

pianoforte /ˌpiænəʊˈfɔːtɪ/ n. Mus. formal or archaic a piano. [It., earlier piano e forte soft and loud, expressing its gradation of tone]

Pianola /piəˈnəʊlə/ n. 1 propr. a kind of automatic piano; a player-piano. 2 (**pianola**) Bridge an easy hand needing no skill. 3 (**pianola**) an easy task. [app. dimin. of PIANO¹]

piano nobile /ˌpjɑːnəʊ ˈnəʊbɪˌleɪ/ n. Archit. the main storey of a large house. [It., = noble floor]

piassava /ˌpiːəˈsɑːvə/ n. 1 a stout fibre obtained from the leaf-stalks of various American and African palm-trees. 2 any of these trees. [Port. f. Tupi piaçába]

piastre /pɪˈæstə(r)/ n. (US **piaster**) a small coin and monetary unit of several Middle Eastern countries. [F piastre f. It. piastra (d'argento) plate (of silver), formed as PLASTER]

piazza /pɪˈætsə/ n. 1 a public square or market-place esp. in an Italian town. 2 US the veranda of a house. [It., formed as PLACE]

pibroch /ˈpiːbrɒx, -brɒk/ n. a series of esp. martial or funerary variations on a theme for the bagpipes. [Gael. piobaireachd art of piping f. piobair piper f. piob f. E PIPE]

pic /pɪk/ n. colloq. a picture, esp. a cinema film. [abbr.]

pica¹ /ˈpaɪkə/ n. Printing 1 a unit of type-size (⅙ inch). 2 a size of letters in typewriting (10 per inch). [AL pica 15th-c. book of rules about church feasts, perh. formed as PIE²]

pica² /ˈpaɪkə/ n. Med. the eating of substances other than normal food. [mod.L or med.L, = magpie]

picador /ˈpɪkəˌdɔː(r)/ n. a mounted man with a lance who goads the bull in a bullfight. [Sp. f. picar prick]

Picardy /ˈpɪkədɪ/ (French **Picardie**) 1 a former province of northern France between Normandy and Flanders, the scene of heavy fighting in the First World War. 2 a region of modern France; pop. (1982) 1,740,300; capital, Amiens.

picaresque /ˌpɪkəˈresk/ adj. (of a style of fiction) dealing with the episodic adventures of rogues etc. [F f. Sp. picaresco f. pícaro rogue]

picaroon /ˌpɪkəˈruːn/ n. 1 a a rogue. b a thief. 2 a a pirate. b a pirate ship. [Sp. picarón (as PICARESQUE)]

Picasso /pɪˈkæsəʊ/, Pablo (1881–1973), Spanish painter. Widely considered to be the most inventive of all 20th-c. painters, his achievement includes major contributions to painting, sculpture, and graphics. His earliest work (1901–4) is known as his Blue Period—pictures of society's outsiders painted predominantly in blue, and redolent of fin-de-siècle melancholia. This gave way, with his permanent settling in Paris (1904), to the less sentimental treatment of circus performers in the Rose Period of 1905–6. From 1907 to 1914 he worked with Georges Braque in the monumental enterprise of cubism which challenged for the first time since the Renaissance the whole function of painting, replacing mimesis with a new self-sufficient pictorial order distinct from everyday visual habits. The 1920s and 1930s saw the protean development of a heavy neoclassical figurative style, designs for Diaghilev's Ballets Russes, pictures using quasi-surrealist imagery, engraved work (particularly, the Minotaur series), and the development of sculpture; 1937 saw the completion of Guernica—his response to the destruction of the Basque capital by Fascist bombs—possibly his greatest and most distinctive single picture. In his later years a certain playfulness imbued his work, but the seemingly inexhaustible imaginative creativity that typified his art never faltered.

picayune /ˌpɪkəˈjuːn/ n. & adj. US —n. 1 colloq. a small coin of little value, esp. a 5-cent piece. 2 an insignificant person or thing. —adj. mean; contemptible; petty. [F picaillon Piedmontese coin, cash, f. Prov. picaioun, of unkn. orig.]

piccalilli /ˌpɪkəˈlɪlɪ/ n. (pl. **piccalillis**) a pickle of chopped vegetables, mustard, and hot spices. [18th c.: perh. f. PICKLE + CHILLI]

piccaninny /ˌpɪkəˈnɪnɪ/ n. & adj. (US **pickaninny**) —n. (pl. -ies) often offens. a small Black or Australian Aboriginal child. —adj. archaic very small. [W.Ind. Negro f. Sp. pequeño or Port. pequeno little]

piccolo /ˈpɪkəˌləʊ/ n. (pl. -os) 1 a small flute sounding an octave higher than the ordinary one. 2 its player. [It., = small (flute)]

pichiciago /ˌpɪtʃɪsɪˈeɪgəʊ/ n. (pl. -os) a small S. American armadillo, Chlamyphorus truncatus. [Sp. pichiciego perh. f. Guarani pichey armadillo + ciego blind f. L caecus]

pick¹ /pɪk/ v. & n. —v.tr. 1 (also absol.) choose carefully from a number of alternatives (picked the pink one; picked a team; picked the right moment to intervene). 2 detach or pluck (a flower, fruit, etc.) from a stem, tree, etc. 3 a probe (the teeth, nose, ears, a pimple, etc.) with the finger, an instrument, etc. to remove unwanted matter. b clear (a bone, carcass, etc.) of scraps of meat etc. 4 (also absol.) (of a person) eat (food, a meal, etc.) in small bits; nibble without appetite. 5 (also absol.) esp. US pluck the strings of (a banjo etc.). 6 remove stalks etc. from (esp. soft fruit) before cooking. 7 a select (a route or path) carefully over difficult terrain by foot. b place (one's steps etc.) carefully. 8 pull apart (pick oakum). 9 (of a bird) take up (grains etc.) in the beak. —n. 1 the act or an instance of picking. 2 a a selection or choice. b the right to select (had first pick of the prizes). 3 (usu. foll. by of) the best (the pick of the bunch). □ **pick and choose** select carefully or fastidiously. **pick at** 1 eat (food) without interest; nibble. 2 = pick on 1 (see PICK¹). **pick a person's brains** extract ideas, information, etc., from a person for one's own use. **pick holes** (or **a hole**) **in** 1 make holes in (material etc.) by plucking, poking, etc. 2 find fault with (an idea etc.). **pick a lock** open a lock with an instrument other than the proper key, esp. with intent to steal. **pick-me-up** 1 a tonic for the nerves etc. 2 a good experience, good news, etc. that cheers. **pick off** 1 pluck (leaves etc.) off. 2 shoot (people etc.) one by one without haste. 3 eliminate (opposition etc.) singly. **pick on** 1 find fault with; nag at. 2 select. **pick out** 1 take from a larger number (picked him out from the others). 2 distinguish from surrounding objects or at a distance (*can just pick out the church spire*). **3** play (a tune) by ear on the piano etc. **4** (often foll. by *in*, *with*) **a** highlight (a painting etc.) with touches of another colour. **b** accentuate (decoration, a painting, etc.) with a contrasting colour (*picked out the handles in red*). **5** make out (the meaning of a passage etc.). **pick over** select the best from. **pick a person's pockets** steal the contents of a person's pockets. **pick a quarrel** start an argument or a fight deliberately. **pick to pieces** = *take to pieces* (see PIECE). **pick up 1** grasp and raise (from the ground etc.) (*picked up his hat*). **2** gain or acquire by chance or without effort (*picked up a cold*). **3 a** fetch (a person, animal, or thing) left in another person's charge. **b** stop for and take along with one, esp. in a vehicle (*pick me up on the corner*). **4** make the acquaintance of (a person) casually, esp. as a sexual overture. **5** (of one's health, the weather, share prices, etc.) recover, prosper, improve. **6** (of a motor engine etc.) recover speed; accelerate. **7** (of the police etc.) take into charge; arrest. **8** detect by scrutiny or with a telescope, searchlight, radio, etc. (*picked up most of the mistakes*; *picked up a distress signal*). **9** (often foll. by *with*) form or renew a friendship. **10** accept the responsibility of paying (a bill etc.). **11** (*refl.*) raise (oneself etc.) after a fall etc. **12** raise (the feet etc.) clear of the ground. **13** *Golf* pick up one's ball, esp. when conceding a hole. **pick-up 1** *sl.* a person met casually, esp. for sexual purposes. **2** a small open motor truck. **3 a** the part of a record-player carrying the stylus. **b** a detector of vibrations etc. **4 a** the act of picking up. **b** something picked up. **pick-your-own** (usu. *attrib.*) (of commercially grown fruit and vegetables) dug or picked by the customer at the place of production. **take one's pick** make a choice. □□ **pickable** *adj.* [ME, earlier *pike*, of unkn. orig.]

pick² /pɪk/ *n. & v.* —*n.* **1** a long-handled tool having a usu. curved iron bar pointed at one or both ends, used for breaking up hard ground, masonry, etc. **2** *colloq.* a plectrum. **3** any instrument for picking, such as a toothpick. —*v.tr.* **1** break the surface of (the ground etc.) with or as if with a pick. **2** make (holes etc.) in this way. [ME, app. var. of PIKE²]

pickaback var. of PIGGYBACK.

pickaninny *US* var. of PICCANINNY.

pickaxe /ˈpɪkæks/ *n. & v.* (*US* **pickax**) —*n.* = PICK² n. 1. —*v.* **1** *tr.* break (the ground etc.) with a pickaxe. **2** *intr.* work with a pickaxe. [ME *pikois* f. OF *picois*, rel. to PIKE²: assim. to AXE]

pickelhaube /ˈpɪkəlˌhaʊbə/ *n. hist.* a German soldier's spiked helmet. [G]

picker /ˈpɪkə(r)/ *n.* **1** a person or thing that picks. **2** (often in *comb.*) a person who gathers or collects (*hop-picker*; *rag-picker*).

pickerel /ˈpɪkər(ə)l/ *n.* (*pl.* same or **pickerels**) a young pike. [ME, dimin. of PIKE¹]

picket /ˈpɪkɪt/ *n. & v.* —*n.* **1** a person or group of people outside a place of work, intending to persuade esp. workers not to enter during a strike etc. **2** a pointed stake or peg driven into the ground to form a fence or palisade, to tether a horse, etc. **3** (also **picquet, piquet**) *Mil.* **a** a small body of troops sent out to watch for the enemy, held in readiness, etc. **b** a party of sentries. **c** an outpost. **d** a camp-guard on police duty in a garrison town etc. —*v.* (**picketed, picketing**) **1 a** *tr.* & *intr.* station or act as a picket. **b** *tr.* beset or guard (a factory, workers, etc.) with a picket or pickets. **2** *tr.* secure (a place) with stakes. **3** *tr.* tether (an animal). □ **picket line** a boundary established by workers on strike, esp. at the entrance to the place of work, which others are asked not to cross. □□ **picketer** *n.* [F *piquet* pointed stake f. *piquer* prick, f. *pic* PICK²]

Pickford /ˈpɪkfəd/, Mary (real name Gladys Mary Smith, 1893–1979), Canadian-born American actress, a star of silent films, usually in the role of innocent young heroine with hair in ringlets, as in *The Little American* (1917) and *Pollyanna* (1920). In 1919 she married Douglas Fairbanks.

pickings /ˈpɪkɪŋz/ *n.pl.* **1** perquisites; pilferings (*rich pickings*). **2** remaining scraps; gleanings.

pickle /ˈpɪk(ə)l/ *n. & v.* —*n.* **1 a** (often in *pl.*) food, esp. vegetables, preserved in brine, vinegar, mustard, etc. and used as a relish. **b** the brine, vinegar, etc. in which food is preserved. **2** *colloq.* a plight (*a fine pickle we are in!*). **3** *Brit. colloq.* a mischievous child.

4 an acid solution for cleaning metal etc. —*v.tr.* **1** preserve in pickle. **2** treat with pickle. **3** (as **pickled** *adj.*) *sl.* drunk. [ME *pekille, pykyl*, f. MDu., MLG *pekel*, of unkn. orig.]

pickler /ˈpɪklə(r)/ *n.* **1** a person who pickles vegetables etc. **2** a vegetable suitable for pickling.

picklock /ˈpɪklɒk/ *n.* **1** a person who picks locks. **2** an instrument for this.

pickpocket /ˈpɪkˌpɒkɪt/ *n.* a person who steals from the pockets of others.

Pickwickian /pɪkˈwɪkɪən/ *adj.* **1** of or like Mr Pickwick in Dickens's *Pickwick Papers* (1836–7), esp. in being jovial, plump, etc. **2** (of words or their sense) misunderstood or misused, esp. to avoid offence.

picky /ˈpɪkɪ/ *adj.* (**pickier, pickiest**) *colloq.* excessively fastidious; choosy. □□ **pickiness** *n.*

picnic /ˈpɪknɪk/ *n. & v.* —*n.* **1** an outing or excursion including a packed meal eaten out of doors. **2** any meal eaten out of doors or without preparation, tables, chairs, etc. **3** (usu. with *neg.*) *colloq.* something agreeable or easily accomplished etc. (*it was no picnic organizing the meeting*). —*v.intr.* (**picnicked, picnicking**) take part in a picnic. □□ **picnicker** *n.* **picnicky** *adj. colloq.* [F *pique-nique*, of unkn. orig.]

pico- /ˈpaɪkəʊ, ˈpiːkəʊ/ *comb. form* denoting a factor of 10^{-12} (*picometre*). [Sp. *pico* beak, peak, little bit]

Pico da Neblina /ˈpiːkəʊ dɑː nɛˈbliːnə/ the highest peak in Brazil, rising to a height of 2,890 m (9,383 ft.) in the Brazilian Highlands close to the Brazil–Venezuela frontier.

picot /ˈpiːkəʊ/ *n.* a small loop of twisted thread in a lace edging etc. [F, dimin. of *pic* peak, point]

picotee /ˌpɪkəˈtiː/ *n.* a type of carnation of which the flowers have a light ground and dark-edged petals. [F *picoté -ée* past part. of *picoter* prick (as PICOT)]

picquet var. of PICKET 3.

picric acid /ˈpɪkrɪk/ *n.* a very bitter yellow compound used in dyeing and surgery and in explosives. □□ **picrate** /-reɪt/ *n.* [Gk *pikros* bitter]

Pict /pɪkt/ *n.* a member of an ancient people, of disputed origin and ethnological affinities, who formerly inhabited parts of northern Britain. In Roman writings (*c.*AD 300) the term *Picti* is applied to the hostile tribes occupying the area north of the Antonine Wall. According to chroniclers the Pictish kingdom was united with the Scottish under Kenneth MacAlpine in 843, and the name of the Picts as a distinct people gradually disappeared. □□ **Pictish** *adj.* [ME f. LL *Picti* perh. = painted people f. *pingere pict-* paint, tattoo, or perh. assim. to native name]

pictograph /ˈpɪktəˌɡrɑːf/ *n.* (also **pictogram** /ˈpɪktəˌɡræm/) **1 a** a pictorial symbol for a word or phrase. **b** an ancient record consisting of these. **2** a pictorial representation of statistics etc. on a chart, graph, etc. □□ **pictographic** /-ˈɡræfɪk/ *adj.* **pictography** /-ˈtɒɡrəfɪ/ *n.* [L *pingere pict-* paint]

pictorial /pɪkˈtɔːrɪəl/ *adj. & n.* —*adj.* **1** of or expressed in a picture or pictures. **2** illustrated. **3** picturesque. —*n.* a journal, postage stamp, etc., with a picture or pictures as the main feature. □□ **pictorially** *adv.* [LL *pictorius* f. L *pictor* painter (as PICTURE)]

picture /ˈpɪktʃə(r)/ *n. & v.* —*n.* **1 a** (often *attrib.*) a painting, drawing, photograph, etc., esp. as a work of art (*picture frame*). **b** a portrait, esp. a photograph, of a person (*does not like to have her picture taken*). **c** a beautiful object (*her hat is a picture*). **2 a** a total visual or mental impression produced; a scene (*the picture looks bleak*). **b** a written or spoken description (*drew a vivid picture of moral decay*). **3 a** a film. **b** (in *pl.*) *Brit.* a showing of films at a cinema (*went to the pictures*). **c** (in *pl.*) films in general. **4** an image on a television screen. **5** *colloq.* **a** esp. *iron.* a person or thing exemplifying something (*he was the picture of innocence*). **b** a person or thing resembling another closely (*the picture of her aunt*). —*v.tr.* **1** represent in a picture. **2** (also *refl.*; often foll. by *to*) imagine, esp. visually or vividly (*pictured it to herself*). **3** describe graphically. □ **get the picture** *colloq.* grasp the tendency or drift of circumstances, information, etc. **in the picture** fully informed or noticed. **out of the picture** uninvolved, inactive;

irrelevant. **picture-book** a book containing many illustrations. **picture-card** a court-card. **picture-gallery** a place containing an exhibition or collection of pictures. **picture-goer** a person who frequents the cinema. **picture hat** a woman's wide-brimmed highly decorated hat as in pictures by Reynolds and Gainsborough. **picture-moulding 1** woodwork etc. used for framing pictures. **2** a rail on a wall used for hanging pictures from. **picture-palace** (or **-theatre**) *Brit. archaic* a cinema. **picture postcard** a postcard with a picture on one side. **picture window** a very large window consisting of one pane of glass. **picture-writing** a mode of recording events etc. by pictorial symbols as in early hieroglyphics etc. [ME f. L *pictura* f. *pingere pict-* paint]

picturesque /ˌpɪktʃəˈresk/ *adj.* **1** (of landscape etc.) beautiful or striking, as in a picture. **2** (of language etc.) strikingly graphic; vivid. □□ **picturesquely** *adv.* **picturesqueness** *n.* [F *pittoresque* f. It. *pittoresco* f. *pittore* painter f. L (as PICTORIAL): assim. to PICTURE]

piddle /ˈpɪd(ə)l/ *v. & n.* —*v.intr.* **1** *colloq.* urinate (used esp. to or by children). **2** work or act in a trifling way. **3** (as **piddling** *adj.*) *colloq.* trivial; trifling. —*n. colloq.* **1** urination. **2** urine (used esp. to or by children). □□ **piddler** *n.* [sense 1 prob. f. PISS + PUDDLE: sense 2 perh. f. PEDDLE]

piddock /ˈpɪdək/ *n.* any rock-boring bivalve mollusc of the family Pholadidae, used for bait. [18th c.: orig. unkn.]

pidgin /ˈpɪdʒɪn/ *n.* a simplified language containing vocabulary from two or more languages, used for communication between people not having a common language. □ **pidgin English** a pidgin in which the chief language is English, used orig. between Chinese and Europeans. [corrupt. of *business*]

pi-dog var. of PYE-DOG.

pie[1] /paɪ/ *n.* **1** a baked dish of meat, fish, fruit, etc., usu. with a top and base of pastry. **2** anything resembling a pie in form (a *mud pie*). □ **easy as pie** very easy. **pie chart** a circle divided into sectors to represent relative quantities. **pie-eater** *Austral. sl.* a person of little account. **pie-eyed** *sl.* drunk. **pie in the sky** an unrealistic prospect of future happiness after present suffering; a misleading promise. [ME, perh. = PIE[2] f. miscellaneous contents compared to objects collected by a magpie]

pie[2] /paɪ/ *n. archaic* **1** a magpie. **2** a pied animal. [ME f. OF f. L *pica*]

pie[3] /paɪ/ *n. & v.* (US **pi**) —*n.* **1** a confused mass of printers' type. **2** chaos. —*v.tr.* (**pieing**) muddle up (type). [perh. transl. F PÂTÉ = PIE[1]]

pie[4] /paɪ/ *n. hist.* a former monetary unit of India equal to one-twelfth of an anna. [Hind. etc. *pā'ī* f. Skr. *pad, padī* quarter]

piebald /ˈpaɪbɔːld/ *adj. & n.* —*adj.* **1** (usu. of an animal, esp. a horse) having irregular patches of two colours, esp. black and white. **2** motley; mongrel. —*n.* a piebald animal, esp. a horse.

piece /piːs/ *n. & v.* —*n.* **1 a** (often foll. by *of*) one of the distinct portions forming part of or broken off from a larger object; a bit; a part (*a piece of string*). **b** each of the parts of which a set or category is composed (*a five-piece band; a piece of furniture*). **2** a coin of specified value (*50p piece*). **3 a** a usu. short literary or musical composition or a picture. **b** a theatrical play. **4** an item, instance, or example (*a piece of impudence; a piece of news*). **5 a** any of the objects used to make moves in board-games. **b** a chessman (strictly, other than a pawn). **6** a definite quantity in which a thing is sold. **7** (often foll. by *of*) an enclosed portion (of land etc.). **8** *derog. sl.* a woman. **9** *US* (foll. by *of*) *sl.* a financial share or investment in (*has a piece of the new production*). —*v.tr.* **1** (usu. foll. by *together*) form into a whole; put together; join (*finally pieced his story together*). **2** (usu. foll. by *out*) **a** eke out. **b** form (a theory etc.) by combining parts etc. **3** (usu. foll. by *up*) patch. **4** join (threads) in spinning. □ **break to pieces** break into fragments. **by the piece** (paid) according to the quantity of work done. **go to pieces** collapse emotionally; suffer a breakdown. **in one piece 1** unbroken. **2** unharmed. **in pieces** broken. **of a piece** (often foll. by *with*) uniform, consistent, in keeping. **piece-goods** fabrics etc. esp. Lancashire cottons, woven in standard lengths. **a piece of cake** see CAKE. **piece of eight** *hist.* a Spanish dollar, equivalent to 8 reals. **piece of goods** *sl. derog.* a woman. **a piece of one's mind** a sharp rebuke or lecture. **piece of**

water a small lake etc. **piece of work** a thing made by working (cf. *nasty piece of work*). **piece-rates** a rate paid according to the amount produced. **piece-work** work paid for by the amount produced. **say one's piece** give one's opinion or make a prepared statement. **take to pieces 1** break up or dismantle. **2** criticize harshly. □□ **piecer** *n.* (in sense 4 of *v.*). [ME f. AF *pece*, OF *piece* f. Rmc, prob. of Gaulish orig.: cf. PEAT]

pièce de résistance /ˌpjes də reɪˈziːstɑ̃s/ *n.* (pl. **pièces de résistance** pronunc. same) **1** the most important or remarkable item. **2** the most substantial dish at a meal. [F]

piecemeal /ˈpiːsmiːl/ *adv. & adj.* —*adv.* piece by piece; gradually. —*adj.* partial; gradual; unsystematic. [ME f. PIECE + -*meal* f. OE *mǽlum* (instr. dative pl. of *mǽl* MEAL[1])]

piecrust /ˈpaɪkrʌst/ *n.* the baked pastry crust of a pie. □ **piecrust table** a table with an indented edge like a piecrust.

pied /paɪd/ *adj.* particoloured. [ME f. PIE[2], orig. of friars]

pied-à-terre /ˌpjeɪdɑːˈteə(r)/ *n.* (pl. **pieds-à-terre** pronunc. same) a usu. small flat, house, etc. kept for occasional use. [F, lit. 'foot to earth']

Piedmont /ˈpiːdmɒnt/ (Italian **Piemonte** /pjeɪˈmɒnteɪ/) a region of NW Italy in the foothills of the Alps; pop. (1981) 4,470,000; capital, Turin. It was united with Italy in 1859. [It. *piemonte* mountain foot]

piedmont /ˈpiːdmɒnt/ *n.* a gentle slope leading from the foot of mountains to a region of flat land. [as PIEDMONT]

pie-dog var. of PYE-DOG.

Pied Piper /paɪd ˈpaɪpə(r)/ the hero of *The Pied Piper of Hamlin*, a poem by Robert Browning (1842), based on an old legend. He rid the town of Hamelin in Brunswick of rats by luring them away with his music, and when refused the promised payment he lured away all the children. The event was long regarded as historical and supposed to have occurred in 1284; the piper's name was Bunting. [= PIED]

pieman /ˈpaɪmən/ *n.* (pl. **-men**) a pie seller.

pier /pɪə(r)/ *n.* **1 a** a structure of iron or wood raised on piles and leading out to sea, a lake, etc., used as a promenade and landing-stage, and often with entertainment arcades etc. **b** a breakwater; a mole. **2 a** a support of an arch or of the span of a bridge; a pillar. **b** solid masonry between windows etc. □ **pier-glass** a large mirror, used orig. to fill wall-space between windows. [ME *per* f. AL *pera*, of unkn. orig.]

Pierce /pɪəs/, Franklin (1804–69), 14th President of the US, 1853–7.

pierce /pɪəs/ *v.* **1** *tr.* **a** (of a sharp instrument etc.) penetrate the surface of. **b** (often foll. by *with*) prick with a sharp instrument, esp. to make a hole in. **c** make (a hole etc.) (*pierced a hole in the belt*). **d** (of cold, grief, etc.) affect keenly or sharply. **e** (of a light, glance, sound, etc.) penetrate keenly or sharply. **2** (as **piercing** *adj.*) (of a glance, intuition, high noise, bright light, etc.) keen, sharp, or unpleasantly penetrating. **3** *tr.* force (a way etc.) through or into (something) (*pierced their way through the jungle*). **4** *intr.* (usu. foll. by *through, into*) penetrate. □□ **piercer** *n.* **piercingly** *adv.* [ME f. OF *percer* f. L *pertundere* bore through (as PER-, *tundere tus-* thrust)]

Piero della Francesca /pɪˈerəʊ ˌdelə frænˈtʃeskə/ (1416–92), Italian painter, for a long time forgotten but regarded in 20th-c. criticism as one of the greatest quattrocento painters. The world of his artistic imagination has clarity, dignity, and order, and the outlines of his figures tend towards the grace and regularity of curves in geometry. His interest in perspective and mathematical relationships is witnessed in an assured naturalism, with protagonists placed firmly in credible landscapes and inhabiting real space. He was capable of investing his art with hieratic solemnity and power by using the severity of frontal or profile poses and formal presentation of the figure (e.g. *The Resurrection*, c.1463).

Pierre /ˈpɪə(r)/ the capital of South Dakota, situated on the Missouri River; pop. (1980) 11,970.

Pierrot /ˈpɪərəʊ, ˈpjerəʊ/ *n.* a stock character in the French and English theatres (*fem.* **Pierrette** /pɪəˈret, pjeˈret/), with whitened face and loose white costume. Originally a robust country bumpkin, he was transformed by the French player Deburau in the 1820s into an ever-hopeful always disappointed lover, a concept which became well known in London. The character was ousted from the harlequinade by the English clown, but regained much of his old vigour when the pierrot troupes, or concert parties, were formed towards the end of the 19th c. [F, dimin. of *Pierre* Peter]

pietà /ˌpɪeˈtɑː/ *n.* a picture or sculpture of the Virgin Mary holding the dead body of Christ on her lap or in her arms. [It. f. L (as PIETY)]

pietas /ˈpaɪəˌtɑːs/ *n.* respect due to an ancestor, a forerunner, etc. [L: see PIETY]

pietism /ˈpaɪəˌtɪz(ə)m/ *n.* **1 a** pious sentiment. **b** an exaggerated or affected piety. **2** (esp. as **Pietism**) *hist.* a movement originated at Frankfurt *c.*1670 by P. J. Spener for the revitalizing of orthodox Lutheranism, with devotional circles for prayer, Bible study, etc. Pietism influenced similar movements elsewhere including that of John Wesley. □□ **pietist** *n.* **pietistic** /-ˈtɪstɪk/ *adj.* **pietistical** /-ˈtɪstɪk(ə)l/ *adj.* [G *Pietismus* (as PIETY)]

piety /ˈpaɪɪtɪ/ *n.* (*pl.* **-ies**) **1** the quality of being pious. **2** a pious act. [ME f. OF *pieté* f. L *pietas -tatis* dutifulness (as PIOUS)]

piezoelectricity /paɪˌiːzəʊˌɪlekˈtrɪsɪtɪ, ˌpiːzəʊ-/ *n.* electric polarization in a substance resulting from the application of mechanical stress, esp. in certain crystals. (See below.) □□ **piezoelectric** /-ɪˈlektrɪk/ *adj.* **piezoelectrically** /-ɪˈlektrɪkəlɪ/ *adv.* [Gk *piezō* press + ELECTRIC]

Piezoelectricity was first discovered by Pierre Curie and his brother in 1880. The converse effect, in which a voltage applied to such a material causes a mechanical deformation, also occurs. These effects are of great practical importance because piezo-electric substances are able to convert mechanical signals (such as sound waves) into electrical signals, and vice versa. They are therefore widely used in microphones, gramophone pick-ups, earphones, etc. They can also be made to resonate very accurately at a fixed frequency, and as such form the basis of accurate time-keeping devices such as quartz clocks.

piezometer /ˌpaɪɪˈzɒmɪtə(r), ˌpiː-/ *n.* an instrument for measuring the magnitude or direction of pressure.

piffle /ˈpɪf(ə)l/ *n. & v. colloq.* —*n.* nonsense; empty speech. —*v.intr.* talk or act feebly; trifle. □□ **piffler** *n.* [imit.]

piffling /ˈpɪflɪŋ/ *adj. colloq.* trivial; worthless.

pig /pɪg/ *n. & v.* —*n.* **1 a** any omnivorous hoofed bristly mammal of the family Suidae, esp. a domesticated kind, *Sus scrofa.* **b** *US* a young pig; a piglet. **c** (often in *comb.*) any similar animal (*guinea-pig*). **2** the flesh of esp. a young or sucking pig as food (*roast pig*). **3** *colloq.* **a** a greedy, dirty, obstinate, sulky, or annoying person. **b** an unpleasant, awkward, or difficult thing, task, etc. **4** an oblong mass of metal (esp. iron or lead) from a smelting-furnace. **5** *sl. derog.* a policeman. —*v.* (**pigged, pigging**) **1** *tr.* (also *absol.*) (of a sow) bring forth (piglets). **2** *tr. colloq.* eat (food) greedily. **3** *intr.* herd together or behave like pigs. □ **bleed like a pig** (or **stuck pig**) bleed copiously. **buy a pig in a poke** buy, accept, etc. something without knowing its value or esp. seeing it. **in pig** (of a sow) pregnant. **in a pig's eye** *colloq.* certainly not. **make a pig of oneself** overeat. **make a pig's ear of** *colloq.* make a mess of; bungle. **pig in the middle** a person who is placed in an awkward situation between two others (after a ball game for three with one in the middle). **pig-iron** see IRON. **pig it** live in a disorderly, untidy, or filthy fashion. **pig-jump** *Austral. sl. n.* a jump made by a horse from all four legs. —*v.intr.* (of a horse) jump in this manner. **pig Latin** a made-up jargon. **pig-meat** *Brit.* pork, ham, or bacon. **pig out** (often foll. by *on*) esp. *US sl.* eat gluttonously. **pigs might fly** *iron.* an expression of disbelief. **pig-sticker** a long sharp knife. **pig's wash** = PIGSWILL. □□ **piggish** *adj.* **piggishly** *adv.* **piggishness** *n.* **piglet** *n.* **piglike** *adj.* **pigling** *n.* [ME *pigge* f. OE *pigga* (unrecorded)]

pigeon[1] /ˈpɪdʒɪn, -dʒ(ə)n/ *n.* **1** any of several large usu. grey and white birds of the family Columbidae, esp. *Columba livia*, often domesticated and bred and trained to carry messages etc.; a dove (cf. *rock-pigeon*). **2** a person easily swindled; a simpleton. □ **pigeon-breast** (or **-chest**) a deformed human chest with a projecting breastbone. **pigeon-breasted** (or **-chested**) having a pigeon-breast. **pigeon-fancier** a person who keeps and breeds fancy pigeons. **pigeon-fancying** this pursuit. **pigeon-hawk** = MERLIN. **pigeon-hearted** cowardly. **pigeon-hole** *n.* **1** each of a set of compartments in a cabinet or on a wall for papers, letters, etc. **2** a small recess for a pigeon to nest in. —*v.tr.* **1** deposit (a document) in a pigeon-hole. **2** put (a matter) aside for future consideration or to forget it. **3** assign (a person or thing) to a preconceived category. **pigeon pair** *Brit.* **1** boy and girl twins. **2** a boy and girl as sole children. **pigeon's milk 1** a secretion from the oesophagus with which pigeons feed their young. **2** an imaginary article for which children are sent on a fool's errand. **pigeon-toed** (of a person) having the toes turned inwards. □□ **pigeonry** *n.* (*pl.* **-ies**). [ME f. OF *pijon* f. LL *pipio -onis* (imit.)]

pigeon[2] /ˈpɪdʒɪn, -dʒ(ə)n/ *n.* **1** = PIDGIN. **2** *colloq.* a particular concern, job, or business (*that's not my pigeon*).

piggery /ˈpɪgərɪ/ *n.* (*pl.* **-ies**) **1** a pig-breeding farm etc. **2** = PIGSTY. **3** piggishness.

Piggott /ˈpɪgət/, Lester Keith (1935–), English flat-racing jockey, who was champion jockey nine times between 1960 and 1971 and won the Derby a record eight times.

piggy /ˈpɪgɪ/ *n. & adj.* —*n.* (also **piggie**) *colloq.* **1** a little pig. **2 a** a child's word for a pig. **b** a child's word for a toe. **3** *Brit.* the game of tipcat. —*adj.* (**piggier, piggiest**) **1** like a pig. **2** (of features etc.) like those of a pig (*little piggy eyes*). □ **piggy bank** a pig-shaped money box. **piggy in the middle** = *pig in the middle.*

piggyback /ˈpɪgɪˌbæk/ *n. & adv.* (also **pickaback** /ˈpɪkəˌbæk/) —*n.* a ride on the back and shoulders of another person. —*adv.* **1** on the back and shoulders of another person. **2** on the back or top of a larger object. [16th c.: orig. unkn.]

pigheaded /pɪgˈhedɪd/ *adj.* obstinate. □□ **pigheadedly** *adv.* **pigheadedness** *n.*

Pig Island *Austral. & NZ sl.* New Zealand.

pigment /ˈpɪgmənt/ *n. & v.* —*n.* **1** colouring-matter used as paint or dye, usu. as an insoluble suspension. **2** the natural colouring-matter of animal or plant tissue, e.g. chlorophyll, haemoglobin. —*v.tr.* colour with or as if with pigment. □□ **pigmental** /-ˈment(ə)l/ *adj.* **pigmentary** *adj.* [ME f. L *pigmentum* f. *pingere* paint]

pigmentation /ˌpɪgmənˈteɪʃ(ə)n/ *n.* **1** the natural colouring of plants, animals, etc. **2** the excessive colouring of tissue by the deposition of pigment.

pigmy var. of PYGMY.

pignut /ˈpɪgnʌt/ *n.* = *earth-nut.*

pigpen /ˈpɪgpen/ *n. US* = PIGSTY.

pigskin /ˈpɪgskɪn/ *n.* **1** the hide of a pig. **2** leather made from this. **3** *US* a football.

pigsticking /ˈpɪgˌstɪkɪŋ/ *n.* **1** the hunting of wild boar with a spear on horseback. **2** the butchering of pigs.

pigsty /ˈpɪgstaɪ/ *n.* (*pl.* **-ies**) **1** a pen or enclosure for a pig or pigs. **2** a filthy house, room, etc.

pigswill /ˈpɪgswɪl/ *n.* kitchen refuse and scraps fed to pigs.

pigtail /ˈpɪgteɪl/ *n.* **1** a plait of hair hanging from the back of the head, or either of a pair at the sides. **2** a thin twist of tobacco. □□ **pigtailed** *adj.*

pigwash /ˈpɪgwɒʃ/ *n.* = PIGSWILL.

pigweed /ˈpɪgwiːd/ *n.* any herb of the genus *Amaranthus*, grown for grain or fodder.

pika /ˈpaɪkə/ *n.* any small rabbit-like mammal of the genus *Ochotona*, with small ears and no tail. [Tungus *piika*]

pike[1] /paɪk/ *n.* (*pl.* same) **1** a large voracious freshwater fish, *Esox lucius*, with a long narrow snout and sharp teeth. **2** any other fish of the family Esocidae. □ **pike-perch** any of various pikelike perches of the genus *Lucioperca* or *Stizostedion*. [ME, = PIKE[2] (because of its pointed jaw)]

pike[2] /paɪk/ *n. & v.* —*n.* **1** *hist.* an infantry weapon with a pointed steel or iron head on a long wooden shaft. **2** *N.Engl.* the peaked top of a hill, esp. in names of hills in the Lake District. —*v.tr.* thrust through or kill with a pike. □ **pike on** *colloq.* withdraw timidly from. [OE *pīc* point, prick: sense 2 perh. f. ON]

pike[3] /paɪk/ n. **1** a toll-gate; a toll. **2** a turnpike road. [abbr. of TURNPIKE]

pike[4] /paɪk/ n. a jackknife position in diving or gymnastics. [20th c.: orig. unkn.]

pikelet /ˈpaɪklɪt/ n. N.Engl. a thin kind of crumpet. [Welsh (bara) pyglyd pitchy (bread)]

pikeman /ˈpaɪkmən/ n. (pl. **-men**) the keeper of a turnpike.

piker /ˈpaɪkə(r)/ n. a cautious, timid, or mean person.

pikestaff /ˈpaɪkstɑːf/ n. **1** the wooden shaft of a pike. **2** a walking-stick with a metal point. □ **plain as a pikestaff** quite plain or obvious (orig. packstaff, a smooth staff used by a pedlar).

pilaster /pɪˈlæstə(r)/ n. a rectangular column, esp. one projecting from a wall. □□ **pilastered** adj. [F pilastre f. It. pilastro f. med.L pilastrum f. L pila pillar]

Pilate /ˈpaɪlət/, Pontius (1st c. AD), the governor of Judaea AD 26–36 who presided at the trial of Jesus Christ.

pilau /pɪˈlaʊ/ n. (also **pilaff** /pɪˈlæf/, **pilaw** /pɪˈlɔː/) a Middle Eastern or Indian dish of spiced rice or wheat with meat, fish, vegetables, etc. [Turk. piláv]

pilch /pɪltʃ/ n. archaic a baby's usu. waterproof garment worn over a nappy. [OE pyl(e)ce f. LL pellicia: see PELISSE]

pilchard /ˈpɪltʃəd/ n. a small marine fish, Sardinia pilchardus of the herring family (see SARDINE). [16th-c. pilcher etc.: orig. unkn.]

pile[1] /paɪl/ n. & v. —n. **1** a heap of things laid or gathered upon one another (a pile of leaves). **2 a** a large imposing building (a stately pile). **b** a large group of tall buildings. **3** colloq. **a** a large quantity. **b** a large amount of money; a fortune (made his pile). **4 a** a series of plates of dissimilar metals laid one on another alternately to produce an electric current. **b** = atomic pile. **5** a funeral pyre. —v. **1** tr. **a** (often foll. by up, on) heap up (piled the plates on the table). **b** (foll. by with) load (piled the bed with coats). **2** intr. (usu. foll. by in, into, on, out of, etc.) crowd hurriedly or tightly (all piled into the car; piled out of the restaurant). □ **pile arms** hist. place (usu. four) rifles with their butts on the ground and the muzzles together. **pile it on** colloq. exaggerate. **pile on the agony** colloq. exaggerate for effect or to gain sympathy etc. **pile up 1** accumulate; heap up. **2** colloq. run (a ship) aground or cause (a vehicle etc.) to crash. **pile-up** n. colloq. a multiple crash of road vehicles. [ME f. OF f. L pila pillar, pier, mole]

pile[2] /paɪl/ n. & v. —n. **1** a heavy beam driven vertically into the bed of a river, soft ground, etc., to support the foundations of a superstructure. **2** a pointed stake or post. **3** Heraldry a wedge-shaped device. —v.tr. **1** provide with piles. **2** drive (piles) into the ground etc. □ **pile-driver** a machine for driving piles into the ground. **pile-dwelling** a dwelling built on piles, esp. in a lake. [OE píl f. L pilum javelin]

pile[3] /paɪl/ n. **1** the soft projecting surface on velvet, plush, etc., or esp. on a carpet; nap. **2** soft hair or down, or the wool of a sheep. [ME prob. f. AF pyle, peile, OF poil f. L pilus hair]

piles /paɪlz/ n.pl. colloq. haemorrhoids. [ME prob. f. L pila ball, f. the globular form of external piles]

pileus /ˈpaɪlɪəs/ n. (pl. **pilei** /-lɪaɪ/) the caplike part of a mushroom or other fungus. □□ **pileate** /-lɪət/ adj. **pileated** /-lɪeɪtɪd/ adj. [L, = felt cap]

pilewort /ˈpaɪlwɜːt/ n. the lesser celandine. [PILES, f. its reputed efficacy against piles]

pilfer /ˈpɪlfə(r)/ v.tr. (also absol.) steal (objects) esp. in small quantities. □□ **pilferage** /-rɪdʒ/ n. **pilferer** n. [ME f. AF & OF pelfrer pillage, of unkn. orig.: assoc. with archaic pill plunder: PELF]

pilgrim /ˈpɪlɡrɪm/ n. & v. —n. **1** a person who journeys to a sacred place for religious reasons. **2** a person regarded as journeying through life etc. **3** a traveller. —v.intr. (**pilgrimed**, **pilgriming**) wander like a pilgrim. □ **Pilgrim Fathers** the pioneers of British colonization of North America, a group of 100 (or according to some reports 102) persons who sailed in the Mayflower and founded a settlement at New Plymouth, Mass., in 1620. The expedition was initiated by a group of English Puritans fleeing religious persecution. □□ **pilgrimize** v.intr. (also **-ise**). [ME pilegrim f. Prov. pelegrin f. L peregrinus stranger: see PEREGRINE]

pilgrimage /ˈpɪlɡrɪmɪdʒ/ n. & v. —n. **1** a pilgrim's journey (go on a pilgrimage). **2** life viewed as a journey. **3** any journey taken for nostalgic or sentimental reasons. —v.intr. go on a pilgrimage. [ME f. Prov. pilgrinatge (as PILGRIM)]

Pilipino /ˌpɪlɪˈpiːnəʊ/ n. the national language of the Philippines. [Tagalog f. Sp. Filipino]

pill /pɪl/ n. **1 a** a solid medicine formed into a ball or a flat disc for swallowing whole. **b** (usu. prec. by the) colloq. a contraceptive pill. **2** an unpleasant or painful necessity; a humiliation (a bitter pill; must swallow the pill). **3** colloq. or joc. a ball, e.g. a football, a cannon-ball. □ **sugar** (or **sweeten**) **the pill** make an unpleasant necessity acceptable. [MDu., MLG pille prob. f. L pilula dimin. of pila ball]

pillage /ˈpɪlɪdʒ/ v. & n. —v.tr. (also absol.) plunder; sack (a place or a person). —n. the act or an instance of pillaging, esp. in war. □□ **pillager** n. [ME f. OF f. piller plunder]

pillar /ˈpɪlə(r)/ n. **1 a** a usu. slender vertical structure of wood, metal, or esp. stone used as a support for a roof etc. **b** a similar structure used for ornament. **c** a post supporting a structure. **2** a person regarded as a mainstay or support (a pillar of the faith; a pillar of strength). **3** an upright mass of air, water, rock, etc. (pillar of salt). **4** a solid mass of coal etc. left to support the roof of a mine. □ **from pillar to post** (driven etc.) from one place to another; to and fro. **pillar-box** Brit. a public postbox shaped like a pillar. **pillar-box red** a bright red colour, as of pillar-boxes. **Pillars of Hercules** see HERCULES. □□ **pillared** adj. **pillaret** n. [ME & AF piler, OF pilier ult. f. L pila pillar]

pillbox /ˈpɪlbɒks/ n. **1** a small shallow cylindrical box for holding pills. **2** a hat of a similar shape. **3** Mil. a small partly underground enclosed concrete fort used as an outpost.

pillion /ˈpɪljən/ n. **1** seating for a passenger behind a motor cyclist. **2** hist. **a** a woman's light saddle. **b** a cushion attached to the back of a saddle for a usu. female passenger. □ **ride pillion** travel seated behind a motor cyclist etc. [Gael. pillean, pillin dimin. of pell cushion f. L pellis skin]

pilliwinks /ˈpɪlɪwɪŋks/ n. hist. an instrument of torture used for squeezing the fingers. [ME pyrwykes, pyrewinkes, of unkn. orig.]

pillock /ˈpɪlək/ n. Brit. sl. a stupid person; a fool. [16th c., = penis (var. of pillicock): 20th c. in sense defined]

pillory /ˈpɪlərɪ/ n. & v. —n. (pl. **-ies**) hist. a wooden framework with holes for the head and hands, into which offenders were formerly locked for exposure to public ridicule or assault. —v.tr. (**-ies, -ied**) **1** expose (a person) to ridicule or public contempt. **2** hist. put in the pillory. [ME f. AL pillorium f. OF pilori etc.: prob. f. Prov. espilori of uncert. orig.]

pillow /ˈpɪləʊ/ n. & v. —n. **1 a** a usu. oblong support for the head, esp. in bed, with a cloth cover stuffed with feathers, flock, foam rubber, etc. **b** any pillow-shaped block or support. **2** = lace-pillow. —v.tr. **1** rest (the head etc.) on or as if on a pillow (pillowed his head on his arms). **2** serve as a pillow for (moss pillowed her head). □ **pillow-fight** a mock fight with pillows, esp. by children. **pillow-lace** lace made on a lace-pillow. **pillow lava** lava forming rounded masses. **pillow talk** romantic or intimate conversation in bed. □□ **pillowy** adj. [OE pyle, pylu, ult. f. L pulvinus cushion]

pillowcase /ˈpɪləʊˌkeɪs/ n. a washable cotton etc. cover for a pillow.

pillowslip /ˈpɪləʊslɪp/ n. = PILLOWCASE.

pillule var. of PILULE.

pillwort /ˈpɪlwɜːt/ n. an aquatic fern, Pilularia globulifera, with small globular spore-producing bracts.

pilose /ˈpaɪləʊz/ adj. (also **pilous** /ˈpaɪləs/) covered with hair. □□ **pilosity** /paɪˈlɒsɪtɪ/ n. [L pilosus f. pilus hair]

pilot /ˈpaɪlət/ n. & v. —n. **1** a person who operates the flying controls of an aircraft. **2** a person qualified to take charge of a ship entering or leaving harbour. **3** (usu. attrib.) an experimental undertaking or test, esp. in advance of a larger one (a pilot project). **4** a guide; a leader. **5** archaic a steersman. —v.tr. (**piloted**, **piloting**) **1** act as a pilot on (a ship) or of (an aircraft). **2** conduct, lead, or initiate as a pilot (piloted the new scheme). □ **pilot balloon** a small balloon used to track air currents etc. **pilot-bird** a rare dark-brown Australian babbler, Pycnoptilus floccosus, with a distinctive loud cry. **pilot chute** a small parachute used to bring the main one into operation. **pilot-cloth** thick blue woollen cloth for seamen's coats etc. **pilot-fish** a small fish, *Naucrates ductor*, said to act as a pilot leading a shark to food. **pilot-house** = wheel-house. **pilot-jacket** = PEA-JACKET. **pilot-light 1** a small gas burner kept alight to light another. **2** an electric indicator light or control light. **pilot officer** *Brit.* the lowest commissioned rank in the RAF. □□ **pilotage** *n.* **pilotless** *adj.* [F *pilote* f. med.L *pilotus*, *pedot(t)a* f. Gk *pēdon* oar]

Pilsen /ˈpɪls(ə)n/ (Czech **Plzeň**) an industrial city in western Czechoslovakia, noted for its lager beer; pop. (1986) 175,000.

Pilsner /ˈpɪlznə(r), -snə(r)/ *n.* (also **Pilsener**) a lager beer brewed or like that brewed at *Pilsen* (Plzeň) in Czechoslovakia.

Piltdown man /ˈpɪltdaʊn/ a fraudulent fossil (*Eoanthropus dawsoni*) composed of a human cranium and an ape jaw that was presented to the scientific community in 1912 as a genuine hominid of great antiquity. The fossil was allegedly discovered in a gravel-pit on Piltdown Common near Lewes, East Sussex, in association with early Pleistocene fossil fauna in addition to stone and bone artefacts of 'pre-Acheulian' type. Although suspicions concerning its genuineness were voiced the fraud was not proved until 1953, when J. S. Weiner and K. P. Oakley demonstrated beyond any doubt, by fluorine dating and other tests, that Piltdown man was a hoax. The problems of human evolution, although still complex and much disputed, were made less difficult with the removal of *Eoanthropus dawsoni* from the competition. Perpetration of the fraud has been variously credited to the skull's 'discoverer' (Charles Dawson) and his friends, who included Samuel Woodhead (county analyst for Sussex), and an unidentified hoaxer.

pilule /ˈpɪljuːl/ *n.* (also **pillule**) a small pill. □□ **pilular** *adj.* **pilulous** *adj.* [F f. L *pilula*: see PILL]

pimento /pɪˈmentəʊ/ *n.* (*pl.* **-os**) **1** a small tropical tree, *Pimenta dioica*, native to Jamaica. **2** the unripe dried berries of this, usu. crushed for culinary use. Also called ALLSPICE. **3** = PIMIENTO. [Sp. *pimiento* (as PIMIENTO)]

pimiento /ˌpɪmɪˈentəʊ, pɪmˈjentəʊ/ *n.* (*pl.* **-os**) = *sweet pepper* (see PEPPER). [Sp. f. L *pigmentum* PIGMENT, in med.L = spice]

pimp /pɪmp/ *n. & v.* —*n.* a man who lives off the earnings of a prostitute or a brothel; a pander; a ponce. —*v.intr.* act as a pimp. [17th c.: orig. unkn.]

pimpernel /ˈpɪmpənel/ *n.* any plant of the genus *Anagallis*, esp. = *scarlet pimpernel*. [ME f. OF *pimpernelle*, *piprenelle* ult. f. L *piper* PEPPER]

pimping /ˈpɪmpɪŋ/ *adj.* **1** small or mean. **2** sickly. [17th c.: orig. unkn.]

pimple /ˈpɪmp(ə)l/ *n.* **1** a small hard inflamed spot on the skin. **2** anything resembling a pimple, esp. in relative size. □□ **pimpled** *adj.* **pimply** *adj.* [ME nasalized f. OE *piplian* break out in pustules]

PIN /pɪn/ *n.* personal identification number (as issued by a bank etc. to validate electronic transactions). [abbr.]

pin /pɪn/ *n. & v.* —*n.* **1 a** a small thin pointed piece of esp. steel wire with a round or flattened head used (esp. in sewing) for holding things in place, attaching one thing to another, etc. **b** any of several types of pin (*drawing-pin*; *safety pin*; *hairpin*). **c** a small brooch (*diamond pin*). **d** a badge fastened with a pin. **2** a peg of wood or metal for various purposes, e.g. a wooden skittle in bowling. **3** something of small value (*don't care a pin*; *for two pins I'd resign*). **4** (in *pl.*) *colloq.* legs (*quick on his pins*). **5** *Med.* a steel rod used to join the ends of fractured bones while they heal. **6** *Chess* a position in which a piece is pinned to another. **7** *Golf* a stick with a flag placed in a hole to mark its position. **8** *Mus.* a peg round which one string of a musical instrument is fastened. **9** a half-firkin cask for beer. —*v.tr.* (**pinned**, **pinning**) **1 a** (often foll. by *to*, *up*, *together*) fasten with a pin or pins (*pinned up the hem*; *pinned the papers together*). **b** transfix with a pin, lance, etc. **2** (usu. foll. by *on*) fix (blame, responsibility, etc.) on a person etc. (*pinned the blame on his friend*). **3** (often foll. by *against*, *on*, etc.) seize and hold fast. **4** *Chess* prevent (an opposing piece) from moving except by exposing a more valuable piece to capture. □ **on pins and needles** in an agitated state of suspense. **pin down**

1 (often foll. by *to*) bind (a person etc.) to a promise, arrangement, etc. **2** force (a person) to declare his or her intentions. **3** restrict the actions or movement of (an enemy etc.). **4** specify (a thing) precisely (*could not pin down his unease to a particular cause*). **5** hold (a person etc.) down by force. **pin one's faith** (or **hopes** etc.) **on** rely implicitly on. **pin-feather** *Zool.* an ungrown feather. **pin-high** *Golf* (of a ball) at the same distance ahead as the pin. **pin-money 1** *hist.* an allowance to a woman for dress etc. from her husband. **2** a very small sum of money, esp. for spending on inessentials (*only works for pin-money*). **pins and needles** a tingling sensation in a limb recovering from numbness. **pin-table** a table used in playing pinball. **pin-tuck** a very narrow ornamental tuck. **pin-up 1** a photograph of a popular or sexually attractive person, designed to be hung on the wall. **2** a person shown in such a photograph. **pin-wheel** a small Catherine wheel. **split pin** a metal cotter pin passed through a hole and held in place by its gaping split end. [OE *pinn* f. L *pinna* point etc., assoc. with *penna* PEN¹]

pina colada /ˌpiːnə kəˈlɑːdə/ *n.* a drink made from pineapple juice, rum, and coconut. [Sp., lit. 'strained pineapple']

pinafore /ˈpɪnəfɔː(r)/ *n.* esp. *Brit.* **1 a** an apron, esp. with a bib. **b** a woman's sleeveless wraparound washable covering for the clothes, tied at the back. **2** (in full **pinafore dress**) a collarless sleeveless dress worn over a blouse or jumper. [PIN + AFORE (because orig. pinned on the front of a dress)]

Pinang see PENANG.

pinaster /paɪˈnæstə(r)/ *n.* = *cluster pine*. [L, = wild pine f. *pinus* pine + -ASTER]

pinball /ˈpɪnbɔːl/ *n.* a game in which small metal balls are shot across a board and score points by striking pins with lights etc.

pince-nez /ˈpænsneɪ, pæsˈneɪ/ *n.* (*pl.* same) a pair of eyeglasses with a nose-clip instead of earpieces. [F, lit. = pinch-nose]

pincers /ˈpɪnsəz/ *n.pl.* **1** (also **pair of pincers**) a gripping-tool resembling scissors but with blunt usu. concave jaws to hold a nail etc. for extraction. **2** the front claws of lobsters and some other crustaceans. □ **pincer movement** *Mil.* a movement by two wings of an army converging on the enemy. [ME *pinsers*, *pinsours* f. AF f. OF *pincier* PINCH]

pincette /pæˈset/ *n.* small pincers; tweezers. [F]

pinch /pɪntʃ/ *v. & n.* —*v.* **1** *tr.* **a** grip (esp. the skin of part of the body or of another person) tightly, esp. between finger and thumb (*pinched my finger in the door*; *stop pinching me*). **b** (often *absol.*) (of a shoe, garment, etc.) constrict (the flesh) painfully. **2** *tr.* (of cold, hunger, etc.) grip (a person) painfully (*she was pinched with cold*). **3** *tr. sl.* **a** steal; take without permission. **b** arrest (a person) (*pinched him for loitering*). **4** (as **pinched** *adj.*) (of the features) drawn, as with cold, hunger, worry, etc. **5 a** *tr.* (usu. foll. by *in*, *of*, *for*, etc.) stint (a person). **b** *intr.* be niggardly with money, food, etc. **6** *tr.* (usu. foll. by *out*, *back*, *down*) *Hort.* remove (leaves, buds, etc.) to encourage bushy growth. **7** *intr.* sail very close to the wind. —*n.* **1** the act or an instance of pinching etc. the flesh. **2** an amount that can be taken up with fingers and thumb (*a pinch of snuff*). **3** the stress or pain caused by poverty, cold, hunger, etc. **4** *sl.* **a** an arrest. **b** a theft. □ **at** (or **in**) **a pinch** in an emergency; if necessary. **feel the pinch** experience the effects of poverty. **pinch-hitter** *US* **1** a baseball player who bats instead of another in an emergency. **2** a person acting as a substitute. [ME f. AF & ONF *pinchier* (unrecorded), OF *pincier*, ult. f. L *pungere* *punct-* prick]

pinchbeck /ˈpɪntʃbek/ *n. & adj.* —*n.* an alloy of copper and zinc resembling gold and used in cheap jewellery etc. —*adj.* **1** counterfeit; sham. **2** cheap; tawdry. [C. *Pinchbeck*, Engl. watchmaker d. 1732]

pinchpenny /ˈpɪntʃˌpenɪ/ *n.* (*pl.* **-ies**) (also *attrib.*) a miserly person.

pincushion /ˈpɪnˌkʊʃ(ə)n/ *n.* a small cushion for holding pins.

Pindar /ˈpɪndə(r)/ (518–438 BC) Greek lyric poet. Of his various works there survive four books of odes in honour of victories won, chiefly by Greek rulers and aristocrats, in athletic contests. They are usually in the form of choral hymns, written in a grand style; the celebration of victory is seen as a religious occasion. □□ **Pindaric** /-ˈdærɪk/ *adj.*

Pindus Mountains /ˈpɪndəs/ (Greek **Pindhos**) a mountain range in west central Greece, stretching from the Gulf of Corinth to the Albanian frontier. The highest peak is Smolikas (2,637 m, 8,136 ft.).

pine¹ /paɪn/ n. **1** any evergreen tree of the genus *Pinus* native to northern temperate regions, with needle-shaped leaves growing in clusters. **2** the soft timber of this, often used to make furniture. Also called DEAL². **3** (*attrib.*) made of pine. **4** = PINEAPPLE. □ **pine cone** the cone-shaped fruit of the pine tree. **pine marten** a weasel-like mammal, *Martes martes*, native to Europe and America, with a dark brown coat and white throat and stomach. **pine nut** the edible seed of various pine trees. □□ **pinery** n. (*pl.* -**ies**). [ME f. OE *pīn* & OF *pin* f. L *pinus*]

pine² /paɪn/ v.intr. **1** (often foll. by *away*) decline or waste away, esp. from grief, disease, etc. **2** (usu. foll. by *for*, *after*, or *to* + infin.) long eagerly; yearn. [OE *pīnian*, rel. to obs. E *pine* punishment, f. Gmc f. med.L *pena*, L *poena*]

pineal /ˈpɪnɪəl, ˈpaɪ-/ adj. shaped like a pine cone. □ **pineal body** (or **gland**) a pea-sized conical mass of tissue behind the third ventricle of the brain, secreting a hormone-like substance in some mammals. [F *pinéal* f. L *pinea* pine cone: see PINE¹]

pineapple /ˈpaɪnˌæp(ə)l/ n. **1** a tropical plant, *Ananas comosus*, with a spiral of sword-shaped leaves and a thick stem bearing a large fruit developed from many flowers. **2** the fruit of this, consisting of yellow flesh surrounded by a tough segmented skin and topped with a tuft of stiff leaves. [PINE¹, from the fruit's resemblance to a pine cone]

Pinero /pɪˈnɪərəʊ/, Sir Arthur Wing (1855–1934), English dramatist, who began as an actor and encouraged by Sir Henry Irving became a prolific author of many successful farces, such as *The Magistrate* (1885), and several more serious plays, including *The Profligate* (1889) and the enduringly popular *The Second Mrs Tanqueray* (1893). In his later years his reputation became eclipsed by the rising popularity of the new theatre of Shaw and Ibsen.

pinetum /paɪˈniːtəm/ n. (*pl.* **pineta** /-tə/) a plantation of pine-trees or other conifers for scientific or ornamental purposes. [L f. *pinus* pine]

pinfold /ˈpɪnfəʊld/ n. & v. —n. a pound for stray cattle etc. —v.tr. confine (cattle) in a pinfold. [OE *pundfald* (as POUND³, FOLD²)]

ping /pɪŋ/ n. & v. —n. a single short high ringing sound. —v.intr. make a ping. [imit.]

pinger /ˈpɪŋə(r)/ n. **1** a device that transmits pings at short intervals for purposes of detection or measurement etc. **2** a device to ring a bell.

pingo /ˈpɪŋgəʊ/ n. (*pl.* -**os**) *Geol.* a dome-shaped mound found in permafrost areas. [Eskimo]

ping-pong /ˈpɪŋpɒŋ/ n. = *table tennis.* [imit. f. the sound of a bat striking a ball]

pinguid /ˈpɪŋgwɪd/ adj. *formal* or *joc.* fat, oily, or greasy. [L *pinguis* fat]

pinhead /ˈpɪnhed/ n. **1** the flattened head of a pin. **2** a very small thing. **3** *colloq.* a stupid or foolish person.

pinheaded /pɪnˈhedɪd/ adj. *colloq.* stupid, foolish. □□ **pinheadedness** n.

pinhole /ˈpɪnhəʊl/ n. **1** a hole made by a pin. **2** a hole into which a peg fits. □ **pinhole camera** a camera with a pinhole aperture and no lens.

pinion¹ /ˈpɪnjən/ n. & v. —n. **1** the outer part of a bird's wing, usu. including the flight feathers. **2** *poet.* a wing; a flight-feather. —v.tr. **1** cut off the pinion of (a wing or bird) to prevent flight. **2 a** bind the arms of (a person). **b** (often foll. by *to*) bind (the arms, a person, etc.) esp. to a thing. [ME f. OF *pignon* ult. f. L *pinna*: see PIN]

pinion² /ˈpɪnjən/ n. **1** a small cog-wheel engaging with a larger one. **2** a cogged spindle engaging with a wheel. [F *pignon* alt. f. obs. *pignol* f. L *pinea* pine-cone (as PINE¹)]

pink¹ /pɪŋk/ n. & adj. —n. **1** a pale red colour (*decorated in pink*). **2 a** a cultivated plant of the genus *Dianthus*, with sweet-smelling white, pink, crimson, etc. flowers. **b** the flower of this plant. **3** (prec. by *the*) the most perfect condition etc. (*the pink of elegance*).

4 (also **hunting-pink**) **a** a fox-hunter's red coat. **b** the cloth for this. **c** a fox-hunter. —adj. **1** (often in *comb.*) of a pale red colour of any of various shades (*rose-pink*; *salmon-pink*). **2** esp. *derog.* tending to socialism. □ **in the pink** *colloq.* in very good health. **pink-collar** (usu. *attrib.*) (of a profession etc.) traditionally associated with women (cf. *white-collar*, *blue-collar* (see BLUE¹)). **pink disease** a disease of young children with pink discoloration of the extremities. **pink elephants** *colloq.* hallucinations caused by alcoholism. **pink-eye** **1** a contagious fever in horses. **2** contagious ophthalmia in humans and some livestock. **pink gin** gin flavoured with angostura bitters. □□ **pinkish** adj. **pinkly** adv. **pinkness** n. **pinky** adj. [perh. f. dial. *pink-eyed* having small eyes]

pink² /pɪŋk/ v.tr. **1** pierce slightly with a sword etc. **2** cut a scalloped or zigzag edge on. **3** (often foll. by *out*) ornament (leather etc.) with perforations. **4** adorn; deck. □ **pinking shears** (or **scissors**) a dressmaker's serrated shears for cutting a zigzag edge. [ME, perh. f. LG or Du.: cf. LG *pinken* strike, peck]

pink³ /pɪŋk/ v.intr. (of a vehicle engine) emit a series of high-pitched explosive sounds caused by faulty combustion. [imit.]

pink⁴ /pɪŋk/ n. *hist.* a sailing-ship, esp. with a narrow stern, orig. small and flat-bottomed. [ME f. MDu. *pin(c)ke*, of unkn. orig.]

pink⁵ /pɪŋk/ n. a yellowish lake pigment made by combining vegetable colouring matter with a white base (*brown pink*; *French pink*). [17th c.: orig. unkn.]

pink⁶ /pɪŋk/ n. *Brit.* **1** a young salmon. **2** *dial.* a minnow. [15th c. *penk*, of unkn. orig.]

Pinkerton /ˈpɪŋkət(ə)n/, Allan (1819–84), American detective. An immigrant from Scotland, Pinkerton established the first American private detective agency in Chicago in 1850 and became a national figure after solving a series of express robberies. In the early years of the American Civil War he served as the secret service chief of the Union general McClellan and was later prominent as a strike-breaker, particularly in the eastern coal industry.

pinkie /ˈpɪŋkɪ/ n. esp. *US* & *Sc.* the little finger. [cf. dial. *pink* small, half-shut (eye)]

Pinkster /ˈpɪŋkstə(r)/ n. *US* Whitsuntide. □ **pinkster flower** the pink azalea, *Rhododendron nudiflorum*. [Du., = Pentecost]

pinna /ˈpɪnə/ n. (*pl.* **pinnae** /-niː/ or **pinnas**) **1** the auricle; the external part of the ear. **2** a primary division of a pinnate leaf. **3** a fin or finlike structure, feather, wing, etc. [L, = *penna* feather, wing, fin]

pinnace /ˈpɪnɪs/ n. *Naut.* a warship's or other ship's small boat, usu. motor-driven, orig. schooner-rigged or eight-oared. [F *pinnace*, *pinasse* ult. f. L *pinus* PINE¹]

pinnacle /ˈpɪnək(ə)l/ n. & v. —n. **1** the culmination or climax (of endeavour, success, etc.). **2** a natural peak. **3** a small ornamental turret usu. ending in a pyramid or cone, crowning a buttress, roof, etc. —v.tr. **1** set on or as if on a pinnacle. **2** form the pinnacle of. **3** provide with pinnacles. [ME *pinacle* f. OF *pin(n)acle* f. LL *pinnaculum* f. *pinna* wing, point (as PIN, -CULE)]

pinnae *pl.* of PINNA.

pinnate /ˈpɪneɪt/ adj. **1** (of a compound leaf) having leaflets arranged on either side of the stem, usu. in pairs opposite each other. **2** having branches, tentacles, etc., on each side of an axis. □□ **pinnated** adj. **pinnately** adv. **pinnation** /-ˈneɪʃ(ə)n/ n. [L *pinnatus* feathered (as PINNA)]

pinni- /ˈpɪnɪ/ comb. form feather, fin. [L *pinna*]

pinniped /ˈpɪnɪped/ adj. & n. —adj. denoting any aquatic mammal with limbs ending in fins. —n. a pinniped mammal. [L *pinna* fin + *pes ped-* foot]

pinnule /ˈpɪnjuːl/ n. **1** the secondary division of a pinnate leaf. **2** a part or organ like a small wing or fin. □□ **pinnular** adj. [L *pinnula* dimin. of *pinna* fin, wing]

pinny /ˈpɪnɪ/ n. (*pl.* -**ies**) *colloq.* a pinafore. [abbr.]

Pinochet /ˈpɪnəʃeɪ/, Augusto (1915–), Chilean general and statesman. Bitterly opposed to the left-wing politics of President Allende, he master-minded a military coup (1973) and took over the presidency. He imposed a harsh repressive military rule until forced to call elections (Dec. 1989) and give way to a democratically elected President.

w we z zoo ʃ she ʒ decision θ thin ð this ŋ ring x loch tʃ chip dʒ jar (*see over for vowels*)

pinochle /'piːˌnɒk(ə)l/ n. US 1 a card-game with a double pack of 48 cards (nine to ace only). 2 the combination of queen of spades and jack of diamonds in this game. [19th c.: orig. unkn.]

pinole /pɪ'nəʊlɪ/ n. US flour made from parched cornflour, esp. mixed with sweet flour made of mesquite beans, sugar, etc. [Amer. Sp. f. Aztec *pinolli*]

piñon /piː'njəʊn/ n. 1 a pine, *Pinus cembra*, bearing edible seeds. 2 the seed of this, a type of pine nut. [Sp. f. L *pinea* pine cone]

pinpoint /'pɪnpɔɪnt/ n. & v. —n. 1 the point of a pin. 2 something very small or sharp. 3 (*attrib.*) **a** very small. **b** precise, accurate. —v.tr. locate with precision (*pinpointed the target*).

pinprick /'pɪnprɪk/ n. 1 a prick caused by a pin. 2 a trifling irritation.

pinstripe /'pɪnstraɪp/ n. 1 a very narrow stripe in (esp. worsted or serge) cloth. 2 a fabric or garment with this.

pint /paɪnt/ n. 1 a measure of capacity for liquids etc., one-eighth of a gallon (in Britain 20 fluid oz. or 4546 cc, in the US 3785 cc). 2 Brit. **a** colloq. a pint of beer. **b** a pint of a liquid, esp. milk. 3 Brit. a measure of shellfish, being the amount containable in a pint mug (*bought a pint of whelks*). □ **pint-pot** a pot, esp. of pewter, holding one pint, esp. of beer. **pint-sized** colloq. very small, esp. of a person. [ME f. OF *pinte*, of unkn. orig.]

pinta /'paɪntə/ n. Brit. colloq. a pint of milk. [corrupt. of *pint of*]

pintail /'pɪnteɪl/ n. a duck, esp. *Anas acuta*, or grouse with a pointed tail.

Pinter /'pɪntə(r)/, Harold (1930–), English playwright. His plays are marked by humorous misunderstandings and often also by a sense of brooding menace, as in *The Caretaker* (1960) and *The Homecoming* (1965).

pintle /'pɪnt(ə)l/ n. a pin or bolt, esp. one on which some other part turns. [OE *pintel* penis, of unkn. orig.: cf. OFris. etc. *pint*]

pinto /'pɪntəʊ, 'piː-/ adj. & n. US —adj. piebald. —n. (pl. **-os**) a piebald horse. [Sp., = mottled, ult. f. L *pictus* past part. of *pingere* paint]

pinworm /'pɪnwɜːm/ n. a small parasitic nematode worm, *Enterobius vermicularis*, of which the female has a pointed tail.

piny /'paɪnɪ/ adj. of, like, or full of pines.

Pinyin /pɪn'jɪn/ n. a system of romanized spelling for transliterating Chinese. [Chin. *pīn-yīn*, lit. 'spell sound']

piolet /pjəʊ'leɪ/ n. a two-headed ice-axe for mountaineering. [F]

pion /'paɪɒn/ n. Physics a meson having a mass approximately 270 times that of an electron. Also called *pi meson* (see PI¹). □□ **pionic** /paɪ'ɒnɪk/ adj. [PI¹ (the letter used as a symbol for the particle) + -ON]

pioneer /ˌpaɪə'nɪə(r)/ n. & v. —n. 1 an initiator of a new enterprise, an inventor, etc. 2 an explorer or settler; a colonist. 3 Mil. a member of an infantry group preparing roads, terrain, etc. for the main body of troops. —v. 1 a tr. initiate or originate (an enterprise etc.). **b** intr. act or prepare the way as a pioneer. 2 tr. Mil. open up (a road etc.) as a pioneer. 3 tr. go before, lead, or conduct (another person or persons). [F *pionnier* foot-soldier, pioneer, OF *paonier, peon(n)ier* (as PEON)]

pious /'paɪəs/ adj. 1 devout; religious. 2 hypocritically virtuous; sanctimonious. 3 dutiful. □ **pious fraud** a deception intended to benefit those deceived, esp. religiously. □□ **piously** adv. **piousness** n. [L *pius* dutiful, pious]

pip¹ n. & v. —n. the seed of an apple, pear, orange, grape, etc. —v.tr. (**pipped, pipping**) remove the pips from (fruit etc.). □□ **pipless** adj. [abbr. of PIPPIN]

pip² /pɪp/ n. Brit. a short high-pitched sound, usu. mechanically produced, esp. as a radio time signal. [imit.]

pip³ /pɪp/ n. 1 any of the spots on a playing-card, dice, or domino. 2 Brit. a star (1–3 according to rank) on the shoulder of an army officer's uniform. 3 a single blossom of a clustered head of flowers. 4 a diamond-shaped segment of the surface of a pineapple. 5 an image of an object on a radar screen. [16th c. *peep*, of unkn. orig.]

pip⁴ /pɪp/ n. 1 a disease of poultry etc. causing thick mucus in the throat and white scale on the tongue. 2 colloq. a fit of disgust or bad temper (esp. *give one the pip*). [ME f. MDu. *pippe*, MLG *pip* prob. ult. f. corrupt. of L *pituita* slime]

pip⁵ /pɪp/ v.tr. (**pipped, pipping**) Brit. colloq. 1 hit with a shot. 2 defeat. 3 blackball. □ **pip at the post** defeat at the last moment. **pip out** die. [PIP² or PIP¹]

pipa /'pɪpə/ n. an aquatic toad, *Pipa pipa*, having a flat body with long webbed feet, the female of which carries her eggs and tadpoles in pockets on her back. Also called SURINAM TOAD. [Surinam Negro *pipál* (masc.), *pipá* (fem.)]

pipal var. of PEEPUL.

pipe /paɪp/ n. & v. —n. 1 a tube of metal, plastic, wood, etc. used to convey water, gas, etc. 2 (also **tobacco-pipe**) **a** a narrow wooden or clay etc. tube with a bowl at one end containing burning tobacco, the smoke from which is drawn into the mouth. **b** the quantity of tobacco held by this (*smoked a pipe*). 3 Mus. **a** a wind instrument consisting of a single tube. **b** any of the tubes by which sound is produced in an organ. **c** (in pl.) = BAGPIPES. **d** (in pl.) a set of pipes joined together, e.g. pan-pipes. 4 a tubal organ, vessel, etc. in an animal's body. 5 a high note or song, esp. of a bird. 6 a cylindrical vein of ore. 7 a cavity in cast metal. 8 **a** a boatswain's whistle. **b** the sounding of this. 9 a cask for wine, esp. as a measure of two hogsheads, usu. equivalent to 105 gallons (about 477 litres). 10 archaic the voice, esp. in singing. —v.tr. 1 (also absol.) play (a tune etc.) on a pipe or pipes. 2 **a** convey (oil, water, gas, etc.) by pipes. **b** provide with pipes. 3 transmit (music, a radio programme, etc.) by wire or cable. 4 (usu. foll. by up, on, to, etc.) Naut. **a** summon (a crew) to a meal, work, etc. **b** signal the arrival of (an officer etc.) on board. 5 utter in a shrill voice; whistle. 6 **a** arrange (icing, cream, etc.) in decorative lines or twists on a cake etc. **b** ornament (a cake etc.) with piping. 7 trim (a dress etc.) with piping. 8 lead or bring (a person etc.) by the sound of a pipe. 9 propagate (pinks etc.) by taking cuttings at the joint of a stem. □ **pipe away** give a signal for (a boat) to start. **pipe-cleaner** a piece of flexible covered wire for cleaning a tobacco-pipe. **pipe down 1** colloq. be quiet or less insistent. 2 Naut. dismiss from duty. **pipe-fish** any of various long slender fish of the family Syngnathidae, with an elongated snout. **pipe-light** a spill for lighting a pipe. **pipe major** an NCO commanding regimental pipers. **pipe-organ** Mus. an organ using pipes instead of or as well as reeds. **pipe-rack** a rack for holding tobacco-pipes. **pipe-rolls** hist. the annual records of the British Exchequer from the 12th–19th c. (prob. because subsidiary documents were rolled in pipe form). **pipe-stem** the shaft of a tobacco-pipe. **pipe-stone** a hard red clay used by US Indians for tobacco-pipes. **pipe up** begin to play, sing, speak, etc. **put that in your pipe and smoke it** colloq. a challenge to another to accept something frank or unwelcome. □□ **pipeful** n. (pl. **-fuls**). **pipeless** adj. **pipy** adj. [OE *pīpe*, *pīpian* & OF *piper* f. Gmc ult. f. L *pipare* peep, chirp]

pipeclay /'paɪpkleɪ/ n. & v. —n. a fine white clay used for tobacco-pipes, whitening leather, etc. —v.tr. 1 whiten (leather etc.) with this. 2 put in order.

pipedream /'paɪpdriːm/ n. an unattainable or fanciful hope or scheme. [orig. as experienced when smoking an opium pipe]

pipeline /'paɪplaɪn/ n. 1 a long, usu. underground, pipe for conveying esp. oil. 2 a channel supplying goods, information, etc. □ **in the pipeline** awaiting completion or processing.

pip emma /pɪp 'emə/ adv. & n. Brit. colloq. = P.M. [formerly signallers' names for letters PM]

Piper /'paɪpə(r)/, John (1903–), English painter and decorative designer. His early paintings were abstract, but in the 1930s he turned to a Romantic naturalism. During the Second World War he was one of the artists commissioned to record the effects of the war upon Britain. He is best known for his water-colours and aquatints of buildings (e.g. Windsor Castle, 1941–2), stage designs at Glyndebourne and elsewhere, and stained glass for Llandaff and Coventry Cathedrals.

piper /'paɪpə(r)/ n. 1 a bagpipe-player. 2 a person who plays a pipe, esp. an itinerant musician. [OE *pīpere* (as PIPE)]

piperidine /pɪ'perɪˌdiːn/ n. Chem. a peppery-smelling liquid formed by the reduction of pyridine. [L *piper* pepper + -IDE + -INE⁴]

pipette /pɪ'pet/ n. & v. —n. a slender tube for transferring or measuring small quantities of liquids esp. in chemistry. —v.tr.

transfer or measure (a liquid) using a pipette. [F, dimin. of *pipe* PIPE]

piping /'paɪpɪŋ/ *n. & adj.* —*n.* **1** the act or an instance of piping, esp. whistling or singing. **2** a thin pipelike fold used to edge hems or frills on clothing, seams on upholstery, etc. **3** ornamental lines of icing, cream, potato, etc. on a cake or other dish. **4** lengths of pipe, or a system of pipes, esp. in domestic use. — *adj.* (of a noise) high; whistling. □ **piping hot** very or suitably hot (esp. as required of food, water, etc.).

pipistrelle /ˌpɪpɪ'strel/ *n.* any bat of the genus *Pipistrellus*, native to temperate regions and feeding on insects. [F f. It. *pipistrello*, *vip-*, f. L *vespertilio* bat f. *vesper* evening]

pipit /'pɪpɪt/ *n.* **1** any of various birds of the family Motacillidae, esp. of the genus *Anthus*, found worldwide and having brown plumage often heavily streaked with a lighter colour. **2** = *meadow pipit.* [prob. imit.]

pipkin /'pɪpkɪn/ *n.* a small earthenware pot or pan. [16th c.: orig. unkn.]

pippin /'pɪpɪn/ *n.* **1 a** an apple grown from seed. **b** a red and yellow dessert apple. **2** *colloq.* an excellent person or thing; a beauty. [ME f. OF *pepin*, of unkn. orig.]

pipsqueak /'pɪpskwiːk/ *n. colloq.* an insignificant or contemptible person or thing. [imit.]

piquant /'piːkənt, -kɑːnt/ *adj.* **1** agreeably pungent, sharp, or appetizing. **2** pleasantly stimulating, or disquieting, to the mind. □□ **piquancy** *n.* **piquantly** *adv.* [F, pres. part. of *piquer* (as PIQUE[1])]

pique[1] /piːk/ *v. & n.* —*v.tr.* (**piques, piqued, piquing**) **1** wound the pride of, irritate. **2** arouse (curiosity, interest, etc.). **3** (*refl.*; usu. foll. by *on*) pride or congratulate oneself. —*n.* ill-feeling; enmity; resentment (*in a fit of pique*). [F *piquer* prick, irritate, f. Rmc]

pique[2] /piːk/ *n. & v.* —*n.* the winning of 30 points on cards and play in piquet before one's opponent scores anything. —*v.* (**piques, piqued, piquing**) **1** *tr.* score a pique against. **2** *intr.* score a pique. [F *pic*, of unkn. orig.]

piqué /'piːkeɪ/ *n.* a stiff ribbed cotton or other fabric. [F, past part. of *piquer*: see PIQUE[1]]

piquet[1] /pɪ'ket/ *n.* a game for two players with a pack of 32 cards (seven to ace only). [F, of unkn. orig.]

piquet[2] var. of PICKET 3.

piracy /'paɪrəsɪ/ *n.* (*pl.* -**ies**) **1** the practice or an act of robbery of ships at sea. **2** a similar practice or act in other forms, esp. hijacking. **3** the infringement of copyright. [med.L *piratia* f. Gk *pirateia* (as PIRATE)]

Piraeus /paɪ'riːəs/ the chief port of Athens in ancient and modern times, 8 km (5 miles) SW of the city; pop. (1981) 196,400.

piragua /pɪ'ræɡwə/ *n.* **1** a long narrow canoe made from a single tree-trunk. **2** a two-masted sailing barge. [Sp. f. Carib, = dug-out]

Pirandello /ˌpɪəræn'deləʊ/, Luigi (1867–1936), Italian dramatist and novelist, born in Sicily, who challenged the conventions of naturalism and greatly influenced European drama. Of his ten plays the best-known include *Six Characters in Search of an Author* (1921) and *Henry IV* (1922), in which he anticipated the theatre of Brecht while probing the conflict between reality and appearance, self and persona, actor and character, face and mask. Among his novels are *The Outcast* (1901), dealing with woman's desire for independence within patriarchal Sicily, *The Late Mattia Pascal* (1904), and *The Old and the Young* (1909). He was awarded the Nobel Prize for literature in 1934.

Piranesi /ˌpɪrə'neɪsɪ/, Giovanni Battista (1720–78), Italian engraver. An enthusiastic devotee of Roman architecture, in his prints he relied on atypical viewpoints and dramatic chiaroscuro to aggrandize its power and scale. His *Prisons* (1745–61) extended this imagery into the realms of fantasy, producing a nightmare vision of claustrophobic space and endless dimensions that prefigured later Romantic concerns.

piranha /pɪ'rɑːnə, -'rɑːnjə/ *n.* (also **piraya** /-'rɑːjə/) any of various freshwater predatory fish of the genera *Pygocentrus*, *Rooseveltiella*, or *Serrasalmus*, native to S. America and having sharp cutting teeth. [Port. f. Tupi, var. of *piraya* scissors]

pirate /'paɪərət/ *n. & v.* —*n.* **1 a** a person who commits piracy. **b** a ship used by pirates. **2** a person who infringes another's copyright or other business rights; a plagiarist. **3** (often *attrib.*) a person, organization, etc., that broadcasts without official authorization (*pirate radio station*). —*v.tr.* **1** appropriate or reproduce (the work or ideas etc. of another) without permission, for one's own benefit. **2** plunder. □□ **piratic** /-'rætɪk/ *adj.* **piratical** /-'rætɪk(ə)l/ *adj.* **piratically** /-'rætɪkəlɪ/ *adv.* [ME f. L *pirata* f. Gk *peiratēs* f. *peiraō* attempt, assault]

piraya var. of PIRANHA.

piripiri /'pɪrɪˌpɪrɪ/ *n.* (*pl.* **piripiris**) NZ a rosaceous plant, *Acaena anserinifolia*, native to New Zealand and having prickly burs. [Maori]

pirogue /pɪ'rəʊɡ/ *n.* = PIRAGUA. [F, prob. f. Galibi]

pirouette /ˌpɪrʊ'et/ *n. & v.* —*n.* a dancer's spin on one foot or the point of the toe. —*v.intr.* perform a pirouette. [F, = spinning-top]

Pisa /'piːzə/ a city in northern Italy; pop. (1981) 104,500. It is noted for its 'Leaning Tower', the campanile of its cathedral. Built at the end of the 12th c., the circular tower in eight storeys is 55 m (181 ft.) high and leans about 5 m (17 ft.) from the perpendicular, part of this inclination dating from its construction. In ancient times Pisa was a port and naval base, but is now about 6 miles (10 km) from the coast because of the silting of the River Arno on which it stands. Its university dates from the mid-14th c., and it was the birthplace of Galileo.

pis aller /ˌpiːz æ'leɪ/ *n.* a course of action followed as a last resort. [F f. *pis* worse + *aller* go]

Pisano[1] /pɪ'sɑːnəʊ/, Andrea (*c.*1290–1348) and Nino (died *c.*1368), Italian sculptors, unrelated to Nicola and Giovanni Pisano. Andrea is first mentioned in 1329, when he received the commission to make a pair of bronze doors for the baptistery at Florence. His son Nino was one of the earliest to specialize in free-standing life-size figures.

Pisano[2] /pɪ'sɑːnəʊ/, Nicola (active *c.*1258–78) and Giovanni, his son (active *c.*1265–1314), Italian sculptors. The father can be seen as one of the greatest medieval sculptors, and he explored the revival of interest in classical form within a Gothic framework. He executed the carvings on the pulpit in Pisa Baptistery (*c.*1260), and reliefs on the pulpit of Siena Cathedral (1265–8); he worked with Giovanni on his last great project, a large fountain in Perugia which was finished in 1278. Giovanni's works show a further refinement of the Gothic ideal, and he is seen as the precursor of the sculptural renaissance which followed. His works include the façade of Siena Cathedral (from 1284), reliefs for the pulpit in S. Andrea at Pistoia (completed in 1301), and what appears to have been his last commission, a monument to Margaret of Luxemburg (1313), in which she is shown not as dead or sleeping but as rising from the grave; since no sculptor hitherto had depicted the flight of the soul in this way, Giovanni's innovation was a dramatic one.

piscary /'pɪskərɪ/ *n.* □ **common of piscary** the right of fishing in another's water in common with the owner and others. [ME f. med.L *piscaria* neut. pl. of L *piscarius* f. *piscis* fish]

piscatorial /ˌpɪskə'tɔːrɪəl/ *adj.* = PISCATORY 1. □□ **piscatorially** *adv.*

piscatory /'pɪskətərɪ/ *adj.* **1** of or concerning fishermen or fishing. **2** addicted to fishing. [L *piscatorius* f. *piscator* fisherman f. *piscis* fish]

Pisces /'paɪsiːz, 'pɪskiːz/ **1** a constellation, traditionally regarded as contained in the figure of fishes. **2** the twelfth sign of the zodiac (the Fishes), which the sun enters about 20 Feb. —*n.* (*pl.* same) a person born when the sun is in this sign. □□ **Piscean** /'paɪsɪən/ *n. & adj.* [ME f. L, pl. of *piscis* fish]

pisciculture /'pɪsɪˌkʌltʃə(r)/ *n.* the artificial rearing of fish. □□ **piscicultural** /-'kʌltʃər(ə)l/ *adj.* **pisciculturist** /-'kʌltʃərɪst/ *n.* [L *piscis* fish, after *agriculture* etc.]

piscina /pɪ'siːnə, -'saɪnə/ *n.* (*pl.* **piscinae** /-niː/ or **piscinas**) **1** a stone basin near the altar in RC and pre-Reformation churches for draining water used in the Mass. **2** a fish-pond. **3** *hist.* a Roman bathing-pond. [L f. *piscis* fish]

piscine[1] /'pɪsaɪn/ *adj.* of or concerning fish. [L *piscis* fish]

piscine[2] /pɪˈsiːn/ n. a bathing-pool. [F (as PISCINA)]

piscivorous /pɪˈsɪvərəs/ adj. fish-eating. [L piscis fish + -VOROUS]

pish /pɪʃ/ int. an expression of contempt, impatience, or disgust. [imit.]

Pishpek see FRUNZE.

Pisidia /paɪˈsɪdɪə/ the ancient name for the region of Asia Minor between Pamphylia and Phrygia. □□ **Pisidian** adj. & n.

pisiform /ˈpɪsɪˌfɔːm/ adj. pea-shaped. □ **pisiform bone** a small bone in the wrist in the upper row of the carpus. [mod.L pisiformis f. pisum pea]

Pisistratus /paɪˈsɪstrətəs/ (6th c. BC) ruler of Athens. He seized power in 561 BC and after twice being expelled ruled continuously from 546 until his death in 527 BC. A benevolent tyrant who also succeeded in placating the nobles, he promoted the financial prosperity and cultural pre-eminence of Athens.

pismire /ˈpɪsˌmaɪə(r)/ n. dial. an ant. [ME f. PISS (from smell of anthill) + obs. mire ant]

piss /pɪs/ v. & n. coarse sl. ¶ Usually considered a taboo word. —v. 1 intr. urinate. 2 tr. a discharge (blood etc.) when urinating. b wet with urine. 3 tr. (as **pissed** adj.) Brit. drunk. —n. 1 urine. 2 an act of urinating. □ **piss about** fool or mess about. **piss artist** 1 a drunkard. 2 a person who fools about. 3 a glib person. **piss down** rain heavily. **piss off** Brit. 1 go away. 2 (often as **pissed off** adj.) annoy; depress. **piss-pot** a chamber-pot. **piss-taker** a person who mocks. **piss-taking** mockery. **piss-up** a drinking spree. **take the piss** (often foll. by out of) mock; deride. [ME f. OF pisser (imit.)]

Pissarro /pɪˈsɑːrəʊ/, Camille (1830–1903), French painter and graphic artist. Born in the West Indies, he moved to France in the 1850s and studied in Paris with Monet. At first heavily influenced by Corot, he later developed a plein-air style that contributed to the formation of impressionism in the 1870s. Always open to new developments, he made use of Seurat's pointillist theories in the 1880s as well as supporting Cézanne and Gauguin in their search for a valid post-impressionist style.

pissoir /piːˈswɑːr/ n. a public urinal. [F]

pistachio /pɪˈstɑːʃɪəʊ/ n. (pl. -os) 1 an evergreen tree, Pistacia vera, bearing small brownish-green flowers and ovoid reddish fruit. 2 (in full **pistachio nut**) the edible pale-green seed of this. 3 a pale green colour. [It. pistaccio and Sp. pistacho f. L pistacium f. Gk pistakion f. Pers. pistah]

piste /piːst/ n. a ski-run of compacted snow. [F, = racetrack]

pistil /ˈpɪstɪl/ n. the female organs of a flower, comprising the stigma, style, and ovary. □□ **pistillary** adj. **pistilliferous** /-ˈlɪfərəs/ adj. **pistilline** /-ˌlaɪn/ adj. [F pistile or L pistillum PESTLE]

pistillate /ˈpɪstɪlət/ adj. 1 having pistils. 2 having pistils but no stamens.

pistol /ˈpɪst(ə)l/ n. & v. —n. 1 a small hand-held firearm. 2 anything of a similar shape. —v.tr. (**pistolled, pistolling**; US **pistoled, pistoling**) shoot with a pistol. □ **hold a pistol to a person's head** coerce a person by threats. **pistol-grip** a handle shaped like a pistol-butt. **pistol-shot** 1 the range of a pistol. 2 a shot fired from a pistol. **pistol-whip** (**-whipped, -whipping**) beat with a pistol. [obs. F f. G Pistole f. Czech pišt'al]

pistole /pɪˈstəʊl/ n. hist. a foreign (esp. Spanish) gold coin. [F pistole abbr. of pistolet, of uncert. orig.]

pistoleer /ˌpɪstəˈlɪə(r)/ n. a soldier armed with a pistol.

piston /ˈpɪst(ə)n/ n. 1 a disc or short cylinder fitting closely within a tube in which it moves up and down against a liquid or gas, used in an internal-combustion engine to impart motion, or in a pump to receive motion. 2 a sliding valve in a trumpet etc. □ **piston-ring** a ring on a piston sealing the gap between the piston and the cylinder wall. **piston-rod** a rod or crankshaft attached to a piston to drive a wheel or to impart motion. [F f. It. pistone var. of pestone augment. of pestello PESTLE]

pit[1] /pɪt/ n. & v. —n. 1 a a usu. large deep hole in the ground. b a hole made in digging for industrial purposes, esp. for coal (chalk pit; gravel pit). c a covered hole as a trap for esp. wild animals. 2 a an indentation left after smallpox, acne, etc. b a hollow in a plant or animal body or on any surface. 3 Brit. Theatr. a = orchestra pit. b usu. hist. seating at the back of the stalls. c

the people in the pit. 4 a (**the pit** or **bottomless pit**) hell. b (**the pits**) sl. a wretched or the worst imaginable place, situation, person, etc. 5 a an area at the side of a track where racing cars are serviced and refuelled. b a sunken area in a workshop floor for access to a car's underside. 6 US the part of the floor of an exchange allotted to special trading (wheat-pit). 7 = COCKPIT. 8 Brit. sl. a bed. —v. (**pitted, pitting**) 1 tr. (usu. foll. by against) a set (one's wits, strength, etc.) in opposition or rivalry. b set (a cock, dog, etc.) to fight, orig. in a pit, against another. 2 tr. (usu. as **pitted** adj.) make pits, esp. scars, in. 3 intr. (of the flesh etc.) retain the impression of a finger etc. when touched. 4 tr. Hort. put (esp. vegetables etc. for storage) into a pit. □ **dig a pit for** try to ensnare. **pit-head** 1 the top of a mineshaft. 2 the area surrounding this. **pit of the stomach** 1 the floor of the stomach. 2 the depression below the bottom of the breastbone. **pit pony** hist. a pony kept underground for haulage in coal-mines. **pit-prop** a balk of wood used to support the roof of a coal mine. **pit-saw** a large saw for use in a saw-pit. **pit viper** any US snake of the family Crotalidae with a pit between the eye and the nostril. [OE pytt ult. f. L puteus well]

pit[2] /pɪt/ n. & v. US —n. the stone of a fruit. —v.tr. (**pitted, pitting**) remove pits from (fruit). [perh. Du., rel. to PITH]

pita var. of PITTA.

pit-a-pat /ˈpɪtəˌpæt/ adv. & n. (also **pitter-patter** /ˈpɪtəˌpætə(r)/) —adv. 1 with a sound like quick light steps. 2 with a faltering sound (heart went pit-a-pat). —n. such a sound. [imit.]

Pitcairn Islands /ˈpɪtkeən/ a British dependency comprising a group of islands in the South Pacific, NE of New Zealand; pop. (1982) about 54. Pitcairn Island, the chief of the group, was discovered in 1767 by a British naval officer and named after the sailor who first sighted it. It remained uninhabited until settled in 1790 by mutineers from HMS Bounty; some of their descendants still dwell there.

pitch[1] /pɪtʃ/ v. & n. —v. 1 tr. (also absol.) erect and fix (a tent, camp, etc.). 2 tr. a throw; fling. b (in games) throw (a flat object) towards a mark. 3 tr. fix or plant (a thing) in a definite position. 4 tr. express in a particular style or at a particular level (pitched his argument at the most basic level). 5 intr. (often foll. by against, into, etc.) fall heavily, esp. headlong. 6 intr. (of a ship etc.) plunge in a longitudinal direction (cf. ROLL v. 8a). 7 tr. Mus. set at a particular pitch. 8 intr. (of a roof etc.) slope downwards. 9 intr. (often foll. by about) move with a vigorous jogging motion, as in a train, carriage, etc. 10 Cricket a tr. cause (a bowled ball) to strike the ground at a specified point etc. b intr. (of a bowled ball) strike the ground. 11 tr. colloq. tell (a yarn or a tale). 12 tr. Golf play (a ball) with a pitch shot. 13 tr. pave (a road) with stones. —n. 1 a the area of play in a field-game. b Cricket the area between the creases. 2 height, degree, intensity, etc. (the pitch of despair; nerves were strung to a pitch). 3 a the steepness of a slope, esp. of a roof, stratum, etc. b the degree of such a pitch. 4 Mus. a that quality of a sound which is governed by the rate of vibrations producing it; the degree of highness or lowness of a tone. b = concert pitch. 5 the pitching motion of a ship etc. 6 Cricket the act or mode of delivery in bowling, or the spot where the ball bounces. 7 colloq. a salesman's advertising or selling approach. 8 Brit. a place where a street vendor sells wares, has a stall, etc. 9 (also **pitch shot**) Golf a high approach shot with a short run. 10 Mech. the distance between successive corresponding points or lines, e.g. between the teeth of a cog-wheel etc. 11 the height to which a falcon etc. soars before swooping on its prey. 12 the delivery of a baseball by a pitcher. □ **pitch-and-toss** a gambling game in which coins are pitched at a mark and then tossed. **pitched battle** 1 a vigorous argument etc. 2 Mil. a battle planned beforehand and fought on chosen ground. **pitched roof** a sloping roof. **pitch in** colloq. set to work vigorously. **pitch into** colloq. 1 attack forcibly with blows, words, etc. 2 assail (food, work, etc.) vigorously. **pitch on** (or **upon**) happen to select. **pitch-pipe** Mus. a small pipe blown to set the pitch for singing or tuning. **pitch up** Cricket bowl (a ball) to bounce near the batsman. **pitch wickets** Cricket fix the stumps in the ground and place the bails. [ME pic(c)he, perh. f. OE picc(e)an (unrecorded: cf. picung stigmata)]

pitch[2] /pɪtʃ/ n. & v. —n. 1 a sticky resinous black or dark-brown substance obtained by distilling tar or turpentine, semi-liquid when hot, hard when cold, and used for caulking the seams of ships etc. **2** any of various bituminous substances including asphalt. —*v.tr.* cover, coat, or smear with pitch. □ **pitch-black** (or **-dark**) very or completely dark. **pitch-pine** any of various pine-trees, esp. *Pinus rigida* or *P. palustris*, yielding much resin. [OE *pic* f. Gmc f. L *pix picis*]

pitchblende /'pɪtʃblend/ *n.* a mineral form of uranium oxide occurring in pitchlike masses and yielding radium. [G *Pechblende* (as PITCH², BLENDE)]

pitcher¹ /'pɪtʃə(r)/ *n.* **1** a large usu. earthenware jug with a lip and a handle, for holding liquids. **2** a modified leaf in pitcher form. **3** (in *pl.*) broken pottery crushed and reused. □ **pitcher-plant** any of various plants, esp. of the family Nepenthaceae or Sarraceniaceae, with pitcher leaves that can hold liquids, trap insects, etc. □□ **pitcherful** *n.* (*pl.* **-fuls**). [ME f. OF *pichier, pechier*, f. Frank.]

pitcher² /'pɪtʃə(r)/ *n.* **1** a person or thing that pitches. **2** *Baseball* a player who delivers the ball to the batter. **3** a stone used for paving.

pitchfork /'pɪtʃfɔːk/ *n.* & *v.* —*n.* a long-handled two-pronged fork for pitching hay etc. —*v.tr.* **1** throw with or as if with a pitchfork. **2** (usu. foll. by *into*) thrust (a person) forcibly into a position, office, etc. [in ME *pickfork*, prob. f. PICK¹ + FORK, assoc. with PITCH¹]

pitchstone /'pɪtʃstəʊn/ *n.* obsidian etc. resembling pitch.

pitchy /'pɪtʃɪ/ *adj.* (**pitchier, pitchiest**) of, like, or dark as pitch.

piteous /'pɪtɪəs/ *adj.* deserving or causing pity; wretched. □□ **piteously** *adv.* **piteousness** *n.* [ME *pito(u)s* etc. f. AF *pitous*, OF *pitos* f. Rmc (as PIETY)]

pitfall /'pɪtfɔːl/ *n.* **1** an unsuspected snare, danger, or drawback. **2** a covered pit for trapping animals etc.

pith /pɪθ/ *n.* & *v.* —*n.* **1** spongy white tissue lining the rind of an orange, lemon, etc. **2** the essential part; the quintessence (*came to the pith of his argument*). **3** the spongy cellular tissue in the stems and branches of dicotyledonous plants. **4 a** physical strength; vigour. **b** force; energy. **5** *archaic* spinal marrow. —*v.tr.* **1** remove the pith or marrow from. **2** slaughter or immobilize (an animal) by severing the spinal cord. □ **pith helmet** a lightweight sun-helmet made from the dried pith of the sola etc. □□ **pithless** *adj.* [OE *pitha* f. WG]

pithecanthrope /ˌpɪθɪˈkænθrəʊp/ *n.* a hominid of the genus *Pithecanthropus*.

Pithecanthropus /ˌpɪθɪˈkænθrəpəs/ *n.* (also called Java man) a genus of hominids first defined on the basis of human fossils found in Java in 1891 within deposits of Middle Pleistocene age, dating from *c.*1,000,000–500,000 years ago. It has now been subsumed under the genus *Homo erectus.* [Gk *pithēkos* ape + *anthrōpos* man]

pithos /'pɪθɒs/ *n.* (*pl.* **pithoi** /-θɔɪ/) *Archaeol.* a large storage jar. [Gk]

pithy /'pɪθɪ/ *adj.* (**pithier, pithiest**) **1** (of style, speech, etc.) condensed, terse, and forcible. **2** of, like, or containing much pith. □□ **pithily** *adv.* **pithiness** *n.*

pitiable /'pɪtɪəb(ə)l/ *adj.* **1** deserving or causing pity. **2** contemptible. □□ **pitiableness** *n.* **pitiably** *adv.* [ME f. OF *piteable, pitoiable* (as PITY)]

pitiful /'pɪtɪfʊl/ *adj.* **1** causing pity. **2** contemptible. **3** *archaic* compassionate. □□ **pitifully** *adv.* **pitifulness** *n.*

pitiless /'pɪtɪlɪs/ *adj.* showing no pity (*the pitiless heat of the desert*). □□ **pitilessly** *adv.* **pitilessness** *n.*

pitman /'pɪtmən/ *n.* **1** (*pl.* **-men**) a collier. **2** *US* (*pl.* **-mans**) a connecting rod in machinery.

piton /'piːtɒn/ *n.* a peg or spike driven into a rock or crack to support a climber or a rope. [F, = eye-bolt]

Pitons /'piːtɒnz/, **the** two conical mountains which rise up out of the Caribbean Sea to the south-west of the island of St Lucia.

Pitot /'piːtəʊ/, Henri (1695–1771), French scientist whose name is used to designate devices based upon his inventions. □ **Pitot tube** a device consisting of an open-ended right-angled tube used to measure the speed or flow of a fluid; a similar device for measuring the airspeed of aircraft.

pitpan /'pɪtpæn/ *n.* a Central American boat made from a tree-trunk. [Miskito]

Pitt¹ /pɪt/, William, 'the Elder', Earl of Chatham (1708–78), British statesman, a brilliant parliamentary orator who made his reputation as an opposition spokesman in the 1740s and, despite earning the King's disfavour, became Secretary of State in 1756 after early military failures in the Seven Years War. As war leader Pitt proved a brilliant success, concentrating on a maritime strategy to defeat France and masterminding the conquest of French possessions overseas, particularly in Canada and India. Forced to resign in 1761, he suffered increasingly from ill health, and although he returned to office in 1766 he never again exercised effective political control.

Pitt² /pɪt/, William, 'the Younger' (1759–1806), British statesman, son of Pitt the Elder. He became Prime Minister in 1783, at 24 the youngest ever to hold this office, and in the ensuing ten years of peace restored the authority of Parliament, with himself in undisputed ascendancy, introduced financial reforms, reduced the enormous national debt which he had inherited, and reformed the administration of India. With Britain's entry into war against France (1793) in the wake of the French Revolution, Pitt became almost entirely occupied as a war leader, proving as successful as his father, and after the Irish uprising in 1798 secured the Union of Great Britain and Ireland (1800). Although he resigned a year later over the issue of Catholic emancipation (which George III refused to accept) he returned to office in 1804 after hostilities with France had been resumed, and died in office early in 1806, his health undermined by the strain of organizing the war.

pitta /'pɪtə/ *n.* (also **pita**) a flat hollow unleavened bread which can be split and filled with salad etc. [mod.Gk, = a cake]

pittance /'pɪt(ə)ns/ *n.* **1** a scanty or meagre allowance, remuneration, etc. (*paid him a mere pittance*). **2** a small number or amount. **3** *hist.* a pious bequest to a religious house for extra food etc. [ME f. OF *pitance* f. med.L *pi(e)tantia* f. L *pietas* PITY]

pitter-patter var. of PIT-A-PAT.

Pitti /'pɪtɪ/ an art gallery and museum in Florence, housed in the Pitti Palace which was begun in 1440 but not completed until after 1549. It contains about 500 masterpieces from the Medici collections, a profusion of art treasures including Gobelin tapestries, and a rich collection of plate, goldsmiths' work, ivories, enamels, etc.

pittosporum /ˌpɪtəʊˈspɔːrəm/ *n.* any evergreen shrub of the family Pittosporaceae, chiefly native to Australasia with many species having fragrant foliage. [Gk *pitta* PITCH² + *sporos* seed]

Pitt-Rivers /pɪtˈrɪvəz/, Augustus Henry Lane Fox (1827–1900), English lieutenant-general, archaeologist, anthropologist, founder of the ethnological museum in Oxford which bears his name. From his studies of weaponry he realized that something analogous to the biological evolution of species could be traced in artefacts, and did pioneering work in establishing typological sequences of objects from different cultures. On retiring in 1882 he began a series of large-scale excavations of the prehistoric, Roman, and Saxon sites on his Wiltshire estate, organized and recorded with meticulous care. His approach greatly advanced the technique of archaeology both because of his thoroughness, in contrast to the sampling or object-seeking common in his day, and through his emphasis on the importance of commonplace objects as distinct from rarities; he is rightly regarded as the father of modern excavation.

Pittsburgh /'pɪtsbɜːg/ an industrial city at the junction of the Allegheny and Monongahela rivers in SW Pennsylvania; pop. (1982) 415,000. Formerly a steel-producing city, Pittsburgh is now a major centre of high technology.

pituitary /pɪˈtjuːɪtərɪ/ *n.* & *adj.* —*n.* (*pl.* **-ies**) (also **pituitary gland** or **body**) a pea-sized ductless gland at the base of the brain, with an important influence on growth and bodily functions, especially through its effect on other glands. Its anterior lobe secretes various hormones including one which stimulates body growth, others regulating the activity of the gonads and the adrenal and thyroid glands, and another which stimulates the growth of the mammary glands and causes them to secrete milk. Its posterior lobe, consisting mainly of nervous tissue, releases two hormones, oxytocin and an antidiuretic hormone which acts on the kidney and may also act on the smooth muscle-tissue of the blood-vessels and affect blood pressure. —*adj.* of or relating to this gland. [L *pituitarius* secreting phlegm f. *pituita* phlegm]

pity /ˈpɪtɪ/ *n. & v.* —*n. (pl.* -**ies**) **1** sorrow and compassion aroused by another's condition (*felt pity for the child*). **2** something to be regretted; grounds for regret (*what a pity!; the pity of it is that he didn't mean it*). —*v.tr.* (-**ies**, -**ied**) feel (often contemptuous) pity for (*they are to be pitied; I pity you if you think that*). □ **for pity's sake** an exclamation of urgent supplication, anger, etc. **more's the pity** so much the worse. **take pity on** feel or act compassionately towards. □□ **pitying** *adj.* **pityingly** *adv.* [ME f. OF *pité* f. L *pietas* (as PIETY)]

pityriasis /ˌpɪtɪˈraɪəsɪs/ *n.* any of a group of skin diseases characterized by the shedding of branlike scales. [mod.L f. Gk *pituriasis* f. *pituron* bran]

più /pjuː/ *adv. Mus.* more (*più piano*). [It.]

pivot /ˈpɪvət/ *n. & v.* —*n.* **1** a short shaft or pin on which something turns or oscillates. **2** a crucial or essential person, point, etc., in a scheme or enterprise. **3** *Mil.* the man or men about whom a body of troops wheels. —*v.* (**pivoted, pivoting**) **1** *intr.* turn on or as if on a pivot. **2** *intr.* (foll. by *on, upon*) hinge on; depend on. **3** *tr.* provide with or attach by a pivot. □□ **pivotable** *adj.* **pivotability** /-ˈbɪlɪtɪ/ *n.* **pivotal** *adj.* [F, of uncert. orig.]

pix[1] /pɪks/ *n.pl. colloq.* pictures, esp. photographs. [abbr.: cf. PIC]

pix[2] var. of PYX.

pixel /ˈpɪks(ə)l/ *n. Electronics* any of the minute areas of uniform illumination of which an image on a display screen is composed. [abbr. of *picture element*: cf. PIX[1]]

pixie /ˈpɪksɪ/ *n.* (also **pixy**) (*pl.* -**ies**) a being like a fairy; an elf. □ **pixie hat** (or **hood**) a child's hat with a pointed crown. [17th c.: orig. unkn.]

pixilated /ˈpɪksɪˌleɪtɪd/ *adj.* (also **pixillated**) **1** bewildered; crazy. **2** drunk. [var. of *pixie-led* (as PIXIE, LED)]

Pizarro /pɪˈzɑːrəʊ/, Francisco (*c.*1478–1541), Spanish conquistador. After service in the Italian wars and under Balboa during the discovery of the Pacific, Pizarro set out from Panama in 1531 with less than 200 men to conquer the Inca empire in Peru. Crossing the mountains, he defeated the Incas and executed their emperor Atahualpa (1533), setting up an Inca puppet monarchy at Cuzco and building his own capital at Lima. Pizarro was then faced by a serious native revolt which was put down in 1537 only after the return of his rival Amalgro from Chile. This was followed by a power struggle between Pizarro and Amalgro which ended in 1538 with the latter's capture and execution. Amalgro's supporters, however, conspired against the ageing Pizarro and assassinated him in his house in Lima.

pizazz /pɪˈzæz/ *n.* (also **pizzazz, pzazz** etc.) *sl.* verve, energy, liveliness, sparkle.

pizza /ˈpiːtsə/ *n.* a flat round base of dough with a topping of tomatoes, cheese, onions, etc. [It., = pie]

pizzeria /ˌpiːtsəˈriːə/ *n.* a place where pizzas are made or sold. [It. (as PIZZA)]

pizzicato /ˌpɪtsɪˈkɑːtəʊ/ *adv., adj., & n. Mus.* —*adv.* plucking the strings of a violin etc. with the finger. —*adj.* (of a note, passage, etc.) performed pizzicato. —*n.* (*pl.* **pizzicatos** or **pizzicati** /-tɪ/) a note, passage, etc. played pizzicato. [It., past part. of *pizzicare* twitch f. *pizzare* f. *pizza* edge]

pizzle /ˈpɪz(ə)l/ *n.* esp. *Austral.* the penis of an animal, esp. a bull, formerly used as a whip. [LG *pesel*, dimin. of MLG *pēse*, MDu. *pēze*]

pk. *abbr.* **1** park. **2** peak. **3** peck(s).

pl. *abbr.* **1** plural. **2** place. **3** plate. **4** esp. *Mil.* platoon.

PLA *abbr.* **1** People's Liberation Army. **2** (in the UK) Port of London Authority.

placable /ˈplækəb(ə)l/ *adj.* easily placated; mild; forgiving. □□

placability /-ˈbɪlɪtɪ/ *n.* **placably** *adv.* [ME f. OF *placable* or L *placabilis* f. *placare* appease]

placard /ˈplækɑːd/ *n. & v.* —*n.* a printed or handwritten poster esp. for advertising. —*v.tr.* /also plæˈkɑːd/ **1** set up placards on (a wall etc.). **2** advertise by placards. **3** display (a poster etc.) as a placard. [ME f. OF *placquart* f. *plaquier* to plaster f. MDu. *placken*]

placate /pləˈkeɪt, ˈplæ-, ˈpleɪ-/ *v.tr.* pacify; conciliate. □□ **placatingly** *adv.* **placation** /pləˈkeɪʃ(ə)n/ *n.* **placatory** /pləˈkeɪtərɪ/ *adj.* [L *placare placat-*]

place /pleɪs/ *n. & v.* —*n.* **1 a** a particular portion of space. **b** a portion of space occupied by a person or thing (*it has changed its place*). **c** a proper or natural position (*he is out of his place; take your places*). **2** a city, town, village, etc. (*was born in this place*). **3** a residence; a dwelling (*has a place in the country; come round to my place*). **4 a** a group of houses in a town etc., esp. a square. **b** a country house with its surroundings. **5** a person's rank or status (*know their place; a place in history*). **6** a space, esp. a seat, for a person (*two places in the coach*). **7** a building or area for a specific purpose (*place of worship; bathing-place*). **8 a** a point reached in a book etc. (*lost my place*). **b** a passage in a book. **9** a particular spot on a surface, esp. of the skin (*a sore place on his wrist*). **10 a** employment or office, esp. government employment (*lost his place at the Ministry*). **b** the duties or entitlements of office etc. (*is his place to hire staff*). **11** a position as a member of a team, a student in a college, etc. **12** *Brit.* any of the first three or sometimes four positions in a race, esp. other than the winner (*backed it for a place*). **13** the position of a figure in a series indicated in decimal or similar notation (*calculated to 50 decimal places*). —*v.tr.* **1** put (a thing etc.) in a particular place or state; arrange. **2** identify, classify, or remember correctly (*cannot place him*). **3** assign to a particular place; locate. **4 a** appoint (a person, esp. a member of the clergy) to a post. **b** find a situation, living, etc. for. **c** (usu. foll. by *with*) consign to a person's care etc. (*placed her with her aunt*). **5** assign rank, importance, or worth to (*place him among the best teachers*). **6 a** dispose of (goods) to a customer. **b** make (an order for goods etc.). **7** (often foll. by *in, on*, etc.) have (confidence etc.). **8** invest (money). **9** *Brit.* state the position of (any of the first three or sometimes four runners) in a race. **10** *tr.* (as **placed** *adj.*) **a** *Brit.* among the first three or sometimes four in a race. **b** *US* second in a race. **11** *Football* get (a goal) by a place-kick. □ **all over the place** in disorder; chaotic. **give place to 1** make room for. **2** yield precedence to. **3** be succeeded by. **go places** *colloq.* be successful. **in place** in the right position; suitable. **in place of** in exchange for; instead of. **in places** at some places or in some parts, but not others. **keep a person in his** or **her place** suppress a person's pretensions. **out of place 1** in the wrong position. **2** unsuitable. **place-bet 1** *Brit.* a bet on a horse to come first, second, third, or sometimes fourth in a race. **2** *US* a bet on a horse to come second. **place-brick** an imperfectly burnt brick from the windward side of the kiln. **place card** a card marking a person's place at a table etc. **place in the sun** a favourable situation, position, etc. **place-kick** *Football* a kick made when the ball is previously placed on the ground. **place-mat** a small mat on a table underneath a person's plate. **place-name** the name of a town, village, hill, field, lake, etc. **place-setting** a set of plates, cutlery, etc. for one person at a meal. **put oneself in another's place** imagine oneself in another's position. **put a person in his** or **her place** deflate or humiliate a person. **take place** occur. **take one's place** go to one's correct position, be seated, etc. **take the place of** be substituted for; replace. □□ **placeless** *adj.* **placement** *n.* [ME f. OF f. L *platea* f. Gk *plateia* (*hodos*) broad (way)]

placebo /pləˈsiːbəʊ/ *n.* (*pl.* -**os**) **1 a** a pill, medicine, etc. prescribed for psychological reasons but having no physiological effect. **b** a placebo used as a control in testing new drugs etc. **c** a blank sample in a test. **2** *RC Ch.* the opening antiphon of the vespers for the dead. [L, = I shall be acceptable or pleasing f. *placēre* please, first word of Ps. 114: 9]

placenta /pləˈsentə/ *n.* (*pl.* **placentae** /-tiː/ or **placentas**) **1** a flattened circular spongy vascular structure that develops in the uterus of pregnant mammals (other than marsupials and monotremes) by interlocking of foetal and maternal tissue, through which the developing foetus is supplied with nutriment and rid of waste products, and to which it is attached by the umbilical cord. **2** (in flowers) part of the ovary wall carrying the ovules. □□ **placental** *adj.* [L f. Gk *plakous -ountos* flat cake f. the root of *plax plakos* flat plate]

placer /ˈpleɪsə(r), ˈplæsə(r)/ *n.* a deposit of sand, gravel, etc., in the bed of a stream etc., containing valuable minerals in particles. [Amer. Sp., rel. to *placel* sandbank f. *plaza* PLACE]

placet /ˈpleɪset/ *n.* an affirmative vote in a church or university assembly. [L, = it pleases]

placid /ˈplæsɪd/ *adj.* **1** (of a person) not easily aroused or disturbed; peaceful. **2** mild; calm; serene. □□ **placidity** /pləˈsɪdɪtɪ/ *n.* **placidly** *adv.* **placidness** *n.* [F *placide* or L *placidus* f. *placēre* please]

placket /ˈplækɪt/ *n.* **1** an opening or slit in a garment, for fastenings or access to a pocket. **2** the flap of fabric under this. [var. of PLACARD]

placoid /ˈplækɔɪd/ *adj. & n.* —*adj.* **1** (of a fish-scale) consisting of a hard base embedded in the skin and a spiny backward projection (cf. CTENOID). **2** (of a fish) covered with these scales. —*n.* a placoid fish, e.g. a shark. [Gk *plax plakos* flat plate]

plafond /plæˈfɔ̃/ *n.* **1 a** an ornately decorated ceiling. **b** such decoration. **2** an early form of contract bridge. [F f. *plat* flat + *fond* bottom]

plagal /ˈpleɪg(ə)l/ *adj. Mus.* (of a church mode) having sounds between the dominant and its octave (cf. AUTHENTIC). □ **plagal cadence** (or **close**) a cadence in which the chord of the subdominant immediately precedes that of the tonic. [med.L *plagalis* f. *plaga* plagal mode f. L *plagius* f. med. Gk *plagios* (in anc. Gk = oblique) f. Gk *plagos* side]

plage /plɑːʒ/ *n.* **1** *Astron.* an unusually bright region on the sun. **2** a sea beach, esp. at a fashionable resort. [F, = beach]

plagiarism /ˈpleɪdʒə‚rɪz(ə)m/ *n.* **1** the act or an instance of plagiarizing. **2** something plagiarized. □□ **plagiarist** *n.* **plagiaristic** /-ˈrɪstɪk/ *adj.*

plagiarize /ˈpleɪdʒə‚raɪz/ *v.tr.* (also **-ise**) (also *absol.*) **1** take and use (the thoughts, writings, inventions, etc. of another person) as one's own. **2** pass off the thoughts etc. of (another person) as one's own. □□ **plagiarizer** *n.* [L *plagiarius* kidnapper f. *plagium* a kidnapping f. Gk *plagion*]

plagio- /ˈpleɪdʒɪəʊ/ *comb. form* oblique. [Gk *plagios* oblique f. *plagos* side]

plagioclase /ˈpleɪdʒɪəʊ‚kleɪz/ *n.* a series of feldspar minerals forming glassy crystals. [PLAGIO- + Gk *klasis* cleavage]

plague /pleɪg/ *n., v., & int.* —*n.* **1** a deadly contagious disease spreading rapidly over a wide area. (See below.) **2** (foll. by *of*) an unusual infestation of a pest etc. (*a plague of frogs*). **3 a** great trouble. **b** an affliction, esp. as regarded as divine punishment. **4** *colloq.* a nuisance. —*v.tr.* (**plagues, plagued, plaguing**) **1** affect with plague. **2** *colloq.* pester or harass continually. —*int. joc.* or *archaic* a curse etc. (*a plague on it!*). □□ **plaguesome** *adj.* [ME f. L *plaga* stroke, wound prob. f. Gk *plaga, plēgē*]

Epidemics of bubonic plague, transmitted to humans by rats' fleas, broke out in Europe in the Middle Ages. The first killed millions in the mid-14th c. (see BLACK DEATH), and the disease re-emerged periodically for several centuries thereafter, the last serious outbreak in Britain killing almost 100,000 inhabitants of London in 1665–6.

plaice /pleɪs/ *n.* (*pl.* same) **1** a European flatfish, *Pleuronectes platessa*, having a brown back with orange spots and a white underside, much used for food. **2** (in full **American plaice**) a N. Atlantic fish, *Hippoglossoides platessoides*. [ME f. OF *plaiz* f. LL *platessa* app. f. Gk *platus* broad]

plaid /plæd/ *n.* **1** (often *attrib.*) chequered or tartan, esp. woollen twilled cloth (*a plaid skirt*). **2** a long piece of plaid worn over the shoulder as part of Highland Scottish costume. □□ **plaided** *adj.* [Gael. *plaide*, of unkn. orig.]

Plaid Cymru /plaɪd ˈkʌmrɪ/ the Welsh nationalist party, founded in 1925 and dedicated to seeking autonomy for Wales. [Welsh, = party of Wales]

plain[1] /pleɪn/ *adj., adv., & n.* —*adj.* **1** clear; evident (*is plain to*

see). **2** readily understood; simple (*in plain words*). **3 a** (of food, sewing, decoration, etc.) uncomplicated; not elaborate; unembellished; simple. **b** without a decorative pattern. **4** (esp. of a woman or girl) ugly. **5** outspoken; straightforward. **6** (of manners, dress, etc.) unsophisticated; homely (*a plain man*). **7** (of drawings etc.) not coloured (*penny plain, twopence coloured*). **8** not in code. —*adv.* **1** clearly; unequivocally (*to speak plain, I don't approve*). **2** simply (*that is plain stupid*). —*n.* **1** a level tract of esp. treeless country. **2** a basic knitting stitch made by putting the needle through the back of the stitch and passing the wool round the front of the needle (opp. PURL[1]). □ **be plain with** speak bluntly to. **plain card** neither a trump nor a court-card. **plain chocolate** dark chocolate without added milk. **plain clothes** ordinary clothes worn esp. as a disguise by policemen etc. **plain-clothes** (*attrib.*) wearing plain clothes. **plain cook** a person competent in plain English cooking. **plain dealing** candour; straightforwardness. **plain flour** flour with no added raising agent. **plain sailing 1** sailing a straightforward course. **2** an uncomplicated situation or course of action. **plain service** *Eccl.* a church service without music. **plain-spoken** outspoken; blunt. **plain suit** a suit that is not trumps. **plain text** a text not in cipher or code. **plain time** time not paid for at overtime rates. **plain weaving** weaving with the weft alternately over and under the warp. □□ **plainly** *adv.* **plainness** /ˈpleɪnnɪs/ *n.* [ME f. OF *plain* (adj. & n.) f. L *planus* (adj.), *planum* (n.)]

plain[2] /pleɪn/ *v.intr. archaic* or *poet.* **1** mourn. **2** complain. **3** make a plaintive sound. [ME f. OF *plaindre* (stem *plaign-*) f. L *plangere planct-* lament]

plainchant /ˈpleɪntʃɑːnt/ *n.* = PLAINSONG.

plainsman /ˈpleɪnzmən/ *n.* (*pl.* **-men**) a person who lives on a plain, esp. in N. America.

Plains of Abraham /pleɪnz, ˈeɪbrə‚hæm/ a plateau in eastern Canada above Quebec City, scene of the decisive battle for North America in 1759. The British army under General Wolfe surprised the French defenders by scaling the heights above the city under cover of darkness, and the city fell. The battle led to British control over Canada, but both Wolfe and the French commander Montcalm died of their wounds.

plainsong /ˈpleɪnsɒŋ/ *n.* traditional church music in medieval modes and in free rhythm depending on accentuation of the words, sung in unison, with a single line of vocal melody to words taken from the liturgy. The chant of the Roman Church is generally known as 'Gregorian', after Pope Gregory the Great (d. 604), but it is likely that the role he played had more to do with organizing and standardizing the various schools of chant then in use than with composing, a role taken up with enthusiasm in the 8th c. by Pepin, king of the Franks, and especially by Charlemagne.

plaint /pleɪnt/ *n.* **1** *Brit. Law* an accusation; a charge. **2** *literary* or *archaic* a complaint; a lamentation. [ME f. OF *plainte* fem. past part. of *plaindre*, and OF *plaint* f. L *planctus* (as PLAIN[2])]

plaintiff /ˈpleɪntɪf/ *n. Law* a person who brings a case against another into court (opp. DEFENDANT). [ME f. OF *plaintif* (adj.) (as PLAINTIVE)]

plaintive /ˈpleɪntɪv/ *adj.* **1** expressing sorrow; mournful. **2** mournful-sounding. □□ **plaintively** *adv.* **plaintiveness** *n.* [ME f. OF (-*if*, -*ive*) f. *plainte* (as PLAINT)]

plait /plæt/ *n. & v.* —*n.* **1** a length of hair, straw, etc., in three or more interlaced strands. **2** = PLEAT. —*v.tr.* form (hair etc.) into a plait. [ME f. OF *pleit* fold ult. f. L *plicare* fold]

plan /plæn/ *n. & v.* —*n.* **1 a** a formulated and esp. detailed method by which a thing is to be done; a design or scheme. **b** an intention or proposed proceeding (*my plan was to distract them; plan of campaign*). **2** a drawing or diagram made by projection on a horizontal plane, esp. showing a building or one floor of a building (cf. ELEVATION). **3** a large-scale detailed map of a town or district. **4 a** a table etc. indicating times, places, etc. of intended proceedings. **b** a scheme or arrangement (*prepared the seating plan*). **5** an imaginary plane perpendicular to the line of vision and containing the objects shown in a picture. —*v.* (**planned, planning**) **1** *tr.* (often foll. by *that* + clause or *to* + *infin.*) arrange (a procedure etc.) beforehand; form a plan (planned to catch the evening ferry). **2** tr. **a** design (a building, new town, etc.). **b** make a plan of (an existing building, an area, etc.). **3** tr. (as **planned** adj.) in accordance with a plan (his planned arrival; planned parenthood). **4** intr. make plans. □ **planning permission** Brit. formal permission for building development etc., esp. from a local authority. **plan on** colloq. aim at doing; intend. □□ **planning** n. [F f. earlier plant, f. It. pianta plan of building: cf. PLANT]

planar /ˈpleɪnə(r)/ adj. Math. of, relating to, or in the form of a plane.

planarian /pləˈneərɪən/ n. any flatworm of the class Turbellaria, usu. living in fresh water. [mod.L Planaria the genus-name, fem. of L planarius lying flat]

planchet /ˈplænʃɪt/ n. a plain metal disc from which a coin is made. [dimin. of planch slab of metal f. OF planche: see PLANK]

planchette /plɑːnˈʃet/ n. a small usu. heart-shaped board on castors with a pencil, said to trace letters etc. at spiritualist seances without conscious direction when one or more persons rest their fingers lightly on the board. [F, dimin. of planche PLANK]

Planck /plæŋk/, Max Karl Ernst Ludwig (1858–1947), German theoretical physicist, the originator of the quantum theory which, with Einstein's general theory of relativity, forms the foundation of 20th-c. physics. During the 1880s he published fundamental papers on thermodynamics before taking up the problem of black-body radiation. The characteristic radiation spectra produced by such, in theory, perfect absorbers of radiant energy had foxed classical physicists. In 1900 he announced his 'radiation law', according to which this electromagnetic radiation was not emitted as a continuous flow but was made up of discrete units or 'quanta' of energy, and mathematical investigation showed that the size of these units involved a fundamental physical constant (Planck's constant). The quantum concept could now be invoked to explain atomic structure. Einstein applied it to the photoelectric effect, and Bohr to his model of the atom. For his achievement Planck received the 1918 Nobel Prize for physics. In his personal life he suffered a series of cruel misfortunes, including the execution of his son, Erwin, by the Nazis in 1944 for his part in the July plot to assassinate Hitler. □ **Planck's constant** (also **Planck constant**) a fundamental constant, equal to the energy of quanta of electromagnetic radiation divided by its frequency, with a value of 6.626×10^{-34} joules.

plane[1] /pleɪn/ n., adj., & v. —n. **1 a** a flat surface on which a straight line joining any two points on it would wholly lie. **b** an imaginary flat surface through or joining etc. material objects. **2** a level surface. **3** colloq. = AEROPLANE. **4** a flat surface producing lift by the action of air or water over and under it (usu. in comb.: hydroplane). **5** (often foll. by of) a level of attainment, thought, knowledge, etc. **6** a flat thin object such as a tabletop. —adj. **1** (of a surface etc.) perfectly level. **2** (of an angle, figure, etc.) lying in a plane. —v.intr. **1** (often foll. by down) travel or glide in an aeroplane. **2** (of a speedboat etc.) skim over water. **3** soar. □ **plane chart** a chart on which meridians and parallels of latitude are represented by equidistant straight lines, used in plane sailing. **plane polarization** a process restricting the vibrations of electromagnetic radiation, esp. light, to one direction. **plane sailing 1** the practice of determining a ship's position on the theory that she is moving on a plane. **2** = plain sailing (see PLAIN[1]). **plane-table** a surveying instrument used for direct plotting in the field, with a circular drawing-board and pivoted alidade. [L planum flat surface, neut. of planus PLAIN[1] (different. f. PLAIN[1] in 17th c.): adj. after F plan, plane]

plane[2] /pleɪn/ n. & v. —n. **1** a tool consisting of a wooden or metal block with a projecting steel blade, used to smooth a wooden surface by paring shavings from it. **2** a similar tool for smoothing metal. —v.tr. **1** smooth (wood, metal, etc.) with a plane. **2** (often foll. by away, down) pare (irregularities) with a plane. **3** archaic level (plane the way). [ME f. OF var. of plaine f. LL plana f. L planus PLAIN[1]]

plane[3] /pleɪn/ n. (in full **plane-tree**) any tree of the genus Platanus often growing to great heights, with maple-like leaves and bark which peels in uneven patches. [ME f. OF f. L platanus f. Gk platanos f. platus broad]

planet /ˈplænɪt/ n. **1** a celestial body moving in an elliptical orbit round a star (see below); the Earth. **2** esp. Astrol. hist. a celestial body distinguished from the fixed stars by having an apparent motion of its own (including the moon and sun), esp. with reference to its supposed influence on people and events. □□ **planetology** /-ˈtɒlədʒɪ/ n. [ME f. OF planete f. LL planeta, planetes f. Gk planētēs wanderer, planet f. planaomai wander]

Planets fall into two main classes, depending on whether they have extensive gaseous atmospheres or are predominantly rocky bodies. The former comprises Jupiter, Saturn, Uranus, and Neptune, all with dense atmospheres of hydrogen-rich gases subject to violent winds and eddies. These giant planets have their own retinues of satellites (some as large as the other planets) and are associated with concentric rings of orbiting small particles. Of the rocky planets, only Earth and Venus have substantial atmospheres, and only Earth has significant amounts of surface water. None but Earth is known to support life.

planetarium /ˌplænɪˈteərɪəm/ n. (pl. **planetariums** or **planetaria** /-rɪə/) **1** a domed building in which images of stars, planets, constellations, etc. are projected for public entertainment or education. **2** the device used for such projection. **3** = ORRERY. [mod.L (as PLANET)]

planetary /ˈplænɪtərɪ/ adj. **1** of or like planets (planetary influence). **2** terrestrial; mundane. **3** wandering; erratic. □ **planetary nebula** a ring-shaped nebula formed by an expanding shell of gas round a star. [LL planetarius (as PLANET)]

planetesimal /ˌplænɪˈtesɪm(ə)l/ n. any of a vast number of minute planets or planetary bodies. □ **planetesimal hypothesis** the theory that planets were formed by the accretion of planetesimals in a cold state. [PLANET, after infinitesimal]

planetoid /ˈplænɪtɔɪd/ n. = ASTEROID.

plangent /ˈplændʒ(ə)nt/ adj. **1** (of a sound) loud and reverberating. **2** (of a sound) plaintive; sad. □□ **plangency** n. [L plangere plangent- lament]

planimeter /pləˈnɪmɪtə(r)/ n. an instrument for mechanically measuring the area of a plane figure. □□ **planimetric** /-ˈmetrɪk/ adj. **planimetrical** /-ˈmetrɪk(ə)l/ adj. **planimetry** n. [F planimètre f. L planus level]

planish /ˈplænɪʃ/ v.tr. flatten (sheet metal, coining-metal, etc.) with a smooth-faced hammer or between rollers. □□ **planisher** n. [ME f. OF planir smooth f. plain PLANE[1] adj.]

planisphere /ˈplænɪˌsfɪə(r)/ n. a map formed by the projection of a sphere or part of a sphere on a plane, esp. to show the appearance of the heavens at a specific time or place. □□ **planispheric** /-ˈsferɪk/ adj. [ME f. med.L planisphaerium (as PLANE[1], SPHERE): infl. by F planisphère]

plank /plæŋk/ n. & v. —n. **1** a long flat piece of timber used esp. in building, flooring, etc. **2** an item of a political or other programme (cf. PLATFORM). —v.tr. **1** provide, cover, or floor, with planks. **2** (usu. foll. by down; also absol.) esp. US colloq. **a** put (a thing, person, etc.) down roughly or violently. **b** pay (money) on the spot or abruptly (planked down £5). □ **plank bed** a bed of boards without a mattress, esp. in prison. **walk the plank** hist. (of a pirate's captive etc.) be made to walk blindfold along a plank over the side of a ship to one's death in the sea. [ME f. ONF planke, OF planche f. LL planca board f. plancus flat-footed]

planking /ˈplæŋkɪŋ/ n. planks as flooring etc.

plankton /ˈplæŋkt(ə)n/ n. the chiefly microscopic organisms drifting or floating in the sea or fresh water (see BENTHOS, NEKTON). □□ **planktonic** /-ˈtɒnɪk/ adj. [G f. Gk plagktos wandering f. plazomai wander]

planner /ˈplænə(r)/ n. **1** a person who controls or plans the development of new towns, designs buildings, etc. **2** a person who makes plans. **3** a list, table, etc., with information helpful in planning.

plano- /ˈpleɪnəʊ/ comb. form level, flat. [L planus flat]

planoconcave /ˌpleɪnəʊˈkɒnkeɪv/ adj. (of a lens etc.) with one surface plane and the other concave.

planoconvex /ˌpleɪnəʊˈkɒnveks/ adj. (of a lens etc.) with one surface plane and the other convex.

planographic /ˌpleɪnəˈgræfɪk/ adj. relating to or produced by a process in which printing is done from a plane surface. □□ **planography** /plə'nɒgrəfɪ/ *n.*

planometer /plə'nɒmɪtə(r)/ *n.* a flat plate used as a gauge for plane surfaces in metalwork.

plant /plɑːnt/ *n. & v.* —*n.* **1 a** any living organism of the kingdom Plantae (see *plant kingdom* below), usu. containing chlorophyll enabling it to live wholly on inorganic substances and lacking specialized sense organs and the power of voluntary movement. **b** a small organism of this kind, as distinguished from a shrub or tree. **2 a** machinery, fixtures, etc., used in industrial processes. **b** a factory. **3** *colloq.* something, esp. incriminating or compromising, positioned or concealed so as to be discovered later. —*v.tr.* **1** place (a seed, bulb, or growing thing) in the ground so that it may take root and flourish. **2** (often foll. by *in, on,* etc.) put or fix in position. **3** deposit (young fish, spawn, oysters, etc.) in a river or lake. **4** station (a person etc.), esp. as a spy or source of information. **5** *refl.* take up a position (*planted myself by the door*). **6** cause (an idea etc.) to be established esp. in another person's mind. **7** deliver (a blow, kiss, etc.) with a deliberate aim. **8** *sl.* position or conceal (something incriminating or compromising) for later discovery. **9 a** settle or people (a colony etc.). **b** found or establish (a city, community, etc.). **10** bury. □ **plant kingdom** the taxonomic group that contains the plants. The term originally included fungi and bacteria as well as green plants, but nowadays these two groups, along with single-celled organisms, are frequently assigned to separate kingdoms and the term 'plant kingdom' restricted to the multicellular green plants, of which the main groups are multicellular algae, mosses, ferns, gymnosperms, and angiosperms (flowering plants). **plant-louse** a small insect that infests plants, esp. an aphis. **plant out** transfer (a plant) from a pot or frame to the open ground; set out (seedlings) at intervals. □□ **plantable** *adj.* **plantlet** *n.* **plantlike** *adj.* [OE *plante* & F *plante* f. L *planta* sprout, slip, cutting]

Plantagenet /plæn'tædʒənɪt/ originally the nickname of Geoffrey, Count of Anjou, father of Henry II of England, probably derived from the sprig of broom (L *planta* plant, *genista* broom) worn as a distinctive mark. It was adopted as a surname (*c.*1460) by Richard, Duke of York, and applied to the royal house which came to the English throne in 1154 (Henry II). In the 15th c. it was divided into two branches, the house of Lancaster and the house of York, which came to an end with the death of Richard III (1485).

plantain¹ /'plæntɪn/ *n.* any shrub of the genus *Plantago,* with broad flat leaves spread out close to the ground and used as food for birds and as a mild laxative. □ **plantain lily** = HOSTA. [ME f. OF f. L *plantago -ginis* f. *planta* sole of the foot (from its broad prostrate leaves)]

plantain² /'plæntɪn/ *n.* **1** a banana plant, *Musa paradisiaca,* widely grown for its fruit. **2** the starchy fruit of this containing less sugar than a dessert banana and chiefly used in cooking. [earlier *platan* f. Sp. *plá(n)tano* plane-tree, prob. assim. f. Galibi *palatana* etc.]

plantar /'plæntə(r)/ *adj.* of or relating to the sole of the foot. [L *plantaris* f. *planta* sole]

plantation /plæn'teɪʃ(ə)n, plɑː-/ *n.* **1** an estate on which cotton, tobacco, etc. is cultivated, esp. in former colonies, formerly by slave labour. **2** an area planted with trees etc. **3** *hist.* a colony; colonization. □ **Plantation of Ireland** the government-sponsored settlement of British families in Ireland, on confiscated land, in the 16th–17th c. **plantation song** a song of the kind formerly sung by Blacks on American plantations. [ME f. OF *plantation* or L *plantatio* (as PLANT)]

planter /'plɑːntə(r)/ *n.* **1** a person who cultivates the soil. **2** the manager or occupier of a coffee, cotton, tobacco, etc. plantation. **3** a large container for decorative plants. **4** a machine for planting seeds etc. (*potato-planter*).

plantigrade /'plæntɪˌgreɪd/ *adj. & n.* —*adj.* (of an animal) walking on the soles of its feet. —*n.* a plantigrade animal, e.g. humans or bears (cf. DIGITIGRADE). [F f. mod.L *plantigradus* f. L *planta* sole + *-gradus* -walking]

plaque /plæk, plɑːk/ *n.* **1** an ornamental tablet of metal, porcelain, etc., esp. affixed to a building in commemoration. **2** a deposit on teeth where bacteria proliferate. **3** *Med.* **a** a patch or eruption of skin etc. as a result of damage. **b** a fibrous lesion in atherosclerosis. **4** a small badge of rank in an honorary order. □□ **plaquette** /plæ'ket/ *n.* [F f. Du. *plak* tablet f. *plakken* stick]

plash¹ /plæʃ/ *n. & v.* —*n.* **1** a splash; a plunge. **2 a** a marshy pool. **b** a puddle. —*v.* **1** *tr.* splash. **2** *tr.* strike the surface of (water). □□ **plashy** *adj.* [OE *plæsc,* prob. imit.]

plash² /plæʃ/ *v.tr.* **1** bend down and interweave (branches, twigs, etc.) to form a hedge. **2** make or renew (a hedge) in this way. [ME f. OF *pla(i)ssier* ult. f. L *plectere* plait: cf. PLEACH]

plasma /'plæzmə/ *n.* (also **plasm** /'plæz(ə)m/) **1** the colourless fluid part of blood, lymph, or milk, in which corpuscles or fat-globules are suspended. **2** = PROTOPLASM. **3 a** a gas in which there are positive ions and free negative electrons, usually in approximately equal numbers throughout and therefore electrically neutral. **b** any analogous collection of charged particles in which one or both kinds are mobile, as the conduction electrons in a metal or the ions in a salt solution. (See below.) **4** a green variety of quartz used in mosaic and for other decorative purposes. □□ **plasmatic** /-'mætɪk/ *adj.* **plasmic** *adj.* [LL, = mould f. Gk *plasma -atos* f. *plassō* to shape]

Plasmas include the following: the hot ionized gases found in the sun, other stars, and artificial fusion reactions; the material of glowing electrical discharges; the gaseous interior of working fluorescent lamps; metals (in which some of the electrons can move freely: see METAL); and molten salts. Salts in the solid state are not included, although they consist of ionized particles, because the particles are not free to move and so cannot conduct electricity. In a narrower sense, however, the term *plasma* frequently refers specifically to the hot ionized gases found in the sun and in fusion reactions. Such plasmas behave differently from ordinary un-ionized gases, notably in being affected by magnetic fields. For this reason they are sometimes regarded as constituting a fourth state of matter alongside solids, liquids, and gases; more than 99 per cent of matter in the universe is estimated to be in this state. The study of plasmas is very important for developing controlled fusion reactions (see NUCLEAR FUSION). Fusion can take place only at extremely high temperatures, which would immediately vaporize any container in which the hydrogen fuel was kept. However, because hydrogen is a plasma at these temperatures, its response to a magnetic field can be utilized to keep it from touching the walls of its container; this property removes one obstacle to the practicability of controlled fusion.

plasmid /'plæzmɪd/ *n.* any genetic structure in a cell that can replicate independently of the chromosomes. [PLASMA + -ID²]

plasmodesma /ˌplæzmə'dezmə/ *n.* (*pl.* **plasmodesmata** /-mətə/) a narrow thread of cytoplasm that passes through cell walls and affords communication between plant cells. [PLASMA + Gk *desma* bond, fetter]

plasmodium /plæz'məʊdɪəm/ *n.* (*pl.* **plasmodia** /-dɪə/) **1** any parasitic protozoan of the genus *Plasmodium,* including those causing malaria in man. **2** a form within the life cycle of various micro-organisms including slime moulds, usu. consisting of a mass of naked protoplasm containing many nuclei. □□ **plasmodial** *adj.* [mod.L f. PLASMA¹ + *-odium*: see -ODE¹]

plasmolyse /'plæzmə,laɪz/ *v.intr. & tr.* (US **plasmolyze**) undergo or subject to plasmolysis.

plasmolysis /plæz'mɒlɪsɪs/ *n.* contraction of the protoplast of a plant cell as a result of loss of water from the cell. [mod.L (as PLASMA, -LYSIS)]

Plassey /'plæsɪ/ a village north-west of Calcutta in former Bengal, scene of a British victory in 1757, when a very small British army under Robert Clive defeated a much larger native force under the Nawab of Bengal partly because Clive had previously bribed some of the Indian generals. The victory established British supremacy in Bengal.

plaster /'plɑːstə(r)/ *n. & v.* —*n.* **1** a soft pliable mixture esp. of lime putty with sand or Portland cement etc. for spreading on walls, ceilings, etc., to form a smooth hard surface when dried. **2** *Brit.* = *sticking-plaster* (see STICK²). **3** *hist.* a curative or protective substance spread on a bandage etc. and applied to the body (*mustard plaster*). —*v.tr.* **1** cover (a wall etc.) with plaster or a similar substance. **2** (often foll. by *with*) coat thickly or to excess; bedaub (*plastered the bread with jam; the wall was plastered with slogans*). **3** stick or apply (a thing) thickly like plaster (*plastered glue all over it*). **4** (often foll. by *down*) make (esp. hair) smooth with water, cream, etc.; fix flat. **5** (as **plastered** *adj.*) *sl.* drunk. **6** apply a medical plaster or plaster cast to. **7** *sl.* bomb or shell heavily. □ **plaster cast 1** a bandage stiffened with plaster of Paris and applied to a broken limb etc. **2** a statue or mould made of plaster. **plaster of Paris** fine white plaster made of gypsum and used for making plaster casts etc. **plaster saint** *iron.* a person regarded as being without moral faults or human frailty. □□ **plasterer** *n.* **plastery** *adj.* [ME f. OE & OF *plastre* or F *plastrer* f. med.L *plastrum* f. L *emplastrum* f. Gk *emplastron*]

plasterboard /ˈplɑːstəˌbɔːd/ *n.* two boards with a filling of plaster used to form or line the inner walls of houses etc.

plastic /ˈplæstɪk/ *n.* & *adj.* —*n.* **1** any of a number of synthetic polymeric substances that can be given any required shape. (See below.) **2** (*attrib.*) made of plastic (*plastic bag*). —*adj.* **1** capable of being moulded; pliant; supple. **2** moulding or giving form to clay, wax, etc. **3** *Biol.* exhibiting an adaptability to environmental changes. **4** (esp. in philosophy) formative, creative. □ **plastic arts** art forms involving modelling or moulding, e.g. sculpture and ceramics, or art involving the representation of solid objects with three-dimensional effects. **plastic bomb** a bomb containing plastic explosive. **plastic explosive** a putty-like explosive capable of being moulded by hand. **plastic surgeon** a qualified practitioner of plastic surgery. **plastic surgery** the process of reconstructing or repairing parts of the body by the transfer of tissue, either in the treatment of injury or for cosmetic reasons. □□ **plastically** *adv.* **plasticity** /-ˈtɪsɪtɪ/ *n.* **plasticize** /-ˌsaɪz/ *v.tr.* (also **-ise**). **plasticization** /-saɪˈzeɪʃ(ə)n/ *n.* **plasticizer** /-ˌsaɪzə(r)/ *n.* **plasticky** *adj.* [F *plastique* or L *plasticus* f. Gk *plastikos* f. *plassō* mould]

Plastics are artificial substances consisting of long chain-like organic molecules (polymers) intertwined with one another. The first plastics, such as celluloid (developed in 1869) used chemically modified forms of cellulose or other natural polymers. In the 20th c., however, polymers made artificially from small molecules became available, leading to the great diversity of plastics available today. The structure of plastics allows them to be softened during manufacture, and thus they can be moulded into many different forms. Other advantages of plastics include toughness, insulating ability, resistance to chemical and biological attack (although this leads to environmental problems), and ability to be given any desired colour. Among the major successes of the plastics industry are celluloid (which became a household name), bakelite (the first heat-proof plastic), and nylon (see entries).

Plasticine /ˈplæstɪˌsiːn/ *n. propr.* a soft plastic material used, esp. by children, for modelling. [PLASTIC + -INE⁴]

plastid /ˈplæstɪd/ *n.* any small organelle in the cytoplasm of a plant cell, containing pigment or food. [G f. Gk *plastos* shaped]

plastron /ˈplæstrən/ *n.* **1 a** a fencer's leather-covered breastplate. **b** a lancer's breast-covering of facings-cloth. **2 a** an ornamental front on a woman's bodice. **b** a man's starched shirt-front. **3 a** the ventral part of the shell of a tortoise or turtle. **b** the corresponding part in other animals. **4** *hist.* a steel breastplate. □□ **plastral** *adj.* [F f. It. *piastrone* augment. of *piastra* breastplate, f. L *emplastrum* PLASTER]

plat¹ /plæt/ *n. US* **1** a plot of land. **2** a plan of an area of land. [16th c.: collateral form of PLOT]

plat² /plæt/ *n.* & *v.* —*n.* = PLAIT *n.* **1**. —*v.tr.* (**platted, platting**) = PLAIT *v.*

platan /ˈplæt(ə)n/ *n.* = PLANE³. [ME f. L *platanus*: see PLANE³]

plat du jour /ˌplɑː duː ˈʒuːə(r)/ *n.* a dish specially featured on a day's menu. [F, = dish of the day]

Plate /pleɪt/, **River** An estuary on the eastern side of South America between Uruguay and Argentina. The chief rivers flowing into it are the Paraná and the Uruguay, and the cities of Buenos Aires and Montevideo stand on its shores. Its name refers to the export of silver (Sp. *plata*) in the Spanish colonial

period. In 1939 it was the scene of a naval battle between British and German warships.

plate /pleɪt/ *n.* & *v.* —*n.* **1 a** a shallow vessel, usu. circular and of earthenware or china, from which food is eaten or served. **b** the contents of this (*ate a plate of sandwiches*). **2** a similar vessel usu. of metal or wood, used esp. for making a collection in a church etc. **3** *US* a main course of a meal, served on one plate. **4** *Austral.* & *NZ* a contribution of cakes, sandwiches, etc., to a social gathering. **5** (*collect.*) **a** utensils of silver, gold, or other metal. **b** objects of plated metal. **6** a piece of metal with a name or inscription for affixing to a door, container, etc. **7** an illustration on special paper in a book. **8** a thin sheet of metal, glass, etc., coated with a sensitive film for photography. **9** a flat thin usu. rigid sheet of metal etc. with an even surface and uniform thickness, often as part of a mechanism. **10 a** a smooth piece of metal etc. for engraving. **b** an impression made from this. **11 a** a silver or gold cup as a prize for a horse-race etc. **b** a race with this as a prize. **12 a** a thin piece of plastic material, moulded to the shape of the mouth and gums, to which artificial teeth or another orthodontic appliance are attached. **b** *colloq.* a complete denture or orthodontic appliance. **13** *Geol.* each of several nearly rigid pieces of the earth's crust which each cover a large area, some of them including whole continents, and which together consitute the surface of the earth. They lie on top of a more plastic region on which they move slowly relative to one another, the boundaries between adjacent plates being associated with well-defined belts of seismic, volcanic, and tectonic activity. **14** *Biol.* a thin flat organic structure or formation. **15** a light shoe for a racehorse. **16** a stereotype, electrotype, or plastic cast of a page of composed movable types, or a metal or plastic copy of filmset matter, from which sheets are printed. **17** *US Baseball* a flat piece of whitened rubber marking the station of a batter or pitcher. **18** *US* the anode of a thermionic valve. **19** a horizontal timber laid along the top of a wall to support the ends of joists or rafters (*window-plate*). —*v.tr.* **1** apply a thin coat esp. of silver, gold, or tin to (another metal). **2** cover (esp. a ship) with plates of metal, esp. for protection. **3** make a plate of (type etc.) for printing. □ **on a plate** *colloq.* available with little trouble to the recipient. **on one's plate** for one to deal with or consider. **plate armour** armour of metal plates, for a man, ship, etc. **plate glass** see GLASS. **plate-rack** *Brit.* a rack in which plates are placed to drain. **plate tectonics** *Geol.* the study of the earth's surface based on the concept of moving 'plates' (see sense 13 of *n.*) forming its structure, and spreading of the sea floor. This theory, which since the 1960s has revolutionized the geological sciences, provides explanations for the phenomenon of continental drift and the distribution of earthquakes, mid-ocean ridges, deep-sea trenches, and mountain chains. **plate tracery** *Archit.* tracery with perforations in otherwise continuous stone. □□ **plateful** *n.* (*pl.* **-fuls**). **plateless** *adj.* **plater** *n.* [ME f. OF f. med.L *plata* plate armour f. *platus* (adj.) ult. f. Gk *platus* flat]

plateau /ˈplætəʊ/ *n.* & *v.* —*n.* (*pl.* **plateaux** /-təʊz/ or **plateaus**) **1** an area of fairly level high ground. **2** a state of little variation after an increase. —*v.intr.* (**plateaus, plateaued**) (often foll. by *out*) reach a level or stable state after an increase. [F f. OF *platel* dimin. of *plat* flat surface]

platelayer /ˈpleɪtˌleɪə(r)/ *n. Brit.* a person employed in fixing and repairing railway rails.

platelet /ˈpleɪtlɪt/ *n.* a small colourless disc of protoplasm found in blood and involved in clotting.

platen /ˈplæt(ə)n/ *n.* **1** a plate in a printing-press which presses the paper against the type. **2** a cylindrical roller in a typewriter against which the paper is held. [OF *platine* a flat piece f. *plat* flat]

plateresque /ˌplætəˈresk/ *adj.* richly ornamented in a style suggesting silverware. [Sp. *plateresco* f. *platero* silversmith f. *plata* silver]

platform /ˈplætfɔːm/ *n.* **1** a raised level surface; a natural or artificial terrace. **2** a raised surface from which a speaker addresses an audience. **3** *Brit.* a raised elongated structure along the side of a track in a railway station. **4** the floor area at the entrance to a bus. **5** a thick sole of a shoe. **6** the declared policy of a political party. □ **platform ticket** a ticket allowing a non-traveller access to a station platform. [F *plateforme* ground-plan f. *plate* flat + *forme* FORM]

Plath /plæθ/, Sylvia (1932–63), American poet and novelist, married in 1956 to the English poet Ted Hughes. In 1960 she published her first volume of poetry *The Colossus*. Her only novel *The Bell Jar* (1963) gives a witty and disturbing account of her nervous breakdown and ECT treatment. Her best-known collection, *Ariel* (1965), published posthumously after her suicide, established her reputation with its courageous and controlled treatment of extreme and painful states of mind.

plating /'pleɪtɪŋ/ n. 1 a coating of gold, silver, etc. 2 racing for plates.

platinic /plə'tɪnɪk/ adj. of or containing (esp. tetravalent) platinum.

platinize /'plætɪˌnaɪz/ v.tr. (also -ise) coat with platinum. □□ **platinization** /-ˈzeɪʃ(ə)n/ n.

platinoid /'plætɪˌnɔɪd/ n. an alloy of copper, zinc, nickel, and tungsten.

platinum /'plætɪnəm/ n. Chem. a rare heavy ductile malleable silvery-white metallic element. (See below.) ¶ Symb.: Pt; atomic number 78. □ **platinum black** platinum in powder form like lampblack. **platinum blonde** (or **blond**) adj. silvery-blond. —n. a person with silvery-blond hair. **platinum metal** any metallic element found with and resembling platinum e.g. osmium, iridium, and palladium. [mod.L f. earlier *platina* f. Sp., dimin. of *plata* silver]

Platinum occurs uncombined in nature, usually alloyed with other metals. It has a high melting-point and is resistant to chemical attack. The pure metal and its alloys have many uses, in jewellery, electrical contacts, and laboratory equipment, and it is an important industrial catalyst.

platitude /'plætɪˌtjuːd/ n. 1 a trite or commonplace remark, esp. one solemnly delivered. 2 the use of platitudes; dullness, insipidity. □□ **platitudinize** /-ˈtjuːdɪˌnaɪz/ v.intr. (also -ise). **platitudinous** /-ˈtjuːdɪnəs/ adj. [F f. *plat* flat, after *certitude*, *multitudinous*, etc.]

Plato /'pleɪtəʊ/ (429–347 BC), Greek philosopher, of aristocratic birth, a disciple of Socrates. His philosophy is presented in the form of dialogues, of high literary merit, with Socrates as the principal speaker. His most famous work, the *Republic*, presents a long inquiry into the best form of life for people and States. Plato's main political principle, that government is a science and requires expert knowledge, led him to the strongest condemnation of democracy. Seeking to discover the real nature of knowledge he developed the doctrine of 'ideas' or 'forms'— abstracts, perfect entities outside the physical world, and of which the material things that we see and handle are ephemeral and imperfect copies. His hypothesis has among its consequences that the soul is immortal; this is elaborately argued in the *Phaedo*. Plato's thought profoundly influenced Christian theology and Western philosophy. He was buried in the grounds of the Academy which he founded in Athens and which he served for 40 years.

Platonic /plə'tɒnɪk/ adj. 1 of or associated with Plato or his ideas. 2 (**platonic**) (of love or friendship) purely spiritual, not sexual. 3 (**platonic**) confined to words or theory; not leading to action; harmless. □ **Platonic solid** (or **body**) any of the five regular solids (tetrahedron, cube, octahedron, dodecahedron, icosahedron). □□ **Platonically** adv. [L *Platonicus* f. Gk *Platōnikos* f. *Platōn* Plato]

Platonism /'pleɪtəˌnɪz(ə)m/ n. 1 the philosophy of Plato or his followers. 2 any of various revivals of these doctrines or related ideas, especially Neoplatonism (3rd–5th c. AD), and Cambridge Platonism (17th c.) centred on Cambridge. 3 (in the philosophy of mathematics) the theory that arithmetical statements are about numbers, entities that exist apart from physical collections of things, and over and above the symbols that represent them. □□ **Platonist** n.

platoon /plə'tuːn/ n. 1 Mil. a subdivision of a company, a tactical unit commanded by a lieutenant and usu. divided into three sections. 2 a group of persons acting together. [F *peloton* small ball, dimin. of *pelote*: see PELLET, -OON]

platteland /'plɑːtəˌlɑːnt/ n. S.Afr. remote country districts. □□ **plattelander** n. [Afrik., = flat land]

platter /'plætə(r)/ n. 1 a large flat dish or plate, esp. for food. 2 colloq. a gramophone record. □ **on a platter** = *on a plate* (see PLATE). [ME & AF *plater* f. AF *plat* PLATE]

platy- /'plætɪ/ comb. form broad, flat. [Gk *platu-* f. *platus* broad, flat]

platyhelminth /ˌplætɪ'hɛlmɪnθ/ n. any invertebrate of the phylum Platyhelminthes, including flatworms, flukes, and tapeworms.

platypus /'plætɪpəs/ n. an Australian aquatic egg-laying mammal, *Ornithorhynchus anatinus*, having a pliable ducklike bill, flat tail, webbed feet, and sleek grey fur. Also called DUCKBILL. When the first complete platypus skin was brought to the British Museum in 1798 it was believed to be a hoax (that was the age of such hoaxes), but four years later a complete carcass arrived and its authenticity was attested.

platyrrhine /'plætɪˌraɪn/ adj. & n. —adj. (of primates) having nostrils far apart and directed forwards or sideways (cf. CATARRHINE). —n. such an animal. [PLATY- + Gk *rhis rhin-* nose]

plaudit /'plɔːdɪt/ n. (usu. in pl.) 1 a round of applause. 2 an emphatic expression of approval. [shortened f. L *plaudite* applaud, imper. pl. of *plaudere plaus-* applaud, said by Roman actors at the end of a play]

plausible /'plɔːzɪb(ə)l/ adj. 1 (of an argument, statement, etc.) seeming reasonable or probable. 2 (of a person) persuasive but deceptive. □□ **plausibility** /-'bɪlɪtɪ/ n. **plausibly** adv. [L *plausibilis* (as PLAUDIT)]

Plautus /'plɔːtəs/, Titus Maccius (c.250–184 BC), Roman comic playwright. His plays, of which 21 survive, are based on models from Greek but with the addition of much specifically Roman material. Fantasy and imagination are more important than realism in the development of the plots; the characters, including stock types such as cunning slaves, boastful soldiers, courtesans, and long-lost daughters, are often larger than life, and the language is correspondingly exuberant.

play /pleɪ/ v. & n. —v. 1 intr. (often foll. by *with*) occupy or amuse oneself pleasantly with some recreation, game, exercise, etc. 2 intr. (foll. by *with*) act light-heartedly or flippantly (with feelings etc.). 3 tr. **a** perform on or be able to perform on (a musical instrument). **b** perform (a piece of music etc.). **c** cause (a record, record-player, etc.) to produce sounds. 4 **a** intr. (foll. by *in*) perform a role in (a drama etc.). **b** tr. perform (a drama or role) on stage, or in a film or broadcast. **c** tr. give a dramatic performance at (a particular theatre or place). 5 tr. act in real life the part of (*play truant*; *play the fool*). 6 tr. (foll. by *on*) perform (a trick or joke etc.) on (a person). 7 tr. (foll. by *for*) regard (a person) as (something specified) (*played me for a fool*). 8 intr. colloq. participate, cooperate; do what is wanted (*they won't play*). 9 intr. gamble. 10 tr. gamble on. 11 tr. **a** take part in (a game or recreation). **b** compete with (another player or team) in a game. **c** occupy a specified position in a team for a game. **d** (foll. by *in*, *on*, *at*, etc.) assign (a player) to a position. 12 tr. move (a piece) or display (a playing-card) in one's turn in a game. 13 tr. (also *absol.*) strike (a ball etc.) or execute (a stroke) in a game. 14 intr. move about in a lively or unrestrained manner. 15 intr. (often foll. by *on*) **a** touch gently. **b** emit light, water, etc. (*fountains gently playing*). 16 tr. allow (a fish) to exhaust itself pulling against a line. 17 intr. (often foll. by *at*) **a** engage in a half-hearted way (in an activity). **b** pretend to be. 18 intr. (of a cricket ground etc.) be conducive to play as specified (*the pitch is playing fast*). 19 intr. colloq. act or behave (as specified) (*play fair*). 20 tr. (foll. by *in*, *out*, etc.) accompany (a person) with music (*were played out with bagpipes*). —n. 1 recreation, amusement, esp. as the spontaneous activity of children and young animals. 2 **a** the playing of a game. **b** the action or manner of this. **c** the status of the ball etc. in a game as being available to be played according to the rules (*in play*; *out of play*). 3 a dramatic piece for the stage etc. 4 activity or operation (*are in full play*; *brought into play*). 5 **a** freedom of movement. **b** space or scope for this. 6 brisk, light, or fitful movement. 7 gambling. 8 an action or manoeuvre, esp. in or as in a game. □ **at play** engaged in recreation. **in play** for amusement; not seriously. **make play** act effectively. **make a**

play for *colloq.* make a conspicuous attempt to acquire. **make play with** use ostentatiously. **play about** (or **around**) behave irresponsibly. **play along** pretend to cooperate. **play back** play (sounds recently recorded), esp. to monitor recording quality etc. **play-back** *n.* a playing back of a sound or sounds. **play ball** see BALL[1]. **play by ear 1** perform (music) without the aid of a score. **2** (also **play it by ear**) proceed instinctively or step by step according to results and circumstances. **play one's cards right** (or **well**) make good use of opportunities; act shrewdly. **play down** minimize the importance of. **play ducks and drakes with** see DUCK[1]. **played out** exhausted of energy or usefulness. **play false** act, or treat a (person), deceitfully or treacherously. **play fast and loose** act unreliably; ignore one's obligations. **play the field** see FIELD. **play for time** seek to gain time by delaying. **play the game** see GAME[1]. **play God** see GOD. **play havoc with** see HAVOC. **play hell with** see HELL. **play hookey** see HOOKEY. **play into a person's hands** act so as unwittingly to give a person an advantage. **play it cool** *colloq.* **1** affect indifference. **2** be relaxed or unemotional. **play the man** = *be a man* (see MAN). **play the market** speculate in stocks etc. **play off** (usu. foll. by *against*) **1** oppose (one person against another), esp. for one's own advantage. **2** play an extra match to decide a draw or tie. **play-off** *n.* a match played to decide a draw or tie. **play on 1** continue to play. **2** take advantage of (a person's feelings etc.). **play oneself in** become accustomed to the prevailing conditions in a game etc. **play on words** a pun. **play-pen** a portable enclosure for young children to play in. **play possum** see POSSUM. **play safe** (or **for safety**) avoid risks. **play-suit** a garment for a young child. **play to the gallery** see GALLERY. **play up 1** behave mischievously. **2** cause trouble; be irritating (*my rheumatism is playing up again*). **3** obstruct or annoy in this way (*played the teacher up*). **4** put all one's energy into a game. **play up to** flatter, esp. to win favour. **play with fire** take foolish risks. □□ **playable** *adj.* **playability** /-'bɪlɪtɪ/ *n.* [OE *plega* (n.), *pleg(i)an* (v.), orig. = (to) exercise]

playa /'plɑːjə/ *n.* a flat dried-up area, esp. a desert basin from which water evaporates quickly. [Sp., = beach, f. LL *plagia*]

play-act /'pleɪækt/ *v.* **1** *intr.* act in a play. **2** *intr.* behave affectedly or insincerely. **3** *tr.* act (a scene, part, etc.). □□ **play-acting** *n.* **play-actor** *n.*

playbill /'pleɪbɪl/ *n.* **1** a poster announcing a theatrical performance. **2** *US* a theatre programme.

playboy /'pleɪbɔɪ/ *n.* an irresponsible pleasure-seeking man, esp. a wealthy one.

player /'pleɪə(r)/ *n.* **1** a person taking part in a sport or game. **2** a person playing a musical instrument. **3** a person who plays a part on the stage; an actor. **4** = *record-player*. □ **player-piano** a piano fitted with an apparatus enabling it to be played automatically. [OE *plegere* (as PLAY)]

Playfair /'pleɪfeə(r)/, John (1748–1819), Scottish mathematician and geologist, a friend of James Hutton. He is chiefly remembered for his *Illustrations of the Huttonian Theory of the Earth* (1802), which presented Hutton's views—and some of his own—in a concise and readable form, enabling them to reach a far wider audience than Hutton's own writings.

playfellow /'pleɪˌfeləʊ/ *n.* a playmate.

playful /'pleɪfʊl/ *adj.* **1** fond of or inclined to play. **2** done in fun; humorous, jocular. □□ **playfully** *adv.* **playfulness** *n.*

playgoer /'pleɪˌgəʊə(r)/ *n.* a person who goes often to the theatre.

playground /'pleɪgraʊnd/ *n.* an outdoor area for children to play on.

playgroup /'pleɪgruːp/ *n.* a group of preschool children who play regularly together at a particular place under supervision.

playhouse /'pleɪhaʊs/ *n.* **1** a theatre. **2** a toy house for children to play in.

playing-card /'pleɪɪŋˌkɑːd/ *n.* each of a set of usu. 52 oblong pieces of card or other material with an identical pattern on one side and different values represented by numbers and symbols on the other, divided into four suits, used to play various games. The origin of playing-cards is uncertain. They were not known to Graeco-Roman antiquity, and though it has been argued that they reached Europe from the Far East, European and Asian cards are so different that there may be no need to assume a common origin. They have been in use in Europe since the 14th c. and in the East for at least as long. From the 14th c. the various suit systems were becoming established in different parts of Europe. The standard pack now contains 52 cards divided into 4 suits of 13 cards each. Each suit has an ace, nine cards numbered 2 to 10, and three picture or 'court cards' (Jack or Knave, Queen, and King); the English pack also includes a Joker. Aces were a Victorian invention (early packs had numbered these cards 1; as ace in most card-games they count the highest). The ornamental ace of spades in English packs dates from the 18th c. when a duty was levied on the cards and this one was selected to bear the government stamp (forging it was an offence punishable by hanging); this duty was not entirely removed until 1960. The signs of the four suits reached England from France in about the 15th c.; since then no major change has been made in the composition of the pack, and figures on the court cards are still clad in the costume of Henry VII's reign. The double head was introduced in the 19th c., for convenience, so that cards laid on the table looked the same way up to players on each side.

playing-field /'pleɪɪŋˌfiːld/ *n.* a field used for outdoor team games.

playlet /'pleɪlɪt/ *n.* a short play or dramatic piece.

playmate /'pleɪmeɪt/ *n.* a child's companion in play.

playschool /'pleɪskuːl/ *n.* a nursery for preschool children.

plaything /'pleɪθɪŋ/ *n.* **1** a toy or other thing to play with. **2** a person treated as a toy.

playtime /'pleɪtaɪm/ *n.* time for play or recreation.

playwright /'pleɪraɪt/ *n.* a person who writes plays.

plaza /'plɑːzə/ *n.* a market-place or open square (esp. in a Spanish town). [Sp., = place]

plc *abbr.* (also **PLC**) Public Limited Company.

plea /pliː/ *n.* **1** an earnest appeal or entreaty. **2** *Law* a formal statement by or on behalf of a defendant. **3** an argument or excuse. □ **plea bargaining** *US* an arrangement between prosecutor and defendant whereby the defendant pleads guilty to a lesser charge in the expectations of leniency. [ME & AF *ple*, *plai*, OF *plait*, *plaid* agreement, discussion f. L *placitum* a decree, neut. past part. of *placēre* to please]

pleach /pliːtʃ/ *v.tr.* entwine or interlace (esp. branches to form a hedge). [ME *pleche* f. OF (as PLASH²)]

plead /pliːd/ *v.* (*past* and *past part.* **pleaded** or esp. *US*, *Sc.*, & *dial.* **pled** /pled/) **1** *intr.* (foll. by *with*) make an earnest appeal to. **2** *intr.* *Law* address a lawcourt as an advocate on behalf of a party. **3** *tr.* maintain (a cause) esp. in a lawcourt. **4** *tr.* *Law* declare to be one's state as regards guilt in or responsibility for a crime (*plead guilty*; *plead insanity*). **5** *tr.* offer or allege as an excuse (*pleaded forgetfulness*). **6** *intr.* make an appeal or entreaty. □□ **pleadable** *adj.* **pleader** *n.* **pleadingly** *adv.* [ME f. AF *pleder*, OF *plaidier* (as PLEA)]

pleading /'pliːdɪŋ/ *n.* (usu. in *pl.*) a formal statement of the cause of an action or defence.

pleasance /'plez(ə)ns/ *n.* a secluded enclosure or part of a garden, esp. one attached to a large house. [ME f. OF *plaisance* (as PLEASANT)]

pleasant /'plez(ə)nt/ *adj.* (**pleasanter**, **pleasantest**) pleasing to the mind, feelings, or senses. □□ **pleasantly** *adv.* **pleasantness** *n.* [ME f. OF *plaisant* (as PLEASE)]

pleasantry /'plezəntrɪ/ *n.* (*pl.* **-ies**) **1** a pleasant or amusing remark, esp. made in casual conversation. **2** a humorous manner of speech. **3** jocularity. [F *plaisanterie* (as PLEASANT)]

please /pliːz/ *v.* **1** *tr.* (also *absol.*) be agreeable to; make glad; give pleasure to (*the gift will please them*; *anxious to please*). **2** *tr.* (in *passive*) **a** (foll. by *to* + infin.) be glad or willing to (*am pleased to help*). **b** (often foll. by *about*, *at*, *with*) derive pleasure or satisfaction (from). **3** *tr.* (with *it* as subject; usu. foll. by *to* + infin.) be the inclination or wish of (*it did not please them to attend*). **4** *intr.* think fit; have the will or desire (*take as many as you please*). **5** *tr.* (short for **may it please you**) used in polite requests (*come* *in, please).* □ **if you please** if you are willing, esp. *iron.* to indicate unreasonableness *(then, if you please, we had to pay).* **pleased as Punch** see PUNCH⁴. **please oneself** do as one likes. □□ **pleased** *adj.* **pleasing** *adj.* **pleasingly** *adv.* [ME *plaise* f. OF *plaisir* f. L *placēre*]

pleasurable /'pleʒərəb(ə)l/ *adj.* causing pleasure; agreeable. □□ **pleasurableness** *n.* **pleasurably** *adv.* [PLEASURE + -ABLE, after *comfortable*]

pleasure /'pleʒə(r)/ *n. & v.* —*n.* **1** a feeling of satisfaction or joy. **2** enjoyment. **3** a source of pleasure or gratification *(painting was my chief pleasure; it is a pleasure to talk to them).* **4** *formal* a person's will or desire *(what is your pleasure?).* **5** sensual gratification or enjoyment *(a life of pleasure).* **6** *(attrib.)* done or used for pleasure *(pleasure-ground).* —*v.* **1** *tr.* give *(esp. sexual)* pleasure to. **2** *intr.* (often foll. by *in*) take pleasure. □ **take pleasure in** like doing. **with pleasure** gladly. [ME & OF *plesir, plaisir* PLEASE, used as a noun]

pleat /pli:t/ *n. & v.* —*n.* a fold or crease, esp. a flattened fold in cloth doubled upon itself. —*v.tr.* make a pleat or pleats in. [ME, var. of PLAIT]

pleb /pleb/ *n. colloq.* usu. *derog.* an ordinary insignificant person. □□ **plebby** *adj.* [abbr. of PLEBEIAN]

plebeian /plɪ'bi:ən/ *n. & adj.* —*n.* a commoner, esp. in ancient Rome. —*adj.* **1** of low birth; of the common people. **2** uncultured. **3** coarse, ignoble. □□ **plebeianism** *n.* [L *plebeius* f. *plebs plebis* the common people]

plebiscite /'plebɪsɪt, -ˌsaɪt/ *n.* **1** the direct vote of all the electors of a State etc. on an important public question, e.g. a change in the constitution. **2** the public expression of a community's opinion, with or without binding force. **3** *Rom.Hist.* a law enacted by the plebeians' assembly. □□ **plebiscitary** /-'bɪsɪtərɪ/ *adj.* [F *plébiscite* f. L *plebiscitum* f. *plebs plebis* the common people + *scitum* decree f. *sciscere* vote for]

plectrum /'plektrəm/ *n.* (*pl.* **plectrums** or **plectra** /-trə/) **1** a thin flat piece of plastic or horn etc. held in the hand and used to pluck a string, esp. of a guitar. **2** the corresponding mechanical part of a harpsichord etc. [L f. Gk *plēktron* f. *plēssō* strike]

pled see PLEAD.

pledge /pledʒ/ *n. & v.* —*n.* **1** a solemn promise or undertaking. **2** a thing given as security for the fulfilment of a contract, the payment of a debt, etc., and liable to forfeiture in the event of failure. **3** a thing put in pawn. **4** a thing given as a token of love, favour, or something to come. **5** the drinking of a person's health; a toast. **6** a solemn undertaking to abstain from alcohol *(sign the pledge).* **7** the state of being pledged *(goods lying in pledge).* —*v.tr.* **1 a** deposit as security. **b** pawn. **2** promise solemnly by the pledge of (one's honour, word, etc.). **3** (often *refl.*) bind by a solemn promise. **4** drink to the health of. □ **pledge one's troth** see TROTH. □□ **pledgeable** *adj.* **pledger** *n.* **pledgor** *n.* [ME *plege* f. OF *plege* f. LL *plebium* f. *plebire* assure]

pledgee /ple'dʒi:/ *n.* a person to whom a pledge is given.

pledget /'pledʒɪt/ *n.* a small wad of lint etc. [16th c.; orig. unkn.]

pleiad /'plaɪəd/ *n.* a brilliant group of (usu. seven) persons or things. [named after PLEIADES]

Pleiades /'plaɪəˌdi:z/ *n.pl.* a cluster of stars in the constellation Taurus, usu. known as 'the Seven Sisters'. They are the best-known galactic cluster in the sky, a beautiful association of some half-dozen stars visible to the naked eye (more if the observer's eyesight is good) but actually containing over two hundred members. [ME f. L *Pleïas* f. Gk *Plēïas -ados*]

Pleistocene /'plaɪstəˌsi:n/ *adj. & n. Geol.* —*adj.* of or relating to the first of the first of the two epochs forming the Quaternary period. The Pleistocene epoch followed the Pliocene and preceded the Holocene (Recent); it lasted from about 2,000,000 to 10,000 years ago, is notable for a succession of ice ages, and also saw the evolution of modern mankind. Towards the end of the epoch many animal species became extinct. —*n.* this epoch or system. Also called *Ice age.* [Gk *pleistos* most + *kainos* new]

plenary /'pli:nərɪ/ *adj.* **1** entire, unqualified, absolute *(plenary indulgence).* **2** (of an assembly) to be attended by all members. [LL *plenarius* f. *plenus* full]

plenipotentiary /ˌplenɪpə'tenʃərɪ/ *n. & adj.* —*n.* (*pl.* **-ies**) a person (esp. a diplomat) invested with the full power of independent action. —*adj.* **1** having this power. **2** (of power) absolute. [med.L *plenipotentiarius* f. *plenus* full + *potentia* power]

plenitude /'plenɪˌtju:d/ *n. literary* **1** fullness, completeness. **2** abundance. [ME f. OF f. LL *plenitudo* f. *plenus* full]

plenteous /'plentɪəs/ *adj. poet.* plentiful. □□ **plenteously** *adv.* **plenteousness** *n.* [ME f. OF *plentivous* f. *plentif -ive* f. *plenté* PLENTY: cf. *bounteous*]

plentiful /'plentɪˌfʊl/ *adj.* abundant, copious. □□ **plentifully** *adv.* **plentifulness** *n.*

plenty /'plentɪ/ *n., adj., & adv.* —*n.* (often foll. by *of*) a great or sufficient quantity or number *(we have plenty; plenty of time).* —*adj. colloq.* existing in an ample quantity. —*adv. colloq.* fully, entirely *(it is plenty large enough).* [ME *plenteth, plente* f. OF *plentet* f. L *plenitas -tatis* f. *plenus* full]

plenum /'pli:nəm/ *n.* **1** a full assembly of people or a committee etc. **2** *Physics* space filled with matter. [L, neut. of *plenus* full]

pleochroic /ˌpli:ə'krəʊɪk/ *adj.* showing different colours when viewed in different directions. □□ **pleochroism** *n.* [Gk *pleiōn* more + -*khroos* f. *khrōs* colour]

pleomorphism /ˌpli:ə'mɔ:fɪz(ə)m/ *n. Biol., Chem., & Mineral.* the occurrence of more than one distinct form. □□ **pleomorphic** *adj.* [Gk *pleiōn* more + *morphē* form]

pleonasm /'pli:əˌnæz(ə)m/ *n.* the use of more words than are needed to give the sense (e.g. *see with one's eyes).* □□ **pleonastic** /-'næstɪk/ *adj.* **pleonastically** /-'næstɪkəlɪ/ *adv.* [LL *pleonasmus* f. Gk *pleonasmos* f. *pleonazō* be superfluous]

plesiosaurus /ˌpli:sɪə'sɔ:rəs/ *n.* (also **plesiosaur** /'pli:sɪəˌsɔ:(r)/) any of a group of extinct marine reptiles with a broad flat body, short tail, long flexible neck, and large paddle-like limbs. [mod.L f. Gk *plēsios* near + *sauros* lizard]

plessor var. of PLEXOR.

plethora /'pleθərə/ *n.* **1** an oversupply, glut, or excess. **2** *Med.* **a** an abnormal excess of red corpuscles in the blood. **b** an excess of any body fluid. □□ **plethoric** /also plɪ'θɒrɪk/ *adj.* **plethorically** /plɪ'θɒrɪkəlɪ/ *adv.* [LL f. Gk *plēthōrē* f. *plēthō* be full]

pleura¹ /'plʊərə/ *n.* (*pl.* **pleurae** /-ri:/) **1** each of a pair of serous membranes lining the thorax and enveloping the lungs in mammals. **2** lateral extensions of the body-wall in arthropods. □□ **pleural** *adj.* [med.L f. Gk, = side of the body, rib]

pleura² *pl.* of PLEURON.

pleurisy /'plʊərɪsɪ/ *n.* inflammation of the pleura, marked by pain in the chest or side, fever, etc. □□ **pleuritic** /-'rɪtɪk/ *adj.* [ME f. OF *pleurisie* f. LL *pleurisis* alt. f. L *pleuritis* f. Gk (as PLEURA¹)]

pleuro- /'plʊərəʊ/ *comb. form* **1** denoting the pleura. **2** denoting the side.

pleuron /'plʊərɒn/ *n.* (*pl.* **pleura** /-rə/) = PLEURA¹ 2. [Gk, = side of the body, rib]

pleuropneumonia /ˌplʊərəʊnju:'məʊnɪə/ *n.* pneumonia complicated with pleurisy.

Pleven /'plev(ə)n/ an industrial town in northern Bulgaria; pop. (1987) 133,750.

Plexiglas /'pleksɪˌglɑːs/ *n. propr.* = PERSPEX. [formed as PLEXOR + GLASS]

plexor /'pleksə(r)/ *n.* (also **plessor** /'plesə(r)/) *Med.* a small hammer used to test reflexes and in percussing. [irreg. f. Gk *plēxis* percussion + -OR¹]

plexus /'pleksəs/ *n.* (*pl.* same or **plexuses**) **1** *Anat.* a network of nerves or vessels in an animal body *(gastric plexus).* **2** any network or weblike formation. □□ **plexiform** *adj.* [L f. *plectere* plex- plait]

pliable /'plaɪəb(ə)l/ *adj.* **1** bending easily; supple. **2** yielding, compliant. □□ **pliability** /-'bɪlɪtɪ/ *n.* **pliableness** *n.* **pliably** *adv.* [F f. *plier* bend: see PLY¹]

pliant /'plaɪənt/ *adj.* = PLIABLE 1. □□ **pliancy** *n.* **pliantly** *adv.* [ME f. OF (as PLIABLE)]

plicate /'plaɪkeɪt/ *adj. Biol. & Geol.* folded, crumpled, corrugated. □□ **plicated** /plɪ'keɪtɪd/ *adj.* [L *plicatus* past part. of *plicare* fold]

plication /plɪ'keɪʃ(ə)n/ *n.* **1** the act of folding. **2** a fold; a folded condition. [ME f. med.L *plicatio* or L *plicare* fold, after *complication*]

plié /'pli:eɪ/ n. Ballet a bending of the knees with the feet on the ground. [F, past part. of plier bend: see PLY[1]]

pliers /'plaɪəz/ n.pl. pincers with parallel flat usu. serrated surfaces for holding small objects, bending wire, etc. [(dial.) ply bend (as PLIABLE)]

plight[1] /plaɪt/ n. a condition or state, esp. an unfortunate one. [ME & AF plit = OF pleit fold: see PLAIT: -gh- by confusion with PLIGHT[2]]

plight[2] /plaɪt/ v. & n. archaic —v.tr. 1 pledge or promise solemnly (one's faith, loyalty, etc.). 2 (foll. by to) engage, esp. in marriage. —n. an engagement or act of pledging. □ **plight one's troth** see TROTH. [orig. as noun, f. OE plint danger f. Gmc]

plimsoll /'plɪms(ə)l/ n. (also **plimsole**) Brit. a rubber-soled canvas sports shoe. [prob. from the resemblance of the side of the sole to a PLIMSOLL LINE]

Plimsoll line /'plɪms(ə)l/ n. (also **Plimsoll mark**) a marking on a ship's side showing the limit of legal submersion under various conditions. It is named after Samuel Plimsoll, the English politician (d. 1898) whose agitation in the 1870s resulted in the Merchant Shipping Act of 1876, putting an end to the practice of sending to sea overloaded and heavily insured old ships from which the owners made a profit if they sank.

plinth /plɪnθ/ n. 1 the lower square slab at the base of a column. 2 a base supporting a vase or statue etc. [F plinthe or L plinthus f. Gk plinthos tile, brick, squared stone]

Pliny[1] /'plɪnɪ/ 'the Elder' (Gaius Plinius Secundus, 23/4–79), Roman statesman, a scholar who combined a busy life in public affairs with prodigious activity in reading and writing. His *Natural History* is a vast encyclopaedia of the natural and human worlds, widely read in later ages. His scientific curiosity led to his death from suffocation while observing the eruption of Vesuvius in AD 79.

Pliny[2] /'plɪnɪ/ 'the Younger' (Gaius Plinius Caecilius Secundus, c.61–c.112), nephew of Pliny the Elder, Roman senator and writer who led a busy public life under a succession of emperors. Nine books of literary letters, carefully edited for publication, deal with a wide variety of public and private affairs; a tenth book contains his correspondence, as governor of Bithynia, with Trajan, and includes one of the earliest pagan accounts of the Christians.

Pliocene /'plaɪəˌsi:n/ adj. & n. Geol. —adj. of or relating to the last epoch of the Tertiary period, following the Miocene and preceding the Pleistocene, lasting from about 5.1 to 2 million years ago. It was a time when world temperatures were falling and many species of mammals that had flourished earlier in the Tertiary were becoming extinct. —n. this epoch or system. [Gk pleiōn more + kainos new]

plissé /'pli:seɪ/ adj. & n. —adj. (of cloth etc.) treated so as to cause permanent puckering. —n. material treated in this way. [F, past part. of plisser pleat]

PLO abbr. Palestine Liberation Organization.

plod /plɒd/ v. & n. —v. (**plodded, plodding**) 1 intr. (often foll. by along, on, etc.) walk doggedly or laboriously; trudge. 2 intr. (often foll. by at) work slowly and steadily. 3 tr. tread or make (one's way) laboriously. —n. the act or a spell of plodding. □□ **plodder** n. **ploddingly** adv. [16th c.: prob. imit.]

-ploid /plɔɪd/ comb. form Biol. forming adjectives denoting the number of sets of chromosomes in a cell (diploid; polyploid). [after HAPLOID]

ploidy /'plɔɪdɪ/ n. the number of sets of chromosomes in a cell. [after DIPLOIDY, POLYPLOIDY, etc.]

Ploiesti /plɔɪ'eʃt/ an oil-refining city in central Romania; pop. (1985) 234,000.

plonk[1] /plɒŋk/ v. & n. —v.tr. 1 set down hurriedly or clumsily. 2 (usu. foll. by down) set down firmly. —n. 1 an act of plonking. 2 a heavy thud. [imit.]

plonk[2] /plɒŋk/ n. colloq. cheap or inferior wine. [orig. Austral.: prob. corrupt. of blanc in F vin blanc white wine]

plop /plɒp/ n., v., & adv. —n. 1 a sound as of a smooth object dropping into water without a splash. 2 an act of falling with this sound. —v. (**plopped, plopping**) intr. & tr. fall or drop with a plop. —adv. with a plop. [19th c.: imit.]

plosion /'pləʊʒ(ə)n/ n. Phonet. the sudden release of breath in the pronunciation of a stop consonant. [EXPLOSION]

plosive /'pləʊsɪv/ adj. & n. Phonet. —adj. pronounced with a sudden release of breath. —n. a plosive sound. [EXPLOSIVE]

plot /plɒt/ n. & v. —n. 1 a defined and usu. small piece of ground. 2 the interrelationship of the main events in a play, novel, film, etc. 3 a conspiracy or secret plan, esp. to achieve an unlawful end. 4 esp. US a graph or diagram. 5 a graph showing the relation between two variables. —v. (**plotted, plotting**) tr. 1 make a plan or map of (an existing object, a place or thing to be laid out, constructed, etc.). 2 (also absol.) plan or contrive secretly (a crime, conspiracy, etc.). 3 mark (a point or course etc.) on a chart or diagram. 4 a mark out or allocate (points) on a graph. b make (a curve etc.) by marking out a number of points. □□ **plotless** adj. **plotlessness** n. **plotter** n. [OE and f. OF complot secret plan: both of unkn. orig.]

Plotinus /plə'taɪnəs/ (c.205–70) Greek philosopher, the founder and leading exponent of Neoplatonism. Born in Upper Egypt, he accompanied the emperor Gordian (d. 243) on a military expedition to Persia to acquaint himself with Eastern thought, and finally settled in Rome in 244, where he set up a school of philosophy. His writings were published after his death by his pupil Porphyry. (See NEOPLATONISM.)

plough /plaʊ/ n. & v. (esp. US **plow**) —n. 1 an implement with a cutting blade fixed in a frame drawn by a tractor or by horses, for cutting furrows in the soil and turning it up. (See below.) 2 an implement resembling this and having a comparable function (snowplough). 3 ploughed land. 4 (**the Plough**) the constellation Ursa Major or its seven bright stars, also known as the Great Bear. —v. 1 tr. (also absol.) turn up (the earth) with a plough, esp. before sowing. 2 tr. (foll. by out, up, down, etc.) turn or extract (roots, weeds, etc.) with a plough. 3 tr. furrow or scratch (a surface) as if with a plough. 4 tr. produce (a furrow or line) in this way. 5 intr. (foll. by through) advance laboriously, esp. through work, a book, etc. 6 intr. (foll. by through, into) move like a plough violently. 7 intr. & tr. Brit. colloq. fail in an examination. □ **plough back** 1 plough (grass etc.) into the soil to enrich it. 2 reinvest (profits) in the business producing them. **Plough Monday** the first Monday after the Epiphany. **put one's hand to the plough** undertake a task (Luke 9: 62). □□ **ploughable** adj. **plougher** n. [OE plōh f. ON plógr f. Gmc]

One of the earliest agricultural tools, the plough is used to loosen and aerate the soil, to bury stubble and weeds, and to expose fresh soil to weathering so that it can be harrowed into a good seed-bed. The essential parts of a plough are a coulter (a vertical knife which cuts a thin vertical slice), a share, which cuts a horizontal slice below the earth to be turned by the mould-board or breast, thus exposing a furrow which is subsequently filled by the next slice of turned earth. The first ploughs were made of wood; later, metal reinforcement was introduced, and finally all-metal ploughs came into use in the 18th c. An important development was the use of chilled cast iron, which resists abrasion, for the ploughshare. Disc ploughs consist of a row of concave discs which break up the surface layer in hard dry soils and leave enough stubble to bind the surface soil and so prevent erosion by wind. Animal traction was used from 2000 BC onwards and is still widespread in developing countries. Steam engines were developed during the 19th c. in England to haul ploughs of up to 8-furrow capacity by means of winches and cables, but were replaced in the 20th c. by tractors. Most modern ploughs are mounted on the rear of a tractor and the depth of the furrow is controlled hydraulically.

ploughman /'plaʊmən/ n. (pl. **-men**) a person who uses a plough. □ **ploughman's lunch** a meal of bread and cheese with pickle or salad. **ploughman's spikenard** a composite fragrant plant, Inula conyzae, with purplish-yellow flowerheads.

ploughshare /'plaʊʃeə(r)/ n. the cutting blade of a plough.

Plovdiv /'plɒvdɪf/ the second-largest city in Bulgaria; pop. (1987) 356,600.

plover /'plʌvə(r)/ n. any plump-breasted wading bird of the family Charadriidae, including the lapwing, usu. having a pigeon-like bill. [ME & AF f. OF plo(u)vier ult. f. L pluvia rain]

plow US var. of PLOUGH.

ploy /plɔɪ/ n. colloq. a stratagem; a cunning manoeuvre to gain an advantage. [orig. Sc., 18th c.: orig. unkn.]

PLP abbr. (in the UK) Parliamentary Labour Party.

PLR abbr. (in the UK) Public Lending Right.

pluck /plʌk/ v. & n. —v. 1 tr. (often foll. by out, off, etc.) remove by picking or pulling out or away. 2 tr. strip (a bird) of feathers. 3 tr. pull at, twitch. 4 intr. (foll. by at) tug or snatch at. 5 tr. sound (the string of a musical instrument) with the finger or plectrum etc. 6 tr. plunder. 7 tr. swindle. —n. 1 courage, spirit. 2 an act of plucking; a twitch. 3 the heart, liver, and lungs of an animal as food. □ **pluck up** summon up (one's courage, spirits, etc.). □□ **plucker** n. **pluckless** adj. [OE ploccian, pluccian, f. Gmc]

plucky /ˈplʌkɪ/ adj. (**pluckier, pluckiest**) brave, spirited. □□ **pluckily** adv. **pluckiness** n.

plug /plʌg/ n. & v. —n. 1 a piece of solid material fitting tightly into a hole, used to fill a gap or cavity or act as a wedge or stopper. 2 **a** a device of metal pins in an insulated casing fitting into holes in a socket for making an electrical connection, esp. between an appliance and the mains. **b** colloq. an electric socket. 3 = sparking-plug (see SPARK[1]). 4 colloq. a piece of (often free) publicity for an idea, product, etc. 5 a mass of solidified lava filling the neck of a volcano. 6 a cake or stick of tobacco; a piece of this for chewing. 7 = fire-plug. —v. (**plugged, plugging**) 1 tr. (often foll. by up) stop (a hole etc.) with a plug. 2 tr. sl. shoot or hit (a person etc.). 3 tr. colloq. seek to popularize (an idea, product, etc.) by constant recommendation. 4 intr. colloq. (often foll. by at) work steadily away (at). □ **plug in** connect electrically by inserting a plug in a socket. **plug-in** adj. able to be connected by means of a plug. **plug-ugly** US sl. n. (pl. **-ies**) a thug or ruffian. —adj. villainous-looking. □□ **plugger** n. [MDu. & MLG plugge, of unkn. orig.]

plum /plʌm/ n. 1 **a** an oval fleshy fruit, usu. purple or yellow when ripe, with sweet pulp and a flattish pointed stone. **b** any deciduous tree of the genus Prunus bearing this. 2 a reddish-purple colour. 3 a dried grape or raisin used in cooking. 4 colloq. the best of a collection; something especially prized (often attrib.: a plum job). □ **plum cake** a cake containing raisins, currants, etc. **plum duff** a plain flour pudding with raisins or currants. **plum pudding** a rich boiled suet pudding with raisins, currants, spices, etc. [OE plūme f. med.L pruna f. L prunum]

plumage /ˈpluːmɪdʒ/ n. a bird's feathers. □□ **plumaged** adj. (usu. in comb.). [ME f. OF (as PLUME)]

plumassier /ˌpluːmæˈsɪə(r)/ n. a person who trades or works in ornamental feathers. [F f. plumasse augment. of plume PLUME]

plumb[1] /plʌm/ n., adv., adj., & v. —n. a ball of lead or other heavy material, esp. one attached to the end of a line for finding the depth of water or determining the vertical on an upright surface. —adv. 1 exactly (plumb in the centre). 2 vertically. 3 US sl. quite, utterly (plumb crazy). —adj. 1 vertical. 2 downright, sheer (plumb nonsense). 3 Cricket (of the wicket) level, true. —v.tr. 1 **a** measure the depth of (water) with a plumb. **b** determine (a depth). 2 test (an upright surface) to determine the vertical. 3 reach or experience in extremes (plumb the depths of fear). 4 learn in detail the facts about (a matter). □ **out of plumb** not vertical. **plumb-line** a line with a plumb attached. **plumb-rule** a mason's plumb-line attached to a board. [ME, prob. ult. f. L plumbum lead, assim. to OF plomb lead]

plumb[2] /plʌm/ v. 1 tr. provide (a building or room etc.) with plumbing. 2 tr. (often foll. by in) fit as part of a plumbing system. 3 intr. work as a plumber. [back-form. f. PLUMBER]

plumbago /plʌmˈbeɪɡəʊ/ n. (pl. **-os**) 1 = GRAPHITE. 2 any plant of the genus Plumbago, with grey or blue flowers. Also called LEADWORT. [L f. plumbum LEAD[2]]

plumbeous /ˈplʌmbɪəs/ adj. 1 of or like lead. 2 lead-glazed. [L plumbeus f. plumbum LEAD[2]]

plumber /ˈplʌmə(r)/ n. a person who fits and repairs the apparatus of a water-supply, heating, etc. [ME plummer etc. f. OF plommier f. L plumbarius f. plumbum LEAD[2]]

plumbic /ˈplʌmbɪk/ adj. 1 Chem. containing lead esp. in its tetravalent form. 2 Med. due to the presence of lead. □□ **plumbism** n. (in sense 2). [L plumbum lead]

plumbing /ˈplʌmɪŋ/ n. 1 the system or apparatus of water-supply, heating, etc., in a building. 2 the work of a plumber. 3 colloq. lavatory installations.

plumbless /ˈplʌmlɪs/ adj. (of a depth of water etc.) that cannot be plumbed.

plumbous /ˈplʌmbəs/ n. Chem. containing lead in its divalent form.

plume /pluːm/ n. & v. —n. 1 a feather, esp. a large one used for ornament. 2 an ornament of feathers etc. attached to a helmet or hat or worn in the hair. 3 something resembling this (a plume of smoke). 4 Zool. a feather-like part or formation. —v. 1 tr. decorate or provide with a plume or plumes. 2 refl. (foll. by on, upon) pride (oneself on esp. something trivial). 3 tr. (of a bird) preen (itself or its feathers). □□ **plumeless** adj. **plumelike** adj. **plumery** n. [ME f. OF f. L pluma down]

plummet /ˈplʌmɪt/ n. & v. —n. 1 a plumb or plumb-line. 2 a sounding-line. 3 a weight attached to a fishing-line to keep the float upright. —v.intr. (**plummeted, plummeting**) fall or plunge rapidly. [ME f. OF plommet dimin. (as PLUMB[1])]

plummy /ˈplʌmɪ/ adj. (**plummier, plummiest**) 1 abounding or rich in plums. 2 colloq. (of a voice) sounding affectedly rich or deep in tone. 3 colloq. good, desirable.

plumose /ˈpluːməʊs/ adj. 1 feathered. 2 feather-like. [L plumosus (as PLUME)]

plump[1] /plʌmp/ adj. & v. —adj. (esp. of a person or animal or part of the body) having a full rounded shape; fleshy; filled out. —v.tr. & intr. (often foll. by up, out) make or become plump; fatten. □□ **plumpish** adj. **plumply** adv. **plumpness** n. **plumpy** adj. [ME plompe f. MDu. plomp blunt, MLG plump, plomp shapeless etc.]

plump[2] /plʌmp/ v., n., adv., & adj. —v. 1 intr. & tr. (often foll. by down) drop or fall abruptly (plumped down on the chair; plumped it on the floor). 2 intr. (foll. by for) decide definitely in favour of (one of two or more possibilities). 3 tr. (often foll. by out) utter abruptly; blurt out. —n. an abrupt plunge; a heavy fall. —adv. colloq. 1 with a sudden or heavy fall. 2 directly, bluntly (I told him plump). —adj. colloq. direct, unqualified (answered with a plump 'no'). [ME f. MLG plumpen, MDu. plompen: orig. imit.]

plumule /ˈpluːmjuːl/ n. 1 the rudimentary shoot or stem of an embryo plant. 2 a down feather on a young bird. □□ **plumulaceous** /ˌpluːmjʊˈleɪʃəs/ adj. (in sense 2). **plumular** /ˈpluːmjʊlə(r)/ adj. (in sense 1). [F plumule or L plumula, dimin. (as PLUME)]

plumy /ˈpluːmɪ/ adj. (**plumier, plumiest**) 1 plumelike, feathery. 2 adorned with plumes.

plunder /ˈplʌndə(r)/ v. & n. —v.tr. 1 rob (a place or person) forcibly of goods, e.g. as in war. 2 rob systematically. 3 (also absol.) steal or embezzle (goods). —n. 1 the violent or dishonest acquisition of property. 2 property acquired by plundering. 3 colloq. profit, gain. □□ **plunderer** n. [LG plündern lit. 'rob of household goods' f. MHG plunder clothing etc.]

plunge /plʌndʒ/ v. & n. —v. 1 (usu. foll. by in, into) **a** tr. thrust forcefully or abruptly. **b** intr. dive; propel oneself forcibly. **c** intr. & tr. enter or cause to enter a certain condition or embark on a certain course abruptly or impetuously (they plunged into a lively discussion; the room was plunged into darkness). 2 tr. immerse completely. 3 intr. **a** move suddenly and dramatically downward. **b** (foll. by down, into, etc.) move with a rush (plunged down the stairs). **c** diminish rapidly (share prices have plunged). 4 intr. (of a horse) start violently forward. 5 intr. (of a ship) pitch. 6 intr. colloq. gamble heavily; run into debt. —n. a plunging action or movement; a dive. □ **plunging** (or **plunge**) **neckline** a low-cut neckline. **take the plunge** colloq. commit oneself to a (usu. risky) course of action. [ME f. OF plungier ult. f. L plumbum plummet]

plunger /ˈplʌndʒə(r)/ n. 1 a part of a mechanism that works with a plunging or thrusting movement. 2 a rubber cup on a handle for clearing blocked pipes by a plunging and sucking action. 3 colloq. a reckless gamble.

plunk /plʌŋk/ n. & v. —n. 1 the sound made by the sharply plucked string of a stringed instrument. 2 US a heavy blow. 3 US = PLONK[1] n. —v. 1 intr. & tr. sound or cause to sound with a plunk. 2 tr. US hit abruptly. 3 tr. US = PLONK[1] v. [imit.]

pluperfect /pluː'pɜːfɪkt/ adj. & n. Gram. —adj. (of a tense) denoting an action completed prior to some past point of time specified or implied, formed in English by had and the past participle, as: he had gone by then. —n. the pluperfect tense. [mod.L plusperfectum f. L plus quam perfectum more than perfect]

plural /'plʊər(ə)l/ adj. & n. —adj. 1 more than one in number. 2 Gram. (of a word or form) denoting more than one, or (in languages with dual number) more than two. —n. Gram. 1 a plural word or form. 2 the plural number. □□ **plurally** adv. [ME f. OF plurel f. L pluralis f. plus pluris more]

pluralism /'plʊərə,lɪz(ə)m/ n. 1 holding more than one office, esp. an ecclesiastical office or benefice, at a time. 2 a form of society in which the members of minority groups maintain their independent cultural traditions. 3 Philos. a system that recognizes more than one ultimate principle or kind of being (cf. MONISM 2); (in moral philosophy) the theory that there is more than one value and that they cannot be reduced one to another. □□ **pluralist** n. **pluralistic** /-'lɪstɪk/ adj. **pluralistically** /-'lɪstɪkəlɪ/ adv.

plurality /plʊə'rælɪtɪ/ n. (pl. -ies) 1 the state of being plural. 2 = PLURALISM 1. 3 a large or the greater number. 4 US a majority that is not absolute. [ME f. OF pluralité f. LL pluralitas (as PLURAL)]

pluralize /'plʊərə,laɪz/ v. (also -ise) 1 tr. & intr. make or become plural. 2 tr. express in the plural. 3 intr. hold more than one ecclesiastical office or benefice.

pluri- /'plʊərɪ/ comb. form several. [L plus pluris more, plures several]

plus /plʌs/ prep., adj., n., & conj. —prep. 1 Math. with the addition of (3 plus 4 equals 7). ¶ Symbol: +. 2 (of temperature) above zero (plus 2° C). 3 colloq. with; having gained; newly possessing (returned plus a new car). —adj. 1 (after a number) at least (fifteen plus). 2 (after a grade etc.) rather better than (beta plus). 3 Math. positive. 4 having a positive electrical charge. 5 (attrib.) additional, extra (plus business). —n. 1 = plus sign. 2 Math. an additional or positive quantity. 3 an advantage (experience is a definite plus). —conj. colloq. disp. also; and furthermore (they arrived late, plus they were hungry). □ **plus sign** the symbol +, indicating addition or a positive value. [L, = more]

plus-fours /plʌs'fɔːz/ n. pl. men's long wide knickerbockers usu. worn for golf etc. [20th c.: so named because the overhang at the knee requires an extra four inches]

plush /plʌʃ/ n. & adj. —n. cloth of silk or cotton etc., with a long soft nap. —adj. 1 made of plush. 2 plushy. □□ **plushly** adv. **plushness** n. [obs. F pluche contr. f. peluche f. OF peluchier f. It. peluzzo dimin. of pelo f. L pilus hair]

plushy /'plʌʃɪ/ adj. (**plushier**, **plushiest**) colloq. stylish, luxurious. □□ **plushiness** n.

Plutarch /'pluːtɑːk/ (Lucius Mestrius Plutarchus, c.46– c.120) Greek Platonist philosopher and biographer, for the latter part of his life a priest at Delphi. He was a prolific writer, producing a varied collection of rhetorical, antiquarian, religious, and philosophical works, including short treatises on themes of popular moral philosophy, derivative in content, with his warm and sympathetic personality never far beneath the surface. His most influential work was the Lives of great men, tantalizing and treacherous to the historian but winning the affection of many generations by his vivid and memorable narrative, a mine of information about the ancient world. Montaigne, Shakespeare, Dryden, and Rousseau are among his debtors.

plutarchy /'pluːtɑːkɪ/ n. (pl. -ies) plutocracy. [Gk ploutos wealth + -arkhia -rule]

Pluto /'pluːtəʊ/ 1 Gk Mythol. see HADES. 2 Astron. the ninth planet of the solar system, discovered in 1930 by Clyde Tombaugh, following analysis of perturbations in the orbit of Neptune which were attributed to the gravitational influence of a then unknown planet. Although these calculations predicted a position close to where Pluto was discovered, it is now believed that Pluto is too small a body (diameter about 2,500 km) to have produced the measured perturbations, so that its discovery may have been serendipitous. Its orbit lies well out of the ecliptic plane in which the other planets lie, and is furthermore highly eccentric, so that its closest approach to the sun brings it within

the orbit of Neptune. It was discovered in 1978 to have one satellite, Charon. [Gk Ploutōn f. ploutos wealth (because wealth comes from the earth)]

plutocracy /pluː'tɒkrəsɪ/ n. (pl. -ies) 1 a government by the wealthy. b a State governed in this way. 2 a wealthy élite or ruling class. □□ **plutocratic** /,pluːtə'krætɪk/ adj. **plutocratically** /,pluːtə'krætɪkəlɪ/ adv. [Gk ploutokratia f. ploutos wealth + -CRACY]

plutocrat /'pluːtə,kræt/ n. derog. or joc. 1 a member of a plutocracy or wealthy élite. 2 a wealthy and influential person.

pluton /'pluːt(ə)n/ n. Geol. a body of plutonic rock. [back-form. f. PLUTONIC]

Plutonian /pluː'təʊnɪən/ adj. 1 infernal. 2 of the infernal regions. [L Plutonius f. Gk Ploutōnios (as PLUTO)]

plutonic /pluː'tɒnɪk/ adj. 1 Geol. a (of rock) formed as igneous rock by solidification below the surface of the earth. b attributing most geological phenomena to the action of internal heat (opp. Neptunian). 2 (**Plutonic**) = PLUTONIAN. [formed as PLUTONIAN]

Plutonist /'pluːtənɪst/ n. a person (esp. in the 18th c.) maintaining the plutonic theory (see PLUTONIC 1 b; opp. Neptunist).

plutonium /pluː'təʊnɪəm/ n. Chem. a dense silvery radioactive metallic transuranic element of the actinide series, first obtained in 1940 by bombarding uranium with deuterons, and since found in trace amounts in nature. There are several isotopes. Plutonium was discovered in the course of the development of the atomic bomb, and the weapon exploded at Nagasaki in 1945 was a plutonium bomb. The use of plutonium as a nuclear fuel is economically important because it can be manufactured in nuclear reactors from the commonest but non-fissile isotope of uranium, 'uranium-238'. ¶ Symb.: Pu; atomic number 94. [PLUTO (as the next planet beyond Neptune) + -IUM]

pluvial /'pluːvɪəl/ adj. & n. —adj. 1 of rain; rainy. 2 Geol. caused by rain; of periods of relatively high average rainfall in low and intermediate latitudes during the geological past (especially in the Pleistocene epoch) which alternated with interpluvial periods in a cycle which may be correlated with or related to the better-known cycle of glacial and interglacial periods in higher latitudes. —n. a period of prolonged rainfall, especially in the Pleistocene epoch. □□ **pluvious** adj. (in sense 1). [L pluvialis f. pluvia rain]

pluviometer /,pluːvɪ'ɒmɪtə(r)/ n. a rain-gauge. □□ **pluviometric** /-ə'metrɪk/ adj. **pluviometrical** /-ə'metrɪk(ə)l/ adj. **pluviometrically** /-ə'metrɪkəlɪ/ adv. [L pluvia rain + -METER]

ply[1] /plaɪ/ n. (pl. -ies) 1 a thickness or layer of certain materials, esp. wood or cloth (three-ply). 2 a strand of yarn or rope etc. [ME f. F pli f. plier, pleier f. L plicare fold]

ply[2] /plaɪ/ v. (-ies, -ied) 1 tr. use or wield vigorously (a tool, weapon, etc.). 2 tr. work steadily at (one's business or trade). 3 tr. (foll. by with) a supply (a person) continuously (with food, drink, etc.). b approach repeatedly (with questions, demands, etc.). 4 a intr. (often foll. by between) (of a vehicle etc.) travel regularly (to and fro between two points). b tr. work (a route) in this way. 5 intr. (of a taxi-driver, boatman, etc.) attend regularly for custom (ply for trade). 6 intr. sail to windward. [ME plye, f. APPLY]

Plymouth[1] /'plɪməθ/ a port and naval base on the Devonshire coast in SW England; pop. (1981) 242,550. Drake is said to have played bowls here before leaving to fight the Spanish Armada (1588), and he and other Elizabethan explorers sailed from Plymouth Sound. In 1620 the Pilgrim Fathers sailed from here in the Mayflower.

Plymouth[2] /'plɪməθ/ the capital of the island of Montserrat in the West Indies; pop. (1985) 3,500.

Plymouth Brethren /'plɪməθ/ n. pl. a Christian denomination with no formal creed and no official order of ministers, named after its first centre, established in 1830 by J. N. Darby at Plymouth in Devon. Its teaching combines elements of Calvinism and Pietism, and emphasis is often placed on an expected millennium. Of austere outlook, members renounce many secular occupations, allowing only those compatible with New Testament standards. Controversies within the movement led in 1849 to a division between the 'Open Brethren' and the 'Exclusive Brethren'.

Plymouth Rock /ˈplɪməθ/ a granite boulder at Plymouth, Mass., on which the Pilgrim Fathers are supposed to have stepped from the *Mayflower*.

plywood /ˈplaɪwʊd/ n. a strong thin board consisting of two or more layers glued and pressed together with the direction of the grain alternating.

PM abbr. **1** Prime Minister. **2** post-mortem. **3** Provost Marshal.

Pm symb. Chem. the element promethium.

p.m. abbr. after noon. [L post meridiem]

PMG abbr. **1** Paymaster General. **2** Postmaster General.

PMT abbr. premenstrual tension.

PNdB abbr. perceived noise decibel(s).

pneumatic /njuːˈmætɪk/ adj. & n. —adj. **1** of or relating to air or wind. **2** containing or operated by compressed air. **3** connected with or containing air cavities esp. in the bones of birds or in fish. □ **pneumatic drill** a drill driven by compressed air, for breaking up a hard surface. **pneumatic trough** a shallow container used in laboratories to collect gases in jars over the surface of water or mercury. **pneumatic tyre** a tyre inflated with air. The first pneumatic tyres, with an air-filled inner tube, were invented in 1845 by a Scottish engineer, R. W. Thomson, but proved expensive to make and awkward to fit; the idea lapsed until 1888 when J. B. Dunlop (see entry) made some for his son's tricycle, and they were soon in wide use. □□ **pneumatically** adv. **pneumaticity** /ˌnjuːməˈtɪsɪtɪ/ n. [F pneumatique or L pneumaticus f. Gk pneumatikos f. pneuma wind f. pneō breathe]

pneumatics /njuːˈmætɪks/ n.pl. (treated as sing.) the science of the mechanical properties of gases.

pneumato- /ˈnjuːmətəʊ/ comb. form denoting: **1** air. **2** breath. **3** spirit. [Gk f. pneuma (as PNEUMATIC)]

pneumatology /ˌnjuːməˈtɒlədʒɪ/ n. **1** the branch of theology concerned with the Holy Ghost and other spiritual concepts. **2** archaic psychology. □□ **pneumatological** /-təˈlɒdʒɪk(ə)l/ adj.

pneumatophore /ˈnjuːmətəˌfɔː(r)/ n. **1** the gaseous cavity of various hydrozoa, such as the Portuguese man-of-war. **2** an aerial root specialized for gaseous exchange found in various plants growing in swampy areas.

pneumo- /ˈnjuːməʊ/ comb. form denoting the lungs. [abbr. of pneumono- f. Gk pneumōn lung]

pneumoconiosis /ˌnjuːməʊˌkɒnɪˈəʊsɪs/ n. a lung disease caused by inhalation of dust or small particles. [PNEUMO- + Gk konis dust]

pneumogastric /ˌnjuːməʊˈgæstrɪk/ adj. of or relating to the lungs and stomach.

pneumonectomy /ˌnjuːməˈnektəmɪ/ n. (pl. -ies) Surgery the surgical removal of a lung or part of a lung.

pneumonia /njuːˈməʊnɪə/ n. a bacterial inflammation of one lung (**single pneumonia**) or both lungs (**double pneumonia**) causing the air sacs to fill with pus and become solid. □□ **pneumonic** /njuːˈmɒnɪk/ adj. [L f. Gk f. pneumōn lung]

pneumonitis /ˌnjuːməˈnaɪtɪs/ n. inflammation of the lungs usu. caused by a virus.

pneumothorax /ˌnjuːməʊˈθɔːræks/ n. the presence of air or gas in the cavity between the lungs and the chest wall.

PNG abbr. Papua New Guinea.

PO abbr. **1** Post Office. **2** postal order. **3** Petty Officer. **4** Pilot Officer.

Po[1] symb. Chem. the element polonium.

Po[2] /pəʊ/ Italy's longest river, flowing eastward for nearly 670 km (416 miles) from the Alps to the Adriatic Sea.

po /pəʊ/ n. (pl. pos) Brit. colloq. a chamber-pot.

POA abbr. (in the UK) Prison Officers' Association.

poach[1] /pəʊtʃ/ v.tr. **1** cook (an egg) without its shell in or over boiling water. **2** cook (fish etc.) by simmering in a small amount of liquid. □□ **poacher** n. [ME f. OF pochier f. poche POKE[2]]

poach[2] /pəʊtʃ/ v. **1** tr. (also absol.) catch (game or fish) illegally. **2** intr. (often foll. by on) trespass or encroach (on another's property, ideas, etc.). **3** tr. appropriate illicitly or unfairly (a person, thing, idea, etc.). **4** tr. Tennis etc. take (a shot) in one's partner's portion of the court. **5 a** tr. trample or cut up (turf) with hoofs. **b** intr. (of land) become sodden by being trampled. □□ **poacher** n. [earlier poche, perh. f. F pocher put in a pocket (as POACH[1])]

Pocahontas /ˌpɒkəˈhɒntəs/ the daughter of Powhatan, an American Indian chief in Virginia. According to the story of an English colonist, Captain John Smith, she rescued him from death at the hands of her father who had captured him. She was seized as a hostage in 1612, and married a colonist, John Rolfe. In 1616 she was taken to England, where she died.

pochard /ˈpəʊtʃəd/ n. any duck of the genus Aythya, esp. A. ferina, the male of which has a bright reddish-brown head and neck and a grey breast. [16th c.: orig. unkn.]

pochette /pɒˈʃet/ n. a woman's envelope-shaped handbag. [F, dimin. of poche pocket: see POKE[2]]

pock /pɒk/ n. (also **pock-mark**) **1** a small pus-filled spot on the skin, esp. caused by chickenpox or smallpox. **2** a mark resembling this. □ **pock-marked** bearing marks resembling or left by such spots. □□ **pocky** adj. [OE poc f. Gmc]

pocket /ˈpɒkɪt/ n. & v. —n. **1** a small bag sewn into or on clothing, for carrying small articles. **2** a pouchlike compartment in a suitcase, car door, etc. **3** one's financial resources (it is beyond my pocket). **4** an isolated group or area (a few pockets of resistance remain). **5 a** a cavity in the earth containing ore, esp. gold. **b** a cavity in rock, esp. filled with foreign matter. **6** a pouch at the corner or on the side of a billiard- or snooker-table into which balls are driven. **7** = air pocket. **8** (attrib.) **a** of a suitable size and shape for carrying in a pocket. **b** smaller than the usual size. —v.tr. (**pocketed, pocketing**) **1** put into one's pocket. **2** appropriate, esp. dishonestly. **3** confine as in a pocket. **4** submit to (an injury or affront). **5** conceal or suppress (one's feelings). **6** Billiards etc. drive (a ball) into a pocket. □ **in pocket 1** having gained in a transaction. **2** (of money) available. **in a person's pocket 1** under a person's control. **2** close to or intimate with a person. **out of pocket** having lost in a transaction. **out-of-pocket expenses** the actual outlay of cash incurred. **pocket battleship** hist. a warship armoured and equipped like, but smaller than, a battleship. **pocket borough** see BOROUGH. **pocket gopher** = GOPHER[1] 1. **pocket knife** a knife with a folding blade or blades, for carrying in the pocket. **pocket money 1** money for minor expenses. **2** Brit. an allowance of money made to a child. **put one's hand in one's pocket** spend or provide money. □□ **pocketable** adj. **pocketless** adj. **pockety** adj. (in sense 5 of n.). [ME f. AF poket(e) dimin. of poke POKE[2]]

pocketbook /ˈpɒkɪtˌbʊk/ n. **1** a notebook. **2** a booklike case for papers or money carried in a pocket. **3** US a purse or handbag. **4** US a paperback or other small book.

pocketful /ˈpɒkɪtˌfʊl/ n. (pl. -fuls) as much as a pocket will hold.

poco /ˈpəʊkəʊ/ adv. Mus. a little; rather (poco adagio). [It.]

pod /pɒd/ n. & v. —n. **1** a long seed-vessel esp. of a leguminous plant, e.g. a pea. **2** the cocoon of a silkworm. **3** the case surrounding locust eggs. **4** a narrow-necked eel-net. **5** a compartment suspended under an aircraft for equipment etc. —v. (**podded, podding**) **1** intr. bear or form pods. **2** tr. remove (peas etc.) from pods. □ **in pod** colloq. pregnant. [back-form. f. dial. podware, podder field crops, of unkn. orig.]

podagra /pəˈdægrə, ˈpɒdəgrə/ n. Med. gout of the foot, esp. the big toe. □□ **podagral** adj. **podagric** adj. **podagrous** adj. [L f. Gk pous podos foot + agra seizure]

podgy /ˈpɒdʒɪ/ adj. (**podgier, podgiest**) **1** (of a person) short and fat. **2** (of a face etc.) plump, fleshy. □□ **podginess** n. [19th c.: f. podge a short fat person]

podiatry /pəˈdaɪətrɪ/ n. US = CHIROPODY. □□ **podiatrist** n. [Gk pous podos foot + iatros physician]

podium /ˈpəʊdɪəm/ n. (pl. **podiums** or **podia** /-dɪə/) **1** a continuous projecting base or pedestal round a room or house etc. **2** a raised platform round the arena of an amphitheatre. **3** a platform or rostrum. [L f. Gk podion dimin. of pous pod- foot]

podzol /ˈpɒdzɒl/ n. (also **podsol** /-sɒl/) a soil with minerals

leached from its surface layers into a lower stratum. □□
podzolize v.tr. & intr. (also **-ise**). [Russ. f. pod under, zola ashes]

Poe /pəʊ/, Edgar Allan (1809-49), American short-story writer, poet, and critic. His first collection Tales of the Grotesque and Arabesque (1839/40) contains his famous gothic romance 'The Fall of the House of Usher'. His poem 'The Raven' (1845) brought him fame but not fortune, and his family suffered continuing poverty and ill health, while Poe struggled with alcohol addiction. His posthumous reputation and influence has been great: Freudian critics have been intrigued by the macabre and pathological elements in his works, ranging from necrophilia in his poem 'Annabel Lee' (1849) to the sadism of 'The Pit and the Pendulum' (1843). His other stories include the first detective story, 'The Murders in the Rue Morgue' (1841). Of his critical writings the most influential was 'The Philosophy of Composition' (1846); 'The Poetic Principle' (1850) preaches a form of 'art for art's sake'.

poem /ˈpəʊɪm/ n. 1 a metrical composition, usu. concerned with feeling or imaginative description. 2 an elevated composition in verse or prose. 3 something with poetic qualities (a poem in stone). [F poème or L poema f. Gk poēma = poiēma f. poieō make]

poesy /ˈpəʊɪzɪ/ n. archaic 1 poetry. 2 the art or composition of poetry. [ME f. OF poesie ult. f. L poesis f. Gk poēsis = poiēsis making, poetry (as POEM)]

poet /ˈpəʊɪt/ n. (fem. **poetess**) 1 a writer of poems. 2 a person possessing high powers of imagination or expression etc. □ **Poet Laureate** see LAUREATE. **Poets' Corner** part of Westminster Abbey where several poets are buried or commemorated. [ME f. OF poete f. L poeta f. Gk poētēs = poiētēs maker, poet (as POEM)]

poetaster /ˌpəʊɪˈtæstə(r)/ n. a paltry or inferior poet. [mod.L (as POET): see -ASTER]

poetic /pəʊˈetɪk/ adj. (also **poetical** /-tɪk(ə)l/) 1 a of or like poetry or poets. b written in verse. 2 elevated or sublime in expression. □ **poetic justice** well-deserved unforeseen retribution or reward. **poetic licence** a writer's or artist's transgression of established rules for effect. □□ **poetically** adv. [F poétique f. L poeticus f. Gk poētikos (as POET)]

poeticize /pəʊˈetɪˌsaɪz/ v.tr. (also **-ise**) make (a theme) poetic.

poetics /pəʊˈetɪks/ n. 1 the art of writing poetry. 2 the study of poetry and its techniques.

poetize /ˈpəʊɪˌtaɪz/ v. (also **-ise**) 1 intr. play the poet. 2 intr. compose poetry. 3 tr. treat poetically. 4 tr. celebrate in poetry. [F poétiser (as POET)]

poetry /ˈpəʊɪtrɪ/ n. 1 the art or work of a poet. 2 poems collectively. 3 a poetic or tenderly pleasing quality. 4 anything compared to poetry. [ME f. med.L poetria f. L poeta POET, prob. after geometry]

po-faced /pəʊˈfeɪsd/ adj. 1 solemn-faced, humourless. 2 smug. [20th c.: perh. f. PO, infl. by poker-faced]

pogo /ˈpəʊgəʊ/ n. (pl. **-os**) (also **pogo stick**) a toy consisting of a spring-loaded stick with rests for the feet, for springing about on. [20th c.: orig. uncert.]

pogrom /ˈpɒgrəm, -rɒm/ n. an organized massacre (orig. of Jews in Russia). [Russ., = devastation f. gromit' destroy]

poignant /ˈpɔɪnjənt/ adj. 1 painfully sharp to the emotions or senses; deeply moving. 2 arousing sympathy. 3 pleasantly pungent in taste or smell. 4 pleasantly piquant. □□ **poignance** n. **poignancy** n. **poignantly** adv. [ME f. OF, pres. part. of poindre prick f. L pungere]

poikilotherm /ˈpɔɪkɪləˌθɜːm/ n. an organism that regulates its body temperature by behavioural means, such as basking or burrowing; a cold-blooded organism (cf. HOMOEOTHERM). □□ **poikilothermal** /-ˈθɜːm(ə)l/ adj. **poikilothermia** /-ˈθɜːmɪə/ n. **poikilothermic** /-ˈθɜːmɪk/ adj. **poikilothermy** n. [Gk poikilos multicoloured, changeable + thermē heat]

poilu /pwaːˈluː/ n. hist. a French private soldier, esp. as a nickname. [F, lit. hairy f. poil hair]

Poincaré /ˈpwæŋkaːˌreɪ/, Jules-Henri (1854-1912), French mathematician and philosopher of science who made far-reaching contributions to pure and applied mathematics. He worked extensively on differential equations which allowed him to transform celestial mechanics (the branch of astronomy concerned with the movement of celestial bodies under the influence of gravitational forces), and was one of the pioneers of algebraic topology. By 1900 he was proposing a relativistic philosophy, suggesting that a consequence of this was the absolute velocity of light which nothing could exceed. His cousin Raymond was President of France during the First World War.

poinciana /ˌpɔɪnsɪˈaːnə/ n. any tropical tree of the genus Poinciana, with bright showy red flowers. [mod.L f. M. de Poinci, 17th-c. governor in the West Indies + -ana fem. suffix]

poind /pɔɪnd/ v. & n. Sc. —v.tr. distrain upon; impound. —n. 1 an act of poinding. 2 an animal or chattel poinded. [ME f. OE pyndan impound]

poinsettia /pɔɪnˈsetɪə/ n. a shrub, Euphorbia pulcherrima, with large showy scarlet or pink bracts surrounding small yellow flowers. [mod.L f. J. R. Poinsett, Amer. diplomat d. 1851]

point /pɔɪnt/ n. & v. —n. 1 the sharp or tapered end of a tool, weapon, pencil, etc. 2 a tip or extreme end. 3 that which in geometry has position but not magnitude, e.g. the intersection of two lines. 4 a particular place or position (Bombay and points east; point of contact). 5 a a precise or particular moment (at the point of death). b the critical or decisive moment (when it came to the point, he refused). 6 a very small mark on a surface. 7 a a dot or other punctuation mark, esp. = full point = FULL¹. b a dot or small stroke used in Semitic languages to indicate vowels or distinguish consonants. 8 = decimal point. 9 a stage or degree in progress or increase (abrupt to the point of rudeness; at that point we gave up). 10 a level of temperature at which a change of state occurs (freezing-point). 11 a single item; a detail or particular (we differ on these points; it is a point of principle). 12 a a unit of scoring in games or of measuring value etc. b an advantage or success in less quantifiable contexts such as an argument or discussion. c a unit of weight (2 mg) for diamonds. d a unit (of varying value) in quoting the price of stocks etc. 13 a (usu. prec. by the) the significant or essential thing; what is actually intended or under discussion (that was the point of the question). b (usu. with neg. or interrog.; often foll. by in) sense or purpose; advantage or value (saw no point in staying). c (usu. prec. by the) a salient feature of a story, joke, remark, etc. (don't see the point). 14 a distinctive feature or characteristic (it has its points; tact is not his good point). 15 pungency, effectiveness (their comments lacked point). 16 a each of 32 directions marked at equal distances round a compass. b the corresponding direction towards the horizon. 17 (usu. in pl.) Brit. a junction of two railway lines, with a pair of linked tapering rails that can be moved laterally to allow a train to pass from one line to the other. 18 Brit. = power point. 19 (usu. in pl.) each of a set of electrical contacts in the distributor of a motor vehicle. 20 Cricket a a fielder on the off side near the batsman. b this position. 21 the tip of the toe in ballet. 22 a promontory. 23 the prong of a deer's antler. 24 the extremities of a dog, horse, etc. 25 Printing a unit of measurement for type bodies (in the UK and US 0.0138 in., in Europe 0.0148 in.). 26 Hunting a a spot to which a straight run is made. b such a run. 27 Heraldry any of nine particular positions on a shield used for specifying the position of charges etc. 28 Boxing the tip of the chin as a spot for a knockout blow. 29 Mil. a small leading party of an advanced guard. 30 hist. a tagged lace for lacing a bodice, attaching a hose to a doublet, etc. 31 Naut. a short piece of cord at the lower edge of a sail for tying up a reef. 32 the act or position of a dog in pointing. —v. 1 (usu. foll. by to, at) a tr. direct or aim (a finger, weapon, etc.). b intr. direct attention in a certain direction (pointed to the house across the road). 2 intr. (foll. by at, towards) a aim or be directed to. b tend towards. 3 intr. (foll. by to) indicate; be evidence of (it all points to murder). 4 tr. give point or force to (words or actions). 5 tr. fill in or repair the joints of (brickwork) with smoothly finished mortar or cement. 6 tr. a punctuate. b insert points in (written Hebrew etc.). c mark (Psalms etc.) with signs for chanting. 7 tr. sharpen (a pencil, tool, etc.). 8 tr. (also absol.) (of a dog) indicate the presence of (game) by acting as pointer. □ **at all points** in every part or respect. **at the point of** (often foll. by verbal noun) on the verge of; about to do (the action specified). **beside the point** irrelevant or irrelevantly. **case in point** an instance that is relevant or (prec. by *the*) under consideration. **have a point** be correct or effective in one's contention. **in point** apposite, relevant. **in point of fact** see FACT. **make** (or **prove**) **a** (or **one's**) **point** establish a proposition; prove one's contention. **make a point of** (often foll. by verbal noun) insist on; treat or regard as essential. **nine points** nine tenths, i.e. nearly the whole (esp. *possession is nine points of the law*). **on** (or **upon**) **the point of** (foll. by verbal noun) about to do (the action specified). **point-duty** the positioning of a police officer or traffic warden at a crossroad or other point to control traffic. **point lace** thread lace made wholly with a needle. **point of honour** an action or circumstance that affects one's reputation. **point of no return** a point in a journey or enterprise at which it becomes essential or more practical to continue to the end. **point of order** a query in a debate etc. as to whether correct procedure is being followed. **point-of-sale** (usu. *attrib.*) denoting publicity etc. associated with the place at which goods are retailed. **point of view 1** a position from which a thing is viewed. **2** a particular way of considering a matter. **point out** (often foll. by *that* + clause) indicate, show; draw attention to. **point-to-point** a steeplechase over a marked course for horses used regularly in hunting. **point up** emphasize; show as important. **score points off** get the better of in an argument etc. **take a person's point** concede that a person has made a valid contention. **to the point** relevant or relevantly. **up to a point** to some extent but not completely. **win on points** *Boxing* win by scoring more points, not by a knockout. [ME f. OF *point, pointer* f. L *punctum* f. *pungere punct-* prick]

point-blank /pɔɪntˈblæŋk/ *adj. & adv.* —*adj.* **1 a** (of a shot) aimed or fired horizontally at a range very close to the target. **b** (of a distance or range) very close. **2** (of a remark, question, etc.) blunt, direct. —*adv.* **1** at very close range. **2** directly, bluntly. [prob. f. POINT + BLANK = white spot in the centre of a target]

Pointe-à-Pitre /ˌpwætaːˈpiːtr/ the largest town in Guadeloupe; pop. (1982) 25,300.

pointed /ˈpɔɪntɪd/ *adj.* **1** sharpened or tapering to a point. **2** (of a remark etc.) having point; penetrating, cutting. **3** emphasized; made evident. □□ **pointedly** *adv.* **pointedness** *n.*

Pointe-Noire /ˌpwætˈnwaː(r)/ the chief seaport and oil terminal of the Congo; pop. (est. 1984) 294,200.

pointer /ˈpɔɪntə(r)/ *n.* **1** a thing that points, e.g. the index hand of a gauge etc. **2** a rod for pointing to features on a map, chart, etc. **3** *colloq.* a hint, clue, or indication. **4 a** a dog of a breed that on scenting game stands rigid looking towards it. **b** this breed. **5** (in *pl.*) **1** two stars (Dubhe and Merak) in the constellation the Great Bear, a straight line through which points nearly to the pole star. **2** the two stars in the Southern Cross which are nearly in a line with the south pole of the heavens.

pointillism /ˈpwæntɪˌlɪz(ə)m/ *n. Art* a technique of impressionist painting, developed by Seurat to give painting greater luminosity, in which pigment is applied in small spots of various pure colours which are blended by the spectator's eye. Under the general title of 'divisionism' the style was influential in France, Holland, and Italy in the 1890s and early 1900s. □□ **pointillist** *n. & adj.* **pointillistic** /-ˈlɪstɪk/ *adj.* [F *pointillisme* f. *pointiller* mark with dots]

pointing /ˈpɔɪntɪŋ/ *n.* **1** cement or mortar filling the joints of brickwork. **2** facing produced by this. **3** the process of producing this.

pointless /ˈpɔɪntlɪs/ *adj.* **1** without a point. **2** lacking force, purpose, or meaning. **3** (in games) without a point scored. □□ **pointlessly** *adv.* **pointlessness** *n.*

pointsman /ˈpɔɪntsmən/ *n.* (*pl.* **-men**) *Brit.* **1** a person in charge of railway points. **2** a policeman or traffic warden on point-duty.

pointy /ˈpɔɪntɪ/ *adj.* (**pointier, pointiest**) having a noticeably sharp end; pointed.

Poirot /ˈpwaːrəʊ/, Hercule. A Belgian private detective in the crime stories of Agatha Christie. Short and bald, with luxuriant moustaches, he constantly advocates orderliness and the use of observation and reasoning.

poise[1] /pɔɪz/ *n. & v.* —*n.* **1** composure or self-possession of

manner. **2** equilibrium; a stable state. **3** carriage (of the head etc.). —*v.* **1** *tr.* balance; hold suspended or supported. **2** *tr.* carry (one's head etc. in a specified way). **3** *intr.* be balanced; hover in the air etc. [ME f. OF *pois, peis, peser* ult. f. L *pensum* weight f. *pendere pens-* weigh]

poise[2] /pɔɪz/ *n. Physics* a unit of dynamic viscosity, such that a tangential force of one dyne per square centimetre causes a velocity change one centimetre per second between two parallel planes in a liquid separated by one centimetre. [J. L. M. *Poiseuille*, Fr. physician d. 1869]

poised /pɔɪzd/ *adj.* **1** composed, self-assured. **2** (often foll. by *for*, or *to* + infin.) ready for action.

poison /ˈpɔɪz(ə)n/ *n. & v.* —*n.* **1** a substance that when introduced into or absorbed by a living organism causes death or injury, esp. one that kills by rapid action even in a small quantity. **2** *colloq.* a harmful influence or principle etc. **3** *Physics & Chem.* a substance that interferes with the normal progress of a nuclear reaction, chain reaction, catalytic reaction, etc. —*v.tr.* **1** administer poison to (a person or animal). **2** kill or injure or infect with poison. **3** infect (air, water, etc.) with poison. **4** (esp. as **poisoned** *adj.*) treat (a weapon) with poison. **5** corrupt or pervert (a person or mind). **6** spoil or destroy (a person's pleasure etc.). **7** render (land etc.) foul and unfit for its purpose by a noxious application etc. □ **poison gas** = GAS *n.* 4. **poison ivy** a N. American climbing plant, *Rhus toxicodendron*, secreting an irritant oil from its leaves. **poison-pen letter** an anonymous libellous or abusive letter. □□ **poisoner** *n.* **poisonous** *adj.* **poisonously** *adv.* [ME f. OF *poison, poisonner* (as POTION)]

Poisson distribution /ˈpwʌsɔ̃/ *n. Statistics* a discrete frequency distribution which gives the probability of events occurring in a fixed time. [S. D. *Poisson*, French mathematician d. 1840]

Poitiers /ˈpwætɪˌeɪ/ a city in west central France, the capital of Poitou-Charentes region; pop. (1982) 82,900. It was the location of a number of important battles: here the Merovingian king Clovis defeated the Visigoths under Alaric in 507, Charles Martel halted the Saracen advance in 732, and Edward the Black Prince defeated the French in 1356.

Poitou /pwæˈtuː/ a former province of west central France now united with Charentes to form Poitou-Charentes region; pop. (1982) 1,568,200; capital, Poitiers.

poke[1] /pəʊk/ *v. & n.* —*v.* **1** (foll. by *in, up, down*, etc.) **a** *tr.* thrust or push with the hand, point of a stick, etc. **b** *intr.* be thrust forward. **2** *intr.* (foll. by *at* etc.) make thrusts with a stick etc. **3** *tr.* thrust the end of a finger etc. against. **4** *tr.* (foll. by *in*) produce (a hole etc. in a thing) by poking. **5** *tr.* thrust forward, esp. obtrusively. **6** *tr.* stir (a fire) with a poker. **7** *intr.* **a** (often foll. by *about, around*) move or act desultorily; potter. **b** (foll. by *about, into*) pry; search casually. **8** *tr. coarse sl.* have sexual intercourse with. **9** *tr.* (foll. by *up*) *colloq.* confine (esp. oneself) in a poky place. —*n.* **1** the act or an instance of poking. **2** a thrust or nudge. **3** a device fastened on cattle etc. to prevent them breaking through fences. **4 a** a projecting brim or front of a woman's bonnet or hat. **b** (in full **poke-bonnet**) a bonnet having this. □ **poke fun at** ridicule, tease. **poke one's nose into** *colloq.* pry or intrude into (esp. a person's affairs). [ME f. MDu. and MLG *poken*, of unkn. orig.]

poke[2] /pəʊk/ *n. dial.* a bag or sack. □ **buy a pig in a poke** see PIG. [ME f. ONF *poke, poque* = OF *poche*; cf. POUCH]

poker[1] /ˈpəʊkə(r)/ *n.* a stiff metal rod with a handle for stirring an open fire. □ **poker-work 1** the technique of burning designs on white wood etc. with a heated metal rod. **2** a design made in this way.

poker[2] /ˈpəʊkə(r)/ *n.* a card-game in which bluff is used as players bet on the value of their hands. □ **poker-dice** dice with card designs from ace to nine instead of spots. **poker-face 1** the impassive countenance appropriate to a poker-player. **2** a person with this. **poker-faced** having a poker-face. [19th c.: orig. unkn.: cf. G *pochen* to brag, *Pochspiel* bragging game]

pokeweed /ˈpəʊkwiːd/ *n.* a tall hardy American plant, *Phytolacca americana*, with spikes of cream flowers and purple berries that yield emetics and purgatives. [*poke*, Amer. Ind. word + WEED]

pokey /ˈpəʊkɪ/ n. US sl. prison. [perh. f. POKY]

poky /ˈpəʊkɪ/ adj. (**pokier**, **pokiest**) (of a room etc.) small and cramped. □□ **pokily** adv. **pokiness** n. [POKE¹ (in colloq. sense 'confine') + -Y¹]

polack /ˈpəʊlæk/ n. US sl. offens. a person of Polish origin. [F Polaque and G Polack f. Pol. Polak]

Poland /ˈpəʊlənd/ a country in eastern Europe with a coastline on the Baltic Sea, bordered by Germany, Czechoslovakia, and the USSR; pop. (est. 1982) 37,958,400; official language, Polish; capital, Warsaw. First united in the 11th c., Poland emerged from a period of internal division to become the dominant East European power in the 16th c. Thereafter it suffered severely from the rise of Russian, Swedish, Prussian, and Austrian power, losing territory and eventually its independent identity in three partitions between 1772 and 1795; the country did not regain full independence until (as a republic) after the First World War. Its invasion by German forces in 1939 precipitated the Second World War, and after 1945 it was dominated to a fluctuating extent, by the USSR until the late 1980s, when the rise of the independent trade union movement Solidarity (see entry), and the eventual introduction of democratic reforms, brought to an end nearly 45 years of Communist rule. The country has deposits of copper and iron, and some of the largest coalfields in the world. Despite rapid advances in urbanization and industrialization, however, Poland is still affected by severe economic problems.

polar /ˈpəʊlə(r)/ **1** adj. **a** of or near a pole of the earth or a celestial body, or of the celestial sphere. **b** (of a species or variety) living in the north polar region. **2** having magnetic polarity. **3 a** (of a molecule) having a positive charge at one end and a negative charge at the other. **b** (of a compound) having electric charges. **4** Geom. of or relating to a pole. **5** directly opposite in character or tendency. □ **polar bear** a white bear, Ursus maritimus, of the Arctic regions. **polar body** a small cell produced from an oocyte during the formation of an ovum, which does not develop further. **polar circle** each of the circles parallel to the equator at a distance of 23° 27′ from either pole. **polar coordinates** a system by which a point can be located with reference to two angles. **polar curve** a curve related in a particular way to a given curve and to a fixed point called a pole. **polar distance** the angular distance of a point on a sphere from the nearest pole. **polar star** = POLE STAR. □□ **polarly** adv. [F polaire or mod.L polaris (as POLE²)]

polari- /ˈpəʊlərɪ/ comb. form polar. [mod.L polaris (as POLAR)]

polarimeter /ˌpəʊləˈrɪmɪtə(r)/ n. an instrument used to measure the polarization of light or the effect of a substance on the rotation of the plane of polarized light. □□ **polarimetric** /-ˈmetrɪk/ adj. **polarimetry** n.

Polaris /pəˈlɑːrɪs/ alpha Ursae Minoris, the North Star or pole star, located within one degree of the celestial north pole, the focal point about which the heavens wheel during the course of a night. The 49th-brightest star in the sky, it is actually a double star, the bright component being a cepheid variable. [as POLAR]

polariscope /pəʊˈlærɪˌskəʊp/ n. = POLARIMETER. □□ **polariscopic** /-ˈskɒpɪk/ adj.

polarity /pəˈlærɪtɪ/ n. (pl. **-ies**) **1** the tendency of a lodestone, magnetized bar, etc., to point with its extremities to the magnetic poles of the earth. **2** the condition of having two poles with contrary qualities. **3** the state of having two opposite tendencies, opinions, etc. **4** the electrical condition of a body (positive or negative). **5** a magnetic attraction towards an object or person.

polarize /ˈpəʊləˌraɪz/ v. (also **-ise**) **1** tr. restrict the vibrations of (a transverse wave, esp. light) to one direction. **2** tr. give magnetic or electric polarity to (a substance or body). **3** tr. reduce the voltage of (an electric cell) by the action of electrolysis products. **4** tr. & intr. divide into two groups of opposing opinion etc. □□ **polarizable** adj. **polarization** /-ˈzeɪʃ(ə)n/ n. **polarizer** n.

polarography /ˌpəʊləˈrɒgrəfɪ/ n. Chem. the analysis by measurement of current-voltage relationships in electrolysis

between mercury electrodes. □□ **polarographic** /-əˈgræfɪk/ adj.

Polaroid /ˈpəʊləˌrɔɪd/ n. propr. **1** material in thin plastic sheets that produces a high degree of plane polarization in light passing through it. **2** a type of camera with internal processing that produces a finished print rapidly after each exposure. **3** (in pl.) sunglasses with lenses made from Polaroid. [POLARI- + -OID]

polder /ˈpəʊldə(r)/ n. a piece of low-lying land reclaimed from the sea or a river, esp. in the Netherlands. [MDu. polre, Du. polder]

Pole /pəʊl/ n. **1** a native or national of Poland. **2** a person of Polish descent. [G f. Pol. Polanie, lit. field-dwellers f. pole field]

pole¹ /pəʊl/ n. & v. —n. **1** a long slender rounded piece of wood or metal, esp. with the end placed in the ground as a support etc. **2** a wooden shaft fitted to the front of a vehicle and attached to the yokes or collars of the draught animals. **3** = PERCH¹ 3. —v.tr. **1** provide with poles. **2** (usu. foll. by off) push off (a punt etc.) with a pole. □ **pole position** the most favourable position at the start of a motor race (orig. next to the inside boundary-fence). **pole-vault** (or **-jump**) n. the athletic sport of vaulting over a high bar with the aid of a long flexible pole held in the hands and giving extra spring. —v.intr. take part in this sport. **pole-vaulter** a person who pole-vaults. **under bare poles** Naut. with no sail set. **up the pole** sl. **1** crazy, eccentric. **2** in difficulty. [OE pāl ult. f. L palus stake]

pole² /pəʊl/ n. **1** (in full **north pole**, **south pole**) **a** each of the two points in the celestial sphere about which the stars appear to revolve. **b** each of the extremities of the axis of rotation of the earth or another body. **c** see magnetic pole. ¶ The spelling is North Pole and South Pole when used as geographical designations. **2** each of the two opposite points on the surface of a magnet at which magnetic forces are strongest. **3** each of two terminals (positive and negative) of an electric cell or battery etc. **4** each of two opposed principles or ideas. **5** Geom. each of two points in which the axis of a circle cuts the surface of a sphere. **6** a fixed point to which others are referred. **7** Biol. an extremity of the main axis of any spherical or oval organ. □ **be poles apart** differ greatly, esp. in nature or opinion. **pole star 1** Astron. = POLARIS. **2 a** a thing or principle serving as a guide. **b** a centre of attraction. □□ **poleward** adj. **polewards** adj. & adv. [ME f. L polus f. Gk polos pivot, axis, sky]

poleaxe /ˈpəʊlæks/ n. & v. —n. **1** a battleaxe. **2** a butcher's axe. —v.tr. hit or kill with or as if with a poleaxe. [ME pol(l)ax, -ex f. MDu. pol(l)aex, MLG pol(l)exe (as POLL¹, AXE)]

polecat /ˈpəʊlkæt/ n. **1** Brit. a small European brownish-black fetid flesh-eating mammal, Mustela putorius, of the weasel family. **2** US a skunk. [pole (unexplained) + CAT]

polemic /pəˈlemɪk/ n. & adj. —n. **1** a controversial discussion. **2** Polit. a verbal or written attack, esp. on a political opponent. —adj. (also **polemical**) involving dispute; controversial. □□ **polemically** adv. **polemicist** /-sɪst/ n. **polemicize** v.tr. (also **-ise**). **polemize** /ˈpɒlɪˌmaɪz/ v.tr. (also **-ise**). [med.L polemicus f. Gk polemikos f. polemos war]

polemics /pəˈlemɪks/ n.pl. the art or practice of controversial discussion.

polenta /pəˈlentə/ n. porridge made of maize meal etc. [It. f. L, = pearl barley]

police /pəˈliːs/ n. & v. —n. **1** (usu. prec. by the) the civil force of a State, responsible for maintaining public order. (See below.) **2** (as pl.) the members of a police force (several hundred police). **3** a force with similar functions of enforcing regulations (military police; railway police). —v.tr. **1** control (a country or area) by means of police. **2** provide with police. **3** keep order in; control. □ **police constable** see CONSTABLE. **police dog** a dog, esp. an Alsatian, used in police work. **police officer** a policeman or policewoman. **police State** a totalitarian State controlled by political police supervising the citizens' activities. **police station** the office of a local police force. [F f. med.L politia POLICY¹]

Police forces are organized along different lines in various parts of the world. Compared with many countries (where the role of the military was not always sharply distinguished from that of the police) Britain was rather tardy in establishing a regular force, the first being that organized in London in 1829 by Sir Robert Peel. From medieval times a petty or parish constable was appointed to preserve the peace in his area and to execute the orders of Justices of the Peace; in towns, the 'watch' patrolled and guarded the streets with varying degrees of diligence. In London in the 18th c. some justices organized bodies of constables, of which the Bow Street Runners were one. The modern British police force is not a national one; a number of forces exist for defined areas, maintained by local police authorities, the Home Office being responsible for the Metropolitan Police.

policeman /pə'li:smən/ n. (pl. **-men**; fem. **policewoman**, pl. **-women**) a member of a police force.

policy[1] /'pɒlɪsɪ/ n. (pl. **-ies**) **1** a course or principle of action adopted or proposed by a government, party, business, or individual etc. **2** prudent conduct; sagacity. [ME f. OF policie f. L politia f. Gk politeia citizenship f. politēs citizen f. polis city]

policy[2] /'pɒlɪsɪ/ n. (pl. **-ies**) **1** a contract of insurance. **2** a document containing this. [F police bill of lading, contract of insurance, f. Prov. poliss(i)a prob. f. med.L apodissa, apodixa, f. L apodixis f. Gk apodeixis evidence, proof (as APO-, deiknumi show)]

policyholder /'pɒlɪsɪ,həʊldə(r)/ n. a person or body holding an insurance policy.

polio /'pəʊlɪəʊ/ n. = POLIOMYELITIS. [abbr.]

poliomyelitis /ˌpəʊlɪəʊˌmaɪɪ'laɪtɪs/ n. Med. an infectious viral disease that affects the central nervous system and which can cause temporary or permanent paralysis. [mod.L f. Gk polios grey + muelos marrow]

Polish /'pəʊlɪʃ/ adj. & n. —adj. **1** of or relating to Poland. **2** of the Poles or their language. —n. the language of Poland, which belongs to the Slavonic language group and is spoken by its 38 million inhabitants and by some 2,500,000 people in the US. □ **Polish Corridor** a belt of territory separating East Prussia from the rest of Germany, granted to Poland after the First World War to ensure access to the Baltic Sea. Historically, it had belonged to Polish Pomerania in the 18th c., but had been colonized by a German minority. Its annexation and the occupation of the rest of Poland by Germany in 1939 precipitated the Second World War. After the war the territory reverted to Poland. **Polish notation** Math. a system of formula notation without brackets and punctuation. [POLE + -ISH[1]]

polish /'pɒlɪʃ/ v. & n. —v. **1** tr. & intr. make or become smooth or glossy by rubbing. **2** (esp. as **polished** adj.) refine or improve; add finishing touches to. —n. **1** a substance used for polishing. **2** smoothness or glossiness produced by friction. **3** the act or an instance of polishing. **4** refinement or elegance of manner, conduct, etc. □ **polish off** finish (esp. food) quickly. **polish up** revise or improve (a skill etc.). □□ **polishable** adj. **polisher** n. [ME f. OF polir f. L polire polit-]

politburo /'pɒlɪt,bjʊərəʊ/ n. (pl. **-os**) the principal policy-making committee of a Communist party, esp. in the USSR. In Moscow, changes made to the governmental structure in 1990 resulted in transference of real power from the Politburo to the presidential council. [Rus. politbyuro f. politícheskoe byuró political bureau]

polite /pə'laɪt/ adj. (**politer**, **politest**) **1** having good manners; courteous. **2** cultivated, cultured. **3** refined, elegant (polite letters). □□ **politely** adv. **politeness** n. [L politus (as POLISH)]

politesse /ˌpɒlɪ'tes/ n. formal politeness. [F f. It. politezza, pulitezza f. pulito polite]

politic /'pɒlɪtɪk/ adj. & v. —adj. **1** (of an action) judicious, expedient. **2** (of a person) prudent, sagacious. **3** political (now only in body politic). —v.intr. (**politicked**, **politicking**) engage in politics. □□ **politicly** adv. [ME f. OF politique f. L politicus f. Gk politikos f. politēs citizen f. polis city]

political /pə'lɪtɪk(ə)l/ adj. **1 a** of or concerning the State or its government, or public affairs generally. **b** of, relating to, or engaged in politics. **c** belonging to or forming part of a civil administration. **2** having an organized form of society or government. **3** taking or belonging to a side in politics. **4** relating to or affecting interests of status or authority in an organization rather than matters of principle (a political decision). □ **political asylum** see ASYLUM. **political economist** a student of or expert in political economy. **political economy** the study of the economic aspects of government. **political geography** that dealing with boundaries and the possessions of States. **political prisoner** a person imprisoned for political beliefs or actions. **political science** the study of the State and systems of government. **political scientist** a specialist in political science. □□ **politically** adv. [L politicus (as POLITIC)]

politician /ˌpɒlɪ'tɪʃ(ə)n/ n. **1** a person engaged in or concerned with politics, esp. as a practitioner. **2** a person skilled in politics. **3** US derog. a person with self-interested political concerns.

politicize /pə'lɪtɪ,saɪz/ v. (also **-ise**) **1** tr. **a** give a political character to. **b** make politically aware. **2** intr. engage in or talk politics. □□ **politicization** /-'zeɪʃ(ə)n/ n.

politico /pə'lɪtɪ,kəʊ/ n. (pl. **-os**) colloq. a politician or political enthusiast. [Sp. or It. (as POLITIC)]

politico- /pə'lɪtɪkəʊ/ comb. form **1** politically. **2** political and (politico-social). [Gk politikos: see POLITIC]

politics /'pɒlɪtɪks/ n.pl. **1** (treated as sing. or pl.) **a** the art and science of government. **b** public life and affairs as involving authority and government. **2** (usu. treated as pl.) **a** a particular set of ideas, principles, or commitments in politics (what are their politics?). **b** activities concerned with the acquisition or exercise of authority or government. **c** an organizational process or principle affecting authority, status, etc. (the politics of the decision).

polity /'pɒlɪtɪ/ n. (pl. **-ies**) **1** a form or process of civil government or constitution. **2** an organized society; a State as a political entity. [L politia f. Gk politeia f. politēs citizen f. polis city]

Polk /pəʊk/, James Knox (1795–1849), 11th President of the US, 1845–9. His term of office resulted in major territorial additions to the US. Texas was admitted to the Union, and the successful outcome of the conflict with Mexico resulted in the annexation of California and the south-west.

polka /'pɒlkə, 'pəʊlkə/ n. & v. —n. **1** a lively dance of Bohemian origin in duple time. **2** the music for this. —v.intr. (**polkas**, **polkaed** /-kəd/ or **polka'd**, **polkaing** /-kəɪŋ/) dance the polka. □ **polka dot** a round dot as one of many forming a regular pattern on a textile fabric etc. [F and G f. Czech půlka half-step f. půl half]

poll[1] /pəʊl/ n. & v. —n. **1 a** the process of voting at an election. **b** the counting of votes at an election. **c** the result of voting. **d** the number of votes recorded (a heavy poll). **2** = GALLUP POLL, opinion poll. **3 a** a human head. **b** the part of this on which hair grows (flaxen poll). **4** a hornless animal, esp. one of a breed of hornless cattle. —v. **1** tr. **a** take the vote or votes of. **b** (in passive) have one's vote taken. **c** (of a candidate) receive (so many votes). **d** give (a vote). **2** tr. record the opinion of (a person or group) in an opinion poll. **3** intr. give one's vote. **4** tr. cut off the top of (a tree or plant), esp. make a pollard of. **5** tr. (esp. as **polled** adj.) cut the horns off (cattle). **6** tr. Computing check the status of (a computer system) at intervals. □ **poll tax 1** hist. a tax levied on every adult. **2** = community charge. □□ **pollee** /pəʊ'li:/ n. (in sense 2 of n.) **pollster** n. [ME, perh. f. LG or Du.]

poll[2] /pɒl/ n. a tame parrot (Pretty poll!). □ **poll parrot** a user of conventional or clichéd phrases and arguments. [Poll, a conventional name for a parrot, alt. f. Moll, a familiar form of Mary]

pollack /'pɒlək/ n. (also **pollock**) a European marine fish, Pollachius pollachius, with a characteristic protruding lower jaw, used for food. [earlier (Sc.) podlock: orig. unkn.]

Pollaiuolo /pɒ'laɪwə,ləʊ/, Antonio (1432–98) and Piero di Benci (1441–96), Florentine brothers who worked as painters, sculptors, and designers. Antonio assisted Ghiberti with the Florence Baptistery doors (1452) and produced the monuments in St Peter's to Popes Sixtus IV and Innocent VIII. His innovatory anatomical studies seem to have determined the composition and choice of subject in his paintings (e.g. Battle of the Naked Men and the Hercules panels). Piero was primarily a painter, producing chastely decorative figures when working independently but collaborating with his brother in the Martyrdom of St Sebastian (1475) and other works.

pollan /'pɒlən/ n. a freshwater fish, Coregonus pollan, found in Irish lakes. [perh. f. Ir. poll deep water]

pollard /'pɒləd/ n. & v. —n. **1** an animal that has lost or cast its horns; an ox, sheep, or goat of a hornless breed. **2** a tree whose branches have been cut off to encourage the growth of new young branches, esp. a riverside willow. **3 a** the bran sifted from flour. **b** a fine bran containing some flour.v.tr. make (a tree) a pollard. [POLL¹ + -ARD]

pollen /'pɒlən/ n. the fine dustlike grains discharged from the male part of a flower containing the gamete that fertilizes the female ovule. □ **pollen analysis** = PALYNOLOGY. **pollen count** an index of the amount of pollen in the air, published esp. for the benefit of those allergic to it. □□ **pollenless** adj. **pollinic** /pə'lɪnɪk/ adj. [L pollen pollinis fine flour, dust]

pollex /'pɒleks/ n. (pl. **pollices** /-lɪˌsiːz/) the innermost digit of a forelimb, usu. the thumb in primates. [L, = thumb or big toe]

pollie var. of POLLY².

pollinate /'pɒlɪˌneɪt/ v.tr. (also absol.) sprinkle (a stigma) with pollen. □□ **pollination** /-'neɪʃ(ə)n/ n. **pollinator** n.

polling /'pəʊlɪŋ/ n. the registering or casting of votes. □ **polling-booth** a compartment in which a voter stands to mark the ballot-paper. **polling-day** the day of a local or general election. **polling-station** a building, often a school, where voting takes place during an election.

pollinic see POLLEN.

polliniferous /ˌpɒlɪ'nɪfərəs/ adj. bearing or producing pollen.

polliwog /'pɒlɪˌwɒg/ n. (also **pollywog**) US dial. a tadpole. [earlier polwigge, polwygle f. POLL¹ + WIGGLE]

Pollock /'pɒlək/, Jackson (1912–56), American painter, the commanding figure of the abstract expressionist movement. He is noted for his 'drip and splash' style, in which he affixed his canvas to a floor or wall and poured or dripped paint on it, manipulating it with sticks, trowels, or knives and sometimes adding sand, broken glass, or other foreign matter; this form of action painting was held by artists and critics alike to result in expression or revelation of the unconscious moods of the artist. His name is also associated with the 'all-over' style of painting, which avoids having points of emphasis or identifiable parts and therefore abandons the traditional idea of composition. Critical assessment of his work has varied from wide-eyed wonder to cynicism.

pollock var. of POLLACK.

pollute /pə'luːt/ v.tr. **1** contaminate or defile (the environment). **2** make foul or filthy. **3** destroy the purity or sanctity of. □□ **pollutant** adj. & n. **polluter** n. **pollution** n. [ME f. L polluere pollut-]

Pollux /'pɒləks/ **1** Gk Mythol. one of the Dioscuri (see entry). **2** Astron. a bright star in the constellation Gemini.

polly¹ /'pɒlɪ/ n. (pl. **-ies**) colloq. a bottle or glass of Apollinaris water. [abbr.]

polly² /'pɒlɪ/ n. (also **pollie**) (pl. **-ies**) Austral. & US a politician. [abbr.]

Pollyanna /ˌpɒlɪ'ænə/ n. a cheerful optimist; an excessively cheerful person. □□ **Pollyannaish** adj. **Pollyannaism** n. [character in a novel (1913) by E. Porter]

pollywog var. of POLLIWOG.

polo /'pəʊləʊ/ n. a four-a-side game resembling hockey, played on horseback with a long-handled mallet (polo-stick). It is of eastern origin, first described in Persia in about 600 BC. Having spread over Asia to China and Japan, by the 19th c. it survived only in a few mountain areas in the NW and NE frontiers of India, where it was discovered by visiting British officers who adopted it with enthusiasm. □ **polo-neck** a high round turned-over collar. **polo-stick** a mallet for playing polo. [Balti, = ball]

polonaise /ˌpɒlə'neɪz/ n. & adj. —n. **1** a dance of Polish origin in triple time. **2** the music for this. **3** hist. a woman's dress consisting of a bodice and a skirt open from the waist downwards to show an underskirt. —adj. cooked in a Polish style. [F, fem. of polonais Polish f. med.L Polonia Poland]

polonium /pə'ləʊnɪəm/ n. Chem. a rare radioactive metallic element, occurring naturally as a product of radioactive decay of uranium. Discovered in 1898 by Marie Curie, occurring in minute amounts in pitchblende, it can now also be created artificially in nuclear reactors. It has some use as an energy source in satellites. ¶ Symb.: Po; atomic number 84. [F & mod.L f. med.L Polonia Poland (the discoverer's native country) + -IUM]

Polonnaruwa /ˌpɒlənə'ruːvə/ a town in eastern Sri Lanka; pop. (1981) 11,000. An ancient capital of Ceylon, it was long deserted until a modern town was built in the 20th c.

polony /pə'ləʊnɪ/ n. (pl. **-ies**) Brit. = BOLOGNA SAUSAGE. [app. corrupt.]

Pol Pot /pɒl 'pɒt/ (?1925–), Cambodian Communist leader. After the Khmer Rouge had seized power he became Prime Minister (1976–9) and presided over the 'reconstruction' of the country in a notorious regime under which as many as two million Cambodians may have been killed. Overthrown in 1979, he led the Khmer Rouge in a guerrilla war against the new Vietnamese-backed government until ill health forced his semi-retirement in 1985.

poltergeist /'pɒltəˌgaɪst/ n. a noisy mischievous ghost, esp. one manifesting itself by physical damage. [G f. poltern create a disturbance + Geist GHOST]

poltroon /pɒl'truːn/ n. a spiritless coward. □□ **poltroonery** n. [F poltron f. It. poltrone perh. f. poltro sluggard]

poly /'pɒlɪ/ n. (pl. **polys**) colloq. polytechnic. [abbr.]

poly-¹ /'pɒlɪ/ comb. form denoting many or much. [Gk polu- f. polus much, polloi many]

poly-² /'pɒlɪ/ comb. form Chem. polymerized (polyunsaturated). [POLYMER]

polyadelphous /ˌpɒlɪə'delfəs/ adj. Bot. having numerous stamens grouped into three or more bundles.

polyamide /ˌpɒlɪ'æmaɪd/ n. Chem. any of a class of condensation polymers produced from the interaction of an amino group of one molecule and a carboxylic acid group of another, and which includes many synthetic fibres such as nylon.

polyandry /'pɒlɪˌændrɪ/ n. **1** polygamy in which a woman has more than one husband. **2** Bot. the state of having numerous stamens. □□ **polyandrous** /-'ændrəs/ adj. [POLY-¹ + andry f. Gk anēr andros male]

polyanthus /ˌpɒlɪ'ænθəs/ n. (pl. **polyanthuses**) a flower cultivated from hybridized primulas. [mod.L, formed as POLY-¹ + Gk anthos flower]

Polybius /pə'lɪbɪəs/ (c.200–after 118 BC) Greek historian of Rome. After an early political career in Greece, he was deported to Rome. His 40 books of Histories (partially extant) chronicled the rise of Rome to world-supremacy from 220 to 146 BC; by ancient standards he is an accurate and honest historian.

polycarbonate /ˌpɒlɪ'kɑːbəˌneɪt/ n. any of a class of polymers in which the units are linked through a carbonate group, mainly used as moulding materials.

Polycarp /'pɒlɪˌkɑːp/, St (traditionally c.69–c.155 but possibly later), bishop of Smyrna in Asia Minor, where he seems to have been the leading Christian figure in the mid-2nd c. He was arrested during a pagan festival, refused to recant his faith, and was burnt to death.

polychaete /'pɒlɪˌkiːt/ n. any aquatic annelid worm of the class Polychaeta, including lugworms and ragworms, having numerous bristles on the fleshy lobes of each body segment. □□ **polychaetan** /-'kiːt(ə)n/ adj. **polychaetous** /-'kiːtəs/ adj.

polychromatic /ˌpɒlɪkrəʊ'mætɪk/ adj. **1** many-coloured. **2** (of radiation) containing more than one wavelength. □□ **polychromatism** /-'krəʊməˌtɪz(ə)m/ n.

polychrome /'pɒlɪˌkrəʊm/ adj. & n. —adj. painted, printed, or decorated in many colours. —n. **1** a work of art in several colours, esp. a coloured statue. **2** varied colouring. □□ **polychromic** /-'krəʊmɪk/ adj. **polychromous** /-'krəʊməs/ adj. [F f. Gk polukhrōmos as POLY-¹, khrōma colour]

polychromy /'pɒlɪˌkrəʊmɪ/ n. the art of painting in several colours, esp. as applied to ancient pottery, architecture, etc. [F polychromie (as POLYCHROME)]

polyclinic /'pɒlɪˌklɪnɪk/ n. a clinic devoted to various diseases; a general hospital.

Polyclitus /ˌpɒlɪˈklaɪtəs/ (5th c. BC) Greek sculptor, who concentrated largely on nude male statues, although his best-known work in contemporary times was a colossal Hera, which was also depicted on coins. Two copies of his works survive, both idealized athletes, 'Doryphoros' (the spear-bearer) and 'Diadumenos' (youth fastening a band round his head). Polyclitus was known for his sensitivity in depicting the varying ages of his models, ideal or human, from young boyhood to maturity.

polycrystalline /ˌpɒlɪˈkrɪstəˌlaɪn/ adj. (of a solid substance) consisting of many crystalline parts at various orientations, e.g. a metal casting.

polycyclic /ˌpɒlɪˈsaɪklɪk/ adj. Chem. having more than one ring of atoms in the molecule.

polydactyl /ˌpɒlɪˈdæktɪl/ adj. & n. —adj. (of an animal) having more than five fingers or toes. —n. a polydactyl animal.

polyester /ˌpɒlɪˈestə(r)/ n. any of a group of condensation polymers used to form synthetic fibres such as Terylene or to make resins.

polyethene /ˈpɒlɪˌeθiːn/ n. Chem. = POLYTHENE.

polyethylene /ˌpɒlɪˈeθɪˌliːn/ n. = POLYTHENE.

polygamous /pəˈlɪɡəməs/ adj. 1 having more than one wife or husband at the same time. 2 having more than one mate. 3 bearing some flowers with stamens only, some with pistils only, some with both, on the same or different plants. □□ **polygamic** /-ˈɡæmɪk/ adj. **polygamist** n. **polygamously** adv. **polygamy** n. [Gk polugamos (as POLY-¹, -gamos marrying)]

polygene /ˈpɒlɪˌdʒiːn/ n. Biol. each of a group of independent genes that collectively affect a characteristic.

polygenesis /ˌpɒlɪˈdʒenɪsɪs/ n. the (usu. postulated) origination of a race or species from several independent stocks. □□ **polygenetic** /-dʒɪˈnetɪk/ adj.

polygeny /pəˈlɪdʒənɪ/ n. the theory that mankind originated from several independent pairs of ancestors. □□ **polygenism** n. **polygenist** n.

polyglot /ˈpɒlɪˌɡlɒt/ adj. & n. —adj. 1 of many languages. 2 (of a person) speaking or writing several languages. 3 (of a book, esp. the Bible) with the text translated into several languages. —n. 1 a polyglot person. 2 a polyglot book, esp. a Bible. □□ **polyglottal** /-ˈɡlɒt(ə)l/ adj. **polyglottic** /-ˈɡlɒtɪk/ adj. **polyglottism** n. [F polyglotte f. Gk poluglōttos (as POLY-¹, glōtta tongue)]

polygon /ˈpɒlɪɡən, -ˌɡɒn/ n. a plane figure with many (usu. a minimum of three) sides and angles. □ **polygon of forces** a polygon that represents by the length and direction of its sides all the forces acting on a body or point. □□ **polygonal** /pəˈlɪɡən(ə)l/ adj. [LL polygonum f. Gk polugōnon (neut. adj.) (as POLY-¹ + -gōnos angled)]

polygonum /pəˈlɪɡənəm/ n. any plant of the genus Polygonum, with small bell-shaped flowers. Also called KNOTGRASS, KNOTWEED. [mod.L f. Gk polugonon]

polygraph /ˈpɒlɪˌɡrɑːf/ n. a machine designed to detect and record changes in physiological characteristics (e.g. rates of pulse and breathing), used esp. as a lie-detector.

polygyny /pəˈlɪdʒɪnɪ/ n. polygamy in which a man has more than one wife. □□ **polygynous** /pəˈlɪdʒɪnəs/ adj. [POLY-¹ + gyny f. Gk gunē woman]

polyhedron /ˌpɒlɪˈhiːdrən, -ˈhedrən/ n. (pl. **polyhedra** /-drə/) a solid figure with many (usu. more than six) faces. □□ **polyhedral** adj. **polyhedric** adj. [Gk poluedron neut. of poluedros (as POLY-¹, hedra base)]

polyhistor /ˌpɒlɪˈhɪstə(r)/ n. = POLYMATH.

Polyhymnia /ˌpɒlɪˈhɪmnɪə/ Gk & Rom. Mythol. the Muse of the mimic art. [Gk, = she of the many hymns]

polymath /ˈpɒlɪˌmæθ/ n. 1 a person of much or varied learning. 2 a great scholar. □□ **polymathic** /ˌpɒlɪˈmæθɪk/ adj. **polymathy** /pəˈlɪməθɪ/ n. [Gk polumathēs (as POLY-¹, math- stem manthanō learn)]

polymer /ˈpɒlɪmə(r)/ n. a compound composed of one or more large molecules that are formed from repeated units of smaller molecules. □□ **polymeric** /-ˈmerɪk/ adj. **polymerism** n.

polymerize v.intr. & tr. (also **-ise**). **polymerization** /-ˈzeɪʃ(ə)n/ n. [G f. Gk polumeros having many parts (as POLY-¹, meros share)]

polymerous /pəˈlɪmərəs/ adj. Biol. having many parts.

polymorphism /ˌpɒlɪˈmɔːfɪz(ə)m/ n. 1 a Biol. the existence of various different forms in the successive stages of the development of an organism. b = PLEOMORPHISM. 2 Chem. = ALLOTROPY. □□ **polymorphic** adj. **polymorphous** adj.

Polynesia /ˌpɒlɪˈniːʒə/ the islands of the central and western Pacific or (more usually) the easternmost of the three great groups of these islands, including New Zealand, Hawaii, and Samoa. □□ **Polynesian** adj. & n. [as POLY- + Gk nēsos island]

polyneuritis /ˌpɒlɪˌnjʊəˈraɪtɪs/ n. any disorder that affects many of the peripheral nerves. □□ **polyneuritic** /-ˈrɪtɪk/ adj.

polynomial /ˌpɒlɪˈnəʊmɪəl/ n. & adj. Math. —n. an expression of more than two algebraic terms, esp. the sum of several terms that contain different powers of the same variable(s). —adj. of or being a polynomial. [POLY-¹ after multinomial]

polynya /pəˈlɪnjə/ n. a stretch of open water surrounded by ice, esp. in the Arctic seas. [Russ. f. pole field]

polyp /ˈpɒlɪp/ n. 1 Zool. an individual coelenterate. 2 Med. a small usu. benign growth protruding from a mucous membrane. [F polype (as POLYPUS)]

polypary /ˈpɒlɪpərɪ/ n. (pl. **-ies**) the common stem or support of a colony of polyps. [mod.L polyparium (as POLYPUS)]

polypeptide /ˌpɒlɪˈpeptaɪd/ n. Biochem. a peptide formed by the combination of about ten or more amino acids. [G Polypeptid (as POLY-², PEPTONE)]

polyphagous /pəˈlɪfəɡəs/ adj. Zool. able to feed on various kinds of food.

polyphase /ˈpɒlɪˌfeɪz/ adj. Electr. (of a device or circuit) designed to supply or use simultaneously several alternating currents of the same voltage but with different phases.

Polyphemus /ˌpɒlɪˈfiːməs/ Gk legend the Cyclops from whom Odysseus and some of his companions escaped by putting out his one eye while he slept.

polyphone /ˈpɒlɪˌfəʊn/ n. Phonet. a symbol or letter that represents several different sounds.

polyphonic /ˌpɒlɪˈfɒnɪk/ adj. 1 Mus. (of vocal music etc.) in two or more relatively independent parts; contrapuntal. 2 Phonet. (of a letter etc.) representing more than one sound. □□ **polyphonically** adv. [Gk poluphōnos (as POLY-¹, phōnē voice, sound)]

polyphony /pəˈlɪfənɪ/ n. (pl. **-ies**) 1 Mus. a polyphonic style in musical composition; counterpoint. b a composition written in this style. 2 Philol. the symbolization of different vocal sounds by the same letter or character. □□ **polyphonous** adj.

polypi pl. of POLYPUS.

polyploid /ˈpɒlɪˌplɔɪd/ n. & adj. Biol. —n. a nucleus or organism that contains more than two sets of chromosomes. —adj. of or being a polyploid. □□ **polyploidy** n. [G (as POLY-¹, -PLOID)]

polypod /ˈpɒlɪˌpɒd/ adj. & n. Zool. —adj. having many feet. —n. a polypod animal. [F polypode (adj.) f. Gk (as POLYPUS)]

polypody /ˈpɒlɪˌpəʊdɪ/ n. (pl. **-ies**) any fern of the genus Polypodium, usu. found in woods growing on trees, walls, and stones. [ME f. L polypodium f. Gk polupodion (as POLYPUS)]

polypoid /ˈpɒlɪˌpɔɪd/ adj. of or like a polyp. □□ **polypous** /-pəs/ adj.

polypropene /ˌpɒlɪˈprəʊpiːn/ n. = POLYPROPYLENE.

polypropylene /ˌpɒlɪˈprəʊpɪˌliːn/ n. Chem. any of various polymers of propylene including thermoplastic materials used for films, fibres, or moulding materials. Also called POLYPROPENE.

polypus /ˈpɒlɪpəs/ n. (pl. **polypi** /-paɪ/ or **polypuses**) Med. = POLYP 2. [ME f. L polypus f. Gk pōlupos, poupous cuttlefish, polyp (as POLY-¹, pous podos foot)]

polysaccharide /ˌpɒlɪˈsækəˌraɪd/ n. any of a group of carbohydrates whose molecules consist of long chains of monosaccharides.

polysemy /ˌpɒlɪˈsiːmɪ, ˈpɒl-/ n. Philol. the existence of many meanings (of a word etc.). □□ **polysemic** /-ˈsiːmɪk/ adj. **polysemous** /-ˈsiːməs/ adj. [POLY-¹ + Gk sēma sign]

polystyrene /ˌpɒlɪˈstaɪəˌriːn/ n. a thermoplastic polymer of styrene, usu. hard and colourless or expanded with a gas to produce a lightweight rigid white substance, used for insulation and in packaging.

polysyllabic /ˌpɒlɪsɪˈlæbɪk/ adj. **1** (of a word) having many syllables. **2** characterized by the use of words of many syllables. □□ **polysyllabically** adv.

polysyllable /ˈpɒlɪˌsɪləb(ə)l/ n. a polysyllabic word.

polytechnic /ˌpɒlɪˈteknɪk/ n. & adj. —n. an institution of higher education offering courses in many (esp. vocational) subjects at degree level or below. The original Polytechnic Institution (in Regent Street, London) was founded in 1838 by George Cayley (see entry) and others. —adj. dealing with or devoted to various vocational or technical subjects. [F polytechnique f. Gk polutekhnos (as POLY-¹ tekhnē art)]

polytetrafluoroethylene /ˌpɒlɪˌtetrəˌfluərəʊ ˈeθɪˌliːn/ n. Chem. a tough translucent polymer resistant to chemicals and used to coat cooking utensils etc. ¶ Abbr.: **PTFE**. [POLY-² + TETRA- + FLUORO- + ETHYLENE]

polytheism /ˈpɒlɪθiːˌɪz(ə)m/ n. the belief in or worship of more than one god. □□ **polytheist** n. **polytheistic** /-ˈɪstɪk/ adj. [F polythéisme f. Gk polutheos of many gods (as POLY-¹, theos god)]

polythene /ˈpɒlɪˌθiːn/ n. Chem. a tough light thermoplastic polymer of ethylene, usu. translucent and flexible or opaque and rigid, used for packaging and insulating materials. Also called POLYETHYLENE, POLYETHENE.

polytonality /ˌpɒlɪtəʊˈnælɪtɪ/ n. Mus. the simultaneous use of two or more keys in a composition. □□ **polytonal** /-ˈtəʊn(ə)l/ adj.

polyunsaturated /ˌpɒlɪʌnˈsætʃəˌreɪtɪd, -tjʊˌreɪtɪd/ adj. Chem. (of a compound, esp. a fat or oil molecule) containing several double or triple bonds and therefore capable of further reaction.

polyurethane /ˌpɒlɪˈjʊərəˌθeɪn/ n. any polymer containing the urethane group, used in adhesives, paints, plastics, rubbers, foams, etc.

polyvalent /ˌpɒlɪˈveɪlənt/ adj. Chem. having a valency of more than two, or several valencies. □□ **polyvalence** n.

polyvinyl acetate /ˌpɒlɪˈvaɪnɪl/ n. Chem. a soft plastic polymer used in paints and adhesives. ¶ Abbr.: **PVA**.

polyvinyl chloride /ˌpɒlɪˈvaɪnɪl/ n. a tough transparent solid polymer of vinyl chloride, easily coloured and used for a wide variety of products including pipes, flooring, etc. ¶ Abbr.: **PVC**.

polyzoan /ˌpɒlɪˈzəʊən/ n. = BRYOZOAN.

pom /pɒm/ n. **1** a Pomeranian dog. **2** Austral. & NZ sl. offens. = POMMY. [abbr.]

pomace /ˈpʌmɪs/ n. **1** the mass of crushed apples in cider-making before or after the juice is pressed out. **2** the refuse of fish etc. after the oil has been extracted, generally used as a fertilizer. [ME f. med.L pomacium cider f. L pomum apple]

pomade /pəˈmɑːd/ n. & v. —n. scented dressing for the hair and the skin of the head. —v.tr. anoint with pomade. [F pommade f. It. pomata f. med.L f. L pomum apple (from which it was orig. made)]

pomander /pəˈmændə(r)/ n. **1** a ball of mixed aromatic substances placed in a cupboard etc. or hist. carried in a box, bag, etc. as a protection against infection. **2** a (usu. spherical) container for this. **3** a spiced orange etc. similarly used. [earlier pom(e)amber f. AF f. OF pome d'embre f. med.L pomum de ambra apple of ambergris]

pomatum /pəˈmɑːtəm/ n. & v.tr. = POMADE. [mod.L f. L pomum apple]

pome /pəʊm/ n. a firm-fleshed fruit in which the carpels from the central core enclose the seeds, e.g. the apple, pear, and quince. □□ **pomiferous** /pəˈmɪfərəs/ adj. [ME f. OF ult. f. poma pl. of L pomum fruit, apple]

pomegranate /ˈpɒmɪˌɡrænɪt, ˈpɒmˌɡrænɪt/ n. **1 a** an orange-sized fruit with a tough golden-orange outer skin containing many seeds in a red pulp. **b** the tree bearing this fruit, Punica granatum, native to N. Africa and W. Asia. **2** an ornamental representation of a pomegranate. [ME f. OF pome grenate (as POME, L granatum having many seeds f. granum seed)]

pomelo /ˈpʌməˌləʊ/ n. (pl. **-os**) **1** = SHADDOCK. **2** US = GRAPEFRUIT. [19th c.: orig. unkn.]

Pomerania /ˌpɒməˈreɪnɪə/ a region along the south shore of the Baltic Sea, between the Oder and Vistula rivers. Most of it is now part of Poland, but the western section is in Germany.

Pomeranian /ˌpɒməˈreɪnɪən/ n. **1** a small dog with long silky hair, a pointed muzzle, and pricked ears. **2** this breed.

pomfret /ˈpɒmfrɪt/ n. **1** any of various fish of the family Stromateidae of the Indian and Pacific Oceans. **2** a dark-coloured deep-bodied marine fish, Brama brama, used as food. [app. f. Port. pampo]

pomfret-cake /ˈpʌmfrɪt, ˈpɒ-/ n. (also **Pontefract-cake** /ˈpɒntɪˌfrækt/) Brit. a small round flat liquorice sweetmeat orig. made at Pontefract (earlier Pomfret) in Yorkshire.

pomiculture /ˈpɒmɪˌkʌltʃə(r)/ n. fruit-growing. [L pomum fruit + CULTURE]

pommel /ˈpʌm(ə)l/ n. & v. —n. **1** a knob, esp. at the end of a sword-hilt. **2** the upward projecting front part of a saddle. —v.tr. (**pommelled, pommelling**; US **pommeled, pommeling**) = PUMMEL. □ **pommel horse** a vaulting horse fitted with a pair of curved handgrips. [ME f. OF pomel f. Rmc pomellum (unrecorded), dimin. of L pomum fruit, apple]

pommy /ˈpɒmɪ/ n. (also **pommie**) (pl. **-ies**) Austral. & NZ sl. offens. a British person, esp. a recent immigrant. [20th c.: orig. uncert.]

pomology /pəˈmɒlədʒɪ/ n. the science of fruit-growing. □□ **pomological** /-məˈlɒdʒɪk(ə)l/ adj. **pomologist** n. [L pomum fruit + -LOGY]

pomp /pɒmp/ n. **1** a splendid display; splendour. **2** (often in pl.) vainglory (the pomps and vanities of this wicked world). [ME f. OF pompe f. L pompa f. Gk pompē procession, pomp f. pempō send]

Pompadour /ˈpɒmpəˌdʊə(r)/, Marquise de. Jeanne Antoinette Poisson le Normant (1721–64), favourite of Louis XV. Pompadour became the king's confidante from 1745 until her death nineteen years later. Although her relationship with the king was platonic, certainly after the first few years, she maintained her hold over him by procuring him young mistresses and became very unpopular with the king's critics, particularly among the nobility who did not approve of her humble origins.

pompadour /ˈpɒmpəˌdʊə(r)/ n. a woman's hairstyle with the hair in a high turned-back roll round the face. [f. Marquise de Pompadour, the mistress of Louis XV of France d. 1764]

pompano /ˈpɒmpɑːnəʊ/ n. (pl. **-os**) any of various fish of the family Carangidae or Stromateidae of the Atlantic and Pacific Oceans, used as food. [Sp. pámpano]

Pompeii /pɒmˈpeɪɪ/ an ancient town SE of Naples. Its sudden end in the Vesuvius eruption of AD 79, described by the Younger Pliny (and in which his uncle, the Elder Pliny, perished), struck the imagination of the ancient world as well as the modern. The site, forgotten in the Middle Ages, was rediscovered in 1748, since when excavation and restoration has proceeded intermittently. The remains, buried and preserved beneath 4–6 metres of volcanic ash, include not only buildings and mosaics but wall-paintings, furniture, graffiti, and personal possessions of the inhabitants, providing an unusually vivid insight into Roman life, art, and architecture of the period.

Pompey /ˈpɒmpɪ/ 'the Great' (Gnaeus Pompeius, 106–48 BC), Roman general and politician. His greatest achievements were the suppression of the Mediterranean pirates (66 BC), and the defeat of Mithridates in the east (63 BC). Disagreement with Caesar ended in civil war and defeat for Pompey at the battle of Pharsalus, after which he fled to Egypt where he was murdered.

pom-pom /ˈpɒmpɒm/ n. an automatic quick-firing gun esp. on a ship. [imit.]

pompon /ˈpɒmpɒn/ n. (also **pompom**) **1** an ornamental ball or bobble made of wool, silk, or ribbons, usu. worn on women's or children's hats or clothing. **2** the round tuft on a soldier's cap, the front of a shako, etc. **3** (often attrib.) a dahlia or chrysanthemum with small tightly-clustered petals. [F, of unkn. orig.]

pompous /ˈpɒmpəs/ n. **1** self-important, affectedly grand or solemn. **2** (of language) pretentious; unduly grand in style. **3**

b but d dog f few g get h he j yes k cat l leg m man n no p pen r red s sit t top v voice

archaic magnificent; splendid. □□ **pomposity** /pɒmˈpɒsɪtɪ/ n. (pl. **-ies**). **pompously** adv. **pompousness** n. [ME f. OF pompeux f. LL pomposus (as POMP)]

'pon /pɒn/ prep. archaic = UPON. [abbr.]

ponce /pɒns/ n. & v. Brit. sl. —n. **1** a man who lives off a prostitute's earnings; a pimp. **2** offens. a homosexual; an effeminate man. —v.intr. act as a ponce. □ **ponce about** move about effeminately or ineffectually. □□ **poncey** adj. (also **poncy**) (in sense 2 of n.). [perh. f. POUNCE¹]

Ponce de Leon /ˈpɒnθeɪ də ˈleɪɒn/, Juan (c.1460–1521), Spanish explorer who accompanied Columbus on his second voyage to the New World in 1493 and in 1510 became Governor of Puerto Rico. He discovered Florida in 1513, but was wounded in a skirmish with natives on a return voyage in 1521 and later died of his injuries in Cuba.

poncho /ˈpɒntʃəʊ/ n. (pl. **-os**) **1** a S. American cloak made of a blanket-like piece of cloth with a slit in the middle for the head. **2** a garment in this style. [S.Amer. Sp., f. Araucan]

pond /pɒnd/ n. & v. —n. **1** a fairly small body of still water formed naturally or by hollowing or embanking. **2** joc. the sea. —v. **1** tr. hold back, dam up (a stream etc.). **2** intr. form a pond. □ **pond-life** animals (esp. invertebrates) that live in ponds. [ME var. of POUND³]

ponder /ˈpɒndə(r)/ v. **1** tr. weigh mentally; think over; consider. **2** intr. (usu. foll. by on, over) think; muse. [ME f. OF ponderer f. pondus -eris weight]

ponderable /ˈpɒndərəb(ə)l/ adj. literary having appreciable weight or significance. □□ **ponderability** /-ˈbɪlɪtɪ/ n. [LL ponderabilis (as PONDER)]

ponderation /ˌpɒndəˈreɪʃ(ə)n/ n. literary the act or an instance of weighing, balancing, or considering. [L ponderatio (as PONDER)]

ponderosa /ˌpɒndəˈrəʊsə/ n. US **1** a N. American pine-tree, Pinus ponderosa. **2** the red timber of this tree. [mod.L, fem. of L ponderosus: see PONDEROUS]

ponderous /ˈpɒndərəs/ adj. **1** heavy; unwieldy. **2** laborious. **3** (of style etc.) dull; tedious. □□ **ponderosity** /-ˈrɒsɪtɪ/ n. **ponderously** adv. **ponderousness** n. [ME f. L ponderosus f. pondus -eris weight]

Pondicherry /ˌpɒndɪˈtʃerɪ/ **1** a Union Territory in SE India, formed from several former French territories incorporated in India in 1954; pop. (1981) 604,100. **2** its capital city; pop. (1981) 251,470.

pondweed /ˈpɒndwiːd/ n. any of various aquatic plants, esp. of the genus Potamogeton, growing in still or running water.

pone¹ /pəʊn/ n. US **1** unleavened maize bread, esp. as made by N. American Indians. **2** a fine light bread made with milk, eggs, etc. **3** a cake or loaf of this. [Algonquian, = bread]

pone² /ˈpəʊnɪ/ n. the dealer's opponent in two-handed card games. [L, 2nd sing. imper. of ponere place]

pong /pɒŋ/ n. & v. Brit. colloq. —n. an unpleasant smell. —v.intr. stink. □□ **pongy** /ˈpɒŋɪ/ adj. (**pongier, pongiest**). [20th c.: orig. unkn.]

pongal /ˈpɒŋ(ə)l/ n. **1** the Tamil New Year festival at which new rice is cooked. **2** a dish of cooked rice. [Tamil poṅkal boiling]

pongee /pɒnˈdʒiː-, pʌn-/ n. **1** a soft usu. unbleached type of Chinese silk fabric. **2** an imitation of this in cotton etc. [perh. f. Chin. dial. pun-chī own loom, i.e. home-made]

pongid /ˈpɒndʒɪd/ n. & adj. —n. any ape of the family Pongidae, including gorillas, chimpanzees, and orang-utans. —adj. of or relating to this family. [mod.L Pongidae f. Pongo the genus-name: see PONGO¹]

pongo¹ /ˈpɒŋgəʊ/ n. (pl. **-os**) **1** an orang-utan. **2** Naut. sl. a soldier. [Congolese mpongo, orig. of African apes]

pongo² /ˈpɒŋgəʊ/ n. (pl. **-os**) Austral. & NZ sl. offens. an Englishman. [20th c.: orig. unkn.]

poniard /ˈpɒnjəd/ n. literary a small slim dagger. [F poignard f. OF poignal f. med.L pugnale f. L pugnus fist]

pons /pɒnz/ n. (pl. **pontes** /ˈpɒntiːz/) Anat. (in full **pons Varolii** /vəˈrəʊlɪaɪ/) the part of the brain stem that links the medulla oblongata and the thalamus. □ **pons asinorum** /ˌæsɪˈnɔːrəm/ any difficult proposition, orig. a rule of geometry from Euclid

('bridge of asses'). [L, = bridge: Varolii f. C. Varoli, It. anatomist d. 1575]

pont /pɒnt/ n. S.Afr. a flat-bottomed ferry-boat. [Du.]

Pont du Gard /pɔ̃ du: ˈgɑːd/ an arched structure built by the Romans c. AD 14 over the River Gard or Gardon in southern France as part of an aqueduct carrying water to Nîmes. Three tiers of limestone arches of diminishing span support the covered water-channel at a height of 55 metres (180 ft.) above the valley. In the 18th c. the lowest tier was widened to form a road bridge that is still in use.

Pontefract-cake var. of POMFRET-CAKE.

pontes pl. of PONS.

Pontianak /ˌpɒntɪˈɑːnæk/ a seaport of Indonesia, capital of the province of West Kalimantan, situated on the west coast of Borneo; pop. (1980) 304,770.

pontifex /ˈpɒntɪˌfeks/ n. (pl. **pontifices** /pɒnˈtɪfɪsiːz/) **1** = PONTIFF. **2** Rom. Antiq. a member of the principal college of priests in Rome. □ **Pontifex Maximus** the head of this. [L pontifex -ficis f. pons pontis bridge + -fex f. facere make]

pontiff /ˈpɒntɪf/ n. RC Ch. (in full **sovereign** or **supreme pontiff**) the Pope. [F pontife (as PONTIFEX)]

pontifical /pɒnˈtɪfɪk(ə)l/ adj. & n. —adj. **1** RC Ch. of or befitting a pontiff; papal. **2** pompously dogmatic; with an attitude of infallibility. —n. **1** an office-book of the Western Church containing rites to be performed by the Pope or bishops. **2** (in pl.) the vestments and insignia of a bishop, cardinal, or abbot. □ **pontifical mass** a high mass, usu. celebrated by a cardinal, bishop, etc. □□ **pontifically** adv. [ME f. F pontifical or L pontificalis (as PONTIFEX)]

pontificate v. & n. —v.intr. /pɒnˈtɪfɪˌkeɪt/ **1 a** play the pontiff; pretend to be infallible. **b** be pompously dogmatic. **2** RC Ch. officiate as bishop, esp. at mass. —n. /pɒnˈtɪfɪkət/ **1** the office of pontifex, bishop, or pope. **2** the period of this. [L pontificatus (as PONTIFEX)]

pontifices pl. of PONTIFEX.

Pontine Marshes /ˈpɒntaɪn/ a reclaimed marshland area in southern central Italy, bordering on the Tyrrhenian Sea. In ancient times it was intensively cultivated, but became malaria-infested until an extensive scheme to drain the marshes began in 1928. It is now a very productive agricultural area with several towns.

pontoon¹ /pɒnˈtuːn/ n. Brit. **1** a card-game in which players try to acquire cards with a face value totalling 21 and no more. **2** = NATURAL n. 4a. [prob. corrupt.]

pontoon² /pɒnˈtuːn/ n. & v. —n. **1** a flat-bottomed boat. **2** each of several boats, hollow metal cylinders, etc., used to support a temporary bridge. **3** = CAISSON 1,2. —v.tr. cross (a river) by means of pontoons. [F ponton f. L ponto -onis f. pons pontis bridge]

Pontormo /pɒnˈtɔːməʊ/, Jacopo da (1494–1557), Florentine painter. Although a pupil of Andrea del Sarto, his admiration for Michelangelo saw the development of strong mannerist tendencies in his work—in particular, dynamic composition, anatomical exaggeration, and abrupt contrasts (e.g. Joseph in Egypt, 1518–19). His portrait style is less exuberant and, with his drawings, justly admired.

Pontus /ˈpɒntəs/ the ancient name for the region in northern Asia Minor north of Cappadocia, stretching along the Black Sea coast.

pony /ˈpəʊnɪ/ n. (pl. **-ies**) **1** a horse of any small breed. **2** a small drinking-glass. **3** (in pl.) sl. racehorses. **4** Brit. sl. £25. □ **pony-tail** a person's hair drawn back, tied, and hanging down like a pony's tail. **pony-trekker** a person who travels across country on a pony for pleasure. **pony-trekking** this as a hobby or activity. [perh. f. poulney (unrecorded) f. F poulenet dimin. of poulain foal]

Pony Express a system of mail delivery in the US in 1860–1, over a distance of 2,900 km (1,800 miles), between St Joseph in Missouri and Sacramento in California, by continuous relays of horse-riders. William Cody ('Buffalo Bill') was one of its riders.

pooch /puːtʃ/ n. esp. US sl. a dog. [20th c.: orig. unkn.]

poodle /ˈpuːd(ə)l/ n. **1 a** a dog of a breed with a curly coat that is usually clipped. **b** this breed. **2** a lackey or servile follower. [G *Pudel(hund)* f. LG *pud(d)eln* splash in water: cf. PUDDLE]

poof /puf, pu:f/ *n.* (also **pouf, poove** /pu:v/) *Brit. sl. derog.* **1** an effeminate man. **2** a male homosexual. □□ **poofy** /ˈpufi/ *adj.* [19th c.: cf. PUFF in sense 'braggart']

poofter /ˈpuftə(r), ˈpu:-/ *n. sl. derog.* = POOF.

pooh /pu:/ *int. & n.* —*int.* expressing impatience or contempt. —*n. sl.* excrement. [imit.]

Pooh-Bah /ˈpu:ba:/ *n.* (also **pooh-bah**) a holder of many offices at once. [a character in W. S. Gilbert's *The Mikado* (1885)]

pooh-pooh /pu:ˈpu:/ *v.tr.* express contempt for; ridicule; dismiss (an idea etc.) scornfully. [redupl. of POOH]

pooja var. of PUJA.

pooka /ˈpu:kə/ *n. Ir.* a hobgoblin. [Ir. *púca*]

pool[1] /pu:l/ *n. & v.* —*n.* **1** a small body of still water, usu. of natural formation. **2** a small shallow body of any liquid. **3** = *swimming-pool* (see SWIM). **4** a deep place in a river. —*v.* **1** *tr.* form into a pool. **2** *intr.* (of blood) become static. [OE *pōl*, MLG, MDu. *pōl*, OHG *pfuol* f. WG]

pool[2] /pu:l/ *n. & v.* —*n.* **1 a** (often *attrib.*) a common supply of persons, vehicles, commodities, etc. for sharing by a group of people (*a typing pool; a pool car*). **b** a group of persons sharing duties etc. **2 a** the collective amount of players' stakes in gambling etc. **b** a receptacle for this. **3 a** a joint commercial venture, esp. an arrangement between competing parties to fix prices and share business to eliminate competition. **b** the common funding for this. **4 a** *US* a game on a billiard-table with usu. 16 balls. **b** *Brit.* a game on a billiard-table in which each player has a ball of a different colour with which to pocket the others in fixed order, the winner taking all of the stakes. **5** a group of contestants who compete against each other in a tournament for the right to advance to the next round. —*v.tr.* **1** put (resources etc.) into a common fund. **2** share (things) in common. **3** (of transport or organizations etc.) share (traffic, receipts). **4** *Austral. sl.* **a** involve (a person) in a scheme etc., often by deception. **b** implicate, inform on. □ **the pools** *Brit.* = *football pool*. [F *poule* (= hen) in same sense: assoc. with POOL[1]]

poolroom /ˈpu:lru:m, -rum/ *n. US* **1** a betting shop. **2** a place for playing pool.

poon /pu:n/ *n.* any E. Indian tree of the genus *Calophyllum*. □ **poon oil** an oil from the seeds of this tree, used in medicine and for lamps. [Sinh. *pūna*]

Poona see PUNE.

poop[1] /pu:p/ *n. & v.* —*n.* the stern of a ship; the aftermost and highest deck. —*v.tr.* **1** (of a wave) break over the stern of (a ship). **2** (of a ship) receive (a wave) over the stern. [ME f. OF *pupe, pope* ult. f. L *puppis*]

poop[2] /pu:p/ *v.tr.* (esp. as **pooped** *adj.*) *US colloq.* exhaust; tire out. [20th c.: orig. unkn.]

poor /puə(r)/ *adj.* **1** lacking adequate money or means to live comfortably. **2** (foll. by *in*) deficient in (a possession or quality) (*the poor in spirit*). **3 a** scanty, inadequate (*a poor crop*). **b** less good than is usual or expected (*poor visibility; is a poor driver; in poor health*). **c** paltry; inferior (*poor condition; came a poor third*). **4 a** deserving pity or sympathy; unfortunate (*you poor thing*). **b** with reference to a dead person (*as my poor father used to say*). **5** spiritless; despicable (*is a poor creature*). **6** often *iron.* or *joc.* humble; insignificant (*in my poor opinion*). □ **poor-box** a collection-box, esp. in church, for the relief of the poor. **Poor Clares** see CLARE. **Poor Law** see separate entry. **poor man's** an inferior or cheaper substitute for. **poor man's weather-glass** the pimpernel. **poor-rate** *hist.* a rate or assessment for relief or support of the poor. **poor relation** an inferior or subordinate member of a family or any other group. **poor-spirited** timid; cowardly. **poor White** *offens.* (esp. used by Blacks) a member of a socially inferior group of White people. **take a poor view of** regard with disfavour or pessimism. [ME & OF *pov(e)re, poure* f. L *pauper*]

poorhouse /ˈpuəhaus/ *n. hist.* = WORKHOUSE 1.

Poor Law *n. hist.* law relating to the support of the poor in England. In Elizabethan times it placed the responsibility for the relief of the poor on the parish, and levied a compulsory rate for the provision of funds. In the 17th–18th c. there was an inefficient system of workhouses and outdoor relief. Successive legislation resulted in a gradual improvement of the system in the 19th c., and in the 20th c. it was finally supplanted by schemes of social security.

poorly /ˈpuəli/ *adv. & adj.* —*adv.* **1** scantily; defectively. **2** with no great success. **3** meanly; contemptibly. —*predic.adj.* unwell.

poorness /ˈpuənis/ *n.* **1** defectiveness. **2** the lack of some good quality or constituent.

poove var. of POOF.

POP *abbr.* Post Office Preferred (size of envelopes etc.).

pop[1] /pɒp/ *n., v., & adv.* —*n.* **1** a sudden sharp explosive sound as of a cork when drawn. **2** *colloq.* an effervescent sweet drink. —*v.* (**popped, popping**) **1** *intr. & tr.* make or cause to make a pop. **2** *intr. & tr.* (foll. by *in, out, up, down*, etc.) go, move, come, or put unexpectedly or in a quick or hasty manner (*pop out to the shops; pop in for a visit; pop it on your head*). **3 a** *intr. & tr.* burst, making a popping sound. **b** *tr.* heat (popcorn etc.) until it pops. **4** *intr.* (often foll. by *at*) *colloq.* fire a gun (at birds etc.). **5** *tr. sl.* pawn. **6** *tr. sl.* inject (a drug etc.). **7** *intr.* (often foll. by *up*) (of a cricket-ball) rise sharply off the pitch. —*adv.* with the sound of a pop (*heard it go pop*). □ **in pop** *Brit. sl.* in pawn. **pop off** *colloq.* **1** die. **2** quietly slip away (cf. sense 2 of *v.*). **pop the question** *colloq.* propose marriage. **pop-shop** *Brit. sl.* a pawnbroker's shop. **pop-up 1** (of a toaster etc.) operating so as to move the object (toast when ready etc.) quickly upwards. **2** (of a book, greetings card, etc.) containing three-dimensional figures, illustrations, etc., that rise up when the page is turned. **3** *Computing* (of a menu) able to be superimposed on the screen being worked on and suppressed rapidly. [ME: imit.]

pop[2] /pɒp/ *adj. & n. colloq.* —*adj.* **1** in a popular or modern style. **2** performing popular music etc. (*pop group; pop star*). —*n.* **1** pop music. **2** a pop record or song (*top of the pops*). □ **pop art** art based on modern popular culture and the mass media, esp. as a critical comment on traditional fine art values. The term is applied specifically to the works of a group of artists who, largely in the mid-1950s and 1960s, were interested in the subject-matter and techniques of commercial culture and mass production, and were opposed to contemporary aesthetic standards. Artists such as Warhol in America and Hockney in Britain produced works including images of media stars, modern transport, and industrial machinery and products. **pop festival** a festival at which popular music etc. is performed. **pop music** modern popular music (e.g. rock music) appealing particularly to younger people. [abbr.]

pop[3] /pɒp/ *n. esp. US colloq.* father. [abbr. of POPPA]

pop. *abbr.* population.

popadam var. of POPPADAM.

popcorn /ˈpɒpkɔ:n/ *n.* **1** Indian corn which bursts open when heated. **2** these kernels when popped.

Pope /pəup/, Alexander (1688–1744), English poet, crippled by a childhood spinal affliction, and largely self-educated, who showed his precocious metrical skill and biting wit in his 'Pastorals', (1709) and his *Essay on Criticism* (1711) which made him known to Addison's literary circle. Later he associated with Swift, Gay, and others. *The Rape of the Lock* 1712) is perhaps his finest achievement, showing his masterful use of the mock heroic. His translation of the *Iliad* (1715–20) into heroic couplets, though not an accurate version of the original, is one of the great poems of the age and, supplemented in 1725–6 by a translation of the *Odyssey*, helped to finance the comfortable house in Twickenham where he spent the remainder of his life.

pope[1] /pəup/ *n.* **1** (as title usu. **Pope**) the head of the Roman Catholic Church (also called the Bishop of Rome). **2** the head of the Coptic Church. **3** = RUFF[2]. □ **pope's eye 1** a lymphatic gland surrounded with fat in the middle of a sheep's leg. **2** *Sc.* a cut of steak. □□ **popedom** *n.* **popeless** *adj.* [OE f. eccl.L *pāpa* bishop, pope f. eccl.Gk *papas* = Gk *pappas* father: cf. PAPA]

pope[2] /pəup/ *n.* a parish priest of the Orthodox Church in Russia etc. [Russ. *pop* f. OSlav. *popŭ* f. WG f. eccl.Gk (as POPE[1])]

Pope Joan /dʒəun/ according to a legend widely believed in the

Middle Ages, a woman in male disguise who (c.1100) became a distinguished scholar and then pope, reigned for more than two years, and died after giving birth to a child during a procession. The legend is rejected by all serious scholars as an invention.

popery /'pəʊpərɪ/ n. derog. the papal system; the Roman Catholic Church.

pop-eyed /'pɒpaɪd/ adj. colloq. **1** having bulging eyes. **2** wide-eyed (with surprise etc.).

popgun /'pɒpgʌn/ n. **1** a child's toy gun which shoots a pellet etc. by the compression of air with a piston. **2** derog. an inefficient firearm.

popinjay /'pɒpɪnˌdʒeɪ/ n. **1** a fop, a conceited person, a coxcomb. **2 a** archaic a parrot. **b** hist. a figure of a parrot on a pole as a mark to shoot at. [ME f. AF papeiaye, OF papingay etc. f. Sp. papagayo f. Arab. babaḡā: assim. to JAY]

popish /'pəʊpɪʃ/ adj. derog. of popery; Roman Catholic. □ **Popish Plot** a fictitious Jesuit plot to kill Charles II of England, massacre Protestants, and put the Catholic Duke of York on the throne, concocted by a Protestant clergyman, Titus Oates, in 1678. The 'discovery' of the plot led to a major panic and the execution of about 35 Catholics, most notably the Primate of Ireland. □□ **popishly** adv.

poplar /'pɒplə(r)/ n. **1** any tree of the genus Populus, with a usu. rapidly growing trunk and tremulous leaves. **2** US = tulip-tree. [ME f. AF popler, OF poplier f. pople f. L populus]

poplin /'pɒplɪn/ n. a plain-woven fabric usu. of cotton, with a corded surface. [obs. F papeline perh. f. It. papalina (fem.) PAPAL, f. the papal town Avignon where it was made]

popliteal /pɒp'lɪtɪəl/ adj. of the hollow at the back of the knee. [mod.L popliteus f. L poples -itis this hollow]

Popocatépetl /ˌpɒpəˌkætə'petl/ a dormant volcano (it last erupted in 1707) 72 km (45 miles) south-east of Mexico City, rising to a height of 5,452 m (17,700 ft.).

poppa /'pɒpə/ n. US colloq. father (esp. as a child's word). [var. of PAPA]

poppadam /'pɒpədəm/ n. (also **poppadom, popadam**) Ind. a thin, crisp, spiced bread eaten with curry etc. [Tamil pappaḍam]

Popper /'pɒpə(r)/, Sir Karl Raimund (1902–), Austrian-born philosopher, originally associated with the Vienna circle, though he was highly critical of some of the main doctrines of its 'logical positivism' (see entry). He left Vienna for New Zealand on Hitler's rise to power, and later came to England, where he was a professor at the London School of Economics 1949–69. Popper's theory of science was that scientific progress is made by imaginative conjecture, by producing a theory and constantly attempting to refute it; its confirmation can only be provisional, its refutation is final. In The Open Society and its Enemies (1945) he strongly attacked the theories of Plato, Hegel, and Karl Marx. Other works include The Self and its Brain (with J. C. Eccles, 1977), in which he argues that the mental cannot be reduced to the physical.

popper /'pɒpə(r)/ n. **1** Brit. colloq. a press-stud. **2** a person or thing that pops. **3** colloq. a small vial of amyl nitrite used for inhalation.

poppet /'pɒpɪt/ n. **1** Brit. colloq. (esp. as a term of endearment) a small or dainty person. **2** (in full **poppet-head**) the head of a lathe. **3** a small square piece of wood fitted inside the gunwale or washstrake of a boat. □ **poppet-head** Brit. the frame at the top of a mine-shaft supporting pulleys for the ropes used in hoisting. **poppet-valve** Engin. a mushroom-shaped valve, lifted bodily from its seat rather than hinged. [ME popet(te), ult. f. L pup(p)a: cf. PUPPET]

popping-crease /'pɒpɪŋˌkriːs/ n. Cricket a line four feet in front of and parallel to the wicket, within which the batsman must keep the bat or one foot grounded to avoid the risk of being stumped. [POP¹, perh. in obs. sense 'strike']

popple /'pɒp(ə)l/ v. & n. —v.intr. (of water) tumble about, toss to and fro. —n. the act or an instance of rolling, tossing, or rippling of water. □□ **popply** adj. [ME prob. f. MDu. popelen murmur, quiver, of imit. orig.]

poppy /'pɒpɪ/ n. (pl. **-ies**) any plant of the genus Papaver, with showy often red flowers and a milky sap with narcotic properties. □ **Poppy Day** Remembrance Sunday, on which artificial poppies are worn (see FLANDERS POPPY). **poppy-head 1** the seed capsule of the poppy. **2** an ornamental top on the end of a church pew. □□ **poppied** adj. [OE popig, papæg, etc. f. med.L papauum f. L papaver]

poppycock /'pɒpɪˌkɒk/ n. sl. nonsense. [Du. dial. pappekak]

popsy /'pɒpsɪ/ n. (also **popsie**) (pl. **-ies**) colloq. (usu. as a term of endearment) a young woman. [shortening of POPPET]

populace /'pɒpjʊləs/ n. **1** the common people. **2** derog. the rabble. [F f. It. popolaccio f. popolo people + -accio pejorative suffix]

popular /'pɒpjʊlə(r)/ adj. **1** liked or admired by many people or by a specified group (popular teachers; a popular hero). **2 a** of or carried on by the general public (popular meetings). **b** prevalent among the general public (popular discontent). **3** adapted to the understanding, taste, or means of the people (popular science; popular medicine). □ **popular music** songs, folk tunes, etc., appealing to popular tastes. □□ **popularism** n. **popularity** /-'lærɪtɪ/ n. **popularly** adv. [ME f. AF populer, OF populeir or L popularis f. populus people]

Popular Front 1 an international political alliance of Communist, radical, and socialist elements formed in 1935 and gaining power in France (1936–8), Spain (1936), and Chile (1938–42). In Europe it was largely ineffective after 1938. **2** (also **popular front**) a similar party or coalition representing left-wing elements.

popularize /'pɒpjʊləˌraɪz/ v.tr. (also **-ise**) **1** make popular. **2** cause (a person, principle, etc.) to be generally known or liked. **3** present (a technical subject, specialized vocabulary, etc.) in a popular or readily understandable form. □□ **popularization** /-'zeɪʃ(ə)n/ n. **popularizer** n.

populate /'pɒpjʊˌleɪt/ v.tr. **1** inhabit; form the population of (a town, country, etc.). **2** supply with inhabitants; people (a densely populated district). [med.L populare populat- (as PEOPLE)]

population /ˌpɒpjʊ'leɪʃ(ə)n/ n. **1 a** the inhabitants of a place, country, etc. referred to collectively. **b** any specified group within this (the Irish population of Liverpool). **2** the total number of any of these (a population of eight million; the seal population). **3** the act or process of supplying with inhabitants (the population of forest areas). **4** Statistics any finite or infinite collection of items under consideration. □ **population explosion** a sudden large increase of population. [LL populatio (as PEOPLE)]

populist /'pɒpjʊlɪst/ n. & adj. —n. a member or adherent of a political party seeking support mainly from the ordinary people. —adj. of or relating to such a political party. □□ **populism** n. **populistic** /-'lɪstɪk/ adj. [L populus people]

populous /'pɒpjʊləs/ adj. thickly inhabited. □□ **populously** adv. **populousness** n. [ME f. LL populosus (as PEOPLE)]

porbeagle /pɔː'biːg(ə)l/ n. a large shark, Lamna nasus, having a pointed snout. [18th-c. Corn. dial., of unkn. orig.]

porcelain /'pɔːsəlɪn/ n. **1** a hard vitrified translucent ceramic. **2** objects made of this. □ **porcelain clay** kaolin. **porcelain-shell** cowrie. □□ **porcellaneous** /ˌpɔːsə'leɪnɪəs/ adj. **porcellanous** /pɔː'selənəs/ adj. [F porcelaine cowrie, porcelain f. It. porcellana f. porcella dimin. of porca (a cowrie being perh. likened to a sow's vulva) f. L porca fem. of porcus pig]

porch /pɔːtʃ/ n. **1** a covered shelter for the entrance of a building. **2** US a veranda. **3** (**the Porch**) = the Stoa (see STOA 2). □□ **porched** adj. **porchless** adj. [ME f. OF porche f. L porticus (transl. Gk stoa) f. porta passage]

porcine /'pɔːsaɪn/ adj. of or like pigs. [F porcin or f. L porcinus f. porcus pig]

porcupine /'pɔːkjʊˌpaɪn/ n. **1** any rodent of the family Hystricidae native to Africa, Asia, and SE Europe, or the family Erethizontidae native to America, having defensive spines or quills. **2** (attrib.) denoting any of various animals or other organisms with spines. □ **porcupine fish** a marine fish, Diodon hystrix, covered with sharp spines and often distending itself into a spherical shape. □□ **porcupinish** adj. **porcupiny** adj. [ME f. OF porc espin f. Prov. porc espi(n) ult. f. L porcus pig + spina thorn]

pore¹ /pɔː(r)/ n. esp. Biol. a minute opening in a surface through which gases, liquids, or fine solids may pass. [ME f. OF f. L *porus* f. Gk *poros* passage, pore]

pore[2] /pɔː(r)/ *v.intr.* (foll. by *over*) **1** be absorbed in studying (a book etc.). **2** meditate on, think intently about (a subject). [ME *pure* etc. perh. f. OE *purian* (unrecorded): cf. PEER[1]]

Poreč /ˈpɒretʃ/ a resort town in NW Yugoslavia, on the Adriatic coast.

porgy /ˈpɔːɡɪ/ *n.* (*pl.* **-ies**) US any usu. marine fish of the family Sparidae, used as food. Also called *sea bream*. [18th c.: orig. uncert.: cf. Sp. & Port. *pargo*]

Pori /ˈpɒrɪ/ a port in SW Finland, on the Gulf of Bothnia; pop. (1987) 77,395.

porifer /ˈpɒrɪfə(r)/ *n.* any aquatic invertebrate of the phylum Porifera, including sponges. [mod.L *Porifera* f. L *porus* PORE[1] + *-fer* bearing]

pork /pɔːk/ *n.* the (esp. unsalted) flesh of a pig, used as food. □ **pork-barrel** US *colloq.* government funds as a source of political benefit. **pork-butcher** a person who slaughters pigs for sale, or who sells pork rather than other meats. **pork pie** a pie of minced pork etc. eaten cold. **pork pie hat** a hat with a flat crown and a brim turned up all round. [ME *porc* f. OF *porc* f. L *porcus* pig]

porker /ˈpɔːkə(r)/ *n.* **1** a pig raised for food. **2** a young fattened pig.

porkling /ˈpɔːklɪŋ/ *n.* a young or small pig.

porky[1] /ˈpɔːkɪ/ *adj.* (**porkier, porkiest**) **1** *colloq.* fleshy, fat. **2** of or like pork.

porky[2] /ˈpɔːkɪ/ *n.* (*pl.* **-ies**) US *colloq.* a porcupine. [abbr.]

porn /pɔːn/ *n.* *colloq.* pornography. [abbr.]

porno /ˈpɔːnəʊ/ *n.* & *adj.* *colloq.* —*n.* pornography. —*adj.* pornographic. [abbr.]

pornography /pɔːˈnɒɡrəfɪ/ *n.* **1** the explicit description or exhibition of sexual activity in literature, films, etc., intended to stimulate erotic rather than aesthetic or emotional feelings. **2** literature etc. characterized by this. □□ **pornographer** *n.* **pornographic** /-nəˈɡræfɪk/ *adj.* **pornographically** /-nəˈɡræfɪkəlɪ/ *adv.* [Gk *pornographos* writing of harlots f. *pornē* prostitute + *graphō* write]

porous /ˈpɔːrəs/ *adj.* **1** full of pores. **2** letting through air, water, etc. **3** (of an argument, security system, etc.) leaky, admitting infiltration. □□ **porosity** /pɔːˈrɒsɪtɪ/ *n.* **porously** *adv.* **porousness** *n.* [ME f. OF *poreux* f. med.L *porosus* f. L *porus* PORE[1]]

porphyria /pɔːˈfɪrɪə/ *n.* any of a group of genetic disorders associated with abnormal metabolism of various pigments. [mod.L f. *porphyrin* purple substance excreted by porphyria patients f. Gk *porphura* purple]

Porphyry /ˈpɔːfɪrɪ/ (c.232–303) Neoplatonist philosopher and opponent of Christianity, a pupil of Plotinus whose works he edited after the latter's death.

porphyry /ˈpɔːfɪrɪ/ *n.* (*pl.* **-ies**) **1** a hard rock quarried in ancient Egypt, composed of crystals of white or red feldspar in a red matrix. **2** *Geol.* an igneous rock with large crystals scattered in a matrix of much smaller crystals. □□ **porphyritic** /-ˈrɪtɪk/ *adj.* [ME ult. f. med.L *porphyreum* f. Gk *porphuritēs* f. *porphura* purple]

porpoise /ˈpɔːpəs/ *n.* any of various small toothed whales of the family Phocaenidae, esp. of the genus *Phocaena*, with a low triangular dorsal fin and a blunt rounded snout. [ME *porpays* etc. f. OF *po(u)rpois* etc. ult. f. L *porcus* pig + *piscis* fish]

porridge /ˈpɒrɪdʒ/ *n.* **1** a dish consisting of oatmeal or another meal or cereal boiled in water or milk. **2** *sl.* imprisonment. □□ **porridgy** *adj.* [16th c.: alt. of POTTAGE]

porringer /ˈpɒrɪndʒə(r)/ *n.* a small bowl, often with a handle, for soup, stew, etc. [earlier *pottinger* f. OF *potager* f. *potage* (see POTTAGE): -n- as in *messenger* etc.]

Porsche /pɔːʃ/, Ferdinand (1875–1952), Austrian designer of cars, of which the best known is the original German Volkswagen (= people's car), planned as a small economical vehicle (and with Adolf Hitler's backing), though Porsche's real passion was for high-performance sports and racing cars.

Porsen(n)a /ˈpɔːsɪnə/, Lars. According to legend (probably based on a confusion of the historical facts) an Etruscan chieftain, who was summoned by the exiled Tarquin the Proud (6th c. BC) and vainly laid siege to Rome.

port[1] /pɔːt/ *n.* **1** a harbour. **2** a place of refuge. **3** a town or place possessing a harbour, esp. one where customs officers are stationed. □ **port of call** a place where a ship or a person stops on a journey. **Port of London Authority** the corporate body controlling the London harbour and docks. [OE f. L *portus* & ME prob. f. OF f. L *portus*]

port[2] /pɔːt/ *n.* (in full **port wine**) a strong, sweet, dark-red (occas. brown or white) fortified wine of Portugal. [shortened form of *Oporto*, city in Portugal from which port is shipped]

port[3] /pɔːt/ *n.* & *v.* —*n.* the left-hand side (looking forward) of a ship, boat, or aircraft (cf. STARBOARD). —*v.tr.* (also *absol.*) turn (the helm) to port. □ **port tack** see TACK[1] **4. port watch** see WATCH *n.* 3b. [prob. orig. the side turned towards PORT[1]]

port[4] /pɔːt/ *n.* **1 a** an opening in the side of a ship for entrance, loading, etc. **b** a porthole. **2** an aperture for the passage of steam, water, etc. **3** *Electr.* a socket or aperture in an electronic circuit, esp. in a computer network, where connections can be made with peripheral equipment. **4** an aperture in a wall etc. for a gun to be fired through. **5** esp. *Sc.* a gate or gateway, esp. of a walled town. [ME & OF *porte* f. L *porta*]

port[5] /pɔːt/ *v.* & *n.* —*v.tr.* *Mil.* carry (a rifle, or other weapon) diagonally across and close to the body with the barrel etc. near the left shoulder (esp. *port arms!*). —*n.* **1** *Mil.* this position. **2** external deportment; carriage; bearing. [ME f. OF *port* ult. f. L *portare* carry]

port[6] /pɔːt/ *n.* *Austral.* **1** a suitcase or travelling bag. **2** a shopping bag, sugar bag, etc. [abbr. of PORTMANTEAU]

portable /ˈpɔːtəb(ə)l/ *adj.* & *n.* —*adj.* **1** easily movable, convenient for carrying (*portable TV*; *portable computer*). **2** (of a right, privilege, etc.) capable of being transferred or adapted in altered circumstances (*portable pension*). —*n.* a portable object, e.g. a radio, typewriter, etc. (*decided to buy a portable*). □□ **portability** /ˌpɔːtəˈbɪlɪtɪ/ *n.* **portableness** *n.* **portably** *adv.* [ME f. OF *portable* or LL *portabilis* f. L *portare* carry]

portage /ˈpɔːtɪdʒ/ *n.* & *v.* —*n.* **1** the carrying of boats or goods between two navigable waters. **2** a place at which this is necessary. **3 a** the act or an instance of carrying or transporting. **b** the cost of this. —*v.tr.* convey (a boat or goods) between navigable waters. [ME f. OF f. *porter*: see PORT[6]]

Portakabin /ˈpɔːtəˌkæbɪn/ *n.* *propr.* a portable room or building designed for quick assembly. [PORTABLE + CABIN]

portal[1] /ˈpɔːt(ə)l/ *n.* a doorway or gate etc., esp. a large and elaborate one. [ME f. OF f. med.L *portale* (neut. adj.): see PORTAL[2]]

portal[2] /ˈpɔːt(ə)l/ *adj.* **1** of or relating to an aperture in an organ through which its associated vessels pass. **2** of or relating to the portal vein. □ **portal vein** a vein conveying blood to the liver from the spleen, stomach, pancreas, and intestines. [mod.L *portalis* f. L *porta* gate]

portamento /ˌpɔːtəˈmentəʊ/ *n.* (*pl.* **portamenti** /-tɪ/) *Mus.* **1** the act or an instance of gliding from one note to another in singing, playing the violin, etc. **2** piano-playing in a manner intermediate between legato and staccato. [It., = carrying]

Port Arthur /ˈɑːθə(r)/ see LÜDA.

portative /ˈpɔːtətɪv/ *adj.* **1** serving to carry or support. **2** *Mus. hist.* (esp. of a small pipe-organ) portable. [ME f. OF *portatif*, app. alt. of *portatil* f. med.L *portatilis* f. L *portare* carry]

Port-au-Prince /ˌpɔːtəʊˈprɪns/ the capital of Haiti; pop. (1982) 763,200.

portcullis /pɔːtˈkʌlɪs/ *n.* **1** a strong heavy grating sliding up and down in vertical grooves, lowered to block a gateway in a fortress etc. **2** (**Portcullis**) *Heraldry* one of the four pursuivants of the English College of Arms, with this as a badge. □□ **portcullised** *adj.* [ME f. OF *porte coleïce* sliding door f. *porte* door f. L *porta* + *col(e)ice* fem. of *couleis* sliding ult. f. L *colare* filter]

Porte /pɔːt/ *n.* (in full the **Sublime** or **Ottoman Porte**) *hist.* the Ottoman court at Constantinople. [F (*la Sublime Porte* = the exalted gate), transl. of Turk. title of the central office of the Ottoman government]

porte-cochère /ˌpɔːtkɒˈʃeə(r)/ n. **1** a porch large enough for vehicles to pass through, usu. into a courtyard. **2** *US* a roofed structure extending from the entrance of a building over a place where vehicles stop to discharge passengers. [F f. *porte* PORT⁴ + *cochère* (fem. adj.) f. *coche* COACH]

Port Elizabeth /ɪˈlɪzəbəθ/ a seaport in Cape Province, South Africa; pop. (1985) 652,000. Founded in 1820, it was named after the wife of the governor of the Cape of Good Hope.

Port el Kantaoui /el kænˈtaʊɪ/ a resort town to the north of Sousse on the east coast of Tunisia.

portend /pɔːˈtend/ v.tr. **1** foreshadow as an omen. **2** give warning of. [ME f. L *portendere portent-* f. *por-* PRO-¹ + *tendere* stretch]

portent /ˈpɔːtent, -t(ə)nt/ n. **1** an omen, a significant sign of something to come. **2** a prodigy; a marvellous thing. [L *portentum* (as PORTEND)]

portentous /pɔːˈtentəs/ adj. **1** like or serving as a portent. **2** pompously solemn. □□ **portentously** adv.

Porter¹ /ˈpɔːtə(r)/, Cole (1891–1964), American composer. He was as set on following a musical career as his parents were against it, and was a skilful enough song composer to make a success of it and live independently of them. His main successes came during and after the 1930s, with a long series of Broadway musicals including *Gay Divorce* (1932), *Anything Goes* (1934), and *Kiss me, Kate* (1948). He wrote his own song lyrics, such as the witty and original 'Begin the Beguine'.

Porter² /ˈpɔːtə(r)/, Katherine Anne (1890–1980), American writer. Her collections of short stories include *Pale Horse, Pale Rider* (1939). Her novel *Ship of Fools* (1962) is an allegorical treatment of a voyage from Mexico to Germany on the eve of Hitler's rise to power.

Porter³ /ˈpɔːtə(r)/, Peter (Neville Frederick) (1929–), Australian poet, who settled in England in 1951 where he has worked from copywriter to full-time critic, broadcaster, and writer. His early collections (*Once Bitten, Twice Bitten*, 1961; *Poems, Ancient and Modern*, 1964; *The Last of England*, 1970) provide a sharply satiric portrait of London in the 1960s. His work became increasingly meditative, complex, and allusive, with a wide range of reference from Italian baroque to classical mythology and German romanticism, which add both richness and obscurity. Later volumes (*The Cost of Seriousness*, 1978; *English Subtitles*, 1981) introduce a new sombre exploration of the poet's conflicting responsibilities to his art and to others.

porter¹ /ˈpɔːtə(r)/ n. **1 a** a person employed to carry luggage etc., esp. a railway, airport, or hotel employee. **b** a hospital employee who moves equipment, trolleys, etc. **2** a dark-brown bitter beer brewed from charred or browned malt (app. orig. made esp. for porters). **3** *US* a sleeping-car attendant. □□ **porterage** n. [ME f. OF *port(e)our* f. med.L *portator -oris* f. *portare* carry]

porter² /ˈpɔːtə(r)/ n. *Brit.* a gatekeeper or doorkeeper, esp. of a large building. [ME & AF, OF *portier* f. LL *portarius* f. *porta* door]

porterhouse /ˈpɔːtəhaʊs/ n. esp. *US* **1** *hist.* a house at which porter and other drinks were retailed. **2** a house where steaks, chops, etc. were served. □ **porterhouse steak** a thick steak cut from the thick end of a sirloin.

portfire /ˈpɔːtˌfaɪə(r)/ n. a device for firing rockets, igniting explosives in mining, etc. [after F *porte-feu* f. *porter* carry + *feu* fire]

portfolio /pɔːtˈfəʊlɪəʊ/ n. (pl. **-os**) **1** a case for keeping loose sheets of paper, drawings, etc. **2** a range of investments held by a person, a company, etc. **3** the office of a minister of State (cf. *minister without portfolio*). **4** samples of an artist's work. [It. *portafogli* f. *portare* carry + *foglio* leaf f. L *folium*]

Port-Gentil /ˌpɔːʒãˈtiː/ the principal port of Gabon; pop. (1983) 123,300.

Port Harcourt /ˈhɑːkɔːt/ the principal seaport of SE Nigeria; pop. (1983) 296,200.

Port Hedland /ˈhedlənd/ a seaport on the NW coast of Western Australia, linked by rail to the iron-ore mines at Newman; pop. (est. 1987) 13,600.

porthole /ˈpɔːthəʊl/ n. **1** an (esp. glazed) aperture in a ship's or aircraft's side for the admission of light. **2** *hist.* an aperture for pointing a cannon through.

portico /ˈpɔːtɪˌkəʊ/ n. (pl. **-oes** or **-os**) a colonnade; a roof supported by columns at regular intervals usu. attached as a porch to a building. [It. f. L *porticus* PORCH]

portière /ˌpɔːtɪˈeə(r)/ n. a curtain hung over a door or doorway. [F f. *porte* door f. L *porta*]

portion /ˈpɔːʃ(ə)n/ n. & v. —n. **1** a part or share. **2** the amount of food allotted to one person. **3** a specified or limited quantity. **4** one's destiny or lot. **5** a dowry. —v.tr. **1** divide (a thing) into portions. **2** (foll. by *out*) distribute. **3** give a dowry to. **4** (foll. by *to*) assign (a thing) to (a person). □□ **portionless** adj. (in sense 5 of n.). [ME f. OF *porcion* portion f. L *portio -onis*]

Portland /ˈpɔːtlənd/ an industrial port on the Williamette River near its junction with the Columbia River in NW Oregon; pop. (1982) 367,500.

Portland cement /ˈpɔːtlənd/ cement manufactured from chalk and clay. It was patented in 1824 by Joseph Aspdin, a bricklayer of Leeds, who fancied that it bore some resemblance to the limestone of the Isle of Portland in Dorset.

Portland stone /ˈpɔːtlənd/ a limestone from the Isle of Portland in Dorset, used in building.

Portland vase /ˈpɔːtlənd/ a Roman vase dating from *c*.1st c. AD, of dark-blue transparent glass with an engraved figured decoration in white opaque glass. Acquired in the 18th c. by the Duchess of Portland from the Barberini Palace in Rome, it is now in the British Museum, where it was damaged by a madman in 1845.

Port Louis /ˈluːɪ/ the capital of Mauritius; pop. (1987) 139,000.

portly /ˈpɔːtlɪ/ adj. (**portlier, portliest**) **1** corpulent; stout. **2** *archaic* of a stately appearance. □□ **portliness** n. [PORT⁵ (in the sense 'bearing') + -LY¹]

portmanteau /pɔːtˈmæntəʊ/ n. (pl. **portmanteaus** /-təʊz/ or **portmanteaux**) a leather trunk for clothes etc., opening into two equal parts. □ **portmanteau word** a word blending the sounds and combining the meanings of two others, e.g. *motel, Oxbridge*. [F *portmanteau* f. *porter* carry f. L *portare* + *manteau* MANTLE]

Port Moresby /ˈmɔːzbɪ/ the capital of Papua New Guinea, situated on the south coast of the island of New Guinea; pop. (1980) 118,400.

Porto see OPORTO.

Pôrto Alegre /ˌpɔːtəʊ əˈlegrə, əˈleɪgreɪ/ a major port on the Guaiba River in SE Brazil; pop. (1980) 1,114,900.

Port-of-Spain the capital of Trinidad and Tobago; pop. (1988) 58,400.

portolan /ˈpɔːtəˌlæn/ n. (also **portolano** /ˌpɔːtəˈlɑːnəʊ/) (pl. **portolans** or **portolanos**) *hist.* a book of sailing directions with charts, descriptions of harbours, etc. [It. *portolano* f. *porto* PORT¹]

Porto Novo /ˌpɔːtəʊ ˈnəʊvəʊ/ a seaport and the capital of Benin, on the Guinea coast of West Africa; pop. (1982) 208,258.

Port Pirie /ˈpɪrɪ/ a port on the Spencer Gulf, north-west of Adelaide, South Australia; pop. (est. 1987) 15,160. Ores mined at Broken Hill in New South Wales are refined in Port Pirie.

portrait /ˈpɔːtrɪt/ n. **1** a representation of a person or animal, esp. of the face, made by drawing, painting, photography, etc. **2** a verbal picture; a graphic description. **3** a person etc. resembling or typifying another (*is the portrait of his father*). **4** (in graphic design etc.) a format in which the height of an illustration etc. is greater than the width (cf. LANDSCAPE). [F, past part. of OF *portraire* PORTRAY]

portraitist /ˈpɔːtrɪtɪst/ n. a person who takes or paints portraits.

portraiture /ˈpɔːtrɪtʃə(r)/ n. **1** the art of painting or taking portraits. **2** graphic description. **3** a portrait. [ME f. OF (as PORTRAIT)]

portray /pɔːˈtreɪ/ v.tr. **1** make a likeness of. **2** describe graphically. □□ **portrayable** adj. **portrayal** n. **portrayer** n. [ME f. OF *portraire* f. *por-* = PRO-¹ + *traire* draw f. L *trahere*]

Port Said /saɪd/ a seaport of Egypt, at the north end of the Suez Canal; pop. (est. 1986) 382,000.

Port Salut /ˌpɔː səˈluː/ n. a pale mild type of cheese. [after the Trappist monastery in France where it was first produced]

Portsmouth /ˈpɔːtsməθ/ a port and naval base on the south coast of England, in Hampshire; pop. (1981) 177,900. It was the birthplace of Charles Dickens.

Port Stanley see STANLEY¹.

Port Sudan the chief port of Sudan, on the Red Sea; pop. (1983) 206,700.

Portugal /ˈpɔːtjʊg(ə)l/ a country occupying the western part of the Iberian peninsula in SW Europe, bordering on the Atlantic Ocean; pop. (est. 1988) 10,388,400; official language, Portuguese; capital, Lisbon. In Roman times the province of Lusitania, the country's history was linked with that of the rest of the peninsula (see SPAIN) until it became an independent kingdom under Alfonso I in the 12th c. Dynastic disputes with the Spanish kingdoms to the east resulted in the formation of Portugal's long-standing alliance with England in the 14th c., and in the following two hundred years it emerged as one of the leading European colonial powers. Independence was lost to Philip II of Spain in 1580 and not regained until 1688, by which time Portugal had been relegated to a position of secondary importance in European affairs, a state of events exacerbated by domestic political instability which has continued through much of the 20th c. A republic since 1911, after the expulsion of the monarchy, the country remains poor by European standards, its economy still largely based on agriculture. Portugal became a member of the EC on 1 Jan. 1986.

Portuguese /ˌpɔːtjʊˈgiːz, ˌpɔːtʃ-/ n. & adj. —n. (pl. same) **1 a** a native or national of Portugal. **b** a person of Portuguese descent. **2** the official language of Portugal and its territories and of Brazil, where it was taken by 15th-c. explorers. It is a Romance language, most closely related to (but clearly distinct from) Spanish, with over 10 million speakers in Portugal and 55 million in Brazil. —adj. of or relating to Portugal or its people or language. □ **Portuguese man-of-war** a dangerous tropical or sub-tropical marine hydrozoan of the genus *Physalia* with a large crest and a poisonous sting. [Port. *portuguez* f. med.L *portugalensis*]

POS abbr. point-of-sale.

pose¹ /pəʊz/ v. & n. —v. **1** intr. assume a certain attitude of body, esp. when being photographed or being painted for a portrait. **2** intr. (foll. by as) set oneself up as or pretend to be (another person etc.) (*posing as a celebrity*). **3** intr. behave affectedly in order to impress others. **4** tr. put forward or present (a question etc.). **5** tr. place (an artist's model etc.) in a certain attitude or position. —n. **1** an attitude of body or mind. **2** an attitude or position, esp. one assumed for effect (*his generosity is a mere pose*). [F *poser* (v.), *pose* (n.) f. LL *pausare* PAUSE: some senses by confusion with L *ponere* place (cf. COMPOSE)]

pose² /pəʊz/ v.tr. puzzle (a person) with a question or problem. [obs. *appose* f. OF *aposer* var. of *oposer* OPPOSE]

Poseidon /pɒˈsaɪd(ə)n/ Gk Mythol. the god of earthquakes and water, and secondarily of the sea, brother of Zeus. In cult he is prominent as the sea-god, displacing Nereus (who is probably a more ancient god) from the position which it would seem that he once held. The Romans identified Neptune with him.

poser /ˈpəʊzə(r)/ n. **1** a person who poses (see POSE¹ v. 3). **2** a puzzling question or problem.

poseur /pəʊˈzɜː(r)/ n. (fem. **poseuse** /pəʊˈzɜːz/) a person who poses for effect or behaves affectedly. [F f. *poser* POSE¹]

posh /pɒʃ/ adj. & adv. colloq. —adj. **1** smart; stylish. **2** of or associated with the upper classes (*spoke with a posh accent*). —adv. in a stylish or upper-class way (*talk posh; act posh*). □ **posh up** smarten up. □□ **poshly** adv. **poshness** n. [20th c.: perh. f. sl. *posh* a dandy: *port out starboard home* (referring to the more comfortable accommodation on ships to and from the East) is a later association and not the true origin]

posit /ˈpɒzɪt/ v. & n. —v.tr. (**posited, positing**) **1** assume as a fact, postulate. **2** put in place or position. —n. Philos. a statement which is made on the assumption that it will prove valid. [L *ponere posit-* place]

position /pəˈzɪʃ(ə)n/ n. & v. —n. **1** a place occupied by a person or thing. **2** the way in which a thing or its parts are placed or arranged (*sitting in an uncomfortable position*). **3** the proper place

(*in position*). **4** the state of being advantageously placed (*jockeying for position*). **5** a person's mental attitude; a way of looking at a question (*changed their position on nuclear disarmament*). **6** a person's situation in relation to others (*puts one in an awkward position*). **7** rank or status; high social standing. **8** paid employment. **9** a place where troops etc. are posted for strategical purposes (*the position was stormed*). **10** the configuration of chessmen etc. during a game. **11** a specific pose in ballet etc. (*hold first position*). **12** Logic **a** a proposition. **b** a statement of proposition. —v.tr. place in position. □ **in a position to** enabled by circumstances, resources, information, etc. to (do, state, etc.). **position paper** orig. US (in business etc.) a written report of attitude or intentions. **position vector** Math. a vector which determines the position of a point. □□ **positional** adj. **positionally** adv. **positioner** n. [ME f. OF *position* or L *positio -onis* (as POSIT)]

positive /ˈpɒzɪtɪv/ adj. & n. —adj. **1** formally or explicitly stated; definite, unquestionable (*positive proof*). **2** (of a person) convinced, confident, or overconfident in his or her opinion (*positive that I was not there*). **3 a** absolute; not relative. **b** Gram. (of an adjective or adverb) expressing a simple quality without comparison (cf. COMPARATIVE, SUPERLATIVE). **4** colloq. downright; complete (*it would be a positive miracle*). **5** constructive; directional (*positive criticism; positive thinking*). **6** marked by the presence rather than absence of qualities or Med. symptoms (*a positive reaction to the plan; the test was positive*). **7** esp. Philos. dealing only with matters of fact; practical (cf. POSITIVISM 1). **8** tending in a direction naturally or arbitrarily taken as that of increase or progress (*clockwise rotation is positive*). **9** greater than zero (*positive and negative integers*) (opp. NEGATIVE). **10** Electr. of, containing, or producing the kind of electrical charge produced by rubbing glass with silk; an absence of electrons. **11** (of a photographic image) showing lights and shades or colours true to the original (opp. NEGATIVE). —n. a positive adjective, photograph, quantity, etc. □ **positive discrimination** the practice of making distinctions in favour of groups considered to be underprivileged. **positive feedback 1** a constructive response to an experiment, questionnaire, etc. **2** Electronics the return of part of an output signal to the input, tending to increase the amplification etc. **positive geotropism** see GEOTROPISM. **positive pole** the north-seeking pole. **positive ray** Physics a canal ray. **positive sign** = plus sign. **positive vetting** Brit. an exhaustive inquiry into the background and character of a candidate for a post in the Civil Service that involves access to secret material. □□ **positively** adv. **positiveness** n. **positivity** /ˌpɒzɪˈtɪvɪtɪ/ n. [ME f. OF *positif -ive* or L *positivus* (as POSIT)]

positivism /ˈpɒzɪtɪˌvɪz(ə)m/ n. **1** the theory (held by Bacon and Hume amongst others, including Comte) that every rationally justifiable assertion can be scientifically verified or is capable of logical or mathematical proof, and that philosophy can do no more than attest to the logical and exact use of language through which such observation or verification can be expressed. **2** logical positivism (see LOGICAL). **3** the theory that laws are to be understood as social rules, valid because they are enacted by the 'sovereign' or derive logically from existing decisions, and that ideal or moral considerations (e.g. that a rule is unjust) should not limit the scope or operation of the law. □□ **positivist** n. **positivistic** /-ˈvɪstɪk/ adj. **positivistically** /-ˈvɪstɪkəlɪ/ adv. [F *positivisme* (as POSITIVE)]

positron /ˈpɒzɪˌtrɒn/ n. Physics an elementary particle with a positive charge equal to the negative charge of an electron and having the same mass as an electron. [POSITIVE + -TRON]

posology /pəˈsɒlədʒɪ/ n. the study of the dosage of medicines. [F *posologie* f. Gk *posos* how much]

posse /ˈpɒsɪ/ n. **1** a strong force or company or assemblage. **2** (in full **posse comitatus** /ˌkɒmɪˈteɪtəs/) **a** a body of constables, law-enforcers, etc. **b** esp. US a body of men summoned by a sheriff etc. to enforce the law. [med.L, = power f. L *posse* be able: *comitatus* = of the county]

possess /pəˈzes/ v.tr. **1** hold as property; own. **2** have (a faculty, quality), etc. (*they possess a special value for us*). **3** (also refl.; foll. by in) maintain (oneself, one's soul, etc.) in a specified state (*possess oneself in patience*). **4 a** (of a demon etc.) occupy; have power over (a person etc.) (*possessed by the devil*). **b** (of an emotion, infatuation, etc.) dominate, be an obsession of (*possessed by fear*). **5** have sexual intercourse with (esp. a woman). □ **be possessed of** own, have. **possess oneself of** take or get for one's own. **what possessed you?** an expression of incredulity. □□ **possessor** *n*. **possessory** *adj*. [OF *possesser* f. L *possidēre possess-* f. *potis* able + *sedēre* sit]

possession /pə'zeʃ(ə)n/ *n*. **1** the act or state of possessing or being possessed. **2** the thing possessed. **3** the act or state of actual holding or occupancy. **4** *Law* power or control similar to lawful ownership but which may exist separately from it (*prosecuted for possession of narcotic drugs*). **5** (in *pl.*) property, wealth, subject territory, etc. **6** *Football* etc. temporary control of the ball by a particular player. □ **in possession 1** (of a person) possessing. **2** (of a thing) possessed. **in possession of 1** having in one's possession. **2** maintaining control over (*in possession of one's wits*). **in the possession of** held or owned by. **possession order** an order made by a court directing that possession of a property be given to the owner. **take possession** (often foll. by *of*) become the owner or possessor (of a thing). □□ **possessionless** *adj*. [ME f. OF *possession* or L *possessio -onis* (as POSSESS)]

possessive /pə'zesɪv/ *adj*. & *n*. —*adj*. **1** showing a desire to possess or retain what one already owns. **2** showing jealous and domineering tendencies towards another person. **3** *Gram*. indicating possession. —*n*. (in full **possessive case**) *Gram*. the case of nouns and pronouns expressing possession. □ **possessive pronoun** each of the pronouns indicating possession (*my, your, his, their*, etc.) or the corresponding absolute forms (*mine, yours, his, theirs*, etc.). □□ **possessively** *adv*. **possessiveness** *n*. [L *possessivus* (as POSSESS), transl. Gk *ktētikē* (*ptōsis* case)]

posset /'pɒsɪt/ *n*. *hist*. a drink made of hot milk curdled with ale, wine, etc., often flavoured with spices, formerly much used as a remedy for colds etc. [ME *poshote*: orig. unkn.]

possibility /ˌpɒsɪ'bɪlɪtɪ/ *n*. (*pl.* **-ies**) **1** the state or fact of being possible, or an occurrence of this (*outside the range of possibility; saw no possibility of going away*). **2** a thing that may exist or happen (*there are three possibilities*). **3** (usu. in *pl.*) the capability of being used, improved, etc.; the potential of an object or situation (esp. *have possibilities*). [ME f. OF *possibilité* or LL *possibilitas -tatis* (as POSSIBLE)]

possible /'pɒsɪb(ə)l/ *adj*. & *n*. —*adj*. **1** capable of existing or happening; that may be managed, achieved, etc. (*came as early as possible; did as much as possible*). **2** that is likely to happen etc. (*few thought their victory possible*). **3** acceptable; potential (*a possible way of doing it*). —*n*. **1** a possible candidate, member of a team, etc. **2** (prec. by *the*) whatever is likely, manageable, etc. **3** the highest possible score, esp. in shooting etc. [ME f. OF *possible* or L *possibilis* f. *posse* be able]

possibly /'pɒsɪblɪ/ *adv*. **1** perhaps. **2** in accordance with possibility (*cannot possibly refuse*).

possum /'pɒsəm/ *n*. **1** *colloq.* = OPOSSUM 1. **2** *Austral.* & *NZ colloq.* a phalanger resembling an American opossum. □ **play possum 1** pretend to be asleep or unconscious when threatened. **2** feign ignorance. [abbr.]

post¹ /pəʊst/ *n*. & *v*. —*n*. **1** a long stout piece of timber or metal set upright in the ground etc.: **a** to support something, esp. in building. **b** to mark a position, boundary, etc. **c** to carry notices. **2** a pole etc. marking the start or finish of a race. —*v.tr.* **1** (often foll. by *up*) **a** attach (a paper etc.) in a prominent place; stick up (*post no bills*). **b** announce or advertise by placard or in a published text. **2** publish the name of (a ship etc.) as overdue or missing. **3** placard (a wall etc.) with bills etc. **4** *US* achieve (a score in a game etc.). □ **post-mill** a windmill pivoted on a post and turning to catch the wind. [OE f. L *postis*: in ME also f. OF etc.]

post² /pəʊst/ *n.*, *v.*, & *adv*. —*n*. **1** *Brit*. the official conveyance of parcels, letters, etc. (*send it by post*). (See below.) **2** *Brit*. a single collection, dispatch, or delivery of these; the letters etc. dispatched (*has the post arrived yet?*). **3** *Brit*. a place where letters etc. are dealt with; a post office or postbox (*take it to the post*). **4** *hist*. **a** one of a series of couriers who carried mail on horseback between fixed stages. **b** a letter-carrier; a mail cart. —*v*. **1** *tr*.

put (a letter etc.) in the post. **2** *tr*. (esp. as **posted** *adj*.) (often foll. by *up*) supply a person with information (*keep me posted*). **3** *tr*. **a** enter (an item) in a ledger. **b** (often foll. by *up*) complete (a ledger) in this way. **c** carry (an entry) from an auxiliary book to a more formal one, or from one account to another. **4** *intr*. **a** travel with haste, hurry. **b** *hist*. travel with relays of horses. —*adv*. express; with haste. □ **post-chaise** *hist*. a travelling carriage hired from stage to stage or drawn by horses hired in this manner. **post exchange** *US Mil*. a shop at a military camp etc. **post-free** *Brit*. carried by post free of charge or with the postage prepaid. **post-haste** with great speed. **post-horn** a valveless horn formerly used to announce the arrival of the post. **Post Office 1** the public department or corporation responsible for postal services and (in some countries) telecommunication. **2** (**post office**) **a** a room or building where postal business is carried on. **b** *US* = *postman's knock*. **post-office box** a numbered place in a post office where letters are kept until called for. **post-paid** on which postage has been paid. **post room** the department of a company that deals with incoming and outgoing mail. **post-town** a town with a post office, esp. one that is not a sub-office of another. [F *poste* (fem.) f. It. *posta* ult. f. L *ponere posit-* place]

In medieval England messengers transported government documents around the country. From the beginning of the 16th c. the term 'post' was applied to men with horses stationed or appointed in places at suitable distances along the routes, the duty of each being to ride with, or forward with all speed to the next stage, the king's 'packet' or mail, and subsequently the letters of other persons also, as well as to furnish horses for use in this. The term corresponds to the *equites dispositi* (L, = posted horsemen) of classical and later times. The corresponding terms in French and Italian are used by Marco Polo of the stations, 40 kilometres (25 miles) apart on the great roads, at which the messengers of the Emperor of China changed horses, and at each of which 300–400 horses are said to have been kept for their service. In 18th-c. England stage-coaches carried the mail, succeeded in the mid-19th c. by the railways. In 1840 the 'penny post' was introduced, and similar developments in other countries led to the establishment of a 'Postal Union' in 1874 which stimulated the development of international mail services. The first regular airmail service (London–Paris) was introduced in 1919.

post³ /pəʊst/ *n*. & *v*. —*n*. **1** a place where a soldier is stationed or which he patrols. **2** a place of duty. **3 a** a position taken up by a body of soldiers. **b** a force occupying this. **c** a fort. **4** a situation, paid employment. **5** = *trading post*. **6** *Naut. hist*. a commission as an officer in command of a vessel of 20 guns or more. —*v.tr.* **1** place or station (soldiers, an employee, etc.). **2** appoint to a post or command. □ **first** (or **last**) **post** *Brit*. a bugle-call giving notice of the hour of retiring at night. **last post** *Brit*. a bugle-call blown at military funerals etc. [F *poste* (masc.) f. It. *posto* f. Rmc *postum* (unrecorded) f. L *ponere posit-* place]

post- /pəʊst/ *prefix* after in time or order. [from or after L *post* (adv. & prep.)]

postage /'pəʊstɪdʒ/ *n*. the amount charged for sending a letter etc. by post, usu. prepaid in the form of a stamp (*£25 including postage & packing*). □ **postage meter** *US* a franking-machine. **postage stamp** an official stamp affixed to or imprinted on a letter etc. indicating the amount of postage paid (see STAMP *n*. 3).

postal /'pəʊst(ə)l/ *adj*. & *n*. —*adj*. **1** of the post. **2** by post (*postal vote*). —*n*. *US* a postcard. □ **postal card** *US* = POSTCARD. **postal code** = POSTCODE. **postal meter** a franking-machine. **postal note** *Austral.* & *NZ* = *postal order*. **postal order** a money order issued by the Post Office, payable to a specified person. **Postal Union** a union of the governments of various countries for the regulation of international postage. □□ **postally** *adv*. [F (*poste* POST²)]

postbag /'pəʊstbæg/ *n*. *Brit*. = MAILBAG.

postbox /'pəʊstbɒks/ *n*. *Brit*. a letter-box.

postcard /'pəʊstkɑːd/ *n*. a card, often with a photograph on one side, for sending a short message by post without an envelope.

post-classical /ˌpəʊstˈklæsɪk(ə)l/ adj. (esp. of Greek and Roman literature) later than the classical period.

postcode /ˈpəʊstkəʊd/ n. a group of letters or letters and figures which are added to a postal address to assist sorting.

post-coital /ˌpəʊstˈkəʊɪt(ə)l/ adj. occurring or existing after sexual intercourse. □□ **post-coitally** adv.

postdate v. & n. —v.tr. /pəʊstˈdeɪt/ affix or assign a date later than the actual one to (a document, event, etc.). —n. /ˈpəʊstdeɪt/ such a date.

post-doctoral /ˌpəʊstˈdɒktər(ə)l/ adj. of or relating to research undertaken after the completion of doctoral research.

post-entry /pəʊstˈentrɪ/ n. (pl. -ies) a late or subsequent entry, esp. in a race or in bookkeeping.

poster /ˈpəʊstə(r)/ n. 1 a placard in a public place. 2 a large printed picture. 3 a billposter. □ **poster paint** a gummy opaque paint.

poste restante /ˌpəʊst reˈstɑ̃t/ n. 1 a direction on a letter to indicate that it should be kept at a specified post office until collected by the addressee. 2 the department in a post office where such letters are kept. [F, = letter(s) remaining]

posterior /pɒˈstɪərɪə(r)/ adj. & n. —adj. 1 later; coming after in series, order, or time. 2 situated at the back. —n. (in sing. or pl.) the buttocks. □□ **posteriority** /pɒˌstɪərɪˈɒrɪtɪ/ n. **posteriorly** adv. [L, compar. of posterus following f. post after]

posterity /pɒˈsterɪtɪ/ n. 1 all succeeding generations. 2 the descendants of a person. [ME f. OF posterité f. L posteritas -tatis f. posterus: see POSTERIOR]

postern /ˈpɒst(ə)n, ˈpəʊ-/ n. 1 a back door. 2 a side way or entrance. [ME f. OF posterne, posterle, f. LL posterula dimin. of posterus: see POSTERIOR]

postfix n. & v. —n. /ˈpəʊstfɪks/ a suffix. —v.tr. /pəʊstˈfɪks/ append (letters) at the end of a word.

postglacial /pəʊstˈɡleɪʃ(ə)l, -sɪəl/ adj. & n. —adj. formed or occurring after a glacial period. —n. a postglacial period or deposit.

postgraduate /pəʊstˈɡrædjʊət/ adj. & n. —adj. 1 (of a course of study) carried on after taking a first degree. 2 of or relating to students following this course of study (postgraduate accommodation). —n. a postgraduate student.

posthumous /ˈpɒstjʊməs/ adj. 1 occurring after death. 2 (of a child) born after the death of its father. 3 (of a book etc.) published after the author's death. □□ **posthumously** adv. [L postumus last (superl. f. post after): in LL posth- by assoc. with humus ground]

postiche /pɒˈstiːʃ/ n. a coil of false hair, worn as an adornment. [F, = false, f. It. posticcio]

postie /ˈpəʊstɪ/ n. colloq. a postman or postwoman. [abbr.]

postil /ˈpɒstɪl/ n. hist. 1 a marginal note or comment, esp. on a text of Scripture. 2 a commentary. [ME f. OF postille f. med.L postilla, of uncert. orig.]

postilion /pɒˈstɪljən/ n. (also **postillion**) the rider on the near (left-hand side) horse drawing a coach etc. when there is no coachman. [F postillon f. It. postiglione post-boy f. posta POST²]

post-impressionism /ˌpəʊstɪmˈpreʃəˌnɪz(ə)m/ n. the artistic aims and methods of a movement in French painting in the late 19th and early 20th c. whose members sought to reveal the subject's structural form without strict fidelity to its natural appearance. The term was unknown to those French painters to whom it is applied (in their day labelled as impressionists, neo-impressionists, or symbolists) being invented by Roger Fry in 1910. In seeking an acceptable title for the 1910 autumn exhibition of modern French painting at the Grafton Gallery in London, Fry settled on what he called this 'somewhat negative title', naming the exhibition 'Manet and the Post-Impressionists' from the fact that they came, chronologically, after impressionism. The term is most readily applied to the three luminaries of that exhibition—Gauguin, Van Gogh, and Cézanne—but it should not be forgotten that Seurat, Denis, Sérusier, and even Matisse were also included. □□ **post-impressionist** n. **post-impressionistic** /-ˈnɪstɪk/ adj.

postindustrial /ˌpəʊstɪnˈdʌstrɪəl/ adj. relating to or characteristic of a society or economy which no longer relies on heavy industry.

postliminy /pəʊstˈlɪmɪnɪ/ n. 1 (in international law) the restoration to their former status of persons and things taken in war. 2 (in Roman law) the right of a banished person or captive to resume civic privileges on return from exile. [L postliminium (as POST-, limen liminis threshold)]

postlude /ˈpəʊstluːd/ n. Mus. a concluding voluntary. [POST-, after PRELUDE]

postman /ˈpəʊstmən/ n. (pl. -men; fem. **postwoman**, pl. -women) a person who is employed to deliver and collect letters etc. □ **postman's knock** Brit. a parlour game in which imaginary letters are delivered in exchange for kisses.

postmark /ˈpəʊstmɑːk/ n. & v. —n. an official mark stamped on a letter, esp. one giving the place, date, etc. of dispatch or arrival, and serving to cancel the stamp. —v.tr. mark (an envelope etc.) with this.

postmaster /ˈpəʊstˌmɑːstə(r)/ n. a man in charge of a post office. □ **postmaster general** the head of a country's postal service. ¶ The office was abolished in the UK in 1969.

post-millennial /ˌpəʊstmɪˈlenɪəl/ adj. following the millennium.

post-millennialism /ˌpəʊstmɪˈlenɪəˌlɪz(ə)m/ n. the doctrine that a second Advent will follow the millennium. □□ **post-millennialist** n.

postmistress /ˈpəʊstˌmɪstrɪs/ n. a woman in charge of a post office.

post-modern /pəʊstˈmɒd(ə)n/ adj. (in literature, architecture, the arts, etc.) denoting a movement reacting against modern tendencies, esp. by drawing attention to former conventions. □□ **post-modernism** n. **post-modernist** n. & adj.

post-mortem /pəʊstˈmɔːtəm/ n., adv., & adj. —n. 1 (in full **post-mortem examination**) an examination made after death, esp. to determine its cause. 2 colloq. a discussion analysing the course and result of a game, election, etc. —adv. & adj. after death. [L]

postnatal /pəʊstˈneɪt(ə)l/ adj. characteristic of or relating to the period after childbirth.

post-nuptial /pəʊstˈnʌpʃ(ə)l/ adj. after marriage.

post-obit /pəʊstˈəʊbɪt/ n. & adj. —n. a bond given to a lender by a borrower securing a sum for payment on the death of another person from whom the borrower expects to inherit. —adj. taking effect after death. [L post obitum f. post after + obitus decease f. obire die]

postoperative /pəʊstˈɒpərətɪv/ adj. relating to or occurring in a period after a surgical operation.

post-partum /pəʊstˈpɑːtəm/ adj. following parturition.

postpone /pəʊstˈpəʊn, pəˈspəʊn/ v.tr. cause or arrange (an event etc.) to take place at a later time. □□ **postponable** adj. **postponement** n. **postponer** n. [L postponere (as POST-, ponere posit- place)]

postposition /ˌpəʊstpəˈzɪʃ(ə)n/ n. 1 a word or particle, esp. an enclitic, placed after the word it modifies, e.g. -ward in homeward and at in the books we looked at. 2 the use of a postposition. □□ **postpositional** adj. & n. **postpositive** /pəʊstˈpɒzɪtɪv/ adj. & n. **postpositively** /-ˈpɒzɪtɪvlɪ/ adv. [LL postpositio (as POSTPONE)]

postprandial /pəʊstˈprændɪəl/ adj. formal or joc. after dinner or lunch. [POST- + L prandium a meal]

postscript /ˈpəʊstskrɪpt, ˈpəʊskrɪpt/ n. 1 an additional paragraph or remark, usu. at the end of a letter after the signature and introduced by 'PS'. 2 any additional information, action, etc. [L postscriptum neut. past part. of postscribere (as POST-, scribere write)]

post-tax /pəʊstˈtæks/ adj. (of income) after the deduction of taxes.

postulant /ˈpɒstjʊlənt/ n. a candidate, esp. for admission into a religious order. [F postulant or L postulans -antis (as POSTULATE)]

postulate v. & n. —v.tr. /ˈpɒstjʊˌleɪt/ 1 (often foll. by that + clause) assume as a necessary condition, esp. as a basis for reasoning; take for granted. 2 claim. 3 (in ecclesiastical law) nominate or elect to a higher rank. —n. /'ppstjʊlət/ 1 a thing postulated. 2 a fundamental prerequisite or condition. 3 Math. an assumption used as a basis for mathematical reasoning. □□ **postulation** /ˌppstjʊ'leɪʃ(ə)n/ n. [L postulare postulat- demand]

postulator /'ppstjʊˌleɪtə(r)/ n. 1 a person who postulates. 2 RC Ch. a person who presents a case for canonization or beatification.

posture /'ppstʃə(r)/ n. & v. —n. 1 the relative position of parts, esp. of the body (in a reclining posture). 2 carriage or bearing (improved by good posture and balance). 3 a mental or spiritual attitude or condition. 4 the condition or state (of affairs etc.) (in more diplomatic postures). —v. 1 intr. assume a mental or physical attitude, esp. for effect (inclined to strut and posture). 2 tr. pose (a person). □□ **postural** adj. **posturer** n. [F f. It. postura f. L positura f. ponere posit- place]

postwar /pəʊst'wɔː(r), 'pəʊst-/ adj. occurring or existing after a war (esp. the most recent major war).

posy /'pəʊzɪ/ n. (pl. -ies) 1 a small bunch of flowers. 2 archaic a short motto, line of verse, etc., inscribed within a ring. □ **posy-ring** a ring with this inscription. [alt. f. POESY]

pot¹ /ppt/ n. & v. —n. 1 a vessel, usu. rounded, of ceramic ware or metal or glass for holding liquids or solids or for cooking in. 2 a a coffee-pot, flowerpot, glue-pot, jam-pot, teapot, etc. b = chimney-pot. c = lobster-pot. 3 a drinking vessel of pewter etc. 4 the contents of a pot (ate a whole pot of jam). 5 the total amount of the bet in a game etc. 6 colloq. a large sum (pots of money). 7 sl. a vessel given as a prize in an athletic contest, esp. a silver cup. 8 = pot-belly. —v.tr. (**potted, potting**) 1 place in a pot. 2 (usu. as **potted** adj.) preserve in a sealed pot (potted shrimps). 3 sit (a young child) on a chamber pot. 4 pocket (a ball) in billiards etc. 5 shoot at, hit, or kill (an animal) with a pot shot. 6 seize or secure. 7 abridge or epitomize (in a potted version; potted wisdom). □ **go to pot** colloq. deteriorate; be ruined. **pot-bellied** having a pot-belly. **pot-belly** (pl. -ies) 1 a protruding stomach. 2 a person with this. 3 a small bulbous stove. **pot-boiler** 1 a work of literature or art done merely to make the writer or artist a living. 2 a writer or artist who does this. **pot-bound** (of a plant) having roots which fill the flowerpot, leaving no room to expand. **pot cheese** US cottage cheese. **pot-herb** any herb grown in a kitchen garden. **pot-hook** 1 a hook over a hearth for hanging a pot etc. on, or for lifting a hot pot. 2 a curved stroke in handwriting, esp. as made in learning to write. **pot-hunter** 1 a person who hunts for game at random. 2 a person who takes part in a contest merely for the sake of the prize. **pot luck** whatever (hospitality etc.) is available. **pot of gold** an imaginary reward; an ideal; a jackpot. **pot pie** a pie of meat etc. or fruit with a crust baked in a pot. **pot plant** a plant grown in a flowerpot. **pot roast** a piece of meat cooked slowly in a covered dish. **pot-roast** v.tr. cook (a piece of meat) in this way. **pot-shot** 1 a random shot. 2 a shot aimed at an animal etc. within easy reach. 3 a shot at a game-bird etc. merely to provide a meal. **pot-valiant** courageous because of drunkenness. **pot-valour** this type of courage. □□ **potful** n. (pl. -fuls). [OE pott, corresp. to OFris., MDu., MLG pot, f. pop.L]

pot² /ppt/ n. sl. marijuana. □ **pot-head** one who smokes this. [prob. f. Mex. Sp. potiguaya]

pot³ /ppt/ n. & v. Austral. & NZ —n. a dropped goal in rugby football. —v.tr. (**potted, potting**) score (a dropped goal). [perh. f. pot-shot]

potable /'pəʊtəb(ə)l/ adj. drinkable. □□ **potability** /-'bɪlɪtɪ/ n. [F potable or LL potabilis f. L potare drink]

potage /pp'tɑːʒ/ n. thick soup. [F (as POTTAGE)]

potamic /pə'tæmɪk/ adj. of rivers. □□ **potamology** /ˌpptə'mɒlɪdʒɪ/ n. [Gk potamos river]

potash /'pptæʃ/ n. an alkaline potassium compound, usu. potassium carbonate or hydroxide. [17th-c. pot-ashes f. Du. pot-asschen (as POT¹, ASH¹): orig. obtained by leaching vegetable ashes and evaporating the solution in iron pots]

potassium /pə'tæsɪəm/ n. Chem. a soft silver-white metallic element first isolated by Sir Humphry Davy in 1807. It is essential to life. The metal itself is very reactive and has few uses, but its compounds are widely used in the manufacture of fertilizers,

soaps, glass, etc. ¶ Symb.: **K**; atomic number 19. □ **potassium chloride** a white crystalline solid used as a fertilizer and in photographic processing. **potassium cyanide** a highly toxic solid that can be hydrolysed to give poisonous hydrogen cyanide gas: also called CYANIDE. **potassium iodide** a white crystalline solid used as an additive to table salt to prevent iodine deficiency. **potassium permanganate** a purple crystalline solid that is used in solution as an oxidizing agent and disinfectant. □□ **potassic** adj. [POTASH + -IUM]

potation /pə'teɪʃ(ə)n/ n. 1 a drink. 2 the act or an instance of drinking. 3 (usu. in pl.) the act or an instance of tippling. □□ **potatory** /pəʊ'teɪtərɪ/ adj. [ME f. OF potation or L potatio f. potare drink]

potato /pə'teɪtəʊ/ n. (pl. -oes) 1 a starchy plant tuber that is cooked and used for food. 2 the plant, Solanum tuberosum, bearing this. Now one of the main food crops of the world, the potato was introduced into Europe c.1570 by the Spaniards who had encountered it in their explorations of South America. 3 colloq. a hole in (esp. the heel of) a sock or stocking. □ **potato chip** = CHIP n. 3. **potato crisp** Brit. = CRISP n. 1. [Sp. patata var. of S. Amer. Indian batata]

pot-au-feu /ˌpptəʊ'fə/ n. 1 a large cooking pot of the kind common in France. 2 the soup or broth cooked in it. 3 the traditional French recipe associated with this. [F, = pot on the fire]

potch /pptʃ/ n. an opal of inferior quality. [19th c.: orig. unkn.]

poteen /pp'tiːn/ n. (also **potheen** /-'tʃiːn/) Ir. alcohol made illicitly, usu. from potatoes. [Ir. poitín dimin. of pota POT¹]

Potemkin /pə'temkɪn/, Grigori Alexandrovich (1739–91), Russian soldier and statesman. The chief favourite of Catherine the Great from 1771, he was responsible for considerable Russian expansion towards the south.

Potemkin /pə'temkɪn/ the battleship whose crew mutinied in the Russian revolution of 1905 when in the Black Sea, bombarding Odessa before seeking asylum in Romania. The incident persuaded the emporer to agree to a measure of reform.

potent¹ /'pəʊt(ə)nt/ adj. 1 powerful; strong. 2 (of a reason) cogent; forceful. 3 (of a male) capable of sexual erection or orgasm. 4 literary mighty. □□ **potence** n. **potency** n. **potently** adv. [L potens -entis pres. part. of posse be able]

potent² /'pəʊt(ə)nt/ adj. & n. Heraldry —adj. 1 with a crutch-head shape. 2 (of a fur) formed by a series of such shapes. —n. this fur. [ME f. OF potence crutch f. L potentia power (as POTENT¹)]

potentate /'pəʊtənˌteɪt/ n. a monarch or ruler. [ME f. OF potentat or L potentatus dominion (as POTENT²)]

potential /pə'tenʃ(ə)l/ adj. & n. —adj. capable of coming into being or action; latent. —n. 1 the capacity for use or development; possibility (achieved its highest potential). 2 usable resources. 3 Physics the quantity determining the energy of mass in a gravitational field or of charge in an electric field. □ **potential barrier** a region of high potential impeding the movement of particles etc. **potential difference** the difference of electric potential between two points. **potential energy** a body's ability to do work by virtue of its position relative to others, stresses within itself, electric charge, etc. □□ **potentiality** /-ʃɪ'ælɪtɪ/ n. **potentialize** v.tr. (also -ise). **potentially** adv. [ME f. OF potencial or LL potentialis f. potentia (as POTENT¹)]

potentiate /pə'tenʃɪˌeɪt/ v.tr. 1 make more powerful, esp. increase the effectiveness of (a drug). 2 make possible. [as POTENT¹ after SUBSTANTIATE]

potentilla /ˌpəʊtən'tɪlə/ n. any plant or shrub of the genus Potentilla; a cinquefoil. [med.L, dimin. of L potens POTENT¹]

potentiometer /pəˌtenʃɪ'ɒmɪtə(r)/ n. an instrument for measuring or adjusting small electrical potentials. □□ **potentiometric** /-ʃɪə'metrɪk/ adj. **potentiometry** /-ʃɪ'ɒmɪtrɪ/ n.

potheen var. of POTEEN.

pother /'ppðə(r)/ n. & v. literary —n. a noise; commotion; fuss. —v. 1 tr. fluster, worry. 2 intr. make a fuss. [16th c.: orig. unkn.]

pothole /'ppthəʊl/ n. & v. —n. 1 Geol. a deep hole or system of caves and underground river-beds formed by the erosion of rock esp. by the action of water. **2** a deep hole in the ground or a river-bed. **3** a hole in a road surface caused by wear or subsidence. —*v.intr. Brit.* explore potholes. □□ **potholer** *n.* **potholing** *n.*

potion /ˈpəʊʃ(ə)n/ *n.* a dose or quantity of medicine, a drug, poison, etc. [ME f. OF f. L *potio -onis* f. *potus* having drunk]

Potiphar /ˈpɒtɪˌfɑː(r)/ an Egyptian officer whose wife tried to seduce Joseph and then falsely accused him of attempting to rape her (Gen. 39).

potlatch /ˈpɒtlætʃ/ *n.* (among N. American Indians) a ceremonial giving away or destruction of property to enhance status. [Chinook f. Nootka *patlatsh* gift]

Potomac /pəˈtəʊmæk/ a river of the US flowing into Chesapeake Bay and forming part of the northern boundary of Virginia.

potoroo /ˌpɒtəˈruː/ *n. Austral.* any small marsupial of the genus *Potorus*, native to Australia and Tasmania; a rat kangaroo. [Aboriginal]

Potosí /ˌpɒtəʊˈsiː/ the chief mining city of southern Bolivia; pop. (1985) 113,000. Situated at an altitude of about 4,205 m (13,780 ft.) it is one of the highest cities in the world.

pot-pourri /ˌpəʊˈpʊərɪ, -ˈriː/ *n.* **1** a mixture of dried petals and spices used to perfume a room etc. **2** a musical or literary medley. [F, = rotten pot]

potrero /pɒˈtreərəʊ/ *n.* (*pl.* **-os**) **1** (in the south-western US and S. America) a paddock or pasture for horses or cattle. **2** (in the south-western US) a narrow steep-sided plateau. [Sp. f. *potro* colt, pony]

Potsdam /ˈpɒtsdæm/ a city in Germany, situated just west of Berlin; pop. (est. 1990) 95,000. In July–August 1945 it was the site of a conference of US, Soviet, and British leaders, following the end of the war in Europe, which established principles for the Allied occupation of Germany. During its session an ultimatum was sent to Japan demanding unconditional surrender.

potsherd /ˈpɒtʃɜːd/ *n.* a broken piece of ceramic material, esp. one found on an archaeological site.

pottage /ˈpɒtɪdʒ/ *n. archaic* soup, stew. [ME f. OF *potage* (as POT[1])]

Potter /ˈpɒtə(r)/, (Helen) Beatrix (1866–1943), English writer for children. *The Tale of Peter Rabbit* (1901) was the first in a series of animal stories, charmingly illustrated in water-colour by the author.

potter[1] /ˈpɒtə(r)/ *v.* (*US* **putter** /ˈpʌtə(r)/) **1** *intr.* **a** (often foll. by *about, around*) work or occupy oneself in a desultory but pleasant manner (*likes pottering about in the garden*). **b** (often foll. by *at, in*) dabble in a subject or occupation. **2** *intr.* go slowly, dawdle, loiter (*pottered up to the pub*). **3** *tr.* (foll. by *away*) fritter away (one's time etc.). □□ **potterer** *n.* [frequent. of dial. *pote* push f. OE *potian*]

potter[2] /ˈpɒtə(r)/ *n.* a maker of ceramic vessels. □ **potter's field** a burial place for paupers, strangers, etc. (after Matt. 27: 7). **potter's wheel** a horizontal revolving disc to carry clay for moulding in making pots. The wheel probably came into use during the 4th millennium BC. At first it was turned by hand (the 'slow wheel'), later by a foot-operated wheel. Known in Mesopotamia by *c.*3500 BC, over a period of centuries it spread to Egypt and other parts of the Near East and to India, reaching Crete and China by about 2000 BC, Europe at varying dates, and southern Britain in the mid-1st c. BC. It was unknown in America until the arrival of European conquerors and settlers. [OE *pottere* (as POT[1])]

pottery /ˈpɒtərɪ/ *n.* (*pl.* **-ies**) **1** vessels etc. made of fired clay. (See below.) **2** a potter's work. **3** a potter's workshop. □ **the Potteries** a district in N. Staffordshire, where the English pottery industry is centred. [ME f. OF *poterie* f. *potier* POTTER[2]]

The shaping and baking of clay vessels is among the oldest and most widely practised of all the crafts: earthenware pottery dating from about 9,000 years ago has been found on the Anatolian plateau of Turkey. At first it was shaped entirely by hand, and many centuries passed before the introduction of the potter's wheel (see POTTER[2]). The brilliant achievements of the Chinese and their neighbours, especially in the field of glazed stoneware and porcelain, were almost unknown in Europe until

the opening up of the direct sea-route in the 16th c., though these wares were not without influence on the Islamic pottery of the Near East. In medieval times pottery was little used at table but by the 18th c. there was an immense demand for table and ornamental wares of all kinds, and new factories appeared in many countries. In Britain, where the Industrial Revolution was beginning, the rise of Staffordshire as the pottery centre saw technical and practical innovations which culminated, during the life of Josiah Wedgwood, in the change from craft to industry.

potting shed /ˈpɒtɪŋ/ *n.* a building in which plants are potted and tools etc. are stored.

pottle /ˈpɒt(ə)l/ *n.* **1** a small punnet or carton for strawberries etc. **2** *archaic* **a** a measure for liquids; a half gallon. **b** a pot etc. containing this. [ME f. OF *potel* (as POT[1])]

potto /ˈpɒtəʊ/ *n.* (*pl.* **-os**) **1** a W. African lemur-like mammal, *Perodicticus potto.* **2** a kinkajou. [perh. f. Guinea dial.]

Pott's fracture /pɒts/ *n.* a fracture of the lower end of the fibula, usu. with dislocation of the ankle. [P. *Pott*, Engl. surgeon d. 1788]

potty[1] /ˈpɒtɪ/ *adj.* (**pottier, pottiest**) *Brit. sl.* **1** foolish or crazy. **2** insignificant, trivial (esp. *potty little*). □□ **pottiness** *n.* [19th c.: orig. unkn.]

potty[2] /ˈpɒtɪ/ *n.* (*pl.* **-ies**) *colloq.* a chamber-pot, esp. for a child.

pouch /paʊtʃ/ *n. & v.* —*n.* **1** a small bag or detachable outside pocket. **2** a baggy area of skin underneath the eyes etc. **3 a** a pocket-like receptacle in which marsupials carry their young during lactation. **b** any of several similar structures in various animals, e.g. in the cheeks of rodents. **4** a soldier's leather ammunition bag. **5** a lockable bag for mail or dispatches. **6** *Bot.* a baglike cavity, esp. the seed-vessel, in a plant. —*v.tr.* **1** put or make into a pouch. **2** take possession of; pocket. **3** make (part of a dress etc.) hang like a pouch. □□ **pouched** *adj.* **pouchy** *adj.* [ME f. ONF *pouche*: cf. POKE[2]]

pouf var. of POOF.

pouffe /puːf/ *n.* (also **pouf**) a large firm cushion used as a low seat or footstool. [F *pouf*; ult. imit.]

poulard /puːˈlɑːd/ *n.* a domestic hen that has been spayed and fattened for eating. [F *poularde* f. *poule* hen]

Poulenc /ˈpuːlæk/, Francis (1899–1963), French composer, a member of the group dubbed 'Les Six'. In his lightness of touch, wit, and adoption of the idioms of popular music (music-hall, jazz, café music, etc.) he was a true disciple of Satie and Cocteau, but his works are also characterized by a lyricism and an almost romantic charm, at its most attractive in his many songs and in such instrumental works as the sonatas for flute (1957), oboe (1962), and clarinet (1962). His works for the theatre include the ballet *Les Biches* (1923) and the large-scale religious opera *Dialogues des Carmélites* (1957) based on events of the French Revolution.

poult[1] /pəʊlt/ *n.* a young domestic fowl, turkey, pheasant, etc. [ME, contr. f. PULLET]

poult[2] /puːlt/ *n.* (in full **poult-de-soie** /ˌpuːdəˈswɑː/) a fine corded silk or taffeta, usu. coloured. [F, of unkn. orig.]

poulterer /ˈpəʊltərə(r)/ *n.* a dealer in poultry and usu. game. [ME *poulter* f. OF *pouletier* (as PULLET)]

poultice /ˈpəʊltɪs/ *n. & v.* —*n.* a soft medicated and usu. heated mass applied to the body and kept in place with muslin etc., for relieving soreness and inflammation. —*v.tr.* apply a poultice to. [orig. *pultes* (pl.) f. L *puls pultis* pottage, pap, etc.]

poultry /ˈpəʊltrɪ/ *n.* domestic fowls (ducks, geese, turkeys, chickens, etc.), esp. as a source of food. [ME f. OF *pouletrie* (as POULTERER)]

pounce[1] /paʊns/ *v. & n.* —*v.intr.* **1** spring or swoop, esp. as in capturing prey. **2** (often foll. by *on, upon*) **a** make a sudden attack. **b** seize eagerly upon an object, remark, etc. (*pounced on what we said*). —*n.* **1** the act or an instance of pouncing. **2** the claw or talon of a bird of prey. □□ **pouncer** *n.* [perh. f. PUNCHEON[1]]

pounce[2] /paʊns/ *n. & v.* —*n.* **1** a fine powder formerly used to prevent ink from spreading on unglazed paper. **2** powdered charcoal etc. dusted over a perforated pattern to transfer the design to the object beneath. —*v.tr.* **1** dust with pounce. **2** transfer (a design etc.) by use of pounce. **3** smooth (paper etc.) with pounce or pumice. □□ **pouncer** *n.* [F *ponce*, *poncer* f. L *pumex* PUMICE]

pouncet-box /ˈpaʊnsɪt/ *n. archaic* a small box with a perforated lid for perfumes etc. [16th c.: perh. orig. erron. f. *pounced* (= perforated) *box*]

Pound /paʊnd/, Ezra Weston Loomis (1885–1972), American poet and critic, who left for Europe in 1908 and in London became a leader of the imagist movement. To this period belong *Ripostes* (1912), 'Homage to Sextus Propertius', and *Hugh Selwyn Mauberley* (1920). Gradually he moved away from imagism, using a wide range of reference including Chinese, Old English, Provençal, Greek, and Latin towards the multicultural world of the *Cantos* (1917–70) on which his reputation rests. He settled in Italy in 1925 where his preoccupation with economics led to anti-Semitism and support for Mussolini; he made anti-democratic broadcasts on Italian radio during the Second World War and in 1945 was charged with treason but adjudged insane and committed to a mental institution until 1958. The tragedies of his later years obscured his reputation, but he is widely accepted as a master of verse form and as the regenerator of the poetic idiom of his day.

pound[1] /paʊnd/ *n.* **1** a unit of weight equal to 16 oz. avoirdupois (0.4536 kg), or 12 oz. troy (0.3732 kg). **2** (in full **pound sterling**) (*pl.* same or **pounds**) the chief monetary unit of the UK and several other countries. □ **pound cake** a rich cake containing a pound (or equal weights) of each chief ingredient. **pound coin** (or **note**) a coin or note worth one pound sterling. **pound of flesh** any legitimate but crippling or morally offensive demand (with allusion to Shylock's demand for a pound of Antonio's flesh, pledged as security for a loan, in Shakespeare's *Merchant of Venice*). **pound Scots** *hist.* 1s. 8d. **pound sign** the sign £, representing a pound. [OE *pund* ult. f. L *pondo* Roman pound weight of 12 ounces]

pound[2] /paʊnd/ *v.* **1** *tr.* **a** crush or beat with repeated heavy blows. **b** thump or pummel, esp. with the fists. **c** grind to a powder or pulp. **2** *intr.* (foll. by *at, on*) deliver heavy blows or gunfire. **3** *intr.* (foll. by *along* etc.) make one's way heavily or clumsily. **4** *intr.* (of the heart) beat heavily. □ **pound out** produce with or as if with heavy blows. □□ **pounder** *n.* [OE *pūnian*, rel. to Du. *puin*, LG *pün* rubbish]

pound[3] /paʊnd/ *n. & v.* —*n.* **1** an enclosure where stray animals or officially removed vehicles are kept until redeemed. **2** a place of confinement. —*v.tr.* enclose (cattle etc.) in a pound. □ **pound lock** a lock with two gates to confine water and often a side reservoir to maintain the water level. [ME f. OE *pund-* in *pundfald*: see PINFOLD]

poundage /ˈpaʊndɪdʒ/ *n.* **1** a commission or fee of so much per pound sterling or weight. **2** a percentage of the total earnings of a business, paid as wages. **3** a person's weight, esp. that which is regarded as excess.

poundal /ˈpaʊnd(ə)l/ *n. Physics* a unit of force equal to the force required to give a mass of one pound an acceleration of one foot per second per second. [POUND[1] + *-al* perh. after *quintal*]

pounder /ˈpaʊndə(r)/ *n.* (usu. in *comb.*) **1** a thing or person weighing a specified number of pounds (*a five-pounder*). **2** a gun carrying a shell of a specified number of pounds. **3** a thing worth, or a person possessing, so many pounds sterling.

pour /pɔː(r)/ *v.* **1** *intr. & tr.* (usu. foll. by *down, out, over,* etc.) flow or cause to flow e.g. downwards in a stream or shower. **2** *tr.* dispense (a drink, e.g. tea) by pouring. **3** *intr.* (of rain, or with *it* as subject) fall heavily. **4** *intr.* (usu. foll. by *in, out,* etc.) come or go in profusion or rapid succession (*the crowd poured out; letters poured in; poems poured from her fertile mind*). **5** *tr.* discharge or send freely (*poured forth arrows*). **6** *tr.* (often foll. by *out*) utter at length or in a rush (*poured out their story; poured scorn on my attempts*). □ **it never rains but it pours** misfortunes rarely come singly. **pour cold water on** see COLD. **pour oil on the waters** (or **on troubled waters**) calm a disagreement or disturbance, esp. with conciliatory words. □□ **pourable** *adj.* **pourer** *n.* [ME: orig. unkn.]

pourboire /pʊəˈbwɑː(r)/ *n.* a gratuity or tip. [F, = *pour boire* (money) for drinking]

Poussin /puːˈsæ̃/, Nicolas (1594–1665), French painter. Although considered the chief representative of French classicism in art, his work could almost be seen as part of the development of painting in Italy from where he took all his inspiration and where he chose to live for thirty-nine of the last forty-one years of his life. At first influenced by Italian mannerist and baroque painting, his study of the antique and the paintings of Raphael and Titian led him to a cogent and lucid style suffused with a rich and vibrant colour sense. His subject-matter ranged over biblical scenes (*The Entombment*), classical mythology (*Arcadia*), and, particularly towards the end of his life, historical landscapes.

poussin /ˈpuːsæ̃/ *n.* a young chicken bred for eating. [F]

pout[1] /paʊt/ *v. & n.* —*v.* **1** *intr.* **a** push the lips forward as an expression of displeasure or sulking. **b** (of the lips) be pushed forward. **2** *tr.* push (the lips) forward in pouting. —*n.* **1** such an action or expression. **2** (**the pouts**) a fit of sulking. □□ **pouter** *n.* **poutingly** *adv.* **pouty** *adj.* [ME, perh. f. OE *putian* (unrecorded) be inflated: cf. POUT[2]]

pout[2] /paʊt/ *n.* **1** = BIB[1] 3. **2** = EELPOUT. [OE *-puta* in *ǣlepūta* eelpout, f. WG]

pouter /ˈpaʊtə(r)/ *n.* **1** a person who pouts. **2** a kind of pigeon able to inflate its crop considerably.

poverty /ˈpɒvətɪ/ *n.* **1** the state of being poor; want of the necessities of life. **2** (often foll. by *of, in*) scarcity or lack. **3** inferiority, poorness, meanness. **4** *Eccl.* renunciation of the right to individual ownership of property. □ **poverty line** the minimum income level needed to secure the necessities of life. **poverty-stricken** extremely poor. **poverty trap** a situation in which an increase of income incurs a loss of State benefits, making real improvement impossible. [ME f. OF *poverte, poverté* f. L *paupertas -tatis* f. *pauper* poor]

POW *abbr.* prisoner of war.

pow /paʊ/ *int.* expressing the sound of a blow or explosion. [imit.]

powder /ˈpaʊdə(r)/ *n. & v.* —*n.* **1** a substance in the form of fine dry particles. **2** a medicine or cosmetic in this form. **3** = GUNPOWDER. —*v.tr.* **1 a** apply powder to (*powder one's nose*). **b** sprinkle or decorate with or as with powder. **2** (esp. as **powdered** *adj.*) reduce to a fine powder (*powdered milk*). □ **keep one's powder dry** be cautious and alert. **powder blue** pale blue. **powder-flask** *hist.* a small case for carrying gunpowder. **powder-keg 1** a barrel of gunpowder. **2** a dangerous or volatile situation. **powder metallurgy** the production of metal as fine powders to make objects. **powder-monkey** *hist.* a boy employed on board ship to carry powder to the guns. **powder-puff** a soft pad for applying powder to the skin, esp. the face. **powder-room** a women's cloakroom or lavatory in a public building. **powder snow** loose dry snow on a ski-run etc. **take a powder** *sl.* depart quickly. □□ **powdery** *adj.* [ME f. OF *poudre* f. L *pulvis pulveris* dust]

Powell /ˈpəʊ(ə)l/, Anthony Dymoke (1905–), English novelist, whose initial reputation as a satirist and comedian rests on five pre-war books beginning with *Afternoon Men* (1931). After the war he embarked on his ambitious sequence of 12 novels (*A Dance to the Music of Time*) beginning with *A Question of Upbringing* (1951) and ending with *Hearing Secret Harmonies* (1975); the whole is seen through the detached eyes of narrator Nicholas Jenkins, whose generation grew up in the shadow of the First World War to find their lives dislocated by the Second, and gives a rich and broad panorama, part humorous, part melancholy, of English life.

power /ˈpaʊə(r)/ *n. & v.* —*n.* **1** the ability to do or act (*will do all in my power; has the power to change colour*). **2** a particular faculty of body or mind (*lost the power of speech; powers of persuasion*). **3 a** government, influence, or authority. **b** political or social ascendancy or control (*the party in power; Black Power*). **4** authorization; delegated authority (*power of attorney; police powers*). **5** (often foll. by *over*) personal ascendancy. **6** an influential person, group, or organization (*the press is a power in the land*). **7 a** military strength.

b a State having international influence, esp. based on military strength (*the leading powers*). **8** vigour, energy. **9** an active property or function (*has a high heating power*). **10** *colloq.* a large number or amount (*has done me a power of good*). **11** the capacity for exerting mechanical force or doing work (*horsepower*). **12** mechanical or electrical energy as distinct from hand-labour (often *attrib.*: *power tools*; *power steering*). **13 a** a public supply of (esp. electrical) energy. **b** a particular source or form of energy (*hydroelectric power*). **14** a mechanical force applied e.g. by means of a lever. **15** *Physics* the rate of energy output. **16** the product obtained when a number is multiplied by itself a certain number of times (*2 to the power of 3 = 8*). **17** the magnifying capacity of a lens. **18 a** a deity. **b** (in *pl.*) the sixth order of the ninefold celestial hierarchy. —*v.tr.* **1** supply with mechanical or electrical energy. **2** (foll. by *up, down*) increase or decrease the power supplied to (a device); switch on or off. □ **in the power of** under the control of. **more power to your elbow!** an expression of encouragement or approval. **power behind the throne** a person who asserts authority or influence without having formal status. **power block** a group of nations constituting an international political force. **power cut** a temporary withdrawal or failure of an electric power supply. **power-dive** *n.* a steep dive of an aircraft with the engines providing thrust. —*v.intr.* perform a power-dive. **power line** a conductor supplying electrical power, esp. one supported by pylons or poles. **power of attorney** see ATTORNEY. **power pack 1** a unit for supplying power. **2** the equipment for converting an alternating current (from the mains) to a direct current at a different (usu. lower) voltage. **power play 1** tactics involving the concentration of players at a particular point. **2** similar tactics in business, politics, etc., involving a concentration of resources, effort, etc. **power point** *Brit.* a socket in a wall etc. for connecting an electrical device to the mains. **power politics** political action based on power or influence. **power-sharing** a policy agreed between parties or within a coalition to share responsibility for decision-making and political action. **power station** a building where electrical power is generated for distribution. **the powers that be** those in authority (Rom. 13:1). **power stroke** the stroke of an internal-combustion engine, in which the piston is moved downward by the expansion of gases. □□ **powered** *adj.* (also in *comb.*). [ME & AF *poer* etc., OF *poeir* ult. f. L *posse* be able]

powerboat /ˈpaʊəˌbəʊt/ *n.* a powerful motor boat.

powerful /ˈpaʊəfʊl/ *adj.* **1** having much power or strength. **2** politically or socially influential. □□ **powerfully** *adv.* **powerfulness** *n.*

powerhouse /ˈpaʊəhaʊs/ *n.* **1** = power station. **2** a person or thing of great energy.

powerless /ˈpaʊəlɪs/ *adj.* **1** without power or strength. **2** (often foll. by *to* + infin.) wholly unable (*powerless to help*). □□ **powerlessly** *adv.* **powerlessness** *n.*

powerplant /ˈpaʊəplɑːnt/ *n.* an apparatus or an installation which provides power for industry, a machine, etc.

powwow /ˈpaʊwaʊ/ *n.* & *v.* —*n.* a conference or meeting for discussion (orig. among N. American Indians). —*v.tr.* hold a powwow. [Algonquian *powah, powwaw* magician (lit. 'he dreams')]

Powys /ˈpəʊɪs, ˈpaʊɪs/ an inland county of Wales; pop. (1981) 110,500; county town, Llandridod Wells.

pox /pɒks/ *n.* **1** any virus disease producing a rash of pimples that become pus-filled and leave pock-marks on healing. **2** *colloq.* = SYPHILIS. **3** a plant disease that causes pocklike spots. □ **a pox on** *archaic* an exclamation of anger or impatience with (a person). [alt. spelling of *pocks* pl. of POCK]

poxy /ˈpɒksɪ/ *adj.* (**poxier, poxiest**) **1** infected by pox. **2** *sl.* of poor quality; worthless.

Poznań /pɒzˈnæn/ an industrial city in western Poland; pop. (1985) 553,000.

pozzolana /ˌpɒtsəˈlɑːnə/ *n.* (also **puzzolana**) a volcanic ash used for mortar or hydraulic cement. [It., f. *pozz(u)olano* (adj.) of *Pozzuoli* near Naples]

pp *abbr.* pianissimo.

pp. *abbr.* pages.

p.p. *abbr.* (also **pp**) *per pro.*

PPE *abbr. Brit.* philosophy, politics, and economics (as a degree course at Oxford University).

p.p.m. *abbr.* parts per million.

PPS *abbr. Brit.* **1** Parliamentary Private Secretary. **2** additional postscript.

PR *abbr.* **1** public relations. **2** proportional representation. **3** *US* Puerto Rico.

Pr *symb. Chem.* the element praseodymium.

pr. *abbr.* pair.

PRA *abbr.* (in the UK) President of the Royal Academy.

praam var. of PRAM².

practicable /ˈpræktɪkəb(ə)l/ *adj.* **1** that can be done or used. **2** possible in practice. □□ **practicability** /-ˈbɪlɪtɪ/ *n.* **practicableness** *n.* **practicably** *adv.* [F *praticable* f. *pratiquer* put into practice (as PRACTICAL)]

practical /ˈpræktɪk(ə)l/ *adj.* & *n.* —*adj.* **1** of or concerned with practice or use rather than theory. **2** suited to use or action; designed mainly to fulfil a function (*practical shoes*). **3** (of a person) inclined to action rather than speculation; able to make things function well. **4 a** that is such in effect though not nominally (*for all practical purposes*). **b** virtual (*in practical control*). **5** feasible; concerned with what is actually possible (*practical politics*). —*n.* a practical examination or lesson. □ **practical joke** a humorous trick played on a person. **practical joker** a person who plays practical jokes. □□ **practicality** /-ˈkælɪtɪ/ *n.* (*pl.* -**ies**). **practicalness** *n.* [earlier *practic* f. obs. F *practique* or LL *practicus* f. Gk *praktikos* f. *prassō* do, act]

practically /ˈpræktɪkəlɪ/ *adv.* **1** virtually, almost (*practically nothing*). **2** in a practical way.

practice /ˈpræktɪs/ *n.* & *v.* —*n.* **1** habitual action or performance (*the practice of teaching*; *makes a practice of saving*). **2** a habit or custom (*has been my regular practice*). **3 a** repeated exercise in an activity requiring the development of skill (*to sing well needs much practice*). **b** a session of this (*time for target practice*). **4** action or execution as opposed to theory. **5** the professional work or business of a doctor, lawyer, etc. (*has a practice in town*). **6** an established method of legal procedure. **7** procedure generally, esp. of a specified kind (*bad practice*). —*v.tr.* & *intr. US* var. of PRACTISE. □ **in practice 1** when actually applied; in reality. **2** skilful because of recent exercise in a particular pursuit. **out of practice** lacking a former skill from lack of recent practice. **put into practice** actually apply (an idea, method, etc.). [ME f. PRACTISE, after *advice, device*]

practician /prækˈtɪʃ(ə)n/ *n.* a worker; a practitioner. [obs. F *practicien* f. *practique* f. med.L *practica* f. Gk *praktikē* fem. of *praktikos*: see PRACTICAL]

practise /ˈpræktɪs/ *v.* (*US* **practice**) **1** *tr.* perform habitually; carry out in action (*practise the same method*; *practise what you preach*). **2** *tr.* & (foll. by *in, on*) *intr.* do repeatedly as an exercise to improve a skill; exercise oneself in or on (an activity requiring skill) (*had to practise in the art of speaking*; *practise your reading*). **3** *tr.* (as **practised** *adj.*) experienced, expert (*a practised liar*; *with a practised hand*). **4** *tr.* **a** pursue or be engaged in (a profession, religion, etc.). **b** (as **practising** *adj.*) currently active or engaged in (a profession or activity) (*a practising Christian*; *a practising lawyer*). **5** *intr.* (foll. by *on, upon*) take advantage of; impose upon. **6** *intr. archaic* scheme, contrive (*when first we practise to deceive*). □□ **practiser** *n.* [ME f. OF *pra(c)tiser* or med.L *practizare* alt. f. *practicare* (as PRACTICAL)]

practitioner /prækˈtɪʃənə(r)/ *n.* a person practising a profession, esp. medicine (*general practitioner*). [obs. *practitian* = PRACTICIAN]

Prado /ˈprɑːdəʊ/ the Spanish national art gallery, in Madrid. Established in 1818 by Ferdinand VII and Isabella of Braganza, it houses the greatest collection in the world of Spanish masters—Velazquez, el Greco, Zurbarán, Ribera, Murillo, Goya—as well as important examples of Flemish and Venetian art collected as a result of political ties with these countries in the reign of Charles V, Philip II, and Philip IV. Work produced after 1850 is deemed ineligible for inclusion.

prae- /priː/ *prefix* = PRE- (esp. in words regarded as Latin or relating to Roman antiquity. [L: see PRE-]

praecipe /ˈpriːsɪpɪ/ *n.* **1** a writ demanding action or an explanation of non-action. **2** an order requesting a writ. [L (the first word of the writ), imper. of *praecipere* enjoin: see PRECEPT]

praecocial /prɪˈkəʊʃ(ə)l/ *adj. & n.* (*US* **precocial**) —*adj.* (of a bird) having young that can feed themselves as soon as they are hatched. —*n.* a praecocial bird (cf. ALTRICIAL). [L *praecox -cocis* (as PRECOCIOUS)]

praemunire /ˌpriːmuːˈnɪərɪ/ *n. hist.* a writ charging a sheriff to summon a person accused of asserting or maintaining papal jurisdiction in England. [med.L, = forewarn, for L *praemonēre* (as PRAE-, *monēre* warn): the words *praemunire facias* that you warn (a person to appear) occur in the writ]

praenomen /priːˈnəʊmen/ *n.* an ancient Roman's first or personal name (e.g. *Marcus* Tullius Cicero). [L f. *prae* before + *nomen* name]

praepostor /prɪˈpɒstə(r)/ *n.* (also **prepostor**) *Brit.* (at some public schools) a prefect or monitor. [*praepositor* alt. f. L *praepositus* past part. of *praeponere* set over (as PRAE-, *ponere posit-* place)]

praesidium var. of PRESIDIUM.

praetor /ˈpriːtə(r), -tɔː(r)/ *n.* (*US* **pretor**) *Rom. Hist.* each of two ancient Roman magistrates ranking below consul. □□ **praetorial** /-ˈtɔːrɪəl/ *adj.* **praetorship** *n.* [ME f. F *préteur* or L *praetor* (perh. as PRAE-, *ire it-* go)]

praetorian /priːˈtɔːrɪən/ *adj. & n.* (*US* **pretorian**) *Rom.Hist.* —*adj.* of or having the powers of a praetor. —*n.* a man of praetorian rank. □ **praetorian guard** the bodyguard of the Roman emperor. [ME f. L *praetorianus* (as PRAETOR)]

pragmatic /prægˈmætɪk/ *adj.* **1** dealing with matters with regard to their practical requirements or consequences. **2** treating the facts of history with reference to their practical lessons. **3** *hist.* of or relating to the affairs of a State. **4** (also **pragmatical**) **a** concerning pragmatism. **b** meddlesome. **c** dogmatic. □ **pragmatic sanction** *hist.* an imperial or royal ordinance issued as a fundamental law, esp. regarding a question of royal succession. (See below.) □□ **pragmaticality** /-ˈkælɪtɪ/ *n.* **pragmatically** *adv.* [LL *pragmaticus* f. Gk *pragmatikos* f. *pragma -matos* deed]

The term Pragmatic Sanction refers specifically to a document drafted by the Emperor Charles VI after the birth of his daughter Maria Theresa in 1717 to allow her to succeed to all his territories should he die without a son. The Sanction was accepted by the Diets of Austria, Hungary, and the Austrian Netherlands in 1720–3, but the campaign to have it recognized by the rest of Europe dominated the international diplomatic scene for two decades afterwards, and, on Charles's death in 1740, led to the War of the Austrian Succession.

pragmatics /prægˈmætɪks/ *n.pl.* (usu. treated as *sing.*) the branch of linguistics dealing with language in use.

pragmatism /ˈprægmətɪz(ə)m/ *n.* **1** a pragmatic attitude or procedure. **2** a philosophy that evaluates assertions solely by their practical consequences and bearing on human interests. □□ **pragmatist** *n.* **pragmatistic** /-ˈtɪstɪk/ *adj.* [Gk *pragma*: see PRAGMATIC]

pragmatize /ˈprægmətaɪz/ *v.tr.* (also **-ise**) **1** represent as real. **2** rationalize (a myth).

Prague /prɑːg/ (Czech **Praha** /ˈprɑːhə/) the capital of Czechoslovakia, situated on the River Vltava; pop. (1986) 1,194,000. It first achieved prominence in the 13th c., when the kings of Bohemia established it as their capital. Its university, founded in 1348 by the future emperor Charles IV, is among the oldest in Europe. □ **Prague Spring** the attempted democratization of Czech political life in 1968 (see DUBČEK).

prahu var. of PROA.

Praia /ˈpraɪə/ the capital of the Cape Verde Islands, situated on the island of São Tiago; pop. (1980) 37,500.

prairie /ˈpreərɪ/ *n.* a large area of usu. treeless grassland esp. in N. America. □ **prairie chicken** (or **hen**) a N. American grouse, *Tympanuchus cupido*. **prairie dog** any N. American rodent of the genus *Cynomys*, living in burrows and making a barking sound.

prairie oyster a seasoned raw egg, swallowed without breaking the yolk. **prairie schooner** *US* a covered wagon used by the 19th-c. pioneers in crossing the N. American prairies. **prairie wolf** = COYOTE. [F f. OF *praerie* ult. f. L *pratum* meadow]

praise /preɪz/ *v. & n.* —*v.tr.* **1** express warm approval or admiration of. **2** glorify (God) in words. —*n.* the act or an instance of praising; commendation (*won high praise; were loud in their praises*). □ **praise be!** an exclamation of pious gratitude. **sing the praises of** commend (a person) highly. □□ **praiseful** *adj.* **praiser** *n.* [ME f. OF *preisier* price, prize, praise, f. LL *pretiare* f. L *pretium* price: cf. PRIZE¹]

praiseworthy /ˈpreɪzˌwɜːðɪ/ *adj.* worthy of praise; commendable. □□ **praiseworthily** *adv.* **praiseworthiness** *n.*

Prakrit /ˈprɑːkrɪt/ *n.* any of the (esp. ancient or medieval) vernacular dialects of North and Central India existing alongside or derived from Sanskrit. [Skr. *prākṛta* unrefined: cf. SANSKRIT]

praline /ˈprɑːliːn/ *n.* a sweet made by browning nuts in boiling sugar. [F f. Marshal de Plessis-*Praslin*, Fr. soldier d. 1675, whose cook invented it]

pralltriller /ˈprɑːlˌtrɪlə(r)/ *n.* a musical ornament consisting of one rapid alternation of the written note with the note immediately above it. [G f. *prallen* rebound + *Triller* TRILL]

pram¹ /præm/ *n. Brit.* a four-wheeled carriage for a baby, pushed by a person on foot. [abbr. of PERAMBULATOR]

pram² /prɑːm/ *n.* (also **praam**) **1** a flat-bottomed gunboat or Baltic cargo-boat. **2** a Scandinavian ship's dinghy. [MDu. *prame*, *praem*, MLG *prām(e)*, f. OSlav. *pramŭ*]

prana /ˈprɑːnə/ *n.* **1** (in Hinduism) breath as a life-giving force. **2** the breath; breathing. [Skr.]

prance /prɑːns/ *v. & n.* —*v.intr.* **1** (of a horse) raise the forelegs and spring from the hind legs. **2** (often foll. by *about*) walk or behave in an elated or arrogant manner. —*n.* **1** the act of prancing. **2** a prancing movement. □□ **prancer** *n.* [ME: orig. unkn.]

prandial /ˈprændɪəl/ *adj. formal* or *joc.* of dinner or lunch. [L *prandium* meal]

Prandtl /ˈprænt(ə)l/, Ludwig (1875–1953), German physicist with a worldwide reputation for his studies on both aerodynamics and hydrodynamics. His work established the existence of a boundary layer (see BOUNDARY) and he made important studies on streamlining. Design of efficient shape, weight, and mass of aircraft and ships owes much to his work.

prang /præŋ/ *v. & n. Brit. sl.* —*v.tr.* **1** crash or damage (an aircraft or vehicle). **2** bomb (a target) successfully. —*n.* the act or an instance of pranging. [imit.]

prank /præŋk/ *n.* a practical joke; a piece of mischief. □□ **prankful** *adj.* **prankish** *adj.* **pranksome** *adj.* [16th c.: orig. unkn.]

prankster /ˈpræŋkstə(r)/ *n.* a person fond of playing pranks.

prase /preɪz/ *n.* a translucent leek-green type of quartz. [F f. L *prasius* f. Gk *prasios* (adj.) leek-green f. *prason* leek]

praseodymium /ˌpreɪzɪəˈdɪmɪəm/ *n. Chem.* a soft silvery metallic element of the lanthanide series, occurring naturally in various minerals, discovered in 1885. The metal is a component of certain alloys and its compounds are used for colouring glass and ceramics. ¶ Symb.: **Pr**; atomic number 59. [G *Praseodym* f. Gk *prasios* (see PRASE) from its green salts, + G *Didym* DIDYMIUM]

prat /præt/ *n. sl.* **1** *Brit.* a silly or foolish person. **2** the buttocks. [16th-c. cant (in sense 2): orig. unkn.]

prate /preɪt/ *v. & n.* —*v.* **1** *intr.* chatter; talk too much. **2** *intr.* talk foolishly or irrelevantly. **3** *tr.* tell or say in a prating manner. —*n.* prating; idle talk. □□ **prater** *n.* **prating** *adj.* [ME f. MDu., MLG *praten*, prob. imit.]

pratfall /ˈprætfɔːl/ *n. US sl.* **1** a fall on the buttocks. **2** a humiliating failure.

pratie /ˈpreɪtɪ/ *n. esp. Ir.* a potato. [corrupt.]

pratincole /ˈprætɪŋkəʊl/ *n.* any of various birds of the subfamily Glareolinae, inhabiting sandy and stony areas and feeding on insects. [mod.L *pratincola* f. L *pratum* meadow + *incola* inhabitant]

pratique /præˈtiːk/ *n.* a licence to have dealings with a port, granted to a ship after quarantine or on showing a clean bill of health. [F, = practice, intercourse, f. It. *pratica* f. med.L *practica*: see PRACTICIAN]

prattle /'præt(ə)l/ v. & n. —v.intr. & tr. chatter or say in a childish way. —n. **1** childish chatter. **2** inconsequential talk. □□ **prattler** n. **prattling** adj. [MLG *pratelen* (as PRATE)]

prau var. of PROA.

prawn /prɔːn/ n. & v. —n. any of various marine crustaceans, resembling a shrimp but usu. larger. —v.intr. fish for prawns. □ **come the raw prawn** see RAW. [ME *pra(y)ne*, of unkn. orig.]

praxis /'præksɪs/ n. **1** accepted practice or custom. **2** the practising of an art or skill. [med.L f. Gk, = doing, f. *prassō* do]

Praxiteles /præk'sɪtəˌliːz/ (mid-4th c. BC) Athenian sculptor. He and Phidias were the greatest Greek sculptors of their age. The *Hermes* (Olympia) is considered a fine example (or copy) of work that justifies his renown, with its physical repose qualified by submerged undercurrents of latent energy—a subtlety that is lost in the copies of his *Sauroctonus* (Apollo slaying a lizard) and Cnidos *Aphrodite* (the first important female nude).

pray /preɪ/ v. (often foll. by *for* or *to* + infin. or *that* + clause) **1** intr. (often foll. by *to*) say prayers (to God etc.); make devout supplication. **2 a** tr. entreat, beseech. **b** tr. & intr. ask earnestly (*prayed to be released*). **3** tr. (as *imper.*) archaic & formal please (*pray tell me*). □ **praying mantis** see MANTIS. [ME f. OF *preier* f. LL *precare* f. L *precari* entreat]

prayer[1] /'preə(r)/ n. **1 a** a solemn request or thanksgiving to God or an object of worship (*say a prayer*). **b** a formula or form of words used in praying (*the Lord's prayer*). **c** the act of praying (*be at prayer*). **d** a religious service consisting largely of prayers (*morning prayers*). **2 a** an entreaty to a person. **b** a thing entreated or prayed for. □ **not have a prayer** US colloq. have no chance (of success etc.). **prayer-book** a book containing the forms of prayer in regular use, esp. the Book of Common Prayer. **prayer-mat** a small carpet used by Muslims when praying. **Prayer of Manasses** /mə'næsiːz/ a book of the Apocrypha consisting of a penitential prayer put into the mouth of Manasseh, king of Judah (2 Kings 21: 1–18). **prayer-wheel** a revolving cylindrical box inscribed with or containing prayers, used esp. by Tibetan Buddhists. □□ **prayerless** adj. [ME f. OF *preiere* ult. f. L *precarius* obtained by entreaty f. *prex precis* prayer]

prayer[2] /'preɪə(r)/ n. a person who prays.

prayerful /'preəˌfʊl/ adj. **1** (of a person) given to praying; devout. **2** (of speech, actions, etc.) characterized by or expressive of prayer. □□ **prayerfully** adv. **prayerfulness** n.

pre- /priː/ *prefix* before (in time, place, order, degree, or importance). [from or after L *prae-* f. *prae* (adv. & prep.)]

preach /priːtʃ/ v. **1 a** intr. deliver a sermon or religious address. **b** tr. deliver (a sermon); proclaim or expound (the Gospel etc.). **2** intr. give moral advice in an obtrusive way. **3** tr. advocate or inculcate (a quality or practice etc.). □□ **preachable** adj. [ME f. OF *prechier* f. L *praedicare* proclaim, in eccl.L preach (as PRAE-, *dicare* declare)]

preacher /'priːtʃə(r)/ n. a person who preaches, esp. a minister of religion. [ME f. AF *prech(o)ur*, OF *prech(e)or* f. eccl.L *praedicator* (as PREACH)]

preachify /'priːtʃɪˌfaɪ/ v.intr. (-ies, -ied) colloq. preach or moralize tediously.

preachment /'priːtʃmənt/ n. usu. derog. preaching, sermonizing.

preachy /'priːtʃɪ/ adj. (**preachier**, **preachiest**) colloq. inclined to preach or moralize. □□ **preachiness** n.

preadolescent /ˌpriːædə'les(ə)nt/ adj. & n. —adj. **1** (of a child) having nearly reached adolescence. **2** of or relating to the two or three years preceding adolescence. —n. a preadolescent child. □□ **preadolescence** n.

preamble /priː'æmb(ə)l, 'priː-/ n. **1** a preliminary statement or introduction. **2** the introductory part of a statute or deed etc. □□ **preambular** /-'æmbjʊlə(r)/ adj. [ME f. OF *preamble* f. med.L *praeambulum* f. LL *praeambulus* (adj.) going before (as PRE-, AMBLE)]

pre-amp /'priːæmp/ n. = PREAMPLIFIER. [abbr.]

preamplifier /priː'æmplɪˌfaɪə(r)/ n. an electronic device that

amplifies a very weak signal (e.g. from a microphone or pickup) and transmits it to a main amplifier. □□ **preamplified** adj.

prearrange /ˌpriːə'reɪndʒ/ v.tr. arrange beforehand. □□ **prearrangement** n.

preatomic /ˌpriːə'tɒmɪk/ adj. existing or occurring before the use of atomic energy.

Preb. abbr. Prebendary.

prebend /'prebənd/ n. **1** the stipend of a canon or member of chapter. **2** a portion of land or tithe from which this is drawn. □□ **prebendal** adj. [ME f. OF *prebende* f. LL *praebenda* pension, neut.pl. gerundive of L *praebēre* grant f. *prae* forth + *habēre* hold]

prebendary /'prebəndərɪ/ n. (pl. -ies) **1** the holder of a prebend. **2** an honorary canon. □□ **prebendaryship** n. [ME f. med.L *praebendarius* (as PREBEND)]

Precambrian /priː'kæmbrɪən/ adj. & n. Geol. —adj. of or relating to the earliest era of geological time, preceding the Cambrian period and Palaeozoic era. The Precambrian era includes the whole of the earth's history from its origin about 4,600 million years ago to the beginning of the Cambrian about 590 million years ago. Fossils of animals with hard skeletons are absent from Precambrian rocks, and the era was once considered to be devoid of organic life, but it is now known that a variety of organisms did exist during that time. The oldest known Precambrian rocks on earth are about 3,800 million years old. —n. this era.

precarious /prɪ'keərɪəs/ adj. **1** uncertain; dependent on chance (*makes a precarious living*). **2** insecure, perilous (*precarious health*). □□ **precariously** adv. **precariousness** n. [L *precarius*: see PRAYER[1]]

precast /priː'kɑːst/ adj. (of concrete) cast in its final shape before positioning.

precative /'prekətɪv/ adj. (of a word or form) expressing a wish or request. [LL *precativus* f. *precari* pray]

precaution /prɪ'kɔːʃ(ə)n/ n. **1** an action taken beforehand to avoid risk or ensure a good result. **2** (in pl.) colloq. the use of contraceptives. □□ **precautionary** adj. [F *précaution* f. LL *praecautio -onis* f. L *praecavēre* (as PRAE-, *cavēre caut-* beware of)]

precede /prɪ'siːd/ v.tr. **1 a** come or go before in time, order, importance, etc. (*preceding generations; the preceding paragraph; sons of barons precede baronets*). **b** walk etc. in front of (*preceded by our guide*). **2** (foll. by *by*) cause to be preceded (*must precede this measure by milder ones*). [OF *preceder* f. L *praecedere* (as PRAE-, *cedere cess-* go)]

precedence /'presɪd(ə)ns/ n. (also **precedency**) **1** priority in time, order, or importance, etc. **2** the right of preceding others on formal occasions. □ **take precedence** (often foll. by *over, of*) have priority (over).

precedent n. & adj. —n. /'presɪd(ə)nt/ a previous case or legal decision etc. taken as a guide for subsequent cases or as a justification. —adj. /prɪ'siːd(ə)nt, 'presɪ-/ preceding in time, order, importance, etc. □□ **precedently** /'priːsɪdəntlɪ, 'presɪ-/ adv. [ME f. OF (n. & adj.) (as PRECEDE)]

precedented /'presɪˌdentɪd/ adj. having or supported by a precedent.

precent /prɪ'sent/ v. **1** intr. act as a precentor. **2** tr. lead the singing of (a psalm etc.). [back-form. f. PRECENTOR]

precentor /prɪ'sentə(r)/ n. **1** a person who leads the singing or (in a synagogue) the prayers of a congregation. **2** a minor canon who administers the musical life of a cathedral. □□ **precentorship** n. [F *précenteur* or L *praecentor* f. *praecinere* (as PRAE-, *canere* sing)]

precept /'priːsept/ n. **1** a command; a rule of conduct. **2** moral instruction (*example is better than precept*). **3 a** a writ or warrant. **b** Brit. an order for collection or payment of money under a local rate. □□ **preceptive** /prɪ'septɪv/ adj. [ME f. L *praeceptum* neut. past part. of *praecipere praecept-* warn, instruct (as PRAE-, *capere* take)]

preceptor /prɪ'septə(r)/ n. a teacher or instructor. □□ **preceptorial** /ˌpriːsep'tɔːrɪəl/ adj. **preceptorship** n. **preceptress** /-trɪs/ n. [L *praeceptor* (as PRECEPT)]

precession /prɪ'seʃ(ə)n/ n. the slow movement of the axis of a spinning body around another axis. □ **precession of the equinoxes 1** the slow retrograde motion of equinoctial points along the ecliptic. **2** the resulting earlier occurrence of equinoxes in each successive sidereal year. As the Earth rotates about its axis it responds to the gravitational attraction of the sun upon its equatorial bulge, so that its axis of rotation describes a circle in the sky. The celestial equator moves backward along the sun's apparent path (the ecliptic), and the points where these two great circles intersect, which define the sun's position at the equinoxes, therefore travel through the constellations of the zodiac once in a period of about 26,000 years. The equinoctial position of the sun at the time of Hipparchus (c.125 BC) was a point in the constellation of Aries; the corresponding position, although now in Pisces, is still known as the First Point of Aries. □□ **precessional** adj. [LL praecessio (as PRECEDE)]

pre-Christian /priːˈkrɪstɪən/ adj. before Christ or the advent of Christianity.

precinct /ˈpriːsɪŋkt/ n. **1** an enclosed or clearly defined area, e.g. around a cathedral, college, etc. **2** a specially designated area in a town, esp. with the exclusion of traffic (shopping precinct). **3** (in pl.) **a** the surrounding area or environs. **b** the boundaries. **4** US **a** a subdivision of a county, city, etc., for police or electoral purposes. **b** (in pl.) a neighbourhood. [ME f. med.L praecinctum neut. past part. of praecingere encircle (as PRAE-, cingere gird)]

preciosity /ˌpreʃɪˈɒsɪtɪ/ n. overrefinement in art or language, esp. in the choice of words. [OF préciosité f. L pretiositas f. pretiosus (as PRECIOUS)]

precious /ˈpreʃəs/ adj. & adv. —adj. **1** of great value or worth. **2** beloved; much prized (precious memories). **3** affectedly refined, esp. in language or manner. **4** colloq. often iron. **a** considerable (a precious lot you know about it). **b** expressing contempt or disdain (you can keep your precious flowers). —adv. colloq. extremely, very (tried precious hard; had precious little left). □ **precious metals** gold, silver, and platinum. **precious stone** a piece of mineral having great value esp. as used in jewellery. □□ **preciously** adv. **preciousness** n. [ME f. OF precios f. L pretiosus f. pretium price]

precipice /ˈpresɪpɪs/ n. **1** a vertical or steep face of a rock, cliff, mountain, etc. **2** a dangerous situation. [F précipice or L praecipitium falling headlong, precipice (as PRECIPITOUS)]

precipitant /prɪˈsɪpɪt(ə)nt/ adj. & n. —adj. = PRECIPITATE adj. —n. Chem. a substance that causes another substance to precipitate. □□ **precipitance** n. **precipitancy** n. [obs. F précipitant pres. part. of précipiter (as PRECIPITATE)]

precipitate v., adj., & n. —v.tr. /prɪˈsɪpɪˌteɪt/ **1** hasten the occurrence of; cause to occur prematurely. **2** (foll. by into) send rapidly into a certain state or condition (were precipitated into war). **3** throw down headlong. **4** Chem. cause (a substance) to be deposited in solid form from a solution. **5** Physics **a** cause (dust etc.) to be deposited from the air on a surface. **b** condense (vapour) into drops and so deposit it. —adj. /prɪˈsɪpɪtət/ **1** headlong; violently hurried (precipitate departure). **2** (of a person or act) hasty, rash, inconsiderate. —n. /prɪˈsɪpɪtət/ **1** Chem. a substance precipitated from a solution. **2** Physics moisture condensed from vapour by cooling and depositing, e.g. rain or dew. □□ **precipitable** /prɪˈsɪpɪtəb(ə)l/ adj. **precipitability** /prɪˌsɪpɪtəˈbɪlɪtɪ/ n. **precipitately** /prɪˈsɪpɪtətlɪ/ adv. **precipitateness** /prɪˈsɪpɪtətnɪs/ n. **precipitator** /prɪˈsɪpɪˌteɪtə(r)/ n. [L praecipitare praecipitat- f. praeceps praecipitis headlong (as PRAE-, caput head)]

precipitation /prɪˌsɪpɪˈteɪʃ(ə)n/ n. **1** the act of precipitating or the process of being precipitated. **2** rash haste. **3 a** rain or snow etc. falling to the ground. **b** a quantity of this. [F précipitation or L praecipitatio (as PRECIPITATE)]

precipitous /prɪˈsɪpɪtəs/ adj. **1 a** of or like a precipice. **b** dangerously steep. **2** = PRECIPITATE adj. □□ **precipitously** adv. **precipitousness** n. [obs. F précipiteux f. L praeceps (as PRECIPITATE)]

précis /ˈpreɪsiː/ n. & v. —n. (pl. same /-siːz/) a summary or abstract, esp. of a text or speech. —v.tr. (**précises** /-siːz/; **précised** /-siːd/; **précising** /-siːɪŋ/) make a précis of. [F, = PRECISE (as n.)]

precise /prɪˈsaɪs/ adj. **1 a** accurately expressed. **b** definite, exact. **2** punctilious; scrupulous in being exact, observing rules, etc. **3** identical, exact (at that precise moment). □□ **preciseness** n. [F précis -ise f. L praecidere praecis- cut short (as PRAE-, caedere cut)]

precisely /prɪˈsaɪslɪ/ adv. **1** in a precise manner; exactly. **2** (as a reply) quite so; as you say.

precisian /prɪˈsɪʒ(ə)n/ n. a person who is rigidly precise or punctilious, esp. in religious observance. □□ **precisianism** n.

precision /prɪˈsɪʒ(ə)n/ n. **1** the condition of being precise; accuracy. **2** the degree of refinement in measurement etc. **3** (attrib.) marked by or adapted for precision (precision instruments; precision timing). □□ **precisionism** n. **precisionist** n. [F précision or L praecisio (as PRECISE)]

preclassical /priːˈklæsɪk(ə)l/ adj. before a period regarded as classical, esp. in music and literature.

preclinical /priːˈklɪnɪk(ə)l/ adj. **1** of or relating to the first, chiefly theoretical, stage of a medical education. **2** (of a stage in a disease) before symptoms can be identified.

preclude /prɪˈkluːd/ v.tr. **1** (foll. by from) prevent, exclude (precluded from taking part). **2** make impossible; remove (so as to preclude all doubt). □□ **preclusion** /-ˈkluːʒ(ə)n/ n. **preclusive** /-ˈkluːsɪv/ adj. [L praecludere praeclus- (as PRAE-, claudere shut)]

precocial US var. of PRAECOCIAL.

precocious /prɪˈkəʊʃəs/ adj. **1** often derog. (of a person, esp. a child) prematurely developed in some faculty or characteristic. **2** (of an action etc.) indicating such development. **3** (of a plant) flowering or fruiting early. □□ **precociously** adv. **precociousness** n. **precocity** /-ˈkɒsɪtɪ/ n. [L praecox -cocis f. praecoquere ripen fully (as PRAE-, coquere cook)]

precognition /ˌpriːkɒgˈnɪʃ(ə)n/ n. **1** (supposed) foreknowledge, esp. of a supernatural kind. **2** Sc. the preliminary examination of witnesses etc., esp. to decide whether there is ground for a trial. □□ **precognitive** /-ˈkɒgnɪtɪv/ adj. [LL praecognitio (as PRE-, COGNITION)]

precoital /priːˈkəʊɪt(ə)l/ adj. preceding sexual intercourse. □□ **precoitally** adv.

pre-Columbian /ˌpriːkəˈlʌmbɪən/ adj. of or relating to the period before the discovery of America by Columbus.

preconceive /ˌpriːkənˈsiːv/ v.tr. form (an idea or opinion etc.) beforehand.

preconception /ˌpriːkənˈsepʃ(ə)n/ n. **1** a preconceived idea. **2** a prejudice.

preconcert /ˌpriːkənˈsɜːt/ v.tr. arrange or organize beforehand.

precondition /ˌpriːkənˈdɪʃ(ə)n/ n. & v. —n. a prior condition, that must be fulfilled before other things can be done. —v.tr. bring into a required condition beforehand.

preconize /ˈpriːkəˌnaɪz/ v.tr. (also **-ise**) **1** proclaim or commend publicly. **2** summon by name. **3** RC Ch. (of the Pope) approve publicly the appointment of (a bishop). □□ **preconization** /-ˈzeɪʃ(ə)n/ n. [ME f. med.L praeconizare f. L praeco -onis herald]

preconscious /priːˈkɒnʃəs/ adj. & n. Psychol. —adj. **1** preceding consciousness. **2** of or associated with a part of the mind below the level of immediate conscious awareness, from which memories and emotions can be recalled. —n. this part of the mind. □□ **preconsciousness** n.

precook /priːˈkʊk/ v.tr. cook in advance.

precool /priːˈkuːl/ v.tr. cool in advance.

precordial /priːˈkɔːdɪəl/ adj. in front of or about the heart.

precostal /priːˈkɒst(ə)l/ adj. in front of the ribs.

precursor /prɪˈkɜːsə(r)/ n. **1 a** a forerunner. **b** a person who precedes in office etc. **2** a harbinger. **3** a substance from which another is formed by decay or chemical reaction etc. [L praecursor f. praecurrere praecurs- (as PRAE-, currere run)]

precursory /prɪˈkɜːsərɪ/ adj. (also **precursive** /-sɪv/) **1** preliminary, introductory. **2** (foll. by of) serving as a harbinger of. [L praecursorius (as PRECURSOR)]

precut /priːˈkʌt/ v.tr. (past and past part. **-cut**) cut in advance.

predacious /prɪˈdeɪʃəs/ adj. (also **predaceous**) **1** (of an animal) predatory. **2** relating to such animals (predacious instincts). □□

predaciousness *n.* **predacity** /-'dæsɪtɪ/ *n.* [L *praeda* booty: cf. *audacious*]

predate /pri:'deɪt/ *v.tr.* exist or occur at a date earlier than.

predation /prɪ'deɪʃ(ə)n/ *n.* **1** (usu. in *pl.*) = DEPREDATION. **2** *Zool.* the natural preying of one animal on others. [L *praedatio -onis* taking of booty f. L *praeda* booty]

predator /'predətə(r)/ *n.* **1** an animal naturally preying on others. **2** a person, State, etc., compared to this. [L *praedator* plunderer f. *praedari* seize as plunder f. *praeda* booty (as PREDACIOUS)]

predatory /'predətərɪ/ *adj.* **1** (of an animal) preying naturally upon others. **2** (of a nation, State, or individual) plundering or exploiting others. □□ **predatorily** *adv.* **predatoriness** *n.* [L *praedatorius* (as PREDATOR)]

predecease /ˌpri:dɪ'si:s/ *v. & n.* —*v.tr.* die earlier than (another person). —*n.* a death preceding that of another.

predecessor /'pri:dɪˌsesə(r)/ *n.* **1** a former holder of an office or position with respect to a later holder (*my immediate predecessor*). **2** an ancestor. **3** a thing to which another has succeeded (*the new plan will share the fate of its predecessor*). [ME f. OF *predecesseur* f. LL *praedecessor* (as PRAE-, *decessor* retiring officer, as DECEASE)]

pre-decimal /ˌpri:'desɪm(ə)l/ *adj.* of or relating to a time before the introduction of a decimal system, esp. of coinage.

predella /prɪ'delə/ *n.* **1** an altar-step, or raised shelf at the back of an altar. **2** a painting or sculpture on this, or any picture forming an appendage to a larger one esp. beneath an altarpiece. [It., = stool]

predestinarian /prɪˌdestɪ'neərɪən/ *n. & adj.* —*n.* a person who believes in predestination. —*adj.* of or relating to predestination.

predestinate *v. & adj.* —*v.tr.* /prɪ'destɪˌneɪt/ = PREDESTINE. —*adj.* /prɪ'destɪnət/ predestined. [ME f. eccl.L *praedestinare praedestinat-* (as PRAE-, *destinare* establish)]

predestination /pri:ˌdestɪ'neɪʃ(ə)n/ *n.* Theol. (as a belief or doctrine) the divine foreordaining of all that will happen, esp. with regard to the salvation of some and not others. [ME f. eccl.L *praedestinatio* (as PREDESTINATE)]

predestine /pri:'destɪn/ *v.tr.* **1** determine beforehand. **2** ordain in advance by divine will or as if by fate. [ME f. OF *predestiner* or eccl.L *praedestinare* PREDESTINATE v.]

predetermine /ˌpri:dɪ'tɜ:mɪn/ *v.tr.* **1** determine or decree beforehand. **2** predestine. □□ **predeterminable** *adj.* **predeterminate** /-nət/ *adj.* **predetermination** /-'neɪʃ(ə)n/ *n.* [LL *praedeterminare* (as PRAE-, DETERMINE)]

predial /'pri:dɪəl/ *adj. & n. hist.* —*adj.* **1 a** of land or farms. **b** rural, agrarian. **c** (of a slave, tenant, etc.) attached to farms or the land. **2** (of a tithe) consisting of agricultural produce. —*n.* a predial slave. [med.L *praedialis* f. L *praedium* farm]

predicable /'predɪkəb(ə)l/ *adj. & n.* —*adj.* that may be predicated or affirmed. —*n.* **1** a predicable thing. **2** (in *pl.*) *Logic* the five classes to which predicates belong: genus, species, difference, property, and accident. □□ **predicability** /-'bɪlɪtɪ/ *n.* [med.L *praedicabilis* that may be affirmed (as PREDICATE)]

predicament /prɪ'dɪkəmənt/ *n.* **1** a difficult, unpleasant, or embarrassing situation. **2** *Philos.* a category in (esp. Aristotelian) logic. [ME (in sense 2) f. LL *praedicamentum* thing predicated: see PREDICATE]

predicant /'predɪkənt/ *adj. & n. hist.* (of a religious order, esp. the Dominicans) engaged in preaching. —*n.* **1** *hist.* a predicant person, esp. a Dominican friar. **2** *S.Afr.* = PREDIKANT. [L *praedicans* part. of *praedicare* (as PREDICATE)]

predicate *v. & n.* —*v.tr.* /'predɪˌkeɪt/ **1** assert or affirm as true or existent. **2** (foll. by *on*) found or base (a statement etc.) on. —*n.* /'predɪkət/ **1** *Gram.* what is said about the subject of a sentence etc. (e.g. *went home* in *John went home*). **2** *Logic* **a** what is predicated. **b** what is affirmed or denied of the subject by means of the copula (e.g. *mortal* in *all men are mortal*). □□ **predication** /-'keɪʃ(ə)n/ *n.* [L *praedicare praedicat-* proclaim (as PRAE-, *dicare* declare)]

predicative /prɪ'dɪkətɪv/ *adj.* **1** *Gram.* (of an adjective or noun) forming or contained in the predicate, as *old* in *the dog is old*

(but not in *the old dog*) and *house* in *there is a large house* (opp. ATTRIBUTIVE). **2** that predicates. □□ **predicatively** *adv.* [L *praedicativus* (as PREDICATE)]

predict /prɪ'dɪkt/ *v.tr.* (often foll. by *that* + clause) make a statement about the future; foretell, prophesy. □□ **predictive** *adj.* **predictively** *adv.* **predictor** *n.* [L *praedicere praedict-* (as PRAE-, *dicere* say)]

predictable /prɪ'dɪktəb(ə)l/ *adj.* that can be predicted or is to be expected. □□ **predictability** /-'bɪlɪtɪ/ *n.* **predictably** *adv.*

prediction /prɪ'dɪkʃ(ə)n/ *n.* **1** the art of predicting or the process of being predicted. **2** a thing predicted; a forecast. [L *praedictio -onis* (as PREDICT)]

predigest /ˌpri:daɪ'dʒest/ *v.tr.* **1** render (food) easily digestible before being eaten. **2** make (reading matter) easier to read or understand. □□ **predigestion** /-'dʒestʃ(ə)n/ *n.*

predikant /ˌpreɪdi:'kɑ:nt/ *n. S.Afr.* a minister of the Dutch Reformed Church. [Du. (as PREDICANT)]

predilection /ˌpri:dɪ'lekʃ(ə)n/ *n.* (often foll. by *for*) a preference or special liking. [F *prédilection* ult. f. L *praediligere praedilect-* prefer (as PRAE-, *diligere* select): see DILIGENT]

predispose /ˌpri:dɪ'spəʊz/ *v.tr.* **1** influence favourably in advance. **2** (foll. by *to*, or *to* + infin.) render liable or inclined beforehand. □□ **predisposition** /-pə'zɪʃ(ə)n/ *n.*

prednisone /'prednɪˌzəʊn/ *n.* a synthetic drug similar to cortisone, used to relieve rheumatic and allergic conditions and to treat leukaemia. [perh. f. *pregnant* + *diene* + *cortisone*]

predominant /prɪ'dɒmɪnənt/ *adj.* **1** predominating. **2** being the strongest or main element. □□ **predominance** *n.* **predominantly** *adv.*

predominate /prɪ'dɒmɪˌneɪt/ *v.intr.* **1** (foll. by *over*) have or exert control. **2** be superior. **3** be the strongest or main element; preponderate (*a garden in which dahlias predominate*). [med.L *praedominari* (as PRAE-, DOMINATE)]

predominately /prɪ'dɒmɪnətlɪ/ *adv.* = PREDOMINANTLY (see PREDOMINANT). [rare *predominate* (adj.) = PREDOMINANT]

predoom /pri:'du:m/ *v.tr.* doom beforehand.

predorsal /pri:'dɔ:s(ə)l/ *adj.* in front of the dorsal region.

predynastic /ˌpri:daɪ'næstɪk/ *adj.* of or relating to a period before the normally recognized dynasties (esp. of ancient Egypt).

pre-echo /pri:'ekəʊ/ *n.* (*pl.* **-oes**) **1** a faint copy heard just before an actual sound in a recording, caused by the accidental transfer of signals. **2** a foreshadowing.

pre-eclampsia /ˌpri:ɪ'klæmpsɪə/ *n.* a condition of pregnancy characterized by high blood pressure and other symptoms associated with eclampsia. □□ **pre-eclamptic** *adj. & n.*

pre-elect /ˌpri:ɪ'lekt/ *v.tr.* elect beforehand.

pre-election /ˌpri:ɪ'lekʃ(ə)n/ *n.* **1** an election held beforehand. **2** (*attrib.*) (esp. of an act or undertaking) done or given before an election.

pre-embryo /pri:'embrɪəʊ/ *n. Med.* a human embryo in the first fourteen days after fertilization. □□ **pre-embryonic** /-'ɒnɪk/ *adj.*

pre-eminent /pri:'emɪnənt/ *adj.* **1** excelling others. **2** outstanding; distinguished in some quality. □□ **pre-eminence** *n.* **pre-eminently** *adv.* [ME f. L *praeeminens* (as PRAE-, EMINENT)]

pre-empt /pri:'empt/ *v.* **1** *tr.* **a** forestall. **b** acquire or appropriate in advance. **2** *tr.* prevent (an attack) by disabling the enemy. **3** *tr.* obtain by pre-emption. **4** *tr.* US take for oneself (esp. public land) so as to have the right of pre-emption. **5** *intr. Bridge* make a pre-emptive bid. □□ **preemptor** *n.* **preemptory** *adj.* [back-form. f. PRE-EMPTION]

pre-emption /pri:'empʃ(ə)n/ *n.* **1 a** the purchase or appropriation by one person or party before the opportunity is offered to others. **b** the right to purchase (esp. public land) in this way. **2** prior appropriation or acquisition. [med.L *praeemptio* (as PRAE-, *emere empt-* buy)]

pre-emptive /pri:'emptɪv/ *adj.* **1** pre-empting; serving to pre-empt. **2** (of military action) intended to prevent attack by disabling the enemy (*a pre-emptive strike*). **3** *Bridge* (of a bid) intended to be high enough to discourage further bidding.

preen /pri:n/ *v.tr. & refl.* **1** (of a bird) tidy (the feathers or itself)

b *but* d *dog* f *few* g *get* h *he* j *yes* k *cat* l *leg* m *man* n *no* p *pen* r *red* s *sit* t *top* v *voice*

with its beak. **2** (of a person) smarten or admire (oneself, one's hair, clothes, etc.). **3** (often foll. by *on*) congratulate or pride (oneself). □ **preen gland** a gland situated at the base of a bird's tail and producing oil used in preening. □□ **preener** *n*. [ME, app. var. of earlier *prune* (perh. rel. to PRUNE²): assoc. with Sc. & dial. *preen* pierce, pin]

pre-engage /ˌpriːɪnˈɡeɪdʒ/ *v.tr.* engage beforehand. □□ **pre-engagement** *n*.

pre-establish /ˌpriːɪˈstæblɪʃ/ *v.tr.* establish beforehand.

pre-exist /ˌpriːɪɡˈzɪst/ *v.intr.* exist at an earlier time. □□ **pre-existence** *n*. **pre-existent** *adj*.

pref. *abbr*. **1** prefix. **2** preface. **3 a** preference. **b** preferred.

prefab /ˈpriːfæb/ *n*. *Brit. colloq.* a prefabricated building, esp. a small house. [abbr.]

prefabricate /priːˈfæbrɪˌkeɪt/ *v.tr.* **1** manufacture sections of (a building etc.) prior to their assembly on a site. **2** produce in an artificially standardized way. □□ **prefabrication** /-ˈkeɪʃ(ə)n/ *n*.

preface /ˈprefəs/ *n. & v.* —*n.* **1** an introduction to a book stating its subject, scope, etc. **2** the preliminary part of a speech. **3** *Eccl.* the introduction to the central part of the Eucharistic service. —*v.tr.* **1** (foll. by *with*) introduce or begin (a speech or event) (*prefaced my remarks with a warning*). **2** provide (a book etc.) with a preface. **3** (of an event etc.) lead up to (another). □□ **prefatorial** /-ˈtɔːrɪəl/ *adj*. **prefatory** /-tərɪ/ *adj*. [ME f. OF f. med.L *praefatia* for L *praefatio* f. *praefari* (as PRAE-, *fari* speak)]

prefect /ˈpriːfekt/ *n*. **1** the chief administrative officer of certain departments, esp. in France. **2** esp. *Brit*. a senior pupil in a school etc. authorized to enforce discipline. **3** *Rom. Antiq.* a senior magistrate or military commander. □□ **prefectoral** /-ˈfektər(ə)l/ *adj*. **prefectorial** /-ˈtɔːrɪəl/ *adj*. [ME f. OF f. L *praefectus* past part. of *praeficere* set in authority over (as PRAE-, *facere* make)]

prefecture /ˈpriːfektjʊə(r)/ *n*. **1** a district under the government of a prefect. **2 a** a prefect's office or tenure. **b** his official residence. □□ **prefectural** /prɪˈfektʃ(ə)r(ə)l/ *adj*. [F *préfecture* or L *praefectura* (as PREFECT)]

prefer /prɪˈfɜː(r)/ *v.tr.* (**preferred**, **preferring**) **1** (often foll. by *to*, or *to* + infin.) choose rather; like better (*would prefer to stay*; *prefers coffee to tea*). **2** submit (information, an accusation, etc.) for consideration. **3** promote or advance (a person). □ **preferred shares** (or **stock**) = *preference shares* or *stock*. [ME f. OF *preferer* f. L *praeferre* (as PRAE-, *ferre* lat- bear)]

preferable /ˈprefərəb(ə)l/ *adj*. **1** to be preferred. **2** more desirable. □□ **preferably** *adv*.

preference /ˈprefərəns/ *n*. **1** the act or an instance of preferring or being preferred. **2** a thing preferred. **3 a** the favouring of one person etc. before others. **b** *Commerce* the favouring of one country by admitting its products at a lower import duty. **4** *Law* a prior right, esp. to the payment of debts. □ **in preference to** as a thing preferred over (another). **preference shares** (or **stock**) *Brit*. shares or stock whose entitlement to dividend takes priority over that of ordinary shares. [F *préférence* f. med.L *praeferentia* (as PREFER)]

preferential /ˌprefəˈrenʃ(ə)l/ *adj*. **1** of or involving preference (*preferential treatment*). **2** giving or receiving a favour. **3** *Commerce* (of a tariff etc.) favouring particular countries. **4** (of voting) in which the voter puts candidates in order of preference. □□ **preferentially** *adv*. [as PREFERENCE, after *differential*]

preferment /prɪˈfɜːmənt/ *n*. promotion to office.

prefigure /priːˈfɪɡə(r)/ *v.tr.* **1** represent beforehand by a figure or type. **2** imagine beforehand. □□ **prefiguration** /-ˈreɪʃ(ə)n/ *n*. **prefigurative** /-rətɪv/ *adj*. **prefigurement** *n*. [ME f. eccl.L *praefigurare* (as PRAE-, FIGURE)]

prefix /ˈpriːfɪks/ *n. & v.* —*n.* **1 a** a verbal element placed at the beginning of a word to adjust or qualify its meaning (e.g. *ex-*, *non-*, *re-*) or (in some languages) as an inflectional formative. **2** a title placed before a name (e.g. *Mr*). —*v.tr.* (often foll. by *to*) **1** add as an introduction. **2** join (a word or element) as a prefix. □□ **prefixation** /-ˈseɪʃ(ə)n/ *n*. **prefixion** /-ˈfɪkʃ(ə)n/ *n*. [earlier as verb: ME f. OF *prefixer* (as PRE-, FIX): (n.) f. L *praefixum*]

preflight /ˈpriːflaɪt/ *attrib.adj.* occurring or provided before an aircraft flight.

preform /priːˈfɔːm/ *v.tr.* form beforehand. □□ **preformation** /-ˈmeɪʃ(ə)n/ *n*.

preformative /priːˈfɔːmətɪv/ *adj. & n.* —*adj.* **1** forming beforehand. **2** prefixed as the formative element of a word. —*n.* a preformative syllable or letter.

prefrontal /priːˈfrʌnt(ə)l/ *adj*. **1** in front of the frontal bone of the skull. **2** in the forepart of the frontal lobe of the brain.

preglacial /priːˈɡleɪʃ(ə)l, -sɪəl/ *adj*. before a glacial period.

pregnable /ˈpreɡnəb(ə)l/ *adj*. able to be captured etc.; not impregnable. [ME f. OF *prenable* takable: see IMPREGNABLE¹]

pregnancy /ˈpreɡnənsɪ/ *n*. (*pl*. **-ies**) the condition or an instance of being pregnant.

pregnant /ˈpreɡnənt/ *adj*. **1** (of a woman or female animal) having a child or young developing in the uterus. **2** full of meaning; significant or suggestive (*a pregnant pause*). **3** (esp. of a person's mind) imaginative, inventive. **4** (foll. by *with*) plentifully provided (*pregnant with danger*). □ **pregnant construction** *Gram.* one in which more is implied than the words express (e.g. *not have a chance* implying *of success* etc.). □□ **pregnantly** *adv*. (in sense 2). [ME f. F *prégnant* or L *praegnans -antis*, earlier *praegnas* (prob. as PRAE-, (g)*nasci* be born)]

preheat /priːˈhiːt/ *v.tr.* heat beforehand.

prehensile /prɪˈhensaɪl/ *adj*. *Zool*. (of a tail or limb) capable of grasping. □□ **prehensility** /-ˈsɪlɪtɪ/ *n*. [F *préhensile* f. L *prehendere prehens-*, *hendere* grasp)]

prehension /prɪˈhenʃ(ə)n/ *n*. **1** grasping, seizing. **2** mental apprehension. [L *prehensio* (as PREHENSILE)]

prehistoric /ˌpriːhɪˈstɒrɪk/ *adj*. **1** of or relating to the period before written records. (See below.) **2** *colloq*. utterly out of date. □□ **prehistorian** /-ˈstɔːrɪən/ *n*. **prehistorically** *adv*. **prehistory** /-ˈhɪstərɪ/ *n*. [F *préhistorique* (as PRE-, HISTORIC)]

The prehistoric era is conventionally divided into a Stone Age, Bronze Age, and Iron Age, on the basis of the material used for weapons and tools. The system was devised by Christian Thomsen (1788–1865) as a means of classifying the collections in the National Museum of Denmark, of which he was curator. It was later elaborated and refined, and confirmed (at least for European areas) by stratification of finds, but is neither a guide to absolute dates nor an essential evolutionary sequence: not all its stages are represented in all parts of the world, and there is often a considerable time-lag between the first appearance of metal artefacts and a fully developed metal-working technology in an area. Until its invention, however, there was no framework into which archaeological discoveries could be fitted, and it remains a convenient terminology.

prehuman /priːˈhjuːmən/ *adj*. existing before the time of man.

pre-ignition /ˌpriːɪɡˈnɪʃ(ə)n/ *n*. the premature firing of the explosive mixture in an internal-combustion engine.

prejudge /priːˈdʒʌdʒ/ *v.tr.* **1** form a premature judgement on (a person, issue, etc.). **2** pass judgement on (a person) before a trial or proper enquiry. □□ **prejudgement** *n*. **prejudication** /-ˌdʒuːdɪˈkeɪʃ(ə)n/ *n*.

prejudice /ˈpredʒʊdɪs/ *n. & v.* —*n.* **1 a** a preconceived opinion. **b** (foll. by *against*, *in favour of*) bias or partiality. **2** harm or injury that results or may result from some action or judgement (*to the prejudice of*). —*v.tr.* **1** impair the validity or force of (a right, claim, statement, etc.). **2** (esp. as **prejudiced** *adj*.) cause (a person) to have a prejudice. □ **without prejudice** (often foll. by *to*) without detriment (to any existing right or claim). [ME f. OF *prejudice* f. L *praejudicium* (as PRAE-, *judicium* judgement)]

prejudicial /ˌpredʒʊˈdɪʃ(ə)l/ *adj*. causing prejudice; detrimental. □□ **prejudicially** *adv*. [ME f. OF *prejudiciel* (as PREJUDICE)]

prelacy /ˈpreləsɪ/ *n*. (*pl*. **-ies**) **1** church government by prelates. **2** (prec. by *the*) prelates collectively. **3** the office or rank of prelate. [ME f. AF *prelacie* f. med.L *prelatia* (as PRELATE)]

prelapsarian /ˌpriːlæpˈseərɪən/ *adj*. before the Fall of man. [PRE- + L *lapsus* (as LAPSE)]

prelate /ˈprelət/ *n*. **1** a high ecclesiastical dignitary, e.g. a bishop. **2** *hist*. an abbot or prior. □□ **prelatic** /prɪˈlætɪk/ *adj*. **prelatical** /prɪˈlætɪk(ə)l/ *adj*. [ME f. OF *prelat* f. med.L *praelatus* past part.: see PREFER]

prelature /ˈprelətjʊə(r)/ *n.* **1** the office of prelate. **2** (prec. by *the*) prelates collectively. [F *prélature* f. med.L *praelatura* (as PRELATE)]

prelim /ˈpriːlɪm, prɪˈlɪm/ *n. colloq.* **1** a preliminary examination, esp. at a university. **2** (in *pl.*) the pages preceding the text of a book. [abbr.]

preliminary /prɪˈlɪmɪnərɪ/ *adj., n.,* & *adv.* —*adj.* introductory, preparatory. —*n.* (*pl.* **-ies**) (usu. in *pl.*) **1** a preliminary action or arrangement (*dispense with the preliminaries*). **2** a preliminary trial or contest. —*adv.* (foll. by *to*) preparatory to; in advance of (*was completed preliminary to the main event*). □□ **preliminarily** *adv.* [mod.L *praeliminaris* or F *préliminaire* (as PRE-, L *limen liminis* threshold)]

preliterate /priːˈlɪtərət/ *adj.* of or relating to a society or culture that has not developed the use of writing.

prelude /ˈpreljuːd/ *n.* & *v.* —*n.* (often foll. by *to*) **1** an action, event, or situation serving as an introduction. **2** the introductory part of a poem etc. **3 a** an introductory piece of music, often preceding a fugue or forming the first piece of a suite or beginning an act of an opera. **b** a short piece of music of a similar type, esp. for the piano. —*v.tr.* **1** serve as a prelude to. **2** introduce with a prelude. □□ **preludial** /prɪˈljuːdɪəl/ *adj.* [F *prélude* or med.L *praeludium* f. L *praeludere praelus-* (as PRE-, *ludere* play)]

premarital /priːˈmærɪt(ə)l/ *adj.* existing or (esp. of sexual relations) occurring before marriage. □□ **premaritally** *adv.*

premature /ˈpremətjʊə(r), -ˈtjʊə(r)/ *adj.* **1 a** occurring or done before the usual or proper time; too early (*a premature decision*). **b** too hasty (*must not be premature*). **2** (of a baby, esp. a viable one) born (esp. three or more weeks) before the end of the full term of gestation. □□ **prematurely** *adv.* **prematureness** *n.* **prematurity** /-ˈtjʊərɪtɪ/ *n.* [L *praematurus* very early (as PRAE-, MATURE)]

premaxillary /ˌpriːmækˈsɪlərɪ/ *adj.* in front of the upper jaw.

premed /priːˈmed/ *n. colloq.* **1** = PREMEDICATION. **2** a premedical course or student. [abbr.]

premedical /priːˈmedɪk(ə)l/ *adj.* of or relating to study in preparation for a course in medicine.

premedication /ˌpriːmedɪˈkeɪʃ(ə)n/ *n.* medication to prepare for an operation or other treatment.

premeditate /priːˈmedɪˌteɪt/ *v.tr.* think out or plan (an action) beforehand (*premeditated murder*). □□ **premeditation** /-ˈteɪʃ(ə)n/ *n.* [L *praemeditari* (as PRAE-, MEDITATE)]

premenstrual /priːˈmenstrʊəl/ *adj.* of, occurring, or experienced before menstruation (*premenstrual tension*). □□ **premenstrually** *adv.*

premier /ˈpremɪə(r)/ *n.* & *adj.* —*n.* (orig. short for *premier minister*; see PRIME MINISTER) a prime minister or other head of government. —*adj.* **1** first in importance, order, or time. **2** earliest creation (*premier earl*). □□ **premiership** *n.* [ME f. OF = first, f. L (as PRIMARY)]

première /ˈpremɪˌeə(r)/ *n.* & *v.* —*n.* the first performance or showing of a play or film. —*v.tr.* give a première of. [F, fem. of *premier* (adj.) (as PREMIER)]

premillennial /ˌpriːmɪˈlenɪəl/ *adj.* existing or occurring before the millennium, esp. with reference to the supposed second coming of Christ. □□ **premillennialism** *n.* **premillennialist** *n.*

premise *n.* & *v.* —*n.* /ˈpremɪs/ **1** *Logic* = PREMISS. **2** (in *pl.*) **a** a house or building with its grounds and appurtenances. **b** *Law* houses, lands, or tenements previously specified in a document etc. —*v.tr.* /prɪˈmaɪz/ say or write by way of introduction. □ **on the premises** in the building etc. concerned. [ME f. OF *premisse* f. med.L *praemissa* (*propositio*) (proposition) set in front f. L *praemittere praemiss-* (as PRAE-, *mittere* send)]

premiss /ˈpremɪs/ *n.* *Logic* a previous statement from which another is inferred. [var. of PREMISE]

premium /ˈpriːmɪəm/ *n.* **1** an amount to be paid for a contract of insurance. **2 a** a sum added to interest, wages, etc.; a bonus. **b** a sum added to ordinary charges. **3** a reward or prize. **4** (*attrib.*) (of a commodity) of best quality and therefore more expensive. □ **at a premium 1** highly valued; above the usual or nominal

price. **2** scarce and in demand. **Premium Bond** (or **Savings Bond**) *Brit.* a government security without interest but with a draw for cash prizes, issued since 1956. **put a premium on 1** provide or act as an incentive to. **2** attach special value to. [L *praemium* booty, reward (as PRAE-, *emere* buy, take)]

premolar /priːˈməʊlə(r)/ *adj.* & *n.* —*adj.* in front of a molar tooth. —*n.* (in an adult human) each of eight teeth situated in pairs between each of the four canine teeth and each first molar.

premonition /ˌpreməˈnɪʃ(ə)n, ˌpriː-/ *n.* a forewarning; a presentiment. □□ **premonitor** /prɪˈmɒnɪtə(r)/ *n.* **premonitory** /prɪˈmɒnɪtərɪ/ *adj.* [F *prémonition* or LL *praemonitio* f. L *praemonēre praemonit-* (as PRAE-, *monēre* warn)]

Premonstratensian /prɪˌmɒnstrəˈtensɪən/ *adj.* & *n. hist.* —*adj.* of or relating to an order of regular canons founded at Prémontré in France in 1120, or of the corresponding order of nuns. —*n.* a member of either of these orders. [med.L *Praemonstratensis* f. *Praemonstratus* the abbey of Prémontré (lit. = foreshown)]

premorse /prɪˈmɔːs/ *adj. Bot.* & *Zool.* with the end abruptly terminated. [L *praemordēre praemors-* bite off (as PRAE-, *mordēre* bite)]

prenatal /priːˈneɪt(ə)l/ *adj.* of or concerning the period before childbirth. □□ **prenatally** *adv.*

prentice /ˈprentɪs/ *n.* & *v. archaic* —*n.* = APPRENTICE. —*v.tr.* (as **prenticed** *adj.*) apprenticed. □ **prentice hand** an inexperienced hand. □□ **prenticeship** *n.* [ME f. APPRENTICE]

preoccupation /priːˌɒkjʊˈpeɪʃ(ə)n/ *n.* **1** the state of being preoccupied. **2** a thing that engrosses the mind. [F *préoccupation* or L *praeoccupatio* (as PREOCCUPY)]

preoccupy /priːˈɒkjʊˌpaɪ/ *v.tr.* (**-ies, -ied**) **1** (of a thought etc.) dominate or engross the mind of (a person) to the exclusion of other thoughts. **2** (as **preoccupied** *adj.*) otherwise engrossed; mentally distracted. **3** occupy beforehand. [PRE- + OCCUPY, after L *praeoccupare* seize beforehand]

preocular /priːˈɒkjʊlə(r)/ *adj.* in front of the eye.

preordain /ˌpriːɔːˈdeɪn/ *v.tr.* ordain or determine beforehand.

prep /prep/ *n. colloq.* **1** *Brit.* **a** the preparation of school work by a pupil. **b** the period when this is done. **2** *US* a student in a preparatory school. [abbr. of PREPARATION]

prep. *abbr.* preposition.

prepack /priːˈpæk/ *v.tr.* (also **pre-package** /-ˈpækɪdʒ/) pack (goods) on the site of production or before retail.

prepaid *past* and *past part.* of PREPAY.

preparation /ˌprepəˈreɪʃ(ə)n/ *n.* **1** the act or an instance of preparing; the process of being prepared. **2** (often in *pl.*) something done to make ready. **3** a specially prepared substance, esp. a food or medicine. **4** work done by school pupils to prepare for a lesson. **5** *Mus.* the sounding of the discordant note in a chord in the preceding chord where it is not discordant, lessening the effect of the discord. [ME f. OF f. L *praeparatio -onis* (as PREPARE)]

preparative /prɪˈpærətɪv/ *adj.* & *n.* —*adj.* preparatory. —*n.* **1** *Mil.* & *Naut.* a signal on a drum, bugle, etc., as an order to make ready. **2** a preparatory act. □□ **preparatively** *adv.* [ME f. OF *preparatif -ive* f. med.L *praeparativus* (as PREPARE)]

preparatory /prɪˈpærətərɪ/ *adj.* & *adv.* —*adj.* (often foll. by *to*) serving to prepare; introductory. —*adv.* (often foll. by *to*) in a preparatory manner (*was packing preparatory to departure*). □ **preparatory school** a usu. private school preparing pupils for a higher school or *US* for college or university. □□ **preparatorily** *adv.* [ME f. LL *praeparatorius* (as PREPARE)]

prepare /prɪˈpeə(r)/ *v.* **1** *tr.* make or get ready for use, consideration, etc. **2** *tr.* make ready or assemble (food, a meal, etc.) for eating. **3 a** *tr.* make (a person or oneself) ready or disposed in some way (*prepares students for university; prepared them for a shock*). **b** *intr.* put oneself or things in readiness; get ready (*prepare to jump*). **4** *tr.* make (a chemical product etc.) by a regular process. **5** *tr. Mus.* lead up to (a discord). □ **be prepared** (often foll. by *for*, or *to* + infin.) be disposed or willing to. □□ **preparer** *n.* [ME f. F *préparer* or L *praeparare* (as PRAE-, *parare* make ready)]

preparedness /prɪˈpeərɪdnɪs/ *n.* a state of readiness, esp. for war.

prepay /priːˈpeɪ/ v.tr. (past and past part. **prepaid**) **1** pay (a charge) in advance. **2** pay postage on (a letter or parcel etc.) before posting. □□ **prepayable** adj. **prepayment** n.

prepense /prɪˈpens/ adj. (usu. placed after noun) esp. Law deliberate, intentional (malice prepense). □□ **prepensely** adv. [earlier prepensed past part. of obs. prepense (v.) alt. f. earlier purpense f. AF & OF purpenser (as PUR-, penser): see PENSIVE]

preplan /priːˈplæn/ v.tr. (**preplanned, preplanning**) plan in advance.

preponderant /prɪˈpɒndərənt/ adj. surpassing in influence, power, number, or importance; predominant, preponderating. □□ **preponderance** n. **preponderantly** adv.

preponderate /prɪˈpɒndəreɪt/ v.intr. (often foll. by over) **1 a** be greater in influence, quantity, or number. **b** predominate. **2 a** be of greater importance. **b** weigh more. [L praeponderare (as PRAE-, PONDER)]

preposition /ˌprepəˈzɪʃ(ə)n/ n. Gram. a word governing (and usu. preceding) a noun or pronoun and expressing a relation to another word or element, as in: 'the man on the platform', 'came after dinner', 'what did you do it for?' □□ **prepositional** adj. **prepositionally** adv. [ME f. L praepositio f. praeponere praeposit- (as PRAE-, ponere place)]

prepositive /priːˈpɒzɪtɪv/ adj. Gram. (of a word, particle, etc.) that should be placed before or prefixed. [LL praepositivus (as PREPOSITION)]

prepossess /ˌpriːpəˈzes/ v.tr. **1** (usu. in passive) (of an idea, feeling, etc.) take possession of (a person); imbue. **2 a** prejudice (usu. favourably and spontaneously). **b** (as **prepossessing** adj.) attractive, appealing. □□ **prepossession** /-ˈzeʃ(ə)n/ n.

preposterous /prɪˈpɒstərəs/ adj. **1** utterly absurd; outrageous. **2** contrary to nature, reason, or common sense. □□ **preposterously** adv. **preposterousness** n. [L praeposterus reversed, absurd (as PRAE-, posterus coming after)]

prepostor var. of PRAEPOSTOR.

prepotent /prɪˈpəʊt(ə)nt/ adj. **1** greater than others in power, influence, etc. **2 a** having a stronger fertilizing influence. **b** dominant in transmitting hereditary qualities. □□ **prepotence** n. **prepotency** n. [ME f. L praepotens -entis, part. of praeposse (as PRAE-, posse be able)]

preppy /ˈprepɪ/ n. & adj. US colloq. — n. (pl. **-ies**) a person attending an expensive private school or who looks like such a person (with short hair, blazer, etc.). — adj. (**preppier, preppiest**) **1** like a preppy. **2** neat and fashionable. [PREP (SCHOOL) + -Y²]

preprandial /priːˈprændɪəl/ adj. formal or joc. before dinner or lunch. [PRE- + L prandium a meal]

pre-preference /priːˈprefərəns/ adj. Brit. (of shares, claims, etc.) ranking before preference shares etc.

preprint /ˈpriːprɪnt/ n. a printed document issued in advance of general publication.

preprocessor /priːˈprəʊsesə(r)/ n. a computer program that modifies data to conform with the input requirements of another program.

prep school /prep/ n. = PREPARATORY SCHOOL. [abbr. of PREPARATORY]

prepublication /ˌpriːpʌblɪˈkeɪʃ(ə)n/ adj. & n. —attrib.adj. produced or occurring before publication. —n. publication in advance or beforehand.

prepuce /ˈpriːpjuːs/ n. **1** = FORESKIN. **2** the fold of skin surrounding the clitoris. □□ **preputial** /priːˈpjuːʃ(ə)l/ adj. [ME f. L praeputium]

prequel /ˈpriːkw(ə)l/ n. a story, film, etc., whose events or concerns precede those of an existing work. [PRE- + SEQUEL]

Pre-Raphaelite /priːˈræfəˌlaɪt/ n. & adj. —n. a member of a group of English 19th-c. artists, emulating the work of Italian artists before the time of Raphael. (See below.) —adj. **1** of or relating to the Pre-Raphaelites. **2** (**pre-Raphaelite**) (esp. of a woman) like a type painted by a Pre-Raphaelite (e.g. with long thick curly auburn hair). □ **Pre-Raphaelite Brotherhood** the chosen name of the Pre-Raphaelites. □□ **pre-Raphaelitism** n.

The Pre-Raphaelite Brotherhood was founded in 1848 by seven young English artists and writers, the major figures being Holman Hunt, Millais, and Rossetti. Abhorring the slickness and sentimentality of much Victorian painting they sought to purify art by a return to the truth and seriousness of the early Renaissance, adopting a minutely detailed method of study from nature and painting in bright colours over a wet white ground. Much criticized for their espousal of 'ugliness', they were defended by Ruskin. The movement began to dissipate in the early 1850s: Millais eloped with Ruskin's wife and became a successful Royal Academician, Rossetti retreated into the world of medieval romance, Hunt went to Palestine to paint biblical scenes, but the style they had created was continued by a number of inferior imitators.

pre-record /ˌpriːrɪˈkɔːd/ v.tr. record (esp. material for broadcasting) in advance.

prerequisite /priːˈrekwɪzɪt/ adj. & n. —adj. required as a precondition. —n. a prerequisite thing.

prerogative /prɪˈrɒgətɪv/ n. **1** a right or privilege exclusive to an individual or class. **2** (in full **royal prerogative**) Brit. the right of the sovereign, theoretically subject to no restriction. [ME f. OF prerogative or L praerogativa privilege (orig. to vote first) f. praerogativus asked first (as PRAE-, rogare ask)]

Pres. abbr. President.

presage n. & v. —n. /ˈpresɪdʒ/ **1** an omen or portent. **2** a presentiment or foreboding. —v.tr. /ˈpresɪdʒ, prɪˈseɪdʒ/ **1** portend, foreshadow. **2** give warning of (an event etc.) by natural means. **3** (of a person) predict or have a presentiment of. □□ **presageful** /prɪˈseɪdʒfʊl/ adj. **presager** n. [ME f. F présage, présager f. L praesagium f. praesagire forebode (as PRAE-, sagire perceive keenly)]

presbyopia /ˌprezbɪˈəʊpɪə/ n. long-sightedness caused by loss of elasticity of the eye lens, occurring esp. in middle and old age. □□ **presbyopic** /-ˈɒpɪk/ adj. [mod.L f. Gk presbus old man + ōps ōpos eye]

presbyter /ˈprezbɪtə(r)/ n. **1** an elder in the early Christian Church. **2** (in the Episcopal Church) a minister of the second order; a priest. **3** (in the Presbyterian Church) an elder. □□ **presbyteral** /-ˈbɪtər(ə)l/ adj. **presbyterate** /-ˈbɪtərət/ n. **presbyterial** /-ˈtɪərɪəl/ adj. **presbytership** n. [eccl.L f. Gk presbuteros elder, compar. of presbus old]

Presbyterian /ˌprezbɪˈtɪərɪən/ adj. & n. —adj. (of a church) governed by elders all of equal rank, esp. with reference to the national Church of Scotland. —n. **1** a member of a Presbyterian Church. **2** an adherent of the Presbyterian system. □□ **Presbyterianism** n. [eccl.L presbyterium (as PRESBYTERY)]

presbytery /ˈprezbɪtərɪ/ n. (pl. **-ies**) **1** the eastern part of a chancel beyond the choir; the sanctuary. **2 a** a body of presbyters, esp. a court next above a Kirk-session. **b** a district represented by this. **3** the house of a Roman Catholic priest. [ME f. OF presbiterie f. eccl.L f. Gk presbuterion (as PRESBYTER)]

preschool /ˈpriːskuːl, priːˈskuːl/ adj. of or relating to the time before a child is old enough to go to school. □□ **preschooler** /-ˈskuːlə(r)/ n.

prescient /ˈpresɪənt/ adj. having foreknowledge or foresight. □□ **prescience** n. **presciently** adv. [L praescire praescient- know beforehand (as PRAE-, scire know)]

prescind /prɪˈsɪnd/ v. **1** tr. (foll. by from) cut off (a part from a whole), esp. prematurely or abruptly. **2** intr. (foll. by from) leave out of consideration. [L praescindere (as PRAE-, scindere cut)]

prescribe /prɪˈskraɪb/ v. **1** tr. **a** advise the use of (a medicine etc.), esp. by an authorized prescription. **b** recommend, esp. as a benefit (prescribed a change of scenery). **2** tr. lay down or impose authoritatively. **3** intr. (foll. by to, for) assert a prescriptive right or claim. □□ **prescriber** n. [L praescribere praescript- direct in writing (as PRAE-, scribere write)]

prescript /ˈpriːskrɪpt/ n. an ordinance, law, or command. [L praescriptum neut. past part.: see PRESCRIBE]

prescription /prɪˈskrɪpʃ(ə)n/ n. **1** the act or an instance of prescribing. **2 a** a doctor's (usu. written) instruction for the composition and use of a medicine. **b** a medicine prescribed. **3** (in full **positive prescription**) uninterrupted use or possession from time immemorial or for the period fixed by law as giving a title or right. **4 a** an ancient custom viewed as authoritative. **b** a claim founded on long use. □ **negative prescription** the time limit within which an action or claim can be raised. [ME f. OF f. L *praescriptio -onis* (as PRESCRIBE)]

prescriptive /prɪˈskrɪptɪv/ *adj.* **1** prescribing. **2** *Linguistics* concerned with or laying down rules of usage. **3** based on prescription (*prescriptive right*). **4** prescribed by custom. □□ **prescriptively** *adv.* **prescriptiveness** *n.* **prescriptivism** *n.* **prescriptivist** *n.* & *adj.* [LL *praescriptivus* (as PRESCRIBE)]

preselect /ˌpriːsɪˈlekt/ *v.tr.* select in advance. □□ **preselection** *n.*

preselective /ˌpriːsɪˈlektɪv/ *adj.* that can be selected or set in advance.

preselector /ˌpriːsɪˈlektə(r)/ *n.* any of various devices for selecting a mechanical or electrical operation in advance of its execution, e.g. of a gear-change in a motor vehicle.

presence /ˈprez(ə)ns/ *n.* **1** the state or condition of being present (*your presence is requested*). **2** a place where a person is (*was admitted to their presence*). **3 a** a person's appearance or bearing, esp. when imposing (*an august presence*). **b** a person's force of personality (*esp. have presence*). **4** a person or thing that is present (*the royal presence; there was a presence in the room*). **5** representation for reasons of political influence (*maintained a presence*). □ **in the presence of** in front of; observed by. **presence chamber** a room in which a monarch or other distinguished person receives visitors. **presence of mind** calmness and self-command in sudden difficulty etc. [ME f. OF f. L *praesentia* (as PRESENT¹)]

present¹ /ˈprez(ə)nt/ *adj.* & *n.* —*adj.* **1** (usu. *predic.*) being in the place in question (*was present at the trial*). **2 a** now existing, occurring, or being such (*the present Duke; during the present season*). **b** now being considered or discussed etc. (*in the present case*). **3** *Gram.* expressing an action etc. now going on or habitually performed (*present participle; present tense*). —*n.* (prec. by *the*) **1** the time now passing (*no time like the present*). **2** *Gram.* the present tense. □ **at present** now. **by these presents** *Law* by this document (*know all men by these presents*). **for the present 1** just now. **2** as far as the present is concerned. **present company excepted** excluding those who are here now. **present-day** *adj.* of this time; modern. [ME f. OF f. L *praesens -entis* part. of *praeesse* be at hand (as PRAE-, *esse* be)]

present² /prɪˈzent/ *v.* & *n.* —*v.tr.* **1** introduce, offer, or exhibit, esp. for public attention or consideration. **2 a** (with a thing as object, foll. by *to*) offer or give as a gift (to a person), esp. formally or ceremonially. **b** (with a person as object, foll. by *with*) make available to; cause to have (*presented them with a new car; that presents us with a problem*). **3 a** (of a company, producer, etc.) put (a form of entertainment) before the public. **b** (of a performer, compère, etc.) introduce or put before an audience. **4** introduce (a person) formally (*may I present my fiancée?; was presented at court*). **5** offer, give (compliments etc.) (*may I present my card; present my regards to your family*). **6 a** (of a circumstance) reveal (some quality etc.) (*this presents some difficulty*). **b** exhibit (an appearance etc.) (*presented a rough exterior*). **7** (of an idea etc.) offer or suggest itself. **8** deliver (a cheque, bill, etc.) for acceptance or payment. **9 a** (usu. foll. by *at*) aim (a weapon). **b** hold out (a weapon) in a position for aiming. **10** (*refl.* or *absol.*) *Med.* (of a patient or illness etc.) come forward for or undergo initial medical examination. **11** (*absol.*) *Med.* (of a part of a foetus) be directed toward the cervix at the time of delivery. **12** (foll. by *to*) *Law* bring formally under notice, submit (an offence, complaint, etc.). **13** (foll. by *to*) *Eccl.* recommend (a clergyman) to a bishop for institution to a benefice. —*n.* the position of presenting arms in salute. □ **present arms** hold a rifle etc. vertically in front of the body as a salute. **present oneself 1** appear. **2** come forward for examination etc. □□ **presenter** *n.* (in sense 3 of *v.*). [ME f. OF *presenter* f. L *praesentare* (as PRESENT¹)]

present³ /ˈprez(ə)nt/ *n.* a gift; a thing given or presented. □ **make a present of** give as a gift. [ME f. OF (as PRESENT¹), orig. in phr. *mettre une chose en present à quelqu'un* put a thing into the presence of a person]

presentable /prɪˈzentəb(ə)l/ *adj.* **1** of good appearance; fit to be presented to other people. **2** fit for presentation. □□

presentability /-ˈbɪlɪtɪ/ *n.* **presentableness** *n.* **presentably** *adv.*

presentation /ˌprezənˈteɪʃ(ə)n/ *n.* **1 a** the act or an instance of presenting; the process of being presented. **b** a thing presented. **2** the manner or quality of presenting. **3** a demonstration or display of materials, information, etc.; a lecture. **4** an exhibition or theatrical performance. **5** a formal introduction. **6** the position of the foetus in relation to the cervix at the time of delivery. □□ **presentational** *adj.* **presentationally** *adv.* [ME f. OF f. LL *praesentatio -onis* (as PRESENT²)]

presentationism /ˌprezənˈteɪʃəˌnɪz(ə)m/ *n. Philos.* the doctrine that in perception the mind has immediate cognition of the object. □□ **presentationist** *n.*

presentative /prɪˈzentətɪv/ *adj.* **1** *Philos.* subject to direct cognition. **2** *hist.* (of a benefice) to which a patron has the right of presentation. [prob. f. med.L (as PRESENTATION)]

presentee /ˌprezənˈtiː/ *n.* **1** the recipient of a present. **2** a person presented. [ME f. AF (as PRESENT²)]

presentient /prɪˈsenʃ(ə)nt, -ˈzenʃ(ə)nt/ *adj.* (often foll. by *of*) having a presentiment. [L *praesentiens* (as PRAE-, SENTIENT)]

presentiment /prɪˈzentɪmənt, -ˈsentɪmənt/ *n.* a vague expectation; a foreboding (esp. of misfortune). [obs. F *présentiment* (as PRE-, SENTIMENT)]

presently /ˈprezəntlɪ/ *adv.* **1** soon; after a short time. **2** esp. *US* & *Sc.* at the present time; now.

presentment /prɪˈzentmənt/ *n.* the act of presenting information, esp. a statement on oath by a jury of a fact known to them. [ME f. OF *presentement* (as PRESENT²)]

preservation /ˌprezəˈveɪʃ(ə)n/ *n.* **1** the act of preserving or process of being preserved. **2** a state of being well or badly preserved (*in an excellent state of preservation*). [ME f. OF f. med.L *praeservatio -onis* (as PRESERVE)]

preservationist /ˌprezəˈveɪʃənɪst/ *n.* a supporter or advocate of preservation, esp. of antiquities and historic buildings.

preservative /prɪˈzɜːvətɪv/ *n.* & *adj.* —*n.* a substance for preserving perishable foodstuffs, wood, etc. —*adj.* tending to preserve. [ME f. OF *preservatif -ive* f. med.L *praeservativus -um* (as PRESERVE)]

preserve /prɪˈzɜːv/ *v.* & *n.* —*v.tr.* **1 a** keep safe or free from harm, decay, etc. **b** keep alive (a name, memory, etc.). **2** maintain (a thing) in its existing state. **3** retain (a quality or condition). **4 a** treat or refrigerate (food) to prevent decomposition or fermentation. **b** prepare (fruit) by boiling it with sugar, for long-term storage. **5** keep (game, a river, etc.) undisturbed for private use. —*n.* (in *sing.* or *pl.*) **1** preserved fruit; jam. **2** a place where game or fish etc. is preserved. **3** a sphere or area of activity regarded as a person's own. □ **well-preserved** (of an elderly person) showing little sign of ageing. □□ **preservable** *adj.* **preserver** *n.* [ME f. OF *preserver* f. LL *praeservare* (as PRAE-, *servare* keep)]

pre-set /priːˈset/ *v.tr.* (**-setting**; *past* and *past part.* **-set**) **1** set or fix (a device) in advance of its operation. **2** settle or decide beforehand.

preshrunk /priːˈʃrʌŋk/ *adj.* (of a fabric or garment) treated so that it shrinks during manufacture and not in use.

preside /prɪˈzaɪd/ *v.intr.* **1** (often foll. by *at*, *over*) be in a position of authority, esp. as the chairperson or president of a meeting. **2 a** exercise control or authority. **b** (foll. by *at*) *colloq.* play an instrument in company (*presided at the piano*). [F *présider* f. L *praesidēre* (as PRAE-, *sedēre* sit)]

presidency /ˈprezɪdənsɪ/ *n.* (*pl.* **-ies**) **1** the office of president. **2** the period of this. [Sp. & Port. *presidencia*, It. *presidenza* f. med.L *praesidentia* (as PRESIDE)]

president /ˈprezɪd(ə)nt/ *n.* **1** the elected head of a republican State. **2** the head of a society or council etc. **3** the head of certain colleges. **4** *US* **a** the head of a university. **b** the head of a company, etc. **5** a person in charge of a meeting, council, etc. □□ **presidential** /-ˈdenʃ(ə)l/ *adj.* **presidentially** /-ˈdenʃəlɪ/ *adv.* **presidentship** *n.* [ME f. OF f. L (as PRESIDE)]

presidium /prɪˈsɪdɪəm, -ˈzɪdɪəm/ *n.* (also **praesidium**) a standing executive committee in a Communist country, esp. that of the Supreme Soviet in the Soviet Union which functions as the ultimate legislative authority when the Soviet itself is not sitting. [Russ. *prezidium* f. L *praesidium* protection etc. (as PRESIDE)]

Presley /ˈprezlɪ/, Elvis Aaron (1935–77), American singer, the dominant personality (known as 'the King') of early rock and roll from the mid-1950s, noted for the vigour and frank sexuality of his style.

presocratic /ˌpriːsəˈkrætɪk/ *adj.* (of philosophy) of the time before Socrates.

press[1] /pres/ *v. & n.* —*v.* **1** *tr.* apply steady force to (a thing in contact) (*press a switch*; *pressed the two surfaces together*). **2** *tr.* **a** compress or apply pressure to a thing to flatten, shape, or smooth it, as by ironing (*got the curtains pressed*). **b** squeeze (a fruit etc.) to extract its juice. **c** manufacture (a gramophone record etc.) by moulding under pressure. **3** *tr.* (foll. by *out of, from,* etc.) squeeze (juice etc.). **4** *tr.* embrace or caress by squeezing (*pressed my hand*). **5** *intr.* (foll. by *on, against,* etc.) exert pressure. **6** *intr.* be urgent; demand immediate action (*time was pressing*). **7** *intr.* (foll. by *for*) make an insistent demand. **8** *intr.* (foll. by *up, round,* etc.) form a crowd. **9** *intr.* (foll. by *on, forward,* etc.) hasten insistently. **10** *tr.* (often in *passive*) (of an enemy etc.) bear heavily on. **11** *tr.* (often foll. by *for,* or *to* + infin.) urge or entreat (*pressed me to stay*; *pressed me for an answer*). **12** *tr.* (foll. by *on, upon*) **a** put forward or urge (an opinion, claim, or course of action). **b** insist on the acceptance of (an offer, a gift, etc.). **13** *tr.* insist on (*did not press the point*). **14** *intr.* (foll. by *on*) produce a strong mental or moral impression; oppress; weigh heavily. **15** *intr. Golf* try too hard for a long shot etc. and so strike the ball imperfectly. —*n.* **1** the act or an instance of pressing (*give it a slight press*). **2 a** a device for compressing, flattening, shaping, extracting juice, etc. (*trouser press*; *flower press*; *wine press*). **b** a machine that applies pressure to a workpiece by means of a tool, in order to punch shapes, bend it, etc. **3** = *printing-press*. **4** (prec. by *the*) **a** the art or practice of printing. **b** newspapers, journalists, etc., generally or collectively (*read it in the press*; *pursued by the press*). **5** a notice or piece of publicity in newspapers etc. (*got a good press*). **6** (**Press**) **a** a printing house or establishment. **b** a publishing company (*Athlone Press*). **7 a** crowding. **b** a crowd (of people etc.). **8** the pressure of affairs. **9** esp. *Ir. & Sc.* a large usu. shelved cupboard for clothes, books, etc., esp. in a recess. □ **at** (or **in**) **press** (or **the press**) being printed. **be pressed for** have barely enough (time etc.). **go** (or **send**) **to press** go or send to be printed. **press agent** a person employed to attend to advertising and press publicity. **press-box** a reporters' enclosure esp. at a sports event. **press the button 1** set machinery in motion. **2** *colloq.* take a decisive initial step. **press-button** *adj.* = *push-button*. **press conference** an interview given to journalists to make an announcement or answer questions. **press gallery** a gallery for reporters esp. in a legislative assembly. **press-on** (of a material) that can be pressed or ironed on. **press release** an official statement issued to newspapers for information. **press-stud** a small fastening device engaged by pressing its two halves together. **press-up** an exercise in which the prone downward-facing body is raised from the legs or trunk upwards by pressing down on the hands to straighten the arms. [ME f. OF *presser, presse* f. L *pressare* frequent. of *premere* press-]

press[2] /pres/ *v. & n.* —*v.tr.* **1** *hist.* force to serve in the army or navy. **2** bring into use as a makeshift (*was pressed into service*). —*n. hist.* compulsory enlistment esp. in the navy. [alt. f. obs. *prest* (v. & n.) f. OF *prest* loan, advance pay f. *prester* f. L *praestare* furnish (as PRAE-, *stare* stand)]

press-gang /ˈpresgæn/ *n. & v.* —*n.* **1** *hist.* a body of men employed to press men into service in the army or navy. **2** any group using similar coercive methods. —*v.tr.* force into service.

pressie /ˈprezɪ/ *n.* (also **prezzie**) *colloq.* a present or gift. [abbr.]

pressing /ˈpresɪŋ/ *adj. & n.* —*adj.* **1** urgent (*pressing business*). **2 a** urging strongly (*a pressing invitation*). **b** persistent, importunate (*since you are so pressing*). —*n.* **1** a thing made by pressing, esp. a gramophone record. **2** a series of these made at one time. **3** the act or an instance of pressing a thing, esp. a gramophone record or grapes etc. (*all at one pressing*). □□ **pressingly** *adv.*

pressman /ˈpresmən/ *n.* (*pl.* **-men**) **1** a journalist. **2** an operator of a printing-press.

pressmark /ˈpresmɑːk/ *n.* a library shelf-mark showing the location of a book etc.

pressure /ˈpreʃə(r)/ *n. & v.* —*n.* **1 a** the exertion of continuous force on or against a body by another in contact with it. **b** the force exerted. **c** the amount of this (expressed by the force on a unit area) (*atmospheric pressure*). **2** urgency; the need to meet a deadline etc. (*work under pressure*). **3** affliction or difficulty (*under financial pressure*). **4** constraining influence (*if pressure is brought to bear*). —*v.tr.* **1** apply (esp. moral) pressure to. **2 a** coerce. **b** (often foll. by *into*) persuade (*was pressured into attending*). □ **pressure-cook** cook in a pressure-cooker. **pressure-cooker** an airtight pan for cooking quickly under steam pressure. The earliest vessel of this kind was described by its French inventor, Denis Papin, in 1681, and called by him 'Papin's Digester'; the diarist John Evelyn describes a supper prepared in it. **pressure gauge** a gauge showing the pressure of steam etc. **pressure group** a group or association formed to promote a particular interest or cause by influencing public policy. **pressure point 1** a point where an artery can be pressed against a bone to inhibit bleeding. **2** a point on the skin sensitive to pressure. **3** a target for political pressure or influence. **pressure suit** an inflatable suit for flying at a high altitude. [ME f. L *pressura* (as PRESS[1])]

pressurize /ˈpreʃəraɪz/ *v.tr.* (also **-ise**) **1** (esp. as **pressurized** *adj.*) maintain normal atmospheric pressure in (an aircraft cabin etc.) at a high altitude. **2** raise to a high pressure. **3** pressure (a person). □ **pressurized-water reactor** a nuclear reactor in which the coolant is water at high pressure. □□ **pressurization** /-ˈzeɪʃ(ə)n/ *n.*

Prestel /ˈprestel/ *n. propr.* (in the UK) the computerized visual information system operated by British Telecom. [PRESS[1] + TELECOMMUNICATION]

Prester John /ˈprestə(r)/ (i.e. 'Presbyter' John) a legendary medieval Christian king of Asia, said to have defeated the Muslims and to be destined to bring help to the Holy Land. The legend spread in Europe in the mid-12th c. He was later identified with a real king of Ethiopia; another theory identifies him with a Chinese prince who defeated the sultan of Persia in 1141. The legend may contain a nucleus of historical fact.

prestidigitator /ˌprestɪˈdɪdʒɪˌteɪtə(r)/ *n. formal* a conjuror. □□ **prestidigitation** /-ˈteɪʃ(ə)n/ *n.* [F *prestidigitateur* f. *preste* nimble (as PRESTO) + L *digitus* finger]

prestige /preˈstiːʒ/ *n.* **1** respect, reputation, or influence derived from achievements, power, associations, etc. **2** (*attrib.*) having or conferring prestige. □□ **prestigeful** *adj.* [F, = illusion, glamour, f. LL *praestigium* (as PRESTIGIOUS)]

prestigious /preˈstɪdʒəs/ *adj.* having or showing prestige. □□ **prestigiously** *adv.* **prestigiousness** *n.* [orig. = deceptive, f. L *praestigiosus* f. *praestigiae* juggler's tricks]

prestissimo /preˈstɪsɪməʊ/ *adv. & n. Mus.* —*adv.* in a very quick tempo. —*n.* (*pl.* **-os**) a movement or passage played in this way. [It., superl. (as PRESTO 1)]

presto /ˈprestəʊ/ *adv. & n.* —*adv.* **1** *Mus.* in quick tempo. **2** (in a conjuror's formula in performing a trick) quickly (*hey presto!*). —*n.* (*pl.* **-os**) *Mus.* a movement to be played in a quick tempo. [It. f. LL *praestus* f. *praesto* ready]

Prestonpans /ˌprestənˈpænz/ a village just east of Edinburgh, near which the first major engagement of the Jacobite Rebellion of 1745 took place. A small Hanoverian army under Sir John Cope was routed by the Highlanders of the equally small Jacobite army, leaving the way clear for the Young Pretender's subsequent invasion of England.

prestressed /priːˈstrest/ *adj.* strengthened by stressing in advance, esp. of concrete by means of stretched rods or wires put in during manufacture.

Prestwick /ˈprestwɪk/ an international airport near Ayr on the west coast of Scotland.

presumably /prɪˈzjuːməblɪ/ *adv.* as may reasonably be presumed.

presume /prɪˈzjuːm/ *v.* **1** *tr.* (often foll. by *that* + clause) suppose to be true; take for granted. **2** *tr.* (often foll. by *to* + infin.) **a** take the liberty; be impudent enough (*presumed to question their authority*). **b** dare, venture (*may I presume to ask?*). **3** *intr.* be presumptuous; take liberties. **4** *intr.* (foll. by *on*, *upon*) take advantage of or make unscrupulous use of (a person's good nature etc.). □□ **presumable** *adj.* **presumedly** *adv.* [ME f. OF *presumer* f. L *praesumere praesumpt-* anticipate, venture (as PRAE-, *sumere* take)]

presuming /prɪˈzjuːmɪŋ/ *adj.* presumptuous. □□ **presumingly** *adv.* **presumingness** *n.*

presumption /prɪˈzʌmpʃ(ə)n/ *n.* **1** arrogance; presumptuous behaviour. **2 a** the act of presuming a thing to be true. **b** a thing that is or may be presumed to be true. **3** a ground for presuming (*a strong presumption against their being guilty*). **4** *Law* an inference from known facts. [ME f. OF *presumpcion* f. L *praesumptio -onis* (as PRESUME)]

presumptive /prɪˈzʌmptɪv/ *adj.* giving grounds for presumption (*presumptive evidence*). □□ **presumptively** *adv.* [F *présómptif -ive* f. LL *praesumptivus* (as PRESUME)]

presumptuous /prɪˈzʌmptjʊəs/ *adj.* unduly or overbearingly confident and presuming. □□ **presumptuously** *adv.* **presumptuousness** *n.* [ME f. OF *presumptueux* f. LL *praesumptuosus, -tiosus* (as PRESUME)]

presuppose /ˌpriːsəˈpəʊz/ *v.tr.* (often foll. by *that* + clause) **1** assume beforehand. **2** imply. [ME f. OF *presupposer*, after med.L *praesupponere* (as PRE-, SUPPOSE)]

presupposition /ˌpriːsʌpəˈzɪʃ(ə)n/ *n.* **1** the act or an instance of presupposing. **2** a thing assumed beforehand as the basis of argument etc. [med.L *praesuppositio* (as PRAE-, *supponere* as SUPPOSE)]

pre-tax /priːˈtæks, ˈpriːtæks/ *adj.* (of income or profits) before the deduction of taxes.

pre-teen /priːˈtiːn/ *adj.* of or relating to a child before the age of thirteen.

pretence /prɪˈtens/ *n.* (US **pretense**) **1** pretending, make-believe. **2 a** a pretext or excuse (*on the slightest pretence*). **b** a false show of intentions or motives (*under the pretence of friendship; under false pretences*). **3** (foll. by *to*) a claim, esp. a false or ambitious one (*has no pretence to any great talent*). **4 a** affectation, display. **b** pretentiousness, ostentation (*stripped of all pretence*). [ME f. AF *pretense* ult. f. med.L *pretensus* pretended (as PRETEND)]

pretend /prɪˈtend/ *v.* & *adj.* —*v.* **1** *tr.* claim or assert falsely so as to deceive (*pretend knowledge; pretended that they were foreigners*). **2** *tr.* imagine to oneself in play (*pretended to be monsters; pretended it was night*). **3** *tr.* **a** profess, esp. falsely or extravagantly (*does not pretend to be a scholar*). **b** (as **pretended** *adj.*) falsely claim to be such (*a pretended friend*). **4** *intr.* (foll. by *to*) **a** lay claim to (a right or title etc.). **b** profess to have (a quality etc.). —*adj. colloq.* pretended; in pretence (*pretend money*). [ME f. F *prétendre* or f. L (as PRAE-, *tendere* tent-, later *tens-* stretch)]

pretender /prɪˈtendə(r)/ *n.* **1** a person who claims a throne or title etc. **2** a person who pretends.

pretense US var. of PRETENCE.

pretension /prɪˈtenʃ(ə)n/ *n.* **1** (often foll. by *to*) **a** an assertion of a claim. **b** a justifiable claim (*has no pretensions to the name; has some pretensions to be included*). **2** pretentiousness. [med.L *praetensio, -tio* (as PRETEND)]

pretentious /prɪˈtenʃəs/ *adj.* **1** making an excessive claim to great merit or importance. **2** ostentatious. □□ **pretentiously** *adv.* **pretentiousness** *n.* [F *prétentieux* (as PRETENSION)]

preter- /ˈpriːtə(r)/ *comb. form* more than. [L *praeter* (adv. & prep.), = past, beyond]

preterite /ˈpretərɪt/ *adj.* & *n.* (US **preterit**) *Gram.* —*adj.* expressing a past action or state. —*n.* a preterite tense or form. [ME f. OF *preterite* or L *praeteritus* past part. of *praeterire* pass (as PRETER-, *ire* it- go)]

preterm /ˈpriːtɜːm/ *adj.* & *adv.* born or occurring prematurely.

pretermit /ˌpriːtəˈmɪt/ *v.tr.* (**pretermitted**, **pretermitting**) *formal* **1** omit to mention (a fact etc.). **2** omit to do or perform; neglect. **3** leave off (a custom or continuous action) for a time. □□ **pretermission** /-ˈmɪʃ(ə)n/ *n.* [L *praetermittere* (as PRETER-, *mittere miss-* let go)]

preternatural /ˌpriːtəˈnætʃər(ə)l/ *adj.* outside the ordinary course of nature; supernatural. □□ **preternaturalism** *n.* **preternaturally** *adv.*

pretext /ˈpriːtekst/ *n.* **1** an ostensible or alleged reason or intention. **2** an excuse offered. □ **on** (or **under**) **the pretext** (foll. by *of*, or *that* + clause) professing as one's object or intention. [L *praetextus* outward display f. *praetexere praetext-* (as PRAE-, *texere* weave)]

pretor US var. of PRAETOR.

Pretoria /prɪˈtɔːrɪə/ the capital of Transvaal and administrative capital of the Republic of South Africa; pop. (1985) approx. 443,000. [A. W. J. *Pretorius* (1799–1853), S.Afr. Boer leader, one of the founders of Transvaal]

pretorian US var. of PRAETORIAN.

prettify /ˈprɪtɪfaɪ/ *v.tr.* (**-ies**, **-ied**) make (a thing or person) pretty esp. in an affected way. □□ **prettification** /-fɪˈkeɪʃ(ə)n/ *n.* **prettifier** *n.*

pretty /ˈprɪtɪ/ *adj., n., v.,* & *adv.* —*adj.* (**prettier, prettiest**) **1** attractive in a delicate way without being truly beautiful or handsome (*a pretty child; a pretty dress; a pretty tune*). **2** fine or good of its kind (*a pretty wit*). **3** *iron.* considerable, fine (*a pretty penny; a pretty mess you have made*). —*adv. colloq.* fairly, moderately (*am pretty well; find it pretty difficult*). —*n.* (*pl.* **-ies**) a pretty person (esp. as a form of address to a child). —*v.tr.* (**-ies**, **-ied**) (often foll. by *up*) make pretty or attractive. □ **pretty much** (or **nearly** or **well**) *colloq.* almost; very nearly. **pretty-pretty** too pretty. **sitting pretty** *colloq.* in a favourable or advantageous position. □□ **prettily** *adv.* **prettiness** *n.* **prettyish** *adj.* **prettyism** *n.* [OE *prættig* f. WG]

pretzel /ˈprets(ə)l/ *n.* (also **bretzel** /ˈbret-/) a crisp knot-shaped or stick-shaped salted biscuit. [G]

prevail /prɪˈveɪl/ *v.intr.* **1** (often foll. by *against*, *over*) be victorious or gain mastery. **2** be the more usual or predominant. **3** exist or occur in general use or experience; be current. **4** (foll. by *on*, *upon*) persuade. □ **prevailing wind** the wind that most frequently occurs at a place. □□ **prevailingly** *adv.* [ME f. L *praevalēre* (as PRAE-, *valēre* have power), infl. by AVAIL]

prevalent /ˈprevələnt/ *adj.* **1** generally existing or occurring. **2** predominant. □□ **prevalence** *n.* **prevalently** *adv.* [as PREVAIL]

prevaricate /prɪˈværɪˌkeɪt/ *v.intr.* **1** speak or act evasively or misleadingly. **2** quibble, equivocate. ¶ Often confused with *procrastinate.* □□ **prevarication** /-ˈkeɪʃ(ə)n/ *n.* **prevaricator** *n.* [L *praevaricari* walk crookedly, practise collusion, in eccl.L transgress (as PRAE-, *varicari* straddle f. *varus* bent, knock-kneed)]

prevenient /prɪˈviːnɪənt/ *adj. formal* preceding something else. [L *praeveniens* pres. part. of *praevenire* (as PREVENT)]

prevent /prɪˈvent/ *v.tr.* **1** (often foll. by *from* + verbal noun) stop from happening or doing something; hinder; make impossible (*the weather prevented me from going*). **2** *archaic* go or arrive before; precede. □□ **preventable** *adj.* (also **preventible**). **preventability** /-təˈbɪlɪtɪ/ *n.* (also **preventibility**). **preventer** *n.* **prevention** *n.* [ME = anticipate, f. L *praevenire praevent-* come before, hinder (as PRAE-, *venire* come)]

preventative /prɪˈventətɪv/ *adj.* & *n.* = PREVENTIVE. □□ **preventatively** *adv.*

preventive /prɪˈventɪv/ *adj.* & *n.* —*adj.* serving to prevent, esp. preventing disease, breakdown, etc. (*preventive medicine; preventive maintenance*). —*n.* a preventive agent, measure, drug, etc. □ **preventive detention** the imprisonment of a criminal for corrective training etc. □□ **preventively** *adv.*

preview /ˈpriːvjuː/ *n.* & *v.* —*n.* **1** the act of seeing in advance. **2 a** the showing of a film, play, exhibition, etc., before it is seen by the general public. **b** (US **prevue**) a film trailer. —*v.tr.* see or show in advance.

Previn /ˈprevɪn/, André George (born Andreas Ludwig Priwin, 1929–), German-born American pianist, conductor, and composer. Once a jazz pianist, he later worked in Hollywood as a composer and arranger of film music. He has composed musicals and orchestral and chamber works but is most famous as a conductor, notably with the London Symphony Orchestra (1968–79) and the Pittsburg Symphony Orchestra (1976–86), and has won popularity as a presenter of classical music on television.

previous /ˈpriːvɪəs/ adj. & adv. —adj. **1** (often foll. by to) coming before in time or order. **2** done or acting hastily. —adv. (foll. by to) before (had called previous to writing). □ **previous question** Parl. a motion concerning the vote on a main question. □□ **previously** adv. **previousness** n. [L praevius (as PRAE-, via way)]

previse /prɪˈvaɪz/ v.tr. literary foresee or forecast (an event etc.). □□ **prevision** /-ˈvɪʒ(ə)n/ n. **previsional** /-ˈvɪʒən(ə)l/ adj. [L praevidēre praevis- (as PRAE-, vidēre see)]

Prévost /preˈvəʊ/, Antoine-François, l'Abbé ('Prévost d'Exiles') (1696–1763), French novelist, successively Jesuit novice, professional soldier, and Benedictine priest. Unfitted for the cloister he fled in 1728 and took refuge in Holland and England. He is remembered for his novel *Manon Lescaut* (1731), the story of a mutually destructive passion between a noble man and a demi-mondaine, which inspired operas by Massenet and Puccini. He wrote many novels and translations of Richardson's major novels which introduced his countrymen to English life and literature.

prevue US var. of PREVIEW n. 2b.

pre-war /priːˈwɔː(r), ˈpriːwɔː(r)/ adj. existing or occurring before a war (esp. the most recent major war).

prey /preɪ/ n. & v. —n. **1** an animal that is hunted or killed by another for food. **2** (often foll. by to) a person or thing that is influenced by or vulnerable to (something undesirable) (became a prey to morbid fears). **3** Bibl. or archaic plunder, booty, etc. —v.intr. (foll. by on, upon) **1** seek or take as prey. **2** make a victim of. **3** (of a disease, emotion, etc.) exert a harmful influence (fear preyed on his mind). □ **beast** (or **bird**) **of prey** an animal (or bird) which hunts animals for food. □□ **preyer** n. [ME f. OF preie f. L praeda booty]

prezzie var. of PRESSIE.

Priam /ˈpraɪæm/ Gk legend the king of Troy at the time of its destruction by the Greeks under Agamemnon. He was slain by Neoptolemus, son of Achilles.

priapic /praɪˈæpɪk/ adj. phallic. [Priapos (as PRIAPISM) + -IC]

priapism /ˈpraɪəˌpɪz(ə)m/ n. **1** lewdness, licentiousness. **2** Med. persistent erection of the penis. [F priapisme f. LL priapismus f. Gk priapismos f. priapizō be lewd f. Priapos PRIAPUS]

Priapus /ˈpraɪəpəs/ Gk Mythol. a god of fertility, whose symbol was the phallus. He was originally worshipped in the Hellespont area and his cult spread to Greece after Alexander's conquest, and thence to Italy. By this time the Greeks had outgrown the more crudely naturalistic worship and Priapus seems to have been found broadly funny. He was adopted as a god of gardens, where his statue (a misshapen little man with enormous genitals) was a sort of combined scarecrow and guardian deity.

price /praɪs/ n. & v. —n. **1 a** the amount of money or goods for which a thing is bought or sold. **b** value or worth (a pearl of great price; beyond price). **2** what is or must be given, done, sacrificed, etc., to obtain or achieve something. **3** the odds in betting (starting price). —v.tr. **1** fix or find the price of (a thing for sale). **2** estimate the value of. □ **above** (or **beyond** or **without**) **price** so valuable that no price can be stated. **at any price** no matter what the cost, sacrifice, etc. (peace at any price). **at a price** at a high cost. **price-fixing** the maintaining of prices at a certain level by agreement between competing sellers. **price-list** a list of current prices of items on sale. **price on a person's head** a reward for a person's capture or death. **price oneself out of the market** lose to one's competitors by charging more than customers are willing to pay. **price-ring** a group of traders acting illegally to control certain prices. **price tag 1** the label on an item showing its price. **2** the cost of an enterprise or undertaking. **price war** fierce competition among traders cutting prices. **set a price** on declare the price of. **what price...?** (often foll. by verbal noun) colloq. **1** what is the chance of...? (what price your finishing the course?). **2** iron. the expected or much boasted... proves disappointing (what price your friendship now?). □□ **priced** adj. (also in comb.). **pricer** n. [(n.) ME f. OF pris f. L pretium: (v.) var. of prise = PRIZE¹]

priceless /ˈpraɪslɪs/ adj. **1** invaluable; beyond price. **2** colloq. very amusing or absurd. □□ **pricelessly** adv. **pricelessness** n.

pricey /ˈpraɪsɪ/ adj. (also **pricy**) (**pricier**, **priciest**) colloq. expensive. □□ **priciness** n.

prick /prɪk/ v. & n. —v. **1** tr. pierce slightly; make a small hole in. **2** tr. (foll. by off, out) mark (esp. a pattern) with small holes or dots. **3** tr. trouble mentally (my conscience is pricking me). **4** intr. feel a pricking sensation. **5** intr. (foll. by at, into, etc.) make a thrust as if to prick. **6** tr. (foll. by in, off, out) plant (seedlings etc.) in small holes pricked in the earth. **7** tr. Brit. archaic mark off (a name in a list, esp. to select a sheriff) by pricking. **8** tr. archaic spur or urge on (a horse etc.). —n. **1** the act or an instance of pricking. **2** a small hole or mark made by pricking. **3** a pain caused as by pricking. **4** a mental pain (felt the pricks of conscience). **5** coarse sl. **a** the penis. **b** derog. (as a term of contempt) a person. ¶ Usually considered a taboo use. **6** archaic a goad for oxen. □ **kick against the pricks** persist in futile resistance. **prick up one's ears 1** (of a dog etc.) make the ears erect when on the alert. **2** (of a person) become suddenly attentive. □□ **pricker** n. [OE prician (v.), pricca (n.)]

pricket /ˈprɪkɪt/ n. **1** Brit. a male fallow deer in its second year, having straight unbranched horns. **2** a spike for holding a candle. [ME f. AL prikettus -um, dimin. of PRICK]

prickle /ˈprɪk(ə)l/ n. & v. —n. **1 a** a small thorn. **b** Bot. a thornlike process developed from the epidermis of a plant. **2** a hard-pointed spine of a hedgehog etc. **3** a prickling sensation. —v.tr. & intr. affect or be affected with a sensation as of pricking. [OE pricel PRICK: (v.) also dimin. of PRICK]

prickly /ˈprɪklɪ/ adj. (**pricklier**, **prickliest**) **1** (esp. in the names of plants and animals) having prickles. **2** (of a person) ready to take offence. **3** tingling. □ **prickly heat** an itchy inflammation of the skin, causing a tingling sensation and common in hot countries. **prickly pear 1** any cactus of the genus Opuntia, native to arid regions of America, bearing barbed bristles and large pear-shaped prickly fruits. **2** its fruit. **prickly poppy** a tropical poppy-like plant, Argemone mexicana, with prickly leaves and yellow flowers. □□ **prickliness** n.

pricy var. of PRICEY.

pride /praɪd/ n. & v. —n. **1 a** a feeling of elation or satisfaction at achievements or qualities or possessions etc. that do one credit. **b** an object of this feeling. **2** a high or overbearing opinion of one's worth or importance. **3** (in full **proper pride**) a proper sense of what befits one's position; self-respect. **4** a group or company (of animals, esp. lions). **5** the best condition; the prime. —v.refl. (foll. by on, upon) be proud of. □ **my, his**, etc. **pride and joy** a thing of which one is very proud. **pride of the morning** a mist or shower at sunrise, supposedly indicating a fine day to come. **pride of place** the most important or prominent position. **take pride** (or **a pride**) **in 1** be proud of. **2** maintain in good condition or appearance. □□ **prideful** adj. **pridefully** adv. **prideless** adj. [OE prȳtu, prȳte, prȳde f. prūd PROUD]

Pride's Purge /praɪdz/ the exclusion or arrest of about 140 Members of Parliament by soldiers under the command of Colonel Pride when, in December 1648, the army, seeking a trial of the captive Charles I, decided to remove those Members likely to vote against it. Following the purge, the remaining Members, known as the Rump Parliament, voted for the trial which resulted in Charles being executed.

prie-dieu /priːˈdjɜː/ n. (pl. **prie-dieux** pronunc. same) a kneeling-desk for prayer. [F, = pray God]

priest /priːst/ n. **1** an ordained minister of the Roman Catholic or Orthodox Church, or of the Anglican Church (above a deacon and below a bishop), authorized to perform certain rites and administer certain sacraments. **2** an official minister of a non-Christian religion. □ **priest's hole** hist. a hiding-place for a Roman Catholic priest during times of religious persecution. □□ **priestless** adj. **priestlike** adj. **priestling** n. [OE prēost, ult. f. eccl.L presbyter: see PRESBYTER]

priestcraft /ˈpriːstkrɑːft/ n. usu. derog. the work and influence of priests.

priestess /ˈpriːstɪs/ n. a female priest of a non-Christian religion.

priesthood /ˈpriːsthʊd/ n. (usu. prec. by the) **1** the office or position of priest. **2** priests in general.

Priestley[1] /ˈpriːstlɪ/, John Boynton (1894–1984), English novelist, playwright, and critic. His good-humoured optimistic novels include The Good Companions (1929). Some of his plays, such as Time and the Conways (1937), are influenced by the time theories of J. W. Dunne. Priestley was a popular broadcaster, known for his forthright down-to-earth comments. His prodigious literary output earned him a fortune and popular esteem, but critical acclaim was more sparing.

Priestley[2] /ˈpriːstlɪ/, Joseph (1733–1804), English chemist, natural philosopher, and theologian, author of about 150 books, mostly theological or educational. He was introduced to the study of electricity (electrostatics) by Franklin, but his most important work was done in 'pneumatic' chemistry (the study of gases), in which, by means of improved techniques, he managed to isolate a number of gases, including ammonia, sulphur dioxide, and nitrous oxide and nitrogen dioxide, but his most significant discovery was of 'dephlogisticated air' in 1774, which he reported to Lavoisier who gave it the modern name of oxygen. He demonstrated the importance of oxygen to animal life, and that plants require sunlight and yield this gas. In his theology he espoused what eventually became known as Unitarianism. His support of the French Revolution provoked so much hostility that he left Birmingham in 1794 and settled in America.

priestly /ˈpriːstlɪ/ adj. of or associated with priests. ☐☐ **priestliness** n. [OE prēostlic (as PRIEST)]

prig /prɪg/ n. a self-righteously correct or moralistic person. ☐☐ **priggery** n. **priggish** adj. **priggishly** adv. **priggishness** n. [16th-c. cant. = tinker: orig. unkn.]

prim /prɪm/ adj. & v. —adj. (**primmer, primmest**) **1** (of a person or manner) stiffly formal and precise. **2** (of a woman or girl) demure. **3** prudish. —v.tr. (**primmed, primming**) **1** form (the face, lips, etc.) into a prim expression. **2** make prim. ☐☐ **primly** adv. **primness** n. [17th c.: prob. orig. cant f. OF prin prime excellent f. L primus first]

prima ballerina /ˌpriːmə ˌbæləˈriːnə/ n. the chief female dancer in a ballet or ballet company. [It.]

primacy /ˈpraɪməsɪ/ n. (pl. **-ies**) **1** pre-eminence. **2** the office of a primate. [ME f. OF primatie or med.L primatia (as PRIMATE)]

prima donna /ˌpriːmə ˈdɒnə/ n. (pl. **prima donnas**) **1** the chief female singer in an opera or opera company. **2** a temperamentally self-important person. ☐☐ **prima donna-ish** adj. [It.]

primaeval var. of PRIMEVAL.

prima facie /ˌpraɪmə ˈfeɪʃiː/ adv. & adj. —adv. at first sight; from a first impression (seems prima facie to be guilty). —adj. (of evidence) based on the first impression (can see a prima facie reason for it). [ME f. L, fem. ablat. of primus first, facies FACE]

primal /ˈpraɪm(ə)l/ adj. **1** primitive, primeval. **2** chief, fundamental. ☐☐ **primally** adv. [med.L primalis f. L primus first]

primary /ˈpraɪmərɪ/ adj. & n. —adj. **1 a** of the first importance; chief (that is our primary concern). **b** fundamental, basic. **2** earliest, original; first in a series. **3** of the first rank in a series; not derived (the primary meaning of a word). **4** designating any of the colours red, green, and blue, or for pigments red, blue, and yellow, from which all other colours can be obtained by mixing. **5** (of a battery or cell) generating electricity by irreversible chemical reaction. **6** (of education) for young children, esp. below the age of 11. **7** (**Primary**) Geol. of the lowest series of strata. **8** Biol. belonging to the first stage of development. **9** (of an industry or source of production) concerned with obtaining or using raw materials. **10** Gram. (of a tense in Latin and Greek) present, future, perfect, or future perfect (cf. HISTORIC). —n. (pl. **-ies**) **1** a thing that is primary. **2** (in full **primary election**) (in the US) a preliminary election to appoint delegates to a party conference or to select the candidates for a principal (esp. presidential) election. **3** = primary planet. **4** (**Primary**) Geol. the Primary period. **5** = primary feather. **6** = primary coil. ☐ **primary coil** a coil to which current is supplied in a transformer. **primary feather** a large flight-feather of a bird's wing. **primary planet** a planet that directly orbits the sun (cf. secondary planet).

primary school a school where young children are taught, esp. below the age of 11. ☐☐ **primarily** /ˈpraɪmərɪlɪ, -ˈmeərɪlɪ/ adv. [ME f. L primarius f. primus first]

primate /ˈpraɪmeɪt/ n. **1** any animal of the order Primates, the highest order of mammals, including tarsiers, lemurs, apes, monkeys, and man. **2** an archbishop. ☐ **Primate of All England** the Archbishop of Canterbury. **Primate of England** the Archbishop of York. ☐☐ **primatial** /-ˈmeɪʃ(ə)l/ adj. **primatology** /-məˈtɒlədʒɪ/ n. (in sense 1). [ME f. OF primat f. L primas -atis (adj.) of the first rank f. primus first, in med.L = primate]

primavera /ˌpriːməˈveərə/ n. **1** a Central American tree, Cybistax donnellsmithii, bearing yellow blooms. **2** the hard light-coloured timber from this. [Sp., = spring (the season) f. L primus first + ver SPRING]

prime[1] /praɪm/ adj. & n. —adj. **1** chief, most important (the prime agent; the prime motive). **2** (esp. of cattle and provisions) first-rate, excellent. **3** primary, fundamental. **4** Math. **a** (of a number) divisible only by itself and unity (e.g. 2, 3, 5, 7, 11). **b** (of numbers) having no common factor but unity. —n. **1** the state of the highest perfection of something (in the prime of life). **2** (prec. by the; foll. by of) the best part. **3** the beginning or first age of anything. **4** Eccl. **a** the second canonical hour of prayer, appointed for the first hour of the day (i.e. 6 a.m.). **b** the office of this. **c** archaic this time. **5** a prime number. **6** Printing a symbol (ʹ) added to a letter etc. as a distinguishing mark, or to a figure as a symbol for minutes or feet. **7** the first of eight parrying positions in fencing. ☐ **prime cost** the direct cost of a commodity in terms of materials, labour, etc. **prime meridian 1** the meridian from which longitude is reckoned, esp. that passing through Greenwich. **2** the corresponding line on a map. **prime minister** see separate entry. **prime mover 1** an initial natural or mechanical source of motive power. **2** the author of a fruitful idea. **prime rate** the lowest rate at which money can be borrowed commercially. **prime time** the time at which a radio or television audience is expected to be at its highest. **prime vertical** the great circle of the heavens passing through the zenith and the E. and W. points of the horizon. ☐☐ **primeness** n. [(n.) OE prīm f. L prima (hora) first (hour), & MF f. OF prime: (adj.) ME f. OF f. L primus first]

prime[2] /praɪm/ v.tr. **1** prepare (a thing) for use or action. **2** prepare (a gun) for firing or (an explosive) for detonation. **3 a** pour (a liquid) into a pump to prepare it for working. **b** inject petrol into (the cylinder or carburettor of an internal-combustion engine). **4** prepare (wood etc.) for painting by applying a substance that prevents paint from being absorbed. **5** equip (a person) with information etc. **6** ply (a person) with food or drink in preparation for something. [16th c.: orig. unkn.]

prime minister n. the head of the executive branch of government in countries with a parliamentary system. In Britain the term was originally merely descriptive and unofficial. In the early 18th c. (perhaps from its prior application to the sole minister of a despotic ruler) it was regarded as odious; it was applied opprobriously to Sir Robert Walpole and disowned by him, as later by Lord North. It was little used in the later part of the 18th c., 'premier' (also 'first minister') being often substituted, but by the middle of the 19th c. it had become usual and began to creep into official use from 1878. In 1905 it was fully recognized and the precedence of the prime minister defined by King Edward VII.

In current use, the terms 'premier' and 'prime minister' are synonymous in Britain, but in Canada and Australia the government of a Province or State is headed by a premier, that of the Federal government by a prime minister. In countries such as France, where the President has an executive function, the prime minister is in a subordinate position.

primer[1] /ˈpraɪmə(r)/ n. **1** a substance used to prime wood etc. **2** a cap, cylinder, etc., used to ignite the powder of a cartridge etc.

primer[2] /ˈpraɪmə(r)/ n. **1** an elementary textbook for teaching children to read. **2** an introductory book. [ME f. AF f. med.L primarius -arium f. L primus first]

primeval /praɪˈmiːv(ə)l/ adj. (also **primaeval**) **1** of or relating

to the first age of the world. **2** ancient, primitive. □□
primevally adv. [L primaevus f. primus first + aevum age]
primigravida /ˌpriːmɪˈgrævɪdə, ˌpraɪmɪ-/ n. (pl.
primigravidae /-ˌdiː/) a woman who is pregnant for the first
time. [mod.L fem. f. L primus first + gravidus pregnant: see
GRAVID]

priming[1] /ˈpraɪmɪŋ/ n. **1** a mixture used by painters for a
preparatory coat. **2** a preparation of sugar added to beer. **3 a**
gunpowder placed in the pan of a firearm. **b** a train of powder
connecting the fuse with the charge in blasting etc.

priming[2] /ˈpraɪmɪŋ/ n. an acceleration of the tides taking place
from the neap to the spring tides. [prime (v.) f. PRIME[1] + -ING[1]]

primipara /praɪˈmɪpərə/ n. (pl. **primiparae** /-ˌriː/) a woman
who is bearing a child for the first time. □□ **primiparous** adj.
[mod.L fem. f. primus first + -parus f. parere bring forth]

primitive /ˈprɪmɪtɪv/ adj. & n. —adj. **1** early, ancient; at an
early stage of civilization (primitive man). **2** undeveloped, crude,
simple (primitive methods). **3** original, primary. **4** Gram. & Philol.
(of words or language) radical; not derivative. **5** Math. (of a line,
figure, etc.) from which another is derived, from which some
construction begins, etc. **6** (of a colour) primary. **7** Geol. of the
earliest period. **8** Biol. appearing in the earliest or a very early
stage of growth or evolution. —n. **1 a** a painter of the period
before the Renaissance. **b** a modern imitator of such. **c** an
untutored painter with a direct naïve style. **d** a picture by such
a painter. **2** a primitive word, line, etc. □ **the Primitive Church**
the Christian Church in its earliest times. □□ **primitively** adv.
primitiveness n. [ME f. OF primitif -ive or L primitivus first of its
kind f. primitus in the first place f. primus first]

primitivism /ˈprɪmɪtɪˌvɪz(ə)m/ n. **1** primitive behaviour. **2**
belief in the superiority of what is primitive. **3** the practice of
primitive art. □□ **primitivist** n. & adj.

primo /ˈpriːməʊ/ n. (pl. **-os**) Mus. the leading or upper part in a
duet etc.

primogenitor /ˌpraɪməʊˈdʒenɪtə(r)/ n. **1** the earliest ancestor
of a people etc. **2** an ancestor. [var. of progenitor, after
PRIMOGENITURE]

primogeniture /ˌpraɪməʊˈdʒenɪtʃə(r)/ n. **1** the fact or condition
of being the first-born child. **2** (in full **right of primogeniture**)
the right of succession belonging to the first-born, esp. the
feudal rule by which the whole real estate of an intestate passes
to the eldest son. □□ **primogenital** adj. **primogenitary** adj.
[med.L primogenitura f. L primo first + genitura f. gignere genit-
beget]

primordial /praɪˈmɔːdɪəl/ adj. **1** existing at or from the beginning, primeval. **2** original, fundamental. □□ **primordiality**
/-ˈælɪtɪ/ n. **primordially** adv. [ME f. LL primordialis (as
PRIMORDIUM)]

primordium /praɪˈmɔːdɪəm/ n. (pl. **primordia** /-dɪə/) Biol. an
organ or tissue in the early stages of development. [L, neut. of
primordius original f. primus first + ordiri begin]

Primorve /ˈpriːmɔːjə/ a territory of the Russian SFSR in SE
Siberia; pop. (1985) 2,136,000; capital, Vladivostock.

primp /prɪmp/ v.tr. **1** make (the hair, one's clothes, etc.) tidy. **2**
refl. make (oneself) smart. [dial. var. of PRIM]

primrose /ˈprɪmrəʊz/ n. **1 a** any plant of the genus Primula,
esp. P. vulgaris, bearing pale yellow flowers. **b** the flower of this.
2 a pale yellow colour. □ **Primrose Day** the anniversary of the
death of Disraeli (19 Apr. 1881). **Primrose League** a political
association, formed in memory of Disraeli (whose favourite
flower was supposedly the primrose) in 1883, to promote and
sustain conservative principles in Britain. It is still in existence
today. **primrose path** the pursuit of pleasure, esp. with disastrous consequences (with ref. to Shakesp. Hamlet I. iii. 50). [ME
primerose, corresp. to OF primerose and med.L prima rosa, lit. first
rose: reason for the name unkn.]

primula /ˈprɪmjʊlə/ n. any plant of the genus Primula, bearing
primrose-like flowers in a wide variety of colours during the
spring, including primroses, cowslips, and polyanthuses.
[med.L, fem. of primulus dimin. of primus first]

primum mobile /ˌpraɪmʊm ˈməʊbɪlɪ/ n. **1** the central or most
important source of motion or action. **2** Astron. in the medieval

version of the Ptolemaic system, an outer sphere supposed to
move round the earth in 24 hours carrying the inner spheres
with it. [med.L, = first moving thing]

Primus /ˈpraɪməs/ n. propr. a brand of portable stove burning
vaporized oil for cooking etc. [L (as PRIMUS)]

primus /ˈpraɪməs/ n. the presiding bishop of the Scottish Episcopal Church. [L, = first]

primus inter pares /ˌpriːməs ˌɪntə ˈpɑːriːz/ n. a first among
equals; the senior or representative member of a group. [L]

prince /prɪns/ n. (as a title usu. **Prince**) **1** a male member of a
royal family other than a reigning king. **2** (in full **prince of the
blood**) a son or grandson of a British monarch. **3** a ruler of a
small State, actually or nominally subject to a king or emperor.
4 (as an English rendering of foreign titles) a noble usu. ranking
next below a duke. **5** (as a courtesy title in some connections) a
duke, marquis, or earl. **6** (often foll. by of) the chief or greatest
(the prince of novelists). □ **prince consort** the husband of a reigning female sovereign who is himself a prince. The title was
conferred on Prince Albert, husband of Queen Victoria, to avoid
the word 'king' as Albert was not regnant. **Prince of Darkness**
Satan. **Prince of Peace** Christ. **Prince of Wales** see separate
entry. **Prince Regent** a prince who acts as regent, esp. George
(afterwards IV) as regent 1811–20. **prince royal** the eldest son
of the reigning monarch. **prince's feather** a tall plant, Amaranthus hypochondriacus, with feathery spikes of small red flowers.
prince's metal a brasslike alloy of copper and zinc. □□
princedom n. **princelet** n. **princelike** adj. **princeship** n. [ME
f. OF f. L princeps principis first, chief, sovereign f. primus first +
capere take]

Prince Charming a fairy-tale hero. The name is a partial
translation of the French Roi Charmant, the name of the hero of
the Comtesse d'Aulnoy's L'Oiseau Bleu (The Blue Bird, 1697). In
English it first appears as that of the hero of Planché's King
Charming or Prince Charming, and was later adopted for the hero
of various fairy-tale pantomimes.

Prince Edward Island the smallest province of Canada
(from 1873), an island in the Gulf of St Lawrence, captured by
the British from the French settlers in 1758; pop. (1986) 126,600;
capital, Charlottetown.

Prince Imperial Napoléon Eugène Louis Jean Joseph (1856–
79), son of Napoleon III. Trained as a soldier in Britain after his
father's overthrow, he was allowed, at his own request, to join
the British forces in the Zulu War and was killed in a skirmish
in Zululand.

princeling /ˈprɪnslɪŋ/ n. a young or petty prince.

princely /ˈprɪnslɪ/ adj. (**princelier**, **princeliest**) **1 a** of or
worthy of a prince. **b** held by a prince. **2** sumptuous, generous,
splendid. □□ **princeliness** n.

Prince of Wales a title, formerly adopted by various Welsh
rulers, usually conferred (since 1301; see EDWARD II) on the heir
apparent to the English (later the British) throne.

Prince Rupert's Land see RUPERT'S LAND.

Princes in the Tower the young sons of Edward IV, supposedly murdered in the Tower of London. Edward, Prince of
Wales, and Richard, Duke of York, were housed in the royal
apartments of the Tower of London following the death of their
father and the seizure of the throne by Richard III. They disappeared soon after their arrival there in 1483, and although
many theories as to their fate were subsequently advanced, it
is generally assumed that they were murdered, either by their
uncle Richard III or by Henry Tudor (later Henry VII).

princess /prɪnˈses/ n. (as a title usu. **Princess** /ˈprɪnses/) **1** the
wife of a prince. **2** a female member of a royal family other than
a reigning queen. **3** (in full **princess of the blood**) a daughter
or granddaughter of a British monarch. **4** a pre-eminent woman
or thing personified as a woman. □ **Princess Regent 1** a
princess who acts as regent. **2** the wife of a Prince Regent.
Princess Royal a monarch's eldest daughter, as a title conferred by the monarch. [ME f. OF princesse (as PRINCE)]

Princeton /ˈprɪnst(ə)n/ a town in the west of New Jersey, named
in 1724 in honour of William III, Prince of Orange-Nassau; pop.

(1980) 12,000. It is the site of the fourth-oldest US university, founded in 1746.

principal /ˈprɪnsɪp(ə)l/ *adj. & n.* —*adj.* **1** (usu. *attrib.*) first in rank or importance; chief (*the principal town of the district*). **2** main, leading (*a principal cause of my success*). **3** (of money) constituting the original sum invested or lent. —*n.* **1** a head, ruler, or superior. **2** the head of some schools, colleges, and universities. **3** the leading performer in a concert, play, etc. **4** a capital sum as distinguished from interest or income. **5** a person for whom another acts as agent etc. **6** (in the UK) a civil servant of the grade below Secretary. **7** the person actually responsible for a crime. **8** a person for whom another is surety. **9** each of the combatants in a duel. **10 a** a main rafter supporting purlins. **b** a main girder. **11** an organ stop sounding an octave above the diapason. **12** *Mus.* the leading player in each section of an orchestra. □ **principal boy** the leading male part in a pantomime, usually played by a woman. **principal girl** the leading female part in a pantomime. **principal clause** *Gram.* a clause to which another clause is subordinate. **principal in the first degree** a person directly responsible for a crime as its actual perpetrator. **principal in the second degree** a person directly responsible for a crime as aiding in its perpetration. **principal parts** *Gram.* the parts of a verb from which all other parts can be deduced. □□ **principalship** *n.* [ME f. OF f. L *principalis* first, original (as PRINCE)]

principality /ˌprɪnsɪˈpælɪtɪ/ *n.* (*pl.* **-ies**) **1** a State ruled by a prince. **2** the government of a prince. **3** (in *pl.*) the fifth order of the ninefold celestial hierarchy. **4** (**the Principality**) *Brit.* Wales. [ME f. OF *principalité* f. LL *principalitas -tatis* (as PRINCIPAL)]

principally /ˈprɪnsɪpəlɪ/ *adv.* for the most part; chiefly.

principate /ˈprɪnsɪpət/ *n.* **1** a State ruled by a prince. **2** *Rom.Hist.* the rule of the early emperors during which some republican forms were retained. [ME f. OF *principat* or L *principatus* first place]

principle /ˈprɪnsɪp(ə)l/ *n.* **1** a fundamental truth or law as the basis of reasoning or action (*arguing from first principles*; *moral principles*). **2 a** a personal code of conduct (*a person of high principle*). **b** (in *pl.*) such rules of conduct (*has no principles*). **3** a general law in physics etc. (*the uncertainty principle*). **4** a law of nature forming the basis for the construction or working of a machine etc. **5** a fundamental source; a primary element (*held water to be the first principle of all things*). **6** *Chem.* a constituent of a substance, esp. one giving rise to some quality, etc. □ **in principle** as regards fundamentals but not necessarily in detail. **on principle** on the basis of a moral attitude (*I refuse on principle*). [ME f. OF *principe* f. L *principium* source, (in *pl.*) foundations (as PRINCE)]

principled /ˈprɪnsɪp(ə)ld/ *adj.* based on or having (esp. praiseworthy) principles of behaviour.

prink /prɪŋk/ *v.* **1** *tr.* (usu. *refl.*) **a** make (oneself etc.) smart. **b** (foll. by *up*) smarten (oneself) up. **c** (of a bird) preen. **2** *intr.* dress oneself up. [16th c.: prob. f. *prank* dress, adorn, rel. to MLG *prank* pomp, Du. *pronk* finery]

print /prɪnt/ *n. & v.* —*n.* **1** an indentation or mark on a surface left by the pressure of a thing in contact with it (*fingerprint*; *footprint*). **2 a** a printed lettering or writing (*large print*). **b** words in printed form. **c** a printed publication, esp. a newspaper. **d** the quantity of a book etc. printed at one time. **e** the state of being printed. **3** a picture or design printed from a block or plate. **4** *Photog.* a picture produced on paper from a negative. **5** a printed cotton fabric. —*v.tr.* **1 a** produce or reproduce (a book, picture, etc.) by applying inked types, blocks, or plates, to paper, vellum, etc. **b** (of an author, publisher, or editor) cause (a book or manuscript etc.) to be produced or reproduced in this way. **2** express or publish in print. **3 a** (often foll. by *on*, *in*) impress or stamp (a mark or figure on a surface). **b** (often foll. by *with*) impress or stamp (a soft surface, e.g. of butter or wax, with a seal, die, etc.). **4** (often *absol.*) write (words or letters) without joining, in imitation of typography. **5** (often foll. by *off*, *out*) *Photog.* produce (a picture) by the transmission of light through a negative. **6** (usu. foll. by *out*) (of a computer etc.) produce output in printed form. **7** mark (a textile fabric) with a decorative design in colours. **8** (foll. by *on*) impress (an idea, scene, etc. on the

mind or memory). **9** transfer (a coloured or plain design) from paper etc. to the unglazed or glazed surface of ceramic ware. □ **appear in print** have one's work published. **in print 1** (of a book etc.) available from the publisher. **2** in printed form. **out of print** no longer available from the publisher. **printed circuit** an electric circuit with thin strips of conductor on a flat insulating sheet, usu. made by a process like printing. □□ **printable** *adj.* **printability** /-təˈbɪlɪtɪ/ *n.* **printless** *adj.* (in sense 1 of *n.*). [ME f. OF *priente*, *preinte*, fem. past part. of *preindre* press f. L *premere*]

printer /ˈprɪntə(r)/ *n.* **1** a person who prints books, magazines, advertising matter, etc. **2** the owner of a printing business. **3** a device that prints, esp. as part of a computer system. □ **printer's devil** an errand-boy in a printer's office. **printer's mark** a device used as a printer's trade mark. **printer's pie** = PIE³ *n.*

printery /ˈprɪntərɪ/ *n.* (*pl.* **-ies**) *US* a printer's office or works.

printhead /ˈprɪnthed/ *n.* the component in a printer (see PRINTER 3) that assembles and prints the characters on the paper.

printing /ˈprɪntɪŋ/ *n.* **1** the production of printed books etc. (See below.) **2** a single impression of a book. **3** printed letters or writing imitating them. □ **printing-press** a machine for printing from types or plates etc.

Printing involves transferring any number of times an image, or group of images, from an original master to a receptive substrate such as paper, board, or cloth. It is most commonly achieved by inking a suitable form of the master image (i.e. printers' type, a rubber stamp, or litho plate) and transferring the ink to the substrate by flat or rolling pressure. The process originated in China in about the 8th c. and spread to Europe in the 15th c. A major advance was Johann Gutenberg's invention of movable type by which each letter is cast separately, allowing words and spaces to be formed into lines and pages, which in turn form relief master images for inking and impressing on to paper. This method has been largely superseded by photographic image-forming techniques and faster rotary printing. Film is now the most universal master-image material, through which the printing-surface is selectively sensitized and etched, ready for the modern rotary printing-press. Multicolour images are formed by superimposing one printed colour upon another in register. A growing method of printing is that whereby master images are held by computer in digital form, and then output on to a suitable substrate by plotting, xerographic, ink-jet, or laser techniques.

printmaker /ˈprɪntˌmeɪkə(r)/ *n.* a person who makes print. □□ **printmaking** *n.*

printout /ˈprɪntaʊt/ *n.* computer output in printed form.

printworks /ˈprɪntwɜːks/ *n.* a factory where fabrics are printed.

prior /ˈpraɪə(r)/ *adj., adv., & n.* —*adj.* **1** earlier. **2** (often foll. by *to*) coming before in time, order, or importance. —*adv.* (foll. by *to*) before (*decided prior to their arrival*). —*n.* **1** the superior officer of a religious house or order. **2** (in an abbey) the officer next under the abbot. □□ **priorate** /-rət/ *n.* **prioress** *n.* **priorship** *n.* [L, = former, elder, compar. of OL *pri* = L *prae* before]

priority /praɪˈɒrɪtɪ/ *n.* (*pl.* **-ies**) **1** the fact or condition of being earlier or antecedent. **2** precedence in rank etc. **3** an interest having prior claim to consideration. □□ **prioritize** *v.tr.* (also **-ise**). **prioritization** /-taɪˈzeɪʃ(ə)n/ *n.* [ME f. OF *priorité* f. med.L *prioritas -tatis* f. L *prior* (as PRIOR)]

priory /ˈpraɪərɪ/ *n.* (*pl.* **-ies**) a monastery governed by a prior or a nunnery governed by a prioress. [ME f. AF *priorie*, med.L *prioria* (as PRIOR)]

Priscian /ˈprɪʃən/ (Priscianus, 6th c.) Byzantine grammarian. His Latin *Grammatical Institutions* was one of the standard grammatical works in the Middle Ages.

prise /praɪz/ *v. & n.* (also **prize**) —*v.tr.* force open or out by leverage (*prised up the lid*; *prised the box open*). —*n.* leverage, purchase. [ME & OF *prise* levering instrument (as PRIZE¹)]

prism /ˈprɪz(ə)m/ *n.* **1** a solid geometric figure whose two ends are similar, equal, and parallel rectilinear figures, and whose sides are parallelograms. **2** a transparent body in this form, usu.

triangular with refracting surfaces at an acute angle with each other, which separates white light into a spectrum of colours. □□ **prismal** /ˈprɪzm(ə)l/ adj. [LL prisma f. Gk prisma prismatos thing sawn f. prizō to saw]

prismatic /prɪzˈmætɪk/ adj. 1 of, like, or using a prism. 2 a (of colours) distributed by or as if by a transparent prism. b (of light) displayed in the form of a spectrum. □□ **prismatically** adv. [F prismatique f. Gk prisma (as PRISM)]

prismoid /ˈprɪzmɔɪd/ n. a body like a prism, with similar but unequal parallel polygonal ends. □□ **prismoidal** /-ˈmɔɪd(ə)l/ adj.

prison /ˈprɪz(ə)n/ n. & v. —n. 1 a place in which a person is kept in captivity, esp. a building to which persons are legally committed while awaiting trial or for punishment; a jail. (See below.) 2 custody, confinement (in prison). —v.tr. poet. (**prisoned**, **prisoning**) put in prison. □ **prison-breaking** escape from prison. **prison camp** a camp for prisoners of war or of State. [ME f. OF prisun, -on f. L prensio -onis f. prehensio f. prehendere prehens- lay hold of]

There have been prisons at all periods of history. Originally imprisonment was not a mode of punishment but a means of holding offenders awaiting trial or execution; it was used also as a means of extorting payment of money, and even by the 19th c. a high proportion of prisoners were debtors. The modern idea of prison grew from the 'house of correction', a place which, in the 16th c., was used for housing beggars and vagrants who threatened the peace of the community, and for setting them to work. By the mid-16th c. such places, modelled on and named after the Bridewell organized in London, were established in every county under the local justices (a similar movement sprang up on the Continent); their original functions were superseded by that of imprisoning petty offenders. Bad insanitary surroundings, oppression, cruelty, and lack of supervision made prison conditions notorious and towards the end of the 18th c. John Howard began a vigorous crusade for reform; this was only one aspect of a European movement. In 1878 the government assumed control of all prisons. Thinking about prisons was affected then and thereafter by the development of penological theory, particularly stressing the individualism of punishment and criticizing imprisonment as not suitable in all cases.

prisoner /ˈprɪznə(r)/ n. 1 a person kept in prison. 2 (in full **prisoner at the bar**) a person in custody on a criminal charge and on trial. 3 a person or thing confined by illness, another's grasp, etc. 4 (in full **prisoner of war**) a person who has been captured in war. □ **prisoner of conscience** see CONSCIENCE. **prisoner of State** (or **State prisoner**) a person confined for political reasons. **prisoner's base** a game played by two groups of children who each occupy a distinct base or home. It was played as a street game in France in the Middle Ages. In England it was prohibited in the avenues of the Palace of Westminster during sessions of Parliament in the reign of Edward III because it interfered with the passage of members. **take prisoner** seize and hold as a prisoner. [ME f. AF prisoner, OF prisonier (as PRISON)]

prissy /ˈprɪsɪ/ adj. (**prissier**, **prissiest**) prim, prudish. □□ **prissily** adv. **prissiness** n. [perh. f. PRIM + SISSY]

Pristina /prɪsˈtiːnə/ the capital of the autonomous province of Kosovo, Yugoslavia; pop. (1981) 210,000.

pristine /ˈprɪstiːn, ˈprɪstaɪn/ adj. 1 in its original condition; unspoilt. 2 disp. spotless; fresh as if new. 3 ancient, primitive. [L pristinus former]

Pritchett /ˈprɪtʃɪt/, Sir Victor Sawdon (1900–), English writer and critic, famous especially for his short stories. His works include two volumes of much-praised autobiography, *The Cab at the Door* (1968; the title refers to his household's frequent removals), and *Midnight Oil* (1971).

prithee /ˈprɪðiː/ int. archaic pray, please. [= I pray thee]

privacy /ˈprɪvəsɪ, ˈpraɪ-/ n. 1 a the state of being private and undisturbed. b a person's right to this. 2 freedom from intrusion or public attention. 3 avoidance of publicity.

private /ˈpraɪvət, -vɪt/ adj. & n. —adj. 1 belonging to an individual; one's own; personal (private property). 2 confidential; not to be disclosed to others (private talks). 3 kept or removed from

public knowledge or observation. 4 a not open to the public. b for an individual's exclusive use (private room). 5 (of a place) secluded; affording privacy. 6 (of a person) not holding public office or an official position. 7 (of education or medical treatment) conducted outside the State system, at the individual's expense. —n. 1 a private soldier. 2 (in pl.) colloq. the genitals. □ **in private** privately; in private company or life. **private bill** a parliamentary bill affecting an individual or corporation only. **private company** Brit. a company with restricted membership and no issue of shares. **private detective** a detective engaged privately, outside an official police force. **private enterprise 1** a business or businesses not under State control. 2 individual initiative. **private eye** colloq. a private detective. **private first class** US a soldier ranking above an ordinary private but below officers. **private hotel** a hotel not obliged to take all comers. **private house** the dwelling-house of a private person, as distinct from a shop, office, or public building. **private law** a law relating to individual persons and private property. **private life** life as a private person, not as an official, public performer, etc. **private means** income from investments etc., apart from earned income. **private member** a member of a legislative body not holding a government office. **private member's bill** a bill introduced by a private member, not part of government legislation. **private parts** the genitals. **private patient** Brit. a patient treated by a doctor other than under the National Health Service. **private practice** Brit. medical practice that is not part of the National Health Service. **private press** a printing establishment operated by a private person or group not primarily for profit and usu. on a small scale. **private school 1** Brit. a school supported wholly by the payment of fees. 2 US a school not supported mainly by the State. **private secretary** a secretary dealing with the personal and confidential concerns of a businessman or businesswoman. **private sector** the part of the economy free of direct State control. **private soldier** an ordinary soldier other than the officers (and US other than recruits). **private view** the viewing of an exhibition (esp. of paintings) before it is open to the public. **private war 1** a feud between persons or families disregarding the law of murder etc. **2** hostilities against members of another State without the sanction of one's own government. **private wrong** an offence against an individual but not against society as a whole. □□ **privately** adv. [ME f. L privatus, orig. past part. of privare deprive]

privateer /ˌpraɪvəˈtɪə(r)/ n. 1 an armed vessel owned and officered by private individuals holding a government commission and authorized to use it against a hostile nation, especially in the capture of merchant shipping. 2 a a commander of such a vessel. b (in pl.) its crew. □□ **privateering** n. [PRIVATE, after volunteer]

privateersman /ˌpraɪvəˈtɪəzmən/ n. (pl. **-men**) = PRIVATEER 2.

privation /praɪˈveɪʃ(ə)n/ n. 1 lack of the comforts or necessities of life (suffered many privations). 2 (often foll. by of) loss or absence (of a quality). [ME f. L privatio (as PRIVATE)]

privative /ˈprɪvətɪv/ adj. 1 consisting in or marked by the loss or removal or absence of some quality or attribute. 2 (of a term) denoting the privation or absence of a quality etc. 3 Gram. (of a particle etc.) expressing privation, as Gk a- = 'not'. □□ **privatively** adv. [F privatif -ive or L privativus (as PRIVATION)]

privatize /ˈpraɪvətaɪz, -vɪˌtaɪz/ v.tr. (also **-ise**) make private, esp. assign (a business etc.) to private as distinct from State control or ownership; de-nationalize. □□ **privatization** /-ˈzeɪʃ(ə)n/ n.

privet /ˈprɪvɪt/ n. any evergreen shrub of the genus Ligustrum, esp. L. vulgare bearing small white flowers and black berries, and much used for hedges. [16th c.: orig. unkn.]

privilege /ˈprɪvɪlɪdʒ/ n. & v. —n. 1 a a right, advantage, or immunity, belonging to a person, class, or office. b the freedom of members of a legislative assembly when speaking at its meetings. 2 a special benefit or honour (it is a privilege to meet you). 3 a monopoly or patent granted to an individual, corporation, etc. 4 US Stock Exch. an option. —v.tr. 1 invest with a privilege. 2 (foll. by to + infin.) allow (a person) as a privilege (to do something). 3 (often foll. by from) exempt (a person from a liability etc.). □□ **privileged** adj. [ME f. OF privilege f. L privilegium bill or law affecting an individual, f. privus private + lex legis law]

privity /'prɪvɪtɪ/ n. (pl. **-ies**) **1** Law a relation between two parties that is recognized by law, e.g. that of blood, lease, or service. **2** (often foll. by to) the state of being privy (to plans etc.). [ME f. OF priveté f. med.L privitas -tatis f. L privus private]

privy /'prɪvɪ/ adj. & n. —adj. **1** (foll. by to) sharing in the secret of (a person's plans etc.). **2** archaic hidden, secret. —n. (pl. **-ies**) **1** US or archaic a lavatory. **2** Law a person having a part or interest in any action, matter, or thing. □ **privy purse** Brit. **1** an allowance from the public revenue for the monarch's private expenses. **2** the keeper of this. **privy seal** (in the UK) a seal formerly affixed to documents that are afterwards to pass the Great Seal or that do not require it. □□ **privily** adv. [ME f. OF privé f. L privatus PRIVATE]

Privy Council 1 (in the UK) a body of advisers appointed by the sovereign (now chiefly on an honorary basis and including present and former government ministers etc.). (See below.) **2** usu. hist. a sovereign's or governor-general's private counsellors. □ **privy counsellor** (or **councillor**) a private adviser, esp. a member of a Privy Council.

In Britain, the Privy Council originated in the Curia Regis (king's council) of the Norman kings. This took two forms: a large council of the realm (which grew into the parliament), and a select body of officials who met regularly to carry on everyday government, becoming known in the 14th c. as the Privy (= private) Council, with political, judicial, and administrative functions. In the 18th c. the importance of the Cabinet increased and the Privy Council's functions became chiefly formal, except in certain judicial capacities. It now consists of about 300 members, chosen by the sovereign (usually as a personal honour) and includes those who hold or have held high political, legal, or ecclesiastical office in the UK or Commonwealth. It is summoned as a body only to sign the proclamation of the accession of a new sovereign, and when the sovereign announces an intention to marry.

prize¹ /praɪz/ n. & v. —n. **1** something that can be won in a competition or lottery etc. **2** a reward given as a symbol of victory or superiority. **3** something striven for or worth striving for (missed all the great prizes of life). **4** (attrib.) **a** to which a prize is awarded (a prize bull; a prize poem). **b** supremely excellent or outstanding of its kind. —v.tr. value highly (a much prized possession). □ **prize-giving** an award of prizes, esp. formally at a school etc. **prize-money** money offered as a prize. **prize-ring 1** an enclosed area (now usu. a square) for prizefighting. **2** the practice of prizefighting. [(n.) ME, var. of PRICE: (v.) ME f. OF prisstem of preisier PRAISE]

prize² /praɪz/ n. & v. —n. **1** a ship or property captured in naval warfare. **2** a find or windfall. —v.tr. make a prize of. □ **prize-court** a department of an admiralty court concerned with prizes. [ME f. OF prise taking, booty, fem. past part. of prendre f. L prehendere prehens- seize: later identified with PRIZE¹]

prize³ var. of PRISE.

prizefight /'praɪzfaɪt/ n. a boxing-match fought for prize-money. □□ **prizefighter** n.

prizeman /'praɪzmən/ n. (pl. **-men**) a winner of a prize, esp. a specified academic one.

prizewinner /'praɪzˌwɪnə(r)/ n. a winner of a prize. □□ **prizewinning** adj.

PRO abbr. **1** Public Record Office. **2** public relations officer.

pro¹ /prəʊ/ n. & adj. colloq. —n. (pl. **-os**) a professional. —adj. professional. □ **pro-am** involving professionals and amateurs. [abbr.]

pro² /prəʊ/ adj., n., & prep. —adj. (of an argument or reason) for; in favour. —n. (pl. **-os**) a reason or argument for or in favour. —prep. in favour of. □ **pros and cons** reasons or considerations for and against a proposition etc. [L, = for, on behalf of]

pro-¹ /prəʊ/ prefix **1** favouring or supporting (pro-government). **2** acting as a substitute or deputy for (proconsul). **3** forwards (produce). **4** forwards and downwards (prostrate). **5** onwards (proceed; progress). **6** in front of (protect). [L pro in front (of), for, on behalf of, instead of, on account of]

pro-² /prəʊ/ prefix before in time, place, order, etc. (problem; proboscis; prophet). [Gk pro before]

proa /'prəʊə/ n. (also **prau, prahu** /'prɑːuː/) a Malay boat, esp. with a large triangular sail and a canoe-like outrigger. [Malay prāū, prāhū]

proactive /prəʊ'æktɪv/ adj. **1** (of a person, policy, etc.) creating or controlling a situation by taking the initiative. **2** of or relating to mental conditioning or a habit etc. which has been learned. □□ **proaction** /-'ækʃ(ə)n/ n. **proactively** adv. **proactivity** /-'tɪvɪtɪ/ n. [PRO-², after REACTIVE]

probability /ˌprɒbə'bɪlɪtɪ/ n. (pl. **-ies**) **1** the state or condition of being probable. **2** the likelihood of something happening. **3** a probable or most probable event (the probability is that they will come). **4** Math. the extent to which an event is likely to occur, measured by the ratio of the favourable cases to the whole number of cases possible. □ **in all probability** most probably. [F probabilité or L probabilitas (as PROBABLE)]

probable /'prɒbəb(ə)l/ adj. & n. —adj. (often foll. by that + clause) that may be expected to happen or prove true; likely (the probable explanation; it is probable that they forgot). —n. a probable candidate, member of a team, etc. □□ **probably** adv. [ME f. OF f. L probabilis f. probare prove]

proband /'prəʊbænd/ n. a person forming the starting-point for the genetic study of a family etc. [L probandus, gerundive of probare test]

probang /'prəʊbæŋ/ n. Surgery a strip of flexible material with a sponge or button etc. at the end for introducing into the throat. [17th c. (named provang by its inventor): orig. unkn., perh. alt. after probe]

probate /'prəʊbeɪt, -bət/ n. & v. —n. **1** the official proving of a will. **2** a verified copy of a will with a certificate as handed to the executors. —v.tr. US establish the validity of (a will). [ME f. L probatum neut. past part. of probare PROVE]

probation /prə'beɪʃ(ə)n/ n. **1** Law a system of suspending the sentence on an offender subject to a period of good behaviour under supervision. **2** a process or period of testing the character or abilities of a person in a certain role, esp. of a new employee. **3** a moral trial or discipline. □ **on probation** undergoing probation, esp. legal supervision. **probation officer** an official supervising offenders on probation. □□ **probational** adj. **probationary** adj. [ME f. OF probation or L probatio (as PROVE)]

probationer /prə'beɪʃənə(r)/ n. **1** a person on probation, e.g. a newly appointed nurse, teacher, etc. **2** an offender on probation. □□ **probationership** n.

probative /'prəʊbətɪv/ adj. affording proof; evidential. [L probativus (as PROVE)]

probe /prəʊb/ n. & v. —n. **1** a penetrating investigation. **2** any small device, esp. an electrode, for measuring, testing, etc. **3** a blunt-ended surgical instrument usu. of metal for exploring a wound etc. **4** (in full **space probe**) an unmanned exploratory spacecraft transmitting information about its environment. —v.tr. **1** examine or enquire into closely. **2** explore (a wound or part of the body) with a probe. **3** penetrate with a sharp instrument. □□ **probeable** adj. **prober** n. **probingly** adv. [LL proba proof, in med.L = examination, f. L probare test]

probit /'prɒbɪt/ n. Statistics a unit of probability based on deviation from the mean of a standard distribution. [probability unit]

probity /'prəʊbɪtɪ, 'prɒb-/ n. uprightness, honesty. [F probité or L probitas f. probus good]

problem /'prɒbləm/ n. **1** a doubtful or difficult matter requiring a solution (how to prevent it is a problem; the problem of ventilation). **2** something hard to understand or accomplish or deal with. **3** (attrib.) **a** causing problems; difficult to deal with (problem child). **b** (of a play, novel, etc.) in which a social or other problem is treated. **4** a Physics & Math. an inquiry starting from given conditions to investigate or demonstrate a fact, result, or law. **b** Geom. a proposition in which something has to be constructed (cf. THEOREM). **5 a** (in various games, esp. chess) an arrangement of men, cards, etc., in which the solver has to achieve a specified result. **b** a puzzle or question for solution. [ME f. OF probleme or L problema f. Gk problēma -matos f. proballō (as PRO-², ballō throw)]

problematic /ˌprɒblə'mætɪk/ adj. (also **problematical**) **1**

attended by difficulty. **2** doubtful or questionable. **3** *Logic* enunciating or supporting what is possible but not necessarily true. □□ **problematically** *adv*. [F *problématique* or LL *problematicus* f. Gk *problēmatíkos* (as PROBLEM)]

proboscidean /ˌprɒbə'sɪdɪən/ *adj*. & *n*. (also **proboscidian**) —*adj*. **1** having a proboscis. **2** of or like a proboscis. **3** of the mammalian order Proboscidea, including elephants and their extinct allies. —*n*. a mammal of this order. [mod.L *Proboscidea* (as PROBOSCIS)]

proboscis /prəʊ'bɒsɪs/ *n*. **1** the long flexible trunk or snout of some mammals, e.g. an elephant or tapir. **2** the elongated mouth parts of some insects. **3** the sucking organ in some worms. **4** *joc.* the human nose. □ **proboscis monkey** a monkey, *Nasalis larvatus*, native to Borneo, the male of which has a large pendulous nose. □□ **proboscidiferous** /-sɪ'dɪfərəs/ *adj*. **proboscidiform** /-'sɪdɪˌfɔ:m/ *adj*. [L *proboscis -cidis* f. Gk *proboskis* f. *proboskō* (as PRO-², *boskō* feed)]

procaine /'prəʊkeɪn/ *n*. (also **procain**) a synthetic compound used as a local anaesthetic. [PRO-¹ + COCAINE]

procaryote var. of PROKARYOTE.

procedure /prə'si:djə(r), -dʒə(r)/ *n*. **1** a way of proceeding, esp. a mode of conducting business or a legal action. **2** a mode of performing a task. **3** a series of actions conducted in a certain order or manner. **4** a proceeding. **5** *Computing* = SUBROUTINE. □□ **procedural** *adj*. **procedurally** *adv*. [F *procédure* (as PROCEED)]

proceed /prə'si:d, prəʊ-/ *v.intr.* **1** (often foll. by *to*) go forward or on further; make one's way. **2** (often foll. by *with*, or *to* + infin.) continue; go on with an activity (*proceeded with their work*; *proceeded to tell the whole story*). **3** (of an action) be carried on or continued (*the case will now proceed*). **4** adopt a course of action (*how shall we proceed?*). **5** go on to say. **6** (foll. by *against*) start a lawsuit (against a person). **7** (often foll. by *from*) come forth or originate (*shouts proceeded from the bedroom*). **8** (foll. by *to*) *Brit.* take the degree of (MA etc.). [ME f. OF *proceder* f. L *procedere* process- (as PRO-¹, *cedere* go)]

proceeding /prə'si:dɪŋ/ *n*. **1** an action or piece of conduct (*a high-handed proceeding*). **2** (in *pl*.) (in full **legal proceedings**) an action at law; a lawsuit. **3** (in *pl*.) a published report of discussions or a conference.

proceeds /'prəʊsi:dz/ *n.pl.* money produced by a transaction or other undertaking. [pl. of obs. *proceed* (n.) f. PROCEED]

process¹ /'prəʊses/ *n*. & *v*. —*n*. **1** a course of action or proceeding, esp. a series of stages in manufacture or some other operation. **2** the progress or course of something (*in process of construction*). **3** a natural or involuntary operation or series of changes (*the process of growing old*). **4** an action at law; a summons or writ. **5** *Anat., Zool.*, & *Bot.* a natural appendage or outgrowth on an organism. —*v.tr.* **1** handle or deal with by a particular process. **2** treat (food, esp. to prevent decay) (*processed cheese*). **3** *Computing* operate on (data) by means of a program. □ **in process of time** as time goes on. **process server** a sheriff's officer who serves writs. □□ **processable** *adj*. [ME f. OF *proces* f. L *processus* (as PROCEED)]

process² /prəʊ'ses/ *v.intr.* walk in procession. [back-form. f. PROCESSION]

procession /prə'seʃ(ə)n/ *n*. **1** a number of people or vehicles etc. moving forward in orderly succession, esp. at a ceremony, demonstration, or festivity. **2** the movement of such a group (*go in procession*). **3** a race in which no competitor is able to overtake another. **4** *Theol.* the emanation of the Holy Spirit. □□ **processionist** *n*. [ME f. OF f. L *processio -onis* (as PROCEED)]

processional /prə'seʃən(ə)l/ *adj*. & *n*. —*adj*. **1** of processions. **2** used, carried, or sung in processions. —*n*. *Eccl.* an office-book of processional hymns etc. [med.L *processionalis* (adj.), *-ale* (n.) (as PROCESSION)]

processor /'prəʊsesə(r)/ *n*. a machine that processes things, esp.: **1** = *central processor*. **2** = *food processor*.

procès-verbal /ˌprɒseɪvɜ:'ba:l/ *n*. (pl. **procès-verbaux** /-'bəʊ/) a written report of proceedings; minutes. [F]

prochronism /'prəʊkrəˌnɪz(ə)m/ *n*. the action of referring an event etc. to an earlier date than the true one. [PRO-² + Gk *khronos* time]

proclaim /prə'kleɪm/ *v.tr.* **1** (often foll. by *that* + clause) announce or declare publicly or officially. **2** declare (a person) to be (a king, traitor, etc.). **3** reveal as being (*an accent that proclaims you a Scot*). □□ **proclaimer** *n*. **proclamation** /ˌprɒklə'meɪʃ(ə)n/ *n*. **proclamatory** /-'klæmətərɪ/ *adj*. [ME *proclame* f. L *proclamare* cry out (as PRO-¹, CLAIM)]

proclitic /prə'klɪtɪk/ *adj*. & *n*. *Gram.* —*adj*. (of a monosyllable) closely attached in pronunciation to a following word and having itself no accent. —*n*. such a word, e.g. *at* in *at home*. □□ **proclitically** *adv*. [mod.L *procliticus* f. Gk *proklinō* lean forward, after LL *encliticus*: see ENCLITIC]

proclivity /prə'klɪvɪtɪ/ *n*. (pl. **-ies**) a tendency or inclination. [L *proclivitas* f. *proclivis* inclined (as PRO-¹, *clivus* slope)]

Procne /'prɒknɪ/ *Gk Mythol.* the sister of Philomel (see entry).

proconsul /prəʊ'kɒns(ə)l/ *n*. **1** *Rom.Hist.* a governor of a province, in the later republic usu. an ex-consul. **2** a governor of a modern colony etc. **3** a deputy consul. □□ **proconsular** /-sjʊlə(r)/ *adj*. **proconsulate** /-sjʊlət/ *n*. **proconsulship** *n*. [ME f. L, earlier *pro consule* (one acting) for the consul]

Procopius /prə'kəʊpɪəs/ (born *c*.500), Byzantine Greek historian from Caesarea in Palestine, who accompanied Justinian's general Belisarius on his compaigns between 527 and 540. In 562 he was made Prefect of the city of Constantinople. His principal works are the *History of the Wars of Justinian*, written from first-hand experience, and *On Justinian's Buildings*, which is panegyric in tone and contains lucid architectural descriptions. The authenticity of another work, the *Secret History*, has often been doubted but is now generally accepted; it is a virulent attack on the whole policy of Justinian, based on court gossip, and also contains scurrilous comments on the dubious morals of the empress Theodora.

procrastinate /prəʊ'kræstɪˌneɪt/ *v.intr.* defer action; be dilatory. ¶ Often confused with *prevaricate*. □□ **procrastination** /-'neɪʃ(ə)n/ *n*. **procrastinative** /-nətɪv/ *adj*. **procrastinator** *n*. **procrastinatory** *adj*. [L *procrastinare procrastinat-* (as PRO-¹, *crastinus* of tomorrow f. *cras* tomorrow)]

procreate /'prəʊkrɪˌeɪt/ *v.tr.* (often *absol.*) bring (offspring) into existence by the natural process of reproduction. □□ **procreant** /'prəʊkrɪənt/ *adj*. **procreative** *adj*. **procreation** /-'eɪʃ(ə)n/ *n*. **procreator** *n*. [L *procreare procreat-* (as PRO-¹, *creare* create)]

Procrustean /prəʊ'krʌstɪən/ *adj*. seeking to enforce uniformity by forceful or ruthless methods. [PROCRUSTES]

Procrustes /prəʊ'krʌsti:z/ *Gk legend* a robber who forced travellers to lie on a bed and made them fit it by stretching their limbs or cutting bits off. Theseus killed him in like manner. [Gk, *Prokroustēs*, lit. stretcher, f. *prokrouō* beat out.]

proctology /prɒk'tɒlədʒɪ/ *n*. the branch of medicine concerned with the anus and rectum. □□ **proctological** /-tə'lɒdʒɪk(ə)l/ *adj*. **proctologist** *n*. [Gk *prōktos* anus + -LOGY]

proctor /'prɒktə(r)/ *n*. **1** *Brit.* an officer (usu. one of two) at certain universities, appointed annually and having mainly disciplinary functions. **2** *US* a supervisor of students in an examination etc. **3** *Law* a person managing causes in a court (now chiefly ecclesiastical) that administers civil or canon law. **4** a representative of the clergy in the Church of England convocation. □ **Queen's** (or **King's**) **Proctor** (in the UK) an official who has the right to intervene in probate, divorce, and nullity cases when collusion or the suppression of facts is alleged. □□ **proctorial** /-'tɔ:rɪəl/ *adj*. **proctorship** *n*. [ME, syncopation of PROCURATOR]

proctoscope /'prɒktəˌskəʊp/ *n*. a medical instrument for inspecting the rectum. [Gk *prōktos* anus + -SCOPE]

procumbent /prə'kʌmbənt/ *adj*. **1** lying on the face; prostrate. **2** *Bot.* growing along the ground. [L *procumbere* fall forwards (as PRO-¹, *cumbere* lay oneself)]

procuration /ˌprɒkjʊ'reɪʃ(ə)n/ *n*. **1** *formal* the action of procuring, obtaining, or bringing about. **2** the function or an authorized action of an attorney. [ME f. OF *procuration* or L *procuratio* (as PROCURE)]

procurator /'prɒkjʊˌreɪtə(r)/ *n*. **1** an agent or proxy, esp. one who has power of attorney. **2** *Rom.Hist.* a treasury officer in an imperial province. □ **procurator fiscal** an officer of a sheriff's court in Scotland, acting as public prosecutor of a district and with other duties similar to those of a coroner. □□ **procuratorial** /-rə'tɔːrɪəl/ adj. **procuratorship** n. [ME f. OF pro-curateur or L procurator administrator, finance-agent (as PROCURE)]

procure /prə'kjʊə(r)/ v.tr. **1** obtain, esp. by care or effort; acquire (managed to procure a copy). **2** bring about (procured their dismissal). **3** (also absol.) obtain (women) for prostitution. □□ **procurable** adj. **procural** n. **procurement** n. [ME f. OF procurer f. L procurare take care of, manage (as PRO-[1], curare see to)]

procurer /prə'kjʊərə(r)/ n. (fem. **procuress** /-rɪs/) a person who obtains women for prostitution. [ME f. AF procurour, OF procureur f. L procurator: see PROCURATOR]

prod /prɒd/ v. & n. —v. (**prodded, prodding**) **1** tr. poke with the finger or a pointed object. **2** tr. stimulate to action. **3** intr. (foll. by at) make a prodding motion. —n. **1** a poke or thrust. **2** a stimulus to action. **3** a pointed instrument. □□ **prodder** n. [16th c.: perh. imit.]

prodigal /'prɒdɪg(ə)l/ adj. & n. —adj. **1** recklessly wasteful. **2** (foll. by of) lavish. —n. **1** a prodigal person. **2** (in full **prodigal son**) a repentant wastrel, returned wanderer, etc. (Luke 15: 11–32). □□ **prodigality** /-'gælɪtɪ/ n. **prodigally** adv. [med.L pro-digalis f. L prodigus lavish]

prodigious /prə'dɪdʒəs/ adj. **1** marvellous or amazing. **2** enormous. **3** abnormal. □□ **prodigiously** adv. **prodigiousness** n. [L prodigiosus (as PRODIGY)]

prodigy /'prɒdɪdʒɪ/ n. (pl. **-ies**) **1** a person endowed with exceptional qualities or abilities, esp. a precocious child. **2** a marvellous thing, esp. one out of the ordinary course of nature. **3** (foll. by of) a wonderful example (of a quality). [L prodigium portent]

prodrome /'prəʊdrəʊm, 'prɒdrəʊm/ n. **1** a preliminary book or treatise. **2** Med. a premonitory symptom. □□ **prodromal** /'prɒdrəʊm(ə)l/ adj. **prodromic** /prə'drɒmɪk/ adj. [F f. mod.L f. Gk prodromos precursor (as PRO-[2], dromos running)]

produce v. & n. —v.tr. /prə'djuːs/ **1** bring forward for consideration, inspection, or use (will produce evidence). **2** manufacture (goods) from raw materials etc. **3** bear or yield (offspring, fruit, a harvest, etc.). **4** bring into existence. **5** cause or bring about (a reaction, sensation, etc.). **6** Geom. extend or continue (a line). **7 a** bring (a play, performer, book, etc.) before the public. **b** supervise the production of (a film, broadcast, etc.). —n. /'prɒdjuːs/ **1 a** what is produced, esp. agricultural and natural products collectively (dairy produce). **b** an amount of this. **2** (often foll. by of) a result (of labour, efforts, etc.). **3** a yield, esp. in the assay of ore. □□ **producible** /prə'djuːsɪb(ə)l/ adj. **producibility** /prə,djuːsɪ'bɪlɪtɪ/ n. [ME f. L producere (as PRO-[1], ducere duct- lead)]

producer /prə'djuːsə(r)/ n. **1** Econ. a person who produces goods or commodities. **2 a** a person generally responsible for the production of a film or play (apart from the direction of the acting). **b** Brit. the director of a play or broadcast programme. □ **producer gas** a combustible gas formed by passing air, or air and steam, through red-hot carbon.

product /'prɒdʌkt/ n. **1** a thing or substance produced by natural process or manufacture. **2** a result (the product of their labours). **3** Math. a quantity obtained by multiplying quantities together. [ME f. L productum, neut. past part. of producere PRODUCE]

production /prə'dʌkʃ(ə)n/ n. **1** the act or an instance of producing; the process of being produced. **2** the process of being manufactured, esp. in large quantities (go into production). **3** a total yield. **4** a thing produced, esp. a literary or artistic work, a film, play, etc. □ **production line** a systematized sequence of mechanical or manual operations involved in producing a commodity. □□ **productional** n. [ME f. OF f. L productio -onis (as PRODUCT)]

productive /prə'dʌktɪv/ adj. **1** of or engaged in the production of goods. **2** producing much (productive soil; a productive writer). **3** Econ. producing commodities of exchangeable value (productive labour). **4** (foll. by of) producing or giving rise to (productive of

great annoyance). □□ **productively** adv. **productiveness** n. [F productif -ive or LL productivus (as PRODUCT)]

productivity /,prɒdʌk'tɪvɪtɪ/ n. **1** the capacity to produce. **2** the quality or state of being productive. **3** the effectiveness of productive effort, esp. in industry. **4** production per unit of effort.

proem /'prəʊɪm/ n. **1** a preface or preamble to a book or speech. **2** a beginning or prelude. □□ **proemial** /-'iːmɪəl/ adj. [ME f. OF proeme or L prooemium f. Gk prooimion prelude (as PRO-[2], oimē song)]

Prof. abbr. Professor.

prof /prɒf/ n. colloq. a professor. [abbr.]

profane /prə'feɪn/ adj. & v. —adj. **1** not belonging to what is sacred or biblical; secular. **2** irreverent, blasphemous. **3** (of a rite etc.) heathen. **4** not initiated into religious rites or any esoteric knowledge. —v.tr. **1** treat (a sacred thing) with irreverence or disregard. **2** violate or pollute (what is entitled to respect). □□ **profanation** /,prɒfə'neɪʃ(ə)n/ n. **profanely** adv. **profaneness** n. **profaner** n. [ME prophane f. OF prophane or med.L prophanus f. L profanus before (i.e. outside) the temple, not sacred (as PRO-[1], fanum temple)]

profanity /prə'fænɪtɪ/ n. (pl. **-ies**) **1** a profane act. **2** profane language; blasphemy. [LL profanitas (as PROFANE)]

profess /prə'fes/ v. **1** tr. claim openly to have (a quality or feeling). **2** tr. (foll. by to + infin.) pretend. **3** tr. declare (profess ignorance). **4** tr. affirm one's faith in or allegiance to. **5** tr. receive into a religious order under vows. **6** tr. have as one's profession or business. **7 a** tr. teach (a subject) as a professor. **b** intr. perform the duties of a professor. [ME f. L profitērī profess- declare publicly (as PRO-[1], fatērī confess)]

professed /prə'fest/ adj. **1** self-acknowledged (a professed Christian). **2** alleged, ostensible. **3** claiming to be duly qualified. **4** (of a monk or nun) having taken the vows of a religious order. □□ **professedly** /-sɪdlɪ/ adv. (in senses 1, 2).

profession /prə'feʃ(ə)n/ n. **1** a vocation or calling, esp. one that involves some branch of advanced learning or science (the medical profession). **2** a body of people engaged in a profession. **3** a declaration or avowal. **4** a declaration of belief in a religion. **5 a** the declaration or vows made on entering a religious order. **b** the ceremony or fact of being professed in a religious order. □ **the oldest profession** colloq. or joc. prostitution. □□ **professionless** adj. [ME f. OF f. L professio -onis (as PROFESS)]

professional /prə'feʃən(ə)l/ adj. & n. —adj. **1** of or belonging to or connected with a profession. **2 a** having or showing the skill of a professional; competent. **b** worthy of a professional (professional conduct). **3** engaged in a specified activity as one's main paid occupation (cf. AMATEUR) (a professional boxer). **4** derog. engaged in a specified activity regarded with disfavour (a professional agitator). —n. a professional person. □ **professional foul** a deliberate foul in football etc., esp. to prevent an opponent from scoring. □□ **professionally** adv.

professionalism /prə'feʃənə,lɪz(ə)m/ n. the qualities or typical features of a profession or of professionals, esp. competence, skill, etc. □□ **professionalize** v.tr. (also **-ise**).

professor /prə'fesə(r)/ n. **1 a** (often as a title) a university academic of the highest rank; the holder of a university chair. **b** US a university teacher. **2** a person who professes a religion. □□ **professorate** n. **professorial** /,prɒfɪ'sɔːrɪəl/ adj. **professorially** /,prɒfɪ'sɔːrɪəlɪ/ adv. **professoriate** /,prɒfɪ'sɔːrɪət/ n. **professorship** n. [ME f. OF professeur or L professor (as PROFESS)]

proffer /'prɒfə(r)/ v. & n. —v.tr. (esp. as **proffered** adj.) offer (a gift, services, a hand, etc.). —n. literary an offer or proposal. [ME f. AF & OF proffrir (as PRO-[1], offrir OFFER)]

proficient /prə'fɪʃ(ə)nt/ adj. & n. —adj. (often foll. by in, at) adept, expert. —n. a person who is proficient. □□ **proficiency** /-sɪ/ n. **proficiently** adv. [L proficiens proficient- (as PROFIT)]

profile /'prəʊfaɪl/ n. & v. —n. **1 a** an outline (esp. of a human face) as seen from one side. **b** a representation of this. **2** a short biographical or character sketch. **3** Statistics a representation by a graph or chart of information (esp. on certain characteristics) recorded in a quantified form. **4** a characteristic personal manner or attitude. **5** a vertical cross-section of a structure. **6** a flat outline piece of scenery on stage. —*v.tr.* **1** represent in profile. **2** give a profile to. □ **in profile** as seen from one side. **keep a low profile** remain inconspicuous. □□ **profiler** *n.* **profilist** *n.* [obs. It. *profilo, profilare* (as PRO-¹, *filare* spin f. L *filare* f. *filum* thread)]

profit /ˈprɒfɪt/ *n.* & *v.* —*n.* **1** an advantage or benefit. **2** financial gain; excess of returns over outlay. —*v.* (**profited, profiting**) **1** *tr.* (also *absol.*) be beneficial to. **2** *intr.* obtain an advantage or benefit (*profited by the experience*). □ **at a profit** with financial gain. **profit and loss account** an account in which gains are credited and losses debited so as to show the net profit or loss at any time. **profit margin** the profit remaining in a business after costs have been deducted. **profit-sharing** the sharing of profits esp. between employer and employees. **profit-taking** the sale of shares etc. at a time when profit will accrue. □□ **profitless** *adj.* [ME f. OF f. L *profectus* progress, profit f. *proficere* *profect-* advance (as PRO-¹, *facere* do)]

profitable /ˈprɒfɪtəb(ə)l/ *adj.* **1** yielding profit; lucrative. **2** beneficial; useful. □□ **profitability** /-ˈbɪlɪtɪ/ *n.* **profitableness** *n.* **profitably** *adv.* [ME f. OF (as PROFIT)]

profiteer /ˌprɒfɪˈtɪə(r)/ *v.* & *n.* —*v.intr.* make or seek to make excessive profits, esp. illegally or in black market conditions. —*n.* a person who profiteers.

profiterole /prəˈfɪtərəʊl/ *n.* a small hollow case of choux pastry usu. filled with cream and covered with chocolate sauce. [F, dimin. of *profit* PROFIT]

profligate /ˈprɒflɪɡət/ *adj.* & *n.* —*adj.* **1** licentious; dissolute. **2** recklessly extravagant. —*n.* a profligate person. □□ **profligacy** /-ɡəsɪ/ *n.* **profligately** *adv.* [L *profligatus* dissolute, past part. of *profligare* overthrow, ruin (as PRO-¹, *fligere* strike down)]

pro forma /prəʊ ˈfɔːmə/ *adv., adj.,* & *n.* —*adv.* & *adj.* as or being a matter of form. —*n.* (in full **pro-forma invoice**) an invoice sent in advance of goods supplied. [L]

profound /prəˈfaʊnd/ *adj.* & *n.* —*adj.* (**profounder, profoundest**) **1 a** having or showing great knowledge or insight (*a profound treatise*). **b** demanding deep study or thought (*profound doctrines*). **2** (of a state or quality) deep, intense, unqualified (*a profound sleep; profound indifference*). **3** at or extending to a great depth (*profound crevasses*). **4** (of a sigh) deep-drawn. **5** (of a disease) deep-seated. —*n.* (prec. by *the*) *poet.* the vast depth (of the ocean, soul, etc.). □□ **profoundly** *adv.* **profoundness** *n.* **profundity** /prəˈfʌndɪtɪ/ *n.* (*pl.* -**ies**). [ME f. AF & OF *profund, profond* f. L *profundus* deep (as PRO-¹, *fundus* bottom)]

profuse /prəˈfjuːs/ *adj.* **1** (often foll. by *in, of*) lavish; extravagant (*was profuse in her generosity*). **2** (of a thing) exuberantly plentiful; abundant (*profuse bleeding; a profuse variety*). □□ **profusely** *adv.* **profuseness** *n.* **profusion** /prəˈfjuːʒ(ə)n/ *n.* [ME f. L *profusus* past part. of *profundere profus-* (as PRO-¹, *fundere fus-* pour)]

progenitive /prəʊˈdʒenɪtɪv/ *adj.* capable of or connected with the production of offspring.

progenitor /prəʊˈdʒenɪtə(r)/ *n.* **1** the ancestor of a person, animal, or plant. **2** a political or intellectual predecessor. **3** the origin of a copy. □□ **progenitorial** /-ˈtɔːrɪəl/ *adj.* **progenitorship** *n.* [ME f. OF *progeniteur* f. L *progenitor -oris* f. *progignere progenit-* (as PRO-¹, *gignere* beget)]

progeniture /prəʊˈdʒenɪtjʊə(r)/ *n.* **1** the act or an instance of procreation. **2** young, offspring.

progeny /ˈprɒdʒɪnɪ/ *n.* **1** the offspring of a person or other organism. **2** a descendant or descendants. **3** an outcome or issue. [ME f. OF *progenie* f. L *progenies* f. *progignere* (as PROGENITOR)]

progesterone /prəʊˈdʒestəˌrəʊn/ *n.* a steroid hormone released by the corpus luteum which stimulates the preparation of the uterus for pregnancy (see also PROGESTOGEN). [*progestin* (as PRO-², GESTATION) + *luteosterone* f. CORPUS LUTEUM + STEROL]

progestogen /prəʊˈdʒestədʒɪn/ *n.* **1** any of a group of steroid hormones (including progesterone) that maintain pregnancy and prevent further ovulation during it. **2** a similar hormone produced synthetically.

proglottis /prəʊˈɡlɒtɪs/ *n.* (*pl.* **proglottides** /-ˌdiːz/) each segment in the strobile of a tapeworm that contains a complete reproductive system. [mod.L f. Gk *proglōssis* (as PRO-², *glōssis* f. *glōssa, glōtta* tongue), from its shape]

prognathous /prɒɡˈneɪθəs, ˈprɒɡnəθəs/ *adj.* **1** having a projecting jaw. **2** (of a jaw) projecting. □□ **prognathic** /prɒɡˈnæθɪk/ *adj.* **prognathism** *n.* [PRO-² + Gk *gnathos* jaw]

prognosis /prɒɡˈnəʊsɪs/ *n.* (*pl.* **prognoses** /-siːz/) **1** a forecast; a prognostication. **2** a forecast of the course of a disease. [LL f. Gk *prognōsis* (as PRO-², *gignōskō* know)]

prognostic /prɒɡˈnɒstɪk/ *n.* & *adj.* —*n.* **1** (often foll. by *of*) an advance indication or omen, esp. of the course of a disease etc. **2** a prediction; a forecast. —*adj.* foretelling; predictive (*prognostic of a good result*). □□ **prognostically** *adv.* [ME f. OF *pronostique* f. L *prognosticum* f. Gk *prognōstikon* neut. of *prognōstikos* (as PROGNOSIS)]

prognosticate /prɒɡˈnɒstɪˌkeɪt/ *v.tr.* **1** (often foll. by *that* + clause) foretell; foresee; prophesy. **2** (of a thing) betoken; indicate (future events etc.). □□ **prognosticable** /-kəb(ə)l/ *adj.* **prognostication** /-ˈkeɪʃ(ə)n/ *n.* **prognosticative** /-kətɪv/ *adj.* **prognosticator** *n.* **prognosticatory** *adj.* [med.L *prognosticare* (as PROGNOSTIC)]

programme /ˈprəʊɡræm/ *n.* & *v.* (*US* **program**) —*n.* **1** a usu. printed list of a series of events, performers, etc. at a public function etc. **2** a radio or television broadcast. **3** a plan of future events (*the programme is dinner and an early night*). **4** a course or series of studies, lectures, etc.; a syllabus. **5** (usu. **program**) a series of coded instructions to control the operation of a computer or other machine. —*v.tr.* (**programmed, programming;** *US* **programed, programing**) **1** make a programme or definite plan of. **2** (usu. **program**) express (a problem) or instruct (a computer) by means of a program. □ **programme music** a piece of music intended to tell a story, evoke images, etc. □□ **programmable** *adj.* **programmability** /-ˈbɪlɪtɪ/ *n.* **programmatic** /-ɡrəˈmætɪk/ *adj.* **programmatically** /-ɡrəˈmætɪkəlɪ/ *adv.* **programmer** *n.* [LL *programma* f. Gk *programma -atos* f. *prographō* write publicly (as PRO-², *graphō* write): spelling after F *programme*]

progress /ˈprəʊɡres/ *n.* & *v.* —*n.* **1** forward or onward movement towards a destination. **2** advance or development towards completion, betterment, etc.; improvement (*has made little progress this term; the progress of civilization*). **3** *Brit. archaic* a State journey or official tour, esp. by royalty. —*v.* **1** *intr.* /prəˈɡres/ move or be moved forward or onward; continue (*the argument is progressing*). **2** *intr.* /prəˈɡres/ advance or develop towards completion, improvement, etc. (*science progresses*). **3** *tr.* cause (work etc.) to make regular progress. □ **in progress** in the course of developing; going on. **progress-chaser** a person employed to check the regular progress of manufacturing work. **progress report** an account of progress made. [ME f. L *progressus* f. *progredi* (as PRO-¹, *gradi* walk: (v.) readopted f. US after becoming obs. in Brit. use in the 17th c.]

progression /prəˈɡreʃ(ə)n/ *n.* **1** the act or an instance of progressing (*a mode of progression*). **2** a succession; a series. **3** *Math.* **a** = *arithmetic progression.* **b** = *geometric progression.* **c** = *harmonic progression.* **4** *Mus.* passing from one note or chord to another. □□ **progressional** *adj.* [ME f. OF *progression* or L *progressio* (as PROGRESS)]

progressionist /prəˈɡreʃənɪst/ *n.* **1** an advocate of or believer in esp. political or social progress. **2** a person who believes in the theory of gradual progression to higher forms of life.

progressive /prəˈɡresɪv/ *adj.* & *n.* —*adj.* **1** moving forward (*progressive motion*). **2** proceeding step by step; cumulative (*progressive drug use*). **3 a** (of a political party, government, etc.) favouring or implementing rapid progress or social reform. **b** modern; efficient (*this is a progressive company*). **4** (of disease, violence, etc.) increasing in severity or extent. **5** (of taxation) at rates increasing with the sum taxed. **6** (of a card-game, dance, etc.) with periodic changes of partners. **7** *Gram.* (of an aspect) expressing an action in progress, e.g. *am writing, was writing.* **8** (of education) informal and without strict discipline, stressing individual needs. —*n.* (also **Progressive**) an advocate of progressive political policies. □□ **progressively** *adv.* **progressiveness** *n.* **progressivism** *n.* **progressivist** *n.* & *adj.* [F *progressif -ive* or med.L *progressivus* (as PROGRESS)]

pro hac vice /ˌprəʊ hɑːk ˈvaɪsɪ/ *adv.* for this occasion (only). [L]

prohibit /prəˈhɪbɪt/ *v.tr.* (**prohibited, prohibiting**) (often foll.

by *from* + verbal noun) **1** formally forbid, esp. by authority. **2** prevent; make impossible (*his accident prohibits him from playing football*). □ **prohibited degrees** degrees of blood relationship within which marriage is forbidden. □□ **prohibiter** *n.* **prohibitor** *n.* [ME f. L *prohibēre* (as PRO-¹, *habēre* hold)]

prohibition /ˌprəʊhɪˈbɪʃ(ə)n, ˌprəʊɪˈb-/ *n.* **1** the act or an instance of forbidding; a state of being forbidden. **2** *Law* **a** an edict or order that forbids. **b** a writ from a superior court forbidding an inferior court from proceeding in a suit deemed to be beyond its cognizance. **3** (usu. **Prohibition**) the prevention by law of the manufacture and sale of alcohol, esp. as established in the US from 1920, after a long campaign, by the 18th Amendment to the Constitution, and repealed in 1933 by the 21st Amendment. □□ **prohibitionary** *adj.* **prohibitionist** *n.* [ME f. OF *prohibition* or L *prohibitio* (as PROHIBIT)]

prohibitive /prəʊˈhɪbɪtɪv/ *adj.* **1** prohibiting. **2** (of prices, taxes, etc.) so high as to prevent purchase, use, abuse, etc. (*published at a prohibitive price*). □□ **prohibitively** *adv.* **prohibitiveness** *n.* **prohibitory** *adj.* [F *prohibitif* *-ive* or L *prohibitivus* (as PROHIBIT)]

project *n.* & *v.* —*n.* /ˈprɒdʒekt/ **1** a plan; a scheme. **2** a planned undertaking. **3** a usu. long-term task undertaken by a student to be submitted for assessment. —*v.* /prəˈdʒekt/ **1** *tr.* plan or contrive (a course of action, scheme, etc.). **2** *intr.* protrude; jut out. **3** *tr.* throw; cast; impel (*projected the stone into the water*). **4** *tr.* extrapolate (results etc.) to a future time; forecast (*I project that we shall produce two million next year*). **5** *tr.* cause (light, shadow, images, etc.) to fall on a surface, screen, etc. **6** *tr.* cause (a sound, esp. the voice) to be heard at a distance. **7** *tr.* (often *refl.* or *absol.*) express or promote (oneself or a positive image) forcefully or effectively. **8** *tr. Geom.* **a** draw straight lines from a centre or parallel lines through every point of (a given figure) to produce a corresponding figure on a surface or a line by intersecting it. **b** draw (such lines). **c** produce (such a corresponding figure). **9** *tr.* make a projection of (the earth, sky, etc.). **10** *tr. Psychol.* **a** (also *absol.*) attribute (an emotion etc.) to an external object or person, esp. unconsciously. **b** (*refl.*) project (oneself) into another's feelings, the future, etc. [ME f. L *projectum* neut. past part. of *projicere* (as PRO-¹, *jacère* throw)]

projectile /prəˈdʒektaɪl/ *n.* & *adj.* —*n.* **1** a missile, esp. fired by a rocket. **2** a bullet, shell, etc. fired from a gun. **3** any object thrown as a weapon. —*adj.* **1** capable of being projected by force, esp. from a gun. **2** projecting or impelling. [mod.L *projectilis* (adj.), *-ile* (n.) (as PROJECT)]

projection /prəˈdʒekʃ(ə)n/ *n.* **1** the act or an instance of projecting; the process of being projected. **2** a thing that projects or obtrudes. **3** the presentation of an image etc. on a surface or screen. **4** **a** a forecast or estimate based on present trends (*a projection of next year's profits*). **b** this process. **5** **a** a mental image or preoccupation viewed as an objective reality. **b** the unconscious transfer of one's own impressions or feelings to external objects or persons. **6** *Geom.* the act or an instance of projecting a figure. **7** the representation on a plane surface of any part of the surface of the earth or a celestial sphere (*Mercator projection*). □□ **projectionist** *n.* (in sense 3). [L *projectio* (as PROJECT)]

projective /prəˈdʒektɪv/ *adj.* **1** *Geom.* **a** relating to or derived by projection. **b** (of a property of a figure) unchanged by projection. **2** *Psychol.* mentally projecting or projected (*a projective imagination*). □ **projective geometry** the study of the projective properties of geometric figures. □□ **projectively** *adv.*

projector /prəˈdʒektə(r)/ *n.* **1** **a** an apparatus containing a source of light and a system of lenses for projecting slides or film on to a screen. **b** an apparatus for projecting rays of light. **2** a person who forms or promotes a project. **3** *archaic* a promoter of speculative companies.

prokaryote /prəʊˈkærɪət/ *n.* (also **procaryote**) an organism in which the chromosomes are not separated from the cytoplasm by a membrane; a bacterium (cf. EUKARYOTE). □□ **prokaryotic** /-ˈɒtɪk/ *adj.* [PRO-² + KARYO- + *-ote* as in ZYGOTE]

Prokofiev /prəˈkɒfɪˌef/, Sergei Sergeevich (1891–1953), Russian composer. His gifts as a composer revealed themselves early, together with a talent for iconoclasm which brought him both fame and a certain notoriety. The wit and vigour of his opera *The Love for Three Oranges* (1921), and the *Lieutenant Kijé* suite (1934), stand in contrast to the opera *War and Peace* (begun 1941), the later symphonies including the deeply pessimistic Sixth (1945–7), and the romantic and widely popular ballet music for *Romeo and Juliet* (1935–6). *Peter and the Wolf* (1936) is perhaps his best-known work, an enduring, touching, and instructive young persons' guide to the orchestra.

prolactin /prəʊˈlæktɪn/ *n.* a hormone released from the anterior pituitary gland that stimulates milk production after childbirth. [PRO-¹ + LACTATION]

prolapse /ˈprəʊlæps/ *n.* & *v.* —*n.* (also **prolapsus** /-ˈlæpsəs/) **1** the forward or downward displacement of a part or organ. **2** the prolapsed part or organ, esp. the womb or rectum. —*v.intr.* undergo prolapse. [L *prolabi prolaps-* (as PRO-¹, *labi* slip)]

prolate /ˈprəʊleɪt/ *adj.* **1** *Geom.* (of a spheroid) lengthened in the direction of a polar diameter (cf. OBLATE²). **2** growing or extending in width. **3** widely spread. **4** *Gram.* = PROLATIVE. □□ **prolately** *adv.* [L *prolatus* past part. of *proferre* prolong (as PRO-¹, *ferre* carry)]

prolative /prəˈleɪtɪv/ *adj. Gram.* serving to continue or complete a predication, e.g. *go* (prolative infinitive) in *you may go*.

prole /prəʊl/ *adj.* & *n. derog. colloq.* —*adj.* proletarian. —*n.* a proletarian. [abbr.]

proleg /ˈprəʊleg/ *n.* a fleshy abdominal limb of a caterpillar or other larva. [PRO-¹ + LEG]

prolegomenon /ˌprəʊlɪˈɡɒmɪnən/ *n.* (*pl.* **prolegomena**) (usu. in *pl.*) an introduction or preface to a book etc., esp. when critical or discursive. □□ **prolegomenary** *adj.* **prolegomenous** *adj.* [L f. Gk, neut. passive pres. part. of *prolegō* (as PRO-², *legō* say)]

prolepsis /prəʊˈlepsɪs, -ˈliːpsɪs/ *n.* (*pl.* **prolepses** /-siːz/) **1** the anticipation and answering of possible objections in rhetorical speech. **2** anticipation. **3** the representation of a thing as existing before it actually does or did so, as in *he was a dead man when he entered*. **4** *Gram.* the anticipatory use of adjectives, as in *paint the town red*. □□ **proleptic** *adj.* [LL f. Gk *prolēpsis* f. *prolambanō* anticipate (as PRO-², *lambanō* take)]

proletarian /ˌprəʊlɪˈteərɪən/ *adj.* & *n.* —*adj.* of or concerning the proletariat. —*n.* a member of the proletariat. □□ **proletarianism** *n.* **proletarianize** *v.tr.* (also **-ise**). [L *proletarius* one who served the State not with property but with offspring (*proles*)]

proletariat /ˌprəʊlɪˈteərɪət/ *n.* (also **proletariate**) **1** **a** *Econ.* wage-earners collectively, esp. those without capital and dependent on selling their labour. **b** esp. *derog.* the lowest class of the community, esp. when considered as uncultured. **2** *Rom.Hist.* the lowest class of citizens. [F *prolétariat* (as PROLETARIAN)]

pro-life /prəʊˈlaɪf/ *adj.* in favour of preserving life, esp. in opposing abortion.

proliferate /prəˈlɪfəˌreɪt/ *v.* **1** *intr.* reproduce; increase rapidly in numbers; grow by multiplication. **2** *tr.* produce (cells etc.) rapidly. □□ **proliferation** /-ˈreɪʃ(ə)n/ *n.* **proliferative** /-rətɪv/ *adj.* [back-form. f. proliferation f. F *prolifération* f. *prolifère* f. PROLIFEROUS)]

proliferous /prəˈlɪfərəs/ *adj.* **1** (of a plant) producing many leaf or flower buds; growing luxuriantly. **2** growing or multiplying by budding. **3** spreading by proliferation. [L *proles* offspring + -FEROUS]

prolific /prəˈlɪfɪk/ *adj.* **1** producing many offspring or much output. **2** (often foll. by *of*) abundantly productive. **3** (often foll. by *in*) abounding, copious. □□ **prolificacy** *n.* **prolifically** *adv.* **prolificness** *n.* [med.L *prolificus* (as PROLIFEROUS)]

prolix /ˈprəʊlɪks, prəˈlɪks/ *adj.* (of speech, writing, etc.) lengthy; tedious. □□ **prolixity** /-ˈlɪksɪtɪ/ *n.* **prolixly** *adv.* [ME f. OF *prolixe* or L *prolixus* poured forth, extended (as PRO-¹, *liquēre* be liquid)]

prolocutor /prəʊləˈkjuːtə(r), prəˈlɒk-/ *n.* **1** *Eccl.* the chairperson esp. of the lower house of convocation of either province of the Church of England. **2** a spokesman. □□ **prolocutorship** *n.* [ME f. L f. *proloqui prolocut-* (as PRO-¹, *loqui* speak)]

prologize /ˈprəʊlɒˌɡaɪz/ *v.intr.* (also **prologuize, -ise**) write or speak a prologue. [med.L *prologizare* f. Gk *prologizō* speak prologue (as PROLOGUE)]

prologue /ˈprəʊlɒg/ n. & v. —n. **1 a** a preliminary speech, poem, etc., esp. introducing a play (cf. EPILOGUE). **b** the actor speaking the prologue. **2** (usu. foll. by to) any act or event serving as an introduction. —v.tr. (**prologues, prologued, prologuing**) introduce with or provide with a prologue. [ME prolog f. OF prologue f. L prologus f. Gk prologos (as PRO-², logos speech)]

prolong /prəˈlɒŋ/ v.tr. **1** extend (an action, condition, etc.) in time or space. **2** lengthen the pronunciation of (a syllable etc.). **3** (as **prolonged** adj.) lengthy, esp. tediously so. □□ **prolongation** /ˌprəʊlɒŋˈgeɪʃ(ə)n/ n. **prolongedly** /-ɪdlɪ/ adv. **prolonger** n. [ME f. OF prolonger & f. LL prolongare (as PRO-¹, longus long)]

prolusion /prəˈljuːʒ(ə)n, -ˈluːʒ(ə)n/ n. formal **1** a preliminary essay or article. **2** a first attempt. □□ **prolusory** /-sərɪ/ adj. [L prolusio f. proludere prolus- practise beforehand (as PRO-¹, ludere lus- play)]

prom /prɒm/ n. colloq. **1** Brit. = PROMENADE n. 1a. **2** Brit. = promenade concert. **3** US = PROMENADE n. 3. [abbr.]

promenade /ˌprɒməˈnɑːd/ n. & v. —n. **1 a** Brit. a paved public walk along the sea front at a resort. **b** any paved public walk. **2** a walk, or sometimes a ride or drive, taken esp. for display, social intercourse, etc. **3** US a school or university ball or dance. **4** a march of dancers in country dancing etc. —v. **1** intr. make a promenade. **2** tr. lead (a person etc.) about a place esp. for display. **3** tr. make a promenade through (a place). □ **promenade concert** a concert at which the audience, or part of it, can stand, sit on the floor, or move about. The most famous series of such concerts is the annual BBC Promenade Concerts ('the Proms'), instituted by Sir Henry Wood, and held (since the Second World War) in the Albert Hall. **promenade deck** an upper deck on a passenger ship where passengers may promenade. [F f. se promener walk, refl. of promener take for a walk]

promenader /ˌprɒməˈnɑːdə(r)/ n. **1** a person who promenades. **2** Brit. a person who attends a promenade concert, esp. regularly.

promethazine /prəʊˈmeθəˌziːn/ n. an antihistamine drug used to treat allergies, motion sickness, etc. [PROPYL + dimethylamine + phenothiazine]

Promethean /prəˈmiːθɪən/ adj. daring or inventive like Prometheus.

Prometheus /prəˈmiːθɪəs/ Gk Mythol. a demigod, one of the Titans, who was worshipped by craftsmen. The two principal tales told of him are (i) that when Zeus hid fire away from man Prometheus stole it by trickery and brought it to earth again, (ii) to punish him Zeus chained him to a rock where an eagle fed each day on his liver which (since he was immortal) grew again each night; he was rescued by Hercules.

promethium /prəˈmiːθɪəm/ n. Chem. a radioactive metallic element of the lanthanide series. Not found in nature, it was first synthesized in a nuclear reactor in the 1940s. Its radiation has been used to power miniature batteries. ¶ Symb.: **Pm**; atomic number 61. [Prometheus: see PROMETHEAN]

prominence /ˈprɒmɪnəns/ n. **1** the state of being prominent. **2** a prominent thing, esp. a jutting outcrop, mountain, etc. **3** Astron. a stream of incandescent gas projecting above the sun's chromosphere. [obs.F f. L prominentia jutting out (as PROMINENT)]

prominent /ˈprɒmɪnənt/ adj. **1** jutting out; projecting. **2** conspicuous. **3** distinguished; important. □□ **prominency** n. **prominently** adv. [L prominēre jut out: cf. EMINENT]

promiscuous /prəˈmɪskjʊəs/ adj. **1 a** (of a person) having frequent and diverse sexual relationships, esp. transient ones. **b** (of sexual relationships) of this kind. **2** of mixed and indiscriminate composition or kinds; indiscriminate (promiscuous hospitality). **3** colloq. carelessly irregular; casual. □□ **promiscuity** /-ˈskjuːɪtɪ/ n. **promiscuously** adv. **promiscuousness** n. [L promiscuus (as PRO-¹, miscēre mix)]

promise /ˈprɒmɪs/ n. & v. —n. **1** an assurance that one will or will not undertake a certain action, behaviour, etc. (a promise of help; gave a promise to be generous). **2** a sign or signs of future achievements, good results, etc. (a writer of great promise). —v.tr. **1** (usu. foll. by to + infin., or that + clause; also absol.) make (a person) a promise, esp. to do, give, or procure (a thing) (I promise you a fair hearing; they promise not to be late; promised that he would be there; cannot positively promise). **2 a** afford expectations of (the discussions promise future problems; promises to be a good cook). **b** (foll. by to + infin.) seem likely to (is promising to rain). **3** colloq. assure, confirm (I promise you, it will not be easy). **4** (usu. in passive) archaic (she is promised to another). □ **the promised land 1** Bibl. Canaan, promised by God to Abraham and his descendants (Gen. 12:7, 17:8, etc.). **2** any desired place, esp. heaven. **promise oneself** look forward to (a pleasant time etc.). **promise well** (or **ill** etc.) hold out good (or bad etc.) prospects. □□ **promisee** /-ˈsiː/ n. esp. Law. **promiser** n. **promisor** n. esp. Law. [ME f. L promissum neut. past part. of promittere put forth, promise (as PRO-¹, mittere send)]

promising /ˈprɒmɪsɪŋ/ adj. likely to turn out well; hopeful; full of promise (a promising start). □□ **promisingly** adv.

promissory /ˈprɒmɪsərɪ/ adj. **1** conveying or implying a promise. **2** (often foll. by of) full of promise. □ **promissory note** a signed document containing a written promise to pay a stated sum to a specified person or the bearer at a specified date or on demand. [med.L promissorius f. L promissor (as PROMISE)]

promo /ˈprəʊməʊ/ n. & adj. colloq. —n. (pl. **-os**) **1** publicity, advertising. **2** a trailer for a television programme. —adj. promotional. [abbr.]

promontory /ˈprɒməntərɪ/ n. (pl. **-ies**) **1** a point of high land jutting out into the sea etc.; a headland. **2** Anat. a prominence or protuberance in the body. [med.L promontorium alt. (after mons montis mountain) f. L promunturium (perh. f. PRO-¹, mons)]

promote /prəˈməʊt/ v.tr. **1** (often foll. by to) advance or raise (a person) to a higher office, rank, etc. (was promoted to captain). **2** help forward; encourage; support actively (a cause, process, desired result, etc.) (promoted women's suffrage). **3** publicize and sell (a product). **4** attempt to ensure the passing of (a private act of parliament). **5** Chess raise (a pawn) to the rank of queen etc. when it reaches the opponent's end of the board. □□ **promotable** adj. **promotability** /-ˈbɪlɪtɪ/ n. **promotion** /-ˈməʊʃ(ə)n/ n. **promotional** /-ˈməʊʃən(ə)l/ adj. **promotive** adj. [ME f. L promovēre promot- (as PRO-¹, movēre move)]

promoter /prəˈməʊtə(r)/ n. **1** a person who promotes. **2** a person who finances, organizes, etc. a sporting event, theatrical production, etc. **3** (in full **company promoter**) a person who promotes the formation of a joint-stock company. **4** Chem. an additive that increases the activity of a catalyst. [earlier promotour f. AF f. med.L promotor (as PROMOTE)]

prompt /prɒmpt/ adj., adv., v., & n. —adj. **1 a** acting with alacrity; ready. **b** made, done, etc. readily or at once (a prompt reply). **2 a** (of a payment) made forthwith. **b** (of goods) for immediate delivery and payment. —adv. punctually (at six o'clock prompt). —v.tr. **1** (usu. foll. by to, or to + infin.) incite; urge (prompted them to action). **2 a** (also absol.) supply a forgotten word, sentence, etc., to (an actor, reciter, etc.). **b** assist (a hesitating speaker) with a suggestion. **3** give rise to; inspire (a feeling, thought, action, etc.). —n. **1 a** an act of prompting. **b** a thing said to help the memory of an actor etc. **c** = PROMPTER 2. **d** Computing an indication or sign on a VDU screen to show that the system is waiting for input. **2** the time limit for the payment of an account, stated on a prompt note. □ **prompt-book** a copy of a play for a prompter's use. **prompt-box** a box in front of the footlights beneath the stage where the prompter sits. **prompt-note** a note sent to a customer as a reminder of payment due. **prompt side** the side of the stage where the prompter sits, usu. to the actor's left. □□ **prompting** n. **promptitude** n. **promptly** adv. **promptness** n. [ME f. OF prompt or L promptus past part. of promere prompt- produce (as PRO-¹, emere take)]

prompter /ˈprɒmptə(r)/ n. **1** a person who prompts. **2** Theatr. a person seated out of sight of the audience who prompts the actors.

promulgate /ˈprɒməlˌgeɪt/ v.tr. **1** make known to the public; disseminate; promote (a cause etc.). **2** proclaim (a decree, news, etc.). □□ **promulgation** /-ˈgeɪʃ(ə)n/ n. **promulgator** n. [L promulgare (as PRO-¹, mulgēre milk, cause to come forth)]

promulge /prəʊˈmʌldʒ/ v.tr. archaic = PROMULGATE. [PROMULGATE]

pronaos /prəʊˈneɪɒs/ n. (pl. **pronaoi** /-ˈneɪɔɪ/) Gk Antiq. the space in front of the body of a temple, enclosed by a portico and projecting side walls. [L f. Gk *pronaos* hall of a temple (as PRO-², NAOS)]

pronate /ˈprəʊneɪt/ v.tr. put (the hand, forearm, etc.) into a prone position (with the palm etc. downwards) (cf. SUPINATE). □□ **pronation** /-ˈneɪʃ(ə)n/ n. [back-form. f. *pronation* (as PRONE)]

pronator /prəʊˈneɪtə(r)/ n. Anat. any muscle producing or assisting in pronation.

prone /prəʊn/ adj. **1 a** lying face downwards (cf. SUPINE). **b** lying flat; prostrate. **c** having the front part downwards, esp. the palm of the hand. **2** (usu. foll. by *to*, or *to* + infin.) disposed or liable, esp. to a bad action, condition, etc. (*is prone to bite his nails*). **3** (usu. in *comb.*) more than usually likely to suffer (*accident-prone*). **4** archaic with a downward slope or direction. □□ **pronely** adv. **proneness** /ˈprəʊnnɪs/ n. [ME f. L *pronus* f. *pro* forwards]

proneur /prəʊˈnɜː(r)/ n. a person who extols; a flatterer. [F *prôneur* f. *prôner* eulogize f. *prône* place in church where addresses were delivered]

prong /prɒŋ/ n. & v. —n. each of two or more projecting pointed parts at the end of a fork etc. —v.tr. **1** pierce or stab with a fork. **2** turn up (soil) with a fork. □ **prong-buck** (or **-horn** or **-horned antelope**) a N. American deerlike ruminant, *Antilocapra americana*, the male of which has horns with forward-pointing prongs. **three-pronged attack** an attack on three separate points at once. □□ **pronged** adj. (also in *comb.*). [ME (also *prang*), perh. rel. to MLG *prange* pinching instrument]

pronominal /prəʊˈnɒmɪn(ə)l/ adj. of, concerning, or being, a pronoun. □□ **pronominalize** v.tr. (also **-ise**). **pronominally** adv. [LL *pronominalis* f. L *pronomen* (as PRO-¹, *nomen, nominis* noun)]

pronoun /ˈprəʊnaʊn/ n. a word used instead of and to indicate a noun already mentioned or known, esp. to avoid repetition (e.g. *we, their, this, ourselves*). [PRO-¹, + NOUN, after F *pronom*, L *pronomen* (as PRO-¹, *nomen* name)]

pronounce /prəˈnaʊns/ v. **1** tr. (also *absol.*) utter or speak (words, sounds, etc.) in a certain way. **2** tr. **a** utter or deliver (a judgement, sentence, curse, etc.) formally or solemnly. **b** proclaim or announce officially (*I pronounce you man and wife*). **3** tr. state or declare, as being one's opinion (*the apples were pronounced excellent*). **4** intr. (usu. foll. by *on, for, against, in favour of*) pass judgement; give one's opinion (*pronounced for the defendant*). □□ **pronounceable** /-səb(ə)l/ adj. **pronouncement** n. **pronouncer** n. [ME f. OF *pronuncier* f. L *pronuntiare* (as PRO-¹, *nuntiare* announce f. *nuntius* messenger)]

pronounced /prəˈnaʊnst/ adj. **1** (of a word, sound, etc.) uttered. **2** strongly marked; decided (*a pronounced flavour; a pronounced limp*). □□ **pronouncedly** /-ˈnaʊnsɪdlɪ/ adv.

pronto /ˈprɒntəʊ/ adv. colloq. promptly, quickly. [Sp. f. L (as PROMPT)]

pronunciation /prənʌnsɪˈeɪʃ(ə)n/ n. **1** the way in which a word is pronounced, esp. with reference to a standard. **2** the act or an instance of pronouncing. **3** a person's way of pronouncing words etc. [ME f. OF *prononciation* or L *pronuntiatio* (as PRONOUNCE)]

proof /pruːf/ n., adj., & v. —n. **1** facts, evidence, argument, etc. establishing or helping to establish a fact (*proof of their honesty; no proof that he was there*). **2** Law the spoken or written evidence in a trial. **3** a demonstration or act of proving (*not capable of proof; in proof of my assertion*). **4** a test or trial (*put them to the proof; the proof of the pudding is in the eating*). **5** the standard of strength of distilled alcoholic liquors. **6** Printing a trial impression taken from type or film, used for making corrections before final printing. **7** the stages in the resolution of a mathematical or philosophical problem. **8** each of a limited number of impressions from an engraved plate before the ordinary issue is printed and usu. (in full **proof before letters**) before an inscription or signature is added. **9** a photographic print made for selection etc. **10** Sc. Law a trial before a judge instead of by a jury. —adj. **1** impervious to penetration, ill effects, etc. (*proof against the severest weather; his soul is proof against corruption*). **2** (in *comb.*) able to withstand damage or destruction by a specified agent (*soundproof; childproof*). **3** being of proof alcoholic strength. **4** (of armour) of tried strength. —v.tr. **1** make (something) proof,

esp. make (fabric) waterproof. **2** make a proof of (a printed work, engraving, etc.). □ **above proof** (of alcohol) having a stronger than standard strength. **proof-plane** a small flat conductor on an insulating handle for measuring the electrification of a body. **proof positive** absolutely certain proof. **proof-sheet** a sheet of printer's proof. **proof spirit** a mixture of alcohol and water having proof strength. □□ **proofless** adj. [ME *prōf prōve*, earlier *prēf* etc. f. OF *proeve, prueve* f. LL *proba* f. L *probare* (see PROVE); adj. and sometimes v. formed app. by ellipsis f. phr. *of proof* = proved to be impenetrable]

proofread /ˈpruːfriːd/ v.tr. (past and past part. **-read** /-red/) read (printer's proofs) and mark any errors. □□ **proofreader** n. **proofreading** n.

prop¹ /prɒp/ n. & v. —n. **1** a rigid support, esp. one not an integral part of the thing supported. **2** a person who supplies support, assistance, comfort, etc. **3** Rugby Football a forward at either end of the front row of a scrum. **4** esp. Austral. a horse's action of propping. —v. (**propped, propping**) **1** tr. (often foll. by *against, up,* etc.) support with or as if with a prop (*propped him against the wall; propped it up with a brick*). **2** intr. esp. Austral. (of a horse etc.) come to a dead stop with the forelegs rigid. [ME prob. f. MDu. *proppe*: cf. MLG, MDu. *proppen* (v.)]

prop² /prɒp/ n. Theatr. colloq. **1** = PROPERTY 3. **2** (in *pl.*) a property man or mistress. [abbr.]

prop³ /prɒp/ n. colloq. an aircraft propeller. □ **prop-jet** a turbo-prop. [abbr.]

prop. abbr. **1** proprietor. **2** proposition.

propaedeutic /ˌprəʊpɪˈdjuːtɪk/ adj. & n. —adj. serving as an introduction to higher study; introductory. —n. (esp. in *pl.*) preliminary learning; a propaedeutic subject, study, etc. □□ **propaedeutical** adj. [PRO-² + Gk *paideutikos* of teaching, after Gk *propaideuō* teach beforehand]

propaganda /ˌprɒpəˈɡændə/ n. **1 a** an organized programme of publicity, selected information, etc., used to propagate a doctrine, practice, etc. **b** usu. derog. the information, doctrines, etc., propagated in this way. **2** (**Propaganda**) RC Ch. a committee of cardinals responsible for foreign missions. [It. f. mod.L *congregatio de propaganda fide* congregation for propagation of the faith]

propagandist /ˌprɒpəˈɡændɪst/ n. a member or agent of a propaganda organization; a person who spreads propaganda. □□ **propagandism** n. **propagandistic** /-ˈdɪstɪk/ adj. **propagandistically** /-ˈdɪstɪkəlɪ/ adv. **propagandize** v.intr. & tr. (also **-ise**).

propagate /ˈprɒpəɡeɪt/ v.tr. **1 a** breed specimens of (a plant, animal, etc.) by natural processes from the parent stock. **b** (refl. or absol.) (of a plant, animal, etc.) reproduce itself. **2** disseminate; spread (a statement, belief, theory, etc.). **3** hand down (a quality etc.) from one generation to another. **4** extend the operation of; transmit (a vibration, earthquake, etc.). □□ **propagation** /-ˈɡeɪʃ(ə)n/ n. **propagative** adj. [L *propagare propagat-* multiply plants from layers, f. *propago* (as PRO-¹, *pangere* fix, layer)]

propagator /ˈprɒpəɡeɪtə(r)/ n. **1** a person or thing that propagates. **2** a small box that can be heated, used for germinating seeds or raising seedlings.

propane /ˈprəʊpeɪn/ n. a gaseous hydrocarbon of the alkane series used as bottled fuel. ¶ Chem. formula: C_3H_8. [PROPIONIC (ACID) + -ANE]

propanoic acid /ˌprəʊpəˈnəʊɪk/ n. Chem. = PROPIONIC ACID. [PROPANE + -IC]

propanone /ˈprəʊpənəʊn/ n. Chem. = ACETONE. [PROPANE + -ONE]

propel /prəˈpel/ v.tr. (**propelled, propelling**) **1** drive or push forward. **2** urge on; encourage. □ **propelling pencil** a pencil with a replaceable lead moved upward by twisting the outer case. [ME, = expel, f. L *propellere* (as PRO-¹, *pellere puls-* drive)]

propellant /prəˈpelənt/ n. **1** a thing that propels. **2** an explosive that fires bullets etc. from a firearm. **3** a substance used as a reagent in a rocket engine etc. to provide thrust.

propellent /prəˈpelənt/ adj. propelling; capable of driving or pushing forward.

æ cat ɑː arm e bed ɜː her ɪ sit iː see ɒ hot ɔː saw ʌ run ʊ put uː too ə ago aɪ my

propeller /prə'pelə(r)/ n. **1** a person or thing that propels. **2** a revolving shaft with blades, esp. for propelling a ship or aircraft (cf. *screw-propeller*). □ **propeller shaft** a shaft transmitting power from an engine to a propeller or to the driven wheels of a motor vehicle. **propeller turbine** a turbo-propeller.

propene /'prəʊpi:n/ n. *Chem.* = PROPYLENE. [PROPANE + ALKENE]

propensity /prə'pensɪtɪ/ n. (pl. **-ies**) an inclination or tendency (*has a propensity for wandering*). [propense f. L propensus inclined, past part. of propendēre (as PRO-¹, pendēre hang)]

proper /'prɒpə(r)/ adj., adv., & n. —adj. **1 a** accurate, correct (*in the proper sense of the word*; *gave him the proper amount*). **b** fit, suitable, right (*at the proper time*; *do it the proper way*). **2** decent; respectable, esp. excessively so (*not quite proper*). **3** (usu. foll. by *to*) belonging or relating exclusively or distinctively (*with the respect proper to them*). **4** (usu. placed after noun) strictly so called; real; genuine (*this is the crypt, not the cathedral proper*). **5** *colloq.* thorough; complete (*had a proper row about it*). **6** (usu. placed after noun) *Heraldry* in the natural, not conventional, colours (*a peacock proper*). **7** *archaic* (of a person) handsome; comely. **8** (usu. with possessive pronoun) *archaic* own (*with my proper eyes*). —adv. *Brit. dial.* or *colloq.* **1** completely; very (*felt proper daft*). **2** (with reference to speech) in a genteel manner (*learn to talk proper*). —n. *Eccl.* the part of a service that varies with the season or feast. □ **proper fraction** a fraction that is less than unity, with the numerator less than the denominator. **proper motion** *Astron.* the part of the apparent motion of a fixed star etc. that is due to its actual movement in space relative to the sun. **proper noun** (or **name**) *Gram.* a name used for an individual person, place, animal, country, title, etc., and spelt with a capital letter, e.g. Jane, London, Everest. **proper psalms** (or **lessons** etc.) psalms or lessons etc. appointed for a particular day. □□ **properness** n. [ME f. OF propre f. L proprius one's own, special]

properly /'prɒpəlɪ/ adv. **1** fittingly; suitably (*do it properly*). **2** accurately; correctly (*properly speaking*). **3** rightly (*he very properly refused*). **4** with decency; respectably (*behave properly*). **5** *colloq.* thoroughly (*they were properly ashamed*).

propertied /'prɒpətɪd/ adj. having property, esp. land.

Propertius /prə'pɜ:ʃəs/, Sextus (c.50–after 16 BC), Roman poet from Assisi. His four books of elegies are largely concerned with the joys and sufferings of his love affair with Cynthia, though the later poems also deal with mythological and historical themes. He is noted for the intensity of his love-poems and for the energetic wit and occasional obscurity of his style.

property /'prɒpətɪ/ n. (pl. **-ies**) **1 a** something owned; a possession, esp. a house, land, etc. **b** *Law* the right to possession, use, etc. **c** possessions collectively, esp. real estate (*has money in property*). **2** an attribute, quality, or characteristic (*has the property of dissolving grease*). **3** a moveable object used on a theatre stage, in a film, etc. **4** *Logic* a quality common to a whole class but not necessary to distinguish it from others. □ **common property** a thing known by most people. **property man** (or **mistress**) a man (or woman) in charge of theatrical properties. **property qualification** a qualification for office, or for the exercise of a right, based on the possession of property. **property tax** a tax levied directly on property. [ME through AF f. OF propriété f. L proprietas -tatis (as PROPER)]

prophase /'prəʊfeɪz/ n. *Biol.* the phase in cell division in which chromosomes contract and each becomes visible as two chromatids. [PRO-² + PHASE]

prophecy /'prɒfɪsɪ/ n. (pl. **-ies**) **1 a** a prophetic utterance, esp. Biblical. **b** a prediction of future events (*a prophecy of massive inflation*). **2** the faculty, function, or practice of prophesying (*the gift of prophecy*). [ME f. OF profecie f. LL prophetia f. Gk prophēteia (as PROPHET)]

prophesy /'prɒfɪˌsaɪ/ v. (**-ies**, **-ied**) **1** tr. (usu. foll. by *that*, *who*, etc.) foretell (an event etc.). **2** intr. speak as a prophet; foretell future events. **3** intr. *archaic* expound the Scriptures. □□ **prophesier** /-ˌsaɪə(r)/ n. [ME f. OF profecier (as PROPHECY)]

prophet /'prɒfɪt/ n. (fem. **prophetess** /-tɪs/) **1** a person regarded as a teacher or interpreter of the will of God. **2** any of the prophetical writers in the Old Testament; **the Prophets** their writings. **major prophets** Isaiah, Jeremiah, Ezekiel, Daniel.

minor prophets Hosea to Malachi, whose surviving writings are not lengthy. **3 a** a person who foretells events. **b** a person who advocates and speaks innovatively for a cause (*a prophet of the new order*). **4** (**the Prophet**) **a** Muhammad. **b** Joseph Smith, founder of the Mormons, or one of his successors. **c** (in pl.) the prophetic writings of the Old Testament. **5** *colloq.* a tipster. □□ **prophethood** n. **prophetism** n. **prophetship** n. [ME f. OF prophete f. L propheta, prophetes f. Gk prophētēs spokesman (as PRO-², phētēs speaker f. phēmi speak)]

prophetic /prə'fetɪk/ adj. **1** (often foll. by *of*) containing a prediction; predicting. **2** of or concerning a prophet. □□ **prophetical** adj. **prophetically** adv. **propheticism** /-ˌsɪz(ə)m/ n. [F prophétique or LL propheticus f. Gk prophētikos (as PROPHET)]

prophylactic /ˌprɒfɪ'læktɪk/ adj. & n. —adj. tending to prevent disease. —n. **1** a preventive medicine or course of action. **2** esp. US a condom. [F prophylactique f. Gk prophulaktikos f. prophulassō (as PRO-², phulassō guard)]

prophylaxis /ˌprɒfɪ'læksɪs/ n. (pl. **prophylaxes** /-siːz/) preventive treatment against disease. [mod.L f. PRO-² + Gk phulaxis act of guarding]

propinquity /prə'pɪŋkwɪtɪ/ n. **1** nearness in space; proximity. **2** close kinship. **3** similarity. [ME f. OF propinquité or L propinquitas f. propinquus near f. prope near to]

propionic acid /ˌprəʊpɪ'ɒnɪk/ n. a colourless sharp-smelling liquid carboxylic acid used for inhibiting the growth of mould in bread. ¶ *Chem.* formula: C_2H_5COOH. Also called PROPANOIC ACID. □□ **propionate** /'prəʊpɪəˌneɪt/ n. [F propionique, formed as PRO-² + Gk piōn fat, as being the first in the series of 'true' fatty acids]

propitiate /prə'pɪʃɪˌeɪt/ v.tr. appease (an offended person etc.). □□ **propitiator** n. [L propitiare (as PROPITIOUS)]

propitiation /prəˌpɪʃɪ'eɪʃ(ə)n/ n. **1** appeasement. **2** *Bibl.* atonement, esp. Christ's. **3** *archaic* a gift etc. meant to propitiate. [ME f. LL propitiatio (as PROPITIATE)]

propitiatory /prə'pɪʃɪətərɪ/ adj. serving or intended to propitiate (*a propitiatory smile*). □□ **propitiatorily** adv. [ME f. LL propitiatorius (as PROPITIATE)]

propitious /prə'pɪʃəs/ adj. **1** (of an omen etc.) favourable. **2** (often foll. by *for*, *to*) (of the weather, an occasion, etc.) suitable. **3** well-disposed (*the fates were propitious*). □□ **propitiously** adv. **propitiousness** n. [ME f. OF propicieus or L propitius]

propolis /'prɒpəlɪs/ n. a red or brown resinous substance collected by bees from buds for use in constructing hives. [L f. Gk propolis suburb, bee-glue, f. PRO-² + polis city]

proponent /prə'pəʊnənt/ n. & adj. —n. a person advocating a motion, theory, or proposal. —adj. proposing or advocating a theory etc. [L proponere (as PROPOUND)]

Propontis /prə'pɒntɪs/ the ancient name for the Sea of Marmara.

proportion /prə'pɔ:ʃ(ə)n/ n. & v. —n. **1 a** a comparative part or share (*a large proportion of the profits*). **b** a comparative ratio (*the proportion of births to deaths*). **2** the correct or pleasing relation of things or parts of a thing (*the house has fine proportions*; *exaggerated out of all proportion*). **3** (in pl.) dimensions; size (*large proportions*). **4** *Math.* **a** an equality of ratios between two pairs of quantities, e.g. 3:5 and 9:15. **b** a set of such quantities. **c** *Math.* = rule of three; see also *direct proportion*, *inverse proportion*. —v.tr. (usu. foll. by *to*) make (a thing etc.) proportionate (*must proportion the punishment to the crime*). □ **in proportion 1** by the same factor. **2** without exaggerating (importance etc.) (*must get the facts in proportion*). □□ **proportioned** adj. (also in comb.). **proportionless** adj. **proportionment** n. [ME f. OF proportion or L proportio (as PRO-¹, PORTION)]

proportionable /prə'pɔ:ʃənəb(ə)l/ adj. = PROPORTIONAL. □□ **proportionably** adv.

proportional /prə'pɔ:ʃən(ə)l/ adj. & n. —adj. in due proportion; comparable (*a proportional increase in the expense*; *resentment proportional to his injuries*). —n. *Math.* each of the terms of a proportion. □ **proportional representation** an electoral system in which all parties gain seats in proportion to the number of votes cast for them. □□ **proportionality** /-'nælɪtɪ/ n. **proportionally** adv.

proportionalist /prə'pɔːʃənəlɪst/ n. an advocate of proportional representation.

proportionate /prə'pɔːʃənət/ adj. = PROPORTIONAL. □□ **proportionately** adv.

proposal /prə'pəʊz(ə)l/ n. **1 a** the act or an instance of proposing something. **b** a course of action etc. so proposed (the proposal was never carried out). **2** an offer of marriage.

propose /prə'pəʊz/ v. **1** tr. (also absol.) put forward for consideration or as a plan. **2** tr. (usu. foll. by to + infin., or verbal noun) intend; purpose (propose to open a restaurant). **3** intr. (usu. foll. by to) offer oneself in marriage. **4** tr. nominate (a person) as a member of a society, for an office, etc. **5** tr. offer (a person's health, a person, etc.) as a subject for a toast. □□ **proposer** n. [ME f. OF proposer f. L proponere (as PROPOUND)]

proposition /ˌprɒpə'zɪʃ(ə)n/ n. & v. —n. **1** a statement or assertion. **2** a scheme proposed; a proposal. **3** Logic a statement consisting of subject and predicate that is subject to proof or disproof. **4** colloq. a problem, opponent, prospect, etc. that is to be dealt with (a difficult proposition). **5** Math. a formal statement of a theorem or problem, often including the demonstration. **6 a** an enterprise etc. with regard to its likelihood of commercial etc. success. **b** a person regarded similarly. **7** colloq. a sexual proposal. —v.tr. colloq. make a proposal (esp. of sexual intercourse) to (he propositioned her). □ **not a proposition** unlikely to succeed. □□ **propositional** adj. [ME f. OF proposition or L propositio (as PROPOUND)]

propound /prə'paʊnd/ v.tr. **1** offer for consideration; propose. **2** Law produce (a will etc.) before the proper authority so as to establish its legality. □□ **propounder** n. [earlier propoune, propone f. L proponere (as PRO-¹, ponere posit- place): cf. compound, expound]

proprietary /prə'praɪətərɪ/ adj. **1 a** of, holding, or concerning property (the proprietary classes). **b** of or relating to a proprietor (proprietary rights). **2** held in private ownership. □ **proprietary medicine** any of several drugs, medicines, etc. produced by private companies under brand names. **proprietary name** (or **term**) a name of a product etc. registered by its owner as a trade mark and not usable by another without permission. [LL proprietarius (as PROPERTY)]

proprietor /prə'praɪətə(r)/ n. (fem. **proprietress**) **1** a holder of property. **2** the owner of a business etc., esp. of a hotel. □□ **proprietorial** /-'tɔːrɪəl/ adj. **proprietorially** /-'tɔːrɪəlɪ/ adv. **proprietorship** n.

propriety /prə'praɪətɪ/ n. (pl. **-ies**) **1** fitness; rightness (doubt the propriety of refusing him). **2** correctness of behaviour or morals (highest standards of propriety). **3** (in pl.) the details or rules of correct conduct (must observe the proprieties). [ME, = ownership, peculiarity f. OF proprieté PROPERTY]

proprioceptive /ˌprəʊprɪə'septɪv/ adj. relating to stimuli produced and perceived within an organism, esp. relating to the position and movement of the body. [L proprius own + RECEPTIVE]

proptosis /prɒp'təʊsɪs/ n. Med. protrusion or displacement, esp. of an eye. [LL f. Gk proptōsis (as PRO-², piptō fall)]

propulsion /prə'pʌlʃ(ə)n/ n. **1** the act or an instance of driving or pushing forward. **2** an impelling influence. □□ **propulsive** /-'pʌlsɪv/ adj. [med.L propulsio f. L propellere (as PROPEL)]

propulsor /prə'pʌlsə(r)/ n. a ducted propeller which can be swivelled to give forward, upward, or downward flight to an airship. [as PROPULSION]

propyl /'prəʊpɪl/ n. Chem. the univalent radical of propane. ¶ Chem. formula: C_3H_7-. [PROPIONIC (ACID) + -YL]

propyla pl. of PROPYLON.

propylaeum /ˌprɒpɪ'liːəm/ n. (pl. **propylaea** /-'liːə/) **1** the entrance to a temple. **2** (**the Propylaeum**) the entrance to the Acropolis at Athens. [L f. Gk propulaion (as PRO-², pulē gate)]

propylene /'prəʊpɪliːn/ n. Chem. a gaseous hydrocarbon of the alkene series used in the manufacture of chemicals. ¶ Chem. formula: C_3H_6. [PROPYL + -ENE]

propylon /'prɒpɪlɒn/ n. (pl. **propylons** or **propyla** /-lə/) = PROPYLAEUM. [L f. Gk propulon (as PRO-², pulē gate)]

pro rata /prəʊ 'rɑːtə, 'reɪtə/ adj. & adv. —adj. proportional. —adv. proportionally. [L, = according to the rate]

prorate /prəʊ'reɪt, 'prəʊ-/ v.tr. allocate or distribute pro rata. □□ **proration** n.

prorogue /prə'rəʊg/ v. (**prorogues**, **prorogued**, **proroguing**) **1** tr. discontinue the meetings of (a parliament etc.) without dissolving it. **2** intr. (of a parliament etc.) be prorogued. □□ **prorogation** /-rə'geɪʃ(ə)n/ n. [ME proroge f. OF proroger, -guer f. L prorogare prolong (as PRO-¹, rogare ask)]

pros- /prɒs/ prefix **1** to, towards. **2** in addition. [Gk f. pros (prep.)]

prosaic /prə'zeɪɪk, prəʊ-/ adj. **1** like prose, lacking poetic beauty. **2** unromantic; dull; commonplace (took a prosaic view of life). □□ **prosaically** adv. **prosaicness** n. [F prosaïque or LL prosaicus (as PROSE)]

prosaist /'prəʊzeɪɪst/ n. **1** a prose-writer. **2** a prosaic person. □□ **prosaism** n. [F prosaïste f. L prosa PROSE]

proscenium /prə'siːnɪəm, prəʊ-/ n. (pl. **prosceniums** or **proscenia** /-nɪə/) **1** the part of the stage in front of the drop or curtain, usu. with the enclosing arch. **2** the stage of an ancient theatre. [L f. Gk proskēnion (as PRO-², skēnē stage)]

prosciutto /prəʊ'ʃuːtəʊ/ n. (pl. **-os**) Italian ham, esp. cured and eaten as an hors-d'œuvre. [It.]

proscribe /prə'skraɪb/ v.tr. **1** banish, exile (proscribed from the club). **2** put (a person) outside the protection of the law. **3** reject or denounce (a practice etc.) as dangerous etc. □□ **proscription** /-'skrɪpʃ(ə)n/ n. **proscriptive** /-'skrɪptɪv/ adj. [L proscribere (as PRO-¹, scribere script- write)]

prose /prəʊz/ n. & v. —n. **1** the ordinary form of the written or spoken language (opp. POETRY, VERSE) (Milton's prose works). **2** a passage of prose, esp. for translation into a foreign language. **3** a tedious speech or conversation. **4** a plain matter-of-fact quality (the prose of existence). **5** Eccl. = SEQUENCE 8. —v. **1** intr. (usu. foll. by about, away, etc.) talk tediously (was prosing away about his dog). **2** tr. turn (a poem etc.) into prose. □ **prose idyll** a short description in prose of a picturesque, esp. rustic, incident, character, etc. **prose poem** (or **poetry**) a piece of imaginative poetic writing in prose. □□ **proser** n. [ME f. OF f. L prosa (oratio) straightforward (discourse), fem. of prosus, earlier prorsus direct]

prosector /prə'sektə(r)/ n. a person who dissects dead bodies in preparation for an anatomical lecture etc. [LL = anatomist, f. prosecare prosect- (as PRO-¹, secare cut), perh. after F prosecteur]

prosecute /'prɒsɪˌkjuːt/ v.tr. **1** (also absol.) **a** institute legal proceedings against (a person). **b** institute a prosecution with reference to (a claim, crime, etc.) (decided not to prosecute). **2** follow up, pursue (an inquiry, studies, etc.). **3** carry on (a trade, pursuit, etc.). □□ **prosecutable** adj. [ME f. L prosequi prosecut- (as PRO-¹, sequi follow)]

prosecution /ˌprɒsɪ'kjuː(ʃ)(ə)n/ n. **1 a** the institution and carrying on of a criminal charge in a court. **b** the carrying on of legal proceedings against a person. **c** the prosecuting party in a court case (the prosecution denied this). **2** the act or an instance of prosecuting (met her in the prosecution of his hobby). [OF prosecution or LL prosecutio (as PROSECUTE)]

prosecutor /'prɒsɪˌkjuːtə(r)/ n. (fem. **prosecutrix** /-trɪks/) a person who prosecutes, esp. in a criminal court. □□ **prosecutorial** /-'tɔːrɪəl/ adj.

proselyte /'prɒsɪˌlaɪt/ n. & v. —n. **1** a person converted, esp. recently, from one opinion, creed, party, etc., to another. **2** a Gentile convert to Judaism. —v.tr. US = PROSELYTIZE. □□ **proselytism** /-lɪˌtɪz(ə)m/ n. [ME f. LL proselytus f. Gk prosēluthos stranger, convert (as PROS-, stem ēluth- of erkhomai come)]

proselytize /'prɒsɪlɪˌtaɪz/ v.tr. (also **-ise**) (also absol.) convert (a person or people) from one belief etc. to another, esp. habitually. □□ **proselytizer** n.

prosenchyma /prɒ'seŋkɪmə/ n. a plant tissue of elongated cells with interpenetrating tapering ends, occurring esp. in vascular tissue. □□ **prosenchymal** adj. **prosenchymatous** /-'kɪmətəs/ adj. [Gk pros toward + egkhuma infusion, after parenchyma]

Proserpine /prə'sɜːpɪnɪ/ the Roman name for Persephone.

prosify /'prəʊzɪˌfaɪ/ v.tr. (**-ies**, **-ied**) **1** tr. turn into prose. **2** tr. make prosaic. **3** intr. write prose.

prosit /'prǝʊzɪt/ *int.* an expression used in drinking a person's health etc. [G f. L, = may it benefit]

prosody /'prɒsǝdɪ/ *n.* **1** the theory and practice of versification; the laws of metre. **2** the study of speech-rhythms. □□ **prosodic** /prǝ'sɒdɪk/ *adj.* **prosodist** *n.* [ME f. L *prosodia* accent f. Gk *prosōidia* (as PROS-, ODE)]

prosopography /ˌprɒsǝ'pɒgrǝfɪ, ˌprɒsǝʊ-/ *n.* (*pl.* **-ies**) **1** a description of a person's appearance, personality, social and family connections, career, etc. **2** the study of such descriptions, esp. in Roman history. □□ **prosopographer** *n.* **prosopographic** /-pǝ'græfɪk/ *adj.* **prosopographical** /-pǝ'græfɪk(ǝ)l/ *adj.* [mod.L *prosopographia* f. Gk *prosōpon* face, person]

prosopopoeia /ˌprɒsǝpǝ'piːǝ/ *n.* the rhetorical introduction of a pretended speaker or the personification of an abstract thing. [L f. Gk *prosōpopoiia* f. *prosōpon* person + *poieō* make]

prospect /'prɒspekt/ *n.* & *v.* —*n.* **1 a** (often in *pl.*) an expectation, esp. of success in a career etc. (*his prospects were brilliant; offers a gloomy prospect; no prospect of success*). **b** something one has to look forward to (*don't relish the prospect of meeting him*). **2** an extensive view of landscape etc. (*a striking prospect*). **3** a mental picture (*a new prospect in his mind*). **4 a** a place likely to yield mineral deposits. **b** a sample of ore for testing. **c** the resulting yield. **5** a possible or probable customer, subscriber, etc. —*v.* /prǝ'spekt/ **1** *intr.* (usu. foll. by *for*) **a** explore a region for gold etc. **b** look out for or search for something. **2** *tr.* **a** explore (a region) for gold etc. **b** work (a mine) experimentally. **c** (of a mine) promise (a specified yield). □ **prospect well** (or **ill** etc.) (of a mine) promise well (or ill etc.). □□ **prospectless** *adj.* **prospector** /prǝ'spektǝ(r)/ *n.* [ME f. L *prospectus*: see PROSPECTUS]

prospective /prǝ'spektɪv/ *adj.* **1** concerned with or applying to the future (*implies a prospective obligation*) (cf. RETROSPECTIVE). **2** some day to be; expected; future (*prospective bridegroom*). □□ **prospectively** *adv.* **prospectiveness** *n.* [obs. F *prospectif* -*ive* or LL *prospectivus* (as PROSPECTUS)]

prospectus /prǝ'spektǝs/ *n.* a printed document advertising or describing a school, commercial enterprise, forthcoming book, etc. [L, = prospect f. *prospicere* (as PRO-¹, *specere* look)]

prosper /'prɒspǝ(r)/ *v.* **1** *intr.* succeed; thrive (*nothing he touches prospers*). **2** *tr.* make successful (*Heaven prosper him*). [ME f. OF *prosperer* or L *prosperare* (as PROSPEROUS)]

prosperity /prɒ'sperɪtɪ/ *n.* a state of being prosperous; wealth or success.

prosperous /'prɒspǝrǝs/ *adj.* **1** successful; rich (*a prosperous merchant*). **2** flourishing; thriving (*a prosperous enterprise*). **3** auspicious (*a prosperous wind*). □□ **prosperously** *adv.* **prosperousness** *n.* [ME f. obs. F *prospereus* f. L *prosper(us)*]

Prost /prɒst/, Alain (1955–), French racing driver. He was the first Frenchman to win the Formula One world championship (1985) and has since won more Grands Prix than any other champion in motor racing.

prostaglandin /ˌprɒstǝ'glændɪn/ *n.* any of a group of hormone-like substances causing contraction of the muscles in mammalian (esp. uterine) tissues etc. [G f. PROSTATE + GLAND¹ + -IN]

prostate /'prɒsteɪt/ *n.* (in full **prostate gland**) a gland surrounding the neck of the bladder in male mammals and releasing a fluid forming part of the semen. □□ **prostatic** /-'stætɪk/ *adj.* [F f. mod.L *prostata* f. Gk *prostatēs* one that stands before (as PRO-², *statos* standing)]

prosthesis /'prɒsθɪsɪs, -'θiːsɪs/ *n.* (*pl.* **prostheses** /-ˌsiːz/) **1 a** an artificial part supplied to remedy a deficiency, e.g. a false breast, leg, tooth, etc. **b** the branch of surgery supplying and fitting prostheses. **2** *Gram.* the addition of a letter or syllable at the beginning of a word, e.g. *be-* in *beloved*. □□ **prosthetic** /-'θetɪk/ *adj.* **prosthetically** /-'θetɪkǝlɪ/ *adv.* [LL f. Gk *prosthesis* f. *prostithēmi* (as PROS-, *tithēmi* place)]

prosthetics /prɒs'θetɪks/ *n.pl.* (usu. treated as *sing.*) = PROSTHESIS 1b.

prostitute /'prɒstɪˌtjuːt/ *n.* & *v.* —*n.* **1 a** a woman who engages in sexual activity for payment. **b** (usu. **male prostitute**) a man or boy who engages in sexual activity, esp. with homosexual men, for payment. **2** a person who debases himself or herself for personal gain. —*v.tr.* **1** (esp. *refl.*) make a prostitute of (esp. oneself). **2 a** misuse (one's talents, skills, etc.) for money. **b** offer (oneself, one's honour, etc.) for unworthy ends, esp. for money. □□ **prostitution** /-'tjuːʃ(ǝ)n/ *n.* **prostitutor** *n.* [L *prostituere prostitut*- offer for sale (as PRO-¹, *statuere* set up, place)]

prostrate *adj.* & *v.* —*adj.* /'prɒstreɪt/ **1 a** lying face downwards, esp. in submission. **b** lying horizontally. **2** overcome, esp. by grief, exhaustion, etc. (*prostrate with self-pity*). **3** *Bot.* growing along the ground. —*v.tr.* /prɒ'streɪt, prǝ-/ **1** lay (a person etc.) flat on the ground. **2** (*refl.*) throw (oneself) down in submission etc. **3** (of fatigue, illness, etc.) overcome; reduce to extreme physical weakness. □□ **prostration** /prɒ'streɪʃ(ǝ)n, prǝ-/ *n.* [ME f. L *prostratus* past part. of *prosternere* (as PRO-¹, *sternere strat*- lay flat)]

prostyle /'prǝʊstaɪl/ *n.* & *adj.* —*n.* a portico with not more than four columns. —*adj.* (of a building) having such a portico. [L *prostylos* having pillars in front (as PRO-², STYLE)]

prosy /'prǝʊzɪ/ *adj.* (**prosier**, **prosiest**) tedious; commonplace; dull (*prosy talk*). □□ **prosily** *adv.* **prosiness** *n.*

Prot. *abbr.* **1** Protectorate. **2** Protestant.

protactinium /ˌprǝʊtæk'tɪnɪǝm/ *n. Chem.* a naturally-occurring radioactive metallic element, first discovered in 1913. It is so named because one of its isotopes decays to form actinium. ¶ Symb.: **Pa**. [G (as PROTO-, ACTINIUM)]

protagonist /prǝʊ'tægǝnɪst/ *n.* **1** the chief person in a drama, story, etc. **2** the leading person in a contest etc.; a principal performer. **3** (usu. foll. by *of, for*) *disp.* an advocate or champion of a cause, course of action, etc. (*a protagonist of women's rights*). [Gk *prōtagōnistēs* (as PROTO-, *agōnistēs* actor)]

protamine /'prǝʊtǝˌmiːn/ *n.* any of a group of proteins found in association with chromosomal DNA in the sperm of birds and fish. [PROTO- + AMINE]

protasis /'prɒtǝsɪs/ *n.* (*pl.* **protases** /-ˌsiːz/) the clause expressing the condition in a conditional sentence. □□ **protatic** /-'tætɪk/ *adj.* [L, f. Gk *protasis* proposition (as PRO-², *teinō* stretch)]

protea /'prǝʊtɪǝ/ *n.* any shrub of the genus *Protea* native to S. Africa, with conelike flower-heads. [mod.L f. PROTEUS, with ref. to the many species]

protean /'prǝʊtɪǝn, -'tiːǝn/ *adj.* **1** variable, taking many forms. **2** (of an artist, writer, etc.) versatile. [after *Proteus*: see PROTEUS]

protease /'prǝʊtɪˌeɪs/ *n.* any enzyme able to hydrolyse proteins and peptides by proteolysis. [PROTEIN + -ASE]

protect /prǝ'tekt/ *v.tr.* **1** (often foll. by *from, against*) keep (a person, thing, etc.) safe; defend; guard (*goggles protected her eyes from dust; guards protected the queen*). **2** *Econ.* shield (home industry) from competition by imposing import duties on foreign goods. **3** *Brit.* provide funds to meet (a bill, draft, etc.). **4** provide (machinery etc.) with appliances to prevent injury from it. [L *protegere protect*- (as PRO-¹, *tegere* cover)]

protection /prǝ'tekʃ(ǝ)n/ *n.* **1 a** the act or an instance of protecting. **b** the state of being protected; defence (*affords protection against the weather*). **c** a thing, person, or animal that provides protection (*bought a dog as protection*). **2** (also **protectionism** /-ˌnɪz(ǝ)m/) *Econ.* the theory or practice of protecting home industries. **3** *colloq.* **a** immunity from molestation obtained by payment to gangsters etc. under threat of violence. **b** (in full **protection money**) the money so paid, esp. on a regular basis. **4** = *safe conduct*. **5** *archaic* the keeping of a woman as a mistress. □□ **protectionist** *n.* [ME f. OF *protection* or LL *protectio* (as PROTECT)]

protective /prǝ'tektɪv/ *adj.* & *n.* —*adj.* **1** protecting; intended or intending to protect. **2** (of food) protecting against deficiency diseases. —*n.* something that protects, esp. a condom. □ **protective clothing** clothing worn to shield the body from dangerous substances or a hostile environment. **protective colouring** colouring disguising or camouflaging a plant or animal. **protective custody** the detention of a person for his or her own protection. □□ **protectively** *adv.* **protectiveness** *n.*

protector /prǝ'tektǝ(r)/ *n.* (*fem.* **protectress** /-trɪs/) **1 a** a person who protects. **b** a guardian or patron. **2** *hist.* a regent in charge of a kingdom during the minority, absence, etc. of the sovereign.

3 (often in *comb.*) a thing or device that protects (*chest-protector*). **4 (Protector)** (in full **Lord Protector of the Commonwealth**) *hist.* the title taken by Oliver Cromwell during his government of Britain in 1653–8 and passed on to his son Richard Cromwell 1658–9. (See PROTECTORATE.) □□ **protectoral** *adj.* **protectorship** *n.* [ME f. OF *protecteur* f. LL *protector* (as PROTECT)]

protectorate /prə'tektərət/ *n.* **1 a** a State that is controlled and protected by another. **b** such a relation of one State to another. **2** *hist.* **a** the office of the protector of a kingdom or State. **b** the period of this, esp. in England under the Cromwells 1653–9. Oliver Cromwell was appointed Lord Protector in December 1653 at the behest of the army and retained the position until his death in September 1658. Although the Protectorate achieved considerable success in foreign wars, it depended almost entirely on its leader's personality at home and was continually threatened by the unstable relationship between the Protector, Parliament, and the army. After the elder Cromwell's death his son Richard proved incapable of holding the regime together, and its subsequent collapse led to the restoration of Charles II.

protégé /'prɒtɪˌʒeɪ, -teˌʒeɪ, 'prəʊ-/ *n.* (*fem.* **protégée** *pronunc.* same) a person under the protection, patronage, tutelage, etc. of another. [F, past part. of *protéger* f. L *protegere* PROTECT]

protein /'prəʊtiːn/ *n.* any of a class of large molecules which form an essential part of all living things. They have many different functions. Some form strong fibres and hold the skeleton together, others are enzymes (see ENZYME), others again are antibodies which prevent disease. Proteins are made from about twenty amino acids which are arranged in different orders in long chains. One or a small number of such chains make one protein molecule, which may be of fibrous or globular shape depending on the type and order of the amino acids present. The information needed for the synthesis of particular proteins comes from the DNA in a cell's nucleus. □□ **proteinaceous** /-ˈneɪʃəs/ *adj.* **proteinic** /-ˈtiːnɪk/ *adj.* **proteinous** /-ˈtiːnəs, -ˈtiːɪnəs/ *adj.* [F *protéine*, G *Protein* f. Gk *prōteios* primary]

pro tem /prəʊ 'tem/ *adj.* & *adv.* *colloq.* = PRO TEMPORE. [abbr.]

pro tempore /prəʊ 'tempərɪ/ *adj.* & *adv.* for the time being. [L]

proteolysis /ˌprəʊtɪ'ɒlɪsɪs/ *n.* the splitting of proteins or peptides by the action of enzymes esp. during the process of digestion. □□ **proteolytic** /-ə'lɪtɪk/ *adj.* [mod.L f. PROTEIN + -LYSIS]

Proterozoic /ˌprəʊtərəʊ'zəʊɪk/ *adj.* & *n.* *Geol.* —*adj.* of or relating to the later part of the Precambrian era, characterized by the oldest forms of life. —*n.* this time. [Gk *proteros* former + *zōē* life, *zōos* living]

protest *n.* & *v.* —*n.* /'prəʊtest/ **1** a statement of dissent or disapproval; a remonstrance (*made a protest*). **2** (often *attrib.*) a usu. public demonstration of objection to government etc. policy (*marched in protest; protest demonstration*). **3** a solemn declaration. **4** *Law* a written declaration, usu. by a notary public, that a bill has been presented and payment or acceptance refused. —*v.* /prə'test/ **1** *intr.* (usu. foll. by *against, at, about*, etc.) make a protest against an action, proposal, etc. **2** *tr.* (often foll. by *that* + clause; also *absol.*) affirm (one's innocence etc.) solemnly, esp. in reply to an accusation etc. **3** *tr.* *Law* write or obtain a protest in regard to (a bill). **4** *tr.* *US* object to (a decision etc.). □ **under protest** unwillingly. □□ **protester** *n.* **protestingly** *adv.* **protestor** *n.* [ME f. OF *protest* (n.), *protester* (v.), f. L *protestari* (as PRO-¹, *testari* assert f. *testis* witness)]

Protestant /'prɒtɪst(ə)nt/ *n.* & *adj.* —*n.* **1** a member or follower of any of the western Christian Churches that are separate from the Roman Catholic Church in accordance with the principles of the Reformation (16th c.; see below). **2** (in *pl.*) *hist.* those German princes and free cities who made a declaration (*Protestatio*) of dissent from the decision of the Diet of Spires (1529) which reaffirmed the edict of the Diet of Worms against the Reformation. **3 (protestant)** /'prɒtɪst(ə)nt, prə'test(ə)nt/ a protesting person. —*adj.* **1** of or relating to any of the Protestant Churches or their members etc. **2 (protestant)** /also prə'test(ə)nt/ protesting. □□ **Protestantism** *n.* **Protestantize** *v.tr.* & *intr.* (also **-ise**). [mod.L *protestans*, part. of L *protestari* (see PROTEST)]

In the 16th c., the name 'Protestant' was generally taken in

Germany by the Lutherans, while the Swiss and French called themselves 'Reformed'. In England the use has varied with time and circumstances. In the 17th c., 'Protestant' was generally accepted and used by members of the Established Church, and was even so applied to the exclusion of Presbyterians, Quakers, and Separatists; it was primarily opposed to 'papist'. Later, it was opposed to 'Roman Catholic' or to 'Catholic', and was viewed with disfavour by those who laid stress on the claim of the Anglican Church to be equally Catholic with the Roman.

protestation /ˌprɒtɪ'steɪʃ(ə)n/ *n.* **1** a strong affirmation. **2** a protest. [ME f. OF *protestation* or LL *protestatio* (as PROTESTANT)]

Proteus /'prəʊtɪəs, -tjuːs/ *Gk Mythol.* a minor sea-god with the power of assuming different shapes. —*n.* **1** a changing or inconstant person or thing. **2 (proteus) a** any bacterium of the genus *Proteus*, usu. found in the intestines and faeces of animals. **b** = OLM.

prothalamium /ˌprəʊθə'leɪmɪəm/ *n.* (also **prothalamion** /-mɪən/) (*pl.* **prothalamia** /-mɪə/) a song or poem to celebrate a forthcoming wedding. [title of a poem by Spenser, after *epithalamium*]

prothallium /prəʊ'θælɪəm/ *n.* (*pl.* **prothallia** /-lɪə/) = PROTHALLUS. [mod.L f. PRO-² + Gk *thallion* dimin. of *thallos*: see PROTHALLUS]

prothallus /prəʊ'θæləs/ *n.* (*pl.* **prothalli** /-laɪ/) *Bot.* the gametophyte of certain plants, esp. a fern. [mod.L f. PRO-² + Gk *thallos* green shoot]

prothesis /'prɒθɪsɪs/ *n.* (*pl.* **protheses** /-ˌsiːz/) **1** *Eccl.* **a** the placing of the Eucharistic elements on the credence table. **b** a credence table. **c** the part of a church where this stands. **2** *Gram.* = PROSTHESIS 2. □□ **prothetic** /prə'θetɪk/ *adj.* [Gk f. *protithēmi* (as PRO-², *tithēmi* place)]

prothonotary var. of PROTONOTARY.

protist /'prəʊtɪst/ *n.* any usu. unicellular organism of the kingdom Protista, not distinguished as animals or plants, including bacteria, algae, and protozoa. □□ **protistology** /-'tɒlədʒɪ/ *n.* [mod.L *Protista* f. Gk *prōtista* neut. pl. superl. f. *prōtos* first]

protium /'prəʊtɪəm/ *n.* the ordinary isotope of hydrogen as distinct from heavy hydrogen (cf. DEUTERIUM, TRITIUM). [mod.L f. PROTO- + -IUM]

proto- /'prəʊtəʊ/ *comb. form* **1** original, primitive (*proto-Germanic; proto-Slavic*). **2** first, original (*protomartyr; protophyte*). [Gk *prōto-* f. *prōtos* first]

protocol /ˌprəʊtə'kɒl/ *n.* & *v.* —*n.* **1 a** official, esp. diplomatic, formality and etiquette observed on State occasions etc. **b** the rules, formalities, etc. of any procedure, group, etc. **2** the original draft of a diplomatic document, esp. of the terms of a treaty agreed to in conference and signed by the parties. **3** a formal statement of a transaction. **4** the official formulae at the beginning and end of a charter, papal bull, etc. **5** *US* a record of experimental observations etc. —*v.* (**protocolled, protocolling**) **1** *intr.* draw up a protocol or protocols. **2** *tr.* record in a protocol. [orig. Sc. *prothocoll* f. OF *prothocole* f. med.L *protocollum* f. Gk *protokollon* flyleaf (as PROTO-, *kolla* glue)]

protomartyr /ˌprəʊtəʊ'maːtə(r)/ *n.* the first martyr in any cause, esp. the first Christian martyr St Stephen.

proton /'prəʊtɒn/ *n.* *Physics* a stable elementary particle with a positive electric charge, equal in magnitude to that of an electron, and occurring in all atomic nuclei. The charge on the proton is equal and opposite to the charge on the electron, although the mass of the proton is 1,836 times greater. The atom of each chemical element has a characteristic number of protons in the nucleus; the common isotope of hydrogen has a nucleus consisting of a single proton. Protons are approximately 10^{-13} cm in diameter, although their size is not sharply defined. The atomic number of each atom is the number of protons it contains and this, together with an equal number of electrons, determines the chemical properties of the corresponding element. Protons, or positively charged ions, are partly responsible for heat radiation, for the conduction of electricity in electrolytes and in hot gases, and also for the gamma radiation from excited nuclei. High-velocity protons are used in particle accelerators to probe the structure of atomic nuclei.

Protons were identified by W. Wien in 1898 and J. J. Thomson in 1910; they were named 'protons' by Rutherford in 1920. □□

protonic /prə'tɒnɪk/ *adj.* [Gk, neut. of *prōtos* first, reflecting their character as primitive constituents of all atomic nuclei; also perhaps suggested by the name of William *Prout* (d. 1850), English chemist and physician, who suggested that hydrogen was a constituent of all the elements]

protonotary /ˌprəutə'nəutəri, prə'tɒnə-/ *n.* (*pl.* **-ies**) (also **prothonotary** /ˌprəuθ-, prə'θɒnə-/) a chief clerk in some law courts, orig. in the Byzantine court. □ **Protonotary Apostolic** (or **Apostolical**) a member of the college of prelates who register papal acts, direct the canonization of saints, etc. [med.L *protonotarius* f. late Gk *protonotarios* (as PROTO-, NOTARY)]

protopectin /ˌprəutə'pektɪn/ *n.* = PECTOSE.

protophyte /'prəutəˌfaɪt/ *n.* a unicellular plant bearing gametes.

protoplasm /'prəutəˌplæz(ə)m/ *n.* the material comprising the living part of a cell, consisting of a nucleus embedded in membrane-enclosed cytoplasm. In the 19th c. protoplasm was thought of as a complex but essentially homogeneous form of matter having the basic properties of life such as irritability and metabolism. With the realization, especially after the invention of the electron microscope, that there is a complex structural organization within cells, the concept of protoplasm as a special substance has lost much of its significance. □□ **protoplasmal** /-'plæzm(ə)l/ *adj.* **protoplasmatic** /-'mætɪk/ *adj.* **protoplasmic** /-'plæzmɪk/ *adj.* [Gk *protoplasma* (as PROTO-, PLASMA)]

protoplast /'prəutəˌplæst/ *n.* the protoplasm of one cell. □□ **protoplastic** /-'plæstɪk/ *adj.* [F *protoplaste* or LL *protoplastus* f. Gk *protoplastos* (as PROTO-, *plassō* mould)]

prototherian /ˌprəutəu'θɪərɪən/ *n.* & *adj.* —*n.* any mammal of the subclass Prototheria, including monotremes. —*adj.* of or relating to this subclass. [PROTO- + Gk *thēr* wild beast]

prototype /'prəutəˌtaɪp/ *n.* **1** an original thing or person of which or whom copies, imitations, improved forms, representations, etc. are made. **2** a trial model or preliminary version of a vehicle, machine, etc. □□ **prototypal** *adj.* **prototypic** /-'tɪpɪk/ *adj.* **prototypical** /-'tɪpɪk(ə)l/ *adj.* **prototypically** /-'tɪpɪkəlɪ/ *adv.* [F *prototype* or LL *prototypus* f. Gk *prototupos* (as PROTO-, TYPE)]

protozoan /ˌprəutə'zəuən/ *n.* & *adj.* —*n.* (also **protozoon** /-'zəuɒn/) (*pl.* **protozoa** /-'zəuə/ or **protozoans**) any usu. unicellular and microscopic organism of the subkingdom Protozoa, including amoebae and ciliates. First observed by Leeuwenhoek in the 17th c., protozoa are ubiquitous in aquatic and damp habitats and there are numerous parasitic species, among them the trypanosomes which cause sleeping sickness, and the malaria parasite. Protozoa display a great variety of form; important groups include the flagellates, amoebas, and ciliates, and some bear shells, the residue of which forms a significant proportion of some limestone rocks. —*adj.* (also **protozoic** /-'zəuɪk/) of or relating to this phylum. □□ **protozoal** *adj.* [mod.L (as PROTO-, Gk *zōion* animal)]

protract /prə'trækt/ *v.tr.* **1** prolong or lengthen in space or esp. time (*protracted their stay for some weeks*). **2** draw (a plan of ground etc.) to scale. □□ **protractedly** *adv.* **protractedness** *n.* [L *protrahere protract-* (as PRO-¹, *trahere* draw)]

protractile /prə'træktaɪl/ *adj.* (of a part of the body etc.) capable of being protruded or extended.

protraction /prə'trækʃ(ə)n/ *n.* **1** the act or an instance of protracting; the state of being protracted. **2** a drawing to scale. **3** the action of a protractor muscle. [F *protraction* or LL *protractio* (as PROTRACT)]

protractor /prə'træktə(r)/ *n.* **1** an instrument for measuring angles, usu. in the form of a graduated semicircle. **2** a muscle serving to extend a limb etc.

protrude /prə'truːd/ *v.* **1** *intr.* extend beyond or above a surface; project. **2** *tr.* thrust or cause to thrust forth. □□ **protrudent** *adj.* **protrusible** *adj.* **protrusion** /-ʒ(ə)n/ *n.* **protrusive** *adj.* [L *protrudere* (as PRO-¹, *trudere trus-* thrust)]

protrusile /prə'truːsaɪl/ *adj.* (of a limb etc.) capable of being thrust forward. [PRO-¹ + EXTRUSILE: see EXTRUDE]

protuberant /prə'tjuːbərənt/ *adj.* bulging out; prominent (*protuberant eyes; a protuberant fact*). □□ **protuberance** *n.* [LL *protuberare* (as PRO-¹, *tuber* bump)]

proud /praud/ *adj.* **1** feeling greatly honoured or pleased (*am proud to know him; proud of his friendship*). **2 a** (often foll. by *of*) valuing oneself, one's possessions, etc. highly, or esp. too highly; haughty; arrogant (*proud of his ancient name*). **b** (often in *comb.*) having a proper pride; satisfied (*house-proud; proud of a job well done*). **3 a** (of an occasion etc.) justly arousing pride (*a proud day for us; a proud sight*). **b** (of an action etc.) showing pride (*a proud wave of the hand*). **4** (of a thing) imposing; splendid. **5** slightly projecting from a surface etc. (*the nail stood proud of the plank*). **6** (of flesh) overgrown round a healing wound. **7** (of water) swollen in flood. □ **do proud** *colloq.* **1** treat (a person) with lavish generosity or honour (*they did us proud on our anniversary*). **2** (*refl.*) act honourably or worthily. **proud-hearted** haughty; arrogant. □□ **proudly** *adv.* **proudness** *n.* [OE *prūt, prūd* f. OF *prud, prod* oblique case of *pruz* etc. valiant, ult. f. LL *prode* f. L *prodesse* be of value (as PRO-¹, *esse* be)]

Proudhon /pruː'dɔ̃/, Pierre Joseph (1809–65), French social reformer, largely self-educated, whose writings argue that property is theft and that for a just society orderly anarchy should replace government.

Proust /pruːst/, Marcel (1871–1922), French novelist, essayist, and critic. In the 1890s he moved in the most fashionable Paris circles. Severe asthma precluded any regular profession; his neurotic disposition, aggravated by efforts to conceal his homosexuality, made him a virtual recluse in his later years. He published a collection of essays, poems, and stories, *Les Plaisirs et les jours* (1896), translations of Ruskin whose artistic ideas influenced his own; he was also influenced by the philosophy of Bergson. Proust explored his own literary aesthetic in *Contre Sainte-Beuve* (1954) where he defines the artist's task as the releasing of creative energies of past experience from the unconscious, an aesthetic which found its most developed literary expression in his novel *À la recherche du temps perdu* (1913–27) which occupied him from c.1907 until his death.

Prov. *abbr.* **1** Proverbs (Old Testament). **2** Province. **3** Provençal.

prove /pruːv/ *v.* (*past part.* **proved** or **proven** /'pruːv(ə)n, 'prəu-/) **1** *tr.* (often foll. by *that* + *clause*) demonstrate the truth of by evidence or argument. **2** *intr.* **a** (usu. foll. by *to* + infin.) be found (*it proved to be untrue*). **b** emerge incontrovertibly as (*will prove the winner*). **3** *tr.* Math. test the accuracy of (a calculation). **4** *tr.* establish the genuineness and validity of (a will). **5** *intr.* (of dough) rise in bread-making. **6** *tr.* = PROOF 6. **7** *tr.* subject (a gun etc.) to a testing process. **8** *tr. archaic* test the qualities of; try. □ **not proven** (in Scottish Law) a verdict that there is insufficient evidence to establish guilt or innocence. **prove oneself** show one's abilities, courage, etc. □□ **provable** *adj.* **provability** /-'bɪlɪtɪ/ *n.* **provably** *adv.* [ME f. OF *prover* f. L *probare* test, approve, demonstrate f. *probus* good]

provenance /'prɒvɪnəns/ *n.* **1** the place of origin or history, esp. of a work of art etc. **2** origin. [F f. *provenir* f. L *provenire* (as PRO-¹, *venire* come)]

Provençal /ˌprɒvɒn'sɑːl, ˌprɒvɑ̃'sæl/ *adj.* & *n.* —*adj.* of or concerning the language, inhabitants, landscape, etc. of Provence. —*n.* **1** a native of Provence. **2 a** the dialect of French used in Provence. **b** a Romance language of this region, closely related to French, Italian, and Catalan. In the 12th–14th c. it was the language of the troubadours and cultured speakers of southern France, but the subsequent spread of the northern dialects of French led to its gradual decline despite attempts to revive it. [F (as PROVINCIAL f. L *provincia* (see PROVENCE)]

Provence /prɒ'vɑ̃s/ a district and former province of SE France east of the lower Rhône, which contains the French Riviera, now part of the region of Provence-Côte d'Azur; pop. (1982) 3,965,200; capital, Marseilles. [L *provincia* province, as L colloq. name for southern Gaul, which was the first Roman province to be established outside Italy]

provender /'prɒvɪndə(r)/ *n.* **1** animal fodder. **2** *joc.* food for human beings. [ME f. OF *provendre, provende* ult. f. L *praebenda* (see PREBEND)]

provenience /prə'viːnɪəns/ *n. US* = PROVENANCE. [L *provenire* f. *venire* come]

proverb /'prɒvɜːb/ *n.* **1** a short pithy saying in general use, held to embody a general truth. **2** a person or thing that is notorious (*he is a proverb for inaccuracy*). **3** (**Proverbs** or **Book of Proverbs**) a didactic poetic Old Testament book of maxims attributed to Solomon and others. [ME f. OF *proverbe* or L *proverbium* (as PRO-¹, *verbum* word)]

proverbial /prə'vɜːbɪəl/ *adj.* **1** (esp. of a specific characteristic etc.) as well-known as a proverb; notorious (*his proverbial honesty*). **2** of or referred to in a proverb (*the proverbial ill wind*). □□ **proverbiality** /-bɪ'ælɪtɪ/ *n.* **proverbially** *adv.* [ME f. L *proverbialis* (as PROVERB)]

provide /prə'vaɪd/ *v.* **1** *tr.* supply; furnish (*provided them with food; provided food for them; provided a chance for escape*). **2** *intr.* **a** (usu. foll. by *for, against*) make due preparation (*provided for any eventuality; provided against invasion*). **b** (usu. foll. by *for*) prepare for the maintenance of a person etc. **3** *tr.* (also *refl.*) equip with necessities (*they had to provide themselves*). **4** *tr.* (usu. foll. by *that*) stipulate in a will, statute, etc. **5** *tr.* (usu. foll. by *to*) *Eccl. hist.* **a** appoint (an incumbent) to a benefice. **b** (of the Pope) appoint (a successor) to a benefice not yet vacant. [ME f. L *providēre* (as PRO-¹, *vidēre vis-* see)]

provided /prə'vaɪdɪd/ *adj. & conj.* —*adj.* supplied, furnished. —*conj.* (often foll. by *that*) on the condition or understanding (that).

Providence /'prɒvɪd(ə)ns/ the capital of the State of Rhode Island; pop. (1980) 156,800.

providence /'prɒvɪd(ə)ns/ *n.* **1** the protective care of God or nature. **2** (**Providence**) God in this aspect. **3** timely care or preparation; foresight; thrift. □ **special providence** a particular instance of God's providence. [ME f. OF *providence* or L *providentia* (as PROVIDE)]

provident /'prɒvɪd(ə)nt/ *adj.* having or showing foresight; thrifty. □ **Provident Society** *Brit.* = *Friendly Society.* □□ **providently** *adv.* [ME f. L (as PROVIDE)]

providential /ˌprɒvɪ'denʃ(ə)l/ *adj.* **1** of or by divine foresight or interposition. **2** opportune, lucky. □□ **providentially** *adv.* [PROVIDENCE + -IAL, after *evidential* etc.]

provider /prə'vaɪdə(r)/ *n.* **1** a person or thing that provides. **2** the breadwinner of a family etc.

providing /prə'vaɪdɪŋ/ *conj.* = PROVIDED *conj.*

province /'prɒvɪns/ *n.* **1** a principal administrative division of a country etc. **2 a** (**the provinces**) the whole of a country outside the capital, esp. regarded as uncultured, unsophisticated, etc. **b** (**the Province**) (in recent use) Northern Ireland. **3** a sphere of action; business (*outside my province as a teacher*). **4** a branch of learning etc. (*in the province of aesthetics*). **5** *Eccl.* a district under an archbishop or a metropolitan. **6** *Rom.Hist.* a territory outside Italy under a Roman governor. [ME f. OF f. L *provincia* charge, province]

provincial /prə'vɪnʃ(ə)l/ *adj. & n.* —*adj.* **1 a** of or concerning a province. **b** of or concerning the provinces. **2** unsophisticated or uncultured in manner, speech, opinion, etc. —*n.* **1** an inhabitant of a province or the provinces. **2** an unsophisticated or uncultured person. **3** *Eccl.* the head or chief of a province or of a religious order in a province. □□ **provinciality** /-ʃɪ'ælɪtɪ/ *n.* **provincialize** *v.tr.* (also **-ise**). **provincially** *adv.* [ME f. OF f. L *provincialis* (as PROVINCE)]

provincialism /prə'vɪnʃəˌlɪz(ə)m/ *n.* **1** provincial manners, fashion, mode of thought, etc., esp. regarded as restricting or narrow. **2** a word or phrase peculiar to a provincial region. **3** concern for one's local area rather than one's country. □□ **provincialist** *n.*

provision /prə'vɪʒ(ə)n/ *n. & v.* —*n.* **1 a** the act or an instance of providing (*made no provision for his future*). **b** something provided (*a provision of bread*). **2** (in *pl.*) food, drink, etc., esp. for an expedition. **3 a** a legal or formal statement providing for something. **b** a clause of this. **4** *Eccl. hist.* an appointment to a

benefice not yet vacant (cf. PROVIDE 5). —*v.tr.* supply (an expedition etc.) with provisions. □□ **provisioner** *n.* **provisionless** *adj.* **provisionment** *n.* [ME f. OF f. L *provisio -onis* (as PROVIDE)]

provisional /prə'vɪʒ(ə)l/ *adj. & n.* —*adj.* **1** providing for immediate needs only; temporary. **2** (**Provisional**) designating the unofficial wing of the IRA established in 1970, advocating terrorism to achieve its aims. The name is taken from the 'Provisional Government of the Republic of Ireland' which was declared in 1916. —*n.* (**Provisional**) a member of the Provisional wing of the IRA. □□ **provisionality** /-'nælɪtɪ/ *n.* **provisionally** *adv.* **provisionalness** *n.*

proviso /prə'vaɪzəʊ/ *n.* (*pl.* **-os**) **1** a stipulation. **2** a clause of stipulation or limitation in a document. [L, neut. ablat. past part. of *providēre* PROVIDE, in med.L phr. *proviso quod* it being provided that]

provisor /prə'vaɪzə(r)/ *n. Eccl.* **1** a deputy of a bishop or archbishop. **2** *hist.* the holder of a provision (see PROVISION *n.* 4). [ME f. AF *provisour* f. L *provisor -oris* (as PROVIDE)]

provisory /prə'vaɪzərɪ/ *adj.* **1** conditional; having a proviso. **2** making provision (*provisory care*). □□ **provisorily** *adv.* [F *provisoire* or med.L *provisorius* (as PROVISOR)]

Provo /'prəʊvəʊ/ *n.* (*pl.* **-os**) *colloq.* a member of the Provisional IRA. [abbr.]

provocation /ˌprɒvə'keɪʃ(ə)n/ *n.* **1** the act or an instance of provoking; a state of being provoked (*did it under severe provocation*). **2** a cause of annoyance. **3** *Law* an action, insult, etc. held to be likely to provoke physical retaliation. [ME f. OF *provocation* or L *provocatio* (as PROVOKE)]

provocative /prə'vɒkətɪv/ *adj. & n.* —*adj.* **1** (usu. foll. by *of*) tending to provoke, esp. anger or sexual desire. **2** intentionally annoying. —*n.* a provocative thing. □□ **provocatively** *adv.* **provocativeness** *n.* [ME f. obs. F *provocatif -ive* f. LL *provocativus* (as PROVOKE)]

provoke /prə'vəʊk/ *v.tr.* **1 a** (often foll. by *to*, or *to* + infin.) rouse or incite (*provoked him to fury*). **b** (as **provoking** *adj.*) exasperating; irritating. **2** call forth; instigate (indignation, an inquiry, a storm, etc.). **3** (usu. foll. by *into* + verbal noun) irritate or stimulate (a person) (*the itch provoked him into scratching*). **4** tempt; allure. **5** cause, give rise to (*will provoke fermentation*). □□ **provokable** *adj.* **provokingly** *adv.* [ME f. OF *provoquer* f. L *provocare* (as PRO-¹, *vocare* call)]

provost /'prɒvəst/ *n.* **1** *Brit.* the head of some colleges esp. at Oxford or Cambridge. **2** *Eccl.* **a** the head of a chapter in a cathedral. **b** *hist.* the head of a religious community. **3** *Sc.* the head of a municipal corporation or burgh. **4** the Protestant minister of the principal church of a town etc. in Germany etc. **5** *US* a high administrative officer in a university. **6** = *provost marshal.* □ **provost guard** *US* a body of soldiers under a provost marshal. **provost marshal 1** the head of military police in camp or on active service. **2** the master-at-arms of a ship in which a court-martial is to be held. □□ **provostship** *n.* [ME f. OE *profost* & AF *provost, prevost* f. med.L *propositus* for *praepositus*: see PRAEPOSTOR]

prow /praʊ/ *n.* **1** the fore-part or bow of a ship adjoining the stem. **2** a pointed or projecting front part. [F *proue* f. Prov. *proa* or It. dial. *prua* f. L *prora* f. Gk *prōira*]

prowess /'praʊɪs/ *n.* **1** skill; expertise. **2** valour; gallantry. [ME f. OF *proesce* f. *prou* valiant]

prowl /praʊl/ *v. & n.* —*v.* **1** *tr.* roam (a place) in search or as if in search of prey, plunder, etc. **2** *intr.* (often foll. by *about, around*) move about like a hunter. —*n.* the act or an instance of prowling. □ **on the prowl** moving about secretively or rapaciously, esp. in search of sexual contact etc. **prowl car** *US* a police squad car. □□ **prowler** *n.* [ME *prolle*, of unkn. orig.]

prox. *abbr.* proximo.

prox. acc. *abbr.* proxime accessit.

proxemics /prɒk'siːmɪks/ *n. Sociol.* the study of socially conditioned spatial factors in ordinary human relations. [PROXIMITY + *-emics*; cf. phonemics]

proximal /'prɒksɪm(ə)l/ *adj.* situated towards the centre of the body or point of attachment. □□ **proximally** *adv.* [L *proximus* nearest]

proximate /ˈprɒksɪmət/ adj. **1** nearest or next before or after (in place, order, time, causation, thought process, etc.). **2** approximate. □□ **proximately** adv. [L proximatus past part. of proximare draw near (as PROXIMAL)]

proxime accessit /ˌprɒksɪmɪ əkˈsiːsɪt/ n. **1** second place in an examination etc. **2** a person gaining this. [L, = came very near]

proximity /prɒkˈsɪmɪtɪ/ n. nearness in space, time, etc. (sat in close proximity to them). □ **proximity fuse** an electronic device causing a projectile to explode when near its target. **proximity of blood** kinship. [ME f. F proximité or L proximitas (as PROXIMAL)]

proximo /ˈprɒksɪˌməʊ/ adj. Commerce of next month (the third proximo). [L proximo mense in the next month]

proxy /ˈprɒksɪ/ n. (pl. **-ies**) (also attrib.) **1** the authorization given to a substitute or deputy (a proxy vote; was married by proxy). **2** a person authorized to act as a substitute etc. **3 a** a document giving the power to act as a proxy, esp. in voting. **b** a vote given by this. [ME f. obs. procuracy f. med.L procuratia (as PROCURATION)]

PRS abbr. **1** (in the UK) President of the Royal Society. **2** Performing Rights Society.

prude /pruːd/ n. a person having or affecting an attitude of extreme propriety or modesty esp. in sexual matters. □□ **prudery** n. (pl. **-ies**). **prudish** adj. **prudishly** adv. **prudishness** n. [F, back form. f. prudefemme fem. of prud'homme good man and true f. prou worthy]

prudent /ˈpruːd(ə)nt/ adj. **1** (of a person or conduct) careful to avoid undesired consequences; circumspect. **2** discreet. □□ **prudence** n. **prudently** adv. [ME f. OF prudent or L prudens = providens PROVIDENT]

prudential /pruːˈdenʃ(ə)l/ adj. & n. —adj. of, involving, or marked by prudence (prudential motives). —n. (in pl.) **1** prudential considerations or matters. **2** US minor administrative or financial matters. □□ **prudentialism** n. **prudentialist** n. **prudentially** adv. [PRUDENT + -IAL, after evidential etc.]

pruinose /ˈpruːɪˌnəʊs/ adj. esp. Bot. covered with white powdery granules; frosted in appearance. [L pruinosus f. pruina hoar-frost]

prune[1] /pruːn/ n. **1** a dried plum. **2** colloq. a silly or disliked person. [ME f. OF ult. f. L prunum f. Gk prou(m)non plum]

prune[2] /pruːn/ v.tr. **1 a** (often foll. by down) trim (a tree etc.) by cutting away dead or overgrown branches etc. **b** (usu. foll. by off, away) lop (branches etc.) from a tree. **2** reduce (costs etc.) (must try to prune expenses). **3 a** (often foll. by of) clear (a book etc.) of superfluities. **b** remove (superfluities). □ **pruning-hook** a long-handled hooked cutting tool used for pruning. □□ **pruner** n. [ME prouyne f. OF pro(o)ignier ult. f. L rotundus ROUND]

prunella[1] /pruːˈnelə/ n. any plant of the genus Prunella, esp. P. vulgaris, bearing pink, purple, or white flower spikes, and formerly thought to cure quinsy. Also called SELF HEAL. [mod.L, = quinsy: earlier brunella dimin. of med.L brunus brown]

prunella[2] /pruːˈnelə/ n. a strong silk or worsted fabric used formerly for barristers' gowns, the uppers of women's shoes, etc. [perh. f. F prunelle, of uncert. orig.]

prurient /ˈprʊərɪənt/ adj. **1** having an unhealthy obsession with sexual matters. **2** encouraging such an obsession. □□ **prurience** n. **pruriency** n. **pruriently** adv. [L prurire itch, be wanton]

prurigo /prʊəˈraɪɡəʊ/ n. a skin disease marked by severe itching. □□ **pruriginous** /prʊəˈrɪdʒɪnəs/ adj. [L prurigo -ginis f. prurire to itch]

pruritus /prʊəˈraɪtəs/ n. severe itching of the skin. □□ **pruritic** /-ˈrɪtɪk/ adj. [L, = itching (as PRURIGO)]

Prussia /ˈprʌʃə/ a former German kingdom, originally centred in NE Europe along the south coast of the Baltic. Prussia rose to prominence in the 17th c. under the Electors of Brandenburg and became the pre-eminent German military power under Frederick the Great in the mid-18th c. Its territory was expanded southwards and westwards by conquest and treaty and in 1866–70 served as the nucleus for the new German empire created by Bismarck under the king of Prussia. Most of the original Prussian territories are now in Poland or the Soviet Union.

Prussian /ˈprʌʃ(ə)n/ adj. & n. —adj. of or relating to Prussia or its rigidly militaristic tradition. —n. a native of Prussia. □ **Old**

Prussian the language spoken in Prussia until the 17th c. **Prussian blue** a deep blue pigment, ferric ferrocyanide, used in painting and dyeing.

prussic /ˈprʌsɪk/ adj. of or obtained from Prussian blue. □ **prussic acid** hydrocyanic acid. [F prussique f. Prusse Prussia]

Prut /pruːt/ (also **Pruth**) a river separating Romania from the Soviet Republic of Moldavia, rising in the Carpathian Mountains and flowing south-east to meet the Danube near Reni.

pry[1] /praɪ/ v.intr. (**pries**, **pried**) **1** (usu. foll. by into) inquire impertinently (into a person's private affairs etc.). **2** (usu. foll. by into, about, etc.) look or peer inquisitively. □□ **prying** adj. **pryingly** adv. [ME prie, of unkn. orig.]

pry[2] /praɪ/ v.tr. (**pries**, **pried**) US (often foll. by out of, open, etc.) = PRISE. [PRISE taken as pries 3rd sing. pres.]

PS abbr. **1** Police Sergeant. **2** postscript. **3** private secretary. **4** prompt side.

Ps. abbr. (pl. **Pss.**) Psalm, Psalms (Old Testament).

psalm /sɑːm/ n. **1 a** (also **Psalm**) any of the sacred songs contained in the Book of Psalms, esp. when set for metrical chanting in a service. **b** (**the Psalms** or **the Book of Psalms**) the book of the Old Testament containing psalms, used in both Jewish and Christian worship. The popular belief that David was the author of the whole Psalter can no longer be sustained, but many of the psalms date from the early years of the monarchy in Israel. **2** a sacred song or hymn. □ **psalm-book** a book containing the Psalms, esp. with metrical settings for worship. □□ **psalmic** adj. [OE (p)sealm f. LL psalmus f. Gk psalmos song sung to a harp f. psallō pluck]

psalmist /ˈsɑːmɪst/ n. **1** the author or composer of a psalm. **2** (**the Psalmist**) David or the author of any of the Psalms. [LL psalmista (as PSALM)]

psalmody /ˈsɑːmədɪ, ˈsæl-/ n. **1** the practice or art of singing psalms, hymns, etc., esp. in public worship. **2 a** the arrangement of psalms for singing. **b** the psalms so arranged. □□ **psalmodic** /sælˈmɒdɪk/ adj. **psalmodist** n. **psalmodize** v.intr. (also **-ise**). [ME f. LL psalmodia f. Gk psalmōidia singing to a harp (as PSALM, ōidē song)]

psalter /ˈsɔːltə(r), ˈsɒl-/ n. **1 a** the Book of Psalms. **b** a version of this (the English Psalter; Prayer-Book Psalter). **2** a copy of the Psalms, esp. for liturgical use. [ME f. AF sauter, OF sautier, & OE (p)saltere f. LL psalterium f. Gk psaltērion stringed instrument (psallō pluck), in eccl.L Book of Psalms]

psalterium /sɔːlˈtɪərɪəm, sɒl-/ n. the third stomach of a ruminant, the omasum. [L (see PSALTER): named from its booklike form]

psaltery /ˈsɔːltərɪ, ˈsɒl-/ n. (pl. **-ies**) an ancient and medieval instrument like a dulcimer but played by plucking the strings with the fingers or a plectrum. [ME f. OF sauterie etc. f. L (as PSALTER)]

PSBR abbr. Brit. public sector borrowing requirement.

psephology /seˈfɒlədʒɪ, pse-/ n. the statistical study of elections, voting, etc. □□ **psephological** /-fəˈlɒdʒɪk(ə)l/ adj. **psephologically** /-fəˈlɒdʒɪkəlɪ/ adv. **psephologist** n. [Gk psēphos pebble, vote + -LOGY]

pseud /sjuːd/ adj. & n. colloq. —adj. intellectually or socially pretentious; not genuine. —n. such a person; a poseur. [abbr. of PSEUDO]

pseud- var. of PSEUDO-.

pseudepigrapha /ˌsjuːdɪˈpɪɡrəfə/ n.pl. **1** Jewish writings ascribed to various Old Testament prophets etc. but written during or just before the early Christian period. **2** spurious writings. □□ **pseudepigraphal** adj. **pseudepigraphic** /-ˈɡræfɪk/ adj. **pseudepigraphical** /-ˈɡræfɪk(ə)l/ adj. [neut. pl. of Gk pseudepigraphos with false title (as PSEUDO-, EPIGRAPH)]

pseudo /ˈsjuːdəʊ/ adj. & n. —adj. **1** sham; spurious. **2** insincere. —n. (pl. **-os**) a pretentious or insincere person. [see PSEUDO-]

pseudo- /ˈsjuːdəʊ/ comb. form (also **pseud-** before a vowel) **1** supposed or purporting to be but not really so; false; not genuine (pseudo-intellectual; pseudepigrapha). **2** resembling or imitating (often in technical applications) (pseudo-language; pseudo-acid). [Gk f. pseudēs false, pseudos falsehood]

pseudocarp /ˈsjuːdəʊˌkɑːp/ *n.* a fruit formed from parts other than the ovary, e.g. the strawberry or fig. [PSEUDO- + Gk *karpos* fruit]

pseudomorph /ˈsjuːdəˌmɔːf/ *n.* **1** a crystal etc. consisting of one mineral with the form proper to another. **2** a false form. □□ **pseudomorphic** /-ˈmɔːfɪk/ *adj.* **pseudomorphism** /-ˈmɔːfɪz(ə)m/ *n.* **pseudomorphous** /-ˈmɔːfəs/ *adj.* [PSEUDO- + Gk *morphē* form]

pseudonym /ˈsjuːdənɪm/ *n.* a fictitious name, esp. one assumed by an author. [F *pseudonyme* f. Gk *pseudōnymos* (as PSEUDO-, *-ōnumos* f. *onoma* name)]

pseudonymous /sjuːˈdɒnɪməs/ *adj.* writing or written under a false name. □□ **pseudonymity** /-ˈnɪmɪti/ *n.* **pseudonymously** *adv.*

pseudopod /ˈsjuːdəʊˌpɒd/ *n.* = PSEUDOPODIUM. [mod.L (as PSEUDOPODIUM)]

pseudopodium /ˌsjuːdəʊˈpəʊdɪəm/ *n.* (*pl.* **pseudopodia** /-dɪə/) (in amoeboid cells) a temporary protrusion of protoplasm for movement, feeding, etc. [mod.L (as PSEUDO-, PODIUM)]

pseudo-science /ˈsjuːdəʊˌsaɪəns/ *n.* a pretended or spurious science. □□ **pseudo-scientific** /-ˈtɪfɪk/ *adj.*

pshaw /pʃɔː, ʃɔː/ *int. archaic* an expression of contempt or impatience. [imit.]

psi /psaɪ/ *n.* **1** the twenty-third letter of the Greek alphabet (Ψ, ψ). **2** supposed parapsychological faculties, phenomena, etc. regarded collectively. [Gk]

p.s.i. *abbr.* pounds per square inch.

psilocybin /ˌsɪləˈsaɪbɪn/ *n.* a hallucinogenic alkaloid found in Mexican mushrooms of the genus *Psilocybe*. [*Psilocybe* f. Gk *psilos* bald + *kubē* head]

psilosis /saɪˈləʊsɪs/ *n.* = SPRUE². [Gk *psilōsis* f. *psilos* bare]

psittacine /ˈsɪtəˌsaɪn/ *adj.* of or relating to parrots; parrot-like. [L *psittacinus* f. *psittacus* f. Gk *psittakos* parrot]

psittacosis /ˌsɪtəˈkəʊsɪs/ *n.* a contagious viral disease of birds transmissible (esp. from parrots) to human beings as a form of pneumonia. [mod.L f. L *psittacus* (as PSITTACINE) + -OSIS]

psoas /ˈsəʊəs/ *n.* either of two muscles used in flexing the hip joint. [Gk, accus. pl. of *psoa*, taken as sing.]

psoriasis /səˈraɪəsɪs/ *n.* a skin disease marked by red scaly patches. □□ **psoriatic** /ˌsɔːrɪˈætɪk/ *adj.* [mod.L f. Gk *psōriasis* f. *psōriaō* have an itch f. *psōra* itch]

psst /pst/ *int.* (also **pst**) a whispered exclamation seeking to attract a person's attention surreptitiously. [imit.]

PST *abbr.* US Pacific Standard Time.

PSV *abbr. Brit.* public service vehicle.

psych /saɪk/ *v.tr. colloq.* **1** (usu. foll. by *up*; often *refl.*) prepare (oneself or another person) mentally for an ordeal etc. **2 a** (usu. foll. by *out*) analyse (a person's motivation etc.) for one's own advantage (*can't psych him out*). **b** subject to psychoanalysis. **3** (often foll. by *out*) influence a person psychologically, esp. negatively; intimidate, frighten. □ **psych out** break down mentally; become confused or deranged. [abbr.]

Psyche /ˈsaɪki/ *Gk mythol.* the soul personified as female, or sometimes represented as a butterfly. She is associated with Eros, either in quiet harmony or being tormented by him as the seat of passions. The allegory of Psyche's love for Cupid is told in the 'Golden Ass' of Apuleius. [as PSYCHE]

psyche /ˈsaɪki/ *n.* **1** the soul; the spirit. **2** the mind. [L f. Gk *psukhē* breath, life, soul]

psychedelia /ˌsaɪkɪˈdiːlɪə/ *n.pl.* **1** psychedelic articles, esp. posters, paintings, etc. **2** psychedelic drugs.

psychedelic /ˌsaɪkɪˈdelɪk/ *adj. & n.* —*adj.* **1 a** expanding the mind's awareness etc., esp. through the use of hallucinogenic drugs. **b** (of an experience) hallucinatory; bizarre. **c** (of a drug) producing hallucinations. **2** *colloq.* **a** producing an effect resembling that of a psychedelic drug; having vivid colours or designs etc. **b** (of colours, patterns, etc.) bright, bold and often abstract. —*n.* a hallucinogenic drug. □□ **psychedelically** *adv.* [irreg. f. Gk (as PSYCHE, *dēlos* clear, manifest)]

psychiatry /saɪˈkaɪətrɪ/ *n.* the study and treatment of mental disease. □□ **psychiatric** /-kɪˈætrɪk/ *adj.* **psychiatrical** /-kɪˈætrɪk(ə)l/ *adj.* **psychiatrically** /-kɪˈætrɪkəlɪ/ *adv.* **psychiatrist** *n.* [as PSYCHE + *iatreia* healing f. *iatros* healer]

psychic /ˈsaɪkɪk/ *adj. & n.* —*adj.* **1 a** (of a person) considered to have occult powers, such as telepathy, clairvoyance, etc. **b** (of a faculty, phenomenon, etc.) inexplicable by natural laws. **2** of the soul or mind. **3** *Bridge* (of a bid) made on the basis of a hand not usually considered strong enough to support it. —*n.* **1 a** person considered to have psychic powers; a medium. **2** *Bridge* a psychic bid. **3** (in *pl.*) the study of psychic phenomena. [Gk *psukhikos* (as PSYCHE)]

psychical /ˈsaɪkɪk(ə)l/ *adj.* **1** concerning psychic phenomena or faculties (*psychical research*). **2** of the soul or mind. □□ **psychically** *adv.* **psychicism** /-ɪˌsɪz(ə)m/ *n.* **psychicist** /-ɪˌsɪst/ *n.*

psycho /ˈsaɪkəʊ/ *n. & adj. colloq.* —*n.* (*pl.* **-os**) a psychopath. —*adj.* psychopathic. [abbr.]

psycho- /ˈsaɪkəʊ/ *comb. form* relating to the mind or psychology. [Gk *psukho-* (as PSYCHE)]

psychoactive /ˌsaɪkəʊˈæktɪv/ *adj.* affecting the mind.

psychoanalysis /ˌsaɪkəʊəˈnælɪsɪs/ *n.* **1** a therapeutic method, originated by Sigmund Freud (see entry) of treating disorders of personality or behaviour by investigating the interaction of conscious and unconscious elements in the mind and bringing repressed fears and conflicts into the conscious mind, e.g. through the free association of ideas, and the analysis and interpretation of dreams, helping the patient to understand his or her condition. **2** a theory of personality and psychical life derived from this, based on concepts of the ego, id, and superego, the conscious, pre-conscious, and unconscious levels of the mind, and the repression of the sexual instinct. □□ **psychoanalyse** /-ˈænəˌlaɪz/ *v.tr.* **psychoanalyst** /-ˈænəlɪst/ *n.* **psychoanalytic** /-ˌænəˈlɪtɪk/ *adj.* **psychoanalytical** /-ˌænəˈlɪtɪk(ə)l/ *adj.* **psychoanalytically** /-ˌænəˈlɪtɪkəlɪ/ *adv.*

psychobabble /ˈsaɪkəʊˌbæb(ə)l/ *n. US colloq. derog.* jargon used in popular psychology.

psychodrama /ˈsaɪkəʊˌdrɑːmə/ *n.* **1** a form of psychotherapy in which patients act out events from their past. **2** a play or film etc. in which psychological elements are the main interest.

psychodynamics /ˌsaɪkəʊdaɪˈnæmɪks/ *n.pl.* (treated as *sing.*) the study of the activity of and the interrelation between the various parts of an individual's personality or psyche. □□ **psychodynamic** *adj.* **psychodynamically** *adv.*

psychogenesis /ˌsaɪkəʊˈdʒenɪsɪs/ *n.* the study of the origin of the mind's development.

psychokinesis /ˌsaɪkəʊkɪˈniːsɪs/ *n.* the movement of objects supposedly by mental effort without the action of natural forces.

psycholinguistics /ˌsaɪkəʊlɪŋˈɡwɪstɪks/ *n.pl.* (treated as *sing.*) the study of the psychological aspects of language and language-learning. □□ **psycholinguist** /-ˈlɪŋɡwɪst/ *n.* **psycholinguistic** *adj.*

psychological /ˌsaɪkəˈlɒdʒɪk(ə)l/ *adj.* **1** of, relating to, or arising in the mind. **2** of or relating to psychology. **3** *colloq.* (of an ailment etc.) having a basis in the mind; imaginary (*her cold is psychological*). □ **psychological block** a mental inability or inhibition caused by emotional factors. **psychological moment** the most appropriate time for achieving a particular effect or purpose. **psychological warfare** a campaign directed at reducing an opponent's morale. □□ **psychologically** *adv.*

psychology /saɪˈkɒlədʒɪ/ *n.* (*pl.* **-ies**) **1** the scientific study of the human mind and its functions, esp. those affecting behaviour in a given context. **2** a treatise on or theory of this. **3 a** the mental characteristics or attitude of a person or group. **b** the mental factors governing a situation or activity (*the psychology of crime*). □□ **psychologist** *n.* **psychologize** *v.tr. & intr.* (also **-ise**). [mod.L *psychologia* (as PSYCHO-, -LOGY)]

psychometrics /ˌsaɪkəʊˈmetrɪks/ *n.pl.* (treated as *sing.*) the science of measuring mental capacities and processes.

psychometry /saɪˈkɒmɪtrɪ/ *n.* **1** the supposed divination of facts about events, people, etc., from inanimate objects associated with them. **2** the measurement of mental abilities. □□

psychometric /-kə'metrɪk/ adj. **psychometrically** /-kə'metrɪkəlɪ/ adv. **psychometrist** n.

psychomotor /ˌsaɪkəʊˌməʊtə(r)/ adj. concerning the study of movement resulting from mental activity.

psychoneurosis /ˌsaɪkəʊnjʊə'rəʊsɪs/ n. neurosis, esp. with the indirect expression of emotions.

psychopath /'saɪkə.pæθ/ n. **1** a person suffering from chronic mental disorder esp. with abnormal or violent social behaviour. **2** a mentally or emotionally unstable person. □□ **psychopathic** /-'pæθɪk/ adj. **psychopathically** /-'pæθɪkəlɪ/ adv.

psychopathology /ˌsaɪkəʊpə'θɒlədʒɪ/ n. **1** the scientific study of mental disorders. **2** a mentally or behaviourally disordered state. □□ **psychopathological** /-ˌpæθə'lɒdʒɪk(ə)l/ adj.

psychopathy /saɪ'kɒpəθɪ/ n. psychopathic or psychologically abnormal behaviour.

psychophysics /ˌsaɪkəʊ'fɪzɪks/ n. the science of the relation between the mind and the body. □□ **psychophysical** adj.

psychophysiology /ˌsaɪkəʊˌfɪzɪ'ɒlədʒɪ/ n. the branch of physiology dealing with mental phenomena. □□ **psychophysiological** /-zɪə'lɒdʒɪk(ə)l/ adj.

psychosexual /ˌsaɪkəʊ'seksjʊəl, -'sekʃʊəl/ adj. of or involving the psychological aspects of the sexual impulse. □□ **psychosexually** adv.

psychosis /saɪ'kəʊsɪs/ n. (pl. **psychoses** /-siːz/) a severe mental derangement, esp. when resulting in delusions and loss of contact with external reality. [Gk psukhōsis f. psukhoō give life to (as PSYCHE)]

psychosocial /ˌsaɪkəʊ'səʊʃ(ə)l/ adj. of or involving the influence of social factors or human interactive behaviour. □□ **psychosocially** adv.

psychosomatic /ˌsaɪkəʊsə'mætɪk/ adj. **1** (of an illness etc.) caused or aggravated by mental conflict, stress, etc. **2** of the mind and body together. □□ **psychosomatically** adv.

psychosurgery /ˌsaɪkəʊ'sɜːdʒərɪ/ n. brain surgery as a means of treating mental disorder. □□ **psychosurgical** adj.

psychotherapy /ˌsaɪkəʊ'θerəpɪ/ n. the treatment of mental disorder by psychological means. □□ **psychotherapeutic** /-'pjuːtɪk/ adj. **psychotherapist** n.

psychotic /saɪ'kɒtɪk/ adj. & n. —adj. of or characterized by a psychosis. —n. a person suffering from a psychosis. □□ **psychotically** adv.

psychotropic /ˌsaɪkəʊ'trɒpɪk/ n. (of a drug) acting on the mind. [PSYCHO- + Gk tropē turning: see TROPIC]

psychrometer /saɪ'krɒmɪtə(r)/ n. a thermometer consisting of a dry bulb and a wet bulb for measuring atmospheric humidity. [Gk psukhros cold + -METER]

PT abbr. physical training.

Pt symb. Chem. the element platinum.

pt. abbr. **1** part. **2** pint. **3** point. **4** port.

PTA abbr. **1** parent-teacher association. **2** Passenger Transport Authority.

Ptah /tɑː/ Egyptian Mythol. an ancient deity of Memphis, originally a god of artisans (the Greeks called him Hephaestus) and creator of the universe. He acquired a solar character and became one of the chief deities of Egypt.

ptarmigan /'tɑːmɪgən/ n. any of various game-birds of the genus Lagopus, esp. L. mutus, with grouselike appearance and black or grey plumage in the summer and white in the winter. [Gael. tàrmachan: p- after Gk words in pt-]

PT boat n. US a motor torpedo-boat. [Patrol Torpedo]

Pte. abbr. Private (soldier).

pteridology /ˌterɪ'dɒlədʒɪ/ n. the study of ferns. □□ **pteridological** /-də'lɒdʒɪk(ə)l/ adj. **pteridologist** n. [Gk pteris -idos fern + -LOGY]

pteridophyte /'terɪdə.faɪt/ n. any flowerless plant of the division Pteridophyta, including ferns, club-mosses, and horsetails. [Gk pteris -idos fern + phuton plant]

ptero- /'terəʊ/ comb. form wing. [Gk pteron wing]

pterodactyl /ˌterə'dæktɪl/ n. a large extinct flying birdlike reptile with a long slender head and neck.

pteropod /'terə.pɒd/ n. a marine gastropod with the middle part of its foot expanded into a pair of winglike lobes. [PTERO- + Gk pous podos foot]

pterosaur /'terə.sɔː(r)/ n. any of a group of extinct flying reptiles with large bat-like wings, including pterodactyls. [PTERO- + Gk saura lizard]

pteroylglutamic acid /ˌterəʊˌaɪlgluː'tæmɪk/ n. = FOLIC ACID. [pteroic acid + -YL + GLUTAMIC (ACID)]

pterygoid process /'terɪ.gɔɪd/ adj. each of a pair of processes from the sphenoid bone in the skull. [Gk pterux -ugos wing]

PTFE abbr. polytetrafluoroethylene.

ptisan /'tɪz(ə)n, tɪ'zæn/ n. a nourishing drink, esp. barley water. [ME & OF tizanne etc. f. L ptisana f. Gk ptisanē peeled barley]

PTO abbr. please turn over.

Ptolemaic /ˌtɒlɪ'meɪɪk/ adj. hist. **1** of or relating to Ptolemy (PTOLEMY²) or his theories. **2** of or relating to the Ptolemies, Macedonian rulers of Egypt from the death of Alexander the Great (323 BC) to the death of Cleopatra (30 BC). (See PTOLEMY¹.) □ **Ptolemaic system** the theory that the earth is the stationary centre of the universe (cf. COPERNICAN SYSTEM). [L Ptolemaeus f. Gk Ptolemaios]

Ptolemy¹ /'tɒlɪmɪ/ the name of all the Macedonian kings of Egypt, a dynasty founded by Ptolemy, the close friend and general of Alexander the Great, who took charge of Egypt after his master's death and declared himself king in 304 BC. The dynasty ended with the death of Cleopatra in 30 BC. Under the Ptolemies their capital, Alexandria, became a leading commercial and cultural centre of the Greek world.

Ptolemy² /'tɒlɪmɪ/ (2nd c.) Greek astronomer and geographer, who worked in Alexandria. His major work, known by its Arabic title the Almagest, was a complete textbook of astronomy based on the geocentric system of Hipparchus. His teachings had enormous influence on medieval thought, the geocentric view of the cosmos being adopted as Church doctrine until the late Renaissance. Besides placing the Earth at the centre of the universe and explaining the motions of the planets by combining individual circular motions, the Almagest included detailed tables of lunar and solar motion with eclipse predictions, and a star catalogue giving the positions and magnitudes (graded from 1 to 6) of 1022 stars. Ptolemy's Geography, giving lists of places with their longitudes and latitudes, was also a standard work for centuries, despite its inaccuracies.

ptomaine /'təʊmeɪn/ n. any of various amine compounds, some toxic, in putrefying animal and vegetable matter. □ **ptomaine poisoning** archaic food poisoning. [F ptomaïne f. It. ptomaina irreg. f. Gk ptōma corpse]

ptosis /'təʊsɪs/ n. a drooping of the upper eyelid due to paralysis etc. □□ **ptotic** /'təʊtɪk/ adj. [Gk ptōsis f. piptō fall]

Pty. abbr. Austral., NZ, & S.Afr. proprietary.

ptyalin /'taɪəlɪn/ n. an enzyme which hydrolyses certain carbohydrates and is found in the saliva of humans and some other animals. [Gk ptualon spittle]

Pu symb. Chem. the element plutonium.

pub /pʌb/ n. colloq. **1** Brit. a public house. **2** Austral. a hotel. □ **pub-crawl** Brit. colloq. a drinking tour of several pubs. [abbr.]

puberty /'pjuːbətɪ/ n. the period during which adolescents reach sexual maturity and become capable of reproduction. □ **age of puberty** the age at which puberty begins, in law usu. 14 in boys and 12 in girls. □□ **pubertal** adj. [ME f. F puberté or L pubertas f. puber adult]

pubes¹ /'pjuːbiːz/ n. (pl. same) the lower part of the abdomen at the front of the pelvis, covered with hair from puberty. [L]

pubes² pl. of PUBIS.

pubescence /pjuː'bes(ə)ns/ n. **1** the time when puberty begins. **2** Bot. soft down on the leaves and stems of plants. **3** Zool. soft down on various parts of animals, esp. insects. □□ **pubescent** adj. [F pubescence or med.L pubescentia f. L pubescere reach puberty]

pubic /'pjuːbɪk/ adj. of or relating to the pubes or pubis.

pubis /'pjuːbɪs/ n. (pl. **pubes** /-biːz/) either of a pair of bones forming the two sides of the pelvis. [L os pubis bone of the PUBES]

public /'pʌblɪk/ adj. & n. —adj. **1** of or concerning the people as a whole (*a public holiday; the public interest*). **2** open to or shared by all the people (*public baths; public library; public meeting*). **3** done or existing openly (*made his views public; a public protest*). **4 a** (of a service, funds, etc.) provided by or concerning local or central government (*public money; public records; public expenditure*). **b** (of a person) in government (*had a distinguished public career*). **5** well-known; famous (*a public institution*). **6** *Brit.* of, for, or acting for, a university (*public examination*). —*n.* **1** (as *sing.* or *pl.*) the community in general, or members of the community. **2** a section of the community having a particular interest or in some special connection (*the reading public; my public demands my loyalty*). **3** *Brit. colloq.* **a** = *public bar.* **b** = *public house.* □ **go public** become a public company. **in public** openly, publicly. **in the public domain** belonging to the public as a whole, esp. not subject to copyright. **in the public eye** famous or notorious. **public act** an act of legislation affecting the public as a whole. **public-address system** loudspeakers, microphones, amplifiers, etc., used in addressing large audiences. **public bar** *Brit.* the least expensive bar in a public house. **public bill** a bill of legislation affecting the public as a whole. **public company** *Brit.* a company that sells shares to all buyers on the open market. **public enemy** a notorious wanted criminal. **public figure** a famous person. **public health** the provision of adequate sanitation, drainage, etc. by government. **public house 1** *Brit.* an inn providing alcoholic drinks for consumption on the premises. **2** an inn. **public law 1** the law of relations between individuals and the State. **2** = *public act.* **public lending right** the right of authors to payment when their books etc. are lent by public libraries. **public libel** a published libel. **public nuisance 1** an illegal act against the public generally. **2** *colloq.* an obnoxious person. **public opinion** views, esp. moral, prevalent among the general public. **public ownership** the State ownership of the means of production, distribution, and exchange. **public prosecutor** a law officer conducting criminal proceedings on behalf of the State or in the public interest. **Public Record Office** an institution keeping official archives, esp. birth, marriage, and death certificates, for public inspection. **public relations** the professional maintenance of a favourable public image, esp. by a company, famous person, etc. **public relations officer** a person employed by a company etc. to promote a favourable public image. **public school** see separate entry. **public sector** that part of an economy, industry, etc., that is controlled by the State. **public servant** a State official. **public spirit** a willingness to engage in community action. **public-spirited** having a public spirit. **public-spiritedly** in a public-spirited manner. **public-spiritedness** the quality of being public-spirited. **public transport** buses, trains, etc., charging set fares and running on fixed routes, esp. when State-owned. **public utility** an organization supplying water, gas, etc. to the community. **public works** building operations etc. done by or for the State on behalf of the community. **public wrong** an offence against society as a whole. □□ **publicly** *adv.* [ME f. OF *public* or L *publicus* f. *pubes* adult]

publican /ˈpʌblɪkən/ *n.* **1 a** *Brit.* the keeper of a public house. **b** *Austral.* the keeper of a hotel. **2** *Rom.Hist. & Bibl.* a tax-collector or tax-farmer. [ME f. OF *publicain* f. L *publicanus* f. *publicum* public revenue (as PUBLIC)]

publication /ˌpʌblɪˈkeɪʃ(ə)n/ *n.* **1 a** the preparation and issuing of a book, newspaper, engraving, music, etc. to the public. **b** a book etc. so issued. **2** the act or an instance of making something publicly known. [ME f. OF f. L *publicatio -onis* (as PUBLISH)]

publicist /ˈpʌblɪsɪst/ *n.* **1** a publicity agent or public relations officer. **2** a journalist, esp. concerned with current affairs. **3** *archaic* a writer or other person skilled in international law. □□ **publicism** *n.* **publicistic** /-ˈsɪstɪk/ *adj.* [F *publiciste* f. L (*jus*) *publicum* public law]

publicity /pʌbˈlɪsɪtɪ/ *n.* **1 a** the professional exploitation of a product, company, person, etc., by advertising or popularizing. **b** material or information used for this. **2** public exposure; notoriety. □ **publicity agent** a person employed to produce or heighten public exposure. [F *publicité* (as PUBLIC)]

publicize /ˈpʌblɪˌsaɪz/ *v.tr.* (also **-ise**) advertise; make publicly known.

public school *n.* **1** *Brit.* a private fee-paying secondary school, esp. for boarders. (See below.) **2** *US, Austral., & Sc.* etc. any non-fee-paying school.
   In England, public schools had their origin in the grammar schools of the Tudor period or earlier, endowed for the use or benefit of the public and carried on under some kind of public management or control; they were contrasted with 'private schools' which were carried on at the risk and for the profit of their proprietors, and with education at home under a tutor. In the 19th c. there was a surge of expansion, as well-to-do members of the middle class sought for their sons the education that they had not had themselves, and of reform, under the influence of headmasters such as Butler of Shrewsbury and Arnold of Rugby, who set new standards of work and behaviour. Among the foremost are Winchester (founded in 1382), Eton (1440), Shrewsbury (1552), Westminster (1560), Rugby (1567), Harrow (1571), and Charterhouse (1611).

publish /ˈpʌblɪʃ/ *v.tr.* **1** (also *absol.*) (of an author, publisher, etc.) prepare and issue (a book, newspaper, engraving, etc.) for public sale. (See below.) **2** make generally known. **3** announce (an edict etc.) formally; read (marriage banns). **4** *Law* communicate (a libel etc.) to a third party. □□ **publishable** *adj.* [ME *puplise* etc. f. OF *puplier, publier* f. L *publicare* (as PUBLIC)]
   The trade in books is now shared by the publisher (who takes the commercial risks on a book's production, and the responsibility for marketing it to booksellers and the public), the printer (who prints the book to a publisher's order), and the bookseller (who offers it to the buying public). Before the invention of printing, texts were 'published' by being read aloud to an audience. In the early days of printing the printer was also publisher and bookseller, but during the 15th-16th c. these functions began to separate and developed into separate trades. Technological developments in the printing industry in the 19th c. dramatically increased output and reduced prices. In the 20th c. the introduction of paperbacks, pioneered in the Penguin series in 1935, tapped a wider market by offering books at an unprecedentedly low price, and after the Second World War social and economic changes, and the spread of university education, resulted in an increased demand for books of all kinds. The advent of computers has changed many aspects of publishing in a technological revolution as important as the invention of printing.

publisher /ˈpʌblɪʃə(r)/ *n.* **1** a person or esp. a company that produces and distributes copies of a book, newspaper, etc. for sale. **2** *US* a newspaper proprietor. **3** a person or thing that publishes.

Puccini /poˈtʃiːnɪ/, Giacomo (1858–1924), Italian composer. He decided to devote his musical gifts to opera after seeing Verdi's *Aida* in 1876, but his first major success did not come until 1893 when *Manon Lescaut* was produced at Turin. His most famous operas followed soon after: *La Bohème* in 1896, *Tosca* in 1900, *Madama Butterfly* in 1904, and *La Fanciulla del West* in 1910. These works, among the most popular in the repertory, are saved from cloying sentimentality by Puccini's sense of the dramatic, his great melodic gift, and the skill and effectiveness of his handling of the orchestra.

puce /pjuːs/ *adj. & n.* dark red or purple-brown. [F, = flea(-colour) f. L *pulex -icis*]

Puck /pʌk/ **1** a merry mischievous sprite or goblin believed, especially in the 16th and 17th c., to haunt the English countryside. He was also called Robin Goodfellow or Hobgoblin. **2** (in earlier superstition) an evil demon. —*n.* (**puck**) any of a class of mischievous or evil sprite. **2** a mischievous child. □□ **puckish** *adj.* **puckishly** *adv.* **puckishness** *n.* **pucklike** *adj.* [OE *pūca*: cf. Welsh *pwca*, Ir. *púca*]

puck /pʌk/ *n.* a rubber disc used as a ball in ice hockey. [19th c.: orig. unkn.]

pucka var. of PUKKA.

pucker /ˈpʌkə(r)/ *v. & n.* —*v.tr. & intr.* (often foll. by *up*) gather or cause to gather into wrinkles, folds, or bulges (*puckered her eyebrows; this seam is puckered up*). —*n.* such a wrinkle, bulge, fold, etc. □□ **puckery** *adj.* [prob. frequent., formed as POKE², POCKET (cf. PURSE)]

pud /pʊd/ *n. colloq.* = PUDDING. [abbr.]

pudding /ˈpʊdɪŋ/ *n.* **1 a** any of various sweet cooked dishes (*plum pudding*; *rice pudding*). **b** a savoury dish containing flour, suet, etc. (*Yorkshire pudding*; *steak and kidney pudding*). **c** the sweet course of a meal. **d** the intestines of a pig etc. stuffed with oatmeal, spices, blood, etc. (*black pudding*). **2** *colloq.* a person or thing resembling a pudding. **3** (*Naut.* **puddening** /ˈpʊdənɪŋ/) a pad or tow binding to prevent chafing etc. □ **in the pudding club** *sl.* pregnant. **pudding-cloth** a cloth used for tying up some puddings for boiling. **pudding face** *colloq.* a large fat face. **pudding-head** *colloq.* a stupid person. **pudding-stone** a conglomerate rock consisting of rounded pebbles in a siliceous matrix. □□ **puddingy** *adj.* [ME *poding* f. OF *boudin* black pudding ult. f. L *botellus* sausage: see BOWEL]

puddle /ˈpʌd(ə)l/ *n. & v.* —*n.* **1** a small pool, esp. of rainwater on a road etc. **2** clay and sand mixed with water and used as a watertight covering for embankments etc. **3** a circular patch of disturbed water made by the blade of an oar at each stroke. —*v.* **1** *tr.* **a** knead (clay and sand) into puddle. **b** line (a canal etc.) with puddle. **2** *intr.* make puddle from clay etc. **3** *tr.* stir (molten iron) to produce wrought iron by expelling carbon. (See CORT.) **4** *intr.* **a** dabble or wallow in mud or shallow water. **b** busy oneself in an untidy way. **5** *tr.* make (water etc.) muddy. **6** *tr.* work (mixed water and clay) to separate gold or opal. □□ **puddler** *n.* **puddly** *adj.* [ME *podel, puddel,* dimin. of OE *pudd* ditch]

pudency /ˈpjuːdənsɪ/ *n. literary* modesty; shame. [LL *pudentia* (as PUDENDUM)]

pudendum /pjuːˈdendəm/ *n.* (*pl.* **pudenda** /-də/) (usu. in *pl.*) the genitals, esp. of a woman. □□ **pudendal** *adj.* **pudic** /ˈpjuːdɪk/ *adj.* [L *pudenda* (*membra* parts), neut. pl. of gerundive of *pudēre* be ashamed]

pudgy /ˈpʌdʒɪ/ *adj.* (**pudgier, pudgiest**) *colloq.* (esp. of a person) plump, thickset. □□ **pudge** *n.* **pudgily** *adv.* **pudginess** *n.* [cf. PODGY]

Pudovkin /puˈdɒfkɪn/, Vsevolod Ilarionovich (1893–1953), Russian film director whose works were consistently successful in the USSR. His three major films *Mother* (1926), *The End of St. Petersburg* (1927), and *The Heir to Ghenghis Khan* (1928) have a warmth that contrasts with the contemporaneous work of Eisenstein. His editing aimed at supporting the narrative by linking images in a meaningful way, the montage drawing the audience along a smooth narrative line.

Puebla /ˈpweblə/ a State of SE central Mexico; pop. (est. 1988) 4,068,000; capital, Puebla de Zaragoza.

Pueblo /ˈpwebləʊ/ *n.* (*pl.* **-os**) a member of certain Indian peoples occupying a pueblo settlement. Their prehistoric period is known as the Anasazi culture. [PUEBLO]

pueblo /ˈpwebləʊ/ *n.* (*pl.* **-os**) a town or village in Latin America, esp. an Indian settlement. [Sp., = people, f. L *populus*]

puerile /ˈpjʊəraɪl/ *adj.* **1** trivial, childish, immature. **2** of or like a child. □ **puerile breathing** breathing characterized by a loud pulmonary murmur as in children, a sign of disease in an adult. □□ **puerilely** *adv.* **puerility** /-ˈrɪlɪtɪ/ *n.* (*pl.* **-ies**). [F *puéril* or L *puerilis* f. *puer* boy]

puerperal /pjuːˈɜːpər(ə)l/ *adj.* of or caused by childbirth. □ **puerperal fever** fever following childbirth and caused by uterine infection. [L *puerperus* f. *puer* child + *-parus* bearing]

Puerto Cortés /ˌpwɜːtəʊ kɔːˈtez/ the principal port of Honduras, on the Caribbean coast; pop. (1986) 40,000.

Puerto Plata /ˌpwɜːtəʊ ˈplɑːtə/ the principal beach resort of the Dominican Republic, with a deep-water harbour for cruise liners; pop. (1986) 96,500.

Puerto Rico /ˌpwɜːtəʊ ˈriːkəʊ/ an island of the Greater Antilles in the West Indies; pop. (est. 1988) 3,358,900; official language, Spanish; capital, San Juan. Discovered in 1493 by Christopher Columbus, the island was one of the earliest Spanish settlements in the New World. It was ceded to the US in 1898 after the Spanish-American war, and was established as a Commonwealth with full powers of local government in 1952. In recent decades there has been considerable progress in industrialization and welfare. □ **Puerto Rico Trench** the deepest section of the North Atlantic, forming a trench that extends in an east-west direction to the north of Puerto Rico and the Leeward Islands. It reaches a depth of 9,220 m (28,397 ft.). □□ **Puerto Rican** *adj. & n.*

puff /pʌf/ *n. & v.* —*n.* **1 a** a short quick blast of breath or wind. **b** the sound of this; a similar sound. **c** a small quantity of vapour, smoke, etc., emitted in one blast (*went up in a puff of smoke*). **2** a cake etc. containing jam, cream, etc., and made of light esp. puff pastry. **3** a gathered mass of material in a dress etc. (*puff sleeve*). **4** a rolled protuberant mass of hair. **5 a** an extravagantly enthusiastic review of a book etc., esp. in a newspaper. **b** an advertisement for goods etc., esp. in a newspaper. **6** = *powder-puff.* **7** *US* an eiderdown. **8** *colloq.* one's life (*in all my puff*). —*v.* **1** *intr.* emit a puff of air or breath; blow with short blasts. **2** *intr.* (usu. foll. by *away, out,* etc.) (of a person smoking, a steam engine, etc.) emit or move with puffs (*puffing away at his cigar; a train puffed out of the station*). **3** *tr.* (usu. in passive; often foll. by *out*) put out of breath (*arrived somewhat puffed; completely puffed him out*). **4** *intr.* breathe hard; pant. **5** *tr.* utter pantingly ('*No more,*' *he puffed*). **6** *intr. & tr.* (usu. foll. by *up, out*) become or cause to become inflated; swell (*his eye was inflamed and puffed up; puffed up the balloon*). **7** *tr.* (usu. foll. by *out, up, away*) blow or emit (dust, smoke, a light object, etc.) with a puff. **8** *tr.* smoke (a pipe etc.) in puffs. **9** *tr.* (usu. as **puffed up** *adj.*) elate; make proud or boastful. **10** *tr.* advertise or promote (goods, a book, etc.) with exaggerated or false praise. □ **puff-adder** a large venomous African viper, *Bitis arietans,* which inflates the upper part of its body and hisses when excited. **puff and blow** = sense 4 of *v.* **puff-ball** any of various fungi having a ball-shaped spore case. **puff pastry** light flaky pastry. **puff-puff** *Brit.* a childish word for a steam-engine or train. **puff up** = sense 9 of *v.* [ME *puf, puffe,* perh. f. OE, imit. of the sound of breath]

puffer /ˈpʌfə(r)/ *n.* **1** a person or thing that puffs. **2** = *puff-puff.* □ **puffer-fish** = *globe-fish.*

puffin /ˈpʌfɪn/ *n.* any of various sea birds of the family Alcidae native to the N. Atlantic and N. Pacific, esp. *Fratercula arctica,* having a large head with a brightly coloured triangular bill, and black and white plumage. [ME *poffin, pophyn,* of unkn. orig.]

puffy /ˈpʌfɪ/ *adj.* (**puffier, puffiest**) **1** swollen, esp. of the face etc. **2** fat. **3** gusty. **4** short-winded; puffed out. □□ **puffily** *adv.* **puffiness** *n.*

pug¹ /pʌg/ *n.* **1** (in full **pug-dog**) **a** a dwarf breed of dog like a bulldog with a broad flat nose and deeply wrinkled face. **b** a dog of this breed. **2** a fox. **3** *Brit.* a small locomotive for shunting etc. □ **pug-nose** a short squat or snub nose. **pug-nosed** having such a nose. □□ **puggish** *adj.* **puggy** *adj.* [16th c.: perh. f. LG or Du.]

pug² /pʌg/ *n. & v.* —*n.* loam or clay mixed and prepared for making bricks, pottery, etc. —*v.tr.* (**pugged, pugging**) **1** prepare (clay) thus. **2** pack (esp. the space under the floor to deaden sound) with pug, sawdust, etc. □ **pug-mill** a mill for preparing pug. □□ **pugging** *n.* [19th c.: orig. unkn.]

pug³ /pʌg/ *n. sl.* a boxer. [abbr. of PUGILIST]

pug⁴ /pʌg/ *n. & v.* —*n.* the footprint of an animal. —*v.tr.* (**pugged, pugging**) track by pugs. [Hindi *pag* footprint]

puggaree /ˈpʌgərɪ/ *n.* **1** an Indian turban. **2** a thin muslin scarf tied round a sun-helmet etc. and shielding the neck. [Hindi *pagṛī* turban]

pugilist /ˈpjuːdʒɪlɪst/ *n.* a boxer, esp. a professional. □□ **pugilism** *n.* **pugilistic** /-ˈlɪstɪk/ *adj.* [L *pugil* boxer]

Pugin /ˈpjuːdʒɪn/, Augustus Welby Northmore (1812–52), English architect, theorist, and designer, whose qualities can be seen in his furniture and decorations for the houses of Parliament designed by Sir Charles Barry. His chief importance lies in his proselytizing zeal as apologist for the Gothic revival in England. Converted to Roman Catholicism in 1835, he championed the Gothic case in *Contrasts* (1836), where medieval Christian society and architecture were favourably compared with the inadequacies of their contemporary equivalents. Other works, e.g. *Principles* (1841) and *Apology* (1843), continued this theoretical assault. His practical schemes, however, although accurate in revivalist detail, appear flimsy overall, indicating perhaps that for all his functionalist justification of Gothic architecture his inspiration was visual rather than structural.

Puglia see APULIA.

pugnacious /pʌgˈneɪʃəs/ adj. quarrelsome; disposed to fight. □□ **pugnaciously** adv. **pugnaciousness** n. **pugnacity** /-ˈnæsɪtɪ/ n. [L pugnax -acis f. pugnare fight f. pugnus fist]

puisne /ˈpjuːnɪ/ adj. Law denoting a judge of a superior court inferior in rank to chief justices. [OF f. puis f. L postea afterwards + né born f. L natus: cf. PUNY]

puissance /ˈpjuːɪs(ə)ns, ˈpwɪs-/ n. 1 /also pwiːˈsɑ̃s/ a test of a horse's ability to jump large obstacles in showjumping. 2 archaic great power, might, or influence. [ME (in sense 2) f. OF (as PUISSANT)]

puissant /ˈpjuːɪs(ə)nt, ˈpwiː:s-, ˈpwɪs-/ adj. literary or archaic having great power or influence; mighty. □□ **puissantly** adv. [ME f. OF f. L posse be able: cf. POTENT¹]

puja /ˈpuːdʒə/ n. (also **pooja**) a Hindu rite of worship; a prayer. [Skr.]

puke /pjuːk/ v. & n. sl. —v.tr. & intr. vomit. —n. vomit. □□ **pukey** adj. [16th c.: prob. imit.]

pukeko /ˈpuːkeˌkəʊ/ n. (pl. **-os**) Austral. & NZ a rail, Porphyrio porphyrio, with blue, black, and white plumage. [Maori]

pukka /ˈpʌkə/ adj. (also **pukkah, pucka**) Anglo-Ind. 1 genuine. 2 of good quality; reliable (did a pukka job). 3 of full weight. [Hindi pakkā cooked, ripe, substantial]

pulchritude /ˈpʌlkrɪˌtjuːd/ n. literary beauty. □□ **pulchritudinous** /-ˈtjuːdɪnəs/ adj. [ME f. L pulchritudo -dinis f. pulcher -chri beautiful]

pule /pjuːl/ v.intr. literary cry querulously or weakly; whine, whimper. [16th c.: prob. imit.: cf. F piauler]

Pulitzer /ˈpʊlɪtsə(r)/, Joseph (1847–1911), American newspaper-owner and editor, of Hungarian origin, one of the founders of American sensational journalism. His object was the remedy of abuses and the reform of social and economic inequalities by the exposure of striking instances and by the vigorous expression of democratic opinion. The success of this appeal to the emotions found many imitators among journalists not actuated by the same creditable motives. □ **Pulitzer prize** (also /ˈpjuː-/) any of a group of money prizes established under his will and offered annually to American citizens for work in music, journalism, American history and biography, poetry, drama, and fiction.

pull /pʊl/ v. & n. —v. 1 tr. exert force upon (a thing) tending to move it to oneself or the origin of the force (stop pulling my hair). 2 tr. cause to move in this way (pulled it nearer; pulled me into the room). 3 intr. exert a pulling force (the horse pulls well; the engine will not pull). 4 tr. extract (a cork or tooth) by pulling. 5 tr. damage (a muscle etc.) by abnormal strain. 6 a tr. move (a boat) by pulling on the oars. b intr. (of a boat etc.) be caused to move, esp. in a specified direction. 7 intr. (often foll. by up) proceed with effort (up a hill etc.). 8 tr. (foll. by on) bring out (a weapon) for use against (a person). 9 a tr. check the speed of (a horse), esp. so as to make it lose the race. b intr. (of a horse) strain against the bit. 10 tr. attract or secure (custom or support). 11 tr. draw (liquor) from a barrel etc. 12 intr. (foll. by at) tear or pluck at. 13 intr. (often foll. by on, at) inhale deeply; draw or suck (on a pipe etc.). 14 tr. (often foll. by up) remove (a plant) by the root. 15 tr. a Cricket strike (the ball) to the leg side. b Golf strike (the ball) widely to the left. 16 tr. print (a proof etc.). 17 tr. colloq. achieve or accomplish (esp. something illicit). —n. 1 the act of pulling. 2 the force exerted by this. 3 a means of exerting influence; an advantage. 4 something that attracts or draws attention. 5 a deep draught of liquor. 6 a prolonged effort, e.g. in going up a hill. 7 a handle etc. for applying a pull. 8 a spell of rowing. 9 a printer's rough proof. 10 Cricket & Golf a pulling stroke. 11 a suck at a cigarette. □ **pull about** 1 treat roughly. 2 pull from side to side. **pull apart** (or **to pieces**) = take to pieces (see PIECE). **pull back** retreat or cause to retreat. **pull-back** n. 1 a retarding influence. 2 a withdrawal of troops. **pull down** 1 demolish (esp. a building). 2 humiliate. 3 colloq.

earn (a sum of money) as wages etc. **pull a face** assume a distinctive or specified (e.g. sad or angry) expression. **pull a fast one** see FAST¹. **pull in** 1 (of a bus, train, etc.) arrive to take passengers. 2 (of a vehicle) move to the side of or off the road. 3 earn or acquire. 4 colloq. arrest. **pull-in** n. Brit. a roadside café or other stopping-place. **pull a person's leg** deceive a person playfully. **pull off** 1 remove by pulling. 2 succeed in achieving or winning. **pull oneself together** recover control of oneself. **pull the other one** colloq. expressing disbelief (with ref. to pull a person's leg). **pull out** 1 take out by pulling. 2 depart. 3 withdraw from an undertaking. 4 (of a bus, train, etc.) leave with its passengers. 5 (of a vehicle) move out from the side of the road, or from its normal position to overtake. **pull-out** n. something that can be pulled out, esp. a section of a magazine. **pull over** (of a vehicle) pull in. **pull the plug on** colloq. defeat, discomfit. **pull one's punches** avoid using one's full force. **pull rank** take unfair advantage of one's seniority. **pull round** (or **through**) recover or cause to recover from an illness. **pull strings** exert (esp. clandestine) influence. **pull the strings** be the real actuator of what another does. **pull together** work in harmony. **pull up** 1 stop or cause to stop moving. 2 pull out of the ground. 3 reprimand. 4 check oneself. **pull one's weight** do one's fair share of work. **pull wires** esp. US = pull strings. □□ **puller** n. [OE (ā)pullian, perh. rel. to LG pūlen, MDu. polen to shell]

pullet /ˈpʊlɪt/ n. a young hen, esp. one less than one year old. [ME f. OF poulet dimin. of poule ult. fem. of L pullus chicken]

pulley /ˈpʊlɪ/ n. & v. —n. (pl. **-eys**) 1 a grooved wheel or set of wheels for a cord etc. to pass over, set in a block and used for changing the direction of a force. 2 a wheel or drum fixed on a shaft and turned by a belt, used esp. to increase speed or power. —v.tr. (**-eys, -eyed**) 1 hoist or work with a pulley. 2 provide with a pulley. [ME f. OF polie prob. ult. f. med. Gk polidion (unrecorded) pivot, dimin. of polos POLE²]

Pullman /ˈpʊlmən/ n. 1 a railway carriage or motor coach affording special comfort. 2 a sleeping-car. [G. M. Pullman, Amer. designer d. 1897]

pullover /ˈpʊlˌəʊvə(r)/ n. a knitted garment put on over the head and covering the top half of the body.

pullulate /ˈpʌljʊˌleɪt/ v.intr. 1 (of a seed, shoot, etc.) bud, sprout, germinate. 2 (esp. of an animal) swarm, throng; breed prolifically. 3 develop; spring up; come to life. 4 (foll. by with) abound. □□ **pullulant** adj. **pullulation** /-ˈleɪʃ(ə)n/ n. [L pullulare sprout f. pullulus dimin. of pullus young of an animal]

pulmonary /ˈpʌlmənərɪ/ adj. 1 of or relating to the lungs. 2 having lungs or lunglike organs. 3 affected with or susceptible to lung disease. □ **pulmonary artery** the artery conveying blood from the heart to the lungs. **pulmonary tuberculosis** a form of tuberculosis caused by inhaling the tubercle bacillus into the lungs. **pulmonary vein** the vein carrying oxygenated blood from the lungs to the heart. □□ **pulmonate** /-nət/ adj. [L pulmonarius f. pulmo -onis lung]

pulmonic /pʌlˈmɒnɪk/ adj. = PULMONARY 1. [F pulmonique or f. mod.L pulmonicus f. L pulmo (as PULMONARY)]

pulp /pʌlp/ n. & v. —n. 1 the soft fleshy part of fruit etc. 2 any soft thick wet mass. 3 a soft shapeless mass derived from rags, wood, etc., used in paper-making. 4 (often attrib.) poor quality (often sensational) writing orig. printed on rough paper (pulp fiction). 5 vascular tissue filling the interior cavity and root canals of a tooth. 6 Mining pulverized ore mixed with water. —v. 1 tr. reduce to pulp. 2 tr. withdraw (a publication) from the market, usu. recycling the paper. 3 tr. remove pulp from. 4 intr. become pulp. □□ **pulper** n. **pulpless** adj. **pulpy** adj. **pulpiness** n. [L pulpa]

pulpit /ˈpʊlpɪt/ n. 1 a raised enclosed platform in a church etc. from which the preacher delivers a sermon. 2 (prec. by the) preachers or preaching collectively. [ME f. L pulpitum scaffold, platform]

pulpwood /ˈpʌlpwʊd/ n. timber suitable for making pulp.

pulque /ˈpʊlkeɪ, ˈpʊlkɪ/ n. a Mexican fermented drink made from the sap of the maguey. □ **pulque brandy** a strong intoxicant made from pulque. [17th c.: Amer. Sp., of unkn. orig.]

pulsar /ˈpʌlsɑː(r)/ n. Astron. a cosmic source from which light or radio waves are emitted in short bursts with great regularity. When discovered in 1968, this regularity was at first attributed to signals from intelligent beings, but is now believed to be due to the interaction of the magnetic field of a rapidly rotating neutron star with circumstellar material, accelerating electrons which radiate energy in a beam; as this beam sweeps past the observer up to hundreds of times a second, the characteristic 'pulsations' in signal strength are noted. [pulsating star, after quasar]

pulsate /pʌlˈseɪt, ˈpʌl-/ v.intr. 1 expand and contract rhythmically; throb. 2 vibrate, quiver, thrill. □□ **pulsation** /-ˈseɪʃ(ə)n/ n. **pulsator** /-ˈseɪtə(r)/ n. **pulsatory** /ˈpʌlsətərɪ/ adj. [L pulsare frequent. of pellere puls- drive, beat]

pulsatile /ˈpʌlsətaɪl/ adj. 1 of or having the property of pulsation. 2 (of a musical instrument) played by percussion. [med.L pulsatilis (as PULSATE)]

pulsatilla /ˌpʌlsəˈtɪlə/ n. any plant of the genus Pulsatilla, esp. the pasque-flower. [mod.L dimin. of pulsata fem. past part. (as PULSATE), because it quivers in the wind]

pulse[1] /pʌls/ n. & v. —n. 1 **a** a rhythmical throbbing of the arteries as blood is propelled through them, esp. as felt in the wrists, temples, etc. **b** each successive beat of the arteries or heart. 2 a throb or thrill of life or emotion. 3 a latent feeling. 4 a single vibration of sound, electric current, light, etc., esp. as a signal. 5 a musical beat. 6 any regular or recurrent rhythm, e.g. of the stroke of oars. —v.intr. 1 pulsate. 2 (foll. by out, in, etc.) transmit etc. by rhythmical beats. □ **pulse code** coding information in pulses. **pulse code modulation** a pulse modulation technique of representing a signal by a sequence of binary codes. **pulse modulation** a type of modulation in which pulses are varied to represent a signal. □□ **pulseless** adj. [ME f. OF pous f. L pulsus f. pellere puls- drive, beat]

pulse[2] /pʌls/ n. (as sing. or pl.) 1 the edible seeds of various leguminous plants, e.g. chick-peas, lentils, beans, etc. 2 the plant or plants producing this. [ME f. OF pols f. L puls pultis porridge of meal etc.]

pulsimeter /pʌlˈsɪmɪtə(r)/ n. an instrument for measuring the rate or force of a pulse.

pulverize /ˈpʌlvəraɪz/ v. (also **-ise**) 1 tr. reduce to fine particles. 2 tr. & intr. crumble to dust. 3 colloq. tr. **a** demolish. **b** defeat utterly. □□ **pulverizable** adj. **pulverization** /-ˈzeɪʃ(ə)n/ n. **pulverizator** n. **pulverizer** n. [ME f. LL pulverizare f. pulvis pulveris dust]

pulverulent /pʌlˈveruʲlənt/ adj. 1 consisting of fine particles; powdery. 2 likely to crumble. [L pulverulentus (as PULVERIZE)]

puma /ˈpjuːmə/ n. a wild American cat, Felis concolor, usu. with a plain greyish-black coat. Also called COUGAR, PANTHER, mountain lion. [Sp. f. Quechua]

pumice /ˈpʌmɪs/ n. & v. —n. (in full **pumice-stone**) 1 a light porous volcanic rock often used as an abrasive in cleaning or polishing substances. 2 a piece of this used for removing hard skin etc. —v.tr. rub or clean with a pumice. □□ **pumiceous** /pjuːˈmɪʃəs/ adj. [ME f. OF pomis f. L pumex pumicis (dial. pom-): cf. POUNCE[2]]

pummel /ˈpʌm(ə)l/ v.tr. (**pummelled, pummelling**; US **pummeled, pummeling**) strike repeatedly esp. with the fist. [alt. f. POMMEL]

pump[1] /pʌmp/ n. & v. —n. 1 a machine, usu. with rotary action or the reciprocal action of a piston, for raising or moving liquids, compressing gases, inflating tyres, etc. 2 an instance of pumping; a stroke of a pump. —v. 1 tr. (often foll. by in, out, into, up, etc.) raise or remove (liquid, gas, etc.) with a pump. 2 tr. (often foll. by up) fill (a tyre etc.) with air. 3 tr. remove (water etc.) with a pump. 4 intr. work a pump. 5 tr. (often foll. by out) cause to move, pour forth, etc., as if by pumping. 6 tr. elicit information from (a person) by persistent questioning. 7 tr. **a** move vigorously up and down. **b** shake (a person's hand) effusively. □ **pump-brake** a handle of a pump, esp. with a transverse bar for several people to work at. **pump-handle** colloq. shake (a person's hand) effusively. **pump iron** colloq. exercise with weights. **pump-priming** 1 introduce fluid etc.

into a pump to prepare it for working. 2 esp. US the stimulation of commerce etc. by investment. **pump room** 1 a room where fuel pumps etc. are stored or controlled. 2 a room at a spa etc. where medicinal water is dispensed. [ME pumpe, pompe (orig. Naut.): prob. imit.]

pump[2] /pʌmp/ n. 1 a plimsoll. 2 a light shoe for dancing etc. 3 US a court shoe. [16th c.: orig. unkn.]

pumpernickel /ˈpʌmpəˌnɪk(ə)l, ˈpʊ-/ n. German wholemeal rye bread. [G, earlier = lout, bumpkin, of uncert. orig.]

pumpkin /ˈpʌmpkɪn/ n. 1 any of various plants of the genus Cucurbita, esp. C. maxima, with large lobed leaves and tendrils. 2 the large rounded yellow fruit of this with a thick rind and edible flesh, used as a vegetable and (in the US) a filling for pies. [alt. f. earlier pompon, pumpion f. obs. F po(m)pon f. L pepo -onis f. Gk pepōn large melon: see PEPO]

pun[1] /pʌn/ n. & v. —n. the humorous use of a word to suggest different meanings, or of words of the same sound and different meanings. —v.intr. (**punned, punning**) (foll. by on) make a pun or puns with (words). □□ **punningly** adv. [17th c.: perh. f. obs. pundigrion, a fanciful formation]

pun[2] /pʌn/ v.tr. (**punned, punning**) Brit. consolidate (earth or rubble) by pounding or ramming. □□ **punner** n. [dial. var. of POUND[2]]

puna /ˈpuːnə/ n. 1 a high plateau in the Peruvian Andes. 2 = mountain sickness. [Quechua, in sense 1]

Punch /pʌntʃ/ a grotesque hook-nosed hump-backed buffoon, the English variant of a stock character derived from Italian popular comedy (Pulcinella; in France Polichinelle; in England Punchinello or Punch). The name is now preserved chiefly as the title of an English humorous weekly periodical (founded in 1841) and in 'Punch and Judy'. □ **as pleased** or **proud as Punch** showing great pleasure or pride. **Punch and Judy** an English puppet-show of uncertain origin, probably introduced into England from the Continent in the 17th c. (Pepys saw a show in 1662). It is presented on the miniature stage of a tall collapsible booth traditionally covered with striped canvas, and was once a familiar sight in large cities and can still be seen in seaside towns. In the standard version of the play Punch, with his humped back and hooked nose, is on the manipulator's right hand, remaining on stage all the time, while the left hand provides a series of characters—baby, wife (Judy), priest, doctor, policeman, hangman—for him to nag, beat, and finally kill. His live dog, Toby, sits on the ledge of the booth. [abbr. Punchinello, f. Neapolitan dial. Polecenella, It. Pulcinella, perh. dimin. of It. pollecena young turkey-cock (with hooked beak which the nose of Punch's mask resembles); f. pulcino chicken ult. f. L pullus; the name of Punch's wife (Judy) is of later date]

punch[1] /pʌntʃ/ v. & n. —v. & tr. 1 strike bluntly, esp. with a closed fist. 2 prod or poke with a blunt object. 3 **a** pierce a hole in (metal, paper, a ticket, etc.) as or with a punch. **b** pierce (a hole) by punching. 4 US drive (cattle) by prodding with a stick etc. —n. 1 a blow with a fist. 2 the ability to deliver this. 3 colloq. vigour, momentum; effective force. □ **punch** (or **punched**) **card** (or **tape**) a card or paper tape perforated according to a code, for conveying instructions or data to a data processor etc. **punch-drunk** stupefied from or as though from a series of heavy blows. **punching-bag** US a suspended stuffed bag used as a punchball. **punch-line** words giving the point of a joke or story. **punch-up** Brit. colloq. a fist-fight; a brawl. □□ **puncher** n. [ME, var. of POUNCE[1]]

punch[2] /pʌntʃ/ n. 1 any of various devices or machines for punching holes in materials (e.g. paper, leather, metal, plaster). 2 a tool or machine for impressing a design or stamping a die on a material. [perh. an abbr. of PUNCHEON[1], or f. PUNCH[1]]

punch[3] /pʌntʃ/ n. a drink of wine or spirits mixed with water, fruit juices, spices, etc., and usu. served hot. □ **punch-bowl** 1 a bowl in which punch is mixed. 2 a deep round hollow in a hill. [17th c.: orig. unkn.]

punch[4] /pʌntʃ/ n. (in full **Suffolk punch**) a short-legged thickset draught horse. [prob. as PUNCH]

punchball /ˈpʌntʃbɔːl/ n. 1 a stuffed or inflated ball suspended or mounted on a stand, for punching as a form of exercise. 2

US a ball game in which a rubber ball is punched with the fist or head.

punched card *n.* a card perforated according to a specified code, used in recording and analysing data. Such cards (introduced by the American engineer Hollerith) were first used in the US census of 1890, and thereafter found widespread use in business and later for scientific and technical purposes. Early computers were often fed with information from punched cards of the Hollerith type.

puncheon[1] /ˈpʌntʃ(ə)n/ *n.* **1** a short post, esp. one supporting a roof in a coal-mine. **2** = PUNCH[2]. [ME f. OF *poinson, po(i)nchon*, ult. f. L *pungere punct-* prick]

puncheon[2] /ˈpʌntʃ(ə)n/ *n. hist.* a large cask for liquids etc. holding from 72 to 120 gallons. [ME f. OF *poinson, po(i)nchon*, of unkn. orig. (prob. not the same as in PUNCHEON[1])]

Punchinello /ˌpʌntʃɪˈneləʊ/ *n.* (*pl.* **-os**) **1** see PUNCH. **2** a short stout person of comical appearance.

punchy /ˈpʌntʃɪ/ *adj.* (**punchier, punchiest**) having punch or vigour; forceful. □□ **punchily** *adv.* **punchiness** *n.*

puncta *pl.* of PUNCTUM.

punctate /ˈpʌŋkteɪt/ *adj. Biol.* marked or studded with points, dots, spots, etc. □□ **punctation** /-ˈteɪʃ(ə)n/ *n.* [L *punctum* (as POINT)]

punctilio /pʌŋkˈtɪlɪəʊ/ *n.* (*pl.* **-os**) **1** a delicate point of ceremony or honour. **2** the etiquette of such points. **3** petty formality. [It. *puntiglio* & Sp. *puntillo* dimin. of *punto* point]

punctilious /pʌŋkˈtɪlɪəs/ *adj.* **1** attentive to formality or etiquette. **2** precise in behaviour. □□ **punctiliously** *adv.* **punctiliousness** *n.* [F *pointilleux* f. *pointille* f. It. (as PUNCTILIO)]

punctual /ˈpʌŋktjʊəl/ *adj.* **1** observant of the appointed time. **2** neither early nor late. **3** *Geom.* of a point. □□ **punctuality** /-ˈælɪtɪ/ *n.* **punctually** *adv.* [ME f. med.L *punctualis* f. L *punctum* POINT]

punctuate /ˈpʌŋktjʊˌeɪt/ *v.tr.* **1** insert punctuation marks in. **2** interrupt at intervals (*punctuated his tale with heavy sighs*). [med.L *punctuare punctuat-* (as PUNCTUAL)]

punctuation /ˌpʌŋktjʊˈeɪʃ(ə)n/ *n.* **1** the system or arrangement of marks used to punctuate a written passage. **2** the practice or skill of punctuating. □ **punctuation mark** any of the marks (e.g. full stop and comma) used in writing to separate sentences and phrases etc. and to clarify meaning. Before the invention of printing, texts were 'published' by being read aloud to an audience from manuscript, and punctuation marks, consisting of simple 'points' or stops, were used to indicate to the reader the pauses which mark off the sense units (phrases, clauses, and sentences) in the spoken language. Since these pauses frequently correlate with a rise or fall in voice pitch, punctuation marks, particularly in liturgical manuscripts, also seem to have been used to indicate changes of intonation, i.e. as a primitive form of musical notation. When printing made the written language directly available to the literate without the intervention of the reader's voice, new punctuation marks were introduced (e.g. brackets, question marks, exclamation and quotation marks) to provide visual clarification of the text. [med.L *punctuatio* (as PUNCTUATE)]

punctum /ˈpʌŋktəm/ *n.* (*pl.* **puncta** /-tə/) *Biol.* a speck, dot, spot of colour, etc., or an elevation or depression on a surface. [L, = POINT]

puncture /ˈpʌŋktʃə(r)/ *n. & v.* —*n.* **1** a prick or pricking, esp. the accidental piercing of a pneumatic tyre. **2** a hole made in this way. —*v.* **1** *tr.* make a puncture in. **2** *intr.* undergo puncture. **3** *tr.* prick or pierce. [ME f. L *punctura* f. *pungere punct-* prick]

pundit /ˈpʌndɪt/ *n.* **1** (also **pandit**) a Hindu learned in Sanskrit and in the philosophy, religion, and jurisprudence of India. **2** often *iron.* a learned expert or teacher. □□ **punditry** *n.* [Hind. *paṇḍit* f. Skr. *paṇḍita* learned]

Pune /ˈpuːnə/ (formerly **Poona**) a city of western India, in Maharashtra State; pop. (1981) 1,685,000.

pungent /ˈpʌndʒ(ə)nt/ *adj.* **1** having a sharp or strong taste or smell, esp. so as to produce a pricking sensation. **2** (of remarks) penetrating, biting, caustic. **3** mentally stimulating. **4** *Biol.*

having a sharp point. □□ **pungency** *n.* **pungently** *adv.* [L *pungent-* pres. part. of *pungere* prick]

Punic /ˈpjuːnɪk/ *adj. & n.* —*adj.* of or relating to ancient Carthage in N. Africa. —*n.* the language of Carthage, related to Phoenician. □ **Punic faith** treachery. **Punic Wars** three wars between Rome and Carthage, which led to the unquestioned dominance of Rome in the western Mediterranean, a position of power which was not endangered for centuries afterwards. In the first (264–241 BC) Rome secured Sicily from Carthage and established herself as a naval power; in the second (218–201 BC) the defeat of Hannibal (largely through the generalship of Fabius Cunctator and Scipio) put an end to Carthage's position as a Mediterranean power; the third (149–146 BC) ended in the total destruction of the city of Carthage. [L *Punicus, Poenicus* f. *Poenus* f. Gk *Phoinix* Phoenician]

punish /ˈpʌnɪʃ/ *v.tr.* **1** cause (an offender) to suffer for an offence. **2** inflict a penalty for (an offence). **3** *colloq.* inflict severe blows on (an opponent). **4 a** tax severely; subject to severe treatment. **b** abuse or treat improperly. □□ **punishable** *adj.* **punisher** *n.* **punishing** *adj.* (in sense 4a). **punishingly** *adv.* [ME f. OF *punir* f. L *punire* = *poenire* f. *poena* penalty]

punishment /ˈpʌnɪʃmənt/ *n.* **1** the act or an instance of punishing; the condition of being punished. **2** the loss or suffering inflicted in this. **3** *colloq.* severe treatment or suffering. [ME f. AF & OF *punissement* f. *punir*]

punitive /ˈpjuːnɪtɪv/ *adj.* (also **punitory** /-tərɪ/) **1** inflicting or intended to inflict punishment. **2** (of taxation etc.) extremely severe. **3** *Law* = VINDICTIVE. □□ **punitively** *adv.* [F *punitif -ive* or med.L *punitivus* (as PUNISHMENT)]

Punjab /pʌnˈdʒɑːb, ˈpʌndʒɑːb/ **1** *hist.* (also **the Punjab**) a former State (later a province; see RANJIT SINGH) of British India, divided in 1947 between Pakistan and India. Its name is derived from Hindustani *pañj* five, *āb* waters, referring to the five rivers Jhelum, Chenab, Ravi, Beas, and Sutlej, tributaries of the Indus, which lay within it. **2** a province of Pakistan; pop. (1981) 47,292,000; capital, Lahore. **3** a State of India; pop. (1981) 16,669,750; capital, Chandigarh. □□ **Punjabi** *adj. & n.*

punk /pʌŋk/ *n. & adj.* —*n.* **1 a** a worthless person or thing (often as a general term of abuse). **b** nonsense. **2 a** (in full **punk rock**) a loud fast-moving form of rock music with crude and aggressive effects. **b** (in full **punk rocker**) a devotee of this. **3** *US* a hoodlum or ruffian. **4** *US* a passive male homosexual. **5** *US* an inexperienced person; a novice. **6** soft crumbly wood that has been attacked by fungus, used as tinder. —*adj.* **1** worthless, rotten. **2** denoting punk rock and its associations. □□ **punky** *adj.* [18th c.: orig. unkn.: cf. SPUNK]

punkah /ˈpʌŋkə/ *n.* **1** (in India) a fan usu. made from the leaf of the palmyra. **2** a large swinging cloth fan on a frame worked by a cord or electrically. □ **punkah-wallah** a person who works a punkah. [Hindi *paṅkhā* fan f. Skr. *pakṣaka* f. *pakṣa* wing]

punnet /ˈpʌnɪt/ *n. Brit.* a small light basket or container for fruit or vegetables. [19th c.: perh. dimin. of dial. *pun* POUND[1]]

punster /ˈpʌnstə(r)/ *n.* a person who makes puns, esp. habitually.

punt[1] /pʌnt/ *n. & v.* —*n.* a long narrow flat-bottomed boat, square at both ends, used mainly for pleasure on rivers and propelled by a long pole. Formerly used for transporting goods and cattle, such boats are now used for pleasure and sometimes for racing. —*v.* **1** *tr.* propel (a punt) with a pole. **2** *intr. & tr.* travel or convey in a punt. □□ **punter** *n.* [ME f. MLG *punte, punto* & MDu. *ponte* ferry-boat f. L *ponto* Gaulish transport vessel]

punt[2] /pʌnt/ *v. & n.* —*v.tr.* kick (a ball, esp. in rugby) after it has dropped from the hands and before it reaches the ground. —*n.* such a kick. □□ **punter** *n.* [prob. f. dial. *punt* push forcibly: cf. BUNT[3]]

punt[3] /pʌnt/ *v. & n.* —*v.intr.* **1** (in some card-games) lay a stake against the bank. **2** *Brit. colloq.* **a** bet on a horse etc. **b** speculate in shares etc. —*n.* **1** a bet. **2** a point in faro. [F *ponter* f. *ponte* player against the bank f. Sp. *punto* POINT]

punt[4] /pʊnt/ *n.* the chief monetary unit of the Republic of Ireland. [Ir., = pound]

Punta Arenas /ˌpʊntə əˈreɪnəs/ the capital of Magallanes province in southern Chile; pop. (est. 1987) 111,700. It is the southernmost city in the world and the only city on the Strait of Magellan.

punter /ˈpʌntə(r)/ n. **1** a person who gambles or lays a bet. **2 a** *colloq.* a customer or client; a member of an audience. **b** *sl.* a prostitute's client. **3** a point in faro.

puny /ˈpjuːnɪ/ adj. (**punier**, **puniest**) **1** undersized. **2** weak, feeble. **3** petty. □□ **punily** adv. **puniness** n. [phonetic spelling of PUISNE]

pup /pʌp/ n. & v. —n. **1** a young dog. **2** a young wolf, rat, seal, etc. **3** *Brit.* an unpleasant or arrogant young man. —v.tr. (**pupped**, **pupping**) (also *absol.*) (of a bitch etc.) bring forth (young). □ **in pup** (of a bitch) pregnant. **sell a person a pup** swindle a person, esp. by selling something worthless. [backform. f. PUPPY as if a dimin. in -Y²]

pupa /ˈpjuːpə/ n. (*pl.* **pupae** /-piː/) an insect in the stage of development between larva and imago. □□ **pupal** adj. [mod.L f. L *pupa* girl, doll]

pupate /pjuːˈpeɪt/ v.intr. become a pupa. □□ **pupation** n.

pupil¹ /ˈpjuːpɪl, -p(ə)l/ n. **1** a person who is taught by another, esp. a schoolchild or student in relation to a teacher. **2** *Sc. Law* a boy less than 14 or a girl less than 12 years in age. □□ **pupillage** n. (also **pupilage**). **pupillary** adj. (also **pupilary**). [ME, orig. = orphan, ward f. OF *pupille* or L *pupillus, -illa,* dimin. of *pupus* boy, *pupa* girl]

pupil² /ˈpjuːpɪl, -p(ə)l/ n. the dark circular opening in the centre of the iris of the eye, varying in size to regulate the passage of light to the retina. □□ **pupillar** adj. (also **pupilar**). **pupillary** adj. (also **pupilary**). [OF *pupille* or L *pupilla,* dimin. of *pūpa* doll (as PUPIL¹): so called from the tiny images visible in the eye]

pupiparous /pjuːˈpɪpərəs/ adj. *Entomol.* bringing forth young which are already in a pupal state. [mod.L *pupipara* neut. pl. of *pupiparus* (as PUPA, *parere* bring forth)]

puppet /ˈpʌpɪt/ n. **1** a small figure representing a human being or animal and moved by various means as entertainment. (See below.) **2** a person whose actions are controlled by another. □ **puppet State** a country that is nominally independent but actually under the control of another power. □□ **puppetry** n. [later form of POPPET]
  Puppetry as a form of theatre is probably as old as the theatre itself. There are hand or glove puppets, rod puppets, marionettes or string puppets, and the flat puppets of the shadowshow. Famous hand puppets include the English Punch, the French Guignol, and the Italian Pulcinella, but the true home of puppetry is the Far East and Eastern Europe, where its uses range from elementary education to cabaret shows.

puppeteer /ˌpʌpɪˈtɪə(r)/ n. a person who works puppets.

puppy /ˈpʌpɪ/ n. (*pl.* **-ies**) **1** a young dog. **2** a conceited or arrogant young man. □ **puppy-fat** temporary fatness of a child or adolescent. **puppy love** = *calf-love* (see CALF¹). □□ **puppyhood** n. **puppyish** adj. [ME perh. f. OF *po(u)pee* doll, plaything, toy f. Rmc (as POPPET)]

pur- /pɜː(r)/ prefix = PRO-¹ (*purchase; pursue*). [AF f. OF *por-, pur-, pour-* f. L *por-, pro-*]

Purana /pʊˈrɑːnə/ n. any of a class of Sanskrit sacred writings on Hindu mythology, folklore, etc., of varying date and origin. The most ancient dates from the 8th c. □□ **Puranic** adj. [Skr. *purāṇa* ancient legend, ancient, f. *purā* formerly]

Purbeck marble /ˈpɜːbek/ n. (also **Purbeck stone**) *Archit.* a hard usu. polished limestone from Purbeck in Dorset, used in pillars, effigies, etc.

purblind /ˈpɜːblaɪnd/ adj. **1** partly blind; dim-sighted. **2** obtuse, dim-witted. □□ **purblindness** n. [ME *pur(e)* blind f. PURE orig. in sense 'utterly', with assim. to PUR-]

Purcell /Xpɜːs(ə)l/, Henry (1659–95), the first English opera composer. His *Dido and Aeneas* (1689) moved away from the tradition of the masque, breaking new dramatic ground and accommodating a wide emotional range. His versatility enabled him to feel equally at home in the composition of religious, occasional, and purely instrumental music. The aptness of Purcell's

treatment of the English language in his vocal music has inspired and influenced British song composers of the 20th c.

purchase /ˈpɜːtʃɪs, -tʃəs/ v. & n. —v.tr. **1** acquire by payment; buy. **2** obtain or achieve at some cost. **3** *Naut.* haul up (an anchor etc.) by means of a pulley, lever, etc. —n. **1** the act or an instance of buying. **2** something bought. **3** *Law* the acquisition of property by one's personal action and not by inheritance. **4 a** a firm hold on a thing to move it or to prevent it from slipping; leverage. **b** a device or tackle for moving heavy objects. **5** the annual rent or return from land. □ **purchase tax** *Brit. hist.* a tax on goods bought, levied at higher rates for non-essential or luxury goods. □□ **purchasable** adj. **purchaser** n. [ME f. AF *purchacer,* OF *pourchacier* seek to obtain (as PUR-, CHASE¹)]

purdah /ˈpɜːdə/ n. *Ind.* **1** a system in certain Muslim and Hindu societies of screening women from strangers by means of a veil or curtain. **2** a curtain in a house, used for this purpose. [Urdu & Pers. *pardah* veil, curtain]

pure /pjʊə(r)/ adj. **1** unmixed, unadulterated (*pure white; pure alcohol*). **2** of unmixed origin or descent (*pure-blooded*). **3** chaste. **4** morally or sexually undefiled; not corrupt. **5** guiltless. **6** sincere. **7** mere, simple, nothing but, sheer (*it was pure malice*). **8** (of a sound) not discordant, perfectly in tune. **9** (of a subject of study) dealing with abstract concepts and not practical application. **10 a** (of a vowel) not joined with another in a diphthong. **b** (of a consonant) not accompanied by another. □ **pure science** a science depending on deductions from demonstrated truths (e.g. mathematics or logic), or one studied without practical applications. □□ **pureness** n. [ME f. OF *pur* pure f. L *purus*]

purée /ˈpjʊəreɪ/ n. & v. —n. a pulp of vegetables or fruit etc. reduced to a smooth cream. —v.tr. (**purées**, **puréed**) make a purée of. [F]

purely /ˈpjʊəlɪ/ adv. **1** in a pure manner. **2** merely, solely, exclusively.

purfle /ˈpɜːf(ə)l/ n. & v. —n. **1** an ornamental border, esp. on a violin etc. **2** *archaic* the ornamental or embroidered edge of a garment. —v.tr. **1** decorate with a purfle. **2** (often foll. by *with*) ornament (the edge of a building). **3** beautify. □□ **purfling** n. [ME f. OF *porfil, porfiler* ult. f. L *filum* thread]

purgation /pɜːˈgeɪʃ(ə)n/ n. **1** purification. **2** purging of the bowels. **3** spiritual cleansing, esp. (*RC Ch.*) of a soul in purgatory. **4** *hist.* the cleansing of oneself from accusation or suspicion by an oath or ordeal. [ME f. OF *purgation* or L *purgatio* (as PURGE)]

purgative /ˈpɜːgətɪv/ adj. & n. —adj. **1** serving to purify. **2** strongly laxative. —n. **1** a purgative thing. **2** a laxative. [ME f. OF *purgatif -ive* or LL *purgativus* (as PURGE)]

purgatory /ˈpɜːgətərɪ/ n. & adj. —n. (*pl.* **-ies**) **1** the condition or supposed place of spiritual cleansing, esp. (*RC & Orthodox Ch.*) of those dying in the grace of God but having to expiate venial sins etc. **2** a place or state of temporary suffering or expiation. —adj. purifying. □□ **purgatorial** /-ˈtɔːrɪəl/ adj. [ME f. AF *purgatorie,* OF *-oire* f. med.L *purgatorium,* neut. of LL *purgatorius* (as PURGE)]

purge /pɜːdʒ/ v. & n. —v.tr. **1** (often foll. by *of, from*) make physically or spiritually clean. **2** remove by a cleansing process. **3** rid (an organization, party, etc.) of persons regarded as undesirable. **4 a** empty (the bowels). **b** empty the bowels of. **5** *Law* atone for or wipe out (an offence, esp. contempt of court). —n. **1** the act or an instance of purging. **2** a purgative. □□ **purger** n. [ME f. OF *purg(i)er* f. L *purgare* purify f. *purus* pure]

purify /ˈpjʊərɪˌfaɪ/ v.tr. (**-ies**, **-ied**) **1** (often foll. by *of, from*) cleanse or make pure. **2** make ceremonially clean. **3** clear of extraneous elements. □□ **purification** /-fɪˈkeɪʃ(ə)n/ n. **purificatory** /-fɪˌkeɪtərɪ/ adj. **purifier** n. [ME f. OF *purifier* f. L *purificare* (as PURE)]

Purim /ˈpjʊərɪm, pjuːˈriːm/ n. a Jewish spring festival commemorating the defeat of Haman's plot to massacre the Jews (Esth. 9). [Heb., pl. of *pūr,* perh. = LOT n. 2]

purine /ˈpjʊəriːn/ n. **1** *Chem.* an organic nitrogenous base forming uric acid on oxidation. **2** any of a group of derivatives with purine-like structure, including the nucleotide constituents adenine and guanine. [G *Purin* L *purus* pure + *uricum* uric acid + *-in* -INE⁴]

purist /ˈpjʊərɪst/ *n.* **1** a stickler for or advocate of scrupulous purity, esp. in language. **2** (**Purist**) an adherent of Purism, an early 20th-c. movement in painting arising out of a rejection of cubism and characterized by a return to the representation of recognizable objects, with emphasis on purity of geometric form. The movement was founded by Le Corbusier and Amédée Ozenfant, launched theoretically in their book *After Cubism* (1918); their pictures, chiefly still-lifes of machine-made objects, are painted in cool muted tones and have the impersonality of the engineer's blueprint. □□ **purism** *n.* **puristic** /-ˈrɪstɪk/ *adj.* [F *puriste* f. *pur* PURE]

Puritan /ˈpjʊərɪt(ə)n/ *n. & adj.* —*n.* **1** a member of the more extreme English Protestants who, dissatisfied with the Elizabethan settlement, sought a further purification of the Church from supposedly unscriptural forms. At first they attacked church ornaments, vestments, organs, etc.; from 1570 the more extreme attacked the institution of episcopacy itself. Puritans were one of the main targets of Archbishop Laud. The Civil War of 1642 and after led to the temporary triumph of Puritanism but also to its proliferation into sects, and the term 'Puritan' ceased to be applicable. —*adj.* of the Puritans. [LL *puritas* (as PURITY) after earlier *Catharan* (see CATHAR)]

puritan /ˈpjʊərɪt(ə)n/ *n. & adj.* —*n.* **1** a purist member of any party. **2** a person practising or affecting extreme strictness in religion or morals. —*adj.* scrupulous and austere in religion or morals. □□ **puritanism** *n.* [PURITAN]

puritanical /ˌpjʊərɪˈtænɪk(ə)l/ *adj.* often *derog.* practising or affecting strict religious or moral behaviour. □□ **puritanically** *adv.*

purity /ˈpjʊərɪtɪ/ *n.* **1** pureness, cleanness. **2** freedom from physical or moral pollution. [ME f. OF *pureté*, with assim. to LL *puritas -tatis* f. L *purus* pure]

purl¹ /pɜːl/ *n. & v.* —*n.* **1** a knitting stitch made by putting the needle through the front of the previous stitch and passing the yarn round the back of the needle. **2** a cord of twisted gold or silver wire for bordering. **3** a chain of minute loops; a picot. **4** the ornamental edges of lace, ribbon, etc. —*v.tr.* (also *absol.*) knit with a purl stitch. [orig. *pyrle*, *pirle* f. Sc. *pirl* twist: the knitting sense may be f. a different word]

purl² /pɜːl/ *v. & n.* —*v.intr.* (of a brook etc.) flow with a swirling motion and babbling sound. —*n.* this motion or sound. [16th c.: prob. imit.: cf. Norw. *purla* bubble up]

purler /ˈpɜːlə(r)/ *n. Brit. colloq.* a headlong fall. [*purl* upset, rel. to PURL¹]

purlieu /ˈpɜːljuː/ *n.* (*pl.* **purlieus**) **1** a person's bounds or limits. **2** a person's usual haunts. **3** *Brit. hist.* a tract on the border of a forest, esp. one earlier included in it and still partly subject to forest laws. **4** (in *pl.*) the outskirts; an outlying region. [ME *purlew*, prob. alt. after F *lieu* place f. AF *purale(e)*, OF *pouralee* a going round to settle the boundaries f. *po(u)raler* traverse]

purlin /ˈpɜːlɪn/ *n.* a horizontal beam along the length of a roof, resting on principals and supporting the common rafters or boards. [ME: orig. uncert.]

purloin /pəˈlɔɪn/ *v.tr. formal* or *joc.* steal, pilfer. □□ **purloiner** *n.* [ME f. AF *purloigner* put away, do away with (as PUR-, *loign* far f. L *longe*)]

purple /ˈpɜːp(ə)l/ *n., adj., & v.* —*n.* **1** a colour intermediate between red and blue. **2** (in full **Tyrian purple**) a crimson dye obtained from some molluscs. **3** a purple robe, esp. as the dress of an emperor or senior magistrate. **4** the scarlet official dress of a cardinal. **5** (prec. by *the*) a position of rank, authority, or privilege. —*adj.* of a purple colour. —*v.tr. & intr.* make or become purple. □ **born in the purple 1** born into a reigning family. **2** belonging to the most privileged class. [tr. L *porphyrogenitus*, orig. used for one born of the imperial family at Constantinople and (it is said) in a chamber called the *Porphyra*] **purple emperor** a large butterfly, *Apatura iris*, with purple wings. **purple heart** *Brit. colloq.* a heart-shaped stimulant tablet, esp. of amphetamine. **Purple Heart** (in the US) a decoration for those wounded in action. **purple passage** (or

patch) **1** an ornate or elaborate passage in a literary composition. **2** *Austral. colloq.* a piece of luck or success. □□ **purpleness** *n.* **purplish** *adj.* **purply** *adj.* [OE alt. f. *purpure* *purpuran* f. L *purpura* (as PURPURA)]

purport *v. & n.* —*v.tr.* /pəˈpɔːt/ **1** profess; be intended to seem (*purports to be the royal seal*). **2** (often foll. by *that* + clause) (of a document or speech) have as its meaning; state. —*n.* /ˈpɜːpɔːt/ **1** the ostensible meaning of something. **2** the sense or tenor (of a document or statement). □□ **purportedly** /pəˈpɔːtɪdlɪ/ *adv.* [ME f. AF & OF *purport*, *porport* f. *purporter* f. med.L *proportare* (as PRO-¹, *portare* carry)]

purpose /ˈpɜːpəs/ *n. & v.* —*n.* **1** an object to be attained; a thing intended. **2** the intention to act. **3** resolution, determination. —*v.tr.* have as one's purpose; design, intend. □ **on purpose** intentionally. **purpose-built** (or **-made**) built or made for a specific purpose. **to no purpose** with no result or effect. **to the purpose 1** relevant. **2** useful. [ME f. OF *porpos*, *purpos* f. L *proponere* (as PROPOUND)]

purposeful /ˈpɜːpəsfʊl/ *adj.* **1** having or indicating purpose. **2** intentional. **3** resolute. □□ **purposefully** *adv.* **purposefulness** *n.*

purposeless /ˈpɜːpəslɪs/ *adj.* having no aim or plan. □□ **purposelessly** *adv.* **purposelessness** *n.*

purposely /ˈpɜːpəslɪ/ *adv.* on purpose; intentionally.

purposive /ˈpɜːpəsɪv/ *adj.* **1** having or serving a purpose. **2** done with a purpose. **3** (of a person or conduct) having purpose or resolution; purposeful. □□ **purposively** *adv.* **purposiveness** *n.*

purpura /ˈpɜːpjʊrə/ *n.* **1** a disease characterized by purple or livid spots on the skin, due to internal bleeding from small blood vessels. **2** any mollusc of the genus *Purpura*, some of which yield a purple dye. □□ **purpuric** /-ˈpjʊərɪk/ *adj.* [L f. Gk *porphura* purple]

purpure /ˈpɜːpjʊə(r)/ *n. & adj. Heraldry* purple. [OE *purpure* & OF *purpre* f. L *purpura* (as PURPURA)]

purpurin /ˈpɜːpjʊrɪn/ *n.* a red colouring-matter occurring naturally in madder roots, or manufactured synthetically.

purr /pɜː(r)/ *v. & n.* —*v.* **1** *intr.* (of a cat) make a low vibratory sound expressing contentment. **2** *intr.* (of machinery etc.) make a similar sound. **3** *intr.* (of a person) express pleasure. **4** *tr.* utter or express (words or contentment) in this way. —*n.* a purring sound. [imit.]

purse /pɜːs/ *n. & v.* —*n.* **1** a small pouch of leather etc. for carrying money on the person. **2** *US* a handbag. **3** a receptacle resembling a purse in form or purpose. **4** money, funds. **5** a sum collected as a present or given as a prize in a contest. —*v.* **1** *tr.* (often foll. by *up*) pucker or contract (the lips). **2** *intr.* become contracted and wrinkled. □ **hold the purse-strings** have control of expenditure. **the public purse** the national treasury. [OE *purs* f. med.L *bursa*, *byrsa* purse f. Gk *bursa* hide, leather]

purser /ˈpɜːsə(r)/ *n.* an officer on a ship who keeps the accounts, esp. the head steward in a passenger vessel. □□ **pursership** *n.*

purslane /ˈpɜːslɪn/ *n.* any of various plants of the genus *Portulaca*, esp. *P. oleracea*, with green or golden leaves, used as a herb and salad vegetable. [ME f. OF *porcelaine* (cf. PORCELAIN) alt. f. L *porcil(l)aca*, *portulaca*]

pursuance /pəˈsjuːəns/ *n.* (foll. by *of*) the carrying out or observance (of a plan, idea, etc.).

pursuant /pəˈsjuːənt/ *adj. & adv.* —*adj.* pursuing. —*adv.* (foll. by *to*) conforming to or in accordance with. □□ **pursuantly** *adv.* [ME, = prosecuting, f. OF *po(u)rsuiant* part. of *po(u)rsu(iv)ir* (as PURSUE): assim. to AF *pursuer* and PURSUE]

pursue /pəˈsjuː/ *v.* (**pursues**, **pursued**, **pursuing**) **1** *tr.* follow with intent to overtake or capture or do harm to. **2** *tr.* continue or proceed along (a route or course of action). **3** *tr.* follow or engage in (study or other activity). **4** *tr.* proceed in compliance with (a plan etc.). **5** *tr.* seek after, aim at. **6** *tr.* continue to investigate or discuss (a topic). **7** *tr.* seek the attention or acquaintance of (a person) persistently. **8** *tr.* (of misfortune etc.) persistently assail. **9** *tr.* persistently attend, stick to. **10** *intr.* go in pursuit. □□ **pursuable** *adj.* **pursuer** *n.* [ME f. AF *pursiwer*, *-suer* = OF *porsivre* etc. ult. f. L *prosequi* follow after]

pursuit /pə'sju:t/ *n.* **1** the act or an instance of pursuing. **2** an occupation or activity pursued. □ **in pursuit of** pursuing. [ME f. OF *poursuite* (as PUR-, SUIT)]

pursuivant /'pɜ:sɪv(ə)nt/ *n.* **1** *Brit.* an officer of the College of Arms ranking below a herald. **2** *archaic* a follower or attendant. [ME f. OF *pursivant* pres. part. of *pursivre* (as PURSUE)]

pursy /'pɜ:sɪ/ *adj.* **1** short-winded; puffy. **2** corpulent. □□ **pursiness** *n.* [ME, earlier *pursive* f. AF *porsif* f. OF *polsif* f. *polser* breathe with difficulty f. L *pulsare* (as PULSATE)]

purulent /'pjuːrʊlənt/ *adj.* **1** consisting of or containing pus. **2** discharging pus. □□ **purulence** *n.* **purulency** *n.* **purulently** *adv.* [F *purulent* or L *purulentus* (as PUS)]

purvey /pə'veɪ/ *v.* **1** *tr.* provide or supply (articles of food) as one's business. **2** *intr.* (often foll. by *for*) **a** make provision. **b** act as supplier. □□ **purveyor** *n.* [ME f. AF *purveier*, OF *porveiir* f. L *providēre* PROVIDE]

purveyance /pə'veɪəns/ *n.* **1** the act of purveying. **2** *Brit. hist.* the right of the sovereign to provisions etc. at a fixed price. [ME f. OF *porveance* f. L *providentia* PROVIDENCE]

purview /'pɜ:vju:/ *n.* **1** the scope or range of a document, scheme, etc. **2** the range of physical or mental vision. [ME f. AF *purveü*, OF *porveü* past part. of *porveiir* (as PURVEY)]

pus /pʌs/ *n.* a thick yellowish or greenish liquid produced from infected tissue. [L *pus puris*]

Pusan /puː'sæn/ a seaport on the SE coast of Korea; pop. (1985) 3,516,700.

Pusey /'pjuːzɪ/, Edward Bouverie (1800–82), leader of the Oxford Movement after the withdrawal of J. H. Newman (1841). He was Professor of Hebrew at Oxford from 1828.

push /pʊʃ/ *v.* & *n.* —*v.* **1** *tr.* exert a force on (a thing) to move it away from oneself or from the origin of the force. **2** *tr.* cause to move in this direction. **3** *intr.* exert such a force (*do not push against the door*). **4** *intr.* & *tr.* **a** thrust forward or upward. **b** project or cause to project (*pushes out new roots; the cape pushes out into the sea*). **5** *intr.* move forward by force or persistence. **6** *tr.* make (one's way) by pushing. **7** *intr.* exert oneself, esp. to surpass others. **8** *tr.* (often foll. by *to*, *into*, or *to* + infin.) urge or impel. **9** *tr.* tax the abilities or tolerance of; press (a person) hard. **10** *tr.* pursue (a claim etc.). **11** *tr.* promote the sale or use or adoption of, e.g. by advertising. **12** *intr.* (foll. by *for*) demand persistently (*pushed hard for reform*). **13** *tr.* *colloq.* sell (a drug) illegally. —*n.* **1** the act or an instance of pushing; a shove or thrust. **2** the force exerted in this. **3** a vigorous effort. **4** a military attack in force. **5** enterprise, determination to succeed. **6** the use of influence to advance a person. **7** the pressure of affairs. **8** a crisis. □ **be pushed for** *colloq.* have very little of (esp. time). **get the push** *colloq.* be dismissed or sent away. **give a person the push** *colloq.* dismiss or send away a person. **push along** (often in *imper.*) *colloq.* depart, leave. **push around** *colloq.* bully. **push-bike** *Brit. colloq.* a bicycle worked by pedals. **push-button 1** a button to be pushed esp. to operate an electrical device. **2** (*attrib.*) operated in this way. **push one's luck 1** take undue risks. **2** act presumptuously. **push off 1** push with an oar etc. to get a boat out into a river etc. **2** (often in *imper.*) *colloq.* go away. **push-pull 1** operated by pushing and pulling. **2** *Electr.* consisting of two valves etc. operated alternately. **push-start** *n.* the starting of a motor vehicle by pushing it to turn the engine. —*v.tr.* start (a vehicle) in this way. **push through** get (a scheme, proposal, etc.) completed or accepted quickly. **push-up** = *press-up*. [ME f. OF *pousser*, *pou(l)ser* f. L *pulsare* (as PULSATE)]

pushcart /'pʊʃkɑ:t/ *n.* a handcart or barrow.

pushchair /'pʊʃtʃeə(r)/ *n.* *Brit.* a folding chair on wheels, for pushing a child in.

pusher /'pʊʃə(r)/ *n.* **1** *colloq.* an illegal seller of drugs. **2** *colloq.* a pushing or pushy person. **3** a child's utensil for pushing food onto a spoon etc.

pushful /'pʊʃfʊl/ *adj.* pushy; arrogantly self-assertive. □□ **pushfully** *adv.*

pushing /'pʊʃɪŋ/ *adj.* **1** pushy; aggressively ambitious. **2** *colloq.* having nearly reached (a specified age). □□ **pushingly** *adv.*

Pushkin /'pʊʃkɪn/, Alexander Sergeevich (1799–1837), the first national poet of Russia, born in Moscow and educated in St Petersburg, but was expelled from the Lyceum in 1820 for writing revolutionary epigrams. He was also expelled from the Civil Service for atheistic writings, and his subsequent seclusion at his mother's estate prevented him from partaking in the unsuccessful revolt of 1825. One of the most influential Russian writers, he wrote prolifically in many genres, including lyric and narrative verse and an epic poem *The Bronze Horseman* (1833). His great verse novel *Eugene Onegin* (1823–31) formed the basis of Tchaikovsky's opera (1879), and his blank-verse historical drama *Boris Godunov* (1825) that of Mussorgsky's opera (1874). He was fatally wounded in a duel with his wife's admirer, Baron Georges D'Anthès.

pushover /'pʊʃəʊvə(r)/ *n.* *colloq.* **1** something that is easily done. **2** a person who can easily be overcome, persuaded, etc.

pushrod /'pʊʃrɒd/ *n.* a rod operated by cams, that opens and closes the valves in an internal-combustion engine.

Pushtu /'pʌʃtuː/ *n.* & *adj.* = PASHTO. [Pers. *puštū*]

pushy /'pʊʃɪ/ *adj.* (**pushier, pushiest**) *colloq.* **1** excessively or unpleasantly self-assertive. **2** selfishly determined to succeed. □□ **pushily** *adv.* **pushiness** *n.*

pusillanimous /ˌpjuːsɪ'lænɪməs/ *adj.* lacking courage; timid. □□ **pusillanimity** /-lə'nɪmɪtɪ/ *n.* **pusillanimously** *adv.* [eccl.L *pusillanimis* f. *pusillus* very small + *animus* mind]

Puskas /'pʊʃkæʃ/, Ferenc (1927–), Hungarian footballer, captain of his national team in their successful years in the 1950s. In 1956 he left Hungary and continued his playing career with further successes for Real Madrid. Always a prolific goal-scorer, he was famous for his left-footed shot.

puss /pʊs/ *n.* *colloq.* **1** a cat (esp. as a form of address). **2** a playful or coquettish girl. **3** a hare. □ **puss moth** a large European moth, *Cerura vinula.* [prob. f. MLG *pūs*, Du. *poes*, of unkn. orig.]

pussy /'pʊsɪ/ *n.* (*pl.* **-ies**) **1** (also **pussy-cat**) *colloq.* a cat. **2** *coarse sl.* the vulva. ¶ Usually considered a taboo use. □ **pussy willow** any of various willows, esp. *Salix discolor*, with furry catkins.

pussyfoot /'pʊsɪfʊt/ *v.intr.* **1** move stealthily or warily. **2** act cautiously or noncommittally. □□ **pussyfooter** *n.*

pustulate *v.* & *adj.* —*v.tr.* & *intr.* /'pʌstjʊˌleɪt/ form into pustules. —*adj.* /-lət/ of or relating to a pustule or pustules. □□ **pustulation** /-'leɪʃ(ə)n/ *n.* [LL *pustulare* f. *pustula*: see PUSTULE]

pustule /'pʌstjuːl/ *n.* a pimple containing pus. □□ **pustular** *adj.* **pustulous** *adj.* [ME f. OF *pustule* or L *pustula*]

put¹ /pʊt/ *v.* & *n.* —*v.* (**putting**; *past* and *past part.* **put**) **1** *tr.* move to or cause to be in a specified place or position (*put it in your pocket; put the children to bed; put your signature here*). **2** *tr.* bring into a specified condition, relation, or state (*puts me in great difficulty; an accident put the car out of action*). **3** *tr.* **a** (often foll. by *on*) impose or assign (*put a tax on beer; where do you put the blame?*). **b** (foll. by *on*, *to*) impose or enforce the existence of (*put a veto on it; put a stop to it*). **4** *tr.* **a** cause (a person) to go or be, habitually or temporarily (*put them at their ease; put them on the right track*). **b** *refl.* imagine (oneself) in a specified situation (*put yourself in my shoes*). **5** *tr.* (foll. by *for*) substitute (one thing for another). **6** *intr.* express (a thought or idea) in a specified way (*to put it mildly*). **7** *tr.* (foll. by *at*) estimate (an amount etc. at a specified amount) (*put the cost at £50*). **8** *tr.* (foll. by *into*) express or translate in (words, or another language). **9** *tr.* (foll. by *into*) invest (money in an asset, e.g. land). **10** *tr.* (foll. by *on*) stake (money) on (a horse etc.). **11** *tr.* (foll. by *to*) apply or devote to a use or purpose (*put it to good use*). **12** *tr.* (foll. by *to*) submit for consideration or attention (*let me put it to you another way; shall now put it to a vote*). **13** *tr.* (foll. by *to*) subject (a person) to (death, suffering, etc.). **14** *tr.* throw (esp. a shot or weight) as an athletic sport or exercise. **15** *tr.* (foll. by *to*) couple (an animal) with (another of the opposite sex) for breeding. **16** *intr.* (foll. by *back, off, out*, etc.) (of a ship etc.) proceed or follow a course in a specified direction. **17** *intr.* *US* (foll. by *in, out of*) (of a river) flow in a specified direction. —*n.* **1** a throw of the shot or weight. **2** *Stock Exch.* the option of selling stock at a fixed price at a given date. □ **not know where to put oneself** feel deeply embarrassed. **put about 1** spread (information, rumour, etc.). **2** *Naut.* turn round; put (a ship) on the opposite tack. **3** trouble, distress. **put across 1** make acceptable or effective. **2** express in an understandable way. **3** (often in **put it (or one) across**) achieve by deceit. **put away 1** put (a thing) back in the place where it is normally kept. **2** lay (money etc.) aside for future use. **3 a** confine or imprison. **b** commit to a home or mental institution. **4** consume (food and drink), esp. in large quantities. **5** put (an old or sick animal) to death. **put back 1** restore to its proper or former place. **2** change (a planned event) to a later date or time. **3** move back the hands of (a clock or watch). **4** check the advance of. **put a bold** etc. **face on it** see FACE. **put the boot in** see BOOT. **put by** lay (money etc.) aside for future use. **put down 1** suppress by force or authority. **2** *colloq.* snub or humiliate. **3** record or enter in writing. **4** enter the name of (a person) on a list, esp. as a member or subscriber. **5** (foll. by *as*, *for*) account or reckon. **6** (foll. by *to*) attribute (*put it down to bad planning*). **7** put (an old or sick animal) to death. **8** preserve or store (eggs etc.) for future use. **9** pay (a specified sum) as a deposit. **10** put (a baby) to bed. **11** land (an aircraft). **12** stop to let (passengers) get off. **put-down** *n. colloq.* a snub or humiliating criticism. **put an end to** see END. **put one's foot down** see FOOT. **put one's foot in it** see FOOT. **put forth 1** (of a plant) send out (buds or leaves). **2** *formal* submit or put into circulation. **put forward 1** suggest or propose. **2** advance the hands of (a clock or watch). **3** (often *refl.*) put into a prominent position; draw attention to. **put in 1 a** enter or submit (a claim etc.). **b** (foll. by *for*) submit a claim for (a specified thing). **2** (foll. by *for*) be a candidate for (an appointment, election, etc.). **3** spend (time). **4** perform (a spell of work) as part of a whole. **5** interpose (a remark, blow, etc.). **put a person in mind of** see MIND. **put it to a person** (often foll. by *that* + clause) challenge a person to deny. **put one's mind to** see MIND. **put off 1 a** postpone. **b** postpone an engagement with (a person). **2** (often foll. by *with*) evade (a person) with an excuse etc. **3** hinder or dissuade. **4** offend, disconcert; cause (a person) to lose interest in something. **put on 1** clothe oneself with. **2** cause (an electrical device, light, etc.) to function. **3** cause (transport) to be available. **4** stage (a play, show, etc.). **5** advance the hands of (a clock or watch). **6 a** pretend to be affected by (an emotion). **b** assume, take on (a character or appearance). **c** (**put it on**) exaggerate one's feelings etc. **7** increase one's weight by (a specified amount). **8** send (a cricketer) on to bowl. **9** (foll. by *to*) make aware of or put in touch with (*put us on to their new accountant*). **put-on** *n. colloq.* a deception or hoax. **put out 1 a** (often as **put out** *adj.*) disconcert or annoy. **b** (often *refl.*) inconvenience (*don't put yourself out*). **2** extinguish (a fire or light). **3** cause (a batsman or side) to be out. **4** dislocate (a joint). **5** exert (strength etc.). **6** lend (money) at interest. **7** allocate (work) to be done off the premises. **8** blind (a person's eyes). **put over 1** make acceptable or effective. **2** express in an understandable way. **3** *US* postpone. **4** *US* achieve by deceit. **put a sock in it** see SOCK[1]. **put store by** see STORE. **put through 1** carry out or complete (a task or transaction). **2** (often foll. by *to*) connect (a person) by telephone to another subscriber. **put to flight** see FLIGHT[2]. **put together 1** assemble (a whole) from parts. **2** combine (parts) to form a whole. **put under** render unconscious by anaesthetic etc. **put up 1** build or erect. **2** raise (a price etc.). **3** take or provide accommodation (*friends put me up for the night*). **4** engage in (a fight, struggle, etc.) as a form of resistance. **5** present (a proposal). **6 a** present oneself for election. **b** propose for election. **7** provide (money) as a backer in an enterprise. **8** display (a notice). **9** publish (banns). **10** offer for sale or competition. **11** cause (game) to rise from cover. **12** put (a sword) back in its sheath. **put-up** *adj.* fraudulently presented or devised. **put upon** *colloq.* make unfair or excessive demands on; take advantage of (a person). **put a person up to 1** inform or instruct a person about. **2** (usu. foll. by verbal noun) instigate a person in (*put them up to stealing the money*). **put up with** endure, tolerate; submit to. **put the wind up** see WIND[1]. **put a person wise** see WISE. **put words into a person's mouth** see MOUTH. □□ **putter** *n*. [ME f. an unrecorded OE form *putian*, of unkn. orig.]

put[2] var. of PUTT.

putative /ˈpjuːtətɪv/ *adj.* reputed, supposed (*his putative father*). □□ **putatively** *adv.* [ME f. OF *putatif -ive* or LL *putativus* f. L *putare* think]

putlog /ˈpʌtlɒg/ *n.* (also **putlock** /-lɒk/) a short horizontal timber projecting from a wall, on which scaffold floorboards rest. [17th c.: orig. uncert.]

put-put /ˈpʌtpʌt/ *n. & v.* —*n.* the rapid intermittent sound of a small petrol engine. —*v.intr.* (**put-putted, put-putting**) make this sound. [imit.]

putrefy /ˈpjuːtrɪˌfaɪ/ *v.* (**-ies, -ied**) **1** *intr. & tr.* become or make putrid; go bad. **2** *intr.* fester, suppurate. **3** *intr.* become morally corrupt. □□ **putrefacient** /-ˈfeɪʃ(ə)nt/ *adj.* **putrefaction** /-ˈfækʃ(ə)n/ *n.* **putrefactive** /-ˈfæktɪv/ *adj.* [ME f. L *putrefacere* f. *puter putris* rotten]

putrescent /pjuːˈtres(ə)nt/ *adj.* **1** in the process of rotting. **2** of or accompanying this process. □□ **putrescence** *n.* [L *putrescere* incept. of *putrēre* (as PUTRID)]

putrid /ˈpjuːtrɪd/ *adj.* **1** decomposed, rotten. **2** foul, noxious. **3** corrupt. **4** *sl.* of poor quality; contemptible; very unpleasant. □□ **putridity** /-ˈrɪdɪti/ *n.* **putridly** *adv.* **putridness** *n.* [L *putridus* f. *putrēre* to rot f. *puter putris* rotten]

putsch /pʊtʃ/ *n.* an attempt at political revolution; a violent uprising. [Swiss G, = thrust, blow]

putt /pʌt/ *v. & n.* (also **put**) —*v.tr.* (**putted, putting**) strike (a golf ball) gently to get it into or nearer to a hole on a putting-green. —*n.* a putting stroke. □ **putting-green** (in golf) the smooth area of grass round a hole. [differentiated f. PUT[1]]

puttee /ˈpʌti/ *n.* **1** a long strip of cloth wound spirally round the leg from ankle to knee for protection and support. **2** *US* a leather legging. [Hindi *paṭṭī* band, bandage]

putter[1] /ˈpʌtə(r)/ *n.* **1** a golf club used in putting. **2** a golfer who putts.

putter[2] /ˈpʌtə(r)/ *n. & v.* = PUT-PUT. [imit.]

putter[3] *US* var. of POTTER[1].

putto /ˈpʊtəʊ/ *n.* (*pl.* **putti** /-ti/) a representation of a naked child (esp. a cherub or a cupid) in (esp. Renaissance) art. [It., = boy, f. L *putus*]

putty /ˈpʌti/ *n. & v.* —*n.* (*pl.* **-ies**) **1** a cement made from whiting and raw linseed oil, used for fixing panes of glass, filling holes in woodwork, etc. **2** a fine white mortar of lime and water, used in pointing brickwork, etc. **3** a polishing powder usu. made from tin oxide, used in jewellery work. —*v.tr.* (**-ies, -ied**) cover, fix, join, or fill up with putty. □ **putty in a person's hands** someone who is overcompliant, or easily influenced. [F *potée*, lit. potful]

puy /pwiː/ *n.* a small extinct volcanic cone, esp. in the Auvergne, France. [F, = hill, f. L *podium*: see PODIUM]

puzzle /ˈpʌz(ə)l/ *n. & v.* —*n.* **1** a difficult or confusing problem; an enigma. **2** a problem or toy designed to test knowledge or ingenuity. —*v.* **1** *tr.* confound or disconcert mentally. **2** *intr.* (usu. foll. by *over* etc.) be perplexed (about). **3** *tr.* (usu. as **puzzling** *adj.*) require much thought to comprehend (*a puzzling situation*). **4** *tr.* (foll. by *out*) solve or understand by hard thought. □□ **puzzlement** *n.* **puzzlingly** *adv.* [16th c.: orig. unkn.]

puzzler /ˈpʌzlə(r)/ *n.* a difficult question or problem.

puzzolana var. of POZZOLANA.

PVA *abbr.* polyvinyl acetate.

PVC *abbr.* polyvinyl chloride.

Pvt. *abbr.* **1** private. **2** *US* private soldier.

PW *abbr.* policewoman.

p.w. *abbr.* per week.

PWR *abbr.* pressurized-water reactor.

PX *abbr. US* post exchange.

pyaemia /paɪˈiːmɪə/ *n.* (*US* **pyemia**) blood-poisoning caused by the spread of pus-forming bacteria in the bloodstream from a source of infection. □□ **pyaemic** *adj.* [mod.L f. Gk *puon* pus + *haima* blood]

pycnic var. of PYKNIC.

pye-dog /ˈpaɪdɒg/ n. (also **pie-dog, pi-dog**) a vagrant mongrel, esp. in Asia. [Anglo-Ind. *pye, paë*, Hindi *pāhī* outsider + DOG]

pyelitis /ˌpaɪəˈlaɪtɪs/ n. inflammation of the renal pelvis. [Gk *puelos* trough, basin + -ITIS]

pyemia US var. of PYAEMIA.

Pygmalion[1] /pɪgˈmeɪlɪən/ Gk legend a legendary king of Cyprus who (according to Ovid) fashioned an ivory statue of a beautiful woman and loved it so deeply that at his prayer Aphrodite gave it life. The woman (at some point named Galatea) bore him a daughter, Paphos.

Pygmalion[2] /pɪgˈmeɪlɪən/ a legendary king of Tyre, brother of Elissa (Dido), whose husband he killed in the hope of obtaining his fortune.

pygmy /ˈpɪgmɪ/ n. (also **pigmy**) (pl. **-ies**) **1** a member of a population whose average male height is not greater than 150 cm (4 ft. 11 in.), e.g. the Bambuti of tropical central Africa (the term 'Negrito' is used of similar populations of SE Asia). **2** a very small person, animal, or thing. **3** an insignificant person. **4** (attrib.) **a** of or relating to pygmies. **b** (of a person, animal, etc.) dwarf. □□ **pygmaean** /-ˈmiːən/ adj. **pygmean** /-ˈmiːən/ adj. [ME f. L *pygmaeus* f. Gk *pugmaios* dwarf f. *pugmē* the length from elbow to knuckles, fist]

pyjamas /pɪˈdʒɑːməz, pə-/ n.pl. (US **pajamas**) **1** a suit of loose trousers and jacket for sleeping in. **2** loose trousers tied round the waist, worn by both sexes in some Asian countries. **3** (**pyjama**) (attrib.) designating parts of a suit of pyjamas (*pyjama jacket; pyjama trousers*). [Urdu *pā(ē)jāma* f. Pers. *pae, pay* leg + Hindi *jāma* clothing]

pyknic /ˈpɪknɪk/ adj. & n. (also **pycnic**) Anthropol. —adj. characterized by a thick neck, large abdomen, and relatively short limbs. —n. a person of this bodily type. [Gk *puknos* thick]

pylon /ˈpaɪlən, -lɒn/ n. **1** a tall structure erected as a support (esp. for electric-power cables) or boundary or decoration. **2** a gateway or gate-tower, esp. the monumental gateway to an Egyptian temple, usually formed by two truncated pyramidal towers connected by a lower architectural member containing the gate. **3** a structure marking a path for aircraft. **4** a structure supporting an aircraft engine. [Gk *pulōn* f. *pulē* gate]

pylorus /paɪˈlɔːrəs/ n. (pl. **pylori** /-raɪ/) Anat. the opening from the stomach into the duodenum. □□ **pyloric** /-ˈlɒrɪk/ adj. [LL f. Gk *pulōros, pulouros* gatekeeper f. *pulē* gate + *ouros* warder]

Pyongyang /pjʌŋˈjaːŋ/ the capital of North Korea; pop. (est. 1984) 2,639,400.

pyorrhoea /ˌpaɪəˈrɪːə/ n. (US **pyorrhea**) **1** a disease of periodontal tissue causing shrinkage of the gums and loosening of the teeth. **2** any discharge of pus. [Gk *puo-* f. *puon* pus + *rhoia* flux f. *rheō* flow]

pyracantha /ˌpaɪrəˈkænθə/ n. any evergreen thorny shrub of the genus *Pyracantha*, having white flowers and bright red or yellow berries. [L f. Gk *purakantha*]

pyramid /ˈpɪrəmɪd/ n. **1** a monumental structure, usu. of stone, with a square base and sloping sides meeting centrally at an apex, esp. an ancient Egyptian royal tomb. (See below.) **2** a solid of this type with a base of three or more sides. **3** a pyramid-shaped thing or pile of things. **4** (in pl.) a game played on a billiard-table with (usu. 15) coloured balls and a cue-ball. □ **pyramid selling** a system of selling goods in which agency rights are sold to an increasing number of distributors at successively lower levels. □□ **pyramidal** /-ˈræmɪd(ə)l/ adj. **pyramidally** /-ˈræmɪdəlɪ/ adv. **pyramidic** /-ˈmɪdɪk/ adj. (also **pyramidical** /-ˈmɪdɪk(ə)l/). **pyramidically** /-ˈmɪdɪkəlɪ/ adv. **pyramidwise** adj. [ME f. L *pyramis* f. Gk *puramis -idos*]

The pyramid is the characteristic tomb built for Egyptian kings from the 3rd Dynasty (c.2649 BC) until c.1640 BC. There are two principal types: the step pyramid (e.g. that of Djoser at Saqqara), consisting of several stepped levels rising to a flat top, and the true pyramid, which developed from this and was introduced in the 4th Dynasty (c.2575 BC, e.g. at Giza). The pyramid was the focal point of a vast funerary complex, including a temple at its side, linked by a causeway to a lower temple near the cultivated land and flood-waters of the river. The internal structure of most true pyramids consists of a series of stepped buttresses

surrounding the central core; these were packed with rubble and finished with casing blocks. Inclined ramps were used in the building process, but the exact procedure, and the mathematical calculations involved, remain (like the reason for the choice of the pyramidal shape) unknown. The hallmark of Egypt, the pyramids are imposing in their austere simplicity; those at Giza were one of the Seven Wonders of the World.

Monuments of similar shape are associated with the civilizations of Mesoamerica and South America c.1200 BC–AD 750. They were built by the Aztecs and Mayas as centres of worship, usually as one component in a complex of courtyards, platforms, and temples.

Pyramus /ˈpɪrəməs/ Rom. legend a Babylonian youth, lover of Thisbe. Their story is almost unknown except from Ovid. Forbidden to marry by their parents, who were neighbours, the lovers conversed through a chink in the wall and agreed to meet at a tomb outside the city. There, Thisbe was frightened away by a lioness coming from its kill, and Pyramus, seeing her bloodstained cloak and supposing her dead, stabbed himself. Thisbe, finding his body when she returned, threw herself upon his sword. Their blood stained a mulberry-tree, whose fruit has ever since been black when ripe, in sign of mourning for them.

pyre /ˈpaɪə(r)/ n. a heap of combustible material esp. a funeral pile for burning a corpse. [L *pyra* f. Gk *pura* f. *pur* fire]

Pyrenees /ˌpɪrəˈniːz/ a range of mountains rising to over 3,380 m (11,000 ft.), separating France from the Iberian Peninsula. □□ **Pyrenean** /-ˈniːən/ adj.

pyrethrin /paɪˈriːθrɪn/ n. any of several active constituents of pyrethrum flowers used in the manufacture of insecticides.

pyrethrum /paɪˈriːθrəm/ n. **1** any of several aromatic chrysanthemums of the genus *Tanacetum*, esp. *T. coccineum*. **2** an insecticide made from the dried flowers of these plants, esp. *Tanacetum cinerariifolium*. [L f. Gk *purethron* feverfew]

pyretic /paɪˈretɪk, pɪ-/ adj. of, for, or producing fever. [mod.L *pyreticus* f. Gk *puretos* fever]

Pyrex /ˈpaɪəreks/ n. propr. a hard heat-resistant type of glass, often used for cookware. [invented word]

pyrexia /paɪˈreksɪə, pɪ-/ n. Med. = FEVER. □□ **pyrexial** adj. **pyrexic** adj. **pyrexical** adj. [mod.L f. Gk *purexis* f. *puressō* be feverish f. *pur* fire]

pyridine /ˈpɪrɪdiːn/ n. Chem. a colourless volatile odorous liquid, formerly obtained from coal tar, used as a solvent and in chemical manufacture. ¶ Chem. formula: C_5H_5N. [Gk *pur* fire + -ID[4] + -INE[4]]

pyridoxine /ˌpɪrɪˈdɒksiːn/ n. a vitamin of the B complex found in yeast, and important in the body's use of unsaturated fatty acids. Also called *vitamin B₆*. [PYRIDINE + OX- + -INE[4]]

pyrimidine /pɪˈrɪmɪdiːn/ n. **1** Chem. an organic nitrogenous base. **2** any of a group of derivatives with similar structure, including the nucleotide constituents uracil, thymine, and cytosine. [G *Pyrimidin* f. *Pyridin* (as PYRIDINE, IMIDE)]

pyrite /ˈpaɪəraɪt/ n. = PYRITES. [F *pyrite* or L (as PYRITES)]

pyrites /paɪˈraɪtiːz/ n. (in full **iron pyrites**) a yellow lustrous form of iron disulphide. □□ **pyritic** /-ˈrɪtɪk/ adj. **pyritiferous** /-rɪˈtɪfərəs/ adj. **pyritize** /ˈpaɪrɪˌtaɪz/ v.tr. (also **-ise**). **pyritous** /ˈpaɪrɪtəs/ adj. [L f. Gk *puritēs* of fire (*pur*)]

pyro /ˈpaɪərəʊ/ n. colloq. = PYROGALLIC ACID.

pyro- /ˈpaɪərəʊ/ comb. form **1** denoting fire. **2** Chem. denoting a new substance formed from another by elimination of water (*pyrophosphate*). **3** Mineral. denoting a mineral etc. showing some property or change under the action of heat, or having a fiery red or yellow colour. [Gk *puro-* f. *pur* fire]

pyroclastic /ˌpaɪərəʊˈklæstɪk/ adj. (of rocks etc.) formed as the result of a volcanic eruption. □□ **pyroclast** n.

pyroelectric /ˌpaɪərəʊɪˈlektrɪk/ adj. having the property of becoming electrically charged when heated. □□ **pyroelectricity** /-ˈtrɪsɪtɪ/ n.

pyrogallic acid /ˌpaɪərəʊˈgælɪk/ n. a weak acid used as a developer in photography, etc.

pyrogallol /ˌpaɪərəʊˈgælɒl/ n. = PYROGALLIC ACID.

pyrogenic /ˌpaɪərəʊˈdʒenɪk/ adj. (also **pyrogenous**

/paɪˈrɒdʒɪnəs/) **1 a** producing heat, esp. in the body. **b** producing fever. **2** produced by combustion or volcanic processes.

pyrography /paɪˈrɒgrəfɪ/ *n.* = *poker-work* (see POKER¹).

pyroligneous /ˌpaɪərəʊˈlɪgnɪəs/ *adj.* produced by the action of fire or heat on wood.

pyrolyse /ˈpaɪərəˌlaɪz/ *v.tr.* (*US* **pyrolyze**) decompose by pyrolysis. [PYROLYSIS after *analyse*]

pyrolysis /paɪˈrɒlɪsɪs/ *n.* chemical decomposition brought about by heat. □□ **pyrolytic** /ˌpaɪrəˈlɪtɪk/ *adj.*

pyromania /ˌpaɪərəʊˈmeɪnɪə/ *n.* an obsessive desire to set fire to things. □□ **pyromaniac** *n.*

pyrometer /paɪˈrɒmɪtə(r)/ *n.* an instrument for measuring high temperatures, esp. in furnaces and kilns. □□ **pyrometric** /-rəˈmetrɪk/ *adj.* **pyrometrically** /-rəˈmetrɪkəlɪ/ *adv.* **pyrometry** /-mɪtrɪ/ *n.*

pyrope /ˈpaɪərəʊp/ *n.* a deep red variety of garnet. [ME f. OF *pirope* f. L *pyropus* f. Gk *purōpos* gold-bronze, lit. fiery-eyed, f. *pur* fire + *ōps* eye]

pyrophoric /ˌpaɪərəʊˈfɒrɪk/ *adj.* (of a substance) liable to ignite spontaneously on exposure to air. [mod.L *pyrophorus* f. Gk *purophoros* fire-bearing f. *pur* fire + *pherō* bear]

pyrosis /paɪˈrəʊsɪs/ *n. Med.* a burning sensation in the lower part of the chest, combined with the return of gastric acid to the mouth. [mod.L f. Gk *purōsis* f. *puroō* set on fire f. *pur* fire]

pyrotechnic /ˌpaɪərəʊˈteknɪk/ *adj.* **1** of or relating to fireworks. **2** (of wit etc.) brilliant or sensational. □□ **pyrotechnical** *adj.* **pyrotechnist** *n.* **pyrotechny** /ˈpaɪrəʊ-/ *n.* [PYRO- + Gk *tekhnē* art]

pyrotechnics /ˌpaɪərəʊˈteknɪks/ *n.pl.* **1** the art of making fireworks. **2** a display of fireworks. **3** any brilliant display.

pyroxene /paɪˈrɒksiːn/ *n.* any of a group of minerals commonly found as components of igneous rocks, composed of silicates of calcium, magnesium, and iron. [PYRO- + Gk *xenos* stranger (because supposed to be alien to igneous rocks)]

pyroxylin /paɪˈrɒksɪlɪn/ *n.* a form of nitrocellulose, soluble in ether and alcohol, used as a basis for lacquers, artificial leather, etc. [F *pyroxyline* (as PYRO-, Gk *xulon* wood)]

Pyrrha /ˈpɪrə/ *Gk Mythol.* the wife of Deucalion (see entry).

pyrrhic¹ /ˈpɪrɪk/ *adj.* (of a victory) won at too great a cost to be of use to the victor. [*Pyrrhus* of Epirus, who defeated the Romans at Asculum in 279 BC, but sustained heavy losses]

pyrrhic² /ˈpɪrɪk/ *n. & adj.* —*n.* a metrical foot of two short or unaccented syllables. —*adj.* written in or based on pyrrhics. [L *pyrrhichius* f. Gk *purrhikhios* (*pous*) pyrrhic (foot)]

Pyrrhonism /ˈpɪrənɪz(ə)m/ *n.* **1** the philosophy of Pyrrho of Elis (*c.*300 BC), maintaining that certainty of knowledge is unattainable. **2** scepticism; philosophic doubt. □□ **Pyrrhonist** *n.* [Gk *Purrhōn* Pyrrho]

pyruvate /paɪˈruːveɪt/ *n. Biochem.* any salt or ester of pyruvic acid.

pyruvic acid /paɪˈruːvɪk/ *n.* an organic acid occurring as an intermediate in many stages of metabolism. [as PYRO- + L *uva* grape]

Pythagoras /paɪˈθægərəs/ (late 6th c. BC) Greek philosopher, founder of a religious, political, and scientific society at Croton in southern Italy. No writings by him survive, his achievements were early confused with those of his followers, and his life is obscured by legend. The Pythagoreans held that the soul is condemned to a cycle of reincarnation, from which it may escape by attaining a state of purity. Pythagoras is said to have discovered the numerical ratios determining the principal intervals of the musical scale, whence he was led to interpret the world as a whole through numbers, the systematic study of which he thus originated. He is the probable discoverer (though not in its Euclidean form) of the geometrical theorem named after him—that the square on the hypotenuse of a right-angled triangle is equal to the sum of the squares on the other two sides. In astronomy, his analysis of the courses of the sun, moon, and stars into circular motions was not set aside until the 17th c. (see KEPLER). □□ **Pythagorean** /-ˈriːən/ *adj.* & *n.*

Pythia /ˈpɪθɪə/ the priestess of Apollo at Delphi in ancient Greece, who delivered the oracles. [as PYTHIAN]

Pythian /ˈpɪθɪən/ *adj. & n.* —*adj.* of or relating to Delphi or its ancient oracle of Apollo. —*n.* Apollo or his priestess at Delphi. □ **Pythian games** those celebrated by the ancient Greeks every four years at Delphi. [L *Pythius* f. Gk *Puthios* f. *Puthō*, an older name of Delphi]

Pythias see DAMON.

python /ˈpaɪθ(ə)n/ *n.* any snake of the family Pythonidae, esp. of the genus *Python*, found throughout the tropics in the Old World. It kills its prey by compressing and asphyxiating it. □□ **pythonic** /-ˈθɒnɪk/ *adj.* [L f. Gk *Puthōn* a huge serpent or monster killed near Delphi (cf. PYTHIAN) by Apollo in myth]

pythoness /ˈpaɪθənɪs/ *n.* **1** the Pythian priestess. **2** a witch. [ME f. OF *phitonise* f. med.L *phitonissa* f. LL *pythonissa* fem. of *pytho* f. Gk *puthōn* soothsaying demon: cf. PYTHON]

pyuria /paɪˈjʊərɪə/ *n. Med.* the presence of pus in urine. [Gk *puon* pus + -URIA]

pyx /pɪks/ *n.* (also **pix**) **1** *Eccl.* the vessel in which the consecrated bread of the Eucharist is kept. **2** (in the UK) a box at the Royal Mint in which specimen gold and silver coins are deposited. □ **trial of the pyx** an annual test of specimen coins at the Royal Mint by a group of members (called a *jury*) of the Goldsmith's Company. [ME f. L (as PYXIS)]

pyxidium /pɪkˈsɪdɪəm/ *n.* (*pl.* **pyxidia** /-dɪə/) *Bot.* a seed-capsule with a top that comes off like the lid of a box. [mod.L f. Gk *puxidion*, dimin. of *puxis*: see PYXIS]

pyxis /ˈpɪksɪs/ *n.* (*pl.* **pyxides** /-ˌdiːz/) **1** a small box or casket. **2** = PYXIDIUM. [ME f. L f. Gk *puxis* f. *puxos* BOX³]

pzazz var. of PIZAZZ.

Q

Q¹ /kjuː/ n. (also **q**) (pl. **Qs** or **Q's**) the seventeenth letter of the alphabet, derived from a Phoenician letter representing a guttural k sound. The letter, followed by v, was used in Latin to represent the double sound kw-, and qu- is used in English to represent this sound in many native English words as well as in those derived from Latin, even when these have now the pronunciation k- (as in words derived through French).

Q² abbr. (also **Q.**) **1** Queen, Queen's. **2** question.

Qantas /ˈkwɒntəs/ n. the international airline of Australia. [abbr. of Queensland and Northern Territory Aerial Services]

QARANC abbr. Queen Alexandra's Royal Army Nursing Corps.

Qatar /ˈkætɑː(r), ˈgæ-/ a sheikdom on a peninsula on the west coast of the Persian Gulf; pop. (est. 1988) 328,000; official language Arabic; capital, Doha. The country became a British protectorate in 1916, and until 1971 (when it became a sovereign independent State) was in special treaty relations with Britain. Oil is the chief source of revenue. □□ **Qatari** adj. & n.

Qattara Depression /kəˈtɑːrə/ a desert basin in the Libyan desert in NE Africa that drops to 133 m (436 ft.) below sea level, the lowest point in Africa.

QB abbr. Queen's Bench.

QC abbr. Law Queen's Counsel.

QED abbr. quod erat demonstrandum.

Q fever /kjuː/ n. a mild febrile disease caused by rickettsiae. [Q = query]

qibla var. of KIBLAH.

Qin /tʃɪn/ (also **Ch'in**) the name of a dynasty that ruled China 221–206 BC.

Qinghai /tʃɪŋˈhaɪ/ (also **Tsinghai**) a mountainous province in west central China; pop. (est. 1986) 4,120,000; capital, Xining (Sining).

Qld. abbr. Queensland.

QM abbr. quartermaster.

QMG abbr. Quartermaster General.

QMS abbr. Quartermaster Sergeant.

QPM abbr. (in the UK) Queen's Police Medal.

qr. abbr. quarter(s).

Q-ship /ˈkjuːʃɪp/ n. an armed and disguised merchant ship used as a decoy or to destroy submarines. [Q = query]

QSO abbr. quasi-stellar object, quasar.

qt. abbr. quart(s).

q.t. n. colloq. quiet (esp. on the q.t.). [abbr.]

qu. abbr. **1** query. **2** question.

qua /kwɑː/ conj. in the capacity of; as being (Napoleon qua general). [L, ablat. fem. sing. of qui who (rel. pron.)]

quack¹ /kwæk/ v. & n. —n. the harsh sound made by ducks. —v.intr. **1** utter this sound. **2** colloq. talk loudly and foolishly. [imit.: cf. Du. kwakken, G quacken croak, quack]

quack² /kwæk/ n. **1 a** an unqualified practiser of medicine. **b** (attrib.) of or characteristic of unskilled medical practice (quack cure). **2** a charlatan. **3** sl. any doctor or medical officer. □□ **quackery** n. **quackish** adj. [abbr. of quacksalver f. Du. (prob. f. obs. quacken prattle + salf SALVE¹)]

quad¹ /kwɒd/ n. colloq. a quadrangle. [abbr.]

quad² /kwɒd/ n. colloq. = QUADRUPLET 1. [abbr.]

quad³ /kwɒd/ n. Printing a piece of blank metal type used in spacing. [abbr. of earlier QUADRAT]

quad⁴ /kwɒd/ n. & adj. —n. quadraphony. —adj. quadraphonic. [abbr.]

quadragenarian /ˌkwɒdrədʒɪˈneərɪən/ n. & adj. —n. a person from 40 to 49 years old. —adj. of this age. [LL quadragenarius f. quadrageni distrib. of quadraginta forty]

Quadragesima /ˌkwɒdrəˈdʒesɪmə/ n. the first Sunday in Lent. [LL, fem. of L quadragesimus fortieth f. quadraginta forty, Lent having 40 days]

quadragesimal /ˌkwɒdrəˈdʒesɪm(ə)l/ adj. **1** (of a fast, esp. in Lent) lasting forty days. **2** Lenten.

quadrangle /ˈkwɒdˌræŋg(ə)l/ n. **1** a four-sided plane figure, esp. a square or rectangle. **2 a** a four-sided court, esp. enclosed by buildings, as in some colleges. **b** such a court with the buildings round it. □□ **quadrangular** /-ˈræŋgjʊlə(r)/ adj. [ME f. OF f. LL quadrangulum square, neut. of quadrangulus (as QUADRI-, ANGLE¹)]

quadrant /ˈkwɒdrənt/ n. **1** a quarter of a circle's circumference. **2** a plane figure enclosed by two radii of a circle at right angles and the arc cut off by them. **3** a quarter of a sphere etc. **4 a** a thing, esp. a graduated strip of metal, shaped like a quarter-circle. **b** an instrument graduated (esp. through an arc of 90°) for taking angular measurements. □□ **quadrantal** /-ˈdrænt(ə)l/ adj. [ME f. L quadrans -antis quarter f. quattuor four]

quadraphonic /ˌkwɒdrəˈfɒnɪk/ adj. (also **quadrophonic**) (of sound reproduction) using four transmission channels. □□ **quadraphonically** adv. **quadraphonics** n.pl. **quadraphony** /-ˈrɒfənɪ/ n. [QUADRI- + STEREOPHONIC]

quadrat /ˈkwɒdrət/ n. Ecol. a small area marked out for study. [var. of QUADRATE]

quadrate adj., n., & v. —adj. /ˈkwɒdrət/ esp. Anat. & Zool. square or rectangular (quadrate bone; quadrate muscle). —n. /ˈkwɒdrət/ **1** a quadrate bone or muscle. **2** a rectangular object. —v. /kwɒˈdreɪt/ **1** tr. make square. **2** intr. & tr. (often foll. by with) conform or make conform. [ME f. L quadrare quadrat- make square f. quattuor four]

quadratic /kwɒˈdrætɪk/ adj. & n. Math. —adj. **1** involving the second and no higher power of an unknown quantity or variable (quadratic equation). **2** square. —n. **1** a quadratic equation. **2** (in pl.) the branch of algebra dealing with these. [F quadratique or mod.L quadraticus (as QUADRATE)]

quadrature /ˈkwɒdrətʃə(r)/ n. **1** Math. the process of constructing a square with an area equal to that of a figure bounded by a curve, e.g. a circle. **2** Astron. **a** each of two points at which the moon is 90° from the sun as viewed from earth. **b** the position of a heavenly body in relation to another 90° away. [F quadrature or L quadratura (as QUADRATE)]

quadrennial /kwɒˈdrenɪəl/ adj. **1** lasting four years. **2** recurring every four years. □□ **quadrennially** adv. [as QUADRENNIUM]

quadrennium /kwɒˈdrenɪəm/ n. (pl. **quadrenniums** or **quadrennia** /-nɪə/) a period of four years. [L quadriennium (as QUADRI-, annus year)]

quadri- /ˈkwɒdrɪ/ comb. form denoting four. [L f. quattuor four]

quadric /ˈkwɒdrɪk/ adj. & n. Geom. —adj. (of a surface) described by an equation of the second degree. —n. a quadric surface. [L quadra square]

quadriceps /ˈkwɒdrɪˌseps/ n. Anat. a four-headed muscle at the front of the thigh. [mod.L (as QUADRI-, BICEPS)]

quadrifid /ˈkwɒdrɪfɪd/ adj. Bot. having four divisions or lobes. [L quadrifidus (as QUADRI-, findere fid- cleave)]

quadrilateral /ˌkwɒdrɪˈlætər(ə)l/ adj. & n. —adj. having four sides. —n. a four-sided figure. [LL quadrilaterus (as QUADRI-, latus lateris side)]

quadrille¹ /kwɒˈdrɪl/ n. **1** a square dance containing usu. five figures. **2** the music for this. [F f. Sp. cuadrilla troop, company f. cuadra square or It. quadriglia f. quadra square]

quadrille² /kwɒˈdrɪl/ n. a card game for four players with forty cards (i.e. an ordinary pack without the 8s, 9s, and 10s), fashionable in the 18th c. [F, perh. f. Sp. cuartillo f. cuarto fourth, assim. to QUADRILLE¹]

quadrillion /kwɒˈdrɪljən/ n. (pl. same or **quadrillions**) a thousand raised to the fifth (or formerly, esp. Brit., the eighth) power (10^{15} and 10^{24} respectively). [F (as QUADRI-, MILLION)]

quadrinomial /ˌkwɒdrɪˈnəʊmɪəl/ n. & adj. Math. —n. an expression of four algebraic terms. —adj. of or being a quadrinomial. [QUADRI- + Gk nomos part, portion]

quadripartite /ˌkwɒdrɪˈpɑːtaɪt/ adj. 1 consisting of four parts. 2 shared by or involving four parties.

quadriplegia /ˌkwɒdrɪˈpliːdʒɪə, -dʒə/ n. Med. paralysis of all four limbs. □□ **quadriplegic** adj. & n. [mod.L (as QUADRI-, Gk plēgē blow, strike)]

quadrivalent /ˌkwɒdrɪˈveɪlənt/ adj. Chem. having a valency of four.

quadrivium /kwɒˈdrɪvɪəm/ n. hist. a medieval university course of arithmetic, geometry, astronomy, and music. [L, = the place where four roads meet (as QUADRI-, via road)]

quadroon /kwɒˈdruːn/ n. the offspring of a White person and a mulatto; a person of one quarter Negro blood. [Sp. cuarterón f. cuarto fourth, assim. to QUADRI-]

quadrophonic var. of QUADRAPHONIC.

quadrumanous /kwɒˈdruːmənəs/ adj. (of primates other than humans) four-handed, i.e. with opposable digits on all four limbs. [mod.L quadrumana neut. pl. of quadrumanus (as QUADRI-, L manus hand)]

quadruped /ˈkwɒdrʊˌped/ n. & adj. —n. a four-footed animal, esp. a four-footed mammal. —adj. four-footed. □□ **quadrupedal** /-ˈruːpɪd(ə)l/ adj. [F quadrupède or L quadrupes -pedis f. quadru- var. of QUADRI- + L pes ped- foot]

quadruple /ˈkwɒdrʊp(ə)l/ adj., n., & v. —adj. 1 fourfold. 2 a having four parts. b involving four participants (quadruple alliance). 3 being four times as many or as much. 4 (of time in music) having four beats in a bar. —n. a fourfold number or amount. —v.tr. & intr. multiply by four; increase fourfold. □ **Quadruple Alliance** an alliance of four powers, (1) that formed in 1718 when Austria joined Britain, the Dutch Republic, and France against Spain (who had seized Sicily and Sardinia); (2) that of 1813 (renewed in 1815) when Britain, Russia, Austria, and Prussia united to defeat Napoleon and to maintain the international order established in Europe by the Peace of Paris at the end of the Napoleonic Wars; (3) that of 1834 between Britain, France, Spain, and Portugal to expel pretenders from the last two named countries. □□ **quadruply** adv. [F f. L quadruplus (as QUADRI-, -plus as in duplus DUPLE)]

quadruplet /ˈkwɒdrʊplɪt, -ˈdruːplɪt/ n. 1 each of four children born at one birth. 2 a set of four things working together. 3 Mus. a group of four notes to be performed in the time of three. [QUADRUPLE, after triplet]

quadruplicate adj. & v. —adj. /kwɒˈdruːplɪkət/ 1 fourfold. 2 of which four copies are made. —v.tr. /kwɒˈdruːplɪˌkeɪt/ 1 multiply by four. 2 make four identical copies of. □ **in quadruplicate** in four identical copies. □□ **quadruplication** /-ˈkeɪʃ(ə)n/ n. [L quadruplicare f. quadruplex -plicis fourfold: cf. QUADRUPED, DUPLEX]

quadruplicity /ˌkwɒdrʊˈplɪsɪtɪ/ n. the state of being fourfold. [L quadruplex -plicis (see QUADRUPLICATE), after duplicity]

quaestor /ˈkwiːstə(r)/ n. either of two ancient Roman magistrates with mainly financial responsibilities. □□ **quaestorial** /-ˈstɔːrɪəl/ adj. [ME f. L f. quaerere quaesit- seek]

quaff /kwɒf, kwɑːf/ v. literary 1 tr. & intr. drink deeply. 2 tr. drain (a cup etc.) in long draughts. □□ **quaffable** adj. **quaffer** n. [16th c.: perh. imit.]

quag /kwæg, kwɒg/ n. a marshy or boggy place. □□ **quaggy** adj. [rel. to dial. quag (v.) = shake: prob. imit.]

quagga /ˈkwægə/ n. an extinct zebra-like mammal, Equus quagga, formerly native to S. Africa, with yellowish-brown stripes on the head, neck, and forebody. [Xhosa-Kaffir iqwara]

quagmire /ˈkwɒgˌmaɪə(r), ˈkwæg-/ n. 1 a soft boggy or marshy area that gives way underfoot. 2 a hazardous or awkward situation. [QUAG + MIRE]

quahog /ˈkwɔːhɒg/ n. (US **quahaug** /-ˈhɔːg/) any of various edible clams of the Atlantic coast of N. America. [Narraganset Indian]

quaich /kweɪx/ n. (also **quaigh**) Sc. a kind of drinking-cup, usu. of wood and with two handles. [Gael. cuach cup, prob. f. L caucus]

Quai d'Orsay /keɪ dɔːˈseɪ/ a riverside street on the left bank of the Seine in Paris. The name is often used to denote the French ministry of foreign affairs, which has its headquarters there.

quail[1] /kweɪl/ n. (pl. same or **quails**) any small migratory bird of the genus Coturnix, with a short tail and allied to the partridge. [ME f. OF quaille f. med.L coacula (prob. imit.)]

quail[2] /kweɪl/ v.intr. flinch; be apprehensive with fear. [ME, of unkn. orig.]

quaint /kweɪnt/ adj. 1 piquantly or attractively unfamiliar or old-fashioned. 2 daintily odd. □□ **quaintly** adv. **quaintness** n. [earlier senses 'wise, cunning': ME f. OF cointe f. L cognitus past part. of cognoscere ascertain]

quake /kweɪk/ v. & n. —v.intr. 1 shake, tremble. 2 rock to and fro. 3 (of a person) shake or shudder (was quaking with fear). —n. 1 colloq. an earthquake. 2 an act of quaking. □ **quaking-grass** any grass of the genus Briza, having slender stalks and trembling in the wind: also called dodder-grass. □□ **quaky** adj. (**quakier**, **quakiest**). [OE cwacian]

Quaker /ˈkweɪkə(r)/ n. a member of the Society of Friends (see entry). □□ **Quakerish** adj. **Quakerism** n. [QUAKE + -ER[1]]

qualification /ˌkwɒlɪfɪˈkeɪʃ(ə)n/ n. 1 the act or an instance of qualifying. 2 an accomplishment fitting a person for a position or purpose. 3 a a circumstance, condition, etc., that modifies or limits (the statement had many qualifications). b a thing that detracts from completeness or absoluteness (their relief had one qualification). 4 a condition that must be fulfilled before a right can be acquired etc. 5 an attribution of a quality (the qualification of our policy as opportunist is unfair). □□ **qualificatory** /ˈkwɒlɪfɪˌkeɪtərɪ/ adj. [F qualification or med.L qualificatio (as QUALIFY)]

qualify /ˈkwɒlɪˌfaɪ/ v. (-ies, -ied) 1 tr. make competent or fit for a position or purpose. 2 tr. make legally entitled. 3 intr. (foll. by for) (of a person) satisfy the conditions or requirements (for a position, award, competition, etc.). 4 tr. add reservations to; modify or make less absolute (a statement or assertion). 5 tr. Gram. (of a word, esp. an adjective) attribute a quality to another word, esp. a noun. 6 tr. moderate, mitigate; make less severe or extreme. 7 tr. alter the strength or flavour of. 8 tr. (foll. by as) attribute a specified quality to, describe as (the idea was qualified as absurd). 9 tr. (as **qualifying** adj.) serving to determine those that qualify (qualifying examination). □□ **qualifiable** adj. **qualifier** n. [F qualifier f. med.L qualificare f. L qualis such as]

qualitative /ˈkwɒlɪtətɪv, -ˌteɪtɪv/ adj. concerned with or depending on quality (led to a qualitative change in society). □ **qualitative analysis** Chem. detection of the constituents, as elements, functional groups, etc., present in a substance (opp. quantitative analysis). □□ **qualitatively** adv. [LL qualitativus (as QUALITY)]

quality /ˈkwɒlɪtɪ/ n. (pl. -ies) 1 the degree of excellence of a thing (of good quality; poor in quality). 2 a general excellence (their work has quality). b (attrib.) of high quality (a quality product). 3 a distinctive attribute or faculty; a characteristic trait. 4 the relative nature or kind or character of a thing (is made in three qualities). 5 the distinctive timbre of a voice or sound. 6 archaic high social standing (people of quality). 7 Logic the property of a proposition's being affirmative or negative. □ **quality control** a system of maintaining standards in manufactured products by testing a sample of the output against the specification. [ME f. OF qualité f. L qualitas -tatis f. qualis of what kind]

qualm /kwɑːm, kwɔːm/ n. 1 a misgiving; an uneasy doubt esp. about one's own conduct. 2 a scruple of conscience. 3 a momentary faint or sick feeling. □□ **qualmish** adj. [16th c.: orig. uncert.]

quandary /ˈkwɒndərɪ/ n. (pl. -ies) 1 a state of perplexity. 2 a difficult situation; a practical dilemma. [16th c.: orig. uncert.]

quango /ˈkwæŋgəʊ/ n. (pl. -os) a semi-public body with financial support from and senior appointments made by the government. The term came into use c.1973 (its full form is found in 1967) in the US. [abbr. of quasi (or quasi-autonomous) non-government(al) organization]

Quant /kwɒnt/, Mary (1934–), English fashion designer, whose most famous innovation was the miniskirt (1965). She was one of the first to design for the ready-to-wear market, and her styles, created especially for the young, did much to make London a leading fashion centre in the 1960s.

quant /kwɒnt/ n. & v. —n. Brit. a punting-pole with a prong at the bottom to prevent it sinking into the mud, as used by Norfolk bargemen etc. —v.tr. (also absol.) propel (a boat) with a quant. [15th c.: perh. f. L contus f. Gk kontos boat-pole]

quanta pl. of QUANTUM.

quantal /ˈkwɒnt(ə)l/ adj. **1** composed of discrete units; varying in steps, not continuously. **2** of or relating to a quantum or quantum theory. □□ **quantally** adv. [L quantus how much]

quantic /ˈkwɒntɪk/ n. Math. a rational integral homogeneous function of two or more variables.

quantify /ˈkwɒntɪˌfaɪ/ v.tr. (-ies, -ied) **1** determine the quantity of. **2** measure or express as a quantity. **3** Logic define the application of (a term or proposition) by the use of all, some, etc., e.g. 'for all x if x is A then x is B'. □□ **quantifiable** adj. **quantifiability** /-ə'bɪlɪtɪ/ n. **quantification** /ˌkwɒntɪfɪ'keɪʃ(ə)n/ n. **quantifier** n. [med.L quantificare (as QUANTAL)]

quantitative /ˈkwɒntɪtətɪv, -ˌteɪtɪv/ adj. **1 a** concerned with quantity. **b** measured or measurable by quantity. **2** of or based on the quantity of syllables. □ **quantitative analysis** Chem. measurement of the amounts of the constituents of a substance (opp. QUALITATIVE ANALYSIS). □□ **quantitatively** adv. [med.L quantitativus (as QUANTITY)]

quantitive /ˈkwɒntɪtɪv/ adj. = QUANTITATIVE. □□ **quantitively** adv.

quantity /ˈkwɒntɪtɪ/ n. (pl. -ies) **1** the property of things that is measurable. **2** the size or extent or weight or amount or number. **3** a specified or considerable portion or number or amount (buys in quantity; the quantity of heat in a body). **4** (in pl.) large amounts or numbers; an abundance (quantities of food; is found in quantities on the shore). **5** the length or shortness of vowel sounds or syllables. **6** Math. **a** a value, component, etc. that may be expressed in numbers. **b** the figure or symbol representing this. □ **quantity mark** a mark put over a vowel etc. to indicate its length. **quantity surveyor** a person who measures and prices building work. **quantity theory** the hypothesis that prices correspond to changes in the monetary supply. [ME f. OF quantité f. L quantitas -tatis f. quantus how much]

quantize /ˈkwɒntaɪz/ v.tr. (also -ise) **1** form into quanta. **2** apply quantum mechanics to. □□ **quantization** /-ˈzeɪʃ(ə)n/ n.

quantum /ˈkwɒntəm/ n. (pl. **quanta** /-tə/) **1** Physics **a** a discrete quantity of energy proportional in magnitude to the frequency of radiation it represents. **b** an analogous discrete amount of any other physical quantity. (See below.) **2 a** a required or allowed amount. **b** a share or portion. □ **quantum jump** (or **leap**) **1** a sudden large increase or advance. **2** Physics an abrupt transition in an atom or molecule from one quantum state to another. **quantum mechanics** a mathematical form of quantum theory dealing with the motion and interaction of (esp. subatomic) particles and incorporating the concept that these particles can also be regarded as waves. **quantum theory** Physics the body of theory based on the existence of quanta of energy. [L, neut. of quantus how much]

The development of quantum theory in the 20th c. has, along with the theory of relativity, revolutionized our understanding of the physical world. The first step occurred in 1900 when Max Planck accounted for certain puzzling characteristics of the electromagnetic radiation given off by hot bodies by postulating that energy could be emitted only in discrete 'lumps' rather than as a continuum—a radical break with traditional views. In 1905 Einstein took this idea further by suggesting that light itself, along with other electromagnetic radiation, could be regarded as consisting of discrete particles or quanta of energy. (These particles are now called photons.) In 1913 Niels Bohr proposed a model of the atom that incorporated quantum theory: electrons are postulated to circle round a central nucleus, but are restricted to particular orbits which correspond to possessing discrete amounts of energy. In 1924 L. de Broglie conjectured that, just as light waves possess some of the attributes of particles, perhaps particles such as electrons also had the properties of waves. This idea was taken up and over the rest of the decade was developed by Schrödinger, Heisenberg, and others into a more sophisticated theory of atomic structure called quantum mechanics, in which the fixed orbits of Bohr's model are replaced by more diffuse 'orbitals', reflecting the dual nature of the electron as behaving both like a wave and like a particle. This 'wave-particle duality' appeared paradoxical to many, as did the so-called 'uncertainty principle' enunciated by Heisenberg in 1927, which set a definite theoretical limit to the accuracy with which properties of a particle, such as position and momentum, can be measured simultaneously. Philosophical debate has continued about whether the uncertainty principle means that there is after all some 'spontaneity' in the physical world, in the sense that not every event is completely determined by previous events. In 1928 quantum mechanics was further refined by P. A. M. Dirac, who incorporated into it the principles of relativity. Since then the ideas of quantum mechanics have been extended to include nuclear physics and the properties of electromagnetic fields. Quantum theory also explains certain properties of solids such as superconductivity, and overall continues to be an extremely successful and accurate account of the fundamental structure of the physical world.

quaquaversal /ˌkweɪkwə'vɜːs(ə)l/ adj. Geol. pointing in every direction. [LL quaquaversus f. quaqua wheresoever + versus towards]

quarantine /ˈkwɒrən,tiːn/ n. & v. —n. **1** isolation imposed on persons or animals that have arrived from elsewhere or been exposed to, and might spread, infectious or contagious disease. **2** the period of this isolation. —v.tr. impose such isolation on, put in quarantine. [It. quarantina forty days f. quaranta forty]

quark[1] /kwɑːk/ n. Physics any of a group of (originally three) postulated components of elementary particles. Quarks are held to carry a charge one-third or two-thirds that of the proton. Many predictions of this theory have been corroborated by experiments but free quarks have yet to be observed. In a sense, quark theory recapitulates at a deeper level efforts earlier this century to explain all atomic properties in terms of electrons, protons, and neutrons. [coined by M. Gell-Mann, 1964, from phrase 'Three quarks for Muster Mark!' in James Joyce's Finnegans Wake (1939)]

quark[2] /kwɑːk/ n. a type of low-fat curd cheese. [G]

quarrel[1] /ˈkwɒr(ə)l/ n. & v. —n. **1** a violent contention or altercation between individuals or with others. **2** a rupture of friendly relations. **3** an occasion of complaint against a person, a person's actions, etc. —v.intr. (**quarrelled, quarrelling**; US **quarreled, quarreling**) **1** (often foll. by with) take exception; find fault. **2** fall out; have a dispute; break off friendly relations. □□ **quarreller** n. [ME f. OF querele f. L querel(l)a complaint f. queri complain]

quarrel[2] /ˈkwɒr(ə)l/ n. hist. a short heavy square-headed arrow or bolt used in a crossbow or arbalest. [ME f. OF quar(r)el ult. f. LL quadrus square]

quarrelsome /ˈkwɒrəlsəm/ adj. given to or characterized by quarrelling. □□ **quarrelsomely** adv. **quarrelsomeness** n.

quarrian /ˈkwɒrɪən/ n. (also **quarrion**) a cockatiel. [prob. Aboriginal]

quarry[1] /ˈkwɒrɪ/ n. & v. —n. (pl. -ies) **1** an excavation made by taking stone etc. for building etc. from its bed. **2** a place from which stone etc. may be extracted. **3** a source of information, knowledge, etc. —v. (-ies, -ied) **1** tr. extract (stone) from a quarry. **2** tr. extract (facts etc.) laboriously from books etc. **3** intr. laboriously search documents etc. [ME f. med.L quare(r)ia f. OF quarriere f. L quadrum square]

quarry[2] /ˈkwɒrɪ/ n. (pl. -ies) **1** the object of pursuit by a bird of prey, hounds, hunters, etc. **2** an intended victim or prey. [ME f. AF f. OF cuiree, couree (assim. to cuir leather and curer disembowel) ult. f. L cor heart: orig. = parts of deer placed on hide and given to hounds]

quarry[3] /ˈkwɒrɪ/ n. (pl. -ies) **1** a diamond-shaped pane of glass as used in lattice windows. **2** (in full **quarry tile**) an unglazed floor-tile. [a later form of QUARREL[2] in the same sense]

quarryman /ˈkwɒrɪmən/ n. (pl. -men) a worker in a quarry.

w we z zoo ʃ she ʒ decision θ thin ð this ŋ ring x loch tʃ chip dʒ jar (see over for vowels)

quart /ˈkwɔːt/ n. **1** a liquid measure equal to a quarter of a gallon; two pints. **2** a vessel containing this amount. **3** US a unit of dry measure, equivalent to one-thirty-second of a bushel (1.1 litre). **4** /kɑːt/ (also **quarte**) the fourth of eight parrying positions in fencing. □ **a quart into a pint pot 1** a large amount etc. fitted into a small space. **2** something difficult or impossible to achieve. [ME f. OF *quarte* f. L *quarta* fem. of *quartus* fourth f. *quattuor* four]

quartan /ˈkwɔːt(ə)n/ adj. (of a fever etc.) recurring every fourth day. [ME f. OF *quartaine* f. L (*febris* fever) *quartana* f. *quartus* fourth]

quarte var. of QUART 4.

quarter /ˈkwɔːtə(r)/ n. & v. —n. **1** each of four equal parts into which a thing is or might be divided. **2** a period of three months, usu. for which payments become due on the quarter day. **3** a point of time 15 minutes before or after any hour. **4** a school or US university term. **5 a** 25 US or Canadian cents. **b** a coin of this denomination. **6** a part of a town, esp. as occupied by a particular class or group (*residential quarter*). **7 a** a point of the compass. **b** a region at such a point. **8** the direction, district, or source of supply etc. (*help from any quarter; came from all quarters*). **9** (in pl.) **a** lodgings; an abode. **b** Mil. the living accommodation of troops etc. **10 a** one fourth of a lunar month. **b** the moon's position between the first and second (**first quarter**) or third and fourth (**last quarter**) of these. **11 a** each of the four parts into which an animal's or bird's carcass is divided, each including a leg or wing. **b** (in pl.) hist. the four parts into which a traitor etc. was cut after execution. **c** (in pl.) = HINDQUARTERS. **12** mercy offered or granted to an enemy in battle etc. on condition of surrender. **13 a** Brit. a grain measure equivalent to 8 bushels. **b** one-fourth of a hundredweight (28 lb. or US 25 lb.). **14 a** each of four divisions on a shield. **b** a charge occupying this, placed in chief. **15** either side of a ship abaft the beam. **16** (in American and Australian football) each of four equal periods into which a match is divided. —v.tr. **1** divide into quarters. **2** hist. divide (the body of an executed person) in this way. **3 a** put (troops etc.) into quarters. **b** station or lodge in a specified place. **4** (foll. by *on*) impose (a person) on another as a lodger. **5** cut (a log) into quarters, and these into planks so as to show the grain well. **6** (esp. of a dog) range or traverse (the ground) in every direction. **7** Heraldry **a** place or bear (charges or coats of arms) on the four quarters of a shield's surface. **b** add (another's coat) to one's hereditary arms. **c** (foll. by *with*) place in alternate quarters with. **d** divide (a shield) into four or more parts by vertical and horizontal lines. □ **quarter-binding** the type of bookbinding in which the spine is bound in one material (usu. leather) and the sides in another. **quarter day** any of the four days on which quarterly payments are due, tenancies begin and end, etc. (in England 25 March, 24 June, 29 Sept., 25 Dec.; in Scotland 2 Feb., 15 May, 1 Aug., 11 Nov.). **quarter-final** a match or round preceding the semifinal. **quarter-hour 1** a period of 15 minutes. **2** = sense 3 of n. **quarter-light** Brit. a window in the side of a motor vehicle, closed carriage, etc. other than the main door-window. **quarter-line** Rugby Football a space enclosed by a line across the ground 22 metres from the goal-line. **quarter note** esp. US Mus. a crotchet. **quarter-plate 1** a photographic plate or film 8.3 × 10.8 cm. **2** a photograph reproduced from it. **quarter sessions** hist. (in the UK) a court of limited criminal and civil jurisdiction and of appeal, usu. held quarterly. **quarter-tone** Mus. half a semitone. [ME f. AF *quarter*, OF *quartier* f. L *quartarius* fourth part (of a measure) f. *quartus* fourth]

quarterage /ˈkwɔːtərɪdʒ/ n. **1** a quarterly payment. **2** a quarter's wages, allowance, pension, etc.

quarterback /ˈkwɔːtəˌbæk/ n. a player in American football who directs attacking play.

quarterdeck /ˈkwɔːtəˌdek/ n. **1** part of a ship's upper deck near the stern, usu. reserved for officers. **2** the officers of a ship or the navy.

quartering /ˈkwɔːtərɪŋ/ n. **1** (in pl.) the coats of arms marshalled on a shield to denote the alliances of a family with the heiresses of others. **2** the provision of quarters for soldiers. **3** the act or an instance of dividing, esp. into four equal parts. **4** timber sawn into lengths, used for high-quality floor-boards etc.

quarterly /ˈkwɔːtəlɪ/ adj., adv., & n. —adj. **1** produced or occurring once every quarter of a year. **2** (of a shield) quartered. —adv. **1** once every quarter of a year. **2** in the four, or in two diagonally opposite, quarters of a shield. —n. (pl. **-ies**) a quarterly review or magazine.

quartermaster /ˈkwɔːtəˌmɑːstə(r)/ n. **1** a regimental officer in charge of quartering, rations, etc. **2** a naval petty officer in charge of steering, signals, etc. □ **Quartermaster General** the head of the army department in charge of quartering etc. **quartermaster sergeant** a sergeant assisting an army quartermaster.

quartern /ˈkwɔːt(ə)n/ n. Brit. archaic a quarter of a pint. □ **quartern loaf** a four-pound loaf. [ME, = quarter f. AF *quartrun*, OF *quart(e)ron* f. QUART fourth or *quartier* QUARTER]

quarterstaff /ˈkwɔːtəˌstɑːf/ n. hist. a stout pole 6–8 feet long, formerly used as a weapon.

quartet /kwɔːˈtet/ n. (also **quartette**) **1** Mus. **a** a composition for four voices or instruments. **b** the performers of such a piece. **2** any group of four. [F *quartette* f. It. *quartetto* f. *quarto* fourth f. L *quartus*]

quartic /ˈkwɑːtɪk/ adj. & n. Math. —adj. involving the fourth and no higher power of an unknown quantity or variable. —n. a quartic equation. [L *quartus* fourth]

quartile /ˈkwɔːtaɪl/ adj. & n. —adj. Astrol. relating to the aspect of two celestial bodies 90° apart. —n. **1** a quartile aspect. **2** Statistics one of three values of a variable dividing a population into four equal groups as regards the value of that variable. [med.L *quartilis* f. L *quartus* fourth]

quarto /ˈkwɔːtəʊ/ n. (pl. **-os**) Printing **1** the size given by folding a (usu. specified) sheet of paper twice. **2** a book consisting of sheets folded in this way. ¶ Abbr.: **4to.** □ **quarto paper** paper folded in this way and cut into sheets. [L (*in*) *quarto* (in) the fourth (of a sheet), ablat. of *quartus* fourth]

quartz /kwɔːts/ n. a mineral form of silica that crystallizes as hexagonal prisms. □ **quartz clock** a clock operated by vibrations of an electrically driven quartz crystal. **quartz lamp** a quartz tube containing mercury vapour and used as a light source. [G *Quarz* f. WSlav. *kwardy*]

quartzite /ˈkwɔːtsaɪt/ n. a metamorphic rock consisting mainly of quartz.

quasar /ˈkweɪzɑː(r), -sɑ:(r)/ n. Astron. any of a class of point-like sources of light visible in large telescopes, often associated with intense radio emission. Their spectra show large red-shifts, suggesting great remoteness and high velocities of recession. If they are indeed at such distances, they must be emitting exceptionally large amounts of energy, the nature of which is not fully understood. [*quasi-stellar*]

quash /kwɒʃ/ v.tr. **1** annul; reject as not valid, esp. by a legal procedure. **2** suppress; crush (a rebellion etc.). [ME f. OF *quasser*, *casser* annul f. LL *cassare* f. *cassus* null, void or f. L *cassare* frequent. of *quatere* shake]

quasi /ˈkweɪzaɪ, ˈkwɑːzɪ/ adv. (introducing an exclamation) that is to say; as it were. [L, = as if, almost]

quasi- /ˈkweɪzaɪ, ˈkwɑːzɪ/ comb. form **1** seemingly; apparently but not really (*quasi-scientific*). **2** being partly or almost (*quasi-independent*). [L *quasi* as if, almost]

Quasimodo[1] /ˌkweɪsɪˈməʊdəʊ/ the deformed bell-ringer of Notre Dame in Victor Hugo's *Notre Dame de Paris* (1831).

Quasimodo[2] /kwɑːzɪˈməʊdəʊ/, Salvatore (1901–68), Italian poet, who was awarded the Nobel Prize for literature in 1959. His early work was influenced by the symbolist movement; his later work is more extrovert and concerned with social issues. Some of his best poetry is inspired by his Sicilian background, for which he felt a nostalgic tenderness.

quassia /ˈkwɒʃə/ n. **1** an evergreen tree, *Quassia amara*, native to S. America. **2** the wood, bark, or root of this tree, yielding a bitter medicinal tonic and insecticide. [G. *Quassi*, 18th-c. Surinam slave, who discovered its medicinal properties]

quatercentenary /ˌkwætəsənˈtiːnərɪ/ n. & adj. —n. (pl. **-ies**) **1** a four-hundredth anniversary. **2** a festival marking this. —adj. of this anniversary. [L *quater* four times + CENTENARY]

quaternary /kwəˈtɜːnərɪ/ adj. & n. —adj. **1** having four parts. **2** (**Quaternary**) Geol. of or relating to the second and most recent period in the Cenozoic era, comprising the Pleistocene and Holocene (Recent) epochs and extending from about 2 million years ago to the present. —n. (pl. **-ies**) **1** a set of four things. **2** (**Quaternary**) Geol. the Quaternary period or system. [ME f. L quaternarius f. quaterni distrib. of quattuor four]

quaternion /kwəˈtɜːnɪən/ n. **1** a set of four. **2** Math. a complex number of the form $w + xi + yj + zk$, where w, x, y, z are real numbers and i, j, k are imaginary units that satisfy certain conditions. [ME f. LL quaternio -onis (as QUATERNARY)]

quatorzain /ˈkætəˌzeɪn/ n. any fourteen-line poem; an irregular sonnet. [F quatorzaine f. quatorze fourteen f. L quattuordecim]

quatorze /kəˈtɔːz/ n. a set of four aces, kings, queens, or jacks, in one hand at piquet, scoring fourteen. [F: see QUATORZAIN]

quatrain /ˈkwɒtreɪn/ n. a stanza of four lines, usu. with alternate rhymes. [F f. quatre four f. L quattuor]

quatrefoil /ˈkætrəˌfɔɪl/ n. a four-pointed or four-leafed figure, esp. as an ornament in architectural tracery, resembling a flower or clover leaf. [ME f. AF f. quatre four: see FOIL²]

quattrocento /ˌkwætrəʊˈtʃentəʊ/ n. the style of Italian art of the 15th c. □□ **quattrocentist** n. [It., = 400 used with reference to the years 1400–99]

quaver /ˈkweɪvə(r)/ v. & n. —v. **1** intr. **a** (esp. of a voice or musical sound) vibrate, shake, tremble. **b** use trills or shakes in singing. **2** tr. **a** sing (a note or song) with quavering. **b** (often foll. by out) say in a trembling voice. —n. **1** Mus. a note having the time value of an eighth of a semibreve or half a crotchet and represented by a large dot with a hooked stem. Also called eighth note. **2** a trill in singing. **3** a tremble in speech. □□ **quaveringly** adv. [ME f. quave, perh. f. OE cwafian (unrecorded: cf. cwacian QUAKE)]

quavery /ˈkweɪvərɪ/ adj. (of a voice etc.) tremulous. □□ **quaveriness** n.

quay /kiː/ n. a solid stationary artificial landing-place lying alongside or projecting into water for loading and unloading ships. □□ **quayage** n. [ME key(e), kay f. OF kay f. Gaulish caio f. OCelt.]

quayside /ˈkiːsaɪd/ n. the land forming or near a quay.

Que. abbr. Quebec.

quean /kwiːn/ n. archaic an impudent or ill-behaved girl or woman. [OE cwene woman: cf. QUEEN]

queasy /ˈkwiːzɪ/ adj. (**-ier, -iest**) **1 a** (of a person) feeling nausea. **b** (of a person's stomach) easily upset, weak of digestion. **2** (of the conscience etc.) overscrupulous, tender. □□ **queasily** adv. **queasiness** n. [ME queysy, coisy perh. f. AF & OF, rel. to OF coisir hurt]

Quebec /kwɪˈbek/ **1** a province of eastern Canada (from 1867, settled by the French and ceded to the British in 1763; pop. (1986) 6,540,300. Its culture remains predominantly French. **2** its capital city, on the St Lawrence river, captured from the French by a British force in 1759 (see PLAINS OF ABRAHAM).

Quechua /ˈketʃwə/ n. (also **Quichua** /ˈkɪ-/) (pl. same) **1** a member of an Indian people of Peru and neighbouring parts of Bolivia, Chile, Colombia, and Ecuador. **2** the language (actually a group of related languages) spoken by this people. It is one of the two official languages of Peru (the other being Spanish). □□ **Quechuan** adj. & n. [Sp. f. Quechua, = plunderer, despoiler]

Queen /kwiːn/, Ellery. The pseudonym of American authors Frederic Dannay (1905–82) and Manfred Lee (1905–71), under which they wrote many detective novels, the first of which was The Roman Hat Mystery (1929) and edited Ellery Queen's Mystery Magazine (1941–).

queen /kwiːn/ n. & v. —n. **1** (as a title usu. **Queen**) a female sovereign etc., esp. the hereditary ruler of an independent State. **2** (in full **queen consort**) a king's wife. **3** a woman, country, or thing pre-eminent or supreme in a specified area or of its kind (tennis queen; the queen of roses). **4** the fertile female among ants, bees, etc. **5** the most powerful piece in chess. **6** a court card with a picture of a queen. **7** sl. a male homosexual, esp. an effeminate one. **8 a** an honoured female, e.g. the Virgin Mary

(Queen of Heaven). **b** an ancient goddess (Venus, Queen of love). **9** a belle or mock sovereign on some occasion (beauty queen; queen of the May). **10** a person's sweetheart, wife, or mistress. **11** (**the Queen**) (in the UK) the national anthem when there is a female sovereign. —v.tr. **1** make (a woman) queen. **2** Chess convert (a pawn) into a queen when it reaches the opponent's side of the board. □ **Queen-Anne** in the style of English architecture, furniture, etc., in or about Queen Anne's time, the early 18th c. **Queen Anne's lace** cow-parsley. **queen bee 1** the fertile female in a hive. **2** the chief or controlling woman in an organization or social group. **queen-cake** a small soft cake often with raisins etc. **queen dowager** the widow of a king. **queen it** play the queen. **queen mother** the dowager who is mother of the sovereign. **queen of the meadows** meadowsweet. **queen of puddings** a pudding made with bread, jam, and meringue. **queen-post** one of two upright timbers between the tie-beam and principal rafters of a roof-truss. **Queen's bench** see BENCH. **queen's bishop, knight**, etc. Chess (of pieces which exist in pairs) the piece starting on the queen's side of the board. **Queen's bounty** see BOUNTY. **Queen's colour** see COLOUR. **Queen's Counsel** see COUNSEL. **the Queen's English** see ENGLISH. **Queen's evidence** see EVIDENCE. **Queen's Guide** see GUIDE. **Queen's highway** see HIGHWAY. **queen-size** (or **-sized**) of an extra-large size, usu. smaller than king-size. **Queen's Messenger** see MESSENGER. **queen's pawn** Chess the pawn in front of the queen at the beginning of a game. **Queen's Proctor** see PROCTOR. **Queen's Scout** see SCOUT¹. **Queen's speech** see SPEECH. **queen's-ware** cream-coloured Wedgwood. □□ **queendom** n. **queenhood** n. **queenless** adj. **queenlike** adj. **queenship** n. [OE cwēn f. Gmc; cf. QUEAN]

queenie /ˈkwiːnɪ/ n. sl. = QUEEN n. 7.

queenly /ˈkwiːnlɪ/ adj. (**queenlier, queenliest**) **1** fit for or appropriate to a queen. **2** majestic; queenlike. □□ **queenliness** n.

Queen Charlotte Islands /ˈʃɑːlət/ an island group off the coast of British Columbia, noted for its timber and fishing resources.

Queen Maud Land /mɔːd/ that part of Antarctica claimed by Norway since 1939.

Queens /kwiːnz/ a borough of New York City, at the west end of Long Island; pop. (1980) 1,891,300.

Queensberry Rules /ˈkwiːnzbərɪ/ n.pl. the standard rules, esp. of boxing, drafted in 1867 under the name and patronage of the Marquess of Queensberry. They formed the basis of modern glove-fighting as distinct from earlier bare-knuckle contests. The rules called for the wearing of gloves, and rounds of 3 minutes' duration interspersed with a minute's rest, and prohibited wrestling.

Queensland /ˈkwiːnzlənd/ a State comprising the north-eastern part of Australia; pop. (1986), 2,649,600; capital, Brisbane. Originally established in 1824 as a penal settlement, it was constituted a separate colony in 1859, having previously formed part of New South Wales, and was federated with the other States of Australia in 1901. □ **Queenslander** n.

queer /kwɪə(r)/ adj., n., & v. —adj. **1** strange; odd; eccentric. **2** shady; suspect; of questionable character. **3 a** slightly ill; giddy; faint. **b** Brit. sl. drunk. **4** derog. sl. (esp. of a man) homosexual. —n. derog. sl. a homosexual. —v.tr. sl. spoil; put out of order. □ **in Queer Street** sl. in a difficulty, in debt or trouble or disrepute. **queer a person's pitch** spoil a person's chances, esp. secretly or maliciously. □□ **queerish** adj. **queerly** adv. **queerness** n. [perh. f. G quer oblique (as THWART)]

quell /kwel/ v.tr. **1 a** crush or put down (a rebellion etc.). **b** reduce (rebels etc.) to submission. **2** suppress (fear, anger, etc.). □□ **queller** n. (also in comb.). [OE cwellan kill f. Gmc]

quench /kwentʃ/ v.tr. **1** satisfy (thirst) by drinking. **2** extinguish (a fire or light etc.). **3** cool, esp. with water (heat, a heated thing). **4** esp. Metallurgy cool (a hot substance) in cold water, air, oil, etc. **5 a** stifle or suppress (desire etc.). **b** Physics & Electronics inhibit or prevent (oscillation, luminescence, etc.) by counteractive means. **6** sl. reduce (an opponent) to silence. □□ **quenchable** adj. **quencher** n. **quenchless** adj. [ME f. OE -cwencan causative f. -cwincan be extinguished]

quenelle /kəˈnel/ n. a seasoned ball or roll of pounded fish or meat. [F, of unkn. orig.]

Quercia /ˈkwɜːʃə/, Jacopo della (1374–1438), Italian sculptor, a native of Siena. His achievement has been overshadowed by his contemporaries, Ghiberti and Donatello, with whom he worked on the Siena Baptistry reliefs (1417–31). His biblical reliefs for the portal of S. Petronio, Bologna (1425) are reckoned to constitute his masterpiece and reveal the pungency and vigour of his mature style.

Querétaro /keˈreɪtəˌrəʊ/ **1** a State of central Mexico; pop. (est. 1988) 952,900. **2** its capital city; pop. (1980) 293,590.

querist /ˈkwɪərɪst/ n. literary a person who asks questions; a questioner. [L quaerere ask]

quern /kwɜːn/ n. **1** a simple apparatus for grinding corn, consisting of two hard stones, the upper of which is rubbed to and fro, or rotated, on the lower one. **2** a small hand-mill for pepper etc. [OE cweorn(e) f. Gmc]

querulous /ˈkwerʊləs/ adj. complaining, peevish. □□ **querulously** adv. **querulousness** n. [LL querulosus or L querulus f. queri complain]

query /ˈkwɪərɪ/ n. & v. —n. (pl. **-ies**) **1** a question, esp. expressing doubt or objection. **2** a question mark, or the word query spoken or written to question accuracy or as a mark of interrogation. —v. (**-ies, -ied**) **1** tr. (often foll. by whether, if, etc. + clause) ask or inquire. **2** tr. call (a thing) in question in speech or writing. **3** tr. dispute the accuracy of. **4** intr. put a question. [Anglicized form of quaere f. L quaerere ask, after INQUIRY]

quest /kwest/ n. & v. —n. **1** a search or the act of seeking. **2** the thing sought, esp. the object of a medieval knight's pursuit. —v. **1** intr. (often foll. by about) **a** (often foll. by for) go about in search of something. **b** (of a dog etc.) search about for game. **2** tr. poet. search for, seek out. □ **in quest of** seeking. □□ **quester** n. **questingly** adv. [ME f. OF queste, quester ult. f. L quaerere quaest-seek]

question /ˈkwestʃ(ə)n/ n. & v. —n. **1** a sentence worded or expressed so as to seek information. **2** a doubt about or objection to a thing's truth, credibility, advisability, etc. (allowed it without question). **b** the raising of such doubt etc. **3** a matter to be discussed or decided or voted on. **4** a problem requiring an answer or solution. **5** (foll. by of) a matter or concern depending on conditions (it's a question of money). —v.tr. **1** ask questions of; interrogate. **2** subject (a person) to examination. **3** throw doubt upon; raise objections to. **4** seek information from the study of (phenomena, facts). □ **be a question of time** be certain to happen sooner or later. **beyond all question** undoubtedly. **come into question** be discussed; become of practical importance. **in question** that is being discussed or referred to (the person in question). **is not the question** is irrelevant. **out of the question** too impracticable etc. to be worth discussing; impossible. **put the question** require supporters and opponents of a proposal to record their votes, divide a meeting. **question mark** a punctuation mark (?) indicating a question. **question-master** Brit. a person who presides over a quiz game etc. **question time** Parl. a period during parliamentary proceedings when MPs may question ministers. □□ **questioner** n. **questioningly** adv. **questionless** adj. [ME f. AF questiun, OF question, questionner f. L quaestio -onis f. quaerere quaest- seek]

questionable /ˈkwestʃənəb(ə)l/ adj. **1** doubtful as regards truth or quality. **2** not clearly in accordance with honesty, honour, wisdom, etc. □□ **questionability** /ˌkwestʃənəˈbɪlɪtɪ/ n. **questionableness** n. **questionably** adv.

questionary /ˈkwestʃənərɪ/ n. (pl. **-ies**) = QUESTIONNAIRE. [med.L quaestionarium or F (as QUESTIONNAIRE)]

questionnaire /ˌkwestʃəˈneə(r), ˌkestjə-/ n. **1** a formulated series of questions, esp. for statistical study. **2** a document containing these. [F f. questionner QUESTION + -aire -ARY¹]

Quetta /ˈkwetə/ a city in western Pakistan, the capital of Baluchistan province; pop. (1981) 285,000. The city was severely damaged by an earthquake in 1935.

quetzal /ˈkwetz(ə)l/ n. **1** any of various brilliantly coloured birds of the family Trogonidae, esp. the Central and S. American Pharomachrus mocinno, the male of which has long green tail coverts. **2** the chief monetary unit of Guatemala. [Sp. f. Aztec f. quetzalli the bird's tail-feather]

Quetzalcóatl /ˌketsəlkəʊˈɑːt(ə)l/ the Plumed Serpent of the Toltec and Aztec civilizations, traditionally known as the god of the morning and evening star, later as the patron of priests, inventor of books and of the calendar, and as the symbol of death and resurrection. His worship involved human sacrifice. Legend said that he would return in another age, and when Montezuma, last king of the Aztecs, received news of the landing of Cortés and his men in 1519, his first thought was that Quetzalcóatl had indeed returned.

queue /kjuː/ n. & v. esp. Brit. —n. **1** a line or sequence of persons, vehicles, etc., awaiting their turn to be attended to or to proceed. **2** a pigtail or plait of hair. —v.intr. (**queues, queued, queuing** or **queueing**) (often foll. by up) (of persons etc.) form a queue; take one's place in a queue. □ **queue-jump** Brit. push forward out of turn in a queue. [F f. L cauda tail]

Quezon City /ˈkeɪsɒn/ a city on the island of Luzon in the northern Philippines; pop. (1980), 1,165,900. Situated on the outskirts of Manila, Quezon City was established in 1940 and named after Manuel Luis Quezon, the first President of the republic. From 1948 to 1976 it was the capital of the Philippines.

Qufu /tʃuːˈfuː/ a small town in Shandong province in eastern China, where Confucius was born (551 BC) and lived for much of his life.

quibble /ˈkwɪb(ə)l/ n. & v. —n. **1** a petty objection; a trivial point of criticism. **2** a play on words; a pun. **3** an evasion; an insubstantial argument which relies on an ambiguity etc. —v.intr. use quibbles. □□ **quibbler** n. **quibbling** adj. **quibblingly** adv. [dimin. of obs. quib prob. f. L quibus dative & ablat. pl. of qui who (familiar from use in legal documents)]

quiche /kiːʃ/ n. an open flan or tart with a savoury filling. [F]

Quichua var. of QUECHUA.

quick /kwɪk/ adj., adv., & n. —adj. **1** taking only a short time (a quick worker). **2** arriving after a short time, prompt (quick action; quick results). **3** with only a short interval (in quick succession). **4** lively, intelligent. **5** acute, alert (has a quick ear). **6** (of a temper) easily roused. **7** archaic living, alive (the quick and the dead). —adv. **1** quickly, at a rapid rate. **2** (as int.) come, go, etc., quickly. —n. **1** the soft flesh below the nails, or the skin, or a sore. **2** the seat of feeling or emotion (cut to the quick). □ **be quick** act quickly. **quick-fire 1** (of repartee etc.) rapid. **2** firing shots in quick succession. **quick-freeze 1** freeze (food) rapidly so as to preserve its natural qualities. **2** this process. **quick march** Mil. **1** a march in quick time. **2** the command to begin this. **quick one** colloq. a drink taken quickly. **quick step** Mil. a step used in quick time (cf. QUICKSTEP). **quick time** Mil. marching at about 120 paces per minute. **quick trick** Bridge **1** a trick in the first two rounds of a suit. **2** the card that should win this. **quick with child** archaic at a stage of pregnancy when movements of the foetus have been felt. □□ **quickly** adv. **quickness** n. [OE cwic(u) alive f. Gmc]

quicken /ˈkwɪkən/ v. **1** tr. & intr. make or become quicker; accelerate. **2** tr. give life or vigour to; rouse; animate; stimulate. **3** intr. **a** (of a woman) reach a stage in pregnancy when movements of the foetus can be felt. **b** (of a foetus) begin to show signs of life. **4** tr. archaic kindle; make (a fire) burn brighter. **5** intr. come to life.

quickie /ˈkwɪkɪ/ n. colloq. **1** a thing done or made quickly or hastily. **2** a drink taken quickly.

quicklime /ˈkwɪklaɪm/ n. = LIME¹ n. 1.

quicksand /ˈkwɪksænd/ n. **1** loose wet sand that sucks in anything placed or falling into it. **2** a bed of this.

quickset /ˈkwɪkset/ adj. & n. —adj. (of a hedge) formed of slips of plants, esp. hawthorn set in the ground to grow. —n. **1** such slips. **2** a hedge formed in this way.

quicksilver /ˈkwɪkˌsɪlvə(r)/ n. & v. —n. **1** mercury. **2** mobility of temperament or mood. —v.tr. coat (a mirror-glass) with an amalgam of tin.

quickstep /ˈkwɪkstep/ n. & v. —n. a fast foxtrot (cf. quick step). —v.intr. (**-stepped, -stepping**) dance the quickstep.

quickthorn /ˈkwɪkθɔːn/ n. a common hawthorn, *Crataegus monogyna*.

quick-witted /kwɪkˈwɪtɪd/ adj. quick to grasp a situation, make repartee, etc. ☐☐ **quick-wittedness** n.

quid[1] /kwɪd/ n. (pl. same) *Brit. sl.* one pound sterling. ☐ **not the full quid** *Austral. sl.* mentally deficient. **quids in** *sl.* in a position of profit. [prob. f. *quid* the nature of a thing f. L *quid* what, something]

quid[2] /kwɪd/ n. a lump of tobacco for chewing. [dial. var. of CUD]

quiddity /ˈkwɪdɪtɪ/ n. (pl. **-ies**) 1 *Philos.* the essence of a person or thing; what makes a thing what it is. 2 a quibble; a trivial objection. [med.L *quidditas* f. L *quid* what]

quidnunc /ˈkwɪdnʌŋk/ n. archaic a newsmonger, a person given to gossip. [L *quid* what + *nunc* now]

quid pro quo /ˌkwɪd prəʊ ˈkwəʊ/ n. 1 a thing given as compensation. 2 return made (for a gift, favour, etc.). [L, = something for something]

quiescent /kwɪˈes(ə)nt/ adj. 1 motionless, inert. 2 silent, dormant. ☐☐ **quiescence** n. **quiescency** n. **quiescently** adv. [L *quiescere* f. *quies* QUIET]

quiet /ˈkwaɪət/ adj., n., & v. —adj. (**quieter**, **quietest**) 1 with little or no sound or motion. 2 of gentle or peaceful disposition. 3 (of a colour, piece of clothing, etc.) unobtrusive; not showy. 4 not overt; private; disguised (*quiet resentment*). 5 undisturbed; uninterrupted; free or far from vigorous action (*a quiet time for prayer*). 6 informal; simple (*just a quiet wedding*). 7 enjoyed in quiet (*a quiet smoke*). 8 tranquil; not anxious or remorseful. —n. 1 silence; stillness. 2 an undisturbed state; tranquillity. 3 a state of being free from urgent tasks or agitation (*a period of quiet at work*). 4 a peaceful state of affairs (*could do with some quiet*). —v. 1 tr. sooth, make quiet. 2 intr. (often foll. by *down*) become quiet or calm. ☐ **be quiet** (esp. in *imper.*) cease talking etc. **keep quiet** 1 refrain from making a noise. 2 (often foll. by *about*) suppress or refrain from disclosing information etc. **on the quiet** unobtrusively; secretly. ☐☐ **quietly** adv. **quietness** n. [ME f. AF *quiete* f. OF *quiet(e)*, *quieté* f. L *quietus* past part. of *quiescere*: see QUIESCENT]

quieten /ˈkwaɪət(ə)n/ v.tr. & intr. *Brit.* (often foll. by *down*) = QUIET v.

quietism /ˈkwaɪətɪz(ə)m/ n. 1 a passive attitude towards life, with devotional contemplation and abandonment of the will, as a form of religious mysticism. 2 the principle of non-resistance. ☐☐ **quietist** n. & adj. **quietistic** /-ˈtɪstɪk/ adj. [It. *quietismo* (as QUIET)]

quietude /ˈkwaɪɪˌtjuːd/ n. a state of quiet.

quietus /kwaɪˈiːtəs/ n. 1 something which quiets or represses. 2 discharge or release from life; death, final riddance. [med.L *quietus est* he is quit (QUIET) used as a form of receipt]

quiff /kwɪf/ n. *Brit.* 1 a man's tuft of hair, brushed upward over the forehead. 2 a curl plastered down on the forehead. [20th c.: orig. unkn.]

quill /kwɪl/ n. & v. —n. 1 (in full **quill-feather**) a large feather in a wing or tail. 2 the hollow stem of this. 3 (in full **quill pen**) a pen made of a quill. 4 (usu. in *pl.*) the spines of a porcupine. 5 a musical pipe made of a hollow stem. —v.tr. form into cylindrical quill-like folds; goffer. ☐ **quill-coverts** the feathers covering the base of quill-feathers. ☐☐ **quilling** n. [ME prob. f. (M)LG *quiele*]

quilt[1] /kwɪlt/ n. & v. —n. 1 a bed-covering made of padding enclosed between layers of cloth etc. and kept in place by cross lines of stitching. 2 a bedspread of similar design (*patchwork quilt*). —v.tr. 1 cover or line with padded material. 2 make or join together (pieces of cloth with padding between) after the manner of a quilt. 3 sew up (a coin, letter, etc.) between two layers of a garment etc. 4 compile (a literary work) out of extracts or borrowed ideas. ☐☐ **quilter** n. **quilting** n. [ME f. OF *coilte*, *cuilte* f. L *culcita* mattress, cushion]

quilt[2] /kwɪlt/ v.tr. *Austral. sl.* thrash; clout. [perh. f. QUILT[1]]

quim /kwɪm/ n. *coarse sl.* the female genitals. [18th c.: orig. unkn.]

quin /kwɪn/ n. esp. *Brit. colloq.* a quintuplet. [abbr.]

quinacrine /ˈkwɪnəˌkriːn, -krɪn/ n. an anti-malarial drug derived from acridine. [*quinine* + *acridine*]

quinary /ˈkwaɪnərɪ/ adj. 1 of the number five. 2 having five parts. [L *quinarius* f. *quini* distrib. of *quinque* five]

quinate /ˈkwaɪneɪt/ adj. *Bot.* (of a leaf) having five leaflets. [L *quini* (as QUINARY)]

quince /kwɪns/ n. 1 a hard acid pear-shaped fruit used as a preserve or flavouring. 2 any shrub or small tree of the genus *Cydonia*, esp. *C. oblonga*, bearing this fruit. [ME, orig. collect. pl. of obs. *quoyn*, *coyn*, f. OF *cooin* f. L *cotoneum* var. of *cydoneum* (apple) of *Cydonia* in Crete]

quincentenary /ˌkwɪnsenˈtiːnərɪ/ n. & adj. —n. (pl. **-ies**) 1 a five-hundredth anniversary. 2 a festival marking this. —adj. of this anniversary. ☐☐ **quincentennial** /-ˈteniəl/ adj. & n. [irreg. f. L *quinque* five + CENTENARY]

quincunx /ˈkwɪnkʌŋks/ n. 1 five objects set so that four are at the corners of a square or rectangle and the fifth is at its centre, e.g. the five on dice or cards. 2 this arrangement, esp. in planting trees. ☐☐ **quincuncial** /kwɪnˈkʌnʃ(ə)l/ adj. **quincuncially** /-ˈkʌnʃəlɪ/ adv. [L, = five-twelfths f. *quinque* five, *uncia* twelfth]

Quine /kwaɪn/, Willard Van Orman (1908–), American philosopher and logician, who developed and revised the work on the foundations of mathematics begun by Frege and Russell. Many of his broader philosophical concerns can be seen as reactions against Carnap, by whom he was greatly influenced. He has argued against the sentence-by-sentence analysis of language, claiming that theories were to be treated as wholes, to which adjustment was to be made on pragmatic grounds. He has been sceptical about the significance of the concepts of meaning and necessity, and raised again traditional questions of existence, claiming that what we take to exist depends upon our choice of language, and that that choice should be made to provide the simplest expression of physics.

quinella /kwɪˈnelə/ n. a form of betting in which the better must select the first two place-winners in a race, not necessarily in the correct order. [Amer. Sp. *quiniela*]

quinine /ˈkwɪniːn, -ˈniːn/ n. 1 an alkaloid found esp. in cinchona bark. 2 a bitter drug containing this, used as a tonic and to reduce fever. [*quina* cinchona bark f. Sp. *quina* f. Quechua *kina* bark]

quinol /ˈkwɪnɒl/ n. = HYDROQUINONE.

quinoline /ˈkwɪnəˌliːn/ n. *Chem.* an oily amine obtained from the distillation of coal tar or by synthesis and used in the preparation of drugs etc.

quinone /ˈkwɪnəʊn, -ˈnəʊn/ n. *Chem.* 1 a yellow crystalline derivative of benzene with the hydrogen atoms on opposite carbon atoms replaced by two of oxygen. 2 any in a class of similar compounds.

quinquagenarian /ˌkwɪŋkwədʒɪˈneərɪən/ n. & adj. —n. a person from 50 to 59 years old. —adj. of or relating to this age. [L *quinquagenarius* f. *quinquageni* distrib. of *quinquaginta* fifty]

Quinquagesima /ˌkwɪŋkwəˈdʒesɪmə/ n. (in full **Quinquagesima Sunday**) the Sunday before the beginning of Lent (fifty days before Easter). [med.L, fem. of L *quinquagesimus* fiftieth f. *quinquaginta* fifty, after QUADRAGESIMA]

quinque- /ˈkwɪŋkwɪ/ comb. form five. [L f. *quinque* five]

quinquennial /kwɪnˈkweniəl/ adj. 1 lasting five years. 2 recurring every five years. ☐☐ **quinquennially** adv. [L *quinquennis* (as QUINQUENNIUM)]

quinquennium /kwɪnˈkweniəm/ n. (pl. **quinquenniums** or **quinquennia** /-nɪə/) a period of five years. [L f. *quinque* five + *annus* year]

quinquereme /ˈkwɪŋkwɪˌriːm/ n. an ancient Roman galley with five files of oarsmen on each side. [L *quinqueremis* (as QUINQUE-, *remus* oar)]

quinquevalent /ˈkwɪnkwəˌveɪlənt/ adj. having a valency of five.

quinsy /ˈkwɪnzɪ/ n. an inflammation of the throat, esp. an abscess in the region around the tonsils. ☐☐ **quinsied** adj. [ME f. OF *quinencie* f. med.L *quinancia* f. Gk *kunagkhē* f. *kun-* dog + *agkhō* throttle]

quint /kwɪnt/ n. 1 a sequence of five cards in the same suit in piquet etc. **2** *US* a quintuplet. □ **quint major** a quint headed by an ace. [F *quinte* f. L *quinta* fem. of *quintus* fifth f. *quinque* five]

quintain /ˈkwɪntɪn/ *n. hist.* **1** a post set up as a mark in tilting, and often provided with a sandbag to swing round and strike an unsuccessful tilter. **2** the medieval military exercise of tilting at such a mark. [ME f. OF *quintaine* perh. ult. f. L *quintana* camp market f. *quintus* (*manipulus*) fifth (maniple)]

quintal /ˈkwɪnt(ə)l/ *n.* **1** a weight of about 100 lb. **2** a hundredweight (112 lb.). **3** a weight of 100 kg. [ME f. OF *quintal*, med.L *quintale* f. Arab. *ḳinṭār*]

quintan /ˈkwɪnt(ə)n/ *adj.* (of a fever etc.) recurring every fifth day. [L *quintana* f. *quintus* fifth]

Quintana Roo /kiːnˌtɑːnə ˈrəʊ/ a State of SE Mexico, on the Yucatán peninsula; pop. (est. 1988) 393,400; capital, Chetumal.

quinte /kæt/ *n.* the fifth of eight parrying positions in fencing. [F: see QUINT]

quintessence /kwɪnˈtes(ə)ns/ *n.* **1** the most essential part of any substance; a refined extract. **2** (usu. foll. by *of*) the purest and most perfect, or most typical, form, manifestation, or embodiment of some quality or class. **3** (in Ancient Philosophy) a fifth substance (beside the four elements) forming heavenly bodies and pervading all things. □□ **quintessential** /ˌkwɪntɪˈsen(ʃ)(ə)l/ *adj.* **quintessentially** /ˌkwɪntɪˈsenʃəlɪ/ *adv.* [ME (in sense 3) f. F f. med.L *quinta essentia* fifth ESSENCE]

quintet /kwɪnˈtet/ *n.* (also **quintette**) **1** *Mus.* **a** a composition for five voices or instruments. **b** the performers of such a piece. **2** any group of five. [F *quintette* f. It. *quintetto* f. *quinto* fifth f. L *quintus*]

Quintilian /kwɪnˈtɪlɪən/ (Marcus Fabius Quintilianus, *c.*30–*c.*96) Roman rhetorician. A famous teacher, whose chief work is his *Education of an Orator*, a comprehensive treatment of the art of rhetoric and of the training of the orator, inspired by a humanist educational ideal of combined technical and moral proficiency. The work was highly influential in the Middle Ages and Renaissance.

quintillion /kwɪnˈtɪljən/ *n.* (*pl.* same or **quintillions**) a thousand raised to the sixth (or formerly, esp. *Brit.*, the tenth) power (10^{18} and 10^{30} respectively). □□ **quintillionth** *adj.* & *n.* [L *quintus* fifth + MILLION]

quintuple /ˈkwɪntjʊp(ə)l/ *adj.*, *n.*, & *v.* —*adj.* **1** fivefold; consisting of five parts. **2** involving five parties. **3** (of time in music) having five beats in a bar. —*n.* a fivefold number or amount. —*v.tr.* & *intr.* multiply by five; increase fivefold. □□ **quintuply** *adv.* [F *quintuple* f. L *quintus* fifth, after QUADRUPLE]

quintuplet /ˈkwɪntjʊplɪt, -ˈtjuːplɪt/ *n.* **1** each of five children born at one birth. **2** a set of five things working together. **3** *Mus.* a group of five notes to be performed in the time of three or four. [QUINTUPLE, after QUADRUPLET, TRIPLET]

quintuplicate *adj.* & *v.* —*adj.* /kwɪnˈtjuːplɪkət/ **1** fivefold. **2** of which five copies are made. —*v.tr.* & *intr.* /kwɪnˈtjuːplɪkeɪt/ multiply by five. □ **in quintuplicate 1** in five identical copies. **2** in groups of five. [F *quintuple* f. L *quintus* fifth, after QUADRUPLICATE]

quip /kwɪp/ *n.* & *v.* —*n.* **1** a clever saying; an epigram; a sarcastic remark etc. **2** a quibble; an equivocation. —*v.intr.* (**quipped**, **quipping**) make quips. □□ **quipster** *n.* [abbr. of obs. *quippy* perh. f. L *quippe* forsooth]

quipu /ˈkiːpuː, ˈkwiːpuː/ *n.* the ancient Peruvians' substitute for writing by variously knotting threads of various colours. [Quechua, = knot]

quire /ˈkwaɪə(r)/ *n.* **1** four sheets of paper etc. folded to form eight leaves, as often in medieval manuscripts. **2** any collection of leaves one within another in a manuscript or book. **3** 25 (also 24) sheets of paper. □ **in quires** unbound; in sheets. [ME f. OF *qua(i)er* ult. f. L *quaterni* set of four (as QUATERNARY)]

quirk /kwɜːk/ *n.* **1** a peculiarity of behaviour. **2** a trick of fate; a freak. **3** a flourish in writing. **4** (often *attrib.*) *Archit.* a hollow in a moulding. □□ **quirkish** *adj.* **quirky** *adj.* (**quirkier**, **quirkiest**). **quirkily** *adv.* **quirkiness** *n.* [16th c.: orig. unkn.]

quirt /kwɜːt/ *n.* & *v.* —*n.* a short-handled riding-whip with a braided leather lash. —*v.tr.* strike with this. [Sp. *cuerda* CORD]

quisling /ˈkwɪzlɪŋ/ *n.* **1** a person cooperating with an occupying enemy; a collaborator or fifth-columnist. **2** a traitor. □□ **quislingite** *adj.* & *n.* [V. Quisling, renegade Norwegian Army officer d. 1945]

quit /kwɪt/ *v.* & *adj.* —*v.tr.* (**quitting**; *past* and *past part.* **quitted** or **quit**) **1** (also *absol.*) give up; let go; abandon (a task etc.). **2** *US* cease; stop (*quit grumbling*). **3 a** leave or depart from (a place, person, etc.). **b** (*absol.*) (of a tenant) leave occupied premises (esp. *notice to quit*). **4** (*refl.*) acquit; behave (*quit oneself well*). —*predic.adj.* (foll. by *of*) rid (*glad to be quit of the problem*). □ **quit hold of** loose. [ME f. OF *quitte, quitter* f. med.L *quittus* f. L *quietus* QUIET]

quitch /kwɪtʃ/ *n.* (in full **quitch-grass**) = COUCH². [OE *cwice*, perh. rel. to QUICK]

quite /kwaɪt/ *adv.* **1** completely; entirely; wholly; to the utmost extent; in the fullest sense. **2** somewhat; rather; to some extent. **3** (often foll. by *so*) said to indicate agreement. □ **quite another** (or **other**) very different (*that's quite another matter*). **quite a few** *colloq.* a fairly large number of. **quite something** a remarkable thing. [ME f. obs. *quite* (adj.) = QUIT]

Quito /ˈkiːtəʊ/ the capital of Ecuador, situated at an altitude of 2,850 m (9,350 ft.) at the foot of the Pichincha volcano; pop. (1982) 1,110,250.

quits /kwɪts/ *predic.adj.* on even terms by retaliation or repayment (*then we'll be quits*). □ **call it** (or **cry**) **quits** acknowledge that things are now even; agree not to proceed further in a quarrel etc. [perh. colloq. abbr. of med.L *quittus*: see QUIT]

quittance /ˈkwɪt(ə)ns/ *n. archaic* or *poet.* **1** (foll. by *from*) a release. **2** an acknowledgement of payment; a receipt. [ME f. OF *quitance* f. *quiter* QUIT]

quitter /ˈkwɪtə(r)/ *n.* **1** a person who gives up easily. **2** a shirker.

quiver¹ /ˈkwɪvə(r)/ *v.* & *n.* —*v.* **1** *intr.* tremble or vibrate with a slight rapid motion, esp.: **a** (usu. foll. by *with*) as the result of emotion (*quiver with anger*). **b** (usu. foll. by *in*) as the result of air currents etc. (*quiver in the breeze*). **2** *tr.* (of a bird, esp. a skylark) make (its wings) quiver. —*n.* a quivering motion or sound. □□ **quiveringly** *adv.* **quivery** *adj.* [ME f. obs. *quiver* nimble: cf. QUAVER]

quiver² /ˈkwɪvə(r)/ *n.* a case for holding arrows. □ **have an arrow** (or **shaft**) **left in one's quiver** not be resourceless. [ME f. OF *quivre* f. WG (cf. OE *cocor*)]

quiverful /ˈkwɪvəfʊl/ *n.* (*pl.* **-fuls**) **1** as much as a quiver can hold. **2** many children of one parent (Ps. 127: 5). [QUIVER²]

qui vive /kiː ˈviːv/ *n.* □ **on the qui vive** on the alert; watching for something to happen. [F, = lit. '(long) live who?', i.e. on whose side are you?, as a sentry's challenge]

Quixote /ˈkwɪksəʊt/, Don. The hero of a romance (1605–15) by Cervantes, written to ridicule books of chivalry. [Sp. *quixote* thigh armour]

quixotic /kwɪkˈsɒtɪk/ *adj.* **1** extravagantly and romantically chivalrous; regardless of material interests in comparison with honour or devotion. **2** visionary; pursuing lofty but unattainable ideals. □□ **quixotically** *adv.* **quixotism** /ˈkwɪksətɪz(ə)m/ *n.* **quixotry** /ˈkwɪksətrɪ/ *n.* [Don QUIXOTE]

quiz¹ /kwɪz/ *n.* & *v.* —*n.* (*pl.* **quizzes**) **1** a test of knowledge, esp. between individuals or teams as a form of entertainment. **2** an interrogation, examination, or questionnaire. —*v.tr.* (**quizzed**, **quizzing**) examine by questioning. □ **quiz-master** a person who presides over a quiz. [19th-c. dial.: orig. unkn.]

quiz² /kwɪz/ *v.* & *n. archaic* —*v.tr.* (**quizzed, quizzing**) **1** look curiously at; observe the ways or oddities of; survey through an eyeglass. **2** make sport of; regard with a mocking air. —*n.* (*pl.* **quizzes**) **1** a hoax, a thing done to burlesque or expose another's oddities. **2 a** an odd or eccentric person; a person of ridiculous appearance. **b** a person given to quizzing. □□ **quizzer** *n.* [18th c.: orig. unkn.]

quizzical /ˈkwɪzɪk(ə)l/ *adj.* **1** expressing or done with mild or amused perplexity. **2** strange; comical. □□ **quizzicality** /-ˈkælɪtɪ/ *n.* **quizzically** *adv.* **quizzicalness** *n.*

Qum /kʊm/ a holy city of Shiite Muslims, in central Iran; pop. (1983) 424,000

Qumran /kʊmˈrɑːn/ a region on the western shore of the Dead

Sea, now in Israel, site of caves in which the Dead Sea scrolls (see entry) were found and of the settlement of an ancient Jewish community to whom these manuscripts belonged.

quod /kwɒd/ n. Brit. sl. prison. [17th c.: orig. unkn.]

quod erat demonstrandum /kwɒd ˌeræt ˌdemən'strændʊm/ (esp. at the conclusion of a proof etc.) which was the thing to be proved. ¶ Abbr.: **QED**. [L]

quodlibet /'kwɒdlɪˌbet/ n. **1** hist. **a** a topic for philosophical or theological discussion. **b** an exercise on this. **2** a light-hearted medley of well-known tunes. □□ **quodlibetarian** /-bɪ'teərɪən/ n. **quodlibetical** /-'betɪk(ə)l/ adj. **quodlibetically** /-'betɪkəlɪ/ adv. [ME f. L f. quod what + libet it pleases one]

quod vide /kwɒd 'viːdeɪ/ which see (in cross-references etc.). ¶ Abbr.: **q.v.** [L]

quoin /kɔɪn/ n. & v. —n. **1** an external angle of a building. **2** a stone or brick forming an angle; a cornerstone. **3** a wedge used for locking type in a forme. **4** a wedge for raising the level of a gun, keeping the barrel from rolling, etc. —v.tr. secure or raise with quoins. □□ **quoining** n. [var. of COIN]

quoit /kɔɪt/ n. & v. —n. **1** a heavy flattish sharp-edged iron ring thrown to encircle an iron peg or to land as near as possible to the peg. **2** (in pl.) a game consisting of aiming and throwing these. It was a well-known game from at least the reign of Richard II, when it was included among the many sports and pastimes that were forbidden because they diverted servants, apprentices, and labourers from recreations of a more warlike character (e.g. archery) at a time of recurring wars against the French. Such edicts were conspicuously unsuccessful. **3** a ring of rope, rubber, etc. for use in a similar game. **4 a** the flat stone of a dolmen. **b** the dolmen itself. —v.tr. fling like a quoit. [ME: orig. unkn.]

quokka /'kwɒkə/ n. a small Australian short-tailed wallaby, Setonix brachyurus. [Aboriginal name]

quondam /'kwɒndæm/ attrib.adj. that once was; sometime; former. [L (adv.), = formerly]

Quonset /'kwɒnsɪt/ n. US propr. a prefabricated metal building with a semicylindrical corrugated roof. [Quonset Point, Rhode Island, where it was first made]

quorate /'kwɔːrət, -reɪt/ adj. Brit. (of a meeting) attended by a quorum. [QUORUM]

quorum /'kwɔːrəm/ n. the fixed minimum number of members that must be present to make the proceedings of an assembly or society valid. [L, = of whom (we wish that you be two, three, etc.), in the wording of commissions]

quota /'kwəʊtə/ n. **1** the share that an individual person or company is bound to contribute to or entitled to receive from a total. **2** a quantity of goods etc. which under official controls must be manufactured, exported, imported, etc. **3** the number of yearly immigrants allowed to enter a country, students allowed to enrol for a course, etc. [med.L quota (pars) how great (a part), fem. of quotus f. quot how many]

quotable /'kwəʊtəb(ə)l/ adj. worth, or suitable for, quoting. □□ **quotability** /-'bɪlɪtɪ/ n.

quotation /kwəʊ'teɪʃ(ə)n/ n. **1** the act or an instance of quoting or being quoted. **2** a passage or remark quoted. **3** Mus. a short passage or tune taken from one piece of music to another. **4** Stock Exch. an amount stated as the current price of stocks or commodities. **5** a contractor's estimate. □ **quotation mark** each of a set of punctuation marks, single (' ') or double (" "), used to mark the beginning and end of a quoted passage, a book title, etc., or words regarded as slang or jargon. [med.L quotatio (as QUOTE)]

quote /kwəʊt/ v. & n. —v.tr. **1** cite or appeal to (an author, book, etc.) in confirmation of some view. **2** repeat a statement by (another person) or copy out a passage from (don't quote me). **3** (often absol.) **a** repeat or copy out (a passage) usu. with an indication that it is borrowed. **b** (foll. by from) cite (an author, book, etc.). **4** (foll. by as) cite (an author etc.) as proof, evidence, etc. **5 a** enclose (words) in quotation marks. **b** (as int.) (in dictation, reading aloud, etc.) indicate the presence of opening quotation marks (he said, quote, 'I shall stay'). **6** (often foll. by at) state the price of (a commodity, bet, etc.) (quoted at 200 to 1). **7** Stock Exch. regularly list the price of. —n. colloq. **1** a passage quoted. **2** a price quoted. **3** (usu. in pl.) quotation marks. [ME, earlier 'mark with numbers', f. med.L quotare f. quot how many, or as QUOTA]

quoth /kwəʊθ/ v.tr. (only in 1st and 3rd person) archaic said. [OE cwæth past of cwethan say f. Gmc]

quotidian /kwɒ'tɪdɪən/ adj. & n. —adj. **1** daily, of every day. **2** commonplace, trivial. —n. (in full **quotidian fever**) a fever recurring every day. [ME f. OF cotidien & L cotidianus f. cotidie daily]

quotient /'kwəʊʃ(ə)nt/ n. a result obtained by dividing one quantity by another. [ME f. L quotiens how many times f. quot how many, by confusion with -ENT]

Qur'an var. of KORAN.

q.v. abbr. quod vide.

Qwaqwa /'kwækwə/ a tribal homeland of the South Sotho people in South Africa; pop. (1985) 183,000.

qwerty /'kwɜːtɪ/ attrib.adj. denoting the standard keyboard on English-language typewriters, word processors, etc., with q, w, e, r, t, and y as the first keys on the top row of letters.

qy. abbr. query.

aʊ how eɪ day əʊ no eə hair ɪə near ɔɪ boy ʊə poor aɪə fire aʊə sour (see over for consonants)

R

R¹ /ɑː(r)/ *n.* (also **r**) (*pl.* **Rs** or **R's**) the eighteenth letter of the alphabet. □ **the r months** the months with r in their names (September to April) as the season for oysters. **the three Rs** see THREE.

R² *abbr.* (also **R.**) **1** Regina (Elizabeth R). **2** Rex. **3** River. **4** (also ®) registered as a trademark. **5** (in names of societies etc.) Royal. **6** Chess rook. **7** Railway. **8** rand. **9** Regiment. **10** Réaumur. **11** radius. **12** rœntgen.

r. *abbr.* (also **r**) **1** right. **2** recto. **3** run(s). **4** radius.

RA *abbr.* **1 a** (in the UK) Royal Academy. **b** (in the UK) Royal Academician. **2** (in the UK) Royal Artillery. **3** right ascension.

Ra¹ /rɑː/ *Egyptian Mythol.* the sun-god (or initially the sun itself), a notable deity to whom other gods could be assimilated. He is often portrayed with a falcon's head bearing the solar disc. He appears travelling in his ship with other gods, crossing the sky by day and journeying through the underworld of the dead at night. From earliest times he was associated with the king.

Ra² *symb. Chem.* the element radium.

RAAF *abbr.* Royal Australian Air Force.

Rabat /rəˈbæt/ the capital and an industrial port of Morocco, on the Atlantic coast; pop. (1982) 518,620.

Rabaul /rəˈbaʊl/ the chief town and port of the island of New Britain, Papua New Guinea; pop. (1980) 14,950.

rabbet /ˈræbɪt/ *n.* & *v.* —*n.* a step-shaped channel etc. cut along the edge or face or projecting angle of a length of wood etc., usu. to receive the edge or tongue of another piece. —*v.tr.* (**rabbeted, rabbeting**) **1** join or fix with a rabbet. **2** make a rabbet in. □ **rabbet plane** a plane for cutting a groove along an edge. [ME f. OF *rab(b)at* abatement, recess f. *rabattre* REBATE]

rabbi /ˈræbaɪ/ *n.* (*pl.* **rabbis**) **1** a Jewish scholar or teacher, esp. of the law. **2** a person appointed as a Jewish religious leader. □ **Chief Rabbi** the religious head of the Jewish communities in Britain. □□ **rabbinate** /ˈræbɪnət/ *n.* [ME & OE f. eccl.L f. Gk *rhabbi* f. Heb. *rabbî* my master f. *raḇ* master + pronominal suffix]

rabbinical /rəˈbɪnɪk(ə)l/ *adj.* (also **rabbinic**) of or relating to rabbis, or to Jewish law or teaching. □□ **rabbinically** *adv.*

rabbit /ˈræbɪt/ *n.* & *v.* —*n.* **1 a** any of various burrowing gregarious plant-eating mammals of the hare family, esp. *Oryctolagus cuniculus*, with long ears and a short tail, varying in colour from brown in the wild to black and white, and kept as a pet or for meat. **b** *US* a hare. **c** the fur of the rabbit. **2** *Brit. colloq.* a poor performer in any sport or game. —*v. intr.* (**rabbited, rabbiting**) **1** hunt rabbits. **2** (often foll. by *on, away*) *Brit. colloq.* talk excessively or pointlessly; chatter (*rabbiting on about his holiday*). □ **rabbit punch** a short chop with the edge of the hand to the nape of the neck. **rabbit warren** an area in which rabbits have their burrows, or are kept for meat etc. □□ **rabbity** *adj.* [ME perh. f. OF: cf. F dial. *rabotte*, Walloon *robète*, Flem. *robbe*]

rabble¹ /ˈræb(ə)l/ *n.* **1** a disorderly crowd; a mob. **2** a contemptible or inferior set of people. **3** (prec. by *the*) the lower or disorderly classes of the populace. □ **rabble-rouser** a person who stirs up the rabble or a crowd of people in agitation for social or political change. **rabble-rousing** *adj.* tending to arouse the emotions of a crowd. —*n.* the act or process of doing this. [ME: orig. uncert.]

rabble² /ˈræb(ə)l/ *n.* an iron bar with a bent end for stirring molten metal etc. [F *râble* f. med.L *rotabulum*, L *rutabulum* fire-shovel f. *ruere rut-* rake up]

Rabelais /ˈræbəˌleɪ/, François (c.1494–1553), French humanist, satirist, and physician, who became successively a monk, priest, bishop's secretary, and Bachelor of Medicine. He travelled in France and Italy, acquiring a widespread reputation for his erudition and medical skill, and enjoyed ecclesiastical and royal patronage. He is remembered for his five great books: *Pantagruel* (1532/3), *Gargantua* (1534), *Tiers Livre* (1546), *Quart Livre* (1548–52),

and *Cinquième Livre* (1562–4) which is of doubtful authenticity. Linked together by a narrative thread the whole provides a vivid panorama of contemporary society through which the author reveals his own humanism, his hatred of asceticism, and his contempt for scholasticism. His command of the vernacular, sustained by an encyclopedic vocabulary, extends beyond French to a dozen contemporary languages. The work was officially condemned for its insulting reference to theologians, and Rabelais is often censured for his lapses into obscenity and coarse wit, but his work gained wide popularity and remains a unique expression of Renaissance energy and plenitude.

Rabelaisian /ˌræbəˈleɪzɪən/ *adj.* & *n.* —*adj.* **1** of or like Rabelais or his writings. **2** marked by exuberant imagination and language, coarse humour, and satire. —*n.* an admirer or student of Rabelais.

rabid /ˈræbɪd, ˈreɪ-/ *adj.* **1** furious, violent (*rabid hate*). **2** unreasoning; headstrong; fanatical (*a rabid anarchist*). **3** (esp. of a dog) affected with rabies; mad. **4** of or connected with rabies. □□ **rabidity** /rəˈbɪdɪtɪ/ *n.* **rabidly** *adv.* **rabidness** *n.* [L *rabidus* f. *rabere* rave]

rabies /ˈreɪbiːz/ *n.* a contagious and fatal viral disease of dogs and other warm-blooded animals, which produces paralysis or a vicious excitability and in man causes a fatal encephalitis with convulsions and with throat spasm on swallowing; hydrophobia. [L f. *rabere* rave]

RAC *abbr.* **1** (in the UK) Royal Automobile Club. **2** (in the UK) Royal Armoured Corps.

raccoon var. of RACOON.

race¹ /reɪs/ *n.* & *v.* —*n.* **1** a contest of speed between runners, horses, vehicles, ships, etc. **2** (in *pl.*) a series of these for horses, dogs, etc. at a fixed time on a regular course. **3** a contest between persons to be first to achieve something. **4 a** a strong or rapid current flowing through a narrow channel in the sea or a river (*a tide race*). **b** the channel of a stream etc. (*a mill-race*). **5** each of two grooved rings in a ball-bearing or roller bearing. **6** *Austral.* a fenced passageway for drafting sheep etc. **7** a passageway along which football players etc. run to enter the field. **8** (in weaving) the channel along which the shuttle moves. **9** *archaic* **a** the course of the sun or moon. **b** the course of life (*has run his race*). —*v.* **1** *intr.* take part in a race. **2** *tr.* have a race with. **3** *tr.* try to surpass in speed. **4** *intr.* (foll. by *with*) compete in speed with. **5** *tr.* cause (a horse, car, etc.) to race. **6 a** *intr.* go at full or (of an engine, propeller, the pulse, etc.) excessive speed. **b** *tr.* cause (a person or thing) to do this (*raced the bill through the House*). **7** *intr.* (usu. as **racing** *adj.*) follow or take part in horse-racing (*a racing man*). □ **not in the race** *Austral. sl.* having no chance. **race meeting** a sequence of horse-races at one place. **racing car** a motor car built for racing on a prepared track. [ME, = running, f. ON *rás*]

race² /reɪs/ *n.* **1** each of the major divisions of mankind, having distinct physical characteristics. The term is often used imprecisely; even among anthropologists there is no generally accepted classification or terminology. (See below.) **2** a tribe, nation, etc., regarded as of a distinct ethnic stock. **3** the fact or concept of division into races (*discrimination based on race*). **4** a genus, species, breed, or variety of animals, plants, or micro-organisms. **5** a group of persons, animals, or plants connected by common descent. **6** any great division of living creatures (*the feathered race; the four-footed race*). **7** descent; kindred (*of noble race; separate in language and race*). **8** a class of persons etc. with some common feature (*the race of poets*). □ **race relations** relations between members of different races usu. in the same country. **race riot** an outbreak of violence due to racial antagonism. [F f. It. *razza*, of unkn. orig.]

The term has been applied to various national or cultural as well as physical groupings (including 'human race' for the entire

---

b **but** d **dog** f **few** g **get** h **he** j **yes** k **cat** l **leg** m **man** n **no** p **pen** r **red** s **sit** t **top** v **voice**

species of mankind). For centuries geographical races were identified by the most observable physical differences, especially the colour of the skin, hair, and eyes. The reason for human variation has been a subject of interest and speculation since antiquity. Christian tradition of the unity of mankind, descended from a common ancestor, became scientific orthodoxy in medieval Europe, with national genealogies traced to a descendant of Noah, but from the time of Paracelsus onwards a diversity of human origins was argued. In the 19th c. a combination of European overseas migration and the heightening of national consciousness strengthened interest in the differences between human groups, generally with the underlying assumption that the 'races' were once separate and that subsequent obscuring of pure racial types had occurred. In the early 20th c. Franz Boas put forward the theory that racial typing on a purely physical basis was arbitrary and argued the cultural origin of mental differences. His approach became dominant, though the Nazis burned his book. Human variation continues to be studied but the notion of 'race' as a rigid classification or genetic system has largely been abandoned.

race³ /reɪs/ n. a ginger root. [OF *rais, raiz* f. L *radix radicis* root]

racecard /ˈreɪskɑːd/ n. a programme of races.

racecourse /ˈreɪskɔːs/ n. a ground or track for horse-racing.

racegoer /ˈreɪsɡəʊə(r)/ n. a person who frequents horse-races.

racehorse /ˈreɪshɔːs/ n. a horse bred or kept for racing.

racemate /ˈræsɪˌmeɪt/ n. *Chem.* a racemic mixture.

raceme /rəˈsiːm/ n. *Bot.* a flower cluster with the separate flowers attached by short equal stalks at equal distances along a central stem (cf. CYME). [L *racemus* grape-bunch]

racemic /rəˈsiːmɪk, -ˈsemɪk/ adj. *Chem.* composed of equal numbers of dextrorotatory and laevorotatory molecules of a compound. □□ **racemize** /ˈræsɪˌmaɪz/ v.tr. & intr. (also **-ise**). [RACEME + -IC, orig. of tartaric acid in grape-juice]

racemose /ˈræsɪˌməʊs/ adj. **1** *Bot.* in the form of a raceme. **2** *Anat.* (of a gland etc.) clustered. [L *racemosus* (as RACEME)]

racer /ˈreɪsə(r)/ n. **1** a horse, yacht, bicycle, etc., of a kind used for racing. **2** a circular horizontal rail along which the traversing-platform of a heavy gun moves. **3** a person or thing that races.

racetrack /ˈreɪstræk/ n. **1** = RACECOURSE. **2** a track for motor-racing.

raceway /ˈreɪsweɪ/ n. **1** a track or channel along which something runs, esp.: **a** a channel for water. **b** a groove in which ball-bearings run. **c** a pipe or tubing enclosing electrical wires. **2** esp. US **a** a track for trotting, pacing, or harness racing. **b** a racecourse.

rachis /ˈreɪkɪs/ n. (pl. **rachides** /-kɪˌdiːz/) **1** *Bot.* **a** a stem of grass etc. bearing flower-stalks at short intervals. **b** the axis of a compound leaf or frond. **2** *Anat.* the vertebral column or the cord from which it develops. **3** *Zool.* a feather-shaft, esp. the part bearing the barbs. □□ **rachidial** /rəˈkɪdɪəl/ adj. [mod.L f. Gk *rhakhis* spine: the E pl. *-ides* is erron.]

rachitis /rəˈkaɪtɪs/ n. rickets. □□ **rachitic** /-ˈkɪtɪk/ adj. [mod.L f. Gk *rhakhitis* (as RACHIS)]

Rachmaninov /rækˈmænɪˌnɒf/, Sergei Vasilyevich (1873–1943), Russian composer. He was a celebrated pianist and his works for the instrument overshadow in fame, if not in importance, his songs, choral works including *The Bells* (1913), and three symphonies. From 1897 he held a conducting post with a private opera company in Moscow (the then unknown Chaliapin was among its members), but in 1917 left Russia for America; until 1933 his music was banned in his native country after he signed a letter attacking the Soviet regime.

Rachmanism /ˈrækməˌnɪz(ə)m/ n. *Brit.* the practices of landlords who buy, at a low price, properties where rents are controlled, and then use unscrupulous methods to evict the tenants (e.g. by intimidating them). This has the effect of removing the legal controls on the properties, which can then be sold at a huge profit. It is named after a London landlord, Peter Rachman (1919–62), who practised it in the early 1960s.

racial /ˈreɪʃ(ə)l/ adj. **1** of or concerning race (*racial diversities*;

racial minority). **2** on the grounds of or connected with difference in race (*racial discrimination*; *racial tension*). □□ **racially** adv.

racialism /ˈreɪʃəˌlɪz(ə)m/ n. = RACISM 1. □□ **racialist** n. & adj.

Racine /ræˈsiːn/, Jean (1639–99), French dramatist, one of the greatest figures of the French classical period. He was admitted to the *Académie* in 1673 and became historiographer to Louis XIV in 1677. His tragedies derive from various sources; from Greek and Roman literature (*Andromaque* 1667, *Iphigénie* 1674, *Phèdre* 1677), from Roman history (*Britannicus* 1669, *Bérénice* 1670, and *Mithridate* 1673), from contemporary Turkish history (*Bajazet* 1672), and from the Bible (*Esther* 1689, *Athalie* 1691); his one comedy *Les Plaideurs* (1668) was drawn from Aristophanes. Central to the majority of his tragedies is a perception of the blind folly of human passion.

racism /ˈreɪsɪz(ə)m/ n. **1 a** a belief in the superiority of a particular race; prejudice based on this. **b** antagonism towards other races, esp. as a result of this. **2** the theory that human abilities etc. are determined by race. □□ **racist** n. & adj.

rack¹ /ræk/ n. & v. —n. **1 a** a framework usu. with rails, bars, hooks, etc., for holding or storing things. **b** a frame for holding animal fodder. **2** a cogged or toothed bar or rail engaging with a wheel or pinion etc., or using pegs to adjust the position of something. **3** *hist.* an instrument of torture stretching the victim's joints by the turning of rollers to which the wrists and ankles were tied. —v.tr. **1** (of disease or pain) inflict suffering on. **2** *hist.* torture (a person) on the rack. **3** place in or on a rack. **4** shake violently. **5** injure by straining. **6** oppress (tenants) by exacting excessive rent. **7** exhaust (the land) by excessive use. □ **on the rack** in distress or under strain. **rack one's brains** make a great mental effort (*racked my brains for something to say*). **rack-railway** a railway with a cogged rail between the bearing rails. **rack-rent** n. **1** a high rent, annually equalling the full value of the property to which it relates. **2** an extortionate rent. —v.tr. exact this from (a tenant) or for (land). **rack-renter** a tenant paying or a landlord exacting an extortionate rent. **rack-up** US achieve (a score etc.). **rack-wheel** a cog-wheel. [ME *rakke* f. MDu., MLG *rak, rek*, prob. f. *recken* stretch]

rack² /ræk/ n. destruction (esp. *rack and ruin*). [var. of WRACK, WRECK]

rack³ /ræk/ n. a joint of lamb etc. including the front ribs. [perh. f. RACK¹]

rack⁴ /ræk/ v.tr. (often foll. by *off*) draw off (wine, beer, etc.) from the lees. [ME f. Prov. *arracar* f. *raca* stems and husks of grapes, dregs]

rack⁵ /ræk/ n. & v. —n. driving clouds. —v.intr. (of clouds) be driven before the wind. [ME, prob. of Scand. orig.: cf. Norw. and Sw. dial. *rak* wreckage etc. f. *reka* drive]

rack⁶ /ræk/ n. & v. —n. a horse's gait between a trot and a canter. —v.intr. progress in this way.

racket¹ /ˈrækɪt/ n. (also **racquet**) **1** a bat with a round or oval frame strung with catgut, nylon, etc., used in tennis, squash, etc. **2** (in pl.) a ball game for two or four persons played with rackets in a plain four-walled court. Each player strikes the ball in turn and tries to keep it rebounding from the end wall of the court. The game in its modern form developed in England in the 19th c., but its origins may be traced to medieval handball. It was played in open courts in the backyards of inns and taverns; the rackets court in the Fleet debtors' prison in London is depicted by Rowlandson and described by Dickens. Indoor courts were built at the Prince's Club, London, in 1853, a development which speeded up the game and (because it was now more expensive to play) altered its social character. The extension of the game to other parts of the world was due largely to the influence of the British Army and the Royal Navy. **3** a snow shoe resembling a racket. □ **racket-ball** a small ball orig. kid-covered ball of cork and string. **racket-press** a press for keeping rackets taut and in shape. **racket-tail** a S. American humming-bird, *Loddigesia mirabilis*, with a racket-shaped tail. [F *racquette* f. It. *racchetta* f. Arab. *rāḥa* palm of the hand]

racket² /ˈrækɪt/ n. **1 a** a disturbance; an uproar; a din. **b** social excitement; gaiety. **2** *sl.* a scheme for obtaining money or attaining other ends by fraudulent and often violent means. **b**

a dodge; a sly game. **3** *colloq.* an activity; a way of life; a line of business (*starting up a new racket*). □□ **rackety** *adj.* [16th c.: perh. imit.]

racketeer /ˌrækɪˈtɪə(r)/ *n.* a person who operates a dishonest business. □□ **racketeering** *n.*

racon /ˈreɪkɒn/ *n.* esp. *US* a radar beacon that can be identified and located by its response to a radar signal from a ship etc. [*radar* + *beacon*]

raconteur /ˌrækɒnˈtɜː(r)/ *n.* (*fem.* **raconteuse** /-ˈtɜːz/) a teller of anecdotes. [F f. *raconter* relate, RECOUNT]

racoon /rəˈkuːn/ *n.* (also **raccoon**) **1** any greyish-brown furry N. American nocturnal flesh-eating mammal of the genus *Procyon*, with a bushy tail and sharp snout. **2** the fur of the racoon. [Algonquian dial.]

racquet var. of RACKET[1].

racy /ˈreɪsɪ/ *adj.* (**racier**, **raciest**) **1** lively and vigorous in style. **2** risqué, suggestive. **3** having characteristic qualities in a high degree (*a racy flavour*). □□ **racily** *adv.* **raciness** *n.* [RACE[2] + -Y[1]]

rad[1] /ræd/ *n.* (*pl.* same) radian. [abbr.]

rad[2] /ræd/ *n. sl.* a political radical. [abbr.]

rad[3] /ræd/ *n. Physics* a unit of absorbed dose of ionizing radiation, corresponding to the absorption of 0.01 joule per kilogram of absorbing material. [*radiation absorbed dose*]

RADA /ˈrɑːdə/ *abbr.* (in the UK) Royal Academy of Dramatic Art.

radar /ˈreɪdɑː(r)/ *n.* **1** a system for detecting the presence of objects at a distance, or ascertaining their position and motion, by transmitting short radio waves and detecting or measuring their return after they are reflected; a similar system in which the return signal consists of radio waves that a suitably equipped target automatically transmits when it receives the outgoing waves. (See below.) **2** an apparatus or installation used for this system. □ **radar trap** an arrangement using radar to detect vehicles etc. travelling faster than the speed limit. [*radio detection and ranging*]

The principle of radar was established when Heinrich Hertz showed (in 1886) that radio waves could be reflected from solid objects, but use of this remained chiefly theoretical until 1922 when Marconi suggested that radio echoes could be used for the detection of ships in bad visibility, and the idea was tested experimentally in the US. Radar systems were developed in Britain, France, Germany, and the US in the 1930s, and used by both sides in the Second World War. They are now widely employed in sea and air navigation.

RADC *abbr.* (in the UK) Royal Army Dental Corps.

Radcliffe /ˈrædklɪf/, Mrs Ann Ward (1764–1823), English writer, the leading exponent of the Gothic novel (see entry). Her works include *The Mysteries of Udolpho* (1794).

raddle /ˈræd(ə)l/ *n. & v.* —*n.* red ochre (often used to mark sheep). —*v.tr.* **1** colour with raddle or too much rouge. **2** (as **raddled** *adj.*) worn out; untidy, unkempt. [var. of RUDDLE]

Radha /ˈrɑːdɑː/ *Hinduism* wife of a cowherd, she was the favourite mistress of the god Krishna, and an incarnation of Lakshmi. In devotional religion she represents the longing of the human soul for God. [Skr., = prosperity]

radial /ˈreɪdɪəl/ *adj. & n.* —*adj.* **1** of, concerning, or in rays. **2 a** arranged like rays or radii; having the position or direction of a radius. **b** having spokes or radiating lines. **c** acting or moving along lines diverging from a centre. **3** *Anat.* relating to the radius (*radial artery*). **4** (in full **radial-ply**) (of a vehicle tyre) having the core fabric layers arranged radially at right angles to the circumference and the tread strengthened. —*n.* **1** *Anat.* the radial nerve or artery. **2** a radial-ply tyre. □ **radial engine** an engine having cylinders arranged along radii. **radial symmetry** symmetry occurring about any number of lines or planes passing through the centre of an organism etc. **radial velocity** esp. *Astron.* the speed of motion along a radial line, esp. between a star etc. and an observer. □□ **radially** *adv.* [med.L *radialis* (as RADIUS)]

radian /ˈreɪdɪən/ *n. Geom.* a unit of angle, equal to an angle at the centre of a circle the arc of which is equal in length to the radius. [RADIUS + -AN]

radiant /ˈreɪdɪənt/ *adj. & n.* —*adj.* **1** emitting rays of light. **2** (of eyes or looks) beaming with joy or hope or love. **3** (of beauty) splendid or dazzling. **4** (of light) issuing in rays. **5** operating radially. **6** extending radially; radiating. —*n.* **1** the point or object from which light or heat radiates, esp. in an electric or gas heater. **2** *Astron.* a radiant point. □ **radiant heat** heat transmitted by radiation, not by conduction or convection. **radiant heater** a heater that works by this method. **radiant point 1** a point from which rays or radii proceed. **2** *Astron.* the apparent focal point of a meteor shower. □□ **radiance** *n.* **radiancy** *n.* **radiantly** *adv.* [ME f. L *radiare* (as RADIUS)]

radiate *v. & adj.* —*v.* /ˈreɪdɪeɪt/ **1** *intr.* **a** emit rays of light, heat, or other electromagnetic waves. **b** (of light or heat) be emitted in rays. **2** *tr.* emit (light, heat, or sound) from a centre. **3** *tr.* transmit or demonstrate (life, love, joy, etc.) (*radiates happiness*). **4** *intr. & tr.* diverge or cause to diverge or spread from a centre. **5** *tr.* (as **radiated** *adj.*) with parts arranged in rays. —*adj.* /ˈreɪdɪət/ having divergent rays or parts radially arranged. □□ **radiately** /-ətlɪ/ *adv.* **radiative** /-ətɪv/ *adj.* [L *radiare radiat-* (as RADIUS)]

radiation /ˌreɪdɪˈeɪʃ(ə)n/ *n.* **1** the act or an instance of radiating; the process of being radiated. **2** *Physics* **a** the emission of energy as electromagnetic waves or as moving particles. **b** the energy transmitted in this way, esp. invisibly. **3** (in full **radiation therapy**) treatment of cancer and other diseases using radiation, such as X-rays or ultraviolet light. □ **radiation chemistry** the study of the chemical effects of radiation on matter. **radiation sickness** sickness caused by exposure to radiation, such as X-rays or gamma rays. □□ **radiational** *adj.* **radiationally** *adv.* [L *radiatio* (as RADIATE)]

radiator /ˈreɪdɪˌeɪtə(r)/ *n.* **1** a person or thing that radiates. **2 a** a device for heating a room etc., consisting of a metal case through which hot water or steam circulates. **b** a usu. portable oil or electric heater resembling this. **3** an engine-cooling device in a motor vehicle or aircraft with a large surface for cooling circulating water. □ **radiator grille** a grille at the front of a motor vehicle allowing air to circulate to the radiator.

radical /ˈrædɪk(ə)l/ *adj. & n.* —*adj.* **1** of the root or roots; fundamental (*a radical error*). **2** far-reaching; thorough; going to the root (*radical change*). **3 a** advocating thorough reform; holding extreme political views; revolutionary. **b** (of a measure etc.) advanced by or according to principles of this kind. **4** forming the basis; primary (*the radical idea*). **5** *Math.* of the root of a number or quantity. **6** (of surgery etc.) seeking to ensure the removal of all diseased tissue. **7** of the roots of words. **8** *Mus.* belonging to the root of a chord. **9** *Bot.* of, or springing direct from, the root. **10** *hist.* belonging to an extreme section of the Liberal Party. **11** *US hist.* seeking extreme anti-South action at the time of the Civil War. —*n.* **1** a person holding radical views or belonging to a radical party. **2** *Chem.* **a** a free radical. **b** an element or atom or a group of these normally forming part of a compound and remaining unaltered during the compound's ordinary chemical changes. **3** the root of a word. **4** a fundamental principle; a basis. **5** *Math.* **a** a quantity forming or expressed as the root of another. **b** a radical sign. □ **radical sign** √, ∛, etc., indicating the square, cube, etc., root of the number following. □□ **radicalism** *n.* **radicalize** *v.tr. & intr.* (also **-ise**). **radicalization** /-ˈzeɪʃ(ə)n/ *n.* **radically** *adv.* **radicalness** *n.* [ME f. LL *radicalis* f. L *radix radicis* root]

radicchio /rəˈdiːkɪəʊ/ *n.* (*pl.* **-os**) a variety of chicory with dark red-coloured leaves. [It., = chicory]

radices *pl.* of RADIX.

radicle /ˈrædɪk(ə)l/ *n.* **1** the part of a plant embryo that develops into the primary root; a rootlet. **2** a rootlike subdivision of a nerve or vein. □□ **radicular** /rəˈdɪkjʊlə(r)/ *adj.* [L *radicula* (as RADIX)]

radii *pl.* of RADIUS.

radio /ˈreɪdɪəʊ/ *n. & v.* —*n.* (*pl.* **-os**) **1** (often *attrib.*) **a** the transmission and reception of sound messages etc. by electromagnetic waves of radio-frequency, without a connecting wire, pioneered by Marconi (see entry and cf. WIRELESS). **b** an apparatus for receiving, broadcasting, or transmitting radio signals. **c** a message sent or received by radio. **2 a** sound broadcasting in general (*prefers the radio*). **b** a broadcasting station or channel (*Radio One*). —*v.* (**-oes, -oed**) **1** *tr.* **a** send (a message) by radio. **b** send a message to (a person) by radio. **2** *intr.* communicate or broadcast by radio. □ **radio astronomy** see separate entry. **radio cab** (or **car**) a cab or car equipped with a two-way radio. **radio fix** the position of an aircraft, ship, etc., found by radio. **radio galaxy** a galaxy emitting radiation in the radio-frequency range of the electromagnetic spectrum. **radio ham** see HAM. **radio star** a small star etc. emitting strong radio waves. **radio telescope** see separate entry. [short for *radio-telegraphy* etc.]

radio- /ˈreɪdɪəʊ/ *comb. form* **1** denoting radio or broadcasting. **2 a** connected with radioactivity. **b** denoting artificially prepared radioisotopes of elements (*radio-caesium*). **3** connected with rays or radiation. **4** *Anat.* belonging to the radius in conjunction with some other part (*radio-carpal*). [RADIUS + -O- or f. RADIO]

radioactive /ˌreɪdɪəʊˈæktɪv/ *adj.* of or exhibiting radioactivity. □□ **radioactively** *adv.*

radioactivity /ˌreɪdɪəʊækˈtɪvɪtɪ/ *n.* the spontaneous disintegration of atomic nucleii, with the emission of usu. penetrating radiation or particles. Radioactivity was discovered in 1896 by Becquerel, who found that uranium salt crystals affected a photographic emulsion. Studies by Rutherford and others from 1898 onwards showed that there are three main types of radiation emitted by radioactive substances: alpha rays, which are identical with nuclei of the element helium; beta rays, which are fast-moving electrons; and gamma radiation, which is electromagnetic radiation of very high energy. Naturally occurring radioactive minerals such as uranium and thorium are believed to be largely responsible for the heating of the earth's core and for volcanic heat; they are also responsible for a large proportion of the background radiation experienced at the surface of the earth. Other contributions come from the radioactivity released in nuclear explosions and in the waste products of nuclear reactors. Although mankind has evolved in an environment which has always had background radiation, severe damage can be caused to living tissue by dosages which are significantly in excess of this background.

radio-assay /ˌreɪdɪəʊəˈseɪ/ *n.* an analysis of a substance based on radiation from a sample.

radio astronomy *n.* the branch of astronomy which monitors radio emission from celestial objects. Long-wavelength radiation originates in such objects as pulsars and super-novae remnants, and radio galaxies and quasars, where poorly understood processes involving large amounts of energy operate. The discovery in 1965 that a uniform background of radiation existed throughout the universe at microwave wavelengths is now believed to be a direct observation of the remnant of radiation from the 'big bang' associated with the formation of the universe. (See RADIO TELESCOPE.)

radiobiology /ˌreɪdɪəʊbaɪˈɒlədʒɪ/ *n.* the biology concerned with the effects of radiation on organisms and the application in biology of radiological techniques. □□ **radiobiological** /-əˈlɒdʒɪk(ə)l/ *adj.* **radiobiologically** /-əˈlɒdʒɪkəlɪ/ *adv.* **radiobiologist** *n.*

radiocarbon /ˌreɪdɪəʊˈkɑːbən/ *n.* a radioactive isotope of carbon, especially carbon 14 which has been used since the late 1940s in a technique of assigning absolute dates to ancient organic material. All living things absorb carbon, either from the carbon dioxide in the atmosphere or by eating plants etc. that contain it. Once they are dead, the proportion of carbon 14 in their remains falls at a steady rate, and by measuring the concentration of this isotope the approximate date of death of the specimen can be calculated. The figure for the half-life of carbon 14 is usually given as 5568 ± 30 years (that is, after 5568 years one half of the C14 will have been lost, after another 5568 years one half of the remainder will have gone, and so on); this figure is subject to correction. The amount of carbon 14 in the atmosphere, however, has not remained constant throughout all time, and carbon 14 dates have been calibrated against dates based on dendrochronology in efforts to produce a secure chronological framework.

radiochemistry /ˌreɪdɪəʊˈkemɪstrɪ/ *n.* the chemistry of radioactive materials. □□ **radiochemical** *adj.* **radiochemist** *n.*

radio-controlled /ˌreɪdɪəʊkənˈtrəʊld/ *adj.* (of a model aircraft etc.) controlled from a distance by radio.

radio-element /ˌreɪdɪəʊˈelɪmənt/ *n.* a natural or artificial radioactive element or isotope.

radio-frequency /ˈreɪdɪəʊˌfriːkwənsɪ/ *n.* (*pl.* **-ies**) the frequency band of telecommunication, ranging from 10^4 to 10^{11} or 10^{12} Hz.

radiogenic /ˌreɪdɪəʊˈdʒenɪk/ *adj.* **1** produced by radioactivity. **2** suitable for broadcasting by radio. □□ **radiogenically** *adv.*

radio-goniometer /ˌreɪdɪəʊˌɡəʊnɪˈɒmɪtə(r)/ *n.* an instrument for finding direction using radio waves.

radiogram /ˈreɪdɪəʊˌɡræm/ *n.* **1** *Brit.* a combined radio and record-player. **2** a picture obtained by X-rays, gamma rays, etc. **3** a radio-telegram. [RADIO- + -GRAM, GRAMOPHONE]

radiograph /ˈreɪdɪəʊˌɡrɑːf/ *n. & v.* —*n.* **1** an instrument recording the intensity of radiation. **2** = RADIOGRAM 2. —*v.tr.* obtain a picture of by X-ray, gamma ray, etc. □□ **radiographer** /-ˈɒɡrəfə(r)/ *n.* **radiographic** /-dɪəˈɡræfɪk/ *adj.* **radiographically** /-dɪəˈɡræfɪkəlɪ/ *adv.* **radiography** /-ˈɒɡrəfɪ/ *n.*

radioimmunology /ˌreɪdɪəʊˌɪmjuːˈnɒlədʒɪ/ *n.* the application of radiological techniques in immunology.

radioisotope /ˌreɪdɪəʊˈaɪsətəʊp/ *n.* a radioactive isotope. □□ **radioisotopic** /-ˈtɒpɪk/ *adj.* **radioisotopically** /-ˈtɒpɪkəlɪ/ *adv.*

radiolarian /ˌreɪdɪəʊˈleərɪən/ *n.* any marine protozoan of the order Radiolaria, having a siliceous skeleton and radiating pseudopodia. [mod.L *radiolaria* f. L *radiolus* dimin. of RADIUS]

radiology /ˌreɪdɪˈɒlədʒɪ/ *n.* the scientific study of X-rays and other high-energy radiation, esp. as used in medicine. □□ **radiologic** /-əˈlɒdʒɪk/ *adj.* **radiological** /-əˈlɒdʒɪk(ə)l/ *adj.* **radiologist** *n.*

radiometer /ˌreɪdɪˈɒmɪtə(r)/ *n.* an instrument for measuring the intensity or force of radiation. □□ **radiometry** *n.*

radiometric /ˌreɪdɪəʊˈmetrɪk/ *adj.* of or relating to the measurement of radioactivity. □ **radiometric dating** a method of dating geological specimens by determining the relative proportions of the isotopes of a radioactive element present in a sample.

radionics /ˌreɪdɪˈɒnɪks/ *n.pl.* (usu. treated as *sing.*) the study and interpretation of radiation believed to be emitted from substances, esp. as a form of diagnosis. [RADIO- + -onics, after ELECTRONICS]

radionuclide /ˌreɪdɪəʊˈnjuːklaɪd/ *n.* a radioactive nuclide.

radiopaque /ˌreɪdɪəʊˈpeɪk/ *adj.* (also **radio-opaque**) opaque to X-rays or similar radiation. □□ **radiopacity** /-ˈpæsɪtɪ/ *n.* [RADIO- + OPAQUE]

radiophonic /ˌreɪdɪəʊˈfɒnɪk/ *adj.* of or relating to synthetic sound, esp. music, produced electronically.

radioscopy /ˌreɪdɪˈɒskəpɪ/ *n.* the examination by X-rays etc. of objects opaque to light. □□ **radioscopic** /-əˈskɒpɪk/ *adj.*

radiosonde /ˈreɪdɪəʊˌsɒnd/ *n.* a miniature radio transmitter broadcasting information about pressure, temperature, etc., from various levels of the atmosphere, carried esp. by balloon. [RADIO- + G *Sonde* probe]

radio-telegram /ˌreɪdɪəʊˈtelɪˌɡræm/ *n.* a telegram sent by radio, usu. from a ship to land.

radio-telegraphy /ˌreɪdɪəʊtɪˈlegrəfɪ/ *n.* telegraphy using radio transmission. □□ **radio-telegraph** /-ˈtelɪˌɡrɑːf/ *n.*

radio-telephony /ˌreɪdɪəʊtɪˈlefənɪ/ *n.* telephony using radio transmission. □□ **radio-telephone** /-ˈtelɪˌfəʊn/ *n.* **radio-telephonic** /-ˌtelɪˈfɒnɪk/ *adj.*

radio telescope *n.* an instrument used to detect radio emissions from the sky, whether from natural celestial objects or from artificial satellites. Most familiar as large dish antennae, like the fully steerable reflector at Jodrell Bank, they may also be constructed as linear arrays of aerials, or as grids of sensitive detectors distributed over large areas of the countryside. Radio signals from outside the Earth's atmosphere were first detected in 1932 by an American radio engineer, Karl Jansky. A few years later Grote Reber, an Illinois engineer, built an apparatus with a parabolic reflector to detect and focus radio waves; the development of radio astronomy had begun.

radiotelex /ˌreɪdɪəʊˈteleks/ n. a telex sent usu. from a ship to land.

radiotherapy /ˌreɪdɪəʊˈθerəpɪ/ n. the treatment of disease by X-rays or other forms of radiation. □□ **radiotherapeutic** /-ˈpjuːtɪk/ adj. **radiotherapist** n.

radish /ˈrædɪʃ/ n. **1** a cruciferous plant, *Raphanus sativus*, with a fleshy pungent root. **2** this root, eaten esp. raw in salads etc. [OE *rædic* f. L *radix radicis* root]

radium /ˈreɪdɪəm/ n. Chem. a radioactive metallic element, discovered in pitchblende in 1898 by Pierre and Marie Curie. Because of its radioactive properties it was formerly used extensively in the treatment of tumours and in luminous materials, but it has now been largely replaced by other substances for these purposes. ¶ Symb.: **Ra**; atomic number 88. □ **radium bomb** a container holding a large quantity of radium and used in radiotherapy as a source of gamma rays. **radium emanation** = RADON. **radium therapy** the treatment of disease by the use of radium. [L *radius* ray]

radius /ˈreɪdɪəs/ n. & v. —n. (pl. **radii** /-dɪˌaɪ/ or **radiuses**) **1** Math. **a** a straight line from the centre to the circumference of a circle or sphere. **b** a radial line from the focus to any point of a curve. **c** the length of the radius of a circle etc. **2** a usu. specified distance from a centre in all directions (*within a radius of 20 miles; has a large radius of action*). **3 a** the thicker and shorter of the two bones in the human forearm (cf. ULNA). **b** the corresponding bone in a vertebrate's foreleg or a bird's wing. **4** any of the five arm-like structures of a starfish. **5 a** any of a set of lines diverging from a point like the radii of a circle. **b** an object of this kind, e.g. a spoke. **6 a** the outer rim of a composite flower-head, e.g. a daisy. **b** a radiating branch of an umbel. —v.tr. give a rounded form to (an edge etc.). □ **radius vector** Math. a variable line drawn from a fixed point to an orbit or other curve, or to any point as an indication of the latter's position. [L, = staff, spoke, ray]

radix /ˈreɪdɪks/ n. (pl. **radices** /-dɪˌsiːz/) **1** Math. a number or symbol used as the basis of a numeration scale (e.g. ten in the decimal system). **2** (usu. foll. by *of*) a source or origin. [L, = root]

radome /ˈreɪdəʊm/ n. a dome or other structure, transparent to radio waves, protecting radar equipment, esp. on the outer surface of an aircraft. [*radar* + *dome*]

radon /ˈreɪdɒn/ n. Chem. a gaseous radioactive inert element arising from the disintegration of radium, and used in radiotherapy. ¶ Symb.: **Rn**. [RADIUM after *argon* etc.]

radula /ˈrædjʊlə/ n. (pl. **radulae** /-liː/) a filelike structure in molluscs for scraping off food particles and drawing them into the mouth. □□ **radular** adj. [L, = scraper f. *radere* scrape]

Raeburn /ˈreɪbɜːn/, Sir Henry (1756–1823), Scottish portrait painter. After moving to London (1784) and travelling in Italy he returned to Edinburgh in 1787 and established a successful portrait practice there, portraying the local intelligentsia and Highland chieftains in a broad and distinctive bravura style. His rising fame was marked by several honours, and he is often considered to be the Scottish equivalent of Sir Joshua Reynolds.

RAF abbr. /colloq. ræf/ (in the UK) Royal Air Force.

Rafferty's rules /ˈræfətɪz/ n. Austral. & NZ colloq. no rules at all, esp. in boxing. [E dial. corrupt. of *refractory*]

raffia /ˈræfɪə/ n. (also **raphia**) **1** a palm-tree, *Raphia ruffia*, native to Madagascar, having very long leaves. **2** the fibre from its leaves used for making hats, baskets, etc., and for tying plants etc. [Malagasy]

raffinate /ˈræfɪˌneɪt/ n. Chem. a refined liquid oil produced by solvent extraction of impurities. [F *raffiner* + -ATE¹]

raffish /ˈræfɪʃ/ adj. **1** disreputable; rakish. **2** tawdry. □□ **raffishly** adv. **raffishness** n. [as RAFT² + -ISH¹]

raffle¹ /ˈræf(ə)l/ n. & v. —n. a fund-raising lottery with goods as prizes. —v.tr. (often foll. by *off*) dispose of by means of a raffle. [ME, a kind of dice-game, f. OF *raf(f)le*, of unkn. orig.]

raffle² /ˈræf(ə)l/ n. **1** rubbish; refuse. **2** lumber; debris. [ME, perh. f. OF *ne rifle, ne rafle* nothing at all]

Raffles¹ /ˈræf(ə)lz/, A. J., a debonair cricket-loving gentleman burglar in novels (1899 onwards) by E. W. Hornung.

Raffles² /ˈræf(ə)lz/, Sir Thomas Stamford Bingley (1781–1826), English colonial administrator, founder of Singapore. Although forced to retire early from the East India Company by ill health, Raffles was responsible for one of the Company's most momentous decisions, persuading it to purchase the undeveloped Singapore Island and then undertaking much of the preliminary work for turning it into an important international port and centre of commerce.

raft¹ /rɑːft/ n. & v. —n. **1** a flat floating structure of timber or other materials for conveying persons or things. **2** a lifeboat or small (often inflatable) boat, esp. for use in emergencies. **3** a floating accumulation of trees, ice, etc. —v. **1** tr. transport as or on a raft. **2** tr. cross (water) on a raft. **3** tr. form into a raft. **4** intr. (often foll. by *across*) work a raft (across water etc.). [ME f. ON *raptr* RAFTER]

raft² /rɑːft/ n. colloq. **1** a large collection. **2** (foll. by *of*) a crowd. [*raff* rubbish, perh. f. Scand. orig.]

rafter¹ /ˈrɑːftə(r)/ n. each of the sloping beams forming the framework of a roof. □□ **raftered** adj. [OE *ræfter*, rel. to RAFT¹]

rafter² /ˈrɑːftə(r)/ n. **1** a person who rafts timber. **2** a person who travels by raft.

raftsman /ˈrɑːftsmən/ n. (pl. **-men**) a worker on a raft.

rag¹ /ræg/ n. **1 a** a torn, frayed, or worn piece of woven material. **b** one of the irregular scraps to which cloth etc. is reduced by wear and tear. **2** (in pl.) old or worn clothes. **3** (collect.) scraps of cloth used as material for paper, stuffing, etc. **4** derog. a newspaper. **b** a flag, handkerchief, curtain, etc. **5** (usu. with neg.) the smallest scrap of cloth etc. (*not a rag to cover him*). **6** an odd scrap; an irregular piece. **7** a jagged projection, esp. on metal. □ **in rags 1** much torn. **2** in old torn clothes. **rag-and-bone man** Brit. an itinerant dealer in old clothes, furniture, etc. **rag-bag 1** a bag in which scraps of fabric etc. are kept for use. **2** a miscellaneous collection. **3** sl. a sloppily-dressed woman. **rag bolt** a bolt with barbs to keep it tight when it has been driven in. **rag book** a children's book made of untearable cloth. **rag doll** a stuffed doll made of cloth. **rag paper** paper made from rags. **rag-picker** a collector and seller of rags. **rags to riches** poverty to affluence. **rag trade** colloq. the business of designing, making, and selling women's clothes. [ME, prob. back-form. f. RAGGED]

rag² /ræg/ n. & v. —n. Brit. **1** a fund-raising programme of stunts, parades, and entertainment organized by students. **2** colloq. a prank. **3 a** a rowdy celebration. **b** a noisy disorderly scene. —v. (**ragged**, **ragging**) **1** tr. tease; torment; play rough jokes on. **2** tr. scold; reprove severely. **3** intr. Brit. engage in rough play; be noisy and riotous. [18th c.: orig. unkn.: cf. BALLYRAG]

rag³ /ræg/ n. **1** a large coarse roofing-slate. **2** any of various kinds of hard coarse sedimentary stone that break into thick slabs. [ME: orig. unkn., but assoc. with RAG¹]

rag⁴ /ræg/ n. Mus. a ragtime composition or tune. [perh. f. RAGGED: see RAGTIME]

raga /ˈrɑːgə/ n. (also **rag** /rɑːg/) Ind. Mus. **1** a pattern of notes used as a basis for improvisation. **2** a piece using a particular raga. [Skr., = colour, musical tone]

ragamuffin /ˈrægəˌmʌfɪn/ n. a person in ragged dirty clothes, esp. a child. [prob. based on RAG¹: cf. 14th-c. *ragamoffyn* the name of a demon]

rage /reɪdʒ/ n. & v. —n. **1** fierce or violent anger. **2** a fit of this (*flew into a rage*). **3** the violent action of a natural force (*the rage of the storm*). **4** (foll. by *for*) **a** a vehement desire or passion. **b** a widespread temporary enthusiasm or fashion. **5** poet. poetic, prophetic, or martial enthusiasm or ardour. **6** sl. a lively frolic. —v.intr. **1** be full of anger. **2** (often foll. by *at*, *against*) speak furiously or madly; rave. **3** (of wind, battle, fever, etc.) be violent; be at its height; continue unchecked. **4** Austral. sl. seek enjoyment; go on a spree. □ **all the rage** popular, fashionable. [ME f. OF *rager* ult. f. L RABIES]

ragee /rɑːˈgiː/ n. (also **raggee**) a coarse cereal, *Eleusine coracana*, forming a staple food in parts of India etc. [Hindi *rāgī*]

ragged /ˈrægɪd/ adj. **1** (of clothes etc.) torn; frayed. **2** rough;

shaggy; hanging in tufts. **3** (of a person) in ragged clothes. **4** with a broken or jagged outline or surface. **5** faulty; imperfect. **6** lacking finish, smoothness, or uniformity (*ragged rhymes*). **7** exhausted (esp. *be run ragged*). □ **ragged robin** a pink-flowered campion, *Lychnis flos-cuculi*, with tattered petals. □□ **raggedly** *adv.* **raggedness** *n.* **raggedy** *adj.* [ME f. ON *roggvathr* tufted]

raggee var. of RAGEE.

raggle-taggle /ˈrægəlˌtæg(ə)l/ *adj.* (also **wraggle-taggle**) ragged; rambling, straggling. [app. fanciful var. of RAGTAG]

raglan /ˈræglən/ *n.* (often *attrib.*) an overcoat without shoulder seams, the sleeves running up to the neck. □ **raglan sleeve** a sleeve of this kind. [Lord *Raglan*, Brit. commander in the Crimea d. 1855]

Ragnarök /ˈrægnərək/ *n. Scand. Mythol.* the great battle between the gods and the powers of evil, the Scandinavian equivalent of the *Götterdämmerung*, the twilight of the gods (see TWILIGHT). [tr. Icel. *ragna rökr* (*rökr* twilight) altered from the original *ragna rök* (= the history or judgement of the gods)]

ragout /ræˈguː/ *n. & v.* —*n.* meat in small pieces stewed with vegetables and highly seasoned. —*v.tr.* cook (food) in this way. [F *ragoût* f. *ragoûter* revive the taste of]

ragstone /ˈrægstəʊn/ *n.* = RAG³ 2.

ragtag /ˈrægtæg/ *n.* (in full **ragtag and bobtail**) *derog.* the rabble or common people. [earlier *tag-rag, tag and rag,* f. RAG¹ + TAG¹]

ragtime /ˈrægtaɪm/ *n. & adj.* —*n.* music characterized by a syncopated melodic line and regularly-accented accompaniment, evolved by American Black musicians in the 1890s and played esp. on the piano. It was the immediate precursor of jazz. —*adj. sl.* disorderly, disreputable, inferior (*a ragtime army*). [prob. f. RAG⁴]

raguly /ˈrægjuːlɪ/ *adj.* Heraldry like a row of sawn-off branches. [perh. f. RAGGED after *nebuly*]

Ragusa /ræˈguːzə/ the Italian name (until 1918) of Dubrovnik. It is the probable source of the word 'argosy' (see entry), referring to the large and richly-freighted merchant ships of Ragusa in the 16th c.

ragweed /ˈrægwiːd/ *n.* **1** = RAGWORT. **2** *US* any plant of the genus *Ambrosia*, with allergenic pollen.

ragwort /ˈrægwɜːt/ *n.* any yellow-flowered ragged-leaved plant of the genus *Senecio*.

rah /rɑː/ *int.* esp. *US colloq.* an expression of encouragement, approval, etc. [shortening of HURRAH]

Rahman see ABDUL RAHMAN.

rah rah /rɑː rɑː/ *n. & adj. US sl.* —*n.* a shout of support and encouragement as for a college team. —*adj.* (as **rah-rah**) marked by the type of enthusiasm or excitement generated in cheer-leading. □ **rah rah skirt** a short flounced skirt similar to those worn by cheer-leaders in the US.

raid /reɪd/ *n. & v.* —*n.* **1** a rapid surprise attack, esp.: **a** by troops, aircraft, etc. in warfare. **b** to commit a crime or do harm. **2** a surprise attack by police etc. to arrest suspected persons or seize illicit goods. **3** *Stock Exch.* an attempt to lower prices by the concerted selling of shares. **4** (foll. by *on, upon*) a forceful or insistent attempt to make a person or thing provide something. —*v.tr.* **1** make a raid on (a person, place, or thing). **2** plunder, deplete. □□ **raider** *n.* [ME, Sc. form of OE *rād* ROAD]

rail¹ /reɪl/ *n. & v.* —*n.* **1** a level or sloping bar or series of bars: **a** used to hang things on. **b** running along the top of a set of banisters. **c** forming part of a fence or barrier as protection against contact, falling over, etc. **2** a steel bar or continuous line of bars laid on the ground, usu. as one of a pair forming a railway track. **3** (often *attrib.*) a railway (*send it by rail; rail fares*). **4** (in *pl.*) the inside boundary fence of a racecourse. **5** a horizontal piece in the frame of a panelled door etc. (cf. STILE²). —*v.tr.* **1** furnish with a rail or rails. **2** (usu. foll. by *in, off*) enclose with rails (*a small space was railed off*). **3** convey (goods) by rail. □ **off the rails** disorganized; out of order; deranged. **over the rails** over the side of a ship. **rail fence** esp. *US* a fence made of posts and rails. **rail gun** an electromagnetic projectile launcher used esp. as an anti-missile weapon. □□ **railage** *n.* **railless** *adj.* [ME f. OF *reille* iron rod f. L *regula* RULE]

rail² /reɪl/ *v.intr.* (often foll. by *at, against*) complain using abusive language; rant. □□ **railer** *n.* **railing** *n. & adj.* [ME f. F *railler* f. Prov. *ralhar* jest, ult. f. L *rugire* bellow]

rail³ /reɪl/ *n.* any bird of the family Rallidae, often inhabiting marshes, esp. the corncrake and water rail. [ME f. ONF *raille* f. Rmc, perh. imit.]

railcar /ˈreɪlkɑː(r)/ *n.* a railway vehicle consisting of a single powered coach.

railcard /ˈreɪlkɑːd/ *n. Brit.* a pass entitling the holder to reduced rail fares.

railhead /ˈreɪlhed/ *n.* **1** the furthest point reached by a railway under construction. **2** the point on a railway at which road transport of goods begins.

railing /ˈreɪlɪŋ/ *n.* **1** (usu. in *pl.*) a fence or barrier made of rails. **2** the material for these.

raillery /ˈreɪlərɪ/ *n.* (*pl.* **-ies**) **1** good-humoured ridicule; rallying. **2** an instance of this. [F *raillerie* (as RAIL²)]

railman /ˈreɪlmən/ *n.* (*pl.* **-men**) = RAILWAYMAN.

railroad /ˈreɪlrəʊd/ *n. & v.* —*n.* esp. *US* = RAILWAY. —*v.tr.* **1** (often foll. by *to, into, through,* etc.) rush or coerce (a person or thing) (*railroaded me into going too*). **2** send (a person) to prison by means of false evidence.

railway /ˈreɪlweɪ/ *n.* **1** a track or set of tracks made of steel rails upon which goods trucks and passenger trains run. (See below.) **2** such a system worked by a single company (*Great Western Railway*). **3** the organization and personnel required for its working. **4** a similar set of tracks for other vehicles etc. □ **railway-yard** the area where rolling-stock is kept and made up into trains.

When a workable steam locomotive was first evolved the idea of a well-laid track of wooden or iron rails on which a 'train' of wagons could be drawn by a horse with less effort than on a rough-surfaced road was already familiar. Such tracks had long been used at collieries, and it was on one of these that Richard Trevithick's steam locomotive ran in 1804. After the success of George Stephenson's definitive *Rocket* in 1830, railways were proposed for many parts of the country. Development was rapid, though opposed by private landowners (who demanded vast payments for a route over their land), and by canal companies (who feared loss of business), but urged by manufacturers and traders who wanted this new form of quick and reliable transport. Railways played a large part in the growing industrial power of Britain in the 19th c., and until the 1860s were an exclusively British industry. By 1920 Britain had 36,800 km (23,000 miles) of track, but after that the railways ceased to grow and road transport began to expand; in recent decades many of the less used lines have been abandoned. Steam locomotives have largely given way to diesel-electric, in which an engine-driven generator supplies power to a number of electric motors driving several axles, and speeds of up to 200 kilometres an hour (125 m.p.h.) are used on main lines. Many busy routes are now electrified, using either insulated overhead wires or an insulated third rail to supply electricity to the motors of the train. Such a system will allow nuclear power to supply the system even when fossil fuels are scarce.

railwayman /ˈreɪlweɪmən/ *n.* (*pl.* **-men**) a railway employee.

raiment /ˈreɪmənt/ *n. archaic* clothing. [ME f. obs. *arrayment* (as ARRAY)]

rain /reɪn/ *n. & v.* —*n.* **1 a** the condensed moisture of the atmosphere falling visibly in separate drops. **b** the fall of such drops. **2** (in *pl.*) **a** rainfalls. **b** (prec. by *the*) the rainy season in tropical countries. **3 a** falling liquid or solid particles or objects. **b** the rainlike descent of these. **c** a large or overwhelming quantity (*a rain of congratulations*). —*v.* **1** *intr.* (prec. by *it* as subject) rain falls (*it is raining; if it rains*). **2 a** *intr.* fall in showers or like rain (*tears rained down their cheeks; blows rain upon him*). **b** *tr.* (prec. by *it* as subject) send in large quantities (*it rained blood; it is raining invitations*). **3** *tr.* send down like rain; lavishly bestow (*rained benefits on us; rained blows upon him*). **4** *intr.* (of the sky, the clouds, etc.) send down rain. □ **rain cats and dogs** see CAT. **rain check** *US* **1** a ticket given for later use when a sporting fixture or other outdoor event is interrupted or postponed by rain. **2** a promise that an offer will be maintained though deferred. **rain-cloud** a cloud bringing rain. **rain forest** luxuriant tropical forest with heavy rainfall. **rain dance** a dance performed by a tribal group etc. in the hope of summoning rain. **rain-gauge** an instrument measuring rainfall. **rain-making** the action of attempting to increase rainfall by artificial means. **rain off** (or *US* **out**) (esp. in *passive*) cause (an event etc.) to be terminated or cancelled because of rain. **rain or shine** whether it rains or not. **rain-shadow** a region shielded from rain by mountains etc. **rain-wash 1** loose material carried away by rain. **2** the movement of this. **rain-worm** the common earthworm. □□ **rainless** *adj.* **raintight** *adj.* [OE *regn, rēn, regnian* f. Gmc]

rainbird /ˈreɪnbɜːd/ *n.* a bird said to foretell rain by its cry, esp. the green woodpecker.

rainbow /ˈreɪnbəʊ/ *n.* & *adj.* —*n.* **1** an arch of colours (conventionally red, orange, yellow, green, blue, indigo, violet) formed in the sky (or across a cataract etc.) opposite the sun by reflection, twofold refraction, and dispersion of the sun's rays in falling rain or in spray or mist. **2** a similar effect formed by the moon's rays. —*adj.* many-coloured. □ **rainbow lorikeet** a small brightly coloured Polynesian parrot, *Trichoglossus haematodus.* **rainbow trout** a large trout, *Salmo gairdneri,* orig. of the Pacific coast of N. America. **secondary rainbow** an additional arch with the colours in reverse order formed inside or outside a rainbow by twofold reflection and twofold refraction. [OE *regnboga* (as RAIN, BOW[1])]

Rainbow Bridge the world's largest bridge of natural rock, situated in San Juan county in southern Utah. Its span is 86 m (278 ft.).

raincoat /ˈreɪnkəʊt/ *n.* a waterproof or water-resistant coat.

raindrop /ˈreɪndrɒp/ *n.* a single drop of rain. [OE *regndropa*]

rainfall /ˈreɪnfɔːl/ *n.* **1** a fall of rain. **2** the quantity of rain falling within a given area in a given time.

Rainier /ˈreɪnɪə(r)/, **Mount** the highest volcanic peak in the Cascade Range in SW Washington, rising to a height of 4,395 m (14,410 ft.).

rainproof /ˈreɪnpruːf/ *adj.* (esp. of a building, garment, etc.) resistant to rainwater.

rainstorm /ˈreɪnstɔːm/ *n.* a storm with heavy rain.

rainwater /ˈreɪnˌwɔːtə(r)/ *n.* water obtained from collected rain, as distinct from a well etc.

rainy /ˈreɪnɪ/ *adj.* (**rainier, rainiest**) **1** (of weather, a climate, day, region, etc.) in or on which rain is falling or much rain usually falls. **2** (of cloud, wind, etc.) laden with or bringing rain. □ **rainy day** a time of special need in the future. □□ **rainily** *adv.* **raininess** *n.* [OE *rēnig* (as RAIN)]

raise /reɪz/ *v.* & *n.* —*v.tr.* **1** put or take into a higher position. **2** (often foll. by *up*) cause to rise or stand up or be vertical; set upright. **3** increase the amount or value or strength of (*raised their prices*). **4** (often foll. by *up*) construct or build up. **5** levy or collect or bring together (*raise money; raise an army*). **6** cause to be heard or considered (*raise a shout; raise an objection*). **7** set going or bring into being; rouse (*raise a protest; raise hopes*). **8** bring up; educate. **9** breed or grow (*raise one's own vegetables*). **10** promote to a higher rank. **11** (foll. by *to*) *Math.* multiply a quantity to a specified power. **12** cause (bread) to rise with yeast. **13** *Cards* **a** bet more than (another player). **b** increase (a stake). **c** *Bridge* make a bid contracting for more tricks in the same suit as (one's partner); increase (a bid) in this way. **14** abandon or force an enemy to abandon (a siege or blockade). **15** remove (a barrier or embargo). **16** cause (a ghost etc.) to appear (opp. LAY[1] 6b). **17** *colloq.* find (a person etc. wanted). **18** establish contact with (a person etc.) by radio or telephone. **19** (usu. as **raised** *adj.*) cause (pastry etc.) to stand without support (*a raised pie*). **20** *Naut.* come in sight of (land, a ship, etc.). **21** make a nap on (cloth). **22** extract from the earth. —*n.* **1** *Cards* an increase in a stake or bid (cf. sense 13 of *v.*). **2** esp. *US* an increase in salary. □ **raise Cain** see CAIN. **raised beach** *Geol.* a beach lying above water level owing to changes since its formation. **raise the devil** *colloq.* make a disturbance. **raise a dust 1** cause turmoil. **2** obscure the truth. **raise one's eyebrows** see EYEBROW. **raise**

one's eyes see EYE. **raise from the dead** restore to life. **raise one's glass to** drink the health of. **raise one's hand to** make as if to strike (a person). **raise one's hat** (often foll. by *to*) remove it momentarily as a gesture of courtesy or respect. **raise hell** *colloq.* make a disturbance. **raise a laugh** cause others to laugh. **raise a person's spirits** give him or her new courage or cheerfulness. **raise one's voice** speak, esp. louder. **raise the wind** *Brit.* procure money for a purpose. □□ **raisable** *adj.* [ME f. ON *reisa,* rel. to REAR[2]]

raisin /ˈreɪz(ə)n/ *n.* a partially dried grape. □□ **raisiny** *adj.* [ME f. OF ult. f. L *racemus* grape-bunch]

raison d'être /ˌreɪzɔ̃ ˈdetr/ *n.* (*pl.* **raisons d'être** pronunc. same) a purpose or reason that accounts for or justifies or originally caused a thing's existence. [F, = reason for being]

raj /rɑːdʒ/ *n.* (prec. by *the*) *hist.* British sovereignty in India. [Hindi *rāj* reign]

raja /ˈrɑːdʒə/ *n.* (also **rajah**) *hist.* **1** an Indian king or prince. **2** a petty dignitary or noble in India. **3** a Malay or Javanese chief. □□ **rajaship** *n.* [Hindi *rājā* f. Skr. *rājan* king]

Rajasthan /ˌrɑːdʒəˈstɑːn/ a State in NW India; pop. (1981) 34,102,900; capital, Jaipur. □□ **Rajasthani** *adj.* & *n.*

raja yoga /ˈrɑːdʒə/ *n.* a form of yoga intended to achieve control over the mind and emotions. [Skr. f. *rājan* king + YOGA]

Rajput /ˈrɑːdʒpʊt, -puːt/ *n.* (also **Rajpoot**) a member of a Hindu soldier caste claiming Kshatriya descent. [Hindi *rājpūt* f. Skr. *rājan* king + *putrá* son]

Rajputana /ˌrɑːdʒpʊˈtɑːnə/ a region of India consisting of a collection of former States which united to form the State of Rajasthan in 1948.

Rajshahi /rɑːdʒˈʃɑːjɪ, ˈrɑːdʒ-/ a port on the Ganges River in western Bangladesh; pop. (1981) 253,700.

rake[1] /reɪk/ *n.* & *v.* —*n.* **1 a** an implement consisting of a pole with a crossbar toothed like a comb at the end, or with several tines held together by a crosspiece, for drawing together hay etc. or smoothing loose soil or gravel. **b** a wheeled implement for the same purpose. **2** a similar implement used for other purposes, e.g. by a croupier drawing in money at a gaming-table. —*v.* **1** *tr.* collect or gather or remove with or as with a rake. **2** *tr.* make tidy or smooth with a rake (*raked it level*). **3** *intr.* use a rake. **4** *tr.* & *intr.* search with or as with a rake, search thoroughly, ransack. **5** *tr.* **a** direct gunfire along (a line) from end to end. **b** sweep with the eyes. **c** (of a window etc.) have a commanding view of. **6** *tr.* scratch or scrape. □ **rake in** *colloq.* amass (profits etc.). **rake-off** *colloq.* a commission or share, esp. in a disreputable deal. **rake up** (or **over**) revive the memory of (past quarrels, grievances, etc.). □□ **raker** *n.* [OE *raca, racu* f. Gmc, partly f. ON *raka* scrape, rake]

rake[2] /reɪk/ *n.* a dissolute man of fashion. □ **rake's progress** a progressive deterioration, esp. through self-indulgence (the title of a series of engravings by Hogarth 1735). [short for archaic *rakehell* in the same sense]

rake[3] /reɪk/ *v.* & *n.* —*v.* **1** *tr.* & *intr.* set or be set at a sloping angle. **2** *intr.* **a** (of a mast or funnel) incline from the perpendicular towards the stern. **b** (of a ship or its bow or stern) project at the upper part of the bow or stern beyond the keel. —*n.* **1** a raking position or build. **2** the amount by which a thing rakes. **3** the slope of the stage or the auditorium in a theatre. **4** the slope of a seat-back etc. **5** the angle of the edge or face of a cutting tool. [17th c.: prob. rel. to G *ragen* project, of unkn. orig.]

raki /rəˈkiː, ˈrækɪ/ *n.* (*pl.* **rakis**) any of various spirits made in E. Europe and the Middle East. [Turk. *raqi*]

rakish[1] /ˈreɪkɪʃ/ *adj.* of or like a rake (see RAKE[2]); dashing; jaunty. □□ **rakishly** *adv.* **rakishness** *n.*

rakish[2] /ˈreɪkɪʃ/ *adj.* (of a ship) smart and fast-looking, seemingly built for speed and therefore open to suspicion of piracy. [RAKE[3], assoc. with RAKE[2]]

raku /ˈrɑːkuː/ *n.* a kind of Japanese earthenware, usu. lead-glazed. [Jap., lit. enjoyment]

rale /rɑːl/ *n.* an abnormal rattling sound heard in the auscultation of unhealthy lungs. [F f. *râler* to rattle]

Raleigh[1] /ˈrɑːlɪ/ the capital of North Carolina; pop. (1980) 150,255.

Raleigh[2] /ˈrɑːlɪ, ˈrɔːlɪ, ˈrælɪ/, Sir Walter (c.1552–1618), explorer and courtier, a favourite of Elizabeth I who conferred a knighthood upon him. He organized several voyages of exploration and colonization to North America, including the first unsuccessful attempt to settle Virginia (now North Carolina); from his expeditions he brought back the potato and the tobacco plant. Raleigh was imprisoned in 1603 by the new king James I on a flimsy charge of conspiracy; while in the Tower of London he wrote his *History of the World*. Released to undertake an expedition in search of the fabled land of El Dorado, he became involved in military action with the Spanish, and on his return empty-handed was executed on the original charge of conspiracy.

rall. /ræl/ *adv. & adj. & n.* = RALLENTANDO. [abbr.]

rallentando /ˌrælənˈtændəʊ/ *adv., adj., & n. Mus.* —*adv. & adj.* with a gradual decrease of speed. —*n.* (pl. **-os** or **rallentandi** /-dɪ/) a passage to be performed in this way. [It.]

ralli car /ˈrælɪ/ *n.* (also **ralli cart**) *hist.* a light two-wheeled horse-drawn vehicle for four persons. [*Ralli*, name of the first purchaser 1885]

ralline /ˈrælaɪn/ *adj.* of the bird-family Rallidae (see RAIL[3]). [mod.L *rallus* RAIL[3]]

rally[1] /ˈrælɪ/ *v. & n.* —*v.* (**-ies, -ied**) **1** *tr. & intr.* (often foll. by *round, behind, to*) bring or come together as support or for concentrated action. **2** *tr. & intr.* bring or come together again after a rout or dispersion. **3 a** *intr.* renew a conflict. **b** *tr.* cause to do this. **4 a** *tr.* revive (courage etc.) by an effort of will. **b** *tr.* rouse (a person or animal) to fresh energy. **c** *intr.* pull oneself together. **5** *intr.* recover after illness or prostration or fear, regain health or consciousness, revive. **6** *intr.* (of share-prices etc.) increase after a fall. —*n.* (pl. **-ies**) **1** an act of reassembling forces or renewing conflict; a reunion for fresh effort. **2** a recovery of energy after or in the middle of exhaustion or illness. **3** a mass meeting of supporters or persons having a common interest. **4** a competition for motor vehicles, usu. over public roads. **5** (in lawn tennis etc.) an extended exchange of strokes between players. □ **rally-cross** motor racing over roads and cross-country. □□ **rallier** *n.* [F *rallier* (as RE-, ALLY[1])]

rally[2] /ˈrælɪ/ *v.tr.* (**-ies, -ied**) subject to good-humoured ridicule. [F *railler*: see RAIL[2]]

RAM *abbr.* **1** (in the UK) Royal Academy of Music. **2** *Computing* random-access memory.

ram /ræm/ *n. & v.* —*n.* **1** an uncastrated male sheep, a tup. **2** (**the Ram**) the zodiacal sign or constellation Aries. **3** *hist.* **a** = *battering ram* (see BATTER[1]). **b** a beak projecting from the bow of a battleship, for piercing the sides of other ships. **c** a battleship with such a beak. **4** the falling weight of a pile-driving machine. **5 a** a hydraulic water-raising or lifting machine. **b** the piston of a hydrostatic press. **c** the plunger of a force-pump. —*v.tr.* (**rammed, ramming**) **1** force or squeeze into place by pressure. **2** (usu. foll. by *down, in, into*) beat down or drive in by heavy blows. **3** (of a ship, vehicle, etc.) strike violently, crash against. **4** (foll. by *against, at, on, into*) dash or violently impel. □ **ram home** stress forcefully (an argument, lesson, etc.). □□ **rammer** *n.* [OE *ram(m)*, perh. rel. to ON *rammr* strong]

Rama /ˈrɑːmə/ the hero of the Indian epic the Ramayana. He is the Hindu model of the ideal man, the seventh incarnation of Vishnu (see entry) and is widely venerated, by some sects as the supreme god. [Skr., = black, dark]

Ramadan /ˈræməˌdæn/ *n.* (also **Ramadhan** /-ˌzæn/) the ninth month of the Muslim year, during which strict fasting is observed from sunrise to sunset. This is one of the five 'Pillars of the Faith' or basic ritual duties. The fast (which entails abstinence from food, water, tobacco, and sexual intercourse) takes place from dawn to sundown every day of the month, and Muslims are enjoined to perform devotions (prayer, reading of the Koran) in addition to the usual five daily ritual sequences of prayer. Emphasis is on Allah's forgiveness and the atonement of sins. Those fasting are expected to live in especial simplicity during the month and to provide more than usual for the needy members of the community. [Arab. *ramaḍān* f. *ramaḍa* be hot; reason for name uncert.]

Ramakrishna /ˌrɑːməˈkrɪʃnə/ Gadadhar Chatterji (1836–86), Indian Hindu mystic. He condemned lust, greed for money, and the caste system, and in his meditations became convinced that all religions are in essence the same and that all are true. His teachings were spread widely in the US and Europe by his most notable disciple Vivekananda (see entry).

ramal /ˈreɪm(ə)l/ *adj. Bot.* of or proceeding from a branch. [L *ramus* branch]

Raman /ˈrɑːmən/, Sir Chandrasekhara Venkata (1888–1970), Indian physicist, discoverer of the Raman effect, that there is a change in the wavelength of light scattered within a substance (e.g. a liquid). His discovery, for which he was awarded the 1930 Nobel Prize for physics, was important for the study of molecular structure.

Ramayana /rɑːˈmaɪənə/ *n.* a Sanskrit epic of India, composed c.300 BC. It describes how Rama, aided by his brother and the monkey Hanuman, rescued his wife Sita from the clutches of Ravana, the ten-headed demon king of Lanka (according to some, modern Sri Lanka). [Skr., = exploits of Rama]

Rambert /ˈrɑːmbeɪr/, Dame Marie (1888–1982), real name Cyvia Rambam, then Miriam Ramberg, Polish-British dancer, teacher, and ballet director. She opened a ballet school in London in 1920, the company being originally called Marie Rambert Dancers, then Ballet Club from 1930 and Ballet Rambert from 1935. One of the pioneers of modern British ballet, she discovered many young choreographers and dancers.

ramble /ˈræmb(ə)l/ *v. & n.* —*v.intr.* **1** walk for pleasure, with or without a definite route. **2** wander in discourse, talk or write disconnectedly. —*n.* a walk taken for pleasure. [prob. f. MDu. *rammelen* (of an animal) wander about in sexual excitement, frequent. of *rammen* copulate with, rel. to RAM]

rambler /ˈræmblə(r)/ *n.* **1** a person who rambles. **2** a straggling or climbing rose (*crimson rambler*).

rambling /ˈræmblɪŋ/ *adj.* **1** peripatetic, wandering. **2** disconnected, desultory, incoherent. **3** (of a house, street, etc.) irregularly arranged. **4** (of a plant) straggling, climbing. □□ **ramblingly** *adv.*

Rambo /ˈræmbəʊ/ the hero of David Morrell's novel *First Blood* (1972, popularized in films), a Vietnam war veteran popularly thought of as macho, self-sufficient, and bent on violent retribution.

rambunctious /ræmˈbʌŋkʃəs/ *adj. US colloq.* **1** uncontrollably exuberant. **2** unruly. □□ **rambunctiously** *adv.* **rambunctiousness** *n.* [19th c.: orig. unkn.]

rambutan /ræmˈbuːt(ə)n/ *n.* **1** a red plum-sized prickly fruit. **2** an East Indian tree, *Nephelium lappaceum*, that bears this. [Malay *rambūtan* f. *rambut* hair, in allusion to its spines]

RAMC *abbr.* (in the UK) Royal Army Medical Corps.

Rameau /rɑːˈməʊ/, Jean-Philippe (1683–1764), French composer, best remembered for his stage works. His first opera was composed in 1733, when he was 50, but the 25 or so such works which followed mark him as a worthy successor to Lully and an important predecessor to Gluck.

ramekin /ˈræmɪkɪn/ *n.* **1** (in full **ramekin case** or **dish**) a small dish for baking and serving an individual portion of food. **2** food served in such a dish, esp. a small quantity of cheese baked with breadcrumbs, eggs, etc. [F *ramequin*, of LG or Du. orig.]

Rameses /ˈræmsiːz/ the name of 11 Egyptian pharaohs:

Rameses II 'the Great' (1290–1224 BC, 19th Dynasty), famed for his numerous self-aggrandizing monuments which are a testimony to Egypt's wealth at the time. For practical reasons, early in his reign he established a new capital in the eastern part of the Nile delta. His major foreign campaign was his offensive against the Hittites, leading his troops in person; the campaign ended indecisively but a treaty followed. Having outlived much of his family Rameses was succeeded by his thirteenth son, Mernepton.

Rameses III (1194–1163 BC, 20th Dynasty), the last great imperial pharaoh. He fought decisive battles against the Libyans and the Sea Peoples who attempted invasions, thus salvaging

Egypt's integrity until the Persian period. After his death the power of Egypt declined steadily.

ramie /'ræmɪ/ n. 1 any of various tall East Asian plants of the genus *Boehmeria*, esp. *B. nivea*. 2 a strong fibre obtained from this, woven into cloth. [Malay *rāmī*]

ramification /ˌræmɪfɪ'keɪʃ(ə)n/ n. 1 the act or an instance of ramifying; the state of being ramified. 2 a subdivision of a complex structure or process comparable to a tree's branches. [F *ramifier*: see RAMIFY]

ramify /'ræmɪˌfaɪ/ v. (-ies, -ied) 1 intr. form branches or subdivisions or offshoots, branch out. 2 tr. (usu. in *passive*) cause to branch out; arrange in a branching manner. [F *ramifier* f. med.L *ramificare* f. L *ramus* branch]

Ramillies /'ræmɪlɪz/ a village in Belgium, scene of a battle in 1706 (see MARLBOROUGH).

ramin /ræ'miːn/ n. 1 any Malaysian tree of the genus *Gonystylus*, esp. *G. bancanus*. 2 the light-coloured hardwood obtained from this tree. [Malay]

ramjet /'ræmdʒet/ n. a type of jet engine in which air is drawn in and compressed by the forward motion of the engine.

rammer see RAM.

rammy /'ræmɪ/ n. (pl. -ies) Sc. sl. a brawl, a fight (esp. between gangs); a quarrel. [perh. f. Sc. *rammle* row, uproar, var. of RAMBLE]

Ramón y Cajal /rə'məʊn iː kə'hɑːl/, Santiago (1852–1934), Spanish histologist who was awarded a Nobel Prize in 1906 (jointly with Golgi) for establishing that the neurone or nerve cell is the fundamental unit of the nervous system.

ramose /'ræməʊs, 'reɪ-/ adj. branched; branching. [L *ramosus* f. *ramus* branch]

ramp¹ /ræmp/ n. & v. —n. 1 a slope or inclined plane, esp. for joining two levels of ground, floor, etc. 2 movable stairs for entering or leaving an aircraft. 3 an upward bend in a stair-rail. 4 *Brit.* a transverse ridge in a road to control the speed of vehicles. —v. 1 tr. furnish or build with a ramp. 2 intr. **a** assume or be in a threatening posture. **b** (often foll. by *about*) storm, rage, rush. **c** *Heraldry* be rampant. 3 intr. *Archit.* (of a wall) ascend or descend to a different level. [ME (as verb in heraldic sense) f. F *rampe* f. OF *ramper* creep, crawl]

ramp² /ræmp/ n. & v. *Brit. sl.* —n. a swindle or racket, esp. one conducted by the levying of exorbitant prices. —v. 1 intr. engage in a ramp. 2 tr. subject (a person etc.) to a ramp. [16th c.: orig. unkn.]

rampage /ræm'peɪdʒ/ v. & n. —v.intr. 1 (often foll. by *about*) rush wildly or violently about. 2 rage, storm. —n. (often 'ræm-/ wild or violent behaviour. □ **on the rampage** rampaging. □□ **rampageous** adj. **rampager** n. [18th c., perh. f. RAMP¹]

rampant /'ræmpənt/ adj. 1 (placed after noun) *Heraldry* (of an animal) standing on its left hind foot with its forefeet raised, right higher than left, facing dexter (*lion rampant*). 2 unchecked, flourishing excessively (*rampant violence*). 3 violent or extravagant in action or opinion (*rampant theorists*). 4 rank, luxuriant. □□ **rampancy** n. **rampantly** adv. [ME f. OF, part. of *ramper*: see RAMP¹]

rampart /'ræmpɑːt/ n. & v. —n. 1 **a** a defensive wall with a broad top and usu. a stone parapet. **b** a walkway on top of such a wall. 2 a defence or protection. —v.tr. fortify or protect with or as with a rampart. [F *rempart*, *rempar* f. *remparer* fortify f. *emparer* take possession of, ult. f. L *ante* before + *parare* prepare]

rampion /'ræmpɪən/ n. 1 a bellflower, *Campanula rapunculus*, with white tuberous roots used as a salad. 2 any of various plants of the genus *Phyteuma*, with clusters of hornlike buds and flowers. [ult. f. med.L *rapuncium*, *rapontium*, prob. f. L *rapum* RAPE²]

ramrod /'ræmrod/ n. 1 a rod for ramming down the charge of a muzzle-loading firearm. 2 a thing that is very straight or rigid.

Ramsay¹ /'ræmzɪ/, Allan (1713–84), Scottish portrait painter. The grace and sensitivity of his style, particularly in his portraits of women (e.g. his wife, Margaret Lindsay, 1755) was much sought after and he was a serious rival to Reynolds in the 1750s. However, in the 1760s he increasingly delegated work to his studio assistants to leave him free to pursue the literary and archaeological interests that dominated his last years.

Ramsay² /'ræmzɪ/, Sir William (1852–1916), Scottish chemist, discoverer of the rare gases of the atmosphere, for which he was awarded the 1904 Nobel Prize for chemistry. This work was initiated after a discussion with Lord Rayleigh (see entry) in 1892 about why nitrogen prepared in the laboratory should be slightly less dense than when isolated from the air, a phenomenon already observed by Cavendish in 1785; Ramsay decided that atmospheric nitrogen must be contaminated by a heavier gas. Between 1894 and 1903 he discovered the existence of five chemically inert gases: argon, helium and, with the help of the chemist Morris William Travers (1872–1961), neon, krypton, and xenon, and determined their atomic weights and places in the periodic table. In 1910 with Soddy and Sir Robert Whytlaw-Gray (1877–1958) he identified the last member of the rare (or noble) gases, radon, the product of radioactive decay.

ramshackle /'ræmˌʃæk(ə)l/ adj. (usu. of a house or vehicle) tumbledown, rickety. [earlier *ramshackled* past part. of obs. *ransackle* RANSACK]

ramsons /'ræms(ə)nz/ n. (usu. treated as *sing.*) 1 a broad-leaved garlic, *Allium ursinum*, with elongate pungent-smelling bulbous roots. 2 the root of this, eaten as a relish. [OE *hramsan* pl. of *hramsa* wild garlic, later taken as sing.]

RAN abbr. Royal Australian Navy.

ran past of RUN.

ranch /rɑːntʃ/ n. & v. —n. 1 **a** a cattle-breeding establishment esp. in the US and Canada. **b** a farm where other animals are bred (*mink ranch*). 2 *US* a single-storey or split-level house. —v.intr. farm on a ranch. [Sp. *rancho* group of persons eating together]

rancher /'rɑːntʃə(r)/ n. 1 a person who farms on a ranch. 2 *US* a modern single-storey house.

ranchero /rɑːn'tʃeərəʊ/ n. (pl. -os) a person who farms or works on a ranch, esp. in Mexico. [Sp. (as RANCH)]

Ranchi /'rɑːntʃɪ/ the summer capital of Bihar State in India; pop. (1981) 501,000.

rancid /'rænsɪd/ adj. smelling or tasting like rank stale fat. □□ **rancidity** /-'sɪdɪtɪ/ n. **rancidness** n. [L *rancidus* stinking]

rancour /'ræŋkə(r)/ n. (*US* **rancor**) inveterate bitterness, malignant hate, spitefulness. □□ **rancorous** adj. **rancorously** adv. [ME f. OF f. LL *rancor -oris* (as RANCID)]

Rand /rænd, rɑːnt/, **the** = WITWATERSRAND.

rand¹ /rænd, rɑːnt/ n. 1 the chief monetary unit of South Africa and some neighbouring countries. 2 *S.Afr.* a ridge of high ground on either side of a river. [Afrik., = edge, rel. to RAND²: sense 1 f. the RAND]

rand² /rænd/ n. a levelling-strip of leather between the heel and sides of a shoe or boot. [OE f. Gmc]

R & B abbr. (also **R. & B.**) rhythm and blues.

R & D abbr. (also **R. & D.**) research and development.

Randers /'rɑːnəz/ a port of Denmark, on the east coast of the Jutland peninsula; pop. (1988) 61,150.

random /'rændəm/ adj. 1 made, done, etc., without method or conscious choice (*random selection*). 2 *Statistics* **a** with equal chances for each item. **b** given by a random process. 3 (of masonry) with stones of irregular size and shape. □ **at random** without aim or purpose or principle. **random-access** *Computing* (of a memory or file) having all parts directly accessible, so that it need not read sequentially. **random error** *Statistics* an error in measurement caused by factors which vary from one measurement to another. □□ **randomize** v.tr. (also -ise). **randomization** /-'zeɪʃ(ə)n/ n. **randomly** adv. **randomness** n. [ME f. OF *randon* great speed f. *randir* gallop]

R and R abbr. (also **R. and R.**) 1 rescue and resuscitation. 2 rest and recreation. 3 rock and roll.

Randstad /'rɔːnstɑːt/ a conurbation in the north-west of The Netherlands that stretches in a horseshoe shape from Dordrecht and Rotterdam round to Utrecht and Amersfoort via The Hague, Leiden, Haarlem, and Amsterdam. The majority of the people of The Netherlands live in this area. Its Dutch name means 'ring of towns'.

randy /'rændɪ/ adj. (**randier, randiest**) 1 lustful; eager for sexual gratification. **2** *Sc.* loud-tongued, boisterous, lusty. □□ **randily** *adv.* **randiness** *n.* [perh. f. obs. *rand* f. obs. Du. *randen, ranten* RANT]

ranee /ˈrɑːniː/ *n.* (also **rani**) *hist.* a raja's wife or widow; a Hindu queen. [Hindi *rānī* = Skr. *rājñī* fem. of *rājan* king]

rang *past of* RING².

rangatira /ˌræŋɡəˈtiːrə/ *n.* NZ a Maori chief or noble. [Maori]

range /reɪndʒ/ *n.* & *v.* —*n.* **1 a** the region between limits of variation, esp. as representing a scope of effective operation (*a voice of astonishing range; the whole range of politics*). **b** such limits. **c** a limited scale or series (*the range of the thermometer readings is about 10 degrees*). **2** the area included in or concerned with something. **3 a** the distance attainable by a gun or projectile (*the enemy are out of range*). **b** the distance between a gun or projectile and its objective. **4** a row, series, line, or tier, esp. of mountains or buildings. **5 a** an open or enclosed area with targets for shooting. **b** a testing-ground for military equipment. **6 a** a fireplace with ovens and hotplates for cooking. **b** *US* an electric or gas cooker. **7** the area over which a thing, esp. a plant or animal, is distributed (*gives the ranges of all species*). **8** the distance that can be covered by a vehicle or aircraft without refuelling. **9** the distance between a camera and the subject to be photographed. **10** the extent of time covered by a forecast etc. **11 a** a large area of open land for grazing or hunting. **b** a tract over which one wanders. **12** lie, direction (*the range of the strata is east and west*). —*v.* **1** *intr.* **a** reach; lie spread out; extend; be found or occur over a specified district; vary between limits (*ages ranging from twenty to sixty*). **b** run in a line (*ranges north and south*). **2** *tr.* (usu. in *passive* or *refl.*) place or arrange in a row or ranks or in a specified situation or order or company (*ranged their troops; ranged themselves with the majority party; trees ranged in ascending order of height*). **3** *intr.* rove, wander (*ranged through the woods; his thoughts range over past, present, and future*). **4** *tr.* traverse in all directions (*ranging the woods*). **5** *Printing* **a** *tr.* make (type) lie flush at the ends of successive lines. **b** *intr.* (of type) line flush. **6** *intr.* **a** (often foll. by *with*) be level. **b** (foll. by *with, among*) rank; find one's right place (*ranges with the great writers*). **7** *intr.* **a** (of a gun) send a projectile over a specified distance (*ranges over a mile*). **b** (of a projectile) cover a specified distance. **c** obtain the range of a target by adjustment after firing past it or short of it. □ **ranging-pole** (or **-rod**) *Surveying* a pole or rod for setting a straight line. [ME f. OF *range* row, rank f. *ranger* f. *rang* RANK¹]

rangé /rãˈʒeɪ/ *adj.* (*fem.* **rangée**) domesticated, orderly, settled. [F]

rangefinder /ˈreɪndʒˌfaɪndə(r)/ *n.* an instrument for estimating the distance of an object, esp. one to be shot at or photographed.

ranger /ˈreɪndʒə(r)/ *n.* **1** a keeper of a royal or national park, or of a forest. **2 a** a member of a body of armed men, esp.: **a a** mounted soldier. **b** *US* a commando. **3** (**Ranger**) *Brit.* a senior Guide. (See GIRL GUIDES ASSOCIATION.) **4** a wanderer. □□ **rangership** *n.*

Rangoon /ræŋˈɡuːn/ (also **Yangon** /jæŋˈɡɔːn/) from 1989 called Yangon, the capital and a seaport of Burma, on the Rangoon river, one of the mouths of the Irrawaddy; pop. (1983) 2,458,712.

rangy /ˈreɪndʒɪ/ *adj.* (**rangier, rangiest**) (of a person) tall and slim.

rani *var.* of RANEE.

Ranjit Singh /ˈrændʒɪt ˈsɪŋ/ (1780–1839), Sikh ruler, who made the Punjab the most powerful State in India and earned himself the nickname 'Lion of the Punjab'. Succeeding his father at the age of 12, he seized Lahore from the Afghans in 1799 and secured the holy city of Amritsar in 1802. By agreement with the British authorities the eastern boundary of his State remained on the Sutlej River, but with his large army, trained by French officers, he expanded his rule westwards, took control of Kashmir, and annexed Peshawar. At the end of the Sikh Wars following his death most of his territory was taken by Britain.

Rank /ræŋk/, Joseph Arthur, 1st Baron (1888–1972), English industrialist and film executive, who built up the Rank Organization, a film production, distribution, and exhibition company, which he founded in 1946. While working in his father's prosperous flour business (Rank Hovis McDougall Ltd.)

he became interested in films when, as a Methodist Sunday School teacher, he realized that they could be an ideal medium for spreading the Gospel. In addition, his patriotic sense was offended by American domination of the British film industry. By the late 1940s the Rank Organization, whose trademark was a muscular man beating an outsize gong, owned or controlled the leading British studios. A shrewd financier, Rank was quick to diversify his interests when cinema output dwindled in the 1950s.

rank¹ /ræŋk/ *n.* & *v.* —*n.* **1 a** a position in a hierarchy, a grade of advancement. **b** a distinct social class, a grade of dignity or achievement (*people of all ranks; in the top rank of performers*). **c** high social position (*persons of rank*). **d** a place in a scale. **2 a** a row or line. **3** a single line of soldiers drawn up abreast. **4** *Brit.* a place where taxis stand to await customers. **5** order, array. **6** *Chess* a row of squares across the board (cf. FILE²). —*v.* **1** *intr.* have rank or place (*ranks next to the king*). **2** *tr.* classify, give a certain grade to. **3** *tr.* arrange (esp. soldiers) in a rank or ranks. **4** *US* **a** *tr.* take precedence of (a person) in respect to rank. **b** *intr.* have the senior position among the members of a hierarchy etc. □ **break rank** fail to remain in line. **close ranks** maintain solidarity. **keep rank** remain in line. **other ranks** soldiers other than commissioned officers. **rank and fashion** high society. **rank and file** ordinary undistinguished people (orig. = *the ranks*). **the ranks** the common soldiers, i.e. privates and corporals. **rise from the ranks 1** (of a private or a non-commissioned officer) receive a commission. **2** (of a self-made man or woman) advance by one's own exertions. [OF *ranc, renc,* f. Gmc, rel. to RING¹]

rank² /ræŋk/ *adj.* **1** too luxuriant, coarse; choked with or apt to produce weeds or excessive foliage. **2 a** foul-smelling, offensive. **b** loathsome, indecent, corrupt. **3** flagrant, virulent, gross, complete, unmistakable, strongly marked (*rank outsider*). □□ **rankly** *adv.* **rankness** *n.* [OE *ranc* f. Gmc]

ranker /ˈræŋkə(r)/ *n.* **1** a soldier in the ranks. **2** a commissioned officer who has been in the ranks.

ranking /ˈræŋkɪŋ/ *n.* & *adj.* —*n.* ordering by rank; classification. —*adj.* *US* having a high rank or position.

rankle /ˈræŋk(ə)l/ *v.intr.* **1** (of envy, disappointment, etc., or their cause) cause persistent annoyance or resentment. **2** *archaic* (of a wound, sore, etc.) fester, continue to be painful. [ME (in sense 2) f. OF *rancler* f. *rancle, draoncle* festering sore f. med.L *d᷂anculus, dracunculus* dimin. of *draco* serpent]

ransack /ˈrænsæk/ *v.tr.* **1** pillage or plunder (a house, country, etc.). **2** thoroughly search (a place, a receptacle, a person's pockets, one's conscience, etc.). □□ **ransacker** *n.* [ME f. ON *rannsaka* f. *rann* house + *-saka* f. *sœkja* seek]

ransom /ˈrænsəm/ *n.* & *v.* —*n.* **1** a sum of money or other payment demanded or paid for the release of a prisoner. **2** the liberation of a prisoner in return for this. —*v.tr.* **1** buy the freedom or restoration of; redeem. **2** hold to ransom. **3** release for a ransom. □□ **ransomer** *n.* (in sense 1 of *v.*). [ME f. OF *ransoun(er)* f. L *redemptio -onis* REDEMPTION]

Ransome /ˈrænsəm/, Arthur Michell (1884–1967), English writer. As a journalist he covered the revolution in Russia, and he published a successful collection of Russian legends and fairy stories. His second wife, Eugenia Shelepin, had been Trotsky's secretary. Ransome is remembered chiefly for his novels for children, beginning with *Swallows and Amazons* (1930) and ending with *Great Northern?* (1947), which reflect his keen interest in sailing, fishing, and the countryside.

rant /rænt/ *v.* & *n.* —*v.* **1** *intr.* use bombastic language. **2** *tr.* & *intr.* declaim, recite theatrically. **3** *tr.* & *intr.* preach noisily. —*n.* **1** a piece of ranting, a tirade. **2** empty turgid talk. □□ **ranter** *n.* **rantingly** *n.* [Du. *ranten* rave]

ranunculaceous /rəˌnʌŋkjʊˈleɪʃəs/ *adj.* of or relating to the family Ranunculaceae of flowering plants, including clematis and delphiniums.

ranunculus /rəˈnʌŋkjʊləs/ *n.* (pl. **ranunculuses** or **ranunculi** /-ˌlaɪ/) any plant of the genus *Ranunculus*, usu. having bowl-shaped flowers with many stamens and carpels, including buttercups and crowfoots. [L, orig. dimin. of *rana* frog]

RAOC *abbr.* (in the UK) Royal Army Ordnance Corps.

rap¹ /ræp/ *n. & v.* —*n.* **1** a smart slight blow. **2** a knock, a sharp tapping sound. **3** *sl.* blame, censure, or punishment. **4** *sl.* a conversation. **5 a** a rhyming monologue recited rhythmically to prerecorded music. **b** (in full **rap music**) a style of rock music with a pronounced beat and words recited rather than sung. —*v.* (**rapped, rapping**) **1** *tr.* strike smartly. **2** *intr.* knock; make a sharp tapping sound (*rapped on the table*). **3** *tr.* criticize adversely. **4** *intr. sl.* talk. □ **beat the rap** *US* escape punishment. **rap on** (or **over**) **the knuckles** a reprimand or reproof. **rap out 1** utter (an oath, order, pun, etc.) abruptly or on the spur of the moment. **2** *Spiritualism* express (a message or word) by raps. **take the rap** suffer the consequences. □□ **rapper** *n.* [ME, prob. imit.]

rap² /ræp/ *n.* a small amount, the least bit (*don't care a rap*). [Ir. *ropaire* Irish counterfeit coin]

rapacious /rə'peɪʃəs/ *adj.* grasping, extortionate, predatory. □□ **rapaciously** *adv.* **rapaciousness** *n.* **rapacity** /rə'pæsɪtɪ/ *n.* [L *rapax -acis* f. *rapere* snatch]

RAPC *abbr.* (in the UK) Royal Army Pay Corps.

rape¹ /reɪp/ *n. & v.* —*n.* **1 a** the act of forcing a woman to have sexual intercourse against her will. **b** forcible sodomy. **2** (often foll. by *of*) violent assault, forcible interference, violation. **3** *poet.* carrying off (esp. of a woman) by force. **4** an instance of rape. —*v.tr.* **1** commit rape on (a person, usu. a woman). **2** violate, assault, pillage. **3** *poet.* take by force. [ME f. AF *rap(er)* f. L *rapere* seize]

rape² /reɪp/ *n.* a plant, *Brassica napus*, grown as food for sheep and for its seed, from which oil is made. Also called COLZA, COLE. □ **rape-cake** rape-seed pressed into a flat shape after the extraction of oil and used as manure or cattle food. **rape-oil** an oil made from rape-seed and used as a lubricant and in foodstuffs. [ME f. L *rapum, rapa* turnip]

rape³ /reɪp/ *n. hist.* (in the UK) any of the six ancient divisions of Sussex. [OE, var. of *rāp* ROPE, with ref. to the fencing-off of land]

rape⁴ /reɪp/ *n.* **1** the refuse of grapes after wine-making, used in making vinegar. **2** a vessel used in vinegar-making. [F *râpe*, med.L *raspa*]

Raphael¹ /'ræfeɪ(ə)l/ one of the seven archangels enumerated in the Book of Enoch. He is said to have 'healed' the earth when it was defiled by the sins of the fallen angels. [Heb., = God has healed]

Raphael² /'ræfeɪ(ə)l/ Raffaello Sanzio (1483–1520), Italian painter whose refined elegant style epitomizes the humanistic spirit of the High Renaissance, influenced by Perugino, Leonardo da Vinci, and Michelangelo. By the age of 25 his reputation was sufficiently established for him to be entrusted with frescos for one of the papal rooms in the Vatican, and in 1514 he was appointed as chief architect of St Peter's. Raphael's numerous versions of the Virgin and Child show a serenity of expression and sense of deep inner integrity; in Rome (probably in 1512) he painted his greatest altarpiece, the *Sistine Madonna*, where Mother and Child appear among the clouds, still triumphantly and splendidly human but transcending the earthly conditions in which he had earlier represented them. His influence was widely spread: he became 'the divine painter', the model of all academies, and through a long tradition his forms and motifs have been used with a steady diminution of their values. In much 20th-c. criticism his naturalism and religious feeling have been at a discount, but his place is secure: in the technical ability to render rounded forms on a two-dimensional surface he remains an unrivalled executant, and he used his great formal sensibility to create memorable symbols of the traditional doctrines of the Christian Church. As well as his frescoes and oil paintings Raphael produced designs for tapestries, mosaics, and architectural projects, including a survey of ancient Rome. His important achievements as an architect, undertaken in later life, should not be underrated, and the elegant classicism of a building such as the Villa Madama has been no less influential on future generations than his painting. Raphael died in Rome in 1520, aged only 37 and at the height of his powers.

raphia var. of RAFFIA.

raphide /'reɪfaɪd/ *n.* a needle-shaped crystal of an irritant substance such as oxalic acid formed in a plant. [back-form. f. *raphides* pl. of *raphis* f. Gk *rhaphis -idos* needle]

rapid /'ræpɪd/ *adj. & n.* —*adj.* (**rapider, rapidest**) **1** quick, swift. **2** acting or completed in a short time. **3** (of a slope) descending steeply. **4** *Photog.* fast. —*n.* (usu. in *pl.*) a steep descent in a river-bed, with a swift current. □ **rapid eye-movement** a type of jerky movement of the eyes beneath closed eyelids during sleep, associated with periods of dreaming. **rapid-fire** (*attrib.*) fired, asked, etc., in quick succession. **rapid transit** (*attrib.*) denoting high-speed urban transport of passengers. □□ **rapidity** /rə'pɪdɪtɪ/ *n.* **rapidly** *adv.* **rapidness** *n.* [L *rapidus* f. *rapere* seize]

rapier /'reɪpɪə(r)/ *n.* a light slender sword used for thrusting. [prob. f. Du. *rapier* or LG *rappir*, f. F *rapière*, of unkn. orig.]

rapine /'ræpaɪn/ *n. rhet.* plundering, robbery. [ME f. OF or f. L *rapina* f. *rapere* seize]

rapist /'reɪpɪst/ *n.* a person who commits rape.

rapparee /,ræpə'riː/ *n. hist.* a 17th-c. Irish irregular soldier or freebooter. [Ir. *rapaire* short pike]

rappee /ræ'piː/ *n.* a coarse kind of snuff. [F (*tabac*) *râpé* rasped (tobacco)]

rappel /ræ'pel/ *n. & v.intr.* (**rappelled, rappelling**; *US* **rappeled, rappeling**) = ABSEIL. [F, = recall, f. *rappeler* (as RE-, APPEAL)]

rapport /ræ'pɔː(r)/ *n.* **1** relationship or communication, esp. when useful and harmonious (*in rapport with; establish a rapport*). **2** *Spiritualism* communication through a medium. [F f. *rapporter* (as RE-, AP-, *porter* f. L *portare* carry)]

rapporteur /,ræpɔː'tɜː(r)/ *n.* a person who prepares an account of the proceedings of a committee etc. for a higher body. [F (as RAPPORT)]

rapprochement /ræ'prɒʃmɑ̃/ *n.* the resumption of harmonious relations, esp. between States. [F f. *rapprocher* (as RE-, APPROACH)]

rapscallion /ræp'skæljən/ *n. archaic* or *joc.* a rascal, scamp, or rogue. [earlier *rascallion*, perh. f. RASCAL]

rapt /ræpt/ *adj.* **1** fully absorbed or intent, enraptured (*listen with rapt attention*). **2** carried away with feeling or lofty thought. **3** carried away bodily. □□ **raptly** *adv.* **raptness** *n.* [ME f. L *raptus* past part. of *rapere* seize]

raptor /'ræptə(r)/ *n.* any bird of prey, e.g. an owl, falcon, etc. [L, = ravisher, plunderer f. *rapere rapt-* seize]

raptorial /ræp'tɔːrɪəl/ *adj. & n.* —*adj.* (of a bird or animal) adapted for seizing prey; predatory. —*n.* **1** = RAPTOR. **2** a predatory animal. [L *raptor:* see RAPTOR]

rapture /'ræptʃə(r)/ *n.* **1 a** ecstatic delight, mental transport. **b** (in *pl.*) great pleasure or enthusiasm or the expression of it. **2** *archaic* the act of transporting a person from one place to another. □ **go into** (or **be in**) **raptures** be enthusiastic; talk enthusiastically. □□ **rapturous** *adj.* **rapturously** *adv.* **rapturousness** *n.* [obs. F *rapture* or med.L *raptura* (as RAPT)]

rara avis /,reərə 'eɪvɪs, ,rɑːrə 'ævɪs/ *n.* (pl. *rarae aves* /-rɪ -viːz/) a rarity; a kind of person or thing rarely encountered. [L, = rare bird]

rare¹ /reə(r)/ *adj.* (**rarer, rarest**) **1** seldom done or found or occurring, uncommon, unusual, few and far between. **2** exceptionally good (*had a rare time*). **3** of less than the usual density, with only loosely packed substance (*the rare atmosphere of the mountain tops*). □ **rare bird** = RARA AVIS. **rare earth** see separate entry. **rare gas** = *noble gas*. □□ **rareness** *n.* [ME f. L *rarus*]

rare² /reə(r)/ *adj.* (**rarer, rarest**) (of meat) underdone. [var. of obs. *rear* half-cooked (of eggs), f. OE *hrēr*]

rarebit /'reəbɪt/ *n.* = *Welsh rabbit*. [RARE¹ + BIT¹]

rare earth *n.* any of a class of 17 chemically similar metallic elements or their oxides, including scandium, yttrium, and the lanthanides (the term is sometimes applied to the lanthanides alone). These elements are not in fact 'rare' compared with many better-known metals, but they tend to occur together in nature and are difficult to separate from one another. It took over a century for all the elements to be identified after the oxide of the first, yttrium, was isolated in 1794. Nowadays mixtures of rare earths, as well as purified individual elements, have a wide variety of specialized uses, notably as industrial catalysts and in alloys.

raree-show /ˈreərɪˌʃəʊ/ n. **1** a show or spectacle. **2** a show carried about in a box; a peep-show. [app. = *rare show* as pronounced by Savoyard showmen]

rarefy /ˈreərɪˌfaɪ/ v. (-ies, -ied) **1** tr. & intr. make or become less dense or solid (*rarefied air*). **2** tr. purify or refine (a person's nature etc.). **3** tr. make (an idea etc.) subtle. □□ **rarefaction** /-ˈfækʃ(ə)n/ n. **rarefactive** /-ˈfæktɪv/ adj. **rarefication** /-fɪˈkeɪʃ(ə)n/ n. [ME f. OF *rarefier* or med.L *rarificare* f. L *rarefacere* f. *rarus* rare + *facere* make]

rarely /ˈreəlɪ/ adv. **1** seldom; not often. **2** in an unusual degree; exceptionally. **3** exceptionally well.

raring /ˈreərɪŋ/ adj. (foll. by *to* + infin.) colloq. enthusiastic, eager (*raring to go*). [part. of rare, dial. var. of ROAR or REAR²]

rarity /ˈreərɪtɪ/ n. (pl. -ies) **1** rareness. **2** an uncommon thing, esp. one valued for being rare. [F *rareté* or L *raritas* (as RARE¹)]

Ras al Khaimah /ˈrɑːs æl ˈkaɪmə/ **1** one of the seven member states of the United Arab Emirates; pop. (1980) 116,470. **2** its capital city (Port Saqr); pop. (1980) 73,880.

rascal /ˈrɑːsk(ə)l/ n. often joc. a dishonest or mischievous person, esp. a child. □□ **rascaldom** n. **rascalism** n. **rascality** /-ˈskælɪtɪ/ n. (pl. -ies). **rascally** adj. [ME f. OF *rascaille* rabble, prob. ult. f. L *radere ras-* scrape]

rase var. of RAZE.

rash¹ /ræʃ/ adj. reckless, impetuous, hasty; acting or done without due consideration. □□ **rashly** adv. **rashness** n. [ME, prob. f. OE *ræsc* (unrecorded) f. Gmc]

rash² /ræʃ/ n. **1** an eruption of the skin in spots or patches. **2** (usu. foll. by *of*) a sudden widespread phenomenon, esp. of something unwelcome (*a rash of strikes*). [18th c.: prob. rel. to OF *ra(s)che* eruptive sores, = It. *raschia* itch]

rasher /ˈræʃə(r)/ n. a thin slice of bacon or ham. [16th c.: orig. unkn.]

rasp /rɑːsp/ n. & v. —n. a coarse kind of file having separate teeth. —v. **1** tr. **a** scrape with a rasp. **b** scrape roughly. **c** (foll. by *off*, *away*) remove by scraping. **2** a intr. make a grating sound. **b** tr. say gratingly or hoarsely. **3** tr. grate upon (a person or a person's feelings), irritate. □□ **raspingly** adv. **raspy** adj. [ME f. OF *raspe(r)* ult. f. WG]

raspberry /ˈrɑːzbərɪ/ n. (pl. -ies) **1 a** a bramble, *Rubus idaeus*, having usu. red berries consisting of numerous drupels on a conical receptacle. **b** this berry. **2** any of various red colours. **3** colloq. **a** a sound made with the lips expressing dislike, derision, or disapproval (orig. *raspberry tart*, rhyming sl. = *fart*). **b** a show of strong disapproval (*got a raspberry from the audience*). □ **raspberry-cane** a raspberry plant. **raspberry vinegar** a kind of syrup made from raspberries. [16th-c. *rasp* (now dial.) f. obs. *raspis*, of unkn. orig., + BERRY]

rasper /ˈrɑːspə(r)/ n. **1** a person or thing that rasps. **2** Hunting a high difficult fence.

Rasputin /ræsˈpuːtɪn/, Grigori Efimovich (1871–1916), Russian religious fanatic who came to exert great influence over Tsar Nicholas II and his family during the First World War by claiming miraculous powers to heal the heir to the throne, who suffered from haemophilia. A libertine and mystic, Rasputin was responsible in a large measure for the Tsar's failure to respond to the rising tide of discontent which eventually resulted in the Russian Revolution. He was murdered by a group of nobles.

Rasta /ˈræstə/ n. & adj. = RASTAFARIAN. [abbr.]

Rastafarian /ˌræstəˈfeərɪən/ n. & adj. —n. a member of the Rastafari sect, of Jamaican origin, which believes that Blacks are the chosen people, that the late Emperor Haile Selassie of Ethiopia was God Incarnate, and that he will secure their repatriation to their homeland in Africa. —adj. of or relating to this sect. □□ **Rastafarianism** n. [the title and name *Ras Tafari* (Amharic, *ras* chief) by which Haile Selassie was known from 1916 until his accession in 1930]

raster /ˈræstə(r)/ n. a pattern of scanning lines for a cathode-ray tube picture. [G, = screen, f. L *rastrum* rake f. *radere ras-* scrape]

rat /ræt/ n. & v. —n. **1 a** any of several rodents of the genus *Rattus* (*brown rat*). **b** any similar rodent (*muskrat*; *water-rat*). **2 a** deserter from a party, cause, difficult situation, etc.; a turncoat (from the superstition that rats desert a sinking ship). **3** colloq. an unpleasant person. **4** a worker who refuses to join a strike, or who blacklegs. **5** (in pl.) sl. an exclamation of contempt, annoyance, etc. —v.intr. (**ratted**, **ratting**) **1** (of a person or dog) hunt or kill rats. **2** colloq. desert a cause, party, etc. **3** (foll. by *on*) **a** betray; let down. **b** inform on. □ **rat-catcher** a person who rids buildings of rats etc. **rat kangaroo** Austral. any of various small ratlike marsupials of the family Potoroidae, having kangaroo-like hind limbs for jumping. **rat race** a fiercely competitive struggle for position, power, etc. **rat's tail** a thing shaped like a rat's tail, e.g. a tapering cylindrical file. **rat-tail 1** the grenadier fish. **2** a horse with a hairless tail. **3** such a tail. **rat-tail** (or **-tailed**) **spoon** a spoon with a tail-like moulding from the handle to the back of the bowl. [OE *ræt* & OF *rat*]

rata /ˈrɑːtə/ n. any large tree of the genus *Metrosideros*, esp. M. *robusta* of New Zealand, with crimson flowers and hard red wood. [Maori]

ratable var. of RATEABLE.

ratafia /ˌrætəˈfiːə/ n. **1** a liqueur flavoured with almonds or kernels of peach, apricot, or cherry. **2** a kind of biscuit similarly flavoured. [F, perh. rel. to TAFIA]

ratan var. of RATTAN.

Ratana /ˈrɑːtənə/, Tahupotiki Wiremu (1870–1939), Maori political and religious leader. He attacked the traditional fears of the power of the spirit-world and sorcery and sought to introduce a heterodox belief in the Christian Trinity. Politically he sought advancement of Maori rights through recognition of the Treaty of Waitangi. Both the religious and the political aspects of this movement survived Ratana's death.

rataplan /ˌrætəˈplæn/ n. & v. —n. a drumming sound. —v. (**rataplanned**, **rataplanning**) **1** tr. play (a tune) on or as on a drum. **2** intr. make a rataplan. [F: imit.]

ratatat (also **rat-a-tat**) var. of RAT-TAT.

ratatouille /ˌrætəˈtuːɪ, -ˈtwiː/ n. a vegetable dish made of stewed onions, courgettes, tomatoes, aubergines, and peppers. [F dial.]

ratbag /ˈrætbæg/ n. sl. an unpleasant or disgusting person.

ratch /rætʃ/ n. **1** a ratchet. **2** a ratchet-wheel. [perh. f. G *Ratsche*: cf. RATCHET]

ratchet /ˈrætʃɪt/ n. & v. —n. **1** a set of teeth on the edge of a bar or wheel in which a device engages to ensure motion in one direction only. **2** (in full **ratchet-wheel**) a wheel with a rim so toothed. —v. (**ratcheted**, **ratcheting**) **1** tr. **a** provide with a ratchet. **b** make into a ratchet. **2** tr. & intr. move as under the control of a ratchet. [F *rochet* blunt lance-head, bobbin, ratchet, etc., prob. ult. f. Gmc]

rate¹ /reɪt/ n. & v. —n. **1** a stated numerical proportion between two sets of things (the second usu. expressed as unity), esp. as a measure of amount or degree (*moving at a rate of 50 miles per hour*) or as the basis of calculating an amount or value (*rate of taxation*). **2** a fixed or appropriate charge or cost or value; a measure of this (*postal rates; the rate for the job*). **3** rapidity of movement or change (*travelling at a great rate; prices increasing at a dreadful rate*). **4** class or rank (*first-rate*). **5** Brit. **a** an assessment levied by local authorities at so much per pound of the assessed value of buildings and land owned or leased. **b** (in pl.) the amount payable by this. Liability to rates originated in the Poor Relief Act of 1801. Domestic rates were replaced in 1989–90 by the *community charge*. —v. **1** tr. **a** estimate the worth or value of (*I do not rate him very highly*). **b** assign a fixed value to (a coin or metal) in relation to a monetary standard. **c** assign a value to (work, the power of a machine, etc.) **2** tr. consider; regard as (*I rate them among my benefactors*). **3** intr. (foll. by *as*) rank or be rated. **4** tr. Brit. **a** subject to the payment of a local rate. **b** value for the purpose of assessing rates. **5** tr. be worthy of, deserve. **6** tr. Naut. place in a specified class (cf. RATING¹). □ **at any rate** in any case, whatever happens. **at this** (or **that**) **rate** if this example is typical or this assumption is true. **rate-capping**

Brit. the imposition of an upper limit on the rate leviable by a local authority. [ME f. OF f. med.L *rata* f. L *pro rata parte* or *portione* according to the proportional share f. *ratus* past part. of *rēri* reckon]

rate² /reɪt/ v.tr. scold angrily. [ME: orig. unkn.]

rate³ var. of RET.

rateable /ˈreɪtəb(ə)l/ adj. (also **ratable**) 1 *Brit.* liable to payment of rates. 2 able to be rated or estimated. □ **rateable value** the value at which a house etc. is assessed for payment of rates. □□ **rateability** /-ˈbɪlɪtɪ/ n. **rateably** adv.

ratel /ˈreɪt(ə)l, ˈrɑː-/ n. an African and Indian nocturnal flesh-eating burrowing mammal, *Mellivora capensis*. Also called *honey-badger*. [Afrik., of unkn. orig.]

ratepayer /ˈreɪtˌpeɪə(r)/ n. *Brit.* a person liable to pay rates.

rathe /reɪð/ adj. *poet.* coming, blooming, etc., early in the year or day. □ **rathe-ripe** 1 ripening early. 2 precocious. [OE *hræth*, *hræd* f. Gmc]

rather /ˈrɑːðə(r)/ adv. 1 (often foll. by *than*) by preference; for choice (*would rather not go; would rather stay than go*). 2 (usu. foll. by *than*) more truly; as a more likely alternative (*is stupid rather than honest*). 3 more precisely (*a book, or rather, a pamphlet*). 4 slightly; to some extent; somewhat (*became rather drunk; I rather think you know him*). 5 /rɑːˈðə(r)/ *Brit.* (as an emphatic response) indeed, assuredly (*Did you like it?—Rather!*). □ **had rather** would rather. [ME f. OE *hrathor*, compar. of *hræthe* (adv.) f. *hræth* (adj.): see RATHE]

Rathlin Island /ˈræθlɪn/ an island off the north coast of Antrim, Northern Ireland.

rathskeller /ˈrɑːtsˌkelə(r)/ n. *US* a beer-saloon or restaurant in a basement. [G, = (restaurant in) town-hall cellar]

ratify /ˈrætɪˌfaɪ/ v.tr. (**-ies, -ied**) confirm or accept (an agreement made in one's name) by formal consent, signature, etc. □□ **ratifiable** adj. **ratification** /-fɪˈkeɪʃ(ə)n/ n. **ratifier** n. [ME f. OF *ratifier* f. med.L *ratificare* (as RATE¹)]

rating¹ /ˈreɪtɪŋ/ n. 1 the act or an instance of placing in a rank or class or assigning a value to. 2 the estimated standing of a person as regards credit etc. 3 *Naut.* **a** *Brit.* a non-commissioned sailor. **b** a person's position or class on a ship's books. 4 *Brit.* an amount fixed as a local rate. 5 the relative popularity of a broadcast programme as determined by the estimated size of the audience. 6 *Naut.* any of the classes into which racing yachts are distributed by tonnage.

rating² /ˈreɪtɪŋ/ n. an angry reprimand.

ratio /ˈreɪʃɪəʊ/ n. (pl. **-os**) the quantitative relation between two similar magnitudes determined by the number of times one contains the other integrally or fractionally (*in the ratio of three to two; the ratios 1:5 and 20:100 are the same*). [L (as RATE¹)]

ratiocinate /ˌrætɪˈɒsɪˌneɪt, ˌræʃɪ-/ v.intr. *literary* go through logical processes, reason, esp. using syllogisms. □□ **ratiocination** /-ˈneɪʃ(ə)n/ n. **ratiocinative** /-nətɪv/ adj. **ratiocinator** n. [L *ratiocinari* (as RATIO)]

ration /ˈræʃ(ə)n/ n. & v. —n. 1 a fixed official allowance of food, clothing, etc., in a time of shortage. 2 (foll. by *of*) a single portion of provisions, fuel, clothing, etc. 3 (usu. in *pl.*) a fixed daily allowance of food, esp. in the armed forces (and formerly of forage for animals). 4 (in *pl.*) provisions. —v.tr. 1 limit (persons or provisions) to a fixed ration. 2 (usu. foll. by *out*) share out (food etc.) in fixed quantities. □ **given out with the rations** *Mil. sl.* awarded without regard to merit. **ration book** (or **card**) a document entitling the holder to a ration. [F f. It. *razione* or Sp. *ración* f. L *ratio -onis* reckoning, RATIO]

rational /ˈræʃən(ə)l/ adj. 1 of or based on reasoning or reason. 2 sensible, sane, moderate; not foolish or absurd or extreme. 3 endowed with reason, reasoning. 4 rejecting what is unreasonable or cannot be tested by reason in religion or custom. 5 *Math.* (of a quantity or ratio) expressible as a ratio of whole numbers. □ **rational dress** *hist.* a style of dress adopted by some women in the late 19th c., including bloomers or knickerbockers. **rational horizon** see HORIZON 1c. □□ **rationality** /-ˈnælɪtɪ/ n. **rationally** adv. [ME f. L *rationalis* (as RATION)]

rationale /ˌræʃəˈnɑːl/ n. 1 (often foll. by *of*) the fundamental reason or logical basis of anything. 2 a reasoned exposition; a statement of reasons. [mod.L, neut. of L *rationalis*: see RATIONAL]

rationalism /ˈræʃənəˌlɪz(ə)m/ n. 1 *Philos.* the theory that reason is the foundation of certainty in knowledge (opp. EMPIRICISM (see EMPIRIC), SENSATIONALISM). 2 *Theol.* the practice of treating reason as the ultimate authority in religion. 3 a belief in reason rather than religion as a guiding principle in life. □□ **rationalist** n. **rationalistic** /-ˈlɪstɪk/ adj. **rationalistically** /-ˈlɪstɪkəlɪ/ adv.

rationalize /ˈræʃənəˌlaɪz/ v. (also **-ise**) 1 **a** tr. offer or subconsciously adopt a rational but specious explanation of (one's behaviour or attitude). **b** intr. explain one's behaviour or attitude in this way. 2 tr. make logical and consistent. 3 tr. make (a business etc.) more efficient by reorganizing it to reduce or eliminate waste of labour, time, or materials. 4 tr. (often foll. by *away*) explain or explain away rationally. 5 tr. *Math.* clear of surds. 6 intr. be or act as a rationalist. □□ **rationalization** /-ˈzeɪʃ(ə)n/ n. **rationalizer** n.

ratite /ˈrætaɪt/ adj. & n. —adj. (of a bird) having a keelless breastbone, and unable to fly (opp. CARINATE). —n. a flightless bird, e.g. an ostrich, emu, cassowary, etc. [L *ratis* raft]

ratline /ˈrætlɪn/ n. (also **ratlin**) (usu. in *pl.*) any of the small lines fastened across a sailing-ship's shrouds like ladder-rungs. [ME: orig. unkn.]

ratoon /rəˈtuːn/ n. & v. —n. a new shoot springing from a root of sugar cane etc. after cropping. —v.intr. send up ratoons. [Sp. *retoño* sprout]

ratsbane /ˈrætsbeɪn/ n. anything poisonous to rats, esp. a plant.

rattan /rəˈtæn/ n. (also **ratan**) 1 any East Indian climbing palm of the genus *Calamus* etc. with long thin jointed pliable stems. 2 a piece of rattan stem used as a walking stick etc. [earlier *rot(t)ang* f. Malay *rōtan* prob. f. *raut* pare]

rat-tat /rætˈtæt/ n. (also **rat-tat-tat** /ˌrættætˈtæt/, **ratatat**, **rat-a-tat** /ˌrætəˈtæt/) a rapping sound, esp. of a knocker. [imit.]

ratter /ˈrætə(r)/ n. 1 a dog or other animal that hunts rats. 2 *sl.* a person who betrays a cause, party, friend, etc.

Rattigan /ˈrætɪgən/, Sir Terence Marvyn (1911–77), English dramatist. His first West End success, the comedy *French Without Tears* (1936), was followed by many other works, including *The Winslow Boy* (1946), *The Browning Version* (1948), and *Ross* (1960), which was based on the life of T. E. Lawrence. In the 1950s and 1960s there was a reaction against the middle-class middlebrow nature of his plays, but later they were again in favour and are still performed.

rattle /ˈræt(ə)l/ v. & n. —v. 1 **a** intr. give out a rapid succession of short sharp hard sounds. **b** tr. make (a chair, window, crockery, etc.) do this. **c** intr. cause such sounds by shaking something (*rattled at the door*). 2 **a** intr. move with a rattling noise. **b** intr. drive a vehicle or ride or run briskly. **c** tr. cause to move quickly (*the bill was rattled through Parliament*). 3 **a** tr. (usu. foll. by *off*) say or recite rapidly. **b** intr. (usu. foll. by *on*) talk in a lively thoughtless way. 4 tr. *colloq.* disconcert, alarm, fluster, make nervous, frighten. —n. 1 a rattling sound. 2 an instrument or plaything made to rattle esp. in order to amuse babies or to give an alarm. 3 the set of horny rings in a rattlesnake's tail. 4 a plant with seeds that rattle in their cases when ripe (*red rattle; yellow rattle*). 5 uproar, bustle, noisy gaiety, racket. 6 **a** a noisy flow of words. **b** empty chatter, trivial talk. 7 *archaic* a lively or thoughtless incessant talker. □ **rattle the sabre** threaten war. □□ **rattly** adj. [ME, prob. f. MDu. & LG *ratelen* (imit.)]

rattlebox /ˈræt(ə)lˌbɒks/ n. 1 a rattle consisting of a box with objects inside. 2 a rickety old vehicle etc.

rattler /ˈrætlə(r)/ n. 1 a thing that rattles, esp. an old or rickety vehicle. 2 *colloq.* a rattlesnake. 3 *sl.* a remarkably good specimen of anything.

rattlesnake /ˈræt(ə)lˌsneɪk/ n. any of various poisonous American snakes of the family Viperidae, esp. of the genus *Crotalus* or *Sistrurus*, with a rattling structure of horny rings in its tail.

rattletrap /ˈræt(ə)lˌtræp/ n. & adj. *colloq.* —n. a rickety old vehicle etc. —adj. rickety.

rattling /ˈrætlɪŋ/ adj. & adv. —adj. 1 that rattles. 2 brisk,

ratty /'rætɪ/ adj. (**rattier, rattiest**) 1 relating to or infested with rats. 2 colloq. irritable or angry. 3 colloq. wretched, nasty. □□ **rattily** adv. **rattiness** n.

raucous /'rɔːkəs/ adj. harsh-sounding, loud and hoarse. □□ **raucously** adv. **raucousness** n. [L raucus]

raunchy /'rɔːntʃɪ/ adj. (**raunchier, raunchiest**) colloq. 1 coarse, earthy, boisterous; sexually provocative. 2 esp. US slovenly, grubby. □□ **raunchily** adv. **raunchiness** n. [20th c.: orig. unkn.]

ravage /'rævɪdʒ/ v. & n. —v.tr. & intr. devastate, plunder. —n. 1 the act or an instance of ravaging; devastation, damage. 2 (usu. in pl.; foll. by of) destructive effect (survived the ravages of winter). □□ **ravager** n. [F ravage(r) alt. f. ravine rush of water]

rave[1] /reɪv/ v. & n. —v. 1 intr. talk wildly or furiously in or as in delirium. 2 intr. (usu. foll. by about, of, over) speak with rapturous admiration; go into raptures. 3 tr. bring into a specified state by raving (raved himself hoarse). 4 tr. utter with ravings (raved their grief). 5 intr. (of the sea, wind, etc.) howl, roar. 6 tr. & intr. colloq. enjoy oneself freely (esp. rave it up). —n. 1 (usu. attrib.) colloq. a highly enthusiastic review of a film, play, etc. (a rave review). 2 sl. an infatuation. 3 (also **rave-up**) colloq. a lively party. 4 the sound of the wind etc. raving. [ME, prob. f. ONF raver, rel. to (M)LG reven be senseless, rave]

rave[2] /reɪv/ n. 1 a rail of a cart. 2 (in pl.) a permanent or removable framework added to the sides of a cart to increase its capacity. [var. of dial. rathe (15th c., of unkn. orig.)]

Ravel /ræ'vel/, Maurice (1875–1937), French composer. The best-known of Debussy's contemporaries, he was equally influenced by the Oriental music brought to Paris in the 1889 World Exhibition and by impressionism, but combined his love of apt descriptive sonorities with a cool classicism and a recognition of Liszt's legacy of brilliance and vigour. His works span all genres: opera, ballet, orchestral music, and song. Among his later works were the two great piano concertos (both 1931); the first is for left hand only, composed for Paul Wittgenstein who lost his right arm in the First World War.

ravel /'ræv(ə)l/ v. & n. —v. (**ravelled, ravelling**; US **raveled, raveling**) 1 tr. & intr. entangle or become entangled or knotted. 2 tr. confuse or complicate (a question or problem). 3 intr. fray out. 4 tr. (often foll. by out) disentangle, unravel, distinguish the separate threads or subdivisions of. —n. 1 a tangle or knot. 2 a complication. 3 a frayed or loose end. [prob. f. Du. ravelen tangle, fray out, unweave]

ravelin /'rævlɪn/ n. hist. an outwork of fortifications, with two faces forming a salient angle. [F f. obs. It. ravellino, of unkn. orig.]

ravelling /'rævəlɪŋ/ n. a thread from fabric which is frayed or unravelled.

raven[1] /'reɪv(ə)n/ n. & adj. —n. a large glossy blue-black crow, Corvus corax, feeding chiefly on carrion etc., having a hoarse cry. —adj. glossy black (raven tresses). [OE hræfn f. Gmc]

raven[2] /'ræv(ə)n/ v. 1 intr. a plunder. b (foll. by after) seek prey or booty. c (foll. by about) go plundering. d prowl for prey (ravening beast). 2 a tr. devour voraciously. b intr. (usu. foll. by for) have a ravenous appetite. c intr. (often foll. by on) feed voraciously. [OF raviner ravage ult. f. L rapina RAPINE]

Ravenna /rə'venə/ a city near the Adriatic coast in NE central Italy; pop. (1981) 138,030. An important centre in Roman times, Ravenna became the capital of the Ostrogothic kingdom of Italy in the 5th c. and afterwards served as capital of the Byzantine Empire of Italy. The richest mosaics of the early Christian period are found there. It became an independent republic in the 13th c. and then a papal possession in 1509, remaining in papal hands until 1859.

ravenous /'rævənəs/ adj. 1 very hungry, famished. 2 (of hunger, eagerness, etc., or of an animal) voracious. 3 rapacious. □□ **ravenously** adv. **ravenousness** n. [ME f. OF ravineus (as RAVEN[2])]

raver /'reɪvə(r)/ n. 1 colloq. an uninhibited pleasure-loving person. 2 a person who raves; a madman or madwoman.

Ravi /'rɑːvi/ a river that rises in the Himalayas in northern India and flows south-west into Pakistan, where it meets the Chenab River. It is one of the 'five rivers' that gave Punjab its name.

ravin /'rævɪn/ n. poet. or rhet. 1 robbery, plundering. 2 the seizing and devouring of prey. 3 prey. □ **beast of ravin** a beast of prey. [ME f. OF ravine f. L rapina RAPINE]

ravine /rə'viːn/ n. a deep narrow gorge or cleft. □□ **ravined** adj. [F (as RAVIN)]

raving /'reɪvɪŋ/ n., adj., & adv. —n. (usu. in pl.) wild or delirious talk. —adj. delirious, frenzied. —adj. & adv. colloq. as an intensive (a raving beauty; raving mad). □□ **ravingly** adv.

ravioli /ˌrævɪ'əʊlɪ/ n. small pasta envelopes containing minced meat etc. [It.]

ravish /'rævɪʃ/ v.tr. 1 commit rape on (a woman). 2 enrapture; fill with delight. 3 archaic a carry off (a person or thing) by force. b (of death, circumstances, etc.) take from life or from sight. □□ **ravisher** n. **ravishment** n. [ME f. OF ravir ult. f. L rapere seize]

ravishing /'rævɪʃɪŋ/ adj. entrancing, delightful. □□ **ravishingly** adv.

raw /rɔː/ adj. & n. —adj. 1 (of food) uncooked. 2 in the natural state; not processed or manufactured (raw sewage). 3 (of alcoholic spirit) undiluted. 4 (of statistics etc.) not analysed or processed. 5 (of a person) inexperienced, untrained; new to an activity (raw recruits). 6 a stripped of skin; having the flesh exposed. b sensitive to the touch from having the flesh exposed. 7 (of the atmosphere, day, etc.) chilly and damp. 8 crude in artistic quality; lacking finish. 9 (of the edge of cloth) without hem or selvage. 10 (of silk) as reeled from cocoons. 11 (of grain) unmalted. —n. a raw place on a person's or horse's body. □ **come the raw prawn** Austral. sl. attempt to deceive. **in the raw** 1 in its natural state without mitigation (life in the raw). 2 naked. **raw-boned** gaunt and bony. **raw deal** harsh or unfair treatment. **raw material** that from which the process of manufacture makes products. **raw sienna** a brownish-yellow ferruginous earth used as a pigment. **raw umber** umber in its natural state, dark yellow in colour. **touch on the raw** upset (a person) on a sensitive matter. □□ **rawish** adj. **rawly** adv. **rawness** n. [OE hrēaw f. Gmc]

Rawalpindi /rɔːl'pɪndɪ/ a city in northern Pakistan, in the foothills of the Himalayas; pop. (1981) 928,000. A former military station, it was the interim capital of Pakistan 1959–67 while Islamabad was being built.

rawhide /'rɔːhaɪd/ n. 1 untanned hide. 2 a rope or whip of this.

Rawlplug /'rɔːlplʌg/ n. propr. a thin cylindrical plug for holding a screw or nail in masonry. [Rawlings, name of the engineers who introduced it]

Rawls /rɔːlz/, John (1921–), American philosopher, author of A Theory of Justice (1972) which presents a systematic moral theory in opposition to utilitarianism. The central claim of the book is that a system is just if and only if it accords with the principles which would be agreed upon by rational people making a kind of social contract. Rawls argues for principles which give weight to basic liberties and improvement for the worst off, in preference to any form of utilitarianism.

Rawson /'rɔːs(ə)n/ a city of southern Argentina, on the Patagonian coast, capital of Chubut province; pop. (1980) 13,000.

Ray[1] /reɪ/, John (1627–1705), English naturalist who developed early systematic classifications of plants and animals. His principal interest was botany, and his major work, the Historia Plantarum, appeared in three volumes between 1686 and 1704. Ray toured Europe in search of specimens. He was the first to classify flowering plants into monocotyledons and dicotyledons, and he established the species as a basic taxonomic unit.

Ray[2] /reɪ/, Man (1890–1976), American painter, designer, and photographer, a prominent figure in the Dada and surrealist movements and a friend of Duchamp. He developed the photographic technique of placing objects directly on sensitized paper and exposing them to light; translucent objects in particular produced striking results. His real name may have been Emanuel Rabinovitch or Rudnitsky; the origin of his pseudonym is unknown.

Ray[3] /riː/, Satyajit (1921–), Indian film director, who won an award for his first film Pather Panchali (On the Road, 1955), which was made in his spare time and with very limited resources, then completed the trilogy with Aparijito (The Unvanquished, 1956) and *Apur Sansar* (*The World of Apur*, 1959). His other films include *Kanchenjunga* (1962), *Days and Nights in the Forest* (1977) and *The Home and the World* (1984). His films have a sensitivity towards eastern and western values that assures him of an audience in both cultures. Music was an important element, and he composed background music himself.

ray[1] /reɪ/ *n. & v.* —*n.* **1** a single line or narrow beam of light from a small or distant source. **2** a straight line in which radiation travels to a given point. **3** (in *pl.*) radiation of a specified type (*gamma rays; X-rays*). **4** a trace or beginning of an enlightening or cheering influence (*a ray of hope*). **5 a** any of a set of radiating lines or parts or things. **b** any of a set of straight lines passing through one point. **6** the marginal portion of a composite flower, e.g. a daisy. **7 a** a radial division of a starfish. **b** each of a set of bones etc. supporting a fish's fin. —*v.* **1** *intr.* (foll. by *forth, out*) (of light, thought, emotion, etc.) issue in or as if in rays. **2** *intr. & tr.* radiate. □ **ray gun** (esp. in science fiction) a gun causing injury or damage by the emission of rays. □□ **rayed** *adj.* **rayless** *adj.* **raylet** *n.* [ME f. OF *rai* f. L *radius*: see RADIUS]

ray[2] /reɪ/ *n.* a large cartilaginous fish of the order Batoidea, with a broad flat body, winglike pectoral fins and a long slender tail, used as food. [ME f. OF *raie* f. L *raia*]

ray[3] /reɪ/ *n.* (also **re**) *Mus.* **1** (in tonic sol-fa) the second note of a major scale. **2** the note D in the fixed-doh system. [ME *re* f. L *resonare*: see GAMUT]

Rayleigh /ˈreɪlɪ/, John William Strutt, 3rd Baron (1842–1919), English physicist who made significant contributions to several branches of the science. In 1877–8 he published a major work on acoustics, *The Theory of Sound*. He studied the scattering of light by small particles, thereby explaining why the sky is blue. In 1879–84 he was director of the Cavendish Laboratory at Cambridge, succeeding James Clerk Maxwell. His researches included the establishment of electrical units of resistance, current, and electromotive force. A brilliant and successful experimentalist, he worked with Sir William Ramsay from 1894, and their accurate measurement of the constituent gases of the atmosphere led to the discovery of argon and other inert gases. In 1904 Rayleigh was awarded the Nobel Prize for physics and Ramsay that for chemistry.

rayon /ˈreɪɒn/ *n.* any of various textile fibres or fabrics made from cellulose. [arbitrary f. RAY[1]]

raze /reɪz/ *v.tr.* (also **rase**) **1** completely destroy; tear down (esp. *raze to the ground*). **2** erase; scratch out (esp. in abstract senses). [ME *rase* = wound slightly f. OF *raser* shave close ult. f. L *radere* *ras-* scrape]

razor /ˈreɪzə(r)/ *n. & v.* —*n.* an instrument with a sharp blade used in cutting hair esp. from the skin. —*v.tr.* **1** use a razor on. **2** shave; cut down close. □ **razor-back** an animal with a sharp ridged back, esp. a rorqual. **razor-bill** an auk, *Alca torda*, with a sharp-edged bill. **razor-blade** a blade used in a razor, esp. a flat piece of metal with a sharp edge or edges used in a safety razor. **razor-cut** a haircut made with a razor. **razor-** (or **razor's**) **edge 1** a keen edge. **2** a sharp mountain-ridge. **3** a critical situation (*found themselves on a razor-edge*). **4** a sharp line of division. **razor-fish** (or **-shell**) any of various bivalve molluscs of the family Solenidae, with a shell like the handle of a cutthroat razor. [ME f. OF *rasor* (as RAZE)]

razz /ræz/ *n. & v. US sl.* —*n.* = RASPBERRY 3. —*v.tr.* tease, ridicule. [*razzberry*, corrupt. of RASPBERRY]

razzle-dazzle /ˈræzəlˌdæz(ə)l/ *n.* (also **razzle**) *sl.* **1 a** a glamorous excitement; bustle. **b** a spree. **2** extravagant publicity. [redupl. of DAZZLE]

razzmatazz /ˌræzməˈtæz/ *n.* (also **razzamatazz** /ˌræzəmə-/) *colloq.* **1** = RAZZLE-DAZZLE. **2** insincere actions; humbug. [prob. alt. f. RAZZLE-DAZZLE]

Rb *symb. Chem.* the element rubidium.

RC *abbr.* **1** Roman Catholic. **2** Red Cross. **3** reinforced concrete.

RCA *abbr.* **1** (in the UK) Royal College of Art. **2** (in the US) Radio Corporation of America.

RCAF *abbr.* Royal Canadian Air Force.

RCM *abbr.* (in the UK) Royal College of Music.

RCMP *abbr.* Royal Canadian Mounted Police.

RCN *abbr.* **1** (in the UK) Royal College of Nursing. **2** Royal Canadian Navy.

RCP *abbr.* (in the UK) Royal College of Physicians.

RCS *abbr.* (in the UK): **1** Royal College of Scientists. **2** Royal College of Surgeons. **3** Royal Corps of Signals.

RCVS *abbr.* (in the UK) Royal College of Veterinary Surgeons.

RD *abbr.* **1** refer to drawer. **2** (in the UK) Royal Naval Reserve Decoration.

Rd. *abbr.* Road (in names).

RDC *abbr. Brit. hist.* Rural District Council.

RDF *abbr.* radio direction-finder.

RE *abbr.* **1** (in the UK) Royal Engineers. **2** religious education.

Re[1] /reɪ/ var. of RA.

Re[2] *symb. Chem.* the element rhenium.

re[1] /reɪ, riː/ *prep.* **1** in the matter of (as the first word in a heading, esp. of a legal document). **2** *colloq.* about, concerning. [L, ablat. of *res* thing]

re[2] var. of RAY[3].

re- /riː, rɪ, re/ *prefix* **1** attachable to almost any verb or its derivative, meaning: **a** once more; afresh, anew (*readjust; renumber*). **b** back; with return to a previous state (*reassemble; reverse*). ¶ A hyphen is usually used when the word begins with *e* (*re-enact*), or to distinguish the compound from a more familiar one-word form (*re-form* = form again). **2** (also **red-** before a vowel, as in *redolent*) in verbs and verbal derivatives denoting: **a** in return; mutually (*react; resemble*). **b** opposition (*repel; resist*). **c** behind or after (*relic; remain*). **d** retirement or secrecy (*recluse; reticence*). **e** off, away, down (*recede; relegate; repress*). **f** frequentative or intensive force (*redouble; refine; resplendent*). **g** negative force (*recant; reveal*). [L re-, red-, again, back, etc.]

reabsorb /ˌriːəbˈsɔːb, -ˈzɔːb/ *v.tr.* absorb again. □□ **reabsorption** *n.*

reaccept /ˌriːəkˈsept/ *v.tr.* accept again. □□ **reacceptance** *n.*

reaccustom /ˌriːəˈkʌstəm/ *v.tr.* accustom again.

reach /riːtʃ/ *v. & n.* —*v.* **1** *intr. & tr.* (often foll. by *out*) stretch out; extend. **2** *intr.* stretch out a limb, the hand, etc.; make a reaching motion or effort. **3** *intr.* (often foll. by *for*) make a motion or effort to touch or get hold of, or to attain (*reached for his pipe*). **4** *tr.* get as far as; arrive at (*reached Lincoln at lunch-time; your letter reached me today*). **5** *tr.* get to or attain (a specified point) on a scale (*the temperature reached 90°; the number of applications reached 100*). **6** *intr.* (foll. by *to*) attain to; be adequate for (*my income will not reach to it*). **7** *tr.* succeed in achieving; attain (*have reached agreement*). **8** *tr.* make contact with the hand etc., or by telephone etc. (*was out all day and could not be reached*). **9** *tr.* succeed in influencing or having the required effect on (*could not manage to reach their audience*). **10** *tr.* hand, pass (*reach me that book*). **11** *tr.* take with an outstretched hand. **12** *intr. Naut.* sail with the wind abeam or abaft the beam. —*n.* **1** the extent to which a hand etc. can be reached out, influence exerted, motion carried out, or mental powers used. **2** an act of reaching out. **3** a continuous extent, esp. a stretch of river between two bends, or the part of a canal between locks. **4** *Naut.* a distance traversed in reaching. □ **out of reach** not able to be reached or attained. **reach-me-down** ready-made. □□ **reachable** *adj.* **reacher** *n.* [OE *ræcan* f. WG]

reacquaint /ˌriːəˈkweɪnt/ *v.tr. & refl.* (usu. foll. by *with*) make (a person or oneself) acquainted again. □□ **reacquaintance** *n.*

reacquire /ˌriːəˈkwaɪə(r)/ *v.tr.* acquire anew. □□ **reacquisition** /-ˌækwɪˈzɪʃ(ə)n/ *n.*

react /rɪˈækt/ *v.* **1** *intr.* (foll. by *to*) respond to a stimulus; undergo a change or show behaviour due to some influence (*how did they react to the news?*). **2** *intr.* (often foll. by *against*) be actuated by repulsion to; tend in a reverse or contrary direction. **3** *intr.* (often foll. by *upon*) produce a reciprocal or responsive effect; act upon the agent (*they react on each other*). **4** *intr.* (foll. by *with*) *Chem. & Physics* (of a substance or particle) be the cause of activity or interaction with another (*nitrous oxide reacts with the metal*). **5** *tr.* (foll. by *with*) *Chem.* cause (a substance) to react with another. **6** *intr. Mil.* make a counter-attack. **7** *intr. Stock Exch.* (of shares) fall after rising. [RE- + ACT or med.L *reagere react-* (as RE-, L *agere do, act*)]

re-act /riːˈækt/ *v.tr.* act (a part) again.

reactance /rɪˈækt(ə)ns/ *n. Electr.* a component of impedance in an AC circuit, due to capacitance or inductance or both.

reactant /rɪˈækt(ə)nt/ *n. Chem.* a substance that takes part in, and undergoes change during a reaction.

reaction /rɪˈækʃ(ə)n/ *n.* **1** the act or an instance of reacting; a responsive or reciprocal action. **2 a** a responsive feeling (*what was your reaction to the news?*). **b** an immediate or first impression. **3** the occurrence of a (physical or emotional) condition after a period of its opposite. **4** a bodily response to an external stimulus, e.g. a drug. **5** a tendency to oppose change or to advocate return to a former system, esp. in politics. **6** the interaction of substances undergoing chemical change. **7** propulsion by emitting a jet of particles etc. in the direction opposite to that of the intended motion. □□ **reactionist** *n. & adj.* [REACT + -ION or med.L *reactio* (as RE-, ACTION)]

reactionary /rɪˈækʃənərɪ/ *adj. & n.* —*adj.* tending to oppose (esp. political) change and advocate return to a former system. —*n.* (*pl.* **-ies**) a reactionary person.

reactivate /rɪˈæktɪˌveɪt/ *v.tr.* restore to a state of activity; bring into action again. □□ **reactivation** /-ˈveɪʃ(ə)n/ *n.*

reactive /rɪˈæktɪv/ *adj.* **1** showing reaction. **2** of or relating to reactance. □□ **reactivity** /-ˈtɪvɪtɪ/ *n.*

reactor /rɪˈæktə(r)/ *n.* **1** a person or thing that reacts. **2** = NUCLEAR REACTOR. **3** *Electr.* a component used to provide reactance, esp. an inductor. **4** an apparatus for the chemical reaction of substances. **5** *Med.* a person who has a reaction to a drug etc.

read /riːd/ *v. & n.* —*v.* (*past and past part.* **read** /red/) **1** *tr.* (also *absol.*) reproduce mentally or (often foll. by *aloud, out, off,* etc.) vocally the written or printed words of (a book, author, etc.) by following the symbols with the eyes or fingers. **2** *tr.* convert or be able to convert into the intended words or meaning (written or other symbols or the things expressed in this way). **3** *tr.* interpret mentally. **4** *tr.* deduce or declare an (esp. accurate) interpretation of (*read the expression on my face*). **5** *tr.* (often foll. by *that* + clause) find (a thing) recorded or stated in print etc. (*I read somewhere that you are leaving*). **6** *tr.* interpret (a statement or action) in a certain sense (*my silence is not to be read as consent*). **7** *tr.* (often foll. by *into*) assume as intended or deducible from a writer's words; find (implications) (*you read too much into my letter*). **8** *tr.* bring into a specified state by reading (*read myself to sleep*). **9** *tr.* (of a meter or other recording instrument) show (a specified figure etc.) (*the thermometer reads 20°*). **10** *intr.* convey meaning in a specified manner when read (*it reads persuasively*). **11** *intr.* sound or affect a hearer or reader as specified when read (*the book reads like a parody*). **12 a** *tr.* study by reading (esp. a subject at university). **b** *intr.* carry out a course of study by reading (*is reading for the Bar*). **13** *tr.* (as **read** /red/ *adj.*) versed in a subject (esp. literature) by reading (*a well-read person; was widely read in law*). **14** *tr.* **a** (of a computer) copy or transfer (data). **b** (foll. by *in, out*) enter or extract (data) in an electronic storage device. **15** *tr.* **a** understand or interpret (a person) by hearing words or seeing signs, gestures, etc. **b** interpret (cards, a person's hand, etc.) as a fortune-teller. **c** interpret (the sky) as an astrologer or meteorologist. **16** *tr. Printing* check the correctness of and emend (a proof). **17** *tr.* (of an editor or text) give as the word or words probably used or intended by an author. —*n.* **1** a spell of reading. **2** *colloq.* a book etc. as regards its readability (*is a really good read*). □ **read between the lines** look for or find hidden meaning (in a document etc.). **read-in** the entry of data in an electronic storage device. **read a person like a book** understand a person's motives etc. **read-only memory** *Computing* a memory read at high speed but not capable of being changed by program instructions. **read out 1** read aloud. **2** *US* expel from a political party etc. **read-out** information retrieved from a computer. **read up** make a special study of (a subject). **read-write** *Computing* capable of reading existing data and accepting alterations or further input (cf. *read-only memory*). [OE *rǣdan* advise, consider, discern f. Gmc]

readable /ˈriːdəb(ə)l/ *adj.* **1** able to be read; legible. **2** interesting

or pleasant to read. □□ **readability** /-ˈbɪlɪtɪ/ *n.* **readableness** *n.* **readably** *adv.*

readapt /ˌriːəˈdæpt/ *v.intr. & tr.* become or cause to become adapted anew. □□ **readaptation** /ˌriːædæpˈteɪʃ(ə)n/ *n.*

readdress /ˌriːəˈdres/ *v.tr.* **1** change the address of (a letter or parcel). **2** address (a problem etc.) anew. **3** speak or write to anew.

Reade /riːd/, Charles (1814–84), English dramatist and novelist who wrote several propagandist novels on social reform, successful stage works, and is chiefly remembered for his historical romance *The Cloister and the Hearth* (1861), set in the 15th c. and relating the adventures of Gerard, whose son became the future Erasmus.

reader /ˈriːdə(r)/ *n.* **1** a person who reads or is reading. **2** a book of extracts for learning, esp. a language. **3** a device for producing an image that can be read from microfilm etc. **4** *Brit.* a university lecturer of the highest grade below professor. **5** a publisher's employee who reports on submitted manuscripts. **6** a printer's proof-corrector. **7** a person appointed to read aloud, esp. parts of a service in a church. **8** a person entitled to use a particular library. [OE (as READ)]

readership /ˈriːdəʃɪp/ *n.* **1** the readers of a newspaper etc. **2** the number or extent of these.

readily /ˈredɪlɪ/ *adv.* **1** without showing reluctance; willingly. **2** without difficulty.

reading /ˈriːdɪŋ/ *n.* **1 a** the act or an instance of reading or perusing (*the reading of the will*). **b** matter to be read (*have plenty of reading with me*). **c** the specified quality of this (*it made exciting reading*). **2** (in *comb.*) used for reading (*reading-lamp; reading-room*). **3** literary knowledge (*a person of wide reading*). **4** an entertainment at which a play, poems, etc., are read (*poetry reading*). **5** a figure etc. shown by a meter or other recording instrument. **6** an interpretation or view taken (*what is your reading of the facts?*). **7** an interpretation made (of drama, music, etc.). **8** each of the successive occasions on which a bill must be presented to a legislature for acceptance (see also *first reading, second reading, third reading*). **9** the version of a text, or the particular wording, conjectured or given by an editor etc. □ **reading age** reading ability expressed as the age for which the same ability is calculated as average (*has a reading age of eight*). [OE (as READ)]

readjust /ˌriːəˈdʒʌst/ *v.tr.* adjust again or to a former state. □□ **readjustment** *n.*

readmit /ˌriːədˈmɪt/ *v.tr.* (**readmitted, readmitting**) admit again. □□ **readmission** *n.*

readopt /ˌriːəˈdɒpt/ *v.tr.* adopt again. □□ **readoption** *n.*

ready /ˈredɪ/ *adj., adv., n., & v.* —*adj.* (**readier, readiest**) (usu. *predic.*) **1** with preparations complete (*dinner is ready*). **2** in a fit state (*are you ready to go?*). **3** willing, inclined, or resolved (*he is always ready to complain; I am ready for anything*). **4** within reach; easily secured (*a ready source of income*). **5** fit for immediate use (*was ready to hand*). **6** immediate, unqualified (*found ready acceptance*). **7** prompt, quick, facile (*is always ready with excuses; has a ready wit*). **8** (foll. by *to* + infin.) about to do something (*a bud just ready to burst*). **9** provided beforehand. —*adv.* **1** beforehand. **2** so as not to require doing when the time comes for use (*the cases are ready packed*). —*n.* (*pl.* **-ies**) *sl.* **1** (prec. by *the*) = *ready money*. **2** (in *pl.*) bank notes. —*v.tr.* (**-ies, -ied**) make ready; prepare. □ **at the ready** ready for action. **make ready** prepare. **ready-mix** (or **-mixed**) (of concrete, paint, food, etc.) having some or all of the constituents already mixed together. **ready money 1** actual coin or notes. **2** payment on the spot. **ready reckoner** a book or table listing standard numerical calculations as used esp. in commerce. **ready, steady** (or **get set**), **go** the usual formula for starting a race. □□ **readiness** *n.* [ME *rædi(g), re(a)di*, f. OE *rǣde* f. Gmc]

ready-made *adj. & n.* —*adj.* (**also ready-to-wear**) (esp. of clothes) made in a standard size, not to measure. —*n.* a type of art-form invented (and named) by Marcel Duchamp, consisting of a mass-produced article selected at random and displayed as a work of art. His first ready-made was a bicycle wheel placed on a kitchen stool; other examples include a bottle rack, and a urinal entitled *Fountain* and signed R. Mutt.

reaffirm /ˌriːəˈfɜːm/ v.tr. affirm again. □□ **reaffirmation** /-ˌæfəˈmeɪʃ(ə)n/ n.

reafforest /ˌriːəˈfɒrɪst/ v.tr. replant (former forest land) with trees. □□ **reafforestation** /-ˈsteɪʃ(ə)n/ n.

Reagan /ˈreɪɡən/, Ronald Wilson (1911–), 40th President of the US 1981–9. A film actor before entering politics, he was governor of California 1966–74. During his presidency taxes and social services were reduced and the national budget deficit rose to record levels. His interventionist policy towards Central American politics was revealed in 1987 (see IRANGATE). Reagan supported the Strategic Defence Initiative (or 'Star Wars'), but towards the end of his term in office successful summit meetings with the Soviet leader, Mikhail Gorbachev, led to a reduction in holdings of nuclear weapons.

reagency /riːˈeɪdʒ(ə)nsɪ/ n. reactive power or operation.

reagent /riːˈeɪdʒ(ə)nt/ n. Chem. **1** a substance used to cause a reaction, esp. to detect another substance. **2** a reactive substance or force. [RE- + AGENT: cf. REACT]

real[1] /rɪəl/ adj. & adv. —adj. **1** actually existing as a thing or occurring in fact. **2** genuine; rightly so called; not artificial or merely apparent. **3** Law consisting of or relating to immovable property such as land or houses (real estate) (cf. personal property). **4** appraised by purchasing power; adjusted for changes in the value of money (real value; income in real terms). **5** Philos. having an absolute and necessary and not merely contingent existence. **6** Math. (of a quantity) having no imaginary part (see IMAGINARY 2). **7** Optics (of an image etc.) such that light actually passes through it. —adv. Sc. & US colloq. really, very. □ **for real** colloq. as a serious or actual concern; in earnest. **real ale** beer regarded as brewed in a traditional way, with secondary fermentation in the cask. **real life** that lived by actual people, as distinct from fiction, drama, etc. **real live** (attrib.) often joc. actual; not pretended or simulated (a real live burglar). **the real McCoy** see McCOY. **real money** current coin or notes; cash. **real tennis** the original form of tennis played on an indoor court. **the real thing** (of an object or emotion) genuine, not inferior. **real time** the actual time during which a process or event occurs. **real-time** (attrib.) Computing (of a system) in which the response time is of the order of milliseconds, e.g. in an airline booking system. □□ **realness** n. [AF = OF reel, LL realis f. L res thing]

real[2] /reɪˈɑːl/ n. hist. a former coin and monetary unit of various Spanish-speaking countries. [Sp., noun use of real (adj.) (as ROYAL)]

realgar /rɪˈælɡə(r)/ n. a mineral of arsenic sulphide used as a pigment and in fireworks. [ME f. med.L f. Arab. rahj al-gār dust of the cave]

realign /ˌriːəˈlaɪn/ v.tr. **1** align again. **2** regroup in politics etc. □□ **realignment** n.

realism /ˈriːəlɪz(ə)m/ n. (usu. opp. IDEALISM) **1** the practice of regarding things in their true nature, and dealing with them as they are; practical views and policy. **2** fidelity of representation, truth to nature, insistence upon details; the showing of life as it is without glossing over what is ugly or painful. **3** Philos. **a** the medieval theory that universals or general ideas have objective existence (cf. NOMINALISM, CONCEPTUALISM). **b** belief that matter as an object of perception has real existence (in the 20th c. the term has been applied to philosophical theories reacting against 19th-c. idealism which, while they agree in affirming that external objects exist independently of the mind, differ in their accounts of appearance, perception, and illusion); the theory that the world has a reality that transcends the mind's analytical capacity, and hence that propositions are to be assessed in terms of their truth in reality rather than in terms of their verifiability. □□ **realist** n.

realistic /rɪəˈlɪstɪk/ adj. **1** regarding things as they are; following a policy of realism. **2** based on facts rather than ideals. □□ **realistically** adv.

reality /rɪˈælɪtɪ/ n. (pl. -ies) **1** what is real or existent or underlies appearances. **2** (foll. by of) the real nature of (a thing). **3** real existence; the state of being real. **4** resemblance to an original (the model was impressive in its reality). □ **in reality** in fact. [med.L realitas or F réalité (as REAL[1])]

realize /ˈrɪəlaɪz/ v.tr. (also **-ise**) **1** (often foll. by that + clause) be fully aware of; conceive as real. **2** understand clearly. **3** present as real; make realistic; give apparent reality to (the story was powerfully realized on stage). **4** convert into actuality; achieve (realized a childhood dream). **5 a** convert into money. **b** acquire (profit). **c** be sold for (a specified price). **6** Mus. reconstruct (a part) in full from a figured bass. □□ **realizable** adj. **realizability** /-ˈbɪlɪtɪ/ n. **realization** /-ˈzeɪʃ(ə)n/ n. **realizer** n.

reallocate /riːˈæləˌkeɪt/ v.tr. allocate again or differently. □□ **reallocation** /-ˈkeɪʃ(ə)n/ n.

reallot /ˌriːəˈlɒt/ v.tr. (**reallotted, reallotting**) allot again or differently. □□ **reallotment** n.

really /ˈrɪəlɪ/ adv. **1** in reality; in fact. **2** positively, assuredly (really useful). **3** (as a strong affirmative) indeed, I assure you. **4** an expression of mild protest or surprise. **5** (in interrog.) (expressing disbelief) is that so? (They're musicians.—Really?).

realm /relm/ n. **1** formal esp. Law a kingdom. **2** a sphere or domain (the realm of imagination). [ME f. OF realme, reaume, f. L regimen -minis (see REGIMEN): infl. by OF reiel ROYAL]

realpolitik /reɪˌɑːlpɒlɪˈtiːk/ n. politics based on realities and material needs, rather than on morals or ideals. [G]

realtor /ˈrɪəltə(r)/ n. US a real-estate agent, esp. (**Realtor**) a member of the National Association of Realtors.

realty /ˈriːəltɪ/ n. Law real estate (opp. PERSONALTY).

ream[1] /riːm/ n. **1** twenty quires or 500 (formerly 480) sheets of paper (or a larger number, to allow for waste). **2** (in pl.) a large quantity of paper or writing (wrote reams about it). [ME rēm, rīm f. OF raime etc., ult. f. Arab. rizma bundle]

ream[2] /riːm/ v.tr. **1** widen (a hole in metal etc.) with a borer. **2** turn over the edge of (a cartridge-case etc.). **3** Naut. open (a seam) for caulking. **4** US squeeze the juice from (fruit). □□ **reamer** n. [19th c.: orig. uncert.]

reanimate /riːˈænɪˌmeɪt/ v.tr. **1** restore to life. **2** restore to activity or liveliness. □□ **reanimation** /-ˈmeɪʃ(ə)n/ n.

reap /riːp/ v.tr. **1** cut or gather (a crop, esp. grain) as a harvest. **2** harvest the crop of (a field etc.). **3** receive as the consequence of one's own or others' actions. [OE ripan, reopan, of unkn. orig.]

reaper /ˈriːpə(r)/ n. **1** a person who reaps. **2** a machine for reaping crops. A crude corn-reaping machine was in use in Roman Gaul in the 1st c. AD, but the first machines of any efficiency date from the early 19th c. □ **the Reaper** (or **grim Reaper**) death personified.

reappear /ˌriːəˈpɪə(r)/ v.intr. appear again or as previously. □□ **reappearance** n.

reapply /ˌriːəˈplaɪ/ v.tr. & intr. (**-ies, -ied**) apply again, esp. submit a further application (for a position etc.). □□ **reapplication** /ˌriːæplɪˈkeɪʃ(ə)n/ n.

reappoint /ˌriːəˈpɔɪnt/ v.tr. appoint again to a position previously held. □□ **reappointment** n.

reapportion /ˌriːəˈpɔːʃ(ə)n/ v.tr. apportion again or differently. □□ **reapportionment** n.

reappraise /ˌriːəˈpreɪz/ v.tr. appraise or assess again. □□ **reappraisal** n.

rear[1] /rɪə(r)/ n. & adj. —n. **1** the back part of anything. **2** the space behind, or position at the back of, anything (a large house with a terrace at the rear). **3** the hindmost part of an army or fleet. **4** colloq. the buttocks. —adj. at the back. □ **bring up the rear** come last. **in the rear** behind; at the back. **rear admiral** a naval officer ranking below vice admiral. **rear commodore** a yacht-club officer below vice commodore. **rear-lamp** (or **-light**) a usu. red light at the rear of a vehicle. **rear sight** the sight nearest to the stock on a firearm. **rear-view mirror** a mirror fixed inside the windscreen of a motor vehicle enabling the driver to see traffic etc. behind. **take in the rear** Mil. attack from behind. [prob. f. (in the) REARWARD or REARGUARD]

rear[2] /rɪə(r)/ v. **1** tr. **a** bring up and educate (children). **b** breed and care for (animals). **c** cultivate (crops). **2** intr. (of a horse etc.) raise itself on its hind legs. **3** tr. **a** set upright. **b** build. **c** hold upwards (rear one's head). **4** intr. extend to a great height. □□ **rearer** n. [OE rǣran f. Gmc]

rearguard /ˈrɪəɡɑːd/ n. **1** a body of troops detached to protect the rear, esp. in retreats. **2** a defensive or conservative element in an organization etc. □ **rearguard action 1** *Mil.* an engagement undertaken by a rearguard. **2** a defensive stand in argument etc., esp. when losing. [OF *rereguarde* (as RETRO-, GUARD)]

rearm /riːˈɑːm/ *v.tr.* (also *absol.*) arm again, esp. with improved weapons. □□ **rearmament** *n.*

rearmost /ˈrɪəməʊst/ *adj.* furthest back.

rearrange /ˌriːəˈreɪndʒ/ *v.tr.* arrange again in a different way. □□ **rearrangement** *n.*

rearrest /ˌriːəˈrest/ *v.* & *n.* —*v.tr.* arrest again. —*n.* an instance of rearresting or being rearrested.

rearward /ˈrɪəwəd/ *n.*, *adj.*, & *adv.* —*n.* rear, esp. in prepositional phrases (*to the rearward of*; *in the rearward*). —*adj.* to the rear. —*adv.* (also **rearwards**) towards the rear. [AF *rerewarde* = REARGUARD]

reascend /ˌriːəˈsend/ *v.tr.* & *intr.* ascend again or to a former position. □□ **reascension** *n.*

reason /ˈriːz(ə)n/ *n.* & *v.* —*n.* **1** a motive, cause, or justification (*has good reasons for doing this*; *there is no reason to be angry*). **2** a fact adduced or serving as this (*I can give you my reasons*). **3** the intellectual faculty by which conclusions are drawn from premisses. **4** sanity (*has lost his reason*). **5** *Logic* a premiss of a syllogism, esp. a minor premiss when given after the conclusion. **6** a faculty transcending the understanding and providing a priori principles; intuition. **7** sense; sensible conduct; what is right or practical or practicable; moderation. —*v.* **1** *intr.* form or try to reach conclusions by connected thought. **2** *intr.* (foll. by *with*) use an argument (with a person) by way of persuasion. **3** *tr.* (foll. by *that* + clause) conclude or assert in argument. **4** *tr.* (foll. by *why, whether, what* + clause) discuss; ask oneself. **5** *tr.* (foll. by *into, out of*) persuade or move by argument (*I reasoned them out of their fears*). **6** *tr.* (foll. by *out*) think or work out (consequences etc.). **7** *tr.* (often as **reasoned** *adj.*) express in logical or argumentative form. **8** *tr.* embody reason in (an amendment etc.). □ **by reason of** owing to. **in** (or **within**) **reason** within the bounds of sense or moderation. **it stands to reason** (often foll. by *that* + clause) it is evident or logical. **listen to reason** be persuaded to act sensibly. **see reason** acknowledge the force of an argument. **with reason** justifiably. □□ **reasoner** *n.* **reasoning** *n.* **reasonless** *adj.* [ME f. OF *reisun, res(o)un, raisoner*, ult. f. L *ratio -onis* f. *rēri rat-* consider]

reasonable /ˈriːzənəb(ə)l/ *adj.* **1** having sound judgement; moderate; ready to listen to reason. **2** in accordance with reason; not absurd. **3 a** within the limits of reason; not greatly less or more than might be expected. **b** inexpensive; not extortionate. **c** tolerable, fair. **4** *archaic* endowed with the faculty of reason. □□ **reasonableness** *n.* **reasonably** *adv.* [ME f. OF *raisonable* (as REASON) after L *rationabilis*]

reassemble /ˌriːəˈsemb(ə)l/ *v.intr.* & *tr.* assemble again or into a former state. □□ **reassembly** *n.*

reassert /ˌriːəˈsɜːt/ *v.tr.* assert again. □□ **reassertion** *n.*

reassess /ˌriːəˈses/ *v.tr.* assess again, esp. differently. □□ **reassessment** *n.*

reassign /ˌriːəˈsaɪn/ *v.tr.* assign again or differently. □□ **reassignment** *n.*

reassume /ˌriːəˈsjuːm/ *v.tr.* take on oneself or undertake again. □□ **reassumption** /-ˈsʌmpʃ(ə)n/ *n.*

reassure /ˌriːəˈʃʊə/ *v.tr.* **1** restore confidence to; dispel the apprehensions of. **2** confirm in an opinion or impression. □□ **reassurance** *n.* **reassurer** *n.* **reassuring** *adj.* **reassuringly** *adv.*

reattach /ˌriːəˈtætʃ/ *v.tr.* attach again or in a former position. □□ **reattachment** *n.*

reattain /ˌriːəˈteɪn/ *v.tr.* attain again. □□ **reattainment** *n.*

reattempt /ˌriːəˈtempt/ *v.tr.* attempt again, esp. after failure.

Réaumur /ˌreɪəʊˈmjʊə(r)/, René Antoine Ferchault de (1683–1757), French entomologist, one of the greatest naturalists of his age, who was put in charge of compiling a list of France's arts, industries, and professions. As a consequence, he suggested improvements in several manufacturing processes, including the making of porcelain, mirrors, tinplate, iron, and steel, but

he is chiefly remembered for his thermometer scale, now obsolete. The traditional Réaumur scale has eighty divisions between 0° (the melting-point of ice) and 80° (the boiling-point of water), but the original alcohol thermometer had only one fixed point, that of melting ice, and its divisions were marked volumetrically rather than lineally.

reave /riːv/ *v.* (*past* and *past part.* **reft** /reft/) *archaic* **1** *tr.* **a** (foll. by *of*) forcibly deprive of. **b** (foll. by *away, from*) take by force or carry off. **2** *intr.* make raids; plunder; = REIVE. [OE *rēafian* f. Gmc: cf. ROB]

reawaken /ˌriːəˈweɪkən/ *v.tr.* & *intr.* awaken again.

rebarbative /rɪˈbɑːbətɪv/ *adj. literary* repellent, unattractive. [F *rébarbatif -ive* f. *barbe* beard]

rebate[1] /ˈriːbeɪt/ *n.* & *v.* —*n.* **1** a partial refund of money paid. **2** a deduction from a sum to be paid; a discount. —*v.tr.* pay back as a rebate. □□ **rebatable** *adj.* **rebater** *n.* [earlier = diminish: ME f. OF *rabattre* (as RE-, ABATE)]

rebate[2] /ˈriːbeɪt/ *n.* & *v.tr.* = RABBET. [respelling of RABBET, after REBATE[1]]

rebec /ˈriːbek/ *n.* (also **rebeck**) *Mus.* a medieval usu. three-stringed instrument played with a bow. [F *rebec* var. of OF *rebebe rubebe* f. Arab. *rabāb*]

rebel *n.*, *adj.*, & *v.* —*n.* /ˈreb(ə)l/ **1** a person who fights against, resists, or refuses allegiance to, the established government. **2** a person or thing that resists authority or control. —*adj.* /ˈreb(ə)l/ (*attrib.*) **1** rebellious. **2** of or concerning rebels. **3** in rebellion. —*v.intr.* /rɪˈbel/ (**rebelled, rebelling**; US **rebeled, rebeling**) (usu. foll. by *against*) **1** act as a rebel; revolt. **2** feel or display repugnance. [ME f. OF *rebelle, rebeller* f. L *rebellis* (as RE-, *bellum* war)]

rebellion /rɪˈbeljən/ *n.* open resistance to authority, esp. organized armed resistance to an established government. [ME f. OF f. L *rebellio -onis* (as REBEL)]

rebellious /rɪˈbeljəs/ *adj.* **1** tending to rebel, insubordinate. **2** in rebellion. **3** defying lawful authority. **4** (of a thing) unmanageable, refractory. □□ **rebelliously** *adv.* **rebelliousness** *n.* [ME f. REBELLION + -OUS or f. earlier *rebellous* + -IOUS]

rebid /ˈriːbɪd/ *v.* & *n.* —*v.* /also riːˈbɪd/ (**rebidding**; *past* and *past part.* **rebid**) *Cards* **1** *intr.* bid again. **2** *tr.* bid (a suit) again at a higher level. —*n.* **1** the act of rebidding. **2** a bid made in this way.

rebind /riːˈbaɪnd/ *v.tr.* (*past* and *past part.* **rebound**) bind (esp. a book) again or differently.

rebirth /riːˈbɜːθ, ˈriː-/ *n.* **1** a new incarnation. **2** spiritual enlightenment. **3** a revival (*the rebirth of learning*). □□ **reborn** /riːˈbɔːn/ *adj.*

reboot /riːˈbuːt/ *v.tr.* (often *absol.*) *Computing* boot up (a system) again.

rebore *v.* & *n.* —*v.tr.* /riːˈbɔː(r)/ make a new boring in, esp. widen the bore of (the cylinder in an internal-combustion engine). —*n.* /ˈriːbɔː(r)/ **1** the process of doing this. **2** a rebored engine.

rebound[1] *v.* & *n.* —*v.intr.* /rɪˈbaʊnd/ **1** spring back after action or impact. **2** (foll. by *upon*) (of an action) have an adverse effect upon (the doer). —*n.* /ˈriːbaʊnd/ **1** the act or an instance of rebounding; recoil. **2** a reaction after a strong emotion. □ **on the rebound** while still recovering from an emotional shock, esp. rejection by a lover. □□ **rebounder** *n.* [ME f. OF *rebonder, rebondir* (as RE-, BOUND[1])]

rebound[2] /riːˈbaʊnd/ *past* and *past part.* of REBIND.

rebroadcast /riːˈbrɔːdkɑːst/ *v.* & *n.* —*v.tr.* (*past* **rebroadcast** or **rebroadcasted**; *past part.* **rebroadcast**) broadcast again. —*n.* a repeat broadcast.

rebuff /rɪˈbʌf/ *n.* & *v.* —*n.* **1** a rejection of one who makes advances, proffers help or sympathy, shows interest or curiosity, makes a request, etc. **2** a repulse; a snub. —*v.tr.* give a rebuff to. [obs. F *rebuffe(r)* f. It. *ribuffo, ribuffare, rabbuffo, rabbuffare* (as RE-, *buffo* puff)]

rebuild /riːˈbɪld/ *v.tr.* (*past* and *past part.* **rebuilt**) build again or differently.

rebuke /rɪˈbjuːk/ *v.* & *n.* —*v.tr.* reprove sharply; subject to protest or censure. —*n.* **1** the act of rebuking. **2** the process of being rebuked. **3** a reproof. □□ **rebuker** *n.* **rebukingly** *adv.* [ME f. AF & ONF *rebuker* (as RE-, OF *buchier* beat, orig. cut down wood f. *busche* log)]

rebury /riːˈbɛrɪ/ *v.tr.* (**-ies, -ied**) bury again. □□ **reburial** *n.*

rebus /ˈriːbəs/ *n.* **1** an enigmatic representation of a word (esp. a name), by pictures etc. suggesting its parts. **2** *Heraldry* a device suggesting the name of its bearer. [F *rébus* f. L *rebus*, ablat. pl. of *res* thing]

rebut /rɪˈbʌt/ *v.tr.* (**rebutted, rebutting**) **1** refute or disprove (evidence or a charge). **2** force or turn back; check. □□ **rebutment** *n.* **rebuttable** *adj.* **rebuttal** *n.* [ME f. AF *rebuter*, OF *rebo(u)ter* (as RE-, BUTT¹)]

rebutter /rɪˈbʌtə(r)/ *n.* **1** a refutation. **2** *Law* a defendant's reply to the plaintiff's surrejoinder. [AF *rebuter* (as REBUT)]

recalcitrant /rɪˈkælsɪtrənt/ *adj. & n.* —*adj.* **1** obstinately disobedient. **2** objecting to restraint. —*n.* a recalcitrant person. □□ **recalcitrance** *n.* **recalcitrantly** *adv.* [L *recalcitrare* (as RE-, *calcitrare* kick out with the heels f. *calx calcis* heel)]

recalculate /riːˈkælkjʊˌleɪt/ *v.tr.* calculate again. □□ **recalculation** /-ˈleɪʃ(ə)n/ *n.*

recalesce /ˌriːkəˈles/ *v.intr.* grow hot again (esp. of iron allowed to cool from white heat, whose temperature rises at a certain point for a short time). □□ **recalescence** *n.* [L *recalescere* (as RE-, *calescere* grow hot)]

recall /rɪˈkɔːl/ *v. & n.* —*v.tr.* **1** summon to return from a place or from a different occupation, inattention, a digression, etc. **2** recollect, remember. **3** bring back to memory; serve as a reminder of. **4** revoke or annul (an action or decision). **5** cancel or suspend the appointment of (an official sent overseas etc.). **6** revive, resuscitate. **7** take back (a gift). —*n.* /also ˈriːkɔl/ **1** the act or an instance of recalling, esp. a summons to come back. **2** the act of remembering. **3** the ability to remember. **4** the possibility of recalling, esp. in the sense of revoking (*beyond recall*). **5** *US* removal of an elected official from office. □□ **recallable** *adj.*

recant /rɪˈkænt/ *v.* **1** *tr.* withdraw and renounce (a former belief or statement) as erroneous or heretical. **2** *intr.* disavow a former opinion, esp. with a public confession of error. □□ **recantation** /ˌriːkænˈteɪʃ(ə)n/ *n.* **recanter** *n.* [L *recantare* revoke (as RE-, *cantare* sing, chant)]

recap /ˈriːkæp/ *v. & n. colloq.* —*v.tr. & intr.* (**recapped, recapping**) recapitulate. —*n.* recapitulation. [abbr.]

recapitalize /riːˈkæpɪtəˌlaɪz/ *v.tr.* (also **-ise**) capitalize (shares etc.) again. □□ **recapitalization** /-ˈzeɪʃ(ə)n/ *n.*

recapitulate /ˌriːkəˈpɪtjʊˌleɪt/ *v.tr.* **1** go briefly through again; summarize. **2** go over the main points or headings of. □□ **recapitulative** /-lətɪv/ *adj.* **recapitulatory** /-lətərɪ/ *adj.* [L *recapitulare* (as RE-, *capitulum* CHAPTER)]

recapitulation /ˌriːkəˌpɪtjʊˈleɪʃ(ə)n/ *n.* **1** the act or an instance of recapitulating. **2** *Biol.* the reappearance in embryos of successive type-forms in the evolutionary line of development. **3** *Mus.* part of a movement, esp. in sonata form, in which themes from the exposition are restated. [ME f. OF *recapitulation* or LL *recapitulatio* (as RECAPITULATE)]

recapture /riːˈkæptʃə(r)/ *v. & n.* —*v.tr.* **1** capture again; recover by capture. **2** re-experience (a past emotion etc.). —*n.* the act or an instance of recapturing.

recast /riːˈkɑːst/ *v. & n.* —*v.tr.* (*past and past part.* **recast**) **1** put into a new form. **2** improve the arrangement of. **3** change the cast of (a play etc.). —*n.* **1** the act or an instance of recasting. **2** a recast form.

recce /ˈrekɪ/ *n. & v. colloq.* —*n.* a reconnaisance. —*v.tr. & intr.* (**recced, recceing**) reconnoitre. [abbr.]

recd. *abbr.* received.

recede /rɪˈsiːd/ *v.intr.* **1** go or shrink back or further off. **2** be left at an increasing distance by an observer's motion. **3** slope backwards (*a receding chin*). **4** decline in force or value. **5** (foll. by *from*) withdraw from (an engagement, opinion, etc.). **6** (of a man's hair) cease to grow at the front, sides, etc. [ME f. L *recedere* (as RE-, *cedere cess-* go)]

re-cede /riːˈsiːd/ *v.tr.* cede back to a former owner.

receipt /rɪˈsiːt/ *n. & v.* —*n.* **1** the act or an instance of receiving or being received into one's possession (*will pay on receipt of the goods*). **2** a written acknowledgement of this, esp. of the payment of money. **3** (usu. in *pl.*) an amount of money etc. received. **4** *archaic* a recipe. —*v.tr.* place a written or printed receipt on (a bill). [ME *receit(e)* f. AF & ONF *receite*, OF *reçoite, recete* f. med.L *recepta* fem. past part. of L *recipere* RECEIVE: *-p-* inserted after L]

receive /rɪˈsiːv/ *v.tr.* **1** take or accept (something offered or given) into one's hands or possession. **2** acquire; be provided with or given (*have received no news; will receive a small fee*). **3** accept delivery of (something sent). **4** have conferred or inflicted on one (*received many honours; received a heavy blow on the head*). **5 a** stand the force or weight of. **b** bear up against; encounter with opposition. **6** consent to hear (a confession or oath) or consider (a petition). **7** (also *absol.*) accept or have dealings with (stolen property knowing of the theft). **8** admit; consent or prove able to hold; provide accommodation for (*received many visitors*). **9** (of a receptacle) be able to hold (a specified amount or contents). **10** greet or welcome, esp. in a specified manner (*how did they receive your offer?*). **11** entertain as a guest etc. **12** admit to membership of a society, organization, etc. **13** be marked more or less permanently with (an impression etc.). **14** convert (broadcast signals) into sound or pictures. **15** *Tennis* be the player to whom the server serves (the ball). **16** (often as **received** *adj.*) give credit to; accept as authoritative or true (*received opinion*). **17** eat or drink (the Eucharistic bread and wine). □ **be at** (or **on**) **the receiving end** *colloq.* bear the brunt of something unpleasant. **received pronunciation** (or **Received Standard**) the form of spoken English based on educated speech in southern England used (with local variations) by the majority of educated English-speaking people. **receiving-order** *Brit.* an order of a court authorizing a receiver (see RECEIVER 3) to act. □□ **receivable** *adj.* [ME f. OF *receivre, reçoivre* f. L *recipere recept-* (as RE-, *capere* take)]

receiver /rɪˈsiːvə(r)/ *n.* **1** a person or thing that receives. **2** the part of a machine or instrument that receives sound, signals, etc. (esp. the part of a telephone that contains the earpiece). **3** (in full **official receiver**) a person appointed by a court to administer the property of a bankrupt or insane person, or property under litigation. **4** a radio or television receiving apparatus. **5** a person who receives stolen goods. **6** *Chem.* a vessel for collecting the products of distillation, chromatography, etc.

receivership /rɪˈsiːvəʃɪp/ *n.* **1** the office of official receiver. **2** the state of being dealt with by a receiver (esp. *in receivership*).

recension /rɪˈsenʃ(ə)n/ *n.* **1** the revision of a text. **2** a particular form or version of a text resulting from such revision. [L *recensio* f. *recensēre* revise (as RE-, *censēre* review)]

recent /ˈriːs(ə)nt/ *adj. & n.* —*adj.* **1** not long past; that happened, appeared, began to exist, or existed lately. **2** not long established; lately begun; modern. **3** (**Recent**) *Geol.* = HOLOCENE. —*n.* (**Recent**) *Geol.* = HOLOCENE. □□ **recency** *n.* **recently** *adv.* **recentness** *n.* [L *recens recentis* or F *récent*]

receptacle /rɪˈseptək(ə)l/ *n.* **1** a containing vessel, place, or space. **2** *Bot.* **a** the common base of floral organs. **b** the part of a leaf or thallus in some algae where the reproductive organs are situated. [ME f. OF *receptacle* or L *receptaculum* (as RECEPTION)]

reception /rɪˈsepʃ(ə)n/ *n.* **1** the act or an instance of receiving or the process of being received, esp. of a person into a place or group. **2** the manner in which a person or thing is received (*got a cool reception*). **3** a social occasion for receiving guests, esp. after a wedding. **4** a formal or ceremonious welcome. **5** a place where guests or clients etc. report on arrival at a hotel, office, etc. **6 a** the receiving of broadcast signals. **b** the quality of this (*we have excellent reception*). □ **reception order** an order authorizing the entry of a patient into a mental hospital. **reception room** a room available or suitable for receiving company or visitors. [ME f. OF *reception* or L *receptio* (as RECEIVE)]

receptionist /rɪˈsepʃənɪst/ *n.* a person employed in a hotel, office, etc., to receive guests, clients, etc.

receptive /rɪˈseptɪv/ *adj.* **1** able or quick to receive impressions or ideas. **2** concerned with receiving stimuli etc. □□ **receptively** *adv.* **receptiveness** *n.* **receptivity** /ˌriːsepˈtɪvɪtɪ/ *n.* [F *réceptif -ive* or med.L *receptivus* (as RECEPTION)]

æ cat ɑː *arm* e bed ɜː *her* ɪ sit iː *see* ɒ hot ɔː *saw* ʌ run ʊ put uː *too* ə *ago* aɪ my

receptor /rɪˈsɛptə(r)/ n. (often attrib.) Biol. **1** an organ able to respond to an external stimulus such as light, heat, or a drug, and transmit a signal to a sensory nerve. **2** a region of a cell, tissue, etc., that responds to a molecule or other substance. [OF receptour or L receptor (as RECEPTIVE)]

recess /rɪˈsɛs, ˈriːsɛs/ n. & v. —n. **1** a space set back in a wall; a niche. **2** (often in pl.) a remote or secret place (the innermost recesses). **3** a temporary cessation from work, esp. of Parliament, or US of a lawcourt or during a school day. **4** Anat. a fold or indentation in an organ. **5** Geog. a receding part of a mountain chain etc. —v. **1** tr. make a recess in. **2** tr. place in a recess; set back. **3** US a intr. take a recess; adjourn. **b** tr. order a temporary cessation from the work of (a court etc.). [L recessus (as RECEDE)]

recession /rɪˈsɛʃ(ə)n/ n. **1** a temporary decline in economic activity or prosperity. **2** a receding or withdrawal from a place or point. **3** a receding part of an object; a recess. □□ **recessionary** adj. [L recessio (as RECESS)]

recessional /rɪˈsɛʃ(ə)n(ə)l/ adj. & n. —adj. sung while the clergy and choir withdraw after a service. —n. a recessional hymn.

recessive /rɪˈsɛsɪv/ adj. **1** tending to recede. **2** Phonet. (of an accent) falling near the beginning of a word. **3** Genetics (of an inherited characteristic) appearing in offspring only when not masked by a dominant characteristic inherited from one parent. □□ **recessively** adv. **recessiveness** n. [RECESS after excessive]

Rechabite /ˈrɛkəbaɪt/ n. **1** a member of a Jewish family, descended from Jonadab son of Rechab, who refused to drink wine or live in houses (Jer. 35: 2–19). **2** a total abstainer; a member of the Independent Order of Rechabites, a benefit society founded in 1835. **recharge** v. & n. —v.tr. /riːˈtʃɑːdʒ/ **1** charge again. **2** reload. —n. /ˈriːtʃɑːdʒ/ **1** a renewed charge. **2** material etc. used for this. □□ **rechargeable** /riːˈtʃɑːdʒəb(ə)l/ adj.

réchauffé /rɪˈʃəʊfeɪ/ n. **1** a warmed-up dish. **2** a rehash. [F past part. of réchauffer (as RE-, CHAFE)]

recheck v. & n. —v.tr. & intr. /riːˈtʃɛk/ check again. —n. /ˈriːtʃɛk/ a second or further check or inspection.

recherché /rəˈʃɛəʃeɪ/ adj. **1** carefully sought out; rare or exotic. **2** far-fetched, obscure. [F, past part. of rechercher (as RE-, chercher seek)]

rechristen /riːˈkrɪs(ə)n/ v.tr. **1** christen again. **2** give a new name to.

recidivist /rɪˈsɪdɪvɪst/ n. a person who relapses into crime. □□ **recidivism** n. **recidivistic** /-ˈvɪstɪk/ adj. [F récidiviste f. récidiver f. med.L recidivare f. L recidivus f. recidere (as RE-, cadere fall)]

Recife /rəˈsiːfeɪ/ (formerly **Pernambuco** /ˌpɜːnæmˈbuːkəʊ/) a port on the Atlantic coast of NE Brazil; pop. (1980) 1,183,400.

recipe /ˈrɛsɪpɪ/ n. **1** a statement of the ingredients and procedure required for preparing cooked food. **2** an expedient; a device for achieving something. **3** a medical prescription. [2nd sing. imper. (as used in prescriptions) of L recipere take, RECEIVE]

recipient /rɪˈsɪpɪənt/ n. & adj. —n. a person who receives something. —adj. **1** receiving. **2** receptive. □□ **recipiency** n. [F récipient f. It. recipiente or L recipiens f. recipere RECEIVE]

reciprocal /rɪˈsɪprək(ə)l/ adj. & n. —adj. **1** in return (offered a reciprocal greeting). **2** mutual (their feelings are reciprocal). **3** Gram. (of a pronoun) expressing mutual action or relation (as in each other). **4** inversely correspondent; complementary (natural kindness matched by a reciprocal severity). —n. Math. an expression or function so related to another that their product is unity (⅓ is the reciprocal of 2). □□ **reciprocality** /-ˈkælɪtɪ/ n. **reciprocally** adv. [L reciprocus ult. f. re- back + pro forward]

reciprocate /rɪˈsɪprəˌkeɪt/ v. **1** tr. return or requite (affection etc.). **2** intr. (foll. by with) offer or give something in return (reciprocated with an invitation to lunch). **3** tr. give and receive mutually; interchange. **4** a intr. (of a part of a machine) move backwards and forwards. **b** tr. cause to do this. □ **reciprocating engine** an engine using a piston or pistons moving up and down in cylinders. □□ **reciprocation** /-ˈkeɪʃ(ə)n/ n. **reciprocator** n. [L reciprocare reciprocat- (as RECIPROCAL)]

reciprocity /ˌrɛsɪˈprɒsɪtɪ/ n. **1** the condition of being reciprocal. **2** mutual action. **3** give and take, esp. the interchange of privileges between countries and organizations. [F réciprocité f. réciproque f. L reciprocus (as RECIPROCATE)]

recirculate /riːˈsɜːkjʊˌleɪt/ v.tr. & intr. circulate again, esp. make available for reuse. □□ **recirculation** /-ˈleɪʃ(ə)n/ n.

recital /rɪˈsaɪt(ə)l/ n. **1** the act or an instance of reciting or being recited. **2** the performance of a programme of music by a solo instrumentalist or singer or by a small group. **3** (foll. by of) a detailed account of (connected things or facts); a narrative. **4** Law the part of a legal document that states the facts. □□ **recitalist** n.

recitation /ˌrɛsɪˈteɪʃ(ə)n/ n. **1** the act or an instance of reciting. **2** a thing recited. [OF recitation or L recitatio (as RECITE)]

recitative /ˌrɛsɪtəˈtiːv/ n. **1** musical declamation of the kind usual in the narrative and dialogue parts of opera and oratorio. **2** the words or part given in this form. [It. recitativo (as RECITE)]

recite /rɪˈsaɪt/ v. **1** tr. repeat aloud or declaim (a poem or passage) from memory, esp. before an audience. **2** intr. give a recitation. **3** tr. mention in order; enumerate. □□ **reciter** n. [ME f. OF reciter or L recitare (as RE-, CITE)]

reck /rɛk/ v. archaic or poet. (only in neg. or interrog.) **1** tr. (foll. by of) pay heed to; take account of; care about. **2** tr. pay heed to. **3** intr. (usu. with it as subject) be of importance (it recks little). [OE reccan, rel. to OHG ruohhen]

reckless /ˈrɛklɪs/ adj. disregarding the consequences or danger etc.; lacking caution; rash. □□ **recklessly** adv. **recklessness** n. [OE recceléas (as RECK)]

reckon /ˈrɛkən/ v. **1** tr. count or compute by calculation. **2** tr. (foll. by in) count in or include in computation. **3** tr. (often foll. by as or to be) consider or regard (reckon him wise; reckon them to be beyond hope). **4** tr. a (foll. by that + clause) conclude after calculation; be of the considered opinion. **b** colloq. (foll. by to + infin.) expect (reckons to finish by Friday). **5** intr. make calculations; add up an account or sum. **6** intr. (foll. by on, upon) rely on, count on, or base plans on. **7** intr. (foll. by with) **a** take into account. **b** settle accounts with. □ **reckon up 1** count up; find the total of. **2** settle accounts. **to be reckoned with** of considerable importance; not to be ignored. [OE (ge)recenian f. WG]

reckoner /ˈrɛkənə(r)/ n. = ready reckoner.

reckoning /ˈrɛkənɪŋ/ n. **1** the act or an instance of counting or calculating. **2** a consideration or opinion. **3 a** the settlement of an account. **b** an account. □ **day of reckoning** the time when something must be atoned for or avenged.

reclaim /rɪˈkleɪm/ v. & n. —v.tr. **1** seek the return of (one's property). **2** claim in return or as a rebate etc. **3** bring under cultivation, esp. from a state of being under water. **4 a** win back or away from vice or error or a waste condition; reform. **b** tame, civilize. —n. the act or an instance of reclaiming; the process of being reclaimed. □□ **reclaimable** adj. **reclaimer** n. **reclamation** /ˌrɛkləˈmeɪʃ(ə)n/ n. [ME f. OF reclamer reclaim- f. L reclamare cry out against (as RE-, clamare shout)]

reclassify /riːˈklæsɪˌfaɪ/ v.tr. (-ies, -ied) classify again or differently. □□ **reclassification** /-fɪˈkeɪʃ(ə)n/ n.

reclinate /ˈrɛklɪˌneɪt/ adj. Bot. bending downwards. [L reclinatus, past part. of reclinare (as RECLINE)]

recline /rɪˈklaɪn/ v. **1** intr. assume or be in a horizontal or leaning position, esp. in resting. **2** tr. cause to recline or move from the vertical. □□ **reclinable** adj. [ME f. OE recliner or L reclinare bend back, recline (as RE-, clinare bend)]

recliner /rɪˈklaɪnə(r)/ n. **1** a comfortable chair for reclining in. **2** a person who reclines.

reclothe /riːˈkləʊð/ v.tr. clothe again or differently.

recluse /rɪˈkluːs/ n. & adj. —n. a person given to or living in seclusion or isolation, esp. as a religious discipline; a hermit. —adj. favouring seclusion; solitary. □□ **reclusion** /rɪˈkluːʒ(ə)n/ n. **reclusive** adj. [ME f. OF reclus recluse past part. of reclure f. L recludere reclus- (as RE-, claudere shut)]

recognition /ˌrɛkəɡˈnɪʃ(ə)n/ n. the act or an instance of recognizing or being recognized. □□ **recognitory** /rɪˈkɒɡnɪtərɪ/ adj. [L recognitio (as RECOGNIZE)]

recognizance /rɪˈkɒɡnɪz(ə)ns/ n. **1** a bond by which a person undertakes before a court or magistrate to observe some condition, e.g. to appear when summoned. **2** a sum pledged as surety for this. [ME f. OF recon(n)issance (as RE-, COGNIZANCE)]

recognizant /rɪˈkɒgnɪz(ə)nt/ *adj.* (usu. foll. by *of*) **1** showing recognition (of a favour etc.). **2** conscious or showing consciousness (of something).

recognize /ˈrekəɡˌnaɪz/ *v.tr.* (also **-ise**) **1** identify (a person or thing) as already known; know again. **2** realize or discover the nature of. **3** (foll. by *that*) realize or admit. **4** acknowledge the existence, validity, character, or claims of. **5** show appreciation of; reward. **6** (foll. by *as, for*) treat or acknowledge. **7** (of a chairperson etc.) allow (a person) to speak in a debate etc. □□ **recognizable** *adj.* **recognizability** /-əˈbɪlɪtɪ/ *n.* **recognizably** *adv.* **recognizer** *n.* [OF *recon(n)iss-* stem of *reconnaistre* f. L *recognoscere recognit-* (as RE-, *cognoscere* learn)]

recoil /rɪˈkɔɪl/ *v. & n.* —*v.intr.* **1** suddenly move or spring back in fear, horror, or disgust. **2** shrink mentally in this way. **3** rebound after an impact. **4** (foll. by *on, upon*) have an adverse reactive effect on (the originator). **5** (of a gun) be driven backwards by its discharge. **6** retreat under an enemy's attack. **7** *Physics* (of an atom etc.) move backwards by the conservation of momentum on emission of a particle. —*n.* /also ˈriːkɔɪl/ **1** the act or an instance of recoiling. **2** the sensation of recoiling. [ME f. OF *reculer* (as RE-, L *culus* buttocks)]

recollect /ˌrekəˈlekt/ *v.tr.* **1** remember. **2** succeed in remembering; call to mind. [L *recolligere recollect-* (as RE-, COLLECT[1])]

re-collect /ˌriːkəˈlekt/ *v.tr.* **1** collect again. **2** (*refl.*) recover control of (oneself).

recollection /ˌrekəˈlekʃ(ə)n/ *n.* **1** the act or power of recollecting. **2** a thing recollected. **3 a** a person's memory (*to the best of my recollection*). **b** the time over which memory extends (*happened within my recollection*). □□ **recollective** *adj.* [F *recollection* or med.L *recollectio* (as RECOLLECT)]

recolonize /riːˈkɒləˌnaɪz/ *v.tr.* (also **-ise**) colonize again. □□ **recolonization** /-ˈzeɪʃ(ə)n/ *n.*

recolour /riːˈkʌlə(r)/ *v.tr.* colour again or differently.

recombinant /riːˈkɒmbɪnənt/ *adj. & n. Biol.* —*adj.* (of a gene etc.) formed by recombination. —*n.* a recombinant organism or cell. □ **recombinant DNA** DNA that has been recombined using constituents from different sources.

recombination /riːˌkɒmbɪˈneɪʃ(ə)n/ *n. Biol.* the rearrangement, esp. by crossing over in chromosomes, of nucleic acid molecules forming a new sequence of the constituent nucleotides.

recombine /ˌriːkəmˈbaɪn/ *v.tr. & intr.* combine again or differently.

recommence /ˌriːkəˈmens/ *v.tr. & intr.* begin again. □□ **recommencement** *n.*

recommend /ˌrekəˈmend/ *v.tr.* **1** suggest as fit for some purpose or use. **2** (often foll. by *that* + clause or to + infin.) advise as a course of action etc. (*I recommend that you stay where you are*). **3** (of qualities, conduct, etc.) make acceptable or desirable. **4** (foll. by *to*) commend or entrust (to a person or a person's care). □□ **recommendable** *adj.* **recommendation** /-ˈdeɪʃ(ə)n/ *n.* **recommendatory** /-dətərɪ/ *adj.* **recommender** *n.* [ME (in sense 4) f. med.L *recommendare* (as RE-, COMMEND)]

recommit /ˌriːkəˈmɪt/ *v.tr.* (**recommitted, recommitting**) **1** commit again. **2** return (a bill etc.) to a committee for further consideration. □□ **recommitment** *n.* **recommittal** *n.*

recompense /ˈrekəmˌpens/ *v. & n.* —*v.tr.* **1** make amends to (a person) or for (a loss etc.). **2** requite; reward or punish (a person or action). —*n.* **1** a reward; requital. **2** retribution; satisfaction given for an injury. [ME f. OF *recompense(r)* f. LL *recompensare* (as RE-, COMPENSATE)]

recompose /ˌriːkəmˈpəʊz/ *v.tr.* compose again or differently.

reconcile /ˈrekənˌsaɪl/ *v.tr.* **1** make friendly again after an estrangement. **2** (usu. in *refl.* or *passive*; foll. by *to*) make acquiescent or contentedly submissive to (something disagreeable or unwelcome) (*was reconciled to failure*). **3** settle (a quarrel etc.). **4 a** harmonize; make compatible. **b** show the compatibility of by argument or in practice (*cannot reconcile your views with the facts*). □□ **reconcilable** *adj.* **reconcilability** /-əˈbɪlɪtɪ/ *n.* **reconcilement** *n.* **reconciler** *n.* **reconciliation** /-ˌsɪlɪˈeɪʃ(ə)n/ *n.* **reconciliatory** /-kənˈsɪlɪətərɪ/ *adj.* [ME f. OF *reconcilier* or L *reconciliare* (as RE-, *conciliare* CONCILIATE)]

recondite /ˈrekənˌdaɪt, rɪˈkɒn-/ *adj.* **1** (of a subject or knowledge) abstruse; out of the way; little known. **2** (of an author or style) dealing in abstruse knowledge or allusions; obscure. □□ **reconditely** *adv.* **reconditeness** *n.* [L *reconditus* (as RE-, *conditus* past part. of *condere* hide)]

recondition /ˌriːkənˈdɪʃ(ə)n/ *v.tr.* **1** overhaul, refit, renovate. **2** make usable again. □□ **reconditioner** *n.*

reconfigure /ˌriːkənˈfɪɡə(r)/ *v.tr.* configure again or differently. □□ **reconfiguration** /-ɡəˈreɪʃ(ə)n/ *n.*

reconfirm /ˌriːkənˈfɜːm/ *v.tr.* confirm, establish, or ratify anew. □□ **reconfirmation** /-kɒnfəˈmeɪʃ(ə)n/ *n.*

reconnaissance /rɪˈkɒnɪs(ə)ns/ *n.* **1** a survey of a region, esp. a military examination to locate an enemy or ascertain strategic features. **2** a preliminary survey or inspection. [F (earlier *-oissance*) f. stem of *reconnaître* (as RECONNOITRE)]

reconnect /ˌriːkəˈnekt/ *v.tr.* connect again. □□ **reconnection** *n.*

reconnoitre /ˌrekəˈnɔɪtə(r)/ *v. & n.* (*US* **reconnoiter**) —*v.* **1** tr. make a reconnaissance of (an area, enemy position, etc.). **2** *intr.* make a reconnaissance. —*n.* a reconnaissance. [obs. F *reconnoître* f. L *recognoscere* RECOGNIZE]

reconquer /riːˈkɒŋkə(r)/ *v.tr.* conquer again. □□ **reconquest** *n.*

reconsider /ˌriːkənˈsɪdə(r)/ *v.tr. & intr.* consider again, esp. for a possible change of decision. □□ **reconsideration** /-ˈreɪʃ(ə)n/ *n.*

reconsign /ˌriːkənˈsaɪn/ *v.tr.* consign again or differently. □□ **reconsignment** *n.*

reconsolidate /ˌriːkənˈsɒlɪˌdeɪt/ *v.tr. & intr.* consolidate again. □□ **reconsolidation** /-ˈdeɪʃ(ə)n/ *n.*

reconstitute /riːˈkɒnstɪˌtjuːt/ *v.tr.* **1** build up again from parts; reconstruct. **2** reorganize. **3** restore the previous constitution of (dried food etc.) by adding water. □□ **reconstitution** /-ˈtjuːʃ(ə)n/ *n.*

reconstruct /ˌriːkənˈstrʌkt/ *v.tr.* **1** build or form again. **2 a** form a mental or visual impression of (past events) by assembling the evidence for them. **b** re-enact (a crime). **3** reorganize. □□ **reconstructable** *adj.* (also **reconstructible**). **reconstructive** *adj.* **reconstructor** *n.*

reconstruction /ˌriːkənˈstrʌkʃ(ə)n/ *n.* **1** the act or a mode of constructing. **2** a thing reconstructed. **3** *US hist.* the reorganization of the Southern States (1865–77) in the aftermath of the American Civil War. Reconstruction Acts passed by the US Congress required the giving of the vote to Blacks and ratification of the Fourteenth Amendment (1868), which extended US citizenship to all persons born or naturalized in the US, as conditions for readmittance to the Union.

reconvene /ˌriːkənˈviːn/ *v.tr. & intr.* convene again, esp. (of a meeting etc.) after a pause in proceedings.

reconvert /ˌriːkənˈvɜːt/ *v.tr.* convert back to a former state. □□ **reconversion** *n.*

record *n. & v.* —*n.* /ˈrekɔːd/ **1 a** a piece of evidence or information constituting an (esp. official) account of something that has occurred, been said, etc. **b** a document preserving this. **2** the state of being set down or preserved in writing or other permanent form (*is a matter of record*). **3 a** (in full **gramophone record**) a thin plastic disc carrying recorded sound in grooves on each surface, for reproduction by a record-player. **b** a trace made on this or some other medium, e.g. magnetic tape. **4 a** an official report of the proceedings and judgement in a court of justice. **b** a copy of the pleadings etc. constituting a case to be decided by a court (see also *court of record*). **5 a** the facts known about a person's past (*has an honourable record of service*). **b** a list of a person's previous criminal convictions. **6** the best performance (esp. in sport) or most remarkable event of its kind on record (often *attrib.: a record attempt*). **7** an object serving as a memorial of a person or thing; a portrait. **8** *Computing* a number of related items of information which are handled as a unit. —*v.tr.* /rɪˈkɔːd/ **1** set down in writing or some other permanent form for later reference, esp. as an official record. **2** convert (sound, a broadcast, etc.) into permanent form for later reproduction. **3** establish or constitute a historical or record of. □ **break** (or **beat**) **the record** outdo all previous performances etc. **for the record** as an official statement etc.

go on record state one's opinion or judgement openly or officially, so that it is recorded. **have a record** be known as a criminal. **a matter of record** a thing established as a fact by being recorded. **off the record** as an unofficial or confidential statement etc. **on record** officially recorded; publicly known. **put** (or **get** or **set** etc.) **the record straight** correct a misapprehension. **recorded delivery** a Post Office service in which the dispatch and receipt of a letter or parcel are recorded. **recording angel** an angel that supposedly registers each person's good and bad actions. **record-player** an apparatus for reproducing sound from gramophone records. (See GRAMOPHONE.) □□ **recordable** adj. [ME f. OF record remembrance, recorder record, f. L recordari remember (as RE-, cor cordis heart)]

recorder /rɪˈkɔːdə(r)/ n. **1** an apparatus for recording, esp. a tape recorder. **2 a** a keeper of records. **b** a person who makes an official record. **3** Brit. **a** a barrister or solicitor of at least ten years' standing, appointed to serve as a part-time judge. **b** hist. a judge in certain courts. **4** Mus. a woodwind instrument like a flute but blown through the end and having a more hollow tone. □□ **recordership** n. (in sense 3). [ME f. AF recordour, OF recordeur & f. RECORD (in obs. sense 'practise a tune')]

recording /rɪˈkɔːdɪŋ/ n. **1** the process by which audio or video signals are recorded for later reproduction. **2** material or a programme recorded.

recordist /rɪˈkɔːdɪst/ n. a person who records sound.

recount /rɪˈkaʊnt/ v.tr. **1** narrate. **2** tell in detail. [ONF & AF reconter (as RE-, COUNT[1])]

re-count v. & n. —v.tr. /riːˈkaʊnt/ count again. —n. /ˈriːkaʊnt/ a re-counting, esp. of votes in an election.

recoup /rɪˈkuːp/ v.tr. **1** recover or regain (a loss). **2** compensate or reimburse for a loss. **3** Law deduct or keep back (part of a sum due). □ **recoup oneself** recover a loss. □□ **recoupable** adj. **recoupment** n. [F recouper (as RE-, couper cut)]

recourse /rɪˈkɔːs/ n. **1** resorting to a possible source of help. **2** a person or thing resorted to. □ **have recourse to** turn to (a person or thing) for help. **without recourse** a formula used by the endorser of a bill etc. to disclaim responsibility for payment. [ME f. OF recours f. L recursus (as RE-, COURSE)]

recover /rɪˈkʌvə(r)/ v. & n. —v. **1** tr. regain possession or use or control of, reclaim. **2** intr. return to health or consciousness or to a normal state or position (have recovered from my illness; the country never recovered from the war). **3** tr. obtain or secure (compensation etc.) by legal process. **4** tr. retrieve or make up for (a loss, setback, etc.). **5** refl. regain composure or consciousness or control of one's limbs. **6** tr. retrieve (reusable substances) from industrial waste. —n. the recovery of a normal position in fencing etc. □□ **recoverable** adj. **recoverability** /-ˈbɪlɪtɪ/ n. **recoverer** n. [ME f. AF recoverer, OF recovrer f. L recuperare RECUPERATE]

re-cover /riːˈkʌvə(r)/ v.tr. **1** cover again. **2** provide (a chair etc.) with a new cover.

recovery /rɪˈkʌvərɪ/ n. (pl. **-ies**) **1** the act or an instance of recovering; the process of being recovered. **2** Golf a stroke bringing the ball out of a bunker etc. [ME f. AF recoverie, OF reco(u)vree (as RECOVER)]

recreant /ˈrekrɪənt/ adj. & n. literary —adj. **1** craven, cowardly. **2** apostate. —n. **1** a coward. **2** an apostate. □□ **recreancy** n. **recreantly** adv. [ME f. OF, part. of recroire f. med.L (se) recredere yield in trial by combat (as RE-, credere entrust)]

re-create /ˌriːkrɪˈeɪt/ v.tr. create over again. □□ **re-creation** n.

recreation /ˌrekrɪˈeɪʃ(ə)n/ n. **1** the process or means of refreshing or entertaining oneself. **2** a pleasurable activity. □ **recreation-ground** public land for games etc. □□ **recreational** adj. **recreationally** adv. **recreative** /ˈrekrɪˌeɪtɪv/ adj. [ME f. OF f. L recreatio -onis f. recreare create again, renew]

recriminate /rɪˈkrɪmɪˌneɪt/ v.intr. make mutual or counter accusations. □□ **recrimination** /-ˈneɪʃ(ə)n/ n. **recriminative** /-nətɪv/ adj. **recriminatory** /-nətərɪ/ adj. [med.L recriminare (as RE-, criminare accuse f. crimen CRIME)]

recross /riːˈkrɒs/ v.tr. & intr. cross or pass over again.

recrudesce /ˌriːkruːˈdes, ˌrek-/ v.intr. (of a disease or difficulty

etc.) break out again, esp. after a dormant period. □□ **recrudescence** n. **recrudescent** adj. [back-form. f. recrudescent, -ence f. L recrudescere (as RE-, crudus raw)]

recruit /rɪˈkruːt/ n. & v. —n. **1** a serviceman or servicewoman newly enlisted and not yet fully trained. **2** a new member of a society or organization. **3** a beginner. —v. **1** tr. enlist (a person) as a recruit. **2** tr. form (an army etc.) by enlisting recruits. **3** intr. get or seek recruits. **4** tr. replenish or reinvigorate (numbers, strength, etc.). □□ **recruitable** adj. **recruiter** n. **recruitment** n. [earlier = reinforcement, f. obs. F dial. recrute ult. f. F recroître increase again f. L recrescere]

recrystallize /riːˈkrɪstəˌlaɪz/ v.tr. & intr. (also **-ise**) crystallize again. □□ **recrystallization** /-ˈzeɪʃ(ə)n/ n.

recta pl. of RECTUM.

rectal /ˈrekt(ə)l/ adj. of or by means of the rectum. □□ **rectally** adv.

rectangle /ˈrekˌtæŋg(ə)l/ n. a plane figure with four straight sides and four right angles, esp. one with the adjacent sides unequal. [F rectangle or med.L rectangulum f. LL rectiangulum f. L rectus straight + angulus ANGLE[1]]

rectangular /rekˈtæŋgʊlə(r)/ adj. **1 a** shaped like a rectangle. **b** having the base or sides or section shaped like a rectangle. **2 a** placed at right angles. **b** having parts or lines placed at right angles. □ **rectangular coordinates** coordinates measured along axes at right angles. **rectangular hyperbola** a hyperbola with rectangular asymptotes. □□ **rectangularity** /-ˈlærɪtɪ/ n. **rectangularly** adv.

recti pl. of RECTUS.

rectifier /ˈrektɪˌfaɪə(r)/ n. **1** a person or thing that rectifies. **2** Electr. an electrical device that allows a current to flow preferentially in one direction by converting an alternating current into a direct one.

rectify /ˈrektɪˌfaɪ/ v.tr. (**-ies**, **-ied**) **1** adjust or make right; correct, amend. **2** purify or refine, esp. by repeated distillation. **3** find a straight line equal in length to (a curve). **4** convert (alternating current) to direct current. □□ **rectifiable** adj. **rectification** /-fɪˈkeɪʃ(ə)n/ n. [ME f. OF rectifier f. med.L rectificare f. L rectus right]

rectilinear /ˌrektɪˈlɪnɪə(r)/ adj. (also **rectilineal** /-nɪəl/) **1** bounded or characterized by straight lines. **2** in or forming a straight line. □□ **rectilinearity** /-ˈærɪtɪ/ n. **rectilinearly** adv. [LL rectilineus f. L rectus straight + linea LINE[1]]

rectitude /ˈrektɪˌtjuːd/ n. **1** moral uprightness. **2** righteousness. **3** correctness. [ME f. OF rectitude or LL rectitudo f. L rectus right]

recto /ˈrektəʊ/ n. (pl. **-os**) **1** the right-hand page of an open book. **2** the front of a printed leaf of paper or manuscript (opp. VERSO). [L recto (folio) on the right (leaf)]

rector /ˈrektə(r)/ n. **1** (in the Church of England) the incumbent of a parish where all tithes formerly passed to the incumbent (cf. VICAR). **2** RC Ch. a priest in charge of a church or religious institution. **3 a** the head of some schools, universities, and colleges. **b** (in Scotland) an elected representative of students on a university's governing body. □□ **rectorate** /-rət/ n. **rectorial** /-ˈtɔːrɪəl/ adj. **rectorship** n. [ME f. OF rectour or L rector ruler f. regere rect- rule]

rectory /ˈrektərɪ/ n. (pl. **-ies**) **1** a rector's house. **2** (in the Church of England) a rector's benefice. [AF & OF rectorie or med.L rectoria (as RECTOR)]

rectrix /ˈrektrɪks/ n. (pl. **rectrices** /-rɪˌsiːz/) a bird's strong tail-feather directing flight. [L, fem. of rector ruler: see RECTOR]

rectum /ˈrektəm/ n. (pl. **rectums** or **recta** /-tə/) the final section of the large intestine, terminating at the anus. [L rectum (intestinum) straight (intestine)]

rectus /ˈrektəs/ n. (pl. **recti** /-taɪ/) Anat. a straight muscle. [L, = straight]

recumbent /rɪˈkʌmbənt/ adj. lying down; reclining. □□ **recumbency** n. **recumbently** adv. [L recumbere recline (as RE-, cumbere lie)]

recuperate /rɪˈkuːpəˌreɪt/ v. **1** intr. recover from illness, exhaustion, loss, etc. **2** tr. regain (health, something lost, etc.). □□ **recuperable** adj. **recuperation** /-ˈreɪʃ(ə)n/ n. **recuperative** /-rətɪv/ adj. **recuperator** n. [L recuperare recuperat- recover]

recur /rɪ'kɜ:(r)/ v.intr. (**recurred, recurring**) **1** occur again; be repeated. **2** (of a thought, idea, etc.) come back to one's mind. **3** (foll. by *to*) go back in thought or speech. □ **recurring decimal** a decimal fraction in which the same figures are repeated indefinitely. [L *recurrere recurs-* (as RE-, *currere* run)]

recurrent /rɪ'kʌrənt/ adj. **1** recurring; happening repeatedly. **2** (of a nerve, vein, branch, etc.) turning back so as to reverse direction. □□ **recurrence** n. **recurrently** adv.

recursion /rɪ'kɜ:ʃ(ə)n/ n. **1** the act or an instance of returning. **2** *Math.* the repeated application of a procedure or definition to a previous result to obtain a series of values. □ **recursion formula** *Math.* an expression giving successive terms of a series etc. □□ **recursive** adj. [LL *recursio* (as RECUR)]

recurve /rɪ'kɜ:v/ v.tr. & intr. bend backwards. □□ **recurvate** /-vət/ adj. **recurvature** n. [L *recurvare recurvat-* (as RE-, *curvare* bend)]

recusant /'rekjʊz(ə)nt/ n. & adj. —n. a person who refuses submission to an authority or compliance with a regulation, esp. *hist.* one who refused to attend services of the Church of England. —adj. of or being a recusant. □□ **recusance** n. **recusancy** n. [L *recusare* refuse]

recycle /ri:'saɪk(ə)l/ v.tr. return (material) to a previous stage of a cyclic process, esp. convert (waste) to reusable material. □□ **recyclable** adj.

red /red/ adj. & n. —adj. **1** of or near the colour seen at the least-refracted end of the visible spectrum, of shades ranging from that of blood to pink or deep orange. **2** flushed in the face with shame, anger, etc. **3** (of the eyes) bloodshot or red-rimmed with weeping. **4** (of the hair) reddish-brown, orange, tawny. **5** involving or having to do with bloodshed, burning, violence, or revolution. **6** *colloq.* communist or socialist. **7** (**Red**) Russian, Soviet (*the Red Army*). **8** (of wine) made from dark grapes and coloured by their skins. —n. **1** a red colour or pigment. **2** red clothes or material (*dressed in red*). **3** *colloq.* a communist or socialist. **4 a** a red ball, piece, etc., in a game or sport. **b** the player using such pieces. **5** the debit side of an account (*in the red*). **6** a red light. □ **red admiral** a butterfly, *Vanessa atalanta*, with red bands on each pair of wings. **red bark** a red kind of cinchona. **red biddy** *colloq.* a mixture of cheap wine and methylated spirits. **red-blooded** virile, vigorous. **red-bloodedness** vigour, spirit. **red card** *Football* a card shown by the referee to a player being sent off the field. **red carpet** privileged treatment of an eminent visitor. **red cedar** an American juniper, *Juniperus virginiana*. **red cell** (or **corpuscle**) an erythrocyte. **red cent** *US* the smallest (orig. copper) coin; a trivial sum. **red cross 1** St George's cross, the national emblem of England. **2** the Christian side in the Crusades. **Red Cross** see separate entry. **red deer** a deer, *Cervus elaphus*, with a rich red-brown summer coat turning dull-brown in winter. **red duster** *Brit. colloq.* = *red ensign*. **red dwarf** an old relatively cool star. **red ensign** see ENSIGN. **red-eye 1** = RUDD. **2** *US sl.* cheap whisky. **red-faced** embarrassed, ashamed. **red flag** see separate entry. **red fox** a native British fox, *Vulpes vulpes*, having a characteristic deep red or fawn coat. **red giant** see separate entry. **red grouse** a subspecies of the willow grouse, native to Britain and familiar as a game-bird. **red gum 1** a teething-rash in children. **2 a** a reddish resin. **b** any of various kinds of eucalyptus yielding this. **red-handed** in or just after the act of committing a crime, doing wrong, etc. **red hat 1** a cardinal's hat. **2** the symbol of a cardinal's office. **red-headed 1** (of a person) having red hair. **2** (of birds etc.) having a red head. **red heat 1** the temperature or state of something so hot as to emit red light. **2** great excitement. **red herring 1** dried smoked herring. **2** a misleading clue or distraction (so called from the practice of using the scent of red herring in training hounds). **red-hot 1** heated until red. **2** highly exciting. **3** (of news) fresh; completely new. **4** intensely excited. **5** enraged. **red-hot poker** any plant of the genus *Kniphofia*, with spikes of usually red or yellow flowers. **Red Indian** *offens.* an American Indian, with reddish skin. **red lead** a red form of lead oxide used as a pigment. **red-letter day** a day that is pleasantly noteworthy or memorable (orig. a festival marked in red on the calendar). **red light 1** a signal to stop on a road, railway, etc. **2** a warning or

refusal. **red-light district** a district containing many brothels. **red man** = *Red Indian*. **red meat** meat that is red when raw (e.g. beef or lamb). **red mullet** a marine fish, *Mullus surmuletus*, valued as food. **red pepper 1** cayenne pepper. **2** the ripe fruit of the capsicum plant, *Capsicum annuum*. **red rag** something that excites a person's rage (so called because red is supposed to provoke bulls). **red rattle** a pink-flowered marsh plant, *Pedicularis palustris*. **red roan** see ROAN[1]. **red rose** the emblem of Lancashire or the Lancastrians. **red shift** the displacement of spectral lines towards longer wavelengths (the red end of the spectrum) in radiation from distant galaxies etc., interpreted as a Doppler shift arising from a velocity of recession. **red spider** any of various mites of the family Tetranychidae infesting hothouse plants esp. vines. **red squirrel** a native British squirrel, *Sciurus vulgaris*, with reddish fur. **Red Star** the emblem of some Communist countries. **red tape** excessive bureaucracy or adherence to formalities esp. in public business. **red-water 1** a bacterial disease of calves, a symptom of which is the passing of reddish urine. **2** a mass of water made red by pigmented plankton, esp. *Gonyanlax tamarensis*. □□ **reddish** adj. **reddy** adj. **redly** adv. **redness** n. [OE *rēad* f. Gmc]

redact /rɪ'dækt/ v.tr. put into literary form; edit for publication. □□ **redactor** n. [L *redigere redact-* (as RE-, *agere* bring)]

redaction /rɪ'dækʃ(ə)n/ n. **1** preparation for publication. **2** revision, editing, rearrangement. **3** a new edition. □□ **redactional** adj. [F *rédaction* f. LL *redactio* (as REDACT)]

redan /rɪ'dæn/ n. a fieldwork with two faces forming a salient angle. [F f. *redent* notching (as RE-, *dent* tooth)]

Red Army 1 the armed forces of the USSR; *orig.* the Russian Bolshevik army. **2** the army of China and other (esp. Communist) countries. **3** a left-wing extremist terrorist organization in Japan. □ **Red Army Faction** an urban guerrilla group in former West Germany, active from 1968 onwards, hostile to US forces and to capitalist society. It was originally led by Andreas Baader (1943–77) and Ulrike Meinhof (1934–76), after whom it was sometimes called the Baader-Meinhof Group.

redbreast /'redbrest/ n. *colloq.* a robin.

redbrick /'redbrɪk/ adj. esp. *Brit.* (of a university) founded relatively recently.

Red Brigades a left-wing terrorist organization based in Italy, who carried out kidnappings, murders, and sabotage from the 1970s onwards. The former Prime Minister of Italy, Aldo Moro, was one of their victims (1978).

redbud /'redbʌd/ n. any American tree of the genus *Cercis*, with pale pink flowers.

redcap /'redkæp/ n. **1** *Brit.* a member of the military police. **2** *US* a railway porter.

redcoat /'redkəʊt/ n. *hist.* a British soldier (so called from the scarlet uniform of most regiments).

Red Crescent an organization that is the equivalent of the Red Cross in Muslim countries.

Red Cross an organization set up, at the instigation of the Swiss philanthropist Henri Dunant (d.1910), according to the Geneva Convention of 1864 for the treatment of the sick and wounded in war and those suffering by large-scale natural disasters. The international organization (which operates through national societies) has twice won the Nobel Peace Prize (1917, 1944). Its headquarters are at Geneva in Switzerland, and its emblem, a red cross on a white ground, is the Swiss flag with its colours reversed. Its national branches include the British Red Cross Society (incorporated in 1908), which undertakes first-aid and welfare work as well as participating in relief work abroad. Muslim countries have adopted a red crescent as their emblem for an equivalent organization.

redcurrant /'red,kʌrənt/ n. **1** a widely cultivated shrub, *Ribes rubrum*. **2** a small red edible berry of this plant.

redd /red/ v.tr. (*past* and *past part.* **redd**) *dial.* **1** clear up. **2** arrange, tidy, compose, settle. [ME: cf. MLG, MDu. *redden*]

redden /'red(ə)n/ v.tr. & intr. make or become red.

reddle /'red(ə)l/ n. red ochre; ruddle. [var. of RUDDLE]

rede /ri:d/ n. & v. *archaic* —n. advice, counsel. —v.tr. **1** advise.

2 read (a riddle or dream). [OE *ræd* f. Gmc, rel. to READ (of which the verb is a ME var. retained for archaic senses)]

redecorate /riːˈdekəˌreɪt/ v.tr. decorate again or differently. □□ **redecoration** /-ˈreɪʃ(ə)n/ n.

redeem /rɪˈdiːm/ v.tr. **1** buy back; recover by expenditure of effort or by a stipulated payment. **2** make a single payment to discharge (a regular charge or obligation). **3** convert (tokens or bonds etc.) into goods or cash. **4** (of God or Christ) deliver from sin and damnation. **5** make up for; be a compensating factor in (*has one redeeming feature*). **6** (foll. by *from*) save from (a defect). **7** *refl.* save (oneself) from blame. **8** purchase the freedom of (a person). **9** save (a person's life) by ransom. **10** save or rescue or reclaim. **11** fulfil (a promise). □□ **redeemable** adj. [ME f. OF *redimer* or L *redimere redempt-* (as RE-, *emere* buy)]

redeemer /rɪˈdiːmə(r)/ n. a person who redeems. □ **the Redeemer** Christ.

redefine /ˌriːdɪˈfaɪn/ v.tr. define again or differently. □□ **redefinition** /-defɪˈnɪʃ(ə)n/ n.

redemption /rɪˈdempʃ(ə)n/ n. **1** the act or an instance of redeeming; the process of being redeemed. **2** man's deliverance from sin and damnation. **3** a thing that redeems. □□ **redemptive** adj. [ME f. OF f. L *redemptio* (as REDEEM)]

redeploy /ˌriːdɪˈplɔɪ/ v.tr. send (troops, workers, etc.) to a new place or task. □□ **redeployment** n.

redesign /ˌriːdɪˈzaɪn/ v.tr. design again or differently.

redetermine /ˌriːdɪˈtɜːmɪn/ v.tr. determine again or differently. □□ **redetermination** /-ˈneɪʃ(ə)n/ n.

redevelop /ˌriːdɪˈveləp/ v.tr. develop anew (esp. an urban area, with new buildings). □□ **redeveloper** n. **redevelopment** n.

redfish /ˈredfɪʃ/ n. **1** a male salmon in the spawning season. **2** a rose-fish.

red flag n. **1** a symbol of danger. **2** the symbol of socialist revolution. □ **The Red Flag** a socialist song (1889) composed by James Connell, secretary to the Workmen's Legal Friendly Society.

Redford /ˈredfəd/, Robert (1936–), American film actor, who co-starred with Paul Newman in *Butch Cassidy and the Sundance Kid* (1969) and *The Sting* (1973), and played the title role in *The Great Gatsby* (1974).

red giant n. an extended star of high luminosity and low surface temperature, generally understood to be in a late stage of evolution when no further hydrogen remains in the central regions to undergo nuclear fusion, but reactions involving hydrogen may continue in a spherical shell. The radius may exceed 150 million km, so that the entire orbit of Earth about the sun could be fitted inside the star's envelope. Temperatures may be as low as 3,000 °C, but the enormous emitting area renders such a star many times more luminous than the sun. Typical examples are Betelgeuse in Orion and Aldebaran in Taurus.

Redgrave /ˈredgreɪv/, Sir Michael Scudamore (1908–), English actor, a major figure in the theatre, who has also appeared in films, including *The Browing Version* (1951) and *The Go-Between* (1971). His daughter Vanessa (1937–) was a successful stage actress before appearing in films that include *Julia* (1976), for which she received an Academy Award. She has also been active in left-wing politics.

Red Guard any of various radical groups and their members, esp. (i) an organized detachment of workers during the Russian Bolshevik Revolution of 1917, (ii) a militant youth movement during the Cultural Revolution in China, 1966–76.

redhead /ˈredhed/ n. a person with red hair.

redial /riːˈdaɪəl/ v.tr. & intr. (**redialled, redialling**; US **redialed, redialing**) dial again.

redid *past* of REDO.

rediffusion /ˌriːdɪˈfjuːʒ(ə)n/ n. the relaying of broadcast programmes esp. by cable from a central receiver.

redingote /ˈredɪŋˌgəʊt/ n. a woman's long coat with a cutaway front or a contrasting piece on the front. [F f. E *riding-coat*]

redintegrate /rɪˈdɪntɪˌgreɪt/ v.tr. **1** restore to wholeness or unity. **2** renew or re-establish in a united or perfect state. □□

redintegration /-ˈgreɪʃ(ə)n/ n. **redintegrative** adj. [ME f. L *redintegrare* (as RE-, INTEGRATE)]

redirect /ˌriːdaɪˈrekt, -dɪˈrekt/ v.tr. direct again, esp. change the address of (a letter). □□ **redirection** n.

rediscover /ˌriːdɪˈskʌvə(r)/ v.tr. discover again. □□ **rediscovery** n. (pl. **-ies**).

redissolve /ˌriːdɪˈzɒlv/ v.tr. & intr. dissolve again. □□ **redissolution** /-ˌdɪsəˈluːʃ(ə)n/ n.

redistribute /ˌriːdɪˈstrɪˌbjuːt, *disp.* riːˈdɪs-/ v.tr. distribute again or differently. □□ **redistribution** /-ˈbjuːʃ(ə)n/ n. **redistributive** /-ˈtrɪbjʊtɪv/ adj.

redivide /ˌriːdɪˈvaɪd/ v.tr. divide again or differently. □□ **redivision** /-ˈvɪʒ(ə)n/ n.

redivivus /ˌredɪˈviːvəs/ adj. (placed after noun) come back to life. [L (as RE-, *vivus* living)]

Redmond /ˈredmənd/, John Edward (1856–1916), Irish statesman who led the Parnellites after Parnell's death. During his leadership the Irish obtained control of local government, and the statutory establishment of an Irish parliament. His aim was to establish a free Ireland within the British Empire, but his moderate approach lost the confidence of his country which passed into the control of extreme nationalists under de Valera.

redneck /ˈrednek/ n. US often *derog.* a working-class White in the southern US, esp. a politically conservative one.

redo /riːˈduː/ v.tr. (3rd sing. present **redoes**; past **redid**; past part. **redone**) **1** do again or differently. **2** redecorate.

redolent /ˈredələnt/ adj. **1** (foll. by *of*, *with*) strongly reminiscent or suggestive or mentally associated. **2** fragrant. **3** having a strong smell; odorous. □□ **redolence** n. **redolently** adv. [ME f. OF *redolent* or L *redolēre* (as RE-, *olēre* smell)]

redouble /riːˈdʌb(ə)l/ v. & n. —v. **1** tr. & intr. make or grow greater or more intense or numerous; intensify, increase. **2** intr. *Bridge* double again a bid already doubled by an opponent. —n. *Bridge* the redoubling of a bid. [F *redoubler* (as RE-, DOUBLE)]

redoubt /rɪˈdaʊt/ n. Mil. an outwork or fieldwork usu. square or polygonal and without flanking defences. [F *redoute* f. obs. It. *ridotta* f. med.L *reductus* refuge f. past part. of L *reducere* withdraw (see REDUCE): *-b-* after DOUBT (cf. REDOUBTABLE)]

redoubtable /rɪˈdaʊtəb(ə)l/ adj. formidable, esp. as an opponent. □□ **redoubtably** adv. [ME f. OF *redoutable* f. *redouter* fear (as RE-, DOUBT)]

redound /rɪˈdaʊnd/ v.intr. **1** (foll. by *to*) (of an action etc.) make a great contribution to (one's credit or advantage etc.). **2** (foll. by *upon*, *on*) come as the final result to; come back or recoil upon. [ME, orig. = overflow, f. OF *redonder* f. L *redundare* surge (as RE-, *unda* wave)]

redox /ˈredɒks, ˈriː-/ n. Chem. (often *attrib.*) oxidation and reduction. [reduction + oxidation]

redpoll /ˈredpɒl/ n. a finch, *Acanthis flammea*, with a red forehead, similar to a linnet.

redraft /riːˈdrɑːft/ v.tr. draft (a writing or document) again.

redraw /riːˈdrɔː/ v.tr. (past **redrew**; past part. **redrawn**) draw again or differently.

redress /rɪˈdres/ v. & n. —v.tr. **1** remedy or rectify (a wrong or grievance etc.). **2** readjust; set straight again. —n. **1** reparation for a wrong. **2** (foll. by *of*) the act or process of redressing (a grievance etc.). □ **redress the balance** restore equality. □□ **redressable** adj. **redressal** n. **redresser** n. (also **redressor**). [ME f. OF *redresse(r), redrecier* (as RE-, DRESS)]

re-dress /riːˈdres/ v.tr. & intr. dress again or differently.

Red River a river that rises in southern China and flows 1,175 km (730 miles) south-east through northern Vietnam to the Gulf of Tonkin.

Red Sea a long narrow land-locked sea separating Africa from the Arabian Peninsula, connected to the Arabian Sea by the Gulf of Aden and to the Mediterranean Sea by the Suez Canal.

redshank /ˈredʃæŋk/ n. either of two sandpipers, *Tringa totanus* and *T. erythropus*, with bright-red legs.

redskin /ˈredskɪn/ n. colloq. offens. an American Indian.

redstart /ˈredstɑːt/ n. **1** any European red-tailed songbird of the genus *Phoenicurus*. **2** any of various similar American warblers of the family Parulidae. [RED + OE *steort* tail]

reduce /rɪˈdjuːs/ *v.* **1** *tr.* & *intr.* make or become smaller or less. **2** *tr.* (foll. by *to*) bring by force or necessity (to some undesirable state or action) (*reduced them to tears*; *were reduced to begging*). **3** *tr.* convert to another (esp. simpler) form (*reduced it to a powder*). **4** *tr.* convert (a fraction) to the form with the lowest terms. **5** *tr.* (foll. by *to*) bring or simplify or adapt by classification or analysis (*the dispute may be reduced to three issues*). **6** *tr.* make lower in status or rank. **7** *tr.* lower the price of. **8** *intr.* lessen one's weight or size. **9** *tr.* weaken (*is in a very reduced state*). **10** *tr.* impoverish. **11** *tr.* subdue; bring back to obedience. **12** *intr.* & *tr. Chem.* **a** combine or cause to combine with hydrogen. **b** undergo or cause to undergo addition of electrons. **13** *tr. Chem.* convert (oxide etc.) to metal. **14** *tr.* **a** (in surgery) restore (a dislocated etc. part) to its proper position. **b** remedy (a dislocation etc.) in this way. **15** *tr. Photog.* make (a negative or print) less dense. **16** *tr. Cookery* boil off excess liquid from. □ **reduced circumstances** poverty after relative prosperity. **reduce to the ranks** demote (an NCO) to the rank of private. **reducing agent** *Chem.* a substance that brings about reduction by oxidation and losing electrons. □□ **reducer** *n.* **reducible** *adj.* **reducibility** /-ˈbɪlɪtɪ/ *n.* [ME in sense 'restore to original or proper position', f. L *reducere reduct-* (as RE-, *ducere* bring)]

reductio ad absurdum /rɪˌdʌktɪəʊ æd æbˈzɜːdəm/ *n.* a method of proving the falsity of a premiss by showing that the logical consequence is absurd; an instance of this. [L, = reduction to the absurd]

reduction /rɪˈdʌkʃ(ə)n/ *n.* **1** the act or an instance of reducing; the process of being reduced. **2** an amount by which prices etc. are reduced. **3** a reduced copy of a picture etc. **4** an arrangement of an orchestral score for piano etc. □□ **reductive** *adj.* [ME f. OF *reduction* or L *reductio* (as REDUCE)]

reductionism /rɪˈdʌkʃəˌnɪz(ə)m/ *n.* **1** the tendency to or principle of analysing complex things into simple constituents. **2** often *derog.* the doctrine that a system can be fully understood in terms of its isolated parts, or an idea in terms of simple concepts. □□ **reductionist** *n.* **reductionistic** /-ˈnɪstɪk/ *adj.*

redundant /rɪˈdʌnd(ə)nt/ *adj.* **1** superfluous; not needed. **2** that can be omitted without any loss of significance. **3** (of a person) no longer needed at work and therefore unemployed. **4** *Engin.* & *Computing* (of a component) not needed but included in case of failure in another component. □□ **redundancy** *n.* (*pl.* **-ies**) **redundantly** *adv.* [L *redundare redundant-* (as REDOUND)]

reduplicate /rɪˈdjuːplɪˌkeɪt/ *v.tr.* **1** make double. **2** repeat. **3** repeat (a letter or syllable or word) exactly or with a slight change (e.g. hurly-burly, see-saw). □□ **reduplication** /-ˈkeɪʃ(ə)n/ *n.* **reduplicative** /-kətɪv/ *adj.* [LL *reduplicare* (as RE-, DUPLICATE)]

redwing /ˈredwɪŋ/ *n.* a thrush, *Turdus iliacus*, with red underwings showing in flight.

redwood /ˈredwʊd/ *n.* **1** an exceptionally large Californian conifer, *Sequoia sempervirens*, yielding red wood. **2** any tree yielding red wood.

reebok /ˈriːbɒk/ *n.* (also **rhebok**) a small S. African antelope, *Pelea capreolus*, with sharp horns. [Du., = roebuck]

re-echo /riːˈekəʊ/ *v.intr.* & *tr.* (**-oes, -oed**) **1** echo. **2** echo repeatedly; resound.

Reed /riːd/, Sir Carol (1906–76), English film director, whose best-known films include *Odd Man Out* (1947), *The Third Man* (1949), *The Fallen Idol* (1948), and the popular musical *Oliver!* (1968).

reed¹ /riːd/ *n.* & *v.* —*n.* **1 a** any of various water or marsh plants with a firm stem, esp. of the genus *Phragmites*. **b** a tall straight stalk of this. **2** (*collect.*) reeds growing in a mass or used as material esp. for thatching. **3** *Brit.* wheat-straw prepared for thatching. **4** a pipe of reed or straw. **5 a** the vibrating part of the mouthpiece of some wind instruments, e.g. the oboe and clarinet, made of reed or other material and producing the sound. **b** (esp. in *pl.*) a reed instrument. **6** a weaver's comblike implement for separating the threads of the warp and correctly positioning the weft. **7** (in *pl.*) a set of semicylindrical adjacent mouldings like reeds laid together. —*v.tr.* **1** thatch with reed.

2 make (straw) into reed. **3** fit (a musical instrument) with a reed. **4** decorate with a moulding of reeds. □ **reed bunting** a small brown bird, *Emberiza schoeniclus*, frequenting reed-beds. **reed-mace** a tall reedlike water-plant, *Typha latifolia*, with straplike leaves and a head of numerous tiny red-brown flowers. **reed-organ** a harmonium etc. with the sound produced by metal reeds. **reed-pipe 1** a wind instrument with sound produced by a reed. **2** an organ-pipe with a reed. **reed-stop** a reeded organ-stop. **reed-warbler** any bird of the genus *Acrocephalus*, esp. *A. scirpaceus*, frequenting reed-beds. [OE *hrēod* f. WG]

reed² /riːd/ *n.* the fourth stomach of a ruminant; the abomasum. [OE *rēada*]

reedbuck /ˈriːdbʌk/ *n.* an antelope, *Redunca redunca*, native to W. Africa.

reeded /ˈriːdɪd/ *adj. Mus.* (of an instrument) having a vibrating reed.

reeding /ˈriːdɪŋ/ *n. Archit.* a small semicylindrical moulding or ornamentation (cf. REED¹ *n.* 7).

re-edit /riːˈedɪt/ *v.tr.* (**-edited, -editing**) edit again or differently. □□ **re-edition** /-ɪˈdɪʃ(ə)n/ *n.*

reedling /ˈriːdlɪŋ/ *n.* a bearded tit. [REED¹]

re-educate /riːˈedjʊˌkeɪt/ *v.tr.* educate again, esp. to change a person's views or beliefs. □□ **re-education** /-ˈkeɪʃ(ə)n/ *n.*

reedy /ˈriːdɪ/ *adj.* (**reedier, reediest**) **1** full of reeds. **2** like a reed, esp. in weakness or slenderness. **3** (of a voice) like a reed instrument in tone; not full. □□ **reediness** *n.*

reef¹ /riːf/ *n.* **1** a ridge of rock or coral etc. at or near the surface of the sea. **2 a** a lode of ore. **b** the bedrock surrounding this. [earlier *riff*(e) f. MDu., MLG *rif, ref,* f. ON *rif* RIB]

reef² /riːf/ *n.* & *v. Naut.* —*n.* each of several strips across a sail, for taking it in or rolling it up to reduce the surface area in a high wind. —*v.tr.* **1** take in a reef or reefs of (a sail). **2** shorten (a topmast or a bowsprit). □ **reefing-jacket** a thick close-fitting double-breasted jacket. **reef-knot** a double knot made symmetrically to hold securely and cast off easily. **reef-point** each of several short pieces of rope attached to a sail to secure it when reefed. [ME *riff, refe* f. Du. *reef, rif* f. ON *rif* RIB, in the same sense: cf. REEF¹]

reefer /ˈriːfə(r)/ *n.* **1** *sl.* a marijuana cigarette. **2** = *reefing-jacket* (see REEF²). **3 a** a person who reefs. **b** *colloq.* a midshipman. [REEF² (in sense 1, = a thing rolled) + -ER¹]

reek /riːk/ *v.* & *n.* —*v.intr.* (often foll. by *of*) **1** smell strongly and unpleasantly. **2** have unpleasant or suspicious associations (*this reeks of corruption*). **3** give off smoke or fumes. —*n.* **1** a foul or stale smell. **2** esp. *Sc.* smoke. **3** vapour; a visible exhalation (esp. from a chimney). □□ **reeky** *adj.* [OE *rēocan* (v.), *rēc* (n.), f. Gmc]

reel /riːl/ *n.* & *v.* —*n.* **1** a cylindrical device on which thread, silk, yarn, paper, film, wire, etc., are wound. **2** a quantity of thread etc. wound on a reel. **3** a device for winding and unwinding a line as required, esp. in fishing. **4** a revolving part in various machines. **5 a** a lively folk or Scottish dance, of two or more couples facing each other. **b** a piece of music for this. —*v.* **1** *tr.* wind (thread, a fishing-line, etc.) on a reel. **2** *tr.* (foll. by *in, up*) draw (fish etc.) in or up by the use of a reel. **3** *intr.* stand or walk or run unsteadily. **4** *intr.* be shaken mentally or physically. **5** *intr.* rock from side to side, or swing violently. **6** *intr.* dance a reel. □ **reel off** say or recite very rapidly and without apparent effort. □□ **reeler** *n.* [OE *hrēol*, of unkn. orig.]

re-elect /ˌriːɪˈlekt/ *v.tr.* elect again, esp. to a further term of office. □□ **re-election** /-ɪˈlekʃ(ə)n/ *n.* **re-eligible** /-ˈelɪdʒɪb(ə)l/ *adj.*

re-embark /ˌriːɪmˈbɑːk/ *v.intr.* & *tr.* go or put on board ship again. □□ **re-embarkation** /-ˈkeɪʃ(ə)n/ *n.*

re-emerge /ˌriːɪˈmɜːdʒ/ *v.intr.* emerge again; come back out. □□ **re-emergence** *n.* **re-emergent** *adj.*

re-emphasize /riːˈemfəˌsaɪz/ *v.tr.* place renewed emphasis on. □□ **re-emphasis** /-ˈemfəsɪs/ *n.*

re-employ /ˌriːɪmˈplɔɪ/ *v.tr.* employ again. □□ **re-employment** *n.*

re-enact /ˌriːɪˈnækt/ *v.tr.* act out (a past event). □□ **re-enactment** *n.*

re-enlist /ˌriːɪnˈlɪst/ v.intr. enlist again, esp. in the armed services. □□ **re-enlister** n.

re-enter /riːˈentə(r)/ v.tr. & intr. enter again; go back in. □□ **re-entrance** /-ˈentrəns/ n.

re-entrant /riːˈentrənt/ adj. & n. —adj. 1 esp. Fortification (of an angle) pointing inwards (opp. SALIENT). 2 Geom. reflex. —n. a re-entrant angle.

re-entry /riːˈentrɪ/ n. (pl. **-ies**) 1 the act of entering again, esp. (of a spacecraft, missile, etc.) re-entering the earth's atmosphere. 2 Law an act of retaking or repossession.

re-equip /ˌriːɪˈkwɪp/ v.tr. & intr. (**-equipped, -equipping**) provide or be provided with new equipment.

re-erect /ˌriːɪˈrekt/ v.tr. erect again.

re-establish /ˌriːɪˈstæblɪʃ/ v.tr. establish again or anew. □□ **re-establishment** n.

re-evaluate /ˌriːɪˈvæljuˌeɪt/ v.tr. evaluate again or differently. □□ **re-evaluation** /-ˈeɪʃ(ə)n/ n.

reeve¹ /riːv/ n. 1 hist. **a** the chief magistrate of a town or district. **b** an official supervising a landowner's estate. **c** any of various minor local officials. 2 Can. the president of a village or town council. [OE (ge)rēfa, girēfa]

reeve² /riːv/ v.tr. (past **rove** /rəʊv/ or **reeved**) Naut. 1 (usu. foll. by through) thread (a rope or rod etc.) through a ring or other aperture. 2 pass a rope through (a block etc.). 3 fasten (a rope or block) in this way. [prob. f. Du. rēven REEF²]

reeve³ /riːv/ n. a female ruff (see RUFF¹). [17th c.: orig. unkn.]

re-examine /ˌriːɪgˈzæmɪn/ v.tr. examine again or further (esp. a witness after cross-examination). □□ **re-examination** /-ˈneɪʃ(ə)n/ n.

re-export v. & n. —v.tr. /ˌriːɪkˈspɔːt/ export again (esp. imported goods after further processing or manufacture). —n. /riːˈekspɔːt/ 1 the process of re-exporting. 2 something re-exported. □□ **re-exportation** /-ˈteɪʃ(ə)n/ n. **re-exporter** /ˌriːɪkˈspɔːtə(r)/ n.

ref /ref/ n. colloq. a referee in sports. [abbr.]

ref. abbr. 1 reference. 2 refer to.

reface /riːˈfeɪs/ v.tr. put a new facing on (a building).

refashion /riːˈfæʃ(ə)n/ v.tr. fashion again or differently.

refection /rɪˈfekʃ(ə)n/ n. literary 1 refreshment by food or drink (we took refection). 2 a light meal. [ME f. OF f. L refectio -onis f. reficere (as REFECTORY)]

refectory /rɪˈfektərɪ, ˈrefɪktərɪ/ n. (pl. **-ies**) a room used for communal meals, esp. in a monastery or college. □ **refectory table** a long narrow table. [LL refectorium f. L reficere refresh (as RE-, facere make)]

refer /rɪˈfɜː(r)/ v. (**referred, referring**) (usu. foll. by to) 1 tr. trace or ascribe (to a person or thing as a cause or source) (referred their success to their popularity). 2 tr. consider as belonging (to a certain date or place or class). 3 tr. send on or direct (a person, or a question for decision) (the matter was referred to arbitration; referred him to her previous answer). 4 intr. make an appeal or have recourse to (some authority or source of information) (referred to his notes). 5 tr. send (a person) to a medical specialist etc. 6 tr. (foll. by back to) send (a proposal etc.) back to (a lower body, court, etc.). 7 intr. (foll. by to) (of a person speaking) make an allusion or direct the hearer's attention (decided not to refer to our other problems). 8 intr. (foll. by to) (of a statement etc.) have a particular relation; be directed (this paragraph refers to the events of last year). 9 tr. (foll. by to) interpret (a statement) as being directed to (a particular context etc.). 10 tr. fail (a candidate in an examination). □ **referred pain** pain felt in a part of the body other than its actual source. **refer to drawer** a banker's note suspending payment of a cheque. □□ **referable** /rɪˈfɜːrəb(ə)l, ˈrefər-/ adj. **referrer** n. [ME f. OF referer f. L referre carry back (as RE-, ferre bring)]

referee /ˌrefəˈriː/ n. & v. —n. 1 an umpire esp. in football or boxing. 2 a person whose opinion or judgement is sought in some connection, or who is referred to for a decision in a dispute etc. 3 a person willing to testify to the character of an applicant for employment etc. —v. (**referees, refereed**) 1 intr. act as referee. 2 tr. be the referee of (a game etc.).

reference /ˈrefərəns/ n. & v. —n. 1 the referring of a matter for decision or settlement or consideration to some authority. 2 the scope given to this authority. 3 (foll. by to) **a** a relation or respect or correspondence (success seems to have little reference to merit). **b** an allusion (made no reference to our problems). **c** a direction to a book etc. (or a passage in it) where information may be found. **d** a book or passage so cited. 4 **a** the act of looking up a passage etc. or looking in a book for information. **b** the act of referring to a person etc. for information. 5 **a** a written testimonial supporting an applicant for employment etc. **b** a person giving this. —v.tr. provide (a book etc.) with references to authorities. □ **reference book** a book intended to be consulted for information on individual matters rather than read continuously. **reference library** a library in which the books are for consultation not loan. **with** (or **in**) **reference to** regarding; as regards; about. **without reference to** not taking account of. □□ **referential** /-ˈrenʃ(ə)l/ adj.

referendum /ˌrefəˈrendəm/ n. (pl. **referendums** or **referenda** /-də/) 1 the process of referring a political question to the electorate for a direct decision by general vote. 2 a vote taken by referendum. [L, gerund or neut. gerundive of referre: see REFER]

referent /ˈrefərənt/ n. the idea or thing that a word etc. symbolizes. [L referens (as REFERENDUM)]

referral /rɪˈfɜːr(ə)l/ n. the referring of an individual to an expert or specialist for advice, esp. the directing of a patient by a GP to a medical specialist.

refill v. & n. —v.tr. /riːˈfɪl/ 1 fill again. 2 provide a new filling for. —n. /ˈriːfɪl/ 1 a new filling. 2 the material for this. □□ **refillable** /-ˈfɪləb(ə)l/ adj.

refine /rɪˈfaɪn/ v. 1 tr. free from impurities or defects; purify, clarify. 2 tr. & intr. make or become more polished or elegant or cultured. 3 tr. & intr. make or become more subtle or delicate in thought, feelings, etc. □□ **refinable** adj. [RE- + FINE¹ v.]

refined /rɪˈfaɪnd/ adj. characterized by polish or elegance or subtlety.

refinement /rɪˈfaɪnmənt/ n. 1 the act of refining or the process of being refined. 2 fineness of feeling or taste. 3 polish or elegance in behaviour or manner. 4 an added development or improvement (a car with several refinements). 5 a piece of subtle reasoning. 6 a fine distinction. 7 a subtle or ingenious example or display (all the refinements of reasoning). [REFINE + -MENT, after F raffinement]

refiner /rɪˈfaɪnə(r)/ n. a person or firm whose business is to refine crude oil, metal, sugar, etc.

refinery /rɪˈfaɪnərɪ/ n. (pl. **-ies**) a place where oil etc. is refined.

refit v. & n. —v.tr. & intr. /riːˈfɪt/ (**refitted, refitting**) make or become fit or serviceable again (esp. of a ship undergoing renewal and repairs). —n. /ˈriːfɪt/ the act or an instance of refitting; the process of being refitted. □□ **refitment** n.

reflag /riːˈflæg/ v.tr. (**reflagged, reflagging**) change the national registration of (a ship).

reflate /riːˈfleɪt/ v.tr. cause reflation of (a currency or economy etc.). [RE- after inflate, deflate]

reflation /riːˈfleɪʃ(ə)n/ n. the inflation of a financial system to restore its previous condition after deflation. [RE- after inflation, deflation]

reflect /rɪˈflekt/ v. 1 tr. **a** (of a surface or body) throw back (heat, light, sound, etc.). **b** cause to rebound (reflected light). 2 tr. (of a mirror) show an image of; reproduce to the eye or mind. 3 tr. correspond in appearance or effect to; have as a cause or source (their behaviour reflects a wish to succeed). 4 tr. **a** (of an action, result, etc.) show or bring (credit, discredit, etc.). **b** (absol.; usu. foll. by on, upon) bring discredit on. 5 **a** intr. (often foll. by on, upon) meditate on; think about. **b** tr. (foll. by that, how, etc. + clause) consider; remind oneself. 6 intr. (usu. foll. by upon, on) make disparaging remarks. □ **reflecting telescope** = REFLECTOR. [ME f. OF reflecter or L reflectere (as RE-, flectere flex- bend)]

reflection /rɪˈflekʃ(ə)n/ n. (also **reflexion**) 1 the act or an instance of reflecting; the process of being reflected. 2 **a** a reflected light, heat, or colour. **b** a reflected image. 3 reconsideration (on reflection). 4 (often foll. by on) discredit or a thing bringing discredit. 5 (often foll. by on, upon) an idea arising in the mind;

a comment or apophthegm. □ **angle of reflection** *Physics* the angle made by a reflected ray with a perpendicular to the reflecting surface. □□ **reflectional** *adj.* [ME f. OF *reflexion* or LL *reflexio* (as REFLECT), with assim. to *reflect*]

reflective /rɪˈflektɪv/ *adj.* **1** (of a surface etc.) giving a reflection or image. **2** (of mental faculties) concerned in reflection or thought. **3** (of a person or mood etc.) thoughtful; given to meditation. □□ **reflectively** *adv.* **reflectiveness** *n.*

reflector /rɪˈflektə(r)/ *n.* **1** a piece of glass or metal etc. for reflecting light in a required direction, e.g. a red one on the back of a motor vehicle or bicycle. **2 a** a telescope etc. using a mirror to produce images. **b** the mirror itself.

reflet /rəˈfleɪ/ *n.* lustre or iridescence, esp. on pottery. [F f. It. *riflesso* reflection, REFLEX]

reflex /ˈriːfleks/ *adj. & n.* —*adj.* **1** (of an action) independent of the will, as an automatic response to the stimulation of a nerve (e.g. a sneeze). **2** (of an angle) exceeding 180°. **3** bent backwards. **4** (of light) reflected. **5** (of a thought etc.) introspective; directed back upon itself or its own operations. **6** (of an effect or influence) reactive; coming back upon its author or source. —*n.* **1** a reflex action. **2** a sign or secondary manifestation (*law is a reflex of public opinion*). **3** reflected light or a reflected image. **4** a word formed by development from an earlier stage of a language. □ **reflex arc** *Anat.* the sequence of nerves involved in a reflex action. **reflex camera** a camera with a ground-glass focusing screen on which the image is formed by a combination of lens and mirror, enabling the scene to be correctly composed and focused. □□ **reflexly** *adv.* [L *reflexus* (as REFLECT)]

reflexible /rɪˈfleksɪb(ə)l/ *adj.* capable of being reflected. □□ **reflexibility** /-ˈbɪlɪtɪ/ *n.*

reflexion *Brit.* var. of REFLECTION.

reflexive /rɪˈfleksɪv/ *adj. & n. Gram.* —*adj.* **1** (of a word or form) referring back to the subject of a sentence (esp. of a pronoun, e.g. *myself*). **2** (of a verb) having a reflexive pronoun as its object (as in *to wash oneself*). —*n.* a reflexive word or form, esp. a pronoun. □□ **reflexively** *adv.* **reflexiveness** *n.* **reflexivity** /-ˈsɪvɪtɪ/ *n.*

reflexology /ˌriːflekˈsɒlədʒɪ/ *n.* **1** a system of massage through reflex points on the feet, hands, and head, used to relieve tension and treat illness. **2** *Psychol.* the scientific study of reflexes. □□ **reflexologist** *n.*

refloat /riːˈfləʊt/ *v.tr.* set (a stranded ship) afloat again.

refluent /ˈrefluənt/ *adj.* flowing back (*refluent tide*). □□ **refluence** *n.* [ME f. L *refluere* (as RE-, *fluere* flow)]

reflux /ˈriːflʌks/ *n. & v.* —*n.* **1** a backward flow. **2** *Chem.* a method of boiling a liquid so that any vapour is liquefied and returned to the boiler. —*v.tr. & intr. Chem.* boil or be boiled under reflux.

refocus /riːˈfəʊkəs/ *v.tr.* (**refocused, refocusing** or **refocussed, refocussing**) adjust the focus of (esp. a lens).

reforest /riːˈfɒrɪst/ *v.tr.* = REAFFOREST. □□ **reforestation** /-ˈsteɪʃ(ə)n/ *n.*

reforge /riːˈfɔːdʒ/ *v.tr.* forge again or differently.

reform /rɪˈfɔːm/ *v. & n.* —*v.* **1** *tr. & intr.* make or become better by the removal of faults and errors. **2** *tr.* abolish or cure (an abuse or malpractice). **3** *tr. US* correct (a legal document). **4** *tr. Chem.* convert (a straight-chain hydrocarbon) by catalytic reaction to a branched-chain form for use as petrol. —*n.* **1** the removal of faults or abuses, esp. of a moral or political or social kind. **2** an improvement made or suggested. □ **Reform Acts** measures of electoral reform undertaken in Britain in the 19th c. The first Reform Bill (1832) disenfranchised various rotten boroughs, redistributed their seats among the counties and newly grown towns, and widened the electorate by about 50 per cent to include most of the upper middle class. The second (1867) carried out a further redistribution of seats and doubled the electorate (to two million) by lowering the property qualification. The third (1884) extended the franchise approved for the towns by the second to cover the entire country, increasing the electorate to about five million. **Reformed Church** any of the Protestant Churches which have accepted the principles of the Reformation, esp. those following Calvinist rather than Lutheran doctrines (see PROTESTANT). **Reform Jew** an adherent

of Reform Judaism. **Reform Judaism** a liberalizing movement, initiated in Germany by the philosopher Moses Mendelssohn (1729–86), to accommodate the Jewish faith to European intellectual enlightenment. **reform school** an institution to which young offenders are sent to be reformed. □□ **reformable** *adj.* [ME f. OF *reformer* or L *reformare* (as RE-, FORM)]

re-form /riːˈfɔːm/ *v.tr. & intr.* form again. □□ **re-formation** /-ˈmeɪʃ(ə)n/ *n.*

reformat /riːˈfɔːmæt/ *v.tr.* (**reformatted, reformatting**) format anew.

reformation /ˌrefəˈmeɪʃ(ə)n/ *n.* the act of reforming or process of being reformed, esp. a radical change for the better in political or religious or social affairs. □ **the Reformation** the movement that led to the division of Western Christendom in the 16th c. Pressure for the reform of medieval Christendom came from many quarters: unease at the political power of the Italian papacy, distress at the externality of much medieval religion, a sense of the gulf between contemporary theology and religious life and that found in the New Testament and Patristic period, made increasingly evident by the access provided by the humanists, especially Erasmus, to the original text of the New Testament and the Fathers. Reluctance by the papacy to allow a reforming council meant that Luther's protest against indulgences led to schism. A parallel movement in Switzerland, led by Zwingli, effected a still more complete break with medieval religion, and the Reformation, influenced in the second generation especially by Calvin, spread to most European countries. All Protestants rejected the authority of the papacy, both religious and political, and found authority in the original text of the Scriptures, made available to all in vernacular translation. The authority of the clergy and the sacramental system was weakened in varying degrees, and the way opened for religious individualism. □□ **Reformational** *adj.* [ME f. OF *reformation* or L *reformatio* (as REFORM)]

re-formation /ˌriːfɔːˈmeɪʃ(ə)n/ *n.* the process or an instance of forming or being formed again.

reformative /rɪˈfɔːmətɪv/ *adj.* tending or intended to produce reform. [OF *reformatif* -*ive* or med.L *reformativus* (as REFORM)]

reformatory /rɪˈfɔːmətərɪ/ *n. & adj.* —*n.* (*pl.* -**ies**) *US & hist.* = reform school. —*adj.* reformative.

reformer /rɪˈfɔːmə(r)/ *n.* a person who advocates or brings about (esp. political or social) reform.

reformism /rɪˈfɔːmɪz(ə)m/ *n.* a policy of reform rather than abolition or revolution. □□ **reformist** *n.*

reformulate /riːˈfɔːmjʊˌleɪt/ *v.tr.* formulate again or differently. □□ **reformulation** /-ˈleɪʃ(ə)n/ *n.*

refract /rɪˈfrækt/ *v.tr.* **1** (of water, air, glass, etc.) deflect (a ray of light etc.) at a certain angle when it enters obliquely from another medium. **2** determine the refractive condition of (the eye). [L *refringere refract-* (as RE-, *frangere* break)]

refraction /rɪˈfrækʃ(ə)n/ *n.* the process by which or the extent to which light is refracted. □ **angle of refraction** the angle made by a refracted ray with the perpendicular to the refracting surface. [F *réfraction* or LL *refractio* (as REFRACT)]

refractive /rɪˈfræktɪv/ *adj.* of or involving refraction. □ **refractive index** the ratio of the velocity of light in a vacuum to its velocity in a specified medium.

refractometer /ˌriːfrækˈtɒmɪtə(r)/ *n.* an instrument for measuring a refractive index. □□ **refractometric** /-təˈmetrɪk/ *adj.* **refractometry** *n.*

refractor /rɪˈfræktə(r)/ *n.* **1** a refracting medium or lens. **2** a telescope using a lens to produce an image.

refractory /rɪˈfræktərɪ/ *adj. & n.* —*adj.* **1** stubborn, unmanageable, rebellious. **2 a** (of a wound, disease, etc.) not yielding to treatment. **b** (of a person etc.) resistant to infection. **3** (of a substance) hard to fuse or work. —*n.* (*pl.* -**ies**) a substance especially resistant to heat, corrosion, etc. □□ **refractorily** *adv.* **refractoriness** *n.* [alt. of obs. *refractary* f. L *refractarius* (as REFRACT)]

refrain[1] /rɪˈfreɪn/ *v.intr.* (foll. by *from*) avoid doing (an action) (*refrain from smoking*). □□ **refrainment** *n.* [ME f. OF *refrener* f. L *refrenare* (as RE-, *frenum* bridle)]

refrain² /rɪˈfreɪn/ n. **1** a recurring phrase or number of lines, esp. at the ends of stanzas. **2** the music accompanying this. [ME f. OF refrain (earlier refrait) ult. f. L refringere (as RE-, frangere break), because the refrain 'broke' the sequence]

refrangible /rɪˈfrændʒɪb(ə)l/ adj. that can be refracted. □□ **refrangibility** /-ˈbɪlɪtɪ/ n. [mod.L refrangibilis f. refrangere = L refringere: see REFRACT]

refreeze /riːˈfriːz/ v.tr. & intr. (past **refroze**; past part. **refrozen**) freeze again.

refresh /rɪˈfreʃ/ v.tr. **1 a** (of food, rest, amusement, etc.) give fresh spirit or vigour to. **b** (esp. refl.) revive with food, rest, etc. (refreshed myself with a short sleep). **2** revive or stimulate (the memory), esp. by consulting the source of one's information. **3** make cool. [ME f. OF refreschi(e)r f. fres fresche FRESH]

refresher /rɪˈfreʃə(r)/ n. **1** something that refreshes, esp. a drink. **2** Law an extra fee payable to counsel in a prolonged case. □ **refresher course** a course reviewing or updating previous studies.

refreshing /rɪˈfreʃɪŋ/ adj. **1** serving to refresh. **2** welcome or stimulating because sincere or untypical (refreshing innocence). □□ **refreshingly** adv.

refreshment /rɪˈfreʃmənt/ n. **1** the act of refreshing or the process of being refreshed in mind or body. **2** (usu. in pl.) food or drink that refreshes. **3** something that refreshes or stimulates the mind. [ME f. OF refreschement (as REFRESH)]

refrigerant /rɪˈfrɪdʒərənt/ n. & adj. —n. **1** a substance used for refrigeration. **2** Med. a substance that cools or allays fever. —adj. cooling. [F réfrigérant f. L refrigerant- (as REFRIGERATE)]

refrigerate /rɪˈfrɪdʒəˌreɪt/ v. **1** tr. make or become cool or cold. **2** tr. subject (food etc.) to cold in order to freeze or preserve it. □□ **refrigeration** /-ˈreɪʃ(ə)n/ n. **refrigerative** /-rətɪv/ adj. [L refrigerare (as RE-, frigus frigoris cold)]

refrigerator /rɪˈfrɪdʒəˌreɪtə(r)/ n. a cabinet or room in which food etc. is refrigerated. A refrigerator contains a chamber that is kept cooler than its surroundings by making use of the cooling effect produced when a liquid is made to evaporate. The liquid (often a fluorine compound) is pumped through a valve that causes it to expand and become a vapour; this vapour is made to condense back to a liquid outside the refrigerator, where it gives up the heat it acquired from the interior when it became a vapour.

Ice-cooled pits or cellars were known in ancient Mesopotamia, Greece, and Rome, and the principle continued in use up to the 19th c.; ice was collected in winter from frozen rivers, and lasted into the summer without melting, while food stored in it stayed fresh for several months. In the mid-19th c. ice was used to cool the air in railway wagons for transporting meat in the US, and by the 1880s refrigerating machines had been developed for use in ships, transporting meat successfully on sea journeys of two or three months. A cooling apparatus had long been used in the brewing industry, and it was from this that the first mechanically operated domestic refrigerator was developed c.1880, powered by a small steam pump. Electric refrigeration was a development of the 1920s.

refrigeratory /rɪˈfrɪdʒərətərɪ/ adj. & n. —adj. serving to cool. —n. (pl. **-ies**) hist. a cold-water vessel attached to a still for condensing vapour. [mod.L refrigeratorium (n.), L refrigeratorius (adj.) (as REFRIGERATE)]

refringent /rɪˈfrɪndʒ(ə)nt/ adj. Physics refracting. □□ **refringence** n. **refringency** n. [L refringere: see REFRACT]

refroze past of REFREEZE.

refrozen past part. of REFREEZE.

reft past part. of REAVE.

refuel /riːˈfjuːəl/ v. (**refuelled**, **refuelling**; US **refueled**, **refueling**) **1** intr. replenish a fuel supply. **2** tr. supply with more fuel.

refuge /ˈrefjuːdʒ/ n. **1** a shelter from pursuit or danger or trouble. **2** a person or place etc. offering this. **3** a person, thing, or course resorted to in difficulties. **4** a traffic island. [ME f. OF f. L refugium (as RE-, fugere flee)]

refugee /ˌrefjʊˈdʒiː/ n. a person taking refuge, esp. in a foreign

country from war or persecution or natural disaster. [F réfugié past part. of (se) réfugier (as REFUGE)]

refulgent /rɪˈfʌldʒ(ə)nt/ adj. literary shining; gloriously bright. □□ **refulgence** n. **refulgently** adv. [L refulgēre (as RE-, fulgēre shine)]

refund v. & n. —v. /rɪˈfʌnd/ tr. (also absol.) **1** pay back (money or expenses). **2** reimburse (a person). —n. /ˈriːfʌnd/ **1** an act of refunding. **2** a sum refunded; a repayment. □□ **refundable** /rɪˈfʌndəb(ə)l/ adj. **refunder** /rɪˈfʌndə(r)/ n. [ME in sense 'pour back', f. OF refonder or L refundere (as RE-, fundere pour), later assoc. with FUND]

re-fund /riːˈfʌnd/ v.tr. fund (a debt etc.) again.

refurbish /riːˈfɜːbɪʃ/ v.tr. **1** brighten up. **2** restore and redecorate. □□ **refurbishment** n.

refurnish /riːˈfɜːnɪʃ/ v.tr. furnish again or differently.

refusal /rɪˈfjuːz(ə)l/ n. **1** the act or an instance of refusing; the state of being refused. **2** (in full **first refusal**) the right or privilege of deciding to take or leave a thing before it is offered to others.

refuse¹ /rɪˈfjuːz/ v. **1** tr. withhold acceptance of or consent to (refuse an offer; refuse orders). **2** tr. (often foll. by to + infin.) indicate unwillingness (I refuse to go; the car refuses to start; I refuse!). **3** tr. (often with double object) not grant (a request) made by (a person) (refused me a day off; I could not refuse them). **4** tr. (also absol.) (of a horse) be unwilling to jump (a fence etc.). □□ **refusable** adj. **refuser** n. [ME f. OF refuser prob. ult. f. L recusare (see RECUSANT) after refutare REFUTE]

refuse² /ˈrefjuːs/ n. items rejected as worthless; waste. [ME, perh. f. OF refusé past part. (as REFUSE)]

re-fuse /riːˈfjuːz/ v.tr. fuse again; provide with a new fuse.

refusenik /rɪˈfjuːznɪk/ n. a Jew in the Soviet Union who has been refused permission to emigrate to Israel. [REFUSE¹ + -NIK]

refute /rɪˈfjuːt/ v.tr. **1** prove the falsity or error of (a statement etc. or the person advancing it). **2** rebut or repel by argument. **3** disp. deny or contradict (without argument). ¶ Often confused in this sense with repudiate. □□ **refutable** adj. **refutal** n. **refutation** /ˌrefjʊˈteɪʃ(ə)n/ n. **refuter** n. [L refutare (as RE-: cf. CONFUTE)]

reg /redʒ/ n. colloq. = registration mark. [abbr.]

regain /rɪˈgeɪn/ v.tr. obtain possession or use of after loss (regain consciousness). [F regagner (as RE-, GAIN)]

regal /ˈriːg(ə)l/ adj. **1** royal; of or by a monarch or monarchs. **2** fit for a monarch; magnificent. □□ **regally** adv. [ME f. OF regal or L regalis f. rex regis king]

regale /rɪˈgeɪl/ v.tr. **1** entertain lavishly with feasting. **2** (foll. by with) entertain or divert with (talk etc.). **3** (of beauty, flowers, etc.) give delight to. □□ **regalement** n. [F régaler f. OF gale pleasure]

regalia /rɪˈgeɪlɪə/ n.pl. **1** the insignia of royalty used at coronations. **2** the insignia of an order or of civic dignity. [med.L, = royal privileges, n. f. L neut. pl. of regalis REGAL]

regalism /ˈriːgəˌlɪz(ə)m/ n. the doctrine of a sovereign's ecclesiastical supremacy.

regality /rɪˈgælɪtɪ/ n. (pl. **-ies**) **1** the state of being a king or queen. **2** an attribute of sovereign power. **3** a royal privilege. [ME f. OF regalité or med.L regalitas (as REGAL)]

regard /rɪˈgɑːd/ v. & n. —v.tr. **1** gaze on steadily (usu. in a specified way) (regarded them suspiciously). **2** give heed to; take into account; let one's course be affected by. **3** look upon or contemplate mentally in a specified way (I regard them kindly; I regard it as an insult). **4** (of a thing) have relation to; have some connection with. —n. **1** a gaze; a steady or significant look. **2** (foll. by to, for) attention or care. **3** (foll. by for) esteem; kindly feeling; respectful opinion. **4** a respect; a point attended to (in this regard). **5** (in pl.) an expression of friendliness in a letter etc.; compliments (sent my best regards). □ **as regards** about, concerning; in respect of. **in** (or **with**) **regard to** as concerns; in respect of. [ME f. OF regard f. regarder (as RE-, garder GUARD)]

regardant /rɪˈgɑːd(ə)nt/ adj. Heraldry looking backwards. [AF & OF (as REGARD)]

regardful /rɪˈɡɑːdfʊl/ *adj.* (foll. by *of*) mindful of; paying attention to.

regarding /rɪˈɡɑːdɪŋ/ *prep.* about, concerning; in respect of.

regardless /rɪˈɡɑːdlɪs/ *adj.* & *adv.* —*adj.* (foll. by *of*) without regard or consideration for (*regardless of the expense*). —*adv.* without paying attention (*carried on regardless*). □□ **regardlessly** *adv.* **regardlessness** *n.*

regather /riːˈɡæðə(r)/ *v.tr.* & *intr.* **1** gather or collect again. **2** meet again.

regatta /rɪˈɡætə/ *n.* a sporting event consisting of a series of boat or yacht races. [It. (Venetian)]

regd. *abbr.* registered.

regelate /ˌriːdʒɪˈleɪt, ˌredʒ-/ *v.intr.* freeze again (esp. of pieces of ice etc. frozen together after temporary thawing of the surfaces). □□ **regelation** /-ˈleɪʃ(ə)n/ *n.* [RE- + L *gelare* freeze]

regency /ˈriːdʒənsɪ/ *n.* (pl. **-ies**) **1** the office of regent. **2** a commission acting as regent. **3 a** the period of office of a regent or regency commission. **b** (**Regency**) a particular period of a regency, esp. the period of 1811–20 in Britain when George, Prince of Wales, acted as regent, or 1715–23 in France with Philip, Duke of Orleans, as regent (often *attrib.*: *Regency costume*). [ME f. med.L *regentia* (as REGENT)]

regenerate *v.* & *adj.* —*v.* /rɪˈdʒenəˌreɪt/ **1** *tr.* & *intr.* bring or come into renewed existence; generate again. **2** *tr.* improve the moral condition of. **3** *tr.* impart new, more vigorous, and spiritually greater life to (a person or institution etc.). **4** *intr.* reform oneself. **5** *tr.* invest with a new and higher spiritual nature. **6** *intr.* & *tr. Biol.* regrow or cause (new tissue) to regrow to replace lost or injured tissue. **7** *tr.* & *intr. Chem.* restore or be restored to an initial state of reaction or process. —*adj.* /rɪˈdʒenərət/ **1** spiritually born again. **2** reformed. □□ **regeneration** /-ˈreɪʃ(ə)n/ *n.* **regenerative** /-rətɪv/ *adj.* **regeneratively** /-rətɪvlɪ/ *adv.* **regenerator** *n.* [L *regenerare* (as RE-, GENERATE)]

regent /ˈriːdʒ(ə)nt/ *n.* & *adj.* —*n.* **1** a person appointed to administer a State because the monarch is a minor or is absent or incapacitated. **2** *US* a member of the governing body of a State university. —*adj.* (placed after noun) acting as regent (*Prince Regent*). □ **regent-bird** an Australian bower bird, *Sericulus chrysocephalus*. [ME f. OF *regent* or L *regere* rule]

regerminate /riːˈdʒɜːmɪˌneɪt/ *v.tr.* & *intr.* germinate again. □□ **regermination** /-ˈneɪʃ(ə)n/ *n.*

reggae /ˈreɡeɪ/ *n.* a kind of music, of Jamaican origin, characterized by a strongly accentuated subsidiary beat and often a prominent bass. [orig. unkn.; perh. rel. to Jamaican English *rege-rege* quarrel, row]

regicide /ˈredʒɪˌsaɪd/ *n.* **1** a person who kills or takes part in killing a king. **2** the act of killing a king. □ **the Regicides** those involved in trying and executing Charles I of England or Louis XVI of France. □□ **regicidal** /-ˈsaɪd(ə)l/ *adj.* [L *rex regis* king + -CIDE]

regild /riːˈɡɪld/ *v.tr.* gild again, esp. to renew faded or worn gilding.

regime /reɪˈʒiːm/ *n.* (also **régime**) **1 a** a method or system of government. **b** *derog.* a particular government. **2** a prevailing order or system of things. **3** the conditions under which a scientific or industrial process occurs. [F *régime* (as REGIMEN)]

regimen /ˈredʒɪˌmen/ *n.* **1** esp. *Med.* a prescribed course of exercise, way of life, and diet. **2** *archaic* a system of government. [L f. *regere* rule]

regiment *n.* & *v.* —*n.* /ˈredʒɪmənt/ **1 a** a permanent unit of an army usu. commanded by a colonel and divided into several companies or troops or batteries and often into two battalions. **b** an operational unit of artillery etc. **2** (usu. foll. by *of*) a large array or number. **3** *archaic* rule, government. —*v.tr.* /ˈredʒɪˌment/ **1** organize (esp. oppressively) in groups or according to a system. **2** form into a regiment or regiments. □□ **regimentation** /-ˈteɪʃ(ə)n/ *n.* [ME (in sense 3) f. OF f. LL *regimentum* (as REGIMEN)]

regimental /ˌredʒɪˈment(ə)l/ *adj.* & *n.* —*adj.* of or relating to a regiment. —*n.* (in *pl.*) military uniform, esp. of a particular regiment. □□ **regimentally** *adv.*

Regina /rɪˈdʒaɪnə/ the capital of Saskatchewan, situated at the centre of the wheat-growing plains of central Canada; pop. (1986) 175,000. Named in 1882 in honour of Queen Victoria, it was the administrative headquarters of the North West Territories until 1905 and the headquarters of the North West (later Royal Canadian) Mounted Police until 1920.

Regina /rɪˈdʒaɪnə/ *n.* the reigning queen (following a name or in the titles of lawsuits, e.g. *Regina v. Jones* the Crown versus Jones). [L, = queen f. *rex regis* king]

region /ˈriːdʒ(ə)n/ *n.* **1** an area of land, or division of the earth's surface, having definable boundaries or characteristics (*a mountainous region*; *the region between London and the coast*). **2** an administrative district esp. in Scotland. **3** a part of the body round or near some organ etc. (*the lumbar region*). **4** a sphere or realm (*the region of metaphysics*). **5 a** a separate part of the world or universe. **b** a layer of the atmosphere or the sea according to its height or depth. □ **in the region of** approximately. □□ **regional** *adj.* **regionalism** *n.* **regionalist** *n.* & *adj.* **regionalize** *v.tr.* (also **-ise**). **regionally** *adv.* [ME f. OF f. L *regio -onis* direction, district f. *regere* direct]

regisseur /ˌreɪʒɪˈsɜː(r)/ *n.* the director of a theatrical production, esp. a ballet. [F *régisseur* stage-manager]

register /ˈredʒɪstə(r)/ *n.* & *v.* —*n.* **1** an official list e.g. of births, marriages, and deaths, of shipping, of professionally qualified persons, or of qualified voters in a constituency. **2** a book in which items are recorded for reference. **3** a device recording speed, force, etc. **4** (in electronic devices) a location in a store of data, used for a specific purpose and with quick access time. **5 a** the compass of a voice or instrument. **b** a part of this compass (*lower register*). **6** an adjustable plate for widening or narrowing an opening and regulating a draught, esp. in a fire-grate. **7 a** a set of organ pipes. **b** a sliding device controlling this. **8** = *cash register* (see CASH[1]). **9** *Linguistics* each of several forms of a language (colloquial, formal, literary, etc.) usually used in particular circumstances. **10** *Printing* the exact correspondence of the position of printed matter on the two sides of a leaf. **11** *Printing* & *Photog.* the correspondence of the position of colour-components in a printed positive. —*v.* **1** *tr.* set down (a name, fact, etc.) formally; record in writing. **2** *tr.* make a mental note of; notice. **3** *tr.* enter or cause to be entered in a particular register. **4** *tr.* entrust (a letter etc.) to a post office for transmission by registered post. **5** *intr.* & *refl.* put one's name on a register, esp. as an eligible voter or as a guest in a register kept by a hotel etc. **6** *tr.* (of an instrument) record automatically; indicate. **7 a** *tr.* express (an emotion) facially or by gesture (*registered surprise*). **b** *intr.* (of an emotion) show in a person's face or gestures. **8** *intr.* make an impression on a person's mind (*did not register at all*). **9** *intr.* & *tr. Printing* correspond or cause to correspond exactly in position. □ **registered nurse** a nurse with a State certificate of competence. **registered post** a postal procedure with special precautions for safety and for compensation in case of loss. **register office** *Brit.* a State office where civil marriages are conducted and births, marriages, and deaths are recorded with the issue of certificates. ¶ The name in official use, and generally preferred to *registry office*. □□ **registrable** *adj.* [ME & OF *registre*, *registre* or med.L *regestrum*, *registrum*, alt. of *regestum* f. LL *regesta* things recorded (as RE-, L *gerere gest-* carry)]

registrar /ˌredʒɪˈstrɑː(r), ˈredʒ-/ *n.* **1** an official responsible for keeping a register or official records. **2** the chief administrative officer in a university. **3** a middle-ranking hospital doctor undergoing training as a specialist. **4** (in the UK) the judicial and administrative officer of the High Court etc. □ **Registrar General** a government official responsible for holding a population census. □□ **registrarship** *n.* [med.L *registrarius* f. *registrum* REGISTER]

registrary /ˈredʒɪstrərɪ/ *n.* (pl. **-ies**) the registrar of Cambridge University.

registration /ˌredʒɪˈstreɪʃ(ə)n/ *n.* the act or an instance of registering; the process of being registered. □ **registration mark** (or **number**) a combination of letters and figures identifying a motor vehicle etc. [obs. F *régistration* or med.L *registratio* (as REGISTRAR)]

registry /'redʒɪstrɪ/ n. (pl. **-ies**) **1** a place or office where registers or records are kept. **2** registration. □ **registry office** = *register office*. [obs. *registery* f. med.L *registerium* (as REGISTER)]

Regius professor /'riːdʒɪəs/ n. *Brit.* the holder of a chair founded by a sovereign (esp. one at Oxford or Cambridge instituted by Henry VIII) or filled by Crown appointment. [L, = royal, f. *rex regis* king]

reglaze /riː'gleɪz/ v.tr. glaze (a window etc.) again.

reglet /'reglɪt/ n. **1** *Archit.* a narrow strip separating mouldings. **2** *Printing* a thin strip of wood or metal separating type. [F *réglet* dimin. of *règle* (as RULE)]

regnal /'regn(ə)l/ adj. of a reign. □ **regnal year** a year reckoned from the date or anniversary of a sovereign's accession. [AL *regnalis* (as REIGN)]

regnant /'regnənt/ adj. **1** reigning (*Queen regnant*). **2** (of things, qualities, etc.) predominant, prevalent. [L *regnare* REIGN]

regolith /'regəlɪθ/ n. *Geol.* unconsolidated solid material covering the bedrock of a planet. [erron. f. Gk *rhēgos* rug, blanket + -LITH]

regorge /rɪ'ɡɔːdʒ/ v. **1** tr. bring up or expel again after swallowing. **2** intr. gush or flow back from a pit, channel, etc. [F *regorger* or RE- + GORGE]

regrade /riː'ɡreɪd/ v.tr. grade again or differently.

regress v. & n. —v. /rɪ'ɡres/ **1** intr. move backwards, esp. (in abstract senses) return to a former state. **2** intr. & tr. *Psychol.* return or cause to return mentally to a former stage of life, esp. through hypnosis or mental illness. —n. /'riːgres/ **1** the act or an instance of going back. **2** reasoning from effect to cause. [ME (as n.) f. L *regressus* f. *regredi* regress- (as RE-, *gradi* step)]

regression /rɪ'ɡreʃ(ə)n/ n. **1** a backward movement, esp. a return to a former state. **2** a relapse or reversion. **3** *Psychol.* a return to an earlier stage of development, esp. through hypnosis or mental illness. **4** *Statistics* a measure of the relation between the mean value of one variable (e.g. output) and corresponding values of other variables (e.g. time and cost). [L *regressio* (as REGRESS)]

regressive /rɪ'ɡresɪv/ adj. **1** regressing; characterized by regression. **2** (of a tax) proportionally greater on lower incomes. □□ **regressively** adv. **regressiveness** n.

regret /rɪ'ɡret/ v. & n. —v.tr. (**regretted**, **regretting**) (often foll. by *that* + clause) **1** feel or express sorrow or repentance or distress over (an action or loss etc.) (*I regret that I forgot; regretted your absence*). **2** (often foll. by *to* + infin. or *that* + clause) acknowledge with sorrow or remorse (*I regret to say that you are wrong; regretted he would not be attending*). —n. **1** a feeling of sorrow, repentance, disappointment, etc., over an action or loss etc. **2** (often in *pl.*) an (esp. polite or formal) expression of disappointment or sorrow at an occurrence, inability to comply, etc. (*refused with many regrets; heard with regret of her death*). □ **give** (or **send**) **one's regrets** formally decline an invitation. [ME f. OF *regreter* bewail]

regretful /rɪ'ɡretfʊl/ adj. feeling or showing regret. □□ **regretfully** adv. **regretfulness** n.

regrettable /rɪ'ɡretəb(ə)l/ adj. (of events or conduct) undesirable, unwelcome; deserving censure. □□ **regrettably** adv.

regroup /riː'ɡruːp/ v.tr. & intr. group or arrange again or differently. □□ **regroupment** n.

regrow /riː'ɡrəʊ/ v.intr. & tr. grow again, esp. after an interval. □□ **regrowth** n.

Regt. abbr. Regiment.

regulable /'regjʊləb(ə)l/ adj. able to be regulated.

regular /'regjʊlə(r)/ adj. & n. —adj. **1** conforming to a rule or principle; systematic. **2** (of a structure or arrangement) harmonious, symmetrical (*regular features*). **3** acting or done or recurring uniformly or calculably in time or manner; habitual, constant, orderly. **4** conforming to a standard of etiquette or procedure; correct; according to convention. **5** properly constituted or qualified; not defective or amateur; pursuing an occupation as one's main pursuit (*cooks as well as a regular cook; has no regular profession*). **6** *Gram.* (of a noun, verb, etc.) following

the normal type of inflection. **7** *colloq.* complete, thorough, absolute (*a regular hero*). **8** *Geom.* **a** (of a figure) having all sides and all angles equal. **b** (of a solid) bounded by a number of equal figures. **9** *Eccl.* (placed before or after noun) **a** bound by religious rule. **b** belonging to a religious or monastic order (*canon regular*). **10** (of forces or troops etc.) relating to or constituting a permanent professional body (*regular soldiers; regular police force*). **11** (of a person) defecating or menstruating at predictable times. **12** *Bot.* (of a flower) having radial symmetry. —n. **1** a regular soldier. **2** *colloq.* a regular customer, visitor, etc. **3** *Eccl.* one of the regular clergy. **4** *colloq.* a person permanently employed. □ **keep regular hours** do the same thing, esp. going to bed and getting up, at the same time each day. □□ **regularity** /-'lærɪtɪ/ n. **regularize** v.tr. (also **-ise**). **regularization** /-'zeɪʃ(ə)n/ n. **regularly** adv. [ME *reguler*, *regular* f. OF *reguler* f. L *regularis* f. *regula* RULE]

regulate /'regjʊ₁leɪt/ v.tr. **1** control by rule. **2** subject to restrictions. **3** adapt to requirements. **4** alter the speed of (a machine or clock) so that it may work accurately. □□ **regulative** /-lətɪv/ adj. **regulator** n. **regulatory** /-lətərɪ/ adj. [LL *regulare* regulat- f. L *regula* RULE]

regulation /₁regjʊ'leɪʃ(ə)n/ n. **1** the act or an instance of regulating; the process of being regulated. **2** a prescribed rule; an authoritative direction. **3** (*attrib.*) **a** in accordance with regulations; of the correct type etc. (*the regulation speed; a regulation tie*). **b** *colloq.* usual (*the regulation soup*).

regulo /'regjʊ₁ləʊ/ n. (usu. foll. by a numeral) each of the numbers of a scale denoting temperature in a gas oven (*cook at regulo 6*). [*Regulo*, propr. term for a thermostatic gas oven control]

regulus /'regjʊləs/ n. (pl. **reguluses** or **reguli** /-₁laɪ/) *Chem.* **1** the purer or metallic part of a mineral that separates by sinking on reduction. **2** an impure metallic product formed during the smelting of various ores. □□ **reguline** /-₁laɪn/ adj. [L, dimin. of *rex regis* king: orig. of a metallic form of antimony, so called because of its readiness to combine with gold]

regurgitate /rɪ'ɡɜːdʒɪ₁teɪt/ v. **1** tr. bring (swallowed food) up again to the mouth. **2** tr. cast or pour out again (*required by the exam to regurgitate facts*). **3** intr. be brought up again; gush back. □□ **regurgitation** /-'teɪʃ(ə)n/ n. [med.L *regurgitare* (as RE-, L *gurges gurgitis* whirlpool)]

rehab /'riːhæb/ n. *colloq.* rehabilitation. [abbr.]

rehabilitate /₁riːhə'bɪlɪ₁teɪt/ v.tr. **1** restore to effectiveness or normal life by training etc., esp. after imprisonment or illness. **2** restore to former privileges or reputation or a proper condition. □□ **rehabilitation** /-'teɪʃ(ə)n/ n. **rehabilitative** /-tətɪv/ adj. [med.L *rehabilitare* (as RE-, HABILITATE)]

rehandle /riː'hænd(ə)l/ v.tr. **1** handle again. **2** give a new form or arrangement to.

rehang /riː'hæŋ/ v.tr. (*past* and *past part.* **rehung**) hang (esp. a picture or a curtain) again or differently.

rehash v. & n. —v.tr. /riː'hæʃ/ put (old material) into a new form without significant change or improvement. —n. /'riːhæʃ/ **1** material rehashed. **2** the act or an instance of rehashing.

rehear /riː'hɪə(r)/ v.tr. (*past* and *past part.* **reheard** /riː'hɜːd/) hear again.

rehearsal /rɪ'hɜːs(ə)l/ n. **1** the act or an instance of rehearsing. **2** a trial performance or practice of a play, recital, etc.

rehearse /rɪ'hɜːs/ v. **1** tr. practise (a play, recital, etc.) for later public performance. **2** intr. hold a rehearsal. **3** tr. train (a person) by rehearsal. **4** tr. recite or say over. **5** tr. give a list of; enumerate. □□ **rehearser** n. [ME f. AF *rehearser*, OF *reherc(i)er*, perh. formed as RE- + *hercer* to harrow f. *herse* harrow: see HEARSE]

reheat v. & n. —v.tr. /riː'hiːt/ heat again. —n. /'riːhiːt/ the process of using the hot exhaust to burn extra fuel in a jet engine and produce extra power. □□ **reheater** /-'hiːtə(r)/ n.

reheel /riː'hiːl/ v.tr. fit (a shoe etc.) with a new heel.

Rehoboam /₁riːhə'bəʊəm/ (10th c. BC) son of Solomon. He succeeded his father as king of Israel, but the northern tribes broke away from his rule and set up a new kingdom under Jeroboam, after which Rehoboam continued as the first king of Judah (1 Kings 11–14).

---

w **we** z **zoo** ʃ **she** ʒ **decision** θ **thin** ð **this** ŋ **ring** x **loch** tʃ **chip** dʒ **jar** (*see over for vowels*)

rehoboam /ˌriːhəˈbəʊəm/ n. a wine bottle of about six times the standard size. [REHOBOAM]

rehouse /riːˈhaʊz/ v.tr. provide with new housing.

rehung past and past part. of REHANG.

rehydrate /ˌriːhaɪˈdreɪt/ v. 1 intr. absorb water again after dehydration. 2 tr. add water to (esp. food) again to restore to a palatable state. □□ **rehydratable** adj. **rehydration** /-ˈdreɪʃ(ə)n/ n.

Reich /raɪx/ n. the German State or commonwealth, especially during the period 1871–1945. □ **Third Reich** the regime under the rule of Hitler and the Nazi party, 1933–45. The German expression was coined with allusion to the former Holy Roman Empire (962–1806) and the Hohenzollern empire (1871–1918). Apart from Third Reich, such collocations with an ordinal do not constitute recognized English historical terminology. [G, = kingdom, realm, State]

Reichstag /ˈraɪxstɑːɡ/ n. 1 the supreme legislature of the former German Empire and of the Republic. 2 the building in Berlin in which this met, burnt down on the Nazi accession to power (1933). [G]

reify /ˈriːɪˌfaɪ/ v.tr. (-ies, -ied) convert (a person, abstraction, etc.) into a thing; materialize. □□ **reification** /-fɪˈkeɪʃ(ə)n/ n. **reificatory** /-fɪˈkeɪtərɪ/ adj. [L res thing + -FY]

reign /reɪn/ v. & n. —v.intr. 1 hold royal office; be king or queen. 2 prevail; hold sway (confusion reigns). 3 (as **reigning** adj.) (of a winner, champion, etc.) currently holding the title etc. —n. 1 sovereignty, rule. 2 the period during which a sovereign rules. [ME f. OF reigne kingdom f. L regnare f. rex regis king]

reignite /ˌriːɪɡˈnaɪt/ v.tr. & intr. ignite again.

Reilly var. of RILEY.

reimburse /ˌriːɪmˈbɜːs/ v.tr. 1 repay (a person who has expended money). 2 repay (a person's expenses). □□ **reimbursable** adj. **reimbursement** n. **reimburser** n. [RE- + obs. imburse put in a purse f. med.L imbursare (as IM-, PURSE)]

reimport v. & n. —v.tr. /ˌriːɪmˈpɔːt/ import (goods processed from exported materials). —n. /riːˈɪmpɔːt/ 1 the act or an instance of reimporting. 2 a reimported item. □□ **reimportation** /-ˈteɪʃ(ə)n/ n.

reimpose /ˌriːɪmˈpəʊz/ v.tr. impose again, esp. after a lapse. □□ **reimposition** /-pəˈzɪʃ(ə)n/ n.

Reims /riːmz/ (also **Rheims**) an ancient cathedral city of northern Fance, capital of Champagne-Ardenne region; pop. (1982) 182,000.

rein /reɪn/ n. & v. —n. (in sing. or pl.) 1 a long narrow strap with each end attached to the bit, used to guide or check a horse etc. in riding or driving. 2 a similar device used to restrain a young child. 3 a means of control. —v.tr. 1 check or manage with reins. 2 (foll. by up, back) pull up or back with reins. 3 (foll. by in) hold in as with reins; restrain. 4 govern, restrain, control. □ **draw rein** 1 stop one's horse. 2 pull up. 3 abandon an effort. **give free rein to** remove constraints from; allow full scope to. **keep a tight rein on** allow little freedom to. □□ **reinless** adj. [ME f. OF rene, reigne, earlier resne, ult. f. L retinēre RETAIN]

reincarnation /ˌriːɪnkɑːˈneɪʃ(ə)n/ n. (in some beliefs) the rebirth of a soul in a new body. □□ **reincarnate** /-ˈkɑːneɪt/ v.tr. **reincarnate** /-ˈkɑːnət/ adj.

reincorporate /ˌriːɪnˈkɔːpəˌreɪt/ v.tr. incorporate afresh. □□ **reincorporation** /-ˈreɪʃ(ə)n/ n.

reindeer /ˈreɪndɪə(r)/ n. (pl. same or **reindeers**) a subarctic deer, Rangifer tarandus, of which both sexes have large antlers, used domestically for drawing sledges and as a source of milk, flesh, and hide. □ **reindeer moss** an arctic lichen, Cladonia rangiferina, with short branched stems growing in clumps. [ME f. ON hreindȳri f. hreinn reindeer + dȳr DEER]

reinfect /ˌriːɪnˈfekt/ v.tr. infect again. □□ **reinfection** /ˌriːɪnˈfekʃ(ə)n/ n.

reinforce /ˌriːɪnˈfɔːs/ v.tr. strengthen or support, esp. with additional personnel or material or by an increase of numbers or quantity or size etc. □ **reinforced concrete** concrete with metal bars or wire etc. embedded to increase its tensile strength. □□ **reinforcer** n. [earlier renforce f. F renforcer]

reinforcement /ˌriːɪnˈfɔːsmənt/ n. 1 the act or an instance of reinforcing; the process of being reinforced. 2 a thing that reinforces. 3 (in pl.) reinforcing personnel or equipment etc.

Reinhardt /ˈraɪnhɑːt/, Max (1873–1943), real name Goldmann, Austrian director and impresario, who dominated the stage in Berlin during the first two decades of the 20th c., mainly as owner of the Deutsches Theater. His integrated productions established the director's pre-eminence, especially in works of symbolism and impressionism. No stage was too big for him, two of his most remarkable productions being Sophocles' Oedipus the King (1910) and Vollmöller's The Miracle (1911).

reinsert /ˌriːɪnˈsɜːt/ v.tr. insert again. □□ **reinsertion** /-ˈsɜːʃ(ə)n/ n.

reinstate /ˌriːɪnˈsteɪt/ v.tr. 1 replace in a former position. 2 restore (a person etc.) to former privileges. □□ **reinstatement** n.

reinsure /ˌriːɪnˈʃʊə(r)/ v.tr. & intr. insure again (esp. of an insurer securing himself by transferring some or all of the risk to another insurer). □□ **reinsurance** n. **reinsurer** n.

reintegrate /riːˈɪntɪˌɡreɪt/ v.tr. 1 = REDINTEGRATE. 2 integrate back into society. □□ **reintegration** /-ˈɡreɪʃ(ə)n/ n.

reinter /ˌriːɪnˈtɜː(r)/ v.tr. inter (a corpse) again. □□ **reinterment** n.

reinterpret /ˌriːɪnˈtɜːprɪt/ v.tr. (**reinterpreted**, **reinterpreting**) interpret again or differently. □□ **reinterpretation** /-ˈteɪʃ(ə)n/ n.

reintroduce /ˌriːɪntrəˈdjuːs/ v.tr. introduce again. □□ **reintroduction** /-ˈdʌkʃ(ə)n/ n.

reinvest /ˌriːɪnˈvest/ v.tr. invest again (esp. money in other property etc.). □□ **reinvestment** n.

reinvigorate /ˌriːɪnˈvɪɡəˌreɪt/ v.tr. impart fresh vigour to. □□ **reinvigoration** /-ˈreɪʃ(ə)n/ n.

reissue /riːˈɪʃuː, -sjuː/ v. & n. —v.tr. (**reissues**, **reissued**, **reissuing**) issue again or in a different form. —n. a new issue, esp. of a previously published book.

reiterate /riːˈɪtəˌreɪt/ v.tr. say or do again or repeatedly. □□ **reiteration** /-ˈreɪʃ(ə)n/ n. **reiterative** /-rətɪv/ adj. [L reiterare (as RE-, ITERATE)]

Reith /riːθ/, John Charles Walsham, 1st Baron Reith (1889–1971), first General Manager and later first Director-General (1927–38) of the BBC. An uncompromising idealist, closely associated with the development of radio broadcasting in Britain, Reith later served in various Cabinet posts during the Second World War.

reive /riːv/ v.intr. esp. Sc. make raids; plunder. □□ **reiver** n. [var. of REAVE]

reject v. & n. —v.tr. /rɪˈdʒekt/ 1 put aside or send back as not to be used or done or complied with etc. 2 refuse to accept or believe in. 3 rebuff or snub (a person). 4 (of a body or digestive system) cast up again; vomit, evacuate. 5 Med. show an immune response to (a transplanted organ or tissue) so that it fails to survive. —n. /ˈriːdʒekt/ a thing or person rejected as unfit or below standard. □□ **rejectable** /rɪˈdʒektəb(ə)l/ adj. **rejecter** /rɪˈdʒektə(r)/ n. (also **rejector**). **rejection** /rɪˈdʒekʃ(ə)n/ n. **rejective** adj. [ME f. L rejicere reject- (as RE-, jacere throw)]

rejig /riːˈdʒɪɡ/ v.tr. (**rejigged**, **rejigging**) 1 re-equip (a factory etc.) for a new kind of work. 2 rearrange.

rejoice /rɪˈdʒɔɪs/ v. 1 intr. feel great joy. 2 intr. (foll. by that + clause or to + infin.) be glad. 3 intr. (foll. by in, at) take delight. 4 intr. celebrate some event. 5 tr. cause joy to. □□ **rejoicer** n. **rejoicingly** adv. [ME f. OF rejoir rejoiss- (as RE-, JOY)]

rejoin[1] /riːˈdʒɔɪn/ v. 1 tr. & intr. join together again; reunite. 2 tr. join (a companion etc.) again.

rejoin[2] /rɪˈdʒɔɪn/ v. 1 tr. say in answer, retort. 2 intr. Law reply to a charge or pleading in a lawsuit. [ME f. OF rejoindre rejoign- (as RE-, JOIN)]

rejoinder /rɪˈdʒɔɪndə(r)/ n. 1 what is said in reply. 2 a retort. 3 Law a reply by rejoining. [AF rejoinder (unrecorded: as REJOIN[2])]

rejuvenate /rɪˈdʒuːvɪˌneɪt/ v.tr. make young or as if young again. □□ **rejuvenation** /-ˈneɪʃ(ə)n/ n. **rejuvenator** n. [RE- + L juvenis young]

rejuvenesce /rɪˌdʒuːvɪˈnes/ v. 1 intr. become young again. 2

Biol. **a** *intr.* (of cells) gain fresh vitality. **b** *tr.* impart fresh vitality to (cells). □□ **rejuvenescent** *adj.* **rejuvenescence** *n.* [LL *rejuvenescere* (as RE-, L *juvenis* young)]

rekindle /riːˈkɪnd(ə)l/ *v.tr. & intr.* kindle again.

-rel /r(ə)l/ *suffix* with diminutive or derogatory force (*cockerel*; *scoundrel*). [from or after OF *-erel(le)*]

relabel /riːˈleɪb(ə)l/ *v.tr.* (**relabelled, relabelling;** US **relabeled, relabeling**) label (esp. a commodity) again or differently.

relapse /rɪˈlæps/ *v. & n.* —*v.intr.* (usu. foll. by *into*) fall back or sink again (into a worse state after an improvement). —*n.* /also ˈriː-/ the act or an instance of relapsing, esp. a deterioration in a patient's condition after a partial recovery. □ **relapsing fever** a bacterial infectious disease with recurrent periods of fever. □□ **relapser** *n.* [L *relabi relaps-* (as RE-, *labi* slip)]

relate /rɪˈleɪt/ *v.* **1** *tr.* narrate or recount (incidents, a story, etc.). **2** *tr.* (in *passive*; often foll. by *to*) be connected by blood or marriage. **3** *tr.* (usu. foll. by *to, with*) bring into relation (with one another); establish a connection between (*cannot relate your opinion to my own experience*). **4** *intr.* (foll. by *to*) have reference to; concern (*see only what relates to themselves*). **5** *intr.* (foll. by *to*) bring oneself into relation to; associate with. □□ **relatable** *adj.* [L *referre relat-* bring back: see REFER]

related /rɪˈleɪtɪd/ *adj.* connected, esp. by blood or marriage. □□ **relatedness** *n.*

relater /rɪˈleɪtə(r)/ *n.* (also **relator**) a person who relates something, esp. a story; a narrator.

relation /rɪˈleɪʃ(ə)n/ *n.* **1 a** what one person or thing has to do with another. **b** the way in which one person stands or is related to another. **c** the existence or effect of a connection, correspondence, contrast, or feeling prevailing between persons or things, esp. when qualified in some way (*bears no relation to the facts; enjoyed good relations for many years*). **2** a relative; a kinsman or kinswoman. **3** (in *pl.*) **a** (foll. by *with*) dealings (with others). **b** sexual intercourse. **4** = RELATIONSHIP. **5 a** narration (*his relation of the events*). **b** a narrative. **6** *Law* the laying of information. □ **in relation to** as regards. [ME f. OF *relation* or L *relatio* (as RELATE)]

relational /rɪˈleɪʃən(ə)l/ *adj.* **1** of, belonging to, or characterized by relation. **2** having relation. □ **relational database** *Computing* a database structured to recognize the relation of stored items of information.

relationship /rɪˈleɪʃənʃɪp/ *n.* **1** the fact or state of being related. **2** *colloq.* **a** a connection or association (*enjoyed a good working relationship*). **b** an emotional (esp. sexual) association between two people. **3** a condition or character due to being related. **4** kinship.

relative /ˈrelətɪv/ *adj. & n.* —*adj.* **1** considered or having significance in relation to something else (*relative velocity*). **2** (foll. by *to*) having existence only as perceived or considered by (*beauty is relative to the eye of the beholder*). **3** (foll. by *to*) proportioned to (something else) (*growth is relative to input*). **4** implying comparison or contextual relation ('*heat*' *is a relative word*). **5** comparative; compared with one another (*their relative advantages*). **6** having mutual relations; corresponding in some way; related to each other. **7** (foll. by *to*) having reference or relating (*the facts relative to the issue*). **8** involving a different but corresponding idea (*the concepts of husband and wife are relative to each other*). **9** *Gram.* **a** (of a word, esp. a pronoun) referring to an expressed or implied antecedent and attaching a subordinate clause to it, e.g. *which, who.* **b** (of a clause) attached to an antecedent by a relative word. **10** *Mus.* (of major and minor keys) having the same key signature. **11** (of a service rank) corresponding in grade to another in a different service. **12** pertinent, relevant; related to the subject (*need more relative proof*). —*n.* **1** a person connected by blood or marriage. **2** a species related to another by common origin (*the apes, man's closest relatives*). **3** *Gram.* a relative word, esp. a pronoun. **4** *Philos.* a relative thing or term. □ **relative atomic mass** the ratio of the average mass of one atom of an element to one-twelfth of the mass of an atom of carbon-12: also called *atomic weight*. **relative density** *Chem.* the ratio of the density of a substance to the density of a standard, usu. water for a liquid or solid, and air for a gas. **relative molecular mass**

the ratio of the average mass of one molecule of an element or compound to one-twelfth of the mass of an atom of carbon-12: also called *molecular weight*. □□ **relatival** /-ˈtaɪv(ə)l/ *adj.* (in sense 3 of *n.*). **relatively** *adv.* **relativeness** *n.* [ME f. OF *relatif -ive* or LL *relativus* having reference or relation (as RELATE)]

relativism /ˈrelətɪˌvɪz(ə)m/ *n.* the doctrine that knowledge is relative, not absolute. □□ **relativist** *n.*

relativistic /ˌrelətɪˈvɪstɪk/ *adj. Physics* (of phenomena etc.) accurately described only by the theory of relativity. □□ **relativistically** *adv.*

relativity /ˌreləˈtɪvɪti/ *n.* **1** the fact or state of being relative. **2** *Physics* **a** (**special theory of relativity**) a theory based on the principle that all motion is relative and that light has constant velocity, regarding space-time as a four-dimensional continuum, and modifying previous conceptions of geometry. (See below.) **b** (**general theory of relativity**) a theory extending this to gravitation and accelerated motion. (See GRAVITATION.)

The special theory of relativity is largely the outcome of experimental and theoretical efforts late last century to produce a coherent theory of electromagnetism. The chief architect of the theory was Einstein, whose investigations led him to reject the idea of a stationary 'ether' pervading space, and the notions of absolute space and time as a common framework of reference for all bodies in the universe. Special relativity places great importance on distinguishing systematically between the viewpoint or framework of the observer and that of the object or process being observed. Fundamental principles of the theory, well confirmed by experiment, are that the measured velocity of every beam of light is the same for all observers, whatever their mutual velocities, and that the mathematical form of those laws of physics which apply to moving objects or systems is independent of the motion of the framework of the observer, provided the latter motion is uniform. Although mathematically the theory is surprisingly uncomplicated its results are far-reaching, changing the basis of physics and undermining intuitive commonsense notions. Among its consequences are the following: nothing can go faster than the speed of light in a vacuum; the mass of a body increases and its length (in the direction of motion) shortens as its speed increases; the time interval between two events occurring in a moving body appears (to a stationary observer) to increase; and mass and energy are equivalent and interconvertible. All of these are well attested by experiment. Their explanation, however, quite eludes modern physics and they tend to be regarded as a basic datum of nature.

relator /rɪˈleɪtə(r)/ *n.* **1** var. of RELATER. **2** *Law* a person who makes a relation (see RELATION 6). [L (as RELATE)]

relax /rɪˈlæks/ *v.* **1** *tr. & intr.* make or become less stiff or rigid or tense. **2** *tr. & intr.* make or become less formal or strict (*rules were relaxed*). **3** *tr.* reduce or abate (one's attention, efforts, etc.). **4** *intr.* cease work or effort. **5** *tr.* (as **relaxed** *adj.*) at ease; unperturbed. □□ **relaxedly** *adv.* **relaxedness** *n.* **relaxer** *n.* [ME f. L *relaxare* (as RE-, LAX)]

relaxant /rɪˈlæks(ə)nt/ *n. & adj.* —*n.* a drug etc. that relaxes and reduces tension. —*adj.* causing relaxation.

relaxation /ˌriːlækˈseɪʃ(ə)n/ *n.* **1** the act of relaxing or state of being relaxed. **2** recreation or rest, esp. after a period of work. **3** a partial remission or relaxing of a penalty, duty, etc. **4** a lessening of severity, precision, etc. **5** *Physics* the restoration of equilibrium following disturbance. [L *relaxatio* (as RELAX)]

relay /ˈriːleɪ/ *n. & v.* —*n.* **1** a fresh set of people or horses substituted for tired ones. **2** a gang of workers, supply of material, etc., deployed on the same basis (*operated in relays*). **3** = *relay race*. **4** a device activating changes in an electric circuit etc. in response to other changes affecting itself. **5 a** a device to receive, reinforce, and transmit a telegraph message, broadcast programme, etc. **b** a relayed message or transmission. —*v.tr.* /ˈriːleɪ, rɪˈleɪ/ **1** receive (a message, broadcast, etc.) and transmit it to others. **2 a** arrange in relays. **b** provide with or replace by relays. □ **relay race** a race between teams of which each member in turn covers part of the distance. [ME f. OF *relai* (n.), *relayer* (v.) (as RE-, *laier* ult. f. L *laxare*): cf. RELAX]

re-lay /riːˈleɪ/ *v.tr.* (*past* and *past part.* **re-laid**) lay again or differently.

relearn /riːˈlɜːn/ v.tr. learn again.

release /rɪˈliːs/ v. & n. —v.tr. **1** (often foll. by *from*) set free; liberate, unfasten. **2** allow to move from a fixed position. **3 a** make (information, a recording, etc.) publicly or generally available. **b** issue (a film etc.) for general exhibition. **4** *Law* **a** remit (a debt). **b** surrender (a right). **c** make over (property or money) to another. —n. **1** deliverance or liberation from a restriction, duty, or difficulty. **2** a handle or catch that releases part of a mechanism. **3** a document or item of information made available for publication (*press release*). **4 a** a film or record etc. that is released. **b** the act or an instance of releasing or the process of being released in this way. **5** *Law* **a** the act of releasing (property, money, or a right) to another. **b** a document effecting this. □□ **releasable** adj. **releasee** /-ˈsiː/ n. (in sense 4 of v.). **releaser** n. **releasor** n. (in sense 4 of v.). [ME f. OF *reles* (n.), *relesser* (v.), *relaiss(i)er* f. L *relaxare*: see RELAX]

relegate /ˈrelɪˌɡeɪt/ v.tr. **1** consign or dismiss to an inferior or less important position; demote. **2** transfer (a sports team) to a lower division of a league etc. **3** banish or send into exile. **4** (foll. by *to*) **a** transfer (a matter) for decision or implementation. **b** refer (a person) for information. □□ **relegable** adj. **relegation** /-ˈɡeɪʃ(ə)n/ n. [L *relegare relegat-* (as RE-, *legare* send)]

relent /rɪˈlent/ v.intr. **1** abandon a harsh intention. **2** yield to compassion. **3** relax one's severity; become less stern. [ME f. med.L *relentare* (unrecorded), formed as RE- + L *lentare* bend f. *lentus* flexible]

relentless /rɪˈlentlɪs/ adj. **1** unrelenting; insistent and uncompromising. **2** continuous; oppressively constant (*the pressure was relentless*). □□ **relentlessly** adv. **relentlessness** n.

re-let /riːˈlet/ v.tr. (**-letting**; *past* and *past part.* **-let**) let (a property) for a further period or to a new tenant.

relevant /ˈrelɪv(ə)nt/ adj. (often foll. by *to*) bearing on or having reference to the matter in hand. □□ **relevance** n. **relevancy** n. **relevantly** adv. [med.L *relevans*, part. of L *relevare* RELIEVE]

reliable /rɪˈlaɪəb(ə)l/ adj. **1** that may be relied on. **2** of sound and consistent character or quality. □□ **reliability** /-ˈbɪlɪtɪ/ n. **reliableness** n. **reliably** adv.

reliance /rɪˈlaɪəns/ n. **1** (foll. by *in*, *on*) trust, confidence (*put full reliance in you*). **2** a thing relied upon. □□ **reliant** adj.

relic /ˈrelɪk/ n. **1** an object interesting because of its age or association. **2** a part of a deceased holy person's body or belongings kept as an object of reverence. **3** a surviving custom or belief etc. from a past age. **4** a memento or souvenir. **5** (in *pl.*) what has survived destruction or wasting or use. **6** (in *pl.*) the dead body or remains of a person. [ME *relike, relique*, etc. f. OF *relique* f. L *reliquiae*: see RELIQUIAE]

relict /ˈrelɪkt/ n. **1 a** a geological or other object surviving in its primitive form. **b** an animal or plant known to have existed in the same form in previous geological ages. **2** (foll. by *of*) *archaic* a widow. [L *relinquere relict-* leave behind (as RE-, *linquere* leave): sense 2 f. OF *relicte* f. L *relicta*]

relief /rɪˈliːf/ n. **1 a** the alleviation of or deliverance from pain, distress, anxiety, etc. **b** the feeling accompanying such deliverance. **2** a feature etc. that diversifies monotony or relaxes tension. **3** assistance (esp. financial) given to those in special need or difficulty (*rent relief*). **4 a** the replacing of a person or persons on duty by another or others. **b** a person or persons replacing others in this way. **5** (usu. *attrib.*) a thing supplementing another in some service, esp. an extra vehicle providing public transport at peak times. **6 a** a method of moulding or carving or stamping in which the design stands out from the surface, with projections proportioned and more (**high relief**) or less (**low relief**) closely approximating to those of the objects depicted (cf. ROUND n. 9). **b** a piece of sculpture etc. in relief. **c** a representation of relief given by an arrangement of line or colour or shading. **7** vividness, distinctness (*brings the facts out in sharp relief*). **8** (foll. by *of*) the reinforcement (esp. the raising of a siege) of a place. **9** esp. *Law* the redress of a hardship or grievance. □ **relief map 1** a map indicating hills and valleys by shading etc. rather than by contour lines alone. **2** a map-model showing elevations and depressions, usu. on an exaggerated relative scale. **relief printing** = LETTERPRESS 2. **relief road** a

road taking traffic around a congested (esp. urban) area. [ME f. AF *relef*, OF *relief* (in sense 6 F *relief* f. It. *rilievo*) f. *relever*: see RELIEVE]

relieve /rɪˈliːv/ v.tr. **1** bring or provide aid or assistance to. **2** alleviate or reduce (pain, suffering, etc.). **3** mitigate the tedium or monotony of. **4** bring military support for (a besieged place). **5** release (a person) from a duty by acting as or providing a substitute. **6** (foll. by *of*) take (a burden or responsibility) away from (a person). **7** bring into relief; cause to appear solid or detached. □ **relieve one's feelings** use strong language or vigorous behaviour when annoyed. **relieve oneself** urinate or defecate. □□ **relievable** adj. **reliever** n. [ME f. OF *relever* f. L *relevare* (as RE-, *levis* light)]

relieved /rɪˈliːvd/ predic.adj. freed from anxiety or distress (*am very relieved to hear it*). □□ **relievedly** adv.

relievo /rɪˈliːvəʊ/ n. (also **rilievo** /riːˈljeɪvəʊ/) (pl. **-os**) = RELIEF 6. [It. *rilievo* RELIEF 6]

relight /riːˈlaɪt/ v.tr. light (a fire etc.) again.

religio- /rɪˈlɪɡɪəʊ, rɪˈlɪdʒɪəʊ/ comb. form **1** religion. **2** religious.

religion /rɪˈlɪdʒ(ə)n/ n. **1** the belief in a superhuman controlling power, esp. in a personal God or gods entitled to obedience and worship. **2** the expression of this in worship. **3** a particular system of faith and worship. **4** life under monastic vows (*the way of religion*). **5** a thing that one is devoted to (*football is their religion*). □ **freedom of religion** the right to follow whatever religion one chooses. □□ **religionless** adj. [ME f. AF *religiun*, OF *religion* f. L *religio -onis* obligation, bond, reverence]

religionism /rɪˈlɪdʒəˌnɪz(ə)m/ n. excessive religious zeal. □□ **religionist** n.

religiose /rɪˈlɪdʒɪəʊs/ adj. excessively religious. [L *religiosus* (as RELIGIOUS)]

religiosity /rɪˌlɪdʒɪˈɒsɪtɪ/ n. the condition of being religious or religiose. [ME f. L *religiositas* (as RELIGIOUS)]

religious /rɪˈlɪdʒəs/ adj. & n. —adj. **1** devoted to religion; pious, devout. **2** of or concerned with religion. **3** of or belonging to a monastic order. **4** scrupulous, conscientious (*a religious attention to detail*). —n. (pl. same) a person bound by monastic vows. □□ **religiously** adv. **religiousness** n. [ME f. AF *religius*, OF *religious* f. L *religiosus* (as RELIGION)]

reline /riːˈlaɪn/ v.tr. renew the lining of (a garment etc.).

relinquish /rɪˈlɪŋkwɪʃ/ v.tr. **1** surrender or resign (a right or possession). **2** give up or cease from (a habit, plan, belief, etc.). **3** relax hold of (an object held). □□ **relinquishment** n. [ME f. OF *relinquir* f. L *relinquere* (as RE-, *linquere* leave)]

reliquary /ˈrelɪkwərɪ/ n. (pl. **-ies**) esp. *Relig.* a receptacle for relics. [F *reliquaire* (as RELIC)]

reliquiae /rɪˈlɪkwɪiː/ n.pl. **1** remains. **2** *Geol.* fossil remains of animals or plants. [L f. *reliquus* remaining, formed as RE- + *linquere liq-* leave]

relish /ˈrelɪʃ/ n. & v. —n. **1** (often foll. by *for*) **a** great liking or enjoyment. **b** keen or pleasurable longing (*had no relish for travelling*). **2 a** an appetizing flavour. **b** an attractive quality (*fishing loses its relish in winter*). **3** a condiment eaten with plainer food to add flavour, esp. a piquant sauce, pickle, etc. **4** (foll. by *of*) a distinctive taste or tinge. —v.tr. **1 a** get pleasure out of; enjoy greatly. **b** look forward to, anticipate with pleasure (*did not relish what lay before her*). **2** add relish to. □□ **relishable** adj. [alt. (with assim. to -ISH²) of obs. *reles* f. OF *reles, relais* remainder f. *relaisser*: see RELEASE]

relive /riːˈlɪv/ v.tr. live (an experience etc.) over again, esp. in the imagination.

reload /riːˈləʊd/ v.tr. (also *absol.*) load (esp. a gun) again.

relocate /ˌriːləʊˈkeɪt/ v. **1** tr. locate in a new place. **2** tr. & intr. move to a new place (esp. to live or work). □□ **relocation** /-ˈkeɪʃən/ n.

reluctant /rɪˈlʌkt(ə)nt/ adj. (often foll. by *to* + infin.) unwilling or disinclined (*most reluctant to agree*). □□ **reluctance** n. **reluctantly** adv. [L *reluctari* (as RE-, *luctari* struggle)]

rely /rɪˈlaɪ/ v.intr. (**-ies**, **-ied**) (foll. by *on*, *upon*) **1** depend on with confidence or assurance (*am relying on your judgement*). **2** be dependent on (*relies on her for everything*). [ME (earlier senses 'rally, be a vassal of') f. OF *relier* bind together f. L *religare* (as RE-, *ligare* bind)]

REM *abbr.* rapid eye-movement.

rem /rem/ *n.* (*pl.* same) a unit of effective absorbed dose of ionizing radiation in human tissue, equivalent to one roentgen of X-rays. [roentgen equivalent man]

remade past and past part. of REMAKE.

remain /rɪˈmeɪn/ *v.intr.* **1** be left over after others or other parts have been removed or used or dealt with. **2** be in the same place or condition during further time; continue to exist or stay; be left behind (*remained at home; it will remain cold*). **3** (foll. by compl.) continue to be (*remained calm; remains President*). [ME f. OF *remain*-stressed stem of *remanoir* or f. OF *remaindre* ult. f. L *remanēre* (as RE-, *manēre* stay)]

remainder /rɪˈmeɪndə(r)/ *n.* & *v.* —*n.* **1** a part remaining or left over. **2** remaining persons or things. **3** a number left after division or subtraction. **4** the copies of a book left unsold when demand has fallen. **5** *Law* an interest in an estate that becomes effective in possession only when a prior interest (devised at the same time) ends. —*v.tr.* dispose of (a remainder of books) at a reduced price. [ME (in sense 5) f. AF, = OF *remaindre*: see REMAIN]

remains /rɪˈmeɪnz/ *n.pl.* **1** what remains after other parts have been removed or used etc. **2** relics of antiquity, esp. of buildings (*Roman remains*). **3** a person's body after death. **4** an author's (esp. unpublished) works left after death.

remake *v.* & *n.* —*v.tr.* /riːˈmeɪk/ (past and past part. **remade**) make again or differently. —*n.* /ˈriːmeɪk/ a thing that has been remade, esp. a cinema film.

reman /riːˈmæn/ *v.tr.* (**remanned, remanning**) **1** equip (a fleet etc.) with new personnel. **2** make courageous again.

remand /rɪˈmɑːnd/ *v.* & *n.* —*v.tr.* return (a prisoner) to custody, esp. to allow further inquiries to be made. —*n.* a recommittal to custody. □ **on remand** in custody pending trial. **remand centre** (in the UK) an institution to which accused persons are remanded pending trial. [ME f. LL *remandare* (as RE-, *mandare* commit)]

remanent /ˈremənənt/ *adj.* **1** remaining, residual. **2** (of magnetism) remaining after the magnetizing field has been removed. □□ **remanence** *n.* [ME f. L *remanēre* REMAIN]

remark /rɪˈmɑːk/ *v.* & *n.* —*v.* **1** *tr.* (often foll. by *that* + clause) **a** say by way of comment. **b** take notice of; regard with attention. **2** *intr.* (usu. foll. by *on, upon*) make a comment. —*n.* **1** a written or spoken comment; anything said. **2 a** the act of noticing or observing (*worthy of remark*). **b** the act of commenting (*let it pass without remark*). [F *remarque, remarquer* (as RE-, MARK¹)]

remarkable /rɪˈmɑːkəb(ə)l/ *adj.* **1** worth notice; exceptional. **2** striking, conspicuous. □□ **remarkableness** *n.* **remarkably** *adv.* [F *remarquable* (as REMARK)]

remarry /riːˈmæri/ *v.intr.* & *tr.* (-ies, -ied) marry again. □□ **remarriage** *n.*

remaster /riːˈmɑːstə(r)/ *v.tr.* make a new master of (a recording), esp. to improve the sound quality.

rematch /ˈriːmætʃ/ *n.* a return match or game.

Rembrandt /ˈrembrænt/ (full name Rembrandt Harmensz van Rijn, 1606–69), the greatest of Dutch painters. The son of a miller, he worked at first in Leyden but from 1632 established himself in Amsterdam. His initial success owed much to highly-finished society portraits, strongly lit in the manner of Caravaggio, and some financial independence came with his marriage to the well-to-do Saskia in 1634. By 1642, when she died, his style was evolving as his art became ever more searching and profound. The great *Night Watch* (1642) transformed the traditional Dutch portrait convention into a haunting mystery. Though his worldly affairs now decayed (he was bankrupted in 1656), yet his imaginative power became ever richer. The emotional resonance of his later work, his ability to paint human flesh as if lit from within by the spirit, in the surrounding darkness, surpasses at its finest the power of any painter in history. The great series of over 60 self-portraits is a unique autobiography in paint, but he found his subjects in genre, religion, and landscape, and in drawing and etching he

is a supreme master. His work is represented in almost all the major art galleries of the Western world.

REME /ˈriːmiː/ *abbr.* (in the UK) Royal Electrical and Mechanical Engineers.

remeasure /riːˈmeʒə(r)/ *v.tr.* measure again. □□ **remeasurement** *n.*

remedial /rɪˈmiːdɪəl/ *adj.* **1** affording or intended as a remedy (*remedial therapy*). **2** (of teaching) for slow or backward children. □□ **remedially** *adv.* [LL *remedialis* f. L *remedium* (as REMEDY)]

remedy /ˈremɪdɪ/ *n.* & *v.* —*n.* (*pl.* **-ies**) (often foll. by *for, against*) **1** a medicine or treatment (for a disease etc.). **2** a means of counteracting or removing anything undesirable. **3** redress; legal or other reparation. **4** the margin within which coins as minted may differ from the standard fineness and weight. —*v.tr.* (**-ies, -ied**) rectify; make good. □□ **remediable** /rɪˈmiːdɪəb(ə)l/ *adj.* [ME f. AF *remedie*, OF *remede* or L *remedium* (as RE-, *medēri* heal)]

remember /rɪˈmembə(r)/ *v.tr.* **1** keep in the memory; not forget. **2 a** (also *absol.*) bring back into one's thoughts, call to mind (knowledge or experience etc.). **b** (often foll. by *to* + infin. or *that* + clause) have in mind (a duty, commitment, etc.) (*will you remember to lock the door?*). **3** think of or acknowledge (a person) in some connection, esp. in making a gift etc. **4** (foll. by *to*) convey greetings from (one person) to (another) (*remember me to your mother*). **5** mention (in prayer). □ **remember oneself** recover one's manners or intentions after a lapse. □□ **rememberer** *n.* [ME f. OF *remembrer* f. LL *rememorari* (as RE-, L *memor* mindful)]

remembrance /rɪˈmembrəns/ *n.* **1** the act of remembering or process of being remembered. **2** a memory or recollection. **3** a keepsake or souvenir. **4** (in *pl.*) greetings conveyed through a third person. □ **Remembrance Day 1** = *Remembrance Sunday*. **2** *hist.* Armistice Day. **Remembrance Sunday** (in the UK) the Sunday nearest 11 Nov., when those who were killed in the First and Second World Wars and in later conflicts are commemorated. [ME f. OF (as REMEMBER)]

remex /ˈriːmeks/ *n.* (*pl.* **remiges** /ˈremɪˌdʒiːz/) a primary or secondary feather in a bird's wing. [L, = rower, f. *remus* oar]

remind /rɪˈmaɪnd/ *v.tr.* **1** (foll. by *of*) cause (a person) to remember or think of. **2** (foll. by *to* + infin. or *that* + clause) cause (a person) to remember (a commitment etc.) (*remind them to pay their subscriptions*).

reminder /rɪˈmaɪndə(r)/ *n.* **1** a thing that reminds, esp. a letter or bill. **2** (often foll. by *of*) a memento or souvenir.

remindful /rɪˈmaɪndfʊl/ *adj.* (often foll. by *of*) acting as a reminder; reviving the memory.

reminisce /ˌremɪˈnɪs/ *v.intr.* indulge in reminiscence. □□ **reminiscer** *n.* [back-form. f. REMINISCENCE]

reminiscence /ˌremɪˈnɪs(ə)ns/ *n.* **1** the act of remembering things past; the recovery of knowledge by mental effort. **2 a** a past fact or experience that is remembered. **b** the process of narrating this. **3** (in *pl.*) a collection in literary form of incidents and experiences that a person remembers. **4** *Philos.* (esp. in Platonism) the theory of the recovery of things known to the soul in previous existences. **5** a characteristic of one thing reminding or suggestive of another. □□ **reminiscential** /-ˈsenʃ(ə)l/ *adj.* [LL *reminiscentia* f. L *reminisci* remember]

reminiscent /ˌremɪˈnɪs(ə)nt/ *adj.* **1** (foll. by *of*) tending to remind one of or suggest. **2** concerned with reminiscence. **3** (of a person) given to reminiscing. □□ **reminiscently** *adv.*

remise /rɪˈmiːz/ *v.* & *n.* —*v.intr.* **1** *Law* surrender or make over (a right or property). **2** *Fencing* make a remise. —*n.* *Fencing* a second thrust made after the first has failed. [F f. *remis, remise* past part. of *remettre* put back: cf. REMIT]

remiss /rɪˈmɪs/ *adj.* careless of duty; lax, negligent. □□ **remissly** *adv.* **remissness** *n.* [ME f. L *remissus* past part. of *remittere* slacken: see REMIT]

remissible /rɪˈmɪsɪb(ə)l/ *adj.* that may be remitted. [F *rémissible* or LL *remissibilis* (as REMIT)]

remission /rɪˈmɪʃ(ə)n/ *n.* **1** the reduction of a prison sentence on account of good behaviour. **2** the remitting of a debt or penalty etc. **3** a diminution of force, effect, or degree (esp. of disease or pain). **4** (often foll. by *of*) forgiveness (of sins etc.). □□ **remissive** *adj.* [ME f. OF *remission* or L *remissio* (as REMIT)]

remit *v. & n.* —*v.* /rɪˈmɪt/ (**remitted, remitting**) **1** *tr.* cancel or refrain from exacting or inflicting (a debt or punishment etc.). **2** *intr. & tr.* abate or slacken; cease or cease from partly or entirely. **3** *tr.* send (money etc.) in payment. **4** *tr.* cause to be conveyed by post. **5** *tr.* **a** (foll. by *to*) refer (a matter for decision etc.) to some authority. **b** *Law* send back (a case) to a lower court. **6** *tr.* **a** (often foll. by *to*) postpone or defer. **b** (foll. by *in, into*) send or put back into a previous state. **7** *tr. Theol.* (usu. of God) pardon (sins etc.). —*n.* /ˈriːmɪt, rɪˈmɪt/ **1** the terms of reference of a committee etc. **2** an item remitted for consideration. □□ **remittable** /rɪˈmɪtəb(ə)l/ *adj.* **remittal** /rɪˈmɪt(ə)l/ *n.* **remittee** /rɪmɪˈtiː/ *n.* **remitter** /rɪˈmɪtə(r)/ *n.* [ME f. L *remittere remiss-* (as RE-, *mittere* send)]

remittance /rɪˈmɪt(ə)ns/ *n.* **1** money sent, esp. by post, for goods or services or as an allowance. **2** the act of sending money. □ **remittance man** *hist.* an emigrant subsisting on remittances from home.

remittent /rɪˈmɪt(ə)nt/ *adj.* (of a fever) that abates at intervals. [L remittent (as REMIT)]

remix *v. & n.* —*v.tr.* /riːˈmɪks/ mix again. —*n.* /ˈriːmɪks/ a sound recording that has been remixed.

remnant /ˈremnənt/ *n.* **1** a small remaining quantity. **2** a piece of cloth etc. left when the greater part has been used or sold. **3** (foll. by *of*) a surviving trace (*a remnant of empire*). [ME (earlier *remenant*) f. OF *remenant* f. *remenoir* REMAIN]

remodel /riːˈmɒd(ə)l/ *v.tr.* (**remodelled, remodelling**; US **remodeled, remodeling**) **1** model again or differently. **2** reconstruct.

remodify /riːˈmɒdɪˌfaɪ/ *v.tr.* (**-ies, -ied**) modify again. □□ **remodification** /-fɪˈkeɪʃ(ə)n/ *n.*

remold US var. of REMOULD.

remonetize /riːˈmʌnɪˌtaɪz/ *v.tr.* (also **-ise**) restore (a metal etc.) to its former position as legal tender. □□ **remonetization** /-ˈzeɪʃ(ə)n/ *n.*

remonstrance /rɪˈmɒnstrəns/ *n.* **1** the act or an instance of remonstrating. **2** an expostulation or protest. **3** (**Remonstrance**) a document drawn up in 1610 by the Arminians of the Dutch Reformed Church, presenting the differences between their doctrines and those of the strict Calvinists. □ **Grand Remonstrance** that presented by the House of Commons to the Crown in 1641. □□ **Remonstrant** *n.* [ME f. obs. F *remonstrance* or med.L *remonstrantia* (as REMONSTRATE)]

remonstrate /ˈremənˌstreɪt/ *v.* **1** *intr.* (foll. by *with*) make a protest; argue forcibly (*remonstrated with them over the delays*). **2** *tr.* (often foll. by *that* + clause) urge protestingly. □□ **remonstrant** /rɪˈmɒnstrənt/ *adj.* **remonstration** /-ˈstreɪʃ(ə)n/ *n.* **remonstrative** /rɪˈmɒnstrətɪv/ *adj.* **remonstrator** *n.* [med.L *remonstrare* (as RE-, *monstrare* show)]

remontant /rɪˈmɒnt(ə)nt/ *adj. & n.* —*adj.* blooming more than once a year. —*n.* a remontant rose. [F f. *remonter* REMOUNT]

remora /ˈremərə/ *n. Zool.* any of various marine fish of the family Echeneidae, which attach themselves by modified sucker-like fins to other fish and to ships. [L, = hindrance (as RE-, *mora* delay, from the former belief that the fish slowed ships down)]

remorse /rɪˈmɔːs/ *n.* **1** deep regret for a wrong committed. **2** compunction; a compassionate reluctance to inflict pain (esp. in *without remorse*). [ME f. OF *remors* f. med.L *remorsus* f. L *remordēre remors-* vex (as RE-, *mordēre* bite)]

remorseful /rɪˈmɔːsfʊl/ *adj.* filled with repentance. □□ **remorsefully** *adv.*

remorseless /rɪˈmɔːslɪs/ *adj.* without compassion or compunction. □□ **remorselessly** *adv.* **remorselessness** *n.*

remortgage /riːˈmɔːgɪdʒ/ *v. & n.* —*v.tr.* (also *absol.*) mortgage again; revise the terms of an existing mortgage on (a property). —*n.* a different or altered mortgage.

remote /rɪˈməʊt/ *adj.* (**remoter, remotest**) **1** far away in place or time. **2** out of the way; situated away from the main centres

of population, society, etc. **3** distantly related (*a remote ancestor*). **4** slight, faint (esp. in *not the remotest chance, idea,* etc.). **5** (of a person) aloof; not friendly. **6** (foll. by *from*) widely different; separate by nature (*ideas remote from the subject*). □ **remote control** control of a machine or apparatus from a distance by means of signals transmitted from a radio or electronic device. **remote-controlled** (of a machine etc.) controlled at a distance. □□ **remotely** *adv.* **remoteness** *n.* [ME f. L *remotus* (as REMOVE)]

remould *v. & n.* (US **remold**) —*v.tr.* /riːˈməʊld/ **1** mould again; refashion. **2** re-form the tread of (a tyre). —*n.* /ˈriːməʊld/ a remoulded tyre.

remount *v. & n.* —*v.* /riːˈmaʊnt/ **1 a** *tr.* mount (a horse etc.) again. **b** *intr.* get on horseback again. **2** *tr.* get on to or ascend (a ladder, hill, etc.) again. **3** *tr.* provide (a person) with a fresh horse etc. **4** *tr.* put (a picture) on a fresh mount. —*n.* /ˈriːmaʊnt/ **1** a fresh horse for a rider. **2** a supply of fresh horses for a regiment.

removal /rɪˈmuːv(ə)l/ *n.* **1** the act or an instance of removing; the process of being removed. **2** the transfer of furniture and other contents on moving house.

remove /rɪˈmuːv/ *v. & n.* —*v.* **1** *tr.* take off or away from the place or position occupied (*remove the top carefully*). **2** *tr.* make a move or take to another place; change the situation of (*will you remove the tea things?*). **b** get rid of; eliminate (*will remove all doubts*). **3** *tr.* cause to be no longer present or available; take away (*all privileges were removed*). **4** *tr.* (often foll. by *from*) dismiss (from office). **5** *tr. colloq.* kill; assassinate. **6** *tr.* (in *passive*; foll. by *from*) distant or remote in condition (*the country is not far removed from anarchy*). **7** *tr.* (as **removed** *adj.*) (esp. of cousins) separated by a specified number of steps of descent (*a first cousin twice removed* = a grandchild of a first cousin). **8** *formal* **a** *intr.* (usu. foll. by *from, to*) change one's home or place of residence. **b** *tr.* conduct the removal of. —*n.* **1** a degree or remoteness; a distance. **2** a stage in a gradation; a degree (*is several removes from what I expected*). **3** *Brit.* a form or division in some schools. □□ **removable** *adj.* **removability** /-ˈbɪlɪtɪ/ *n.* **remover** *n.* (esp. in sense 8b of v.). [ME f. OF *removeir* f. L *removēre remot-* (as RE-, *movēre* move)]

remunerate /rɪˈmjuːnəˌreɪt/ *v.tr.* **1** reward; pay for services rendered. **2** serve as or provide recompense for (toil etc.) or to (a person). □□ **remuneration** /-ˈreɪʃ(ə)n/ *n.* **remunerative** /-rətɪv/ *adj.* **remuneratory** /-rətərɪ/ *adj.* [L *remunerari* (as RE-, *munus muneris* gift)]

Remus /ˈriːməs/ *Rom. legend* the twin brother of Romulus (see entry).

Renaissance /rɪˈneɪs(ə)ns, rəˈn-, -sãs/ *n.* **1** the revival of art and learning under the influence of classical models which began in Italy in the late Middle Ages and reached its peak at the end of the 15th c. before spreading northwards into the rest of Europe. **2** the period of this. **3** the culture and style of art, architecture, etc. developed during this era. **4** (**renaissance**) any similar revival. [F *renaissance* (as RE-, F *naissance* birth f. L *nascentia* or F *naître naiss-* be born f. Rmc: cf. NASCENT)]

renal /ˈriːn(ə)l/ *adj.* of or concerning the kidneys. [F *rénal* f. LL *renalis* f. L *renes* kidneys]

rename /riːˈneɪm/ *v.tr.* name again; give a new name to.

Renan /rəˈnã/, Ernest (1823–92), French historian and philologist,. He was educated for the priesthood but his scepticism of the divine inspiration of the Bible and the fundamental doctrines of orthodox religion found him unable to take his vows. His controversial *Vie de Jésus* (1863) rejects the supernatural element in Jesus' life. Through the persuasive force of his reasoning and his erudition he became a major representative of 19th-c. French thought. His belief that the future of the world lay in the progress of science found expression in *L'Avenir de la science* (1890).

renascence /rɪˈnæs(ə)ns/ *n.* **1** rebirth; renewal. **2** = RENAISSANCE. [RENASCENT]

renascent /rɪˈnæs(ə)nt/ *adj.* springing up anew; being reborn. [L *renasci* (as RE-, *nasci* be born)]

Renault /ˈrenəʊ/, Mary (pseudonym of Mary Challans, 1905–83), British novelist, born in South Africa, known especially for her historical novels set in ancient Greec or Asia Minor. They include *The King must Die* (1958) and *The Bull from the Sea* (1962), both recalling the legend of Theseus, and the Alexander trilogy — *Fire from Heaven* (1970), *The Persian Boy* (1972), and *Funeral Games* (1981) — set in the time of Alexander the Great.

rencontre /rɛnˈkɒntə(r)/ *n. archaic* = RENCOUNTER. [F (as RENCOUNTER)]

rencounter /rɛnˈkaʊntə(r)/ *n. & v. —n.* **1** an encounter; a chance meeting. **2** a battle, skirmish, or duel. *—v.tr.* encounter; meet by chance. [F *rencontre(r)* (as RE-, ENCOUNTER)]

rend /rɛnd/ *v.* (past and past part. **rent** /rɛnt/) *archaic* or *rhet.* **1** *tr.* (foll. by *off*, *from*, *away*, etc.; also *absol.*) tear or wrench forcibly. **2** *tr. & intr.* split or divide in pieces or into factions (*a country rent by civil war*). **3** *tr.* cause emotional pain to (the heart etc.). □ **rend the air** sound piercingly. **rend one's garments** (or **hair**) display extreme grief or rage. [OE *rendan*, rel. to MLG *rende*]

Rendell /ˈrɛnd(ə)l/, Ruth (1930–), English writer of crime thrillers and short stories, for which she has won many awards. Her novels, often portraying characters with sick or weak minds, include *From Doon with Death* (1964), the grim *A Judgement in Stone* (1977), and *The Bridesmaid* (1989).

render /ˈrɛndə(r)/ *v.tr.* **1** cause to be or become; make (*rendered us helpless*). **2** give or pay (money, service, etc.), esp. in return or as a thing due (*render thanks; rendered good for evil*). **3** (often foll. by *to*) **a** give (assistance) (*rendered aid to the injured man*). **b** show (obedience etc.). **c** do (a service etc.). **4** submit; send in; present (an account, reason, etc.). **5 a** represent or portray artistically, musically, etc. **b** act (a role); represent (a character, idea, etc.) (*the dramatist's conception was well rendered*). **c** *Mus.* perform; execute. **6** translate (*rendered the poem into French*). **7** (often foll. by *down*) melt down (fat etc.) esp. to clarify; extract by melting. **8** cover (stone or brick) with a coat of plaster. **9** *archaic* **a** give back; hand over; deliver, give up, surrender (*render to Caesar the things that are Caesar's*). **b** show (obedience). □ **render-set** *v.tr.* (**-setting**; past and past part. **-set**) plaster (a wall etc.) with two coats. *—n.* a plastering of two coats. *—adj.* of two coats. □□ **renderer** *n.* [ME f. OF *rendre* ult. f. L *reddere reddit-* (as RE-, *dare* give)]

rendering /ˈrɛndərɪŋ/ *n.* **1 a** the act or an instance of performing music, drama, etc.; an interpretation or performance (*an excellent rendering of the part*). **b** a translation. **2 a** the act or an instance of plastering stone, brick, etc. **b** this coating. **3** the act or an instance of giving, yielding, or surrendering.

rendezvous /ˈrɒndɪˌvuː, -deɪˌvuː/ *n. & v. —n.* (pl. same /-ˌvuːz/) **1** an agreed or regular meeting-place. **2** a meeting by arrangement. **3** a place appointed for assembling troops, ships, etc. *—v.intr.* (**rendezvouses** /-ˌvuːz/; **rendezvoused** /-ˌvuːd/; **rendezvousing** /-ˌvuːɪŋ/) meet at a rendezvous. [F *rendez-vous* present yourselves f. *rendre*: see RENDER]

rendition /rɛnˈdɪʃ(ə)n/ *n.* (often foll. by *of*) **1** an interpretation or rendering of a dramatic role, piece of music, etc. **2** a visual representation. [obs. F f. *rendre* RENDER]

renegade /ˈrɛnɪˌɡeɪd/ *n. & v. —n.* **1** a person who deserts a party or principles. **2** an apostate; a person who abandons one religion for another. *—v.intr.* be a renegade. [Sp. *renegado* f. med.L *renegatus* (as RE-, L *negare* deny)]

renegado /ˌrɛnɪˈɡeɪdəʊ/ *n.* (pl. **-oes**) *archaic* = RENEGADE. [Sp. (as RENEGADE)]

renege /rɪˈniːɡ, -ˈneɡ, -ˈneɪɡ/ *v.* (also **renegue**) **1** *intr.* **a** go back on one's word; change one's mind; recant. **b** (foll. by *on*) go back on (a promise or undertaking or contract). **2** *tr.* deny, renounce, abandon (a person, faith, etc.). **3** *intr. Cards* revoke. □□ **reneger** *n.* **reneguer** *n.* [med.L *renegare* (as RE-, L *negare* deny)]

renegotiate /ˌriːnɪˈɡəʊʃɪˌeɪt/ *v.tr.* (also *absol.*) negotiate again or on different terms. □□ **renegotiable** *adj.* **renegotiation** /-ˈeɪʃ(ə)n/ *n.*

renew /rɪˈnjuː/ *v.tr.* **1** revive; regenerate; make new again; restore to the original state. **2** reinforce; resupply; replace. **3** repeat or re-establish; resume after an interruption (*renewed our acquaintance; a renewed attack*). **4** get, begin, make, say, give, etc. anew. **5** (also *absol.*) grant or be granted a continuation of or continued validity of (a licence, subscription, lease, etc.). **6**

recover (one's youth, strength, etc.). □□ **renewable** *adj.* **renewability** /-əˈbɪlɪtɪ/ *n.* **renewal** *n.* **renewer** *n.*

reniform /ˈriːnɪˌfɔːm/ *adj. esp. Med.* kidney-shaped. [L *ren* kidney + -FORM]

Rennes /rɛn/ an industrial city of Brittany in NW France; pop. (1982) 200,400.

rennet /ˈrɛnɪt/ *n.* **1** curdled milk found in the stomach of an unweaned calf, used in curdling milk for cheese, junket, etc. **2** a preparation made from the stomach-membrane of a calf or from certain fungi, used for the same purpose. [ME, prob. f. an OE form *rynet* (unrecorded), rel. to RUN]

Rennie /ˈrɛnɪ/, John (1761–1821), Scottish civil engineer, much of whose work can still be seen. He built some distinguished bridges, including three in London, the Waterloo, Southwark, and New London bridges, of which Southwark remains, and many docks including some in London, Hull, Malta, and Bermuda, while his great breakwater at Plymouth (1811–48) is an enduring monument.

rennin /ˈrɛnɪn/ *n. Biochem.* an enzyme secreted into the stomach of unweaned mammals causing the clotting of milk. [RENNET + -IN]

Renoir[1] /rəˈnwɑː(r), ˈrɛn-/, Jean (1894–1979), French film director, second son of Pierre Auguste Renoir. His fame is based chiefly on the deeply moving films that he made in France in the 1930s, including *La Grande Illusion* (1937) and his masterpiece *La Règle du Jeu* (1939). All his works are notable for their humanity, grace, and style.

Renoir[2] /rəˈnwɑː(r), ˈrɛn-/, Pierre Auguste (1841–1919), French impressionist painter, a close friend of Monet and Sisley. He introduced the so-called 'rainbow palette' restricted to pure tones at maximum intensity with no use of black, and a more thorough use of divisionism and the subordination of outline. The human figure played a larger part in his painting than in that of his colleagues, and he delighted in the intrinsic charm of lovely women, children, flowers, and beautiful scenes; nowhere in his landscape is there a suggestion of sadness or melancholy. His later subjects are mostly female nudes of a fine fleshiness and sensuality. Among his best-known works are *Les grandes baigneuses* (1885–7), *Les grandes laveuses* (1912), and *Le jugement de Paris* (c.1914).

renominate /riːˈnɒmɪˌneɪt/ *v.tr.* nominate for a further term of office. □□ **renomination** /-ˈneɪʃ(ə)n/ *n.*

renounce /rɪˈnaʊns/ *v.* **1** *tr.* consent formally to abandon; surrender; give up (a claim, right, possession, etc.). **2** *tr.* repudiate; refuse to recognize any longer (*renouncing their father's authority*). **3** *tr.* **a** decline further association or disclaim relationship with (*renounced my former friends*). **b** withdraw from; discontinue; forsake. **4** *intr. Law* refuse or resign a right or position esp. as an heir or trustee. **5** *intr. Cards* follow with a card of another suit when having no card of the suit led (cf. REVOKE). □ **renounce the world** abandon society or material affairs. □□ **renounceable** *adj.* **renouncement** *n.* **renouncer** *n.* [ME f. OF *renoncer* f. L *renuntiare* (as RE-, *nuntiare* announce)]

renovate /ˈrɛnəˌveɪt/ *v.tr.* **1** restore to good condition; repair. **2** make new again. □□ **renovation** /-ˈveɪʃ(ə)n/ *n.* **renovative** *adj.* **renovator** *n.* [L *renovare* (as RE-, *novus* new)]

renown /rɪˈnaʊn/ *n.* fame; high distinction; celebrity (*a city of great renown*). [ME f. AF *ren(o)un*, OF *renon, renom* f. *renomer* make famous (as RE-, L *nominare* NOMINATE)]

renowned /rɪˈnaʊnd/ *adj.* famous; celebrated.

rent[1] /rɛnt/ *n. & v. —n.* **1** a tenant's periodical payment to an owner or landlord for the use of land or premises. **2** payment for the use of a service, equipment, etc. *—v.* **1** *tr.* (often foll. by *from*) take, occupy, or use at a rent (*rented a cottage from the local farmer*). **2** *tr.* (often foll. by *out*) let or hire (a thing) for rent. **3** *intr.* (foll. by *at*) be let or hired out at a specified rate (*the land rents at £100 per month*). □ **for rent** *US* available to be rented. **rent-a-** (in *comb.*) often *joc.* denoting availability for hire (*rent-a-van; rent-a-crowd*). **rent-boy** a young male prostitute. **rent-free** with exemption from rent. **rent-roll** the register of a landlord's lands etc. with the rents due from them; the sum of one's income from rent. [ME f. OF *rente* f. Rmc (as RENDER)]

rent[2] /rent/ n. **1** a large tear in a garment etc. **2** an opening in clouds etc. **3** a cleft, fissure, or gorge. [obs. *rent* var. of REND]

rent[3] past and past part. of REND.

rentable /ˈrentəb(ə)l/ adj. **1** available or suitable for renting. **2** giving an adequate ratio of profit to capital. □□ **rentability** /-ˈbɪlɪtɪ/ n.

rental /ˈrent(ə)l/ n. **1** the amount paid or received as rent. **2** the act of renting. **3** an income from rents. **4** US a rented house etc. □ **rental library** US a library which rents books for a fee. [ME f. AF *rental* or AL *rentale* (as RENT[1])]

renter /ˈrentə(r)/ n. **1** a person who rents. **2** *Cinematog.* (in the UK) a person who distributes cinema films. **3** sl. a male prostitute.

rentier /ˈrɑ̃tɪˌeɪ/ n. a person living on dividends from property, investments, etc. [F f. *rente* dividend]

renumber /riːˈnʌmbə(r)/ v.tr. change the number or numbers given or allocated to.

renunciation /rɪˌnʌnsɪˈeɪʃ(ə)n/ n. **1** the act or an instance of renouncing or giving up. **2** self-denial. **3** a document expressing renunciation. □□ **renunciant** /rɪˈnʌnsɪənt/ n. & adj. **renunciative** /rɪˈnʌnsɪətɪv/ adj. **renunciatory** /rɪˈnʌnʃətərɪ/ adj. [ME f. OF *renonciation* or LL *renuntiatio* (as RENOUNCE)]

renvoi /rɑ̃ˈvwʌ/ n. *Law* the act or an instance of referring a case, dispute, etc. to a different jurisdiction. [F f. *renvoyer* send back]

reoccupy /riːˈɒkjʊˌpaɪ/ v.tr. (**-ies**, **-ied**) occupy again. □□ **reoccupation** /-ˈpeɪʃ(ə)n/ n.

reoccur /ˌriːəˈkɜː(r)/ v.intr. (**reoccurred**, **reoccurring**) occur again or habitually. □□ **reoccurrence** /-ˈkʌrəns/ n.

reopen /riːˈəʊpən/ v.tr. & intr. open again.

reorder /riːˈɔːdə(r)/ v. & n. —v.tr. order again. —n. a renewed or repeated order for goods.

reorganize /riːˈɔːgəˌnaɪz/ v.tr. (also **-ise**) organize differently. □□ **reorganization** /-ˈzeɪʃ(ə)n/ n. **reorganizer** n.

reorient /riːˈɔːrɪˌent, -ˈɒrɪˌent/ v.tr. **1** give a new direction to (ideas etc.); redirect (a thing). **2** help (a person) find his or her bearings again. **3** change the outlook of (a person). **4** (refl., often foll. by *to*) adjust oneself to or come to terms with something.

reorientate /riːˈɔːrɪənˌteɪt/ v.tr. = REORIENT. □□ **reorientation** /-ˈteɪʃ(ə)n/ n.

Rep. abbr. US **1** a Representative in Congress. **2** a Republican.

rep[1] /rep/ n. colloq. a representative, esp. a commercial traveller. [abbr.]

rep[2] /rep/ n. colloq. **1** repertory. **2** a repertory theatre or company. [abbr.]

rep[3] /rep/ n. (also **repp**) a textile fabric with a corded surface, used in curtains and upholstery. [F *reps*, of unkn. orig.]

rep[4] /rep/ n. US sl. reputation. [abbr.]

repack /riːˈpæk/ v.tr. pack again.

repackage /riːˈpækɪdʒ/ v.tr. **1** package again or differently. **2** present in a new form. □□ **repackaging** n.

repaginate /riːˈpædʒɪˌneɪt/ v.tr. paginate again; renumber the pages of. □□ **repagination** /-ˈneɪʃ(ə)n/ n.

repaid past and past part. of REPAY.

repaint v. & n. —v.tr. /riːˈpeɪnt/ **1** paint again or differently. **2** restore the paint or colouring of. —n. /ˈriːpeɪnt/ **1** the act of repainting. **2** a repainted thing, esp. a golf ball.

repair[1] /rɪˈpeə(r)/ v. & n. —v.tr. **1** restore to good condition after damage or wear. **2** renovate or mend by replacing or fixing parts or by compensating for loss or exhaustion. **3** set right or make amends for (loss, wrong, error, etc.). —n. **1** the act or an instance of restoring to sound condition (*in need of repair*; *closed during repair*). **2** the result of this (*the repair is hardly visible*). **3** good or relative condition for working or using (*must be kept in repair*; *in good repair*). □□ **repairable** adj. **repairer** n. [ME f. OF *reparer* f. L *reparare* (as RE-, *parare* make ready)]

repair[2] /rɪˈpeə(r)/ v. & n. —v.intr. (foll. by *to*) resort; have recourse; go often or in great numbers or for a specific purpose (*repaired to Spain*). —n. archaic **1** resort (*have repair to*). **2** a place of frequent resort. **3** popularity (*a place of great repair*). [ME f. OF *repaire(r)* f. LL *repatriare* REPATRIATE]

repairman /rɪˈpeəmən/ n. (pl. **-men**) a man who repairs machinery etc.

repand /rɪˈpænd/ adj. *Bot.* with an undulating margin; wavy. [L *repandus* (as RE-, *pandus* bent)]

repaper /riːˈpeɪpə(r)/ v.tr. paper (a wall etc.) again.

reparable /ˈrepərəb(ə)l/ adj. (of a loss etc.) that can be made good. □□ **reparability** /-ˈbɪlɪtɪ/ n. **reparably** adv. [F f. L *reparabilis* (as REPAIR[1])]

reparation /ˌrepəˈreɪʃ(ə)n/ n. **1** the act or an instance of making amends. **2 a** compensation. **b** (esp. in pl.) compensation for war damage paid by the defeated State. **3** the act or an instance of repairing or being repaired. □□ **reparative** /ˈrepərətɪv, rɪˈpærətɪv/ adj. [ME f. OF f. LL *reparatio -onis* (as REPAIR)]

repartee /ˌrepɑːˈtiː/ n. **1** the practice or faculty of making witty retorts; sharpness or wit in quick reply. **2 a** a witty retort. **b** witty retorts collectively. [F *repartie* fem. past part. of *repartir* start again, reply promptly (as RE-, *partir* PART)]

repartition /ˌriːpɑːˈtɪʃ(ə)n/ v.tr. partition again.

repass /riːˈpɑːs/ v.tr. & intr. pass again, esp. on the way back. [ME f. OF *repasser*]

repast /rɪˈpɑːst/ n. formal **1** a meal, esp. of a specified kind (*a light repast*). **2** food and drink supplied for or eaten at a meal. [ME f. OF *repaistre* f. LL *repascere repast-* feed]

repat /ˈriːpæt, rɪˈpæt/ n. colloq. **1** a repatriate. **2** repatriation. [abbr.]

repatriate /riːˈpætrɪˌeɪt/ v. & n. —v. **1** tr. restore (a person) to his or her native land. **2** intr. return to one's own native land. —n. a person who has been repatriated. □□ **repatriation** /-ˈeɪʃ(ə)n/ n. [LL *repatriare* (as RE-, L *patria* native land)]

repay /riːˈpeɪ/ v. (past and past part. **repaid**) **1** tr. pay back (money). **2** tr. return (a blow, visit, etc.). **3** tr. make repayment to (a person). **4** tr. make return for; requite (a service, action, etc.) (*must repay their kindness*; *the book repays close study*). **5** tr. (often foll. by *for*) give in recompense. **6** intr. make repayment. □□ **repayable** adj. **repayment** n. [OF *repaier* (as RE-, PAY[1])]

repeal /rɪˈpiːl/ v. & n. —v.tr. revoke, rescind, or annul (a law, act of parliament, etc.). —n. the act or an instance of repealing. □□ **repealable** adj. [ME f. AF *repeler*, OF *rapeler* (as RE-, APPEAL)]

repeat /rɪˈpiːt/ v. & n. —v. **1** tr. say or do over again. **2** tr. recite, rehearse, report, or reproduce (something from memory) (*repeated a poem*). **3** tr. imitate (an action etc.). **4** intr. recur; appear again, perhaps several times (*a repeating pattern*). **5** tr. used for emphasis (*am not, repeat not, going*). **6** intr. (of food) be tasted intermittently for some time after being swallowed as a result of belching or indigestion. **7** intr. (of a watch etc.) strike the last quarter etc. over again when required. **8** intr. (of a firearm) fire several shots without reloading. **9** intr. US illegally vote more than once in an election. —n. **1 a** the act or an instance of repeating. **b** a thing repeated (often attrib.: *repeat prescription*). **2** a repeated broadcast. **3** *Mus.* **a** a passage intended to be repeated. **b** a mark indicating this. **4** a pattern repeated in wallpaper etc. **5** *Commerce* **a** a consignment similar to a previous one. **b** an order given for this; a reorder. □ **repeating decimal** a recurring decimal. **repeat itself** recur in the same form. **repeat oneself** say or do the same thing over again. □□ **repeatable** adj. **repeatability** /-ˈbɪlɪtɪ/ n. **repeatedly** adv. [ME f. OF *repeter* f. L *repetere* (as RE-, *petere* seek)]

repeater /rɪˈpiːtə(r)/ n. **1** a person or thing that repeats. **2** a firearm which fires several shots without reloading. **3** a watch or clock which repeats its last strike when required. **4** a device for the automatic re-transmission or amplification of an electrically transmitted message. **5** a signal lamp indicating the state of another that is invisible.

repêchage /ˌrepɪˈʃɑːʒ/ n. (in rowing etc.) an extra contest in which the runners-up in the eliminating heats compete for a place in the final. [F *repêcher* fish out, rescue]

repel /rɪˈpel/ v.tr. (**repelled**, **repelling**) **1** drive back; ward off; repulse. **2** refuse admission or approach or acceptance to (*repel an assailant*). **3** be repulsive or distasteful to. □□ **repeller** n. [ME f. L *repellere* (as RE-, *pellere puls-* drive)]

repellent /rɪˈpelənt/ adj. & n. —adj. **1** that repels. **2** disgusting, repulsive. —*n.* a substance that repels esp. insects etc. □□ **repellence** *n.* **repellency** *n.* **repellently** *adv.* [L *repellere* (as REPEL)]

repent[1] /rɪˈpent/ *v.* **1** *intr.* (often foll. by *of*) feel deep sorrow about one's actions etc. **2** *tr.* (also *absol.*) wish one had not done, regret (one's wrong, omission, etc.); resolve not to continue (a wrongdoing etc.). **3** *refl.* (often foll. by *of*) *archaic* feel regret or penitence about one (*now I repent me*). □□ **repentance** *n.* **repentant** *adj.* **repenter** *n.* [ME f. OF *repentir* (as RE-, *pentir* ult. f. L *paenitēre*)]

repent[2] /ˈriːpənt/ *adj. Bot.* creeping, esp. growing along the ground or just under the surface. [L *repere* creep]

repeople /riːˈpiːp(ə)l/ *v.tr.* people again; increase the population of.

repercussion /ˌriːpəˈkʌʃ(ə)n/ *n.* **1** (often foll. by *of*) an indirect effect or reaction following an event or action (*consider the repercussions of moving*). **2** the recoil after impact. **3** an echo or reverberation. □□ **repercussive** /-ˈkʌsɪv/ *adj.* [ME f. OF *repercussion* or L *repercussio* (as RE-, PERCUSSION)]

repertoire /ˈrepətwɑː(r)/ *n.* **1** a stock of pieces etc. that a company or a performer knows or is prepared to give. **2** a stock of regularly performed pieces, regularly used techniques, etc. (*went through his repertoire of excuses*). [F *répertoire* f. LL (as REPERTORY)]

repertory /ˈrepətərɪ/ *n.* (pl. **-ies**) **1** = REPERTOIRE. **2** the theatrical performance of various plays for short periods by one company. **3 a** a repertory company. **b** repertory theatres regarded collectively. **4** a store or collection, esp. of information, instances, etc. □ **repertory company** a theatrical company that performs plays from a repertoire. [LL *repertorium* f. L *reperire repert-* find]

repetend /ˈrepɪtend/ *n.* **1** the recurring figures of a decimal. **2** the recurring word or phrase; a refrain. [L *repetendum* (as REPEAT)]

répétiteur /reˌpetiˈtɜː(r)/ *n.* **1** a tutor or coach of musicians, esp. opera singers. **2** a person who supervises ballet rehearsals etc. [F]

repetition /ˌrepɪˈtɪʃ(ə)n/ *n.* **1 a** the act or an instance of repeating or being repeated. **b** the thing repeated. **2** a copy or replica. **3** a piece to be learned by heart. **4** the ability of a musical instrument to repeat a note quickly. □□ **repetitional** *adj.* **repetitionary** *adj.* [F *répétition* or L *repetitio* (as REPEAT)]

repetitious /ˌrepɪˈtɪʃəs/ *adj.* characterized by repetition, esp. when unnecessary or tiresome. □□ **repetitiously** *adv.* **repetitiousness** *n.*

repetitive /rɪˈpetɪtɪv/ *adj.* = REPETITIOUS. □□ **repetitively** *adv.* **repetitiveness** *n.*

rephrase /riːˈfreɪz/ *v.tr.* express in an alternative way.

repine /rɪˈpaɪn/ *v.intr.* (often foll. by *at*, *against*) fret; be discontented. [RE- + PINE[2], after *repent*]

repique /rɪˈpiːk/ *n.* & *v.* —*n.* (in piquet) the winning of 30 points on cards alone before beginning to play. —*v.* (**repiques, repiqued, repiquing**) **1** *intr.* score repique. **2** *tr.* score repique against (another person). [F *repic* (as RE-, PIQUE[2])]

replace /rɪˈpleɪs/ *v.tr.* **1** put back in place. **2** take the place of; succeed; be substituted for. **3** find or provide a substitute for. **4** (often foll. by *with*, *by*) fill up the place of. **5** (in *passive*, often foll. by *by*) be succeeded or have one's place filled by another; be superseded. □□ **replaceable** *adj.* **replacer** *n.*

replacement /rɪˈpleɪsmənt/ *n.* **1** the act or an instance of replacing or being replaced. **2** a person or thing that takes the place of another.

replan /riːˈplæn/ *v.tr.* (**replanned, replanning**) plan again or differently.

replant /riːˈplɑːnt/ *v.tr.* **1** transfer (a plant etc.) to a larger pot, a new site, etc. **2** plant (ground) again; provide with new plants.

replay *v.* & *n.* —*v.tr.* /riːˈpleɪ/ play (a match, recording, etc.) again. —*n.* /ˈriːpleɪ/ the act or an instance of replaying a match, a recording, or a recorded incident in a game etc.

replenish /rɪˈplenɪʃ/ *v.tr.* **1** (often foll. by *with*) fill up again. **2** renew (a supply etc.). **3** (as **replenished** *adj.*) filled; fully stored or stocked; full. □□ **replenisher** *n.* **replenishment** *n.* [ME f. OF *replenir* (as RE-, *plenir* f. *plein* full f. L *plenus*)]

replete /rɪˈpliːt/ *adj.* (often foll. by *with*) **1** filled or well-supplied with. **2** stuffed; gorged; sated. □□ **repleteness** *n.* **repletion** *n.* [ME f. OF *replet replete* or L *repletus* past part. of *replēre* (as RE-, *plēre plet-* fill)]

replevin /rɪˈplevɪn/ *n. Law* **1** the provisional restoration or recovery of distrained goods pending the outcome of trial and judgement. **2** a writ granting this. **3** the action arising from this process. [ME f. AF f. OF *replevir* (as REPLEVY)]

replevy /rɪˈplevɪ/ *v.tr.* (**-ies, -ied**) *Law* recover by replevin. [OF *replevir* recover f. Gmc]

replica /ˈreplɪkə/ *n.* **1** a duplicate of a work made by the original artist. **2** a facsimile, an exact copy. **3** a copy or model, esp. on a smaller scale. [It. f. *replicare* REPLY]

replicate *v., adj.,* & *n.* —*v.tr.* /ˈreplɪˌkeɪt/ **1** repeat (an experiment etc.). **2** make a replica of. **3** fold back. —*adj.* /ˈreplɪkət/ *Bot.* folded back on itself. —*n.* /ˈreplɪkət/ *Mus.* a tone one or more octaves above or below the given tone. □□ **replicable** /ˈreplɪkəb(ə)l/ *adj.* (in sense 1 of *v.*). **replicability** /ˌreplɪkəˈbɪlɪtɪ/ *n.* (in sense 1 of *v.*). **replicative** /ˈreplɪkətɪv/ *adj.* [L *replicare* (as RE-, *plicare* fold)]

replication /ˌreplɪˈkeɪʃ(ə)n/ *n.* **1** a reply or response, esp. a reply to an answer. **2** *Law* the plaintiff's reply to the defendant's plea. **3 a** the act or an instance of copying. **b** a copy. **c** the process by which genetic material of a living organism gives rise to a copy of itself. [ME f. OF *replicacion* f. L *replicatio -onis* (as REPLICATE)]

reply /rɪˈplaɪ/ *v.* & *n.* —*v.* (**-ies, -ied**) **1** *intr.* (often foll. by *to*) make an answer, respond in word or action. **2** *tr.* say in answer (*he replied, 'Please yourself'*). —*n.* (pl. **-ies**) **1** the act of replying (*what did they say in reply?*). **2** what is replied; a response. **3** *Law* = REPLICATION. □ **reply coupon** a coupon exchangeable for stamps in any country for prepaying the reply to a letter. **reply paid 1** *hist.* (of a telegram) with the cost of a reply prepaid by the sender. **2** (of an envelope etc.) for which the addressee undertakes to pay postage. □□ **replier** *n.* [ME f. OF *replier* f. L (as REPLICATE)]

repoint /riːˈpɔɪnt/ *v.tr.* point (esp. brickwork) again.

repolish /riːˈpɒlɪʃ/ *v.tr.* polish again.

repopulate /riːˈpɒpjʊˌleɪt/ *v.tr.* populate again or increase the population of. □□ **repopulation** /-ˈleɪʃ(ə)n/ *n.*

report /rɪˈpɔːt/ *v.* & *n.* —*v.* **1** *tr.* **a** bring back or give an account of. **b** state as fact or news, narrate or describe or repeat, esp. as an eyewitness or hearer etc. **c** relate as spoken by another. **2** *tr.* make an official or formal statement about. **3** *tr.* (often foll. by *to*) name or specify (an offender or offence) (*shall report you for insubordination; reported them to the police*). **4** *intr.* (often foll. by *to*) present oneself to a person as having returned or arrived (*report to the manager on arrival*). **5** *tr.* (also *absol.*) take down word for word or summarize or write a description of for publication. **6** *intr.* make or draw up or send in a report. **7** *intr.* (often foll. by *to*) be responsible (to a superior, supervisor, etc.) (*reports directly to the managing director*). **8** *tr. Parl.* (of a committee chairman) announce that the committee has dealt with (a bill). **9** *intr.* (often foll. by *of*) give a report to convey that one is well, badly, etc. impressed (*reports well of the prospects*). —*n.* **1** an account given or opinion formally expressed after investigation or consideration. **2** a description, summary, or reproduction of a scene or speech or law case, esp. for newspaper publication or broadcast. **3** common talk; rumour. **4** the way a person or thing is spoken of (*I hear a good report of you*). **5** a periodical statement on (esp. a school pupil's) work, conduct, etc. **6** the sound of an explosion. □ **report back** deliver a report to the person, organization, etc. for whom one acts etc. **reported speech** the speaker's words with the changes of person, tense, etc. usual in reports, e.g. *he said that he would go* (opp. *direct speech*). **report progress** state what has been done so far. **report stage** (in the UK) the debate on a bill in the House of Commons or House of Lords after it is reported. □□ **reportable** *adj.* **reportedly** *adv.* [ME f. OF *reporter* f. L *reportare* (as RE-, *portare* bring)]

reportage /ˌrepɔːˈtɑːʒ/ *n.* **1** the describing of events, esp. the reporting of news etc. for the press and for broadcasting. **2** the typical style of this. **3** factual presentation in a book etc. [REPORT, after F]

reporter /rɪˈpɔːtə(r)/ n. **1** a person employed to report news etc. for newspapers or broadcasts. **2** a person who reports.

reportorial /ˌrɪpɔːˈtɔːrɪəl/ adj. US of newspaper reporters. □□ **reportorially** adv. [REPORTER, after editorial]

repose[1] /rɪˈpəʊz/ n. & v. —n. **1** the cessation of activity or excitement or toil. **2** sleep. **3** a peaceful or quiescent state; stillness; tranquillity. **4** Art a restful effect; harmonious combination. **5** composure or ease of manner. —v. **1** intr. & refl. lie down in rest (reposed on a sofa). **2** tr. (often foll. by on) lay (one's head etc.) to rest (on a pillow etc.). **3** intr. (often foll. by in, on) lie, be lying or laid, esp. in sleep or death. **4** tr. give rest to; refresh with rest. **5** intr. (foll. by on, upon) be supported or based on. **6** intr. (foll. by on) (of memory etc.) dwell on. □□ **reposal** n. **reposeful** adj. **reposefully** adv. **reposefulness** n. [ME f. OF repos(er) f. LL repausare (as RE-, pausare PAUSE)]

repose[2] /rɪˈpəʊz/ v.tr. (foll. by in) place (trust etc.) in. □□ **reposal** n. [RE- + POSE[1] after L reponere reposit-]

reposition /ˌriːpəˈzɪʃ(ə)n/ v. **1** tr. move or place in a different position. **2** intr. adjust or alter one's position.

repository /rɪˈpɒzɪtərɪ/ n. (pl. **-ies**) **1** a place where things are stored or may be found, esp. a warehouse or museum. **2** a receptacle. **3** (often foll. by of) **a** a book, person, etc. regarded as a store of information etc. **b** the recipient of confidences or secrets. [obs. F repositoire or L repositorium (as REPOSE[2])]

repossess /ˌriːpəˈzez/ v.tr. regain possession of (esp. property or goods on which repayment of a debt is in arrears). □□ **repossession** n. **repossessor** n.

repot /riːˈpɒt/ v.tr. (**repotted**, **repotting**) put (a plant) in another, esp. larger, pot.

repoussé /rəˈpuːseɪ/ adj. & n. —adj. hammered into relief from the reverse side. —n. ornamental metalwork fashioned in this way. [F, past part. of repousser (as RE-, pousser PUSH)]

repp var. of REP[3].

repped /rept/ adj. having a surface like rep.

repr. abbr. **1** represent, represented, etc. **2** reprint, reprinted.

reprehend /ˌreprɪˈhend/ v.tr. rebuke; blame; find fault with. □□ **reprehension** n. [ME f. L reprehendere (as RE-, prehendere seize)]

reprehensible /ˌreprɪˈhensɪb(ə)l/ adj. deserving censure or rebuke; blameworthy. □□ **reprehensibility** /-ˈbɪlɪtɪ/ n. **reprehensibly** adv. [LL reprehensibilis (as REPREHEND)]

represent /ˌreprɪˈzent/ v.tr. **1** stand for or correspond to (the comment does not represent all our views). **2** (often in passive) be a specimen or example of; exemplify (all types of people were represented in the audience). **3** act as an embodiment of; symbolize (the sovereign represents the majesty of the State; numbers are represented by letters). **4** call up in the mind by description or portrayal or imagination; place a likeness of before the mind or senses. **5** serve or be meant as a likeness of. **6 a** state by way of expostulation or persuasion (represented the rashness of it). **b** (foll. by to) try to bring (the facts influencing conduct) home to (represented the risks to his client). **7** (often foll. by as, to be) describe or depict as; declare or make out (represented them as martyrs; not what you represent it to be). **8** (foll. by that + clause) allege. **9** show, or play the part of, on stage. **10** fill the place of; be a substitute or deputy for; be entitled to act or speak for (the Queen was represented by the Princess of Wales). **11** be elected as a member of Parliament, a legislature, etc. by (represents a rural constituency). □□ **representable** adj. **representability** /-ˈbɪlɪtɪ/ n. [ME f. OF representer or f. L repraesentare (as RE-, PRESENT[2])]

representation /ˌreprɪzenˈteɪʃ(ə)n/ n. **1** the act or an instance of representing or being represented. **2** a thing (esp. a painting etc.) that represents another. **3** (esp. in pl.) a statement made by way of allegation or to convey opinion. [ME f. OF representation or L repraesentatio (as REPRESENT)]

representational /ˌreprɪzenˈteɪʃən(ə)l/ adj. of representation. □ **representational art** art seeking to portray the physical appearance of a subject. □□ **representationalism** n. **representationalist** adj. & n.

representationism /ˌreprɪzenˈteɪʃəˌnɪz(ə)m/ n. the doctrine that perceived objects are only a representation of real external objects. □□ **representationist** n.

representative /ˌreprɪˈzentətɪv/ adj. & n. —adj. **1** typical of a class or category. **2** containing typical specimens of all or many classes (a representative sample). **3 a** consisting of elected deputies etc. **b** based on the representation of a nation etc. by such deputies (representative government). **4** (foll. by of) serving as a portrayal or symbol of (representative of their attitude to work). **5** that presents or can present ideas to the mind (imagination is a representative faculty). **6** (of art) representational. —n. **1** (foll. by of) a sample, specimen, or typical embodiment or analogue of. **2 a** the agent of a person or society. **b** a commercial traveller. **3** a delegate; a substitute. **4** a deputy in a representative assembly. **5** (of art) Representation. □ **House of Representatives** see CONGRESS. □□ **representatively** adv. **representativeness** n. [ME f. OF representatif -ive or med.L repraesentativus (as REPRESENT)]

repress /rɪˈpres/ v.tr. **1 a** check; restrain; keep under; quell. **b** suppress; prevent from sounding, rioting, or bursting out. **2** Psychol. actively exclude (an unwelcome thought) from conscious awareness. **3** (usu. as **repressed** adj.) subject (a person) to the suppression of his or her thoughts or impulses. □□ **represser** n. **repressible** adj. **repression** /-ˈpreʃ(ə)n/ n. **repressive** adj. **repressively** adv. **repressiveness** n. **repressor** n. [ME f. L reprimere (as RE-, premere PRESS[1])]

reprice /riːˈpraɪs/ v.tr. price again or differently.

reprieve /rɪˈpriːv/ v. & n. —v.tr. **1** remit, commute, or postpone the execution of (a condemned person). **2** give respite to. —n. **1 a** the act or an instance of reprieving or being reprieved. **b** a warrant for this. **2** respite; a respite or temporary escape. [ME as past part. repryed f. AF & OF repris past part. of reprendre (as RE-, prendre f. L prehendere take): 16th-c. -v- unexpl.]

reprimand /ˈreprɪˌmɑːnd/ n. & v. —n. (often foll. by for) an official or sharp rebuke (for a fault etc.). —v.tr. administer this to. [F réprimande(r) f. Sp. reprimanda f. L reprimenda neut. pl. gerundive of reprimere REPRESS]

reprint v. & n. —v.tr. /riːˈprɪnt/ print again. —n. /ˈriːprɪnt/ **1** the act or an instance of reprinting a book etc. **2** the book etc. reprinted. **3** the quantity reprinted. □□ **reprinter** n.

reprisal /rɪˈpraɪz(ə)l/ n. **1** an act of retaliation. **2** hist. the forcible seizure of a foreign subject or his or her goods as an act of retaliation. [ME (in sense 2) f. AF reprisaille f. med.L reprisalia f. repraehensalia (as REPREHEND)]

reprise /rɪˈpriːz/ n. **1** a repeated passage in music. **2** a repeated item in a musical programme. [F, fem. past part. of reprendre (see REPRIEVE)]

repro /ˈriːprəʊ/ n. (pl. **-os**) (often attrib.) a reproduction or copy. [abbr.]

reproach /rɪˈprəʊtʃ/ v. & n. —v.tr. **1** express disapproval to (a person) for a fault etc. **2** scold; rebuke; censure. **3** archaic rebuke (an offence). —n. **1** a rebuke or censure (heaped reproaches on them). **2** (often foll. by to) a thing that brings disgrace or discredit (their behaviour is a reproach to us all). **3** a disgraced or discredited state (live in reproach and ignominy). **4** (in pl.) RC Ch. a set of antiphons and responses for Good Friday representing the reproaches of Christ to his people. □ **above** (or **beyond**) **reproach** perfect. □□ **reproachable** adj. **reproacher** n. **reproachingly** adv. [ME f. OF reproche(r) f. Rmc (as RE-, L prope near)]

reproachful /rɪˈprəʊtʃfʊl/ adj. full of or expressing reproach. □□ **reproachfully** adv. **reproachfulness** n.

reprobate /ˈreprəˌbeɪt/ n., adj., & v. —n. **1** an unprincipled person; a person of highly immoral character. **2** a person who is condemned by God. —adj. **1** immoral. **2** hardened in sin. —v.tr. **1** express or feel disapproval of; censure. **2** (of God) condemn; exclude from salvation. □□ **reprobation** /-ˈbeɪʃ(ə)n/ n. [ME f. L reprobare reprobat- disapprove (as RE-, probare approve)]

reprocess /riːˈprəʊses/ v.tr. process again or differently.

reproduce /ˌriːprəˈdjuːs/ v. **1** tr. produce a copy or representation of. **2** tr. cause to be seen or heard etc. again (tried to reproduce the sound exactly). **3** intr. produce further members of the same species by natural means. **4** refl. produce offspring (reproduced itself several times). **5** intr. give a specified quality or result when copied (reproduces badly in black and white). **6** tr. Biol. form afresh (a lost part etc. of the body). □□ **reproducer** n.

reproducible *adj.* **reproducibility** /-'bɪlɪtɪ/ *n.* **reproducibly** *adv.*

reproduction /ˌriːprə'dʌkʃ(ə)n/ *n.* **1** the act or an instance of reproducing. **2** a copy of a work of art, esp. a print or photograph of a painting. **3** (*attrib.*) (of furniture etc.) made in imitation of a certain style or of an earlier period. □□ **reproductive** *adj.* **reproductively** *adv.* **reproductiveness** *n.*

reprogram /riː'prəʊɡræm/ *v.tr.* (also **reprogramme**) (**reprogrammed**, **reprogramming**; *US* **reprogramed**, **reprograming**) program (esp. a computer) again or differently. □□ **reprogrammable** *adj.* (also **reprogramable**).

reprography /rɪ'prɒɡrəfɪ/ *n.* the science and practice of copying documents by photography, xerography, etc. □□ **reprographer** *n.* **reprographic** /ˌriːprə'ɡræfɪk/ *adj.* **reprographically** /ˌriːprə'ɡræfɪkəlɪ/ *adv.* [REPRODUCE + -GRAPHY]

reproof[1] /rɪ'pruːf/ *n.* **1** blame (*a glance of reproof*). **2** a rebuke; words expressing blame. [ME f. OF *reprove* f. *reprover* REPROVE]

reproof[2] /rɪ'pruːf/ *v.tr.* **1** render (a coat etc.) waterproof again. **2** make a fresh proof of (printed matter etc.).

reprove /rɪ'pruːv/ *v.tr.* rebuke (a person, a person's conduct, etc.). □□ **reprovable** *adj.* **reprover** *n.* **reprovingly** *adv.* [ME f. OF *reprover* f. LL *reprobare* disapprove: see REPROBATE]

reptant /'rept(ə)nt/ *adj.* (of a plant or animal) creeping. [L *reptare* *reptant-* frequent. of *repere* crawl]

reptile /'reptaɪl/ *n.* & *adj.* —*n.* **1** any cold-blooded scaly animal of the class Reptilia, including snakes, lizards, crocodiles, turtles, and tortoises. Reptiles, which first appeared in the Carboniferous period, probably evolved from amphibians, but they differ from them in several important respects. They breathe air all their lives, they are protected from desiccation by a scaly skin, and their eggs have shells, so that they can be laid on land without drying up; the young when hatched resemble their parents and do not undergo metamorphosis. Present-day reptiles are cold-blooded; there are about 6,000 living species, but there were formerly many more, especially in the Mesozoic era (284–265 million years ago), when dinosaurs dominated the earth. The closest living relatives of the now extinct dinosaurs are the crocodiles and the birds, which descended from one group of bipedal dinosaurs. **2** a mean, grovelling, or repulsive person. —*adj.* **1** (of an animal) creeping. **2** mean, grovelling. □□ **reptilian** /-'tɪlɪən/ *adj.* & *n.* [ME f. LL *reptilis* f. L *repere* *rept-* crawl]

Repton /'rept(ə)n/, Humphry (1752–1818), English landscape gardner. Repton's reconstructions of estates often used regular bedding and straight paths close to the house but his parks were carefully informal, like those of 'Capability' Brown, his acknowledged master. From about 1795 to 1803 he joined forces with the architect John Nash. The park at Cobham in Kent is a fine example of a Repton landscape, but his most complete creation is Sheringham Hall, Norfolk, and its surroundings (1812).

republic /rɪ'pʌblɪk/ *n.* **1** a State in which supreme power is held by the people or their elected representatives or by an elected or nominated president, not by a monarch etc. **2** a society with equality between its members (*the literary republic*). □ **Republic Day** the day on which the foundation of a republic is commemorated; in India 26 January. [F *république* f. L *respublica* f. *res* concern + *publicus* PUBLIC]

republican /rɪ'pʌblɪkən/ *adj.* & *n.* —*adj.* **1** of or constituted as a republic. **2** characteristic of a republic. **3** advocating or supporting republican government. —*n.* **1** a person advocating or supporting republican government. **2** (**Republican**) (in the US) a member or supporter of the Republican Party. **3** an advocate of a united Ireland. □□ **republicanism** *n.*

Republican Party one of the two chief political parties in the US (the other being the Democratic Party). It was formed in 1854 to resist the extension of slave territory; Abraham Lincoln was the first of its leaders to become President. It is now chiefly identified with business interests and favours restrictions on central power.

republish /riː'pʌblɪʃ/ *v.tr.* (also *absol.*) publish again or in a new edition etc. □□ **republication** /-'keɪʃ(ə)n/ *n.*

repudiate /rɪ'pjuːdɪeɪt/ *v.tr.* **1 a** disown; disavow; reject. **b** refuse dealings with. **c** deny. **2** refuse to recognize or obey (authority or a treaty). **3** refuse to discharge (an obligation or debt). **4** (esp. of the ancients or non-Christians) divorce (one's wife). □□ **repudiable** *adj.* **repudiation** /-'eɪʃ(ə)n/ *n.* **repudiator** *n.* [L *repudiare* f. *repudium* divorce]

repugnance /rɪ'pʌɡnəns/ *n.* (also **repugnancy**) **1** (usu. foll. by *to*, *against*) antipathy; aversion. **2** (usu. foll. by *of*, *between*, *to*, *with*) inconsistency or incompatibility of ideas, statements, etc. [ME (in sense 2) f. F *répugnance* or L *repugnantia* f. *repugnare* oppose (as RE-, *pugnare* fight)]

repugnant /rɪ'pʌɡnənt/ *adj.* **1** (often foll. by *to*) extremely distasteful. **2** (often foll. by *to*) contradictory. **3** (often foll. by *with*) incompatible. **4** *poet.* refractory; resisting. □□ **repugnantly** *adv.* [ME f. F *répugnant* or L (as REPUGNANCE)]

repulse /rɪ'pʌls/ *v.* & *n.* —*v.tr.* **1** drive back (an attack or attacking enemy) by force of arms. **2 a** rebuff (friendly advances or their maker). **b** refuse (a request or offer or its maker). **3** be repulsive to, repel. **4** foil in controversy. —*n.* **1** the act or an instance of repulsing or being repulsed. **2** a rebuff. [L *repellere* *repuls-* drive back (as REPEL)]

repulsion /rɪ'pʌlʃ(ə)n/ *n.* **1** aversion; disgust. **2** esp. *Physics* the force by which bodies tend to repel each other or increase their mutual distance (opp. ATTRACTION). [LL *repulsio* (as REPEL)]

repulsive /rɪ'pʌlsɪv/ *adj.* **1** causing aversion or loathing; loathsome, disgusting. **2** *Physics* exerting repulsion. **3** *archaic* (of behaviour etc.) cold, unsympathetic. □□ **repulsively** *adv.* **repulsiveness** *n.* [F *répulsif* *-ive* or f. REPULSE]

repurchase /riː'pɜːtʃɪs/ *v.* & *n.* —*v.tr.* purchase again. —*n.* the act or an instance of purchasing again.

repurify /riː'pjʊərɪˌfaɪ/ *v.tr.* (**-ies**, **-ied**) purify again. □□ **repurification** /-fɪ'keɪʃ(ə)n/ *n.*

reputable /'repjʊtəb(ə)l/ *adj.* of good repute; respectable. □□ **reputably** *adv.* [obs. F or f. med.L *reputabilis* (as REPUTE)]

reputation /ˌrepjʊ'teɪʃ(ə)n/ *n.* **1** what is generally said or believed about a person's or thing's character or standing (*has a reputation for dishonesty*). **2** the state of being well thought of; distinction; respectability (*have my reputation to think of*). **3** (foll. by *of*, *for* + verbal noun) credit or discredit (*has the reputation of driving hard bargains*). [ME f. L *reputatio* (as REPUTE)]

repute /rɪ'pjuːt/ *n.* & *v.* —*n.* reputation (*known by repute*). —*v.tr.* **1** (as **reputed** *adj.*) (often foll. by *to* + infin.) be generally considered or reckoned (*is reputed to be the best*). **2** (as **reputed** *adj.*) passing as being, but probably not being (*his reputed father*). □□ **reputedly** *adv.* [ME f. OF *reputer* or L *reputare* (as RE-, *putare* think)]

request /rɪ'kwest/ *n.* & *v.* —*n.* **1** the act or an instance of asking for something; a petition (*came at his request*). **2** a thing asked for. **3** the state of being sought after; demand (*in great request*). **4** a letter etc. asking for a particular record etc. to be played on a radio programme, often with a personal message. —*v.tr.* **1** ask to be given or allowed or favoured with (*request a hearing*; *requests your presence*). **2** (foll. by *to* + infin.) ask (a person) to do something (*requested her to answer*). **3** (foll. by *that* + clause) ask that. □ **by** (or **on**) **request** in response to an expressed wish. **request programme** a programme composed of items requested by the audience. **request stop** a bus-stop at which a bus stops only on a passenger's request. □□ **requester** *n.* [ME f. OF *requeste(r)* ult. f. L *requaerere* (as REQUIRE)]

requiem /'rekwɪem/ *n.* **1** (**Requiem**) (also *attrib.*) *chiefly RC Ch.* a mass for the repose of the souls of the dead. **2** *Mus.* the musical setting for this. [ME f. accus. of L *requies* rest, the initial word of the mass]

requiescat /ˌrekwɪ'eskæt/ *n.* a wish or prayer for the repose of a dead person. [L, = may he or she rest (in peace)]

require /rɪ'kwaɪə(r)/ *v.tr.* **1** need; depend on for success or fulfilment (*the work requires much patience*). **2** lay down as an imperative (*did all that was required by law*). **3** command; instruct (a person etc.). **4** order; insist on (an action or measure). **5** (often foll. by *of*, *from*, or *that* + clause) demand (of or from a person)

as a right. **6** wish to have (*is there anything else you require?*). □□
requirer n. **requirement** n. [ME f. OF *requere* ult. f. L *requirere*
(as RE-, *quaerere* seek)]

requisite /'rekwɪzɪt/ adj. & n. —adj. required by circumstances;
necessary to success etc. —n. (often foll. by *for*) a thing needed
(for some purpose). □□ **requisitely** adv. [ME f. L *requisitus* past
part. (as REQUIRE)]

requisition /ˌrekwɪ'zɪʃ(ə)n/ n. & v. —n. **1** an official order laying
claim to the use of property or materials. **2** a formal written
demand that some duty should be performed. **3** being called or
put into service. —v.tr. demand the use or supply of, esp. by
requisition order. □ **under** (or **in**) **requisition** being used or
applied. □□ **requisitioner** n. **requisitionist** n. [F *réquisition* or
L *requisitio* (as REQUIRE)]

requite /rɪ'kwaɪt/ v.tr. **1** make return for (a service). **2** (often
foll. by *with*) reward or avenge (a favour or injury). **3** (often foll.
by *for*) make return to (a person). **4** (often foll. by *for, with*) repay
with good or evil (*requite like for like; requite hate with love*). □□
requital n. [RE- + *quite* var. of QUIT]

reran past of RERUN.

reread /riː'riːd/ v. & n. —v.tr. (*past* and *past part.* **reread** /-'red/)
read again. —n. an instance of reading again. □□ **re-readable**
adj.

reredos /'rɪədos/ n. *Eccl.* an ornamental screen covering the wall
at the back of an altar. [ME f. AF f. OF *areredos* f. *arere* behind +
dos back: cf. ARREARS]

re-release /ˌriːrɪ'liːs/ v. & n. —v.tr. release (a record, film, etc.)
again. —n. a re-released record, film, etc.

re-route /riː'ruːt/ v.tr. (**-routeing**) send or carry by a different
route.

rerun /riː'rʌn/ v. & n. —v.tr. (**rerunning**; *past* **reran**; *past part.*
rerun) run (a race, film, etc.) again. —n. /'riːrʌn/ **1** the act or
an instance of rerunning. **2** a film etc. shown again.

resale /riː'seɪl/ n. the sale of a thing previously bought. □ **resale
price maintenance** a manufacturer's practice of setting a minimum resale price for goods. □□ **resalable** adj.

resat past and past part. of RESIT.

reschedule /riː'ʃedjuːl, -'skedʒʊəl/ v.tr. alter the schedule of;
replan.

rescind /rɪ'sɪnd/ v.tr. abrogate, revoke, cancel. □□ **rescindable**
adj. **rescindment** n. **rescission** /-'sɪʒ(ə)n/ n. [L *rescindere* resciss-
(as RE-, *scindere* cut)]

rescript /riː'skrɪpt/ n. **1** a Roman emperor's written reply to an
appeal for guidance, esp. on a legal point. **2** *RC Ch.* the Pope's
decision on a question of doctrine or papal law. **3** an official
edict or announcement. **4 a** the act or an instance of rewriting.
b the thing rewritten. [L *rescriptum*, neut. past part. of *rescribere*
rescript- (as RE-, *scribere* write)]

rescue /'reskjuː/ v. & n. —v.tr. (**rescues, rescued, rescuing**) **1**
(often foll. by *from*) save or set free or bring away from attack,
custody, danger, or harm. **2** *Law* **a** unlawfully liberate (a person).
b forcibly recover (property). —n. the act or an instance of
rescuing or being rescued; deliverance. □ **rescue bid** *Bridge* a
bid made to get one's partner out of a difficult situation. □□
rescuable adj. **rescuer** n. [ME *rescowe* f. OF *rescoure* f. Rmc,
formed as RE- + L *excutere* (as EX-¹, *quatere* shake)]

reseal /riː'siːl/ v.tr. seal again. □□ **resealable** adj.

research /rɪ'sɜːtʃ, disp. 'riːsɜːtʃ/ n. & v. —n. **1 a** the systematic
investigation into and study of materials, sources, etc., in order
to establish facts and reach new conclusions. **b** (usu. in *pl.*) an
endeavour to discover new or collate old facts etc. by the scientific study of a subject or by a course of critical investigation.
2 (*attrib.*) engaged in or intended for research (*research assistant*).
—v. **1** tr. do research into or for. **2** intr. make researches. □
research and development (in industry etc.) work directed
towards the innovation, introduction, and improvement of
products and processes. □□ **researchable** adj. **researcher** n.
[obs. F *recerche* (as RE-, SEARCH)]

reseat /riː'siːt/ v.tr. **1** (also *refl.*) seat (oneself, a person, etc.) again.
2 provide with a fresh seat or seats.

resect /rɪ'sekt/ v.tr. *Surgery* **1** cut out part of (a lung etc.). **2** pare

down (bone, cartilage, etc.). □□ **resection** n. **resectional** adj.
resectionist n. [L *resecare resect-* (as RE-, *secare* cut)]

reseda /'resɪdə/ n. **1** any plant of the genus *Reseda*, with sweet-
scented flowers, e.g. a mignonette. **2** /also 'rez-/ the pale green
colour of mignonette flowers. [L, perh. f. imper. of *resedare*
assuage, with ref. to its supposed curative powers]

reselect /ˌriːsɪ'lekt/ v.tr. select again or differently. □□
reselection n.

resell /riː'sel/ v.tr. (*past* and *past part.* **resold**) sell (an object etc.)
after buying it.

resemblance /rɪ'zembləns/ n. (often foll. by *to, between, of*) a
likeness or similarity. □□ **resemblant** adj. [ME f. AF (as
RESEMBLE)]

resemble /rɪ'zemb(ə)l/ v.tr. be like; have a similarity to, or features in common with, or the same appearance as. □□
resembler n. [ME f. OF *resembler* (as RE-, *sembler* f. L *similare* f.
similis like)]

resent /rɪ'zent/ v.tr. show or feel indignation at; be aggrieved by
(a circumstance, action, or person) (*we resent being patronized*).
[obs. F *resentir* (as RE-, L *sentire* feel)]

resentful /rɪ'zentfʊl/ adj. feeling resentment. □□ **resentfully**
adv. **resentfulness** n.

resentment /rɪ'zentmənt/ n. (often foll. by *at, of*) indignant or
bitter feelings; anger. [It. *risentimento* or F *ressentiment* (as RESENT)]

reserpine /rɪ'sɜːpiːn/ n. an alkaloid obtained from plants of the
genus *Rauwolfia*, used as a tranquillizer and in the treatment of
hypertension. [G *Reserpin* f. mod.L Rauwolfia (f. L. *Rauwolf*, Ger.
botanist d. 1596) *serpentina*]

reservation /ˌrezə'veɪʃ(ə)n/ n. **1** the act or an instance of reserving or being reserved. **2** a booking (of a room, berth, seat, etc.).
3 the thing booked, e.g. a room in a hotel. **4** an express or tacit
limitation or exception to an agreement etc. (*had reservations
about the plan*). **5** *Brit.* a strip of land between the carriageways
of a road. **6** an area of land reserved for occupation by American
Indians, African Blacks, or Australian Aboriginals, etc. **7 a** a
right or interest retained in an estate being conveyed. **b** the
clause reserving this. **8** *Eccl.* **a** the practice of retaining for some
purpose a portion of the Eucharistic elements (esp. the bread)
after celebration. **b** *RC Ch.* the power of absolution reserved to
a superior. **c** *RC Ch.* the right reserved to the Pope of nomination
to a vacant benefice. [ME f. OF *reservation* or LL *reservatio* (as
RESERVE)]

reserve /rɪ'zɜːv/ v. & n. —v.tr. **1** postpone, put aside, keep back
for a later occasion or special use. **2** order to be specially retained
or allocated for a particular person or at a particular time. **3**
retain or secure, esp. by formal or legal stipulation (*reserve the
right to*). **4** postpone delivery of (judgement etc.) (*reserved my
comments until the end*). —n. **1** a thing reserved for future use;
an extra stock or amount (*a great reserve of strength; huge energy
reserves*). **2** a limitation, qualification, or exception attached to
something (*accept your offer without reserve*). **3 a** self-restraint;
reticence; lack of cordiality (*difficult to overcome his reserve*). **b** (in
artistic or literary expression) absence from exaggeration or
ill-proportioned effects. **4** a company's profit added to capital.
5 (in *sing.* or *pl.*) assets kept readily available as cash or at a
central bank, or as gold or foreign exchange (*reserve currency*). **6**
(in *sing.* or *pl.*) **a** troops withheld from action to reinforce or
protect others. **b** forces in addition to the regular army, navy,
airforce, etc., but available in an emergency. **7** a member of the
military reserve. **8** an extra player chosen to be a possible
substitute in a team. **9** a pláce reserved for special use, esp. as
a habitat for a native tribe or for wildlife (*game reserve; nature
reserve*). **10** the intentional suppression of the truth (*exercised a
certain amount of reserve*). **11** (in the decoration of ceramics or
textiles) an area which still has the original colour of the material or the colour of the background. □ **in reserve** unused and
available if required. **reserve grade** *Austral.* a second-grade
team. **reserve price** the lowest acceptable price stipulated for
an item sold at an auction. **with all** (or **all proper**) **reserve**
without endorsing. □□ **reservable** adj. **reserver** n. [ME f. OF
reserver f. L *reservare* (as RE-, *servare* keep)]

re-serve /riː'sɜːv/ v.tr. & intr. serve again.

reserved /rɪˈzɜːvd/ *adj.* **1** reticent; slow to reveal emotion or opinions; uncommunicative. **2 a** set apart, destined for some use or fate. **b** (often foll. by *for*, *to*) left by fate for; falling first or only to. □ **reserved occupation** an occupation from which a person will not be taken for military service. □□ **reservedly** /-vɪdlɪ/ *adv.* **reservedness** *n.*

reservist /rɪˈzɜːvɪst/ *n.* a member of the reserve forces.

reservoir /ˈrezəˌvwɑː(r)/ *n.* **1** a large natural or artificial lake used as a source of water supply. **2 a** any natural or artificial receptacle esp. for or of fluid. **b** a place where fluid etc. collects. **3** a part of a machine etc. holding fluid. **4** (usu. foll. by *of*) a reserve or supply esp. of information. [F *réservoir* f. *réserver* RESERVE]

reset /riːˈset/ *v.tr.* (**resetting**; *past* and *past part.* **reset**) set (a broken bone, gems, a mechanical device, etc.) again or differently. □□ **resettable** *adj.* **resettability** /-ˈbɪlɪtɪ/ *n.*

resettle /riːˈset(ə)l/ *v.tr.* & *intr.* settle again. □□ **resettlement** *n.*

reshape /riːˈʃeɪp/ *v.tr.* shape or form again or differently.

reshuffle /riːˈʃʌf(ə)l/ *v.* & *n.* —*v.tr.* **1** shuffle (cards) again. **2** interchange the posts of (government ministers etc.). —*n.* the act or an instance of reshuffling.

reside /rɪˈzaɪd/ *v.intr.* **1** (often foll. by *at*, *in*, *abroad*, etc.) (of a person) have one's home, dwell permanently. **2** (of power, a right, etc.) rest or be vested in. **3** (of an incumbent official) be in residence. **4** (foll. by *in*) (of a quality) be present or inherent in. [ME, prob. back-form. f. RESIDENT infl. by F *résider* or L *residēre* (as RE-, *sedēre* sit)]

residence /ˈrezɪd(ə)ns/ *n.* **1** the act or an instance of residing. **2 a** the place where a person resides; an abode. **b** a mansion; the official house of a government minister etc. **c** a house, esp. one of considerable pretension (*returned to their London residence*). □ **in residence** dwelling at a specified place, esp. for the performance of duties or work. [ME f. OF *residence* or med.L *residentia* f. L *residēre*: see RESIDE]

residency /ˈrezɪdənsɪ/ *n.* (*pl.* **-ies**) **1** = RESIDENCE 1, 2a. **2** *US* a period of specialized medical training; the position of a resident. **3** *hist.* the official residence of the Governor-General's representative or other government agent at an Indian native court; the territory supervised by this official. **4** a musician's regular engagement at a club etc. **5** a group or organization of intelligence agents in a foreign country.

resident /ˈrezɪd(ə)nt/ *n.* & *adj.* —*n.* **1** (often foll. by *of*) **a** a permanent inhabitant (of a town or neighbourhood). **b** a bird belonging to a species that does not migrate. **2** a guest in a hotel etc. staying overnight. **3** *hist.* a British government agent in any semi-independent State, esp. the Governor-General's agent at an Indian native court. **4** *US* a medical graduate engaged in specialized practice under supervision in a hospital. **5** an intelligence agent in a foreign country. —*adj.* **1** residing; in residence. **2 a** having quarters on the premises of one's work etc. (*resident housekeeper*; *resident doctor*). **b** working regularly in a particular place. **3** located in; inherent (*powers of feeling are resident in the nerves*). **4** (of birds etc.) non-migratory. □□ **residentship** *n.* (in sense 3 of *n.*). [ME f. OF *resident* or L: see RESIDE]

residential /ˌrezɪˈdenʃ(ə)l/ *adj.* **1** suitable for or occupied by private houses (*residential area*). **2** used as a residence (*residential hotel*). **3** based on or connected with residence (*the residential qualification for voters*; *a residential course of study*). □□ **residentially** *adv.*

residentiary /ˌrezɪˈdenʃərɪ/ *adj.* & *n.* —*adj.* of, subject to, or requiring, official residence. —*n.* (*pl.* **-ies**) an ecclesiastic who must officially reside in a place. [med.L *residentiarius* (as RESIDENCE)]

residua *pl.* of RESIDUUM.

residual /rɪˈzɪdjʊəl/ *adj.* & *n.* —*adj.* **1** remaining; left as a residue or residuum. **2** *Math.* resulting from subtraction. **3** (in calculation) still unaccounted for or not eliminated. —*n.* **1 a** quantity left over or *Math.* resulting from subtraction. **2** an error in calculation not accounted for or eliminated. □□ **residually** *adv.*

residuary /rɪˈzɪdjʊərɪ/ *adj.* **1** of the residue of an estate (*residuary bequest*). **2** of or being a residuum; residual; still remaining.

residue /ˈrezɪˌdjuː/ *n.* **1** what is left over or remains; a remainder; the rest. **2** *Law* what remains of an estate after the payment of charges, debts, and bequests. **3** esp. *Chem.* a residuum. [ME f. OF *residu* f. L *residuum*: see RESIDUUM]

residuum /rɪˈzɪdjʊəm/ *n.* (*pl.* **residua** /-djʊə/) **1** *Chem.* a substance left after combustion or evaporation. **2** a remainder or residue. [L, neut. of *residuus* remaining f. *residēre*: see RESIDE]

resign /rɪˈzaɪn/ *v.* **1** *intr.* **a** (often foll. by *from*) give up office, one's employment, etc. (*resigned from the Home Office*). **b** (often foll. by *as*) retire (*resigned as chief executive*). **2** *tr.* (often foll. by *to*, *into*) relinquish; surrender; hand over (a right, charge, task, etc.). **3** *tr.* give up (hope etc.). **4** *refl.* (usu. foll. by *to*) **a** reconcile (oneself, one's mind, etc.) to the inevitable (*have resigned myself to the idea*). **b** surrender (oneself to another's guidance). **5** *intr.* *Chess* etc. discontinue play and admit defeat. □□ **resigner** *n.* [ME f. OF *resigner* f. L *resignare* unseal, cancel (as RE-, *signare* sign, seal)]

re-sign /riːˈsaɪn/ *v.tr.* & *intr.* sign again.

resignation /ˌrezɪɡˈneɪʃ(ə)n/ *n.* **1** the act or an instance of resigning, esp. from one's job or office. **2** the document etc. conveying this intention. **3** the state of being resigned; the uncomplaining endurance of a sorrow or difficulty. [ME f. OF f. med.L *resignatio* (as RESIGN)]

resigned /rɪˈzaɪnd/ *adj.* (often foll. by *to*) having resigned oneself; submissive, acquiescent. □□ **resignedly** /-nɪdlɪ/ *adv.* **resignedness** *n.*

resile /rɪˈzaɪl/ *v.intr.* **1** (of something stretched or compressed) recoil to resume a former size and shape; spring back. **2** have or show resilience or recuperative power. **3** (usu. foll. by *from*) withdraw from a course of action. [obs. F *resilir* or L *resilire* (as RE-, *salire* jump)]

resilient /rɪˈzɪlɪənt/ *adj.* **1** (of a substance etc.) recoiling; springing back; resuming its original shape after bending, stretching, compression, etc. **2** (of a person) readily recovering from shock, depression, etc.; buoyant. □□ **resilience** *n.* **resiliency** *n.* **resiliently** *adv.* [L *resiliens resilient-* (as RESILE)]

resin /ˈrezɪn/ *n.* & *v.* —*n.* **1** an adhesive inflammable substance insoluble in water, secreted by some plants, and often extracted by incision, esp. from fir and pine (cf. GUM¹). **2** (in full **synthetic resin**) a solid or liquid organic compound made by polymerization etc. and used in plastics etc. —*v.tr.* (**resined**, **resining**) rub or treat with resin. □□ **resinate** /-nət/ *n.* **resinate** /-ˌneɪt/ *v.tr.* **resinoid** *adj.* & *n.* **resinous** *adj.* [ME *resyn*, *rosyn* f. L *resina* & med.L *rosina*, *rosinum*]

resist /rɪˈzɪst/ *v.* & *n.* —*v.* **1** *tr.* withstand the action or effect of; repel. **2** *tr.* stop the course or progress of; prevent from reaching, penetrating, etc. **3** *tr.* abstain from (pleasure, temptation, etc.). **4** *tr.* strive against; try to impede; refuse to comply with (*resist arrest*). **5** *intr.* offer opposition; refuse to comply. —*n.* a protective coating of a resistant substance, applied esp. to parts of calico that are not to take dye or to parts of pottery that are not to take glaze or lustre. □ **cannot** (or **could not** etc.) **resist 1** (foll. by verbal noun) feel obliged or strongly inclined to (*cannot resist teasing me about it*). **2** is certain to be amused, attracted, etc., by (*can't resist children's clothes*). □□ **resistant** *adj.* **resister** *n.* **resistible** *adj.* **resistibility** /-ˈbɪlɪtɪ/ *n.* [ME f. OF *resister* or L *resistere* (as RE-, *sistere* stop, redupl. of *stare* stand)]

resistance /rɪˈzɪst(ə)ns/ *n.* **1** the act or an instance of resisting; refusal to comply. **2** the power of resisting (*showed resistance to wear and tear*). **3** *Biol.* the ability to withstand adverse conditions. **4** the impeding, slowing, or stopping effect exerted by one material thing on another. **5** *Physics* **a** the property of hindering the conduction of electricity, heat, etc. **b** the measure of this in a body. ¶ Symb.: **R**. **6** a resistor. **7** (in full **resistance movement**) a secret organization resisting authority, esp. in a conquered or enemy-occupied country. [ME f. F *résistance*, *résistence* f. LL *resistentia* (as RESIST)]

resistive /rɪˈzɪstɪv/ *adj.* **1** able to resist. **2** *Electr.* of or concerning resistance.

resistivity /ˌrɪzɪˈstɪvɪtɪ/ *n.* *Electr.* a measure of the resisting power of a specified material to the flow of an electric current.

resistless /rɪˈzɪstlɪs/ adj. archaic poet. **1** irresistible; relentless. **2** unresisting. □□ **resistlessly** adv.

resistor /rɪˈzɪstə(r)/ n. Electr. a device having resistance to the passage of an electrical current.

resit v. & n. —v.tr. /riːˈsɪt/ (**resitting**; past and past part. **resat**) sit (an examination) again after failing. —n. /ˈriːsɪt/ **1** the act or an instance of resitting an examination. **2** an examination held specifically to enable candidates to resit.

re-site /riːˈsaɪt/ v.tr. place on another site; relocate.

resold past and past part. of RESELL.

resoluble /rɪˈzɒljʊb(ə)l/ adj. **1** that can be resolved. **2** (foll. by into) analysable. [F résoluble or L resolubilis (as RESOLVE, after soluble)]

re-soluble /riːˈsɒljʊb(ə)l/ adj. that can be dissolved again.

resolute /ˈrezəˌluːt, -ˌljuːt/ adj. (of a person or a person's mind or action) determined; decided; firm of purpose; not vacillating. □□ **resolutely** adv. **resoluteness** n. [L resolutus past part. of resolvere (see RESOLVE)]

resolution /ˌrezəˈluːʃ(ə)n, -ˈljuːʃ(ə)n/ n. **1** a resolute temper or character; boldness and firmness of purpose. **2** a thing resolved on; an intention (New Year's resolutions). **3 a** a formal expression of opinion or intention by a legislative body or public meeting. **b** the formulation of this (passed a resolution). **4** (usu. foll. by of) the act or an instance of solving doubt or a problem or question (towards a resolution of the difficulty). **5 a** separation into components; decomposition. **b** the replacing of a single force etc. by two or more jointly equivalent to it. **6** (foll. by into) analysis; conversion into another form. **7** Mus. the act or an instance of causing discord to pass into concord. **8** Physics etc. the smallest interval measurable by a scientific instrument; the resolving power. **9** Med. the disappearance of inflammation etc. without suppuration. **10** Prosody the substitution of two short syllables for one long. [ME f. L resolutio (as RESOLVE)]

resolutive /ˈrezəˌluːtɪv, -ˌljuːtɪv/ adj. Med. having the power or ability to dissolve. □ **resolutive condition** Law a condition whose fulfilment terminates a contract etc. [med.L resolutivus (as RESOLVE)]

resolve /rɪˈzɒlv/ v. & n. —v. **1** intr. make up one's mind; decide firmly (resolve to do better). **2** tr. (of circumstances etc.) cause (a person) to do this (events resolved him to leave). **3** tr. (foll. by that + clause) (of an assembly or meeting) pass a resolution by vote (the committee resolved that immediate action should be taken). **4** intr. & tr. (often foll. by into) separate or cause to separate into constituent parts; disintegrate; analyse; dissolve. **5** tr. (of optical or photographic equipment) separate or distinguish between closely adjacent objects. **6** tr. & intr. (foll. by into) convert or be converted. **7** tr. & intr. (foll. by into) reduce by mental analysis into. **8** tr. solve; explain; clear up; settle (doubt, argument, etc.). **9** tr. & intr. Mus. convert or be converted into concord. **10** tr. Med. remove (inflammation etc.) without suppuration. **11** tr. Prosody replace (a long syllable) by two short syllables. **12** tr. Mech. replace (a force etc.) by two or more jointly equivalent to it. —n. **1 a** a firm mental decision or intention; a resolution (made a resolve not to go). **b** US a formal resolution by a legislative body or public meeting. **2** resoluteness; steadfastness. □ **resolving power** an instrument's ability to distinguish very small or very close objects. □□ **resolvable** adj. **resolvability** /-ˈbɪlɪtɪ/ n. **resolver** n. [ME f. L resolvere resolut- (as RE-, SOLVE)]

resolved /rɪˈzɒlvd/ adj. resolute, determined. □□ **resolvedly** /-vɪdlɪ/ adv. **resolvedness** n.

resolvent /rɪˈzɒlv(ə)nt/ adj. & n. esp. Med. —adj. (of a drug, application, substance, etc.) effecting the resolution of a tumour etc. —n. such a drug etc.

resonance /ˈrezənəns/ n. **1** the reinforcement or prolongation of sound by reflection or synchronous vibration. **2** Mech. a condition in which an object or system is subjected to an oscillating force having a frequency close to its own natural frequency. **3** Chem. the property of a molecule having a structure best represented by two or more forms rather than a single structural formula. **4** Physics a short-lived elementary particle that is an excited state of a more stable particle. [OF f. L resonantia echo (as RESONANT)]

resonant /ˈrezənənt/ adj. **1** (of sound) echoing, resounding; continuing to sound; reinforced or prolonged by reflection or synchronous vibration. **2** (of a body, room, etc.) tending to reinforce or prolong sounds esp. by synchronous vibration. **3** (often foll. by with) (of a place) resounding. **4** of or relating to resonance. □□ **resonantly** adv. [F résonnant or L resonare resonant- (as RE-, sonare sound)]

resonate /ˈrezəˌneɪt/ v.intr. produce or show resonance; resound. [L resonare resonat- (as RESONANT)]

resonator /ˈrezəˌneɪtə(r)/ n. Mus. **1** an instrument responding to a single note and used for detecting it in combinations. **2** an appliance for giving resonance to sound or other vibrations.

resorb /rɪˈsɔːb/ v.tr. absorb again. □□ **resorbence** n. **resorbent** adj. [L resorbēre resorpt- (as RE-adj., sorbēre absorb)]

resorcin /rɪˈzɔːsɪn/ n. = RESORCINOL. [RESIN + ORCIN]

resorcinol /rɪˈzɔːsɪˌnɒl/ n. Chem. a crystalline organic compound usu. made by synthesis and used in the production of dyes, drugs, resins, etc.

resorption /rɪˈzɔːpʃ(ə)n/ n. **1** the act or an instance of resorbing; the state of being resorbed. **2** the absorption of tissue within the body. □□ **resorptive** /-tɪv/ adj. [RESORB after absorption]

resort /rɪˈzɔːt/ n. & v. —n. **1** a place frequented esp. for holidays or for a specified purpose or quality (seaside resort; health resort). **2 a** a thing to which one has recourse; an expedient or measure (a taxi was our best resort). **b** (foll. by to) recourse to; use of (without resort to violence). **c** (foll. by to) frequent or be frequented (places of great resort). —v.intr. **1** (foll. by to) turn to as an expedient (resorted to threats). **2** (foll. by to) go often or in large numbers to. □ **in the** (or **as a**) **last resort** when all else has failed. □□ **resorter** n. [ME f. OF resortir (as RE-, sortir come or go out)]

re-sort /riːˈsɔːt/ v.tr. sort again or differently.

resound /rɪˈzaʊnd/ v. **1** intr. (often foll. by with) (of a place) ring or echo (the hall resounded with laughter). **2** intr. (of a voice, instrument, sound, etc.) produce echoes; go on sounding; fill the place with sound. **3** intr. **a** (of fame, a reputation, etc.) be much talked of. **b** (foll. by through) produce a sensation (the call resounded through Europe). **4** tr. (often foll. by of) proclaim or repeat loudly (the praises) of a person or thing (resounded the praises of Greece). **5** tr. (of a place) re-echo (a sound). [ME f. RE- + SOUND[1] v., after OF resoner or L resonare: see RESONANT]

resounding /rɪˈzaʊndɪŋ/ adj. **1** in senses of RESOUND. **2** unmistakable; emphatic (was a resounding success). □□ **resoundingly** adv.

resource /rɪˈsɔːs, -ˈzɔːs/ n. **1** an expedient or device (escape was their only resource). **2** (usu. in pl.) **a** the means available to achieve an end, fulfil a function, etc. **b** a stock or supply that can be drawn on. **c** US available assets. **3** (in pl.) a country's collective wealth or means of defence. **4** a leisure occupation (reading is a great resource). **5 a** a skill in devising expedients (a person of great resource). **b** practical ingenuity; quick wit (full of resource). **6** archaic the possibility of aid (lost without resource). □ **one's own resources** one's own abilities, ingenuity, etc. □□ **resourceful** adj. **resourcefully** adv. **resourcefulness** n. **resourceless** adj. **resourcelessness** n. [F ressource, ressource, fem. past part. of OF dial. resourdre (as RE-, L surgere rise)]

respect /rɪˈspekt/ n. & v. —n. **1** deferential esteem felt or shown towards a person or quality. **2 a** (foll. by of, for) heed or regard. **b** (foll. by to) attention to or consideration of (without respect to the results). **3** an aspect, detail, particular, etc. (correct except in this one respect). **4** reference, relation (a morality that has no respect to religion). **5** (in pl.) a person's polite messages or attentions (give my respects to your mother). —v.tr. **1** regard with deference, esteem, or honour. **2 a** avoid interfering with, harming, degrading, insulting, injuring, or interrupting. **b** treat with consideration. **c** refrain from offending, corrupting, or tempting (a person, a person's feelings, etc.). □ **in respect of** as concerns; with reference to. **in respect that** because. **with** (or **with all due**) **respect** a mollifying formula preceding an expression of disagreement with another's views. □□ **respecter** n. [ME f. OF respect or L respectus f. respicere (as RE-, specere look at) or f. respectare frequent. of respicere]

respectability /rɪˌspektəˈbɪlɪtɪ/ n. **1** the state of being respectable. **2** those who are respectable.

respectable /rɪˈspektəb(ə)l/ adj. **1** deserving respect. **2 a** of fair social standing. **b** having the qualities necessary for such standing. **3** honest and decent in conduct etc. **4** of some merit or importance. **5** tolerable, passable, fairly good or competent (a respectable try). **6** (of activities, clothes, etc.) presentable; befitting a respectable person. **7** reasonably good in condition or appearance. **8** appreciable in number, size, amount, etc. **9** primly conventional. □□ **respectably** adv.

respectful /rɪˈspektfʊl/ adj. showing deference (stood at a respectful distance). □□ **respectfully** adv. **respectfulness** n.

respecting /rɪˈspektɪŋ/ prep. with reference or regard to; concerning.

respective /rɪˈspektɪv/ adj. concerning or appropriate to each of several individually; proper to each (go to your respective places). [F respectif -ive f. med.L respectivus (as RESPECT)]

respectively /rɪˈspektɪvlɪ/ adv. for each separately or in turn, and in the order mentioned (she and I gave £10 and £1 respectively).

respell /riːˈspel/ v.tr. (past and past part. **respelt** or **respelled**) spell again or differently, esp. phonetically.

Respighi /reˈspiːgɪ/, Ottorino (1879–1936), Italian composer, string-player, and pianist. His highly popular suites Fountains of Rome (1914–16) and Pines of Rome (1923–4) reveal his gifts for bright evocative orchestration, which can be seen also in his arrangements of other composers' music. In his operas he reacted against the 'realism' of Puccini, but some of his most tender and exquisite work is to be found in his shorter vocal pieces.

respirable /ˈrespərəb(ə)l, rɪˈspaɪrəb(ə)l/ adj. (of air, gas, etc.) able or fit to be breathed. [F respirable or LL respirabilis (as RESPIRE)]

respirate /ˈrespɪˌreɪt/ v.tr. subject to artificial respiration. [back-form. f. RESPIRATION]

respiration /ˌrespɪˈreɪʃ(ə)n/ n. **1 a** the act or an instance of breathing. **b** a single inspiration or expiration; a breath. **2** Biol. in living organisms, the process involving the release of energy and carbon dioxide from the oxidation of complex organic substances. [ME f. F respiration or L respiratio (as RESPIRE)]

respirator /ˈrespɪˌreɪtə(r)/ n. **1** an apparatus worn over the face to prevent poison gas, cold air, dust particles, etc., from being inhaled. **2** Med. an apparatus for maintaining artificial respiration.

respire /rɪˈspaɪə(r)/ v. **1** intr. breathe air. **2** intr. inhale and exhale air. **3** intr. (of a plant) carry out respiration. **4** tr. breathe (air etc.). **5** intr. breathe again; take a breath. **6** intr. get rest or respite; recover hope or spirit. □□ **respiratory** /rɪˈspɪrətərɪ, ˈrespəˌreɪtərɪ/ adj. [ME f. OF respirer or f. L respirare (as RE-, spirare breathe)]

respite /ˈrespaɪt, -pɪt/ n. & v. —n. **1** an interval of rest or relief. **2** a delay permitted before the discharge of an obligation or the suffering of a penalty. —v.tr. **1** grant respite to; reprieve (a condemned person). **2** postpone the execution or exaction of (a sentence, obligation, etc.). **3** give temporary relief from (pain or care) or to (a sufferer). [ME f. OF respit f. L respectus RESPECT]

resplendent /rɪˈsplend(ə)nt/ adj. brilliant, dazzlingly or gloriously bright. □□ **resplendence** n. **resplendency** n. **resplendently** adv. [ME f. L resplendēre (as RE-, splendēre glitter)]

respond /rɪˈspɒnd/ v. & n. —v. **1** intr. answer, give a reply. **2** intr. act or behave in an answering or corresponding manner. **3** intr. (usu. foll. by to) show sensitiveness to by behaviour or change (does not respond to kindness). **4** intr. (of a congregation) make answers to a priest etc. **5** intr. Bridge make a bid on the basis of a partner's preceding bid. **6** tr. say (something) in answer. —n. **1** Archit. a half-pillar or half-pier attached to a wall to support an arch, esp. at the end of an arcade. **2** Eccl. a responsory; a response to a versicle. □□ **respondence** n. **respondency** n. **responder** n. [ME f. OF respondre answer ult. f. L respondēre respons- answer (as RE-, spondēre pledge)]

respondent /rɪˈspɒnd(ə)nt/ n. & adj. —n. **1** a defendant, esp. in an appeal or divorce case. **2** a person who makes an answer or defends an argument etc. —adj. **1** making answer. **2** (foll. by to) responsive. **3** in the position of defendant.

response /rɪˈspɒns/ n. **1** an answer given in word or act; a reply. **2** a feeling, movement, change, etc., caused by a stimulus or influence. **3** (often in pl.) Eccl. any part of the liturgy said or sung in answer to the priest; a responsory. **4** Bridge a bid made in responding. [ME f. OF respons(e) or L responsum neut. past part. of respondēre RESPOND]

responsibility /rɪˌspɒnsɪˈbɪlɪtɪ/ n. (pl. **-ies**) **1 a** (often foll. by for, of) the state or fact of being responsible (refuses all responsibility for it; will take the responsibility of doing it). **b** authority; the ability to act independently and make decisions (a job with more responsibility). **2** the person or thing for which one is responsible (the food is my responsibility). □ **on one's own responsibility** without authorization.

responsible /rɪˈspɒnsɪb(ə)l/ adj. **1** (often foll. by to, for) liable to be called to account (to a person or for a thing). **2** morally accountable for one's actions; capable of rational conduct. **3** of good credit, position, or repute; respectable; evidently trustworthy. **4** (often foll. by for) being the primary cause (a short circuit was responsible for the power failure). **5** (of a ruler or government) not autocratic. **6** involving responsibility (a responsible job). □□ **responsibleness** n. **responsibly** adv. [obs. F f. L respondēre: see RESPOND]

responsive /rɪˈspɒnsɪv/ adj. **1** (often foll. by to) responding readily (to some influence). **2** sympathetic; impressionable. **3 a** answering. **b** by way of answer. **4** (of a liturgy etc.) using responses. □□ **responsively** adv. **responsiveness** n. [F responsif -ive or LL responsivus (as RESPOND)]

responsory /rɪˈspɒnsərɪ/ n. (pl. **-ies**) an anthem said or sung by a soloist and choir after a lesson. [ME f. LL responsorium (as RESPOND)]

respray v. & n. —v.tr. /riːˈspreɪ/ spray again (esp. to change the colour of the paint on a vehicle). —n. /ˈriːspreɪ/ the act or an instance of respraying.

rest[1] /rest/ v. & n. —v. **1** intr. cease, abstain, or be relieved from exertion, action, movement, or employment; be tranquil. **2** intr. be still or asleep, esp. to refresh oneself or recover strength. **3** tr. give relief or repose to; allow to rest (a chair to rest my legs). **4** intr. (foll. by on, upon, against) lie on; be supported by; be spread out on; be propped against. **5** intr. (foll. by on, upon) depend, be based, or rely on. **6** intr. (foll. by on, upon) (of a look) alight or be steadily directed on. **7** tr. (foll. by on, upon) place for support or foundation. **8** intr. (of a problem or subject) be left without further investigation or discussion (let the matter rest). **9** intr. **a** lie in death. **b** (foll. by in) lie buried in (a churchyard etc.). **10** tr. (as **rested** adj.) refreshed or reinvigorated by resting. **11** intr. US conclude the calling of witnesses in a law case (the prosecution rests). **12** intr. (of land) lie fallow. **13** intr. (foll. by in) repose trust in (am content to rest in God). —n. **1** repose or sleep, esp. in bed at night (get a good night's rest). **2** freedom from or the cessation of exertion, worry, activity, etc. (give the subject a rest). **3** a period of resting (take a 15-minute rest). **4** a support or prop for holding or steadying something. **5** Mus. **a** an interval of silence of a specified duration. **b** the sign denoting this. **6** a place of resting or abiding, esp. a lodging place or shelter provided for sailors, cabmen, etc. **7** a pause in elocution. **8** a caesura in verse. □ **at rest** not moving; not agitated or troubled; dead. **be resting** Brit. euphem. (of an actor) be out of work. **rest-baulk** a ridge left unploughed between furrows. **rest one's case** conclude one's argument etc. **rest-cure** a rest usu. of some weeks as a medical treatment. **rest-day 1** a day spent in rest. **2** = day of rest. **rest (or God rest) his (or her) soul** may God grant his (or her) soul repose. **rest-home** a place where old or frail people can be cared for. **rest-house** Ind. a house for travellers to rest in. **resting-place** a place provided or used for resting. **rest mass** Physics the mass of a body when at rest. **rest on one's laurels** see LAUREL. **rest on one's oars** see OAR. **rest room** esp. US a public lavatory in a factory, shop, etc. **rest up** US rest oneself thoroughly. **set at rest** settle or relieve (a question, a person's mind, etc.). □□ **rester** n. [OE ræst, rest (n.), ræstan, restan (v.)]

rest[2] /rest/ n. & v. —n. (prec. by the) **1** the remaining part or parts; the others; the remainder of some quantity or number (finish what you can and leave the rest). **2** Brit. Econ. the reserve fund, esp. of the Bank of England. **3** hist. a rally in tennis.

—v.intr. 1 remain in a specified state (*rest assured*). **2** (foll. by *with*) be left in the hands or charge of (*the final arrangements rest with you*). □ **and all the rest** (or **the rest of it**) and all else that might be mentioned; etcetera. **for the rest** as regards anything else. [ME f. OF *reste rester* f. L *restare* (as RE-, *stare* stand)]

restart *v. & n.* —*v.tr. & intr.* /riː'staːt/ begin again. —*n.* /'riːstaːt/ a new beginning.

restate /riː'steɪt/ *v.tr.* express again or differently, esp. more clearly or convincingly. □□ **restatement** *n.*

restaurant /'restə‚rɒnt, -‚rɔ̃/ *n.* public premises where meals or refreshments may be bought and eaten. □ **restaurant car** *Brit.* a dining-car on a train. [F f. *restaurer* RESTORE]

restaurateur /‚restərə'tɜː(r)/ *n.* a restaurant-keeper. [F (as RESTAURANT)]

restful /'restfʊl/ *adj.* **1** favourable to quiet or repose. **2** free from disturbing influences. **3** soothing. □□ **restfully** *adv.* **restfulness** *n.*

rest-harrow /'rest‚hærəʊ/ *n.* any tough-rooted plant of the genus *Ononis*, native to Europe and the Mediterranean. [obs. *rest* (v.) = ARREST (in sense 'stop') + HARROW]

restitution /‚resti'tjuːʃ(ə)n/ *n.* **1** (often foll. by *of*) the act or an instance of restoring a thing to its proper owner. **2** reparation for an injury (esp. *make restitution*). **3** esp. *Theol.* the restoration of a thing to its original state. **4** the resumption of an original shape or position because of elasticity. □□ **restitutive** /'resti‚tjuːtɪv/ *adj.* [ME f. OF *restitution* or L *restitutio* f. *restituere restitut-* restore (as RE-, *statuere* establish)]

restive /'restɪv/ *adj.* **1** fidgety; restless. **2** (of a horse) refusing to advance, stubbornly standing still or moving backwards or sideways; jibbing; refractory. **3** (of a person) unmanageable; rejecting control. □□ **restively** *adv.* **restiveness** *n.* [ME f. OF *restif -ive* f. Rmc (as REST²)]

restless /'restlɪs/ *adj.* **1** finding or affording no rest. **2** uneasy; agitated. **3** constantly in motion, fidgeting, etc. □□ **restlessly** *adv.* **restlessness** *n.* [OE *restlēas* (as REST, -LESS)]

restock /riː'stɒk/ *v.tr.* (also *absol.*) stock again or differently.

restoration /‚restə'reɪʃ(ə)n/ *n.* **1** the act or an instance of restoring or being restored. **2** a model or drawing representing the supposed original form of an extinct animal, ruined building, etc. **3 a** the re-establishment of a monarch etc. **b** the period of this. **4** (**Restoration**) *hist.* **a** (prec. by *the*) the re-establishment of the Stuart monarchy in Britain with the return of Charles II to the throne in 1660. After the death of Oliver Cromwell in 1658, his son Richard proved incapable of maintaining the Protectorate, and, with no other viable form of government possible, a faction led by General Monck organized the King's return from exile. **b** (often *attrib.*) the literary period following this (*Restoration comedy*). [17th-c. alt. (after RESTORE) of *restauration*, ME f. OF *restauration* or LL *restauratio* (as RESTORE)]

restorative /rɪ'stɒrətɪv/ *adj. & n.* —*adj.* tending to restore health or strength. —*n.* a restorative medicine, food, etc. (*needs a restorative*). □□ **restoratively** *adv.* [ME var. of obs. *restaurative* f. OF *restauratif -ive* (as RESTORE)]

restore /rɪ'stɔː(r)/ *v.tr.* **1** bring back or attempt to bring back to the original state by rebuilding, repairing, repainting, emending, etc. **2** bring back to health etc.; cure. **3** give back to the original owner etc.; make restitution of. **4** reinstate; bring back to dignity or right. **5** replace; put back; bring back to a former condition. **6** make a representation of the supposed original state of (a ruin, extinct animal, etc.). **7** reinstate by conjecture (missing words in a text, missing pieces, etc.). □□ **restorable** *adj.* **restorer** *n.* [ME f. OF *restorer* f. L *restaurare*]

restrain /rɪ'streɪn/ *v.tr.* **1** (often *refl.*, usu. foll. by *from*) check or hold in; keep in check or under control or within bounds. **2** repress; keep down. **3** confine; imprison. □□ **restrainable** *adj.* **restrainer** *n.* [ME f. OF *restrei(g)n-* stem of *restreindre* f. L *restringere restrict-* (as RE-, *stringere* tie)]

re-strain /riː'streɪn/ *v.tr.* strain again.

restrainedly /rɪ'streɪnɪdlɪ/ *adv.* with self-restraint.

restraint /rɪ'streɪnt/ *n.* **1** the act or an instance of restraining or being restrained. **2** a stoppage; a check; a controlling agency or influence. **3 a** self-control; avoidance of excess or exaggeration. **b** austerity of literary expression. **4** reserve of manner. **5** confinement, esp. because of insanity. **6** something which restrains or holds in check. □ **in restraint of** in order to restrain. **restraint of trade** action seeking to interfere with free-market conditions. [ME f. OF *restreinte* fem. past part. of *restreindre*: see RESTRAIN]

restrict /rɪ'strɪkt/ *v.tr.* (often foll. by *to, within*) **1** confine, bound, limit (*restricted parking; restricted them to five days a week*). **2** subject to limitation. **3** withhold from general circulation or disclosure. □ **restricted area 1** *Brit.* an area in which there is a special speed limit for vehicles. **2** *US* an area which military personnel are not allowed to enter. □□ **restrictedly** *adv.* **restrictedness** *n.* [L *restringere*: see RESTRAIN]

restriction /rɪ'strɪkʃ(ə)n/ *n.* **1** the act or an instance of restricting; the state of being restricted. **2** a thing that restricts. **3** a limitation placed on action. □□ **restrictionist** *adj. & n.* [ME f. OF *restriction* or L *restrictio* (as RESTRICT)]

restrictive /rɪ'strɪktɪv/ *adj.* imposing restrictions. □ **restrictive clause** *Gram.* a relative clause, usu. without surrounding commas. **restrictive practice** *Brit.* an agreement to limit competition or output in industry. □□ **restrictively** *adv.* **restrictiveness** *n.* [ME f. OF *restrictif -ive* or med.L *restrictivus* (as RESTRICT)]

restring /riː'strɪŋ/ *v.tr.* (*past* and *past part.* **restrung**) **1** fit (a musical instrument) with new strings. **2** thread (beads etc.) on a new string.

restructure /riː'strʌktʃə(r)/ *v.tr.* give a new structure to; rebuild; rearrange.

restudy /riː'stʌdɪ/ *v.tr.* (**-ies, -ied**) study again.

restyle /riː'staɪl/ *v.tr.* **1** reshape; remake in a new style. **2** give a new designation to (a person or thing).

result /rɪ'zʌlt/ *n. & v.* —*n.* **1** a consequence, issue, or outcome of something. **2** a satisfactory outcome; a favourable result (*gets results*). **3** a quantity, formula, etc., obtained by calculation. **4** (in *pl.*) a list of scores or winners etc. in an examination or sporting event. —*v.intr.* **1** (often foll. by *from*) arise as the actual consequence or follow as a logical consequence (from conditions, causes, etc.). **2** (often foll. by *in*) have a specified end or outcome (*resulted in a large profit*). □ **without result** in vain; fruitless. □□ **resultful** *adj.* **resultless** *adj.* [ME f. med.L *resultare* f. L (as RE-, *saltare* frequent. of *salire* jump)]

resultant /rɪ'zʌlt(ə)nt/ *adj. & n.* —*adj.* resulting, esp. as the total outcome of more or less opposed forces. —*n.* *Math.* a force etc. equivalent to two or more acting in different directions at the same point.

resume /rɪ'zjuːm/ *v. & n.* —*v.* **1** *tr. & intr.* begin again or continue after an interruption. **2** *tr. & intr.* begin to speak, work, or use again; recommence. **3** *tr.* get back; take back; recover; reoccupy (*resume one's seat*). —*n.* = RÉSUMÉ. □□ **resumable** *adj.* [ME f. OF *resumer* or L *resumere resumpt-* (as RE-, *sumere* take)]

résumé /'rezjʊ‚meɪ/ *n.* **1** a summary. **2** *US* a curriculum vitae. [F past part. of *résumer* (as RESUME)]

resumption /rɪ'zʌmpʃ(ə)n/ *n.* the act or an instance of resuming (*ready for the resumption of negotiations*). □□ **resumptive** *adj.* [ME f. OF *resumption* or LL *resumptio* (as RESUME)]

resupinate /rɪ'sjuːpɪnət/ *adj.* (of a leaf etc.) upside down. [L *resupinatus* past part. of *resupinare* bend back: see SUPINE]

resurface /riː'sɜːfɪs/ *v.* **1** *tr.* lay a new surface on (a road etc.). **2** *intr.* rise or arise again; turn up again.

resurgent /rɪ'sɜːdʒ(ə)nt/ *adj.* **1** rising or arising again. **2** tending to rise again. □□ **resurgence** *n.* [L *resurgere resurrect-* (as RE-, *surgere* rise)]

resurrect /‚rezə'rekt/ *v.* **1** *tr. colloq.* revive the practice, use, or memory of. **2** *tr.* take from the grave; exhume. **3** *tr.* dig up. **4** *tr. & intr.* raise or rise from the dead. [back-form. f. RESURRECTION]

resurrection /‚rezə'rekʃ(ə)n/ *n.* **1** the act or an instance of rising from the dead. **2** (**Resurrection**) **a** Christ's rising from the dead. **b** the rising of the dead at the Last Judgement. **3** a revival after disuse, inactivity, or decay. **4** exhumation. **5** the unearthing of a lost or forgotten thing; restoration to vogue or memory. □ **resurrection plant** any of various plants, including clubmosses of the genus *Selaginella* and the Rose of Jericho, unfolding when moistened after being dried. □□ **resurrectional** adj. [ME f. OF f. LL *resurrectio -onis* (as RESURGENT)]

resurvey v. & n. —v.tr. /ˌriːsəˈveɪ/ survey again; reconsider. —n. /ˈriːsɜːveɪ/ the act or an instance of resurveying.

resuscitate /rɪˈsʌsɪˌteɪt/ v.tr. & intr. 1 revive from unconsciousness or apparent death. 2 return or restore to vogue, vigour, or vividness. □□ **resuscitation** /-ˈteɪʃ(ə)n/ n. **resuscitative** adj. **resuscitator** n. [L *resuscitare* (as RE-, *suscitare* raise)]

ret /ret/ v. (also **rate** /reɪt/) (**retted, retting**) 1 tr. soften (flax, hemp, etc.) by soaking or by exposure to moisture. 2 intr. (often as **retted** adj.) (of hay etc.) be spoilt by wet or rot. [ME, rel. to ROT]

ret. abbr. retired; returned.

retable /rɪˈteɪb(ə)l/ n. 1 a frame enclosing decorated panels above the back of an altar. 2 a shelf. [F *rétable*, *retable* f. Sp. *retablo* f. med.L *retrotabulum* rear table (as RETRO-, TABLE)]

retail /ˈriːteɪl/ n., adj., adv., & v. —n. the sale of goods in relatively small quantities to the public, and usu. not for resale (cf. WHOLESALE). —adj. & adv. by retail; at a retail price (*do you buy wholesale or retail?*). —v. /also rɪˈteɪl/ 1 tr. sell (goods) in retail trade. 2 intr. (often foll. by *at, of*) (of goods) be sold in this way (esp. for a specified price) (*retails at £4.95*). 3 tr. recount; relate details of. □ **retail price index** an index of the variation in the prices of retail goods. □□ **retailer** n. [ME f. OF *retaille* a piece cut off f. *retaillier* (as RE-, TAIL²)]

retain /rɪˈteɪn/ v.tr. 1 **a** keep possession of; not lose; continue to have, practise, or recognize. **b** not abolish, discard, or alter. 2 keep in one's memory. 3 keep in place; hold fixed. 4 secure the services of (a person, esp. a barrister) with a preliminary payment. □ **retaining fee** a fee paid to secure a person, service, etc. **retaining wall** a wall supporting and confining a mass of earth or water. □□ **retainable** adj. **retainability** /-ˈbɪlɪtɪ/ n. **retainment** n. [ME f. AF *retei(g)n-* f. stem of OF *retenir* ult. f. L *retinēre retent-* (as RE-, *tenēre* hold)]

retainer /rɪˈteɪnə(r)/ n. 1 a person or thing that retains. 2 *Law* a fee for retaining a barrister etc. 3 **a** hist. a dependant or follower of a person of rank. **b** joc. an old and faithful friend or servant (esp. *old retainer*). 4 *Brit.* a reduced rent paid to retain accommodation during a period of non-occupancy.

retake v. & n. —v.tr. /riːˈteɪk/ (*past* **retook**; *past part.* **retaken**) 1 take again. 2 recapture. —n. /ˈriːteɪk/ 1 **a** the act or an instance of retaking. **b** a thing retaken, e.g. an examination. 2 **a** the act or an instance of filming a scene or recording music etc. again. **b** the scene or recording obtained in this way.

retaliate /rɪˈtælɪˌeɪt/ v. 1 intr. repay an injury, insult, etc., in kind; attack in return; make reprisals. 2 tr. **a** (usu. foll. by *upon*) cast (an accusation) back upon a person. **b** repay (an injury or insult) in kind. □□ **retaliation** /-ˈeɪʃ(ə)n/ n. **retaliative** /-ˈtælɪətɪv/ adj. **retaliator** n. **retaliatory** /-ˈtælɪətərɪ/ adj. [L *retaliare* (as RE-, *talis* such)]

retard /rɪˈtɑːd/ v. & n. —v.tr. 1 make slow or late. 2 delay the progress, development, arrival, or accomplishment of. —n. retardation. □ **in retard** delayed, in the rear. □□ **retardant** adj. & n. **retardation** /ˌriːtɑːˈdeɪʃ(ə)n/ n. **retardative** adj. **retardatory** adj. **retarder** n. **retardment** n. [F *retarder* f. L *retardare* (as RE-, *tardus* slow)]

retardate /rɪˈtɑːdeɪt/ adj. & n. *US* —adj. mentally retarded. —n. a mentally retarded person. [L *retardare*: see RETARD]

retarded /rɪˈtɑːdɪd/ adj. backward in mental or physical development.

retch /retʃ, riːtʃ/ v. & n. —v.intr. make a motion of vomiting esp. involuntarily and without effect. —n. such a motion or the sound of it. [var. of (now dial.) *reach* f. OE *hrǣcan* spit, ON *hrækja* f. Gmc, of imit. orig.]

retd. abbr. 1 retired. 2 returned.

rete /ˈriːtɪ/ n. (pl. **retia** /-tɪə, -ʃɪə/) *Anat.* an elaborate network or plexus of blood vessels and nerve cells. [L *rete* net]

reteach /riːˈtiːtʃ/ v.tr. (*past* and *past part.* **retaught**) teach again or differently.

retell /riːˈtel/ v.tr. (*past* and *past part.* **retold**) tell again or in a different version.

retention /rɪˈtenʃ(ə)n/ n. 1 **a** the act or an instance of retaining; the state of being retained. **b** the ability to retain things experienced or learned; memory. 2 *Med.* the failure to evacuate urine or another secretion. [ME f. OF *retention* or L *retentio* (as RETAIN)]

retentive /rɪˈtentɪv/ adj. 1 (often foll. by *of*) tending to retain (moisture etc.). 2 (of memory or a person) not forgetful. 3 *Surgery* (of a ligature etc.) serving to keep something in place. □□ **retentively** adv. **retentiveness** n. [ME f. OF *retentif -ive* or med.L *retentivus* (as RETAIN)]

retexture /riːˈtekstʃə(r)/ v.tr. treat (material, a garment, etc.) so as to restore its original texture.

rethink v. & n. —v.tr. /riːˈθɪŋk/ (*past* and *past part.* **rethought**) think about (something) again, esp. with a view to making changes. —n. /ˈriːθɪŋk/ a reassessment; a period of rethinking.

Rethymnon /ˈreθɪmˌnɒn/ a port on the north coast of Crete; pop. (1981) 17,700.

retia pl. of RETE.

retiarius /ˌretɪˈɑːrɪəs/ n. (pl. **retiarii** /-rɪˌaɪ/) a Roman gladiator using a net to trap his opponent. [L f. *rete* net]

reticence /ˈretɪs(ə)ns/ n. 1 the avoidance of saying all one knows or feels, or of saying more than is necessary; reserve in speech. 2 a disposition to silence; taciturnity. 3 the act or an instance of holding back some fact. 4 abstinence from overemphasis in art. □□ **reticent** adj. **reticently** adv. [L *reticentia* f. *reticēre* (as RE-, *tacēre* be silent)]

reticle /ˈretɪk(ə)l/ n. a network of fine threads or lines in the focal plane of an optical instrument to help accurate observation. [L *reticulum*: see RETICULUM]

reticula pl. of RETICULUM.

reticulate v. & adj. —v.tr. & intr. /rɪˈtɪkjʊˌleɪt/ 1 divide or be divided in fact or appearance into a network. 2 arrange or be arranged in small squares or with intersecting lines. —adj. /rɪˈtɪkjʊlət/ reticulated. □□ **reticulately** /rɪˈtɪkjʊlətlɪ/ adv. **reticulation** /-ˈleɪʃ(ə)n/ n. [L *reticulatus* reticulated (as RETICULUM)]

reticule /ˈretɪˌkjuːl/ n. 1 = RETICLE. 2 usu. hist. a woman's netted or other bag, esp. with a drawstring, carried or worn to serve the purpose of a pocket. [F *réticule* f. L (as RETICULUM)]

reticulum /rɪˈtɪkjʊləm/ n. (pl. **reticula** /-lə/) 1 a netlike structure; a fine network, esp. of membranes etc. in living organisms. 2 a ruminant's second stomach. □□ **reticular** adj. **reticulose** adj. [L, dimin. of *rete* net]

retie /riːˈtaɪ/ v.tr. (**retying**) tie again.

retiform /ˈriːtɪˌfɔːm/ adj. netlike, reticulated. [L *rete* net + -FORM]

retina /ˈretɪnə/ n. (pl. **retinas, retinae** /-ˌniː/) a layer at the back of the eyeball sensitive to light, and triggering nerve impulses via the optic nerve to the brain where the visual image is formed. □□ **retinal** adj. [ME f. med.L f. L *rete* net]

retinitis /ˌretɪˈnaɪtɪs/ n. inflammation of the retina.

retinol /ˈretɪˌnɒl/ n. a vitamin found in green and yellow vegetables, egg-yolk, and fish-liver oil, essential for growth and vision in dim light. Also called *vitamin A*. [RETINA + -OL¹]

retinue /ˈretɪˌnjuː/ n. a body of attendants accompanying an important person. [ME f. OF *retenue* fem. past part. of *retenir* RETAIN]

retiral /rɪˈtaɪər(ə)l/ n. esp. *Sc.* retirement from office etc.

retire /rɪˈtaɪə(r)/ v. 1 **a** intr. leave office or employment, esp. because of age (*retire from the army; retire on a pension*). **b** tr. cause (a person) to retire from work. 2 intr. withdraw; go away; retreat. 3 intr. seek seclusion or shelter. 4 intr. go to bed. 5 tr. withdraw (troops). 6 intr. & tr. *Cricket* (of a batsman) voluntarily end or be compelled to suspend one's innings (*retired hurt*). 7 tr. *Econ.* withdraw (a bill or note) from circulation or currency. □ **retire from the world** become a recluse. **retire into oneself** become uncommunicative or unsociable. **retiring age** the age at which most people normally retire from work. □□ **retirer** n. [F *retirer* (as RE-, *tirer* draw)]

retired /rɪˈtaɪəd/ adj. 1 **a** having retired from employment (a retired *teacher*). **b** relating to a retired person (*received retired pay*). **2** withdrawn from society or observation; secluded (*lives a retired life*). □□ **retiredness** *n*.

retirement /rɪˈtaɪəmənt/ *n*. **1 a** the act or an instance of retiring. **b** the condition of having retired. **2 a** seclusion or privacy. **b** a secluded place. □ **retirement pension** *Brit*. a pension paid by the State to retired people above a certain age.

retiring /rɪˈtaɪərɪŋ/ *adj*. shy; fond of seclusion. □□ **retiringly** *adv*.

retold *past* and *past part*. of RETELL.

retook *past* of RETAKE.

retool /riːˈtuːl/ *v.tr*. equip (a factory etc.) with new tools.

retort[1] /rɪˈtɔːt/ *n. & v.* —*n.* **1** an incisive or witty or angry reply. **2** the turning of a charge or argument against its originator. **3** a piece of retaliation. —*v.* **1 a** *tr.* say by way of a retort. **b** *intr.* make a retort. **2** *tr.* repay (an insult or attack) in kind. **3** *tr.* (often foll. by *on*, *upon*) return (mischief, a charge, sarcasm, etc.) to its originator. **4** *tr.* (often foll. by *against*) make (an argument) tell against its user. **5** *tr.* (as **retorted** *adj*.) recurved; twisted or bent backwards. [L *retorquēre retort-* (as RE-, *torquēre* twist)]

retort[2] /rɪˈtɔːt/ *n. & v.* —*n.* **1** a vessel usu. of glass with a long recurved neck used in distilling liquids. **2** a vessel for heating mercury for purification, coal to generate gas, or iron and carbon to make steel. —*v.tr.* purify (mercury) by heating in a retort. [F *retorte* f. med.L *retorta* fem. past part. of *retorquēre*: see RETORT[1]]

retortion /rɪˈtɔːʃ(ə)n/ *n*. **1** the act or an instance of bending back; the condition of being bent back. **2** retaliation by a State on the subjects of another. [RETORT[1], perh. after *contortion*]

retouch /riːˈtʌtʃ/ *v. & n.* —*v.tr.* improve or repair (a composition, picture, photographic negative or print, etc.) by fresh touches or alterations. —*n.* the act or an instance of retouching. □□ **retoucher** *n*. [prob. f. F *retoucher* (as RE-, TOUCH)]

retrace /rɪˈtreɪs/ *v.tr.* **1** go back over (one's steps etc.). **2** trace back to a source or beginning. **3** recall the course of in one's memory. [F *retracer* (as RE-, TRACE[1])]

retract /rɪˈtrækt/ *v.* **1** *tr.* (also *absol.*) withdraw or revoke (a statement or undertaking). **2 a** *tr. & intr.* (esp. with ref. to part of the body) draw or be drawn back or in. **b** *tr.* draw (an undercarriage etc.) into the body of an aircraft. □□ **retractable** *adj.* **retraction** *n.* **retractive** *adj.* [L *retrahere* or (in sense 1) *retractare* (as RE-, *trahere tract-* draw)]

retractile /rɪˈtræktaɪl/ *adj.* capable of being retracted. □□ **retractility** /-ˈtɪlɪtɪ/ *n.* [RETRACT, after *contractile*]

retractor /rɪˈtræktə(r)/ *n.* **1** a muscle used for retracting. **2** a device for retracting.

retrain /riːˈtreɪn/ *v.tr. & intr.* train again or further, esp. for new work.

retral /ˈriːtr(ə)l/ *adj. Biol.* hinder, posterior; at the back. [RETRO- + -AL]

retranslate /ˌriːtrænzˈleɪt, -sˈleɪt, ˌriːtrɑːn-/ *v.tr.* translate again, esp. back into the original language. □□ **retranslation** *n.*

retransmit /ˌriːtrænzˈmɪt, -sˈmɪt, ˌriːtrɑːn-/ *v.tr.* (**retransmitted**, **retransmitting**) transmit (esp. radio signals or broadcast programmes) back again or to a further distance. □□ **retransmission** /-ˈmɪʃ(ə)n/ *n.*

retread *v. & n.* —*v.tr.* /riːˈtred/ (*past* **retrod**; *past part.* **retrodden** or (in sense 2) **retreaded**) **1** tread (a path etc.) again. **2** put a fresh tread on (a tyre). —*n.* /ˈriːtred/ a retreaded tyre.

retreat /rɪˈtriːt/ *v. & n.* —*v.* **1 a** *intr.* (esp. of military forces) go back, retire; relinquish a position. **b** *tr.* cause to retreat; move back. **2** *intr.* (esp. of features) recede; slope back. —*n.* **1 a** the act or an instance of retreating. **b** *Mil.* a signal for this. **2** withdrawal into privacy or security. **3** a place of shelter or seclusion. **4** a period of seclusion for prayer and meditation. **5** *Mil.* a bugle-call at sunset. **6** a place for the reception of the elderly or others in need of care. [ME f. OF *retret* (n.), *retraiter* (v.) f. L *retrahere*: see RETRACT]

retrench /rɪˈtrentʃ/ *v.* **1 a** *tr.* reduce the amount of (costs). **b** *intr.* cut down expenses; introduce economies. **2** *tr.* shorten or abridge. □□ **retrenchment** *n.* [obs. F *retrencher* (as RE-, TRENCH)]

retrial /riːˈtraɪəl/ *n.* a second or further (judicial) trial.

retribution /ˌretrɪˈbjuːʃ(ə)n/ *n.* requital usu. for evil done; vengeance. □□ **retributive** /rɪˈtrɪbjʊtɪv/ *adj.* **retributory** /rɪˈtrɪbjʊtərɪ/ *adj.* [ME f. LL *retributio* (as RE-, *tribuere tribut-* assign)]

retrieve /rɪˈtriːv/ *v. & n.* —*v.tr.* **1 a** regain possession of. **b** recover by investigation or effort of memory. **2 a** restore to knowledge or recall to mind. **b** obtain (information stored in a computer etc.). **3** (of a dog) find and bring in (killed or wounded game etc.). **4** (foll. by *from*) recover or rescue (esp. from a bad state). **5** restore to a flourishing state; revive. **6** repair or set right (a loss or error etc.) (*managed to retrieve the situation*). —*n.* the possibility of recovery (*beyond retrieve*). □□ **retrievable** *adj.* **retrieval** *n.* [ME f. OF *retroeve-* stressed stem of *retrover* (as RE-, *trover* find)]

retriever /rɪˈtriːvə(r)/ *n.* **1 a** a dog of a breed used for retrieving game. **b** this breed. **2** a person who retrieves something.

retro- /ˈretrəʊ/ *comb. form* **1** denoting action back or in return (*retroact*; *retroflex*). **2** *Anat. & Med.* denoting location behind. [L *retro* backwards]

retroact /ˌretrəʊˈækt/ *v.intr.* **1** operate in a backward direction. **2** have a retrospective effect. **3** react. □□ **retroaction** *n.*

retroactive /ˌretrəʊˈæktɪv/ *adj.* (esp. of legislation) having retrospective effect. □□ **retroactively** *adv.* **retroactivity** /-ˈtɪvɪtɪ/ *n.*

retrocede /ˌretrəʊˈsiːd/ *v.* **1** *intr.* move back; recede. **2** *tr.* cede back again. □□ **retrocedence** *n.* **retrocedent** *adj.* **retrocession** /-ˈseʃ(ə)n/ *n.* **retrocessive** /-ˈsesɪv/ *adj.* [L *retrocedere* (as RETRO-, *cedere cess-* go)]

retrochoir /ˈretrəʊˌkwaɪə(r)/ *n.* the part of a cathedral or large church behind the high altar. [med.L *retrochorus* (as RETRO-, CHOIR)]

retrod *past* of RETREAD.

retrodden *past part.* of RETREAD.

retrofit /ˈretrəʊfɪt/ *v.tr.* (**-fitted**, **-fitting**) modify (machinery, vehicles, etc.) to incorporate changes and developments introduced after manufacture. [RETROACTIVE + REFIT]

retroflex /ˈretrəˌfleks/ *adj.* (also **retroflexed**) **1** *Anat., Med., & Bot.* turned backwards. **2** *Phonet.* = CACUMINAL. □□ **retroflexion** /-ˈflekʃ(ə)n/ *n.* [L *retroflectere retroflex-* (as RETRO-, *flectere* bend)]

retrogradation /ˌretrəʊɡrəˈdeɪʃ(ə)n/ *n. Astron.* **1** the apparent backward motion of a planet in the zodiac. **2** the apparent motion of a celestial body from east to west. **3** backward movement of the lunar nodes on the ecliptic. [LL *retrogradatio* (as RETRO-, GRADATION)]

retrograde /ˈretrəˌɡreɪd/ *adj., n., & v.* —*adj.* **1** directed backwards; retreating. **2** reverting esp. to an inferior state; declining. **3** inverse, reversed (*in retrograde order*). **4** *Astron.* in or showing retrogradation. —*n.* a degenerate person. —*v.intr.* **1** move backwards; recede, retire. **2** decline, revert. **3** *Astron.* show retrogradation. □□ **retrogradely** *adv.* [ME f. L *retrogradus* (as RETRO-, *gradus* step, *gradi* walk)]

retrogress /ˌretrəˈɡres/ *v.intr.* **1** go back; move backwards. **2** deteriorate. □□ **retrogressive** *adj.* [RETRO-, after PROGRESS v.]

retrogression /ˌretrəˈɡreʃ(ə)n/ *n.* **1** backward or reversed movement. **2** a return to a less advanced state; a reversal of development; a decline or deterioration. **3** *Astron.* = RETROGRADATION. □□ **retrogressive** /-sɪv/ *adj.* [RETRO-, after *progression*]

retroject /ˈretrəʊˌdʒekt/ *v.tr.* throw back (usu. opp. PROJECT). [RETRO-, after PROJECT n.]

retro-rocket /ˈretrəʊˌrɒkɪt/ *n.* an auxiliary rocket for slowing down a spacecraft etc., e.g. when re-entering the earth's atmosphere.

retrorse /rɪˈtrɔːs/ *adj. Biol.* turned back or down. □□ **retrorsely** *adv.* [L *retrorsus* = *retroversus* (as RETRO-, *versus* past part. of *vertere* turn)]

retrospect /ˈretrəˌspekt/ *n.* **1** (foll. by *to*) regard or reference to precedent or authority, or to previous conditions. **2** a survey of past time or events. □ **in retrospect** when looked back on. [RETRO-, after PROSPECT n.]

retrospection /ˌretrəˈspekʃ(ə)n/ *n.* **1** the action of looking back esp. into the past. **2** an indulgence or engagement in retrospect. [prob. f. *retrospect* (v.) (as RETROSPECT)]

retrospective /ˌretrəʊˈspektɪv/ *adj.* & *n.* —*adj.* **1** looking back on or dealing with the past. **2** (of an exhibition, recital, etc.) showing an artist's development over his or her lifetime. **3** (of a statute etc.) applying to the past as well as the future; retroactive. **4** (of a view) lying to the rear. —*n.* a retrospective exhibition, recital, etc. □□ **retrospectively** *adv.*

retrosternal /ˌretrəʊˈstɜːn(ə)l/ *adj.* Anat. & Med. behind the breastbone.

retroussé /rəˈtruːseɪ/ *adj.* (of the nose) turned up at the tip. [F, past part. of *retrousser* tuck up (as RE-, TRUSS)]

retrovert /ˈretrəʊvɜːt/ *v.tr.* **1** turn backwards. **2** Med. (as **retroverted** *adj.*) (of the womb) having a backward inclination. □□ **retroversion** /-ˈvɜːʃ(ə)n/ *n.* [LL *retrovertere* (as RETRO-, *vertere* *vers-* turn)]

retrovirus /ˈretrəʊˌvaɪərəs/ *n.* Biol. any of a group of RNA viruses which form DNA during the replication of their RNA. [mod.L f. initial letters of *reverse transcriptase* + VIRUS]

retry /riːˈtraɪ/ *v.tr.* (**-ies, -ied**) try (a defendant or lawsuit) a second or further time. □□ **retrial** *n.*

retsina /retˈsiːnə/ *n.* a Greek white wine flavoured with resin. [mod. Gk]

retune /riːˈtjuːn/ *v.tr.* **1** tune (a musical instrument) again or differently. **2** tune (a radio etc.) to a different frequency.

returf /riːˈtɜːf/ *v.tr.* provide with new turf.

return /rɪˈtɜːn/ *v.* & *n.* —*v.* **1** *intr.* come or go back. **2** *tr.* bring or put or send back to the person or place etc. where originally belonging or obtained (*returned the fish to the river; have you returned my scissors?*). **3** *tr.* pay back or reciprocate; give in response (*decided not to return the compliment*). **4** *tr.* yield (a profit). **5** *tr.* say in reply; retort. **6** *tr.* (in cricket or tennis etc.) hit or send (the ball) back after receiving it. **7** *tr.* state or mention or describe officially, esp. in answer to a writ or formal demand. **8** *tr.* (of an electorate) elect as an MP, government, etc. **9** *tr.* Cards **a** lead (a suit) previously led or bid by a partner. **b** lead (a suit or card) after taking a trick. **10** *tr.* Archit. continue (a wall etc.) in a changed direction, esp. at right angles. —*n.* **1** the act or an instance of coming or going back. **2 a** the act or an instance of giving or sending or putting or paying back. **b** a thing given or sent back. **3** (in full **return ticket**) esp. *Brit.* a ticket for a journey to a place and back to the starting-point. **4** (in *sing.* or *pl.*) **a** the proceeds or profit of an undertaking. **b** the acquisition of these. **5** a formal report or statement compiled or submitted by order (*an income-tax return*). **6** (in full **return match** or **game**) a second match etc. between the same opponents. **7** *Electr.* a conductor bringing a current back to its source. **8** *Brit.* a sheriff's report on a writ. **9** esp. *Brit.* **a** a person's election as an MP etc. **b** a returning officer's announcement of this. **10** *Archit.* a part receding from the line of the front, e.g. the side of a house or of a window-opening. □ **by return (of post)** by the next available post in the return direction. **in return** as an exchange or reciprocal action. **many happy returns (of the day)** a greeting on a birthday. **return crease** *Cricket* each of two lines joining the popping-crease and bowling-crease at right angles to the bowling-crease and extending beyond it. **returning officer** *Brit.* an official conducting an election in a constituency and announcing the results. **return thanks** express thanks esp. in a grace at meals or in response to a toast or condolence. □□ **returnable** *adj.* **returner** *n.* **returnless** *adj.* [ME f. OF *returner* (as RE-, TURN)]

returnee /rɪtɜːˈniː/ *n.* a person who returns home from abroad, esp. after war service.

retuse /rɪˈtjuːs/ *adj.* esp. *Bot.* having a broad end with a central depression. [L *retundere retus-* (as RE-, *tundere* beat)]

retying *pres. part.* of RETIE.

retype /riːˈtaɪp/ *v.tr.* type again, esp. to correct errors.

Reuben /ˈruːbən/ **1** a Hebrew patriarch, eldest son of Jacob and Leah (Gen. 29: 32). **2** the tribe of Israel traditionally descended from him.

reunify /riːˈjuːnɪˌfaɪ/ *v.tr.* (**-ies, -ied**) restore (esp. separated territories) to a political unity. □□ **reunification** /-fɪˈkeɪʃ(ə)n/ *n.*

Réunion /ˌreruːnˈjɔ̃/ an island in the Indian Ocean east of Madagascar; pop. (est. 1988) 557,400; capital, Saint-Denis. A French

possession since 1638, the island became an overseas department of France in 1946 and an administrative region in 1974.

reunion /riːˈjuːnjən, -nɪən/ *n.* **1 a** the act or an instance of reuniting. **b** the condition of being reunited. **2** a social gathering esp. of people formerly associated. [F *réunion* or AL *reunio* f. L *reunire* unite (as RE-, UNION)]

reunite /ˌriːjuːˈnaɪt/ *v.tr.* & *intr.* bring or come back together.

reupholster /ˌriːʌpˈhəʊlstə(r)/ *v.tr.* upholster anew. □□ **reupholstery** *n.*

reuse *v.* & *n.* —*v.tr.* /riːˈjuːz/ use again or more than once. —*n.* /riːˈjuːs/ a second or further use. □□ **reusable** /-ˈjuːzəb(ə)l/ *adj.*

Reuter /ˈrɔɪtə(r)/, Paul Julius, Baron von (1816–99), pioneer in the use of the telegraph for international news. In 1851 he established in London the headquarters of a press service (Reuters) which still operates throughout the world.

reutilize /riːˈjuːtɪˌlaɪz/ *v.tr.* (also **-ise**) utilize again or for a different purpose. □□ **reutilization** /-ˈzeɪʃ(ə)n/ *n.*

Rev. *abbr.* **1** Reverend. **2** Revelation (New Testament).

rev /rev/ *n.* & *v.* colloq. —*n.* (in *pl.*) the number of revolutions of an engine per minute (*running at 3,000 revs*). —*v.* (**revved, revving**) **1** *intr.* (of an engine) revolve; turn over. **2** *tr.* (also *absol.*; often foll. by *up*) cause (an engine) to run quickly. □ **rev counter** = *revolution counter*. [abbr.]

revaccinate /riːˈvæksɪˌneɪt/ *v.tr.* vaccinate again. □□ **revaccination** /-ˈneɪʃ(ə)n/ *n.*

revalue /riːˈvæljuː/ *v.tr.* (**revalues, revalued, revaluing**) Econ. give a different value to, esp. give a higher value to (a currency) in relation to other currencies or gold (opp. DEVALUE). □□ **revaluation** /-ˈeɪʃ(ə)n/ *n.*

revamp /riːˈvæmp/ *v.tr.* **1** renovate, revise, improve. **2** patch up. [RE- + VAMP[1]]

revanchism /rɪˈvæntʃɪz(ə)m/ *n.* Polit. a policy of seeking to retaliate, esp. to recover lost territory. □□ **revanchist** *n.* & *adj.* [F *revanche* (as REVENGE)]

revarnish /riːˈvɑːnɪʃ/ *v.tr.* varnish again.

Revd *abbr.* Reverend.

reveal[1] /rɪˈviːl/ *v.tr.* **1** display or show; allow to appear. **2** (often as **revealing** *adj.*) disclose, divulge, betray (*revealed his plans; a revealing remark*). **3** *tr.* (in *refl.* or *passive*) come to sight or knowledge. **4** *Relig.* (esp. of God) make known by inspiration or supernatural means. □ **revealed religion** a religion based on revelation (opp. *natural religion*). □□ **revealable** *adj.* **revealer** *n.* **revealingly** *adv.* [ME f. OF *reveler* or L *revelare* (as RE-, *velum* veil)]

reveal[2] /rɪˈviːl/ *n.* an internal side surface of an opening or recess, esp. of a doorway or window-aperture. [obs. *revale* (v.) lower f. OF *revaler* f. *avaler* (as RE-, VAIL)]

reveille /rɪˈvælɪ, rɪˈvelɪ/ *n.* a military waking-signal sounded in the morning on a bugle or drums etc. [F *réveillez* imper. pl. of *réveiller* awaken (as RE-, *veiller* f. L *vigilare* keep watch)]

revel /ˈrev(ə)l/ *v.* & *n.* —*v.* (**revelled, revelling**; *US* **reveled, reveling**) **1** *intr.* have a good time; be extravagantly festive. **2** *intr.* (foll. by *in*) take keen delight in. **3** *tr.* (foll. by *away*) throw away (money or time) in revelry. —*n.* (in *sing.* or *pl.*) the act or an instance of revelling. □□ **reveller** *n.* **revelry** *n.* (pl. **-ies**). [ME f. OF *reveler* riot f. L *rebellare* REBEL *v.*]

revelation /ˌrevəˈleɪʃ(ə)n/ *n.* **1 a** the act or an instance of revealing, esp. the supposed disclosure of knowledge to humankind by a divine or supernatural agency. **b** knowledge disclosed in this way. **2** a striking disclosure (*it was a revelation to me*). **3** (**Revelation** or colloq. **Revelations**) (in full **the Revelation of St John the Divine**) the last book of the New Testament (see APOCALYPSE 1) describing visions of heaven. □□ **revelational** *adj.* [ME f. OF *revelation* or LL *revelatio* (as REVEAL[1])]

revelationist /ˌrevəˈleɪʃənɪst/ *n.* a believer in divine revelation.

revelatory /ˌrevəˈleɪtərɪ/ *adj.* serving to reveal, esp. something significant. [L *revelare*: see REVEAL[1]]

revenant /ˈrevənənt/ *n.* a person who has returned, esp. supposedly from the dead. [F, pres. part. of *revenir*: see REVENUE]

revenge /rɪˈvendʒ/ *n.* & *v.* —*n.* **1** retaliation for an offence or injury. **2** an act of retaliation. **3** the desire for this; a vindictive feeling. **4** (in games) a chance to win after an earlier defeat.

—*v.* **1** *tr.* (in *refl.* or *passive*; often foll. by *on*, *upon*) inflict retaliation for an offence. **2** *tr.* take revenge for (an offence). **3** *tr.* avenge (a person). **4** *intr.* take vengeance. □□ **revenger** *n.* [ME f. OF *revenger*, *revencher* f. LL *revindicare* (as RE-, *vindicare* lay claim to)]

revengeful /rɪ'vendʒfʊl/ *adj.* eager for revenge. □□ **revengefully** *adv.* **revengefulness** *n.*

revenue /'revə,njuː/ *n.* **1 a** income, esp. of a large amount, from any source. **b** (in *pl.*) items constituting this. **2** a State's annual income from which public expenses are met. **3** the department of the civil service collecting this. □ **revenue tax** a tax imposed to raise revenue, rather than to affect trade. [ME f. OF *revenu(e)* past part. of *revenir* f. L *revenire* return (as RE-, *venire* come)]

reverb /rɪ'vɜːb, 'riːvɜːb/ *n. Mus. colloq.* **1** reverberation. **2** a device to produce this. [abbr.]

reverberate /rɪ'vɜːbə,reɪt/ *v.* **1 a** *intr.* (of sound, light, or heat) be returned or echoed or reflected repeatedly. **b** *tr.* return (a sound etc.) in this way. **2** *intr.* (of a story, rumour, etc.) be heard much or repeatedly. □ **reverberating furnace** a furnace constructed to throw heat back on to the substance exposed to it. □□ **reverberant** *adj.* **reverberantly** *adv.* **reverberation** /-'reɪʃ(ə)n/ *n.* **reverberative** /-rətɪv/ *adj.* **reverberator** *n.* **reverberatory** /-rətəri/ *adj.* [L *reverberare* (as RE-, *verberare* lash f. *verbera* (pl.) scourge)]

Revere /rɪ'vɪə(r)/, Paul (1735–1818), American patriot, famous for his midnight ride from Charlestown to Lexington in April 1775 to warn fellow American revolutionaries of the approach of British troops from Boston.

revere /rɪ'vɪə(r)/ *v.tr.* hold in deep and usu. affectionate or religious respect; venerate. [F *révérer* or L *reverēri* (as RE-, *verēri* fear)]

reverence /'revərəns/ *n.* & *v.* —*n.* **1 a** the act of revering or the state of being revered (*hold in reverence*; *feel reverence for*). **b** the capacity for revering (*lacks reverence*). **2** *archaic* a gesture showing that one reveres; a bow or curtsy. **3** (**Reverence**) a title used of or to some members of the clergy. —*v.tr.* regard or treat with reverence. [ME f. OF f. L *reverentia* (as REVERE)]

reverend /'revərənd/ *adj.* & *n.* —*adj.* (esp. as the title of a clergyman) deserving reverence. —*n. colloq.* a clergyman. □ **Most Reverend** the title of an archbishop or an Irish Roman Catholic bishop. **Reverend Mother** the title of the Mother Superior of a convent. **Right Reverend** the title of a bishop. **Very Reverend** the title of a dean etc. [ME f. OF *reverend* or L *reverendus* gerundive of *reverēri*: see REVERE]

reverent /'revərənt/ *adj.* feeling or showing reverence. □□ **reverently** *adv.* [ME f. L *reverens* (as REVERE)]

reverential /,revə'renʃ(ə)l/ *n.* of the nature of, due to, or characterized by reverence. □□ **reverentially** *adv.* [med.L *reverentialis* (as REVERE)]

reverie /'revəri/ *n.* **1** a fit of abstracted musing (*was lost in a reverie*). **2** *archaic* a fantastic notion or theory; a delusion. **3** *Mus.* an instrumental piece suggesting a dreamy or musing state. [obs. F *resverie* f. OF *reverie* rejoicing, revelry f. *rever* be delirious, of unkn. orig.]

revers /rɪ'vɪə(r)/ *n.* (*pl.* same /-'vɪəz/) **1** the turned-back edge of a garment revealing the under-surface. **2** the material on this surface. [F, = REVERSE]

reverse /rɪ'vɜːs/ *v.*, *adj.*, & *n.* —*v.* **1** *tr.* turn the other way round or up or inside out. **2** *tr.* change to the opposite character or effect (*reversed the decision*). **3** *intr.* & *tr.* travel or cause to travel backwards. **4** *tr.* make (an engine etc.) work in a contrary direction. **5** *tr.* revoke or annul (a decree, act, etc.). **6** *intr.* (of a dancer, esp. in a waltz) revolve in the opposite direction. —*adj.* **1** placed or turned in an opposite direction or position. **2** opposite or contrary in character or order; inverted. —*n.* **1** the opposite or contrary (*the reverse is the case*; *is the reverse of the truth*). **2** the contrary of the usual manner. **3** an occurrence of misfortune; a disaster, esp. a defeat in battle (*suffered a reverse*). **4** reverse gear or motion. **5** the reverse side of something. **6 a** the side of a coin or medal etc. bearing the secondary design. **b** this design (cf. OBVERSE). **7** the verso of a leaf. □ **reverse arms** hold a rifle with the butt upwards. **reverse the charges** *Brit.* make the recipient of a telephone call responsible for payment. **reverse**

gear a gear used to make a vehicle etc. travel backwards. **reversing light** a white light at the rear of a vehicle operated when the vehicle is in reverse gear. **reverse Polish notation** see *Polish notation*. **reverse strata** *Geol.* a fault in which the overlying side of a mass of rock is displaced upward in relation to the underlying side. □□ **reversal** *n.* **reversely** *adv.* **reverser** *n.* **reversible** *adj.* **reversibility** /-'bɪlɪtɪ/ *n.* **reversibly** *adv.* [ME f. OF *revers* (n.), *reverser* (v.), f. L *revertere revers-* (as RE-, *vertere* turn)]

reversion /rɪ'vɜːʃ(ə)n/ *n.* **1 a** the legal right (esp. of the original owner, or his or her heirs) to possess or succeed to property on the death of the present possessor. **b** property to which a person has such a right. **2** *Biol.* a return to ancestral type. **3** a return to a previous state, habit, etc. **4** a sum payable on a person's death, esp. by way of life insurance. □□ **reversional** *adj.* **reversionary** *adj.* [ME f. OF *reversion* or L *reversio* (as REVERSE)]

revert /rɪ'vɜːt/ *v.* **1** *intr.* (foll. by *to*) return to a former state, practice, opinion, etc. **2** *intr.* (of property, an office, etc.) return by reversion. **3** *intr.* fall back into a wild state. **4** *tr.* turn (one's eyes or steps) back. □□ **reverter** *n.* (in sense 2). [ME f. OF *revertir* or L *revertere* (as REVERSE)]

revertible /rɪ'vɜːtɪb(ə)l/ *adj.* (of property) subject to reversion.

revet /rɪ'vet/ *v.tr.* (**revetted**, **revetting**) face (a rampart, wall, etc.) with masonry, esp. in fortification. [F *revêtir* f. OF *revestir* f. LL *revestire* (as RE-, *vestire* clothe f. *vestis*)]

revetment /rɪ'vetmənt/ *n.* a retaining wall or facing. [F *revêtement* (as REVET)]

review /rɪ'vjuː/ *n.* & *v.* —*n.* **1** a general survey or assessment of a subject or thing. **2** a retrospect or survey of the past. **3** revision or reconsideration (*is under review*). **4** a display and formal inspection of troops etc. **5** a published account or criticism of a book, play, etc. **6** a periodical publication with critical articles on current events, the arts, etc. **7** a second view. —*v.tr.* **1** survey or look back on. **2** reconsider or revise. **3** hold a review of (troops etc.). **4** write a review of (a book, play, etc.). **5** view again. □ **court of review** a court before which sentences etc. come for revision. □□ **reviewable** *adj.* **reviewal** *n.* **reviewer** *n.* [obs. F *reveue* f. *revoir* (as RE-, *voir* see)]

revile /rɪ'vaɪl/ *v.* **1** *tr.* abuse; criticize abusively. **2** *intr.* talk abusively; rail. □□ **revilement** *n.* **reviler** *n.* **reviling** *n.* [ME f. OF *reviler* (as RE-, VILE)]

revise /rɪ'vaɪz/ *v.* & *n.* —*v.tr.* **1** examine or re-examine and improve or amend (esp. written or printed matter). **2** consider and alter (an opinion etc.). **3** (also *absol.*) *Brit.* read again (work learnt or done) to improve one's knowledge, esp. for an examination. —*n. Printing* a proof-sheet including corrections made in an earlier proof. □□ **Revised Standard Version** the revision published in 1946, 1952, 1957 of the American Standard Version (the latter was based on the English RV and published in 1901). **Revised Version** the revision published in 1881, 1885, 1895 of the Authorized Version of the Bible. □□ **revisable** *adj.* **revisal** *n.* **reviser** *n.* **revisory** *adj.* [F *réviser* look at, or L *revisere* (as RE-, *visere* intensive of *vidēre vis-* see)]

revision /rɪ'vɪʒ(ə)n/ *n.* **1** the act or an instance of revising; the process of being revised. **2** a revised edition or form. □□ **revisionary** *adj.* [OF *revision* or LL *revisio* (as REVISE)]

revisionism /rɪ'vɪʒə,nɪz(ə)m/ *n.* often *derog.* a policy of revision or modification, esp. of Marxism on evolutionary socialist (rather than revolutionary) or pluralist principles. □□ **revisionist** *n.* & *adj.*

revisit /riː'vɪzɪt/ *v.tr.* (**revisited**, **revisiting**) visit again.

revitalize /riː'vaɪtə,laɪz/ *v.tr.* (also **-ise**) imbue with new life and vitality. □□ **revitalization** /-'zeɪʃ(ə)n/ *n.*

revival /rɪ'vaɪv(ə)l/ *n.* **1** the act or an instance of reviving; the process of being revived. **2** a new production of an old play etc. **3** a revived use of an old practice, custom, etc. **4 a** a reawakening of religious fervour. **b** a series of evangelistic meetings to promote this. **5** restoration to bodily or mental vigour or to life or consciousness.

revivalism /rɪ'vaɪvə,lɪz(ə)m/ *n.* belief in or the promotion of a revival, esp. of religious fervour. □□ **revivalist** *n.* **revivalistic** /-'lɪstɪk/ *adj.*

revive /rɪ'vaɪv/ *v.intr.* & *tr.* **1** come or bring back to consciousness or life or strength. **2** come or bring back to existence, use, notice, etc. □□ **revivable** *adj.* [ME f. OF *revivre* or LL *revivere* (as RE-, L *vivere* live)]

reviver /rɪˈvaɪvə(r)/ *n.* **1** a person or thing that revives. **2** *colloq.* a stimulating drink. **3** a preparation used for restoring faded colours etc.

revivify /rɪˈvɪvɪˌfaɪ/ *v.tr.* (**-ies, -ied**) restore to animation, activity, vigour, or life. □□ **revivification** /-fɪˈkeɪʃ(ə)n/ *n.* [F *revivifier* or LL *revivificare* (as RE-, VIVIFY)]

revoke /rɪˈvəʊk/ *v. & n.* —*v.* **1** *tr.* rescind, withdraw, or cancel (a decree or promise etc.). **2** *intr. Cards* fail to follow suit when able to do so. —*n. Cards* the act of revoking. □□ **revocable** /ˈrevəkəb(ə)l/ *adj.* **revocability** /ˌrevəkəˈbɪlɪtɪ/ *n.* **revocation** /ˌrevəˈkeɪʃ(ə)n/ *n.* **revocatory** /ˈrevəkətərɪ/ *adj.* **revoker** *n.* [ME f. OF *revoquer* or L *revocare* (as RE-, *vocare* call)]

revolt /rɪˈvəʊlt/ *v. & n.* —*v.* **1** *intr.* **a** rise in rebellion against authority. **b** (as **revolted** *adj.*) having revolted. **2 a** *tr.* (often in *passive*) affect with strong disgust; nauseate (*was revolted by the thought of it*). **b** *intr.* (often foll. by *at, against*) feel strong disgust. —*n.* **1** an act of rebelling. **2** a state of insurrection (*in revolt*). **3** a sense of loathing. **4** a mood of protest or defiance. [F *révolter* f. It. *rivoltare* ult. f. L *revolvere* (as REVOLVE)]

revolting /rɪˈvəʊltɪŋ/ *adj.* disgusting, horrible. □□ **revoltingly** *adv.*

revolute /ˈrevəˌluːt/ *adj. Bot.* etc. having a rolled-back edge. [L *revolutus* past part. of *revolvere*: see REVOLVE]

revolution /ˌrevəˈluːʃ(ə)n/ *n.* **1 a** the forcible overthrow of a government or social order, in favour of a new system; (in English history) the Glorious Revolution of 1688 (see GLORIOUS); (in American history) the overthrow of British supremacy (see WAR OF AMERICAN INDEPENDENCE); (in French history) the French Revolution (see separate entry); (in Russian history) a series of revolutionary movements in Russia in 1917, beginning with a revolt of workers, peasants, and soldiers in March (February Old Style, whence 'February Revolution') and the formation of a provisional government, and culminating in the Bolshevik Revolution in November (October Old Style, whence 'October Revolution') which led to the establishment of the USSR. **b** (in Marxism) the replacement of one ruling class by another; the class struggle which is expected to lead to political change and the triumph of communism. **2** any fundamental change or reversal of conditions. **3** the act or an instance of revolving. **4 a** motion in orbit or a circular course or round an axis or centre; rotation. **b** the single completion of an orbit or rotation. **c** the time taken for this. **5 a** cyclic recurrence. □ **revolution counter** a device for indicating the number or rate of revolutions of an engine etc. □□ **revolutionism** *n.* **revolutionist** *n.* [ME f. OF *revolution* or LL *revolutio* (as REVOLVE)]

revolutionary /ˌrevəˈluːʃənərɪ/ *adj. & n.* —*adj.* **1** involving great and often violent change. **2** of or causing political revolution. **3** (**Revolutionary**) of or relating to a particular revolution, esp. the War of American Independence. —*n.* (*pl.* **-ies**) an instigator or supporter of political revolution.

revolutionize /ˌrevəˈluːʃəˌnaɪz/ *v.tr.* (also **-ise**) introduce fundamental change to.

revolve /rɪˈvɒlv/ *v.* **1** *intr. & tr.* turn or cause to turn round, esp. on an axis; rotate. **2** *intr.* move in a circular orbit. **3** *tr.* ponder (a problem etc.) in the mind. □ **revolving credit** credit that is automatically renewed as debts are paid off. **revolving door** a door with usu. four partitions turning round a central axis. □□ **revolvable** *adj.* [ME f. L *revolvere* (as RE-, *volvere* roll)]

revolver /rɪˈvɒlvə(r)/ *n.* a pistol with revolving chambers enabling several shots to be fired without reloading.

revue /rɪˈvjuː/ *n.* a theatrical entertainment of a series of short items—songs, dances, sketches, monologues—which are normally unrelated. The players reappear in various items throughout the programme, and the material is usually topical. In France revues were seen in the 1820s, but it was not until the end of the 19th c. that they spread to England and America. The genre declined largely because satirical programmes on television were able to achieve a topicality impossible in the theatre. [F, = REVIEW *n.*]

revulsion /rɪˈvʌlʃ(ə)n/ *n.* **1** abhorrence; a sense of loathing. **2** a sudden violent change of feeling. **3** a sudden reaction in taste, fortune, trade, etc. **4** *Med.* counterirritation; the treatment of one disordered organ etc. by acting upon another. [F *revulsion* or L *revulsio* (as RE-, *vellere vuls-* pull)]

revulsive /rɪˈvʌlsɪv/ *adj. & n. Med.* —*adj.* producing revulsion. —*n.* a revulsive substance.

reward /rɪˈwɔːd/ *n. & v.* **1 a** a return or recompense for service or merit. **b** requital for good or evil; retribution. **2** a sum offered for the detection of a criminal, the restoration of lost property, etc. —*v.tr.* give a reward to (a person) or for (a service etc.). □□ **rewardless** *adj.* [ME f. AF, ONF *reward* = OF *reguard* REGARD]

rewarding /rɪˈwɔːdɪŋ/ *adj.* (of an activity etc.) well worth doing; providing satisfaction. □□ **rewardingly** *adv.*

rewarewa /ˈreɪwəˌreɪwə/ *n.* a tall red-flowered tree, *Knightia excelsa*, of New Zealand. [Maori]

rewash /riːˈwɒʃ/ *v.tr.* wash again.

reweigh /riːˈweɪ/ *v.tr.* weigh again.

rewind /riːˈwaɪnd/ *v.tr.* (*past* and *past part.* **rewound**) wind (a film or tape etc.) back to the beginning. □□ **rewinder** *n.*

rewire /riːˈwaɪə(r)/ *v.tr.* provide (a building etc.) with new wiring. □□ **rewirable** *adj.*

reword /riːˈwɜːd/ *v.tr.* change the wording of.

rewound *past* and *past part.* of REWIND.

rewrap /riːˈræp/ *v.tr.* (**rewrapped, rewrapping**) wrap again or differently.

rewrite *v. & n.* —*v.tr.* /riːˈraɪt/ (*past* **rewrote**; *past part.* **rewritten**) write again or differently. —*n.* /ˈriːraɪt/ **1** the act or an instance of rewriting. **2** a thing rewritten.

Rex /reks/ *n.* the reigning king (following a name or in the titles of lawsuits, e.g. *Rex v. Jones* the Crown versus Jones). [L]

Rexine /ˈreksiːn/ *n. propr.* an artificial leather used in upholstery, bookbinding, etc. [20th c.: orig. unkn.]

Reykjavik /ˈreɪkjəvɪk/ the capital of Iceland; pop. (1987) 93,245.

Reynard /ˈrenɑːd, ˈreɪ-/ *n.* a fox (esp. as a proper name in stories). □ **Reynard the Fox** the central character in the *Roman de Renart*, a series of popular satirical fables written in France at various times *c.*1175–1250.

Reynolds /ˈren(ə)ldz/, Sir Joshua (1723–92), English painter and first President of the Royal Academy. He spent three years in Italy (1749–52) studying antique, Renaissance, and Baroque art, and laying the foundations for the philosophy of art that he would develop practically in his portraits and theoretically in the *Discourses* delivered at the Royal Academy between 1769 and 1790—the lofty calling of the artist and the intellectual nobility of painting. These concerns are evident in his formal portraits where the dignity of history painting adds an extra dimension of solemnity to the sitter (e.g. *Mrs Siddons as the Tragic Muse*). As President of the Royal Academy and a member of London's intellectual circle he did a great deal to advance the whole profession of painting in England.

Reynolds number /ˈrenəldz/ *n. Physics* a quantity indicating the degree of turbulence of flow past an obstacle etc. [O. *Reynolds*, Engl. physicist d. 1912]

Rf *symb. Chem.* the element rutherfordium.

r.f. *abbr.* radio frequency.

RFA *abbr.* (in the UK) Royal Fleet Auxiliary.

RFC *abbr.* **1** Rugby Football Club. **2** *hist.* Royal Flying Corps.

RGS *abbr.* Royal Geographical Society.

Rh[1] *symb. Chem.* the element rhodium.

Rh[2] *abbr.* **1** Rhesus. **2** Rhesus factor.

r.h. *abbr.* right hand.

RHA *abbr.* (in the UK) Royal Horse Artillery.

rhabdomancy /ˈræbdəˌmænsɪ/ *n.* the use of a divining-rod, esp. for discovering subterranean water or mineral ore. [Gk *rhabdomanteia* f. *rhabdos* rod: see -MANCY]

Rhadamanthine /ˌrædəˈmænθɪn/ *adj.* stern and incorruptible in judgement, like Rhadamanthus.

Rhadamanthus /ˌrædəˈmænθəs/ *Gk Mythol.* the son of Zeus and Europa, and brother of Minos. He did not die but went to

Elysium where he is represented as a ruler and judge of the dead, renowned for his justice.

Rhaeto-Romance /ˌriːtəʊrəʊˈmæns/ adj. & n. (also **Rhaeto-Romanic** /-ˈmænɪk/) —adj. of or in any of the Romance dialects of SE Switzerland and Tyrol, esp. Romansh and Ladin. —n. any of these dialects. [L *Rhaetus* of Rhaetia in the Alps + ROMANIC]

rhapsode /ˈræpsəʊd/ n. a reciter of epic poems, esp. of Homer in ancient Greece. [Gk *rhapsōidos* f. *rhaptō* stitch + *ōidē* song, ODE]

rhapsodist /ˈræpsədɪst/ n. **1** a person who rhapsodizes. **2** = RHAPSODE.

rhapsodize /ˈræpsəˌdaɪz/ v.intr. (also **-ise**) talk or write rhapsodies.

rhapsody /ˈræpsədɪ/ n. (pl. **-ies**) **1** an enthusiastic or extravagant utterance or composition. **2** Mus. a piece of music in one extended movement, usu. emotional in character. **3** Gk Antiq. an epic poem, or part of it, of a length for one recitation. □□ **rhapsodic** /ræpˈsɒdɪk/ adj. **rhapsodical** /ræpˈsɒdɪk(ə)l/ adj. (in senses 1, 2). [L *rhapsodia* f. Gk *rhapsōidia* (as RHAPSODE)]

rhatany /ˈrætənɪ/ n. (pl. **-ies**) **1** either of two American shrubs, *Krameria trianda* and *K. argentea*, having an astringent root when dried. **2** the root of either of these. [mod.L *rhatania* f. Port. *ratanha*, Sp. *ratania*, f. Quechua *rataña*]

Rhea /ˈriːə/ Gk Mythol. one of the Titans, wife of Cronus and mother of Zeus, Demeter, Poseidon, and Hades.

rhea /ˈriːə/ n. any of several S. American flightless birds of the family Rheidae, like but smaller than an ostrich. [mod.L genus name f. L f. Gk RHEA]

rhebok var. of REEBOK.

Rheims see REIMS.

Rhein see RHINE.

Rhenish /ˈriːnɪʃ, ˈren-/ adj. & n. —adj. of the Rhine and the regions adjoining it. —n. wine from this area. [ME *rynis, rynisch* etc., f. AF *reneis*, OF *r(a)inois* f. L *Rhenanus* f. *Rhenus* Rhine]

Rhenish Slate Mountains a mountainous region of the Rhineland-Palatinate on the western frontier of Germany.

rhenium /ˈriːnɪəm/ n. Chem. a rare metallic element of the manganese group, discovered in 1925. It is not found uncombined in nature. The metal and its alloys have a number of specialized uses, including in the manufacture of superconducting alloys. ¶ Symb.: **Re**; atomic number 75. [mod.L f. L *Rhenus* Rhine]

rheology /riːˈɒlədʒɪ/ n. the science dealing with the flow and deformation of matter. □□ **rheological** /-əˈlɒdʒɪk(ə)l/ adj. **rheologist** n. [Gk *rheos* stream + -LOGY]

rheostat /ˈriːəˌstæt/ n. Electr. an instrument used to control a current by varying the resistance. □□ **rheostatic** /-ˈstætɪk/ adj. [Gk *rheos* stream + -STAT]

rhesus /ˈriːsəs/ n. (in full **rhesus monkey**) a small catarrhine monkey, *Macaca mulatta*, common in N. India. □ **rhesus baby** an infant with a haemolytic disorder caused by the incompatibility of its own rhesus-positive blood with its mother's rhesus-negative blood. **rhesus factor** an antigen occurring on the red blood cells of most humans and some other primates (as in the rhesus monkey, in which it was first observed). **rhesus negative** lacking the rhesus factor. **rhesus positive** having the rhesus factor. [mod.L, arbitrary use of L *Rhesus* f. Gk *Rhēsos*, mythical king of Thrace]

rhetor /ˈriːtə(r)/ n. **1** an ancient Greek or Roman teacher or professor of rhetoric. **2** usu. derog. an orator. [ME f. LL *rethor* f. L *rhetor* f. Gk *rhētōr*]

rhetoric /ˈretərɪk/ n. **1** the art of effective or persuasive speaking or writing. **2** language designed to persuade or impress (often with an implication of insincerity or exaggeration etc.). [ME f. OF *rethorique* f. L *rhetorica, -ice* f. Gk *rhētorikē (tekhnē)* (art) of rhetoric (as RHETOR)]

rhetorical /rɪˈtɒrɪk(ə)l/ adj. **1** expressed with a view to persuasive or impressive effect; artificial or extravagant in language. **2** of the nature of rhetoric. **3 a** of or relating to the art of rhetoric. **b** given to rhetoric; oratorical. □ **rhetorical**

question a question asked not for information but to produce an effect, e.g. *who cares?* for *nobody cares.* □□ **rhetorically** adv. [ME f. L *rhetoricus* f. Gk *rhētorikos* (as RHETOR)]

rhetorician /ˌretəˈrɪʃ(ə)n/ n. **1** an orator. **2** a teacher of rhetoric. **3** a rhetorical speaker or writer. [ME f. OF *rethoricien* (as RHETORICAL)]

rheum /ruːm/ n. a watery discharge from a mucous membrane, esp. of the eyes or nose. [ME f. OF *reume* ult. f. Gk *rheuma -atos* stream f. *rheō* flow]

rheumatic /ruːˈmætɪk/ adj. & n. —adj. **1** of, relating to, or suffering from rheumatism. **2** producing or produced by rheumatism. —n. a person suffering from rheumatism. □ **rheumatic fever** a non-infectious fever with inflammation and pain in the joints. □□ **rheumatically** adv. **rheumaticky** adj. colloq. [ME f. OF *reumatique* or L *rheumaticus* f. Gk *rheumatikos* (as RHEUM)]

rheumatics /ruːˈmætɪks/ n.pl. (treated as sing.; often prec. by the) colloq. rheumatism.

rheumatism /ˈruːməˌtɪz(ə)m/ n. any disease marked by inflammation and pain in the joints, muscles, or fibrous tissue, esp. rheumatoid arthritis. [F *rhumatisme* or L *rheumatismus* f. Gk *rheumatismos* f. *rheumatizō* f. *rheuma* stream]

rheumatoid /ˈruːməˌtɔɪd/ adj. having the character of rheumatism. □ **rheumatoid arthritis** a chronic progressive disease causing inflammation and stiffening of the joints.

rheumatology /ˌruːməˈtɒlədʒɪ/ n. the study of rheumatic diseases. □□ **rheumatological** /-təˈlɒdʒɪk(ə)l/ adj. **rheumatologist** n.

RHG abbr. (in the UK) Royal Horse Guards.

rhinal /ˈraɪn(ə)l/ adj. Anat. of a nostril or the nose. [Gk *rhis rhin-*: see RHINO-]

Rhine /raɪn/ (German **Rhein**) a river of Western Europe flowing from the Swiss Alps to the North Sea in The Netherlands. Most of its course (1,320 km, 820 miles) lies within western Germany and it forms part of an important inland waterway network.

Rhineland /ˈraɪnlænd/ the region of western Germany through which the Rhine flows, especially the part to the west of the river. The area was demilitarized as part of the Versailles Treaty in 1919 but was reoccupied by Hitler in 1936. □ **Rhineland-Palatinate** (German **Rheinland-Pfalz** /-fælts/) a 'Land' (State) in the west of Germany; pop. (1987) 3,606,000; capital, Mainz.

rhinestone /ˈraɪnstəʊn/ n. an imitation diamond. [*Rhine*, river and region in Germany + STONE]

rhinitis /raɪˈnaɪtɪs/ n. inflammation of the mucous membrane of the nose. [Gk *rhis rhinos* nose]

rhino[1] /ˈraɪnəʊ/ n. (pl. same or **-os**) colloq. a rhinoceros. [abbr.]

rhino[2] /ˈraɪnəʊ/ n. Brit. sl. money. [17th c.: orig. unkn.]

rhino- /ˈraɪnəʊ/ comb. form Anat. the nose. [Gk *rhis rhinos* nostril, nose]

rhinoceros /raɪˈnɒsərəs/ n. (pl. same or **rhinoceroses**) any of various large thick-skinned plant-eating ungulates of the family Rhinocerotidae of Africa and S. Asia, with one horn or in some cases two horns on the nose and plated or folded skin. □ **rhinoceros bird** = ox-pecker. **rhinoceros horn** a mass of keratinized fibres, reputed to have medicinal or aphrodisiac powers. □□ **rhinocerotic** /raɪˌnɒsəˈrɒtɪk/ adj. [ME f. L f. Gk *rhinokerōs* (as RHINO-, *keras* horn)]

rhinopharyngeal /ˌraɪnəʊfəˈrɪndʒɪəl/ adj. of or relating to the nose and pharynx.

rhinoplasty /ˈraɪnəʊˌplæstɪ/ n. plastic surgery of the nose. □□ **rhinoplastic** adj.

rhizo- /ˈraɪzəʊ/ comb. form Bot. a root. [Gk *rhiza* root]

rhizocarp /ˈraɪzəʊˌkɑːp/ n. a plant with a perennial root but stems that wither. [RHIZO- + Gk *karpos* fruit]

rhizoid /ˈraɪzɔɪd/ adj. & n. Bot. —adj. rootlike. —n. a root-hair or filament in mosses, ferns, etc.

rhizome /ˈraɪzəʊm/ n. an underground rootlike stem bearing both roots and shoots. [Gk *rhizōma* f. *rhizoō* take root (as RHIZO-)]

rhizopod /ˈraɪzəʊˌpɒd/ n. any protozoa of the class Rhizopodea, forming rootlike pseudopodia.

rho /rəʊ/ n. the seventeenth letter of the Greek alphabet (P, ρ). [Gk]

rhodamine /ˈrəʊdəmɪn/ n. Chem. any of various red synthetic dyes used to colour textiles. [RHODO- + AMINE]

Rhode Island /rəʊd/ a State in the north-eastern US, on the Atlantic coast, settled from England in the 17th c.; pop. (est. 1985) 947,150; capital, Providence. It was one of the original 13 States of the US. □ **Rhode Island Red** an orig. American breed of reddish-black domestic fowl.

Rhodes[1] /rəʊdz/ the largest of the Dodecanese Islands in the SE Aegean, off the Turkish coast, acquired by Italy from Turkey in 1912 and returned to Greece in 1947; pop. (1971) 66,606.

Rhodes[2] /rəʊdz/, Cecil John (1853–1902), South African statesman. Born in Britain, Rhodes went to South Africa for reasons of health and made a huge fortune in diamond mining. A convinced imperialist, he was instrumental in extending British territory in South Africa and in the development of Rhodesia, and served as Premier of the Cape Colony from 1890 until forced to resign in 1896 as a result of implication in the Jameson Raid. Much of his fortune was used to set up the system of Rhodes Scholarships to allow students from the Empire, the United States, and Germany to study at Oxford University.

Rhodes[3] /rəʊdz/, Wilfred (1877–1973), English all-round cricketer, who played for Yorkshire and for England in a career that extended from 1898 to 1930. He achieved the 'double' of 1000 runs and 100 wickets in the same season a record number of sixteen times between 1903 and 1926.

Rhodesia /rəʊˈdiːʃə/ **1** the former name of a large area of southern Africa south of Zaïre, divided into Northern Rhodesia and Southern Rhodesia. The region was developed by Sir Cecil Rhodes and the British South Africa Company, which administered it until Southern Rhodesia became a self-governing British colony in 1923 and Northern Rhodesia a British protectorate in 1924. From 1953 to 1963 Northern and Southern Rhodesia were united with Nyasaland (now Malawi) to form the Federation of Rhodesia and Nyasaland. **2** the name adopted by Southern Rhodesia when Northern Rhodesia left the Federation in 1963 to become the independent republic of Zambia. For its subsequent history see ZIMBABWE. □□ **Rhodesian** adj. & n.

rhodium /ˈrəʊdɪəm/ n. Chem. a hard white metallic element of the platinum group, usually found associated with platinum. It is chiefly used in alloys with platinum, where it increases hardness, but the pure metal is used in electroplating for decorative purposes and to form reflecting surfaces. ¶ Symb.: **Rh**; atomic number 45. [Gk rhodon rose (from the colour of the solution of its salts)]

rhodo- /ˈrəʊdəʊ/ comb. form esp. Mineral. & Chem. rose-coloured. [Gk rhodon rose]

rhodochrosite /ˌrəʊdəʊˈkrəʊsaɪt/ n. a mineral form of manganese carbonate occurring in rose-red crystals. [Gk rhodokhrous rose-coloured]

rhododendron /ˌrəʊdəˈdendrən/ n. any evergreen shrub of the genus Rhododendron, with large clusters of trumpet-shaped flowers. [L, = oleander, f. Gk (as RHODO-, dendron tree)]

Rhodope Mountains /ˈrɒdəpɪ/ a range of mountains on the frontier between Bulgaria and Greece, rising to a height of 2,925 m (9,596 ft.) at Musala.

rhodopsin /rəʊˈdɒpsɪn/ n. = visual purple. [Gk rhodon rose + opsis sight]

rhodora /rəˈdɔːrə/ n. a N. American pink-flowered shrub, Rhodora canadense. [mod.L f. L plant-name f. Gk rhodon rose]

rhomb /rɒm/ n. = RHOMBUS. □□ **rhombic** adj. [F rhombe or L rhombus]

rhombi pl. of RHOMBUS.

rhombohedron /ˌrɒmbəˈhiːdrən/ n. (pl. **-hedrons** or **-hedra** /-drə/) **1** a solid bounded by six equal rhombuses. **2** a crystal in this form. □□ **rhombohedral** adj. [RHOMBUS, after polyhedron etc.]

rhomboid /ˈrɒmbɔɪd/ adj. & n. —adj. (also **rhomboidal** /-ˈbɔɪd(ə)l/) having or nearly having the shape of a rhombus. —n. a quadrilateral of which only the opposite sides and angles are equal. [F rhomboïde or LL rhomboides f. Gk rhomboeidēs (as RHOMB)]

rhomboideus /rɒmˈbɔɪdɪəs/ n. (pl. **rhomboidei** /-dɪˌaɪ/) Anat. a muscle connecting the shoulder-blade to the vertebrae. [mod.L rhomboideus RHOMBOID]

rhombus /ˈrɒmbəs/ n. (pl. **rhombuses** or **rhombi** /-baɪ/) Geom. a parallelogram with oblique angles and equal sides. [L f. Gk rhombos]

Rhondda /ˈrɒndə/ a district of Mid Glamorgan, South Wales, formerly noted for the mining district which extended along the Rhondda Fawr and Rhondda Fach valleys.

Rhône /rəʊn/ a river rising in the Swiss Alps and flowing west and south 812 km (505 miles) through France to the Mediterranean Sea. The cities of Geneva, Lyons, and Avignon lie along its course.

RHS abbr. **1** Royal Historical Society. **2** Royal Horticultural Society. **3** Royal Humane Society.

rhubarb /ˈruːbɑːb/ n. **1 a** any of various plants of the genus Rheum, esp. R. rhaponticum, producing long fleshy dark-red leaf-stalks used cooked as food. **b** the leaf-stalks of this. (See below.) **2 a** a root of a Chinese and Tibetan plant of the genus Rheum. **b** a purgative made from this. **3 a** colloq. a murmurous conversation or noise, esp. the repetition of the word 'rhubarb' by crowd actors. **b** sl. nonsense; worthless stuff. **4** US sl. a heated dispute. [ME f. OF r(e)ubarbe, shortening of med.L r(h)eubarbarum, alt. (by assoc. with Gk rhēon rhubarb) of rhabarbarum foreign 'rha', ult. f. Gk rha + barbaros foreign]

The earliest use of rhubarb was medicinal; the dried rootstock, principally of Chinese species imported via Russia and the Levant, was employed as a purgative. Culinary use of the leaf-stalks (the plants now used are of hybrid origin) dates only from the mid-18th c., and it did not become popular until the introduction of forced rhubarb in the early 19th c.

rhumb /rʌm/ n. Naut. **1** any of the 32 points of the compass. **2** the angle between two successive compass-points. **3** (in full **rhumb-line**) **a** a line cutting all meridians at the same angle. **b** the line followed by a ship sailing in a fixed direction. [F rumb prob. f. Du. ruim room, assoc. with L rhombus: see RHOMBUS]

rhumba var. of RUMBA.

rhyme /raɪm/ n. & v. —n. **1** identity of sound between words or the endings of words, esp. in verse. **2** (in sing. or pl.) verse having rhymes. **3 a** the use of rhyme. **b** a poem having rhymes. **4** a word providing a rhyme. —v. **1** intr. **a** (of words or lines) produce a rhyme. **b** (foll. by with) act as a rhyme (with another). **2** intr. make or write rhymes; versify. **3** tr. put or make (a story etc.) into rhyme. **4** tr. (foll. by with) treat (a word) as rhyming with another. □ **rhyming slang** slang that replaces words by rhyming words or phrases, e.g. stairs by apples and pears, often with the rhyming element omitted (as in TITFER). **without rhyme or reason** lacking discernible sense or logic. □□ **rhymeless** adj. **rhymer** n. **rhymist** n. [ME rime f. OF rime f. med.L rithmus, rythmus f. L f. Gk rhuthmos RHYTHM]

rhymester /ˈraɪmstə(r)/ n. a writer of (esp. simple) rhymes.

rhyolite /ˈraɪəˌlaɪt/ n. a fine-grained volcanic rock of granitic composition. [G Rhyolit f. Gk rhuax lava-stream + lithos stone]

Rhys /riːs/, Jean (Gwendolen Rees Williams, ?1890–1970), British novelist and writer of short stories, born in Dominica. Her novels include Voyage in the Dark (1934) and Wide Sargasso Sea (1966). The latter, set in Dominica and Jamaica in the 1830s, presents the life of the mad Mrs Rochester from Charlotte Brontë's Jane Eyre, ending with her imprisonment in the attic in Thornfield Hall.

rhythm /ˈrɪð(ə)m/ n. **1** a measured flow of words and phrases in verse or prose determined by various relations of long and short or accented and unaccented syllables. **2** the aspect of musical composition concerned with periodical accent and the duration of notes. **3** Physiol. movement with a regular succession of strong and weak elements. **4** a regularly recurring sequence of events. **5** Art a harmonious correlation of parts. □ **rhythm and blues** popular music with a blues theme and a strong rhythm. **rhythm method** birth control by avoiding sexual intercourse when ovulation (which recurs regularly) is likely to occur. **rhythm section** the part of a dance band or jazz band mainly supplying rhythm, usu. consisting of piano, bass, and drums. □□ **rhythmless** adj. [F rhythme or L rhythmus f. Gk rhuthmos, rel. to rheō flow]

rhythmic /ˈrɪðmɪk/ adj. (also **rhythmical**) **1** relating to or characterized by rhythm. **2** regularly occurring. □□ **rhythmically** adv. [F rhythmique or L rhythmicus (as RHYTHM)]

rhythmicity /rɪðˈmɪsɪtɪ/ n. **1** rhythmical quality or character. **2** the capacity for maintaining a rhythm.

RI abbr. **1** King and Emperor. **2** Queen and Empress. **3** US Rhode Island (also in official postal use). **4** Royal Institute or Institution. [sense 1 f. L rex et imperator: sense 2 f. L regina et imperatrix]

ria /ˈrɪə/ n. Geog. a long narrow inlet formed by the partial submergence of a river valley. [Sp. ría estuary]

rial /ˈriːɑːl/ n. (also **riyal**) the monetary unit of Iran, equal to 100 dinars. [Pers. f. Arab. riyal f. Sp. real ROYAL]

Rialto /rɪˈæltəʊ/ an island and district of Venice, containing the old mercantile quarter. The Rialto Bridge, completed in 1591, crosses the Grand Canal in a single span between Rialto and San Marco islands.

rib /rɪb/ n. & v. —n. **1** each of the curved bones articulated in pairs to the spine and protecting the thoracic cavity and its organs. **2** a joint of meat from this part of an animal. **3** a ridge or long raised piece often of stronger or thicker material across a surface or through a structure serving to support or strengthen it. **4** any of a ship's transverse curved timbers forming the framework of the hull. **5** Knitting a combination of plain and purl stitches producing a ribbed somewhat elastic fabric. **6** each of the hinged rods supporting the fabric of an umbrella. **7** a vein of a leaf or an insect's wing. **8** Aeron. a structural member in an aerofoil. —v.tr. (**ribbed, ribbing**) **1** provide with ribs; act as the ribs of. **2** colloq. make fun of; tease. **3** mark with ridges. **4** plough with spaces between the furrows. □□ **ribless** adj. [OE rib, ribb f. Gmc]

RIBA abbr. Royal Institute of British Architects.

ribald /ˈrɪb(ə)ld/ adj. & n. —adj. (of language or its user) coarsely or disrespectfully humorous; scurrilous. —n. a user of ribald language. [ME (earlier sense 'low-born retainer') f. OF ribau(l)d f. riber pursue licentious pleasures f. Gmc]

ribaldry /ˈrɪbəldrɪ/ n. ribald talk or behaviour.

riband /ˈrɪbənd/ n. a ribbon. [ME f. OF riban, prob. f. a Gmc compound of BAND[1]]

Ribatejo /ˌriːbəˈteɪʒəʊ/ a fertile province of central Portugal in the lower valley of the Tagus River. The region is celebrated for its horses and fighting-bulls.

ribbed /rɪbd/ adj. having ribs or riblike markings.

Ribbentrop /ˈrɪbənˌtrɒp/, Joachim von (1893–1946), German Nazi: politician, a close associate of Hitler. He was Foreign Minister 1938–45.

ribbing /ˈrɪbɪŋ/ n. **1** ribs or a riblike structure. **2** colloq. the act or an instance of teasing.

ribbon /ˈrɪbən/ n. **1 a** a narrow strip or band of fabric, used esp. for trimming or decoration. **b** material in this form. **2** a ribbon of a special colour etc. worn to indicate some honour or membership of a sports team etc. **3** a long narrow strip of anything, e.g. impregnated material forming the inking agent in a typewriter. **4** (in pl.) ragged strips (torn to ribbons). □ **ribbon development** the building of houses along a main road, usu. one leading out of a town or village. **ribbon worm** a nemertean. □□ **ribboned** adj. [var. of RIBAND]

ribbonfish /ˈrɪbənfɪʃ/ n. any of various long slender flat fishes of the family Trachypteridae.

ribcage /ˈrɪbkeɪdʒ/ n. the wall of bones formed by the ribs round the chest.

Ribera /ˈriːbərə/, José (Jusepe) de (1591–1652), Spanish painter and etcher. In 1616 he settled in Naples (at that time a Spanish possession) where because of his small stature he gained the sobriquet Il Spagnoletto (the little Spaniard). His early paintings, chiefly of religious subjects and scenes of everyday life, show dramatic chiaroscuro effects, and his penchant for martyrdoms and the realistic depiction of torture prompted Byron's line 'Il

Spagnoletto tainted his brush with all the blood of all the Sainted'; his later paintings show a softer style and have a spiritual quality.

riboflavin /ˌraɪbəʊˈfleɪvɪn/ n. (also **riboflavine** /-viːn/) a vitamin of the B complex, found in liver, milk, and eggs, essential for energy production. Also called vitamin B₂. [RIBOSE + L flavus yellow]

ribonucleic acid /ˌraɪbənjuːˈkliːɪk/ n. a nucleic acid yielding ribose on hydrolysis. It is present in all cells and has several functions, one of which is to act as a 'messenger' carrying instructions from DNA for controlling the synthesis of proteins (see DNA). In some viruses it is RNA, not DNA, that carries the genetic information. ¶ Abbr.: RNA. [RIBOSE + NUCLEIC ACID]

ribose /ˈraɪbəʊs/ n. a sugar found in many nucleosides and in several vitamins and enzymes. [G, alt. f. Arabinose a related sugar]

ribosome /ˈraɪbəˌsəʊm/ n. Biochem. each of the minute particles consisting of RNA and associated proteins found in the cytoplasm of living cells, concerned with the synthesis of proteins. □□ **ribosomal** adj. [RIBONUCLEIC (ACID) + -SOME[3]]

ribwort /ˈrɪbwɜːt/ n. a kind of plantain (see PLANTAIN[1]) with long narrow ribbed leaves.

rice /raɪs/ n. & v.tr. **1** a swamp grass, Oryza sativa, cultivated in marshes, esp. in Asia. **2** the grains of this, used as cereal food. —v.tr. US sieve (cooked potatoes etc.) into thin strings. □ **rice-bowl** an area producing much rice. **rice-paper** edible paper made from the pith of an oriental tree and used for painting and in cookery. □□ **ricer** n. [ME rys f. OF ris f. It. riso, ult. f. Gk oruza, of oriental orig.]

ricercar /ˌriːʃeəˈkɑː(r)/ n. (also **ricercare** /-ˈkɑːre/) an elaborate contrapuntal instrumental composition in fugal or canonic style, esp. of the 16th–18th c. [It., = seek out]

rich /rɪtʃ/ adj. **1** having much wealth. **2** (often foll. by in, with) splendid, costly, elaborate (rich tapestries; rich with lace). **3** valuable (rich offerings). **4** copious, abundant, ample (a rich harvest; a rich supply of ideas). **5** (often foll. by in, with) (of soil or a region etc.) abounding in natural resources or means of production; fertile (rich in nutrients; rich with vines). **6** (of food or diet) containing a large proportion of fat, oil, eggs, spice, etc. **7** (of the mixture in an internal-combustion engine) containing a high proportion of fuel. **8** (of colour or sound or smell) mellow and deep, strong and full. **9 a** (of an incident or assertion etc.) highly amusing or ludicrous; outrageous. **b** (of humour) earthy. □□ **richen** v.intr. & tr. **richness** n. [OE ríce f. Gmc f. Celt., rel. to L rex king: reinforced in ME f. OF riche rich, powerful, of Gmc orig.]

Richard /ˈrɪtʃəd/ the name of three kings of England:

Richard I (1157–99), son of Henry II, reigned 1189–99. Richard's military exploits won him the nickname 'Coeur de Lion' (Lionheart) and made him a medieval legend, but he was absent from his kingdom too frequently to govern effectively. In his youth he twice rebelled against his father and soon after succeeding him he left to take part in the Third Crusade. He defeated Saladin at Arsuf, but failed to capture Jerusalem, and was captured on his way home by Duke Leopold of Austria. Held captive at the behest of the Emperor Henry VI, Richard was released in 1194 only after the payment of a huge ransom. After staying in England for little more than a matter of weeks he embarked on a campaign against Philip II Augustus of France, eventually dying from wounds received at the siege of the castle of Châlus.

Richard II (1367–1400), son of the Black Prince, reigned 1377–99. Though Richard behaved bravely when still a minor during the Peasants' Revolt, he proved a weak king, heavily dependent on favourites and on his uncle John of Gaunt. In 1386–8 noble opponents of his administration, known as the Lords Appellant, successfully removed many of the King's confidants. Ten years later Richard exacted revenge, executing or banishing most of his former opponents, but when he confiscated John of Gaunt's estate after the latter's death, the dispossessed heir returned from exile to overthrow Richard and reign in his place as Henry IV. Richard died in prison in Pontefract Castle, apparently of starvation.

Richard III (1452–85), brother of Edward IV, reigned 1483–5.

He succeeded his brother after the latter's heir Edward V had been declared (on dubious grounds) to be illegitimate. Historical opinion on the popular picture of Richard as a bloodthirsty usurper is still divided; what is certain is that, after suppressing several plots in the early months of his reign, he ruled with some success for a brief period before being defeated and killed at Bosworth in 1485 by Henry Tudor, who then took the throne as Henry VII.

Richards /ˈrɪtʃədz/, Sir Gordon (1904–86), English jockey, who between 1925 and 1953 was champion jockey 26 times.

Richardson /ˈrɪtʃəds(ə)n/, Samuel (1689–1761), English novelist, of humble background, who became a prosperous printer. A request by two booksellers for a series of model letters on the problems and concerns of everyday life resulted in his first novel *Pamela* (1740–1) which, in spite of his rival Fielding's stinging parodies, was a successful and pioneering novel in epistolary form. This technique he further developed in his masterpiece, *Clarissa Harlowe* (1747–8), about a heroine of rare beauty and virtue, and in his final novel, *Sir Charles Grandison* (1754), an attempted portrayal of the ideal Christian gentleman. In these works he explored, with psychological intensity, moral issues in a detailed social context, and greatly influenced the development of future fiction.

Richelieu /ˈriːʃljaː/ (Armand Jean du Plessis, 1585–1642), French Cardinal and statesman. Chief minister of Louis XIII from 1624 until his death in 1642, Richelieu completely dominated French government, establishing a strong central government at home, and pursuing an aggressive foreign policy, particularly against Spain, which made France indisputably the strongest nation in Europe.

riches /ˈrɪtʃɪz/ *n.pl.* abundant means; valuable possessions. [ME *richesse* f. OF *richeise* f. *riche* RICH, taken as pl.]

richly /ˈrɪtʃlɪ/ *adv.* 1 in a rich way. 2 fully, thoroughly (*richly deserves success*).

Richmond /ˈrɪtʃmənd/ the capital of Virginia; pop. (1980) 219,215. During the American Civil War it was made the Confederate capital from 1861 until its capture in 1865.

Richter /ˈrɪktə(r), ˈrɪx-/, Johann Friedrich, see JEAN PAUL.

Richter scale /ˈrɪktə/ *n.* a scale of 0 to 10 for representing the strength of an earthquake. [C. F. *Richter*, Amer. seismologist d. 1985]

ricin /ˈrɪsɪn/ *n.* a toxic substance obtained from castor oil beans and causing gastroenteritis, jaundice, and heart failure. [mod.L *ricinus communis* castor oil]

rick[1] /rɪk/ *n. & v.* —*n.* a stack of hay, corn, etc., built into a regular shape and usu. thatched. —*v.tr.* form into a rick or ricks. [OE *hrēac*, of unkn. orig.]

rick[2] /rɪk/ *n. & v.* (also **wrick**) —*n.* a slight sprain or strain. —*v.tr.* sprain or strain slightly. [ME *wricke* f. MLG *wricken* move about, sprain]

rickets /ˈrɪkɪts/ *n.* (treated as *sing.* or *pl.*) a disease of children with softening of the bones (esp. the spine) and bow-legs, caused by a deficiency of vitamin D. [17th c.: orig. uncert., but assoc. by medical writers with Gk *rhakhitis* RACHITIS]

rickettsia /rɪˈketsɪə/ *n.* a parasitic micro-organism of the genus *Rickettsia* causing typhus and other febrile diseases. □□ **rickettsial** *adj.* [mod.L f. H. T. *Ricketts*, Amer. pathologist d. 1910]

rickety /ˈrɪkɪtɪ/ *adj.* 1 a insecure or shaky in construction; likely to collapse. b feeble. 2 a suffering from rickets. b resembling or of the nature of rickets. □□ **ricketiness** *n.* [RICKETS + -Y[1]]

rickey /ˈrɪkɪ/ *n.* (pl. **-eys**) a drink of spirit (esp. gin), lime-juice, etc. [20th c.: prob. f. the surname *Rickey*]

rickrack var. of RICRAC.

rickshaw /ˈrɪkʃɔː/ *n.* (also **ricksha** /-ʃə/) a light two-wheeled hooded vehicle drawn by one or more persons. [abbr. of *jinricksha, jinrikshaw* f. Jap. *jinrikisha* f. *jin* person + *riki* power + *sha* vehicle]

ricochet /ˈrɪkəˌʃeɪ, -ˌʃet/ *n. & v.* —*n.* 1 the action of a projectile, esp. a shell or bullet, in rebounding off a surface. 2 a hit made after this. —*v.intr.* (**ricocheted** /-ˌʃeɪd/; **ricocheting** /-ˌʃeɪɪŋ/ or **ricochetted** /-ˌʃetɪd/; **ricochetting** /-ˌʃetɪŋ/) (of a projectile) rebound one or more times from a surface. [F, of unkn. orig.]

ricotta /rɪˈkɒtə/ *n.* a soft Italian cheese. [It., = recooked, f. L *recoquere* (as RE-, *coquere* COOK)]

ricrac /ˈrɪkræk/ *n.* (also **rickrack**) a zigzag braided trimming for garments. [redupl. of RACK[1]]

RICS *abbr.* Royal Institution of Chartered Surveyors.

rictus /ˈrɪktəs/ *n. Anat. & Zool.* the expanse or gape of a mouth or beak. □□ **rictal** *adj.* [L, = open mouth f. *ringi rict-* to gape]

rid /rɪd/ *v.tr.* (**ridding**; *past* and *past part.* **rid** or *archaic* **ridded**) (foll. by *of*) make (a person or place) free of something unwanted. □ **be** (or **get**) **rid of** be freed or relieved of (something unwanted); dispose of. [ME, earlier = 'clear (land etc.)' f. ON *rythja*]

riddance /ˈrɪd(ə)ns/ *n.* the act of getting rid of something. □ **good riddance** welcome relief from an unwanted person or thing.

ridden *past part.* of RIDE.

riddle[1] /ˈrɪd(ə)l/ *n. & v.* —*n.* 1 a question or statement testing ingenuity in divining its answer or meaning. 2 a puzzling fact or thing or person. —*v.* 1 *intr.* speak in or propound riddles. 2 *tr.* solve or explain (a riddle). □□ **riddler** *n.* [OE *rǣdels, rǣdelse* opinion, riddle, rel. to READ]

riddle[2] /ˈrɪd(ə)l/ *v. & n.* —*v.tr.* (usu. foll. by *with*) 1 make many holes in, esp. with gunshot. 2 (in *passive*) fill; spread through; permeate (*was riddled with errors*). 3 pass through a riddle. —*n.* a coarse sieve. [OE *hriddel*, earlier *hrīder*: cf. *hrīdrian* sift]

riddling /ˈrɪdlɪŋ/ *adj.* expressed in riddles; puzzling. □□ **riddlingly** *adv.*

ride /raɪd/ *v. & n.* —*v.* (*past* **rode** /rəʊd/; *past part.* **ridden** /ˈrɪd(ə)n/) 1 *tr.* travel or be carried on (a bicycle etc.) or esp. *US* in (a vehicle). 2 *intr.* (often foll. by *on, in*) travel or be conveyed (on a bicycle or in a vehicle). 3 *tr.* sit on and control or be carried by (a horse etc.). 4 *intr.* (often foll. by *on*) be carried (on a horse etc.). 5 *tr.* be carried or supported by (*the ship rides the waves*). 6 *tr.* a traverse on horseback etc., ride over or through (*ride 50 miles; rode the prairie*). b compete or take part in on horseback etc. (*rode a good race*). 7 *intr.* a be at anchor; float buoyantly. b (of the moon) seem to float. 8 *intr.* (foll. by *in, on*) rest in or on while moving. 9 *tr.* yield to (a blow) so as to reduce its impact. 10 *tr.* give a ride to; cause to ride (*rode the child on his back*). 11 *tr.* (of a rider) cause (a horse etc.) to move forward (*rode their horses at the fence*). 12 *tr.* a (in *passive*; foll. by *by, with*) be oppressed or dominated by; be infested with (*was ridden with guilt*). b (as **ridden** *adj.*) infested or afflicted (usu. in *comb.*: *a rat-ridden cellar*). 13 *intr.* (of a thing normally level or even) project or overlap. 14 *tr.* mount (a female) in copulation. 15 *tr. US* annoy or seek to annoy. —*n.* 1 an act or period of travel in a vehicle. 2 a spell of riding on a horse, bicycle, person's back, etc. 3 a path (esp. through woods) for riding on. 4 the quality of sensations when riding (*gives a bumpy ride*). □ **let a thing ride** leave it alone; let it take its natural course. **ride again** reappear, esp. unexpectedly and reinvigorated. **ride down** overtake or trample on horseback. **ride for a fall** act recklessly risking defeat or failure. **ride herd on** see HERD. **ride high** be elated or successful. **ride out** come safely through (a storm etc., or a danger or difficulty). **ride roughshod over** see ROUGHSHOD. **ride to hounds** see HOUND. **ride up** (of a garment, carpet, etc.) work or move out of its proper position. **take for a ride** *colloq.* hoax or deceive. □□ **ridable** *adj.* [OE *rīdan*]

rider /ˈraɪdə(r)/ *n.* 1 a person who rides (esp. a horse). 2 a an additional clause amending or supplementing a document. b *Brit. Parl.* an addition or amendment to a bill at its third reading. c a corollary. d *Brit.* a recommendation etc. added to a judicial verdict. 3 *Math.* a problem arising as a corollary of a theorem etc. 4 a piece in a machine etc. that surmounts or bridges or works on or over others. 5 (in *pl.*) an additional set of timbers or iron plates strengthening a ship's frame. □□ **riderless** *adj.* [OE *rīdere* (as RIDE)]

ridge /rɪdʒ/ *n. & v.* —*n.* 1 the line of the junction of two surfaces sloping upwards towards each other (*the ridge of a roof*). 2 a long narrow hilltop, mountain range, or watershed. 3 any narrow elevation across a surface. 4 *Meteorol.* an elongated region of high barometric pressure. 5 *Agriculture* a raised strip of arable land, usu. one of a set separated by furrows. 6 *Hort.* a raised hotbed for melons etc. —*v.* **1** *tr.* mark with ridges. **2** *tr. Agriculture* break up (land) into ridges. **3** *tr. Hort.* plant (cucumbers etc.) in ridges. **4** *tr. & intr.* gather into ridges. □ **ridge-piece** (or **-tree**) a beam along the ridge of a roof. **ridge-pole 1** the horizontal pole of a long tent. **2** = *ridge-piece.* **ridge-tile** a tile used in making a roof-ridge. □□ **ridgy** *adj.* [OE *hrycg* f. Gmc]

ridgeway /ˈrɪdʒweɪ/ *n.* a road or track along a ridge.

ridicule /ˈrɪdɪˌkjuːl/ *n. & v.* —*n.* subjection to derision or mockery. —*v.tr.* make fun of; subject to ridicule; laugh at. [F or f. L *ridiculum* neut. of *ridiculus* laughable f. *ridēre* laugh]

ridiculous /rɪˈdɪkjʊləs/ *adj.* **1** deserving or inviting ridicule. **2** unreasonable, absurd. □□ **ridiculously** *adv.* **ridiculousness** *n.* [L *ridiculosus* (as RIDICULE)]

riding[1] /ˈraɪdɪŋ/ *n.* **1** in senses of RIDE *v.* **2** the practice or skill of riders of horses. **3** = RIDE *n.* 3. □ **riding-light** (or **-lamp**) a light shown by a ship at anchor. **riding-school** an establishment teaching skills in horsemanship.

riding[2] /ˈraɪdɪŋ/ *n.* **1** each of three former administrative divisions (**East Riding, North Riding, West Riding**) of Yorkshire. **2** an electoral division of Canada. [OE *thriding* (unrecorded) f. ON *thrithjungr* third part f. *thrithi* THIRD: *th-* was lost owing to the preceding *-t* or *-th* of *east* etc.]

Ridley /ˈrɪdlɪ/, Nicholas (*c*.1500–55), English Protestant martyr. One of Archbishop Cranmer's chaplains, he rose to become successively Bishop of Rochester and of London and one of the leaders of the Protestant Reformation in the reign of Edward VI. He opposed the Catholic policies of Edward's sister and successor Mary I and was imprisoned and eventually burnt for heresy at Oxford.

Riemann /ˈriːmən/, (Georg Friedrich) Bernhard (1826–66), German mathematician whose achievements are characterized by their outstandingly imaginative character. Riemann surfaces are the modifications of the complex number plane required for a proper understanding of algebraic and other many-valued functions; Riemannian geometry is the study of intrinsic properties of curved space, now fundamental to the relativistic description of our universe. His name is attached to several other concepts and theorems in mathematics, of which the most famous is an assertion about the complex numbers which are roots of a certain transcendental equation. This assertion, known as the Riemann hypothesis, has many deep implications, particularly about the distribution of prime numbers, but after more than 100 years it remains one of the greatest of the unsolved problems of mathematics.

Riesling /ˈriːzlɪŋ, -slɪŋ/ *n.* **1** a kind of dry white wine produced in Germany, Austria, and elsewhere. **2** the variety of grape from which this is produced. [G]

rife /raɪf/ *predic.adj.* **1** of common occurrence; widespread. **2** (foll. by *with*) abounding in; teeming with. □□ **rifeness** *n.* [OE *rȳfe* prob. f. ON *rífr* acceptable f. *reifa* enrich, *reifr* cheerful]

riff /rɪf/ *n. & v.* —*n.* a short repeated phrase in jazz etc. —*v.intr.* play riffs. [20th c.: abbr. of RIFFLE *n.*]

riffle /ˈrɪf(ə)l/ *v. & n.* —*v.* **1** *tr.* **a** turn (pages) in quick succession. **b** shuffle (playing-cards) esp. by flexing and combining the two halves of a pack. **2** *intr.* (often foll. by *through*) leaf quickly (through pages). —*n.* **1** the act or an instance of riffling. **2** (in gold-washing) a groove or slat set in a trough or sluice to catch gold particles. **3** US **a** a shallow part of a stream where the water flows brokenly. **b** a patch of waves or ripples on water. [perh. var. of RUFFLE]

riff-raff /ˈrɪfræf/ *n.* (often prec. by *the*) rabble; disreputable or undesirable persons. [ME *riff and raff* f. OF *rif et raf*]

rifle[1] /ˈraɪf(ə)l/ *n. & v.* —*n.* **1** a gun with a long rifled barrel, esp. one fired from shoulder-level. **2** (in *pl.*) riflemen. —*v.tr.* make spiral grooves in (a gun or its barrel or bore) to make a bullet spin. □ **rifle bird** any dark green Australian bird of paradise of the genus *Ptiloris.* **rifle-range** a place for rifle-practice. **rifle-shot 1** the distance coverable by a shot from a rifle. **2** a shot fired with a rifle. [OF *rifler* graze, scratch f. Gmc]

rifle[2] /ˈraɪf(ə)l/ *v.tr. & (foll. by through) intr.* **1** search and rob, esp. of all that can be found. **2** carry off as booty. [ME f. OF *rifler* graze, scratch, plunder f. ODu. *riffelen*]

rifleman /ˈraɪf(ə)lmən/ *n.* (*pl.* **-men**) **1** a soldier armed with a rifle. **2** a small yellow and green New Zealand bird, *Acanthisitta chloris.*

rifling /ˈraɪflɪŋ/ *n.* the arrangement of grooves on the inside of a gun's barrel.

Rif Mountains /rɪf/ (also **Er Rif**) a mountain range of northern Morocco, running parallel to the Mediterranean for about 290 km (180 miles) from Tangier to near the Algerian frontier.

rift /rɪft/ *n. & v.* —*n.* **1 a** a crack or split in an object. **b** an opening in a cloud etc. **2** a cleft or fissure in earth or rock. **3** a disagreement; a breach in friendly relations. —*v.tr.* tear or burst apart. □ **rift-valley** a steep-sided valley formed by subsidence of the earth's crust between nearly parallel faults. □□ **riftless** *adj.* **rifty** *adj.* [ME, of Scand. orig.]

rig[1] /rɪg/ *v. & n.* —*v.tr.* (**rigged, rigging**) **1 a** provide (a sailing ship) with sails, rigging, etc. **b** prepare ready for sailing. **2** (often foll. by *out, up*) fit with clothes or other equipment. **3** (foll. by *up*) set up hastily or as a makeshift. **4** assemble and adjust the parts of (an aircraft). —*n.* **1** the arrangement of masts, sails, rigging, etc., of a sailing ship. **2** equipment for a special purpose, e.g. a radio transmitter. **3** = *oil rig.* **4** a person's or thing's look as determined by clothing, equipment, etc., esp. uniform. □ **in full rig** *colloq.* smartly or ceremonially dressed. **rig-out** *Brit. colloq.* an outfit of clothes. □□ **rigged** *adj.* (also in *comb.*). [ME, perh. of Scand. orig.: cf. Norw. *rigga* bind or wrap up]

rig[2] /rɪg/ *v. & n.* —*v.tr.* (**rigged, rigging**) manage or conduct fraudulently (*they rigged the election*). —*n.* **1** a trick or dodge. **2** a way of swindling. □ **rig the market** cause an artificial rise or fall in prices. □□ **rigger** *n.* [19th c.: orig. unkn.]

Riga /ˈriːgə/ a port on the Baltic Sea, capital of the republic of Latvia; pop. (est. 1987) 900,000.

rigadoon /ˌrɪgəˈduːn/ *n.* **1** a lively dance in duple or quadruple time for two persons. **2** the music for this. [F *rigodon, rigaudon*, perh. f. its inventor *Rigaud*]

Rigel /ˈraɪg(ə)l/ the seventh-brightest star in the sky, found in the constellation Orion. Its name is derived from an Arabic phrase meaning 'left leg of the Great One'. Blue in colour, it is a supergiant star nearly sixty thousand times as luminous as our sun.

rigger /ˈrɪgə(r)/ *n.* **1** a person who rigs or who arranges rigging. **2** (of a rowing-boat) = OUTRIGGER 5a. **3** a ship rigged in a specified way. **4** a worker on an oil rig.

rigging /ˈrɪgɪŋ/ *n.* **1** a ship's spars, ropes, etc., supporting and controlling the sails. **2** the ropes and wires supporting the structure of an airship or biplane.

right /raɪt/ *adj., n., v., adv., & int.* —*adj.* **1** (of conduct etc.) just, morally or socially correct (*it is only right to tell you; I want to do the right thing*). **2** true, correct; not mistaken (*the right time; you were right about the weather*). **3** less wrong or not wrong (*which is the right way to town?*). **4** more or most suitable or preferable (*the right person for the job; along the right lines*). **5** in a sound or normal condition; physically or mentally healthy; satisfactory (*the engine doesn't sound right*). **6 a** on or towards the side of the human body which corresponds to the position of east if one regards oneself as facing north. **b** on or towards that part of an object which is analogous to a person's right side or (with opposite sense) which is nearer to a spectator's right hand. **7** (of a side of fabric etc.) meant for display or use (*turn it right side up*). **8** *colloq.* or *archaic* real; properly so called (*made a right mess of it; a right royal welcome*). —*n.* **1** that which is morally or socially correct or just; fair treatment (often in *pl.*: *the rights and wrongs of the case*). **2** (often foll. by *to*, or *to* + *infin.*) a justification or fair claim (*has no right to speak like that*). **3** a thing one may legally or morally claim; the state of being entitled to a privilege or immunity or authority to act (*a right of reply; human rights*). **4** the right-hand part or region or direction. **5** *Boxing* **a** the right hand. **b** a blow with this. **6** (often **Right**) *Polit.* **a** a group or section favouring conservatism (orig. the more conservative section of a continental legislature, seated on the president's right). **b** such conservatives collectively. **7** the side of a stage which is to the right of a person facing the audience. **8** (esp. in marching) the right foot. **9** the right wing of an army. —*v.tr.* **1**

(often *refl.*) restore to a proper or straight or vertical position. **2 a** correct (mistakes etc.); set in order. **b** avenge (a wrong or a wronged person); make reparation for or to. **c** vindicate, justify, rehabilitate. —*adv.* **1** straight (*go right on*). **2** *colloq.* immediately; without delay (*I'll be right back*; *do it right now*). **3 a** (foll. by *to*, *round*, *through*, etc.) all the way (*sank right to the bottom*; *ran right round the block*). **b** (foll. by *off*, *out*, etc.) completely (*came right off its hinges*; *am right out of butter*). **4** exactly, quite (*right in the middle*). **5** justly, properly, correctly, truly, satisfactorily (*did not act right*; *not holding it right*; *if I remember right*). **6** on or to the right side. **7** *archaic* very; to the full (*am right glad to hear it*; *dined right royally*). —*int. colloq.* expressing agreement or assent. □ **as right as rain** perfectly sound and healthy. **at right angles** placed to form a right angle. **by right** (or **rights**) if right were done. **do right by** act dutifully towards (a person). **in one's own right** through one's own position or effort etc. **in the right** having justice or truth on one's side. **in one's right mind** sane; competent to think and act. **of** (or **as of**) **right** having legal or moral etc. entitlement. **on the right side of 1** in the favour of (a person etc.). **2** somewhat less than (a specified age). **put** (or **set**) **right 1** restore to order, health, etc. **2** correct the mistaken impression etc. of (a person). **put** (or **set**) **to rights** make correct or well ordered. **right about** (or **about-turn** or **about-face**) **1** a right turn continued to face the rear. **2** a reversal of policy. **3** a hasty retreat. **right and left** (or **right, left, and centre**) on all sides. **right angle** an angle of 90°, made by lines meeting with equal angles on either side. **right-angled 1** containing or making a right angle. **2** involving right angles, not oblique. **right arm** one's most reliable helper. **right ascension** see ASCENSION. **right away** (or **off**) immediately. **right bank** the bank of a river on the right facing downstream. **right bower** see BOWER³. **right field** *Baseball* the part of the outfield to the right of the batter as he faces the pitcher. **right hand 1** = *right-hand man*. **2** the most important position next to a person (*stand at God's right hand*). **right-hand** *adj.* **1** on or towards the right side of a person or thing (*right-hand drive*). **2** done with the right hand (*right-hand blow*). **3** (of a screw) = RIGHT-HANDED 4b. **right-hand man** an indispensable or chief assistant. **Right Honourable** *Brit.* a title given to certain high officials, e.g. Privy Counsellors. **right-minded** (or **-thinking**) having sound views and principles. **right of search** *Naut.* see SEARCH. **right of way 1** a right established by usage to pass over another's ground. **2** a path subject to such a right. **3** the right of one vehicle to proceed before another. **right oh!** (or **ho!**) = RIGHTO. **right on!** *colloq.* an expression of strong approval or encouragement. **a right one** *Brit. colloq.* a silly or foolish person. **Right Reverend** see REVEREND. **rights of man** = human rights (see HUMAN). The phrase is associated with the declaration of the rights of man and of the citizen adopted by the French National Assembly in 1789 and serving as a preface to the French Constitution of 1791. Other declarations to the same effect include the American Declaration of Independence. **right sphere** *Astron.* see SPHERE. **right turn** a turn that brings one's front to face as one's right side did before. **right whale** any large-headed whale of the family Balaenidae, rich in whalebone and easily captured. **right wing 1** the right side of a football etc. team on the field. **2** the conservative section of a political party or system. **right-wing** *adj.* conservative or reactionary. **right-winger** a person on the right wing. **right you are!** *colloq.* an exclamation of assent. **she's** (or **she'll be**) **right** *Austral. colloq.* that will be all right. **too right** *sl.* an expression of agreement. **within one's rights** not exceeding one's authority or entitlement. □□ **rightable** *adj.* **righter** *n.* **rightish** *adj.* **rightless** *adj.* **rightlessness** *n.* **rightness** *n.* [OE *riht* (adj.), *rihtan* (v.), *rihte* (adv.)]

righten /ˈraɪt(ə)n/ *v.tr.* make right or correct.

righteous /ˈraɪtʃəs/ *adj.* (of a person or conduct) morally right; virtuous, law-abiding. □□ **righteously** *adv.* **righteousness** *n.* [OE *rihtwīs* (as RIGHT *n.* + -WISE or RIGHT *adj.* + WISE²), assim. to *bounteous* etc.]

rightful /ˈraɪtfʊl/ *adj.* **1 a** (of a person) legitimately entitled to (a position etc.) (*the rightful heir*). **b** (of status or property etc.) that one is entitled to. **2** (of an action etc.) equitable, fair. □□ **rightfully** *adv.* **rightfulness** *n.* [OE *rihtful* (as RIGHT *n.*)]

right-handed /raɪtˈhændɪd/ *adj.* **1** using the right hand by preference as more serviceable than the left. **2** (of a tool etc.) made to be used with the right hand. **3** (of a blow) struck with the right hand. **4** a turning to the right; towards the right. **b** (of a screw) advanced by turning to the right (clockwise). □□ **right-handedly** *adv.* **right-handedness** *n.*

right-hander /raɪtˈhændə(r)/ *n.* **1** a right-handed person. **2** a right-handed blow.

rightism /ˈraɪtɪz(ə)m/ *n. Polit.* the principles or policy of the right. □□ **rightist** *n. & adj.*

rightly /ˈraɪtlɪ/ *adv.* justly, properly, correctly, justifiably.

rightmost /ˈraɪtməʊst/ *adj.* furthest to the right.

righto /ˈraɪtəʊ, raɪˈtəʊ/ *int. Brit. colloq.* expressing agreement or assent.

rightward /ˈraɪtwəd/ *adv. & adj.* —*adv.* (also **rightwards** /-wədz/) towards the right. —*adj.* going towards or facing the right.

rigid /ˈrɪdʒɪd/ *adj.* **1** not flexible; that cannot be bent (*a rigid frame*). **2** (of a person, conduct, etc.) inflexible, unbending, strict, harsh, punctilious (*a rigid disciplinarian*; *rigid economy*). □□ **rigidity** /-ˈdʒɪdɪtɪ/ *n.* **rigidly** *adv.* **rigidness** *n.* [F *rigide* or L *rigidus* f. *rigēre* be stiff]

rigidify /rɪˈdʒɪdɪˌfaɪ/ *v.tr. & intr.* (**-ies**, **-ied**) make or become rigid.

rigmarole /ˈrɪɡməˌrəʊl/ *n.* **1** a lengthy and complicated procedure. **2 a** a rambling or meaningless account or tale. **b** such talk. [orig. *ragman roll* = a catalogue, of unkn. orig.]

rigor¹ /ˈrɪɡə(r), ˈraɪɡɔː(r)/ *n. Med.* **1** a sudden feeling of cold with shivering accompanied by a rise in temperature, preceding a fever etc. **2** rigidity of the body caused by shock or poisoning etc. [ME f. L f. *rigēre* be stiff]

rigor² *US var. of* RIGOUR.

rigor mortis /ˌrɪɡə ˈmɔːtɪs/ *n.* stiffening of the body after death. [L, = stiffness of death]

rigorous /ˈrɪɡərəs/ *adj.* **1** characterized by or showing rigour; strict, severe. **2** strictly exact or accurate. **3** (of the weather) cold, severe. □□ **rigorously** *adv.* **rigorousness** *n.* [OF *rigorous* or LL *rigorosus* (as RIGOR¹)]

rigour /ˈrɪɡə(r)/ *n.* (*US* **rigor**) **1 a** severity, strictness, harshness. **b** (in *pl.*) harsh measures or conditions. **2** logical exactitude. **3** strict enforcement of rules etc. (*the utmost rigour of the law*). **4** austerity of life; puritanical discipline. [ME f. OF *rigour* f. L *rigor* (as RIGOR¹)]

Rig-Veda /rɪɡˈveɪdə, -ˈviːdə/ *n.* a collection of hymns in Old Sanskrit used in the Vedic religion by the priest in charge of invoking the gods at the ritual sacrifice. Composed in the 2nd millenium BC, this is the oldest and most important of the four Vedas. [Skr. *r̥gvēda* f. *r̥c* praise + *vēda* VEDA]

Rijeka /riːˈekə/ (Italian **Fiume** /fiˈuːmeɪ/) the largest port of Yugoslavia, situated on the Adriatic coast of Croatia; pop. (1981) 193,000.

Rijksmuseum /ˈraɪksmuˌzeɪəm/ the national gallery of The Netherlands, in Amsterdam. Established in the late 19th c. and developed from the collection of the House of Orange, it now contains the most representative collection of Dutch art in the world.

Rila Mountains /ˈriːlə/ a range of mountains in western Bulgaria, forming the NW part of the Rhodope Mountains.

rile /raɪl/ *v.tr.* **1** *colloq.* anger, irritate. **2** *US* make (water) turbulent or muddy. [var. of ROIL]

Riley¹ /ˈraɪlɪ/ *n.* (also **Reilly**) □ **the life of Riley** *colloq.* a carefree existence. [20th c.: orig. unkn.]

Riley² /ˈraɪlɪ/, Bridget Louise (1931–), English painter, whose work belongs to the category known as op art. Her earlier works are in black and white (e.g. *Movement in Squares*, 1961; *Fall*, 1963), and through graded greys she advanced to colour compositions which arrived at similar effects.

rilievo var. of RELIEVO.

Rilke /ˈrɪlkə/, Rainer Maria (1875–1926), German lyric poet, born in Prague. He visited Russia, where he met Tolstoy, and travelled in Europe; in 1901 he married a pupil of the French sculptor

Rodin, and became the latter's secretary for a time, then after further travels he settled in Switzerland. Rilke's *Duino Elegies*, begun shortly before the First World War and completed afterwards, arose from his endeavour to discover a satisfactory spiritual position amid the decay of reality, and his *Sonnets to Orpheus* (1923) are the jubilant outcome of that endeavour. His poetry has been translated into many languages.

rill /rɪl/ *n.* **1** a small stream. **2** a shallow channel cut in the surface of soil or rocks by running water. **3** var. of RILLE. [LG *ril*, *rille*]

rille /rɪl/ *n.* (also **rill**) *Astron.* a cleft or narrow valley on the moon's surface. [G (as RILL)]

rim /rɪm/ *n.* & *v.* —*n.* **1 a** a raised edge or border. **b** a margin or verge, esp. of something circular. **2** the part of a pair of spectacles surrounding the lenses. **3** the outer edge of a wheel, on which the tyre is fitted. **4** a boundary line (*the rim of the horizon*). —*v.tr.* (**rimmed**, **rimming**) **1 a** provide with a rim. **b** be a rim for or to. **2** edge, border. □ **rim-brake** a brake acting on the rim of a wheel. □□ **rimless** *adj.* **rimmed** *adj.* (also in *comb.*). [OE *rima* edge: cf. ON *rimi* ridge (the only known cognate)]

Rimbaud /ˈræmbəʊ/, Arthur (1854–91), French poet of precocious genius, who at the age of 17 had written his most famous poem 'Le bateau ivre'. In the same year he began a passionate relationship with the poet Paul Verlaine and the pair led a dissolute life in Brussels and London until they quarrelled violently. He undertook a programme of 'disorientation of the senses' in an attempt to become a visionary, and his prose poems *Une Saison en enfer* (1873) and *Les Illuminations* (1886) explored the possibilities of this. By the age of 19 his poetic career was over and he succumbed to a vagabond life in Europe and in NE Africa, but he had become one of the most revolutionary figures in 19th-c. literature, whose verse was fiercely independent of religious, political, and literary orthodoxy.

rime[1] /raɪm/ *n.* & *v.* —*n.* **1** frost, esp. formed from cloud or fog. **2** *poet.* hoar-frost. —*v.tr.* cover with rime. [OE *hrīm*]

rime[2] *archaic* var. of RHYME.

Rimmon /ˈrɪmən/ a deity worshipped in ancient Damascus (2 Kings 5: 18). □ **bow down in the house of Rimmon** compromise one's convictions.

rimose /ˈraɪməʊz/ *adj.* (also **rimous** /-məs/) esp. *Bot.* full of chinks or fissures. [L *rimosus* f. *rima* chink]

Rimsky-Korsakov /ˌrɪmskɪˈkɔːsəkɒf/, Nikolai Andreievich (1844–1908), Russian composer. Born of an aristocratic family he attended the Corps of Naval Cadets in St Petersburg, at the same time pursuing his interest in music which, though he lacked formal training, was keen enough to lead him to compose a much acclaimed First Symphony in 1861–5. He was appointed professor of composition at the St Petersburg Conservatory in 1871 and followed his early success with such works as the symphonic suite *Scheherazade* (1888). In 1905 his involvement with revolutionary students led to temporary suspension from the Conservatory; his attitude to autocracy found expression in his opera *The Golden Cockerel* (1909), after Pushkin's poem. He was a fine orchestrator, but today his versions of such works as Mussorgsky's *Khovanshchina* and *Boris Godunov* find less favour than do the originals.

rimu /ˈriːmuː/ *n.* NZ a softwood tree, *Dacrydium cupressinum*, native to New Zealand. [Maori]

rimy /ˈraɪmɪ/ *adj.* (**rimier**, **rimiest**) frosty; covered with frost.

rind /raɪnd/ *n.* & *v.* —*n.* **1** the tough outer layer or covering of fruit and vegetables, cheese, bacon, etc. **2** the bark of a tree or plant. —*v.tr.* strip the bark from. □□ **rinded** *adj.* (also in *comb.*). **rindless** *adj.* [OE *rind(e)*]

rinderpest /ˈrɪndəˌpest/ *n.* a virulent infectious disease of ruminants (esp. cattle). [G f. *Rinder* cattle + *Pest* PEST]

ring[1] /rɪŋ/ *n.* & *v.* —*n.* **1** a circular band, usu. of precious metal, worn on a finger as an ornament or a token of marriage or betrothal. **2** a circular band of any material. **3** the rim of a cylindrical or circular object, or a line or band round it. **4** a mark or part having the form of a circular band (*had rings round his eyes*; *smoke rings*). **5** = *annual ring.* **6 a** an enclosure for a circus performance, betting at races, the showing of cattle, etc.

b (prec. by *the*) bookmakers collectively. **c** a roped enclosure for boxing or wrestling. **7 a** a group of people or things arranged in a circle. **b** such an arrangement. **8** a combination of traders, bookmakers, spies, politicians, etc. acting together usu. illicitly for the control of operations or profit. **9** a circular or spiral course. **10** = *gas ring.* **11** *Astron.* **a** a thin band or disc of particles etc. round a planet. **b** a halo round the moon. **12** *Archaeol.* a circular prehistoric earthwork usu. of a bank and ditch. **13** *Chem.* a group of atoms each bonded to two others in a closed sequence. **14** *Math.* a set of elements with two binary operations, addition and multiplication, the second being distributive over the first and associative. —*v.tr.* **1** make or draw a circle round. **2** (often foll. by *round*, *about*, *in*) encircle or hem in (game or cattle). **3** put a ring on (a bird etc.) or through the nose of (a pig, bull, etc.). **4** cut (fruit, vegetables, etc.) into rings. □ **ring-binder** a loose-leaf binder with ring-shaped clasps that can be opened to pass through holes in the paper. **ring circuit** an electrical circuit serving a number of power points with one fuse in the supply to the circuit. **ring-dove 1** the woodpigeon. **2** the collared dove. **ringed plover** either of two small plovers, *Charadrius hiaticula* and *C. dubius.* **ring finger** the finger next to the little finger, esp. of the left hand, on which the wedding ring is usu. worn. **ring main 1** an electrical supply serving a series of consumers and returning to the original source, so that each consumer has an alternative path in the event of a failure. **2** = *ring circuit.* **ring-neck** any of various ring-necked birds esp. a type of pheasant, *Phasianus colchicus*, with a white neck-ring. **ring-necked** *Zool.* having a band or bands of colour round the neck. **ring ouzel** a thrush, *Turdus torquatus*, with a white crescent across its breast. **ring-pull** (of a tin) having a ring for pulling to break its seal. **ring road** a bypass encircling a town. **ring-tailed 1** (of monkeys, lemurs, racoons, etc.) having a tail ringed in alternate colours. **2** with the tail curled at the end. **run** (or **make**) **rings round** *colloq.* outclass or outwit (another person). □□ **ringed** *adj.* (also in *comb.*). **ringless** *adj.* [OE *hring* f. Gmc]

ring[2] /rɪŋ/ *v.* & *n.* —*v.* (*past* **rang** /ræŋ/; *past part.* **rung** /rʌŋ/) **1** *intr.* (often foll. by *out* etc.) give a clear resonant or vibrating sound of or as of a bell (*a shot rang out*; *a ringing laugh*; *the telephone rang*). **2** *tr.* **a** make (esp. a bell) ring. **b** (*absol.*) call for service or attention by ringing a bell (*you rang, madam?*). **3** *tr.* (also *absol.*; often foll. by *up*) *Brit.* call by telephone (*will ring you on Monday*; *did you ring?*). **4** *tr.* (usu. foll. by *with*, *to*) (of a place) resound or be permeated with a sound, or an attribute, e.g. fame (*the theatre rang with applause*). **5** *intr.* (of the ears) be filled with a sensation of ringing. **6** *tr.* **a** sound (a peal etc.) on bells. **b** (of a bell) sound (the hour etc.). **7** *tr.* (foll. by *in*, *out*) usher in or out with bell-ringing (*ring in the May*; *rang out the Old Year*). **8** *intr.* (of sentiments etc.) convey a specified impression (*words rang hollow*). —*n.* **1** a ringing sound or tone. **2 a** the act of ringing a bell. **b** the sound caused by this. **3** *colloq.* a telephone call (*give me a ring*). **4** a specified feeling conveyed by an utterance (*had a melancholy ring*). **5** a set of esp. church bells. □ **ring back** make a return telephone call to (a person who has telephoned earlier). **ring a bell** see BELL[1]. **ring the changes** (on) see CHANGE. **ring down** (or **up**) **the curtain 1** cause the curtain to be lowered or raised. **2** (foll. by *on*) mark the end or the beginning of (an enterprise etc.). **ring in 1** report or make contact by telephone. **2** *Austral.* & *NZ sl.* substitute fraudulently. **ring in one's ears** (or **heart** etc.) linger in the memory. **ringing tone** a sound heard by a telephone caller when the number dialled is being rung. **ring off** *Brit.* end a telephone call by replacing the receiver. **ring true** (or **false**) convey an impression of truth or falsehood. **ring up 1** *Brit.* call by telephone. **2** record (an amount etc.) on a cash register. □□ **ringed** *adj.* (also in *comb.*). **ringer** *n.* **ringing** *adj.* **ringingly** *adv.* [OE *hringan*]

ringbark /ˈrɪŋbɑːk/ *v.tr.* cut a ring in the bark of (a tree) to kill it or retard its growth and thereby improve fruit production.

ringbolt /ˈrɪŋbɒlt/ *n.* a bolt with a ring attached for fitting a rope to etc.

ringer /ˈrɪŋə(r)/ *n. sl.* **1 a** esp. *US* an athlete or horse entered in a competition by fraudulent means, esp. as a substitute. **b** a person's double, esp. an imposter. **2** *Austral.* **a** the fastest shearer in a shed. **b** a stockman or station hand. **3** a person who rings, esp. a bell-ringer. □ **be a ringer** (or **dead ringer) for** resemble (a person) exactly. [RING² + -ER¹]

ringhals /'rɪŋhæls/ n. a large venomous snake, *Hemachatus hemachatus*, of southern Africa, with a white ring or two across the neck. [Afrik. *rinkhals* f. *ring* RING¹ + *hals* neck]

ringleader /'rɪŋˌliːdə(r)/ n. a leading instigator in an illicit or illegal activity.

ringlet /'rɪŋlɪt/ n. **1** a curly lock of hair, esp. a long one. **2** a butterfly, *Aphantopus hyperantus*, with spots on its wings. □□ **ringleted** adj. **ringlety** adj.

ringmaster /'rɪŋˌmɑːstə(r)/ n. the person directing a circus performance.

ringside /'rɪŋsaɪd/ n. the area immediately beside a boxing ring or circus ring etc. (often attrib.: *a ringside seat; a ringside view*). □□ **ringsider** n.

ringster /'rɪŋstə(r)/ n. a person who participates in a political or commercial ring (see RING¹ n. 8).

ringtail /'rɪŋteɪl/ n. **1** a ring-tailed opossum, lemur, or phalanger. **2** a golden eagle up to its third year. **3** a female hen-harrier.

ringworm /'rɪŋwɜːm/ n. any of various fungous infections of the skin causing circular inflamed patches, esp. on a child's scalp.

rink /rɪŋk/ n. **1** an area of natural or artificial ice for skating or the game of curling etc. **2** an enclosed area for roller-skating. **3** a building containing either of these. **4** Bowls a strip of the green used for playing a match. **5** a team in bowls or curling. [ME (orig. Sc.), = jousting-ground: perh. orig. f. OF *renc* RANK¹]

rinse /rɪns/ v. & n. —v.tr. (often foll. by *through, out*) **1** wash with clean water. **2** apply liquid to. **3** wash lightly. **4** put (clothes etc.) through clean water to remove soap or detergent. **5** (foll. by *out, away*) clear (impurities) by rinsing. —n. **1** the act or an instance of rinsing (*give it a rinse*). **2** a solution for cleansing the mouth. **3** a dye for the temporary tinting of hair (*a blue rinse*). □□ **rinser** n. [ME f. OF *rincer, raincier*, of unkn. orig.]

Rio de Janeiro /'riːəʊ də dʒəˈnɪəˌrəʊ/ the chief port, second-largest city, and former capital of Brazil; pop. (1980) 5,094,396.

Rio de la Plata /'riːəʊ də lɑː 'plɑːtə/ the River Plate.

Rio de Oro /'riːəʊ diː 'ɔːrəʊ/ the southern region of Western Sahara (formerly Spanish Sahara). Its chief town is Dakhla.

Rio Grande /ˌriːəʊ 'grænd/ a river of North America which rises in Colorado and flows 3,030 km (1,880 miles) SE to the Gulf of Mexico. It forms the US–Mexico frontier from El Paso to the sea.

Rioja /riːˈɒxə/, **La** an autonomous region of northern Spain, in the wine-producing valley of the River Ebro; pop. (1986) 262,600; capital, Logroño.

Rio Muni /ˌriːəʊ 'muːnɪ/ the part of Equatorial Guinea that lies on the mainland of West Africa. Its chief town is Bata.

riot /'raɪət/ n. & v. —n. **1 a** a disturbance of the peace by a crowd; an occurrence of public disorder. **b** (attrib.) involved in suppressing riots (*riot police; riot shield*). **2** uncontrolled revelry; noisy behaviour. **3** (foll. by *of*) a lavish display or enjoyment (*a riot of emotion; a riot of colour and sound*). **4** colloq. a very amusing thing or person. —v.intr. **1** make or engage in a riot. **2** live wantonly; revel. □ **read the Riot Act** insist that noise or insubordination etc. must cease. **Riot Act** an Act passed in 1715 by the Whig government in the wake of anti-Hanoverian rioting, which made it a felony for an assembly of more than twelve people to refuse to disperse after being ordered to do so, with a specified portion of the Act being read, by lawful authority. It was repealed in 1967. **run riot 1** throw off all restraint. **2** (of plants) grow or spread uncontrolled. □□ **rioter** n. **riotless** adj. [ME f. OF *riote, rioter, rihoter*, of unkn. orig.]

riotous /'raɪətəs/ adj. **1** marked by or involving rioting. **2** characterized by wanton conduct. **3** wildly profuse. □□ **riotously** adv. **riotousness** n. [ME f. OF (as RIOT)]

RIP abbr. may he or she or they rest in peace. [L *requiescat* (pl. *requiescant*) *in pace*]

rip¹ /rɪp/ v. & n. —v.tr. & intr. (**ripped, ripping**) **1** tr. tear or cut (a thing) quickly or forcibly away or apart (*ripped out the lining;*

ripped the book up). **2** tr. **a** make (a hole etc.) by ripping. **b** make a long tear or cut in. **3** intr. come violently apart; split. **4** intr. rush along. —n. **1** a long tear or cut. **2** an act of ripping. □ **let rip** colloq. **1** act or proceed without restraint. **2** speak violently. **3** not check the speed of or interfere with (a person or thing). **rip-cord** a cord for releasing a parachute from its pack. **rip into** attack (a person) verbally. **rip off** colloq. defraud, steal. **rip-off** n. colloq. **1** a fraud or swindle. **2** financial exploitation. [ME: orig. unkn.]

rip² /rɪp/ n. a stretch of rough water in the sea or in a river, caused by the meeting of currents. □ **rip current** (or **tide**) **1** a strong surface current from the shore. **2** a state of conflicting psychological forces. [18th c.: perh. rel. to RIP¹]

rip³ /rɪp/ n. **1** a dissolute person. **2** a rascal. **3** a worthless horse. [perh. f. *rep*, abbr. of REPROBATE]

riparian /raɪˈpeərɪən/ adj. & n. esp. Law —adj. of or on a river-bank (*riparian rights*). —n. an owner of property on a river-bank. [L *riparius* f. *ripa* bank]

ripe /raɪp/ adj. **1** (of grain, fruit, cheese, etc.) ready to be reaped or picked or eaten. **2** mature; fully developed (*ripe in judgement; a ripe beauty*). **3** (of a person's age) advanced. **4** (often foll. by *for*) fit or ready (*when the time is ripe; land ripe for development*). **5** (of the complexion etc.) red and full like ripe fruit. □□ **ripely** adv. **ripeness** n. [OE *rīpe* f. WG]

ripen /'raɪpən/ v.tr. & intr. make or become ripe.

ripieno /rɪˈpjeɪnəʊ/ n. (pl. **-os** or **ripieni** /-nɪ/) Mus. a body of accompanying instruments in baroque concerto music. [It. (as RE-, *pieno* full)]

riposte /rɪˈpɒst/ n. & v. —n. **1** a quick sharp reply or retort. **2** a quick return thrust in fencing. —v.intr. deliver a riposte. [F *ri(s)poste, ri(s)poster* f. It. *risposta* RESPONSE]

ripper /'rɪpə(r)/ n. **1** a person or thing that rips. **2** a murderer who rips the victims' bodies.

ripping /'rɪpɪŋ/ adj. Brit. archaic colloq. very enjoyable (*a ripping good yarn*). □□ **rippingly** adv.

ripple¹ /'rɪp(ə)l/ n. & v. —n. **1** a ruffling of the water's surface, a small wave or series of waves. **2** a gentle lively sound that rises and falls, e.g. of laughter or applause. **3** a wavy appearance in hair, material, etc. **4** Electr. a slight variation in the strength of a current etc. **5** ice-cream with added syrup giving a coloured ripple effect (*raspberry ripple*). **6** US a riffle in a stream. —v. **1 a** intr. form ripples; flow in ripples. **b** tr. cause to do this. **2** intr. show or sound like ripples. □ **ripple mark** a ridge or ridged surface left on sand, mud, or rock by the action of water or wind. □□ **ripplet** n. **ripply** adj. [17th c.: orig. unkn.]

ripple² /'rɪp(ə)l/ n. & v. —n. a toothed implement used to remove seeds from flax. —v.tr. treat with a ripple. [corresp. to MDu. & MLG *repel(en)*, OHG *riffila, rifilōn*]

riprap /'rɪpræp/ n. US a collection of loose stone as a foundation for a structure. [redupl. of RAP¹]

rip-roaring /'rɪpˌrɔːrɪŋ/ adj. **1** wildly noisy or boisterous. **2** excellent, first-rate. □□ **rip-roaringly** adv.

ripsaw /'rɪpsɔː/ n. a coarse saw for sawing wood along the grain.

ripsnorter /'rɪpˌsnɔːtə(r)/ n. colloq. an energetic, remarkable, or excellent person or thing. □□ **ripsnorting** adj. **ripsnortingly** adv.

Rip van Winkle /'wɪŋk(ə)l/ the good-for-nothing hero of a story (1820) by Washington Irving. He fell asleep in the Catskill Mountains north-west of New York, and awoke after 20 years to find the world completely changed.

rise /raɪz/ v. & n. —v.intr. (past **rose** /rəʊz/; past part. **risen** /'rɪz(ə)n/) **1** move from a lower position to a higher one; come or go up. **2** grow, project, expand, or incline upwards; become higher. **3** (of the sun, moon, or stars) appear above the horizon. **4 a** get up from lying or sitting or kneeling (*rose to their feet; rose from the table*). **b** get out of bed, esp. in the morning (*do you rise early?*). **5** recover a standing or vertical position; become erect (*rose to my full height*). **6** (of a meeting etc.) cease to sit for business; adjourn (*Parliament rises next week; the court will rise*). **7** reach a higher position or level or amount (*the flood has risen; prices are rising*). **8** develop greater intensity, strength, volume, or pitch (*the colour rose in her cheeks; the wind is rising; their voices rose with excitement*). **9** make progress; reach a higher social position (*rose from the ranks*). **10 a** come to the surface of liquid (*bubbles rose from the bottom; waited for the fish to rise*). **b** (of a person) react to provocation (*rise to the bait*). **11** become or be visible above the surroundings etc., stand prominently (*mountains rose to our right*). **12 a** (of buildings etc.) undergo construction from the foundations (*office blocks were rising all around*). **b** (of a tree etc.) grow to a (usu. specified) height. **13** come to life again (*rise from the ashes; risen from the dead*). **14** (of dough) swell by the action of yeast etc. **15** (often foll. by *up*) cease to be quiet or submissive; rebel (*rise in arms*). **16** originate; have as its source (*the river rises in the mountains*). **17** (of wind) start to blow. **18** (of a person's spirits) become cheerful. **19** (of a barometer) show a higher atmospheric pressure. **20** (of a horse) rear (*rose on its hind legs*). **21** (of a bump, blister, etc.) form. **22** (of the stomach) show nausea. —*n.* **1** an act or manner or amount of rising. **2** an upward slope or hill or movement (*a rise in the road; the house stood on a rise; the rise and fall of the waves*). **3** an increase in sound or pitch. **4 a** an increase in amount, extent, etc. (*a rise in unemployment*). **b** *Brit.* an increase in salary, wages, etc. **5** an increase in status or power. **6** social, commercial, or political advancement; upward progress. **7** the movement of fish to the surface. **8** origin. **9 a** the vertical height of a step, arch, incline, etc. **b** = RISER 2. □ **get** (or **take**) **a rise out of** *colloq.* provoke an emotional reaction from (a person), esp. by teasing. **on the rise** on the increase. **rise above 1** be superior to (petty feelings etc.). **2** show dignity or strength in the face of (difficulty, poor conditions, etc.). **rise and shine** (usu. as *imper.*) *colloq.* get out of bed smartly; wake up. **rise in the world** attain a higher social position. **rise to** develop powers equal to (an occasion). **rise with the sun** (or **lark**) get up early in the morning. [OE *rīsan* f. Gmc]

riser /ˈraɪzə(r)/ *n.* **1** a person who rises esp. from bed (*an early riser*). **2** a vertical section between the treads of a staircase. **3** a vertical pipe for the flow of liquid or gas.

rishi /ˈrɪʃɪ/ *n.* (*pl.* **rishis**) a Hindu sage or saint. [Skr. ṛṣi]

risible /ˈrɪzɪb(ə)l/ *adj.* **1** laughable, ludicrous. **2** inclined to laugh. **3** *Anat.* relating to laughter (*risible nerves*). □□ **risibility** /-ˈbɪlɪtɪ/ *n.* **risibly** *adv.* [LL *risibilis* f. L *rīdēre ris-* laugh]

rising /ˈraɪzɪŋ/ *adj.* & *n.* —*adj.* **1** going up; getting higher. **2** increasing (*rising costs*). **3** advancing to maturity or high standing (*the rising generation; a rising young lawyer*). **4** approaching a specified age (*the rising fives*). **5** (of ground) sloping upwards. —*n.* a revolt or insurrection. □ **rising damp** moisture absorbed from the ground into a wall.

risk /rɪsk/ *n.* & *v.* —*n.* **1** a chance or possibility of danger, loss, injury, or other adverse consequences (*a health risk; a risk of fire*). **2** a person or thing causing a risk or regarded in relation to risk (*is a poor risk*). —*v.tr.* **1** expose to risk. **2** accept the chance of (*could not risk getting wet*). **3** venture on. □ **at risk** exposed to danger. **at one's (own) risk** accepting responsibility, agreeing to make no claims. **at the risk of** with the possibility of (an adverse consequence). **put at risk** expose to danger. **risk capital** money put up for speculative business investment. **risk one's neck** put one's own life in danger. **run a** (or **the**) **risk** (often foll. by *of*) expose oneself to danger or loss etc. **take** (or **run**) **a risk** chance the possibility of danger etc. [F *risque, risquer* f. It. *risco* danger, *riscare* run into danger]

risky /ˈrɪskɪ/ *adj.* (**riskier, riskiest**) **1** involving risk. **2** = RISQUÉ. □□ **riskily** *adv.* **riskiness** *n.*

Risorgimento /rɪˌsɔːdʒɪˈmentəʊ/ *n. hist.* a movement for the unification and independence of Italy (achieved in 1870). It is associated with the names of Cavour, Mazzini, and Garibaldi. [It., = resurrection]

risotto /rɪˈzɒtəʊ/ *n.* (*pl.* **-os**) an Italian dish of rice cooked in stock with meat, onions, etc. [It.]

risqué /ˈrɪskeɪ, -ˈkeɪ/ *adj.* (of a story etc.) slightly indecent or liable to shock. [F, past part. of *risquer* RISK]

rissole /ˈrɪsəʊl/ *n.* a compressed mixture of meat and spices, coated in breadcrumbs and fried. [F f. OF *ruissole, roussole* ult. f. LL *russeolus* reddish f. L *russus* red]

rit. /rɪt/ *abbr. Mus.* ritardando.

ritardando /ˌrɪtɑːˈdændəʊ/ *adv.* & *n. Mus.* (*pl.* **-os** or **ritardandi** /-dɪ/) = RALLENTANDO. [It.]

rite /raɪt/ *n.* **1** a religious or solemn observance or act (*burial rites*). **2** an action or procedure required or usual in this. **3** a body of customary observances characteristic of a Church or a part of it (*the Latin rite*). □ **rite of passage** (often in *pl.*) a ritual or event marking a stage of a person's advance through life, e.g. marriage. □□ **riteless** *adj.* [ME f. OF *rit, rite* or L *ritus* (esp. religious) usage]

ritenuto /ˌrɪtɛˈnuːtəʊ/ *adv.* & *n. Mus.* —*adv.* with immediate reduction of speed. —*n.* (*pl.* **-os** or **ritenuti** /-tɪ/) a passage played in this way. [It.]

ritornello /ˌrɪtɔːˈnɛləʊ/ *n. Mus.* (*pl.* **-os** or **ritornelli** /-lɪ/) a short instrumental refrain, interlude, etc., in a vocal work. [It., dimin. of *ritorno* RETURN]

ritual /ˈrɪtjʊəl/ *n.* & *adj.* —*n.* **1** a prescribed order of performing rites. **2** a procedure regularly followed. —*adj.* of or done as a ritual or rites (*ritual murder*). □□ **ritualize** *v.tr.* & *intr.* (also **-ise**). **ritualization** /-ˈzeɪʃ(ə)n/ *n.* (also **-isation**). **ritually** *adv.* [L *ritualis* (as RITE)]

ritualism /ˈrɪtjʊəˌlɪz(ə)m/ *n.* the regular or excessive practice of ritual. □□ **ritualist** *n.* **ritualistic** /-ˈlɪstɪk/ *adj.* **ritualistically** /-ˈlɪstɪkəlɪ/ *adv.*

ritzy /ˈrɪtzɪ/ *adj.* (**ritzier, ritziest**) *colloq.* **1** high-class, luxurious. **2** ostentatiously smart. □□ **ritzily** *adv.* **ritziness** *n.* [*Ritz*, the name of luxury hotels f. C. *Ritz*, Swiss hotel-owner d. 1918]

rival /ˈraɪv(ə)l/ *n.* & *v.* —*n.* **1** a person competing with another for the same objective. **2** a person or thing that equals another in quality. **3** (*attrib.*) being a rival or rivals (*a rival firm*). —*v.tr.* (**rivalled, rivalling**; *US* **rivaled, rivaling**) **1** be the rival of or comparable to. **2** seem or claim to be as good as. [L *rivalis*, orig. = using the same stream, f. *rivus* stream]

rivalry /ˈraɪv(ə)lrɪ/ *n.* (*pl.* **-ies**) the state or an instance of being rivals; competition.

rive /raɪv/ *v.* (*past* **rived**; *past part.* **riven** /ˈrɪv(ə)n/) *archaic or poet.* **1** tr. split or tear apart violently. **2 a** tr. split (wood or stone). **b** *intr.* be split. [ME f. ON *rīfa*]

river /ˈrɪvə(r)/ *n.* **1** a copious natural stream of water flowing in a channel to the sea or a lake etc. **2** a copious flow (*a river of lava; rivers of blood*). **3** (*attrib.*) (in the names of animals, plants, etc.) living in or associated with the river. □ **river blindness** a tropical disease of the skin caused by a parasitic worm, the larvae of which can migrate into the eye and cause blindness. **river capture** the diversion of the upper headwaters of a river into a tain stream into a more powerful one. **sell down the river** *colloq.* betray or let down. □□ **rivered** *adj.* (also in *comb.*). **riverless** *adj.* [ME f. AF *river, rivere*, OF *riviere* river or river-bank ult. f. L *riparius* f. *ripa* bank]

Rivera /rɪˈveərə/, Diego (1886–1957), Mexican painter, the most celebrated figure in the revival of monumental fresco painting that is Mexico's most distinctive contribution to modern art. His most ambitious scheme, in the National Palace, portrays the history of Mexico; begun in 1929 and left unfinished at his death, it contains some of his most magnificent work, frankly didactic and intended to inspire a sense of nationalist and socialist identity.

riverine /ˈrɪvəraɪn/ *adj.* of or on a river or river-bank; riparian.

riverside /ˈrɪvəsaɪd/ *n.* the ground along a river-bank.

rivet /ˈrɪvɪt/ *n.* & *v.* —*n.* a nail or bolt for holding together metal plates etc., its headless end being beaten out or pressed down when in place. —*v.tr.* (**riveted, riveting**) **1 a** join or fasten with rivets. **b** beat out or press down the end of (a nail or bolt). **c** fix; make immovable. **2 a** (foll. by *on, upon*) direct intently (one's eyes or attention etc.). **b** (esp. as **riveting** *adj.*) engross (a person or the attention). □□ **riveter** *n.* [ME f. OF f. *river* clench, of unkn. orig.]

Riviera /ˌrɪvɪˈeərə/ **1** that part of the Mediterranean coastal region of southern France and northern Italy extending from Nice to La Spezia, famous for its scenic beauty, fertility, and mild climate, and with many fashionable resorts. **2** a region resembling this. [It., = sea-shore]

rivière /riːˈvjeə(r), ˈrɪvɪˌeə(r)/ n. a gem necklace. [F, = RIVER]

rivulet /ˈrɪvjʊlɪt/ n. a small stream. [obs. *riveret* f. F, dimin. of *rivière* RIVER, perh. after It. *rivoletto* dimin. of *rivolo* dimin. of *rivo* f. L *rivus* stream]

Riyadh /riːˈɑːd/ the capital of Saudi Arabia; pop. (est. 1986) 1,500,000.

riyal var. of RIAL.

RL abbr. Rugby League.

rly. abbr. railway.

RM abbr. **1** (in the UK) Royal Marines. **2** Resident Magistrate. **3** (in the UK) Royal Mail.

rm. abbr. room.

RMA abbr. Royal Military Academy.

r.m.s. abbr. Math. root-mean-square.

RMT abbr. (in the UK) National Union of Rail, Maritime and Transport Workers. ¶ Formed in 1990 by a merger of the NUR and NUS (sense 1).

RN abbr. **1** (in the UK) Royal Navy. **2** (in the UK) Registered Nurse.

Rn symb. Chem. the element radon.

RNA abbr. ribonucleic acid (see entry).

RNAS abbr. (in the UK) Royal Naval Air Service (or Station).

RNLI abbr. (in the UK) Royal National Lifeboat Institution.

RNZAF abbr. Royal New Zealand Air Force.

RNZN abbr. Royal New Zealand Navy.

roach[1] /rəʊtʃ/ n. (pl. same) a small freshwater fish, esp. *Rutilus rutilus*, allied to the carp. [ME f. OF *roc(h)e*, of unkn. orig.]

roach[2] /rəʊtʃ/ n. **1** US colloq. a cockroach. **2** sl. the butt of a marijuana cigarette. [abbr.]

roach[3] /rəʊtʃ/ n. Naut. an upward curve in the foot of a square sail. [18th c.: orig. unkn.]

road[1] /rəʊd/ n. **1 a** a path or way with a specially prepared surface, used by vehicles, pedestrians, etc. **b** the part of this used by vehicles (*don't step in the road*). **2** one's way or route (*our road took us through unexplored territory*). **3** an underground passage in a mine. **4** US a railway. **5** (usu. in pl.) a partly sheltered piece of water near the shore in which ships can ride at anchor. □ **by road** using transport along roads. **get out of the** (or **my** etc.) **road** colloq. cease to obstruct a person. **in the** (or **my** etc.) **road** colloq. obstructing a person or thing. **one for the road** colloq. a final (esp. alcoholic) drink before departure. **on the road** travelling, esp. as a firm's representative, itinerant performer, or vagrant. **road fund** Brit. hist. a fund for the construction and maintenance of roads and bridges. **road fund licence** Brit. a disc displayed on a vehicle certifying payment of road tax. **road-hog** colloq. a reckless or inconsiderate road-user, esp. a motorist. **road-holding** the capacity of a moving vehicle to remain stable when cornering at high speeds etc. **road-house** an inn or club on a major road. **road hump** = *sleeping policeman* (see SLEEP). **road-manager** the organizer and supervisor of a musicians' tour. **road-map** a map showing the roads of a country or area. **road-metal** broken stone used in road-making or for railway ballast. **road sense** a person's capacity for safe behaviour on the road, esp. in traffic. **road show 1 a** a performance given by a touring company, esp. a group of pop musicians. **b** a company giving such performances. **2** a radio or television programme done on location. **road sign** a sign giving information or instructions to road users. **road tax** a periodic tax payable on road vehicles. **road test** a test of the performance of a vehicle on the road. **road-test** v.tr. test (a vehicle) on the road. **the road to** the way of getting to or achieving (*the road to London*; *the road to ruin*). **road train** a large lorry pulling one or more trailers. **rule of the road** the custom or law regulating which side of the road is to be taken by vehicles (also riders or ships) meeting or passing each other. **take the road** set out. □□ **roadless** adj. [OE *rād* f. *rīdan* RIDE]

road[2] /rəʊd/ v.tr. (also absol.) (of a dog) follow up (a game-bird) by the scent of its trail. [19th c.: orig. unkn.]

roadbed /ˈrəʊdbed/ n. **1** the foundation structure of a railway. **2** the material laid down to form a road. **3** US the part of a road on which vehicles travel.

roadblock /ˈrəʊdblɒk/ n. a barrier or barricade on a road, esp. one set up by the authorities to stop and examine traffic.

roadie /ˈrəʊdɪ/ n. colloq. an assistant employed by a touring band of musicians to erect and maintain equipment.

roadman /ˈrəʊdmən/ n. (pl. **-men**) a man employed to repair or maintain roads.

roadroller /ˈrəʊdˌrəʊlə(r)/ n. a motor vehicle with a heavy roller, used in road-making.

roadrunner /ˈrəʊdˌrʌnə(r)/ n. a bird of Mexican and US deserts, *Geococcyx californianus*, related to the cuckoo, and a poor flier but fast runner.

roadside /ˈrəʊdsaɪd/ n. the strip of land beside a road.

roadstead /ˈrəʊdsted/ n. = ROAD[1] 5. [ROAD[1] + *stead* in obs. sense 'place']

roadster /ˈrəʊdstə(r)/ n. **1** an open car without rear seats. **2** a horse or bicycle for use on the road.

Road Town the capital of the British Virgin Islands, situated on the island of Tortola; pop. (1980) 3,000.

roadway /ˈrəʊdweɪ/ n. **1** a road. **2** = ROAD[1] 1b. **3** the part of a bridge or railway used for traffic.

roadwork /ˈrəʊdwɜːk/ n. **1** (in pl.) the construction or repair of roads, or other work involving digging up a road surface. **2** athletic exercise or training involving running on roads.

roadworthy /ˈrəʊdˌwɜːðɪ/ adj. **1** fit to be used on the road. **2** (of a person) fit to travel. □□ **roadworthiness** n.

roam /rəʊm/ v. & n. —v. **1** intr. ramble, wander. **2** tr. travel unsystematically over, through, or about. —n. an act of roaming; a ramble. □□ **roamer** n. [ME: orig. unkn.]

roan[1] /rəʊn/ adj. & n. —adj. (of an animal, esp. a horse or cow) having a coat of which the prevailing colour is thickly interspersed with hairs of another colour, esp. bay or sorrel or chestnut mixed with white or grey. —n. a roan animal. □ **blue roan** adj. black mixed with white. —n. a blue roan animal. **red roan** adj. bay mixed with white or grey. —n. a red roan animal. **strawberry roan** adj. chestnut mixed with white or grey. —n. a strawberry roan animal. [OF, of unkn. orig.]

roan[2] /rəʊn/ n. soft sheepskin leather used in bookbinding as a substitute for morocco. [ME, perh. f. *Roan*, old name of ROUEN]

roar /rɔː(r)/ n. & v. —n. **1** a loud deep hoarse sound, as made by a lion, a person in pain or rage or excitement, thunder, a loud engine, etc. **2** a loud laugh. —v. **1** intr. **a** utter or make a roar. **b** utter loud laughter. **c** (of a horse) make a loud noise in breathing as a symptom of disease. **2** travel in a vehicle at high speed, esp. with the engine roaring. **3** tr. (often foll. by *out*) say, sing, or utter (words, an oath, etc.) in a loud tone. □□ **roarer** n. [OE *rārian*, of imit. orig.]

roaring /ˈrɔːrɪŋ/ adj. in senses of ROAR v. □ **roaring drunk** very drunk and noisy. **roaring forties** stormy ocean tracts between lat. 40° and 50° S. **roaring trade** (or **business**) very brisk trade or business. **roaring twenties** the decade of the 1920s (with ref. to its postwar buoyancy). □□ **roaringly** adv.

roast /rəʊst/ v., adj., & n. —v. **1** tr. **a** cook (food, esp. meat) in an oven or by exposure to open heat. **b** heat (coffee beans) before grinding. **2** tr. heat (the ore of metal) in a furnace. **3** tr. **a** expose (a torture victim) to fire or great heat. **b** tr. or refl. expose (oneself or part of oneself) to warmth. **4** tr. criticize severely, denounce. **5** intr. undergo roasting. —attrib.adj. (of meat or a potato, chestnut, etc.) roasted. —n. **1 a** a roast meat. **b** a dish of this. **c** a piece of meat for roasting. **2** the process of roasting. **3** US a party where roasted food is eaten. [ME f. OF *rost*, *rostir*, f. Gmc]

roaster /ˈrəʊstə(r)/ n. **1** a person or thing that roasts. **2 a** an oven or dish for roasting food in. **b** an ore-roasting furnace. **c** a coffee-roasting apparatus. **3** something fit for roasting.

roasting /ˈrəʊstɪŋ/ adj. & n. —adj. very hot. —n. **1** in senses of ROAST v. **2** a severe criticism or denunciation.

rob /rɒb/ v.tr. (**robbed, robbing**) (often foll. by *of*) **1** take unlawfully from, esp. by force or threat of force (*robbed the safe*; *robbed her of her jewels*). **2** deprive of what is due or normal (*was robbed of my sleep*). **3** (absol.) commit robbery. □ **rob Peter to pay Paul** take away from one to give to another, discharge one debt by incurring another. [ME f. OF *rob(b)er* f. Gmc: cf. REAVE]

robber /ˈrɒbə(r)/ n. a person who commits robbery. □ **robber baron 1** a plundering feudal lord. **2** an unscrupulous plutocrat. [ME f. AF & OF (as ROB)]

robbery /ˈrɒbəri/ n. (pl. **-ies**) **1 a** the act or process of robbing, esp. with force or threat of force. **b** an instance of this. **2** excessive financial demand or cost (set us back £20—it was sheer robbery). [ME f. OF roberie (as ROB)]

Robbia /ˈrɒbɪə/, **della.** The name of a family of Florentine sculptors and ceramists of whom Luca (1400–82) is the most famous. His Singing Gallery for Florence Cathedral (1431–8) reinterpreted in marble relief antique motifs of singing and dancing youths with a delightful tenderness and sympathy, and it is this quality in his work that characterizes his output, particularly his half-length Madonna and Child in glazed white terracotta on blue ground. His nephew Andrea (1435–1525) carried on the family business; the roundels of infants on the Foundling Hospital in Florence (1463–6) have been attributed to him.

Robbins /ˈrɒbɪnz/, Jerome (1918–), American choreographer and director, originally a dancer. His adaptation of his first ballet Fancy Free (1944) as the musical On the Town led to a long series of successful musicals including The King and I (1951), West Side Story (1957), Funny Girl (1964), and Fiddler on the Roof (1964). Though much of his work draws on jazz and modern dance he has also created a number of ballets with music by classical composers.

robe /rəʊb/ n. & v. —n. **1** a long loose outer garment. **2** esp. US a dressing-gown. **3** a baby's outer garment esp. at a christening. **4** (often in pl.) a long outer garment worn as an indication of the wearer's rank, office, profession, etc.; a gown or vestment. **5** US a blanket or wrap of fur. —v. **1** tr. clothe (a person) in a robe; dress. **2** intr. put on one's robes or vestments. [ME f. OF f. Gmc (as ROB, orig. sense 'booty')]

Robert /ˈrɒbət/ the name of three kings of Scotland:
Robert I 'the Bruce' (1274–1329), reigned 1306–29. One of several competitors for the Scottish throne, Bruce eventually took up the leadership of the struggle against the English after the death of Sir William Wallace. Initially he suffered a series of defeats at the hands of Edward I and various Scottish rivals, but after several years as a fugitive he returned to lead a successful campaign against Edward II, culminating in his great victory at Bannockburn. He then went on to re-establish Scotland as a kingdom in its own right and to force the Plantagenets, at least temporarily, to give up their claim to overlordship.
Robert II 'the Steward' (1316–90), grandson of Robert the Bruce, reigned 1371–90. The first of the Stuart line, he succeeded his uncle David II at an advanced age and proved incapable of strong government. By the time of Robert's death the lawlessness of the Scottish nobility, which was to dominate the country's affairs for more than a century, had already become a serious problem.
Robert III (c.1337–1406), illegitimate son of Robert II, reigned 1390–1406, he changed his name from John to Robert on coming to the throne. Like his father, Robert III was senescent by the time he became king and proved unable to check the spread of noble lawlessness, in which his own brother Alexander, 'the Wolf of Badenoch', was a prime culprit. He described himself on his deathbed as 'the worst of kings and most miserable of men'.

Roberts /ˈrɒbəts/, Frederick Sleigh, 1st Earl Roberts of Kandahar (1832–1914), British military leader, whose career spanned the great age of British imperialism. He won a Victoria Cross during the Indian Mutiny and in 1880 commanded the British army which ended the Second Afghan War with a victory at Kandahar. In 1899 he was appointed Commander-in-Chief in South Africa and planned the successful march on the Boer capital of Pretoria.

Robeson /ˈrəʊbs(ə)n/, Paul Bustill (1898–1976), American Black actor and singer. His singing of 'Ole Man River' in the London production of Show Boat (1928) first revealed his superb bass voice, and he gave many recitals of Negro spirituals. He did much to further the interests of Blacks but his visit to Russia in 1963 as an avowed Communist aroused much controversy.

Robespierre /ˈrəʊbzpjeə(r)/, Maximilien François Marie Isidore de (1758–94), French revolutionary. A lawyer of some distinction, Robespierre entered politics in the early days of the French Revolution, and, although initially a moderate, drifted gradually towards the extreme left. Allying himself with the radical Jacobins, he purged the more moderate Girondins and instituted the Terror to rid himself of political opponents. As the pace of executions quickened, many of Robespierre's Revolutionary colleagues began to fear that he had gone mad and eventually they rose against him, sending him to the guillotine in July 1794.

Robey /ˈrəʊbɪ/, Sir George (1869–1954), the name adopted by George Edward Wade, British music-hall comedian, who became known as 'the Prime Minister of mirth'.

robin /ˈrɒbɪn/ n. **1** (also **robin redbreast**) a small brown European bird, Erithacus rubecula, the adult of which has a red throat and breast. **2** US a red-breasted thrush, Turdus migratorius. **3** a bird similar in appearance etc. to either of these. [ME f. OF, familiar var. of the name Robert]

Robin Goodfellow /ˌrɒbɪn ˈɡʊdfeləʊ/ see PUCK.

Robin Hood /ˌrɒbɪn ˈhʊd/ a semi-legendary English medieval outlaw, reputed to have robbed the rich and helped the poor. Although generally associated with Sherwood Forest in Nottinghamshire in the legends which sprang up around him, it seems likely that the real Robin Hood operated further north, in Yorkshire, most probably in the early decades of the 13th c.

robinia /rəˈbɪnɪə/ n. any N. American tree or shrub of the genus Robinia, e.g. a locust tree or false acacia. [mod.L, f. J. Robin, 17th-c. French gardener]

Robinson¹ /ˈrɒbɪns(ə)n/, Edward G. (real name Emanuel Goldenberg, 1893–1972), Romanian-born American actor. After playing the part of a gangster in Little Caesar (1930) he became particularly associated with racketeer or tough-guy characters in the 1930s, but later played a wider range of roles.

Robinson² /ˈrɒbɪns(ə)n/, Sugar Ray (real name Walker Smith, 1920–89), American boxer, world welterweight champion 1946–51 and middleweight champion five times between 1951 and 1960.

Robinson Crusoe /ˌrɒbɪns(ə)n ˈkruːsəʊ/ the hero of a novel (1719) by Defoe, based on an adventure of Alexander Selkirk who lived alone on the uninhabited Pacific Island of Juan Fernandez for five years (1704–9).

roborant /ˈrəʊbərənt, ˈrɒb-/ adj. & n. Med. —adj. strengthening. —n. a strengthening drug. [L roborare f. robur -oris strength]

robot /ˈrəʊbɒt/ n. **1** a machine with a human appearance or functioning like a human. **2** a machine capable of carrying out a complex series of actions automatically. **3** a person who works mechanically and efficiently but insensitively. **4** S.Afr. an automatic traffic-signal. □□ **robotic** /-ˈbɒtɪk/ adj. **robotize** v.tr. (also **-ise**). [Czech (in K. Čapek's play R.U.R. (Rossum's Universal Robots) 1920), f. robota forced labour]

robotics /rəʊˈbɒtɪks/ n.pl. the study of robots; the art or science of their design, construction, operation, and application. The term originated in the science fiction stories of Isaac Asimov, American scientist and writer, but is now used of automatic processes in industry. The discipline is concerned with building robots, programmable devices consisting of fixed or mobile mechanical manipulators and sensory organs, which are linked to a computer. Simple robots are widely used in production engineering, especially where a variety of goods is to be produced with minimum changeover time. Such robots have very little (if any) sensory capability and follow a fixed but reprogrammable sequence of instructions. Important goals of robotics research in artifical intelligence are (i) to program robots off line using a high-level computing language, especially including a degree of automatic planning and recovery from errors, and (ii) to provide the robot with sensors—typically a television camera—and to use sensory perception to guide it in a flexible manner. Goals of robotic research in mechanical and production engineering are to improve dynamic performance and to design robot systems able to handle the assembly of complex objects.

Rob Roy /rɒb ˈrɔɪ/ (Robert MacGregor, 1671–1734), Scottish highland bandit, popularized in Sir Walter Scott's novel of the same name, who was heavily involved in blackmail and cattle theft in the area north of Loch Lomond. He proclaimed his support for the Old Pretender in 1715, but failed to commit his men to battle.

Robsart /ˈrɒbsɑːt/, Amy (1532–60), the first wife of Robert Dudley (later Earl of Leicester), a favourite of Queen Elizabeth I. Her mysterious death at Cumnor Place, a country house near Oxford, aroused suspicions that her husband had had her killed (with or without Elizabeth's connivance) so that he could be free to marry the Queen. Sir Walter Scott's novel *Kenilworth* (1821) is based on the tradition of her tragic fate.

Robson /ˈrɒbs(ə)n/, Dame Flora (1902–85), English actress, an outstanding player of parts demanding controlled nervous tension.

robust /rəʊˈbʌst/ *adj.* (**robuster**, **robustest**) **1** (of a person, animal, or thing) strong and sturdy, esp. in physique or construction. **2** (of exercise, discipline, etc.) vigorous, requiring strength. **3** (of intellect or mental attitude) straightforward, not given to nor confused by subtleties. **4** (of a statement, reply, etc.) bold, firm, unyielding. **5** (of wine etc.) full-bodied. □□ **robustly** *adv.* **robustness** *n.* [F *robuste* or L *robustus* firm and hard f. *robus*, *robur* oak, strength]

ROC *abbr.* (in the UK) Royal Observer Corps.

roc /rɒk/ *n.* a gigantic bird of Eastern legend. [Sp. *rocho* ult. f. Arab *ruḵ*]

rocaille /rəʊˈkaɪ/ *n.* **1** an 18th-c. style of ornamentation based on rock and shell motifs. **2** a rococo style. [F f. *roc* (as ROCK[1])]

rocambole /ˈrɒkəmˌbəʊl/ *n.* an alliaceous plant, *Allium scorodoprasum*, with a garlic-like bulb used for seasoning. [F f. G *Rockenbolle*]

roche moutonnée /ˌrɒʃ muːˈtɒneɪ/ *n.* Geol. a small bare outcrop of rock shaped by glacial erosion, with one side smooth and gently sloping and the other steep, rough and irregular. [F, = fleecy rock]

Rochester /ˈrɒtʃɪstə(r)/, John Wilmot, 2nd Earl of (1647–80), English poet, one of the 'court wits' surrounding Charles II. According to Samuel Johnson he 'blazed out his youth and health in lavish voluptuousness'; at the end of his short life he had moved towards religious conversion. His poems (often erotic and sometimes pornographic) combine a brilliant wit with an emotional complexity, and with his social and literary verse satires he was one of the first Augustans. These works include his tough self-dramatization 'The Maimed Debauchee', the grimly funny 'Upon Nothing', and the *Satyr against Mankind* (1675).

rochet /ˈrɒtʃɪt/ *n.* a vestment resembling a surplice, used chiefly by bishops and abbots. [ME f. OF, dimin. f. Gmc]

rock[1] /rɒk/ *n.* **1 a** the hard material of the earth's crust, exposed on the surface or underlying the soil. **b** a similar material on other planets. **2** Geol. any natural material, hard or soft (e.g. clay), consisting of one or more minerals. **3 a** a mass of rock projecting and forming a hill, cliff, reef, etc. **b** (**the Rock**) Gibraltar. **4** a large detached stone. **5** US a stone of any size. **6** a firm and dependable support or protection. **7** a source of danger or destruction. **8** Brit. a hard usu. cylindrical stick of confectionery made from sugar with flavouring esp. of peppermint. **9** (in *pl.*) US sl. money. **10** sl. a precious stone, esp. a diamond. **11** sl. a solid form of cocaine. **12** (in *pl.*) *coarse sl.* the testicles. □ **get one's rocks off** *coarse sl.* **1** achieve sexual satisfaction. **2** obtain enjoyment. **on the rocks** *colloq.* **1** short of money. **2** broken down. **3** (of a drink) served undiluted with ice-cubes. **rock-bed** a base of rock or a rocky bottom. **rock-bottom** *adj.* (of prices etc.) the very lowest. —*n.* the very lowest level. **rock-bound** (of a coast) rocky and inaccessible. **rock-cake** a small currant cake with a hard rough surface. **rock-candy** US = sense 8 of *n.* **rock cress** = ARABIS. **rock-crystal** transparent colourless quartz usu. in hexagonal prisms. **rock-dove** a wild dove, *Columba livia*, frequenting rocks, supposed ancestor of the domestic pigeon. **rock-face** a vertical surface of natural rock. **rock-fish** a rock-frequenting goby, bass, wrasse, catfish, etc. **rock-garden** an artificial mound or bank of earth and stones planted with rock-plants etc.; a garden in which rockeries are the chief feature. **rock-pigeon** = *rock-dove*. **rock-pipit** a species

of pipit, *Anthus spinoletta*, frequenting rocky shores. **rock-plant** any plant growing on or among rocks. **rock python** any large snake of the family Boidae, esp. the African python *Python sebae*. **rock-rabbit** any of several species of hyrax. **rock rose** any plant of the genus *Cistus*, *Helianthemum*, etc., with rose-like flowers. **rock-salmon 1** any of several fishes, esp. *Brit.* (as a commercial name) the catfish and dogfish. **2** US an amberjack. **rock-salt** common salt as a solid mineral. **rock-wool** inorganic material made into matted fibre esp. for insulation or soundproofing. □□ **rockless** *adj.* **rocklet** *n.* **rocklike** *adj.* [ME f. OF *ro(c)que*, *roche*, med.L *rocca*, of unkn. orig.]

rock[2] /rɒk/ *v. & n.* —*v.* **1** *tr.* move gently to and fro in or as if in a cradle; set or maintain such motion (*rock him to sleep*; *the ship was rocked by the waves*). **2** *intr.* be or continue in such motion (*sat rocking in his chair*; *the ship was rocking on the waves*). **3 a** *intr.* sway from side to side; shake, oscillate, reel (*the house rocks*). **b** *tr.* cause to do this (*an earthquake rocked the house*). **4** *tr.* distress, perturb. **5** *intr.* dance to or play rock music. —*n.* **1** a rocking movement (*gave the chair a rock*). **2** a spell of rocking (*had a rock in his chair*). **3 a** = *rock and roll*. **b** any of a variety of types of modern popular music with a rocking or swinging beat, derived from rock and roll. (See below.) □ **rock and** (or **rock 'n'**) **roll** a type of popular dance-music originating in the 1950s, characterized by a heavy beat and simple melodies, often with a blues element. **rock and** (or **rock 'n'**) **roller** a devotee of rock and roll. **rock the boat** *colloq.* disturb the equilibrium of a situation. **rocking-chair** a chair mounted on rockers or springs for gently rocking in. **rocking-horse** a model of a horse on rockers or springs for a child to rock on. **rocking-stone** a poised boulder easily rocked. **rock-shaft** a shaft that oscillates about an axis without making complete revolutions. [OE *roccian*, prob. f. Gmc]

Rock and roll, developed in the 1950s, was an amalgam of the styles of American White country music and Black rhythm and blues; its most famous figure was Elvis Presley (see entry), and its established format was the short (three-minute) song. In the 1960s and 1970s styles became more diverse, with much improvisation and experimentation, with emphasis on themes of youth protest and sometimes with cryptic references to hallucinogenic drugs. Amplified singing, electric instruments, and a prominent rhythm section have been elements throughout, in a style intended to encourage people to dance, and its appeal is chiefly to the young. The term 'rock' applies strictly to the style that emerged in the mid-1960s, but is used more widely to include 'rock and roll' too, and now frequently encompasses most modern popular music ('pop') with a rocking or swinging beat.

rockabilly /ˈrɒkəˌbɪlɪ/ *n.* a type of popular music combining elements of rock and roll and hill-billy music. [blend of *rock and roll* and *hill-billy*]

Rockall /ˈrɒkɔːl/ a rocky islet in the North Atlantic, about 400 km (250 miles) north-west of Ireland.

rockburst /ˈrɒkbɜːst/ *n.* a sudden rupture or collapse of highly stressed rock in a mine.

Rockefeller /ˈrɒkəˌfelə(r)/, John Davison (1839–1937), American industrialist. One of the first to recognize the industrial possibilities of oil, Rockefeller established the Standard Oil Company and by the end of the 1870s exercised a virtual monopoly over oil refining and transportation in the US. Early in the 20th c. he handed over his business interests to his son and devoted his immense private fortune to various philanthropic projects.

rocker /ˈrɒkə(r)/ *n.* **1** a person or thing that rocks. **2** a curved bar or similar support, on which something can rock. **3** a rocking-chair. **4** Brit. a young devotee of rock music, characteristically associated with leather clothing and motor cycles. **5** a skate with a highly curved blade. **6** a switch constructed on a pivot mechanism operating between the 'on' and 'off' positions. **7** any rocking device forming part of a mechanism. □ **off one's rocker** *sl.* crazy.

rockery /ˈrɒkərɪ/ *n.* (*pl.* **-ies**) a heaped arrangement of rough stones with soil between them for growing rock-plants on.

rocket[1] /ˈrɒkɪt/ *n. & v.* —*n.* **1** a cylindrical projectile that can be propelled to a great height or distance by combustion of its contents, used esp. as a firework or signal. **2** an engine using a similar principle but not dependent on air intake for its operation. **3** a rocket-propelled missile, spacecraft, etc. (See below.) **4** *Brit. sl.* a severe reprimand. —*v.* (**rocketed, rocketing**) **1** *tr.* bombard with rockets. **2** *intr.* **a** move rapidly upwards or away. **b** increase rapidly (*prices rocketed*). [F *roquette* f. It. *rochetto* dimin. of *rocca* ROCK², with ref. to its cylindrical shape]

The use of rockets (probably of the fireworks type) as a weapon of war dates from the 13th c. in both China and Europe. They were developed and used in warfare over the centuries, but by the mid-19th c. could not compete with improved artillery. In 1926 the work of the American physicist R. H. Goddard resulted in the launching of the first rocket to use liquid fuel, an important development in the history of rocketry. The Germans devoted considerable effort towards rocket research and experimentation in the 1930s, and used both guided and ballistic missiles (the V1 and V2) during the Second World War, after which von Braun and others of the German research team were recruited by the Americans to assist in the development of rockets which eventually launched vehicles into space.

rocket² /ˈrɒkɪt/ *n.* **1** (also **sweet rocket**) any of various fast-growing plants, esp. of the genus *Hesperis* or *Sisymbrium*. **2** a cruciferous annual plant, *Eruca sativa*, grown for salad. □ **wall-rocket** a yellow-flowered weed, *Diplotaxis muralis*, emitting a foul smell when crushed. **yellow rocket** winter cress. [F *roquette* f. It. *rochetta, ruchetta* dimin. of *ruca* f. L *eruca* downy-stemmed plant]

rocketeer /ˌrɒkɪˈtɪə(r)/ *n.* **1** a discharger of rockets. **2** a rocket expert or enthusiast.

rocketry /ˈrɒkɪtrɪ/ *n.* the science or practice of rocket propulsion.

rockfall /ˈrɒkfɔːl/ *n.* **1** a descent of loose rocks. **2** a mass of fallen rock.

Rockhampton /rɒkˈhæmpt(ə)n/ a town in Queensland, Australia, the centre of Australia's largest beef-producing area; pop. (est. 1987) 60,400.

rockhopper /ˈrɒkˌhɒpə(r)/ *n.* a small penguin, *Eudyptes crestatus*, of the Antarctic and New Zealand, with a crest of feathers on the forehead.

rockling /ˈrɒklɪŋ/ *n.* any of various small marine fish of the cod family, esp. of the genus *Ciliata* and *Rhinomenus*, found in pools among rocks.

rocky¹ /ˈrɒkɪ/ *adj.* (**rockier, rockiest**) **1** of or like rock. **2** full of or abounding in rock or rocks (*a rocky shore*). □□ **rockiness** *n.*

rocky² /ˈrɒkɪ/ *adj.* (**rockier, rockiest**) *colloq.* unsteady, tottering. □□ **rockily** *adv.* **rockiness** *n.* [ROCK²]

Rocky Mountains (also **Rockies**) the great mountain system of western North America extending from the US–Mexico border to the Yukon Territory of Canada. Several peaks rise to over 4,300 m (14,000 ft.).

rococo /rəˈkəʊkəʊ/ *adj. & n.* —*adj.* **1** of a late baroque style of decoration prevalent in 18th-c. continental Europe, with asymmetrical patterns involving scroll-work, shell motifs, etc. **2** (of literature, music, architecture, and the decorative arts) highly ornamented, florid. —*n.* the rococo style. [F, joc. alt. f. ROCAILLE]

rod /rɒd/ *n.* **1** a slender straight bar esp. of wood or metal. **2** this as a symbol of office. **3 a** a stick or bundle of twigs used in caning or flogging. **b** (prec. by *the*) the use of this. **4 a** *=fishing-rod.* **b** an angler using a rod. **5 a** a slender straight round stick growing as a shoot on a tree. **b** this when cut. **6** (as a measure) a perch or square perch (see PERCH¹ and GUNTER). **7** *US sl.* = hot rod. **8** *US sl.* a pistol or revolver. **9** *Anat.* any of numerous rod-shaped structures in the eye, detecting dim light. □ **make a rod for one's own back** act in a way that will bring one trouble later. □□ **rodless** *adj.* **rodlet** *n.* **rodlike** *adj.* [OE *rodd*, prob. rel. to ON *rudda* club]

rode¹ *past of* RIDE.

rode² /rəʊd/ *v.intr.* **1** (of wildfowl) fly landwards in the evening. **2** (of woodcock) fly in the evening during the breeding season. [18th c.: orig. unkn.]

rodent /ˈrəʊd(ə)nt/ *n. & adj.* —*n.* any mammal of the order Rodentia with strong incisors and no canine teeth, e.g. rat, mouse, squirrel, beaver, porcupine. —*adj.* **1** of the order Rodentia. **2** gnawing (esp. *Med.* of slow-growing ulcers). □ **rodent officer** *Brit.* an official dealing with rodent pests. □□ **rodential** /-ˈdenʃ(ə)l/ *adj.* [L *rodere* ros- gnaw]

rodenticide /rəˈdentɪˌsaɪd/ *n.* a poison used to kill rodents.

rodeo /ˈrəʊdɪəʊ, rəˈdeɪəʊ/ *n.* (*pl.* **-os**) **1** an exhibition or entertainment involving cowboys' skills in handling animals. Rodeo was born in the southern States of the US after the Civil War, when Texan cowboys, driving their cattle to the north and west in search of new markets, had to find their own amusements. They did so with riding and roping contests, which presently became public entertainments. **2** an exhibition of other skills, e.g. in motor cycling. **3 a** a round-up of cattle on a ranch for branding etc. **b** an enclosure for this. [Sp. f. *rodear* go round ult. f. L *rotare* ROTATE¹]

Rodgers /ˈrɒdʒəz/, Richard (1902–79), American song-writer. He collaborated with Lorenz Hart on musical shows such as *The Girl Friend* (1926). After Hart's death in 1943, Oscar Hammerstein II became his lyric-writer and together they produced such triumphs as *Oklahoma!* (1943), *Carousel* (1945), *South Pacific* (1949), *The King and I* (1951), and *The Sound of Music* (1959).

rodham /ˈrɒdəm/ *n.* a raised bank in the Fen district of E. Anglia, formed on the bed of a dry river-course. [20th c.: orig. uncert.]

Rodin /ˈrəʊdæ̃/, Auguste (1840–1917), the most celebrated sculptor of the French Romantic school, primarily a modeller rather than a carver in spite of being deeply influenced by Michelangelo. His sketchy unfinished figures are reminiscent of contemporary impressionist paintings. Rodin began as a mason, but visited Italy in 1875, and first became known with a life-sized nude called *Bronze Age* (1877). Like that of his most famous work, the huge *Gate of Hell* (1880, unfinished), the title is virtually meaningless (the latter derives from Ghiberti's *Door of Paradise*); it is actually a collection of nude figures, including one reused as *The Thinker* (1904). His works exist in many replicas; there are large collections in Paris (Musée Rodin), London, and Philadelphia.

rodomontade /ˌrɒdəmɒnˈteɪd/ *n., adj., & v.* —*n.* **1** boastful or bragging talk or behaviour. **2** an instance of this. —*adj.* boastful or bragging. —*v.intr.* brag, talk boastfully. [F f. obs. It. *rodomontada* f. F *rodomont* & It. *rodomonte* f. the name of a boastful character in the *Orlando* epics]

roe¹ /rəʊ/ *n.* **1** (also **hard roe**) the mass of eggs in a female fish's ovary. **2** (also **soft roe**) the milt of a male fish. □ **roe-stone** oolite. □□ **roed** *adj.* (also in *comb.*). [ME *row(e)*, rough, f. MLG, MDu. *roge(n)*, OHG *rogo, rogan*, ON *hrogn*]

roe² /rəʊ/ *n.* (*pl.* same or **roes**) (also **roe-deer**) a small European and Asian deer, *Capreolus capreolus*. [OE *rā(ha)*]

roebuck /ˈrəʊbʌk/ *n.* a male roe.

roentgen /ˈrʌntjən/ *n.* a unit of ionizing radiation, the amount producing one electrostatic unit of positive or negative ionic charge in one cubic centimetre of air under standard conditions. □ **roentgen rays** X-rays. [W. C. RÖNTGEN]

roentgenography /ˌrʌntjəˈnɒɡrəfɪ/ *n.* photography using X-rays.

roentgenology /ˌrʌntjəˈnɒlədʒɪ/ *n.* = RADIOLOGY.

Roeselare /ˌruːsəˈlɑːrə/ (French **Roulers** /ruːˈleə(r)/) a textile-manufacturing town in Belgium, 12 km (20 miles) south-west of Bruges; pop. (1988) 52,100.

rogation /rəʊˈɡeɪʃ(ə)n/ *n.* (usu. in *pl.*) *Eccl.* a solemn supplication consisting of the litany of the saints chanted on the three Rogation days before Ascension day. □ **Rogation Days** certain days prescribed in the Western Church for prayer and fasting, on which intercession is made especially for the harvest. The Major Rogation (25 Apr.) is a Christianized version of pagan ritual processions through the cornfields to pray for the preservation of the crops from mildew. The Minor Rogations are kept on the three days before Ascension Day, and originated in 5th-c. Gaul to protect the land against earthquakes and other perils; these days (only) are prescribed in the Book of Common Prayer. In England the traditional ceremony of beating the parish bounds is associated with this observance. **Rogation Sunday** the Sunday before Ascension Day. □□ **rogational** adj. [ME f. L rogatio f. rogare ask]

roger /ˈrɒdʒə(r)/ int. & v. —int. **1** your message has been received and understood (used in radio communication etc.). **2** sl. I agree. —v. coarse sl. **1** intr. have sexual intercourse. **2** tr. have sexual intercourse with (a woman). [the name Roger, code for R]

rogue /rəʊg/ n. & v. —n. **1** a dishonest or unprincipled person. **2** joc. a mischievous person, esp. a child. **3** (usu. attrib.) **a** a wild animal driven away or living apart from the herd and of fierce temper (rogue elephant). **b** a stray, irresponsible, or undisciplined person or thing (rogue trader). **4** an inferior or defective specimen among many acceptable ones. —v.tr. remove rogues (sense 4 of n.) from. □ **rogues' gallery** a collection of photographs of known criminals etc., used for identification of suspects. [16th-c. cant word: orig. unkn.]

roguery /ˈrəʊgərɪ/ n. (pl. **-ies**) conduct or an action characteristic of rogues.

roguish /ˈrəʊgɪʃ/ adj. **1** playfully mischievous. **2** characteristic of rogues. □□ **roguishly** adv. **roguishness** n.

roil /rɔɪl/ v.tr. **1** make (a liquid) turbid by agitating it. **2** US = RILE 1. [perh. f. OF ruiler mix mortar f. LL regulare regulate]

roister /ˈrɔɪstə(r)/ v.intr. (esp. as **roistering** adj.) revel noisily; be uproarious. □□ **roisterer** n. **roistering** n. **roisterous** adj. [obs. roister roisterer f. F rustre ruffian var. of ruste f. L rusticus RUSTIC]

Roland /ˈrəʊlənd/ the most famous of Charlemagne's paladins, hero of the Chanson de Roland (12th c.) and other (esp. French and Italian) medieval romances. He is said to have become a friend of Oliver, another paladin, after contending with him in single combat in which neither won. Roland was killed in a rearguard action at Roncesvalles (see entry). □ **a Roland for an Oliver 1** an effective retort. **2** a well-balanced combat or exchange.

role /rəʊl/ n. (also **rôle**) **1** an actor's part in a play, film, etc. **2** a person's or thing's characteristic or expected function (the role of the tape recorder in language-learning). □ **role model** a person looked to by others as an example in a particular role. **role-playing** an exercise in which participants act the part of another character, used in psychotherapy, language-teaching, etc. [F rôle and obs. F roule, rolle, = ROLL n.]

roll /rəʊl/ v. & n. —v. **1 a** intr. move or go in some direction by turning over and over on an axis (the ball rolled under the table; a barrel started rolling). **b** tr. cause to do this (rolled the barrel into the cellar). **2** tr. make revolve between two surfaces (rolled the clay between his palms). **3 a** intr. (foll. by along, by, etc.) move or advance on or (of time etc.) as if on wheels etc. (the bus rolled past; the pram rolled off the pavement; the years rolled by). **b** tr. cause to do this (rolled the tea trolley into the kitchen). **c** intr. (of a person) be conveyed in a vehicle (the farmer rolled by on his tractor). **4 a** tr. turn over and over on itself to form a more or less cylindrical or spherical shape (rolled a newspaper). **b** tr. make by forming material into a cylinder or ball (rolled a cigarette; rolled a huge snowball). **c** tr. accumulate into a mass (rolled the dough into a ball). **d** intr. (foll. by into) make a specified shape of itself (the hedgehog rolled into a ball). **5** tr. flatten or form by passing a roller etc. over or by passing between rollers (roll the lawn; roll pastry; roll thin foil). **6** intr. & tr. change or cause to change direction by rotatory movement (his eyes rolled; he rolled his eyes). **7** intr. **a** wallow, turn about in a fluid or a loose medium (the dog rolled in the dust). **b** (of a horse etc.) lie on its back and kick about, esp. in an attempt to dislodge its rider. **8** intr. **a** (of a moving ship, aircraft, or vehicle) sway to and fro on an axis parallel to the direction of motion. **b** walk with an unsteady swaying gait (they rolled out of the pub). **9 a** intr. undulate, show or go with an undulating surface or motion (rolling hills; rolling mist; the waves roll in). **b** tr. carry or propel with such motion (the river rolls its waters to the sea). **10 a** intr. (of machinery) start functioning or moving (the cameras rolled; the train began to roll). **b** tr. cause (machinery) to do this. **11** intr. & tr. sound or utter with a vibratory or trilling effect (words rolled off his tongue; thunder rolled in the distance; he rolls his rs). **12** US sl. **a** overturn (a car etc.). **b** intr. (of a car etc.) overturn. **13** tr. US throw (dice). **14** tr. sl. rob (esp. a helpless victim). —n. **1** a rolling motion or gait; undulation (the roll of

the hills). **2 a** a spell of rolling (a roll in the mud). **b** a gymnastic exercise in which the body is rolled into a tucked position and turned in a forward or backward circle. **c** (esp. **a roll in the hay**) colloq. an act of sexual intercourse or erotic fondling. **3** the continuous rhythmic sound of thunder or a drum. **4** Aeron. a complete revolution of an aircraft about its longitudinal axis. **5 a** a cylinder formed by turning flexible material over and over on itself without folding (a roll of carpet; a roll of wallpaper). **b** a filled cake or pastry of similar form (fig roll; sausage roll). **6 a** a small portion of bread individually baked. **b** this with a specified filling (ham roll). **7 a** a more or less cylindrical or semicylindrical straight or curved mass of something (rolls of fat; a roll of hair). **8 a** an official list or register (the electoral roll). **b** the total numbers on this (the schools' rolls have fallen). **c** a document, esp. an official record, in scroll form. **9** a cylinder or roller, esp. to shape metal in a rolling-mill. **10** Archit. **a** a moulding of convex section. **b** a spiral scroll of an Ionic capital. **11** US & Austral. money, esp. as banknotes rolled together. □ **be rolling** colloq. be very rich. **be rolling in** colloq. have plenty of (esp. money). **on a roll** US sl. experiencing a bout of success or progress; engaged in a period of intense activity. **roll back** US cause (esp. prices) to decrease. **roll-back** n. a reduction (esp. in price). **roll bar** an overhead metal bar strengthening the frame of a vehicle (esp. in racing) and protecting the occupants if the vehicle overturns. **roll-call** a process of calling out a list of names to establish who is present. **rolled gold** gold in the form of a thin coating applied to a baser metal by rolling. **rolled into one** combined in one person or thing. **rolled oats** oats that have been husked and crushed. **roll in** arrive in great numbers or quantity. **rolling barrage** = creeping barrage. **rolling drunk** swaying or staggering from drunkenness. **rolling-mill** a machine or factory for rolling metal into shape. **rolling-pin** a cylinder for rolling out pastry, dough, etc. **rolling-stock 1** the locomotives, carriages, or other vehicles, used on a railway. **2** US the road vehicles of a company. **rolling stone** a person who is unwilling to settle for long in one place. **rolling strike** industrial action through a series of limited strikes by consecutive groups. **roll-neck** (of a garment) having a high loosely turned-over neck. **roll of honour** a list of those honoured, esp. the dead in war. **roll on** v.tr. **1** put on or apply by rolling. **2** (in imper.) colloq. (of a time, in eager expectation) come quickly (roll on Friday!). **roll-on** (attrib.) (of deodorant etc.) applied by means of a rotating ball in the neck of the container. —n. a light elastic corset. **roll-off** (of a ship, a method of transport, etc.) in which vehicles are driven directly on at the start of the voyage and off at the end of it. **roll over 1** send (a person) sprawling or rolling. **2** Econ. finance the repayment of (maturing stock etc.) by an issue of new stock. **roll-over** n. **1** Econ. the extension or transfer of a debt or other financial relationship. **2** colloq. the overturning of a vehicle etc. **roll-top desk** a desk with a flexible cover sliding in curved grooves. **roll up 1** colloq. arrive in a vehicle; appear on the scene. **2** make into or form a roll. **3** Mil. drive the flank of (an enemy line) back and round so that the line is shortened or surrounded. **roll-up** (or **roll-your-own**) n. a hand-rolled cigarette. **roll up one's sleeves** see SLEEVE. **strike off the rolls** debar (esp. a solicitor) from practising after dishonesty etc. □□ **rollable** adj. [ME f. OF rol(l)er, rouler, ro(u)lle f. L rotulus dimin. of rota wheel]

Rolland /rɒˈlɑ̃/, Romain (1866–1944), French writer and critic of art and music, who published an Histoire de l'opéra (1895) and achieved success with a lyrically written life of Beethoven (1903) and similar studies on Michelangelo (1908) and Tolstoy (1911). His stage works include three dramas of the Revolution; his best-known work Jean-Christophe (1906–12) is a roman-fleuve about a German composer. Rolland's pamphlet Au-dessus de la mêlée (1915) was an appeal to both sides to agitate for peace in days of fanatical patriotism; it aroused resentment in many quarters. He was awarded the Nobel Prize for literature in 1915.

rollaway /ˈrəʊləˌweɪ/ adj. US (of a bed etc.) that can be removed on wheels or castors.

roller /ˈrəʊlə(r)/ n. **1 a** a hard revolving cylinder for smoothing the ground, spreading ink or paint, crushing or stamping, rolling up cloth on, hanging a towel on, etc., used alone or as a rotating part of a machine. **b** a cylinder for diminishing friction when moving a heavy object. **2** a small cylinder on which hair is rolled for setting. **3** a long swelling wave. **4** (also **roller bandage**) a long surgical bandage rolled up for convenient application. **5** a kind of tumbler-pigeon. **6 a** any brilliantly plumaged bird of the family Coraciidae, with characteristic tumbling display-flight. **b** a breed of canary with a trilling song. □ **roller bearing** a bearing like a ball-bearing but with small cylinders instead of balls. **roller-coaster** *n.* a switchback at a fair etc. —*adj.* that goes up and down, or changes, suddenly and repeatedly. —*v.intr.* (or **roller-coast**) go up and down or change in this way. **roller-skate** see SKATE¹. Although a primitive form of roller-skate was known in The Netherlands from the 18th c., the first practical four-wheel skate was patented in the US in 1863. Its original purpose was to enable ice-skaters to practise when there was no natural ice, but roller-skating quickly developed as an independent sport. **roller-skater** a person who roller-skates. **roller towel** a towel with the ends joined, hung on a roller.

rollerball /ˈrəʊləˌbɔːl/ *n.* a ball-point pen using thinner ink than other ball-points.

rollick /ˈrɒlɪk/ *v. & n.* —*v.intr.* (esp. as **rollicking** *adj.*) be jovial or exuberant, indulge in high spirits, revel. —*n.* **1** exuberant gaiety. **2** a spree or escapade. [19th-c., prob. dial.: perh. f. ROMP + FROLIC]

Rolling Stones, the an English group playing rock music, formed in 1962–3, whose members include the vocalist Mick Jagger (1943–). They became noted for their defiance of established social conventions and for the exhibitionism which was a feature of their performances and of other groups who sought to emulate them.

rollmop /ˈrəʊlmɒp/ *n.* a rolled uncooked pickled herring fillet. [G *Rollmops*]

Rolls /rəʊlz/, Charles Stewart (1877–1910), English motoring and aviation pioneer, one of the founder members of the Royal Automobile Club and the Royal Aero Club. In 1906 he and Royce (see entry) formed the company Rolls-Royce Ltd. with Royce as chief engineer and Rolls himself as demonstrator-salesman. He was the first Englishman to fly across the English Channel, and made the first double crossing in 1910 shortly before he was killed in an air crash, the first English victim of aviation.

roly-poly /ˌrəʊlɪˈpəʊlɪ/ *n. & adj.* —*n.* (*pl.* **-ies**) **1** (also **roly-poly pudding**) a pudding made of a strip of suet pastry covered with jam etc., formed into a roll, and boiled or baked. **2** *US* a tumbler toy. **3** *Austral.* a bushy plant, esp. *Salsola kali*, that breaks off and is rolled by the wind. —*adj.* (usu. of a child) podgy, plump. [prob. formed on ROLL]

ROM /rɒm/ *n. Computing* read-only memory. [abbr.]

Rom /rɒm/ *n.* (*pl.* **Roma** /ˈrəʊmə/) a male gypsy. [Romany, = man, husband]

Rom. *abbr.* Romans (New Testament).

rom. *abbr.* roman (type).

Roma see ROME.

Romaic /rəʊˈmeɪɪk/ *n. & adj.* —*n.* the vernacular language of modern Greece. —*adj.* of or relating to this language. [Gk *Rhōmaïkos* Roman (used esp. of the Eastern Empire)]

romaine /rəˈmeɪn/ *n. US* a cos lettuce. [F, fem. of *romain* (as ROMAN)]

romaji /ˈrəʊmədʒɪ/ *n.* a system of Romanized spelling used to transliterate Japanese. [Jap.]

Roman /ˈrəʊmən/ *adj. & n.* —*adj.* **1** of ancient Rome or its territory or people. **b** *archaic* of its language. **2** of medieval or modern Rome. **3** of papal Rome, esp. = ROMAN CATHOLIC. **4** of a kind ascribed to the early Romans (*Roman honesty*; *Roman virtue*). **5** surviving from a period of Roman rule (*Roman road*). **6** (**roman**) (of type) of a plain upright kind used in ordinary print (opp. *Gothic* or *black letter*, and *italic*). **7** (of the alphabet etc.) based on the ancient Roman system with letters A–Z. —*n.* **1 a** a citizen of the ancient Roman republic or Empire. **b** a soldier of the Roman Empire. **2** a citizen of modern Rome. **3** = ROMAN CATHOLIC. **4** (**roman**) roman type. **5** (in *pl.*) the Christians of ancient Rome; (**Epistle to the**) **Romans** a book of the New Testament,

an epistle of St Paul to the Church at Rome. □ **Roman candle** a firework discharging a series of flaming coloured balls and sparks. **Roman Catholic** *adj.* of the Roman Catholic Church (see separate entry). —*n.* a member of this Church. **Roman Catholicism** the beliefs and practice of this Church. **Roman Empire** see separate entry. **Roman holiday** enjoyment derived from others' discomfiture. **Roman law** the law-code developed by the ancient Romans and forming the basis of many modern codes. **Roman nose** one with a high bridge; an aquiline nose. **roman numeral** any of the Roman letters representing numbers: I = 1, V = 5, X = 10, L = 50, C = 100, D = 500, M = 1000. [ME f. OF *Romain* (n. & adj.) f. L *Romanus* f. *Roma* Rome]

roman-à-clef /rəʊˌmɑːnaːˈkleɪ/ *n.* (*pl.* **romans-à-clef** *pronunc.* same) a novel in which real persons or events appear with invented names. [F, = novel with a key]

Roman Catholic Church that part of the Christian Church which acknowledges the pope as its head, especially that which has developed since the Reformation. It has an elaborately organized hierarchy of bishops and priests, basing its claims on the power entrusted by Christ to his Apostles, particularly to St Peter, whose successors the popes are traditionally regarded as being. In doctrine, it is characterized by strict adherence to tradition combined with acceptance of the living voice of the Church and belief in its infallibility. The classic definition of its position was made in response to the Reformation at the Council of Trent (1545–63). During the Enlightenment the Church increasingly saw itself as an embattled defender of ancient truth, something that culminated in the proclamation of Papal Infallibility in 1870. The 20th c. has seen a great change as the Church has become more open to the world, a change given effect in the decrees of the 2nd Vatican Council (1962–5).

Romance /rəʊˈmæns/ *adj. & n.* —*adj.* of the group of European languages descended from Latin. —*n.* this group, of which the main languages are French, Spanish, Portuguese, Italian, and Romanian. With the spread of the Roman Empire, Latin was introduced as the language of administration; with its decline the languages of separate areas began to develop in different ways, and the Latin from which they developed seems to have been not the classical Latin of Rome but the informal Latin of the soldiers. [ME f. OF *romanz*, *-ans*, *-ance*, ult. f. L *Romanicus* ROMANIC)]

romance /rəʊˈmæns/ *n. & v.* —*n.* / also *disp.* ˈrəʊ-/ **1** an atmosphere or tendency characterized by a sense of remoteness from or idealization of everyday life. **2 a** a prevailing sense of wonder or mystery surrounding the mutual attraction in a love affair. **b** sentimental or idealized love. **c** a love affair. **3 a** a literary genre with romantic love or highly imaginative unrealistic episodes forming the central theme. **b** a work of this genre. **4** a medieval tale, usu. in verse, of some hero of chivalry, of the kind common in the Romance languages. **5 a** exaggeration or picturesque falsehood. **b** an instance of this. **6** *Mus.* a short informal piece. —*v.* **1** *intr.* exaggerate or distort the truth, esp. fantastically. **2** *tr.* court, woo. [ROMANCE]

romancer /rəʊˈmænsə(r)/ *n.* **1** a writer of romances, esp. in the medieval period. **2** a liar who resorts to fantasy.

Roman Empire the period of ancient Roman history from 27 BC, when Octavian took power as what was effectively a constitutional monarch with the title of Augustus, until the barbarian invasions of the 4th–5th c. (which followed the death of Constantine) ended with the deposition of the last Roman emperor, Romulus Augustulus, in 476. At its greatest extent Roman rule or influence extended from Armenia and Mesopotamia in the east to the Iberian peninsula in the west, and from the Rhine and Danube in the north to Egypt and provinces on the Mediterranean coast of North Africa. The empire was divided by Theodosius (AD 395) into the Western or Latin and Eastern or Greek Empire, of which the Eastern lasted until 1453 and the Western, after lapsing in 476, was revived in 800 by Charlemagne and continued to exist as the Holy Roman Empire until 1806.

Romanesque /ˌrəʊməˈnesk/ *n. & adj.* —*n.* a style of architecture prevalent in Europe *c*.900–1200, with massive vaulting and round arches. Although disseminated throughout Europe, the style reached its fullest development in central and northern France; the English version is usually termed Norman. —*adj.* of the Romanesque style of architecture. [F f. *roman* ROMANCE]

roman-fleuve /ˌrəʊmãˈflɜːv/ *n.* (pl. **romans-fleuves** pronunc. same) **1 a** a novel featuring the leisurely description of the lives of members of a family etc. **2** a sequence of self-contained novels. [F, = river novel]

Romania /rəʊˈmeɪnɪə/ (also **Rumania** /ruː-/) a country in SE Europe with the USSR on its northern frontier and a coastline on the Black Sea; pop. (est.1988) 23,040,900; official language, Romanian; capital, Bucharest. In Roman times Romania formed the imperial province of Dacia, and in the Middle Ages the principalities of Walachia and Moldavia, each of which was swallowed up by the Ottoman empire in the 15th–16th c. The two principalities were unified in 1859 and gained independence in 1878, and although conquered in 1916 by the Central Powers, Romania emerged from the peace settlement with fresh territorial gains in Bessarabia and Transylvania. The present boundaries are a result of the Second World War (its oilfields were of vital importance to Germany, which it supported), after which Romania became a Communist State under Soviet influence. The end of 1989 saw the fall of Communism with virtual civil war, but the previous governmental structure survived elections held in May 1990.

Romanian /rəʊˈmeɪnɪən/ *n.* & *adj.* (also **Rumanian** /ruː-/) —*n.* **1 a** a native or national of Romania. **b** a person of Romanian descent. **2** the official language of Romania, the only Romance language spoken in eastern Europe, which developed from the Latin introduced by Trajan when he conquered the area in the 2nd c. AD and has kept its Latin character, being lightly influenced by the Slavonic languages. It is spoken by over 23 million people in Romania itself and by the majority of the population of the Moldavian SSR. —*adj.* of or relating to Romania or its people or language.

Romanic /rəʊˈmænɪk/ *n.* & *adj.* —*n.* = ROMANCE *n.* 6. —*adj.* **1 a** of or relating to Romance. **b** Romance-speaking. **2** descended from the ancient Romans or inheriting aspects of their social or political life. [L *Romanicus* (as ROMAN)]

Romanism /ˈrəʊmənɪz(ə)m/ *n.* Roman Catholicism.

Romanist /ˈrəʊmənɪst/ *n.* **1** a student of Roman history or law or of the Romance languages. **2 a** a supporter of Roman Catholicism. **b** a Roman Catholic. [mod.L *Romanista* (as ROMAN)]

romanize /ˈrəʊmənaɪz/ *v.tr.* (also **-ise**) **1** make Roman or Roman Catholic in character. **2** put into the Roman alphabet or into roman type. □□ **romanization** /-ˈzeɪʃ(ə)n/ *n.*

Romano /rəʊˈmɑːnəʊ/ *n.* a strong-tasting hard cheese, orig. made in Italy. [It., = ROMAN]

Romano- /rəʊˈmɑːnəʊ/ *comb. form* Roman; Roman and (*Romano-British*).

Romanov /ˈrəʊmənɒf/ the name of a dynasty that ruled in Russia from the accession of Michael Romanov in 1613 until the overthrow of the last tsar, Nicholas II, in 1917.

Romansh /rəʊˈmænʃ, -ˈmɑːnʃ/ *n.* & *adj.* (also **Rumansh** /ruː-/) —*n.* the Rhaeto-Romanic dialects, esp. as spoken in the Swiss canton of Grisons. —*adj.* of these dialects. [Romansh *Ruman(t)sch, Roman(t)sch* f. med.L *romanice* (adv.) (as ROMANCE)]

romantic /rəʊˈmæntɪk/ *adj.* & *n.* —*adj.* **1** of, characterized by, or suggestive of an idealized, sentimental, or fantastic view of reality; remote from experience (*a romantic picture; a romantic setting*). **2** inclined towards or suggestive of romance in love (*a romantic woman; a romantic evening; romantic words*). **3** (of a person) imaginative, visionary, idealistic. **4 a** (of style in art, music, etc.) concerned more with feeling and emotion than with form and aesthetic qualities; preferring grandeur or picturesqueness to finish and proportion. **b** (also **Romantic**) of or relating to the 18th–19th-c. romantic movement or style in the European arts. (See below.) **5** (of a project etc.) unpractical, fantastic. —*n.* **1 a** romantic person. **2** a romanticist. **3** (also **Romantic**) a composer etc. in the Romantic style. □□ **romantically** *adv.* [*romant* tale of chivalry etc. f. OF f. *romanz* ROMANCE]

The Romantic movement originated in the 18th c. It was a reaction to the Enlightenment, with its rejection of authoritarianism, and recognized the claims of passion and emotion and the sense of mystery in life; the critical was replaced by the creative spirit, and wit by humour, pathos, and gentle melancholy. In music, the period embraces much of the 19th c., with Weber, Schubert, Schumann, Liszt, and Wagner (some critics would include Beethoven). In literature, the movement is usually dated from the publication of *Lyrical Ballads* (1798) by Wordsworth and Coleridge; other writers include Byron, Shelley, Keats, and Scott. In Germany the Romantic writers included Goethe, Schiller, and the philosophical criticism of A. W. Schlegel, and in France, where the tone of Romanticism was shaped by Rousseau's *Julie* (1761), they included Chateaubriand and Victor Hugo. A state of mind rather than a style, it included, in painting, such stylistically diverse artists as Blake, Turner, Delacroix, and Goya. In its implications for the idea of an artist as an isolated misunderstood genius the Romantic movement has not yet ended.

romanticism /rəʊˈmæntɪˌsɪz(ə)m/ *n.* (also **Romanticism**) adherence to a romantic style in art, music, etc.

romanticist /rəʊˈmæntɪsɪst/ *n.* (also **Romanticist**) a writer or artist of the romantic school.

romanticize /rəʊˈmæntɪˌsaɪz/ *v.* (also **-ise**) **1 tr. a** make or render romantic or unreal (*a romanticized account of war*). **b** describe or portray in a romantic fashion. **2** *intr.* indulge in romantic thoughts or actions. □□ **romanticization** /-ˈzeɪʃ(ə)n/ *n.*

Romany /ˈrɒmənɪ, ˈrəʊ-/ *n.* & *adj.* —*n.* (*pl.* **-ies**) **1** a Gypsy. **2** the distinctive language of the Gypsies, which shares common features with Sanskrit and the later Indian languages (indicating an origin in the Indian subcontinent), with regional variations reflecting the incorporation of loanwords and other local linguistic features absorbed in their travels. —*adj.* **1** of or concerning Gypsies. **2** of the Romany language. [Romany *Romani* fem. and pl. of *Romano* (adj.) (ROM)]

Romberg /ˈrɒmbɜːg/, Sigmund (1887–1951), Hungarian-born composer who settled in New York in 1913. He wrote a succession of popular operettas, including *Maytime* (1917), *The Student Prince* (1924), *The Desert Song* (1926), and *New Moon* (1928).

Rome /rəʊm/ (Italian **Roma** /ˈrəʊmə/ the capital of Italy, situated on the River Tiber about 25 km (16 miles) inland; pop. (1981) 2,830,569. The name is used allusively of the ancient Roman republic (see below) and Empire, and (as the see of the pope) of the Roman Catholic Church. The ancient city, traditionally founded by Romulus in 753 BC, was ruled by kings until the expulsion of Tarquin the Proud in 510 BC. An aristocratic republic was established, and its history in the next 250 years was marked by internal class-struggle and external conflict with the surrounding peoples. By the mid-2nd c. BC Rome had subdued the whole of Italy; her power brought her into conflict with Carthaginian interests in the western Mediterranean and with the Hellenistic world in the east. Success in the Punic Wars gave Rome her first overseas possessions, and the Macedonian wars eventually left her dominant over Greece and much of Asia Minor. From about 135 BC provincial unrest, and dissatisfaction at home with the Senate's control of government, brought a series of ambitious military leaders to the fore in open rivalry, each able to count on the support of a devoted soldiery, until civil wars culminated in the defeat of Pompey by Julius Caesar. Caesar's brief dictatorship established the principle of personal autocracy, and after his assassination by republican conspirators another round of civil war ended with Octavian's assumption of authority as a kind of constitutional monarch. (See ROMAN EMPIRE.) During the Middle Ages Rome emerged as the seat of the papacy and the spiritual capital of western Christianity, and became a centre of the Renaissance. It remained under papal control until 1871 when it was made the capital of a unified Italy. □ **Treaty of Rome** a treaty signed at Rome on 25 March 1957, setting up the European Economic Community.

Romeo /ˈrəʊmɪˌəʊ/ *n.* (*pl.* **-os**) a passionate male lover or seducer. [the hero of Shakespeare's romantic tragedy *Romeo and Juliet*]

---

romer /'rəʊmə(r)/ n. a small piece of plastic or card marked with scales along two edges meeting at a right angle, or (if transparent) bearing a grid, used for measuring grid references on a map. [name of C. Romer (d.1951), British barrister, its inventor]

Romish /'rəʊmɪʃ/ adj. usu. derog. Roman Catholic.

Rommel /'rɒm(ə)l/, Erwin (1891–1944), German general, best known for his victories as commander of the Afrika Korps in the Second World War. The Italian army had been all but defeated in its attempt to secure Egypt and the Suez Canal when Rommel assumed command in 1941. The Arabs saw him as a liberator, and his audacious attacks earned him his enemies' respect and the nickname of the 'Desert Fox'. He drove the Allied forces east to 96 km (60 miles) from Alexandria, only to be defeated there at El Alamein (1942) and forced to withdraw, handicapped by the difficulty of maintaining his supply lines for so great a distance from friendly territory when the Allies held superiority in the air; in 1943 he was withdrawn from Africa to assume command of the Channel coastline. A professional soldier, he saw the inevitability of Germany's defeat. The discovery of his involvement with the conspirators who unsuccessfully attempted to assassinate Hitler in 1944, and who would have had Rommel succeed him as head of State, led to his enforced suicide.

Romney /'rɒmnɪ/, George (1734–1802), English portrait painter. He left his north country practice for London in 1762 and worked there for most of his professional life. In his day he was almost as popular as Reynolds and Gainsborough, and the elegance of his pictures with their lucid presentation and delicate colour was a distinctive contribution to 18th–c. portraiture.

romneya /'rɒmnɪə/ n. any shrub of the genus Romneya, bearing poppy-like flowers. [T. Romney Robinson, Brit. astronomer d. 1882]

romp /rɒmp/ v. & n. —v.intr. 1 play about roughly and energetically. 2 (foll. by along, past, etc.) colloq. proceed without effort. —n. a spell of romping or boisterous play. □ **romp in** (or **home**) colloq. finish as the easy winner. □□ **rompingly** adv. **rompy** adj. (**rompier**, **rompiest**). [perh. var. of RAMP[1]]

romper /'rɒmpə(r)/ n. (usu. in pl.) (also **romper suit**) a young child's one-piece garment covering legs and trunk.

Romulus /'rɒmjʊləs/ Rom. legend the founder of Rome, one of the twin sons of Mars by the Vestal Virgin Rhea Silvia, exposed at birth with his brother Remus and found and suckled by a she-wolf. He was worshipped after his death as Quirinus.

Roncesvalles /'rɒnsəˌvæl/ (also **Roncevaux** /-ˌvəʊ/) a mountain pass in the Pyrenees, scene of the defeat of the rearguard of Charlemagne's army by native tribesmen in 778 and of the heroic death of one of his nobles, Roland, an event much celebrated in medieval literature.

rondavel /rɒn'dɑːvel/ n. S.Afr. 1 a round tribal hut usu. with a thatched conical roof. 2 a similar building, esp. as a holiday cottage, or as an outbuilding on a farm etc. [Afrik. rondawel]

ronde /rɒnd/ n. 1 a dance in which the dancers move in a circle. 2 a course of talk, activity, etc. [F, fem. of rond ROUND adj.]

rondeau /'rɒndəʊ/ n. (pl. **rondeaux** pronunc. same or /-əʊz/) a poem of ten or thirteen lines with only two rhymes throughout and with the opening words used twice as a refrain. [F, earlier rondel: see RONDEL]

rondel /'rɒnd(ə)l/ n. a rondeau, esp. one of special form. [ME f. OF f. rond ROUND: cf. ROUNDEL]

rondo /'rɒndəʊ/ n. (pl. **-os**) Mus. a form with a recurring leading theme, often found in the final movement of a sonata or concerto etc. [It. f. F rondeau: see RONDEAU]

Rondônia /rɒn'dɒnjə/ a State of NW Brazil; pop. (est. 1987) 981,800; capital, Pôrto Velho.

rone /rəʊn/ n. Sc. a gutter for carrying off rain from a roof.

ronin /'rəʊnɪn/ n. hist. (in feudal Japan) a lordless wandering samurai; an outlaw. [Jap.]

Röntgen /'rʌntjən/, Wilhelm Conrad von (1845–1923), German physicist, the discoverer of X-rays, for which he was awarded the first Nobel Prize for physics in 1901. Röntgen was trained as a mechanical engineer before taking up an academic career in physics, and he was a skilful experimenter. He worked on a variety of topics but the two pieces of research for which he is famous were outside his normal scope. In 1888 he demonstrated the existence of a magnetic field caused by the motion of electrostatic charges, predicted by Maxwell's electromagnetic theory and important for future electrical theory; then in 1895 he observed by chance that a fluorescent screen began to glow brightly as soon as a current was passed through a Crookes' vacuum tube some distance away. He investigated the properties of this invisible radiation, which he called X-rays because of their unknown origin, and startled the world with the photograph of the bones of his wife's hand, taken on 22 Dec. 1895. The roentgen (see entry) was named in his honour.

röntgen etc. var. of ROENTGEN etc.

roo /ruː/ n. (also **'roo**) Austral. colloq. a kangaroo. [abbr.]

rood /ruːd/ n. 1 a crucifix, esp. one raised on a screen or beam at the entrance to the chancel. 2 a quarter of an acre. □ **rood-loft** a gallery on top of a rood-screen. **rood-screen** a wooden or stone carved screen separating the nave from the chancel in a church, found in England and on the Continent especially in the 14th–mid-16th c. [OE rōd]

roof /ruːf/ n. & v. —n. (pl. **roofs** or disp. **rooves** /ruːvz/) 1 a the upper covering of a building, usu. supported by its walls. b the top of a covered vehicle. c the top inner surface of an oven, refrigerator, etc. 2 the overhead rock in a cave or mine etc. 3 the branches or the sky etc. overhead. 4 (of prices etc.) the upper limit or ceiling. —v.tr. 1 (often foll. by in, over) cover with or as with a roof. 2 be the roof of. □ **go through the roof** colloq. (of prices etc.) reach extreme or unexpected heights. **hit** (or **go through** or **raise**) **the roof** colloq. become very angry. **roof-garden** a garden on the flat roof of a building. **roof of the mouth** the palate. **a roof over one's head** somewhere to live. **roof-rack** a framework for carrying luggage etc. on the roof of a vehicle. **roof-tree** the ridge-piece of a roof. **under one roof** in the same building. **under a person's roof** in a person's house (esp. with ref. to hospitality). □□ **roofed** adj. (also in comb.). **roofless** adj. [OE hrōf]

roofage /'ruːfɪdʒ/ n. the expanse of a roof or roofs.

roofer /'ruːfə(r)/ n. a person who constructs or repairs roofs.

roofing /'ruːfɪŋ/ n. 1 material for constructing a roof. 2 the process of constructing a roof or roofs.

roofscape /'ruːfskeɪp/ n. a scene or view of roofs.

rooftop /'ruːftɒp/ n. 1 the outer surface of a roof. 2 (esp. in pl.) the level of a roof.

rooibos /'rɔɪbɒs/ n. S.Afr. 1 an evergreen shrub of the genus Aspalathus, with leaves used to make tea. 2 a shrub or small tree, Combretum apiculatum, with spikes of scented yellow flowers. [Afrik., = red bush]

rooinek /'rɔɪnek, 'rəʊ-/ n. S.Afr. sl. offens. a British or English-speaking South African. [Afrik., = red-neck]

rook[1] /rʊk/ n. & v. —n. 1 a black European and Asiatic bird, Corvus frugilegus, of the crow family, nesting in colonies in tree-tops. 2 a sharper, esp. at dice or cards; a person who lives off inexperienced gamblers etc. —v.tr. 1 charge (a customer) extortionately. 2 win money from (a person) at cards etc. esp. by swindling. [OE hrōc]

rook[2] /rʊk/ n. a chess piece with its top in the shape of a battlement. [ME f. OF roc(k) ult. f. Arab. rukk, orig. sense uncert.]

rookery /'rʊkərɪ/ n. (pl. **-ies**) 1 a colony of rooks. b a clump of trees having rooks' nests. 2 a colony of sea birds (esp. penguins) or seals.

rookie /'rʊkɪ/ n. sl. 1 a new recruit, esp. in the army or police. 2 US a new member of a sports team. [corrupt. of recruit, after ROOK[1]]

room /ruːm, rʊm/ n. & v. —n. 1 a space that is or might be occupied by something; capaciousness or ability to accommodate contents (it takes up too much room; there is plenty of room; we have no room for idlers). b space in or on (houseroom; shelf-room). 2 a a part of a building enclosed by walls or partitions, floor and ceiling. b (in pl.) a set of these occupied by a person or family; apartments or lodgings. **c** persons present in a room (*the room fell silent*). **3** (in *comb.*) a room or area for a specified purpose (*auction-room*). **4** (foll. by *for*, or *to* + infin.) opportunity or scope (*room to improve things; no room for dispute*). —*v.intr. US* have a room or rooms; lodge, board. □ **make room** (often foll. by *for*) clear a space (for a person or thing) by removal of others; make way, yield place. **not** (or **no**) **room to swing a cat** a very confined space. **rooming-house** a lodging house. **room-mate** a person occupying the same room as another. **room service** (in a hotel etc.) service of food or drink taken to a guest's room. □□ **-roomed** *adj.* (in *comb.*). **roomful** *n.* (*pl.* **-fuls**). [OE *rūm* f. Gmc]

roomer /ˈruːmə(r), ˈrʊmə(r)/ *n. US* a lodger occupying a room or rooms without board.

roomette /ruːˈmet, rʊ-/ *n. US* **1** a private single compartment in a sleeping-car. **2** a small bedroom for letting.

roomie /ˈruːmɪ/ *n. US colloq.* a room-mate.

roomy /ˈruːmɪ/ *adj.* (**roomier**, **roomiest**) having much room, spacious. □□ **roomily** *adv.* **roominess** *n.*

Roosevelt[1] /ˈrəʊzəˌvelt/, Franklin Delano (1882–1945), 32nd President of the US 1933–45. His New Deal (see entry) successfully lifted the US out of the Great Depression, and after the American entry into the Second World War he played a vital part in the coordination of the Allied war effort. In 1940 he became the first President to be elected for a third term in office, and four years later he was once again successful at the polls, but died of a cerebral haemorrhage several months later.

Roosevelt[2] /ˈrəʊzəvelt/, Theodore (1858–1919), 26th President of the US 1901–8. After a varied early career in politics, Roosevelt won national fame for his service in the Spanish-American War. Elected Vice-President in 1900, he succeeded McKinley following the latter's assassination in 1901 and won re-election in 1904. At home he was notable for his antitrust activities; while abroad, he successfully engineered the American bid to build the Panama Canal and won a Nobel Peace Prize for bringing the Russo-Japanese War to an end. He retired temporarily from politics in 1908 and was unsuccessful in his attempt to regain the Presidency in 1912 at the head of his own 'Bull Moose' party. The 'teddy-bear' is named after him, with allusion to his bear-hunting activities.

roost[1] /ruːst/ *n. & v.* —*n.* **1** a branch or other support on which a bird perches, esp. a place where birds regularly settle to sleep. **2** a place offering temporary sleeping-accommodation. —*v.* **1** *intr.* **a** (of a bird) settle for rest or sleep. **b** (of a person) stay for the night. **2** *tr.* provide with a sleeping-place. □ **come home to roost** (of a scheme etc.) recoil unfavourably upon the originator. [OE *hrōst*]

roost[2] /ruːst/ *n.* a tidal race in the Orkneys and Shetlands. [ON *rōst*]

rooster /ˈruːstə(r)/ *n.* esp. *US* a domestic cock.

root[1] /ruːt/ *n. & v.* —*n.* **1 a** the part of a plant normally below the ground, attaching it to the earth and conveying nourishment to it from the soil. **b** (in *pl.*) such a part divided into branches or fibres. **c** the corresponding organ of an epiphyte; the part attaching ivy to its support. **d** the permanent underground stock of a plant. **e** any small plant with a root for transplanting. **2 a** any plant, e.g. a turnip or carrot, with an edible root. **b** such a root. **3** (in *pl.*) the sources of or reasons for one's long-standing emotional attachment to a place, community, etc. **4 a** the embedded part of a bodily organ or structure, e.g. hair, tooth, nail, etc. **b** the part of a thing attaching it to a greater or more fundamental whole. **c** (in *pl.*) the base of a mountain etc. **5 a** the basic cause, source, or origin (*love of money is the root of all evil; has its roots in the distant past*). **b** (*attrib.*) (of an idea etc.) from which the rest originated. **6** the basis of something, its means of continuance or growth (*has its root(s) in selfishness; has no root in the nature of things*). **7** the essential substance or nature of something (*get to the root of things*). **8** *Math.* **a** a number or quantity that when multiplied by itself a usu. specified number of times gives a specified number or quantity (*the cube root of eight is two*). **b** a square root. **c** a value of an unknown quantity satisfying a given equation. **9** *Philol.* any ultimate unanalysable

element of language; a basis, not necessarily surviving as a word in itself, on which words are made by the addition of prefixes or suffixes or by other modification. **10** *Mus.* the fundamental note of a chord. **11** *Bibl.* a scion, an offshoot (*there shall be a root of Jesse*). **12** *Austral. & NZ coarse sl.* **a** an act of sexual intercourse. **b** a (female) sexual partner. —*v.* **1 a** *intr.* take root or grow roots. **b** *tr.* cause to do this (*take care to root them firmly*). **2** *tr.* **a** fix firmly; establish (*fear rooted him to the spot*). **b** (as **rooted** *adj.*) firmly established (*her affection was deeply rooted; rooted objection to*). **3** *tr.* (usu. foll. by *out, up*) drag or dig up by the roots. **4** *tr. Austral. coarse sl.* **a** have sexual intercourse with (a woman). **b** exhaust, frustrate. □ **pull up by the roots 1** uproot. **2** eradicate, destroy. **put down roots 1** begin to draw nourishment from the soil. **2** become settled or established. **root and branch** thorough(ly), radical(ly). **root beer** *US* an effervescent drink made from an extract of roots. **root-mean-square** *Math.* the square root of the arithmetic mean of the squares of a set of values. **root out** find and get rid of. **root sign** *Math.* = *radical sign.* **strike at the root** (or **roots**) **of** set about destroying. **strike** (or **take**) **root 1** begin to grow and draw nourishment from the soil. **2** become fixed or established. □□ **rootage** *n.* **rootedness** *n.* **rootless** *adj.* **rootlet** *n.* **rootlike** *adj.* **rooty** *adj.* [OE *rōt* f. ON *rót*, rel. to WORT & L *radix*: see RADIX]

root[2] /ruːt/ *v.* **1 a** *intr.* (of an animal, esp. a pig) turn up the ground with the snout, beak, etc., in search of food. **b** *tr.* (foll. by *up*) turn up (the ground) by rooting. **2 a** *intr.* (foll. by *around, in,* etc.) rummage. **b** *tr.* (foll. by *out* or *up*) find or extract by rummaging. **3** *intr.* (foll. by *for*) *US sl.* encourage by applause or support. □□ **rooter** *n.* (in sense 3). [earlier *wroot* f. OE *wrōtan* & ON *róta*: rel. to OE *wrōt* snout]

rootle /ˈruːt(ə)l/ *v.intr. & tr. Brit.* = ROOT[2] 1, 2. [ROOT[2]]

rootstock /ˈruːtstɒk/ *n.* **1** a rhizome. **2** a plant into which a graft is inserted. **3** a primary form from which offshoots have arisen.

rooves see ROOF.

rope /rəʊp/ *n. & v.* —*n.* **1 a** a stout cord made by twisting together strands of hemp, sisal, flax, cotton, nylon, wire, or similar material. **b** a piece of this. **c** *US* a lasso. **2** (foll. by *of*) a quantity of onions, ova, or pearls strung together. **3** (in *pl.*, prec. by *the*) **a** the conditions in some sphere of action (*know the ropes; show a person the ropes*). **b** the ropes enclosing a boxing- or wrestling-ring or cricket ground. **4** (prec. by *the*) **a** a halter for hanging a person. **b** execution by hanging. —*v.* **1** *tr.* fasten, secure, or catch with rope. **2** *tr.* (usu. foll. by *off, in*) enclose (a space) with rope. **3** *Mountaineering* **a** *tr.* connect (a party) with a rope; attach (a person) to a rope. **b** (*absol.*) put on a rope. **c** *intr.* (foll. by *down, up*) climb down or up using a rope. □ **give a person plenty of rope** (or **enough rope to hang himself** or **herself**) give a person enough freedom of action to bring about his or her own downfall. **on the rope** *Mountaineering* roped together. **on the ropes 1** *Boxing* forced against the ropes by the opponent's attack. **2** near defeat. **rope in** persuade to take part. **rope into** persuade to take part in (*was roped into doing the washing-up*). **rope-ladder** two long ropes connected by short crosspieces, used as a ladder. **rope-moulding** a moulding cut spirally in imitation of rope-strands. **rope of sand** delusive security. **rope's end** *hist.* a short piece of rope used to flog (formerly, esp. a sailor) with. **rope-walk** a long piece of ground where ropes are made. **rope-walker** a performer on a tightrope. **rope-walking** the action of performing on a tightrope. **rope-yard** a rope-making establishment. **rope-yarn 1** material obtained by unpicking rope-strands, or used for making them. **2** a piece of this. **3** a mere trifle. [OE *rāp* f. Gmc]

ropeable /ˈrəʊpəb(ə)l/ *adj.* (also **ropable**) **1** capable of being roped. **2** *Austral. & NZ sl.* angry.

ropemanship /ˈrəʊpmənʃɪp/ *n.* skill in rope-walking or climbing with ropes.

ropeway /ˈrəʊpweɪ/ *n.* a cable railway.

roping /ˈrəʊpɪŋ/ *n.* a set or arrangement of ropes.

ropy /ˈrəʊpɪ/ *adj.* (also **ropey**) (**ropier**, **ropiest**) **1** *Brit. colloq.* poor in quality. **2** (of wine, bread, etc.) forming viscous or gelatinous threads. **3** like a rope. □□ **ropily** *adv.* **ropiness** *n.*

roque /rəʊk/ n. US croquet played on a hard court surrounded by a bank. [alt. form of ROQUET]

Roquefort /ˈrɒkfɔː(r)/ n. propr. **1** a soft blue cheese originally made at Roquefort, a town in southern France, usually from ewes' milk and ripened in limestone caves, with a strong characteristic flavour. **2** a salad-dressing made of this.

roquet /ˈrəʊkeɪ, -kɪ/ v. & n. Croquet —v. (**roqueted, roqueting**) **1** tr. **a** cause one's ball to strike (another ball). **b** (of a ball) strike (another). **2** intr. strike another ball thus. —n. an instance of roqueting. [app. arbitr. f. CROQUET v., orig. used in the same sense]

Roraima /rɔːˈraɪmə/ the highest peak of the Guiana Highlands, South America, rising to a height of 2,774 m (9,094 ft.) at the junction of the frontiers of Venezuela, Brazil, and Guyana.

ro-ro /ˈrəʊrəʊ/ adj. roll-on roll-off. [abbr.]

rorqual /ˈrɔːkw(ə)l/ n. any of various whales of the family Balaenopteridae esp. Balaenoptera musculus, having a dorsal fin. Also called fin-back, fin whale. [F f. Norw. røyrkval f. Olcel. reythr the specific name + hvalr WHALE¹]

Rorschach test /ˈrɔːʃɑːk/ n. Psychol. a type of personality test in which a standard set of ink-blots is presented one by one to the subject, who is asked to describe what they suggest or resemble. [H. Rorschach, Swiss psychiatrist d. 1922, who first devised such a test]

rort /rɔːt/ n. Austral. sl. **1** a trick, a fraud; a dishonest practice. **2** a wild party. [back-form. f. RORTY]

rorty /ˈrɔːtɪ/ adj. (**rortier, rortiest**) Brit. sl. **1** splendid; boisterous, rowdy (had a rorty time). **2** coarse, earthy. [19th c.: orig. unkn.]

Rosa /ˈrəʊzə/, Salvator (1615–73), Italian painter and etcher, born in Naples but active chiefly in Rome. His wide artistic abilities—including music and poetry—coupled with his colourful and dramatic life made him the epitome of the Romantic artist for the 18th and 19th c. His reputation now rests on his invention of a type of landscape, often peopled with bandits and containing scenes of violence, whose form and atmosphere blend together to create an overall feeling of sublime terror. These landscapes were, with those of Claude and Poussin, one of the determinants of 18th-c. taste and had a profound influence on Romantic art in England.

rosace /ˈrəʊzeɪs/ n. **1** a rose-window. **2** a rose-shaped ornament or design. [F f. L rosaceus: see ROSACEOUS]

rosaceous /rəʊˈzeɪʃəs/ adj. Bot. of the large plant family Rosaceae, which includes the rose. [L rosaceus f. rosa rose]

rosaline /ˈrəʊzəˌliːn/ n. a variety of fine needlepoint or pillow lace. [prob. F]

rosaniline /rəʊˈzænɪˌliːn, -lɪn, -ˌlaɪn/ n. **1 a** an organic base derived from aniline. **b** a red dye obtained from this. **2** fuchsine. [ROSE¹ + ANILINE]

rosarian /rəˈzeərɪən/ n. a person who cultivates roses, esp. professionally. [L rosarium ROSARY]

Rosario /rəʊˈsɑːrɪˌəʊ/ a port on the Paraná River in east central Argentina; pop. (1980) 954,600.

rosarium /rəˈzeərɪəm/ n. a rose-garden. [L (as ROSARY)]

rosary /ˈrəʊzərɪ/ n. (pl. **-ies**) **1** RC Ch. **a** a form of devotion in which five (or fifteen) decades of Hail Marys are repeated, each decade preceded by an Our Father and followed by a Glory Be. **b** a string of 55 (or 165) beads for keeping count in this. **c** a book containing this devotion. According to a tradition current since the 15th c., the devotion was founded by St Dominic, but in fact it seems to have developed gradually. **2** a similar form of bead-string used in other religions. **3** a rose-garden or rose-bed. [ME f. L rosarium rose-garden, neut. of rosarius (as ROSE¹)]

Roscius /ˈrɒskɪəs/ (Quintus Roscius Gallus, d. 62 BC) the most famous Roman actor of his day, whose talents brought him wealth and the friendship of the great (including Cicero). His name became synonymous with all that was best in acting. Shakespeare referred to him in Hamlet, and many outstanding actors were nicknamed with reference to him (the African, Scottish etc. Roscius).

roscoe /ˈrɒskəʊ/ n. US sl. a gun, esp. a pistol or revolver. [the name Roscoe]

Roscommon /rɒsˈkɒmən/ **1** a county in the province of Connaught, Republic of Ireland; pop. (1986) 54,550. **2** its capital city; pop. (1981) 1,673.

rose¹ /rəʊz/ n., adj., & v. —n. **1** any prickly bush or shrub of the genus Rosa, bearing usu. fragrant flowers generally of a red, pink, yellow, or white colour. **2** this flower. **3** any flowering plant resembling this (Christmas rose; rock rose). **4 a** a light crimson colour, pink. **b** (usu. in pl.) a rosy complexion (roses in her cheeks). **5 a** a representation of the flower in heraldry or decoration (esp. as the national emblem of England). **b** a rose-shaped design, e.g. on a compass card or on the sound-hole of a lute etc. **6** the sprinkling-nozzle of a watering-can or hose. **7** a circular mounting on a ceiling through which the wiring of an electric light passes. **8 a** a rose diamond. **b** a rose-window. **9** (in pl.) used in various phrases to express favourable circumstances, ease, success, etc. (roses all the way; everything's roses). **10** an excellent person or thing, esp. a beautiful woman (English rose; rose between two thorns; not the rose but near it). —adj. = rose-coloured 1. —v.tr. (esp. as **rosed** adj.) make (one's face, a snow-slope, etc.) rosy. □ **rose-apple 1** a tropical tree of the genus Eugenia, cultivated for its foliage and fragrant fruit. **2** this fruit. **rose-bush** a rose plant. **rose-chafer** a green or copper-coloured beetle, Cetonia aurata, frequenting roses. **rose-colour** the colour of a pale red rose, warm pink. **rose-coloured 1** of rose-colour. **2** optimistic, sanguine, cheerful (takes rose-coloured views). **rose comb** a flat fleshy comb of a fowl. **rose-cut** cut as a rose diamond. **rose diamond** a hemispherical diamond with the curved part cut in triangular facets. **rose-engine** an appendage to a lathe for engraving curved patterns. **rose-fish** a bright red food fish, Sebastes marinus, of the N. Atlantic. **rose geranium** a pink-flowered sweet-scented pelargonium, Pelargonium graveolus. **rose-hip** = HIP². **rose-leaf** (pl. **-leaves**) **1** a petal of a rose. **2** a leaf of a rose. **rose madder** a pale pink pigment. **rose-mallow** = HIBISCUS. **rose nail** a nail with a head shaped like a rose diamond. **rose of Jericho** a resurrection plant, Anastatica hierochuntica. **rose of Sharon 1** a species of hypericum, Hypericum calycinum, with dense foliage and golden-yellow flowers: also called AARON'S BEARD. **2** Bibl. a flowering plant of unknown identity. **rose-pink** = rose-colour, rose-coloured. **rose-point** a point lace with a design of roses. **rose-red** adj. red like a rose, rose-coloured. —n. this colour. **rose-root** a yellow-flowered plant, Rhodiola rosea, with roots smelling like a rose when dried or bruised. **rose-tinted** = rose-coloured. **rose-tree** a rose plant, esp. a standard rose. **rose-water** perfume made from roses. **rose-window** a circular window, usu. with roselike or spokelike tracery. **see through rose-coloured (or -tinted) spectacles** regard (circumstances etc.) with unfounded favour or optimism. **under the rose** in confidence; under pledge of secrecy. **Wars of the Roses** hist. the 15th-c. civil wars between Yorkists with a white rose as an emblem and Lancastrians with a red rose. □□ **roseless** adj. **roselike** adj. [ME f. OE rōse f. L rosa]

rose² past of RISE.

rosé /ˈrəʊzeɪ/ n. any light pink wine, coloured by only brief contact with red grape-skins. [F, = pink]

roseate /ˈrəʊzɪət/ adj. **1** = rose-coloured (see ROSE¹). **2** having a partly pink plumage (roseate spoonbill; roseate tern). [L roseus rosy (as ROSE¹)]

Roseau /rəʊˈzəʊ/ the capital of Dominica in the West Indies; pop. (est. 1981) 20,000.

rosebay /ˈrəʊzbeɪ/ n. an oleander, rhododendron, or willow-herb.

Rosebery /ˈrəʊzbərɪ/, Archibald Philip Primrose, 5th Earl of (1847–1929), British Liberal statesman, who was briefly Prime Minister in 1894–5 at the wish of Queen Victoria rather than of the Liberal Party. His support for British imperialism alienated many Liberal supporters.

rosebowl /ˈrəʊzbəʊl/ n. a bowl for displaying cut roses.

rosebud /ˈrəʊzbʌd/ n. **1** a bud of a rose. **2** a pretty young woman.

rosella /rəˈzelə/ n. **1** any brightly coloured Australian parakeet of the genus Platycercus. **2** Austral. an easily-shorn sheep. [corrupt. of Rosehill, NSW, where the bird was first found]

rosemaling /ˈrəʊzə͵mɑːlɪŋ, -͵mɔːlɪŋ/ n. the art of painting wooden furniture etc. with flower motifs. [Norw., = rose painting]

rosemary /ˈrəʊzmərɪ/ n. an evergreen fragrant shrub, *Rosmarinus officinalis*, with leaves used as a culinary herb, in perfumery, etc., and taken as an emblem of remembrance. [ME, earlier *rosmarine* ult. f. L *ros marinus* f. *ros* dew + *marinus* MARINE, with assim. to ROSE¹ and *Mary* name of the Virgin]

roseola /rəʊˈziːələ/ n. 1 a rosy rash in measles and similar diseases. 2 a mild febrile disease of infants. ◻◻ **roseolar** adj. **roseolous** adj. [mod. var. of RUBEOLA f. L *roseus* rose-coloured]

rosery /ˈrəʊzərɪ/ n. (pl. **-ies**) a rose-garden.

Rosetta stone /rəʊˈzetə/ an inscribed stone found near Rosetta on the western mouth of the Nile by one of Napoleon's officers in 1799. Its text, a decree commemorating the accession of Ptolemy V (reigned 205–180 BC) is written in two languages and three scripts: hieroglyphic and demotic Egyptian, and Greek. The decipherment of the Egyptian parts of the inscription by J.-F. Champollion in 1822 led to the interpretation of all the other early records of Egyptian civilization. The stone is now in the British Museum.

rosette /rəʊˈzet/ n. 1 a rose-shaped ornament made usu. of ribbon and worn esp. as a supporter's badge, or as an award or the symbol of an award in a competition, esp. by a prizewinning animal. 2 *Archit.* **a** a carved or moulded ornament resembling or representing a rose. **b** a rose-window. 3 an object or symbol or arrangement of parts resembling a rose. 4 *Biol.* **a** a roselike cluster of parts. **b** markings resembling a rose. 5 a rose diamond. ◻◻ **rosetted** adj. [F dimin. of *rose* ROSE¹]

rosewood /ˈrəʊzwʊd/ n. any of several fragrant close-grained woods used in making furniture.

Rosh Hashana /rɒʃ ͵hɑːʃɑːˈnɑː, rəʊʃ həˈʃəʊnəʊ/ n. (also **Rosh Hashanah**) the Jewish New Year. [Heb., = beginning (lit. 'head') of the year]

Roshi /ˈrəʊʃi/ n. (pl. **Roshis**) the spiritual leader of a community of Zen Buddhist monks. [Jap.]

Rosicrucian /͵rəʊzɪˈkruːʃ(ə)n/ n. & adj. —n. 1 *hist.* a member of certain secret societies who venerated the emblems of the Rose and the Cross as twin symbols of Christ's Resurrection and Redemption. Early in the 17th c. two anonymous writings were published in Germany relating the fabulous story of one Christian Rosenkreutz, who having learnt the wisdom of the Arabs founded a secret society devoted to the study of the hidden things of nature. The books were meant to be satirical but were taken seriously, and a number of societies with alchemistic tendencies sprang up under this title. 2 a member of any of several later organizations deriving from this. —adj. of or relating to the Rosicrucians. ◻◻ **Rosicrucianism** n. [mod.L *rosa crucis* (or *crux*), as Latinization of G *Rosenkreuz*]

rosin /ˈrɒzɪn/ n. & v. —n. resin, esp. the solid residue after distillation of oil of turpentine from crude turpentine. —v.tr. (**rosined, rosining**) 1 rub (esp. the bow of a violin etc.) with rosin. 2 smear or seal up with rosin. ◻◻ **rosiny** adj. [ME, alt. f. RESIN]

Rosinante /͵rɒsɪˈnæntɪ/ the name of Don Quixote's horse.

Roskilde /ˈrɒskɪlə/ a port of Denmark, on the island of Zealand; pop. (1981) 39,650. It was the seat of Danish kings from c.1020 and the capital of Denmark until 1443.

rosolio /rəˈzəʊlɪəʊ/ n. (also **rosoglio**) (pl. **-os**) a sweet cordial of spirits, sugar, and flavouring. [It., f. mod.L *ros solis* dew of the sun]

RoSPA /ˈrɒspə/ abbr. (in the UK) Royal Society for the Prevention of Accidents.

Ross¹ /rɒs/, Sir James Clark (1800–62), English polar explorer. A nephew of Sir John Ross, he served his apprenticeship as a polar explorer in the 1820s under both Parry and his uncle. In 1831 he discovered the north magnetic pole and in 1838 undertook a magnetic survey of the United Kingdom. Between 1839 and 1843 Ross commanded the *Erebus* and the *Terror* on an expedition to the Antarctic (where Ross Sea, Ross Barrier, and Ross Island all now bear his name), for which he was knighted.

Ross² /rɒs/, Sir John (1777–1856), Scottish polar explorer. After

serving with distinction in the Napoleonic Wars, Ross led an expedition to Baffin Bay in 1818 and another in search of the North-west Passage between 1829 and 1833, during which he surveyed King William Land, Boothia Peninsula, and the Gulf of Boothia (the last two named in honour of the expedition's patron, Sir Felix Booth (d. 1850), head of a firm of distillers).

Ross Dependency that part of Antarctica explored by Sir James Ross and claimed by New Zealand.

Rossellini /͵rɒseˈliːnɪ/, Roberto (1906–77), Italian film director, noted for his 'neo-realist' style. Among his most successful films are those on the theme of the Italian resistance movement during the German occupation — *Open City* (1945), which incorporated documentary material filmed during the Second World War, and *General Della Rovere* (1959).

Rossetti¹ /rəˈzetɪ/, Christina Georgina (1830–94), English poet, sister of D. G. Rossetti (see entry). She was deeply influenced by the Oxford Movement and her devotion to the Anglican faith is reflected in the religious poetry which constitutes the greater part of her prolific output. Marked by recurrent themes of melancholy, frustrated love and premature resignation, and great technical virtuosity, her work includes poems of fantasy, love lyrics, and poems for the young. Her first published work *Goblin Market and other Poems* (1862) shows a literary expression of Pre-Raphaelite ideals.

Rossetti² /rəˈzetɪ/, Dante Gabriel (Gabriel Charles Dante Rossetti, 1828–82), English poet and painter, son of a cultured Italian patriot. A founder-member of the Pre-Raphaelite brotherhood (1848), he contributed something of the mystic religiosity of quattrocento painting to the movement. Some of his poems appeared in the Pre-Raphaelite journal *The Germ* in 1850, including 'The Blessed Damozel' which was the subject of a later painting. *Poems* (1870) was attacked for its impurity and obscenity, but some readers have enjoyed the erotic and emotional power of his poetry.

Rossini /rɒˈsiːnɪ/, Gioachino Antonio (1792–1868), Italian composer, a precociously musical child who by the age of 31 was a successful enough opera composer for Stendhal (admittedly a partial witness) to declare 'The glory of the man is limited only by the limits of civilization'. Almost all of his works were written in the first half of his life. His combination of deft sophisticated humour and brilliant orchestral writing was to find its finest expression in *The Barber of Seville* (1816). Ranking equally with this work, however, is the grand opera *William Tell* (1829), a powerful recounting of the William Tell legend. A fine cook, Rossini also left to posterity a recipe for fillet steaks with artichoke hearts, *foie gras*, truffles, and Madeira sauce—tournedos Rossini.

Rosslare /rɒsˈleə(r)/ a ferry port in County Wexford in the Republic of Ireland.

Rostand /rɒˈstɑ̃/, Edmond (1868–1918), French playwright, who won sudden fame with his poetic drama *Cyrano de Bergerac* (1897) which remains his most popular and successful work, reviving in romantic guise the 17th-c. soldier and duellist of the title.

roster /ˈrɒstə(r), ˈrəʊstə(r)/ n. & v. —n. a list or plan showing turns of duty or leave for individuals or groups esp. of a military force. —v.tr. place on a roster. [Du. *rooster* list, orig. gridiron f. *roosten* ROAST, with ref. to its parallel lines]

Rostock /ˈrɒstɒk/ an industrial port on the Baltic coast of Germany; pop. (1986) 245,600.

Rostov-on-Don /ˈrɒstɒf/ a city of the Soviet Union on the River Don near its point of entry into the Sea of Azov; pop. (est. 1987) 1,004,000.

rostra pl. of ROSTRUM.

rostral /ˈrɒstr(ə)l/ adj. 1 *Zool.* & *Bot.* of or on the rostrum. 2 *Anat.* **a** nearer the hypophysial area in the early embryo. **b** nearer the region of the nose and mouth in post-embryonic life. 3 (of a column etc.) adorned with the beaks of ancient war-galleys or with representations of these. ◻◻ **rostrally** adv.

rostrated /rɒˈstreɪtɪd/ adj. 1 *Zool.* & *Bot.* having or ending in a rostrum. 2 = ROSTRAL 3. [L *rostratus* (as ROSTRUM)]

rostrum /ˈrɒstrəm/ n. (pl. **rostra** /-strə/ or **rostrums**) 1 **a** a platform for public speaking. **b** a conductor's platform facing the orchestra. **c** a similar platform for other purposes, e.g. for supporting a film or television camera. **2** *Zool. & Bot.* a beak, stiff snout, or beaklike part, esp. of an insect or arachnid. **3** *Rom. Antiq.* the beak of a war-galley. □□ (all in sense 2) **rostrate** /-strət/ *adj.* **rostriferous** /-ˈstrɪfərəs/ *adj.* **rostriform** *adj.* [L, = beak f. *rodere ros-* gnaw: orig. *rostra* (pl., in sense 1a) in the Roman forum adorned with beaks of captured galleys]

rosy /ˈrəʊzɪ/ *adj.* (**rosier, rosiest**) **1** coloured like a pink or red rose (esp. of the complexion as indicating good health, of a blush, wine, the sky, light, etc.). **2** optimistic, hopeful, cheerful (*a rosy future; a rosy attitude to life*). □□ **rosily** *adv.* **rosiness** *n.*

rot /rɒt/ *v., n., & int.* —*v.* (**rotted, rotting**) **1** *intr.* **a** (of animal or vegetable matter) lose its original form by the chemical action of bacteria, fungi, etc.; decay. **b** (foll. by *off, away*) crumble or drop from a stem etc. through decomposition. **2** *intr.* **a** (of society, institutions, etc.) gradually perish from lack of vigour or use. **b** (of a prisoner etc.) waste away (*left to rot in prison*); (of a person) languish. **3** *tr.* cause to rot, make rotten. **4** *tr. Brit. sl.* tease, abuse, denigrate. **5** *intr. Brit. sl.* joke. —*n.* **1** the process or state of rotting. **2** *sl.* nonsense; an absurd or foolish statement, argument, or proposal. **3** a sudden series of (usu. unaccountable) failures; a rapid decline in standards etc. (*a rot set in; we must try to stop the rot*). **4** (often prec. by *the*) a virulent liver-disease of sheep. —*int.* expressing incredulity or ridicule. □ **rot-gut** *sl.* cheap harmful alcoholic liquor. [OE *rotian* (v.): (n.) ME, perh. f. Scand.: cf. Icel., Norw. *rot*]

rota /ˈrəʊtə/ *n.* **1** esp. *Brit.* a list of persons acting, or duties to be done, in rotation; a roster. **2** (**Rota**) *RC Ch.* the supreme ecclesiastical and secular court. [L, = wheel]

Rotarian /rəʊˈteərɪən/ *n. & adj.* —*n.* a member of Rotary. —*adj.* of Rotary. [ROTARY + -AN]

rotary /ˈrəʊtərɪ/ *adj. & n.* —*adj.* acting by rotation (*rotary drill; rotary pump*). —*n.* (*pl.* **-ies**) **1** a rotary machine. **2** *US* a traffic roundabout. **3** (**Rotary**) (in full **Rotary International**) a worldwide society for business and professional men having as its aim the promotion of unselfish service and international goodwill. Its name derives from the fact that the first local group, formed at Chicago in 1905, met at each member's premises in rotation. □ **Rotary Club** a local branch of Rotary. **rotary-wing** (of an aircraft) deriving lift from rotary aerofoils. [med.L *rotarius* (as ROTA)]

rotate[1] /rəʊˈteɪt/ *v.* **1** *intr. & tr.* move round an axis or centre, revolve. **2 a** *tr.* take or arrange in rotation. **b** *intr.* act or take place in rotation (*the chairmanship will rotate*). □□ **rotatable** *adj.* **rotative** /ˈrəʊtətɪv/ *adj.* **rotatory** /ˈrəʊtətərɪ, -ˈteɪtərɪ/ *adj.* [L *rotare* f. *rota* wheel]

rotate[2] /ˈrəʊteɪt/ *adj. Bot.* wheel-shaped. [formed as ROTA]

rotation /rəʊˈteɪʃ(ə)n/ *n.* **1** the act or an instance of rotating or being rotated. **2** a recurrence; a recurrent series or period; a regular succession of various members of a group in office etc. **3** a system of growing different crops in regular order to avoid exhausting the soil. □□ **rotational** *adj.* **rotationally** *adv.* [L *rotatio*]

rotator /rəʊˈteɪtə(r)/ *n.* **1** a machine or device for causing something to rotate. **2** *Anat.* a muscle that rotates a limb etc. **3** a revolving apparatus or part. [L (as ROTATE[1])]

Rotavator /ˈrəʊtəˌveɪtə(r)/ *n.* (also **Rotovator**) *propr.* a machine with a rotating blade for breaking up or tilling the soil. □□ **rotavate** *v.tr.* [ROTARY + CULTIVATOR]

rote /rəʊt/ *n.* (usu. prec. by *by*) mechanical or habitual repetition (with ref. to acquiring knowledge). [ME: orig. unkn.]

rotenone /ˈrəʊtəˌnəʊn/ *n.* a toxic crystalline substance obtained from the roots of derris and other plants, used as an insecticide. [Jap. *rotenon* f. *roten* derris]

Roth /rəʊθ/, Philip (1933–), American novelist, whose complex relationship with his Jewish background is reflected in many of his works. His best-known novel is *Portnoy's Complaint* (1969), which records the intimate confessions of Alexander Portnoy to his psychiatrist.

Rothko /ˈrɒθkəʊ/, Mark (born Marcus Rothkovich, 1903–70), American painter, born in Latvia of Russian-Jewish parents. After about 1948 he became a leading figure in the abstract

expressionist movement, his characteristic idiom being large rectangular bands of colour arranged parallel to each other, usually in a vertical format. The edges of these shapes are softly uneven, giving them a hazy pulsating quality, as if they were suspended and floating on the canvas. The overall effect of these often enormous canvases is one of calmness and contemplation, as opposed to the frenzied energy of the action painters.

Rothschild /ˈrɒtʃaɪld/ the name of a famous Jewish banking-house, first established in Frankfurt at the end of the 18th c. and eventually spreading its operations all over western Europe.

rotifer /ˈrəʊtɪfə(r)/ *n.* any minute aquatic animal of the phylum Rotifera, with rotatory organs used in swimming and feeding. [mod.L *rotiferus* f. L *rota* wheel + *-fer* bearing]

rotisserie /rəʊˈtɪsərɪ/ *n.* **1** a restaurant etc. where meat is roasted or barbecued. **2** a cooking appliance with a rotating spit for roasting and barbecuing meat. [F *rôtisserie* (as ROAST)]

rotogravure /ˌrəʊtəɡrəˈvjʊə(r)/ *n.* **1** a printing system using a rotary press with intaglio cylinders, usu. running at high speed. **2** a sheet etc. printed with this system. [G *Rotogravur* (name of a company) assim. to PHOTOGRAVURE]

rotor /ˈrəʊtə(r)/ *n.* **1** a rotary part of a machine, esp. in the distributor of an internal-combustion engine. **2** a set of radiating aerofoils round a hub on a helicopter, providing lift when rotated. [irreg. for ROTATOR]

Rotorua /ˌrəʊtəˈruːə/ a health resort on North Island, New Zealand, at the centre of a region of thermal springs and geysers; pop. (1988) 53,000.

Rotovator var. of ROTAVATOR.

rotten /ˈrɒt(ə)n/ *adj.* (**rottener, rottenest**) **1** rotting or rotted; falling to pieces or liable to break or tear from age or use. **2** morally, socially, or politically corrupt. **3** *sl.* **a** disagreeable, unpleasant (*had a rotten time*). **b** (of a plan etc.) ill-advised, unsatisfactory (*a rotten idea*). **c** disagreeably ill (*feel rotten today*). □ **rotten borough** *hist.* (before 1832) an English borough able to elect an MP though having very few voters. **rotten-stone** decomposed siliceous limestone used as a powder for polishing metals. □□ **rottenly** *adv.* **rottenness** *n.* [ME f. ON *rotinn*, rel. to ROT, RET]

rotter /ˈrɒtə(r)/ *n.* esp. *Brit. sl.* an objectionable, unpleasant, or reprehensible person. [ROT]

Rotterdam /ˈrɒtəˌdæm/ a city and the principal port of The Netherlands, on the River Meuse; pop. (1987) 574,300.

Rottweiler /ˈrɒtˌvaɪlə(r), -ˌwaɪlə(r)/ *n.* **1** a dog of a tall black-and-tan breed. **2** this breed. [G f. *Rottweil* in SW Germany]

rotund /rəʊˈtʌnd/ *adj.* **1 a** circular, round. **b** (of a person) large and plump, podgy. **2** (of speech, literary style, etc.) sonorous, grandiloquent. □□ **rotundity** *n.* **rotundly** *adv.* [L *rotundus* f. *rotare* ROTATE[1]]

rotunda /rəʊˈtʌndə/ *n.* **1** a building with a circular ground-plan, esp. one with a dome. **2** a circular hall or room. [earlier *rotonda* f. It. *rotonda* (*camera*) round (chamber), fem. of *rotondo* round (as ROTUND)]

rouble /ˈruːb(ə)l/ *n.* (also **ruble**) the chief monetary unit of the USSR. [f f. Russ.]

roué /ˈruːeɪ/ *n.* a debauchee, esp. an elderly one; a rake. [F, past part. of *rouer* break on wheel, = one deserving this]

Rouen /ruːˈɑ̃/ a port on the River Seine in NW France, capital of the region of Upper Normandy (Haute-Normandie); pop. (1982) 105,100. It was in English possession from the time of the Norman Conquest (1066) until captured by the French in 1204, returning briefly to English rule (1419–49) after its capture by Henry V. Joan of Arc was tried and burnt at the stake here in 1431.

rouge /ruːʒ/ *n. & v.* —*n.* **1** a red powder or cream used for colouring the cheeks. **2** powdered ferric oxide etc. as a polishing agent esp. for metal. —*v.* **1** *tr.* colour with rouge. **2** *intr.* **a** apply rouge to one's cheeks. **b** become red, blush. □ **rouge-et-noir** /ˌruːʒeɪˈnwɑː(r)/ a gambling game using a table with red and black marks, on which players place stakes. [F, = red, f. L *rubeus*, rel. to RED]

rough /rʌf/ *adj., adv., n., & v.* —*adj.* **1 a** having an uneven or irregular surface, not smooth or level or polished. **b** *Tennis* applied to the side of a racket from which the twisted gut projects. **2** (of ground, country, etc.) having many bumps, obstacles, etc. **3 a** hairy, shaggy. **b** (of cloth) coarse in texture. **4 a** (of a person or behaviour) not mild or quiet or gentle; boisterous, unrestrained (*rough manners; rough play*). **b** (of language etc.) coarse, indelicate. **c** (of wine etc.) sharp or harsh in taste. **5** (of the sea, weather, etc.) violent, stormy. **6** disorderly, riotous (*a rough part of town*). **7** harsh, insensitive, inconsiderate (*rough words; rough treatment*). **8 a** unpleasant, severe, demanding (*had a rough time*). **b** unfortunate, unreasonable, undeserved (*had rough luck*). **c** (foll. by *on*) hard or unfair towards. **9** lacking finish, elaboration, comfort, etc. (*rough lodgings; a rough welcome*). **10** incomplete, rudimentary (*a rough attempt; a rough makeshift*). **11 a** inexact, approximate, preliminary (*a rough estimate; a rough sketch*). **b** (of stationery etc.) for use in writing rough notes etc. **12** *colloq.* **a** ill, unwell (*am feeling rough*). **b** depressed, dejected. —*adv.* in a rough manner (*the land should be ploughed rough; play rough*). —*n.* **1** (usu. prec. by *the*) a hard part or aspect of life; hardship (*take the rough with the smooth*). **2** rough ground (*over rough and smooth*). **3** a rough or violent person (*met a bunch of roughs*). **4** *Golf* rough ground off the fairway between tee and green. **5** an unfinished or provisional or natural state (*have written it in rough; shaped from the rough*). **6** (prec. by *the*) the general way or tendency (*is true in the rough*). —*v.tr.* **1** (foll. by *up*) ruffle (feathers, hair, etc.) by rubbing against the grain. **2 a** (foll. by *out*) shape or plan roughly. **b** (foll. by *in*) sketch roughly. **3** give the first shaping to (a gun, lens, etc.). □ **rough-and-ready** rough or crude but effective; not elaborate or over-particular. **rough-and-tumble** *adj.* irregular, scrambling, disorderly. —*n.* a haphazard fight; a scuffle. **rough breathing** see BREATHING. **rough coat** a first coat of plaster applied to a surface. **rough copy 1** a first or original draft. **2** a copy of a picture etc. showing only the essential features. **rough deal** hard or unfair treatment. **rough diamond 1** an uncut diamond. **2** a person of good nature but rough manners. **rough-dry** (**-dries**, **-dried**) dry (clothes) without ironing. **the rough edge** (or **side**) **of one's tongue** severe or harsh words. **rough-handle** treat or handle roughly. **rough-hew** (*past part.* **-hewed** or **-hewn**) shape out roughly; give crude form to. **rough-hewn** uncouth, unrefined. **rough house** *sl.* a disturbance or row; boisterous play. **rough-house** *v. sl.* **1** *tr.* handle (a person) roughly. **2** *intr.* make a disturbance; act violently. **rough it** do without basic comforts. **rough justice 1** treatment that is approximately fair. **2** treatment that is not at all fair. **rough passage 1** a crossing over rough sea. **2** a difficult time or experience. **rough ride** a difficult time or experience. **rough-rider** a person who breaks in or can ride unbroken horses. **rough stuff** *colloq.* boisterous or violent behaviour. **rough tongue** a habit of rudeness in speaking. **rough trade** *sl.* a tough or sadistic element among male homosexuals. **rough up** *sl.* treat (a person) with violence; attack violently. **rough work 1** preliminary or provisional work. **2** *colloq.* violence. **3** a task requiring the use of force. **sleep rough** sleep outdoors, or not in a proper bed. □□ **roughness** *n*. [OE *rūh* f. WG]

roughage /'rʌfidʒ/ *n.* **1** coarse material with a high fibre content, the part of food which stimulates digestion. **2** coarse fodder. [ROUGH + -AGE 3]

roughcast /'rʌfkɑːst/ *n., adj., & v.* —*n.* plaster of lime and gravel, used on outside walls. —*adj.* **1** (of a wall etc.) coated with roughcast. **2** (of a plan etc.) roughly formed, preliminary. —*v.tr.* (*past* and *past part.* **-cast**) **1** coat (a wall) with roughcast. **2** prepare (a plan, essay, etc.) in outline.

roughen /'rʌf(ə)n/ *v.tr. & intr.* make or become rough.

roughie /'rʌfi/ *n. dial. sl.* **1** a rough; a hooligan. **2** *Austral.* **a** an outsider. **b** an unfair or unreasonable act.

roughish /'rʌfiʃ/ *adj.* somewhat rough.

roughly /'rʌfli/ *adv.* **1** in a rough manner. **2** approximately (*roughly 20 people attended*). □ **roughly speaking** in an approximate sense (*it is, roughly speaking, a square*).

roughneck /'rʌfnek/ *n. colloq.* **1** a rough or rowdy person. **2** a worker on an oil rig.

roughshod /'rʌfʃɒd/ *adj.* (of a horse) having shoes with nail-heads projecting to prevent slipping. □ **ride roughshod over** treat inconsiderately or arrogantly.

roughy /'rʌfi/ *n.* (*pl.* **-ies**) *Austral. & NZ* a fish, *Arripis georgianus*, of the perch family. [perh. f. ROUGH]

roulade /ruːˈlɑːd/ *n.* **1** a dish cooked or served in the shape of a roll, esp. a rolled piece of meat or sponge with a filling. **2** a florid passage of runs etc. in solo vocal music, usu. sung to one syllable. [F f. *rouler* to roll]

rouleau /'ruːləʊ/ *n.* (*pl.* **rouleaux** or **rouleaus** /-əʊz/) **1** a cylindrical packet of coins. **2** a coil or roll of ribbon etc., esp. as trimming. [F f. *rôle* ROLL *n.*]

Roulers see ROESELARE.

roulette /ruːˈlet/ *n.* **1** a gambling game using a table in which a ball is dropped on to a revolving wheel with numbered compartments, players betting on the number at which the ball comes to rest. Its origins are obscure but probably French; it was only in the late 18th or early 19th c. that it became a fashionable attraction in the casinos of Europe. **2** *Math.* a curve generated by a point on a curve rolling on another. **3 a** a revolving toothed wheel used in engraving. **b** a similar wheel for making perforations between postage stamps in a sheet. □□ **rouletted** *adj.* (in sense 3b). [F, dimin. of *rouelle* f. LL *rotella* dimin. of L *rota* wheel]

Roumelia /ruːˈmiːliə/ (also **Rumelia**) *hist.* the European territory of the Ottoman empire, including Macedonia, Thrace, and Albania. [Turk. *Rumeli* land of the Romans]

round /raʊnd/ *adj., n., adv., prep., & v.* —*adj.* **1** shaped like or approximately like a circle, sphere, or cylinder; having a convex or circular outline or surface; curved, not angular. **2** done with or involving circular motion. **3 a** entire, continuous, complete (*a round dozen*); fully expressed or developed; all together, not broken or defective or scanty. **b** (of a sum of money) considerable. **4** genuine, candid, outspoken; (of a statement etc.) categorical, unmistakable. **5** (usu. *attrib.*) (of a number) expressed for convenience or as an estimate in fewer significant numerals or with a fraction removed (*spent £297.32, or in round figures £300*). **6 a** (of a style) flowing. **b** (of a voice) not harsh. **7** *Phonet.* (of a vowel) pronounced with rounded lips. —*n.* **1** a round object or form. **2 a** a revolving motion, a circular or recurring course (*the earth in its yearly round*). **b** a regular recurring series of activities or functions (*one's daily round; a continuous round of pleasure*). **c** a recurring succession or series of meetings for discussion etc. (*a new round of talks on disarmament*). **3 a** a fixed route on which things are regularly delivered (*milk round*). **b** a route or sequence by which people or things are regularly supervised or inspected (*a watchman's round; a doctor's rounds*). **4** an allowance of something distributed or measured out, esp.: **a** a single provision of drinks etc. to each member of a group. **b** ammunition to fire one shot; the act of firing this. **5 a** a slice across a loaf of bread. **b** a sandwich made from whole slices of bread. **c** a thick disc of beef cut from the haunch as a joint. **6** each of a set or series, a sequence of actions by each member of a group in turn, esp. **a** one spell of play in a game etc. **b** one stage in a competition. **7** *Golf* the playing of all the holes in a course once. **8** *Archery* a fixed number of arrows shot from a fixed distance. **9** (**the round**) a form of sculpture in which the figure stands clear of any ground (cf. RELIEF 6a). **10** *Mus.* a canon for three or more unaccompanied voices singing at the same pitch or in octaves. **11** (in *pl.*) *Mil.* **a** a watch that goes round inspecting sentries. **b** a circuit made by this. **12** a rung of a ladder. **13** (foll. by *of*) the circumference, bounds, or extent of (*in all the round of Nature*). —*adv.* **1** with circular motion (*wheels go round*). **2** with return to the starting-point or an earlier state (*summer soon comes round*). **3 a** with rotation, or change to an opposite position (*he turned round to look*). **b** with change to an opposite opinion etc. (*they were angry but I soon won them round*). **4** to, at, or affecting all or many points of a circumference or an area or the members of a company etc. (*tea was then handed round; may I look round?*). **5** in every direction from a centre or within a radius (*spread destruction round; everyone for a mile round*). **6** by a circuitous way (*will you jump over or go round?; go a long way round*). **7 a** to a person's house etc. (*ask him round*; *will be round soon*). **b** to a more prominent or convenient position (*brought the car round*). **8** measuring (a specified distance) in girth. —*prep.* **1** so as to encircle or enclose (*tour round the world*; *has a blanket round him*). **2** at or to points on the circumference of (*sat round the table*). **3** with successive visits to (*hawks them round the cafés*). **4** in various directions from or with regard to (*towns round Birmingham*; *shells bursting round them*). **5** having as an axis of revolution or as a central point (*turns round its centre of gravity*; *write a book round an event*). **6 a** so as to double or pass in a curved course (*go round the corner*). **b** having passed in this way (*be round the corner*). **c** in the position that would result from this (*find them round the corner*). **7** so as to come close from various sides but not into contact. —*v.* **1 a** *tr.* give a round shape to. **b** *intr.* assume a round shape. **2** *tr.* double or pass round (a corner, cape, etc.). **3** *tr.* express (a number) in a less exact but more convenient form (also foll. by *down* when the number is decreased and *up* when it is increased). **4** *tr.* pronounce (a vowel) with rounded lips. □ **go the round** (or **rounds**) (of news etc.) be passed on from person to person. **in the round 1** with all features shown; all things considered. **2** *Theatr.* with the audience round at least three sides of the stage. **3** (of sculpture) with all sides shown; not in relief. **make the round of** go round. **make** (or **go**) **one's rounds** take a customary route for inspection etc. **round about 1** in a ring (about); all round; on all sides (of). **2** with a change to an opposite position. **3** approximately (*cost round about £50*). **round and round** several times round. **round-arm** *Cricket* (of bowling) with the arm swung horizontally. **round the bend** see BEND¹. **round brackets** brackets of the form (). **round dance 1** a dance in which couples move in circles round the ballroom. **2** a dance in which the dancers form one large circle. **round down** see sense 3 of *v.* **round off** (or **out**) **1** bring to a complete or symmetrical or well-ordered state. **2** smooth out; blunt the corners or angles of. **round on a person** make a sudden verbal attack on or unexpected retort to a person. **round out** = *round off* 1. **round peg in a square hole** = *square peg in a round hole* (see PEG). **round robin 1** a petition esp. with signatures written in a circle to conceal the order of writing. **2** *US* a tournament in which each competitor plays in turn against every other. **round-shouldered** with shoulders bent forward so that the back is rounded. **Round Table 1** the table at which King Arthur and his knights sat so that none should have precedence. **2** an international charitable association which holds discussions, debates, etc., and undertakes community service. **3** (**round table**) an assembly for discussion, esp. at a conference (often *attrib.*: *round-table talks*). **round trip** a trip to one or more places and back again (esp. by a circular route). **round the twist** see TWIST. **round up** collect or bring together, esp. by going round (see also sense 3 of *v.*). **round-up** *n.* **1** a systematic rounding up of people or things. **2** a summary; a résumé of facts or events. □□ **roundish** *adj.* **roundness** *n.* [ME f. OF *ro(u)nd-* stem of *ro(o)nt*, *reont* f. L *rotundus* ROTUND]

roundabout /ˈraʊndəˌbaʊt/ *n. & adj.* —*n.* **1** *Brit.* a road junction at which traffic moves in one direction round a central island. **2** *Brit.* **a** a large revolving device in a playground, for children to ride on. **b** = MERRY-GO-ROUND 1. —*adj.* circuitous, circumlocutory, indirect.

roundel /ˈraʊnd(ə)l/ *n.* **1** a small disc, esp. a decorative medallion. **2** a circular identifying mark painted on military aircraft, esp. the red, white, and blue of the RAF. **3** a poem of eleven lines in three stanzas. [ME f. OF *rondel(le)* (as ROUND)]

roundelay /ˈraʊndɪˌleɪ/ *n.* a short simple song with a refrain. [F *rondelet* (as RONDEL), with assim. to LAY³ or *virelay*]

rounder /ˈraʊndə(r)/ *n.* **1** (in *pl.*; treated as *sing.*) a game with a bat and ball in which players after hitting the ball run through a round of bases. **2** a complete run of a player through all the bases as a unit of scoring in rounders.

Roundhead /ˈraʊndhed/ *n. hist.* a member of the party (also known as *Parliamentarians*) opposing the king (Charles I) in the English Civil War, so called because of the style in which the Puritans, who were an important element in the forces, wore their hair.

roundhouse /ˈraʊndhaʊs/ *n.* **1** a circular repair-shed for railway locomotives, built round a turntable. **2** *sl.* **a** a blow given with a wide sweep of the arm. **b** *US Baseball* a pitch made with a sweeping sidearm motion. **3** *hist.* a prison; a place of detention. **4** *Naut.* a cabin or set of cabins on the after part of the quarterdeck, esp. on a sailing-ship.

roundly /ˈraʊndlɪ/ *adv.* **1** bluntly, in plain language, severely (*was roundly criticized*; *told them roundly that he refused*). **2** in a thoroughgoing manner (*go roundly to work*). **3** in a circular way (*swells out roundly*).

roundsman /ˈraʊndzmən/ *n.* (*pl.* **-men**) **1** *Brit.* a tradesman's employee going round delivering and taking orders. **2** *US* a police officer in charge of a patrol. **3** *Austral.* a journalist covering a specified subject (*political roundsman*).

roundworm /ˈraʊndwɜːm/ *n.* a worm, esp. a nematode, with a rounded body.

roup¹ /raʊp/ *n. & v. Sc. & N.Engl.* —*n.* an auction. —*v.tr.* sell by auction. [ME 'to shout', of Scand. orig.]

roup² /ruːp/ *n.* an infectious poultry-disease, esp. of the respiratory tract. □□ **roupy** *adj.* [16th c.: orig. unkn.]

rouse /raʊz/ *v.* **1 a** *tr.* (often foll. by *from*, *out of*) bring out of sleep, wake. **b** *intr.* (often foll. by *up*) cease to sleep, wake up. **2** (often foll. by *up*) **a** *tr.* stir up, make active or excited, startle out of inactivity or confidence or carelessness (*roused them from their complacency*; *was roused to protest*). **b** *intr.* become active. **3** *tr.* provoke to anger (*is terrible when roused*). **4** *tr.* evoke (feelings). **5** *tr.* (usu. foll. by *in*, *out*, *up*) *Naut.* haul vigorously. **6** *tr.* startle (game) from a lair or cover. **7** *tr.* stir (liquid, esp. beer while brewing). □ **rouse oneself** overcome one's indolence. □□ **rousable** *adj.* **rouser** *n.* [orig. as a hawking and hunting term, so prob. f. AF: orig. unkn.]

rouseabout /ˈraʊzəˌbaʊt/ *n. Austral. & NZ* an unskilled labourer or odd jobber, esp. on a farm.

rousing /ˈraʊzɪŋ/ *adj.* **1** exciting, stirring (*a rousing cheer*; *a rousing song*). **2** (of a fire) blazing strongly. □□ **rousingly** *adv.*

Rousse see RUSE.

Rousseau¹ /ˈruːsəʊ/, Henri Julien (1844–1910), French painter known as 'Le Douanier' from his job as a Parisian toll-inspector. He began painting in 1885 in a naïve style that was to appeal to Apollinaire's circle (including Jarry and Picasso) in its often dreamlike intensity and simplicity of vision. The unique stylization and authority of his pictures—e.g. *Sleeping Gypsy* (1897) and *Tropical Storm with Tiger* (1891)—have caused him to be considered a modern master and the doyen of all naïve painters.

Rousseau² /ˈruːsəʊ/, Jean-Jacques (1712–78), philosopher and novelist, born in Geneva. Lacking in stability of character he led an unsettled life, sometimes aided by benefactors (including Hume) whose kindness he ill repaid, sometimes occupying humble situations, as footman or music-master, living for twenty-five years with a kitchen-maid and (she claimed) depositing their five babies at the Foundling Hospital. He came into notice by the works in which he expounded his revolt against the existing social order. Believing in the original goodness of human nature he considered that the rise of property and human pride (*amour propre*) had corrupted the 'noble savage'. His novel *Émile* (1762) lays down principles for a new scheme of education in which the child is to be allowed full scope for individual development in natural surroundings, shielded from the harmful influences of civilization. His most important work, the *Social Contract* (1762) set forth the theory that society is founded on a contract: the people sacrifice their natural rights to the general will in return for protection, and the head of the State is their mandatary not their master. These views had an effect on the American Declaration of Independence and were wildly acclaimed during the French Revolution, when his body was brought to Paris and reburied with pomp in the Panthéon.

Rousseau³ /ˈruːsəʊ/, Théodore (1812–67), French landscape painter. His fruitless attempts to get his pictures accepted in the French Academy—an opponent of its *plein-air* aesthetic and bold handling—earned him the nickname of 'Le Grand Refusé', but the more liberal circumstances following the 1848 revolution saw the beginning of public recognition. In that year he settled at Barbizon in Fontainebleau Forest and worked in the company of others of the Barbizon school. His style ranged between luminous realism and deeply felt responses to the melancholy of nature.

roust /raʊst/ *v.tr.* **1** (often foll. by *up, out*) **a** a rouse, stir up. **b** root out. **2** *US sl.* jostle, harass, rough up. □ **roust around** rummage. [perh. alt. of ROUSE]

roustabout /ˈraʊstəˌbaʊt/ *n.* **1** a labourer on an oil rig. **2** an unskilled or casual labourer. **3** *US* a dock labourer or deck hand. **4** *Austral.* = ROUSEABOUT.

rout[1] /raʊt/ *n. & v.* —*n.* **1** a disorderly retreat of defeated troops. **2 a** an assemblage or company esp. of revellers or rioters. **b** *Law* an assemblage of three or more persons who have made a move towards committing an illegal act. **3** riot, tumult, disturbance, clamour, fuss. **4** *Brit. archaic* a large evening party or reception. —*v.tr.* put to rout. □ **put to rout** put to flight, defeat utterly. [ME f. AF *rute*, OF *route* ult. f. L *ruptus* broken]

rout[2] /raʊt/ *v.* **1** *intr. & tr.* = ROOT[2]. **2** *tr.* cut a groove, or any pattern not extending to the edges, in (a wooden or metal surface). □ **rout out** force or fetch out of bed or from a house or hiding-place. [var. of ROOT[2]]

route /ruːt, *Mil.* also raʊt/ *n. & v.* —*n.* **1** a way or course taken (esp. regularly) in getting from a starting-point to a destination. **2** *US* a round travelled in delivering, selling, or collecting goods. **3** *Mil. archaic* marching orders. —*v.tr.* (**routeing**) send or forward or direct to be sent by a particular route. □ **route man** *US* = ROUNDSMAN 1. **route march** a training-march for troops. [ME f. OF r(o)*ute* road ult. f. L *ruptus* broken]

router /ˈraʊtə(r)/ *n.* a type of plane with two handles used in routing.

routine /ruːˈtiːn/ *n., adj., & v.* —*n.* **1** a regular course or procedure, an unvarying performance of certain acts. **2** a set sequence in a performance, esp. a dance, comedy act, etc. **3** *Computing* a sequence of instructions for performing a task. —*adj.* **1** performed as part of a routine (*routine duties*). **2** of a customary or standard kind. —*v.tr.* organize according to a routine. □□ **routinely** *adv.* [F (as ROUTE)]

routinism /ruːˈtiːnɪz(ə)m/ *n.* the prevalence of routine. □□ **routinist** *n. & adj.*

routinize /ruːˈtiːnaɪz/ *v.tr.* (also **-ise**) subject to a routine; make into a matter of routine. □□ **routinization** /-ˈzeɪʃ(ə)n/ *n.*

roux /ruː/ *n.* (*pl.* same) a mixture of fat (esp. butter) and flour used in making sauces etc. [F, = browned (butter): see RUSSET]

Rovaniemi /ˌrɒvænˈjeɪmɪ/ the principal town of Finnish Lapland; pop. (1987) 32,911.

rove[1] /rəʊv/ *v. & n.* —*v.* **1** *intr.* wander without a settled destination, roam, ramble. **2** *intr.* (of eyes) look in changing directions. **3** *tr.* wander over or through. —*n.* an act of roving (*on the rove*). □ **rove-beetle** any long-bodied beetle of the family Staphylinidae, usu. found in decaying animal and vegetable matter. **roving commission** authority given to a person or persons conducting an inquiry to travel as may be necessary. **roving eye** a tendency to ogle or towards infidelity. [ME, orig. a term in archery = shoot at a casual mark with the range not determined, perh. f. dial. *rave* stray, prob. of Scand. orig.]

rove[2] *past of* REEVE[2].

rove[3] /rəʊv/ *n. & v.* —*n.* a sliver of cotton, wool, etc., drawn out and slightly twisted. —*v.tr.* form into roves. [18th c.: orig. unkn.]

rove[4] /rəʊv/ *n.* a small metal plate or ring for a rivet to pass through and be clenched over, esp. in boat-building. [ON *ró*, with excrescent *v*]

rover[1] /ˈrəʊvə(r)/ *n.* **1** a roving person; a wanderer. **2** *Croquet* **a** a ball that has passed all the hoops but not pegged out. **b** a player whose ball is a rover. **3** *Archery* **a** a mark chosen at undetermined range. **b** a mark for long-distance shooting. **4** (**Rover**) *Brit.* a senior Scout. ¶ Now called *Venture Scout*. (See SCOUT ASSOCIATION.)

rover[2] /ˈrəʊvə(r)/ *n.* a sea robber, a pirate. [ME f. MLG, MDu. *rōver* f. *rōven* rob, rel. to REAVE]

rover[3] /ˈrəʊvə(r)/ *n.* a person or machine that makes roves of fibre.

row[1] /rəʊ/ *n.* **1** a number of persons or things in a more or less straight line. **2** a line of seats across a theatre etc. (*in the front row*). **3** a street with a continuous line of houses along one or each side. **4** a line of plants in a field or garden. **5** a horizontal line of entries in a table etc. □ **a hard row to hoe** a difficult task. **in a row 1** forming a row. **2** *colloq.* in succession (*two Sundays in a row*). **row-house** *US* a terrace house. [ME *raw, row*, f. OE f. Gmc]

row[2] /rəʊ/ *v. & n.* —*v.* **1** *tr.* propel (a boat) with oars. Rowing dates back to ancient times when it provided motive power for warships. The earliest literary reference to rowing as a sport occurs in Virgil's *Aeneid*, at the funeral games arranged by Aeneas in honour of his father. **2** *tr.* convey (a passenger) in a boat in this way. **3** *intr.* propel a boat in this way. **4** *tr.* make (a stroke) or achieve (a rate of striking) in rowing. **5** *tr.* compete in (a race) by rowing. **6** *tr.* row a race with. —*n.* **1** a spell of rowing. **2** an excursion in a rowing-boat. □ **row-boat** *US* = *rowing-boat*. **row down** overtake in a rowing, esp. bumping, race. **rowing-boat** *Brit.* a small boat propelled by oars. **rowing-machine** a device for exercising the muscles used in rowing. **row out** exhaust by rowing (*the crew were completely rowed out at the finish*). **row over** complete the course of a boat race with little effort, owing to the absence or inferiority of competitors. □□ **rower** *n.* [OE *rōwan* f. Gmc, rel. to RUDDER, L *remus* oar]

row[3] /raʊ/ *n. & v. colloq.* —*n.* **1** a loud noise or commotion. **2** a fierce quarrel or dispute. **3 a** a severe reprimand. **b** the condition of being reprimanded (*shall get into a row*). —*v.* **1** *intr.* make or engage in a row. **2** *tr.* reprimand. □ **make** (or **kick up**) **a row 1** raise a noise. **2** make a vigorous protest. [18th-c. sl.: orig. unkn.]

rowan /ˈrəʊən, ˈraʊ-/ *n.* (in full **rowan-tree**) **1** *Sc. & N.Engl.* the mountain ash. **2** a similar tree, *Sorbus americana*, native to America. **3** (in full **rowan-berry**) the scarlet berry of either of these trees. [Scand., corresp. to Norw. *rogn, raun*, Icel. *reynir*]

rowdy /ˈraʊdɪ/ *adj. & n.* —*adj.* (**rowdier, rowdiest**) noisy and disorderly. —*n.* (*pl.* -**ies**) a rowdy person. □□ **rowdily** *adv.* **rowdiness** *n.* **rowdyism** *n.* [19th-c. US, orig. = lawless backwoodsman: orig. unkn.]

Rowe /rəʊ/, Nicholas (1674–1718), English dramatist, who abandoned the legal profession for the theatre. His best-known tragedies were *The Fair Penitent* (1703) and *Jane Shore* (1714), both of which provided Mrs Siddons with celebrated roles, and *Tamerlane* (1701). They are marked by pathos and female suffering, and their strong moral tone is in sharp contrast to the licentiousness of the drama of the preceding 50 years.

rowel /ˈraʊəl/ *n. & v.* —*n.* **1** a spiked revolving disc at the end of a spur. **2** a circular piece of leather etc. with a hole in the centre inserted between a horse's skin and flesh to discharge an exudate. —*v.tr.* (**rowelled, rowelling**; *US* **roweled, roweling**) **1** urge with a rowel. **2** insert a rowel in. [ME f. OF *roel(e)* f. LL *rotella* dimin. of L *rota* wheel]

rowen /ˈraʊən/ *n.* (in *sing.* or *pl.*) *US* a second growth of grass, an aftermath. [ME f. OF *regain* (as GAIN)]

Rowlandson /ˈrəʊlənds(ə)n/, Thomas (1756–1827), English draughtsman and print-maker. He trained at the Royal Academy in the 1770s and set up in London as a portrait painter in 1777, but is remembered today as one of the finest and most acute commentators on contemporary English mores, satirizing the manners, morals, and occupations of English society, e.g. in *Vauxhall Gardens* (1784) and his illustrations to William Combe's *Tours of Dr Syntax* (1812–20). His style was essentially illustrative, a combination of graceful outline and delicate colour washes.

rowlock /ˈrɒlək, ˈrʌlək/ *n.* a device on a boat's gunwale, esp. a pair of thole-pins, serving as a fulcrum for an oar and keeping it in place. [alt. of earlier OARLOCK, after ROW[2]]

Rowntree /ˈraʊntriː/, Joseph (1801–59), English businessman and philanthropist. A Quaker, he founded the family cocoa and chocolate manufacturing firm in York. He had three sons, of whom Joseph Rowntree (1836–1925) was also distinguished for his philanthropy and for his care of employees' welfare; Benjamin Seebohm Rowntree (1871–1904) is known for his surveys of poverty in York and for his studies of management.

Rowton house /ˈraʊt(ə)n/ n. Brit. hist. a type of lodging-house for poor men, providing better conditions than a common lodging-house. [Lord *Rowton*, English social reformer d. 1903]

royal /ˈrɔɪəl/ adj. & n. —adj. **1** of or suited to or worthy of a king or queen. **2** in the service or under the patronage of a king or queen. **3** belonging to the king or queen (*the royal hands; the royal anger*). **4** of the family of a king or queen. **5** kingly, majestic, stately, splendid. **6** on a great scale, of exceptional size or quality, first-rate (*gave us royal entertainment; in royal spirits; had a royal time*). —n. **1** colloq. a member of the royal family. **2** a royal sail or mast. **3** a royal stag. **4** a size of paper, about 620 × 500 mm (25 × 20 in.). **5** (**the Royals**) the Royal Marines. □ **royal assent** see ASSENT. **royal blue** Brit. a deep vivid blue. **royal burgh** hist. (in Scotland) a burgh holding a charter from the Crown. **Royal Commission** see COMMISSION. **royal duke** see DUKE. **royal family** the family to which a sovereign belongs. **royal fern** a fern, *Osmunda regalis*, with huge spreading fronds. **royal flush** see FLUSH³. **royal icing** a hard white icing made from icing sugar and egg-whites. **royal jelly** a substance secreted by honey-bee workers and fed by them to future queen bees. **royal mast** a mast above a topgallant mast. **royal oak** a sprig of oak worn on 29 May to commemorate the restoration of Charles II (1660), who hid in an oak after the battle of Worcester (1651). **royal plural** the first person plural 'we' used by a single person. **royal road to** way of attaining without trouble. **royal sail** a sail above a topgallant sail. **royal stag** a stag with a head of 12 or more points. **royal standard** a banner bearing royal heraldic arms. **royal tennis** real tennis. **Royal Victorian Chain** (in the UK) an order founded by Edward VII in 1902 and conferred by the sovereign on special occasions. **Royal Victorian Order** (in the UK) an order founded by Queen Victoria in 1896 and conferred usu. for great service rendered to the sovereign. **royal warrant** a warrant authorizing a tradesperson to supply goods to a specified royal person. □□ **royally** adv. [ME f. OF *roial* f. L *regalis* REGAL]

Royal Academy of Arts (London) an institution established with the sanction of George III in 1768. Its original purpose was to cultivate and improve the arts of painting, sculpture, and architecture; this implied raising the artist's social and economic status by demonstrating the seriousness of his calling—a task that Reynolds, its first President, emphasized in his annual lectures. Like most 18th-c. academies its schools instructed students in drawing from life and the antique, and an annual open exhibition selected by its own jury was established as a showcase for artistic talent. Its premises were successively in Pall Mall, Somerset Palace (1780), and with the National Gallery in Trafalgar Square from 1837, moving to Burlington House, Piccadilly, in 1867. Although it became increasingly unrepresentative of modernist tendencies (and often at odds with new talent), it is now seen as the repository of mainstream art in England and its annual summer exhibition (May–August) is something of a social event. The Royal Scottish Academy received its royal charter in 1838 as a regional focus for Scottish art but has never matched its English counterpart in prestige.

Royal Air Force the British air force, formed in 1918 by amalgamation of the Royal Flying Corps (1912) and the Royal Naval Air Service (1914).

Royal British Legion a national association of ex-members of the British armed forces, founded in 1921.

Royal Canadian Mounted Police the Canadian police force, founded in 1873 as the North West Mounted Police.

Royal Engineers the engineering branch of the British Army.

Royal Institution a society founded in London in 1799 for the dissemination of scientific knowledge.

royalist /ˈrɔɪəlɪst/ n. **1 a** a supporter of monarchy. **b** hist. (also **Royalist**) a supporter of the royal side in the English Civil War. **2** US a reactionary, esp. a reactionary business tycoon. □□ **royalism** n.

Royal Marines a British armed service founded in 1664 for service on land and at sea. It is primarily a military force trained also for naval and amphibious operations and providing commandos, landing-craft and crews, frogmen, etc.

Royal Mint the establishment (since 1850, the only one) responsible for the manufacture of British coins. Set up in 1810 in a building near the Tower of London, it moved in 1968 to Llantrisant in South Wales. It also mints coins on behalf of certain foreign and Commonwealth governments, as well as medals, decorations, and seals. Since 1869 the office of Master Worker and Warden of the Mint has been nominally held by the Chancellor of the Exchequer, who has control of the establishment.

Royal Navy the British navy, whose origin dates from the fleet of warships created by King Alfred to defend the southern coast of England against Viking invaders in the 9th c. (see NAVY).

Royal Society the oldest and most prestigious scientific society in Britain, formed to promote scientific discussion especially in the physical sciences. Such societies had stormy beginnings in 16th-c. Italy, for scientific discoveries, such as those of Galileo, contradicted the accepted ideas of the time and were frowned on by the Church. The Royal Society, which received its charter from Charles II in 1662, had originated privately among the followers of Francis Bacon, and numbered among its members such famous scientists as Boyle, Wren, and Newton, who was its president from 1703 to 1727. Its *Philosophical Transactions*, founded in 1665 and still published, is the earliest scientific journal.

royalty /ˈrɔɪəltɪ/ n. (pl. **-ies**) **1** the office or dignity or power of a king or queen, sovereignty. **2 a** royal persons. **b** a member of a royal family. **3** a sum paid to a patentee for the use of a patent or to an author etc. for each copy of a book etc. sold or for each public performance of a work. **4 a** a royal right (now esp. over minerals) granted by the sovereign to an individual or corporation. **b** a payment made by a producer of minerals, oil, or natural gas to the owner of the site or of the mineral rights over it. [ME f. OF *roialté* (as ROYAL)]

Royce /rɔɪs/, Sir Frederick Henry (1863–1933), English engine designer who founded the company of Rolls-Royce Ltd. with C. S. Rolls in 1906, after having started his own successful electrical manufacturing business in 1884 and designing and building his own car and engine in 1903. He became famous as the designer of the Rolls-Royce Silver Ghost motor car (produced 1906–25). His first aircraft engine was the Eagle, used extensively in the First World War, and subsequent designs included the Merlin, used in Spitfires and Hurricanes of the Second World War. A genius as an engineer, he was noted for his extraordinary modesty and remarkable memory. The symbol 'RR' on the front of Rolls-Royce motor cars was originally in maroon, but was changed to black because this often clashed with the colour scheme ordered by buyers. The decision to make the change had been taken shortly before Royce died but the fact that it was implemented after his death gave rise to the legend that the change was made in mourning.

rozzer /ˈrɒzə(r)/ n. Brit. sl. a policeman. [19th c.: orig. unkn.]

RP abbr. received pronunciation.

RPI abbr. retail price index.

r.p.m. abbr. **1** revolutions per minute. **2** resale price maintenance.

RPO abbr. Royal Philharmonic Orchestra.

RR abbr. US **1** railroad. **2** rural route.

RS abbr. **1** (in the UK) Royal Society. **2** US Received Standard. **3** (in the UK) Royal Scots.

Rs. abbr. rupee(s).

RSA abbr. **1** (in the UK) Royal Society of Arts. **2** Royal Scottish Academy; Royal Scottish Academician.

RSC abbr. **1** (in the UK) Royal Shakespeare Company. **2** (in the UK) Royal Society of Chemistry.

RSFSR abbr. Russian Soviet Federative Socialist Republic.

RSJ abbr. rolled steel joist.

RSM abbr. Regimental Sergeant-Major.

RSPB abbr. (in the UK) Royal Society for the Protection of Birds.

RSPCA abbr. (in the UK) Royal Society for the Prevention of Cruelty to Animals.

RSV abbr. Revised Standard Version (of the Bible).

æ cat ɑː arm e bed ɜː her ɪ sit iː see ɒ hot ɔː saw ʌ run ʊ put uː too ə ago aɪ my

RSVP *abbr.* (in an invitation etc.) please answer. [F *répondez s'il vous plaît*]

RT *abbr.* **1** radio telegraphy. **2** radio telephony.

rt. *abbr.* right.

Rt. Hon. *abbr. Brit.* Right Honourable.

Rt. Revd. *abbr.* (also **Rt. Rev.**) Right Reverend.

RU *abbr.* Rugby Union.

Ru *symb. Chem.* the element ruthenium.

rub¹ /rʌb/ v. & n. —v. (**rubbed, rubbing**) **1** *tr.* move one's hand or another object with firm pressure over the surface of. **2** *tr.* (usu. foll. by *against, in, on, over*) apply (one's hand etc.) in this way. **3** *tr.* clean or polish or make dry or bare by rubbing. **4** *tr.* (often foll. by *over*) apply (polish, ointment, etc.) by rubbing. **5** *tr.* (foll. by *in, into, through*) use rubbing to make (a substance) go into or through something. **6** *tr.* (often foll. by *together*) move or slide (objects) against each other. **7** *intr.* (foll. by *against, on*) move with contact or friction. **8** *tr.* chafe or make sore by rubbing. **9** *intr.* (of cloth, skin, etc.) become frayed or worn or sore or bare with friction. **10** *tr.* reproduce the design of (a sepulchral brass or a stone) by rubbing paper laid on it with heelball or coloured chalk etc. **11** *tr.* (foll. by *to*) reduce to powder etc. by rubbing. **12** *intr. Bowls* (of a bowl) be slowed or diverted by the unevenness of the ground. —n. **1** a spell or an instance of rubbing (*give it a rub*). **2 a** an impediment or difficulty (*there's the rub*). **b** *Bowls* an inequality of the ground impeding or diverting a bowl; the diversion or hindering of a bowl by this. □ **rub along** *colloq.* cope or manage without undue difficulty. **rub down** dry or smooth or clean by rubbing. **rub-down** *n.* an instance of rubbing down. **rub elbows with** *US* = **rub shoulders with**. **rub one's hands** rub one's hands together usu. in sign of keen satisfaction, or for warmth. **rub it in** (or **rub a person's nose in it**) emphasize or repeat an embarrassing fact etc. **rub noses** rub one's nose against another's in greeting. **rub off 1** (usu. foll. by *on*) be transferred by contact, be transmitted (*some of his attitudes have rubbed off on me*). **2** remove by rubbing. **rub of** (or **on**) **the green** *Golf* an accidental interference with the course or position of a ball. **rub on** *colloq.* = **rub along**. **rub out 1** erase with a rubber. **2** esp. *US sl.* kill, eliminate. **rub shoulders with** associate or come into contact with (another person). **rub up 1** polish (a tarnished object). **2** brush up (a subject or one's memory). **3** mix (pigment etc.) into paste by rubbing. **rub-up** *n.* the act or an instance of rubbing up. **rub up the wrong way** irritate or repel as by stroking a cat against the lie of its fur. [ME *rubben*, perh. f. LG *rubben*, of unkn. orig.]

rub² /rʌb/ *n.* = RUBBER². [abbr.]

rubato /ru:ˈbɑːtəʊ/ *adj. & n. Mus.* —n. (pl. **-os** or **rubati** /-tɪ/) the temporary disregarding of strict tempo. —adj. performed with a flexible tempo. [It., = robbed]

rubber¹ /ˈrʌbə(r)/ *n.* **1** a tough elastic polymeric substance made from the latex of plants or synthetically. **2** esp. *Brit.* a piece of this or another substance for erasing pencil or ink marks. **3** *colloq.* a condom. **4** (in *pl.*) *US* galoshes. **5** a person who rubs; a masseur or masseuse. **6 a** an implement used for rubbing. **b** part of a machine operating by rubbing. □ **rubber band** a loop of rubber for holding papers etc. together. **rubber plant 1** an evergreen plant, *Ficus elastica*, with dark-green shiny leaves, often cultivated as a house-plant. **2** (also **rubber tree**) any of various tropical trees yielding latex, esp. *Hevea brasiliensis*. **rubber solution** a liquid drying to a rubber-like material, used esp. as an adhesive in mending rubber articles. **rubber stamp 1** a device for inking and imprinting on a surface. **2 a** a person who mechanically copies or agrees to others' actions. **b** an indication of such agreement. **rubber-stamp** *v.tr.* approve automatically without proper consideration. □□ **rubbery** *adj.* **rubberiness** *n.* [RUB¹ + -ER¹, from its early use to rub out pencil marks]

rubber² /ˈrʌbə(r)/ *n.* **1** a match of three or five successive games between the same sides or persons at whist, bridge, cricket, lawn tennis, etc. **2** (prec. by *the*) **a** the act of winning two games in a rubber. **b** a third game when each side has won one. [orig. unkn.: used as a term in bowls from *c.*1600]

rubberize /ˈrʌbəˌraɪz/ *v.tr.* (also **-ise**) treat or coat with rubber.

rubberneck /ˈrʌbəˌnek/ *n. & v. colloq.* —n. a person who stares inquisitively or stupidly. —v.intr. act in this way.

rubbing /ˈrʌbɪŋ/ *n.* **1** in senses of RUB¹ *v.* **2** an impression or copy made by rubbing (see RUB¹ *v.* 10).

rubbish /ˈrʌbɪʃ/ *n. & v.* —n. esp. *Brit.* **1** waste material; debris, refuse, litter. **2** worthless material or articles; trash. **3** (often as *int.*) absurd ideas or suggestions; nonsense. —v.tr. *colloq.* **1** criticize severely. **2** reject as worthless. □□ **rubbishy** *adj.* [ME f. AF *rubbous* etc., perh. f. RUBBLE]

rubble /ˈrʌb(ə)l/ *n.* **1** waste or rough fragments of stone or brick etc. **2** pieces of undressed stone used, esp. as filling-in, for walls. **3** *Geol.* loose angular stones etc. as the covering of some rocks. **4** water-worn stones. □□ **rubbly** *adj.* [ME *robyl, rubel*, of uncert. orig.: cf. OF *robe* spoils]

Rubbra /ˈrʌbrə/, Edmund (1901–86), English composer and pianist. Recognition came with the performance of his first symphony (1935–7). His prolific output includes ten symphonies, a piano concerto, a viola concerto, choral works, songs, and chamber music; among these is a large amount of religious music. His symphonies have a musical substance and spiritual grandeur which have still not been fully appreciated.

rube /ruːb/ *n. US colloq.* a country bumpkin. [abbr. of the name *Reuben*]

rubefy /ˈruːbɪˌfaɪ/ *v.tr.* (also **rubify**) (**-ies, -ied**) **1** make red. **2** *Med.* (of a counterirritant) stimulate (the skin etc.) to redness. □□ **rubefacient** /-ˈfeɪʃ(ə)nt/ *adj. & n.* **rubefaction** /ˌruːbɪˈfækʃ(ə)n/ *n.* [ME f. OF *rubifier, rubefier* f. med.L *rubificare* f. L *rubefacere* f. *rubeus* red]

rubella /ruːˈbelə/ *n. Med.* an acute infectious virus disease with a red rash; German measles. [mod.L, neut. pl. of L *rubellus* reddish]

rubellite /ˈruːbəˌlaɪt/ *n.* a red variety of tourmaline. [L *rubellus* reddish]

Rubens /ˈruːbɪnz/, Sir Peter Paul (1577–1640), Flemish painter, the supreme master of northern baroque. He trained in Antwerp, but in Italy (1600–8) and Spain studied profoundly the work of Italian old masters, especially Titian. Based in Antwerp from 1609, his output from a superbly organized workshop was prodigious—in fresh departures in portraiture, in landscape, in religious subjects no less than historical or mythological scenes. His appetite for the female nude was robustly large, and he defined an enduringly valid type of feminine beauty (of his wives Isabella Brant, and secondly Hélène Fourment). In person sophisticated, handsome, of a learned but deftly worldly intelligence, he served also as a diplomat in Spain and in England: a prince amongst painters. The ease and vitality, the copious but sinuous rush of his strokes, are inexhaustibly influential, while his work is to be found amongst almost all the major galleries of the world.

rubeola /ruːˈbiːələ/ *n. Med.* measles. [med.L f. L *rubeus* red]

Rubicon /ˈruːbɪˌkɒn/ a stream in NE Italy marking the ancient boundary between Italy and Cisalpine Gaul. By taking his army across it (i.e. outside his own province) in 49 BC Julius Caesar committed himself to war against the Senate and Pompey. —n. **1** a boundary which once crossed betokens irrevocable commitment; a point of no return. **2** (**rubicon**) the act of winning a game in piquet before an opponent has scored 100.

rubicund /ˈruːbɪˌkʌnd/ *adj.* (of a face, complexion, or person in these respects) ruddy, high-coloured. □□ **rubicundity** /-ˈkʌndɪtɪ/ *n.* [F *rubicond* or L *rubicundus* f. *rubēre* be red]

rubidium /ruːˈbɪdɪəm/ *n. Chem.* a soft silvery element occurring naturally in various minerals and as the radioactive isotope rubidium-87. First discovered spectroscopically by R. W. Bunsen and G. R. Kirchhoff in 1861, it has few commercial uses. ¶ Symb.: **Rb**; atomic number 37. [L *rubidus* red (with ref. to its spectral lines)]

rubify var. of RUBEFY.

rubiginous /ruːˈbɪdʒɪnəs/ *adj. formal* rust-coloured. [L *rubiginis* rust]

Rubik's cube /ˈruːbɪks/ *n.* a puzzle in which the aim is to restore the faces of a composite cube to single colours by rotating layers of constituent smaller cubes. [E. *Rubik*, its Hungarian inventor]

aʊ *how* eɪ *day* əʊ *no* eə *hair* ɪə *near* ɔɪ *boy* ʊə *poor* aɪə *fire* aʊə *sour* (see over for consonants)

Rubinstein /'ru:bɪn,staɪn/, Anton Grigorievich (1829–94), Russian composer and pianist, who founded the St Petersburg Conservatory in 1862 and was its director 1862–7 and 1887–91. Tchaikovsky was among his pupils. Rubinstein composed symphonies, operas, songs, and piano music, including the popular *Melody in F* (1852). His brother Nikolai (1835–81), pianist and composer, was likewise a key figure in Moscow's musical life and a close friend of Tchaikovsky.

ruble var. of ROUBLE.

rubric /'ru:brɪk/ n. 1 a direction for the conduct of divine service inserted in a liturgical book. 2 a heading or passage in red or special lettering. 3 explanatory words. 4 an established custom. □□ **rubrical** adj. [ME f. OF *rubrique*, *rubrice* or L *rubrica (terra)* red (earth or ochre) as writing-material, rel. to *rubeus* red]

rubricate /'ru:brɪ,keɪt/ v.tr. 1 mark with red; print or write in red. 2 provide with rubrics. □□ **rubrication** /-'keɪʃ(ə)n/ n. **rubricator** n. [L *rubricare* f. *rubrica*: see RUBRIC]

ruby /'ru:bɪ/ n., adj., & v. —n. (pl. -ies) 1 a rare precious stone consisting of corundum with a colour varying from deep crimson or purple to pale rose. 2 a glowing purple-tinged red colour. —adj. of this colour. —v.tr. (-ies, -ied) dye or tinge ruby-colour. □ **ruby glass** glass coloured with oxides of copper, iron, lead, tin, etc. **ruby-tail** a wasp, *Chrysis ignita*, with a ruby-coloured hinder part. **ruby wedding** the fortieth anniversary of a wedding. [ME f. OF *rubi* f. med.L *rubinus (lapis)* red (stone), rel. to L *rubeus* red]

RUC abbr. Royal Ulster Constabulary.

ruche /ru:ʃ/ n. a frill or gathering of lace etc. as a trimming. □□ **ruched** adj. **ruching** n. [F f. med.L *rusca* tree-bark, of Celt. orig.]

ruck¹ /rʌk/ n. 1 (prec. by *the*) the main body of competitors not likely to overtake the leaders. 2 an undistinguished crowd of persons or things. 3 *Rugby Football* a loose scrum with the ball on the ground. 4 *Austral. Rules* a group of three mobile players. [ME, = stack of fuel, heap, rick: app. Scand., = Norw. *ruka* in the same senses]

ruck² /rʌk/ v. & n. —v.tr. & intr. (often foll. by *up*) make or become creased or wrinkled. —n. a crease or wrinkle. [ON *hrukka*]

ruckle /'rʌk(ə)l/ v. & n. Brit. = RUCK².

rucksack /'rʌksæk, 'rʊk-/ n. a bag slung by straps from both shoulders and resting on the back. [G f. *rucken* dial. var. of *Rücken* back + *Sack* SACK¹]

ruckus /'rʌkəs/ n. esp. US a row or commotion. [cf. RUCTION, RUMPUS]

ruction /'rʌkʃ(ə)n/ n. colloq. 1 a disturbance or tumult. 2 (in pl.) unpleasant arguments or reactions. [19th c.: orig. unkn.]

rudaceous /ru:'deɪʃəs/ adj. (of rock) composed of fragments of relatively large size. [L *rudus* rubble]

rudbeckia /rʌd'bekɪə/ n. a composite garden plant of the genus *Rudbeckia*, native to N. America. [mod.L f. O. *Rudbeck*, Sw. botanist d. 1740]

rudd /rʌd/ n. (pl. same) a freshwater fish, *Scardinius erythrophthalmus*, resembling a roach and having red fins. [app. rel. to *rud* red colour f. OE *rudu*, rel. to RED]

rudder /'rʌdə(r)/ n. 1 a a flat piece hinged vertically to the stern of a ship for steering. b a vertical aerofoil pivoted from the tailplane of an aircraft, for controlling its horizontal movement. 2 a guiding principle etc. □□ **rudderless** adj. [OE *rōther* f. WG *rōthra-* f. the stem of ROW²]

ruddle /'rʌd(ə)l/ n. & v. —n. a red ochre, esp. of a kind used for marking sheep. —v.tr. mark or colour with or as with ruddle. [rel. to obs. *rud*: see RUDD]

ruddock /'rʌdək/ n. dial. the robin redbreast. [OE *rudduc* (as RUDDLE)]

ruddy /'rʌdɪ/ adj. & v. —adj. (ruddier, ruddiest) 1 a (of a person or complexion) freshly or healthily red. b (of health, youth, etc.) marked by this. 2 reddish. 3 Brit. colloq. bloody, damnable. —v.tr. & intr. (-ies, -ied) make or grow ruddy. □□ **ruddily** adv. **ruddiness** n. [OE *rudig* (as RUDD)]

rude /ru:d/ adj. 1 (of a person, remark, etc.) impolite or offensive. 2 roughly made or done; lacking subtlety or accuracy (a *rude* plough). 3 primitive or uneducated (*rude chaos*; *rude simplicity*). 4 abrupt, sudden, startling, violent (a *rude awakening*; a *rude reminder*). 5 colloq. indecent, lewd (a *rude joke*). 6 vigorous or hearty (*rude health*). □ **be rude to** speak impolitely to; insult. □□ **rudely** adv. **rudeness** n. **rudery** n. **rudish** adj. [ME f. OF f. L *rudis* unwrought]

ruderal /'ru:dər(ə)l/ adj. & n. —adj. (of a plant) growing on or in rubbish or rubble. —n. a ruderal plant. [mod.L *ruderalis* f. L *rudera* pl. of *rudus* rubble]

rudiment /'ru:dɪmənt/ n. 1 (in pl.) the elements or first principles of a subject. 2 (in pl.) an imperfect beginning of something undeveloped or yet to develop. 3 a part or organ imperfectly developed as being vestigial or having no function (e.g. the breast in males). [F *rudiment* or L *rudimentum* (as RUDE, after *elementum* ELEMENT)]

rudimentary /,ru:dɪ'mentərɪ/ adj. 1 involving basic principles; fundamental. 2 incompletely developed; vestigial. □□ **rudimentarily** /-'mentərɪlɪ/ adv. **rudimentariness** /-'mentərɪnɪs/ n.

Rudolf /'ru:dɒlf/, **Lake** the former name of Lake Turkana in NW Kenya.

Rudra /'rʊdrə/ 1 (in the Rig-Veda) a minor god, associated with the storm, father of the Maruts. A destructive force, his arrows brought disease and disaster. 2 *Hinduism* one of the names of Siva, who may have evolved from the earlier deity. [Skr., = howler (*rud* howl, roar)]

rue¹ /ru:/ v. & n. —v.tr. (**rues, rued, rueing** or **ruing**) repent of; bitterly feel the consequences of; wish to be undone or non-existent (esp. *rue the day*). —n. archaic 1 repentance; dejection at some occurrence. 2 compassion or pity. [OE *hrēow*, *hrēowan*]

rue² /ru:/ n. a perennial evergreen shrub, *Ruta graveolens*, with bitter strong-scented leaves formerly used in medicine. [ME f. OF f. L *ruta* f. Gk *rhutē*]

rueful /'ru:fʊl/ adj. expressing sorrow, genuine or humorously affected. □□ **ruefully** adv. **ruefulness** n. [ME, f. RUE¹]

rufescent /ru:'fes(ə)nt/ adj. Zool. etc. reddish. □□ **rufescence** n. [L *rufescere* f. *rufus* reddish]

ruff¹ /rʌf/ n. 1 a projecting starched frill worn round the neck esp. in the 16th c. 2 a projecting or conspicuously coloured ring of feathers or hair round a bird's or animal's neck. 3 a domestic pigeon like a jacobin. 4 (fem. **reeve** /ri:v/) a wading bird, *Philomachus pugnax*, of which the male has a ruff and ear-tufts in the breeding season. □□ **rufflike** adj. [perh. f. *ruff* = ROUGH]

ruff² /rʌf/ n. (also **ruffe**) any of various fish, esp. a perch-like freshwater fish, *Gymnocephalus cernua*, found in European lakes and rivers. [ME, prob. f. ROUGH]

ruff³ /rʌf/ v. & n. —v.intr. & tr. trump at cards. —n. an act of ruffing. [orig. the name of a card-game: f. OF *roffle*, *rouffle*, = It. *ronfa* (perh. alt. of *trionfo* TRUMP¹)]

ruffian /'rʌfɪən/ n. a violent lawless person. □□ **ruffianism** n. **ruffianly** adv. [F *ruff(i)an* f. It. *ruffiano*, perh. f. dial. *rofia* scurf]

ruffle /'rʌf(ə)l/ v. & n. —v. 1 tr. disturb the smoothness or tranquillity of. 2 tr. upset the calmness of (a person). 3 tr. gather (lace etc.) into a ruffle. 4 tr. (often foll. by *up*) (of a bird) erect (its feathers) in anger, display, etc. 5 intr. undergo ruffling. 6 intr. lose smoothness or calmness. —n. 1 an ornamental gathered or goffered frill of lace etc. worn at the opening of a garment esp. round the wrist, breast, or neck. 2 perturbation, bustle. 3 a rippling effect on water. 4 the ruff of a bird etc. (see RUFF¹ 2). 5 Mil. a vibrating drum-beat. [ME: orig. unkn.]

rufous /'ru:fəs/ adj. (esp. of animals) reddish-brown. [L *rufus* red, reddish]

rug /rʌg/ n. 1 a floor-mat of shaggy material or thick pile. 2 a thick woollen coverlet or wrap. □ **pull the rug from under** deprive of support; weaken, unsettle. [prob. f. Scand.: cf. Norw. dial. *rugga* coverlet, Sw. *rugg* ruffled hair: rel. to RAG¹]

Rugby /'rʌgbɪ/ n. (in full **Rugby football**) a form of football played with an oval ball which may be carried as well as kicked. It is named after Rugby School in Warwickshire where it was developed, though the exact date when the distinctive practice originated (in 1823 or later) of running while carrying the ball is in dispute. The oval ball owes its shape to the inflated pig's bladder which was used in ball games for many centuries before being given (by the 16th c.) a leather outer cover. □ **Rugby League** a partly professional form of the game with teams of 13. It dates from 1895 when a group of northern clubs, exasperated by repeated refusals of the ruling body to allow them to compensate players for money lost by taking time off from work to play football, decided to break away from the Rugby Union. **Rugby Union** an amateur form with teams of 15.

Rügen /ˈruːgən/ an island in the Baltic Sea to the north of the German port of Rostock, linked to the mainland by a causeway.

rugged /ˈrʌgɪd/ adj. **1** (of ground or terrain) having a rough uneven surface. **2** (of features) strongly marked; irregular in outline. **3 a** unpolished; lacking gentleness or refinement (*rugged grandeur*). **b** harsh in sound. **c** austere, unbending (*rugged honesty*). **d** involving hardship (*a rugged life*). **4** (esp. of a machine) robust, sturdy. □□ **ruggedly** adv. **ruggedness** n. [ME, prob. f. Scand.: cf. RUG, and Sw. *rugga*, roughen]

rugger /ˈrʌgə(r)/ n. Brit. colloq. Rugby football.

rugose /ˈruːgəʊs, -gəʊz/ adj. esp. Biol. wrinkled, corrugated. □□ **rugosely** adv. **rugosity** /-ˈgɒsɪtɪ/ n. [L *rugosus* f. *ruga* wrinkle]

Ruhr /rʊə(r)/ a tributary of the Rhine in the west of Germany, which has given its name to this region of coalmining and heavy industry.

ruin /ˈruːɪn/ n. & v. —n. **1** a destroyed or wrecked state. **2** a person's or thing's downfall or elimination (*the ruin of my hopes*). **3 a** the complete loss of one's property or position (*bring to ruin*). **b** a person who has suffered ruin. **4** (in *sing.* or *pl.*) the remains of a building etc. that has suffered ruin (*an old ruin; ancient ruins*). **5** a cause of ruin (*will be the ruin of us*). —v. **1** tr. **a** bring to ruin (*your extravagance has ruined me*). **b** utterly impair or wreck (*the rain ruined my hat*). **2** tr. (esp. as **ruined** adj.) reduce to ruins. **3** intr. poet. fall headlong or with a crash. □ **in ruins 1** in a state of ruin. **2** completely wrecked (*their hopes were in ruins*). [ME f. OF *ruine* f. L *ruina* f. *ruere* fall]

ruination /ˌruːɪˈneɪʃ(ə)n/ n. **1** the act of bringing to ruin. **2** the act of ruining or the state of being ruined. [obs. *ruinate* (as RUIN)]

ruinous /ˈruːɪnəs/ adj. **1** bringing ruin; disastrous (*at ruinous expense*). **2** in ruins; dilapidated. □□ **ruinously** adv. **ruinousness** n. [ME f. L *ruinosus* (as RUIN)]

Ruisdael /ˈrɔɪsdɑːl/, Jacob Isaacksz van (1628/9–82), the most important Dutch landscape painter of the 17th c. Born in Haarlem, he painted the surrounding landscape from the mid-1640s until his move to Amsterdam in 1657, where he spent the rest of his life. His subdued palette suited his typical subject-matter of low horizons, dominant cloudscapes, and wind-blown silvery atmosphere. His painting demonstrates the possibilities of investing landscape with an emotional quality that ranges from the subtlest intimations of mood to a sense of tragedy and transcendence (e.g. *Jewish Cemetery*, 1660s). Hobbema was his most famous pupil. His influence continued as far as the 18th and 19th c. affecting, among others, Gainsborough, Constable, and the Barbizon school.

Ruiz de Alascón y Mendoza /ruˈiːθ dɪ ælɑːsˈkɒn iː meɪnˈdəʊθə/, Juan (1580–1639), Spanish playwright, born in Mexico City. His most famous play, the moral comedy *La verdad sospechosa (The suspicious Truth*, published in 1630) was the basis of Corneille's *Le menteur (The Liar)*.

rule /ruːl/ n. & v. —n. **1** a principle to which an action conforms or is required to conform. **2** a prevailing custom or standard; the normal state of things. **3** government or dominion (*under British rule; the rule of law*). **4** a graduated straight measure used in carpentry etc.; a ruler. **5** *Printing* **a** a thin strip of metal for separating headings, columns, etc. **b** a thin line or dash. **6** a code of discipline of a religious order. **7** *Law* an order made by a judge or court with reference to a particular case only. **8** (**Rules**) *Austral.* = *Australian Rules*. —v. **1** tr. exercise decisive influence over; keep under control. **2** tr. & (foll. by *over*) intr. have sovereign control of (*rules over a vast kingdom*). **3** tr. (often foll. by *that* + clause) pronounce authoritatively (*was ruled out*

of order). **4** tr. **a** make parallel lines across (paper). **b** make (a straight line) with a ruler etc. **5** intr. (of prices or goods etc. in regard to price or quality etc.) have a specified general level; be for the most part (*the market ruled high*). **6** tr. (in *passive*; foll. by *by*) consent to follow (advice etc.); be guided by. □ **as a rule** usually; more often than not. **by rule** in a regulation manner; mechanically. **rule of the road** see ROAD¹. **rule of three** a method of finding a number in the same ratio to one given as exists between two others given. **rule of thumb** a rule for general guidance, based on experience or practice rather than theory. **rule out** exclude; pronounce irrelevant or ineligible. **rule the roost** (or **roast**) be in control. **run the rule over** examine cursorily for correctness or adequacy. □□ **ruleless** adj. [ME f. OF *reule, reuler* f. LL *regulare* f. L *regula* straight stick]

ruler /ˈruːlə(r)/ n. **1** a person exercising government or dominion. **2** a straight usu. graduated strip or cylinder of wood, metal, etc., used to draw lines or measure distance. □□ **rulership** n.

ruling /ˈruːlɪŋ/ n. & adj. —n. an authoritative decision or announcement. —adj. prevailing; currently in force (*ruling prices*). □ **ruling passion** a motive that habitually directs one's actions.

rum¹ /rʌm/ n. **1** a spirit distilled from sugar-cane residues or molasses. **2** *US* intoxicating liquor. □ **rum baba** see BABA. [17th c.: perh. abbr. of contemporary forms *rumbullion, rumbustion*, of unkn. orig.]

rum² /rʌm/ adj. Brit. colloq. **1** odd, strange, queer. **2** difficult, dangerous. □ **rum go** (or **start**) colloq. a surprising occurrence or unforeseen turn of affairs. □□ **rumly** adv. **rumness** n. [16th-c. cant, orig. = fine, spirited, perh. var. of ROM]

Rumania, RUMANIAN see ROMANIA, ROMANIAN.

Rumansh var. of ROMANSH.

rumba /ˈrʌmbə/ n. & v. (also **rhumba**) —n. **1** a ballroom dance of Cuban origin, danced on the spot with a pronounced movement of the hips. **2** the music for it. —v.tr. (**rumbas**, **rumbaed** /-bəd/ or **rumba'd**, **rumbaing** /-bəɪŋ/) dance the rumba. [Amer. Sp.]

rumble /ˈrʌmb(ə)l/ v. & n. —v. **1** intr. make a continuous deep resonant sound as of distant thunder. **2** intr. (foll. by *along, by, past*, etc.) (of a person or vehicle) move with a rumbling noise. **3** tr. (often foll. by *out*) utter or say with a rumbling sound. **4** tr. Brit. sl. find out about (esp. something illicit). —n. **1** a rumbling sound. **2** *US sl.* a street-fight between gangs. □ **rumble seat** *US* an uncovered folding seat in the rear of a motor car. □□ **rumbler** n. [ME *romble*, prob. f. MDu. *rommelen, rummelen* (imit.)]

rumbustious /rʌmˈbʌstʃəs/ adj. colloq. boisterous, noisy, uproarious. □□ **rumbustiously** adv. **rumbustiousness** n. [prob. var. of *robustious* boisterous, ROBUST]

Rumelia see ROUMELIA.

rumen /ˈruːmen/ n. (*pl.* **rumens** or **rumina** /-mɪnə/) the first stomach of a ruminant, in which food, esp. cellulose, is partly digested by bacteria. [L *rumen ruminis* throat]

Rumi /ˈruːmiː/, Jalal al-Din (1207–73), Persian Islamic poet and mystic, also called Mevlana or Maulana, founder of the whirling dervishes (see DERVISH). He was born in Balkh (in modern Afghanistan), but lived for most of his life at Konya in Turkey, where he is buried.

ruminant /ˈruːmɪnənt/ n. & adj. —n. an animal that chews the cud regurgitated from its rumen. —adj. **1** of or belonging to ruminants. **2** contemplative; given to or engaged in meditation. [L *ruminari ruminant-* (as RUMEN)]

ruminate /ˈruːmɪˌneɪt/ v. **1** tr. & (foll. by *over, on*, etc.) intr. meditate, ponder. **2** intr. (of ruminants) chew the cud. □□ **rumination** /-ˈneɪʃ(ə)n/ n. **ruminative** /-nətɪv/ adj. **ruminatively** /-nətɪvlɪ/ adv. **ruminator** n.

rummage /ˈrʌmɪdʒ/ v. & n. —v. **1** tr. & (foll. by *in, through, among*) intr. search, esp. untidily and unsystematically. **2** tr. (foll. by *out, up*) find among other things. **3** tr. (foll. by *about*) disarrange; make untidy in searching. —n. **1** an instance of rummaging. **2** things found by rummaging; a miscellaneous accumulation. □ **rummage sale** esp. *US* a jumble sale. □□ **rummager** n. [earlier as noun in obs. sense 'arranging of casks etc. in a hold': OF *arrumage* f. *arrumer* stow (as AD-, *run* ship's hold f. MDu. *ruim* ROOM)]

rummer /ˈrʌmə(r)/ *n.* a large drinking-glass. [rel. to Du. *roemer*, LG *römer* f. *roemen* praise, boast]

rummy[1] /ˈrʌmɪ/ *n.* a card-game played usu. with two packs, in which the players try to form sets and sequences of cards. [20th c.: orig. unkn.]

rummy[2] /ˈrʌmɪ/ *adj. Brit. colloq.* = RUM[2].

rumour /ˈruːmə(r)/ *n. & v.* (US **rumor**) —*n.* **1** general talk or hearsay of doubtful accuracy. **2** (often foll. by *of*, or *that* + clause) a current but unverified statement or assertion (*heard a rumour that you are leaving*). —*v.tr.* (usu. in *passive*) report by way of rumour (*it is rumoured that you are leaving; you are rumoured to be leaving*). [ME f. OF *rumur*, *rumor* f. L *rumor -oris* noise]

rump /rʌmp/ *n.* **1** the hind part of a mammal, esp. the buttocks. **2 a** a small or contemptible remnant of a parliament or similar body. **b** (**the Rump**) *hist.* the Rump Parliament. □ **Rump Parliament** that part of the Long Parliament which continued to sit after Pride's Purge in 1648. Dissolved by Cromwell in 1653, the Rump was briefly reconvened in 1659 but voted its own dissolution early in 1660. **rump steak** a cut of beef from the rump. □□ **rumpless** *adj.* [ME, prob. f. Scand.]

rumple /ˈrʌmp(ə)l/ *v.tr. & intr.* make or become creased or ruffled. □□ **rumply** *adj.* [obs. *rumple* (n.) f. MDu. *rompel* f. *rompe* wrinkle]

rumpus /ˈrʌmpəs/ *n. colloq.* a disturbance, brawl, row, or uproar. □ **rumpus room** US a room in the basement of a house for games and play. [18th c.: prob. fanciful]

run /rʌn/ *v. & n.* —*v.* (**running**; *past* **ran** /ræn/; *past part.* **run**) **1** *intr.* go with quick steps on alternate feet, never having both or all feet on the ground at the same time. **2** *intr.* flee, abscond. **3** *intr.* go or travel hurriedly, briefly, etc. **4** *intr.* **a** advance by or as by rolling or on wheels, or smoothly or easily. **b** be in action or operation (*left the engine running*). **5** *intr.* be current or operative; have duration (*the lease runs for 99 years*). **6** *intr.* (of a bus, train, etc.) travel or be travelling on its route (*the train is running late*). **7** *intr.* (of a play, exhibition, etc.) be staged or presented (*is now running at the Apollo*). **8** *intr.* extend; have a course or order or tendency (*the road runs by the coast; prices are running high*). **9 a** *intr.* compete in a race. **b** *intr.* finish a race in a specified position. **c** *tr.* compete in (a race). **10** *intr.* (often foll. by *for*) seek election (*ran for president*). **11 a** *intr.* (of a liquid etc. or its container) flow or be wet; drip. **b** *tr.* flow with. **12** *tr.* **a** cause (water etc.) to flow. **b** fill (a bath) with water. **13** *intr.* spread rapidly or beyond the proper place (*ink ran over the table; a shiver ran down my spine*). **14** *intr. Cricket* (of a batsman) run from one wicket to the other in scoring a run. **15** *tr.* traverse or make one's way through or over (a course, race, or distance). **16** *tr.* perform (an errand). **17** *tr.* publish (an article etc.) in a newspaper or magazine. **18 a** *tr.* cause (a machine or vehicle etc.) to operate. **b** *intr.* (of a mechanism or component etc.) move or work freely. **19** *tr.* direct or manage (a business etc.). **20** *tr.* own and use (a vehicle) regularly. **21** *tr.* take (a person) for a journey in a vehicle (*shall I run you to the shops?*). **22** *tr.* cause to run or go in a specified way (*ran the car into a tree*). **23** *tr.* enter (a horse etc.) for a race. **24** *tr.* smuggle (guns etc.). **25** *tr.* chase or hunt. **26** *tr.* allow (an account) to accumulate for a time before paying. **27** *intr. Naut.* (of a ship etc.) go straight and fast. **28** *intr.* (of salmon) go up river from the sea. **29** *intr.* (of a colour in a fabric) spread from the dyed parts. **30 a** *intr.* (of a thought, the eye, the memory, etc.) pass in a transitory or cursory way (*ideas ran through my mind*). **b** *tr.* cause (one's eye) to look cursorily (*ran my eye down the page*). **31** *intr.* (of hosiery) ladder. **32** *intr.* (of a candle) gutter. **33** *intr.* (of an orifice, esp. the eyes or nose) exude liquid matter. **34** *tr.* sew (fabric) loosely or hastily with running stitches. **35** *tr.* turn (cattle etc.) out to graze. —*n.* **1** an act or spell of running. **2** a short trip or excursion, esp. for pleasure. **3** a distance travelled. **4** a general tendency of development or movement. **5** a rapid motion. **6** a regular route. **7** a continuous or long stretch or spell or course (*a metre's run of wiring; had a run of bad luck*). **8** (often foll. by *on*) **a** a high general demand (for a commodity, currency, etc.) (*a run on the dollar*). **b** a sudden demand for repayment by a large number of customers of (a bank). **9** a quantity produced in one period of production (*a print run*). **10** a general or average type or class (*not typical of the general run*). **11 a** *Cricket* a point scored by the batsmen each running to the other's wicket, or an equivalent point awarded for some other reason. **b** *Baseball* a point scored usu. by the batter returning to the plate after touching the other bases. **12** (foll. by *of*) free use of or access to (*had the run of the house*). **13 a** an animal's regular track. **b** an enclosure for fowls. **c** a range of pasture. **14** a ladder in hosiery. **15** *Mus.* a rapid scale passage. **16** a class or line of goods. **17** a batch or drove of animals born or reared together. **18** a shoal of fish in motion. **19** a trough for water to run in. **20** US a small stream or brook. **21 a** a single journey, esp. by an aircraft. **b** (of an aircraft) a flight on a straight and even course at a constant speed before or while dropping bombs. **c** an offensive military operation. □ **at a** (or **the**) **run** running. **on the run 1** escaping, running away. **2** hurrying about from place to place. **run about 1** bustle; hurry from one person or place to another. **2** (esp. of children) play or wander without restraint. **run across 1** happen to meet. **2** (foll. by *to*) make a brief journey or a flying visit (to a place). **run after 1** pursue with attentions; seek the society of. **2** give much time to (a pursuit etc.). **3** pursue at a run. **run against** happen to meet. **run along** *colloq.* depart. **run around 1** *Brit.* take from place to place by car etc. **2** deceive or evade repeatedly. **3** (often foll. by *with*) *sl.* engage in sexual relations (esp. casually or illicitly). **run-around** *n.* (esp. in phr. **give a person the run-around**) deceit or evasion. **run at** attack by charging or rushing. **run away 1** get away by running; flee, abscond. **2** elope. **3** (of a horse) bolt. **run away with 1** carry off (a person, stolen property, etc.). **2** win (a prize) easily. **3** accept (a notion) hastily. **4** (of expense etc.) consume (money etc.). **5** (of a horse) bolt with (a rider, a carriage or its occupants). **run a blockade** see BLOCKADE. **run down 1** knock down or collide with. **2** reduce the strength or numbers of (resources). **3** (of an unwound clock etc.) stop. **4** (of a person or a person's health) become feeble from overwork or underfeeding. **5** discover after a search. **6** disparage. **run-down** *n.* **1** a reduction in numbers. **2** a detailed analysis. —*adj.* **1** decayed after prosperity. **2** enfeebled through overwork etc. **run dry** cease to flow, be exhausted. **run for it** seek safety by fleeing. **a run** (or **a good run**) **for one's money 1** vigorous competition. **2** pleasure derived from an activity. **run foul of** collide or become entangled with (another vessel etc.). **run the gauntlet** see GAUNTLET[2]. **run a person hard** (or **close**) press a person severely in a race or competition, or in comparative merit. **run high 1** (of the sea) have a strong current with a high tide. **2** (of feelings) be strong. **run in 1** run (a new engine or vehicle) carefully in the early stages. **2** *colloq.* arrest. **3** (of a combatant) rush to close quarters. **4** incur (a debt). **run-in** *n.* **1** the approach to an action or event. **2** a quarrel. **run in the family** (of a trait) be common in the members of a family. **run into 1** collide with. **2** encounter. **3** reach as many as (a specified figure). **4** fall into (a practice, absurdity, etc.). **5** be continuous or coalesce with. **run into the ground** *colloq.* bring (a person) to exhaustion etc. **run it fine** see FINE[1]. **run its course** follow its natural progress; be left to itself. **run low** (or **short**) become depleted, have too little (*our tea ran short; we ran short of tea*). **run off 1** flee. **2** produce (copies etc.) on a machine. **3** decide (a race or other contest) after a series of heats or in the event of a tie. **4** flow or cause to flow away. **5** write or recite fluently. **6** digress suddenly. **run-off** *n.* **1** an additional competition, election, race, etc., after a tie. **2** an amount of rainfall that is carried off an area by streams and rivers. **3** *NZ* a separate area of land where young animals etc. are kept. **run off one's feet** very busy. **run-of-the-mill** ordinary, undistinguished. **run on 1** (of written characters) be joined together. **2** continue in operation. **3** elapse. **4** speak volubly. **5** talk incessantly. **6** *Printing* continue on the same line as the preceding matter. **run out 1** come to an end; become used up. **2** (foll. by *of*) exhaust one's stock of. **3** put down the wicket of (a batsman who is running). **4** escape from a containing vessel. **5** (of rope) pass out; be paid out. **6** jut out. **7** come out of a contest in a specified position etc. or complete a required score etc. (*they ran out worthy winners*). **8** complete (a race). **9** advance (a gun etc.) so as to project. **10** exhaust oneself by running. **run-out** *n.* the dismissal of a batsman by being run out. **run out on** *colloq.*

desert (a person). **run over 1** overflow. **2** study or repeat quickly. **3** (of a vehicle or its driver) pass over, knock down or crush. **4** touch (the notes of a piano etc.) in quick succession. **5** (often foll. by *to*) go quickly by a brief journey or for a flying visit. **run ragged** exhaust (a person). **run rings round** see RING[1]. **run riot** see RIOT. **run a** (or **the**) **risk** see RISK. **run the show** *colloq.* dominate in an undertaking etc. **run a temperature** be feverish. **run through 1** examine or rehearse briefly. **2** peruse. **3** deal successively with. **4** consume (an estate etc.) by reckless or quick spending. **5** traverse. **6** pervade. **7** pierce with a sword etc. **8** draw a line through (written words). **run-through** *n.* **1** a rehearsal. **2** a brief survey. **run to 1** have the money or ability for. **2** reach (an amount or number). **3** (of a person) show a tendency to (*runs to fat*). **4 a** be enough for (some expense or undertaking). **b** have the resources or capacity for. **5** fall into (ruin). **run to earth 1** *Hunting* chase to its lair. **2** discover after a long search. **run to meet** anticipate (one's troubles etc.). **run to seed** see SEED. **run up 1** accumulate (a debt etc.) quickly. **2** build or make hurriedly. **3** raise (a flag). **4** grow quickly. **5** rise in price. **6** (foll. by *to*) amount to. **7** force (a rival bidder) to bid higher. **8** add up (a column of figures). **9** (foll. by *to*) go quickly by a brief journey or for a flying visit. **run-up** *n.* **1** (often foll. by *to*) the period preceding an important event. **2** *Golf* a low approach shot. **run up against** meet with (a difficulty or difficulties). **run upon** (of a person's thoughts etc.) be engrossed by; dwell upon. **run wild** grow or stray unchecked or undisciplined or untrained. □□ **runnable** *adj.* [OE *rinnan*]

runabout /ˈrʌnəˌbaʊt/ *n.* a light car or aircraft.

runaway /ˈrʌnəˌweɪ/ *n.* **1** a fugitive. **2** an animal or vehicle that is running out of control. **3** (*attrib.*) **a** that is running away or out of control (*runaway inflation; had a runaway success*). **b** done or performed after running away (*a runaway wedding*).

runcible spoon /ˈrʌnsɪb(ə)l/ *n.* a fork curved like a spoon, with three broad prongs, one edged. [nonsense word used by E. Lear, Engl. humorist d. 1888, perh. after *rouncival* large pea]

runcinate /ˈrʌnsɪnət/ *adj. Bot.* (of a leaf) saw-toothed, with lobes pointing towards the base. [mod.L *runcinatus* f. L *runcina* PLANE[2] (formerly taken to mean saw)]

rune /ruːn/ *n.* **1** any of the letters of the earliest Germanic alphabet used by Scandinavians and Anglo-Saxons from about the 3rd c. and formed by modifying Roman or Greek characters to suit carving. **2** any letter of a similar alphabet used by 8th-c. Mongolian Turks. **3** a similar mark of mysterious or magic significance. **4** a Finnish poem or a division of it. □ **rune-staff 1** a magic wand inscribed with runes. **2** a runic calendar. □□ **runic** *adj.* [ON *rún* (only in pl. *rúnar*) magic sign, rel. to OE *rūn*]

rung[1] /rʌŋ/ *n.* **1** each of the horizontal supports of a ladder. **2** a strengthening crosspiece in the structure of a chair etc. □□ **runged** *adj.* **rungless** *adj.* [OE *hrung*]

rung[2] *past part.* of RING[2].

runlet /ˈrʌnlɪt/ *n.* a small stream.

runnel /ˈrʌn(ə)l/ *n.* **1** a brook or rill. **2** a gutter. [later form (assim. to RUN) of *rinel* f. OE *rynel* (as RUN)]

runner /ˈrʌnə(r)/ *n.* **1** a person who runs, esp. in a race. **2 a** a creeping plant-stem that can take root. **b** a twining plant. **3** a rod or groove or blade on which a thing slides. **4** a sliding ring on a rod etc. **5** a messenger, scout, collector, or agent for a bank etc.; a tout. **6** *hist.* a police officer. **7** a running bird. **8 a** a smuggler. **b** = *blockade-runner*. **9** a revolving millstone. **10** *Naut.* a rope in a single block with one end round a tackle-block and the other having a hook. **11** (in full **runner bean**) *Brit.* a twining bean plant, *Phaseolus multiflorus*, with red flowers and long green seed pods. Also called *scarlet runner*. **12** each of the long pieces on the underside of a sledge etc. that forms the contact in sliding. **13** a roller for moving a heavy article. **14** a long narrow ornamental cloth or rug. □ **do a runner** *sl.* leave hastily; flee. **runner-up** (*pl.* **runners-up** or **runner-ups**) the competitor or team taking second place.

running /ˈrʌnɪŋ/ *n. & adj.* —*n.* **1** the action of runners in a race etc. **2** the way a race etc. proceeds. —*adj.* **1** continuing on an essentially continuous basis though changing in detail (*a running battle*). **2** consecutive; one after another (*three days running*).

3 done with a run (*a running jump*). □ **in** (or **out of**) **the running** (of a competitor) with a good (or poor) chance of winning. **make** (or **take up**) **the running** take the lead; set the pace. **running account** a current account. **running-board** a footboard on either side of a vehicle. **running commentary** an oral description of events as they occur. **running fire** successive shots from a line of troops etc. **running gear** the moving or running parts of a machine, esp. the wheels and suspension of a vehicle. **running hand** writing in which the pen etc. is not lifted after each letter. **running head** (or **headline**) a heading printed at the top of a number of consecutive pages of a book etc. **running knot** a knot that slips along the rope etc. and changes the size of a noose. **running light 1** = *navigation light*. **2** each of a small set of lights on a motor vehicle that remain illuminated while the vehicle is running. **running mate** *US* **1** a candidate for a secondary position in an election. **2** a horse entered in a race in order to set the pace for another horse from the same stable which is intended to win. **running repairs** minor or temporary repairs etc. to machinery while in use. **running rope** a rope that is freely movable through a pulley etc. **running sore** a suppurating sore. **running stitch 1** a line of small non-overlapping stitches for gathering etc. **2** one of these stitches. **running water** water flowing in a stream or from a tap etc. **take a running jump** (esp. as *int.*) *sl.* go away.

runny /ˈrʌnɪ/ *adj.* (**runnier, runniest**) **1** tending to run or flow. **2** excessively fluid.

Runnymede /ˈrʌnɪˌmiːd/ a meadow at Egham on the south bank of the Thames near Windsor, famous for its association with Magna Carta which was signed by King John in the meadow or on the island near by.

runt /rʌnt/ *n.* **1** a small pig, esp. the smallest in a litter. **2** a weakling; an undersized person. **3** a large domestic pigeon. **4** a small ox or cow, esp. of various Scottish Highland or Welsh breeds. □□ **runty** *adj.* [16th c.: orig. unkn.]

runway /ˈrʌnweɪ/ *n.* **1** a specially prepared surface along which aircraft take off and land. **2** a trail to an animals' watering-place. **3** an incline down which logs are slid. **4** a raised gangway in a theatre, fashion display, etc.

Runyon /ˈrʌnjən/, (Alfred) Damon (1884–1946), American journalist and sports writer, famous also for his short stories about New York City's Broadway and underworld characters, written in a highly individual style with much use of colourful slang idiom. His stories were the inspiration for the musical comedy *Guys and Dolls* (1950).

rupee /ruːˈpiː/ *n.* the chief monetary unit of India, Pakistan, Sri Lanka, Nepal, Mauritius, and the Seychelles. [Hind. *rūpiyah* f. Skr. *rūpya* wrought silver]

Rupert /ˈruːpət/, Prince (1619–82), a Royalist general of the English Civil War, son of the Elector Palatine and nephew of Charles I. Rupert was one of the most innovative and accomplished soldiers of his day, with a particular reputation as a dashing leader of cavalry. After being victorious in a series of engagements in the early years of the war, he was defeated by superior Parliamentarian forces at Marston Moor (1644) and Naseby (1645) and finally dismissed by the King for surrendering Bristol. Banished by Parliament, he led a series of expeditions against English shipping from the Low Countries before returning to Britain with Charles II to become one of the admirals in the Restoration Navy. Rupert was an active dilettante of science and the arts; an amateur etcher, he introduced mezzotint engraving to England. □ **Prince Rupert's drops** pear-shaped drops of glass with a long tail, made by dropping melted glass into water, and remarkable for the property, due to internal strain, of disintegrating explosively into powder when the tail is broken off or the surface scratched. **Prince Rupert's metal** a gold-coloured alloy of about three parts copper and one part zinc.

Rupert's Land (also **Prince Rupert's Land**) an area of northern and western Canada, granted in 1670 by Charles II to Hudson's Bay Company and purchased from it by the Dominion of Canada in 1869. It is named after Prince Rupert, the first governor of the Company.

aʊ *how* eɪ *day* əʊ *no* eə *hair* ɪə *near* ɔɪ *boy* ʊə *poor* aɪə *fire* aʊə *sour* (*see over for consonants*)

rupiah /ruːˈpiːə/ n. the chief monetary unit of Indonesia. [as RUPEE]

rupture /ˈrʌptʃə(r)/ n. & v. —n. **1** the act or an instance of breaking; a breach. **2** a breach of harmonious relations; a disagreement and parting. **3** *Med.* an abdominal hernia. —v. **1** *tr.* break or burst (a cell or membrane etc.). **2** *tr.* sever (a connection). **3** *intr.* undergo a rupture. **4** *tr. & intr.* affect with or suffer a hernia. □□ **rupturable** *adj.* [ME f. OF *rupture* or L *ruptura* f. *rumpere rupt-* break]

rural /ˈrʊər(ə)l/ *adj.* in, of, or suggesting the country (opp. URBAN); pastoral or agricultural (*in rural seclusion; a rural constituency*). □ **rural dean** see DEAN¹. **rural district** *Brit. hist.* a group of country parishes governed by an elected council. □□ **ruralism** *n.* **ruralist** *n.* **rurality** /-ˈrælɪtɪ/ *n.* **ruralize** *v.* (also **-ise**). **ruralization** /-laɪˈzeɪʃ(ə)n/ *n.* **rurally** *adv.* [ME f. OF *rural* or LL *ruralis* f. *rus ruris* the country]

Rurik /ˈruːrɪk/ the name of a dynasty that ruled in Russia from the 9th c. until 1598, reputedly founded by a Varangian chief who settled in Novgorod in 862. The Ruriks established themselves as rulers of the principality of Moscow and gradually extended their dominions into the surrounding territory.

Ruritania /ˌrʊərɪˈteɪnɪə/ an imaginary Central-European kingdom used as a fictional background for court romances with chivalry and intrigue in a modern setting, as in the novels of Sir Anthony Hope (Hawkins) *The Prisoner of Zenda* (1894) and *Rupert of Hentzau* (1898). □□ **Ruritanian** *adj. & n.* [as RURAL, after *Lusitania*]

rusa /ˈruːsə/ n. any of various E. Indian deer of the genus *Cervus*. esp a sambur. [mod.L f. Malay]

Ruse /ˈruːseɪ/ (also **Rousse** /ˈruːsə/) an industrial city on the Danube in northern Bulgaria; pop. (1987) 190,450.

ruse /ruːz/ n. a stratagem or trick. [ME f. OF f. *ruser* drive back, perh. ult. f. L *rursus* backwards: cf. RUSH¹]

rush¹ /rʌʃ/ v. & n. —v. **1** *intr.* go, move, or act precipitately or with great speed. **2** *tr.* move or transport with great haste (*was rushed to hospital*). **3** *intr.* (foll. by *at*) **a** move suddenly and quickly towards. **b** begin impetuously. **4** *tr.* perform or deal with hurriedly (*don't rush your dinner; the bill was rushed through Parliament*). **5** *tr.* force (a person) to act hastily. **6** *tr.* attack or capture by sudden assault. **7** *tr. sl.* overcharge (a customer). **8** *tr. US* pay attentions to (a person) with a view to securing acceptance of a proposal. **9** *tr.* pass (an obstacle) with a rapid dash. **10** *intr.* flow, fall, spread, or roll impetuously or fast (*felt the blood rush to my face; the river rushes past*). —n. **1** an act of rushing; a violent advance or attack. **2** a period of great activity. **3** (*attrib.*) done with great haste or speed (*a rush job*). **4** a sudden migration of large numbers. **5** (foll. by *on, for*) a sudden strong demand for a commodity. **6** (in pl.) *colloq.* the first prints of a film after a period of shooting. **7** *Football* **a** a combined dash by several players with the ball. **b** *US* the act of carrying the ball. □ **rush one's fences** act with undue haste. **rush hour** a time each day when traffic is at its heaviest. □□ **rusher** *n.* **rushingly** *adv.* [ME f. AF *russher*, = OF *ruser, russer*: see RUSE]

rush² /rʌʃ/ n. **1 a** any marsh or waterside plant of the family Juncaceae, with naked slender tapering pith-filled stems (properly leaves) formerly used for strewing floors and still used for making chair-bottoms and plaiting baskets etc. **b** a stem of this. **c** (*collect.*) rushes as a material. **2** *archaic* a thing of no value (*not worth a rush*). □ **rush candle** a candle made by dipping the pith of a rush in tallow. □□ **rushlike** *adj.* **rushy** *adj.* [OE *rysc, rysce,* corresp. to MLG, MHG *rusch*]

Rushdie /ˈrʌʃdɪ/, (Ahmed) Salman (1947–), Indian-born British novelist, author of 'magic realist' novels. His prizewinning *Midnight's Children* (1981) views the development of modern India through the eyes of a telepathic child born at the very moment of the country's independence. The publication of his novel *The Satanic Verses* (1988), an ambitious fantasy on good and evil and on the migrant experience, gave rise to an international crisis; regarded by many Muslims as blasphemous, it led to an Islamic *fatwa* which was in effect a death sentence.

rushlight /ˈrʌʃlaɪt/ n. a rush candle.

Rushmore /ˈrʌʃmɔː(r)/, **Mount** a mountain in the Black Hills

of South Dakota, noted for its giant busts of four US presidents —Washington, Jefferson, Lincoln, and Theodore Roosevelt— carved (1927–41) under the direction of the sculptor Gutzon Borglum.

rusk /rʌsk/ n. a slice of bread rebaked usu. as a light biscuit, esp. as food for babies. [Sp. or Port. *rosca* twist, coil, roll of bread]

Ruskin /ˈrʌskɪn/, John (1819–1900), English art and social critic. His voluminous writings profoundly influenced 19th-c. opinion and the development of the Labour movement. He was a champion of the painter Turner, who was then a controversial figure, and of Gothic architecture, which he saw as a religious expression of the piety of the Middle Ages: *The Stones of Venice* (1851–3), in its attacks on 'the pestilent art of the Renaissance', led on to his later attacks on capitalism in his lectures on 'The Political Economy of Art' (1857), and on utilitarianism in *Unto This Last* (1860). His *Fors Clavigera* (1871–8) or 'Letters to the Workmen and Labourers of Great Britain' was an attempt to spread his notions of social justice, coupled with aesthetic improvement; his religious and philanthropic instincts also expressed themselves in the founding of the Guild of St George in 1871, a major contribution to the Arts and Crafts movement, and in other public causes. His unfinished autobiography *Praeterita* (1885–9) was written in his final years of mental infirmity and semi-isolation.

Russell¹ /ˈrʌs(ə)l/, Bertrand Arthur William (1873–1970), 3rd Earl (though he rejected the title), British philosopher, mathematician, and reformer, important especially for his work on mathematical logic, which had great influence on symbolic logic and on set theory in mathematics. In *Principia Mathematica* (1910–13), written with A. N. Whitehead, he followed Frege in seeking to provide a secure foundation for mathematics by showing how its axioms could be deduced from those of logic. Although his philosophical views underwent continual development and revision, he remained constant in his admiration of physics and his belief that science provides the best understanding of all that exists. Kept from a traditional academic career by his radical views, he became widely known to the general public through campaigns and writings in favour of progressive views in politics, morals, education, and religion. He campaigned for women's suffrage, opposed the First World War, ran a progressive school, and demonstrated in favour of nuclear disarmament. He was awarded the Nobel Prize for literature in 1950, and retained his lucidity and wit to the end of his long life.

Russell² /ˈrʌs(ə)l/, George William (1867–1935), Irish poet who wrote under the pseudonym 'AE'. He met W. B. Yeats in 1886 and became interested in theosophy and mysticism, evident in his volume of verse, *Homeward; Songs by the Way* (1894). After the performance of *Deirdre* (1902) he became an established figure in the Irish literary revival. His interests extended to public affairs and he successfully edited *The Irish Homestead* (1905–23) and *The Irish Statesman* (1923–30).

Russell³ /ˈrʌs(ə)l/, John, 1st Earl Russell (1792–1878), British Whig statesman who introduced the Reform Bill of 1832 into Parliament. He was Prime Minister 1846–52 and 1865–6. His government was overshadowed by the dominant personality of his Foreign Secretary, Lord Palmerston.

russet /ˈrʌsɪt/ adj. & n. —adj. **1** reddish-brown. **2** *archaic* rustic, homely, simple. —n. **1** a reddish-brown colour. **2** a kind of rough-skinned russet-coloured apple. **3** *hist.* a coarse homespun reddish-brown or grey cloth used for simple clothing. □□ **russety** *adj.* [ME f. AF f. OF *rosset, rousset,* dimin. of *roux* red f. Prov. *ros,* It. *rosso* f. L *russus* red]

Russia /ˈrʌʃə/ a country in northern Asia and eastern Europe. The modern State originated from the expansion of Muscovy under the Rurik and Romanov dynasties, westwards towards Poland and Hungary, southwards to the Black Sea, and eastwards to the Pacific Ocean. Russia played an increasing role in Europe from the time of Peter the Great in the early 18th c. and pursued imperial ambitions in the east in the second half of the 19th c. Social and economic problems, exacerbated by the First World War, led to the overthrow of the Tsar in 1917 and the establishment of a Communist government. (See UNION OF

b *but* d *dog* f *few* g *get* h *he* j *yes* k *cat* l *leg* m *man* n *no* p *pen* r *red* s *sit* t *top* v *voice*

SOVIET SOCIALIST REPUBLICS.) □ **Russia leather** a durable book-binding leather from skins impregnated with birch-bark oil.

Russian /ˈrʌʃ(ə)n/ n. & adj. —n. **1 a** a native or national of Russia or the Soviet Union. **b** a person of Russian descent. **2** the language of Russia and the official language of the Soviet Union, the most important of the Slavonic languages, spoken in the USSR as a first language by about 142 million people and by another 42 million as a second language. It is written in the Cyrillic alphabet. —adj. **1** of or relating to Russia. **2** of or in Russian. □ **Russian boot** a boot that loosely encloses the calf. **Russian olive** = OLEASTER. **Russian roulette 1** an act of daring in which one (usu. with others in turn) squeezes the trigger of a revolver held to one's head with one chamber loaded, having first spun the chamber. **2** a potentially dangerous enterprise. **Russian salad** a salad of mixed diced vegetables with mayonnaise. □□ **Russianize** v.tr. (also **-ise**). **Russianization** /-naɪˈzeɪʃ(ə)n/ n. **Russianness** n. [med.L *Russianus*]

Russian Soviet Federative Socialist Republic the largest and most important of the constituent republics of the Soviet Union; pop. (est. 1987) 145,311,000; capital, Moscow. It occupies more than three-quarters of the total area of the Union, contains more than half its population, and consists of twelve autonomous republics and numerous provinces.

Russify /ˈrʌsɪˌfaɪ/ v.tr. (**-ies**, **-ied**) make Russian in character. □□ **Russification** /-fɪˈkeɪʃ(ə)n/ n.

Russki /ˈrʌskɪ/ n. (also **Russky**) (pl. **Russkis** or **-ies**) often offens. a Russian or Soviet. [RUSSIAN after Russ. surnames ending in -ski]

Russo- /ˈrʌsəʊ/ comb. form Russian; Russian and. □ **Russo-Japanese War** a war of 1904–5, caused by conflict of Russian and Japanese interests in Manchuria and Korea. Russia suffered a series of defeats, and by the peace settlement Japan gained the ascendancy in that region.

Russophile /ˈrʌsəʊˌfaɪl/ n. a person who is fond of Russia or the Russians.

rust /rʌst/ n. & v. —n. **1 a** a reddish or yellowish-brown coating formed on iron or steel by oxidation, esp. as a result of moisture. **b** a similar coating on other metals. **2 a** any of various plant-diseases with rust-coloured spots caused by fungi of the order *Uredinales*. **b** the fungus causing this. **3** an impaired state due to disuse or inactivity. —v. **1** tr. & intr. affect or be affected with rust; undergo oxidation. **2** intr. (of bracken etc.) become rust-coloured. **3** intr. (of a plant) be attacked by rust. **4** intr. lose quality or efficiency by disuse or inactivity. □□ **rustless** adj. [OE *rūst* f. Gmc]

rustic /ˈrʌstɪk/ adj. & n. —adj. **1** having the characteristics of or associations with the country or country life. **2** unsophisticated, simple, unrefined. **3** of rude or country workmanship. **4** made of untrimmed branches or rough timber (a *rustic bench*). **5** (of lettering) freely formed. **6** Archit. with rough-hewn or roughened surface or with sunk joints. **7** archaic rural. —n. a person from or living in the country, esp. a simple unsophisticated one. □□ **rustically** adv. **rusticity** /-ˈtɪsɪtɪ/ n. [ME f. L *rusticus* f. *rus* the country]

rusticate /ˈrʌstɪˌkeɪt/ v. **1** tr. send down (a student) temporarily from university. **2** intr. retire to or live in the country. **3** tr. make rural. **4** tr. mark (masonry) with sunk joints or a roughened surface. □□ **rustication** /-ˈkeɪʃ(ə)n/ n. [L *rusticari* live in the country (as RUSTIC)]

rustle /ˈrʌs(ə)l/ v. & n. —v. **1** intr. & tr. make or cause to make a gentle sound as of dry leaves blown in a breeze. **2** intr. (often foll. by *along* etc.) move with a rustling sound. **3** tr. (also absol.) steal (cattle or horses). **4** intr. US colloq. hustle. —n. a rustling sound or movement. □ **rustle up** colloq. produce quickly when needed. □□ **rustler** n. (esp. in sense 3 of v.). [ME *rustel* etc. (imit.): cf. obs. Flem. *ruysselen*, Du. *ritselen*]

rustproof /ˈrʌstpruːf/ adj. & v. —adj. (of a metal) not susceptible to corrosion by rust. —v.tr. make rustproof.

rustre /ˈrʌstə(r)/ n. Heraldry a lozenge with a round hole. [F]

rusty /ˈrʌstɪ/ adj. (**rustier**, **rustiest**) **1** rusted or affected by rust. **2** stiff with age or disuse. **3** (of knowledge etc.) faded or impaired by neglect (my *French is a bit rusty*). **4** rust-coloured. **5** (of black

clothes) discoloured by age. **6 a** of antiquated appearance. **b** antiquated or behind the times. **7** (of a voice) croaking or creaking. □□ **rustily** adv. **rustiness** n. [OE *rūstig* (as RUST)]

rut¹ /rʌt/ n. & v. —n. **1** a deep track made by the passage of wheels. **2** an established (esp. tedious) mode of practice or procedure. —v.tr. (**rutted**, **rutting**) mark with ruts. □ **in a rut** following a fixed (esp. tedious or dreary) pattern of behaviour that is difficult to change. □□ **rutty** adj. [prob. f. OF *rote* (as ROUTE)]

rut² /rʌt/ n. & v. —n. the periodic sexual excitement of a male deer, goat, ram, etc. —v.intr. (**rutted**, **rutting**) be affected with rut. □□ **ruttish** adj. [ME f. OF *rut*, *ruit* f. L *rugitus* f. *rugire* roar]

rutabaga /ˌruːtəˈbɑːgə/ n. a swede. [Sw. dial. *rotabagge*]

Ruth¹ /ruːθ/ a book of the Old Testament telling the story of Ruth, a Moabite woman, who married her husband's kinsman Boaz. King David (and therefore Christ, Matt. 1: 5) are descended from them.

Ruth² /ruːθ/, George Herman ('Babe') (1895–1948), American professional baseball player, the most famous player during the period between the two World Wars.

Ruthenia /ruːˈθiːnɪə/ a region of central Europe that is now part of the Ukrainian SSR. **Ruthenian** adj. & n.

ruthenium /ruːˈθiːnɪəm/ n. Chem. a rare hard white metallic transition element, chemically related to platinum. First isolated in the pure state in the 1840s, the metal is used in powdered form as a catalyst, and in alloys to increase the hardness of platinum and palladium. ¶ Symb.: **Ru**; atomic number 44. [med.L *Ruthenia* Russia (from its discovery in ores from the Urals)]

Rutherford¹ /ˈrʌðəfəd/, Sir Ernest, 1st Baron Rutherford of Nelson (1871–1937), British physicist, born in New Zealand, successively professor at Montreal, Manchester, and Cambridge, widely regarded as the founder of nuclear physics, his researches having led to major discoveries concerning the nature of the atom. An experimental genius with a strategic approach to research, Rutherford had an unrivalled capacity for isolating a problem until there were only a small number of possible explanations, and then devising a series of simple experiments until all but one possibility had been eliminated. While studying radioactivity he established the nature of alpha and beta particles, and (with Soddy) proposed the laws of radioactive decay. From further experiments he concluded that the positive charge in an atom, and virtually all its mass, is concentrated in a central nucleus with negatively charged electrons in orbit round it; in essence his view is still held today. In 1919, after spending the war years developing means of detecting German submarines, Rutherford announced the first artificial transmutation of matter—an experiment which caught the public imagination: he bombarded nitrogen gas with alpha particles produced by natural radioactive substances, and found that the disruption of the nuclei had changed the nitrogen atoms into oxygen. For his considerable services to science he received many honours, including the Nobel Prize for chemistry in 1908, a knighthood in 1914, and a peerage in 1931. The artificial element rutherfordium is named in his honour.

Rutherford² /ˈrʌðəfəd/, Dame Margaret (1892–1972), English stage and film actress, noted for her roles as a formidable but jovial eccentric. She played Miss Prism in *The Importance of Being Earnest* (1939, 1952) and the bicycling medium in *Blithe Spirit* (1941, 1945), and is remembered especially for her later films which include *Passport to Pimlico* (1949), several films of Agatha Christie novels in which she played the elderly dectective, Miss Marple, and *The VIPs* (1963), for which she won an Academy Award.

rutherfordium /ˌrʌðəˈfɔːdɪəm/ n. Chem. the American name for an artificially made transuranic metallic element produced by bombarding an isotope of californium. ¶ Symb.: **Rf**; atomic number 104. Also called KURCHATOVIUM. The preferred name for it is now *unnilquadium*. [E. *Rutherford*, Engl. physicist d. 1937]

ruthless /ˈruːθlɪs/ adj. having no pity or compassion. □□ **ruthlessly** adv. **ruthlessness** n. [ME, f. *ruth* compassion f. RUE¹]

w we z zoo ʃ she ʒ decision θ thin ð this ŋ ring x loch tʃ chip dʒ jar (see over for vowels)

rutile /ˈruːtaɪl/ n. a mineral form of titanium dioxide. [F *rutile* or G *Rutil* f. L *rutilus* reddish]

Ruwenzori /ˌruːenˈzɔːrɪ/ a national park in the Rift Valley of SW Uganda, established in 1952 as the Queen Elizabeth National Park.

RV abbr. Revised Version (of the Bible).

Rwanda /ruːˈændə/ a country of central Africa east of Zaïre; pop. (est. 1988) 7,058,350; official languages, Rwanda (a Bantu language) and French; capital, Kigali. The area was claimed by Germany from 1890, and after the First World War it became part of a Belgian trust territory, gaining independence as a republic in 1962. □□ **Rwandan** adj. & n.

Ry. abbr. Railway.

-ry /rɪ/ suffix = -ERY (*infantry*; *rivalry*). [shortened f. -ERY, or by analogy]

Ryazan /rɪəˈzæn/ a city of the Soviet Union, situated to the south-east of Moscow on the River Oka; pop. (est. 1987) 508,000.

Ryder Cup /ˈraɪdə(r)/ a golf tournament played between teams of men professionals of the US and of Great Britain and Ireland (and, since 1979, other European players), held every second year in September, alternately in the US and Great Britain, from 1927; the trophy for this, donated by Samuel Ryder, a British seed-merchant.

rye /raɪ/ n. **1 a** a cereal plant, *Secale cereale*, with spikes bearing florets which yield wheatlike grains. **b** the grain of this used for bread and fodder. **2** (in full **rye whisky**) whisky distilled from fermented rye. [OE *ryge* f. Gmc]

ryegrass /ˈraɪɡrɑːs/ n. any forage or lawn grass of the genus *Lolium*, esp. *L. perenne*. [obs. *ray-grass*, of unkn. orig.]

Ryle[1] /raɪl/, Gilbert (1900–76), English philosopher, professor of metaphysical philosophy at Oxford 1945–68. His most famous work *The Concept of Mind* (1949) is a strong attack on the mind-and-body dualism of Descartes, referred to by Ryle as 'the dogma of the Ghost in the Machine', which postulates that mental events exist alongside physical events but in a non-material mental 'world'. He was a cousin of the astronomer Sir Martin Ryle (see RYLE[2]).

Ryle[2] /raɪl/, Sir Martin (1918–84), English physicist and astronomer, noted for his work on radio astronomy in the 1950s. His surveys played an important role in the current cosmological debates, helping to establish the 'big bang' as opposed to 'steady state' theory of the universe. Ryle was Astronomer Royal 1972–82 and was awarded the Nobel Prize for physics in 1974, the first astronomer to be so honoured.

ryokan /rɪˈɒkən/ n. a traditional Japanese inn. [Jap.]

ryot /ˈraɪət/ n. an Indian peasant. [Urdu *raʿiyat* f. Arab. *raʿiya* flock, subjects f. *raʿā* to pasture]

Rysy /ˈrɪsɪ/ the highest mountain in Poland, a peak in the Tatra Mountains which rises to a height of 2,499 m (8,197 ft.).

Ryukyu Islands /rɪˈuːkjuː/ a chain of islands in the western Pacific, stretching for about 960 km (600 miles) from the southern tip of Kyushu Island, Japan, to Taiwan. The islands were placed under US military control in 1945 and returned to Japan in 1972.

S

S¹ /es/ *n.* (also **s**) (*pl.* **Ss** or **S's** /'esɪz/) **1** the nineteenth letter of the alphabet. **2** an S-shaped object or curve.

S² *abbr.* (also **S.**) **1** Saint. **2** siemens. **3** Society. **4** South, Southern.

S³ *symb. Chem.* the element sulphur.

s. *abbr.* **1** second(s). **2** shilling(s). [orig. f. L *solidus*: see SOLIDUS] **3** singular. **4** son. **5** succeeded.

's /s; z after a vowel sound or voiced consonant/ *abbr.* **1** is, has (*he's; it's; John's; Charles's*). **2** us (*let's*). **3** *colloq.* does (*what's he say?*).

-s¹ /s; z after a vowel sound or voiced consonant, e.g. *ways, bags*/ *suffix* denoting the plurals of nouns (cf. -ES¹). [OE *-as* pl. ending]

-s² /s; z after a vowel sound or voiced consonant, e.g. *ties, begs*/ *suffix* forming the 3rd person sing. present of verbs (cf. -ES²). [OE dial., prob. f. OE 2nd person sing. present ending *-es, -as*]

-s³ /s; z after a vowel sound or voiced consonant, e.g. *besides*/ *suffix* **1** forming adverbs (*afterwards; besides*). **2** forming possessive pronouns (*hers; ours*). [formed as -'s¹]

-s⁴ /s; z after a vowel sound or voiced consonant/ *suffix* forming nicknames or pet names (*Fats; ducks*). [after -s¹]

-s' /s; z after a vowel sound or voiced consonant/ *suffix* denoting the possessive case of plural nouns and sometimes of singular nouns ending in *s* (*the boys' shoes; Charles' book*). [as -'s¹]

's- /s, z/ *prefix archaic* (esp. in oaths) God's ('*sblood; 'struth*). [abbr.]

-'s¹ /s; z after a vowel sound or voiced consonant/ *suffix* denoting the possessive case of singular nouns and of plural nouns not ending in *-s* (*John's book; the book's cover; the children's shoes*). [OE genit. sing. ending]

-'s² /s; z after a vowel sound or voiced consonant/ *suffix* denoting the plural of a letter or symbol (*S's; 8's*). [as -s¹]

SA *abbr.* **1** Salvation Army. **2** sex appeal. **3 a** South Africa. **b** South America. **c** South Australia. **4** *hist.* Sturmabteilung (the paramilitary force of the Nazi party; see BROWNSHIRTS).

Saar /sɑ:(r)/ (French **Sarre**) a river of western Europe, rising in the Vosges Mountains in eastern France and flowing 240 km (150 miles) to join the Moselle River in Germany.

Saarland /'sɑ:lænd/ a 'Land' (State) in the west of Germany, through which the River Saar flows; pop. (1987) 1,041,000; capital, Saarbrücken.

Saba /'sɑ:bə/ the smallest island of the Netherlands Antilles; pop. (1981) 963; chief town, Leverock.

sabadilla /ˌsæbə'dɪlə/ *n.* **1** a Mexican plant, *Schoenocaulon officinale*, with seeds yielding veratrine. **2** a preparation of these seeds, used in medicine and agriculture. [Sp. *cebadilla* dimin. of *cebada* barley]

Sabaean /sə'bi:ən/ *n. & adj.* —*n.* a member of a Semitic-speaking people who by the 3rd c. AD had established an elaborate system of government and succeeded in uniting southern Arabia into a single State, overthrown by the Abyssinians in AD 525. —*adj.* of or relating to the Sabaeans. [L *Sabaeus* f. Gk *Sabaios*, ult. f. Heb. *Sheba* people of Yemen (see SHEBA)]

Sabah /'sɑ:bɑ:/ a State of Malaysia, comprising North Borneo and some offshore islands pop. (1980) 998,800; capital, Kota Kinabalu. A British protectorate from 1888, it gained independence and joined Malaysia in 1963.

Sabaoth /sæ'beɪɒθ, 'sæ-/ *n.pl. Bibl.* heavenly hosts (see HOST¹ 2) (*Lord of Sabaoth*). [ME f. LL f. Gk *Sabaōth* f. Heb. *ṣᵊbāōt* pl. of *ṣābā* host (of heaven)]

Sabbatarian /ˌsæbə'teərɪən/ *n. & adj.* —*n.* **1** a strict sabbath-keeping Jew. **2** a Christian who favours observing Sunday strictly as the sabbath. **3** a Christian who observes Saturday as the sabbath. —*adj.* relating to or holding the tenets of Sabbatarians. □□ **Sabbatarianism** *n.* [LL *sabbatarius* f. L *sabbatum*: see SABBATH]

sabbath /'sæbəθ/ *n.* **1** (in full **sabbath day**) **a** a religious rest-day appointed for Jews on the last day of the week (Saturday). **b** Sunday as a Christian day of abstinence from work and play. **2** (in full **witches' sabbath**) a supposed general midnight meeting of witches with the Devil. [OE *sabat*, L *sabbatum*, & OF *sabbat*, f. Gk *sabbaton* f. Heb. *šabbāt* f. *šābat* to rest]

sabbatical /sə'bætɪk(ə)l/ *adj. & n.* —*adj.* **1** of or appropriate to the sabbath. **2** (of leave) granted at intervals to a university teacher for study or travel, orig. every seventh year. —*n.* a period of sabbatical leave. □ **sabbatical year 1** *Bibl.* every seventh year, prescribed by the Mosaic law to be observed as a 'sabbath', during which the land was allowed to rest. **2** a year's sabbatical leave. □□ **sabbatically** *adv.* [LL *sabbaticus* f. Gk *sabbatikos* of the sabbath]

Sabellian¹ /sə'belɪən/ *n. & adj.* —*n.* a member of a group of tribes in ancient Italy (including Sabines, Samnites, Campanians, etc.), or their language or dialects. —*adj.* of or relating to the Sabellians or their language or dialects. [L *Sabellus*]

Sabellian² /sə'belɪən/ *n. & adj.* —*n.* a holder of the doctrine of Sabellius (3rd c.), African heretic, that the Father, Son, and Holy Spirit are merely aspects of one divine Person. —*adj.* of or relating to the Sabellians.

saber US var. of SABRE.

Sabian /'seɪbɪən/ *n. & adj.* —*n.* **1** an adherent of a religious sect mentioned in the Koran and by later Arabian writers. In the Koran, the Sabians are classed with Muslims, Jews, and Christians as believers in the true God. On account of the toleration extended to them by Muslims the name of Sabians, was some centuries after Muhammad, assumed not only by a half-Christian Gnostic sect, the Mandaeans (whose religion was perhaps akin to that of true Sabians), but also by certain actual polytheists. **2** a member of a group of Syrian pagan star-worshipers. —*adj.* of or relating to the Sabians. f. [Arab. *ṣābi'*, prob. as Heb. *ṣābā* host]

sabicu /'sæbɪˌku:/ *n.* **1** a W. Indian tree, *Lysiloma latisiliqua*, grown for timber. **2** the mahogany-like wood of this tree. [Cuban Sp. *sabicú*]

Sabin /'seɪbɪn/, Albert Bruce (1906–), Russian-born American microbiologist who in 1955 developed an orally administered vaccine, named after him, against poliomyelitis.

Sabine /'sæbaɪn/ *n. & adj.* —*n.* a member of a people of ancient Italy of the area NE of Rome, renowned in antiquity for their frugal and hardy character and their superstitious practices, finally conquered by Rome in 290 BC. The (unhistorical) legend of the Rape of the Sabine Women (said to have been carried off by the Romans at a spectacle to which the Sabines had been invited) reflects the early intermingling of Romans and Sabines; some Roman religious institutions were said to have a Sabine origin. —*adj.* of or relating to the Sabines. [L *Sabinus*]

sable¹ /'seɪb(ə)l/ *n.* **1 a** a small brown-furred flesh-eating mammal, *Martes zibellina*, of N. Europe and parts of N. Asia, related to the marten. **b** its skin or fur. **2** a fine paintbrush made of sable fur. [ME f. OF f. med.L *sabelum* f. Slav.]

sable² /'seɪb(ə)l/ *n. & adj.* —*n.* **1** esp. *poet.* black. **2** (in *pl.*) mourning garments. **3** (in full **sable antelope**) a large stout-horned African antelope, *Hippotragus niger*, the males of which are mostly black in old age. —*adj.* **1** (usu. placed after noun) *Heraldry* black. **2** esp. *poet.* dark, gloomy. □□ **sabled** *adj.* **sably** *adv.* [ME f. OF (in Heraldry): gen. taken to be identical with SABLE¹, although sable fur is dark brown]

sabot /'sæbəʊ, 'sæbəʊ/ *n.* **1** a kind of simple shoe hollowed out from a block of wood. **2** a wooden-soled shoe. **3** *Austral.* a small snub-nosed yacht. □□ **saboted** /'sæbəʊd/ *adj.* [F, blend of *savate* shoe + *botte* boot]

sabotage /'sæbəˌtɑ:ʒ/ *n. & v.* —*n.* deliberate damage to productive capacity, esp. as a political act. —*v.tr.* **1** commit sabotage on. **2** destroy, spoil; make useless (*sabotaged my plans*). [F f. *saboter* make a noise with sabots, bungle, wilfully destroy: see SABOT]

saboteur /ˌsæbəˈtɜː(r)/ n. a person who commits sabotage. [F]

sabra /ˈsæbrə/ n. a Jew born in Israel. [mod. Heb. *sābrāh* opuntia fruit]

sabre /ˈseɪbə(r)/ n. & v. (US **saber**) —n. 1 a cavalry sword with a curved blade. 2 a cavalry soldier and horse. 3 a light fencing-sword with a tapering blade. —v.tr. cut down or wound with a sabre. □ **sabre-bill** any S. American bird of the genus *Campylorhamphus* with a long curved bill. **sabre-cut** 1 a blow with a sabre. 2 a wound made or a scar left by this. **sabre-rattling** a display or threat of military force. **sabre-toothed** designating any of various extinct mammals having long sabre-shaped upper canines. **sabre-wing** a S. American humming-bird, *Campylopterus falcatus*, with curved wings. [F, earlier *sable* f. G *Sabel*, *Säbel*, *Schabel* f. Pol. *szabla* or Magyar *szablya*]

sabretache /ˈsæbətæʃ/ n. a flat satchel on long straps worn by some cavalry officers from the left of the waist-belt. [F f. G *Säbeltasche* (as SABRE, *Tasche* pocket)]

sabreur /sæˈbrɜː(r)/ n. a user of the sabre, esp. a cavalryman. [F f. *sabrer* SABRE v.]

SAC abbr. (in the UK) Senior Aircraftman.

sac /sæk/ n. 1 a baglike cavity, enclosed by a membrane, in an animal or plant. 2 the distended membrane surrounding a hernia, cyst, tumour, etc. [F *sac* or L *saccus* SACK[1]]

saccade /sæˈkɑːd/ n. a brief rapid movement of the eye between fixation points. □□ **saccadic** /səˈkædɪk/ adj. [F, = violent pull, f. OF *saquer*, *sachier* pull]

saccate /ˈsækeɪt/ adj. Bot. 1 dilated into a bag. 2 contained in a sac.

saccharide /ˈsækəˌraɪd/ n. Chem. = SUGAR 2. [mod.L *saccharum* sugar + -IDE]

saccharimeter /ˌsækəˈrɪmɪtə(r)/ n. any instrument, esp. a polarimeter, for measuring the sugar content of a solution. [F *saccharimètre* (as SACCHARIDE)]

saccharin /ˈsækərɪn/ n. a very sweet substance used as a non-fattening substitute for sugar. [G (as SACCHARIDE) + -IN]

saccharine /ˈsækəˌriːn/ adj. 1 sugary. 2 of, containing, or like sugar. 3 unpleasantly over-polite, sentimental, etc.

saccharo- /ˈsækərəʊ/ comb. form sugar; sugar and. [Gk *sakkharon* sugar]

saccharogenic /ˌsækərəʊˈdʒenɪk/ adj. producing sugar.

saccharometer /ˌsækəˈrɒmɪtə(r)/ n. any instrument, esp. a hydrometer, for measuring the sugar content of a solution.

saccharose /ˈsækəˌrəʊs, -ˌrəʊz/ n. sucrose. [mod.L *saccharum* sugar + -OSE[2]]

sacciform /ˈsæksɪˌfɔːm/ adj. sac-shaped. [L *saccus* sac + -FORM]

saccule /ˈsækjuːl/ n. a small sac or cyst. □□ **saccular** adj. [L *sacculus* (as SAC)]

sacerdotal /ˌsækəˈdəʊt(ə)l/ adj. 1 of priests or the priestly office; priestly. 2 (of a doctrine etc.) ascribing sacrificial functions and supernatural powers to ordained priests; claiming excessive authority for the priesthood. □□ **sacerdotalism** n. **sacerdotalist** n. **sacerdotally** adv. [ME f. OF *sacerdotal* or L *sacerdotalis* f. *sacerdos -dotis* priest]

sachem /ˈseɪtʃəm/ n. 1 the supreme chief of some American Indian tribes. 2 US a political leader. [Narraganset, = SAGAMORE]

sachet /ˈsæʃeɪ/ n. 1 a small bag or packet containing a small portion of a substance, esp. shampoo. 2 a small perfumed bag. 3 a dry perfume for laying among clothes etc. b a packet of this. [F, dimin. of *sac* f. L *saccus*]

Sachs /sæks, zæks/, Hans (1494–1576), German writer, by trade a shoemaker of Nuremberg, prolific author of verse and some 200 plays. He became renowned in the Guild of Meistersinger, writing many songs using their elaborate technique, and celebrated Luther in a poem and the Protestant cause in prose dialogues. Despised in the 17th c., he was restored to fame by Goethe in his poem *Hans Sachsens poetische Sendung* (1776), and Wagner raised him to legendary status in *Die Meistersinger von Nürnberg* (1868).

sack[1] /sæk/ n. & v. —n. 1 a a large strong bag, usu. made of hessian, paper, or plastic, for storing or conveying goods. b (usu. foll. by *of*) this with its contents (*a sack of potatoes*). c a quantity contained in a sack. 2 (prec. by *the*) colloq. dismissal from employment. 3 (prec. by *the*) US sl. bed. 4 a a woman's short loose dress with a sacklike appearance. b archaic or hist. a woman's loose gown, or a silk train attached to the shoulders of this. 5 a man's or woman's loose-hanging coat not shaped to the back. —v.tr. 1 put into a sack or sacks. 2 colloq. dismiss from employment. □ **sack race** a race between competitors in sacks up to the waist or neck. □□ **sackful** n. (pl. **-fuls**). **sacklike** adj. [OE *sacc* f. L *saccus* f. Gk *sakkos*, of Semitic orig.]

sack[2] /sæk/ v. & n. —v.tr. 1 plunder and destroy (a captured town etc.). 2 steal valuables from (a place). —n. the sacking of a captured place. [orig. as noun, f. F *sac* in phr. *mettre à sac* put to sack, f. It. *sacco* SACK[1]]

sack[3] /sæk/ n. hist. a white wine formerly imported into Britain from Spain and the Canaries (*sherry sack*). [16th-c. *wyne seck*, f. F *vin sec* dry wine]

sackbut /ˈsækbʌt/ n. an early form of trombone. [F *saquebute*, earlier *saqueboute* hook for pulling a man off a horse f. *saquer* pull, *boute* (as BUTT[1])]

sackcloth /ˈsækklɒθ/ n. 1 a coarse fabric of flax or hemp. 2 clothing made of this, formerly worn as a penance or in mourning (esp. *sackcloth and ashes*).

sacking /ˈsækɪŋ/ n. material for making sacks; sackcloth.

Sackville-West /ˌsækvɪlˈwest/, Hon. Victoria (Mary) (1892–1962), English novelist and poet. Her poem *The Land* (1927) is a fine evocation of the English countryside. She is said to be portrayed in her friend Virginia Woolf's novel *Orlando* (1928).

sacra pl. of SACRUM.

sacral /ˈseɪkr(ə)l/ adj. 1 Anat. of or relating to the sacrum. 2 Anthropol. of or for sacred rites. [E or L *sacrum*: see SACRUM]

sacrament /ˈsækrəmənt/ n. 1 a religious ceremony or act of the Christian Churches regarded as an outward and visible sign of inward and spiritual grace. The term is applied by the Eastern, pre-Reformation Western, and Roman Catholic Churches to the seven rites of baptism, confirmation, the Eucharist, penance, extreme unction, ordination, and matrimony, but restricted by most Protestants to baptism and the Eucharist. 2 a thing of mysterious and sacred significance; a sacred influence, symbol, etc. 3 (also **Blessed** or **Holy Sacrament**) (prec. by *the*) a the Eucharist. b the consecrated elements, esp. the bread or Host. 4 an oath or solemn engagement taken. [ME f. OF *sacrement* f. L *sacramentum* solemn oath etc. f. *sacrare* hallow f. *sacer* SACRED, used in Christian L as transl. of Gk *mustērion* MYSTERY[1]]

sacramental /ˌsækrəˈment(ə)l/ adj. & n. —adj. 1 of or of the nature of a sacrament or the sacrament. 2 (of a doctrine etc.) attaching great importance to the sacraments. —n. an observance analogous to but not reckoned among the sacraments, e.g. the use of holy water or the sign of the cross. □□ **sacramentalism** n. **sacramentalist** n. **sacramentality** /-ˈtælɪtɪ/ n. **sacramentally** adv. [ME f. F *sacramental* or LL *sacramentalis* (as SACRAMENT)]

Sacramento /ˌsækrəˈmentəʊ/ the capital of California, situated 115 km (72 miles) north-east of San Francisco, on the Sacramento River; pop. (1980) 274,100.

sacrarium /səˈkreərɪəm/ n. (pl. **sacraria** /-rɪə/) 1 the sanctuary of a church. 2 RC Ch. a piscina. 3 Rom. Antiq. a shrine; the room (in a house) containing the penates. [L f. *sacer sacri* holy]

sacred /ˈseɪkrɪd/ adj. 1 a (often foll. by *to*) exclusively dedicated or appropriated (to a god or to some religious purpose). b made holy by religious association. c connected with religion; used for a religious purpose (*sacred music*). 2 a safeguarded or required by religion, reverence, or tradition. b sacrosanct. 3 (of writings etc.) embodying the laws or doctrines of a religion. □ **Sacred College** RC Ch. the body of cardinals. **sacred cow** colloq. an idea or institution unreasonably held to be above criticism (with ref. to the Hindus' respect for the cow as a holy animal). **Sacred Heart** RC Ch. the heart of Christ (or *of* Mary) as an object of devotion. **sacred number** a number associated with religious symbolism, e.g. 7. □□ **sacredly** adv. **sacredness** n. [ME, past part. of obs. *sacre* consecrate f. OF *sacrer* f. L *sacrare* f. *sacer sacri* holy]

sacrifice /ˈsækrɪˌfaɪs/ n. & v. —n. 1 a the act of giving up something valued for the sake of something else more important or worthy. **b** a thing given up in this way. **c** the loss entailed in this. **2 a** the slaughter of an animal or person or the surrender of a possession as an offering to a deity. **b** an animal, person, or thing offered in this way. **3** an act of prayer, thanksgiving, or penitence as propitiation. **4** *Theol.* **a** Christ's offering of himself in the Crucifixion. **b** the Eucharist as either a propitiatory offering of the body and blood of Christ or an act of thanksgiving. **5** (in games) a loss incurred deliberately to avoid a greater loss or to obtain a compensating advantage. —*v.* **1** *tr.* give up (a thing) as a sacrifice. **2** *tr.* (foll. by *to*) devote or give over to. **3** *tr.* (also *absol.*) offer or kill as a sacrifice. □□ **sacrificial** /-'fɪʃ(ə)l/ *adj.* **sacrificially** /-'fɪʃəlɪ/ *adv.* [ME f. OF f. L *sacrificium* f. *sacrificus* (as SACRED)]

sacrilege /'sækrɪlɪdʒ/ *n.* the violation or misuse of what is regarded as sacred. □□ **sacrilegious** /-'lɪdʒəs/ *adj.* **sacrilegiously** /-'lɪdʒəslɪ/ *adv.* [ME f. OF f. L *sacrilegium* f. *sacrilegus* stealer of sacred things, f. *sacer sacri* sacred + *legere* take possession of]

sacring /'seɪkrɪŋ/ *n.* *archaic* **1** the consecration of the Eucharistic elements. **2** the ordination and consecration of a bishop, sovereign, etc. □ **sacring bell** a bell rung at the elevation of the elements in the Eucharist. [ME f. obs. *sacre*: see SACRED]

sacristan /'sækrɪst(ə)n/ *n.* **1** a person in charge of a sacristy and its contents. **2** *archaic* the sexton of a parish church. [ME f. med.L *sacristanus* (as SACRED)]

sacristy /'sækrɪstɪ/ *n.* (*pl.* **-ies**) a room in a church, where the vestments, sacred vessels, etc., are kept and the celebrant can prepare for a service. [F *sacristie* or It. *sacrestia* or med.L *sacristia* (as SACRED)]

sacro- /'seɪkrəʊ/ *comb. form* denoting the sacrum (*sacro-iliac*).

sacrosanct /'sækrəʊˌsæŋkt/ *adj.* (of a person, place, law, etc.) most sacred; inviolable. □□ **sacrosanctity** /-'sæŋktɪtɪ/ *n.* [L *sacrosanctus* f. *sacro* ablat. of *sacrum* sacred rite (see SACRED) + *sanctus* (as SAINT)]

sacrum /'seɪkrəm/ *n.* (*pl.* **sacra** /-krə/ or **sacrums**) *Anat.* a triangular bone formed from fused vertebrae and situated between the two hip-bones of the pelvis. [L *os sacrum* transl. Gk *hieron osteon* sacred bone (from its sacrificial use)]

SACW *abbr.* (in the UK) Senior Aircraftwoman.

SAD *abbr.* seasonal affective disorder.

sad /sæd/ *adj.* (**sadder**, **saddest**) **1** unhappy; feeling sorrow or regret. **2** causing or suggesting sorrow (*a sad story*). **3** regrettable. **4** shameful, deplorable (*is in a sad state*). **5** (of a colour) dull, neutral-tinted. **6** (of dough etc.) heavy, having failed to rise. □ **sad-iron** a solid flat-iron. **sad sack** *US colloq.* a very inept person. □□ **saddish** *adj.* **sadly** *adv.* **sadness** *n.* [OE *sæd* f. Gmc, rel. to L *satis*]

Sadat /sæ'dæt/, Muhammad Anwar al- (1918–81), Egyptian statesman, President of Egypt 1970–81. By 1972 he had dismissed the Soviet military mission to Egypt, installed by President Nasser, and in 1974 he recovered the Suez Canal zone from Israel. For his efforts to negotiate peace in the Middle East he, together with Menachem Begin, Prime Minister of Israel, was awarded a Nobel Peace Prize (1978), but opposition within the Arab world led to his assassination in 1981.

Saddam Hussein see HUSSEIN².

sadden /'sæd(ə)n/ *v.tr.* & *intr.* make or become sad.

saddle /'sæd(ə)l/ *n.* & *v.* —*n.* **1** a seat of leather etc., usu. raised at the front and rear, fastened on a horse etc. for riding. **2** a seat for the rider of a bicycle etc. **3** a joint of meat consisting of the two loins. **4** a ridge rising to a summit at each end. **5** the part of a draught-horse's harness to which the shafts are attached. **6** a part of an animal's back resembling a saddle in shape or marking. **7** the rear part of a male fowl's back. **8** a support for a cable or wire on top of a suspension-bridge, pier, or telegraph-pole. **9** a fireclay bar for supporting ceramic ware in a kiln. —*v.tr.* **1** put a saddle on (a horse etc.). **2 a** (foll. by *with*) burden (a person) with a task, responsibility, etc. **b** (foll. by *on*, *upon*) impose (a burden) on a person. **3** (of a trainer) enter (a horse) for a race. □ **in the saddle 1** mounted. **2** in office or control. **saddle-bag 1** each of a pair of bags laid across a horse

etc. behind the saddle. **2** a bag attached behind the saddle of a bicycle or motor cycle. **saddle-bow** the arched front or rear of a saddle. **saddle-cloth** a cloth laid on a horse's back under the saddle. **saddle-horse** a horse for riding. **saddle-sore** chafed by riding on a saddle. **saddle stitch** a stitch of thread or a wire staple passed through the centre of a magazine or booklet. **saddle-tree 1** the frame of a saddle. **2** a tulip-tree (with saddle-shaped leaves). □□ **saddleless** *adj.* [OE *sadol, sadul* f. Gmc]

saddleback /'sæd(ə)lˌbæk/ *n.* **1** *Archit.* a tower-roof with two opposite gables. **2** a hill with a concave upper outline. **3** a black pig with a white stripe across the back. **4** any of various birds with a saddle-like marking esp. a New Zealand bird, *Philesturnus carunculatus.* □□ **saddlebacked** *adj.*

saddler /'sædlə(r)/ *n.* a maker of or dealer in saddles and other equipment for horses.

saddlery /'sædlərɪ/ *n.* (*pl.* **-ies**) **1** the saddles and other equipment of a saddler. **2** a saddler's business or premises.

Sadducee /'sædjʊˌsiː/ *n.* a member of a Jewish sect or party of the time of Christ that denied the resurrection of the dead, the existence of spirits, and the obligation of oral tradition, emphasizing acceptance of the written Law only. (Cf. PHARISEE, ESSENE.) □□ **Sadducean** /-'siːən/ *adj.* [OE *sadducæas* f. LL *Sadducaeus* f. Gk *Saddoukaios* f. Heb. *ṣᵊḏûḳî*, prob. = descendant of Zadok (2 Sam. 8: 17)]

Sade /saːd/, Donatien-Alphonse-François, Comte (known as Marquis) de (1740–1814), French novelist and pornographer. His career as a cavalry officer was destroyed by the criminal debauchery of his life. During his prolonged periods of imprisonment for sexual offences he wrote his licentious novels *Justine ou les Malheurs de la vertu* (1791), *La philosophie dans le boudoir* (1795), and *Nouvelle Justine* (1797). Their obsession with the minutiae of sexual pathology and their hedonistic nihilism have persuaded recent critics that they anticipate Nietzsche and Freud. The word 'sadism' owes its origin to his name, referring to the sexual perversions which he described.

sadhu /'saːduː/ *n.* (in India) a holy man, sage, or ascetic. [Skr., = holy man]

Sadi /'saːdɪ/ Muslih ibn abd Allah (late 13th c.), Persian poet, whose principal works were the collections of verse known as the 'Gulistan' or Rose Garden, and the 'Bustan' or Tree Garden.

sadism /'seɪdɪz(ə)m/ *n.* **1** a form of sexual perversion characterized by the enjoyment of inflicting pain or suffering on others (cf. MASOCHISM). **2** *colloq.* the enjoyment of cruelty to others. □□ **sadist** *n.* **sadistic** /sə'dɪstɪk/ *adj.* **sadistically** /sə'dɪstɪkəlɪ/ *adv.* [F *sadisme* f. Count or 'Marquis' de SADE]

Sadler's Wells Theatre /'sædləz welz/ a London theatre so called because in 1683 Thomas Sadler discovered a medicinal spring in his garden and established a pleasure-garden which became known as Sadler's Wells. A wooden music room built there in 1685 became a theatre in 1753, whose stone-built successor remained in use until 1906. In 1927 Lilian Baylis took over the derelict building, erecting a new theatre which opened in 1931. At first drama, ballet, and opera productions alternated between Sadler's Wells and the Old Vic, but from 1934 Sadler's Wells became the home only of opera and ballet. In 1946 the ballet company moved to Covent Garden, and in 1990 to Birmingham, becoming known as the Birmingham Royal Ballet; opera remained until 1968, when the company moved to the Coliseum as the English National Opera. The theatre has since housed visiting companies.

sado-masochism /ˌseɪdəʊ'mæsəˌkɪz(ə)m/ *n.* the combination of sadism and masochism in one person. □□ **sado-masochist** *n.* **sado-masochistic** /-'kɪstɪk/ *adj.*

s.a.e. *abbr.* stamped addressed envelope.

safari /sə'faːrɪ/ *n.* (*pl.* **safaris**) **1** a hunting or scientific expedition, esp. in E. Africa (*go on safari*). **2** a sightseeing trip to see African animals in their natural habitat. □ **safari park** an enclosed area where lions etc. are kept in relatively open spaces for public viewing from vehicles driven through. **safari suit** a lightweight suit usu. with short sleeves and four pleated pockets in the jacket. [Swahili f. Arab. *safara* to travel]

safe /seɪf/ *adj.* & *n.* —*adj.* **1 a** free of danger or injury. **b** (often foll. by *from*) out of or not exposed to danger (*safe from their enemies*). **2** affording security or not involving danger or risk (*put it in a safe place*). **3** reliable, certain; that can be reckoned on (*a safe catch; a safe method; is safe to win*). **4** prevented from escaping or doing harm (*have got him safe*). **5** (also **safe and sound**) uninjured; with no harm done. **6** cautious and unenterprising; consistently moderate. —*n.* **1** a strong lockable cabinet etc. for valuables. **2** = *meat safe.* □ **on the safe side** with a margin of security against risks. **safe bet** a bet that is certain to succeed. **safe-breaker** (or **-blower** or **-cracker**) a person who breaks open and robs safes. **safe conduct 1** a privilege of immunity from arrest or harm, esp. on a particular occasion. **2** a document securing this. **safe deposit** a building containing strongrooms and safes let separately. **safe house** a place of refuge or rendezvous for spies etc. **safe keeping** preservation in a safe place. **safe light** *Photog.* a filtered light for use in a darkroom. **safe period** the time during and near the menstrual period when conception is least likely. **safe seat** a seat in Parliament etc. that is usually won with a large margin by a particular party. **safe sex** sexual activity in which precautions are taken to reduce the risk of spreading sexually transmitted diseases, esp. Aids. □□ **safely** *adv.* **safeness** *n.* [ME f. AF *saf*, OF *sauf* f. L *salvus* uninjured: (n.) orig. *save* f. SAVE[1]]

safeguard /ˈseɪfgɑːd/ *n. & v.* —*n.* **1** a proviso, stipulation, quality, or circumstance, that tends to prevent something undesirable. **2** a safe conduct. —*v.tr.* guard or protect (rights etc.) by a precaution or stipulation. [ME f. AF *salve garde*, OF *sauve garde* (as SAFE, GUARD)]

safety /ˈseɪftɪ/ *n.* (*pl.* **-ies**) **1** the condition of being safe; freedom from danger or risks. **2** (*attrib.*) **a** designating any of various devices for preventing injury from machinery (*safety bar; safety lock*). **b** designating items of protective clothing (*safety helmet*). □ **safety-belt** = *seat-belt.* **2** a belt or strap securing a person to prevent injury. **safety-catch** a contrivance for locking a gun-trigger or preventing the accidental operation of machinery. **safety curtain** a fireproof curtain that can be lowered to cut off the auditorium in a theatre from the stage. **safety factor** (or **factor of safety**) **1** the ratio of a material's strength to an expected strain. **2** a margin of security against risks. **safety film** a cinematographic film on a slow-burning or non-flammable base. **safety first** a motto advising caution. **safety fuse 1** a fuse (see FUSE[2]) containing a slow-burning composition for firing detonators from a distance. **2** *Electr.* a protective fuse (see FUSE[1]). **safety glass** glass that will not splinter when broken. **safety harness** a system of belts or restraints to hold a person to prevent falling or injury. **safety lamp** a miner's lamp so protected as not to ignite firedamp. **safety match** a match igniting only on a specially prepared surface. **safety net** a net placed to catch an acrobat etc. in case of a fall. **safety pin** see separate entry. **safety razor** a razor with a guard to reduce the risk of cutting the skin. **safety-valve 1** (in a steam boiler) a valve opening automatically to relieve excessive pressure. **2** a means of giving harmless vent to excitement etc. **safety zone** *US* an area of a road marked off for pedestrians etc. to wait safely. [ME *sauvete* f. OF *sauveté* f. med.L *salvitas -tatis* f. L *salvus* (as SAFE)]

safety pin *n.* a pin with a point that is bent back to the head and can be held in a guard so that the user may not be pricked nor the pin come out unintentionally. Fasteners made on the same principle, consisting of a single length of metal wire coiled on itself at its middle point so as to form a spring, are known from the Bronze Age (13th c. BC) and seem to have been a European invention. The modern type (with a clasp) was re-invented and patented in the US by Walter Ireland Hunt in 1849.

safflower /ˈsæflaʊə(r)/ *n.* **1 a** a thistle-like plant, *Carthamus tinctorius*, yielding a red dye. **b** its dried petals. **2** a dye made from these, used in rouge etc. [Du. *saffloer* or G *Safflor* f. OF *saffleur* f. obs. It. *saffiore*, of unkn. orig.]

saffron /ˈsæfrən/ *n. & adj.* —*n.* **1** an orange flavouring and food colouring made from the dried stigmas of the crocus, *Crocus sativus*. **2** the colour of this. **3** = *meadow saffron.* —*adj.* saffron-coloured. □□ **saffrony** *adj.* [ME f. OF *safran* f. Arab. *za'farān*]

safranine /ˈsæfrəniːn/ *n.* (also **safranin** /-nɪn/) any of a large group of mainly red dyes used in biological staining etc. [F *safranine* (as SAFFRON): orig. of dye from saffron]

sag /sæg/ *v. & n.* —*v.intr.* (**sagged, sagging**) **1** sink or subside under weight or pressure, esp. unevenly. **2** have a downward bulge or curve in the middle. **3** fall in price. **4** (of a ship) drift from its course, esp. to leeward. —*n.* **1 a** the amount that a rope etc. sags. **b** the distance from the middle of its curve to a straight line between its supports. **2** a sinking condition; subsidence. **3** a fall in price. **4** *Naut.* a tendency to leeward. □□ **saggy** *adj.* [ME f. MLG *sacken*, Du. *zakken* subside]

saga /ˈsɑːgə/ *n.* **1** a long story of heroic achievement, esp. a medieval Icelandic or Norwegian prose narrative. **2** a series of connected books giving the history of a family etc. **3** a long involved story. [ON, = narrative, rel. to SAW[3]]

sagacious /səˈgeɪʃ(ə)s/ *adj.* **1** mentally penetrating; gifted with discernment; having practical wisdom. **2** acute-minded, shrewd. **3** (of a saying, plan, etc.) showing wisdom. **4** (of an animal) exceptionally intelligent; seeming to reason or deliberate. □□ **sagaciously** *adv.* **sagacity** /səˈgæsɪtɪ/ *n.* [L *sagax sagacis*]

sagamore /ˈsægəmɔː(r)/ *n.* = SACHEM 1. [Penobscot *sagamo*]

sage[1] /seɪdʒ/ *n.* **1** an aromatic herb, *Salvia officinalis*, with dull greyish-green leaves. **2** its leaves used in cookery. □ **sage and onion** (or **onions**) a stuffing used with poultry, pork, etc. **sage Derby** (or **cheese**) a cheese made with an infusion of sage which flavours and mottles it. **sage-green** the colour of sage-leaves. **sage tea** a medicinal infusion of sage-leaves. □□ **sagy** *adj.* [ME f. OF *sauge* f. L *salvia* healing plant f. *salvus* safe]

sage[2] /seɪdʒ/ *n. & adj.* —*n.* **1** often *iron.* a profoundly wise man. **2** any of the ancients traditionally regarded as the wisest of their time. —*adj.* **1** profoundly wise, esp. from experience. **2** of or indicating profound wisdom. **3** often *iron.* wise-looking; solemn-faced. □□ **sagely** *adv.* **sageness** *n.* **sageship** *n.* [ME f. OF ult. f. L *sapere* be wise]

sagebrush /ˈseɪdʒbrʌʃ/ *n.* **1** a growth of shrubby aromatic plants of the genus *Artemisia*, esp. *A. tridentata*, found in some semi-arid regions of western N. America. **2** this plant.

saggar /ˈsægə(r)/ *n.* (also **sagger**) a protective fireclay box enclosing ceramic ware while it is being fired. [prob. contr. of SAFEGUARD]

sagittal /ˈsædʒɪt(ə)l/ *adj. Anat.* **1** of or relating to the suture between the parietal bones of the skull. **2** in the same plane as this, or in a parallel plane. [F f. med.L *sagittalis* f. *sagitta* arrow]

Sagittarius /ˌsædʒɪˈteərɪəs/ **1** a constellation, traditionally regarded as contained in the figure of an archer. **2** the ninth sign of the zodiac (the Archer), which the sun enters about 22 Nov. —*n.* a person born when the sun is in this sign. □□ **Sagittarian** *adj. & n.* [ME f. L, = archer, f. *sagitta* arrow]

sagittate /ˈsædʒɪteɪt/ *adj. Bot. & Zool.* shaped like an arrowhead.

sago /ˈseɪgəʊ/ *n.* (*pl.* **-os**) **1** a kind of starch, made from the powdered pith of the sago palm and used in puddings etc. **2** (in full **sago palm**) any of several tropical palms and cycads, esp. *Cycas circinalis* and *Metroxylon sagu*, from which sago is made. [Malay *sāgū* (orig. through Port.)]

saguaro /sæˈgwɑːrəʊ/ *n.* (also **sahuaro** /sæˈwɑːrəʊ/) (*pl.* **-os**) a giant cactus, *Carnegiea gigantea*, of the SW United States and Mexico. [Mex. Sp.]

Saguia el Hamra /səˈgiːə el ˈhæmrə/ **1** a river in the north of Western Sahara. **2** the region through which it flows.

Sahara /səˈhɑːrə/ a great desert of North Africa, the largest in the world, covering an area of about 9,065,000 sq. km (3,500,000 square miles) from the Atlantic to the Red Sea. In recent years it has been increasing its southerly extent. □ **Western Sahara** see separate entry. [Arab., = desert]

Sahel /səˈhel/ the belt of dry savannah south of the Sahara in West Africa, comprising parts of Senegal, Mauritania, Mali, Niger, and Chad. □□ **Sahelian** /səˈhiːlɪən/ *adj.*

sahib /sɑːb, ˈsɑːhɪb/ *n.* **1** *hist.* (in India) a form of address, often placed after the name, to European men. **2** *colloq.* a gentleman (*pukka sahib*). [Urdu f. Arab. *ṣāḥib* friend, lord]

said past and past part. of SAY[1].

Saida see SIDON.

saiga /ˈsaɪgə, ˈseɪ-/ n. an antelope, *Saiga tatarica*, of the Asian steppes. [Russ.]

Saigon /saɪˈgɒn/ the former name of Ho Chi Minh City.

sail /seɪl/ n. & v. —n. **1** a piece of material (orig. canvas, now usu. nylon etc.) extended on rigging to catch the wind and propel a boat or ship. **2** a ship's sails collectively. **3 a** a voyage or excursion in a sailing-ship. **b** a voyage of specified duration. **4** a ship, esp. as discerned from its sails. **5** (*collect.*) ships in a squadron or company (*a fleet of twenty sail*). **6** (in *pl.*) *Naut.* **a** *sl.* a maker or repairer of sails. **b** *hist.* a chief petty officer in charge of rigging. **7** a wind-catching apparatus, usu. a set of boards, attached to the arm of a windmill. **8 a** the dorsal fin of a sailfish. **b** the tentacle of a nautilus. **c** the float of a Portuguese man-of-war. —v. **1** *intr.* travel on water by the use of sails or engine-power. **2** *tr.* **a** navigate (a ship etc.). **b** travel on (a sea). **3** *tr.* set (a toy boat) afloat. **4** *intr.* glide or move smoothly or in a stately manner. **5** *intr.* (often foll. by *through*) *colloq.* succeed easily (*sailed through the exams*). □ **sail-arm** the arm of a windmill. **sail close to** (or **near**) **the wind 1** sail as nearly against the wind as possible. **2** come close to indecency or dishonesty; risk over-stepping the mark. **sail-fluke** = MEGRIM². **sailing-boat** (or **-ship** or **-vessel**) a vessel driven by sails. **sailing-master** an officer navigating a ship, esp. *Brit.* a yacht. **sailing orders** instructions to a captain regarding departure, destination, etc. **sail into** *colloq.* attack physically or verbally with force. **take in sail 1** furl the sail or sails of a vessel. **2** moderate one's ambitions. **under sail** with sails set. □□ **sailable** adj. **sailed** adj. (also in *comb.*). **sailless** adj. [OE *segel* f. Gmc]

sailboard /ˈseɪlbɔːd/ n. a board with a mast and sail, used in windsurfing. □□ **sailboarder** n. **sailboarding** n.

sailboat /ˈseɪlbəʊt/ n. US a boat driven by sails.

sailcloth /ˈseɪlklɒθ/ n. **1** canvas for sails. **2** a canvas-like dress material.

sailer /ˈseɪlə(r)/ n. a ship of specified sailing-power (*a good sailer*).

sailfish /ˈseɪlfɪʃ/ n. **1** any fish of the genus *Istiophorus*, with a large dorsal fin. **2** a basking shark.

sailor /ˈseɪlə(r)/ n. **1** a seaman or mariner, esp. one below the rank of officer. **2** a person considered as liable or not liable to seasickness (*a good sailor*). □ **sailor hat 1** a straw hat with a straight narrow brim and flat top. **2** a hat with a turned-up brim in imitation of a sailor's, worn by women and children. □□ **sailoring** n. **sailorless** adj. **sailorly** adj. [var. of SAILER]

sailplane /ˈseɪlpleɪn/ n. a glider designed for sustained flight.

Saimaa Canal /ˈsaɪmɑː/ a waterway linking Lake Saimaa in SW Finland with the Gulf of Finland.

sainfoin /ˈseɪnfɔɪn, ˈsæn-/ n. a leguminous plant, *Onobrychis viciifolia*, grown for fodder and having pink flowers. [obs. F *saintfoin* f. mod.L *sanum foenum* wholesome hay (because of its medicinal properties)]

Sainsbury /ˈseɪnzbəri/, John James (1844–1928), English founder of the grocery and provision firm that bears his name.

saint /seɪnt, before a name usu. sənt/ n. & v. —n. (*abbr.* **St** or **S**; *pl.* **Sts** or **SS**) **1** a holy person, one declared (in the Roman Catholic or Orthodox Church) worthy of veneration, whose intercession may be publicly sought. (See below, and under names of individual saints.) **2** (**Saint** or **St**) the title of such a person or of an archangel, hence used in the name of a church etc. (*St Paul's*) or in the name of a church not named after a saint (*St Saviour's, St Cross*), or (often with the loss of the apostrophe) in the name of a town etc. (*St Andrews; St Albans*). **3** a very virtuous person; a person of great real or affected holiness (*would try the patience of a saint*). **4** a member of the company of heaven (*with all the angels and saints*). **5** (*Bibl.*, *archaic*, and used by Puritans, Mormons, etc.) one of God's chosen people; a member of the Christian Church or one's own branch of it. —v.tr. **1** canonize; admit to the calendar of saints. **2** call or regard as a saint. **3** (as **sainted** adj.) sacred; of a saintly life; worthy to be regarded as a saint. □ **my sainted aunt** see AUNT. **saint's day** a Church festival in memory of a saint. □□ **saintdom** n. **sainthood** n. **saintlike** adj. **saintling** n. **saintship** n. [ME f. OF *seint, saint* f. L *sanctus* holy, past part. of *sancire* consecrate]

The original ideal of the saint (in sense 1) in Christianity was the martyr. The cessation of persecution in the 4th c. led to the transformation of this ideal: the monk tended to take the place of the martyr. A saint in this sense is one who is close to God and can therefore intercede with God on behalf of other Christians, and one through whom divine power is therefore manifest. A cult of the saints, focused on their physical remains, has early attestation (e.g. Polycarp, 2nd c.), and developed rapidly from the 4th c. onwards. Procedures for the approval of such veneration (called canonization) were gradually formalized, being eventually vested in the papacy in the West and episcopal synods in the East: miracles and a life of heroic sanctity are the criteria for canonization. At the Reformation the cult of the saints was attacked as blurring the unique status of Christ and as the occasion of deplorable religious commercialization. The persecution of Christians in some countries in the 20th c. has to an extent restored the primitive ideal of the saint as martyr.

St Andrews /ˈændruːz/ a town in east Scotland, on the coast of Fife; pop. (1981) 11,350. Its university, founded in 1411, is the oldest in Scotland. St Andrews Royal and Ancient Golf Club is the ruling authority on the game of golf.

St Andrew's cross /ˈændruːz/ n. an X-shaped cross.

St Anthony cross /ˈæntəni/ n. (also **St Anthony's cross** /ˈæntənɪz/) a T-shaped cross.

St Anthony's fire /ˈæntənɪz/ n. erysipelas or ergotism.

St Bernard /ˈbɜːnəd/ n. (in full **St Bernard dog**) **1** a very large dog of a breed orig. kept to rescue travellers by the monks of the Hospice on the Great St Bernard pass in the Alps. (See BERNARD³.) **2** this breed.

St Christopher and Nevis see ST KITTS AND NEVIS.

St Croix /krɔɪ/ an island in the West Indies, the largest of the US Virgin Islands; pop. (1980) 49,000; chief town, Christiansted (formerly the capital of the Danish West Indies).

Saint-Denis /sædəˈniː/ the capital of the island of Réunion in the Indian Ocean; pop. (1982) 109,000.

Sainte-Beuve /sæˈtbɜːv/, Charles-Augustin (1804–69), French critic, who studied medicine before turning to literature. His modest creative output included volumes of verse, a novel *Volupté* (1834), and love poems addressed to Victor Hugo's wife Adèle with whom he fell in love. *Port-Royal* (1840–59) is a remarkable study of Jansenism, and *Causeries du lundi* (1851–62) a collection of weekly critical and biographical essays. He is one of the founders of modern criticism and these works illustrate the range of his reading and the breadth of his views. His approach to criticism was objective and re-creative rather than dogmatic, believing that formative influences on the authors' characters be considered before reaching any conclusions.

St Elmo's fire /ˈelməʊz/ n. a corposant.

St Emilion /sæt eˈmiːljən/ a small town situated to the north of the Dordogne River in SW France, that gives its name to a group of Bordeaux wines.

St-Étienne /ˌsæt etiˈen/ an industrial city in SE central France; pop. (1982) 206,700.

Saint Eustatius /juːˈsteɪʃəs/ a small island in the Caribbean Sea forming part of the Netherlands Antilles; pop. (1981) 1,428; chief town, Oranjestad.

St George's /ˈdʒɔːdʒɪz/ the capital of the island of Grenada in the West Indies; pop. (1981) 29,369.

St George's Channel a channel linking the Irish Sea with the Atlantic Ocean and separating Ireland from mainland Britain.

St George's cross /ˈdʒɔːdʒɪz/ n. a +-shaped cross, red on a white background.

St Gottard Pass /ˈgɒtɑːd/ a high Alpine pass linking Switzerland and Italy. Beneath it is a railway tunnel (constructed in 1872–80) and a road tunnel (opened in 1980). The route is believed to be named after a former chapel and hospice built on the summit, dedicated to St Godehard or Gotthard (d. 1038), bishop of Hildesheim in Germany.

St Helena /hɪˈliːnə/ a solitary island in the South Atlantic, a British dependency, famous as the place of Napoleon's exile

(1815–21) and death; pop. (est. 1988) 8,620; official language, English; capital, Jamestown. The island was discovered by the Portuguese in 1502 on 21 May, feast day of St Helena, mother of Constantine.

St Helens /ˈhelɪnz/, **Mount** an active volcano in the Cascade Range, SW Washington, US. A dramatic eruption in May 1980 killed 100 people and reduced the height of the mountain from 2,950 m (9,578 ft.) to 2,560 m (8,312 ft.).

St Helier /ˈhelɪə(r)/ a resort town and capital of the Channel Islands, on the island of Jersey; pop. (1981) 25,700.

St James's Palace /ˈdʒeɪmzɪz/ the old Tudor palace of the monarchs of England in London, built by Henry VIII on the site of an earlier leper hospital dedicated to St James the Less. The palace was the chief royal residence in London from 1697 (when Whitehall was burnt down) until Queen Victoria made Buckingham Palace the monarch's London residence. □ **Court of St James's** the official title of the British court, to which ambassadors from foreign countries are accredited.

St John /dʒɒn/ an island in the West Indies, one of the three principal islands of the US Virgin Islands; pop. (1980) 2,360.

St John Ambulance an organization providing first aid, nursing, ambulance, and welfare services. (See KNIGHTS HOSPITALLERS.)

St John's[1] /dʒɒnz/ the capital of Newfoundland; pop. (1986) 161,900. In 1901 the first transatlantic wireless message was received at St John's (see MARCONI) and from here the first transatlantic flight was made in 1919 (see BROWN[1]).

St John's[2] /dʒɒnz/ the capital of Antigua and Barbuda, situated on the island of Antigua; pop. (1982) 30,000.

St John's wort /dʒɒnz/ n. any yellow-flowered plant of the genus Hypericum, esp. H. androsaemum.

St Kilda /ˈkɪldə/ a group of five uninhabited islands of the Outer Hebrides group in the Atlantic Ocean, 64 km (40 miles) west of Lewis and Harris. They are the most westerly group of islands in Scotland. The last inhabitants left the island in 1930.

St Kitts and Nevis /kɪts, ˈniːvɪs/ a State in association with Britain (who has responsibility for defence and foreign affairs) consisting of two adjoining islands (St Kitts and Nevis) of the Leeward Islands in the West Indies; pop. (St Kitts) 35,000, (Nevis) 9,300; official language, English; capital, Basseterre (on St Kitts). St Kitts was discovered in 1493 by Columbus. He named it after his patron saint, St Christopher, but the name was shortened by settlers from England who arrived in 1623 and established the first successful English colony in the West Indies. Nevis, which consists almost entirely of a mountain, gained its name from the resemblance of the clouds around its peak to snow (Sp. las nieves the snows). A union between St Kitts, Nevis, and Anguilla was created in 1967, but Anguilla seceded within three months.

St Laurent /sæ lɔːˈrɑ̃/, Yves (1936–), French couturier, who was Dior's partner from 1954 and later succeeded him, opening his own establishment in 1962.

St Lawrence /ˈlɒrəns/ a river of North America flowing from Lake Ontario to the Atlantic Ocean. The St Lawrence Seaway, which includes a number of artificial sections to bypass rapids, was inaugurated by Canada and the US in 1959 and enables large vessels to navigate the entire length of the river.

St Leger /ˈledʒə(r)/ an annual horse-race for 3-year-old colts and fillies, held in September at Doncaster, S.Yorks, instituted by Lieutenant-General St Leger in 1776.

St Louis /ˈluːɪ/ a city and port that is a major transportation centre on the Mississippi River in eastern Missouri; pop. (1982) 437,350. Founded as a fur-trading post in 1763, the city was dedicated to Louis XV of France by Pierre Laclede who named it after his 'name' saint, Louis IX of France.

St Lucia /ˈluːʃə/ an island of the West Indies, one of the Windward Islands; pop. (1988) 146,600; official language, English; capital, Castries. Possession of the island was long disputed with France, and it did not pass finally into British hands until the early 19th c. Since 1979 it has been an independent State within the Commonwealth. □□ **St Lucian** adj. & n.

St Luke's summer /luːks/ n. Brit. see LUKE.

saintly /ˈseɪntlɪ/ adj. (**saintlier**, **saintliest**) very holy or virtuous. □□ **saintliness** n.

St Mark's Cathedral /mɑːks/ the church in Venice, its cathedral church since 1807, built in the 9th c. to house the relics of St Mark brought from Alexandria, and rebuilt in the 11th c. It is lavishly decorated with mosaics (11th–13th c.) and sculptures.

Saint Martin /sæ mɑːˈtæ/ a small island in the Caribbean Sea, of which the southern section (Dutch Sint Maarten) forms part of the Netherlands Antilles and the larger northern section forms part of the French overseas department of Guadeloupe; pop. (1982); chief town, Philipsburg, situated in the south of the island.

St Martin's summer /ˈmɑːtɪnz/ n. Brit. see MARTIN.

St Moritz /sæ mɒˈriːts/ a resort and winter sports centre in SE Switzerland. The Winter Olympics of 1928 and 1948 were held here.

St Nazaire /sæ næˈzeə(r)/ a seaport and industrial town in NW France, at the mouth of the River Loire; pop. (1982) 68,970.

Saint Nicolas /ˈnɪkələs/ (Flemish **Sint Niklaas** /sɪnt ˈnɪklɑːs/) an industrial town in East Flanders, whose market square is the largest in Belgium; pop. (1988) 68,000.

St Paul /pɔːl/ the capital of Minnesota, on the Mississippi River; pop. (1980) 270,230.

saintpaulia /səntˈpɔːlɪə/ n. any plant of the genus Saintpaulia, esp. the African violet. [Baron W. von Saint Paul, Ger. soldier d. 1910, its discoverer]

St Paul's Cathedral /pɔːlz/ a cathedral on Ludgate Hill, London, built between 1675 and 1711 by Sir Christopher Wren to replace a medieval cathedral largely destroyed in the Great Fire.

St Peter's Basilica /ˈpiːtəz/ the Roman Catholic basilica in the Vatican City, Rome, the largest church in Christendom. The present 16th-c. building replaced a much older basilican structure, erected by Constantine on the supposed site of St Peter's crucifixion. A succession of architects (Bramante, Raphael, Peruzzi, Sangallo) in turn made drastic changes in the design; the dome closely follows a design of Michelangelo. The building was consecrated in 1626.

St Petersburg /ˈpiːtəzbɜːg/ see LENINGRAD.

St Pierre and Miquelon /sæ pɪˈeɔr, ˈmiːkəˌlɔ̃/ a group of eight small islands in the north Atlantic, south of Newfoundland, which form the last remnants of the once extensive French possessions in North America; pop. (1988) 6,400. Since 1985 the islands have been a Territorial Collectivity of France. The chief settlement is St Pierre.

Saint-Saëns /sæˈsɑ̃/, Camille (1835–1921), French composer, pianist, and organist. Born in Paris, he became an important figure in musical life there. He devoted much time and energy to the composition of opera (notably Samson et Dalila, 1877) and oratorio, but is best known today for his Third Symphony (with organ, 1886), the symphonic poem Danse macabre (1874), and the light, witty Carnaval des animaux (1886).

Saint-Simon[1] /ˌsæsiˈmɔ̃/, Claude-Henri de Rouvroy, Comte de (1760–1825), French social scientist. An aristocrat (his father was a cousin of the Duc de Saint-Simon), reduced to poverty by profligacy, Saint-Simon devoted the last twenty years of his life to writing, promulgating a new theory of social organization in reaction to the chaos engendered by the French Revolution, arguing that society ought to be organized in an industrial order, controlled by leaders of industry and given spiritual direction by scientists. Such works as L'Industrie (1816), Du système industriel (1821), and Nouveau Christianisme (1825) were of great influence on later French social thinkers, earning Saint-Simon a reputation as the founder of French socialism.

Saint-Simon[2] /ˌsæsiːˈmɔ̃/, Louis de Rouvroy, Duc de (1675–1755), French writer. His Mémoires describe people and events of the latter years of Louis XIV's reign in graphic detail, although they are not the work of a critical and accurate historian.

St Sophia /səˈfiːə, -ˈfaɪə/ a church at Constantinople (now Istanbul), dedicated to the 'Holy Wisdom' (i.e. the Person of Christ), built by order of Justinian (532–7) and inaugurated in 537. The key monument of Byzantine architecture, its chief feature is the enormous dome, supported by piers, arches, and pendentives and pierced by 40 windows, which crowns the basilica. In 1453, on the day of the Turkish invasion, orders were given for its conversion into a mosque; the mosaics which adorned its interior were covered and partly destroyed, and minarets were added. It was used as a mosque until 1935, when Atatürk converted it into a museum.

St Stephens /ˈstiːvənz/ the House of Commons, so called from the ancient chapel of St Stephen, Westminster, in which the House used to sit (1537–1834).

St Thomas /ˈtɒməs/ an island in the West Indies, the second-largest of the US Virgin Islands; pop. (1980) 44,200.

St Trinian's /ˈtrɪnɪənz/ the name of a girls' school invented by the cartoonist Ronald Searle (1920–) in 1941, whose pupils are characterized by hoydenish behaviour, ungainly appearance, and unattractive school uniform. (Searle's daughters attended St Trinnean's school in Edinburgh.)

St Tropez /sæ trəʊˈpeɪ/ a fishing port and resort on the Côte d'Azur in southern France; pop. (1985) 6,250.

St Vincent /ˈvɪns(ə)nt/ an island State in the Windward Islands in the West Indies, consisting of the island of St Vincent and some of the Grenadines; pop. (est. 1988) 107,400; official language, English; capital, Kingstown. The French, Dutch, and British all made attempts at settlements in the 18th c., and it finally fell to British possession early in the 19th c. The State obtained full independence with a limited form of membership of the Commonwealth in 1979. It is the world's chief producer of arrowroot.

St Vitus's dance /ˈvaɪtəsɪz/ n. = Sydenham's chorea (see CHOREA and St VITUS).

saith /seθ/ archaic 3rd sing. present of SAY[1].

saithe /seɪθ/ n. Sc. a codlike fish, Pollachius virens, with skin that soils fingers like wet coal. Also called COALFISH, COLEY, POLLACK. [ON seithr]

Sakai /saːˈkaɪ/ an industrial city of Japan, on the east coast of Osaka Bay, Honshu Island; pop. (1987) 808,000.

sake[1] /seɪk/ n. (esp. **for the sake of** or **for one's sake**) **1** out of consideration for; in the interest of; because of; owing to (for my own sake as well as yours). **2** in order to please, honour, get, or keep (for the sake of uniformity). □ **for Christ's** (or **God's** or **goodness'** or **Heaven's** or **Pete's** etc.) **sake** an expression of urgency, impatience, supplication, anger, etc. **for old times' sake** in memory of former times. [OE sacu contention, charge, fault, sake f. Gmc]

sake[2] /ˈsaːkɪ/ n. a Japanese alcoholic drink made from rice. [Jap.]

saker /ˈseɪkə(r)/ n. **1** a large falcon, Falco cherrug, used in hawking, esp. the larger female bird. **2** hist. an old form of cannon. [ME f. OF sacre (in both senses), f. Arab. ṣaḳr]

Sakhalin /ˌsaːxəˈliːn/ an island in the Sea of Okhotsk, separated by the Tatar Strait from the east coast of the Soviet Union. In 1875 it was ceded to Russia by Japan in exchange for the Kuril Islands; between 1905 and 1946 the island was again occupied by Japan.

Sakharov /ˈsæxəˌrɒf/, Andrei Dmitrievich (1921–89), Russian nuclear physicist, a man of immense intellectual achievement and moral courage. Having played a decisive role in developing the Soviet hydrogen bomb (1953), after 1958 he campaigned against nuclear proliferation and called for Soviet-American cooperation. He fought courageously for reform and human rights in the USSR at a time when such an approach was extremely dangerous, and in recognition of his efforts he was awarded the Nobel Peace Prize in 1975. His international repute as a scientist kept him out of jail, but in 1980 he was banished to Gorky and kept under police surveillance. Freedom came eventually with the new spirit of 'glasnost', and at his death he was honoured in his own country as well as in the West.

Saki /ˈsaːkɪ/ pseudonym of Hector Hugh Munro (1870–1916), a writer known principally for his short stories. He was killed in France in the First World War. His stories include the satiric, comic, macabre, and supernatural, and show a marked interest in the use of animals as agents of revenge upon mankind.

saki /ˈsaːkɪ/ n. (pl. **sakis**) any monkey of the genus Pithecia or Chiropotes, native to S. America, having coarse fur and a long non-prehensile tail. [F f. Tupi çahy]

Sakta /ˈʃaːktə/ n. a member of a Hindu sect worshipping the Sakti. [Skr. śākta relating to power or to the SAKTI]

Sakti /ˈʃæktɪ/ n. (also **sakti**) Hinduism **1** the power of the male god, usually Siva, personified as a goddess. **2** the goddess as supreme deity (Devi). □□ **Saktism** n. [Skr. śakti power, divine energy]

sal /saːl/ n. a N. Indian tree, Shorea robusta, yielding teaklike timber and dammar resin. [Hindi sāl]

salaam /səˈlaːm/ n. & v. —n. **1** the oriental salutation 'Peace'. **2** an Indian obeisance, with or without the salutation, consisting of a low bow of the head and body with the right palm on the forehead. **3** (in pl.) respectful compliments. —v. **1** tr. make a salaam to (a person). **2** intr. make a salaam. [Arab. salām]

salable var. of SALEABLE.

salacious /səˈleɪʃəs/ adj. **1** lustful; lecherous. **2** (of writings, pictures, talk, etc.) tending to cause sexual desire. □□ **salaciously** adv. **salaciousness** n. **salacity** /səˈlæsɪtɪ/ n. [L salax salacis f. salire leap]

salad /ˈsæləd/ n. **1** a cold dish of various mixtures of raw or cooked vegetables or herbs, usu. seasoned with oil, vinegar, etc. **2** a vegetable or herb suitable for eating raw. □ **salad cream** creamy salad-dressing. **salad days** a period of youthful inexperience. **salad-dressing** a mixture of oil, vinegar, etc., used with salad. [ME f. OF salade f. Prov. salada ult. f. L sal salt]

salade var. of SALLET.

Saladin /ˈsælədɪn/ (1137–93), sultan of Egypt, who successfully invaded the Holy Land and reconquered Jerusalem from the Crusaders before fighting off the Third Crusade, the leaders of which included Richard I. Saladin won a reputation not only for military skill but for honesty and chivalry, and was generally a match for his European opponents.

Salam /səˈlaːm/, Abdus (1926–), Pakistani physicist, noted for his work on interaction of elementary particles. In 1979 he received a Nobel Prize for physics, the first person from his country to win a Nobel Prize.

Salamanca /ˌsæləˈmæŋkə/ a city in western Spain, scene of a victory of the British under Wellington over the French in 1812, during the Peninsular War; pop. (1981) 153,980.

salamander /ˈsæləˌmændə(r)/ n. **1** Zool. any tailed newtlike amphibian of the order Urodela, esp. the genus Salamandra, once thought able to endure fire. **2** a mythical lizard-like creature credited with this property. **3** US = GOPHER[1] 1. **4** an elemental spirit living in fire. **5** a red-hot iron used for lighting pipes, gunpowder, etc. **6** a metal plate heated and placed over food to brown it. □□ **salamandrian** /-ˈmændrɪən/ adj. **salamandrine** /-ˈmændrɪn/ adj. **salamandroid** /-ˈmændrɔɪd/ adj. & n. (in sense 1). [ME f. OF salamandre f. L salamandra f. Gk salamandra]

salami /səˈlaːmɪ/ n. (pl. **salamis**) a highly-seasoned orig. Italian sausage often flavoured with garlic. [It., pl. of salame, f. LL salare (unrecorded) to salt]

Salamis /ˈsæləmɪs/ an island in the Saronic Gulf in Greece. In the straits between it and the western coast of Attica the Greek fleet crushingly defeated the Persian fleet of Xerxes in 480 BC.

sal ammoniac /ˌsæl əˈməʊnɪˌæk/ n. ammonium chloride, a white crystalline salt. [L sal ammoniacus 'salt of Ammon', said to have been made from camels' dung near the Roman temple of Ammon in N. Africa]

Salang Pass /ˈsaːlæŋ/ a high-altitude route across the Hindu Kush mountain range in Afghanistan. The Salang Pass and tunnel were built by the Soviet Union during the 1960s in an attempt to improve the supply route from the Soviet frontier to Kabul.

salariat /səˈleərɪət/ n. the salaried class. [F f. salaire (see SALARY), after prolétariat]

salary /ˈsælərɪ/ n. & v. —n. (pl. **-ies**) a fixed regular payment, usu. monthly or quarterly, made by an employer to an employee, esp. a professional or white-collar worker (cf. WAGE n. 1). —v.tr. (**-ies**, **-ied**) (usu. as **salaried** adj.) pay a salary to. [ME f. AF salarie, OF salaire f. L salarium orig. soldier's salt-money f. sal salt]

sale /seɪl/ n. **1** the exchange of a commodity for money etc.; an act or instance of selling. **2** the amount sold (*the sales were enormous*). **3** the rapid disposal of goods at reduced prices for a period esp. at the end of a season etc. **4 a** an event at which goods are sold. **b** a public auction. □ **on** (or **for**) **sale** offered for purchase. **sale of work** an event where goods made by parishioners etc. are sold for charity. **sale or return** an arrangement by which a purchaser takes a quantity of goods with the right of returning surplus goods without payment. **sale-ring** a circle of buyers at an auction. **sales clerk** US a salesman or saleswoman in a shop. **sales department** etc. the section of a firm concerned with selling as opposed to manufacturing or dispatching goods. **sales engineer** a salesperson with technical knowledge of the goods and their market. **sales resistance** the opposition or apathy of a prospective customer etc. to be overcome by salesmanship. **sales talk** persuasive talk to promote the sale of goods or the acceptance of an idea etc. **sales tax** a tax on sales or on the receipts from sales. [OE *sala* f. ON]

saleable /ˈseɪləb(ə)l/ adj. (also **salable**) fit to be sold; finding purchasers. □□ **saleability** /-ˈbɪlɪtɪ/ n.

Salem[1] /ˈseɪləm/ the capital of Oregon; pop. (1980) 58,220.

Salem[2] /ˈseɪləm/ a city and port in NE Massachusetts; pop. (1980) 38,300. It was the scene of a series of witchcraft trials in 1692, and was the birthplace of Nathaniel Hawthorne.

Salem[3] /ˈseɪləm/ an industrial city in Tamil Nadu in southern India; pop. (1981) 515,000.

salep /ˈsæləp/ n. a starchy preparation of the dried tubers of various orchids, used in cookery and formerly medicinally. [F f. Turk. *sālep* f. Arab. (ḳuṣa-'l-) *ta'lab* fox, fox's testicles]

saleratus /ˌsæləˈreɪtəs/ n. US an ingredient of baking powder consisting mainly of potassium or sodium bicarbonate. [mod.L *sal aeratus* aerated salt]

saleroom /ˈseɪlruːm, -rʊm/ n. esp. *Brit.* a room in which items are sold at auction.

salesgirl /ˈseɪlzɡɜːl/ n. a saleswoman.

Salesian /səˈliːʒ(ə)n/ n. & adj. —n. a member of an educational religious order within the RC Church, founded near Turin in 1859, named after St Francis de Sales (d. 1622), French bishop of Geneva. —adj. of or relating to this order.

saleslady /ˈseɪlzˌleɪdɪ/ n. (pl. **-ies**) a saleswoman.

salesman /ˈseɪlzmən/ n. (pl. **-men**; fem. **saleswoman**, pl. **-women**) **1** a person employed to sell goods in a shop, or as an agent between the producer and retailer. **2** US a commercial traveller.

salesmanship /ˈseɪlzmənʃɪp/ n. **1** skill in selling. **2** the techniques used in selling.

salesperson /ˈseɪlzˌpɜːs(ə)n/ n. a salesman or saleswoman (used as a neutral alternative).

salesroom /ˈseɪlzruːm, -rʊm/ n. US = SALEROOM.

Salian /ˈseɪlɪən/ adj. & n. —adj. of or relating to the Salii, a 4th-c. Frankish people living near the River IJssel, from which the Merovingians were descended. —n. a member of this people. [LL *Salii*]

Salic /ˈsælɪk, ˈseɪ-/ adj. = SALIAN. □ **Salic law** hist. **1** a Frankish law-book extant in Merovingian and Carolingian times. **2** a law excluding females from dynastic succession, especially an alleged fundamental law of French monarchy (based on a quotation, not referring to such succession, from the law-book). In the 14th c. Edward III's claim to the French throne, based on descent from his mother, a Capetian princess, was denied by the French on the authority of this law and brought on the Hundred Years War. [F *Salique* or med.L *Salicus* f. *Salii* (as SALIAN)]

salicet /ˈsælɪsɪt/ n. an organ stop like a salicional but one octave higher. [as SALICIONAL]

salicin /ˈsælɪsɪn/ n. (also **salicine** /-ˌsiːn/) a bitter crystalline glucoside with analgesic properties, obtained from poplar and willow bark. [F *salicine* f. L *salix -icis* willow]

salicional /səˈlɪʃ(ə)n(ə)l/ n. an organ stop with a soft reedy tone like that of a willow-pipe. [G f. L *salix* as SALICIN]

salicylic acid /ˌsælɪˈsɪlɪk/ n. a bitter chemical used as a fungicide and in the manufacture of aspirin and dyestuffs. □□

salicylate /səˈlɪsɪˌleɪt/ n. [*salicyl* its radical f. F *salicyle* (as SALICIN)]

salient /ˈseɪlɪənt/ adj. & n. —adj. **1** jutting out; prominent; conspicuous, most noticeable. **2** (of an angle, esp. in fortification) pointing outwards (opp. RE-ENTRANT). **3** *Heraldry* (of a lion etc.) standing on its hind legs with the forepaws raised. **4** *archaic* **a** leaping or dancing. **b** (of water etc.) jetting forth. —n. a salient angle or part of a work in fortification; an outward bulge in a line of military attack or defence. □ **salient point** archaic the initial stage, origin, or first beginning. □□ **salience** n. **saliency** n. **saliently** adv. [L *salire* leap]

salientian /ˌseɪlɪˈenʃ(ə)n/ adj. & n. = ANURAN. [mod.L *Salientia* (as SALIENT)]

Salieri /ˌsælɪˈeəri/, Antonio (1750–1825), Italian composer, who wrote over forty operas, four oratorios, much church music, and many vocal and instrumental pieces. He taught Beethoven, Schubert, and Liszt. Salieri was hostile to Mozart but there is no truth in the legend that he poisoned him.

saliferous /səˈlɪfərəs/ adj. *Geol.* (of rock etc.) containing much salt. [L *sal* salt + -FEROUS]

salina /səˈlaɪnə/ n. a salt lake. [Sp. f. med.L, = salt pit (as SALINE)]

saline /ˈseɪlaɪn/ adj. & n. —adj. **1** (of natural waters, springs, etc.) impregnated with or containing salt or salts. **2** (of food or drink etc.) tasting of salt. **3** of chemical salts. **4** of the nature of a salt. **5** (of medicine) containing a salt or salts of alkaline metals or magnesium. —n. **1** a salt lake, spring, marsh, etc. **2** a salt-pan or salt-works. **3** a saline substance, esp. a medicine. **4** a solution of salt in water. □□ **salinity** /səˈlɪnɪtɪ/ n. **salinization** /ˌsælɪnaɪˈzeɪʃ(ə)n/ n. **salinometer** /ˌsælɪˈnɒmɪtə(r)/ n. [ME f. L *sal* salt]

Salinger /ˈsælɪndʒə(r)/, Jerome David (1919–), American novelist and writer of short stories, best known for his novel of adolescence *The Catcher in the Rye* (1951). His other works include *Franny and Zooey* (1961).

Salisbury[1] /ˈsɔːlzbəri/ a town in Wiltshire, noted for its 13th-c. cathedral whose spire is the highest in England; pop. (1981) 37,830.

Salisbury[2] /ˈsɔːlzbəri/ the former name of Harare.

Salisbury[3] /ˈsɔːlzbəri/, Robert Arthur Talbot Gascoigne-Cecil, 3rd Marquess of (1830–1903), British Conservative statesman, Prime Minister 1885–6, 1886–92, and 1895–1902. In foreign affairs he supported the policies which resulted in the second Boer War (1899–1902).

saliva /səˈlaɪvə/ n. liquid secreted into the mouth by glands to provide moisture and facilitate chewing and swallowing. □ **saliva test** a scientific test requiring a saliva sample. □□ **salivary** /səˈlaɪ-, ˈsælɪ-/ adj. [ME f. L]

salivate /ˈsælɪˌveɪt/ v. **1** intr. secrete or discharge saliva esp. in excess or in greedy anticipation. **2** tr. produce an unusual secretion of saliva in (a person) usu. with mercury. □□ **salivation** /ˌsælɪˈveɪʃ(ə)n/ n. [L *salivare* (as SALIVA)]

Salk vaccine /sɔːlk/ n. the first vaccine developed against poliomyelitis, named after J. E. Salk (1914–), US virologist, who developed the vaccine in 1954.]

sallee /ˈsæliː/ n. (also **sally**) (pl. **-ees** or **-ies**) *Austral.* any of several eucalypts and acacias resembling the willow. [Aboriginal]

sallet /ˈsælɪt/ n. (also **salade** /səˈlɑːd/) hist. a light helmet with an outward-curving rear part. [F *salade* ult. f. L *caelare* engrave f. *caelum* chisel]

sallow[1] /ˈsæləʊ/ adj. & v. —adj. (**sallower**, **sallowest**) (of the skin or complexion, or of a person) of a sickly yellow or pale brown. —v.tr. & intr. make or become sallow. □□ **sallowish** adj. **sallowness** n. [OE *salo* dusky f. Gmc]

sallow[2] /ˈsæləʊ/ n. **1** a willow-tree, esp. one of a low-growing or shrubby kind. **2** the wood or a shoot of this. □□ **sallowy** adj. [OE *salh salg-* f. Gmc, rel. to OHG *salaha*, ON *selja*, L *salix*]

Sallust /ˈsæləst/ (Gaius Sallustius Crispus, 86–35 BC) Roman historian, who retired to write after an unsuccessful political career. He is a moralizing historian, with a pessimistic view of the political and moral decline of Rome, a process which he dates from the fall of Carthage.

Sally /ˈsælɪ/ n. (pl. **-ies**) colloq. **1** (usu. prec. by the) the Salvation Army. **2** a member of this. [abbr.]

sally¹ /ˈsælɪ/ n. & v. —n. (pl. **-ies**) **1** a sudden charge from a fortification upon its besiegers; a sortie. **2** a going forth; an excursion. **3** a witticism; a piece of banter; a lively remark esp. by way of attack upon a person or thing or of a diversion in argument. **4** a sudden start into activity; an outburst. **5** archaic an escapade. —v.intr. (**-ies**, **-ied**) **1** (usu. foll. by out, forth) go for a walk, set out on a journey etc. **2** (usu. foll. by out) make a military sally. **3** archaic issue or come out suddenly. □ **sally-port** an opening in a fortification for making a sally from. [F saillie fem. past part. of saillir issue f. OF salir f. L salire leap]

sally² /ˈsælɪ/ n. (pl. **-ies**) **1** the part of a bell-rope prepared with inwoven wool for holding. **2 a** the first movement of a bell when set for ringing. **b** the bell's position when set. □ **sally-hole** the hole through which the bell-rope passes. [perh. f. SALLY¹ in sense 'leaping motion']

sally³ var. of SALLEE.

Sally Lunn /ˌsælɪ ˈlʌn/ n. Brit. a sweet light teacake, properly served hot. [perh. f. the name of a woman selling them at Bath c.1800]

salmagundi /ˌsælməˈɡʌndɪ/ n. (pl. **salmagundis**) **1** a dish of chopped meat, anchovies, eggs, onions, etc., and seasoning. **2** a general mixture; a miscellaneous collection of articles, subjects, qualities, etc. [F salmigondis of unkn. orig.]

salmanazar /ˌsælməˈneɪzə(r)/ n. a wine bottle of about 12 times the standard size. [Shalmaneser king of Assyria (2 Kings 17–18)]

salmi /ˈsælmɪ/ n. (pl. **salmis**) a ragout or casserole esp. of partly roasted game-birds. [F, abbr. formed as SALMAGUNDI]

salmon /ˈsæmən/ n. & adj. —n. (pl. same or (esp. of types) **salmons**) **1** any anadromous fish of the family Salmonidae, esp. of the genus Salmo, much prized for its (often smoked) pink flesh. **2** Austral. & NZ the barramundi or a similar fish. —adj. salmon-pink. □ **salmon-ladder** (or **-leap**) a series of steps or other arrangement incorporated in a dam to allow salmon to pass upstream. **salmon-pink** the colour of salmon flesh. **salmon trout** a large silver-coloured trout, Salmo trutta. □□ **salmonoid** adj. & n. (in sense 1). **salmony** adj. [ME f. AF sa(u)-moun, OF saumon f. L salmo -onis]

salmonella /ˌsælməˈnelə/ n. (pl. **salmonellae** /-liː/) **1** any bacterium of the genus Salmonella, esp. any of various serotypes causing food poisoning. **2** food poisoning caused by infection with salmonellae. □□ **salmonellosis** /-ˈləʊsɪs/ n. [mod.L f. D. E. Salmon, Amer. veterinary surgeon d. 1914]

Salome /səˈləʊmɪ/ the name given by Josephus to the daughter of Herodias, who is mentioned but not named in the Gospels. She danced before Herod Antipas, and St John the Baptist was beheaded at her request.

Salon /ˈsælɔ̃/ the name given to the exhibitions of the French Royal Academy of Painting and Sculpture founded in the 17th c. by Colbert and Lebrun. The name derived from the fact that exhibitions were held in the Salon d'Apollon in the Louvre. Even after its reorganization in 1881 it retained its traditional hostility to new and creative artists.

salon /ˈsælɒn, -lɔ̃/ n. **1** the reception room of a large, esp. French or continental, house. **2** a room or establishment where a hairdresser, beautician, etc., conducts trade. **3** hist. a meeting of eminent people in the reception room of a (esp. Parisian) lady of fashion. □ **salon music** light music for the drawing-room etc. [F: see SALOON]

Salonica /səˈlɒnɪkə/ (Greek **Thessaloniki** /ˌθesələˈniːkɪ/, the ancient Thessalonica) a seaport in NE Greece, the capital of Macedonia and second-largest city of Greece; pop. (1981) 706,100. It was the scene of a campaign in the First World War by the French and British in support of Serbia, during which they occupied Salonica (Oct. 1915).

saloon /səˈluːn/ n. **1 a** a large room or hall, esp. in a hotel or public building. **b** a public room or gallery for a specified purpose (billiard-saloon; shooting-saloon). **2** (in full **saloon car**) a motor car with a closed body and no partition behind the driver. **3** a public room on a ship. **4** US a drinking-bar. **5** (in full **saloon bar**) Brit. the more comfortable bar in a public house. **6** (in full

saloon car) Brit. a luxurious railway carriage serving as a lounge etc. □ **saloon deck** a deck for passengers using the saloon. **saloon-keeper** US a publican or bartender. **saloon pistol** (or **rifle**) a pistol or rifle adapted for short-range practice in a shooting-saloon. [F salon f. It. salone augment. of sala hall]

Salopian /səˈləʊpɪən/ n. & adj. —n. a native or inhabitant of Shropshire. —adj. of or relating to Shropshire. [AF Salopesberia f. ME f. OE Scrobbesbyrig Shrewsbury]

salpiglossis /ˌsælpɪˈɡlɒsɪs/ n. any solanaceous plant of the genus Salpiglossis, cultivated for its funnel-shaped flowers. [mod.L, irreg. f. Gk salpigx trumpet + glōssa tongue]

salping- /ˈsælpɪŋ/ comb. form Med. denoting the Fallopian tubes. [Gk salpigx salpiggos, lit. 'trumpet']

salpingectomy /ˌsælpɪŋˈdʒektəmɪ/ n. (pl. **-ies**) Med. the surgical removal of the Fallopian tubes.

salpingitis /ˌsælpɪŋˈdʒaɪtɪs/ n. Med. inflammation of the Fallopian tubes.

salsa /ˈsælsə/ n. **1** a kind of dance music of Latin American origin, incorporating jazz and rock elements. **2** a dance performed to this music. [Sp. (as SAUCE)]

salsify /ˈsælsɪfɪ, -ˌfaɪ/ n. (pl. **-ies**) **1** a European plant, Tragopogon porrifolius, with long cylindrical fleshy roots. **2** this root used as a vegetable. □ **black salsify** scorzonera. [F salsifis f. obs. It. salsefica, of unkn. orig.]

SALT /sɔːlt, sɒlt/ abbr. Strategic Arms Limitation Talks (or Treaty), organized from 1968 onwards and involving esp. the US and the Soviet Union, aimed at the limitation or reduction of nuclear armaments.

salt /sɔːlt, sɒlt/ n., adj., & v. —n. **1** (also **common salt**) sodium chloride, the substance that gives sea water its characteristic taste, got in crystalline form by mining from strata consisting of it or by the evaporation of sea water, and used for seasoning or preserving food, or for other purposes. **2** a chemical compound formed from the reaction of an acid with a base, with all or part of the hydrogen of the acid replaced by a metal or metal-like radical. **3** sting; piquancy; pungency; wit (added salt to the conversation). **4** (in sing. or pl.) **a** a substance resembling salt in taste, form, etc. (bath salts; Epsom salts; smelling-salts). **b** (esp. in pl.) this type of substance used as a laxative. **5** a marsh, esp. one flooded by the tide, often used as a pasture or for collecting water for salt-making. **6** (also **old salt**) an experienced sailor. **7** (in pl.) an exceptional rush of sea water up river. —adj. **1** impregnated with, containing, tasting of, or tasting of salt; cured or preserved or seasoned with salt. **2** (of a plant) growing in the sea or in salt marshes. **3** (of tears etc.) bitter. **4** (of wit) pungent. —v.tr. **1** cure or preserve with salt or brine. **2** season with salt. **3** make (a narrative etc.) piquant. **4** sprinkle (the ground etc.) with salt esp. in order to melt snow etc. **5** treat with a solution of salt or mixture of salts. **6** (as **salted** adj.) (of a horse or person) hardened or proof against diseases etc. caused by the climate or by special conditions. □ **eat salt with** be a guest of. **in salt** sprinkled with salt or immersed in brine as a preservative. **not made of salt** not disconcerted by wet weather. **put salt on the tail of** capture (with ref. to jocular directions given to children for catching a bird). **salt an account** sl. set an extremely high or low price for articles. **salt-and-pepper** (of materials etc. and esp. of hair) with light and dark colours mixed together. **salt away** (or **down**) sl. put money etc. by. **salt the books** sl. show receipts as larger than they really have been. **salt-cat** a mass of salt mixed with gravel, urine, etc., to attract pigeons and keep them at home. **salt dome** a mass of salt forced up into sedimentary rocks. **salt fish** W.Ind. preserved cod. **salt-glaze** a hard stoneware glaze produced by throwing salt into a hot kiln containing the ware. **salt-grass** US grass growing in salt meadows or in alkaline regions. **salt horse** Naut. sl. **1** salt beef. **2** a naval officer with general duties. **salt lake** a lake of salt water. **salt-lick 1** a place where animals go to lick salt from the ground. **2** this salt. **salt-marsh** = sense 5 of n. **salt meadow** a meadow subject to flooding with salt water. **salt a mine** sl. introduce extraneous ore, material, etc., to make the source seem rich. **the salt of the earth** a person or people of great worthiness, reliability, honesty, etc.; those whose qualities keep society wholesome (Matt. 5: 13). **salt-pan** a vessel, or a depression near the sea, used for getting salt by evaporation. **salt-shaker** *US* a container of salt for sprinkling on food. **salt-spoon** a small spoon usu. with a short handle and a roundish deep bowl for taking table salt. **salt water 1** sea water. **2** *sl.* tears. **salt-water** *adj.* of or living in the sea. **salt-well** a bored well yielding brine. **salt-works** a place where salt is produced. **take with a pinch (or grain) of salt** regard as exaggerated; be incredulous about; believe only part of. **worth one's salt** efficient, capable. □□ **saltish** *adj.* **saltless** *adj.* **saltly** *adv.* **saltness** *n.* [OE *s(e)alt s(e)altan*, OS, ON, Goth. *salt*, OHG *salz* f. Gmc]

saltarello /ˌsæltəˈreləʊ/ *n.* (*pl.* **-os** or **saltarelli** /-lɪ/) an Italian and Spanish dance for one couple, with sudden skips. [It. *salterello*, Sp. *saltarelo*, rel. to It. *saltare* and Sp. *saltar* leap, dance f. L *saltare* (as SALTATION)]

saltation /sælˈteɪʃ(ə)n/ *n.* **1** the act or an instance of leaping or dancing; a jump. **2** a sudden transition or movement. □□ **saltatory** /ˈsæltətərɪ/ *adj.* **saltatorial** /ˌsæltəˈtɔːrɪəl/ *adj.* [L *saltatio* f. *saltare* frequent. of *salire* salt- leap]

saltbush /ˈsɔːltbʊʃ, ˈsɒlt-/ *n.* = ORACHE.

salt-cellar /ˈsɔːltˌselə(r), ˈsɒlt-/ *n.* **1** a vessel holding salt for table use. **2** *colloq.* an unusually deep hollow above the collarbone, esp. found in women. [SALT + obs. *saler* f. AF f. OF *salier* salt-box f. L (as SALARY), assim. to CELLAR]

salter /ˈsɔːltə(r), ˈsɒl-/ *n.* **1** a manufacturer or dealer in salt. **2** a workman at a salt-works. **3** a person who salts fish etc. **4** = *dry-salter*. [OE *sealtere* (as SALT)]

saltern /ˈsɔːlt(ə)n, ˈsɒl-/ *n.* **1** a salt-works. **2** a set of pools for the natural evaporation of sea water. [OE *sealtærn* (as SALT, *ærn* building)]

saltigrade /ˈsæltɪˌɡreɪd/ *adj.* & *n.* *Zool.* —*adj.* (of arthropods) moving by leaping or jumping. —*n.* a saltigrade arthropod, e.g. a spider, sand-hopper, etc. [mod.L *Saltigradae* f. L *saltus* leap f. *salire* salt- + *-gradus* walking]

salting /ˈsɔːltɪŋ, ˈsɒl-/ *n.* **1** in senses of SALT *v.* **2** (esp. in *pl.*) *Geol.* a salt marsh; a marsh overflowed by the sea.

saltire /ˈsɔːlˌtaɪə(r)/ *n.* *Heraldry* an ordinary formed by a bend and a bend sinister crossing like a St Andrew's cross. □ **in saltire** arranged in this way. □□ **saltirewise** *adv.* [ME f. OF *sau(l)toir* etc. stirrup-cord, stile, saltire, f. med.L *saltatorium* (as SALTATION)]

Salt Lake City the capital and largest city of Utah; pop. (1980) 163,000. Founded in 1847 by Brigham Young for the Mormon community, the city is the world headquarters of the Church of Jesus Christ of Latter-Day Saints.

saltpetre /ˌsɒltˈpiːtə(r), ˌsɔːlt-/ *n.* (*US* **saltpeter**) potassium nitrate, a white crystalline salty substance used in preserving meat and as a constituent of gunpowder. [ME f. OF *salpetre* f. med.L *salpetra* prob. for *sal petrae* (unrecorded) salt of rock (i.e. found as an incrustation): assim. to SALT]

saltus /ˈsæltəs/ *n.* *literary* a sudden transition; a breach of continuity. [L, = leap]

saltwort /ˈsɔːltwɜːt, ˈsɒlt-/ *n.* any plant of the genus *Salsola*; glasswort.

salty /ˈsɔːltɪ, ˈsɒl-/ *adj.* (**saltier**, **saltiest**) tasting of, containing, or preserved with salt. □□ **saltiness** *n.*

salubrious /səˈluːbrɪəs, səˈljuː-/ *adj.* **1** health-giving; healthy. **2** (of surroundings etc.) pleasant; agreeable. □□ **salubriously** *adv.* **salubriousness** *n.* **salubrity** *n.* [L *salubris* f. *salus* health]

saluki /səˈluːkɪ/ *n.* (*pl.* **salukis**) **1** a tall swift slender dog of a silky-coated breed with large ears and a fringed tail and feet. **2** this breed. [Arab. *salūkī*]

salutary /ˈsæljʊtərɪ/ *adj.* **1** producing good effects; beneficial. **2** *archaic* health-giving. [ME f. F *salutaire* or L *salutaris* f. *salus -utis* health]

salutation /ˌsæljuːˈteɪʃ(ə)n/ *n.* **1** a sign or expression of greeting or recognition of another's arrival or departure. **2** words spoken or written to enquire about another's health or well-being. □□ **salutational** *adj.* [ME f. OF *salutation* or L *salutatio* (as SALUTE)]

salutatory /səˈljuːtətərɪ, səˈluː-/ *adj.* & *n.* —*adj.* of salutation. —*n.* (*pl.* **-ies**) *US* an oration, esp. as given by a member of a graduating class, often the second-ranking member. □□

salutatorian /-ˈtɔːrɪən/ *n.* (in sense of *n.*). [L *salutatorius* (as SALUTE)]

salute /səˈluːt, -ˈljuːt/ *n.* & *v.* —*n.* **1** a gesture of respect, homage, or courteous recognition, esp. made to or by a person when arriving or departing. **2 a** *Mil.* & *Naut.* a prescribed or specified movement of the hand or of weapons or flags as a sign of respect or recognition. **b** (prec. by *the*) the attitude taken by an individual soldier, sailor, policeman, etc., in saluting. **3** the discharge of a gun or guns as a formal or ceremonial sign of respect or celebration. **4** *Fencing* the formal performance of certain guards etc. by fencers before engaging. —*v.* **1 a** *tr.* make a salute to. **b** *intr.* (often foll. by *to*) perform a salute. **2** *tr.* greet; make a salutation to. **3** *tr.* (foll. by *with*) receive or greet with (a smile etc.). **4** *tr. archaic* hail as (king etc.). □ **take the salute 1** (of the highest officer present) acknowledge it by gesture as meant for him. **2** receive ceremonial salutes by members of a procession. □□ **saluter** *n.* [ME f. L *salutare* f. *salus -utis* health]

Salvador[1] /ˌsælvəˈdɔː(r)/ (also **Bahía** /bɑːˈiːə/) a port on the Atlantic coast of NE Brazil; pop. (1980) 1,491,600. It was the capital of the Portuguese colony from 1549, when it was founded, until 1763, when the seat of government was transferred to Rio de Janeiro. During the colonial period it was a major port of entry for slaves shipped from Africa.

Salvador[2], **El** see EL SALVADOR. □□ **Salvadorean** /ˌsælvəˈdɔːrɪən/ *adj.* & *n.*

salvage /ˈsælvɪdʒ/ *n.* & *v.* —*n.* **1** the rescue of a ship, its cargo, or other property, from loss at sea, destruction by fire, etc. **2** the property etc. saved in this way. **3 a** the saving and utilization of waste paper, scrap material, etc. **b** the materials salvaged. **4** payment made or due to a person who has saved a ship or its cargo. —*v.tr.* **1** save from a wreck, fire, etc. **2** retrieve or preserve (something favourable) in adverse circumstances (*tried to salvage some dignity*). □□ **salvageable** *adj.* **salvager** *n.* [F f. med.L *salvagium* f. L *salvare* SAVE[1]]

salvation /sælˈveɪʃ(ə)n/ *n.* **1** the act of saving or being saved; preservation from loss, calamity, etc. **2** deliverance from sin and its consequences and admission to heaven, brought about by Christ. **3** a religious conversion. **4** a person or thing that saves (*was the salvation of*). □□ **salvationism** *n.* **salvationist** *n.* (both nouns esp. with ref. to the Salvation Army). [ME f. OF *sauvacion, salvacion*, f. eccl.L *salvatio -onis* f. *salvare* SAVE[1], transl. Gk *sōtēria*]

Salvation Army an international organization for evangelistic and social work, founded in 1865 by William Booth. It is organized on a military basis, headed by a General, and exacts unquestioning obedience from its members, who wear a distinctive uniform on public occasions. Public worship consists of open-air meetings marked by brass bands and banners. The Army is active in all kinds of social work, including the care of criminals and drunkards, soup kitchens, workers' hostels, and night shelters. Its headquarters are in London.

salve[1] /sælv, sɑːv/ *n.* & *v.* —*n.* **1** a healing ointment. **2** (often foll. by *for*) a thing that is soothing or consoling for wounded feelings, an uneasy conscience, etc. **3** *archaic* a thing that explains away a discrepancy or palliates a fault. —*v.tr.* **1** soothe (pride, self-love, conscience, etc.). **2** *archaic* anoint (a wound etc.). **3** *archaic* smooth over, make good, vindicate, harmonize, etc. [OE *s(e)alf(e), s(e)alfian* f. Gmc; senses 1 and 3 of *v.* partly f. L *salvare* SAVE[1]]

salve[2] /sælv/ *v.tr.* **1** save (a ship or its cargo) from loss at sea. **2** save (property) from fire. □□ **salvable** *adj.* [back-form. f. SALVAGE]

salver /ˈsælvə(r)/ *n.* a tray usu. of gold, silver, brass, or electroplate, on which drinks, letters, etc., are offered. [F *salve* tray for presenting food to the king f. Sp. *salva* assaying of food f. *salvar* SAVE: assoc. with *platter*]

Salve Regina /ˌsælveɪ rəˈdʒiːnə/ *n.* **1** a Roman Catholic hymn or prayer said or sung after compline and after the Divine Office from Trinity Sunday to Advent. **2** the music for this. [f. the opening words *salve regina* hail (holy) queen]

salvia /ˈsælvɪə/ *n.* any plant of the genus *Salvia*, esp. *S. splendens* with red or blue flowers. [L, = SAGE[1]]

Salvo /ˈsælvəʊ/ n. (pl. **-os**) Austral. sl. a member of the Salvation Army. [abbr.]

salvo¹ /ˈsælvəʊ/ n. (pl. **-oes** or **-os**) **1** the simultaneous firing of artillery or other guns esp. as a salute, or in a sea-fight. **2** a number of bombs released from aircraft at the same moment. **3** a round or volley of applause. [earlier salve f. F f. It. salva salutation (as SAVE¹)]

salvo² /ˈsælvəʊ/ n. (pl. **-os**) **1** a saving clause; a reservation (with an express salvo of their rights). **2** a tacit reservation. **3** a quibbling evasion; a bad excuse. **4** an expedient for saving reputation or soothing pride or conscience. [L, ablat. of salvus SAFE as used in salvo jure without prejudice to the rights of (a person)]

sal volatile /ˌsæl vɒˈlætɪlɪ/ n. ammonium carbonate, esp. in the form of a flavoured solution in alcohol used as smelling-salts. [mod.L, = volatile salt]

salvor /ˈsælvə(r)/ n. a person or ship making or assisting in salvage. [SALVE²]

Salween /ˈsælwiːn, sælˈwiːn/ a river of SE Asia which rises in Tibet and flows south-east and south through Burma to the Gulf of Martaban, an inlet of the Andaman Sea.

Salyut /sælˈjuːt, ˈsæ-/ any of a series of Soviet manned space stations, of which the first was launched into Earth orbit in 1971.

Salzburg /ˈsæltsbɜːg, ˈsɑː-/ **1** a province of central Austria; pop. (1981) 441,842. **2** its capital city (pop. 139,400), noted for its music festivals, one of which is dedicated to the composer Mozart who was born in the city.

SAM abbr. surface-to-air missile.

Sam. abbr. Samuel (Old Testament).

samadhi /səˈmɑːdɪ/ n. Buddhism & Hinduism **1** a state of concentration induced by meditation. **2** a state into which a perfected holy man is said to pass at his apparent death. [Skr. samādhi contemplation]

Samar /ˈsɑːmɑː(r)/ the third-largest island of the Philippines; pop. (1980) 2,717,215.

samara /ˈsæmərə, səˈmɑː-/ n. Bot. a winged seed from the sycamore, ash, etc. [mod.L f. L, = elm-seed]

Samaria /səˈmeərɪə/ **1** the ancient capital of the northern kingdom of the Hebrews (see ISRAEL¹ 2). In 721 BC it was captured by the Assyrians and resettled with pagans from other parts of their empire (2 Kings 17, 18). **2** the region surrounding this, west of the Jordan, bounded by Galilee and Judaea.

Samarinda /ˌsæməˈrɪndə/ a city of Indonesia, capital of the province of East Kalimantan; pop. (1980) 264,700.

Samaritan /səˈmærɪt(ə)n/ n. & adj. —n. **1** (in full good Samaritan) a charitable or helpful person (with ref. to Luke 10:33 etc.). **2** a member of an organization (the Samaritans) founded in 1953 by the Revd Chad Varah to enable help, compassion, and friendship to be given (especially through the telephone service) to the suicidal and despairing. **3** a native of Samaria. According to Jewish tradition, the Samaritans were descendants of the pagan settlers established by the Assyrians in 721 BC; the hostility of the Jews to them was proverbial. A few still survive, living near Nablus (now in Israel), and bear a striking resemblance to the Assyrians depicted on ancient monuments. **4** the Aramaic dialect formerly spoken in Samaria. **5** an adherent of the Samaritan religious system, accepting only the Samaritan Pentateuch. —adj. of Samaria or the Samaritans. □ **Samaritan Pentateuch** a recension used by Samaritans of which the MSS are in archaic characters. □□ **Samaritanism** n. [LL Samaritanus f. Gk Samareitēs f. Samareia Samaria]

samarium /səˈmeərɪəm/ n. Chem. a soft silvery metallic element of the lanthanide series, first discovered in 1879. The pure metal is used as a catalyst and its compounds are used in computer hardware, some types of electrode, special glasses, etc. ¶ Symb.: **Sm**; atomic number 82. [samarskite the mineral in which its spectrum was first observed, f. Samarski name of a 19th-c. Russ. official]

Samarkand /ˌsæmɑːˈkænd/ a city in central Asia. Destroyed by Alexander the Great in 329 BC, Samarkand later rose to fame as the centre of the silk trade, becoming the subject of much

legend in the West. It was destroyed again by Genghis Khan in 1221 but later became the capital of Tamerlane's empire. By 1700 it was almost deserted, but in 1868 it was taken by Russia and in 1924 was incorporated into the Uzbek Soviet Socialist Republic, briefly becoming its capital.

Samarra /səˈmærə/ a city of Iraq, on the River Tigris, north of Baghdad. It is a place of Shiite pilgrimage.

Sama-Veda /ˌsɑːməˈveɪdə, -ˈviːdə/ n. one of the four Vedas, a collection of liturgical chants in Old Sanskrit used in the Vedic religion by the priest in charge of chanting aloud at the sacrifice. Its material is drawn largely from the Rig-Veda. [Skr. sāmavēda f. sāma chant + vēda VEDA]

samba /ˈsæmbə/ n. & v. —n. **1** a Brazilian dance of African origin. **2** a ballroom dance imitative of this. **3** the music for this. —v.intr. (**sambas, sambaed** /-bəd/ or **samba'd, sambaing** /-bəɪŋ/) dance the samba. [Port., of Afr. orig.]

sambar /ˈsæmbə(r)/ n. (also **samba, sambhar**) either of two large deer, Cervus unicolor or C. equinus, native to S. Asia. [Hindi sā(m)bar]

Sambo /ˈsæmbəʊ/ n. (pl. **-os** or **-oes**) **1** sl. offens. a Black person. **2** (sambo) hist. a person of mixed race esp. of Negro and Indian or Negro and European blood. [Sp. zambo perh. = zambo bandy-legged; sense 1 perh. a different word f. Foulah sambo uncle]

Sam Browne /sæm ˈbraʊn/ n. (in full **Sam Browne belt**) a belt with a supporting strap that passes over the right shoulder, worn by commissioned officers of the British Army and also by members of various police forces etc. [Sir Samuel J. Browne, its inventor, Brit. military commander d. 1901]

same /seɪm/ adj., pron., & adv. —adj. **1** (often prec. by the) identical; not different; unchanged (everyone was looking in the same direction; the same car was used in another crime; saying the same thing over and over). **2** unvarying, uniform, monotonous (the same old story). **3** (usu. prec. by this, these, that, those) (of a person or thing) previously alluded to; just mentioned; aforesaid (this same man was later my husband). —pron. (prec. by the) **1** the same person or thing (the others asked for the same). **2** Law or archaic the person or thing just mentioned (detected the youth breaking in and apprehended the same). —adv. (usu. prec. by the) similarly; in the same way (we all feel the same; I want to go, the same as you do). □ **all** (or **just**) **the same 1** emphatically the same. **2** in spite of changed conditions, adverse circumstances, etc. (but you should offer, all the same). **at the same time 1** simultaneously. **2** notwithstanding; in spite of circumstances etc. **be all** (or **just**) **the same to** an expression of indifference or impartiality (it's all the same to me what we do). **by the same token** see TOKEN. **same here** colloq. the same applies to me. **the same to you!** may you do, have, find, etc., the same thing; likewise. **the very same** emphatically the same. □□ **sameness** n. [ME f. ON sami, sama, with Gmc cognates]

samey /ˈseɪmɪ/ adj. (**samier, samiest**) colloq. lacking in variety; monotonous. □□ **sameyness** n.

samfu /ˈsæmfuː/ n. a suit consisting of a jacket and trousers, worn by Chinese women and sometimes men. [Cantonese]

Samhain /saʊn, ˈsaʊɪn/ n. Brit. 1 Nov., celebrated by the Celts as a festival marking the beginning of winter. [Ir. Samhain]

Samian /ˈseɪmɪən/ n. & adj. —n. **1** a native or inhabitant of Samos **2** (in full **Samian pottery** or **ware**) a kind of glossy red pottery made in Gaul in the 1st–4th c. and common on archaeological sites of this period. It is also called terra sigillata; 'Samian' is a misnomer, deriving from a supposed but non-existent connection with Samos. —adj. of Samos. □ **Samian ware** fine red pottery from various parts of the Roman Empire, esp. Gaulish pottery often found on Roman sites in Britain. [L Samius f. Gk Samios Samos]

samisen /ˈsæmɪsɪn/ n. a long three-stringed Japanese guitar, played with a plectrum. [Jap. f. Chin. san-hsien f. san three + hsien string]

samite /ˈsæmaɪt, ˈseɪ-/ n. hist. a rich medieval dress-fabric of silk occas. interwoven with gold. [ME f. OF samit f. med.L examitum f. med. Gk hexamiton f. Gk hexa- six + mitos thread]

samizdat /ˈsæmɪzˌdæt, -ˈdæt/ n. a system of clandestine publication of banned literature in the USSR. [Russ., = self-publishing house]

Samnite /ˈsæmnaɪt/ n. & adj. —n. 1 a member of a people of ancient Italy often at war with republican Rome. 2 the language of this people. —adj. of this people or their language. [ME f. L Samnites (pl.), rel. to Sabinus SABINE]

Samoa /səˈməʊə/ a group of Polynesian Islands of which the eastern part is a US territory. □ **Western Samoa** see separate entry. □□ **Samoan** adj. & n.

Samos /ˈseɪmɒs/ a Greek island in the Aegean Sea; pop. (1981) 40,500.

samosa /səˈməʊsə/ n. a triangular pastry fried in ghee or oil, containing spiced vegetables or meat. [Hind.]

samovar /ˈsæməˌvɑː(r)/ n. a Russian urn for making tea, with an internal heating tube to keep water at boiling-point. [Russ., = self-boiler]

Samoyed /ˈsæməˌjed/ n. 1 a member of a people of northern Siberia. 2 the language of this people. 3 (also **samoyed**) a a dog of a white Arctic breed. b this breed. [Russ. samoed]

Samoyedic /ˌsæməˈjedɪk/ n. & adj. —n. the language of the Samoyeds. —adj. of or relating to the Samoyeds.

samp /sæmp/ n. US 1 coarsely-ground maize. 2 porridge made of this. [Algonquin nasamp softened by water]

sampan /ˈsæmpæn/ n. a small boat used on the rivers and coasts of China, Japan, and neighbouring islands, rowed with a scull (or two sculls) from the stern and usually having a sail of matting and an awning. [Chin. san-ban f. san three + ban board]

samphire /ˈsæmˌfaɪə(r)/ n. 1 an umbelliferous maritime rock plant, Crithmum maritimum, with aromatic fleshy leaves used in pickles. 2 the glasswort. [earlier samp(i)ere f. F (herbe de) Saint Pierre St Peter('s herb)]

sample /ˈsɑːmp(ə)l/ n. & v. —n. 1 a small part or quantity intended to show what the whole is like. 2 a small amount of fabric, food, or other commodity, esp. given to a prospective customer. 3 a specimen, esp. one taken for scientific testing or analysis. 4 an illustrative or typical example. —v.tr. 1 take or give samples of. 2 try the qualities of. 3 get a representative experience of. □ **sample bag** Austral. an (orig. free) bag of advertisers' samples. [ME f. AF assample, OF essample EXAMPLE]

sampler[1] /ˈsɑːmplə(r)/ n. a piece of embroidery worked in various stitches as a specimen of proficiency (often displayed on a wall etc.). [OF essamplaire (as EXEMPLAR)]

sampler[2] /ˈsɑːmplə(r)/ n. 1 a person who samples. 2 US a collection of representative items etc.

samsara /sʌmˈsɑːrə/ n. Ind. Philos. the endless cycle of death and rebirth to which life in the material world is bound. □□ **samsaric** adj. [Skr. saṃsāra a wandering through]

samskara /sʌnˈskɑːrə/ n. Ind. Philos. 1 a purificatory ceremony or rite marking an event in one's life. 2 a mental impression, instinct, or memory. [Skr. samskāra a making perfect, preparation]

Samson /ˈsæms(ə)n/ (prob. 11th c. BC) an Israelite leader famous for his strength (Judges 13–16). He confided to a woman, Delilah, that his strength lay in his hair, and she betrayed him to the Philistines. They cut off his hair while he slept and captured and blinded him, but when his hair grew again his strength returned and he pulled down the pillars of a house, destroying himself and a large concourse of Philistines —n. a person of great strength or resembling Samson in some respect. □ **Samson-** (or **Samson's-**) **post 1** a strong pillar passing through the hold of a ship or between decks. 2 a post in a whaleboat to which a harpoon rope is attached.

Samuel /ˈsæmjʊ(ə)l/ 1 a Hebrew prophet who rallied the Israelites after their defeat by the Philistines and became their ruler. 2 either of two books of the Old Testament covering the history of Israel from Samuel's birth to the end of the reign of David.

samurai /ˈsæmʊˌraɪ, -jʊˌraɪ/ n. (pl. same) 1 a Japanese army officer. 2 hist. a member of the feudal warrior class of Japan which was bound by the code of bushido, emphasizing qualities of loyalty, bravery, and endurance. The samurai dominated Japanese society until the demise of the feudal order in the 19th c. [Jap.]

san /sæn/ n. = SANATORIUM 2. [abbr.]

Sana'a /sæˈnɑː, ˈsɑːnə/ the capital of the Yemeni Republic and of the former Yemen Arab Republic (1967–90); pop. (1986) 427,150.

San Andreas fault /sæn ænˈdreɪəs/ a fault line or fracture of the earth's crust extending for some 965 km (600 miles) through the length of California. Seismic activity is common along its course and is ascribed to movement of two sections of the earth's crust—the eastern Pacific plate and the North American plate—which abut against each other in this region (see PLATE TECTONICS). The city of San Francisco lies close to the fault, and such movement caused the devastating earthquake of 1906 and a further convulsion in 1989.

San Andrés /sæn ænˈdreɪs/ a small Colombian island in the Caribbean Sea off the coast of Nicaragua.

San Antonio /sæn ænˈtəʊnɪˌəʊ/ an industrial city in south central Texas, site of the Alamo (see entry); pop. (1982) 819,000.

sanative /ˈsænətɪv/ adj. 1 healing; curative. 2 of or tending to physical or moral health. [ME f. OF sanatif or LL sanativus f. L sanare cure]

sanatorium /ˌsænəˈtɔːrɪəm/ n. (pl. **sanatoriums** or **sanatoria** /-rɪə/) 1 an establishment for the treatment of invalids, esp. of convalescents and the chronically sick. 2 Brit. a room or building for sick people in a school etc. [mod.L (as SANATIVE)]

San Carlos de Bariloche /sæn ˈkɑːlɒs deɪ ˌbærɪˈləʊtʃɪ/ the principal Andean skiing resort of Argentina, situated in the province of Río Negro; pop. (1980) 48,200.

Sanchi /ˈsɑːntʃɪ/ the site in central India, in Madhya Pradesh, of several well-preserved Buddhist stupas. The largest of these was probably begun by the emperor Asoka in the 3rd c. BC.

Sancho Panza /ˌsænkəʊ ˈpænzə/ the squire of Don Quixote (see entry), who accompanies the latter on his adventures. He is an ignorant and credulous peasant but has a store of proverbial wisdom, and is thus a foil to his master.

sanctify /ˈsænktɪˌfaɪ/ v.tr. (**-ies, -ied**) 1 consecrate; set apart or observe as holy. 2 purify or free from sin. 3 make legitimate or binding by religious sanction; justify; give the colour of morality or innocence to. 4 make productive of or conducive to holiness. □□ **sanctification** /-fɪˈkeɪʃ(ə)n/ n. **sanctifier** n. [ME f. OF saintifier f. eccl.L sanctificare f. L sanctus holy]

sanctimonious /ˌsænktɪˈməʊnɪəs/ adj. making a show of sanctity or piety. □□ **sanctimoniously** adv. **sanctimoniousness** n. **sanctimony** /ˈsænktɪmənɪ/ n. [L sanctimonia sanctity (as SAINT)]

sanction /ˈsænkʃ(ə)n/ n. & v. —n. 1 approval or encouragement given to an action etc. by custom or tradition; express permission. 2 confirmation or ratification of a law etc. 3 a a penalty for disobeying a law or rule, or a reward for obeying it. b a clause containing this. 4 Ethics a consideration operating to enforce obedience to any rule of conduct. 5 (esp. in pl.) military or esp. economic action by a State to coerce another to conform to an international agreement or norms of conduct. 6 Law hist. a law or decree. —v.tr. 1 authorize, countenance, or agree to (an action etc.). 2 ratify; attach a penalty or reward to; make binding. □□ **sanctionable** adj. [F f. L sanctio -onis f. sancire sanct-make sacred]

sanctitude /ˈsænktɪˌtjuːd/ n. archaic saintliness. [ME f. L sanctitudo (as SAINT)]

sanctity /ˈsænktɪtɪ/ n. (pl. **-ies**) 1 holiness of life; saintliness. 2 sacredness; the state of being hallowed. 3 inviolability. 4 (in pl.) sacred obligations, feelings, etc. [ME f. OF sain(c)tité or L sanctitas (as SAINT)]

sanctuary /ˈsænktjʊərɪ/ n. (pl. **-ies**) 1 a holy place; a church, temple, etc. 2 a the inmost recess or holiest part of a temple etc. b the part of the chancel containing the high altar. 3 a place where birds, wild animals, etc., are bred and protected. 4 a place of refuge, esp. for political refugees. 5 a immunity from arrest. b the right to offer this. 6 hist. a sacred place where a fugitive from the law or a debtor was secured by medieval Church law against arrest or violence. □ **take sanctuary** resort to a place of refuge. [ME f. AF *sanctuarie*, OF *sanctuaire* f. L *sanctuarium* (as SAINT)]

sanctum /ˈsæŋktəm/ n. (pl. **sanctums**) 1 a holy place. 2 colloq. a person's private room, study, or den. □ **sanctum sanctorum** /sæŋkˈtɔːrəm/ 1 the holy of holies in the Jewish temple. 2 = sense 2 of n. 3 an inner retreat. 4 an esoteric doctrine etc. [L, neut. of *sanctus* holy, past part. of *sancire* consecrate: *sanctorum* genit. pl. in transl. of Heb. *ḳōdeš haḳḳoḏāšîm* holy of holies]

sanctus /ˈsæŋktəs/ n. (also **Sanctus**) 1 the prayer or hymn (from Isa. 6: 3) beginning 'Sanctus, sanctus, sanctus' or 'Holy, holy, holy', forming the conclusion of the Eucharistic preface. 2 the music for this. □ **sanctus bell** a handbell or the bell in the turret at the junction of the nave and the chancel, rung at the sanctus or at the elevation of the Eucharist. [ME f. L, = holy]

Sand /sɑ̃/, George (pseudonym of Amandine-Aurore Lucille Dupin, Baronne Dudevant, 1804–76), French novelist, who left her husband to lead an independent literary life in Paris. She wrote romantic novels portraying women's struggles against conventional morals, including *Indiana* (1832) and *Lélia* (1833), and idyllic works of rustic life such as *La mare au diable* (1846) and *François le champi* (1850). *Elle et lui* (1859) is a fictionalized account of her affair with Alfred de Musset; *Un hiver à Majorque* (1841) describes an unhappy episode during her passionate liaison with Chopin.

sand /sænd/ n. & v. —n. 1 a loose granular substance resulting from the wearing down of esp. siliceous rocks and found on the seashore, river-beds, deserts, etc. 2 (in pl.) grains of sand. 3 (in pl.) an expanse or tracts of sand. 4 a light yellow-brown colour like that of sand. 5 (in pl.) a sandbank. 6 US colloq. firmness of purpose; grit. —v.tr. 1 smooth or polish with sandpaper or sand. 2 sprinkle or overlay with, or bury under, sand. 3 adulterate (sugar etc.) with sand. □ **sand bar** a sandbank at the mouth of a river or US on the coast. **sand-bath** a vessel of heated sand to provide uniform heating. **sand-bed** a stratum of sand. **sand-cloud** driving sand in a simoom. **sand-crack 1** a fissure in a horse's hoof. 2 a crack in the human foot from walking on hot sand. 3 a crack in brick due to imperfect mixing. **sand dollar** US any of various round flat sea urchins, esp. of the order Clypeasteroida. **sand-dune** (or **-hill**) a mound or ridge of sand formed by the wind. **sand eel** any eel-like fish of the family Ammodytidae or Hypotychidae: also called LAUNCE. **sand-flea** a chigoe or sand-hopper. **sand-glass** = HOURGLASS. **sand-groper** Austral. 1 a gold-rush pioneer. 2 joc. a Western Australian. **sand-hill** a dune. **sand-hopper** any of various small jumping crustaceans of the order Amphipoda, burrowing on the seashore. **sand-martin** a swallow-like bird, *Riparia riparia*, nesting in the side of a sandy bank etc. **the sands are running out** the allotted time is nearly at an end. **sand-shoe** a shoe with a canvas, rubber, hemp, etc., sole for use on sand. **sand-skipper** = *sand-hopper*. **sand-yacht** a boat on wheels propelled along a beach by wind. □□ **sander** n. **sandlike** adj. [OE *sand* f. Gmc]

sandal[1] /ˈsænd(ə)l/ n. & v. —n. 1 a light shoe with an openwork upper or no upper, attached to the foot usu. by straps. 2 a strap for fastening a low shoe, passing over the instep or around the ankle. —v.tr. (**sandalled, sandalling**; US **sandaled, sandaling**) 1 (esp. as **sandalled** adj.) put sandals on (a person, his feet). 2 fasten or provide (a shoe) with a sandal. [ME f. L *sandalium* f. Gk *sandalion* dimin. of *sandalon* wooden shoe, prob. of Asiatic orig.]

sandal[2] /ˈsænd(ə)l/ n. = SANDALWOOD. □ **sandal-tree** any tree yielding sandalwood, esp. the white sandalwood, *Santalum album*, of India. [ME f. med.L *sandalum*, ult. f. Skr. *candana*]

sandalwood /ˈsænd(ə)l‚wʊd/ n. 1 the scented wood of a sandal-tree. 2 a perfume derived from this. □ **red sandalwood** the red wood from either of two SE Asian trees, *Adenanthera pavonina* and *Pterocarpus santalinus*, used as timber and to produce a red dye. **sandalwood oil** a yellow aromatic oil made from the sandal-tree.

Sandalwood Island see SUMBA.

sandarac /ˈsændə‚ræk/ n. (also **sandarach**) 1 the gummy resin of a N. African conifer, *Tetraclinis articulata*, used in making varnish. 2 = REALGAR. [L *sandaraca* f. Gk *sandarakē*, of Asiatic orig.]

sandbag /ˈsændbæg/ n. & v. —n. a bag filled with sand for use: 1 (in fortification) for making temporary defences or for the protection of a building etc. against blast and splinters or floodwaters. 2 as ballast esp. for a boat or balloon. 3 as a weapon to inflict a heavy blow without leaving a mark. 4 to stop a draught from a window or door. —v.tr. (**-bagged, -bagging**) 1 barricade or defend. 2 place sandbags against (a window, chink, etc.). 3 fell with a blow from a sandbag. 4 US coerce by harsh means. □□ **sandbagger** n.

sandbank /ˈsændbæŋk/ n. a deposit of sand forming a shallow place in the sea or a river.

sandblast /ˈsændblɑːst/ v. & n. —v.tr. roughen, treat, or clean with a jet of sand driven by compressed air or steam. —n. this jet. □□ **sandblaster** n.

sandbox /ˈsændbɒks/ n. 1 *Railways* a box of sand on a locomotive for sprinkling slippery rails. 2 *Golf* a container for sand used in teeing. 3 a sandpit enclosed in a box. 4 *hist.* a device for sprinkling sand to dry ink.

sandboy /ˈsændbɔɪ/ n. □ **happy as a sandboy** extremely happy or carefree. [prob. = a boy hawking sand for sale]

sandcastle /ˈsænd‚kɑːs(ə)l/ n. a shape like a castle made in sand, usu. by a child on the seashore.

sanderling /ˈsændəlɪŋ/ n. a small wading bird, *Calidris alba*, of the sandpiper family. [perh. f. an OE form *sandyrthling* (unrecorded, as SAND + *yrthling* ploughman, also the name of a bird)]

sanders /ˈsændəz/ n. (also **saunders** /ˈsɔː-/) sandalwood, esp. red sandalwood. [ME f. OF *sandre* var. of *sandle* SANDAL[2]]

sandfly /ˈsændflaɪ/ n. (pl. **-ies**) 1 any midge of the genus *Simulium*. 2 any biting fly of the genus *Phlebotomus* transmitting the viral disease leishmaniasis.

sandhi /ˈsændi/ n. *Gram.* the process whereby the form of a word changes as a result of its position in an utterance (e.g. the change from *a* to *an* before a vowel). [Skr. *saṃdhi* putting together]

sandhog /ˈsændhɒg/ n. US a person who works underwater laying foundations, constructing tunnels, etc.

Sandhurst /ˈsændhɜːst/ (in full 'The Royal Military Academy, Sandhurst') a training college, now at Camberley, Surrey, for officers for the British Army. It was formed in 1946 from an amalgamation of the Royal Military College at Sandhurst in Berkshire (founded 1799) and the Royal Military Academy at Woolwich, London (founded 1741).

San Diego /sæn dɪˈeɪgəʊ/ an industrial city and US naval port on the Pacific coast of southern California; pop. (1982) 916,000.

Sandinista /‚sændɪˈniːstə/ n. a member of a revolutionary Nicaraguan guerrilla organization founded by the nationalist leader A. C. Sandino (1893–1934), or of a similar organization founded in his name and in power from 1979.

sandiver /ˈsændɪvə(r)/ n. liquid scum formed in glass-making. [ME app. f. F *suin de verre* exhalation of glass f. *suer* to sweat]

sandlot /ˈsændlɒt/ n. US a piece of unoccupied sandy land used for children's games.

sandman /ˈsændmæn/ n. the personification of tiredness causing children's eyes to smart towards bedtime.

sand-painting n. 1 an American Indian ceremonial art form, using coloured sands, also called *dry painting*. 2 an example of this. Although sand-painting had largely died out by the early 20th c., it continues to be an important ritual among the Navajos (where it is associated with healing practices) and the Pueblos. The designs are executed with traditional gestures; the gods are represented in conventionalized form; the colours used are traditional, and the greater part of the design follows patterns handed down from memory, each sand-painting being destroyed after the ceremony.

sandpaper /ˈsænd‚peɪpə(r)/ n. paper with sand or another abrasive stuck to it for smoothing or polishing.

sandpiper /ˈsænd‚paɪpə(r)/ n. any of various wading birds of the family Scolopacidae, frequenting moorland and coastal areas.

sandpit /ˈsændpɪt/ n. a hollow partly filled with sand, usu. for children to play in.

Sandringham House /ˈsændrɪŋəm/ a holiday residence of

the Royal Family, NE of King's Lynn in Norfolk. The estate was acquired in 1861 by Edward VII, then Prince of Wales.

sandsoap /ˈsændsəʊp/ n. heavy-duty gritty soap.

sandstock /ˈsændstɒk/ n. brick made with sand dusted on the surface.

sandstone /ˈsændstəʊn/ n. **1** any clastic rock containing particles visible to the naked eye. **2** a sedimentary rock of consolidated sand commonly red, yellow, brown, grey, or white.

sandstorm /ˈsændstɔːm/ n. a desert storm of wind with clouds of sand.

sandwich /ˈsænwɪdʒ, -wɪtʃ/ n. & v. —n. **1** two or more slices of usu. buttered bread with a filling of meat, cheese, etc., between them. **2** a cake of two or more layers with jam or cream between (*bake a sponge sandwich*). —v.tr. **1** put (a thing, statement, etc.) between two of another character. **2** squeeze in between others (*sat sandwiched in the middle*). □ **sandwich-board** one of two advertisement boards carried by a sandwich-man. **sandwich course** a course of training with alternate periods of practical experience and theoretical instruction. **sandwich-man** (*pl.* **-men**) a man who walks the streets with sandwich-boards hanging before and behind. [4th Earl of *Sandwich*, Engl. nobleman d. 1792, said to have eaten food in this form so as not to leave the gaming-table for 24 hours]

sandwort /ˈsændwɜːt/ n. any low-growing plant of the genus *Arenaria*, usu. bearing small white flowers.

sandy /ˈsændɪ/ adj. (**sandier**, **sandiest**) **1** having the texture of sand. **2** having much sand. **3 a** (of hair) yellowish-red. **b** (of a person) having sandy hair. □ **sandy blight** *Austral.* conjunctivitis with sandlike grains in the eye. □□ **sandiness** n. **sandyish** adj. [OE *sandig* (as SAND)]

sane /seɪn/ adj. **1** of sound mind; not mad. **2** (of views etc.) moderate; sensible. □□ **sanely** adv. **saneness** n. [L *sanus* healthy]

San Francisco /frænˈsɪskəʊ/ a city and seaport on the coast of California, with a magnificent land-locked harbour entered by a channel called the Golden Gate; pop. (1983) 3,250,630.

sang past of SING.

sangar /ˈsæŋgə(r)/ n. (also **sanga** /ˈsæŋgə/) a stone breastwork round a hollow. [Pashto *sangar*]

sangaree /ˌsæŋgəˈriː/ n. a cold drink of wine diluted and spiced. [Sp. *sangría* SANGRIA]

sang-froid /sɑ̃ˈfrwɑː/ n. composure, coolness, etc., in danger or under agitating circumstances. [F, = cold blood]

sangha /ˈsɑːŋə/ n. the Buddhist monastic order, including monks, nuns, and novices. [Hind. *saṅgha* f. Skr. *saṃgha* community f. *sam* together + *han* come in contact]

sangrail /sænˈgreɪl/ n. = GRAIL. [ME f. OF *saint graal* (as SAINT, GRAIL)]

sangria /sænˈgriːə/ n. a Spanish drink of red wine with lemonade, fruit, etc. [Sp., = bleeding: cf. SANGAREE]

sanguinary /ˈsæŋgwɪnərɪ/ adj. **1** accompanied by or delighting in bloodshed. **2** bloody; bloodthirsty. **3** (of laws) inflicting death freely. □□ **sanguinarily** adv. **sanguinariness** n. [L *sanguinarius* f. *sanguis -inis* blood]

sanguine /ˈsæŋgwɪn/ adj. & n. —adj. **1** optimistic; confident. **2** (of the complexion) florid; bright; ruddy. **3** *hist.* of a ruddy complexion with a courageous and hopeful amorous disposition. **4** *hist.* of the temperament in which blood predominates over the other humours. **5** *Heraldry* or *literary* blood red. **6** *archaic* bloody; bloodthirsty. —n. **1** a blood-red colour. **2** a crayon of chalk coloured red or flesh with iron oxide. □□ **sanguinely** adv. **sanguineness** n. (both in sense 1 of n.). [ME f. OF *sanguin -ine* blood-red f. L *sanguineus* (as SANGUINARY)]

sanguineous /sæŋˈgwɪnɪəs/ adj. **1** sanguinary. **2** *Med.* of or relating to blood. **3** blood-red. **4** full-blooded; plethoric. [L *sanguineus* (as SANGUINE)]

Sanhedrin /ˈsænɪdrɪn/ n. (also **Sanhedrim** /-rɪm/) the highest court of justice and the supreme council at Jerusalem in New Testament times, with 71 members. It pronounced sentence of death on Christ. [late Heb. *sanhedrin* f. Gk *sunedrion* (as SYN-, *hedra* seat)]

sanicle /ˈsænɪk(ə)l/ n. any umbelliferous plant of the genus

Sanicula, esp. *S. europaea*, formerly believed to have healing properties. [ME ult. f. med.L *sanicula* perh. f. L *sanus* healthy]

sanify /ˈsænɪˌfaɪ/ v.tr. (**-ies**, **-ied**) make healthy; improve the sanitary state of. [L *sanus* healthy]

sanitarium /ˌsænɪˈteərɪəm/ n. (*pl.* **sanitariums** or **sanitaria** /-rɪə/) *US* = SANATORIUM. [pseudo-L f. L *sanitas* health]

sanitary /ˈsænɪtərɪ/ adj. **1** of the conditions that affect health, esp. with regard to dirt and infection. **2** hygienic; free from or designed to kill germs, infection, etc. □ **sanitary engineer** a person dealing with systems needed to maintain public health. **sanitary towel** (*US* **napkin**) an absorbent pad used during menstruation. **sanitary ware** porcelain for lavatories etc. □□ **sanitarian** /-ˈteərɪən/ n. & adj. **sanitarily** adv. **sanitariness** n. [F *sanitaire* f. L *sanitas*: see SANITY]

sanitation /ˌsænɪˈteɪʃ(ə)n/ n. **1** sanitary conditions. **2** the maintenance or improving of these. **3** the disposal of sewage and refuse from houses etc. □□ **sanitate** /ˈsænɪˌteɪt/ v.tr. & intr. **sanitationist** n. [irreg. f. SANITARY]

sanitize /ˈsænɪˌtaɪz/ v.tr. (also **-ise**) **1** make sanitary; disinfect. **2** *US colloq.* render (information etc.) more acceptable by removing improper or disturbing material. □□ **sanitizer** n.

sanity /ˈsænɪtɪ/ n. **1 a** the state of being sane. **b** mental health. **2** the tendency to avoid extreme views. [ME f. L *sanitas* (as SANE)]

San José[1] /sæn xəʊˈzeɪ, həʊ-/ the capital and chief port of Costa Rica; pop. (1984) 241,450.

San José[2] /sæn xəʊˈzeɪ, həʊ-/ a city in western California at the centre of 'Silicon Valley'; pop. (1982) 659,200.

San Juan /sæn ˈxwɑːn, ˈhwɑːn/ the capital and chief port of Puerto Rico; pop. (est. 1986) 431,200.

sank past of SINK.

San Luis Potosí /sæn luːˈiːs ˌpɒtəʊˈsiː/ **1** a State of north central Mexico; pop. (est. 1988) 2,020,700. **2** its capital, a silver-mining city; pop. (1980) 406,630.

San Marino /sæn məˈriːnəʊ/ a small landlocked republic near the Adriatic near Rimini, Italy, with a capital of the same name; pop. (est. 1988) 23,000; official language, Italian. It is perhaps Europe's oldest State, claiming to have been independent almost continuously since its foundation in the 4th c.

San Martín /sæn mɑːˈtiːn/, José de (1778–1850), South American soldier and statesman. Having assisted in the liberation of Argentina from Spanish rule (1812–13) he went on to liberate Chile (1817–18) and Peru (1820–1), and was appointed Protector of Peru in 1821. He resigned a year later, having refused to oppose the ambitions of the other great liberator Bolivar, who, because of San Martín's retiring ways, has always received a disproportionate share of the credit for liberating South America.

sannyasi /sʌnˈjɑːsɪ/ n. (also **sanyasi**) (*pl.* same) a Hindu religious mendicant. [Hindi & Urdu *sannyāsī* f. Skr. *saṃnyāsin* laying aside f. *sam* together, *ni* down, *as* throw]

San Pedro Sula /sæn ˌpedrəʊ ˈsuːlə/ the second-largest city in Honduras; pop. (1986) 399,700.

sans /sænz, sɑ̃/ prep. archaic or joc. without. [ME f. OF *san(z)*, *sen(s)* ult. f. L *sine*, infl. by L *absentia* in the absence of]

San Salvador /sæn ˈsælvəˌdɔː(r)/ the capital of El Salvador; pop. (1984) 452,600.

sansculotte /ˌsænzkjʊˈlɒt, ˌsɑ̃kjʊ-/ n. **1** *hist.* a republican of the poorer classes in Paris during the French Revolution. **2** an extreme republican or revolutionary. □□ **sansculottism** n. [F, lit. = without knee-breeches; usu. explained as one wearing trousers instead of the knee-breeches of the aristocracy]

sanserif /sænˈserɪf/ n. & adj. (also **sans-serif**) *Printing* —n. a form of type without serifs. —adj. without serifs. [app. f. SANS + SERIF]

Sanskrit /ˈsænskrɪt/ n. & adj. —n. the ancient language of Hindus in India, belonging to a branch of the Indo-European family of languages. It flourished in India as the language of learning for more than three millenniums, well into the 19th c., but has been gradually eclipsed by English and the modern Indian languages (e.g. Hindi, Bengali, Gujarati) to which, as a spoken language, it gave rise, and is now used only for religious purposes. It is written in the Devanagari script. —*adj.* of or in this language. □□ **Sanskritic** /-ˈskrɪtɪk/ *adj.* **Sanskritist** *n.* [Skr. *saṃskṛta* composed, elaborated, f. *saṃ* together, *kṛ* make, *-ta* past part. ending]

Sansovino /ˌsænsəˈviːnəʊ/, Jacopo Tatti (1486–1570), Italian sculptor and architect, city architect of Venice from 1529, where his buildings include St Mark's Library, the Loggia of the Campanile, and the Palazzo Corner, all of which show the influence of his early training in Rome and the development of antique architectural style for contemporary use. His sculpture includes reliefs for the Campanile Loggia and the sacristy doors of St Mark's, and the colossal *Mars* and *Neptune* for the staircase of the Ducal Palace.

Santa Ana /ˌsæntə ˈænə/ **1** the second-largest city in El Salvador. **2** the highest volcano in El Salvador, situated south-west of the city, rising to a height of 2,381 m (7,730 ft.).

Santa Claus /ˌsæntə ˈklɔːz/ *n.* (also *colloq.* **Santa**) a person said to bring children presents on the night before Christmas. (See FATHER CHRISTMAS.) [orig. US f. Du. dial. *Sante Klaas* St Nicholas]

Santa Cruz /ˌsæntə ˈkruːz/ a leading commercial city in the agricultural central region of Bolivia; pop. (1985) 441,700.

Santa Fé /ˌsæntə ˈfeɪ/ the capital of New Mexico; pop. (1980) 48,950.

Santander /ˌsæntænˈdeə(r)/ the principal ferry port of northern Spain, capital of the region of Cantabria; pop. (1986) 188,500.

Santiago de Compostela /ˌsæntiˈɑːgəʊ deɪ ˌkɒmpəʊˈstelə/ a city of NW Spain, capital of Galicia region; pop. (1986) 104,000. It is named after St James the Great (Spanish *Sant Iago*) whose relics were said to have been brought here (see JAMES⁴ 1). During the 10th–16th centuries his tomb was the principal centre of Christian pilgrimage after Jerusalem and Rome; from *c.*1100 the city became the centre of the national and Christian movement against Spain's Muslim rulers.

Santiago de Cuba /ˌsæntiˈɑːgəʊ deɪ ˈkjuːbə/ the second-largest city on the island of Cuba; pop. (est. 1986) 358,800.

Santo Domingo /ˌsæntəʊ dəˈmɪŋgəʊ/ the capital and chief port of the Dominican Republic; pop. (1981) 1,550,739. Founded in 1496 by a brother of Christopher Columbus, it is the oldest city in the New World.

santolina /ˌsæntəˈliːnə/ *n.* any aromatic shrub of the genus *Santolina*, with finely divided leaves and small usu. yellow flowers. [mod.L, var. of SANTONICA]

santonica /sænˈtɒnɪkə/ *n.* **1** a shrubby wormwood plant, *Artemisia cina*, yielding santonin. **2** the dried flower-heads of this used as an anthelmintic. [L f. *Santones* an Aquitanian tribe]

santonin /ˈsæntənɪn/ *n.* a toxic drug extracted from santonica and other plants of the genus *Artemisia*, used as an anthelmintic. [SANTONICA + -IN]

Santorini /ˌsæntəˈriːnɪ/ (Greek **Thera** or **Thira** /ˈθɪərə/) a volcanic island in the Cyclades group in the Aegean Sea. It is named after St Irene of Salonica who died here in exile in 304.

sanyasi var. of SANNYASI.

Saône /səʊn/ a river rising in the Vosges Mountains in eastern France and flowing 430 km (268 miles) south-west to join the Rhône near Lyons.

São Paulo /saʊ ˈpaʊləʊ/ the largest city in Brazil and second-largest in South America; pop. (1980) 7,032,500.

São Tomé and Principe /saʊ tɒˈmeɪ, ˈprɪnsɪpə/ a country consisting of two islands in the Gulf of Guinea, formerly an overseas province of Portugal; pop. (est. 1988) 117,400; official language, Portuguese; capital, São Tomé. The islands became independent in 1975. Cacao is the main product.

sap¹ /sæp/ *n. & v.* —*n.* **1** the vital juice circulating in plants. **2** vigour; vitality. **3** = SAPWOOD. **4** *US sl.* a bludgeon (orig. one made from a sapling). —*v.tr.* (**sapped, sapping**) **1** drain or dry (wood) of sap. **2** exhaust the vigour of (*my energy had been sapped by disappointment*). **3** remove the sapwood from (a log). **4** *US sl.* hit with a sap. □ **sap-green** *n.* **1** the pigment made from buckthorn berries. **2** the colour of this. —*adj.* of this colour. □□ **sapful** *adj.* **sapless** *adj.* [OE *sæp* prob. f. Gmc]

sap² /sæp/ *n. & v.* —*n.* **1** a tunnel or trench to conceal assailants'

approach to a fortified place; a covered siege-trench. **2** an insidious or slow undermining of a belief, resolution, etc. —*v.* (**sapped, sapping**) **1** *intr.* **a** dig a sap or saps. **b** approach by a sap. **2** *tr.* undermine; make insecure by removing the foundations. **3** *tr.* destroy insidiously. [ult. f. It. *zappa* spade, spadework, in part through F *sappe sap(p)er*, prob. of Arab. orig.]

sap³ /sæp/ *n. sl.* a foolish person. [abbr. of *sapskull* f. SAP¹ = sapwood + SKULL]

sapanwood var. of SAPPANWOOD.

sapele /səˈpiːlɪ/ *n.* **1** any of several large W. African hardwood trees of the genus *Entandrophragma*. **2** the reddish-brown mahogany-like timber of these trees. [W. Afr. name]

sapid /ˈsæpɪd/ *adj. literary* **1** having (esp. an agreeable) flavour; savoury; palatable; not insipid. **2** *literary* (of talk, writing, etc.) not vapid or uninteresting. □□ **sapidity** /səˈpɪdɪtɪ/ *n.* [L *sapidus* f. *sapere* taste]

sapient /ˈseɪpɪənt/ *adj. literary* **1** wise. **2** aping wisdom; of fancied sagacity. □□ **sapience** *n.* **sapiently** *adv.* [ME f. OF *sapient* or L part. stem of *sapere* be wise]

sapiential /ˌseɪpɪˈenʃ(ə)l, ˌsæ-/ *adj. literary* of or relating to wisdom. [ME f. F *sapiential* or eccl.L *sapientialis* f. L *sapientia* wisdom]

Sapir /ˈsæpɪə(r)/, Edward (1884–1939), American linguistics scholar and anthropologist who, like Bloomfield, had an important role in the creation of American linguistic structuralism. He was immensely learned in a number of subjects and left important works on American-Indian languages and linguistic theory (e.g. his book *Language*, 1921). His approach is characterized by constant awareness of the links between language and culture, language and psychology, etc.

sapling /ˈsæplɪŋ/ *n.* **1** a young tree. **2** a youth. **3** a greyhound in its first year.

sapodilla /ˌsæpəˈdɪlə/ *n.* a large evergreen tropical American tree, *Manilkara zapota*, with edible fruit and durable wood, and sap from which chicle is obtained. □ **sapodilla plum** the fruit of this tree. [Sp. *zapotillo* dimin. of *zapote* f. Aztec *tzápotl*]

saponaceous /ˌsæpəˈneɪʃəs/ *adj.* **1** of, like, or containing soap; soapy. **2** *joc.* unctuous; flattering. [mod.L *saponaceus* f. L *sapo -onis* soap]

saponify /səˈpɒnɪˌfaɪ/ *v.* (**-ies, -ied**) **1** *tr.* turn (fat or oil) into soap by reaction with an alkali. **2** *tr.* convert (an ester) to an acid and alcohol. **3** *intr.* become saponified. □□ **saponifiable** *adj.* **saponification** /-fɪˈkeɪʃ(ə)n/ *n.* [F *saponifier* (as SAPONACEOUS)]

saponin /ˈsæpənɪn/ *n.* any of a group of plant glycosides, esp. those derived from the bark of the tree *Quillaja saponaria*, that foam when shaken with water and are used in detergents and fire extinguishers. [F *saponine* f. L *sapo -onis* soap]

sapor /ˈseɪpɔː(r)/ *n.* **1** a quality perceptible by taste, e.g. sweetness. **2** the distinctive taste of a substance. **3** the sensation of taste. [ME f. L *sapere* taste]

sappanwood /ˈsæpənˌwʊd/ *n.* (also **sapanwood**) the heartwood of an E. Indian tree, *Caesalpinia sappan*, formerly used as a source of red dye. [Du. *sapan* f. Malay *sapang*, of S. Indian orig.]

sapper /ˈsæpə(r)/ *n.* **1** a person who digs saps. **2** *Brit.* a soldier of the Royal Engineers (esp. as the official term for a private).

Sapphic /ˈsæfɪk/ *adj. & n.* —*adj.* **1** of or relating to Sappho or her poetry. **2** lesbian. —*n.* (in *pl.*) (**sapphics**) verse in a metre associated with Sappho. [F *sa(p)phique* f. L *Sapphicus* f. Gk *Sapphikos* f. *Sapphō*]

sapphire /ˈsæfaɪə(r)/ *n. & adj.* —*n.* **1** a transparent blue precious stone consisting of corundum. **2** precious transparent corundum of any colour. **3** the bright blue of a sapphire. **4** a humming-bird with bright blue colouring. —*adj.* of sapphire blue. □ **sapphire wedding** a 45th wedding anniversary. □□ **sapphirine** /ˈsæfɪˌraɪn/ *adj.* [ME f. OF *safir* f. L *sapphirus* f. Gk *sappheiros* prob. = lapis lazuli]

Sappho /ˈsæfəʊ/ (early 7th c. BC) Greek lyric poetess from the island of Lesbos. The fragments of her poems, written in her local dialect, are chiefly on personal subjects; many concern young girls in her circle, and her affection and love for them.

Sapporo /səˈpɔːrəʊ/ a city in northern Japan, the capital of Hokkaido region; pop. (1987) 1,555,000.

w we z zoo ʃ she ʒ decision θ thin ð this ŋ ring x loch tʃ chip dʒ jar (*see over for vowels*)

sappy /ˈsæpɪ/ adj. (**sappier, sappiest**) 1 full of sap. 2 young and vigorous. □□ **sappily** adv. **sappiness** n.

sapro- /ˈsæprəʊ/ comb. form Biol. rotten, putrefying. [Gk sapros putrid]

saprogenic /ˌsæprəˈdʒenɪk/ adj. causing or produced by putrefaction.

saprophagous /sæˈprɒfəgəs/ adj. feeding on decaying matter.

saprophile /ˈsæprəˌfaɪl/ n. a bacterium inhabiting putrid matter. □□ **saprophilous** /-ˈprɒfɪləs/ adj.

saprophyte /ˈsæprəˌfaɪt/ n. any plant or micro-organism living on dead or decayed organic matter. □□ **saprophytic** /-ˈfɪtɪk/ adj.

sapwood /ˈsæpwʊd/ n. the soft outer layers of recently formed wood between the heartwood and the bark.

Saqqara /səˈkɑːrə/ a vast necropolis of ancient Memphis, with monuments dating from the early dynastic period (3rd millennium BC) to the Graeco-Roman age, including the step pyramid of King Djoser (c.2700 BC), the earliest type of pyramid and the first known building entirely of stone.

saraband /ˈsærəˌbænd/ n. 1 a stately old Spanish dance. 2 music for this or in its rhythm, usu. in triple time often with a long note on the second beat of the bar. [F sarabande f. Sp. & It. zarabanda]

Saracen /ˈsærəs(ə)n/ n. & adj. hist. —n. 1 an Arab or Muslim at the time of the Crusades. 2 a nomad of the Syrian and Arabian desert. —adj. of the Saracens. □ **Saracen corn** Brit. archaic buckwheat. **Saracen's head** the head of a Saracen or Turk as a heraldic charge or inn-sign. □□ **Saracenic** /ˌsærəˈsenɪk/ adj. [ME f. OF sar(r)azin, sar(r)acin f. LL Saracenus f. late Gk Sarakēnos perh. f. Arab. šarḳī eastern]

Saragossa /ˌsærəˈgɒsə/ (Spanish **Zaragoza** /ˌθærəˈgɒθə/) a city of northern Spain, the capital of Aragon region; pop. (1986) 596,000. □ **Maid of Saragossa** María Augustín, noted for her heroism in the siege of Saragossa by the French (1808–9) during the Peninsular War. Her exploits are described in Byron's poem 'Childe Harold'.

Sarah /ˈseərə/ the wife of Abraham and mother of Isaac (Gen. 17: 15 ff.).

Sarajevo /ˌsærəˈjervəʊ/ a city in Yugoslavia, formerly capital of the Balkan province of Bosnia, now capital of the republic of Bosnia and Hercegovina; pop. (1981) 448,500. In this city the Archduke Franz Ferdinand (heir to the Austrian throne) and his wife were assassinated on 28 June 1914, an event which triggered off the First World War. The city was a centre of Slav opposition to Austrian rule, and connections between Bosnian nationalists and Serbian agents were used by the Austrians as a pretext for war with Serbia. Each side was supported by its European allies, so that within a few weeks most of the Continent was at war.

sarangi /səˈræŋɡɪ/ n. (pl. **sarangis**) an Indian stringed instrument played with a bow. [Hindi sāraṅgī]

sarape var. of SERAPE.

Saratoga /ˌsærəˈtəʊgə/ a city and spa in New York State; pop. (1980) 23,900. Near this city two battles were fought (1777) in the War of American Independence. The Americans were victorious in both, and in the second battle the British forces, under General Burgoyne, were decisively defeated. The defeat encouraged French support of the Americans and destroyed the best British opportunity to end the rebellion.

Saratov /səˈrætɒf/ an industrial city of the Soviet Union, on the River Volga; pop. (est. 1987) 918,000.

Sarawak /səˈrɑːwək/ a State of Malaysia on the NW coast of Borneo; pop. (1980) 1,307,600; capital, Kuching.

sarcasm /ˈsɑːˌkæz(ə)m/ n. 1 a bitter or wounding remark. 2 a taunt, esp. one ironically worded. 3 language consisting of such remarks. 4 the faculty of using this. □□ **sarcastic** /sɑːˈkæstɪk/ adj. **sarcastically** /sɑːˈkæstɪkəlɪ/ adv. [F sarcasme or f. LL sarcasmus f. late Gk sarkasmos f. Gk sarkazō tear flesh, in late Gk gnash the teeth, speak bitterly f. sarx sarkos flesh]

sarcenet var. of SARSENET.

sarcoma /sɑːˈkəʊmə/ n. (pl. **sarcomas** or **sarcomata** /-mətə/) a malignant tumour of connective or other non-epithelial tissue.

□□ **sarcomatosis** /-ˈtəʊsɪs/ n. **sarcomatous** adj. [mod.L f. Gk sarkōma f. sarkoō become fleshy f. sarx sarkos flesh]

sarcophagus /sɑːˈkɒfəgəs/ n. (pl. **sarcophagi** /-ˌgaɪ, -ˌdʒaɪ/) a stone coffin, esp. one adorned with a sculpture or inscription. [L f. Gk sarkophagos flesh-consuming (as SARCOMA, -phagos -eating)]

sarcoplasm /ˈsɑːkəˌplæz(ə)m/ n. Anat. the cytoplasm in which muscle fibrils are embedded. [Gk sarx sarkos flesh + PLASMA]

sarcous /ˈsɑːkəs/ adj. consisting of flesh or muscle. [Gk sarx sarkos flesh]

sard /sɑːd/ n. a yellow or orange-red cornelian. [ME f. F sarde or L sarda = LL sardius f. Gk sardios prob. f. Sardō Sardinia]

Sardanapalus /ˌsɑːdəˈnæpələs/ the name given by ancient Greek historians to the last king of Assyria (died c.626 BC), portrayed as being notorious for his wealth and sensuality. It may not represent a specific historical person. [Gk Sardanapalos]

sardelle /sɑːˈdel/ n. any of several fish resembling the sardine. [It. sardella dimin. of sarda f. L (as SARDINE[1])]

sardine[1] /sɑːˈdiːn/ n. a young pilchard or similar young or small herring-like marine fish. □ **like sardines** crowded close together (as sardines are in tins). [ME f. OF sardine = It. sardina f. L f. sarda f. Gk, perh. f. Sardō Sardinia]

sardine[2] /ˈsɑːdaɪn/ n. a precious stone mentioned in Rev. 4: 3. [ME f. LL sardinus f. Gk sardinos var. of sardios SARD]

Sardinia /sɑːˈdɪnɪə/ (Italian **Sardegna** /sɑːˈdeɪnjə/) a large island in the Mediterranean Sea west of Italy, which became part of the kingdom of Italy in 1861; pop. (1981) 1,594,200; capital, Cagliari. □□ **Sardinian** adj. & n.

Sardis /ˈsɑːdɪs/ an ancient city that was the capital of Lydia.

sardius /ˈsɑːdɪəs/ n. Bibl. etc. a precious stone. [ME f. LL f. Gk sardios sard]

sardonic /sɑːˈdɒnɪk/ adj. 1 grimly jocular. 2 (of laughter etc.) bitterly mocking or cynical. □□ **sardonically** adv. **sardonicism** /-ˌsɪz(ə)m/ n. [F sardonique, earlier sardonien f. L sardonius f. Gk sardonios of Sardinia, substituted for Homeric sardanios (epithet of bitter or scornful laughter) because of belief that eating a Sardinian plant could result in convulsive laughter ending in death]

sardonyx /ˈsɑːdənɪks/ n. onyx in which white layers alternate with sard. [ME f. L f. Gk sardonux (prob. as SARD, ONYX)]

saree var. of SARI.

sargasso /sɑːˈgæsəʊ/ n. (also **sargassum**) (pl. **-os** or **-oes** or **sargassa**) any seaweed of the genus Sargassum, with berry-like air-vessels, found floating in island-like masses, esp. in the Sargasso Sea. Also called GULFWEED. [Port. sargaço, of unkn. orig.]

Sargasso Sea /sɑːˈgæsəʊ/ a region of the western Atlantic Ocean between the Azores and the West Indies, around latitude 35 °N, so called because of the prevalence in it of floating sargasso seaweed. It is the breeding-place of eels from the rivers of Europe and eastern North America.

sarge /sɑːdʒ/ n. sl. sergeant. [abbr.]

Sargent /ˈsɑːdʒ(ə)nt/, John Singer (1856–1925), American portrait painter. Born in Florence, he travelled and studied widely in Europe as a youth. In the 1870s he painted some impressionist landscapes, but it was in portraiture that he developed the loaded brush and bravura handling typical of his style. A painterly painter—he had profited from studying Manet, Hals, and Velazquez—his virtuoso technique was much in demand in Parisian circles, but the scandal over the supposed eroticism of Madame Gautreau (1884) made him move to London, where he dominated society portraiture for over twenty years. In about 1910 he produced a small number of water-colour landscapes and later worked as an official war artist, revealing an unexpected side to his talents in the enormous Gassed (1918) which has remarkable tragic power and is one of the greatest pictures inspired by the First World War.

Sargodha /sɑːˈgəʊdə/ a city in northern Pakistan, on the lower Jhelum Canal; pop. (1981) 294,000.

Sargon /ˈsɑːgɒn/ (2334–2279 BC) the semi-legendary founder of the ancient kingdom of Akkad.

Sargon II /ˈsɑːgɒn/ (d. 705 BC) king of Assyria 722–705 BC, who

æ cat ɑː arm e bed ɜː her ɪ sit iː see ɒ hot ɔː saw ʌ run ʊ put uː too ə ago aɪ my

adopted the name of Sargon of Akkad (see entry) and is famous for his conquest of a number of cities in Syria and Palestine.

sari /ˈsɑːriː/ n. (also **saree**) (pl. **saris** or **sarees**) a length of cotton or silk draped round the body, traditionally worn as a main garment by Indian women. [Hindi sāṛ(h)ī]

sark /sɑːk/ n. Sc. & N.Engl. a shirt or chemise. [ME serk f. ON serkr f. Gmc]

sarking /ˈsɑːkɪŋ/ n. boarding between the rafters and the roof. [SARK + -ING¹]

sarky /ˈsɑːki/ adj. (**sarkier**, **sarkiest**) Brit. sl. sarcastic. □□ **sarkily** adv. **sarkiness** n. [abbr.]

Sarmatia /sɑːˈmeɪʃə/ the name in ancient times of a region north of the Black Sea inhabited by ancestors of the Slavs, used occasionally by English poets to signify Poland. □□ **Sarmatian** adj. & n.

sarmentose /ˈsɑːmənˌtəʊs/ adj. (also **sarmentous** /-ˈmentəs/) Bot. having long thin trailing shoots. [L sarmentosus f. sarmenta (pl.) twigs, brushwood, f. sarpere to prune]

sarnie /ˈsɑːni/ n. Brit. colloq. a sandwich. [abbr.]

sarong /səˈrɒŋ/ n. **1** a Malay and Javanese garment consisting of a long strip of (often striped) cloth worn by both sexes tucked round the waist or under the armpits. **2** a woman's garment resembling this. [Malay, lit. 'sheath']

saros /ˈsɑːrɒs/ n. Astron. a period of about 18 years between repetitions of eclipses. [Gk f. Babylonian šār(u) 3,600 (years)]

Sarre see SAAR.

sarrusophone /səˈruːsəˌfəʊn/ n. a metal wind instrument played with a double reed like an oboe. [Sarrus, 19th-c. Fr. inventor]

sarsaparilla /ˌsɑːsəpəˈrɪlə/ n. **1** a preparation of the dried roots of various plants, esp. smilax, used to flavour some drinks and medicines and formerly as a tonic. **2** any of the plants yielding this. [Sp. zarzaparilla f. zarza bramble, prob. + dimin. of parra vine]

sarsen /ˈsɑːs(ə)n/ n. Geol. a sandstone boulder carried by ice during a glacial period. [prob. var. of SARACEN]

sarsenet /ˈsɑːsənɪt/ n. (also **sarcenet**) a fine soft silk material used esp. for linings. [ME f. AF sarzinett perh. dimin. of sarzin SARACEN after OF drap sarrasinois Saracen cloth]

sartorial /sɑːˈtɔːrɪəl/ adj. **1** of a tailor or tailoring. **2** of men's clothes. □□ **sartorially** adv. [L sartor tailor f. sarcire sart- patch]

sartorius /sɑːˈtɔːrɪəs/ n. Anat. the long narrow muscle running across the front of each thigh. [mod.L f. L sartor tailor (the muscle being used in adopting a tailor's cross-legged posture)]

Sartre /sɑːtr/, Jean-Paul (1905–80), French philosopher, novelist, dramatist, and critic, a nephew of Albert Schweitzer. During the Second World War he was a prisoner of war and an active member of the Resistance. In his philosophy and literature, which established him as the leading figure in the existentialist movement, he set out to show that the human situation is characterized by lack of a permanent nature, essence, or divinely bestowed destiny, and as a result possesses a terrifying freedom of choice. His later philosophy, cast in a Marxist mould, explores the social setting of human relationships conditioned by material scarcity. His works include the treatise *Being and Nothingness* (1943), the novels *Nausea* (1938) and the trilogy *Les Chemins de la liberté* (*Roads to Freedom*, 1945–9), and the plays *Les Mouches* (*The Flies*, 1943) and *Huis clos* (*No Exit*, 1944). In 1964 he was offered but refused the Nobel Prize for literature. The novelist Simone de Beauvoir was his friend and lover throughout much of his life.

Sarum /ˈseərəm/ the ecclesiastical name of Salisbury, Wilts., and its diocese. □ **Old Sarum** a hill 3 km (2 miles) from Salisbury on which a Norman castle and town were built, now deserted. **Sarum use** the form of liturgy used in the diocese of Salisbury from the 11th c. to the Reformation. [med.L, perh. f. misreading of abbreviated form of L Sarisburia Salisbury]

SAS abbr. (in the UK) Special Air Service, a special section of the armed forces trained in commando techniques of warfare. (Cf. SBS.)

s.a.s.e. abbr. US self-addressed stamped envelope.

sash¹ /sæʃ/ n. a long strip or loop of cloth etc. worn over one shoulder usu. as part of a uniform or insignia, or worn round the waist, usu. by a woman or child. □□ **sashed** adj. [earlier shash f. Arab. šāš muslin, turban]

sash² /sæʃ/ n. **1** a frame holding the glass in a sash-window and usu. made to slide up and down in the grooves of a window aperture. **2** the glazed sliding light of a glasshouse or garden frame. □ **sash-cord** a strong cord attaching the sash-weights to a sash. **sash-tool** a glazier's or painter's brush for work on sash-windows. **sash-weight** a weight attached to each end of a sash to balance it at any height. **sash-window** a window with one or two sashes of which one or each can be slid vertically over the other to make an opening. □□ **sashed** adj. [sashes corrupt. of CHASSIS, mistaken for pl.]

sashay /ˈsæʃeɪ/ v.intr. esp. US colloq. walk or move ostentatiously, casually, or diagonally. [corrupt. of CHASSÉ]

sashimi /ˈsæʃɪmi/ n. a Japanese dish of garnished raw fish in thin slices. [Jap.]

sasin /ˈsæsɪn/ n. = BLACKBUCK. [Nepali]

sasine /ˈseɪsɪn/ n. Sc. Law **1** the possession of feudal property. **2** an act or document granting this. [var. of SEISIN]

Sask. abbr. Saskatchewan.

Saskatchewan /səˈskætʃɪwən/ **1** a province of central Canada (from 1905), settled by the Hudson's Bay Company; pop. (1986) 1,010,200; capital, Regina. **2** a river of Canada, flowing from the Rocky Mountains to Lake Winnipeg.

Saskatoon /ˌsæskəˈtuːn/ an industrial city in south central Saskatchewan, at the heart of the great plains of central Canada; pop. (1986) 177,600; metropolitan area pop. 200,650.

sasquatch /ˈsæskwætʃ/ n. a supposed yeti-like animal of NW America. [Amer. Ind.]

sass /sæs/ n. & v. US colloq. —n. impudence, cheek. —v.tr. be impudent to, cheek. [var. of SAUCE]

sassaby /ˈsæsəbi/ n. (pl. **-ies**) a S. African antelope, Damaliscus lunatus, similar to the hartebeest. [Tswana tsessébe, -ábi]

sassafras /ˈsæsəˌfræs/ n. **1** a small tree, Sassafras albidum, native to N. America, with aromatic leaves and bark. **2** a preparation of oil extracted from the leaves, or from its bark, used medicinally or in perfumery. [Sp. sasafrás or Port. sassafraz, of unkn. orig.]

Sassanian /sæˈseɪnɪən/ n. & adj. (also **Sassanid** /ˈsæsənɪd/) —n. a member of (esp. a king) of the dynasty ruling the Persian empire from 224 until driven from Mesopotamia by the Arabs (637–51). —adj. of or relating to this dynasty. [Sasan, grandfather of the first Sassanian, Ardashir]

Sassenach /ˈsæsəˌnæx, -ˌnæk/ n. & adj. Sc. & Ir. usu. derog. —n. an English person. —adj. English. [Gael. Sasunnoch, Ir. Sasanach f. L Saxones Saxons]

Sassoon /səˈsuːn/, Siegfried Louvain (1886–1967), English poet and prose writer, remembered for his starkly realistic poems written in the trenches during the First World War. In hospital, recovering from shell-shock, he met and inspired the poet Wilfred Owen. After the war his poetry became increasingly religious and he became a successful prose writer with *Memoirs of a Fox-Hunting Man* (1928), *Memoirs of an Infantry Officer* (1930), *Sherston's Progress* (1936), three volumes of autobiography, and an important biography of George Meredith (1948). His later works reflect his attachment to the countryside.

sassy /ˈsæsi/ adj. (**sassier**, **sassiest**) esp. US colloq. = SAUCY. □□ **sassily** adv. **sassiness** n. [var. of SAUCY]

sastrugi /sæˈstruːgi/ n.pl. wavelike irregularities on the surface of hard polar snow, caused by winds. [Russ. zastrugi small ridges]

Sat. abbr. Saturday.

sat past and past part. of SIT.

Satan /ˈseɪt(ə)n/ the Devil; Lucifer. [OE f. LL f. Gk f. Heb. śāṭān lit. 'adversary' f. śaṭan oppose, plot against]

satanic /səˈtænɪk/ adj. **1** of, like, or befitting Satan. **2** diabolical, hellish. □□ **satanically** adv.

Satanism /ˈseɪtəˌnɪz(ə)m/ n. **1** the worship of Satan, with a travesty of Christian forms. **2** the pursuit of evil for its own sake. **3** deliberate wickedness. □□ **Satanist** n. **Satanize** v.tr. (also **-ise**).

Satanology /ˌseɪtəˈnɒlədʒɪ/ n. **1** beliefs concerning the Devil. **2** a history or collection of these.

satay /ˈsæteɪ/ n. (also **satai, saté**) an Indonesian and Malaysian dish consisting of small pieces of meat grilled on a skewer and usu. served with spiced sauce. [Malayan *satai sate*, Indonesian *sate*]

SATB abbr. Mus. soprano, alto, tenor, and bass (as a combination of voices).

satchel /ˈsætʃ(ə)l/ n. a small bag usu. of leather and hung from the shoulder with a strap, for carrying books etc. esp. to and from school. [ME f. OF *sachel* f. L *saccellus* (as SACK[1])]

sate /seɪt/ v.tr. **1** gratify (desire, a desirous person) to the full. **2** cloy, surfeit, weary with over-abundance (*sated with pleasure*). □□ **sateless** adj. poet. [prob. f. dial. *sade*, OE *sadian* (as SAD), assim. to SATIATE]

sateen /sæˈtiːn/ n. cotton fabric woven like satin with a glossy surface. [*satin* after *velveteen*]

satellite /ˈsætəˌlaɪt/ n. & adj. —n. **1** a celestial body orbiting the Earth or another planet. **2** an artificial body placed in orbit round the Earth or other planet for purposes of observation, research, navigation or communications. The first artificial satellite (Sputnik I) was launched by the USSR on 4 Oct. 1957, but the idea had been put forward much earlier, e.g. in Jules Verne's *Begum's Fortune* (tr. 1880). **3** a follower; a hanger-on. **4** an underling; a member of an important person's staff or retinue. **5** (in full **satellite State**) a small country etc. nominally independent but controlled by or dependent on another. —adj. **1** transmitted by satellite (*satellite communications*; *satellite television*). **2** esp. Computing secondary; dependent; minor (*networks of small satellite computers*). □ **satellite dish** a concave dish-shaped aerial for receiving broadcasting signals transmitted by satellite. **satellite town** a small town economically or otherwise dependent on a nearby larger town. □□ **satellitic** /-ˈlɪtɪk/ adj. **satellitism** n. [F *satellite* or L *satelles satellitis* attendant]

Sati /ˈsɒtiː/ Hinduism the wife of Siva, reborn as Parvati. According to some accounts, she died by throwing herself into the sacred fire, hence the custom of suttee. [Skr., = virtuous woman, chaste wife]

sati var. of SUTTEE.

satiate /ˈseɪʃɪˌeɪt/ adj. & v. —adj. archaic satiated. —v.tr. = SATE. □□ **satiable** /-ʃəb(ə)l/ adj. archaic. **satiation** /-ˈeɪʃ(ə)n/ n. [L *satiatus* past part. of *satiare* f. *satis* enough]

Satie /ˈsɑːtiː/, Erik (1866–1925), French composer. He formed the centre of an irreverent avant-garde artistic set, associated not only with the composers of the group known as Les Six but also with Cocteau, Dadaism, and surrealism. He was fond of giving facetious titles to his short irresistibly naïve works: the *Trois Pièces en forme de poire* (1903), for example, is in fact a set of six pieces. One of his few large-scale works is the symphonic drama *Socrate* (1919) to a libretto based on Plato and scored for four sopranos and orchestra.

satiety /səˈtaɪɪtɪ/ n. **1** the state of being glutted or satiated. **2** the feeling of having too much of something. **3** (foll. by *of*) a cloyed dislike of. □ **to satiety** to an extent beyond what is desired. [obs. F *sacieté* f. L *satietas -tatis* f. *satis* enough]

satin /ˈsætɪn/ n., adj., & v. —n. a fabric of silk or various man-made fibres, with a glossy surface on one side produced by a twill weave with the weft-threads almost hidden. —adj. smooth as satin. —v.tr. (**satined, satining**) give a glossy surface to (paper). □ **satin finish 1** a polish given to silver etc. with a metallic brush. **2** any effect resembling satin in texture produced on materials in various ways. **satin paper** fine glossy writing paper. **satin spar** a fibrous variety of gypsum. **satin stitch** a long straight embroidery stitch, giving the appearance of satin. **satin white** a white pigment of calcium sulphate and alumina. □□ **satinized** adj. (also **-ised**). **satiny** adj. [ME f. OF f. Arab. *zaytūnī* of *Tseutung* in China]

satinette /ˌsætɪˈnet/ n. (also **satinet**) a satin-like fabric made partly or wholly of cotton or synthetic fibre.

satinflower /ˈsætɪnˌflaʊə(r)/ n. **1** any plant of the genus *Clarkia*, with pink or lavender flowers. **2** = HONESTY 3.

satinwood /ˈsætɪnˌwʊd/ n. **1 a** (in full **Ceylon satinwood**) a tree, *Chloroxylon swietenia*, native to central and southern India and Sri Lanka (formerly Ceylon). **b** (in full **West Indian satinwood**) a tree, *Fagara flava*, native to the West Indies, Bermuda, the Bahamas, and southern Florida. **2** the yellow glossy timber of either of these trees.

satire /ˈsætaɪə(r)/ n. **1** the use of ridicule, irony, sarcasm, etc., to expose folly or vice or to lampoon an individual. **2** a work or composition in prose or verse using satire. **3** this branch of literature. **4** a thing that brings ridicule upon something else. **5** Rom. Antiq. a poetic medley, esp. a poem ridiculing prevalent vices or follies. [F *satire* or L *satira* later form of *satura* medley]

satiric /səˈtɪrɪk/ adj. **1** of satire or satires. **2** containing satire (*wrote a satiric review*). **3** writing satire (*a satiric poet*). [F *satirique* or LL *satiricus* (as SATIRE)]

satirical /səˈtɪrɪk(ə)l/ adj. **1** = SATIRIC. **2** given to the use of satire in speech or writing or to cynical observation of others; sarcastic; humorously critical. □□ **satirically** adv.

satirist /ˈsætərɪst/ n. **1** a writer of satires. **2** a satirical person.

satirize /ˈsætɪˌraɪz/ v.tr. (also **-ise**) **1** assail or ridicule with satire. **2** write a satire upon. **3** describe satirically. □□ **satirization** /-ˈzeɪʃ(ə)n/ n. [F *satiriser* (as SATIRE)]

satisfaction /ˌsætɪsˈfækʃ(ə)n/ n. **1** the act or an instance of satisfying; the state of being satisfied (*heard this with great satisfaction*). **2** a thing that satisfies desire or gratifies feeling (*is a great satisfaction to me*). **3** a thing that settles an obligation or pays a debt. **4 a** (foll. by *for*) atonement; compensation (*demanded satisfaction*). **b** Theol. Christ's atonement for the sins of mankind. □ **to one's satisfaction** so that one is satisfied. [ME f. OF f. L *satisfactio -onis* (as SATISFY)]

satisfactory /ˌsætɪsˈfæktərɪ/ adj. **1** adequate; causing or giving satisfaction (*was a satisfactory pupil*). **2** satisfying expectations or needs; leaving no room for complaint (*a satisfactory result*). □□ **satisfactorily** adv. **satisfactoriness** n. [F *satisfactoire* or med.L *satisfactorius* (as SATISFY)]

satisfy /ˈsætɪsˌfaɪ/ v. (**-ies, -ied**) **1** tr. **a** meet the expectations or desires of; comply with (a demand). **b** be accepted by (a person, his taste) as adequate; be equal to (a preconception etc.). **2** tr. put an end to (an appetite or want) by supplying what was required. **3** tr. rid (a person) of an appetite or want in a similar way. **4** intr. give satisfaction; leave nothing to be desired. **5** tr. pay (a debt or creditor). **6** tr. adequately meet, fulfil, or comply with (conditions, obligations, etc.) (*has satisfied all the legal conditions*). **7** tr. (often foll. by *of, that*) provide with adequate information or proof, convince (*satisfied the others that they were right*; *satisfy the court of their innocence*). **8** tr. Math. (of a quantity) make (an equation) true. **9** tr. (in passive) **a** (foll. by *with*) contented or pleased with. **b** (foll. by *to*) demand no more than or consider it enough to do. □ **satisfy the examiners** reach the standard required to pass an examination. **satisfy oneself** (often foll. by *that* + clause) be certain in one's own mind. □□ **satisfiable** adj. **satisfiability** /-əˈbɪlɪtɪ/ n. **satisfiedly** adv. **satisfying** adj. **satisfyingly** adv. [ME f. OF *satisfier* f. L *satisfacere satisfact-* f. *satis* enough]

satori /səˈtɔːrɪ/ n. Buddhism sudden enlightenment. [Jap.]

satrap /ˈsætræp/ n. **1** a provincial governor in the ancient Persian empire. **2** a subordinate ruler, colonial governor, etc. [ME f. OF *satrape* or L *satrapa* f. Gk *satrapēs* f. OPers. *xšathra-pāvan* country-protector]

satrapy /ˈsætrəpɪ/ n. (pl. **-ies**) a province ruled over by a satrap.

satsuma /ˈsætsʊmə/ n. **1** /also sætˈsuːmə/ a variety of tangerine orig. grown in Japan. **2** (**Satsuma**) (in full **Satsuma ware**) cream-coloured Japanese pottery. [*Satsuma* a province in Japan]

saturate /ˈsætʃəˌreɪt, -tjʊˌreɪt/ v.tr. **1** fill with moisture; soak thoroughly. **2** (often foll. by *with*) fill to capacity. **3** cause (a substance, solution, vapour, metal, or air) to absorb, hold, or combine with the greatest possible amount of another substance, or of moisture, magnetism, electricity, etc. **4** cause (a substance) to combine with the maximum of another substance. **5** supply (a market) beyond the point at which the demand for a product is satisfied. **6** (foll. by *with*, *in*) imbue with or steep in (learning, tradition, prejudice, etc.). **7** overwhelm (enemy defences, a target area, etc.) by concentrated bombing. **8** (as **saturated** *adj.*) **a** (of colour) full; rich; free from an admixture of white. **b** (of fat molecules) containing the greatest number of hydrogen atoms. □□ **saturate** /-rət/ *adj. literary.* **saturable** /-rəb(ə)l/ *adj.* **saturant** /-rənt/ *n. & adj.* [L *saturare* f. *satur* full]

saturation /ˌsætʃəˈreɪʃ(ə)n, -tjʊˈreɪʃ(ə)n/ *n.* the act or an instance of saturating; the state of being saturated. □ **saturation point** the stage beyond which no more can be absorbed or accepted.

Saturday /ˈsætədeɪ, -dɪ/ *n. & adv.* —*n.* the seventh day of the week, following Friday. —*adv. colloq.* **1** on Saturday. **2** (**Saturdays**) on Saturdays; each Saturday. [OE *Sætern(es) dæg* transl. of L *Saturni dies* day of Saturn]

Saturn /ˈsætə(ə)n/ **1** *Rom. Mythol.* an ancient god whose festival was 17 Dec., often interpreted (but not with certainty) as a god of agriculture, and also identified with the Greek Cronus (see entry). In historical times his festival was the merriest of the year, when slaves were allowed temporary liberty to do as they liked and presents were exchanged. By about the 4th c. AD much of this had been transferred to what was then New Year's Day, and so became one of the elements in the traditional celebrations of Christmas. **2 a** *Astron.* a ringed planet of the solar system, sixth in distance from the sun, with a mean orbital radius of 1,427 million km. The planet has a radius of 60,000 km, but the rings, extending out to a distance twice as great, make this planet a glorious sight in any moderate to large telescope. Galileo recognized from his observations that the planet departed from sphericity, but could not provide the explanation. We now know that several thousand individual rings, composed of small icy particles, occupy a wide band of orbits, broken here and there by the so-called 'gaps', which are not true gaps in the particle distribution, but only regions of smaller particle density. The planet itself has a dense hydrogen-rich atmosphere, similar to that of Jupiter, but with more vigorous atmospheric circulation. There are at least fifteen moons, ranging in radius from the 2,560 km of Titan, which itself has a dense atmosphere of methane, to the few kilometres radius of the small moons which travel close to the outermost thin ring, 'shepherding' it into place. **b** *Astrol.* Saturn as a supposed astrological influence on those born under its sign, characterized by coldness and gloominess. —*n. Alchemy* the metal lead. □□ **Saturnian** /səˈtɜːnɪən/ *adj.*

saturnalia /ˌsætəˈneɪlɪə/ *n.* (*pl.* same or **saturnalias**) **1** (usu. **Saturnalia**) *Rom.Hist.* the festival of Saturn in December, characterized by unrestrained merrymaking for all, the predecessor of Christmas. **2** (as *sing.* or *pl.*) a scene of wild revelry or tumult; an orgy. □□ **saturnalian** *adj.* [L, neut. pl. of *Saturnalis* (as SATURN)]

saturnic /səˈtɜːnɪk/ *adj. Med.* affected with lead-poisoning. □□ **saturnism** /ˈsætənɪz(ə)m/ [SATURN 2]

saturniid /sæˈtɜːnɪd/ *n.* any large moth of the family Saturniidae, including emperor moths. [mod.L]

saturnine /ˈsætənaɪn/ *adj.* **1 a** of a sluggish gloomy temperament. **b** (of looks etc.) dark and brooding. **2** *archaic* **a** of the metal lead. **b** *Med.* of or affected by lead-poisoning. □□ **saturninely** *adv.* [ME f. OF *saturnin* f. med.L *Saturninus* (as SATURN)]

satyagraha /sʌtjɑːgrəˈhɑː/ *n. Ind.* **1** *hist.* a policy of passive resistance to British rule advocated by Gandhi. **2** passive resistance as a policy. [Skr. f. *satya* truth + *āgraha* obstinacy]

satyr /ˈsætə(r)/ *n.* **1** *Gk Mythol.* any of a class of woodland spirits, bestial in their desires and behaviour, in Hellenistic art and poetry, associated with Dionysus. In Greek art of the pre-Roman period they are represented with the tail and ears of a horse. Roman sculptors assimilated the satyr in some degree to the faun of their native mythology, giving it the ears, tail, and legs of a goat, with budding horns. **2** a lustful or sensual man. **3** = SATYRID. [ME f. OF *satyre* or L *satyrus* f. Gk *saturos*]

satyriasis /ˌsætɪˈraɪəsɪs/ *n. Med.* excessive sexual desire in men. [LL f. Gk *satyriasis* (as SATYR)]

satyric /səˈtɪrɪk/ *adj.* (in Greek mythology) of or relating to

satyrs. □ **satyric drama** a kind of ancient Greek comic play with a chorus of satyrs. [L *satyricus* f. Gk *saturikos* (as SATYR)]

satyrid /səˈtɪrɪd/ *n.* any butterfly of the family Satyridae, with distinctive eyelike markings on the wings. [mod.L *Satyridae* f. the genus-name *Satyrus* (as SATYR)]

sauce /sɔːs/ *n. & v.* —*n.* **1** any of various liquid or semi-solid preparations taken as a relish with food; the liquid constituent of a dish (*mint sauce; tomato sauce; chicken in a lemon sauce*). **2** something adding piquancy or excitement. **3** *colloq.* impudence, impertinence, cheek. **4** *US* stewed fruit etc. eaten as dessert or used as a garnish. —*v.tr.* **1** *colloq.* be impudent to; cheek. **2** *archaic* **a** season with sauce or condiments. **b** add excitement to. □ **sauce-boat** a kind of jug or dish used for serving sauces etc. **sauce for the goose** what is appropriate in one case (by implication appropriate in others). □□ **sauceless** *adj.* [ME f. OF ult. f. L *salsus* f. *salere* *sals-* to salt f. *sal* salt]

saucepan /ˈsɔːspən/ *n.* a usu. metal cooking pan, usu. round with a lid and a long handle at the side, used for boiling, stewing, etc., on top of a cooker. □□ **saucepanful** *n.* (*pl.* **-fuls**)

saucer /ˈsɔːsə(r)/ *n.* **1** a shallow circular dish used for standing a cup on and to catch drips. **2** any similar dish used to stand a plant pot etc. on. □□ **saucerful** *n.* (*pl.* **-fuls**). **saucerless** *adj.* [ME, = condiment-dish, f. OF *saussier(e)* sauce-boat, prob. f. LL *salsarium* (as SAUCE)]

saucy /ˈsɔːsɪ/ *adj.* (**saucier, sauciest**) **1** impudent, cheeky. **2** *colloq.* smart-looking (*a saucy hat*). **3** *colloq.* smutty, suggestive. □□ **saucily** *adv.* **sauciness** *n.* [earlier sense 'savoury', f. SAUCE]

Saudi /ˈsaʊdɪ/ *n. & adj.* (also **Saudi Arabian**) —*n.* (*pl.* **Saudis**) **1 a** a native or national of Saudi Arabia. **b** a person of Saudi descent. **2** a member of the dynasty founded by King Saud. —*adj.* of or relating to Saudi Arabia or the Saudi dynasty. [A. Ibn-*Saud*, Arab. king d. 1953]

Saudi Arabia /ˌsaʊdɪ əˈreɪbɪə/ a country in SW Asia occupying most of the Arabian peninsula; pop. (est. 1988) 15,452,100; official language, Arabic; capital, Riyadh. The birthplace of Islam, Saudi Arabia emerged from the Arab revolt against the Turks during the First World War to become an independent kingdom in 1932. Since the Second World War the economy has been revolutionized by the exploitation of the area's oil resources, the export of oil now accounting for 85% of the government's revenue and making Saudi Arabia the largest oil producer in the Middle East. Ruled along traditional Islamic lines, the country has exercised a conservative influence over Middle Eastern politics, although the position of the ruling house of Saud was severely threatened by the brief seizure of the Great Mosque in Mecca by Islamic fanatics in 1979. In 1987 violence in Mecca during an Iranian political demonstration in which over 400 people were killed and many others injured led to strained relations with Iran. □□ **Saudi Arabian** *adj. & n.*

sauerkraut /ˈsaʊəkraʊt/ *n.* a German dish of chopped pickled cabbage. [G f. *sauer* SOUR + *Kraut* vegetable]

sauger /ˈsɔːgə(r)/ *n. US* a small American pike-perch. [19th c.: orig. unkn.]

Saul /sɔːl/ **1** the first king of Israel (11th c. BC). **2** (also **Saul of Tarsus**) the original name of St Paul.

sauna /ˈsɔːnə/ *n.* **1** a Finnish-style steam bath. **2** a building used for this. [Finn.]

saunders var. of SANDERS.

saunter /ˈsɔːntə(r)/ *v. & n.* —*v.intr.* **1** walk slowly; amble, stroll. **2** proceed without hurry or effort. —*n.* **1** a leisurely ramble. **2** a slow gait. □□ **saunterer** *n.* [ME, = muse: orig. unkn.]

saurian /ˈsɔːrɪən/ *adj.* of or like a lizard. [mod.L *Sauria* f. Gk *saura* lizard]

sauropod /ˈsɔːrəʊˌpɒd/ *n.* any of a group of plant-eating dinosaurs with a long neck and tail, and four thick limbs. [Gk *saura* lizard + *pous pod-* foot]

saury /ˈsɔːrɪ/ *n.* (*pl.* **-ies**) a long-beaked marine fish, *Scomberesox saurus*, of temperate waters. [perh. f. LL f. Gk *sauros* horse-mackerel]

sausage /ˈsɒsɪdʒ/ *n.* **1 a** minced pork, beef, or other meat seasoned and often mixed with other ingredients, encased in cylindrical form in a skin, for cooking and eating hot or cold. **b** a length of this. **2** a sausage-shaped object. □ **not a sausage** *colloq.* nothing at all. **sausage dog** *Brit. colloq.* a dachshund. **sausage machine 1** a sausage-making machine. **2** a relentlessly uniform process. **sausage meat** minced meat used in sausages or as a stuffing etc. **sausage roll** *Brit.* sausage meat enclosed in a pastry roll and baked. [ME f. ONF *saussiche* f. med.L *salsicia* f. L *salsus*: see SAUCE]

Saussure /sɒˈsjʊə(r), səʊ-/, Ferdinand de (1857–1913), Swiss linguistics scholar often treated as the founder of modern linguistics. The contrast he established between a synchronic and a diachronic approach to language and the priority he gave to the former also allowed him to treat language as a system in which each element is defined in terms of the other elements (see STRUCTURALISM). In his lifetime he published works of fundamental importance for Indo-European studies, but his theoretical work, *Cours de linguistique générale*, appeared posthumously (1916) and was put together from lecture-notes.

sauté /ˈsəʊteɪ/ *adj., n., & v.* —*adj.* (esp. of potatoes etc.) quickly fried in a little hot fat. —*n.* food cooked in this way. —*v.tr.* (**sautéd** or **sautéed**) cook in this way. [F, past part. of *sauter* jump]

Sauternes /səʊˈtɜːn/ *n.* a sweet white wine from Sauternes in the Bordeaux region of France.

Sauveterrian /səʊvˈtɛrɪən/ *adj. & n.* —*adj.* of an early mesolithic industry of France and western Europe, named after the type-site at Sauveterre-la-Lémance, France. —*n.* this industry.

savage /ˈsævɪdʒ/ *adj., n., & v.* —*adj.* **1** fierce; cruel (*savage persecution; a savage blow*). **2** wild; primitive (*savage tribes; a savage animal*). **3** *archaic* (of scenery etc.) uncultivated (*a savage scene*). **4** *colloq.* angry; bad-tempered (*in a savage mood*). **5** *Heraldry* (of the human figure) naked. —*n.* **1** *Anthropol. derog.* a member of a primitive tribe. **2** a cruel or barbarous person. —*v.tr.* **1** (esp. of a dog, wolf, etc.) attack and bite or trample. **2** (of a critic etc.) attack fiercely. □□ **savagedom** *n.* **savagely** *adv.* **savageness** *n.* **savagery** *n.* (*pl.* -**ies**). [ME f. OF *sauvage* wild f. L *silvaticus* f. *silva* a wood]

savannah /səˈvænə/ *n.* (also **savanna**) a grassy plain in tropical and subtropical regions, with few or no trees. [Sp. *zavana* perh. of Carib orig.]

Savannakhet /ˌsævænəˈket/ a town in southern Laos on the Mekong River, close to the Thailand frontier; pop. 50,700.

savant /ˈsæv(ə)nt, sæˈvɑ̃/ *n.* (*fem.* **savante** /ˈsæv(ə)nt or sæˈvɑ̃t/) a learned person, esp. a distinguished scientist etc. [F, part. of *savoir* know (as SAPIENT)]

savate /səˈvɑːt/ *n.* a form of boxing in which feet and fists are used. [F, orig. a kind of shoe: cf. SABOT]

save[1] /seɪv/ *v. & n.* —*v.* **1** *tr.* (often foll. by *from*) rescue, preserve, protect, or deliver from danger, harm, discredit, etc. (*saved my life; saved me from drowning*). **2** *tr.* (often foll. by *up*) keep for future use; reserve; refrain from spending (*saved up £150 for a new bike; likes to save plastic bags*). **3** *tr.* (often *refl.*) **a** relieve (another person or oneself) from spending (money, time, trouble, etc.); prevent exposure to (annoyance etc.) (*saved myself £50; a word processor saves time*). **b** obviate the need or likelihood of (*soaking saves scrubbing*). **4** *tr.* preserve from damnation; convert (*saved her soul*). **5** *tr. & refl.* husband or preserve (one's strength, health, etc.) (*saving himself for the last lap; save your energy*). **6** *intr.* (often foll. by *up*) save money for future use. **7** *tr.* **a** avoid losing (a game, match, etc.). **b** prevent an opponent from scoring (a goal etc.). **c** stop (a ball etc.) from entering the goal. —*n.* **1** *Football* etc. the act of preventing an opponent's scoring etc. **2** *Bridge* a sacrifice-bid to prevent unnecessary losses. □ **save-all 1** a device to prevent waste. **2** *hist.* a pan with a spike for burning up candle-ends. **save appearances** present a prosperous, respectable, etc. appearance. **save-as-you-earn** *Brit.* a method of saving by regular deduction from earnings at source. **save one's breath** not waste time speaking to no effect. **save a person's face** see FACE. **save the situation** (or **day**) find or provide a solution to difficulty or disaster. **save one's skin** (or **neck** or **bacon**) avoid loss, injury, or death; escape from danger. **save the tide** get in or out (of port etc.) while it lasts. **save the**

trouble avoid useless or pointless effort. □□ **savable** *adj.* (also **saveable**). [ME f. AF *sa(u)ver*, OF *salver*, *sauver* f. LL *salvare* f. L *salvus* SAFE]

save[2] /seɪv/ *prep. & conj. archaic or poet.* —*prep.* except; but (*all save him*). —*conj.* (often foll. by *for*) unless; but; except (*happy save for one want; is well save that he has a cold*). [ME f. OF *sauf sauve* f. L *salvo, salva,* ablat. sing. of *salvus* SAFE]

saveloy /ˈsævəˌlɔɪ/ *n.* a seasoned red pork sausage, dried and smoked, and sold ready to eat. [corrupt. of F *cervelas, -at,* f. It. *cervellata* (*cervello* brain)]

saver /ˈseɪvə(r)/ *n.* **1** a person who saves esp. money. **2** (often in *comb.*) a device for economical use (of time etc.) (*found the short cut a time-saver*). **3** *Racing sl.* a hedging bet.

Savery /ˈseɪvərɪ/, Thomas ('Captain') (*c.*1650–1715), English inventor of a partially successful engine for raising water 'by the Impellent Force of Fire', patented in 1698. It was described as being suitable for raising water from mines, supplying towns with water, and operating mills. Its use of high-pressure steam made it very dangerous, but the patent covered the type of engine developed by Thomas Newcomen, who was therefore obliged to join Savery in its exploitation.

savin /ˈsævɪn/ *n.* (also **savine**) **1** a bushy juniper, *Juniperus sabina,* usu. spreading horizontally, and yielding oil formerly used in the treatment of amenorrhoea. **2** *US* = red cedar. [OE f. OF *savine* f. L *sabina* (*herba*) Sabine (herb)]

saving /ˈseɪvɪŋ/ *adj., n., & prep.* —*adj.* (often in *comb.*) making economical use of (*labour-saving*). —*n.* **1** anything that is saved. **2** an economy (*a saving in expenses*). **3** (usu. in *pl.*) money saved. —*prep.* **1** with the exception of; except (*all saving that one*). **2** without offence to (*saving your presence*). □ **saving clause** *Law* a clause containing a stipulation of exemption etc. **saving grace 1** the redeeming grace of God. **2** a redeeming quality or characteristic. **savings account** a deposit account. **savings bank** a bank receiving small deposits at interest and returning the profits to the depositors. **savings certificate** *Brit.* an interest-bearing document issued by the Government for the benefit of savers. [ME f. SAVE[1]: prep. prob. f. SAVE[2] after *touching*]

saviour /ˈseɪvjə(r)/ *n.* (*US* **savior**) **1** a person who saves or delivers from danger, destruction, etc. (*the saviour of the nation*). **2** (**Saviour**) (prec. by *the, our*) Christ. [ME f. OF *sauvéour* f. eccl.L *salvator -oris* (transl. Gk *sōtēr*) f. LL *salvare* SAVE[1]]

savoir faire /ˌsævwɑː ˈfeə(r)/ *n.* the ability to act suitably in any situation; tact. [F, = know how to do]

Savonarola /ˌsævənəˈrəʊlə/, Girolamo (1452–98), Italian preacher and reformer. A Dominican monk and severe ascetic, in 1482 he moved to Florence, where he attracted great attention as a preacher by his passionate denunciations of the immorality of the people of Florence and of the clergy, and by his apocalyptic prophecies. He became virtual ruler of Florence in 1494–5, but his severity made him many enemies, and in 1495 the Pope forbade him to preach and summoned him to Rome. His refusal to comply with these orders led to his excommunication in 1497; he was hanged as a schismatic and heretic.

Savonlinna /ˌsɑːvɒnˈliːnə/ (Swedish **Nyslott** /ˈniːslɒt/) a town in Mikkeli province, SE Finland; pop. (1987) 28,510. Once a resort of the Russian tsars, the town is now famous for its annual opera festival.

savor *US* var. of SAVOUR.

savory[1] /ˈseɪvərɪ/ *n.* (*pl.* -**ies**) any herb of the genus *Satureia,* esp. *S. hortensis* and *S. montana,* used esp. in cookery. [ME *saverey,* perh. f. OE *sætherie* f. L *satureia*]

savory[2] *US* var. of SAVOUR.

savour /ˈseɪvə(r)/ *n. & v.* (*US* **savor**) —*n.* **1** a characteristic taste, flavour, relish, etc. **2** a quality suggestive of or containing a small amount of another. **3** *archaic* a characteristic smell. —*v.* **1** *tr.* **a** appreciate and enjoy the taste of (food). **b** enjoy or appreciate (an experience etc.). **2** *intr.* (foll. by *of*) **a** suggest by taste, smell, etc. (*savours of mushrooms*). **b** imply or suggest a specified quality (*savours of impertinence*). □□ **savourless** *adj.* [ME f. OF f. L *sapor -oris* f. *sapere* to taste]

savoury /ˈseɪvərɪ/ *adj. & n.* (*US* **savory**) —*adj.* **1** having an appetizing taste or smell. **2** (of food) salty or piquant, not sweet (a *savoury omelette*). **3** pleasant; acceptable. —*n.* (*pl.* **-ies**) *Brit.* a savoury dish served as an appetizer or at the end of dinner. □□ **savourily** *adv.* **savouriness** *n.* [ME f. OF *savouré* past part. (as SAVOUR)]

Savoy /sə'vɔɪ/ a former duchy of SE France bordering on NW Italy, ruled by the counts of Savoy from the 11th c. although frequently invaded and fought over by neighbouring States. In 1720 Savoy was formed with Sardinia and Piedmont into the Kingdom of Sardinia. In the mid-19th c. Sardinia served as the nucleus for the formation of a unified Italy, but at the time of unification (1860) Savoy itself was ceded to France.

savoy /sə'vɔɪ/ *n.* a hardy variety of cabbage with wrinkled leaves. [*Savoy* in SE France]

Savoyard /sə'vɔɪɑːd, ˌsævɔɪ'ɑːd/ *n.* & *adj.* —*n.* a native of Savoy in SE France. —*adj.* of or relating to Savoy or its people etc. [F f. *Savoie* Savoy]

Savu Sea /'sɑːvuː/ part of the Indian Ocean lying to the south of the island of Flores, Indonesia.

savvy /'sævɪ/ *v.*, *n.*, & *adj. sl.* —*v.intr.* & *tr.* (**-ies**, **-ied**) know. —*n.* knowingness; shrewdness; understanding. —*adj.* (**savvier**, **savviest**) *US* knowing; wise. [orig. Black & Pidgin E after Sp. *sabe usted* you know]

saw[1] /sɔː/ *n.* & *v.* —*n.* **1 a** a hand tool having a toothed blade used to cut esp. wood with a to-and-fro movement. **b** any of several mechanical power-driven devices with a toothed rotating disk or moving band, for cutting. **2** *Zool.* etc. a serrated organ or part. —*v.* (*past part.* **sawn** /sɔːn/ or **sawed**) **1** *tr.* **a** cut (wood etc.) with a saw. **b** make (boards etc.) with a saw. **2** *intr.* use a saw. **3 a** *intr.* move to and fro with a motion as of a saw or person sawing (*sawing away on his violin*). **b** *tr.* divide (the air etc.) with gesticulations. □ **saw-doctor** a machine for making the teeth of a saw. **saw-edged** with a jagged edge like a saw. **saw-frame** a frame in which a saw-blade is held taut. **saw-gate** = *saw-frame*. **saw-gin** = *cotton-gin*. **saw-horse** a rack supporting wood for sawing. **sawn-off** (*US* **sawed-off**) **1** (of a gun) having part of the barrel sawn off to make it easier to handle and give a wider field of fire. **2** *colloq.* (of a person) short. **saw-pit** a pit in which the lower of two men working a pit-saw stands. **saw-set** a tool for wrenching saw-teeth in alternate directions to allow the saw to work freely. **saw-wort** a composite plant, *Serratula tinctoria*, yielding a yellow dye from its serrated leaves. □□ **sawlike** *adj.* [OE *saga* f. Gmc]

saw[2] past of SEE[1].

saw[3] /sɔː/ *n.* a proverb; a maxim (*that's just an old saw*). [OE *sagu* f. Gmc, rel. to SAY: cf. SAGA]

sawbill /'sɔːbɪl/ *n.* a merganser.

sawbones /'sɔːbəʊnz/ *n. sl.* a doctor or surgeon.

sawbuck /'sɔːbʌk/ *n. US* **1** a saw-horse. **2** *sl.* a $10 note.

sawdust /'sɔːdʌst/ *n.* powdery particles of wood produced in sawing.

sawfish /'sɔːfɪʃ/ *n.* any large marine fish of the family Pristidae, with a toothed flat snout used as a weapon.

sawfly /'sɔːflaɪ/ *n.* (*pl.* **-flies**) any insect of the superfamily Tenthredinidae, with a serrated ovipositor, the larvae of which are injurious to plants.

sawmill /'sɔːmɪl/ *n.* a factory in which wood is sawn mechanically into planks or boards.

sawn *past part.* of SAW[1].

sawtooth /'sɔːtuːθ/ *adj.* **1** (also **sawtoothed** /-tuːθt/) (esp. of a roof, wave, etc.) shaped like the teeth of a saw with one steep and one slanting side. **2** (of a wave-form) showing a slow linear rise and rapid linear fall.

sawyer /'sɔːjə(r)/ *n.* **1** a person who saws timber professionally. **2** *US* an uprooted tree held fast by one end in a river. **3** *NZ* a large wingless horned grasshopper whose grubs bore in wood. [ME, earlier *sawer*, f. SAW[1]]

sax[1] /sæks/ *n. colloq.* **1** a saxophone. **2** a saxophone-player. □□ **saxist** *n.* [abbr.]

sax[2] /sæks/ *n.* (also **zax** /zæks/) a slater's chopper, with a point for making nail-holes. [OE *seax* knife f. Gmc]

saxatile /'sæksəˌtaɪl, -tɪl/ *adj.* living or growing on or among rocks. [F *saxatile* or L *saxatilis* f. *saxum* rock]

saxboard /'sæksbɔːd/ *n.* the uppermost strake of an open boat. [SAX[2] + BOARD]

saxe /sæks/ *n.* (in full **saxe blue**) (often *attrib.*) a lightish blue colour with a greyish tinge. [F, = Saxony, the source of a dye of this colour]

Saxe-Coburg-Gotha /'sæksˌkəʊbɜːg'gəʊθə/ the name of the British royal house from the accession of Edward VII (1901), whose father Prince Albert, consort of Queen Victoria, was a prince of the German duchy of Saxe-Coburg and Gotha. In 1917, with anti-German feeling running high during the First World War, George V changed the family name to Windsor.

saxhorn /'sækshɔːn/ *n.* any of a series of different-sized brass wind instruments with valves and a funnel-shaped mouthpiece, used mainly in military and brass bands usually held with its mouth upwards. It was evolved by the Belgian instrument-maker A. Sax (d. 1894) and patented by him in 1846. [*Sax* + HORN]

saxicoline /sæk'sɪkəˌlaɪn/ *adj.* (also **saxicolous**) *Biol.* = SAXATILE. [mod.L *saxicolus* f. *saxum* rock + *colere* inhabit]

saxifrage /'sæksɪˌfreɪdʒ/ *n.* any plant of the genus *Saxifraga*, growing on rocky or stony ground and usu. bearing small white, yellow, or red flowers. [ME f. OF *saxifrage* or LL *saxifraga* (*herba*) f. L *saxum* rock + *frangere* break]

Saxon /'sæks(ə)n/ *n.* & *adj.* —*n.* **1** *hist.* **a** a member of a north German tribe, originally inhabitants of the area round the mouth of the Elbe, one branch of which, along with the Angles and the Jutes, conquered and colonized much of southern Britain in the 5th and 6th centuries. **b** (usu. **Old Saxon**) the language of this people. **2** = ANGLO-SAXON. **3** a native of modern Saxony. **4** the Germanic (as opposed to Latin or Romance) elements of English. —*adj.* **1** *hist.* of or concerning the Saxons. **2** belonging to or originating from the Saxon language or Old English. **3** of or concerning modern Saxony or Saxons. □ **Saxon architecture** the form of Romanesque architecture preceding the Norman in England. **Saxon blue** a solution of indigo in sulphuric acid as a dye. □□ **Saxondom** *n.* **Saxonism** *n.* **Saxonist** *n.* **Saxonize** /-ˌnaɪz/ *v.tr.* & *intr.* (also **-ise**). [ME f. OF f. LL *Saxo -onis* f. Gk *Saxones* (pl.) f. WG: cf. OE *Seaxan*, *Seaxe* (pl.)]

Saxony /'sæksənɪ/ **1** a former province of east central Germany on the upper reaches of the Elbe, earlier part of the large Kingdom of Saxony. **2** a 'Land' (State) of Germany; pop. (est. 1990) 5,000,000; capital, Dresden. □ **Lower Saxony** a 'Land' (State) of NW Germany; pop. (est. 1987) 7,189,000; capital, Hanover.

saxony /'sæksənɪ/ *n.* **1** a fine kind of wool. **2** cloth made from this. [*Saxony* in Germany f. LL *Saxonia* (as SAXON)]

Saxony-Anhalt /'ɑːnhɑːlt/ a 'Land' (State) of Germany on the plains of the Elbe and the Saale rivers; pop. (est. 1990) 3,000,000; capital, Magdeburg.

saxophone /'sæksəˌfəʊn/ *n.* **1** a keyed brass reed instrument in several sizes and registers, used esp. in jazz and dance music. It was invented *c.*1840 by A. Sax (see SAXHORN) and patented in 1846. **2** a saxophone-player. □□ **saxophonic** /-'fɒnɪk/ *adj.* **saxophonist** /-'sɒfənɪst, -əˌfəʊnɪst/ *n.* [*Sax* (as SAXHORN) + -PHONE]

say /seɪ/ *v.* & *n.* —*v.* (*3rd sing. present* **says** /sez/; *past and past part.* **said** /sed/) **1** *tr.* (often foll. by *that* + clause) **a** utter (specified words) in a speaking voice; remark (*said 'Damn!'*; *said that he was satisfied*). **b** put into words; express (*that was well said*; *cannot say what I feel*). **2** *tr.* (often foll. by *that* + clause) **a** state; promise or prophesy (*says that there will be war*). **b** have specified wording; indicate (*says here that he was killed*; *the clock says ten to six*). **3** *tr.* (in *passive*; usu. foll. by *to* + infin.) be asserted or described (*is said to be 93 years old*). **4** *tr.* (foll. by *to* + infin.) *colloq.* tell a person to do something (*he said to bring the car*). **5** *tr.* convey (information) (*spoke for an hour but said little*). **6** *tr.* put forward as an argument or excuse (*much to be said in favour of it*; *what have you to say for yourself?*). **7** *tr.* (often *absol.*) form and give an opinion or decision as to (*who did it I cannot say*; *do say which you prefer*). **8** *tr.* select, assume, or take as an example or (a specified number etc.) as near enough (*shall we say this one?*; *paid, say, £20*). **9** *tr.* **a** speak the words of (prayers, Mass, a grace, etc.). **b** repeat (a lesson etc.); recite (*can't say his tables*). **10** *tr.* *Art* etc. convey (inner meaning or intention) (*what is the director saying in this film?*). **11** *intr.* **a** speak; talk. **b** (in *imper.*) *poet.* tell me (*what is your name, say!*). **12** *tr.* (**the said**) *Law* or *joc.* the previously mentioned (*the said witness*). **13** *intr.* (as *int.*) *US* an exclamation of surprise, to attract attention, etc. —*n.* **1 a** an opportunity for stating one's opinion etc. (*let him have his say*). **b** a stated opinion. **2** a share in a decision (*had no say in the matter*). □ **how say you?** *Law* how do you find? (addressed to the jury requesting its verdict). **I** etc. **cannot** (or **could not**) **say** I etc. do not know. **I'll say** *colloq.* yes indeed. **I say!** *Brit.* an exclamation expressing surprise, drawing attention, etc. **it is said** the rumour is that. **not to say** and indeed; or possibly even (*his language was rude not to say offensive*). **said he** (or **I** etc.) *colloq.* or *poet.* he etc. said. **say for oneself** say by way of conversation, oratory, etc. **say much** (or **something**) **for** indicate the high quality of. **say no** refuse or disagree. **say out** express fully or candidly. **says I** (or **he** etc.) *colloq.* I, he, etc., said (used in reporting conversation). **say-so 1** the power of decision. **2** mere assertion (*cannot proceed merely on his say-so*). **say something** make a short speech. **says you!** *colloq.* I disagree. **say when** *colloq.* indicate when enough drink or food has been given. **say the word 1** indicate that you agree or give permission. **2** give the order etc. **say yes** agree. **that is to say 1** in other words, more explicitly. **2** or at least. **they say** it is rumoured. **to say nothing of** = *not to mention* (see MENTION). **what do** (or **would**) **you say to?** would you like? **when all is said and done** after all, in the long run. **you can say that again!** (or **you said it!**) *colloq.* I agree emphatically. **you don't say so** *colloq.* an expression of amazement or disbelief. □□ **sayable** *adj.* **sayer** *n.* [OE *secgan* f. Gmc]

SAYE *abbr. Brit.* save-as-you-earn.

Sayers /ˈseɪəz/, Dorothy Leigh (1893–1957), English writer whose detective fiction, introducing the hero amateur detective Lord Peter Wimsey, is among the classics of the genre. In this she reached her peak with *Murder Must Advertise* (1933) and *The Nine Tailors* (1934). Her religious plays showed her as a formidable theological polemicist. She left unfinished a translation of Dante's *Divine Comedy* (1949–55).

saying /ˈseɪɪŋ/ *n.* **1** the act or an instance of saying. **2** a maxim, proverb, adage, etc. □ **as the saying goes** (or **is**) an expression used in introducing a proverb, cliché, etc. **go without saying** be too well known or obvious to need mention. **there is no saying** it is impossible to know.

Sb *symb. Chem.* the element antimony. [L *stibium*]

SBN *abbr.* Standard Book Number (cf. ISBN).

SBS *abbr.* (in the UK) Special Boat Service (*formerly* Squadron) a nautical counterpart of the land-based SAS, provided by the Royal Marines.

S. by E. *abbr.* South by East.

S. by W. *abbr.* South by West.

SC *abbr.* **1** *US* South Carolina (also in official postal use). **2** special constable.

Sc *symb. Chem.* the element scandium.

sc. *abbr.* scilicet.

s.c. *abbr.* small capitals.

scab /skæb/ *n. & v.* —*n.* **1** a dry rough crust formed over a cut, sore, etc. in healing. **2** (often *attrib.*) *colloq. derog.* a person who refuses to strike or join a trade union, or who tries to break a strike by working; a blackleg. **3** the mange or a similar skin disease esp. in animals. **4** a fungous plant-disease causing scablike roughness. **5** a dislikeable person. —*v.intr.* (**scabbed, scabbing**) **1** act as a scab. **2** (of a wound etc.) form a scab; heal over. □□ **scabbed** *adj.* **scabby** *adj.* (**scabbier, scabbiest**). **scabbiness** *n.* **scablike** *adj.* [ME f. ON *skabbr* (unrecorded), corresp. to OE *sceabb*]

scabbard /ˈskæbəd/ *n.* **1** *hist.* a sheath for a sword, bayonet, etc. **2** *US* a sheath for a revolver etc. □ **scabbard-fish** any of various silvery-white marine fish shaped like a sword-scabbard, esp. *Lepidopus caudatus*. [ME *sca(u)berc* etc. f. AF prob. f. Frank.]

scabies /ˈskeɪbiːz/ *n.* a contagious skin disease causing severe itching (cf. ITCH). [ME f. L *scabere* scratch]

scabious /ˈskeɪbɪəs/ *n. & adj.* —*n.* any plant of the genus *Scabiosa, Knautia,* etc., with pink, white, or esp. blue pincushion-shaped flowers. —*adj.* affected with mange; scabby. [ME f. med.L *scabiosa (herba)* formerly regarded as a cure for skin disease: see SCABIES]

scabrous /ˈskeɪbrəs/ *adj.* **1** having a rough surface; bearing short stiff hairs, scales, etc.; scurfy. **2** (of a subject, situation, etc.) requiring tactful treatment; hard to handle with decency. **3 a** indecent, salacious. **b** behaving licentiously. □□ **scabrously** *adv.* **scabrousness** *n.* [F *scabreux* or LL *scabrosus* f. L *scaber* rough]

scad /skæd/ *n.* any fish of the family Carangidae native to tropical and subtropical seas, usu. having an elongated body and very large spiky scales. [17th c.: orig. unkn.]

scads /skædz/ *n.pl. US colloq.* large quantities. [19th c.: orig. unkn.]

Scafell Pike /skɔːˈfel/ the highest peak in England, in the Lake District in Cumbria, rising to a height of 978 m (3,210 ft.).

scaffold /ˈskæfəʊld, -f(ə)ld/ *n. & v.* —*n.* **1 a** *hist.* a raised wooden platform used for the execution of criminals. **b** a similar platform used for drying tobacco etc. **2** = SCAFFOLDING. **3** (prec. by *the*) death by execution. —*v.tr.* attach scaffolding to (a building). □□ **scaffolder** *n.* [ME f. AF f. OF (*e*)*schaffaut*, earlier *escadafaut*: cf. CATAFALQUE]

scaffolding /ˈskæfəʊldɪŋ, -fəldɪŋ/ *n.* **1 a** a temporary structure formed of poles, planks, etc., erected by workmen and used by them while building or repairing a house etc. **b** materials used for this. **2** a temporary conceptual framework used for constructing theories etc.

scagliola /skæˈljəʊlə/ *n.* imitation stone or plaster mixed with glue. [It. *scagliuola* dimin. of *scaglia* SCALE¹]

scalable /ˈskeɪləb(ə)l/ *adj.* capable of being scaled or climbed. □□ **scalability** /-ˈbɪlɪtɪ/ *n.*

scalar /ˈskeɪlə(r)/ *adj. & n. Math. & Physics* —*adj.* (of a quantity) having only magnitude, not direction. —*n.* a scalar quantity (cf. VECTOR). [L *scalaris* f. *scala* ladder; see SCALE³]

scalawag var. of SCALLYWAG.

scald¹ /skɔːld, skɒld/ *v. & n.* —*v.tr.* **1** burn (the skin etc.) with hot liquid or steam. **2** heat (esp. milk) to near boiling-point. **3** (usu. foll. by *out*) clean (a pan etc.) by rinsing with boiling water. **4** treat (poultry etc.) with boiling water to remove feathers etc. —*n.* **1** a burn etc. caused by scalding. **2** a skin disease caused esp. by air pollution etc. affecting the fruits of some plants. □ **like a scalded cat** moving unusually fast. **scalded cream** a dessert made from milk scalded and allowed to stand. **scalding tears** hot bitter tears of grief etc. □□ **scalder** *n.* [ME f. AF, ONF *escalder*, OF *eschalder* f. LL *excaldare* (as EX-¹, L *calidus* hot)]

scald² var. of SKALD.

scale¹ /skeɪl/ *n. & v.* —*n.* **1** each of the small thin bony or horny overlapping plates protecting the skin of fish and reptiles. **2** something resembling a fish-scale, esp.: **a** a pod or husk. **b** a flake of skin; a scab. **c** a rudimentary leaf, feather, or bract. **d** each of the structures covering the wings of butterflies and moths. **e** *Bot.* a layer of a bulb. **3 a** a flake formed on the surface of rusty iron. **b** a thick white deposit formed in a kettle, boiler, etc. by the action of heat on water. **4** plaque formed on teeth. —*v.* **1** *tr.* remove scale or scales from (fish, nuts, iron, etc.). **2** *tr.* remove plaque from (teeth) by scraping. **3** *intr.* **a** (of skin, metal, etc.) form, come off in, or drop, scales. **b** (usu. foll. by *off*) (of scales) come off. □ **scale-armour** *hist.* armour formed of metal scales attached to leather etc. **scale-board** very thin wood used for the back of a mirror, picture, etc. **scale-bug** = *scale insect.* **scale-fern** any of various spleenworts, esp. *Asplenium ceterach.* **scale insect** any of various insects, esp. of the family Coccidae, clinging to plants and secreting a shieldlike scale as covering. **scale-leaf** a modified leaf resembling a scale. **scale-moss** a type of liverwort with scalelike leaves. **scales fall from a person's eyes** a person is no longer deceived (cf. Acts 9: 18). **scale-winged** lepidopterous. **scale-work** an overlapping arrangement. □□ **scaled** *adj.* (also in *comb.*). **scaleless** /ˈskeɪllɪs/ *adj.* **scaler** *n.* [ME f. OF *escale* f. Gmc, rel. to SCALE²]

scale² /skeɪl/ *n. & v.* —*n.* **1 a** (often in *pl.*) a weighing machine or device (*bathroom scales*). **b** (also **scale-pan**) each of the dishes on a simple scale balance. **2 (the Scales)** the zodiacal sign or constellation Libra. —*v.tr.* (of something weighed) show (a specified weight) in the scales. □ **pair of scales** a simple balance. **throw into the scale** cause to be a factor in a contest, debate, etc. **tip** (or **turn**) **the scales 1** (usu. foll. by *at*) outweigh the opposite scale-pan (at a specified weight); weigh. **2** (of a motive, circumstance, etc.) be decisive. [ME f. ON *skál* bowl f. Gmc]

scale³ /skeɪl/ *n. & v.* —*n.* **1** a series of degrees; a graded classification system (*pay fees according to a prescribed scale*; *high on the social scale*; *seven points on the Richter scale*). **2 a** (often *attrib.*) *Geog. & Archit.* a ratio of size in a map, model, picture, etc. (*on a scale of one centimetre to the kilometre*; *a scale model*). **b** relative dimensions or degree (*generosity on a grand scale*). **3** *Mus.* an arrangement of all the notes in any system of music in ascending or descending order of pitch (*chromatic scale*; *major scale*). In Western music the 12 notes of the chromatic scale which make up the octave have been organized as three seven-note scale types, the major and the harmonic and melodic minor, since the 17th c., superseding the modes of earlier music. **4 a** a set of marks on a line used in measuring, reducing, enlarging, etc. **b** a rule determining the distances between these. **c** a piece of metal, apparatus, etc. on which these are marked. **5** (in full **scale of notation**) *Math.* the ratio between units in a numerical system (*decimal scale*). —*v.* **1** *tr.* **a** (also *absol.*) climb (a wall, height, etc.) esp. with a ladder. **b** climb (the social scale, heights of ambition, etc.). **2** *tr.* represent in proportional dimensions; reduce to a common scale. **3** *intr.* (of quantities etc.) have a common scale; be commensurable. □ **economies of scale** proportionate savings gained by using larger quantities. **in scale** (of drawing etc.) in proportion to the surroundings etc. **play** (or **sing**) **scales** *Mus.* perform the notes of a scale as an exercise for the fingers or voice. **scale down** make smaller in proportion; reduce in size. **scale up** make larger in proportion; increase in size. **scaling-ladder** *hist.* a ladder used to climb esp. fortress walls, esp. to break a siege. **to scale** with a uniform reduction or enlargement. □□ **scaler** *n.* [(n.) ME (= ladder): (v.) ME f. OF *escaler* or med.L *scalare* f. L *scala* f. *scandere* climb]

scalene /ˈskeɪliːn/ *adj. & n.* —*adj.* (esp. of a triangle) having sides unequal in length. —*n.* **1** (in full **scalene muscle**) = SCALENUS. **2** a scalene triangle. □ **scalene cone** (or **cylinder**) a cone (or cylinder) with the axis not perpendicular to the base. [LL *scalenus* f. Gk *skalēnos* unequal, rel. to *skolios* bent]

scalenus /skəˈliːnəs/ *n.* (*pl.* **scaleni** /-naɪ/) any of several muscles extending from the neck to the first and second ribs. [mod.L: see SCALENE]

Scaliger /ˈskælɪdʒə(r)/, Julius Caesar (1484–1558), Italian classical scholar and physician. Besides polemical works directed against Erasmus (1531) he wrote a long Latin treatise on poetics, scientific commentaries on botanical works, and a philosophical treatise, all showing encyclopaedic knowledge and acute observation marred by arrogance and vanity. His son Joseph Justus Scaliger (1540–1609), the greatest scholar of the Renaissance, has been described as 'the founder of historical criticism'. His edition of Manilius (1579) and his *De Emendatione Temporum* revolutionized understanding of ancient chronology by recognizing the historical material relating to the Jews, Persians, Babylonians, and Egyptians.

scallawag var. of SCALLYWAG.

scallion /ˈskæljən/ *n.* a shallot or spring onion; any long-necked onion with a small bulb. [ME f. AF *scal(o)un* = OF *escalo(i)gne* ult. f. L *Ascalonia* (*caepa*) (onion) of *Ascalon* in anc. Palestine]

scallop /ˈskæləp, ˈskɒl-/ *n. & v.* (also **scollop** /ˈskɒl-/) —*n.* **1** any of various bivalve molluscs of the family Pectinidae, esp. of the genus *Chlamys* or *Pecten*, much prized as food. **2** (in full **scallop shell**) **a** a single valve from the shell of a scallop, with grooves and ridges radiating from the middle of the hinge and edged with small rounded lobes, often used for cooking or serving food. **b** *hist.* a representation of this shell worn as a pilgrim's badge. **3** (in *pl.*) an ornamental edging cut in material in imitation of a scallop-edge. **4** a small pan or dish shaped like a scallop shell and used for baking or serving food. —*v.tr.* (**scalloped**, **scalloping**) **1** cook in a scallop. **2** ornament (an edge or material)

with scallops or scalloping. □□ **scalloper** *n.* **scalloping** *n.* (in sense 3 of *n.*). [ME f. OF *escalope* prob. f. Gmc]

scallywag /ˈskælɪˌwæg/ *n.* (also **scalawag**, **scallawag** /ˈskælə-/) a scamp; a rascal. [19th-c. US sl.: orig. unkn.]

scalp /skælp/ *n. & v.* —*n.* **1** the skin covering the top of the head, with the hair etc. attached. **2 a** *hist.* the scalp of an enemy cut or torn away as a trophy by an American Indian. **b** a trophy or symbol of triumph, conquest, etc. **3** *Sc.* a bare rock projecting above water etc. —*v.tr.* **1** *hist.* take the scalp of (an enemy). **2** criticize savagely. **3** *US* defeat; humiliate. **4** *US colloq.* resell (shares, tickets, etc.) at a high or quick profit. □□ **scalpless** *adj.* [ME, prob. of Scand. orig.]

scalpel /ˈskælp(ə)l/ *n.* a surgeon's small sharp knife shaped for holding like a pen. [F *scalpel* or L *scalpellum* dimin. of *scalprum* chisel f. *scalpere* scratch]

scalper /ˈskælpə(r)/ *n.* **1** a person or thing that scalps (esp. in sense 4 of *v.*). **2** (also **scauper**, **scorper** /ˈskɔːpə(r)/) an engraver's tool for hollowing out woodcut or linocut designs. [SCALP + -ER¹: sense 2 also f. L *scalper* cutting tool f. *scalpere* carve]

scaly /ˈskeɪlɪ/ *adj.* (**scalier**, **scaliest**) covered in or having many scales or flakes. □□ **scaliness** *n.*

scam /skæm/ *n. US sl.* **1** a trick or swindle; a fraud. **2** a story or rumour. [20th c.: orig. unkn.]

scammony /ˈskæmənɪ/ *n.* (*pl.* -**ies**) an Asian plant, *Convolvulus scammonia*, bearing white or pink flowers, the dried roots of which are used as a purgative. [ME f. OF *scamonee*, *escamonie* or L *scammonia* f. Gk *skammōnia*]

scamp¹ /skæmp/ *n. colloq.* a rascal; a rogue. □□ **scampish** *adj.* [*scamp* rob on highway, prob. f. MDu. *schampen* decamp f. OF *esc(h)amper* (as EX-¹, L *campus* field)]

scamp² /skæmp/ *v.tr.* do (work etc.) in a perfunctory or inadequate way. [perh. formed as SCAMP¹: cf. SKIMP]

scamper /ˈskæmpə(r)/ *v. & n.* —*v.intr.* (usu. foll. by *about*, *through*) run and skip impulsively or playfully. —*n.* the act or an instance of scampering. [prob. formed as SCAMP¹]

scampi /ˈskæmpɪ/ *n.pl.* **1** large prawns. **2** (often treated as *sing.*) a dish of these, usu. fried. [It.]

scan /skæn/ *v. & n.* —*v.* (**scanned**, **scanning**) **1** *tr.* look at intently or quickly (*scanned the horizon*; *rapidly scanned the speech for errors*). **2** *intr.* (of a verse etc.) be metrically correct; be capable of being recited etc. metrically (*this line doesn't scan*). **3** *tr.* **a** examine all parts of (a surface etc.) to detect radioactivity etc. **b** cause (a particular region) to be traversed by a radar etc. beam. **4** *tr.* resolve (a picture) into its elements of light and shade in a prearranged pattern for the purposes esp. of television transmission. **5** *tr.* test the metre of (a line of verse etc.) by reading with the emphasis on its rhythm, or by examining the number of feet etc. **6** *tr.* **a** make a scan of (the body or part of it). **b** examine (a patient etc.) with a scanner. —*n.* **1** the act or an instance of scanning. **2** an image obtained by scanning or with a scanner. □□ **scannable** *adj.* [ME f. L *scandere* climb: in LL = scan verses (from the raising of one's foot in marking rhythm)]

scandal /ˈskænd(ə)l/ *n.* **1 a** a thing or a person causing general public outrage or indignation. **b** the outrage etc. so caused, esp. as a subject of common talk. **c** malicious gossip or backbiting. **2** *Law* a public affront, esp. an irrelevant abusive statement in court. □ **scandal sheet** *derog.* a newspaper etc. giving prominence to esp. malicious gossip. □□ **scandalous** *adj.* **scandalously** *adv.* **scandalousness** *n.* [ME f. OF *scandale* f. eccl.L *scandalum* f. Gk *skandalon* snare, stumbling-block]

scandalize /ˈskændəˌlaɪz/ *v.tr.* (also -**ise**) offend the moral feelings, sensibilities, etc. of; shock. [ME in sense 'make a scandal of' f. F *scandaliser* or eccl.L *scandalizo* f. Gk *skandalizō* (as SCANDAL)]

scandalmonger /ˈskænd(ə)l̩ˌmʌŋgə(r)/ *n.* a person who spreads malicious scandal.

Scandinavian /ˌskændɪˈneɪvɪən/ *n. & adj.* —*n.* **1 a** a native or inhabitant of Scandinavia. **b** a person of Scandinavian descent. **2** the North Germanic branch of the Indo-European family of languages, including Danish, Norwegian, Swedish, and Icelandic, all descended from Old Norse. —*adj.* of or relating to Scandinavia or its people or languages. [L *Scandinavia*]

scandium /ˈskændɪəm/ n. *Chem.* a rare soft silver-white metallic element occurring naturally in lanthanide ores. It was first discovered in 1879, after its existence had been predicted by Mendeleev on the basis of his periodic table. The metal and its compounds have at present few commercial uses. ¶ Symb.: **Sc**; atomic number 21. [mod.L f. *Scandia* Scandinavia (source of the minerals containing it)]

scannable see SCAN.

scanner /ˈskænə(r)/ n. **1** a device for scanning or systematically examining all the parts of something. **2** a machine for measuring the intensity of radiation, ultrasound reflections, etc., from the body as a diagnostic aid. **3** a person who scans or examines critically. **4** a person who scans verse.

scansion /ˈskænʃ(ə)n/ n. **1** the metrical scanning of verse. **2** the way a verse etc. scans. [L *scansio* (LL of metre) f. *scandere scans*-climb]

scant /skænt/ adj. & v. —adj. barely sufficient; deficient (*with scant regard for the truth*; *scant of breath*). —v.tr. archaic provide (a supply, material, a person, etc.) grudgingly; skimp; stint. □□ **scantly** adv. **scantness** n. [ME f. ON *skamt* neut. of *skammr* short]

scantling /ˈskæntlɪŋ/ n. **1 a** a timber beam of small cross-section. **b** a size to which a stone or timber is to be cut. **2 a** set of standard dimensions for parts of a structure, esp. in shipbuilding. **3** (usu. foll. by *of*) archaic **a** a specimen or sample. **b** one's necessary supply; a modicum or small amount. [alt. after -LING¹ f. obs. *scantlon* f. OF *escantillon* sample]

scanty /ˈskæntɪ/ adj. (**scantier**, **scantiest**) **1** of small extent or amount. **2** barely sufficient. □□ **scantily** adv. **scantiness** n. [obs. *scant* scanty supply f. ON *skamt* neut. adj.: see SCANT]

Scapa Flow /ˌskɑːpə ˈfləʊ/ a stretch of sea in the Orkney Islands, Scotland, an important British naval base in the First World War. The entire German High Seas Fleet, which was interned here after its surrender, was scuttled in 1919 as an act of defiance against the terms of the Versailles peace settlement. In October 1939 the defences of Scapa Flow were penetrated when a German U-boat sank HMS *Royal Oak*.

scape /skeɪp/ n. **1** a long flower-stalk coming directly from the root. **2** the base of an insect's antenna. [L *scapus* f. Gk *skapos*, rel. to SCEPTRE]

-scape /skeɪp/ comb. form forming nouns denoting a view or a representation of a view (*moonscape*; *seascape*). [after LANDSCAPE]

scapegoat /ˈskeɪpgəʊt/ n. & v. —n. **1** a person bearing the blame for the sins, shortcomings, etc. of others, esp. as an expedient. **2** *Bibl.* a goat sent into the wilderness after the Jewish chief priest had symbolically laid the sins of the people upon it (Lev. 16). —v.tr. make a scapegoat of. □□ **scapegoater** n. [*scape* (archaic, = escape) + GOAT, = the goat that escapes]

scapegrace /ˈskeɪpgreɪs/ n. a rascal; a scamp, esp. a young person or child. [*scape* (as SCAPEGOAT) + GRACE = one who escapes the grace of God]

scaphoid /ˈskæfɔɪd/ adj. & n. *Anat.* = NAVICULAR. [mod.L *scaphoides* f. Gk *skaphoeidēs* f. *skaphos* boat]

scapula /ˈskæpjʊlə/ n. (pl. **scapulae** /-ˌliː/ or **scapulas**) the shoulder-blade. [LL, sing. of L *scapulae*]

scapular /ˈskæpjʊlə(r)/ adj. & n. —adj. of or relating to the shoulder or shoulder-blade. —n. **1 a** a monastic short cloak covering the shoulders. **b** a symbol of affiliation to an ecclesiastical order, consisting of two strips of cloth hanging down the breast and back and joined across the shoulders. **2** a bandage for or over the shoulders. **3** a scapular feather. □ **scapular feather** a feather growing near the insertion of the wing. [(adj.) f. SCAPULA: (n.) f. LL *scapulare* (as SCAPULA)]

scapulary /ˈskæpjʊlərɪ/ n. (pl. **-ies**) **1** = SCAPULAR n. 1. **2** = SCAPULAR n. 3. [ME f. OF *eschapeloyre* f. med.L *scapelorium*, *scapularium* (as SCAPULA)]

scar¹ /skɑː(r)/ n. & v. —n. **1** a usu. permanent mark on the skin left after the healing of a wound, burn, or sore. **2** the lasting effect of grief etc. on a person's character or disposition. **3** a mark left by damage etc. (*the table bore many scars*). **4** a mark left on the stem etc. of a plant by the fall of a leaf etc. —v. (**scarred**, **scarring**) **1** tr. (esp. as **scarred** adj.) mark with a scar or scars (*was scarred for life*). **2** intr. heal over; form a scar. **3** tr. form a

scar on. □□ **scarless** adj. [ME f. OF *eschar(r)e* f. LL *eschara* f. Gk *eskhara* scab]

scar² /skɑː(r)/ n. (also **scaur** /skɔː(r)/) a steep craggy outcrop of a mountain or cliff. [ME f. ON *sker* low reef in the sea]

scarab /ˈskærəb/ n. **1 a** the sacred dung-beetle of ancient Egypt. **b** = SCARABAEID. **2** an ancient Egyptian gem cut in the form of a beetle and engraved with symbols on its flat side, used as a signet etc. [L *scarabaeus* f. Gk *skarabeios*]

scarabaeid /ˌskærəˈbiːɪd/ n. any beetle of the family Scarabaeidae, including the dung-beetle, cockchafer, etc. [mod.L *Scarabaeidae* (as SCARAB)]

scaramouch /ˈskærəˌmaʊtʃ/ n. archaic a boastful coward; a braggart. [It. *Scaramuccia* stock character in Italian farce f. *scaramuccia* = SKIRMISH, infl. by F form *Scaramouche*]

scarce /skeəs/ adj. & adv. —adj. **1** (usu. predic.) (esp. of food, money, etc.) insufficient for the demand; scanty. **2** hard to find; rare. —adv. archaic or literary scarcely. □ **make oneself scarce** colloq. keep out of the way; surreptitiously disappear. □□ **scarceness** n. [ME f. AF & ONF (e)*scars*, OF *eschars* f. L *excerpere*: see EXCERPT]

scarcely /ˈskeəslɪ/ adv. **1** hardly; barely; only just (*I scarcely know him*). **2** surely not (*he can scarcely have said so*). **3** a mild or apologetic or ironical substitute for 'not' (*I scarcely expected to be insulted*).

scarcity /ˈskeəsɪtɪ/ n. (pl. **-ies**) (often foll. by *of*) a lack or inadequacy, esp. of food.

scare /skeə(r)/ v. & n. —v. **1** tr. frighten, esp. suddenly (*his expression scared us*). **2** tr. (as **scared** adj.) (usu. foll. by *of*, or *to* + infin.) frightened; terrified (*scared of his own shadow*). **3** tr. (usu. foll. by *away*, *off*, *up*, etc.) drive away by frightening. **4** intr. become scared (*they don't scare easily*). —n. **1** a sudden attack of fright (*gave me a scare*). **2** a general, esp. baseless, fear of war, invasion, epidemic, etc. (*a measles scare*). **3** a financial panic causing share-selling etc. □ **scaredy-cat** /ˈskeədɪˌkæt/ colloq. a timid person. **scare-heading** (or **-head**) a shockingly sensational newspaper headline. **scare up** (or **out**) esp. US **1** frighten (game etc.) out of cover. **2** colloq. manage to find; discover (*see if we can scare up a meal*). □□ **scarer** n. [ME *skerre* f. ON *skirra* frighten f. *skjarr* timid]

scarecrow /ˈskeəˌkrəʊ/ n. **1** a human figure dressed in old clothes and set up in a field to scare birds away. **2** colloq. a badly-dressed, grotesque-looking, or very thin person. **3** archaic an object of baseless fear.

scaremonger /ˈskeəˌmʌŋgə(r)/ n. a person who spreads frightening reports or rumours. □□ **scaremongering** n.

scarf¹ /skɑːf/ n. (pl. **scarves** /skɑːvz/ or **scarfs**) a square, triangular, or esp. long narrow strip of material worn round the neck, over the shoulders, or tied round the head (of a woman), for warmth or ornament. □ **scarf-pin** (or **-ring**) Brit. an ornamental device for fastening a scarf. **scarf-skin** the outermost layer of the skin constantly scaling off, esp. that at the base of the nails. **scarf-wise** worn diagonally across the body from shoulder to hip. □□ **scarfed** adj. [prob. alt. of *scarp* (infl. by SCARF²) f. ONF *escarpe* = OF *escherpe* sash]

scarf² /skɑːf/ v. & n. —v.tr. join the ends of (pieces of esp. timber, metal, or leather) by bevelling or notching them to fit and then bolting, brazing, or sewing them together; cut the blubber of (a whale). —n. **1** a joint made by scarfing. **2** a cut on a whale made by scarfing. [ME (earlier as noun) prob. f. OF *escarf* (unrecorded) perh. f. ON]

scarifier /ˈskærɪˌfaɪə(r), ˈskeə-/ n. **1** a thing or person that scarifies. **2** a machine with prongs for loosening soil without turning it. **3** a spiked road-breaking machine.

scarify¹ /ˈskærɪˌfaɪ, ˈskeə-/ v.tr. (**-ies**, **-ied**) **1 a** make superficial incisions in. **b** cut off skin from. **2** hurt by severe criticism etc. **3** loosen (soil) with a scarifier. □□ **scarification** /-fɪˈkeɪʃ(ə)n/ n. [ME f. F *scarifier* f. LL *scarificare* f. L *scarifare* f. Gk *skariphaomai* f. *skariphos* stylus]

scarify² /ˈskeərɪˌfaɪ/ v.tr. & intr. (**-ies**, **-ied**) colloq. scare; terrify.

scarious /ˈskeərɪəs/ adj. (of a part of a plant etc.) having a dry membranous appearance; thin and brittle. [F *scarieux* or mod.L *scariosus*]

scarlatina /ˌskɑːləˈtiːnə/ n. = scarlet fever. [mod.L f. It. scarlattina (febbre fever) dimin. of scarlatto SCARLET]

Scarlatti /skɑːˈlætɪ/, Alessandro (1660–1725), Italian composer, an important and prolific composer of operas. Over 70 survive, and in them can be found the elements which carried Italian opera through the baroque period and into the classical, together with a fine sense of the dramatic in music. His son Domenico (1685–1757) is best known today for over 500 keyboard sonatas, lively invigorating pieces in one movement.

scarlet /ˈskɑːlɪt/ n. & adj. —n. 1 a brilliant red colour tinged with orange. 2 clothes or material of this colour (dressed in scarlet). —adj. of a scarlet colour. □ **scarlet fever** an infectious bacterial fever, affecting esp. children, with a scarlet rash. **scarlet hat** RC Ch. a cardinal's hat as a symbol of rank. **scarlet pimpernel** a small annual wild plant, Anagallis arvensis, with small esp. scarlet flowers closing in rainy or cloudy weather: also called poor man's weather-glass. **scarlet rash** = ROSEOLA 1. **scarlet runner** 1 a runner bean. 2 a scarlet-flowered climber bearing this bean. **scarlet woman** derog. a notoriously promiscuous woman, a prostitute. [ME f. OF escarlate: ult. orig. unkn.]

Scarlet Pimpernel the name assumed by the hero of a series of novels by Baroness Orczy. He was a dashing but elusive English nobleman who rescued potential victims of the French Reign of Terror and smuggled them out of France.

scaroid /ˈskærɔɪd, ˈskeə-/ n. & adj. —n. any colourful marine fish of the family Scaridae, native to tropical and temperate seas, including the scarus. —adj. of or relating to this family.

scarp /skɑːp/ n. & v. —n. 1 the inner wall or slope of a ditch in a fortification (cf. COUNTERSCARP). 2 a steep slope. —v.tr. 1 make (a slope) perpendicular or steep. 2 provide (a ditch) with a steep scarp and counterscarp. 3 (as **scarped** adj.) (of a hillside etc.) steep; precipitous. [It. scarpa]

scarper /ˈskɑːpə(r)/ v.intr. Brit. sl. run away; escape. [prob. f. It. scappare escape, infl. by rhyming sl. Scapa Flow = go]

scarus /ˈskeərəs/ n. any fish of the genus Scarus, with brightly coloured scales, and teeth fused to form a parrot-like beak used for eating coral. Also called parrot-fish. [L f. Gk skaros]

scarves pl. of SCARF[1].

scary /ˈskeərɪ/ adj. (**scarier**, **scariest**) colloq. scaring, frightening. □□ **scarily** adv.

scat[1] /skæt/ v. & int. colloq. —v.intr. (**scatted**, **scatting**) depart quickly. —int. go! [perh. abbr. of SCATTER]

scat[2] /skæt/ n. & v. —n. improvised jazz singing using sounds imitating instruments, instead of words. —v.intr. (**scatted**, **scatting**) sing scat. [prob. imit.]

scathe /skeɪð/ v. & n. —v.tr. 1 poet. injure esp. by blasting or withering. 2 (as **scathing** adj.) witheringly scornful (scathing sarcasm). 3 (with neg.) do the least harm to (shall not be scathed) (cf. UNSCATHED). —n. (usu. with neg.) archaic harm; injury (without scathe). □□ **scatheless** predic.adj. **scathingly** adv. [(v.) ME f. ON skatha = OE sceathian: (n.) OE f. ON skathi = OE sceatha malefactor, injury, f. Gmc]

scatology /skæˈtɒlədʒɪ/ n. 1 a a morbid interest in excrement. b a preoccupation with obscene literature, esp. that concerned with the excretory functions. c such literature. 2 the study of fossilized dung. 3 the study of excrement for esp. diagnosis. □□ **scatological** /-təˈlɒdʒɪk(ə)l/ adj. [Gk skōr skatos dung + -LOGY]

scatophagous /skæˈtɒfəgəs/ adj. feeding on dung. [as SCATOLOGY + Gk -phagos -eating]

scatter /ˈskætə(r)/ v. & n. —v. 1 tr. a throw here and there; strew (scattered gravel on the road). b cover by scattering (scattered the road with gravel). 2 tr. & intr. a move or cause to move in flight etc.; disperse (scattered to safety at the sound). b disperse or cause (hopes, clouds, etc.) to disperse. 3 tr. (as **scattered** adj.) not clustered together; wide apart; sporadic (scattered villages). 4 tr. Physics deflect or diffuse (light, particles, etc.). 5 a intr. (of esp. a shotgun) fire a charge of shot diffusely. b tr. fire (a charge) in this way. —n. 1 the act or an instance of scattering. 2 a small amount scattered. 3 the extent of distribution of esp. shot. □ **scatter cushions** (or **rugs**, etc.) cushions, rugs, etc., placed here

and there for effect. **scatter-shot** n. & adj. US firing at random. □□ **scatterer** n. [ME, prob. var. of SHATTER]

scatterbrain /ˈskætəˌbreɪn/ n. a person given to silly or disorganized thought with lack of concentration. □□ **scatterbrained** adj.

scatty /ˈskætɪ/ adj. (**scattier**, **scattiest**) Brit. colloq. scatterbrained; disorganized. □□ **scattily** adv. **scattiness** n. [abbr.]

scaup /skɔːp/ n. any diving duck of the genus Aythya. [scaup Sc. var. of scalp mussel-bed, which it frequents]

scauper var. of SCALPER 2.

scaur var. of SCAR[2].

scavenge /ˈskævɪndʒ/ v. 1 tr. & intr. (usu. foll. by for) search for and collect (discarded items). 2 tr. remove unwanted products from (an internal-combustion engine cylinder etc.). [back-form. f. SCAVENGER]

scavenger /ˈskævɪndʒə(r)/ n. 1 a person who seeks and collects discarded items. 2 an animal, esp. a beetle, feeding on carrion, refuse, etc. 3 Brit. archaic a person employed to clean the streets etc. □□ **scavengery** n. [ME scavager f. AF scawager f. scawage f. ONF escauwer inspect f. Flem. scauwen, rel. to SHOW: for -n- cf. MESSENGER]

scazon /ˈskeɪz(ə)n, ˈskæz-/ n. Prosody a Greek or Latin metre of limping character, esp. a trimeter of two iambuses and a spondee or trochee. [L f. Gk skazōn f. skazō limp]

Sc.D. abbr. Doctor of Science. [L scientiae doctor]

SCE abbr. Scottish Certificate of Education.

scena /ˈʃeɪnɑː/ n. Mus. 1 a scene or part of an opera. 2 an elaborate dramatic solo usu. including recitative. [It. f. L: see SCENE]

scenario /sɪˈnɑːrɪəʊ, -ˈneərɪəʊ/ n. (pl. -os) 1 an outline of the plot of a play, film, opera, etc., with details of the scenes, situations, etc. 2 a postulated sequence of future events. □□ **scenarist** n. (in sense 1). [It. (as SCENA)]

scend /send/ n. & v. Naut. —n. 1 the impulse given by a wave or waves (scend of the sea). 2 a plunge of a vessel. —v.intr. (of a vessel) plunge or pitch owing to the impulse of a wave. [alt. f. SEND or DESCEND]

scene /siːn/ n. 1 a place in which events in real life, drama, or fiction occur; the locality of an event etc. (the scene was set in India; the scene of the disaster). 2 a an incident in real life, fiction, etc. (distressing scenes occurred). b a description or representation of an incident etc. (scenes of clerical life). 3 a public incident displaying emotion, temper, etc., esp. when embarrassing to others (made a scene in the restaurant). 4 a a continuous portion of a play in a fixed setting and usu. without a change of personnel; a subdivision of an act. b a similar section of a film, book, etc. 5 a any of the pieces of scenery used in a play. b these collectively. 6 a landscape or a view (a desolate scene). 7 colloq. a an area of action or interest (not my scene). b a way of life; a milieu (well-known on the jazz scene). 8 archaic the stage of a theatre. □ **behind the scenes** 1 Theatr. among the actors, scenery, etc. offstage. 2 not known to the public; secret. **behind-the-scenes** (attrib.) secret, using secret information (a behind-the-scenes investigation). **change of scene** a variety of surroundings esp. through travel. **come on the scene** arrive. **quit the scene** die; leave. **scene-dock** a space for storing scenery near the stage. **scene-shifter** a person who moves scenery in a theatre. **scene-shifting** this activity. **set the scene** 1 describe the location of events. 2 give preliminary information. [L scena f. Gk skēnē tent, stage]

scenery /ˈsiːnərɪ/ n. 1 the general appearance of the natural features of a landscape, esp. when picturesque. 2 Theatr. structures (such as painted representations of landscape, rooms, etc.) used on a theatre stage to represent features in the scene of the action. Stage scenery is a comparatively recent innovation, Greek plays being acted against a stage wall. Modern scenery originated with the masque, which used a decorative proscenium arch behind which sets of side scenes framed the back scene on either side. □ **change of scenery** = change of scene (see SCENE). [earlier scenary f. It. SCENARIO: assim. to -ERY]

scenic /ˈsiːnɪk/ adj. 1 a picturesque; impressive or beautiful (took the scenic route). b of or concerning natural scenery (flatness is the *main scenic feature*). **2** (of a picture etc.) representing an incident. **3** *Theatr.* of or on the stage (*scenic performances*). □ **scenic railway 1** a miniature railway running through artificial scenery at funfairs etc. **2** = *big dipper* 1. □□ **scenically** *adv.* [L *scenicus* f. Gk *skēnikos* of the stage (as SCENE)]

scent /sent/ *n. & v.* —*n.* **1** a distinctive, esp. pleasant, smell (*the scent of hay*). **2 a** a scent trail left by an animal perceptible to hounds etc. **b** clues etc. that can be followed like a scent trail (*lost the scent in Paris*). **c** the power of detecting or distinguishing smells etc. or of discovering things (*some dogs have little scent; the scent for talent*). **3** *Brit.* = PERFUME 2. **4** a trail laid in a paper-chase. —*v.* **1** *tr.* **a** discern by scent (*the dog scented game*). **b** sense the presence of (*scent treachery*). **2** *tr.* make fragrant or foul-smelling. **3** *tr.* (as **scented** *adj.*) having esp. a pleasant smell (*scented soap*). **4** *intr.* exercise the sense of smell (*goes scenting about*). **5** *tr.* apply the sense of smell to (*scented the air*). □ **false scent 1** a scent trail laid to deceive. **2** false clues etc. intended to deflect pursuers. **on the scent** having a clue. **put** (or **throw**) **off the scent** deceive by false clues etc. **scent-bag** a bag of aniseed etc. used to lay a trail in drag-hunting. **scent-gland** (or **-organ**) a gland in some animals secreting musk, civet, etc. **scent out** discover by smelling or searching. □□ **scentless** *adj.* [ME *sent* f. OF *sentir* perceive, smell, f. L *sentire*; *-c-* (17th c.) unexpl.]

scepsis /ˈskepsɪs/ *n.* (*US* **skepsis**) **1** philosophic doubt. **2** sceptical philosophy. [Gk *skepsis* inquiry, doubt f. *skeptomai* consider]

scepter *US* var. of SCEPTRE.

sceptic /ˈskeptɪk/ *n. & adj.* (*US* **skeptic**) —*n.* **1** a person inclined to doubt all accepted opinions; a cynic. **2** a person who doubts the truth of Christianity and other religions. **3** *hist.* a person who accepts the philosophy of Pyrrhonism. —*adj.* = SCEPTICAL. □□ **scepticism** /-ˌsɪz(ə)m/ *n.* [F *sceptique* or L *scepticus* f. Gk *skeptikos* (as SCEPSIS)]

sceptical /ˈskeptɪk(ə)l/ *adj.* (*US* **skeptical**) **1** inclined to question the truth or soundness of accepted ideas, facts, etc.; critical; incredulous. **2** *Philos.* of or accepting the philosophy of Pyrrhonism, denying the possibility of knowledge. □□ **sceptically** *adv.*

sceptre /ˈseptə(r)/ *n.* (*US* **scepter**) **1** a staff borne esp. at a coronation as a symbol of sovereignty. **2** royal or imperial authority. □□ **sceptred** *adj.* [ME f. OF (s)*ceptre* f. L *sceptrum* f. Gk *skēptron* f. *skēptō* lean on]

sch. *abbr.* **1** scholar. **2** school. **3** schooner.

schadenfreude /ˈʃɑːdənˌfrɔɪdə/ *n.* the malicious enjoyment of another's misfortunes. [G f. *Schaden* harm + *Freude* joy]

schappe /ˈʃæpə/ *n.* fabric or yarn made from waste silk. [G, = waste silk]

schedule /ˈʃedjuːl, ˈske-/ *n. & v.* —*n.* **1 a** a list or plan of intended events, times, etc. **b** a plan of work (*not on my schedule for next week*). **2** a list of rates or prices. **3** *US* a timetable. **4** a tabulated inventory etc. esp. as an appendix to a document. —*v.tr.* **1** include in a schedule. **2** make a schedule of. **3** *Brit.* include (a building) in a list for preservation or protection. □ **according to schedule** (or **on schedule**) as planned; on time. **behind schedule** behind time. **scheduled flight** (or **service** etc.) a public flight, service, etc., according to a regular timetable. **scheduled territories** *hist.* = *sterling area*. □□ **scheduler** *n.* [ME f. OF *cedule* f. LL *schedula* slip of paper, dimin. of *scheda* f. Gk *skhedē* papyrus-leaf]

scheelite /ˈʃiːlaɪt/ *n. Mineral.* calcium tungstate in its mineral crystalline form. [K. W. *Scheele*, Sw. chemist d. 1786]

Scheherazade /ʃəˌherəˈzɑːd/ the female narrator of the *Arabian Nights*.

Scheldt /skelt/ (also **Schelde** /ˈskeltə/, French **Escaut** /esˈkoʊ/) a river that rises in northern France and flows 432 km (270 miles) through Belgium into The Netherlands where it meets the North Sea. The city of Antwerp lies upon it.

schema /ˈskiːmə/ *n.* (*pl.* **schemata** /-mətə/ or **schemas**) **1** a synopsis, outline, or diagram. **2** a proposed arrangement. **3** *Logic* a syllogistic figure. **4** (in Kantian philosophy) a conception of what is common to all members of a class; a general type or essential form. [Gk *skhēma -atos* form, figure]

schematic /skɪˈmætɪk, skiː-/ *adj. & n.* —*adj.* **1** of or concerning a scheme or schema. **2** representing objects by symbols etc.

—*n.* a schematic diagram, esp. of an electronic circuit. □□ **schematically** *adv.*

schematism /ˈskiːməˌtɪz(ə)m/ *n.* a schematic arrangement or presentation. [mod.L *schematismus* f. Gk *skhēmatismos* (as SCHEMATIZE)]

schematize /ˈskiːməˌtaɪz/ *v.tr.* (also **-ise**) **1** put in a schematic form; arrange. **2** represent by a scheme or schema. □□ **schematization** /-ˈzeɪʃ(ə)n/ *n.*

scheme /skiːm/ *n. & v.* —*n.* **1 a** a systematic plan or arrangement for work, action, etc. **b** a proposed or operational systematic arrangement (*a colour scheme*). **2** an artful or deceitful plot. **3** a timetable, outline, syllabus, etc. —*v.* **1** *intr.* (often foll. by *for*, or *to* + infin.) plan esp. secretly or deceitfully; intrigue. **2** *tr.* plan to bring about, esp. artfully or deceitfully (*schemed their downfall*). □□ **schemer** *n.* [L *schema* f. Gk (as SCHEMA)]

scheming /ˈskiːmɪŋ/ *adj. & n.* —*adj.* artful, cunning, or deceitful. —*n.* plots; intrigues. □□ **schemingly** *adv.*

schemozzle var. of SHEMOZZLE.

scherzando /skeəˈtsændəʊ/ *adv., adj., & n. Mus.* —*adv. & adj.* in a playful manner. —*n.* (*pl.* **scherzandos** or **scherzandi** /-dɪ/) a passage played in this way. [It., gerund of *scherzare* to jest (as SCHERZO)]

scherzo /ˈskeətsəʊ/ *n.* (*pl.* **-os**) *Mus.* a vigorous, light, or playful composition, usu. as a movement in a symphony, sonata, etc. [It., lit. 'jest']

Schiaparelli /ˌskiːəpəˈrelɪ/, Elsa (1896–1973), Italian-born couturière, who settled in Paris in the late 1920s and became a leader in haute couture. She introduced padded shoulders in her designs of 1932, and the vivid shade known as 'shocking pink' in 1937.

Schiller /ˈʃɪlə(r)/, Johann Christoph Friedrich von (1759–1805), German dramatist and poet. His early play *Die Räuber* (*The Robbers*, 1781) established him as the leading figure of this period of German literature; *Kabale und Liebe* (*Intrigue and Love*, 1784), on which Verdi based his opera *Luisa Miller*, attacked contemporary society. His historical plays include *Wallenstein* (1799), his greatest success, *Mary Stuart* (1800), and *Die Jungfrau von Orleans* (*The Maid of Orleans*, 1801); his last completed play was *Wilhelm Tell* (1804). These plays are concerned with the problem of freedom and responsibility either political, personal, or moral. Among his best-known poems are 'Die Künstler' ('The Artists'), on the humanizing influence of art, 'Das Ideal und das Leben' ('The Ideal and Life'), and 'An die Freude' ('Ode to Joy'), which Beethoven set to music in his 9th Symphony. His many essays on aesthetics include *Über naive und sentimentalische Dichtung* (*On Naïve and Reflective Poetry*, 1795–6), in which he contrasts his own 'modern' reflective style with Goethe's more 'antique' un selfconscious genius.

schilling /ˈʃɪlɪŋ/ *n.* **1** the chief monetary unit of Austria. **2** a coin equal to the value of one schilling. [G (as SHILLING)]

schipperke /ˈskɪpəki, ˈʃɪp-/ *n.* **1** a small black tailless dog of a breed with a ruff of fur round its neck. **2** this breed. [Du. dial., = little boatman, f. its use as a watchdog on barges]

schism /ˈsɪz(ə)m, ˈskɪ-/ *n.* **1 a** the division of a group into opposing sections or parties. **b** any of the sections so formed. **2 a** the separation of a Church into two Churches or the secession of a group owing to doctrinal, disciplinary, etc., differences. **b** the offence of causing or promoting such a separation. □ **Great Schism** see separate entry. [ME f. OF s(c)*isme* f. eccl.L *schisma* f. Gk *skhisma -atos* cleft f. *skhizō* to split]

schismatic /sɪzˈmætɪk, skɪz-/ *adj. & n.* (also **schismatical**) —*adj.* inclining to, concerning, or guilty of, schism. —*n.* **1** a holder of schismatic opinions. **2** a member of a schismatic faction or a seceded branch of a Church. □□ **schismatically** *adv.* [ME f. OF *scismatique* f. eccl.L *schismaticus* f. eccl.Gk *skhismatikos* (as SCHISM)]

schist /ʃɪst/ *n.* a foliated metamorphic rock composed of layers of different minerals and splitting into thin irregular plates. □□ **schistose** *adj.* [F *schiste* f. L *schistos* f. Gk *skhistos* split (as SCHISM)]

schistosome /ˈʃɪstəˌsəʊm/ *n.* = BILHARZIA 1. [Gk *skhistos* divided (as SCHISM) + *sōma* body]

schistosomiasis /ˌʃɪstəsəˈmaɪəsɪs/ n. = BILHARZIASIS. [mod.L *Schistosoma* (the genus-name, as SCHISTOSOME)]

schizanthus /skɪˈzænθəs/ n. any plant of the genus *Schizanthus*, with showy flowers in various colours, and finely-divided leaves. [mod.L f. Gk *skhizō* to split + *anthos* flower]

schizo /ˈskɪtsəʊ/ adj. & n. colloq. —adj. schizophrenic. —n. (pl. **-os**) a schizophrenic. [abbr.]

schizocarp /ˈskɪzəˌkɑːp/ n. Bot. any of a group of dry fruits that split into single-seeded parts when ripe. □□ **schizocarpic** /-ˈkɑːpɪk/ adj. **schizocarpous** /-ˈkɑːpəs/ adj. [Gk *skhizō* to split + *karpos* fruit]

schizoid /ˈskɪtsɔɪd/ adj. & n. —adj. (of a person or personality etc.) tending to or resembling schizophrenia or a schizophrenic, but usu. without delusions. —n. a schizoid person.

schizomycete /ˌskɪtsəˈmaɪsiːt/ n. a former name for a bacterium. [Gk *skhizō* to split + *mukēs -ētos* mushroom]

schizophrenia /ˌskɪtsəˈfriːnɪə/ n. a mental disease marked by a breakdown in the relation between thoughts, feelings, and actions, frequently accompanied by delusions and retreat from social life. □□ **schizophrenic** /-ˈfrenɪk, -ˈfriːnɪk/ adj. & n. [mod.L f. Gk *skhizō* to split + *phrēn* mind]

schizothymia /ˌskɪtsəʊˈθaɪmɪə, ˌskɪz-/ n. Psychol. an introvert condition with a tendency to schizophrenia. □□ **schizothymic** adj. [mod.L (as SCHIZOPHRENIA + Gk *thumos* temper)]

schlemiel /ʃləˈmiːl/ n. US colloq. a foolish or unlucky person. [Yiddish *shlumiel*]

schlep /ʃlep/ v. & n. (also **schlepp**) colloq. —v. (**schlepped**, **schlepping**) 1 tr. carry, drag. 2 intr. go or work tediously or effortfully. —n. esp. US trouble or hard work. [Yiddish *shlepn* f. G *schleppen* drag]

Schleswig /ˈʃlɛsvɪk/ a former duchy of the Danish Crown, acquired by conquest by Prussia in 1864 and incorporated into the province of Schleswig-Holstein. The northern part of this territory was returned to Denmark in 1920 after a plebiscite held in accordance with the Treaty of Versailles.

Schleswig-Holstein /ˈhɒlʃtaɪn/ a 'Land' (State) of NW Germany; pop. (1987) 2,612,000; capital, Kiel.

Schliemann /ˈʃliːmən/, Heinrich (1822–90), German archaeologist. During the early part of his life he was very successfully engaged in commerce, and did not begin archaeological work until he was nearly 50. Convinced that if the city of Troy had existed remains of it must surely survive, he ignored the open derision of scholars and in 1871 began excavating, at his own expense, the mound of Hissarlik on the NE Aegean coast of Turkey. The remains of nine consecutive cities faced him, and (there being at that time no accepted method of scientifically excavating a complex site) he incorrectly identified the second oldest as Homer's Troy, and romantically called a hoard of jewellery (which he smuggled out of Turkey and had photographed adorning his wife) 'Priam's Treasure'. He subsequently excavated at Mycenae, where he believed he had discovered Agamemnon's tomb, and at other sites of mainland Greece. Schliemann is recognized as the discoverer of the Mycenaean civilization and the bringer of a new romance and excitement to archaeology.

schlieren /ˈʃliərən/ n. 1 a visually discernible area or stratum of different density in a transparent medium. 2 Geol. an irregular streak of mineral in igneous rock. [G, pl. of *Schliere* streak]

schlock /ʃlɒk/ n. US colloq. inferior goods; trash. [Yiddish *shlak* a blow]

schmaltz /ʃmɔːlts, ʃmælts/ n. esp. US colloq. sentimentality, esp. in music, drama, etc. □□ **schmaltzy** adj. (**schmaltzier, schmaltziest**). [Yiddish f. G *Schmalz* dripping, lard]

schmuck /ʃmʌk/ n. esp. US sl. a foolish or contemptible person. [Yiddish]

schnapps /ʃnæps/ n. any of various spirits drunk in N. Europe. [G, = dram of liquor f. LG & Du. *snaps* mouthful (as SNAP)]

schnauzer /ˈʃnaʊtsə(r), ˈʃnaʊzə(r)/ n. 1 a dog of a German breed with a close wiry coat and heavy whiskers round the muzzle. 2 this breed. [G f. *Schnauze* muzzle, SNOUT]

Schneider /ˈʃnaɪdə(r)/, Jacques (1879–1928), French flying enthusiast, who donated a trophy, the Jacques Schneider Maritime Cup, which he presented in 1913 to the winner of an international competition for seaplanes comprising an air race and seaworthiness trials. It was contested annually (with certain exceptions) until won outright by Great Britain in 1931.

schnitzel /ˈʃnɪtz(ə)l/ n. an escalope of veal. □ **Wiener** (or **Vienna**) **schnitzel** a breaded, fried, and garnished schnitzel. [G, = slice]

schnorkel var. of SNORKEL.

schnorrer /ˈʃnɔːrə(r)/ n. esp. US sl. a beggar or scrounger; a layabout. [Yiddish f. G *Schnurrer*]

Schoenberg /ˈʃɜːnbɜːg/, Arnold (1874–1951), one of the most influential figures in the history of music. Born in Vienna, he worked as a professor of music there and in Berlin until 1933 when, after having his music branded (together with that of his pupils Berg and Webern) 'degenerate art' by Hitler, he emigrated to the US. His dedication to the development of the musical language inherited from the late 19th c. led in 1908 to a break with tonal writing and the concept of atonality and, later, serialism. Such early works as the symphonic poem for string sextet *Verklärte Nacht* (1899) reveal the chromatic idiom being stretched to its limits; his first atonal works, the Five Orchestral Pieces, the monodrama *Erwartung* (both 1909), and the song cycle *Pierrot lunaire* (1912), are expressionist and intense in their exploration of fundamental human emotion and violence; with the serial works Schoenberg returned to classical formal moulds and a quieter manner. One of the last works written by him before leaving Germany was *Moses und Aron* (1930–2), an opera reflecting his concern with religion at that time (he returned to the Jewish faith of his upbringing in 1933); it was left unfinished with its central problem unresolved at his death.

scholar /ˈskɒlə(r)/ n. 1 a learned person, esp. in language, literature, etc.; an academic. 2 the holder of a scholarship. 3 a a person with specified academic ability (*is a poor scholar*). b a person who learns (*am a scholar of life*). 4 archaic colloq. a person able to read and write. 5 archaic a schoolboy or schoolgirl. □ **scholar's mate** see MATE². □□ **scholarly** adv. **scholarliness** n. [ME f. OE *scol(i)ere* & OF *escol(i)er* f. LL *scholaris* f. L *schola* SCHOOL¹]

scholarship /ˈskɒləʃɪp/ n. 1 a academic achievement; learning of a high level. b the methods and standards characteristic of a good scholar (*shows great scholarship*). 2 payment from the funds of a school, university, local government, etc., to maintain a student in full-time education, awarded on the basis of scholarly achievement.

scholastic /skəˈlæstɪk/ adj. & n. —adj. 1 of or concerning universities, schools, education, teachers, etc. 2 pedantic; formal (*shows scholastic precision*). 3 Philos. hist. of, resembling, or concerning the schoolmen, esp. in dealing with logical subtleties. —n. 1 a student. 2 Philos. hist. a schoolman. 3 a theologian of scholastic tendencies. 4 RC Ch. a member of any of several religious orders, who is between the novitiate and the priesthood. □□ **scholastically** adv. [L *scholasticus* f. Gk *skholastikos* studious f. *skholazō* be at leisure, formed as SCHOOL¹]

scholasticism /skəˈlæstɪˌsɪz(ə)m/ n. 1 the educational tradition of the medieval 'schools' (i.e. universities), especially a method of philosophical and theological speculation which aimed at a better understanding of the revealed truths of Christianity by defining, systematizing, and reasoning. Its theoretical foundations were laid by St Augustine and Boethius, and among its most famous figures were St Anselm and Abelard (who perfected the technique). Of decisive importance was the introduction of the works of Aristotle into Western Europe, and the crowning achievement of scholastic theology was the work of Aquinas, whose *Summa Theologica* drew the line between faith and reason with the utmost clarity. From this time scholasticism declined, undermined by the writings of William of Occam, but it never wholly lost its vitality, and interest in it revived at the end of the 19th c. 2 narrow or unenlightened insistence on traditional doctrines etc.

scholiast /ˈskəʊlɪˌæst/ n. hist. an ancient or medieval scholar, esp. a grammarian, who annotated ancient literary texts. □□ **scholiastic** /-ˈæstɪk/ adj. [med.Gk *skholiastēs* f. *skholiazō* write scholia: see SCHOLIUM]

scholium /ˈskəʊliəm/ n. (pl. **scholia** /-liə/) a marginal note or explanatory comment, esp. by an ancient grammarian on a classical text. [mod.L f. Gk *skholion* f. *skholē* disputation: see SCHOOL]

school[1] /skuːl/ n. & v. —n. **1 a** an institution for educating or giving instruction, esp. Brit. for children under 19 years, or US for any level of instruction including college or university. **b** (*attrib.*) associated with or for use in school (*a school bag; school dinners*). **2 a** the buildings used by such an institution. **b** the pupils, staff, etc. of a school. **c** the time during which teaching is done, or the teaching itself (*no school today*). **3 a** a branch of study with separate examinations at a university; a department or faculty (*the history school*). **b** Brit. the hall in which university examinations are held. **c** (in *pl.*) Brit. such examinations. **4 a** the disciples, imitators, or followers of a philosopher, artist, etc. (*the school of Epicurus*). **b** a group of artists etc. whose works share distinctive characteristics. **c** a group of people sharing a cause, principle, method, etc. (*school of thought*). **5** Brit. a group of gamblers or of persons drinking together (*a poker school*). **6** *colloq.* instructive or disciplinary circumstances, occupation, etc. (*the school of adversity; learnt in a hard school*). **7** *hist.* a medieval lecture-room. **8** *Mus.* (usu. foll. by *of*) a handbook or book of instruction (*school of counterpoint*). **9** (in *pl.*; prec. by *the*) *hist.* medieval universities, their teachers, disputations, etc. —v.tr. **1** send to school; provide for the education of. **2** (often foll. by *to*) discipline; train; control. **3** (as **schooled** *adj.*) (foll. by *in*) educated or trained (*schooled in humility*). □ **at** (*US* **in**) **school** attending lessons etc. **go to school 1** begin one's education. **2** attend lessons. **leave school** finish one's education. **of the old school** according to former and esp. better tradition (*a gentleman of the old school*). **school age** the age-range in which children normally attend school. **school board** US or hist. a board or authority for local education. **school-days** the time of being at school, esp. in retrospect. **school-inspector** a government official reporting on the efficiency, teaching standards, etc. of schools. **school-leaver** Brit. a child leaving school esp. at the minimum specified age. **school-leaving age** the minimum age at which a schoolchild may leave school. **school-ma'm** (or **-marm**) US *colloq.* a schoolmistress. **school-marmish** *colloq.* prim and fussy. **school-ship** a training-ship. **school-time 1** lesson-time at school or at home. **2** school-days. **school year** = *academic year*. [ME f. OE *scōl, scolu*, & f. OF *escole* ult. f. L *schola* school f. Gk *skholē* leisure, disputation, philosophy, lecture-place]

school[2] /skuːl/ n. & v. —n. (often foll. by *of*) a shoal of fish, porpoises, whales, etc. —v.intr. form schools. [ME f. MLG, MDu. *schōle* f. WG]

schoolable /ˈskuːləb(ə)l/ adj. liable by age etc. to compulsory education.

schoolboy /ˈskuːlbɔɪ/ n. a boy attending school.

schoolchild /ˈskuːltʃaɪld/ n. a child attending school.

schoolfellow /ˈskuːlˌfeləʊ/ n. a past or esp. present member of the same school.

schoolgirl /ˈskuːlgɜːl/ n. a girl attending school.

schoolhouse /ˈskuːlhaʊs/ n. Brit. **1** a building used as a school, esp. in a village. **2** a dwelling-house adjoining a school.

schoolie /ˈskuːli/ n. Austral. sl. & dial. a schoolteacher.

schooling /ˈskuːlɪŋ/ n. **1** education, esp. at school. **2** training or discipline, esp. of an animal.

schoolman /ˈskuːlmən/ n. (pl. **-men**) **1** hist. a teacher in a medieval European university. **2** RC Ch. hist. a theologian seeking to deal with religious doctrines by the rules of Aristotelian logic. (See SCHOLASTICISM.) **3** US a male teacher.

schoolmaster /ˈskuːlˌmɑːstə(r)/ n. a head or assistant male teacher. □□ **schoolmasterly** adj.

schoolmastering /ˈskuːlˌmɑːstərɪŋ/ n. teaching as a profession.

schoolmate /ˈskuːlmeɪt/ n. = SCHOOLFELLOW.

schoolmistress /ˈskuːlˌmɪstrɪs/ n. a head or assistant female teacher.

schoolmistressy /ˈskuːlˌmɪstrɪsi/ adj. *colloq.* prim and fussy.

schoolroom /ˈskuːlruːm, -rʊm/ n. a room used for lessons in a school or esp. in a private house.

schoolteacher /ˈskuːlˌtiːtʃə(r)/ n. a person who teaches in a school. □□ **schoolteaching** n.

schooner /ˈskuːnə(r)/ n. **1** a fore-and-aft rigged ship with two or more masts, the foremast being smaller than the other masts. **2 a** Brit. a measure or glass for esp. sherry. **b** US & Austral. a tall beer-glass. **3** US hist. = *prairie schooner*. [18th c.: orig. uncert.]

Schopenhauer /ˈʃəʊpənˌhaʊə(r), ˈʃɒp-/, Arthur (1788–1860), German author of a pessimistic philosophy which is an adaptation of Kant's and is embodied in his principal work *The World as Will and Idea* (1818). According to Schopenhauer the will, of which we have direct intuition, is the only reality and the means by which all other things are understood; what is real is one vast will, appearing in the whole natural world, animate and inanimate alike. This 'cosmic will' is a malignant thing, which inveigles us into reproducing and perpetuating life. Asceticism and chastity are the duty of man, with a view to terminating the evil. As a stage towards this goal he found a transient place of rest in the realms of poetry, art, and above all music. His theory of the predominance of the will anticipated that of Freud and later psychologists; in his ethical doctrines he was influenced by Buddhism. In private life he made no attempt to put into practice the asceticism which he extolled, but he bequeathed what material wealth he had to the relief of suffering.

schorl /ʃɔːl/ n. black tourmaline. [G *Schörl*]

schottische /ʃɒˈtiːʃ/ n. **1** a kind of slow polka. **2** the music for this. [G *der schottische Tanz* the Scottish dance]

Schottky effect /ˈʃɒtki/ n. *Electronics* the increase in thermionic emission from a solid surface due to the presence of an external electric field. [W. Schottky, Ger. physicist d. 1976]

Schrödinger /ˈʃrɜːdɪŋə(r)/, Erwin (1887–1961), Austrian theoretical physicist who in the 1920s developed wave mechanics, a mathematical theory which describes the structure and properties of atoms and the particles they contain. He shared the 1933 Nobel Prize for physics with Dirac, and (an ardent anti-Nazi) moved to Oxford. He spent the Second World War in Dublin, and wrote a book *What is Life?* which was the inspiration of many physicists who became molecular biologists. □ **Schrödinger equation**. *Physics* a differential equation used in quantum mechanics for the wave function of a particle.

Schubert /ˈʃuːbɜːt/, Franz (1797–1828), Austrian composer. During his short life he produced over 600 songs, 9 symphonies, 15 string quartets, and 21 piano sonatas, as well as operas, church music, and a host of single-movement pieces for piano, chamber ensemble, etc. Schubert can be considered equally the most approachable and lovable of composers for his gift for exquisite miniatures and a master of sustained thought on a larger scale, particularly in the works of his last years. He has been criticized both for setting inferior verse and for missing the deeper implications of more serious poets, but to look for a refined literary sensibility in such a composer is to miss the essence of his genius. His response to poetry was immediate and overpowering in its intensity, allowing no time for meditation or qualification; as Richard Capell wrote in his study of the songs (1928), 'Schubert . . . knew nothing but the rapture and poignancy of first sensations, the loss of which is the beginning of wisdom'.

Schulz /ʃʊlts/, Charles (1922–), American cartoonist, creator of the 'Peanuts' comic strip (originally entitled 'Li'l Folks'), featuring the child Charlie Brown and the beagle hound Snoopy, which first appeared in 1950.

Schumann /ˈʃuːmən/, Robert Alexander (1810–56), German composer, who studied law before embarking on a musical career. He had ambitions to become a concert pianist but damaged his hand with a device intended to aid finger control; in 1840 he married Clara Wieck, the daughter of his piano teacher and herself a celebrated pianist. In 1854 Schumann attempted suicide by drowning, and his last two years were passed in a private asylum near Bonn. His most productive years were those following his marriage to Clara: in 1840 he composed the bulk of his many songs; 1841 saw the start of his symphonic writing, and in 1842 he produced much chamber music. His symphonies,

Piano Concerto (1845), and chamber works have much to recommend them, but he was at his best on a smaller scale, as in the loosely linked miniatures for piano of *Papillons* (1829–31), *Carnaval* (1834–5), and *Waldscenen* (1848–9) and especially in the songs, where he reveals his sensitivity to the romanticism of contemporary poets.

schuss /ʃʊs/ *n. & v.* —*n.* a straight downhill run on skis. —*v.intr.* make a schuss. [G, lit. 'shot']

Schütz /ʃuːts/, Heinrich (1585–1672), German composer and organist, one of the greatest of Bach's predecessors. A visit to Italy in 1609–13 for a period of study provided an important influence, seen for example in the settings of *Psalmens Davids* (1619), and he composed what is thought to have been the first opera by a German (*Dafne*, now lost). His three settings of the Passion story represent a turning towards a simple meditative style, eschewing instrumental accompaniment and relying on voices alone for his depiction of Christ's suffering and crucifixion.

schwa /ʃwɑː, ʃvɑː/ *n.* (also **sheva** /ʃəˈvɑː/) *Phonet.* **1** the indistinct unstressed vowel sound as in *a* moment *ago*. **2** the symbol /ə/ representing this in the International Phonetic Alphabet. [G f. Heb. *šʷā*, app. f. *šaw* emptiness]

Schwarzkopf /ˈʃvɑːtskɒpf/, Elisabeth (1915–), German operatic soprano singer, famous especially for roles in works by Richard Strauss and Mascagni's *Cavalleria Rusticana*.

Schwarzwald see BLACK FOREST.

Schweitzer /ˈʃwaɪtsə(r), ˈʃvaɪ-/, Albert (1875–1965), theologian, musician, and physician, born in Alsace-Lorraine (then part of Germany), who devoted the early part of his life to learning and music and the remainder to the service of others. His book *The Quest of the Historical Jesus* (1906) ended an epoch of attempts to unearth an authentic portrait of Jesus from the Gospels by historical-critical research, showing that many such portraits were conditioned by 19th-c. ideals, and argued that Jesus was a more alien figure who had believed that the end of the world was imminent. Schweitzer was an accomplished organist and interpreter of Bach, on whom he wrote a monograph (1908). In 1913 he abandoned his academic career to become a doctor and missionary at Lambaréné in French Equatorial Africa (now Gabon). After being interned in France during the First World War he returned to restore his hospital and continue the work which embodied his ethical principle of 'reverence for life'. One of the greatest humanitarians of the 20th c., Schweitzer was awarded the Nobel Peace Prize in 1952.

Schwerin /ˈʃʊərɪn/ a city in NE Germany, capital of Mecklenburg-West Pomerania; pop. (est. 1990) 130,000.

Schwyz /ʃviːts/ the capital of a canton of the same name in central Switzerland; pop. (1980) 12,100. Schwyz was one of the three original districts of the anti-Hapsburg league, formed in 1291, that developed into the Swiss Confederation. Because of its leadership in this league its name and its flag were adapted by the whole country.

sciagraphy /skaɪˈægrəfɪ/ *n.* (also **skiagraphy**) the art of shading in drawing etc. □□ **sciagram** /ˈskaɪəˌgræm/ *n.* **sciagraph** /ˈskaɪəˌgrɑːf/ *n. & v.tr.* **sciagraphic** /ˌskaɪəˈgræfɪk/ *adj.* [F *sciagraphie* f. L *sciagraphia* f. Gk *skiagraphia* f. *skia* shadow]

sciamachy /saɪˈæməkɪ/ *n.* (also **skiamachy** /skaɪ-/) *formal* **1** fighting with shadows. **2** imaginary or futile combat. [Gk *skiamakhia* (as SCIAGRAPHY, *-makhia* -fighting)]

sciatic /saɪˈætɪk/ *adj.* **1** of the hip. **2** of or affecting the sciatic nerve. **3** suffering from or liable to sciatica. □ **sciatic nerve** the largest nerve in the human body, running from the pelvis to the thigh. □□ **sciatically** *adv.* [F *sciatique* f. LL *sciaticus* f. L *ischiadicus* f. Gk *iskhiadikos* subject to sciatica f. *iskhion* hip-joint]

sciatica /saɪˈætɪkə/ *n.* neuralgia of the hip and thigh; a pain in the sciatic nerve. [ME f. LL *sciatica* (*passio*) fem. of *sciaticus*: see SCIATIC]

science /ˈsaɪəns/ *n.* **1** a branch of knowledge conducted on objective principles involving the systematized observation of and experiment with phenomena, esp. concerned with the material and functions of the physical universe (see also *natural science*). **2 a** systematic and formulated knowledge, esp. of a

specified type or on a specified subject (*political science*). **b** the pursuit or principles of this. **3** an organized body of knowledge on a subject (*the science of philology*). **4** skilful technique rather than strength or natural ability. **5** *archaic* knowledge of any kind. □ **science park** an area devoted to scientific research or the development of science-based industries. [ME f. OF f. L *scientia* f. *scire* know]

science fiction *n.* a class of prose narrative which assumes an imaginary technological or scientific advance, portrays space travel or life on other planets, or depends upon a spectacular change in the human environment. Although examples exist from the time of Lucian (2nd c. AD), it was not until the end of the 19th c. that the form emerged as we know it today. The works of Jules Verne are notable examples, but the first successful English author was H. G. Wells, using themes of invasion from outer space (*The War of the Worlds*, 1898), biological change or catastrophe (*The Food of the Gods*, 1904), time travel (*The Time Machine*, 1895), and air warfare (*The War in the Air*, 1908). Since the Second World War scientific developments and their possible consequences have been reflected in fictional forms often carrying apocalyptic undertones; the destruction of the world as a result of its own technological achievements is a favourite theme. The literary quality of the genre is extremely variable, ranging from violent strip cartoons in pulp magazines, through respectable 'domestic' novels, to more challenging intellectual ventures and philosophical inquiry into the nature of mankind and human behaviour. The impact of its tradition on films and television has been enormous, with products ranging from children's programmes to cinema epics.

scienter /saɪˈentə(r)/ *adv. Law* intentionally; knowingly. [L f. *scire* know]

sciential /saɪˈenʃ(ə)l/ *adj.* concerning or having knowledge. [LL *scientialis* (as SCIENCE)]

scientific /ˌsaɪənˈtɪfɪk/ *adj.* **1 a** (of an investigation etc.) according to rules laid down in exact science for performing observations and testing the soundness of conclusions. **b** systematic, accurate. **2** used in, engaged in, or relating to (esp. natural) science (*scientific discoveries*; *scientific terminology*). **3** assisted by expert knowledge. □□ **scientifically** *adv.* [F *scientifique* or LL *scientificus* (as SCIENCE)]

scientism /ˈsaɪənˌtɪz(ə)m/ *n.* **1 a** a method or doctrine regarded as characteristic of scientists. **b** the use or practice of this. **2** often *derog.* an excessive belief in or application of scientific method. □□ **scientistic** /-ˈtɪstɪk/ *adj.*

scientist /ˈsaɪəntɪst/ *n.* **1** a person with expert knowledge of a (usu. physical or natural) science. **2** a person using scientific methods.

scientology /ˌsaɪənˈtɒlədʒɪ/ *n.* a religious system based on self-improvement and promotion through grades of esp. self-knowledge. It was founded in 1951 by the American writer of science fiction, L. Ron Hubbard (1911–86). □□ **scientologist** *n.* [L *scientia* knowledge + -LOGY]

sci-fi /ˈsaɪfaɪ, saɪˈfaɪ/ *n.* (often *attrib.*) *colloq.* science fiction. [abbr.: cf. HI-FI]

scilicet /ˈsaɪlɪˌset, ˈskiːlɪˌket/ *adv.* to wit; that is to say; namely (introducing a word to be supplied or an explanation of an ambiguity). [ME f. L, = *scire licet* one is permitted to know]

scilla /ˈsɪlə/ *n.* any liliaceous plant of the genus *Scilla*, related to the bluebell, usu. bearing small blue star-shaped or bell-shaped flowers and having long glossy straplike leaves. [L f. Gk *skilla*]

Scilly Islands /ˈsɪlɪ/ (also **Scillies**) a group of about 40 small islands off the western extremity of Cornwall; pop. 1,850; capital, Hugh Town (on St Mary's). □□ **Scillonian** /sɪˈləʊnɪən/ *adj. & n.*

scimitar /ˈsɪmɪtə(r)/ *n.* an oriental curved sword usu. broadening towards the point. [F *cimeterre*, It. *scimitarra*, etc., of unkn. orig.]

scintigram /ˈsɪntɪˌgræm/ *n.* an image of an internal part of the body, produced by scintigraphy.

scintigraphy /sɪnˈtɪgrəfɪ/ *n.* the use of a radioisotope and a scintillation counter to get an image or record of a bodily organ etc. [SCINTILLATION + -GRAPHY]

scintilla /sɪn'tɪlə/ n. **1** a trace. **2** a spark. [L]

scintillate /'sɪntɪˌleɪt/ v.intr. **1** (esp. as **scintillating** adj.) talk cleverly or wittily; be brilliant. **2** sparkle; twinkle; emit sparks. **3** Physics fluoresce momentarily when struck by a charged particle etc. □□ **scintillant** adj. **scintillatingly** adv. [L scintillare (as SCINTILLA)]

scintillation /ˌsɪntɪ'leɪʃ(ə)n/ n. **1** the process or state of scintillating. **2** the twinkling of a star. **3** a flash produced in a material by an ionizing particle etc. □ **scintillation counter** a device for detecting and recording scintillation.

scintiscan /'sɪntɪˌskæn/ n. an image or other record showing the distribution of radioactive traces in parts of the body, used in the detection and diagnosis of various diseases. [SCINTILLATION + SCAN]

sciolist /'saɪəlɪst/ n. a superficial pretender to knowledge. □□ **sciolism** /-'lɪz(ə)m/ n. **sciolistic** /-'lɪstɪk/ adj. [LL sciolus smatterer f. L scire know]

scion /'saɪən/ n. **1** (US **cion**) a shoot of a plant etc., esp. one cut for grafting or planting. **2** a descendant; a younger member of (esp. a noble) family. [ME f. OF ciun, cion, sion shoot, twig, of unkn. orig.]

Scipio[1] /'skɪpɪˌəʊ/ (Publius Cornelius Scipio Africanus Major, 236–184/3 BC) Roman general and politician. His tactical reforms of the army and offensive strategy were successful in concluding the second Punic War, firstly by the defeat of the Carthaginians in Spain in 206 BC, and then by the defeat of Hannibal in Africa in 202 BC (after which he was given the name Africanus); his victories pointed the way to Roman hegemony in the Mediterranean. His son was the adoptive father of Scipio[2].

Scipio[2] /'skɪpɪˌəʊ/ (Publius Cornelius Scipio Aemilianus Africanus, 185/4–129 BC), Roman general and politician. He achieved distinction in the third Punic War, and blockaded and destroyed Carthage in 146 BC. His successful campaign in Spain (133 BC) ended organized resistance in that country. Returning to Rome in triumph, he provoked a major political storm by initiating moves against the reforms introduced by his brother-in-law Tiberius Gracchus. Scipio's sudden death at the height of the crisis gave rise to the rumour that he had been murdered.

scire facias /ˌsaɪərɪ 'feɪʃɪˌæs/ n. Law a writ to enforce or annul a judgement, patent, etc. [L, = let (him) know]

scirocco var. of SIROCCO.

scirrhus /'sɪrəs, 'skɪ-/ n. (pl. **scirrhi** /-raɪ/) a carcinoma which is hard to the touch. □□ **scirrhoid** adj. **scirrhosity** /sɪ'rɒsɪtɪ/ n. **scirrhous** adj. [mod.L f. Gk skir(r)os f. skiros hard]

scissel /'skɪs(ə)l/ n. waste clippings etc. of metal produced during coin manufacture. [F cisaille f. cisailler clip with shears]

scissile /'sɪsaɪl/ adj. able to be cut or divided. [L scissilis f. scindere sciss- cut]

scission /'sɪʃ(ə)n/ n. **1** the act or an instance of cutting; the state of being cut. **2** a division or split. [ME f. OF scission or LL scissio (as SCISSILE)]

scissor /'sɪzə(r)/ v.tr. **1** (usu. foll. by off, up, into, etc.) cut with scissors. **2** (usu. foll. by out) clip out (a newspaper cutting etc.).

scissors /'sɪzəz/ n.pl. **1** (also **pair of scissors** sing.) an instrument for cutting fabric, paper, hair, etc., having two pivoted blades with finger and thumb holes in the handles, operating by closing on the material to be cut. (See below.) **2** (treated as sing.) **a** a method of high jumping with a forward and backward movement of the legs. **b** a hold in wrestling in which the opponent's body or esp. head is gripped between the legs. □ **scissor-bill** = SKIMMER 4. **scissor-bird** (or **-tail**) a fork-tailed flycatcher, Tyrannus forficatus. **scissors and paste** a method of compiling a book, article, etc., from extracts from others or without independent research. □□ **scissorwise** adv. [ME sisoures f. OF cisoires f. LL cisoria pl. of cisorium cutting instrument (as CHISEL): assoc. with L scindere sciss- cut]

Scissors with overlapping blades and with a C-shaped spring at the handle end (like tongs) probably date from the Bronze Age; they were used in Europe until the end of the Middle Ages, and the design survived still later for some specific purposes (e.g. sheep-shearing). Scissors pivoted between handle and blade were used in Roman Europe and the Far East 2,000 years ago.

In Europe they came into domestic use in the 16th c.; large-scale production dates from 1761 when Robert Hinchcliffe of Sheffield began to use cast steel in their manufacture.

sciurine /'saɪjʊˌraɪn/ adj. **1** of or relating to the family Sciuridae, including squirrels and chipmunks. **2** squirrel-like. □□ **sciuroid** adj. [L sciurus f. Gk skiouros squirrel f. skia shadow + oura tail]

sclera /'sklɪərə/ n. the white of the eye; a white membrane coating the eyeball. □□ **scleral** adj. **scleritis** /sklɪə'raɪtɪs/ n. **sclerotomy** /-'rɒtəmɪ/ n. (pl. **-ies**). [mod.L f. fem. of Gk sklēros hard]

sclerenchyma /sklɪə'reŋkɪmə/ n. the woody tissue found in a plant, formed from lignified cells and usu. providing support. [mod.L f. Gk sklēros hard + egkhuma infusion, after parenchyma]

scleroid /'sklɪərɔɪd/ adj. Bot. & Zool. having a hard texture; hardened. [Gk sklēros hard]

scleroma /sklɪə'rəʊmə/ n. (pl. **scleromata** /-mətə/) an abnormal patch of hardened skin or mucous membrane. [mod.L f. Gk sklērōma (as SCLEROSIS)]

sclerometer /sklɪə'rɒmɪtə(r)/ n. an instrument for determining the hardness of materials. [Gk sklēros hard + -METER]

sclerophyll /'sklɪərəfɪl/ n. any woody plant with leathery leaves retaining water. □□ **sclerophyllous** /-'rɒfɪləs/ adj. [Gk sklēros hard + phullon leaf]

scleroprotein /ˌsklɪərəʊ'prəʊtiːn/ n. Biochem. any insoluble structural protein. [Gk sklēros hard + PROTEIN]

sclerosed /'sklɪəˌrəʊst, -ˌrəʊzd/ adj. affected by sclerosis.

sclerosis /sklɪə'rəʊsɪs/ n. **1** an abnormal hardening of body tissue (see also ARTERIOSCLEROSIS, ATHEROSCLEROSIS). **2** (in full **multiple** or **disseminated sclerosis**) a chronic and progressive disease of the nervous system resulting in symptoms including paralysis and speech defects. **3** Bot. the hardening of a cell-wall with lignified matter. [ME f. med.L f. Gk sklērōsis f. sklēroō harden]

sclerotic /sklɪə'rɒtɪk/ adj. & n. —adj. **1** of or having sclerosis. **2** of or relating to the sclera. —n. = SCLERA. □□ **sclerotitis** /-rə'taɪtɪs/ n. [med.L sclerotica (as SCLEROSIS)]

sclerous /'sklɪərəs/ adj. Physiol. hardened; bony. [Gk sklēros hard]

SCM abbr. (in the UK) **1** State Certified Midwife. **2** Student Christian Movement.

scoff[1] /skɒf/ v. & n. —v.intr. (usu. foll. by at) speak derisively, esp. of serious subjects; mock; be scornful. —n. **1** mocking words; a taunt. **2** an object of ridicule. □□ **scoffer** n. **scoffingly** adv. [perh. f. Scand.: cf. early mod. Da. skuf, skof jest, mockery]

scoff[2] /skɒf/ v. & n. colloq. —v.tr. & intr. eat greedily. —n. food; a meal. [(n.) f. Afrik. schoff repr. Du. schoft quarter of a day (hence, meal): (v.) orig. var. of dial. scaff, assoc. with the noun]

scold /skəʊld/ v. & n. —v. **1** tr. rebuke (esp. a child, employee, or inferior). **2** intr. find fault noisily; complain; rail. —n. archaic a nagging or grumbling woman. □□ **scolder** n. **scolding** n. [ME (earlier as noun), prob. f. ON skáld SKALD]

scolex /'skəʊleks/ n. (pl. **scoleces** /-'liːsiːz/ or **scolices** /-lɪˌsiːz/) the head of a larval or adult tapeworm. [mod.L f. Gk skōlēx worm]

scoliosis /ˌskɒlɪ'əʊsɪs/ n. an abnormal lateral curvature of the spine. □□ **scoliotic** /-'ɒtɪk/ adj. [mod.L f. Gk f. skolios bent]

scollop var. of SCALLOP.

scolopendrium /ˌskɒlə'pendrɪəm/ n. any of various ferns, esp. hart's tongue. [mod.L f. Gk skolopendrion f. skolopendra millipede (because of the supposed resemblance)]

scomber /'skɒmbə(r)/ n. any marine fish of the family Scombridae, including mackerels, tunas, and bonitos. □□ **scombrid** n. **scombroid** adj. & n. [L f. Gk skombros]

sconce[1] /skɒns/ n. **1** a flat candlestick with a handle. **2** a bracket candlestick to hang on a wall. [ME f. OF esconse lantern or med.L sconsa f. L absconsa fem. past part. of abscondere hide: see ABSCOND]

sconce[2] /skɒns/ n. **1** a small fort or earthwork usu. defending a ford, pass, etc. **2** archaic a shelter or screen. [Du. schans brushwood f. MHG schanze]

Scone /skuːn/ a village in Tayside, the ancient Scottish capital where their kings were crowned. □ **stone of Scone** see CORONATION STONE.

scone /skɒn, skəʊn/ n. a small sweet or savoury cake of flour, fat, and milk, baked quickly in an oven. [orig. Sc., perh. f. MDu. *schoon(broot)*, MLG *schon(brot)* fine (bread)]

scoop /skuːp/ n. & v. —n. **1** any of various objects resembling a spoon, esp.: **a** a short-handled deep shovel used for transferring grain, sugar, coal, coins, etc. **b** a large long-handled ladle used for transferring liquids. **c** the excavating part of a digging-machine etc. **d** Med. a long-handled spoonlike instrument used for scraping parts of the body etc. **e** an instrument used for serving portions of mashed potato, ice-cream, etc. **2** a quantity taken up by a scoop. **3** a movement of or resembling scooping. **4** a piece of news published by a newspaper etc. in advance of its rivals. **5** a large profit made quickly or by anticipating one's competitors. **6** Mus. a singer's exaggerated portamento. **7** a scooped-out hollow etc. —v.tr. **1** (usu. foll. by *out*) hollow out with or as if with a scoop. **2** (usu. foll. by *up*) lift with or as if with a scoop. **3** forestall (a rival newspaper, reporter, etc.) with a scoop. **4** secure (a large profit etc.) esp. suddenly. □ **scoop-neck** the rounded low-cut neck of a garment. **scoop-net** a net used for sweeping a river bottom, or for catching bait. □□ **scooper** n. **scoopful** n. (pl. **-fuls**). [ME f. MDu., MLG *schōpe* bucket etc., rel. to SHAPE]

scoot /skuːt/ v. & n. colloq. —v.intr. run or dart away, esp. quickly. —n. the act or an instance of scooting. [19th-c. US (earlier *scout*): orig. unkn.]

scooter /ˈskuːtə(r)/ n. & v. —n. **1 a** a child's toy consisting of a footboard mounted on two wheels and a long steering-handle, propelled by resting one foot on the footboard and pushing the other against the ground. **2** (in full **motor scooter**) a light two-wheeled open motor vehicle with a shieldlike protective front. **3** US a sailboat able to travel on both water and ice. —v.intr. travel or ride on a scooter. □□ **scooterist** n.

scopa /ˈskəʊpə/ n. (pl. **scopae** /-piː/) a small brushlike tuft of hairs, esp. on the leg of a bee for collecting pollen. [sing. of L *scopae* = twigs, broom]

scope¹ /skəʊp/ n. **1 a** the extent to which it is possible to range; the opportunity for action etc. (*this is beyond the scope of our research*). **b** the sweep or reach of mental activity, observation, or outlook (*an intellect limited in its scope*). **2** Naut. the length of cable extended when a ship rides at anchor. **3** archaic a purpose, end, or intention. [It. *scopo* aim f. Gk *skopos* target f. *skeptomai* look at]

scope² /skəʊp/ n. colloq. a telescope, microscope, or other device ending in *-scope*. [abbr.]

-scope /skəʊp/ comb. form forming nouns denoting: **1** a device looked at or through (*kaleidoscope*; *telescope*). **2** an instrument for observing or showing (*gyroscope*; *oscilloscope*). □□ **-scopic** /ˈskɒpɪk/ comb. form forming adjectives. [from or after mod.L *-scopium* f. Gk *skopeō* look at]

scopolamine /skəˈpɒləmɪn, -ˌmiːn/ n. = HYOSCINE. [*Scopolia* genus-name of the plants yielding it, f. G. A. *Scopoli*, It. naturalist d. 1788 + AMINE]

scopula /ˈskɒpjʊlə/ n. (pl. **scopulae** /-ˌliː/) any of various small brushlike structures, esp. on the legs of spiders. [LL, dimin. of L *scopa*: see SCOPA]

-scopy /skəpɪ/ comb. form indicating viewing or observation, usu. with an instrument ending in *-scope* (*microscopy*).

scorbutic /skɔːˈbjuːtɪk/ adj. & n. —adj. relating to, resembling, or affected with scurvy. —n. a person affected with scurvy. □□ **scorbutically** adv. [mod.L *scorbuticus* f. med.L *scorbutus* scurvy, perh. f. MLG *schorbūk* f. *schoren* break + *būk* belly]

scorch /skɔːtʃ/ v. & n. —v. **1** tr. **a** burn the surface of with flame or heat so as to discolour, parch, injure, or hurt. **b** affect with the sensation of burning. **2** intr. become discoloured etc. with heat. **3** tr. (as **scorching** adj.) colloq. **a** (of the weather) very hot. **b** (of criticism etc.) stringent; harsh. **4** intr. colloq. (of a motorist etc.) go at excessive speed. —n. **1** a mark made by scorching. **2** colloq. a spell of fast driving etc. □ **scorched earth policy** the burning of crops etc. and the removing or destroying of anything that might be of use to an enemy force occupying a country. □□ **scorchingly** adv. [ME, perh. rel. to *skorkle* in the same sense]

scorcher /ˈskɔːtʃə(r)/ n. **1** a person or thing that scorches. **2** colloq. **a** a very hot day. **b** a fine specimen.

score /skɔː(r)/ n. & v. —n. **1 a** the number of points, goals, runs, etc., made by a player, side, etc., in some games. **b** the total number of points etc. at the end of a game (*the score was five–nil*). **c** the act of gaining esp. a goal (*a superb score there!*). **2** (pl. same or **scores**) twenty or a set of twenty. **3** (in pl.) a great many (*scores of people arrived*). **4 a** a reason or motive (*rejected on the score of absurdity*). **b** topic, subject (*no worries on that score*). **5** Mus. **a** a usu. printed copy of a composition showing all the vocal and instrumental parts arranged one below the other. **b** the music composed for a film or play, esp. for a musical. **6** colloq. **a** a piece of good fortune. **b** the act or an instance of scoring off another person. **7** colloq. the state of affairs; the present situation (*asked what the score was*). **8** a notch, line, etc. cut or scratched into a surface. **9 a** an amount due for payment. **b** a running account kept by marks against a customer's name. **10** Naut. a groove in a block or dead-eye to hold a rope. —v. **1** tr. **a** win or gain (a goal, run, points, etc., or success etc.) (*scored a century*). **b** count for a score of (points in a game etc.) (*a bull's-eye scores most points*). **c** allot a score to (a competitor etc.). **d** make a record of (a point etc.). **2** intr. **a** make a score in a game (*failed to score*). **b** keep the tally of points, runs, etc. in a game. **3** tr. mark with notches, incisions, lines, etc.; slash; furrow (*scored his name on the desk*). **4** intr. secure an advantage by luck, cunning, etc. (*that is where he scores*). **5** tr. Mus. **a** orchestrate (a piece of music). **b** (usu. foll. by *for*) arrange for an instrument or instruments. **c** write the music for (a film, musical, etc.). **d** write out in a score. **6** tr. **a** (usu. foll. by *up*) mark (a total owed etc.) in a score (see sense 9b of n.). **b** (usu. foll. by *against*, *to*) enter (an item of debt to a customer). **7** intr. sl. **a** obtain drugs illegally. **b** (of a man) make a sexual conquest. **8** tr. (usu. foll. by *against*, *to*) mentally record (an offence etc.). **9** tr. US criticize (a person) severely. □ **keep score** (or **the score**) register the score as it is made. **know the score** colloq. be aware of the essential facts. **on the score of** for the reason that; because of. **on that score** so far as that is concerned. **score-book** (or **-card** or **-sheet**) a book etc. prepared for entering esp. cricket scores in. **score draw** a draw in football in which goals are scored. **score off** (or **score points off**) colloq. humiliate, esp. verbally in repartee etc. **score out** draw a line through (words etc.). **score under** underline. □□ **scorer** n. **scoring** n. Mus. [(n.) f. OE: sense 5 f. the line or bar drawn through all staves: (v.) partly f. ON *skora* f. ON *skor* notch, tally, twenty, f. Gmc: see SHEAR]

scoreboard /ˈskɔːbɔːd/ n. a large board for publicly displaying the score in a game or match.

scoria /ˈskɔːrɪə/ n. (pl. **scoriae** /-rɪˌiː/) **1** cellular lava, or fragments of it. **2** the slag or dross of metals. □□ **scoriaceous** /-ˈeɪʃəs/ adj. [L f. Gk *skōria* refuse f. *skōr* dung]

scorify /ˈskɔːrɪˌfaɪ/ v.tr. (**-ies**, **-ied**) **1** reduce to dross. **2** assay (precious metal) by treating a portion of its ore fused with lead and borax. □□ **scorification** /-fɪˈkeɪʃ(ə)n/ n. **scorifier** n.

scorn /skɔːn/ n. & v. —n. **1** disdain, contempt, derision. **2** an object of contempt etc. (*the scorn of all onlookers*). —v.tr. **1** hold in contempt or disdain. **2** (often foll. by *to* + infin.) abstain from or refuse to do as unworthy (*scorns lying*; *scorns to lie*). □ **think scorn of** despise. □□ **scorner** n. [ME f. OF *esc(h)arn(ir)* ult. f. Gmc: cf. OS *skern* MOCKERY]

scornful /ˈskɔːnfʊl/ adj. (often foll. by *of*) full of scorn; contemptuous. □□ **scornfully** adv. **scornfulness** n.

scorper var. of SCALPER 2.

Scorpio /ˈskɔːpɪˌəʊ/ **1** a constellation, traditionally regarded as contained in the figure of a scorpion. It is noteworthy for its brightest member, the red giant star Antares, and its X-ray source Sco X-1 which is the brightest object in the X-ray sky. **2** the eighth sign of the zodiac (the Scorpion), which the sun enters about 23 Oct.). —n. (pl. **-os**) a person born when the sun is in this sign. □□ **Scorpian** adj. & n. [ME f. L (as SCORPION)]

scorpioid /ˈskɔːpɪˌɔɪd/ adj. & n. —adj. **1** Zool. of, relating to, or resembling a scorpion; of the scorpion order. **2** Bot. (of an inflorescence) curled up at the end, and uncurling as the flowers develop. —n. this type of inflorescence. [Gk *skorpioeidēs* (as SCORPIO)]

scorpion /ˈskɔːpɪən/ n. **1** an arachnid of the order Scorpionida, with lobster-like pincers and a jointed tail that can be bent over to inflict a poisoned sting on prey held in its pincers. **2** (in full **false scorpion**) a similar arachnid of the order Pseudo-scorpionida, smaller and without a tail. **3** (**the Scorpion**) the zodiacal sign or constellation Scorpio. **4** Bibl. a whip with metal points (1 Kings 12: 11). □ **scorpion fish** any of various marine fish of the family Scorpaenidae, with venomous spines on the head and gills. **scorpion fly** any insect of the order Mecoptera, esp. of the family Panorpidae, the males of which have a swollen abdomen curved upwards like a scorpion's sting. **scorpion grass** = forget-me-not. [ME f. OF f. L scorpio -onis f. scorpius f. Gk skorpios]

scorzonera /ˌskɔːzəˈnɪərə/ n. **1** a composite plant, Scorzonera hispanica, with long tapering purple-brown roots. **2** the root used as a vegetable. [It. f. scorzone venomous snake ult f. med.L curtio]

Scot /skɒt/ n. **1 a** a native of Scotland. **b** a person of Scottish descent. **2** hist. a member of a Gaelic people that migrated from Ireland to Scotland around the 6th c. [OE Scottas (pl.) f. LL Scottus]

scot /skɒt/ n. hist. a payment corresponding to a modern tax, rate, etc. □ **pay scot and lot** share the financial burdens of a borough etc. (and so be allowed to vote). **scot-free** unharmed; unpunished; safe. [ME f. ON skot & f. OF escot, of Gmc orig.: cf. SHOT¹]

Scotch /skɒtʃ/ adj. & n. —adj. var. of SCOTTISH or SCOTS. (See below.) —n. **1** var. of SCOTTISH or SCOTS. **2** Scotch whisky. □ **Scotch broth** a soup made from beef or mutton with pearl barley etc. **Scotch cap** = BONNET n. 1b. **Scotch catch** Mus. a short note on the beat followed by a long one. **Scotch egg** a hard-boiled egg enclosed in sausage meat and fried. **Scotch fir** (or **pine**) a pine tree, Pinus sylvestris, native to Europe and Asia. **Scotch kale** a variety of kale with purplish leaves. **Scotch mist 1** a thick drizzly mist common in the Highlands. **2** a retort made to a person implying that he or she has imagined or failed to understand something. **Scotch pebble** agate, jasper, cairngorm, etc., found in Scotland. **Scotch pine** = Scotch fir. **Scotch snap** = Scotch catch. **Scotch terrier 1** a small terrier of a rough-haired short-legged breed. **2** this breed. **Scotch whisky** whisky distilled in Scotland, esp. from malted barley. [contr. of SCOTTISH]

In recent years the word Scotch has been falling into disuse in England as well as in Scotland, out of deference to the Scotsman's supposed dislike of it; except for certain fixed collocations, such as those listed above, Scottish (less frequently Scots) is now the usual adjective, and Scots (pl.) designates the inhabitants of Scotland.

scotch¹ /skɒtʃ/ v. & n. —v.tr. **1** put an end to; frustrate (injury scotched his attempt). **2** archaic **a** wound without killing; slightly disable. **b** make incisions in; score. —n. **1** archaic a slash. **2** a line on the ground for hopscotch. [ME: orig. unkn.]

scotch² /skɒtʃ/ n. & v. —n. a wedge or block placed against a wheel etc. to prevent its slipping. —v.tr. hold back (a wheel, barrel, etc.) with a scotch. [17th c.: perh. = scatch stilt f. OF escache]

Scotchman /ˈskɒtʃmən/ n. (pl. **-men**; fem. **Scotchwoman**, pl. **-women**) = SCOTSMAN. ¶ Scotsman etc. are generally preferred in Scotland.

scoter /ˈskəʊtə(r)/ n. (pl. same or **scoters**) a large marine duck of the genus Melanitta. [17th c.: orig. unkn.]

scotia /ˈskəʊʃə/ n. a concave moulding, esp. at the base of a column. [L f. Gk skotia f. skotos darkness, with ref. to the shadow produced]

Scoticism var. of SCOTTICISM.

Scoticize var. of SCOTTICIZE.

Scotland /ˈskɒtlənd/ the northern part of Great Britain and of the United Kingdom; pop. (1981) 5,130,735; capital, Edinburgh. Early inhabitants were the Picts, and Celtic peoples arrived from the Continent during the Bronze and early Iron Age. The limit of Roman subjugation of Britain was marked by Hadrian's Wall except for a period of about 40 years at the more northerly line of the Antonine Wall. An independent country in the Middle Ages, after the unification of various small Dark Age kingdoms between the 9th and 11th c. Scotland successfully resisted English attempts at domination but was amalgamated with her southern neighbour as a result of the union of the crowns in 1603 and of the parliaments in 1707. The northern part of the country is lightly populated, but the south and south-west benefited from the Industrial Revolution in the 18th and 19th c., although they have suffered badly from the effects of economic recession in the 20th c. while the discovery of North Sea oil has led to a boom on the east coast.

Scotland Yard 1 the headquarters of the London Metropolitan Police, situated from 1829 to 1890 in Great Scotland Yard, a short street off Whitehall in London, from then until 1967 in New Scotland Yard on the Thames Embankment, and from 1967 in New Scotland Yard, Broadway, Westminster. **2** the detective department of the London Metropolitan Police force.

scotoma /skɒˈtəʊmə/ n. (pl. **scotomata** /-mətə/) a partial loss of vision or blind spot in an otherwise normal visual field. [LL f. Gk skotōma f. skotoō darken f. skotos darkness]

Scots /skɒts/ adj. & n. esp. Sc. —adj. **1** = SCOTTISH adj. **2** in the dialect, accent, etc., of (esp. Lowlands) Scotland. —n. **1** = SCOTTISH n. **2** the form of English spoken in (esp. Lowlands) Scotland. [ME orig. Scottis, north. var. of SCOTTISH]

Scotsman /ˈskɒtsmən/ n. (pl. **-men**; fem. **Scotswoman**, pl. **-women**) **1** a native of Scotland. **2** a person of Scottish descent.

Scott¹ /skɒt/, Sir George Gilbert (1811–78), English architect. The most prolific Gothic revivalist, he built or 'improved' over 400 churches, 39 cathedrals, 25 university buildings, and fulfilled many private commissions. In 1858 he confronted Palmerston over the design for the new Foreign Office, the so-called 'Battle of Styles', and was compelled to adopt a classical solution; but his Albert Memorial (1872) reflects more accurately his preferred aesthetic. Although many of his alterations to religious buildings have been criticized for their excess, there is no doubt as to his qualities as an architect. His grandson, Sir Giles Scott (1880–1960), also worked as a revivalist architect and is best known for Liverpool Cathedral (begun in 1903), the last Gothic building to be built in England.

Scott² /skɒt/, Sir Peter Markham (1909–89), English naturalist, son of the Antarctic explorer Robert Falcon Scott. He is best known for his activities in wildlife conservation and for his paintings of birds; in 1946 he founded the Wildfowl Trust, based at Slimbridge in Gloucestershire.

Scott³ /skɒt/, Robert Falcon (1868–1912), English polar explorer. Entering the Royal Navy in 1881, Scott commanded the National Antarctic Expedition of 1900–4, surveying the interior of the continent, charting the Ross Sea, and discovering King Edward VII Land. On a second expedition (1910–12) Scott and four companions (Wilson, Oates, Bowers, and Evans) made a journey to the South Pole by sled, arriving there in January 1912 to discover that the Norwegian explorer Amundsen had beaten them to their goal by a month. On the journey back to base Scott and his companions were hampered by bad weather and illness, the last three finally dying of starvation and exposure in March. Their bodies and diaries were discovered by a search party eight months later. Scott, a national hero, was posthumously knighted.

Scott⁴ /skɒt/, Sir Walter (1771–1832), Scottish novelist and poet, nicknamed 'the Wizard of the North'. Deeply influenced by the old and romantic poetry of France and Italy, and by the modern German poets, he developed an interest in the old Border tales and ballads which he collected (with imitations) in The Minstrelsy of the Scottish Border (1802). Among his original works were the romantic poem The Lay of the Last Minstrel (1805), The Lady of the Lake (1810), and Rokeby (1813). As a poet he was eclipsed by Byron, and found expression for his wide erudition, humour, and sympathies in the historical novel. Of these the Scottish Waverley novels were his masterpieces: Waverley (1814), The Antiquary (1816), Old Mortality (1816), and The Heart of Midlothian (1818). In 1826 the firm of booksellers, James Ballantyne & Co., in which Scott was a partner, became involved in bankruptcy, and he henceforth worked strenuously and prolifically to pay off his creditors. His influence as a novelist was incalculable: he established the form of the historical novel which was imitated throughout the 19th c., as was his treatment of rural themes; he influenced the development of the short story. His other works include plays, historical, literary, and antiquarian works, and editions of Swift and Dryden.

Scotticism /ˈskɒtɪˌsɪz(ə)m/ n. (also **Scoticism**) a Scottish phrase, word, or idiom. [LL Scot(t)icus]

Scotticize /ˈskɒtɪˌsaɪz/ v. (also **Scoticize, -ise**) 1 tr. imbue with or model on Scottish ways etc. 2 intr. imitate the Scottish in idiom or habits.

Scottie /ˈskɒtɪ/ n. colloq. 1 (also **Scottie dog**) a Scotch terrier. 2 a Scot.

Scottish /ˈskɒtɪʃ/ adj. & n. —adj. of or relating to Scotland or its inhabitants. —n. (prec. by the; treated as pl.) the people of Scotland (see also SCOTS). □ **Scottish National Party** a political party formed in 1934 by an amalgamation of the National Party of Scotland and the Scottish Party, which seeks autonomous government for Scotland. **Scottish Nationalist** a member of this party. □□ **Scottishness** n.

scoundrel /ˈskaʊndr(ə)l/ n. an unscrupulous villain; a rogue. □□ **scoundreldom** n. **scoundrelism** n. **scoundrelly** adj. [16th c.: orig. unkn.]

scour¹ /ˈskaʊə(r)/ v. & n. —v.tr. 1 a cleanse or brighten by rubbing, esp. with soap, chemicals, sand, etc. b (usu. foll. by away, off, etc.) clear (rust, stains, reputation, etc.) by rubbing, hard work, etc. (scoured the slur from his name). 2 (of water, or a person with water) clear out (a pipe, channel, etc.) by flushing through. 3 hist. purge (the bowels) drastically. —n. 1 the act or an instance of scouring; the state of being scoured, esp. by a swift water current (the scour of the tide). 2 diarrhoea in cattle. 3 a substance used for scouring. □ **scouring-rush** any of various horsetail plants with a rough siliceous coating used for polishing wood etc. □□ **scourer** n. [ME f. MDu., MLG schüren f. F escurer f. LL excurare clean (off) (as EX-¹, CURE)]

scour² /ˈskaʊə(r)/ v. 1 tr. hasten over (an area etc.) searching thoroughly (scoured the streets for him; scoured the pages of the newspaper). 2 intr. range hastily esp. in search or pursuit. [ME: orig. unkn.]

scourge /skɜːdʒ/ n. & v. —n. 1 a whip used for punishment, esp. of people. 2 a person or thing seen as punishing, esp. on a large scale (the scourge of famine; Genghis Khan, the scourge of Asia). —v.tr. 1 whip. 2 punish; afflict; oppress. □□ **scourger** n. [ME f. OF escorge (n.), escorgier (v.) (ult. as EX-¹, L corrigia thong, whip)]

Scouse /skaʊs/ n. & adj. colloq. —n. 1 the dialect of Liverpool. 2 (also **Scouser** /ˈskaʊsə(r)/) a native of Liverpool. 3 (scouse) = LOBSCOUSE. —adj. of or relating to Liverpool. [abbr. of LOBSCOUSE]

scout¹ /skaʊt/ n. & v. —n. 1 a person, esp. a soldier, sent out to get information about the enemy's position, strength, etc. 2 the act of seeking (esp. military) information (on the scout). 3 = talent-scout. 4 (**Scout**) a member of the Scout Association (see entry). 5 a college servant, esp. at Oxford University. 6 colloq. a person; a fellow. 7 a ship or aircraft designed for reconnoitring, esp. a small fast aircraft. —v. 1 intr. act as a scout. 2 intr. (foll. by about, around) make a search. 3 tr. (often foll. by out) colloq. explore to get information about (territory etc.). □ **Queen's** (or **King's**) **Scout** a Scout who has reached the highest standard of proficiency. □□ **scouter** n. **scouting** n. [ME f. OF escouter listen, earlier ascolter ult. f. L auscultare]

scout² /skaʊt/ v.tr. reject (an idea etc.) with scorn. [Scand.: cf. ON skúta, skúti taunt]

Scout Association an organization (originally called the Boy Scouts) founded in 1908 by Lord Baden-Powell for helping boys to develop character by training them in open-air activities. Its motto 'Be Prepared' reflects the initials of the founder's name; much of the uniform was adopted from the South African constabulary. The word 'Boy' was dropped from the Association's title in 1967, and its sections (Wolf Cubs, Scouts, and Rover Scouts) were subsequently known as Cub Scouts (8–11 years), Scouts (11–16 years), and Venture Scouts (16–20 years). From 1990 girls were admitted as members.

Scouter /ˈskaʊtə(r)/ n. an adult leader in the Scout Association.

Scoutmaster /ˈskaʊtˌmɑːstə(r)/ n. a person in charge of a group of Scouts.

scow /skaʊ/ n. esp. US a flat-bottomed boat used as a lighter etc. [Du. schouw ferry-boat]

scowl /skaʊl/ n. & v. —n. a severe frown producing a sullen, bad-tempered, or threatening look on a person's face. —v.intr. make a scowl. □□ **scowler** n. [ME, prob. f. Scand.: cf. Da. skule look down or sidelong]

SCPS abbr. (in the UK) Society of Civil and Public Servants.

SCR abbr. Brit. Senior Common (or Combination) Room.

scr. abbr. scruple(s) (of weight).

scrabble /ˈskræb(ə)l/ v. & n. —v.intr. (often foll. by about, at) scratch or grope to find or collect or hold on to something. —n. 1 an act of scrabbling. 2 (**Scrabble**) propr. a game in which players build up words from letter-blocks on a board. [MDu. schrabbelen frequent. of schrabben SCRAPE]

scrag /skræg/ n. & v. —n. 1 (also **scrag-end**) the inferior end of a neck of mutton. 2 a skinny person or animal. 3 colloq. a person's neck. —v.tr. (**scragged, scragging**) sl. 1 strangle, hang. 2 seize roughly by the neck. 3 handle roughly; beat up. [perh. alt. f. dial. crag neck, rel. to MDu. crāghe, MLG krage]

scraggly /ˈskræglɪ/ adj. sparse and irregular.

scraggy /ˈskrægɪ/ adj. (**scraggier, scraggiest**) thin and bony. □□ **scraggily** adv. **scragginess** n.

scram /skræm/ v.intr. (**scrammed, scramming**) (esp. in imper.) colloq. go away. [20th c.: perh. f. SCRAMBLE]

scramble /ˈskræmb(ə)l/ v. & n. —v. 1 intr. make one's way over rough ground, rocks, etc., by clambering, crawling, etc. 2 intr. (foll. by for, at) struggle with competitors (for a thing or share of it). 3 intr. move with difficulty, hastily, or anxiously. 4 tr. a mix together indiscriminately. b jumble or muddle. 5 tr. cook (eggs) by heating them when broken and well mixed with butter, milk, etc. 6 tr. change the speech frequency of (a broadcast transmission or telephone conversation) so as to make it unintelligible without a corresponding decoding device. 7 intr. move hastily. 8 tr. colloq. execute (an action etc.) awkwardly and inefficiently. 9 intr. (of fighter aircraft or their pilots) take off quickly in an emergency or for action. —n. 1 an act of scrambling. 2 a difficult climb or walk. 3 (foll. by for) an eager struggle or competition. 4 a motor-cycle race over rough ground. (See MOTO-CROSS.) 5 an emergency take-off by fighter aircraft. □ **scrambled egg** colloq. gold braid on a military officer's cap. [16th c. (imit.): cf. dial. synonyms scamble, cramble]

scrambler /ˈskræmblə(r)/ n. a device for scrambling telephone conversations.

scran /skræn/ n. sl. 1 food, eatables. 2 remains of food. □ **bad scran** Ir. bad luck. [18th c.: orig. unkn.]

scrap¹ /skræp/ n. & v. —n. 1 a small detached piece; a fragment or remnant. 2 rubbish or waste material. 3 an extract or cutting from something written or printed. 4 discarded metal for reprocessing (often attrib.: scrap metal). 5 (with neg.) the smallest piece or amount (not a scrap of food left). 6 (in pl.) a odds and ends. b bits of uneaten food. 7 (in sing. or pl.) a residuum of melted fat or of fish with the oil expressed. —v.tr. (**scrapped, scrapping**) discard as useless. □ **scrap heap 1** a pile of scrap materials. 2 a state of uselessness. **scrap merchant** a dealer in scrap. [ME f. ON skrap, rel. to skrapa SCRAPE]

scrap² /skræp/ n. & v. colloq. —n. a fight or rough quarrel, esp. a spontaneous one. —v.tr. (**scrapped, scrapping**) (often foll. by with) have a scrap. □□ **scrapper** n. [perh. f. SCRAPE]

scrapbook /ˈskræpbʊk/ n. a book of blank pages for sticking cuttings, drawings, etc., in.

scrape /skreɪp/ v. & n. —v. 1 tr. a move a hard or sharp edge across (a surface), esp. to make something smooth. b apply (a hard or sharp edge) in this way. 2 tr. (foll. by away, off, etc.) remove (a stain, projection, etc.) by scraping. 3 tr. a rub (a surface) harshly against another. b scratch or damage by scraping. 4 tr. make (a hollow) by scraping. 5 a tr. draw or move with a sound of, or resembling, scraping. b intr. emit or produce such a sound. c tr. produce such a sound from. 6 intr. (often foll. by along, by, through, etc.) move or pass along while almost touching close or surrounding features, obstacles, etc. (*the car scraped through the narrow lane*). **7** *tr.* just manage to achieve (a living, an examination pass, etc.). **8** *intr.* (often foll. by *by, through*) **a** barely manage. **b** pass an examination etc. with difficulty. **9** *tr.* (foll. by *together, up*) contrive to bring or provide; amass with difficulty. **10** *intr.* be economical. **11** *intr.* draw back a foot in making a clumsy bow. **12** *tr.* clear (a ship's bottom) of barnacles etc. **13** *tr.* completely clear (a plate) of food. **14** *tr.* (foll. by *back*) draw (the hair) tightly back off the forehead. —*n.* **1** the act or sound of scraping. **2** a scraped place (on the skin etc.). **3** a thinly applied layer of butter etc. on bread. **4** the scraping of a foot in bowing. **5** *colloq.* an awkward predicament, esp. resulting from an escapade. □ **scrape acquaintance with** contrive to get to know (a person). **scrape the barrel** *colloq.* be reduced to one's last resources. [ME f. ON *skrapa* or MDu. *schrapen*]

scraper /ˈskreɪpə(r)/ *n.* a device used for scraping, esp. for removing dirt etc. from a surface.

scraperboard /ˈskreɪpəˌbɔːd/ *n. Brit.* cardboard or board with a blackened surface which can be scraped off for making white-line drawings.

scrapie /ˈskreɪpɪ/ *n.* a viral disease of sheep involving the central nervous system and characterized by lack of coordination causing affected animals to rub against trees etc. for support.

scraping /ˈskreɪpɪŋ/ *n.* **1** in senses of SCRAPE *v.* & *n.* **2** (esp. in *pl.*) a fragment produced by this.

scrappy /ˈskræpɪ/ *adj.* (**scrappier, scrappiest**) **1** consisting of scraps. **2** incomplete; carelessly arranged or put together. □□ **scrappily** *adv.* **scrappiness** *n.*

scrapyard /ˈskræpjɑːd/ *n.* a place where (esp. metal) scrap is collected.

scratch /skrætʃ/ *v., n., & adj.* —*v.* **1** *tr.* score or mark the surface of with a sharp or pointed object. **2** *tr.* **a** make a long narrow superficial wound in (the skin). **b** cause (a person or part of the body) to be scratched (*scratched himself on the table*). **3** *tr.* (also *absol.*) scrape without marking, esp. with the hand to relieve itching (*stood there scratching*). **4** *tr.* make or form by scratching. **5** *tr.* scribble; write hurriedly or awkwardly (*scratched a quick reply; scratched a large A*). **6** *tr.* (foll. by *together, up*, etc.) obtain (a thing) by scratching or with difficulty. **7** *tr.* (foll. by *out, off, through*) cancel or strike (out) with a pencil etc. **8** *tr.* (also *absol.*) withdraw (a competitor, candidate, etc.) from a race or competition. **9** *intr.* (often foll. by *about, around*, etc.) **a** scratch the ground etc. in search. **b** look around haphazardly (*they were scratching about for evidence*). —*n.* **1** a mark or wound made by scratching. **2** a sound of scratching. **3** a spell of scratching oneself. **4** *colloq.* a superficial wound. **5** a line from which competitors in a race (esp. those not receiving a handicap) start. **6** (in *pl.*) a disease of horses in which the pastern appears scratched. **7** *sl.* money. —*attrib.adj.* **1** collected by chance. **2** collected or made from whatever is available; heterogeneous (*a scratch crew*). **3** with no handicap given (*a scratch race*). □ **from scratch 1** from the beginning. **2** without help or advantage. **scratch along** make a living etc. with difficulty. **scratch one's head** be perplexed. **scratch my back and I will scratch yours 1** do me a favour and I will return it. **2** used in reference to mutual aid or flattery. **scratch pad 1** esp. *US* a pad of paper for scribbling. **2** *Computing* a small fast memory for the temporary storage of data. **scratch the surface** deal with a matter only superficially. **up to scratch** up to the required standard. □□ **scratcher** *n.* [ME, prob. f. synonymous ME *scrat* & *cratch*, both of uncert. orig.: cf. MLG *kratsen*, OHG *krazzōn*]

scratchings /ˈskrætʃɪŋz/ *n.pl.* the crisp residue of pork fat left after rendering lard (*pork scratchings*).

scratchy /ˈskrætʃɪ/ *adj.* (**scratchier, scratchiest**) **1** tending to make scratches or a scratching noise. **2** (esp. of a garment) tending to cause itchiness. **3** (of a drawing etc.) done in scratches or carelessly. □□ **scratchily** *adv.* **scratchiness** *n.*

scrawl /skrɔːl/ *v. & n.* —*v.* **1** *tr.* & *intr.* write in a hurried untidy way. **2** *tr.* (foll. by *out*) cross out by scrawling over. —*n.* **1** a piece of hurried writing. **2** a scrawled note. □□ **scrawly** *adj.* [perh. f. obs. *scrawl* sprawl, alt. of CRAWL]

scrawny /ˈskrɔːnɪ/ *adj.* (**scrawnier, scrawniest**) lean, scraggy.

□□ **scrawniness** *n.* [var. of dial. *scranny*: cf. archaic *scrannel* (of sound) weak, feeble]

scream /skriːm/ *n. & v.* —*n.* **1** a loud high-pitched piercing cry expressing fear, pain, extreme fright, etc. **2** the act of emitting a scream. **3** *colloq.* an irresistibly funny occurrence or person. —*v.* **1** *intr.* emit a scream. **2** *tr.* speak or sing (words etc.) in a screaming tone. **3** *intr.* make or move with a shrill sound like a scream. **4** *intr.* laugh uncontrollably. **5** *intr.* be blatantly obvious or conspicuous. **6** *intr. colloq.* turn informer. [OE or MDu.]

screamer /ˈskriːmə(r)/ *n.* **1** a person or thing that screams. **2** any S. American goose-like bird of the family Anhimidae, frequenting marshland and having a characteristic shrill cry. **3** *colloq.* a tale that raises screams of laughter. **4** *US colloq.* a sensational headline.

scree /skriː/ *n.* (in *sing.* or *pl.*) **1** small loose stones. **2** a mountain slope covered with these. [prob. back-form. f. *screes* (pl.) ult. f. ON *skritha* landslip, rel. to *skritha* glide]

screech /skriːtʃ/ *n. & v.* —*n.* a harsh high-pitched scream. —*v.tr.* & *intr.* utter with or make a screech. □ **screech-owl** any owl that screeches instead of hooting, esp. a barn-owl or a small American owl, *Otus asio.* □□ **screecher** *n.* **screechy** *adj.* (**screechier, screechiest**). [16th-c. var. of ME *scritch* (imit.)]

screed /skriːd/ *n.* **1** a long usu. tiresome piece of writing or speech. **2 a** a strip of plaster or other material placed on a surface as a guide to thickness. **b** a levelled layer of material (e.g. cement) applied to a floor or other surface. [ME, prob. var. of SHRED]

screen /skriːn/ *n. & v.* —*n.* **1** a fixed or movable upright partition for separating, concealing, or sheltering from draughts or excessive heat or light. **2** a thing used as a shelter, esp. from observation. **3 a** a measure adopted for concealment. **b** the protection afforded by this (*under the screen of night*). **4 a** a blank usu. white or silver surface on which a photographic image is projected. **b** (prec. by *the*) the cinema industry. **5** the surface of a cathode-ray tube or similar electronic device, esp. of a television, VDU, etc., on which images appear. **6** = *sight-screen*. **7** = WIND-SCREEN. **8** a frame with fine wire netting to keep out flies, mosquitoes, etc. **9** *Physics* a body intercepting light, heat, electric or magnetic induction, etc., in a physical apparatus. **10** *Photog.* a piece of ground glass in a camera for focusing. **11** a large sieve or riddle, esp. for sorting grain, coal, etc., into sizes. **12** a system of checking for the presence or absence of a disease, ability, attribute, etc. **13** *Printing* a transparent finely-ruled plate or film used in half-tone reproduction. **14** *Mil.* a body of troops, ships, etc., detached to warn of the presence of an enemy force. —*v.tr.* **1** (often foll. by *from*) **a** afford shelter to; hide partly or completely. **b** protect from detection, censure, etc. **2** (foll. by *off*) shut off or hide behind a screen. **3 a** show (a film etc.) on a screen. **b** broadcast (a television programme). **4** prevent from causing, or protect from, electrical interference. **5 a** test (a person or group) for the presence or absence of a disease. **b** check on (a person) for the presence or absence of a quality, esp. reliability or loyalty. **6** pass (grain, coal, etc.) through a screen. □ **screen printing** a process like stencilling with ink forced through a prepared sheet of fine material (orig. silk). **screen test** an audition for a part in a cinema film. □□ **screenable** *adj.* **screener** *n.* [ME f. ONF *escren, escran*: cf. OHG *skrank* barrier]

screenings /ˈskriːnɪŋz/ *n.pl.* refuse separated by sifting.

screenplay /ˈskriːnpleɪ/ *n.* the script of a film, with acting instructions, scene directions, etc.

screenwriter /ˈskriːnˌraɪtə(r)/ *n.* a person who writes a screenplay.

screw /skruː/ *n. & v.* —*n.* **1** a thin cylinder or cone with a spiral ridge or thread running round the outside (**male screw**) or the inside (**female screw**). (See below.) **2** (in full **wood-screw**) a metal male screw with a slotted head and a sharp point for fastening things, esp. in carpentry, by being rotated to form a thread in wood etc. **3** (in full **screw-bolt**) a metal male screw with a blunt end on which a nut is threaded to bolt things together. **4** a wooden or metal straight screw used to exert pressure. **5** (in *sing.* or *pl.*) an instrument of torture acting in this way. **6** (in full **screw-propeller**) a form of propeller with

twisted blades acting like a screw on the water or air. **7** one turn of a screw. **8** (foll. by *of*) *Brit.* a small twisted-up paper (of tobacco etc.). **9** *Brit.* (in billiards etc.) an oblique curling motion of the ball. **10** *sl.* a prison warder. **11** *Brit. sl.* an amount of salary or wages. **12** *coarse sl.* **a** an act of sexual intercourse. **b** a partner in this. ¶ Usually considered a taboo use. **13** *sl.* a mean or miserly person. **14** *sl.* a worn-out horse. —*v.* **1** *tr.* fasten or tighten with a screw or screws. **2** *tr.* turn (a screw). **3** *intr.* twist or turn round like a screw. **4** *intr.* (of a ball etc.) swerve. **5** *tr.* **a** put psychological etc. pressure on to achieve an end. **b** oppress. **6** *tr.* (foll. by *out of*) extort (consent, money, etc.) from (a person). **7** *tr.* (also *absol.*) *coarse sl.* have sexual intercourse with. ¶ Usually considered a taboo use. **8** *intr.* (of a rolling ball, or of a person etc.) take a curling course; swerve. **9** *intr.* (often foll. by *up*) make tenser or more efficient. □ **have one's head screwed on the right way** *colloq.* have common sense. **have a screw loose** *colloq.* be slightly crazy. **put the screws on** *colloq.* exert pressure, esp. to extort or intimidate. **screw cap** = *screw top.* **screw-coupling** a female screw with threads at both ends for joining lengths of pipes or rods. **screw eye** a screw with a loop for passing cord etc. through instead of a slotted head. **screw gear** an endless screw with a cog-wheel or pinion. **screw hook** a hook to hang things on, with a screw point for fastening it. **screw-jack** a vehicle jack (see JACK¹) worked by a screw device. **screw pine** any plant of the genus *Pandanus*, with its leaves arranged spirally and resembling those of a pineapple. **screw-plate** a steel plate with threaded holes for making male screws. **screw-tap** a tool for making female screws. **screw top** (also (with hyphen) *attrib.*) a cap or lid that can be screwed on to a bottle, jar, etc. **screw up** **1** contract or contort (one's face etc.). **2** contract and crush into a tight mass (a piece of paper etc.). **3** summon up (one's courage etc.). **4** *sl.* **a** bungle or mismanage. **b** spoil or ruin (an event, opportunity, etc.). **screw-up** *n. sl.* a bungle, muddle, or mess. **screw valve** a stopcock opened and shut by a screw. □□ **screwable** *adj.* **screwer** *n.* [ME f. OF *escroue* female screw, nut, f. L *scrofa* sow]
    The principle of the screw was used by the ancient Greeks in a water-raising device (see ARCHIMEDEAN SCREW), and from the 1st c. AD for exerting pressure in wine- and olive-presses. As fasteners, metal screws and nuts appear in the 16th c., turned with a box-wrench; some of those found in 16th-c. armour may have been turned with a pronged device. The metal screw for fixing various materials to wood is described by a German mining-engineer of the mid-16th c., but may have been in use for some time. The screwdriver as a hand-tool appears from c.1800.

screwball /ˈskruːbɔːl/ *n. & adj. US sl.* —*n.* a crazy or eccentric person. —*adj.* crazy.

screwdriver /ˈskruːˌdraɪvə(r)/ *n.* a tool with a shaped tip to fit into the head of a screw to turn it.

screwed /skruːd/ *adj.* **1** twisted. **2** *sl.* **a** ruined; rendered ineffective. **b** drunk.

screwy /ˈskruːɪ/ *adj.* (**screwier**, **screwiest**) *sl.* **1** crazy or eccentric. **2** absurd. □□ **screwiness** *n.*

Scriabin var. of SKRYABIN.

scribble¹ /ˈskrɪb(ə)l/ *v. & n.* —*v.* **1** *tr. & intr.* write carelessly or hurriedly. **2** *intr.* often *derog.* be an author or writer. **3** *intr. & tr.* draw carelessly or meaninglessly. —*n.* **1** a scrawl. **2** a hasty note etc. **3** careless handwriting. □□ **scribbler** *n.* **scribbly** *adj.* [ME f. med.L *scribillare* dimin. of L *scribere* write]

scribble² /ˈskrɪb(ə)l/ *v.tr.* card (wool, cotton, etc.) coarsely. [prob. f. LG: cf. G *schrubbeln* (in the same sense), frequent. f. LG *schrubben*: see SCRUB¹]

scribe /skraɪb/ *n. & v.* —*n.* **1** a person who writes out documents, esp. an ancient or medieval copyist of manuscripts. **2** *Bibl.* an ancient Jewish record-keeper or professional theologian and jurist. **3** (in full **scribe-awl**) a pointed instrument for making marks on wood, bricks, etc., to guide a saw, or in sign-writing. **4** *US colloq.* a writer, esp. a journalist. —*v.tr.* mark (wood etc.) with a scribe (see sense 3 of *n.*). □□ **scribal** *adj.* **scriber** *n.* [(n.) ME f. L *scriba* f. *scribere* write: (v.) perh. f. DESCRIBE]

scrim /skrɪm/ *n.* open-weave fabric for lining or upholstery etc. [18th c.: orig. unkn.]

scrimmage /ˈskrɪmɪdʒ/ *n. & v.* —*n.* **1** a rough or confused struggle; a brawl. **2** *Amer. Football* a sequence of play beginning with the placing of the ball on the ground with its longest axis at right angles to the goal-line. —*v.* **1** *intr.* engage in a scrimmage. **2** *tr. Amer. Football* put (the ball) into a scrimmage. □□ **scrimmager** *n.* [var. of SKIRMISH]

scrimp /skrɪmp/ *v.* **1** *intr.* be sparing or parsimonious. **2** *tr.* use sparingly. □□ **scrimpy** *adj.* [18th c., orig. Sc.: perh. rel. to SHRIMP]

scrimshank /ˈskrɪmʃæŋk/ *v.intr. Brit. sl. esp. Mil.* shirk duty. □□ **scrimshanker** *n.* [19th c.: orig. unkn.]

scrimshaw /ˈskrɪmʃɔː/ *v. & n.* —*v.tr.* (also *absol.*) adorn (shells, ivory, etc.) with carved or coloured designs (as sailors' pastime at sea). —*n.* work or a piece of work of this kind. [19th c.: perh. f. a surname]

scrip /skrɪp/ *n.* **1** a provisional certificate of money subscribed to a bank or company etc. entitling the holder to a formal certificate and dividends. **2** (*collect.*) such certificates. **3** an extra share or shares instead of a dividend. [abbr. of *subscription receipt*]

script /skrɪpt/ *n. & v.* —*n.* **1** handwriting as distinct from print; written characters. **2** type imitating handwriting. **3** an alphabet or system of writing (*the Russian script*). **4** the text of a play, film, or broadcast. **5** an examinee's set of written answers. **6** *Law* an original document as distinct from a copy. —*v.tr.* write a script for (a film etc.). [ME, = thing written, f. OF *escri(p)t* f. L *scriptum*, neut. past part. of *scribere* write]

scriptorium /ˌskrɪpˈtɔːrɪəm/ *n.* (*pl.* **scriptoria** /-rɪə/ or **scriptoriums**) a room set apart for writing, esp. in a monastery. □□ **scriptorial** *adj.* [med.L (as SCRIPT)]

scriptural /ˈskrɪptʃər(ə)l, -tʃʊər(ə)l/ *adj.* **1** of or relating to a scripture, esp. the Bible. **2** having the authority of a scripture. □□ **scripturally** *adv.* [LL *scripturalis* f. L *scriptura*: see SCRIPTURE]

scripture /ˈskrɪptʃə(r)/ *n.* **1** sacred writings. **2** (**Scripture** or **the Scriptures**) the sacred writings of the Christians (the Old and New Testaments) or the Jews (the Old Testament). (See TESTAMENT.) [ME f. L *scriptura* (as SCRIPT)]

scriptwriter /ˈskrɪptˌraɪtə(r)/ *n.* a person who writes a script for a film, broadcast, etc. □□ **scriptwriting** *n.*

scrivener /ˈskrɪvənə(r)/ *n. hist.* **1** a copyist or drafter of documents. **2** a notary. **3** a broker. **4** a moneylender. [ME f. obs. *scrivein* f. OF *escrivein* ult. f. L (as SCRIBE)]

scrobiculate /skrəˈbɪkjʊlət/ *adj. Bot. & Zool.* pitted, furrowed. [L *scrobiculus* f. *scrobis* trench]

scrod /skrɒd/ *n. US* a young cod or haddock, esp. as food. [19th c.: perh. rel. to SHRED]

scrofula /ˈskrɒfjʊlə/ *n. archaic* a disease with glandular swellings, prob. a form of tuberculosis. Also called *king's evil*. □□ **scrofulous** *adj.* [ME f. med.L (sing.) f. LL *scrofulae* (pl.) scrofulous swelling, dimin. of L *scrofa* a sow]

scroll /skrəʊl/ *n. & v.* —*n.* **1** a roll of parchment or paper esp. with writing on it. **2** a book in the ancient roll form. **3** an ornamental design or carving imitating a roll of parchment. —*v.* **1** *tr.* (often foll. by *down*, *up*) move (a display on a VDU screen) in order to view new material. **2** *tr.* inscribe in or like a scroll. **3** *intr.* curl up like paper. □ **scroll saw** a saw for cutting along curved lines in ornamental work. [ME *scrowle* alt. f. *rowle* ROLL, perh. after *scrow* (in the same sense), formed as ESCROW]

scrolled /skrəʊld/ *adj.* having a scroll ornament.

scrollwork /ˈskrəʊlwɜːk/ *n.* decoration of spiral lines, esp. as cut by a scroll saw.

Scrooge /skruːdʒ/, Ebenezer. A miserly curmudgeon in Charles Dickens's novel *A Christmas Carol* (1843). —*n.* a mean or miserly person.

scrotum /ˈskrəʊtəm/ *n.* (*pl.* **scrota** /-tə/ or **scrotums**) a pouch of skin containing the testicles. □□ **scrotal** *adj.* **scrotitis** /-ˈtaɪtɪs/ *n.* [L]

scrounge /skraʊndʒ/ *v. & n. colloq.* —*v.* **1** *tr.* (also *absol.*) obtain (things) illicitly or by cadging. **2** *intr.* search about to find something at no cost. —*n.* an act of scrounging. □ **on the scrounge** engaged in scrounging. □□ **scrounger** *n.* [var. of dial. *scrunge* steal]

scrub[1] /skrʌb/ v. & n. —v. (**scrubbed**, **scrubbing**) **1** tr. rub hard so as to clean, esp. with a hard brush. **2** intr. use a brush in this way. **3** intr. (often foll. by up) (of a surgeon etc.) thoroughly clean the hands and arms by scrubbing, before operating. **4** tr. colloq. scrap or cancel (a plan, order, etc.). **5** tr. use water to remove impurities from (gas etc.). —n. the act or an instance of scrubbing; the process of being scrubbed. □ **scrubbing-brush** (US **scrub-brush**) a hard brush for scrubbing floors. **scrub round** colloq. circumvent, avoid. [ME prob. f. MLG, MDu. schrobben, schrubben]

scrub[2] /skrʌb/ n. **1 a** vegetation consisting mainly of brushwood or stunted forest growth. **b** an area of land covered with this. **2** (of livestock) of inferior breed or physique (often attrib.: scrub horse). **3** a small or dwarf variety (often attrib.: scrub pine). **4** US Sport colloq. a team or player not of the first class. □ **scrub turkey** a megapode. **scrub typhus** a rickettsial disease of the W. Pacific transmitted by mites. □□ **scrubby** adj. [ME, var. of SHRUB[1]]

scrubber /ˈskrʌbə(r)/ n. **1** an apparatus using water or a solution for purifying gases etc. **2** sl. derog. a sexually promiscuous woman.

scruff[1] /skrʌf/ n. the back of the neck as used to grasp and lift or drag an animal or person by (esp. scruff of the neck). [alt. of scuff, perh. f. ON skoft hair]

scruff[2] /skrʌf/ n. colloq. an untidy or scruffy person. [orig. = SCURF, later 'worthless thing', or back-form. f. SCRUFFY]

scruffy /ˈskrʌfɪ/ adj. (**scruffier**, **scruffiest**) colloq. shabby, slovenly, untidy. □□ **scruffily** adv. **scruffiness** n. [scruff var. of SCURF + -Y[1]]

scrum /skrʌm/ n. **1** Rugby Football an arrangement of the forwards of each team in two opposing groups, each with arms interlocked and heads down, with the ball thrown in between them to restart play. **2** colloq. a milling crowd. □ **scrum-half** a half-back who puts the ball into the scrum. [abbr. of SCRUMMAGE]

scrummage /ˈskrʌmɪdʒ/ n. Rugby Football = SCRUM 1. [as SCRIMMAGE]

scrump /skrʌmp/ v.tr. Brit. colloq. steal (fruit) from an orchard or garden. [cf. SCRUMPY]

scrumple /ˈskrʌmp(ə)l/ v.tr. crumple, wrinkle. [var. of CRUMPLE]

scrumptious /ˈskrʌmpʃəs/ adj. colloq. **1** delicious. **2** pleasing, delightful. □□ **scrumptiously** adv. **scrumptiousness** n. [19th c.: orig. unkn.]

scrumpy /ˈskrʌmpɪ/ n. Brit. colloq. rough cider, esp. as made in the West Country of England. [dial. scrump small apple]

scrunch /skrʌntʃ/ v. & n. —v.tr. & intr. **1** (usu. foll. by up) make or become crushed or crumpled. **2** make or cause to make a crunching sound. —n. the act or an instance of scrunching. [var. of CRUNCH]

scruple /ˈskruːp(ə)l/ n. & v. —n. **1** (in sing. or pl.) **a** regard to the morality or propriety of an action. **b** a feeling of doubt or hesitation caused by this. **2** Brit. hist. an apothecaries' weight of 20 grains. **3** archaic a very small quantity. —v.intr. **1** (foll. by to + infin.; usu. with neg.) be reluctant because of scruples (did not scruple to stop their allowance). **2** feel or be influenced by scruples. [F scrupule or L scrupulus f. scrupus rough pebble, anxiety]

scrupulous /ˈskruːpjʊləs/ adj. **1** conscientious or thorough even in small matters. **2** careful to avoid doing wrong. **3** punctilious; over-attentive to details. □□ **scrupulosity** /-ˈlɒsɪtɪ/ n. **scrupulously** adv. **scrupulousness** n. [ME f. F scrupuleux or L scrupulosus (as SCRUPLE)]

scrutineer /ˌskruːtɪˈnɪə(r)/ n. a person who scrutinizes or examines something, esp. the conduct and result of a ballot.

scrutinize /ˈskruːtɪnaɪz/ v.tr. (also **-ise**) look closely at; examine with close scrutiny. □□ **scrutinizer** n.

scrutiny /ˈskruːtɪnɪ/ n. (pl. **-ies**) **1** a critical gaze. **2** a close investigation or examination of details. **3** an official examination of ballot-papers to check their validity or accuracy of counting. [ME f. L scrutinium f. scrutari search f. scruta rubbish: orig. f. rag-collectors]

scry /skraɪ/ v.intr. (**-ies**, **-ied**) divine by crystal-gazing. □□ **scryer** n. [shortening f. DESCRY]

scuba /ˈskuːbə, ˈskjuː-/ n. (pl. **scubas**) an aqualung. [acronym f. self-contained underwater breathing apparatus]

scuba-diving /ˈskuːbəˌdaɪvɪŋ, ˈskjuː-/ n. swimming underwater using a scuba, esp. as a sport. □□ **scuba-dive** v.intr. **scuba-diver** n.

scud /skʌd/ v. & n. —v.intr. (**scudded**, **scudding**) **1** fly or run straight, fast, and lightly; skim along. **2** Naut. run before the wind. —n. **1** a spell of scudding. **2** a scudding motion. **3** vapoury driving clouds. **4** a driving shower; a gust. **5** wind-blown spray. [perh. alt. of SCUT, as if to race like a hare]

scuff /skʌf/ v. & n. —v. **1** tr. graze or brush against. **2** tr. mark or wear down (shoes) in this way. **3** intr. walk with dragging feet; shuffle. —n. a mark of scuffing. [imit.]

scuffle /ˈskʌf(ə)l/ n. & v. —n. a confused struggle or disorderly fight at close quarters. —v.intr. engage in a scuffle. [prob. f. Scand.: cf. Sw. skuffa to push, rel. to SHOVE]

sculduggery var. of SKULDUGGERY.

scull /skʌl/ n. & v. —n. **1** either of a pair of small oars used by a single rower. **2** an oar placed over the stern of a boat to propel it, usu. by a twisting motion. **3** (in pl.) a race between boats with single pairs of oars. —v.tr. propel (a boat) with sculls. [ME: orig. unkn.]

sculler /ˈskʌlə(r)/ n. **1** a user of sculls. **2** a boat intended for sculling.

scullery /ˈskʌlərɪ/ n. (pl. **-ies**) a small kitchen or room at the back of a house for washing dishes etc. [ME f. AF squillerie, OF escuelerie f. escuele dish f. L scutella salver dimin. of scutra wooden platter]

scullion /ˈskʌljən/ n. archaic **1** a cook's boy. **2** a person who washes dishes etc. [ME: orig. unkn.]

sculpin /ˈskʌlpɪn/ n. any of numerous fish of the family Cottidae, native to non-tropical regions, having large spiny heads. [perh. f. obs. scorpene f. L scorpaena f. Gk skorpaina a fish]

sculpt /skʌlpt/ v.tr. & intr. (also **sculp**) sculpture. [F sculpter f. sculpteur SCULPTOR: now regarded as an abbr.]

sculptor /ˈskʌlptə(r)/ n. (fem. **sculptress** /-trɪs/) an artist who makes sculptures. [L (as SCULPTURE)]

sculpture /ˈskʌlptʃə(r)/ n. & v. —n. **1** the art of making forms, often representational, in the round or in relief by chiselling stone, carving wood, modelling clay, casting metal, etc. **2** a work or works of sculpture. **3** Zool. & Bot. raised or sunken markings on a shell etc. —v. **1** tr. represent in or adorn with sculpture. **2** intr. practise sculpture. □□ **sculptural** adj. **sculpturally** adv. **sculpturesque** adj. [ME f. L sculptura f. sculpere sculpt- carve]

scum /skʌm/ n. & v. —n. **1** a layer of dirt, froth, or impurities etc. forming at the top of liquid, esp. in boiling or fermentation. **2** (foll. by of) the most worthless part of something. **3** colloq. a worthless person or group. —v. (**scummed**, **scumming**) **1** tr. remove scum from; skim. **2** tr. be or form a scum on. **3** intr. (of a liquid) develop scum. □□ **scummy** adj. (**scummier**, **scummiest**) adj. [ME f. MLG, MDu. schūm, OHG scūm f. Gmc]

scumble /ˈskʌmb(ə)l/ v. & n. —v.tr. **1** modify (a painting) by applying a thin opaque coat of paint to give a softer or duller effect. **2** modify (a drawing) similarly with light pencilling etc. —n. **1** material used in scumbling. **2** the effect produced by scumbling. [perh. frequent. of SCUM v.tr.]

scuncheon /ˈskʌntʃ(ə)n/ n. the inside face of a door-jamb, window-frame, etc. [ME f. OF escoinson (as EX-[1], COIN)]

scunge /skʌndʒ/ n. Austral. & NZ colloq. **1** dirt, scum. **2** a dirty or disagreeable person. □□ **scungy** adj. (**scungier**, **scungiest**). [perh. f. E dial. scrunge steal: cf. SCROUNGE]

scunner /ˈskʌnə(r)/ v. & n. Sc. —v.intr. feel disgust or nausea. —n. **1** a strong dislike (esp. take a scunner at or against). **2** an object of loathing. [14th c.: orig. uncert.]

scup /skʌp/ n. an E. American fish, Stenotomus chrysops, a kind of porgy. [Narraganset mishcup thick-scaled f. mishe large + cuppi scale]

scupper[1] /ˈskʌpə(r)/ n. a hole in a ship's side to carry off water from the deck. [ME (perh. f. AF) f. OF escopir f. Rmc skuppire (unrecorded) to spit: orig. imit.]

scupper² /ˈskʌpə(r)/ v.tr. Brit. sl. **1** sink (a ship or its crew). **2** defeat or ruin (a plan etc.). **3** kill. [19th c.: orig. unkn.]

scurf /skɜːf/ n. **1** flakes on the surface of the skin, cast off as fresh skin develops below, esp. those of the head; dandruff. **2** any scaly matter on a surface. □□ **scurfy** adj. [OE, prob. f. ON & earlier OE sceorf, rel. to sceorfan gnaw, sceorfian cut to shreds]

scurrilous /ˈskʌrɪləs/ adj. **1** (of a person or language) grossly or indecently abusive. **2** given to or expressed with low humour. □□ **scurrility** /-ˈrɪlɪtɪ/ n. (pl. **-ies**). **scurrilously** adv. **scurrilousness** n. [F scurrile or L scurrilus f. scurra buffoon]

scurry /ˈskʌrɪ/ v. & n. (**-ies**, **-ied**) run or move hurriedly, esp. with short quick steps; scamper. —n. (pl. **-ies**) **1** the act or sound of scurrying. **2** bustle, haste. **3** a flurry of rain or snow. [abbr. of hurry-scurry redupl. of HURRY]

scurvy /ˈskɜːvɪ/ n. & adj. —n. a disease caused by a deficiency of vitamin C, characterized by swollen bleeding gums and the opening of previously healed wounds, esp. formerly affecting sailors. —adj. (**scurvier**, **scurviest**) paltry, low, mean, dishonourable, contemptible. □ **scurvy grass** any cresslike seaside plant of the genus Cochlearia, orig. taken as a cure for scurvy. □□ **scurvied** adj. **scurvily** adv. [SCURF + -Y¹: noun sense by assoc. with F scorbut (cf. SCORBUTIC)]

scut /skʌt/ n. a short tail, esp. of a hare, rabbit, or deer. [ME: orig. unkn.: cf. obs. scut short, shorten]

scuta pl. of SCUTUM.

scutage /ˈskjuːtɪdʒ/ n. hist. money paid by a feudal landowner instead of personal service. [ME f. med.L scutagium f. L scutum shield]

Scutari¹ /ˈskuːtərɪ/ **1** (also **Shkodër** /ˈʃkəʊdə(r)/ **a** a province of NW Albania. **b** its capital city. **2** a lake on the frontier between NW Albania and the republic of Montenegro, Yugoslavia.

Scutari² /skuːˈtɑːrɪ/ the former name of Üsküdar, a suburb of Istanbul on the Asian side of the Bosporus. It was the British Army base during the Crimean War; a corner of the barracks was used by Florence Nightingale as a hospital.

scutch /skʌtʃ/ v.tr. dress (fibrous material, esp. retted flax) by beating. □□ **scutcher** n. [OF escouche, escoucher (dial.), escousser, ult. f. L excutere excuss- (as EX-¹, quatere shake)]

scutcheon /ˈskʌtʃ(ə)n/ n. **1** = ESCUTCHEON. **2** an ornamented brass etc. plate round or over a keyhole. **3** a plate for a name or inscription. [ME f. ESCUTCHEON]

scute /skjuːt/ n. Zool. etc. = SCUTUM. [L (as SCUTUM)]

scutellum /skjʊˈteləm/ n. (pl. **scutella** /-lə/) Bot. & Zool. a scale, plate, or any shieldlike formation on a plant, insect, bird, etc., esp. one of the horny scales on a bird's foot. □□ **scutellate** /ˈskjuːtələt/ adj. **scutellation** /ˌskjuːtəˈleɪʃ(ə)n/ n. [mod.L dimin. of L scutum shield]

scutter /ˈskʌtə(r)/ v. & n. —v.intr. colloq. scurry. —n. the act or an instance of scuttering. [perh. alt. of SCUTTLE²]

scuttle¹ /ˈskʌt(ə)l/ n. **1** a receptacle for carrying and holding a small supply of coal. **2** Brit. the part of a motor-car body between the windscreen and the bonnet. [ME f. ON skutill, OHG scuzzila f. L scutella dish]

scuttle² /ˈskʌt(ə)l/ v. & n. —v.intr. **1** scurry; hurry along. **2** run away; flee from danger or difficulty. —n. **1** a hurried gait. **2** a precipitate flight or departure. [cf. dial. scuddle frequent. of SCUD]

scuttle³ /ˈskʌt(ə)l/ n. & v. —n. a hole with a lid in a ship's deck or side. —v.tr. let water into (a ship) to sink it, esp. by opening the seacocks. [ME, perh. f. obs. F escoutille f. Sp. escotilla hatchway dimin. of escota cutting out cloth]

scuttlebutt /ˈskʌt(ə)lˌbʌt/ n. **1** a water-butt on the deck of a ship, for drinking from. **2** colloq. rumour, gossip.

scutum /ˈskjuːtəm/ n. (pl. **scuta** /-tə/) each of the shieldlike plates or scales forming the bony covering of a crocodile, sturgeon, turtle, armadillo, etc. □□ **scutal** adj. **scutate** adj. [L, = oblong shield]

Scylla /ˈsɪlə/ Gk Mythol. a female sea-monster who devoured men from ships when they tried to navigate the narrow channel between her cave and the whirlpool Charybdis. Later legend substituted a dangerous rock for the monster and located it on the Italian side of the Strait of Messina.

scyphozoan /ˌsaɪfəˈzəʊən/ n. & adj. —n. any marine jellyfish of the class Scyphozoa, with tentacles bearing stinging cells. —adj. of or relating to this class. [as SCYPHUS + Gk zōion animal]

scyphus /ˈsaɪfəs/ n. (pl. **scyphi** /-faɪ/) **1** Gk Antiq. a footless drinking-cup with two handles below the level of the rim. **2** Bot. a cup-shaped part as in a narcissus flower or in lichens. □□ **scyphose** adj. [mod.L f. Gk skuphos]

scythe /saɪð/ n. & v. —n. a mowing and reaping implement with a long curved blade swung over the ground by a long pole with two short handles projecting from it. —v.tr. cut with a scythe. [OE sīthe f. Gmc]

Scythia /ˈsɪðɪə/ the name given by the ancient Greeks to a country on the north shore of the Black Sea. Its inhabitants were an Indo-European people of Central Asian origin, skilful horsemen and craftsmen, known for their distinctive 'animal style' art. They were eventually absorbed by the Goths and other immigrants during the 3rd and 2nd c. BC. □□ **Scythian** adj. & n.

SD abbr. US South Dakota (in official postal use).

S.Dak. abbr. South Dakota.

SDI abbr. Strategic Defence Initiative.

SDLP abbr. Social Democratic and Labour Party, a political party in Northern Ireland, founded in 1970.

SDP abbr. hist. (in the UK) Social Democratic Party.

SDR abbr. special drawing right (from the International Monetary Fund).

SE abbr. **1** south-east. **2** south-eastern.

Se symb. Chem. the element selenium.

se- /sə, sɪ/ prefix apart, without (seclude; secure). [L f. OL se (prep. & adv.)]

SEA abbr. Single European Act (see SINGLE).

sea /siː/ n. **1** the expanse of salt water that covers most of the earth's surface and surrounds its land masses. **2** any part of this as opposed to land or fresh water. **3** a particular (usu. named) tract of salt water partly or wholly enclosed by land (the North Sea; the Dead Sea). **4** a large inland lake (the Sea of Galilee). **5** the waves of the sea, esp. with reference to their local motion or state (a choppy sea). **6** (foll. by of) a vast quantity or expanse (a sea of troubles; a sea of faces). **7** (attrib.) living or used in, on, or near the sea (often prefixed to the name of a marine animal, plant, etc., having a superficial resemblance to what it is named after) (sea lettuce). □ **at sea 1** in a ship on the sea. **2** (also **all at sea**) perplexed, confused. **by sea** in a ship or ships. **go to sea** become a sailor. **on the sea 1** in a ship at sea. **2** situated on the coast. **put** (or **put out**) **to sea** leave land or port. **sea anchor** a device such as a heavy bag dragged in the water to retard the drifting of a ship. **sea anemone** any of various coelenterates of the order Actiniaria having a polypoid body bearing a ring of tentacles around the mouth. **sea-angel** an angel-fish. **sea bass** any of various marine fishes like the bass, esp. Centropristis striatus. **sea bird** a bird frequenting the sea or the land near the sea. **sea bream** = PORGY. **sea breeze** a breeze blowing towards the land from the sea, esp. during the day (cf. land breeze). **sea buckthorn** a maritime shrub, Hippophaë rhamnoides with orange berries. **sea change** a notable or unexpected transformation (with ref. to Shakesp. Tempest I. ii. 403). **sea-chest** a sailor's storage-chest. **sea coal** archaic mineral coal, as distinct from charcoal etc. **sea cow 1** a sirenian. **2** a walrus. **sea cucumber** a holothurian, esp. a bêche-de-mer. **sea dog** an old or experienced sailor. **Sea Dyak** see IBAN. **sea eagle** any fish-eating eagle esp. of the genus Haliaëtus. **sea-ear** = ORMER. **sea elephant** any large seal of the genus Mirounga, the male of which has a proboscis: also called elephant seal. **sea fan** any colonial coral of the order Gorgonacea supported by a fanlike horny skeleton. **sea front** the part of a coastal town directly facing the sea. **sea-girt** literary surrounded by sea. **sea gooseberry** any marine animal of the phylum Ctenophora, with an ovoid body bearing numerous cilia. **sea-green** bluish-green (as of the sea). **sea hare** any of various marine molluscs of the order Anaspidea, having an internal shell and long extensions from its foot. **sea holly** a spiny-leaved blue-flowered evergreen plant, Eryngium maritimum. **sea horse 1** any of various small upright marine fish of the family Syngnathidae, esp. *Hippocampus hippocampus*, having a body suggestive of the head and neck of a horse. **2** a mythical creature with a horse's head and a tail that can be wrapped round a support. **sea-island cotton** a fine-quality long-stapled cotton grown on islands off the southern US. **sea lavender** any maritime plant of the genus *Limonium*, with small brightly-coloured funnel-shaped flowers. **sea legs** the ability to keep one's balance and avoid seasickness when at sea. **sea level** the mean level of the sea's surface, used in reckoning the height of hills etc. and as a barometric standard. **sea lily** any of various sessile echinoderms, esp. of the class Crinoidea, with long jointed stalks and feather-like arms for trapping food. **sea lion** any large, eared seal of the Pacific, esp. of the genus *Zalophus* or *Otaria*. **sea loch** = LOCH 2. **Sea Lord** (in the UK) a naval member of the Admiralty Board. **sea mile** = *nautical mile*. **sea mouse** any iridescent marine annelid of the genus *Aphrodite*. **sea onion** = SQUILL 2. **sea otter** a Pacific otter, *Enhydra lutris*, using a stone balanced on its abdomen to crack bivalve molluscs. **sea pink** a maritime plant, *Armeria maritima*, with bright pink flowers: also called THRIFT. **sea purse** the egg-case of a skate or shark. **sea room** clear space at sea for a ship to turn or manoeuvre in. **sea salt** salt produced by evaporating sea water. **Sea Scout** a member of the maritime branch of the Scout Association. **sea serpent** (or **snake**) **1** a snake of the family Hydrophidae, living in the sea. **2** an enormous legendary serpent-like sea monster. **sea shell** the shell of a salt-water mollusc. **sea snail 1** a small slimy fish of the family Liparididae, with a ventral sucker. **2** any spiral-shelled mollusc, e.g. a whelk. **sea squirt** any marine turnicate of the class Ascidiacea, consisting of a bag-like structure with apertures for the flow of water. **sea trout** = *salmon trout*. **sea urchin** a small marine echinoderm of the class Echinoidea, with a spherical or flattened spiny shell. **sea wall** a wall or embankment erected to prevent encroachment by the sea. **sea water** water in or taken from the sea. [OE *sæ* f. Gmc]

seabed /ˈsiːbed/ *n.* the ground under the sea; the ocean floor.

seaboard /ˈsiːbɔːd/ *n.* **1** the seashore or coastal region. **2** the line of a coast.

seaborne /ˈsiːbɔːn/ *adj.* transported by sea.

seacock /ˈsiːkɒk/ *n.* a valve below a ship's water-line for letting water in or out.

seafarer /ˈsiːˌfeərə(r)/ *n.* **1** a sailor. **2** a traveller by sea.

seafaring /ˈsiːˌfeərɪŋ/ *adj. & n.* travelling by sea, esp. regularly.

seafood /ˈsiːfuːd/ *n.* edible sea fish or shellfish.

seagoing /ˈsiːˌɡəʊɪŋ/ *adj.* **1** (of ships) fit for crossing the sea. **2** (of a person) seafaring.

seagull /ˈsiːɡʌl/ *n.* = GULL[1].

seakale /ˈsiːkeɪl/ *n.* a cruciferous maritime plant, *Crambe maritima*, having coarsely-toothed leaves and used as a vegetable. □ **seakale beet** = CHARD.

seal[1] /siːl/ *n. & v.* —*n.* **1** a piece of wax, lead, paper, etc., with a stamped design, attached to a document as a guarantee of authenticity. **2** a similar material attached to a receptacle, envelope, etc., affording security by having to be broken to allow access to the contents. **3** an engraved piece of metal, gemstone, etc., for stamping a design on a seal. **4 a** a substance or device used to close an aperture or act as a fastening. **b** an amount of water standing in the trap of a drain to prevent foul air from rising. **5** an act or gesture or event regarded as a confirmation or guarantee. **6** a significant or prophetic mark (*has the seal of death in his face*). **7** a decorative adhesive stamp. **8** esp. *Eccl.* a vow of secrecy; an obligation to silence. —*v.tr.* **1** close securely or hermetically. **2** stamp or fasten with a seal. **3** fix a seal to. **4** certify as correct with a seal or stamp. **5** (often foll. by *up*) confine or fasten securely. **6** settle or decide (*their fate is sealed*). **7** (foll. by *off*) put barriers round (an area) to prevent entry and exit, esp. as a security measure. **8** apply a non-porous coating to (a surface) to make it impervious. □ **Great Seal** (in the UK) the seal in the charge of the Lord Chancellor or Lord Keeper used in sealing important State papers. **one's lips are sealed** one is obliged to keep a secret. **sealed-beam** (*attrib.*) designating a vehicle headlamp with a sealed unit consisting of the light source, reflector, and lens. **sealed book** see BOOK. **sealed**

orders orders for procedure not to be opened before a specified time. **sealing-wax** a mixture of shellac and rosin with turpentine and pigment, softened by heating and used to make seals. **seal ring** a finger ring with a seal. **seals of office** (in the UK) those held during tenure esp. by the Lord Chancellor or a Secretary of State. **set one's seal to** (or **on**) authorize or confirm. □□ **sealable** *adj.* [ME f. AF *seal*, OF *seel* f. L *sigillum* dimin. of *signum* SIGN]

seal[2] /siːl/ *n. & v.* —*n.* any fish-eating amphibious sea mammal of the family Phocidae or Otariidae, with flippers and webbed feet. —*v.intr.* hunt for seals. [OE *seolh seol-* f. Gmc]

sealant /ˈsiːlənt/ *n.* material for sealing, esp. to make something airtight or watertight.

sealer /ˈsiːlə(r)/ *n.* a ship or person engaged in hunting seals.

sealery /ˈsiːləri/ *n.* (*pl.* **-ies**) a place for hunting seals.

sealskin /ˈsiːlskɪn/ *n.* **1** the skin or prepared fur of a seal. **2** (often *attrib.*) a garment made from this.

Sealyham /ˈsiːlɪəm/ *n.* (in full **Sealyham terrier**) **1** a terrier of a wire-haired short-legged breed. **2** this breed. [*Sealyham* in S. Wales]

seam /siːm/ *n. & v.* —*n.* **1** a line where two edges join, esp. of two pieces of cloth etc. turned back and stitched together, or of boards fitted edge to edge. **2** a fissure between parallel edges. **3** a wrinkle or scar. **4** a stratum of coal etc. —*v.tr.* **1** join with a seam. **2** (esp. as **seamed** *adj.*) mark or score with or as with a seam. □ **bursting at the seams** full to overflowing. **seam bowler** *Cricket* a bowler who makes the ball deviate by bouncing off its seam. □□ **seamer** *n.* **seamless** *adj.* [OE *seam* f. Gmc]

seaman /ˈsiːmən/ *n.* (*pl.* **-men**) **1** a sailor, esp. one below the rank of officer. **2** a person regarded in terms of skill in navigation (*a poor seaman*). □□ **seamanlike** *adj.* **seamanly** *adj.* [OE *sæman* (as SEA, MAN)]

seamanship /ˈsiːmənʃɪp/ *n.* skill in managing a ship or boat.

seamstress /ˈsemstrɪs/ *n.* (also **sempstress**) a woman who sews, esp. professionally; a needlewoman. [OE *sēamestre* fem. f. *sēamere* tailor, formed as SEAM + -STER + -ESS[1]]

seamy /ˈsiːmɪ/ *adj.* (**seamier**, **seamiest**) **1** marked with or showing seams. **2** unpleasant, disreputable (esp. *the seamy side*). □□ **seaminess** *n.*

Seanad /ˈʃænəð/ *n.* the upper House of Parliament in the Republic of Ireland, composed of 60 members, of whom 11 are nominated by the Taoiseach and 49 are elected by institutions etc. [Ir., = senate]

seance /ˈseɪɑ̃s/ *n.* (also **séance**) a meeting at which spiritualists attempt to make contact with the dead. [F *séance* f. OF *seoir* f. L *sedēre* sit]

Sea Peoples (also) **Peoples of the Sea** groups of invaders who encroached on the Levant and Egypt by land and by sea in the late 13th c. Their identity is still being debated. In the Levant they are associated with destruction; the Egyptians were successful in driving them away. Some, including the Philistines, settled in Palestine.

seaplane /ˈsiːpleɪn/ *n.* an aircraft designed to take off from and land and float on water, using floats instead of an undercarriage. It differs from a flying boat in that its hull does not support it in the water.

seaport /ˈsiːpɔːt/ *n.* a town with a harbour for seagoing ships.

SEAQ *abbr.* Stock Exchange Automated Quotations (computerized access to share information).

seaquake /ˈsiːkweɪk/ *n.* an earthquake under the sea.

sear /sɪə(r)/ *v. & adj.* —*v.tr.* **1 a** scorch, esp. with a hot iron; cauterize, brand. **b** (as **searing** *adj.*) scorching, burning (*searing pain*). **2** cause pain or great anguish to. **3** brown (meat) quickly at a high temperature so that it will retain its juices in cooking. **4** make (one's conscience, feelings, etc.) callous. **5** *archaic* blast, wither. —*adj.* (also **sere**) *literary* (esp. of a plant etc.) withered, dried up. [OE *sēar* (adj.), *sēarian* (v.), f. Gmc]

search /sɜːtʃ/ *v. & n.* —*v.* **1** *tr.* look through or go over thoroughly to find something. **2** *tr.* examine or feel over (a person) to find anything concealed. **3** *tr.* **a** probe or penetrate into. **b** examine or question (one's mind, conscience, etc.) thoroughly.

b **but** d **dog** f **few** g **get** h **he** j **yes** k **cat** l **leg** m **man** n **no** p **pen** r **red** s **sit** t **top** v **voice**

4 *intr.* (often foll. by *for*) make a search or investigation. **5** *intr.* (as **searching** *adj.*) (of an examination) thorough; leaving no loopholes. **6** *tr.* (foll. by *out*) look probingly for; seek out. —*n.* **1** an act of searching. **2** an investigation. □ **in search of** trying to find. **right of search** a belligerent's right to stop a neutral vessel and search it for prohibited goods. **search me!** *colloq.* I do not know. **search-party** a group of people organized to look for a lost person or thing. **search warrant** an official authorization to enter and search a building. □□ **searchable** *adj.* **searcher** *n.* **searchingly** *adv.* [ME f. AF *sercher*, OF *cerchier* f. LL *circare* go round (as CIRCUS)]

searchlight /'sɜːtʃlaɪt/ *n.* **1** a powerful outdoor electric light with a concentrated beam that can be turned in any direction. **2** the light or beam from this.

seascape /'siːskeɪp/ *n.* a picture or view of the sea.

seashore /'siːʃɔː(r)/ *n.* **1** land close to or bordering on the sea. **2** *Law* the area between high and low water marks.

seasick /'siːsɪk/ *adj.* suffering from sickness or nausea from the motion of a ship at sea. □□ **seasickness** *n.*

seaside /'siːsaɪd/ *n.* the sea-coast, esp. as a holiday resort.

season /'siːz(ə)n/ *n.* & *v.* —*n.* **1** each of the four divisions of the year (spring, summer, autumn, and winter) associated with a type of weather and a stage of vegetation. **2** a time of year characterized by climatic or other features (*the dry season*). **3 a** the time of year when a plant is mature or flowering etc. **b** the time of year when an animal breeds or is hunted. **4** a proper or suitable time. **5** a time when something is plentiful or active or in vogue. **6** (usu. prec. by *the*) = *high season*. **7** the time of year regularly devoted to an activity (*the football season*). **8** the time of year dedicated to social life generally (*went up to London for the season*). **9** a period of indefinite or varying length. **10** *Brit. colloq.* = *season ticket*. —*v.* **1** *tr.* flavour (food) with salt, herbs, etc. **2** *tr.* enhance with wit, excitement, etc. **3** *tr.* temper or moderate. **4** *tr.* & *intr.* **a** make or become suitable or in the desired condition, esp. by exposure to the air or weather; mature. **b** make or become experienced or accustomed (*seasoned soldiers*). □ **in season 1** (of foodstuff) available in plenty and in good condition. **2** (of an animal) on heat. **3** timely. **season ticket** a ticket entitling the holder to any number of journeys, admittances, etc., in a given period. □□ **seasoner** *n.* [ME f. OF *seson* f. L *satio -onis* (in Rmc sense 'seed-time') f. *serere sat- sow*]

seasonable /'siːzənəb(ə)l/ *adj.* **1** suitable to or usual in the season. **2** opportune. **3** meeting the needs of the occasion. □□ **seasonableness** *n.* **seasonably** *adv.*

seasonal /'siːzən(ə)l/ *adj.* of, depending on, or varying with the season. □ **seasonal affective disorder** a depressive state associated with late autumn and winter and thought to be caused by a lack of light. □□ **seasonality** /-'nælɪtɪ/ *n.* **seasonally** *adv.*

seasoning /'siːzənɪŋ/ *n.* condiments added to food.

seat /siːt/ *n.* & *v.* —*n.* **1** a thing made or used for sitting on; a chair, stool, saddle, etc. **2** the buttocks. **3** the part of the trousers etc. covering the buttocks. **4** the part of a chair etc. on which the sitter's weight directly rests. **5** a place for one person in a theatre, vehicle, etc. **6** the occupation of a seat. **7** esp. *Brit.* **a** the right to occupy a seat, esp. as a Member of the House of Commons. **b** a member's constituency. **8** the part of a machine that supports or guides another part. **9** a site or location of something specified (*a seat of learning; the seat of the emotions*). **10** a country mansion, esp. with large grounds. **11** the manner of sitting on a horse etc. —*v.tr.* **1** cause to sit. **2 a** provide sitting accommodation for (*the cinema seats 500*). **b** provide with seats. **3** (as **seated** *adj.*) sitting. **4** put or fit in position. □ **be seated** sit down. **by the seat of one's pants** *colloq.* by instinct rather than logic or knowledge. **seat-belt** a belt securing a person in the seat of a car or aircraft. **take a** (or **one's**) **seat** sit down. □□ **seatless** *adj.* [ME f. ON *sæti* (= OE *gesete* f. Gmc)]

-seater /'siːtə(r)/ *n.* (in *comb.*) having a specified number of seats (*a 16-seater bus*).

seating /'siːtɪŋ/ *n.* **1** seats collectively. **2** sitting accommodation.

SEATO /'siːtəʊ/ *abbr.* South-East Asia Treaty Organization.

Seattle /sɪ'æt(ə)l/ a port and industrial city in the State of Washington, the largest city in the north-western US; pop. (1982) 490,000.

seaward /'siːwəd/ *adv., adj.,* & *n.* —*adv.* (also **seawards**) towards the sea. —*adj.* going or facing towards the sea. —*n.* such a direction or position.

seaway /'siːweɪ/ *n.* **1** an inland waterway open to seagoing ships. **2** a ship's progress. **3** a ship's path across the sea.

seaweed /'siːwiːd/ *n.* any of various algae growing in the sea or on the rocks on a shore.

seaworthy /'siː,wɜːðɪ/ *adj.* (esp. of a ship) fit to put to sea. □□ **seaworthiness** *n.*

sebaceous /sɪ'beɪʃəs/ *adj.* fatty; of or relating to tallow or fat. □ **sebaceous gland** (or **follicle** or **duct**) a gland etc. secreting or conveying oily matter to lubricate the skin and hair. [L *sebaceus* f. *sebum* tallow]

Sebastian /sɪ'bæstɪən/, St (late 3rd c.), Roman martyr. According to legend he was sentenced by Diocletian to be shot by archers but recovered, confronted the Emperor, and was clubbed to death. Feast day, 20 Jan.

Sebastopol /sɪ'bæstəp(ə)l/ (Russian **Sevastopol** /sɪ'væ-/) a Soviet fortress and naval base in the Crimea; pop. (est. 1987) 350,000. It was the focal point of military operations during the Crimean War, falling eventually to Anglo-French forces in September 1855 after year-long siege.

seborrhoea /,sebə'rɪə/ *n.* (US **seborrhea**) excessive discharge of sebum from the sebaceous glands. □□ **seborrhoeic** *adj.* [SEBUM after *gonorrhoea* etc.]

sebum /'siːbəm/ *n.* the oily secretion of the sebaceous glands. [mod.L f. L *sebum* grease]

Sec. *abbr.* secretary.

sec /sek/ *adj.* (of wine) dry. [F f. L *siccus*]

sec¹ *abbr.* secant.

sec² /sek/ *n. colloq.* (in phrases) a second (of time). [abbr.]

sec. *abbr.* second(s).

secant /'siːkənt, 'se-/ *adj.* & *n. Math.* —*adj.* cutting (*secant line*). —*n.* **1** a line cutting a curve at one or more points. **2** the ratio of the hypotenuse to the shorter side adjacent to an acute angle (in a right-angled triangle). ¶ Abbr.: **sec.** [F *sécant(e)* f. L *secare secant- cut*]

secateurs /,sekə'tɜːz/ *n.pl.* esp. *Brit.* a pair of pruning clippers for use with one hand. [F *sécateur* cutter, irreg. f. L *secare* cut]

secco /'sekəʊ/ *n.* the technique of painting on dry plaster with pigments mixed in water. [It., = dry, f. L *siccus*]

secede /sɪ'siːd/ *v.intr.* (usu. foll. by *from*) withdraw formally from membership of a political federation or a religious body. □□ **seceder** *n.* [L *secedere secess-* (as SE-, *cedere* go)]

secession /sɪ'seʃ(ə)n/ *n.* **1** the act or an instance of seceding. **2** (**Secession**) *hist.* the withdrawal of eleven southern States from the US Union in 1860, leading to the Civil War. □□ **secessional** *adj.* **secessionism** *n.* **secessionist** *n.* [F *sécession* or L *secessio* (as SECEDE)]

Sechuana var. of SETSWANA.

seclude /sɪ'kluːd/ *v.tr.* (also *refl.*) **1** keep (a person or place) retired or away from company. **2** (esp. as **secluded** *adj.*) hide or screen from view. [ME f. L *secludere seclus-* (as SE-, *claudere* shut)]

seclusion /sɪ'kluːʒ(ə)n/ *n.* **1** a secluded state; retirement, privacy. **2** a secluded place. □□ **seclusionist** *n.* **seclusive** /-sɪv/ *adj.* [med.L *seclusio* (as SECLUDE)]

second¹ /'sekənd/ *n., adj.,* & *v.* —*n.* **1** the position in a sequence corresponding to that of the number 2 in the sequence 1–2. **2** something occupying this position. **3** the second person etc. in a race or competition. **4** *Mus.* **a** an interval or chord spanning two consecutive notes in the diatonic scale (e.g. C to D). **b** a note separated from another by this interval. **5** = *second gear*. **6** another person or thing in addition to one previously mentioned or considered (*the policeman was then joined by a second*). **7** (in *pl.*) **a** goods of a second or inferior quality. **b** coarse flour, or bread made from it. **8** (in *pl.*) *colloq.* **a** a second helping of food at a meal. **b** the second course of a meal. **9** an attendant assisting a combatant in a duel, boxing-match, etc. **10 a** a place in the second class of an examination. **b** a person having this. —*adj.*

1 that is the second; next after first. 2 additional, further; other besides one previously mentioned or considered (*ate a second cake*). 3 subordinate in position or importance etc.; inferior. 4 *Mus.* performing a lower or subordinate part (*second violins*). 5 such as to be comparable to; closely reminiscent of (*a second Callas*). —*v.tr.* 1 supplement, support; back up. 2 formally support or endorse (a nomination or resolution etc., or its proposer). □ **at second hand** by hearsay, not direct observation etc. **in the second place** as a second consideration etc. **second advent** a supposed return of Christ to earth. **second ballot** a deciding ballot between candidates coming first (without an absolute majority) and second in a previous ballot. **second-best** *adj.* next after best. —*n.* a less adequate or desirable alternative. **second cause** *Logic* a cause that is itself caused. **second chamber** the upper house of a bicameral parliament. **second class** the second-best group or category, esp. of hotel or train accommodation or (in the UK) of postal services. **second-class** *adj.* 1 of or belonging to the second class. 2 inferior in quality, status, etc. (*second-class citizens*). —*adv.* by second-class post, train, etc. (*travelled second-class*). **second coming** *Theol.* the second advent of Christ on earth. **second cousin** see COUSIN. **second-degree** *Med.* denoting burns that cause blistering but not permanent scars. **second fiddle** see FIDDLE. **second floor 1** *Brit.* the floor two levels above the ground floor. 2 *US* the floor above the ground floor. **second gear** the second (and next to lowest) in a sequence of gears. **second-generation** denoting the offspring of a first generation, esp. of immigrants. **second-guess** *colloq.* 1 anticipate or predict by guesswork. 2 judge or criticize with hindsight. **second honeymoon** a holiday like a honeymoon, taken by a couple after some years of marriage. **second in command** the officer next in rank to the commanding or chief officer. **second lieutenant** an army officer next below lieutenant or *US* first lieutenant. **second name** a surname. **second nature** (often foll. by *to*) an acquired tendency that has become instinctive (*is second nature to him*). **second officer** an assistant mate on a merchant ship. **second person** *Gram.* see PERSON. **second-rate** of mediocre quality; inferior. **second-rater** a person or thing that is second-rate. **second reading** a second presentation of a bill to a legislative assembly, in the UK to approve its general principles and in the US to debate committee reports. **second self** a close friend or associate. **second sight** the supposed power of being able to perceive future or distant events. **second-sighted** having the gift of second sight. **second string** an alternative course of action, means of livelihood, etc., invoked if the main one is unsuccessful. **second teeth** the teeth that replace the milk teeth in a mammal. **second thoughts** a new opinion or resolution reached after further consideration. **second to none** surpassed by no other. **second wind 1** recovery of the power of normal breathing during exercise after initial breathlessness. 2 renewed energy to continue an effort. **Second World War** see WORLD WAR. □□ **seconder** *n.* (esp. in sense 2 of *v.*). [ME f. OF f. L *secundus* f. *sequi* follow]

second² /ˈsekənd/ *n.* 1 a sixtieth of a minute of time or angular distance. ¶ *Symb.*: ″. 2 the SI unit of time, established in 1967 for international use, the duration of 9,192,631,770 periods of the radiation of a certain transition of the caesium-133 atom. Originally the second was defined as the fraction 1/86,400 of the mean solar day, exact definition of which was left to astronomers, but this was shown to be insufficiently accurate on account of irregularities in the rotation of the Earth. ¶ *Abbr.*: **s.** 3 *colloq.* a very short time (*wait a second*). □ **second-hand** an extra hand in some watches and clocks, recording seconds. [F f. med.L *secunda* (*minuta*) secondary (minute)]

second³ /sɪˈkɒnd/ *v.tr.* *Brit.* transfer (a military officer or other official or worker) temporarily to other employment or to another position. □□ **secondment** *n.* [F *en second* in the second rank (of officers)]

secondary /ˈsekəndərɪ/ *adj. & n.* —*adj.* 1 coming after or next below what is primary. 2 derived from or depending on or supplementing what is primary. 3 (of education, a school, etc.) for those who have had primary education, usu. from 11 to 18 years. 4 *Electr.* **a** (of a cell or battery) having a reversible chemical reaction and therefore able to store energy. **b** denoting a device

using electromagnetic induction, esp. a transformer. —*n.* (*pl.* **-ies**) 1 a secondary thing. 2 a secondary device or current. □ **secondary colour** the result of mixing two primary colours. **secondary feather** a feather growing from the second joint of a bird's wing. **secondary picketing** the picketing of premises of a firm not otherwise involved in the dispute in question. **secondary planet** a satellite of a planet (cf. *primary planet*). **secondary sexual characteristics** those distinctive of one sex but not directly related to reproduction. □□ **secondarily** *adv.* **secondariness** *n.* [ME f. L *secundarius* (as SECOND¹)]

seconde /səˈkɔ̃d/ *n.* Fencing the second of eight parrying positions. [F, fem. of *second* SECOND¹]

second-hand /ˌsekəndˈhænd/ *adj. & adv.* —*adj.* /also ˈsek-/ **1 a** (of goods) having had a previous owner; not new. **b** (of a shop etc.) where such goods can be bought. 2 (of information etc.) accepted on another's authority and not from original investigation. —*adv.* 1 on a second-hand basis. 2 at second hand; not directly.

secondly /ˈsekəndlɪ/ *adv.* 1 furthermore; in the second place. 2 as a second item.

secondo /sɪˈkɒndəʊ/ *n.* (*pl.* **secondi** /-dɪ/) *Mus.* the second or lower part in a duet etc. [It.]

secrecy /ˈsiːkrɪsɪ/ *n.* 1 the keeping of secrets as a fact, habit, or faculty. 2 a state in which all information is withheld (*was done in great secrecy*). □ **sworn to secrecy** having promised to keep a secret. [ME f. *secretie* f. obs. *secre* (adj.) or SECRET adj.]

secret /ˈsiːkrɪt/ *adj. & n.* —*adj.* 1 kept or meant to be kept private, unknown, or hidden from all or all but a few. 2 acting or operating secretly. 3 fond of, prone to, or able to preserve secrecy. 4 (of a place) hidden, completely secluded. —*n.* 1 a thing kept or meant to be kept secret. 2 a thing known only to a few. 3 a mystery. 4 a valid but not commonly known or recognized method of achieving or maintaining something (*what's their secret?*; *correct breathing is the secret of good health*). 5 *RC Ch.* a prayer concluding the offertory of the mass. □ **in secret** secretly. **in** (or **in on**) **the secret** among the number of those who know it. **keep a secret** not reveal it. **secret agent** a spy acting for a country. **secret ballot** a ballot in which votes are cast in secret. **secret police** a police force operating in secret for political purposes. **secret service** a government department concerned with espionage. **secret society** a society whose members are sworn to secrecy about it. □□ **secretly** *adv.* [ME f. OF f. L *secretus* (adj.) separate, set apart f. *secernere secret-* (as SE-, *cernere* sift)]

secretaire /ˌsekrɪˈteə(r)/ *n.* an escritoire. [F (as SECRETARY)]

secretariat /ˌsekrəˈteərɪət/ *n.* 1 a permanent administrative office or department, esp. a governmental one. 2 its members or premises. 3 the office of secretary. [F *secrétariat* f. med.L *secretariatus* (as SECRETARY)]

secretary /ˈsekrɪtərɪ, ˈsekrətrɪ/ *n.* (*pl.* **-ies**) 1 a person employed by an individual or in an office etc. to assist with correspondence, keep records, make appointments, etc. 2 an official appointed by a society etc. to conduct its correspondence, keep its records, etc. 3 (in the UK) the principal assistant of a government minister, ambassador, etc. □ **secretary bird** a long-legged snake-eating African bird, *Sagittarius serpentarius*, with a crest likened to a quill pen stuck over a writer's ear. **Secretary-General** the principal administrator of an organization. **Secretary of State 1** (in the UK) the head of a major government department. The title occurs first during the reign of Queen Elizabeth I; it probably indicates the beginning of the development by which the monarch's secretary (sense 1 above) became a minister invested with governing functions. 2 (in the US) the chief government official responsible for foreign affairs. □□ **secretarial** /-ˈteərɪəl/ *adj.* **secretaryship** *n.* [ME f. LL *secretarius* (as SECRET)]

secrete¹ /sɪˈkriːt/ *v.tr.* *Biol.* (of a cell, organ, etc.) produce by secretion. □□ **secretor** *n.* **secretory** *adj.* [back-form. f. SECRETION]

secrete² /sɪˈkriːt/ *v.tr.* conceal; put into hiding. [obs. *secret* (v.) f. SECRET]

secretion /sɪˈkriːʃ(ə)n/ *n.* 1 *Biol.* **a** a process by which substances are produced and discharged from a cell for a function in the organism or for excretion. **b** the secreted substance. **2** the act or an instance of concealing (*the secretion of stolen goods*). [F *sécretion* or L *secretio* separation (as SECRET)]

secretive /ˈsiːkrɪtɪv/ *adj.* inclined to make or keep secrets; uncommunicative. ☐☐ **secretively** *adv.* **secretiveness** *n.* [back-form. f. *secretiveness* after F *secrétivité* (as SECRET)]

sect /sekt/ *n.* **1 a** a body of people subscribing to religious doctrines usu. different from those of an established Church from which they have separated. **b** usu. *derog.* a nonconformist or other Church. **c** a party or faction in a religious body. **d** a religious denomination. **2** the followers of a particular philosopher or philosophy, or school of thought in politics etc. [ME f. OF *secte* or L *secta* f. the stem of *sequi secut-* follow]

sect. *abbr.* section.

sectarian /sekˈteərɪən/ *adj.* & *n.* —*adj.* **1** of or concerning a sect. **2** bigoted or narrow-minded in following the doctrines of one's sect. —*n.* **1** a member of a sect. **2** a bigot. ☐☐ **sectarianism** *n.* **sectarianize** *v.tr.* (also **-ise**). [SECTARY]

sectary /ˈsektərɪ/ *n.* (*pl.* **-ies**) a member of a religious or political sect. [med.L *sectarius* adherent (as SECT)]

section /ˈsekʃ(ə)n/ *n.* & *v.* —*n.* **1** a part cut off or separated from something. **2** each of the parts into which a thing is divided (actually or conceptually) or divisible or out of which a structure can be fitted together. **3** a distinct group or subdivision of a larger body of people (*the wind section of an orchestra*). **4** a subdivision of a book, document, statute, etc. **5** *US* **a** an area of land. **b** one square mile of land. **c** a particular district of a town (*residential section*). **6** a subdivision of an army platoon. **7** esp. *Surgery* a separation by cutting. **8** *Biol.* a thin slice of tissue etc., cut off for microscopic examination. **9 a** the cutting of a solid by or along a plane. **b** the resulting figure or the area of this. **10** a representation of the internal structure of something as if cut across along a vertical or horizontal plane. **11** *Biol.* a group, esp. a subgenus. —*v.tr.* **1** arrange in or divide into sections. **2** *Brit.* cause (a person) to be compulsorily committed to a psychiatric hospital in accordance with a section of a mental health act. **3** *Biol.* cut into thin slices for microscopic examination. ☐ **section-mark** the sign (§) used as a reference mark to indicate the start of a section of a book etc. [F *section* or L *sectio* f. *secare sect-* cut]

sectional /ˈsekʃən(ə)l/ *adj.* **1 a** relating to a section, esp. of a community. **b** partisan. **2** made in sections. **3** local rather than general. ☐☐ **sectionalism** *n.* **sectionalist** *n.* & *adj.* **sectionalize** *v.tr.* (also **-ise**). **sectionally** *adv.*

sector /ˈsektə(r)/ *n.* **1** a distinct part or branch of an enterprise, or of society, the economy, etc. **2** *Mil.* a subdivision of an area for military operations, controlled by one commander or headquarters. **3** the plane figure enclosed by two radii of a circle, ellipse, etc., and the arc between them. **4** a mathematical instrument consisting of two arms hinged at one end and marked with sines, tangents, etc., for making diagrams etc. ☐☐ **sectoral** *adj.* [LL, techn. use of L *sector* cutter (as SECTION)]

sectorial /sekˈtɔːrɪəl/ *adj.* **1** of or like a sector or sectors. **2** = CARNASSIAL.

secular /ˈsekjʊlə(r)/ *adj.* & *n.* —*adj.* **1** concerned with the affairs of this world; not spiritual or sacred. **2** (of education etc.) not concerned with religion or religious belief. **3 a** not ecclesiastical or monastic. **b** (of clergy) not bound by a religious rule. **4** occurring once in an age or century. **5** lasting for or occurring over an indefinitely long time. —*n.* a secular priest. ☐ **secular variation** *Astron.* variation compensated over a long period of time. ☐☐ **secularism** *n.* **secularist** *n.* **secularity** /-ˈlærɪtɪ/ *n.* **secularize** *v.tr.* (also **-ise**). **secularization** /-ˈzeɪʃ(ə)n/ *n.* **secularly** *adv.* [ME (in senses 1-3 f. OF *seculer*) f. L *saecularis* f. *saeculum* generation, age]

secund /sɪˈkʌnd/ *adj.* arranged on one side only (as the flowers of lily of the valley). ☐☐ **secundly** *adv.* [L *secundus* (as SECOND)]

secure /sɪˈkjʊə(r)/ *adj.* & *v.* —*adj.* **1** untroubled by danger or fear. **2** safe against attack; impregnable. **3** reliable; certain not to fail (*the plan is secure*). **4** fixed or fastened so as not to give way

or get loose or be lost (*made the door secure*). **5 a** (foll. by *of*) certain to achieve (*secure of victory*). **b** (foll. by *against*, *from*) safe, protected (*secure against attack*). —*v.tr.* **1** make secure or safe; fortify. **2** fasten, close, or confine securely. **3** succeed in obtaining or achieving (*have secured front seats*). **4** guarantee against loss (*a loan secured by property*). **5** compress (a blood-vessel) to prevent bleeding. ☐ **secure arms** *Mil.* hold a rifle with the muzzle downward and the lock in the armpit to guard it from rain. ☐☐ **securable** *adj.* **securely** *adv.* **securement** *n.* [L *securus* (as SE-, *cura* care)]

Securitate /seˌkjʊərɪˈtɑːteɪ/ *n. hist.* the internal security force of Romania, set up in 1948 and officially disbanded during the revolution of Dec. 1989. [Romanian, = security]

security /sɪˈkjʊərɪtɪ/ *n.* (*pl.* **-ies**) **1** a secure condition or feeling. **2** a thing that guards or guarantees. **3 a** the safety of a State, company, etc., against espionage, theft, or other danger. **b** an organization for ensuring this. **4** a thing deposited or pledged as a guarantee of the fulfilment of an undertaking or the payment of a loan, to be forfeited in case of default. **5** (often in *pl.*) a certificate attesting credit or the ownership of stock, bonds, etc. ☐ **on security of** using as a guarantee. **security blanket** **1** an official sanction on information in the interest of security. **2** a blanket or other familiar object given as a comfort to a child. **security guard** a person employed to protect the security of buildings, vehicles, etc. **security risk** a person whose presence may threaten security. [ME f. OF *securité* or L *securitas* (as SECURE)]

Security Council a principal council of the UN consisting of 15 members, of which five (China, France, UK, USA, USSR) are permanent and the rest are elected for two-year terms, charged with the duty of maintaining security and peace between nations.

Sedan /sɪˈdæn/ a town on the River Meuse in NE France; pop. (1982) 24,535. It was the site of the decisive battle (1870) in the Franco-Prussian war of 1870-1, in which the Prussian army succeeded in surrounding a smaller French army under Napoleon III and forcing it to surrender, opening the way for a Prussian advance on Paris and marking the end of the Second Empire.

sedan /sɪˈdæn/ *n.* **1** (in full **sedan chair**) an enclosed chair for conveying one person, carried between horizontal poles by two porters, common in the 17th-18th c. **2** *US* an enclosed motor car for four or more people. [perh. alt. f. It. dial., ult. f. L *sella* saddle f. *sedēre* sit]

sedate¹ /sɪˈdeɪt/ *adj.* tranquil and dignified; equable, serious. ☐☐ **sedately** *adv.* **sedateness** *n.* [L *sedatus* past part. of *sedare* settle f. *sedēre* sit]

sedate² /sɪˈdeɪt/ *v.tr.* put under sedation. [back-form. f. SEDATION]

sedation /sɪˈdeɪʃ(ə)n/ *n.* a state of rest or sleep esp. produced by a sedative drug. [F *sédation* or L *sedatio* (as SEDATE¹)]

sedative /ˈsedətɪv/ *n.* & *adj.* —*n.* a drug, influence, etc., that tends to calm or soothe. —*adj.* calming, soothing; inducing sleep. [ME f. OF *sedatif* or med.L *sedativus* (as SEDATE¹)]

sedentary /ˈsedəntərɪ/ *adj.* **1** sitting (*a sedentary posture*). **2** (of work etc.) characterized by much sitting and little physical exercise. **3** (of a person) spending much time seated. **4** *Zool.* not migratory, free-swimming, etc. ☐☐ **sedentarily** *adv.* **sedentariness** *n.* [F *sédentaire* or L *sedentarius* f. *sedēre* sit]

Seder /ˈseɪdə(r)/ *n.* the ritual for the first night or first two nights of the Passover. [Heb. *sēder* order]

sederunt /sɪˈdeərənt/ *n. Sc.* a sitting of an ecclesiastical assembly or other body. [L, = (the following persons) sat f. *sedēre* sit]

sedge /sedʒ/ *n.* **1** any grasslike plant of the genus *Carex* with triangular stems, usu. growing in wet areas. **2** an expanse of this plant. ☐ **sedge-warbler** (or **-wren**) a small warbler, *Acrocephalus schoenobaenus*, that breeds in sedge. ☐☐ **sedgy** *adj.* [OE *secg* f. Gmc]

Sedgemoor /ˈsedʒmʊə(r)/ a plain in Somerset, scene of a battle (1685) in which Monmouth, who had landed on the Dorset coast as champion of the Protestant party, was defeated by James II's troops. Monmouth himself was captured, and was executed soon afterwards.

sedile /sɪˈdaɪlɪ/ *n.* (*pl.* **sedilia** /-ˈdɪlɪə/) (usu. in *pl.*) *Eccl.* each of usu. three stone seats for priests in the south wall of a chancel, often canopied and decorated. [L, = seat f. *sedēre* sit]

sediment /ˈsedɪmənt/ n. **1** matter that settles to the bottom of a liquid; dregs. **2** *Geol.* matter that is carried by water or wind and deposited on the surface of the land, and may in time become consolidated into rock. □□ **sedimentation** /-ˈteɪʃ(ə)n/ n. [F *sédiment* or L *sedimentum* (as SEDILE)]

sedimentary /ˌsedɪˈmentərɪ/ adj. **1** of or like sediment. **2** (of rock) formed from sediment (cf. IGNEOUS, METAMORPHIC). Such rocks are characteristically laid down in strata which are initially horizontal or nearly so. It is through the study of sequences of sedimentary rocks and the fossils associated with them that the geological time-scale was established. By volume, sedimentary rocks constitute only 5 % of the known crust of the earth, igneous rocks contributing the other 95 %.

sedition /sɪˈdɪʃ(ə)n/ n. **1** conduct or speech inciting to rebellion or a breach of public order. **2** agitation against the authority of a State. □□ **seditious** adj. **seditiously** adv. [ME f. OF *sedition* or L *seditio* f. *sed-* = SE- + *ire* it- go]

seduce /sɪˈdjuːs/ v.tr. **1** tempt or entice into sexual activity or into wrongdoing. **2** coax or lead astray; tempt (*seduced by the smell of coffee*). □□ **seducer** n. **seducible** adj. [L *seducere seduct-* (as SE-, *ducere* lead)]

seduction /sɪˈdʌkʃ(ə)n/ n. **1** the act or an instance of seducing; the process of being seduced. **2** something that tempts or allures. [F *séduction* or L *seductio* (as SEDUCE)]

seductive /sɪˈdʌktɪv/ adj. tending to seduce; alluring, enticing. □□ **seductively** adv. **seductiveness** n. [SEDUCTION after *inductive* etc.]

seductress /sɪˈdʌktrɪs/ n. a female seducer. [obs. *seductor* male seducer (as SEDUCE)]

sedulous /ˈsedjʊləs/ adj. **1** persevering, diligent, assiduous. **2** (of an action etc.) deliberately and consciously continued; painstaking. □□ **sedulity** /sɪˈdjuːlɪtɪ/ n. **sedulously** adv. **sedulousness** n. [L *sedulus* zealous]

sedum /ˈsiːdəm/ n. any plant of the genus *Sedum*, with fleshy leaves and star-shaped yellow, pink, or white flowers, e.g. stonecrop. [L, = houseleek]

see[1] /siː/ v. (*past* **saw** /sɔː/; *past part.* **seen** /siːn/) **1** tr. discern by use of the eyes; observe; look at (*can you see that spider?; saw him fall over*). **2** intr. have or use the power of discerning objects with the eyes (*sees best at night*). **3** tr. discern mentally; understand (*I see what you mean; could not see the joke*). **4** tr. watch; be a spectator of (a film, game, etc.). **5** tr. ascertain or establish by inquiry or research or reflection (*I will see if the door is open*). **6** tr. consider; deduce from observation (*I see that you are a brave man*). **7** tr. contemplate; foresee mentally (*we saw that no good would come of it; can see myself doing this job indefinitely*). **8** tr. look at for information (usu. in *imper.* as a direction in or to a book: *see page 15*). **9** tr. meet or be near and recognize (*I saw your mother in town*). **10** tr. **a** meet socially (*sees her sister most weeks*). **b** meet regularly as a boyfriend or girlfriend; court (*is still seeing that tall man*). **11** tr. give an interview to (*the doctor will see you now*). **12** tr. visit to consult (*went to see the doctor*). **13** tr. find out or learn, esp. from a visual source (*I see the match has been cancelled*). **14** intr. reflect; consider further; wait until one knows more (*we shall have to see*). **15** tr. interpret or have an opinion of (*I see things differently now*). **16** tr. experience; have presented to one's attention (*I never thought I would see this day*). **17** tr. recognize as acceptable; foresee (*do you see your daughter marrying this man?*). **18** tr. observe without interfering (*stood by and saw them squander my money*). **19** tr. find attractive (*can't think what she sees in him*). **20** intr. (usu. foll. by *to*, or *that* + *infin.*) make provision for; ensure; attend to (*shall see to your request immediately; see that he gets home safely*) (cf. *see to it*). **21** tr. escort or conduct (to a place etc.) (*saw them home*). **22** tr. be a witness of (an event etc.) (*see the New Year in*). **23** tr. supervise (an action etc.) (*will stay and see the doors locked*). **24** tr. **a** (in gambling, esp. poker) equal (a bet). **b** equal the bet of (a player), esp. to see the player's cards. □ **as far as I can see** to the best of my understanding or belief. **as I see it** in my opinion. **do you see?** do you understand? **has seen better days** has declined from former prosperity, good condition, etc. **I'll be seeing you** colloq. an expression on parting. **I see** I understand (referring to an explanation etc.). **let me see** an appeal for time to think before speaking etc. **see about** attend to. **see after 1** take care of. **2** = *see about*. **see the back of** colloq. be rid of (an unwanted person or thing). **see a person damned first** colloq. refuse categorically and with hostility to do what a person wants. **see eye to eye** see EYE. **see fit** see FIT[1]. **see here!** = *look here*. **see into** investigate. **see life** gain experience of the world, often by enjoying oneself. **see the light 1** realize one's mistakes etc. **2** suddenly see the way to proceed. **3** undergo religious conversion. **see the light of day** (usu. with *neg.*) come into existence. **see off 1** be present at the departure of (a person) (*saw them off at Heathrow*). **2** colloq. ward off, get the better of (*managed to see off an investigation into their working methods*). **see out 1** accompany out of a building etc. **2** finish (a project etc.) completely. **3** remain awake, alive, etc., until the end of (a period). **4** last longer than; outlive. **see over** inspect; tour and examine. **see reason** see REASON. **see red** become suddenly enraged. **see a person right** make sure that a person is rewarded, safe, etc. **see service** see SERVICE. **see stars** colloq. see lights before one's eyes as a result of a blow on the head. **see things** have hallucinations or false imaginings. **see through 1** not be deceived by; detect the true nature of. **2** penetrate visually. **see-through** adj. (esp. of clothing) translucent. **see a person through** support a person during a difficult time. **see a thing through** persist with it until it is completed. **see to it** (foll. by *that* + clause) ensure (*see to it that I am not disturbed*) (cf. sense 20 of v.). **see one's way clear to** feel able or entitled to. **see the world** see WORLD. **see you** (or **see you later**) colloq. an expression on parting. **we shall see 1** let us await the outcome. **2** a formula for declining to act at once. **will see about it** a formula for declining to act at once. **you see 1** you understand. **2** you will understand when I explain. □□ **seeable** adj. [OE *sēon* f. Gmc]

see[2] /siː/ n. **1** the area under the authority of a bishop or archbishop, a diocese (*the see of Norwich*). **2** the office or jurisdiction of a bishop or archbishop (*fill a vacant see*). □ **See of Rome** the papacy, the Holy See. [ME f. AF *se(d)* ult. f. L *sedes* seat f. *sedēre* sit]

seed /siːd/ n. & v. —n. **1 a** a flowering plant's unit of reproduction (esp. in the form of grain) capable of developing into another such plant. **b** seeds collectively, esp. as collected for sowing (*is full of seed; to be kept for seed*). **2 a** semen. **b** milt. **3** (foll. by *of*) prime cause, beginning, germ (*seeds of doubt*). **4** archaic offspring, progeny, descendants (*the seed of Abraham*). **5** *Sport* a seeded player. **6** a small seedlike container for the application of radium etc. **7** a seed crystal. —v. **1** tr. **a** place seeds in. **b** sprinkle with or as with seed. **2** intr. sow seeds. **3** intr. produce or drop seed. **4** tr. remove seeds from (fruit etc.). **5** tr. place a crystal or crystalline substance in (a solution etc.) to cause crystallization or condensation (esp. in a cloud to produce rain). **6** tr. *Sport* **a** assign to (a strong competitor in a knockout competition) a position in an ordered list so that strong competitors do not meet each other in early rounds (*is seeded seventh*). **b** arrange (the order of play) in this way. **7** intr. go to seed. □ **go** (or **run**) **to seed 1** cease flowering as seed develops. **2** become degenerate, unkempt, ineffective, etc. **raise up seed** archaic beget children. **seed-bed 1** a bed of fine soil in which to sow seeds. **2** a place of development. **seed-cake** cake containing whole seeds esp. of caraway as flavouring. **seed-coat** the outer integument of a seed. **seed-corn 1** good quality corn kept for seed. **2** assets reused for future profit or benefit. **seed crystal** a crystal used to initiate crystallization. **seed-eater** a bird (esp. a finch) living mainly on seeds. **seed-fish** a fish that is ready to spawn. **seed-leaf** a cotyledon. **seed-lip** a basket for seed in sowing by hand. **seed money** money allocated to initiate a project. **seed-pearl** a very small pearl. **seed-plot** a place of development. **seed-potato** a potato kept for seed. **seed-time** the sowing season. **seed-vessel** a pericarp. □□ **seedless** adj. [OE *sǣd* f. Gmc, rel. to sow[1]]

seeder /ˈsiːdə(r)/ n. **1** a person or thing that seeds. **2** a machine for sowing seed, esp. a drill. **3** an apparatus for seeding raisins etc. **4** *Brit.* a spawning fish.

seedling /ˈsiːdlɪŋ/ n. a young plant, esp. one raised from seed and not from a cutting etc.

seedsman /'si:dzmən/ n. (pl. **-men**) a dealer in seeds.

seedy /'si:dɪ/ adj. (**seedier, seediest**) 1 full of seed. 2 going to seed. 3 shabby-looking, in worn clothes. 4 colloq. unwell. □□ **seedily** adv. **seediness** n.

seeing /'si:ɪŋ/ conj. & n. —conj. (usu. foll. by that + clause) considering that, inasmuch as, because (seeing that you do not know it yourself). —n. Astron. the quality of observed images as determined by atmospheric conditions.

seek /si:k/ v. (past and past part. **sought** /sɔ:t/) 1 a tr. make a search or inquiry for. b intr. (foll. by for, after) make a search or inquiry. 2 tr. a try or want to find or get. b ask for; request (sought help from him; seeks my aid). 3 tr. (foll. by to + infin.) endeavour or try. 4 tr. make for or resort to (a place or person, for advice, health, etc.) (sought his bed; sought a fortune-teller; sought the shore). 5 tr. archaic aim at, attempt. 6 intr. (foll. by to) archaic resort. □ **seek dead** an order to a retriever to find killed game. **seek out** 1 search for and find. 2 single out for companionship, etc. **sought-after** much in demand; generally desired or courted. **to seek** (or **much to seek** or **far to seek**) deficient, lacking, or not yet found (the reason is not far to seek; an efficient leader is yet to seek). □□ **seeker** n. (also in comb.). [OE sēcan f. Gmc]

seel /si:l/ v.tr. archaic close (a person's eyes). [obs. sile f. F ciller, siller, or med.L ciliare f. L cilium eyelid]

seem /si:m/ v.intr. 1 give the impression or sensation of being (seems ridiculous; seems certain to win). 2 (foll. by to + infin.) appear or be perceived or ascertained (he seems to be breathing; they seem to have left). □ **can't seem to** colloq. seem unable to. **do not seem to** colloq. somehow do not (I do not seem to like him). **it seems** (or **would seem**) (often foll. by that + clause) it appears to be true or the fact (in a hesitant, guarded, or ironical statement). [ME f. ON sœma honour f. sœmr fitting]

seeming¹ /'si:mɪŋ/ adj. 1 apparent but perhaps not real (with seeming sincerity). 2 apparent only; ostensible (the seeming and the real; seeming-virtuous). □□ **seemingly** adv.

seeming² /'si:mɪŋ/ n. literary 1 appearance, aspect. 2 deceptive appearance.

seemly /'si:mlɪ/ adj. (**seemlier, seemliest**) conforming to propriety or good taste; decorous, suitable. □□ **seemliness** n. [ME f. ON sœmiligr (as SEEM)]

seen past part. of SEE¹.

seep /si:p/ v. & n. —v.intr. ooze out; percolate slowly. —n. US a place where petroleum etc. oozes slowly out of the ground. [perh. dial. form of OE sipian to soak]

seepage /'si:pɪdʒ/ n. 1 the act of seeping. 2 the quantity that seeps out.

seer¹ /'si:ə(r), sɪə(r)/ n. 1 a person who sees. 2 a prophet; a person who sees visions; a person of supposed supernatural insight esp. as regards the future. [ME f. SEE¹]

seer² /sɪə(r)/ n. an Indian (varying) measure of weight (about one kilogram) or liquid measure (about one litre). [Hindi ser]

seersucker /'sɪə,sʌkə(r)/ n. material of linen, cotton, etc., with a puckered surface. [Pers. šir o šakar, lit. 'milk and sugar']

see-saw /'si:sɔ:/ n., v., adj., & adv. —n. 1 a a device consisting of a long plank balanced on a central support for children to sit on at each end and move up and down by pushing the ground with their feet. b a game played on this. 2 an up-and-down or to-and-fro motion. 3 a contest in which the advantage repeatedly changes from one side to the other. —v.intr. 1 play on a see-saw. 2 move up and down as on a see-saw. 3 vacillate in policy, emotion, etc. —adj. & adv. with up-and-down or backward-and-forward motion (see-saw motion). □ **go see-saw** vacillate or alternate. [redupl. of SAW¹]

seethe /si:ð/ v. 1 intr. boil, bubble over. 2 intr. be very agitated, esp. with anger (seething with discontent; I was seething inwardly). 3 tr. & intr. archaic cook by boiling. □□ **seethingly** adv. [OE sēothan f. Gmc]

segment /'segmənt/ n. & v. —n. 1 each of several parts into which a thing is or can be divided or marked off. 2 Geom. a part of a figure cut off by a line or plane intersecting it, esp.: a the part of a circle enclosed between an arc and a chord. b the part of a line included between two points. c the part of a sphere

cut off by any plane not passing through the centre. 3 the smallest distinct part of a spoken utterance. 4 Zool. each of the longitudinal sections of the body of certain animals (e.g. worms). —v. /usu. -'ment/ 1 intr. & tr. divide into segments. 2 intr. Biol. (of a cell) undergo cleavage or divide into many cells. □□ **segmental** /-'ment(ə)l/ adj. **segmentalize** /-'mentə,laɪz/ v.tr. (also **-ise**). **segmentalization** /-,mentəlaɪ'zeɪʃ(ə)n/ n. **segmentally** /-'mentəlɪ/ adv. **segmentary** adj. **segmentation** /-'teɪʃ(ə)n/ n. [L segmentum f. secare cut]

sego /'si:gəʊ/ n. (pl. **-os**) (in full **sego lily**) a N. American plant, Calochortus nuttallii, with green and white bell-shaped flowers. [Paiute]

Segovia /se'gəʊvɪə/, Andrés (1893–1987), Spanish guitarist and composer. More than any other person he is responsible for the revival of interest in the guitar as a 'classical' instrument, elevating it to use as a major concert instrument rather than for a small room only.

segregate¹ /'segrɪ,geɪt/ v. 1 tr. put apart from the rest; isolate. 2 tr. enforce racial segregation on (persons) or in (a community etc.). 3 intr. separate from a mass and collect together. 4 intr. Biol. (of alleles) separate into dominant and recessive groups. □□ **segregable** /-gəb(ə)l/ adj. **segregative** adj. [L segregare (as SE-, grex gregis flock)]

segregate² /'segrɪgət/ adj. 1 Zool. simple or solitary, not compound. 2 archaic set apart, separate. [L segregatus past part. (as SEGREGATE¹)]

segregation /,segrɪ'geɪʃ(ə)n/ n. 1 enforced separation of racial groups in a community etc. 2 the act or an instance of segregating; the state of being segregated. □□ **segregational** adj. **segregationist** n. & adj. [LL segregatio (as SEGREGATE¹)]

segue /'segweɪ/ v. & n. esp. Mus. —v.intr. (**segues, segued, seguing**) (usu. foll. by into) go on without a pause. —n. an uninterrupted transition from one song or melody to another. [It., = follows]

seguidilla /,segɪ'dɪljə/ n. 1 a Spanish dance in triple time. 2 the music for this. [Sp. f. seguida following f. seguir follow]

Sehnsucht /'zeɪnzu:xt/ n. yearning, wistful longing. [G]

sei /seɪ/ n. a small rorqual, Balaenoptera borealis. [Norw. sejhval sei whale]

seicento /seɪ'tʃentəʊ/ n. the style of Italian art and literature of the 17th c. □□ **seicentist** n. **seicentoist** n. [It., = 600, used with ref. to the years 1600–99]

seiche /seɪʃ/ n. a fluctuation in the water-level of a lake etc., usu. caused by changes in barometric pressure. [Swiss F]

Seidlitz powder /'sedlɪts/ n. (US **Seidlitz powders**) a laxative medicine of two powders mixed separately with water and then poured together to effervesce. [named with ref. to the mineral water of Seidlitz in Bohemia]

seif /si:f, seɪf/ n. (in full **seif dune**) a sand-dune in the form of a long narrow ridge. [Arab. saif sword (from its shape)]

seigneur /seɪ'njɜ:(r)/ n. (also **seignior** /'seɪnjə(r)/) a feudal lord; the lord of a manor. □ **grand seigneur** /grã/ a person of high rank or noble presence. □□ **seigneurial** adj. **seigniorial** /-'njɔ:rɪəl/ adj. [ME f. OF seigneur, seignor f. L SENIOR]

seigniorage /'seɪnjərɪdʒ/ n. (also **seignorage**) 1 a profit made by issuing currency, esp. by issuing coins rated above their intrinsic value. b hist. the Crown's right to a percentage on bullion brought to a mint for coining. 2 hist. something claimed by a sovereign or feudal superior as a prerogative. [ME f. OF seignorage, seigneurage (as SEIGNEUR)]

seigniory /'seɪnjərɪ/ n. (pl. **-ies**) 1 lordship, sovereign authority. 2 (also **seigneury**) a seigneur's domain. [ME f. OF seigniorie (as SEIGNEUR)]

Seikan Tunnel /'seɪkən/ the world's longest underwater tunnel, linking the Japanese islands of Hokkaido and Honshu which are separated by the Tsungaru Strait. Completed in 1988, the tunnel is 51.7 km (32.3 miles) in length.

Seine /seɪn/ a river of northern France flowing 761 km (473 miles) from Burgundy to the English Channel near Le Havre. The cities of Paris and Rouen lie along its course.

seine /seɪn/ n. & v. —n. (also **seine-net**) a fishing-net for encircling fish, with floats at the top and weights at the bottom edge, and usu. hauled ashore. —v.intr. & tr. fish or catch with a seine. □□ **seiner** n. [ME f. OF saïne, & OE segne f. WG f. L sagena f. Gk sagēnē]

seise var. of SEIZE 9.

seisin /ˈsiːzɪn/ n. (also **seizin**) Law **1** possession of land by freehold. **2** the act of taking such possession. **3** what is so held. [ME f. AF sesine, OF seisine, saisine (as SEIZE)]

seismic /ˈsaɪzmɪk/ adj. of or relating to an earthquake or earthquakes or similar vibrations. □ **seismic survey** the use of artificially generated seismic waves to explore the structure of underground rocks etc., used in mining and in the oil and gas extraction industries. □□ **seismal** adj. **seismical** adj. **seismically** adv. [Gk seismos earthquake f. seiō shake]

seismo- /ˈsaɪzməʊ/ comb. form earthquake. [Gk seismos]

seismogram /ˈsaɪzməˌɡræm/ n. a record given by a seismograph.

seismograph /ˈsaɪzməˌɡrɑːf/ n. an instrument that records the force, direction, etc., of earthquakes. □□ **seismographic** /-ˈɡræfɪk/ adj. **seismographical** /-ˈɡræfɪk(ə)l/ adj.

seismology /saɪzˈmɒlədʒɪ/ n. the scientific study and recording of earthquakes and related phenomena. □□ **seismological** /-məˈlɒdʒɪk(ə)l/ adj. **seismologically** /-məˈlɒdʒɪkəlɪ/ adv. **seismologist** n.

seize /siːz/ v. **1** tr. take hold of forcibly or suddenly. **2** tr. take possession of forcibly (seized the fortress; seized power). **3** tr. take possession of (contraband goods, documents, etc.) by warrant or legal right, confiscate, impound. **4** tr. affect suddenly (panic seized us; was seized by apoplexy; was seized with remorse). **5** tr. take advantage of (an opportunity). **6** tr. comprehend quickly or clearly. **7** intr. (usu. foll. by on, upon) **a** take hold forcibly or suddenly. **b** take advantage eagerly (seized on a pretext). **8** intr. (usu. foll. by up) (of a moving part in a machine) become stuck or jammed from undue heat, friction, etc. **9** tr. (also **seise**) (usu. foll. by of) Law put in possession of. **10** tr. Naut. fasten or attach by binding with turns of yarn etc. □ **seized** (or **seised**) **of 1** possessing legally. **2** aware or informed of. □□ **seizable** adj. **seizer** n. [ME f. OF seizir, saisir give seisin f. Frank. f. L sacire f. Gmc]

seizin var. of SEISIN.

seizing /ˈsiːzɪŋ/ n. Naut. a cord or cords used for seizing (see SEIZE 10).

seizure /ˈsiːʒə(r)/ n. **1** the act or an instance of seizing; the state of being seized. **2** a sudden attack of apoplexy etc., a stroke.

sejant /ˈsiːdʒ(ə)nt/ adj. (placed after noun) Heraldry (of an animal) sitting upright on its haunches. [properly seiant f. OF var. of seant sitting f. seoir f. L sedēre sit]

Sekhmet /ˈsekmet/ Egyptian Mythol. a ferocious lioness-goddess, counterpart of the gentle cat-goddess Bastet, and wife of Ptah at Memphis. Her messengers were fearful creatures who could inflict disease and other scourges upon mankind.

Sekt /zekt/ n. a German sparkling white wine. [G]

selachian /sɪˈleɪkɪən/ n. & adj. —n. any fish of the subclass Selachii, including sharks and dogfish. —adj. of or relating to this subclass. [mod.L Selachii f. Gk selakhos shark]

seladang /səˈlɑːdæŋ/ n. a Malayan gaur. [Malay]

selah /ˈsiːlə/ int. often used at the end of a verse in Psalms and Habakkuk, supposed to be a musical direction. [Heb. se·lāh]

Selangor /səˈlæŋɡə(r)/ a State of Malaysia, on the west coast of the Malay peninsula; pop. (1980) 1,515,500; capital, Shah Alam.

seldom /ˈseldəm/ adv. & adj. —adv. rarely, not often. —adj. rare, uncommon. [OE seldan f. Gmc]

select /sɪˈlekt/ v. & adj. —v.tr. choose, esp. as the best or most suitable. —adj. **1** chosen for excellence or suitability; choice. **2** (of a society etc.) exclusive, cautious in admitting members. □ **select committee** see COMMITTEE. □□ **selectable** adj. **selectness** n. [L seligere select- (as SE-, legere choose)]

selectee /ˌsɪlekˈtiː/ n. US a conscript.

selection /sɪˈlekʃ(ə)n/ n. **1** the act or an instance of selecting; the state of being selected. **2** a selected person or thing. **3** things from which a choice may be made. **4** Biol. the process in which environmental and genetic influences determine which types

of organism thrive better than others, regarded as a factor in evolution. □□ **selectional** adj. **selectionally** adv. [L selectio (as SELECT)]

selective /sɪˈlektɪv/ adj. **1** using or characterized by selection. **2** able to select, esp. (of a radio receiver) able to respond to a chosen frequency without interference from others. □ **selective service** US hist. service in the armed forces under conscription. □□ **selectively** adv. **selectiveness** n. **selectivity** /ˌsɪlekˈtɪvɪtɪ, ˌsel-, ˌsiːl-/ n.

selector /sɪˈlektə(r)/ n. **1** a person who selects, esp. one who selects a representative team in a sport. **2** a device that selects, esp. a device in a vehicle that selects the required gear.

Selene /sɪˈliːnɪ/ Gk Mythol. the goddess of the moon, identified with Artemis, perhaps because both had been identified with Hecate. She has few myths (for the best known see ENDYMION) and little cult in Greece; it is the moon itself rather than the goddess that played a role in Greek magic, folklore, and poetry. [Gk selēnē moon]

selenite /ˈselɪˌnaɪt/ n. a form of gypsum occurring as transparent crystals or thin plates. □□ **selenitic** /-ˈnɪtɪk/ adj. [L selenites f. Gk selēnītēs lithos moonstone f. selēnē moon]

selenium /sɪˈliːnɪəm/ n. Chem. a non-metallic element occurring naturally in various metallic sulphide ores and characterized by the variation of its electrical resistivity with intensity of illumination. It occurs in a number of red, black, and grey allotropic forms. Selenium (which is a semiconductor) has various applications in electronics. It is used in rectifiers and photoelectric cells, and for colouring glass and ceramics. ¶ Symb.: Se; atomic number 34. □ **selenium cell** a piece of this used as a photoelectric device. □□ **selenate** /ˈselɪˌneɪt/ n. **selenic** /sɪˈliːnɪk/ adj. **selenious** adj. [mod.L f. Gk selēnē moon + -IUM]

seleno- /sɪˈliːnəʊ/ comb. form moon. [Gk selēnē moon]

selenography /ˌsiːlɪˈnɒɡrəfɪ/ n. the study or mapping of the moon. □□ **selenographer** n. **selenographic** /-nəˈɡræfɪk/ adj.

selenology /ˌsiːlɪˈnɒlədʒɪ/ n. the scientific study of the moon. □□ **selenologist** n.

Seleucid /sɪˈluːsɪd/ adj. & n. —adj. of the dynasty founded by Seleucus Nicator, one of the generals of Alexander the Great, ruling over Syria and a great part of western Asia 312–65 BC. Its capital was at Antioch. —n. a member of this dynasty.

self /self/ n. & adj. —n. (pl. **selves** /selvz/) **1** a person's or thing's own individuality or essence (showed his true self). **2** a person or thing as the object of introspection or reflexive action (the consciousness of self). **3 a** one's own interests or pleasure (cares for nothing but self). **b** concentration on these (self is a bad guide to happiness). **4** Commerce or colloq. myself, yourself, himself, etc. (cheque drawn to self; ticket admitting self and friend). **5** used in phrases equivalent to myself, yourself, himself, etc. (his very self; your good selves). **6** (pl. **selfs**) a flower of uniform colour, or of the natural wild colour. —adj. **1** of the same colour as the rest or throughout. **2** (of a flower) of the natural wild colour. **3** (of colour) uniform, the same throughout. □ **one's better self** one's nobler impulses. **one's former** (or **old**) **self** oneself as one formerly was. [OE f. Gmc]

self- /self/ comb. form expressing reflexive action: **1** of or directed towards oneself or itself (self-respect; self-cleaning). **2** by oneself or itself, esp. without external agency (self-evident). **3** on, in, for, or relating to oneself or itself (self-absorbed; self-confident).

self-abandon /ˌselfəˈbænd(ə)n/ n. (also **self-abandonment**) the abandonment of oneself, esp. to passion or an impulse. □□ **self-abandoned** adj.

self-abasement /ˌselfəˈbeɪsmənt/ n. the abasement of oneself; self-humiliation; cringing.

self-abhorrence /ˌselfəbˈhɒrəns/ n. the abhorrence of oneself; self-hatred.

self-abnegation /ˌselfˌæbnɪˈɡeɪʃ(ə)n/ n. the abnegation of oneself, one's interests, needs, etc.; self-sacrifice.

self-absorption /ˌselfəbˈzɔːpʃ(ə)n/ n. **1** absorption in oneself. **2** Physics the absorption, by a body, of radiation emitted within it. □□ **self-absorbed** /-ˈzɔːbd/ adj.

self-abuse /ˌselfəˈbjuːs/ n. **1** the reviling or abuse of oneself. **2** archaic masturbation.

self-accusation /selfˌækjuːˈzeɪʃ(ə)n/ n. the accusing of oneself. □□ **self-accusatory** /-əˈkjuːzətərɪ/ adj.

self-acting /selfˈæktɪŋ/ adj. acting without external influence or control; automatic. □□ **self-action** /-ˈækʃ(ə)n/ n. **self-activity** /-ækˈtɪvɪtɪ/ n.

self-addressed /ˌselfəˈdrest/ adj. (of an envelope etc.) having one's own address on for return communication.

self-adhesive /ˌselfədˈhiːsɪv/ adj. (of an envelope, label, etc.) adhesive, esp. without being moistened.

self-adjusting /ˌselfəˈdʒʌstɪŋ/ adj. (of machinery etc.) adjusting itself. □□ **self-adjustment** n.

self-admiration /selfˌædməˈreɪʃ(ə)n/ n. the admiration of oneself; pride; conceit.

self-advancement /ˌselfədˈvɑːnsmənt/ n. the advancement of oneself.

self-advertisement /ˌselfədˈvɜːtɪsmənt/ n. the advertising or promotion of oneself. □□ **self-advertiser** /-ˈædvəˌtaɪzə(r)/ n.

self-affirmation /selfˌæfəˈmeɪʃ(ə)n/ n. Psychol. the recognition and assertion of the existence of the conscious self.

self-aggrandizement /ˌselfəˈgrændɪzmənt/ n. the act or process of enriching oneself or making oneself powerful. □□ **self-aggrandizing** /-ˈgrændaɪzɪŋ/ adj.

self-analysis /ˌselfəˈnæləsɪs/ n. Psychol. the analysis of oneself, one's motives, character, etc. □□ **self-analysing** /-ˈænəˌlaɪzɪŋ/ adj.

self-appointed /ˌselfəˈpɔɪntɪd/ adj. designated so by oneself, not authorized by another (a self-appointed guardian).

self-appreciation /ˌselfəˌpriːʃɪˈeɪʃ(ə)n/ n. a good opinion of oneself; conceit.

self-approbation /selfˌæprəˈbeɪʃ(ə)n/ n. = SELF-APPRECIATION.

self-approval /ˌselfəˈpruːv(ə)l/ n. = SELF-APPRECIATION.

self-assertion /ˌselfəˈsɜːʃ(ə)n/ n. the aggressive promotion of oneself, one's views, etc. □□ **self-asserting** adj. **self-assertive** adj. **self-assertiveness** n.

self-assurance /ˌselfəˈʃʊərəns/ n. confidence in one's own abilities etc. □□ **self-assured** adj. **self-assuredly** adv.

self-aware /ˌselfəˈweə(r)/ adj. conscious of one's character, feelings, motives, etc. □□ **self-awareness** n.

self-begotten /ˌselfbɪˈgɒt(ə)n/ adj. produced by oneself or itself; not made externally.

self-betrayal /ˌselfbɪˈtreɪəl/ n. **1** the betrayal of oneself. **2** the inadvertent revelation of one's true thoughts etc.

self-binder /selfˈbaɪndə(r)/ n. a reaping machine with an automatic mechanism for binding the sheaves.

self-born /selfˈbɔːn/ adj. produced by itself or oneself; not made externally.

self-catering /selfˈkeɪtərɪŋ/ adj. (esp. of a holiday or holiday premises) providing rented accommodation with cooking facilities but without food.

self-censorship /selfˈsensəʃɪp/ n. the censoring of oneself.

self-centred /selfˈsentəd/ adj. preoccupied with one's own personality or affairs. □□ **self-centredly** adv. **self-centredness** n.

self-certification /selfˌsɜːtɪfɪˈkeɪʃ(ə)n/ n. the practice by which an employee declares in writing that an absence from work was due to illness.

self-cleaning /selfˈkliːnɪŋ/ adj. (esp. of an oven) cleaning itself when heated etc.

self-closing /selfˈkləʊzɪŋ/ adj. (of a door etc.) closing automatically.

self-cocking /selfˈkɒkɪŋ/ adj. (of a gun) with the hammer raised by the trigger, not by hand.

self-collected /ˌselfkəˈlektɪd/ adj. composed, serene, self-assured.

self-coloured /selfˈkʌləd/ adj. **1 a** having the same colour throughout (buttons and belt are self-coloured). **b** (of material) natural; undyed. **2 a** (of a flower) of uniform colour. **b** having its colour unchanged by cultivation or hybridization.

self-command /ˌselfkəˈmɑːnd/ n. = SELF-CONTROL.

self-communion /ˌselfkəˈmjuːnɪən/ n. meditation upon one's own character, conduct, etc.

self-conceit /ˌselfkənˈsiːt/ n. = SELF-SATISFACTION. □□ **self-conceited** adj.

self-condemnation /selfˌkɒndemˈneɪʃ(ə)n/ n. **1** the blaming of oneself. **2** the inadvertent revelation of one's own sin, crime, etc. □□ **self-condemned** /-kənˈdemd/ adj.

self-confessed /ˌselfkənˈfest/ adj. openly admitting oneself to be (a self-confessed thief).

self-confidence /selfˈkɒnfɪd(ə)ns/ n. = SELF-ASSURANCE. □□ **self-confident** adj. **self-confidently** adv.

self-congratulation /ˌselfkənˌgrætjʊˈleɪʃ(ə)n/ n. = SELF-SATISFACTION. □□ **self-congratulatory** /-kənˈgrætʊlətərɪ/ adj.

self-conquest /selfˈkɒŋkwest/ n. the overcoming of one's worst characteristics etc.

self-conscious /selfˈkɒnʃəs/ adj. **1** socially inept through embarrassment or shyness. **2** Philos. having knowledge of one's own existence; self-contemplating. □□ **self-consciously** adv. **self-consciousness** n.

self-consistent /ˌselfkənˈsɪst(ə)nt/ adj. (of parts of the same whole etc.) consistent; not conflicting. □□ **self-consistency** n.

self-constituted /selfˈkɒnstɪˌtjuːtɪd/ adj. (of a person, group, etc.) assuming a function without authorization or right; self-appointed.

self-contained /ˌselfkənˈteɪnd/ adj. **1** (of a person) uncommunicative; independent. **2** Brit. (esp. of living-accommodation) complete in itself. □□ **self-containment** n.

self-contempt /ˌselfkənˈtempt/ n. contempt for oneself. □□ **self-contemptuous** adj.

self-content /ˌselfkənˈtent/ n. satisfaction with oneself, one's life, achievements, etc. □□ **self-contented** adj.

self-contradiction /selfˌkɒntrəˈdɪkʃ(ə)n/ n. internal inconsistency. □□ **self-contradictory** adj.

self-control /ˌselfkənˈtrəʊl/ n. the power of controlling one's external reactions, emotions, etc. □□ **self-controlled** adj.

self-convicted /ˌselfkənˈvɪktɪd/ adj. = SELF-CONDEMNED (see SELF-CONDEMNATION).

self-correcting /ˌselfkəˈrektɪŋ/ adj. correcting itself without external help.

self-created /ˌselfkrɪˈeɪtɪd/ adj. created by oneself or itself. □□ **self-creation** /-ˈeɪʃ(ə)n/ n.

self-critical /selfˈkrɪtɪk(ə)l/ adj. critical of oneself, one's abilities, etc. □□ **self-criticism** /-ˌsɪz(ə)m/ n.

self-deception /ˌselfdɪˈsepʃ(ə)n/ n. deceiving oneself esp. concerning one's true feelings etc. □□ **self-deceit** /-ˈdiːsiːt/ n. **self-deceiver** /-dɪˈsiːvə(r)/ n. **self-deceiving** /-dɪˈsiːvɪŋ/ adj. **self-deceptive** adj.

self-defeating /ˌselfdɪˈfiːtɪŋ/ adj. (of an attempt, action, etc.) doomed to failure because of internal inconsistencies etc.

self-defence /ˌselfdɪˈfens/ n. **1** an aggressive act, speech, etc., intended as defence (had to hit him in self-defence). **2** (usu. **the noble art of self-defence**) boxing. □□ **self-defensive** adj.

self-delight /ˌselfdɪˈlaɪt/ n. delight in oneself or one's existence.

self-delusion /ˌselfdɪˈluːʒ(ə)n, -ˈljuːʒ(ə)n/ n. the act or an instance of deluding oneself.

self-denial /ˌselfdɪˈnaɪəl/ n. = SELF-ABNEGATION. □ **self-denying ordinance** hist. a resolution of the Long Parliament 1645 depriving Members of Parliament of civil and military office. □□ **self-denying** adj.

self-dependence /ˌselfdɪˈpend(ə)ns/ adj. dependence only on oneself or itself; independence. □□ **self-dependent** adj.

self-deprecation /selfˌdeprɪˈkeɪʃ(ə)n/ n. the act of disparaging or belittling oneself. □□ **self-deprecating** /-ˈdeprɪˌkeɪtɪŋ/ adj. **self-deprecatingly** /-ˈdeprɪˌkeɪtɪŋlɪ/ adv.

self-despair /ˌselfdɪˈspeə(r)/ n. despair with oneself.

self-destroying /ˌselfdɪˈstrɔɪɪŋ/ adj. destroying oneself or itself.

self-destruct /ˌselfdɪˈstrʌkt/ v. & adj. esp. US —v.intr. (of a spacecraft, bomb, etc.) explode or disintegrate automatically, esp. when pre-set to do so. —attrib.adj. enabling a thing to self-destruct (a self-destruct device).

self-destruction /ˌselfdɪ'strʌkʃ(ə)n/ n. **1** the process or an act of destroying oneself or itself. **2** esp. *US* the process or an act of self-destructing. □□ **self-destructive** adj. **self-destructively** adv.

self-determination /ˌselfdɪˌtɜːmɪ'neɪʃ(ə)n/ n. **1** a nation's right to determine its own allegiance, government, etc. **2** the ability to act with free will, as opposed to fatalism etc. □□ **self-determined** /-'tɜːmɪnd/ adj. **self-determining** /-'tɜːmɪnɪŋ/ adj.

self-development /ˌselfdɪ'veləpmənt/ n. the development of oneself, one's abilities, etc.

self-devotion /ˌselfdɪ'vəʊʃ(ə)n/ n. the devotion of oneself to a person or cause.

self-discipline /self'dɪsɪplɪn/ n. the act of or ability to apply oneself, control one's feelings, etc.; self-control. □□ **self-disciplined** adj.

self-discovery /ˌselfdɪ'skʌvərɪ/ n. the process of acquiring insight into oneself, one's character, desires, etc.

self-disgust /ˌselfdɪs'gʌst/ n. disgust with oneself.

self-doubt /self'daʊt/ n. lack of confidence in oneself, one's abilities, etc.

self-drive /self'draɪv/ adj. (of a hired vehicle) driven by the hirer.

self-educated /self'edjuːˌkeɪtɪd/ adj. educated by oneself by reading etc., without formal instruction. □□ **self-education** /-'keɪʃ(ə)n/ n.

self-effacing /ˌselfɪ'feɪsɪŋ/ adj. retiring; modest; timid. □□ **self-effacement** n. **self-effacingly** adv.

self-elective /ˌselfɪ'lektɪv/ adj. (of a committee etc.) proceeding esp. by co-opting members etc.

self-employed /ˌselfɪm'plɔɪd/ adj. working for oneself, as a freelance or owner of a business etc.; not employed by an employer. □□ **self-employment** n.

self-esteem /ˌselfɪ'stiːm/ n. a good opinion of oneself.

self-evident /self'evɪd(ə)nt/ adj. obvious; without the need of evidence or further explanation. □□ **self-evidence** n. **self-evidently** adv.

self-examination /ˌselfɪgˌzæmɪ'neɪʃ(ə)n/ n. **1** the study of one's own conduct, reasons, etc. **2** the examining of one's body for signs of illness etc.

self-executing /self'eksɪˌkjuːtɪŋ/ adj. *Law* (of a law, legal clause, etc.) not needing legislation etc. to be enforced; automatic.

self-existent /ˌselfɪg'zɪst(ə)nt/ adj. existing without prior cause; independent.

self-explanatory /ˌselfɪk'splænətərɪ/ adj. easily understood; not needing explanation.

self-expression /ˌselfɪk'spreʃ(ə)n/ n. the expression of one's feelings, thoughts, etc., esp. in writing, painting, music, etc. □□ **self-expressive** adj.

self-faced /self'feɪst/ adj. (of stone) unhewn; undressed.

self-feeder /self'fiːdə(r)/ n. **1** a furnace, machine, etc., that renews its own fuel or material automatically. **2** a device for supplying food to farm animals automatically. □□ **self-feeding** adj.

self-fertile /self'fɜːtaɪl/ adj. (of a plant etc.) self-fertilizing. □□ **self-fertility** /-'tɪlɪtɪ/ n.

self-fertilization /self,fɜːtɪlaɪ'zeɪʃ(ə)n/ n. the fertilization of plants by their own pollen, not from others. □□ **self-fertilized** /-'fɜːtɪˌlaɪzd/ adj. **self-fertilizing** /-'fɜːtɪˌlaɪzɪŋ/ adj.

self-financing /self'faɪnænsɪŋ/ adj. that finances itself, esp. (of a project or undertaking) that pays for its own implementation or continuation. □□ **self-finance** v.tr.

self-flattery /self'flætərɪ/ n. = SELF-APPRECIATION. □□ **self-flattering** adj.

self-forgetful /ˌselffə'getfʊl/ adj. unselfish. □□ **self-forgetfulness** n.

self-fulfilling /ˌselffʊl'fɪlɪŋ/ adj. (of a prophecy, forecast, etc.) bound to come true as a result of actions brought about by its being made.

self-fulfilment /ˌselffʊl'fɪlmənt/ n. (*US* **-fulfillment**) the fulfilment of one's own hopes and ambitions.

self-generating /self'dʒenəˌreɪtɪŋ/ adj. generated by itself or oneself, not externally.

self-glorification /self,glɔːrɪfɪ'keɪʃ(ə)n/ n. the proclamation of oneself, one's abilities, etc.; self-satisfaction.

self-government /self'gʌvənmənt/ n. **1** (esp. of a former colony etc.) government by its own people. **2** = SELF-CONTROL. □□ **self-governed** adj. **self-governing** adj.

self-hate /self'heɪt/ n. = SELF-HATRED.

self-hatred /self'heɪtrɪd/ n. hatred of oneself, esp. of one's actual self when contrasted with one's imagined self.

self-heal /self'hiːl/ n. any of several plants, esp. *Prunella vulgaris*, believed to have healing properties.

self-help /self'help/ n. **1** the theory that individuals should provide for their own support and improvement in society. **2** the act or faculty of providing for or improving oneself.

selfhood /'selfhʊd/ n. personality, separate and conscious existence.

self-image /self'ɪmɪdʒ/ n. one's own idea or picture of oneself, esp. in relation to others.

self-importance /ˌselfɪm'pɔːt(ə)ns/ n. a high opinion of oneself; pompousness. □□ **self-important** adj. **self-importantly** adv.

self-imposed /ˌselfɪm'pəʊzd/ adj. (of a task or condition etc.) imposed on and by oneself, not externally (*self-imposed exile*).

self-improvement /ˌselfɪm'pruːvmənt/ n. the improvement of one's own position or disposition by one's own efforts.

self-induced /ˌselfɪn'djuːst/ adj. **1** induced by oneself or itself. **2** *Electr.* produced by self-induction.

self-inductance /ˌselfɪn'dʌkt(ə)ns/ n. *Electr.* the property of an electric circuit that causes an electromotive force to be generated in it by a change in the current flowing through it (cf. *mutual inductance*).

self-induction /ˌselfɪn'dʌkʃ(ə)n/ n. *Electr.* the production of an electromotive force in a circuit when the current in that circuit is varied. □□ **self-inductive** adj.

self-indulgent /ˌselfɪn'dʌldʒ(ə)nt/ adj. indulging or tending to indulge oneself in pleasure, idleness, etc. □□ **self-indulgence** n. **self-indulgently** adv.

self-inflicted /ˌselfɪn'flɪktɪd/ adj. (esp. of a wound, damage, etc.) inflicted by and on oneself, not externally.

self-interest /self'ɪntrəst, -trɪst/ n. one's personal interest or advantage. □□ **self-interested** adj.

selfish /'selfɪʃ/ adj. **1** deficient in consideration for others; concerned chiefly with one's own personal profit or pleasure; actuated by self-interest. **2** (of a motive etc.) appealing to self-interest. □□ **selfishly** adv. **selfishness** n.

self-justification /self,dʒʌstɪfɪ'keɪʃ(ə)n/ n. the justification or excusing of oneself, one's actions, etc.

self-knowledge /self'nɒlɪdʒ/ n. the understanding of oneself, one's motives, etc.

selfless /'selflɪs/ adj. disregarding oneself or one's own interests; unselfish. □□ **selflessly** adv. **selflessness** n.

self-loading /self'ləʊdɪŋ/ adj. (esp. of a gun) loading itself. □□ **self-loader** n.

self-locking /self'lɒkɪŋ/ adj. locking itself.

self-love /self'lʌv/ n. **1** selfishness; self-indulgence. **2** *Philos.* regard for one's own well-being and happiness.

self-made /'selfmeɪd/ adj. **1** successful or rich by one's own effort. **2** made by oneself.

self-mastery /self'mɑːstərɪ/ n. = SELF-CONTROL.

selfmate /'selfmeɪt/ n. *Chess* checkmate in which a player forces the opponent to achieve checkmate.

self-mocking /self'mɒkɪŋ/ adj. mocking oneself or itself.

self-motion /self'məʊʃ(ə)n/ n. motion caused by oneself or itself, not externally. □□ **self-moving** /-'muːvɪŋ/ adj.

self-motivated /self'məʊtɪˌveɪtɪd/ adj. acting on one's own initiative without external pressure. □□ **self-motivation** /-'veɪʃ(ə)n/ n.

self-murder /self'mɜːdə(r)/ *n.* = SUICIDE. □□ **self-murderer** *n.*

self-neglect /ˌselfnɪ'glekt/ *n.* neglect of oneself.

selfness /'selfnɪs/ *n.* **1** individuality, personality, essence. **2** selfishness or self-regard.

self-opinionated /ˌselfə'pɪnjə͜neɪtɪd/ *adj.* **1** stubbornly adhering to one's own opinions. **2** arrogant. □□ **self-opinion** *n.*

self-perpetuating /ˌselfpə'petjuːˌeɪtɪŋ/ *adj.* perpetuating itself or oneself without external agency. □□ **self-perpetuation** /-'eɪʃ(ə)n/ *n.*

self-pity /self'pɪtɪ/ *n.* extreme sorrow for one's own troubles etc. □□ **self-pitying** *adj.* **self-pityingly** *adv.*

self-pollination /ˌselfˌpɒlɪ'neɪʃ(ə)n/ *n.* the pollination of a flower by pollen from the same plant. □□ **self-pollinated** *adj.* **self-pollinating** *adj.* **self-pollinator** *n.*

self-portrait /self'pɔːtrɪt/ *n.* a portrait or description of an artist, writer, etc., by himself or herself.

self-possessed /ˌselfpə'zest/ *adj.* habitually exercising self-control; composed. □□ **self-possession** /-'zeʃ(ə)n/ *n.*

self-praise /self'preɪz/ *n.* boasting; self-glorification.

self-preservation /ˌselfˌprezə'veɪʃ(ə)n/ *n.* **1** the preservation of one's own life, safety, etc. **2** this as a basic instinct of human beings and animals.

self-proclaimed /ˌselfprə'kleɪmd/ *adj.* proclaimed by oneself or itself to be such.

self-propagating /self'prɒpəˌɡeɪtɪŋ/ *adj.* (esp. of a plant) able to propagate itself.

self-propelled /ˌselfprə'peld/ *adj.* (esp. of a motor vehicle etc.) moving or able to move without external propulsion. □□ **self-propelling** *adj.*

self-protection /ˌselfprə'tekʃ(ə)n/ *n.* protecting oneself or itself. □□ **self-protective** *adj.*

self-raising /self'reɪzɪŋ/ *adj.* Brit. (of flour) having a raising agent already added.

self-realization /selfˌrɪəlaɪ'zeɪʃ(ə)n/ *n.* **1** the development of one's faculties, abilities, etc. **2** this as an ethical principle.

self-recording /ˌselfrɪ'kɔːdɪŋ/ *adj.* (of a scientific instrument etc.) automatically recording its measurements.

self-regard /ˌselfrɪ'ɡɑːd/ *n.* **1** a proper regard for oneself. **2 a** selfishness. **b** conceit.

self-registering /self'redʒɪstərɪŋ/ *adj.* (of a scientific instrument etc.) automatically registering its measurements.

self-regulating /self'reɡjuˌleɪtɪŋ/ *adj.* regulating oneself or itself without intervention. □□ **self-regulation** /-'leɪʃ(ə)n/ *n.* **self-regulatory** /-lətərɪ/ *adj.*

self-reliance /ˌselfrɪ'laɪəns/ *n.* reliance on one's own resources etc.; independence. □□ **self-reliant** *adj.* **self-reliantly** *adv.*

self-renewal /ˌselfrɪ'njuːəl/ *n.* the act or process of renewing oneself or itself.

self-renunciation /ˌselfrɪˌnʌnsɪ'eɪʃ(ə)n/ *n.* **1** = SELF-SACRIFICE. **2** unselfishness.

self-reproach /ˌselfrɪ'prəʊtʃ/ *n.* reproach or blame directed at oneself. □□ **self-reproachful** *adj.*

self-respect /ˌselfrɪ'spekt/ *n.* respect for oneself, a feeling that one is behaving with honour, dignity, etc. □□ **self-respecting** *adj.*

self-restraint /ˌselfrɪ'streɪnt/ *n.* = SELF-CONTROL. □□ **self-restrained** *adj.*

self-revealing /ˌselfrɪ'viːlɪŋ/ *adj.* revealing one's character, motives, etc., esp. inadvertently. □□ **self-revelation** /-ˌrevə'leɪʃ(ə)n/ *n.*

Selfridge /'selfrɪdʒ/, Harry Gordon (?1864–1947), US-born businessman, founder of the shop in Oxford Street, London, that bears his name. It opened in 1909.

self-righteous /self'raɪtʃəs/ *adj.* excessively conscious of or insistent on one's rectitude, correctness, etc. □□ **self-righteously** *adv.* **self-righteousness** *n.*

self-righting /self'raɪtɪŋ/ *adj.* (of a boat) righting itself when capsized.

self-rising /self'raɪzɪŋ/ *adj.* US = SELF-RAISING.

self-rule /self'ruːl/ *n.* = SELF-GOVERNMENT 1.

self-sacrifice /self'sækrɪˌfaɪs/ *n.* the negation of one's own interests, wishes, etc., in favour of those of others. □□ **self-sacrificing** *adj.*

selfsame /'selfseɪm/ *attrib.adj.* (prec. by *the*) the very same (*the selfsame village*).

self-satisfaction /selfˌsætɪs'fækʃ(ə)n/ *n.* excessive and unwarranted satisfaction with oneself, one's achievements, etc.; complacency. □□ **self-satisfied** /-'sætɪsˌfaɪd/ *adj.* **self-satisfiedly** /-'sætɪsˌfaɪdlɪ/ *adv.*

self-sealing /self'siːlɪŋ/ *adj.* **1** (of a pneumatic tyre, fuel tank, etc.) automatically able to seal small punctures. **2** (of an envelope) self-adhesive.

self-seeking /'self'siːkɪŋ/ *adj.* & *n.* seeking one's own welfare before that of others. □□ **self-seeker** *n.*

self-selection /ˌselfsɪ'lekʃ(ə)n/ *n.* the act of selecting oneself or itself. □□ **self-selecting** *adj.*

self-service /self'sɜːvɪs/ *adj.* & *n.* —*adj.* (often *attrib.*) **1** (of a shop, restaurant, garage, etc.) where customers serve themselves and pay at a checkout counter etc. **2** (of a machine) serving goods after the insertion of coins. —*n.* *colloq.* a self-service store, garage, etc.

self-serving /self'sɜːvɪŋ/ *adj.* = SELF-SEEKING.

self-slaughter /self'slɔːtə(r)/ *n.* = SUICIDE.

self-sown /self'səʊn/ *adj.* grown from seed scattered naturally.

self-starter /self'stɑːtə(r)/ *n.* **1** an electric appliance for starting a motor vehicle engine without the use of a crank. **2** an ambitious person who needs no external motivation.

self-sterile /self'steraɪl/ *adj.* Biol. not being self-fertile. □□ **self-sterility** /-stə'rɪlɪtɪ/ *n.*

self-styled /'selfstaɪld/ *adj.* called so by oneself; would-be; pretended (*a self-styled artist*).

self-sufficient /ˌselfsə'fɪʃ(ə)nt/ *adj.* **1 a** needing nothing; independent. **b** (of a person, nation, etc.) able to supply one's needs for a commodity, esp. food, from one's own resources. **2** content with one's own opinion; arrogant. □□ **self-sufficiency** *n.* **self-sufficiently** *adv.* **self-sufficing** /-sə'faɪsɪŋ/ *adj.*

self-suggestion /ˌselfsə'dʒestʃ(ə)n/ *n.* = AUTO-SUGGESTION.

self-supporting /ˌselfsə'pɔːtɪŋ/ *adj.* **1** capable of maintaining oneself or itself financially. **2** staying up or standing without external aid. □□ **self-support** *n.*

self-surrender /ˌselfsə'rendə(r)/ *n.* the surrender of oneself or one's will etc. to an influence, emotion, or other person.

self-sustaining /ˌselfsə'steɪnɪŋ/ *adj.* sustaining oneself or itself. □□ **self-sustained** *adj.*

self-taught /self'tɔːt/ *adj.* educated or trained by oneself, not externally.

self-torture /self'tɔːtʃə(r)/ *n.* the inflicting of pain, esp. mental, on oneself.

self-willed /self'wɪld/ *adj.* obstinately pursuing one's own wishes. □□ **self-will** *n.*

self-winding /self'waɪndɪŋ/ *adj.* (of a watch etc.) having an automatic winding apparatus.

self-worth /self'wɜːθ/ *n.* = SELF-ESTEEM.

Seljuk /'seldʒʊk/ *n.* & *adj.* —*n.* a member of the Turkish dynasty which ruled Asia Minor in the 11th–13th c., successfully invading the Byzantine Empire and defending the Holy Land against the Crusaders. —*adj.*. of or relating to the Seljuks. □□ **Seljukian** /-'dʒuːkɪən/ *adj.* & *n.* [Turk. *seljūq* (name of their reputed ancestor)]

Selkirk /'selkɜːk/, Alexander (1676–1721), Scottish sailor. While on a privateering expedition, Selkirk quarrelled with his captain and was put ashore, at his own request, on one of the uninhabited Juan Fernandez Islands in the South Pacific, where he remained from 1704 to 1709 before being rescued. His experiences later formed the basis of Defoe's novel *Robinson Crusoe*.

sell /sel/ *v.* & *n.* —*v.* (*past* and *past part.* **sold** /səʊld/) **1** *tr.* make over or dispose of in exchange for money. **2** *tr.* keep a stock of for sale or be a dealer in (*do you sell candles?*). **3** *intr.* (of goods) be purchased (*will never sell; these are selling well*). **4** *intr.* (foll. by *at,* *for*) have a specified price (*sells at £5*). **5** *tr.* betray for money or other reward (*sell one's country*). **6** *tr.* offer dishonourably for money or other consideration; make a matter of corrupt bargaining (*sell justice; sell oneself; sell one's honour*). **7** *tr.* **a** advertise or publish the merits of. **b** give (a person) information on the value of something, inspire with a desire to buy or acquire or agree to something. **8** *tr.* cause to be sold (*the author's name alone will sell many copies*). **9** *tr. sl.* disappoint by not keeping an engagement etc., by failing in some way, or by trickery (*sold again!*). —*n. colloq.* **1** a manner of selling (*soft sell*). **2** a deception or disappointment. □ **sell-by date** the latest recommended date of sale marked on the packaging of esp. perishable food. **sell down the river** see RIVER. **sell the** (or **a**) **dummy** see DUMMY. **selling-point** an advantageous feature. **selling-race** a horse-race after which the winning horse must be auctioned. **sell one's life dear** (or **dearly**) do great injury before being killed. **sell off** sell the remainder of (goods) at reduced prices. **sell out 1 a** sell all one's stock-in-trade, one's shares in a company, etc. **b** sell (all or some of one's stock, shares, etc.). **2 a** betray. **b** be treacherous or disloyal. **sell-out** *n.* **1** a commercial success, esp. the selling of all tickets for a show. **2** a betrayal. **sell the pass** see PASS². **sell a pup** see PUP. **sell short** disparage, underestimate. **sell up** *Brit.* **1** sell one's business, house, etc. **2** sell the goods of (a debtor). **sold on** *colloq.* enthusiastic about. □□ **sellable** *adj.* [OE *sellan* f. Gmc]

Sellafield /ˈseləˌfiːld/ an industrial site near the coast of Cumbria in NW England, formerly the site of a Royal Ordnance Factory and now belonging to British Nuclear Fuels. The name was changed to Windscale in 1947 and reverted officially to Sellafield in 1981. (See WINDSCALE.)

seller /ˈselə(r)/ *n.* **1** a person who sells. **2** a commodity that sells well or badly. □ **seller's** (or **sellers'**) **market** an economic position in which goods are scarce and expensive.

Sellotape /ˈseləˌteɪp/ *n. & v.* —*n. propr.* adhesive usu. transparent cellulose or plastic tape. Tape of this kind was first developed in the US (where it was called Scotch tape) in 1928. —*v.tr.* (**sellotape**) fix with Sellotape. [CELLULOSE + TAPE]

Selous /səˈluː/, Frederick Court (1851–1917), English hunter, soldier, naturalist, and explorer in south central Africa. A game reserve named after him, in SE Tanzania, is the largest wildlife sanctuary in Africa and has the most numerous elephant population in the world.

seltzer /ˈseltsə(r)/ *n.* (in full **seltzer water**) **1** medicinal mineral water from Nieder-Selters in Germany. **2** an artificial substitute for this; soda water. [G *Selterser* (adj.) f. *Selters*]

selvage /ˈselvɪdʒ/ *n.* (also **selvedge**) **1 a** an edging that prevents cloth from unravelling (either an edge along the warp or a specially woven edging). **b** a border of different material or finish intended to be removed or hidden. **2** *Geol.* an alteration zone at the edge of a rock mass. **3** the edge-plate of a lock with an opening for the bolt. [ME f. SELF + EDGE, after Du. *selfegghe*]

Selvas /ˈselvəs/ a name given to the equatorial rainforest of the Amazon basin in South America.

selves *pl.* of SELF.

semanteme /sɪˈmæntiːm/ *n. Linguistics* a fundamental element expressing an image or idea. [F *sémantème* (as SEMANTIC)]

semantic /sɪˈmæntɪk/ *adj.* relating to meaning in language; relating to the connotations of words. □□ **semantically** *adv.* [F *sémantique* f. Gk *sēmantikos* significant f. *sēmainō* signify f. *sēma* sign]

semantics /sɪˈmæntɪks/ *n.pl.* (usu. treated as *sing.*) the branch of linguistics concerned with meaning. □□ **semantician** /-ˈtɪʃ(ə)n/ *n.* **semanticist** /-tɪsɪst/ *n.*

semaphore /ˈseməˌfɔː(r)/ *n. & v.* —*n.* **1** *Mil.* etc. a system of sending messages by holding the arms or two flags in certain positions according to an alphabetic code. **2** a signalling apparatus consisting of a post with a movable arm or arms, lanterns, etc., for use (esp. on railways) by day or night. —*v.intr. & tr.* signal or send by semaphore. □□ **semaphoric** /-ˈfɔrɪk/ *adj.* **semaphorically** /-ˈfɔrɪkəlɪ/ *adv.* [F *sémaphore*, irreg. f. Gk *sēma* sign + *-phoros* -PHORE]

Semarang /səˈmɑːræŋ/ a port and the capital of the province of Central Java, Indonesia; pop. (1980) 1,026,600.

semasiology /sɪˌmeɪsɪˈɒlədʒɪ/ *n.* semantics. □□ **semasiological** /-əˈlɒdʒɪk(ə)l/ *adj.* [G *Semasiologie* f. Gk *sēmasia* meaning f. *sēmainō* signify]

sematic /sɪˈmætɪk/ *adj. Zool.* (of colouring, markings, etc.) significant; serving to warn off enemies or attract attention. [Gk *sēma sēmatos* sign]

semblable /ˈsembləb(ə)l/ *n. & adj.* —*n.* a counterpart or equal. —*adj. archaic* having the semblance of something, seeming. [ME f. OF (as SEMBLANCE)]

semblance /ˈsembləns/ *n.* **1** the outward or superficial appearance of something (*put on a semblance of anger*). **2** resemblance. [ME f. OF f. *sembler* f. L *similare, simulare* SIMULATE]

semé /ˈsemɪ, ˈsemeɪ/ *adj.* (also **semée**) *Heraldry* covered with small bearings of indefinite number (e.g. stars, fleurs-de-lis) arranged all over the field. [F, past part. of *semer* to sow]

semeiology var. of SEMIOLOGY.

semeiotics var. of SEMIOTICS.

Semele /ˈsemɪlɪ/ *Gk Mythol.* the mother, by Zeus, of Dionysus. She entreated Zeus to come to her in his full majesty and the fire of his thunderbolts killed her but made her child immortal.

sememe /ˈsemiːm, ˈsiːm-/ *n. Linguistics* the unit of meaning carried by a morpheme. [as SEMANTIC]

semen /ˈsiːmən/ *n.* the reproductive fluid of male animals, containing spermatozoa in suspension. [ME f. L *semen seminis* seed f. *serere* to sow]

semester /sɪˈmestə(r)/ *n.* a half-year course or term in (esp. German and US) universities. [G f. L *semestris* six-monthly f. *sex* six + *mensis* month]

semi /ˈsemɪ/ *n.* (*pl.* **semis**) *colloq.* **1** *Brit.* a semi-detached house. **2** *US* a semi-trailer. [abbr.]

semi- /ˈsemɪ/ *prefix* **1** half (*semicircle*). **2** partly; in some degree or particular (*semi-official; semi-detached*). **3** almost (*a semi-smile*). **4** occurring or appearing twice in a specified period (*semi-annual*). [F, It., etc. or L, corresp. to Gk HEMI-, Skr. *sāmi*]

semi-annual /ˌsemɪˈænjʊəl/ *adj.* occurring, published, etc., twice a year. □□ **semi-annually** *adv.*

semi-automatic /ˌsemɪˌɔːtəˈmætɪk/ *adj.* **1** partially automatic. **2** (of a firearm) having a mechanism for continuous loading but not for continuous firing.

semi-basement /ˌsemɪˈbeɪsmənt/ *n.* a storey partly below ground level.

semi-bold /ˌsemɪˈbəʊld/ *adj. Printing* printed in a type darker than normal but not as dark as bold.

semibreve /ˈsemɪˌbriːv/ *n. Mus.* the longest note now in common use, having the time value of two minims or four crochets, and represented by a ring with no stem. Also called *whole note*.

semicircle /ˈsemɪˌsɜːk(ə)l/ *n.* **1** half of a circle or of its circumference. **2** a set of objects ranged in, or an object forming, a semicircle. [L *semicirculus* (as SEMI-, CIRCLE)]

semicircular /ˌsemɪˈsɜːkjʊlə(r)/ *adj.* **1** forming or shaped like a semicircle. **2** arranged as or in a semicircle. □ **semicircular canal** any of three fluid-filled channels in the ear giving information to the brain to help maintain balance. [LL *semicircularis* (as SEMICIRCLE)]

semi-civilized /ˌsemɪˈsɪvɪˌlaɪzd/ *adj.* partially civilized.

semicolon /ˌsemɪˈkəʊlɒn, -lɒn/ *n.* a punctuation mark (;) of intermediate value between a comma and full stop.

semiconducting /ˌsemɪkənˈdʌktɪŋ/ *adj.* having the properties of a semiconductor.

semiconductor /ˌsemɪkənˈdʌktə(r)/ *n.* a solid substance that is a non-conductor when pure or at a low temperature but has a conductivity between that of insulators and that of most metals when containing a suitable impurity or at a higher temperature. Modern electronics now relies principally upon devices made of semiconductors such as silicon and germanium, and increasing miniaturization of such devices has been achieved. The significance of semiconductors lies not only in their overall degree of conductivity but also in the fact that, in comparison with metals, their conductivity is liable to be much more sensitive to factors such as heat, light, applied voltage, and traces of impurities. This sensitivity means that the performance of transistors and other semiconductor devices can be very precisely controlled—control which is a prerequisite of creating electronic circuits that are able to process complicated information, as in a computer. Semiconductors are seldom used in the pure state but are normally mixed with traces of special impurities which increase conductivity and also help to determine its character.

semi-conscious /ˌsemɪˈkɒnʃəs/ *adj.* partly or imperfectly conscious.

semicylinder /ˌsemɪˈsɪlɪndə(r)/ *n.* half of a cylinder cut longitudinally. □□ **semicylindrical** /-ˈlɪndrɪk(ə)l/ *adj.*

semidemisemiquaver /ˈsemɪˌdemɪˌsemɪ ˌkweɪvə(r)/ *n. Mus.* = HEMIDEMISEMIQUAVER. [SEMI- + DEMISEMIQUAVER]

semi-deponent /ˌsemɪdɪˈpəʊnənt/ *adj. Gram.* (of a Latin verb) having active forms in present tenses and passive forms with active sense in perfect tenses.

semi-detached /ˌsemɪdɪˈtætʃt/ *adj. & n.* —*adj.* (of a house) joined to another by a party-wall on one side only. —*n.* a semi-detached house.

semidiameter /ˌsemɪdaɪˈæmɪtə(r)/ *n.* half of a diameter. [LL (as SEMI-, DIAMETER)]

semi-documentary /ˌsemɪˌdɒkjʊˈmentərɪ/ *adj. & n.* —*adj.* (of a film) having a factual background and a fictitious story. —*n.* (*pl.* **-ies**) a semi-documentary film.

semi-dome /ˈsemɪˌdəʊm/ *n.* **1** a half-dome formed by vertical section. **2** a part of a structure more or less resembling a dome.

semi-double /ˌsemɪˈdʌb(ə)l/ *adj.* (of a flower) intermediate between single and double in having only the outer stamens converted to petals.

semifinal /ˌsemɪˈfaɪn(ə)l/ *n.* a match or round immediately preceding the final.

semifinalist /ˌsemɪˈfaɪnəlɪst/ *n.* a competitor in a semifinal.

semi-finished /ˌsemɪˈfɪnɪʃt/ *adj.* prepared for the final stage of manufacture.

semi-fitted /ˌsemɪˈfɪtɪd/ *adj.* (of a garment) shaped to the body but not closely fitted.

semifluid /ˌsemɪˈfluːɪd/ *adj. & n.* —*adj.* of a consistency between solid and liquid. —*n.* a semifluid substance.

semi-infinite /ˌsemɪˈɪnfɪnɪt/ *adj. Math.* limited in one direction and stretching to infinity in the other.

semi-invalid /ˌsemɪˈɪnvəˌliːd, -lɪd/ *n.* a person somewhat enfeebled or partially disabled.

semi-liquid /ˌsemɪˈlɪkwɪd/ *adj. & n.* = SEMIFLUID.

semi-lunar /ˌsemɪˈluːnə(r)/ *adj.* shaped like a half moon or crescent. □ **semi-lunar bone** a bone of this shape in the carpus. **semi-lunar cartilage** a cartilage of this shape in the knee. **semi-lunar valve** a valve of this shape in the heart. [mod.L *semilunaris* (as SEMI-, LUNAR)]

semi-metal /ˌsemɪˈmet(ə)l/ *n.* a substance with some of the properties of metals. [mod.L *semimetallum* (as SEMI-, METAL)]

semi-monthly /ˌsemɪˈmʌnθlɪ/ *adj. & adv.* —*adj.* occurring, published, etc., twice a month. —*adv.* twice a month.

seminal /ˈsemɪn(ə)l/ *adj.* **1** of or relating to seed, semen, or reproduction. **2** germinal. **3** rudimentary, undeveloped. **4** (of ideas etc.) providing the basis for future development. □ **seminal fluid** semen. □□ **seminally** *adv.* [ME f. OF *seminal* or L *seminalis* (as SEMEN)]

seminar /ˈsemɪˌnɑː(r)/ *n.* **1** a small class at a university etc. for discussion and research. **2** a short intensive course of study. **3** a conference of specialists. [G (as SEMINARY)]

seminary /ˈsemɪnərɪ/ *n.* (*pl.* **-ies**) **1** a training-college for priests, rabbis, etc. **2** a place of education or development. □□ **seminarist** *n.* [ME f. L *seminarium* seed-plot, neut. of *seminarius* (adj.) (as SEMEN)]

seminiferous /ˌsemɪˈnɪfərəs/ *adj.* **1** bearing seed. **2** conveying semen. [L *semin-* f. SEMEN + -FEROUS]

semi-official /ˌsemɪəˈfɪʃ(ə)l/ *adj.* **1** partly official; rather less than official. **2** (of communications to newspapers etc.) made by an official with the stipulation that the source should not be revealed. □□ **semi-officially** *adv.*

semiology /ˌsiːmɪˈɒlədʒɪ, ˌsem-/ *n.* (also **semeiology**) = SEMIOTICS. □□ **semiological** /-əˈlɒdʒɪk(ə)l/ *adj.* **semiologist** *n.* [Gk *sēmeion* sign f. *sēma* mark]

semi-opaque /ˌsemɪəʊˈpeɪk/ *adj.* not fully transparent.

semiotics /ˌsiːmɪˈɒtɪks, ˌsem-/ *n.* (also **semeiotics**) **1** the study of signs and symbols in various fields, esp. language. **2** *Med.* symptomatology. □□ **semiotic** *adj.* **semiotical** *adj.* **semiotically** *adv.* **semiotician** /-ˈtɪʃ(ə)n/ *n.* [Gk *sēmeiōtikos* of signs (as SEMIOLOGY)]

semi-permanent /ˌsemɪˈpɜːmənənt/ *adj.* rather less than permanent.

semi-permeable /ˌsemɪˈpɜːmɪəb(ə)l/ *adj.* (of a membrane etc.) allowing small molecules, but not large ones, to pass through.

semi-plume /ˈsemɪˌpluːm/ *n.* a feather with a firm stem but a downy web.

semiprecious /ˌsemɪˈpreʃəs/ *adj.* (of a gem) less valuable than a precious stone.

semi-pro /ˌsemɪˈprəʊ/ *adj. & n.* (*pl.* **-os**) *US colloq.* = SEMI-PROFESSIONAL.

semi-professional /ˌsemɪprəˈfeʃ(ə)n(ə)l/ *adj. & n.* —*adj.* **1** receiving payment for an activity but not relying on it for a living. **2** involving semi-professionals. —*n.* a semi-professional musician, sportsman, etc.

semiquaver /ˈsemɪˌkweɪvə(r)/ *n. Mus.* a note having the time value of half a quaver and represented by a large dot with a two-hooked stem. Also called *sixteenth note.*

Semiramis /sɪˈmɪrəmɪs/ *Gk legend* the daughter of a Syrian goddess. Exposed at birth, she was tended by doves until found by shepherds. Her second husband was Ninus, king of Assyria, after whose death she ruled for many years, renowned in war and (allegedly) as a builder of Babylon; at death she was changed into a dove. The historical figure behind this legend is almost certainly Sammuramat, wife of the Assyrian king Shamshi-Adad V, and herself regent 810–805 BC during the minority of her son.

semi-rigid /ˌsemɪˈrɪdʒɪd/ *adj.* (of an airship) having a stiffened keel attached to a flexible gas container.

semi-skilled /ˌsemɪˈskɪld/ *adj.* (of work or a worker) having or needing some training but less than for a skilled worker.

semi-smile /ˈsemɪˌsmaɪl/ *n.* an expression that is not quite a smile.

semi-solid /ˌsemɪˈsɒlɪd/ *adj.* viscous, semifluid.

semi-sweet /ˈsemɪˌswiːt/ *adj.* (of biscuits etc.) slightly sweetened.

semi-synthetic /ˌsemɪsɪnˈθetɪk/ *adj. Chem.* (of a substance) that is prepared synthetically but derives from a naturally occurring material.

Semite /ˈsiːmaɪt, ˈsem-/ *n.* a member of any of the peoples supposed to be descended from Shem, son of Noah (Gen. 10: 21 ff.), including esp. the Jews, Arabs, Assyrians, and Phoenicians. □□ **Semitism** /ˈsemɪˌtɪz(ə)m/ *n.* **Semitist** /ˈsemɪtɪst/ *n.* **Semitize** /ˈsemɪˌtaɪz/ *v.tr.* (also **-ise**). **Semitization** /ˌsemɪtaɪˈzeɪʃ(ə)n/ *n.* [mod.L *Semita* f. LL f. Gk *Sēm* Shem]

Semitic /sɪˈmɪtɪk/ *adj.* **1** of or relating to the Semites, esp. the Jews. **2** of or relating to the languages of the family that includes Hebrew, Arabic, and Aramaic, and certain ancient languages such as Phoenician, Assyrian, and Babylonian. They are closely related both in structure and in vocabulary. Almost all Semitic words are derived from verbs consisting of three consonants. [mod.L *Semiticus* (as SEMITE)]

semitone /ˈsemɪˌtəʊn/ *n. Mus.* the smallest interval used in classical European music; half a tone.

semi-trailer /ˌsemɪˈtreɪlə(r)/ *n.* a trailer having wheels at the back but supported at the front by a towing vehicle.

semi-transparent /ˌsemɪˌtrænsˈpærənt, ˌsemɪˌtrɑːn-, -ˈpeərənt/ *adj.* partially or imperfectly transparent.

semi-tropics /ˌsemɪˈtrɒpɪks/ *n.pl.* = SUBTROPICS. □□ **semi-tropical** *adj.*

semi-vowel /ˈsemɪˌvaʊəl/ *n.* **1** a sound intermediate between a vowel and a consonant (e.g. *w*, *y*). **2** a letter representing this. [after L *semivocalis*]

semi-weekly /ˌsemɪˈwiːklɪ/ *adj. & adv.* —*adj.* occurring, published, etc., twice a week. —*adv.* twice a week.

Semmelweis /ˈseməlˌvaɪs/, Ignaz Philipp (1818–65), Austro-Hungarian obstetrician who discovered the infectious septic character of puerperal fever, a major cause of maternal mortality. He demonstrated that the infection was transmitted by the hands of doctors who examined patients after carrying out work in the dissecting room, and advocated rigorous cleanliness and the use of antiseptics. His results were spectacular, but though the younger medical men accepted his discoveries the weight of authority was against him; Virchow and others rejected his views, and his involvement in the 1848 revolution hindered his career. Disheartened and depressed by the years of opposition, he died in a mental hospital.

semmit /ˈsemɪt/ *n. Sc.* an undershirt. [ME: orig. unkn.]

semolina /ˌseməˈliːnə/ *n.* **1** the hard grains left after the milling of flour, used in puddings etc. and in pasta. **2** a pudding etc. made of this. [It. *semolino* dimin. of *semola* bran f. L *simila* flour]

sempiternal /ˌsempɪˈtɜːn(ə)l/ *adj. rhet.* eternal, everlasting. □□ **sempiternally** *adv.* **sempiternity** *n.* [ME f. OF *sempiternel* f. LL *sempiternalis* f. L *sempiternus* f. *semper* always + *aeternus* eternal]

semplice /ˈsemplɪˌtʃeɪ, -tʃɪ/ *adv. Mus.* in a simple style of performance. [It., = SIMPLE]

sempre /ˈsempreɪ, -rɪ/ *adv. Mus.* throughout, always (*sempre forte*). [It.]

sempstress var. of SEAMSTRESS.

Semtex /ˈsemteks/ *n. propr.* very malleable odourless plastic explosive. [prob. f. *Semtín* village in E. Bohemia, Czechoslovakia, where manufactured + *explosive* or *export*]

SEN *abbr.* (in the UK) State Enrolled Nurse.

Sen. *abbr.* **1** Senior. **2** *US* **a** Senator. **b** Senate.

Senanyake /ˌsenəˈnaɪəkə/, Don Stephen (1884–1952), Sinhalese statesman, chief architect of Sri Lanka's independence and the country's first Prime Minister (1947–52).

senarius /sɪˈneərɪəs/ *n.* (*pl.* **senarii** /-ɪˌaɪ/) *Prosody* a verse of six feet, esp. an iambic trimeter. [L: see SENARY]

senary /ˈsiːnərɪ, ˈsen-/ *adj.* of six, by sixes. [L *senarius* f. *seni* distrib. of *sex* six]

senate /ˈsenɪt/ *n.* **1** a legislative body, esp. the upper and smaller assembly in the US, France, and other countries, in the States of the US, etc. **2** the governing body of a university or (in the US) a college. **3** *Rom.Hist.* the State council of the republic and empire composed (after the early period) of ex-magistrates, sharing legislative power with the popular assemblies, administration with the magistrates, and judicial power with the knights. [ME f. OF *senat* f. L *senatus* f. *senex* old man]

senator /ˈsenətə(r)/ *n.* **1** a member of a senate. **2** (in Scotland) a Lord of Session. □□ **senatorial** /-ˈtɔːrɪəl/ *adj.* **senatorship** *n.* [ME f. OF *senateur* f. L *senator -oris* (as SENATE)]

send /send/ *v.* (*past and past part.* **sent** /sent/) **1** *tr.* **a** order or cause to go or be conveyed (*send a message to headquarters*; *sent me a book*; *sends goods all over the world*). **b** propel; cause to move (*send a bullet*; *sent him flying*). **c** cause to go or become (*send into raptures*; *send to sleep*). **d** dismiss with or without force (*sent her away*; *sent him about his business*). **2** *intr.* send a message or letter (*he sent to warn me*). **3** *tr.* (of God, providence, etc.) grant or bestow or inflict; bring about; cause to be (*send rain*; *send a judgement*; *send her victorious!*). **4** *tr. sl.* affect emotionally, put into ecstasy. □ **send away for** send an order to a dealer for (goods). **send down** *Brit.* **1** rusticate or expel from a university. **2** sentence to imprisonment. **3** *Cricket* bowl (a ball or an over). **send for** **1** summon. **2** order by post. **send in** **1** cause to go in. **2** submit (an entry etc.) for a competition etc. **send off** **1** get (a letter, parcel, etc.) dispatched. **2** attend the departure of (a person) as a sign of respect etc. **3** *Sport* (of a referee) order (a player) to leave the field and take no further part in the game. **send-off** *n.* a demonstration of goodwill etc. at the departure of a person, the start of a project, etc. **send off for** = *send away for*. **send on** transmit to a further destination or in advance of one's own arrival. **send**

a person to Coventry see COVENTRY. **send up** **1** cause to go up. **2** transmit to a higher authority. **3** *Brit. colloq.* satirize or ridicule, esp. by mimicking. **4** *US* sentence to imprisonment. **send-up** *n. Brit. colloq.* a satire or parody. **send word** send information. □□ **sendable** *adj.* **sender** *n.* [OE *sendan* f. Gmc]

Sendai /senˈdaɪ/ a city of Japan, capital of Tohoku region, Honshu Island; pop. (1987) 686,000.

sendal /ˈsend(ə)l/ *n. hist.* **1** a thin rich silk material. **2** a garment of this. [ME f. OF *cendal*, ult. f. Gk *sindōn*]

senecio /sɪˈniːʃɪəʊ/ *n.* any composite plant of the genus *Senecio*, including many cultivated species as well as groundsel and ragwort. [L *senecio* old man, groundsel, with ref. to the hairy fruits]

Senegal /ˌsenɪˈɡɔːl/ a country on the west coast of Africa, with the River Senegal as its northern boundary and the Gambia forming a narrow strip within its territory; pop. (est. 1988) 7,281,000; official language, French; capital, Dakar. Part of the Mali empire in the 14th and 15th c., the area was colonized by the French in the second half of the 19th c. Senegal became part of French West Africa in 1895, a member of the French community in 1958, and part of the Federation of Mali in 1959 before becoming an independent republic in 1960. The economy is largely based on groundnuts, although the capital, Dakar, is industrialized. □□ **Senegalese** /-ˈliːz/ *adj. & n.*

senesce /sɪˈnes/ *v.intr.* grow old. □□ **senescence** *n.* **senescent** *adj.* [L *senescere* f. *senex* old]

seneschal /ˈsenɪʃ(ə)l/ *n.* **1** the steward or major-domo of a medieval great house. **2** a judge in Sark. [ME f. OF f. med.L *seniscalus* f. Gmc, = old servant]

senhor /seɪnˈjɔː(r)/ *n.* a title used of or to a Portuguese or Brazilian man. [Port. f. L *senior*: see SENIOR]

senhora /seɪnˈjɔːrə/ *n.* a title used of or to a Portuguese woman or a Brazilian married woman. [Port., fem. of SENHOR]

senhorita /ˌseɪnjəˈriːtə/ *n.* a title used of or to a Brazilian unmarried woman. [Port., dimin. of SENHORA]

senile /ˈsiːnaɪl/ *adj. & n.* —*adj.* **1** of or characteristic of old age (*senile apathy*; *senile decay*). **2** having the weaknesses or diseases of old age. —*n.* a senile person. □□ **senility** /sɪˈnɪlɪtɪ/ *n.* [F *sénile* or L *senilis* f. *senex* old man]

senior /ˈsiːnɪə(r)/ *adj. & n.* —*adj.* **1** (often foll. by *to*) more or most advanced in age or standing. **2** of high or highest position. **3** (placed after a person's name) senior to another of the same name. **4** (of a school) having pupils in an older age-range (esp. over 11). **5** *US* of the final year at a university, high school, etc. —*n.* **1** a person of advanced age or comparatively long service etc. **2** one's elder, or one's superior in length of service, membership, etc. (*is my senior*). **3** a senior student. □ **senior citizen** an elderly person, esp. an old-age pensioner. **senior college** *US* a college in which the last two years' work for a bachelor's degree is done. **senior common** (or **combination**) **room** *Brit.* a room for use by senior members of a college. **senior nursing officer** the person in charge of nursing services in a hospital. **senior officer** an officer to whom a junior is responsible. **senior partner** the head of a firm. **senior service** *Brit.* the Royal Navy as opposed to the Army. **senior tutor** *Brit.* a college tutor in charge of the teaching arrangements. □□ **seniority** /ˌsiːnɪˈɒrɪtɪ/ *n.* [ME f. L, = older, older man, compar. of *senex senis* old man, old]

senna /ˈsenə/ *n.* **1** a cassia tree. **2** a laxative prepared from the dried pods of this. [med.L *sena* f. Arab. *sanā*]

Sennacherib /sɪˈnækərɪb/ king of Assyria 704–681 BC, who rebuilt the city of Nineveh, making it his capital. He was obliged to devote much of his reign to suppressing revolts in various parts of his empire, including Babylon which he sacked in 689 BC. In 701 BC he put down a Jewish rebellion, exacting tribute from Hezekiah and laying siege to Jerusalem but sparing it from destruction, according to 2 Kings 19: 35, after an epidemic of illness amongst his forces.

sennet[1] /ˈsenɪt/ *n. hist.* a signal call on a trumpet or cornet (in the stage directions of Elizabethan plays). [perh. var. of SIGNET]

sennet[2] var. of SINNET.

sennight /ˈsenaɪt/ *n. archaic* a week. [OE *seofon nihta* seven nights]

sennit /ˈsenɪt/ n. 1 hist. plaited straw, palm leaves, etc., used for making hats. 2 = SINNET. [var. of SINNET]

señor /senˈjɔː(r)/ n. (pl. **señores** /-rez/) a title used of or to a Spanish-speaking man. [Sp. f. L senior: see SENIOR]

señora /senˈjɔːrə/ n. a title used of or to a Spanish-speaking married woman. [Sp., fem. of SEÑOR]

señorita /ˌsenjəˈriːtə/ n. a title used of or to a Spanish-speaking unmarried woman. [Sp., dimin. of SEÑORA]

Senr. abbr. Senior.

sensate /ˈsenseɪt/ adj. perceived by the senses. [LL sensatus having senses (as SENSE)]

sensation /senˈseɪʃ(ə)n/ n. 1 the consciousness of perceiving or seeming to perceive some state or condition of one's body or its parts or senses or of one's mind or its emotions; an instance of such consciousness (lost all sensation in my left arm; had a sensation of giddiness; a sensation of pride; in search of a new sensation). 2 a a stirring of emotions or intense interest esp. among a large group of people (the news caused a sensation). b a person, event, etc., causing such interest. 3 the sensational use of literary etc. material. [med.L sensatio f. L sensus SENSE]

sensational /senˈseɪʃən(ə)l/ adj. 1 causing or intended to cause great public excitement etc. 2 of or causing sensation. □□ **sensationalize** v.tr. **sensationally** adv.

sensationalism /senˈseɪʃənəˌlɪz(ə)m/ n. 1 the use of or interest in the sensational in literature, political agitation, etc. 2 Philos. the theory that ideas are derived solely from sensation (opp. RATIONALISM). □□ **sensationalist** n. & adj. **sensationalistic** /-ˈlɪstɪk/ adj.

sense /sens/ n. & v. —n. 1 a any of the special bodily faculties by which sensation is roused (has keen senses; has a dull sense of smell). b sensitiveness of all or any of these. 2 the ability to perceive or feel or to be conscious of the presence or properties of things. 3 (foll. by of) consciousness (sense of having done well; sense of one's own importance). 4 (often foll. by of) a quick or accurate appreciation, understanding, or instinct regarding a specified matter (sense of the ridiculous; road sense; the moral sense). b the habit of basing one's conduct on such instinct. 5 practical wisdom or judgement, common sense; conformity to these (has plenty of sense; what is the sense of talking like that?; has more sense than to do that). 6 a a meaning; the way in which a word etc. is to be understood (the sense of the word is clear; I mean that in the literal sense). b intelligibility or coherence or possession of a meaning. 7 the prevailing opinion among a number of people. 8 (in pl.) a person's sanity or normal state of mind. 9 Math. etc. a a direction of movement. b that which distinguishes a pair of entities which differ only in that each is the reverse of the other. —v.tr. 1 perceive by a sense or senses. 2 be vaguely aware of. 3 realize. 4 (of a machine etc.) detect. 5 US understand. □ **bring a person to his** or **her senses** 1 cure a person of folly. 2 restore a person to consciousness. **come to one's senses** 1 regain consciousness. 2 become sensible after acting foolishly. **the five senses** sight, hearing, smell, taste, and touch. **in a** (or **one**) **sense** if the statement is understood in a particular way (what you say is true in a sense). **in one's senses** sane. **make sense** be intelligible or practicable. **make sense of** show or find the meaning of. **man of sense** a sagacious man. **out of one's senses** in or into a state of madness (is out of her senses; frightened him out of his senses). **sense-datum** (pl. **-data**) Philos. an element of experience received through the senses. **sense of direction** the ability to know without guidance the direction in which one is or should be moving. **sense of humour** see HUMOUR. **sense-organ** a bodily organ conveying external stimuli to the sensory system. **take leave of one's senses** go mad. **take the sense of the meeting** ascertain the prevailing opinion. **under a sense of wrong** feeling wronged. [ME f. L sensus faculty of feeling, thought, meaning, f. sentire sens- feel]

senseless /ˈsenslɪs/ adj. 1 unconscious. 2 wildly foolish. 3 without meaning or purpose. 4 incapable of sensation. □□ **senselessly** adv. **senselessness** n.

sensibility /ˌsensɪˈbɪlɪti/ n. (pl. **-ies**) 1 capacity to feel (little finger lost its sensibility). 2 a openness to emotional impressions, susceptibility, sensitiveness (sensibility to kindness). b an exceptional or excessive degree of this (sense and sensibility). 3 (in pl.) a tendency to feel offended etc. [ME f. LL sensibilitas (as SENSIBLE)]

sensible /ˈsensɪb(ə)l/ adj. 1 having or showing wisdom or common sense; reasonable, judicious (a sensible person; a sensible compromise). 2 a perceptible by the senses (sensible phenomena). b great enough to be perceived; appreciable (a sensible difference). 3 (of clothing etc.) practical and functional. 4 (foll. by of) aware; not unmindful (was sensible of his peril). □ **sensible horizon** see HORIZON 1b. □□ **sensibleness** n. **sensibly** adv. [ME f. OF sensible or L sensibilis (as SENSE)]

sensitive /ˈsensɪtɪv/ adj. & n. —adj. 1 (often foll. by to) very open to or acutely affected by external stimuli or mental impressions; having sensibility. 2 (of a person) easily offended or emotionally hurt. 3 (often foll. by to) (of an instrument etc.) responsive to or recording slight changes. 4 (often foll. by to) a (of photographic materials) prepared so as to respond (esp. rapidly) to the action of light. b (of any material) readily affected by or responsive to external action. 5 (of a topic etc.) subject to restriction of discussion to prevent embarrassment, ensure security, etc. 6 (of a market) liable to quick changes of price. —n. a person who is sensitive (esp. to supposed occult influences). □ **sensitive plant** 1 a plant whose leaves curve downwards and leaflets fold together when touched, esp. mimosa. 2 a sensitive person. □□ **sensitively** adv. **sensitiveness** n. [ME, = sensory, f. OF sensitif -ive or med.L sensitivus, irreg. f. L sentire sens- feel]

sensitivity /ˌsensɪˈtɪvɪti/ n. the quality or degree of being sensitive.

sensitize /ˈsensɪˌtaɪz/ v.tr. (also **-ise**) 1 make sensitive. 2 Photog. make sensitive to light. 3 make (an organism etc.) abnormally sensitive to a foreign substance. □□ **sensitization** /-ˈzeɪʃ(ə)n/ n. **sensitizer** n.

sensitometer /ˌsensɪˈtɒmɪtə(r)/ n. Photog. a device for measuring sensitivity to light.

sensor /ˈsensə(r)/ n. a device giving a signal for the detection or measurement of a physical property to which it responds. [SENSORY, after MOTOR]

sensorium /senˈsɔːrɪəm/ n. (pl. **sensoria** /-rɪə/ or **sensoriums**) 1 the seat of sensation, the brain, brain and spinal cord, or grey matter of these. 2 Biol. the whole sensory apparatus including the nerve-system. □□ **sensorial** adj. **sensorially** adv. [LL f. L sentire sens- feel]

sensory /ˈsensəri/ adj. of sensation or the senses. □□ **sensorily** adv. [as SENSORIUM]

sensual /ˈsensjʊəl, ˈsenʃʊəl/ adj. 1 a of or depending on the senses only and not on the intellect or spirit; carnal, fleshly (sensual pleasures). b given to the pursuit of sensual pleasures or the gratification of the appetites; self-indulgent sexually or in regard to food and drink; voluptuous, licentious. c indicative of a sensual nature (sensual lips). 2 of sense or sensation, sensory. 3 Philos. of, according to, or holding the doctrine of, sensationalism. □□ **sensualism** n. **sensualist** n. **sensualize** v.tr. (also **-ise**). **sensually** adv. [ME f. LL sensualis (as SENSE)]

sensuality /ˌsensjʊˈælɪti, ˌsenʃʊ-/ n. gratification of the senses, self-indulgence. [ME f. F sensualité f. LL sensualitas (as SENSUAL)]

sensum /ˈsensəm/ n. (pl. **sensa** /-sə/) Philos. a sense-datum. [mod.L, neut. past part. of L sentire feel]

sensuous /ˈsensjʊəs/ adj. of or derived from or affecting the senses, esp. aesthetically rather than sensually. □□ **sensuously** adv. **sensuousness** n. [L sensus sense]

sent past and past part. of SEND.

sentence /ˈsent(ə)ns/ n. & v. —n. 1 a a set of words complete in itself as the expression of a thought, containing or implying a subject and predicate, and conveying a statement, question, exclamation, or command. b a piece of writing or speech between two full stops or equivalent pauses, often including several grammatical sentences (e.g. I went; he came). 2 a a decision of a lawcourt, esp. the punishment allotted to a person convicted in a criminal trial. b the declaration of this. 3 Logic a series of signs or symbols expressing a proposition in an artificial or logical language. —v.tr. 1 declare the sentence of (a convicted criminal etc.). **2** (foll. by *to*) declare (such a person) to be condemned to a specified punishment. □ **under sentence of** having been condemned to (*under sentence of death*). [ME f. OF f. L *sententia* opinion f. *sentire* be of opinion]

sentential /sen'tenʃ(ə)l/ *adj. Gram. & Logic* of a sentence. [L *sententialis* (as SENTENCE)]

sententious /sen'tenʃəs/ *adj.* **1** (of a person) fond of pompous moralizing. **2** (of a style) affectedly formal. **3** aphoristic, pithy, given to the use of maxims, affecting a concise impressive style. □□ **sententiously** *adv.* **sententiousness** *n.* [L *sententiosus* (as SENTENCE)]

sentient /'senʃ(ə)nt/ *adj.* having the power of perception by the senses. □□ **sentience** *n.* **sentiency** *n.* **sentiently** *adv.* [L *sentire* feel]

sentiment /'sentɪmənt/ *n.* **1** a mental feeling (*the sentiment of pity*). **2 a** the sum of what one feels on some subject. **b** a verbal expression of this. **3** the expression of a view or desire esp. as formulated for a toast (*concluded his speech with a sentiment*). **4** an opinion as distinguished from the words meant to convey it (*the sentiment is good though the words are injudicious*). **5** a view or tendency based on or coloured with emotion (*animated by noble sentiments*). **6** such views collectively, esp. as an influence (*sentiment unchecked by reason is a bad guide*). **7** the tendency to be swayed by feeling rather than by reason. **8 a** mawkish tenderness. **b** the display of this. **9** an emotional feeling conveyed in literature or art. [ME f. OF *sentement* f. med.L *sentimentum* f. L *sentire* feel]

sentimental /ˌsentɪ'ment(ə)l/ *adj.* **1** of or characterized by sentiment. **2** showing or affected by emotion rather than reason. **3** appealing to sentiment. □ **sentimental value** the value of a thing to a particular person because of its associations. □□ **sentimentalism** *n.* **sentimentalist** *n.* **sentimentality** /-'tælɪtɪ/ *n.* **sentimentalize** *v.intr. & tr.* (also **-ise**). **sentimentalization** /-laɪ'zeɪʃ(ə)n/ *n.* **sentimentally** *adv.*

sentinel /'sentɪn(ə)l/ *n. & v.* —*n.* a sentry or lookout. —*v.tr.* (**sentinelled, sentinelling;** *US* **sentineled, sentineling**) **1** station sentinels at or in. **2** *poet.* keep guard over or in. [F *sentinelle* f. It. *sentinella*, of unkn. orig.]

sentry /'sentrɪ/ *n.* (*pl.* **-ies**) a soldier etc. stationed to keep guard. □ **sentry-box** a wooden cabin intended to shelter a standing sentry. **sentry-go** the duty of pacing up and down as a sentry. [perh. f. obs. *centrinel*, var. of SENTINEL]

Senussi /se'nu:sɪ/ *n.* **1** a Muslim religious fraternity founded in 1837 by Sidi Mohammad ibn Ali es-Senussi. **2** a member of this fraternity.

Seoul /səʊl/ the capital of the Republic of Korea; pop. (1985) 9,645,800. It was the venue of the 1988 Olympic Games.

sepal /'sep(ə)l, 'si:-/ *n. Bot.* each of the divisions or leaves of the calyx. [F *sépale*, mod.L *sepalum*, perh. formed as SEPARATE + PETAL]

separable /'sepərəb(ə)l/ *adj.* **1** able to be separated. **2** *Gram.* (of a prefix, or a verb in respect of a prefix) written as a separate word in some collocations. □□ **separability** /-'bɪlɪtɪ/ *n.* **separableness** *n.* **separably** *adv.* [F *séparable* or L *separabilis* (as SEPARATE)]

separate *adj., n., & v.* —*adj.* /'sepərət/ (often foll. by *from*) forming a unit that is or may be regarded as apart or by itself; physically disconnected, distinct, or individual (*living in separate rooms; the two questions are essentially separate*). —*n.* /'sepərət/ **1** (in *pl.*) separate articles of clothing suitable for wearing together in various combinations. **2** an offprint. —*v.* /'sepəˌreɪt/ **1** *tr.* make separate, sever, disunite. **2** *tr.* prevent union or contact of. **3** *intr.* go different ways, disperse. **4** *intr.* cease to live together as a married couple. **5** *intr.* (foll. by *from*) secede. **6** *tr.* **a** divide or sort (milk, ore, fruit, light, etc.) into constituent parts or sizes. **b** (often foll. by *out*) extract or remove (an ingredient, waste product, etc.) by such a process for use or rejection. **7** *tr. US* discharge, dismiss. □□ **separately** *adv.* **separateness** *n.* **separative** /-rətɪv/ *adj.* **separatory** /-rətərɪ/ *adj.* [L *separare separat-* (as SE-, *parare* make ready)]

separation /ˌsepə'reɪʃ(ə)n/ *n.* **1** the act or an instance of separating; the state of being separated. **2** (in full **judicial**

separation or **legal separation**) an arrangement by which a husband and wife remain married but live apart. **3** any of three or more monochrome reproductions of a coloured picture which can combine to reproduce the full colour of the original. □ **separation order** an order of court for judicial separation. [ME f. OF f. L *separatio -onis* (as SEPARATE)]

separatist /'sepərətɪst/ *n.* a person who favours separation, esp. for political or ecclesiastical independence (opp. UNIONIST 2). □□ **separatism** *n.*

separator /'sepəˌreɪtə(r)/ *n.* a machine for separating, e.g. cream from milk.

Sephardi /sɪ'fɑ:dɪ/ *n.* (*pl.* **Sephardim** /-dɪm/) a Jew of Spanish or Portuguese descent (cf. ASHKENAZI). □□ **Sephardic** *adj.* [LHeb., f. s'pāraḏ, a country mentioned in Obad. 20 and held in late Jewish tradition to be Spain]

sepia /'si:pɪə/ *n.* **1** a dark reddish-brown colour. **2 a** a brown pigment prepared from a black fluid secreted by cuttlefish, used in monochrome drawing and in water-colours. **b** a brown tint used in photography. **3** a drawing done in sepia. **4** the fluid secreted by cuttlefish. [L f. Gk *sēpia* cuttlefish]

sepoy /'si:pɔɪ/ *n. hist.* a native Indian soldier under European, esp. British, discipline. [Urdu & Pers. *sipāhī* soldier f. *sipāh* army]

seppuku /se'pu:ku:/ *n.* hara-kiri. [Jap.]

sepsis /'sepsɪs/ *n.* **1** the state of being septic. **2** blood-poisoning. [mod.L f. Gk *sēpsis* f. *sēpō* make rotten]

Sept. *abbr.* **1** September. **2** Septuagint.

sept /sept/ *n.* a clan, esp. in Ireland. [prob. alt. of SECT]

sept- var. of SEPTI-.

septa *pl.* of SEPTUM.

septal[1] /'sept(ə)l/ *adj.* **1** of a septum or septa. **2** *Archaeol.* (of a stone or slab) separating compartments in a burial chamber. [SEPTUM]

septal[2] /'sept(ə)l/ *adj.* of a sept or septs.

septate /'septeɪt/ *adj. Bot., Zool., & Anat.* having a septum or septa; partitioned. □□ **septation** /-'teɪʃ(ə)n/ *n.*

septcentenary /ˌseptsen'ti:nərɪ/ *n. & adj.* —*n.* (*pl.* **-ies**) **1** a seven-hundredth anniversary. **2** a festival marking this. —*adj.* of or concerning a septcentenary.

September /sep'tembə(r)/ *n.* the ninth month of the year. [ME f. L *September* f. *septem* seven: orig. the seventh month of the Roman year]

septenarius /ˌseptɪ'neərɪəs/ *n.* (*pl.* **septenarii** /-rɪˌaɪ/) *Prosody* a verse of seven feet, esp. a trochaic or iambic tetrameter catalectic. [L f. *septeni* distributive of *septem* seven]

septenary /sep'ti:nərɪ, 'septɪn-/ *adj. & n.* —*adj.* of seven, by sevens, on the basis of seven. —*n.* (*pl.* **-ies**) **1** a group or set of seven (esp. years). **2** a septenarius. [L *septenarius* (as SEPTENARIUS)]

septenate /'septɪˌneɪt/ *adj. Bot.* **1** growing in sevens. **2** having seven divisions. [L *septeni* (as SEPTENARIUS)]

septennial /sep'tenɪəl/ *adj.* **1** lasting for seven years. **2** recurring every seven years. [LL *septennis* f. L *septem* seven + *annus* year]

septennium /sep'tenɪəm/ *n.* (*pl.* **septenniums** or **septennia** /-nɪə/) a period of seven years.

septet /sep'tet/ *n.* (also **septette**) **1** *Mus.* **a** a composition for seven performers. **b** the performers of such a composition. **2** any group of seven. [G *Septett* f. L *septem* seven]

septfoil /'setfɔɪl/ *n.* **1** a seven-lobed ornamental figure. **2** *archaic* tormentil. [LL *septifolium* after CINQUEFOIL, TREFOIL]

septi- /'septɪ/ *comb. form* (also **sept-** before a vowel) seven. [L f. *septem* seven]

septic /'septɪk/ *adj.* contaminated with bacteria from a festering wound etc., putrefying. □ **septic tank** a tank in which the organic matter in sewage is disintegrated through bacterial activity, making it liquid enough to drain away. □□ **septically** *adv.* **septicity** /-'tɪsɪtɪ/ *n.* [L *septicus* f. Gk *sēptikos* f. *sēpō* make rotten]

septicaemia /ˌseptɪ'si:mɪə/ *n.* (*US* **septicemia**) blood-poisoning. □□ **septicaemic** *adj.* [mod.L f. Gk *sēptikos* + *haima* blood]

septillion /sep'tɪljən/ *n.* (*pl.* same) a thousand raised to the

æ cat ɑ: arm e bed ɜ: her ɪ sit i: see ɒ hot ɔ: saw ʌ run ʊ put u: too ə ago aɪ my

eighth (or formerly, esp. *Brit.*, the fourteenth) power (10^{24} and 10^{42} respectively). [F f. *sept* seven, after *billion* etc.]

septimal /ˈseptɪm(ə)l/ *adj.* of the number seven. [L *septimus* seventh f. *septem* seven]

septime /ˈseptiːm/ *n.* *Fencing* the seventh of the eight parrying positions. [L *septimus* (as SEPTIMAL)]

Septimius Severus /sepˈtɪmɪəs sɪˈvɪərəs/, Lucius (145/6–211), Roman emperor 193–211. After an unsuccessful invasion of Britain he died at York. He was active in reforms of the imperial administration and of the army, which he recognized as the real basis of imperial power.

septivalent /sepˈtɪvələnt/ *adj.* (also **septavalent**) *Chem.* having a valency of seven.

septuagenarian /ˌseptjʊəˈdʒɪˈneərɪən/ *n.* & *adj.* —*n.* a person from 70 to 79 years old. —*adj.* of this age. [L *septuagenarius* f. *septuageni* distributive of *septuaginta* seventy]

Septuagesima /ˌseptjʊəˈdʒesɪmə/ *n.* (in full **Septuagesima Sunday**) the Sunday before Sexagesima. [ME f. L, = seventieth (day), formed as SEPTUAGINT, perh. after QUINQUAGESIMA or with ref. to the period of 70 days from Septuagesima to the Saturday after Easter]

Septuagint /ˈseptjʊəˌdʒɪnt/ *n.* a Greek version of the Old Testament including the Apocrypha, made for the use of Jewish communities in Egypt whose native language was Greek. It derives its name from the tradition that it was the work of about 70 translators who were said to have worked in separate cells, each translating the whole, and whose versions were found to be identical, thereby showing the work to be divinely inspired. Internal evidence shows that the work was divided between a number of translators and spread over the 3rd–2nd c. BC. The early Christian Church, whose language was Greek, used the Septuagint as its Bible, and it is still the standard version of the Old Testament in the Greek Church. [L *septuaginta* seventy]

septum /ˈseptəm/ *n.* (*pl.* **septa** /-tə/) *Anat.*, *Bot.*, & *Zool.* a partition such as that between the nostrils or the chambers of a poppy-fruit or of a shell. [L *s(a)eptum* f. *saepire saept-* enclose f. *saepes* hedge]

septuple /ˈseptjʊp(ə)l/ *adj.*, *n.*, & *v.* —*adj.* 1 sevenfold, having seven parts. 2 being seven times as many or as much. —*n.* a sevenfold number or amount. —*v.tr.* & *intr.* multiply by seven. [LL *septuplus* f. L *septem* seven]

septuplet /ˈsepˌtjʊplɪt, sepˈtjuːplɪt/ *n.* 1 one of seven children born at one birth. 2 *Mus.* a group of seven notes to be played in the time of four or six. [as SEPTUPLE, after TRIPLET etc.]

sepulchral /sɪˈpʌlkr(ə)l/ *adj.* 1 of a tomb or interment (*sepulchral mound*; *sepulchral customs*). 2 suggestive of the tomb, funereal, gloomy, dismal (*sepulchral look*). □□ **sepulchrally** *adv.* [F *sépulchral* or L *sepulchralis* (as SEPULCHRE)]

sepulchre /ˈsepəlkə(r)/ *n.* & *v.* (*US* **sepulcher**) —*n.* a tomb esp. cut in rock or built of stone or brick, a burial vault or cave. —*v.tr.* 1 lay in a sepulchre. 2 serve as a sepulchre for. □ **the Holy Sepulchre** the tomb in which Christ was laid. **whited sepulchre** a hypocrite (with ref. to Matt. 23: 27). [ME f. OF f. L *sepulc(h)rum* f. *sepelire sepult-* bury]

sepulture /ˈsepəltʃə(r)/ *n.* *literary* the act or an instance of burying or putting in the grave. [ME f. OF f. L *sepultura* (as SEPULCHRE)]

seq. *abbr.* (*pl.* **seqq.**) the following. [L *sequens* etc.]

sequacious /sɪˈkweɪʃəs/ *adj.* 1 (of reasoning or a reasoner) not inconsequent, coherent. 2 *archaic* inclined to follow, lacking independence or originality, servile. □□ **sequaciously** *adv.* **sequacity** /sɪˈkwæsɪtɪ/ *n.* [L *sequax* f. *sequi* follow]

sequel /ˈsiːkw(ə)l/ *n.* 1 what follows (esp. as a result). 2 a novel, film, etc., that continues the story of an earlier one. □ **in the sequel** as things developed afterwards. [ME f. OF *sequelle* or L *sequel(l)a* f. *sequi* follow]

sequela /sɪˈkwiːlə/ *n.* (*pl.* **sequelae** /-liː/) *Med.* (esp. in *pl.*) a morbid condition or symptom following a disease. [L f. *sequi* follow]

sequence /ˈsiːkwəns/ *n.* & *v.* —*n.* 1 succession, coming after or next. 2 order of succession (*shall follow the sequence of events*; *give the facts in historical sequence*). 3 a set of things belonging next to one another on some principle of order; a series without gaps. 4 a part of a film dealing with one scene or topic. 5 a set of poems on one theme. 6 a set of three or more playing-cards next to one another in value. 7 *Mus.* repetition of a phrase or melody at a higher or lower pitch. 8 *Eccl.* a hymn said or sung after the Gradual or Alleluia that precedes the Gospel. 9 succession without implication of causality (opp. CONSEQUENCE). —*v.tr.* 1 arrange in a definite order. 2 *Biochem.* ascertain the sequence of monomers in (esp. a polypeptide or nucleic acid). □ **sequence of tenses** *Gram.* the dependence of the tense of a subordinate verb on the tense of the principal verb, according to certain rules (e.g. *I think you are*, *thought you were*, *wrong*). □□ **sequencer** *n.* [ME f. LL *sequentia* f. L *sequens* pres. part. of *sequi* follow]

sequent /ˈsiːkwənt/ *adj.* 1 following as a sequence or consequence. 2 consecutive. □□ **sequently** *adv.* [OF *sequent* or L *sequens* (as SEQUENCE)]

sequential /sɪˈkwenʃ(ə)l/ *adj.* forming a sequence or consequence or sequela. □□ **sequentiality** /-ʃɪˈælɪtɪ/ *n.* **sequentially** *adv.* [SEQUENCE, after CONSEQUENTIAL]

sequester /sɪˈkwestə(r)/ *v.tr.* 1 (esp. as **sequestered** *adj.*) seclude, isolate, set apart (*sequester oneself from the world*; *a sequestered life*; *a sequestered cottage*). 2 = SEQUESTRATE. 3 *Chem.* bind (a metal ion) so that it cannot react. [ME f. OF *sequestrer* or LL *sequestrare* commit for safe keeping f. L *sequester* trustee]

sequestrate /sɪˈkwestreɪt, ˈsiːkwɪ-/ *v.tr.* 1 confiscate, appropriate. 2 *Law* take temporary possession of (a debtor's estate etc.). 3 *Eccl.* apply (the income of a benefice) to clearing the incumbent's debts or accumulating a fund for the next incumbent. □□ **sequestrable** *adj.* **sequestration** /ˌsiːkwɪˈstreɪʃ(ə)n/ *n.* **sequestrator** /ˈsiːkwɪˌstreɪtə(r)/ *n.* [LL *sequestrare* (as SEQUESTER)]

sequestrum /sɪˈkwestrəm/ *n.* (*pl.* **sequestra** /-trə/) a piece of dead bone or other tissue detached from the surrounding parts. □□ **sequestral** *adj.* **sequestrotomy** /ˌsiːkwɪsˈtrɒtəmɪ/ *n.* (*pl.* **-ies**). [mod.L, neut. of L *sequester* standing apart]

sequin /ˈsiːkwɪn/ *n.* 1 a circular spangle for attaching to clothing as an ornament. 2 *hist.* a Venetian gold coin. □□ **sequinned** *adj.* (also **sequined**). [F f. It. *zecchino* f. *zecca* a mint f. Arab. *sikka* a die]

sequoia /sɪˈkwɔɪə/ *n.* a Californian evergreen coniferous tree, *Sequoia sempervirens*, of very great height. [mod.L genus-name, f. *Sequoiah*, the name of a Cherokee]

sera *pl.* of SERUM.

serac /seˈræk/ *n.* any of the tower-shaped masses into which a glacier is divided at steep points by crevasses crossing it. [Swiss F *sérac*, orig. the name of a compact white cheese]

seraglio /seˈrɑːlɪəʊ, sɪ-/ *n.* (*pl.* **-os**) 1 a harem. 2 *hist.* a Turkish palace, esp. that of the Sultan with government offices etc. at Constantinople. [It. *serraglio* f. Turk. f. Pers. *sarāy* palace: cf. SERAI]

serai /seˈraɪ, seˈrɑːɪ/ *n.* a caravanserai. [Turk. f. Pers. (as SERAGLIO)]

Seraing /səˈræ̃/ an industrial town on the River Meuse in east Belgium, 7 km (4 miles) south-west of Liège; pop. (1988) 61,400. The first locomotive in Europe was built here at an ironworks established in 1817 by an Englishman, John Cockerill.

Seram Sea see CERAM SEA.

serang /səˈræŋ/ *n.* *Anglo-Ind.* a native head of a Lascar crew. [Hindi f. Pers. *sarhang* commander]

serape /seˈrɑːpeɪ/ *n.* (also **sarape** /sæ-/, **zarape** /zæ-/) a shawl or blanket worn as a cloak by Spanish Americans. [Mexican Sp.]

seraph /ˈserəf/ *n.* (*pl.* **seraphim** /-fɪm/ or **seraphs**) an angelic being, one of the highest order of the ninefold celestial hierarchy gifted esp. with love and associated with light, ardour, and purity. [back-form. f. *seraphim* (cf. CHERUB) (pl.) f. LL f. Gk *seraphim* f. Heb. *ś'rāpīm*]

seraphic /səˈræfɪk/ *adj.* 1 of or like the seraphim. 2 ecstatically adoring, fervent, or serene. □ **the Seraphic Doctor** the nickname of St Bonaventura. □□ **seraphically** *adv.* [med.L *seraphicus* f. LL (as SERAPH)]

Serapis /səˈreɪpɪs/ *Egyptian Mythol.* a god whose cult arose at

Memphis in the temple where the deceased Apis bulls were entombed. Ptolemy I sought to make this an imperial cult, a combination of the Apis with Osiris, to unite Greeks and Egyptians in a common worship.

seraskier /ˌserəˈskɪə(r)/ n. hist. the Turkish Commander-in-Chief and minister of war. [Turk. f. Pers. sar askar head of army]

Serb /sɜːb/ n. & adj. —n. 1 a native of Serbia. 2 a person of Serbian descent. —adj. = SERBIAN. [Serbian Srb]

Serbia /ˈsɜːbɪə/ a constituent republic of Yugoslavia, formed from a former Balkan kingdom; pop. (1981) 9,313,700; capital, Belgrade. It was conquered by the Turks in the 14th c., but with the decline of Ottoman power in the 19th c., the Serbs successfully pressed for independence, finally winning nationhood in 1878. Subsequent Serbian ambitions to found a South Slav nation State brought the country into rivalry with the Austro-Hungarian empire and eventually contributed to the outbreak of the First World War. Despite early successes against the Austrians, Serbia was occupied by the Central Powers and never regained its pre-war identity, being absorbed into the new State of Yugoslavia after the end of hostilities. □□ **Serbian** adj. & n.

Serbo- /ˈsɜːbəʊ/ comb. form Serbian.

Serbo-Croat /ˌsɜːbəʊˈkrəʊæt/ n. & adj. (also **Serbo-Croatian** /-krəʊˈeɪʃ(ə)n/) —n. the language of the Serbs and Croats, generally considered to be one language (the differences between Serbian and Croatian are cultural rather than linguistic). Serbian is spoken by 10 million Serbs in Yugoslavia who belong to the Eastern Orthodox religion and so use the Cyrillic alphabet; Croat is spoken by the 5 million Croats who live in the same country and are Roman Catholic and use the Roman alphabet. Both belong to the Slavonic group of languages. —adj. of or relating to this language.

SERC abbr. (in the UK) Science and Engineering Research Council.

sere[1] /sɪə(r)/ n. a catch of a gunlock holding the hammer at half or full cock. [prob. f. OF serre lock, bolt, grasp, f. serrer (see SERRIED)]

sere[2] var. of SEAR adj.

sere[3] /sɪə(r)/ n. Ecol. a sequence of animal or plant communities. [L serere join in a series]

serein /səˈræ̃/ n. a fine rain falling in tropical climates from a cloudless sky. [F f. OF serain ult. f. L serum evening f. serus late]

serenade /ˌserəˈneɪd/ n. & v. —n. 1 a piece of music sung or played at night, esp. by a lover under his lady's window, or suitable for this. 2 = SERENATA. —v.tr. sing or play a serenade to. □□ **serenader** n. [F sérénade f. It. serenata f. sereno SERENE]

serenata /ˌserəˈnɑːtə/ n. Mus. 1 a cantata with a pastoral subject. 2 a simple form of suite for orchestra or wind band. [It. (as SERENADE)]

serendipity /ˌserənˈdɪpɪtɪ/ n. the faculty of making happy and unexpected discoveries by accident. □□ **serendipitous** adj. **serendipitously** adv. [coined by Horace Walpole (1754) after The Three Princes of Serendip (Sri Lanka), a fairy-tale]

serene /sɪˈriːn, səˈriːn/ adj. & n. —adj. (**serener**, **serenest**) 1 a (of the sky, the air, etc.) clear and calm. b (of the sea etc.) unruffled. 2 placid, tranquil, unperturbed. —n. poet. a serene expanse of sky, sea, etc. □ **all serene** Brit. sl. all right. **Serene Highness** a title used in addressing and referring to members of some European royal families (His Serene Highness; Their Serene Highnesses; Your Serene Highness). □□ **serenely** adv. **sereneness** n. [L serenus]

Serengeti /ˌserənˈɡetɪ/ a vast plain lying to the west of the Great Rift Valley in Tanzania. In 1951 a national park was created to protect large numbers of migrating wildebeest, zebra, and Thomson's gazelle.

serenity /sɪˈrenɪtɪ, səˈr-/ n. (pl. **-ies**) 1 tranquillity, being serene. 2 (**Serenity**) a title used in addressing and referring to a reigning prince or similar dignitary (your Serenity). [F sérénité or L serenitas (as SERENE)]

serf /sɜːf/ n. 1 hist. a labourer who could not be removed (except by manumission) from his lord's land on which he worked, and was transferred with it when it passed to another owner. Though free, he was restricted in his movements and in the disposal of his property, and was inferior in status to a free tenant. Serfdom in England lasted until the 14th or 15th c., but was not abolished in eastern Europe until the 19th c. 2 an oppressed person, a drudge. □□ **serfage** n. **serfdom** n. **serfhood** n. [OF f. L servus slave]

serge /sɜːdʒ/ n. a durable twilled worsted etc. fabric. [ME f. OF sarge, serge ult. f. L serica (lana): see SILK]

sergeant /ˈsɑːdʒ(ə)nt/ n. 1 a non-commissioned Army or Air Force officer next below warrant officer. 2 a police officer ranking below (Brit.) inspector or (US) captain. □ **company sergeant-major** Mil. the highest non-commissioned officer of a company. **Sergeant Baker** Austral. a large brightly-coloured marine fish, Aulopus purpurissatus. **sergeant-fish** a marine fish, Rachycentron canadum, with lateral stripes suggesting a chevron. **sergeant-major** Mil. 1 (in full **regimental sergeant-major**) Brit. a warrant-officer assisting the adjutant of a regiment or battalion. 2 US the highest-ranking non-commissioned officer. □□ **sergeancy** n. (pl. **-ies**). **sergeantship** n. [ME f. OF sergent f. L serviens -entis servant f. servire SERVE]

Sergius /ˈsɜːdʒɪəs/, St (1314–92), Russian monastic reformer and mystic, who founded the monastery of the Holy Trinity near Moscow, and thereby re-established monasticism, which had been lost in Russia through the Tartar invasion. His influence was great: he stopped four civil wars between Russian princes, and inspired the resistance which saved Russia from the Tartars in 1380. Altogether, Sergius founded forty monasteries. He is regarded as the greatest of Russian Saints. Feast day, 25 Sept.

Sergt. abbr. Sergeant.

serial /ˈsɪərɪəl/ n. & adj. —n. 1 a story, play, or film which is published, broadcast, or shown in regular instalments. 2 a periodical. —adj. 1 of or in or forming a series. 2 (of a story etc.) in the form of a serial. 3 Mus. using transformations of a fixed series of notes (see SERIES 8 and SERIAL COMPOSITION). 4 (of a publication) appearing in successive parts published usu. at regular intervals, periodical. □ **serial killer** a person who murders continuously with no apparent motive. **serial number** a number showing the position of an item in a series. **serial rights** the right to publish a story or book as a serial. □□ **seriality** /-ˈælɪtɪ/ n. **serially** adv. [SERIES + -AL]

serial composition n. a technique used in composing music whereby the twelve notes of the chromatic scale are arranged in a fixed order and form the basic core of a piece, generating melodies and harmonies and, strictly speaking, subject to change only in specific ways, such as by inversion or retrograde motion. Serialism was designed to combat the potential anarchy of atonality, which overthrew the traditional harmonic thinking associated with scale and key, and the first fully serial movements appeared in 1923 in works by Schoenberg. For some composers, notably Boulez and Stockhausen, serialism remains an important concept, but in general composers have looked elsewhere for means of musical integration.

serialist /ˈsɪərɪəlɪst/ n. a composer or advocate of serial music. □□ **serialism** n.

serialize /ˈsɪərɪəˌlaɪz/ v.tr. (also **-ise**) 1 publish or produce in instalments. 2 arrange in a series. 3 Mus. compose according to a serial technique. □□ **serialization** /-ˈzeɪʃ(ə)n/ n.

seriate adj. & v. —adj. /ˈsɪərɪɪt/ in the form of a series; in orderly sequence. —v.tr. /ˈsɪərɪˌeɪt/ arrange in a seriate manner. □□ **seriation** /-ˈeɪʃ(ə)n/ n.

seriatim /ˌsɪərɪˈeɪtɪm, ˌser-/ adv. point by point; taking one subject etc. after another in regular order (consider seriatim). [med.L f. L series, after LITERATIM etc.]

Seric /ˈsɪərɪk/ adj. archaic Chinese. [L sericus; see SILK]

sericeous /sɪˈrɪʃəs/ adj. Bot. & Zool. covered with silky hairs. [LL sericeus silken]

sericulture /ˈserɪˌkʌltʃ(ə)r/ n. 1 silkworm-breeding. 2 the production of raw silk. □□ **sericultural** /-ˈkʌltʃ(ə)r(ə)l/ adj. **sericulturist** /-ˈkʌltʃərɪst/ n. [F sériciculture f. LL sericum: see SILK, CULTURE]

seriema /ˌserɪˈiːmə/ n. (also **cariama** /ˌkærɪˈɑːmə/) Zool. any S.

American bird of the family Cariamidae, having a long neck and legs and a crest above the bill. [mod.L f. Tupi *siriema* etc. crested]

series /ˈsɪəriːz, -rɪz/ *n.* (*pl.* same) **1** a number of things of which each is similar to the preceding or in which each successive pair are similarly related; a sequence, succession, order, row, or set. **2** a set of successive games between the same teams. **3** a set of programmes with the same actors etc. or on related subjects but each complete in itself. **4** a set of lectures by the same speaker or on the same subject. **5 a** a set of successive issues of a periodical, of articles on one subject or by one writer, etc., esp. when numbered separately from a preceding or following set (*second series*). **b** a set of independent books in a common format or under a common title or supervised by a common general editor. **6** *Philately* a set of stamps, coins, etc., of different denominations but issued at one time, in one reign, etc. **7** *Geol.* **a** a set of strata with a common characteristic. **b** the rocks deposited during a specific epoch. **8** *Mus.* an arrangement of the twelve notes of the chromatic scale as a basis for serial music. **9** *Electr.* **a** a set of circuits or components arranged so that the current passes through each successively. **b** a set of batteries etc. having the positive electrode of each connected with the negative electrode of the next. **10** *Chem.* a set of elements with common properties or of compounds related in composition or structure. **11** *Math.* a set of quantities constituting a progression or having the several values determined by a common relation. □ **arithmetical** (or **geometrical**) **series** a series in arithmetical (or geometrical) progression. **in series 1** in ordered succession. **2** *Electr.* (of a set of circuits or components) arranged so that the current passes through each successively. [L, = row, chain f. *serere* join, connect]

serif /ˈserɪf/ *n.* a slight projection finishing off a stroke of a letter as in T contrasted with T (cf. SANSERIF). □□ **seriffed** *adj.* [perh. f. Du. *schreef* dash, line f. Gmc]

serigraphy /səˈrɪɡrəfi/ *n.* the art or process of printing designs by means of a silk screen. □□ **serigraph** /ˈserɪˌɡrɑːf/ *n.* **serigrapher** *n.* [irreg. f. L *sericum* SILK]

serin /ˈserɪn/ *n.* any small yellow Mediterranean finch of the genus *Serinus*, esp. the wild canary *S. serinus*. [F, of uncert. orig.]

serinette /ˌserɪˈnet/ *n.* an instrument for teaching cage-birds to sing. [F (as SERIN)]

seringa /səˈrɪŋɡə/ *n.* **1** = SYRINGA. **2** any of various rubber-trees of the genus *Hevea*, native to Brazil. [F (as SYRINGA)]

serio-comic /ˌsɪərɪəʊˈkɒmɪk/ *adj.* combining the serious and the comic, jocular in intention but simulating seriousness or vice versa. □□ **serio-comically** *adv.*

serious /ˈsɪərɪəs/ *adj.* **1** thoughtful, earnest, sober, sedate, responsible, not reckless or given to trifling (*has a serious air; a serious young person*). **2** important, demanding consideration (*this is a serious matter*). **3** not slight or negligible (*a serious injury; a serious offence*). **4** sincere, in earnest, not ironical or joking (*are you serious?*). **5** (of music and literature) not merely for amusement (opp. LIGHT² 5a). **6** not perfunctory (*serious thought*). **7** not to be trifled with (*a serious opponent*). **8** concerned with religion or ethics (*serious subjects*). □□ **seriousness** *n.* [ME f. OF *serieux* or LL *seriosus* f. L *serius*]

seriously /ˈsɪərɪəslɪ/ *adv.* **1** in a serious manner (esp. introducing a sentence, implying that irony etc. is now to cease). **2** to a serious extent.

serjeant /ˈsɑːdʒ(ə)nt/ *n.* **1** (in full **serjeant-at-law**, *pl.* **serjeants-at-law**) *hist.* a barrister of the highest rank. **2** *Brit.* (in official lists) a sergeant in the Army. □ **Common Serjeant** *Brit.* a circuit judge of the Central Criminal Court with duties in the City of London. **serjeant-at-arms** (*pl.* **serjeants-at-arms**) **1** an official of a court or city or parliament, with ceremonial duties. **2** (in Britain) an officer of each House of Parliament with the duty of enforcing the commands of the house, arresting offenders, etc. □□ **serjeantship** *n.* [var. of SERGEANT]

sermon /ˈsɜːmən/ *n.* **1** a spoken or written discourse on a religious or moral subject, esp. a discourse based on a text or passage of Scripture and delivered in a service by way of religious instruction or exhortation. **2** a piece of admonition or reproof, a lecture. **3** a moral reflection suggested by natural objects etc. (*sermons in stones*). □ **Sermon on the Mount** the discourse of Christ recorded in Matt. 5–7. [ME f. AF *sermun*, OF *sermon* f. L *sermo -onis* discourse, talk]

sermonette /ˌsɜːməˈnet/ *n.* a short sermon.

sermonize /ˈsɜːməˌnaɪz/ *v.* (also **-ise**) **1** *tr.* deliver a moral lecture to. **2** *intr.* deliver a moral lecture. □□ **sermonizer** *n.*

serology /sɪəˈrɒlədʒɪ/ *n.* the scientific study of blood sera and their effects. □□ **serological** /-rəˈlɒdʒɪk(ə)l/ *adj.* **serologist** *n.*

serosa /səˈrəʊsə/ *n.* a serous membrane. [mod.L, fem. of med.L *serosus* SEROUS]

serotine /ˈserətɪn/ *n.* a chestnut-coloured European bat, *Eptesicus serotinus*. [F *sérotine* f. L *serotinus* late, of the evening, f. *serus* late]

serotonin /ˌsɪərəˈtəʊnɪn/ *n.* *Biol.* a compound present in blood serum, which constricts the blood vessels and acts as a neurotransmitter. [SERUM + TONIC + -IN]

serous /ˈsɪərəs/ *adj.* of or like or producing serum; watery. □ **serous gland** (or **membrane**) a gland or membrane with a serous secretion. □□ **serosity** /-ˈrɒsɪtɪ/ *n.* [F *séreux* or med.L *serosus* (as SERUM)]

serpent /ˈsɜːpənt/ *n.* **1** usu. *literary.* **a** a snake, esp. of a large kind. **b** a scaly limbless reptile. **2** a sly or treacherous person, esp. one who exploits a position of trust to betray it. **3** *Mus.* an old type of wind instrument, about 20 cm (8 inches) long and roughly S-shaped (whence its name), made of wood or sometimes of metal and giving a powerful deep note. First introduced towards the end of the 16th c. in France, where it was used in church, it became a popular military-band instrument and was used in English church bands until the mid-19th c. **4** (**the Serpent**) *Bibl.* Satan (see Gen. 3, Rev. 20). [ME f. OF f. L *serpens -entis* part. of *serpere* creep]

serpentine /ˈsɜːpənˌtaɪn/ *adj., n.,* & *v.* —*adj.* **1** of or like a serpent. **2** coiling, tortuous, sinuous, meandering, writhing (*the serpentine windings of the stream*). **3** cunning, subtle, treacherous. —*n.* **1** a soft rock mainly of hydrated magnesium silicate, usu. dark green and sometimes mottled or spotted like a serpent's skin, taking a high polish and used as a decorative material. **2** *Skating* a figure of three circles in a line. —*v.intr.* move sinuously, meander. □ **serpentine verse** a metrical line beginning and ending with the same word. [ME f. OF *serpentin* f. LL *serpentinus* (as SERPENT)]

serpiginous /sɜːˈpɪdʒɪnəs/ *adj.* (of a skin-disease etc.) creeping from one part to another. [med.L *serpigo -ginis* ringworm f. L *serpere* creep]

SERPS /sɜːps/ *abbr.* (in the UK) State earnings-related pension scheme.

serpula /ˈsɜːpjʊlə/ *n.* (*pl.* **serpulae** /-liː/) any of various marine worms of the family Serpulidae, living in intricately twisted shell-like tubes. [LL, = small serpent, f. L *serpere* creep]

serra /ˈserə/ *n.* (*pl.* **serrae** /-riː/) a serrated organ, structure, or edge. [L, = saw]

serradilla /ˌserəˈdɪlə/ *n.* (*pl.* **serradillae** /-liː/) a clover, *Ornithopus sativus*, grown as fodder. [Port., dimin. of *serrado* serrated]

serran /ˈserən/ *n.* any marine fish of the family Serranidae. [mod.L *serranus* f. L *serra* saw]

serrate *v.* & *adj.* —*v.tr.* /seˈreɪt/ (usu. as **serrated** *adj.*) provide with a sawlike edge. —*adj.* /ˈserɪt/ esp. *Anat., Bot.,* & *Zool.* notched like a saw. □□ **serration** *n.* [LL *serrare serrat-* f. L *serra* saw]

serried /ˈserɪd/ *adj.* (of ranks of soldiers, rows of trees, etc.) pressed together; without gaps; close. [past part. of *serry* press close prob. f. F *serré* past part. of *serrer* close ult. f. L *sera* lock, or past part. of obs. *serr* f. OF *serrer*]

serrulate /ˈserʊˌleɪt/ *adj.* esp. *Anat., Bot.,* & *Zool.* finely serrate; with a series of small notches. □□ **serrulation** /-ˈleɪʃ(ə)n/ *n.* [mod.L *serrulatus* f. L *serrula* dimin. of *serra* saw]

serum /ˈsɪərəm/ *n.* (*pl.* **sera** /-rə/ or **serums**) **1 a** an amber-coloured liquid that separates from a clot when blood coagulates. **b** whey. **2** *Med.* blood serum (usu. from a non-human mammal) as an antitoxin or therapeutic agent, esp. in inoculation. **3** a watery fluid in animal bodies. □ **serum sickness** a reaction to an injection of serum, characterized by skin eruption, fever, etc. [L, = whey]

serval /ˈsɜːv(ə)l/ n. a tawny black-spotted long-legged African cat, *Felis serval*. [F f. Port. *cerval* deerlike f. *cervo* deer f. L *cervus*]

servant /ˈsɜːv(ə)nt/ n. **1** a person who has undertaken (usu. in return for stipulated pay) to carry out the orders of an individual or corporate employer, esp. a person employed in a house on domestic duties or as a personal attendant. **2** a devoted follower, a person willing to serve another (*a servant of Jesus Christ*). □ **your humble servant** *Brit. archaic* a formula preceding a signature or expressing ironical courtesy. **your obedient servant** *Brit.* a formula preceding a signature, now used only in certain formal letters. [ME f. OF (as SERVE)]

serve /sɜːv/ v. & n. —v. **1** tr. do a service for (a person, community, etc.). **2** tr. (also *absol.*) be a servant to. **3** intr. carry out duties (*served on six committees*). **4** intr. **a** (foll. by *in*) be employed in (an organization, esp. the armed forces, or a place, esp. a foreign country) (*served in the air force*). **b** be a member of the armed forces. **5 a** tr. be useful to or serviceable for; meet the needs of; do what is required for (*serve a purpose; one packet serves him for a week*). **b** intr. meet requirements; perform a function (*a sofa serving as a bed*). **c** intr. (foll. by *to* + infin.) avail, suffice (*his attempt served only to postpone the inevitable; it serves to show the folly of such action*). **6** tr. go through a due period of (office, apprenticeship, a prison sentence, etc.). **7** tr. set out or present (food) for those about to eat it (*asparagus served with butter; dinner was then served*). **8** intr. (in full **serve at table**) act as a waiter. **9** tr. **a** attend to (a customer in a shop). **b** (foll. by *with*) supply with (goods) (*was serving a customer with apples; served the town with gas*). **10** tr. treat or act towards (a person) in a specified way (*has served me shamefully; you may serve me as you will*). **11** tr. **a** (often foll. by *on*) deliver (a writ etc.) to the person concerned in a legally formal manner (*served a warrant on him*). **b** (foll. by *with*) deliver a writ etc. to (a person) in this way (*served her with a summons*). **12** tr. *Tennis* etc. **a** (also *absol.*) deliver (a ball etc.) to begin or resume play. **b** produce (a fault etc.) by doing this. **13** tr. *Mil.* keep (a gun, battery, etc.) firing. **14** tr. (of an animal, esp. a stallion etc. hired for the purpose) copulate with (a female). **15** tr. distribute (*served the ammunition out; served the rations round*). **16** tr. render obedience to (a deity etc.). **17** *Eccl.* **a** intr. act as a server. **b** tr. act as a server at (a service). **18** intr. (of a tide) be suitable for a ship to leave harbour etc. **19** tr. *Naut.* bind (a rope etc.) with thin cord to strengthen it. **20** tr. play (a trick etc.) on. —n. **1** *Tennis* etc. **a** the act or an instance of serving. **b** a manner of serving. **c** a person's turn to serve. **2** *Austral. sl.* a reprimand. □ **it will serve** it will be adequate. **serve one's needs** (or **need**) be adequate. **serve out** retaliate on. **serve the purpose of** take the place of, be used as. **serve a person right** be a person's deserved punishment or misfortune. **serve one's time 1** hold office for the normal period. **2** (also **serve time**) undergo imprisonment, apprenticeship, etc. **serve one's** (or **the**) **turn** be adequate. **serve up** offer for acceptance. [ME f. OF *servir* f. L *servire* f. *servus* slave]

server /ˈsɜːvə(r)/ n. **1** a person who serves. **2** *Eccl.* a person assisting the celebrant at a service, esp. the Eucharist.

servery /ˈsɜːvərɪ/ n. (pl. -**ies**) a room from which meals etc. are served and in which utensils are kept.

Servian[1] /ˈsɜːvɪən/ adj. & n. former var. of SERBIAN.

Servian[2] /ˈsɜːvɪən/ adj. of Servius Tullius, the semi-legendary sixth king of ancient Rome (6th c. BC). □ **Servian Wall** the wall said to have been built by him round Rome.

service[1] /ˈsɜːvɪs/ n. & v. —n. **1** the act of helping or doing work for another or for a community etc. **2** work done in this way. **3** assistance or benefit given to someone. **4** the provision or system of supplying a public need, e.g. transport, or (often in *pl.*) the supply of water, gas, electricity, telephone, etc. **5 a** the fact or status of being a servant. **b** employment or a position as a servant. **6** a state or period of employment doing work for an individual or organization (*resigned after 15 years' service*). **7 a** a public or Crown department or organization employing officials working for the State (*civil service; secret service*). **b** employment in this. **8** (in *pl.*) the armed forces. **9** (*attrib.*) of the kind issued to the armed forces (*a service revolver*). **10 a** a ceremony of worship

according to prescribed forms. **b** a form of liturgy for this. **11 a** the provision of what is necessary for the installation and maintenance of a machine etc. or operation. **b** a periodic routine maintenance of a motor vehicle etc. **12** assistance or advice given to customers after the sale of goods. **13 a** the act or process of serving food, drinks, etc. **b** an extra charge nominally made for this. **14** a set of dishes, plates, etc., used for serving meals (*a dinner service*). **15** *Tennis* etc. **a** the act or an instance of serving. **b** a person's turn to serve. **c** the manner or quality of serving. **d** (in full **service game**) a game in which a particular player serves. —v.tr. **1** provide service or services for, esp. maintain. **2** maintain or repair (a car, machine, etc.). **3** pay interest on (a debt). **4** supply with a service. □ **at a person's service** ready to serve or assist a person. **be of service** be available to assist. **in service 1** employed as a servant. **2** available for use. **on active service** serving in the armed forces in wartime. **out of service** not available for use. **see service 1** have experience of service, esp. in the armed forces. **2** (of a thing) be much used. **service area 1** an area beside a major road for the supply of petrol, refreshments, etc. **2** the area served by a broadcasting station. **service-book** a book of authorized forms of worship of a Church. **service bus** (or **car**) *Austral.* & *NZ* a motor coach. **service charge** an additional charge for service in a restaurant, hotel, etc. **service dress** ordinary military etc. uniform. **service flat** a flat in which domestic service and sometimes meals are provided by the management. **service industry** one providing services not goods. **service line** (in tennis etc.) a line marking the limit of the area into which the ball must be served. **service road** a road parallel to a main road, serving houses, shops, etc. **service station** an establishment beside a road selling petrol and oil etc. to motorists and often able to carry out maintenance. **take service with** become a servant to. [ME f. OF *service* or L *servitium* f. *servus* slave]

service[2] /ˈsɜːvɪs/ n. (in full **service tree**) a European tree of the genus *Sorbus*, esp. *S. domestica* with toothed leaves, cream-coloured flowers, and small round or pear-shaped fruit eaten when overripe. □ **service-berry 1** the fruit of the service tree. **2 a** any American shrub of the genus *Amelanchier*. **b** the edible fruit of this. [earlier *serves*, pl. of obs. *serve* f. OE *syrfe* f. Gmc *surbhjōn* ult. f. L *sorbus*]

serviceable /ˈsɜːvɪsəb(ə)l/ adj. **1** useful or usable. **2** able to render service. **3** durable; capable of withstanding difficult conditions. **4** suited for ordinary use rather than ornament. □□ **serviceability** /-ˈbɪlɪtɪ/ n. **serviceableness** n. **serviceably** adv. [ME f. OF *servisable* (as SERVICE[1])]

serviceman /ˈsɜːvɪsmən/ n. (pl. -**men**) **1** a man serving in the armed forces. **2** a man providing service or maintenance.

servicewoman /ˈsɜːvɪsˌwʊmən/ n. (pl. -**women**) a woman serving in the armed forces.

serviette /ˌsɜːvɪˈet/ n. esp. *Brit.* a napkin for use at table. [ME f. OF f. *servir* SERVE]

servile /ˈsɜːvaɪl/ adj. **1** of or being or like a slave or slaves. **2** slavish; fawning; completely dependent. □□ **servilely** adv. **servility** /-ˈvɪlɪtɪ/ n. [ME f. L *servilis* f. *servus* slave]

serving /ˈsɜːvɪŋ/ n. a quantity of food served to one person.

servitor /ˈsɜːvɪt(ə)r/ n. **1** *archaic* **a** a servant. **b** an attendant. **2** *hist.* an Oxford undergraduate performing menial duties in exchange for assistance from college funds. □□ **servitorship** n. [ME f. OF f. LL (as SERVE)]

servitude /ˈsɜːvɪˌtjuːd/ n. **1** slavery. **2** subjection (esp. involuntary); bondage. **3** *Law* the subjection of property to an easement. [ME f. OF f. L *servitudo -inis* f. *servus* slave]

servo /ˈsɜːvəʊ/ n. (pl. -**os**) **1** (in full **servo-mechanism**) a powered mechanism producing motion or forces at a higher level of energy than the input level, e.g. in the brakes and steering of large motor vehicles, esp. where feedback is employed to make the control automatic. **2** (in full **servo-motor**) the motive element in a servo-mechanism. **3** (in comb.) of or involving a servo-mechanism (*servo-assisted*). [L *servus* slave]

sesame /ˈsesəmɪ/ n. *Bot.* **1** an E. Indian herbaceous plant, *Sesamum indicum*, with seeds used as food and yielding an edible oil. **2** its seeds. □ **open sesame** a means of acquiring or achieving what is normally unattainable (from the magic words used in the *Arabian Nights* to cause a door to open). [L *sesamum* f. Gk *sēsamon*, *sēsamē*]

sesamoid /ˈsesəˌmɔɪd/ *adj. & n.* —*adj.* shaped like a sesame seed; nodular (esp. of small independent bones developed in tendons passing over an angular structure such as the kneecap and the navicular bone). —*n.* a sesamoid bone.

Sesotho /seˈsuːtuː/ *n.* a Bantu language spoken by members of the Sotho people, one of the official languages of Lesotho. [Bantu, = language of the Sotho]

sesqui- /ˈseskwɪ/ *comb. form* **1** denoting one and a half. **2** *Chem.* (of a compound) in which there are three equivalents of a named element or radical to two others. [L (as SEMI-, *-que* and)]

sesquicentenary /ˌseskwɪsenˈtiːnərɪ/ *n.* (*pl.* **-ies**) a one-hundred-and-fiftieth anniversary.

sesquicentennial /ˌseskwɪsenˈtenɪəl/ *n. & adj.* —*n.* = SES-QUICENTENARY. —*adj.* of or relating to a sesquicentennial.

sess var. of CESS[1].

sessile /ˈsesaɪl/ *adj.* **1** *Bot. & Zool.* (of a flower, leaf, eye, etc.) attached directly by its base without a stalk or peduncle. **2** fixed in one position; immobile. □ **sessile oak** = DURMAST. [L *sessilis* f. *sedēre sess-* sit]

session /ˈseʃ(ə)n/ *n.* **1** the process of assembly of a deliberative or judicial body to conduct its business. **2** a single meeting for this purpose. **3** a period during which such meetings are regularly held. **4 a** an academic year. **b** the period during which a school etc. has classes. **5** a period devoted to an activity (*poker session*; *recording session*). **6** the governing body of a Presbyterian Church. □ **in session** assembled for business; not on vacation. **petty sessions 1** a meeting of two or more magistrates for the summary trial of certain offences. **2** = *quarter sessions*. □□ **sessional** *adj.* [ME f. OF *session* or L *sessio -onis* (as SESSILE)]

sesterce /ˈsestɜːs/ *n.* (also **sestertius** /seˈstɜːʃəs/) (*pl.* **sesterces** /ˈsestəˌsiːz/ or **sestertii** /-ˈstɜːʃɪɪ/) an ancient Roman coin and monetary unit equal to one quarter of a denarius. [L *sestertius* (*nummus* coin) = 2½ f. *semis* half + *tertius* third]

sestet /sesˈtet/ *n.* **1** the last six lines of a sonnet. **2** a sextet. [It. *sestetto* f. *sesto* f. L *sextus* a sixth]

sestina /sesˈtiːnə/ *n.* a form of rhymed or unrhymed poem with six stanzas of six lines and a final triplet, all stanzas having the same six words at the line-ends in six different sequences. [It. (as SESTET)]

set[1] /set/ *v.* (**setting**; *past* and *past part.* **set**) **1** *tr.* put, lay, or stand (a thing) in a certain position or location (*set it on the table*; *set it upright*). **2** *tr.* (foll. by *to*) apply (one thing) to (another) (*set pen to paper*). **3** *tr.* **a** fix ready or in position. **b** dispose suitably for use, action, or display. **4** *tr.* **a** adjust the hands of (a clock or watch) to show the right time. **b** adjust (an alarm clock) to sound at the required time. **5** *tr.* **a** fix, arrange, or mount. **b** insert (a jewel in a ring, framework, etc. **6** *tr.* make (a device) ready to operate. **7** *tr.* lay (a table) for a meal. **8** *tr.* arrange (the hair) while damp so that it dries in the required style. **9** *tr.* (foll. by *with*) ornament or provide (a surface, esp. a precious item) (*gold set with gems*). **10** *tr.* bring by placing or arranging or other means into a specified state; cause to be (*set things in motion*; *set it on fire*). **11** *intr. & tr.* harden or solidify (*the jelly is set*; *the cement has set*). **12** *intr.* (of the sun, moon, etc.) appear to move towards and below the earth's horizon (as the earth rotates). **13** *tr.* represent (a story, play, scene, etc.) as happening in a certain time or place. **14** *tr.* **a** (foll. by *to* + infin.) cause or instruct (a person) to perform a specified activity (*set them to work*). **b** (foll. by *pres. part.*) start (a person or thing) doing something (*set him chatting*; *set the ball rolling*). **15** *tr.* present or impose as work to be done or a matter to be dealt with (*set them an essay*). **16** *tr.* exhibit as a type or model (*set a good example*). **17** *tr.* initiate; take the lead in (*set the fashion*; *set the pace*). **18** *tr.* establish (a record etc.). **19** *tr.* determine or decide (*the itinerary is set*). **20** *tr.* appoint or establish (*set them in authority*). **21** *tr.* join, attach, or fasten. **22** *tr.* **a** put parts of (a broken or dislocated bone, limb, etc.) into the correct position for healing. **b** deal with (a fracture or dislocation) in this way. **23** *tr.* (in full **set to music**) provide (words etc.) with

music for singing. **24** *tr.* (often foll. by *up*) *Printing* **a** arrange or produce (type or film etc.) as required. **b** arrange the type or film etc. for (a book etc.). **25** *intr.* (of a tide, current, etc.) have a certain motion or direction. **26** *intr.* (of a face) assume a hard expression. **27** *tr.* **a** cause (a hen) to sit on eggs. **b** place (eggs) for a hen to sit on. **28** *tr.* put (a seed, plant, etc.) in the ground to grow. **29** *tr.* give the teeth of (a saw) an alternate outward inclination. **30** *tr. esp. US* start (a fire). **31** *intr.* (of eyes etc.) become motionless. **32** *intr.* feel or show a certain tendency (*opinion is setting against it*). **33** *intr.* **a** (of blossom) form into fruit. **b** (of fruit) develop from blossom. **c** (of a tree) develop fruit. **34** *intr.* (in full **set to partner**) (of a dancer) take a position facing one's partner. **35** *intr.* (of a hunting dog) take a rigid attitude indicating the presence of game. **36** *intr. dial.* or *sl. sit.* □ **set about 1** begin or take steps towards. **2** *colloq.* attack. **set (a person or thing) against (another) 1** consider or reckon (a thing) as a counterpoise or compensation for. **2** cause to oppose. **set apart** separate, reserve, differentiate. **set aside** see ASIDE. **set back 1** place further back in place or time. **2** impede or reverse the progress of. **3** *colloq.* cost (a person) a specified amount. **set-back** *n.* **1** a reversal or arrest of progress. **2** a relapse. **set by** *archaic* save for future use. **set down 1** record in writing. **2** allow to alight from a vehicle. **3** (foll. by *to*) attribute to. **4** (foll. by *as*) explain or describe to oneself as. **set eyes on** see EYE. **set one's face against** see FACE. **set foot on** (or **in**) see FOOT. **set forth 1** begin a journey. **2** make known; expound. **set forward** begin to advance. **set free** release. **set one's hand to** see HAND. **set one's heart** (or **hopes**) **on** want or hope for eagerly. **set in 1** (of weather, a condition, etc.) begin (and seem likely to continue), become established. **2** insert (esp. a sleeve etc. into a garment). **set little** by consider to be of little value. **set a person's mind at rest** see MIND. **set much by** consider to be of much value. **set off 1** begin a journey. **2** detonate (a bomb etc.). **3** initiate, stimulate. **4** cause (a person) to start laughing, talking, etc. **5** serve as an adornment or foil to; enhance. **6** (foll. by *against*) use as a compensating item. **set-off** *n.* **1** a thing set off against another. **2** a thing of which the amount or effect may be deducted from that of another or opposite tendency. **3** a counterpoise. **4** a counter-claim. **5** a thing that embellishes; an adornment to something. **6** *Printing* = OFFSET 7. **set on** (or **upon**) **1** attack violently. **2** cause or urge to attack. **set out 1** begin a journey. **2** (foll. by *to* + infin.) aim or intend. **3** demonstrate, arrange, or exhibit. **4** mark out. **5** declare, state. **set sail 1** hoist the sails. **2** begin a voyage. **set the scene** see SCENE. **set store by** (or **on**) see STORE. **set one's teeth 1** clench them. **2** summon one's resolve. **set to** begin doing something vigorously, esp. fighting, arguing, or eating. **set-to** *n.* (*pl.* **-tos**) *colloq.* a fight or argument. **set up 1** place in position or view. **2** organize or start (a business etc.). **3** establish in some capacity. **4** supply the needs of. **5** begin making (a loud sound). **6** cause or make arrangements for (a condition or situation). **7** prepare (a task etc. for another). **8** restore or enhance the health of (a person). **9** establish (a record). **10** propound (a theory). **11** *colloq.* put (a person) in a dangerous or vulnerable position. **set-up** *n.* **1** an arrangement or organization. **2** the manner or structure or position of this. **set oneself up as** make pretensions to being. [OE *settan* f. Gmc]

set[2] /set/ *n.* **1** a number of things or persons that belong together or resemble one another or are usually found together. **2** a collection or group. **3** a section of society consorting together or having similar interests etc. **4** a collection of implements, vessels, etc., regarded collectively and needed for a specified purpose (*cricket set*; *teaset*; *a set of teeth*). **5** a piece of electric or electronic apparatus, esp. a radio or television receiver. **6** (in tennis etc.) a group of games counting as a unit towards a match for the player or side that wins a defined number or proportion of the games. **7** *Math. & Logic* a collection of distinct entities, individually specified or satisfying specified conditions, forming a unit. **8** a group of pupils or students having the same average ability. **9 a** a slip, shoot, bulb, etc., for planting. **b** a young fruit just set. **10 a** a habitual posture or conformation; the way the head etc. is carried or a dress etc. flows. **b** (also **dead set**) a setter's pointing in the presence of game. **11** the way, drift, or tendency (of a current, public opinion, state of mind, etc.) (*the set of public feeling is against it*). **12** the way in which a machine, device, etc., is set or adjusted. **13** esp. *Austral. & NZ colloq.* a grudge. **14 a** the alternate outward deflection of the teeth of a saw. **b** the amount of this. **15** the last coat of plaster on a wall. **16** *Printing* **a** the amount of spacing in type controlling the distance between letters. **b** the width of a piece of type. **17** a warp or bend or displacement caused by continued pressure or a continued position. **18** a setting, including stage furniture etc., for a play or film etc. **19** a sequence of songs or pieces performed in jazz or popular music. **20** the setting of the hair when damp. **21** (also **sett**) a badger's burrow. **22** (also **sett**) a granite paving-block. **23** a predisposition or expectation influencing a response. **24** a number of people making up a square dance. □ **make a dead set at 1** make a determined attack on. **2** seek to win the affections of. **set point** *Tennis* etc. **1** the state of a game when one side needs only one more point to win the set. **2** this point. **set theory** see separate entry. [sense 1 (and related senses) f. OF *sette* f. L *secta* SECT: other senses f. SET[1]]

set[3] /set/ *adj.* **1** in senses of SET[1]. **2** prescribed or determined in advance. **3** fixed, unchanging, unmoving. **4** (of a phrase or speech etc.) having invariable or predetermined wording; not extempore. **5** prepared for action. **6** (foll. by *on, upon*) determined to acquire or achieve etc. **7** (of a book etc.) specified for reading in preparation for an examination. **8** (of a meal) served according to a fixed menu. □ **set fair** (of the weather) fine without a sign of breaking. **set phrase** an invariable or usual arrangement of words. **set piece 1** a formal or elaborate arrangement, esp. in art or literature. **2** fireworks arranged on scaffolding etc. **set screw** a screw for adjusting or clamping parts of a machine. **set scrum** *Rugby Football* a scrum ordered by the referee. **set square** a right-angled triangular plate for drawing lines, esp. at 90°, 45°, 60°, or 30°. [past part. of SET[1]]

seta /ˈsiːtə/ *n.* (*pl.* **setae** /-tiː/) *Bot. & Zool.* stiff hair; bristle. □□ **setaceous** /-ˈteɪʃəs/ *adj.* [L, = bristle]

Seth /seθ/ *Egyptian Mythol.* the personification of evil, who appears in the myth of Osiris as the wicked brother who murders Osiris and wounds Osiris's son Horus. He was probably the beneficent deity of the people of Upper Egypt before he became absorbed into the Osiris myth. Seth is represented with the head of a beast with a long pointed snout.

set theory *n.* the branch of mathematics which deals with sets (i.e. things grouped together as forming a unit) without regard to the nature of their individual constituents. It was originated by Cantor (and, less explicitly, Dedekind) in the years 1873–1900 and now exists both as a sophisticated subject, closely related to mathematical logic, which is extensively studied for its sake, and as an excellent language in which other parts of mathematics may be easily and precisely expressed.

setiferous /sɪˈtɪfərəs/ *adj.* (also **setigerous** /sɪˈtɪdʒərəs/) having bristles. [L *seta* bristle, *setiger* bristly + -FEROUS, -GEROUS]

seton /ˈsiːt(ə)n/ *n.* *Surgery* a skein of cotton etc. passed below the skin and left with the ends protruding to promote drainage etc. [ME f. med.L *seto, seta* silk, app. f. L *seta* bristle]

setose /ˈsiːtəʊz/ *adj.* *Biol.* bristly. [L *seta* bristle]

Setswana var. of TSWANA (and the preferred form for the language).

sett var. of SET[2] 21, 22.

settee /seˈtiː/ *n.* a seat (usu. upholstered), with a back and usu. arms, for more than one person. [18th c.: perh. a fanciful var. of SETTLE[2]]

setter /ˈsetə(r)/ *n.* **1 a** a dog of a large long-haired breed trained to stand rigid when scenting game (see SET[1] 35). **b** this breed. **2** a person or thing that sets.

setting /ˈsetɪŋ/ *n.* **1** the position or manner in which a thing is set. **2** the immediate surroundings (of a house etc.). **3** the surroundings of any object regarded as its framework; the environment of a thing. **4** the place and time, scenery, etc., of a story, drama, etc. **5** a frame in which a jewel is set. **6** the music to which words of a poem, song, etc., are set. **7** a set of cutlery and other accessories for one person at a table. **8** the way in which

or level at which a machine is set to operate. □ **setting lotion** lotion used to prepare the hair for being set.

settle[1] /ˈset(ə)l/ *v.* **1** *tr. & intr.* (often foll. by *down*) establish or become established in a more or less permanent abode or way of life. **2** *intr. & tr.* (often foll. by *down*) **a** cease or cause to cease from wandering, disturbance, movement, etc. **b** adopt a regular or secure style of life. **c** (foll. by *to*) apply oneself (to work, an activity, a way of life, etc.) (*settled down to writing letters*). **3 a** *intr.* sit or come down to stay for some time. **b** *tr.* cause to do this. **4** *tr. & intr.* bring to or attain fixity, certainty, composure, or quietness. **5** *tr.* determine or decide or agree upon (*shall we settle a date?*). **6** *tr.* **a** resolve (a dispute etc.). **b** deal with (a matter) finally. **7** *tr.* terminate (a lawsuit) by mutual agreement. **8** *intr.* **a** (foll. by *for*) accept or agree to (esp. an alternative not one's first choice). **b** (foll. by *on*) decide on. **9** *tr.* (also *absol.*) pay (a debt, an account, etc.). **10** *intr.* (as **settled** *adj.*) not likely to change for a time (*settled weather*). **11** *tr.* **a** aid the digestion of (food). **b** remedy the disordered state of (nerves, the stomach, etc.). **12** *tr.* **a** colonize. **b** establish colonists in. **13** *intr.* subside; fall to the bottom or on to a surface (*the foundations have settled; wait till the sediment settles; the dust will settle*). **14** *intr.* (of a ship) begin to sink. **15** *tr.* get rid of the obstruction of (a person) by argument or conflict or killing. □ **settle one's affairs** make any necessary arrangements (e.g. write a will) when death is near. **settle a person's hash** see HASH[1]. **settle in** become established in a place. **settle up 1** (also *absol.*) pay (an account, debt, etc.). **2** finally arrange (a matter). **settle with 1** pay all or part of an amount due to (a creditor). **2** get revenge on. **settling day** the fortnightly pay-day on the Stock Exchange. □□ **settleable** *adj.* [OE *setlan* (as SETTLE[2]) f. Gmc]

settle[2] /ˈset(ə)l/ *n.* a bench with a high back and arms and often with a box fitted below the seat. [OE *setl* place to sit f. Gmc]

settlement /ˈsetəlmənt/ *n.* **1** the act or an instance of settling; the process of being settled. **2 a** the colonization of a region. **b** a place or area occupied by settlers. **c** a small village. **3 a** a political or financial etc. agreement. **b** an arrangement ending a dispute. **4 a** the terms on which property is given to a person. **b** a deed stating these. **c** the amount of property given. **d** = *marriage settlement*. **5** the process of settling an account. **6** subsidence of a wall, house, soil, etc. □ **Act of Settlement** the statute of 1701 that established the Hanoverian succession to the British throne. It vested the Crown in Sophia of Hanover (granddaughter of James I of England) and her heirs; her son became George I.

settler /ˈsetlə(r)/ *n.* a person who goes to settle in a new country or place; an early colonist.

settlor /ˈsetlə(r)/ *n.* *Law* a person who makes a settlement esp. of a property.

Seurat /sɜːˈrɑː/, Georges (1859–91), French painter, the founder of neo-impressionism. He became interested in scientific theories of colour vision and colour combination, and set himself to systematize the 'additive' method of juxtaposing colours to be combined through the seeing eye, a technique which had been to some extent anticipated by the impressionists and by Corot (see POINTILLISM). Among his major paintings was *Un Dimanche d'été à la Grande-Jatte*.

Sevastopol see SEBASTOPOL.

seven /ˈsev(ə)n/ *n. & adj.* —*n.* **1** one more than six, or three less than ten; the sum of four units and three units. **2** a symbol for this (7, vii, VII). **3** a size etc. denoted by seven. **4** a set or team of seven individuals. **5** the time of seven o'clock (*is it seven yet?*). **6** a card with seven pips. —*adj.* that amount to seven. □ **the seven deadly sins** see DEADLY. **seven-league boots** (in the fairy story of Hop-o'-my-Thumb) boots enabling the wearer to go seven leagues at each stride. **the seven seas** the oceans of the world: the Arctic, Southern or Antarctic, N. Pacific, S. Pacific, N. Atlantic, S. Atlantic, and Indian Oceans. **the Seven Sisters** the Pleiades. **the seven wonders of the world** see separate entry. **seven year itch** a supposed tendency to infidelity after seven years of marriage. [OE *seofon* f. Gmc]

sevenfold /ˈsev(ə)nfəʊld/ *adj. & adv.* **1** seven times as much or as many. **2** consisting of seven parts.

Seven Sages a traditional list (found in Plato) of seven wise

Greeks of the 6th c. BC, to each of whom a moral saying is attributed. The seven are: Bias, Chilon, Cleobulus, Periander, Pittacus, Solon, Thales.

Seven Sleepers in early Christian legend, seven noble Christian youths of Ephesus who fell asleep in a cave while fleeing from the Decian persecution and awoke 187 years later. The legend was translated from the Syriac by Gregory of Tours (6th c.), and is also given by other authors; it occurs in the Koran.

seventeen /ˌsevən'tiːn/ n. & adj. —n. **1** one more than sixteen, or seven more than ten. **2** a symbol for this (17, xvii, XVII). **3** a size etc. denoted by seventeen. —adj. that amount to seventeen. □□ **seventeenth** adj. & n. [OE seofontīene]

seventh /'sev(ə)nθ/ n. & adj. —n. **1** the position in a sequence corresponding to the number 7 in the sequence 1–7. **2** something occupying this position. **3** one of seven equal parts of a thing. **4** Mus. **a** an interval or chord spanning seven consecutive notes in the diatonic scale (e.g. C to B). **b** a note separated from another by this interval. —adj. that is the seventh. □ **in seventh heaven** see HEAVEN. **Seventh-Day Adventist** a member of a sect of Adventists who originally expected the second coming of Christ in 1844 and still preach that his return is imminent. They are strict Protestants and are notable for observing Saturday as the Sabbath. **seventh heaven 1** a state of intense joy. **2** the highest of seven heavens in Muslim and some Jewish systems. □□ **seventhly** adv.

seventy /'sevəntɪ/ n. & adj. —n. (pl. **-ies**) **1** the product of seven and ten. **2** a symbol for this (70, lxx, LXX). **3** (in pl.) the numbers from 70 to 79, esp. the years of a century or of a person's life. —adj. that amount to seventy. □ **seventy-first, -second**, etc. the ordinal numbers between seventieth and eightieth. **seventy-one, -two**, etc. the cardinal numbers between seventy and eighty. □□ **seventieth** adj. & n. **seventyfold** adj. & adv. [OE -seofontig]

Seven Wonders of the World the seven most spectacular man-made structures of the ancient world. The earliest extant list of these dates from the 2nd c.; traditionally they comprise (1) the pyramids of Egypt, especially those at Giza; (2) the Hanging Gardens of Babylon (see HANGING); (3) the Mausoleum of Halicarnassus; (4) the temple of Diana (Artemis) at Ephesus in Asia Minor, rebuilt in 356 BC, measuring 90 × 45 m (300 × 150 ft.) and with 127 columns; (5) the Colossus of Rhodes; (6) the huge ivory and gold statue of Zeus at Olympia in the Peloponnese, made by Phidias c.430 BC; (7) the Pharos of Alexandria (or in some lists, the walls of Babylon).

Seven Years War a war (1756–63) which ranged Britain, Prussia, and Hanover against Austria, France, Russia, Saxony, Sweden, and Spain. Its main issues were the struggle between Britain and France for supremacy overseas, and that between Prussia and Austria for the domination of Germany. After some early setbacks, the British made substantial gains over France abroad, capturing (under Wolfe) French Canada and (under Clive) undermining French influence in India. On the Continent, the war was most notable for the brilliant campaigns of Frederick the Great of Prussia against converging enemy armies. The war was ended by the Treaties of Paris and Hubertusburg in 1763, leaving Britain the supreme European naval and colonial power and Prussia in an appreciably stronger position than before in central Europe.

sever /'sevə(r)/ v. **1** tr. & intr. (often foll. by from) divide, break, or make separate, esp. by cutting. **2** tr. & intr. break off or away; separate, part, divide (severed our friendship). **3** tr. end the employment contract of (a person). □□ **severable** adj. [ME f. AF severer, OF sevrer ult. f. L separare SEPARATE v.]

several /'sevr(ə)l/ adj. & n. —adj. & n. more than two but not many. —adj. **1** separate or respective; distinct (all went their several ways). **2** Law applied or regarded separately (opp. JOINT). □□ **severally** adv. [ME f. AF f. AL separalis f. L separ SEPARATE adj.]

severalty /'sevrəltɪ/ n. **1** separateness. **2** the individual or unshared tenure of an estate etc. (esp. in severalty). [ME f. AF severalte (as SEVERAL)]

severance /'sevərəns/ n. **1** the act or an instance of severing. **2** a severed state. □ **severance pay** an amount paid to an employee on the early termination of a contract.

severe /sɪ'vɪə(r)/ adj. **1** rigorous, strict, and harsh in attitude or treatment (a severe critic; severe discipline). **2** serious, critical (a severe shortage). **3** vehement or forceful (a severe storm). **4** extreme (in an unpleasant quality) (a severe winter; severe cold). **5** arduous or exacting; making great demands on energy, skill, etc. (severe competition). **6** unadorned; plain in style (severe dress). □□ **severely** adv. **severity** /-'verɪtɪ/ n. [F sévère or L severus]

Severn /'sevɜːn/ the longest river of Britain, rising on Mount Plynlimon in eastern Wales and flowing about 300 km (220 miles) to the Bristol Channel.

severy /'sevərɪ/ n. (pl. **-ies**) Archit. a space or compartment in a vaulted ceiling. [ME f. OF civoire (as CIBORIUM)]

Seville /'sevɪl/ (Spanish **Sevilla** /se'viːljə/) a city in southern Spain, the capital of Andalusia region; pop. (1986) 668,350. □ **Seville orange** a bitter orange used for marmalade.

Sèvres /seɪvr/ n. porcelain made at Sèvres, south-west of Paris. The factory founded in 1738 in the Château de Vincennes, east of Paris, moved to Sèvres in 1756 and three years later was purchased by Louis XV to save it from closure; thereafter it became a subsidized royal venture, and its pieces display an opulence matching court life. In 1793 the French Republic took over the factory; it created a sophisticated style at the beginning of the 19th c., but the great designs faded and the factory took to producing copies of 18th-c. wares.

sew /səʊ/ v.tr. (past part. **sewn** /səʊn/ or **sewed**) **1** (also absol.) fasten, join, etc., by making stitches with a needle and thread or a sewing-machine. **2** make (a garment etc.) by sewing. **3** (often foll. by on, in, etc.) attach by sewing (shall I sew on your buttons?). □ **sew up 1** join or enclose by sewing. **2** colloq. (esp. in passive) satisfactorily arrange or finish dealing with (a project etc.). **3** esp. US obtain exclusive use of. □□ **sewer** n. [OE si(o)wan]

sewage /'suːɪdʒ, 'sjuː-/ n. waste matter, esp. excremental, conveyed in sewers. □ **sewage farm** (or **works**) a place where sewage is treated, esp. to produce manure.

sewen var. of SEWIN.

sewer /'suːə(r), 'sjuː-/ n. a conduit, usu. underground, for carrying off drainage water and sewage. (See below.) □ **sewer rat** the common brown rat. [ME f. AF sever(e), ONF se(u)wiere channel to carry off the overflow from a fishpond, ult. f. L ex- out of + aqua water]

Sewers were known in the ancient world: the earliest that survives is at Mohenjodaro in the Indus valley (c.2500 BC) and there were elaborate domestic arrangements at the Palace of Minos in Crete (c.2000 BC). Many Roman cities had underground sewers, but after the decline of Roman power these were allowed to deteriorate. In medieval Europe there was no proper drainage system and the water-supply was inadequate and insanitary; disease was rife. When the Industrial Revolution swelled the numbers of people living in towns it became essential to devise a system of waste-disposal. The first underground sewers were constructed at Hamburg in Germany in 1843.

sewerage /'suːərɪdʒ, 'sjuː-/ n. a system of or drainage by sewers.

sewin /'sjuːɪn/ n. (also **sewen**) a salmon trout of Welsh etc. rivers. [16th c.: orig. unkn.]

sewing /'səʊɪŋ/ n. a piece of material or work to be sewn.

sewing-machine n. a machine for sewing or stitching things. The earliest patents for mechanical sewing were taken out in England by Charles Weisenthal in 1755 and Thomas Saint in 1790. The first chain-stitch machine was invented in 1829 by Barthélemy Thimonnier, a French tailor, but when (some years later) a number of these were put into operation to make French army uniforms they were smashed by rioting tailors alarmed at this threat to their livelihood. Independent efforts in the US led to the design and patenting of machines producing a lock stitch, and though the style and powering of modern machines varies the basic principle remains the same. The success of Isaac Singer (see entry) was due not only to the worth of his machine but to the astuteness of his lawyer, who fought his patent-battles and pioneered selling by hire purchase. Gandhi, who learned to use a sewing-machine while in prison, declared that it was one of the few useful things ever invented, and exempted it from his ban on the import of Western machinery.

sewn *past part.* of SEW.

sex /seks/ *n., adj., & v.* —*n.* **1** either of the main divisions (male and female) into which living things are placed on the basis of their reproductive functions. **2** the fact of belonging to one of these. **3** males or females collectively. **4** sexual instincts, desires, etc., or their manifestation. **5** *colloq.* sexual intercourse. —*adj.* **1** of or relating to sex (*sex education*). **2** arising from a difference or consciousness of sex (*sex antagonism; sex urge*). —*v.tr.* **1** determine the sex of. **2** (as **sexed** *adj.*) **a** having a sexual appetite (*highly sexed*). **b** having sexual characteristics. □ **sex act** (usu. prec. by *the*) the (or an) act of sexual intercourse. **sex appeal** sexual attractiveness. **sex change** an apparent change of sex by surgical means and hormone treatment. **sex chromosome** a chromosome concerned in determining the sex of an organism, which in most animals are of two kinds, the X-chromosome and the Y-chromosome. **sex hormone** a hormone affecting sexual development or behaviour. **sex kitten** *colloq.* a young woman who asserts her sex appeal. **sex life** a person's activity related to sexual instincts. **sex-linked** *Genetics* carried on or by a sex chromosome. **sex maniac** *colloq.* a person needing or seeking excessive gratification of the sexual instincts. **sex object** a person regarded mainly in terms of sexual attractiveness. **sex-starved** lacking sexual gratification. **sex symbol** a person widely noted for sex appeal. □□ **sexer** *n.* [ME f. OF *sexe* or L *sexus*]

sexagenarian /ˌseksədʒɪˈneərɪən/ *n. & adj.* —*n.* a person from 60 to 69 years old. —*adj.* of this age. [L *sexagenarius* f. *sexageni* distrib. of *sexaginta* sixty]

Sexagesima /ˌseksəˈdʒesɪmə/ *n.* the Sunday before Quinquagesima. [ME f. eccl.L. = sixtieth (day), prob. named loosely as preceding QUINQUAGESIMA]

sexagesimal /ˌseksəˈdʒesɪm(ə)l/ *adj. & n.* —*adj.* **1** of sixtieths. **2** of sixty. **3** reckoning or reckoned by sixtieths. —*n.* (in full **sexagesimal fraction**) a fraction with a denominator equal to a power of 60 as in the divisions of the degree and hour. □□ **sexagesimally** *adv.* [L *sexagesimus* (as SEXAGESIMA)]

sexcentenary /ˌseksenˈtiːnərɪ/ *n. & adj.* —*n.* (*pl.* **-ies**) **1** a six-hundredth anniversary. **2** a celebration of this. —*adj.* **1** of or relating to a sexcentenary. **2** occurring every six hundred years.

sexennial /sekˈsenɪəl/ *adj.* **1** lasting six years. **2** recurring every six years. [SEXI- + L *annus* year]

sexfoil /ˈseksfɔɪl/ *n.* a six-lobed ornamental figure. [SEXI-, after CINQUEFOIL, TREFOIL]

sexi- /ˈseksɪ/ *comb. form* (also **sex-** before a vowel) six. [L *sex* six]

sexism /ˈseksɪz(ə)m/ *n.* prejudice or discrimination, esp. against women, on the grounds of sex. □□ **sexist** *adj. & n.*

sexivalent /ˈseksɪˌveɪlənt/ *adj.* (also **sexvalent**) *Chem.* having a valency of six.

sexless /ˈsekslɪs/ *adj.* **1** *Biol.* neither male nor female. **2** lacking in sexual desire or attractiveness. □□ **sexlessly** *adv.* **sexlessness** *n.*

sexology /sekˈsɒlədʒɪ/ *n.* the study of sexual life or relationships, esp. in human beings. □□ **sexological** /-əˈlɒdʒɪk(ə)l/ *adj.* **sexologist** *n.*

sexpartite /seksˈpɑːtaɪt/ *adj.* divided into six parts.

sexploitation /ˌseksplɔɪˈteɪʃ(ə)n/ *n. colloq.* the exploitation of sex, esp. commercially.

sexpot /ˈsekspɒt/ *n. colloq.* a sexy person (esp. a woman).

sext /sekst/ *n. Eccl.* **1** the canonical hour of prayer appointed for the sixth daytime hour (i.e. noon). **2** the office of sext. [ME f. L *sexta hora* sixth hour f. *sextus* sixth]

sextant /ˈsekst(ə)nt/ *n.* an instrument with a graduated arc of 60° used in navigation and surveying for measuring the angular distance of objects by means of mirrors. The instrument was first described by Robert Hooke in 1667 and was re-invented independently by John Hadley in England (1731) and Thomas Godfrey in America. [L *sextans -ntis* sixth part f. *sextus* sixth]

sextet /sekˈstet/ *n.* (also **sextette**) **1** *Mus.* a composition for six voices or instruments. **2** the performers of such a piece. **3** any group of six. [alt. of SESTET after L *sex* six]

sextillion /seksˈtɪljən/ *n.* (*pl.* same or **sextillions**) a thousand raised to the seventh (or formerly, esp. *Brit.*, the twelfth) power (10^{21} and 10^{36} respectively) (cf. BILLION). □□ **sextillionth** [F f. L *sex* six, after *septillion* etc.]

sexto /ˈsekstəʊ/ *n.* (*pl.* **-os**) **1** a size of book or page in which each leaf is one-sixth that of a printing-sheet. **2** a book or sheet of this size. [L *sextus* sixth, as QUARTO]

sextodecimo /ˌsekstəʊˈdesɪməʊ/ *n.* (*pl.* **-os**) **1** a size of book or page in which each leaf is one-sixteenth that of a printing-sheet. **2** a book or sheet of this size. [L *sextus decimus* 16th (as QUARTO)]

sexton /ˈsekst(ə)n/ *n.* a person who looks after a church and churchyard, often acting as bell-ringer and gravedigger. □ **sexton beetle** any beetle of the genus *Necrophorus*, burying carrion to serve as a nidus for its eggs. [ME *segerstane* etc., f. AF, OF *segerstein, secrestein* f. med.L *sacristanus* SACRISTAN]

sextuple /ˈsekstjuːp(ə)l/ *adj., n., & v.* —*adj.* **1** sixfold. **2** having six parts. **3** being six times as many or much. —*n.* a sixfold number or amount. —*v.tr. & intr.* multiply by six; increase sixfold. □□ **sextuply** *adv.* [med.L *sextuplus*, irreg. f. L *sex* six, after LL *quintuplus* QUINTUPLE]

sextuplet /ˈsekstjʊplɪt, -ˈtjuːplɪt/ *n.* **1** each of six children born at one birth. **2** *Mus.* a group of six notes to be played in the time of four. [SEXTUPLE, after *triplet* etc.]

sexual /ˈseksjʊəl/ *adj.* **1** of or relating to sex, or to the sexes or the relations between them. **2** *Bot.* (of classification) based on the distinction of sexes in plants. **3** *Biol.* having a sex. □ **sexual intercourse** the insertion of a man's erect penis into a woman's vagina, usu. followed by the ejaculation of semen. □□ **sexuality** /-ˈælɪtɪ/ *n.* **sexually** *adv.* [LL *sexualis* (as SEX)]

sexvalent var. of SEXIVALENT.

sexy /ˈseksɪ/ *adj.* (**sexier, sexiest**) **1** sexually attractive or stimulating. **2** sexually aroused. **3** concerned with or engrossed in sex. □□ **sexily** *adv.* **sexiness** *n.*

Seychelles /seɪˈʃelz/ a country in the Indian Ocean, a member State of the Commonwealth, consisting of a group of about 90 islands about 1,000 km (600 miles) NE of Madagascar; pop. (est. 1988) 68,600; official languages, English and French; capital, Victoria. The islands are said to have been named the 'Isles of Gold' by visiting Arab seafarers, perhaps in the 9th c. The Portuguese, who arrived there in the 16th c., called them the 'Seven Sisters', by which name they were known until the French annexed and settled them in the mid-18th c. They formed an excellent hide-out for pirates until these were hunted down by the British and French. The Seychelles were captured by Britain during the Napoleonic Wars and administered from Mauritius before becoming a separate colony in 1903 and finally an independent republic in 1976. Noted for their beauty, the islands attract a considerable tourist trade; the economy is also supported by exports of copra and cinnamon. □□ **Seychellois** /-ʃelˈwɑː/ *adj. & n.*

Seymour /ˈsiːmɔː(r)/, Jane (*c.*1509–37), the third wife of Henry VIII, and mother of Edward VI. Jane Seymour finally provided the king with the male heir he wanted, and, although she died little over a year after her wedding, probably made the ageing king happier than any of his other wives. After her demise Henry donned mourning and ordered that she be buried beside him.

sez /sez/ *sl.* says (*sez you*). [phonetic repr.]

SF *abbr.* science fiction.

sf *abbr. Mus.* sforzando.

SFA *abbr.* Scottish Football Association.

Sfax /sfæks/ a seaport on the east coast of Tunisia; pop. (1984) 231,900. The city, which is the second-largest in Tunisia, is a major centre of phosphate processing.

sforzando /sfɔːˈtsændəʊ/ *adj., adv., & n.* (also **sforzato** /-ˈtsɑːtəʊ/) —*adj. & adv. Mus.* with sudden emphasis. —*n.* (*pl.* **-os** or **sforzandi** /-dɪ/) **1** a note or group of notes especially emphasized. **2** an increase in emphasis and loudness. [It., verbal noun and past part. of *sforzare* use force]

sfumato /sfuːˈmɑːtəʊ/ *adj. & n. Painting.* —*adj.* with indistinct outlines. —*n.* the technique of allowing tones and colours to shade gradually into one another. [It., past part. of *sfumare* shade off f. s- = EX-1 + *fumare* smoke]

sfz *abbr. Mus.* sforzando.

SG *abbr.* **1** *US* senior grade. **2** *Law* Solicitor-General. **3** specific gravity.

sgd. *abbr.* signed.

sgraffito /sgrɑːˈfiːtəʊ/ *n.* (*pl.* **sgraffiti** /-tɪ/) a form of decoration made by scratching through wet plaster on a wall or through slip on ceramic ware, showing a different-coloured under-surface. [It., past part. of *sgraffire* scratch f. *s-* = EX-¹ + *graffio* scratch]

's-Gravenhage see The HAGUE.

Sgt. *abbr.* Sergeant.

sh *int.* calling for silence. [var. of HUSH]

sh. *abbr. Brit. hist.* shilling(s).

Shaanxi /ʃɑːnˈʃiː/ (also **Shensi** /ʃenˈsiː/) a province in north central China; pop. (est. 1986) 30,430,000; capital, Xian.

Shaba /ˈʃɑːbə/ a copper-mining region of SE Zaïre; pop. (1984) 3,874,000; capital, Lubumbashi.

shabby /ˈʃæbɪ/ *adj.* (**shabbier, shabbiest**) **1** in bad repair or condition; faded and worn, dingy, dilapidated. **2** dressed in old or worn clothes. **3** of poor quality. **4** contemptible, dishonourable (*a shabby trick*). □□ **shabbily** *adv.* **shabbiness** *n.* **shabbyish** *adj.* [*shab* scab f. OE *sceabb* f. ON, rel. to SAB]

shabrack /ˈʃæbræk/ *n. hist.* a cavalry saddle-cloth. [G *Schabracke* of E. European orig.: cf. Russ. *shabrak*]

shack /ʃæk/ *n. & v.* —*n.* a roughly built hut or cabin. —*v.intr.* (foll. by *up*) *sl.* cohabit, esp. as lovers. [perh. f. Mex. *jacal*, Aztec *xacatli* wooden hut]

shackle /ˈʃæk(ə)l/ *n. & v.* —*n.* **1** a metal loop or link, closed by a bolt, to connect chains etc. **2** a fetter enclosing the ankle or wrist. **3** (usu. in *pl.*) a restraint or impediment. —*v.tr.* fetter, impede, restrain. □ **shackle-bolt 1** a bolt for closing a shackle. **2** a bolt with a shackle at its end. [OE *sc(e)acul* fetter, corresp. to LG *shäkel* link, coupling, ON *skökull* wagon-pole f. Gmc]

Shackleton /ˈʃæk(ə)lt(ə)n/, Sir Ernest Henry (1874–1922), Irish-born polar explorer. A junior officer on Scott's first polar expedition of 1900–4, Shackleton commanded an expedition of his own in 1909, getting within 155 km (97 miles) of the South Pole (the farthest south anyone had reached at that time). On a second expedition to the Antarctic (1914–16) his ship the *Endurance* was crushed in the ice. Extracting his crew with great difficulty, Shackleton set out with five others from Elephant Island in an open boat on an epic 1300 km (800-mile) voyage to South Georgia to get help. On a final expedition to the Antarctic in 1920–2 he died on South Georgia.

shad /ʃæd/ *n.* (*pl.* same or **shads**) *Zool.* any deep-bodied edible marine fish of the genus *Alosa*, spawning in fresh water. [OE *sceadd*, of unkn. orig.]

shaddock /ˈʃædək/ *n. Bot.* **1** the largest citrus fruit, with a thick yellow skin and bitter pulp. Also called POMELO. **2** the tree, *Citrus grandis*, bearing these. [Capt. *Shaddock*, who introduced it to the W. Indies in the 17th c.]

shade /ʃeɪd/ *n. & v.* —*n.* **1** comparative darkness (and usu. coolness) caused by shelter from direct light and heat. **2** a place or area sheltered from the sun. **3** a darker part of a picture etc. **4** a colour, esp. with regard to its depth or as distinguished from one nearly like it. **5** comparative obscurity. **6** a slight amount (*am a shade better today*). **7** a translucent cover for a lamp etc. **8** a screen excluding or moderating light. **9** an eye-shield. **10** (in *pl.*) esp. *US colloq.* sunglasses. **11** a slightly differing variety (*all shades of opinion*). **12** *literary* **a** a ghost. **b** (in *pl.*) Hades. **13** (in *pl.*; foll. by *of*) suggesting reminiscence or unfavourable comparison (*shades of Dr Johnson!*). —*v.* **1** *tr.* screen from light. **2** *tr.* cover, moderate, or exclude the light of. **3** *tr.* darken, esp. with parallel pencil lines to represent shadow etc. **4** *intr. & tr.* (often foll. by *away, off, into*) pass or change by degrees. □ **in the shade** in comparative obscurity. □□ **shadeless** *adj.* [OE *sc(e)adu* f. Gmc]

shading /ˈʃeɪdɪŋ/ *n.* **1** the representation of light and shade, e.g. by pencilled lines, on a map or drawing. **2** the graduation of tones from light to dark to create a sense of depth.

shadoof /ʃəˈduːf/ *n.* a pole with a bucket and counterpoise used esp. in Egypt for drawing water from a river etc.. [Egypt. Arab. *šādūf*]

shadow /ˈʃædəʊ/ *n. & v.* —*n.* **1** shade or a patch of shade. **2** a dark figure projected by a body intercepting rays of light, often regarded as an appendage. **3** an inseparable attendant or companion. **4** a person secretly following another. **5** the slightest trace (*not the shadow of a doubt*). **6** a weak or insubstantial remnant or thing (*a shadow of his former self*). **7** (*attrib.*) *Brit.* denoting members of a political party in opposition holding responsibilities parallel to those of the government (*shadow Home Secretary; shadow Cabinet*). **8** the shaded part of a picture. **9** a substance used to colour the eyelids. **10** gloom or sadness. —*v.tr.* **1** cast a shadow over. **2** secretly follow and watch the movements of. □ **shadow-boxing** boxing against an imaginary opponent as a form of training. □□ **shadower** *n.* **shadowless** *adj.* [repr. OE *scead(u)we*, oblique case of *sceadu* SHADE]

shadowgraph /ˈʃædəʊˌɡrɑːf/ *n.* **1** an image or photograph made by means of X-rays; = RADIOGRAM 2. **2** a picture formed by a shadow cast on a lighted surface. **3** an image formed by light refracted differently by different densities of a fluid.

shadow-show *n.* a form of puppetry in which flat jointed figures pass between a strong light and a translucent screen, while the audience, in front of the screen, sees only their shadows. It originated in the Far East, spread to Turkey and Greece, and as *les Ombres Chinoises* was popular in Paris for about 100 years. In the streets of London shadow-shows, known as the galanty show, were given until the end of the 19th c., usually in Punch and Judy booths. The shadow-show survives in its traditional form in Java and Bali.

shadowy /ˈʃædəʊɪ/ *adj.* **1** like or having a shadow. **2** full of shadows. **3** vague, indistinct. □□ **shadowiness** *n.*

shady /ˈʃeɪdɪ/ *adj.* (**shadier, shadiest**) **1** giving shade. **2** situated in shade. **3** (of a person or behaviour) disreputable; of doubtful honesty. □□ **shadily** *adv.* **shadiness** *n.*

shaft /ʃɑːft/ *n. & v.* —*n.* **1 a** an arrow or spear. **b** the long slender stem of these. **2** a remark intended to hurt or provoke (*a shaft of malice; shafts of wit*). **3** (foll. by *of*) **a** a ray (of light). **b** a bolt (of lightning). **4** the stem or handle of a tool, implement, etc. **5** a column, esp. between the base and capital. **6** a long narrow space, usu. vertical, for access to a mine, a lift in a building, for ventilation, etc. **7** a long and narrow part supporting or connecting or driving a part or parts of greater thickness etc. **8** each of the pair of poles between which a horse is harnessed to a vehicle. **9** the central stem of a feather. **10** *Mech.* a large axle or revolving bar transferring force by belts or cogs. **11** *US colloq.* harsh or unfair treatment. —*v.tr. US colloq.* treat unfairly. □ **shaft grave** a type of grave found in Late Bronze Age Greece and Crete in which the burial chamber is approached by a vertical shaft sometimes lined with stones and roofed over with beams, as seen in the more elaborate examples of the famous six at Mycenae. [OE *scæft, sceaft* f. Gmc]

Shaftesbury /ˈʃɑːftsbərɪ/, Anthony Ashley Cooper, 7th Earl (1801–85), British philanthropist and social reformer. Shaftesbury was one of the dominating figures of the 19th-c. movement towards social reform, inspiring much of the legislation designed to improve the lot of the large working class created by Britain's Industrial Revolution.

shafting /ˈʃɑːftɪŋ/ *n. Mech.* **1** a system of connected shafts for transmitting motion. **2** material from which shafts are cut.

shag¹ /ʃæɡ/ *n.* **1** a rough growth or mass of hair etc. **2** a coarse kind of cut tobacco. **3** a cormorant, esp. the crested cormorant, *Phalacrocorax aristotelis*. [OE *sceacga*, rel. to ON *skegg* beard, OE *sceaga* coppice]

shag² /ʃæɡ/ *v.tr.* (**shagged, shagging**) *coarse sl.* ¶ Usually considered a taboo word. **1** have sexual intercourse with. **2** (usu. in *passive*; often foll. by *out*) exhaust; tire out. [18th c.: orig. unkn.]

shaggy /ˈʃæɡɪ/ *adj.* (**shaggier, shaggiest**) **1** hairy, rough-haired. **2** unkempt. **3** (of the hair) coarse and abundant. **4** *Biol.* having a hairlike covering. □ **shaggy-dog story** a long rambling story amusing only by its being inconsequential. □□ **shaggily** *adv.* **shagginess** *n.*

shagreen /ʃæˈɡriːn/ *n.* **1** a kind of untanned leather with a rough granulated surface. **2** a sharkskin rough with natural papillae, used for rasping and polishing. [var. of CHAGRIN in the sense 'rough skin']

shah /ʃɑː/ *n. hist.* a title of the former monarch of Iran. □□

shahdom *n.* [Pers. šāh f. OPers. kšāy}tiya king]

shaikh var. of SHEIKH.

shake /ʃeɪk/ *v. & n.* —*v.* (*past* **shook** /ʃʊk/; *past part.* **shaken** /ˈʃeɪkən/) **1** *tr. & intr.* move forcefully or quickly up and down or to and fro. **2 a** *intr.* tremble or vibrate markedly. **b** *tr.* cause to do this. **3** *tr.* a agitate or shock. **b** *colloq.* upset the composure of. **4** *tr.* weaken or impair; make less convincing or firm or courageous (*shook his confidence*). **5** *intr.* (of a voice, note, etc.) make tremulous or rapidly alternating sounds; trill (*his voice shook with emotion*). **6** *tr.* brandish; make a threatening gesture with (one's fist, a stick, etc.). **7** *intr. colloq.* shake hands (*they shook on the deal*). **8** *tr.* esp. *US colloq.* = *shake off.* —*n.* **1** the act or an instance of shaking; the process of being shaken. **2** a jerk or shock. **3** (in *pl.*; prec. by *the*) a fit of or tendency to trembling or shivering. **4** *Mus.* a trill. **5** = *milk shake.* □ **in two shakes (of a lamb's** or **dog's tail)** very quickly. **no great shakes** *colloq.* not very good or significant. **shake a person by the hand** = *shake hands.* **shake down 1** settle or cause to fall by shaking. **2** settle down. **3** become established; get into harmony with circumstances, surroundings, etc. **4** *US sl.* extort money from. **shake the dust off one's feet** depart indignantly or disdainfully. **shake hands** (often foll. by *with*) clasp right hands at meeting or parting, in reconciliation or congratulation, or over a concluded bargain. **shake one's head** move one's head from side to side in refusal, denial, disapproval, or concern. **shake in one's shoes** tremble with apprehension. **shake a leg 1** begin dancing. **2** make a start. **shake off 1** get rid of (something unwanted). **2** manage to evade (a person who is following or pestering one). **shake out 1** empty by shaking. **2** spread or open (a sail, flag, etc.) by shaking. **shake-out** *n.* = *shake-up.* **shake up 1** mix (ingredients) by shaking. **2** restore to shape by shaking. **3** disturb or make uncomfortable. **4** rouse from lethargy, apathy, conventionality, etc. **shake-up** *n.* an upheaval or drastic reorganization. □□ **shakeable** *adj.* (also **shakable**). [OE *sc(e)acan* f. Gmc]

shakedown /ˈʃeɪkdaʊn/ *n.* **1** a makeshift bed. **2** *US sl.* a swindle; a piece of extortion. **3** (*attrib.*) *US colloq.* denoting a voyage, flight, etc., to test a new ship or aircraft and its crew.

shaken *past part.* of SHAKE.

shaker /ˈʃeɪkə(r)/ *n.* **1** a person or thing that shakes. **2** a container for shaking together the ingredients of cocktails etc. **3** (**Shaker**) a member of an American religious sect living simply, in celibate mixed communities. □□ **Shakeress** *n.* (in sense 3). **Shakerism** *n.* (in sense 3). [ME, f. SHAKE: sense 3 from religious dances]

Shakespeare /ˈʃeɪkspɪə(r)/, William (1564–1616), English dramatist, born in Stratford-upon-Avon, the son of a merchant, and probably educated at the local grammar school. His wife Anne Hathaway (see entry) remained in Stratford while he pursued a successful career in London as actor, poet, and dramatist, initially under the patronage of the Earl of Southampton, to whom his *Sonnets* (1609) may have been dedicated. Little is known of his life but his plays, many of which were not printed in his lifetime, have subsequently made him the world's most famous dramatist. These include early comedies such as *Love's Labour's Lost*, which sparkle with verbal ingenuity; the more mature and complex comedies such as *Twelfth Night* and *As You Like It*; several highly theatrical historical plays, including *Henry IV Parts 1 and 2* which introduced perhaps his best-known comic character, Falstaff; the Roman plays, which include *Julius Caesar*; the so-called 'problem plays', enigmatic comedies which include *All's Well that Ends Well* and *Measure for Measure*; his great tragedies, *Hamlet, Othello, King Lear, Macbeth*, and *Antony and Cleopatra*; and the group of autumnal romantic tragicomedies with which he ended his career, his last work being *The Tempest*, in which, like Prospero, he bids his imagined world farewell.

Shakespearian /ʃeɪkˈspɪərɪən/ *adj. & n.* (also **Shakespearean**) —*adj.* **1** of or relating to William Shakespeare. **2** in the style of Shakespeare. —*n.* a student of Shakespeare's works etc.

shako /ˈʃeɪkəʊ/ *n.* (*pl.* **-os**) a cylindrical peaked military hat with a plume. [F *schako* f. Magyar *csákó (süveg)* peaked (cap) f. *csák* peak f. G *Zacken* spike]

shakuhachi /ˌʃækuːˈhætʃi/ *n.* (*pl.* **shakuhachis**) a Japanese bamboo flute. [Jap. f. *shaku* a measure of length + *hachi* eight (tenths)]

shaky /ˈʃeɪkɪ/ *adj.* (**shakier, shakiest**) **1** unsteady; apt to shake; trembling. **2** unsound, infirm (*a shaky hand*). **3** unreliable, wavering (*a shaky promise; got off to a shaky start*). □□ **shakily** *adv.* **shakiness** *n.*

shale /ʃeɪl/ *n.* soft finely stratified rock that splits easily, consisting of consolidated mud or clay. □ **shale oil** oil obtained from bituminous shale. □□ **shaly** *adj.* [prob. f. G *Schale* f. OE *sc(e)alu* rel. to ON *skál* (see SCALE²)]

shall /ʃæl, ʃ(ə)l/ *v.aux.* (3rd sing. present **shall**; archaic 2nd sing. present **shalt** as below; past **should** /ʃʊd, ʃəd/ (foll. by infin. without *to*, or *absol.*; present and past only in use) **1** (in the 1st person) expressing the future tense (*I shall return soon*) or (with *shall* stressed) emphatic intention (*I shall have a party*). **2** (in the 2nd and 3rd persons) expressing a strong assertion or command rather than a wish (cf. WILL¹) (*you shall not catch me again; they shall go to the party*). ¶ For the other persons in senses 1, 2 see WILL¹. **3** expressing a command or duty (*thou shalt not steal; they shall obey*). **4** (in 2nd-person questions) expressing an enquiry, esp. to avoid the form of a request (cf. WILL¹) (*shall you go to France?*). □ **shall I?** do you want me to? [OE *sceal* f. Gmc]

shallot /ʃəˈlɒt/ *n.* an onion-like plant, *Allium ascalonicum*, with a cluster of small bulbs. [*eschalot* f. F *eschalotte* alt. of OF *eschaloigne*: see SCALLION]

shallow /ˈʃæləʊ/ *adj., n., & v.* —*adj.* **1** of little depth. **2** superficial, trivial (*a shallow mind*). —*n.* (often in *pl.*) a shallow place. —*v.intr. & tr.* become or make shallow. □□ **shallowly** *adv.* **shallowness** *n.* [ME, prob. rel. to *schald*, OE *sceald* SHOAL²]

Shalmaneser III /ˌʃælməˈniːzə(r)/ (9th c. BC), king of Assyria 859–824 BC. According to Assyrian records (though it is unmentioned in the Bible) he defeated an alliance of Syrian kings and Ahab, king of Israel, in a battle at Qarqar on the Orontes in 853 BC. The Black Obelisk, now in the British Museum, shows a number of kings including Jehu of Israel (or his representative) doing obeisance before Shalmaneser.

shalom /ʃəˈlɒm/ *n. & int.* a Jewish salutation at meeting or parting. [Heb. *šālôm* peace]

shalt /ʃælt/ archaic 2nd person sing. of SHALL.

sham /ʃæm/ *v., n., & adj.* —*v.* (**shammed, shamming**) **1** *intr.* feign, pretend. **2** *tr.* **a** pretend to be. **b** simulate (*is shamming sleep*). —*n.* **1** imposture, pretence. **2** a person or thing pretending or pretended to be what he or she or it is not. —*adj.* pretended, counterfeit. □□ **shammer** *n.* [perh. north. dial. var. of SHAME]

shaman /ˈʃæmən/ *n.* (in primitive religions) a person regarded as having direct access to, and influence in, the spiritual world which is usually manifested during a trance and empowers him or her to guide souls, cure illnesses, etc. The general pattern of beliefs, rituals, techniques, etc., associated with a shaman is found almost universally in primitive cultures at the food-gathering stage of development. □□ **shamanism** *n.* **shamanist** *n. & adj.* **shamanistic** /-ˈnɪstɪk/ *adj.* [G *Schamane* & Russ. *shaman* f. Tungusian *samán*]

shamateur /ˈʃæmətɜː(r)/ *n. derog.* a sports player who makes money from sporting activities though classed as an amateur. □□ **shamateurism** *n.* [SHAM + AMATEUR]

shamble /ˈʃæmb(ə)l/ *v. & n.* —*v.intr.* walk or run with a shuffling or awkward gait. —*n.* a shambling gait. [prob. f. dial. *shamble* (adj.) ungainly, perh. f. *shamble legs* with ref. to straddling trestles: see SHAMBLES]

shambles /ˈʃæmb(ə)lz/ *n.pl.* (usu. treated as *sing.*) **1** *colloq.* a mess or muddle (*the room was a shambles*). **2** a butcher's slaughterhouse. **3** a scene of carnage. [pl. of *shamble* stool, stall f. OE *sc(e)amul* f. WG f. L *scamellum* dimin. of *scamnum* bench]

shambolic /ʃæmˈbɒlɪk/ *adj. colloq.* chaotic, unorganized. [SHAMBLES, prob. after SYMBOLIC]

shame /ʃeɪm/ *n. & v.* —*n.* **1** a feeling of distress or humiliation caused by consciousness of the guilt or folly of oneself or an associate. **2** a capacity for experiencing this feeling, esp. as imposing a restraint on behaviour (*has no sense of shame*). **3** a state of disgrace, discredit, or intense regret. **4 a** a person or thing that brings disgrace etc. **b** a thing or action that is wrong or regrettable. —*v.tr.* **1** bring shame on; make ashamed; put to shame. **2** (foll. by *into, out of*) force by shame (*was shamed into confessing*). □ **for shame!** a reproof to a person for not showing shame. **put to shame** disgrace or humiliate by revealing superior qualities etc. **shame on you!** you should be ashamed. **what a shame!** how unfortunate! [OE *sc(e)amu*]

shamefaced /ʃeɪmˈfeɪst, ˈʃeɪm-/ *adj.* **1** showing shame. **2** bashful, diffident. □□ **shamefacedly** /*also* -sɪdlɪ/ *adv.* **shamefacedness** *n.* [16th-c. alt. of *shamefast*, by assim. to FACE]

shameful /ˈʃeɪmfʊl/ *adj.* **1** that causes or is worthy of shame. **2** disgraceful, scandalous. □□ **shamefully** *adv.* **shamefulness** *n.* [OE *sc(e)amful* (as SHAME, -FUL)]

shameless /ˈʃeɪmlɪs/ *adj.* **1** having or showing no sense of shame. **2** impudent. □□ **shamelessly** *adv.* **shamelessness** *n.* [OE *sc(e)amlēas* (as SHAME, -LESS)]

shammy /ˈʃæmɪ/ *n.* (*pl.* **-ies**) (in full **shammy leather**) *colloq.* = CHAMOIS 2. [repr. corrupted pronunc.]

shampoo /ʃæmˈpuː/ *n.* & *v.* —*n.* **1** liquid or cream used to lather and wash the hair. **2** a similar substance for washing a car or carpet etc. **3** an act or instance of cleaning with shampoo. —*v.tr.* (**shampoos, shampooed**) wash with shampoo. [Hind. *chhāmpo*, imper. of *chhāmpnā* to press]

shamrock /ˈʃæmrɒk/ *n.* any of various plants with trifoliate leaves, esp. *Trifolium repens* or *Medicago lupulina*, used as the national emblem of Ireland. [Ir. *seamróg* trefoil, dimin. of *seamar* clover + *og* young]

shamus /ˈʃeɪməs/ *n.* US *sl.* a detective. [20th c.: orig. uncert.]

Shandong /ʃænˈtʌŋ/ (also **Shantung** /ʃænˈtʌŋ/) a province of eastern China; pop. (est. 1986) 77,760,000; capital, Jinan.

shandy /ˈʃændɪ/ *n.* (*pl.* **-ies**) a mixture of beer with lemonade or ginger beer. [19th c.: orig. unkn.]

Shang /ʃæŋ/ the name of a dynasty which ruled China during part of the 2nd millennium BC, probably 16th–11th c. BC. The discovery of inscriptions on bone oracles confirmed literary references to the existence of the Shang dynasty, which witnessed the invention of Chinese ideographic script and the discovery and development of bronze casting.

Shanghai /ʃæŋˈhaɪ/ a port and the largest city in China; pop. (est. 1986) 6,980,000.

shanghai /ʃæŋˈhaɪ/ *v.* & *n.* —*v.tr.* (**shanghais, shanghaied, shanghaiing**) **1** force (a person) to be a sailor on a ship by using drugs or other trickery. **2** *colloq.* put into detention or an awkward situation by trickery. **3** *Austral.* & *NZ* shoot with a catapult. —*n.* (*pl.* **shanghais**) *Austral.* & *NZ* a catapult. [SHANGHAI]

Shangri La /ˌʃæŋgrɪ ˈlɑː/ a Tibetan utopia in James Hilton's novel *Lost Horizon* (1933). —*n.* an earthly paradise, a place of retreat from the worries of modern civilization. [Tibetan *la* mountain pass]

shank /ʃæŋk/ *n.* **1 a** the leg. **b** the lower part of the leg; the leg from knee to ankle. **c** the shin-bone. **2** the lower part of an animal's foreleg, esp. as a cut of meat. **3** a shaft or stem. **4 a** the long narrow part of a tool etc. joining the handle to the working end. **b** the stem of a key, spoon, anchor, etc. **c** the straight part of a nail or fish-hook. **5** the narrow middle of the sole of a shoe. □ **shanks's mare** (or **pony**) one's own legs as a means of conveyance. □□ **shanked** *adj.* (also in comb.). [OE *sceanca* f. WG]

Shankar /ˈʃæŋkɑː(r)/, Ravi (1920–), Indian sitar player and composer, who toured Europe and North America giving sitar recitals which awakened interest in Indian music. From 1951 he and the violinist Yehudi Menuhin collaborated in musical ventures, including some joint performances (1966–7).

Shannon¹ /ˈʃænən/ the chief river of Ireland, flowing 390 km (240 miles) to its estuary on the Atlantic.

Shannon² /ˈʃænən/, Claude Elwood (1916–), American engineer, pioneer of mathematical communication theory (see INFORMATION THEORY).

shanny /ˈʃænɪ/ *n.* (*pl.* **-ies**) a long-bodied olive-green European marine fish, *Blennius pholis*. [19th c.: orig. unkn.: cf. 18th-c. *shan*]

Shansi see SHANXI.

shan't /ʃɑːnt/ *contr.* shall not.

Shantung see SHANDONG.

shantung /ʃænˈtʌŋ/ *n.* soft undressed Chinese silk, usu. undyed. [SHANTUNG]

shanty¹ /ˈʃæntɪ/ *n.* (*pl.* **-ies**) **1** a hut or cabin. **2** a crudely built shack. □ **shanty town** a poor or depressed area of a town, consisting of shanties. [19th c., orig. N.Amer.: perh. f. Can.F *chantier*]

shanty² /ˈʃæntɪ/ *n.* (also **chanty**) (*pl.* **-ies**) (in full **sea shanty**) a song with alternating solo and chorus, of a kind orig. sung by sailors while hauling ropes etc. [prob. F *chantez*, imper. pl. of *chanter* sing: see CHANT]

Shanxi /ʃænˈʃiː/ (also **Shansi** /ʃænˈsiː/) a province of north central China; pop. (est. 1986) 26,550,000; capital, Taiyuan.

SHAPE /ʃeɪp/ *abbr.* Supreme Headquarters Allied Powers Europe.

shape /ʃeɪp/ *n.* & *v.* —*n.* **1** the total effect produced by the outlines of a thing. **2** the external form or appearance of a person or thing. **3** a specific form or guise. **4** a description or sort or way (*not on offer in any shape or form*). **5** a definite or proper arrangement (*must get our ideas into shape*). **6 a** condition, as qualified in some way (*in good shape; in poor shape*). **b** (when unqualified) good condition (*back in shape*). **7** a person or thing as seen, esp. indistinctly or in the imagination (*a shape emerged from the mist*). **8** a mould or pattern. **9** a jelly etc. shaped in a mould. **10** a piece of material, paper, etc., made or cut in a particular form. —*v.* **1** *tr.* give a certain shape or form to; fashion, create. **2** *tr.* (foll. by *to*) adapt or make conform. **3** *tr.* give signs of a future shape or development. **4** *tr.* frame mentally; imagine. **5** *intr.* assume or develop into a shape. **6** *tr.* direct (one's life, course, etc.). □ **lick** (or **knock**) **into shape** make presentable or efficient. **shape up 1** take a (specified) form. **2** show promise; make good progress. **shape up well** be promising. □□ **shapable** *adj.* (also **shapeable**). **shaped** *adj.* (also in comb.). **shaper** *n.* [OE *gesceap* creation f. Gmc]

shapeless /ˈʃeɪplɪs/ *adj.* lacking definite or attractive shape. □□ **shapelessly** *adv.* **shapelessness** *n.*

shapely /ˈʃeɪplɪ/ *adj.* (**shapelier, shapeliest**) **1** well formed or proportioned. **2** of elegant or pleasing shape or appearance. □□ **shapeliness** *n.*

shard /ʃɑːd/ *n.* **1** a broken piece of pottery or glass etc. **2** = POTSHERD. **3** a fragment of volcanic rock. **4** the wing-case of a beetle. [OE *sceard*: sense 3 f. *shard-borne* (Shakesp.) = born in a shard (dial., = cow-dung), wrongly taken as 'borne on shards']

share¹ /ʃeə(r)/ *n.* & *v.* —*n.* **1** a portion that a person receives from or gives to a common amount. **2 a** a part contributed by an individual to an enterprise or commitment. **b** a part received by an individual from this (*got a large share of the credit*). **3** part-proprietorship of property held by joint owners, esp. any of the equal parts into which a company's capital is divided entitling its owner to a proportion of the profits. —*v.* **1** *tr.* get or have or give a share of. **2** *tr.* use or benefit from jointly with others. **3** *intr.* have a share; be a sharer (*shall I share with you?*). **4** *intr.* (foll. by *in*) participate. **5** *tr.* (often foll. by *out*) **a** divide and distribute. **b** give away part of. □ **share and share alike** make an equal division. **share-farmer** *Austral.* & *NZ* a tenant farmer who receives a share of the profits from the owner. □□ **shareable** *adj.* (also **sharable**). **sharer** *n.* [ME f. OE *scearu* division, rel. to SHEAR]

share² /ʃeə(r)/ *n.* = PLOUGHSHARE. [OE *scear, scær* f. Gmc]

sharecropper /ˈʃeəkrɒpə(r)/ *n.* esp. *US* a tenant farmer who gives a part of each crop as rent. □□ **sharecrop** *v.tr.* & *intr.* (**-cropped, -cropping**).

shareholder /ˈʃeəhəʊldə(r)/ *n.* an owner of shares in a company.

shariah /ʃəˈriːə/ *n.* the sacred law of Islam, including the teachings of the Koran and the traditional sayings of Muhammad, prescribing religious and other duties. [Arab. *šarīʿa*]

sharif /ʃəˈriːf/ n. (also **shereef, sherif**) **1** a descendant of Muhammad through his daughter Fatima, entitled to wear a green turban or veil. **2** a Muslim leader. [Arab. *šarīf* noble f. *šarafa* be exalted]

Sharjah /ˈʃɑːdʒə/ (Arabic **Ash-Shariqah** /ˌæʃʃɑːˈriːkə/) **1** the third-largest of the member States of the United Arab Emirates; pop. (1980) 125,150. Its Arabic name means 'The Eastern'. **2** its capital city (Port Khalid), on the Persian Gulf.

shark[1] /ʃɑːk/ n. any of various large usu. voracious marine fish with a long body and prominent dorsal fin. [16th c.: orig. unkn.]

shark[2] /ʃɑːk/ n. colloq. a person who unscrupulously exploits or swindles others. [16th c.: orig. perh. f. G *Schurke* worthless rogue: infl. by SHARK[1]]

sharkskin /ˈʃɑːkskɪn/ n. **1** the skin of a shark. **2** a smooth dull-surfaced fabric.

Sharon /ˈʃeərən/ a fertile coastal plain in Israel, lying between the Mediterranean Sea and the hills of Samaria.

Sharp /ʃɑːp/, Cecil (James) (1859–1924), English collector of folk-songs and folk-dances, whose enthusiasm inspired others to emulate him. He founded the English Folk Dance Society in 1911.

sharp /ʃɑːp/ adj., n., adv., & v. —adj. **1** having an edge or point able to cut or pierce. **2** tapering to a point or edge. **3** abrupt, steep, angular (*a sharp fall; a sharp turn*). **4** well-defined, clean-cut. **5 a** severe or intense (*has a sharp temper*). **b** (of food etc.) pungent, keen (*a sharp appetite*). **c** (of a frost) severe, hard. **6** (of a voice or sound) shrill and piercing. **7** (of sand etc.) composed of angular grains. **8** (of words or temper etc.) harsh or acrimonious (*had a sharp tongue*). **9** (of a person) acute; quick to perceive or comprehend. **10** quick to take advantage; artful, unscrupulous, dishonest. **11** vigorous or brisk. **12** Mus. **a** above the normal pitch. **b** (of a key) having a sharp or sharps in the signature. **c** (C, F, etc., **sharp**) a semitone higher than C, F, etc. **13** colloq. stylish or flashy with regard to dress. —n. **1** Mus. **a** a note raised a semitone above natural pitch. **b** the sign (#) indicating this. **2** colloq. a swindler or cheat. **3** a fine sewing-needle. —adv. **1** punctually (*at nine o'clock sharp*). **2** suddenly, abruptly, promptly (*pulled up sharp*). **3** at a sharp angle. **4** Mus. above the true pitch (*sings sharp*). —v. **1** intr. archaic cheat or swindle at cards etc. **2** tr. US Mus. make sharp. □ **sharp end** colloq. **1** the bow of a ship. **2** the scene of direct action or decision. **sharp practice** dishonest or barely honest dealings. **sharp-set 1** set with a sharp edge. **2** hungry. □□ **sharply** adv. **sharpness** n. [OE sc(e)arp f. Gmc]

sharpen /ˈʃɑːpən/ v.tr. & intr. make or become sharp. □□ **sharpener** n.

sharper /ˈʃɑːpə(r)/ n. a swindler, esp. at cards.

Sharpeville /ˈʃɑːpvɪl/ a South African Black township in southern Transvaal, scene of an incident on 21 March 1960 when security forces fired on a crowd demonstrating against apartheid laws, killing 67 Africans and wounding about 180. There was widespread international condemnation.

sharpish /ˈʃɑːpɪʃ/ adj. & adv. colloq. —adj. fairly sharp. —adv. **1** fairly sharply. **2** quite quickly.

sharpshooter /ˈʃɑːpˌʃuːtə(r)/ n. a skilled marksman. □□ **sharpshooting** n. & adj.

sharp-witted /ʃɑːpˈwɪtɪd/ adj. keenly perceptive or intelligent. □□ **sharp-wittedly** adv. **sharp-wittedness** n.

shashlik /ˈʃæʃlɪk/ n. (in Asia and E. Europe) a kebab of mutton and garnishings. [Russ. *shashlyk*, ult. f. Turk. *šiš* spit, skewer: cf. SHISH KEBAB]

Shasta /ˈʃæstə/ n. (in full **Shasta daisy**) a European plant, *Chrysanthemum maximum*, with large daisy-like flowers. [*Shasta* in California]

Shastra /ˈʃɑːstrə/ n. Hindu sacred writings. [Hindi *šāstr*, Skr. *śāstra*]

Shatt al-Arab /ʃæt æl ˈærəb/ a river of SE Iraq, formed by the confluence of the Tigris and Euphrates Rivers, flowing about 195 km (120 miles) south-east to the Persian Gulf.

shatter /ˈʃætə(r)/ v. **1** tr. & intr. break suddenly in pieces. **2** tr. severely damage or utterly destroy (*shattered hopes*). **3** tr. greatly upset or discompose. **4** tr. (usu. as **shattered** adj.) exhaust. □□ **shatterer** n. **shattering** adj. **shatteringly** adv. **shatter-proof** adj. [ME, rel. to SCATTER]

shave /ʃeɪv/ v. & n. —v.tr. (past part. **shaved** or (as adj.) **shaven**) **1** remove (bristles or hair) from the face etc. with a razor. **2** (also absol.) remove bristles or hair with a razor from the face etc. of (a person) or (a part of the body). **3 a** reduce by a small amount. **b** take (a small amount) away from. **4** cut thin slices from the surface of (wood etc.) to shape it. **5** pass close to without touching; miss narrowly. —n. **1** an act of shaving or the process of being shaved. **2** a close approach without contact. **3** a narrow miss or escape; = *close shave* (see CLOSE[1]). **4** a tool for shaving wood etc. [OE sc(e)afan (sense 4 of noun f. OE *sceafa*) f. Gmc]

shaveling /ˈʃeɪvlɪŋ/ n. archaic **1** a shaven person. **2** a monk, friar, or priest.

shaven see SHAVE.

shaver /ˈʃeɪvə(r)/ n. **1** a person or thing that shaves. **2** an electric razor. **3** colloq. a young lad.

Shavian /ˈʃeɪvɪən/ adj. & n. —adj. of or in the manner of G. B. Shaw, or his ideas. —n. an admirer of Shaw. [*Shavius*, Latinized form of *Shaw*]

shaving /ˈʃeɪvɪŋ/ n. **1** a thin strip cut off the surface of wood etc. **2** (attrib.) used in shaving the face (*shaving-cream*).

Shavuoth /ʃəˈvuːəs, ˌʃɑːvuːˈɒt/ n. (also **Shavuot**) the Jewish Pentecost. [Heb. *šāḇūˈôt*, = weeks, with ref. to the weeks between Passover and Pentecost]

Shaw /ʃɔː/, George Bernard (1856–1950), Irish playwright who moved to London in 1876 and began his literary career as a critic and unsuccessful novelist. An active member of the Fabian Society, he was already well known as a socialist and public speaker when his first play was performed in 1892. After a slow start, Shaw was soon recognized as one of the wittiest, most provocative, and prolific writers of the age, whose intellectual comedies (e.g. *Man and Superman*, 1903; *Major Barbara*, 1907; *Pygmalion*, 1913; *Heartbreak House*, 1919) attacked conventional morality and thought with epigram, paradox, and a great fertility of theatrical invention. Shaw also wrote many prose works, including the lengthy Prefaces to his plays, and generously supported many progressive causes, including feminism. He was awarded the Nobel Prize for literature in 1925. Abstemious, vegetarian, and indefatigable, he continued to work until the very end of his long life.

shaw /ʃɔː/ n. esp. Brit. the stalks and leaves of potatoes, turnips, etc. [perh. = SHOW n.]

shawl /ʃɔːl/ n. a piece of fabric, usu. rectangular and often folded into a triangle, worn over the shoulders or head or wrapped round a baby. □ **shawl collar** a rolled collar extended down the front of a garment without lapel notches. □□ **shawled** adj. [Urdu etc. f. Pers. *šāl*, prob. f. *Shāliāt* in India]

shawm /ʃɔːm/ n. Mus. a medieval double-reed wind instrument with a sharp penetrating tone. [ME f. OF *chalemie, chalemel, chalemeaus* (pl.), ult. f. L *calamus* f. Gk *kalamos* reed]

shchi /ʃiː/ n. a Russian cabbage soup. [Russ.]

she /ʃiː/ pron. & n. —pron. (obj. **her**; poss. **her**; pl. **they**) **1** the woman or girl or female animal previously named or in question. **2** a thing regarded as female, e.g. a vehicle or ship. **3** Austral. & NZ colloq. it; the state of affairs (*she'll be right*). —n. **1** a female; a woman. **2** (in comb.) female (*she-goat*). □ **she-devil** a malicious or spiteful woman. [ME *scæ, sche*, etc., f. OE fem. demonstr. pron. & adj. *sīo, sēo*, acc. *sīe*]

s/he pron. a written representation of 'he or she' used to indicate both sexes.

shea /ʃiː/ n. a W. African tree, *Vitellaria paradoxa*, bearing nuts containing a large amount of fat. □ **shea-butter** a butter made from this fat. [Mandingo *si, se, sye*]

sheading /ˈʃiːdɪŋ/ n. each of the six administrative divisions of the Isle of Man. [SHED[1] + -ING[1]]

sheaf /ʃiːf/ n. & v. —n. (pl. **sheaves** /ʃiːvz/) a group of things laid lengthways together and usu. tied, esp. a bundle of cornstalks tied after reaping, or a collection of papers. —v.tr. make into sheaves. [OE *scēaf* f. Gmc (as SHOVE)]

shealing var. of SHIELING.

shear /ʃɪə(r)/ v. & n. —v. (past **sheared**, archaic except Austral. & NZ **shore** /ʃɔː(r)/; past part. **shorn** /ʃɔːn/ or **sheared**) **1** tr. cut with scissors or shears etc. **2** tr. remove or take off by cutting. **3** tr. clip the wool off (a sheep etc.). **4** tr. (foll. by *of*) **a** strip bare. **b** deprive. **5** tr. & intr. (often foll. by *off*) distort or be distorted, or break, from a structural strain. —n. **1** Mech. & Geol. a strain produced by pressure in the structure of a substance, when its layers are laterally shifted in relation to each other. **2** (in pl.) (also **pair of shears** sing.) a large clipping or cutting instrument shaped like scissors for use in gardens etc. □□ **shearer** n. [OE *sceran* f. Gmc]

Shearer /ˈʃɪərə(r)/, Moira (full name Moira Shearer King, 1926–), Scottish dancer, who became a ballerina with Sadler's Wells ballet. She created roles in a number of ballets by Sir Frederick Ashton. Her greatest international success was her portrayal of a dedicated ballerina in the film *The Red Shoes* (1948).

shearling /ˈʃɪəlɪŋ/ n. **1** a sheep that has been shorn once. **2** wool from a shearling.

shearwater /ˈʃɪəˌwɔːtə(r)/ n. **1** any long-winged sea bird of the genus *Puffinus*, usu. flying near the surface of the water. **2** = SKIMMER 4.

sheatfish /ˈʃiːtfɪʃ/ n. (pl. same or **sheatfishes**) a large freshwater catfish, *Silurus glanis*, native to European waters. [earlier *sheathfish*, prob. after G *Scheid*]

sheath /ʃiːθ/ n. (pl. **sheaths** /ʃiːðz, ʃiːθs/) **1** a close-fitting cover, esp. for the blade of a knife or sword. **2** a condom. **3** Bot., Anat., & Zool. an enclosing case or tissue. **4** the protective covering round an electric cable. **5** a woman's close-fitting dress. □ **sheath knife** a dagger-like knife carried in a sheath. □□ **sheathless** adj. [OE *scæth, scēath*]

sheathe /ʃiːð/ v.tr. **1** put into a sheath. **2** encase; protect with a sheath. [ME f. SHEATH]

sheathing /ˈʃiːðɪŋ/ n. a protective casing or covering.

sheave[1] /ʃiːv/ v.tr. make into sheaves.

sheave[2] /ʃiːv/ n. a grooved wheel in a pulley-block etc., for a rope to run on. [ME f. OE *scife* (unrecorded) f. Gmc]

sheaves pl. of SHEAF.

Sheba /ˈʃiːbə/ the Biblical name of Saba, an ancient country in SW Arabia, famous for its trade in gold and spices. The Queen of Sheba visited King Solomon in Jerusalem. The Hebrew word is the name of the people (Sabaeans), but was erroneously assumed by Greek and Roman writers to be a place-name.

shebang /ʃɪˈbæŋ/ n. US sl. **1** a matter or affair (esp. *the whole shebang*). **2** a shed or hut. [19th c.: orig. unkn.]

shebeen /ʃɪˈbiːn/ n. esp. Ir. an unlicensed house selling alcoholic liquor. [Anglo-Ir. *síbín* f. *séibe* mugful]

shed[1] /ʃed/ n. **1** a one-storeyed structure usu. of wood for storage or shelter for animals etc., or as a workshop. **2** a large roofed structure with one open side open, for storing or maintaining machinery etc. **3** Austral. & NZ an open-sided building for shearing sheep or milking cattle. [app. var. of SHADE[1]]

shed[2] /ʃed/ v.tr. (**shedding**; past and past part. **shed**) **1** let or cause to fall off (*trees shed their leaves*). **2** take off (clothes). **3** reduce (an electrical power load) by disconnection etc. **4** cause to fall or flow (*shed blood; shed tears*). **5** disperse, diffuse, radiate (*shed light*). □ **shed light on** see LIGHT[1]. [OE *sc(e)adan* f. Gmc]

she'd /ʃiːd, ʃɪd/ contr. **1** she had. **2** she would.

shedder /ˈʃedə(r)/ n. **1** a person or thing that sheds. **2** a female salmon after spawning.

shedhand /ˈʃedhænd/ n. Austral. & NZ an unskilled assistant in a shearing shed.

sheela-na-gig /ˈʃiːlənəˌɡɪɡ/ n. a medieval carved stone female figure, sometimes found on churches or castles in Britain and Ireland, shown nude, in frontal aspect, and with the hands indicating the genitalia. [Ir. *Síle na gcíoch*, perh. = lady of the breasts]

sheen /ʃiːn/ n. **1** a gloss or lustre on a surface. **2** radiance, brightness. □□ **sheeny** adj. [obs. *sheen* beautiful, resplendent f. OE *scēne*: sense assim. to SHINE]

sheep /ʃiːp/ n. (pl. same) **1** any ruminant mammal of the genus *Ovis* with a thick woolly coat, esp. kept in flocks for its wool or meat, and noted for its timidity. **2** a bashful, timid, or silly person. **3** (usu. in pl.) **a** a member of a minister's congregation. **b** a parishioner. □ **separate the sheep from the goats** divide into superior and inferior groups (cf. Matt. 25: 33). **sheep-dip 1** a preparation for cleansing sheep of vermin or preserving their wool. **2** the place where sheep are dipped in this. **sheep-run** an extensive sheepwalk, esp. in Australia. **sheep's-bit** a plant, *Jasione montana*, resembling a scabious. □□ **sheeplike** adj. [OE *scēp, scæp, scēap*]

sheepdog /ˈʃiːpdɒɡ/ n. **1** a dog trained to guard and herd sheep. **2 a** a dog of various breeds suitable for this. **b** any of these breeds.

sheepfold /ˈʃiːpfəʊld/ n. an enclosure for penning sheep.

sheepish /ˈʃiːpɪʃ/ adj. **1** bashful, shy, reticent. **2** embarrassed through shame. □□ **sheepishly** adv. **sheepishness** n.

sheepshank /ˈʃiːpʃæŋk/ n. a knot used to shorten a rope temporarily.

sheepskin /ˈʃiːpskɪn/ n. **1** a garment or rug of sheep's skin with the wool on. **2** leather from a sheep's skin used in bookbinding.

sheepwalk /ˈʃiːppwɔːk/ n. Brit. a tract of land on which sheep are pastured.

sheer[1] /ʃɪə(r)/ adj. & adv. —adj. **1** no more or less than; mere, unqualified, absolute (*sheer luck; sheer determination*). **2** (of a cliff or ascent etc.) perpendicular; very steep. **3** (of a textile) very thin; diaphanous. —adv. **1** directly, outright. **2** perpendicularly. □□ **sheerly** adv. **sheerness** n. [ME *schere* prob. f. dial. *shire* pure, clear f. OE *scīr* f. Gmc]

sheer[2] /ʃɪə(r)/ v. & n. —v.intr. **1** esp. Naut. swerve or change course. **2** (foll. by *away, off*) go away, esp. from a person or topic one dislikes or fears. —n. Naut. a deviation from a course. [perh. f. MLG *scheren* = SHEAR v.]

sheer[3] /ʃɪə(r)/ n. the upward slope of a ship's lines towards the bow and stern. [prob. f. SHEAR n.]

sheerlegs /ˈʃɪəleɡz/ n.pl. (treated as sing.) a hoisting apparatus made from poles joined at or near the top and separated at the bottom for masting ships, installing engines, etc. [*sheer*, var. of SHEAR n. + LEG]

sheet[1] /ʃiːt/ n. & v. —n. **1** a large rectangular piece of cotton or other fabric, used esp. in pairs as inner bedclothes. **2 a** a broad usu. thin flat piece of material (e.g. paper or metal). **b** (attrib.) made in sheets (*sheet iron*). **3** a wide continuous surface or expanse of water, ice, flame, falling rain, etc. **4** a set of unseparated postage stamps. **5** derog. a newspaper, esp. a disreputable one. **6** a complete piece of paper of the size in which it was made, for printing and folding as part of a book. —v. **1** tr. provide or cover with sheets. **2** tr. form into sheets. **3** intr. (of rain etc.) fall in sheets. □ **sheet lightning** a lightning flash with its brightness diffused by reflection. **sheet metal** metal formed into thin sheets by rolling, hammering, etc. **sheet music** music published in cut or folded sheets, not bound. [OE *scēte, scīete* f. Gmc]

sheet[2] /ʃiːt/ n. **1** a rope or chain attached to the lower corner of a sail for securing or controlling it. **2** (in pl.) the space at the bow or stern of an open boat. □ **flowing sheets** sheets eased for free movement in the wind. **sheet anchor 1** a second anchor for use in emergencies. **2** a person or thing depended on in the last resort. **sheet bend** a method of temporarily fastening one rope through the loop of another. [ME f. OE *scēata*, ON *skaut* (as SHEET[1])]

sheeting /ˈʃiːtɪŋ/ n. material for making bed linen.

Sheffield /ˈʃefiːld/ an industrial city in South Yorkshire; pop. (1981) 477,250. From medieval times onwards it was noted for metal-working, and became famous especially for the manufacture of cutlery and silverware and, after the establishment of a works by Henry Bessemer (see entry), for the production of steel.

sheikh /ʃeɪk/ n. (also **shaikh, sheik**) **1** a chief or head of an Arab tribe, family, or village. **2** a Muslim leader. □□ **sheikhdom** n. [ult. f. Arab. *šayk* old man, sheikh, f. *šāka* be or grow old]

sheila /ˈʃiːlə/ n. Austral. & NZ sl. a girl or young woman. [orig. *shaler* (of unkn. orig.): assim. to the name *Sheila*]

shekel /ˈʃek(ə)l/ n. **1** the chief monetary unit of modern Israel. **2** hist. a silver coin and unit of weight used in ancient Israel and the Middle East. **3** (in pl.) colloq. money; riches. [Heb. šeķel f. šāķal weigh]

shelduck /ˈʃeldʌk/ n. (pl. same or **shelducks**; masc. **sheldrake**, pl. same or **sheldrakes**) any bright-plumaged coastal wild duck of the genus Tadorna, esp. T. tadorna. [ME prob. f. dial. sheld pied, rel. to MDu. schillede variegated, + DUCK¹, DRAKE]

shelf¹ /ʃelf/ n. (pl. **shelves** /ʃelvz/) **1 a** a thin flat piece of wood or metal etc. projecting from a wall, or as part of a unit, used to support books etc. **b** a flat-topped recess in a wall etc. used for supporting objects. **2 a** a projecting horizontal ledge in a cliff face etc. **b** a reef or sandbank under water. **c** = continental shelf. □ **on the shelf 1** (of a woman) past the age when she might expect to be married. **2** (esp. of a retired person) no longer active or of use. **shelf-life** the amount of time for which a stored item of food etc. remains usable. **shelf-mark** a notation on a book showing its place in a library. **shelf-room** available space on a shelf. □□ **shelved** /ʃelvd/ adj. **shelfful** n. (pl. -**fuls**). **shelflike** adj. [ME f. (M)LG schelf, rel. to OE scylfe partition, scylf crag]

shelf² /ʃelf/ n. & v. Austral. sl. —n. an informer. —v.tr. inform upon. [20th c.: orig. uncert.]

shell /ʃel/ n. & v. —n. **1 a** the hard outer case of many marine molluscs (cockle shell). **b** the esp. hard but fragile outer covering of a bird's, reptile's, etc. egg. **c** the usu. hard outer case of a nut-kernel, seed, etc. **d** the carapace of a tortoise, turtle, etc. **e** the wing-case or pupa-case of many insects etc. **2 a** an explosive projectile or bomb for use in a big gun or mortar. **b** a hollow metal or paper case used as a container for fireworks, explosives, cartridges, etc. **c** US a cartridge. **3** a mere semblance or outer form without substance. **4** any of several things resembling a shell in being an outer case, esp.: **a** a light racing-boat. **b** a hollow pastry case. **c** the metal framework of a vehicle body etc. **d** the walls of an unfinished or gutted building, ship, etc. **e** an inner or roughly-made coffin. **f** a building shaped like a conch. **g** the handguard of a sword. **5** a group of electrons with almost equal energy in an atom. —v. **1** tr. remove the shell or pod from. **2** tr. bombard (a town, troops, etc.) with shells. **3** tr. provide or cover with a shell or shells. **4** intr. (usu. foll. by off) (of metal etc.) come off in scales. **5** intr. (of a seed etc.) be released from a shell. □ **come out of one's shell** cease to be shy; become communicative. **shell-bit** a gouge-shaped boring bit. **shell company** an unimportant firm made the subject of a take-over bid because of its status on the Stock Exchange etc. **shell egg** an egg still in its shell, not dried etc. **shell-heap** (or -**mound**) hist. a kitchen midden. **shell-jacket** an army officer's tight-fitting undress jacket reaching to the waist. **shell-keep** a form of Norman keep built on a mound, usually on the site of an older fortress. **shell-lime** fine quality lime produced by burning sea shells. **shell-money** shells used as a medium of exchange, e.g. wampum. **shell out** (also absol.) colloq. **1** pay (money). **2** hand over (a required sum). **shell-out** n. **1** the act of shelling out. **2** a game of snooker etc. played by three or more people. **shell-pink** a delicate pale pink. **shell-shock** a nervous breakdown resulting from exposure to battle. **shell-shocked** suffering from shell-shock. **shell suit** a track suit with a soft lining and a weather-proof outer nylon 'shell', used for leisure wear. **shell-work** ornamentation consisting of shells cemented on to wood etc. □□ **shelled** adj. **shell-less** adj. **shell-like** adj. **shellproof** adj. (in sense 2a of n.). **shelly** adj. [OE sc(i)ell f. Gmc: cf. SCALE¹]

she'll /ʃiːl, ʃɪl/ contr. she will; she shall.

shellac /ʃəˈlæk/ n. & v. —n. lac resin melted into thin flakes and used for making varnish (cf. LAC¹). —v.tr. (**shellacked**, **shellacking**) **1** varnish with shellac. **2** US sl. defeat or thrash soundly. [SHELL + LAC, transl. F laque en écailles lac in thin plates]

shellback /ˈʃelbæk/ n. sl. an old sailor.

Shelley¹ /ˈʃeli/, Mary Wollstonecraft (1797–1851), English novelist, daughter of W. Godwin and Mary Wollstonecraft. She eloped with P. B. Shelley in 1814 and married him in 1816. She is chiefly remembered as the author of Frankenstein, or the Modern Prometheus (1818). Her other works include the novels The Last

Man (1826) and Lodore (1835), short stories (some with science fiction elements, others Gothic or historical), biographies, and an edition of her husband's poems (1830).

Shelley² /ˈʃeli/, Percy Bysshe (1792–1822), English poet. His pamphlet The Necessity of Atheism (1811; with T. J. Hogg) caused his expulsion from Oxford. This period of political activism, during which he married Harriet Westbrook (1811), is reflected in his ideological poem Queen Mab (1813). His marriage collapsed in 1814 and he eloped abroad with Mary Godwin and her stepsister 'Claire' Clairmont, marrying Mary in 1816 after Harriet had drowned herself. From 1818 he settled permanently in Italy where, in spite of his increasingly troubled domestic situation, he composed his greatest works, including Prometheus Unbound (1820), a lyrical drama on his aspirations and contradictions as a poet and radical, The Mask of Anarchy (1819), a poem of political protest, 'Ode to the West Wind' (1820), The Cenci (1819), a verse tragedy, his famous prose work The Defence of Poetry (1821), vindicating the role of poetry in a progressive industrial society, and Adonais (1821), an elegy on the death of Keats. Shelley was drowned in a boating accident. Spectacular lyric powers, and his intellectual courage and originality, have earned him a high place among the Romantic poets.

shellfish /ˈʃelfɪʃ/ n. **1** an aquatic shelled mollusc, e.g. an oyster, winkle, etc. **2** a crustacean, e.g. a crab, shrimp, etc.

Shelta /ˈʃeltə/ n. an ancient hybrid secret language used by Irish gypsies and pipers, Irish and Welsh travelling tinkers, etc. It is composed partly of Irish or Gaelic words, mostly disguised by inversion or by arbitrary alteration of initial consonants. [19th c.: orig. unkn.]

shelter /ˈʃeltə(r)/ n. & v. —n. **1** anything serving as a shield or protection from danger, bad weather, etc. **2 a** a place of refuge provided esp. for the homeless etc. **b** US an animal sanctuary. **3** a shielded condition; protection (took shelter under a tree). —v. **1** tr. act or serve as shelter to; protect; conceal; defend (sheltered them from the storm; had a sheltered upbringing). **2** intr. & refl. find refuge; take cover (sheltered under a tree; sheltered themselves behind the wall). □ **shelter-belt** a line of trees etc. planted to protect crops from the wind. □□ **shelterer** n. **shelterless** adj. [16th c.: perh. f. obs. sheltron phalanx f. OE scieldtruma (as SHIELD, truma troop)]

sheltie /ˈʃelti/ n. (also **shelty**) (pl. -**ies**) a Shetland pony or sheepdog. [prob. repr. ON Hjalti Shetlander as pronounced in Orkney]

shelve¹ /ʃelv/ v.tr. **1** put (books etc.) on a shelf. **2 a** abandon or defer (a plan etc.). **b** remove (a person) from active work etc. **3** fit (a cupboard etc.) with shelves. □□ **shelver** n. **shelving** n. [shelves pl. of SHELF]

shelve² /ʃelv/ v.intr. (of ground etc.) slope in a specified direction (land shelved away to the horizon). [perh. f. shelvy (adj.) having underwater reefs f. shelve (n.) ledge, f. SHELVE¹]

shelves pl. of SHELF.

Shem /ʃem/ a son of Noah (Gen. 10: 21), traditional ancestor of the Semites.

Shema /ʃeˈmɑː/ n. a Hebrew text forming an important part of Jewish evening and morning prayer and used as a Jewish confession of faith, beginning 'Hear, O Israel, the Lord our God is one Lord'. [Heb., = hear]

shemozzle /ʃɪˈmɒz(ə)l/ n. (also **schemozzle**) sl. **1** a brawl or commotion. **2** a muddle. [Yiddish after LHeb. šel-lō'-mazzāl of no luck]

Shenandoah /ˌʃenənˈdəʊə/ a river of West Virginia which rises on both sides of the Blue Ridge Mountains and flows about 240 km (150 miles) to enter the Potomac River at Harpers Ferry.

shenanigan /ʃɪˈnænɪgən/ n. (esp. in pl.) colloq. **1** high-spirited behaviour; nonsense. **2** trickery; dubious manoeuvres. [19th c.: orig. unkn.]

Shensi see SHAANXI.

Shenyang /ʃenˈjæŋ/ (formerly **Mukden** /ˈmʊkd(ə)n/) the fourth-largest city in China, a former Manchu capital and now the capital of Liaoning province; pop. (est. 1986) 4,200,000.

Shenzhen /ʃenˈʒen/ an industrial city developed as a special economic zone near Canton in southern China; pop. (est. 1984) 191,400.

Sheol /'ʃiːəʊl, -ɒl/ n. (in the Old Testament) the underworld, the abode of the dead. [Heb. šʾôl]

shepherd /'ʃepəd/ n. & v. —n. 1 (fem. **shepherdess** /'ʃepədɪs/) a person employed to tend sheep, esp. at pasture. 2 a member of the clergy etc. who cares for and guides a congregation. — v.tr. 1 a tend (sheep etc.) as a shepherd. b guide (followers etc.). 2 marshal or drive (a crowd etc.) like sheep. □ **the Good Shepherd** Christ. **shepherd dog** a sheepdog. **shepherd's crook** a staff with a hook at one end used by shepherds. **shepherd's needle** a white-flowered common plant, *Scandix pecten-veneris*, with spiny fruit. **shepherd's pie** a dish of minced meat under a layer of mashed potato. **shepherd's plaid 1** a small black and white check pattern. 2 woollen cloth with this pattern. **shepherd's purse** a white-flowered hairy cornfield plant, *Capsella bursa-pastoris*, with triangular or cordate pods. [OE *scēaphierde* (as SHEEP, HERD)]

sherardize /'ʃerə‚daɪz/ v.tr. (also **-ise**) coat (iron or steel) with zinc by heating in contact with zinc dust. [*Sherard* Cowper-Coles, Engl. inventor d. 1936]

Sheraton /'ʃerət(ə)n/ n. (often *attrib.*) a style of furniture introduced in England *c*.1790, with delicate and graceful forms. [T. *Sheraton*, Engl. furniture-maker d. 1806]

sherbet /'ʃɜːbət/ n. 1 a a flavoured sweet effervescent powder or drink. b *US* a water-ice. 2 a cooling drink of sweet diluted fruit-juices esp. in Arab countries. 3 *Austral. joc.* beer. [Turk. *şerbet*, Pers. *šerbet* f. Arab. *šarba* drink f. *šariba* to drink: cf. SHRUB², SYRUP]

sherd /ʃɜːd/ n. = POTSHERD. [var. of SHARD]

shereef (also **sherif**) var. of SHARIF.

Sheridan /'ʃerɪd(ə)n/, Richard Brinsley (1751–1816), Anglo-Irish dramatist, son of an actor-manager. After eloping to France with the beautiful singer Eliza Linley whom he married in 1773, he established his reputation with *The Rivals* (1775) which included the famous Mrs Malaprop among its characters, and continued his success with his masterpiece *The School for Scandal* (1777), both comedies of manners, skilfully constructed with great wit and elegance and continuously popular. He became principal director of Drury Lane Theatre in 1776 and sole proprietor in 1779. Already politically ambitious, Sheridan became the friend and supporter of Charles James Fox; he entered Parliament in 1780, where he became a celebrated orator, held senior government posts, and won the friendship of the Prince Regent. Meanwhile financial problems associated with Drury Lane became crushing; he died in poverty, but was given a magnificent funeral in Westminster Abbey.

sheriff /'ʃerɪf/ n. 1 *Brit.* a (also **High Sheriff**) the chief executive officer of the Crown in a county, nominally charged with keeping the peace, administering justice through the courts, executing writs by deputy, presiding over elections, etc. b an honorary officer elected annually in some towns. 2 *US* an elected officer in a county, responsible for keeping the peace. □ **sheriff court** *Sc.* a county court. **sheriff-depute** *Sc.* the chief judge of a county or district. □□ **sheriffalty** n. (pl. **-ies**). **sheriffdom** n. **sheriffhood** n. **sheriffship** n. [OE *scīr-gerēfa* (as SHIRE, REEVE¹)]

Sherlock /'ʃɜːlɒk/ n. 1 a person who investigates mysteries or shows great perceptiveness. 2 a private detective. [*Sherlock* HOLMES]

Sherman /'ʃɜːmən/, William Tecumseh (1820–91), one of the great generals of the American Civil War. In March 1864 he succeeded Grant as chief commander in the west, and crushed the Confederate forces in his march through Georgia. Ordering his troops to live off the land, by deliberate and disciplined destruction he not only wiped out the South's sources of supply but sought to break the spirit of civilians as well as soldiers. In 1869 he became commander of the US army, a post he filled until his retirement in 1884.

Sherpa /'ʃɜːpə/ n. (pl. same or **Sherpas**) a member of a Himalayan people living on the borders of Nepal and Tibet, and skilled in mountaineering. [native name]

Sherrington /'ʃerɪŋt(ə)n/, Sir Charles Scott (1857–1952), English physiologist whose researches opened up a new chapter in

the understanding of the central nervous system. For his study of the neuron he shared the 1932 Nobel Prize for medicine.

sherry /'ʃerɪ/ n. (pl. **-ies**) 1 a fortified wine orig. from S. Spain. 2 a glass of this. □ **sherry cobbler** see COBBLER 2. **sherry-glass** a small wineglass used for sherry. [earlier *sherris* f. Sp. (*vino de*) *Xeres* (now Jerez de la Frontera) in Andalusia]

's-Hertogenbosch /‚seətɒxen'bɒs/ (French **Bois-le-Duc** /‚bwɑːlə'djuːk/) a city in The Netherlands, the capital of North Brabant; pop. (1987) 90,000. It was the birthplace of the painter Hieronymus Bosch.

she's /ʃiːz, ʃɪz/ contr. 1 she is. 2 she has.

Shetland /'ʃetlənd/ an islands area of Scotland consisting of the Shetland Islands; pop. (1981) 22,400; chief town, Lerwick. —adj. of the Shetland Islands. □ **Shetland Islands** (also **Shetlands**) a group of about 100 Scottish islands NNE of the Orkneys, which have become important bases for the exploitation of oil and gas in the North Sea. (See also ORKNEY.) **Shetland lace** openwork woollen trimming. **Shetland pony 1** a pony of a small hardy rough-coated breed. 2 this breed. **Shetland sheepdog 1** a small dog of a collie-like breed. 2 this breed. **Shetland wool** a fine loosely twisted wool from Shetland sheep. □□ **Shetlander** n.

sheva var. of SCHWA.

shew *archaic* var. of SHOW.

shewbread /'ʃəʊbred/ n. twelve loaves that were displayed in a Jewish temple and renewed each sabbath.

Shiah /'ʃiːə/ n. one of the two main branches of Islam, esp. in Iran, that rejects the first three Sunni Caliphs and regards Ali as Muhammad's first successor. (See below.) [Arab. *šīʾa* party (of Ali, Muhammad's cousin and son-in-law)]
The Shiites followed a succession of imams, whom they believed to possess a Divine Light giving them special wisdom—indeed, infallibility—in matters of the faith and community of believers. There exist several subgroups, depending on which imam they believe to be the final one, regarded as forced to go into hiding through the repressive political rule of the majority community and expected to return and to triumph over injustice. 2 a Shiite.

shiatsu /ʃɪ'ætsuː/ n. a kind of therapy of Japanese origin, in which pressure is applied with the fingers to certain points of the body. [Jap., = finger pressure]

shibboleth /'ʃɪbə‚leθ/ n. a long-standing formula, doctrine, or phrase, etc., held to be true by a party or sect, regarded as revealing a person's orthodoxy (*must abandon outdated shibboleths*). [ME f. Heb. *šibbōleṯ* ear of corn, used as a test of nationality for its difficult pronunciation (Judg. 12: 6)]

shicer /'ʃaɪsə(r)/ n. *Austral.* 1 *Mining* an unproductive claim or mine. 2 *sl.* a a swindler, welsher, or cheat. b a worthless thing; a failure. [G *Scheisser* contemptible person]

shicker /'ʃɪkə(r)/ adj. (also **shickered** /'ʃɪkəd/) *Austral.* & *NZ sl.* drunk. [Yiddish *shiker* f. Heb. *šikkôr* f. *šākar* be drunk]

shied past and past part. of SHY¹, SHY².

shield /ʃiːld/ n. & v. —n. 1 a esp. *hist.* a piece of armour of esp. metal, carried on the arm or in the hand to deflect blows from the head or body. b a thing serving to protect (*insurance is a shield against disaster*). 2 a thing resembling a shield, esp.: a a trophy in the form of a shield. b a protective plate or screen in machinery etc. c a shieldlike part of an animal, esp. a shell. d a similar part of a plant. e *Geol.* a large rigid area of the earth's crust, usu. of Precambrian rock, which has been unaffected by later orogenic episodes. The largest example is the Canadian shield, which occupies over two-fifths of the land area of Canada; it is drained by rivers flowing into Hudson Bay. f *US* a policeman's shield-shaped badge. 3 *Heraldry* a stylized representation of a shield used for displaying a coat of arms etc. —v.tr. protect or screen, esp. from blame or lawful punishment. □ **shield fern** 1 any common fern of the genus *Polystichum*, with shield-shaped indusia. 2 = BUCKLER 2. □□ **shieldless** adj. [OE *sc(i)eld* f. Gmc: prob. orig. = board, rel. to SCALE¹]

shieling /'ʃiːlɪŋ/ n. (also **shealing**) *Sc.* 1 a roughly constructed hut orig. esp. for pastoral use. 2 pasture for cattle. [Sc. *shiel* hut: ME, of unkn. orig.]

shier *compar.* of SHY¹.

shiest *superl.* of SHY¹.

shift /ʃɪft/ *v.* & *n.* —*v.* **1** *intr.* & *tr.* change or move or cause to change or move from one position to another. **2** *tr.* remove, esp. with effort (*washing won't shift the stains*). **3** *sl.* **a** *intr.* hurry (*we'll have to shift!*). **b** *tr.* consume (food or drink) hastily or in bulk. **c** *tr.* sell (esp. dubious goods). **4** *intr.* contrive or manage as best one can. **5** *US* **a** *tr.* change (gear) in a vehicle. **b** *intr.* change gear. **6** *intr.* (of cargo) get shaken out of place. **7** *intr. archaic* be evasive or indirect. —*n.* **1 a** the act or an instance of shifting. **b** the substitution of one thing for another; a rotation. **2 a** a relay of workers (*the night shift*). **b** the time for which they work (*an eight-hour shift*). **3 a** a device, stratagem, or expedient. **b** a dodge, trick, or evasion. **4 a** a woman's straight unwaisted dress. **b** *archaic* a loose-fitting undergarment. **5** a displacement of spectral lines (see also *red shift*). **6** (also **sound shift**) a systematic change in pronunciation as a language evolves. **7** a key on a keyboard used to switch between lower and upper case etc. **8** *Bridge* **a** a change of suit in bidding. **b** *US* a change of suit in play. **9** the positioning of successive rows of bricks so that their ends do not coincide. **10** *US* **a** a gear lever in a motor vehicle. **b** a mechanism for this. □ **make shift** manage or contrive; get along somehow (*made shift without it*). **shift for oneself** rely on one's own resources. **shift one's ground** take up a new position in an argument etc. **shift off** get rid of (responsibility etc.) to another. □□ **shiftable** *adj.* **shifter** *n.* [OE *sciftan* arrange, divide, etc., f. Gmc]

shiftless /ˈʃɪftlɪs/ *adj.* lacking resourcefulness; lazy; inefficient. □□ **shiftlessly** *adv.* **shiftlessness** *n.*

shifty /ˈʃɪftɪ/ *adj. colloq.* (**shiftier, shiftiest**) not straightforward; evasive; deceitful. □□ **shiftily** *adv.* **shiftiness** *n.*

shigella /ʃɪˈgelə/ *n.* any airborne bacterium of the genus *Shigella*, some of which cause dysentery. [mod.L f. K. *Shiga*, Jap. bacteriologist d. 1957 + dimin. suffix]

shih-tzu /ˈʃiːˈtsuː/ *n.* **1** a dog of a breed with long silky erect hair and short legs. **2** this breed. [Chin. *shizi* lion]

Shiite /ˈʃiːaɪt/ *n.* & *adj.* —*n.* an adherent of the Shiah branch of Islam. —*adj.* of or relating to Shiah. □□ **Shiism** /ˈʃiːɪz(ə)m/ *n.*

Shijiazhuang /ˌʃiːdʒɪəˈdʒwæŋ/ a city in NE central China, capital of Hebei province; pop. (est. 1986) 1,160,000.

shikar /ʃɪˈkɑː(r)/ *n.* Ind. hunting. [Urdu f. Pers. *šikār*]

Shikoku /ʃɪˈkəʊkuː/ the smallest of the four main islands of Japan; pop. (1986) 4,226,000; capital, Matsuyama.

shiksa /ˈʃɪksə/ *n.* often *offens.* (used by Jews) a gentile girl or woman. [Yiddish *shikse* f. Heb. *šiqṣâ* f. *sheqeṣ* detested thing + *-â fem. suffix*]

shill /ʃɪl/ *n. US* a person employed to decoy or entice others into buying, gambling, etc. [prob. f. earlier *shillaber*, of unkn. orig.]

shillelagh /ʃɪˈleɪlə, -lɪ/ *n.* a thick stick of blackthorn or oak used in Ireland esp. as a weapon. [*Shillelagh* in Co. Wicklow, Ireland]

shilling /ˈʃɪlɪŋ/ *n.* **1** *hist.* a former British coin and monetary unit worth one-twentieth of a pound or twelve pence. **2** a monetary unit in Kenya, Tanzania, and Uganda. □ **shilling-mark** *hist.* = SOLIDUS. **take the King's** (or **Queen's**) **shilling** *hist.* enlist as a soldier (formerly a soldier was paid a shilling on enlisting). [OE *scilling*, f. Gmc]

shilly-shally /ˈʃɪlɪˌʃælɪ/ *v., adj.,* & *n.* —*v.intr.* (**-ies, -ied**) hesitate to act or choose; be undecided; vacillate. —*adj.* vacillating. —*n.* indecision; vacillation. □□ **shilly-shallyer** *n.* (also **-shallier**). [orig. *shill I, shall I*, redupl. of *shall I?*]

shily var. of SHYLY (see SHY¹).

shim /ʃɪm/ *n.* & *v.* —*n.* a thin strip of material used in machinery etc. to make parts fit. —*v.tr.* (**shimmed, shimming**) fit or fill up with a shim. [18th c.: orig. unkn.]

shimmer /ˈʃɪmə(r)/ *v.* & *n.* —*v.intr.* shine with a tremulous or faint diffused light. —*n.* such a light. □□ **shimmeringly** *adv.* **shimmery** *adj.* [OE *scymrian* f. Gmc: cf. SHINE]

shimmy /ˈʃɪmɪ/ *n.* & *v.* —*n.* (*pl.* **-ies**) **1** *hist.* a kind of ragtime dance in which the whole body is shaken. **2** *archaic colloq.* = CHEMISE. **3** *US* an abnormal vibration of esp. the front wheels of a motor vehicle. —*v.intr.* (**-ies, -ied**) **1 a** *hist.* dance a shimmy.

b move in a similar manner. **2** shake or vibrate abnormally. [20th c.: orig. uncert.]

shin /ʃɪn/ *n.* & *v.* —*n.* **1** the front of the leg below the knee. **2 a** cut of beef from the lower foreleg. —*v.tr.* & (usu. foll. by *up, down*) *intr.* (**shinned, shinning**) climb quickly by clinging with the arms and legs. □ **shin-bone** = TIBIA. **shin-pad** (or **-guard**) a protective pad for the shins, worn when playing football etc. [OE *sinu*]

shindig /ˈʃɪndɪg/ *n. colloq.* **1** a festive, esp. noisy, party. **2** = SHINDY 1. [prob. f. SHINDY]

shindy /ˈʃɪndɪ/ *n.* (*pl.* **-ies**) *colloq.* **1** a brawl, disturbance, or noise (*kicked up a shindy*). **2** = SHINDIG 1. [perh. alt. of SHINTY]

shine /ʃaɪn/ *v.* & *n.* —*v.* (*past* and *past part.* **shone** /ʃɒn/ or **shined**) **1** *intr.* emit or reflect light; be bright; glow (*the lamp was shining; his face shone with gratitude*). **2** *intr.* (of the sun, a star, etc.) not be obscured by clouds etc.; be visible. **3** *tr.* cause (a lamp etc.) to shine. **4** *tr.* (*past* and *past part.* **shined**) make bright; polish (*shined his shoes*). **5** *intr.* be brilliant in some respect; excel (*does not shine in conversation; is a shining example*). —*n.* **1** light; brightness, esp. reflected. **2** a high polish; lustre. **3** *US* the act or an instance of shining esp. shoes. □ **shine up to** *US* seek to ingratiate oneself with. **take the shine out of 1** spoil the brilliance or newness of. **2** throw into the shade by surpassing. **take a shine to** *colloq.* take a fancy to; like. □□ **shiningly** *adv.* [OE *scīnan* f. Gmc]

shiner /ˈʃaɪnə(r)/ *n.* **1** a thing that shines. **2** *colloq.* a black eye. **3** *US* any of various small silvery freshwater fish, esp. of the genus *Notropis*. **4** (usu. in *pl.*) *sl.* **a** *archaic* money. **b** a jewel.

shingle¹ /ˈʃɪŋg(ə)l/ *n.* (in *sing.* or *pl.*) small rounded pebbles, esp. on a sea-shore. □□ **shingly** *adj.* [16th c.: orig. uncert.]

shingle² /ˈʃɪŋg(ə)l/ *n.* & *v.* —*n.* **1** a rectangular wooden tile used on roofs, spires, or esp. walls. **2** *archaic* **a** shingled hair. **b** the act of shingling hair. **3** *US* a small signboard, esp. of a doctor, lawyer, etc. —*v.tr.* **1** roof or clad with shingles. **2** *archaic* **a** cut (a woman's hair) very short. **b** cut the hair of (a person or head) in this way. [ME app. f. L *scindula*, earlier *scandula*]

shingles /ˈʃɪŋg(ə)lz/ *n.pl.* (usu. treated as *sing.*) an acute painful viral inflammation of the nerve ganglia, with a skin eruption often forming a girdle around the middle of the body. [ME f. med.L *cingulus* f. L *cingulum* girdle f. *cingere* gird]

shinny /ˈʃɪnɪ/ *v.intr.* (**-ies, -ied**) (usu. foll. by *up, down*) *US colloq.* shin (up or down a tree etc.).

Shinto /ˈʃɪntəʊ/ *n.* a Japanese religion revering ancestors and nature-spirits and embodying the beliefs and attitudes that are in accordance with this. The name was applied to the indigenous polytheistic religion of Japan of the 6th c. AD to distinguish it from Buddhism. Its oral traditions are recorded in the *Kojiki* (Records of Ancient Matters) and *Nihon Shoki* (Chronicles of Japan), both written *c.*712–20. Central to the religion is the belief in sacred power (*kami*) in both animate and inanimate things; in its mythology the sun-goddess was the ancestress of the imperial household. Shinto became closely associated with the State, a position that it held until after the Second World War, when it was disestablished and the Emperor Hirohito disavowed his claim to divine descent. □□ **Shintoism** *n.* **Shintoist** *n.* [Jap. f. Chin. *shen dao* way of the gods]

shinty /ˈʃɪntɪ/ *n.* (*pl.* **-ies**) *Brit.* **1** a game like hockey played with a ball and curved sticks, and taller goalposts, brought to Scotland by the invading Irish Gaels and sharing its history with hurling (see entry) until the mid-14th c. **2** a stick or ball used in shinty. [earlier *shinny*, app. f. the cry used in the game *shin ye, shin you, shin t' ye*, of unkn. orig.]

shiny /ˈʃaɪnɪ/ *adj.* (**shinier, shiniest**) **1** having a shine; glistening; polished; bright. **2** (of clothing, esp. the seat of trousers etc.) having the nap worn off. □□ **shinily** *adv.* **shininess** *n.* [SHINE]

ship /ʃɪp/ *n.* & *v.* —*n.* **1 a** any large seagoing vessel. (See below.) **b** a sailing-vessel with a bowsprit and three, four, or five square-rigged masts. **2** *US* an aircraft. **3** a spaceship. **4** *colloq.* a boat, esp. a racing-boat. —*v.* (**shipped, shipping**) **1** *tr.* put, take, or send away (goods, passengers, sailors, etc.) on board ship. **2** *tr.* **a** take in (water) over the side of a ship, boat, etc. **b** take (oars) from the rowlocks and lay them inside a boat. **c** fix (a rudder etc.) in its place on a ship etc. **d** step (a mast). **3** *intr.* **a** take ship; embark. **b** (of a sailor) take service on a ship (*shipped for Africa*). **4** *tr.* deliver (goods) to a forwarding agent for conveyance. □ **ship-breaker** a contractor who breaks up old ships. **ship-broker** an agent in shipping goods and insuring ships. **ship burial** *Archaeol.* burial in a wooden ship under a mound. The practice is found in Scandinavia and parts of the British Isles in the pagan Anglo-Saxon and Viking periods (6th–11th c. AD). **ship-canal** a canal large enough for ships to pass inland. **ship** (or **ship's**) **chandler** see CHANDLER. **ship-fever** typhus. **ship-money** *hist.* a tax raised to provide ships for the navy in the 17th c. **ship of the desert** the camel. **ship off 1** send or transport by ship. **2** *colloq.* send (a person) away. **ship of the line** *hist.* a large battleship with powerful enough armament to fight in the front line of battle. **ship-rigged** square-rigged. **ship's articles** the terms on which seamen take service on a ship. **ship's biscuit** *hist.* a hard coarse kind of biscuit kept and eaten on board ship. **ship's boat** a small boat carried on board a ship. **ship's company** a ship's crew. **ship's corporal** see CORPORAL[1] **2**. **ship a sea** be flooded by a wave. **ship's husband** an agent appointed by the owners to see to the provisioning of a ship in port. **ship's papers** documents establishing the ownership, nationality, nature of the cargo, etc., of a ship. **take ship** embark. **when a person's ship comes home** (or **in**) when a person's fortune is made. □□ **shipless** *adj.* **shippable** *adj.* [OE *scip, scipian* f. Gmc]

Ships is the generic name for sea-going vessels (as opposed to *boats*), originally personified as masculine but by the 16th c. almost universally expressed as feminine. Their origin is lost in the mists of antiquity, beginning when people discovered that wood and bundles of reeds would float and thought of using a river or the sea to convey themselves and their goods, probably on a roughly-constructed raft. The need to acquire additional buoyancy and stowage-space was met first by the use of a hollowed-out tree trunk, then by development of stem and stern pieces fixed to a keel, and with ribs to support the two sides. Among the most ancient vessels known are a dugout canoe found at Pese in Holland, dating from the 8th millennium BC, and the oared funeral ship, buried beside his tomb, of the Egyptian pharaoh Cheops (4th millennium BC). Early ships were propelled by sail, sometimes supplemented by oars. They were built of wood, but iron was introduced and then steel, which is now universal, though ships have also been made of concrete, glass-reinforced plastics, and light alloy. Steamships were evolved in the 19th c. using reciprocating steam engines and later steam turbines; these in turn have been replaced by turbo-charged diesel engines or gas turbines. Modern ships are worked with small crews through extensive use of automatic control systems. The price of fuel oil and problems of its supply have led to renewed interest in the use of sail.

-ship /ʃɪp/ *suffix* forming nouns denoting: **1** a quality or condition (*friendship; hardship*). **2** status, office, or honour (*authorship; lordship*). **3** a tenure of office (*chairmanship*). **4** a skill in a certain capacity (*workmanship*). **5** the collective individuals of a group (*membership*). [OE *-scipe* etc. f. Gmc]

shipboard /ʃɪpbɔːd/ *n.* (usu. *attrib.*) used or occurring on board a ship (*a shipboard romance*). □ **on shipboard** on board ship.

shipbuilder /ʃɪpˌbɪldə(r)/ *n.* a person, company, etc., that constructs ships. □□ **shipbuilding** *n.*

shiplap /ʃɪplæp/ *v. & n.* —*v.tr.* fit (boards) together for cladding etc. so that each overlaps the one below. —*n.* such cladding.

shipload /ʃɪpləʊd/ *n.* a quantity of goods forming a cargo.

shipmaster /ʃɪpˌmɑːstə(r)/ *n.* a ship's captain.

shipmate /ʃɪpmeɪt/ *n.* a fellow member of a ship's crew.

shipment /ʃɪpmənt/ *n.* **1** an amount of goods shipped; a consignment. **2** the act or an instance of shipping goods etc.

shipowner /ʃɪpˌəʊnə(r)/ *n.* a person owning a ship or ships or shares in ships.

shipper /ʃɪpə(r)/ *n.* a person or company that sends or receives goods by ship, or *US* by land or air. [OE *scipere* (as SHIP)]

shipping /ʃɪpɪŋ/ *n.* **1** the act or an instance of shipping goods etc. **2** ships, esp. the ships of a country, port, etc. □ **shipping-agent** a person acting for a ship or ships at a port etc. **shipping-articles** = *ship's articles.* **shipping-bill** *Brit.* a manifest of goods shipped. **shipping-master** *Brit.* an official presiding at the signing of ship's articles, paying off of seamen, etc. **shipping-office** the office of a shipping-agent or -master.

shipshape /ʃɪpʃeɪp/ *adv. & predic.adj.* in good order; trim and neat.

shipway /ʃɪpweɪ/ *n.* a slope on which a ship is built and down which it slides to be launched.

shipworm /ʃɪpwɜːm/ *n.* = TEREDO.

shipwreck /ʃɪprek/ *n. & v.* —*n.* **1 a** the destruction of a ship by a storm, foundering, etc. **b** a ship so destroyed. **2** (often foll. by *of*) the destruction of hopes, dreams, etc. —*v.* **1** *tr.* inflict shipwreck on (a ship, a person's hopes, etc.). **2** *intr.* suffer shipwreck.

shipwright /ʃɪpraɪt/ *n.* **1** a shipbuilder. **2** a ship's carpenter.

shipyard /ʃɪpjɑːd/ *n.* a place where ships are built, repaired, etc.

shiralee /ʃɪrəˌliː/ *n. Austral.* a tramp's swag or bundle. [20th c.: orig. unkn.]

Shiraz /ʃɪəˈræz/ a city in SW central Iran, capital of Fars province; pop. (1986) 425,800.

shire /ʃaɪə(r)/ *n.* **1** *Brit.* a county. (See below.) **2 (the Shires) a** a group of English counties with names ending or formerly ending in *-shire*, extending NE from Hampshire and Devon. **b** the midland counties of England. **c** the fox-hunting district of mainly Leicestershire and Northants. **3** *Austral.* a rural area with its own elected council. □ **shire-horse** a heavy powerful type of draught-horse with long white hair covering the lower part of the leg, bred chiefly in the midland counties of England. **shire-moot** the judicial assembly of the shire in Old English times. [OE *scír*, OHG *scíra* care, official charge: orig. unkn.]

In pre-Norman times a shire was an administrative district made up of a number of smaller districts ('hundreds' or 'wapentakes'). Under Norman rule this division was retained but the term *shire* was replaced by French *comté* (= country). Until the local government reorganization of 1974 'shire' and 'county' were generally synonymous, indicating the major rural area of local government, but since that date the term 'shire county' has been applied to the non-metropolitan counties (see METROPOLITAN COUNTY).

-shire /ʃə(r), ʃɪə(r)/ *suffix* forming the names of counties (*Derbyshire; Hampshire*).

shirk /ʃɜːk/ *v. & n.* —*v.tr.* (also *absol.*) shrink from; avoid; get out of (duty, work, responsibility, fighting, etc.). —*n.* a person who shirks. □□ **shirker** *n.* [obs. *shirk* (n.) sponger, perh. f. G *Schurke* scoundrel]

shirr /ʃɜː(r)/ *n. & v.* —*n.* **1** two or more rows of esp. elastic gathered threads in a garment etc. forming smocking. **2** elastic webbing. —*v.tr.* **1** gather (material) with parallel threads. **2** *US* bake (eggs) without shells. □□ **shirring** *n.* [19th c.: orig. unkn.]

shirt /ʃɜːt/ *n.* **1** a man's upper-body garment of cotton etc., having a collar, sleeves, and esp. buttons down the front, and often worn under a jacket or sweater. **2** a similar garment worn by a woman; a blouse. **3** = NIGHTSHIRT. □ **keep one's shirt on** *colloq.* keep one's temper. **put one's shirt on** *colloq.* bet all one has on; be sure of. **shirt blouse** = sense 2 of *n.* **shirt-dress** = SHIRTWAISTER. **shirt-front** the breast of a shirt, esp. of a stiffened evening shirt. **the shirt off one's back** *colloq.* one's last remaining possessions. **shirt-tail** the lower curved part of a shirt below the waist. □□ **shirted** *adj.* **shirting** *n.* **shirtless** *adj.* [OE *scyrte*, corresp. to ON *skyrta* (cf. SKIRT) f. Gmc: cf. SHORT]

shirtsleeve /ʃɜːtsliːv/ *n.* (usu. in *pl.*) the sleeve of a shirt. □ **in shirtsleeves** wearing a shirt with no jacket etc. over it.

shirtwaist /ʃɜːtweɪst/ *n.* esp. *US* a woman's blouse resembling a shirt.

shirtwaister /ʃɜːtˌweɪstə(r)/ *n. US* a woman's dress with a bodice like a shirt. [SHIRT, WAIST]

shirty /ʃɜːtɪ/ *adj.* (**shirtier, shirtiest**) *colloq.* angry; annoyed. □□ **shirtily** *adv.* **shirtiness** *n.*

shish kebab /ˌʃɪʃ kɪˈbæb/ *n.* a dish of pieces of marinated meat and vegetables cooked and served on skewers. [Turk. şiş kebabı f. şiş skewer, KEBAB roast meat]

shit /ʃɪt/ *v.*, *n.*, & *int.* coarse sl. ¶ Usually considered a taboo word. —*v.* (**shitting**; *past* and *past part.* **shitted** or **shit**) *intr.* & *tr.* expel faeces from the body or cause (faeces etc.) to be expelled. —*n.* **1** faeces. **2** an act of defecating. **3** a contemptible or worthless person or thing. **4** nonsense. **5** an intoxicating drug, esp. cannabis. —*int.* an exclamation of disgust, anger, etc. [OE *scītan* (unrecorded) f. Gmc]

shitty /ˈʃɪtɪ/ *adj.* (**shittier**, **shittiest**) coarse sl. **1** disgusting, contemptible. **2** covered with excrement.

Shiva var. of SIVA.

shivaree esp. *US* var. of CHARIVARI.

shiver¹ /ˈʃɪvə(r)/ *v.* & *n.* —*v.intr.* **1** tremble with cold, fear, etc. **2** suffer a quick trembling movement of the body; shudder. —*n.* **1** a momentary shivering movement. **2** (in *pl.*) an attack of shivering, esp. from fear or horror (*got the shivers in the dark*). □□ **shiverer** *n.* **shiveringly** *adv.* **shivery** *adj.* [ME *chivere*, perh. f. *chavele* chatter (as JOWL¹)]

shiver² /ˈʃɪvə(r)/ *n.* & *v.* —*n.* (esp. in *pl.*) each of the small pieces into which esp. glass is shattered when broken; a splinter. —*v.tr.* & *intr.* break into shivers. □ **shiver my timbers** a reputed piratical curse. [ME *scifre*, rel. to OHG *scivaro* splinter f. Gmc]

shivoo /ʃɪˈvuː/ *n.* Austral. colloq. a party or celebration.

shoal¹ /ʃəʊl/ *n.* & *v.* —*n.* **1** a great number of fish swimming together (cf. SCHOOL²). **2** a multitude; a crowd (*shoals of letters*). —*v.intr.* (of fish) form shoals. [prob. re-adoption of MDu. *schōle* SCHOOL²]

shoal² /ʃəʊl/ *n.*, *v.*, & *adj.* —*n.* **1 a** an area of shallow water. **b** a submerged sandbank visible at low water. **2** (esp. in *pl.*) hidden danger or difficulty. —*v.* **1** *intr.* (of water) get shallower. **2** *tr.* (of a ship etc.) move into a shallower part of (water). —*adj.* archaic (of water) shallow. □□ **shoaly** *adj.* [OE *sceald* f. Gmc, rel. to SHALLOW]

shoat /ʃəʊt/ *n.* US a young pig, esp. newly weaned. [ME: cf. W.Flem. *schote*]

shock¹ /ʃɒk/ *n.* & *v.* —*n.* **1** a violent collision, impact, tremor, etc. **2** a sudden and disturbing effect on the emotions, physical reactions, etc. (*the news was a great shock*). **3** an acute state of prostration following a wound, pain, etc., esp. when much blood is lost (*died of shock*). **4** = *electric shock*. **5** a disturbance in stability causing fluctuations in an organization, monetary system, etc. —*v.* **1** *tr.* **a** affect with shock; horrify; outrage; disgust; sadden. **b** (*absol.*) cause shock. **2** *tr.* (esp. in *passive*) affect with an electric or pathological shock. **3** *intr.* experience shock (*I don't shock easily*). **4** *intr.* archaic collide violently. □ **shock absorber** a device on a vehicle etc. for absorbing shocks, vibrations, etc. **shock-brigade** (or **-workers**) a body of esp. voluntary workers in the USSR engaged in an especially arduous task. **shock stall** excessive strain produced by air resistance on an aircraft approaching the speed of sound. **shock tactics 1** sudden and violent action. **2** *Mil.* a massed cavalry charge. **shock therapy** (or **treatment**) *Psychol.* a method of treating depressive patients by electric shock or drugs inducing coma and convulsions. **shock troops** troops specially trained for assault. **shock wave** a sharp change of pressure in a narrow region travelling through air etc. caused by explosion or by a body moving faster than sound. □□ **shockable** *adj.* **shockability** /-ˈbɪlɪtɪ/ *n.* [F *choc*, *choquer*, of unkn. orig.]

shock² /ʃɒk/ *n.* & *v.* —*n.* a group of usu. twelve corn-sheaves stood up with their heads together in a field. —*v.tr.* arrange (corn) in shocks. [ME, perh. repr. OE *sc(e)oc* (unrecorded)]

shock³ /ʃɒk/ *n.* an unkempt or shaggy mass of hair. [cf. obs. *shock(-dog)*, earlier *shough*, shaggy-haired poodle]

shocker /ˈʃɒkə(r)/ *n.* colloq. **1** a shocking, horrifying, unacceptable, etc. person or thing. **2** hist. a sordid or sensational novel etc. **3** a shock absorber.

shocking /ˈʃɒkɪŋ/ *adj.* & *adv.* —*adj.* **1** causing indignation or disgust. **2** colloq. very bad (*shocking weather*). —*adv.* colloq. shockingly (*shocking bad manners*). □ **shocking pink** a vibrant shade of pink. □□ **shockingly** *adv.* **shockingness** *n.*

shockproof /ˈʃɒkpruːf/ *adj.* resistant to the effects of (esp. physical) shock.

shod *past* and *past part.* of SHOE.

shoddy /ˈʃɒdɪ/ *adj.* & *n.* —*adj.* (**shoddier**, **shoddiest**) **1** trashy; shabby; poorly made. **2** counterfeit. —*n.* (*pl.* **-ies**) **1 a** an inferior cloth made partly from the shredded fibre of old woollen cloth. **b** such fibre. **2** any thing of shoddy quality. □□ **shoddily** *adv.* **shoddiness** *n.* [19th c.: orig. dial.]

shoe /ʃuː/ *n.* & *v.* —*n.* **1** either of a pair of protective foot-coverings of leather, plastic, etc., having a sturdy sole and, in Britain, not reaching above the ankle. **2** a metal rim nailed to the hoof of a horse etc.; a horseshoe. **3** anything resembling a shoe in shape or use, esp.: **a** a drag for a wheel. **b** = *brake shoe* (see BRAKE¹). **c** a socket. **d** a ferrule, esp. on a sledge-runner. **e** a mast-step. **f** a box from which cards are dealt in casinos at baccarat etc. —*v.tr.* (**shoes**, **shoeing**; *past* and *past part.* **shod** /ʃɒd/) **1** fit (esp. a horse etc.) with a shoe or shoes. **2** protect (the end of a pole etc.) with a metal shoe. **3** (as **shod** *adj.*) (in *comb.*) having shoes etc. of a specified kind (*dry-shod*; *roughshod*). □ **be in a person's shoes** be in his or her situation, difficulty, etc. **dead men's shoes** property or a position etc. coveted by a prospective successor. **if the shoe fits** US = *if the cap fits* (see CAP). **shoe-bill** an African stork-like bird, *Balaeniceps rex*, with a large flattened bill for catching aquatic prey. **shoe-buckle** a buckle worn as ornament or as a fastening on a shoe. **shoe-leather** leather for shoes, esp. when worn through by walking. **shoe-tree** a shaped block for keeping a shoe in shape when not worn. **where the shoe pinches** where one's difficulty or trouble is. □□ **shoeless** *adj.* [OE *scōh*, *scōg(e)an* f. Gmc]

shoeblack /ˈʃuːblæk/ *n.* a person who cleans the shoes of passers-by for payment.

shoebox /ˈʃuːbɒks/ *n.* **1** a box for packing shoes. **2** a very small space or dwelling.

shoehorn /ˈʃuːhɔːn/ *n.* a curved piece of horn, metal, etc., for easing the heel into a shoe.

shoelace /ˈʃuːleɪs/ *n.* a cord for lacing up shoes.

shoemaker /ˈʃuːˌmeɪkə(r)/ *n.* a maker of boots and shoes. □□ **shoemaking** *n.*

shoeshine /ˈʃuːʃaɪn/ *n.* esp. *US* a polish given to shoes.

shoestring /ˈʃuːstrɪŋ/ *n.* **1** a shoelace. **2** colloq. a small esp. inadequate amount of money (*living on a shoestring*). **3** (*attrib.*) barely adequate; precarious (*a shoestring majority*).

shofar /ˈʃəʊfə(r)/ *n.* (*pl.* **shofroth** /ˈʃəʊfrəʊt/) a ram's-horn trumpet used by Jews in religious ceremonies and as an ancient battle-signal. [Heb. *šōp̄ar*, pl. *šōp̄ārôt*]

shogun /ˈʃəʊgʊn/ *n.* hist. any of a succession of Japanese hereditary Commanders-in-Chief and virtual rulers in feudal Japan. Because of the military power concentrated in his hands, and the consequent weakness of the nominal head of State (Mikado or Emperor), the shogun was generally the real ruler of the country until feudalism was abolished in 1867. □□ **shogunate** /-nət/ *n.* [Jap., = general, f. Chin. *jiang jun*]

Sholapur /ˌʃəʊləˈpʊə(r)/ a city of western India, in the State of Maharashtra; pop. (1981) 514,000.

Shona /ˈʃəʊnə/ *n.* & *adj.* —*n.* (*pl.* **Shona** or **Shonas**) **1** a member of a group of Bantu peoples living in parts of Zimbabwe and Mozambique. **2** any of the languages of these peoples. —*adj.* of or relating to the Shona or their languages. [native name]

shone *past* and *past part.* of SHINE.

shonky /ˈʃɒŋkɪ/ *adj.* (**shonkier**, **shonkiest**) Austral. sl. unreliable, dishonest. [perh. E dial. *shonk* smart]

shoo /ʃuː/ *int.* & *v.* —*int.* an exclamation used to frighten away birds, children, etc. —*v.* (**shoos**, **shooed**) **1** *intr.* utter the word 'shoo!'. **2** *tr.* (usu. foll. by *away*) drive (birds etc.) away by shooing. □ **shoo-in** US something easy or certain to succeed. [imit.]

shook¹ /ʃʊk/ *past* of SHAKE. —*predic.adj.* colloq. **1** (foll. by *up*) emotionally or physically disturbed; upset. **2** (foll. by *on*) Austral.

& *NZ* keen on; enthusiastic about (*not too shook on the English climate*).

shook² /ʃʊk/ *n. US* a set of staves and headings for a cask, ready for fitting together. [18th c.: orig. unkn.]

shoot /ʃuːt/ *v., n.,* & *int.* —*v.* (*past* and *past part.* **shot** /ʃɒt/) **1** *tr.* **a** cause (a gun, bow, etc.) to fire. **b** discharge (a bullet, arrow, etc.) from a gun, bow, etc. **c** kill or wound (a person, animal, etc.) with a bullet, arrow, etc. from a gun, bow, etc. **2** *intr.* discharge a gun etc. esp. in a specified way (*shoots well*). **3** *tr.* send out, discharge, propel, etc., esp. violently or swiftly (*shot out the contents; shot a glance at his neighbour*). **4** *intr.* (often foll. by *out, along, forth,* etc.) come or go swiftly or vigorously. **5** *intr.* **a** (of a plant etc.) put forth buds etc. **b** (of a bud etc.) appear. **6** *intr.* **a** hunt game etc. with a gun. **b** (usu. foll. by *over*) shoot game over an estate etc. **7** *tr.* shoot game in or on (coverts, an estate, etc.). **8** *tr.* film or photograph (a scene, film, etc.). **9** *tr.* (also *absol.*) esp. *Football* **a** score (a goal). **b** take a shot at (the goal). **10** *tr.* (of a boat) sweep swiftly down or under (a bridge, rapids, falls, etc.). **11** *tr.* move (a door-bolt) to fasten or unfasten a door etc. **12** *tr.* let (rubbish, a load, etc.) fall or slide from a container, lorry, etc. **13** *intr.* **a** (usu. foll. by *through, up,* etc.) (of a pain) pass with a stabbing sensation. **b** (of part of the body) be intermittently painful. **14** *intr.* (often foll. by *out*) project abruptly (*the mountain shoots out against the sky*). **15** *tr.* (often foll. by *up*) *sl.* inject esp. oneself with (a drug). **16** *tr. US colloq.* **a** play a game of (craps, pool, etc.). **b** throw (a die or dice). **17** *tr. Golf colloq.* make (a specified score) for a round or hole. **18** *tr. colloq.* pass (traffic-lights at red). **19** *tr.* plane (the edge of a board) accurately. **20** *intr. Cricket* (of a ball) dart along the ground after pitching. —*n.* **1** the act or an instance of shooting. **2 a** a young branch or sucker. **b** the new growth of a plant. **3** *Brit.* **a** a hunting party, expedition, etc. **b** land shot over for game. **4** = CHUTE¹. **5** a rapid in a stream. —*int. colloq.* **1** a demand for a reply, information, etc. **2** *US euphem.* an exclamation of disgust, anger, etc. (see SHIT). □ **shoot ahead** come quickly to the front of competitors etc. **shoot one's bolt** see BOLT¹. **shoot down 1** kill (a person) by shooting. **2** cause (an aircraft, its pilot, etc.) to crash by shooting. **3** argue effectively against (a person, argument, etc.). **shoot it out** *sl.* engage in a decisive gun-battle. **shoot a line** *sl.* talk pretentiously. **shoot one's mouth off** *sl.* talk too much or indiscreetly. **shoot-out** *colloq.* a decisive gun battle. **shoot through** *Austral.* & *NZ sl.* depart; escape, abscond. **shoot up 1** grow rapidly, esp. (of a person) grow taller. **2** rise suddenly. **3** terrorize (a district) by indiscriminate shooting. **4** *sl.* = sense 15 of *v.* **the whole shoot** = *the whole shooting match* (see SHOOTING). □□ **shootable** *adj.* [OE scēotan f. Gmc: cf. SHEET¹, SHOT¹, SHUT]

shooter /ʃuːtə(r)/ *n.* **1** a person or thing that shoots. **2 a** (in *comb.*) a gun or other device for shooting (*peashooter; six-shooter*). **b** *sl.* a pistol etc. **3** a player who shoots or is able to shoot a goal in football, netball, etc. **4** *Cricket* a ball that shoots. **5** a person who throws a die or dice.

shooting /ʃuːtɪŋ/ *n.* & *adj.* —*n.* **1** the act or an instance of shooting. **2 a** the right of shooting over an area of land. **b** an estate etc. rented to shoot over. —*adj.* moving, growing, etc. quickly (*a shooting pain in the arm*). □ **shooting-box** *Brit.* a lodge used to house persons taking part in the shooting-season. **shooting-brake** (or **-break**) *Brit.* an estate car. **shooting-coat** (or **-jacket**) a coat designed to be worn when shooting game. **shooting-gallery** a place used for shooting at targets with rifles etc. **shooting-iron** esp. *US colloq.* a firearm. **shooting-range** a ground with butts for rifle practice. **shooting star** a small meteor moving rapidly and burning up on entering the earth's atmosphere. **shooting-stick** a walking-stick with a foldable seat. **shooting war** a war in which there is shooting (opp. *cold war, war of nerves* etc.). **the whole shooting match** *colloq.* everything.

shop /ʃɒp/ *n.* & *v.* —*n.* **1** a building, room, etc., for the retail sale of goods or services (*chemist's shop; betting-shop*). **2** a place in which manufacture or repairing is done; a workshop (*engineering-shop*). **3** a profession, trade, business, etc., esp. as a subject of conversation (*talk shop*). **4** *colloq.* an institution, establishment, place of business, etc. —*v.* (**shopped, shopping**) **1** *intr.* **a** go to a shop or shops to buy goods. **b** *US* = *window-shop*.

2 *tr.* esp. *Brit. sl.* inform against (a criminal etc.). □ **all over the shop** *colloq.* **1** in disorder (*scattered all over the shop*). **2** in every place (*looked for it all over the shop*). **3** wildly (*hitting out all over the shop*). **set up shop** establish oneself in business etc. **shop around** look for the best bargain. **shop assistant** *Brit.* a person who serves customers in a shop. **shop-boy** (or **-girl**) an assistant in a shop. **shop-floor** workers in a factory etc. as distinct from management. **shop-soiled 1** (of an article) soiled or faded by display in a shop. **2** (of a person, idea, etc.) grubby; tarnished; no longer fresh or new. **shop steward** a person elected by workers in a factory etc. to represent them in dealings with management. **shop-window 1** a display window in a shop. **2** an opportunity for displaying skills, talents, etc. **shop-worn** = *shop-soiled.* □□ **shopless** *adj.* **shoppy** *adj.* [ME f. AF & OF *eschoppe* booth f. MLG *schoppe*, OHG *scopf* porch]

shopkeeper /ʃɒpˌkiːpə(r)/ *n.* the owner and manager of a shop. □□ **shopkeeping** *n.*

shoplifter /ʃɒpˌlɪftə(r)/ *n.* a person who steals goods while appearing to shop. □□ **shoplifting** *n.*

shopman /ʃɒpmən/ *n.* (*pl.* **-men**) **1** *Brit.* a shopkeeper or shop-keeper's assistant. **2** a workman in a repair shop.

shopper /ʃɒpə(r)/ *n.* **1** a person who makes purchases in a shop. **2** a shopping bag or trolley. **3** *sl.* an informer.

shopping /ʃɒpɪŋ/ *n.* **1** (often *attrib.*) the purchase of goods etc. (*shopping expedition*). **2** goods purchased (*put the shopping on the table*). □ **shopping centre** an area or complex of shops, with associated facilities.

shopwalker /ʃɒpˌwɔːkə(r)/ *n. Brit.* an attendant in a large shop who directs customers, supervises assistants, etc.

shoran /ʃɔːræn/ *n.* a system of aircraft navigation using the return of two radar signals by two ground stations. [*short range navigation*]

shore¹ /ʃɔː(r)/ *n.* **1** the land that adjoins the sea or a large body of water. **2** (usu. in *pl.*) a country; a sea-coast (*often visits these shores; on a distant shore*). **3** *Law* land between ordinary high and low water marks. □ **in shore** on the water near or nearer to the shore (cf. INSHORE). **on shore** ashore. **shore-based** operating from a base on shore. **shore leave** *Naut.* **1** permission to go ashore. **2** a period of time ashore. □□ **shoreless** *adj.* **shoreward** *adj.* & *adv.* **shorewards** *adv.* [ME f. MDu., MLG *schōre*, perh. f. the root of SHEAR]

shore² /ʃɔː(r)/ *v.* & *n.* —*v.tr.* (often foll. by *up*) support with or as if with a shore or shores; hold up. —*n.* a prop or beam set obliquely against a ship, wall, tree, etc., as a support. □□ **shoring** *n.* [ME f. MDu., MLG *schōre* prop, of unkn. orig.]

shore³ see SHEAR.

shoreline /ʃɔːlaɪn/ *n.* the line along which a stretch of water, esp. a sea or lake, meets the shore.

shoreweed /ʃɔːwiːd/ *n.* a stoloniferous plant, *Littorella uniflora,* growing in shallow water.

shorn *past part.* of SHEAR.

short /ʃɔːt/ *adj., adv., n.,* & *v.* —*adj.* **1 a** measuring little; not long from end to end (*a short distance*). **b** not long in duration; brief (*a short time ago; had a short life*). **c** seeming less than the stated amount (*a few short years of happiness*). **2** of small height; not tall (*a short square tower; was shorter than average*). **3 a** (usu. foll. by *of, on*) having a partial or total lack; deficient; scanty (*short of spoons; is rather short on sense*). **b** not far-reaching; acting or being near at hand (*within short range*). **4 a** concise; brief (*kept his speech short*). **b** curt; uncivil (*was short with her*). **5** (of the memory) unable to remember distant events. **6** *Phonet.* & *Prosody* (of a vowel or syllable): **a** having the lesser of the two recognized durations. **b** unstressed. **c** (of an English vowel) having a sound other than that called long (cf. LONG¹ *adj.* 8). **7 a** (of pastry) crumbling; not holding together. **b** (of clay) having poor plasticity. **8** esp. *Stock Exch.* **a** (of stocks, a stockbroker, crops, etc.) sold or selling when the amount is not in hand, with reliance on getting the deficit in time for delivery. **b** (of a bill of exchange) maturing at an early date. **9** *Cricket* **a** (of a ball) pitching relatively near the bowler. **b** (of a fielder or his position) relatively near the batsman. **10** (of a drink of spirits) undiluted. —*adv.* **1** before the natural or expected time or place; abruptly (*pulled up short;*

cut short the celebrations). **2** rudely; uncivilly (*spoke to him short*). —*n.* **1** *colloq.* a short drink, esp. spirits. **2** a short circuit. **3** a short film. **4** *Stock Exch.* **a** a person who sells short. **b** (in *pl.*) short-dated stocks. **5** *Phonet.* **a** a short syllable or vowel. **b** a mark indicating that a vowel is short. **6** (in *pl.*) a mixture of bran and coarse flour. —*v.tr. & intr.* short-circuit. □ **be caught** (or **taken**) **short 1** be put at a disadvantage. **2** *colloq.* urgently need to urinate or defecate. **bring up** (or **pull up**) **short** check or pause abruptly. **come short** be inadequate or disappointing. **come short of** fail to reach or amount to. **for short** as a short name (*Tom for short*). **get** (or **have**) **by the short hairs** *colloq.* be in complete control of (a person). **go short** (often foll. by *of*) not have enough. **in short** to use few words; briefly. **in short order** *US* immediately. **in the short run** over a short period of time. **in short supply** scarce. **in the short term** = *in the short run*. **make short work of** accomplish, dispose of, destroy, consume, etc. quickly. **short and sweet** esp. *iron.* brief and pleasant. **short-arm** (of a blow etc.) delivered with the arm not fully extended. **short back and sides** a haircut in which the hair is cut short at the back and the sides. **short change** insufficient money given as change. **short-change** *v.tr.* rob or cheat by giving short change. **short circuit** an electric circuit through small resistance, esp. instead of the resistance of a normal circuit. **short-circuit 1** cause a short circuit or a short circuit in. **2** shorten or avoid (a journey, work, etc.) by taking a more direct route etc. **short commons** insufficient food. **short cut 1** a route shortening the distance travelled. **2** a quick way of accomplishing something. **short date** an early date for the maturing of a bill etc. **short-dated** due for early payment or redemption. **short-day** (of a plant) needing the period of light each day to fall below some limit to cause flowering. **short division** *Math.* division in which the quotient is written directly without being worked out in writing. **short drink** a strong alcoholic drink served in small measures. **short-eared owl** an owl, *Asio flammeus*, frequenting open country and hunting at dawn or dusk. **short for** an abbreviation for ('*Bob' is short for 'Robert'*). **short fuse** a quick temper. **short game** *Golf* approaching and putting. **short-handed** undermanned or understaffed. **short haul 1** the transport of goods over a short distance. **2** a short-term effort. **short head** *Racing* a distance less than the length of a horse's head. **short-head** *v.tr.* beat by a short head. **short hundredweight** see HUNDREDWEIGHT. **short list** *Brit.* a list of selected candidates from which a final choice is made. **short-list** *v.tr. Brit.* put on a short list. **short-lived** ephemeral; not long-lasting. **short mark** = BREVE 2. **short measure** less than the professed amount. **short metre** *Prosody* a hymn stanza of four lines with 6, 6, 8, and 6 syllables. **short notice** an insufficient length of warning time. **short odds** nearly equal stakes or chances in betting. **short of 1** see sense 3a of *adj.* **2** less than (*nothing short of a miracle*). **3** distant from (*two miles short of home*). **4** without going so far as; except (*did everything short of destroying it*). **short of breath** panting, short-winded. **short on** *colloq.* see sense 3a of *adj.* **short order** *US* an order in a restaurant for quickly cooked food. **Short Parliament** the first of two Parliaments summoned by Charles I in 1640. Owing to its insistence on seeking a general redress of grievances against the King before granting him the money he required, Charles dismissed it after only three weeks. **short-pitched** *Cricket* (of a ball) pitching relatively near the bowler. **short-range 1** having a short range. **2** relating to a fairly immediate future time (*short-range possibilities*). **short rib** = *floating rib.* **short score** *Mus.* a score not giving all parts. **short shrift** curt or dismissive treatment. **short sight** the inability to focus except on comparatively near objects. **short-sleeved** with sleeves not reaching below the elbow. **short-staffed** having insufficient staff. **short story** a story with a fully developed theme but shorter than a novel. **short suit** a suit of less than four cards. **short temper** self-control soon or easily lost. **short-tempered** quick to lose one's temper; irascible. **short-term** occurring in or relating to a short period of time. **short time** the condition of working fewer than the regular hours per day or days per week. **short title** an abbreviated form of a title of a book etc. **short ton** see TON. **short view** a consideration of the present only, not the future. **short waist 1** a high or shallow waist of a dress.

2 a short upper body. **short wave** a radio wave of frequency greater than 3 MHz. **short weight** weight less than it is alleged to be. **short whist** whist with ten or five points to a game. **short wind** quickly exhausted breathing-power. **short-winded 1** having short wind. **2** incapable of sustained effort. □□ **shortish** *adj.* **shortness** *n.* [OE *sceort* f. Gmc: cf. SHIRT, SKIRT]

shortage /ˈʃɔːtɪdʒ/ *n.* (often foll. by *of*) a deficiency; an amount lacking (*a shortage of 100 tons*).

shortbread /ˈʃɔːtbred/ *n.* a crisp rich crumbly type of biscuit made with butter, flour, and sugar.

shortcake /ˈʃɔːtkeɪk/ *n.* **1** = SHORTBREAD. **2** a cake made of short pastry and filled with fruit and cream.

shortcoming /ˈʃɔːtˌkʌmɪŋ/ *n.* failure to come up to a standard; a defect.

shortcrust /ˈʃɔːtkrʌst/ *n.* (in full **shortcrust pastry**) a type of crumbly pastry made with flour and fat.

shorten /ˈʃɔːt(ə)n/ *v.* **1** *intr. & tr.* become or make shorter or short; curtail. **2** *tr. Naut.* reduce the amount of (sail spread). **3** *intr. & tr.* (with reference to gambling odds, prices, etc.) become or make shorter; decrease.

shortening /ˈʃɔːtənɪŋ/ *n.* fat used for making pastry, esp. for making short pastry.

shortfall /ˈʃɔːtfɔːl/ *n.* a deficit below what was expected.

shorthand /ˈʃɔːthænd/ *n.* **1** (often *attrib.*) a method of rapid writing in abbreviations and symbols esp. for taking dictation. (See below.) **2** an abbreviated or symbolic mode of expression. □ **shorthand typist** *Brit.* a typist qualified to take and transcribe shorthand.

The use of shortened handwriting dates at least from ancient Roman times: Cicero's secretary devised a system for recording his speeches. Modern shorthand in England can be traced back to 1588 when Dr Timothy Bright published a system; it was difficult to learn, for nearly every word had its own special sign. Other systems were produced, based on the alphabet (Samuel Pepys kept his diaries in shorthand), but were gradually superseded by phonetic systems of which the best was that of Samuel Taylor (1786). Its brevity and simplicity attracted the attention of Sir Isaac Pitman (1813–97), who presently began anew on his own lines and issued his *Stenographic Sound-Hand* in 1837. His system is still widely used, though others are in common use; in the US the system devised in 1888 by J. R. Gregg (1867–1948) is the most popular. Shorthand writing has become less essential in many contexts with the technological development of recordings of various kinds.

shorthorn /ˈʃɔːthɔːn/ *n.* **1** an animal of a breed of cattle with short horns. **2** this breed.

shortie var. of SHORTY.

shortly /ˈʃɔːtlɪ/ *adv.* **1** (often foll. by *before, after*) before long; soon (*will arrive shortly; arrived shortly after him*). **2** in a few words; briefly. **3** curtly. [OE *scortlice* (as SHORT, -LY²)]

shorts /ʃɔːts/ *n.pl.* **1** trousers reaching only to the knees or higher. **2** *US* underpants.

short-sighted /ʃɔːtˈsaɪtɪd, ˈʃɔːt-/ *adj.* **1** having short sight. **2** lacking imagination or foresight. □□ **short-sightedly** *adv.* **short-sightedness** *n.*

shortstop /ˈʃɔːtstɒp/ *n.* a baseball fielder between second and third base.

shorty /ˈʃɔːtɪ/ *n.* (also **shortie**) (*pl.* -ies) *colloq.* **1** a person shorter than average. **2** a short garment, esp. a nightdress or raincoat.

Shostakovich /ˌʃɒstəˈkəʊvɪtʃ/, Dmitri (1906–75), Russian composer. Born in St Petersburg, he lived there through the October Revolution and the forming of the Soviet State. His life was marked by conflict between his desire to serve the people of his country and the volatile response of the authorities to his music. His first brush with the authorities concerned an opera, *The Lady Macbeth of the Mtsensk District*, which had been praised on its first performance in 1934 but was criticized in *Pravda* two years later in an article entitled 'Chaos instead of Music'. A previous opera, *The Nose* (1930), had found favour for its biting mockery of bureaucracy, but in *The Lady Macbeth* Shostakovich had portrayed the life of a Soviet woman in music of uncompromising modernity. In subsequent works he successfully attempted a less formidable style, but another attack, this time on the Ninth Symphony (1945, written to celebrate the end of the war), caused a further retreat which was to end only with Stalin's death in 1953. From then on Shostakovich produced many works in which he expressed his most personal feelings, often despairing, including the last six symphonies and, in his last year, the Viola Sonata.

shot[1] /ʃɒt/ *n.* **1** the act or an instance of firing a gun, cannon, etc. (*several shots were heard*). **2** an attempt to hit by shooting or throwing etc. (*took a shot at him*). **3 a** a single non-explosive missile for a cannon, gun, etc. **b** (*pl.* same or **shots**) a small lead pellet used in quantity in a single charge or cartridge in a shotgun. **c** (as *pl.*) these collectively. **4 a** a photograph. **b** a film sequence photographed continuously by one camera. **5 a** a stroke or a kick in a ball game. **b** *colloq.* an attempt to guess or do something (*let him have a shot at it*). **6** *colloq.* a person having a specified skill with a gun etc. (*is not a good shot*). **7** a heavy ball thrown by a shot-putter. **8** the launch of a space rocket (a *moonshot*). **9** the range, reach, or distance to or at which a thing will carry or act (*out of earshot*). **10** a remark aimed at a person. **11** *colloq.* **a** a drink of esp. spirits. **b** an injection of a drug, vaccine, etc. (*has had his shots*). □ **like a shot** *colloq.* without hesitation; willingly. **make a bad shot** guess wrong. **not a shot in one's** (or **the**) **locker 1** no money left. **2** not a chance left. **shot-blasting** the cleaning of metal etc. by the impact of a stream of shot. **shot-firer** a person who fires a blasting-charge in a mine etc. **shot in the arm** *colloq.* **1** stimulus or encouragement. **2** an alcoholic drink. **shot in the dark** a mere guess. **shot-put** an athletic contest in which a shot is thrown a great distance. **shot-putter** an athlete who puts the shot. **shot-tower** *hist.* a tower in which shot was made from molten lead poured through sieves at the top and falling into water at the bottom. □□ **shotproof** *adj.* [OE *sc(e)ot, gesc(e)ot* f. Gmc: cf. SHOOT]

shot[2] /ʃɒt/ *past* and *past part.* of SHOOT. —*adj.* **1** (of coloured material) woven so as to show different colours at different angles. **2** *colloq.* **a** exhausted; finished. **b** drunk. **3** (of a board-edge) accurately planed. □ **be** (or **get**) **shot of** *sl.* be (or get) rid of. **shot through** permeated or suffused. [past part. of SHOOT]

shot[3] /ʃɒt/ *n. colloq.* a reckoning, a bill, esp. at an inn etc. (*paid his shot*). [ME, = SHOT[1]: cf. OE *scēotan* shoot, pay, contribute, and SCOT]

shotgun /ˈʃɒtgʌn/ *n.* a smooth-bore gun for firing small shot at short range. □ **shotgun marriage** (or **wedding**) *colloq.* an enforced or hurried wedding, esp. because of the bride's pregnancy.

shotten herring /ˈʃɒt(ə)n/ *n.* **1** a herring that has spawned. **2** *archaic* a weakened or dispirited person. [ME, archaic past part. of SHOOT]

should /ʃʊd, ʃəd/ *v.aux.* (*3rd sing.* **should**) *past* of SHALL, used esp.: **1** in reported speech, esp. with the reported element in the 1st person (*I said I should be home by evening*). ¶ Cf. WILL[1], WOULD, now more common in this sense, esp. to avoid implications of sense 2. **2 a** to express a duty, obligation, or likelihood; = OUGHT[1] (*I should tell you; you should have been more careful; they should have arrived by now*). **b** (in the 1st person) to express a tentative suggestion (*I should like to say something*). **3 a** expressing the conditional mood in the 1st person (cf. WOULD) (*I should have been killed if I had gone*). **b** forming a conditional protasis or indefinite clause (*if you should see him; should they arrive, tell them where to go*). **4** expressing purpose = MAY, MIGHT[1] (*in order that we should not worry*).

shoulder /ˈʃəʊldə(r)/ *n. & v.* —*n.* **1 a** the part of the body at which the arm, foreleg, or wing is attached. **b** (in full **shoulder joint**) the end of the upper arm joining with the collar-bone and blade-bone. **c** either of the two projections below the neck from which the arms depend. **2** the upper foreleg and shoulder blade of a pig, lamb, etc. when butchered. **3** (often in *pl.*) **a** the upper part of the back and arms. **b** this part of the body regarded as capable of bearing a burden or blame, providing comfort, etc. (*needs a shoulder to cry on*). **4** a strip of land next to a metalled road (*pulled over on to the shoulder*). **5** a part of a garment covering the shoulder. **6** a part of anything resembling a shoulder in

form or function, as in a bottle, mountain, tool, etc. —*v.* **1 a** *tr.* push with the shoulder; jostle. **b** *intr.* make one's way by jostling (*shouldered through the crowd*). **2** *tr.* take (a burden etc.) on one's shoulders (*shouldered the family's problems*). □ **put** (or **set**) **one's shoulder to the wheel** make an effort. **shoulder arms** hold a rifle with the barrel against the shoulder and the butt in the hand. **shoulder-bag** a woman's handbag that can be hung from the shoulder. **shoulder-belt** a bandolier or other strap passing over one shoulder and under the opposite arm. **shoulder-blade** *Anat.* either of the large flat bones of the upper back; the scapula. **shoulder-high** up to or as high as the shoulders. **shoulder-holster** a gun holster worn in the armpit. **shoulder-knot** a knot of ribbon, metal, lace, etc. worn as part of a ceremonial dress. **shoulder-length** (of hair etc.) reaching to the shoulders. **shoulder loop** *US* the shoulder-strap of an army, air-force, or marines officer. **shoulder mark** *US* the shoulder-strap of a naval officer. **shoulder-note** *Printing* a marginal note at the top of a page. **shoulder-of-mutton sail** = *leg-of-mutton sail*. **shoulder-pad** a pad sewn into a garment to bulk out the shoulder. **shoulder-strap 1** a strip of fabric, leather, etc. suspending a bag or garment from the shoulder. **2** a strip of cloth from shoulder to collar on a military uniform bearing a symbol of rank etc. **3** a similar strip on a raincoat. **shoulder to shoulder 1** side by side. **2** with closed ranks or united effort. □□ **shouldered** *adj.* (also in *comb.*). [OE *sculdor* f. WG]

shouldn't /ˈʃʊd(ə)nt/ *contr.* should not.

shout /ʃaʊt/ *v. & n.* —*v.* **1** *intr.* make a loud cry or vocal sound; speak loudly (*shouted for attention*). **2** *tr.* say or express loudly; call out (*shouted that the coast was clear*). **3** *tr.* (also *absol.*) *Austral. & NZ colloq.* treat (another person) to drinks etc. —*n.* **1** a loud cry expressing joy etc. or calling attention. **2** *colloq.* one's turn to order a round of drinks etc. (*your shout I think*). □ **all over bar** (or **but**) **the shouting** *colloq.* the contest is virtually decided. **shout at** speak loudly to etc. **shout down** reduce to silence by shouting. **shout for** call for by shouting. **shout-up** *colloq.* a noisy argument. □□ **shouter** *n.* [ME, perh. rel. to SHOOT: cf. ON *skúta* SCOUT]

shove /ʃʌv/ *v. & n.* —*v.* **1** *tr.* (also *absol.*) push vigorously; move by hard or rough pushing (*shoved him out of the way*). **2** *intr.* (usu. foll. by *along, past, through*, etc.) make one's way by pushing (*shoved through the crowd*). **3** *tr. colloq.* put somewhere (*shoved it in the drawer*). —*n.* an act of shoving or of prompting a person into action. □ **shove-halfpenny** a form of shovelboard played with coins etc. on a table esp. in licensed premises. **shove off 1** start from the shore in a boat. **2** *sl.* depart; go away (*told him to shove off*). [OE *scūfan* f. Gmc]

shovel /ˈʃʌv(ə)l/ *n. & v.* —*n.* **1 a** a spadelike tool for shifting quantities of coal, earth, etc., esp. having the sides curved upwards. **b** the amount contained in a shovel; a shovelful. **2 a** machine or part of a machine having a similar form or function. —*v.tr.* (**shovelled**, **shovelling**; *US* **shoveled**, **shoveling**) **1** shift or clear (coal etc.) with or as if with a shovel. **2** *colloq.* move (esp. food) in large quantities or roughly (*shovelled peas into his mouth*). □ **shovel hat** a broad-brimmed hat esp. worn by some clergymen. □□ **shovelful** *n.* (*pl.* **-fuls**). [OE *scofl* f. Gmc (see SHOVE)]

shovelboard /ˈʃʌv(ə)lˌbɔːd/ *n.* a game played esp. on a ship's deck by pushing discs with the hand or with a long-handled shovel over a marked surface. [earlier *shoveboard* f. SHOVE + BOARD]

shovelhead /ˈʃʌv(ə)lˌhed/ *n.* a shark, *Sphyrna tiburo*, like the hammerhead but smaller. Also called BONNETHEAD.

shoveller /ˈʃʌvələ(r)/ *n.* (also **shoveler**) **1** a person or thing that shovels. **2** a duck, *Anas clypeata*, with a broad shovel-like beak. [SHOVEL: sense 2 earlier *shovelard* f. -ARD, perh. after *mallard*]

show /ʃəʊ/ *v. & n.* —*v.* (*past part.* **shown** /ʃəʊn/ or **showed**) **1** *intr. & tr.* be, or allow or cause to be, visible; manifest; appear (*the buds are beginning to show; white shows the dirt*). **2** *tr.* (often foll. by *to*) offer, exhibit, or produce (a thing) for scrutiny etc. (*show your tickets please; showed him my poems*). **3** *tr.* **a** indicate (one's feelings) by one's behaviour etc. (*showed mercy to him*). **b** indicate (one's feelings) to a person etc.) (*showed him particular favour*).

4 *intr.* (of feelings etc.) be manifest (*his dislike shows*). **5** *tr.* **a** demonstrate; point out; prove (*has shown it to be false*; *showed that he knew the answer*). **b** (usu. foll. by *how to* + infin.) cause (a person) to understand or be capable of doing (*showed them how to knit*). **6** *tr.* (*refl.*) exhibit oneself as being (*showed herself to be fair*). **7** *tr.* & *intr.* (with ref. to a film) be presented or cause to be presented. **8** *tr.* exhibit (a picture, animal, flower, etc.) in a show. **9** *tr.* (often foll. by *in*, *out*, *up*, etc.) conduct or lead (*showed them to their rooms*). **10** *intr.* = show up 3 (*waited but he didn't show*). **11** *intr.* US finish in the first three in a race. —*n.* **1** the act or an instance of showing; the state of being shown. **2 a** a spectacle, display, exhibition, etc. (*a fine show of blossom*). **b** a collection of things etc. shown for public entertainment or in competition (*dog show*; *flower show*). **3 a** a play etc., esp. a musical. **b** a light entertainment programme on television etc. **c** any public entertainment or performance. **4 a** an outward appearance, semblance, or display (*made a show of agreeing*; *a show of strength*). **b** empty appearance; mere display (*did it for show*; *that's all show*). **5** *colloq.* an undertaking, business, etc. (*sold the whole show*). **6** *colloq.* an opportunity of acting, defending oneself, etc. (*gave him a fair show*; *made a good show of it*). **7** *Med.* a discharge of blood etc. from the vagina at the onset of childbirth. □ **give the show** (or **whole show**) **away** demonstrate the inadequacies or reveal the truth. **good** (or **bad** or **poor**) **show!** *colloq.* **1** that was well (or badly) done. **2** that was lucky (or unlucky). **nothing to show for** no visible result of (effort etc.). **on show** being exhibited. **show business** *colloq.* the theatrical profession. **show-card** a card used for advertising. **show one's cards** = show one's hand. **show cause** *Law* allege with justification. **show a clean pair of heels** *colloq.* retreat speedily; run away. **show one's colours** make one's opinion clear. **show a person the door** dismiss or eject a person. **show one's face** make an appearance; let oneself be seen. **show fight** be persistent or belligerent. **show the flag** see FLAG¹. **show forth** *archaic* exhibit; expound. **show one's hand 1** disclose one's plans. **2** reveal one's cards. **show house** (or **flat** etc.) a furnished and decorated house (or flat etc.) on a new estate shown to prospective buyers. **show in** see sense 9 of *v.* **show a leg** *colloq.* get out of bed. **show off 1** display to advantage. **2** *colloq.* act pretentiously; display one's wealth, knowledge, etc. **show-off** *n. colloq.* a person who shows off. **show of force** proof that one is prepared to use force. **show of hands** raised hands indicating a vote for or against, usu. without being counted. **show oneself 1** be seen in public. **2** see sense 6 of *v.* **show out** see sense 9 of *v.* **show-piece 1** an item of work presented for exhibition or display. **2** an outstanding example or specimen. **show-place** a house etc. that tourists go to see. **show round** take (a person) to places of interest; act as guide for (a person) in a building etc. **show-stopper** *colloq.* a performance receiving prolonged applause. **show one's teeth** reveal one's strength; be aggressive. **show through 1** be visible although supposedly concealed. **2** (of real feelings etc.) be revealed inadvertently. **show trial** esp. *hist.* a judicial trial designed by the State to terrorize or impress the public. **show up 1** make or be conspicuous or clearly visible. **2** expose (a fraud, impostor, inferiority, etc.). **3** *colloq.* appear; be present; arrive. **4** *colloq.* embarrass or humiliate (*don't show me up by wearing jeans*). **show the way 1** indicate what has to be done etc. by attempting it first. **2** show others which way to go etc. **show the white feather** appear cowardly (see also *white feather*). **show willing** display a willingness to help etc. **show-window** a window for exhibiting goods etc. [ME f. OE *scēawian* f. WG: cf. SHEEN]

showbiz /ˈʃəʊbɪz/ *n. colloq.* = show business.

showboat /ˈʃəʊbəʊt/ *n.* US a river steamer on which theatrical performances are given.

showcase /ˈʃəʊkeɪs/ *n.* & *v.* —*n.* **1** a glass case used for exhibiting goods etc. **2** a place or medium for presenting (esp. attractively) to general attention. —*v.tr.* display in or as if in a showcase.

showdown /ˈʃəʊdaʊn/ *n.* **1** a final test or confrontation; a decisive situation. **2** the laying down face up of the players' cards in poker.

shower /ˈʃaʊə(r)/ *n.* & *v.* —*n.* **1** a brief fall of esp. rain, hail, sleet, or snow. **2 a** a brisk flurry of arrows, bullets, dust, stones,

sparks, etc. **b** a similar flurry of gifts, letters, honours, praise, etc. **3** (in full **shower-bath**) **a** a cubicle, bath, etc. in which one stands under a spray of water. **b** the apparatus etc. used for this. **c** the act of bathing in a shower. **4** a group of particles initiated by a cosmic-ray particle in the earth's atmosphere. **5** US a party for giving presents to a prospective bride, etc. **6** Brit. *sl.* a contemptible or unpleasant person or group of people. —*v.* **1** *tr.* discharge (water, missiles, etc.) in a shower. **2** *intr.* use a shower-bath. **3** *tr.* (usu. foll. by *on*, *upon*) lavishly bestow (gifts etc.). **4** *intr.* descend or come in a shower (*it showered on and off all day*). □□ **showery** *adj.* [OE *scūr* f. Gmc]

showerproof /ˈʃaʊəpruːf/ *adj.* & *v.* —*adj.* resistant to light rain. —*v.tr.* render showerproof.

showgirl /ˈʃəʊɡɜːl/ *n.* an actress who sings and dances in musicals, variety shows, etc.

showing /ˈʃəʊɪŋ/ *n.* **1** the act or an instance of showing. **2** a usu. specified quality of performance (*made a poor showing*). **3** the presentation of a case; evidence (*on present showing it must be true*). [OE *scēawung* (as SHOW)]

showjumping /ˈʃəʊˌdʒʌmpɪŋ/ *n.* the sport of riding horses over a course of fences and other obstacles, with penalty points for errors. □□ **showjump** *v.intr.* **showjumper** *n.*

showman /ˈʃəʊmən/ *n.* (*pl.* **-men**) **1** the proprietor or manager of a circus etc. **2** a person skilled in self-advertisement or publicity. □□ **showmanship** *n.*

shown *past part.* of SHOW.

showroom /ˈʃəʊruːm, -rʊm/ *n.* a room in a factory, office building, etc. used to display goods for sale.

showy /ˈʃəʊɪ/ *adj.* (**showier**, **showiest**) **1** brilliant; gaudy; esp. vulgarly so. **2** striking. □□ **showily** *adv.* **showiness** *n.*

s.h.p. *abbr.* shaft horsepower.

shrank *past* of SHRINK.

shrapnel /ˈʃræpn(ə)l/ *n.* **1** fragments of a bomb etc. thrown out by an explosion. **2** a shell containing bullets or pieces of metal timed to burst short of impact. [Gen. H. *Shrapnel*, Brit. soldier d. 1842, inventor of the shell]

shred /ʃred/ *n.* & *v.* —*n.* **1** a scrap, fragment, or strip of esp. cloth, paper, etc. **2** the least amount, remnant (*not a shred of evidence*). —*v.tr.* (**shredded**, **shredding**) tear or cut into shreds. □ **tear to shreds** completely refute (an argument etc.). [OE *scrēad* (unrecorded) piece cut off, *scrēadian* f. WG: see SHROUD]

shredder /ˈʃredə(r)/ *n.* **1** a machine used to reduce documents to shreds. **2** any device used for shredding.

shrew /ʃruː/ *n.* **1** any small usu. insect-eating mouselike mammal of the family Soricidae, with a long pointed snout. **2** a bad-tempered or scolding woman. □□ **shrewish** *adj.* (in sense 2). **shrewishly** *adv.* **shrewishness** *n.* [OE *scrēawa*, *scrēwa* shrew-mouse: cf. OHG *scrawaz* dwarf, MHG *schrawaz* etc. devil]

shrewd /ʃruːd/ *adj.* **1 a** showing astute powers of judgement; clever and judicious (*a shrewd observer*; *made a shrewd guess*). **b** (of a face etc.) shrewd-looking. **2** *archaic* **a** (of pain, cold, etc.) sharp, biting. **b** (of a blow, thrust, etc.) severe, hard. **c** mischievous; malicious. □□ **shrewdly** *adv.* **shrewdness** *n.* [ME, = malignant, f. SHREW in sense 'evil person or thing', or past part. of obs. *shrew* to curse, f. SHREW]

shriek /ʃriːk/ *v.* & *n.* —*v.* **1** *intr.* **a** utter a shrill screeching sound or words esp. in pain or terror. **b** (foll. by *of*) provide a clear or blatant indication of. **2** *tr.* **a** utter (sounds or words) by shrieking (*shrieked his name*). **b** indicate clearly or blatantly. —*n.* a high-pitched piercing cry or sound; a scream. □ **shriek out** say in shrill tones. **shriek with laughter** laugh uncontrollably. □□ **shrieker** *n.* [imit.: cf. dial. *screak*, ON *skrækja*, and SCREECH]

shrieval /ˈʃriːv(ə)l/ *adj.* of or relating to a sheriff. [*shrieve* obs. var. of SHERIFF]

shrievalty /ˈʃriːvəltɪ/ *n.* (*pl.* **-ies**) **1** a sheriff's office or jurisdiction. **2** the tenure of this. [as SHRIEVAL + -*alty* as in mayoralty etc.]

shrift /ʃrɪft/ *n. archaic* **1** confession to a priest. **2** confession and absolution. □ **short shrift 1** curt treatment. **2** *archaic* little time between condemnation and execution or punishment. [OE *scrift* (verbal noun) f. SHRIVE]

shrike /ʃraɪk/ n. any bird of the family Laniidae, with a strong hooked and toothed bill, that impales its prey of small birds and insects on thorns. Also called *butcher-bird*. [perh. rel. to OE *scric* thrush, MLG *schrīk* corncrake (imit.): cf. SHRIEK]

shrill /ʃrɪl/ adj. & v. —adj. **1** piercing and high-pitched in sound. **2** derog. (esp. of a protester) sharp, unrestrained, unreasoning. —v. **1** intr. (of a cry etc.) sound shrilly. **2** tr. (of a person etc.) utter or send out (a song, complaint, etc.) shrilly. □□ **shrilly** adv. **shrillness** n. [ME, rel. to LG *schrell* sharp in tone or taste f. Gmc]

shrimp /ʃrɪmp/ n. & v. —n. **1** (pl. same or **shrimps**) any of various small (esp. marine) edible crustaceans, with ten legs, grey-green when alive and pink when boiled. **2** colloq. a very small slight person. —v.intr. go catching shrimps. □ **shrimp plant** an evergreen shrub, *Justicia brandegeana*, bearing small white flowers in clusters of pinkish-brown bracts. □□ **shrimper** n. [ME, prob. rel. to MLG *schrempen* wrinkle, MHG *schrimpfen* contract, and SCRIMP]

shrine /ʃraɪn/ n. & v. —n. **1** esp. RC Ch. **a** a chapel, church, altar, etc., sacred to a saint, holy person, relic, etc. **b** the tomb of a saint etc. **c** a casket esp. containing sacred relics; a reliquary. **d** a niche containing a holy statue etc. **2** a place associated with or containing memorabilia of a particular person, event, etc. **3** a Shinto place of worship —v.tr. poet. enshrine. [OE *scrīn* f. Gmc f. L *scrinium* case for books etc.]

shrink /ʃrɪŋk/ v. & n. —v. (past **shrank** /ʃræŋk/; past part. **shrunk** /ʃrʌŋk/ or (esp. as adj.) **shrunken** /ˈʃrʌŋkən/) **1** tr. & intr. make or become smaller; contract, esp. by the action of moisture, heat, or cold. **2** intr. (usu. foll. by *from*) **a** retire; recoil; flinch; cower (*shrank from her touch*). **b** be averse from doing (*shrinks from meeting them*). **3** (as **shrunken** adj.) (esp. of a face, person, etc.) having grown smaller esp. because of age, illness, etc. —n. **1** the act or an instance of shrinking; shrinkage. **2** sl. a psychiatrist (from 'head-shrinker'). □ **shrinking violet** an exaggeratedly shy person. **shrink into oneself** become withdrawn. **shrink on** slip (a metal tyre etc.) on while expanded with heat and allow to tighten. **shrink-resistant** (of textiles etc.) resistant to shrinkage when wet etc. **shrink-wrap** (-**wrapped**, -**wrapping**) enclose (an article) in (esp. transparent) film that shrinks tightly on to it. □□ **shrinkable** adj. **shrinker** n. **shrinkingly** adv. **shrink-proof** adj. [OE *scrincan*: cf. *skrynka* to wrinkle]

shrinkage /ˈʃrɪŋkɪdʒ/ n. **1 a** the process or fact of shrinking. **b** the degree or amount of shrinking. **2** an allowance made for the reduction in takings due to wastage, theft, etc.

shrive /ʃraɪv/ v.tr. (past **shrove** /ʃrəʊv/; past part. **shriven** /ˈʃrɪv(ə)n/) RC Ch. archaic **1** (of a priest) hear the confession of, assign penance to, and absolve. **2** (refl.) (of a penitent) submit oneself to a priest for confession etc. [OE *scrīfan* impose as penance, WG f. L *scribere* write]

shrivel /ˈʃrɪv(ə)l/ v.tr. & intr. (**shrivelled**, **shrivelling** or US **shriveled**, **shriveling**) contract or wither into a wrinkled, folded, rolled-up, contorted, or dried-up state. [perh. f. ON: cf. Sw. dial. *skryvla* to wrinkle]

shriven past part. of SHRIVE.

Shropshire /ˈʃrɒpʃɪə(r)/ a west midland county of England; pop. (1981) 380,600; county town, Shrewsbury.

shroud /ʃraʊd/ n. & v. —n. **1** a sheetlike garment for wrapping a corpse for burial. **2** anything that conceals like a shroud (*wrapped in a shroud of mystery*). **3** (in pl.) Naut. a set of ropes forming part of the standing rigging and supporting the mast or topmast. —v.tr. **1** clothe (a body) for burial. **2** cover, conceal, or disguise (*hills shrouded in mist*). □ **shroud-laid** (of a rope) having four strands laid right-handed on a core. □□ **shroudless** adj. [OE *scrūd* f. Gmc: see SHRED]

shrove past of SHRIVE.

Shrovetide /ˈʃrəʊvtaɪd/ n. Shrove Tuesday and the two days preceding it when it was formerly customary to be shriven. [ME *shrove* abnormally f. SHROVE]

Shrove Tuesday /ʃrəʊv/ n. the day before Ash Wednesday.

shrub[1] /ʃrʌb/ n. a woody plant smaller than a tree and having a very short stem with branches near the ground. □□ **shrubby**

adj. [ME f. OE *scrubb*, *scrybb* shrubbery: cf. NFris. *skrobb* brushwood, WFlem. *schrobbe* vetch, Norw. *skrubba* dwarf cornel, and SCRUB[2]]

shrub[2] /ʃrʌb/ n. a cordial made of sweetened fruit-juice and spirits, esp. rum. [Arab. *šurb*, *šarāb* f. *šariba* to drink: cf. SHERBET, SYRUP]

shrubbery /ˈʃrʌbərɪ/ n. (pl. -**ies**) an area planted with shrubs.

shrug /ʃrʌg/ v. & n. —v. (**shrugged**, **shrugging**) **1** intr. slightly and momentarily raise the shoulders to express indifference, helplessness, contempt, etc. **2** tr. **a** raise (the shoulders) in this way. **b** shrug the shoulders to express (indifference etc.) (*shrugged his consent*). —n. the act or an instance of shrugging. □ **shrug off** dismiss as unimportant etc. by or as if by shrugging. [ME: orig. unkn.]

shrunk (also **shrunken**) past part. of SHRINK.

shtick /ʃtɪk/ n. sl. a theatrical routine, gimmick, etc. [Yiddish f. G *Stück* piece]

shuck /ʃʌk/ n. & v. US —n. **1** a husk or pod. **2** the shell of an oyster or clam. **3** (in pl.) colloq. an expression of contempt or regret or self-deprecation in response to praise. —v.tr. remove the shucks of; shell. □□ **shucker** n. [17th c.: orig. unkn.]

shudder /ˈʃʌdə(r)/ v. & n. —v.intr. **1** shiver esp. convulsively from fear, cold, repugnance, etc. **2** feel strong repugnance etc. (*shudder to think what might happen*). **3** (of a machine etc.) vibrate or quiver. —n. **1** the act or an instance of shuddering. **2** (in pl.; prec. by *the*) colloq. a state of shuddering. □□ **shudderingly** adv. **shuddery** adj. [ME *shod(d)er* f. MDu. *schūderen*, MLG *schōderen* f. Gmc]

shuffle /ˈʃʌf(ə)l/ v. & n. —v. **1** tr. & intr. move with a scraping, sliding, or dragging motion (*shuffles along; shuffling his feet*). **2** tr. **a** (also absol.) rearrange (a pack of cards) by sliding them over each other quickly. **b** rearrange; intermingle; confuse (*shuffled the documents*). **3** tr. (usu. foll. by *on, off, into*) assume or remove (clothes, a burden, etc.) esp. clumsily or evasively (*shuffled on his clothes; shuffled off responsibility*). **4** intr. **a** equivocate; prevaricate. **b** continually shift one's position; fidget. **5** intr. (foll. by *out of*) escape evasively (*shuffled out of the blame*). —n. **1** a shuffling movement. **2** the act or an instance of shuffling cards. **3** a general change of relative positions. **4** a piece of equivocation; sharp practice. **5** a quick scraping movement of the feet in dancing (see also *double shuffle*). □ **shuffle-board** = SHOVELBOARD. **shuffle the cards** change policy etc. □□ **shuffler** n. [perh. f. LG *schuffeln* walk clumsily f. Gmc: cf. SHOVE]

shufti /ˈʃʊftɪ/ n. (pl. **shuftis**) Brit. colloq. a look or glimpse. [Arab. *šaffa* try to see]

Shumen /ˈʃuːmen/ a city in NE Bulgaria, noted for its 17th-c. mosque and medieval fortress; pop. (1987) 106,500.

shun /ʃʌn/ v.tr. (**shunned**, **shunning**) avoid; keep clear of (*shuns human company*). [OE *scunian*, of unkn. orig.]

shunt /ʃʌnt/ v. & n. —v. **1** intr. & tr. diverge or cause (a train) to be diverted esp. on to a siding. **2** tr. Electr. provide (a current) with a shunt. **3** tr. **a** postpone or evade. **b** divert (a decision etc.) on to another person etc. —n. **1** the act or an instance of shunting on to a siding. **2** Electr. a conductor joining two points of a circuit, through which more or less of a current may be diverted. **3** Surgery an alternative path for the circulation of the blood. **4** sl. a motor accident, esp. a collision of vehicles travelling one close behind another. □□ **shunter** n. [ME, perh. f. SHUN]

shush /ʃʊʃ, ʃʌʃ/ int. & v. —int. = HUSH int. —v. **1** intr. **a** call for silence by saying shush. **b** be silent (*they shushed at once*). **2** tr. make or attempt to make silent. [imit.]

shut /ʃʌt/ v. (**shutting**; past and past part. **shut**) **1** tr. **a** move (a door, window, lid, lips, etc.) into position so as to block an aperture (*shut the lid*). **b** close or seal (a room, window, box, eye, mouth, etc.) by moving a door etc. (*shut the box*). **2** intr. become or be capable of being closed or sealed (*the door shut with a bang; the lid shuts automatically*). **3** intr. & tr. become or make (a shop, business, etc.) closed for trade (*the shops shut at five; shuts his shop at five*). **4** tr. bring (a book, hand, telescope, etc.) into a folded-up or contracted state. **5** tr. (usu. foll. by *in, out*) keep (a person, sound, etc.) in or out of a room etc. by shutting a door etc. (*shut out the noise; shut them in*). **6** tr. (usu. foll. by *in*) catch (a finger, dress, etc.) by shutting something on it (*shut her finger in the door*). **7** *tr.* bar access to (a place etc.) (*this entrance is shut*). □ **be** (or **get**) **shut of** *sl.* be (or get) rid of (*were glad to get shut of him*). **shut the door on** refuse to consider; make impossible. **shut down 1** stop (a factory, nuclear reactor, etc.) from operating. **2** (of a factory etc.) stop operating. **3** push or pull (a window-sash etc.) down into a closed position. **shut-down** *n.* the closure of a factory etc. **shut-eye** *colloq.* sleep. **shut one's eyes** (or **ears** or **heart** or **mind**) **to** pretend not, or refuse, to see (or hear or feel sympathy for or think about). **shut in** (of hills, houses, etc.) encircle, prevent access etc. to or escape from (*were shut in by the sea on three sides*) (see also sense **5**). **shut off 1** stop the flow of (water, gas, etc.) by shutting a valve. **2** separate from society etc. **shut-off** *n.* **1** something used for stopping an operation. **2** a cessation of flow, supply, or activity. **shut out 1** exclude (a person, light, etc.) from a place, situation, etc. **2** screen (landscape etc.) from view. **3** prevent (a possibility etc.). **4** block (a painful memory etc.) from the mind. **5** *US* prevent (an opponent) from scoring (see also sense **5**). **shut-out bid** *Bridge* a pre-emptive bid. **shut to 1** close (a door etc.). **2** (of a door etc.) close as far as it will go. **shut up 1** close all doors and windows of (a house etc.); bolt and bar. **2** imprison (a person). **3** close (a box etc.) securely. **4** *colloq.* reduce to silence by rebuke etc. **5** put (a thing) away in a box etc. **6** (esp. in *imper.*) *colloq.* stop talking. **shut up shop 1** close a business, shop, etc. **2** cease business etc. permanently. **shut your face** (or **head** or **mouth** or **trap**)! *sl.* an impolite request to stop talking. [OE *scyttan* f. WG: cf. SHOOT]

Shute /ʃuːt/, Nevil (Nevil Shute Norway, 1899–1960), English novelist, by profession an aeronautical engineer. After the Second World War he settled in Australia, which provides the setting for a number of his novels, including *A Town Like Alice* (1950). In all his works, which are peopled by wholly credible characters, he excelled at showing how ordinary people act in extraordinary situations. *On the Beach* (1957), set in Australia and brilliantly effective in its understatement, portrays a community facing the gradual destruction of mankind in the aftermath of a nuclear war.

shutter /ˈʃʌtə(r)/ *n. & v.* —*n.* **1** a person or thing that shuts. **2 a** each of a pair or set of panels fixed inside or outside a window for security or privacy or to keep the light in or out. **b** a structure of slats on rollers used for the same purpose. **3** a device that exposes the film in a photographic camera. **4** *Mus.* the blind of a swell-box in an organ used for controlling the sound-level. —*v.tr.* **1** put up the shutters of. **2** provide with shutters. □ **put up the shutters 1** cease business for the day. **2** cease business etc. permanently. □□ **shutterless** *adj.*

shuttering /ˈʃʌtərɪŋ/ *n.* **1** a temporary structure usu. of wood, used to hold concrete during setting. **2** material for making shutters.

shuttle /ˈʃʌt(ə)l/ *n. & v.* —*n.* **1 a** a bobbin with two pointed ends used for carrying the weft-thread across between the warp-threads in weaving. **b** a bobbin carrying the lower thread in a sewing-machine. **2** a train, bus, etc., going to and fro over a short route continuously. **3** = SHUTTLECOCK. **4** = *space shuttle.* —*v.* **1** *intr.* & *tr.* move or cause to move to and fro like a shuttle. **2** *intr.* travel in a shuttle. □ **shuttle armature** *Electr.* an armature with a single coil wound on an elongated iron bobbin. **shuttle diplomacy** negotiations conducted by a mediator who travels successively to several countries. Henry Kissinger (see entry) was a noted exponent of this system. **shuttle service** a train or bus etc. service operating to and fro over a short route. [OE *scytel* dart f. Gmc: cf. SHOOT]

shuttlecock /ˈʃʌt(ə)l,kɒk/ *n.* **1** a cork with a ring of feathers, or a similar device of plastic, struck to and fro with a battledore in the old game of battledore and shuttlecock, and with a racket in badminton. **2** a thing passed repeatedly back and forth. [SHUTTLE + COCK[1], prob. f. the flying motion]

shy[1] /ʃaɪ/ *adj., v., & n.* —*adj.* (**shyer, shyest** or **shier, shiest**) **1 a** diffident or uneasy in company; timid. **b** (of an animal, bird, etc.) easily startled; timid. **2** (foll. by *of*) avoiding; chary of (*shy of his aunt; shy of going to meetings*). **3** (in *comb.*) showing fear of or distaste for (*gun-shy; work-shy*). **4** (often foll. by *of, on*) *colloq.* having

lost; short of (*I'm shy three quid; shy of the price of admission*). —*v.intr.* (**shies, shied**) **1** (usu. foll. by *at*) (esp. of a horse) start suddenly aside (at an object, noise, etc.) in fright. **2** (usu. foll. by *away from, at*) avoid accepting or becoming involved in (a proposal etc.) in alarm. —*n.* a sudden startled movement. □□ **shyer** *n.* **shyly** *adv.* (also **shily**). **shyness** *n.* [OE *sceoh* f. Gmc]

shy[2] /ʃaɪ/ *v. & n.* —*v.tr.* (**shies, shied**) (also *absol.*) fling or throw (a stone etc.). —*n.* (*pl.* **shies**) the act or an instance of shying. □ **have a shy at** *colloq.* **1** try to hit with a stone etc. **2** make an attempt at. **3** jeer at. □□ **shyer** *n.* [18th c.: orig. unkn.]

Shylock /ˈʃaɪlɒk/ a hard-hearted Jewish money-lender in Shakespeare's *Merchant of Venice.*

shyster /ˈʃaɪstə(r)/ *n.* esp. *US colloq.* a person, esp. a lawyer, who uses unscrupulous methods. [19th c.: orig. uncert.]

SI *abbr.* **1** (Order of the) Star of India. **2** the international system of units of measurement (F *Système International*). (See INTERNATIONAL SYSTEM OF UNITS.)

Si *symb. Chem.* the element silicon.

si /siː/ *n. Mus.* = TE. [F f. It., perh. f. the initials of *Sancte Iohannes*: see GAMUT]

Siachen Glacier /siˈɑːtʃ(ə)n/ one of the world's longest glaciers, situated at an altitude of *c.*5,500 m (17,800 ft.) in the Karakoram Range of eastern Kashmir in NW India. The occupation of the glacier by Indian troops in 1984 precipitated a high-altitude armed conflict between India and Pakistan.

sial /ˈsaɪəl/ *n.* **1** the discontinuous upper layer of the earth's crust represented by the continental masses, which are composed of relatively light rocks rich in silica and alumina and may be regarded as floating on a lower crustal layer of sima. **2** the material of which these masses are composed. [SILICON + ALUMINA]

Sialkot /siˈɑːlkɒt/ a city in Punjab province, Pakistan; pop. (1981) 296,000.

sialogogue /ˈsaɪələ,ɡɒɡ/ *n. & adj.* —*n.* a medicine inducing the flow of saliva. —*adj.* inducing such a flow. [F f. Gk *sialon* saliva + *agōgos* leading]

Siam /saɪˈæm/ the name until 1939 of Thailand. □ **Gulf of Siam** = Gulf of Thailand.

siamang /ˈsaɪə,mæŋ, ˈsiːə,mæŋ/ *n.* a large black gibbon, *Hylobates syndactylus*, native to Sumatra and the Malay peninsula. [Malay]

Siamese /,saɪəˈmiːz/ *n. & adj.* —*n.* (*pl.* same) **1 a** a native of Siam (now Thailand) in SE Asia. **b** the language of Siam (also called Thai; see entry). **2** (in full **Siamese cat**) **a** a cat of a cream-coloured short-haired breed with a brown face and ears and blue eyes. **b** this breed. —*adj.* of or concerning Siam, its people, or language. □ **Siamese twins 1** identical twins that are physically conjoined at birth. The condition ranges from those joined only by the umbilical blood-vessels to those in whom the conjoined heads or trunks are inseparable. The name refers to two Siamese men (1811–74) joined by a fleshy band in the region of the waist; despite this conjunction they each married, and fathered several children. **2** any closely associated pair.

sib /sɪb/ *n. & adj.* —*n.* **1** a brother or sister (cf. SIBLING). **2** a blood relative. **3** a group of people recognized by an individual as his or her kindred. —*adj.* (usu. foll. by *to*) esp. *Sc.* related; akin. [OE *sib(b)*]

Sibelius /sɪˈbeɪlɪəs/, Jean (1865–1957), Finnish composer. In 1885 he went to Helsinki, where he studied first law then music. He went on to further studies in Berlin and Vienna but maintained a deep feeling for his native country, revealed in his choice of the epic *Kalevala* as inspiration for many of his greatest works (the symphonic poem *Kullervo*, 1892; the four Lemminkäinen works which include *The Swan of Tuonela*, 1893; and *Pohjola's Daughter*, 1906). His seven symphonies move towards a cool but heartfelt purity of style and form the most substantial feature of his *œuvre*, but should not be allowed to detract from his songs (over 100), many of which set Swedish texts. The picture of him as an ascetic bleak figure is not supported by the facts of his far from austere life, nor is his music the 'cold, forbidding' art which some writers have portrayed.

æ *cat* ɑː *arm* e *bed* ɜː *her* ɪ *sit* iː *see* ɒ *hot* ɔː *saw* ʌ *run* ʊ *put* uː *too* ə *ago* aɪ *my*

Siberia /saɪˈbɪərɪə/ a region of the USSR in northern Asia, forming the larger part of the RSFSR. It has long been used as a place of exile for offenders. □□ **Siberian** adj. & n.

sibilant /ˈsɪbɪlənt/ adj. & n. —adj. **1** (of a letter or set of letters, as s, sh) sounded with a hiss. **2** hissing (a sibilant whisper). —n. a sibilant letter or letters. □□ **sibilance** n. **sibilancy** n. [L sibilare sibilant- hiss]

sibilate /ˈsɪbɪˌleɪt/ v.tr. & intr. pronounce with or utter a hissing sound. □□ **sibilation** /-ˈleɪʃ(ə)n/ n.

sibling /ˈsɪblɪŋ/ n. each of two or more children having one or both parents in common. [SIB + -LING¹]

sibship /ˈsɪbʃɪp/ n. **1** the state of belonging to a sib or the same sib. **2** a group of children having the same two parents.

sibyl /ˈsɪbɪl/ n. **1** any of the women who in ancient times acted as the reputed mouthpiece of a god, uttering prophecies and oracles, the most famous of whom was the sibyl of Cumae in south Italy who guided Aeneas through the underworld. **2** a prophetess, fortune-teller, or witch. [ME f. OF Sibile or med.L Sibilla f. L Sibylla f. Gk Sibulla]

sibylline /ˈsɪbɪˌlaɪn/ adj. **1** of or from a sibyl. **2** oracular; prophetic. □ **the Sibylline books** a collection of prophecies in Greek hexameter verses, ascribed to the sibyls, belonging to the State of ancient Rome and consulted by its magistrates for guidance in times of national calamity. They were destroyed in 83 BC in the burning of the Capitol and a new collection, from various sources, replaced them; these were later recopied (with many Jewish and Christian interpolations). The last known consultation of the books was in 363. [L Sibyllinus (as SIBYL)]

sic /sɪk/ adv. (usu. in brackets) used, spelt, etc., as written (confirming, or calling attention to, the form of quoted or copied words). [L, = so, thus]

siccative /ˈsɪkətɪv/ n. & adj. —n. a substance causing drying, esp. mixed with oil-paint etc. for quick drying. —adj. having such properties. [LL siccativus f. siccare to dry]

sice¹ /saɪs/ n. the six on dice. [ME f. OF sis f. L sex six]

sice² var. of SYCE.

Sichuan /sɪtʃˈwɑːn/ (also **Szechuan** /setʃˈwɑːn/) a province of central China; pop. (est. 1986) 103,200,000; capital, Chengdu.

Sicilian Vespers the massacre of the French inhabitants of Sicily in 1282, after a riot which began near Palermo while the vesper-bell was ringing. The ensuing war resulted in the unpopular Angevin dynasty being replaced by the Spanish House of Aragon.

siciliano /ˌsɪtʃɪˈljɑːnəʊ/ n. (pl. -os) (also **siciliana** /-nə/) a dance, song, or instrumental piece in 6/8 or 12/8 time, often in a minor key, and evoking a pastoral mood. [It., = Sicilian]

Sicily /ˈsɪsɪlɪ/ a large triangular island in the Mediterranean Sea, separated from the 'toe' of Italy by the Strait of Messina; pop. (1981) 4,906,900; capital, Palermo. Settled successively by Phoenicians, Greeks, and Carthaginians, it became a Roman province in 241 BC after the first Punic War. After various struggles Sicily and southern Italy became a Norman kingdom towards the end of the 11th c. It was conquered by Charles of Anjou in 1266, but the unpopularity of the Angevin regime led to the uprising known as the Sicilian Vespers (see entry) and the establishment in Sicily of the Spanish House of Aragon in its place; southern Italy remained under Angevin rule until reunited with Sicily in 1442. In 1816 the two areas were officially merged when the Spanish Bourbon Ferdinand styled himself King of the Two Sicilies. The island was liberated by Garibaldi in 1860 and finally incorporated into the new State of Italy. The Sicilian economy is predominantly agricultural and the island remains relatively backward in comparison with the Italian mainland. □□ **Sicilian** /sɪˈsɪljən, -lɪən/ adj. & n.

sick¹ /sɪk/ adj., n., & v. —adj. **1** (often in comb.) esp. Brit. vomiting or tending to vomit (feels sick; has been sick; seasick). **2** esp. US ill; affected by illness (has been sick for a week; a sick man; sick with measles). **3 a** (often foll. by at) esp. mentally perturbed; disordered (the product of a sick mind; sick at heart). **b** (often foll. by for, or in comb.) pining; longing (sick for a sight of home; lovesick). **4** (often foll. by of) colloq. **a** disgusted; surfeited (sick of chocolates). **b** angry, esp. because of surfeit (am sick of being teased). **5** colloq. (of humour

etc.) jeering at misfortune, illness, death, etc.; morbid (sick joke). **6** (of a ship) needing repair (esp. of a specified kind) (paint-sick). —n. Brit. colloq. vomit. —v.tr. (usu. foll. by up) Brit. colloq. vomit (sicked up his dinner). □ **go sick** report oneself as ill. **look sick** colloq. be unimpressive or embarrassed. **sick at** (or **to**) **one's stomach** US vomiting or tending to vomit. **sick-benefit** Brit. an allowance made by the State to a person absent from work through sickness. **sick building syndrome** a high incidence of illness in office workers, attributed to the immediate working surroundings. **sick-call 1** a visit by a doctor to a sick person etc. **2** Mil. a summons for sick men to attend. **sick-flag** a yellow flag indicating disease at a quarantine station or on ship. **sick headache** a migraine headache with vomiting. **sick-leave** leave of absence granted because of illness. **sick-list** a list of the sick, esp. in a regiment, ship, etc. **sick-making** colloq. sickening. **sick nurse** = NURSE. **sick-pay** pay given to an employee etc. on sick-leave. **take sick** colloq. be taken ill. □□ **sickish** adj. [OE sēoc f. Gmc]

sick² /sɪk/ v.tr. (usu. in imper.) (esp. to a dog) set upon (a rat etc.). [19th c., dial. var. of SEEK]

sickbay /ˈsɪkbeɪ/ n. **1** part of a ship used as a hospital. **2** any room etc. for sick people.

sickbed /ˈsɪkbed/ n. **1** an invalid's bed. **2** the state of being an invalid.

sicken /ˈsɪkən/ v. **1** tr. affect with loathing or disgust. **2** intr. **a** (often foll. by for) show symptoms of illness (is sickening for measles). **b** (often foll. by at, or to + infin.) feel nausea or disgust (he sickened at the sight). **3** (as **sickening** adj.) **a** loathsome, disgusting. **b** colloq. very annoying. □□ **sickeningly** adv.

Sickert /ˈsɪkət/, Walter Richard (1860–1942), English painter, who was a pupil of Whistler and also worked with Degas. His subjects were mainly urban scenes and figure compositions, particularly pictures of the theatre and music hall and drab domestic interiors, avoiding the conventionally picturesque, eliciting rare beauty from the sordid, and lending enchantment to the commonplace. His most famous painting, Ennui, portrays a stagnant marriage.

sickie /ˈsɪkɪ/ n. Austral. & NZ colloq. a period of sick-leave, usu. taken with insufficient medical reason.

sickle /ˈsɪk(ə)l/ n. **1** a short-handled farming tool with a semicircular blade, used for cutting corn, lopping, or trimming. **2** anything sickle-shaped, esp. the crescent moon. □ **sickle-bill** any of various curlews with a sickle-shaped bill. **sickle-cell** a sickle-shaped blood-cell, esp. as found in a type of severe hereditary anaemia. **sickle-feather** one of the long middle feathers of a cock's tail. [OE sicol, sicel f. L secula f. secare cut]

sickly /ˈsɪklɪ/ adj. (**sicklier, sickliest**) **1 a** of weak health; apt to be ill. **b** (of a person's complexion, look, etc.) languid, faint, or pale, suggesting sickness (a sickly smile). **c** (of light or colour) faint, pale, feeble. **2** causing ill health (a sickly climate). **3** (of a book etc.) sentimental or mawkish. **4** inducing or connected with nausea (a sickly taste). **5** (of a colour etc.) of an unpleasant shade inducing nausea (a sickly green). □□ **sickliness** n. [ME, prob. after ON sjúkligr (as SICK¹)]

sickness /ˈsɪknɪs/ n. **1** the state of being ill; disease. **2** a specified disease (sleeping sickness). **3** vomiting or a tendency to vomit. □ **sickness benefit** (in the UK) benefit paid by the State for sickness interrupting paid employment. [OE sēocnesse (as SICK¹, -NESS)]

sickroom /ˈsɪkruːm, -rʊm/ n. **1** a room occupied by a sick person. **2** a room adapted for sick people.

sidalcea /sɪˈdælsɪə/ n. any mallow-like plant of the genus Sidalcea, bearing racemes of white, pink, or purple flowers. [mod.L f. Sida + Alcea, names of related genera]

Siddons /ˈsɪd(ə)nz/, Sarah (1755–1831), née Kemble, English actress. Her first London appearance, in 1775, was a failure, but after her second, in 1782, she was acclaimed as an incomparable tragic actress with beauty, tenderness, and nobility. She retained her pre-eminence until her retirement in 1812.

side /saɪd/ n. & v. —n. **1 a** each of the more or less flat surfaces bounding an object (a cube has six sides; this side up). **b** a more or less vertical inner or outer plane or surface (the side of a house; a *mountainside*). **c** such a vertical lateral surface or plane as distinct from the top or bottom, front or back, or ends (*at the side of the house*). **2 a** the half of a person or animal that is on the right or the left, esp. of the torso (*has a pain in his right side*). **b** the left or right half or a specified part of a thing, area, building, etc. (*put the box on that side*). **c** (often in *comb.*) a position next to a person or thing (*grave-side; seaside; stood at my side*). **d** a specified direction relating to a person or thing (*on the north side of; came from all sides*). **e** half of a butchered carcass (*a side of bacon*). **3 a** either surface of a thing regarded as having two surfaces. **b** the amount of writing needed to fill one side of a sheet of paper (*write three sides*). **4** any of several aspects of a question, character, etc. (*many sides to his character; look on the bright side*). **5 a** each of two sets of opponents in war, politics, games, etc. (*the side that bats first; much to be said on both sides*). **b** a cause or philosophical position etc. regarded as being in conflict with another (*on the side of right*). **6 a** a part or region near the edge and remote from the centre (*at the side of the room*). **b** (*attrib.*) a subordinate, peripheral, or detached part (*a side-road; a side-table*). **7 a** each of the bounding lines of a plane rectilinear figure (*a hexagon has six sides*). **b** each of two quantities stated to be equal in an equation. **8** a position nearer or farther than, or right or left of, a dividing line (*on this side of the Alps; on the other side of the road*). **9** a line of hereditary descent through the father or the mother. **10** (in full **side spin**) *Brit.* a spinning motion given to a billiard-ball etc. by hitting it on one side, not centrally. **11** *Brit. sl.* boastfulness; swagger (*has no side about him*). **12** *Brit. colloq.* a television channel (*shall we try another side?*). —*v.intr.* (usu. foll. by *with*) take part or be on the same side as a disputant etc. (*sided with his father*). □ **by the side of 1** close to. **2** compared with. **from side to side 1** right across. **2** alternately each way from a central line. **let the side down** fail one's colleagues, esp. by frustrating their efforts or embarrassing them. **on one side 1** not in the main or central position. **2** aside (*took him on one side to explain*). **on the . . . side** fairly, somewhat (qualifying an adjective: *on the high side*), **on the side 1** as a sideline; in addition to one's regular work etc. **2** secretly or illicitly. **3** *US* as a side dish. **on this side of the grave** in life. **side-arms** swords, bayonets, or pistols. **side-band** a range of frequencies near the carrier frequency of a radio wave, concerned in modulation. **side-bet** a bet between opponents, esp. in card-games, over and above the ordinary stakes. **side-bone** either of the small forked bones under the wings of poultry. **side by side** standing close together, esp. for mutual support. **side-car 1** a small car for a passenger or passengers attached to the side of a motor cycle. **2** a cocktail of orange liqueur, lemon juice, and brandy. **3** a jaunting car. **side-chapel** a chapel in the aisle or at the side of a church. **side dish** an extra dish subsidiary to the main course. **side-door 1** a door in or at the side of a building. **2** an indirect means of access. **side-drum** a small double-headed drum in a jazz or military band or in an orchestra (orig. hung at the drummer's side). **side-effect** a secondary, usu. undesirable, effect. **side-glance** a sideways or brief glance. **side-issue** a point that distracts attention from what is important. **side-note** a marginal note. **side-on** *adv.* from the side. —*adj.* **1** from or towards one side. **2** (of a collision) involving the side of a vehicle. **side-road** a minor or subsidiary road, esp. joining or diverging from a main road. **side-saddle** *n.* a saddle for a woman rider with both feet on the same side of the horse. —*adv.* sitting in this position on a horse. **side salad** a salad served as a side dish. **side-seat** a seat in a vehicle etc. in which the occupant has his back to the side of the vehicle. **side-slip** *n.* **1** a skid. **2** *Aeron.* a sideways movement instead of forward. —*v.intr.* **1** skid. **2** *Aeron.* move sideways instead of forward. **side-splitting** causing violent laughter. **side-street** a minor or subsidiary street. **side-stroke 1** a stroke towards or from a side. **2** an incidental action. **3** a swimming stroke in which the swimmer lies on his or her side. **side-swipe** *n.* **1** a glancing blow along the side. **2** incidental criticism etc. —*v.tr.* hit with or as if with a side-swipe. **side-table** a table placed at the side of a room or apart from the main table. **side-trip** a minor excursion during a voyage or trip; a detour. **side valve** a valve in a vehicle engine, operated from the side of the cylinder. **side-view 1** a view obtained

sideways. **2** a profile. **side-wheeler** *US* a steamer with paddle-wheels. **side-whiskers** whiskers growing on the cheeks. **side wind 1** wind from the side. **2** an indirect agency or influence. **take sides** support one or other cause etc. □□ **sideless** *adj.* [OE *sīde* f. Gmc]

sideboard /ˈsaɪdbɔːd/ *n.* a table or esp. a flat-topped cupboard at the side of a dining-room for supporting and containing dishes, table linen, decanters, etc.

sideboards /ˈsaɪdbɔːdz/ *n.pl. Brit. colloq.* hair grown by a man down the sides of his face; side-whiskers.

sideburns /ˈsaɪdbɜːnz/ *n.pl.* = SIDEBOARDS. [*burnsides* pl. of *burn-side* f. Amer. General *Burnside* d. 1881 who affected this style]

sided /ˈsaɪdɪd/ *adj.* **1** having sides. **2** (in *comb.*) having a specified side or sides (*one-sided*). □□ **-sidedly** *adv.* **sidedness** *n.* (also in *comb.*).

sidehill /ˈsaɪdhɪl/ *n. US* a hillside.

sidekick /ˈsaɪdkɪk/ *n. colloq.* a close associate.

sidelight /ˈsaɪdlaɪt/ *n.* **1** a light from the side. **2** incidental information etc. **3** *Brit.* a light at the side of the front of a motor vehicle to warn of its presence. **4** *Naut.* the red port or green starboard light on a ship under way.

sideline /ˈsaɪdlaɪn/ *n. & v.* —*n.* **1** work etc. done in addition to one's main activity. **2** (usu. in *pl.*) **a** a line bounding the side of a hockey-pitch, tennis-court, etc. **b** the space next to these where spectators etc. sit. —*v.tr. US* remove (a player) from a team through injury, suspension, etc. □ **on** (or **from**) **the sidelines** in (or from) a position removed from the main action.

sidelong /ˈsaɪdlɒŋ/ *adj. & adv.* —*adj.* inclining to one side; oblique (*a sidelong glance*). —*adv.* obliquely (*moved sidelong*). [*sideling* (as SIDE, -LING²): see -LONG]

sidereal /saɪˈdɪərɪəl/ *adj.* of or concerning the constellations or fixed stars. □ **sidereal clock** a clock showing sidereal time. **sidereal day** the time between successive meridional transits of a star or esp. of the first point of Aries, about four minutes shorter than the solar day. **sidereal time** time measured by the apparent diurnal motion of the stars. **sidereal year** a year longer than the solar year by 20 minutes 23 seconds because of precession. [L *sidereus* f. *sidus sideris* star]

siderite /ˈsaɪdəˌraɪt/ *n.* **1** a mineral form of ferrous carbonate. **2** a meteorite consisting mainly of nickel and iron. [Gk *sidēros* iron]

siderostat /ˈsaɪdərəˌstæt/ *n.* an instrument used for keeping the image of a celestial body in a fixed position. [L *sidus sideris* star, after *heliostat*]

sideshow /ˈsaɪdʃəʊ/ *n.* **1** a minor show or attraction in an exhibition or entertainment. **2** a minor incident or issue.

sidesman /ˈsaɪdzmən/ *n.* (*pl.* **-men**) an assistant churchwarden, who shows worshippers to their seats, takes the collection, etc.

sidestep /ˈsaɪdstep/ *n. & v.* —*n.* a step taken sideways. —*v.tr.* (**-stepped, -stepping**) **1** esp. *Football* avoid (esp. a tackle) by stepping sideways. **2** evade. □□ **sidestepper** *n.*

sidetrack /ˈsaɪdtræk/ *n. & v.* —*n.* a railway siding. —*v.tr.* **1** turn into a siding; shunt. **2 a** postpone, evade, or divert treatment or consideration. **b** divert (a person) from considering etc.

sidewalk /ˈsaɪdwɔːk/ *n. US* a pedestrian path at the side of a road; a pavement.

sideward /ˈsaɪdwəd/ *adj. & adv.* —*adj.* = SIDEWAYS. —*adv.* (also **sidewards** /-wədz/) = SIDEWAYS.

sideways /ˈsaɪdweɪz/ *adv. & adj.* —*adv.* **1** to or from a side (*moved sideways*). **2** with one side facing forward (*sat sideways on the bus*). —*adj.* to or from a side (*a sideways movement*). □□ **sidewise** *adv. & adj.*

sidewinder /ˈsaɪdˌwaɪndə(r)/ *n.* **1** a desert rattlesnake, *Crotalus cerastes*, native to N. America, moving with a lateral motion. **2** *US* a sideways blow.

siding /ˈsaɪdɪŋ/ *n.* **1** a short track at the side of and opening on to a railway line, used for shunting trains. **2** *US* cladding material for the outside of a building.

sidle /ˈsaɪd(ə)l/ *v. & n.* —*v.intr.* (usu. foll. by *along*, *up*) walk in a timid, furtive, stealthy, or cringing manner. —*n.* the act or an instance of sidling. [back-form. f. *sideling*, SIDELONG]

b but d dog f few g get h he j yes k cat l leg m man n no p pen r red s sit t top v voice

Sidney /ˈsɪdnɪ/, Sir Philip (1554–86), English soldier and poet. Generally considered to represent the apotheosis of the Elizabethan courtier, Sidney was one of the leading poets of the age, his most famous work being *Arcadia* (1580). He died of wounds received in the Low Countries while fighting the Spanish.

Sidon /ˈsaɪd(ə)n/ (Arabic **Saida** /ˈsaɪdə/) a city and seaport of the Phoenicians, now in Lebanon; pop. (1980) 24,740.

Sidra /ˈsɪdrə/, **Gulf of** (also **Gulf of Sirte** /ˈsɜːtɪ/) a bay on the Mediterranean coast of Libya, between the towns of Benghazi and Misratah.

SIDS *abbr.* sudden infant death syndrome; = *cot-death* (see COT[1]).

siege /siːdʒ/ *n.* **1 a** a military operation in which an attacking force seeks to compel the surrender of a fortified place by surrounding it and cutting off supplies etc. **b** a similar operation by police etc. to force the surrender of an armed person. **c** the period during which a siege lasts. **2** a persistent attack or campaign of persuasion. □ **lay siege to** esp. *Mil.* conduct the siege of. **raise the siege of** abandon or cause the abandonment of an attempt to take (a place) by siege. **siege-gun** *hist.* a heavy gun used in sieges. **siege-train** artillery and other equipment for a siege, with vehicles etc. [ME f. OF *sege* seat f. *assegier* BESIEGE]

Siegfried /ˈsiːɡfriːd/ the hero of the first part of the Nibelungenlied, who forged the Nothung sword, slew Fafner, the dragon guarding the stolen Rhine gold, and helped Gunther to win Brunhild. He was treacherously slain by Hagen, a Burgundian retainer, who was eventually slain with Siegfried's sword.

Siegfried Line /ˈsiːɡfriːd/ **1** the Hindenburg Line (see entry). **2** the line of defence constructed along the western frontier of Germany before the Second World War.

Siemens /ˈsiːmənz/, Ernst Werner von (1816–92), German electrical engineer, who developed electroplating and an electric generator using an electromagnet rather than a permanent magnetic field. He set up a factory in Berlin which manufactured telegraph systems and electric cables and pioneered electrical traction. His brother Karl Wilhelm (Charles William, 1823–83), was sent to England at the age of 20 and remained there all his life. He developed the open-hearth steel furnace, which was widely used, and designed the cable-laying steamship *Faraday* and one of the first electric railways in the UK, built at Portrush in Northern Ireland. A third brother Friedrich (1826–1904) worked both with Werner in Germany and with Charles in England; he applied the principles of the open-hearth furnace to glassmaking.

siemens /ˈsiːmənz/ *n.* *Electr.* the SI unit of conductance, equal to one reciprocal ohm. ¶ Abbr.: **S**. [E. W. von SIEMENS]

Siena /sɪˈenə/ a city of Tuscany in west central Italy, noted for its medieval architecture and for its school of art, which flourished in the 13th–14th centuries; pop. (1985) 60,670. □□ **Sienese** /-ˈniːz/ *adj.* & *n.*

sienna /sɪˈenə/ *n.* **1** a kind of ferruginous earth used as a pigment in paint. **2** its colour of yellowish-brown (**raw sienna**) or reddish-brown (**burnt sienna**). [It. (*terra di*) *Sienna* (earth of) Siena]

sierra /sɪˈerə/ *n.* a long jagged mountain chain, esp. in Spain or Spanish America. [Sp. f. L *serra* saw]

Sierra Leone /sɪˌerə lɪˈəʊn/ a country on the coast of West Africa, a member State of the Commonwealth; pop. (est. 1988) 3,963,300; official language, English; capital, Freetown. An area of British influence from the late 18th c., the district around Freetown on the coast became a colony in 1807 but the large inland territory was not declared a protectorate until 1896. Sierra Leone achieved independence in 1961 and is now a one-party State. Its economy, though largely agricultural, benefits from iron mining and diamond exports. □□ **Sierra Leonian** *adj.* & *n.*

siesta /sɪˈestə/ *n.* an afternoon sleep or rest esp. in hot countries. [Sp. f. L *sexta* (*hora*) sixth hour]

sieve /sɪv/ *n.* & *v.* —*n.* a utensil having a perforated or meshed bottom for separating solids or coarse material from liquids or fine particles, or for reducing a soft solid to a fine pulp. —*v.tr.* **1** put through or sift with a sieve. **2** examine (evidence etc.) to

select or separate. □ **head like a sieve** *colloq.* a memory that retains little. □□ **sievelike** *adj.* [OE *sife* f. WG]

siffleur /siːˈflɜːr/ *n.* (*fem.* **siffleuse** /-ˈflɜːz/) a professional whistler. [F f. *siffler* whistle]

sift /sɪft/ *v.* **1** *tr.* sieve (material) into finer and coarser parts. **2** *tr.* (usu. foll. by *from*, *out*) separate (finer or coarser parts) from material. **3** *tr.* sprinkle (esp. sugar) from a perforated container. **4** *tr.* examine (evidence, facts, etc.) in order to assess authenticity etc. **5** *intr.* (of snow, light, etc.) fall as if from a sieve. □ **sift through** examine by sifting. □□ **sifter** *n.* (also in *comb.*). [OE *siftan* f. WG]

Sig. *abbr.* Signor.

sigh /saɪ/ *v.* & *n.* —*v.* **1** *intr.* emit a long deep audible breath expressive of sadness, weariness, longing, relief, etc. **2** *intr.* (foll. by *for*) yearn for (a lost person or thing). **3** *tr.* utter or express with sighs ('*Never!*' he sighed). **4** *intr.* (of the wind etc.) make a sound like sighing. —*n.* **1** the act or an instance of sighing. **2** a sound made in sighing (*a sigh of relief*). [ME *sihen* etc., prob. back-form. f. *sihte* past of *sihen* f. OE *sican*]

sight /saɪt/ *n.* & *v.* —*n.* **1 a** the faculty of seeing with the eyes (*lost his sight*). **b** the act or an instance of seeing; the state of being seen. **2** a thing seen; a display, show, or spectacle (*not a pretty sight*; *a beautiful sight*). **3** a way of looking at or considering a thing (*in my sight he can do no wrong*). **4** a range of space within which a person etc. can see or an object be seen (*he's out of sight*; *they are just coming into sight*). **5** (usu. in *pl.*) noteworthy features of a town, area, etc. (*went to see the sights*). **6 a** a device on a gun or optical instrument used for assisting the precise aim or observation. **b** the aim or observation so gained (*got a sight of him*). **7** *colloq.* a person or thing having a ridiculous, repulsive, or dishevelled appearance (*looked a perfect sight*). **8** *colloq.* a great quantity (*will cost a sight of money*; *is a sight better than he was*). —*v.tr.* **1** get sight of, esp. by approaching (*they sighted land*). **2** observe the presence of (esp. aircraft, animals, etc.) (*sighted buffalo*). **3** take observations of (a star etc.) with an instrument. **4 a** provide (a gun, quadrant, etc.) with sights. **b** adjust the sight of (a gun etc.). **c** aim (a gun etc.) with sights. □ **at first sight** on first glimpse or impression. **at** (or **on**) **sight** as soon as a person or a thing has been seen (*plays music at sight*; *liked him on sight*). **catch** (or **lose**) **sight of** begin (or cease) to see or be aware of. **get a sight of** manage to see; glimpse. **have lost sight of** no longer know the whereabouts of. **in sight 1** visible. **2** near at hand (*salvation is in sight*). **in** (or **within**) **sight of** so as to see or be seen from. **lower one's sights** become less ambitious. **out of my sight!** go at once! **out of sight 1** not visible. **2** *colloq.* excellent; delightful. **out of sight out of mind** we forget the absent. **put out of sight** hide, ignore. **set one's sights on** aim at (*set her sights on a directorship*). **sight for the gods** (or **sight for sore eyes**) a welcome person or thing, esp. a visitor. **sight-glass** a transparent device for observing the interior of apparatus etc. **sighting shot** an experimental shot to guide riflemen in adjusting their sights. **sight-line** a hypothetical line from a person's eye to what is seen. **sight-read** (*past* and *past part.* **-read** /-red/) read and perform (music) at sight. **sight-reader** a person who sight-reads. **sight-screen** *Cricket* a large white screen on wheels placed near the boundary in line with the wicket to help the batsman see the ball. **sight-sing** sing (music) at sight. **sight unseen** without previous inspection. □□ **sighter** *n.* [OE (*ge*)*sihth*]

sighted /ˈsaɪtɪd/ *adj.* **1** capable of seeing; not blind. **2** (in *comb.*) having a specified kind of sight (*long-sighted*).

sightless /ˈsaɪtlɪs/ *adj.* **1** blind. **2** *poet.* invisible. □□ **sightlessly** *adv.* **sightlessness** *n.*

sightly /ˈsaɪtlɪ/ *adj.* attractive to the sight; not unsightly. □□ **sightliness** *n.*

sightseer /ˈsaɪtˌsiːə(r)/ *n.* a person who visits places of interest; a tourist. □□ **sightsee** *v.intr.* & *tr.* **sightseeing** *n.*

sightworthy /ˈsaɪtˌwɜːðɪ/ *adj.* worth seeing.

sigillate /ˈsɪdʒɪlət/ *adj.* **1** (of pottery) having impressed patterns. **2** *Bot.* having seal-like marks. [L *sigillatus* f. *sigillum* seal dimin. of *signum* sign]

siglum /ˈsɪɡləm/ *n.* (*pl.* **sigla** /-lə/) a letter (esp. an initial) or other symbol used to denote a word in a book, esp. to refer to a particular text. [LL *sigla* (pl.), perh. f. *singula* neut. pl. of *singulus* single]

sigma /'sɪgmə/ *n.* the eighteenth letter of the Greek alphabet (Σ,σ, or, when final, ς). [L f. Gk]

sigmate /'sɪgmət/ *adj.* **1** sigma-shaped. **2** S-shaped.

sigmoid /'sɪgmɔɪd/ *adj. & n.* —*adj.* **1** curved like the uncial sigma (ϲ); crescent-shaped. **2** S-shaped. —*n.* (in full **sigmoid flexure**) *Anat.* the curved part of the intestine between the colon and the rectum. [Gk *sigmoeidēs* (as SIGMA)]

sign /saɪn/ *n. & v.* —*n.* **1 a** a thing indicating or suggesting a quality or state etc.; a thing perceived as indicating a future state or occurrence (*violence is a sign of weakness; shows all the signs of decay*). **b** a miracle evidencing supernatural power; a portent (*did signs and wonders*). **2 a** a mark, symbol, or device used to represent something or to distinguish the thing on which it is put (*marked the jar with a sign*). **b** a technical symbol used in algebra, music, etc. (*a minus sign; a repeat sign*). **3** a gesture or action used to convey information, an order, request, etc. (*gave him a sign to leave; conversed by signs*). **4** a publicly displayed board etc. giving information; a signboard or signpost. **5** any objective evidence of a disease, usu. specified (*Babinski's sign*). **6** a password (*advanced and gave the sign*). **7** any of the twelve divisions of the zodiac, named from the constellations formerly situated in them (*the sign of Cancer*). **8** *US* the trail of a wild animal. **9** *Math.* etc. the positiveness or negativeness of a quantity. **10** = *sign language.* —*v.* **1** *tr.* **a** (also *absol.*) write (one's name, initials, etc.) on a document etc. indicating that one has authorized it. **b** write one's name etc. on (a document) as authorization. **2** *intr. & tr.* communicate by gesture (*signed to me to come; signed their assent*). **3** *tr. & intr.* engage or be engaged by signing a contract etc. (see also *sign on, sign up*). **4** *tr.* mark with a sign (esp. with the sign of the cross in baptism). □ **make no sign** seem unconscious; not protest. **sign and countersign** secret words etc. used as passwords. **sign away** convey (one's right, property, etc.) by signing a deed etc. **sign for** acknowledge receipt of by signing. **sign language** a system of communication by visual gestures, used esp. by the deaf. **sign of the cross** a Christian sign made in blessing or prayer, by tracing a cross from the forehead to the chest and to each shoulder, or in the air. **sign off 1** end work, broadcasting, a letter, etc., esp. by writing or speaking one's name. **2 a** end a period of employment, contract, etc. **b** end the period of employment or contract of (a person). **3** *Brit.* stop receiving unemployment benefit after finding work. **4** *Bridge* indicate by a conventional bid that one is seeking to end the bidding. **sign-off** *n. Bridge* such a bid. **sign of the times** a portent etc. showing a likely trend. **sign on 1** agree to a contract, employment, etc. **2** begin work, broadcasting, etc., esp. by writing or announcing one's name. **3** employ (a person). **4** *Brit.* register as unemployed. **sign-painter** (or **-writer**) a person who paints signboards etc. **sign up 1** engage or employ (a person). **2** enlist in the armed forces. **3 a** commit (another person or oneself) by signing etc. (*signed you up for dinner*). **b** enrol (*signed up for evening classes*). □□ **signable** *adj.* **signer** *n.* [ME f. OF *signe, signer* f. L *signum, signare*]

Signac /siː'njæk/, Paul (1863–1935), French neo-impressionist painter, an ardent disciple of the views and methods of Seurat, though his own work had a liveliness and spontaneity not altogether in keeping with these. In 1899 he published a manifesto in defence of the movement, *D'Eugène Delacroix aux néoimpressionisme*.

signal[1] /'sɪgn(ə)l/ *n. & v.* —*n.* **1 a** a usu. prearranged sign conveying information, guidance, etc. esp. at a distance (*waved as a signal to begin*). **b** a message made up of such signs (*signals made with flags*). **2** an immediate occasion or cause of movement, action, etc. (*the uprising was a signal for repression*). **3** *Electr.* **a** an electrical impulse or impulses or radio waves transmitted as a signal. **b** a sequence of these. **4** a light, semaphore, etc., on a railway giving instructions or warnings to train-drivers etc. **5** *Bridge* a prearranged mode of bidding or play to convey information to one's partner. —*v.* (**signalled, signalling**; *US* **signaled, signaling**) **1** *intr.* make signals. **2** *tr.* **a** (often foll. by *to* + infin.) make signals to; direct. **b** transmit (an order, information, etc.)

by signal; announce (*signalled her agreement; signalled that the town had been taken*). □ **signal-book** a list of signals arranged for sending esp. naval and military messages. **signal-box** *Brit.* a building beside a railway track from which signals are controlled. **signal of distress** esp. *Naut.* an appeal for help, esp. from a ship by firing guns. **signal-tower** *US* = *signal-box.* □□ **signaller** *n.* [ME f. OF f. Rmc & med.L *signale* neut. of LL *signalis* f. L *signum* SIGN]

signal[2] /'sɪgn(ə)l/ *adj.* remarkably good or bad; noteworthy (*a signal victory*). □□ **signally** *adv.* [F *signalé* f. It. past part. *segnalato* distinguished f. *segnale* SIGNAL[1]]

signalize /'sɪgnə,laɪz/ *v.tr.* (also **-ise**) **1** make noteworthy or remarkable. **2** lend distinction or lustre to. **3** indicate.

signalman /'sɪgn(ə)lmən/ *n.* (*pl.* **-men**) **1** a railway employee responsible for operating signals and points. **2** a person who displays or receives naval etc. signals.

signary /'sɪgnərɪ/ *n.* (*pl.* **-ies**) a list of signs constituting the syllabic or alphabetic symbols of a language. [L *signum* SIGN + -ARY[1], after *syllabary*]

signatory /'sɪgnətərɪ/ *n. & adj.* —*n.* (*pl.* **-ies**) a party or esp. a State that has signed an agreement or esp. a treaty. —*adj.* having signed such an agreement etc. [L *signatorius* of sealing f. *signare signat-* mark]

signature /'sɪgnətʃə(r)/ *n.* **1 a** a person's name, initials, or mark used in signing a letter, document, etc. **b** the act of signing a document etc. **2** *archaic* a distinctive action, characteristic, etc. **3** *Mus.* **a** = *key signature.* **b** = *time signature.* **4** *Printing* **a** a letter or figure placed at the foot of one or more pages of each sheet of a book as a guide for binding. **b** such a sheet after folding. **5** *US* directions given to a patient as part of a medical prescription. □ **signature tune** esp. *Brit.* a distinctive tune used to introduce a particular programme or performer on television or radio. [med.L *signatura* (LL = marking of sheep), as SIGNATORY]

signboard /'saɪnbɔːd/ *n.* a board with a name or symbol etc. displayed outside a shop or hotel etc.

signet /'sɪgnɪt/ *n.* **1** a seal used instead of or with a signature as authentication. **2** (prec. by *the*) the royal seal formerly used for special purposes in England and Scotland, and in Scotland later as the seal of the Court of Session. □ **signet-ring** a ring with a seal set in it. [ME f. OF *signet* or med.L *signetum* (as SIGN)]

significance /sɪg'nɪfɪkəns/ *n.* **1** importance; noteworthiness (*his opinion is of no significance*). **2** a concealed or real meaning (*what is the significance of his statement?*). **3** the state of being significant. **4** *Statistics* the extent to which a result deviates from a hypothesis such that the difference is due to more than errors in sampling. [OF *significance* or L *significantia* (as SIGNIFY)]

significant /sɪg'nɪfɪkənt/ *adj.* **1** having a meaning; indicative. **2** having an unstated or secret meaning; suggestive (*refused it with a significant gesture*). **3** noteworthy; important; consequential (*a significant figure in history*). **4** *Statistics* of or relating to the significance in the difference between an observed and calculated result. □ **significant figure** *Math.* a digit conveying information about a number containing it, and not a zero used simply to fill vacant space at the beginning or end. □□ **significantly** *adv.* [L *significare*: see SIGNIFY]

signification /,sɪgnɪfɪ'keɪʃ(ə)n/ *n.* **1** the act of signifying. **2** (usu. foll. by *of*) exact meaning or sense, esp. of a word or phrase. [ME f. OF f. L *significatio -onis* (as SIGNIFY)]

significative /sɪg'nɪfɪkətɪv/ *adj.* **1** (esp. of a symbol etc.) signifying. **2** having a meaning. **3** (usu. foll. by *of*) serving as a sign or evidence. [ME f. OF *significatif -ive*, or LL *significativus* (as SIGNIFY)]

signify /'sɪgnɪ,faɪ/ *v.* (**-ies, -ied**) **1** *tr.* be a sign or indication of (*a yawn signifies boredom*). **2** *tr.* mean; have as its meaning (*'Dr' signifies 'doctor'*). **3** *tr.* communicate; make known (*signified their agreement*). **4** *intr.* be of importance; matter (*it signifies little*). □□ **signifier** *n.* [ME f. OF *signifier* f. L *significare* (as SIGN)]

signing /'saɪnɪŋ/ *n.* a person who has signed a contract, esp. to join a professional sports team.

signor /'siːnjɔː(r)/ *n.* (*pl.* **signori** /-'njɔːriː/) **1** a title or form of address used of or to an Italian-speaking man, corresponding to Mr or sir. **2** an Italian man. [It. f. L *senior*: see SENIOR]

signora /siːˈnjɔːrə/ n. **1** a title or form of address used of or to an Italian-speaking married woman, corresponding to Mrs or madam. **2** a married Italian woman. [It., fem. of SIGNOR]

signorina /ˌsiːnjəˈriːnə/ n. **1** a title or form of address used of or to an Italian-speaking unmarried woman. **2** an Italian unmarried woman. [It., dimin. of SIGNORA]

signory /ˈsiːnjərɪ/ n. (pl. **-ies**) **1** = SEIGNIORY. **2** hist. the governing body of a medieval Italian republic. [ME f. OF s(e)ignorie (as SEIGNEUR)]

signpost /ˈsaɪnpəʊst/ n. & v. —n. **1** a sign on posts erected at a crossroads or road junction, roundabout, etc., indicating the direction to and sometimes also the distance from various places. **2** a means of guidance; an indication. —v.tr. **1** provide with a signpost or signposts. **2** indicate (a course of action, direction, etc.).

sika /ˈsiːkə/ n. a small forest-dwelling deer, Cervus nippon, native to Japan. [Jap. shika]

Sikh /siːk, sɪk/ n. an adherent of Sikhism. There are over 10 million Sikhs, most of whom live in Punjab. □ **Sikh Wars** wars between the Sikhs and the British in 1845 and 1848–9, culminating in the British annexation of the Punjab. [Hindi, = disciple, f. Skr. sishya]

Sikhism /ˈsiːkɪz(ə)m, ˈsɪk-/ n. a monotheistic religion founded in the Punjab in the 15th c. by Guru Nanak. It combines elements of Hinduism and Islam, accepting the Hindu concepts of karma and reincarnation but rejecting the caste system, and has one sacred scripture, the Adi Granth. The tenth and last of the series of gurus, Gobind Singh, prescribed the distinctive outward forms (the so-called five Ks)—long hair (to be covered by a turban) and uncut beard (kesh), comb (kangha), short sword (kirpan), steel bangle (kara), and short trousers for horse-riding (kaccha). Originating as a religion, Sikhism became a militant political movement within the Punjab.

Sikkim /ˈsɪkɪm/ a State of India (since 1975) in the eastern Himalayas, previously an Indian protectorate; pop. (1981) 315,680; capital, Gangtok. □□ **Sikkimese** /-ˈmiːz/ adj. & n.

Sikorsky /sɪˈkɔːskɪ/, Igor Ivan (1889–1972), Russian-born aircraft designer who studied aeronautics in Paris before returning to Russia to build the world's first large four-engined aircraft, the Grand, in 1913. After experimenting unsuccessfully with helicopters he emigrated to New York (1919), where he established the Sikorski Aero Engineering Co. (1923) and produced many famous amphibious aircraft and flying boats. In the 1930s he again turned his attention to helicopters and personally flew the prototype of the world's first mass-produced helicopter in 1939; his name is closely associated with their subsequent development.

silage /ˈsaɪlɪdʒ/ n. & v. —n. **1** storage in a silo. **2** green fodder that has been stored in a silo. —v.tr. put into a silo. [alt. of ENSILAGE after silo]

sild /sɪlt/ n. a small immature herring, esp. one caught in N. European seas. [Da. & Norw.]

silence /ˈsaɪləns/ n. & v. —n. **1** absence of sound. **2** abstinence from speech or noise. **3** the avoidance of mentioning a thing, betraying a secret, etc. **4** oblivion; the state of not being mentioned. —v.tr. make silent, esp. by coercion or superior argument. □ **in silence** without speech or other sound. **reduce (or put) to silence** refute in argument. [ME f. OF f. L silentium (as SILENT)]

silencer /ˈsaɪlənsə(r)/ n. any of various devices for reducing the noise emitted by the exhaust of a motor vehicle, a gun, etc.

silent /ˈsaɪlənt/ adj. **1** not speaking; not uttering or making or accompanied by any sound. **2** (of a letter) written but not pronounced, e.g. b in doubt. **3** (of a film) without a synchronized soundtrack. **4** (of a person) taciturn; speaking little. **5** saying or recording nothing on some subject (the records are silent on the incident). **6** (of spirits) unflavoured. □ **silent majority** those of moderate opinions who rarely assert them. **silent partner** US = sleeping partner (see SLEEP). □□ **silently** adv. [L silēre silent- be silent]

Silenus /saɪˈliːnəs/ Gk Mythol. one of the sileni (see SILENUS) with many weaknesses but also with intellectual talents, who was

entrusted with the education of Dionysus. He is depicted either as dignified, inspired, and musical, or as an old drunkard. Portraits of Socrates and idealized heads of Silenus show great similarity.

silenus /saɪˈliːnəs/ n. (pl. **sileni** /-naɪ/) Gk Mythol. any of a class of woodland spirits, usually shown in art as old and with horse-ears, similar to the satyrs. [L f. Gk seilēnos]

Silesia /saɪˈliːzjə/ a region of central Europe (now largely in SW Poland), an ancient district and duchy, partitioned at various times between the States of Prussia, Austria-Hungary, Poland, and Czechoslovakia. □□ **Silesian** adj. & n.

silex /ˈsaɪleks/ n. a kind of glass made of fused quartz. [L (as SILICA)]

silhouette /ˌsɪluːˈet/ n. & v. —n. **1** a representation of a person or thing showing the outline only, usu. done in solid black on white or cut from paper. (See below.) **2** the dark shadow or outline of a person or thing against a lighter background. —v.tr. represent or (usu. in passive) show in silhouette. □ **in silhouette** seen or placed in outline. [Étienne de Silhouette, Fr. author and politician (d. 1767), amateur maker of paper cut-outs]

The method of silhouette painting is seen in Egyptian and Greek art, but its main vogue was from the mid-18th c. to mid-19th c., when such portraiture was popularized by neoclassical taste until the introduction of photography relegated it to a position of curiosity value.

silica /ˈsɪlɪkə/ n. silicon dioxide, occurring as quartz etc. and as a principal constituent of sandstone and other rocks. □ **silica gel** hydrated silica in a hard granular form used as a desiccant. □□ **siliceous** /-ˈlɪʃəs/ adj. (also **silicious**). **silicic** /-ˈlɪsɪk/ adj. **silicify** /-ˈlɪsɪˌfaɪ/ v.tr. & intr. (**-ies**, **-ied**) **silicification** /-sɪfɪˈkeɪʃ(ə)n/ n. [L silex -icis flint, after alumina etc.]

silicate /ˈsɪlɪˌkeɪt/ n. any of the many insoluble compounds of a metal combined with silicon and oxygen, occurring widely in the rocks of the earth's crust.

silicon /ˈsɪlɪkən/ n. Chem. a non-metallic element occurring widely in silica and silicates, the most abundant element in the earth's crust after oxygen. ¶ Symb.: **Si**; atomic number 14. □ **silicon chip** a silicon microchip. **silicon carbide** = CARBORUNDUM. **Silicon Valley** an area with a high concentration of electronics industries, esp. the Santa Clara valley south-east of San Francisco. [L silex -icis flint (after carbon, boron), alt. of earlier silicium]

Silicon was first isolated and described as an element by Berzelius in 1823. It does not occur uncombined in nature, but most rocks of the earth's crust consist primarily of silica or silicates. Pure silicon, which can exist in a dark-grey crystalline form or as an amorphous powder, is used in some alloys and (as a semiconductor) as the basis of many microelectronic devices, where it has largely replaced the chemically similar element germanium (which was used for the first transistors). Silicon compounds have for centuries been widely used: glass, pottery, and bricks are largely composed of silicate minerals.

silicone /ˈsɪlɪˌkəʊn/ n. any of the many polymeric organic compounds of silicon and oxygen with high resistance to cold, heat, water, and the passage of electricity, used in polishes, paints, lubricants, etc.

silicosis /ˌsɪlɪˈkəʊsɪs/ n. lung fibrosis caused by the inhalation of dust containing silica. □□ **silicotic** /-ˈkɒtɪk/ adj.

siliqua /ˈsɪlɪkwə/ n. (also **silique** /sɪˈliːk/) (pl. **siliquae** /-kwiː/ or **siliques** /sɪˈliːks/) the long narrow seed-pod of a cruciferous plant. □□ **siliquose** /-ˌkwəʊs/ adj. **siliquous** /-kwəs/ adj. [L, = pod]

silk /sɪlk/ n. **1** a fine strong soft lustrous fibre produced by silkworms in making cocoons. **2** a similar fibre spun by some spiders etc. **3 a** thread or cloth made from silk fibre. **b** a thread or fabric resembling silk. **4** (in pl.) kinds of silk cloth or garments made from it, esp. as worn by a jockey in a horse-owner's colours. **5** Brit. colloq. Queen's (or King's) Counsel, as having the right to wear a silk gown. **6** (attrib.) made of silk (silk blouse). **7** the silky styles of the female maize-flower. □ **silk cotton** kapok or a similar substance. **silk-fowl** a breed of fowl with a silky plumage. **silk-gland** a gland secreting the substance produced as silk. **silk hat** a tall cylindrical hat covered with silk plush. **silk moth** any of various large moths of the family Saturniidae, esp. *Hyalophora cecropia*. **silk-screen printing** = *screen printing*. **take silk** *Brit.* become a Queen's (or King's) Counsel. □□ **silklike** *adj.* [OE *sioloc*, *seolec* (cf. ON *silki*) f. LL *sericum* neut. of L *sericus* f. *seres* f. Gk *Sēres* an oriental people]

silken /'sɪlkən/ *adj.* **1** made of silk. **2** wearing silk. **3** soft or lustrous as silk. **4** (of a person's manner etc.) suave or insinuating. [OE *seolcen* (as SILK)]

Silk Road (also **Silk Route**) an ancient caravan route linking China with the West, used from Roman times onwards and taking its name from the silk which was a major Chinese export. By this route also Christianity and (from India) Buddhism reached China. A 'North Road' skirted the northern edge of the Taklimakan Desert before heading westwards into Turkestan (and thence to the Levant), while a 'South Road' followed a more southerly route through the high passes of the Kunlun and Pamir mountains into India. A railway (completed in 1963) follows the northern route from Xian to Urumchi.

silkworm /'sɪlkwɜːm/ *n.* the caterpillar of the moth *Bombyx mori*, which spins its cocoon of silk.

silky /'sɪlkɪ/ *adj.* (**silkier, silkiest**) **1** like silk in smoothness, softness, fineness, or lustre. **2** (of a person's manner etc.) suave, insinuating. □□ **silkily** *adv.* **silkiness** *n.*

sill /sɪl/ *n.* (also **cill**) **1** a shelf or slab of stone, wood, or metal at the foot of a window or doorway. **2** a horizontal timber at the bottom of a dock or lock entrance, against which the gates close. **3** *Geol.* a tabular sheet of igneous rock intruded between other rocks and parallel with their planar structure. [OE *syll*, *sylle*]

sillabub var. of SYLLABUB.

sillimanite /'sɪlɪməˌnaɪt/ *n.* an aluminium silicate occurring in orthorhombic crystals or fibrous masses. [B. *Silliman*, Amer. chemist d. 1864]

Sillitoe /'sɪlɪˌtəʊ/, Alan (1928–), English writer of novels, poems, short stories, and plays. His much-praised first novel *Saturday Night and Sunday Morning* (1958) describes the life of a dissatisfied young nottingham factory worker. His other works include *The Loneliness of the Long-Distance Runner* (1959), portraying a rebellious and anarchic Borstal boy, and the semi-autobiographical *Raw Material* (1972), a vivid evocation of his own family background and of working-class attitudes to the First World War and the Depression.

silly /'sɪlɪ/ *adj.* & *n.* —*adj.* (**sillier, silliest**) **1** lacking sense; foolish, imprudent, unwise. **2** weak-minded. **3** *Cricket* (of a fielder or position) very close to the batsman (*silly mid-off*). **4** *archaic* innocent, simple, helpless. —*n.* (*pl.* **-ies**) *colloq.* a foolish person. □ **silly billy** *colloq.* a foolish person. **the silly season** high summer as the season when newspapers often publish trivial material for lack of important news. □□ **sillily** *adv.* **silliness** *n.* [later form of ME *sely* (dial. *seely*) happy, repr. OE *sǣlig* (recorded in *unsǣlig* unhappy) f. Gmc]

silo /'saɪləʊ/ *n.* & *v.* —*n.* (*pl.* **-os**) **1** a pit or airtight structure in which green crops are pressed and kept for fodder, undergoing fermentation. **2** a pit or tower for the storage of grain, cement, etc. **3** an underground chamber in which a guided missile is kept ready for firing. —*v.tr.* (**-oes, -oed**) make silage of. [Sp. f. L *sirus* f. Gk *siros* corn-pit]

Siloam /saɪˈləʊəm/ a spring and pool of water near ancient Jerusalem, where the man born blind was bidden to wash (John 9: 7).

silt /sɪlt/ *n.* & *v.* —*n.* sediment deposited by water in a channel, harbour, etc. —*v.tr.* & *intr.* (often foll. by *up*) choke or be choked with silt. □□ **siltation** /-'teɪʃ(ə)n/ *n.* **silty** *adj.* [ME, perh. rel. to Da., Norw. *sylt*, OLG *sulta*, OHG *sulza* salt marsh, formed as SALT]

siltstone /'sɪltstəʊn/ *n.* rock of consolidated silt.

Silurian /saɪˈljʊərɪən/ *adj.* & *n.* *Geol.* —*adj.* of or relating to the third period of the Palaeozoic era, following the Ordovician and preceding the Devonian, lasting from about 438 to 408 million years ago. The first land plants and the first true fish (with jaws) appeared during this period. —*n.* this period or system. [L *Silures*, a people of ancient SE Wales]

silva var. of SYLVA.

silvan var. of SYLVAN.

silver /'sɪlvə(r)/ *n.*, *adj.*, & *v.* —*n.* *Chem.* **1** a greyish-white lustrous malleable ductile precious metallic element. (See below.) ¶ Symb.: **Ag**; atomic number 47. **2** the colour of silver. **3** silver or cupro-nickel coins. **4** esp. *Sc.* money. **5** silver vessels or implements, esp. cutlery. **6** household cutlery of any material. **7** = *silver medal*. —*adj.* **1** made wholly or chiefly of silver. **2** coloured like silver. —*v.* **1** *tr.* coat or plate with silver. **2** *tr.* provide (a mirror-glass) with a backing of tin amalgam etc. **3** *tr.* (of the moon or a white light) give a silvery appearance to. **4 a** *tr.* turn (the hair) grey or white. **b** *intr.* (of the hair) turn grey or white. □ **silver age** a period regarded as inferior to a golden age, e.g. that of post-classical Latin literature in the early Imperial period. **silver band** *Brit.* a band playing silver-plated instruments. **silver birch** a common birch, *Betula alba*, with silver-coloured bark. **silver fir** any fir of the genus *Abies*, with the under-sides of its leaves coloured silver. **silver fox 1** an American red fox at a time when its fur is black with white tips. **2** its fur. **silver gilt 1** gilded silver. **2** an imitation gilding of yellow lacquer over silver leaf. **silver-grey** a lustrous grey. **silver jubilee 1** the 25th anniversary of a sovereign's accession. **2** any other 25th anniversary. **silver Latin** see LATIN. **silver-leaf** a fungal disease of fruit trees. **silver lining** a consolation or hopeful feature in misfortune. **silver medal** a medal of silver, usu. awarded as second prize. **silver nitrate** a colourless solid that is soluble in water and formerly used in photography. **silver paper 1** a fine white tissue-paper for wrapping silver. **2** aluminium or tin foil. **silver plate** vessels, spoons, etc., of copper etc. plated with silver. **silver salmon** a coho. **silver sand** a fine pure sand used in gardening. **silver screen** (usu. prec. by *the*) motion pictures collectively. **silver solder** solder containing silver. **silver spoon** a sign of future prosperity. **silver standard** a system by which the value of a currency is defined in terms of silver, for which the currency may be exchanged. **silver thaw** a glassy coating of ice formed on the ground or an exposed surface, caused by freezing rain or a sudden light frost. **silver tongue** eloquence. **silver wedding** the 25th anniversary of a wedding. **silver weed** a plant with silvery leaves, esp. a potentilla, *Potentilla anserina*, with silver-coloured leaves. [OE *seolfor* f. Gmc]

Silver is found in the uncombined state in nature as well as in a number of ores. It has been used for jewellery and other ornaments since ancient times and it is also used in coins, cutlery, the coatings of mirrors, and dental amalgams; a further use is in printed circuits, as silver is a very good electrical conductor. The metal is generally resistant to corrosion but tarnishes in air through a reaction with small quantities of hydrogen sulphide gas. Silver salts are used in photographic films as they decompose when exposed to light, depositing metallic silver.

silverfish /'sɪlvəfɪʃ/ *n.* (*pl.* same or **-fishes**) **1** any small silvery wingless insect of the order Thysanura, esp. *Lepisma saccharina* in houses and other buildings. **2** a silver-coloured fish, esp. a colourless variety of goldfish.

silvern /'sɪlv(ə)n/ *adj.* *archaic* or *poet.* = SILVER *adj.* [OE *seolfren*, *silfren* (as SILVER)]

silver-point *n.* the process (now largely obsolete) of drawing with a silver-pointed instrument on paper coated with a special ground of powdered bone or zinc white. Fragments of metal deposited on the paper produce a very delicate fine line that does not smudge and cannot be erased. It was widely used in the 15th and 16th c. in Italy, The Netherlands, and Germany. Points of other metals, such as lead, were also used.

silverside /'sɪlvəˌsaɪd/ *n.* *Brit.* the upper side of a round of beef from the outside of the leg.

silversmith /'sɪlvəsmɪθ/ *n.* a worker in silver; a manufacturer of silver articles. □□ **silversmithing** *n.*

Silverstone /'sɪlvəˌstəʊn/ a motor-racing circuit near Towcester in Northamptonshire, built on a disused airfield after the Second World War.

silverware /'sɪlvəˌweə(r)/ *n.* articles made of or coated with silver.

silvery /ˈsɪlvəri/ adj. **1** like silver in colour or appearance. **2** having a clear gentle ringing sound. **3** (of the hair) white and lustrous. □□ **silveriness** n.

silviculture /ˈsɪlvɪˌkʌltʃə(r)/ n. (also **sylviculture**) the growing and tending of trees as a branch of forestry. □□ **silvicultural** /-ˈkʌltʃər(ə)l/ adj. **silviculturist** /-ˈkʌltʃərɪst/ n. [F f. L silva a wood + F culture CULTURE]

sima /ˈsaɪmə/ n. the continuous basal layer of the earth's crust, composed of relatively heavy basic rocks rich in silica and magnesia, that underlies the sial of the continental masses and forms the crust under the oceans; the material of which it is composed. The lower limit of the sima is generally taken to be the Mohorovičić discontinuity. [SILICON + MAGNESIUM]

Simenon /ˈsiːməˌnɔ̃/, Georges (1903–89), Belgian-French novelist, a prolific writer, who produced some 300 works between 1920 and 1973. His popularity rests on the series of detective novels featuring Commissaire Maigret, introduced in 1931, who sets out to discover, with great insight and sensitivity to local atmosphere, the human motives behind the crime.

Simeon /ˈsɪmɪən/ **1** Hebrew patriarch, son of Jacob and Leah (Gen. 29: 33). **2** the tribe of Israel traditionally descended from him.

Simeon Stylites /ˈsɪmɪən staɪˈlaɪtiːz/, St (c.390–459) a hermit in northern Syria, the first ascetic to live on top of a pillar (Gk stulos). The pillar eventually reached 40 cubits (c.20 m) in height. This novel form of austerity attracted many pilgrims and imitators in the East.

simian /ˈsɪmɪən/ adj. & n. —adj. **1** of or concerning the anthropoid apes. **2** like an ape or monkey (a simian walk). —n. an ape or monkey. [L simia ape, perh. f. L simus f. Gk simos flat-nosed]

similar /ˈsɪmɪlə(r)/ adj. **1** like, alike. **2** (often foll. by to) having a resemblance. **3** of the same kind, nature, or amount. **4** Geom. shaped alike. □□ **similarity** /-ˈlærɪti/ n. (pl. **-ies**). **similarly** adv. [F similaire or med.L similaris f. L similis like]

simile /ˈsɪmɪli/ n. **1** a figure of speech involving the comparison of one thing with another of a different kind, as an illustration or ornament (e.g. as brave as a lion). **2** the use of such comparison. [ME f. L, neut. of similis like]

similitude /sɪˈmɪlɪˌtjuːd/ n. **1** the likeness, guise, or outward appearance of a thing or person. **2** a comparison or the expression of a comparison. **3** archaic a counterpart or facsimile. [ME f. OF similitude or L similitudo (as SIMILE)]

simmer /ˈsɪmə(r)/ v. & n. —v. **1** intr. & tr. be or keep bubbling or boiling gently. **2** intr. be in a state of suppressed anger or excitement. —n. a simmering condition. □ **simmer down** become calm or less agitated. [alt. of ME (now dial.) simper, perh. imit.]

Simnel /ˈsɪmn(ə)l/, Lambert (c.1475–1525), the son of an Irish baker, trained by Yorkists to impersonate the Earl of Warwick in an attempt to overthrow Henry VII. He was crowned in Dublin in 1487 as Edward VI but captured in the Yorkist uprising when the rebels were defeated at Stoke-on-Trent. As there was no real danger of his being taken to be the real Warwick (who was imprisoned in the Tower), he was not executed, but was given a menial post in the royal household.

simnel cake /ˈsɪmn(ə)l/ n. Brit. a rich fruit cake, usu. with a marzipan layer and decoration, eaten esp. at Easter or during Lent. [ME f. OF simenel, ult. f. L simila or Gk semidalis fine flour]

Simon[1] /ˈsaɪmən/, (Marvin) Neil (1927–), American playwright, most of whose plays are wry comedies portraying aspects of middle-class life. They include Barefoot in the Park (1963), The Odd Couple (1965), and The Sunshine Boys (1972). He also wrote the musicals Sweet Charity (1966) and They're Playing Our Song (1978).

Simon[2] /ˈsaɪmən/, St (1st c. AD), one of the twelve Apostles, who may have been a member of the Zealots. According to one tradition he preached and was martyred in Persia along with St Jude. Feast day (with St Jude), 28 Oct.

Simonides /saɪˈmɒnɪˌdiːz/ (c.556–468 BC) Greek lyric and elegiac poet, admired for his sweet and harmonious style. He wrote for the ruling men in Athens, Thessaly, and Syracuse, and composed verse inscriptions for the fallen of Marathon and for the Spartans who died at Thermopylae.

simon-pure /ˌsaɪmənˈpjʊə(r)/ adj. real, genuine. [(the real) Simon Pure, a character in Centlivre's Bold Stroke for a Wife (1717)]

simony /ˈsaɪmənɪ, ˈsɪm-/ n. the buying or selling of ecclesiastical privileges, e.g. pardons or benefices. □□ **simoniac** /-ˈməʊnɪˌæk/ adj. & n. **simoniacal** /-ˈnaɪək(ə)l/ adj. [ME f. OF simonie f. LL simonia f. Simon Magus (Acts 8: 18), with allusion to his offer of money to the Apostles to purchase the power of giving the Holy Ghost by the laying on of hands)]

simoom /sɪˈmuːm/ n. (also **simoon** /-muːn/) a hot dry dust-laden wind blowing at intervals esp. in the Arabian desert. [Arab. samūm f. samma to poison]

simp /sɪmp/ n. US colloq. a simpleton. [abbr.]

simpatico /sɪmˈpætɪˌkəʊ/ adj. congenial, likeable. [It. & Sp. (as SYMPATHY)]

simper /ˈsɪmpə(r)/ v. & n. —v. **1** intr. smile in a silly or affected way. **2** tr. express by or with simpering. —n. such a smile. □□ **simperingly** adv. [16th c.: cf. Du. and Scand. semper, simper, G zimp(f)er elegant, delicate]

simple /ˈsɪmp(ə)l/ adj. & n. —adj. **1** easily understood or done; presenting no difficulty (a simple explanation; a simple task). **2** not complicated or elaborate; without luxury or sophistication. **3** not compound; consisting of or involving only one element or operation etc. **4** absolute, unqualified, straightforward (the simple truth; a simple majority). **5** foolish or ignorant; gullible, feeble-minded (am not so simple as to agree to that). **6** plain in appearance or manner; unsophisticated, ingenuous, artless. **7** of low rank; humble, insignificant (simple people). **8** Bot. **a** consisting of one part. **b** (of fruit) formed from one pistil. —n. archaic **1** a herb used medicinally. **2** a medicine made from it. □ **simple eye** an eye of an insect, having only one lens. **simple fracture** a fracture of the bone only, without a skin wound. **simple harmonic motion** see HARMONIC. **simple interest** interest payable on a capital sum only (cf. compound interest (see COMPOUND)). **simple interval** Mus. an interval of one octave or less. **simple machine** any of the basic mechanical devices for applying a force (e.g. an inclined plane, wedge, or lever). **simple sentence** a sentence with a single subject and predicate. **Simple Simon** a foolish person (from the nursery-rhyme character). **simple time** Mus. a time with two, three, or four beats in a bar. □□ **simpleness** n. [ME f. OF f. L simplus]

simple-minded /ˌsɪmp(ə)lˈmaɪndɪd/ adj. **1** natural, unsophisticated. **2** feeble-minded. □□ **simple-mindedly** adv. **simple-mindedness** n.

simpleton /ˈsɪmp(ə)lt(ə)n/ n. a foolish, gullible, or halfwitted person. [SIMPLE after surnames f. place-names in -ton]

simplex /ˈsɪmpleks/ adj. & n. —adj. **1** simple; not compounded. **2** Computing (of a circuit) allowing transmission of signals in one direction only. —n. a simple or uncompounded thing, esp. a word. [L, = single, var. of simplus simple]

simplicity /sɪmˈplɪsɪtɪ/ n. the fact or condition of being simple. □ **be simplicity itself** be extremely easy. [OF simplicité or L simplicitas (as SIMPLEX)]

simplify /ˈsɪmplɪˌfaɪ/ v.tr. (**-ies**, **-ied**) make simple; make easy or easier to do or understand. □□ **simplification** /-fɪˈkeɪʃ(ə)n/ n. [F simplifier f. med.L simplificare (as SIMPLE)]

simplism /ˈsɪmplɪz(ə)m/ n. **1** affected simplicity. **2** the unjustifiable simplification of a problem etc.

simplistic /sɪmˈplɪstɪk/ adj. **1** excessively or affectedly simple. **2** oversimplified so as to conceal or distort difficulties. □□ **simplistically** adv.

Simplon /ˈsæplɔ̃/ a pass in the Alps in southern Switzerland reaching an altitude of 2,028 m (6,591 ft.). The nearby railway tunnel connecting Switzerland and Italy is the longest main-line railway tunnel in the world (19 km, 12 miles).

simply /ˈsɪmplɪ/ adv. **1** in a simple manner. **2** absolutely; without doubt (simply astonishing). **3** merely (was simply trying to please).

Simpson[1] /ˈsɪmps(ə)n/, Sir James Young (1811–71), Scottish surgeon and obstetrician who discovered the usefulness of chloroform as an anaesthetic by experimentation on himself and his colleagues shortly after the first use of ether. He was active in the debate over which of the two was the best agent to use in surgery, and made a famous attack on Lister and antisepsis. Simpson was also a distinguished antiquarian and historian, publishing monographs on archaeology and the history of medicine.

Simpson[2] /ˈsɪmps(ə)n/, Wallis (born Wallis Warfield, 1896–1986; later Duchess of Windsor), see EDWARD VIII.

Simpson Desert /ˈsɪmps(ə)n/ a desert in central Australia, situated between Alice Springs and the Channel Country to the east. It was named in 1929 after A. A. Simpson, who was President of the Royal Geographical Society of Australia at that time.

simulacrum /ˌsɪmjʊˈleɪkrəm/ n. (pl. **simulacra** /-krə/) **1** an image of something. **2 a** a shadowy likeness; a deceptive substitute. **b** mere pretence. [L (as SIMULATE)]

simulate /ˈsɪmjʊˌleɪt/ v.tr. **1 a** pretend to have or feel (an attribute or feeling). **b** pretend to be. **2** imitate or counterfeit. **3 a** imitate the conditions of (a situation etc.), e.g. for training. **b** produce a computer model of (a process). **4** (as **simulated** adj.) made to resemble the real thing but not genuinely such (*simulated fur*). **5** (of a word) take or have an altered form suggested by (a word wrongly taken to be its source, e.g. *amuck*). □□ **simulation** /-ˈleɪʃ(ə)n/ n. **simulative** /-lətɪv/ adj. [L *simulare* f. *similis* like]

simulator /ˈsɪmjʊˌleɪtə(r)/ n. **1** a person or thing that simulates. **2** a device designed to simulate the operations of a complex system, used esp. in training.

simulcast /ˈsɪmlˌkɑːst/ n. simultaneous transmission of the same programme on radio and television. [SIMULTANEOUS + BROADCAST]

simultaneous /ˌsɪmlˈteɪnɪəs/ adj. (often foll. by *with*) occurring or operating at the same time. □ **simultaneous equations** equations involving two or more unknowns that are to have the same values in each equation. □□ **simultaneity** /-təˈneɪɪtɪ/ n. **simultaneously** adv. **simultaneousness** n. [med.L *simultaneus* f. L *simul* at the same time, prob. after *instantaneus* etc.]

simurg /sɪˈmɜːɡ/ n. a monstrous bird of Persian myth, with the power of reasoning and speech. [Pers. *sīmurĝ* f. Pahlavi *sīn* eagle + *murĝ* bird]

sin[1] /sɪn/ n. & v. —n. **1 a** the breaking of divine or moral law, esp. by a conscious act. **b** such an act. **2** an offence against good taste or propriety etc. —v. (**sinned**, **sinning**) **1** intr. commit a sin. **2** intr. (foll. by *against*) offend. **3** tr. archaic commit (a sin). □ **as sin** colloq. extremely (*ugly as sin*). **for one's sins** joc. as a judgement on one for something or other. **like sin** colloq. vehemently or forcefully. **live in sin** colloq. live together without being married. **sin bin** colloq. **1** Ice Hockey a penalty box. **2** a place set aside for offenders of various kinds. □□ **sinless** adj. **sinlessly** adv. **sinlessness** n. [OE *syn(n)*]

sin[2] /saɪn/ abbr. sine.

Sinai /ˈsaɪnaɪ, -nɪaɪ/ a peninsula, mostly desert, at the north end of the Red Sea, now part of Egypt. In the south is Mount Sinai where according to Exod. 19–34 the Ten Commandments and the Tables of the Law were given to Moses. □□ **Sinaitic** /-ˈɪtɪk/ adj.

Sinaloa /ˌsiːnəˈləʊə/ a State of western Mexico; pop. (est. 1988) 2,367,600; capital, Culiacán Rosales.

Sinanthropus /sɪnˈænθrəpəs/ n. the name formerly applied to a genus of fossil hominids now classified as a species of *Homo erectus*. (See PEKING MAN.) [mod.L, as SINO- Chinese (remains having been found near Peking) + Gk *anthrōpos* man]

Sinatra /sɪˈnɑːtrə/, Francis Albert ('Frank') (1915–   ), American singer and film actor, whose career spanned more than forty years. His films include *From Here to Eternity* (1953), for which he won an Academy Award. His many successful songs include 'Night and Day' and later 'My Way'.

since /sɪns/ prep., conj., & adv. —prep. throughout, or at a point in, the period between (a specified time, event, etc.) and the time present or being considered (*must have happened since yesterday; has been going on since June; the greatest composer since Beethoven*). —conj. **1** during or in the time after (*what have you been doing since we met?; has not spoken since the dog died*). **2** for the reason that, because; inasmuch as (*since you are drunk I will drive you home*). **3** (ellipt.) as being (*a more useful, since better designed, tool*). —adv. **1** from that time or event until now or the time being considered (*have not seen them since; had been healthy ever since; has since been cut down*). **2** ago (*happened many years since*). [ME, reduced form of obs. *sithence* or f. dial. *sin* (f. *sithen*) f. OE *siththon*]

sincere /sɪnˈsɪə(r)/ adj. (**sincerer**, **sincerest**) **1** free from pretence or deceit; the same in reality as in appearance. **2** genuine, honest, frank. □□ **sincereness** n. **sincerity** /-ˈserɪtɪ/ n. [L *sincerus* clean, pure]

sincerely /sɪnˈsɪəlɪ/ adv. in a sincere manner. □ **yours sincerely** a formula for ending an informal letter.

sinciput /ˈsɪnsɪˌpʌt/ n. Anat. the front of the skull from the forehead to the crown. □□ **sincipital** /-ˈsɪpɪt(ə)l/ adj. [L f. *semi-* half + *caput* head]

Sind /sɪnd/ a province of southern Pakistan, formerly part of British India after its acquisition by Britain in 1843; pop. (1981) 19,029,000; capital, Karachi.

Sindbad /ˈsɪndbæd/ (also **Sinbad the Sailor**) hero of one of the tales in the *Arabian Nights*, who relates his fantastic adventures in a number of voyages.

sindonology /ˌsɪndəˈnɒlədʒɪ/ n. study of the Holy Shroud of Turin, in which the body of Christ was reputedly wrapped. [OF or L f. Gk *sindōn* linen fabric, shroud + -LOGY]

sine /saɪn/ n. Math. **1** the trigonometric function that is equal to the ratio of the side opposite a given angle (in a right-angled triangle) to the hypotenuse. **2** a function of the line drawn from one end of an arc perpendicularly to the radius through the other. □ **sine curve** (or **wave**) a curve representing periodic oscillations of constant amplitude as given by a sine function: also called SINUSOID. [L *sinus* curve, fold of a toga, used in med.L as transl. of Arab. *jayb* bosom, sine]

sinecure /ˈsaɪnɪˌkjʊə(r), ˈsɪn-/ n. a position that requires little or no work but usu. yields profit or honour. □□ **sinecurism** n. **sinecurist** n. [L *sine cura* without care]

sine die /ˌsaɪnɪ ˈdaɪiː, ˌsɪneɪ ˈdiːeɪ/ adv. (of business adjourned indefinitely) with no appointed date. [L, = without day]

sine qua non /ˌsaɪneɪ kwɑː ˈnɒn/ n. an indispensable condition or qualification. [L, = without which not]

sinew /ˈsɪnjuː/ n. & v. —n. **1** tough fibrous tissue uniting muscle to bone; a tendon. **2** (in pl.) muscles; bodily strength; wiriness. **3** (in pl.) that which forms the strength or framework of a plan, city, organization, etc. —v.tr. poet. serve as the sinews of; sustain; hold together. □ **the sinews of war** money. □□ **sinewless** adj. **sinewy** adj. [OE *sin(e)we* f. Gmc]

sinfonia /ˌsɪnfəˈnɪə, sɪnˈfəʊnɪə/ n. Mus. **1** a symphony. **2** (in Baroque music) an orchestral piece used as an introduction to an opera, cantata, or suite. **3** (**Sinfonia**; usu. in names) a small symphony orchestra. [It., = SYMPHONY]

sinfonietta /ˌsɪnfəˈnjetə/ n. Mus. **1** a short or simple symphony. **2** (**Sinfonietta**; usu. in names) a small symphony orchestra. [It., dimin. of *sinfonia*: see SINFONIA]

sinful /ˈsɪnfʊl/ adj. **1** (of a person) committing sin, esp. habitually. **2** (of an act) involving or characterized by sin. □□ **sinfully** adv. **sinfulness** n. [OE *synfull* (as SIN, -FUL)]

sing /sɪŋ/ v. & n. —v. (past **sang** /sæŋ/; past part. **sung** /sʌŋ/) **1** intr. utter musical sounds with the voice, esp. words with a set tune. **2** tr. utter or produce by singing (*sing another song*). **3** intr. (of the wind, a kettle, etc.) make inarticulate melodious or humming, buzzing, or whistling sounds. **4** intr. (of the ears) be affected as with a buzzing sound. **5** intr. sl. turn informer; confess. **6** intr. archaic compose poetry. **7** tr. & (foll. by *of*) intr. celebrate in verse. **8** tr. (foll. by *in, out*) usher (esp. the new or old year) in or out with singing. **9** tr. bring to a specified state by singing (*sang the child to sleep*). —n. **1** an act or spell of singing. **2** US a meeting for amateur singing. □ **sing-along** a tune etc. to which one can sing in accompaniment. **singing hinny** see HINNY[2]. **singing saw** = *musical saw*. **sing out** call out loudly; shout. **sing the praises of** see PRAISE. **sing up** sing more loudly. □□ **singable** adj. **singer** n. **singingly** adv. [OE *singan* f. Gmc]

sing. abbr. singular.

Singapore /ˌsɪŋgəˈpɔ:(r)/ a country in SE Asia, a member State of the Commonwealth, consisting of the island of Singapore and about 54 smaller islands, lying just north of the equator off the southern tip of the Malay Peninsula to which it is linked by a causeway carrying a road and railway; pop. (est. 1988) 2,645,400; official languages, Malay, Chinese, Tamil, and English. Sir Stamford Raffles established a trading post under the East India Company in 1819, and it was incorporated with Penang and Malacca to form the Straits Settlements in 1826; these became a Crown Colony in the following year. Singapore rapidly grew, by virtue of its large protected harbour, to become the most important commercial centre and naval base in SE Asia. It fell to the Japanese in 1942, and after liberation became first a British Crown Colony in 1946 and then a self-governing State in 1959. Federated with Malaysia in 1963, it regained full independence two years later and remains a world trade and financial centre; it also has an important oil-refining industry. □□ **Singaporean** /-ˈpɔ:rɪən/ adj. & n.

singe /sɪndʒ/ v. & n. —v. (**singeing**) **1** tr. & intr. burn superficially or lightly. **2** tr. burn the bristles or down off (the carcass of a pig or fowl) to prepare it for cooking. **3** tr. burn off the tips of (the hair) in hairdressing. —n. a superficial burn. □ **singe one's wings** suffer some harm esp. in a risky attempt. [OE sencgan f. WG]

Singer[1] /ˈsɪŋə(r)/, Isaac Bashevis (1904–), Polish-born American author of short stories and novels, written in Yiddish, whose work portrays with colourful intensity and much realistic detail the lives of Polish Jews of many periods of Poland's history. He was awarded a Nobel Prize for literature in 1978.

Singer[2] /ˈsɪŋə(r)/, Isaac Merrit (1811–75), American inventor, who in 1857 designed and built the first commercially successful sewing-machine (see entry).

Singh /sɪŋ/ n. **1** a title adopted by the warrior castes of N. India. **2** a surname adopted by male Sikhs. [Hind. siṅgh f. Skr. siṅhá lion]

Singhalese var. of SINHALESE.

single /ˈsɪŋg(ə)l/ adj., n., & v. —adj. **1** one only, not double or multiple. **2** united or undivided. **3 a** designed or suitable for one person (single room). **b** used or done by one person etc. or one set or pair. **4** one by itself; not one of several (a single tree). **5** regarded separately (every single thing). **6** not married. **7** Brit. (of a ticket) valid for an outward journey only, not for the return. **8** (with neg. or interrog.) even one; not to speak of more (did not see a single person). **9** (of a flower) having only one circle of petals. **10** lonely, unaided. **11** archaic free from duplicity, sincere, consistent, guileless, ingenuous. —n. **1** a single thing, or item in a series. **2** Brit. a single ticket. **3** a short pop record with one piece of music etc. on each side. **4** Cricket a hit for one run. **5** (usu. in pl.) a game with one player on each side. **6** an unmarried person (young singles). **7** sl. US a one-dollar note. —v.tr. (foll. by out) choose as an example or as distinguishable or to serve some purpose. □ **single acrostic** see ACROSTIC. **single-acting** (of an engine etc.) having pressure applied only to one side of the piston. **single-breasted** (of a coat etc.) having only one set of buttons and buttonholes, not overlapping. **single combat** a duel. **single cream** thin cream with a relatively low fat-content. **single cut** (of a file) with grooves cut in one direction only, not crossing. **single-decker** esp. Brit. a bus having only one deck. **single entry** a system of bookkeeping in which each transaction is entered in one account only. **Single European Act** the decree approved by the European Council in Dec. 1985, which came into force on 1 July 1987, with provisions which objective is to make concrete progress towards European unity. **single file** a line of people or things arranged one behind another. **single-handed** adv. **1** without help from another. **2** with one hand. —adj. **1** done etc. single-handed. **2** for one hand. **single-handedly** in a single-handed way. **single-lens reflex** denoting a reflex camera in which a single lens serves the film and the viewfinder. **single-line** with movement of traffic in only one direction at a time. **single parent** a person bringing up a child or children without a partner. **singles bar** a bar for single people seeking company. **single-seater** a vehicle with one seat. **single stick 1** a basket-hilted stick of about a sword's

length. **2** one-handed fencing with this. **single-tree** US = SWINGLETREE. □□ **singleness** n. **singly** adv. [ME f. OF f. L singulus, rel. to simplus SIMPLE]

single-minded /ˌsɪŋg(ə)lˈmaɪndɪd/ adj. having or intent on only one purpose. □□ **single-mindedly** adv. **single-mindedness** n.

singlet /ˈsɪŋglɪt/ n. **1** Brit. a garment worn under or instead of a shirt; a vest. **2** a single unresolvable line in a spectrum. [SINGLE + -ET[1], after doublet, the garment being unlined]

singleton /ˈsɪŋg(ə)lt(ə)n/ n. **1** one card only of a suit, esp. as dealt to a player. **2 a** a single person or thing. **b** an only child. **3** a single child or animal born, not a twin etc. [SINGLE, after simpleton]

Sing Sing /sɪŋ ˈsɪŋ/ a New York State Prison, built in 1825–8 at Ossining village on the Hudson River and formerly notorious for its severe discipline. It is now called Ossining Correctional Facility.

singsong /ˈsɪŋsɒŋ/ adj., n., & v. —adj. uttered with a monotonous rhythm or cadence. —n. **1** a singsong manner. **2** Brit. an informal gathering for singing. —v.intr. & tr. (past and past part. **singsonged**) speak or recite in a singsong manner.

singular /ˈsɪŋgjʊlə(r)/ adj. & n. —adj. **1** unique; much beyond the average; extraordinary. **2** eccentric or strange. **3** Gram. (of a word or form) denoting or referring to a single person or thing. **4** Math. possessing unique properties. **5** single, individual. —n. Gram. **1** a singular word or form. **2** the singular number. □□ **singularly** adv. [ME f. OF singuler f. L singularis (as SINGLE)]

singularity /ˌsɪŋgjʊˈlærɪtɪ/ n. (pl. **-ies**) **1** the state or condition of being singular. **2** an odd trait or peculiarity. **3** Physics & Math. a point at which a function takes an infinite value, esp. in space-time when matter is infinitely dense. [ME f. OF singularité f. LL singularitas (as SINGULAR)]

singularize /ˈsɪŋgjʊləˌraɪz/ v.tr. (also **-ise**) **1** distinguish, individualize. **2** make singular. □□ **singularization** /-ˈzeɪʃ(ə)n/ n.

sinh /ʃaɪn, saɪˈneɪtʃ/ abbr. Math. hyperbolic sine. [sine + hyperbolic]

Sinhalese /ˌsɪnhəˈliːz, ˌsɪnəˈliːz/ n. & adj. (also **Singhalese** /ˌsɪŋg-/) —n. (pl. same) **1** a member of an Aryan people deriving from northern India and forming the majority of the population in Sri Lanka. **2** their language, spoken by 9 million people in Sri Lanka. It is descended from Sanskrit and was brought by settlers from northern India in the 5th c. BC; its alphabet resembles that of the Dravidian languages of southern India. —adj. of or relating to this people or language. [Skr. siṅhalam Sri Lanka (Ceylon) + -ESE]

sinister /ˈsɪnɪstə(r)/ adj. **1** suggestive of evil; looking malignant or villainous. **2** wicked or criminal (a sinister motive). **3** of evil omen. **4** Heraldry of or on the left-hand side of a shield etc. (i.e. to the observer's right). **5** archaic left-hand. □□ **sinisterly** adv. **sinisterness** n. [ME f. OF sinistre or L sinister left]

sinistral /ˈsɪnɪstr(ə)l/ adj. & n. —adj. **1** left-handed. **2** of or on the left. **3** (of a flat-fish) with the left side uppermost. **4** (of a spiral shell) with whorls rising to the left and not (as usually) to the right. □□ **sinistrality** /-ˈtrælɪtɪ/ n. **sinistrally** adv.

sinistrorse /ˈsɪnɪˌstrɔːs/ adj. rising towards the left, esp. of the spiral stem of a plant. [L sinistrorsus f. sinister left + vorsus past part. of vertere turn]

sink /sɪŋk/ v. & n. —v. (past **sank** /sæŋk/ or **sunk** /sʌŋk/; past part. **sunk** or **sunken**) **1** intr. fall or come slowly downwards. **2** intr. disappear below the horizon (the sun is sinking). **3** intr. **a** go or penetrate below the surface esp. of a liquid. **b** (of a ship) go to the bottom of the sea etc. **4** intr. settle down comfortably (sank into a chair). **5** intr. **a** gradually lose strength or value or quality etc.; decline (my heart sank). **b** (of the voice) descend in pitch or volume. **c** (of a sick person) approach death. **6** tr. send (a ship) to the bottom of the sea etc. **7** tr. cause or allow to sink or penetrate (sank its teeth into my leg). **8** tr. cause the failure of (a plan etc.) or the discomfiture of (a person). **9** tr. dig (a well) or bore (a shaft). **10** tr. engrave (a die) or inlay (a design). **11** tr. **a** invest (money) (sunk a large sum into the business). **b** lose (money) by investment. **12** tr. **a** cause (a ball) to enter a pocket in billiards, a hole at golf, etc. **b** achieve this by (a stroke). **13** tr. overlook or forget; keep in the background (*sank their differences*). **14** *intr.* (of a price etc.) become lower. **15** *intr.* (of a storm or river) subside. **16** *intr.* (of ground) slope down, or reach a lower level by subsidence. **17** *intr.* (foll. by *on, upon*) (of darkness) descend (on a place). **18** *tr.* lower the level of. **19** *tr.* (usu. in *passive*; foll. by *in*) absorb; hold the attention of (*be sunk in thought*). —*n.* **1** a fixed basin with a water-supply and outflow pipe. **2** a place where foul liquid collects. **3** a place of vice or corruption. **4** a pool or marsh in which a river's water disappears by evaporation or percolation. **5** *Physics* a body or process used to absorb or dissipate heat. **6** (in full **sink-hole**) *Geol.* a cavity in limestone etc. into which a stream etc. disappears. □ **sink in 1** penetrate or make its way in. **2** become gradually comprehended (*paused to let the words sink in*). **sinking feeling** a bodily sensation caused by hunger or apprehension. **sinking fund** money set aside for the gradual repayment of a debt. **sink or swim** even at the risk of complete failure (*determined to try, sink or swim*). **sunk fence** a fence formed by, or along the bottom of, a ditch. □□ **sinkable** *adj.* **sinkage** *n.* [OE *sincan* f. Gmc]

sinker /ˈsɪŋkə(r)/ *n.* **1** a weight used to sink a fishing-line or sounding-line. **2** *US* a doughnut.

Sinkiang see XINJIANG.

sinner /ˈsɪnə(r)/ *n.* a person who sins, esp. habitually.

sinnet /ˈsɪnɪt/ *n.* (also **sennit**) *Naut.* braided cordage made in flat or round or square form from 3 to 9 cords. [17th c.: orig. unkn.]

Sinn Fein /ʃɪn ˈfeɪn/ *n.* an Irish movement founded in 1905 by Arthur Griffith (1872–1922), Irish journalist and politician, originally aiming at the independence of Ireland and a revival of Irish culture and language and now dedicated to the political unification of Northern Ireland and the Republic of Ireland. Sinn Fein became increasingly republican with the failure of the Home Rule movement. After the failure of the Easter rising it began to win Irish seats in Parliament, its members refusing to go to Westminster and setting up their own Parliament in Ireland in 1919. The republican section of the party supported De Valera in his rejection of the Anglo-Irish Treaty, most of it joining his Fianna Fáil party on its formation in 1926. The remainder of the party began to function as the political wing of the IRA, and in 1969 split like the IRA into Official and Provisional wings. □□ **Sinn Feiner** *n.* [Ir. *sinn féin* we ourselves]

Sino- /ˈsaɪnəʊ/ *comb. form* Chinese; Chinese and (*Sino-American*). [Gk *Sinai* the Chinese]

Sino-Japanese Wars wars fought between China and Japan. The first, in 1894–5, caused by rivalry over Korea, was ended by Treaty of Shimonoseki in Japan's favour. Poor Chinese performance in the war was a factor in the eventual overthrow of the Manchus in 1912. The second was in 1937–45; Japanese expansionism led to trouble in Manchuria in 1931 and to the establishment of a Japanese puppet State (Manchukuo) a year later. Hostilities began in earnest in 1937, but after two years of dramatic Japanese successes degenerated into stalemate. The Japanese position was gradually eroded by Communist guerrilla successes and finally collapsed at the end of the Second World War.

sinologue /ˈsaɪnəˌlɒg, ˈsɪ-/ *n.* an expert in sinology. [F, formed as SINO- + Gk *-logos* speaking]

sinology /saɪˈnɒlədʒɪ, sɪ-/ *n.* the study of Chinese language, history, customs, etc. □□ **sinological** /-nəˈlɒdʒɪk(ə)l/ *adj.* **sinologist** *n.*

Sino-Tibetan /ˌsaɪnəʊtɪˈbet(ə)n/ *adj.* of a language group which includes Chinese, Burmese, Tibetan, Nepalese, and Thai. They are tonal languages, but the exact relationships between them are far from clear. —*n.* this group of languages.

sinter /ˈsɪntə(r)/ *n.* & *v.* —*n.* **1** a siliceous or calcareous rock formed by deposition from springs. **2** a substance formed by sintering. —*v.intr.* & *tr.* coalesce or cause to coalesce from powder into solid by heating. [G, = E *sinder* CINDER]

Sint Niklaas see SAINT NICOLAS.

Sintra /ˈsiːntrə/ (also **Cintra**) a small town in central Portugal, formerly the summer residence of the Portuguese royal family; pop. (1981) 20,000.

sinuate /ˈsɪnjʊət/ *adj.* esp. *Bot.* wavy-edged; with distinct inward

and outward bends along the edge. [L *sinuatus* past part. of *sinuare* bend]

sinuosity /ˌsɪnjʊˈɒsɪtɪ/ *n.* (*pl.* **-ies**) **1** the state of being sinuous. **2** a bend, esp. in a stream or road. [F *sinuosité* or med.L *sinuositas* (as SINUOUS)]

sinuous /ˈsɪnjʊəs/ *adj.* with many curves; tortuous, undulating. □□ **sinuously** *adv.* **sinuousness** *n.* [F *sinueux* or L *sinuosus* (as SINUS)]

sinus /ˈsaɪnəs/ *n.* **1** a cavity of bone or tissue, esp. in the skull connecting with the nostrils. **2** *Med.* a fistula esp. to a deep abscess. **3** *Bot.* the curve between the lobes of a leaf. [L, = bosom, recess]

sinusitis /ˌsaɪnəˈsaɪtɪs/ *n.* inflammation of a nasal sinus.

sinusoid /ˈsaɪnəˌsɔɪd/ *n.* **1** a curve having the form of a sine wave. **2** a small irregular-shaped blood-vessel, esp. found in the liver. □□ **sinusoidal** /-ˈsɔɪd(ə)l/ *adj.* [F *sinusoïde* f. L *sinus*: see SINUS]

Sion var. of ZION.

-sion /ʃ(ə)n, ʒ(ə)n/ *suffix* forming nouns (see -ION) from Latin participial stems in *-s-* (*mansion*; *mission*; *persuasion*).

Sioux /suː/ *n.* & *adj.* —*n.* (*pl.* same) **1** a member of a group of N. American Indian peoples. **2** the language of this group. —*adj.* of or relating to this people or language. □□ **Siouan** /ˈsuːən/ *adj.* & *n.* [F f. a native name]

sip /sɪp/ *v.* & *n.* —*v.tr.* & *intr.* (**sipped, sipping**) drink in one or more small amounts or by spoonfuls. —*n.* **1** a small mouthful of liquid (*a sip of brandy*). **2** the act of taking this. □□ **sipper** *n.* [ME: perh. a modification of SUP¹]

sipe /saɪp/ *n.* a groove or channel in the tread of a tyre to improve its grip. [dial. *sipe* to ooze f. OE *sīpian*, MLG *sīpen*, of unkn. orig.]

siphon /ˈsaɪf(ə)n/ *n.* & *v.* (also **syphon**) —*n.* **1** a pipe or tube shaped like an inverted V or U with unequal legs to convey a liquid from a container to a lower level by atmospheric pressure. **2** (in full **siphon-bottle**) an aerated-water bottle from which liquid is forced out through a tube by the pressure of gas. **3** *Zool.* **a** a canal or conduit esp. in cephalopods. **b** the sucking-tube of some insects etc. —*v.tr.* & *intr.* (often foll. by *off*) **1** conduct or flow through a siphon. **2** divert or set aside (funds etc.). □□ **siphonage** *n.* **siphonal** *adj.* **siphonic** /-ˈfɒnɪk/ *adj.* [F *siphon* or L *sipho -onis* f. Gk *siphōn* pipe]

siphonophore /saɪˈfɒnəˌfɔː(r)/ *n.* any usu. translucent marine hydrozoan of the order Siphonophora, e.g. the Portuguese man-of-war. [Gk *siphōno-* (as SIPHON, -PHORE)]

sippet /ˈsɪpɪt/ *n.* **1** a small piece of bread etc. soaked in liquid. **2** a piece of toast or fried bread as a garnish. **3** a fragment. [app. dimin. of SOP]

sir /sɜː(r)/ *n.* **1** a polite or respectful form of address or mode of reference to a man. **2** (**Sir**) a titular prefix to the forename of a knight or baronet. [ME, reduced form of SIRE]

sirdar /ˈsɜːdɑː(r)/ *n.* *Ind.* etc. **1** a person of high political or military rank. **2** a Sikh. [Urdu *sardār* f. Pers. *sar* head + *dār* possessor]

sire /ˈsaɪə(r)/ *n.* & *v.* —*n.* **1** the male parent of an animal, esp. a stallion kept for breeding. **2** *archaic* a respectful form of address, now esp. to a king. **3** *archaic poet.* a father or male ancestor. —*v.tr.* (esp. of a stallion) beget. [ME f. OF ult. f. L *senior*: see SENIOR]

siren /ˈsaɪərən/ *n.* **1 a** a device for making a loud prolonged signal or warning sound, esp. by revolving a perforated disc over a jet of compressed air or steam. **b** the sound made by this. **2** *Gk Mythol.* any of the creatures (two or three in number) who had the power of luring seafarers to destruction on dangerous rocks by their song. (This was the original meaning. See below.) **3** a sweet singer. **4 a** a dangerously fascinating woman; a temptress. **b** a tempting pursuit etc. **5** (*attrib.*) irresistibly tempting. **6** an eel-shaped tailed amphibian of the family Sirenidae. □ **siren suit** a one-piece garment for the whole body, easily put on or taken off, orig. for use in air-raid shelters. [ME f. OF *sereine*, *sirene* f. LL *Sirena* fem. f. L f. Gk *Seirēn*]

When definite locations began to be attached to Homeric geography the sirens were associated with the coast of Italy, and were worshipped in Naples, Sorrentum, and Sicily. Their appearance is not described by Homer, but in art they are represented as half women and half birds, though in early examples male bearded sirens preponderate. The rapacious monsters of the archaic period are ennobled in classical art to mournful beautiful beings; in Hellenistic art and literature they are representative of music.

sirenian /saɪˈriːnɪən/ adj. & n. —adj. of the order Sirenia of large aquatic plant-eating mammals, e.g. the manatee and dugong. —n. any mammal of this order. [mod.L Sirenia (as SIREN)]

sirgang /ˈsɜːɡæŋ/ n. an Asian magpie, Kitta chinensis, having mainly green plumage with red wings. [a name in the E. Indies]

Sirius /ˈsɪrɪəs/ the Dog Star, alpha Canis Majoris, the brightest of the fixed stars, an unmistakable jewel in the winter sky of the northern hemisphere, apparently following on the heels of the hunter Orion. It was important to the ancient Egyptians as its heliacal rising coincided with the season of flooding of the Nile. It has a dim companion, Sirius B or the Pup, which is a white dwarf. The pronounced twinkling of Sirius, familiar to observers in northern latitudes, arises from atmospheric refraction and is not a property of the star itself.

sirloin /ˈsɜːlɔɪn/ n. the upper and choicer part of a loin of beef. [OF (as SUR-¹, LOIN)]

sirocco /sɪˈrɒkəʊ/ n. (also **scirocco**) (pl. **-os**) 1 a Saharan simoom reaching the northern shores of the Mediterranean. 2 a warm sultry rainy wind in S. Europe. [F f. It. scirocco, ult. f. Arab. šarūḳ east wind]

sirrah /ˈsɪrə/ n. archaic = SIR (as a form of address). [prob. f. ME sīrē SIR]

sirree /sɪˈriː/ int. US colloq. as an emphatic, esp. after yes or no. [SIR + emphatic suffix]

Sirte, Gulf of see Gulf of SIDRA.

sirup US var. of SYRUP.

SIS abbr. Secret Intelligence Service, the British Secret Service controlling overseas agents (see DI and M.I.6).

sis /sɪs/ n. colloq. a sister. [abbr.]

sisal /ˈsaɪs(ə)l/ n. 1 a Mexican plant, Agave sisalana, with large fleshy leaves. 2 the fibre made from this plant, used for cordage, ropes, etc. [Sisal, the port of Yucatan, Mexico]

siskin /ˈsɪskɪn/ n. a dark-streaked yellowish-green songbird, Carduelis spinus, allied to the goldfinch. [MDu. siseken dimin., rel. to MLG sīsek, MHG zīse, zīsec, of Slav. origin]

Sisley /ˈsɪslɪ/, Alfred (1839–99), French-born painter, of English parentage. His development towards impressionism from his early Corot-influenced landscapes was gradual and greatly indebted to Monet. He is chiefly remembered for his paintings of the Seine in the 1870s, with their concentration on reflecting surfaces, tonal mastery, and careful orchestration of fluid brush work.

sissy /ˈsɪsɪ/ n. & adj. (also **cissy**) colloq. —n. (pl. **-ies**) an effeminate or cowardly person. —adj. (**sissier, sissiest**) effeminate; cowardly. □□ **sissified** adj. **sissiness** n. **sissyish** adj. [SIS + -Y²]

sister /ˈsɪstə(r)/ n. 1 a woman or girl in relation to sons and other daughters of her parents. 2 a (often as a form of address) a close female friend or associate. b a female fellow member of a trade union, class, sect, or the human race. 3 a senior female nurse. 4 a member of a female religious order. 5 (attrib.) of the same type or design or origin etc. (sister ship; prose, the younger sister of verse). □ **sister german** see GERMAN. **sister-in-law** (pl. **sisters-in-law**) 1 the sister of one's wife or husband. 2 the wife of one's brother. 3 the wife of one's brother-in-law. **Sister of Mercy** a member of an educational or charitable order of women, esp. that founded in Dublin in 1827. **sister uterine** see UTERINE. □□ **sisterless** adj. **sisterly** adj. **sisterliness** n. [ME sister (f. ON), suster etc. (repr. OE sweoster f. Gmc)]

sisterhood /ˈsɪstəhʊd/ n. 1 a the relationship between sisters. b sisterly friendliness; companionship; mutual support. 2 a a society or association of women, esp. when bound by monastic vows or devoting themselves to religious or charitable work or the feminist cause. b its members collectively.

Sistine /ˈsɪstiːn, ˈsɪstaɪn/ adj. of any of the popes called Sixtus, esp. Sixtus IV (pope 1471–84). □ **Sistine Chapel** a chapel in the Vatican, built by Pope Sixtus IV, containing Michelangelo's painted ceiling and his fresco of the Last Judgement, and also frescos by Botticelli, Ghirlandaio, and others. It is used for the principal papal ceremonies and also by the cardinals when meeting for the election of a new pope. [It. Sistino f. Sisto Sixtus]

sistrum /ˈsɪstrəm/ n. (pl. **sistra** /-trə/) a jingling metal instrument used by the ancient Egyptians esp. in the worship of Isis. [ME f. L f. Gk seistron f. seiō shake]

Sisyphean /ˌsɪsɪˈfiːən/ adj. as of Sisyphus; endlessly laborious.

Sisyphus /ˈsɪsɪfəs/ Gk Mythol. the son of Aeolus, condemned for his misdeeds to Hades where his eternal task was to roll a large stone to the top of a hill from which it always rolled down again.

sit /sɪt/ v. & n. —v. (**sitting**; past and past part. **sat** /sæt/) 1 intr. adopt or be in a position in which the body is supported more or less upright by the buttocks resting on the ground or a raised seat etc., with the thighs usu. horizontal. 2 tr. cause to sit; place in a sitting position. 3 intr. a (of a bird) perch. b (of an animal) rest with the hind legs bent and the body close to the ground. 4 intr. (of a bird) remain on its nest to hatch its eggs. 5 intr. a be engaged in an occupation in which the sitting position is usual. b (of a committee, legislative body, etc.) be engaged in business. c (of an individual) be entitled to hold some office or position (sat as a magistrate). 6 intr. (usu. foll. by for) pose in a sitting position (for a portrait). 7 intr. (foll. by for) be a Member of Parliament for (a constituency). 8 tr. & (foll. by for) intr. Brit. be a candidate for (an examination). 9 intr. be in a more or less permanent position or condition (esp. of inactivity or being out of use or out of place). 10 intr. (of clothes etc.) fit or hang in a certain way. 11 tr. keep or have one's seat on (a horse etc.). 12 intr. act as a babysitter. 13 intr. (often foll. by before) (of an army) take a position outside a city etc. to besiege it. —n. the way a dress etc. sits on a person. □ **be sitting pretty** be comfortably or advantageously placed. **make a person sit up** colloq. surprise or interest a person. **sit at a person's feet** be a person's pupil. **sit at home** be inactive. **sit back** relax one's efforts. **sit by** look on without interfering. **sit down** 1 sit after standing. 2 cause to sit. 3 (foll. by under) submit tamely to (an insult etc.). **sit-down** adj. (of a meal) eaten sitting at a table. **sit-down strike** a strike in which workers refuse to leave their places of work. **sit heavy on the stomach** take a long time to be digested. **sit in** 1 occupy a place as a protest. 2 (foll. by for) take the place of. 3 (foll. by on) be present as a guest or observer at (a meeting etc.). **sit-in** n. a protest involving sitting in. **sit in judgement** assume the right of judging others; be censorious. **sit loosely on** not be very binding. **sit on** 1 be a member of (a committee etc.). 2 hold a session or inquiry concerning. 3 colloq. delay action about (the government has been sitting on the report). 4 colloq. repress or rebuke or snub (felt rather sat on). **sit on the fence** see FENCE. **sit on one's hands** 1 take no action. 2 refuse to applaud. **sit out** 1 take no part in (a dance etc.). 2 stay till the end of (esp. an ordeal). 3 sit outdoors. 4 outstay (other visitors). **sit tight** colloq. 1 remain firmly in one's place. 2 not be shaken off or move away or yield to distractions. **sit up** 1 rise from a lying to a sitting position. 2 sit firmly upright. 3 go to bed later than the usual time. 4 colloq. become interested or aroused etc. **sit-up** n. a physical exercise in which a person sits up without raising the legs from the ground. **sit up and take notice** colloq. have one's interest aroused, esp. suddenly. **sit-upon** colloq. the buttocks. **sit well** have a good seat in riding. **sit well on** suit or fit. [OE sittan f. Gmc]

Sita /ˈsiːtɑː/ (in the Ramayana) the wife of Rama. She is the Hindu model of the ideal woman, an incarnation of Lakshmi [Skr., = furrow]

sitar /ˈsɪtɑː(r), sɪˈtɑː(r)/ n. a long-necked Indian lute with movable frets, of Persian origin, one of the most important of Indian music and now well known also in the West. The name derives from the Persian sehtar, 'three-stringed', and originally there were three melody strings (from four to seven are now common), together with a dozen or more 'sympathetic strings' (made of metal and providing a special background resonance) and two or three drone strings. The strings are plucked with a plectrum. □□ **sitarist** /sɪ'tɑːrɪst/ n. [Hindi *sitār*]

sitcom /'sɪtkɒm/ n. *colloq.* a situation comedy. [abbr.]

site /saɪt/ n. & v. **1** the ground chosen or used for a town or building. **2** a place where some activity is or has been conducted (*camping site; launching site*). —*v.tr.* **1** locate or place. **2** provide with a site. [ME f. AF *site* or L *situs* local position]

Sitka /'sɪtkə/ n. (in full **Sitka spruce**) a fast-growing spruce, *Picea sitchensis*, native to N. America and yielding timber. [*Sitka* in Alaska]

sitrep /'sɪtrep/ n. a report on the current military situation in an area. [*situation report*]

sits vac /sɪts 'væk/ abbr. situations vacant.

Sittang /'sɪtæŋ/ a river that rises in east central Burma and flows south into the Bay of Bengal at the Gulf of Martaban.

sitter /'sɪtə(r)/ n. **1** a person who sits, esp. for a portrait. **2** = BABYSITTER (see BABYSIT). **3** *colloq.* **a** an easy catch or shot. **b** an easy task. **4** a sitting hen.

sitting /'sɪtɪŋ/ n. & adj. —n. **1** a continuous period of being seated, esp. engaged in an activity (*finished the book in one sitting*). **2** a time during which an assembly is engaged in business. **3** a session in which a meal is served (*dinner will be served in two sittings*). **4** *Brit.* = TERM 5c. **5** a clutch of eggs. —adj. **1** having sat down. **2** (of an animal or bird) not running or flying. **3** (of a hen) engaged in hatching. □ **sitting duck** (or **target**) *colloq.* a vulnerable person or thing. **sitting pretty** see PRETTY. **sitting-room 1** a room in a house for relaxed sitting in. **2** space enough to accommodate seated persons. **sitting tenant** a tenant already in occupation of premises.

situate v. & adj. —v.tr. /'sɪtjʊˌeɪt/ (usu. in *passive*) **1** put in a certain position or circumstances (*is situated at the top of a hill; how are you situated at the moment?*). **2** establish or indicate the place of; put in a context. —adj. /'sɪtjʊət/ *Law* or *archaic* situated. [med.L *situare situat-* f. L *situs* site]

situation /ˌsɪtjʊ'eɪʃ(ə)n/ n. **1** a place and its surroundings (*the house stands in a fine situation*). **2** a set of circumstances; a position in which one finds oneself; a state of affairs (*came out of a difficult situation with credit*). **3** an employee's position or job. **4** a critical point or complication in a drama. □ **situation comedy** a comedy in which the humour derives from the situations the characters are placed in. **situations vacant** (or **wanted**) headings of lists of employment offered and sought. □□ **situational** adj. [ME f. F *situation* or med.L *situatio* (as SITUATE)]

Sitwell /'sɪtwel/, Dame Edith (Louisa) (1887–1964), English poet and critic. Light-hearted and experimental, her early verse, like that of her brothers Osbert (1892–1969) and Sacheverell (1897–88), marked a revolt against the prevailing Georgian style of the day; *Façade*, a group of her poems in notated rhythm declaimed to music by Sir William Walton, was performed in 1923. Her later verse is graver and more profound.

sitz-bath /'sɪtsbɑːθ/ n. a hip-bath. [partial transl. of G *Sitzbad* f. *sitzen* sit + *Bad* bath]

Siva /'siːvə, 'ʃiːvə/ n. (also **Shiva** /'ʃiːvə/) *Hinduism* one of the major gods, perhaps a later development of the Vedic god Rudra. He is worshipped in many aspects: as fierce destroyer, naked ascetic, lord of the cosmic dance, lord of beasts and, most commonly, in the form of the phallus (linga). In his beneficent aspect, he lives in the Himalayas with his wife Parvati and their two sons, Ganesha and Skanda. His mount is the bull Nandi. Typically, Siva is depicted with a third eye in the middle of his forehead, wearing a crescent moon in his matted hair and a necklace of skulls at his throat, entwined with live snakes, and carrying a trident. □□ **Sivaism** n. **Sivaite** n. & adj. [Skr. *Śiva*, lit. the auspicious one]

Siwalik Hills /sɪ'wɑːlɪk/ foothills of the Himalayas in northern India and Nepal.

six /sɪks/ n. & adj. —n. **1** one more than five, or four less than ten; the product of two units and three units. **2** a symbol for this (6, vi, VI). **3** a size etc. denoted by six. **4** a set or team of six individuals. **5** *Cricket* a hit scoring six runs by clearing the boundary without bouncing. **6** the time of six o'clock (*is it six yet?*). **7** a card etc. with six pips. —adj. that amount to six. □

the Six (chiefly as the French phrase **Les Six** /leɪ 'siːs/) a Parisian group of six composers (Durey, Honegger, Milhaud, Tailleferre, Auric, and Poulenc), formed after the First World War, whose music represents a reaction against romanticism and impressionism. **at sixes and sevens** in confusion or disagreement. **knock for six** *colloq.* utterly surprise or overcome (a person). **the Six Counties** the Ulster counties of Antrim, Down, Armagh, Londonderry, Tyrone, and Fermanagh, which since 1960 have comprised the province of Northern Ireland. **Six Day(s) War** an Arab-Israeli war, 5–10 June 1967 (known to the Arabs as the June War), in which Israel occupied Sinai, east Jerusalem (the Old City), the West Bank, and the Golan Heights. **six-gun** = *six-shooter*. **six of one and half a dozen of the other** a situation of little real difference between the alternatives. **six-shooter** a revolver with six chambers. [OE *siex* etc. f. Gmc]

sixain /'sɪkseɪn/ n. a six-line stanza. [F f. *six* six]

sixer /'sɪksə(r)/ n. **1** the leader of a group of six Brownies or Cubs. **2** *Cricket* a hit for six runs.

sixfold /'sɪksfəʊld/ adj. & adv. **1** six times as much or as many. **2** consisting of six parts.

sixpence /'sɪkspəns/ n. *Brit.* **1** the sum of six pence, esp. before decimalization. **2** *hist.* a coin worth six old pence (2½p).

sixpenny /'sɪkspənɪ/ adj. *Brit.* costing or worth six pence, esp. before decimalization.

sixte /sɪkst/ n. *Fencing* the sixth of the eight parrying positions. [F f. L *sextus* sixth]

sixteen /ˌsɪks'tiːn, 'sɪks-/ n. & adj. —n. **1** one more than fifteen, or six more than ten. **2** a symbol for this (16, xvi, XVI). **3** a size etc. denoted by sixteen. —adj. that amount to sixteen. □ **sixteenth note** *US Mus.* = SEMIQUAVER. □□ **sixteenth** adj. & n. [OE *sixtiene* (as SIX, -TEEN)]

sixteenmo /sɪks'tiːnməʊ/ n. (pl. **-os**) sextodecimo. [English reading of the symbol 16mo]

sixth /sɪksθ/ n. & adj. —n. **1** the position in a sequence corresponding to that of the number 6 in the sequence 1–6. **2** something occupying this position. **3** any of six equal parts of a thing. **4** *Mus.* **a** an interval or chord spanning six consecutive notes in the diatonic scale (e.g. C to A). **b** a note separated from another by this interval. —adj. that is the sixth. □ **sixth form** *Brit.* a form in a secondary school for pupils over 16. **sixth-form college** *Brit.* a college for pupils over 16. **sixth-former** a pupil in the sixth form. **sixth sense 1** a supposed faculty giving intuitive or extrasensory knowledge. **2** such knowledge. □□ **sixthly** adv. [SIX]

Sixtine /'sɪkstiːn, -taɪn/ adj. = SISTINE. [mod.L *Sixtinus* f. *Sixtus*]

sixty /'sɪkstɪ/ n. & adj. —n. (pl. **-ies**) **1** the product of six and ten. **2** a symbol for this (60, lx, LX). **3** (in pl.) the numbers from 60 to 69, esp. the years of a century or of a person's life. **4** a set of sixty persons or things. —adj. that amount to sixty. □ **sixty-first, -second,** etc. the ordinal numbers between sixtieth and seventieth. **sixty-fourmo** /ˌsɪkstɪ'fɔːməʊ/ (pl. **-os**) **1** a size of book in which each leaf is one-sixty-fourth of a printing-sheet. **2** a book of this size (*after* DUO-DECIMO etc.). **sixty-fourth note** esp. *US Mus.* = HEMIDEMISEMIQUAVER. **sixty-four thousand** (or **sixty-four**) **dollar question** a difficult and crucial question (from the top prize in a broadcast quiz show). **sixty-one, -two,** etc. the cardinal numbers between sixty and seventy. □□ **sixtieth** adj. & n. **sixtyfold** adj. & adv. [OE *sixtig* (as SIX, -TY²)]

sizable var. of SIZEABLE.

sizar /'saɪzə(r)/ n. a student at Cambridge or at Trinity College, Dublin, paying reduced fees and formerly having certain menial duties. □□ **sizarship** n. [SIZE¹ = ration]

size¹ /saɪz/ n. & v. —n. **1** the relative bigness or extent of a thing, dimensions, magnitude (*is of vast size; size matters less than quality*). **2** each of the classes, usu. numbered, into which things otherwise similar, esp. garments, are divided according to size (*is made in several sizes; takes size 7 in gloves; is three sizes too big*). —v.tr. sort or group in sizes or according to size. □ **of a size** having the same size. **of some size** fairly large. **the size of** as big as. **the size of it** *colloq.* a true account of the matter (*that is the size of it*). **size-stick** a shoemaker's measure for taking the length of a foot. **size up 1** estimate the size of. **2** *colloq.* form a judgement of. **what size?** how big? □□ **sized** *adj.* (also in *comb.*). **sizer** *n.* [ME f. OF *sise* f. *assise* ASSIZE, or f. ASSIZE]

size² /saɪz/ *n.* & *v.* —*n.* a gelatinous solution used in glazing paper, stiffening textiles, preparing plastered walls for decoration, etc. —*v.tr.* glaze or stiffen or treat with size. [ME, perh. = SIZE¹]

sizeable /ˈsaɪzəb(ə)l/ *adj.* (also **sizable**) large or fairly large. □□ **sizeably** *adv.*

sizzle /ˈsɪz(ə)l/ *v.* & *n.* —*v.intr.* **1** make a sputtering or hissing sound as of frying. **2** *colloq.* be in a state of great heat or excitement or marked effectiveness. —*n.* **1** a sizzling sound. **2** *colloq.* a state of great heat or excitement. □□ **sizzler** *n.* **sizzling** *adj.* & *adv.* (*sizzling hot*). [imit.]

SJ *abbr.* Society of Jesus.

SJAA *abbr.* (in the UK) St John Ambulance Association.

SJAB *abbr.* (in the UK) St John Ambulance Brigade.

Sjaelland see ZEALAND.

sjambok /ˈʃæmbɒk/ *n.* & *v.* —*n.* (in S. Africa) a rhinoceros-hide whip. —*v.tr.* flog with a sjambok. [Afrik. f. Malay *samboq*, *chambok* f. Urdu *chābuk*]

SJC *abbr.* (in the US) Supreme Judicial Court.

Skaggerak /ˈskægəˌræk/ a strait separating south Norway from north Denmark and linking the Baltic to the North Sea.

skald /skɔːld, skɒld/ *n.* (also **scald**) (in ancient Scandinavia) a composer and reciter of poems honouring heroes and their deeds. □□ **skaldic** *adj.* [ON *skáld*, of unkn. orig.]

Skara Brae /ˌskɑːrə ˈbreɪ/ a late neolithic (3rd millennium BC) settlement on the main island (Mainland) of Orkney, consisting of stone-built rooms with slab-shelves, chests, and hearths.

skat /skɑːt/ *n.* a three-handed card-game with bidding. [G f. It. *scarto* a discard f. *scartare* discard]

skate¹ /skeɪt/ *n.* & *v.* —*n.* **1** each of a pair of steel blades (or of boots with blades attached) for gliding on ice. **2** (in full **roller skate**) each of a pair of metal frames with small wheels, fitted to shoes for riding on a hard surface. **3** a device on which a heavy object moves. —*v.* **1 a** *intr.* move on skates. **b** *tr.* perform (a specified figure) on skates. **2** *intr.* (foll. by *over*) refer fleetingly to, disregard. □ **get one's skates on** *Brit. sl.* make haste. **skate on thin ice** *colloq.* behave rashly, risk danger, esp. by dealing with a subject needing tactful treatment. **skating-rink** a piece of ice artificially made, or a floor used, for skating. □□ **skater** *n.* [orig. *scates* (pl.) f. Du. *schaats* (sing.) f. ONF *escace*, OF *eschasse* stilt]

skate² /skeɪt/ *n.* (*pl.* same or **skates**) any cartilaginous marine fish of the family *Rajidae*, esp. *Raja batis*, a large flat rhomboidal fish used as food. [ME f. ON *skata*]

skate³ /skeɪt/ *n. sl.* a contemptible, mean, or dishonest person (esp. *cheap skate*). [19th c.: orig. uncert.]

skateboard /ˈskeɪtbɔːd/ *n.* & *v.* —*n.* a short narrow board on roller-skate wheels for riding on while standing. Skateboards were introduced in California in the early 1960s and later achieved worldwide popularity. —*v.intr.* ride on a skateboard. □□ **skateboarder** *n.* [SKATE¹, after *surfboard*]

skean /skiːn, ˈskiːən/ *n. hist.* a Gaelic dagger formerly used in Ireland and Scotland. □ **skean-dhu** /-ˈduː/ *n.* a dagger worn in the stocking as part of Highland costume. [Gael. *sgian* knife, *dubh* black]

sked /sked/ *n.* & *v. colloq.* —*n.* = SCHEDULE. —*v.tr.* (**skedded**, **skedding**) = SCHEDULE. [abbr.]

skedaddle /skɪˈdæd(ə)l/ *v.* & *n. colloq.* —*v.intr.* run away, depart quickly, flee. —*n.* a hurried departure or flight. [19th c.: orig. unkn.]

skeet /skiːt/ *n.* a shooting sport in which a clay target is thrown from a trap to simulate the flight of a bird. [ON *skjóta* SHOOT]

skeeter¹ /ˈskiːtə(r)/ *n. US & Austral. sl.* a mosquito. [abbr.]

skeeter² var. of SKITTER.

skeg /skeg/ *n.* **1** a fin underneath the rear of a surfboard. **2** the after part of a vessel's keel or a projection from it. [ON *skeg* beard, perh. via Du. *scheg(ge)*]

skein /skeɪn/ *n.* **1** a loosely-coiled bundle of yarn or thread. **2** a flock of wild geese etc. in flight. **3** a tangle or confusion. [ME f. OF *escaigne*, of unkn. orig.]

skeleton /ˈskelɪt(ə)n/ *n.* **1 a** a hard internal or external framework of bones, cartilage, shell, woody fibre, etc., supporting or containing the body of an animal or plant. **b** the dried bones of a human being or other animal fastened together in the same relative positions as in life. **2** the supporting framework or structure or essential part of a thing. **3** a very thin or emaciated person or animal. **4** the remaining part of anything after its life or usefulness is gone. **5** an outline sketch, an epitome or abstract. **6** (*attrib.*) having only the essential or minimum number of persons, parts, etc. (*skeleton plan*; *skeleton staff*). □ **skeleton at the feast** something that spoils one's pleasure; an intrusive worry. **skeleton in the cupboard** (*US* **closet**) a discreditable or embarrassing fact kept secret. **skeleton key** a key designed to fit many locks by having the interior of the bit hollowed. □□ **skeletal** *adj.* **skeletally** *adv.* **skeletonize** *v.tr.* (also **-ise**). [mod.L f. Gk, neut. of *skeletos* dried-up f. *skellō* dry up]

Skeleton Coast a name given to the arid Atlantic coast of Namibia.

Skelton /ˈskelt(ə)n/, John (?1460–1529), English poet, who was created 'poet-laureate' by Oxford, Cambridge, and Louvain Universities and became tutor to the future Henry VIII. His principal works include *The Bowge of Courte*, a satire on the court of Henry VII, *Collyn Cloute*, *Speke Parrot*, and a morality play *Magnyfycence*. His satires contained attacks on Cardinal Wolsey, setting forth the evil consequences of his dominating position, and as a result Skelton was obliged to take sanctuary at Westminster, where he died. His favourite metre was designated 'a headlong voluble breathless doggerel', short lines with two or three stresses and quick recurring rhymes, now known as 'skeltonic'.

skep /skep/ *n.* **1 a** a wooden or wicker basket of any of various forms. **b** the quantity contained in this. **2** a straw or wicker beehive. [ME f. ON *skeppa*]

skepsis *US* var. of SCEPSIS.

skeptic *US* var. of SCEPTIC.

skeptical *US* var. of SCEPTICAL.

skerrick /ˈskerɪk/ *n.* (usu. with *neg.*) *US & Austral. colloq.* the smallest bit (*not a skerrick left*). [N.Engl. dial.; orig. uncert.]

skerry /ˈskerɪ/ *n.* (*pl.* **-ies**) *Sc.* a reef or rocky island. [Orkney dial. f. ON *sker*: cf. SCAR²]

sketch /sketʃ/ *n.* & *v.* —*n.* **1** a rough, slight, merely outlined, or unfinished drawing or painting, often made to assist in making a more finished picture. **2** a brief account without many details conveying a general idea of something, a rough draft or general outline. **3** a very short play, usu. humorous and limited to one scene. **4** a short descriptive piece of writing. **5** a musical composition of a single movement. **6** *colloq.* a comical person or thing. —*v.* **1** *tr.* make or give a sketch of. **2** *intr.* draw sketches esp. of landscape (*went out sketching*). **3** *tr.* (often foll. by *in*, *out*) indicate briefly or in outline. □ **sketch-book** (or **-block**) a pad of drawing-paper for doing sketches on. **sketch-map** a roughly-drawn map with few details. □□ **sketcher** *n.* [Du. *schets* or G *Skizze* f. It. *schizzo* f. *schizzare* make a sketch ult. f. Gk *skhedios* extempore]

sketchy /ˈsketʃɪ/ *adj.* (**sketchier**, **sketchiest**) **1** giving only a slight or rough outline, like a sketch. **2** *colloq.* unsubstantial or imperfect esp. through haste. □□ **sketchily** *adv.* **sketchiness** *n.*

skeuomorph /ˈskjuːəʊˌmɔːf/ *n.* **1** an object or feature copying the design of a similar artefact in another material. **2** an ornamental design resulting from the nature of the material used or the method of working it. □□ **skeuomorphic** /-ˈmɔːfɪk/ *adj.* [Gk *skeuos* vessel, implement + *morphē* form]

skew /skjuː/ *adj.*, *n.*, & *v.* —*adj.* **1** oblique, slanting, set askew. **2** *Math.* **a** lying in three dimensions (*skew curve*). **b** (of lines) not coplanar. **c** (of a statistical distribution) not symmetrical. —*n.* **1** a slant. **2** *Statistics* skewness. —*v.* **1** *tr.* make skew. **2** *tr.* distort. **3** *intr.* move obliquely. **4** *intr.* twist. □ **on the skew** askew. **skew arch** (or **bridge**) an arch (or bridge) with the line of the arch not at right angles to the abutment. **skew chisel** a chisel with an oblique edge. **skew-eyed** *Brit.* squinting. **skew gear** a gear consisting of two cog-wheels having non-parallel, non-intersecting axes. **skew-whiff** /skjuː'wɪf/ *Brit. colloq.* askew. □□ **skewness** *n.* [ONF *eskiu(w)er* (v.) = OF *eschuer*: see ESCHEW]

skewback /'skjuːbæk/ *n.* the sloping face of the abutment on which an extremity of an arch rests.

skewbald /'skjuːbɔːld/ *adj.* & *n.* —*adj.* (of an animal) with irregular patches of white and another colour (properly not black) (cf. PIEBALD). —*n.* a skewbald animal, esp. a horse. [ME *skued* (orig. uncert.), after PIEBALD]

skewer /'skjuːə(r)/ *n.* & *v.* —*n.* a long pin designed for holding meat compactly together while cooking. —*v.tr.* fasten together or pierce with or as with a skewer. [17th c., var. of dial. *skiver*: orig. unkn.]

ski /skiː/ *n.* & *v.* —*n.* (*pl.* **skis** or **ski**) **1** each of a pair of long narrow pieces of wood etc., usu. pointed and turned up at the front, fastened under the feet for travelling over snow. (See below.) **2** a similar device under a vehicle or aircraft. **3** = WATER-SKI. **4** (*attrib.*) for wear when skiing (*ski boots*). —*v.* (**skis**, **ski'd** or **skied** /skiːd/; **skiing**) **1** *intr.* travel on skis. **2** *tr.* ski at (a place). □ **ski-bob** *n.* a machine like a bicycle with skis instead of wheels. —*v.intr.* (**-bobbed**, **-bobbing**) ride a ski-bob. **ski-bobber** a person who ski-bobs. **ski-jump 1** a steep slope levelling off before a sharp drop to allow a skier to leap through the air. **2** a jump made from this. **ski-jumper** a person who takes part in ski-jumping. **ski-jumping** the sport of leaping off a ski-jump with marks awarded for style and distance attained. **ski-lift** a device for carrying skiers up a slope, usu. on seats hung from an overhead cable. **ski-plane** an aeroplane having its undercarriage fitted with skis for landing on snow or ice. **ski-run** a slope prepared for skiing. □□ **skiable** *adj.* [Norw. f. ON *skíth* billet, snow-shoe]

The oldest skis that have been found, preserved in bogs in Sweden and Finland, date from the 3rd millennium BC, and a rock-carving in northern Norway of two men on skis from *c*.2000 BC; there are references to skis in Norse mythology. The Vikings used skis in the 10th–11th c., and ski troops were used in Scandinavia, Poland, and Russia in the 15th–16th c. The type of ski evolved in these countries, however, was unsuited to steep Alpine mountains, and skiing was virtually unknown in central Europe until it was introduced by Scandinavian and British visitors as a sport and recreation in the mid-19th and 20th c. Competitive skiing falls into two categories: Nordic (cross-country racing and jumping) and Alpine (downhill or straight racing, and slalom and giant slalom racing between series of set gates).

skiagraphy var. of SCIAGRAPHY.

skiamachy var. of SCIAMACHY.

skid /skɪd/ *v.* & *n.* —*v.* (**skidded**, **skidding**) **1** *intr.* (of a vehicle, a wheel, or a driver) slide on slippery ground, esp. sideways or obliquely. **2** *tr.* cause (a vehicle etc.) to skid. **3** *intr.* slip, slide. **4** *intr. colloq.* fail or decline or err. **5** *tr.* support or move or protect or check with a skid. —*n.* **1** the act or an instance of skidding. **2** a piece of wood etc. serving as a support, ship's fender, inclined plane, etc. **3** a braking device, esp. a wooden or metal shoe preventing a wheel from revolving or used as a drag. **4** a runner beneath an aircraft for use when landing. □ **hit the skids** *colloq.* enter a rapid decline or deterioration. **on the skids** *colloq.* **1** about to be discarded or defeated. **2** ready for launching. **put the skids under** *colloq.* **1** hasten the downfall or failure of. **2** cause to hasten. **skid-lid** *sl.* a crash-helmet. **skid-pan** *Brit.* **1** a slippery surface prepared for vehicle-drivers to practise control of skidding. **2** a braking device. **skid road** *US* **1** a road for hauling logs along. **2** a part of a town frequented by loggers or vagrants. **skid row** *US* a part of a town frequented by vagrants, alcoholics, etc. [17th c.: orig. unkn.]

skiddoo /skɪ'duː/ *v.intr.* (also **skidoo**) (**-oos**, **-ooed**) *US sl.* go away; depart. [perh. f. SKEDADDLE]

skier[1] /'skiːə(r)/ *n.* a person who skis.

skier[2] var. of SKYER.

skiff /skɪf/ *n.* a light rowing-boat or sculling-boat. [F *esquif* f. It. *schifo*, rel. to SHIP]

skiffle /'skɪf(ə)l/ *n.* a kind of folk music played by a small group,

mainly with a rhythmic accompaniment to a singing guitarist etc. [perh. imit.]

ski-joring /'skiːˌdʒɔːrɪŋ, ʃiː'jɔːrɪŋ/ *n.* a winter sport in which a skier is towed by a horse or vehicle. □□ **ski-jorer** *n.* [Norw. *skíkjøring* (as SKI, *kjøre* drive)]

skilful /'skɪlfʊl/ *adj.* (*US* **skillful**) (often foll. by *at, in*) having or showing skill; practised, expert, adroit, ingenious. □□ **skilfully** *adv.* **skilfulness** *n.*

skill /skɪl/ *n.* (often foll. by *in*) expertness, practised ability, facility in an action; dexterity or tact. □□ **skill-less** *adj.* (*archaic* **skilless**). [ME f. ON *skil* distinction]

skilled /skɪld/ *adj.* **1** (often foll. by *in*) having or showing skill; skilful. **2** (of a worker) highly trained or experienced. **3** (of work) requiring skill or special training.

skillet /'skɪlɪt/ *n.* **1** *Brit.* a small metal cooking-pot with a long handle and usu. legs. **2** *US* a frying-pan. [ME, perh. f. OF *escuelete* dimin. of *escuele* platter f. LL *scutella*]

skillful *US* var. of SKILFUL.

skilly /'skɪlɪ/ *n. Brit.* **1** a thin broth or soup or gruel (usu. of oatmeal and water flavoured with meat). **2** an insipid beverage; tea or coffee. [abbr. f. *skilligalee*, prob. fanciful]

skim /skɪm/ *v.* & *n.* —*v.* (**skimmed**, **skimming**) **1** *tr.* **a** take scum or cream or a floating layer from the surface of (a liquid). **b** take (cream etc.) from the surface of a liquid. **2** *tr.* **a** keep touching lightly or nearly touching (a surface) in passing over. **b** deal with or treat (a subject) superficially. **3** *intr.* **a** (often foll. by *over, along*) go lightly over a surface, glide along in the air. **b** (foll. by *over*) = sense 2b of *v.* **4 a** *tr.* read superficially, look over cursorily, gather the salient facts contained in. **b** *intr.* (usu. foll. by *through*) read or look over cursorily. **5** *tr. US sl.* conceal or divert (income) to avoid paying tax. —*n.* **1** the act or an instance of skimming. **2** a thin covering on a liquid (*skim of ice*). □ **skim the cream off** take the best part of. **skim** (or **skimmed**) **milk** milk from which the cream has been skimmed. [ME, back-form. f. SKIMMER]

skimmer /'skɪmə(r)/ *n.* **1** a device for skimming liquids. **2** a person who skims. **3** a flat hat, esp. a broad-brimmed straw hat. **4** any long-winged marine bird of the genus *Rynchops* that feeds by skimming over water with its knifelike lower mandible immersed. **5** a hydroplane, hydrofoil, hovercraft, or other vessel that has little or no displacement at speed. **6** *US* a sheath-like dress. [ME f. OF *escumoir* f. *escumer* f. *escume* SCUM]

skimmia /'skɪmɪə/ *n.* any evergreen shrub of the genus *Skimmia*, native to E. Asia, with red berries. [mod.L f. Jap.]

skimp /skɪmp/ *v.*, *adj.*, & *n.* —*v.* **1** *tr.* (often foll. by *in*) supply (a person etc.) meagrely with food, money, etc. **2** *tr.* use a meagre or insufficient amount of, stint (material, expenses, etc.). **3** *intr.* be parsimonious. —*adj.* scanty. —*n. colloq.* a small or scanty thing, esp. a skimpy garment. [18th c.: orig. unkn.: cf. SCRIMP]

skimpy /'skɪmpɪ/ *adj.* (**skimpier**, **skimpiest**) meagre; not ample or sufficient. □□ **skimpily** *adv.* **skimpiness** *n.*

skin /skɪn/ *n.* & *v.* —*n.* **1** the flexible continuous covering of a human or other animal body. (See below.) **2 a** the skin of a flayed animal with or without the hair etc. **b** a material prepared from skins esp. of smaller animals (opp. HIDE[2]). **3** a person's skin with reference to its colour or complexion (*has a fair skin*). **4** an outer layer or covering, esp. the coating of a plant, fruit, or sausage. **5** a film like skin on the surface of a liquid etc. **6** a container for liquid, made of an animal's whole skin. **7 a** the planking or plating of a ship or boat, inside or outside the ribs. **b** the outer covering of any craft or vehicle, esp. an aircraft or spacecraft. **8** *Brit. sl.* a skinhead. **9** *US Cards* a game in which each player has one card which he bets will not be the first to be matched by a card dealt from the pack. **10** = *gold-beater's skin*. **11** a duplicating stencil. —*v.* (**skinned**, **skinning**) **1** *tr.* remove the skin from. **2** (often foll. by *over*) **a** *tr.* cover (a sore etc.) with or as with skin. **b** *intr.* (of a wound etc.) become covered with new skin. **3** *tr. sl.* fleece or swindle. □ **be skin and bone** be very thin. **by** (or **with**) **the skin of one's teeth** by a very narrow margin. **change one's skin** undergo an impossible change of character etc. **get under a person's skin** *colloq.* interest or annoy a person intensely. **have a thick** (or **thin**) **skin** be insensitive (or sensitive) to criticism etc. **no skin off one's nose** *colloq.* a matter of indifference or even benefit to one. **skin-deep** (of a wound, or of an emotion, an impression, beauty, etc.) superficial, not deep or lasting. **skin-diver** a person who swims underwater without a diving-suit, usu. in deep water with an aqualung and flippers. **skin-diving** such swimming. **skin effect** *Electr.* the tendency of a high-frequency alternating current to flow through the outer layer only of a conductor. **skin-flick** *sl.* an explicitly pornographic film. **skin-food** a cosmetic intended to improve the condition of the skin. **skin friction** friction at the surface of a solid and a fluid in relative motion. **skin game** *US sl.* a swindling game. **skin-graft 1** the surgical transplanting of skin. **2** a piece of skin transferred in this way. **skin test** a test to determine whether an immune reaction is elicited when a substance is applied to or injected into the skin. **skin-tight** (of a garment) very close-fitting. **to the skin** through all one's clothing (*soaked to the skin*). **with a whole skin** unwounded. □□ **skinless** *adj.* **skin-like** *adj.* **skinned** *adj.* (also in *comb.*). [OE *scin(n)* f. ON *skinn*]

Skin protects the rest of the body from external injury, excessive heat or cold, fluid loss, and infection, and acts as a sense-organ, providing the body with information about the environment through special nerve-endings (temperature, touch, pressure, and pain receptors). Heat and water are lost through the skin, which thus plays an important part in controlling the temperature of the body and in maintaining the balance of body fluid. The skin's outer layer, the epidermis, itself consists of four layers, of which the innermost consists of continuously dividing cells; the other three are continually renewed as these are pushed outwards and become progressively impregnated with keratin. The outermost layer contains dead cells whose cytoplasm has been entirely replaced by keratin, and which are gradually sloughed off. The inner layer or true skin, the dermis, is a thick layer of living tissue within which are blood capillaries and lymph vessels, sensory nerve-endings, sweat glands and their ducts, sebaceous glands, and smooth muscle fibres.

skinflint /ˈskɪnflɪnt/ *n.* a miserly person.

skinful /ˈskɪnfʊl/ *n.* (*pl.* **-fuls**) *colloq.* enough alcoholic liquor to make one drunk.

skinhead /ˈskɪnhed/ *n.* **1** *Brit.* a youth with close-cropped hair, esp. one of an aggressive gang. **2** *US* a recruit in the Marines.

skink /skɪŋk/ *n.* any small lizard of the family Scincidae. [F *scinc* or L *scincus* f. Gk *skigkos*]

Skinner /ˈskɪnə(r)/, Burrhus Frederic (1904–90), American psychologist, ardent promoter of the view that the proper study of psychology should be to predict, and hence be able to control, behaviour. His experiments on animals demonstrated that arbitrary responses could be obtained provided that certain outcomes ('reinforcements') were made contingent upon them: rewards increased the frequency of response, punishments decreased it. He applied similar techniques in both clinical and educational practice, devising (in the 1930s) one of the first teaching machines, and was involved in the development of programmed learning. Skinner also attempted to account for the nature and development of language as being a response to conditioning.

skinner /ˈskɪnə(r)/ *n.* **1** a person who skins animals or prepares skins. **2** a dealer in skins, a furrier. **3** *Austral. Racing sl.* a result very profitable to bookmakers.

skinny /ˈskɪnɪ/ *adj.* (**skinnier**, **skinniest**) **1** thin or emaciated. **2** (of clothing) tight-fitting. **3** made of or like skin. □ **skinny-dipping** esp. *US colloq.* bathing in the nude. □□ **skinniness** *n.*

skint /skɪnt/ *adj. Brit. sl.* having no money left. [= *skinned*, past part. of SKIN]

skip[1] /skɪp/ *v. & n.* —*v.* (**skipped**, **skipping**) **1** *intr.* **a** move along lightly, esp. by taking two steps with each foot in turn. **b** jump lightly from the ground, esp. so as to clear a skipping-rope. **c** jump about, gambol, caper, frisk. **2** *intr.* (often foll. by *from*, *off*, *to*) move quickly from one point, subject, or occupation to another; be desultory. **3** *tr.* (also *absol.*) omit in dealing with a series or in reading (*skip every tenth row; always skips the small*

print). **4** *tr. colloq.* not participate in. **5** *tr. colloq.* depart quickly from; leave hurriedly. **6** *intr.* (often foll. by *out, off*) *colloq.* make off, disappear. **7** *tr.* make (a stone) ricochet on the surface of water. —*n.* **1** a skipping movement or action. **2** *Computing* the action of passing over part of a sequence of data or instructions. **3** *US colloq.* a person who defaults or absconds. □ **skip it** *sl.* **1** abandon a topic etc. **2** make off, disappear. **skipping-rope** (*US* **skip-rope**) a length of rope revolved over the head and under the feet while jumping as a game or exercise. **skip zone** the annular region round a broadcasting station where neither direct nor reflected waves are received. [ME, prob. f. Scand.]

skip[2] /skɪp/ *n.* **1** a large container for builders' refuse etc. **2** a cage, bucket, etc., in which men or materials are lowered and raised in mines and quarries. **3** = SKEP. [var. of SKEP]

skip[3] /skɪp/ *n. & v.* —*n.* the captain or director of a side at bowls or curling. —*v.tr.* (**skipped, skipping**) be the skip of. [abbr. of SKIPPER[1]]

skipjack /ˈskɪpdʒæk/ *n.* **1** (in full **skipjack tuna**) a small striped Pacific tuna, *Katsuwonus pelamus*, used as food. **2** a click beetle. **3** a kind of sailing-boat used off the East coast of the US. [SKIP[1] + JACK[1]]

skipper[1] /ˈskɪpə(r)/ *n. & v.* —*n.* **1** a sea captain, esp. the master of a small trading or fishing vessel. **2** the captain of an aircraft. **3** the captain of a side in games. —*v.tr.* act as captain of. [ME f. MDu., MLG *schipper* f. *schip* SHIP]

skipper[2] /ˈskɪpə(r)/ *n.* **1** a person who skips. **2** any brown thick-bodied butterfly of the family Hesperiidae.

skippet /ˈskɪpɪt/ *n.* a small round wooden box to enclose and protect a seal attached to a document. [ME: orig. unkn.]

skirl /skɜːl/ *n. & v.* —*n.* the shrill sound characteristic of bagpipes. —*v.intr.* make a skirl. [prob. Scand.: ult. imit.]

skirmish /ˈskɜːmɪʃ/ *n. & v.* —*n.* **1** a piece of irregular or unpremeditated fighting esp. between small or outlying parts of armies or fleets, a slight engagement. **2** a short argument or contest of wit etc. —*v.intr.* engage in a skirmish. □□ **skirmisher** *n.* [ME f. OF *eskirmir, escremir* f. Frank.]

skirr /skɜː(r)/ *v.intr.* move rapidly esp. with a whirring sound. [perh. rel. to SCOUR[1] or SCOUR[2]]

skirret /ˈskɪrɪt/ *n.* a perennial umbelliferous plant, *Sium sisarum*, formerly cultivated in Europe for its edible root. [ME *skirwhit(e)*, perh. formed as SHEER[1], WHITE]

skirt /skɜːt/ *n. & v.* —*n.* **1** a woman's outer garment hanging from the waist. **2** the part of a coat etc. that hangs below the waist. **3** a hanging part round the base of a hovercraft. **4** (in *sing.* or *pl.*) an edge, border, or extreme part. **5** (also **bit of skirt**) *sl. offens.* a woman regarded as an object of sexual desire. **6** (in full **skirt of beef** etc.) **a** the diaphragm and other membranes as food. **b** *Brit.* a cut of meat from the lower flank. **7** a flap of a saddle. **8** a surface that conceals or protects the wheels or underside of a vehicle or aircraft. —*v.* **1** *tr.* go along or round or past the edge of. **2** *tr.* be situated along. **3** *tr.* avoid dealing with (an issue etc.). **4** *intr.* (foll. by *along*) go along the coast, a wall, etc. □ **skirt-dance** a dance with graceful manipulation of a full skirt. □□ **skirted** *adj.* (also in *comb.*). **skirtless** *adj.* [ME f. ON *skyrta* shirt, corresp. to OE *scyrte*: see SHIRT]

skirting /ˈskɜːtɪŋ/ *n.* (in full **skirting-board**) *Brit.* a narrow board etc. along the bottom of the wall of a room.

skit[1] /skɪt/ *n.* (often foll. by *on*) a light, usu. short, piece of satire or burlesque. [rel. to *skit* move lightly and rapidly, perh. f. ON (cf. *skjóta* SHOOT)]

skit[2] /skɪt/ *n. colloq.* **1** a large number, a crowd. **2** (in *pl.*) heaps, lots. [20th c.: cf. SCADS]

skite /skaɪt/ *v. & n.* —*v.intr. Austral. & NZ colloq.* boast, brag. —*n.* **1** *Austral. & NZ colloq.* **a** a boaster. **b** boasting; boastfulness. **2** *Sc.* a drinking-bout; a spree (*on the skite*). [Sc. & N.Engl. dial., = a person regarded with contempt: cf. BLATHERSKITE]

skitter /ˈskɪtə(r)/ *v.intr.* (also **skeeter** /ˈskiːtə(r)/) **1 a** (usu. foll. by *along, across*) move lightly or hastily. **b** (usu. foll. by *about, off*) hurry about, dart off. **2** fish by drawing bait jerkily across the surface of the water. [app. frequent. of dial. *skite*, perh. formed as SKIT[1]]

skittery /ˈskɪtərɪ/ adj. skittish, restless.

skittish /ˈskɪtɪʃ/ adj. **1** lively, playful. **2** (of a horse etc.) nervous, inclined to shy, fidgety. □□ **skittishly** adv. **skittishness** n. [ME, perh. formed as SKIT¹]

skittle /ˈskɪt(ə)l/ n. & v. —n. **1** a pin used in the game of skittles. **2** (in pl.; usu. treated as sing.) **a** a game like ninepins played with usu. nine wooden pins set up at the end of an alley to be bowled down usu. with wooden balls or a wooden disc. **b** (in full **table skittles**) a game played with similar pins set up on a board to be knocked down by swinging a suspended ball. **c** colloq. chess not played seriously. —v.tr. (often foll. by out) Cricket get (batsmen) out in rapid succession. [17th c. (also kittle-pins): orig. unkn.]

skive /skaɪv/ v. & n. —v. **1** tr. split or pare (hides, leather, etc.). **2** intr. Brit. sl. **a** evade a duty, shirk. **b** (often foll. by off) avoid work by absenting oneself, play truant. —n. sl. **1** an instance of shirking. **2** an easy option. □□ **skiver** n. [ON skífa, rel. to ME schīve slice]

skivvy /ˈskɪvɪ/ n. & v. —n. (pl. -ies) **1** Brit. colloq. derog. a female domestic servant. **2** US **a** a thin high-necked long-sleeved garment. **b** (in pl.) underwear of vest and underpants —v. (-ies, -ied) Brit. work as or like a skivvy. [20th c.: orig. unkn.]

skol /skɒl, skəʊl/ n. (also **skoal**) used as a toast in drinking. [Da. skaal, Sw. skål, f. ON skál bowl]

Skopje /ˈskɒpjeɪ/ the capital of the republic of Macedonia Yugoslavia; pop. (1981) 506,500.

Skryabin /skrɪˈɑːbɪn/, Alexander (1872–1915), Russian composer, born in Moscow where he studied at the Conservatory before embarking on a career as a concert pianist. Much of his music is influenced by the mystic theories he encountered in Brussels in 1908, especially the best known of his works, the symphonic poem Prometheus, or The Poem of Fire (1909–10), which is scored for orchestra, piano, optional choir, and 'keyboard of light' (projecting colours on to a screen) and is based on the chord he called 'mystic'.

skua /ˈskjuːə/ n. any large predatory sea bird of the family Stercorariidae which pursues other birds and makes them disgorge the fish they have caught. [mod.L f. Faroese skúgvur, ON skúfr]

skulduggery /skʌlˈdʌgərɪ/ n. (also **sculduggery**, **skullduggery**) trickery; unscrupulous behaviour. [earlier sculduddery, orig. Sc. = unchastity (18th c.: orig. unkn.)]

skulk /skʌlk/ v. & n. —v.intr. **1** move stealthily, lurk, or keep oneself concealed, esp. in a cowardly or sinister way. **2** stay or sneak away in time of danger. **3** shirk duty. —n. **1** a person who skulks. **2** a company of foxes. □□ **skulker** n. [ME f. Scand.: cf. Norw. skulka lurk, Da. skulke, Sw. skolka shirk]

skull /skʌl/ n. **1** the bony case of the brain of a vertebrate. **2 a** the part of the skeleton corresponding to the head. **b** this with the skin and soft internal parts removed. **c** a representation of this. **3** the head as the seat of intelligence. □ **out of one's skull** sl. out of one's mind, crazy. **skull and crossbones** a representation of a skull with two thigh-bones crossed below it as an emblem of piracy or death. **skull session** US sl. a discussion or conference. □□ **skulled** adj. (also in comb.). [ME scolle: orig. unkn.]

skullcap /ˈskʌlkæp/ n. **1** a small close-fitting peakless cap. **2** the top part of the skull. **3** any plant of the genus Scutellaria, with helmet-shaped bilabiate flowers.

skunk /skʌŋk/ n. & v. —n. **1 a** any of various cat-sized flesheating mammals of the family Mustelidae, esp. Mephitis mephitis having a distinctive black and white striped fur and able to emit a powerful stench from a liquid secreted by its anal glands as a defence. **b** its fur. **2** colloq. a thoroughly contemptible person. —v.tr. **1** US sl. defeat. **2** fail to pay (a bill etc.). □ **skunk-bear** US a wolverine. **skunk-cabbage** US a herbaceous plant, Lysichiton americanum, with an offensive-smelling spathe. [Amer. Ind. segankw, segongw]

sky /skaɪ/ n. & v. —n. (pl. skies) (in sing. or pl.) **1** the region of the atmosphere and outer space seen from the earth. **2** the weather or climate evidenced by this. —v.tr. (skies, skied) **1** Cricket etc. hit (a ball) high into the air. **2** hang (a picture) high on a wall. □ **sky-blue** adj. & n. a bright clear blue. **sky-blue pink**

an imaginary colour. **sky-clad** sl. naked (esp. in witchcraft). **sky cloth** Theatr. a backcloth painted or coloured to represent the sky. **sky-high** adv. & adj. as if reaching the sky, very high. **the sky is the limit** there is practically no limit. **sky pilot** sl. a clergyman. **sky-rocket** n. a rocket exploding high in the air. —v.intr. (**-rocketed, -rocketing**) (esp. of prices etc.) rise very steeply or rapidly. **sky-shouting** the sending of messages from an aircraft to the ground by means of a loudspeaker. **sky-sign** an advertisement on the roof of a building. **sky wave** a radio wave reflected from the ionosphere. **sky-writing** legible smoke-trails made by an aeroplane esp. for advertising. **to the skies** very highly; without reserve (praised to the skies). **under the open sky** out of doors. □□ **skyey** adj. **skyless** adj. [ME ski(es) cloud(s) f. ON ský]

skydiving /ˈskaɪˌdaɪvɪŋ/ n. the sport of performing acrobatic manoeuvres under free fall with a parachute. □□ **skydive** v.intr. **skydiver** n.

Skye /skaɪ/ the largest of the Inner Hebrides in NW Scotland. Much of the island is mountainous, especially the rugged Cuillin Hills. —n. (in full **Skye terrier**) a small long-bodied shortlegged long-haired slate or fawn coloured variety of Scotch terrier.

skyer /ˈskaɪə(r)/ n. (also **skier**) Cricket a high hit.

skyjack /ˈskaɪdʒæk/ v. & n. sl. —v.tr. hijack (an aircraft). —n. an act of skyjacking. □□ **skyjacker** n. [SKY + HIJACK]

Skylab /ˈskaɪlæb/ a space laboratory (Skylab 1) launched into Earth orbit by the US in 1973, where experiments were conducted in conditions of zero gravity. It was manned until 1974 and disintegrated in the atmosphere in 1979 after its orbit had become unstable, some parts crashing to earth in the desert of Western Australia.

skylark /ˈskaɪlɑːk/ n. & v. —n. a lark, Alauda arvensis of Eurasia and N. Africa, that sings while hovering in flight. —v.intr. play tricks or practical jokes, indulge in horseplay, frolic. [SKY + LARK¹: (v.) with pun on LARK¹, LARK²]

skylight /ˈskaɪlaɪt/ n. a window set in the plane of a roof or ceiling.

skyline /ˈskaɪlaɪn/ n. the outline of hills, buildings, etc., defined against the sky; the visible horizon.

skysail /ˈskaɪseɪl, -s(ə)l/ n. a light sail above the royal in a squarerigged ship.

skyscape /ˈskaɪskeɪp/ n. **1** a picture chiefly representing the sky. **2** a view of the sky.

skyscraper /ˈskaɪˌskreɪpə(r)/ n. a very tall building with many storeys, especially the type of office building that dominates Manhattan Island, New York, and the centres of other large American cities. Skyscrapers were first built because of the high cost of land in congested urban areas, and subsequently also for their prestige value even when they were not economical. They were made possible technically by the development of the steelframe construction and the invention of the electric lift. Leroy S. Buffington, a Minneapolis architect, designed the first skyscraper in 1880, but the first one actually erected was the Home Insurance Building in Chicago, a 10-storey structure completed in 1885.

skyward /ˈskaɪwəd/ adv. & adj. —adv. (also **skywards**) towards the sky. —adj. moving skyward.

skywatch /ˈskaɪwɒtʃ/ n. the activity of watching the sky for aircraft etc.

skyway /ˈskaɪweɪ/ n. **1** a route used by aircraft. **2** the sky as a medium of transport.

slab /slæb/ n. & v. —n. **1** a flat broad fairly thick usu. square or rectangular piece of solid material, esp. stone. **2** a large flat piece of cake, chocolate, etc. **3** (of timber) an outer piece sawn from a log. **4** Brit. a mortuary table. —v.tr. (**slabbed, slabbing**) remove slabs from (a log or tree) to prepare it for sawing into planks. [ME: orig. unkn.]

slack¹ /slæk/ adj., n., v., & adv. —adj. **1** (of rope etc.) not taut. **2** inactive or sluggish. **3** negligent or remiss. **4** (of tide etc.) neither ebbing nor flowing. **5** (of trade or business or a market) with little happening. **6** loose. **7** Phonet. lax. **8** relaxed, languid. —n. **1** the slack part of a rope (haul in the slack). **2** a slack time in trade etc. **3** *colloq.* a spell of inactivity or laziness. **4** (in *pl.*) full-length loosely-cut trousers for informal wear. —*v.* **1 a** *tr.* & *intr.* slacken. **b** *tr.* loosen (rope etc.). **2** *intr. colloq.* take a rest, be lazy. **3** *tr.* slake (lime). —*adv.* **1** slackly. **2** slowly or insufficiently (*dry slack*; *bake slack*). □ **slack hand** lack of full control in riding or governing. **slack lime** slaked lime. **slack off 1** loosen. **2** lose or cause to lose vigour. **slack rein** = *slack hand*. **slack suit** *US* casual clothes of slacks and a jacket or shirt. **slack up** reduce the speed of a train etc. before stopping. **slack water** a time near the turn of the tide, esp. at low tide. **take up the slack** use up a surplus or make up a deficiency; avoid an undesirable lull. □□ **slackly** *adv.* **slackness** *n.* [OE *slæc* f. Gmc]

slack² /slæk/ *n.* coal-dust or small pieces of coal. [ME prob. f. LG or Du.]

slacken /'slækən/ *v.tr.* & *intr.* make or become slack. □ **slacken off** = *slack off* (see SLACK¹).

slacker /'slækə(r)/ *n.* a shirker; an indolent person.

slag /slæg/ *n.* & *v.* —*n.* **1** vitreous refuse left after ore has been smelted, dross separated in a fused state in the reduction of ore, clinkers. **2** volcanic scoria. **3** *sl. derog.* **a** a prostitute or promiscuous woman. **b** a worthless or insignificant person. —*v.* (**slagged, slagging**) **1** *intr.* **a** form slag. **b** cohere into a mass like slag. **2** *tr.* (often foll. by *off*) *sl.* criticize, insult. □ **slag-heap** a hill of refuse from a mine etc. **slag-wool** = *mineral wool*. □□ **slaggy** *adj.* (**slaggier, slaggiest**). [MLG *slagge*, perh. f. *slagen* strike, with ref. to fragments formed by hammering]

slain *past part.* of SLAY¹.

slainte /'slɑːntʃə/ *int.* a Gaelic toast: good health! [Gael. *sláinte*, lit. 'health']

slake /sleɪk/ *v.tr.* **1** assuage or satisfy (thirst, revenge, etc.). **2** disintegrate (quicklime) by chemical combination with water. [OE *slacian* f. *slæc* SLACK¹]

slalom /'slɑːləm/ *n.* **1** a ski-race down a zigzag course defined by artificial obstacles. **2** an obstacle race in canoes or cars or on skateboards or water-skis. [Norw., lit. 'sloping track']

slam¹ /slæm/ *v.* & *n.* —*v.* (**slammed, slamming**) **1** *tr.* & *intr.* shut forcefully and loudly. **2** *tr.* put down (an object) with a similar sound. **3** *intr.* move violently (*he slammed out of the room*). **4** *tr.* & *intr.* put or come into sudden action (*slam the brakes on*). **5** *tr. sl.* criticize severely. **6** *tr. sl.* hit. **7** *tr. sl.* gain an easy victory over. —*n.* **1** a sound of or as of a slammed door. **2** the shutting of a door etc. with a loud bang. **3** (usu. prec. by *the*) *US sl.* prison. [prob. f. Scand.: cf. ON *slam(b)ra*]

slam² /slæm/ *n.* *Cards* the winning of every trick in a game. □ **grand slam 1** *Bridge* the winning of 13 tricks. **2** the winning of all of a group of championships or matches in a sport. **small** (or **little**) **slam** *Bridge* the winning of 12 tricks. [orig. name of a card-game: perh. f. obs. *slampant* trickery]

slambang /slæm'bæŋ/ *adv.* & *adj.* —*adv.* with the sound of a slam. —*adj. colloq.* impressive, exciting, or energetic.

slammer /'slæmə(r)/ *n.* (usu. prec. by *the*) *sl.* prison.

slander /'slɑːndə(r)/ *n.* & *v.* —*n.* **1** a malicious, false, and injurious statement spoken about a person. **2** the uttering of such statements; calumny. **3** *Law* false oral defamation (cf. LIBEL). —*v.tr.* utter slander about; defame falsely. □□ **slanderer** *n.* **slanderous** *adj.* **slanderously** *adv.* [ME *sclaundre* f. AF *esclaundre*, OF *esclandre* alt. f. *escandle* f. LL *scandalum*: see SCANDAL]

slang /slæŋ/ *n.* & *v.* —*n.* words, phrases, and uses that are regarded as very informal and are often restricted to special contexts or are peculiar to a specified profession, class, etc. (*racing slang*; *schoolboy slang*). (See below.) —*v.* **1** *tr.* use abusive language to. **2** *intr.* use such language. □ **slanging-match** a prolonged exchange of insults. [18th-c. cant: orig. unkn.]

Some words originally regarded as slang (e.g. *clever, fun, frisky, mob*, which were disliked by Dr Johnson and others in the 18th c.) have now passed into standard non-colloquial usage; others (e.g. *quid* = £1) have remained in the category of slang. Slang is used sometimes for fun, or to be concise or picturesque, or to express feelings and attitudes (e.g. of hostility, ridicule, or affection) better than dignified words would do; it can make light of a serious or tragic situation, or refer to it by paraphrase; it can shock or attract attention; in particular, it can identify

its users as members of a special group. Writers such as Dryden and Swift (17th–18th c.) thought that slang words and phrases were allowed too easy an entrance to the English language and proposed an Academy on the French model which they hoped might 'regulate' grammar and vocabulary. The proposal, however, came to nothing.

slangy /'slæŋɪ/ *adj.* (**slangier, slangiest**) **1** of the character of slang. **2** fond of using slang. □□ **slangily** *adv.* **slanginess** *n.*

slant /slɑːnt/ *v.*, *n.*, & *adj.* —*v.* **1** *intr.* slope; diverge from a line; lie or go obliquely to a vertical or horizontal line. **2** *tr.* cause to do this. **3** *tr.* (often as **slanted** *adj.*) present (information) from a particular angle esp. in a biased or unfair way. —*n.* **1** a slope; an oblique position. **2** a way of regarding a thing; a point of view, esp. a biased one. □ **on a** (or **the**) **slant** aslant. **slant-eyed** having slanting eyes. **slant height** the height of a cone from the vertex to the periphery of the base. [aphetic form of ASLANT: (v.) rel. to ME *slent* f. ON *sletta* dash, throw]

slantwise /'slɑːntwaɪz/ *adv.* aslant.

slap /slæp/ *v.*, *n.*, & *adv.* —*v.* (**slapped, slapping**) **1** *tr.* & *intr.* strike with the palm of the hand or a flat object, or so as to make a similar noise. **2** *tr.* lay forcefully (*slapped the money on the table*; *slapped a writ on the offender*). **3** *tr.* put hastily or carelessly (*slap some paint on the walls*). **4** *tr.* (often foll. by *down*) *colloq.* reprimand or snub. —*n.* **1** a blow with the palm of the hand or a flat object. **2** a slapping sound. —*adv.* **1** with the suddenness or effectiveness or true aim of a blow, suddenly, fully, directly (*ran slap into him*; *hit me slap in the eye*). **2** = *slap-bang*. □ **slap and tickle** *Brit. colloq.* light-hearted amorous amusement. **slap-bang** violently, noisily, headlong. **slap-happy** *colloq.* **1** cheerfully casual or flippant. **2** punch-drunk. **slap in the face** a rebuff or affront. **slap on the back** *n.* congratulations. —*v.tr.* congratulate. **slap-up** esp. *Brit. colloq.* excellent, lavish; done regardless of expense (*slap-up meal*). [LG *slapp* (imit.)]

slapdash /'slæpdæʃ/ *adj.* & *adv.* —*adj.* hasty and careless. —*adv.* in a slapdash manner.

slapjack /'slæpdʒæk/ *n.* *US* a kind of pancake cooked on a griddle. [SLAP + JACK¹]

slapstick /'slæpstɪk/ *n.* **1** boisterous knockabout comedy. **2** a flexible divided lath used by a clown. [SLAP + STICK¹]

slash /slæʃ/ *v.* & *n.* —*v.* **1** *intr.* make a sweeping or random cut or cuts with a blade, sword, whip, etc. **2** *tr.* make such a cut or cuts at. **3** *tr.* make a long narrow gash or gashes in. **4** *tr.* reduce (prices etc.) drastically. **5** *tr.* censure vigorously. **6** *tr.* make (one's way) by slashing. **7** *tr.* **a** lash (a person etc.) with a whip. **b** crack (a whip). —*n.* **1 a** a slashing cut or stroke. **b** a wound or slit made by this. **2** an oblique stroke; a solidus. **3** *Brit. sl.* an act of urinating. **4** *US* debris resulting from the felling or destruction of trees. □ **slash-and-burn** (of cultivation) in which vegetation is cut down, allowed to dry, and then burned off before seeds are planted. □□ **slasher** *n.* [ME perh. f. OF *esclachier* break in pieces]

slashed /slæʃt/ *adj.* (of a sleeve etc.) having slits to show a lining or puffing of other material.

slashing /'slæʃɪŋ/ *adj.* vigorously incisive or effective.

slat /slæt/ *n.* a thin narrow piece of wood or plastic or metal, esp. used in an overlapping series as in a fence or Venetian blind. [ME *s(c)lat* f. OF *esclat* splinter etc. f. *esclater* split f. Rmc]

slate /sleɪt/ *n.*, *v.*, & *adj.* —*n.* **1** a fine-grained grey, green, or bluish-purple metamorphic rock easily split into flat smooth plates. **2** a piece of such a plate used as roofing-material. **3** a piece of such a plate used for writing on, usu. framed in wood. **4** the colour of slate. **5** *US* a list of nominees for office etc. —*v.tr.* **1** cover with slates esp. as roofing. **2** *Brit. colloq.* criticize severely; scold. **3** *US* make arrangements for (an event etc.). **4** *US* propose or nominate for office etc. —*adj.* made of slate. □ **on the slate** *Brit.* recorded as a debt to be paid. **slate-blue** (or **-black**) a shade of blue (or black) occurring in slate. **slate-colour** a dark bluish or greenish grey. **slate-coloured** of this colour. **slate-grey** a shade of grey occurring in slate. **slate-pencil** a small rod of soft slate used for writing on slate. **wipe the slate clean** forgive or cancel the record of past offences. □□ **slating** n. **slaty** adj. [ME s(c)late f. OF esclate, fem. form of esclat SLAT]

slater /ˈsleɪtə(r)/ n. **1** a person who slates roofs etc. **2** a woodlouse or similar crustacean.

slather /ˈslæðə(r)/ n. & v. —n. **1** (usu. in pl.) US colloq. a large amount. **2** (often **open slather**) Austral. & NZ sl. unrestricted scope for action. —v.tr. US colloq. **1** spread thickly. **2** squander. [19th c.: orig. unkn.]

slatted /ˈslætɪd/ adj. having slats.

slattern /ˈslæt(ə)n/ n. a slovenly woman. □□ **slatternly** adj. **slatternliness** n. [17th c.: rel. to slattering slovenly, f. dial. slatter to spill, slop, waste, frequent. of slat strike]

slaughter /ˈslɔːtə(r)/ n. & v. —n. **1** the killing of an animal or animals for food. **2** the killing of many persons or animals at once or continuously; carnage, massacre. —v.tr. **1** kill (people) in a ruthless manner or on a great scale. **2** kill for food, butcher. **3** colloq. defeat utterly. □□ **slaughterer** n. **slaughterous** adj. [ME slahter ult. f. ON slátr butcher's meat, rel. to SLAY[1]]

slaughterhouse /ˈslɔːtəˌhaʊs/ n. **1** a place for the slaughter of animals as food. **2** a place of carnage.

Slav /slɑːv/ n. & adj. —n. a member of a group of peoples in Central and Eastern Europe (including the Russians, Poles, Czechs, Bulgarians, Serbo-Croats, and others) speaking Slavonic languages. —adj. **1** of or relating to the Slavs. **2** Slavonic. □□ **Slavism** n. [ME Sclave f. med.L Sclavus, late Gk Sklabos, & f. med.L Slavus]

slave /sleɪv/ n. & v. —n. **1** a person who is the legal property of another or others and is bound to absolute obedience, a human chattel. **2** a drudge, a person working very hard. **3** (foll. by of, to) a helpless victim of some dominating influence (slave of fashion; slave to duty). **4** a machine, or part of one, directly controlled by another. —v. **1** intr. (often foll. by at, over) work very hard. **2** tr. (foll. by to) subject (a device) to control by another. □ **slave-bangle** a bangle of gold, glass, etc., worn by a woman usu. above the elbow. **slave-born** born in slavery, born of slave parents. **slave-bracelet** = slave-bangle. **slave-drive** (past -drove; past part. -driven) work (a person) hard, esp. excessively. **slave-driver 1** an overseer of slaves at work. **2** a person who works others hard. **slave labour** forced labour. **slave ship** hist. a ship transporting slaves, esp. from Africa. **Slave State** hist. any of the southern States of the US in which slavery was legal before the Civil War. **slave-trade** hist. the procuring, transporting, and selling of human beings, esp. African Blacks, as slaves. **slave-trader** hist. a person engaged in the slave-trade. [ME f. OF esclave = med.L sclavus, sclava Slav (captive): see SLAV]

slaver[1] /ˈsleɪvə(r)/ n. hist. a ship or person engaged in the slave-trade.

slaver[2] /ˈslævə(r)/ n. & v. —n. **1** saliva running from the mouth. **2** a fulsome or servile flattery. **b** drivel, nonsense. —v.intr. **1** let saliva run from the mouth, dribble. **2** (foll. by over) show excessive sentimentality over, or desire for. [ME prob. f. LG or Du.: cf. SLOBBER]

slavery /ˈsleɪvərɪ/ n. **1** the condition of a slave. **2** exhausting labour; drudgery. **3** the custom of having slaves.

A widespread institution in ancient times, slavery had died out in England by the 12th c. The transportation of slaves from Africa to the Americas by European traders began on a large scale in the 16th and 17th c., and although slavery became illegal in Britain in 1772, it remained an important feature of the economy of the Empire until the 19th c., the slave-trade being abolished in 1807 and slavery itself throughout the Empire in 1833. In the American South slavery was an essential part of the cotton-based economy, and the abolition campaign waged during the first half of the 19th c. eventually led to the American Civil War and to final emancipation. In some parts of the world chattel slavery, the ownership of one person by another, continues to exist.

slavey /ˈsleɪvɪ/ n. (pl. -eys) colloq. a maidservant, esp. a hard-worked one.

Slavic /ˈslɑːvɪk/ adj. & n. = SLAVONIC.

slavish /ˈsleɪvɪʃ/ adj. **1** of, like, or as of slaves. **2** showing no

attempt at originality or development. **3** abject, servile, base. □□ **slavishly** adv. **slavishness** n.

Slavonic /sləˈvɒnɪk/ adj. & n. —adj. **1** of or relating to the group of Indo-European languages including Russian, Polish, and Czech. **2** of or relating to the Slavs. —n. the Slavonic group of languages, a main division of the Indo-European family, including Russian, Czech, Serbo-Croat, Bulgarian, and Polish. The common Slavonic language from which they are all descended probably broke away from the main Indo-European family before Christian times. They have many characteristics in common: nouns and adjectives are highly inflected (Russian and Polish have as many as seven cases), verbs have few tenses but preserve an ancient distinction (called aspect) between actions thought of as finished or limited in time and those regarded as continuous, and final syllables are varied to show subtle changes of meaning. The two principal alphabets used are the Cyrillic and the Latin. □ **Church** or **Old (Church) Slavonic** the earliest written Slavonic language, surviving as a liturgical language in the Orthodox Church. It was a South Slavonic dialect from the region of Macedonia, used in the 9th c. by St Cyril and his brother St Methodius for their missionary purposes in the Slav countries of Moravia and Pannonia. Throughout the Middle Ages it was the language of culture for the Orthodox peoples of eastern Europe, playing a role similar to that of Latin in the West. Two different alphabets were used, Glagolitic and Cyrillic. [med.L S(c)lavonicus f. S(c)lavonia country of Slavs f. Sclavus SLAV]

slaw /slɔː/ n. coleslaw. [Du. sla, shortened f. salade SALAD]

slay[1] /sleɪ/ v.tr. (past **slew** /sluː/; past part. **slain** /sleɪn/) **1** literary or joc. kill. **2** sl. overwhelm with delight; convulse with laughter. □□ **slayer** n. [OE slēan f. Gmc]

slay[2] var. of SLEY.

SLBM abbr. submarine-launched ballistic missile.

SLD abbr. (in the UK) Social and Liberal Democrats. ¶ In 1989 officially replaced by Liberal Democrats.

sleaze /sliːz/ n. & v. colloq. —n. **1** sleaziness. **2** a person of low moral standards. —v.intr. move in a sleazy fashion. [back-form. f. SLEAZY]

sleazy /ˈsliːzɪ/ adj. (**sleazier**, **sleaziest**) **1** squalid, tawdry. **2** slatternly. **3** (of textiles etc.) flimsy. □□ **sleazily** adv. **sleaziness** n. [17th c.: orig. unkn.]

sled /sled/ n. & v. US —n. a sledge. —v.intr. (**sledded**, **sledding**) ride on a sledge. [MLG sledde, rel. to SLIDE]

sledge[1] /sledʒ/ n. & v. —n. **1** a vehicle on runners for conveying loads or passengers esp. over snow, drawn by horses, dogs, or reindeer or pushed or pulled by one or more persons. **2** a toboggan. —v.intr. & tr. travel or convey by sledge. [MDu. sleedse, rel. to SLED]

sledge[2] /sledʒ/ n. = SLEDGEHAMMER.

sledgehammer /ˈsledʒˌhæmə(r)/ n. **1** a large heavy hammer used to break stone etc. **2** (attrib.) heavy or powerful (a sledgehammer blow). [OE slecg, rel. to SLAY[1]]

sleek /sliːk/ adj. & v. —adj. **1** (of hair, fur, or skin, or an animal or person with such hair etc.) smooth and glossy. **2** looking well-fed and comfortable. **3** ingratiating. **4** (of a thing) smooth and polished. —v.tr. make sleek, esp. by stroking or pressing down. □□ **sleekly** adv. **sleekness** n. **sleeky** adj. [later var. of SLICK]

sleep /sliːp/ n. & v. —n. **1** a condition of body and mind such as that which normally recurs for several hours every night, in which the nervous system is inactive, the eyes closed, the postural muscles relaxed, and consciousness practically suspended. (See below.) **2** a period of sleep (shall try to get a sleep). **3** a state like sleep, such as rest, quiet, negligence, or death. **4** the prolonged inert condition of hibernating animals. **5** a substance found in the corners of the eyes after sleep. —v. (past and past part. **slept** /slept/) **1** intr. **a** be in a state of sleep. **b** fall asleep. **2** intr. (foll. by at, in, etc.) spend the night. **3** tr. provide sleeping accommodation for (the house sleeps six). **4** intr. (foll. by with, together) have sexual intercourse, esp. in bed. **5** intr. (foll. by on, over) not decide (a question) until the next day. **6** intr. (foll. by through) fail to be woken by. **7** intr. be inactive or dormant. **8** intr. be dead; lie in the grave. **9** tr. **a** (foll. by off) remedy by

sleeping (*slept off his hangover*). **b** (foll. by *away*) spend in sleeping (*sleep the hours away*). **10** *intr.* (of a top) spin so steadily as to seem motionless. □ **get to sleep** manage to fall asleep. **go to sleep 1** enter a state of sleep. **2** (of a limb) become numbed by pressure. **in one's sleep** while asleep. **last sleep** death. **let sleeping dogs lie** avoid stirring up trouble. **put to sleep 1** anaesthetize. **2** kill (an animal) painlessly. **sleep around** *colloq.* be sexually promiscuous. **sleep in 1** remain asleep later than usual in the morning. **2** sleep by night at one's place of work. **sleeping-bag** a lined or padded bag to sleep in esp. when camping etc. **Sleeping Beauty** a fairy-tale heroine who slept for 100 years. **sleeping-car** (or **-carriage**) a railway coach provided with beds or berths. **sleeping-draught** a drink to induce sleep. **sleeping partner** a partner not sharing in the actual work of a firm. **sleeping-pill** a pill to induce sleep. **sleeping policeman** a ramp etc. in the road intended to cause traffic to reduce speed. **sleeping sickness** see separate entry. **sleeping-suit** a child's one-piece night-garment. **sleep-learning** learning by hearing while asleep. **sleep like a log** (or *top*) sleep soundly. **the sleep of the just** sound sleep. **sleep out** sleep by night out of doors, or not at one's place of work. **sleep-out** *n. Austral. & NZ* a veranda, porch, or outbuilding providing sleeping accommodation. [OE *slǣp, slæp* (n.), *slēpan, slǣpan* (v.) f. Gmc]
The capacity for sleep is very general. Most animals have it, and many insects show a marked difference between their daytime and night-time levels of activity. The pattern of sleep in mammals is usually related to their general habits and the importance of their different senses, with those dependent principally on vision for finding food etc. active by day and asleep at night, but some (e.g. lions, horses, and sheep) show no clearcut rhythm and may sleep at any time. Sleep varies not only in duration but in depth. The physiology of sleep has been studied by analysing the electrical activity of the human brain: the relatively fast electrical rhythm of the waking brain disappears during sleep and is replaced by slow waves and occasional bursts of fast activity. There is evidence that electrical activity of the brain changes when a sleeper dreams, and this is associated with rapid movements of the eyes. There is no general agreement, however, about why sleep is a feature of life.

sleeper /ˈsliːpə(r)/ *n.* **1** a person or animal that sleeps. **2** *Brit.* a wooden or concrete beam laid horizontally as a support, esp. for railway track. **3 a** a sleeping-car. **b** a berth in this. **4** *Brit.* a ring worn in a pierced ear to keep the hole from closing. **5** a thing that is suddenly successful after being undistinguished. **6** a sleeping-suit. **7** a spy or saboteur etc. who remains inactive while establishing a secure position.

sleeping sickness *n.* any of several similar diseases caused by trypanosomes transmitted by the bite of the tsetse fly and characterized by changes in the central nervous system leading to apathy, coma, and death. Such diseases are prevalent in tropical Africa. The characteristic feature of the areas where they occur is a dense shade cast by thickly growing shrubs and small trees, such as may be found on the banks of watercourses and water-holes; there the fly flourishes, and one of the principal control methods is to eliminate such vegetation, especially around villages, fords, and other places where people congregate.

sleepless /ˈsliːplɪs/ *adj.* **1** characterized by lack of sleep (*a sleepless night*). **2** unable to sleep. **3** continually active or moving. □□ **sleeplessly** *adv.* **sleeplessness** *n.*

sleepwalk /ˈsliːpwɔːk/ *v.intr.* walk or perform other actions while asleep. □□ **sleepwalker** *n.*

sleepy /ˈsliːpɪ/ *adj.* (**sleepier, sleepiest**) **1** drowsy; ready for sleep; about to fall asleep. **2** lacking activity or bustle (*a sleepy little town*). **3** habitually indolent, unobservant, etc. □ **sleepy sickness** encephalitis lethargica, an infection of the brain with drowsiness and sometimes a coma. □□ **sleepily** *adv.* **sleepiness** *n.*

sleepyhead /ˈsliːpɪˌhed/ *n.* (esp. as a form of address) a sleepy or inattentive person.

sleet /sliːt/ *n. & v.* —*n.* **1** a mixture of snow and rain falling together. **2** hail or snow melting as it falls. **3** *US* a thin coating of ice. —*v.intr.* (prec. by *it* as subject) sleet falls (*it is sleeting; if it*

sleets). □□ **sleety** *adj.* [ME prob. f. OE: rel. to MLG *slōten* (pl.) hail, MHG *slōz(e)* f. Gmc]

sleeve /sliːv/ *n.* **1** the part of a garment that wholly or partly covers an arm. **2** the cover of a gramophone record. **3** a tube enclosing a rod or smaller tube. **4 a** a wind-sock. **b** a drogue towed by an aircraft. □ **roll up one's sleeves** prepare to fight or work. **sleeve-board** a small ironing-board for pressing sleeves. **sleeve-coupling** a tube for connecting shafts or pipes. **sleeve-link** a cuff-link. **sleeve-note** a descriptive note on a record-sleeve. **sleeve-nut** a long nut with right-hand and left-hand screw-threads for drawing together pipes or shafts conversely threaded. **sleeve-valve** a valve in the form of a cylinder with a sliding movement. **up one's sleeve** concealed but ready for use, in reserve. □□ **sleeved** *adj.* (also in *comb.*). **sleeveless** *adj.* [OE *slēfe, sliefe, slȳf*]

sleeving /ˈsliːvɪŋ/ *n.* tubular covering for electric cable etc.

sleigh /sleɪ/ *n. & v.* —*n.* a sledge, esp. one for riding on. —*v.intr.* travel on a sleigh. □ **sleigh-bell** any of a number of tinkling bells attached to the harness of a sleigh-horse etc. [orig. US, f. Du. *slee*, rel. to SLED]

sleight /slaɪt/ *n. archaic* **1** a deceptive trick or device or movement. **2** dexterity. **3** cunning. □ **sleight of hand 1** dexterity esp. in conjuring or fencing. **2** a display of dexterity, esp. a conjuring trick. [ME *sleghth* f. ON *slœgth* f. *slœgr* SLY]

slender /ˈslendə(r)/ *adj.* (**slenderer, slenderest**) **1 a** of small girth or breadth (*a slender pillar*). **b** gracefully thin (*a slender waist*). **2** relatively small or scanty; slight, meagre, inadequate (*slender hopes; slender resources*). □ **slender loris** see LORIS. □□ **slenderly** *adv.* **slenderness** *n.* [ME: orig. unkn.]

slenderize /ˈslendəˌraɪz/ *v.* (also **-ise**) **1** *tr.* **a** make (a thing) slender. **b** make (one's figure) appear slender. **2** *intr.* make oneself slender; slim.

slept *past* and *past part.* of SLEEP.

sleuth /sluːθ/ *n. & v. colloq.* —*n.* a detective. —*v.* **1** *intr.* act as a detective. **2** *tr.* investigate. □ **sleuth-hound 1** a bloodhound. **2** *colloq.* a detective, an investigator. [orig. in *sleuth-hound*: ME f. *sleuth* f. ON *slóth* track, trail: cf. SLOT[2]]

slew[1] /sluː/ *v. & n.* (also **slue**) —*v.tr. & intr.* (often foll. by *round*) turn or swing forcibly or with effort out of the forward or ordinary position. —*n.* such a change of position. [18th-c. Naut.: orig. unkn.]

slew[2] *past* of SLAY[1].

slew[3] /sluː/ *n.* esp. *US colloq.* a large number or quantity. [Ir. *sluagh*]

sley /sleɪ/ *n.* (also **slay**) a weaver's reed. [OE *slege*, rel. to SLAY[1]]

slice /slaɪs/ *n. & v.* —*n.* **1** a thin broad piece or wedge cut off or out esp. from meat or bread or a cake, pie, or large fruit. **2** a share; a part taken or allotted or gained (*a slice of territory; a slice of the profits*). **3** an implement with a broad flat blade for serving fish etc. or for scraping or chipping. **4** *Golf & Lawn Tennis* a slicing stroke. —*v.* **1** *tr.* (often foll. by *up*) cut into slices. **2** *tr.* (foll. by *off*) cut (a piece) off. **3** *intr.* (foll. by *into, through*) cut with or like a knife. **4** *tr.* (also *absol.*) **a** *Golf* strike (the ball) so that it deviates away from the striker. **b** (in other sports) propel (the ball) forward at an angle. **5** *tr.* go through (air etc.) with a cutting motion. □ **slice of life** a realistic representation of everyday experience. □□ **sliceable** *adj.* **slicer** *n.* (also in *comb.*). [ME f. OF *esclice, esclicier* splinter f. Frank. *slītjan*, rel. to SLIT]

slick /slɪk/ *adj., n., & v.* —*adj. colloq.* **1 a** (of a person or action) skilful or efficient; dextrous (*gave a slick performance*). **b** superficially or pretentiously smooth and dextrous. **c** glib. **2 a** sleek, smooth. **b** slippery. —*n.* **1** a smooth patch of oil etc., esp. on the sea. **2** *Motor Racing* a smooth tyre. **3** *US* a glossy magazine. **4** *US sl.* a slick person. —*v.tr. colloq.* **1** make sleek or smart. **2** (usu. foll. by *down*) flatten (one's hair etc.). □□ **slickly** *adv.* **slickness** *n.* [ME *slike(n),* prob. f. OE: cf. SLEEK]

slicker /ˈslɪkə(r)/ *n. US* **1** *colloq.* **a** a plausible rogue. **b** a smart and sophisticated city-dweller (cf. *city slicker*). **2** a raincoat of smooth waterproof material.

slide /slaɪd/ *v. & n.* —*v.* (*past* and *past part.* **slid** /slɪd/) **1 a** *intr.* move along a smooth surface with continuous contact on the same part of the thing moving (cf. ROLL). **b** *tr.* cause to do this (*slide the drawer into place*). **2** *intr.* move quietly; glide; go smoothly along. **3** *intr.* pass gradually or imperceptibly. **4** *intr.* glide over ice on one or both feet without skates (under gravity or with momentum got by running). **5** *intr.* (foll. by *over*) barely touch upon (a delicate subject etc.). **6** *intr.* & *tr.* (often foll. by *into*) move or cause to move quietly or unobtrusively (*slid his hand into mine*). **7** *intr.* take its own course (*let it slide*). —*n.* **1 a** the act or an instance of sliding. **b** a rapid decline. **2** an inclined plane down which children, goods, etc., slide; a chute. **3 a** a track made by or for sliding, esp. on ice. **b** a slope prepared with snow or ice for tobogganing. **4** a part of a machine or instrument that slides, esp. a slide-valve. **5 a** a thing slid into place, esp. a piece of glass holding an object for a microscope. **b** a mounted transparency usu. placed in a projector for viewing on a screen. **6** *Brit.* = hair-slide. **7** a part or parts of a machine on or between which a sliding part works. □ **let things slide** be negligent; allow deterioration. **slide fastener** *US* a zip-fastener. **slide-rule** a ruler with a sliding central strip, graduated logarithmically for making rapid calculations, esp. multiplication and division. **slide-valve** a sliding piece that opens and closes an aperture by sliding across it. **sliding door** a door drawn across an aperture on a slide, not turning on hinges. **sliding keel** *Naut.* a centreboard. **sliding roof** a part of a roof (esp. in a motor car) made able to slide and so form an aperture. **sliding scale** a scale of fees, taxes, wages, etc., that varies as a whole in accordance with variation of some standard. **sliding seat** a seat able to slide to and fro on runners etc., esp. in a racing-boat to adjust the length of a stroke. □□ **slidable** *adj.* **slidably** *adv.* **slider** *n.* [OE *slīdan*]

slideway /ˈslaɪdweɪ/ *n.* = SLIDE *n.* 7.

slight /slaɪt/ *adj.*, *v.*, & *n.* —*adj.* **1 a** inconsiderable; of little significance (*has a slight cold; the damage is very slight*). **b** barely perceptible (*a slight smell of gas*). **c** not much or great or thorough, inadequate, scanty (*a conclusion based on very slight observation; paid him slight attention*). **2** slender, frail-looking (*saw a slight figure approaching; supported by a slight framework*). **3** (in *superl.*, with *neg.* or *interrog.*) any whatever (*paid not the slightest attention*). —*v.tr.* **1** treat or speak of (a person etc.) as not worth attention, fail in courtesy or respect towards, markedly neglect. **2** *hist.* make militarily useless, raze (a fortification etc.). —*n.* a marked piece of neglect, a failure to show due respect. □ **not in the slightest** not at all. **put a slight upon** = sense 1 of *v.* □□ **slightingly** *adv.* **slightish** *adj.* **slightly** *adv.* **slightness** *n.* [ME *slyght*, *sleght* f. ON *slēttr* level, smooth f. Gmc]

Sligo /ˈslaɪɡəʊ/ **1** a county of western Ireland, in Connaught province; pop. (est. 1986) 56,000. **2** its county town, a seaport on the Atlantic.

slily var. of SLYLY (see SLY).

slim /slɪm/ *adj.*, *v.*, & *n.* —*adj.* (**slimmer, slimmest**) **1 a** of small girth or thickness; of long narrow shape. **b** gracefully thin, slenderly built. **c** not fat or overweight. **2** small, insufficient (*a slim chance of success*). **3** clever, artful, crafty, unscrupulous. —*v.* (**slimmed, slimming**) **1** *intr.* make oneself slimmer by dieting, exercise, etc. **2** *tr.* make slim or slimmer. —*n.* a course of slimming. □□ **slimly** *adv.* **slimmer** *n.* **slimming** *n.* & *adj.* **slimmish** *adj.* **slimness** *n.* [LG or Du. f. Gmc]

slime /slaɪm/ *n.* & *v.* —*n.* thick slippery mud or a substance of similar consistency, e.g. liquid bitumen or a mucus exuded by fish etc. —*v.tr.* cover with slime. □ **slime mould** a spore-bearing micro-organism secreting slime. [OE *slīm* f. Gmc, rel. to L *limus* mud, Gk *limnē* marsh]

slimline /ˈslɪmlaɪn/ *adj.* of slender design.

slimy /ˈslaɪmɪ/ *adj.* (**slimier, slimiest**) **1** of the consistency of slime. **2** covered, smeared with, or full of slime. **3** disgustingly dishonest, meek, or flattering. **4** slippery, hard to hold. □□ **slimily** *adv.* **sliminess** *n.*

sling¹ /slɪŋ/ *n.* & *v.* —*n.* **1** a strap, belt, etc., used to support or raise a hanging weight, e.g. a rifle, a ship's boat, or goods being transferred. **2** a bandage looped round the neck to support an injured arm. **3** a strap or string used with the hand to give impetus to a small missile, esp. a stone. **4** *Austral.* *sl.* a tip or bribe. —*v.tr.* (*past* and *past part.* **slung** /slʌŋ/) **1** (also *absol.*) hurl (a stone etc.) from a sling. **2** *colloq.* throw. **3** suspend with a

sling, allow to swing suspended, arrange so as to be supported from above, hoist or transfer with a sling. □ **sling-back 1** a shoe held in place by a strap above the heel. **2** (in full **sling-back chair**) a chair with a fabric seat suspended from a rigid frame. **sling-bag** a bag with a long strap which may be hung from the shoulder. **sling one's hook** see HOOK. **sling off at** *Austral.* & *NZ sl.* disparage; mock; make fun of. **slung shot** a metal ball attached by a thong etc. to the wrist and used esp. by criminals as a weapon. [ME, prob. f. ON *slyngva* (v.)]

sling² /slɪŋ/ *n.* a sweetened drink of spirits (esp. gin) and water. [18th c.: orig. unkn.]

slinger /ˈslɪŋə(r)/ *n.* a person who slings, esp. the user of a sling.

slingshot /ˈslɪŋʃɒt/ *n.* *US* a catapult.

slink¹ /slɪŋk/ *v.intr.* (*past* and *past part.* **slunk** /slʌŋk/) (often foll. by *off*, *away*, *by*) move in a stealthy or guilty or sneaking manner. [OE *slincan* crawl]

slink² /slɪŋk/ *v.* & *n.* —*v.tr.* (also *absol.*) (of an animal) produce (young) prematurely. —*n.* **1** an animal, esp. a calf, so born. **2** its flesh. [app. f. SLINK¹]

slinky /ˈslɪŋkɪ/ *adj.* (**slinkier, slinkiest**) **1** stealthy. **2** (of a garment) close-fitting and flowing, sinuous. **3** gracefully slender. □□ **slinkily** *adv.* **slinkiness** *n.*

slip¹ /slɪp/ *v.* & *n.* —*v.* (**slipped, slipping**) **1** *intr.* slide unintentionally esp. for a short distance; lose one's footing or balance or place by unintended sliding. **2** *intr.* go or move with a sliding motion (*as the door closes the catch slips into place; slipped into her nightdress*). **3** *intr.* escape restraint or capture by being slippery or hard to hold or by not being grasped (*the eel slipped through his fingers*). **4** *intr.* make one's or its way unobserved or quietly or quickly (*just slip across to the baker's; errors will slip in*). **5** *intr.* **a** make a careless or casual mistake. **b** fall below the normal standard, deteriorate, lapse. **6** *tr.* insert or transfer stealthily or casually or with a sliding motion (*slipped a coin into his hand; slipped the papers into his pocket*). **7** *tr.* **a** release from restraint (*slipped the greyhounds from the leash*). **b** detach (an anchor) from a ship. **c** *Brit.* detach (a carriage) from a moving train. **d** release (the clutch of a motor vehicle) for a moment. **e** (of an animal) produce (young) prematurely. **8** *tr.* move (a stitch) to the other needle without knitting it. **9** *tr.* (foll. by *on*, *off*) pull (a garment) hastily on or off. **10** *tr.* escape from; give the slip to (*the dog slipped its collar; point slipped my mind*). —*n.* **1** the act or an instance of slipping. **2** an accidental or slight error. **3** a loose covering or garment, esp. a petticoat or pillowcase. **4 a** a reduction in the movement of a pulley etc. due to slipping of the belt. **b** a reduction in the distance travelled by a ship or aircraft arising from the nature of the medium in which its propeller revolves. **5** (in *sing.* or *pl.*) **a** an artificial slope of stone etc. on which boats are landed. **b** an inclined structure on which ships are built or repaired. **6** *Cricket* **a** a fielder stationed for balls glancing off the bat to the off side. **b** (in *sing.* or *pl.*) the position of such a fielder (*caught in the slips; caught at slip*). **7** a leash to slip dogs. □ **give a person the slip** escape from or evade him or her. **let slip 1** release accidentally or deliberately, esp. from a leash. **2** miss (an opportunity). **3** utter inadvertently. **let slip the dogs of war** *poet.* open hostilities. **let slip through one's fingers 1** lose hold of. **2** miss the opportunity of having. **slip away** depart without leave-taking etc. **slip-carriage** *Brit.* a railway carriage on an express for detaching at a station where the rest of the train does not stop. **slip-case** a close-fitting case for a book. **slip-coach** *Brit.* = *slip-carriage.* **slip-cover 1 a** a calico etc. cover for furniture out of use. **b** *US* = *loose cover.* **2** a jacket or slip-case for a book. **slip form** a mould in which a structure of uniform cross-section is cast by filling it with concrete and continually moving and refilling it. **slip-hook** a hook with a contrivance for releasing it readily when necessary. **slip-knot 1** a knot that can be undone by a pull. **2** a running knot. **slip off** depart without leave-taking etc. **slip of the pen** (or **tongue**) a small mistake in which something is written (or said) unintentionally. **slip-on** *adj.* (of shoes or clothes) that can be easily slipped on and off. —*n.* a slip-on shoe or garment. **slip-over** (of a garment) to be slipped on over the head. **slipped disc** a disc between vertebrae that has become displaced and causes lumbar pain. **slip-ring** a ring for sliding contact in a dynamo or electric motor. **slip-road** *Brit.* a road for entering or leaving a motorway etc. **slip-rope** *Naut.* a rope with both ends on board so that casting loose either end frees the ship from her moorings. **slip sheet** *Printing* a sheet of paper placed between newly printed sheets to prevent set-off or smudging. **slip something over on** *colloq.* outwit. **slip-stitch** *n.* **1** a loose stitch joining layers of fabric and not visible externally. **2** a stitch moved to the other needle without being knitted. —*v.tr.* sew with slip-stitch. **slip up** *colloq.* make a mistake. **slip-up** *n.* *colloq.* a mistake, a blunder. **there's many a slip 'twixt cup and lip** nothing is certain till it has happened. [ME prob. f. MLG *slippen*: cf. SLIPPERY]

slip[2] /slɪp/ *n.* **1 a** a small piece of paper esp. for writing on. **b** a long narrow strip of thin wood, paper, etc. **c** a printer's proof on such paper; a galley proof. **2** a cutting taken from a plant for grafting or planting, a scion. □ **slip of a** small and slim (*a slip of a girl*). [ME, prob. f. MDu., MLG *slippe* cut, strip, etc.]

slip[3] /slɪp/ *n.* clay in a creamy mixture with water, used mainly for decorating earthenware. □ **slip casting** the manufacture of ceramic ware by allowing slip to solidify in a mould. **slip-ware** ware decorated with slip. [OE *slipa, slyppe* slime: cf. COWSLIP]

slipover /ˈslɪpˌəʊvə(r)/ *n.* a pullover, usu. without sleeves.

slippage /ˈslɪpɪdʒ/ *n.* **1** the act or an instance of slipping. **2 a** a decline, esp. in popularity or value. **b** failure to meet a deadline or fulfil a promise; delay.

slipper /ˈslɪpə(r)/ *n. & v.* —*n.* **1** a light loose comfortable indoor shoe. **2** a light slip-on shoe for dancing etc. —*v.tr.* beat or strike with a slipper. □ **slipper bath** *Brit.* a bath shaped like a slipper, with a covered end. □□ **slippered** *adj.*

slipperwort /ˈslɪpəˌwɜːt/ *n.* calceolaria.

slippery /ˈslɪpərɪ/ *adj.* **1** difficult to hold firmly because of smoothness, wetness, sliminess, or elusive motion. **2** (of a surface) difficult to stand on, causing slips by its smoothness or muddiness. **3** unreliable, unscrupulous, shifty. **4** (of a subject) requiring tactful handling. □ **slippery elm 1** the N. American red elm, *Ulmus fulva*. **2** the medicinal inner bark of this. **slippery slope** a course leading to disaster. □□ **slipperily** *adv.* **slipperiness** *n.* [prob. coined by Coverdale (1535) after Luther's *schlipfferig*, MHG *slipferig* f. *slipfern, slipfen* f. Gmc: partly f. *slipper* slippery (now dial.) f. OE *slipor* f. Gmc]

slippy /ˈslɪpɪ/ *adj.* (**slippier, slippiest**) *colloq.* slippery. □ **look** (or **be**) **slippy** *Brit.* look sharp; make haste. □□ **slippiness** *n.*

slipshod /ˈslɪpʃɒd/ *adj.* **1** (of speech or writing, a speaker or writer, a method of work, etc.) careless, unsystematic; loose in arrangement. **2** slovenly. **3** having shoes down at heel.

slipstream /ˈslɪpstriːm/ *n. & v.* —*n.* **1** a current of air or water driven back by a revolving propeller or a moving vehicle. **2** an assisting force regarded as drawing something along with or behind something else. —*v.tr.* **1** follow closely behind (another vehicle). **2** pass after travelling in another's slipstream.

slipway /ˈslɪpweɪ/ *n.* a slip for building ships or landing boats.

slit /slɪt/ *n. & v.* —*n.* **1** a long straight narrow incision. **2** a long narrow opening comparable to a cut. —*v.tr.* (**slitting**; *past* and *past part.* **slit**) **1** make a slit in; cut or tear lengthwise. **2** cut into strips. □ **slit-eyed** having long narrow eyes. **slit-pocket** a pocket with a vertical opening giving access to the pocket or to a garment beneath. **slit trench** a narrow trench for a soldier or a weapon. □□ **slitter** *n.* [ME *slitte*, rel. to OE *slītan*, f. Gmc]

slither /ˈslɪðə(r)/ *v. & n.* —*v.intr.* slide unsteadily; go with an irregular slipping motion. —*n.* an instance of slithering. □□ **slithery** *adj.* [ME var. of *slidder* (now dial.) f. OE *slid(e)rian* frequent. f. *slid-*, weak grade of *slīdan* SLIDE]

slitty /ˈslɪtɪ/ *adj.* (**slittier, slittiest**) (of the eyes) long and narrow.

Sliven /ˈsliːv(ə)n/ a commercial city in central Bulgaria; pop. (1987) 106,600.

sliver /ˈslɪvə(r), ˈslaɪvə(r)/ *n. & v.* —*n.* **1** a long thin piece cut or split off. **2** a piece of wood torn from a tree or from timber. **3** a splinter, esp. from an exploded shell. **4** a strip of loose textile fibres after carding. —*v.tr. & intr.* **1** break off as a sliver. **2** break up into slivers. **3** form into slivers. [ME, rel. to *slive* cleave (now dial.) f. OE]

slivovitz /ˈslɪvəvɪts/ *n.* a plum brandy made esp. in Yugoslavia and Romania. [Serbo-Croat *šljivovica* f. *šljiva* plum]

Sloane[1] /sləʊn/ *n.* (in full **Sloane Ranger**) *Brit. sl.* a fashionable and conventional upper-class young person, esp. living in London. □□ **Sloaney** *adj.* [*Sloane* Square, London + Lone *Ranger*, a cowboy hero]

Sloane[2] /sləʊn/, Sir Hans (1660–1753), English physician and naturalist. He purchased the manor of Chelsea and endowed the Chelsea Physic Garden. His collections (including a large number of books and manuscripts) were purchased by the nation and placed in Montague House (afterwards the British Museum); the geological and zoological specimens formed the basis of the Natural History Museum in South Kensington, opened in 1881.

slob /slɒb/ *n.* **1** *colloq.* a stupid, careless, coarse, or fat person. **2** *Ir.* muddy land. □□ **slobbish** *adj.* [Ir. *slab* mud f. E *slab* ooze, sludge, prob. f. Scand.]

slobber /ˈslɒbə(r)/ *v. & n.* —*v.intr.* **1** slaver. **2** (foll. by *over*) show excessive sentiment. —*n.* saliva running from the mouth; slaver. □□ **slobbery** *adj.* [ME, = Du. *slobbern*, of imit. orig.]

sloe /sləʊ/ *n.* **1** = BLACKTHORN. **2** its small bluish-black fruit with a sharp sour taste. □ **sloe-eyed 1** having eyes of this colour. **2** slant-eyed. **sloe-gin** a liqueur of sloes steeped in gin. [OE *slā(h)* f. Gmc]

slog /slɒg/ *v. & n.* —*v.* (**slogged, slogging**) **1** *intr. & tr.* hit hard and usu. wildly esp. in boxing or at cricket. **2** *intr.* (often foll. by *away, on*) walk or work doggedly. —*n.* **1** a hard random hit. **2 a** hard steady work. **b** a spell of this. □□ **slogger** *n.* [19th c.: orig. unkn.: cf. SLUG[2]]

slogan /ˈsləʊgən/ *n.* **1** a short catchy phrase used in advertising etc. **2** a party cry; a watchword or motto. **3** *hist.* a Scottish Highland war-cry. [Gael. *sluagh-ghairm* f. *sluagh* army + *gairm* shout]

sloop /sluːp/ *n.* **1** a small one-masted fore-and-aft-rigged vessel with mainsail and jib. **2** (in full **sloop of war**) *Brit. hist.* a small warship with guns on the upper deck only. □ **sloop-rigged** rigged like a sloop. [Du. *sloep(e)*, of unkn. orig.]

sloosh /sluːʃ/ *n. & v. colloq.* —*n.* a pouring or pouring sound of water. —*v.intr.* **1** flow with a rush. **2** make a heavy splashing or rushing noise. [imit.]

sloot /sluːt/ *n.* (also **sluit**) *S.Afr.* a deep gully formed by heavy rain. [Afrik. f. Du. *sloot* ditch]

slop[1] /slɒp/ *v. & n.* —*v.* (**slopped, slopping**) **1** (often foll. by *over*) **a** *intr.* spill or flow over the edge of a vessel. **b** *tr.* allow to do this. **2** *tr.* make (the floor, clothes, etc.) wet or messy by slopping, spill or splash liquid on. **3** *intr.* (usu. foll. by *over*) gush; be effusive or maudlin. —*n.* **1** a quantity of liquid spilled or splashed. **2** weakly sentimental language. **3** (in *pl.*) waste liquid, esp. dirty water or the waste contents of kitchen, bedroom, or prison vessels. **4** (in *sing.* or *pl.*) unappetizing weak liquid food. **5** *Naut.* a choppy sea. □ **slop about** move about in a slovenly manner. **slop-basin** *Brit.* a basin for the dregs of cups at table. **slop out** carry slops out (in prison etc.). **slop-pail** a pail for removing bedroom or kitchen slops. [earlier sense 'slush', prob. rel. to *slyppe*: cf. COWSLIP]

slop[2] /slɒp/ *n.* **1** a workman's loose outer garment. **2** (in *pl.*) ready-made or cheap clothing. **3** (in *pl.*) clothes and bedding supplied to sailors in the navy. **4** (in *pl.*) *archaic* wide baggy trousers esp. as worn by sailors. [ME: cf. OE *oferslop* surplice f. Gmc]

slope /sləʊp/ *n. & v.* —*n.* **1** an inclined position or direction; a state in which one end or side is at a higher level than another; a position in a line neither parallel nor perpendicular to level ground or to a line serving as a standard. **2** a piece of rising or falling ground. **3 a** a difference in level between the two ends or sides of a thing (*a slope of 5 metres*). **b** the rate at which this increases with distance etc. **4** a place for skiing on the side of a hill or mountain. **5** (prec. by *the*) the position of a rifle when sloped. —*v.* **1** *intr.* have or take a slope; slant esp. up or down; lie or tend obliquely, esp. to ground level. **2** *tr.* place or arrange or make in or at a slope. □ **slope arms** place one's rifle in a sloping position against one's shoulder. **slope off** *sl.* go away, esp. to evade work etc. [shortening of ASLOPE]

sloppy /ˈslɒpɪ/ *adj.* (**sloppier, sloppiest**) **1 a** (of the ground) wet with rain; full of puddles. **b** (of food etc.) watery and disagreeable. **c** (of a floor, table, etc.) wet with slops, having water etc. spilt on it. **2** unsystematic, careless, not thorough. **3** (of a garment) ill-fitting or untidy. **4** (of sentiment or talk) weakly emotional, maudlin. **5** *colloq.* (of the sea) choppy. □□ **sloppily** *adv.* **sloppiness** *n.*

slosh /slɒʃ/ *v. & n.* —*v.* **1** *intr.* (often foll. by *about*) splash or flounder about, move with a splashing sound. **2** *tr. Brit. sl.* hit esp. heavily. **3** *tr. colloq.* **a** pour (liquid) clumsily. **b** pour liquid on. —*n.* **1** slush. **2 a** an instance of splashing. **b** the sound of this. **3** *Brit. sl.* a heavy blow. **4** a quantity of liquid. [var. of SLUSH]

sloshed /slɒʃt/ *adj. Brit. sl.* drunk.

sloshy /ˈslɒʃɪ/ *adj.* (**sloshier, sloshiest**) **1** slushy. **2** sloppy, sentimental.

slot[1] /slɒt/ *n. & v.* —*n.* **1** a slit or other aperture in a machine etc. for something (esp. a coin) to be inserted. **2** a slit, groove, channel, or long aperture into which something fits or in which something works. **3** an allotted place in an arrangement or scheme, esp. in a broadcasting schedule. —*v.* (**slotted, slotting**) **1** *tr. & intr.* place or be placed into or as if into a slot. **2** *tr.* provide with a slot or slots. □ **slot-machine** a machine worked by the insertion of a coin, esp.: **1** one for automatic retail of small articles. **2** one allowing a spell of play at a pin-table etc. **3** *US* = *fruit machine*. [ME, = hollow of the breast, f. OF *esclot*, of unkn. orig.]

slot[2] /slɒt/ *n.* **1** the track of a deer etc. esp. as shown by footprints. **2** a deer's foot. [OF *esclot* hoof-print of a horse, prob. f. ON *slóth* trail: cf. SLEUTH]

sloth /sləʊθ/ *n.* **1** laziness or indolence; reluctance to make an effort. **2** any slow-moving nocturnal mammal of the family Bradypodidae or Megalonychidae of S. America, having long limbs and hooked claws for hanging upside down from branches of trees. □ **sloth bear** a large-lipped black shaggy bear, *Melursus ursinus*, of India. [ME f. SLOW + -TH[2]]

slothful /ˈsləʊθfʊl/ *adj.* lazy; characterized by sloth. □□ **slothfully** *adv.* **slothfulness** *n.*

slouch /slaʊtʃ/ *v. & n.* —*v.* **1** *intr.* stand or move or sit in a drooping ungainly fashion. **2** *tr.* bend one side of the brim of (a hat) downwards (opp. COCK[1]). **3** *intr.* droop, hang down loosely. —*n.* **1** a slouching posture or movement, a stoop. **2** a downward bend of a hat-brim (opp. COCK[1]). **3** *sl.* an incompetent or slovenly worker or operator or performance. □ **slouch hat** a hat with a wide flexible brim. □□ **slouchy** *adj.* (**slouchier, slouchiest**). [16th c.: orig. unkn.]

slough[1] /slaʊ/ *n.* a swamp; a miry place; a quagmire. □ **Slough of Despond 1** (in Bunyan's *Pilgrim's Progress*) a deep miry place between the City of Destruction and the wicket gate at the beginning of Christian's journey. **2** a state of hopeless depression. □□ **sloughy** *adj.* [OE *slōh*, *slō(g)*]

slough[2] /slʌf/ *n. & v.* —*n.* **1** a part that an animal casts or moults, esp. a snake's cast skin. **2** dead tissue that drops off from living flesh etc. **3** a habit etc. that has been abandoned. —*v.* **1** *tr.* cast off as a slough. **2** *intr.* (often foll. by *off*) drop off as a slough. **3** *intr.* cast off a slough. **4** *intr.* (often foll. by *away, down*) (of soil, rock, etc.) collapse or slide into a hole or depression. □□ **sloughy** *adj.* [ME, perh. rel. to LG *slu(we)* husk]

Slovak /ˈsləʊvæk/ *n. & adj.* —*n.* **1** a member of a Slavonic people inhabiting Slovakia (formerly part of Hungary, now the Slovak Republic, one of the two constituent republics of Czechoslovakia). **2** the language of this people, one of the two official languages of Czechoslovakia. —*adj.* of or relating to this people or language. [Slovak etc. *Slovák*, rel. to SLOVENE]

sloven /ˈslʌv(ə)n/ *n.* a person who is habitually untidy or careless. [ME perh. f. Flem. *sloef* dirty or Du. *slof* careless]

Slovenia /sləˈviːnɪə/ a constituent republic of Yugoslavia; pop. (1981) 1,891,800; capital, Ljubljana. In Dec. 1990 the people of Slovenia voted to become an independent State unless a looser form of confederation was organized within Yugoslavia, **Slovene** /ˈsləʊviːn/ *adj. & n.* **Slovenian** *adj. & n.*

slovenly /ˈslʌvənlɪ/ *adj. & adv.* —*adj.* careless and untidy; unmethodical. —*adv.* in a slovenly manner. □□ **slovenliness** *n.*

slow /sləʊ/ *adj., adv., & v.* —*adj.* **1 a** taking a relatively long time to do a thing or cover a distance (also foll. by *of*: *slow of speech*). **b** not quick; acting or moving or done without speed. **2** gradual; obtained over a length of time (*slow growth*). **3** not producing, allowing, or conducive to speed (*in the slow lane*). **4** (of a clock etc.) showing a time earlier than is the case. **5** (of a person) not understanding readily; not learning easily. **6** dull; uninteresting; tedious. **7** slack or sluggish (*business is slow*). **8** (of a fire or oven) giving little heat. **9** *Photog.* (of a film) needing long exposure. **b** (of a lens) having a small aperture. **10 a** reluctant; tardy (*not slow to defend himself*). **b** not hasty or easily moved (*slow to take offence*). **11** (of a cricket-pitch, tennis-court, putting-green, etc.) on which the ball bounces or runs slowly. —*adv.* **1** at a slow pace; slowly. **2** (in *comb.*) (*slow-moving traffic*). —*v.* (usu. foll. by *down, up*) **1** *intr. & tr.* reduce one's speed or the speed of (a vehicle etc.). **2** *intr.* reduce one's pace of life; live or work less intensely. □ **slow and sure** of the attitude that haste is risky. **slow but sure** achieving the required result eventually. **slow-down** the action of slowing down; a go-slow. **slow handclap** slow clapping by an audience as a sign of displeasure or boredom. **slow loris** see LORIS. **slow march** the marching time adopted by troops in a funeral procession etc. **slow-match** a slow-burning match for lighting explosives etc. **slow motion 1** the operation or speed of a film using slower projection or more rapid exposure so that actions etc. appear much slower than usual. **2** the simulation of this in real action. **slow neutron** a neutron with low kinetic energy esp. after moderation (cf. *fast neutron* (see FAST[1])). **slow poison** a poison eventually causing death by repeated doses. **slow puncture** a puncture causing only slow deflation of the tyre. **slow reactor** *Physics* a nuclear reactor using mainly slow neutrons (cf. *fast reactor* (see FAST[1])). **slow virus** a progressive disease caused by a virus or virus-like organism that multiplies slowly in the host organism and has a long incubation period, such as scrapie or BSE. □□ **slowish** *adj.* **slowly** *adv.* **slowness** *n.* [OE *slāw* f. Gmc]

slowcoach /ˈsləʊkəʊtʃ/ *n. Brit.* **1** a slow or lazy person. **2** a dull-witted person. **3** a person behind the times in opinions etc.

slowpoke /ˈsləʊpəʊk/ *n. US* = SLOWCOACH.

slow-worm /ˈsləʊwɜːm/ *n.* a small European legless lizard, *Anguis fragilis*, giving birth to live young. Also called BLINDWORM. [OE *slā-wyrm*: first element of uncert. orig., assim. to SLOW]

SLR *abbr.* **1** *Photog.* single-lens reflex. **2** self-loading rifle.

slub[1] /slʌb/ *n. & adj.* —*n.* **1** a lump or thick place in yarn or thread. **2** fabric woven from thread etc. with slubs. —*adj.* (of material etc.) with an irregular appearance caused by uneven thickness of the warp. [19th c.: orig. unkn.]

slub[2] /slʌb/ *n. & v.* —*n.* wool slightly twisted in preparation for spinning. —*v.tr.* (**slubbed, slubbing**) twist (wool) in this way. [18th c.: orig. unkn.]

sludge /slʌdʒ/ *n.* **1** thick greasy mud. **2** muddy or slushy sediment. **3** sewage. **4** *Mech.* an accumulation of dirty oil, esp. in the sump of an internal-combustion engine. **5** *Geol.* sea-ice newly formed in small pieces. **6** (usu. *attrib.*) a muddy colour (*sludge green*). □□ **sludgy** *adj.* [cf. SLUSH]

slue var. of SLEW[1].

slug[1] /slʌg/ *n.* **1** a small shell-less mollusc of the class Gastropoda often destructive to plants. **2 a** a bullet esp. of irregular shape. **b** a missile for an airgun. **3** *Printing* **a** a metal bar used in spacing. **b** a line of type in Linotype printing. **4** esp. *US* a tot of liquor. **5** a unit of mass, given an acceleration of 1 foot per second per second by a force of 1 lb. **6** a roundish lump of metal. [ME *slug(g)e* sluggard, prob. f. Scand.]

slug[2] /slʌg/ *v. & n. US* —*v.tr.* (**slugged, slugging**) strike with a hard blow. —*n.* a hard blow. □ **slug it out 1** fight it out. **2** endure; stick it out. □□ **slugger** *n.* [19th c.: orig. unkn.]

slugabed /ˈslʌgəˌbed/ *n. archaic* a lazy person who lies late in bed. [slug (v.) (see SLUGGARD) + ABED]

sluggard /ˈslʌgəd/ *n.* a lazy sluggish person. □□ **sluggardly**

adv. **sluggardliness** n. [ME f. slug (v.) be slothful (prob. f. Scand.: cf. SLUG¹) + -ARD]

sluggish /ˈslʌgɪʃ/ adj. inert; inactive; slow-moving; torpid; indolent (a sluggish circulation; a sluggish stream). □□ **sluggishly** adv. **sluggishness** n. [ME f. SLUG¹ or slug (v.): see SLUGGARD]

sluice /sluːs/ n. & v. —n. 1 (also **sluice-gate**, **sluice-valve**) a sliding gate or other contrivance for controlling the volume or flow of water. 2 (also **sluice-way**) an artificial water-channel esp. for washing ore. 3 a place for rinsing. 4 the act or an instance of rinsing. 5 the water above or below or issuing through a floodgate. —v. 1 tr. provide or wash with a sluice or sluices. 2 tr. rinse, pour or throw water freely upon. 3 tr. (foll. by out, away) wash out or away with a flow of water. 4 tr. flood with water from a sluice. 5 intr. (of water) rush out from a sluice, or as if from a sluice. [ME f. OF escluse ult. f. L excludere EXCLUDE]

sluit var. of SLOOT.

slum /slʌm/ n. & v. —n. 1 an overcrowded and squalid back street, district, etc., usu. in a city and inhabited by very poor people. 2 a house or building unfit for human habitation. —v.intr. (**slummed**, **slumming**) 1 live in slumlike conditions. 2 go about the slums through curiosity, to examine the condition of the inhabitants, or for charitable purposes. □ **slum clearance** the demolition of slums and rehousing of their inhabitants. **slum it** colloq. put up with conditions less comfortable than usual. □□ **slummy** adj. (**slummier**, **slummiest**). **slumminess** n. [19th c.: orig. cant]

slumber /ˈslʌmbə(r)/ v. & n. poet. rhet. —v.intr. 1 sleep, esp. in a specified manner. 2 be idle, drowsy, or inactive. —n. a sleep, esp. of a specified kind (fell into a fitful slumber). □ **slumber away** spend (time) in slumber. **slumber-wear** nightclothes. □□ **slumberer** n. **slumberous** adj. **slumbrous** adj. [ME slūmere etc. f. slūmen (v.) or slūme (n.) f. OE slūma: -b- as in number]

slump /slʌmp/ n. & v. —n. 1 a sudden severe or prolonged fall in prices or values of commodities or securities. 2 a sharp or sudden decline in trade or business usu. bringing widespread unemployment. 3 a lessening of interest or commitment in a subject or undertaking. —v.intr. 1 undergo a slump; fail; fall in price. 2 sit or fall heavily or limply (slumped into a chair). 3 lean or subside. [17th c., orig. 'sink in a bog': imit.]

slung past and past part. of SLING¹.

slunk past and past part. of SLINK¹.

slur /slɜː(r)/ v. & n. —v. (**slurred**, **slurring**) 1 tr. & intr. pronounce or write indistinctly so that the sounds or letters run into one another. 2 tr. Mus. **a** perform (a group of two or more notes) legato. **b** mark (notes) with a slur. 3 tr. archaic or US put a slur on (a person or a person's character); make insinuations against. 4 tr. (usu. foll. by over) pass over (a fact, fault, etc.) lightly; conceal or minimize. —n. 1 an imputation of wrongdoing; blame; stigma (a slur on my reputation). 2 the act or an instance of slurring in pronunciation, singing, or writing. 3 Mus. a curved line to show that two or more notes are to be sung to one syllable or played or sung legato. [17th c.: orig. unkn.]

slurp /slɜːp/ v. & n. —v.tr. eat or drink noisily. —n. the sound of this; a slurping gulp. [Du. slurpen, slorpen]

slurry /ˈslʌrɪ/ n. (pl. **-ies**) 1 a semi-liquid mixture of fine particles and water; thin mud. 2 thin liquid cement. 3 a fluid form of manure. 4 a residue of water and particles of coal left at pit-head washing plants. [ME, rel. to dial. slur thin mud]

slush /slʌʃ/ n. 1 watery mud or thawing snow. 2 silly sentiment. □ **slush fund** reserve funding esp. as used for political bribery. [17th c., also sludge and slutch: orig. unkn.]

slushy /ˈslʌʃɪ/ adj. (**slushier**, **slushiest**) like slush; watery. □□ **slushiness** n.

slut /slʌt/ n. derog. a slovenly woman; a slattern; a hussy. □□ **sluttish** adj. **sluttishness** n. [ME: orig. unkn.]

sly /slaɪ/ adj. (**slyer**, **slyest**) 1 cunning; crafty; wily. 2 **a** (of a person) practising secrecy or stealth. **b** (of an action etc.) done etc. in secret. 3 hypocritical; ironical. 4 knowing; arch; bantering; insinuating. 5 Austral. & NZ sl. (esp. of liquor) illicit. □ **on the sly** privately; covertly; without publicity (smuggled some through on the sly). **sly dog** colloq. a person who is discreet about mistakes or pleasures. □□ **slyly** adv. (also **slily**). **slyness** n. [ME

sleh etc. f. ON slœgr cunning, orig. 'able to strike' f. slóg- past stem of slá strike: cf. SLEIGHT]

slyboots /ˈslaɪbuːts/ n. colloq. a sly person.

slype /slaɪp/ n. a covered way or passage between a cathedral etc. transept and the chapter house or deanery. [perh. = slipe a long narrow piece of ground, = SLIP² 1]

SM abbr. 1 sadomasochism. 2 Sergeant-Major.

Sm symb. Chem. the element samarium.

smack¹ /smæk/ n., v., & adv. —n. 1 a sharp slap or blow esp. with the palm of the hand or a flat object. 2 a hard hit at cricket etc. 3 a loud kiss (gave her a hearty smack). 4 a loud sharp sound (heard the smack as it hit the floor). —v. 1 tr. strike with the open hand etc. 2 tr. part (one's) lips noisily in eager anticipation or enjoyment of food or another delight. 3 tr. crack (a whip). 4 tr. & intr. move, hit, etc., with a smack. —adv. colloq. 1 with a smack. 2 suddenly; directly; violently (landed smack on my desk). 3 exactly (hit it smack in the centre). □ **have a smack at** colloq. make an attempt, attack, etc., at. **a smack in the eye** (or **face**) colloq. a rebuff; a setback. [MDu. smack(en) of imit. orig.]

smack² /smæk/ v. & n. (foll. by of) —v.intr. 1 have a flavour of; taste of (smacked of garlic). 2 suggest the presence or effects of (it smacks of nepotism). —n. 1 a flavour; a taste that suggests the presence of something. 2 (in a person's character etc.) a barely discernible quality (just a smack of superciliousness). 3 (in food etc.) a very small amount (add a smack of ginger). [OE smæc]

smack³ /smæk/ n. a single-masted sailing-boat for coasting or fishing. [Du. smak f. earlier smacke; orig. unkn.]

smack⁴ /smæk/ n. sl. a hard drug, esp. heroin, sold or used illegally. [prob. alt. of Yiddish schmeck sniff]

smacker /ˈsmækə(r)/ n. sl. 1 a loud kiss. 2 a resounding blow. 3 **a** Brit. £1. **b** US $1.

small /smɔːl/ adj., n., & adv. —adj. 1 not large or big. 2 slender; thin. 3 not great in importance, amount, number, strength, or power. 4 not much; trifling (a small token; paid small attention). 5 insignificant; unimportant (a small matter; from small beginnings). 6 consisting of small particles (small gravel; small shot). 7 doing something on a small scale (a small farmer). 8 socially undistinguished; poor or humble. 9 petty; mean; ungenerous; paltry (a small spiteful nature). 10 young; not fully grown or developed (a small child). —n. 1 the slenderest part of something (esp. small of the back). 2 (in pl.) Brit. colloq. small items of laundry, esp. underwear. —adv. into small pieces (chop it small). □ **feel** (or **look**) **small** be humiliated; appear mean or humiliated. **in a small way** unambitiously; on a small scale. **no small** considerable; a good deal of (no small excitement about it). **small arms** portable firearms, esp. rifles, pistols, light machine-guns, sub-machine-guns, etc. **small beer** 1 a trifling matter; something unimportant. 2 weak beer. **small-bore** (of a firearm) with a narrow bore, in international and Olympic shooting usu. .22 inch calibre (5.6 millimetre bore). **small capital** a capital letter which is of the same dimensions as the lower-case letters in the same typeface minus ascenders and descenders, as THIS. **small change** 1 money in the form of coins as opposed to notes. 2 trivial remarks. **small circle** see CIRCLE. **small claims court** Brit. a local tribunal in which claims for small amounts can be heard and decided quickly and cheaply without legal representation. **small craft** a general term for small boats and fishing vessels. **small fry** 1 young children or the young of various species. 2 small or insignificant things or people. **small hours** the early hours of the morning after midnight. **small intestine** see INTESTINE. **small letter** (in printed material) a lower-case letter. **small mercy** a minor concession, benefit, etc. (be grateful for small mercies). **small potatoes** an insignificant person or thing. **small print** 1 printed matter in small type. 2 inconspicuous and usu. unfavourable limitations etc. in a contract. **small profits and quick returns** the policy of a cheap shop etc. relying on large trade. **small-scale** made or occurring in small amounts or to a lesser degree. **small slam** see SLAM². **small-sword** a light tapering thrusting-sword, esp. hist. for duelling. **small talk** light social conversation. **small-time** colloq. unimportant or petty. **small-timer** colloq. a small-time operator; an insignificant person. **small-town**

relating to or characteristic of a small town; unsophisticated; provincial. **small wonder** not very surprising. □□ **smallish** *adj.* **smallness** *n.* [OE *smæl* f. Gmc]

smallgoods /ˈsmɔːlgʊdz/ *n. Austral.* delicatessen meats.

smallholder /ˈsmɔːlˌhəʊldə(r)/ *n. Brit.* a person who farms a smallholding.

smallholding /ˈsmɔːlˌhəʊldɪŋ/ *n. Brit.* an agricultural holding smaller than a farm.

small-minded /smɔːˈmaɪndɪd/ *adj.* petty; of rigid opinions or narrow outlook. □□ **small-mindedly** *adv.* **small-mindedness** *n.*

smallpox /ˈsmɔːlpɒks/ *n.* an acute contagious virus disease with fever and pustules usually leaving permanent scars, the main devastating disease of the 17th and 18th c. Because it seldom attacked the same person more than once, it had been the practice in the East deliberately to infect healthy people with a mild form of the disease in order to confer upon them immunity from a more dangerous form, and this was introduced into England by the traveller and letter-writer Lady Mary Wortley Montagu (1689–1762). In 1796 Edward Jenner observed that the mild disease cowpox gave immunity from smallpox, and established the practice of vaccination; its systematic application resulted in the worldwide eradication of smallpox by 1979.

smalt /smɒlt, smɔːlt/ *n.* **1** glass coloured blue with cobalt. **2** a pigment made by pulverizing this. [F f. It. *smalto* f. Gmc, rel. to SMELT[1]]

smarm /smɑːm/ *v.tr. colloq.* **1** (often foll. by *down*) smooth, plaster down (hair etc.) usu. with cream or oil. **2** flatter fulsomely. [orig. dial. (also *smalm*), of uncert. orig.]

smarmy /ˈsmɑːmɪ/ *adj.* (**smarmier, smarmiest**) *colloq.* ingratiating; flattering; obsequious. □□ **smarmily** *adv.* **smarminess** *n.*

smart /smɑːt/ *adj., v., n.,* & *adv.* —*adj.* **1 a** clever; ingenious; quickwitted (*a smart talker; gave a smart answer*). **b** keen in bargaining; quick to take advantage. **c** (of transactions etc.) unscrupulous to the point of dishonesty. **2** well-groomed; neat; bright and fresh in appearance (*a smart suit*). **3** in good repair; showing bright colours, new paint, etc. (*a smart red bicycle*). **4** stylish; fashionable; prominent in society (*in all the smart restaurants; the smart set*). **5** quick; brisk (*set a smart pace*). **6** painfully severe; sharp; vigorous (*a smart blow*). —*v.intr.* **1** (of a person or a part of the body) feel or give acute pain or distress (*my eye smarts; smarting from the insult*). **2** (of an insult, grievance, etc.) rankle. **3** (foll. by *for*) suffer the consequences of (*you will smart for this*). —*n.* a bodily or mental sharp pain; a stinging sensation. —*adv.* smartly; in a smart manner. □ **look smart** make haste. **smart-arse** (or **-ass**) = SMART ALEC. **smart-money 1** money paid or exacted as a penalty or compensation. **2** money invested by persons with expert knowledge. □□ **smartingly** *adv.* **smartish** *adj.* & *adv.* **smartly** *adv.* **smartness** *n.* [OE *smeart*, *smeortan*]

smart alec /ˈælɪk/ *n.* (also **aleck, alick**) *colloq.* a person displaying ostentatious or smug cleverness. □□ **smart-alecky** *adj.* [SMART + *Alec*, dimin. of the name *Alexander*]

smarten /ˈsmɑːt(ə)n/ *v.tr.* & *intr.* (usu. foll. by *up*) make or become smart or smarter.

smarty /ˈsmɑːtɪ/ *n.* (pl. **-ies**) *colloq.* **1** a know-all; a smart alec. **2** a smartly-dressed person; a member of a smart set. □ **smarty-boots** (or **-pants**) = SMARTY 1. [SMART]

smash /smæʃ/ *v., n.,* & *adv.* —*v.* **1** *tr.* & *intr.* (often foll. by *up*) **a** break into pieces; shatter. **b** bring or come to sudden or complete destruction, defeat, or disaster. **2** *tr.* (foll. by *into, through*) (of a vehicle etc.) move with great force and impact. **3** *tr.* & *intr.* (foll. by *in*) break in with a crushing blow (*smashed in the window*). **4** *tr.* (in tennis, squash, etc.) hit (a ball etc.) with great force, esp. downwards (*smashed it back over the net*). **5** *intr.* (of a business etc.) go bankrupt, come to grief. **6** *tr.* (as **smashed** *adj.*) *sl.* intoxicated. —*n.* **1** the act or an instance of smashing; a violent fall, collision, or disaster. **2** the sound of this. **3** (in full **smash hit**) a very successful play, song, performer, etc. **4** a stroke in tennis, squash, etc., in which the ball is hit esp. downwards with great force. **5** a violent blow with a fist etc. **6** bankruptcy; a series of

commercial failures. **7** a mixture of spirits (usu. brandy) with flavoured water and ice. —*adv.* with a smash (*fell smash on the floor*). □ **go to smash** be ruined etc. **smash-and-grab** (of a robbery etc.) in which the thief smashes a shop-window and seizes goods. **smash-up** a violent collision; a complete smash. [18th c., prob. imit. after *smack, smite* and *bash, mash,* etc.]

smasher /ˈsmæʃə(r)/ *n.* **1** *colloq.* a very beautiful or pleasing person or thing. **2** a person or thing that smashes.

smashing /ˈsmæʃɪŋ/ *adj. colloq.* superlative; excellent; wonderful; beautiful. □□ **smashingly** *adv.*

smatter /ˈsmætə(r)/ *n.* (also **smattering**) a slight superficial knowledge of a language or subject. □□ **smatterer** *n.* [ME *smatter* talk ignorantly, prate: orig. unkn.]

smear /smɪə(r)/ *v.* & *n.* —*v.tr.* **1** daub or mark with a greasy or sticky substance or with something that stains. **2** blot; smudge; obscure the outline of (writing, artwork, etc.). **3** defame the character of; slander; attempt to or succeed in discrediting (a person or his name) publicly. —*n.* **1** the act or an instance of smearing. **2** *Med.* **a** material smeared on a microscopic slide etc. for examination. **b** a specimen of this. □ **smear test** = *cervical smear.* □□ **smearer** *n.* **smeary** *adj.* [OE *smierwan* f. Gmc]

smegma /ˈsmɛgmə/ *n.* a sebaceous secretion in the folds of the skin, esp. of the foreskin. □□ **smegmatic** /-ˈmætɪk/ *adj.* [L f. Gk *smēgma -atos* detergent f. *smēkhō* cleanse]

smell /smɛl/ *n.* & *v.* —*n.* **1** the faculty of perceiving odours or scents (*has a fine sense of smell*). **2** the quality in substances that is perceived by this (*the smell of thyme; this rose has no smell*). **3** an unpleasant odour. **4** the act of inhaling to ascertain smell. —*v.* (*past* and *past part.* **smelt** /smɛlt/ or **smelled**) **1** *tr.* perceive the smell of; examine by smell (*thought I could smell gas*). **2** *intr.* emit odour. **3** *intr.* seem by smell to be (*this milk smells sour*). **4** *intr.* (foll. by *of*) **a** be redolent of (*smells of fish*). **b** be suggestive of (*smells of dishonesty*). **5** *intr.* stink; be rank. **6** *tr.* perceive as if by smell; detect, discern, suspect (*smell a bargain; smell blood*). **7** *intr.* have or use a sense of smell. **8** *intr.* (foll. by *about*) sniff or search about. **9** *intr.* (foll. by *at*) inhale the smell of. □ **smelling-bottle** a small bottle of smelling-salts. **smelling-salts** ammonium carbonate mixed with scent to be sniffed as a restorative in faintness etc. **smell out 1** detect by smell; find out by investigation. **2** (of a dog etc.) hunt out by smell. **smell a rat** begin to suspect trickery etc. □□ **smellable** *adj.* **smeller** *n.* **smell-less** *adj.* [ME *smel(le),* prob. f. OE]

smelly /ˈsmɛlɪ/ *adj.* (**smellier, smelliest**) having a strong or unpleasant smell. □□ **smelliness** *n.*

smelt[1] /smɛlt/ *v.tr.* **1** extract metal from (ore) by melting. **2** extract (metal) from ore by melting. □□ **smelter** *n.* **smeltery** *n.* (pl. **-ies**). [MDu., MLG *smelten,* rel. to MELT]

smelt[2] *past* and *past part.* of SMELL.

smelt[3] /smɛlt/ *n.* (pl. same or **smelts**) any small green and silver fish of the genus *Osmerus* etc. allied to salmon and used as food. [OE, of uncert. orig.: cf. SMOLT]

Smersh /smɜːʃ/ the popular name for the Russian counter-espionage organization, originating during the Second World War, responsible for maintaining security within the Soviet armed and intelligence services. [Russ. abbr. of *smert[1] shpionam,* lit. 'death to spies']

Smetana /ˈsmɛtənə/, Bedřich (1824–84), Bohemian composer regarded as the founder of Czech music. His dedication to Czech nationalism is apparent in his operas (notably *The Bartered Bride,* 1866, and *Dalibor,* 1868) and in the cycle of symphonic poems *My Country* (1874–9). He also contributed to the cause through his work as conductor of the Provisional Theatre in Prague. Smetana died in an asylum after 10 years of suffering from the onset of syphilis, which had left him completely deaf in 1881, and was buried as a national hero.

smew /smjuː/ *n.* a small merganser, *Mergus albellus.* [17th c., rel. to *smeath, smee* = smew, widgeon, etc.]

smidgen /ˈsmɪdʒ(ə)n/ *n.* (also **smidgin** /-dʒɪn/) *colloq.* a small bit or amount. [perh. f. *smitch* in the same sense: cf. dial. *smitch* wood-smoke]

smilax /ˈsmaɪlæks/ *n.* **1** any climbing shrub of the genus *Smilax,* the roots of some species of which yield sarsaparilla. **2** a climbing kind of asparagus, *Asparagus medeoloides*, used decoratively by florists. [L f. Gk, = bindweed]

smile /smaɪl/ *v. & n.* —*v.* **1** *intr.* relax the features into a pleased or kind or gently sceptical expression or a forced imitation of these, usu. with the lips parted and the corners of the mouth turned up. **2** *tr.* express by smiling (*smiled their consent*). **3** *tr.* give (a smile) of a specified kind (*smiled a sardonic smile*). **4** *intr.* (foll. by *on*, *upon*) adopt a favourable attitude towards; encourage (*fortune smiled on me*). **5** *intr.* have a bright or favourable aspect (*the smiling countryside*). **6** *tr.* (foll. by *away*) drive (a person's anger etc.) away (*smiled their tears away*). **7** *intr.* (foll. by *at*) **a** ridicule or show indifference to (*smiled at my feeble attempts*). **b** favour; smile on. **8** *tr.* (foll. by *into*, *out of*) bring (a person) into or out of a specified mood etc. by smiling (*smiled them into agreement*). —*n.* **1** the act or an instance of smiling. **2** a smiling expression or aspect. □ **come up smiling** *colloq.* recover from adversity and cheerfully face what is to come. □□ **smileless** *adj.* **smiler** *n.* **smiley** *adj.* **smilingly** *adv.* [ME perh. f. Scand., rel. to SMIRK: cf. OHG *smīlenter*]

Smiley /ˈsmaɪlɪ/, George. A quiet scholarly senior officer in the British intelligence bureaucracy in novels by John le Carré.

smiley /ˈsmaɪlɪ/ *adj.* showing a smile, esp. of a cartoon-style representation of a face.

smirch /smɜːtʃ/ *v. & n.* —*v.tr.* mark, soil, or smear (a thing, a person's reputation, etc.). —*n.* **1** a spot or stain. **2** a blot (on one's character etc.). [ME: orig. unkn.]

smirk /smɜːk/ *n. & v.* —*n.* an affected, conceited, or silly smile. —*v.intr.* put on or wear a smirk. □□ **smirker** *n.* **smirkingly** *adv.* **smirky** *adj.* **smirkily** *adv.* [OE *sme(a)rcian*]

smit /smɪt/ *archaic past part.* of SMITE.

smite /smaɪt/ *v. & n.* —*v.* (*past* **smote** /sməʊt/; *past part.* **smitten** /ˈsmɪt(ə)n/) *archaic or literary* **1** *tr.* strike or hit. **2** *tr.* chastise; defeat. **3** *tr.* (in *passive*) **a** have a sudden strong effect on (*was smitten by his conscience*). **b** infatuate, fascinate (*was smitten by her beauty*). **4** *intr.* (foll. by *on*, *upon*) come forcibly or abruptly upon. —*n.* a blow or stroke. □□ **smiter** *n.* [OE *smītan* smear f. Gmc]

Smith¹ /smɪθ/, Adam (1723–90), Scottish philosopher and economist, founder of modern political economy, whose work marks a highly significant turning-point in the breakdown of mercantilist orthodoxy and the spread of *laissez-faire* ideas. A notable participant in the Scottish Enlightenment of the 18th c., with a considerable reputation as a philosopher, Smith retired from academic life to produce his seminal *Inquiry into the Nature and Causes of the Wealth of Nations* (1776), establishing theories of labour, distribution, wages, prices, and money, and putting forward a theory of the natural liberty of trade and commerce which was to prove highly influential in terms not only of economic but also of political theory in the following century. It appeared on the actual date of the Declaration of Independence of the American rebels, and contained the prophecy 'They will be one of the foremost nations of the world'.

Smith² /smɪθ/, Bessie (1894–1937), American jazz and blues singer, known as the 'Empress of the Blues'. She became a leading artist in the 1920s and made over 150 recordings, including some with Benny Goodman and Louis Armstrong. She died from injuries received in a car accident, reportedly after being refused admission to a 'Whites only' hospital.

Smith³ /smɪθ/, Ian Douglas (1919–), Rhodesian statesman. Smith became Prime Minister of the White minority government of Rhodesia in 1964, and, after Britain refused to give the country its independence under his administration, unilaterally declared independence in 1965. He was forced to resign in 1979 to make way for majority Black rule. After the transformation of the country into the independent State of Zimbabwe he remained active in politics, leading the party that represented the interests of those Whites who chose to remain.

Smith⁴ /smɪθ/, Joseph (1805–44), founder of the Mormon sect.

Smith⁵ /smɪθ/, Stevie (Florence Margaret) (1902–71), English poet. She wrote three novels, including *Novel on Yellow Paper* (1936), but is more widely recognized for her witty, caustic, and enigmatic verse, often illustrated by her own comic drawings,

in volumes which include *A Good Time was Had By All* (1937) and *Not Waving But Drowning* (1957). Her *Collected Poems* (1975) appeared posthumously.

Smith⁶, Sydney (1771–1845), English churchman, essayist, and wit, author of the *Letters of Peter Plymley* (1807), in defence of Catholic emancipation.

Smith⁷, William (1769–1839), English land-surveyor and self-taught geologist, one of the founders of stratigraphical geology, long known as the father of English geology. Working initially in the area around Bath, he discovered that rock strata could be distinguished on the basis of their characteristic assemblages of fossils, and that the identity of strata exposed in different places could thereby be established. Smith later travelled extensively in Britain, accumulating data which enabled him to produce the first geological map of the whole of England and Wales. Many of the names he devised for particular strata are still in use.

smith /smɪθ/ *n. & v.* —*n.* **1** (esp. in *comb.*) a worker in metal (*goldsmith*; *tinsmith*). **2** a person who forges iron; a blacksmith. **3** a craftsman (*wordsmith*). —*v.tr.* make or treat by forging. [OE f. Gmc]

smithereens /ˌsmɪðəˈriːnz/ *n.pl.* (also **smithers** /ˈsmɪðəz/) small fragments (*smash them to smithereens*). [19th c.: orig. unkn.]

smithery /ˈsmɪθərɪ/ *n.* (*pl.* **-ies**) **1** a smith's work. **2** (esp. in naval dockyards) a smithy.

Smithfield /ˈsmɪθfiːld/ originally, an open area outside the NW walls of the City of London, a market for cattle and horses, which later became the central meat-market. In the 16th c. it was the scene of the burning of heretics.

Smithsonian Institution /smɪθˈsəʊnɪən/ the oldest US foundation for scientific research, established by Congress in 1838 and opened in 1846 in Washington, DC. It originated in a £100,000 bequest in the will of James Smithson (1765–1829), English chemist and mineralogist, for 'an establishment for the increase and diffusion of knowledge among men'.

smithy /ˈsmɪðɪ/ *n.* (*pl.* **-ies**) a blacksmith's workshop; a forge. [ME f. ON *smithja*]

smitten *past part.* of SMITE.

smock /smɒk/ *n. & v.* —*n.* **1** a loose shirtlike garment with the upper part closely gathered in smocking. **2** (also **smock-frock**) a loose overall, esp. *hist.* a field-labourer's outer linen garment. —*v.tr.* adorn with smocking. [OE *smoc*, prob. rel. to OE *smūgan* creep, ON *smjúga* put on a garment]

smocking /ˈsmɒkɪŋ/ *n.* an ornamental effect on cloth made by gathering the material tightly into pleats, often with stitches in a honeycomb pattern.

smog /smɒg/ *n.* fog intensified by smoke. □□ **smoggy** *adj.* (**smoggier**, **smoggiest**). [portmanteau word]

smoke /sməʊk/ *n. & v.* —*n.* **1** a visible suspension of carbon etc. in air, emitted from a burning substance. **2** an act or period of smoking tobacco (*had a quiet smoke*). **3** *colloq.* a cigarette or cigar (*got a smoke?*). **4** (**the Smoke**) *Brit. & Austral. colloq.* a big city, esp. London. —*v.* **1** *intr.* **a** emit smoke or visible vapour (*smoking ruins*). **b** (of a lamp etc.) burn badly with the emission of smoke. **c** (of a chimney or fire) discharge smoke into the room. **2 a** *intr.* inhale and exhale the smoke of a cigarette or cigar or pipe. **b** *intr.* do this habitually. **c** *tr.* use (a cigarette etc.) in this way. **3** *tr.* darken or preserve by the action of smoke (*smoked salmon*). **4** *tr.* spoil the taste of in cooking. **5** *tr.* **a** rid of insects etc. by the action of smoke. **b** subdue (insects, esp. bees) in this way. **6** *tr. archaic* make fun of. **7** *tr.* bring (oneself) into a specified state by smoking. □ **go up in smoke** *colloq.* **1** be destroyed by fire. **2** (of a plan etc.) come to nothing. **no smoke without fire** rumours are not entirely baseless. **smoke-ball 1** a puff-ball. **2** a projectile filled with material emitting dense smoke, used to conceal military operations etc. **smoke bomb** a bomb that emits dense smoke on exploding. **smoke-bush** = *smoke-plant*. **smoked glass** glass darkened with smoke. **smoke-dried** cured in smoke. **smoke-ho** *Austral. & NZ colloq.* = SMOKO. **smoke out 1** drive out by means of smoke. **2** drive out of hiding or secrecy etc. **smoke-plant** (or **-tree**) any ornamental shrub of the genus *Cotinus*, with feathery smokelike fruit-stalks.

smoke-ring smoke from a cigarette etc. exhaled in the shape of a ring. **smoke-room** *Brit.* = SMOKING-ROOM. **smoke-stone** cairngorm. **smoke-tunnel** a form of wind-tunnel using smoke filaments to show the motion of air. □□ **smokable** *adj.* (also **smokeable**). [OE *smoca* f. weak grade of the stem of *smēocan* emit smoke]

smokeless /ˈsməʊklɪs/ *adj.* having or producing little or no smoke. □ **smokeless zone** a district in which it is illegal to create smoke and where only smokeless fuel may be used.

smoker /ˈsməʊkə(r)/ *n.* **1** a person or thing that smokes, esp. a person who habitually smokes tobacco. **2** a compartment on a train, in which smoking is allowed. **3** esp. *US* an informal social gathering of men. □ **smoker's cough** an ailment caused by excessive smoking.

smokescreen /ˈsməʊkskriːn/ *n.* **1** a cloud of smoke diffused to conceal (esp. military) operations. **2** a device or ruse for disguising one's activities.

smokestack /ˈsməʊkstæk/ *n.* **1** a chimney or funnel for discharging the smoke of a locomotive or steamer. **2** a tall chimney.

smoking-jacket /ˈsməʊkɪŋˌdʒækɪt/ *n.* an ornamental jacket formerly worn by men while smoking.

smoking-room /ˈsməʊkɪŋˌruːm, -ˌrʊm/ *n.* a room in a hotel or house, kept for smoking in.

smoko /ˈsməʊkəʊ/ *n.* (*pl.* **-os**) *Austral.* & *NZ colloq.* **1** a stoppage of work for a rest and a smoke. **2** a tea break.

smoky /ˈsməʊkɪ/ *adj.* (**smokier, smokiest**) **1** emitting, veiled or filled with, or obscured by, smoke (*smoky fire; smoky room*). **2** stained with or coloured like smoke (*smoky glass*). **3** having the taste or flavour of smoked food (*smoky bacon*). □□ **smokily** *adv.* **smokiness** *n.*

smolder *US* var. of SMOULDER.

Smolensk /sməˈlensk/ a city in the west of the Soviet Union, on the River Dneiper; pop. (est. 1987) 338,000.

Smollett /ˈsmɒlɪt/, Tobias George (1721–71), Scottish novelist, who became a surgeon's mate in the Navy and was present at the abortive attack on Cartagena which is described in his first novel *Roderick Random* (1748). His other novels were *Peregrine Pickle* (1751), *Count Fathom* (1753), *Sir Launcelot Greaves* (1760–1), the story of an 18th-c. Don Quixote, and his most famous work *Humphrey Clinker* (1771) in epistolary form. These works are often described as picaresque and are characterized by fast-moving narrative, humorous caricature, and incident which sometimes distorts Smollett's professed moral purpose. He also edited periodicals, produced political pamphlets (often controversial), poems, plays, a *Complete History of England* (1757–8), and translations of Voltaire, Cervantes, and A.-R. Lesage.

smolt /sməʊlt/ *n.* a young salmon migrating to the sea for the first time. [ME (orig. Sc. & N.Engl.): orig. unkn.]

smooch /smuːtʃ/ *n.* & *v. colloq.* —*n.* **1** *Brit.* a period of slow dancing close together. **2** a spell of kissing and caressing. —*v.intr.* engage in a smooch. □□ **smoocher** *n.* **smoochy** *adj.* (**smoochier, smoochiest**). [dial. *smouch* imit.]

smoodge /smuːdʒ/ *v.intr.* (also **smooge**) *Austral.* & *NZ* **1** behave in a fawning or ingratiating manner. **2** behave amorously. [prob. var. of dial. *smudge* kiss, sidle up to, beg in a sneaking way]

smooth /smuːð/ *adj., v., n.,* & *adv.* —*adj.* **1** having a relatively even and regular surface; free from perceptible projections, lumps, indentations, and roughness. **2** not wrinkled, pitted, scored, or hairy (*smooth skin*). **3** that can be traversed without check. **4** (of liquids) of even consistency; without lumps (*mix to a smooth paste*). **5** (of the sea etc.) without waves or undulations. **6** (of a journey, passage, progress, etc.) untroubled by difficulties or adverse conditions. **7** having an easy flow or correct rhythm (*smooth breathing; a smooth metre*). **8 a** not harsh in sound or taste. **b** (of wine etc.) not astringent. **9** (of a person, his or her manner, etc.) suave, conciliatory, flattering, unruffled, or polite (*a smooth talker; he's very smooth*). **10** (of movement etc.) not suddenly varying; not jerky. —*v.* **1** *tr.* & *intr.* (often foll. by *out, down*) make or become smooth. **2** *tr.* (often foll. by *out, down, over, away*) **a** *tr.* reduce or get rid of (differences, faults, difficulties, etc.) in fact or appearance. **b** *intr.* (of difficulties etc.) diminish, become less obtrusive (*it will all smooth over*). **3** *tr.* modify (a graph, curve, etc.)

so as to lessen irregularities. **4** *tr.* free from impediments or discomfort (*smooth the way; smooth the declining years*). —*n.* **1** a smoothing touch or stroke (*gave his hair a smooth*). **2** the easy part of life (*take the rough with the smooth*). —*adv.* smoothly (*the course of true love never did run smooth*). □ **in smooth water** having passed obstacles or difficulties. **smooth-bore** a gun with an unrifled barrel. **smooth-faced** hypocritically friendly. **smoothing-iron** *hist.* a flat-iron. **smoothing-plane** a small plane for finishing the planing of wood. **smooth muscle** a muscle without striations, usu. occurring in hollow organs and performing involuntary functions. **smooth talk** *colloq.* bland specious language. **smooth-talk** *v.tr.* address or persuade with this. **smooth-tongued** insincerely flattering. □□ **smoothable** *adj.* **smoother** *n.* **smoothish** *adj.* **smoothly** *adv.* **smoothness** *n.* [OE *smōth*]

smoothie /ˈsmuːðɪ/ *n. colloq.* a person who is smooth (see SMOOTH *adj.* 9). [SMOOTH]

smorgasbord /ˈsmɔːɡəsˌbɔːd/ *n.* open sandwiches served with delicacies as hors d'œuvres or a buffet. [Sw. f. *smör* butter + *gås* goose, lump of butter + *bord* table]

smorzando /smɔːˈtsændəʊ/ *adj., adv.,* & *n. Mus.* —*adj.* & *adv.* dying away. —*n.* (*pl.* **-os** or **smorzandi** /-dɪ/) a smorzando passage. [It., gerund of *smorzare* extinguish]

smote *past* of SMITE.

smother /ˈsmʌðə(r)/ *v.* & *n.* —*v.* **1** *tr.* suffocate; stifle; kill by stopping the breath of or excluding air from. **2** *tr.* (foll. by *with*) overwhelm with (kisses, gifts, kindness, etc.) (*smothered with affection*). **3** *tr.* (foll. by *in, with*) cover entirely in or with (*chicken smothered in mayonnaise*). **4** *tr.* extinguish or deaden (a fire or flame) by covering it or heaping it with ashes etc. **5** *intr.* **a** die of suffocation. **b** have difficulty breathing. **6** *tr.* (often foll. by *up*) suppress or conceal; keep from notice or publicity. **7** *tr. US* defeat rapidly or utterly. —*n.* **1** a cloud of dust or smoke. **2** obscurity caused by this. □ **smothered mate** *Chess* checkmate in which the king, having no vacant square to move to, is checkmated by a knight. [ME *smorther* f. the stem of OE *smorian* suffocate]

smothery /ˈsmʌðərɪ/ *adj.* tending to smother; stifling.

smoulder /ˈsmoʊldə(r)/ *v.* & *n.* (*US* **smolder**) —*v.intr.* **1** burn slowly with smoke but without a flame; slowly burn internally or invisibly. **2** (of emotions etc.) exist in a suppressed or concealed state. **3** (of a person) show silent or suppressed anger, hatred, etc. —*n.* a smouldering or slow-burning fire. [ME, rel. to LG *smöln*, MDu. *smölen*]

smriti /ˈsmrɪtɪ/ *n.* Hindu traditional teachings on religion etc. [Skr. *smṛti* remembrance]

smudge[1] /smʌdʒ/ *n.* & *v.* —*n.* **1** a blurred or smeared line or mark; a blot; a smear of dirt. **2** a stain or blot on a person's character etc. —*v.* **1** *tr.* make a smudge on. **2** *intr.* become smeared or blurred (*smudges easily*). **3** *tr.* smear or blur the lines of (writing, drawing, etc.) (*smudge the outline*). **4** *tr.* defile, sully, stain, or disgrace (a person's name, character, etc.). □□ **smudgeless** *adj.* [ME: orig. unkn.]

smudge[2] /smʌdʒ/ *n. US* an outdoor fire with dense smoke made to keep off insects, protect plants against frost, etc. □ **smudge-pot** a container holding burning material that produces a smudge. [*smudge* (v.) cure (herring) by smoking (16th c.: orig. unkn.)]

smudgy /ˈsmʌdʒɪ/ *adj.* (**smudgier, smudgiest**) **1** smudged. **2** likely to produce smudges. □□ **smudgily** *adv.* **smudginess** *n.*

smug /smʌɡ/ *adj.* (**smugger, smuggest**) self-satisfied; complacent. □□ **smugly** *adv.* **smugness** *n.* [16th c., orig. 'neat' f. LG *smuk* pretty]

smuggle /ˈsmʌɡ(ə)l/ *v.tr.* **1** (also *absol.*) import or export (goods) illegally esp. without payment of customs duties. **2** (foll. by *in, out*) convey secretly. **3** (foll. by *away*) put into concealment. □□ **smuggler** *n.* **smuggling** *n.* [17th c. (also *smuckle*) f. LG *smukkeln, smuggelen*]

smut /smʌt/ *n.* & *v.* —*n.* **1** a small flake of soot etc. **2** a spot or smudge made by this. **3** obscene or lascivious talk, pictures, or stories. **4 a** a fungous disease of cereals in which parts of the ear change to black powder. **b** any fungus of the order

Ustilaginales causing this. —v. (**smutted, smutting**) 1 tr. mark with smuts. 2 tr. infect (a plant) with smut. 3 intr. (of a plant) contract smut. □ **smut-ball** Agriculture grain affected by smut. **smut-mill** a machine for freeing grain from smut. □□ **smutty** adj. (**smuttier, smuttiest**) (esp. in sense 3 of n.). **smuttily** adv. **smuttiness** n. [rel. to LG smutt, MHG smutz(en) etc.: cf. OE smitt(ian) smear, and SMUDGE[1]]

Smuts /smʌts/, Jan Christiaan (1870–1950), South African soldier, statesman, and philosopher. A lawyer by training, Smuts played an important part in the Boer War, leading a Boer guerrilla group in the Cape area, but afterwards supported Botha's policy of Anglo-Boer cooperation and was one of the founders of the Union of South Africa. During the First World War he became that country's foremost soldier, leading Imperial troops against the Germans in East Africa in 1916 and acting as South African representative in the British War Cabinet in 1917–18, during which time he played a crucial role in the formation of the Royal Air Force. After the war he held a series of high posts in the South African government, including that of Prime Minister in 1919–24 and 1939–48. During the Second World War he commanded the South African troops. As a statesman Smuts was respected internationally; he helped to found the League of Nations, drafted the preamble to the UN charter, and put forward the idea that the British Empire should evolve into a commonwealth of equal nations. In South Africa itself, however, he failed to grasp the strength of Afrikaner nationalism, and his support of Britain aroused resentment.

Smyrna see IZMIR.

Sn symb. Chem. the element tin.

snack /snæk/ n. & v. —n. 1 a light, casual, or hurried meal. 2 a small amount of food eaten between meals. 3 Austral. sl. something easy to accomplish. —v.intr. eat a snack. □ **snack bar** a place where snacks are sold. [ME, orig. a snap or bite, f. MDu. snac(k) f. snacken (v.), var. of snappen]

snaffle /ˈsnæf(ə)l/ n. & v. —n. (in full **snaffle-bit**) a simple bridle-bit without a curb and usu. with a single rein. —v.tr. 1 put a snaffle on. 2 colloq. steal; seize; appropriate. [prob. f. LG or Du.: cf. MLG, MDu. snavel beak, mouth]

snafu /snæˈfuː/ adj. & n. sl. —adj. in utter confusion or chaos. —n. this state. [acronym for 'situation normal: all fouled (or fucked) up']

snag[1] /snæg/ n. & v. —n. 1 an unexpected or hidden obstacle or drawback. 2 a jagged or projecting point or broken stump. 3 a tear in material etc. 4 a short tine of an antler. —v.tr. (**snagged, snagging**) 1 catch or tear on a snag. 2 clear (land, a waterway, a tree-trunk, etc.) of snags. 3 US catch or obtain by quick action. □□ **snagged** adj. **snaggy** adj. [prob. f. Scand.: cf. Norw. dial. snag(e) sharp point]

snag[2] /snæg/ n. (usu. in pl.) Austral. sl. a sausage. [20th c.: orig. unkn.]

snaggle-tooth /ˈsnæg(ə)l/ n. (pl. **snaggle-teeth**) an irregular or projecting tooth. □□ **snaggle-toothed** adj. [SNAG[1] + -LE[2]]

snail /sneɪl/ n. any slow-moving gastropod mollusc with a spiral shell able to enclose the whole body. □ **snail's pace** a very slow movement. □□ **snail-like** adj. [OE snæg(e)l f. Gmc]

snake /sneɪk/ n. & v. —n. 1 **a** any long limbless reptile of the suborder Serpentes, including boas, pythons, and poisonous forms such as cobras and vipers. **b** a limbless lizard or amphibian. 2 (also **snake in the grass**) a treacherous person or secret enemy. 3 (prec. by the) a system of interconnected exchange rates for the EEC currencies. —v.intr. move or twist like a snake. □ **snake bird** a fish-eating bird, Anhinga anhinga, with a long slender neck. **snake-charmer** a person appearing to make snakes move by music etc. **snake-pit 1** a pit containing snakes. 2 a scene of vicious behaviour. **snakes and ladders** a game with counters moved along a board with advances up 'ladders' or returns down 'snakes' depicted on the board. **snake's head** a bulbous plant, Fritillaria meleagris, with bell-shaped pendent flowers. □□ **snakelike** adj. [OE snaca]

snakeroot /ˈsneɪkruːt/ n. any of various N. American plants, esp. Cimicifuga racemosa, with roots reputed to contain an antidote to snake's poison.

snaky /ˈsneɪkɪ/ adj. 1 of or like a snake. 2 winding; sinuous. 3 showing coldness, ingratitude, venom, or guile. 4 **a** infested with snakes. **b** (esp. of the hair of the Furies) composed of snakes. 5 Austral. sl. angry; irritable. □□ **snakily** adv. **snakiness** n.

snap /snæp/ v., n., adv., & adj. —v. (**snapped, snapping**) 1 intr. & tr. break suddenly or with a snap. 2 intr. & tr. emit or cause to emit a sudden sharp sound or crack. 3 intr. & tr. open or close with a snapping sound (the bag snapped shut). 4 **a** intr. (often foll. by at) speak irritably or spitefully (to a person) (did not mean to snap at you). **b** tr. say irritably or spitefully. 5 intr. (often foll. by at) (esp. of a dog etc.) make a sudden audible bite. 6 tr. & intr. move quickly (snap into action). 7 tr. take a snapshot of. 8 tr. Amer. Football put (the ball) into play on the ground by a quick backward movement. —n. 1 an act or sound of snapping. 2 a crisp biscuit or cake (brandy snap; ginger snap). 3 a snapshot. 4 (in full **cold snap**) a sudden brief spell of cold weather. 5 Brit. **a** a card-game in which players call 'snap' when two similar cards are exposed. **b** (as int.) on noticing the (often unexpected) similarity of two things. 6 crispness of style; fresh vigour or liveliness in action; zest; dash; spring. 7 US sl. an easy task (it was a snap). —adv. with the sound of a snap (heard it go snap). —adj. done or taken on the spur of the moment, unexpectedly, or without notice (snap decision). □ **snap at** accept (bait, a chance, etc.) eagerly (see also senses 4a and 5 of v.). **snap bean** US a bean grown for its pods which are broken into pieces and eaten. **snap-bolt** (or **-lock**) a bolt etc. which locks automatically when a door or window closes. **snap-brim** (of a hat) with a brim that can be turned up and down at opposite sides. **snap-fastener** = press-stud (see PRESS[1]). **snap one's fingers 1** make an audible fillip, esp. in rhythm to music etc. 2 (often foll. by at) defy; show contempt for. **snap-hook** (or **-link**) a hook or link with a spring allowing the entrance but barring the escape of a cord, link, etc. **snap off** break off or bite off. **snap off a person's head** address a person angrily or rudely. **snap out** say irritably. **snap out of** sl. get rid of (a mood, habit, etc.) by a sudden effort. **snapping turtle** any large American freshwater turtle of the family Chelydridae which seizes prey with a snap of its jaws. **snap up 1** accept (an offer, a bargain) quickly or eagerly. 2 pick up or catch hastily or smartly. 3 interrupt (another person) before he or she has finished speaking. □□ **snappable** adj. **snappingly** adv. [prob. f. MDu. or MLG snappen, partly imit.]

snapdragon /ˈsnæpˌdrægən/ n. a plant, Antirrhinum majus, with a bag-shaped flower like a dragon's mouth.

snapper /ˈsnæpə(r)/ n. 1 a person or thing that snaps. 2 any of several fish of the family Lutjanidae, used as food. 3 a snapping turtle. 4 US a cracker (as a toy).

snappish /ˈsnæpɪʃ/ adj. 1 (of a person's manner or a remark) curt; ill-tempered; sharp. 2 (of a dog etc.) inclined to snap. □□ **snappishly** adv. **snappishness** n.

snappy /ˈsnæpɪ/ adj. (**snappier, snappiest**) colloq. 1 brisk, full of zest. 2 neat and elegant (a snappy dresser). 3 snappish. □ **make it snappy** be quick about it. □□ **snappily** adv. **snappiness** n.

snapshot /ˈsnæpʃɒt/ n. a casual photograph taken quickly with a small hand-camera.

snare /sneə(r)/ n. & v. —n. 1 a trap for catching birds or animals, esp. with a noose of wire or cord. 2 a thing that acts as a temptation. 3 a device for tempting an enemy etc. to expose himself or herself to danger, failure, loss, capture, defeat, etc. 4 (in sing. or pl.) Mus. twisted strings of gut, hide, or wire stretched across the lower head of a side-drum to produce a rattling sound. 5 (in full **snare drum**) a drum fitted with snares. 6 Surgery a wire loop for extracting polyps etc. —v.tr. 1 catch (a bird etc.) in a snare. 2 ensnare; lure or trap (a person) with a snare. □□ **snarer** n. (also in comb.). [OE sneare f. ON snara: senses 4 & 5 prob. f. MLG or MDu.]

snark /snɑːk/ n. a fabulous animal, orig. the subject of a nonsense poem. [The Hunting of the Snark (1876) by Lewis Carroll]

snarl[1] /snɑːl/ v. & n. —v. 1 intr. (of a dog) make an angry growl with bared teeth. 2 intr. (of a person) speak cynically; make bad-tempered complaints or criticisms. 3 tr. (often foll. by out) **a** utter in a snarling tone. **b** express (discontent etc.) by snarling. —n. the act or sound of snarling. □□ **snarler** n. **snarlingly**

adv. **snarly** *adj.* (**snarlier, snarliest**). [earlier *snar* f. (M)LG, MHG *snarren*]

snarl² /snɑːl/ *v. & n.* —*v.* **1** *tr.* (often foll. by *up*) twist; entangle; confuse and hamper the movement of (traffic etc.). **2** *intr.* (often foll. by *up*) become entangled, congested, or confused. **3** *tr.* adorn the exterior of (a narrow metal vessel) with raised work. —*n.* a knot or tangle. □ **snarling iron** an implement used for snarling metal. **snarl-up** *colloq.* a traffic jam; a muddle; a mistake. [ME f. *snare* (n. & v.): sense 3 perh. f. noun in dial. sense 'knot in wood']

snatch /snætʃ/ *v. & n.* —*v.tr.* **1** seize quickly, eagerly, or unexpectedly, esp. with outstretched hands. **2** steal (a wallet, handbag, etc.). **3** secure with difficulty (*snatched an hour's rest*). **4** (foll. by *away, from*) take away or from esp. suddenly (*snatched away my hand*). **5** (foll. by *from*) rescue narrowly (*snatched from the jaws of death*). **6** (foll. by *at*) **a** try to seize by stretching or grasping suddenly. **b** take (an offer etc.) eagerly. —*n.* **1** an act of snatching (*made a snatch at it*). **2** a fragment of a song or talk etc. (*caught a snatch of their conversation*). **3** *US sl.* a kidnapping. **4** (in weight-lifting) the rapid raising of a weight from the floor to above the head. **5** a short spell of activity etc. □ **in** (or **by**) **snatches** in fits and starts. □□ **snatcher** *n.* (esp. in sense 3 of *n.*). **snatchy** *adj.* [ME *snecchen, sna(c)che,* perh. rel. to SNACK]

snavel /ˈsnæv(ə)l/ *v.tr.* (also **snavle, snavvle**) *Austral. sl.* catch; take; steal. [E dial. (as SNAFFLE)]

snazzy /ˈsnæzɪ/ *adj.* (**snazzier, snazziest**) *sl.* smart or attractive esp. in an ostentatious way. □□ **snazzily** *adv.* **snazziness** *n.* [20th c.: orig. unkn.]

sneak /sniːk/ *v., n., & adj.* —*v.* **1** *intr. & tr.* (foll. by *in, out, past, away,* etc.) go or convey furtively; slink. **2** *tr. sl.* steal unobserved; make off with. **3** *intr. Brit. school sl.* tell tales; turn informer. **4** *intr.* (as **sneaking** *adj.*) **a** furtive; undisclosed (*have a sneaking affection for him*). **b** persistent in one's mind; nagging (*a sneaking feeling that it is not right*). —*n.* **1** a mean-spirited cowardly underhand person. **2** *Brit. school sl.* a tell-tale. —*adj.* acting or done without warning; secret (*a sneak attack*). □ **sneak-thief** a thief who steals without breaking in; a pickpocket. □□ **sneakingly** *adv.* [16th c., prob. dial.: perh. rel. to ME *snike,* OE *snīcan* creep]

sneaker /ˈsniːkə(r)/ *n. sl.* each of a pair of soft-soled canvas etc. shoes.

sneaky /ˈsniːkɪ/ *adj.* (**sneakier, sneakiest**) given to or characterized by sneaking; furtive, mean. □□ **sneakily** *adv.* **sneakiness** *n.*

sneck /snek/ *n. & v. Sc. & N.Engl.* —*n.* a latch. —*v.tr.* latch (a door etc.); close or fasten with a sneck. [ME, rel. to SNATCH]

Sneek /sneɪk/ a market-town and water-sports centre in The Netherlands, with the largest yachting harbour in the country; pop. (1987) 29,337.

sneer /snɪə(r)/ *n. & v.* —*n.* a derisive smile or remark. —*v.* **1** *intr.* (often foll. by *at*) smile derisively. **2** *tr.* say sneeringly. **3** *intr.* (often foll. by *at*) speak derisively esp. covertly or ironically (*sneered at his attempts*). □□ **sneerer** *n.* **sneeringly** *adv.* [16th c.: orig. unkn.]

sneeze /sniːz/ *n. & v.* —*n.* **1** a sudden involuntary expulsion of air from the nose and mouth caused by irritation of the nostrils. **2** the sound of this. —*v.intr.* make a sneeze. □ **not to be sneezed at** *colloq.* not contemptible; considerable; notable. □□ **sneezer** *n.* **sneezy** *adj.* [ME *snese,* app. alt. of obs. *fnese* f. OE *-fnēsan,* ON *fnýsa* & replacing earlier and less expressive *nese*]

sneezewort /ˈsniːzwɜːt/ *n.* a kind of yarrow, *Achillea ptarmica,* whose dried leaves are used to induce sneezing.

Snell's law /snelz/ *n. Physics* the law that the ratio of the sines of the angles of incidence and refraction of a wave are constant when it passes between two given media. [W. *Snell,* Du. mathematician d. 1626]

snib /snɪb/ *v. & n. Sc. & Ir.* —*v.tr.* (**snibbed, snibbing**) bolt, fasten, or lock (a door etc.). —*n.* a lock, catch, or fastening for a door or window. [19th c.: orig. uncert.]

snick /snɪk/ *v. & n.* —*v.tr.* **1** cut a small notch in. **2** make a small incision in. **3** *Cricket* deflect (the ball) slightly with the bat. —*n.* **1** a small notch or cut. **2** *Cricket* a slight deflection of the ball by the bat. [18th c.: prob. f. *snick-a-snee* fight with knives]

snicker /ˈsnɪkə(r)/ *v. & n.* —*v.intr.* **1** = SNIGGER *v.* **2** whinny, neigh. —*n.* **1** = SNIGGER *n.* **2** a whinny, a neigh. □□ **snickeringly** *adv.* [imit.]

snide /snaɪd/ *adj. & n.* —*adj.* **1** sneering; slyly derogatory; insinuating. **2** counterfeit; bogus. **3** *US* mean; underhand. —*n.* a snide person or remark. □□ **snidely** *adv.* **snideness** *n.* [19th-c. colloq.: orig. unkn.]

sniff /snɪf/ *v. & n.* —*v.* **1** *intr.* draw up air audibly through the nose to stop it running or to detect a smell or as an expression of contempt. **2** *tr.* (often foll. by *up*) draw in (a scent, drug, liquid, or air) through the nose. **3** *tr.* draw in the scent of (food, drink, flowers, etc.) through the nose. —*n.* **1** an act or sound of sniffing. **2** the amount of air etc. sniffed up. □ **sniff at 1** try the smell of; show interest in. **2** show contempt for or discontent with. **sniff out** detect; discover by investigation. □□ **sniffingly** *adv.* [ME, imit.]

sniffer /ˈsnɪfə(r)/ *n.* **1** a person who sniffs, esp. one who sniffs a drug or toxic substances (often in *comb.*: *glue-sniffer*). **2** *sl.* the nose. **3** *colloq.* any device for detecting gas, radiation, etc. □ **sniffer-dog** *colloq.* a dog trained to sniff out drugs or explosives.

sniffle /ˈsnɪf(ə)l/ *v. & n.* —*v.intr.* sniff slightly or repeatedly. —*n.* **1** the act of sniffling. **2** (in *sing.* or *pl.*) a cold in the head causing a running nose and sniffling. □□ **sniffler** *n.* **sniffly** *adj.* [imit.: cf. SNIVEL]

sniffy /ˈsnɪfɪ/ *adj.* (**sniffier, sniffiest**) **1** inclined to sniff. **2** disdainful; contemptuous. □□ **sniffily** *adv.* **sniffiness** *n.*

snifter /ˈsnɪftə(r)/ *n.* **1** *sl.* a small drink of alcohol. **2** *US* a balloon glass for brandy. □ **snifter-valve** a valve in a steam engine to allow air in or out. [dial. *snift* sniff, perh. f. Scand.: imit.]

snig /snɪg/ *v.tr.* (**snigged, snigging**) *Austral. & NZ* drag with a jerk. □ **snigging chain** a chain used to move logs. [E dial.]

snigger /ˈsnɪgə(r)/ *n. & v.* —*n.* a half-suppressed secretive laugh. —*v.intr.* utter such a laugh. □□ **sniggerer** *n.* **sniggeringly** *adv.* [var. of SNICKER]

sniggle /ˈsnɪg(ə)l/ *v.intr.* fish (for eels) by pushing bait into a hole. [ME *snig* small eel, of unkn. orig.]

snip /snɪp/ *v. & n.* —*v.tr.* (**snipped, snipping**) (also *absol.*) cut (cloth, a hole, etc.) with scissors or shears, esp. in small quick strokes. —*n.* **1** an act of snipping. **2** a piece of material etc. snipped off. **3** *sl.* **a** something easily achieved. **b** *Brit.* a bargain; something cheaply acquired. **4** (in *pl.*) hand-shears for metal cutting. □ **snip at** make snipping strokes at. □□ **snipping** *n.* [LG & Du. *snippen* imit.]

snipe /snaɪp/ *n. & v.* —*n.* (*pl.* same or **snipes**) any of various wading birds, esp. of the genus *Gallinago,* with a long straight bill and frequenting marshes. —*v.* **1** *intr.* fire shots from hiding usu. at long range. **2** *tr.* kill by sniping. **3** *intr.* (foll. by *at*) make a sly critical attack. **4** *intr.* go snipe-shooting. □ **snipe eel** any eel of the family Nemichthyidae, having a long slender snout. **snipe fish** any marine fish of the family Macrorhamphosidae, with a long slender snout. □□ **sniper** *n.* [ME, prob. f. Scand.: cf. Icel. *mýrisnípa,* & MDu., MLG *snippe,* OHG *snepfa*]

snippet /ˈsnɪpɪt/ *n.* **1** a small piece cut off. **2** (usu. in *pl.*; often foll. by *of*) **a** a scrap or fragment of information, knowledge, etc. **b** a short extract from a book, newspaper, etc. □□ **snippety** *adj.*

snippy /ˈsnɪpɪ/ *adj.* (**snippier, snippiest**) *colloq.* fault-finding; snappish, sharp. □□ **snippily** *adv.* **snippiness** *n.*

snit /snɪt/ *n. US* a rage; a sulk (esp. *in a snit*). [20th c.: orig. unkn.]

snitch /snɪtʃ/ *v. & n.* —*v. sl.* **1** *tr.* steal. **2** *intr.* (often foll. by *on*) inform on a person. —*n.* an informer. [17th c.: orig. unkn.]

snivel /ˈsnɪv(ə)l/ *v. & n.* —*v.intr.* (**snivelled, snivelling;** *US* **sniveled, sniveling**) **1** weep with sniffling. **2** run at the nose; make a repeated sniffing sound. **3** show weak or tearful sentiment. —*n.* **1** running mucus. **2** hypocritical talk; cant. □□ **sniveller** *n.* **snivelling** *adj.* **snivellingly** *adv.* [ME f. OE *snyflan* (unrecorded) f. *snofl* mucus: cf. SNUFFLE]

snob /snɒb/ *n.* **1 a** a person with an exaggerated respect for social position or wealth and who despises socially inferior connections. **b** (*attrib.*) related to or characteristic of this attitude. **2** a person who behaves with servility to social superiors. **3** a person who despises others whose (usu. specified) tastes or attainments are considered inferior (*an intellectual snob; a wine snob*). □□ **snobbery** *n*. (*pl*. **-ies**). **snobbish** *adj*. **snobbishly** *adv*. **snobbishness** *n*. **snobby** *adj*. (**snobbier**, **snobbiest**). [18th c. (now dial.) 'cobbler': orig. unkn.]

snoek /snuːk/ *n*. *S.Afr*. a barracouta. [Afrik. f. Du., = PIKE¹, f. MLG *snōk*, prob. rel. to SNACK]

snog /snɒg/ *v*. & *n*. *Brit*. *sl*. —*v.intr*. (**snogged**, **snogging**) engage in kissing and caressing. —*n*. a spell of snogging. [20th c.: orig. unkn.]

snood /snuːd/ *n*. **1** an ornamental hairnet usu. worn at the back of the head. **2** a ring of woollen etc. material worn as a hood. **3** a short line attaching a hook to a main line in sea fishing. **4** *hist*. a ribbon or band worn by unmarried women in Scotland to confine their hair. [OE *snōd*]

snook¹ /snuːk/ *n*. *sl*. a contemptuous gesture with the thumb to the nose and the fingers spread out. □ **cock a snook** (often foll. by *at*) **1** make this gesture. **2** register one's contempt (for a person, establishment, etc.). [19th c.: orig. unkn.]

snook² /snuːk/ *n*. a marine fish, *Centropomus undecimalis*, used as food. [Du. *snoek*: see SNOEK]

snooker /ˈsnuːkə(r)/ *n*. & *v*. —*n*. **1** a game played with cues on a rectangular baize-covered table in which the players use a cue-ball (white) to pocket the other balls (15 red and 6 coloured) in a set order. (See below.) **2** a position in this game in which a direct shot at a permitted ball is impossible. —*v.tr*. **1** (also *refl*.) subject (oneself or another player) to a snooker. **2** (esp. as **snookered** *adj*.) *sl*. defeat; thwart. [19th c.: orig. unkn.]

The game of snooker is a combination of pool and pyramids (see PYRAMID 4), developed in the 1870s by British army officers in India. The sport did not overtake billiards in skill or popularity until the arrival of Joe Davis (see DAVIS²) in the 1920s, but it was the development of colour television in the 1960s, and the BBC's series 'Pot Black', that made snooker one of the most popular sports both for participants and for spectators.

snoop /snuːp/ *v*. & *n*. *colloq*. —*v.intr*. **1** pry into matters one need not be concerned with. **2** (often foll. by *about*, *around*) investigate in order to find out transgressions of the law etc. —*n*. **1** an act of snooping. **2** a person who snoops; a detective. □□ **snooper** *n*. **snoopy** *adj*. [Du. *snoepen* eat on the sly]

snooperscope /ˈsnuːpəˌskəʊp/ *n*. *US* a device which converts infrared radiation into a visible image, esp. used for seeing in the dark.

snoot /snuːt/ *n*. *sl*. the nose. [var. of SNOUT]

snooty /ˈsnuːtɪ/ *adj*. (**snootier**, **snootiest**) *colloq*. supercilious; conceited. □□ **snootily** *adv*. **snootiness** *n*. [20th c.: orig. unkn.]

snooze /snuːz/ *n*. & *v*. *colloq*. —*n*. a short sleep, esp. in the daytime. —*v.intr*. take a snooze. □□ **snoozer** *n*. **snoozy** *adj*. (**snoozier**, **snooziest**). [18th-c. *sl*.: orig. unkn.]

snore /snɔː(r)/ *n*. & *v*. —*n*. a snorting or grunting sound in breathing during sleep. —*v.intr*. make this sound. □ **snore away** pass (time) sleeping or snoring. □□ **snorer** *n*. **snoringly** *adv*. [ME, prob. imit.: cf. SNORT]

Snorkel /ˈsnɔːk(ə)l/ *n*. [*propr*.] a piece of apparatus consisting of a platform which may be elevated and extended, used in fighting fires in tall buildings.

snorkel /ˈsnɔːk(ə)l/ *n*. & *v*. (also **schnorkel** /ˈʃnɔː-/) —*n*. **1** a breathing-tube for an underwater swimmer. **2** a device for supplying air to a submerged submarine. —*v.intr*. (**snorkelled**, **snorkelling**; *US* **snorkeled**, **snorkeling**) use a snorkel. □□ **snorkeller** *n*. [G *Schnorchel*]

Snorri Sturluson /ˌsnɔːrɪ ˈstɜːləs(ə)n/ (1178–1241), Icelandic historian, the most important figure in Old Icelandic literature, author of the prose *Edda* and the *Heimskringla*, a history of the kings of Norway, through which works he popularized Norse myth and Old Norse poetry. He was involved in the chief political intrigues of his time and King Hákon of Norway ordered his assassination.

snort /snɔːt/ *n*. & *v*. —*n*. **1** an explosive sound made by the sudden forcing of breath through the nose, esp. expressing indignation or incredulity. **2** a similar sound made by an engine etc. **3** *colloq*. a small drink of liquor. **4** *sl*. an inhaled dose of a (usu. illegal) powdered drug. —*v*. **1** *intr*. make a snort. **2** *intr*.

(of an engine etc.) make a sound resembling this. **3** *tr*. (also *absol*.) *sl*. inhale (a usu. illegal narcotic drug, esp. cocaine or heroin). **4** *tr*. express (defiance etc.) by snorting. □ **snort out** express (words, emotions, etc.) by snorting. [ME, prob. imit.: cf. SNORE]

snorter /ˈsnɔːtə(r)/ *n*. *colloq*. **1** something very impressive or difficult. **2** something vigorous or violent.

snot /snɒt/ *n*. *sl*. **1** nasal mucus. **2** a term of contempt for a person. □ **snot-rag** a handkerchief. [prob. f. MDu., MLG *snotte*, MHG *snuz*, rel. to SNOUT]

snotty /ˈsnɒtɪ/ *adj*. (**snottier**, **snottiest**) *sl*. **1** running or foul with nasal mucus. **2** contemptible. **3** supercilious, conceited. □□ **snottily** *adv*. **snottiness** *n*.

snout /snaʊt/ *n*. **1** the projecting nose and mouth of an animal. **2** *derog*. a person's nose. **3** the pointed front of a thing; a nozzle. **4** *Brit*. *sl*. tobacco or a cigarette. □ **snout-beetle** a weevil. □□ **snouted** *adj*. (also in *comb*.). **snoutlike** *adj*. **snouty** *adj*. [ME f. MDu., MLG *snūt*]

Snow /snəʊ/, Charles Percy (1905–80), English novelist, scientist, and administrator. His sequence of novels *Strangers and Brothers* deals with moral dilemmas and power-struggles in the academic world, and includes *The Masters* (1951) and *The Affair* (1960). He was created a life peer in 1964.

snow /snəʊ/ *n*. & *v*. —*n*. **1** atmospheric vapour frozen into ice crystals and falling to earth in light white flakes. **2** a fall of this, or a layer of it on the ground. **3** a thing resembling snow in whiteness or texture. **4** a mass of flickering white spots on a television or radar screen, caused by interference or a poor signal. **5** *sl*. cocaine. **6** a dessert or other dish resembling snow. **7** frozen carbon dioxide. —*v*. **1** *intr*. (prec. by *it* as subject) snow falls (*it is snowing; if it snows*). **2** *tr*. (foll. by *in*, *over*, *up*, etc.) confine or block with large quantities of snow. **3** *tr*. & *intr*. sprinkle or scatter or fall as or like snow. **4** *intr*. come in large numbers or quantities. **5** *tr*. *US sl*. deceive or charm with plausible words. □ **be snowed under** be overwhelmed, esp. with work. **snow-blind** temporarily blinded by the glare of light reflected by large expanses of snow. **snow-blindness** this blindness. **snow-blink** the reflection in the sky of snow or ice fields. **snow boot** an overboot of rubber and cloth. **snow-broth** melted or melting snow. **snow bunting** a mainly white finch, *Plectrophenax nivalis*. **snow goose** a white Arctic goose, *Anser caerulescens*, with black-tipped wings. **snow-ice** opaque white ice formed from melted snow. **snow leopard** = OUNCE². **snow owl** = *snowy owl*. **snow partridge** a mainly white partridge, *Lerwa lerwa*. **snow-slip** an avalanche. **snow-white** pure white. □□ **snowless** *adj*. **snowlike** *adj*. [OE *snāw* f. Gmc]

snowball /ˈsnəʊbɔːl/ *n*. & *v*. —*n*. **1** snow pressed together into a ball, esp. for throwing in play. **2** anything that grows or increases rapidly like a snowball rolled on snow. —*v*. **1** *intr*. & *tr*. throw or pelt with snowballs. **2** *intr*. increase rapidly. □ **snowball-tree** a guelder rose.

snowberry /ˈsnəʊbərɪ/ *n*. (*pl*. **-ies**) any shrub of the genus *Symphoricarpos*, with white berries.

snowblower /ˈsnəʊˌbləʊə(r)/ *n*. a machine that clears snow by blowing it to the side of the road etc.

snowbound /ˈsnəʊbaʊnd/ *adj*. prevented by snow from going out or travelling.

snowcap /ˈsnəʊkæp/ *n*. **1** the tip of a mountain when covered with snow. **2** a white-crowned humming-bird, *Microchera albocoronata*, native to Central America. □□ **snowcapped** *adj*.

Snowdon /ˈsnəʊd(ə)n/ the highest mountain of Wales (1,085 m, 3,560 ft.).

snowdrift /ˈsnəʊdrɪft/ *n*. a bank of snow heaped up by the action of the wind.

snowdrop /ˈsnəʊdrɒp/ *n*. a bulbous plant, *Galanthus nivalis*, with white drooping flowers in the early spring.

snowfall /ˈsnəʊfɔːl/ *n*. **1** a fall of snow. **2** *Meteorol*. the amount of snow that falls on one occasion or on a given area within a given time.

snowfield /ˈsnəʊfiːld/ *n*. a permanent wide expanse of snow in mountainous or polar regions.

snowflake /ˈsnəʊfleɪk/ n. **1** each of the small collections of crystals in which snow falls. **2 a** any bulbous plant of the genus *Leucojum*, with snowdrop-like flowers. **b** the white flower of this plant.

snowline /ˈsnəʊlaɪn/ n. the level above which snow never melts entirely.

snowman /ˈsnəʊmæn/ n. (*pl.* **-men**) a figure resembling a man, made of compressed snow.

snowmobile /ˈsnəʊməˌbiːl/ n. a motor vehicle, esp. with runners or Caterpillar tracks, for travelling over snow.

snowplough /ˈsnəʊplaʊ/ n. (*US* **snowplow**) **1** a device, or a vehicle equipped with one, for clearing roads of thick snow. **2** a skiing movement turning the points of the skis inwards so as to stop.

snowshoe /ˈsnəʊʃuː/ n. & v. —n. a flat device like a racket attached to a boot for walking on snow without sinking in. —v.intr. travel on snowshoes. □□ **snowshoer** n.

snowstorm /ˈsnəʊstɔːm/ n. a heavy fall of snow, esp. with a high wind.

snowy /ˈsnəʊɪ/ adj. (**snowier**, **snowiest**) **1** of or like snow. **2** (of the weather etc.) with much snow. □ **snowy owl** a large white owl, *Nyctea scandiaca*, native to the Arctic. □□ **snowily** adv. **snowiness** n.

SNP abbr. Scottish National Party.

Snr. abbr. Senior.

snub /snʌb/ v., n., & adj. —v.tr. (**snubbed**, **snubbing**) **1** rebuff or humiliate with sharp words or a marked lack of cordiality. **2** check the movement of (a boat, horse, etc.) esp. by a rope wound round a post etc. —n. an act of snubbing; a rebuff. —adj. short and blunt in shape. □ **snub nose** a short turned-up nose. **snub-nosed** having a snub nose. □□ **snubber** n. **snubbingly** adv. [ME f. ON *snubba* chide, check the growth of]

snuff[1] /snʌf/ n. & v. —n. the charred part of a candle-wick. —v.tr. trim the snuff from (a candle). □ **snuff it** Brit. sl. die. **snuff out 1** extinguish by snuffing. **2** kill; put an end to. [ME *snoffe*, *snuffe*: orig. unkn.]

snuff[2] /snʌf/ n. & v. —n. powdered tobacco or medicine taken by sniffing it up the nostrils. —v.intr. take snuff. □ **snuff-coloured** dark yellowish-brown. **up to snuff** colloq. **1** Brit. knowing; not easily deceived. **2** up to standard. [Du. *snuf* (*tabak* tobacco) f. MDu. *snuffen* snuffle]

snuffbox /ˈsnʌfbɒks/ n. a small usu. ornamental box for holding snuff.

snuffer /ˈsnʌfə(r)/ n. **1** a small hollow cone with a handle used to extinguish a candle. **2** (in pl.) an implement like scissors used to extinguish a candle or trim its wick.

snuffle /ˈsnʌf(ə)l/ v. & n. —v. **1** intr. make sniffing sounds. **2 a** intr. speak nasally, whiningly, or like one with a cold. **b** tr. (often foll. by out) say in this way. **3** intr. breathe noisily as through a partially blocked nose. **4** intr. sniff. —n. **1** a snuffling sound or tone. **2** (in pl.) a partial blockage of the nose causing snuffling. **3** a sniff. □□ **snuffler** n. **snuffly** adj. [prob. f. LG & Du. *snuffelen* (as SNUFF[2]): cf. SNIVEL]

snuffy[1] /ˈsnʌfɪ/ adj. (**snuffier**, **snuffiest**) **1** annoyed. **2** irritable. **3** supercilious or contemptuous. [SNUFF[1] + -Y[1]]

snuffy[2] /ˈsnʌfɪ/ adj. like snuff in colour or substance. [SNUFF[2] + -Y[2]]

snug /snʌg/ adj. & n. —adj. (**snugger**, **snuggest**) **1 a** cosy, comfortable, sheltered; well enclosed or placed or arranged. **b** cosily protected from the weather or cold. **2** (of an income etc.) allowing comfort and comparative ease. —n. Brit. a small room in a pub or inn. □□ **snugly** adv. **snugness** n. [16th c. (orig. Naut.): prob. of LG or Du. orig.]

snuggery /ˈsnʌgərɪ/ n. (*pl.* **-ies**) **1** a snug place, esp. a person's private room or den. **2** Brit. = SNUG n.

snuggle /ˈsnʌg(ə)l/ v.intr. & tr. (usu. foll. by *down*, *up*, *together*) settle or draw into a warm comfortable position. [SNUG + -LE[4]]

So. abbr. South.

so[1] /səʊ/ adv. & conj. —adv. **1** (often foll. by *that* + clause) to such an extent, or to the extent implied (*why are you so angry?*; *do stop complaining so*; *they were so pleased that they gave us a bonus*).

2 (with *neg.*; often foll. by *as* + clause) to the extent to which ... is or does etc., or to the extent implied (*was not so late as I expected*; *am not so eager as you*). ¶ In positive constructions *as ... as ...* is used: see AS[1]. **3** (foll. by *that* or *as* + clause) to the degree or in the manner implied (*so expensive that few can afford it*; *so small as to be invisible*; *am not so foolish as to agree to that*). **4** (adding emphasis) to that extent; in that or a similar manner (*I want to leave and so does she*; *you said it was good, and so it is*). **5** to a great or notable degree (*I am so glad*). **6** (with verbs of state) in the way described (*am not very fond of it but may become so*). **7** (with verb of saying or thinking etc.) as previously mentioned or described (*I think so*; *so he said*; *so I should hope*). —conj. (often foll. by *that* + clause) **1** with the result that (*there was none left, so we had to go without*). **2** in order that (*came home early so that I could see you*). **3** and then; as the next step (*so then the car broke down*; *and so to bed*). **4 a** (introducing a question) then; after that (*so what did you tell them?*). **b** (*absol.*) = *so what?* □ **and so on** (or **forth**) **1** and others of the same kind. **2** and in other similar ways. **so as** (foll. by *to* + infin.) in order to (*did it so as to get it finished*). **so be it** an expression of acceptance or resignation. **so-called** commonly designated or known as, often incorrectly. **so far** see FAR. **so far as** see FAR. **so far so good** see FAR. **so long!** colloq. goodbye till we meet again. **so long as** see LONG[1]. **so much 1** a certain amount (of). **2** a great deal of (*is so much nonsense*). **3** (with *neg.*) **a** less than; to a lesser extent (*not so much forgotten as ignored*). **b** not even (*didn't give me so much as a penny*). **so much for** that is all that need be done or said about. **so so** adj. (usu. *predic.*) indifferent; not very good. —adv. indifferently; only moderately well. **so to say** (or **speak**) an expression of reserve or apology for an exaggeration or neologism etc. **so what?** colloq. why should that be considered significant? [OE *swā* etc.]

so[2] var. of SOH.

-so /səʊ/ comb. form = -SOEVER.

soak /səʊk/ v. & n. —v. **1** tr. & intr. make or become thoroughly wet through saturation with or in liquid. **2** tr. (of rain etc.) drench. **3** tr. (foll. by *in*, *up*) **a** absorb (liquid). **b** acquire (knowledge etc.) copiously. **4** refl. (often foll. by *in*) steep (oneself) in a subject of study etc. **5** intr. (foll. by *in*, *into*, *through*) (of liquid) make its way or penetrate by saturation. **6** tr. colloq. extract money from by an extortionate charge, taxation, etc. (*soak the rich*). **7** intr. colloq. drink persistently, booze. **8** tr. (as **soaked** adj.) very drunk. —n. **1** the act of soaking or the state of being soaked. **2** a drinking-bout. **3** colloq. a hard drinker. □□ **soakage** n. **soaking** n. & adj. [OE *socian* rel. to *soc* sucking at the breast, *sūcan* SUCK]

soakaway /ˈsəʊkəˌweɪ/ n. an arrangement for disposing of waste water by letting it percolate through the soil.

so-and-so /ˈsəʊəndˌsəʊ/ n. (*pl.* **so-and-so's**) **1** a particular person or thing not needing to be specified (*told me to do so-and-so*). **2** colloq. a person disliked or regarded with disfavour (*the so-and-so left me behind*).

Soane /səʊn/, Sir John (1753–1837), English architect. His highly individualistic manipulation of the classical canon makes him something of a Romantic classicist. From 1788 he was architect of the Bank of England and there developed his characteristic style of simple masses defined by flat surfaces and articulated with incised lines. By 1810 his style had become more severe, avoiding unnecessary ornament and adopting structural necessity as the basis of design. His picture collection, amassed as a result of his professional success, is housed in his self-designed home, the Sir John Soane Museum, London.

soap /səʊp/ n. & v. —n. **1** a cleansing agent that is a compound of fatty acid with soda or potash or (**insoluble soap**) with another metallic oxide, of which the soluble kinds when rubbed in water yield a lather used in washing. **2** colloq. = *soap opera*. —v.tr. **1** apply soap to. **2** scrub or rub with soap. □ **soap flakes** soap in the form of thin flakes, for washing clothes etc. **soap opera** a broadcast drama, usu. serialized in many episodes, dealing with sentimental domestic themes (so called because orig. sponsored in the US by soap manufacturers). **soap powder** powdered soap esp. with additives. □□ **soapless** adj. **soaplike** adj. [OE *sāpe* f. WG]

soapbark /'səʊpbɑːk/ n. an American tree, *Quillaja saponaria*, with bark yielding saponin.

soapberry /'səʊpˌberɪ/ n. (pl. **-ies**) any of various tropical American shrubs, esp. of the genus *Sapindus*, with fruits yielding saponin.

soapbox /'səʊpbɒks/ n. **1** a box for holding soap. **2** a makeshift stand for a public speaker.

soapstone /'səʊpstəʊn/ n. steatite.

soapsuds /'səʊpsʌdz/ n.pl. = SUDS 1.

soapwort /'səʊpwɜːt/ n. a European plant, *Saponaria officinalis*, with pink or white flowers and leaves yielding a soapy substance.

soapy /'səʊpɪ/ adj. (**soapier, soapiest**) **1** of or like soap. **2** containing or smeared with soap. **3** (of a person or manner) unctuous or flattering. □□ **soapily** adv. **soapiness** n.

soar /sɔː(r)/ v.intr. **1** fly or rise high. **2** reach a high level or standard (*prices soared*). **3** maintain height in the air without flapping the wings or using power. □□ **soarer** n. **soaringly** adv. [ME f. OF *essorer* ult. f. L (as EX-¹, *aura* breeze)]

sob /sɒb/ v. & n. —v. (**sobbed, sobbing**) **1** intr. draw breath in convulsive gasps usu. with weeping under mental distress or physical exhaustion. **2** tr. (usu. foll. by *out*) utter with sobs. **3** tr. bring (oneself) to a specified state by sobbing (*sobbed themselves to sleep*). —n. a convulsive drawing of breath, esp. in weeping. □ **sob story** a story or explanation appealing mainly to the emotions. **sob-stuff** colloq. sentimental talk or writing. □□ **sobber** n. **sobbingly** adv. [ME *sobbe* (prob. imit.)]

sober /'səʊbə(r)/ adj. & n. —adj. (**soberer, soberest**) **1** not affected by alcohol. **2** not given to excessive drinking of alcohol. **3** moderate, well-balanced, tranquil, sedate. **4** not fanciful or exaggerated (*the sober truth*). **5** (of a colour etc.) quiet and inconspicuous. —v.tr. & intr. (often foll. by *down, up*) make or become sober or less wild, reckless, enthusiastic, etc. (*a sobering thought*). □ **as sober as a judge** completely sober. □□ **soberingly** adv. **soberly** adv. [ME f. OF *sobre* f. L *sobrius*]

Sobers /'səʊbəz/, Sir Garfield St Aubrun ('Gary') (1936–), West Indian all-round cricketer, who captained the West Indies and Nottinghamshire and also played for South Australia. He holds the record for the number of runs (365 not out) scored in test-match cricket, and in 1968 became the first batsman to score 36 runs off a six-ball over.

sobriety /sə'braɪətɪ/ n. the state of being sober. [ME f. OF *sobrieté* or L *sobrietas* (as SOBER)]

sobriquet /'səʊbrɪˌkeɪ/ n. (also **soubriquet** /'suː-/) **1** a nickname. **2** an assumed name. [F, orig. = 'tap under the chin']

Soc. abbr. **1** Socialist. **2** Society.

socage /'sɒkɪdʒ/ n. (also **soccage**) a feudal tenure of land involving payment of rent or other non-military service to a superior. [ME f. AF *socage* f. *soc* f. OE *sōcn* SOKE]

soccer /'sɒkə(r)/ n. Association football. [ASSOC. + -ER³]

sociable /'səʊʃəb(ə)l/ adj. & n. —adj. **1** fitted for or liking the society of other people; ready and willing to talk and act with others. **2** (of a person's manner or behaviour etc.) friendly. **3** (of a meeting etc.) marked by friendliness, not stiff or formal. —n. **1** an open carriage with facing side seats. **2** an S-shaped couch for two occupants partly facing each other. **3** US a social. □□ **sociability** /-'bɪlɪtɪ/ n. **sociableness** n. **sociably** adv. [F *sociable* or L *sociabilis* f. *sociare* to unite f. *socius* companion]

social /'səʊʃ(ə)l/ adj. & n. —adj. **1** of or relating to society or its organization. **2** concerned with the mutual relations of human beings or of classes of human beings. **3** living in organized communities; unfitted for a solitary life (*man is a social animal*). **4 a** needing companionship; gregarious, interdependent. **b** cooperative; practising the division of labour. **5** existing only as a member of a compound organism. **6 a** (of insects) living together in organized communities. **b** (of birds) nesting near each other in communities. **7** (of plants) growing thickly together and monopolizing the ground they grow on. —n. a social gathering, esp. one organized by a club, congregation, etc. □ **social anthropology** the comparative study of peoples through their culture and kinship systems. **social climber**

derog. a person anxious to gain a higher social status. **social contract** (or **compact**) an agreement to cooperate for social benefits, e.g. by sacrificing some individual freedom for State protection. **social credit** the economic theory that the profits of industry should be distributed to the general public. **social democracy** a socialist system achieved by democratic means. **social democrat** a person who advocates social democracy. **social order** the network of human relationships in society. **social realism** the expression of social or political views in art. **social science a** the scientific study of human society and social relationships. **b** a branch of this (e.g. politics or economics). **social scientist** a student of or expert in the social sciences. **social secretary** a person who makes arrangements for the social activities of a person or organization. **social security** State assistance to those lacking in economic security and welfare, e.g. the aged and the unemployed. **social service** philanthropic activity. **social services** services provided by the State for the community, esp. education, health, and housing. **social war** hist. a war fought between allies. **social work** work of benefit to those in need of help or welfare, esp. done by specially trained personnel. **social worker** a person trained to do social work. □□ **sociality** /ˌsəʊʃɪ'ælɪtɪ/ n. **socially** adv. [F *social* or L *socialis* allied f. *socius* friend]

Social Democratic Party a UK political party with moderate socialist aims, founded in 1981 by a group of former Labour MPs and disbanded in 1990 after political regroupings.

socialism /'səʊʃəˌlɪz(ə)m/ n. **1** a political and economic theory of social organization which advocates that the community as a whole should own and control the means of production, distribution, and exchange. (See below.) **2** policy or practice based on this theory. □□ **socialist** n. & adj. **socialistic** /-'lɪstɪk/ adj. **socialistically** /-'lɪstɪkəlɪ/ adv. [F *socialisme* (as SOCIAL)]

In its earliest forms, socialism tended to be little more than a romantic vision held by a minority of social reformers, many of them well-to-do philanthropists. It was revolutionized as a political ideal by Karl Marx in the mid-19th c., becoming a mass movement aimed at the transformation of society, but both the methods by which this transformation was to be achieved and the manner in which the new society was to be run have remained the subject of considerable disagreement and have produced a wide variety of socialist parties, ranging from moderate reformers to ultra-left-wing Communists dedicated to upheaval by violent revolution.

socialite /'səʊʃəˌlaɪt/ n. a person prominent in fashionable society.

socialize /'səʊʃəˌlaɪz/ v. (also **-ise**) **1** intr. act in a sociable manner. **2** tr. make social. **3** tr. organize on socialistic principles. □ **socialized medicine** US the provision of medical services for all from public funds. □□ **socialization** /-'zeɪʃ(ə)n/ n.

society /sə'saɪətɪ/ n. (pl. **-ies**) **1** the sum of human conditions and activity regarded as a whole functioning interdependently. **2** a social community (*all societies must have firm laws*). **3 a** a social mode of life. **b** the customs and organization of an ordered community. **4** Ecol. a plant community. **5 a** the socially advantaged or prominent members of a community (*society would not approve*). **b** this, or a part of it, qualified in some way (*is not done in polite society*). **6** participation in hospitality; other people's homes or company (*avoids society*). **7** companionship, company (*avoids the society of such people*). **8** an association of persons united by a common aim or interest or principle (*formed a music society*). □□ **societal** adj. (esp. in sense 1). **societally** adv. [F *société* f. L *societas -tatis* f. *socius* companion]

Society Islands a group of islands in French Polynesia, including Tahiti; pop. (1982) 143,000. They were named by Captain Cook in honour of the Royal Society.

Society of Friends a body of Christians, also called Quakers, founded by George Fox. They were organized as a distinctive group in 1668, and began to engage in missionary work; in 1682 William Penn founded Pennsylvania on a Quaker basis. Until the Toleration Act of 1689 they were much persecuted, refusing to meet in secret, laying stress on outward observances in speech and in plainness of dress, and cutting themselves off from cultural life, which they regarded as frivolous. Their main activities were trade and philanthropic pursuits, for which they became famous. Central to their belief is the doctrine of the 'Inner Light', or sense of Christ's direct working in the soul; this has led them to reject the sacraments, the ministry, and all set forms of worship. Their meetings begin in silence until some member feels stirred to speak. They have a strong commitment to pacifism. Refusal of military service and of oaths has often brought members into conflict with the authorities, but their devotion to social and educational work (and, more recently, to international relief) has earned them general respect.

Society of Jesus see JESUIT.

socio- /ˈsəʊsɪəʊ, -ʃɪəʊ/ *comb. form* **1** of society (and). **2** of or relating to sociology (and). [L *socius* companion]

sociobiology /ˌsəʊsɪəʊbaɪˈɒlədʒɪ, ˌsəʊʃɪəʊ-/ *n.* the scientific study of the biological aspects of social behaviour in animals and in humans. It gives special emphasis to social systems considered as ecological adaptations, and attempts a mechanistic explanation of social behaviour in terms of modern biological and, in particular, evolutionary theory. According to its supporters the apparent altruism of certain social animals and insects is an attempt at 'survival' by choosing the course or action that will enable their genes (rather than themselves or their group) to survive. One of the bulwarks of the theory is the work of the biologist W. D. Hamilton (1936–) on the breeding system of social insects such as ants, which means that a worker's sisters acquire a higher proportion of the same genes than its own offspring would; it therefore pays, from the viewpoint of evolutionary survival, to ensure that the queen produces offspring while the female workers remain sterile. The theory as a whole is regarded as controversial. (See also the entries for E. O. WILSON and R. DAWKINS.) □□ **sociobiological** /-ˌbaɪəˈlɒdʒɪk(ə)l/ *adj.* **sociobiologically** /-ˌbaɪəˈlɒdʒɪkəlɪ/ *adv.* **sociobiologist** *n.*

sociocultural /ˌsəʊsɪəʊˈkʌltʃər(ə)l, ˌsəʊʃɪəʊ-/ *adj.* combining social and cultural factors. □□ **socioculturally** *adv.*

socio-economic /ˌsəʊsɪəʊˌiːkəˈnɒmɪk, ˌsəʊʃɪəʊ-/ *adj.* relating to or concerned with the interaction of social and economic factors. □□ **socio-economically** *adv.*

sociolinguistic /ˌsəʊsɪəʊlɪŋˈɡwɪstɪk, ˌsəʊʃɪəʊ-/ *adj.* relating to or concerned with language in its social aspects. □□ **sociolinguist** *n.* **sociolinguistically** *adv.*

sociolinguistics /ˌsəʊsɪəʊlɪŋˈɡwɪstɪks, ˌsəʊʃɪəʊ-/ *n.* the study of language in relation to social factors.

sociology /ˌsəʊsɪˈɒlədʒɪ, ˌsəʊʃɪ-/ *n.* **1** the study of the development, structure, and functioning of human society. **2** the study of social problems. □□ **sociological** /-əˈlɒdʒɪk(ə)l/ *adj.* **sociologically** /-əˈlɒdʒɪkəlɪ/ *adv.* **sociologist** *n.* [F *sociologie* (as SOCIO-, -LOGY)]

sociometry /ˌsəʊsɪˈɒmɪtrɪ, ˌsəʊʃɪ-/ *n.* the study of relationships within a group of people. □□ **sociometric** /-əˈmetrɪk/ *adj.* **sociometrically** /-əˈmetrɪkəlɪ/ *adv.* **sociometrist** *n.*

sock¹ /sɒk/ *n.* (*pl.* **socks** or *informal & Commerce* **sox** /sɒks/) **1** a short knitted covering for the foot, usu. not reaching the knee. **2** a removable inner sole put into a shoe for warmth etc. **3** an ancient Greek or Roman comic actor's light shoe. **4** comic drama. □ **pull one's socks up** *Brit. colloq.* make an effort to improve. **put a sock in it** *Brit. sl.* be quiet. [OE *socc* f. L *soccus* comic actor's shoe, light low-heeled slipper, f. Gk *sukkhos*]

sock² /sɒk/ *v. & n. colloq.* —*v.tr.* hit (esp. a person) forcefully. —*n.* **1** a hard blow. **2** *US* the power to deliver a blow. □ **sock it to** attack or address (a person) vigorously. [*c.*1700 (cant): orig. unkn.]

socket /ˈsɒkɪt/ *n. & v.* —*n.* **1** a natural or artificial hollow for something to fit into or stand firm or revolve in. **2** *Electr.* a device receiving a plug, light-bulb, etc., to make a connection. **3** *Golf* the part of an iron club into which the shaft is fitted. —*v.tr.* (**socketed, socketing**) **1** place in or fit with a socket. **2** *Golf* hit (a ball) with the socket of a club. [ME f. AF, dimin. of OF *soc* ploughshare, prob. f. Celt. orig.]

sockeye /ˈsɒkaɪ/ *n.* a blue-backed salmon of Alaska etc., *Oncorhynchus nerka.* [Salish *sukai* fish of fishes]

socle /ˈsəʊk(ə)l/ *n. Archit.* a plain low block or plinth serving as a

support for a column, urn, statue, etc., or as the foundation of a wall. [F f. It. *zoccolo* orig. 'wooden shoe' f. L *socculus* f. *soccus* SOCK¹]

Socotra /səʊˈkəʊtrə/ an island belonging to Yemen in the Arabian Sea near the mouth of the Gulf of Aden; capital, Tamridah.

Socrates /ˈsɒkrəˌtiːz/ (469–399 BC) Athenian philosopher. His interests lay not in the natural-philosophical speculation of earlier thinkers but in the question of how men should conduct their lives, an inquiry pursued through the method of cross-questioning those he met. Self-denying in his own life, he was the centre of a circle of devoted friends who included the great and the rich. Although he wrote nothing himself, he was immensely influential, particularly on Plato, in whose *Dialogues* he is the principal interlocutor. He was condemned to death by an Athenian jury on charges of introducing strange gods and corrupting the young.

Socratic /səˈkrætɪk/ *adj. & n.* —*adj.* of or relating to the Greek philosopher Socrates (d. 399 BC) or his philosophy, esp. the method associated with him of seeking the truth by a series of questions and answers. —*n.* a follower of Socrates. □ **Socratic irony** see IRONY. □□ **Socratically** *adv.* [L *Socraticus* f. Gk *Sōkratikos* f. *Sōkratēs*]

sod¹ /sɒd/ *n. & v.* —*n.* **1** turf or a piece of turf. **2** the surface of the ground. —*v.tr.* (**sodded, sodding**) cover (the ground) with sods. □ **under the sod** in the grave. [ME f. MDu., MLG *sode*, of unkn. orig.]

sod² /sɒd/ *n. & v. esp. Brit. coarse sl.* ¶ Often considered a taboo word. —*n.* **1** an unpleasant or awkward person or thing. **2** a person of a specified kind; a fellow (*the lucky sod*). —*v.tr.* (**sodded, sodding**) **1** (often *absol.* or as *int.*) an exclamation of annoyance (*sod them, I don't care!*). **2** (as **sodding** *adj.*) a general term of contempt. □ **sod off** go away. **Sod's Law** = MURPHY'S LAW. [abbr. of SODOMITE]

soda /ˈsəʊdə/ *n.* **1** any of various compounds of sodium in common use, e.g. washing soda, caustic soda. **2** (in full **soda water**) water made effervescent by impregnation with carbon dioxide under pressure and used alone or with spirits etc. as a drink (orig. made with sodium bicarbonate). **3** esp. *US* a sweet effervescent drink. □ **soda bread** bread leavened with baking-soda. **soda fountain 1** a device supplying soda water. **2** a shop or counter equipped with this. **soda lime** a mixture of calcium oxide and sodium hydroxide. [med.L, perh. f. *sodanum* glasswort (used as a remedy for headaches) f. *soda* headache f. Arab. *ṣudā'* f. *ṣada'a* split]

sodality /səʊˈdælɪtɪ/ *n.* (*pl.* **-ies**) a confraternity or association, esp. a Roman Catholic religious guild or brotherhood. [F *sodalité* or L *sodalitas* f. *sodalis* comrade]

sodden /ˈsɒd(ə)n/ *adj. & v.* —*adj.* **1** saturated with liquid; soaked through. **2** rendered stupid or dull etc. with drunkenness. **3** (of bread etc.) doughy; heavy and moist. —*v.intr. & tr.* become or make sodden. □□ **soddenly** *adv.* **soddenness** *n.* [archaic past part. of SEETHE]

Soddy /ˈsɒdɪ/, Frederick (1877–1956), English physicist who was awarded the 1921 Nobel Prize for chemistry for his work with Rutherford in Canada on radioactive decay, and especially for his theory of isotopes (the word was coined by him in 1913). He also assisted Ramsey in London in the discovery of helium. He wrote on economics, and later concentrated on creating an awareness of the social relevance of science.

sodium /ˈsəʊdɪəm/ *n. Chem.* a soft silver-white reactive metallic element, first isolated by Sir Humphry Davy in 1807. Sodium, which is essential to all living things, occurs commonly in the earth's crust, notably as rock salt (sodium chloride). Although very reactive, the liquid metal is used as a coolant in some types of nuclear reactor. Sodium compounds have many industrial uses. ¶ Symb.: Na; atomic number 11. □ **sodium bicarbonate** a white soluble powder used in the manufacture of fire extinguishers and effervescent drinks. **sodium carbonate** a white powder with many commercial applications including the manufacture of soap and glass. **sodium chloride** a colourless crystalline compound occurring naturally in sea water and halite; common salt. **sodium hydroxide** a deliquescent compound which is strongly alkaline and used in the manufacture of salt and pepper: also called *caustic soda*. **sodium nitrate** a white powdery compound used mainly in the manufacture of fertilizers. **sodium-vapour lamp** (or **sodium lamp**) a lamp using an electrical discharge in sodium vapour and giving a yellow light. □□ **sodic** *adj*. [SODA + -IUM]

Sodom /ˈsɒdəm/ a town of ancient Palestine, probably south of the Dead Sea, destroyed by fire from heaven (according to Genesis 19: 24), along with Gomorrah, for the wickedness of its inhabitants.

sodomite /ˈsɒdəˌmaɪt/ *n*. a person who practises sodomy. [ME f. OF f. LL *Sodomita* f. Gk *Sodomitēs* inhabitant of Sodom f. *Sodoma* Sodom]

sodomy /ˈsɒdəmɪ/ *n*. = BUGGERY. □□ **sodomize** *v.tr*. (also **-ise**). [ME f. med.L *sodomia* f. LL *peccatum Sodomiticum* sin of Sodom: see SODOM]

Sodor /ˈsəʊdə(r)/ a medieval diocese comprising the Hebrides and the Isle of Man, originally the 'southern isles' (Norse *Sudhreyjar*) of the kingdom of Norway. The Hebrides were separated in 1334, but *Sodor and Man* has been the official name for the Anglican diocese of the Isle of Man since 1684.

soever /səʊˈevə(r)/ *adv*. *literary* of any kind; to any extent (*how great soever it may be*).

-soever /səʊˈevə(r)/ *comb. form* (added to relative pronouns, adverbs, and adjectives) of any kind; to any extent (*whatsoever; howsoever*).

sofa /ˈsəʊfə/ *n*. a long upholstered seat with a back and arms, for two or more people. □ **sofa bed** a sofa that can be converted into a temporary bed. [F, ult. f. Arab. *suffa*]

Sofala see BEIRA².

soffit /ˈsɒfɪt/ *n*. the under-surface of an architrave, arch, balcony, etc. [F *soffite* or It. *soffitta*, *-itto* ult. f. L *suffixus* (as SUFFIX)]

Sofia /ˈsəʊfɪə, səˈfiːə/ (also **Sophia**) the capital of Bulgaria; pop. (1987) 1,128,850.

S. of S. *abbr*. Song of Songs (Old Testament).

soft /sɒft/ *adj*., *adv*., & *n*. —*adj*. **1** (of a substance, material, etc.) lacking hardness or firmness; yielding to pressure; easily cut. **2** (of cloth etc.) having a smooth surface or texture; not rough or coarse. **3** (of air etc.) mellow, mild, balmy; not noticeably cold or hot. **4** (of water) free from mineral salts and therefore good for lathering. **5** (of a light or colour etc.) not brilliant or glaring. **6** (of a voice or sounds) gentle and pleasing. **7** *Phonet*. **a** (of a consonant) sibilant or palatal (as *c* in *ice*, *g* in *age*). **b** voiced or unaspirated. **8** (of an outline etc.) not sharply defined. **9** (of an action or manner etc.) gentle, conciliatory, complimentary, amorous. **10** (of the heart or feelings etc.) compassionate, sympathetic. **11** (of a person's character or attitude etc.) feeble, lenient, silly, sentimental. **12** *colloq*. (of a job etc.) easy. **13** (of drugs) mild; not likely to cause addiction. **14** (of radiation) having little penetrating power. **15** (also **soft-core**) (of pornography) suggestive or erotic but not explicit. **16** *Stock Exch*. (of currency, prices, etc.) likely to fall in value. **17** *Polit*. moderate; willing to compromise (*the soft left*). **18** peaceful (*soft slumbers*). **19** *Brit*. (of the weather etc.) rainy or moist or thawing. —*adv*. softly (*play soft*). —*n*. a silly weak person. □ **be soft on** *colloq*. **1** be lenient towards. **2** be infatuated with. **have a soft spot for** be fond of or affectionate towards (a person). **soft answer** a good-tempered answer to abuse or an accusation. **soft-boiled** (of an egg) lightly boiled with the yolk soft or liquid. **soft-centred** (of a person) soft-hearted, sentimental. **soft coal** bituminous coal. **soft detergent** a biodegradable detergent. **soft drink** a non-alcoholic drink. **soft focus** *Photog*. the slight deliberate blurring of a picture. **soft fruit** *Brit*. small stoneless fruit (strawberry, currant, etc.). **soft furnishings** *Brit*. curtains, rugs, etc. **soft goods** *Brit*. textiles. **soft-headed** feeble-minded. **soft-headedness** feeble-mindedness. **soft-land** make a soft landing. **soft landing** a landing by a spacecraft without its suffering major damage. **soft option** the easier alternative. **soft palate** the rear part of the palate. **soft-paste** denoting an 'artificial' porcelain containing glassy materials and fired at a comparatively low temperature. **soft pedal** a pedal on a piano that makes the tone softer. **soft-pedal** *v.tr*. & (often foll. by *on*)

intr. (**-pedalled**, **-pedalling**; *US* **-pedaled**, **-pedaling**) **1** refrain from emphasizing; be restrained (about). **2** play with the soft pedal down. **soft roe** see ROE¹. **soft sell** restrained or subtly persuasive salesmanship. **soft-sell** *v.tr*. (*past* and *past part*. **-sold**) sell by this method. **soft soap 1** a semifluid soap made with potash. **2** *colloq*. persuasive flattery. **soft-soap** *v.tr*. *colloq*. persuade (a person) with flattery. **soft-spoken** speaking with a gentle voice. **soft sugar** granulated or powdered sugar. **soft tack** bread or other good food (opp. *hard tack*). **soft tissues** tissues of the body that are not bony or cartilaginous. **soft touch** *colloq*. a gullible person, esp. over money. **soft wicket** a wicket with moist or sodden turf. □□ **softish** *adj*. **softness** *n*. [OE *sōfte* agreeable, earlier *sēfte* f. WG]

softa /ˈsɒftə/ *n*. a Muslim student of sacred law and theology. [Turk. f. Pers. *sūkta* burnt, afire]

softball /ˈsɒftbɔːl/ *n*. **1** a ball like a baseball but softer and larger. **2** a modified form of baseball using this.

soften /ˈsɒf(ə)n/ *v*. **1** *tr*. & *intr*. make or become soft or softer. **2** *tr*. (often foll. by *up*) **a** reduce the strength of (defences) by bombing or some other preliminary attack. **b** reduce the resistance of (a person). □ **softening of the brain** a morbid degeneration of the brain, esp. in old age. □□ **softener** *n*.

soft-hearted /sɒftˈhɑːtɪd/ *adj*. tender, compassionate; easily moved. □□ **soft-heartedness** *n*.

softie /ˈsɒftɪ/ *n*. (also **softy**) *colloq*. a weak or silly or soft-hearted person.

softly /ˈsɒftlɪ/ *adv*. in a soft, gentle, or quiet manner. □ **softly softly** (of an approach or strategy) cautious; discreet and cunning.

software /ˈsɒftweə(r)/ *n*. the programs and other operating information used by a computer (opp. HARDWARE 3).

softwood /ˈsɒftwʊd/ *n*. the wood of pine, spruce, or other conifers, easily sawn.

softy var. of SOFTIE.

SOGAT /ˈsəʊɡæt/ *abbr*. (in the UK) Society of Graphical and Allied Trades. ¶ From 1982 officially called SOGAT 82.

soggy /ˈsɒɡɪ/ *adj*. (**soggier**, **soggiest**) sodden, saturated, dank. □□ **soggily** *adv*. **sogginess** *n*. [dial. *sog* a swamp]

soh /səʊ/ *n*. (also **so**, **sol** /sɒl/) *Mus*. **1** (in tonic sol-fa) the fifth note of a major scale. **2** the note G in the fixed-doh system. [*sol* f. ME *sol* f. L *solve*: see GAMUT]

soi-disant /ˌswɑːdiːˈzɑ̃/ *adj*. self-styled or pretended. [F f. *soi* oneself + *disant* saying]

soigné /ˈswɑːnjeɪ/ *adj*. (*fem*. **soignée** *pronunc*. same) carefully finished or arranged; well-groomed. [past part. of F *soigner* take care of f. *soin* care]

soil¹ /sɔɪl/ *n*. **1** the upper layer of earth in which plants grow, consisting of disintegrated rock usu. with an admixture of organic remains (*alluvial soil*; *rich soil*). **2** ground belonging to a nation; territory (*on British soil*). □ **soil mechanics** the study of the properties of soil as affecting its use in civil engineering. **soil science** pedology. □□ **soilless** *adj*. **soily** *adj*. [ME f. AF, perh. f. L *solium* seat, taken in sense of L *solum* ground]

soil² /sɔɪl/ *v*. & *n*. —*v.tr*. **1** make dirty; smear or stain with dirt (*soiled linen*). **2** tarnish, defile; bring discredit to (*would not soil my hands with it*). —*n*. **1** a dirty mark; a stain, smear, or defilement. **2** filth; refuse matter. □ **soil pipe** the discharge-pipe of a lavatory. [ME f. OF *suiller*, *soiller*, etc., ult. f. L *sucula* dimin. of *sus* pig]

soil³ /sɔɪl/ *v.tr*. feed (cattle) on fresh-cut green fodder (orig. for purging). [perh. f. SOIL²]

soirée /ˈswɑːreɪ/ *n*. an evening party, usu. in a private house, for conversation or music. [F f. *soir* evening]

soixante-neuf /ˌswɑːsɑ̃tˈnɜːf/ *n. sl*. sexual activity between two people involving mutual oral stimulation of the genitals. [F, = sixty-nine, from the position of the couple]

sojourn /ˈsɒdʒ(ə)n, -dʒɜːn, ˈsʌ-/ *n*. & *v*. —*n*. a temporary stay. —*v.intr*. stay temporarily. □□ **sojourner** *n*. [ME f. OF *sojorn* etc. f. LL SUB- + *diurnum* day]

soke /səʊk/ *n*. *Brit. hist*. **1** a right of local jurisdiction. **2** a district under a particular jurisdiction and administration. [ME f. AL *sōca* f. OE *sōcn* prosecution f. Gmc]

Sol /sɒl/ n. Rom. Mythol. the sun, esp. as a personification. [ME f. L]

sol¹ var. of SOH.

sol² /sɒl/ n. Chem. a liquid suspension of a colloid. [abbr. of SOLUTION]

sola¹ /ˈsəʊlə/ n. a pithy-stemmed E. Indian swamp plant, *Aeschynomene indica*. □ **sola topi** an Indian sun-helmet made from its pith. [Urdu & Bengali *solā*, Hindi *sholā*]

sola² fem. of SOLUS.

solace /ˈsɒləs/ n. & v. —n. comfort in distress, disappointment, or tedium. —v.tr. give solace to. □ **solace oneself with** find compensation or relief in. [ME f. OF *solas* f. L *solatium* f. *solari* CONSOLE¹]

solan /ˈsəʊlən/ n. (in full **solan goose**) a gannet, *Sula bassana*. [prob. f. ON *súla* gannet + *önd, and-* duck]

solanaceous /ˌsɒləˈneɪʃəs/ adj. of or relating to the plant family Solanaceae, including potatoes, nightshades, and tobacco. [mod.L *solanaceae* f. L *sōlānum* nightshade]

solar /ˈsəʊlə(r)/ adj. & n. of, relating to, or reckoned by the sun (*solar eclipse; solar time*). —n. **1** a solarium. **2** an upper chamber in a medieval house. □ **solar battery** (or **cell**) a device converting solar radiation into electricity. **solar constant** the quantity of heat reaching the earth from the sun. **solar day** the interval between successive meridian transits of the sun at a place. **solar month** one-twelfth of the solar year. **solar myth** a tale explained as symbolizing solar phenomena. **solar panel** a panel designed to absorb the sun's rays as a source of energy for operating electricity or heating. **solar plexus** a complex of radiating nerves at the pit of the stomach. **solar system** see separate entry. **solar wind** the continuous flow of charged particles from the sun. **solar year** the time taken for the Earth to travel once round the sun, equal to 365 days, 5 hours, 48 minutes, and 46 seconds. [ME f. L *solaris* f. *sol* sun]

solarium /səˈleərɪəm/ n. (pl. **solaria** /-rɪə/) a room equipped with sun-lamps or fitted with extensive areas of glass for exposure to the sun. [L, = sundial, sunning-place (as SOLAR)]

solarize /ˈsəʊləˌraɪz/ v.intr. & tr. (also **-ise**) Photog. undergo or cause to undergo change in the relative darkness of parts of an image by long exposure. □□ **solarization** /-ˈzeɪʃ(ə)n/ n.

solar system n. the collection of nine planets and their moons in orbit round the sun, together with smaller bodies in the form of asteroids, meteors, and comets. Most of these objects lie within or close to the plane of the ecliptic, suggesting that the solar system originated in the collapse to a disc of a primordial gaseous nebula which fragmented to produce a large massive star at the centre of a group of orbiting inert bodies. It remains a mystery why the planets, with mass much less than that of the sun, should contain most of the angular momentum of the system.

solatium /səˈleɪʃɪəm/ n. (pl. **solatia** /-ʃɪə/) a thing given as a compensation or consolation. [L, = SOLACE]

sold past and past part. of SELL.

soldanella /ˌsɒldəˈnelə/ n. any dwarf Alpine plant of the genus *Soldanella*, having bell-shaped flowers with fringed petals. [mod.L f. It.]

solder /ˈsəʊldə(r), ˈsɒ-/ n. & v. —n. **1** a fusible alloy used to join less fusible metals or wires etc. **2** a cementing or joining agency. —v.tr. join with solder. □ **soldering iron** a tool used for applying solder. □□ **solderable** n. **solderer** n. [ME f. OF *soudure* f. *souder* f. L *solidare* fasten f. *solidus* SOLID]

soldier /ˈsəʊldʒə(r)/ n. & v. —n. **1** a person serving in or having served in an army. **2** (in full **common soldier**) a private or NCO in an army. **3** a military commander of specified ability (*a great soldier*). **4** (in full **soldier ant**) a wingless ant or termite with a large head and jaws for fighting in defence of its colony. **5** (in full **soldier beetle**) a reddish-coloured beetle, *Rhagonycha fulva*, with flesh-eating larvae. —v.intr. serve as a soldier (*was off soldiering*). □ **soldier of Christ** an active or proselytizing Christian. **soldier of fortune** an adventurous person ready to take service under any State or person; a mercenary. **soldier on** colloq. persevere doggedly. □□ **soldierly** adj. **soldiership** n.

[ME *souder* etc. f. OF *soudier, soldier* f. *soulde* (soldier's) pay f. L *solidus*: see SOLIDUS]

soldiery /ˈsəʊldʒərɪ/ n. (pl. **-ies**) **1** soldiers, esp. of a specified character. **2** a group of soldiers.

sole¹ /səʊl/ n. & v. —n. **1** the under-surface of the foot. **2** the part of a shoe, sock, etc., corresponding to this (esp. excluding the heel). **3** the lower surface or base of an implement, e.g. a plough, golf-club head, etc. **4** the floor of a ship's cabin. —v.tr. provide (a shoe etc.) with a sole. □ **sole-plate** the bedplate of an engine etc. □□ **-soled** adj. (in comb.). [OF ult. f. L *solea* sandal, sill: cf. OE unrecorded *solu* or *sola* f. *solum* bottom, pavement, sole]

sole² /səʊl/ n. any flatfish of the family Soleidae, esp. *Solea solea* used as food. [ME f. OF f. Prov. *sola* ult. f. L *solea* (as SOLE¹, named from its shape)]

sole³ /səʊl/ adj. **1** (attrib.) one and only; single, exclusive (*the sole reason; has the sole right*). **2** archaic or Law (esp. of a woman) unmarried. **3** archaic alone, unaccompanied. □□ **solely** adv. [ME f. OF *soule* f. L *sola* fem. of *solus* alone]

solecism /ˈsɒlɪˌsɪz(ə)m/ n. **1** a mistake of grammar or idiom; a blunder in the manner of speaking or writing. **2** a piece of bad manners or incorrect behaviour. □□ **solecist** n. **solecistic** /-ˈsɪstɪk/ adj. [F *solécisme* or L *soloecismus* f. Gk *soloikismos* f. *soloikos* speaking incorrectly]

solemn /ˈsɒləm/ adj. **1** serious and dignified (*a solemn occasion*). **2** formal; accompanied by ceremony (*a solemn oath*). **3** mysteriously impressive. **4** (of a person) serious or cheerless in manner (*looks rather solemn*). **5** full of importance; weighty (*a solemn warning*). **6** grave, sober, deliberate; slow in movement or action (*a solemn promise; solemn music*). □ **solemn mass** = high mass (see MASS²). □□ **solemnly** adv. **solemness** n. [ME f. OF *solemne* f. L *sol(l)emnis* customary, celebrated at a fixed date f. *sollus* entire]

solemnity /səˈlemnɪtɪ/ n. (pl. **-ies**) **1** the state of being solemn; a solemn character or feeling; solemn behaviour. **2** a rite or celebration; a piece of ceremony. [ME f. OF *solem(p)nité* f. L *sollemnitas -tatis* (as SOLEMN)]

solemnize /ˈsɒləmˌnaɪz/ v.tr. (also **-ise**) **1** duly perform (a ceremony esp. of marriage). **2** celebrate (a festival etc.). **3** make solemn. □□ **solemnization** /-ˈzeɪʃ(ə)n/ n. [ME f. OF *solem(p)niser* f. med.L *solemnizare* (as SOLEMN)]

Solemn League and Covenant an agreement of 1643 between the Parliamentarians and the Scots during the English Civil War. The Scots were to send 21,000 men to assist the English rebels, who would pay them, and in return a presbyterian system was to be established in England and Ireland. Scottish support was crucial; the arrival of their troops transferred the centre of operations from London to York, and after the battle of Marston Moor the loyal North passed under Scottish control. The conversion of the Church of England to Presbyterianism, however, was prevented by the action of Cromwell's army which in 1647 expelled the principal Presbyterian leaders from Parliament.

solen /ˈsəʊlən/ n. any razor-shell of the genus *Solen*. [L f. Gk *sōlēn* tube, shellfish]

solenoid /ˈsəʊləˌnɔɪd, ˈsɒl-/ n. a cylindrical coil of wire acting as a magnet when carrying electric current. □□ **solenoidal** /-ˈnɔɪd(ə)l/ adj. [F *solénoïde* (as SOLEN)]

Solent /ˈsəʊlənt/ the west part of the channel between the Isle of Wight and the mainland of England.

sol-fa /ˈsɒlfɑː/ n. & v. —n. = SOLMIZATION; (cf. *tonic sol-fa*). —v.tr. (**-fas, -faed**) sing (a tune) with sol-fa syllables. [SOL¹ + FA]

solfatara /ˌsɒlfəˈtɑːrə/ n. a volcanic vent emitting only sulphurous and other vapours. [name of a volcano near Naples, f. It. *solfo* sulphur]

solfeggio /sɒlˈfedʒɪəʊ/ n. (pl. **solfeggi** /-dʒiː/) Mus. **1** an exercise in singing using sol-fa syllables. **2** solmization. [It. (as SOL-FA)]

soli pl. of SOLO.

solicit /səˈlɪsɪt/ v. (**solicited, soliciting**) **1** tr. & (foll. by *for*) intr. ask repeatedly or earnestly for or seek or invite (business etc.). **2** tr. (often foll. by *for*) make a request or petition to (a person).

3 *tr.* accost (a person) and offer one's services as a prostitute. □□ **solicitation** /-'teɪʃ(ə)n/ *n.* [ME f. OF *solliciter* f. L *sollicitare* agitate f. *sollicitus* anxious f. *sollus* entire + *citus* past part., = set in motion]

solicitor /sə'lɪsɪtə(r)/ *n.* **1** *Brit.* a member of the legal profession qualified to deal with conveyancing, draw up wills, etc., and to advise clients and instruct barristers. **2** a person who solicits. **3** *US* a canvasser. **4** *US* the chief law officer of a city etc. □ **Solicitor-General 1** (in the UK) the Crown law officer below the Attorney-General or (in Scotland) below the Lord Advocate. **2** (in the US) the law officer below the Attorney-General. [ME f. OF *solliciteur* (as SOLICIT)]

solicitous /sə'lɪsɪtəs/ *adj.* **1** (often foll. by *of*, *about*, etc.) showing interest or concern. **2** (foll. by *to* + infin.) eager, anxious. □□ **solicitously** *adv.* **solicitousness** *n.* [L *sollicitus* (as SOLICIT)]

solicitude /sə'lɪsɪtjuːd/ *n.* **1** the state of being solicitous; solicitous behaviour. **2** anxiety or concern. [ME f. OF *sollicitude* f. L *sollicitudo* (as SOLICITOUS)]

solid /'sɒlɪd/ *adj.* & *n.* —*adj.* (**solider**, **solidest**) **1** firm and stable in shape; not liquid or fluid (*solid food; water becomes solid at 0°C*). **2** of such material throughout, not hollow or containing cavities (*a solid sphere*). **3** of the same substance throughout (*solid silver*). **4** of strong material or construction or build, not flimsy or slender etc. **5 a** having three dimensions. **b** concerned with solids (*solid geometry*). **6 a** sound and reliable; genuine (*solid arguments*). **b** staunch and dependable (*a solid Tory*). **7** sound but without any special flair etc. (*a solid piece of work*). **8** financially sound. **9** (of time) uninterrupted, continuous (*spend four solid hours on it*). **10 a** unanimous, undivided (*support has been pretty solid so far*). **b** (foll. by *for*) united in favour of. **11** (of printing) without spaces between the lines etc. **12** (of a tyre) without a central air space. **13** (foll. by *with*) *US colloq.* on good terms. **14** *Austral.* & *NZ colloq.* severe, unreasonable. —*n.* **1** a solid substance or body. **2** (in *pl.*) solid food. **3** *Geom.* a body or magnitude having three dimensions. □ **solid angle** an angle formed by planes etc. meeting at a point. **solid colour** colour covering the whole of an object, without a pattern etc. **solid-drawn** (of a tube etc.) pressed or drawn out from a solid bar of metal. **solid solution** solid material containing one substance uniformly distributed in another. **solid state** see separate entry. □□ **solidly** *adv.* **solidness** *n.* [ME f. OF *solide* f. L *solidus*, rel. to *salvus* safe, *sollus* entire]

Solidarity /ˌsɒlɪ'dærɪtɪ/ an independent trade-union movement in Poland, registered in Sept. 1980, officially banned in Oct. 1982, and legalized again in 1989. The union itself declined, but its name became a powerful symbol in Polish life. (See also Lech WALESA.) [tr. Polish *Solidarność*]

solidarity /ˌsɒlɪ'dærɪtɪ/ *n.* **1** unity or agreement of feeling or action, esp. among individuals with a common interest. **2** mutual dependence. [F *solidarité* f. *solidaire* f. *solide* SOLID]

solidi *pl.* of SOLIDUS.

solidify /sə'lɪdɪfaɪ/ *v.tr.* & *intr.* (**-ies**, **-ied**) make or become solid. □□ **solidification** /-fɪ'keɪʃ(ə)n/ *n.* **solidifier** *n.*

solidity /sə'lɪdɪtɪ/ *n.* the state of being solid; firmness.

solid state *n.* a state of matter in which the constituent atoms or molecules occupy fixed positions with respect to each other and cannot move freely. (See below.) **solid-state** *adj.* of or relating to the solid state; using the electronic properties of solids, especially semiconductors, to replace those of valves.

The solid state is one of the fundamental states in which matter can exist, along with the liquid, gas, and plasma states. The atoms in a solid differ from those in a liquid and in a gas in that they are bound together at definite sites in the solid. When such an atom is displaced a little from its equilibrium position restoring forces are called into play which resist the displacement. This explains why solids oppose deforming forces and also why solid bodies do not easily penetrate each other. Solids may be roughly classified into crystalline and amorphous. In crystalline solids, such as ice, the atoms are arranged in an orderly and repeating manner. In amorphous solids, such as amorphous sulphur, this order is absent over distances large compared with inter-atomic distances, but there may still be some short-range crystalline structure.

solidus /'sɒlɪdəs/ *n.* (*pl.* **solidi** /-ˌdaɪ/) **1** an oblique stroke (/) used in writing fractions (3/4), to separate other figures and letters, or to denote alternatives (*and/or*) and ratios (*miles/day*). **2** (in full **solidus curve**) a curve in a graph of the temperature and composition of a mixture, below which the substance is entirely solid. **3** *hist.* a gold coin of the later Roman Empire. [ME (in sense 3) f. L: see SOLID]

solifluction /ˌsɒlɪ'flʌkʃ(ə)n, ˌsɒl-/ *n.* the gradual movement of wet soil etc. down a slope. [L *solum* soil + L *fluctio* flowing f. *fluere fluct-* flow]

soliloquy /sə'lɪləkwɪ/ *n.* (*pl.* **-ies**) **1** the act of talking when alone or regardless of any hearers, esp. in drama. **2** part of a play involving this. □□ **soliloquist** *n.* **soliloquize** *v.intr.* (also **-ise**). [LL *soliloquium* f. L *solus* alone + *loqui* speak]

soliped /'sɒlɪˌped/ *adj.* & *n.* —*adj.* (of an animal) solid-hoofed. —*n.* a solid-hoofed animal. [F *solipède* or mod.L *solipes -pedis* f. L *solidipes* f. *solidus* solid + *pes* foot]

solipsism /'sɒlɪpˌsɪz(ə)m/ *n. Philos.* the view that the self is all that exists or can be known. □□ **solipsist** *n.* **solipsistic** /-'sɪstɪk/ *adj.* **solipsistically** /-'sɪstɪkəlɪ/ *adv.* [L *solus* alone + *ipse* self]

solitaire /'sɒlɪˌteə(r)/ *n.* **1** a diamond or other gem set by itself. **2** a ring having a single gem. **3** a game for one player played by removing pegs etc. one at a time from a board by jumping others over them until only one is left. **4** *US* = PATIENCE **4**. **5** any of various extinct dodo-like flightless birds of the family Raphidae. **6** any American thrush of the genus *Myadestes*. [F f. L *solitarius* (as SOLITARY)]

solitary /'sɒlɪtərɪ/ *adj.* & *n.* —*adj.* **1** living alone; not gregarious; without companions; lonely (*a solitary existence*). **2** (of a place) secluded or unfrequented. **3** single or sole (*a solitary instance*). **4** (of an insect) not living in communities. **5** *Bot.* growing singly, not in a cluster. —*n.* (*pl.* **-ies**) **1** a recluse or anchorite. **2** *colloq.* = *solitary confinement*. □ **solitary confinement** isolation of a prisoner in a separate cell as a punishment. □□ **solitarily** *adv.* **solitariness** *n.* [ME f. L *solitarius* f. *solus* alone]

solitude /'sɒlɪˌtjuːd/ *n.* **1** the state of being solitary. **2** a lonely place. [ME f. OF *solitude* or L *solitudo* f. *solus* alone]

solmization /ˌsɒlmɪ'zeɪʃ(ə)n/ *n. Mus.* a system of associating each note of a scale with a particular syllable, now usu. *doh ray me fah soh lah te*, with doh as C in the fixed-doh system and as the keynote in the movable-doh or tonic sol-fa system. □□ **solmizate** /'sɒlmɪˌzeɪt/ *v.intr.* & *tr.* [F *solmisation* (as SOL¹, MI)]

solo /'səʊləʊ/ *n.*, *v.*, & *adv.* —*n.* (*pl.* **-os**) **1** (*pl.* **-os** or **soli** /-lɪ/) **a** a vocal or instrumental piece or passage, or a dance, performed by one person with or without accompaniment. **b** (*attrib.*) performed or performing as a solo (*solo passage; solo violin*). **2 a** an unaccompanied flight by a pilot in an aircraft. **b** anything done by one person unaccompanied. **c** (*attrib.*) unaccompanied, alone. **3** (in full **solo whist**) **a** a card-game like whist in which one player may oppose the others. **b** a declaration or the act of playing to win five tricks at this. —*v.* (**-oes**, **-oed**) **1** *intr.* perform a solo, esp. a solo flight. **2** *tr.* perform or achieve as a solo. —*adv.* unaccompanied, alone (*flew solo for the first time*). □ **solo stop** an organ stop especially suitable for imitating a solo performance on another instrument. [It. f. L *solus* alone]

soloist /'səʊləʊɪst/ *n.* a performer of a solo, esp. in music.

Solomon /'sɒləmən/ king of Israel *c.*970–930 BC, son of David, famed for his wisdom and magnificence. His grandiose schemes, including the building of the Temple with which his name is associated, and the fortifying of strategic cities, led to a system of levies and enforced labour, and the resulting discontent culminated in the secession of the northern tribes (see ISRAEL¹). □ **Judgement of Solomon** his proposal to cut in two the baby claimed by two women (1 Kings 3: 16–28), which he then gave to the woman who showed concern for its life. **Solomon's seal 1** a figure like the Star of David. **2** any liliaceous plant of the genus *Polygonatum*, with arching stems and drooping green and white flowers. □□ **Solomonic** /ˌsɒlə'mɒnɪk/ *adj.* **Song of Solomon** (also called the *Song of Songs* or *Canticles*) an anthology of love poems ascribed to Solomon but dating from a much later period. From an early date Jewish and Christian writers interpreted the book allegorically, in the Talmud as God's dealings with the congregation of Israel and in Christian exegesis as God's relations with the Church or the individual soul. **Wisdom of Solomon** a book of the Apocrypha containing a meditation on wisdom which has given it its name. The ascription to Solomon is now believed to be a literary device; it probably dates from about 1st c. BC–1st c. AD.

Solomon Islands /'sɒləmən/ a country consisting of a group of islands in the South Pacific, SE of the Bismarck Archipelago; pop. (est. 1988) 312,200; official language, English; capital, Honiara. Discovered by the Spanish in 1658, the islands were divided between Britain and Germany in the late 19th c.; the southern islands became a British protectorate in 1893 while the north remained German until mandated to Australia in 1920. The scene of heavy fighting in 1942–3, the Solomons achieved self-government in 1976 and full independence as a member State of the Commonwealth two years later, with the exception of the northern part of the chain which is now part of Papua New Guinea. Copra and timber are the main exports.

Solon /'səʊlɒn/ (early 6th c. BC) Athenian statesman and poet, one of the traditional Seven Sages. His economic reforms included the abolition of serfdom and of slavery for debt; his constitutional reforms, by which he divided the citizens into four classes based on wealth with a corresponding division of political responsibility, laid the foundations of the future democracy. His poetry is largely concerned with his political interests.

solstice /'sɒlstɪs/ n. **1** either of the times when the sun is furthest from the equator. **2** the point in its ecliptic reached by the sun at a solstice. □ **summer solstice** the time at which the sun is furthest north from the equator, about 21 June in the northern hemisphere. **winter solstice** the time at which the sun is furthest south from the equator, about 22 Dec. in the northern hemisphere. Since these events mark the turn of the seasons, they have been celebrated since prehistoric times by traditional festivities, and it is no coincidence that the feast of Christmas occurs so close to the winter solstice. □□ **solstitial** /sɒl'stɪʃ(ə)l/ adj. [ME f. OF f. L solstitium f. sol sun + sistere stit- make stand]

solubilize /'sɒljʊbɪˌlaɪz/ v.tr. (also **-ise**) make soluble or more soluble. □□ **solubilization** /-'zeɪʃ(ə)n/ n.

soluble /'sɒljʊb(ə)l/ adj. **1** that can be dissolved, esp. in water. **2** that can be solved. □ **soluble glass** = water-glass. □□ **solubility** /-'bɪlɪtɪ/ n. [ME f. OF f. LL solubilis (as SOLVE)]

solus /'səʊləs/ predic.adj. (fem. **sola** /-lə/) (esp. in a stage direction) alone, unaccompanied. [L]

solute /'sɒljuːt/ n. a dissolved substance. [L solutum, neut. of solutus: see SOLVE]

solution /sə'luːʃ(ə)n, -'ljuːʃ(ə)n/ n. **1** the act or a means of solving a problem or difficulty. **2 a** the conversion of a solid or gas into a liquid by mixture with a liquid solvent. **b** the state resulting from this (held in solution). **3** the act of dissolving or the state of being dissolved. **4** the act of separating or breaking. **5** = rubber solution (see RUBBER[1]). □ **solution set** Math. the set of all the solutions of an equation or condition. [ME f. OF f. L solutio -onis (as SOLVE)]

Solutrean /sə'luːtrɪən/ adj. & n. (also **Solutrian**) —adj. of an upper palaeolithic industry of central and SW France and parts of Iberia, following the Aurignacian and preceding the Magdalenian, dated to c.19,000–18,000 BC. It is named after the type-site of Solutré in eastern France. —n. this industry.

solvate /'sɒlveɪt/ v.intr. & tr. enter or cause to enter combination with a solvent. □□ **solvation** /-'veɪʃ(ə)n/ n.

Solvay process /'sɒlveɪ/ n. a manufacturing process for obtaining sodium carbonate (= washing-soda) from limestone, ammonia, and brine. [E. Solvay (d. 1922), Belgian chemist, who developed the process]

solve /sɒlv/ v.tr. find an answer to, or an action or course that removes or effectively deals with (a problem or difficulty). □□ **solvable** adj. **solver** n. [ME, = loosen, f. L solvere solut- unfasten, release]

solvent /'sɒlv(ə)nt/ adj. & n. —adj. **1** able to dissolve or form a solution with something. **2** having enough money to meet

one's liabilities. —n. **1** a solvent liquid etc. **2** a dissolving or weakening agent. □□ **solvency** n. (in sense 2).

Solway Firth /'sɒlweɪ/ an inlet of the Irish Sea, formed by the estuary of the Esk and Eden rivers, separating Cumbria (England) from Dumfries and Galloway (Scotland).

Solzhenitsyn /ˌsɒlʒə'nɪtsɪn/, Alexander (1918–), Russian novelist, whose criticism of Stalin in 1945 led to his imprisonment for eight years, three of which were spent in a labour camp. After his release, his novel One Day in the Life of Ivan Denisovich (1962), describing life in such a camp, received international acclaim and was widely sold in the USSR, where it coincided with the de-Stalinization campaign begun in 1956. In 1963, however, he was again in conflict with the authorities and thereafter had difficulty in getting his books published in the Soviet Union. He was awarded the Nobel Prize for literature in 1970. The publication abroad of the first part of The Gulag Archipelago (1973–5) resulted in his deportation to West Germany in 1974, since when he has lived in the US.

Som. abbr. Somerset.

soma[1] /'səʊmə/ n. **1** the body as distinct from the soul. **2** the body of an organism as distinct from its reproductive cells. [Gk sōma -atos body]

soma[2] /'səʊmə/ n. **1** an intoxicating drink used in Vedic ritual. **2** a plant yielding this. [Skr. sōma]

Somali /sə'mɑːlɪ/ n. & adj. —n. **1** (pl. same or **Somalis**) a member of a Hamitic Muslim people of Somalia in NE Africa. **2** their language, which belongs to the Cushitic branch of the Hamito-Semitic family of languages and is the official language of Somalia. —adj. of or relating to this people or their language. □□ **Somalian** adj. [native name]

Somalia /sə'mɑːlɪə/ a country in NE Africa, with a coastline on the Indian Ocean; pop. (est. 1988) 7,990,000; official language, Somali; capital, Mogadishu. The economy is largely agricultural, dependent upon nomadic stock-raising and (in the southern part of the country) some irrigated plantation-farming. Livestock, skins, and hides form the main export; the second-largest export is the banana crop, most of which is imported by Italy. The area of the Horn of Africa was divided between British and Italian spheres of influence in the late 19th c., and the modern Somali Republic (which became an independent member of the United Nations in 1960) is a result of the unification of the former British Somaliland and Italian Somalia. Since independence, Somalia has been involved in border disputes with Kenya and Ethiopia, the latter leading to an intermittent war over the Ogaden Desert. Civil war broke out in Somalia in 1988 and has continued, with many casualties.

somatic /sə'mætɪk/ adj. of or relating to the body, esp. as distinct from the mind. □ **somatic cell** any cell of a living organism except the reproductive cells. □□ **somatically** adv. [Gk sōmatikos (as SOMA[1])]

somato- /'səʊmətəʊ/ comb. form the human body. [Gk sōma -atos body]

somatogenic /ˌsəʊmətəʊ'dʒenɪk/ adj. originating in the body.

somatology /ˌsəʊmə'tɒlədʒɪ/ n. the science of living bodies physically considered.

somatotonic /ˌsəʊmətəʊ'tɒnɪk/ adj. like a mesomorph in temperament, with predominantly physical interests.

somatotrophin /ˌsəʊmətəʊ'trəʊfɪn/ n. a growth hormone secreted by the pituitary gland. [as SOMATO-, TROPHIC]

somatotype /'səʊmətəʊˌtaɪp/ n. physique expressed in relation to various extreme types.

sombre /'sɒmbə(r)/ adj. (also US **somber**) **1** dark, gloomy (a sombre sky). **2** oppressively solemn or sober. **3** dismal, foreboding (a sombre prospect). □□ **sombrely** adv. **sombreness** n. [F sombre f. OF sombre (n.) ult. f. L SUB- + umbra shade]

sombrero /sɒm'breərəʊ/ n. (pl. **-os**) a broad-brimmed felt or straw hat worn esp. in Mexico and the south-west US. [Sp. f. sombra shade (as SOMBRE)]

some /sʌm/ adj., pron., & adv. —adj. **1** an unspecified amount or number of (some water; some apples; some of them). **2** that is unknown or unnamed (will return some day; some fool has locked the door; to some extent). **3** denoting an approximate number (waited some twenty minutes). **4** a considerable amount or number of (went to some trouble). **5** (usu. stressed) **a** at least a small amount of (do have some consideration). **b** such to a certain extent (that is some help). **c** colloq. notably such (I call that some story). —pron. some people or things, some number or amount (I have some already; would you like some more?). —adv. colloq. to some extent (we talked some; do it some more). □ **and then some** sl. and plenty more than that. **some few** see FEW. [OE sum f. Gmc]

-some¹ /səm/ suffix forming adjectives meaning: **1** adapted to; productive of (cuddlesome; fearsome). **2** characterized by being (fulsome; lithesome). **3** apt to (tiresome; meddlesome). [OE -sum]

-some² /səm/ suffix forming nouns from numerals, meaning 'a group of (so many)' (foursome). [OE sum SOME, used after numerals in genit. pl.]

-some³ /səʊm/ comb. form denoting a portion of a body, esp. of a cell (chromosome; ribosome). [Gk sōma body]

somebody /ˈsʌmbədɪ/ pron. & n. —pron. some person. —n. (pl. -ies) a person of importance (is really somebody now).

someday /ˈsʌmdeɪ/ adv. at some time in the future.

somehow /ˈsʌmhaʊ/ adv. **1** for some reason or other (somehow I never liked them). **2** in some unspecified or unknown way (he somehow dropped behind). **3** no matter how (must get it finished somehow).

someone /ˈsʌmwʌn/ n. & pron. = SOMEBODY.

someplace /ˈsʌmpleɪs/ adv. US colloq. = SOMEWHERE.

somersault /ˈsʌməˌsɒlt/ n. & v. (also **summersault**) —n. an acrobatic movement in which a person turns head over heels in the air or on the ground and lands on the feet. —v.intr. perform a somersault. [OF sombresault alt. f. sobresault ult. f. L supra above + saltus leap f. salire to leap]

Somerset /ˈsʌməˌset/ a county of SW England; pop. (1981) 430,800; county town, Taunton.

something /ˈsʌmθɪŋ/ n., pron., & adv. —n. & pron. **1 a** some unspecified or unknown thing (have something to tell you; something has happened). **b** (in full **something or other**) as a substitute for an unknown or forgotten description (a student of something or other). **2** a known or understood but unexpressed quantity, quality, or extent (there is something about it I do not like; is something of a fool). **3** colloq. an important or notable person or thing (the party was quite something). —adv. archaic in some degree. □ **or something** or some unspecified alternative possibility (must have run away or something). **see something of** encounter (a person) briefly or occasionally. **something else 1** something different. **2** colloq. something exceptional. **something like 1** an amount in the region of (left something like a million pounds). **2** somewhat like (shaped something like a cigar). **3** colloq. impressive; a fine specimen of. **something of** to some extent; in some sense (is something of an expert). [OE sum thing (as SOME, THING)]

sometime /ˈsʌmtaɪm/ adv. & adj. —adv. **1** at some unspecified time. **2** formerly. —adj. former (the sometime mayor).

sometimes /ˈsʌmtaɪmz/ adv. at some times; occasionally.

somewhat /ˈsʌmwɒt/ adv., n., & pron. —adv. to some extent (behaviour that was somewhat strange; answered somewhat hastily). —n. & pron. archaic something (loses somewhat of its force). □ **more than somewhat** colloq. very (was more than somewhat perplexed).

somewhen /ˈsʌmwen/ adv. colloq. at some time.

somewhere /ˈsʌmweə(r)/ adv. & pron. —adv. in or to some place. —pron. some unspecified place. □ **get somewhere** colloq. achieve success. **somewhere about** approximately.

somite /ˈsəʊmaɪt/ n. each body-division of a metamerically segmented animal. □□ **somitic** /səʊˈmɪtɪk/ adj. [Gk sōma body + -ITE¹]

Somme /sɒm/ a river of NE France, running into the English Channel, the scene of heavy fighting in the First World War, especially in July–Nov. 1916.

sommelier /ˈsɒməˌljeɪ/ n. a wine waiter. [F, = butler, f. somme pack (as SUMPTER)]

somnambulism /sɒmˈnæmbjʊˌlɪz(ə)m/ n. **1** sleepwalking. **2** a condition of the brain inducing this. □□ **somnambulant** adj. **somnambulantly** adv. **somnambulist** n. **somnambulistic**

/-ˈlɪstɪk/ adj. **somnambulistically** /-ˈlɪstɪkəlɪ/ adv. [L somnus sleep + ambulare walk]

somniferous /sɒmˈnɪfərəs/ adj. inducing sleep; soporific. [L somnifer f. somnium dream]

somnolent /ˈsɒmnələnt/ adj. **1** sleepy, drowsy. **2** inducing drowsiness. **3** Med. in a state between sleeping and waking. □□ **somnolence** n. **somnolency** n. **somnolently** adv. [ME f. OF sompnolent or L somnolentus f. somnus sleep]

son /sʌn/ n. **1** a boy or man in relation to either or both of his parents. **2 a** a male descendant. **b** (foll. by of) a male member of a family, nation, etc. **3** a person regarded as inheriting an occupation, quality, etc., or associated with a particular attribute (sons of freedom; sons of the soil). **4** (in full **my son**) a form of address esp. to a boy. **5** (**the Son**) (in Christian belief) the second person of the Trinity. □ **son-in-law** (pl. **sons-in-law**) the husband of one's daughter. **son of a bitch** sl. a general term of contempt. **son of a gun** colloq. a jocular or affectionate form of address or reference. □□ **sonless** adj. **sonship** n. [OE sunu f. Gmc]

sonant /ˈsəʊnənt/ adj. & n. Phonet. —adj. (of a sound) voiced and syllabic. —n. a voiced sound, esp. other than a vowel and capable of forming a syllable, e.g. l, m, n, ng, r. □□ **sonancy** n. [L sonare sonant- sound]

sonar /ˈsəʊnə(r)/ n. **1** a system for the underwater detection of objects by reflected or emitted sound. **2** an apparatus for this. The 'hydrophone' (a kind of underwater microphone) was used in the 1890s to detect sounds such as the operation of engines or propellers, but by 1918 a system of transmitting a pulse of sound and using its rebounding echo to detect a stationary submerged craft had been developed. It became known as 'asdic' (see entry) and later as 'sonar' (from the initials of the US development), and was widely used in the Second World War. Such apparatus also has civil applications, as in the location of shoals of fish. [sound navigation and ranging, after radar]

sonata /səˈnɑːtə/ n. a composition for one instrument or two (one usu. being a piano accompaniment), usu. in several movements with one (esp. the first) or more in sonata form. (See below.) □ **sonata form** a type of composition in three sections (exposition, development, and recapitulation) in which two themes (or subjects) are explored according to set key relationships. [It., = sounded (orig. as distinct from sung): fem. past part. of sonare sound]

The classical sonata has clear formal implications of a four-movement work, each movement of a standard type and in a particular order, and is scored for one or two solo instruments, such as piano, piano and violin; earlier uses of the term, however, have a common factor only in their use of instruments rather than voices. In the Romantic period the sonata lost its pre-eminence in favour of shorter pieces which depended on extra-musical rather than formal considerations for their integrity.

sonatina /ˌsɒnəˈtiːnə/ n. a simple or short sonata. [It., dimin. of SONATA]

sonde /sɒnd/ n. a device sent up to obtain information about atmospheric conditions, esp. = RADIOSONDE. [F, = sounding(-line)]

Sondheim /ˈsɒndhaɪm/, Stephen Joshua (1930–), American composer and lyric-writer. He became famous on Broadway by writing the lyrics for Bernstein's West Side Story (1957), and later composed successful musicals including A Funny Thing Happened on the Way to the Forum (1962), A Little Night Music (1973), and Sweeney Todd (1979).

sone /səʊn/ n. a unit of subjective loudness, equal to 40 phons. [L sonus sound]

son et lumière /ˌsɒneɪˈluːmjeə(r)/ n. an entertainment by night at a historic monument, building, etc., using lighting effects and recorded sound to give a dramatic narrative of its history. [F, = sound and light]

song /sɒŋ/ n. **1** a short poem or other set of words set to music or meant to be sung. **2** singing or vocal music (burst into song). **3** a musical composition suggestive of a song. **4** the musical cry of some birds. **5** a short poem in rhymed stanzas. **6** archaic poetry or verse. □ **for a song** *colloq.* very cheaply. **on song** *Brit. colloq.* performing exceptionally well. **song and dance** *colloq.* a fuss or commotion. **song cycle** a set of musically linked songs on a romantic theme. **Song of Songs** (i.e. greatest song; cf. *holy of holies*) the Song of Solomon (see SOLOMON). **Song of the Three (Holy Children)** a book of the Apocrypha, telling of the three Hebrew exiles thrown into the fiery furnace by Nebuchadnezzar. **song sparrow** a N. American sparrow, *Melospiza melodia*, with a characteristic musical song. **song thrush** a thrush, *Turdus philomelos*, of Europe and W. Asia, with a song partly mimicked from other birds. □□ **songless** *adj.* [OE *sang* f. Gmc (as SING)]

songbird /ˈsɒŋbɜːd/ *n.* a bird with a musical call.

songbook /ˈsɒŋbʊk/ *n.* a collection of songs with music.

songsmith /ˈsɒŋsmɪθ/ *n.* a writer of songs.

songster /ˈsɒŋstə(r)/ *n.* (*fem.* **songstress**) /-strɪs/ **1** a singer, esp. a fluent and skilful one. **2** a songbird. **3** a poet. **4** *US* a songbook. [OE *sangestre* (as SONG, -STER)]

songwriter /ˈsɒŋˌraɪtə(r)/ *n.* a writer of songs or the music for them.

sonic /ˈsɒnɪk/ *adj.* of or relating to or using sound or sound waves. □ **sonic bang** (or **boom**) a loud explosive noise caused by the shock wave from an aircraft when it passes the speed of sound. **sonic barrier** = *sound barrier* (see SOUND¹). **sonic mine** a mine exploded by the sound of a passing ship. □□ **sonically** *adv.* [L *sonus* sound]

sonnet /ˈsɒnɪt/ *n.* & *v.* —*n.* a poem of 14 lines (usu. pentameters) using any of a number of formal rhyme schemes, in English usu. having ten syllables per line. —*v.* (**sonneted**, **sonneting**) **1** *intr.* write sonnets. **2** *tr.* address sonnets to. [F *sonnet* or It. *sonetto* dimin. of *suono* SOUND¹]

sonneteer /ˌsɒnɪˈtɪə(r)/ *n.* usu. *derog.* a writer of sonnets.

sonny /ˈsʌnɪ/ *n. colloq.* a familiar form of address to a young boy.

sonobuoy /ˈsəʊnəˌbɔɪ/ *n.* a buoy for detecting underwater sounds and transmitting them by radio. [L *sonus* sound + BUOY]

sonometer /səˈnɒmɪtə(r)/ *n.* **1** an instrument for measuring the vibration frequency of a string etc. **2** an audiometer. [L *sonus* sound + -METER]

Sonora /səˈnɔːrə/ a State of NW Mexico; pop. (est. 1988) 1,799,600; capital, Hermosillo.

sonorous /ˈsɒnərəs, səˈnɔːrəs/ *adj.* **1** having a loud, full, or deep sound; resonant. **2** (of a speech, style, etc.) imposing, grand. □□ **sonority** /səˈnɒrɪtɪ/ *n.* **sonorously** *adv.* **sonorousness** *n.* [L *sonorus* f. *sonor* sound]

sonsy /ˈsɒnsɪ/ *adj.* (also **sonsie**) (**sonsier, sonsiest**) *Sc.* **1** plump, buxom. **2** of a cheerful disposition. **3** bringing good fortune. [ult. f. Ir. & Gael. *sonas* good fortune f. *sona* fortunate]

sook /sʊk/ *n. Austral. & NZ sl.* **1** *derog.* a timid bashful person; a coward or sissy. **2** a hand-reared calf. [E dial. *suck*, call-word for a calf]

sool /suːl/ *v.tr. Austral. & NZ sl.* **1** (of a dog) attack or worry (an animal). **2** (often foll. by *on*) urge or goad. □□ **sooler** *n.* [var. of 17th-c. (now dial.) *sowl* seize roughly, of unkn. orig.]

soon /suːn/ *adv.* **1** after no long interval of time (*shall soon know the result*). **2** relatively early (*must you go so soon?*). **3** (*prec. by how*) early (with relative rather than distinctive sense) (*how soon will it be ready?*). **4** readily or willingly (in expressing choice or preference: *which would you sooner do?*; *would as soon stay behind*). □ **as** (or **so**) **soon as** (implying a causal or temporal connection) at the moment that; not later than; as early as (*came as soon as I heard about it*; *disappears as soon as it's time to pay*). **no sooner ... than** at the very moment that (*we no sooner arrived than the rain stopped*). **sooner or later** at some future time; eventually. □□ **soonish** *adv.* [OE *sōna* f. WG]

soot /sʊt/ *n.* & *v.* —*n.* a black carbonaceous substance rising in fine flakes in the smoke of wood, coal, oil, etc., and deposited on the sides of a chimney etc. —*v.tr.* cover with soot. [OE *sōt* f. Gmc]

sooth /suːθ/ *n. archaic* truth, fact. □ **in sooth** really, truly. [OE *sōth* (orig. adj., = true) f. Gmc]

soothe /suːð/ *v.tr.* **1** calm (a person or feelings). **2** soften or

mitigate (pain). **3** *archaic* flatter or humour. □□ **soother** *n.* **soothing** *adj.* **soothingly** *adv.* [OE *sōthian* verify f. *sōth* true: see SOOTH]

soothsayer /ˈsuːθˌseɪə(r)/ *n.* a diviner or seer. [ME, = one who says the truth: see SOOTH]

sooty /ˈsʊtɪ/ *adj.* (**sootier, sootiest**) **1** covered with or full of soot. **2** (esp. of an animal or bird) black or brownish-black. □ **sooty albatross** an albatross, *Diomedia chrysostoma*, with grey-brown plumage. □□ **sootily** *adv.* **sootiness** *n.*

sop /sɒp/ *n.* & *v.* —*n.* **1** a piece of bread etc. dipped in gravy etc. **2** a thing given or done to pacify or bribe. —*v.* (**sopped, sopping**) **1** *intr.* be drenched (*came home sopping*; *sopping wet clothes*). **2** *tr.* (foll. by *up*) absorb (liquid) in a towel etc. **3** *tr.* wet thoroughly; soak. [OE *sopp*, corresp. to MLG *soppe*, OHG *sopfa* bread and milk, prob. f. a weak grade of the base of OE *sūpan*: see SUP¹]

Sophia see SOFIA.

sophism /ˈsɒfɪz(ə)m/ *n.* a false argument, esp. one intended to deceive. [ME f. OF *sophime* f. L f. Gk *sophisma* clever device f. *sophizomai* become wise f. *sophos* wise]

Sophist /ˈsɒfɪst/ *n.* **1** a member of the last generations of Greek philosophers before Plato, of the period *c.*450 BC to *c.*400 BC. Their name (= 'expert') was originally a descriptive term, not a term of abuse. They were in business offering the equivalent of university education: for a hefty fee they would teach, in particular, rhetoric—how to argue a case in a lawcourt or an assembly. But they were also thinkers with argued views. Perhaps most important was the contrast they emphasized between *phusis*, what exists by nature, and *nomos*, what exists only by human convention. This led not only to moral relativism (what is right here depends entirely on what this society thinks right) but to amoralism (morality is a matter merely of conventions, which the intelligent and strong man will disregard). Such views, together with the thought that they taught how to make the worse case appear the better, made the word become an uncomplimentary one. **2** (**sophist**) one who reasons with clever but fallacious arguments. □□ **sophistic** /-ˈfɪstɪk/ *adj.* **sophistical** /səˈfɪstɪk(ə)l/ *adj.* **sophistically** /səˈfɪstɪkəlɪ/ *adv.* [L *sophistes* f. Gk *sophistēs* f. *sophizomai*: see SOPHISM]

sophisticate *v.*, *adj.*, & *n.* —*v.* /səˈfɪstɪˌkeɪt/ **1** *tr.* make (a person etc.) educated, cultured, or refined. **2** *tr.* make (equipment or techniques etc.) highly developed or complex. **3** *tr.* **a** involve (a subject) in sophistry. **b** mislead (a person) by sophistry. **4** *tr.* deprive (a person or thing) of its natural simplicity, make artificial by worldly experience etc. **5** *tr.* tamper with (a text etc.) for purposes of argument etc. **6** *tr.* adulterate (wine etc.). **7** *intr.* use sophistry. —*adj.* /səˈfɪstɪkət/ sophisticated. —*n.* /səˈfɪstɪkət/ a sophisticated person. □□ **sophistication** /-ˈkeɪʃ(ə)n/ *n.* [med.L *sophisticare* tamper with f. *sophisticus* (as SOPHISM)]

sophisticated /səˈfɪstɪˌkeɪtɪd/ *adj.* **1** (of a person) educated and refined; discriminating in taste and judgement. **2** (of a thing, idea, etc.) highly developed and complex. □□ **sophisticatedly** *adv.*

sophistry /ˈsɒfɪstrɪ/ *n.* (*pl.* **-ies**) **1** the use of sophisms. **2** a sophism.

Sophocles /ˈsɒfəˌkliːz/ (*c.*496–406 BC) Greek dramatist. The second of the three great tragedians (the others were Aeschylus and Euripides), he took an active part in the political and religious life of contemporary Athens. His introduction of a third actor allowed the greater complexity of plot and fuller depiction of character for which his seven surviving plays are notable (*Antigone*, *Electra*, *Oedipus Tyrannus*, *Oedipus at Colonus*, *Philoctetes*, *Trachiniae*), as well as for their examination of the relationship between man and the divine order of the world.

sophomore /ˈsɒfəˌmɔː(r)/ *n. US* a second-year university or high-school student. □□ **sophomoric** /-ˈmɒrɪk/ *adj.* [earlier *sophumer* f. *sophum*, obs. var. of SOPHISM]

Sophy /ˈsəʊfɪ/ *n.* (*pl.* **-ies**) *hist.* a ruler of Persia in the 16th–17th c. [Pers. *safī* surname of the dynasty, f. Arab. *safī-ud-dīn* pure of religion, title of the founder's ancestor]

soporific /ˌsɒpəˈrɪfɪk/ *adj.* & *n.* —*adj.* tending to produce sleep.

—n. a soporific drug or influence. □□ **soporiferous** *adj.* **soporifically** *adv.* [L *sopor* sleep + -FIC]

sopping /ˈsɒpɪŋ/ *adj.* (also **sopping wet**) soaked with liquid; wet through. [pres. part. of SOP *v.*]

soppy /ˈsɒpɪ/ *adj.* (**soppier, soppiest**) **1** *Brit. colloq.* **a** silly or foolish in a feeble or self-indulgent way. **b** mawkishly sentimental. **2** *Brit. colloq.* (foll. by *on*) foolishly infatuated with. **3** soaked with water. □□ **soppily** *adv.* **soppiness** *n.* [SOP + -Y¹]

sopranino /ˌsɒprəˈniːnəʊ/ *n.* (*pl.* **-os**) *Mus.* an instrument higher than soprano, esp. a recorder or saxophone. [It., dimin. of SOPRANO]

soprano /səˈprɑːnəʊ/ *n.* (*pl.* **-os** or **soprani** /-nɪ/) **1 a** the highest singing-voice. **b** a female or boy singer with this voice. **c** a part written for it. **2 a** an instrument of a high or the highest pitch in its family. **b** its player. □ **soprano-clef** an obsolete clef placing middle C on the lowest line of the staff. [It. f. *sopra* above f. L *supra*]

Sopwith /ˈsɒpwɪθ/, Sir Thomas Octave Murdoch (1888–1989), English aircraft designer, famous especially for the biplane the Sopwith Camel, designed and built by his firm and used in the First World War.

sora /ˈsɔːrə/ *n.* (in full **sora rail**) a bird, *Porzana carolina*, frequenting the marshes of N. and S. Carolina etc. in the autumn and used as food. [prob. a native name]

sorb /sɔːb/ *n.* **1** = *service tree* (see SERVICE²). **2** (in full **sorb-apple**) its fruit. [F *sorbe* or L *sorbus* service tree, *sorbum* service-berry]

sorbefacient /ˌsɔːbɪˈfeɪʃ(ə)nt/ *adj.* & *n.* *Med.* —*adj.* causing absorption. —*n.* a sorbefacient drug etc. [L *sorbēre* suck in + -FACIENT]

sorbet /ˈsɔːbeɪ, -bɪt/ *n.* **1** a water-ice. **2** sherbet. [F f. It. *sorbetto* f. Turk. *şerbet* f. Arab. *šarba* to drink: cf. SHERBET]

Sorbo /ˈsɔːbəʊ/ *n.* *Brit. propr.* (in full **Sorbo rubber**) a spongy rubber. [ABSORB + -O]

Sorbonne /sɔːˈbɒn/ originally a theological college founded in Paris by Robert de Sorbon, chaplain to Louis IX, *c.*1257; later, the faculty of theology in the University of Paris, suppressed in 1792; now, the seat of the faculties of science and letters of the University of Paris.

sorcerer /ˈsɔːsərə(r)/ *n.* (*fem.* **sorceress** /-rɪs/) a person who claims to use magic powers; a magician or wizard. □□ **sorcerous** *adj.* **sorcery** *n.* (*pl.* **-ies**). [obs. *sorcer* f. OF *sorcier* ult. f. L *sors sortis* lot]

sordid /ˈsɔːdɪd/ *adj.* **1** dirty or squalid. **2** ignoble, mean, or mercenary. **3** mean or niggardly. **4** dull-coloured. □□ **sordidly** *adv.* **sordidness** *n.* [F *sordide* or L *sordidus* f. *sordēre* be dirty]

sordino /sɔːˈdiːnəʊ/ *n.* (*pl.* **sordini** /-nɪ/) *Mus.* a mute for a bowed or wind instrument. [It. f. *sordo* mute f. L *surdus*]

sore /sɔː(r)/ *adj.*, *n.*, & *adv.* —*adj.* **1** (of a part of the body) painful from injury or disease (*has a sore arm*). **2** (of a person) suffering pain. **3** (often foll. by *about*, *at*) aggrieved or vexed. **4** *archaic* grievous or severe (*in sore need*). —*n.* **1** a sore place on the body. **2** a source of distress or annoyance (*reopen old sores*). —*adv.* *archaic* grievously, severely. □ **sore point** a subject causing distress or annoyance. **sore throat** an inflammation of the lining membrane at the back of the mouth etc. □□ **soreness** *n.* [OE *sār* (n. & adj.), *sāre* (adv.), f. Gmc]

sorehead /ˈsɔːhed/ *n.* US a touchy or disgruntled person.

sorel /ˈsɒr(ə)l/ *n.* *Brit.* a male fallow deer in its third year. [var. of SORREL²]

sorely /ˈsɔːlɪ/ *adv.* **1** extremely, badly (*am sorely tempted; sorely in need of repair*). **2** severely (*am sorely vexed*). [OE *sārlīce* (as SORE, -LY²)]

sorghum /ˈsɔːgəm/ *n.* any tropical cereal grass of the genus *Sorghum*, e.g. durra. [mod.L f. It. *sorgo*, perh. f. unrecorded Rmc *syricum* (*gramen*) Syrian (grass)]

sori *pl.* of SORUS.

Soroptimist /səˈrɒptɪmɪst/ *n.* a member of the Soroptimist Club, an international club for professional and business women, founded in California in 1921 with the aim of providing service to the community. [L *soror* sister + OPTIMIST (as OPTIMISM)]

sorority /səˈrɒrɪtɪ/ *n.* (*pl.* **-ies**) US a female students' society in a university or college. [med.L *sororitas* or L *soror* sister, after *fraternity*]

sorosis /səˈrəʊsɪs/ *n.* (*pl.* **soroses** /-siːz/) *Bot.* a fleshy compound fruit, e.g. a pineapple or mulberry. [mod.L f. Gk *sōros* heap]

sorption /ˈsɔːpʃ(ə)n/ *n.* absorption or adsorption happening jointly or separately. [back-form. f. *absorption, adsorption*]

sorrel¹ /ˈsɒr(ə)l/ *n.* any acid-leaved herb of the genus *Rumex*, used in salads and for flavouring. [ME f. OF *surele, sorele* f. Gmc]

sorrel² /ˈsɒr(ə)l/ *adj.* & *n.* —*adj.* of a light reddish-brown colour. —*n.* **1** this colour. **2** a sorrel animal, esp. a horse. **3** *Brit.* a sorrel. [ME f. OF *sorel* f. *sor* yellowish f. Frank.]

Sorrento /səˈrentəʊ/ a town of central Italy situated on a peninsula separating the Bay of Naples, which it faces, from the Gulf of Salerno; pop. (1981) 17,300. It has been a resort since Roman times (Latin *Surrentum*), noted for its climate and the beauty of the surrounding scenery.

sorrow /ˈsɒrəʊ/ *n.* & *v.* —*n.* **1** mental distress caused by loss or disappointment etc. **2** a cause of sorrow. **3** lamentation. —*v.intr.* **1** feel sorrow. **2** mourn. □□ **sorrower** *n.* **sorrowing** *adj.* [OE *sorh, sorg*]

sorrowful /ˈsɒrəʊfʊl/ *adj.* **1** feeling or showing sorrow. **2** distressing, lamentable. □□ **sorrowfully** *adv.* **sorrowfulness** *n.* [OE *sorhful* (as SORROW, -FUL)]

sorry /ˈsɒrɪ/ *adj.* (**sorrier, sorriest**) **1** (*predic.*) pained or regretful or penitent (*were sorry for what they had done; am sorry that you have to go*). **2** (*predic.*; foll. by *for*) feeling pity or sympathy for (a person). **3** as an expression of apology. **4** wretched; in a poor state (*a sorry sight*). □ **sorry for oneself** dejected. □□ **sorrily** *adv.* **sorriness** *n.* [OE *sārig* f. WG (as SORE, -Y²)]

sort /sɔːt/ *n.* & *v.* —*n.* **1** a group of things etc. with common attributes; a class or kind. **2** (foll. by *of*) roughly of the kind specified (*is some sort of doctor*). **3** *colloq.* a person of a specified character or kind (*a good sort*). **4** *Printing* a letter or piece in a fount of type. **5** *Computing* the arrangement of data in a prescribed sequence. **6** *archaic* a manner or way. —*v.tr.* (often foll. by *out, over*) arrange systematically or according to type, class, etc. □ **after a sort** after a fashion. **in some sort** to a certain extent. **of a sort** (or **of sorts**) *colloq.* not fully deserving the name (*a holiday of sorts*). **out of sorts 1** slightly unwell. **2** in low spirits; irritable. **sort of** *colloq.* as it were; to some extent (*I sort of expected it*). **sort out 1** separate into sorts. **2** select (things of one or more sorts) from a miscellaneous group. **3** disentangle or put into order. **4** resolve (a problem or difficulty). **5** *colloq.* deal with or reprimand (a person). □□ **sortable** *adj.* **sorter** *n.* **sorting** *n.* [ME f. OF *sorte* ult. f. L *sors sortis* lot, condition]

sortie /ˈsɔːtɪ/ *n.* & *v.* —*n.* **1** a sally, esp. from a besieged garrison. **2** an operational flight by a single military aircraft. —*v.intr.* (**sorties, sortied, sortieing**) make a sortie; sally. [F, fem. past part. of *sortir* go out]

sortilege /ˈsɔːtɪlɪdʒ/ *n.* divination by lots. [ME f. OF f. med.L *sortilegium* sorcery f. L *sortilegus* sorcerer (as SORT, *legere* choose)]

sorus /ˈsɔːrəs/ *n.* (*pl.* **sori** /-raɪ/) *Bot.* a heap or cluster, esp. of spore-cases on the under-surface of a fern-leaf, or in a fungus or lichen. [mod.L f. Gk *sōros* heap]

SOS /ˌesəʊˈes/ *n.* (*pl.* **SOSs**) **1** an international code-signal of extreme distress, used esp. by ships at sea. **2** an urgent appeal for help. **3** *Brit.* a message broadcast to an untraceable person in an emergency. [chosen as being easily transmitted and recognized in Morse code]

Sosnowiec /sɒsˈnɒvjets/ a mining town in Poland; pop. (1985) 255,000.

sostenuto /ˌsɒstəˈnuːtəʊ/ *adv.*, *adj.*, & *n.* *Mus.* —*adv.* & *adj.* in a sustained or prolonged manner. —*n.* (*pl.* **-os**) a passage to be played in this way. [It., past part. of *sostenere* SUSTAIN]

sot /sɒt/ *n.* & *v.* —*n.* a habitual drunkard. —*v.intr.* (**sotted, sotting**) tipple. □□ **sottish** *adj.* [OE *sott* & OF *sot* foolish, f. med.L *sottus*, of unkn. orig.]

soteriology /sɒˌtɪərɪˈɒlədʒɪ/ *n.* *Theol.* the doctrine of salvation. [Gk *sōtēria* salvation + -LOGY]

Sothic /ˈsəʊθɪk/ *adj.* of or relating to the dog-star. □ **Sothic**

year the ancient Egyptian year of 365¼ days, fixed by the heliacal rising of the dog-star. **Sothic cycle** a cycle (first fixed in AD 139) of 1460 Sothic years, after which the 365-day calendar year gives the same date for this rising. [Gk *Sōthis* f. the Egypt. name of the dog-star]

Sotho /ˈsuːtuː/ *n. & adj.* —*n.* **1** a subdivision of the Bantu people which includes tribes living chiefly in Botswana, Lesotho, and the Transvaal. **2** their Bantu languages. —*adj.* of this people or their languages. [native name]

sotto voce /ˌsɒtəʊ ˈvəʊtʃɪ/ *adv.* in an undertone or aside. [It. *sotto* under + *voce* voice]

sou /suː/ *n.* **1** *hist.* a former French coin of low value. **2** (usu. with *neg.*) *colloq.* a very small amount of money (*hasn't a sou*). [F, orig. pl. *sous* f. OF *sout* f. L SOLIDUS]

soubrette /suːˈbret/ *n.* **1** a pert maidservant or similar female character in a comedy. **2** an actress taking this part. [F f. Prov. *soubreto* fem. of *soubret* coy f. *sobrar* f. L *superare* be above]

soubriquet var. of SOBRIQUET.

souchong /ˈsuːʃɒŋ/ *n.* a fine black kind of China tea. [Chin. *xiao* small + *zhong* sort]

souffle /ˈsuːf(ə)l/ *n. Med.* a low murmur heard in the auscultation of various organs etc. [F f. *souffler* blow f. L *sufflare*]

soufflé /ˈsuːfleɪ/ *n. & adj.* —*n.* **1** a light spongy dish usu. made with flavoured egg yolks added to stiffly beaten whites of eggs and baked (*cheese soufflé*). **2** any of various light sweet or savoury dishes made with beaten egg whites. —*adj.* **1** light and frothy or spongy (*omelette soufflé*). **2** (of ceramics) decorated with small spots. [F past part. (as SOUFFLE)]

Soufrière /ˌsuːfrɪˈeə(r)/ a volcanic peak rising to a height of 1,234 m (4,006 ft.) on the island of St Vincent in the West Indies.

sough /saʊ, sʌf/ *v. & n.* —*v.intr.* make a moaning, whistling, or rushing sound as of the wind in trees etc. —*n.* this sound. [OE *swōgan* resound]

sought past and past part. of SEEK.

souk /suːk/ *n.* (also **suk, sukh, suq**) a market-place in Muslim countries. [Arab. *sūk*]

soul /səʊl/ *n.* **1** the spiritual or immaterial part of a human being, often regarded as immortal. **2** the moral or emotional or intellectual nature of a person or animal. **3** the personification or pattern of something (*the very soul of discretion*). **4** an individual (*not a soul in sight*). **5 a** a person regarded with familiarity or pity etc. (*the poor soul was utterly confused*). **b** a person regarded as embodying moral or intellectual qualities (*left that to meaner souls*). **6** a person regarded as the animating or essential part of something (*the life and soul of the party*). **7** emotional or intellectual energy or intensity, esp. as revealed in a work of art (*pictures that lack soul*). **8** Black American culture or music etc. □ **soul-destroying** (of an activity etc.) deadeningly monotonous. **soul food** the traditional food of American Blacks. **soul mate** a person ideally suited to another. **soul music** a kind of music incorporating elements of rhythm and blues and gospel music, popularized by American Blacks. **the soul of honour** a person incapable of dishonourable conduct. **soul-searching** *n.* the examination of one's emotions and motives. —*adj.* characterized by this. **upon my soul** an exclamation of surprise. □□ **-souled** *adj.* (in *comb.*). [OE *sāwol, sāwel, sāwl,* f. Gmc]

soulful /ˈsəʊlfʊl/ *adj.* **1** having or expressing or evoking deep feeling. **2** *colloq.* over-emotional. □□ **soulfully** *adv.* **soulfulness** *n.*

soulless /ˈsəʊllɪs/ *adj.* **1** lacking sensitivity or noble qualities. **2** having no soul. **3** undistinguished or uninteresting. □□ **soullessly** *adv.* **soullessness** *n.*

sound¹ /saʊnd/ *n. & v.* —*n.* **1** a sensation caused in the ear by the vibration of the surrounding air or other medium. **2 a** vibrations causing this sensation. **b** similar vibrations whether audible or not. (See below.) **3** what is or may be heard. **4** an idea or impression conveyed by words (*don't like the sound of that*). **5** mere words (*sound and fury*). **6** (in full **musical sound**) sound produced by continuous and regular vibrations (opp. NOISE *n.* 3). **7** any of a series of articulate utterances (*vowel and consonant sounds*). **8** music, speech, etc., accompanying a film or other visual presentation. **9** (often *attrib.*) broadcasting by radio as

distinct from television. —*v.* **1** *intr. & tr.* emit or cause to emit sound. **2** *tr.* utter or pronounce (*sound a note of alarm*). **3** *intr.* convey an impression when heard (*you sound worried*). **4** *tr.* give an audible signal for (an alarm etc.). **5** *tr.* test (the lungs etc.) by noting the sound produced. **6** *tr.* cause to resound; make known (*sound their praises*). □ **sound barrier** the high resistance of air to objects moving at speeds near that of sound. **sound bite** a short extract from a recorded interview, chosen for its pungency or appropriateness. **sound effect** a sound other than speech or music made artificially for use in a play, film, etc. **sound engineer** an engineer dealing with acoustics etc. **sound-hole** an aperture in the belly of some stringed instruments. **sound off** talk loudly or express one's opinions forcefully. **sound-post** a small prop between the belly and back of some stringed instruments. **sound shift** see SHIFT *n.* 6. **sound spectrograph** an instrument for analysing sound into its frequency components. **sound wave** a wave of compression and rarefaction, by which sound is propagated in an elastic medium, e.g. air. □□ **soundless** *adj.* **soundlessly** *adv.* **soundlessness** *n.* [ME f. AF *soun*, OF *son* (n.), AF *suner*, OF *soner* (v.) f. L *sonus*]

Sound consists of longitudinal waves of pressure (see WAVE) passing through solids, liquids, or gases; it cannot travel through a vacuum. The speed of sound tends to be independent of its frequency and to be a constant for any particular medium: for example, the speed of sound in air is about 344 metres (1,128 ft.) per second. In general, sound travels faster through solids than through liquids, and faster through liquids than through gases, although density and temperature are also important. The human ear responds to frequencies of sound that are between about 20 Hz and 20,000 Hz. Frequency is perceived as pitch: if one sound has twice the frequency of another, it is perceived (in musical terms) as being an octave above it. Most musical tones, however, are complex in form, including many higher frequencies or 'harmonics' as well as the fundamental frequency. Frequencies below and above the range of human hearing are called infrasonic and ultrasonic respectively. Some animals, such as dogs, bats, and dolphins, can hear frequencies in the ultrasonic range. Although the properties of sound waves do not suddenly change above 20,000 Hz, sound of very high frequency can be formed into a powerful beam, and ultrasound has a number of practical applications: it is used to form emulsions between immiscible liquids, as an alternative to X-rays in medical diagnosis, as a means of underwater detection, and for many other purposes.

sound² /saʊnd/ *adj. & adv.* —*adj.* **1** healthy; not diseased or injured. **2** (of an opinion or policy etc.) correct, orthodox, well-founded, judicious. **3** financially secure (*a sound investment*). **4** undisturbed (*a sound sleeper*). **5** severe, hard (*a sound blow*). —*adv.* soundly (*sound asleep*). □□ **soundly** *adv.* **soundness** *n.* [ME *sund, isund* f. OE *gesund* f. WG]

sound³ /saʊnd/ *v. & n.* —*v.tr. & intr.* **1** *tr.* test the depth or quality of the bottom of (the sea or a river etc.). **2** *tr.* (often foll. by *out*) inquire (esp. cautiously or discreetly) into the opinions or feelings of (a person). **3** *tr.* find the depth of water in (a ship's hold). **4** *tr.* get records of temperature, humidity, pressure, etc. from (the upper atmosphere). **5** *tr.* examine (a person's bladder etc.) with a probe. **6** *intr.* (of a whale or fish) dive to the bottom. —*n.* a surgeon's probe. □□ **sounder** *n.* [ME f. OF *sonder* ult. f. L SUB- + *unda* wave]

sound⁴ /saʊnd/ *n.* **1 a** a narrow passage of water connecting two seas or a sea with a lake etc. **b** an arm of the sea. **2** a fish's swim-bladder. □ **the Sound** see ØRESUND. [OE *sund*, = ON *sund* swimming, strait, f. Gmc (as SWIM)]

soundboard /ˈsaʊndbɔːd/ *n.* a thin sheet of wood over which the strings of a piano etc. pass to increase the sound produced.

soundbox /ˈsaʊndbɒks/ *n.* the hollow chamber providing resonance and forming the body of a stringed musical instrument.

sounding¹ /ˈsaʊndɪŋ/ *n.* **1 a** the action or process of measuring the depth of water, now usu. by means of echo. **b** an instance of this (*took a sounding*). **2** (in *pl.*) **a** a region close to the shore of the right depth for sounding. **b** *Naut.* measurements taken by sounding. **c** cautious investigation (*made soundings as to his suitability*). **3 a** the determination of any physical property at a depth in the sea or at a height in the atmosphere. **b** an instance of this. □ **sounding-balloon** a balloon used to obtain information about the upper atmosphere. **sounding-line** a line used in sounding the depth of water. **sounding-rod** a rod used in finding the depth of water in a ship's hold (see SOUND³).

sounding² /ˈsaʊndɪŋ/ adj. **1** giving forth (esp. loud or resonant) sound (*sounding brass*). **2** emptily boastful, resonant, or imposing (*sounding promises*).

sounding-board /ˈsaʊndɪŋˌbɔːd/ n. **1** a canopy over a pulpit etc. to direct sound towards the congregation. **2** = SOUNDBOARD. **3 a** a means of causing opinions etc. to be more widely known (*used his students as a sounding-board*). **b** a person etc. used as a trial audience.

soundproof /ˈsaʊndpruːf/ adj. & v. —adj. impervious to sound. —v.tr. make soundproof.

soundtrack /ˈsaʊndtræk/ n. **1** the recorded sound element of a film. **2** this recorded on the edge of a film in optical or magnetic form.

soup /suːp/ n. & v. —n. **1** a usu. savoury liquid dish made by boiling meat, fish, or vegetables etc. in stock or water. **2** US sl. nitroglycerine or gelignite, esp. for safe-breaking. **3** sl. the chemicals in which film is developed. **4** colloq. fog; thick cloud. —v.tr. (usu. foll. by up) colloq. **1** increase the power and efficiency of (an engine). **2** increase the power or impact of (writing, music, etc.). □ **in the soup** colloq. in difficulties. **soup and fish** colloq. evening dress. **soup-kitchen** a place dispensing soup etc. to the poor. **soup-plate** a deep wide-rimmed plate for serving soup. **soup-spoon** a large round-bowled spoon for drinking soup. [F *soupe* sop, broth, f. LL *suppa* f. Gmc: cf. SOP, SUP¹]

soupçon /ˈsuːpsɒ̃/ n. a very small quantity; a dash. [F f. OF *sou(s)peçon* f. med.L *suspectio -onis*: see SUSPICION]

soupy /ˈsuːpɪ/ adj. (**soupier, soupiest**) **1** of or resembling soup. **2** colloq. sentimental; mawkish. □□ **soupily** adv. **soupiness** n.

sour /ˈsaʊə(r)/ adj., n., & v. —adj. **1** having an acid taste like lemon or vinegar, esp. because of unripeness (*sour apples*). **2 a** (of food, esp. milk or bread) bad because of fermentation. **b** smelling or tasting rancid or unpleasant. **3** (of a person, temper, etc.) harsh; morose; bitter. **4** (of a thing) unpleasant; distasteful. **5** (of the soil) deficient in lime and usually dank. —n. **1** US a drink with lemon- or lime-juice (*whisky sour*). **2** an acid solution used in bleaching etc. —v.tr. & intr. make or become sour (*soured the cream; soured by misfortune*). □ **go** (or **turn**) **sour 1** (of food etc.) become sour. **2** turn out badly (*the job went sour on him*). **3** lose one's keenness. **sour cream** cream deliberately fermented by adding bacteria. **sour grapes** resentful disparagement of something one cannot personally acquire. (From the fable of the fox who wanted some grapes but found that they were out of reach and so pretended that they were sour and undesirable anyway.) **sour mash** US a brewing- or distilling-mash made acid to promote fermentation. □□ **sourish** adj. **sourly** adv. **sourness** n. [OE *sūr* f. Gmc]

source /sɔːs/ n. & v. —n. **1** a spring or fountain-head from which a stream issues (*the sources of the Nile*). **2** a place, person, or thing from which something originates (*the source of all our troubles*). **3** a person or document etc. providing evidence (*reliable sources of information; historical source material*). **4 a** a body emitting radiation etc. **b** Physics a place from which a fluid or current flows. **c** Electronics a part of a transistor from which carriers flow into the interelectrode channel. —v.tr. obtain (esp. components) from a specified source. □ **at source** at the point of origin or issue. **source-criticism** the evaluation of different, esp. successive, literary or historical sources. [ME f. OF *sors, sourse*, past part. of *sourdre* rise f. L *surgere*]

sourcebook /ˈsɔːsbʊk/ n. a collection of documentary sources for the study of a subject.

sourdough /ˈsaʊəˌdəʊ/ n. US **1** fermenting dough, esp. that left over from a previous baking, used as leaven. **2** an old-timer in Alaska etc. [dial., = leaven, in allusion to piece of sour dough for raising bread baked in winter]

sourpuss /ˈsaʊəˌpʊs/ n. colloq. a sour-tempered person. [SOUR + PUSS = face]

soursop /ˈsaʊəˌsɒp/ n. **1** a W. Indian evergreen tree, *Annona muricata*. **2** the large succulent fruit of this tree.

sous- /suː(z)/ prefix (in words adopted from French) subordinate, under (*sous-chef*). [F]

Sousa /ˈsuːzə/, John Philip (1854–1932), American composer and conductor. He became director of the US Marine Band (1880) and then formed his own band in 1892. His works include over 100 marches, for example *The Stars and Stripes, King Cotton*, and *Hands Across the Sea*. The sousaphone (see entry) was named in his honour on its invention in 1898.

sousaphone /ˈsuːzəˌfəʊn/ n. a large brass bass wind instrument encircling the player's body. □□ **sousaphonist** n. [J. P. SOUSA, after *saxophone*]

souse /saʊs/ v. & n. —v. **1** tr. put (gherkins, fish, etc.) in pickle. **2** tr. & intr. plunge into liquid. **3** tr. (as **soused** adj.) colloq. drunk. **4** tr. (usu. foll. by *in*) soak (a thing) in liquid. **5** tr. (usu. foll. by *over*) throw (liquid) over a thing. —n. **1 a** a pickle made with salt. **b** US food, esp. a pig's head etc., in pickle. **2** a dip, plunge, or drenching in water. **3** colloq. **a** a drinking-bout. **b** a drunkard. [ME f. OF *sous, souz* pickle f. OS *sultia*, OHG *sulza* brine f. Gmc: cf. SALT]

Sousse /suːs/ a port and resort on the east coast of Tunisia; pop. (1984) 83,500.

soutache /suːˈtæʃ/ n. a narrow flat ornamental braid used to trim garments. [F f. Magyar *sujtás*]

soutane /suːˈtɑːn/ n. RC Ch. a cassock worn by a priest. [F f. It. *sottana* f. *sotto* under f. L *subtus*]

souteneur /ˌsuːtəˈnɜː(r)/ n. a pimp. [F, = protector]

souter /ˈsuːtə(r)/ n. Sc. & N.Engl. a shoemaker; a cobbler. [OE *sūtere* f. L *sutor* f. *suere* sut- sew]

souterrain /ˈsuːtəˌreɪn/ n. esp. Archaeol. an underground chamber or passage. [F f. *sous* under + *terre* earth]

south /saʊθ/ n., adj., adv., & v. —n. **1** the point of the horizon 90° clockwise from east. **2** the compass point corresponding to this. **3** the direction in which this lies. **4** (usu. **the South**) **a** the part of the world or a country or a town lying to the south. **b** the Southern States of the US. **5** Bridge a player occupying the position designated 'south'. —adj. **1** towards, at, near, or facing the south (*a south wall; south country*). **2** coming from the south (*south wind*). —adv. **1** towards, at, or near the south (*they travelled south*). **2** (foll. by *of*) further south than. —v.intr. **1** move towards the south. **2** (of a celestial body) cross the meridian. □ **south by east** (or **west**) between south and south-east (or south-south-west). **south pole** see POLE². **south-south-east** the point or direction midway between south and south-east. **south-south-west** the point or direction midway between south and south-west. **south wind** a wind blowing from the south. **to the south** (often foll. by *of*) in a southerly direction. [OE *sūth*]

South Africa a country occupying the southernmost part of the continent of Africa; pop. (est. 1988) 35,094,000; official languages, English and Afrikaans; administrative capital, Pretoria; seat of legislature, Cape Town. Settled by the Dutch in the 17th c., the Cape area later came under British occupation, setting in motion a series of conflicting political and economic developments leading to inland expansion, the subjugation of the native population, and finally war between the British and the Boer (Dutch) settlers at the end of the 19th c. The defeated Boer republics of the Transvaal and the Orange Free State were annexed as British Crown Colonies in 1902, but joined with the colonies of Natal and the Cape to form the self-governing Union of South Africa in 1910. After supporting Britain in both World Wars, in 1960–1 South Africa became a republic and left the Commonwealth. The dominant economic power in the southern half of the continent as a result of her well-developed agricultural and economic base and gold and diamond resources, South Africa has pursued a policy of White minority rule (apartheid), with (until 1991) only a limited liberalization, which has kept her in conflict with her Black African neighbours and complicated her international position. □□ **South African** adj. & n.

South America the southern half of the American land mass, connected to North America by the Isthmus of Panama, bordered by the Atlantic Ocean to the east and the Pacific Ocean to the west. (See AMERICA.) Colonized largely by the Spanish in the 16th c. (although the British, Dutch, and Portuguese were particularly active in the north-east), much of the continent remained part of Spain's overseas empire until liberated under the leadership of Bolívar and San Martín in the 1820s. Both culturally and ethnically the continent is now a mixture of native Indian and imported Hispanic influences, modified slightly by North European and North American penetration in the 19th and 20th centuries. Although many South American countries are still hampered by economic underdevelopment and political instability, a minority have emerged as world industrial powers in their own right.

Southampton /saʊθˈhæmpt(ə)n/ an industrial city and seaport on the south coast of England, situated on a peninsula between the estuaries of the Rivers Test and Itchen in Hampshire; pop. (1981) 204,600. From here the *Mayflower* set sail for North America in 1620, and the *Titanic* sailed on her disastrous maiden voyage on 10 April 1912.

South Australia a State comprising the central southern part of Australia; pop. (1986) 1,388,100; capital, Adelaide. In 1836 it was constituted as a hybrid of a Crown colony and chartered colony, to which no convicts were to be sent. After financial collapse it lost its semi-independent status and became a regular Crown colony in 1841. It was federated with the other States of Australia in 1901.

southbound /ˈsaʊθbaʊnd/ adj. travelling or leading southwards.

South Carolina /ˌkærəˈlaɪnə/ a State of the US on the Atlantic coast; pop. (est. 1985) 3,122,700; capital, Columbia. Settled by the Spanish and English in the 16th–17th c. and named after Charles I, it became one of the original 13 States of the US in 1788.

South China Sea see CHINA SEA.

South Dakota /dəˈkəʊtə/ a State in the north central US; pop. (est. 1985) 690,800; capital, Pierre. Acquired partly by the Louisiana Purchase in 1803, it became the 40th State of the US in 1889.

Southdown /ˈsaʊθdaʊn/ n. 1 a sheep of a breed raised esp. for mutton, orig. on the South Downs of Hampshire and Sussex. 2 this breed.

south-east n., adj., & adv. —n. 1 the point of the horizon midway between south and east. 2 the compass point corresponding to this. 3 the direction in which this lies. 4 (**South-East**) the part of a country or town lying to the south-east. —adj. of, towards, or coming from the south-east. —adv. towards, at, or near the south-east. □□ **south-easterly** adj. & adv. **south-eastern** adj.

South-East Asia Treaty Organization a defence alliance established in 1954 for countries of SE Asia and part of the SW Pacific, to further a US policy of containment of communism. Its members were Australia, Britain, France, New Zealand, Pakistan, the Philippines, Thailand, and the US. The Organization was dissolved in 1977.

southeaster /saʊθˈiːstə(r)/ n. a south-east wind.

Southend-on-Sea /saʊθˌendɒnˈsiː/ a resort town in Essex, on the Thames estuary; pop. (1981) 155,000.

souther /ˈsaʊðə(r)/ n. a south wind.

southerly /ˈsʌðəlɪ/ adj., adv., & n. —adj. & adv. 1 in a southern position or direction. 2 (of a wind) blowing from the south. —n. (pl. **-ies**) a southerly wind.

southern /ˈsʌð(ə)n/ adj. esp. Geog. 1 of or in the south; inhabiting the south. 2 lying or directed towards the south (at the southern end). □ **Southern hemisphere** the half of the earth below the equator. **southern lights** the aurora australis. **Southern States** the States in the south, esp. the south-east, of the US. □□ **southernmost** adj. [OE sūtherne (as SOUTH, -ERN)]

Southern Cross a constellation in the southern sky, also known as Crux Australis, the smallest of the constellations officially recognized by the International Astronomical Union.

It contains some noteworthy objects, such as Acrux, the 14th-brightest star in the sky, and the beautiful galactic cluster of kappa Crucis (the Jewel Box).

southerner /ˈsʌðənə(r)/ n. a native or inhabitant of the south.

Southern Ocean the body of water surrounding the continent of Antarctica.

Southern Rhodesia see ZIMBABWE.

southernwood /ˈsʌð(ə)nwʊd/ n. a bushy kind of wormwood, *Artemisia abrotanum.*

Southey /ˈsʌðɪ/, Robert (1774–1843), English poet and prose writer. His early revolutionary ideas, which he shared with his friends Coleridge and Wordsworth, later moderated and he became a leading contributor to the Tory *Quarterly Review*. His voluminous works include the long poems *Thalaba* (1801), *Madoc* (1805), and *Roderick* (1814), and the historical work *The Life of Nelson* (1813), but he is better remembered for his shorter poems, such as the ballad 'The Inchcape Rock' and 'The Battle of Blenheim'. In his verse he introduced metrical innovations; he was appointed Poet Laureate in 1813.

South Georgia a barren island in the South Atlantic, 1,120 km (700 miles) south-east of the Falkland Islands from where it is administered.

South Glamorgan /gləˈmɔːgən/ a county of South Wales; pop. (1981) 389,900; county town, Cardiff.

southing /ˈsaʊθɪŋ/ n. 1 a southern movement. 2 Naut. the distance travelled or measured southward. 3 Astron. the angular distance of a star etc. south of the celestial equator.

South Orkney Islands a group of uninhabited islands in the South Atlantic, lying to the north-east of the Antarctic Peninsula. Discovered by Captain G. Powell in 1821, they are now administered as part of the British Antarctic Territory.

South Pacific Commission an agency established in 1947 to promote the economic and social stability of the islands in the South Pacific. There are 27 member governments and administrations, and the agency provides advice etc. in matters such as marine resources, rural management and technology, and community and education services. Its headquarters are in Noumea, New Caledonia.

southpaw /ˈsaʊθpɔː/ n. & adj. colloq. —n. a left-handed person, esp. in boxing. —adj. left-handed.

South Sandwich Islands a group of barren uninhabited islands in the South Atlantic lying 480 km (300 miles) south-east of South Georgia, with which it is administered from the Falkland Islands.

South Sea hist. the southern Pacific Ocean. □ **South Sea bubble** the fever of speculation in stock of the South Sea Company (1720). The Company had been formed in 1711 to trade with Spanish America. In 1720 it assumed responsibility for the National Debt in return for a guaranteed profit, but the speculative boom in this and in ever more implausible projects was quickly followed by the Company's collapse and a general financial catastrophe; there were matching disasters in Paris and Amsterdam. The subsequent inquiry revealed corruption among the King's ministers. The situation was saved by Sir Robert Walpole, who transferred the South Sea stock to the Bank of England and the East India Company. A statute was passed severely restricting joint-stock companies for the future.

South Shetland Islands a group of uninhabited islands in the South Atlantic, lying immediately north of the Antarctic Peninsula. Discovered in 1819 by Captain W. Smith, they are now administered as part of the British Antarctic Territory.

southward /ˈsaʊθwəd/ adj., adv., & n. —adj. & adv. (also **southwards**) towards the south. —n. a southward direction or region.

south-west n., adj., & adv. —n. 1 the point of the horizon midway between south and west. 2 the compass point corresponding to this. 3 the direction in which this lies. 4 (**South-West**) the part of a country or town lying to the south-west. —adj. of, towards, or coming from the south-west. —adv. towards, at, or near the south-west. □□ **south-westerly** adj. & adv. **south-western** adj.

southwester /ˌsaʊθ'westə(r)/ n. a south-west wind.

South Yorkshire a metropolitan county of northern England; pop. (1981) 1,317,000.

souvenir /ˌsuːvə'nɪə(r)/ n. & v. —n. (often foll. by of) a memento of an occasion, place, etc. —v.tr. sl. take as a 'souvenir'; pilfer, steal. [F f. souvenir remember f. L subvenire occur to the mind (as SUB-, venire come)]

souvlaki /suː'vlɑːkɪ/ n. (pl. **souvlakia** /-kɪə/) a Greek dish of pieces of meat grilled on a skewer. [mod. Gk]

sou'wester /saʊ'westə(r)/ n. **1** = SOUTHWESTER. **2** a waterproof hat with a broad flap covering the neck.

sov. /sɒv/ abbr. Brit. sovereign.

sovereign /'sɒvrɪn/ n. & adj. —n. **1** a supreme ruler, esp. a monarch. **2** Brit. hist. a gold coin nominally worth £1. —adj. **1 a** supreme (sovereign power). **b** unmitigated (sovereign contempt). **2** excellent; effective (a sovereign remedy). **3** possessing sovereign power (a sovereign State). **4** royal (our sovereign lord). □ **the sovereign good** the greatest good, esp. for a State, its people, etc. **sovereign pontiff** see PONTIFF. □□ **sovereignly** adv. **sovereignty** n. (pl. **-ies**). [ME f. OF so(u)verain f. L: -g- by assoc. with reign]

soviet /'səʊvɪət, 'sɒ-/ n. & adj. —n. **1** an elected local, district, or national council in the USSR. **2** (**Soviet**) a citizen of the USSR. **3** hist. a revolutionary council of workers, peasants, etc. before 1917. —adj. (usu. **Soviet**) of or concerning the Soviet Union. □ **Supreme Soviet** the governing council of the USSR or of any of its constituent republics. As the highest legislative authority in the Soviet Union the Supreme Soviet is responsible for electing the Presidium, the supreme authority when the Soviet is not sitting. It is composed of two equal chambers: the Soviet of Union, composed of one delegate for every 300,000 citizens, and the Soviet of Nationalities, elected on a regional basis in the component republics and areas. □□ **Sovietize** v.tr. (also **-ise**). **Sovietization** /-taɪ'zeɪʃ(ə)n/ n. [Russ. sovet council]

sovietologist /ˌsəʊvɪə'tɒlədʒɪst, ˌsɒ-/ n. a person who studies the Soviet Union.

Soviet Union the Union of Soviet Socialist Republics.

sow[1] /səʊ/ v.tr. (past **sowed** /səʊd/; past part. **sown** /səʊn/ or **sowed**) **1** (also absol.) **a** scatter (seed) on or in the earth. **b** (often foll. by with) plant (a field etc.) with seed. **2** initiate; arouse (sowed doubt in her mind). **3** (foll. by with) cover thickly with. □ **sow the seed** (or **seeds**) **of** first give rise to; implant (an idea etc.). □□ **sower** n. **sowing** n. [OE sāwan f. Gmc]

sow[2] /saʊ/ n. **1 a** a female adult pig, esp. after farrowing. **b** a female guinea-pig. **c** the female of some other species. **2 a** the main trough through which molten iron runs into side-channels to form pigs. **b** a large block of iron so formed. **3** (in full **sow bug**) esp. US a woodlouse. [OE sugu]

sowback /'saʊbæk/ n. a low ridge of sand etc.

sowbread /'saʊbred/ n. a tuberous plant, Cyclamen hederifolium, with solitary nodding flowers.

Soweto /sə'weɪtəʊ/ a large predominantly Black urban area, south-west of Johannesburg, that is an amalgamation of several townships, where in June 1976 Black schoolchildren and students demonstrated against legislation proposing to make Afrikaans the compulsory language of instruction. Violence followed, and by the end of the year some 500 Blacks and Coloureds had been killed, many of them children. The plans for compulsory teaching in Afrikaans were dropped. Anniversaries of the demonstrations have been marked by further violence on both sides. [South West Township]

sown past part. of SOW[1].

sowthistle /'saʊˌθɪs(ə)l/ n. any plant of the genus Sonchus with thistle-like leaves and milky juice.

sox informal or Commerce pl. of SOCK[1].

soy /sɔɪ/ n. (also **soya** /'sɔɪjə/) **1** (also **soy sauce**) a sauce made in Japan and China from pickled soya beans. **2** (in full **soy bean**) = soya bean. [Jap. shō-yu f. Chin. shi-you f. shi salted beans + you oil]

soya /'sɔɪə/ n. (in full **soya bean**) **1 a** a leguminous plant, Glycine soja, orig. of SE Asia, cultivated for the edible oil and flour it

yields, and used as a replacement for animal protein in certain foods. **b** the seed of this. **2** (also **soya sauce**) = SOY 1. [Du. soja f. Malay soi (as SOY)]

Soyinka /ʃɔɪ'ɪŋkə/, Wole (1934–), Nigerian playwright and novelist, educated in Nigeria and England. His play A Dance of the Forests (1960) is a half-satirical, half-fantastic celebration of Nigeria's independence. His first novel, The Interpreters (1965), captures the idealism of young Nigerians seeking the development of a new Africa; Death and the King's Housemen (1975) embodies his post-Biafran cultured philosophy, expressed in Myth, Literature and the African World (1976) of the need for the distinct aesthetics of Africa and Europe to cross-fertilize each other. Soyinka was awarded the Nobel Prize for literature in 1986.

sozzled /'sɒz(ə)ld/ adj. colloq. very drunk. [past part. of dial. sozzle mix sloppily (prob. imit.)]

SP abbr. starting price.

spa /spɑː/ n. **1** a curative mineral spring. **2** a place or resort with this. [Spa in Belgium, celebrated since medieval times for the curative properties of its mineral springs]

space /speɪs/ n. & v. —n. **1 a** a continuous unlimited area or expanse which may or may not contain objects etc. **b** an interval between one, two, or three-dimensional points or objects (a space of 10 metres). **c** an empty area; room (clear a space in the corner; occupies too much space). **2** a large unoccupied region (the wide open spaces). **3** = outer space. **4** an interval of time (in the space of an hour). **5** the amount of paper used in writing etc. (hadn't the space to discuss it). **6 a** a blank between printed, typed, or written words, etc. **b** a piece of metal providing this. **7** Mus. each of the blanks between the lines of a staff. —v.tr. **1** set or arrange at intervals. **2** put spaces between (esp. words, letters, lines, etc. in printing, typing, or writing). **3** (as **spaced** adj.) (often foll. by out) sl. in a state of euphoria, esp. from taking drugs. □ **space age** the era when space travel has become possible. **space-bar** a long key in a typewriter for making a space between words etc. **space flight 1** a journey through space. **2** = space travel. **space out** put more or wider spaces or intervals between. **space probe** = PROBE n. 4. **space rocket** a rocket used to launch a spacecraft. **space-saving** occupying little space. **space shuttle** a rocket for repeated use esp. between the earth and a space station. (See SPACECRAFT.) **space station** an artificial satellite used as a base for operations in space. **space-time** (or **space-time continuum**) the fusion of the concepts of space and time, esp. as a four-dimensional continuum. **space travel** travel through outer space. **space traveller** a traveller in outer space; an astronaut. **space vehicle** = SPACECRAFT. **space walk** any physical activity by an astronaut in space outside a spacecraft. □□ **spacer** n. **spacing** n. (esp. in sense 2 of v.). [ME f. OF espace f. L spatium]

spacecraft n. a vehicle for travelling in outer space. The first spacecraft to be launched into orbit was the Soviet Sputnik I, launched on 4 Oct. 1957, the fortieth anniversary of the start of the Russian Revolution. The first manned spacecraft took the Soviet pilot Yuri Gagarin into orbit on 12 Apr. 1961, and on 21 July 1969 two US astronauts landed on the moon. The first reusable spacecraft was the American space shuttle which made its first mission in 1981.

spaceman /'speɪsmæn/ n. (pl. **-men**; fem. **spacewoman**, pl. **-women**) = space traveller.

spaceship /'speɪsʃɪp/ n. a spacecraft, esp. one controlled by its crew.

spacesuit /'speɪssjuːt, -suːt/ n. a garment designed to allow an astronaut to survive in space.

spacial var. of SPATIAL.

spacious /'speɪʃəs/ adj. having ample space; covering a large area; roomy. □□ **spaciously** adv. **spaciousness** n. [ME f. OF spacios or L spatiosus (as SPACE)]

spade[1] /speɪd/ n. & v. —n. **1** a tool used for digging or cutting the ground etc., with a sharp-edged metal blade and a long handle. **2** a tool of a similar shape for various purposes, e.g. for removing the blubber from a whale. **3** anything resembling a spade. —v.tr. dig over (ground) with a spade. □ **call a spade a**

spade speak plainly or bluntly. **spade beard** an oblong-shaped beard. **spade foot** a square spadelike enlargement at the end of a chair-leg. □□ **spadeful** n. (pl. **-fuls**). [OE spadu, spada]

spade² /speɪd/ n. **1 a** a playing-card of a suit denoted by black inverted heart-shaped figures with small stalks. **b** (in pl.) this suit. **2** sl. offens. a Black. □ **in spades** sl. to a high degree, with great force. **spade guinea** hist. a guinea of George III's reign with a spade-shaped shield on the reverse. [It. spade pl. of spada sword f. L spatha f. Gk spathē, rel. to SPADE¹: assoc. with the shape of a pointed spade]

spadework /ˈspeɪdwɜːk/ n. hard or routine preparatory work.

spadille /spəˈdɪl/ n. **1** the ace of spades in ombre and quadrille. **2** the highest trump, esp. the ace of spades. [F f. Sp. espadilla dimin. of espada sword (as SPADE²)]

spadix /ˈspeɪdɪks/ n. (pl. **spadices** /-ˌsiːz/) Bot. a spike of flowers closely arranged round a fleshy axis and usu. enclosed in a spathe. □□ **spadiceous** /-ˈdɪʃəs/ adj. [L f. Gk, = palm-branch]

spae /speɪ/ v.intr. & tr. Sc. foretell; prophesy. [ME f. ON spá]

spaewife /ˈspeɪwaɪf/ n. Sc. a female fortune-teller or witch.

spaghetti /spəˈgetɪ/ n. pasta made in solid strings, between macaroni and vermicelli in thickness. □ **spaghetti Bolognese** /ˌbɒləˈneɪz/ spaghetti served with a sauce of minced beef, tomato, onion, etc. **spaghetti junction** a multi-level road junction, esp. on a motorway. **spaghetti western** a western film made cheaply in Italy. [It., pl. of dimin. of spago string: Bolognese It., = of Bologna]

spahi /ˈspɑːhiː/ n. hist. **1** a member of the Turkish irregular cavalry. **2** a member of the Algerian cavalry in French service. [Turk. sipāhī formed as SEPOY]

Spain /speɪn/ a country in SW Europe, occupying the greater part of the Iberian peninsula; pop. (est. 1988) 39,209,750; official language, Spanish; capital, Madrid. Conquered successively by the Carthaginians, Romans, Visigoths, and Arabs, Spain was reunited by the marriage of Ferdinand of Aragon and Isabella of Castile at the end of the 15th c. and emerged under the Hapsburg kings of the 16th c. to become the dominant European power. Thereafter it declined, suffering as a result of the War of the Spanish Succession and the Napoleonic War, and losing most of its overseas empire in the early 19th c. Endemic political instability finally resulted in the Spanish Civil War (1936–9) and the establishment of a Fascist dictatorship under Franco. Franco's death in 1975 was followed by the re-establishment of a constitutional monarchy and a pronounced liberalization of the State, but the country's political problems have yet to be finally resolved. Despite some industrialization and a massive development of the tourist trade, Spain remains predominantly agricultural and, in European terms, economically under-developed. It became a member of the European Community on 1 Jan. 1986.

spake /speɪk/ archaic past of SPEAK.

spall /spɔːl/ n. & v. —n. a splinter or chip, esp. of rock. —v.intr. & tr. break up or cause (ore) to break up in preparation for sorting. [ME (also spale): orig. unkn.]

spallation /spɔːˈleɪʃ(ə)n/ n. Physics the breakup of a bombarded nucleus into several parts.

spalpeen /spælˈpiːn/ n. Ir. **1** a rascal; a villain. **2** a youngster. [Ir. spailpín, of unkn. orig.]

Spam /spæm/ n. propr. a tinned meat product made mainly from ham. [spiced ham]

span¹ /spæn/ n. & v. —n. **1** the full extent from end to end in space or time (the span of a bridge; the whole span of history). **2** each arch or part of a bridge between piers or supports. **3** the maximum lateral extent of an aeroplane, its wing, a bird's wing, etc. **4 a** the maximum distance between the tips of the thumb and little finger. **b** this as a measurement, equal to 9 inches. **5** a short distance or time (our life is but a span). —v. (**spanned**, **spanning**) **1** tr. **a** (of a bridge, arch, etc.) stretch from side to side of; extend across (the bridge spanned the river). **b** (of a builder etc.) bridge (a river etc.). **2** tr. extend across (space or a period of time etc.). **3** tr. measure or cover the extent of (a thing) with one's hand with the fingers stretched (spanned a tenth on the piano). **4** intr. US move in distinct stretches like the span-worm.

□ **span roof** a roof with two inclined sides (opp. PENTHOUSE 2, lean-to (see LEAN¹)). **span-worm** US the caterpillar of the geometer moth. [OE span(n) or OF espan]

span² /spæn/ n. **1** Naut. a rope with both ends fastened to take purchase in a loop. **2** US a matched pair of horses, mules, etc. **3** S.Afr. a team of two or more pairs of oxen. [LG & Du. span f. spannen unite]

span³ see SPICK AND SPAN.

span⁴ /spæn/ archaic past of SPIN.

spandrel /ˈspændrɪl/ n. Archit. **1** the almost triangular space between one side of the outer curve of an arch, a wall, and the ceiling or framework. **2** the space between the shoulders of adjoining arches and the ceiling or moulding above. □ **spandrel wall** a wall built on the curve of an arch, filling in the spandrel. [perh. f. AF spaund(e)re, or f. espaundre EXPAND]

spang /spæŋ/ adv. US colloq. exactly; completely (spang in the middle). [20th c.: orig. unkn.]

spangle /ˈspæŋg(ə)l/ n. & v. —n. **1 a** small thin piece of glittering material esp. used in quantity to ornament a dress etc.; a sequin. **2** a small sparkling object. **3** (in full **spangle gall**) a spongy excrescence on oak-leaves. —v.tr. (esp. as **spangled** adj.) cover with or as with spangles (star-spangled; spangled costume). □□ **spangly** /-ŋglɪ/ adj. [ME f. spang f. MDu. spange, OHG spanga, ON spöng brooch f. Gmc]

Spaniard /ˈspænjəd/ n. **1 a** a native or national of Spain. **b** a person of Spanish descent. **2** NZ a spear grass. [ME f. OF Espaignart f. Espaigne Spain]

spaniel /ˈspænj(ə)l/ n. **1 a** a dog of any of various breeds with a long silky coat and drooping ears. **b** any of these breeds. **2** an obsequious or fawning person. [ME f. OF espaigneul Spanish (dog) f. Rmc Hispaniolus (unrecorded) f. Hispania Spain]

Spanish /ˈspænɪʃ/ adj. & n. —adj. of or relating to Spain or its people or language. —n. **1** the language of Spain and Spanish America. (See below.) **2** (prec. by the; treated as pl.) the people of Spain. □ **Spanish America** those parts of America orig. settled by Spaniards, including Central and South America and part of the West Indies. **Spanish Armada** hist. the Spanish war fleet sent against England in 1588. (See ARMADA.) **Spanish bayonet** a yucca, Yucca aloifolia, with stiff sharp-pointed leaves. **Spanish chestnut** = CHESTNUT n. 1b. **Spanish fly** a bright green beetle, Lytta vesicatoria, formerly dried and used for raising blisters, as a supposed aphrodisiac, etc. **Spanish goat** a goat, Capra pyrenaica, inhabiting the Pyrenees. **Spanish guitar** the standard six-stringed acoustic guitar, used esp. for classical and folk music. **Spanish mackerel** any of various large mackerels, esp. Scomber colias or S. maculatus. **Spanish Main** hist. the NE coast of South America between the Orinoco River and Panama, and adjoining parts of the Caribbean Sea. **Spanish omelette** an omelette containing chopped vegetables and often not folded. **Spanish onion** a large mild-flavoured onion. **Spanish windlass** the use of a stick as a lever for tightening ropes etc. [ME f. Spain, with shortening of the first element]

Spanish is the most widely spoken of the Romance languages, with many Arabic words dating from the time when the Moors dominated Spain (8th–15th c.); there are in all about 225 million speakers. It is the official language of Spain and of every South American republic except Brazil and Guyana, and is widely spoken in the Southern States of the US. In sound it is very like Italian, with a strong 'r' sound and with many masculine words ending in -o and feminine words in -a; the ñ sound /-nj-/ is characteristic. A variety of Spanish known as Ladino is spoken in Turkey and Israel by descendants of Jews expelled from Spain in 1492.

Spanish-American War the war between Spain and the US in the Caribbean and the Philippines in 1898. American public opinion having been aroused by Spanish atrocities in Cuba and the destruction of the US warship Maine in Santiago harbour, the United States declared war and destroyed the Spanish fleets in both the Pacific and the West Indies before successfully invading Cuba, Puerto Rico, and the Philippines, all of which Spain gave up by the Treaty of Paris, signed at the end of the year.

Spanish Sahara see WESTERN SAHARA.

Spanish Succession, War of the (1701–14), a European war, provoked by the death of the Spanish king Charles II without issue, marking the end of Louis XIV's attempts to establish French dominance over Europe. The Grand Alliance of Britain, Holland, and the Holy Roman Emperor, largely through the victories of Marlborough, threw back the French invasion of the Low Countries, and, although the Treaty of Utrecht (1713–14) confirmed the accession of a Bourbon king in Spain, it prevented Spain and France being united under one crown.

Spanish Town the second-largest town of Jamaica; pop. (1982) 89,100.

spank /spæŋk/ v. & n. —v. 1 tr. slap esp. on the buttocks with the open hand, a slipper, etc. 2 intr. (of a horse etc.) move briskly, esp. between a trot and a gallop. —n. a slap esp. with the open hand on the buttocks. [perh. imit.]

spanker /'spæŋkə(r)/ n. 1 a person or thing that spanks. 2 Naut. a fore-and-aft sail set on the after side of the mizen-mast. 3 a fast horse. 4 colloq. a person or thing of notable size or quality.

spanking /'spæŋkɪŋ/ adj., adv., & n. —adj. 1 (esp. of a horse) moving quickly; lively; brisk (at a spanking trot). 2 colloq. striking; excellent. —adv. colloq. very, exceedingly (spanking clean). —n. the act or an instance of slapping, esp. on the buttocks as a punishment for children.

spanner /'spænə(r)/ n. 1 Brit. an instrument for turning or gripping a nut on a screw etc. (cf. WRENCH). 2 the cross-brace of a bridge etc. □ **a spanner in the works** Brit. colloq. a drawback or impediment. [G spannen draw tight: see SPAN²]

spar¹ /spɑː(r)/ n. 1 a stout pole esp. used for the mast, yard, etc. of a ship. 2 the main longitudinal beam of an aeroplane wing. □ **spar-buoy** a buoy made of a spar with one end moored so that the other stands up. **spar-deck** the light upper deck of a vessel. [ME sparre, sperre f. OF esparre or ON sperra or direct f. Gmc: cf. MDu., MLG sparre, OS, OHG sparro]

spar² /spɑː(r)/ v. & n. —v.intr. (**sparred, sparring**) 1 (often foll. by at) make the motions of boxing without landing heavy blows. 2 engage in argument (they are always sparring). 3 (of a gamecock) fight with the feet or spurs. —n. 1 a sparring motion. b a boxing-match. 2 a cock-fight. 3 an argument or dispute. □ **sparring partner** 1 a boxer employed to engage in sparring with another as training. 2 a person with whom one enjoys arguing. [ME f. OE sperran, spyrran, of unkn. orig.: cf. ON sperrask kick out]

spar³ /spɑː(r)/ n. any crystalline, easily cleavable and non-lustrous mineral, e.g. calcite or fluorspar. □□ **sparry** adj. [MLG, rel. to OE spæren of plaster, spærstān gypsum]

sparable /'spærəb(ə)l/ n. a headless nail used for the soles and heels of shoes. [contr. of sparrow-bill, also used in this sense]

sparaxis /spə'ræksɪs/ n. any S. African iridaceous plant of the genus Sparaxis, with showy flowers and jagged spathes. [mod.L f. Gk, = laceration, f. sparassō tear]

spare /speə(r)/ adj., n., & v. —adj. 1 a not required for ordinary use; extra (have no spare cash; spare time). b reserved for emergency or occasional use (slept in the spare room). 2 lean; thin. 3 scanty; frugal; not copious (a spare diet; a spare prose style). 4 colloq. not wanted or used by others (a spare seat in the front row). —n. 1 Brit. a spare part; a duplicate. 2 Bowling the knocking-down of all the pins with the first two balls. —v. 1 tr. afford to give or do without; dispense with (cannot spare him just now; can spare you a couple). 2 tr. a abstain from killing, hurting, wounding, etc. (spared his feelings; spared her life). b abstain from inflicting or causing; relieve from (spare me this talk; spare my blushes). 3 tr. be frugal or grudging of (no expense spared). 4 intr. archaic be frugal. □ **go spare** colloq. 1 Brit. become extremely angry or distraught. 2 be unwanted by others. **not spare oneself** exert one's utmost efforts. **spare part** a duplicate part to replace a lost or damaged part of a machine etc. **spare tyre 1** an extra tyre carried in a motor vehicle for emergencies. **2** Brit. colloq. a roll of fat round the waist. **to spare** left over; additional (an hour to spare). □□ **sparely** adv. **spareness** n. **sparer** n. [OE spær, sparian f. Gmc]

spare-rib /speə'rɪb/ n. closely-trimmed ribs of esp. pork. [prob. f. MLG ribbesper, by transposition and assoc. with SPARE]

sparge /spɑːdʒ/ v.tr. moisten by sprinkling, esp. in brewing. □□ **sparger** n. [app. f. L spargere sprinkle]

sparing /'speərɪŋ/ adj. **1** inclined to save; economical. **2** restrained; limited. □□ **sparingly** adv. **sparingness** n.

Spark /spɑːk/, Muriel (1918–), British author, of Scottish-Jewish descent. She became a Roman Catholic in 1954. Her novels include Memento Mori (1959), a comic and macabre study of old age; The Ballad of Peckham Rye (1960), a bizarre tale of the underworld; The Prime of Miss Jean Brodie (1961), a disturbing portrait of an Edinburgh schoolmistress and her favoured pupils; and Loitering with Intent (1981), on the problems of biography and autobiography. Her novels, with the exception of The Mandelbaum Gate (1965), are short, elegant, eccentric, and sophisticated, with touches of the bizarre and the perverse, and her use of narrative omniscience is highly distinctive.

spark¹ /spɑːk/ n. & v. —n. **1 a** a fiery particle thrown off from a fire, or alight in ashes, or produced by a flint, match, etc. **2** (often foll. by of) a particle of a quality etc. (not a spark of life; a spark of interest). **3** Electr. **a** a light produced by a sudden disruptive discharge through the air etc. **b** such a discharge serving to ignite the explosive mixture in an internal-combustion engine. **4 a** a flash of wit etc. **b** anything causing interest, excitement, etc. **c** (also **bright spark**) a witty or lively person. **5** a small bright object or point, e.g. in a gem. **6** (**Sparks**) a nickname for a radio operator or an electrician. —v. **1** intr. emit sparks of fire or electricity. **2** tr. (often foll. by off) stir into activity; initiate (a process) suddenly. **3** intr. Electr. produce sparks at the point where a circuit is interrupted. □ **spark chamber** an apparatus designed to show ionizing particles. **spark-gap** the space between electric terminals where sparks occur. **sparking-plug** Brit. = spark-plug. **spark-plug** a device for firing the explosive mixture in an internal-combustion engine. □□ **sparkless** adj. **sparky** adj. [ME f. OE spærca, spearca]

spark² /spɑːk/ n. & v. —n. **1** a lively young fellow. **2** a gallant, a beau. —v.intr. play the gallant. □□ **sparkish** adj. [prob. a fig. use of SPARK¹]

sparkle /'spɑːk(ə)l/ v. & n. —v.intr. **1 a** emit or seem to emit sparks; glitter; glisten (her eyes sparkled). **b** be witty; scintillate (sparkling repartee). **2** (of wine etc.) effervesce (cf. STILL¹ adj. 4). —n. a gleam, spark. □□ **sparkly** adj. [ME f. SPARK¹ + -LE⁴]

sparkler /'spɑːklə(r)/ n. **1** a person or thing that sparkles. **2** a hand-held sparkling firework. **3** colloq. a diamond or other gem.

sparling /'spɑːlɪŋ/ n. a European smelt, Osmerus eperlanus. [ME f. OF esperlinge, of Gmc orig.]

sparoid /'spærɔɪd/ n. & adj. —n. any marine fish of the family Sparidae, e.g. a porgy. —adj. of or concerning the Sparidae. [mod.L Sparoides f. L sparus f. Gk sparos sea-bream]

sparrow /'spærəʊ/ n. **1** any small brownish-grey bird of the genus Passer, esp. the house sparrow and tree sparrow. **2** any of various birds of similar appearance such as the hedge sparrow. □ **sparrow-grass** dial. or colloq. asparagus. [OE spearwa f. Gmc]

sparrowhawk /'spærəʊˌhɔːk/ n. a small hawk, Accipiter nisus, preying on small birds.

sparse /spɑːs/ adj. thinly dispersed or scattered; not dense (sparse population; sparse greying hair). □□ **sparsely** adv. **sparseness** n. **sparsity** n. [L sparsus past part. of spargere scatter]

Sparta /'spɑːtə/ a city in the southern Peloponnese in Greece, capital of the prefecture of Lakonia; pop. 11,900. After enslaving the surrounding populations as helots, in the 5th c. BC Sparta became the chief rival of Athens, whom she defeated in the Peloponnesian War. The ancient Spartans were renowned for the military organization of their State and for their rigorous discipline, courage, and austerity.

Spartacus /'spɑːtəkəs/ (1st c. BC) Thracian gladiator who led a revolt against Rome in 73 BC. He defeated the Romans in a number of engagements in Italy; his army increased to a total of 90,000. He was eventually defeated by Crassus in 71 BC.

Spartan /'spɑːt(ə)n/ adj. & n. —adj. **1** of or relating to ancient Sparta. **2 a** possessing the qualities of courage, endurance, stern frugality, etc., associated with Sparta. **b** (of a regime, conditions, etc.) lacking comfort; austere. —*n.* a citizen of Sparta. [ME f. L *Spartanus* f. *Sparta* f. Gk *Sparta*, *-tē*]

spartina /spɑːˈtiːnə/ *n.* any grass of the genus *Spartina*, with rhizomatous roots and growing in wet or marshy ground. [Gk *spartinē* rope]

spasm /ˈspæz(ə)m/ *n.* **1** a sudden involuntary muscular contraction. **2** a sudden convulsive movement or emotion etc. (*a spasm of coughing*). **3** (usu. foll. by *of*) *colloq.* a brief spell of an activity. [ME f. OF *spasme* or L *spasmus* f. Gk *spasmos*, *spasma* f. *spaō* pull]

spasmodic /spæzˈmɒdɪk/ *adj.* **1** of, caused by, or subject to, a spasm or spasms (*a spasmodic jerk; spasmodic asthma*). **2** occurring or done by fits and starts (*spasmodic efforts*). □□ **spasmodically** *adv.* [mod.L *spasmodicus* f. Gk *spasmōdēs* (as SPASM)]

spastic /ˈspæstɪk/ *adj.* & *n.* —*adj.* **1** *Med.* suffering from cerebral palsy with spasm of the muscles. **2** *offens.* weak, feeble, incompetent. **3** spasmodic. —*n.* *Med.* a spastic person. □□ **spastically** *adv.* **spasticity** /-ˈtɪsɪtɪ/ *n.* [L *spasticus* f. Gk *spastikos* pulling f. *spaō* pull]

spat[1] *past* and *past part.* of SPIT.

spat[2] /spæt/ *n.* **1** (usu. in *pl.*) *hist.* a short cloth gaiter protecting the shoe from mud etc. **2** a cover for an aircraft wheel. [abbr. of SPATTERDASH]

spat[3] /spæt/ *n.* & *v.* *US colloq.* —*n.* **1** a petty quarrel. **2** a slight amount. —*v.intr.* (**spatted**, **spatting**) quarrel pettily. [prob. imit.]

spat[4] /spæt/ *n.* & *v.* —*n.* the spawn of shellfish, esp. the oyster. —*v.* (**spatted**, **spatting**) **1** *intr.* (of an oyster) spawn. **2** *tr.* shed (spawn). [AF, of unkn. orig.]

spatchcock /ˈspætʃkɒk/ *n.* & *v.* —*n.* a chicken or esp. game bird split open and grilled. —*v.tr.* **1** treat (poultry) in this way. **2** *colloq.* insert or interpolate (a phrase, sentence, story, etc.) esp. incongruously. [orig. in Ir. use, expl. by Grose (1785) as f. *dispatch-cock*, but cf. SPITCHCOCK]

spate /speɪt/ *n.* **1** a river-flood (*the river is in spate*). **2** a large or excessive amount (*a spate of enquiries*). [ME, Sc. & N.Engl.: orig. unkn.]

spathe /speɪð/ *n.* *Bot.* a large bract or pair of bracts enveloping a spadix or flower-cluster. □□ **spathaceous** /spəˈθeɪʃəs/ *adj.* [L f. Gk *spathē* broad blade etc.]

spathic /ˈspæθɪk/ *adj.* (of a mineral) like spar (see SPAR[3]), esp. in cleavage. □ **spathic iron ore** = SIDERITE. □□ **spathose** *adj.* [*spath* spar f. G *Spath*]

spatial /ˈspeɪʃ(ə)l/ *adj.* (also **spacial**) of or concerning space (*spatial extent*). □□ **spatiality** /-ʃɪˈælɪtɪ/ *n.* **spatialize** *v.tr.* (also **-ise**). **spatially** *adv.* [L *spatium* space]

spatio-temporal /ˌspeɪʃɪəʊˈtempər(ə)l/ *adj.* *Physics* & *Philos.* belonging to both space and time or to space-time. □□ **spatio-temporally** *adv.* [formed as SPATIAL + TEMPORAL]

spatter /ˈspætə(r)/ *v.* & *n.* —*v.* **1** *tr.* **a** (often foll. by *with*) splash (a person etc.) (*spattered him with mud*). **b** scatter or splash (liquid, mud, etc.) here and there. **2** *intr.* (of rain etc.) fall here and there (*glass spattered down*). **3** *tr.* slander (a person's honour etc.). —*n.* **1** (usu. foll. by *of*) a splash (*a spatter of mud*). **2** a quick pattering sound. [frequent. f. base as in Du., LG *spatten* burst, spout]

spatterdash /ˈspætədæʃ/ *n.* **1** (usu. in *pl.*) *hist.* a cloth or other legging to protect the stockings etc. from mud etc. **2** *US* = ROUGHCAST.

spatula /ˈspætjʊlə/ *n.* **1** a broad-bladed knife-like implement used for spreading, stirring, mixing (paints), etc. **2** a doctor's instrument for pressing the tongue down or to one side. [L, var. of *spathula*, dimin. of *spatha* SPATHE]

spatulate /ˈspætjʊlət/ *adj.* **1** spatula-shaped. **2** (esp. of a leaf) having a broad rounded end. [SPATULA]

spavin /ˈspævɪn/ *n.* *Vet.* a disease of a horse's hock with a hard bony tumour or excrescence. □ **blood** (or **bog**) **spavin** a distension of the joint by effusion of lymph or fluid. **bone spavin** a deposit of bony substance uniting the bones. □□ **spavined** *adj.* [ME f. OF *espavin*, var. of *esparvain* f. Gmc]

spawn /spɔːn/ *v.* & *n.* —*v.* **1 a** *tr.* (also *absol.*) (of a fish, frog, mollusc, or crustacean) produce (eggs). **b** *intr.* be produced as eggs or young. **2** *tr. derog.* (of people) produce (offspring). **3** *tr.* produce or generate, esp. in large numbers. —*n.* **1** the eggs of fish, frogs, etc. **2** *derog.* human or other offspring. **3** a white fibrous matter from which fungi are produced; mycelium. □□ **spawner** *n.* [ME f. AF *espaundre* shed roe, OF *espandre* EXPAND]

spay /speɪ/ *v.tr.* sterilize (a female animal) by removing the ovaries. [ME f. AF *espeier*, OF *espeer* cut with a sword f. *espee* sword f. L *spatha*: see SPATHE]

SPCK *abbr.* Society for Promoting Christian Knowledge.

speak /spiːk/ *v.* (*past* **spoke** /spəʊk/; *past part.* **spoken** /ˈspəʊkən/) **1** *intr.* make articulate verbal utterances in an ordinary (not singing) voice. **2** *tr.* **a** utter (words). **b** make known or communicate (one's opinion, the truth, etc.) in this way (*never speaks sense*). **3** *intr.* **a** (foll. by *to, with*) hold a conversation (*spoke to him for an hour; spoke with them about their work*). **b** (foll. by *of*) mention in writing etc. (*speaks of it in his novel*). **c** (foll. by *for*) articulate the feelings of (another person etc.) in speech or writing (*speaks for our generation*). **4** *intr.* (foll. by *to*) **a** address; converse with (a person etc.). **b** speak in confirmation of or with reference to (*spoke to the resolution; can speak to his innocence*). **c** *colloq.* reprove (*spoke to them about their lateness*). **5** *intr.* make a speech before an audience etc. (*spoke for an hour on the topic; has a good speaking voice*). **6** *tr.* use or be able to use (a specified language) (*cannot speak French*). **7** *intr.* (of a gun, a musical instrument, etc.) make a sound. **8** *intr.* (usu. foll. by *to*) *poet.* communicate feeling etc., affect, touch (*the sunset spoke to her*). **9** *intr.* (of a hound) bark. **10** *tr.* hail and hold communication with (a ship). **11** *tr. archaic* **a** (of conduct etc.) show (a person) to be (*his conduct speaks him generous*). **b** be evidence of (*the loud laugh speaks the vacant mind*). □ **not** (or **nothing**) **to speak of** not (or nothing) worth mentioning; practically not (or nothing). **speak for itself** need no supporting evidence. **speak for oneself 1** give one's own opinions. **2** not presume to speak for others. **speak one's mind** speak bluntly or frankly. **speak out** speak loudly or freely, give one's opinion. **speak up** = *speak out*. **speak volumes** (of a fact etc.) be very significant. **speak volumes** (or **well** etc.) **for 1** be abundant evidence of. **2** place in a favourable light. □□ **speakable** *adj.* [OE *sprecan*, later *specan*]

speakeasy /ˈspiːkˌiːzɪ/ *n.* (*pl.* **-ies**) *US hist. sl.* an illicit liquor shop or drinking club during Prohibition.

speaker /ˈspiːkə(r)/ *n.* **1** a person who speaks, esp. in public. **2** a person who speaks a specified language (esp. in *comb.*: a *French-speaker*). **3** (**Speaker**) the presiding officer in a legislative assembly, esp. the House of Commons. (See below.) **4** = LOUDSPEAKER. □□ **speakership** *n.*

The Speaker of the House of Commons is a member of that House, chosen to act as its representative (to 'speak' for it, whence the title) and to preside over its debates. The first person formally mentioned as holding the office was Sir Thomas de Hungerford in 1376–7. Originally a royal nominee, the Speaker has been elected since the late 17th c., and although no longer holding ministerial office or taking part in debate remains chairman of the House with the casting vote and the power to censure, suspend, or expel members. On appointment the Speaker is ceremonially dragged to his chair, the simulated reluctance being due to the fact that nine previous holders of this office were beheaded. In the House of Lords the Speaker (who does not hold disciplinary powers) is now the Lord Chancellor or one acting as his deputy or substitute.

speaking /ˈspiːkɪŋ/ *n.* & *adj.* —*n.* the act or an instance of uttering words etc. —*adj.* **1** that speaks; capable of articulate speech. **2** (of a portrait) lifelike; true to its subject (*a speaking likeness*). **3** (in *comb.*) speaking or capable of speaking a specified foreign language (*French-speaking*). **4** with a reference or from a point of view specified (*roughly speaking; professionally speaking*). □ **on speaking terms** (foll. by *with*) **1** slightly acquainted. **2** on friendly terms. **speaking acquaintance 1** a person one knows slightly. **2** this degree of familiarity. **speaking clock** *Brit.* a telephone service giving the correct time in words. **speaking-trumpet** *hist.* an instrument for making the voice carry. **speaking-tube** a tube for conveying the voice from one room, building, etc., to another.

spear /ˈspɪə(r)/ *n.* & *v.* —*n.* **1** a thrusting or throwing weapon with a pointed usu. steel tip and a long shaft. **2** a similar barbed instrument used for catching fish etc. **3** *archaic* a spearman. **4** a pointed stem of asparagus etc. —*v.tr.* pierce or strike with or as if with a spear (*speared an olive*). □ **spear gun** a gun used to propel a spear in underwater fishing. **spear side** the male side of a family. [OE *spere*]

spearhead /ˈspɪəhed/ *n. & v.* —*n.* **1** the point of a spear. **2** an individual or group chosen to lead a thrust or attack. —*v.tr.* act as the spearhead of (an attack etc.).

spearman /ˈspɪəmən/ *n.* (*pl.* **-men**) *archaic* a person, esp. a soldier, who uses a spear.

spearmint /ˈspɪəmɪnt/ *n.* a common garden mint, *Mentha spicata*, used in cookery and to flavour chewing-gum.

spearwort /ˈspɪəwɜːt/ *n.* an aquatic plant, *Ranunculus lingua*, with thick hollow stems, long narrow spear-shaped leaves, and yellow flowers.

spec[1] /spek/ *n. colloq.* a commercial speculation or venture. □ **on spec** in the hope of success; as a gamble, on the off chance. [abbr. of SPECULATION]

spec[2] /spek/ *n. colloq.* a detailed working description; a specification. [abbr. of SPECIFICATION]

special /ˈspeʃ(ə)l/ *adj. & n.* —*adj.* **1 a** particularly good; exceptional; out of the ordinary (*bought them a special present; took special trouble*). **b** peculiar; specific; not general (*lacks the special qualities required; the word has a special sense*). **2** for a particular purpose (*sent on a special assignment*). **3** in which a person specializes (*statistics is his special field*). **4** denoting education for children with particular needs, e.g. the handicapped. —*n.* a special person or thing, e.g. a special constable, train, examination, edition of a newspaper, dish on a menu, etc. □ **special area** *Brit.* a district for which special economic provision is made in legislation. **Special Branch** (in the UK) a police department dealing with political security. **special case 1** a written statement of fact presented by litigants to a court. **2** an exceptional or unusual case. **special constable** *Brit.* a policeman sworn in to assist in times of emergency etc. **special correspondent** a journalist writing for a newspaper on special events or a special area of interest. **special delivery** a delivery of mail in advance of the regular delivery. **special drawing rights** the right to purchase extra foreign currency from the International Monetary Fund. **special edition** an extra edition of a newspaper including later news than the ordinary edition. **special effects** scenic illusions created by props and camera-work. **special intention** see INTENTION. **special jury** a jury with members of a particular social standing (cf. *common jury*). **special licence** *Brit.* a marriage licence allowing immediate marriage without banns, or at an unusual time or place. **special pleading 1** *Law* pleading with reference to new facts in a case. **2** (in general use) a specious or unfair argument favouring the speaker's point of view. **special verdict** *Law* a verdict stating the facts as proved but leaving the court to draw conclusions from them. □□ **specially** *adv.* **specialness** *n.* [ME f. OF *especial* ESPECIAL or L *specialis* (as SPECIAL)]

specialist /ˈspeʃəlɪst/ *n.* (usu. foll. by *in*) **1** a person who is trained in a particular branch of a profession, esp. medicine (*a specialist in dermatology*). **2** a person who specially or exclusively studies a subject or a particular branch of a subject. □□ **specialism** /-ˌlɪz(ə)m/ *n.* **specialistic** /-ˈlɪstɪk/ *adj.*

speciality /ˌspeʃɪˈælɪtɪ/ *n.* (*pl.* **-ies**) **1** a special pursuit, product, operation, etc., to which a company or a person gives special attention. **2** a special feature, characteristic, or skill. [ME f. OF *especialité* or LL *specialitas* (as SPECIAL)]

specialize /ˈspeʃəˌlaɪz/ *v.* (also **-ise**) **1** *intr.* (often foll. by *in*) **a** be or become a specialist (*specializes in optics*). **b** devote oneself to an area of interest, skill, etc. (*specializes in insulting people*). **2** *Biol.* **a** *tr.* (esp. in *passive*) adapt or set apart (an organ etc.) for a particular purpose. **b** *intr.* (of an organ etc.) become adapted etc. in this way. **3** *tr.* make specific or individual. **4** *tr.* modify or limit (an idea, statement, etc.). □□ **specialization** /-ˈzeɪʃ(ə)n/ *n.* [F *spécialiser* (as SPECIAL)]

specialty /ˈspeʃəltɪ/ *n.* (*pl.* **-ies**) **1** esp. *US* = SPECIALITY. **2** *Law*

an instrument under seal; a sealed contract. [ME f. OF (*e*)*specialté* (as SPECIAL)]

speciation /ˌspiːsɪˈeɪʃən, ˌspiːʃ-/ *n. Biol.* the formation of a new species in the course of evolution.

specie /ˈspiːʃiː, -ʃɪ/ *n.* coin money as opposed to paper money. [L, ablat. of SPECIES in phrase *in specie*]

species /ˈspiːʃiːz, -ʃɪz, ˈspiːs-/ *n.* (*pl.* same) **1** a class of things having some common characteristics. **2** *Biol.* a category in the system of classification of living organisms consisting of similar individuals capable of exchanging genes or interbreeding. **3** a kind or sort. **4** *Logic* a group subordinate to a genus and containing individuals agreeing in some common attribute(s) and called by a common name. **5** *Law* a form or shape given to materials. **6** *Eccl.* the visible form of each of the elements of consecrated bread and wine in the Eucharist. [L, = appearance, kind, beauty, f. *specere* look]

specific /spɪˈsɪfɪk/ *adj. & n.* —*adj.* **1** clearly defined; definite (*has no specific name; told me so in specific terms*). **2** relating to a particular subject; peculiar (*a style specific to that*). **3 a** of or concerning a species (*the specific name for a plant*). **b** possessing, or concerned with, the properties that characterize a species (*the specific forms of animals*). **4** (of a duty or a tax) assessed by quantity or amount, not by the value of goods. —*n.* **1** *archaic* a specific medicine or remedy. **2** a specific aspect or factor (*shall we discuss specifics?*). □ **specific cause** the cause of a particular form of a disease. **specific difference** a factor that differentiates a species. **specific disease** a disease caused by one identifiable agent. **specific gravity** = *relative density*. **specific heat capacity** the heat required to raise the temperature of the unit mass of a given substance by a given amount (usu. one degree). **specific medicine** a medicine having a distinct effect in curing a certain disease. **specific performance** *Law* the performance of a contractual duty, as ordered in cases where damages would not be adequate remedy. □□ **specifically** *adv.* **specificity** /-ˈfɪsɪtɪ/ *n.* **specificness** *n.* [LL *specificus* (as SPECIES)]

specification /ˌspesɪfɪˈkeɪʃ(ə)n/ *n.* **1** the act or an instance of specifying; the state of being specified. **2** (esp. in *pl.*) a detailed description of the construction, workmanship, materials, etc., of work done or to be done, prepared by an architect, engineer, etc. **3** a description by an applicant for a patent of the construction and use of his invention. **4** *Law* the conversion of materials into a new product not held to be the property of the owner of the materials. [med.L *specificatio* (as SPECIFY)]

specify /ˈspesɪˌfaɪ/ *v.tr.* (**-ies**, **-ied**) **1** (also *absol.*) name or mention expressly (*specified the type he needed*). **2** (usu. foll. by *that* + clause) name as a condition (*specified that he must be paid at once*). **3** include in specifications (*a French window was not specified*). □□ **specifiable** *adj.* **specifier** *n.* [ME f. OF *specifier* or LL *specificare* (as SPECIFIC)]

specimen /ˈspesɪmən/ *n.* **1** an individual or part taken as an example of a class or whole, esp. when used for investigation or scientific examination (*specimens of copper ore; a specimen of your handwriting*). **2** *Med.* a sample of urine for testing. **3** *colloq.* usu. *derog.* a person of a specified sort. [L f. *specere* look]

speciology /ˌspiːsɪˈɒlədʒɪ/ *n.* the scientific study of species or of their origin etc. □□ **speciological** /-əˈlɒdʒɪk(ə)l/ *adj.*

specious /ˈspiːʃəs/ *adj.* **1** superficially plausible but actually wrong (*a specious argument*). **2** misleadingly attractive in appearance. □□ **speciosity** /-ˈɒsɪtɪ/ *n.* **speciously** *adv.* **speciousness** *n.* [ME, = beautiful, f. L *speciosus* (as SPECIES)]

speck /spek/ *n. & v.* —*n.* **1** a small spot, dot, or stain. **2** (foll. by *of*) a particle (*speck of dirt*). **3** a rotten spot in fruit. —*v.tr.* (esp. as **specked** *adj.*) marked with specks. □□ **speckless** *adj.* [OE *specca*: cf. SPECKLE]

speckle /ˈspek(ə)l/ *n. & v.* —*n.* a small spot, mark, or stain, esp. in quantity on the skin, a bird's egg, etc. —*v.tr.* (esp. as **speckled** *adj.*) mark with speckles or patches. [ME f. MDu. *spekkel*]

specs /speks/ *n.pl. colloq.* a pair of spectacles. [abbr.]

spectacle /ˈspektək(ə)l/ *n.* **1** a public show, ceremony, etc. **2** anything attracting public attention (*a charming spectacle; a disgusting spectacle*). □ **make a spectacle of oneself** make oneself an object of ridicule. [ME f. OF f. L *spectaculum* f. *spectare* frequent. of *specere* look]

spectacled /ˈspektək(ə)ld/ *adj.* **1** wearing spectacles. **2** (of an animal) having facial markings resembling spectacles. □ **spectacled bear** a S. American bear, *Tremarctos ornatus*. **spectacled cobra** the Indian cobra.

spectacles /ˈspektək(ə)lz/ *n.pl.* (also **pair of spectacles** *sing.*) a pair of lenses in a frame resting on the nose and ears, used to correct defective eyesight or protect the eyes.

Spectacles seem to have been invented in Europe and in China at about the same time (c.1300). In Europe they originated in Italy, and for centuries were the mark of the learned man, since most people were unable to read and defective eyesight was not a great handicap. An early design shows a type of pince-nez; side-pieces came later. A portrait of St Jerome by Ghirlandaio (15th c.) shows the saint at a desk from which spectacles dangle, and he became the patron saint of the spectacle-maker's guild. With the increase of books and the spread of literacy the spectacle trade grew rapidly in the 16th c. The early rims were of horn or leather; metal ones date from *c.*1600. Bifocals worn on the nose are known from *c.*1760, when a pair was made for the American statesman Benjamin Franklin. During the 19th c. only the elderly and scholarly made use of spectacles, but with the spread of education and general health care spectacles have become common.

spectacular /spekˈtækjʊlə(r)/ *adj. & n.* —*adj.* **1** of or like a public show; striking, amazing, lavish. **2** strikingly large or obvious (*a spectacular increase in output*). —*n.* an event intended to be spectacular, esp. a musical film or play. □□ **spectacularly** *adv.* [SPECTACLE, after *oracular* etc.]

spectate /spekˈteɪt/ *v.intr.* be a spectator, esp. at a sporting event. [back-form. f. SPECTATOR]

spectator /spekˈteɪtə(r)/ *n.* a person who looks on at a show, game, incident, etc. □ **spectator sport** a sport attracting spectators rather than participants. □□ **spectatorial** /-təˈtɔːrɪəl/ *adj.* [F *spectateur* or L *spectator* f. *spectare*: see SPECTACLE]

spectra *pl.* of SPECTRUM.

spectral /ˈspektr(ə)l/ *adj.* **1 a** of or relating to spectres or ghosts. **b** ghostlike. **2** of or concerning spectra or the spectrum (*spectral colours; spectral analysis*). □□ **spectrally** *adv.*

spectre /ˈspektə(r)/ *n.* (US **specter**) **1** a ghost. **2** a haunting presentiment or preoccupation (*the spectre of war*). **3** (in *comb.*) used in the names of some animals because of their thinness, transparency, etc. (*spectre-bat; spectre-crab*). [F *spectre* or L *spectrum*: see SPECTRUM]

spectro- /ˈspektrəʊ/ *comb. form* a spectrum.

spectrochemistry /ˌspektrəʊˈkemɪstrɪ/ *n.* chemistry based on the study of the spectra of substances.

spectrogram /ˈspektrəʊˌɡræm/ *n.* a record obtained with a spectrograph.

spectrograph /ˈspektrəʊˌɡrɑːf/ *n.* an apparatus for photographing or otherwise recording spectra. □□ **spectrographic** /-ˈɡræfɪk/ *adj.* **spectrographically** /-ˈɡræfɪkəlɪ/ *adv.* **spectrography** /spekˈtrɒɡrəfɪ/ *n.*

spectroheliograph /ˌspektrəʊˈhiːlɪəˌɡrɑːf/ *n.* an instrument for taking photographs of the sun in the light of one wavelength only.

spectrohelioscope /ˌspektrəʊˈhiːlɪəˌskəʊp/ *n.* a device similar to a spectroheliograph, for visual observation.

spectrometer /spekˈtrɒmɪtə(r)/ *n.* an instrument used for the measurement of observed spectra. □□ **spectrometric** /ˌspektrəˈmetrɪk/ *adj.* **spectrometry** *n.* [G *Spektrometer* or F *spectromètre* (as SPECTRO-, -METER)]

spectrophotometer /ˌspektrəʊfəʊˈtɒmɪtə(r)/ *n.* an instrument for measuring and recording the intensity of light in various parts of the spectrum. □□ **spectrophotometric** /-təˈmetrɪk/ *adj.* **spectrophotometry** *n.*

spectroscope /ˈspektrəˌskəʊp/ *n.* an instrument for producing and recording spectra for examination. □□ **spectroscopic** /-ˈskɒpɪk/ *adj.* **spectroscopical** /-ˈskɒpɪk(ə)l/ *adj.* **spectroscopist** /-ˈtrɒskəpɪst/ *n.* [G *Spektroskop* or F *spectroscope* (as SPECTRO-, -SCOPE)]

spectroscopy /spekˈtrɒskəpɪ/ *n.* the examination and investigation of spectra (see SPECTRUM). The technique was initiated by the German scientists Kirchhoff and Bunsen after the former's discovery in 1859 that each pure substance has its own characteristic spectrum. It led to the discovery of the elements caesium and rubidium, and has been used in the study of the structures of atoms and molecules and in the investigation of celestial bodies.

spectrum /ˈspektrəm/ *n.* (*pl.* **spectra** /-trə/) **1** the band of colours, as seen in a rainbow etc., arranged in a progressive series according to their refrangibility or wavelength. The parts are arranged according to wavelength, ranging continuously from red (the longest wavelength) to violet (the shortest). It was Sir Isaac Newton who first analysed light in this way. **2** the entire range of wavelengths of electromagnetic radiation. **3 a** an image or distribution of parts of electromagnetic radiation arranged in a progressive series according to wavelength. **b** this as characteristic of a body or substance when emitting or absorbing radiation. **4** a similar image or distribution of energy, mass, etc., arranged according to frequency, charge, etc. **5** the entire range or a wide range of anything arranged by degree or quality etc. **6** (in full **ocular spectrum**) an after-image. □ **spectrum** (or **spectral**) **analysis** chemical analysis by means of a spectroscope. [L, = image, apparition f. *specere* look]

specula *pl.* of SPECULUM.

specular /ˈspekjʊlə(r)/ *adj.* **1** of or having the nature of a speculum. **2** reflecting. □ **specular iron ore** lustrous haematite. [L *specularis* (as SPECULUM)]

speculate /ˈspekjʊˌleɪt/ *v.* **1** *intr.* (usu. foll. by *on*, *upon*, *about*) form a theory or conjecture, esp. without a firm factual basis; meditate (*speculated on their prospects*). **2** *tr.* (foll. by *that*, *how*, etc. + clause) conjecture, consider (*speculated how he might achieve it*). **3** *intr.* **a** invest in stocks etc. in the hope of gain but with the possibility of loss. **b** gamble recklessly. □□ **speculator** *n.* [L *speculari* spy out, observe f. *specula* watch-tower f. *specere* look]

speculation /ˌspekjʊˈleɪʃ(ə)n/ *n.* **1** the act or an instance of speculating; a theory or conjecture (*made no speculation as to her age; is given to speculation*). **2 a** a speculative investment or enterprise (*bought it as a speculation*). **b** the practice of business speculating. **3** a game in which trump cards are bought or sold. [ME f. OF *speculation* or LL *speculatio* (as SPECULATE)]

speculative /ˈspekjʊlətɪv/ *adj.* **1** of, based on, engaged in, or inclined to speculation. **2** (of a business investment) involving the risk of loss (*a speculative builder*). □□ **speculatively** *adv.* **speculativeness** *n.* [ME f. OF *speculatif* -*ive* or LL *speculativus* (as SPECULATE)]

speculum /ˈspekjʊləm/ *n.* (*pl.* **specula** /-lə/) **1** *Surgery* an instrument for dilating the cavities of the human body for inspection. **2** a mirror, usu. of polished metal, esp. in a reflecting telescope. **3** *Ornithol.* a lustrous coloured area on the wing of some birds, esp. ducks. □ **speculum-metal** an alloy of copper and tin used as a mirror, esp. in a telescope. [L, = mirror, f. *specere* look]

sped *past* and *past part.* of SPEED.

speech /spiːtʃ/ *n.* **1** the faculty or act of speaking. **2** a formal public address. **3** a manner of speaking (*a man of blunt speech*). **4** a remark (*after this speech he was silent*). **5** the language of a nation, region, group, etc. **6** *Mus.* the act of sounding in an organ-pipe etc. □ **the Queen's** (or **King's**) **Speech** a statement including the Government's proposed measures read by the sovereign at the opening of Parliament. **speech day** *Brit.* an annual prize-giving day in many schools, usu. marked by speeches etc. **speech-reading** lip-reading. **speech therapist** a person who practises speech therapy. **speech therapy** treatment to improve defective speech. **speech-writer** a person employed to write speeches for a politician etc. to deliver. □□ **speechful** *adj.* [OE *sprǣc*, later *spēc* f. WG, rel. to SPEAK]

speechify /ˈspiːtʃɪˌfaɪ/ *v.intr.* (**-ies**, **-ied**) *joc.* or *derog.* make esp. boring or long speeches. □□ **speechification** /-fɪˈkeɪʃ(ə)n/ *n.* **speechifier** *n.*

speechless /ˈspiːtʃlɪs/ *adj.* **1** temporarily unable to speak because of emotion etc. (*speechless with rage*). **2** dumb. □□

speechlessly adv. **speechlessness** n. [OE spǣclēas (as SPEECH, -LESS)]

speed /spi:d/ n. & v. —n. **1** rapidity of movement (with all speed; at full speed). **2** a rate of progress or motion over a distance in time (attains a high speed). **3 a** a gear appropriate to a range of speeds of a bicycle. **b** US or archaic such a gear in a motor vehicle. **4** Photog. **a** the sensitivity of film to light. **b** the light-gathering power of a lens. **c** the duration of an exposure. **5** sl. an amphetamine drug, esp. methamphetamine. **6** archaic success, prosperity (send me good speed). —v. (past and past part. sped /sped/) **1** intr. go fast (sped down the street). **2** (past and past part. speeded) **a** intr. (of a motorist etc.) travel at an illegal or dangerous speed. **b** tr. regulate the speed of (an engine etc.). **c** tr. cause (an engine etc.) to go at a fixed speed. **3** tr. send fast or on its way (speed an arrow from the bow). **4** intr. & tr. archaic be or make prosperous or successful (how have you sped?; God speed you!). □ **at speed** moving quickly. **speed bump** (or **hump**) a transverse ridge in the road to control the speed of vehicles. **speed limit** the maximum speed at which a road vehicle may legally be driven in a particular area etc. **speed merchant** colloq. a motorist who enjoys driving fast. **speed up** move or work at greater speed. **speed-up** n. an increase in the speed or rate of working. □□ **speeder** n. [OE spēd, spēdan f. Gmc]

speedball /'spi:dbɔ:l/ n. sl. a mixture of cocaine with heroin or morphine.

speedboat /'spi:dbəʊt/ n. a motor boat designed for high speed.

speedo /'spi:dəʊ/ n. (pl. **-os**) colloq. = SPEEDOMETER. [abbr.]

speedometer /spi:'dɒmɪtə(r)/ n. an instrument on a motor vehicle etc. indicating its speed to the driver. [SPEED + METER[1]]

speedway /'spi:dweɪ/ n. **1 a** motor-cycle racing. **b** a stadium or track used for this. **2** US a road or track used for fast motor traffic.

speedwell /'spi:dwel/ n. any small herb of the genus Veronica, with a creeping or ascending stem and tiny blue or pink flowers. [app. f. SPEED + WELL[1]]

speedy /'spi:dɪ/ adj. (**speedier**, **speediest**) **1** moving quickly; rapid. **2** done without delay; prompt (a speedy answer). □□ **speedily** adv. **speediness** n.

speiss /spaɪs/ n. a compound of arsenic, iron, etc., formed in smelting certain lead ores. [G Speise food, amalgam]

Speke /spi:k/, John Hanning (1827–64), English explorer who accompanied (Sir) Richard Burton on expeditions to trace the source of the Nile. After they had discovered Lake Tanganyika Speke went on alone and reached a great lake which he correctly identified as the 'source reservoir' of the Nile, and named it in honour of Queen Victoria. His claim to have found the Nile source was disputed, and on the day when he was to have debated the subject publicly with Richard Burton he was killed by his own gun in a shooting accident.

speleology /ˌspi:lɪ'ɒlədʒɪ, ˌspe-/ n. **1** the scientific study of caves. **2** the exploration of caves. □□ **speleological** /-ə'lɒdʒɪk(ə)l/ adj. **speleologist** n. [F spéléologie f. L spelaeum f. Gk spēlaion cave]

spell[1] /spel/ v.tr. (past and past part. **spelt** or **spelled**) **1** (also absol.) write or name the letters that form (a word etc.) in correct sequence (spell 'exaggerate'; cannot spell properly). **2 a** (of letters) make up or form (a word etc.). **b** (of circumstances, a scheme, etc.) result in; involve (spell ruin). □ **spell out** (or **over**) **1** make out (words, writing, etc.) letter by letter. **2** explain in detail (spelled out what the change would mean). □□ **spellable** adj. [ME f. OF espel(l)er, f. Frank. (as SPELL[2])]

spell[2] /spel/ n. **1** a form of words used as a magical charm or incantation. **2** an attraction or fascination exercised by a person, activity, quality, etc. □ **under a spell** mastered by or as if by a spell. [OE spel(l) f. Gmc]

spell[3] /spel/ n. & v. —n. **1** a short or fairly short period (a cold spell in April). **2** a turn of work (did a spell of woodwork). **3** Austral. a period of rest from work. —v. **1** tr. **a** relieve or take the place of (a person) in work etc. **b** allow to rest briefly. **2** intr. Austral. take a brief rest. [earlier as verb: later form of dial. spele take place of f. OE spelian, of unkn. orig.]

spell[4] /spel/ n. a splinter of wood etc. [perh. f. obs. speld]

spellbind /'spelbaɪnd/ tr. (past and past part. **spellbound**) **1**

bind with or as if with a spell; entrance. **2** (as **spellbound** adj.) entranced, fascinated, esp. by a speaker, activity, quality, etc. □□ **spellbinder** n. **spellbindingly** adv.

speller /'spelə(r)/ n. **1** a person who spells esp. in a specified way (is a poor speller). **2** a book on spelling.

spellican var. of SPILLIKIN.

spelling /'spelɪŋ/ n. **1** the process or activity of writing or naming the letters of a word etc. **2** the way a word is spelled. **3** the ability to spell (his spelling is weak). □ **spelling-bee** a spelling competition.

spelt[1] past and past part. of SPELL[1].

spelt[2] /spelt/ n. a species of wheat, Triticum aestivum. [OE f. OS spelta (OHG spelza), ME f. MLG, MDu. spelte]

spelter /'speltə(r)/ n. impure zinc, esp. for commercial purposes. [corresp. to OF espeautre, MDu. speauter, G Spialter, rel. to PEWTER]

spelunker /spɪ'lʌŋkə(r)/ n. US a person who explores caves, esp. as a hobby. □□ **spelunking** n. [obs. spelunk cave f. L spelunca]

Spence /spens/, Sir Basil Urwin (1907–76), English architect, born in Bombay. He became known internationally in 1951 when he produced the winning design for the rebuilding of Coventry cathedral. Later he designed the 'Beehive' extension to the New Zealand Parliament building in Wellington.

spence /spens/ n. archaic a buttery or larder. [ME f. OF despense f. L dispensa fem. past part. of dispendere: see DISPENSE]

Spencer[1] /'spensə(r)/, Herbert (1820–1903), English philosopher, the leading English exponent of agnosticism in the 19th c. He worked for some years as a railway engineer and later as a sub-editor of The Economist, advocating a policy of laissez-faire. Spencer greeted Darwin's work with enthusiasm, coined the phrase 'survival of the fittest' (1864), and sought to trace an evolutionary principle in all branches of knowledge. In 1860 he published his Programme of a System of Synthetic Philosophy, to the elaboration of which he devoted the remainder of his life. Essentially an individualist, in his moral and political philosophy he deprecated State intervention and championed individual rights.

Spencer[2] /'spensə(r)/, Sir Stanley (1891–1959), English painter, best known for the pictures in which he set biblical events in his native village of Cookham in Berkshire. For him the Christian religion was a living and present reality and his visionary attitude has been compared to that of William Blake. His greatest public successes were The Resurrection: Cookham (1924–6) and the series of murals (1927–32) for the Sandham Memorial Chapel in Hampshire which depict with deep human feeling the life of the common soldier.

spencer[1] /'spensə(r)/ n. **1** a short close-fitting jacket. **2** a woman's thin usu. woollen under-bodice worn for extra warmth in winter. [prob. f. the 2nd Earl Spencer, Engl. politician d. 1834]

spencer[2] /'spensə(r)/ n. Naut. a trysail. [perh. f. K. Spencer (early 19th c.)]

spend /spend/ v.tr. (past and past part. **spent** /spent/) **1** (usu. foll. by on) **a** (also absol.) pay out (money) in making a purchase etc. (spent £5 on a new pen). **b** pay out (money) for a particular person's benefit or for the improvement of a thing (had to spend £200 on the car). **2 a** use or consume (time or energy) (shall spend no more effort; how do you spend your Sundays?). **b** (also refl.) use up; exhaust; wear out (their ammunition was all spent; his anger was soon spent; spent herself campaigning for justice). **3** tr. (as **spent** adj.) having lost its original force or strength; exhausted (the storm is spent; spent bullets). □ **spending money** pocket money. **spend a penny** Brit. colloq. urinate or defecate (from the coin-operated locks of public lavatories). □□ **spendable** adj. **spender** n. [OE spendan f. L expendere (see EXPEND): in ME perh. also f. obs. dispend f. OF despendre expend f. L dispendere: see DISPENSE]

Spender /'spendə(r)/, Sir Stephen (1909–85), English poet and critic, a contemporary at Oxford with Auden, MacNeice, and Day Lewis, whose left-wing political convictions he shared. A period spent in Germany sharpened his political consciousness. During the Spanish Civil War he actively supported the Republicans, a period reflected in The Still Centre (1939). His Poems (1933) contained both personal and political poems including the notorious 'The Pylons' which gave the nickname of 'Pylon Poets' to himself and his friends; his critical work *The Destructive Element* (1935) argues the importance of 'politico-moral' subjects in literature. A gradual shift in his political allegiance is seen in his poetry and critical works, and in his autobiography *World Within World* (1951) he gives an account of his association with the Communist Party. His interest in the public and social duty of the writer has tended to obscure the essentially tender and private nature of much of his poetry.

spendthrift /'spendθrɪft/ n. & adj. —n. an extravagant person; a prodigal. —adj. extravagant; prodigal.

Spengler /'spɛŋglə(r)/, Oswald (1880–1936), German philosopher, whose fame rests on his book *Der Untergang des Abendlande* (1918–22; translated as *The Decline of the West*, 1926–8), in which he argued that civilizations are subject to growth, flowering, and decay in a way that is analogous to that of biological species.

Spenser /'spensə(r)/, Edmund (c.1552–99), English poet. He dedicated his first major poem, *The Shepheardes Calendar* (1579) in twelve eclogues (one for each month of the year), to Sir Philip Sidney, nephew of his patron the Earl of Leicester. His greatest work is the allegorical romance, *The Faerie Queene* (1590, 1596). The general scheme is expounded in his introductory letter to Sir Walter Raleigh: by the Faerie Queene the poet celebrates Glory in the abstract and Queen Elizabeth in particular, and twelve knights were to represent the different virtues but only 6 of the 12 books were ever written. The poem is written in the stanza invented by Spenser (in which a ninth line of 12 syllables is added to 8 lines of 10 syllables); its chief beauties lie in the particular episodes with which the allegory is varied, and in the imaginative and musical descriptions such as in the Cave of Mammon. Spenser has been a major influence on many succeeding poets including Milton and Keats. He died in poverty but was buried in honour at Westminster Abbey.

Spenserian /spen'sɪərɪən/ adj. of, relating to, or in the style of Edmund Spenser. □ **Spenserian stanza** the stanza used by Spenser in the *Faerie Queene*, with eight iambic pentameters and an alexandrine, rhyming ababbcbcc.

spent past and past part. of SPEND.

sperm /spɜːm/ n. (pl. same or **sperms**) **1** = SPERMATOZOON. **2** the male reproductive fluid containing spermatozoa; semen. **3** = *sperm whale*. **4** = SPERMACETI. **5** = *sperm oil*. □ **sperm bank** a supply of semen stored for use in artificial insemination. **sperm count** the number of spermatozoa in one ejaculation or a measured amount of semen. **sperm oil** an oil obtained from the head of a sperm whale, and used as a lubricant. **sperm whale** a large whale, *Physeter macrocephalus*, hunted for the spermaceti and sperm oil contained in its bulbous head, and for the ambergris found in its intestines: also called CACHALOT. [ME f. LL *sperma* f. Gk *sperma -atos* seed f. *speirō* sow: in *sperm whale* an abbr. of SPERMACETI]

spermaceti /ˌspɜːməˈsetɪ/ n. a white waxy substance produced by the sperm whale to aid buoyancy, and used in the manufacture of candles, ointments, etc. □□ **spermacetic** adj. [ME f. med.L f. LL *sperma* sperm + *ceti* genit. of *cetus* f. Gk *kētos* whale, from the belief that it was whale-spawn]

spermary /'spɜːmərɪ/ n. (pl. **-ies**) an organ in which human or animal sperms are generated. [mod.L *spermarium* (as SPERM)]

spermatic /spɜːˈmætɪk/ adj. of or relating to a sperm or spermary. □ **spermatic cord** a bundle of nerves, ducts, and blood vessels passing to the testicles. [LL *spermaticus* f. Gk *spermatikos* (as SPERM)]

spermatid /'spɜːmətɪd/ n. Biol. an immature male sex cell formed from a spermatocyte, which may develop into a spermatozoon. □□ **spermatidal** /-'taɪd(ə)l/ adj.

spermato- /'spɜːmətəʊ/ comb. form Biol. a sperm or seed.

spermatocyte /'spɜːmətəʊˌsaɪt/ n. a cell produced from a spermatogonium and which may divide by meiosis into spermatids.

spermatogenesis /ˌspɜːmətəʊˈdʒenɪsɪs/ n. the production or development of mature spermatozoa. □□ **spermatogenetic** /-dʒɪˈnetɪk/ adj.

spermatogonium /ˌspɜːmətəʊˈɡəʊnɪəm/ n. (pl. **spermatogonia** /-nɪə/) a cell produced at an early stage in the formation of spermatozoa, from which spermatocytes develop. [SPERM + mod.L *gonium* f. Gk *gonos* offspring, seed]

spermatophore /'spɜːmətəʊˌfɔː(r)/ n. an albuminous capsule containing spermatozoa found in various invertebrates. □□ **spermatophoric** /-ˈfɔːrɪk/ adj.

spermatophyte /'spɜːmətəʊˌfaɪt/ n. any seed-bearing plant.

spermatozoid /ˌspɜːmətəʊˈzɔɪd/ n. the mature motile male sex cell of some plants.

spermatozoon /ˌspɜːmətəʊˈzəʊɒn/ n. (pl. **spermatozoa** /-ˈzəʊə/) the mature motile sex cell in animals. □□ **spermatozoal** adj. **spermatozoan** adj. **spermatozoic** adj. [SPERM + Gk *zōion* animal]

spermicide /'spɜːmɪˌsaɪd/ n. a substance able to kill spermatozoa. □□ **spermicidal** /-ˈsaɪd(ə)l/ adj.

spermo- /'spɜːməʊ/ comb. form = SPERMATO-.

spew /spjuː/ v. (also **spue**) **1** tr. & intr. vomit. **2** (often foll. by *out*) **a** tr. expel (contents) rapidly and forcibly. **b** intr. (of contents) be expelled in this way. □□ **spewer** n. [OE *spīwan*, *spēowan* f. Gmc]

sp. gr. abbr. specific gravity.

sphagnum /'sfægnəm/ n. (pl. **sphagna** /-nə/) (in full **sphagnum moss**) any moss of the genus *Sphagnum*, growing in bogs and peat, and used as packing esp. for plants, as fertilizer, etc. [mod.L f. Gk *sphagnos* a moss]

sphalerite /'sfæləraɪt/ n. = BLENDE. [Gk *sphaleros* deceptive: cf. BLENDE]

spheno- /'sfiːnəʊ/ comb. form Anat. the sphenoid bone. [Gk f. *sphēn* wedge]

sphenoid /'sfiːnɔɪd/ adj. & n. —adj. **1** wedge-shaped. **2** of or relating to the sphenoid bone. —n. (in full **sphenoid bone**) a large compound bone forming the base of the cranium behind the eyes. □□ **sphenoidal** /-ˈnɔɪd(ə)l/ adj. [mod.L *sphenoides* f. Gk *sphēnoeidēs* f. *sphēn* wedge]

sphere /sfɪə(r)/ n. & v. —n. **1** a solid figure, or its surface, with every point on its surface equidistant from its centre. **2** an object having this shape; a ball or globe. **3 a** any celestial body. **b** a globe representing the earth. **c** poet. the heavens; the sky. **d** the sky perceived as a vault upon or in which celestial bodies are represented as lying. **e** hist. each of a series of revolving concentrically arranged spherical shells in which celestial bodies were formerly thought to be set in a fixed relationship. **4 a** a field of action, influence, or existence (*have done much within their own sphere*). **b** a (usu. specified) stratum of society or social class (*moves in quite another sphere*). —v.tr. archaic or poet. **1** enclose in or as in a sphere. **2** form into a sphere. □ **music** (or **harmony**) **of the spheres** the natural harmonic tones supposedly produced by the movement of the celestial spheres (see sense 3e of n.) or the bodies fixed in them. **oblique** (or **parallel** or **right**) **sphere** the sphere of the apparent heavens at a place where there is an oblique, zero, or right angle between the equator and the horizon. **sphere of influence** the claimed or recognized area of a State's interests, an individual's control, etc. □□ **spheral** adj. [ME *sper(e)* f. OF *espere* f. LL *sphera*, L f. Gk *sphaira* ball]

-sphere /sfɪə(r)/ comb. form **1** having the form of a sphere (*bathysphere*). **2** a region round the earth (*atmosphere*).

spheric /'sfɪərɪk/ adj. = SPHERICAL. □□ **sphericity** /-ˈrɪsɪtɪ/ n.

spherical /'sferɪk(ə)l/ adj. **1** shaped like a sphere; globular. **2** of or relating to the properties of spheres (*spherical geometry*). **b** formed inside or on the surface of a sphere (*spherical triangle*). □ **spherical aberration** a loss of definition in the image produced by a spherically curved mirror or lens. **spherical angle** an angle formed by the intersection of two great circles of a sphere. □□ **spherically** adv. [LL *sphaericus* f. Gk *sphairikos* (as SPHERE)]

spheroid /'sfɪərɔɪd/ n. **1** a spherelike but not perfectly spherical body. **2** a solid generated by a half-revolution of an ellipse about its major axis (**prolate spheroid**) or minor axis (**oblate spheroid**). □□ **spheroidal** /sfɪəˈrɔɪd(ə)l/ adj. **spheroidicity** /-ˈdɪsɪtɪ/ n.

spherometer /sfɪəˈrɒmɪtə(r)/ n. an instrument for finding the radius of a sphere and for the exact measurement of the thickness of small bodies. [F *sphéromètre* (as SPHERE, -METER)]

spherule /ˈsferuːl/ n. a small sphere. □□ **spherular** adj. [LL sphaerula dimin. of L sphaera (as SPHERE)]

spherulite /ˈsferəˌlaɪt/ n. a vitreous globule as a constituent of volcanic rocks. □□ **spherulitic** /-ˈlɪtɪk/ adj.

sphincter /ˈsfɪŋktə(r)/ n. Anat. a ring of muscle surrounding and serving to guard or close an opening or tube, esp. the anus. □□ **sphincteral** adj. **sphinctered** adj. **sphincterial** /-ˈtɪərɪəl/ adj. **sphincteric** /-ˈterɪk/ adj. [L f. Gk sphigktēr f. sphiggō bind tight]

sphingid /ˈsfɪŋgɪd/ n. any hawk moth of the family Sphingidae. [as SPHINX + -ID³]

sphinx /sfɪŋks/ n. 1 a mythological monster with a human head and the body of a lion. Originating in Egypt, it became known early to Syrians, Phoenicians, and Mycenaean Greeks. In Greek literature it is a female being. One tale associates it with Thebes, where it propounded a riddle about the three ages of man and devoured whoever failed to solve this until Oedipus was successful and the sphinx committed suicide (or was killed by him). In classical art the sphinx is humanized with a beautiful serious face, and becomes the wise, enigmatic, and musical messenger of divine justice. 2 (in Egypt) a figure with a couchant lion's body and a man's or animal's head. The colossal figure of a sphinx at Giza is part of the complex of funerary monuments of the pharaoh Chephren (4th Dynasty, 3rd millennium BC). It is carved from the natural rock and completed with masonry; the beard and nose have disappeared because the monument was used as a target by a Mameluke sultan. It is believed to be an effigy of Chephren, but it came to be identified with a god whom the Greeks called Harmachis (= Horus in the horizon), and received its own cult; the Arabs called it Abu Hol (= father of terror). 3 an enigmatic or inscrutable person. 4 **a** a hawk moth. **b** a species of baboon, Papio sphinx. [L f. Gk Sphigx, app. f. sphiggō draw tight]

sphragistics /sfrəˈdʒɪstɪks/ n.pl. (also treated as sing.) the study of engraved seals. [F sphragistique (n. & adj.) f. Gk sphragistikos f. sphragis seal]

sphygmo- /ˈsfɪgməʊ/ comb. form Physiol. a pulse or pulsation. [Gk sphygmo- f. sphugmos pulse f. sphuzō to throb]

sphygmogram /ˈsfɪgməʊˌgræm/ n. a record produced by a sphygmograph.

sphygmograph /ˈsfɪgməʊˌɡrɑːf/ n. an instrument for showing the character of a pulse in a series of curves. □□ **sphygmographic** /-ˈgræfɪk/ adj. **sphygmographically** /-ˈgræfɪkəlɪ/ adv. **sphygmography** /-ˈmɒɡrəfɪ/ n.

sphygmology /sfɪgˈmɒlədʒɪ/ n. the scientific study of the pulse. □□ **sphygmological** /-məˈlɒdʒɪk(ə)l/ adj.

sphygmomanometer /ˌsfɪgməʊməˈnɒmɪtə(r)/ n. an instrument for measuring blood pressure. □□ **sphygmomanometric** /-nəˈmetrɪk/ adj.

spica /ˈspaɪkə/ n. 1 Bot. a spike or spikelike form. 2 Surgery a spiral bandage with reversed turns, suggesting an ear of corn. □□ **spicate** /-keɪt/ adj. **spicated** /-ˈkeɪtɪd/ adj. [L, = spike, ear of corn, rel. to spina SPINE: in sense 2 after Gk stakhus]

spiccato /spɪˈkɑːtəʊ/ n., adj., & adv. Mus. —n. (pl. **-os**) 1 a style of staccato playing on stringed instruments involving bouncing the bow on the strings. 2 a passage in this style. —adj. performed or to be performed in this style. —adv. in this style. [It., = detailed, distinct]

spice /spaɪs/ n. & v. —n. 1 an aromatic or pungent vegetable substance used to flavour food, e.g. cloves, pepper, or mace. 2 spices collectively (a dealer in spice). 3 **a** an interesting or piquant quality. **b** (foll. by of) a slight flavour or suggestion (a spice of malice). —v.tr. 1 flavour with spice. 2 add an interesting or piquant quality to (a book spiced with humour). [ME f. OF espice(r) f. L species specific kind: in LL pl. = merchandise]

spicebush /ˈspaɪsbʊʃ/ n. any aromatic shrub of the genus Lindera or Calycanthus, native to America.

Spice Islands see MOLUCCA ISLANDS.

spick and span /ˌspɪk ənd ˈspæn/ adj. 1 smart and new. 2 neat and clean. [16th-c. spick and span new, emphatic extension of ME span new f. ON spán-nýr f. spánn chip + nýr new]

spicknel /ˈspɪkn(ə)l/ n. = BALDMONEY. [var. of SPIGNEL]

spicule /ˈspɪkjuːl/ n. 1 any small sharp-pointed body. 2 Zool. a small hard calcareous or siliceous body, esp. in the framework of a sponge. 3 Bot. a small or secondary spike. 4 Astron. a spikelike prominence, esp. one appearing as a jet of gas in the sun's corona. □□ **spicular** adj. **spiculate** /-lət/ adj. [mod.L spicula, spiculum, dimins. of SPICA]

spicy /ˈspaɪsɪ/ adj. (**spicier**, **spiciest**) 1 of, flavoured with, or fragrant with spice. 2 piquant, pungent; sensational or improper (a spicy story). □□ **spicily** adv. **spiciness** n.

spider /ˈspaɪdə(r)/ n. & v. —n. 1 **a** any eight-legged arthropod of the order Araneae with a round unsegmented body, many of which spin webs for the capture of insects as food. **b** any of various similar or related arachnids, e.g. a red spider. 2 any object comparable to a spider, esp. as having numerous or prominent legs or radiating spokes. 3 Brit. a radiating series of elastic ties used to hold a load in place on a vehicle etc. —v.intr. 1 move in a scuttling manner suggestive of a spider (fingers spidered across the map). 2 cause to move or appear in this way. 3 (as **spidering** adj.) spiderlike in form, manner, or movement (spidering streets). □ **spider crab** any of various crabs of the family Majidae with a pear-shaped body and long thin legs. **spider monkey** any S. American monkey of the genus Ateles, with long limbs and a prehensile tail. **spider plant** any of various house plants with long narrow striped leaves. □□ **spiderish** adj. [OE spīthra (as SPIN)]

spiderman /ˈspaɪdəˌmæn/ n. (pl. **-men**) Brit. colloq. a person who works at great heights in building construction.

spiderwort /ˈspaɪdəˌwɜːt/ n. any plant of the genus Tradescantia, esp. T. virginiana, having flowers with long hairy stamens.

spidery /ˈspaɪdərɪ/ adj. elongated and thin (spidery handwriting).

spiegeleisen /ˈspiːɡ(ə)lˌaɪz(ə)n/ n. an alloy of iron and manganese, used in steel-making. [G f. Spiegel mirror + Eisen iron]

spiel /ʃpiːl/ n. & v. sl. —n. a glib speech or story, esp. a salesman's patter. —v. 1 intr. speak glibly; hold forth. 2 tr. reel off (patter etc.). [G, = play, game]

Spielberg /ˈspɪəlbɜːɡ/, Steven (1947–), American film director, whose immensely successful films include Jaws (1975), Close Encounters of the Third Kind (1977), and ET (1982).

spieler /ˈʃpiːlə(r)/ n. sl. 1 esp. US a person who spiels. 2 Austral. a gambler; a swindler. [G (as SPIEL)]

spiffing /ˈspɪfɪŋ/ adj. archaic sl. 1 excellent. 2 smart, handsome. [19th c.: orig. unkn.]

spiffy /ˈspɪfɪ/ adj. (**spiffier**, **spiffiest**) esp. US sl. = SPIFFING. □□ **spiffily** adv.

spiflicate /ˈspɪflɪˌkeɪt/ v.tr. (also **spifflicate**) esp. joc. 1 destroy. 2 beat (in a fight etc.). [18th c.: fanciful]

spignel /ˈspɪgn(ə)l/ n. = BALDMONEY. [perh. f. ME spigurnel plant-name, f. med.L spigurnellus, of unkn. orig.]

spigot /ˈspɪɡət/ n. 1 a small peg or plug, esp. for insertion into the vent-hole of a cask. 2 **a** US a tap. **b** a device for controlling the flow of liquid in a tap. 3 the plain end of a pipe-section fitting into the socket of the next one. [ME, perh. f. Prov. espigou(n) f. L spiculum dimin. of spicum = SPICA]

spike¹ /spaɪk/ n. & v. —n. 1 **a** a sharp point. **b** a pointed piece of metal, esp. the top of an iron railing etc. 2 **a** any of several metal points set into the sole of a running-shoe to prevent slipping. **b** (in pl.) a pair of running-shoes with spikes. 3 **a** a pointed metal rod standing on a base and used for filing news items etc. esp. when rejected for publication. **b** a similar spike used for bills etc. 4 a large stout nail esp. as used for railways. 5 sl. a hypodermic needle. 6 Brit. sl. a doss-house. 7 Electronics a pulse of very short duration in which a rapid increase in voltage is followed by a rapid decrease. —v.tr. 1 **a** fasten or provide with spikes. **b** fix on or pierce with spikes. 2 (of a newspaper editor etc.) reject (a story) by filing it on a spike. 3 colloq. **a** lace (a drink) with alcohol, a drug, etc. **b** contaminate (a substance) with something added. 4 make useless, put an end to, thwart (an idea etc.). 5 hist. plug up the vent of (a gun) with a spike. □ **spike a person's guns** spoil his or her plans. **spike heel** a high tapering heel of a shoe. [ME perh. f. MLG, MDu. spiker, rel. to SPOKE¹]

spike[2] /spaɪk/ n. Bot. **1** a flower-cluster formed of many flower-heads attached closely on a long stem. **2** a separate sprig of any plant in which flowers form a spikelike cluster. □□ **spikelet** n. [ME, = ear of corn, f. L SPICA]

spikenard /ˈspaɪknɑːd/ n. **1** Bot. an Indian plant, Nardostachys grandiflora. **2** hist. a costly perfumed ointment made from this. [ME ult. f. med.L spica nardi (as SPIKE[2], NARD) after Gk nardostakhus]

spiky[1] /ˈspaɪkɪ/ adj. (**spikier**, **spikiest**) **1** like a spike; having many spikes. **2** colloq. easily offended; prickly. □□ **spikily** adv. **spikiness** n.

spiky[2] /ˈspaɪkɪ/ adj. Bot. having spikes or ears.

spile /spaɪl/ n. & v. —n. **1** a wooden peg or spigot. **2** a large timber or pile for driving into the ground. **3** US a small spout for tapping the sap from a sugar-maple etc. —v.tr. make a spike-hole in (a cask etc.) in order to draw off liquid. [MDu., MLG, = wooden peg etc.: in sense 'pile' app. alt. of PILE[2]]

spill[1] /spɪl/ v. & n. —v. (past and past part. **spilt** or **spilled**) **1** intr. & tr. fall or run or cause (a liquid, powder, etc.) to fall or run out of a vessel, esp. unintentionally. **2 a** tr. & intr. throw (a person etc.) from a vehicle, saddle, etc. **b** intr. (esp. of a crowd) tumble out quickly from a place etc. (the fans spilled into the street). **3** tr. sl. disclose (information etc.). **4** tr. Naut. **a** empty (a sail) of wind. **b** lose (wind) from a sail. —n. **1 a** the act or an instance of spilling or being spilt. **b** a quantity spilt. **2** a tumble or fall, esp. from a horse etc. (had a nasty spill). **3** Austral. the vacating of all or several posts of a parliamentary party to allow reorganization. □ **spill the beans** colloq. divulge information etc., esp. unintentionally or indiscreetly. **spill blood** be guilty of bloodshed. **spill the blood of** kill or injure (a person). **spill over 1** overflow. **2** (of a surplus population) be forced to move (cf. OVERSPILL). □□ **spillage** /-ɪdʒ/ n. **spiller** n. [OE spillan kill, rel. to OE spildan destroy: orig. unkn.]

spill[2] /spɪl/ n. a thin strip of wood, folded or twisted paper, etc., used for lighting a fire, candles, a pipe, etc. [ME, rel. to SPILE]

spillikin /ˈspɪlɪkɪn/ n. (also **spellican** /ˈspelɪkən/) **1** a splinter of wood, bone, etc. **2** (in pl.) a game in which a heap of spillikins is to be removed one at a time without moving the others. [SPILL[2] + -KIN]

spillover /ˈspɪlˌəʊvə(r)/ n. **1 a** the process or an instance of spilling over. **b** a thing that spills over. **2** a consequence, repercussion, or by-product.

spillway /ˈspɪlweɪ/ n. a passage for surplus water from a dam.

spilt past and past part. of SPILL[1].

spilth /spɪlθ/ n. **1** material that is spilled. **2** the act or an instance of spilling. **3** an excess or surplus.

spin /spɪn/ v. & n. —v. (**spinning**; past and past part. **spun** /spʌn/) **1** intr. & tr. turn or cause (a person or thing) to turn or whirl round quickly. **2** tr. (also absol.) **a** draw out and twist (wool, cotton, etc.) into threads. **b** make (yarn) in this way. **c** make a similar type of thread from (a synthetic substance etc.). **3** tr. (of a spider, silkworm, etc.) make (a web, gossamer, a cocoon, etc.) by extruding a fine viscous thread. **4** tr. tell or write (a story, essay, article, etc.) (spins a good tale). **5** tr. impart spin to (a ball). **6** intr. (of a person's head etc.) be dizzy through excitement, astonishment, etc. **7** tr. shape (metal) on a mould in a lathe etc. **8** intr. esp. Cricket (of a ball) move through the air with spin. **9** tr. (as **spun** adj.) converted into threads (spun glass; spun gold; spun sugar). **10** tr. fish in (a stream, pool, etc.) with a spinner. **11** tr. toss (a coin). **12** tr. = spin-dry. —n. **1** a spinning motion; a whirl. **2** an aircraft's diving descent combined with rotation. **3 a** a revolving motion through the air, esp. in a rifle bullet or in a billiard, tennis, or table tennis ball struck aslant. **b** Cricket a twisting motion given to the ball in bowling. **4** colloq. a brief drive in a motor vehicle, aeroplane, etc., esp. for pleasure. **5** Physics the intrinsic angular momentum of an elementary particle. **6** Austral. & NZ sl. a piece of good or bad luck. □ **spin bowler** Cricket an expert at bowling with spin. **spin-drier** n. a machine for drying wet clothes etc. centrifugally in a revolving drum. **spin-dry** (**-dries**, **-dried**) dry (clothes etc.) in this way. **spin off** throw off by centrifugal force in spinning. **spin-off** n. an incidental result or results esp. as a side benefit from

industrial technology. **spin out 1** prolong (a discussion etc.). **2** make (a story, money, etc.) last as long as possible. **3** spend or consume (time, one's life, etc., by discussion or in an occupation etc.). **4** Cricket dismiss (a batsman or side) by spin bowling. **spin a yarn** orig. Naut. tell a story. **spun silk** a cheap material made of short-fibred and waste silk. **spun yarn** Naut. a line formed of rope-yarns twisted together. [OE spinnan]

spina bifida /ˌspaɪnə ˈbɪfɪdə/ n. a congenital defect of the spine, in which part of the spinal cord and its meninges are exposed through a gap in the backbone. [mod.L (as SPINE, BIFID)]

spinach /ˈspɪnɪdʒ, -ɪtʃ/ n. **1** a green garden vegetable, Spinacia oleracea, with succulent leaves. **2** the leaves of this plant used as food. □ **spinach beet** a variety of beetroot cultivated for its edible leaves. □□ **spinaceous** /-ˈneɪʃəs/ adj. **spinachy** adj. [prob. MDu. spinaetse, spinag(i)e, f. OF espinage, espinache f. med.L spinac(h)ia etc. f. Arab. 'isfānāk f. Pers. ispānāk: perh. assim. to L spina SPINE, with ref. to its prickly seeds]

spinal /ˈspaɪn(ə)l/ adj. of or relating to the spine (spinal curvature; spinal disease). □ **spinal canal** a cavity through the vertebrae containing the spinal cord. **spinal column** the spine. **spinal cord** a cylindrical structure of the central nervous system enclosed in the spine, connecting all parts of the body with the brain. □□ **spinally** adv. [LL spinalis (as SPINE)]

spindle /ˈspɪnd(ə)l/ n. & v. —n. **1 a** a pin in a spinning-wheel used for twisting and winding the thread. **b** a small bar with tapered ends used for the same purpose in hand-spinning. **c** a pin bearing the bobbin of a spinning-machine. **2** a pin or axis that revolves or on which something revolves. **3** a turned piece of wood used as a banister, chair leg, etc. **4** Biol. a spindle-shaped mass of microtubules formed when a cell divides. **5** a 'varying measure of length for yarn. **6** a slender person or thing. —v.intr. have, or grow into, a long slender form. □ **spindle berry** the fruit of the spindle tree. **spindle-shanked** having long thin legs. **spindle-shanks** a person with such legs. **spindle-shaped** having a circular cross-section and tapering towards each end. **spindle side** = distaff side. **spindle tree** any shrub or small tree of the genus Euonymus, esp. E. europaeus with greenish-white flowers, pink or red berries, and hard wood used for spindles. [OE spinel (as SPIN)]

spindly /ˈspɪndlɪ/ adj. (**spindlier**, **spindliest**) long or tall and thin; thin and weak.

spindrift /ˈspɪndrɪft/ n. spray blown along the surface of the sea. [Sc. var. of spoondrift f. spoon run before wind or sea + DRIFT]

spine /spaɪn/ n. **1** a series of vertebrae extending from the skull to the small of the back, enclosing the spinal cord and providing support for the thorax and abdomen; the backbone. **2** Zool. & Bot. any hard pointed process or structure. **3** a sharp ridge or projection, esp. of a mountain range or slope. **4** a central feature, main support, or source of strength. **5** the part of a book's jacket or cover that encloses the page-fastening part and usu. faces outwards on a shelf. □ **spine-chiller** a frightening story, film, etc. **spine-chilling** (esp. of a story etc.) frightening. □□ **spined** adj. [ME f. OF espine f. L spina thorn, backbone]

spinel /spɪˈnel/ n. **1** any of a group of hard crystalline minerals of various colours, consisting chiefly of oxides of magnesium and aluminium. **2** any substance of similar composition or properties. □ **spinel ruby** a deep-red variety of spinel used as a gem. [F spinelle f. It. spinella, dimin. of spina: see SPINE]

spineless /ˈspaɪnlɪs/ adj. **1 a** having no spine; invertebrate. **b** (of a fish) having no fin-spines. **2** (of a person) lacking energy or resolution; weak and purposeless. □□ **spinelessly** adv. **spinelessness** n.

spinet /spɪˈnet, ˈspɪnɪt/ n. Mus. hist. a small harpsichord with oblique strings. [obs. F espinette f. It. spinetta virginal, spinet, dimin. of spina thorn etc. (as SPINE), with ref. to the plucked strings]

spinifex /ˈspɪnɪˌfeks/ n. any Australian grass of the genus Spinifex, with coarse, spiny leaves. [mod.L f. L spina SPINE + -fex maker f. facere make]

spinnaker /ˈspɪnəkə(r)/ n. a large triangular sail carried opposite the mainsail of a racing-yacht running before the wind.

[fanciful f. *Sphinx*, name of yacht first using it, perh. after *spanker*]

spinner /ˈspɪnə(r)/ *n*. **1** a person or thing that spins. **2** *Cricket* **a** a spin bowler. **b** a spun ball. **3** a spin-drier. **4 a** a real or artificial fly for esp. trout-fishing. **b** revolving bait. **5** a manufacturer or merchant engaged in (esp. cotton-) spinning. **6** = SPINNERET. **7** *archaic* a spider.

spinneret /ˈspɪnəˌret/ *n*. **1** the spinning-organ in a spider, silkworm, etc. **2** a device for forming filaments of synthetic fibre.

spinney /ˈspɪnɪ/ *n*. (*pl.* **-eys**) *Brit.* a small wood; a thicket. [OF *espinei* f. L *spinetum* thicket f. *spina* thorn]

spinning /ˈspɪnɪŋ/ *n*. the act or an instance of spinning. □ **spinning-jenny** *hist.* a machine for spinning with more than one spindle at a time. (see HARGREAVES.) **spinning-machine** a machine that spins fibres continuously. **spinning-top** = TOP². **spinning-wheel** a household machine for spinning yarn or thread, with a spindle driven by a wheel operated originally by hand, later by a crank or treadle. The device is thought to have been introduced into Europe from India in the early 14th c.

spinose /ˈspaɪnəʊs/ *adj*. (also **spinous** /-nəs/) *Bot.* (of a plant) having many spines.

Spinoza /spɪˈnəʊzə/, Baruch (Benedict) de (1632–77), Dutch rationalist philosopher of Jewish descent. Expelled from the Amsterdam synagogue in 1656 for his unorthodox views, he made his living by grinding and polishing lenses. Rejecting the Cartesian dualism of spirit and matter he saw only one infinite substance, of which finite existences are modes or limitations: God is all and all is God. For him, God was the immanent cause of the universe, not a ruler outside it; among his conclusions are determinism and a denial of personal immortality. Spinoza's *Ethics*, published posthumously, founded morality on the 'intellectual love of God', which becomes possible after the complete victory over the passions; virtue is its own reward. His political doctrine involved a 'social contract' in which man surrenders part of his natural rights to the State in order to obtain security. Spinoza's influence was at its height in the 19th c., especially in Germany.

spinster /ˈspɪnstə(r)/ *n*. **1** an unmarried woman. **2** a woman, esp. elderly, thought unlikely to marry. □□ **spinsterhood** *n*. **spinsterish** *adj*. **spinsterishness** *n*. [ME, orig. = woman who spins]

spinthariscope /spɪnˈθærɪˌskəʊp/ *n*. an instrument with a fluorescent screen showing the incidence of alpha particles by flashes. [irreg. f. Gk *spintharis* spark + -SCOPE]

spinule /ˈspɪnjuːl/ *n*. *Bot.* & *Zool.* a small spine. □□ **spinulose** *adj*. **spinulous** *adj*. [L *spinula* dimin. of *spina* SPINE]

spiny /ˈspaɪnɪ/ *adj*. (**spinier**, **spiniest**) **1** full of spines; prickly. **2** perplexing, troublesome, thorny. □ **spiny anteater** = ECHIDNA. **spiny lobster** any of various large edible crustaceans of the family Palinuridae, esp. *Palinuris vulgaris*, with a spiny shell and no large anterior claws. □□ **spininess** *n*.

spiracle /ˈspaɪərək(ə)l/ *n*. (also **spiraculum** /ˌspaɪəˈrækjʊləm/) (*pl.* **spiracles** or **spiracula** /-lə/) an external respiratory opening in insects, whales, and some fish. □□ **spiracular** /-ˈrækjʊlə(r)/ *adj*. [L *spiraculum* f. *spirare* breathe]

spiraea /ˌspaɪəˈriːə/ *n*. (*US* **spirea**) any rosaceous shrub of the genus *Spiraea*, with clusters of small white or pink flowers. [L f. Gk *speiraia* f. *speira* coil]

spiral /ˈspaɪər(ə)l/ *adj*., *n*., & *v*. —*adj*. **1** winding about a centre in an enlarging or decreasing continuous circular motion, either on a flat plane or rising in a cone; coiled. **2** winding continuously along or as if along a cylinder, like the thread of a screw. —*n*. **1** a plane or three-dimensional spiral curve. **2** a spiral spring. **3** a spiral formation in a shell etc. **4** a spiral galaxy. **5** a progressive rise or fall of prices, wages, etc., each responding to an upward or downward stimulus provided by the other (*a spiral of rising prices and wages*). —*v*. (**spiralled**, **spiralling**; *US* **spiraled**, **spiraling**) **1** *intr.* move in a spiral course, esp. upwards or downwards. **2** *tr.* make spiral. **3** *intr.* esp. *Econ.* (of prices, wages, etc.) rise or fall, esp. rapidly (cf. sense 5 of *n*.). □ **spiral balance** a device for measuring weight by the torsion of a spiral spring. **spiral galaxy** a galaxy in which the

matter is concentrated mainly in one or more spiral arms. **spiral staircase** a staircase rising in a spiral round a central axis. □□ **spirality** /-ˈrælɪtɪ/ *n*. **spirally** *adv*. [F *spiral* or med.L *spiralis* (as SPIRE²)]

spirant /ˈspaɪərənt/ *adj*. & *n*. *Phonet.* —*adj*. (of a consonant) uttered with a continuous expulsion of breath, esp. fricative. —*n*. such a consonant. [L *spirare spirant-* breathe]

spire¹ /ˈspaɪə(r)/ *n*. & *v*. —*n*. **1** a tapering cone- or pyramid-shaped structure built esp. on a church tower (cf. STEEPLE). **2** the continuation of a tree trunk above the point where branching begins. **3** any tapering thing, e.g. the spike of a flower. —*v.tr.* provide with a spire. □□ **spiry** /ˈspaɪərɪ/ *adj*. [OE *spīr*]

spire² /ˈspaɪə(r)/ *n*. **1 a** a spiral; a coil. **b** a single twist of this. **2** the upper part of a spiral shell. [F f. L *spira* f. Gk *speira* coil]

spirea *US* var. of SPIRAEA.

spirillum /ˌspaɪˈrɪləm/ *n*. (*pl.* **spirilla** /-lə/) **1** any bacterium of the genus *Spirillum*, characterized by a rigid spiral structure. **2** any bacterium with a similar shape. [mod.L, irreg. dimin. of L *spira* SPIRE²]

spirit /ˈspɪrɪt/ *n*. & *v*. —*n*. **1 a** the vital animating essence of a person or animal (*was sadly broken in spirit*). **b** the intelligent non-physical part of a person; the soul. **2 a** a rational or intelligent being without a material body. **b** a supernatural being such as a ghost, fairy, etc. (*haunted by spirits*). **3** a prevailing mental or moral condition or attitude; a mood; a tendency (*public spirit; took it in the wrong spirit*). **4 a** (usu. in *pl.*) strong distilled liquor, e.g. brandy, whisky, gin, rum. **b** a distilled volatile liquid (*wood spirit*). **c** purified alcohol (*methylated spirit*). **d** a solution of a volatile principle in alcohol; a tincture (*spirit of ammonia*). **5 a** a person's mental or moral nature or qualities, usu. specified (*has an unbending spirit*). **b** a person viewed as possessing these (*is an ardent spirit*). **c** (in full **high spirit**) courage, energy, vivacity, dash (*played with spirit; infused him with spirit*). **6** the real meaning as opposed to lip service or verbal expression (*the spirit of the law*). **7** *archaic* an immaterial principle thought to govern vital phenomena (*animal spirits*). —*v.tr.* (**spirited, spiriting**) (usu. foll. by *away, off*, etc.) convey rapidly and secretly by or as if by spirits. □ **in** (or **in the**) **spirit** inwardly (*shall be with you in spirit*). **spirit duplicator** a duplicator using an alcoholic solution to reproduce copies from a master sheet. **spirit gum** a quick-drying solution of gum used esp. for attaching false hair. **spirit-lamp** a lamp burning methylated or other volatile spirits instead of oil. **spirit-level** a device consisting of a sealed glass tube nearly filled with liquid and containing an air-bubble, used to test levelness by the position of this bubble. Such devices were used on telescopes in the 17th c., but did not become a carpenter's and builder's tool until the mid-19th c. **the spirit moves a person** he or she feels inclined (to do something) (orig. in Quaker use). **spirit** (or **spirits**) **of wine** *archaic* purified alcohol. **spirits of salt** *archaic* hydrochloric acid. **spirit up** animate or cheer (a person). [ME f. AF *(e)spirit*, OF *esp(e)rit*, f. L *spiritus* breath, spirit f. *spirare* breathe]

spirited /ˈspɪrɪtɪd/ *adj*. **1** full of spirit; animated, lively, brisk, or courageous (*a spirited attack; a spirited translation*). **2** having a spirit or spirits of a specified kind (*high-spirited; mean-spirited*). □□ **spiritedly** *adv*. **spiritedness** *n*.

spiritless /ˈspɪrɪtlɪs/ *adj*. lacking courage, vigour, or vivacity. □□ **spiritlessly** *adv*. **spiritlessness** *n*.

spiritual /ˈspɪrɪtjʊəl/ *adj*. & *n*. —*adj*. **1** of or concerning the spirit as opposed to matter. **2** concerned with sacred or religious things; holy; divine; inspired (*the spiritual life; spiritual songs*). **3** (of the mind etc.) refined, sensitive; not concerned with the material. **4** (of a relationship etc.) concerned with the soul or spirit etc., not with external reality (*his spiritual home*). —*n.* = *Negro spiritual*. □ **spiritual courts** ecclesiastical courts. □□ **spirituality** /-ˈælɪtɪ/ *n*. **spiritually** *adv*. **spiritualness** *n*. [ME f. OF *spirituel* f. L *spiritualis* (as SPIRIT)]

spiritualism /ˈspɪrɪtjʊəˌlɪz(ə)m/ *n*. **1 a** the belief that the spirits of the dead can communicate with the living, esp. through mediums. (See below.) **b** the practice of this. **2** *Philos.* the doctrine that the spirit exists as distinct from matter, or that spirit is the only reality (cf. MATERIALISM). □□ **spiritualist** *n*. **spiritualistic** /-ˈlɪstɪk/ *adj*.

Belief that spirits of the dead can and do communicate with the living is very ancient and is an element in most primitive and some higher religions. Saul clandestinely consulted the woman of Endor (1 Sam. 28) in order to speak with the dead prophet Samuel, but the Jewish prophets disapproved of the practice and this repugnance was maintained by Christianity. In 1848 three sisters, Fox by name, living in New York State, heard strange rappings in their home and devised a simple code which, they asserted, was answered by rappings in such a way as to prove that they were made by an intelligent being. The news caused a sensation, and from this the modern spiritualistic movement had its origin. Hitherto most Christians had believed that spirits were evil and invoked only to do harm; now it was proclaimed that they dwelt in lands far better than this world, and were continually progressing. The impulse to make psychic communication the basis of a new religion comes from the natural longing (particularly evident after the two World Wars) to know what happens to people after death. In England the Society for Psychical Research was founded in 1882 for objective investigation not only of communication with the dead but of visions, telepathy, hauntings, etc. Although mediums appear to have access (in varying degrees) to knowledge beyond the ordinary, how it comes to them is still a mystery; it may proceed from some deep activity of the human mind, and any postulated type of 'communication' remains a hypothesis formulated to explain such knowledge.

spiritualize /ˈspɪrɪtjʊəˌlaɪz/ v.tr. (also **-ise**) **1** make (a person or a person's character, thoughts, etc.) spiritual; elevate. **2** attach a spiritual as opposed to a literal meaning to. □□ **spiritualization** /-ˈzeɪʃ(ə)n/ n.

spirituel /ˌspɪrɪtjʊˈel/ adj. (also **spirituelle**) (of the mind) refined and yet spirited; witty. [F spirituel, fem. -elle (as SPIRITUAL)]

spirituous /ˈspɪrɪtjʊəs/ adj. **1** containing much alcohol. **2** distilled, as whisky, rum, etc. (spirituous liquor). □□ **spirituousness** n. [L spiritus spirit, or F spiritueux]

spiro-¹ /ˈspaɪərəʊ/ comb. form a coil. [L spira, Gk speira coil]

spiro-² /ˈspaɪərəʊ/ comb. form breath. [irreg. f. L spirare breathe]

spirochaete /ˈspaɪərəʊˌkiːt/ n. (US **spirochete**) any of various flexible spiral-shaped bacteria. [SPIRO-¹ + Gk khaitē long hair]

spirograph /ˈspaɪərəˌɡrɑːf/ n. an instrument for recording breathing movements. □□ **spirographic** /-ˈɡræfɪk/ adj. **spirographically** /-ˈɡræfɪkəlɪ/ adv.

spirogyra /ˌspaɪərəʊˈdʒaɪərə/ n. any freshwater alga of the genus Spirogyra, with cells containing spiral bands of chlorophyll. [mod.L f. SPIRO-¹ + Gk guros gura round]

spirometer /spaɪˈrɒmɪtə(r)/ n. an instrument for measuring the air capacity of the lungs.

spirt var. of SPURT.

spit¹ /spɪt/ v. & n. —v. (**spitting**; past and past part. **spat** /spæt/ or **spit**) **1** intr. **a** eject saliva from the mouth. **b** do this as a sign of hatred or contempt (spat at him). **2** tr. (usu. foll. by out) **a** eject (saliva, blood, food, etc.) from the mouth (spat the meat out). **b** utter (oaths, threats, etc.) vehemently ('Damn you!' he spat). **3** intr. (of a fire, pen, pan, etc.) send out sparks, ink, hot fat, etc. **4** intr. (of rain) fall lightly (it's only spitting). **5** intr. (esp. of a cat) make a spitting or hissing noise in anger or hostility. —n. **1** spittle. **2** the act or an instance of spitting. **3** the foamy liquid secretion of some insects used to protect their young. □ **the spit** (or **very spit**) **of** colloq. the exact double of (cf. spitting image). **spit and polish 1** the cleaning and polishing duties of a soldier etc. **2** exaggerated neatness and smartness. **spit chips** Austral. sl. **1** feel extreme thirst. **2** be angry or frustrated. **spit it out** colloq. say what is on one's mind. **spitting cobra** the African black-necked cobra, Naja nigricollis, that ejects venom by spitting, not striking. **spitting distance** a very short distance. **spitting image** (foll. by of) colloq. the exact double of (another person or thing). □□ **spitter** n. [OE spittan, of imit. orig.: cf. SPEW]

spit² /spɪt/ n. & v. —n. **1** a slender rod on which meat is skewered before being roasted on a fire etc.; a skewer. **2 a** a small point of land projecting into the sea. **b** a long narrow underwater bank. —v.tr. (**spitted, spitting**) **1** thrust a spit through (meat etc.). **2** pierce or transfix with a sword etc. □ **spit-roast** cook on a spit. □□ **spitty** adj. [OE spitu f. WG]

spit³ /spɪt/ n. (pl. same or **spits**) a spade-depth of earth (dig it two spit deep). [MDu. & MLG, = OE spittan dig with spade, prob. rel. to SPIT²]

spitball /ˈspɪtbɔːl/ n. & v. —n. US **1** a ball of chewed paper etc. used as a missile. **2** a baseball moistened by the pitcher to impart spin. —v.intr. throw out suggestions for discussion. □□ **spitballer** n.

spitchcock /ˈspɪtʃkɒk/ n. & v. —n. an eel split and broiled. —v.tr. prepare (an eel, fish, bird, etc.) in this way. [16th c.: orig. unkn.: cf. SPATCHCOCK]

spite /spaɪt/ n. & v. —n. **1** ill will, malice towards a person (did it from spite). **2** a grudge. —v.tr. thwart, mortify, annoy (does it to spite me). □ **in spite of** notwithstanding. **in spite of oneself** etc. though one would rather have done otherwise. [ME f. OF despit DESPITE]

spiteful /ˈspaɪtfʊl/ adj. motivated by spite; malevolent. □□ **spitefully** adv. **spitefulness** n.

spitfire /ˈspɪtˌfaɪə(r)/ n. a person of fiery temper.

Spitsbergen /ˈspɪtsbɜːɡən/ an archipelago in the Arctic Ocean, north of Norway, under Norwegian sovereignty.

spittle /ˈspɪt(ə)l/ n. saliva, esp. as ejected from the mouth. □□ **spittly** adj. [alt. of ME (now dial.) spattle = OE spātl f. spǣtan to spit, after SPIT¹]

spittoon /spɪˈtuːn/ n. a metal or earthenware pot with esp. a funnel-shaped top, used for spitting into.

Spitz /spɪts/, Mark Andrew (1950–), American swimmer, winner of seven gold medals in the 1972 Olympic Games at Munich.

spitz /spɪts/ n. **1** a small type of dog with a pointed muzzle, esp. a Pomeranian. **2** this breed. [G Spitz(hund) f. spitz pointed + Hund dog]

spiv /spɪv/ n. Brit. colloq. a man, often characterized by flashy dress, who makes a living by illicit or unscrupulous dealings. □□ **spivvish** adj. **spivvy** adj. [20th c.: orig. unkn.]

splanchnic /ˈsplæŋknɪk/ adj. of or relating to the viscera; intestinal. [mod.L splanchnicus f. Gk splagkhnikos f. splagkhna entrails]

splash /splæʃ/ v. & n. —v. **1** intr. & tr. spatter or cause (liquid) to spatter in small drops. **2** tr. cause (a person) to be spattered with liquid etc. (splashed them with mud). **3** intr. **a** (of a person) cause liquid to spatter (was splashing about in the bath). **b** (usu. foll. by across, along, etc.) move while spattering liquid etc. (splashed across the carpet in his boots). **c** step, fall, or plunge etc. into a liquid etc. so as to cause a splash (splashed into the sea). **4** tr. display (news) prominently. **5** tr. decorate with scattered colour. **6** tr. spend (money) ostentatiously. —n. **1** the act or an instance of splashing. **2 a** a quantity of liquid splashed. **b** the resulting noise (heard a splash). **3** a spot of dirt etc. splashed on to a thing. **4** a prominent news feature etc. **5** a daub or patch of colour, esp. on an animal's coat. **6** Brit. colloq. a small quantity of liquid, esp. of soda water etc. to dilute spirits. □ **make a splash** attract much attention, esp. by extravagance. **splash out** colloq. spend money freely. □□ **splashy** adj. (**splashier, splashiest**). [alt. of PLASH¹]

splashback /ˈsplæʃbæk/ n. a panel behind a sink etc. to protect the wall from splashes.

splashdown /ˈsplæʃdaʊn/ n. the alighting of a spacecraft on the sea.

splat¹ /splæt/ n. a flat piece of thin wood in the centre of a chair-back. [splat (v.) split up, rel. to SPLIT]

splat² /splæt/ n., adj., & v. colloq. —n. a sharp cracking or slapping sound (hit the wall with a splat). —adv. with a splat (fell splat on his head). —v.intr. & tr. (**splatted, splatting**) fall or hit with a splat. [abbr. of SPLATTER]

splatter /ˈsplætə(r)/ v. & n. —v.tr. & intr. **1** splash esp. with a continuous noisy action. **2** US spatter. —n. a noisy splashing sound. [imit.]

splay /spleɪ/ v., n., & adj. —v. **1** tr. (usu. foll. by out) spread (the elbows, feet, etc.) out. **2** intr. (of an aperture or its sides) diverge in shape or position. **3** tr. construct (a window, doorway, aperture, etc.) so that it diverges or is wider at one side of the wall than the other. —*n.* a surface making an oblique angle with another, e.g. the splayed side of a window or embrasure. —*adj.* **1** wide and flat. **2** turned outward. □ **splay-foot** a broad flat foot turned outward. **splay-footed** having such feet. [ME f. DISPLAY]

spleen /spliːn/ *n.* **1** an abdominal organ involved in maintaining the proper condition of blood in most vertebrates. **2** lowness of spirits; moroseness, ill temper, spite (from the earlier belief that the spleen was the seat of such feelings) (*a fit of spleen; vented their spleen*). □□ **spleenful** *adj.* **spleeny** *adj.* [ME f. OF *esplen* f. L *splen* f. Gk *splēn*]

spleenwort /ˈspliːnwɜːt/ *n.* any fern of the genus *Asplenium*, formerly used as a remedy for disorders of the spleen.

splen- /spliːn/ *comb. form Anat.* the spleen. [Gk (as SPLEEN)]

splendent /ˈsplend(ə)nt/ *adj. formal.* **1** shining; lustrous. **2** illustrious. [ME f. L *splendēre* to shine]

splendid /ˈsplendɪd/ *adj.* **1** magnificent, gorgeous, brilliant, sumptuous (*a splendid palace; a splendid achievement*). **2** dignified; impressive (*splendid isolation*). **3** excellent; fine (*a splendid chance*). □□ **splendidly** *adv.* **splendidness** *n.* [F *splendide* or L *splendidus* (as SPLENDENT)]

splendiferous /splenˈdɪfərəs/ *adj. colloq.* or *joc.* splendid. □□ **splendiferously** *adv.* **splendiferousness** *n.* [irreg. f. SPLENDOUR]

splendour /ˈsplendə(r)/ *n.* (US **splendor**) **1** great or dazzling brightness. **2** magnificence; grandeur. [ME f. AF *splendeur* or L *splendor* (as SPLENDENT)]

splenectomy /spliːˈnektəmɪ/ *n.* (*pl.* **-ies**) the surgical excision of the spleen.

splenetic /splɪˈnetɪk/ *adj.* & *n.* —*adj.* **1** ill-tempered; peevish. **2** of or concerning the spleen. —*n.* a splenetic person. □□ **splenetically** *adv.* [LL *spleneticus* (as SPLEEN)]

splenic /ˈsplenɪk, ˈspliː-/ *adj.* of or in the spleen. □ **splenic fever** anthrax. □□ **splenoid** /ˈspliːnɔɪd/ *adj.* [F *splénique* or L *splenicus* f. Gk *splēnikos* (as SPLEEN)]

splenitis /splɪˈnaɪtɪs/ *n.* inflammation of the spleen.

splenius /ˈspliːnɪəs/ *n.* (*pl.* **splenii** /-nɪaɪ/) *Anat.* either section of muscle on each side of the neck and back serving to draw back the head. □□ **splenial** *adj.* [mod.L f. Gk *splēnion* bandage]

splenology /spliːˈnɒlədʒɪ/ *n.* the scientific study of the spleen.

splenomegaly /ˌspliːnəˈmegəlɪ/ *n.* a pathological enlargement of the spleen. [SPLENO- + *megaly* (as MEGALO-)]

splenotomy /spliːˈnɒtəmɪ/ *n.* (*pl.* **-ies**) a surgical incision into or dissection of the spleen.

splice /splaɪs/ *v.* & *n.* —*v.tr.* **1** join the ends of (ropes) by interweaving strands. **2** join (pieces of timber, magnetic tape, film, etc.) in an overlapping position. **3** (esp. as **spliced** *adj.*) *colloq.* join in marriage. —*n.* a joint consisting of two ropes, pieces of wood, film, etc., made by splicing, e.g. the handle and blade of a cricket bat. □ **splice the main brace** *Naut. hist.* issue an extra tot of rum. □□ **splicer** *n.* [prob. f. MDu. *splissen*, of uncert. orig.]

spliff /splɪf/ *n.* (also **splif**) *sl.* a cannabis cigarette. [20th c.: orig. unkn.]

spline /splaɪn/ *n.* & *v.* —*n.* **1** a rectangular key fitting into grooves in the hub and shaft of a wheel and allowing longitudinal play. **2** a slat. **3** a flexible wood or rubber strip used esp. in drawing large curves. —*v.tr.* fit with a spline (sense 1). [orig. E. Anglian dial., perh. rel. to SPLINTER]

splint /splɪnt/ *n.* & *v.* —*n.* **1 a** a strip of rigid material used for holding a broken bone etc. when set. **b** a rigid or flexible strip of esp. wood used in basketwork etc. **2** a tumour or bony excrescence on the inside of a horse's leg. **3** a thin strip of wood etc. used to light a fire, pipe, etc. **4** = *splint-bone.* —*v.tr.* secure (a broken limb etc.) with a splint or splints. □ **splint-bone 1** either of two small bones in a horse's foreleg lying behind and close to the cannon-bone. **2** the human fibula. **splint-coal** hard bituminous laminated coal burning with great heat. [ME *splent(e)* f. MDu. *splinte* or MLG *splinte, splente* metal plate or pin, rel. to SPLINTER]

splinter /ˈsplɪntə(r)/ *v.* & *n.* —*v.tr.* & *intr.* break into fragments.

—*n.* a small thin sharp-edged piece broken off from wood, stone, etc. □ **splinter-bar** *Brit.* a crossbar in a vehicle to which traces are attached; a swingletree. **splinter group** (or **party**) a group or party that has broken away from a larger one. **splinter-proof** proof against splinters e.g. from bursting shells or bombs. □□ **splintery** *adj.* [ME f. MDu. (= LG) *splinter, splenter*, rel. to SPLINT]

Split /splɪt/ a seaport on the Adriatic coast of Croatia in western Yugoslavia; pop. (1981) 235,900.

split /splɪt/ *v.* & *n.* —*v.* (**splitting;** *past* and *past part.* **split**) **1** *intr.* & *tr.* **a** break or cause to break with the grain or into halves. **b** (often foll. by *up*) divide into parts (*split into groups; split up the money equally*). **2** *tr.* & *intr.* (often foll. by *off, away*) remove or be removed by breaking, separating, or dividing (*split the top off the bottle; split away from the main group*). **3** *intr.* & *tr.* **a** (usu. foll. by *up, on, over*, etc.) separate esp. through discord (*split up after ten years; they were split on the question of picketing*). **b** (foll. by *with*) quarrel or cease association with (another person etc.). **4** *tr.* cause the fission of (an atom). **5** *intr.* & *tr. sl.* leave, esp. suddenly. **6** *intr.* (usu. foll. by *on*) *colloq.* betray secrets; inform (*split on them to the police*). **7** *intr.* **a** (as **splitting** *adj.*) (esp. of a headache) very painful; acute. **b** (of the head) suffer great pain from a headache, noise, etc. **8** *intr.* (of a ship) be wrecked. **9** *tr. US colloq.* dilute (whisky etc.) with water. —*n.* **1** the act or an instance of splitting; the state of being split. **2** a fissure, vent, crack, cleft, etc. **3** a separation into parties; a schism. **4** (in *pl.*) *Brit.* the athletic feat of leaping in the air or sitting down with the legs at right angles to the body in front and behind, or at the sides with the trunk facing forwards. **5** a split osier etc. used for parts of basketwork. **6** each strip of steel, cane, etc., of the reed in a loom. **7** a single thickness of split hide. **8** the turning up of two cards of equal value in faro, so that the stakes are divided. **9 a** half a bottle of mineral water. **b** half a glass of liquor. **10** *colloq.* a division of money, esp. the proceeds of crime. □ **split the difference** take the average of two proposed amounts. **split gear** (or **pulley** or **wheel**) a gear etc. made in halves for removal from a shaft. **split hairs** make small and insignificant distinctions. **split infinitive** a phrase consisting of an infinitive with an adverb etc. inserted between *to* and the verb, e.g. *seems to really like it.* **split-level** (of a building) having a room or rooms a fraction of a storey higher than other parts. **split mind** = SCHIZOPHRENIA. **split pea** a pea dried and split in half for cooking. **split personality** the alteration or dissociation of personality occurring in some mental illnesses, esp. schizophrenia and hysteria. **split pin** a metal cotter passed through a hole and held by the pressing back of the two ends. **split ring** a small steel ring with two spiral turns, such as a key-ring. **split-screen** a screen on which two or more separate images are displayed. **split second** a very brief moment of time. **split shift** a shift comprising two or more separate periods of duty. **split shot** (or **stroke**) *Croquet* a stroke driving two touching balls in different directions. **split one's sides** be convulsed with laughter. **split the ticket** (or **one's vote**) *US* vote for candidates of more than one party. **split the vote** *Brit.* (of a candidate or minority party) attract votes from another so that both are defeated by a third. □□ **splitter** *n.* [orig. Naut. f. MDu. *splitten*, rel. to *spletten, splīten*, MHG *splīzen*]

splodge /splɒdʒ/ *n.* & *v. colloq.* —*n.* a daub, blot, or smear. —*v.tr.* make a large, esp. irregular, spot or patch on. □□ **splodgy** *adj.* [imit., or alt. of SPLOTCH]

splosh /splɒʃ/ *v.* & *n. colloq.* —*v.tr.* & *intr.* move with a splashing sound. —*n.* **1** a splashing sound. **2** a splash of water etc. **3** *sl.* money. [imit.]

splotch /splɒtʃ/ *n.* & *v.tr.* = SPLODGE. □□ **splotchy** *adj.* [perh. f. SPOT + obs. *plotch* BLOTCH]

splurge /splɜːdʒ/ *n.* & *v. colloq.* —*n.* **1** an ostentatious display or effort. **2** an instance of sudden great extravagance. —*v.intr.* **1** (usu. foll. by *on*) spend effort or esp. large sums of money (*splurged on new furniture*). **2** splash heavily. [19th-c. US: prob. imit.]

splutter /ˈsplʌtə(r)/ *v.* & *n.* —*v.* **1** *intr.* **a** speak in a hurried, vehement, or choking manner. **b** emit particles from the mouth, sparks, hot oil, etc., with spitting sounds. **2** *tr.* **a** speak or utter (words, threats, a language, etc.) rapidly or incoherently. **b** emit (food, sparks, hot oil, etc.) with a spitting sound. —*n.* spluttering speech. □□ **splutterer** *n.* **splutteringly** *adv.* [SPUTTER by assoc. with *splash*]

Spock /spɒk/, Benjamin McLane (1903–), American paediatrician, whose book *The Common Sense Book of Baby and Child Care* (1946), advocating a relaxed and gentle approach to the upbringing of children, was widely read and immensely influential.

Spode /spəʊd/ *n.* a kind of fine pottery or porcelain named after the English potter Josiah Spode (1754–1827), its original maker.

spoil /spɔɪl/ *v.* & *n.* —*v.* (*past* and *past part.* **spoilt** or **spoiled**) **1** *tr.* **a** damage; diminish the value of (*was spoilt by the rain; will spoil all the fun*). **b** reduce a person's enjoyment etc. of (*the news spoiled his dinner*). **2** *tr.* injure the character of (esp. a child, pet, etc.) by excessive indulgence. **3** *intr.* **a** (of food) go bad, decay; become unfit for eating. **b** (usu. in *neg.*) (of a joke, secret, etc.) become stale through long keeping. **4** *tr.* render (a ballot paper) invalid by improper marking. **5** *tr.* (foll. by *of*) *archaic* or *literary* plunder or deprive (a person of a thing) by force or stealth (*spoiled him of all his possessions*). —*n.* **1** (usu. in *pl.*) **a** plunder taken from an enemy in war, or seized by force. **b** esp. *joc.* profit or advantages gained by succeeding to public office, high position, etc. **2** earth etc. thrown up in excavating, dredging, etc. □ **be spoiling for** aggressively seek (a fight etc.). **spoils system** *US* the practice of giving public office to the adherents of a successful party. **spoilt for choice** having so many choices that it is difficult to choose. [ME f. OF *espoillier, espoille* f. L *spoliare* f. *spolium* spoil, plunder, or f. DESPOIL]

spoilage /ˈspɔɪlɪdʒ/ *n.* **1** paper spoilt in printing. **2** the spoiling of food etc. by decay.

spoiler /ˈspɔɪlə(r)/ *n.* **1** a person or thing that spoils. **2 a** a device on an aircraft to retard its speed by interrupting the air flow. **b** a similar device on a vehicle to improve its road-holding at speed.

spoilsman /ˈspɔɪlzmən/ *n.* (*pl.* **-men**) *US* esp. *Polit.* **1** an advocate of the spoils system. **2** a person who seeks to profit by it.

spoilsport /ˈspɔɪlspɔːt/ *n.* a person who spoils others' pleasure or enjoyment.

spoilt *past* and *past part.* of SPOIL.

spoke[1] /spəʊk/ *n.* & *v.* —*n.* **1** each of the bars running from the hub to the rim of a wheel. **2** a rung of a ladder. **3** each radial handle of the wheel of a ship etc. —*v.tr.* **1** provide with spokes. **2** obstruct (a wheel etc.) by thrusting a spoke in. □ **put a spoke in a person's wheel** *Brit.* thwart or hinder a person. **spoke-bone** the radius of the forearm. □□ **spokewise** *adv.* [OE *spāca* f. WG]

spoke[2] *past* of SPEAK.

spoken /ˈspəʊkən/ *past part.* of SPEAK. —*adj.* (in *comb.*) speaking in a specified way (*smooth-spoken; well-spoken*). □ **spoken for** claimed, requisitioned (*this seat is spoken for*).

spokeshave /ˈspəʊkʃeɪv/ *n.* a blade set between two handles, used for shaping spokes and other esp. curved work where an ordinary plane is not suitable.

spokesman /ˈspəʊksmən/ *n.* (*pl.* **-men**; *fem.* **spokeswoman**, *pl.* **-women**) **1** a person who speaks on behalf of others, esp. in the course of public relations. **2** a person deputed to express the views of a group etc. [irreg. f. SPOKE[2] after *craftsman* etc.]

spokesperson /ˈspəʊks₁pɜːs(ə)n/ *n.* (*pl.* **-persons** or **-people**) a spokesman or spokeswoman.

Spoleto /spəˈleɪtəʊ/ a town of Umbria in central Italy; pop. (1981) 20,000. A festival of music, art, and drama is held here each summer.

spoliation /₁spəʊlɪˈeɪʃ(ə)n/ *n.* **1 a** plunder or pillage, esp. of neutral vessels in war. **b** extortion. **2** *Eccl.* the taking of the fruits of a benefice under a pretended title etc. **3** *Law* the destruction, mutilation, or alteration, of a document to prevent its being used as evidence. □□ **spoliator** /ˈspəʊ-/ *n.* **spoliatory** /ˈspəʊlɪətərɪ/ *adj.* [ME f. L *spoliatio* (as SPOIL)]

spondaic /spɒnˈdeɪɪk/ *adj.* **1** of or concerning spondees. **2** (of a hexameter) having a spondee as a fifth foot. [F *spondaïque* or LL *spondaicus* = LL *spondiacus* f. Gk *spondeiakos* (as SPONDEE)]

spondee /ˈspɒndiː/ *n. Prosody* a foot consisting of two long (or stressed) syllables. [ME f. OF *spondee* or L *spondeus* f. Gk *spondeios* (*pous* foot) f. *spondē* libation, as being characteristic of music accompanying libations]

spondulicks /spɒnˈdjuːlɪks/ *n.pl. sl.* money. [19th c.: orig. unkn.]

spondylitis /₁spɒndɪˈlaɪtɪs/ *n.* inflammation of the vertebrae. [L *spondylus* vertebra f. Gk *spondulos* + -ITIS]

sponge /spʌndʒ/ *n.* & *v.* —*n.* **1** any aquatic animal of the phylum Porifera, with pores in its body wall and a rigid internal skeleton. **2 a** the skeleton of a sponge, esp. the soft light elastic absorbent kind used in bathing, cleansing surfaces, etc. **b** a piece of porous rubber or plastic etc. used similarly. **3** a thing of spongelike absorbency or consistency, e.g. a sponge pudding, cake, porous metal, etc. (*lemon sponge*). **4** = SPONGER. **5** *colloq.* a person who drinks heavily. **6** cleansing with or as with a sponge (*had a quick sponge this morning*). —*v.* **1** *tr.* wipe or cleanse with a sponge. **2** *tr.* (also *absol.*; often foll. by *down, over*) sluice water over (the body, a car, etc.). **3** *tr.* (often foll. by *out, away,* etc.) wipe off or efface (writing, a memory, etc.) with or as with a sponge. **4** *tr.* (often foll. by *up*) absorb with or as with a sponge. **5** *intr.* (often foll. by *on, off*) live as a parasite; be meanly dependent upon (another person). **6** *tr.* obtain (drink etc.) by sponging. **7** *intr.* gather sponges. **8** *tr.* apply paint with a sponge to (walls, furniture, etc.). □ **sponge bag** a waterproof bag for toilet articles. **sponge cake** a very light cake with a spongelike consistency. **sponge cloth 1** soft, lightly-woven cloth with a slightly wrinkled surface. **2** a thin spongy material used for cleaning. **sponge pudding** *Brit.* a steamed or baked pudding of fat, flour, and eggs with a usu. specified flavour. **sponge rubber** liquid rubber latex processed into a spongelike substance. **sponge tree** a spiny tropical acacia, *Acacia farnesiana*, with globose heads of fragrant yellow flowers yielding a perfume: also called OPOPANAX. □□ **spongeable** *adj.* **spongelike** *adj.* **spongiform** *adj.* (esp. in senses 1, 2). [OE f. L *spongia* f. Gk *spoggia, spoggos*]

sponger /ˈspʌndʒə(r)/ *n.* a person who contrives to live at another's expense.

spongy /ˈspʌndʒɪ/ *adj.* (**spongier**, **spongiest**) **1** like a sponge, esp. in being porous, compressible, elastic, or absorbent. **2** (of metal) finely divided and loosely coherent. □□ **spongily** *adv.* **sponginess** *n.*

sponsion /ˈspɒnʃ(ə)n/ *n.* **1** being a surety for another. **2** a pledge or promise made on behalf of the State by an agent not authorized to do so. [L *sponsio* f. *spondēre spons-* promise solemnly]

sponson /ˈspɒns(ə)n/ *n.* **1** a projection from the side of a warship or tank to enable a gun to be trained forward and aft. **2** a short subsidiary wing to stabilize a seaplane. **3** a triangular platform supporting the wheel on a paddle-steamer. [19th c.: orig. unkn.]

sponsor /ˈspɒnsə(r)/ *n.* & *v.* —*n.* **1** a person who supports an activity done for charity by pledging money in advance. **2 a** a person or organization that promotes or supports an artistic or sporting activity etc. **b** esp. *US* a business organization that promotes a broadcast programme in return for advertising time. **3** an organization lending support to an election candidate. **4** a person who introduces a proposal for legislation. **5** a godparent at baptism or esp. *RC Ch.* a person who presents a candidate for confirmation. **6** a person who makes himself or herself responsible for another. —*v.tr.* be a sponsor for. □□ **sponsorial** /spɒnˈsɔːrɪəl/ *adj.* **sponsorship** *n.* [L (as SPONSION)]

spontaneous /spɒnˈteɪnɪəs/ *adj.* **1** acting or done or occurring without external cause. **2** voluntary, without external incitement (*made a spontaneous offer of his services*). **3** *Biol.* (of structural changes in plants and muscular activity esp. in young animals) instinctive, automatic, prompted by no motive. **4** (of bodily movement, literary style, etc.) gracefully natural and unconstrained. **5** (of sudden movement etc.) involuntary, not due to conscious volition. **6** growing naturally without cultivation. □ **spontaneous combustion** the ignition of a mineral or vegetable substance (e.g. a heap of rags soaked with oil, a mass of wet coal) from heat engendered within itself, usu. by rapid oxidation. **spontaneous generation** the supposed production of living from non-living matter as inferred from the appearance of life (due in fact to bacteria etc.) in some infusions; abiogenesis. **spontaneous suggestion** suggestion from association of ideas without conscious volition. □□ **spontaneity** /ˌspɒntəˈniːɪtɪ, -ˈneɪtɪ/ n. **spontaneously** adv. **spontaneousness** n. [LL *spontaneus* f. *sponte* of one's own accord]

spoof /spuːf/ n. & v. colloq. —n. **1** a parody. **2** a hoax or swindle. —v.tr. **1** parody. **2** hoax, swindle. □□ **spoofer** n. **spoofery** n. [invented by A. Roberts, English comedian d. 1933]

spook /spuːk/ n. & v. —n. **1** colloq. a ghost. **2** US sl. a spy. —v. US sl. **1** tr. frighten, unnerve, alarm. **2** intr. take fright, become alarmed. [Du., = MLG *spōk*, of unkn. orig.]

spooky /ˈspuːkɪ/ adj. (**spookier**, **spookiest**) **1** colloq. ghostly, eerie. **2** US sl. nervous; easily frightened. **3** US sl. of spies or espionage. □□ **spookily** adv. **spookiness** n.

spool /spuːl/ n. & v. —n. **1 a** a reel for winding magnetic tape, photographic film, etc., on. **b** a reel for winding yarn or US thread on. **c** a quantity of tape, yarn, etc., wound on a spool. **2** the revolving cylinder of an angler's reel. —v.tr. wind on a spool. [ME f. OF *espole* or f. MLG *spōle*, MDu. *spoele*, OHG *spuolo*, of unkn. orig.]

spoon /spuːn/ n. & v. —n. **1 a** a utensil consisting of an oval or round bowl and a handle for conveying food (esp. liquid) to the mouth, for stirring, etc. **b** a spoonful, esp. of sugar. **c** (in pl.) Mus. a pair of spoons held in the hand and beaten together rhythmically. **2** a spoon-shaped thing, esp.: **a** (in full **spoon-bait**) a bright revolving piece of metal used as a lure in fishing. **b** an oar with a broad curved blade. **c** a wooden-headed golf club. **3** colloq. **a** a silly or demonstratively fond lover. **b** a simpleton. —v. **1** tr. (often foll. by up, out) take (liquid etc.) with a spoon. **2** tr. hit (a ball) feebly upwards. **3** colloq. **a** intr. behave in an amorous way, esp. foolishly. **b** tr. archaic woo in a silly or sentimental way. **4** intr. fish with a spoon-bait. □ **born with a silver spoon in one's mouth** born in affluence. **spoon-bread** US soft maize bread. □□ **spooner** n. **spoonful** n. (pl. **-fuls**). [OE *spōn* chip of wood f. Gmc]

spoonbill /ˈspuːnbɪl/ n. **1** any large wading bird of the subfamily Plataleidae, having a bill with a very broad flat tip. **2** a shoveller duck.

spoonerism /ˈspuːnəˌrɪz(ə)m/ n. a transposition, usu. accidental, of the initial letters etc. of two or more words, e.g. *you have hissed the mystery lectures*. [Revd W. A. *Spooner*, English scholar d. 1930, reputed to make such errors in speaking]

spoonfeed /ˈspuːnfiːd/ v.tr. (past and past part. **-fed**) **1** feed (a baby etc.) with a spoon. **2** provide help, information, etc., to (a person) without requiring any effort on the recipient's part. **3** artificially encourage (an industry) by subsidies or import duties.

spoony /ˈspuːnɪ/ adj. & n. colloq. archaic —adj. (**spoonier**, **spooniest**) **1** (often foll. by on) sentimental, amorous. **2** foolish, silly. —n. (pl. **-ies**) a simpleton. □□ **spoonily** adv. **spooniness** n.

spoor /spʊə(r)/ n. & v. —n. the track or scent of an animal. —v.tr. & intr. follow by the spoor. □□ **spoorer** n. [Afrik. f. MDu. *spo(o)r* f. Gmc]

Sporades /ˈspɒrəˌdiːz/ (Greek **Sporádhes** /spɒˈrɑːdiːz/) two separate groups of Greek islands in the Aegean Sea. The Northern Sporades, which lie to the east of mainland Greece, include the islands of Euboea, Skiros, Skiathos, Skópelos, and Iliodhrómia. The Southern Sporades, off the west coast of Turkey, include Rhodes and the Dodecanese Islands.

sporadic /spəˈrædɪk/ adj. occurring only here and there or occasionally, separate, scattered. □□ **sporadically** adv. [med.L *sporadicus* f. Gk *sporadikos* f. *sporas -ados* scattered: cf. *speirō* to sow]

sporangium /spəˈrændʒɪəm/ n. (pl. **sporangia** /-dʒɪə/) Bot. a receptacle in which spores are found. □□ **sporangial** adj. [mod.L f. Gk *spora* SPORE + *aggeion* vessel]

spore /spɔː(r)/ n. **1** a specialized reproductive cell of many plants and micro-organisms. **2** these collectively. [mod.L *spora* f. Gk *spora* sowing, seed f. *speirō* sow]

sporo- /ˈspɔːrəʊ/ comb. form Biol. a spore. [Gk *spora* (as SPORE)]

sporogenesis /ˌspɔːrəˈdʒenɪsɪs/ n. the process of spore formation.

sporogenous /spəˈrɒdʒɪnəs/ adj. producing spores.

sporophyte /ˈspɔːrəˌfaɪt/ n. a spore-producing form of plant with alternating sexual and asexual generations. □□ **sporophytic** /-ˈfɪtɪk/ adj. **sporophytically** /-ˈfɪtɪkəlɪ/ adv.

sporran /ˈspɒrən/ n. a pouch, usu. of leather or sealskin covered with fur etc., worn by a Highlander in front of the kilt. [Gael. *sporan* f. med.L *bursa* PURSE]

sport /spɔːt/ n. & v. —n. **1 a** a game or competitive activity, esp. an outdoor one involving physical exertion, e.g. cricket, football, racing, hunting. **b** such activities collectively (the world of sport). **2** (in pl.) Brit. **a** a meeting for competing in sports, esp. athletics (school sports). **b** athletics. **3** amusement, diversion, fun. **4** colloq. **a** a fair or generous person. **a** a person behaving in a specified way, esp. regarding games, rules, etc. (a bad sport at tennis). **c** Austral. a form of address, esp. between males. **d** US a playboy. **5** Biol. an animal or plant deviating suddenly or strikingly from the normal type. **6** a plaything or butt (was the sport of Fortune). —v. **1** intr. divert oneself, take part in a pastime. **2** tr. wear, exhibit, or produce, esp. ostentatiously (sported a gold tie-pin). **3** intr. Biol. become or produce a sport. □ **have good sport** be successful in shooting, fishing, etc. **in sport** jestingly. **make sport of** make fun of, ridicule. **the sport of kings** horse-racing (less often war, hunting, or surfing). **sports car** an open, low-built fast car. **sports coat** (or **jacket**) a man's jacket for informal wear. **sports writer** a person who writes (esp. as a journalist) on sports. □□ **sporter** n. [ME f. DISPORT]

sporting /ˈspɔːtɪŋ/ adj. **1** interested in sport (a sporting man). **2** sportsmanlike, generous (a sporting offer). **3** concerned in sport (a sporting dog; sporting news). □ **a sporting chance** some possibility of success. **sporting house** US a brothel. □□ **sportingly** adv.

sportive /ˈspɔːtɪv/ adj. playful. □□ **sportively** adv. **sportiveness** n.

sportscast /ˈspɔːtskɑːst/ n. US a broadcast of a sports event or information about sport. □□ **sportscaster** n.

sportsman /ˈspɔːtsmən/ n. (pl. **-men**; fem. **sportswoman**, pl. **-women**) **1** a person who takes part in much sport, esp. professionally. **2** a person who behaves fairly and generously. □□ **sportsmanlike** adj. **sportsmanly** adj. **sportsmanship** n.

sportswear /ˈspɔːtsweə(r)/ n. clothes worn for sport or casual outdoor use.

sporty /ˈspɔːtɪ/ adj. (**sportier**, **sportiest**) colloq. **1** fond of sport. **2** rakish, showy. □□ **sportily** adv. **sportiness** n.

sporule /ˈspɔːruːl/ n. a small spore or a single spore. □□ **sporular** adj. [F *sporule* or mod.L *sporula* (as SPORE)]

spot /spɒt/ n. & v. —n. **1 a** a small part of the surface of a thing distinguished by colour, texture, etc., usu. round or less elongated than a streak or stripe (a blue tie with pink spots). **b** a small mark or stain. **c** a pimple. **d** a small circle or other shape used in various numbers to distinguish faces of dice, playing-cards in a suit, etc. **e** a moral blemish or stain (without a spot on his reputation). **2 a** a particular place; a definite locality (dropped it on this precise spot; the spot where William III landed). **b** a place used for a particular activity (often in comb.: nightspot). **c** (prec. by the) Football the place from which a penalty kick is taken. **3** a particular part of one's body or aspect of one's character. **4 a** colloq. one's esp. regular position in an organization, programme of events, etc. **b** a place or position in a performance or show (did the spot before the interval). **5** Brit. **a** colloq. a small quantity of anything (a spot of lunch; a spot of trouble). **b** a drop (a spot of rain). **c** colloq. a drink. **6** = SPOTLIGHT. **7** (usu. attrib.) money paid or goods delivered immediately after a sale (spot cash; spot silver). **8** Billiards etc. **a** a small round black patch to mark the position where a ball is placed at certain times. **b** (in full **spot-ball**) the white ball distinguished from the other by two black spots. —v. (**spotted**, **spotting**) **1** tr. **a** colloq. single out beforehand (the winner of a race etc.). **b** colloq. recognize the identity, nationality, etc., of (spotted him at once as the murderer). **c** watch for and take note of (trains, talent, etc.). **d** colloq. catch sight of. **e** Mil. locate (an enemy's position), esp. from the air. **2 a** tr. & intr. mark or become marked with spots. **b** tr. stain, soil (a person's character etc.). **3** intr. make spots, rain slightly (it was spotting with rain). **4** tr. Billiards place (a ball) on a spot. □ **in**

a spot (or **in a tight** etc. **spot**) *colloq.* in difficulty. **on the spot 1** at the scene of an action or event. **2** *colloq.* in a position such that response or action is required. **3** without delay or change of place, then and there. **4** (of a person) wide awake, equal to the situation, in good form at a game etc. **put on the spot** *US sl.* decide to murder. **running on the spot** raising the feet alternately as in running but without moving forwards or backwards. **spot check** a test made on the spot or on a randomly-selected subject. **spot height 1** the altitude of a point. **2** a figure on a map showing this. **spot on** *Brit. colloq. adj.* precise; on target. —*adv.* precisely. **spot weld** a weld made in spot welding. **spot-weld** *v.tr.* join by spot welding. **spot welder** a person or device that spot-welds. **spot welding** welding two surfaces together in a series of discrete points. [ME, perh. f. MDu. *spotte*, LG *spot*, ON *spotti* small piece]

spotless /ˈspɒtlɪs/ *adj.* immaculate; absolutely clean or pure. □□ **spotlessly** *adv.* **spotlessness** *n.*

spotlight /ˈspɒtlaɪt/ *n. & v.* —*n.* **1** a beam of light directed on a small area, esp. on a particular part of a theatre stage or of the road in front of a vehicle. **2** a lamp projecting this. **3** full attention or publicity. —*v.tr.* (*past* and *past part.* **-lighted** or **-lit**) **1** direct a spotlight on. **2** make conspicuous, draw attention to.

spotted /ˈspɒtɪd/ *adj.* marked or decorated with spots. □ **spotted dick** (or **dog**) **1** *Brit.* a suet pudding containing currants. **2** a Dalmatian dog. **spotted fever 1** cerebrospinal meningitis. **2** typhus. □□ **spottedness** *n.*

spotter /ˈspɒtə(r)/ *n.* **1** (often in *comb.*) a person who spots people or things (*train-spotter*). **2** an aviator or aircraft employed in locating enemy positions etc.

spotty /ˈspɒtɪ/ *adj.* (**spottier, spottiest**) **1** marked with spots. **2** patchy, irregular. □□ **spottily** *adv.* **spottiness** *n.*

spouse /spaʊz, spaʊs/ *n.* a husband or wife. [ME *spūs(e)* f. OF *sp(o)us* (masc.), *sp(o)use* (fem.), vars. of *espous(e)* f. L *sponsus sponsa* past part. of *spondēre* betroth]

spout /spaʊt/ *n. & v.* —*n.* **1 a** a projecting tube or lip through which a liquid etc. is poured from a teapot, kettle, jug, etc., or issues from a fountain, pump, etc. **b** a sloping trough down which a thing may be shot into a receptacle. **c** *hist.* a lift serving a pawnbroker's storeroom. **2** a jet or column of liquid, grain, etc. **3** (in full **spout-hole**) a whale's blow-hole. —*v.tr. & intr.* **1** discharge or issue forcibly in a jet. **2** utter (verses etc.) or speak in a declamatory manner, speechify. □ **up the spout** *sl.* **1** useless, ruined, hopeless. **2** pawned. **3** pregnant. □□ **spouter** *n.* **spoutless** *adj.* [ME f. MDu. *spouten*, orig. imit.]

SPQR *abbr.* **1** *hist.* the Senate and people of Rome. **2** small profits and quick returns. [sense 1 f. L *Senatus Populusque Romanus*]

Spr. *abbr.* (in the UK) Sapper.

sprag /spræg/ *n.* **1** a thick piece of wood or similar device used as a brake. **2** a support-prop in a coal mine. [19th c.: orig. unkn.]

sprain /spreɪn/ *v. & n.* —*v.tr.* wrench (an ankle, wrist, etc.) violently so as to cause pain and swelling but not dislocation. —*n.* **1** such a wrench. **2** the resulting inflammation and swelling. [17th c.: orig. unkn.]

sprang past of SPRING.

sprat /spræt/ *n. & v.* —*n.* **1** a small European herring-like fish, *Sprattus sprattus*, much used as food. **2** a similar fish, e.g. a sand eel or a young herring. —*v.intr.* (**spratted, spratting**) fish for sprats. □ **a sprat to catch a mackerel** a small risk to gain much. □□ **spratter** *n.* **spratting** *n.* [OE *sprot*]

Spratly Islands /ˈsprætlɪ/ a group of islets and coral reefs in the South China Sea between Vietnam and Borneo. Dispersed over a distance of some 965 km (600 miles), the islands are claimed in whole or in part by China, Taiwan, Vietnam, the Philippines, and Malaysia.

sprauncy /ˈsprɔːnsɪ/ *adj.* (**sprauncier, spraunciest**) *Brit. sl.* smart or showy. [20th c.: perh. rel. to dial. *sprouncey* cheerful]

sprawl /sprɔːl/ *v. & n.* —*v.* **1 a** *intr.* sit or lie or fall with limbs flung out or in an ungainly way. **b** *tr.* spread (one's limbs) in this way. **2** *intr.* (of handwriting, a plant, a town, etc.) be of irregular or straggling form. —*n.* **1** a sprawling movement or attitude. **2** a straggling group or mass. **3** the straggling expansion of an urban or industrial area. □□ **sprawlingly** *adv.* [OE *spreawlian*]

spray[1] /spreɪ/ *n. & v.* —*n.* **1** water or other liquid flying in small drops from the force of the wind, the dashing of waves, or the action of an atomizer etc. **2** a liquid preparation to be applied in this form with an atomizer etc., esp. for medical purposes. **3** an instrument or apparatus for such application. —*v.tr.* (also *absol.*) **1** throw (liquid) in the form of spray. **2** sprinkle (an object) with small drops or particles, esp. (a plant) with an insecticide. **3** (*absol.*) (of a tom-cat) mark its environment with the smell of its urine, as an attraction to females. □ **spray-dry** (**-dries, -dried**) dry (milk etc.) by spraying into hot air etc. **spray-gun** a gunlike device for spraying paint etc. **spray-paint** paint (a surface) by means of a spray. □□ **sprayable** *adj.* **sprayer** *n.* [earlier *spry*, perh. rel. to MDu. *spra(e)yen*, MHG *spræjen* sprinkle]

spray[2] /spreɪ/ *n.* **1** a sprig of flowers or leaves, or a branch of a tree with branchlets or flowers, esp. a slender or graceful one. **2** an ornament in a similar form (*a spray of diamonds*). □□ **sprayey** /ˈspreɪɪ/ *adj.* [ME f. OE *spræg* (unrecorded)]

spread /spred/ *v. & n.* —*v.* (*past* and *past part.* **spread**) **1** *tr.* (often foll. by *out*) **a** open or extend the surface of. **b** cause to cover a larger surface (*spread butter on bread*). **c** display to the eye or the mind (*the view was spread out before us*). **2** *intr.* (often foll. by *out*) have a wide or specified or increasing extent (*on every side spread a vast desert; spreading trees*). **3** *intr. & tr.* become or make widely known, felt, etc. (*rumours are spreading; spread a little happiness*). **4** *tr.* **a** cover the surface of (*spread the wall with paint; a meadow spread with daisies*). **b** lay (a table). —*n.* **1** the act or an instance of spreading. **2** capability of expanding (*has a large spread*). **3** diffusion (*spread of learning*). **4** breadth, compass (*arches of equal spread*). **5** an aircraft's wing-span. **6** increased bodily girth (*middle-aged spread*). **7** the difference between two rates, prices, etc. **8** *colloq.* an elaborate meal. **9** a sweet or savoury paste for spreading on bread etc. **10** a bedspread. **11** printed matter spread across two facing pages or across more than one column. **12** *US* a ranch with extensive land. □ **spread eagle 1** a representation of an eagle with legs and wings extended as an emblem. **2** *hist.* a person secured with arms and legs spread out, esp. to be flogged. **spread-eagle** *v.tr.* (usu. as **spread-eagled** *adj.*) **1** place (a person) in this position. **2** defeat utterly. **3** spread out. —*adj. US* bombastic, esp. noisily patriotic. **spread oneself** be lavish or discursive. **spread one's wings** see WING. □□ **spreadable** *adj.* **spreader** *n.* [OE *-sprǣdan* f. WG]

spreadsheet /ˈspredʃiːt/ *n.* a computer program allowing manipulation and flexible retrieval of esp. tabulated numerical data.

Sprechgesang /ˈʃprexgəˌzɑːŋ/ *n. Mus.* a style of dramatic vocalization between speech and song. [G, lit. 'speech song']

spree /spriː/ *n. & v. colloq.* —*n.* **1** a lively extravagant outing (*shopping spree*). **2** a bout of fun or drinking etc. —*v.intr.* (**sprees, spreed**) have a spree. □ **on the spree** engaged in a spree. [19th c.: orig. unkn.]

sprig[1] /sprɪg/ *n. & v.* —*n.* **1** a small branch or shoot. **2** an ornament resembling this, esp. on fabric. **3** usu. *derog.* a youth or young man (*a sprig of the nobility*). —*v.tr.* (**sprigged, sprigging**) **1** ornament with sprigs (*a dress of sprigged muslin*). **2** (usu. as **sprigging** *n.*) decorate (ceramic ware) with ornaments in applied relief. □□ **spriggy** *adj.* [ME f. or rel. to LG *sprick*]

sprig[2] /sprɪg/ *n.* a small tapering headless tack. [ME: orig. unkn.]

sprightly /ˈspraɪtlɪ/ *adj.* (**sprightlier, sprightliest**) vivacious, lively, brisk. □□ **sprightliness** *n.* [*spright* var. of SPRITE + -LY[1]]

spring /sprɪŋ/ *v. & n.* —*v.* (*past* **sprang** /spræŋ/ or *US* **sprung** /sprʌŋ/; *past part.* **sprung**) **1** *intr.* jump; move rapidly or suddenly (*sprang from his seat; sprang through the gap; sprang to their assistance*). **2** *intr.* move rapidly as from a constrained position or by the action of a spring (*the branch sprang back; the door sprang to*). **3** *intr.* (usu. foll. by *from*) originate or arise (*springs from an old family; their actions spring from a false conviction*). **4** *intr.* (usu. foll. by *up*) come into being; appear, esp. suddenly (*a breeze sprang up; the belief has sprung up*). **5** *tr.* cause to act suddenly, esp. by means of a spring (*spring a trap*). **6** *tr.* (often foll. by *on*) produce or develop or make known suddenly or unexpectedly (*has sprung a new theory*; *loves to spring surprises*). **7** *tr. sl.* contrive the escape or release of. **8** *tr.* rouse (game) from earth or covert. **9 a** *intr.* become warped or split. **b** *tr.* split, crack (wood or a wooden implement). **10** *tr.* (usu. as **sprung** *adj.*) provide (a motor vehicle etc.) with springs. **11 a** *tr. colloq.* spend (money). **b** *intr.* (usu. foll. by *for*) *US* & *Austral. sl.* pay for a treat. **12** *tr.* cause (a mine) to explode. —*n.* **1** a jump (*took a spring*; *rose with a spring*). **2** a backward movement from a constrained position; a recoil, e.g. of a bow. **3** elasticity; ability to spring back strongly (*a mattress with plenty of spring*). **4** a resilient device usu. of bent or coiled metal used esp. to drive clockwork or for cushioning in furniture or vehicles. **5 a** the season in which vegetation begins to appear, the first season of the year, in the N. hemisphere from March to May and in the S. hemisphere from September to November. **b** *Astron.* the period from the vernal equinox to the summer solstice. **c** (often foll. by *of*) the early stage of life etc. **d** = **spring tide**. **6** a place where water, oil, etc., wells up from the earth; the basin or flow so formed (*hot springs*; *mineral springs*). **7** the motive for or origin of an action, custom, etc. (*the springs of human action*). **8** *sl.* an escape or release from prison. **9** the upward curve of a beam etc. from a horizontal line. **10** the splitting or yielding of a plank etc. under strain. □ **spring balance** a balance that measures weight by the tension of a spring. **spring bed** a bed with a spring mattress. **spring chicken 1** a young fowl for eating (orig. available only in spring). **2** (esp. with *neg.*) a young person (*she's no spring chicken*). **spring-clean** *n.* a thorough cleaning of a house or room, esp. in spring. —*v.tr.* clean (a house or room) in this way. **spring fever** a restless or lethargic feeling sometimes associated with spring. **spring greens** the leaves of young cabbage plants. **spring a leak** develop a leak (orig. *Naut.*, from timbers springing out of position). **spring-loaded** containing a compressed or stretched spring pressing one part against another. **spring mattress** a mattress containing or consisting of springs. **spring onion** an onion taken from the ground before the bulb has formed, and eaten raw in salad. **spring roll** a Chinese snack consisting of a pancake filled with vegetables etc. and fried. **spring tide** a tide just after new and full moon when there is the greatest difference between high and low water. **spring water** water from a spring, as opposed to river or rain water. **sprung rhythm** a poetic metre approximating to speech, each foot having one stressed syllable followed by a varying number of unstressed. The term was invented by G. M. Hopkins (see HOPKINS[2]) to describe his own idiosyncratic poetic metre. □□ **springless** *adj.* **springlet** *n.* **springlike** *adj.* [OE *springan* f. Gmc]

springboard /ˈsprɪŋbɔːd/ *n.* **1** a springy board giving impetus in leaping, diving, etc. **2** a source of impetus in any activity. **3** *US* & *Austral.* a platform inserted in the side of a tree, on which a lumberjack stands to chop at some height from the ground.

springbok /ˈsprɪŋbɒk/ *n.* **1** a southern African gazelle, *Antidorcas marsupialis*, with the ability to run with high springing jumps. **2** (**Springbok**) a South African, esp. one who has played for South Africa in international sporting competitions. [Afrik. f. Du. *springen* SPRING + *bok* antelope]

springe /sprɪndʒ/ *n.* a noose or snare for catching small game. [ME, rel. to obs. *sprenge*, and SPRING]

springer /ˈsprɪŋə(r)/ *n.* **1** a person or thing that springs. **2 a** a small spaniel of a breed used to spring game. **b** this breed. **3** *Archit.* **a** the part of an arch where the curve begins. **b** the lowest stone of this. **c** the bottom stone of the coping of a gable. **d** a rib of a groined roof or vault. **4** a springbok.

Springfield /ˈsprɪŋfiːld/ the capital of Illinois; pop. (1980) 99,640. It was the home and burial place of Abraham Lincoln.

springtail /ˈsprɪŋteɪl/ *n.* any wingless insect of the order Collembola, leaping by means of a springlike caudal part.

springtide /ˈsprɪŋtaɪd/ *n. poet.* = SPRINGTIME.

springtime /ˈsprɪŋtaɪm/ *n.* **1** the season of spring. **2** a time compared to this.

springy /ˈsprɪŋɪ/ *adj.* (**springier**, **springiest**) **1** springing back quickly when squeezed or stretched, elastic. **2** (of movements) as of a springy substance. □□ **springily** *adv.* **springiness** *n.*

sprinkle /ˈsprɪŋk(ə)l/ *v.* & *n.* —*v.tr.* **1** scatter (liquid, ashes,

crumbs, etc.) in small drops or particles. **2** (often foll. by *with*) subject (the ground or an object) to sprinkling with liquid etc. **3** (of liquid etc.) fall on in this way. **4** distribute in small amounts. —*n.* (usu. foll. by *of*) **1** a light shower. **2** = SPRINKLING. [ME, perh. f. MDu. *sprenkelen*]

sprinkler /ˈsprɪŋklə(r)/ *n.* a person or thing that sprinkles, esp. a device for sprinkling water on a lawn or to extinguish fires.

sprinkling /ˈsprɪŋklɪŋ/ *n.* (usu. foll. by *of*) a small thinly distributed number or amount.

sprint /sprɪnt/ *v.* & *n.* —*v.* **1** *intr.* run a short distance at full speed. **2** *tr.* run (a specified distance) in this way. —*n.* **1** such a run. **2** a similar short spell of maximum effort in cycling, swimming, motor racing, etc. □□ **sprinter** *n.* [ON *sprinta* (unrecorded), of unkn. orig.]

sprit /sprɪt/ *n.* a small spar reaching diagonally from the mast to the upper outer corner of the sail. [OE *sprēot* pole, rel. to SPROUT]

sprite /spraɪt/ *n.* an elf, fairy, or goblin. [ME f. *sprit* var. of SPIRIT]

spritsail /ˈsprɪts(ə)l, -seɪl/ *n.* **1** a sail extended by a sprit. **2** *hist.* a sail extended by a yard set under the bowsprit.

spritz /sprɪts/ *v.* & *n. US* —*v.tr.* sprinkle, squirt, or spray. —*n.* the act or an instance of spritzing. [G *spritzen* to squirt]

spritzer /ˈsprɪtsə(r)/ *n.* a mixture of wine and soda water. [G *Spritzer* a splash]

sprocket /ˈsprɒkɪt/ *n.* **1** each of several teeth on a wheel engaging with links of a chain, e.g. on a bicycle, or with holes in film or tape or paper. **2** (also **sprocket-wheel**) a wheel with sprockets. [16th c.: orig. unkn.]

sprog /sprɒg/ *n. sl.* a child; a baby. [orig. services' sl., = new recruit: perh. f. obs. *sprag* lively young man]

sprout /spraʊt/ *v.* & *n.* —*v.* **1** *tr.* put forth, produce (shoots, hair, etc.) (*has sprouted a moustache*). **2** *intr.* begin to grow, put forth shoots. **3** *intr.* spring up, grow to a height. —*n.* **1** a shoot of a plant. **2** = BRUSSELS SPROUT. [OE *sprūtan* (unrecorded) f. WG]

spruce[1] /spruːs/ *adj.* & *v.* —*adj.* neat in dress and appearance; trim, smart. —*v.tr.* & *intr.* (also *refl.*; usu. foll. by *up*) make or become smart. □□ **sprucely** *adv.* **spruceness** *n.* [perh. f. SPRUCE[2] in obs. sense 'Prussian', in the collocation *spruce (leather) jerkin*]

spruce[2] /spruːs/ *n.* **1** any coniferous tree of the genus *Picea*, with dense foliage growing in a distinctive conical shape. **2** the wood of this tree used as timber. □ **spruce beer** a fermented beverage using spruce twigs and needles as flavouring. [alt. of obs. *Pruce* Prussia: cf. PRUSSIAN]

spruce[3] /spruːs/ *v. Brit. sl.* **1** *tr.* deceive. **2** *intr.* lie, practise deception. **3** *intr.* evade a duty, malinger. □□ **sprucer** *n.* [20th c.: orig. unkn.]

sprue[1] /spruː/ *n.* **1** a channel through which metal or plastic is poured into a mould. **2** a piece of metal or plastic which has filled a sprue and solidified there. [19th c.: orig. unkn.]

sprue[2] /spruː/ *n.* a tropical disease with ulceration of the mucous membrane of the mouth and chronic enteritis. [Du. *spruw* THRUSH[2]; cf. Flem. *spruwen* sprinkle]

spruik /spruːk/ *v.intr. Austral.* & *NZ sl.* speak in public, esp. as a showman. □□ **spruiker** *n.* [20th c.: orig. unkn.]

spruit /spreɪt/ *n. S.Afr.* a small watercourse, usu. dry except during the rainy season. [Du., rel. to SPROUT]

sprung see SPRING.

spry /spraɪ/ *adj.* (**spryer**, **spryest**) active, lively. □□ **spryly** *adv.* **spryness** *n.* [18th c., dial. & US: orig. unkn.]

spud /spʌd/ *n.* & *v.* —*n.* **1** *sl.* a potato. **2** a small narrow spade for cutting the roots of weeds etc. —*v.tr.* (**spudded**, **spudding**) **1** (foll. by *up*, *out*) remove (weeds) with a spud. **2** (also *absol.*; often foll. by *in*) make the initial drilling for (an oil well). □ **spud-bashing** *Brit. sl.* a lengthy spell of peeling potatoes. [ME: orig. unkn.]

spue var. of SPEW.

spumante /spuːˈmæntɪ/ *n.* an Italian sparkling white wine (cf. ASTI). [It., = 'sparkling']

spume /spjuːm/ *n.* & *v.intr.* froth, foam. □□ **spumous** *adj.* **spumy** *adj.* (**spumier**, **spumiest**). [ME f. OF (*e*)*spume* or L *spuma*]

spumoni /spu:ˈməʊnɪ/ n. US a kind of ice-cream dessert. [It. *spumone* f. *spuma* SPUME]

spun past and past part. of SPIN.

spunk /spʌŋk/ n. **1** touchwood. **2** *colloq.* courage, mettle, spirit. **3** *coarse sl.* semen. ¶ Usually considered a taboo use. [16th c.: orig. unkn.: cf. PUNK]

spunky /ˈspʌŋkɪ/ adj. (**spunkier**, **spunkiest**) *colloq.* brave, spirited. □□ **spunkily** adv.

spur /spɜː(r)/ n. & v. —n. **1** a device with a small spike or a spiked wheel worn on a rider's heel for urging a horse forward. **2** a stimulus or incentive. **3** a spur-shaped thing, esp.: **a** a projection from a mountain or mountain range. **b** a branch road or railway. **c** a hard projection on a cock's leg. **d** a steel point fastened to the leg of a gamecock. **e** a climbing-iron. **f** a small support for ceramic ware in a kiln. **4** *Bot.* **a** a slender hollow projection from part of a flower. **b** a short fruit-bearing shoot. —v. (**spurred**, **spurring**) **1** *tr.* prick (a horse) with spurs. **2** *tr.* **a** (often foll. by *on*) incite (a person) (*spurred him on to greater efforts; spurred her to try again*). **b** stimulate (interest etc.). **3** *intr.* (often foll. by *on, forward*) ride a horse hard. **4** *tr.* (esp. as **spurred** adj.) provide (a person, boots, a gamecock) with spurs. □ **on the spur of the moment** on a momentary impulse; impromptu. **put** (or **set**) **spurs to 1** spur (a horse). **2** stimulate (resolution etc.). **spur-gear** = *spur-wheel*. **spur royal** *hist.* a 15-shilling coin of James I bearing a spurlike sun with rays. **spur-wheel** a cog-wheel with radial teeth. □□ **spurless** adj. [OE *spora, spura* f. Gmc, rel. to SPURN]

spurge /spɜːdʒ/ n. any plant of the genus *Euphorbia*, exuding an acrid milky juice once used medicinally as a purgative. □ **spurge laurel** any shrub of the genus *Daphne*, esp. *D. laureola*, with small yellow flowers. [ME f. OF *espurge* f. *espurgier* f. L *expurgare* (as EX-¹, PURGE)]

spurious /ˈspjʊərɪəs/ adj. **1** not genuine, not being what it purports to be, not proceeding from the pretended source (*a spurious excuse*). **2** having an outward similarity of form or function only. **3** (of offspring) illegitimate. □□ **spuriously** adv. **spuriousness** n. [L *spurius* false]

spurn /spɜːn/ v. & n. —v.tr. **1** reject with disdain; treat with contempt. **2** repel or thrust back with one's foot. —n. an act of spurning. □□ **spurner** n. [OE *spurnan, spornan*, rel. to SPUR]

spurrier /ˈspʌrɪə(r)/ n. a spur-maker.

spurry /ˈspʌrɪ/ n. (also **spurrey**) (pl. **-ies** or **-eys**) a slender plant of the genus *Spergula*, esp. the corn-spurry, a white-flowered weed in cornfields etc. [Du. *spurrie*, prob. rel. to med.L *spergula*]

spurt /spɜːt/ v. & n. —v. **1** (also **spirt**) **a** *intr.* gush out in a jet or stream. **b** *tr.* cause (liquid etc.) to do this. **2** *intr.* make a sudden effort. —n. **1** (also **spirt**) a sudden gushing out, a jet. **2** a short sudden effort or increase of pace esp. in racing. [16th c.: orig. unkn.]

sputnik /ˈspʊtnɪk, ˈspʌt-/ n. each of a series of Soviet artificial satellites orbiting the Earth. The first of these was launched on 4 Oct. 1957. [Russ., = fellow-traveller]

sputter /ˈspʌtə(r)/ v. & n. —v. **1** *intr.* emit spitting sounds, esp. when being heated. **2** *intr.* (often foll. by *at*) speak in a hurried or vehement fashion. **3** *tr.* emit with a spitting sound. **4** *tr.* speak or utter (words, threats, a language, etc.) rapidly or incoherently. **5** *tr. Physics* deposit (metal) by using fast ions etc. to eject particles of it from a target. —n. a sputtering sound, esp. sputtering speech. □□ **sputterer** n. [Du. *sputteren* (imit.)]

sputum /ˈspjuːtəm/ n. (pl. **sputa** /-tə/) **1** saliva, spittle. **2** a mixture of saliva and mucus expectorated from the respiratory tract, usu. a sign of disease. [L, neut. past part. of *spuere* spit]

spy /spaɪ/ n. & v. —n. (pl. **spies**) **1** a person who secretly collects and reports information on the activities, movements, etc., of an enemy, competitor, etc. **2** a person who keeps watch on others, esp. furtively. —v. (**spies, spied**) **1** *tr.* discern or make out, esp. by careful observation (*spied a house in the distance*). **2** *intr.* (often foll. by *on*) act as a spy, keep a close and secret watch. **3** *intr.* (often foll. by *into*) pry. □ **I spy** a children's game of guessing a visible object from the initial letter of its name. **spy-master** *colloq.* the head of an organization of spies. **spy**

out explore or discover, esp. secretly. [ME f. OF *espie* espying, *espier* espy f. Gmc]

spyglass /ˈspaɪglɑːs/ n. a small telescope.

spyhole /ˈspaɪhəʊl/ n. a peep-hole.

sq. *abbr.* square.

Sqn. Ldr. *abbr.* Squadron Leader.

squab /skwɒb/ n. & adj. —n. **1** a short fat person. **2** a young esp. unfledged pigeon or other bird. **3 a** a stuffed cushion. **b** *Brit.* the padded back or side of a car-seat. **4** a sofa or ottoman. —adj. short and fat, squat. □ **squab-chick** an unfledged bird. **squab pie 1** pigeon pie. **2** a pie of mutton, pork, onions, and apples. [17th c.: orig. unkn.: cf. obs. *quab* shapeless thing, Sw. dial. *sqvabba* fat woman]

squabble /ˈskwɒb(ə)l/ n. & v. —n. a petty or noisy quarrel. —v.intr. engage in a squabble. □□ **squabbler** n. [prob. imit.: cf. Sw. dial. *sqvabbel* a dispute]

squabby /ˈskwɒbɪ/ adj. (**squabbier**, **squabbiest**) short and fat; squat.

squad /skwɒd/ n. **1** a small group of people sharing a task etc. **2** *Mil.* a small number of men assembled for drill etc. **3** *Sport* a group of players forming a team. **4 a** (often in *comb.*) a specialized unit within a police force (*drug squad*). **b** = *flying squad*. **5** a group or class of people of a specified kind (*the awkward squad*). □ **squad car** a police car having a radio link with headquarters. [F *escouade* var. of *escadre* f. It. *squadra* SQUARE]

squaddie /ˈskwɒdɪ/ n. (also **squaddy**) (pl. **-ies**) *Brit. Mil. sl.* **1** a recruit. **2** a private.

squadron /ˈskwɒdrən/ n. **1** an organized body of persons. **2** a principal division of a cavalry regiment or armoured formation, consisting of two troops. **3** a detachment of warships employed on a particular duty. **4** a unit of the Royal Air Force with 10 to 18 aircraft. □ **Squadron Leader** the commander of a squadron of the Royal Air Force, the officer next below Wing Commander. [It. *squadrone* (as SQUAD)]

squail /skweɪl/ n. **1** (in *pl.*) a game with small wooden discs propelled across a table or board. **2** each of these discs. □ **squail-board** a board used in squails. [19th c.: orig. unkn.: cf. dial. *kayles* skittles]

squalid /ˈskwɒlɪd/ adj. **1** filthy, repulsively dirty. **2** mean or poor in appearance. **3** wretched, sordid. □□ **squalidity** n. /-ˈlɪdɪtɪ/ **squalidly** adv. **squalidness** n. [L *squalidus* f. *squalēre* be rough or dirty]

squall /skwɔːl/ n. & v. —n. **1** a sudden or violent gust or storm of wind, esp. with rain or snow or sleet. **2** a discordant cry; a scream (esp. of a baby). **3** (esp. in *pl.*) trouble, difficulty. —v. **1** *intr.* utter a squall; scream, cry out violently as in fear or pain. **2** *tr.* utter in a screaming or discordant voice. □□ **squally** adj. [prob. f. SQUEAL after BAWL]

squalor /ˈskwɒlə(r)/ n. the state of being filthy or squalid. [L, as SQUALID]

squama /ˈskweɪmə/ n. (pl. **squamae** /-miː/) **1** a scale on an animal or plant. **2** a thin scalelike plate of bone. **3** a scalelike feather. □□ **squamate** /-meɪt/ adj. **squamose** adj. **squamous** adj. **squamule** n. [L *squama*]

squander /ˈskwɒndə(r)/ v.tr. **1** spend (money, time, etc.) wastefully. **2** dissipate (a fortune etc.) wastefully. □□ **squanderer** n. [16th c.: orig. unkn.]

square /skweə(r)/ n., adj., adv., & v. —n. **1** an equilateral rectangle. **2 a** an object of this shape or approximately this shape. **b** a small square area on a game-board. **c** a square scarf. **d** an academic cap with a stiff square top; a mortarboard. **3 a** an open (usu. four-sided) area surrounded by buildings, esp. one planted with trees etc. and surrounded by houses. **b** an open area at the meeting of streets. **c** *Cricket* a closer-cut area at the centre of a ground, any strip of which may be prepared as a wicket. **d** an area within barracks etc. for drill. **e** *US* a block of buildings bounded by four streets. **4** the product of a number multiplied by itself (*81 is the square of 9*). **5** an L-shaped or T-shaped instrument for obtaining or testing right angles. **6** *sl.* a conventional or old-fashioned person, one ignorant of or opposed to current trends. **7** a square arrangement of letters, figures,

æ cat ɑː arm e bed ɜː her ɪ sit iː see ɒ hot ɔː saw ʌ run ʊ put uː too ə ago aɪ my

etc. **8** a body of infantry drawn up in rectangular form. **9** a unit of 100 sq. ft. as a measure of flooring etc. **10** *US* a square meal (*three squares a day*). —*adj.* **1** having the shape of a square. **2** having or in the form of a right angle (*table with square corners*). **3** angular and not round; of square section (*has a square jaw*). **4** designating a unit of measure equal to the area of a square whose side is one of the unit specified (*square metre*). **5** (often foll. by *with*) **a** level, parallel. **b** on a proper footing; even, quits. **6 a** (usu. foll. by *to*) at right angles. **b** *Cricket* on a line through the stumps at right angles to the wicket. **7** having the breadth more nearly equal to the length or height than is usual (*a man of square frame*). **8** properly arranged; in good order, settled (*get things square*). **9** (also **all square**) **a** not in debt, with no money owed. **b** having equal scores, esp. *Golf* having won the same number of holes as one's opponent. **c** (of scores) equal. **10** fair and honest (*his dealings are not always quite square*). **11** uncompromising, direct, thorough (*was met with a square refusal*). **12** *sl.* conventional or old-fashioned, unsophisticated, conservative (cf. sense 6 of *n.*). **13** *Mus.* (of rhythm) simple, straightforward. —*adv.* **1** squarely (*sat square on his seat*). **2** fairly, honestly (*play square*). —*v.* **1** *tr.* make square or rectangular, give a rectangular cross-section to (timber etc.). **2** *tr.* multiply (a number) by itself (*3 squared is 9*). **3** *tr.* & *intr.* (usu. foll. by *to*, *with*) adjust; make or be suitable or consistent; reconcile (*the results do not square with your conclusions*). **4** *tr.* mark out in squares. **5** *tr.* settle or pay (a bill etc.). **6** *tr.* place (one's shoulders etc.) squarely facing forwards. **7** *tr. colloq.* **a** pay or bribe. **b** secure the acquiescence etc. of (a person) in this way. **8** *tr.* (also *absol.*) make the scores of (a match etc.) all square. **9** *intr.* assume the attitude of a boxer. **10** *tr. Naut.* **a** lay (yards) at right angles with the keel making them at the same time horizontal. **b** get (dead-eyes) horizontal. **c** get (ratlines) horizontal and parallel to one another. □ **back to square one** *colloq.* back to the starting-point with no progress made. **get square with** pay or compound with (a creditor). **on the square** *adj.* **1** *colloq.* honest, fair. **2** having membership of the Freemasons. —*adv. colloq.* honestly, fairly (*can be trusted to act on the square*). **out of square** not at right angles. **perfect square** = *square number*. **square accounts with** see ACCOUNT. **square away** *US* tidy up. **square-bashing** *Brit. Mil. sl.* drill on a barrack-square. **square brackets** brackets of the form []. **square-built** of comparatively broad shape. **square the circle 1** construct a square equal in area to a given circle (a problem incapable of a purely geometrical solution). **2** do what is impossible. **square dance** a dance with usu. four couples facing inwards from four sides. **square deal** a fair bargain, fair treatment. **squared paper** paper marked out in squares, esp. for plotting graphs. **square-eyed** *joc.* affected by or given to excessive viewing of television. **square leg** *Cricket* **1** the fielding position at some distance on the batsman's leg side and nearly opposite the stumps. **2** a fielder in this position. **square meal** a substantial and satisfying meal. **square measure** measure expressed in square units. **square number** the square of an integer e.g. 1, 4, 9, 16. **square off 1** *US* assume the attitude of a boxer. **2** *Austral.* placate or conciliate. **3** mark out in squares. **square peg in a round hole** see PEG. **square piano** an early type of piano, small and oblong in shape. **square-rigged** with the principal sails at right angles to the length of the ship and extended by horizontal yards slung to the mast by the middle (opp. *fore-and-aft rigged*). **square root** the number that multiplied by itself gives a specified number (*3 is the square root of 9*). **square sail** a four-cornered sail extended on a yard slung to the mast by the middle. **square-shouldered** with broad and not sloping shoulders (cf. *round-shouldered*). **square-toed 1** (of shoes or boots) having square toes. **2** wearing such shoes or boots. **3** formal, prim. **square up** settle an account etc. **square up to 1** move towards (a person) in a fighting attitude. **2** face and tackle (a difficulty etc.) resolutely. **square wave** *Physics* a wave with periodic sudden alternations between only two values of quantity. □□ **squarely** *adv.* **squareness** *n.* **squarer** *n.* **squarish** *adj.* [ME f. OF *esquare*, *esquarré*, *esquarrer*, ult. f. EX-[1] + L *quadra* square]

Squarial /ˈskweəriəl/ *n. propr.* a diamond-shaped satellite dish. [SQUARE + AERIAL]

squarrose /ˈskwɒrəʊs/ *adj. Bot.* & *Zool.* rough with scalelike projections. [L *squarrosus* scurfy, scabby]

squash[1] /skwɒʃ/ *v.* & *n.* —*v.* **1** *tr.* crush or squeeze flat or into pulp. **2** *intr.* (often foll. by *into*) make one's way by squeezing. **3** *tr.* pack tight, crowd. **4** *tr.* **a** silence (a person) with a crushing retort etc. **b** dismiss (a proposal etc.). **c** quash (a rebellion). —*n.* **1** a crowd; a crowded assembly. **2** a sound of or as of something being squashed, or of a soft body falling. **3** *Brit.* a concentrated drink made of crushed fruit etc., diluted with water. **4** squash rackets (see separate entry). **5** a squashed thing or mass. □ **squash tennis** *US* a game similar to squash, played with a lawn-tennis ball. □□ **squashy** *adj.* (**squashier**, **squashiest**). **squashily** *adv.* **squashiness** *n.* [alt. of QUASH]

squash[2] /skwɒʃ/ *n.* (pl. same or **squashes**) **1** any of various trailing plants of the genus *Cucurbita*, esp. *C. maxima*, *C. moschata*, and *C. pepo*, having pumpkin-like fruits. **2** the fruit of these cooked and eaten as a vegetable. [obs. (i)*squoutersquash* f. Narraganset *asquutasquash* f. *asq* uncooked + *squash* green]

squash rackets *n.* a game played with rackets and a small fairly soft ball in a closed court. It is derived from the game of rackets (see entry), and originated at Harrow School in England, the word *squash* being derived from the softer hollow 'squashy' ball used.

squat /skwɒt/ *v.*, *adj.*, & *n.* —*v.* (**squatted**, **squatting**) **1** *intr.* **a** crouch with the hams resting on the backs of the heels. **b** sit on the ground etc. with the knees drawn up and the heels close to or touching the hams. **2** *tr.* put (a person) into a squatting position. **3** *intr. colloq.* sit down. **4** *intr.* act as a squatter. **b** *tr.* occupy (a building) as a squatter. **5** *intr.* (of an animal) crouch close to the ground. —*adj.* (**squatter**, **squattest**) **1** (of a person etc.) short and thick, dumpy. **2** in a squatting posture. —*n.* **1** a squatting posture. **2 a** a place occupied by a squatter or squatters. **b** being a squatter. □□ **squatly** *adv.* **squatness** *n.* [ME f. OF *esquatir* flatten f. *es-* EX-[1] + *quatir* press down, crouch ult. f. L *coactus* past part. of *cogere* compel: see COGENT]

squatter /ˈskwɒtə(r)/ *n.* **1** a person who takes unauthorized possession of unoccupied premises. **2** *Austral.* **a** a sheep-farmer esp. on a large scale. **b** *hist.* a person who gets the right of pasturage from the government on easy terms. **3** a person who settles on new esp. public land without title. **4** a person who squats.

squaw /skwɔː/ *n.* a N. American Indian woman or wife. □ **squaw-man** a White married to a squaw. **squaw winter** (in N. America) a brief wintry spell before an Indian Summer. [Narraganset *squaws*, Massachusetts *squaw* woman]

squawk /skwɔːk/ *n.* & *v.* —*n.* **1** a loud harsh cry esp. of a bird. **2** a complaint. —*v.intr.* utter a squawk. □ **squawk-box** *colloq.* a loudspeaker or intercom. □□ **squawker** *n.* [imit.]

squeak /skwiːk/ *n.* & *v.* —*n.* **1 a** a short shrill cry as of a mouse. **b** a slight high-pitched sound as of an unoiled hinge. **2** (also **narrow squeak**) a narrow escape, a success barely attained. —*v.* **1** *intr.* make a squeak. **2** *tr.* utter (words) shrilly. **3** *intr.* (foll. by *by*, *through*) *colloq.* pass narrowly. **4** *intr. sl.* turn informer. [ME, imit.: cf. SQUEAL, SHRIEK, and Sw. *skväka* croak]

squeaker /ˈskwiːkə(r)/ *n.* **1** a person or thing that squeaks. **2** a young bird, esp. a pigeon.

squeaky /ˈskwiːkɪ/ *adj.* (**squeakier**, **squeakiest**) making a squeaking sound. □ **squeaky clean 1** completely clean. **2** above criticism; beyond reproach. □□ **squeakily** *adv.* **squeakiness** *n.*

squeal /skwiːl/ *n.* & *v.* —*n.* a prolonged shrill sound, esp. a cry of a child or a pig. —*v.* **1** *intr.* make a squeal. **2** *tr.* utter (words) with a squeal. **3** *intr. sl.* turn informer. **4** *intr. sl.* protest loudly or excitedly. □□ **squealer** *n.* [ME, imit.]

squeamish /ˈskwiːmɪʃ/ *adj.* **1** easily nauseated or disgusted. **2** fastidious or overscrupulous in questions of propriety, honesty, etc. □□ **squeamishly** *adv.* **squeamishness** *n.* [ME var. of *squeamous* (now dial.), f. AF *escoymos*, of unkn. orig.]

squeegee /ˈskwiːdʒiː/ *n.* & *v.* —*n.* **1** a rubber-edged implement set on a long handle and used for cleaning windows, etc. **2** a small similar instrument or roller used in photography. —*v.tr.* (**squeegees**, **squeegeed**) treat with a squeegee. [*squeege*, strengthened form of SQUEEZE]

squeeze /skwiːz/ v. & n. —v. 1 tr. **a** exert pressure on from opposite or all sides, esp. in order to extract moisture or reduce size. **b** compress with one's hand or between two bodies. **c** reduce the size of or alter the shape of by squeezing. 2 tr. (often foll. by out) extract (moisture) by squeezing. 3 **a** tr. force (a person or thing) into or through a small or narrow space. **b** intr. make one's way by squeezing. **c** tr. make (one's way) by squeezing. 4 tr. **a** harass by exactions; extort money etc. from. **b** constrain; bring pressure to bear on. **c** (usu. foll. by out of) obtain (money etc.) by extortion, entreaty, etc. **d** Bridge subject (a player) to a squeeze. 5 tr. press (a person's hand) with one's own as a sign of sympathy, affection, etc. 6 tr. (often foll. by out) produce with effort (squeezed out a tear). —n. 1 an instance of squeezing; the state of being squeezed. 2 Brit. a close embrace. 3 a crowd or crowded state; a crush. 4 a small quantity produced by squeezing (a squeeze of lemon). 5 a sum of money extorted or exacted, esp. an illicit commission. 6 Econ. a restriction on borrowing, investment, etc., in a financial crisis. 7 an impression of a coin etc. taken by pressing damp paper, wax, etc., against it. 8 (in full **squeeze play**) **a** Bridge leading winning cards until an opponent is forced to discard an important card. **b** Baseball hitting a ball short to the infield to enable a runner on third base to start for home as soon as the ball is pitched. □ **put the squeeze on** colloq. coerce or pressure (a person). **squeeze bottle** a flexible container whose contents are extracted by squeezing it. **squeeze-box** sl. an accordion or concertina. □□ **squeezable** adj. **squeezer** n. [earlier squise, intensive of obs. queise, of unkn. orig.]

squelch /skweltʃ/ v. & n. —v. 1 intr. **a** make a sucking sound as of treading in thick mud. **b** move with a squelching sound. 2 tr. **a** disconcert, silence. **b** stamp on, crush flat, put an end to. —n. an instance of squelching. □□ **squelcher** n. **squelchy** adj. [imit.]

squib /skwɪb/ n. & v. —n. 1 a small firework burning with a hissing sound and usu. with a final explosion. 2 a short satirical composition, a lampoon. —v. (**squibbed, squibbing**) 1 tr. US Football kick (the ball) a comparatively short distance on a kick-off; execute (a kick) in this way. 2 archaic **a** intr. write lampoons. **b** tr. lampoon. [16th c.: orig. unkn.: perh. imit.]

squid /skwɪd/ n. & v. —n. 1 any of various ten-armed cephalopods, esp. of the genus Loligo, used as bait or food. 2 artificial bait for fish imitating a squid in form. —v.intr. (**squidded, squidding**) fish with squid as bait. [17th c.: orig. unkn.]

squidgy /ˈskwɪdʒɪ/ adj. (**squidgier, squidgiest**) colloq. squashy, soggy. [imit.]

squiffed /skwɪft/ adj. sl. = SQUIFFY.

squiffy /ˈskwɪfɪ/ adj. (**squiffier, squiffiest**) esp. Brit. sl. slightly drunk. [19th c.: orig. unkn.]

squiggle /ˈskwɪg(ə)l/ n. & v. —n. a short curly line, esp. in handwriting or doodling. —v. 1 tr. write in a squiggly manner; scrawl. 2 intr. wriggle, squirm. □□ **squiggly** adj. [imit.]

squill /skwɪl/ n. 1 any bulbous plant of the genus Scilla, esp. S. autumnalis. 2 a seashore plant, Urginea maritima, having bulbs used in diuretic and purgative preparations. Also called sea onion. 3 any crustacean of the genus Squilla. [ME f. L squilla, scilla f. Gk skilla]

squinch /skwɪntʃ/ n. a straight or arched structure across an interior angle of a square tower to carry a superstructure, e.g. a dome. [var. of obs. scunch, abbr. of SCUNCHEON]

squint /skwɪnt/ v., n., & adj. —v. 1 intr. have the eyes turned in different directions, have a squint. 2 intr. (often foll. by at) look obliquely or with half-closed eyes. 3 tr. close (one's eyes) quickly, hold (one's eyes) half-shut. —n. 1 = STRABISMUS. 2 a stealthy or sidelong glance. 3 colloq. a glance or look (had a squint at it). 4 an oblique opening through the wall of a church affording a view of the altar. 5 a leaning or inclination towards a particular object or aim. —adj. 1 squinting. 2 looking different ways. □ **squint-eyed** 1 squinting. 2 malignant, ill-willed. □□ **squinter** n. **squinty** adj. [ASQUINT: (adj.) perh. f. squint-eyed f. obs. squint (adv.) f. ASQUINT]

squire /ˈskwaɪə(r)/ n. & v. —n. 1 a country gentleman, esp. the chief landowner in a country district. 2 hist. a knight's attendant.

3 Brit. colloq. a jocular form of address to a man. 4 US a magistrate or lawyer. 5 Austral. a young snapper fish. —v.tr. (of a man) attend upon or escort (a woman). □□ **squiredom** n. **squirehood** n. **squirelet** n. **squireling** n. **squirely** adj. **squireship** n. [ME f. OF esquier ESQUIRE]

squirearch /ˈskwaɪəˌrɑːk/ n. a member of the squirearchy. □□ **squirearchical** /-ˈrɑːkɪk(ə)l/ adj. (also **squirarchical**). [back-form. f. SQUIREARCHY, after MONARCH]

squirearchy /ˈskwaɪəˌrɑːkɪ/ n. (also **squirarchy**) (pl. **-ies**) landowners collectively, esp. as a class having political or social influence; a class or body of squires. [SQUIRE, after HIERARCHY etc.]

squireen /ˌskwaɪəˈriːn/ n. Brit. the owner of a small landed property esp. in Ireland.

squirl /skwɜːl/ n. colloq. a flourish or twirl, esp. in handwriting. [perh. f. SQUIGGLE + TWIRL or WHIRL]

squirm /skwɜːm/ v. & n. —v.intr. 1 wriggle, writhe. 2 show or feel embarrassment or discomfiture. —n. a squirming movement. □□ **squirmer** n. **squirmy** adj. (**squirmier, squirmiest**). [imit., prob. assoc. with WORM]

squirrel /ˈskwɪr(ə)l/ n. & v. —n. 1 any rodent of the family Sciuridae, e.g. the red squirrel, grey squirrel, etc., often of arboreal habits, with a bushy tail arching over its back, and pointed ears. 2 the fur of this animal. 3 a person who hoards objects, food, etc. —v. (**squirrelled, squirrelling**; US **squirreled, squirreling**) 1 tr. (often foll. by away) hoard (objects, food, time, etc.) (squirrelled it away in the cupboard). 2 intr. (often foll. by around) bustle about. □ **squirrel cage** 1 a small cage containing a revolving cylinder like a treadmill, on which a captive squirrel may exercise. 2 a form of rotor used in small electric motors, resembling the cylinder of a squirrel cage. 3 a monotonous or repetitive way of life. **squirrel** (or **squirrel-tail**) **grass** a grass, Hordeum jubatum, with bushy spikelets. **squirrel-monkey** a small yellow-haired monkey, Saimiri sciureus, native to S. America. [ME f. AF esquirel, OF esquireul, ult. f. L sciurus f. Gk skiouros f. skia shade + oura tail]

squirrelly /ˈskwɪrəlɪ/ adj. 1 like a squirrel. 2 **a** inclined to bustle about. **b** (of a person) unpredictable, nervous, demented.

squirt /skwɜːt/ v. & n. —v. 1 tr. eject (liquid or powder) in a jet as from a syringe. 2 intr. (of liquid or powder) be discharged in this way. 3 tr. splash with liquid or powder ejected by squirting. —n. 1 **a** a jet of water etc. **b** a small quantity produced by squirting. 2 **a** a syringe. **b** (in full **squirt-gun**) a kind of toy syringe. 3 colloq. an insignificant but presumptuous person. □□ **squirter** n. [ME, imit.]

squish /skwɪʃ/ n. & v. —n. a slight squelching sound. —v. 1 intr. move with a squish. 2 tr. colloq. squash, squeeze. □□ **squishy** adj. (**squishier, squishiest**). [imit.]

squit /skwɪt/ n. Brit. 1 sl. a small or insignificant person. 2 dial. nonsense. [cf. dial. squirt insignificant person, and squit to squirt]

squitch /skwɪtʃ/ n. couch grass. [alt. f. QUITCH]

squiz /skwɪz/ n. Austral. & NZ sl. a look or glance. [prob. f. QUIZ²]

Sr symb. Chem. the element strontium.

Sr. abbr. 1 Senior. 2 Señor. 3 Signor. 4 Eccl. Sister.

sr abbr. steradian(s).

SRC abbr. (in the UK) Science Research Council.

Sri Lanka /ʃriː ˈlaŋkə, ʃri, sr-/ (formerly Ceylon) an island off the SE coast of India; pop. (est. 1988) 16,639,700; official language, Sinhalese; capital, Colombo. The economy is largely dependent on exports of tea, rubber, and coconuts. A centre of Buddhist culture from the 3rd c. BC, the island was ruled by a strong native dynasty from the 12th c. but was successively dominated by the Portuguese, Dutch, and British from the 16th c. and finally annexed by the last in 1815. A Commonwealth State from 1948, the country became an independent republic in 1972, taking the name of Sri Lanka (= resplendent island). Its political stability has been continually threatened by trouble between the Sinhalese and Tamil parts of the population. □□ **Sri Lankan** adj. & n.

Srinagar /ˈsriːnəgə(r)/ the summer capital of the State of Jammu and Kashmir in NW India; pop. (est. 1981) 520,000.

SRN *abbr.* (in the UK) State Registered Nurse.

SRO *abbr.* standing room only.

SS *abbr.* **1** Saints. **2** steamship. **3** *hist.* Nazi special police force (German **Schutz-Staffel**), the élite corps of the German Nazi Party. Founded in 1925 by Hitler as a personal bodyguard, the SS was schooled in absolute loyalty and obedience and in total ruthlessness towards opponents. From 1929 until 1945 it was headed by Heinrich Himmler. A section of the SS served as a combat troop alongside but independent of the armed forces; it also administered the concentration camps.

SSAFA *abbr.* (in the UK) Soldiers', Sailors', and Airmen's Families Association.

SSC *abbr.* (in Scotland) Solicitor to the Supreme Court.

SSE *abbr.* south-south-east.

SSP *abbr.* (in the UK) statutory sick pay.

SSR *abbr.* Soviet Socialist Republic.

SSSI *abbr.* (in the UK) Site of Special Scientific Interest.

SST *abbr.* supersonic transport.

SSW *abbr.* south-south-west.

St *abbr.* **1** Saint. **2** stokes.

St. *abbr.* Street.

st. *abbr.* **1** stone (in weight). **2** *Cricket* stumped by.

-st var. of -EST[2].

Sta. *abbr.* Station.

stab /stæb/ *v. & n.* —*v.* (**stabbed, stabbing**) **1** *tr.* pierce or wound with a (usu. short) pointed tool or weapon e.g. a knife or dagger. **2** *intr.* (often foll. by *at*) aim a blow with such a weapon. **3** *intr.* cause a sensation like being stabbed (*stabbing pain*). **4** *tr.* hurt or distress (a person, feelings, conscience, etc.). **5** *intr.* (foll. by *at*) aim a blow at a person's reputation, etc. —*n.* **1 a** an instance of stabbing. **b** a blow or thrust with a knife etc. **2** a wound made in this way. **3** a blow or pain inflicted on a person's feelings. **4** *colloq.* an attempt, a try. □ **stab in the back** *n.* a treacherous or slanderous attack. —*v.tr.* slander or betray. □□ **stabber** *n.* [ME: cf. dial. *stob* in sense 1 of *v.*]

Stabat Mater /ˌstɑːbæt ˈmɑːtə(r)/ *n.* **1** a Latin hymn on the suffering of the Virgin Mary at the Crucifixion. **2** a musical setting for this. [the opening words, L *Stabat mater dolorosa* 'Stood the mother, full of grief']

stabile /ˈsteɪbaɪl, -bɪl/ *n.* a rigid, free-standing abstract sculpture or structure of wire, sheet metal, etc. [L *stabilis* STABLE[1], after MOBILE]

stability /stəˈbɪlɪtɪ/ *n.* the quality or state of being stable. [ME f. OF *stableté* f. L *stabilitas* f. *stabilis* STABLE[1]]

stabilize /ˈsteɪbɪˌlaɪz/ *v.tr. & intr.* (also **-ise**) make or become stable. □□ **stabilization** /-ˈzeɪʃ(ə)n/ *n.*

stabilizer /ˈsteɪbɪˌlaɪzə(r)/ *n.* (also **-iser**) a device or substance used to keep something stable, esp.: **1** a gyroscope device to prevent rolling of a ship. **2** *US* the horizontal tailplane of an aircraft. **3** (in *pl.*) a pair of small wheels fitted to the rear wheel of a child's bicycle.

stable[1] /ˈsteɪb(ə)l/ *adj.* (**stabler, stablest**) **1** firmly fixed or established; not easily adjusted, destroyed, or altered (*a stable structure; a stable government*). **2** firm, resolute; not wavering or fickle (*a stable and steadfast friend*). **3** *Chem.* (of a compound) not readily decomposing. **4** *Physics* (of an isotope) not subject to radioactive decay. □ **stable equilibrium** a state in which a body when disturbed tends to return to equilibrium. □□ **stableness** *n.* **stably** *adv.* [ME f. AF *stable*, OF *estable* f. L *stabilis* f. *stare* stand]

stable[2] /ˈsteɪb(ə)l/ *n. & v.* —*n.* **1** a building set apart and adapted for keeping horses. **2** an establishment where racehorses are kept and trained. **3** the racehorses of a particular stable. **4** persons, products, etc., having a common origin or affiliation. **5** such an origin or affiliation. —*v.tr.* put or keep (a horse) in a stable. □ **stable-boy** a boy employed in a stable. **stable-companion** (or **-mate**) **1** a horse of the same stable. **2** a member of the same organization. **stable-girl** a girl employed in a stable. **stable-lad** a person employed in a stable. □□ **stableful** *n.* (*pl.* **-fuls**). [ME f. OF *estable* f. L *stabulum* f. *stare* stand]

stableman /ˈsteɪb(ə)lmən/ *n.* (*pl.* **-men**) a person employed in a stable.

stabling /ˈsteɪblɪŋ/ *n.* accommodation for horses.

stablish /ˈstæblɪʃ/ *v.tr. archaic* fix firmly; establish; set up. [var. of ESTABLISH]

staccato /stəˈkɑːtəʊ/ *adv., adj., & n. esp. Mus.* —*adv. & adj.* with each sound or note sharply detached or separated from the others (cf. LEGATO, TENUTO). —*n.* (*pl.* **-os**) **1** a staccato passage in music etc. **2** staccato delivery or presentation. □ **staccato mark** a dot or stroke above or below a note, indicating that it is to be played staccato. [It., past part. of *staccare* = *distaccare* DETACH]

stack /stæk/ *n. & v.* —*n.* **1** a pile or heap, esp. in orderly arrangement. **2** a circular or rectangular pile of hay, straw, etc., or of grain in sheaf, often with a sloping thatched top, a rick. **3** *colloq.* a large quantity (*a stack of work; has stacks of money*). **4 a** = *chimney-stack*. **b** = SMOKESTACK. **c** a tall factory chimney. **5** a stacked group of aircraft. **6** (also **stack-room**) a part of a library where books are compactly stored, esp. one to which the public does not have direct access. **7** *Brit.* a high detached rock esp. off the coast of Scotland and the Orkneys. **8** a pyramidal group of rifles, a pile. **9** *Computing* a set of storage locations which store data in such a way that the most recently stored item is the first to be retrieved. **10** *Brit.* a measure for a pile of wood of 108 cu. ft. (30.1 cubic metres). —*v.tr.* **1** pile in a stack or stacks. **2 a** arrange (cards) secretly for cheating. **b** manipulate (circumstances etc.) to one's advantage. **3** cause (aircraft) to fly round the same point at different levels while waiting to land at an airport. □ **stack arms** *hist.* = *pile arms*. **stack up** *US colloq.* present oneself, measure up. **stack-yard** an enclosure for stacks of hay, straw, etc. □□ **stackable** *adj.* **stacker** *n.* [ME f. ON *stakkr* haystack f. Gmc]

stacte /ˈstæktiː/ *n.* a sweet spice used by the ancient Jews in making incense. [ME f. L f. Gk *staktē* f. *stazō* drip]

staddle /ˈstæd(ə)l/ *n.* a platform or framework supporting a rick etc. □ **staddle-stone** a stone supporting a staddle or rick etc. [OE *stathol* base f. Gmc, rel. to STAND]

stadium /ˈsteɪdɪəm/ *n.* (*pl.* **stadiums**) **1** an athletic or sports ground with tiers of seats for spectators. **2** (*pl.* **stadiums** or **stadia** /-dɪə/) *Antiq.* **a** a course for a foot-race or chariot-race. **b** a measure of length, about 185 metres. **3** a stage or period of development etc. [ME f. L f. Gk *stadion*]

stadtholder /ˈstɑːdˌhəʊldə(r), ˈstɑːt-, ˈstæ-/ *n.* (also **stadholder**) *hist.* **1** the chief magistrate of the United Provinces of The Netherlands. **2** the viceroy or governor of a province or town in The Netherlands. □□ **stadtholdership** *n.* [Du. *stadhouder* deputy f. *stad* STEAD + *houder* HOLDER, after med.L LOCUM TENENS]

Staël /stɑːl/, Anne-Louise-Germaine Necker, Mme de (1766–1817), French writer, who occupied a central place in French intellectual life for three decades but aroused the hostility of Napoleon. Her most important work, *De l'Allemagne* (1810), which she banned, introduced German writers and thinkers of the end of the 18th c. to France. She also wrote two novels, *Delphine* (1802) and *Corinne* (1807). She was a major precursor of French Romanticism.

staff[1] /stɑːf/ *n. & v.* —*n.* **1 a** a stick or pole for use in walking or climbing or as a weapon. **b** a stick or pole as a sign of office or authority. **c** a person or thing that supports or sustains. **d** a flagstaff. **e** *Surveying* a rod for measuring distances, heights, etc. **f** a token given to an engine-driver on a single-track railway as authority to proceed over a given section of line. **g** a spindle in a watch. **2 a** a body of persons employed in a business etc. (*editorial staff of a newspaper*). **b** those in authority within an organization, esp. the teachers in a school. **c** *Mil.* etc. a body of officers assisting an officer in high command and concerned with an army, regiment, fleet, or air force as a whole (*general staff*). **d** (usu. **Staff**) *Mil.* = *staff sergeant*. **3** (*pl.* **staffs** or **staves** /steɪvz/) *Mus.* a set of usu. five parallel lines on any one or between any adjacent two of which a note is placed to indicate its pitch. —*v.tr.* provide (an institution etc.) with staff. □ **staff college** *Brit. Mil.* etc. a college at which officers are trained for staff duties. **staff notation** *Mus.* notation by means of a staff, esp. as distinct from tonic sol-fa. **staff nurse** *Brit.* a nurse ranking just below a sister. **staff officer** *Mil.* an officer serving on the staff of an army etc. **staff sergeant 1** *Brit.* the senior sergeant of a non-infantry company. **2** *US* a non-commissioned officer ranking just above sergeant. □□ **staffed** *adj.* (also in *comb.*). [OE *stæf* f. Gmc]

staff[2] /stɑːf/ *n.* a mixture of plaster of Paris, cement, etc., as a temporary building-material. [19th c.: orig. unkn.]

Staffa /ˈstæfə/ a small uninhabited island of the Inner Hebrides, west of Mull. It is the site of Fingal's Cave.

staffage /stəˈfɑːʒ/ *n.* accessory items in a painting, esp. figures or animals in a landscape picture. [G f. *staffieren* decorate, perh. f. OF *estoffer*: see STUFF]

staffer /ˈstɑːfə(r)/ *n. US* a member of a staff, esp. of a newspaper.

Staffordshire /ˈstæfədˌʃɪə(r)/ a county of central England; pop. (1981) 1,019,400; county town, Stafford.

Staffs. *abbr.* Staffordshire.

stag /stæg/ *n. & v.* —*n.* **1** an adult male deer, esp. one with a set of antlers. **2** *Brit. Stock Exch.* a person who applies for shares of a new issue with a view to selling at once for a profit. **3** a man who attends a social gathering unaccompanied by a woman. —*v.tr.* (**stagged, stagging**) *Brit. Stock Exch.* deal in (shares) as a stag. □ **stag beetle** any beetle of the family Lucanidae, the male of which has large branched mandibles resembling a stag's antlers. **stag-** (or **stag's-**) **horn 1** the horn of a stag, used to make knife-handles, snuff-boxes, etc. **2** any of various ferns, esp. of the genus *Platycerium*, having fronds like antlers. **stag-night** (or **-party**) an all-male celebration, esp. in honour of a man about to marry. [ME f. OF *stacga, stagga* (unrecorded): cf. *docga* dog, *frogga* frog, etc., and ON *staggr, staggi* male bird]

stage /steɪdʒ/ *n. & v.* —*n.* **1** a point or period in a process or development (*reached a critical stage; is in the larval stage*). **2 a** a raised floor or platform, esp. one on which plays etc. are performed before an audience. **b** (prec. by *the*) the acting or theatrical profession, dramatic art or literature, the drama. **c** the scene of action (*the stage of politics*). **d** = *landing-stage*. **3 a** a regular stopping-place on a route. **b** the distance between two stopping-places. **c** *Brit.* = *fare-stage*. **4** *Astronaut.* a section of a rocket with a separate engine, jettisoned when its propellant is exhausted. **5** *Geol.* a range of strata forming a subdivision of a series. **6** *Electronics* a single amplifying transistor or valve with the associated equipment. **7** the surface on which an object is placed for inspection through a microscope. —*v.tr.* **1** present (a play etc.) on stage. **2** arrange the occurrence of (*staged a demonstration; staged a comeback*). □ **go on the stage** become an actor. **hold the stage** dominate a conversation etc. **stage direction** an instruction in the text of a play as to the movement, position, tone, etc., of an actor, or sound effects etc. **stage door** an actors' and workmen's entrance from the street to a theatre behind the stage. **stage effect 1** an effect produced in acting or on the stage. **2** an artificial or theatrical effect produced in real life. **stage fright** nervousness on facing an audience esp. for the first time. **stage-hand** a person handling scenery etc. during a performance on stage. **stage left** (or **right**) on the left (or right) side of the stage, facing the audience. **stage-manage 1** be the stage-manager of. **2** arrange and control for effect. **stage-management** the job or craft of a stage-manager. **stage-manager** the person responsible for lighting and other mechanical arrangements for a play etc. **stage name** a name assumed for professional purposes by an actor. **stage play** a play performed on stage rather than broadcast etc. **stage rights** exclusive rights to perform a particular play. **stage-struck** filled with an inordinate desire to go on the stage. **stage whisper 1** an aside. **2** a loud whisper meant to be heard by others than the person addressed. □□ **stageable** *adj.* **stageability** /-dʒəˈbɪlɪtɪ/ *n.* **stager** *n.* [ME f. OF *estage* dwelling ult. f. L *stare* stand]

stagecoach /ˈsteɪdʒkəʊtʃ/ *n. hist.* a large closed horse-drawn coach running regularly by stages between two places. Such coaches were used in England from the mid-17th c. and reached their heyday in the early 19th c. as roads improved; in the US they were often the only method available for long-distance travel. By the mid-19th c. their use was lapsing as they were superseded by the newly developed railways.

stagecraft /ˈsteɪdʒkrɑːft/ *n.* skill or experience in writing or staging plays.

stagey var. of STAGY.

stagflation /stægˈfleɪʃ(ə)n/ *n. Econ.* a state of inflation without a corresponding increase of demand and employment. [STAG-NATION (as STAGNATE) + INFLATION]

stagger /ˈstægə(r)/ *v. & n.* —*v.* **1 a** *intr.* walk unsteadily, totter. **b** *tr.* cause to totter (*was staggered by the blow*). **2 a** *tr.* shock, confuse; cause to hesitate or waver (*the question staggered them; they were staggered at the suggestion*). **b** *intr.* hesitate; waver in purpose. **3** *tr.* arrange (events, hours of work, etc.) so that they do not coincide. **4** *tr.* arrange (objects) so that they are not in line, esp.: **a** arrange (a road-crossing) so that the side-roads are not in line. **b** set (the spokes of a wheel) to incline alternately to right and left. —*n.* **1** a tottering movement. **2** (in *pl.*) **a** a disease of the brain and spinal cord esp. in horses and cattle, causing staggering. **b** giddiness. **3** an overhanging or slantwise or zigzag arrangement of like parts in a structure etc. □□ **staggerer** *n.* [alt. of ME *stacker* (now dial.) f. ON *stakra* frequent. of *staka* push, stagger]

staggering /ˈstægərɪŋ/ *adj.* **1** astonishing, bewildering. **2** that staggers. □□ **staggeringly** *adv.*

staghound /ˈstæghaʊnd/ *n.* **1** any large dog of a breed used for hunting deer by sight or scent. **2** this breed.

staging /ˈsteɪdʒɪŋ/ *n.* **1** the presentation of a play etc. **2 a** a platform or support or scaffolding, esp. temporary. **b** shelves for plants in a greenhouse. □ **staging area** an intermediate assembly point for troops in transit. **staging post** a regular stopping-place, esp. on an air route.

stagnant /ˈstægnənt/ *adj.* **1** (of liquid) motionless, having no current. **2** (of life, action, the mind, business, a person) showing no activity, dull, sluggish. □□ **stagnancy** *n.* **stagnantly** *adv.* [L *stagnare stagnant-* f. *stagnum* pool]

stagnate /stægˈneɪt/ *v.intr.* be or become stagnant. □□ **stagnation** *n.*

stagy /ˈsteɪdʒɪ/ *adj.* (also **stagey**) (**stagier, stagiest**) theatrical, artificial, exaggerated. □□ **stagily** *adv.* **staginess** *n.*

staid /steɪd/ *adj.* of quiet and steady character; sedate. □□ **staidly** *adv.* **staidness** *n.* [= *stayed*, past part. of STAY[1]]

stain /steɪn/ *v. & n.* —*v.* **1** *tr. & intr.* discolour or be discoloured by the action of liquid sinking in. **2** *tr.* sully, blemish, spoil, damage (a reputation, character, etc.). **3** *tr.* colour (wood, glass, etc.) by a process other than painting or covering the surface. **4** *tr.* impregnate (a specimen) for microscopic examination with colouring matter that makes the structure visible by being deposited in some parts more than in others. **5** *tr.* print colours on (wallpaper). —*n.* **1** a discoloration, a spot or mark caused esp. by contact with foreign matter and not easily removed (*a cloth covered with tea-stains*). **2 a** a blot or blemish. **b** damage to a reputation etc. (*a stain on one's character*). **3** a substance used in staining. □ **stained glass** pieces of glass, either dyed or superficially coloured, set in a framework (usually of lead) to form decorative or pictorial designs. The art began in the service of the Christian Church and is of Byzantine origin, but its highest achievements are seen in the west and north of Europe. □□ **stainable** *adj.* **stainer** *n.* [ME f. *distain* f. OF *desteindre desteign-* (as DIS-, TINGE)]

Stainer /ˈsteɪnə(r)/, Sir John (1840–1901), English composer, scholar, and teacher. He wrote a considerable amount of church music, including hymn tunes, and an oratorio *The Crucifixion* (1887) which achieved enormous popularity.

stainless /ˈsteɪnlɪs/ *adj.* **1** (esp. of a reputation) without stains. **2** not liable to stain. □ **stainless steel** chrome steel not liable to rust or tarnish under ordinary conditions.

stair /steə(r)/ *n.* **1** each of a set of fixed indoor steps (*on the top stair but one*). **2** (usu. in *pl.*) a set of indoor steps (*passed him on the stairs; down a winding stair*). **3** (in *pl.*) a landing-stage. □ **stair-rod** a rod for securing a carpet in the angle between two steps. [OE *stæger* f. Gmc]

staircase /ˈsteəkeɪs/ *n.* **1** a flight of stairs and the supporting structure. **2** a part of a building containing a staircase.

stairhead /ˈsteəhed/ *n.* a level space at the top of stairs.

stairway /ˈsteəweɪ/ *n.* **1** a flight of stairs, a staircase. **2** the way up this.

æ cat ɑː arm e bed ɜː her ɪ sit iː see ɒ hot ɔː saw ʌ run ʊ put uː too ə ago aɪ my

stairwell /ˈsteəwel/ n. the shaft in which a staircase is built.

staithe /steɪð/ n. Brit. a wharf, esp. a waterside coal depot equipped for loading vessels. [ME f. ON stöth landing-stage f. Gmc, rel. to STAND]

stake[1] /steɪk/ n. & v. —n. 1 a stout stick or post sharpened at one end and driven into the ground as a support, boundary mark, etc. 2 hist. a the post to which a person was tied to be burnt alive. b (prec. by the) death by burning as a punishment (was condemned to the stake). 3 a long vertical rod in basket-making. 4 a metalworker's small anvil fixed on a bench by a pointed prop. —v.tr. 1 fasten, secure, or support with a stake or stakes. 2 (foll. by off, out) mark off (an area) with stakes. 3 state or establish (a claim). □ pull (or pull up) stakes depart; go to live elsewhere. stake-boat a boat anchored to mark the course for a boat race etc. stake-body (pl. -ies) US a body for a lorry etc. having a flat open platform with removable posts along the sides. stake-net a fishing-net hung on stakes. stake out colloq. 1 place under surveillance. 2 place (a person) to maintain surveillance. stake-out n. esp. US colloq. a period of surveillance. [OE staca f. WG, rel. to STICK[2]]

stake[2] /steɪk/ n. & v. —n. 1 a sum of money etc. wagered on an event, esp. deposited with a stakeholder. 2 (often foll. by in) an interest or concern, esp. financial. 3 (in pl.) a money offered as a prize esp. in a horse-race. b such a race (maiden stakes; trial stakes). —v.tr. 1 a wager (staked £5 on the next race). b risk (staked everything on convincing him). 2 US colloq. give financial or other support to. □ at stake 1 risked, to be won or lost (life itself is at stake). 2 at issue, in question. □□ staker n. [16th c.: perh. f. STAKE[1]]

stakeholder /ˈsteɪkˌhəʊldə(r)/ n. an independent party with whom each of those who make a wager deposits the money etc. wagered.

Stakhanovite /stəˈkɑːnəˌvaɪt/ n. a worker who is exceptionally hard-working and productive. The term was first applied to a worker in the USSR during the 1930s and 1940s whose productivity exceeded the norms and who thus earned special privileges and rewards. □□ **Stakhanovism** /-ˌvɪz(ə)m/ n. **Stakhanovist** /-vɪst/ n. [A. G. Stakhanov (d. 1977), who in 1935 produced a phenomenal amount of coal by a combination of new methods and great energy, an achievement publicized by the Soviet authorities in their campaign to increase industrial output]

stalactite /ˈstæləkˌtaɪt, stəˈlæk-/ n. a deposit of calcium carbonate having the shape of a large icicle, formed by the trickling of water from the roof of a cave, etc. □□ **stalactic** /-ˈlæktɪk/ adj. **stalactiform** /-ˈlæktɪˌfɔːm/ adj. **stalactitic** /-ˈtɪtɪk/ adj. [mod.L stalactites f. Gk stalaktos dripping f. stalassō drip]

Stalag /ˈstælæɡ/ n. hist. a German prison camp, esp. for non-commissioned officers and privates. [G f. Stamm base, main stock, Lager camp]

stalagmite /ˈstæləɡˌmaɪt/ n. a deposit of calcium carbonate formed by the dripping of water into the shape of a large inverted icicle rising from the floor of a cave etc., often uniting with a stalactite. □□ **stalagmitic** /-ˈmɪtɪk/ adj. [mod.L stalagmites f. Gk stalagma a drop f. stalassō drip (as STALACTITE)]

stale[1] /steɪl/ adj. & v. —adj. 1 a not fresh, not quite new (stale bread is best for toast). b musty, insipid, or otherwise the worse for age or use. 2 trite or unoriginal (a stale joke; stale news). 3 (of an athlete or other performer) having ability impaired by excessive exertion or practice. 4 Law (esp. of a claim) having been left dormant for an unreasonably long time. —v.tr. & intr. make or become stale. □□ **stalely** adv. **staleness** n. [ME, prob. f. AF & OF f. estaler halt: cf. STALL[1]]

stale[2] /steɪl/ n. & v. —n. the urine of horses and cattle. —v.intr. (esp. of horses and cattle) urinate. [ME, perh. f. OF estaler adopt a position (cf. STALE[1])]

stalemate /ˈsteɪlmeɪt/ n. & v. —n. 1 Chess a position counting as a draw, in which a player is not in check but cannot move except into check. 2 a deadlock or drawn contest. —v.tr. 1 Chess bring (a player) to a stalemate. 2 bring to a standstill. [obs. stale (f. AF estale f. estaler be placed: cf. STALE[1]) + MATE[2]]

Stalin /ˈstɑːlɪn/ the name adopted by Joseph Vissarionovich

Dzhugashvili (1879–1953), Russian dictator. An early member of the Bolshevik Party, he was imprisoned in 1913 and released only after the start of the Russian Revolution, when he rose rapidly to become one of Lenin's right-hand men. After Lenin's death, Stalin won a long struggle with Trotsky for the leadership and went on to become sole dictator. His large-scale purges gravely weakened the Soviet Union and the country only just survived Hitler's attack in 1941, but under Stalin's leadership it eventually went on to win the titanic struggle on the Eastern Front. Stalin stayed in power until his death, following his policy of removing anyone whose power might threaten his own. He was later denounced by Khruschev.

Stalingrad see VOLGOGRAD.

Stalinism /ˈstɑːlɪˌnɪz(ə)m/ n. 1 the policies followed by Stalin in the government of the USSR, esp. centralization, total-itarianism, and the pursuit of socialism. 2 any rigid centralized authoritarian form of socialism. □□ **Stalinist** n.

stalk[1] /stɔːk/ n. 1 the main stem of a herbaceous plant. 2 the slender attachment or support of a leaf, flower, fruit, etc. 3 a similar support for an organ etc. in an animal. 4 a slender support or linking shaft in a machine, object, etc., e.g. the stem of a wineglass. 5 the tall chimney of a factory etc. □ **stalk-eyed** (of crabs, snails, etc.) having the eyes mounted on stalks. □□ **stalked** adj. (also in comb.). **stalkless** adj. **stalklet** n. **stalklike** adj. **stalky** adj. [ME stalke, prob. dimin. of (now dial.) stale rung of a ladder, long handle, f. OE stalu]

stalk[2] /stɔːk/ v. & n. —v. 1 a tr. pursue or approach (game or an enemy) stealthily. b intr. steal up to game under cover. 2 intr. stride, walk in a stately or haughty manner. —n. 1 the stalking of game. 2 an imposing gait. □ **stalking-horse 1** a horse behind which a hunter is concealed. 2 a pretext concealing one's real intentions or actions. □□ **stalker** n. (also in comb.). [OE f. Gmc, rel. to STEAL]

stall[1] /stɔːl/ n. & v. —n. 1 a a trader's stand or booth in a market etc., or out of doors. b a compartment in a building for the sale of goods. c a table in this on which goods are exposed. 2 a a stable or cowhouse. b a compartment for one animal in this. 3 a a fixed seat in the choir or chancel of a church, more or less enclosed at the back and sides and often canopied, esp. one appropriated to a clergyman (canon's stall; dean's stall). b the office or dignity of a canon etc. 4 (usu. in pl.) Brit. each of a set of seats in a theatre, usu. on the ground floor. 5 a a compartment for one person in a shower-bath, lavatory, etc. b a compartment for one horse at the start of a race. 6 a the stalling of an engine or aircraft. b the condition resulting from this. 7 a receptacle for one object (finger-stall). —v. 1 a intr. (of a motor vehicle or its engine) stop because of an overload on the engine or an inadequate supply of fuel to it. b intr. (of an aircraft or its pilot) reach a condition where the speed is too low to allow effective operation of the controls. c tr. cause (an engine or vehicle or aircraft) to stall. 2 tr. a put or keep (cattle etc.) in a stall or stalls esp. for fattening (a stalled ox). b furnish (a stable etc.) with stalls. 3 intr. a (of a horse or cart) stick fast as in mud or snow. b US be snowbound. □ **stall-feed** fatten (cattle) in a stall. [OE steall f. Gmc, rel. to STAND: partly f. OF estal f. Frank.]

stall[2] /stɔːl/ v. & n. —v. 1 intr. play for time when being questioned etc. 2 tr. delay, obstruct, block. —n. an instance of stalling. □ **stall off** evade or deceive. [stall pickpocket's confederate, orig. 'decoy' f. AF estal(e), prob. rel. to STALL[1]]

stallage /ˈstɔːlɪdʒ/ n. Brit. 1 space for a stall or stalls in a market etc. 2 the rent for such a stall. 3 the right to erect such a stall. [ME f. OF estalage f. estal STALL[1]]

stallholder /ˈstɔːlˌhəʊldə(r)/ n. a person in charge of a stall at a market etc.

stallion /ˈstæljən/ n. an uncastrated adult male horse, esp. one kept for breeding. [ME f. OF estalon ult. f. a Gmc root rel. to STALL[1]]

stalwart /ˈstɔːlwət/ adj. & n. —adj. 1 strongly built, sturdy. 2 courageous, resolute, determined (stalwart supporters). —n. a stalwart person, esp. a loyal uncompromising partisan. □□ **stalwartly** adv. **stalwartness** n. [Sc. var. of obs. stalworth f. OE stælwierthe f. stæl place, WORTH]

Stamboul /stæm'buːl/ an obsolete name for Istanbul.

stamen /'steɪmən/ n. the male fertilizing organ of a flowering plant, including the anther containing pollen. □□ **staminiferous** /ˌstæmɪ'nɪfərəs/ adj. [L stamen staminis warp in an upright loom, thread]

stamina /'stæmɪnə/ n. the ability to endure prolonged physical or mental strain; staying power, power of endurance. [L, pl. of STAMEN in sense 'warp, threads spun by the Fates']

staminate /'stæmɪnət/ adj. (of a plant) having stamens, esp. stamens but not pistils.

stammer /'stæmə(r)/ v. & n. —v. 1 intr. speak (habitually, or on occasion from embarrassment etc.) with halting articulation, esp. with pauses or rapid repetitions of the same syllable. 2 tr. (often foll. by out) utter (words) in this way (stammered out an excuse). —n. 1 a tendency to stammer. 2 an instance of stammering. □□ **stammerer** n. **stammeringly** adv. [OE stamerian f. WG]

stamp /stæmp/ v. & n. —v. 1 a tr. bring down (one's foot) heavily on the ground etc. b tr. crush, flatten, or bring into a specified state in this way (stamped down the earth round the plant). c intr. bring down one's foot heavily; walk with heavy steps. 2 tr. a impress (a pattern, mark, etc.) on metal, paper, butter, etc., with a die or similar instrument of metal, wood, rubber, etc. b impress (a surface) with a pattern etc. in this way. 3 tr. affix a postage or other stamp to (an envelope or document). 4 tr. assign a specific character to; characterize; mark out (stamps the story an invention). 5 tr. crush or pulverize (ore etc.). —n. 1 an instrument for stamping a pattern or mark. 2 a a mark or pattern made by this. b the impression of an official mark required to be made for revenue purposes on deeds, bills of exchange, etc., as evidence of payment of tax. 3 a small adhesive piece of paper indicating that a price, fee, or tax has been paid, esp. a postage stamp. (See below.) 4 a mark impressed on or label etc. affixed to a commodity as evidence of quality etc. 5 a a heavy downward blow with the foot. b the sound of this. 6 a a characteristic mark or impress (bears the stamp of genius). b character, kind (avoid people of that stamp). 7 the block that crushes ore in a stamp-mill. □ **Stamp Act** an act concerned with stamp-duty, esp. that imposing the duty on the American colonies in 1765 and repealed in 1766. **stamp-collecting** the collecting of postage stamps as objects of interest or value. **stamp-collector** a person engaged in stamp-collecting. **stamp-duty** a duty imposed on certain kinds of legal document. **stamp-hinge** see HINGE. **stamping-ground** a favourite haunt or place of action. **stamp-machine** a coin-operated machine for selling postage stamps. **stamp-mill** a mill for crushing ore etc. **stamp-office** an office for the issue of government stamps and the receipt of stamp-duty etc. **stamp on 1** impress (an idea etc.) on (the memory etc.). **2** suppress. **stamp out 1** produce by cutting out with a die etc. **2** put an end to, crush, destroy. **stamp-paper 1** paper with the government revenue stamp. **2** the gummed marginal paper of a sheet of postage stamps. □□ **stamper** n. [prob. f. OE stampian (v.) (unrecorded) f. Gmc: infl. by OF estamper (v.) and F estampe (n.) also f. Gmc]

The world's first postage stamps were the penny black and twopence blue, issued by Great Britain in May 1840 and showing the head of Queen Victoria in profile. The system of their use was introduced on the initiative of Sir Rowland Hill (1795–1879). Proposing the reform, in 1837 he described the invention as 'a bit of paper just large enough to bear the stamp, and covered at the back with glutinous wash'. He adopted the notion from Charles Knight's proposal in 1834 that the postage of newspapers should be collected by means of uniformly stamped wrappers. The system was subsequently adopted throughout the world.

The name stamp was originally applied to the marks stamped or impressed by the Post Office on letters, to state whether they were 'prepaid', 'unpaid', 'free', etc. When adhesive labels were introduced in 1840 and took the place of these marks they appear to have been called 'postage stamps' from the first, though the official name was 'postage label', and the marks which continued to be impressed by the Post Office to show the

place and date of postage, and to obliterate the 'label' so that it could not be reused, became called 'postmarks'.

stampede /stæm'piːd/ n. & v. —n. 1 a sudden flight and scattering of a number of horses, cattle, etc. 2 a sudden flight or hurried movement of people due to interest or panic. 3 US the spontaneous response of many persons to a common impulse. —v. 1 intr. take part in a stampede. 2 tr. cause to do this. 3 tr. cause to act hurriedly or unreasoningly. □□ **stampeder** n. [Sp. estampida crash, uproar, ult. f. Gmc, rel. to STAMP]

stance /stɑːns, stæns/ n. 1 an attitude or position of the body esp. when hitting a ball etc. 2 a standpoint; an attitude of mind. 3 Sc. a site for a market, taxi rank, etc. [F f. It. stanza: see STANZA]

stanch[1] /stɑːntʃ, stɔːntʃ/ v.tr. (also **staunch**) 1 restrain the flow of (esp. blood). 2 restrain the flow from (esp. a wound). [ME f. OF estanchier f. Rmc]

stanch[2] var. of STAUNCH[1].

stanchion /'stɑːnʃ(ə)n/ n. & v. —n. 1 a post or pillar, an upright support, a vertical strut. 2 an upright bar, pair of bars, or frame, for confining cattle in a stall. —v.tr. 1 supply with a stanchion. 2 fasten (cattle) to a stanchion. [ME f. AF stanchon, OF estanchon f. estance prob. ult. f. L stare stand]

stand /stænd/ v. & n. —v. (past and past part. **stood** /stʊd/) 1 intr. have or take or maintain an upright position, esp. on the feet or a base. 2 intr. be situated or located (here once stood a village). 3 intr. be of a specified height (stands six foot three). 4 intr. be in a specified condition (stands accused; the thermometer stood at 90°; the matter stands as follows; stood in awe of them). 5 tr. place or set in an upright or specified position (stood it against the wall). 6 intr. a move to and remain in a specified position (stand aside). b take a specified attitude (stand aloof). 7 intr. maintain a position; avoid falling or moving or being moved (the house will stand for another century; stood for hours arguing). 8 intr. assume a stationary position; cease to move (now stand still). 9 intr. remain valid or unaltered; hold good (the former conditions must stand). 10 intr. Naut. hold a specified course (stand in for the shore; you are standing into danger). 11 tr. endure without yielding or complaining; tolerate (cannot stand the pain; how can you stand him?). 12 tr. provide for another or others at one's own expense (stood him a drink). 13 intr. (often foll. by for) Brit. be a candidate (for an office, legislature, or constituency) (stood for Parliament; stood for Finchley). 14 intr. act in a specified capacity (stood proxy). 15 tr. undergo (trial). 16 intr. Cricket act as umpire. 17 intr. (of a dog) point, set. 18 intr. (in full **stand at stud**) (of a stallion) be available for breeding. —n. 1 a cessation from motion or progress, a stoppage (was brought to a stand). 2 a a halt made, or a stationary condition assumed, for the purpose of resistance. b resistance to attack or compulsion (esp. make a stand). c Cricket a prolonged period at the wicket by two batsmen. 3 a a position taken up (took his stand near the door). b an attitude adopted. 4 a rack, set of shelves, table, etc., on or in which things may be placed (music stand; hatstand). 5 a a small open-fronted structure for a trader outdoors or in a market etc. b a structure occupied by a participating organization at an exhibition. 6 a standing-place for vehicles (cab-stand). 7 a raised structure for persons to sit or stand on. b US a witness-box (take the stand). 8 Theatr. etc. each halt made on a tour to give one or more performances. 9 a group of growing plants (stand of trees; stand of clover). □ **as it stands 1** in its present condition, unaltered. 2 in the present circumstances. **be at a stand** archaic be unable to proceed, be in perplexity. **it stands to reason** see REASON. **stand alone** be unequalled. **stand and deliver!** hist. a highwayman's order to hand over valuables etc. **stand at bay** see BAY[5]. **stand back 1** withdraw; take up a position further from the front. **2** withdraw psychologically in order to take an objective view. **stand by 1** stand nearby; look on without interfering (will not stand by and see him ill-treated). **2** uphold, support, side with (a person). **3** adhere to, abide by (terms or promises). **4** Naut. stand ready to take hold of or operate (an anchor etc.). **stand-by** n. (pl. **-bys**) 1 a person or thing ready if needed in an emergency etc. 2 readiness for duty (on stand-by). —adj. 1 ready for immediate use. 2 (of air travel) not booked in advance but allocated on the basis of earliest availability. **stand camera** a camera for use on a tripod, not hand-held. **stand a chance** see CHANCE. **stand**

corrected accept correction. **stand down 1** withdraw (a person) or retire from a team, witness-box, or similar position. **2** *Brit.* cease to be a candidate etc. **3** *Brit. Mil.* go off duty. **stand easy!** see EASY. **stand for 1** represent, signify, imply (*'US' stands for 'United States'*; *democracy stands for a great deal more than that*). **2** (often with *neg.*) *colloq.* endure, tolerate, acquiesce in. **3** espouse the cause of. **stand one's ground** maintain one's position, not yield. **stand high** be high in status, price, etc. **stand in** (usu. foll. by *for*) deputize; act in place of another. **stand-in** *n.* a deputy or substitute, esp. for an actor when the latter's acting ability is not needed. **stand in the breach** see BREACH. **stand in good stead** see STEAD. **stand in with** be in league with. **stand of arms** *Brit. Mil.* a complete set of weapons for one man. **stand of colours** *Brit. Mil.* a regiment's flags. **stand off 1** move or keep away, keep one's distance. **2** *Brit.* temporarily dispense with the services of (an employee). **stand-off** *n.* **1** *US* a deadlock. **2** = *stand-off half*. **stand-off half** *Rugby Football* a half-back who forms a link between the scrum-half and the three-quarters. **stand on 1** insist on, observe scrupulously (*stand on ceremony*; *stand on one's dignity*). **2** *Naut.* continue on the same course. **stand on me** *sl.* rely on me; believe me. **stand on one's own feet** (or **legs**) be self-reliant or independent. **stand out 1** be prominent or conspicuous or outstanding. **2** (usu. foll. by *against, for*) hold out; persist in opposition or support or endurance. **stand over 1** stand close to (a person) to watch, control, threaten, etc. **2** be postponed, be left for later settlement etc. **stand pat** see PAT². **stand to 1** *Mil.* stand ready for an attack (esp. before dawn or after dark). **2** abide by, adhere to (terms or promises). **3** be likely or certain to (*stands to lose everything*). **4** uphold, support, or side with (a person). **stand treat** bear the expense of entertainment etc. **stand up 1 a** rise to one's feet from a sitting or other position. **b** come to or remain in or place in a standing position. **2** (of an argument etc.) be valid. **3** *colloq.* fail to keep an appointment with. **stand-up** *attrib.adj.* **1** (of a meal) eaten standing. **2** (of a fight) violent, thorough, or fair and square. **3** (of a collar) upright, not turned down. **4** (of a comedian) performing by standing before an audience and telling jokes. **stand up for** support, side with, maintain (a person or cause). **stand upon** = *stand on*. **stand up to 1** meet or face (an opponent) courageously. **2** be resistant to the harmful effects of (wear, use, etc.). **stand well** (usu. foll. by *with*) be on good terms or in good repute. **take one's stand** base one's argument etc. on, rely on. □□ **stander** *n.* [OE *standan* f. Gmc]

standalone /ˌstændəˈləʊn/ *adj.* (of a computer) operating independently of a network or other system.

standard /ˈstændəd/ *n. & adj.* —*n.* **1** an object or quality or measure serving as a basis or example or principle to which others conform or should conform or by which the accuracy or quality of others is judged (*by present-day standards*). **2 a** the degree of excellence etc. required for a particular purpose (*not up to standard*). **b** average quality (*of a low standard*). **3** the ordinary procedure, or quality or design of a product, without added or novel features. **4** a distinctive flag, esp. the flag of a cavalry regiment as distinct from the *colours* of an infantry regiment. **5 a** an upright support. **b** an upright water or gas pipe. **6 a** a tree or shrub that stands alone without support. **b** a shrub grafted on an upright stem and trained in tree form (*standard rose*). **7 a** document specifying nationally or internationally agreed properties for manufactured goods etc. (*British Standard*). **8** a thing recognized as a model for imitation etc. **9** a tune or song of established popularity. **10 a** a system by which the value of a currency is defined in terms of gold or silver or both. **b** the prescribed proportion of the weight of fine metal in gold or silver coins. **11** a measure for timber, equivalent to 165 cu. ft. (4.7 cubic metres). **12** *Brit. hist.* a grade of classification in elementary schools. —*adj.* **1** serving or used as a standard (*a standard size*). **2** of a normal or prescribed quality or size etc. **3** having recognized and permanent value; authoritative (*the standard book on the subject*). **4** (of language) conforming to established educated usage (*Standard English*). □ **multiple standard** a standard of value obtained by averaging the prices of a number of products. **raise a standard** take up arms; rally support (*raised the standard of revolt*). **standard-bearer 1** a soldier who carries

a standard. **2** a prominent leader in a cause. **standard deviation** see DEVIATION. **standard lamp** *Brit.* a lamp set on a tall upright with its base standing on the floor. **standard of living** the degree of material comfort available to a person or class or community. **standard time** a uniform time for places in approximately the same longitude, established in a country or region by law or custom. [ME f. AF *estaundart*, OF *estendart* f. *estendre*, as EXTEND: in senses 5 and 6 of *n.* affected by association with STAND]

Standardbred /ˈstændədˌbred/ *n.* *US* **1** a horse of a breed able to attain a specified speed, developed esp. for trotting. **2** this breed.

standardize /ˈstændəˌdaɪz/ *v.tr.* (also **-ise**) **1** cause to conform to a standard. **2** determine the properties of by comparison with a standard. □□ **standardizable** *adj.* **standardization** /-ˈzeɪʃ(ə)n/ *n.* **standardizer** *n.*

standee /stænˈdiː/ *n.* *colloq.* a person who stands, esp. when all seats are occupied.

standing /ˈstændɪŋ/ *n. & adj.* —*n.* **1** esteem or repute, esp. high; status, position (*people of high standing*; *is of no standing*). **2** duration (*a dispute of long standing*). **3** length of service, membership, etc. —*adj.* **1** that stands, upright. **2 a** established, permanent (*a standing rule*). **b** not made, raised, etc., for the occasion (*a standing army*). **3** (of a jump, start, race, etc.) performed from rest or from a standing position. **4** (of water) stagnant. **5** (of corn) unreaped. **6** (of a stallion) that stands at stud. **7** *Printing* (formerly, of type) not yet distributed after use. □ **all standing** *Naut.* without time to lower the sails. **2** taken by surprise. **in good standing** fully paid-up as a member etc. **leave a person standing** make far more rapid progress than he or she. **standing committee** see COMMITTEE. **standing joke** an object of permanent ridicule. **standing order** an instruction to a banker to make regular payments, or to a newsagent etc. for a regular supply of a periodical etc. **standing orders** the rules governing the manner in which all business shall be conducted in a parliament, council, society, etc. **standing ovation** see OVATION. **standing rigging** rigging which is fixed in position. **standing-room** space to stand in. **standing wave** *Physics* the vibration of a system in which some particular points remain fixed while others between them vibrate with the maximum amplitude (cf. *travelling wave*).

standoffish /stændˈɒfɪʃ/ *adj.* cold or distant in manner. □□ **standoffishly** *adv.* **standoffishness** *n.*

standout /ˈstændaʊt/ *n.* *US* a remarkable person or thing.

standpipe /ˈstændpaɪp/ *n.* a vertical pipe extending from a water supply, esp. one connecting a temporary tap to the mains.

standpoint /ˈstændpɔɪnt/ *n.* **1** the position from which a thing is viewed. **2** a mental attitude.

standstill /ˈstændstɪl/ *n.* a stoppage; an inability to proceed.

Stanhope /ˈstænəp/, Lady Hester Lucy (1776–1839), niece of William Pitt the Younger, for whom she kept house from 1803 until his death in 1806, gaining a reputation as a brilliant political hostess. Becoming disillusioned with life in England she set out for the Middle East in 1810, and four years later established herself for the rest of her life at a ruined convent on Mount Lebanon, where she lived with a semi-oriental retinue which she ruled despotically. For several years her high rank and imperious character enabled her to meddle effectively in Middle Eastern politics, but later her debts accumulated, her eccentricity increased, and she sought to replace her waning political prestige by an undefined spiritual authority based on claims to be an inspired prophetess and mistress of occult sciences. She became a legendary figure in her lifetime and was visited by many distinguished European travellers.

stanhope /ˈstænhəʊp/ *n.* a light open carriage for one with two or four wheels. [Fitzroy *Stanhope*, Engl. clergyman d. 1864, for whom the first one was made]

staniel /ˈstænj(ə)l/ *n.* a kestrel. [OE *stāngella* 'stone-yeller' f. *stān* stone + *gellan* yell]

Stanislaus /ˈstænɪsˌlɔːs/, St (1030–79), the patron saint of Poland, who became bishop of Cracow in 1072. He came into conflict with King Boleslav II who (according to tradition) slew

Stanislaus, while the latter was offering Mass, with his own hand. Feast day, 7 May.

Stanislavsky /ˌstænɪsˈlæfskɪ/, Konstantin Sergeivich (Konstantin Alexeyev, 1863–1938), Russian director, actor, and teacher of acting. In 1898 he helped to found the Moscow Art Theatre, which opened a new epoch in Russian theatre. He trained his actors in a new way of acting, basing his methods on the psychological development of character and the drawing out of latent powers of self-expression. A whole system of actor training was built up on his theories, particularly in the US where his system was elaborated into the 'method' (see entry). Among his greatest achievements were his productions of the plays of Chekhov and Gorky.

stank past of STINK.

Stanley[1] /ˈstænlɪ/ (also **Port Stanley**) the chief port and town of the Falkland Islands, situated on the island of East Falkland; pop. 1,000.

Stanley[2] /ˈstænlɪ/, Sir Henry Morton (1841–1904), explorer of central Africa. Born in Wales as John Rowlands, after a hard and unhappy youth he sailed to America as a cabin boy and changed his name to that of an American merchant who befriended him. He became a successful newspaper correspondent and in 1869 was dispatched to find the Scottish missionary-explorer, David Livingstone (see entry), in Central Africa. After Livingstone's death Stanley continued his exploration work in Africa and in 1874–7 traced the course of the Congo and crossed the continent. Supported by Belgium, he helped to organize and develop the Congo region, and laid the foundations for the establishment of the Congo Free State. In 1887 he led an expedition to rescue Emin Pasha during the Mahdist advance on the Sudan. A popular figure with the public, he was accorded many honours and his books on his travels had an immense sale. From 1895 until 1900 he was a Member of Parliament.

stannary /ˈstænərɪ/ n. (pl. **-ies**) Brit. 1 a tin-mine. 2 (usu. in pl.) a tin-mining district in Cornwall and Devon. □ **stannary court** a legal body for the regulation of tin-miners in the stannaries. [med.L stannaria (pl.) f. LL stannum tin]

stannic /ˈstænɪk/ adj. Chem. of or relating to tetravalent tin (stannic acid; stannic chloride). [LL stannum tin]

stannous /ˈstænəs/ adj. Chem. of or relating to bivalent tin (stannous salts; stannous chloride).

Stansted /ˈstænsted/ the site, in Essex, of London's third international airport.

stanza /ˈstænzə/ n. 1 the basic metrical unit in a poem or verse consisting of a recurring group of lines (often four lines and usu. not more than twelve) which may or may not rhyme. 2 a group of four lines in some Greek and Latin metres. □□ **stanza'd** adj. (also **stanzaed**) (also in comb.). **stanzaic** /-ˈzeɪɪk/ adj. [It., = standing-place, chamber, stanza, ult. f. L stare stand]

stapelia /stəˈpiːlɪə/ n. any S. African plant of the genus Stapelia, with flowers having an unpleasant smell. [mod.L f. J. B. von Stapel, Du. botanist d. 1636]

stapes /ˈsteɪpiːz/ n. (pl. same) a small stirrup-shaped bone in the ear of a mammal. [mod.L f. med.L stapes stirrup]

staphylococcus /ˌstæfɪləˈkɒkəs/ n. (pl. **staphylococci** /-kaɪ/) any bacterium of the genus Staphylococcus, occurring in grapelike clusters, and sometimes causing pus formation usu. in the skin and mucous membranes of animals. □□ **staphylococcal** adj. [mod.L f. Gk staphulē bunch of grapes + kokkos berry]

staple[1] /ˈsteɪp(ə)l/ n. & v. —n. a U-shaped metal bar or piece of wire with pointed ends for driving into, securing, or fastening together various materials or for driving through and clenching papers, netting, electric wire, etc. —v.tr. provide or fasten with a staple. □ **staple gun** a hand-held device for driving in staples. □□ **stapler** n. [OE stapol f. Gmc]

staple[2] /ˈsteɪp(ə)l/ n., adj., & v. —n. 1 the principal or an important article of commerce (the staples of British Industry). 2 the chief element or a main component, e.g. of a diet. 3 a raw material. 4 the fibre of cotton or wool etc. as determining its quality (cotton of fine staple). —adj. 1 main or principal (staple commodities). 2 important as a product or an export. —v.tr. sort or classify

(wool etc.) according to fibre. [ME f. OF estaple market f. MLG, MDu. stapel market (as STAPLE[1])]

star /stɑː(r)/ n. & v. —n. 1 a celestial body appearing as a luminous point in the night sky. (See below.) 2 (in full **fixed star**) such a body so far from the Earth as to appear motionless (cf. PLANET, COMET). 3 a large naturally luminous gaseous body such as the sun is. 4 a celestial body regarded as influencing a person's fortunes etc. (born under a lucky star). 5 a thing resembling a star in shape or appearance. 6 a star-shaped mark, esp. a white mark on a horse's forehead. 7 a figure or object with radiating points esp. as the insignia of an order, as a decoration or mark of rank, or showing a category of excellence (a five-star hotel; was awarded a gold star). 8 a a famous or brilliant person; the principal or most prominent performer in a play, film, etc. (the star of the show). b (attrib.) outstanding; particularly brilliant (star pupil). 9 (in full **star connection**) Electr. a Y-shaped arrangement of three-phase windings. 10 = star prisoner. —v. (**starred**, **starring**) 1 a tr. (of a film etc.) feature as a principal performer. b intr. (of a performer) be featured in a film etc. 2 (esp. as **starred** adj.) a mark, set, or adorn with a star or stars. b put an asterisk or star beside (a name, an item in a list, etc.). □ **my stars!** colloq. an expression of surprise. **star-apple** an edible purple apple-like fruit (with a starlike cross-section) of a tropical evergreen tree, Chrysophyllum cainito. **star-crossed** archaic ill-fated. **star fruit** = CARAMBOLA. **star-gaze** 1 gaze at or study the stars. 2 gaze intently. **star-gazer** 1 colloq. usu. derog. or joc. an astronomer or astrologer. 2 Austral. sl. a horse that turns its head when galloping. **star of Bethlehem** any of various plants with starlike flowers esp. Ornithogalum umbellatum with white star-shaped flowers striped with green on the outside (see Matt. 2: 9). **Star of David** a figure consisting of two interlaced equilateral triangles used as a symbol of Judaism and of the State of Israel. **star prisoner** Brit. sl. a convict serving a first prison sentence. **star route** US a postal delivery route served by private contractors. **star sapphire** a cabochon sapphire reflecting a star-like image due to its regular internal structure. **star shell** an explosive projectile designed to burst in the air and light up the enemy's position. **star-spangled** (esp. of the US national flag) covered or glittering with stars. **star stream** a systematic drift of stars. **star-studded** containing or covered with many stars, esp. featuring many famous performers. **star turn** the principal item in an entertainment or performance. **Star Wars** colloq. the Strategic Defense Initiative (see STRATEGIC). □□ **stardom** n. **starless** adj. **starlike** adj. [OE steorra f. Gmc]

Stars are now known to be gaseous spheres, primarily of hydrogen and helium, in equilibrium between the force of self-gravity, which exerts a compressional force, and the pressure of radiation produced deep within the interior as a result of thermonuclear fusion reactions of the sort occurring in hydrogen bombs. Apart from the sun, the star nearest to Earth is Proxima Centauri, at a distance of some four light-years. Most are much further away than this, so that they appear hardly to change their relative positions in the sky. Some six thousand stars are visible to the naked eye; the actual number existing is vastly greater, more than a hundred thousand million in our own Galaxy, while billions of galaxies are known.

Stara Zagora /ˌstɑːrə zəˈɡɔːrə/ a manufacturing city in east central Bulgaria; pop. (1987) 156,400.

starboard /ˈstɑːbəd/ n. & v. Naut. & Aeron. —n. the right-hand side (looking forward) of a ship, boat, or aircraft (cf. PORT[3]). —v.tr. (also absol.) turn (the helm) to starboard. □ **starboard tack** see TACK[1] 4. **starboard watch** see WATCH n. 3b. [OE stēorbord = rudder side (see STEER, BOARD), early Teutonic ships being steered with a paddle over the right side]

starch /stɑːtʃ/ n. & v. —n. 1 an odourless tasteless polysaccharide occurring widely in plants and obtained chiefly from cereals and potatoes, forming an important constituent of the human diet. 2 a preparation of this for stiffening fabric before ironing. 3 stiffness of manner; formality. —v.tr. stiffen (clothing) with starch. □ **starch-reduced** (esp. of food) containing less than the normal proportion of starch. □□ **starcher** n. [earlier as verb: ME sterche f. OE stercan (unrecorded) stiffen f. Gmc: cf. STARK]

Star Chamber 1 an apartment in the royal palace at Westminster (said to have had gilt stars on the ceiling) where, in the 14th–15th c., the Privy Council in its judicial capacity tried civil and criminal cases, especially those affecting Crown interests. Under the Tudors and early Stuarts the court (**Court of Star Chamber**) became an instrument of tyranny, notorious for its arbitrary and oppressive judgements. It was abolished by Parliament in 1641. **2** any arbitrary or oppressive tribunal. **3** *colloq.* a committee appointed to arbitrate between the Treasury and the spending departments of the British Government.

starchy /ˈstɑːtʃɪ/ *adj.* (**starchier, starchiest**) **1 a** of or like starch. **b** containing much starch. **2** (of a person) precise, prim. □□ **starchily** *adv.* **starchiness** *n.*

stardust /ˈstɑːdʌst/ *n.* **1** a twinkling mass. **2** a romantic mystical look or sensation. **3** a multitude of stars looking like dust.

stare /steə(r)/ *v. & n.* —*v.* **1** *intr.* (usu. foll. by *at*) look fixedly with eyes open, esp. as the result of curiosity, surprise, bewilderment, admiration, horror, etc. (*sat staring at the door; stared in amazement*). **2** *intr.* (of eyes) be wide open and fixed. **3** *intr.* be unpleasantly prominent or striking. **4** *tr.* (foll. by *into*) reduce (a person) to a specified condition by staring (*stared me into silence*). —*n.* a staring gaze. □ **stare down** (or **out**) outstare. **stare a person in the face** be evident or imminent. □□ **starer** *n.* [OE *starian* f. Gmc]

starfish /ˈstɑːfɪʃ/ *n.* an echinoderm of the class Asteroidea with five or more radiating arms.

stark /stɑːk/ *adj. & adv.* —*adj.* **1** desolate, bare (*a stark landscape*). **2** sharply evident (*in stark contrast*). **3** downright, sheer (*stark madness*). **4** completely naked. **5** *archaic* strong, stiff, rigid. —*adv.* completely, wholly (*stark mad; stark naked*). □□ **starkly** *adv.* **starkness** *n.* [OE *stearc* f. Gmc: stark naked f. earlier *start-naked* f. obs. *start* tail: cf. REDSTART]

Stark effect /stɑːk/ *n. Physics* the splitting of a spectrum line into several components by the application of an electric field. [J. *Stark*, Ger. physicist d. 1957]

starkers /ˈstɑːkəz/ *adj. Brit. sl.* stark naked.

starlet /ˈstɑːlɪt/ *n.* **1** a promising young performer, esp. a woman. **2** a little star.

starlight /ˈstɑːlaɪt/ *n.* **1** the light of the stars (*walked home by starlight*). **2** (*attrib.*) = STARLIT (*a starlight night*).

starling¹ /ˈstɑːlɪŋ/ *n.* **1** a small gregarious partly migratory bird, *Sturnus vulgaris*, with blackish-brown speckled lustrous plumage, chiefly inhabiting cultivated areas. **2** any similar bird of the family Sturnidae. [OE *stærlinc* f. *stær* starling f. Gmc: cf. -LING¹]

starling² /ˈstɑːlɪŋ/ *n.* piles built around or upstream of a bridge or pier to protect it from floating rubbish etc. [perh. corrupt. of (now dial.) *staddling* STADDLE]

starlit /ˈstɑːlɪt/ *adj.* **1** lighted by stars. **2** with stars visible.

starry /ˈstɑːrɪ/ *adj.* (**starrier, starriest**) **1** covered with stars. **2** resembling a star. □ **starry-eyed** *colloq.* **1** visionary: enthusiastic but impractical. **2** euphoric. □□ **starrily** *adv.* **starriness** *n.*

Stars and Bars the popular name of the flag of the Confederate States of the US.

Stars and Stripes the popular name of the flag of the US. Originally it contained 13 alternating red and white stripes and 13 stars, representing the 13 States of the Union. Today it retains the 13 stripes, but has 50 stars, Hawaii having brought the number of States to 50 in 1959.

Star-spangled Banner a song with words composed by Francis Scott Key and a tune adapted from that of *To Anacreon in Heaven* (by the English composer J. Stafford Smith), inspired by the heroic defence of Fort McHenry in Baltimore harbour against the British in 1814 and officially adopted as the US national anthem in 1931.

START /stɑːt/ *abbr.* Strategic Arms Reduction Treaty (or Talks).

start /stɑːt/ *v. & n.* —*v.* **1** *tr. & intr.* begin; commence (*started work; started crying; started to shout; the play starts at eight*). **2** *tr.* set (proceedings, an event, etc.) in motion (*start the meeting; started a fire*). **3** *intr.* (often foll. by *on*) make a beginning (*started on a new project*). **4** *intr.* (often foll. by *after, for*) set oneself in motion or

action ('*wait!*' *he shouted, and started after her*). **5** *intr.* set out; begin a journey etc. (*we start at 6 a.m.*). **6** (often foll. by *up*) **a** *intr.* (of a machine) begin operating (*the car wouldn't start*). **b** *tr.* cause (a machine etc.) to begin operating (*tried to start the engine*). **7** *tr.* **a** cause or enable (a person) to make a beginning (with something) (*started me in business with £10,000*). **b** (foll. by pres. part.) cause (a person) to begin (doing something) (*the smoke started me coughing*). **c** *Brit. colloq.* complain or be critical (*don't you start*). **8** *tr.* (often foll. by *up*) found or establish; originate. **9** *intr.* (foll. by *at, with*) have as the first of a series of items, e.g. in a meal (*we started with soup*). **10** *tr.* give a signal to (competitors) to start in a race. **11** *intr.* (often foll. by *up, from,* etc.) make a sudden movement from surprise, pain, etc. (*started at the sound of my voice*). **12** *intr.* (foll. by *out, up, from,* etc.) spring out, up, etc. (*started up from the chair*). **13** *tr.* conceive (a baby). **14** *tr.* rouse (game etc.) from its lair. **15 a** *intr.* (of timbers etc.) spring from their proper position; give way. **b** *tr.* cause or experience (timbers etc.) to do this. **16** *intr.* (foll. by *out, to,* etc.) (of a thing) move or appear suddenly (*tears started to his eyes*). **17** *intr.* (foll. by *from*) (of eyes, usu. with exaggeration) burst forward (from their sockets etc.). **18** *tr.* pour out (liquor) from a cask. —*n.* **1** a beginning of an event, action, journey, etc. (*missed the start; an early start tomorrow; made a fresh start*). **2** the place from which a race etc. begins. **3** an advantage given at the beginning of a race etc. (*a 15-second start*). **4** an advantageous initial position in life, business, etc. (*a good start in life*). **5** a sudden movement of surprise, pain, etc. (*you gave me a start*). **6** an intermittent or spasmodic effort or movement (esp. *in* or *by fits and starts*). **7** *colloq.* a surprising occurrence (*a queer start; a rum start*). □ **for a start** *colloq.* as a beginning; in the first place. **get the start of** gain an advantage over. **start a hare** see HARE. **start in** *colloq.* **1** begin. **2** (foll. by *on*) US make a beginning on. **start off 1** begin; commence (*started off on a lengthy monologue*). **2** begin to move (*it's time we started off*). **start out 1** begin a journey. **2** *colloq.* (foll. by *to* + infin.) proceed as intending (to do something). **start over** US begin again. **start school** attend school for the first time. **start something** *colloq.* cause trouble. **start up** arise; occur. **to start with 1** in the first place; before anything else is considered (*should never have been there to start with*). **2** at the beginning (*had six members to start with*). [OE (orig. in sense 11) f. Gmc]

starter /ˈstɑːtə(r)/ *n.* **1** a person or thing that starts. **2** an esp. automatic device for starting the engine of a motor vehicle etc. **3** a person giving the signal for the start of a race. **4** a horse or competitor starting in a race (*a list of probable starters*). **5** the first course of a meal. **6** the initial action etc. □ **for starters** *sl.* to start with. **under starter's orders** (of racehorses etc.) in a position to start a race and awaiting the starting-signal.

starting /ˈstɑːtɪŋ/ *n.* in senses of START *v.* □ **starting-block** a shaped rigid block for bracing the feet of a runner at the start of a race. **starting-gate** a movable barrier for securing a fair start in horse-races. **starting-handle** *Brit. Mech.* a crank for starting a motor engine. **starting pistol** a pistol used to give the signal for the start of a race. **starting-point** the point from which a journey, process, argument, etc. begins. **starting post** the post from which competitors start in a race. **starting price** the odds ruling at the start of a horse-race. **starting stall** a compartment for one horse at the start of a race.

startle /ˈstɑːt(ə)l/ *v.tr.* give a shock or surprise to; cause (a person etc.) to start with surprise or sudden alarm. □□ **startler** *n.* [OE *steartlian* (as START, -LE⁴)]

startling /ˈstɑːtlɪŋ/ *adj.* **1** surprising. **2** alarming (*startling news*). □□ **startlingly** *adv.*

starve /stɑːv/ *v.* **1** *intr.* die of hunger; suffer from malnourishment. **2** *tr.* cause to die of hunger or suffer from lack of food. **3** *intr.* suffer from extreme poverty. **4** *intr. colloq.* feel very hungry (*I'm starving*). **5** *intr.* **a** suffer from mental or spiritual want. **b** (foll. by *for*) feel a strong craving for (sympathy, amusement, knowledge, etc.). **6** *tr.* **a** (foll. by *of*) deprive of; keep scantily supplied with (*starved of affection*). **b** cause to suffer from mental or spiritual want. **7** *tr.* **a** (foll. by *into*) compel by starving (*starved into submission*). **b** (foll. by *out*) compel to surrender etc. by starving (*starved them out*). **8** *intr. archaic* or *dial.* perish with or suffer from cold. □□ **starvation** /-ˈveɪʃ(ə)n/ *n.* [OE *steorfan* die]

starveling /'stɑːvlɪŋ/ n. & adj. archaic —n. a starving or ill-fed person or animal. —adj. **1** starving. **2** meagre.

starwort /'stɑːwɜːt/ n. a plant of the genus Stellaria with star-like flowers.

stash /stæʃ/ v. & n. colloq. —v.tr. (often foll. by away) **1** conceal; put in a safe or hidden place. **2** hoard, stow, store. —n. **1** a hiding-place or hide-out. **2** a thing hidden; a cache. [18th c.: orig. unkn.]

Stasi /'ʃtɑːzɪ/ n. hist. the internal security force of the German Democratic Republic (East Germany). [G, acronym f. Staatssicherheits(dienst) State security service]

stasis /'steɪsɪs, 'stæsɪs/ n. (pl. **stases** /-siːz/) **1** inactivity; stagnation; a state of equilibrium. **2** a stoppage of circulation of any of the body fluids. [mod.L f. Gk f. sta- STAND]

-stasis /'stæsɪs, 'steɪsɪs/ comb. form (pl. **-stases** /-siːz/) Physiol. forming nouns denoting a slowing or stopping (haemostasis). □□ **-static** comb. form forming adjectives.

-stat /stæt/ comb. form forming nouns with ref. to keeping fixed or stationary (rheostat). [Gk statos stationary]

state /steɪt/ n. & v. —n. **1** the existing condition or position of a person or thing (in a bad state of repair; in a precarious state of health). **2** colloq. **a** an excited, anxious, or agitated mental condition (esp. in a state). **b** an untidy condition. **3** (usu. **State**) **a** an organized political community under one government; a commonwealth; a nation. **b** such a community forming part of a federal republic, esp. the United States of America. **c** (**the States**) the US. **4** (usu. **State**) (attrib.) **a** of, for, or concerned with the State (State documents). **b** reserved for or done on occasions of ceremony (State apartments; State visit). **c** involving ceremony (State opening of Parliament). **5** (usu. **State**) civil government (Church and State; Secretary of State). **6** pomp, rank, dignity (as befits their state). **7** (**the States**) the legislative body in Jersey, Guernsey, and Alderney. **8** Bibliog. one of two or more variant forms of a single edition of a book. **9 a** an etched or engraved plate at a particular stage of its progress. **b** an impression taken from this. —v.tr. **1** express, esp. fully or clearly, in speech or writing (have stated my opinion; must state full particulars). **2** fix, specify (at stated intervals). **3** Law specify the facts of (a case) for consideration. **4** Mus. play (a theme etc.) so as to make it known to the listener. □ **in state** with all due ceremony. **of State** concerning politics or government. **State capitalism** a system of State control and use of capital. **State Department** (in the US) the department of foreign affairs. **State Enrolled Nurse** (in the UK) a nurse enrolled on a State register and having a qualification lower than that of a State Registered Nurse. **State-house** US the building where the legislature of a State meets. **State house** NZ a private house built at the government's expense. **state of the art 1** the current stage of development of a practical or technological subject. **2** (usu. **state-of-the-art**) (attrib.) using the latest techniques or equipment (state-of-the-art weaponry). **state of grace** the condition of being free from grave sin. **state of life** rank and occupation. **state of things** (or **affairs** or **play**) the circumstances; the current situation. **State of the Union message** a yearly address delivered by the President of the US to Congress, giving the Administration's view of the state of the nation and plans for legislation. **state of war** the situation when war has been declared or is in progress. **State prisoner** see PRISONER. **State Registered Nurse** (in the UK) a nurse enrolled on a State register and more highly qualified than a State Enrolled Nurse. **State school** a school managed and funded by the public authorities. **State's evidence** see EVIDENCE. **States General** hist. the legislative body in The Netherlands, and in France before 1789. **State socialism** a system of State control of industries and services. **States' rights** US the rights and powers not assumed by the United States but reserved to its individual States. **State trial** prosecution by the State. **State university** US a university managed by the public authorities of a State. □□ **statable** adj. **statedly** adv. **statehood** n. [ME: partly f. ESTATE, partly f. L STATUS]

statecraft /'steɪtkrɑːft/ n. the art of conducting affairs of state.

stateless /'steɪtlɪs/ adj. **1** (of a person) having no nationality or citizenship. **2** without a State. □□ **statelessness** n.

stately /'steɪtlɪ/ adj. (**statelier**, **stateliest**) dignified; imposing; grand. □ **stately home** Brit. a large magnificent house, esp. one open to the public. □□ **stateliness** n.

statement /'steɪtmənt/ n. **1** the act or an instance of stating or being stated; expression in words. **2** a thing stated; a declaration (that statement is unfounded). **3** a formal account of facts, esp. to the police or in a court of law (make a statement). **4** a record of transactions in a bank account etc. **5** a formal notification of the amount due to a tradesman etc.

Staten Island /'stɑːt(ə)n/ a borough of New York City, named by early Dutch settlers after the Stahten or States General of The Netherlands; pop. (1980) 352,100.

stater /'steɪtə(r)/ n. an ancient Greek gold or silver coin. [ME f. LL f. Gk statēr]

stateroom /'steɪtruːm, -rʊm/ n. **1** a state apartment in a palace, hotel, etc. **2** a private compartment in a passenger ship or US train.

Stateside /'steɪtsaɪd/ adj. US colloq. of, in, or towards the United States.

statesman /'steɪtsmən/ n. (pl. **-men**; fem. **stateswoman**, pl. **-women**) **1** a person skilled in affairs of State, esp. one taking an active part in politics. **2** a distinguished and capable politician. □□ **statesmanlike** adj. **statesmanly** adj. **statesmanship** n. [= state's man after F homme d'état]

statewide /'steɪtwaɪd/ adj. US so as to include or cover a whole State.

static /'stætɪk/ adj. & n. —adj. **1** stationary; not acting or changing; passive. **2** Physics **a** concerned with bodies at rest or forces in equilibrium (opp. DYNAMIC). **b** acting as weight but not moving (static pressure). **c** of statics. —n. **1** static electricity. **2** atmospherics. □ **static electricity** electricity not flowing as a current. **static line** a length of cord attached to an aircraft etc. which releases a parachute without the use of a ripcord. [mod.L staticus f. Gk statikos f. sta- stand]

statical /'stætɪk(ə)l/ adj. = STATIC. □□ **statically** adv.

statice /'statɪsɪ/ n. **1** sea lavender. **2** sea pink. [L f. Gk, fem. of statikos STATIC (with ref. to stanching of blood)]

statics /'stætɪks/ n.pl. (usu. treated as sing.) **1** the science of bodies at rest or of forces in equilibrium (opp. DYNAMICS). **2** = STATIC. [STATIC n. in the same senses + -ICS]

station /'steɪʃ(ə)n/ n. & v. —n. **1 a** a regular stopping place on a railway line, with a platform and usu. administrative buildings. **b** these buildings (see also bus station, coach station). **2** a place or building etc. where a person or thing stands or is placed, esp. habitually or for a definite purpose. **3 a** a designated point or establishment where a particular service or activity is based or organized (police station; polling station). **b** US a subsidiary post office. **4** an establishment involved in radio or television broadcasting. **5 a** a military or naval base esp. hist. in India. **b** the inhabitants of this. **6** position in life; rank or status (ideas above your station). **7** Austral. & NZ a large sheep or cattle farm. **8** Bot. a particular place where an unusual species etc. grows. —v.tr. **1** assign a station to. **2** put in position. □ **station-bill** Naut. a list showing the prescribed stations of a ship's crew for various drills or in an emergency. **station break** US a pause between broadcast programmes for an announcement of the identity of the station transmitting them. **station hand** Austral. a worker on a large sheep or cattle farm. **station house** US a police station. **station-keeping** the maintenance of one's proper relative position in a moving body of ships etc. **Stations of the Cross** see separate entry. **station pointer** Naut. a ship's navigational instrument, often a three-armed protractor, for fixing one's place on a chart from the angle in the horizontal plane between two land- or sea-marks. **station sergeant** Brit. the sergeant in charge of a police station. **station-wagon** an estate car. [ME, = standing, f. OF f. L statio -onis f. stare stand]

stationary /'steɪʃ(ə)nərɪ/ adj. **1** remaining in one place, not moving (hit a stationary car). **2** not meant to be moved; not portable (stationary troops; stationary engine). **3** not changing in magnitude, number, quality, efficiency, etc. (stationary temperature). **4** (of a planet) having no apparent motion in longitude. □ **stationary air** air remaining in the lungs during ordinary respiration. **stationary bicycle** a fixed exercise-machine resembling a bicycle. **stationary point** *Math.* a point on a curve where the gradient is zero. **stationary wave** = *standing wave.* □□

stationariness *n.* [ME f. L *stationarius* (as STATION)]

stationer /ˈsteɪʃənə(r)/ *n.* a person who sells writing materials etc. □ **Stationers' Hall** *Brit.* the hall of the Stationers' Company in London, at which a book was formerly registered for purposes of copyright. [ME, = bookseller (as STATIONARY in med.L sense 'shopkeeper', esp. bookseller, as opposed to pedlar)]

stationery /ˈsteɪʃənərɪ/ *n.* writing materials etc. sold by a stationer. □ **Stationery Office** (in the UK) the Government's publishing house which also provides stationery for Government offices.

stationmaster /ˈsteɪʃ(ə)n,mɑːstə(r)/ *n.* the official in charge of a railway station.

Stations of the Cross a series·of 14 pictures or carvings, representing events in Christ's passion, before which devotions are performed in some Churches. The custom probably arose out of the practice, attested from an early date, of pilgrims at Jerusalem following the traditional route from Pilate's house to Calvary.

statism /ˈsteɪtɪz(ə)m/ *n.* centralized State administration and control of social and economic affairs.

statist /ˈsteɪtɪst, ˈstætɪst/ *n.* 1 a statistician. 2 a supporter of statism. [orig. 'politician' f. It. *statista* (as STATE)]

statistic /stəˈtɪstɪk/ *n.* & *adj.* —*n.* a statistical fact or item. —*adj.* = STATISTICAL. [G *statistisch, Statistik* f. *Statist* (as STATIST)]

statistical /stəˈtɪstɪk(ə)l/ *adj.* of or relating to statistics. □ **statistical physics** physics as it is concerned with large numbers of particles to which statistics can be applied. **statistical significance** = SIGNIFICANCE 4. □□ **statistically** *adv.*

statistics /stəˈtɪstɪks/ *n.pl.* 1 (usu. treated as *sing.*) the science of collecting and analysing numerical data, esp. in or for large quantities, and usu. inferring proportions in a whole from proportions in a representative sample. 2 any systematic collection or presentation of such facts. □□ **statistician** /ˌstætɪˈstɪʃ(ə)n/ *n.*

Statius /ˈsteɪʃəs/, Publius Papinius (c.AD 45–96), Roman poet who flourished at the court of Domitian. His works include the *Silvae* (lit. = 'bits of raw material'), which are a miscellany of poems addressed to friends, and the *Thebais*, an epic written in a colourful and rhetorical style. His works were much admired in the Middle Ages. Statius was regarded by Dante as a Christian, and was a favourite of Chaucer's.

stator /ˈsteɪtə(r)/ *n. Electr.* the stationary part of a machine, esp. of an electric motor or generator. [STATIONARY, after ROTOR]

statoscope /ˈstætə,skəʊp/ *n.* an aneroid barometer used to show minute variations of pressure, esp. to indicate the altitude of an aircraft. [Gk *statos* fixed f. *sta-* stand + -SCOPE]

statuary /ˈstætjʊərɪ/ *adj.* & *n.* —*adj.* of or for statues (*statuary art*). —*n.* (*pl.* -ies) 1 statues collectively. 2 the art of making statues. 3 a sculptor. □ **statuary marble** fine-grained white marble. [L *statuarius* (as STATUE)]

statue /ˈstætjuː, ˈstætʃuː/ *n.* a sculptured, cast, carved, or moulded figure of a person or animal, esp. life-size or larger (cf. STATUETTE). □ **Statue of Liberty** see LIBERTY. □□ **statued** *adj.* [ME f. OF f. L *statua* f. *stare* stand]

statuesque /ˌstætjʊˈesk, ˌstætʃʊˈesk/ *adj.* like, or having the dignity or beauty of a statue. □□ **statuesquely** *adv.* **statuesqueness** *n.* [STATUE + -ESQUE, after *picturesque*]

statuette /ˌstætjʊˈet, ˌstætʃʊˈet/ *n.* a small statue; a statue less than life-size. [F, dimin. of *statue*]

stature /ˈstætʃə(r)/ *n.* 1 the height of a (esp. human) body. 2 a degree of eminence, social standing, or advancement (*recruit someone of his stature*). □□ **statured** *adj.* (also in *comb.*). [ME f. OF f. L *statura* f. *stare* stat- stand]

status /ˈsteɪtəs/ *n.* 1 rank, social position, relation to others, relative importance (*not sure of their status in the hierarchy*). 2 a superior social etc. position (*considering your status in the business*). 3 *Law* a person's legal standing which determines his or her rights and duties, e.g. citizen, alien, commoner, civilian, etc. 4 the position of affairs (*let me know if the status changes*). □ **status symbol** a possession etc. taken to indicate a person's high status. [L, = standing f. *stare* stand]

status quo /ˌsteɪtəs ˈkwəʊ/ *n.* the existing state of affairs. [L, = the state in which]

statutable /ˈstætjʊtəb(ə)l/ *adj.* = STATUTORY, esp. in amount or value. □□ **statutably** *adv.*

statute /ˈstætjuːt/ *n.* 1 a written law passed by a legislative body, e.g. an Act of Parliament. 2 a rule of a corporation, founder, etc., intended to be permanent (*against the University Statutes*). 3 divine law (*kept thy statutes*). □ **statute-barred** (of a case etc.) no longer legally enforceable by reason of the lapse of time. **statute-book** 1 a book or books containing the statute law. 2 the body of a country's statutes. **statute law** 1 (*collect.*) the body of principles and rules of law laid down in statutes as distinct from rules formulated in practical application (cf. *common law, case-law* (see CASE[1])). 2 a statute. **statute mile** see MILE 1. **statute-roll** 1 the rolls in the Public Records Office containing the statutes of the Parliament of England. 2 = *statute-book*. **statutes at large** the statutes as originally enacted, regardless of later modifications. [ME f. OF *statut* f. LL *statutum* neut. past part. of L *statuere* set up f. *status*: see STATUS]

statutory /ˈstætjʊtərɪ/ *adj.* required, permitted, or enacted by statute (*statutory minimum; statutory provisions*). □ **statutory rape** *US* the act of sexual intercourse with a minor. □□ **statutorily** *adv.*

staunch[1] /stɔːntʃ, stɑːntʃ/ *adj.* (also **stanch**) 1 trustworthy, loyal (*my staunch friend and supporter*). 2 (of a ship, joint, etc.) strong, watertight, airtight, etc. □□ **staunchly** *adv.* **staunchness** *n.* [ME f. OF *estanche* fem. of *estanc* f. Rmc: see STANCH[1]]

staunch[2] var. of STANCH[1].

Stavanger /stəˈvæŋgə(r)/ a seaport in SW Norway; pop. (1988) 96,440.

stave /steɪv/ *n.* & *v.* —*n.* 1 each of the curved pieces of wood forming the sides of a cask, pail, etc. 2 = STAFF[1] n. 3. 3 a stanza or verse. 4 the rung of a ladder. —*v.tr.* (*past* and *past part.* **stove** /stəʊv/ or **staved**) 1 break a hole in. 2 crush or knock out of shape. 3 fit or furnish (a cask etc.) with staves. □ **stave in** crush by forcing inwards. **stave off** avert or defer (danger or misfortune). **stave rhyme** alliteration, esp. in old Germanic poetry. [ME, back-form. f. *staves*, pl. of STAFF[1]]

staves pl. of STAFF[1] n. 3.

stavesacre /ˈsteɪvz,eɪkə(r)/ *n.* a larkspur, *Delphinium staphisagria*, yielding seeds used as poison for vermin. [ME f. L *staphisagria* f. Gk *staphis agria* wild raisin]

stay[1] /steɪ/ *v.* & *n.* —*v.* 1 *intr.* continue to be in the same place or condition; not depart or change (*stay here until I come back*). 2 *intr.* **a** (often foll. by *at, in, with*) have temporary residence as a visitor etc. (*stayed with them for Christmas*). **b** *Sc.* & *S.Afr.* dwell permanently. 3 *archaic* or *literary* **a** *tr.* stop or check (progress, the inroads of a disease, etc.). **b** *intr.* (esp. in *imper.*) pause in movement, action, speech, etc. (*Stay! You forget one thing*). 4 *tr.* postpone (judgement, decision, etc.). 5 *tr.* assuage (hunger etc.) esp. for a short time. 6 **a** *intr.* show endurance. **b** *tr.* show endurance to the end of (a race etc.). 7 *tr.* (often foll. by *up*) *literary* support, prop up (as or with a buttress etc.). 8 *intr.* (foll. by *for, to*) wait long enough to share or join in an activity etc. (*stay to supper; stay for the film*). —*n.* 1 **a** the act or an instance of staying or dwelling in one place. **b** the duration of this (*just a ten-minute stay; a long stay in London*). 2 a suspension or postponement of a sentence, judgement, etc. (*was granted a stay of execution*). 3 *archaic* or *literary* a check or restraint (*will endure no stay; a stay upon his activity*). 4 endurance, staying power. 5 a prop or support. 6 (in *pl.*) *hist.* a corset esp. with whalebone etc. stiffening, and laced. □ **has come** (or **is here**) **to stay** *colloq.* must be regarded as permanent. **stay-at-home** *adj.* remaining habitually at home. —*n.* a person who does this. **stay-bar** (or **-rod**) a support used in building or in machinery. **stay the course** pursue a course of action or endure a struggle etc. to the end. **stay one's hand** see HAND. **stay in** remain indoors or at home, esp. in school after hours as a punishment. **staying power** endurance, stamina. **stay-in strike** = *sit-down strike.* **stay the night** remain until the next day. **stay put** *colloq.* remain where it is placed or where one is. **stay up** not go to bed (until late at night). □□ **stayer** *n.* [AF *estai-* stem of OF *ester* f. L *stare* stand: sense 5 f. OF *estaye(r)* prop, formed as STAY[2]]

stay[2] /steɪ/ n. & v. —n. **1** Naut. a rope or guy supporting a mast, spar, flagstaff, etc. **2** a tie-piece in an aircraft etc. —v.tr. **1** support (a mast etc.) by stays. **2** put (a ship) on another tack. □ **be in stays** (of a sailing ship) be head to the wind while tacking. **miss stays** fail to be in stays. [OE stæg be firm, f. Gmc]

staysail /ˈsteɪseɪl, ˈsteɪs(ə)l/ n. a triangular fore-and-aft sail extended on a stay.

STD abbr. **1** subscriber trunk dialling. **2** Doctor of Sacred Theology. [sense 2 f. L Sanctae Theologiae Doctor]

stead /sted/ n. □ **in a person's** or **thing's stead** as a substitute; instead of him or her or it. **stand a person in good stead** be advantageous or serviceable to him or her. [OE stede f. Gmc]

steadfast /ˈstedfɑːst, ˈstedfəst/ adj. constant, firm, unwavering. □□ **steadfastly** adv. **steadfastness** n. [OE stedefæst (as STEAD, FAST[1])]

steading /ˈstedɪŋ/ n. Brit. a farmstead.

steady /ˈstedɪ/ adj., v., adv., int., & n. —adj. **(steadier, steadiest)** **1** firmly fixed or supported or standing or balanced; not tottering, rocking, or wavering. **2** done or operating or happening in a uniform and regular manner (a steady pace; a steady increase). **3 a** constant in mind or conduct; not changeable. **b** persistent. **4** (of a person) serious and dependable in behaviour; of industrious and temperate habits; safe; cautious. **5** regular, established (a steady girlfriend). **6** accurately directed; not faltering (a steady hand; a steady eye). **7** (of a ship) on course and upright. —v.tr. & intr. **(-ies, -ied)** make or become steady (steady the boat). —adv. steadily (hold it steady). —int. as a command or warning to take care. —n. (pl. **-ies**) colloq. a regular boyfriend or girlfriend. □ **go steady** (often foll. by with) colloq. have as a regular boyfriend or girlfriend. **steady down** become steady. **steady-going** staid; sober. **steady on!** a call to take care. **steady state** see separate entry. □□ **steadier** n. **steadily** adv. **steadiness** n. [STEAD = place, + -Y[1]]

steady state n. an unvarying condition, especially in a physical process. The term is used specifically of a cosmological theory put forward by Sir James Jeans c.1920, again (revised) by Hermann Bondi and Thomas Gold in 1948, and further developed by Fred Hoyle, postulating that the universe maintains a constant average density, with more matter continuously created to fill the void left by galaxies that are known to be receding from one another. The theory has now largely been abandoned in favour of the 'big bang' theory, and an evolving universe, as a result of two major discoveries: (i) that the most distant quasars are very different in nature from nearby galaxies, and (ii) the discovery of the microwave radiation background, by use of radio telescopes, appears to provide direct evidence for very hot radiation in an early stage of the universe, immediately following the big bang.

steak /steɪk/ n. **1** a thick slice of meat (esp. beef) or fish, often cut for grilling, frying, etc. **2** beef cut for stewing or braising. □ **steak-house** a restaurant specializing in serving beefsteaks. **steak-knife** a knife with a serrated steel blade for eating steak. [ME f. ON steik rel. to steikja roast on spit, stikna be roasted]

steal /stiːl/ v. & n. —v. (past **stole** /stəʊl/; past part. **stolen** /ˈstəʊlən/) **1** tr. (also absol.) **a** take (another person's property) illegally. **b** take (property etc.) without right or permission, esp. in secret with the intention of not returning it. **2** tr. obtain surreptitiously or by surprise (stole a kiss). **3** tr. **a** gain insidiously or artfully. **b** (often foll. by away) win or get possession of (a person's affections etc.), esp. insidiously (stole her heart away). **4** intr. (foll. by in, out, away, up, etc.) **a** move, esp. silently or stealthily (stole out of the room). **b** (of a sound etc.) become gradually perceptible. **5** tr. **a** (in various sports) gain (a run, the ball, etc.) surreptitiously or by luck. **b** Baseball reach (a base) by deceiving the fielders. —n. **1** US colloq. the act or an instance of stealing or theft. **2** colloq. an unexpectedly easy task or good bargain. □ **steal a march on** get an advantage over by surreptitious means; anticipate. **steal the show** outshine other performers, esp. unexpectedly. **steal a person's thunder** see THUNDER. □□ **stealer** n. (also in comb.). [OE stelan f. Gmc]

stealth /stelθ/ n. **1** secrecy, a secret procedure. **2 (Stealth)** a type of US military aircraft capable of extremely high speed and designed to evade detection, esp. by enemy radar, while in flight. □ **by stealth** surreptitiously. [ME f. OE (as STEAL, -TH[2])]

stealthy /ˈstelθɪ/ adj. **(stealthier, stealthiest) 1** (of an action) done with stealth; proceeding imperceptibly. **2** (of a person or thing) moving with stealth. □□ **stealthily** adv. **stealthiness** n.

steam /stiːm/ n. & v. —n. **1 a** the gas into which water is changed by boiling, used as a source of power by virtue of its expansion of volume. **b** a mist of liquid particles of water produced by the condensation of this gas. **2** any similar vapour. **3 a** energy or power provided by a steam engine or other machine. **b** colloq. power or energy generally. —v. **1** tr. **a** cook (food) in steam. **b** soften or make pliable (timber etc.) or otherwise treat with steam. **2** intr. give off steam or other vapour, esp. visibly. **3** intr. **a** move under steam power (the ship steamed down the river). **b** (foll. by ahead, away, etc.) colloq. proceed or travel fast or with vigour. **4** tr. & intr. (usu. foll. by up) **a** cover or become covered with condensed steam. **b** (as **steamed up** adj.) colloq. angry or excited. **5** tr. (foll. by open etc.) apply steam to the gum of (a sealed envelope) to get it open. □ **get up steam 1** generate enough power to work a steam engine. **2** work oneself into an energetic or angry state. **let off steam** relieve one's pent up feelings or energy. **run out of steam** lose one's impetus or energy. **steam age** the era when trains were drawn by steam locomotives. **steam bath** a room etc. filled with steam for bathing in. **steam boiler** a vessel (in a steam engine etc.) in which water is boiled to generate steam. **steam engine** see separate entry. **steam gauge** a pressure gauge attached to a steam boiler. **steam hammer** a forging-hammer powered by steam. **steam-heat** the warmth given out by steam-heated radiators etc. **steam iron** an electric iron that emits steam from its flat surface, to improve its pressing ability. **steam-jacket** a casing for steam round a cylinder, for heating its contents. **steam organ** a fairground pipe-organ driven by a steam engine and played by means of a keyboard or a system of punched cards. **steam power** the force of steam applied to machinery etc. **steam shovel** an excavator powered by steam. **steam-tight** impervious to steam. **steam train** a train driven by a steam engine. **steam tug** a steamer for towing ships etc. **steam turbine** a turbine in which a high-velocity jet of steam rotates a bladed disc or drum. **under one's own steam** without assistance; unaided. [OE stēam f. Gmc]

steamboat /ˈstiːmbəʊt/ n. a boat propelled by a steam engine, especially a paddle-wheel craft used widely on rivers in the 19th c. Such boats were constructed experimentally in the 1780s, following James Watt's improvements of the steam engine; earlier attempts had been less effective. John Fitch launched his invention on the Delaware River in 1787, but the most successful pioneer was Robert Fulton (see entry). In the US the most famous steamboats were those on the Mississippi, noted for their ornate fittings and for the risk of fire and other hazards to which they were prone. The classic account of them is Mark Twain's Life on the Mississippi (1883), telling of his experiences as a river-boat pilot. (See also STEAMSHIP.)

steam engine n. **1** an engine in which the successive expansion and rapid condensation of steam forces a piston (or pistons) to move up and down in a cylinder (or cylinders) to produce motive power, which is transmitted to a crank by means of a connecting-rod. **2** a locomotive powered by this. The power of steam had been demonstrated by Hero of Alexandria in AD 100, and condensed steam was made to drive a piston in experiments in the 18th c. The steam engine proper, the first successful form of heat engine, was developed and successively improved in the 18th c. by Newcomen, Watt, and others, after an early form had been invented by Captain Savery, and has changed little in its essentials since c.1820. It had reached its highest development by c.1900, when it was by far the most important heat engine in existence: large stationary steam engines provided the power for factories and blast furnaces, while smaller engines drove locomotives and tractors. It made possible the Industrial Revolution, being used first for pumping water from mines, later for driving machinery in mills, then for railway locomotives and for steamships. It has now been largely replaced by the steam turbine and the internal-combustion engine, but may again become popular because it can use coal rather than oil as a fuel.

steamer /ˈstiːmə(r)/ n. **1** a person or thing that steams. **2** a vessel propelled by steam, esp. a ship. **3** a vessel in which things are steamed, esp. cooked by steam. □ **steamer rug** US a travelling-rug.

steamroller /'sti:m,rəʊlə(r)/ n. & v. —n. **1** a heavy slow-moving vehicle with a roller, used to flatten new-made roads. **2** a crushing power or force. —v.tr. **1** crush forcibly or indiscriminately. **2** (foll. by *through*) force (a measure etc.) through a legislature by overriding opposition.

steamship /'sti:mʃɪp/ n. a ship propelled by a steam engine. (See also SHIP and STEAMBOAT.) From the early 19th c. steam engines were used to power ships. At first they were used as auxiliary engines on what were essentially sailing-ships, but in 1832 HMS *Rhadamanthus* crossed the Atlantic entirely under steam power, stopping at intervals to desalt the boilers, and in 1838 the *Sirius* crossed under continuous steam power, burning the cabin furniture, spare yards, and one mast en route in order to keep up steam in the boiler. Several steamship lines were established to exploit the profitable Atlantic route. The disadvantage of steamships for long journeys was that they were obliged to carry large amounts of fuel, and sailing-ships for carrying cargo survived into the 20th c.

steamy /'sti:mɪ/ adj. (**steamier, steamiest**) **1** like or full of steam. **2** colloq. erotic, salacious. □□ **steamily** adv. **steaminess** n.

stearic /'stɪərɪk/ adj. derived from stearin. □ **stearic acid** a solid saturated fatty acid obtained from animal or vegetable fats. □□ **stearate** /-,reɪt/ n. [F *stéarique* f. Gk *stear steatos* tallow]

stearin /'stɪərɪn/ n. **1** a glyceryl ester of stearic acid, esp. in the form of a white crystalline constituent of tallow etc. **2** a mixture of fatty acids used in candle-making. [F *stéarine* f. Gk *stear steatos* tallow]

steatite /'stɪətaɪt/ n. a soapstone or other impure form of talc. □□ **steatitic** /-'tɪtɪk/ adj. [L *steatitis* f. Gk *steatitēs* f. *stear steatos* tallow]

steatopygia /,stɪətəʊ'pɪdʒɪə/ n. an excess of fat on the buttocks. □□ **steatopygous** /-'paɪɡəs, -'tɒpɪɡəs/ adj. [mod.L (as STEATITE + Gk *pugē* rump)]

steed /sti:d/ n. archaic or poet. a horse, esp. a fast powerful one. [OE *stēda* stallion, rel. to STUD²]

steel /sti:l/ n., adj., & v. —n. **1** any of various alloys of iron and carbon with other elements increasing strength and malleability, much used for making tools, weapons, etc., and capable of being tempered to many different degrees of hardness. (See below.) **2** hardness of character; strength, firmness (*nerves of steel*). **3 a** a rod of steel, usu. roughened and tapering, on which knives are sharpened. **b** a strip of steel for expanding a skirt or stiffening a corset. **4** (not in pl.) literary a sword, lance, etc. (*foemen worthy of their steel*). —adj. **1** made of steel. **2** like or having the characteristics of steel. —v.tr. & refl. harden or make resolute (*steeled myself for a shock*). □ **cold steel** cutting or thrusting weapons. **pressed steel** steel moulded under pressure. **steel band** a group of usu. W. Indian musicians with percussion instruments made from oil drums. **steel-clad** wearing armour. **steel engraving** the process of engraving on or an impression taken from a steel-coated copper plate. **steel wool** an abrasive substance consisting of a mass of fine steel shavings. [OE *stȳle*, *stēli* f. Gmc, rel. to STAY²]

In antiquity (c.1200 BC) steel surfaces were produced on iron weapons and tools by heating them over red-hot charcoal so that carbon was absorbed from the coals. By c.200 BC steel production had started in India, where iron fragments and wood chips were sealed into clay containers and heated until the iron had absorbed carbon—a process that later lapsed until it reappeared in 1740, when the 'crucible' method was developed in Sheffield. The basis of modern steelmaking is the removal of a large proportion of the non-ferrous elements from molten pig-iron by making them combine with oxygen. This can be done by any of several processes, including the Bessemer process, the open-hearth process, and (from c.1900) the electric-arc furnace, in which heat is provided by an electric arc. The most popular modern process, superseding the open-hearth, uses oxygen instead of air to reduce the carbon content without introducing impurities. The chief uses of steel are for structural purposes

(e.g. girders), reinforcement for concrete, railways, ships, motor vehicles, machine tools, fastenings, and food containers.

Steele /sti:l/, Sir Richard (1672–1729), British essayist and dramatist, born in Dublin in the same year as Addison, with whom he was educated. He wrote several not very successful comedies, including *The Funeral* (1701) which broke away from Restoration drama in its true portrayal of virtue and vice. Today he is remembered for his essays in *The Tatler* (1709–11) which he founded, and *The Spectator* (1711–12) which he conducted with Addison; these had an important influence on the manners, morals, and literature of the time. He edited several other periodicals and in 1713 was elected MP, but his pamphlet *The Crisis* (1714) in favour of the Hanoverian succession led to his expulsion from the House. On the accession of George I he was appointed supervisor of Drury Lane Theatre and to other official posts; he was knighted in 1715.

steelhead /'sti:lhed/ n. a large N. American rainbow trout.

steelwork /'sti:lwɜːk/ n. articles of steel.

steelworks /'sti:lwɜːks/ n.pl. (usu. treated as *sing.*) a place where steel is manufactured. □□ **steelworker** n.

steely /'sti:lɪ/ adj. (**steelier, steeliest**) **1** of, or hard as, steel. **2** inflexibly severe; cold; ruthless (*steely composure; steely-eyed glance*). □□ **steeliness** n.

steelyard /'sti:ljɑːd/ n. a kind of balance with a short arm to take the item to be weighed and a long graduated arm along which a weight is moved until it balances.

steenbok /'steɪnbɒk, 'sti:n-/ n. an African dwarf-antelope, *Raphicerus campestris*. [Du. f. *steen* STONE + *bok* BUCK¹]

steep¹ /sti:p/ adj. & n. —adj. **1** sloping sharply; almost perpendicular (*a steep hill; steep stairs*). **2** (of a rise or fall) rapid (*a steep drop in share prices*). **3** (predic.) colloq. **a** (of a demand, price, etc.) exorbitant; unreasonable (esp. *a bit steep*). **b** (of a story etc.) exaggerated; incredible. —n. a steep slope; a precipice. □□ **steepen** v.intr. & tr. **steepish** adj. **steeply** adv. **steepness** n. [OE *stēap* f. WG, rel. to STOOP¹]

steep² /sti:p/ v. & n. —v.tr. soak or bathe in liquid. —n. **1** the act or process of steeping. **2** the liquid for steeping. □ **steep in 1** pervade or imbue with (*steeped in misery*). **2** make deeply acquainted with (a subject etc.) (*steeped in the classics*). [ME f. OE f. Gmc (as STOUP)]

steeple /'sti:p(ə)l/ n. a tall tower, esp. one surmounted by a spire, above the roof of a church. □ **steeple-crowned** (of a hat) with a tall pointed crown. □□ **steepled** adj. [OE *stēpel stȳpel* f. Gmc (as STEEP¹)]

steeplechase /'sti:p(ə)l,tʃeɪs/ n. **1** a horse-race (orig. with a steeple as the goal) across the countryside or over a racecourse with ditches, hedges, etc., to jump. (See below.) **2** a cross-country foot-race. □□ **steeplechaser** n. **steeplechasing** n.

Steeplechasing is believed to have begun in Ireland in the 18th c., with matches between two horses across country, using steeples as landmarks, over a distance of four or five miles. The new sport soon spread to England, but it was not until 1830 that annual steeplechase fixtures began.

steeplejack /'sti:p(ə)l,dʒæk/ n. a person who climbs tall chimneys, steeples, etc. to do repairs etc.

steer¹ /stɪə(r)/ v. & n. —v. **1** tr. **a** guide (a vehicle, aircraft, etc.) by a wheel etc. **b** guide (a vessel) by a rudder or helm. **2** intr. guide a vessel or vehicle in a specified direction (*tried to steer left*). **3** tr. direct (one's course). **4** intr. direct one's course in a specified direction (*steered for the railway station*). **5** tr. guide the movement or trend of (*steered them into the garden; steered the conversation away from that subject*). —n. US steering; guidance. □ **steer clear of** take care to avoid. **steering-column** the shaft or column which connects the steering-wheel, handlebars, etc. of a vehicle to the rest of the steering-gear. **steering committee** a committee deciding the order of dealing with business, or priorities and the general course of operations. **steering-wheel** a wheel by which a vehicle etc. is steered. □□ **steerable** adj. **steerer** n. **steering** n. (esp. in senses 1, 2 of v.). [OE *stieran* f. Gmc]

steer² /stɪə(r)/ n. a young male bovine animal, esp. one castrated and raised for beef. [OE *stēor* f. Gmc]

steerage /'stɪərɪdʒ/ n. **1** the act of steering. **2** the effect of the helm on a ship. **3** *archaic* the part of a ship allotted to passengers travelling at the cheapest rate. **4** *hist.* (in a warship) quarters assigned to midshipmen etc. just forward of the wardroom. □ **steerage-way** the amount of headway required by a vessel to enable her to be controlled by the helm.

steersman /ˈstɪəzmən/ n. (pl. **-men**) a person who steers a vessel.

steeve[1] /stiːv/ n. & v. Naut. —n. the angle of the bowsprit in relation to the horizontal. —v. **1** intr. (of a bowsprit) make an angle with the horizontal. **2** tr. cause (the bowsprit) to do this. [17th c.: orig. unkn.]

steeve[2] /stiːv/ n. & v. Naut. —n. a long spar used in stowing cargo. —v.tr. stow with a steeve. [ME f. OF estiver or Sp. estivar f. L stipare pack tight]

stegosaurus /ˌstegəˈsɔːrəs/ n. any of a group of plant-eating dinosaurs with a double row of large bony plates along the spine. [mod. L f. Gk stegē covering + sauros lizard]

Steiermark see STYRIA.

Stein /staɪn/, Gertrude (1874–1946), American writer. From 1903 she lived mainly in Paris, where her home became a focus for the avant-garde between the two World Wars, attracting writers such as Hemingway and F. M. Ford and artists including Picasso (who painted her portrait), Matisse, and Georges Brague. Her highly idiosyncratic poetry includes the famous line 'A rose is a rose is a rose is a rose'; her flowing unpunctuated prose is a version of the stream-of-consciousness technique. Stein's works include essays, sketches of life in France, works of literary theory, short stories, portraits of her friends, a lyric drama *Four Saints in Three Acts* (1929), and *Wars I have Seen* (1945), a personal account of German-occupied Paris. Because of her opaque style the only book to reach a wide public was *The Autobiography of Alice B. Toklar* (1933), actually her own autobiography, Toklar being the friend and companion with whom she had lived since 1912.

stein /staɪn/ n. a large earthenware mug, esp. for beer. [G, lit. 'stone']

Steinbeck /ˈstaɪnbek/, John Ernst (1902–68), American novelist. His best work deals sympathetically and realistically with the poor and oppressed, especially the migrant agricultural workers of California, as in *The Grapes of Wrath* (1939).

steinbock /ˈstaɪnbɒk/ n. **1** an ibex native to the Alps. **2** = STEENBOK. [G f. Stein STONE + Bock BUCK[1]]

Steinway /ˈstaɪnweɪ/, Henry Engelhard (1797–1871), German piano-builder. His name is used to designate a piano manufactured by him or by the firm which he founded in New York in 1853.

stela /ˈstiːlə/ n. (pl. **stelae** /-liː/) Archaeol. an upright slab or pillar usu. with an inscription and sculpture, esp. as a gravestone. [L f. Gk (as STELE)]

stele /stiːl, ˈstiːliː/ n. **1** Bot. the axial cylinder of vascular tissue in the stem and roots of most plants. **2** Archaeol. = STELA. □□ **stelar** adj. [Gk stēlē standing block]

Stella /ˈstelə/, Frank Philip (1936–), American painter, who in the late 1950s broke away from abstract expressionism without reverting to figural painting, and became recognized as a leading figure in the 'minimal art' movement. He often used notched and shaped canvases; in his 'black' paintings series of thin white stripes followed the shape of the format, and later he painted in flat bands of bright colour. In the 1970s he experimented with paintings that included cut-out shapes in relief.

stellar /ˈstelə(r)/ adj. of or relating to a star or stars. □□ **stelliform** adj. [LL stellaris f. L stella star]

stellate /ˈstelət/ adj. (also **stellated** /steˈleɪtɪd/) **1** arranged like a star; radiating. **2** Bot. (of leaves) surrounding the stem in a whorl. [L stellatus f. stella star]

stellular /ˈsteljʊlə(r)/ adj. shaped like, or set with, small stars. [LL stellula dimin. of L stella star]

stem[1] /stem/ n. & v. —n. **1** the main body or stalk of a plant or shrub, usu. rising into light, but occasionally subterranean. **2** the stalk supporting a fruit, flower, or leaf, and attaching it to a larger branch, twig, or stalk. **3** a stem-shaped part of an object:

a the slender part of a wineglass between the body and the foot. **b** the tube of a tobacco-pipe. **c** a vertical stroke in a letter or musical note. **d** the winding-shaft of a watch. **4** Gram. the root or main part of a noun, verb, etc., to which inflections are added; the part that appears unchanged throughout the cases and derivatives of a noun, persons of a tense, etc. **5** Naut. the main upright timber or metal piece at the bow of a ship to which the ship's sides are joined at the fore end (from stem to stern). **6** a line of ancestry, branch of a family, etc. (descended from an ancient stem). **7** (in full **drill stem**) a rotating rod, cylinder, etc., used in drilling. —v. (**stemmed**, **stemming**) **1** intr. (foll. by from) spring or originate from (stems from a desire to win). **2** tr. remove the stem or stems from (fruit, tobacco, etc.). **3** tr. (of a vessel etc.) hold its own or make headway against (the tide etc.). □ **stem cell** Biol. an undifferentiated cell from which specialized cells develop. **stem stitch** an embroidery stitch used for narrow stems etc. **stem-winder** US a watch wound by turning a head on the end of a stem rather than by a key. □□ **stemless** adj. **stemlet** n. **stemlike** adj. **stemmed** adj. (also in comb.). [OE stemn, stefn f. Gmc, rel. to STAND]

stem[2] /stem/ v. & n. —v. (**stemmed**, **stemming**) **1** tr. check or stop. **2** tr. dam up (a stream etc.). **3** intr. slide the tail of one ski or both skis outwards usu. in order to turn or slow down. —n. an act of stemming on skis. □ **stem-turn** a turn on skis made by stemming with one ski. [ON stemma f. Gmc: cf. STAMMER]

stemma /ˈstemə/ n. (pl. **stemmata** /ˈstemətə/) **1** a family tree; a pedigree. **2** the line of descent e.g. of variant texts of a work. **3** Zool. a simple eye; a facet of a compound eye. [L f. Gk stemma wreath f. stephō wreathe]

stemple /ˈstemp(ə)l/ n. each of several crossbars in a mineshaft serving as supports or steps. [17th c.: orig. uncert.: cf. MHG stempfel]

stemware /ˈstemweə(r)/ n. US glasses with stems.

stench /stentʃ/ n. an offensive or foul smell. □ **stench trap** a trap in a sewer etc. to prevent the upward passage of gas. [OE stenc smell f. Gmc, rel. to STINK]

stencil /ˈstensɪl/ n. & v. —n. **1** (in full **stencil-plate**) a thin sheet of plastic, metal, card, etc., in which a pattern or lettering is cut, used to produce a corresponding pattern on the surface beneath it by applying ink, paint, etc. **2** the pattern, lettering, etc., produced by a stencil-plate. **3** a waxed sheet etc. from which a stencil is made by means of a typewriter. —v.tr. (**stencilled**, **stencilling**; US **stenciled**, **stenciling**) **1** (often foll. by on) produce (a pattern) with a stencil. **2** decorate or mark (a surface) in this way. [ME f. OF estanceler sparkle, cover with stars, f. estencele spark ult. f. L scintilla]

Stendhal /ˈstɑ̃daːl/ (pseudonym of Henri Beyle, 1783–1842), French novelist who served under Napoleon in Italy, Germany, and Russia, and later held consular posts in Italy. His two recognized masterpieces are *Le Rouge et le Noir* (1830) and *La Chartreuse de Parme* (1839); each is remarkable for its political dimension, for the variety of experience portrayed, for the energy and passion of the principal characters, and for his penetrating psychological analysis. As well as novels he wrote studies of music, musicians, and Italian painting, travel books, three volumes of autobiography, and much journalism. His study *De l'amour* (1822) considers the passion both psychologically and in relation to historical and social questions, and with *Racine et Shakespeare* (1823, 1825) he linked himself with the Romantics in the Classic-Romantic controversy.

Sten gun /sten/ n. a type of lightweight sub-machine-gun. [S and T (the initials of the inventors' surnames, Shepherd and Turpin) + -en after BREN]

Steno /ˈstiːnəʊ/, Nicolaus (1638–86), Danish-born anatomist, geologist, and physician (Danish name Niels Steensen), who worked and studied in a number of European cities. He is remembered for proposing several ideas which are now part of modern geological thought: that fossils are the petrified remains of living organisms, that many rocks arise from consolidation of sediments, and that such rocks occur in layers in the order in which they were laid down, thereby constituting a record of the geological history of the earth. Steno later turned from science to religion, and ended his days as a bishop.

b but   d dog   f few   g get   h he   j yes   k cat   l leg   m man   n no   p pen   r red   s sit   t top   v voice

steno /ˈstenəʊ/ n. (pl. -os) US colloq. a stenographer. [abbr.]

stenography /steˈnɒgrəfɪ/ n. shorthand or the art of writing this. □□ **stenographer** n. **stenographic** /-nəˈgræfɪk/ adj. [Gk stenos narrow + -GRAPHY]

stenosis /stɪˈnəʊsɪs/ n. Med. the abnormal narrowing of a passage in the body. □□ **stenotic** /-ˈnɒtɪk/ adj. [mod.L f. Gk stenōsis narrowing f. stenoō make narrow f. stenos narrow]

stenotype /ˈstenəˌtaɪp/ n. **1** a machine like a typewriter for recording speech in syllables or phonemes. **2** a symbol or the symbols used in this process. □□ **stenotypist** n. [STENOGRAPHY + TYPE]

Stentor /ˈstentə(r)/ n. (also **stentor**) a person with a powerful voice. □□ **stentorian** /-ˈtɔːrɪən/ adj. [Gk Stentōr, herald in the Trojan War (Homer, Iliad v. 785)]

step /step/ n. & v. —n. **1 a** the complete movement of one leg in walking or running (took a step forward). **b** the distance covered by this. **2** a unit of movement in dancing. **3** a measure taken, esp. one of several in a course of action (took steps to prevent it; considered it a wise step). **4 a** a surface on which a foot is placed on ascending or descending a stair or tread. **b** a block of stone or other platform before a door, altar, etc. **c** the rung of a ladder. **d** a notch cut for a foot in ice-climbing. **e** a platform etc. in a vehicle provided for stepping up or down. **5** a short distance (only a step from my door). **6** the sound or mark made by a foot in walking etc. (heard a step on the stairs). **7** the manner of walking etc. as seen or heard (know her by her step). **8 a** a degree in the scale of promotion, advancement, or precedence. **b** one of a series of fixed points on a payscale etc. **9 a** stepping (or not stepping) in time with others or music (esp. in or out of step). **b** the state of conforming to what others are doing (refuses to keep step with the team). **10** (in pl.) (also **pair of steps** sing.) = STEPLADDER. **11** esp. US Mus. a melodic interval of one degree of the scale, i.e. a tone or semitone. **12** Naut. a block, socket, or platform supporting a mast. —v. (**stepped, stepping**) **1** intr. lift and set down one's foot or alternate feet in walking. **2** intr. come or go in a specified direction by stepping. **3** intr. make progress in a specified way (stepped into a new job). **4** tr. (foll. by off, out) measure (distance) by stepping. **5** tr. perform (a dance). **6** tr. Naut. set up (a mast) in a step. □ **in a person's steps** following a person's example. **mind** (or **watch**) **one's step** be careful. **step by step** gradually; cautiously; by stages or degrees. **step-cut** (of a gem) cut in straight facets round the centre. **step down 1** resign from a position etc. **2** Electr. decrease (voltage) by using a transformer. **step in 1** enter a room, house, etc. **2 a** intervene to help or hinder. **b** act as a substitute for an indisposed colleague etc. **step-in** attrib.adj. (of a garment) put on by being stepped into without unfastening. —n. such a garment. **step it** dance. **step on it** (or **on the gas** etc.) colloq. **1** accelerate a motor vehicle. **2** hurry up. **step out 1** leave a room, house, etc. **2** be active socially. **3** take large steps. **stepping-stone 1** a raised stone, usu. one of a set in a stream, muddy place, etc., to help in crossing. **2** a means or stage of progress to an end. **step this way** a deferential formula meaning 'follow me'. **step up 1** increase, intensify (must step up production). **2** Electr. increase (voltage) using a transformer. **turn one's steps** go in a specified direction. □□ **steplike** adj. **stepped** adj. **stepwise** adv. & adj. [OE stæpe, stepe (n.), stæppan, steppan (v.), f. Gmc]

step- /step/ comb. form denoting a relationship like the one specified but resulting from a parent's remarriage. [OE stēop-orphan-]

Stepanakert /ˌstepənəˈkɜːt/ the capital of the autonomous Soviet republic of Nagorno-Kharabakh; pop. (1985) 33,000. The city is named after a Baku communist revolutionary, Stepan Shaumyan.

stepbrother /ˈstepˌbrʌðə(r)/ n. a son of a step-parent by a marriage other than with one's father or mother.

stepchild /ˈsteptʃaɪld/ n. a child of one's husband or wife by a previous marriage. [OE stēopcild (as STEP-, CHILD)]

stepdaughter /ˈstepˌdɔːtə(r)/ n. a female stepchild. [OE stēopdohtor (as STEP-, DAUGHTER)]

stepfather /ˈstepˌfɑːðə(r)/ n. a male step-parent. [OE stēopfæder (as STEP-, FATHER)]

stephanotis /ˌstefəˈnəʊtɪs/ n. any climbing tropical plant of the genus Stephanotis, cultivated for its fragrant waxy usu. white flowers. [mod.L f. Gk, = fit for a wreath f. stephanos wreath]

Stephen[1] /ˈstiːvən/ (c.1097–1154), grandson of William I, king of England 1135–54. Stephen seized the throne of England from Matilda, the only legitimate child of Henry I, a few months after the latter's death in 1135. More popular with the English nobility than his rival, he forced her to flee the kingdom, but failed to restore royal authority in a time of great domestic unrest and was eventually obliged to recognize Matilda's son, the future Henry II, as heir to the throne.

Stephen[2] /ˈstiːvən/, St (d c.35), the first Christian martyr. One of the original seven deacons in Jerusalem appointed by the Apostles, he incurred the hostility of the Jews and was charged with blasphemy before the Sanhedrin and stoned; Saul (the future St Paul) was present at his execution. Feast day (in the Western Church) 26 Dec., in the Eastern Church) 27 Dec.

Stephen[3] /ˈstiːvən/, St (c.997–1038), the first king and patron saint of Hungary, who on his accession to the throne in 997 set out to christianize his country. Feast day, 2 Sept., but in Hungary 20 Aug., the day of the translation of his relics, is kept as his principal festival.

Stephenson /ˈstiːvəns(ə)n/, George (1781–1848), English engineer, generally regarded as the father of railways. Stephenson started as a colliery engineman and so had early acquaintance with steam power, which he proceeded to apply to haulage of coal wagons by cable. His first locomotive, the Blucher, was built in 1814. He became engineer to a company laying a railway track between Stockton and Darlington, and, having persuaded them to use steam power instead of horse-drawn wagons, in 1825 drove the first train upon it, with a locomotive of his own design, at a speed of 19km an hour. His son Robert (1803–59) assisted him in the building of engines and of the Liverpool-Manchester railway for which they built the famous locomotive Rocket (1829), the prototype for all future steam locomotives. George invented a miner's safety lamp at about the same time as Sir Humphry Davy, while Robert became famous as both a locomotive builder and a bridge designer, notably the box-girder Britannia tubular bridge over the Menai Strait in Wales and other major bridges at Conway, Berwick, Newcastle, in Egypt, and at Montreal.

stepladder /ˈstepˌlædə(r)/ n. a short ladder with flat steps and a folding prop, used without being leant against a surface.

stepmother /ˈstepˌmʌðə(r)/ n. a female step-parent. [OE stēopmōdor (as STEP-, MOTHER)]

step-parent /ˈstepˌpeərənt/ n. a mother's or father's later husband or wife.

steppe /step/ n. a level grassy unforested plain, esp. in SE Europe and Siberia. [Russ. step']

stepsister /ˈstepˌsɪstə(r)/ n. a daughter of a step-parent by a marriage other than with one's father or mother.

stepson /ˈstepsʌn/ n. a male stepchild. [OE stēopsunu (as STEP-, SON)]

-ster /stə(r)/ suffix denoting a person engaged in or associated with a particular activity or thing (brewster; gangster; youngster). [OE -estre etc. f. Gmc]

steradian /stəˈreɪdɪən/ n. the SI unit of solid angle, equal to the angle at the centre of a sphere subtended by a part of the surface equal in area to the square of the radius. ¶ Abbr.: sr. [Gk stereos solid + RADIAN]

stercoraceous /ˌstɜːkəˈreɪʃ(ə)s/ adj. **1** consisting of or resembling dung or faeces. **2** living in dung. [L stercus -oris dung]

stere /stɪə(r)/ n. a unit of volume equal to one cubic metre. [F stère f. Gk stereos solid]

stereo /ˈsterɪəʊ, ˈstɪə-/ n. & adj. —n. (pl. -os) **1 a** a stereophonic record-player, tape recorder, etc. **b** = STEREOPHONY (see STEREOPHONIC). **2** = STEREOSCOPE. —adj. **1** = STEREOPHONIC. **2** = STEREOSCOPIC (see STEREOSCOPE). [abbr.]

stereo- /ˈsterɪəʊ, ˈstɪə-/ comb. form solid; having three dimensions. [Gk stereos solid]

stereobate /ˈsterɪəˌbeɪt/ n. Archit. a solid mass of masonry as a foundation for a building. [F *stéréobate* f. L *stereobata* f. Gk *stereobatēs* (as STEREO-, *bainō* walk)]

stereochemistry /ˌsterɪəʊˈkemɪstrɪ, ˌstɪə-/ n. the branch of chemistry dealing with the three-dimensional arrangement of atoms in molecules.

stereography /ˌsterɪˈɒɡrəfɪ/ n. the art of depicting solid bodies in a plane.

stereoisomer /ˌsterɪəʊˈaɪsəmə(r)/ n. *Chem.* any of two or more compounds differing only in their spatial arrangement of atoms.

stereometry /ˌsterɪˈɒmɪtrɪ/ n. the measurement of solid bodies.

stereophonic /ˌsterɪəʊˈfɒnɪk, ˌstɪə-/ adj. (of sound reproduction) using two or more channels so that the sound has the effect of being distributed and of reaching the listener from more than one direction, thus seeming more realistic. □□ **stereophonically** adv. **stereophony** /-ˈɒfənɪ/ n.

stereoscope /ˈsterɪəˌskəʊp, ˈstɪə-/ n. a device by which two photographs of the same object taken at slightly different angles are viewed together, giving an impression of depth and solidity as in ordinary human vision. □□ **stereoscopic** /-ˈskɒpɪk/ adj. **stereoscopically** /-ˈskɒpɪkəlɪ/ adv. **stereoscopy** /-ˈɒskəpɪ/ n.

stereotype /ˈsterɪəʊˌtaɪp, ˈstɪə-/ n. & v. —n. **1 a** a person or thing that conforms to an unjustifiably fixed, usu. standardized, mental picture. **b** such an impression or attitude. **2** a printing-plate cast from a mould of composed type. —v.tr. **1** (esp. as **stereotyped** adj.) formalize, standardize; cause to conform to a type. **2 a** print from a stereotype. **b** make a stereotype of. □□ **stereotypic** /-ˈtɪpɪk/ adj. **stereotypical** /-ˈtɪpɪk(ə)l/ adj. **stereotypically** /-ˈtɪpɪkəlɪ/ adv. **stereotypy** n. [F *stéréotype* (adj.) (as STEREO-, TYPE)]

steric /ˈstɪərɪk/ adj. *Chem.* relating to the spatial arrangement of atoms in a molecule. □ **steric hindrance** the inhibiting of a chemical reaction by the obstruction of reacting atoms. [irreg. f. Gk *stereos* solid]

sterile /ˈsteraɪl/ adj. **1** not able to produce crop or fruit or (of an animal) young; barren. **2** unfruitful, unproductive (*sterile discussions*). **3** free from living micro-organisms etc. **4** lacking originality or emotive force; mentally barren. □□ **sterilely** adv. **sterility** /stəˈrɪlɪtɪ/ n. [F *stérile* or L *sterilis*]

sterilize /ˈsterɪˌlaɪz/ v.tr. (also **-ise**) **1** make sterile. **2** deprive of the power of reproduction. □□ **sterilizable** adj. **sterilization** /-ˈzeɪʃ(ə)n/ n. **sterilizer** n.

sterlet /ˈstɜːlɪt/ n. a small sturgeon, *Acipenser ruthenus*, found in the Caspian Sea area and yielding fine caviare. [Russ. *sterlyad'*]

sterling /ˈstɜːlɪŋ/ adj. & n. —adj. **1** of or in British money (*pound sterling*). **2** (of a coin or precious metal) genuine; of standard value or purity. **3** (of a person or qualities etc.) of solid worth; genuine, reliable (*sterling work*). —n. **1** British money (*paid in sterling*). **2** *Austral. Hist.* an English-born Australian person, as distinct from Australian-born (called *currency*). □ **sterling area** a group of countries with currencies tied to British sterling and holding reserves mainly in sterling. **sterling silver** silver of 92½% purity. □□ **sterlingness** n. [prob. f. late OE *steorling* (unrecorded) f. *steorra* star + -LING¹ (because some early Norman pennies bore a small star): recorded earlier in OF *esterlin*]

stern¹ /stɜːn/ adj. severe, grim, strict; enforcing discipline or submission (*a stern expression; stern treatment*). □ **the sterner sex** men. □□ **sternly** adv. **sternness** n. [OE *styrne*, prob. f. a Gmc root = be rigid]

stern² /stɜːn/ n. **1** the rear part of a ship or boat. **2** any rear part. □ **stern foremost** moving backwards. **stern on** with the stern presented. **stern-post** the central upright support at the stern, usu. bearing the rudder. □□ **sterned** adj. (also in *comb.*). **sternmost** adj. **sternward** adj. & adv. **sternwards** adv. [ME prob. f. ON *stjórn* steering f. *stýra* STEER¹]

sternal /ˈstɜːn(ə)l/ adj. of or relating to the sternum. □ **sternal rib** = *true rib*.

Sterne /stɜːn/, Laurence (1713–68), British novelist, born in Ireland, who became a clergyman and prebendary of York cathedral (1741). He was fêted by London society after the publication of the first two volumes of his greatest novel *Tristram*

Shandy (1759–67) in which he parodies the developing conventions of the still new 'novel' form and its problems in presenting reality, space, and time; in this Sterne excels as an innovator of the highest virtuosity, and in his use of the stream-of-consciousness technique he acknowledges his debt to Locke. He had been suffering from tuberculosis and in 1762 left for France in the hope of recuperation. His travels in France and Italy provided material for *A Sentimental Journey through France and Italy* (1767).

sternum /ˈstɜːnəm/ n. (pl. **sternums** or **sterna** /-nə/) the breastbone. [mod.L f. Gk *sternon* chest]

sternutation /ˌstɜːnjʊˈteɪʃ(ə)n/ n. *Med.* or *joc.* a sneeze or attack of sneezing. [L *sternutatio* f. *sternutare* frequent. of *sternuere* sneeze]

sternutator /ˈstɜːnjʊˌteɪtə(r)/ n. a substance, esp. poison gas, that causes nasal irritation, violent coughing, etc. □□ **sternutatory** /-ˈnjuːtətərɪ/ adj. & n. (pl. **-ies**).

sternway /ˈstɜːnweɪ/ n. *Naut.* a backward motion or impetus of a ship.

steroid /ˈstɪərɔɪd, ˈste-/ n. *Biochem.* any of a group of organic compounds with a characteristic structure of four rings of carbon atoms, including many hormones, alkaloids, and vitamins. □□ **steroidal** /-ˈrɔɪd(ə)l/ adj. [STEROL + -OID]

sterol /ˈsterɒl/ n. *Chem.* any of a group of naturally occurring steroid alcohols. [CHOLESTEROL, ERGOSTEROL, etc.]

stertorous /ˈstɜːtərəs/ adj. (of breathing etc.) laboured and noisy; sounding like snoring. □□ **stertorously** adv. **stertorousness** n. [*stertor*, mod.L f. L *stertere* snore]

stet /stet/ v. (**stetted, stetting**) **1** intr. (usu. as an instruction written on a proof-sheet etc.) ignore or cancel the correction or alteration; let the original form stand. **2** tr. write 'stet' against; cancel the correction of. [L = let it stand, f. *stare* stand]

stethoscope /ˈsteθəˌskəʊp/ n. an instrument used in listening to sounds within the body, e.g. those of the action of the heart and lungs. The French physician R. T. H. Laennec in 1816 introduced a perforated wooden cylinder which concentrated the sounds of air flowing in and out of the lungs, and described the sounds which it revealed. The modern form, with two earpieces connected to the chest-piece by flexible tubes, developed later in the 19th c.. □□ **stethoscopic** /-ˈskɒpɪk/ adj. **stethoscopically** /-ˈskɒpɪkəlɪ/ adv. **stethoscopist** /-ˈθɒskəpɪst/ n. **stethoscopy** /-ˈθɒskəpɪ/ n. [F *stéthoscope* f. Gk *stēthos* breast: see -SCOPE]

stetson /ˈstets(ə)n/ n. a slouch hat with a very wide brim and a high crown. [J. B. *Stetson*, Amer. hat-maker d. 1906]

Stettin see SZCZECIN.

stevedore /ˈstiːvəˌdɔː(r)/ n. a person employed in loading and unloading ships. [Sp. *estivador* f. *estivar* stow a cargo f. L *stipare*: see STEEVE²]

stevengraph /ˈstiːv(ə)nˌɡrɑːf/ n. a colourful woven silk picture. [T. *Stevens*, Engl. weaver d. 1888, whose firm made them]

Stevens /ˈstiːv(ə)nz/, Wallace (1878–1955), American poet, who for many years worked as a lawyer on the staff of a large insurance company. His first volume of poems, *Harmonium* (1923), was followed by other collections, which slowly brought him recognition.

Stevenson /ˈstiːv(ə)ns(ə)n/, Robert Louis Balfour (1850–94), British novelist, born in Edinburgh, where he studied law. He suffered from a chronic bronchial condition and spent much of his life abroad, in France, the US, and the South Seas, finally settling in Samoa. He published a number of essays, short stories, and travel pieces; his poems include *A Child's Garden of Verses* (1885). His first full length fictional work, the adventure story *Treasure Island* (1883), brought him fame which continued with *The Strange Case of Dr. Jekyll and Mr. Hyde* (1886), *Kidnapped* (1886), its sequel *Catriona* (1893), and *The Master of Ballantrae* (1889); his masterpiece *Weir of Hermiston* (1896) is unfinished. In these works critics have detected beneath a lightness of touch a dark sense of apprehension, but his critical reputation has been obscured by his vivid personality and adventurous life.

stew¹ /stjuː/ v. & n. —v. **1** tr. & intr. cook by long simmering in a closed vessel with liquid. **2** intr. *colloq.* be oppressed by heat or humidity, esp. in a confined space. **3** *intr. colloq.* **a** suffer prolonged embarrassment, anxiety, etc. **b** (foll. by *over*) fret or be anxious. **4** *tr.* make (tea) bitter or strong with prolonged brewing. **5** *tr.* (as **stewed** *adj.*) *colloq.* drunk. **6** *intr.* (often foll. by *over*) *colloq.* study hard. —*n.* **1** a dish of stewed meat etc. **2** *colloq.* an agitated or angry state (*be in a stew*). **3** *archaic* **a** a hot bath. **b** (in *pl.*) a brothel. □ **stew in one's own juice** be left to suffer the consequences of one's own actions. [ME f. OF *estuve, estuver* prob. ult. f. EX-¹ + Gk *tuphos* smoke, steam]

stew² /stjuː/ *n. Brit.* **1** an artificial oyster-bed. **2** a pond or large tank for keeping fish for eating. [ME f. F *estui* f. *estoier* confine ult. f. L *studium*: see STUDY]

steward /ˈstjuːəd/ *n. & v.* **1** a passengers' attendant on a ship or aircraft or train. **2** an official appointed to keep order or supervise arrangements at a meeting or show or demonstration etc. **3** = *shop steward.* **4** a person responsible for supplies of food etc. for a college or club etc. **5** a person employed to manage another's property. **6** *Brit.* the title of several officers of State or the royal household. —*v.tr.* act as a steward of (*will steward the meeting*). □ **Lord High Steward of England** a high officer of State presiding at coronations. □□ **stewardship** *n.* [OE *stīweard* f. *stig* prob. = house, hall + *weard* WARD]

stewardess /ˌstjuːəˈdes, ˈstjuːədɪs/ *n.* a female steward, esp. on a ship or aircraft.

Stewart¹ var. of STUART¹.

Stewart² /ˈstjuːət/, John Young ('Jackie') (1939–), British motor-racing driver, world champion in 1969, 1971, and 1973.

Stewart Island /ˈstjuːət/ an island separated from the south coast of South Island, New Zealand, by the Foveaux Strait; chief settlement, Oban. It is named after Captain William Stewart, whaler and sealer, who made a survey of the island in 1809.

stg. *abbr.* sterling.

Sth. *abbr.* South.

sthenic /ˈstheɪnɪk/ *adj. Med.* (of a disease etc.) with a morbid increase of vital action esp. of the heart and arteries. [Gk *sthenos* strength, after *asthenic*]

stick¹ /stɪk/ *n.* **1 a** a short slender branch or length of wood broken or cut from a tree. **b** this trimmed for use as a support or weapon. **2** a thin rod or spike of wood etc. for a particular purpose (*cocktail stick*). **3 a** an implement used to propel the ball in hockey or polo etc. **b** (in *pl.*) the raising of the stick above the shoulder in hockey. **4** a gear lever. **5** a conductor's baton. **6 a** a slender piece of a thing, e.g. celery, dynamite, deodorant, etc. **b** a number of bombs or paratroops released rapidly from aircraft. **7** (often prec. by *the*) punishment, esp. by beating. **8** *colloq.* adverse criticism; censure, reproof (*took a lot of stick*). **9** *colloq.* a piece of wood as part of a house or furniture (*a few sticks of furniture*). **10** *colloq.* a person, esp. one who is dull or unsociable (*a funny old stick*). **11** (in *pl.*; prec. by *the*) *colloq.* remote rural areas. **12** (in *pl.*) *Austral. sl.* goalposts. **13** *Naut. sl.* a mast or spar. □ **stick insect** any usu. wingless female insect of the family Phasmidae with a twiglike body. **up sticks** *colloq.* go to live elsewhere. □□ **stickless** *adj.* **sticklike** *adj.* [OE *sticca* f. WG]

stick² /stɪk/ *v.* (*past* and *past part.* **stuck** /stʌk/) **1** *tr.* (foll. by *in, into, through*) insert or thrust (a thing or its point) (*stuck a finger in my eye; stick a pin through it*). **2** *tr.* insert a pointed thing into; stab. **3** *tr. & intr.* (foll. by *in, into, on, etc.*) **a** fix or be fixed on a pointed thing. **b** fix or be fixed by or as by a pointed end. **4** *tr. & intr.* fix or become or remain fixed by or as by adhesive etc. (*stick a label on it; the label won't stick*). **5** *intr.* endure; make a continued impression (*the scene stuck in my mind; the name stuck*). **6** *intr.* lose or be deprived of the power of motion or action through adhesion or jamming or other impediment. **7** *colloq.* **a** *tr.* put in a specified position or place, esp. quickly or haphazardly (*stick them down anywhere*). **b** *intr.* remain in a place (*stuck indoors*). **8** *colloq.* **a** *intr.* (of an accusation etc.) be convincing or regarded as valid (*could not make the charges stick*). **b** *tr.* (foll. by *on*) place the blame for (a thing) on (a person). **9** *tr. colloq.* endure, tolerate (*could not stick it any longer*). **10** *tr.* (foll. by *at*) *colloq.* persevere with. □ **be stuck for** be at a loss for or in need of. **be stuck on** *colloq.* be infatuated with. **be stuck with** *colloq.* be unable to get rid of or escape from; be permanently involved

with. **get stuck in** (or **into**) *sl.* begin in earnest. **stick around** *colloq.* linger; remain at the same place. **stick at it** *colloq.* persevere. **stick at nothing** allow nothing, esp. no scruples, to deter one. **stick by** (or **with** or **to**) stay loyal or close to. **stick 'em up!** *colloq.* hands up! **stick fast** adhere or become firmly fixed or trapped in a position or place. **stick in one's gizzard** see GIZZARD. **sticking-plaster** an adhesive plaster for wounds etc. **sticking-point** the limit of progress, agreement, etc. **stick-in-the-mud** *colloq.* an unprogressive or old-fashioned person. **stick in one's throat** be against one's principles. **stick it on** *sl.* **1** make high charges. **2** tell an exaggerated story. **stick it out** *colloq.* put up with or persevere with a burden etc. to the end. **stick one's neck** (or **chin**) **out** expose oneself to censure etc. by acting or speaking boldly. **stick out** protrude or cause to protrude or project (*stuck his tongue out; stick out your chest*). **stick out for** persist in demanding. **stick out a mile** (or **like a sore thumb**) *colloq.* be very obvious or incongruous. **stick pigs** engage in pigsticking. **stick to 1** remain close to or fixed on or to. **2** remain faithful to. **3** keep to (a subject etc.) (*stick to the point*). **stick to a person's fingers** *colloq.* (of money) be embezzled by a person. **stick together** *colloq.* remain united or mutually loyal. **stick to one's guns** see GUN. **stick to it** persevere. **stick to one's last** see LAST³. **stick up 1** be or make erect or protruding upwards. **2** fasten to an upright surface. **3** *colloq.* rob or threaten with a gun. **stick-up** *n. colloq.* an armed robbery. **stick up for** support or defend or champion (a person or cause). **stick up to** be assertive in the face of; offer resistance to. **stick with** *colloq.* remain in touch with or faithful to. **stuck-up** *colloq.* affectedly superior and aloof, snobbish. □□ **stickability** /-kəˈbɪlɪtɪ/ *n.* [OE *stician* f. Gmc]

sticker /ˈstɪkə(r)/ *n.* **1** an adhesive label or notice etc. **2** a person or thing that sticks. **3** a persistent person.

stickleback /ˈstɪk(ə)l.bæk/ *n.* any small fish of the family Gasterosteidae, esp. *Gasterosteus aculeatus*, with sharp spines along the back. [ME f. OE *sticel* thorn, sting + *bæc* BACK]

stickler /ˈstɪklə(r)/ *n.* (foll. by *for*) a person who insists on something (*a stickler for accuracy*). [obs. *stickle* be umpire, ME *stightle* control, frequent. of *stight* f. OE *stiht(i)an* set in order]

stickpin /ˈstɪkpɪn/ *n. US* an ornamental tie-pin.

stickweed /ˈstɪkwiːd/ *n. US* = RAGWEED 2.

sticky /ˈstɪkɪ/ *adj.* (**stickier, stickiest**) **1** tending or intended to stick or adhere. **2** glutinous, viscous. **3** (of the weather) humid. **4** *colloq.* awkward or uncooperative; intransigent (*was very sticky about giving me leave*). **5** *colloq.* difficult, awkward (*a sticky problem*). **6** *colloq.* very unpleasant or painful (*came to a sticky end*). □ **sticky wicket 1** *Cricket* a pitch that has been drying after rain and is difficult for the batsman. **2** *colloq.* difficult or awkward circumstances. □□ **stickily** *adv.* **stickiness** *n.*

stickybeak /ˈstɪkɪˌbiːk/ *n. & v. Austral. & NZ sl.* —*n.* an inquisitive person. —*v.intr.* pry.

stiff /stɪf/ *adj. & n.* —*adj.* **1** rigid; not flexible. **2** hard to bend or move or turn etc.; not working freely. **3** hard to cope with; needing strength or effort (*a stiff test; a stiff climb*). **4** severe or strong (*a stiff breeze; a stiff penalty*). **5** (of a person or manner) formal, constrained; lacking spontaneity. **6** (of a muscle or limb etc., or a person affected by these) aching when used, owing to previous exertion, injury, etc. **7** (of an alcoholic or medicinal drink) strong. **8** (*predic.*) *colloq.* to an extreme degree (*bored stiff; scared stiff*). **9** (foll. by *with*) *colloq.* abounding in (*a place stiff with tourists*). —*n. sl.* **1** a corpse. **2** a foolish or useless person (*you big stiff*). □ **stiff neck** a rheumatic condition in which the head cannot be turned without pain. **stiff-necked** obstinate or haughty. **stiff upper lip** firmness, fortitude. □□ **stiffish** *adj.* **stiffly** *adv.* **stiffness** *n.* [OE *stíf* f. Gmc]

stiffen /ˈstɪf(ə)n/ *v.tr. & intr.* make or become stiff. □□ **stiffener** *n.* **stiffening** *n.*

stifle¹ /ˈstaɪf(ə)l/ *v.* **1** *tr.* smother, suppress (*stifled a yawn*). **2** *intr. & tr.* experience or cause to experience constraint of breathing (*stifling heat*). **3** *tr.* kill by suffocating. □□ **stifler** /-flə(r)/ *n.* **stiflingly** *adv.* [perh. alt. of ME *stuffe, stuffle* f. OF *estouffer*]

stifle² /ˈstaɪf(ə)l/ *n.* (in full **stifle-joint**) a joint in the legs of horses, dogs, etc., equivalent to the knee in humans. □ **stifle-bone** the bone in front of this joint. [ME: orig. unkn.]

stigma /'stɪgmə/ n. (pl. **stigmas** or esp. in sense 4 **stigmata** /-mətə, -'mɑːtə/) **1** a mark or sign of disgrace or discredit. **2** (foll. by of) a distinguishing mark or characteristic. **3** the part of a pistil that receives the pollen in pollination. **4** (in pl.) Eccl. (in Christian belief) marks corresponding to those left on Christ's body by the nails and spear at his Crucifixion. Such marks are attributed to divine favour; they are first recorded as occurring on the person of St Francis of Assisi. **5** a mark or spot on the skin or on a butterfly-wing. **6** Med. a visible sign or characteristic of a disease. **7** an insect's spiracle. [L f. Gk stigma -atos a mark made by a pointed instrument, a brand, a dot: rel. to STICK¹]

stigmatic /stɪg'mætɪk/ adj. & n. —adj. **1** of or relating to a stigma or stigmas. **2** = ANASTIGMATIC. —n. Eccl. a person bearing stigmata. □□ **stigmatically** adv.

stigmatist /'stɪgmətɪst/ n. Eccl. = STIGMATIC n.

stigmatize /'stɪgmətaɪz/ v.tr. (also **-ise**) **1** (often foll. by as) describe as unworthy or disgraceful. **2** Eccl. produce stigmata on. □□ **stigmatization** /-'zeɪʃ(ə)n/ n. [F stigmatiser or med.L stigmatizo f. Gk stigmatizō (as STIGMA)]

Stijl /staɪl/ n. a 20th-c. Dutch art movement which took its name from the Dutch periodical De Stijl (1917–32) founded by Theo van Doesburg and Piet Mondrian, devoted to the principles of neoplasticism. Its adherents sought an interdisciplinary application of their ideas and theory to painting, sculpture, architecture, and even poetry: form was reduced to the geometric simplicity of horizontals and verticals, and colour (which was used not as decoration but as an ancillary to special definition) was restricted to primary colours and black, white, and grey. Architects in the group included J. J. P. Oud (1890–1963), and Gerrit Rietveld (1888–1965). In the 1920s and 1930s De Stijl was influential in a European context, particularly on the Bauhaus and the constructivist movements and on Parisian purism. [Du., = the style]

stilb /stɪlb/ n. a unit of luminance equal to one candela per square centimetre. [F f. Gk stilbō glitter]

stilbene /'stɪlbiːn/ n. Chem. an aromatic hydrocarbon forming phosphorescent crystals. [as STILB + -ENE]

stilboestrol /stɪl'biːstrɒl/ n. (US **stilbestrol**) a powerful synthetic oestrogen derived from stilbene. [STILBENE + OESTRUS]

stile¹ /staɪl/ n. an arrangement of steps allowing people but not animals to climb over a fence or wall. [OE stigel f. a Gmc root stig- (unrecorded) climb]

stile² /staɪl/ n. a vertical piece in the frame of a panelled door, wainscot, etc. (cf. RAIL¹ n. 5). [prob. f. Du. stijl pillar, doorpost]

stiletto /stɪ'letəʊ/ n. (pl. **-os**) **1** a short dagger with a thick blade. **2** a pointed instrument for making eyelets etc. **3** (in full **stiletto heel**) **a** a long tapering heel of a shoe. **b** a shoe with such a heel. [It., dimin. of stilo dagger (as STYLUS)]

still¹ /stɪl/ adj., n., adv., & v. —adj. **1** not or hardly moving. **2** with little or no sound; calm and tranquil (a still evening). **3** (of sounds) hushed, stilled. **4** (of a drink) not effervescing. —n. **1** deep silence (in the still of the night). **2** an ordinary static photograph (as opposed to a motion picture), esp. a single shot from a cinema film. —adv. **1** without moving (stand still). **2** even now or at a particular time (they still did not understand; why are you still here?). **3** nevertheless; all the same. **4** (with compar. etc.) even, yet, increasingly (still greater efforts; still another explanation). —v.tr. & intr. make or become still; quieten. □ **still and all** colloq. nevertheless. **still life** (pl. **still lifes**) **1** a painting or drawing of inanimate objects such as fruit or flowers. **2** this genre of painting. **still waters run deep** a quiet manner conceals depths of feeling or knowledge or cunning. □□ **stillness** n. [OE stille (adj. & adv.), stillan (v.), f. WG]

still² /stɪl/ n. an apparatus for distilling spirituous liquors etc. □ **still-room** Brit. **1** a room for distilling. **2** a housekeeper's storeroom in a large house. [obs. still (v.), ME f. DISTIL]

stillage /'stɪlɪdʒ/ n. a bench, frame, etc., for keeping articles off the floor while draining, drying, waiting to be packed, etc. [app. f. Du. stellagie scaffold f. stellen to place + F -age]

stillbirth /'stɪlbɜːθ/ n. the birth of a dead child.

stillborn /'stɪlbɔːn/ adj. **1** (of a child) born dead. **2** (of an idea, plan, etc.) abortive; not able to succeed.

Stillson /'stɪls(ə)n/ n. (in full **Stillson wrench**) a large wrench with jaws that tighten as pressure is increased. [D. C. Stillson, its inventor d. 1899]

stilly /'stɪlɪ/ adv. & adj. —adv. in a still manner. —adj. poet. still, quiet. [(adv.) OE stillīce: (adj.) f. STILL¹]

stilt /stɪlt/ n. **1** either of a pair of poles with supports for the feet enabling the user to walk at a distance above the ground. **2** each of a set of piles or posts supporting a building etc. **3** **a** any wading bird of the genus Himantopus with long legs. **b** (in comb.) denoting a long-legged kind of bird (stilt-petrel). **4** a three-legged support for ceramic ware in a kiln. □ **on stilts** **1** supported by stilts. **2** bombastic, stilted. □□ **stiltless** adj. [ME & LG stilte f. Gmc]

stilted /'stɪltɪd/ adj. **1** (of a literary style etc.) stiff and unnatural; bombastic. **2** standing on stilts. **3** Archit. (of an arch) with pieces of upright masonry between the imposts and the springers. □□ **stiltedly** adv. **stiltedness** n.

Stilton /'stɪlt(ə)n/ n. propr. a kind of strong rich cheese, often with blue veins, orig. made at various places in Leicestershire and formerly sold to travellers at a coaching inn at Stilton (now in Cambridgeshire) on the Great North Road from London.

stimulant /'stɪmjʊlənt/ adj. & n. —adj. that stimulates, esp. bodily or mental activity. —n. **1** a stimulant substance, esp. a drug or alcoholic drink. **2** a stimulating influence. [L stimulare stimulant- urge, goad]

stimulate /'stɪmjʊleɪt/ v.tr. **1** apply or act as a stimulus to. **2** animate, excite, arouse. **3** be a stimulant to. □□ **stimulating** adj. **stimulatingly** adv. **stimulation** /-'leɪʃ(ə)n/ n. **stimulative** /-lətɪv/ adj. **stimulator** n.

stimulus /'stɪmjʊləs/ n. (pl. **stimuli** /-ˌlaɪ/) **1** a thing that rouses to activity or energy. **2** a stimulating or rousing effect. **3** a thing that evokes a specific functional reaction in an organ or tissue. [L, = goad, spur, incentive]

stimy var. of STYMIE.

sting /stɪŋ/ n. & v. —n. **1** a sharp often poisonous wounding organ of an insect, snake, nettle, etc. **2** **a** the act of inflicting a wound with this. **b** the wound itself or the pain caused by it. **3** a wounding or painful quality or effect (the sting of hunger; stings of remorse). **4** pungency, sharpness, vigour (a sting in the voice). **5** sl. a swindle or robbery. —v. (past and past part. **stung** /stʌŋ/) **1** **a** tr. wound or pierce with a sting. **b** intr. be able to sting; have a sting. **2** intr. & tr. feel or cause to feel a tingling physical or sharp mental pain. **3** tr. (foll. by into) incite by a strong or painful mental effect (was stung into replying). **4** tr. sl. swindle or charge exorbitantly. □ **stinging-nettle** a nettle, Urtica dioica, having stinging hairs. **sting in the tail** unexpected pain or difficulty at the end. □□ **stingingly** adv. **stingless** adj. **stinglike** adj. [OE sting (n.), stingan (v.), f. Gmc]

stingaree /ˈstɪŋɡəriː, ˌstɪŋɡəˈriː/ n. US & Austral. = STINGRAY.

stinger /'stɪŋə(r)/ n. **1** a stinging insect, snake, nettle, etc. **2** a sharp painful blow.

stingray /'stɪŋreɪ/ n. any of various broad flat-fish esp. of the family Dasyatidae, having a long poisonous serrated spine at the base of its tail.

stingy /'stɪndʒɪ/ adj. (**stingier, stingiest**) niggardly, mean. □□ **stingily** adv. **stinginess** n. [perh. f. dial. stinge STING]

stink /stɪŋk/ v. & n. —v. (past **stank** /stæŋk/ or **stunk** /stʌŋk/; past part. **stunk**) **1** intr. emit a strong offensive smell. **2** (often foll. by out) fill (a place) with a stink. **3** tr. (foll. by out etc.) drive (a person) out etc. by a stink. **4** intr. colloq. be or seem very unpleasant, contemptible, or scandalous. **5** intr. (foll. by of) colloq. have plenty of (esp. money). —n. **1** a strong or offensive smell; a stench. **2** colloq. a row or fuss (the affair caused quite a stink). □ **like stink** colloq. intensely; extremely hard or fast etc. (working like stink). **stink bomb** a device emitting a stink when exploded. [OE stincan ult. f. WG: cf. STENCH]

stinker /'stɪŋkə(r)/ n. **1** a person or thing that stinks. **2** sl. an objectionable person or thing. **3** sl. **a** a difficult task. **b** a letter etc. conveying strong disapproval.

stinkhorn /'stɪŋkhɔːn/ n. any foul-smelling fungus of the order Phallales.

stinking /'stɪŋkɪŋ/ adj. & adv. —adj. **1** that stinks. **2** sl. very objectionable. —adv. sl. extremely and usu. objectionably (stinking rich). □ **stinking badger** a teledu. □□ **stinkingly** adv.

stinko /'stɪŋkəʊ/ adj. sl. drunk.

stinkpot /'stɪŋkpɒt/ n. sl. **1** a term of contempt for a person. **2** a vehicle or boat that emits foul exhaust fumes.

stinkweed /'stɪŋkwiːd/ n. = wall-rocket (see ROCKET²).

stinkwood /'stɪŋkwʊd/ n. an African tree, Ocotea bullata, with foul-smelling timber.

stint /stɪnt/ v. & n. —v.tr. **1** supply (food or aid etc.) in a niggardly amount or grudgingly. **2** (often refl.) supply (a person etc.) in this way. —n. **1** a limitation of supply or effort (without stint). **2** a fixed or allotted amount of work (do one's stint). **3** a small sandpiper, esp. a dunlin. □□ **stinter** n. **stintless** adj. [OE styntan to blunt, dull, f. Gmc, rel. to STUNT¹]

stipe /staɪp/ n. Bot. & Zool. a stalk or stem, esp. the support of a carpel, the stalk of a frond, the stem of a fungus, or an eye-stalk. □□ **stipiform** adj. **stipitate** /'stɪpɪˌteɪt/ adj. **stipitiform** /stɪ'pɪtɪˌfɔːm/ adj. [F f. L stipes: see STIPES]

stipel /'staɪp(ə)l/ n. Bot. a secondary stipule at the base of the leaflets of a compound leaf. □□ **stipellate** /-ˌleɪt/ adj. [F stipelle f. mod.L stipella dimin. (as STIPULE)]

stipend /'staɪpend/ n. a fixed regular allowance or salary, esp. paid to a clergyman. [ME f. OF stipend(i)e or L stipendium f. stips wages + pendere to pay]

stipendiary /staɪ'pendjərɪ, stɪ-/ adj. & n. —adj. **1** receiving a stipend. **2** working for pay, not voluntarily. —n. (pl. **-ies**) a person receiving a stipend. □ **stipendiary magistrate** a paid professional magistrate. [L stipendiarius (as STIPEND)]

stipes /'staɪpiːz/ n. (pl. **stipites** /'stɪpɪˌtiːz/) = STIPE. [L, = log, tree-trunk]

stipple /'stɪp(ə)l/ v. & n. —v. **1** tr. & intr. draw or paint or engrave etc. with dots instead of lines. **2** tr. roughen the surface of (paint, cement, etc.). —n. **1** the process or technique of stippling. **2** the effect of stippling. □□ **stippler** n. **stippling** n. [Du. stippelen frequent. of stippen to prick f. stip point]

stipulate¹ /'stɪpjʊˌleɪt/ v.tr. **1** demand or specify as part of a bargain or agreement. **2** (foll. by for) mention or insist upon as an essential condition. **3** (as **stipulated** adj.) laid down in the terms of an agreement. □□ **stipulation** /-'leɪʃ(ə)n/ n. **stipulator** n. [L stipulari]

stipulate² /'stɪpjʊlət/ adj. Bot. having stipules. [L stipula (as STIPULE)]

stipule /'stɪpjuːl/ n. a small leaflike appendage to a leaf, usu. at the base of a leaf-stem. □□ **stipular** adj. [F stipule or L stipula straw]

stir¹ /stɜː(r)/ v. & n. —v. (**stirred**, **stirring**) **1** tr. move a spoon or other implement round and round in (a liquid etc.) to mix the ingredients or constituents. **2 a** tr. cause to move or be disturbed, esp. slightly (a breeze stirred the lake). **b** intr. be or begin to be in motion (not a creature was stirring). **c** refl. rouse (oneself), esp. from a lethargic state. **3** intr. rise from sleep (is still not stirring). **4** intr. (foll. by out of) leave; go out of (esp. one's house). **5** tr. arouse or inspire or excite (the emotions etc., or a person as regards these) (was stirred to anger; it stirred the imagination). —n. **1** an act of stirring (give it a good stir). **2** commotion or excitement; public attention (caused quite a stir). **3** the slightest movement (not a stir). □ **not stir a finger** make no effort to help. **stir the blood** inspire enthusiasm etc. **stir in** mix (an added ingredient) with a substance by stirring. **stir one's stumps** colloq. **1** begin to move. **2** become active. **stir up 1** mix thoroughly by stirring. **2** incite (trouble etc.) (loved stirring things up). **3** stimulate, excite, arouse (stirred up their curiosity). □□ **stirless** adj. **stirrer** n. [OE styrian f. Gmc]

stir² /stɜː(r)/ n. sl. a prison (esp. in stir). □ **stir-crazy** deranged from long imprisonment. [19th c.: orig. unkn.]

stir-fry /'stɜːfraɪ/ v.tr. (**-ies, -ied**) fry rapidly while stirring and tossing.

stirk /stɜːk/ n. Brit. dial. a yearling bullock or heifer. [OE stirc, perh. dimin. of stēor STEER²: see -OCK]

Stirling¹ /'stɜːlɪŋ/ a royal burgh in central Scotland, capital of Central region; pop. (1981) 38,800.

Stirling² /'stɜːlɪŋ/, James (1692–1770), Scottish mathematician. The formula named after him, giving the approximate value of the factorial of a large number, was first worked out by Abraham de Moivre (d. 1754).

Stirling³ /'stɜːlɪŋ/, Robert (1796–1878), minister of the Presbyterian Church of Scotland, co-inventor with his brother James in 1816–17 of a type of external-combustion engine known as the Stirling engine. This engine achieved a modest success in the 1890s but development lapsed until 1938, and has not achieved commercial success despite postwar efforts.

stirps /stɜːps/ n. (pl. **stirpes** /-piːz/) **1** Biol. a classificatory group. **2** Law **a** a branch of a family. **b** its progenitor. [L, = stock]

stirrer /'stɜːrə(r)/ n. **1** a thing or a person that stirs. **2** colloq. a troublemaker; an agitator.

stirring /'stɜːrɪŋ/ adj. **1** stimulating, exciting, rousing. **2** actively occupied (lead a stirring life). □□ **stirringly** adv. [OE styrende (as STIR¹)]

stirrup /'stɪrəp/ n. **1** each of a pair of devices attached to each side of a horse's saddle, in the form of a loop with a flat base to support the rider's foot. **2** (attrib.) having the shape of a stirrup. **3** (in full **stirrup bone**) = STAPES. □ **stirrup-cup** a cup of wine etc. offered to a person about to depart, orig. on horseback. **stirrup-iron** the metal loop of a stirrup. **stirrup-leather** (or **-strap**) the strap attaching a stirrup to a saddle. **stirrup-pump** a hand-operated water-pump with a foot-rest, used to extinguish small fires. [OE stigrāp f. stigan climb (as STILE¹) + ROPE]

stitch /stɪtʃ/ n. & v. —n. **1 a** (in sewing or knitting or crocheting etc.) a single pass of a needle or the thread or loop etc. resulting from this. **b** a particular method of sewing or knitting etc. (am learning a new stitch). **2** (usu. in pl.) Surgery each of the loops of material used in sewing up a wound. **3** the least bit of clothing (hadn't a stitch on). **4** an acute pain in the side of the body induced by running etc. —v.tr. **1** sew; make stitches (in). **2** join or close with stitches. □ **in stitches** colloq. laughing uncontrollably. **a stitch in time** a timely remedy. **stitch up 1** join or mend by sewing or stitching. **2** sl. betray or cheat. □□ **stitcher** n. **stitchery** n. **stitching** n. **stitchless** adj. [OE stice f. Gmc, rel. to STICK²]

stitchwort /'stɪtʃwɜːt/ n. any plant of the genus Stellaria, esp. S. media with an erect stem and white starry flowers, once thought to cure a stitch in the side.

stiver /'staɪvə(r)/ n. the smallest quantity or amount (don't care a stiver). [Du. stuiver a small coin, prob. rel. to STUB]

stoa /'stəʊə/ n. (pl. **stoas**) **1** a portico or roofed colonnade in ancient Greek architecture. **2** (**the Stoa**) the Stoic school of philosophy. [Gk: cf. STOIC]

stoat /stəʊt/ n. a flesh-eating mammal, Mustela erminea, of the weasel family, having brown fur in the summer turning mainly white in the winter. Also called ERMINE. [ME: orig. unkn.]

stochastic /stə'kæstɪk/ adj. **1** determined by a random distribution of probabilities. **2** (of a process) characterized by a sequence of random variables. **3** governed by the laws of probability. □□ **stochastically** adv. [Gk stokhastikos f. stokhazomai aim at, guess f. stokhos aim]

stock /stɒk/ n., adj., & v. —n. **1** a store of goods etc. ready for sale or distribution etc. **2** a supply or quantity of anything for use (lay in winter stocks of fuel; a great stock of information). **3** equipment or raw material for manufacture or trade etc. (rolling-stock; paper stock). **4 a** farm animals or equipment. **b** = FATSTOCK. **5 a** the capital of a business company. **b** shares in this. **6** one's reputation or popularity (his stock is rising). **7 a** money lent to a government at fixed interest. **b** the right to receive such interest. **8** a line of ancestry; family origins (comes of Cornish stock). **9** liquid made by stewing bones, vegetables, fish, etc., as a basis for soup, gravy, sauce, etc. **10** any of various fragrant-flowered cruciferous plants of the genus Matthiola or Malcolmia (orig. stock-gillyflower, so-called because it had a stronger stem than the clove gillyflower). **11** a plant into which a graft is inserted. **12** the main trunk of a tree etc. **13** (in pl.) hist. a timber frame with holes for the feet and occas. the hands and head, in which offenders were locked as a public punishment. **14** *US* **a** = stock company. **b** the repertory of this. **15 a** a base or support or handle for an implement or machine. **b** the crossbar of an anchor. **16** the butt of a rifle etc. **17 a** = HEADSTOCK. **b** = TAILSTOCK. **18** (in *pl.*) the supports for a ship during building. **19** a band of material worn round the neck esp. in horse-riding or below a clerical collar. **20** hard solid brick pressed in a mould. —*adj.* **1** kept in stock and so regularly available (*stock sizes*). **2** perpetually repeated; hackneyed, conventional (*a stock answer*). —*v.tr.* **1** have or keep (goods) in stock. **2 a** provide (a shop or a farm etc.) with goods, equipment, or livestock. **b** fill with items needed (*shelves well-stocked with books*). **3** fit (a gun etc.) with a stock. □ **in stock** available immediately for sale etc. **on the stocks** in construction or preparation. **out of stock** not immediately available for sale. **stock-book** a book showing amounts of goods acquired and disposed of. **stock-car 1** a specially strengthened production car for use in racing in which collision occurs. **2** *US* a railway truck for transporting livestock. **stock company** *US* a repertory company performing mainly at a particular theatre. **stock dove** a European wild pigeon, *Columba oenas*, with a shorter tail and squarer head than a wood pigeon and breeding in tree-trunks. **Stock Exchange** see separate entry. **stock-in-trade 1** all the requisites of a trade or profession. **2** a ready supply of characteristic phrases, attitudes, etc. **stock market 1** = STOCK EXCHANGE. **2** transactions on this. **stock-still** motionless. **stock up 1** provide with or get stocks or supplies. **2** (foll. by *with*) get in or gather a stock of (food, fuel, etc.). **take stock 1** make an inventory of one's stock. **2** (often foll. by *of*) make a review or estimate of (a situation etc.). **3** (foll. by *in*) concern oneself with. □□ **stocker** *n.* **stockless** *adj.* [OE *stoc, stocc* f. Gmc]

stockade /stɒ'keɪd/ *n. & v.* —*n.* a line or enclosure of upright stakes. —*v.tr.* fortify with a stockade. [obs. F *estocade*, alt. of *estacade* f. Sp. *estacada*: rel. to STAKE¹]

stockbreeder /'stɒk,briːdə(r)/ *n.* a farmer who raises livestock. □□ **stockbreeding** *n.*

stockbroker /'stɒk,brəʊkə(r)/ *n.* = BROKER 2. □ **stockbroker belt** *Brit.* an affluent residential area, esp. near a business centre such as London. □□ **stockbrokerage** *n.* **stockbroking** *n.*

stock exchange *n.* a place where stocks and shares are publicly bought and sold. □ **the Stock Exchange 1** an association of dealers in stocks, conducting business according to fixed rules. **2** the building occupied by these. An association was not formed in London until late in the 18th c., although dealings had previously taken place among bankers, brokers, and financial houses. Members of the new association met regularly at a coffee-house known as 'Jonathan's', and early in the 19th c. acquired a building of their own. The New York Stock Exchange had even humbler beginnings, for it started (at the end of the 18th c.) as a street market under a spreading tree in Lower Wall Street. That in London (now officially called the International Stock Exchange) formerly made a rigid division of membership between the jobbers or dealers and those who acted as brokers; this was abolished in 1986 (see BIG BANG).

stockfish /'stɒkfɪʃ/ *n.* cod or a similar fish split and dried in the open air without salt.

Stockhausen /'stɒkhaʊz(ə)n/, Karlheinz (1928–), German composer. In 1952 he went to Paris for a year to study with Messiaen and Milhaud and work at the electronic music studios of Radio France. On his return to Cologne he joined the staff of West German Radio, becoming director in 1963. His experience with electronic music bore fruit in such works as the *Gesang der Jünglinge* (1955–6), which combines electrical sounds with the voice of a boy soprano altered by echo-effects, filters, etc. Another important early interest was in the serial works of Webern, and in *Gruppen* (1955–7) and *Momente* (1961–72), for example, he takes serialism to its limits, allowing it to govern every possible aspect of performance. In other works of the 1960s he concentrated on different timbres, frequently leaving the realization of details to the performers. From 1977 onwards he has worked on his *Licht* ('Light') cycle of musical ceremonies.

stockholder /'stɒk,həʊldə(r)/ *n.* an owner of stocks or shares. □□ **stockholding** *n.*

Stockholm /'stɒkhəʊm/ the capital of Sweden since 1634 and a major port; pop. (1987) 666,800.

stockinet /,stɒkɪ'net/ *n.* (also **stockinette**) an elastic knitted material. [prob. f. *stocking-net*]

stocking /'stɒkɪŋ/ *n.* **1 a** either of a pair of long separate coverings for the legs and feet, usu. close-woven in wool or nylon and worn esp. by women and girls. **b** esp. *US* = SOCK¹. **2** any close-fitting garment resembling a stocking (*bodystocking*). **3** a differently-coloured, usu. white, lower part of the leg of a horse etc. □ **in one's stocking** (or **stockinged**) **feet** without shoes (esp. while being measured). **stocking cap** a knitted usu. conical cap. **stocking-filler** *Brit.* a small present suitable for a Christmas stocking. **stocking-stitch** *Knitting* a stitch of alternate rows of plain and purl, making a plain smooth surface on one side. □□ **stockinged** *adj.* (also in *comb.*). **stockingless** *adj.* [STOCK in (now dial.) sense 'stocking' + -ING¹]

stockist /'stɒkɪst/ *n. Brit.* a dealer who stocks goods of a particular type for sale.

stockjobber /'stɒk,dʒɒbə(r)/ *n.* **1** *Brit.* = JOBBER 1. **2** *US* = JOBBER 2b. □□ **stockjobbing** *n.*

stocklist /'stɒklɪst/ *n. Brit.* a regular publication stating a dealer's stock of goods with current prices etc.

stockman /'stɒkmən/ *n.* (*pl.* **-men**) **1 a** *Austral.* a man in charge of livestock. **b** *US* an owner of livestock. **2** *US* a person in charge of a stock of goods in a warehouse etc.

stockpile /'stɒkpaɪl/ *n. & v.* —*n.* an accumulated stock of goods, materials, weapons, etc., held in reserve. —*v.tr.* accumulate a stockpile of. □□ **stockpiler** *n.*

stockpot /'stɒkpɒt/ *n.* a pot for cooking stock for soup etc.

stockroom /'stɒkruːm, -rʊm/ *n.* a room for storing goods in stock.

stocktaking /'stɒk,teɪkɪŋ/ *n.* **1** the process of making an inventory of stock in a shop etc. **2** a review of one's position and resources.

stocky /'stɒkɪ/ *adj.* (**stockier**, **stockiest**) (of a person, plant, or animal) short and strongly built; thickset. □□ **stockily** *adv.* **stockiness** *n.*

stockyard /'stɒkjɑːd/ *n.* an enclosure with pens etc. for sorting or temporary keeping of cattle.

stodge /stɒdʒ/ *n. & v. colloq.* —*n.* **1** food esp. of a thick heavy kind. **2** an unimaginative person or idea. —*v.tr.* stuff with food etc. [earlier as verb: imit., after *stuff* and *podge*]

stodgy /'stɒdʒɪ/ *adj.* (**stodgier**, **stodgiest**) **1** (of food) heavy and indigestible. **2** dull and uninteresting. **3** (of a literary style etc.) turgid and dull. □□ **stodgily** *adv.* **stodginess** *n.*

stoep /stuːp/ *n. S.Afr.* a terraced veranda in front of a house. [Du., rel. to STEP]

stogy /'stəʊgɪ/ *n.* (also **stogie**) (*pl.* **-ies**) *US* **1** a long narrow roughly-made cigar. **2** a rough heavy boot. [orig. *stoga*, short for *Conestoga* in Pennsylvania]

Stoic /'stəʊɪk/ *n. & adj.* —*n.* **1** a member of the ancient Greek school of philosophy named after the *Stoa Poikilē* (painted colonnade) in Athens in which its founder Zeno (early 3rd c. BC) used to lecture. They taught that virtue, the highest good, is based on knowledge, and that only the wise man is truly virtuous; the wise man lives in harmony with the divine Reason (also identified with Fate and Providence) that governs nature, and is indifferent to the vicissitudes of fortune and to pleasure and pain (and hence 'stoic' in the popular sense). Stoicism was particularly influential among the Roman upper classes, numbering Seneca and Marcus Aurelius among its followers. —*adj.* of or like the Stoics. [ME f. L *stoicus* f. Gk *stōïkos* f. STOA]

stoic /'stəʊɪk/ *n. & adj.* —*n.* a stoical person. —*adj.* = STOICAL. [STOIC]

stoical /'stəʊɪk(ə)l/ *adj.* having or showing great self-control in adversity. □□ **stoically** *adv.*

stoichiometry /,stɔɪkɪ'ɒmɪtrɪ/ *n.* (also **stoichometry** /stɔɪ'kɒmɪtrɪ/) *Chem.* **1** the fixed, usu. rational numerical relationship between the relative quantities of substances in a reaction or compound. **2** the determination or measurement of these quantities. □□ **stoichiometric** /-kɪə¹metrɪk/ adj. [Gk stoikheion element + -METRY]

Stoicism /¹stəʊɪˌsɪz(ə)m/ n. **1** the philosophy of the Stoics. **2** (**stoicism**) a stoical attitude.

stoke /stəʊk/ v. (often foll. by up) **1 a** tr. feed and tend (a fire or furnace etc.). **b** intr. act as a stoker. **2** intr. colloq. consume food, esp. steadily and in large quantities. [back-form. f. STOKER]

stokehold /¹stəʊkhəʊld/ n. a compartment in a steamship, containing its boilers and furnace.

stokehole /¹stəʊkhəʊl/ n. a space for stokers in front of a furnace.

Stoke-on-Trent /ˌstəʊkɒn¹trent/ a pottery-manufacturing city on the River Trent in Staffordshire; pop. (1981) 252,500.

Stoker /¹stəʊkə(r)/, Abraham ('Bram') (1847–1912), Irish novelist, for several years business manager of the actor Sir Henry Irving. He is remembered as the author of the vampire story *Dracula* (see entry).

stoker /¹stəʊkə(r)/ n. a person who tends to the furnace on a steamship. [Du. f. *stoken* stoke f. MDu. *stoken* push, rel. to STICK[1]]

stokes /stəʊks/ n. (pl. same) the cgs unit of kinematic viscosity, corresponding to a dynamic viscosity of 1 poise and a density of 1 gram per cubic centimetre, equivalent to 10^{-4} square metres per second. [Sir G. G. *Stokes*, Brit. physicist d. 1903]

Stokowski /stɒ¹kɒfskɪ/, Leopold (1882–1977), English-born conductor, who settled in the US. He championed new American music, including that of Ives, conducted the music for Walt Disney's *Fantasia* (1940) in which music and cartoons were allied, and made transcriptions of Bach for a large symphony orchestra. Assessments of his work vary, for he took unusual liberties in order to obtain the effects he required.

STOL abbr. Aeron. short take-off and landing.

stole[1] /stəʊl/ n. **1** a woman's long garment like a scarf, worn over the shoulders. **2** a strip of silk etc. worn similarly as a vestment by a priest. [OE *stol*, *stole* (orig. a long robe) f. L *stola* f. Gk *stolē* equipment, clothing]

stole[2] past of STEAL.

stolen past part. of STEAL.

stolid /¹stɒlɪd/ adj. **1** lacking or concealing emotion or animation. **2** not easily excited or moved. □□ **stolidity** /-¹lɪdɪtɪ/ n. **stolidly** adv. **stolidness** n. [obs. F *stolide* or L *stolidus*]

stolon /¹stəʊlɒn/ n. **1** Bot. a horizontal stem or branch that takes root at points along its length, forming new plants. **2** Zool. a branched stemlike structure in some invertebrates such as corals. □□ **stolonate** /-ˌneɪt/ adj. **stoloniferous** /-¹nɪfərəs/ adj. [L *stolo -onis*]

stoma /¹stəʊmə/ n. (pl. **stomas** or **stomata** /-mətə/) **1** Bot. a minute pore in the epidermis of a leaf. **2 a** Zool. a small mouth-like opening in some lower animals. **b** Surgery a similar artificial orifice made in the stomach. □□ **stomal** adj. [mod.L f. Gk *stoma -atos* mouth]

stomach /¹stʌmək/ n. & v. —n. **1 a** the internal organ in which the first part of digestion occurs, being in man a pear-shaped enlargement of the alimentary canal linking the oesophagus to the small intestine. **b** any of several such organs in animals, esp. ruminants, in which there are four (cf. RUMEN, RETICULUM, OMASUM, ABOMASUM). **2 a** the belly, abdomen, or lower front of the body (*pit of the stomach*). **b** a protuberant belly (*what a stomach he has got!*). **3** (usu. foll. by *for*) **a** an appetite (for food). **b** liking, readiness, or inclination (for controversy, conflict, danger, or an undertaking) (*had no stomach for the fight*). —v.tr. **1** find sufficiently palatable to swallow or keep down. **2** submit to or endure (an affront etc.) (usu. with neg.: *cannot stomach it*). □ **muscular stomach** any organ that grinds or squeezes to aid digestion, such as a gizzard. **on an empty stomach** not having eaten recently. **on a full stomach** soon after a large meal. **stomach-ache** a pain in the belly or bowels. **stomach-pump** a syringe for forcing liquid etc. into or out of the stomach. **stomach-tube** a tube introduced into the stomach via the gullet for cleansing or emptying it. **stomach upset** (or **upset stomach**) a temporary slight disorder of the digestive system. □□ **stomachful** n. (pl. **-fuls**). **stomachless** adj. [ME *stomak* f. OF

stomaque, *estomac* f. L *stomachus* f. Gk *stomakhos* gullet f. *stoma* mouth]

stomacher /¹stʌməkə(r)/ n. hist. **1** a pointed front-piece of a woman's dress covering the breast and pit of the stomach, often jewelled or embroidered. **2** an ornament worn on the front of a bodice. [ME, prob. f. OF *estomacher* (as STOMACH)]

stomachic /stə¹mækɪk/ adj. & n. —adj. **1** of or relating to the stomach. **2** promoting the appetite or assisting digestion. —n. a medicine or stimulant for the stomach. [F *stomachique* or L *stomachicus* f. Gk *stomakhikos* (as STOMACH)]

stomata pl. of STOMA.

stomatitis /ˌstəʊmə¹taɪtɪs/ n. Med. inflammation of the mucous membrane of the mouth.

stomatology /ˌstəʊmə¹tɒlədʒɪ/ n. the scientific study of the mouth or its diseases. □□ **stomatological** /-tə¹lɒdʒɪk(ə)l/ adj. **stomatologist** n.

stomp /stɒmp/ v. & n. —v.intr. tread or stamp heavily. —n. a lively jazz dance with heavy stamping. □□ **stomper** n. [US dial. var. of STAMP]

stone /stəʊn/ n. & v. —n. **1 a** solid non-metallic mineral matter, of which rock is made. **b** a piece of this, esp. a small piece. **2** Building **a** = LIMESTONE (*Portland stone*). **b** = SANDSTONE (*Bath stone*). **3** Mineral. = precious stone. **4** a stony meteorite, an aerolite. **5** (often in *comb.*) a piece of stone of a definite shape or for a particular purpose (*tombstone*; *stepping-stone*). **6 a** a thing resembling stone in hardness or form, e.g. the hard case of the kernel in some fruits. **b** Med. (often in pl.) a hard morbid concretion in the body esp. in the kidney or gall-bladder (*gallstones*). **7** (pl. same) Brit. a unit of weight equal to 14 lb. (6.35 kg). **8** (attrib.) made of stone. **b** of the colour of stone. —v.tr. **1** pelt with stones. **2** remove the stones from (fruit). **3** face or pave etc. with stone. □ **cast** (or **throw**) **stones** (or **the first stone**) make aspersions on a person's character etc. **leave no stone unturned** try all possible means. **Stone Age** See separate entry. **stone-coal** anthracite. **stone-cold** completely cold. **stone-cold sober** completely sober. **stone the crows** Brit. sl. an exclamation of surprise or disgust. **stone curlew** any mottled brown and grey wader of the family Burhinidae, esp. *Burhinus oedicnemus*, inhabiting esp. stony open country. **stone-dead** completely dead. **stone-deaf** completely deaf. **stone-fruit** a fruit with flesh or pulp enclosing a stone. **stone parsley** an umbelliferous hedge-plant, *Sison amomum*, with aromatic seeds. **stone pine** a S. European pine-tree, *Pinus pinea*, with branches at the top spreading like an umbrella. **stone-pit** a quarry. **a stone's throw** a short distance. □□ **stoned** adj. (also in *comb.*). **stoneless** adj. **stoner** n. [OE *stān* f. Gmc]

Stone Age the first stage in the three-era classification of prehistoric periods (see PREHISTORY) when weapons and tools were made out of stone or of organic materials such as bone, wood, or horn. It is subdivided into the palaeolithic (formerly called the Old Stone Age), mesolithic (Middle Stone Age), and neolithic (New Stone Age).

stonechat /¹stəʊntʃæt/ n. any small brown bird of the thrush family with black and white markings, esp. *Saxicola torquata* with a call like stones being knocked together.

stonecrop /¹stəʊnkrɒp/ n. any succulent plant of the genus *Sedum*, usu. having yellow or white flowers and growing amongst rocks or in walls.

stonecutter /¹stəʊnˌkʌtə(r)/ n. a person or machine that cuts or carves stone.

stoned /stəʊnd/ adj. sl. under the influence of alcohol or drugs.

stonefish /¹stəʊnfɪʃ/ n. (pl. same) a venomous tropical fish, *Synanceia verrucosa*, with poison glands underlying its erect dorsal spines. Also called DEVILFISH.

stonefly /¹stəʊnflaɪ/ n. (pl. **-flies**) any insect of the order Plecoptera, with aquatic larvae found under stones.

stoneground /¹stəʊngraʊnd/ adj. (of flour) ground with millstones.

stonehatch /¹stəʊnhætʃ/ n. a ringed plover.

Stonehenge /stəʊn¹hendʒ/ a unique megalithic monument on Salisbury Plain in Wiltshire, England. Its alleged connection with the Druids dates from the 17th c., when people's ideas about what constituted 'the past' were very vague. In the 12th c. it was believed to be a monument over King Arthur's grave; other theories have attributed it to the Phoenicians, Romans, Vikings, and visitors from other worlds (see also DRUID); modern theory inclines to the view that it was a temple. Scientific study and excavation have identified three main constructional phases between c.3000 BC and c.1500 BC, i.e. it was completed in the Bronze Age. The circular bank and ditch, double circle of 'bluestones' (spotted dolerite), and circle of sarsen stones (some with stone lintels), are concentric, and the main axis is aligned on the midsummer sunrise—an orientation that was probably for ritual rather than scientific purposes.

stonemason /ˈstəʊnˌmeɪs(ə)n/ n. a person who cuts, prepares, and builds with stone. □□ **stonemasonry** n.

stonewall /ˈstəʊnwɔːl/ v. 1 tr. & intr. obstruct (discussion or investigation) or be obstructive with evasive answers or denials etc. 2 intr. Cricket bat with excessive caution. □□ **stonewaller** n. **stonewalling** n.

stoneware /ˈstəʊnweə(r)/ n. ceramic ware which is impermeable and partly vitrified but opaque.

stonewashed /ˈstəʊnwɒʃd/ adj. (of a garment or fabric, esp. denim) washed with abrasives to produce a worn or faded appearance.

stoneweed /ˈstəʊnwiːd/ n. = GROMWELL.

stonework /ˈstəʊnwɜːk/ n. 1 masonry. 2 the parts of a building made of stone. □□ **stoneworker** n.

stonewort /ˈstəʊnwɜːt/ n. 1 = stone parsley. 2 any plant of the genus Chara, with a calcareous deposit on the stem.

stonkered /ˈstɒŋkəd/ adj. Austral. & NZ sl. utterly defeated or exhausted. [20th c.: orig. unkn.]

stony /ˈstəʊnɪ/ adj. (**stonier, stoniest**) 1 full of or covered with stones (stony soil; a stony road). 2 a hard, rigid. b cold, unfeeling, uncompromising (a stony stare; a stony silence). □ **stony-broke** Brit. sl. entirely without money. **stony-hearted** unfeeling, obdurate. □□ **stonily** adv. **stoniness** n. [OE stānig (as STONE)]

stood past and past part. of STAND.

stooge /stuːdʒ/ n. & v. colloq. —n. 1 a butt or foil, esp. for a comedian. 2 an assistant or subordinate, esp. for routine or unpleasant work. 3 a compliant person; a puppet. —v.intr. 1 (foll. by for) act as a stooge for. 2 (foll. by about, around, etc.) move about aimlessly. [20th c.: orig. unkn.]

stook /stuːk, stʊk/ n. & v. —n. a group of sheaves of grain stood on end in a field. —v.tr. arrange in stooks. [ME stouk, from or rel. to MLG stūke]

stool /stuːl/ n. & v. —n. 1 a seat without a back or arms, usu. for one person and consisting of a wooden slab on three or four short legs. 2 a = FOOTSTOOL. b a low bench for kneeling on. 3 (usu. in pl.) = FAECES. 4 the root or stump of a tree or plant from which the shoots spring. 5 US a decoy-bird in hunting. —v.intr. (of a plant) throw up shoots from the root. □ **fall between two stools** fail from vacillation between two courses etc. **stool-pigeon** 1 a person acting as a decoy (orig. a decoy of a pigeon fixed to a stool). 2 a police informer. [OE stōl f. Gmc, rel. to STAND]

stoolball /ˈstuːlbɔːl/ n. an old game resembling cricket, still played in Sussex etc. especially by women and girls. Forms of it were played in Elizabethan times, when it was a hand-game, not using bats, and the 'stool' or wicket may have been an ordinary stool.

stoolie /ˈstuːlɪ/ n. US sl. a person acting as a stool-pigeon.

stoop[1] /stuːp/ v. & n. —v. 1 tr. bend (one's head or body) forwards and downwards. 2 intr. carry one's head and shoulders bowed forward. 3 intr. (foll. by to + infin.) deign or condescend. 4 intr. (foll. by to) descend or lower oneself to (some conduct) (has stooped to crime). 5 intr. (of a hawk etc.) swoop on its prey. —n. 1 a stooping posture. 2 the downward swoop of a hawk etc. [OE stūpian f. Gmc, rel. to STEEP[1]]

stoop[2] /stuːp/ n. US a porch or small veranda or set of steps in front of a house. [Du. stoep: see STOEP]

stoop[3] var. of STOUP.

stop /stɒp/ v. & n. —v. (**stopped, stopping**) 1 tr. a put an end to (motion etc.); completely check the progress or motion or operation of. b effectively hinder or prevent (stopped them playing so loudly). c discontinue (an action or sequence of actions) (stopped playing; stopped my visits). 2 intr. come to an end; cease (supplies suddenly stopped). 3 intr. cease from motion or speaking or action; make a halt or pause (the car stopped at the lights; he stopped in the middle of a sentence; my watch has stopped). 4 tr. cause to cease action; defeat. 5 tr. sl. receive (a blow etc.). 6 intr. remain; stay for a short time. 7 tr. (often foll. by up) block or close up (a hole or leak etc.). 8 tr. not permit or supply as usual; discontinue or withhold (shall stop their wages). 9 tr. (in full **stop payment of** or **on**) instruct a bank to withhold payment on (a cheque). 10 tr. Brit. put a filling in (a tooth). 11 tr. obtain the required pitch from (the string of a violin etc.) by pressing at the appropriate point with the finger. 12 tr. plug the upper end of (an organ-pipe), giving a note an octave lower. 13 tr. Bridge be able to prevent opponents from taking all the tricks in (a suit). 14 tr. make (a sound) inaudible. 15 tr. Boxing a parry (a blow). b knock out (an opponent). 16 tr. Hort. pinch back (a plant). 17 tr. make (a clock, factory, etc.) cease working. 18 tr. Brit. provide with punctuation. 19 tr. Naut. make fast; stopper (a cable etc.). —n. 1 the act or an instance of stopping; the state of being stopped (put a stop to; the vehicle was brought to a stop). 2 a place designated for a bus or train etc. to stop. 3 a punctuation mark, esp. = full stop (see FULL[1]). 4 a device for stopping motion at a particular point. 5 a change of pitch effected by stopping a string. 6 a (in an organ) a row of pipes of one character. b a knob etc. operating these. 7 a manner of speech adopted to produce a particular effect. 8 Optics & Photog. = DIAPHRAGM 3. 9 a the effective diameter of a lens. b a device for reducing this. c a unit of change of relative aperture or exposure (with a reduction of one stop equivalent to halving it). 10 (of sound) = PLOSIVE. 11 (in telegrams etc.) a full stop (see FULL[1]). 12 Bridge a card or cards stopping a suit. 13 Naut. a small line used as a lashing. □ **put a stop to** cause to end, esp. abruptly. **stop at nothing** be ruthless. **stop by** (also absol.) call at (a place). **stop dead** (or **short**) cease abruptly. **stop down** Photog. reduce the aperture of (a lens) with a diaphragm. **stop-drill** a drill with a shoulder limiting the depth of penetration. **stop one's ears** 1 put one's fingers in one's ears to avoid hearing. 2 refuse to listen. **stop a gap** serve to meet a temporary need. **stop-go** 1 alternate stopping and restarting of progress. 2 Brit. the alternate restriction and stimulation of economic demand. **stop-knob** a knob controlling an organ stop. **stop lamp** a light on the rear of a vehicle showing when the brakes are applied. **stop light 1** a red traffic-light. **2** = stop lamp. **stop a person's mouth** induce a person by bribery or other means to keep silence about something. **stop off** (or **over**) break one's journey. **stop out 1** stay out. **2** cover (part of an area) to prevent printing, etching, etc. **stop payment** declare oneself insolvent. **stop press** Brit. 1 (often attrib.) late news inserted in a newspaper after printing has begun. 2 a column in a newspaper reserved for this. **stop valve** a valve closing a pipe against the passage of liquid. **stop-volley** (esp. in lawn tennis) a checked volley close to the net, dropping the ball dead on the other side. **with all the stops out** exerting extreme effort. □□ **stopless** adj. **stoppable** adj. [ME f. OE -stoppian f. LL stuppare STUFF: see ESTOP]

stopbank /ˈstɒpbæŋk/ n. Austral. & NZ an embankment built to prevent river-flooding.

stopcock /ˈstɒpkɒk/ n. an externally operated valve regulating the flow of a liquid or gas through a pipe etc.

stope /stəʊp/ n. a steplike part of a mine where ore etc. is being extracted. [app. rel. to STEP n.]

Stopes /stəʊps/, Marie Charlotte Carmichael (1880–1958), advocate of birth control, born in Scotland. She studied botany and specialized in fossil plants, establishing a considerable academic reputation, but after the failure in 1916 of her first marriage devoted herself to sex education and family planning, founding the first birth-control clinic in London in 1921.

stopgap /ˈstɒpgæp/ n. (often attrib.) a temporary substitute.

stopoff /ˈstɒpɒf/ n. a break in one's journey.

stopover /ˈstɒpˌəʊvə(r)/ n. = STOPOFF.

stoppage /'stɒpɪdʒ/ n. **1** the condition of being blocked or stopped. **2** a stopping (of pay). **3** a stopping or interruption of work in a factory etc.

Stoppard /'stɒpɑːd/, Tom (1937–), Czech-born English playwright, author of *Rosencrantz and Guildenstern are Dead* (1966) and other comedies. His plays are noted for their bizarre conjunctions and verbal dexterity.

stopper /'stɒpə(r)/ n. & v. —n. **1** a plug for closing a bottle etc. **2** a person or thing that stops something. **3** Naut. a rope or clamp etc. for checking and holding a rope cable or chain cable. —v.tr. close or secure with a stopper. □ **put a stopper on 1** put an end to (a thing). **2** keep (a person) quiet.

stopping /'stɒpɪŋ/ n. Brit. a filling for a tooth.

stopple /'stɒp(ə)l/ n. & v. —n. a stopper or plug. —v.tr. close with a stopple. [ME: partly f. STOP + -LE¹, partly f. ESTOPPEL]

stopwatch /'stɒpwɒtʃ/ n. a watch with a mechanism for recording elapsed time, used to time races etc.

storage /'stɔːrɪdʒ/ n. **1 a** the storing of goods etc. **b** a particular method of storing or the space available for it. **2** the cost of storing. **3** the electronic retention of data in a computer etc. □ **storage battery** (or **cell**) a battery (or cell) for storing electricity. **storage heater** Brit. an electric heater accumulating heat outside peak hours for later release.

storax /'stɔːræks/ n. **1 a** a fragrant resin, obtained from the tree *Styrax officinalis* and formerly used in perfume. **b** this tree. **2** (in full **Levant** or **liquid storax**) a balsam obtained from the tree *Liquidambar orientalis*. [L f. Gk, var. of STYRAX]

store /stɔː(r)/ n. & v. —n. **1** a quantity of something kept available for use (*a store of wine; a store of wit*). **2** (in pl.) **a** articles for a particular purpose accumulated for use (*naval stores*). **b** a supply of these or the place where they are kept. **3 a** = *department store*. **b** esp. US any retail outlet or shop. **c** (often in pl.) a shop selling basic necessities (*general stores*). **4** a warehouse for the temporary keeping of furniture etc. **5** a device in a computer for storing retrievable data; a memory. —v.tr. **1** put (furniture etc.) in store. **2** (often foll. by up, away) accumulate (stores, energy, electricity, etc.) for future use. **3** stock or provide with something useful (*a mind stored with facts*). **4** (of a receptacle) have storage capacity for. **5** enter or retain (data) for retrieval. □ **in store 1** kept in readiness. **2** coming in the future. **3** (foll. by for) destined or intended. **set** (or **lay** or **put**) **store by** (or **on**) consider important or valuable. □□ **storable** adj. **storer** n. [ME f. obs. *astore* (n. & v.) f. OF *estore, estorer* f. L *instaurare* renew: cf. RESTORE]

storefront /'stɔːfrʌnt/ n. esp. US **1** the side of a shop facing the street. **2** a room at the front of a shop.

storehouse /'stɔːhaʊs/ n. a place where things are stored.

storekeeper /'stɔːˌkiːpə(r)/ n. **1** a storeman. **2** US a shopkeeper.

storeman /'stɔːmən/ n. (pl. **-men**) a person responsible for stored goods.

storeroom /'stɔːruːm, -rʊm/ n. a room in which items are stored.

storey /'stɔːrɪ/ n. (also **story**) (pl. **-eys** or **-ies**) **1** any of the parts into which a building is divided horizontally; the whole of the rooms etc. having a continuous floor (*a third-storey window; a house of five storeys*). **2** a thing forming a horizontal division. □□ **-storeyed** (in comb.) (also **-storied**). [ME f. AL *historia* HISTORY (perh. orig. meaning a tier of painted windows or sculpture)]

storiated /'stɔːrɪˌeɪtɪd/ adj. decorated with historical, legendary, or emblematic designs. □□ **storiation** /-'eɪʃ(ə)n/ n. [shortening of HISTORIATED]

storied /'stɔːrɪd/ adj. literary celebrated in or associated with stories or legends.

stork /stɔːk/ n. **1** any long-legged large wading bird of the family Ciconiidae, esp. *Ciconia ciconia* with white plumage, black wing-tips, a long reddish beak, and red feet, nesting esp. on tall buildings. **2** this bird as the pretended bringer of babies. □ **stork's-bill** a plant of the genus *Pelargonium* or *Erodium*. [OE *storc*, prob. rel. to STARK (from its rigid posture)]

storm /stɔːm/ n. & v. —n. **1** a violent disturbance of the atmosphere with strong winds and usu. with thunder and rain or snow etc. **2** Meteorol. a wind intermediate between gale and hurricane, esp. (on the Beaufort scale) of 55–72 m.p.h. **3** a violent disturbance of the established order in human affairs. **4** (foll. by of) **a** a violent shower of missiles or blows. **b** an outbreak of applause, indignation, hisses, etc. (*they were greeted by a storm of abuse*). **5 a** a direct assault by troops on a fortified place. **b** the capture of a place by such an assault. —v. **1** intr. (often foll. by at, away) talk violently, rage, bluster. **2** intr. (usu. foll. by in, out of, etc.) move violently or angrily (*stormed out of the meeting*). **3** tr. attack or capture by storm. **4** intr. (of wind, rain, etc.) rage; be violent. □ **storm-bird** = *storm petrel*. **storm centre 1** the point to which the wind blows spirally inward in a cyclonic storm. **2** a subject etc. upon which agitation or disturbance is concentrated. **storm cloud 1** a heavy rain-cloud. **2** a threatening state of affairs. **storm-cock** a mistle-thrush. **storm-collar** a high coat-collar that can be turned up and fastened. **storm cone** Brit. a tarred-canvas cone hoisted as a warning of high wind, upright for the north and inverted for the south. **storm-door** an additional outer door for protection in bad weather or winter. **storm-finch** Brit. = *storm petrel*. **storm-glass** a sealed tube containing a solution of which the clarity is thought to change when storms approach. **storming-party** a detachment of troops ordered to begin an assault. **storm in a teacup** Brit. great excitement over a trivial matter. **storm-lantern** Brit. a hurricane lamp. **storm petrel 1** a small petrel, *Hydrobates pelagicus*, of the North Atlantic, with black and white plumage. **2** a person causing unrest. **storm-sail** a sail of smaller size and stouter canvas than the corresponding one used in ordinary weather. **storm-signal** a device warning of an approaching storm. **storm trooper 1** (also **Storm Trooper**) hist. a member of the Nazi political militia. **2** a member of the shock troops. **storm troops 1** = *shock troops* (see SHOCK¹). **2** (also **Storm Troops**) hist. the Nazi political militia. (See BROWNSHIRTS.) **storm window** an additional outer sash-window used like a storm-door. **take by storm 1** capture by direct assault. **2** rapidly captivate (a person, audience, etc.). □□ **stormless** adj. **stormproof** adj. [OE f. Gmc]

stormbound /'stɔːmbaʊnd/ adj. prevented by storms from leaving port or continuing a voyage.

Stormont /'stɔːmənt/ a suburb of the east side of Belfast, the seat of the parliament of Northern Ireland (suspended since the imposition of direct rule from London in 1972).

stormy /'stɔːmɪ/ adj. (**stormier, stormiest**) **1** of or affected by storms. **2** (of a wind etc.) violent, raging, vehement. **3** full of angry feeling or outbursts; lively, boisterous (*a stormy meeting*). □ **stormy petrel** = *storm petrel*. □□ **stormily** adv. **storminess** n.

story¹ /'stɔːrɪ/ n. (pl. **-ies**) **1** an account of imaginary or past events; a narrative, tale, or anecdote. **2** the past course of the life of a person or institution etc. (*my story is a strange one*). **3** (in full **story-line**) the narrative or plot of a novel or play etc. **4** facts or experiences that deserve narration. **5** colloq. a fib or lie. **6** a narrative or descriptive item of news. □ **the old** (or **same old**) **story** the familiar or predictable course of events. **story-book 1** a book of stories for children. **2** (attrib.) unreal, romantic (*a story-book ending*). **the story goes** it is said. **to cut** (or **make**) **a long story short** a formula excusing the omission of details. [ME *storie* f. AF *estorie* (OF *estoire*) f. L *historia* (as HISTORY)]

story² var. of STOREY.

storyboard /'stɔːrɪˌbɔːd/ n. a displayed sequence of pictures etc. outlining the plan of a film, television advertisement, etc.

storyteller /'stɔːrɪˌtelə(r)/ n. **1** a person who tells stories. **2** colloq. a liar. □□ **storytelling** n. & adj.

stoup /stuːp/ n. (also **stoop**) **1** a holy-water basin. **2** archaic a flagon, beaker, or drinking-vessel. [ME f. ON *staup* (= OE *stēap*) f. Gmc, rel. to STEEP²]

stoush /staʊʃ/ v. & n. Austral. & NZ sl. —v.tr. **1** hit; fight with. **2** attack verbally. —n. a fight; a beating. [19th c.: orig. uncert.]

stout /staʊt/ adj. & n. —adj. **1** rather fat; corpulent; bulky. **2** of considerable thickness or strength (*a stout stick*). **3** brave, resolute, vigorous (*a stout fellow; put up stout resistance*). —n. a strong dark beer brewed with roasted malt or barley. □ **a stout heart** courage, resolve. **stout-hearted** courageous. **stout-heartedly**

courageously. **stout-heartedness** courage. □□ **stoutish** adj. **stoutly** adv. **stoutness** n. [ME f. AF & dial. OF stout f. WG, perh. rel. to STILT]

stove[1] /stəʊv/ n. & v. —n. **1** a closed apparatus burning fuel or electricity for heating or cooking. **2** Brit. Hort. a hothouse with artificial heat. —v.tr. Brit. force or raise (plants) in a stove. □ **stove-enamel** a heatproof enamel produced by the treatment of enamelled objects in a stove. **stove-pipe** a pipe conducting smoke and gases from a stove to a chimney. **stove-pipe hat** colloq. a tall silk hat. [ME = sweating-room, f. MDu., MLG stove, OHG stuba f. Gmc, perh. rel. to STEW[1]]

stove[2] past and past part. of STAVE v.

stow /stəʊ/ v.tr. **1** pack (goods etc.) tidily and compactly. **2** Naut. place (a cargo or provisions) in its proper place and order. **3** fill (a receptacle) with articles compactly arranged. **4** (usu. in imper.) sl. abstain or cease from (stow the noise!). □ **stow away 1** place (a thing) where it will not cause an obstruction. **2** be a stowaway on a ship etc. [ME, f. BESTOW: in Naut. use perh. infl. by Du. stouwen]

stowage /ˈstəʊɪdʒ/ n. **1** the act or an instance of stowing. **2** a place for this.

stowaway /ˈstəʊəˌweɪ/ n. a person who hides on board a ship or aircraft etc. to get free passage.

Stowe /stəʊ/, Mrs Harriet Beecher (1811–96), American novelist who won fame with her anti-slavery novel Uncle Tom's Cabin (1852) which stirred up great public feeling in its powerful and melodramatic descriptions of the sufferings of slaves. The novel's success brought her to England where she was rapturously received and honoured by Queen Victoria, though she later alienated British opinion by her Lady Byron Vindicated (1870) which charged Byron with incestuous relations with his half-sister.

STP abbr. **1** Professor of Sacred Theology. **2** standard temperature and pressure.

str. abbr. **1** strait. **2** stroke (of an oar).

Strabane /strəˈbæn/ a town in Co. Tyrone, Northern Ireland; pop. (1981) 10,300.

strabismus /strəˈbɪzməs/ n. Med. the abnormal condition of one or both eyes not correctly aligned in direction; a squint. □□ **strabismal** adj. **strabismic** adj. [mod.L f. Gk strabismos f. strabizō squint f. strabos squinting]

Strabo /ˈstreɪbəʊ/ (64/3 BC–after AD 21) Greek historian and geographer. His historical writing is lost; his Geography, probably written for the use of public figures, deals with theoretical and philosophical matters (he himself was a Stoic) before presenting a detailed physical and historical geography of the ancient world.

Strachey /ˈstreɪtʃɪ/, (Giles) Lytton (1880–1932), English biographer, a prominent member of the Bloomsbury Group. He achieved recognition with Eminent Victorians (1918) which attacked the Victorian establishment through satirical biographies of Cardinal Manning, Florence Nightingale, Dr Thomas Arnold, General Gordon, and others. He influenced the development of biography with his irreverent biography of Queen Victoria (1921), and Elizabeth and Essex (1928) reveals his debt to Freud.

Strad /stræd/ n. colloq. a Stradivarius. [abbr.]

straddle /ˈstræd(ə)l/ v. & n. —v. **1** tr. **a** sit or stand across (a thing) with the legs wide apart. **b** be situated across or on both sides of (the town straddles the border). **2** intr. **a** sit or stand in this way. **b** (of the legs) be wide apart. **3** tr. part (one's legs) widely. **4** tr. drop shots or bombs short of and beyond (a target). **5** tr. vacillate between two policies etc. regarding (an issue). —n. **1** the act or an instance of straddling. **2** Stock Exch. an option giving the holder the right of either calling for or delivering stock at a fixed price. □□ **straddler** n. [alt. of striddle, back-form. f. striddlings astride f. strid- = STRIDE]

Stradivarius /ˌstrædɪˈveərɪəs/ n. a violin or other stringed instrument made by Antonio Stradivari (?1644–1737), the greatest of a family of violin-makers of Cremona in northern Italy, or his followers. Antonio Stradivari trained in the workshop of Nicolò Amati and produced over 1,100 instruments, of which perhaps 400 are known still to exist. Among the many famous Stradivarius violins are those nicknamed the 'Betts' (1704), now in the Library of Congress, and the 'Messie' (Messiah, named by the French violinist Alard on being shown 'what one waits for always but which never appears'; 1716), now in the Ashmolean Museum, Oxford. Stradivari's finest instruments are those dating from c.1700 onwards. [Latinized f. Stradivari]

strafe /strɑːf, streɪf/ v. & n. —v.tr. **1** bombard; harass with gunfire. **2** reprimand. **3** abuse. **4** thrash. —n. an act of strafing. [joc. adaptation of G catchword (1914) Gott strafe England may God punish England]

straggle /ˈstræg(ə)l/ v. & n. —v.intr. **1** lack or lose compactness or tidiness. **2** be or become dispersed or sporadic. **3** trail behind others in a march or race etc. **4** (of a plant, beard, etc.) grow long and loose. —n. a body or group of straggling or scattered persons or things. □□ **straggler** n. **straggly** adj. (**stragglier**, **straggliest**). [ME, perh. rel. to dial. strake go, rel. to STRETCH]

straight /streɪt/ adj., n., & adv. —adj. **1 a** extending uniformly in the same direction; without a curve or bend etc. **b** Geom. (of a line) lying on the shortest path between any two of its points. **2** successive, uninterrupted (three straight wins). **3** in proper order or place or condition; duly arranged; level, symmetrical (is the picture straight?; put things straight). **4** honest, candid; not evasive (a straight answer). **5** (of thinking etc.) logical, unemotional. **6** (of drama etc.) serious as opposed to popular or comic; employing the conventional techniques of its art form. **7 a** unmodified. **b** (of a drink) undiluted. **8** colloq. (of music) classical. **9** colloq. **a** (of a person etc.) conventional or respectable. **b** heterosexual. **10** (of an arch) flat-topped. **11** (of a person's back) not bowed. **12** (of the hair) not curly or wavy. **13** (of a knee) not bent. **14** (of the legs) not bandy or knock-kneed. **15** (of a garment) not flared. **16** coming direct from its source. **17** (of an aim, look, blow, or course) going direct to the mark. —n. **1** the straight part of something, esp. the concluding stretch of a racecourse. **2** a straight condition. **3** a sequence of five cards in poker. **4** colloq. a conventional person; a heterosexual. —adv. **1** in a straight line; direct; without deviation or hesitation or circumlocution (came straight from Paris; I told them straight). **2** in the right direction, with a good aim (shoot straight). **3** correctly (can't see straight). **4** archaic at once or immediately. □ **go straight** live an honest life after being a criminal. **the straight and narrow** morally correct behaviour. **straight angle** an angle of 180°. **straight away** at once; immediately. **straight-bred** not cross-bred. **straight-cut** (of tobacco) cut lengthwise into long silky fibres. **straight-edge** a bar with one edge accurately straight, used for testing. **straight-eight 1** an internal-combustion engine with eight cylinders in line. **2** a vehicle having this. **straight eye** the ability to detect deviation from the straight. **straight face** an intentionally expressionless face, esp. avoiding a smile though amused. **straight-faced** having a straight face. **straight fight** Brit. Polit. a direct contest between two candidates. **straight flush** see FLUSH[3]. **straight from the shoulder 1** (of a blow) well delivered. **2** (of a verbal attack) frank or direct. **straight man** a comedian's stooge. **straight off** colloq. without hesitation, deliberation, etc. (cannot tell you straight off). **straight-out** US **1** uncompromising. **2** straightforward, genuine. **straight razor** US a cutthroat razor. **straight up** Brit. sl. truly, really (straight up, I couldn't find it). □□ **straightly** adv. **straightness** n. [ME, past part. of STRETCH]

straightaway /ˈstreɪtəˌweɪ/ adj. US **1** (of a course etc.) straight. **2** straightforward.

straighten /ˈstreɪt(ə)n/ v.tr. & intr. **1** (often foll. by out) make or become straight. **2** (foll. by up) stand erect after bending. □□ **straightener** n.

straightforward /streɪtˈfɔːwəd/ adj. **1** honest or frank. **2** (of a task etc.) uncomplicated. □□ **straightforwardly** adv. **straightforwardness** n.

straightway /ˈstreɪtweɪ/ adv. archaic = straight away.

strain[1] /streɪn/ v. & n. —v. **1** tr. & intr. stretch tightly; make or become taut or tense. **2** tr. exercise (oneself, one's senses, a thing, etc.) intensely or excessively, press to extremes. **3 a** intr. make an intensive effort. **b** intr. (foll. by after) strive intensely for (straining after perfection). **4** intr. (foll. by at) tug, pull (the dog strained at the leash). **5** intr. hold out with difficulty under pressure (straining under the load). **6** tr. **a** distort from the true intention or meaning. **b** apply (authority, laws, etc.) beyond their province or in violation of their true intention. **7** tr. overtask or injure by overuse or excessive demands (strain a muscle; strained their loyalty). **8 a** tr. clear (a liquid) of solid matter by passing it through a sieve etc. **b** tr. (foll. by out) filter (solids) out from a liquid. **c** intr. (of a liquid) percolate. **9** tr. hug or squeeze tightly. **10** tr. use (one's ears, eyes, voice, etc.) to the best of one's power. —n. **1 a** the act or an instance of straining. **b** the force exerted in this. **2** an injury caused by straining a muscle etc. **3 a** a severe demand on physical or mental strength or resources. **b** the exertion needed to meet this (is suffering from strain). **4** (in sing. or pl.) a snatch or spell of music or poetry. **5** a tone or tendency in speech or writing (more in the same strain). **6** Physics **a** the condition of a body subjected to stress; molecular displacement. **b** a quantity measuring this, equal to the amount of deformation usu. divided by the original dimension. □ **at strain** (or **full strain**) exerted to the utmost. **strain every nerve** make every possible effort. **strain oneself 1** injure oneself by effort. **2** make undue efforts. □□ **strainable** adj. [ME f. OF estreindre estreign- f. L stringere strict- draw tight]

strain² /streɪn/ n. **1** a breed or stock of animals, plants, etc. **2** a moral tendency as part of a person's character (a strain of aggression). [ME, = progeny, f. OE strēon (recorded in ġestrēonan beget), rel. to L struere build]

strained /streɪnd/ adj. **1** constrained, forced, artificial. **2** (of a relationship) mutually distrustful or tense. **3** (of an interpretation) involving an unreasonable assumption; far-fetched, laboured.

strainer /ˈstreɪnə(r)/ n. a device for straining liquids, vegetables, etc.

strait /streɪt/ n. & adj. —n. **1** (in sing. or pl.) a narrow passage of water connecting two seas or large bodies of water. **2** (usu. in pl.) difficulty, trouble, or distress (usu. in dire or desperate straits). —adj. archaic **1** narrow, limited; confined or confining. **2** strict or rigorous. □ **strait-laced** severely virtuous; morally scrupulous; puritanical. □□ **straitly** adv. **straitness** n. [ME streit f. OF estreit tight, narrow f. L strictus STRICT]

straiten /ˈstreɪt(ə)n/ v. **1** tr. restrict in range or scope. **2** tr. (as **straitened** adj.) of or marked by poverty. **3** tr. & intr. archaic make or become narrow.

strait-jacket /ˈstreɪtˌdʒækɪt/ n. & v. —n. **1** a strong garment with long arms for confining the arms of a violent prisoner, mental patient, etc. **2** restrictive measures. —v.tr. (**-jacketed**, **-jacketing**) **1** restrain with a strait-jacket. **2** severely restrict.

strake /streɪk/ n. **1** a continuous line of planking or plates from the stem to the stern of a ship. **2** a section of the iron rim of a wheel. [ME: prob. rel. to OE streccan STRETCH]

stramonium /strəˈməʊnɪəm/ n. **1** datura. **2** the dried leaves of this plant used in the treatment of asthma. [mod.L, perh. f. Tartar turman horse-medicine]

strand¹ /strænd/ v. & n. —v. **1** tr. & intr. run aground. **2** tr. (as **stranded** adj.) in difficulties, esp. without money or means of transport. —n. rhet. or poet. the margin of a sea, lake, or river, esp. the foreshore. [OE]

strand² /strænd/ n. & v. —n. **1** each of the threads or wires twisted round each other to make a rope or cable. **2 a** a single thread or strip of fibre. **b** a constituent filament. **3** a lock of hair. **4** an element or strain in any composite whole. —v.tr. **1** break a strand in (a rope). **2** arrange in strands. [ME: orig. unkn.]

strange /streɪndʒ/ adj. **1** unusual, peculiar, surprising, eccentric, novel. **2 a** (often foll. by to) unfamiliar, alien, foreign (lost in a strange land). **b** not one's own (strange gods). **3** (foll. by to) unaccustomed. **4** not at ease; out of one's element (felt strange in such company). □ **feel strange** be unwell. **strange particle** Physics an elementary particle classified as having a non-zero value for strangeness. **strange to say** it is surprising or unusual (that). □□ **strangely** adv. [ME f. OF estrange f. L extraneus EXTRANEOUS]

strangeness /ˈstreɪndʒnɪs/ n. **1** the state or fact of being strange

or unfamiliar etc. **2** Physics a property of certain elementary particles that is conserved in strong interactions.

stranger /ˈstreɪndʒə(r)/ n. **1** a person who does not know or is not known in a particular place or company. **2** (often foll. by to) a person one does not know (was a complete stranger to me). **3** (foll. by to) a person entirely unaccustomed to (a feeling, experience, etc.) (no stranger to controversy). **4** a floating tea-leaf etc. held to foretell the arrival of a visitor. **5** Parl. a person who is not a member or official of the House of Commons. [ME f. OF estrangier ult. f. L (as STRANGE)]

strangle /ˈstræŋg(ə)l/ v.tr. **1** squeeze the windpipe or neck of, esp. so as to kill. **2** hamper or suppress (a movement, impulse, cry, etc.). □□ **strangler** n. [ME f. OF estrangler f. L strangulare f. Gk straggalaō f. straggalē halter: cf. straggos twisted]

stranglehold /ˈstræŋg(ə)lˌhəʊld/ n. **1** a wrestling hold that throttles an opponent. **2** a deadly grip. **3** complete and exclusive control.

strangles /ˈstræŋg(ə)lz/ n.pl. (usu. treated as sing.) an infectious streptococcal fever, esp. affecting the respiratory tract, in a horse, ass, etc. [pl. of strangle (n.) f. STRANGLE]

strangulate /ˈstræŋgjʊˌleɪt/ v.tr. Surgery **1** prevent circulation through (a vein, intestine, etc.) by compression. **2** remove (a tumour etc.) by binding with a cord. □ **strangulated hernia** Med. a hernia in which the protruding part is constricted, preventing circulation. [L strangulare strangulat- (as STRANGLE)]

strangulation /ˌstræŋgjʊˈleɪʃ(ə)n/ n. **1** the act of strangling or the state of being strangled. **2** the act of strangulating. [L strangulatio (as STRANGULATE)]

strangury /ˈstræŋgjʊrɪ/ n. a condition in which urine is passed painfully and in drops. □□ **strangurious** /-ˈgjʊərɪəs/ adj. [ME f. L stranguria f. Gk straggouria f. stragx -ggos drop squeezed out + ouron urine]

strap /stræp/ n. & v. —n. **1** a strip of leather or other flexible material, often with a buckle or other fastening for holding things together etc. **2** a thing like this for keeping a garment in place. **3** a loop for grasping to steady oneself in a moving vehicle. **4 a** a strip of metal used to secure or connect. **b** a leaf of a hinge. **5** Bot. a tongue-shaped part in a floret. **6** (prec. by the) punishment by beating with a strap. —v.tr. (**strapped**, **strapping**) **1** (often foll. by down, up, etc.) secure or bind with a strap. **2** beat with a strap. **3** (esp. as **strapped** adj.) colloq. subject to a shortage. **4** (often foll. by up) close (a wound) or bind (a part) with adhesive plaster. □ **strap-work** ornamentation imitating plaited straps. □□ **strapper** n. **strappy** adj. [dial. form of STROP]

straphanger /ˈstræpˌhæŋə(r)/ n. sl. a standing passenger in a bus or train. □□ **straphang** v.intr.

strapless /ˈstræplɪs/ adj. (of a garment) without straps, esp. shoulder-straps.

strappado /strəˈpɑːdəʊ/ n. (pl. **-os**) hist. a form of torture in which the victim is secured to a rope and made to fall from a height almost to the ground then stopped with a jerk; an application of this; the instrument used. [F (e)strapade f. It. strappata f. strappare snatch]

strapping /ˈstræpɪŋ/ adj. (esp. of a person) large and sturdy.

Strasbourg /ˈstræzbʊəg/ a city in NE France, capital of Alsace region; pop. (1982) 252,250. Meetings of the Council of Europe and sessions of the European Parliament are held in this city.

strata pl. of STRATUM.

stratagem /ˈstrætədʒəm/ n. **1** a cunning plan or scheme, esp. for deceiving an enemy. **2** trickery. [ME f. F stratagème f. L stratagema f. Gk stratēgēma f. stratēgeō be a general (stratēgos) f. stratos army + agō lead]

stratal see STRATUM.

strategic /strəˈtiːdʒɪk/ adj. **1** of or serving the ends of strategy (strategic considerations). **2** (of materials) essential in fighting a war. **3** (of bombing or weapons) done or for use against an enemy's home territory as a longer-term military objective (opp. TACTICAL). □ **Strategic Arms Limitation Talks** see SALT. **Strategic Defense Initiative** a proposed US defence system (popularly known as Star Wars) against potential nuclear attack. Based partly in space, it is intended to protect the US from intercontinental ballistic missiles by intercepting and destroying them before they reach their targets. □□ **strategical** adj. **strategically** adv. **strategics** n.pl. (usu. treated as sing.). [F stratégique f. Gk stratēgikos (as STRATAGEM)]

strategy /'strætɪdʒɪ/ n. (pl. **-ies**) **1** the art of war. **2 a** the management of an army or armies in a campaign. **b** the art of moving troops, ships, aircraft, etc. into favourable positions (cf. TACTICS). **c** an instance of this or a plan formed according to it. **3** a plan of action or policy in business or politics etc. (economic strategy). □□ **strategist** n. [F stratégie f. Gk stratēgia generalship f. stratēgos: see STRATAGEM]

Stratford-upon-Avon /'strætfədʊ,pɒn'eɪv(ə)n/ a market town on the River Avon in Warwickshire, where William Shakespeare was born and is buried; pop. (1981) 20,100.

strath /stræθ/ n. Sc. a broad mountain valley. [Gael. srath]

Strathclyde /stræθ'klaɪd/ a local government region in western Scotland; pop. (1981) 2,332,500; capital, Glasgow.

strathspey /stræθ'speɪ/ n. **1** a slow Scottish dance. **2** the music for this. [Strathspey, valley of the river Spey]

strati pl. of STRATUS.

straticulate /strə'tɪkjʊlət/ adj. Geol. (of rock-formations) arranged in thin strata. [STRATUM, after vermiculate etc.]

stratify /'strætɪ,faɪ/ v.tr. (**-ies, -ied**) **1** (esp. as **stratified** adj.) arrange in strata. **2** construct in layers, social grades, etc. □□ **stratification** /-fɪ'keɪʃ(ə)n/ n. [F stratifier (as STRATUM)]

stratigraphy /strə'tɪgrəfɪ/ n. Geol. & Archaeol. **1** the order and relative position of strata. **2** the study of this as a means of historical interpretation. □□ **stratigraphic** /,strætɪ'græfɪk/ adj. **stratigraphical** /,strætɪ'græfɪk(ə)l/ adj. [STRATUM + -GRAPHY]

strato- /'strætəʊ/ comb. form stratus.

stratocirrus /,strætəʊ'sɪrəs/ n. clouds combining stratus and cirrus features.

stratocracy /strə'tɒkrəsɪ/ n. (pl. **-ies**) **1** a military government. **2** domination by soldiers. [Gk stratos army + -CRACY]

stratocumulus /,strætəʊ'kju:mjʊləs/ n. clouds combining cumulus and stratus features.

stratopause /'strætəʊ,pɔ:z/ n. the interface between the stratosphere and the ionosphere.

stratosphere /'strætə,sfɪə(r)/ n. a layer of atmospheric air above the troposphere extending to about 50 km above the earth's surface, in which the lower part changes little in temperature and the upper part increases in temperature with height (cf. IONOSPHERE). □□ **stratospheric** /-'sferɪk/ adj. [STRATUM + SPHERE after atmosphere]

stratum /'strɑːtəm, 'streɪ-/ n. (pl. **strata** /-tə/) **1** esp. Geol. a layer or set of successive layers of any deposited substance. **2** an atmospheric layer. **3** a layer of tissue etc. **4 a** a social grade, class, etc. (the various strata of society). **b** Statistics each of the groups into which a population is divided in stratified sampling. □□ **stratal** adj. [L, = something spread or laid down, neut. past part. of sternere strew]

stratus /'streɪtəs, 'strɑː-/ n. (pl. **strati** /-taɪ/) a continuous horizontal sheet of cloud. [L, past part. of sternere: see STRATUM]

Strauss[1] /straʊs/, Johann (II) (1825–99), Austrian composer, who was born and died in Vienna. He was the son of a composer of dance music, particularly waltzes, also named Johann (I) (1804–49), and became known himself as 'the waltz king' after such successes as The Blue Danube (1867) and Tales from the Vienna Woods (1868). In 1874 he composed the ever popular operetta Die Fledermaus (The Bat, 1874), a triumph which was followed in 1885 with Der Zigeunerbaron (The Gipsy Baron), equally masterly in its combination of comic opera and operetta. He was a friend and admirer of Wagner, who, like Brahms and other composers including Schoenberg, were what we should now call 'fans' of Strauss, recognizing a supreme master of a genre who composed with style, elegance, taste, and wit.

Strauss[2] /straʊs/, Richard (1864–1949), German composer. His early works include a series of symphonic poems which remain among the staple fare of orchestras; Don Juan (1888–9) established him as the natural successor to Wagner, whose widow took a great interest in his career. He married the soprano

Pauline de Ahna in 1894, and wrote many songs for her, appearing as her accompanist. In 1905 he produced the opera Salome, based on Oscar Wilde's play, and followed it in 1909 with Elektra: the two works both shocked and fascinated the musical public with music perfectly matched to the studies of emotional extremes and psychological abnormality. His subsequent operas were quite different in intention and effect, including the deliciously Viennese Der Rosenkavalier (1911), the combination of mythology and comedy of Ariadne auf Naxos (1912), and Capriccio (1942), which turns over, but does not resolve, the perennial question of whether the music should be master of the words or vice versa in opera.

Stravinsky /strə'vɪnskɪ/, Igor (1882–1971), Russian-born composer. In 1910 he began his travels with Diaghilev's ballet company, composing for it the ballets The Firebird (1909–10), Petrushka (1910–11), and, of course, The Rite of Spring (1911–13), which shocked Paris with its angular rhythms and liberal use of dissonance. He was prevented from returning to his native land by the 1917 revolution, but many works of this period have their roots in Russian folk-song, notably another ballet Les Noces (1914–23). He was fascinated also by the idioms of Western music and derived inspiration for his own neoclassical works from the baroque and classical periods. Stravinsky had moved from Paris to Los Angeles on the outbreak of the Second World War, and in the 1950s turned to serialism in such works as the cantatas Canticum sacrum (1955) and Threni (1957–8). In his final years he wrote short bare works, many of them religious in feeling and form. The overriding feature of his music is rhythm, and the sense of theatre and of the dance is never wholly absent even from his most austere works.

straw /strɔ:/ n. **1** dry cut stalks of grain for use as fodder or as material for thatching, packing, making hats, etc. **2** a single stalk or piece of straw. **3** a thin hollow paper or plastic tube for sucking drink from a glass etc. **4** an insignificant thing (not worth a straw). **5** the pale yellow colour of straw. **6** a straw hat. □ **catch** (or **grasp**) **at a straw** resort to an utterly inadequate expedient in desperation, like a person drowning. **straw boss** US an assistant foreman. **straw-colour** pale yellow. **straw-coloured** of pale yellow. **straw in the wind** a slight hint of future developments. **straw vote** (or **poll**) an unofficial ballot as a test of opinion. **straw-worm** a caddis-worm. □□ **strawy** adj. [OE strēaw f. Gmc, rel. to STREW]

strawberry /'strɔːbərɪ/ n. (pl. **-ies**) **1 a** any plant of the genus Fragaria, esp. any of various cultivated varieties, with white flowers, trifoliate leaves, and runners. **b** the pulpy red edible fruit of this, having a seed-studded surface. **2** a deep pinkish-red colour. □ **strawberry blonde 1** pinkish-blonde hair. **2** a woman with such hair. **strawberry mark** a soft reddish birthmark. **strawberry pear 1** a W. Indian cactaceous plant, Hylocereus undatus. **2** the fruit of this. **strawberry roan** see ROAN[1]. **strawberry-tree** an evergreen tree, Arbutus unedo, bearing strawberry-like fruit. [OE strēa(w)berige, strēowberige (as STRAW, BERRY): reason for the name unkn.]

strawboard /'strɔːbɔːd/ n. a coarse cardboard made of straw pulp.

stray /streɪ/ v., n., & adj. —v.intr. **1** wander from the right place; become separated from one's companions etc.; go astray. **2** deviate morally. **3** (as **strayed** adj.) that has gone astray. —n. **1** a person or thing that has strayed, esp. a domestic animal. **2** (esp. in pl.) electrical phenomena interfering with radio reception. —adj. **1** strayed or lost. **2** isolated; found or occurring occasionally (a stray customer or two; hit by a stray bullet). **3** Physics wasted or unwanted (eliminate stray magnetic fields). □□ **strayer** n. [ME f. AF & OF estrayer (v.), AF strey (n. & adj.) f. OF estraié (as ASTRAY)]

streak /stri:k/ n. & v. —n. **1** a long thin usu. irregular line or band, esp. distinguished by colour (black with red streaks; a streak of light above the horizon). **2** a strain or element in a person's character (has a streak of mischief). **3** a spell or series (a winning streak). **4** a line of bacteria etc. placed on a culture medium. —v. **1** tr. mark with streaks. **2** intr. move very rapidly. **3** intr. colloq. run naked in a public place as a stunt. □ **streak of lightning** a

sudden prominent flash of lightning. □□ **streaker** n. **streaking**
n. [OE *strica* pen-stroke f. Gmc: rel. to STRIKE]

streaky /'stri:kɪ/ adj. (**streakier, streakiest**) **1** full of streaks. **2**
(of bacon) with alternate streaks of fat and lean. □□ **streakily**
adv. **streakiness** n.

stream /stri:m/ n. & v. —n. **1** a flowing body of water, esp. a
small river. **2 a** the flow of a fluid or of a mass of people (*a stream
of lava*). **b** (in *sing.* or *pl.*) a large quantity of something that flows
or moves along. **3** a current or direction in which things are
moving or tending (*against the stream*). **4** *Brit.* a group of schoolchildren taught together as being of similar ability for a given
age. —v. **1** intr. flow or move as a stream. **2** intr. run with liquid
(*my eyes were streaming*). **3** intr. (of a banner or hair etc.) float or
wave in the wind. **4** tr. emit a stream of (blood etc.). **5** tr. *Brit.*
arrange (schoolchildren) in streams. □ **go with the stream**
do as others do. **on stream** (of a factory etc.) in operation.
stream-anchor an anchor intermediate in size between a
bower and a kedge, esp. for use in warping. **stream of
consciousness 1** *Psychol.* a person's thoughts and conscious
reactions to events perceived as a continuous flow. **2** a literary
style depicting events in such a flow in the mind of a character,
as in James Joyce's novel *Ulysses*. □□ **streamless** adj. **streamlet**
n. [OE *strēam* f. Gmc]

streamer /'stri:mə(r)/ n. **1** a long narrow flag. **2** a long narrow
strip of ribbon or paper, esp. in a coil that unrolls when thrown.
3 a banner headline. **4** (in *pl.*) the aurora borealis or australis.

streamline /'stri:mlaɪn/ v. & n. —v.tr. **1** give (a vehicle etc.) the
form which presents the least resistance to motion. **2** make (an
organization, process, etc.) simple or more efficient or better
organized. —n. **1** the natural course of water or air currents.
2 (often *attrib.*) the shape of an aircraft, car, etc., calculated to
cause the least resistance to motion.

street /stri:t/ n. **1 a** a public road in a city, town, or village. **b**
this with the houses or other buildings on each side. **2** the
persons who live or work on a particular street. □ **in the street
1** in the area outside the houses. **2** (of Stock Exchange business)
done after closing-time. **not in the same street with** *colloq.*
utterly inferior to in ability etc. **on the streets 1** living by
prostitution. **2** homeless. **street Arab 1** a homeless child. **2** an
urchin. **street credibility** (or *colloq.* **cred**) familiarity with a
fashionable urban subculture. **street cries** *Brit.* the cries of
street hawkers. **street door** a main outer house-door opening
on the street. **street jewellery** enamel advertising plates as
collectors' items. **streets ahead** (often foll. by *of*) *colloq.* much
superior (to). **street value** the value of drugs sold illicitly. **up**
(or **right up**) **one's street** *colloq.* **1** within one's range of interest
or knowledge. **2** to one's liking. □□ **streeted** adj. (also in *comb.*).
streetward adj. & adv. [OE *strǣt* f. LL *strāta* (*via*) paved (way),
fem. past part. of *sternere* lay down]

streetcar /'stri:tkɑ:(r)/ n. *US* a tram.

streetwalker /'stri:t,wɔ:kə(r)/ n. a prostitute seeking customers
in the street. □□ **streetwalking** n. & adj.

streetwise /'stri:twaɪz/ n. esp. *US* familiar with the ways of
modern urban life.

strength /strɛŋθ, strɛŋkθ/ n. **1** the state of being strong; the
degree or respect in which a person or thing is strong. **2 a** a
person or thing affording strength or support. **b** an attribute
making for strength of character (*patience is your great strength*). **3**
the number of persons present or available. **4** a full complement
(*below strength*). □ **from strength** from a strong position. **from
strength to strength** with ever-increasing success. **in
strength** in large numbers. **on the strength of** relying on; on
the basis of. **the strength of** the essence or main features of.
□□ **strengthless** adj. [OE *strengthu* f. Gmc (as STRONG)]

strengthen /'strɛŋθ(ə)n, -ŋkθ(ə)n/ v.tr. & intr. make or become
stronger. □ **strengthen a person's hand** (or **hands**) encourage
a person to vigorous action. □□ **strengthener** n.

strenuous /'strɛnjʊəs/ adj. **1** requiring or using great effort. **2**
energetic or unrelaxing. □□ **strenuously** adv. **strenuousness**
n. [L *strenuus* brisk]

strep /strep/ n. *colloq.* = STREPTOCOCCUS. [abbr.]

streptococcus /,streptə'kɒkəs/ n. (*pl.* **streptococci** /-'kɒkaɪ/)
any bacterium of the genus *Streptococcus*, usu. occurring in
chains, some of which cause infectious diseases. □□
streptococcal adj. [Gk *streptos* twisted f. *strephō* turn + COCCUS]

streptomycin /,streptəʊ'maɪsɪn/ n. an antibiotic produced by
the bacterium *Streptomyces griseus*, effective against many
disease-producing bacteria. [Gk *streptos* (as STREPTOCOCCUS) +
mukēs fungus]

stress /stres/ n. & v. —n. **1 a** pressure or tension exerted on a
material object. **b** a quantity measuring this. **2 a** demand on
physical or mental energy. **b** distress caused by this (*suffering
from stress*). **3 a** emphasis (*the stress was on the need for success*). **b**
accentuation; emphasis laid on a syllable or word. **c** an accent,
esp. the principal one in a word (*the stress is on the first syllable*).
4 *Mech.* force per unit area exerted between contiguous bodies
or parts of a body. —v.tr. **1** lay stress on; emphasize. **2** subject
to mechanical or physical or mental stress. □ **lay stress on**
indicate as important. **stress disease** a disease resulting from
continuous mental stress. □□ **stressless** adj. [ME f. DISTRESS,
or partly f. OF *estresse* narrowness, oppression, ult. f. L *strictus*
STRICT]

stressful /'stresfʊl/ adj. causing stress; mentally tiring (*had a
stressful day*). □□ **stressfully** adv. **stressfulness** n.

stretch /stretʃ/ v. & n. —v. **1** tr. & intr. draw or be drawn or
admit of being drawn out into greater length or size. **2** tr. &
intr. make or become taut. **3** tr. & intr. place or lie at full length
or spread out (*with a canopy stretched over them*). **4** tr. (also *absol.*)
a extend (an arm, leg, etc.). **b** (often *refl.*) thrust out one's limbs
and tighten one's muscles after being relaxed. **5** intr. have a
specified length or extension; extend (*farmland stretches for many
miles*). **6** tr. strain or exert extremely or excessively; exaggerate
(*stretch the truth*). **7** intr. (as **stretched** adj.) lying at full length.
—n. **1** a continuous extent or expanse or period (*a stretch of open
road*). **2** the act or an instance of stretching; the state of being
stretched. **3** (*attrib.*) able to stretch; elastic (*stretch fabric*). **4 a**
colloq. a period of imprisonment. **b** a period of service. **5** *US* the
straight side of a racetrack. **6** *Naut.* the distance covered on one
tack. □ **at full stretch** working to capacity. **at a stretch 1** in
one continuous period (*slept for two hours at a stretch*). **2** with
much effort. **stretch one's legs** exercise oneself by walking.
stretch marks marks on the skin resulting from a gain of
weight, or on the abdomen after pregnancy. **stretch out 1** tr.
extend (a hand or foot etc.). **2** intr. & tr. last for a longer period;
prolong. **3** tr. make (money etc.) last for a sufficient time. **stretch
a point** agree to something not normally allowed. **stretch
one's wings** see WING. □□ **stretchable** adj. **stretchability**
/-ə'bɪlɪtɪ/ n. **stretchy** adj. **stretchiness** n. [OE *streccan* f. WG: cf.
STRAIGHT]

stretcher /'stretʃə(r)/ n. & v. —n. **1** a framework of two poles
with canvas etc. between, for carrying sick, injured, or dead
persons in a lying position. **2** a brick or stone laid with its long
side along the face of a wall (cf. HEADER). **3** a board in a boat
against which a rower presses the feet. **4** a rod or bar as a tie
between chair-legs etc. **5** a wooden frame over which a canvas
is stretched ready for painting. **6** *archaic sl.* an exaggeration or
lie. —v.tr. (often foll. by *off*) convey (a sick or injured person) on
a stretcher. □ **stretcher-bearer** a person who helps to carry a
stretcher, esp. in war or at a major accident.

stretto /'stretəʊ/ adv. *Mus.* in quicker time. [It., = narrow]

strew /stru:/ v.tr. (*past part.* **strewn** or **strewed**) **1** scatter or
spread about over a surface. **2** (usu. foll. by *with*) spread (a
surface) with scattered things. □□ **strewer** n. [OE *stre(o)wian*]

'strewth var. of 'STRUTH.

stria /'straɪə/ n. (*pl.* **-ae** /-i:/) **1** *Anat., Zool., Bot.,* & *Geol.* **a** a linear
mark on a surface. **b** a slight ridge, furrow, or score. **2** *Archit.* a
fillet between the flutes of a column. [L]

striate adj. & v. —adj. /'straɪɪt/ (also **striated** /-eɪtɪd/) *Anat., Zool.,
Bot.,* & *Geol.* marked with striae. —v.tr. /'straɪeɪt/ mark with
striae. □□ **striation** /straɪ'eɪʃ(ə)n/ n.

stricken /'strɪkən/ adj. **1** affected or overcome with illness or
misfortune etc. (*stricken with measles; grief-stricken*). **2** levelled with
a strickle. **3** (often foll. by *from* etc.) *US Law* deleted. □ **stricken
in years** *archaic* enfeebled by age. [archaic past part. of STRIKE]

strickle /ˈstrɪk(ə)l/ n. **1** a rod used in strike-measure. **2** a whetting tool. [OE *stricel*, rel. to STRIKE]

strict /strɪkt/ adj. **1** precisely limited or defined; without exception or deviation (*lives in strict seclusion*). **2** requiring complete compliance or exact performance; enforced rigidly (*gave strict orders*). □□ **strictness** n. [L *strictus* past part. of *stringere* tighten]

strictly /ˈstrɪktlɪ/ adv. **1** in a strict manner. **2** (also **strictly speaking**) applying words in their strict sense (*he is, strictly, an absconder*). **3** esp. US colloq. definitely.

stricture /ˈstrɪktʃə(r)/ n. **1** (usu. in pl.; often foll. by *on, upon*) a critical or censorious remark. **2** Med. a morbid narrowing of a canal or duct in the body. □□ **strictured** adj. [ME f. L *strictura* (as STRICT)]

stride /straɪd/ v. & n. —v. (*past* **strode** /strəʊd/; *past part.* **stridden** /ˈstrɪd(ə)n/) **1** intr. & tr. walk with long firm steps. **2** tr. cross with one step. **3** tr. bestride; straddle. —n. **1 a** a single long step. **b** the length of this. **2** a person's gait as determined by the length of stride. **3** (usu. in pl.) progress (*has made great strides*). **4** a settled rate of progress (*get into one's stride; be thrown out of one's stride*). **5** (in pl.) sl. trousers. **6** the distance between the feet parted either laterally or as in walking. □ **take in one's stride 1** clear (an obstacle) without changing one's gait to jump. **2** manage without difficulty. □□ **strider** n. [OE *strīdan*]

strident /ˈstraɪd(ə)nt/ adj. loud and harsh. □□ **stridency** n. **stridently** adv. [L *stridere strident-* creak]

stridulate /ˈstrɪdjʊˌleɪt/ v.intr. (of insects, esp. the cicada and grasshopper) make a shrill sound by rubbing esp. the legs or wing-cases together. □□ **stridulant** adj. **stridulation** /-ˈleɪʃ(ə)n/ n. [F *striduler* f. L *stridulus* creaking (as STRIDENT)]

strife /straɪf/ n. **1** conflict; struggle between opposed persons or things. **2** Austral. colloq. trouble of any kind. [ME f. OF *estrif*; cf. OF *estriver* STRIVE]

strigil /ˈstrɪdʒɪl/ n. **1** Gk & Rom. Antiq. a skin-scraper used by bathers after exercise. **2** a structure on the leg of an insect used to clean its antennae etc. [L *strigilis* f. *stringere* graze]

strigose /ˈstraɪgəʊs/ adj. **1** (of leaves etc.) having short stiff hairs or scales. **2** (of an insect etc.) streaked, striped, or ridged. [L *striga* swath, furrow]

strike /straɪk/ v. & n. —v. (*past* **struck** /strʌk/; *past part.* **struck** or *archaic* **stricken** /ˈstrɪkən/) **1 a** tr. subject to an impact. **b** tr. deliver (a blow) or inflict a blow on. **2** tr. come or bring sharply into contact with (*the ship struck a rock*). **3** tr. propel or divert with a blow (*struck the ball into the pond*). **4** intr. (foll. by *at*) try to hit. **5** tr. penetrate or cause to penetrate (*struck terror into him*). **6** tr. ignite (a match) or produce (sparks etc.) by rubbing. **7** tr. make (a coin) by stamping. **8** tr. produce (a musical note) by striking. **9 a** tr. (also *absol.*) (of a clock) indicate (the time) by the sounding of a chime etc. **b** intr. (of time) be indicated in this way. **10** tr. **a** attack suddenly (*was struck with sudden terror*). **b** (of a disease) afflict. **11** tr. cause to become suddenly (*was struck dumb*). **12** tr. reach or achieve (*strike a balance*). **13** tr. agree on (a bargain). **14** tr. assume (an attitude) suddenly and dramatically. **15** tr. **a** discover or come across. **b** find (oil etc.) by drilling. **c** encounter (an unusual thing etc.). **16** come to the attention of or appear to (*it strikes me as silly; an idea suddenly struck me*). **17 a** intr. (of employees) engage in a strike; cease work as a protest. **b** tr. US act in this way against (an employer). **18 a** tr. lower or take down (a flag or tent etc.). **b** intr. signify surrender by striking a flag; surrender. **19** intr. take a specified direction (*struck east*). **20** tr. (also *absol.*) secure a hook in the mouth of (a fish) by jerking the tackle. **21** tr. (of a snake) wound with its fangs. **22** intr. (of oysters) attach themselves to a bed. **23 a** tr. insert (the cutting of a plant) in soil to take root. **b** tr. (also *absol.*) (of a plant or cutting etc.) put forth (roots). **24** tr. level (grain etc. or the measure) in strike-measure. **25** tr. **a** ascertain (a balance) by deducting credit or debit from the other. **b** arrive at (an average, state of balance) by equalizing all items. **26** compose (a jury) esp. by allowing both sides to reject the same number. —n. **1** the act or an instance of striking. **2 a** the organized refusal by employees to work until some grievance is remedied. The first strike on record took place in Egypt in the mid-12th c. BC, in the reign of Rameses III, when tomb workers at Thebes downed

tools because their rations had not arrived; it caused considerable alarm. **b** a similar refusal to participate in some other expected activity. **3** a sudden find or success (*a lucky strike*). **4** an attack, esp. from the air. **5** Baseball a batter's unsuccessful attempt to hit a pitched ball, or another event counting equivalently against a batter. **6** the act of knocking down all the pins with the first ball in bowling. **7** horizontal direction in a geological structure. **8** a strickle. □ **on strike** taking part in an industrial etc. strike. **strike at the root** (or **roots**) **of** see ROOT¹. **strike back 1** strike or attack in return. **2** (of a gas-burner) burn from an internal point before the gas has become mixed with air. **strike down 1** knock down. **2** bring low; afflict (*struck down by a virus*). **strike home 1** deal an effective blow. **2** have an intended effect (*my words struck home*). **strike in 1** intervene in a conversation etc. **2** (of a disease) attack the interior of the body from the surface. **strike it rich** colloq. find a source of abundance or success. **strike a light 1** produce a light by striking a match. **2** Brit. sl. an expression of surprise, disgust, etc. **strike lucky** have a lucky success. **strike-measure** measurement by passing a rod across the top of a heaped vessel to ensure that it is exactly full. **strike off 1** remove with a stroke. **2** delete (a name etc.) from a list. **3** produce (copies of a document). **strike oil 1** find petroleum by sinking a shaft. **2** attain prosperity or success. **strike out 1** hit out. **2** act vigorously. **3** delete (an item or name etc.). **4** set off or begin (*struck out eastwards*). **5** use the arms and legs in swimming. **6** forge or devise (a plan etc.). **7** Baseball **a** dismiss (a batter) by means of three strikes. **b** be dismissed in this way. **strike pay** an allowance paid to strikers by their trade union. **strike through** delete (a word etc.) with a stroke of one's pen. **strike up 1** start (an acquaintance, conversation, etc.) esp. casually. **2** (also *absol.*) begin playing (a tune etc.). **strike upon 1** have (an idea etc.) luckily occur to one. **2** (of light) illuminate. **strike while the iron is hot** act promptly at a good opportunity. **struck on** colloq. infatuated with. □□ **strikable** adj. [OE *strīcan* go, stroke f. WG]

strikebound /ˈstraɪkbaʊnd/ adj. immobilized or closed by a strike.

strikebreaker /ˈstraɪkˌbreɪkə(r)/ n. a person working or employed in place of others who are on strike. □□ **strikebreak** v.intr.

striker /ˈstraɪkə(r)/ n. **1** a person or thing that strikes. **2** an employee on strike. **3** Sport the player who is to strike, or who is to be the next to strike, the ball. **4** Football an attacking player positioned well forward in order to score goals. **5** a device striking the primer in a gun.

striking /ˈstraɪkɪŋ/ adj. & n. —adj. **1** impressive; attracting attention. **2** (of a clock) making a chime to indicate the hours etc. —n. the act or an instance of striking. □ **striking-circle** (in hockey) an elongated semicircle in front of the goal, from within which the ball must be hit in order to score. **striking-force** a military body ready to attack at short notice. **within striking distance** near enough to hit or achieve. □□ **strikingly** adv. **strikingness** n.

Strindberg /ˈstrɪndbɜːg/, (Johan) August (1849–1912), Swedish dramatist and novelist. The bitterness and misogyny of his starkly naturalistic earlier plays, notably *The Father* (1887), reflect his unhappy marriage and increasing paranoia. A more tranquil later period following a mental breakdown evoked expressionistic 'dream plays' as well as notable historical dramas.

Strine /straɪn/ n. **1** a comic transliteration of Australian speech, e.g. *Emma Chissitt* = 'How much is it?' **2** (esp. uneducated) Australian English. [= *Australian* in Strine]

string /strɪŋ/ n. & v. —n. **1** twine or narrow cord. **2** a piece of this or of similar material used for tying or holding together, pulling, etc. **3** a length of catgut or wire etc. on a musical instrument, producing a note by vibration. **4 a** (in pl.) the stringed instruments in an orchestra etc. **b** (*attrib.*) relating to or consisting of stringed instruments (*string quartet*). **5** (in pl.) an awkward condition or complication (*the offer has no strings*). **6** a set of things strung together; a series or line of persons or things (*a string of beads; a string of oaths*). **7** a group of racehorses trained at one stable. **8** a tough piece connecting the two halves of a bean-pod etc. **9** a piece of catgut etc. interwoven with others

æ cat ɑ: arm e bed ɜ: her ɪ sit iː see ɒ hot ɔ: saw ʌ run ʊ put uː too ə ago aɪ my

to form the head of a tennis etc. racket. **10** = STRINGBOARD. —*v.* (*past* and *past part.* **strung** /strʌŋ/) **1** *tr.* supply with a string or strings. **2** *tr.* tie with string. **3** *tr.* thread (beads etc.) on a string. **4** *tr.* arrange in or as a string. **5** *tr.* remove the strings from (a bean). **6** *tr.* place a string ready for use on (a bow). **7** *tr.* *colloq.* hoax. **8** *intr.* (of glue etc.) become stringy. **9** *intr.* *Billiards* make the preliminary strokes that decide which player begins. □ **on a string** under one's control or influence. **string along** *colloq.* **1** deceive, esp. by appearing to comply with (a person). **2** (often foll. by *with*) keep company (with). **string bass** *Mus.* a double-bass. **string bean 1** any of various beans eaten in their fibrous pods, esp. runner beans or French beans. **2** *colloq.* a tall thin person. **string-course** a raised horizontal band or course of bricks etc. on a building. **string out** extend; prolong (esp. unduly). **string-piece** a long timber supporting and connecting the parts of a framework. **string tie** a very narrow necktie. **string up 1** hang up on strings etc. **2** kill by hanging. **3** make tense. **string vest** a vest with large meshes. □□ **stringless** *adj.* **stringlike** *adj.* [OE *streng* f. Gmc: cf. STRONG]

stringboard /ˈstrɪŋbɔːd/ *n.* a supporting timber or skirting in which the ends of a staircase steps are set.

stringed /strɪŋd/ *adj.* (of musical instruments) having strings (also in *comb.*: *twelve-stringed guitar*).

stringendo /strɪnˈdʒɛndəʊ/ *adj.* & *adv.* *Mus.* with increasing speed. [It. f. *stringere* press: see STRINGENT]

stringent /ˈstrɪndʒ(ə)nt/ *adj.* **1** (of rules etc.) strict, precise; requiring exact performance; leaving no loophole or discretion. **2** (of a money market etc.) tight; hampered by scarcity; unaccommodating; hard to operate in. □□ **stringency** *n.* **stringently** *adv.* [L *stringere* draw tight]

stringer /ˈstrɪŋə(r)/ *n.* **1** a longitudinal structural member in a framework, esp. of a ship or aircraft. **2** *colloq.* a newspaper correspondent not on the regular staff. **3** = STRINGBOARD.

stringhalt /ˈstrɪŋhɒlt/ *n.* spasmodic movement of a horse's hind leg.

stringy /ˈstrɪŋɪ/ *adj.* (**stringier**, **stringiest**) **1** (of food etc.) fibrous, tough. **2** of or like string. **3** (of a person) tall, wiry, and thin. **4** (of a liquid) viscous; forming strings. □ **stringy-bark** *Austral.* any of various eucalyptus trees with tough fibrous bark. □□ **stringily** *adv.* **stringiness** *n.*

strip[1] /strɪp/ *v.* & *n.* —*v.* (**stripped**, **stripping**) **1** *tr.* (often foll. by *of*) remove the clothes or covering from (a person or thing). **2** *intr.* (often foll. by *off*) undress oneself. **3** *tr.* (often foll. by *of*) deprive (a person) of property or titles. **4** *tr.* leave bare of accessories or fittings. **5** *tr.* remove bark and branches from (a tree). **6** *tr.* (often foll. by *down*) remove the accessory fittings of or take apart (a machine etc.) to inspect or adjust it. **7** *tr.* milk (a cow) to the last drop. **8** *tr.* remove the old hair from (a dog). **9** *tr.* remove the stems from (tobacco). **10** *tr.* tear the thread from (a screw). **11** *tr.* tear the teeth from (a gearwheel). **12** *tr.* remove (paint) or remove paint from (a surface) with solvent. **13** *tr.* (often foll. by *from*) pull or tear (a covering or property etc.) off (*stripped the masks from their faces*). **14** *intr.* (of a screw) lose its thread. **15** *intr.* (of a bullet) issue from a rifled gun without spin owing to a loss of surface. —*n.* **1** an act of stripping, esp. of undressing in striptease. **2** *colloq.* the identifying outfit worn by the members of a sports team while playing. □ **strip club** a club at which striptease performances are given. **strip mine** *US* a mine worked by removing the material that overlies the ore etc. **strip-search** *n.* a search of a person involving the removal of all clothes. —*v.tr.* search in this way. [ME f. OE *bestrīepan* plunder f. Gmc]

strip[2] /strɪp/ *n.* **1** a long narrow piece (*a strip of land*). **2** a narrow flat bar of iron or steel. **3** (in full **strip cartoon**) = comic strip. □ **strip light** a tubular fluorescent lamp. **strip mill** a mill in which steel slabs are rolled into strips. **tear a person off a strip** *colloq.* angrily rebuke a person. [ME, from or rel. to MLG *strippe* strap, thong, prob. rel. to STRIPE]

stripe /straɪp/ *n.* **1** a long narrow band or strip differing in colour or texture from the surface on either side of it (*black with a red stripe*). **2** *Mil.* a chevron etc. denoting military rank. **3** *US* a category of character, opinion, etc. (*a man of that stripe*). **4** (usu.

in *pl.*) *archaic* a blow with a scourge or lash. **5** (in *pl.*, treated as *sing.*) *colloq.* a tiger. [perh. back-form. f. *striped*: cf. MDu., MLG *strīpe*, MHG *strīfe*]

striped /straɪpt/ *adj.* marked with stripes (also in *comb.*: *red-striped*).

stripling /ˈstrɪplɪŋ/ *n.* a youth not yet fully grown. [ME, prob. f. STRIP[2] + -LING[1], in the sense of having a figure not yet filled out]

stripper /ˈstrɪpə(r)/ *n.* **1** a person or thing that strips something. **2** a device or solvent for removing paint etc. **3** a striptease performer.

striptease /ˈstrɪptiːz/ *n.* & *v.* —*n.* an entertainment in which the performer gradually undresses before the audience. —*v.intr.* perform a striptease. □□ **stripteaser** *n.*

stripy /ˈstraɪpɪ/ *adj.* (**stripier**, **stripiest**) striped; having many stripes.

strive /straɪv/ *v.intr.* (*past* **strove** /strəʊv/; *past part.* **striven** /ˈstrɪv(ə)n/) **1** (often foll. by *for*, or *to* + infin.) try hard, make efforts (*strive to succeed*). **2** (often foll. by *with*, *against*) struggle or contend. □□ **striver** *n.* [ME f. OF *estriver*, rel. to *estrif* STRIFE]

strobe /strəʊb/ *n.* *colloq.* **1** a stroboscope. **2** a stroboscopic lamp. [abbr.]

strobila /strəˈbaɪlə/ *n.* (*pl.* **strobilae** /-liː/) **1** a chain of proglottids in a tapeworm. **2** a sessile polyp-like form which divides horizontally to produce jellyfish larvae. [mod.L f. Gk *strobilē* twisted lint-plug f. *strephō* twist]

strobile /ˈstrəʊbaɪl/ *n.* **1** the cone of a pine etc. **2** the layered flower of the hop. [F *strobile* or LL *strobilus* f. Gk *strobilos* f. *strephō* twist]

strobilus /ˈstrəʊbɪləs/ *n.* (*pl.* **strobili** /-ˌlaɪ/) *Bot.* = STROBILE 1. [LL (as STROBILE)]

stroboscope /ˈstrəʊbəˌskəʊp/ *n.* **1** *Physics* an instrument for determining speeds of rotation etc. by shining a bright light at intervals so that a rotating object appears stationary. **2** a lamp made to flash intermittently, esp. for this purpose. □□ **stroboscopic** /-ˈskɒpɪk/ *adj.* **stroboscopical** /-ˈskɒpɪk(ə)l/ *adj.* **stroboscopically** /-ˈskɒpɪkəlɪ/ *adv.* [Gk *strobos* whirling + -SCOPE]

strode *past* of STRIDE.

Stroganoff /ˈstrɒɡəˌnɒf/ *adj.* (of meat) cut into strips and cooked in sour-cream sauce (*beef Stroganoff*). [P. *Stroganoff*, 19th-c. Russ. diplomat]

stroke /strəʊk/ *n.* & *v.* —*n.* **1** the act or an instance of striking; a blow or hit (*with a single stroke*; *a stroke of lightning*). **2** a sudden disabling attack or loss of consciousness caused by an interruption in the flow of blood to the brain, esp. through thrombosis; apoplexy. **3 a** an action or movement esp. as one of a series. **b** the time or way in which such movements are done. **c** the slightest such action (*has not done a stroke of work*). **4** the whole of the motion (of a wing, oar, etc.) until the starting-position is regained. **5** (in rowing) the mode or action of moving the oar (*row a fast stroke*). **6** the whole motion (of a piston) in either direction. **7** *Golf* the action of hitting (or hitting at) a ball with a club, as a unit of scoring. **8** a mode of moving the arms and legs in swimming. **9** a method of striking with the bat etc. in games etc. (*played some unorthodox strokes*). **10** a specially successful or skilful effort (*a stroke of diplomacy*). **11 a** a mark made by the movement in one direction of a pen or pencil or paintbrush. **b** a similar mark printed. **12** a detail contributing to the general effect in a description. **13** the sound made by a striking clock. **14** (in full **stroke oar**) the oar or oarsman nearest the stern, setting the time of the stroke. **15** the act or a spell of stroking. —*v.tr.* **1** pass one's hand gently along the surface of (hair or fur etc.); caress lightly. **2** act as the stroke of (a boat or crew). □ **at a stroke** by a single action. **finishing stroke** a *coup de grâce*; a final and fatal stroke. **off one's stroke** not performing as well as usual. **on the stroke** punctually. **on the stroke of nine** etc. with the clock about to strike nine etc. **stroke a person down** appease a person's anger. **stroke of business** a profitable transaction. **stroke of genius** an original or strikingly successful idea. **stroke of luck** (or **good luck**) an unforeseen opportune occurrence. **stroke play** *Golf* play in which the score is reckoned by counting the number of strokes taken for the round (cf. *match play* (see MATCH[1])). **stroke a person** (or a **person's hair) the wrong way** irritate a person. [OE *strācian* f. Gmc, rel. to STRIKE]

stroll /strəʊl/ *v. & n.* —*v.intr.* saunter or walk in a leisurely way. —*n.* a short leisurely walk (*go for a stroll*). □ **strolling players** actors etc. going from place to place to give performances. [orig. of a vagrant, prob. f. G *strollen, strolchen* f. *Strolch* vagabond, of unkn. orig.]

stroller /ˈstrəʊlə(r)/ *n.* **1** a person who strolls. **2** *US* a pushchair.

stroma /ˈstrəʊmə/ *n.* (*pl.* **stromata** /-mətə/) *Biol.* **1** the framework of an organ or cell. **2** a fungous tissue containing spore-producing bodies. □□ **stromatic** /-ˈmætɪk/ *adj.* [mod.L f. LL f. Gk *strōma* coverlet]

Stromboli /ˈstrɒmbəlɪ, strɒmˈbəʊlɪ/ an active volcano forming one of the Lipari Islands, off the NE coast of Sicily, noted for its perpetual state of mild activity.

strong /strɒŋ/ *adj. & adv.* —*adj.* (**stronger** /ˈstrɒŋɡə(r)/; **strongest** /ˈstrɒŋɡɪst/) **1** having the power of resistance; able to withstand great force or opposition; not easily damaged or overcome (*strong material; strong faith; a strong character*). **2** (of a person's constitution) able to overcome, or not liable to, disease. **3** (of a person's nerves) proof against fright, irritation, etc. **4** (of a patient) restored to health. **5** (of a market) having steadily high or rising prices. **6** capable of exerting great force or of doing much; muscular, powerful. **7** forceful or powerful in effect (*a strong wind; a strong protest*). **8** decided or firmly held (*a strong suspicion; strong views*). **9** (of an argument etc.) convincing or striking. **10** powerfully affecting the senses or emotions (*a strong light; strong acting*). **11** powerful in terms of size or numbers or quality (*a strong army*). **12** capable of doing much when united (*a strong combination*). **13** formidable; likely to succeed (*a strong candidate*). **14** (of a solution or drink etc.) containing a large proportion of a substance in water or another solvent (*strong tea*). **15** *Chem.* (of an acid or base) fully ionized into cations and anions in aqueous solution. **16** (of a group) having a specified number (*200 strong*). **17** (of a voice) loud or penetrating. **18** (of food or its flavour) pungent. **19** (of a person's breath) ill-smelling. **20** (of a literary style) vivid and forceful. **21** (of a measure) drastic. **22** *Gram.* in Germanic languages: **a** (of a verb) forming inflections by change of vowel within the stem rather than by the addition of a suffix (e.g. *swim, swam*). **b** (of a noun or adjective) belonging to a declension in which the stem originally ended otherwise than in *-n* (opp. WEAK 9). —*adv.* strongly (*the tide is running strong*). □ **come it strong** *colloq.* go to great lengths; use exaggeration. **going strong** *colloq.* continuing action vigorously; in good health or trim. **strong-arm** using force (*strong-arm tactics*). **strong drink** see DRINK. **strong grade** the stressed ablaut-form. **strong interaction** *Physics* interaction between certain elementary particles that is very strong but is effective only at short distances. **strong language** forceful language; swearing. **strong meat** a doctrine or action acceptable only to vigorous or instructed minds. **strong-minded** having determination. **strong-mindedness** determination. **strong point 1** a thing at which one excels. **2** a specially fortified defensive position. **strong stomach** a stomach not easily affected by nausea. **strong suit 1** a suit at cards in which one can take tricks. **2** a thing at which one excels. □□ **strongish** *adj.* **strongly** *adv.* [OE f. Gmc: cf. STRING]

strongbox /ˈstrɒŋbɒks/ *n.* a strongly made small chest for valuables.

stronghold /ˈstrɒŋhəʊld/ *n.* **1** a fortified place. **2** a secure refuge. **3** a centre of support for a cause etc.

strongroom /ˈstrɒŋruːm, -rʊm/ *n.* a room designed to protect valuables against fire and theft.

strontia /ˈstrɒnʃə/ *n. Chem.* strontium oxide. [*strontian* native strontium carbonate f. Strontian in the Highland Region of Scotland, where it was discovered]

strontium /ˈstrɒntɪəm/ *n. Chem.* a soft silver-white metallic element occurring naturally in various minerals, first detected in 1787 and isolated by Sir Humphry Davy in 1808. The metal has few uses, but strontium salts are used in fireworks and flares because they give a brilliant red light. The radioactive

isotope strontium 90 is a particularly dangerous component of nuclear fallout as it can become concentrated in bones and teeth. ¶ Symb.: **Sr**; atomic number 38. □ **strontium-90** a radioactive isotope of strontium concentrated selectively in bones and teeth when taken into the body. **strontium oxide** a white compound used in the manufacture of fireworks. [STRONTIA + -IUM]

strop /strɒp/ *n. & v.* —*n.* **1** a device, esp. a strip of leather, for sharpening razors. **2** *Naut.* a collar of leather or spliced rope or iron used for handling cargo. —*v.tr.* (**stropped, stropping**) sharpen on or with a strop. [ME f. MDu., MLG *strop*, OHG *strupf*, WG f. L *stroppus*]

strophanthin /strəˈfænθɪn/ *n.* a white crystalline poisonous glucoside extracted from various tropical plants of the genus *Strophanthus* and used as a heart-tonic. [mod.L *strophanthus* f. Gk *strophos* twisted cord + *anthos* flower]

strophe /ˈstrəʊfɪ/ *n.* **1 a** a turn in dancing made by an ancient Greek chorus. **b** lines recited during this. **c** the first section of an ancient Greek choral ode or of one division of it. **2** a group of lines forming a section of a lyric poem. □□ **strophic** *adj.* [Gk *strophē*, lit. turning, f. *strephō* turn]

stroppy /ˈstrɒpɪ/ *adj.* (**stroppier, stroppiest**) *Brit. colloq.* bad-tempered; awkward to deal with. □□ **stroppily** *adv.* **stroppiness** *n.* [20th c.: perh. abbr. of OBSTREPEROUS]

strove *past of* STRIVE.

strow /strəʊ/ *v.tr.* (*past part.* **strown** /strəʊn/ or **strowed**) *archaic* = STREW. [var. of STREW]

struck *past and past part. of* STRIKE.

structural /ˈstrʌktʃər(ə)l/ *adj.* of, concerning, or having a structure. □ **structural engineering** the branch of civil engineering concerned with large modern buildings etc. **structural formula** *Chem.* a formula showing the arrangement of atoms in the molecule of a compound. **structural linguistics** the study of language as a system of interrelated elements, without regard to their historical development. **structural psychology** the study of the arrangement and composition of mental states and conscious experiences. **structural steel** strong mild steel in shapes suited to construction work. □□ **structurally** *adv.*

structuralism /ˈstrʌktʃərəˌlɪz(ə)m/ *n.* **1** the doctrine that structure rather than function is important. (See below.) **2** structural linguistics. **3** structural psychology. □□ **structuralist** *n.*

The term has been applied to such theories or methods in various disciplines, and subsequently to theories concerned with analysing the surface structures of a system in terms of its underlying structure. In *Psychology* (see *structural psychology*) it is connected especially with the American psychologist E. B. Titchener (1867–1927); in *Linguistics* it became popular after the work of F. de Saussure (see entry); in *Anthropology* and *Sociology* it refers to theories or methods of analysis concerned with the structure or form of human society or social life, and (following the work of Claude Lévi-Strauss; see entry) with the deeper structures of communication from which the surface structures or 'models' evolve.

structure /ˈstrʌktʃə(r)/ *n. & v.* —*n.* **1 a** a whole constructed unit, esp. a building. **b** the way in which a building etc. is constructed (*has a flimsy structure*). **2** a set of interconnecting parts of any complex thing; a framework (*the structure of a sentence; a new wages structure*). —*v.tr.* give structure to; organize; frame. □□ **structured** *adj.* (also in *comb.*). **structureless** *adj.* [ME f. OF *structure* or L *structura* f. *struere struct-* build]

strudel /ˈstruːd(ə)l/ *n.* a confection of thin pastry rolled up round a filling and baked (*apple strudel*). [G]

struggle /ˈstrʌɡ(ə)l/ *v. & n.* —*v.intr.* **1** make forceful or violent efforts to get free of restraint or constriction. **2** (often foll. by *for*, or *to* + *infin.*) make violent or determined efforts under difficulties; strive hard (*struggled for supremacy; struggled to get the words out*). **3** (foll. by *with, against*) contend; fight strenuously (*struggled with the disease; struggled against superior numbers*). **4** (foll. by *along, up*, etc.) make one's way with difficulty (*struggled to my feet*). **5** (esp. as **struggling** *adj.*) have difficulty in gaining recognition or a living (*a struggling artist*). —*n.* **1** the act or a spell of struggling. **2** a hard or confused contest. **3** a determined effort under difficulties. □ **the struggle for existence** (or **life**) the competition between organisms esp. as an element in natural selection, or between persons seeking a livelihood. □□ **struggler** n. [ME *strugle* frequent. of uncert. orig. (perh. imit.)]

strum /strʌm/ v. & n. —v.tr. (**strummed, strumming**) **1** play on (a stringed or keyboard instrument), esp. carelessly or unskilfully. **2** play (a tune etc.) in this way. —n. the sound made by strumming. □□ **strummer** n. [imit.: cf. THRUM¹]

struma /ˈstruːmə/ n. (pl. **strumae** /-miː/) **1** Med. **a** = SCROFULA. **b** = GOITRE. **2** Bot. a cushion-like swelling of an organ. □□ **strumose** adj. **strumous** adj. [L, = scrofulous tumour]

strumpet /ˈstrʌmpɪt/ n. archaic or rhet. a prostitute. [ME: orig. unkn.]

strung past and past part. of STRING.

strut /strʌt/ n. & v. —n. **1** a bar forming part of a framework and designed to resist compression. **2** a strutting gait. —v. (**strutted, strutting**) **1** intr. walk with a pompous or affected stiff erect gait. **2** tr. brace with a strut or struts. □□ **strutter** n. **struttingly** adv. [ME 'bulge, swell, strive', earlier *stroute* f. OE *strūtian* be rigid (?)]

'struth /struːθ/ int. (also **'strewth**) colloq. a mild oath. [God's truth]

struthious /ˈstruːθɪəs/ adj. of or like an ostrich. [L *struthio* ostrich]

Struwwelpeter /ˈstruːəlˌpiːtə(r)/ a character in a children's book of the same name by Heinrich Hoffmann (1809–94), with long thick unkempt hair.

strychnine /ˈstrɪkniːn/ n. a vegetable alkaloid obtained from plants of the genus *Strychnos* (esp. nux vomica), bitter and highly poisonous, used as a stimulant and (in small amounts) a tonic. □□ **strychnic** adj. [F f. L *strychnos* f. Gk *strukhnos* a kind of nightshade]

Sts abbr. Saints.

Stuart¹ /ˈstjuːət/ the name of the royal house of Scotland from the accession (1371) of Robert II, one of the hereditary stewards of Scotland, and of Britain from the accession of James VI of Scotland to the English throne as James I (1603) to the death of Queen Anne (1714).

Charles Edward Stuart (1720–88), 'the Young Pretender', elder son of James Stuart (see below). A far more dashing and romantic figure than his father, on whose behalf he led the Jacobite uprising of 1745–6, Charles was not really able enough to face the task of overthrowing a reasonably well established Hanoverian regime. He made little impact on events after his flight from Scotland in the aftermath of Culloden and eventually succumbed to alcoholism, dying in obscurity in Rome.

James Stuart (1688–1766), 'the Old Pretender', only son of James II of Britain, Jacobite claimant to the throne following his father's death. He spent his entire life in exile, failing to restore his fortunes as much because of the weakness of his political position as because of his lack of charisma and decisiveness. Arriving in Scotland too late to alter the outcome of the 1715 uprising, he left the leadership of a second major attempt in 1745 to his son Charles.

Stuart² /ˈstjuːət/ John McDouall (1815–66), Scottish emigrant to Australia who crossed the continent in 1861–2, at his sixth attempt, from south to north and back again. He was a man of indomitable courage and tenacity, who in all his journeys never lost a man of his expeditions, though his own health was destroyed as a result of the hardships he had suffered.

stub /stʌb/ n. & v. —n. **1** the remnant of a pencil or cigarette etc. after use. **2** the counterfoil of a cheque or receipt etc. **3** a stunted tail etc. **4** the stump of a tree, tooth, etc. **5** (attrib.) going only part of the way through (*stub-mortise*; *stub-tenon*). —v.tr. (**stubbed, stubbing**) **1** strike (one's toe) against something. **2** (usu. foll. by *out*) extinguish (a lighted cigarette) by pressing the lighted end against something. **3** (foll. by *up*) grub up by the roots. **4** clear (land) of stubs. □ **stub-axle** an axle supporting only one wheel of a pair. [OE *stub, stubb* f. Gmc]

stubble /ˈstʌb(ə)l/ n. **1** the cut stalks of cereal plants left sticking up after the harvest. **2 a** cropped hair or a cropped beard. **b** a short growth of unshaven hair. □□ **stubbled** adj. **stubbly** adj.

[ME f. AF *stuble*, OF *estuble* f. L *stupla, stupula* var. of *stipula* straw]

stubborn /ˈstʌbən/ adj. **1** unreasonably obstinate. **2** unyielding, obdurate, inflexible. **3** refractory, intractable. □□ **stubbornly** adj. **stubbornness** n. [ME *stiborn, stoburn,* etc., of unkn. orig.]

Stubbs¹ /stʌbz/, George (1724–1806), English animal painter and engraver. Largely self-taught, he worked as a portrait painter in Leeds and studied anatomy at York. In 1759 he moved to London and there published his *Anatomy of the Horse* (1766), illustrated with his own engravings, which established his reputation. He was widely admired as a painter of horses, not only for his anatomical and observational knowledge but also for his ability to convey their spirit and dignity. His imaginative compositions, especially the horse and lion confrontations, show his proto-romantic nature, while the neoclassical purity of his line is evident in his mare and foals series.

Stubbs² /stʌbz/, William (1825–1901), English historian, Regius Professor of Modern History at Oxford (1866–1901), Bishop of Chester (1884) and of Oxford (1888). He showed his supreme professional skill, acquired from the German academic method, in his great *Constitutional History of England* (1874–8) which, together with his *Select Charters and other Illustrations of English Constitutional History to 1307* (1870), imposed a pattern and a method on the teaching of English history in British universities which lasted until the middle of the 20th c.

stubby /ˈstʌbɪ/ adj. & n. —adj. (**stubbier, stubbiest**) short and thick. —n. (pl. **-ies**) Austral. colloq. a small squat bottle of beer. □□ **stubbily** adv. **stubbiness** n.

stucco /ˈstʌkəʊ/ n. & v. —n. (pl. **-oes**) plaster or cement used for coating wall surfaces or moulding into architectural decorations. —v.tr. (**-oes, -oed**) coat with stucco. [It., of Gmc orig.]

stuck past and past part. of STICK².

stuck-up see STICK².

stud¹ /stʌd/ n. & v. —n. **1** a large-headed nail, boss, or knob, projecting from a surface esp. for ornament. **2** a double button esp. for use with two buttonholes in a shirt-front. **3** a small object projecting slightly from a road-surface as a marker etc. **4** a rivet or crosspiece in each link of a chain-cable. **5 a** a post to which laths are nailed. **b** US the height of a room as indicated by the length of this. —v.tr. (**studded, studding**) **1** set with or as with studs. **2** (as **studded** adj.) (foll. by *with*) thickly set or strewn (*studded with diamonds*). **3** be scattered over or about (a surface). [OE *studu, stuthu* post, prop, rel. to G *stützen* to prop]

stud² /stʌd/ n. **1 a** a number of horses kept for breeding etc. **b** a place where these are kept. **2** (in full **stud-horse**) a stallion. **3** colloq. a young man (esp. one noted for sexual prowess). **4** (in full **stud poker**) a form of poker with betting after the dealing of successive rounds of cards face up. □ **at stud** (of a male horse) publicly available for breeding on payment of a fee. **stud-book** a book containing the pedigrees of horses. **stud-farm** a place where horses are bred. [OE *stōd* f. Gmc: rel. to STAND]

studding /ˈstʌdɪŋ/ n. the woodwork of a lath-and-plaster wall.

studding-sail /ˈstʌns(ə)l/ n. a sail set on a small extra yard and boom beyond the leech of a square sail in light winds. [16th c.: orig. uncert.: perh. f. MLG, MDu. *stōtinge* a thrusting]

student /ˈstjuːd(ə)nt/ n. **1** a person who is studying, esp. at university or another place of higher education. **2** (attrib.) studying in order to become (*a student nurse*). **3** a person of studious habits. **4** Brit. a graduate recipient of a stipend from the foundation of a college, esp. a fellow of Christ Church, Oxford. □□ **studentship** n. [ME f. L *studēre* f. *studium* STUDY]

studio /ˈstjuːdɪəʊ/ n. (pl. **-os**) **1** the workroom of a painter or photographer etc. **2** a place where cinema films or recordings are made or where television or radio programmes are made or produced. □ **studio couch** a couch that can be converted into a bed. **studio flat** a flat containing a room suitable as an artist's studio, or only one main room. [It. f. L (as STUDY)]

studious /ˈstjuːdɪəs/ adj. **1** devoted to or assiduous in study or reading. **2** studied, deliberate, painstaking (*with studious care*). **3** (foll. by *to* + infin. or *in* + verbal noun) showing care or attention. **4** (foll. by *of* + verbal noun) anxiously desirous. □□ **studiously** adv. **studiousness** n. [ME f. L *studiosus* (as STUDY)]

study /ˈstʌdɪ/ n. & v. —n. (pl. **-ies**) **1** the devotion of time and attention to acquiring information or knowledge, esp. from books. **2** (in *pl.*) the pursuit of academic knowledge (*continued their studies abroad*). **3** a room used for reading, writing, etc. **4** a piece of work, esp. a drawing, done for practice or as an experiment (*a study of a head*). **5** the portrayal in literature or another art form of an aspect of behaviour or character etc. **6** a musical composition designed to develop a player's skill. **7** a thing worth observing closely (*your face was a study*). **8** a thing that is or deserves to be investigated. **9** *Theatr.* **a** the act of memorizing a role. **b** a person who memorizes a role. **10** *archaic* a thing to be secured by pains or attention. —*v.* (**-ies, -ied**) **1** *tr.* make a study of; investigate or examine (a subject) (*study law*). **2** *intr.* (often foll. by *for*) apply oneself to study. **3** *tr.* scrutinize or earnestly contemplate (a visible object) (*studied their faces*). **4** *tr.* try to learn (the words of one's role etc.). **5** *tr.* take pains to achieve (a result) or pay regard to (a subject or principle etc.). **6** *tr.* (as **studied** *adj.*) deliberate, intentional, affected (*with studied politeness*). **7** *tr.* read (a book) attentively. **8** *tr.* (foll. by *to* + infin.) *archaic* **a** be on the watch. **b** try constantly to manage. □ **in a brown study** in a reverie; absorbed in one's thoughts. **make a study of** investigate carefully. **study group** a group of people meeting from time to time to study a particular subject or topic. □□ **studiedly** *adv.* **studiedness** *n.* [ME f. OF *estudie* f. L *studium* zeal, study]

stuff /stʌf/ *n.* & *v.* —*n.* **1** the material that a thing is made of; material that may be used for some purpose. **2** a substance or things or belongings of an indeterminate kind or a quality not needing to be specified (*there's a lot of stuff about it in the newspapers*). **3** a particular knowledge or activity (*know one's stuff*). **4** woollen fabric (esp. as distinct from silk, cotton, and linen). **5** valueless matter, trash, refuse, nonsense (*take that stuff away*). **6** (prec. by *the*) **a** *colloq.* an available supply of something, esp. drink or drugs. **b** *sl.* money. —*v.* **1** *tr.* pack (a receptacle) tightly (*stuff a cushion with feathers; a head stuffed with weird notions*). **2** *tr.* (foll. by *in, into*) force or cram (a thing) (*stuffed the socks in the drawer*). **3** *tr.* fill out the skin of (an animal or bird etc.) with material to restore the original shape (*a stuffed owl*). **4** *tr.* fill (poultry etc.) with a savoury or sweet mixture, esp. before cooking. **5 a** *tr.* & *refl.* fill (a person or oneself) with food. **b** *tr.* & *intr.* eat greedily. **6** *tr.* push, esp. hastily or clumsily (*stuffed the note behind the cushion*). **7** *tr.* (usu. in *passive*; foll. by *up*) block up (a person's nose etc.). **8** *tr. sl.* (esp. as an expression of contemptuous dismissal) dispose of as unwanted (*you can stuff the job*). **9** *tr. US* place bogus votes in (a ballot-box). **10** *tr. coarse sl. offens.* have sexual intercourse with (a woman). □ **bit of stuff** *sl. offens.* a woman regarded as an object of sexual desire. **do one's stuff** *colloq.* do what one has to. **get stuffed** *sl.* an exclamation of dismissal, contempt, etc. **stuff and nonsense** an exclamation of incredulity or ridicule. **stuffed shirt** *colloq.* a pompous person. **stuff gown** *Brit.* a gown worn by a barrister who has not taken silk. **stuff it** *sl.* an expression of rejection or disdain. **that's the stuff** *colloq.* that is what is wanted. □□ **stuffer** *n.* (also in *comb.*). [ME *stoffe* f. OF *estoffe* (n.), *estoffer* (v.) equip, furnish f. Gk *stuphō* draw together]

stuffing /stʌfɪŋ/ *n.* **1** padding used to stuff cushions etc. **2** a mixture used to stuff poultry etc., esp. before cooking. □ **knock** (or **take**) **the stuffing out of** *colloq.* make feeble or weak; defeat. **stuffing-box** a box packed with material, to allow the working of an axle while remaining airtight.

stuffy /stʌfɪ/ *adj.* (**stuffier, stuffiest**) **1** (of a room or the atmosphere in it) lacking fresh air or ventilation; close. **2** dull or uninteresting. **3** (of a person's nose etc.) stuffed up. **4** (of a person) dull and conventional. □□ **stuffily** *adv.* **stuffiness** *n.*

stultify /stʌltɪˌfaɪ/ *v.tr.* (**-ies, -ied**) **1** make ineffective, useless, or futile, esp. as a result of tedious routine (*stultifying boredom*). **2** cause to appear foolish or absurd. **3** negate or neutralize. □□ **stultification** /-fɪˈkeɪʃ(ə)n/ *n.* **stultifier** *n.* [LL *stultificare* f. L *stultus* foolish]

stum /stʌm/ *n.* & *v.* —*n.* unfermented grape-juice; must. —*v.tr.* (**stummed, stumming**) **1** prevent from fermenting, or secure (wine) against further fermentation in a cask, by the use of sulphur etc. **2** renew the fermentation of (wine) by adding stum. [Du. *stommen* (v.), *stom* (n.) f. *stom* (adj.) dumb]

stumble /stʌmb(ə)l/ *v.* & *n.* —*v.* **1** *intr.* lurch forward or have a partial fall from catching or striking or misplacing one's foot. **2** *intr.* (often foll. by *along*) walk with repeated stumbles. **3** *intr.* make a mistake or repeated mistakes in speaking etc. **4** *intr.* (foll. by *on, upon, across*) find or encounter by chance (*stumbled on a disused well*). —*n.* an act of stumbling. □ **stumbling-block** an obstacle or circumstance causing difficulty or hesitation. □□ **stumbler** *n.* **stumblingly** *adv.* [ME *stumble* (with euphonic *b*) corresp. to Norw. *stumla*: rel. to STAMMER]

stumblebum /stʌmb(ə)lˌbʌm/ *n. US colloq.* a clumsy or inept person.

stumer /stjuːmə(r)/ *n. Brit. sl.* **1** a worthless cheque; a counterfeit coin or note. **2** a sham or fraud. **3** a failure. [19th c.: orig. unkn.]

stump /stʌmp/ *n.* & *v.* —*n.* **1** the projecting remnant of a cut or fallen tree. **2** the similar remnant of anything else (e.g. a branch or limb) cut off or worn down. **3** *Cricket* each of the three uprights of a wicket. **4** (in *pl.*) *joc.* the legs. **5** the stump of a tree, or other place, used by an orator to address a meeting. **6** a cylinder of rolled paper or other material with conical ends for softening pencil-marks and other uses in drawing. —*v.* **1** *tr.* (of a question etc.) be too hard for; puzzle. **2** *tr.* (as **stumped** *adj.*) at a loss; baffled. **3** *tr. Cricket* (esp. of a wicket-keeper) put (a batsman) out by touching the stumps with the ball while the batsman is out of the crease. **4** *intr.* walk stiffly or noisily as on a wooden leg. **5** *tr.* (also *absol.*) *US* traverse (a district) making political speeches. **6** *tr.* use a stump on (a drawing, line, etc.). □ **on the stump** *colloq.* engaged in political speech-making or agitation. **stump up** *Brit. colloq.* pay or produce (the money required). **up a stump** *US* in difficulties. [ME *stompe·* f. MDu. *stomp*, OHG *stumpf*]

stumper /stʌmpə(r)/ *n. colloq.* **1** a puzzling question. **2** a wicket-keeper.

stumpy /stʌmpɪ/ *adj.* (**stumpier, stumpiest**) short and thick. □□ **stumpily** *adv.* **stumpiness** *n.*

stun /stʌn/ *v.tr.* (**stunned, stunning**) **1** knock senseless; stupefy. **2** bewilder or shock. **3** (of a sound) deafen temporarily. [ME f. OF *estoner* ASTONISH]

stung past and past part. of STING.

stunk past and past part. of STINK.

stunner /stʌnə(r)/ *n. colloq.* a stunning person or thing.

stunning /stʌnɪŋ/ *adj. colloq.* extremely impressive or attractive. □□ **stunningly** *adv.*

stunsail /stʌns(ə)l/ *n.* (also **stuns'l**) = STUDDING-SAIL.

stunt[1] /stʌnt/ *v.tr.* **1** retard the growth or development of. **2** dwarf, cramp. □□ **stuntedness** *n.* [*stunt* foolish (now dial.), MHG *stunz*, ON *stuttr* short f. Gmc, perh. rel. to STUMP]

stunt[2] /stʌnt/ *n.* & *v.* —*n.* **1** something unusual done to attract attention. **2** a trick or daring manoeuvre. **3** a display of concentrated energy. —*v.intr.* perform stunts, esp. aerobatics. □ **stunt man** a man employed to take an actor's place in performing dangerous stunts. [orig. unkn.: first used in 19th-c. US college athletics]

stupa /stuːpə/ *n.* a round usu. domed building erected as a Buddhist shrine. [Skr. *stūpa*]

stupe[1] /stjuːp/ *n.* & *v.* —*n.* a flannel etc. soaked in hot water, wrung out, and applied as a fomentation. —*v.tr.* treat with this. [ME f. L f. Gk *stupē* tow]

stupe[2] /stjuːp/ *n. sl.* a foolish or stupid person.

stupefy /stjuːpɪˌfaɪ/ *v.tr.* (**-ies, -ied**) **1** make stupid or insensible (*stupefied with drink*). **2** stun with astonishment (*the news was stupefying*). □□ **stupefacient** /-ˈfeɪʃ(ə)nt/ *adj.* & *n.* **stupefaction** /-ˈfækʃ(ə)n/ *n.* **stupefactive** *adj.* **stupefier** *n.* **stupefying** *adj.* **stupefyingly** *adv.* [F *stupéfier* f. L *stupefacere* f. *stupēre* be amazed]

stupendous /stjuːˈpendəs/ *adj.* amazing or prodigious, esp. in terms of size or degree (*a stupendous achievement*). □□ **stupendously** *adv.* **stupendousness** *n.* [L *stupendus* gerundive of *stupēre* be amazed at]

stupid /stjuːpɪd/ *adj.* (**stupider, stupidest**) *adj.* & *n.* —*adj.* **1** unintelligent, slow-witted, foolish (*a stupid fellow*). **2** typical of stupid persons (*put it in a stupid place*). **3** uninteresting or boring. **4** in a state of stupor or lethargy. **5** obtuse; lacking in sensibility.

—*n. colloq.* a stupid person. □□ **stupidity** /-'pɪdɪtɪ/ *n.* (*pl.* **-ies**). **stupidly** *adv.* [F *stupide* or L *stupidus* (as STUPENDOUS)]

stupor /'stju:pə(r)/ *n.* a dazed, torpid, or helplessly amazed state. □□ **stuporous** *adj.* [ME f. L (as STUPENDOUS)]

sturdy /'stɜ:dɪ/ *adj. & n.* —*adj.* (**sturdier, sturdiest**) **1** robust; strongly built. **2** vigorous and determined (*sturdy resistance*). —*n.* vertigo in sheep caused by a tapeworm larva encysted in the brain. □□ **sturdied** *adj.* (in sense of *n.*). **sturdily** *adv.* **sturdiness** *n.* [ME 'reckless, violent', f. OF *esturdi, estourdi* past part. of *estourdir* stun, daze ult. f. L *ex* EX-¹ + *turdus* thrush (taken as a type of drunkenness)]

sturgeon /'stɜ:dʒ(ə)n/ *n.* any large mailed sharklike fish of the family Acipenseridae etc. swimming up river to spawn, used as food and a source of caviare and isinglass. [ME f. AF *sturgeon*, OF *esturgeon* ult. f. Gmc]

Sturm und Drang /ˌʃtʊəm ʊnt 'dræŋ/ *n.* a literary and artistic movement in Germany in the late 18th c., characterized by the expression of emotional unrest and strong feeling. [G, = storm and stress]

Sturt /stɜ:t/, Charles (1795–1869), English explorer of Australia. Secretary to the Governor of New South Wales in 1827, he led several expeditions into the interior, discovering the Darling River and becoming surveyor-general for South Australia in 1833. He went blind during his third expedition in 1846 and returned to England, where he was Colonial Secretary in 1849–51.

stutter /'stʌtə(r)/ *v. & n.* —*v.* **1** *intr.* stammer, esp. by involuntarily repeating the first consonants of words. **2** *tr.* (often foll. by *out*) utter (words) in this way. —*n.* **1** the act or habit of stuttering. **2** an instance of stuttering. □□ **stutterer** *n.* **stutteringly** *adv.* [frequent. of ME (now dial.) *stut* f. Gmc]

Stuttgart /'ʃtʊtgɑ:t/ a motor-manufacturing city in the west of Germany, capital of Baden-Württemberg; pop. (1987) 565,200. The philosopher Hegel was born here in 1770.

sty¹ /staɪ/ *n. & v.* —*n.* (*pl.* **sties**) **1** a pen or enclosure for pigs. **2** a filthy room or dwelling. **3** a place of debauchery. —*v.tr. & intr.* (**sties, stied**) lodge in a sty. [OE *stī*, prob. = *stig* hall (cf. STEWARD), f. Gmc]

sty² /staɪ/ *n.* (also **stye**) (*pl.* **sties** or **styes**) an inflamed swelling on the edge of an eyelid. [*styany* (now dial.) = *styan eye* f. OE *stīgend* sty, lit. 'riser' f. *stīgan* rise + EYE, shortened as if = *sty on eye*]

Stygian /'stɪdʒɪən/ *adj.* **1** *Gk Mythol.* of or relating to the Styx or Hades. **2** *literary* dark, gloomy, indistinct. [L *stugius* f. Gk *stugios* f. *Stux -ugos* Styx f. *stugnos* hateful, gloomy]

style /staɪl/ *n. & v.* —*n.* **1** a kind or sort, esp. in regard to appearance and form (*an elegant style of house*). **2** a manner of writing or speaking or performing (*written in a florid style; started off in fine style*). **3** the distinctive manner of a person or school or period, esp. in relation to painting, architecture, furniture, dress, etc. **4** the correct way of designating a person or thing. **5 a** a superior quality or manner (*do it in style*). **b** = FORM *n.* 9 (*bad style*). **6** a particular make, shape, or pattern (*in all sizes and styles*). **7** a method of reckoning dates (*old style; new style*). **8 a** an ancient writing-implement, a small rod with a pointed end for scratching letters on wax-covered tablets and a blunt end for obliterating them. **b** a thing of a similar shape esp. for engraving, tracing, etc. **9** the gnomon of a sundial. **10** *Bot.* the narrow extension of the ovary supporting the stigma. **11** (in *comb.*) = -WISE. —*v.tr.* **1** design or make etc. in a particular (esp. fashionable) style. **2** designate in a specified way. □□ **styleless** *adj.* **stylelessness** *n.* **styler** *n.* [ME f. OF *stile, style* f. L *stilus*: spelling *style* due to assoc. with Gk *stulos* column]

stylet /'staɪlɪt/ *n.* **1** a slender pointed instrument; a stiletto. **2** *Med.* the stiffening wire of a catheter; a probe. [F *stilet* f. It. STILETTO]

styli *pl.* of STYLUS.

stylish /'staɪlɪʃ/ *adj.* **1** fashionable; elegant. **2** having a superior quality, manner, etc. □□ **stylishly** *adv.* **stylishness** *n.*

stylist /'staɪlɪst/ *n.* **1 a** a designer of fashionable styles etc. **b** a hairdresser. **2 a** a writer noted for or aspiring to good literary style. **b** (in sport or music) a person who performs with style.

stylistic /staɪ'lɪstɪk/ *adj.* of or concerning esp. literary style. □□ **stylistically** *adv.* [STYLIST + -IC, after G *stilistisch*]

stylistics /staɪ'lɪstɪks/ *n.* the study of literary style.

stylite /'staɪlaɪt/ *n. Eccl. hist.* an ancient or medieval ascetic living on top of a pillar, esp. in Syria in the 5th c. (See SIMEON STYLITES.) [eccl.Gk *stulitēs* f. *stulos* pillar]

stylize /'staɪlaɪz/ *v.tr.* (also **-ise**) (esp. as **stylized** *adj.*) paint, draw, etc. (a subject) in a conventional non-realistic style. □□ **stylization** /-'zeɪʃ(ə)n/ *n.* [STYLE + -IZE, after G *stilisieren*]

stylo /'staɪləʊ/ *n.* (*pl.* **-os**) *colloq.* = STYLOGRAPH. [abbr.]

stylobate /'staɪləˌbeɪt/ *n. Archit.* a continuous base supporting a row of columns. [L *stylobata* f. Gk *stulobatēs* f. *stulos* pillar, *bainō* walk]

stylograph /'staɪləˌgrɑ:f/ *n.* a kind of fountain pen having a point instead of a split nib. □□ **stylographic** /-'græfɪk/ *adj.* [STYLUS + -GRAPH]

styloid /'staɪlɔɪd/ *adj. & n.* —*adj.* resembling a stylus or pen. —*n.* (in full **styloid process**) a spine of bone, esp. that projecting from the base of the temporal bone. [mod.L *styloides* f. Gk *stuloeidēs* f. *stulos* pillar]

stylus /'staɪləs/ *n.* (*pl.* **-li** /-laɪ/ or **-luses**) **1 a** a hard, esp. diamond or sapphire, point following a groove in a gramophone record and transmitting the recorded sound for reproduction. **b** a similar point producing such a groove when recording sound. **2** = STYLE *n.* 8, 9. [erron. spelling of L *stilus*: cf. STYLE]

stymie /'staɪmɪ/ *n. & v.* (also **stimy**) —*n.* (*pl.* **-ies**) **1** *Golf* a situation where an opponent's ball lies between the player and the hole, forming a possible obstruction to play (*lay a stymie*). **2** a difficult situation. —*v.tr.* (**stymies, stymied, stymying** or **stymieing**) **1** obstruct; thwart. **2** *Golf* block (an opponent, his ball, or oneself) with a stymie. [19th c.: orig. unkn.]

styptic /'stɪptɪk/ *adj. & n.* —*adj.* (of a drug etc.) that checks bleeding. —*n.* a styptic drug or substance. [ME f. L *stypticus* f. Gk *stuptikos* f. *stuphō* contract]

styrax /'staɪəræks/ *n.* **1** storax resin. **2** any tree or shrub of the genus *Styrax*, e.g. the storax-tree. [L f. Gk *sturax*: cf. STORAX]

styrene /'staɪəri:n/ *n. Chem.* a liquid hydrocarbon easily polymerized and used in making plastics etc. [STYRAX + -ENE]

Styria /'stɪrɪə/ (German **Steiermark** /'ʃteɪəˌmɑ:k/) a province of SE Austria; pop. (1981) 1,187,500; capital, Graz.

Styx /stɪks/ *Gk Mythol.* one of the nine rivers of the underworld, over which Charon ferried the souls of the dead.

suable /'su:əb(ə)l, 'sju:-/ *adj.* capable of being sued. □□ **suability** /-'bɪlɪtɪ/ *n.*

suasion /'sweɪʒ(ə)n/ *n. formal* persuasion as opposed to force (*moral suasion*). □□ **suasive** /'sweɪsɪv/ *adj.* [ME f. OF *suasion* or L *suasio* f. *suadēre suas-* urge]

suave /swɑ:v/ *adj.* **1** (of a person, esp. a man) smooth; polite; sophisticated. **2** (of a wine etc.) bland, smooth. □□ **suavely** *adv.* **suaveness** *n.* **suavity** /-vɪtɪ/ *n.* (*pl.* **-ies**). [F *suave* or L *suavis* agreeable: cf. SWEET]

sub /sʌb/ *n. & v. colloq.* —*n.* **1** a submarine. **2** a subscription. **3** a substitute. **4** a sub-editor. **5** *Mil.* a subaltern. **6** *Brit.* an advance or loan against expected income. —*v.* (**subbed, subbing**) **1** *intr.* (usu. foll. by *for*) act as a substitute for a person. **2** *tr. Brit.* lend or advance (a sum) to (a person) against expected income. **3** *tr.* sub-edit. [abbr.]

sub- /sʌb, səb/ *prefix* (also **suc-** before *c*, **suf-** before *f*, **sug-** before *g*, **sup-** before *p*, **sur-** before *r*, **sus-** before *c, p, t*) **1** at or to or from a lower position (*subordinate; submerge; subtract; subsoil*). **2** secondary or inferior in rank or position (*subclass; subcommittee; sub-lieutenant; subtotal*). **3** somewhat, nearly; more or less (*subacid; subarctic; subaquatic*). **4** (forming verbs) denoting secondary action (*subdivide; sublet*). **5** denoting support (*subvention*). **6** *Chem.* (of a salt) basic (*subacetate*). [from or after L *sub-* f. *sub* under, close to, towards]

subabdominal /ˌsʌbæb'dɒmɪn(ə)l/ *adj.* below the abdomen.

subacid /sʌb'æsɪd/ *adj.* moderately acid or tart (*subacid fruit; a subacid remark*). □□ **subacidity** /ˌsʌbə'sɪdɪtɪ/ *n.* [L *subacidus* (as SUB-, ACID)]

subacute /ˌsʌbəˈkjuːt/ adj. Med. (of a condition) between acute and chronic.

subagency /sʌbˈeɪdʒənsɪ/ n. (pl. **-ies**) a secondary or subordinate agency. □□ **subagent** n.

subalpine /sʌbˈælpaɪn/ adj. of or situated in the higher slopes of mountains just below the timberline.

subaltern /ˈsʌbəlt(ə)n/ n. & adj. —n. Brit. Mil. an officer below the rank of captain, esp. a second lieutenant. —adj. **1** of inferior rank. **2** Logic (of a proposition) particular, not universal. [LL subalternus f. alternus ALTERNATE adj.]

subantarctic /ˌsʌbænˈtɑːktɪk/ adj. of or like regions immediately north of the Antarctic Circle.

sub-aqua /sʌbˈækwə/ adj. of or concerning underwater swimming or diving.

subaquatic /sʌbəˈkwætɪk/ adj. **1** of more or less aquatic habits or kind. **2** underwater.

subaqueous /sʌbˈeɪkwɪəs/ adj. **1** existing, formed, or taking place under water. **2** lacking in substance or strength; wishy-washy.

subarctic /sʌbˈɑːktɪk/ adj. of or like regions immediately south of the Arctic Circle.

subastral /sʌbˈæstr(ə)l/ adj. terrestrial.

subatomic /ˌsʌbəˈtɒmɪk/ adj. occurring in or smaller than an atom.

subaudition /ˌsʌbɔːˈdɪʃ(ə)n/ n. **1** the act of mentally supplying an omitted word or words in speech. **2** the act or process of understanding the unexpressed; reading between the lines. [LL subauditio f. subaudire understand (as SUB-, AUDITION)]

subaxillary /ˌsʌbækˈzɪlərɪ/ adj. **1** Bot. in or growing beneath the axil. **2** beneath the armpit.

sub-basement /ˈsʌbˌbeɪsmənt/ n. a storey below a basement.

sub-branch /ˈsʌbbrɑːntʃ/ n. a secondary or subordinate branch.

sub-breed /ˈsʌbbriːd/ n. a secondary or inferior breed.

subcategory /ˈsʌbˌkætɪgərɪ/ n. (pl. **-ies**) a secondary or subordinate category. □□ **subcategorize** v.tr. (also **-ise**). **subcategorization** /-ˈzeɪʃ(ə)n/ n.

subcaudal /sʌbˈkɔːd(ə)l/ adj. of or concerning the region under the tail or the back part of the body.

subclass /ˈsʌbklɑːs/ n. **1** a secondary or subordinate class. **2** Biol. a taxonomic category below a class.

sub-clause /ˈsʌbklɔːz/ n. **1** esp. Law a subsidiary section of a clause. **2** Gram. a subordinate clause.

subclavian /sʌbˈkleɪvɪən/ adj. & n. —adj. (of an artery etc.) lying or extending under the collar-bone. —n. such an artery. [mod.L subclavius (as SUB-, clavis key): cf. CLAVICLE]

subclinical /sʌbˈklɪnɪk(ə)l/ adj. Med. (of a disease) not yet presenting definite symptoms.

subcommissioner /ˈsʌbkəˌmɪʃənə(r)/ n. a deputy commissioner.

subcommittee /ˈsʌbkəˌmɪtɪ/ n. a secondary committee.

subconical /sʌbˈkɒnɪk(ə)l/ adj. approximately conical.

subconscious /sʌbˈkɒnʃəs/ adj. & n. —adj. of or concerning the part of the mind which is not fully conscious but influences actions etc. —n. this part of the mind. □□ **subconsciously** adv. **subconsciousness** n.

subcontinent /ˈsʌbˌkɒntɪnənt/ n. **1** a large land mass, smaller than a continent. **2** a large geographically or politically independent part of a continent. □□ **subcontinental** /-ˈnent(ə)l/ adj.

subcontract v. & n. —v. /ˌsʌbkənˈtrækt/ **1** tr. employ a firm etc. to do (work) as part of a larger project. **2** intr. make or carry out a subcontract. —n. /sʌbˈkɒntrækt/ a secondary contract, esp. to supply materials, labour, etc. □□ **subcontractor** /-ˈtræktə(r)/ n.

subcontrary /sʌbˈkɒntrərɪ/ adj. & n. Logic —adj. (of a proposition) incapable of being false at the same time as another. —n. (pl. **-ies**) such a proposition. [LL subcontrarius (as SUB-, CONTRARY), transl. Gk hupenantios]

subcordate /sʌbˈkɔːdeɪt/ adj. approximately heart-shaped.

subcortical /sʌbˈkɔːtɪk(ə)l/ adj. Anat. below the cortex.

subcostal /sʌbˈkɒst(ə)l/ adj. Anat. below the ribs.

subcranial /sʌbˈkreɪnɪəl/ adj. Anat. below the cranium.

subcritical /sʌbˈkrɪtɪk(ə)l/ adj. Physics of less than critical mass etc.

subculture /ˈsʌbˌkʌltʃə(r)/ n. a cultural group within a larger culture, often having beliefs or interests at variance with those of the larger culture. □□ **subcultural** /-ˈkʌltʃər(ə)l/ adj.

subcutaneous /ˌsʌbkjuːˈteɪnɪəs/ adj. under the skin. □□ **subcutaneously** adv.

subdeacon /sʌbˈdiːkən/ n. Eccl. a minister of the order next below a deacon. □□ **subdiaconate** /-daɪˈækəˌneɪt, -daɪˈækənət/ n.

subdean /sʌbˈdiːn/ n. an official ranking next below, or acting as a deputy for, a dean. □□ **subdeanery** n. (pl. **-ies**). **subdecanal** /-dɪˈkeɪn(ə)l/ adj.

subdelirious /ˌsʌbdɪˈlɪrɪəs/ adj. capable of becoming delirious; mildly delirious. □□ **subdelirium** n.

subdivide /ˈsʌbdɪˌvaɪd, -ˈvaɪd/ v.tr. & intr. divide again after a first division. [ME f. L subdividere (as SUB-, DIVIDE)]

subdivision /ˈsʌbdɪˌvɪʒ(ə)n, -ˈvɪʒ(ə)n/ n. **1** the act or an instance of subdividing. **2** a secondary or subordinate division. **3** US & Austral. an area of land divided into plots for sale.

subdominant /sʌbˈdɒmɪnənt/ n. Mus. the fourth note of the diatonic scale of any key.

subdue /səbˈdjuː/ v.tr. (**subdues**, **subdued**, **subduing**) **1** conquer, subjugate, or tame (an enemy, nature, one's emotions, etc.). **2** (as **subdued** adj.) softened; lacking in intensity; toned down (subdued light; in a subdued mood). □□ **subduable** adj. **subdual** n. [ME sodewe f. OF so(u)duire f. L subducere (as SUB-, ducere lead, bring) used with the sense of subdere conquer (as SUB-, -dere put)]

sub-editor /sʌbˈedɪtə(r)/ n. **1** an assistant editor. **2** Brit. a person who edits material for printing in a book, newspaper, etc. □□ **sub-edit** v.tr. (**-edited**, **-editing**). **sub-editorial** /-ˈtɔːrɪəl/ adj.

suberect /ˌsʌbɪˈrekt/ adj. (of an animal, plant, etc.) almost erect.

subereous /sjuːˈbɪərɪəs/ adj. (also **suberic** /sjuːˈberɪk/, **suberose** /ˈsjuːbəˌrəʊs/) **1** of or concerning cork. **2** corky. [L suber cork, cork-oak]

subfamily /ˈsʌbˌfæmɪlɪ/ n. (pl. **-ies**) **1** Biol. a taxonomic category below a family. **2** any subdivision of a group.

subfloor /ˈsʌbflɔː(r)/ n. a foundation for a floor in a building.

subform /ˈsʌbfɔːm/ n. a subordinate or secondary form.

subfusc /ˈsʌbfʌsk/ adj. & n. —adj. formal dull; dusky; gloomy. —n. formal clothing at some universities. [L subfuscus f. fuscus dark brown]

subgenus /sʌbˈdʒiːnəs/ n. (pl. **subgenera** /-ˈdʒenərə/) Biol. a taxonomic category below a genus. □□ **subgeneric** /-dʒɪˈnerɪk/ adj.

subglacial /sʌbˈgleɪʃ(ə)l, -sɪəl/ adj. next to or at the bottom of a glacier.

subgroup /ˈsʌbgruːp/ n. Math. etc. a subset of a group.

subhead /ˈsʌbhed/ n. (also **subheading**) **1** a subordinate heading or title in a chapter, article, etc. **2** a subordinate division in a classification.

subhuman /sʌbˈhjuːmən/ adj. **1** (of an animal) closely related to man. **2** (of behaviour, intelligence, etc.) less than human.

subjacent /sʌbˈdʒeɪs(ə)nt/ adj. underlying; situated below. [L subjacēre (as SUB-, jacēre lie)]

subject n., adj., adv., & v. —n. /ˈsʌbdʒɪkt/ **1 a** a matter, theme, etc. to be discussed, described, represented, dealt with, etc. **b** (foll. by for) a person, circumstance, etc., giving rise to specified feeling, action, etc. (a subject for congratulation). **2** a department or field of study (his best subject is geography). **3** Gram. a noun or its equivalent about which a sentence is predicated and with which the verb agrees. **4 a** any person except a monarch living under a monarchy or any other form of government (the ruler and his subjects). **b** any person owing obedience to another. **5** Philos. **a** a thinking or feeling entity; the conscious mind; the ego, esp. as opposed to anything external to the mind. **b** the central substance or core of a thing as opposed to its attributes. **6** Mus. a theme of a fugue or sonata; a leading phrase or motif.

7 a person of specified mental or physical tendencies (*a hysterical subject*). **8** *Logic* the part of a proposition about which a statement is made. **9** (in full **subject for dissection**) a dead body. —*adj.* /ˈsʌbdʒɪkt/ **1** (often foll. by *to*) owing obedience to a government, colonizing power, force, etc.; in subjection. **2** (foll. by *to*) liable, exposed, or prone to (*is subject to infection*). **3** (foll. by *to*) conditional upon; on the assumption of (*the arrangement is subject to your approval*). —*adv.* /ˈsʌbdʒɪkt/ (foll. by *to*) conditionally upon (*subject to your consent, I propose to try again*). —*v.tr.* /səbˈdʒekt/ **1** (foll. by *to*) make liable; expose; treat (*subjected us to hours of waiting*). **2** (usu. foll. by *to*) subdue (a nation, person, etc.) to one's sway etc. □ **on the subject of** concerning, about. **subject and object** *Psychol.* the ego or self and the non-ego; consciousness and that of which it is or may be conscious. **subject catalogue** a catalogue, esp. in a library, arranged according to the subjects treated. **subject-heading** a heading in an index collecting references to a subject. **subject-matter** the matter treated of in a book, lawsuit, etc. □□ **subjection** /səbˈdʒekʃ(ə)n/ *n.* **subjectless** /ˈsʌbdʒɪktlɪs/ *adj.* [ME *soget* etc. f. OF *suget* etc. f. L *subjectus* past part. of *subicere* (as SUB-, *jacere* throw)]

subjective /səbˈdʒektɪv/ *adj.* & *n.* —*adj.* **1** (of art, literature, written history, a person's views, etc.) proceeding from personal idiosyncrasy or individuality; not impartial or literal. **2** esp. *Philos.* proceeding from or belonging to the individual consciousness or perception; imaginary, partial, or distorted. **3** *Gram.* of or concerning the subject. —*n. Gram.* the subjective case. □ **subjective case** *Gram.* the nominative. □□ **subjectively** *adv.* **subjectiveness** *n.* **subjectivity** /ˌsʌbdʒekˈtɪvɪtɪ/ *n.* [ME f. L *subjectivus* (as SUBJECT)]

subjectivism /səbˈdʒektɪˌvɪz(ə)m/ *n. Philos.* the doctrine that knowledge is merely subjective and that there is no external or objective truth. □□ **subjectivist** *n.*

subjoin /sʌbˈdʒɔɪn/ *v.tr.* add or append (an illustration, anecdote, etc.) at the end. [obs. F *subjoindre* f. L *subjungere* (as SUB-, *jungere* *junct-* join)]

subjoint /ˈsʌbdʒɔɪnt/ *n.* a secondary joint (in an insect's leg etc.).

sub judice /sʌb ˈdʒuːdɪsɪ, sʊb ˈjuːdɪˌkeɪ/ *adj. Law* under judicial consideration and therefore prohibited from public discussion elsewhere. [L, = under a judge]

subjugate /ˈsʌbdʒʊˌgeɪt/ *v.tr.* bring into subjection; subdue; vanquish. □□ **subjugable** /-gəb(ə)l/ *adj.* **subjugation** /-ˈgeɪʃ(ə)n/ *n.* **subjugator** *n.* [ME f. LL *subjugare* bring under the yoke (as SUB-, *jugum* yoke)]

subjunctive /səbˈdʒʌŋktɪv/ *adj.* & *n. Gram.* —*adj.* (of a mood) denoting what is imagined or wished or possible (e.g. *if I were you, God help you, be that as it may*). —*n.* **1** the subjunctive mood. **2** a verb in this mood. □□ **subjunctively** *adv.* [F *subjonctif -ive* or LL *subjunctivus* f. L (as SUBJOIN), transl. Gk *hupotaktikos*, as being used in subjoined clauses]

subkingdom /ˈsʌbˌkɪŋdəm/ *n. Biol.* a taxonomic category below a kingdom.

sublease *n.* & *v.* —*n.* /ˈsʌbliːs/ a lease of a property by a tenant to a subtenant. —*v.tr.* /sʌbˈliːs/ lease (a property) to a subtenant.

sublessee /ˌsʌbleˈsiː/ *n.* a person who holds a sublease.

sublessor /ˌsʌbleˈsɔː(r)/ *n.* a person who grants a sublease.

sublet *n.* & *v.* —*n.* /ˈsʌblet/ = SUBLEASE *n.* —*v.tr.* /sʌbˈlet/ (**-letting**; *past* and *past part.* **-let**) = SUBLEASE *v.*

sub-lieutenant /ˌsʌblefˈtenənt/ *n. Brit.* an officer ranking next below lieutenant.

sublimate *v., adj.,* & *n.* —*v.tr.* /ˈsʌblɪˌmeɪt/ **1** divert the energy of (a primitive impulse, esp. sexual) into a culturally higher activity. **2** *Chem.* convert (a substance) from the solid state directly to its vapour by heat, and usu. allow it to solidify again. **3** refine; purify; idealize. —*adj.* /ˈsʌblɪmət/ **1** *Chem.* (of a substance) sublimated. **2** purified, refined. —*n.* /ˈsʌblɪmət/ *Chem.* **1** a sublimated substance. **2** = *corrosive sublimate*. □□ **sublimation** /-ˈmeɪʃ(ə)n/ *n.* [L *sublimare sublimat-* SUBLIME *v.*]

sublime /səˈblaɪm/ *adj.* & *v.* —*adj.* (**sublimer, sublimest**) **1** of the most exalted, grand, or noble kind; awe-inspiring (*sublime genius*). **2** (of indifference, impudence, etc.) arrogantly unruffled. —*v.* **1** *tr.* & *intr. Chem.* = SUBLIMATE *v.* **2** *tr.* purify or elevate by or as if by sublimation; make sublime. **3** *intr.* become pure

by or as if by sublimation. □ **Sublime Porte** see PORTE. □□ **sublimely** *adv.* **sublimity** /-ˈlɪmɪtɪ/ *n.* [L *sublimis* (as SUB-, second element perh. rel. to *limen* threshold, *limus* oblique)]

subliminal /səbˈlɪmɪn(ə)l/ *adj. Psychol.* (of a stimulus etc.) below the threshold of sensation or consciousness. □ **subliminal advertising** the use of subliminal images in advertising on television etc. to influence the viewer at an unconscious level. **subliminal self** the part of one's personality outside conscious awareness. □□ **subliminally** *adv.* [SUB- + L *limen -inis* threshold]

sublingual /sʌbˈlɪŋgw(ə)l/ *adj.* under the tongue. [SUB- + L *lingua* tongue]

sublittoral /sʌbˈlɪtər(ə)l/ *adj.* **1** (of plants, animals, deposits, etc.) living or found on the seashore just below the low-water mark. **2** of or concerning the seashore.

Sub-Lt. *abbr. Brit.* Sub-Lieutenant.

sublunary /sʌbˈluːnərɪ, -ˈljuːnərɪ/ *adj.* **1** beneath the moon. **2** *Astron.* **a** within the moon's orbit. **b** subject to the moon's influence. **3** of this world; earthly. [LL *sublunaris* (as SUB-, LUNAR)]

sub-machine-gun /ˌsʌbməˈʃiːngʌn/ *n.* a hand-held lightweight machine-gun.

subman /ˈsʌbmæn/ *n.* (*pl.* **-men**) *derog.* an inferior, brutal, or stupid man.

submarginal /sʌbˈmɑːdʒɪn(ə)l/ *adj.* **1** esp. *Econ.* not reaching minimum requirements. **2** (of land) that cannot be farmed profitably.

submarine /ˌsʌbməˈriːn, ˈsʌb-/ *n.* & *adj.* —*n.* a vessel, esp. a warship, capable of operating under water and usu. equipped with torpedoes, missiles, and a periscope. (See below.) —*adj.* existing, occurring, done, or used under the surface of the sea (*submarine cable*). □□ **submariner** /-ˈmærɪnə(r)/ *n.*

Ancient Greek and Roman writers mention attempts to build submersible craft of various kinds, but the first authenticated vessel to be built seems to have been that of Cornelius Drebbel, a Dutch inventor (working for James I) who in the 1620s successfully manoeuvred his craft 4–5 metres below the surface of the River Thames. In the following century a number of types were patented and the principle of buoyancy tanks devised. The submarine's use in naval warfare dates from the War of American Independence, when a one-man craft, the *Turtle*, devised by the American inventor David Bushnell, attempted an underwater attack on a British warship. Robert Fulton experimented with submarines, but although initially backed by Napoleon his designs were not successful enough to attract serious attention. By the early 20th c. the invention of the internal-combustion engine, the electric motor, and new designs of torpedo enabled real progress to be made with the design of an effective war vessel, and submarines played a significant part in both World Wars, especially the Second. The greatest development in submarine construction came after the war, when the first nuclear-powered submarine, the *Nautilus*, was built. Since a nuclear reactor functions without the use of oxygen from the air, it enables the submarine to proceed submerged at or near her maximum speed for an indefinite period. The inertial navigation system enables a vessel to fix its position without surfacing at intervals to take navigational observations of heavenly bodies. Speeds greatly in excess of anything previously attained have been made possible by streamlining of the hull and adoption of a 'teardrop' design. The arming of nuclear-powered submarines with ballistic missiles capable of being fired while the vessel is submerged is one of the great engineering feats of the 20th century, with significant implications for international attack.

submaster /ˈsʌbˌmɑːstə(r)/ *n.* an assistant master or assistant headmaster in a school.

submaxillary /ˌsʌbmækˈsɪlərɪ/ *adj.* beneath the lower jaw.

submediant /sʌbˈmiːdɪənt/ *n. Mus.* the sixth note of the diatonic scale of any key.

submental /sʌbˈment(ə)l/ *adj.* under the chin.

submerge /səbˈmɜːdʒ/ *v.* **1** *tr.* **a** place under water; flood; inundate. **b** flood or inundate with work, problems, etc. **2** *intr.* (of a submarine, its crew, a diver, etc.) dive below the surface of water. □ **the submerged tenth** the supposed fraction of the population permanently living in poverty. □□ **submergence** n.

submergible adj. **submersion** /-ˈmɜːʃ(ə)n/ n. [L submergere (as SUB-, mergere mers- dip)]

submersible /səbˈmɜːsɪb(ə)l/ n. & adj. —n. a craft capable of operating under water for short periods. —adj. capable of being submerged. [submerse (v.) = SUBMERGE]

submicroscopic /sʌbˌmaɪkrəˈskɒpɪk/ adj. too small to be seen by means of an ordinary microscope.

subminiature /sʌbˈmɪnɪtʃə(r)/ adj. **1** of greatly reduced size. **2** (of a camera) very small and using 16-mm film.

submission /səbˈmɪʃ(ə)n/ n. **1 a** the act or an instance of submitting; the state of being submitted. **b** anything that is submitted. **2** humility, meekness, obedience, submissiveness (showed great submission of spirit). **3** Law a theory etc. submitted by counsel to a judge or jury. **4** (in wrestling) the surrender of a participant yielding to the pain of a hold. [ME f. OF submission or L submissio (as SUBMIT)]

submissive /səbˈmɪsɪv/ adj. **1** humble; obedient. **2** yielding to power or authority; willing to submit. □□ **submissively** adv. **submissiveness** n. [SUBMISSION after remissive etc.]

submit /səbˈmɪt/ v. (**submitted, submitting**) **1** (usu. foll. by to) **a** intr. cease resistance; give way; yield (had to submit to defeat; will never submit). **b** refl. surrender (oneself) to the control of another etc. **2** tr. present for consideration or decision. **3** tr. (usu. foll. by to) subject (a person or thing) to an operation, process, treatment, etc. (submitted it to the flames). **4** tr. esp. Law urge or represent esp. deferentially (that, I submit, is a misrepresentation). □□ **submitter** n. [ME f. L submittere (as SUB-, mittere miss- send)]

submultiple /sʌbˈmʌltɪp(ə)l/ n. & adj. —n. a number that can be divided exactly into a specified number. —adj. being such a number.

subnormal /sʌbˈnɔːm(ə)l/ adj. **1** (esp. as regards intelligence) below normal. **2** less than normal. □□ **subnormality** /-ˈmælɪtɪ/ n.

subnuclear /sʌbˈnjuːklɪə(r)/ adj. Physics occurring in or smaller than an atomic nucleus.

subocular /sʌbˈɒkjʊlə(r)/ adj. situated below or under the eyes.

suborbital /sʌbˈɔːbɪt(ə)l/ adj. **1** situated below the orbit of the eye. **2** (of a spaceship etc.) not completing a full orbit of the earth.

suborder /ˈsʌbɔːdə(r)/ n. a taxonomic category between an order and a family. □□ **subordinal** /-ˈɔːdɪn(ə)l/ adj.

subordinary /sʌbˈɔːdɪnərɪ/ n. (pl. **-ies**) Heraldry a device or bearing that is common but less so than ordinaries.

subordinate adj., n., & v. —adj. /səˈbɔːdɪnət/ (usu. foll. by to) of inferior importance or rank; secondary, subservient. —n. /səˈbɔːdɪnət/ a person working under another's control or orders. —v.tr. /səˈbɔːdɪneɪt/ (usu. foll. by to) **1** make subordinate; treat or regard as of minor importance. **2** make subservient. □ **subordinate clause** a clause serving as an adjective, adverb, or noun in a main sentence because of its position or a preceding conjunction. □□ **subordinately** /səˈbɔːdɪnətlɪ/ adv. **subordination** /-ˈneɪʃ(ə)n/ n. **subordinative** /səˈbɔːdɪnətɪv/ adj. [med.L subordinare, subordinat- (as SUB-, L ordinare ordain)]

suborn /səˈbɔːn/ v.tr. induce by bribery etc. to commit perjury or any other unlawful act. □□ **subornation** /ˌsʌbɔːˈneɪʃ(ə)n/ n. **suborner** n. [L subornare incite secretly (as SUB-, ornare equip)]

suboxide /sʌbˈɒksaɪd/ n. Chem. an oxide containing the smallest proportion of oxygen.

subphylum /sʌbˈfaɪləm/ n. (pl. **subphyla** /-lə/) Biol. a taxonomic category below a phylum.

sub-plot /ˈsʌbplɒt/ n. a subordinate plot in a play etc.

subpoena /səbˈpiːnə, səˈpiːnə/ n. & v. —n. a writ ordering a person to attend a lawcourt. —v.tr. (past and past part. **subpoenaed** or **subpoena'd**) serve a subpoena on. [ME f. L sub poena under penalty (the first words of the writ)]

subregion /ˈsʌbriːdʒ(ə)n/ n. a division of a region, esp. with regard to natural life. □□ **subregional** /-ˈriːdʒən(ə)l/ adj.

subreption /səbˈrepʃ(ə)n/ n. formal the obtaining of a thing by surprise or misrepresentation. [L subreptio purloining f. subripere (as SUB-, rapere snatch)]

subrogation /ˌsʌbrəˈgeɪʃ(ə)n/ n. Law the substitution of one party for another as creditor, with the transfer of rights and duties. □□ **subrogate** /ˈsʌbrəˌgeɪt/ v.tr. [LL subrogatio f. subrogare choose as substitute (as SUB-, rogare ask)]

sub rosa /sʌb ˈrəʊzə/ adj. & adv. (of communication, consultation, etc.) in secrecy or confidence. [L, lit. 'under the rose', as emblem of secrecy]

subroutine /ˈsʌbruːˌtiːn/ n. Computing a routine designed to perform a frequently used operation within a program.

subscribe /səbˈskraɪb/ v. **1** (usu. foll. by to, for) **a** tr. & intr. contribute (a specified sum) or make or promise a contribution to a fund, project, charity, etc., esp. regularly. **b** intr. enter one's name in a list of contributors to a charity etc. **c** tr. raise or guarantee raising (a sum) by so subscribing. **2** intr. (usu. foll. by to) express one's agreement with an opinion, resolution, etc. (cannot subscribe to that). **3** tr. **a** write (esp. one's name) at the foot of a document etc. (subscribed a motto). **b** write one's name at the foot of, sign (a document, picture, etc.). □ **subscribe for** agree to take a copy or copies of (a book) before publication. **subscribe oneself** sign one's name as. **subscribe to** arrange to receive (a periodical etc.) regularly. [ME f. L subscribere (as SUB-, scribere script- write)]

subscriber /səbˈskraɪbə(r)/ n. **1** a person who subscribes. **2** a person paying for the hire of a telephone line. □ **subscriber trunk dialling** Brit. the automatic connection of trunk calls by dialling without the assistance of an operator.

subscript /ˈsʌbskrɪpt/ adj. & n. —adj. written or printed below the line, esp. Math. (of a symbol) written below and to the right of another symbol. —n. a subscript number or symbol. [L subscriptus (as SUBSCRIBE)]

subscription /səbˈskrɪpʃ(ə)n/ n. **1 a** the act or an instance of subscribing. **b** money subscribed. **2** Brit. a fee for the membership of a society etc., esp. paid regularly. **3 a** an agreement to take and pay for usu. a specified number of issues of a newspaper, magazine, etc. **b** the money paid by this. **4** a signature on a document etc. **5** the offer of a reduced price to those ordering a book before publication. □ **subscription concert** etc. each of a series of concerts etc. for which tickets are sold in advance. [ME f. L subscriptio (as SUBSCRIBE)]

subsection /ˈsʌbˌsekʃ(ə)n/ n. a division of a section.

subsellium /səbˈselɪəm/ n. (pl. **subsellia** /-lɪə/) = MISERICORD 1. [L f. sella seat]

subsequence /ˈsʌbsɪkwəns/ n. a subsequent incident; a consequence.

sub-sequence /ˈsʌbˌsiːkwəns/ n. a sequence forming part of a larger one.

subsequent /ˈsʌbsɪkwənt/ adj. (usu. foll. by to) following a specified event etc. in time, esp. as a consequence. □□ **subsequently** adv. [ME f. OF subsequent or L subsequi (as SUB-, sequi follow)]

subserve /səbˈsɜːv/ v.tr. serve as a means in furthering (a purpose, action, etc.). [L subservire (as SUB-, SERVE)]

subservient /səbˈsɜːvɪənt/ adj. **1** cringing; obsequious. **2** (usu. foll. by to) serving as a means; instrumental. **3** (usu. foll. by to) subordinate. □□ **subservience** n. **subserviency** n. **subserviently** adv. [L subserviens subservient- (as SUBSERVE)]

subset /ˈsʌbset/ n. **1** a secondary part of a set. **2** Math. a set all the elements of which are contained in another set.

subshrub /ˈsʌbʃrʌb/ n. a low-growing or small shrub.

subside /səbˈsaɪd/ v.intr. **1** cease from agitation; become tranquil; abate (excitement subsided). **2** (of water, suspended matter, etc.) sink. **3** (of the ground) cave in; sink. **4** (of a building, ship, etc.) sink lower in the ground or water. **5** (of a swelling etc.) become less. **6** usu. joc. (of a person) sink into a sitting, kneeling, or lying posture. □□ **subsidence** /-ˈsaɪd(ə)ns, ˈsʌbsɪd(ə)ns/ n. [L subsidere (as SUB-, sidere settle rel. to sedēre sit)]

subsidiary /səbˈsɪdɪərɪ/ adj. & n. —adj. **1** serving to assist or supplement; auxiliary. **2** (of a company) controlled by another. **3** (of troops): **a** paid for by subsidy. **b** hired by another nation.

—*n.* (*pl.* **-ies**) **1** a subsidiary thing or person; an accessory. **2** a subsidiary company. □□ **subsidiarily** *adv.* **subsidiarity** /-ˈærɪtɪ/ *n.* [L *subsidiarius* (as SUBSIDY)]

subsidize /ˈsʌbsɪˌdaɪz/ *v.tr.* (also **-ise**) **1** pay a subsidy to. **2** reduce the cost of by subsidy (*subsidized lunches*). □□ **subsidization** /-ˈzeɪʃ(ə)n/ *n.* **subsidizer** *n.*

subsidy /ˈsʌbsɪdɪ/ *n.* (*pl.* **-ies**) **1 a** money granted by the State or a public body etc. to keep down the price of commodities etc. (*housing subsidy*). **b** money granted to a charity or other undertaking held to be in the public interest. **c** any grant or contribution of money. **2** money paid by one State to another in return for military, naval, or other aid. **3** *hist.* **a** a parliamentary grant to the sovereign for State needs. **b** a tax levied on a particular occasion. [ME f. AF *subsidie*, OF *subside* f. L *subsidium* assistance]

subsist /səbˈsɪst/ *v.* **1** *intr.* (often foll. by *on*) keep oneself alive; be kept alive (*subsists on vegetables*). **2** *intr.* remain in being; exist. **3** *intr.* (foll. by *in*) be attributable to (*its excellence subsists in its freshness*). **4** *tr. archaic* provide sustenance for. □□ **subsistent** *adj.* [L *subsistere* stand firm (as SUB-, *sistere* set, stand)]

subsistence /səbˈsɪst(ə)ns/ *n.* **1** the state or an instance of subsisting. **2 a** the means of supporting life; a livelihood. **b** a minimal level of existence or the income providing this (*a bare subsistence*). □ **subsistence allowance** (or **money**) esp. *Brit.* an allowance or advance on pay granted esp. as travelling expenses. **subsistence farming** farming which directly supports the farmer's household without producing a significant surplus for trade. **subsistence level** (or **wage**) a standard of living (or wage) providing only the bare necessities of life.

subsoil /ˈsʌbsɔɪl/ *n.* soil lying immediately under the surface soil (opp. TOPSOIL).

subsonic /sʌbˈsɒnɪk/ *adj.* relating to speeds less than that of sound. □□ **subsonically** *adv.*

subspecies /ˈsʌbˌspiːʃiːz, -ʃɪz/ *n.* (*pl.* same) *Biol.* a taxonomic category below a species, usu. a fairly permanent geographically isolated variety. □□ **subspecific** /-spəˈsɪfɪk/ *adj.*

substance /ˈsʌbst(ə)ns/ *n.* **1 a** the essential material, esp. solid, forming a thing (*the substance was transparent*). **b** a particular kind of material having uniform properties (*this substance is salt*). **2 a** reality; solidity (*ghosts have no substance*). **b** seriousness or steadiness of character (*there is no substance in him*). **3** the theme or subject of esp. a work of art, argument, etc. (*prefer the substance to the style*). **4** the real meaning or essence of a thing. **5** wealth and possessions (*a woman of substance*). **6** *Philos.* the essential nature underlying phenomena, which is subject to changes and accidents. □ **in substance** generally; apart from details. [ME f. OF f. L *substantia* (as SUB-, *stare* stand)]

substandard /sʌbˈstændəd/ *adj.* **1** of less than the required or normal quality or size; inferior. **2** (of language) not conforming to standard usage.

substantial /səbˈstænʃ(ə)l/ *adj.* **1 a** of real importance or value (*made a substantial contribution*). **b** of large size or amount (*awarded substantial damages*). **2** of solid material or structure; stout (*a man of substantial build; a substantial house*). **3** commercially successful; wealthy. **4** essential; true in large part (*substantial truth*). **5** having substance; real. □□ **substantiality** /-ʃɪˈælɪtɪ/ *n.* **substantially** *adv.* [ME f. OF *substantiel* or LL *substantialis* (as SUBSTANCE)]

substantialism /səbˈstænʃəˌlɪz(ə)m/ *n.* *Philos.* the doctrine that behind phenomena there are substantial realities. □□ **substantialist** *n.*

substantialize /səbˈstænʃəˌlaɪz/ *v.tr.* & *intr.* (also **-ise**) invest with or acquire substance or actual existence.

substantiate /səbˈstænʃɪˌeɪt/ *v.tr.* prove the truth of (a charge, statement, claim, etc.); give good grounds for. □□ **substantiation** /-ˈeɪʃ(ə)n/ *n.* [med.L *substantiare* give substance to (as SUBSTANCE)]

substantive /ˈsʌbstəntɪv/ *adj.* & *n.* —*adj.* /also səbˈstæntɪv/ **1** having separate and independent existence. **2** *Law* relating to rights and duties. **3** (of an enactment, motion, resolution, etc.) made in due form as such; not amended. **4** *Gram.* expressing existence. **5** (of a dye) not needing a mordant. **6** *Mil.* (of a rank etc.) permanent, not acting or temporary. **7** *archaic* denoting a

substance. —*n.* *Gram.* = NOUN. □ **the substantive verb** the verb 'to be'. □□ **substantival** /-ˈtaɪv(ə)l/ *adj.* **substantivally** *adv.* esp. *Gram.* [ME f. OF *substantif* -*ive*, or LL *substantivus* (as SUBSTANCE)]

substation /ˈsʌbˌsteɪʃ(ə)n/ *n.* a subordinate station, esp. one reducing the high voltage of electric power transmission to that suitable for supply to consumers.

substituent /sʌbˈstɪtjʊənt/ *adj.* & *n.* *Chem.* —*adj.* (of a group of atoms) replacing another atom or group in a compound. —*n.* such a group. [L *substituere substituent-* (as SUBSTITUTE)]

substitute /ˈsʌbstɪˌtjuːt/ *n.* & *v.* —*n.* **1 a** (also *attrib.*) a person or thing acting or serving in place of another. **b** an artificial alternative to a natural substance (*butter substitute*). **2** *Sc. Law* a deputy. —*v.* **1** *intr.* & *tr.* (often foll. by *for*) act or cause to act as a substitute; put or serve in exchange (*substituted for her mother; substituted it for the broken one*). **2** *tr.* (usu. foll. by *by*, *with*) *colloq.* replace (a person or thing) with another. **3** *tr.* *Chem.* replace (an atom or group in a molecule) with another. □□ **substitutable** *adj.* **substitutability** /-ˈbɪlɪtɪ/ *n.* **substitution** /-ˈtjuːʃ(ə)n/ *n.* **substitutional** /-ˈtjuːʃən(ə)l/ *adj.* **substitutionary** /-ˈtjuːʃənərɪ/ *adj.* **substitutive** *adj.* [ME f. L *substitutus* past part. of *substituere* (as SUB-, *statuere* set up)]

substrate /ˈsʌbstreɪt/ *n.* **1** = SUBSTRATUM. **2** a surface to be painted, printed, etc., on. **3** *Biol.* **a** the substance upon which an enzyme acts. **b** the surface or material on which any particular organism grows. [Anglicized f. SUBSTRATUM]

substratum /ˈsʌbˌstrɑːtəm, -ˌstreɪtəm/ *n.* (*pl.* **substrata** /-tə/) **1** an underlying layer or substance. **2** a layer of rock or soil beneath the surface. **3** a foundation or basis (*there is a substratum of truth in it*). [mod.L, past part. of L *substernere* (as SUB-, *sternere* strew); cf. STRATUM]

substructure /ˈsʌbˌstrʌktʃə(r)/ *n.* an underlying or supporting structure. □□ **substructural** *adj.*

subsume /səbˈsjuːm/ *v.tr.* (usu. foll. by *under*) include (an instance, idea, category, etc.) in a rule, class, category, etc. □□ **subsumable** *adj.* **subsumption** /-ˈsʌmpʃ(ə)n/ *n.* [med.L *subsumere* (as SUB-, *sumere sumpt-* take)]

subtenant /ˈsʌbˌtenənt/ *n.* a person who leases a property from a tenant. □□ **subtenancy** *n.*

subtend /sʌbˈtend/ *v.tr.* **1 a** (usu. foll. by *at*) (of a line, arc, figure, etc.) form (an angle) at a particular point when its extremities are joined at that point. **b** (of an angle or chord) have bounding lines or points that meet or coincide with those of (a line or arc). **2** *Bot.* (of a bract etc.) extend under so as to embrace or enfold. [L *subtendere* (as SUB-, *tendere* stretch)]

subterfuge /ˈsʌbtəˌfjuːdʒ/ *n.* **1 a** an attempt to avoid blame or defeat esp. by lying or deceit. **b** a statement etc. resorted to for such a purpose. **2** this as a practice or policy. [F *subterfuge* or LL *subterfugium* f. L *subterfugere* escape secretly f. *subter* beneath + *fugere* flee]

subterminal /sʌbˈtɜːmɪn(ə)l/ *adj.* nearly at the end.

subterranean /ˌsʌbtəˈreɪnɪən/ *adj.* **1** existing, occurring, or done under the earth's surface. **2** secret, underground, concealed. □□ **subterraneously** *adv.* [L *subterraneus* (as SUB-, *terra* earth)]

subtext /ˈsʌbtekst/ *n.* an underlying often distinct theme in a piece of writing or conversation.

subtilize /ˈsʌtɪˌlaɪz/ *v.* (also **-ise**) **1** *tr.* **a** make subtle. **b** elevate; refine. **2** *intr.* (usu. foll. by *upon*) argue or reason subtly. □□ **subtilization** /-ˈzeɪʃ(ə)n/ *n.* [F *subtiliser* or med.L *subtilizare* (as SUBTLE)]

subtitle /ˈsʌbˌtaɪt(ə)l/ *n.* & *v.* —*n.* **1** a secondary or additional title of a book etc. **2** a printed caption at the bottom of a film etc., esp. translating dialogue. —*v.tr.* provide with a subtitle or subtitles.

subtle /ˈsʌt(ə)l/ *adj.* (**subtler**, **subtlest**) **1** evasive or mysterious; hard to grasp (*subtle charm; a subtle distinction*). **2** (of scent, colour, etc.) faint, delicate, elusive (*subtle perfume*). **3 a** capable of making fine distinctions; perceptive; acute (*subtle intellect; subtle senses*). **b** ingenious; elaborate; clever (*a subtle device*). **4** *archaic* crafty, cunning. □□ **subtleness** *n.* **subtly** *adv.* [ME f. OF *sotil* f. L *subtilis*]

subtlety /ˈsʌtəltɪ/ n. (pl. **-ies**) **1** something subtle. **2** a fine distinction; an instance of hairsplitting. [ME f. OF s(o)utilté f. L subtilitas -tatis (as SUBTLE)]

subtonic /sʌbˈtɒnɪk/ n. Mus. the note below the tonic, the seventh note of the diatonic scale of any key.

subtopia /sʌbˈtəʊpɪə/ n. Brit. derog. unsightly and sprawling suburban development. □□ **subtopian** adj. [SUBURB, UTOPIA]

subtotal /ˈsʌbˌtəʊt(ə)l/ n. the total of one part of a group of figures to be added.

subtract /səbˈtrækt/ v.tr. (often foll. by from) deduct (a part, quantity, or number) from another. □□ **subtracter** n. (cf. SUBTRACTOR). **subtraction** /-ˈtrækʃ(ə)n/ n. **subtractive** adj. [L subtrahere subtract- (as SUB-, trahere draw)]

subtractor /səbˈtræktə(r)/ n. Electronics a circuit or device that produces an output dependent on the difference of two inputs.

subtrahend /ˈsʌbtrəˌhend/ n. Math. a quantity or number to be subtracted. [L subtrahendus gerundive of subtrahere: see SUBTRACT]

subtropics /sʌbˈtrɒpɪks/ n.pl. the regions adjacent to or bordering on the tropics. □□ **subtropical** adj.

subulate /ˈsʌbjʊlət/ adj. Bot. & Zool. slender and tapering. [L subula awl]

suburb /ˈsʌbɜːb/ n. an outlying district of a city, esp. residential. [ME f. OF suburbe or L suburbium (as SUB-, urbs urbis city)]

suburban /səˈbɜːbən/ adj. **1** of or characteristic of suburbs. **2** derog. provincial, uncultured, or naïve. □□ **suburbanite** n. **suburbanize** v.tr. (also **-ise**). **suburbanization** /-ˈzeɪʃ(ə)n/ n. [L suburbanus (as SUBURB)]

suburbia /səˈbɜːbɪə/ n. often derog. the suburbs, their inhabitants, and their way of life.

subvention /səbˈvenʃ(ə)n/ n. a grant of money from a government etc.; a subsidy. [ME f. OF f. LL subventio -onis f. L subvenire subvent- assist (as SUB-, venire come)]

subversive /səbˈvɜːsɪv/ adj. & n. —adj. (of a person, organization, activity, etc.) seeking to subvert (esp. a government). —n. a subversive person; a revolutionary. □□ **subversion** /-ˈvɜːʃ(ə)n/ n. **subversively** adv. **subversiveness** n. [med.L subversivus (as SUBVERT)]

subvert /səbˈvɜːt/ v.tr. esp. Polit. overturn, overthrow, or upset (religion, government, the monarchy, morality, etc.). □□ **subverter** n. [ME f. OF subvertir or L subvertere (as SUB-, vertere vers- turn)]

subway /ˈsʌbweɪ/ n. **1 a** a tunnel beneath a road etc. for pedestrians. **b** an underground passage for pipes, cables, etc. **2** esp. US an underground railway.

subzero /sʌbˈzɪərəʊ/ adj. (esp. of temperature) lower than zero.

suc- /sʌk, sək/ prefix assim. form of SUB- before c.

succedaneum /ˌsʌksɪˈdeɪnɪəm/ n. (pl. **succedanea** /-nɪə/) a substitute, esp. for a medicine or drug. □□ **succedaneous** adj. [mod.L, neut. of L succedaneus (as SUCCEED)]

succeed /səkˈsiːd/ v. **1** intr. **a** (often foll. by in) accomplish one's purpose; have success; prosper (succeeded in his ambition). **b** (of a plan etc.) be successful. **2 a** tr. follow in order; come next after (night succeeded day). **b** intr. (foll. by to) come next; be subsequent. **3** intr. (often foll. by to) come by an inheritance, office, title, or property (succeeded to the throne). **4** tr. take over an office, property, inheritance, etc. from (succeeded his father; succeeded the manager). □ **nothing succeeds like success** one success leads to others. □□ **succeeder** n. [ME f. OF succeder or L succedere (as SUB-, cedere cess- go)]

succentor /səkˈsentə(r)/ n. Eccl. a precentor's deputy in some cathedrals. □□ **succentorship** n. [LL f. L succinere (as SUB-, canere sing)]

succès de scandale /sʊkˌseɪ də skɒ̃ˈdɑːl/ n. a book, play, etc. having great success because of its scandalous nature or associations. [F]

success /səkˈses/ n. **1** the accomplishment of an aim; a favourable outcome (their efforts met with success). **2** the attainment of wealth, fame, or position (spoilt by success). **3** a thing or person that turns out well. **4** archaic a usu. specified outcome of an undertaking (ill success). □ **success story** a person's rise from poverty to wealth etc. [L successus (as SUCCEED)]

successful /səkˈsesfʊl/ adj. having success; prosperous. □□ **successfully** adv. **successfulness** n.

succession /səkˈseʃ(ə)n/ n. **1 a** the process of following in order; succeeding. **b** a series of things or people in succession. **2 a** the right of succeeding to the throne, an office, inheritance, etc. **b** the act or process of so succeeding. **c** those having such a right. **3** Biol. the order of development of a species or community; = SERE³. □ **in quick succession** following one another at short intervals. **in succession** one after another, without intervention. **in succession to** as the successor of. **law of succession** the law regulating inheritance. **settle the succession** determine who shall succeed. **Succession State** a State resulting from the partition of a previously existing country. □□ **successional** adj. [ME f. OF succession or L successio (as SUCCEED)]

successive /səkˈsesɪv/ adj. following one after another; running, consecutive. □□ **successively** adv. **successiveness** n. [ME f. med.L successivus (as SUCCEED)]

successor /səkˈsesə(r)/ n. (often foll. by to) a person or thing that succeeds to another. [ME f. OF successour f. L successor (as SUCCEED)]

succinct /səkˈsɪŋkt/ adj. briefly expressed; terse, concise. □□ **succinctly** adv. **succinctness** n. [ME f. L succinctus past part. of succingere tuck up (as SUB-, cingere gird)]

succinic acid /sʌkˈsɪnɪk/ n. Chem. a crystalline dibasic acid derived from amber etc. □□ **succinate** /ˈsʌksɪˌneɪt/ n. [F succinique f. L succinum amber]

succor US var. of SUCCOUR.

succory /ˈsʌkərɪ/ n. = CHICORY 1. [alt. f. cicoree etc., early forms of CHICORY]

succotash /ˈsʌkəˌtæʃ/ n. US a dish of green maize and beans boiled together. [Narraganset msiquatash]

Succoth /sʊˈkəʊt, ˈsʌkəθ/ n. the Jewish autumn thanksgiving festival commemorating the sheltering in the wilderness. [Heb. sukkôt pl. of sukkāh thicket, hut]

succour /ˈsʌkə(r)/ n. & v. (US **succor**) —n. **1** aid; assistance, esp. in time of need. **2** (in pl.) archaic reinforcements of troops. —v.tr. assist or aid (esp. a person in danger or distress). □□ **succourless** adj. [ME f. OF socours f. med.L succursus f. L succurrere (as SUB-, currere curs- run)]

succubus /ˈsʌkjʊbəs/ n. (pl. **succubi** /-ˌbaɪ/) a female demon believed to have sexual intercourse with sleeping men. [LL succuba prostitute, med.L succubus f. succubare (as SUB-, cubare lie)]

succulent /ˈsʌkjʊlənt/ adj. & n. —adj. **1** juicy; palatable. **2** colloq. desirable. **3** Bot. (of a plant, its leaves, or stems) thick and fleshy. —n. Bot. a succulent plant, esp. a cactus. □□ **succulence** n. **succulently** adv. [L succulentus f. succus juice]

succumb /səˈkʌm/ v.intr. (usu. foll. by to) **1** be forced to give way; be overcome (succumbed to temptation). **2** be overcome by death (succumbed to his injuries). [ME f. OF succomber or L succumbere (as SUB-, cumbere lie)]

succursal /səˈkɜːs(ə)l/ adj. Eccl. (of a chapel etc.) subsidiary. [F succursale f. med.L succursus (as SUCCOUR)]

such /sʌtʃ/ adj. & pron. —adj. **1** (often foll. by as) of the kind or degree in question or under consideration (such a person; such people; people such as these). **2** (usu. foll. by as to + infin. or that + clause) so great; in such high degree (not such a fool as to believe them; had such a fright that he fainted). **3** of a more than normal kind or degree (we had such an enjoyable evening; such horrid language). **4** of the kind or degree already indicated, or implied by the context (there are no such things; such is life). **5** Law or formal the aforesaid; of the aforesaid kind. —pron. **1** the thing or action in question or referred to (such were his words; such was not my intention). **2 a** Commerce or colloq. the aforesaid thing or things; it, they, or them (those without tickets should purchase such). **b** similar things; suchlike (brought sandwiches and such). □ **as such** as being what has been indicated or named (a stranger is welcomed as such; there is no theatre as such). **such-and-such** adj. of a particular kind but not needing to be specified. —n. a person or thing of this kind. **such-and-such a person** someone; so-and-so. **such as 1** of a kind that; like (a person such as we all admire). **2** for example (insects, such as moths and bees). **3** those who (such as don't need help). **such as it is** despite its shortcomings (you are welcome to *it, such as it is*). **such a one 1** (usu. foll. by *as*) such a person or such a thing. **2** *archaic* some person or thing unspecified. [OE *swilc, swylc* f. Gmc: cf. LIKE¹]

suchlike /ˈsʌtʃlaɪk/ *adj. & n. colloq.* —*adj.* of such a kind. —*n.* things, people, etc. of such a kind.

suck /sʌk/ *v. & n.* —*v.* **1** *tr.* draw (a fluid) into the mouth by making a partial vacuum. **2** *tr.* (also *absol.*) **a** draw milk or other fluid from or through (the breast etc. or a container). **b** extract juice from (a fruit) by sucking. **3** *tr.* **a** draw sustenance, knowledge, or advantage from (a book etc.). **b** imbibe or gain (knowledge, advantage, etc.) as if by sucking. **4** *tr.* roll the tongue round (a sweet, teeth, one's thumb, etc.). **5** *intr.* make a sucking action or sound (*sucking at his pipe*). **6** *intr.* (of a pump etc.) make a gurgling or drawing sound. **7** *tr.* (usu. foll. by *down, in*) engulf, smother, or drown in a sucking movement. —*n.* **1** the act or an instance of sucking, esp. the breast. **2** the drawing action or sound of a whirlpool etc. **3** (often foll. by *of*) a small draught of liquor. **4** (in *pl.*; esp. as *int.*) *colloq.* **a** an expression of disappointment. **b** an expression of derision or amusement at another's discomfiture. □ **give suck** *archaic* (of a mother, dam, etc.) suckle. **suck dry 1** exhaust the contents of (a bottle, the breast, etc.) by sucking. **2** exhaust (a person's sympathy, resources, etc.) as if by sucking. **suck in 1** absorb. **2** = sense 7 of *v.* **3** involve (a person) in an activity etc. esp. against his or her will. **suck up 1** (often foll. by *to*) *colloq.* behave obsequiously esp. for one's own advantage. **2** absorb. [OE *sūcan*, = L *sugere*]

sucker /ˈsʌkə(r)/ *n. & v.* —*n.* **1 a** a person or thing that sucks. **b** a sucking-pig, newborn whale, etc. **2** *sl.* **a** a gullible or easily deceived person. **b** (foll. by *for*) a person especially susceptible to. **3 a** a rubber cup etc. that adheres to a surface by suction. **b** an organ enabling an organism to cling to a surface by suction. **4** *Bot.* a shoot springing from the rooted part of a stem, from the root at a distance from the main stem, from an axil, or occasionally from a branch. **5** any of various fish that has a mouth capable of or seeming to be capable of adhering by suction. **6 a** the piston of a suction-pump. **b** a pipe through which liquid is drawn by suction. **7** *US colloq.* a lollipop. —*v. Bot.* **1** *tr.* remove suckers from. **2** *intr.* produce suckers.

sucking /ˈsʌkɪŋ/ *adj.* **1** (of a child, animal, etc.) not yet weaned. **2** *Zool.* unfledged (*sucking dove*). □ **sucking-disc** an organ used for adhering to a surface. **sucking-fish** = REMORA.

suckle /ˈsʌk(ə)l/ *v.* **1** *tr.* **a** feed (young) from the breast or udder. **b** nourish (*suckled his talent*). **2** *intr.* feed by sucking the breast etc. □□ **suckler** *n.* [ME, prob. back-form. f. SUCKLING]

Suckling /ˈsʌklɪŋ/, Sir John (1609–41), English poet and dramatist, who lived at court from 1632 and was a leader of the supporters of Charles I in the Civil War. His poems include the 'Ballad upon a Wedding'. According to Aubrey, Suckling invented the game of cribbage.

suckling /ˈsʌklɪŋ/ *n.* an unweaned child or animal.

Sucre¹ /ˈsuːkreɪ/ the legal capital and seat of the judiciary of Bolivia; pop. (1985) 86,600.

Sucre² /suːkreɪ/, Antonio José de (1795–1830), South American revolutionary. As Bolivar's chief of staff he defeated the Spanish forces remaining in Peru (1824) and drove the last of these from Bolivia in 1825; a year later he became that country's first elected President, but was driven out after an invasion of Peruvian troops in 1828, and later assassinated.

sucrose /ˈsuːkrəʊz, ˈsjuː-/ *n. Chem.* sugar, a disaccharide obtained from sugar cane, sugar beet, etc. [F *sucre* SUGAR]

suction /ˈsʌkʃ(ə)n/ *n.* **1** the act or an instance of sucking. **2 a** the production of a partial vacuum by the removal of air etc. in order to force in liquid etc. or procure adhesion. **b** the force produced by this process (*suction keeps the lid on*). □ **suction-pump** a pump for drawing liquid through a pipe into a chamber emptied by a piston. [LL *suctio* f. L *sugere suct-* SUCK]

suctorial /sʌkˈtɔːrɪəl/ *adj. Zool.* **1** adapted for or capable of sucking. **2** having a sucker for feeding or adhering. □□ **suctorian** *n.* [mod.L *suctorius* (as SUCTION)]

Sudan /suːˈdɑːn, su-/ a country in NE Africa south of Egypt, with a coastline on the Red Sea; pop. (est. 1988) 24,014,500; official language, Arabic; capital, Khartoum. The NE area was part of ancient Nubia. Under Arab rule from the 13th c., the country was conquered by Egypt in 1820–2. The Sudan was separated from its northern neighbour by the Mahdist revolt of 1881–98, and administered after the reconquest of 1898 as an Anglo-Egyptian condominium. It became an independent republic in 1956, but has suffered as a result of north-south tension within the country. Cotton, grown in the irrigated areas of the south, forms the country's most important export. □□ **Sudanese** /ˌsuːdəˈniːz/ *adj. & n.* [Arab. *sūdān* (pl. of *sūdā* black), = country of the Blacks]

sudarium /sjuːˈdeərɪəm, su-/ *n.* (*pl.* **sudaria** /-rɪə/) **1** a cloth for wiping the face. **2** *RC Ch.* = VERONICA 2. [L, = napkin f. *sudor* sweat]

sudatorium /ˌsjuːdəˈtɔːrɪəm, ˌsu-/ *n.* (*pl.* **sudatoria** /-rɪə/) esp. *Rom. Antiq.* **1** a hot-air or steam bath. **2** a room where such a bath is taken. [L, neut. of *sudatorius*: see SUDATORY]

sudatory /ˈsjuːdətərɪ, ˈsu-/ *adj. & n.* —*adj.* promoting perspiration. —*n.* (*pl.* **-ies**) **1** a sudatory drug. **2** = SUDATORIUM. [L *sudatorius* f. *sudare* sweat]

Sudbury /ˈsʌdbərɪ/ a city in central Ontario, at the centre of Canada's largest mining region; pop. (1986) 88,700; metropolitan area pop. 148,900. This region is the world's largest source of nickel.

sudd /sʌd/ *n.* floating vegetation impeding the navigation of the White Nile. [Arab., = obstruction]

sudden /ˈsʌd(ə)n/ *adj. & n.* —*adj.* occurring or done unexpectedly or without warning; abrupt, hurried, hasty (*a sudden storm; a sudden departure*). —*n.* *archaic* a hasty or abrupt occurrence. □ **all of a sudden** unexpectedly; hurriedly; suddenly. **on a sudden** *archaic* suddenly. **sudden death** *colloq.* a decision in a tied game etc. dependent on one move, card, toss of a coin, etc. **sudden infant death syndrome** *Med.* = cot-death (see COT¹). □□ **suddenly** *adv.* **suddenness** /-dənnɪs/ *n.* [ME f. AF *sodein, sudein,* OF *soudain* f. LL *subitanus* f. L *subitaneus* f. *subitus* sudden]

Sudetenland /suˈdeɪtənˌlænd/ an area of Bohemia adjacent to the German border, allocated to the new State of Czechoslovakia after the First World War despite the presence of three million German-speaking inhabitants. The Sudetenland became the first object of German expansionist policies after the Nazis came to power, and, after war was threatened, was ceded to Germany as a result of the Munich Agreement of September 1938. In 1945 the area was returned to Czechoslovakia, and the German inhabitants were expelled and replaced by Czechs.

sudoriferous /ˌsuːdəˈrɪfərəs, ˌsu-/ *adj.* (of a gland etc.) secreting sweat. [LL *sudorifer* f. L *sudor* sweat]

sudorific /ˌsjuːdəˈrɪfɪk/ *adj. & n.* —*adj.* (of a drug) causing sweating. —*n.* a sudorific drug. [mod.L *sudorificus* f. L *sudor* sweat]

Sudra /ˈsuːdrə/ *n.* a member of the lowest of the four great Hindu classes (the labourer class), whose function is to serve the other three varnas. [Skr. *śūdra*]

suds /sʌdz/ *n. & v.* —*n.pl.* **1** froth of soap and water. **2** *US colloq.* beer. —*v.* **1** *intr.* form suds. **2** *tr.* lather, cover, or wash in soapy water. □□ **sudsy** *adj.* [orig. = fen waters etc., of uncert. orig.: cf. MDu., MLG *sudde,* MDu. *sudse* marsh, bog, prob. rel. to SEETHE]

sue /suː, sjuː/ *v.* (**sues, sued, suing**) **1** *tr.* (also *absol.*) *Law* institute legal proceedings against (a person). **2** *tr.* (also *absol.*) entreat (a person). **3** *intr.* (often foll. by *to, for*) *Law* make application to a lawcourt for redress. **4** *intr.* (often foll. by *to, for*) make entreaty to a person for a favour. **5** *tr.* (often foll. by *out*) make a petition in a lawcourt for and obtain (a writ, pardon, etc.). □□ **suer** *n.* [ME f. AF *suer, siwer,* etc. f. OF *siu-* etc. stem of *sivre* f. L *sequi* follow]

suede /sweɪd/ *n.* (often *attrib.*) **1** leather, esp. kidskin, with the flesh side rubbed to make a velvety nap. **2** (also **suede-cloth**) a woven fabric resembling suede. [F (*gants de*) *Suède* (gloves of) Sweden]

suet /ˈsuːɪt, ˈsjuːɪt/ *n.* the hard white fat on the kidneys or loins of oxen, sheep, etc., used to make dough etc. □ **suet pudding** a pudding of suet etc., usu. boiled or steamed. □□ **suety** *adj.* [ME f. AF f. OF *seu* f. L *sebum* tallow]

Suetonius /ˌsuːˈiːtəʊnɪəs/ (Gaius Suetonius Tranquillus, born *c.*69) Roman scholar and biographer. His surviving works include biographies of the first twelve Caesars, from Julius Caesar to Domitian, which detail the good and bad qualities and deeds of their subjects in a schematic but objective manner, and which provided a model for biography in the Middle Ages and Renaissance.

Suez /ˈsuːɪz/ an isthmus connecting Egypt to the Sinai peninsula, site of the **Suez Canal,** a shipping canal 171 km (106 miles) long connecting the Mediterranean (at Port Said) with the Red Sea, constructed in 1859–69 by Ferdinand de Lesseps. The Canal, now important for Egypt's economy as providing the shortest route for international sea traffic travelling between Europe and Asia, came under British control after British acquired majority shares in it, at Disraeli's instigation, in 1875, and after 1888 Britain acted as guarantor of its neutral status. It was nationalized by Egypt in 1956 and an Anglo-French attempt at intervention was called off after international protest.

suf- /sʌf, səf/ *prefix* assim. form of SUB- before *f.*

suffer /ˈsʌfə(r)/ *v.* **1** *intr.* undergo pain, grief, damage, etc. (*suffers acutely; your reputation will suffer; suffers from neglect*). **2** *tr.* undergo, experience, or be subjected to (pain, loss, grief, defeat, change, etc.) (*suffered banishment*). **3** *tr.* put up with; tolerate (*does not suffer fools gladly*). **4** *intr.* undergo martyrdom. **5** *intr.* (usu. foll. by to + infin.) *archaic* allow. □□ **sufferable** *adj.* **sufferer** *n.* **suffering** *n.* [ME f. AF *suffrir*, *soeffrir*, OF *sof(f)rir* f. L *sufferre* (as SUB-, *ferre* bear)]

sufferance /ˈsʌfərəns/ *n.* **1** tacit consent, abstinence from objection. **2** *archaic* submissiveness. □ **on sufferance** with toleration implied by lack of consent or objection. [ME f. AF, OF *suffraunce* f. LL *sufferentia* (as SUFFER)]

suffice /səˈfaɪs/ *v.* **1** *intr.* (often foll. by *for*, or *to* + infin.) be enough or adequate (*that will suffice for our purpose; suffices to prove it*). **2** *tr.* meet the needs of; satisfy (*six sufficed him*). □ **suffice it to say** I shall content myself with saying. [ME f. OF *suffire* (*suffis-*) f. L *sufficere* (as SUB-, *facere* make)]

sufficiency /səˈfɪʃənsɪ/ *n.* (*pl.* **-ies**) **1** (often foll. by *of*) an adequate amount or adequate resources. **2** *archaic* being sufficient; ability; efficiency. [LL *sufficientia* (as SUFFICIENT)]

sufficient /səˈfɪʃ(ə)nt/ *adj.* **1** sufficing, adequate, enough (*is sufficient for a family; didn't have sufficient funds*). **2** = SELF-SUFFICIENT. **3** *archaic* competent; of adequate ability, resources, etc. □□ **sufficiently** *adv.* [ME f. OF *sufficient* or L *sufficiens* (as SUFFICE)]

suffix /ˈsʌfɪks/ *n.* & *v.* —*n.* **1** a verbal element added at the end of a word to form a derivative (e.g. -*ation,* -*fy,* -*ing,* -*itis*). **2** *Math.* = SUBSCRIPT. —*v.tr.* /also səˈfɪks/ append, esp. as a suffix. □□ **suffixation** /-ˈseɪʃ(ə)n/ *n.* [*suffixum, suffixus* past part. of L *suffigere* (as SUB-, *figere* fix- fasten)]

suffocate /ˈsʌfəkeɪt/ *v.* **1** *tr.* choke or kill by stopping breathing, esp. by pressure, fumes, etc. **2** *tr.* (often foll. by *by, with*) produce a choking or breathless sensation in, esp. by excitement, terror, etc. **3** *intr.* be or feel suffocated or breathless. □□ **suffocating** *adj.* **suffocatingly** *adv.* **suffocation** /-ˈkeɪʃ(ə)n/ *n.* [L *suffocare* (as SUB-, *fauces* throat)]

Suffolk /ˈsʌfək/ a county of eastern England; pop. (1981) 604,600; county town, Ipswich. —*n.* **1** a sheep of a black-faced breed. **2** this breed. □ **Suffolk punch** see PUNCH⁴ 2.

suffragan /ˈsʌfrəgən/ *n.* (in full **suffragan bishop** or **bishop suffragan**) **1** a bishop appointed to help a diocesan bishop in the administration of a diocese. **2** a bishop in relation to his archbishop or metropolitan. □ **suffragan see** the see of a suffragan bishop. □□ **suffraganship** *n.* [ME f. AF & OF, repr. med.L *suffraganeus* assistant (bishop) f. L *suffragium* (see SUFFRAGE): orig. of a bishop summoned to vote in synod]

suffrage /ˈsʌfrɪdʒ/ *n.* **1 a** the right of voting in political elections (*full adult suffrage*). **b** a view expressed by voting; a vote (*gave their suffrages for and against*). **c** opinion in support of a proposal etc. **2** (esp. in *pl.*) *Eccl.* **a** a prayer made by a priest in the liturgy. **b** a short prayer made by a congregation esp. in response to a

priest. **c** *archaic* an intercessory prayer. [ME f. L *suffragium*, partly through F *suffrage*]

suffragette /ˌsʌfrəˈdʒet/ *n. hist.* a woman seeking the right to vote through organized protest. Under the leadership of the Pankhursts the Women's Suffrage Movement became an important political force in Britain in the early 20th c., eventually winning (in 1918) the vote for women over 30. Ten years later British women were given full equality with men in voting rights. [SUFFRAGE + -ETTE]

suffragist /ˈsʌfrədʒɪst/ *n.* esp. *hist.* a person who advocates the extension of the suffrage, esp. to women. □□ **suffragism** *n.*

suffuse /səˈfjuːz/ *v.tr.* **1** (of colour, moisture, etc.) spread from within to colour or moisten (*a blush suffused her cheeks*). **2** cover with colour etc. □□ **suffusion** /-ˈfjuːʒ(ə)n/ *n.* [L *suffundere suffus-* (as SUB-, *fundere* pour)]

Sufi /ˈsuːfɪ/ *n.* (*pl.* **Sufis**) a Muslim ascetic and mystic; a member of any of several orders of Islamic mystics. (See below.) □□ **Sufic** *adj.* **Sufism** *n.* [Arab. *ṣūfī,* perh. f. *ṣūf* wool (from the woollen garment worn)]

Sufism is the esoteric dimension of the Islamic faith, the inner way or spiritual path to mystical union with God. Its followers may be ascetics who isolate themselves from society, more usually they are members of a Sufi order. The many orders have each been founded by a devout individual, and the movement (which seems to have begun in the late 7th c., perhaps in response to the increasing worldliness of the expanding Muslim community) reached its peak in the 13th c. The devotional practices of various orders differ widely (see DERVISH). The Sufi have been responsible for worldwide missionary activity, and their mystical ideas spread through Persian and Arab poetry. In the 19th–20th c. Sufic orders have often taken on overtly political roles; the Sanusiyya of Libya led resistance to the Italian colonial occupation and founded the independent State after the Second World War.

sug- /sʌg, səg/ *prefix* assim. form of SUB- before *g.*

sugar /ˈʃʊgə(r)/ *n.* & *v.* —*n.* **1** a sweet crystalline substance obtained from various plants, esp. the sugar cane and sugar beet, used in cookery, confectionery, brewing, etc.; sucrose. (See below.) **2** *Chem.* any of a group of soluble usu. sweet-tasting crystalline carbohydrates found esp. in plants, e.g. glucose. **3** esp. *US colloq.* darling, dear (used as a term of address). **4** sweet words; flattery. **5** anything comparable to sugar encasing a pill in reconciling a person to what is unpalatable. **6** *sl.* a narcotic drug, esp. heroin or LSD (taken on a lump of sugar). —*v.tr.* **1** sweeten with sugar. **2** make (one's words, meaning, etc.) more pleasant or welcome. **3** coat with sugar (*sugared almond*). **4** spread a sugar mixture on (a tree) to catch moths. □ **sugar beet** a beet, *Beta vulgaris,* from which sugar is extracted. **sugar-candy** see CANDY 1. **sugar cane** *Bot.* any perennial tropical grass of the genus *Saccharum,* esp. *S. officinarum,* with tall stout jointed stems from which sugar is made. **sugar-coated 1** (of food) enclosed in sugar. **2** made superficially attractive. **sugar-daddy** (*pl.* **-ies**) *sl.* an elderly man who lavishes gifts on a young woman. **sugar-gum** *Bot.* an Australian eucalyptus, *Eucalyptus cladocalyx,* with sweet foliage eaten by cattle. **sugar loaf** a conical moulded mass of sugar. **sugar-maple** any of various trees, esp. *Acer saccharum,* from the sap of which sugar is made. **sugar of lead** *Chem.* = *lead acetate* (see LEAD²). **sugar-pea** a variety of pea eaten whole including the pod. **sugar the pill** see PILL. **sugar soap** an alkaline compound for cleaning or removing paint. □□ **sugarless** *adj.* [ME f. OF *çukre, sukere* f. It. *zucchero* prob. f. med.L *succarum* f. Arab. *sukkar*]

Cane-sugar was known in India in prehistoric times. In Europe it was known from the Roman period but only as a rare spice obtained from the East; the Venetian merchants later became prominent in this trade. In 1493 the plant was taken to the West Indies by Christopher Columbus, and has since been introduced into every tropical country. Sugar beet (which will grow in colder climates) was long used as a vegetable and cattle-food. In 1747 the German chemist Andreas Marggraf found a way of extracting from it sugar in crystalline form, and its development as the basis of a successful industry dates from the period of

æ cat ɑː arm e bed ɜː her ɪ sit iː see ɒ hot ɔː saw ʌ run ʊ put uː too ə ago aɪ my

the Napoleonic Wars, when the British blockade prevented the importing of cane-sugar from the West Indies.

Sugar Loaf Mountain a rocky peak rising to a height of 2,074 m (1,296 ft.) north-east of Copacabana Beach, Rio de Janeiro.

sugarplum /ˈʃʊgəˌplʌm/ n. *archaic* a small round sweet of flavoured boiled sugar.

sugary /ˈʃʊgərɪ/ adj. **1** containing or resembling sugar. **2** excessively sweet or esp. sentimental. **3** falsely sweet or pleasant (*sugary compliments*). □□ **sugariness** n.

suggest /səˈdʒest/ v.tr. **1** (often foll. by *that* + clause) propose (a theory, plan, or hypothesis) (*suggested to them that they should wait; suggested a different plan*). **2 a** cause (an idea, memory, association, etc.) to present itself; evoke (*poem suggests peace*). **b** hint at (*his behaviour suggests guilt*). □ **suggest itself** (of an idea etc.) come into the mind. □□ **suggester** n. [L *suggerere* suggest- (as SUB-, *gerere* bring)]

suggestible /səˈdʒestɪb(ə)l/ adj. **1** capable of being suggested. **2** open to suggestion; easily swayed. □□ **suggestibility** /-ˈbɪlɪtɪ/ n.

suggestion /səˈdʒestʃ(ə)n/ n. **1** the act or an instance of suggesting; the state of being suggested. **2** a theory, plan, etc., suggested (*made a helpful suggestion*). **3** a slight trace; a hint (*a suggestion of garlic*). **4** *Psychol.* **a** the insinuation of a belief etc. into the mind. **b** such a belief etc. [ME f. OF f. L *suggestio -onis* (as SUGGEST)]

suggestive /səˈdʒestɪv/ adj. **1** (usu. foll. by *of*) conveying a suggestion; evocative. **2** (esp. of a remark, joke, etc.) indecent; improper. □□ **suggestively** adv. **suggestiveness** n.

suicidal /ˌsuːɪˈsaɪd(ə)l, ˌsjuː-/ adj. **1** inclined to commit suicide. **2** of or concerning suicide. **3** self-destructive; fatally or disastrously rash. □□ **suicidally** adv.

suicide /ˈsuːɪˌsaɪd, ˈsjuː-/ n. & v. —n. **1 a** the intentional killing of oneself. **b** a person who commits suicide. **2** a self-destructive action or course (*political suicide*). **3** (*attrib.*) *Mil.* designating a highly dangerous or deliberately suicidal operation etc. (*a suicide mission*). —v.intr. commit suicide. □ **suicide pact** an agreement between two or more people to commit suicide together. [mod.L *suicida, suicidium* f. L *sui* of oneself]

sui generis /ˌsjuːaɪ ˈdʒenərɪs, ˌsuːɪ ˈgen-/ adj. of its own kind; unique. [L]

sui juris /ˌsjuːaɪ ˈdʒʊərɪs, ˌsuːɪ ˈjʊə-/ adj. *Law* of age; independent. [L]

suilline /ˈsuːɪˌlaɪn/ adj. of the pig family Suidae. [L *suillus* f. *sus* pig]

suint /swɪnt/ n. the natural grease in sheep's wool. [F f. *suer* sweat]

suit /suːt, sjuːt/ n. & v. —n. **1 a** a set of outer clothes of matching material for men, consisting usu. of a jacket, trousers, and sometimes a waistcoat. **b** a similar set of clothes for women usu. having a skirt instead of trousers. **c** (esp. in *comb.*) a set of clothes for a special occasion, occupation, etc. (*play-suit; swim-suit*). **2 a** any of the four sets (spades, hearts, diamonds, clubs) into which a pack of cards is divided. **b** a player's holding in a suit (*his strong suit was clubs*). **c** *Bridge* one of the suits as proposed trumps in bidding, frequently as opposed to no trumps. **3** (in full **suit at law**) a lawsuit (*criminal suit*). **4 a** a petition esp. to a person in authority. **b** the process of courting a woman (*paid suit to her*). **5** (usu. foll. by *of*) a set of sails, armour, etc. —v. **1** tr. go well with (a person's figure, features, character, etc.); become. **2** tr. (also *absol.*) meet the demands or requirements of; satisfy; agree with (*does not suit all tastes; that date will suit*). **3** tr. make fitting or appropriate; accommodate; adapt (*suited his style to his audience*). **4** tr. (as **suited** adj.) appropriate; well-fitted (*not suited to be an engineer*). **5** intr. (usu. foll. by *with*) go well with the appearance etc. of a person (*red hair suits with her complexion*). □ **suit the action to the word** carry out a promise or threat at once. **suit oneself 1** do as one chooses. **2** find something that satisfies one. [ME f. AF *siute*, OF *si(e)ute* f. fem. past part. of Rmc *sequere* (unrecorded) follow: see SUE]

suitable /ˈsuːtəb(ə)l, ˈsjuː-/ adj. (usu. foll. by *to, for*) well fitted for the purpose; appropriate. □□ **suitability** /-ˈbɪlɪtɪ/ n. **suitableness** n. **suitably** adv. [SUIT + -ABLE, after *agreeable*]

suitcase /ˈsuːtkeɪs, ˈsjuː-/ n. a usu. oblong case for carrying clothes etc., having a handle and a flat hinged lid. □□ **suitcaseful** n. (pl. **-fuls**).

suite /swiːt/ n. **1** a set of things belonging together, esp.: **a** a set of rooms in a hotel etc. **b** a sofa, armchairs, etc., of the same design. **2** *Mus.* **a** a set of instrumental compositions, orig. in dance style, to be played in succession. During the 17th–18th c. the suite was one of the most important forms of instrumental music. It was superseded in importance by the sonata and the symphony, and the title was given to works of a lighter type and assemblages of movements from opera or ballet scores; 20th-c. neoclassical composers (e.g. Stravinsky) have revived the term. **b** a set of selected pieces from an opera, musical, etc., arranged to be played as one instrumental work. **3** a set of people in attendance; a retinue. [F (as SUIT)]

suiting /ˈsuːtɪŋ, ˈsjuː-/ n. cloth used for making suits.

suitor /ˈsuːtə(r), ˈsjuː-/ n. **1** a man seeking to marry a specified woman; a wooer. **2** a plaintiff or petitioner in a lawsuit. [ME f. AF *seutor, suitour*, etc., f. L *secutor -oris* f. *sequi secut-* follow]

suk (also **sukh**) var. of SOUK.

Sukarno /suːˈkɑːnəʊ/, Achmad (1901–70), Indonesian statesman, a radical nationalist leader and founder of Indonesia's independence. In 1945 he claimed the title of President, and remained in office after the legal transfer of power from Holland in 1949, becoming a leading statesman of the area, but after about 1955 his position was undermined by economic and diplomatic problems and resistance to his dictatorial tendencies. He lost power to the army in 1965 and was officially stripped of power in 1967.

Sukhotai /ˌsʊkəˈtaɪ/ a town in western Thailand, formerly the capital of an independent State that flourished from the mid-13th to mid-14th c. Its Thai name means 'dawn of happiness'.

sukiyaki /ˌsʊkɪˈjɑːkɪ/ n. a Japanese dish of sliced meat simmered with vegetables and sauce. [Jap.]

Sukkur /sʊˈkʊə(r)/ a city on the Indus River in SE Pakistan; pop. (1981) 191,000. Nearby is the Sukkar Barrage, nearly 1.6 km (1 mile) long, completed in 1932, built across the river and feeding irrigation canals which direct its water to over 12 million hectares (5 million acres) of the Indus valley.

Sulawesi /ˌsʊləˈweɪsɪ/ a large island of Indonesia, east of Borneo, formerly called Celebes; pop. (1980) 9,909,500.

sulcate /ˈsʌlkeɪt/ adj. grooved, fluted, channelled. [L *sulcatus*, past part. of *sulcare* furrow (as SULCUS)]

sulcus /ˈsʌlkəs/ n. (pl. **sulci** /-saɪ/) *Anat.* a groove or furrow, esp. on the surface of the brain. [L]

Suleiman I /ˈsʊlɪmˌɑːn, -leɪˌmɑːn/ 'the Magnificent', (?1495–1566), sultan of Turkey 1520–66, under whom the Ottoman empire reached its peak in military power and in cultural achievements.

sulfa US var. of SULPHA.

sulfanilamide US var. of SULPHANILAMIDE.

sulfate etc. US var. of SULPHATE etc.

sulfur etc. US var. of SULPHUR etc.

sulk /sʌlk/ v. & n. —v.intr. indulge in a sulk, be sulky. —n. (also in pl., prec. by *the*) a period of sullen esp. resentful silence (*having a sulk; got the sulks*). □□ **sulker** n. [perh. back-form. f. SULKY]

sulky /ˈsʌlkɪ/ adj. & n. —adj. (**sulkier, sulkiest**) **1** sullen, morose, or silent, esp. from resentment or ill temper. **2** sluggish. —n. (pl. **-ies**) a light two-wheeled horse-drawn vehicle for one, esp. used in trotting-races. □□ **sulkily** adv. **sulkiness** n. [perh. f. obs. *sulke* hard to dispose of]

Sulla /ˈsʌlə/ (Lucius Cornelius Sulla Felix, *c.*138–78 BC) Roman general and politician. In 88 BC he marched on Rome and ousted the supporters of Marius. After concluding the war in the east by a peace with Mithridates, Sulla invaded Italy in 88 BC and instituted ruthless proscriptions of his enemies. Elected dictator, he pushed through constitutional reforms in favour of the Senate, but resigned in 79 BC and returned to private status. Sulla never aimed at permanent tyranny, but he set the precedent for the use of military force against the State—and for its success.

sullage /ˈsʌlɪdʒ/ n. filth, refuse, sewage. [perh. f. AF *suillage* f. *souiller* SOIL²]

sullen /ˈsʌlən/ adj. & n. —adj. **1** morose, resentful, sulky, unforgiving, unsociable. **2 a** (of a thing) slow-moving. **b** dismal, melancholy (*a sullen sky*). —n. (in pl., usu. prec. by *the*) archaic a sullen frame of mind; depression. □□ **sullenly** adv. **sullenness** /-ənnɪs/ n. [16th-c. alt. of ME *solein* f. AF f. *sol* SOLE⁹]

Sullivan /ˈsʌlɪv(ə)n/, Sir Arthur Seymour (1842–1900), English composer. He first collaborated with the librettist W. S. Gilbert in 1871, and they produced a string of highly popular light operas, many of them for Richard D'Oyly Carte's company at the Savoy theatre. Among the best known are *Trial by Jury* (1875), *HMS Pinafore* (1878), *The Pirates of Penzance* (1879), *Patience* (1881), *The Mikado* (1885), *Ruddigore* (1887), and *The Gondoliers* (1889). He also composed the hymn 'Onward, Christian Soldiers' (1871) and the song *The Lost Chord* (1877).

sully /ˈsʌlɪ/ v.tr. (**-ies**, **-ied**) **1** disgrace or tarnish (a person's reputation or character, a victory, etc.). **2** *poet.* dirty; soil. [perh. f. F *souiller* (as SOIL²)]

sulpha /ˈsʌlfə/ n. (US **sulfa**) any drug derived from sulphanilamide (often *attrib.*: *sulpha drug*). [abbr.]

sulphamic acid /sʌlˈfæmɪk/ n. (US **sulfamic**) a strong acid used in weed-killer, an amide of sulphuric acid. □□ **sulphamate** /ˈsʌlfəˌmeɪt/ n. [SULPHUR + AMIDE]

sulphanilamide /ˌsʌlfəˈnɪləˌmaɪd/ n. (US **sulfanilamide**) a colourless sulphonamide drug with anti-bacterial properties. [*sulphanilic* (SULPHUR, ANILINE) + AMIDE]

sulphate /ˈsʌlfeɪt/ n. (US **sulfate**) a salt or ester of sulphuric acid. [F *sulfate* f. L *sulphur*]

sulphide /ˈsʌlfaɪd/ n. (US **sulfide**) *Chem.* a binary compound of sulphur.

sulphite /ˈsʌlfaɪt/ n. (US **sulfite**) *Chem.* a salt or ester of sulphurous acid. [F *sulfite* alt. of *sulfate* SULPHATE]

sulphonamide /sʌlˈfonəˌmaɪd/ n. (US **sulfonamide**) a substance derived from an amide of a sulphonic acid, able to prevent the multiplication of some pathogenic bacteria. [SULPHONE + AMIDE]

sulphonate /ˈsʌlfəˌneɪt/ n. & v. *Chem.* —n. a salt or ester of sulphonic acid. —v.tr. convert into a sulphonate by reaction with sulphuric acid.

sulphone /ˈsʌlfəʊn/ n. (US **sulfone**) an organic compound containing the SO₂ group united directly to two carbon atoms. □□ **sulphonic** /-ˈfonɪk/ adj. [G *Sulfon* (as SULPHUR)]

sulphur /ˈsʌlfə(r)/ n. & v. (US **sulfur**) —n. **1 a** a pale-yellow non-metallic element having crystalline and amorphous forms (See below). ¶ Symb.: S; atomic number 16. **b** (*attrib.*) like or containing sulphur. **2** the material of which hell-fire and lightning were believed to consist. **3** any yellow butterfly of the family Pieridae. **4** a pale greenish yellow colour. —v.tr. **1** treat with sulphur. **2** fumigate with sulphur. □ **sulphur candle** a candle burnt to produce sulphur dioxide for fumigating. **sulphur dioxide** a colourless pungent gas formed by burning sulphur in air and used as a food preservative. **sulphur spring** a spring impregnated with sulphur or its compounds. □□ **sulphury** adj. [ME f. AF *sulf(e)re*, OF *soufre* f. L *sulfur*, *sulp(h)ur*]

Sulphur, formerly also called brimstone, can occur uncombined in nature and has been known since ancient times. It was recognized as an element in 1777. Elemental sulphur, which can exist in a number of allotropic forms, burns with a blue flame and a suffocating smell, and is used in making gunpowder, matches, and as an antiseptic and fungicide. The most important compound of sulphur, produced in huge amounts, is sulphuric acid, much of which is in turn converted into other compounds. Sulphur compounds of one kind or another play a role in most manufacturing processes, and the element is also essential to living organisms.

sulphurate /ˈsʌlfjʊˌreɪt/ v.tr. (US **sulfurate**) impregnate, fumigate, or treat with sulphur, esp. in bleaching. □□ **sulphuration** /-ˈreɪʃ(ə)n/ n. **sulphurator** n.

sulphureous /sʌlˈfjʊərɪəs/ adj. (US **sulfureous**) **1** of, like, or suggesting sulphur. **2** sulphur-coloured; yellow. [L *sulphureus* f. SULPHUR]

sulphuretted /ˌsʌlfjʊˈretɪd/ adj. (US **sulfureted**) archaic containing sulphur in combination. □ **sulphuretted hydrogen** hydrogen sulphide. [*sulphuret* sulphide f. mod.L *sulphuretum*]

sulphuric /sʌlˈfjʊərɪk/ adj. (US **sulfuric**) *Chem.* containing sexivalent sulphur. □ **sulphuric acid** a dense oily colourless highly acid and corrosive fluid much used in the chemical industry. ¶ Chem. formula: H₂SO₄. [F *sulfurique* (as SULPHUR)]

sulphurize /ˈsʌlfjʊəˌraɪz/ v.tr. (also **-ise**, US **sulfurize**) = SULPHURATE. □□ **sulphurization** /-ˈzeɪʃ(ə)n/ n. [F *sulfuriser* (as SULPHUR)]

sulphurous /ˈsʌlfərəs/ adj. (US **sulfurous**) **1** relating to or suggestive of sulphur, esp. in colour. **2** *Chem.* containing quadrivalent sulphur. □ **sulphurous acid** an unstable weak acid used as a reducing and bleaching acid. [L *sulphurosus* f. SULPHUR]

sultan /ˈsʌlt(ə)n/ n. **1 a** a Muslim sovereign. **b** (**the Sultan**) *hist.* the sultan of Turkey. **2** a variety of white domestic fowl from Turkey. □□ **sultanate** /-ˌneɪt/ n. [F *sultan* or med.L *sultanus* f. Arab. *sulṭān* power, ruler f. *saluṭa* rule]

sultana /sʌlˈtɑːnə/ n. **1 a** a seedless raisin used in puddings, cakes, etc. **b** the small pale yellow grape producing this. **2** the mother, wife, concubine, or daughter of a sultan. [It., fem. of *sultano* = SULTAN]

sultry /ˈsʌltrɪ/ adj. (**sultrier**, **sultriest**) **1** (of the atmosphere or the weather) hot or oppressive; close. **2** (of a person, character, etc.) passionate; sensual. □□ **sultrily** adv. **sultriness** n. [obs. *sulter* SWELTER]

Sulu Sea /ˈsuːluː/ an arm of the South China Sea separating the islands of the Philippines from NE Borneo.

sum /sʌm/ n. & v. —n. **1** the total amount resulting from the addition of two or more items, facts, ideas, feelings, etc. (*the sum of two and three is five; the sum of their objections is this*). **2** a particular amount of money (*paid a large sum for it*). **3 a** an arithmetical problem (*could not work out the sum*). **b** (esp. *pl.*) *colloq.* arithmetic work, esp. at an elementary level (*was good at sums*). —v.tr. (**summed**, **summing**) find the sum of. □ **in sum** in brief. **summing-up 1** a review of evidence and a direction given by a judge to a jury. **2** a recapitulation of the main points of an argument, case, etc. **sum total** = sense 1 of n. **sum up 1** (esp. of a judge) recapitulate or review the evidence in a case etc. **2** form or express an idea of the character of (a person, situation, etc.). **3** collect into or express as a total or whole. [ME f. OF *summe*, *somme* f. L *summa* main part, fem. of *summus* highest]

sumac /ˈsuːmæk, ˈʃuː-, ˈsjuː-/ n. (also **sumach**) **1** any shrub or tree of the genus *Rhus*, having reddish cone-shaped fruits used as a spice in cooking. **2** the dried and ground leaves of this used in tanning and dyeing. [ME f. OF *sumac* or med.L *sumac(h)* f. Arab. *summāk*]

Sumatra /sʊˈmɑːtrə/ (also **Sumatera**) a large island of Indonesia, separated from the Malay Peninsula by the Strait of Malacca; pop. (1980) 28,016,160.

Sumba /ˈsʊmbə/ (also **Sandalwood Island**) an island of the Lesser Sundas, Indonesia, lying to the south of the islands of Flores and Sumbawa; chief town, Waingapu.

Sumbawa /sʊmˈbɑːwə/ an island in the Lesser Sundas, Indonesia, situated to the east of Lombok; chief town, Raba.

Sumer /ˈsuːmə(r)/ the name used in antiquity from the 3rd millennium BC for southern Mesopotamia, the region inhabited by Sumerian-speaking people and later known as Babylonia.

Sumerian /suːˈmɪərɪən, sjuː-/ adj. & n. —adj. of or relating to a non-Semitic language, people, and civilization native to Sumer in the 4th millennium BC and possibly earlier. —n. **1** a member of this people. **2** their language. The Sumerians were a hybrid stock, speaking an agglutinative language related structurally to Turkish, Hungarian, Finnish, and several Caucasian dialects. As the first historically attested civilization they are credited with the invention of cuneiform writing, the sexagesimal system of mathematics, and the socio-political institution of the city-state with bureaucracies, legal codes, division of labour, and a money economy. Their art, literature, and theology had a profound cultural and religious influence on the rest of Mesopotamia and beyond, which continued long after the Sumerian

b but d dog f few g get h he j yes k cat l leg m man n no p pen r red s sit t top v voice

demise *c*.2000 BC, as the prototype of Akkadian, Hurrian, Canaanite, Hittite, and eventually, biblical literature.

Sumgait /ˌsʊmgɑːˈiːt/ an industrial city of the Soviet republic of Azerbaijan on the western shore of the Caspian Sea; pop. (est. 1987) 234,000.

summa /ˈsʌmə/ *n.* (*pl.* **summae** /-miː/) a summary of what is known of a subject. [ME f. L: see SUM]

summa cum laude /ˌsʊmə kʊm ˈlaʊdeɪ/ *adv. & adj.* esp. *US* (of a degree, diploma, etc.) of the highest standard; with the highest distinction. [L, = with highest praise]

summarize /ˈsʌməˌraɪz/ *v.tr.* (also **-ise**) make or be a summary of; sum up. □□ **summarist** *n.* **summarizable** *adj.* **summarization** /-ˈzeɪʃ(ə)n/ *n.* **summarizer** *n.*

summary /ˈsʌmərɪ/ *n. & adj.* —*n.* (*pl.* **-ies**) a brief account; an abridgement. —*adj.* **1** dispensing with needless details or formalities; brief (*a summary account*). **2** *Law* (of a trial etc.) without the customary legal formalities (*summary justice*). □ **summary conviction** a conviction made by a judge or magistrates without a jury. **summary jurisdiction** the authority of a court to use summary proceedings and arrive at a judgement. **summary offence** an offence within the scope of a summary court. □□ **summarily** *adv.* **summariness** *n.* [ME f. L *summarium* f. L *summa* SUM]

summation /sʌˈmeɪʃ(ə)n/ *n.* **1** the finding of a total or sum; an addition. **2** a summing-up. □□ **summational** *adj.*

summer[1] /ˈsʌmə(r)/ *n. & v.* —*n.* **1** the warmest season of the year, in the N. hemisphere from June to August and in the S. hemisphere from December to February. **2** *Astron.* the period from the summer solstice to the autumnal equinox. **3** the hot weather typical of summer. **4** (often foll. by *of*) the mature stage of life; the height of achievement, powers, etc. **5** (esp. in *pl.*) *poet.* a year (esp. of a person's age) (*a child of ten summers*). **6** (*attrib.*) characteristic of or suitable for summer (*summer clothes*). —*v.* **1** *intr.* (usu. foll. by *at, in*) pass the summer. **2** *tr.* (often foll. by *at, in*) pasture (cattle). □ **summer-house** a light building in a garden etc. used for sitting in in fine weather. **summer lightning** sheet lightning without thunder, resulting from a distant storm. **Summer Palace** a palace (now in ruins) of the Chinese emperors near Peking. **summer pudding** *Brit.* a pudding of soft summer fruit encased in bread or sponge. **summer school** a course of lectures etc. held during the summer vacation, esp. at a university. **summer solstice** see SOLSTICE. **summer time** *Brit.* the period between March and October during which the clocks are advanced an hour (cf. SUMMERTIME). **summer-weight** (of clothes) suitable for use in summer, esp. because of their light weight. □□ **summerless** *adj.* **summerly** *adv.* **summery** *adj.* [OE *sumor*]

summer[2] /ˈsʌmə(r)/ *n.* (in full **summer-tree**) a horizontal bearing beam, esp. one supporting joists or rafters. [ME f. AF *sumer*, *somer* packhorse, beam, OF *somier* f. LL *sagmarius* f. *sagma* f. Gk *sagma* pack-saddle]

summersault var. of SOMERSAULT.

summertime /ˈsʌməˌtaɪm/ *n.* the season or period of summer (cf. *summer time*).

summit /ˈsʌmɪt/ *n.* **1** the highest point, esp. of a mountain; the apex. **2** the highest degree of power, ambition, etc. **3** (in full **summit meeting**, **talks**, etc.) a discussion, esp. on disarmament etc., between heads of government. □□ **summitless** *adj.* [ME f. OF *somet*, *som(m)ete* f. *som* top f. L *summum* neut. of *summus*]

summon /ˈsʌmən/ *v.tr.* **1** call upon to appear, esp. as a defendant or witness in a lawcourt. **2** (usu. foll. by *to* + infin.) call upon (*summoned her to assist*). **3** call together for a meeting or some other purpose (*summoned the members to attend*). □ **summon up** (often foll. by *to, for*) gather (courage, spirits, resources, etc.) (*summoned up her strength for the task*). □□ **summonable** *adj.* **summoner** *n.* [ME f. OF *somondre* f. L *summonēre* (as SUB-, *monēre* warn)]

summons /ˈsʌmənz/ *n. & v.* —*n.* (*pl.* **summonses**) **1** an authoritative or urgent call to attend on some occasion or do something. **2 a** a call to appear before a judge or magistrate. **b** the writ containing such a summons. —*v.tr.* esp. *Law* serve with a summons. [ME f. OF *somonce*, *sumunse* f. L *summonita* fem. past part. of *summonēre*: see SUMMON]

summum bonum /ˌsʊməm ˈbɒnəm, ˈbəʊ-/ *n.* the highest good, esp. as the end or determining principle in an ethical system. [L]

sumo /ˈsuːməʊ/ *n.* (*pl.* **-os**) **1** a style of Japanese wrestling, in which a participant is defeated by touching the ground with any part of the body except the soles of the feet or by moving outside the marked area. **2** a sumo wrestler. [Jap.]

sump /sʌmp/ *n.* **1** a pit, well, hole, etc. in which superfluous liquid collects in mines, machines, etc. **2** a cesspool. [ME, = marsh f. MDu., MLG *sump*, or (mining) G *Sumpf*, rel. to SWAMP]

sumpter /ˈsʌmptə(r)/ *n. archaic* **1** a packhorse. **2** any pack-animal (*sumpter-mule*). [ME f. OF *som(m)etier* f. LL f. Gk *sagma* *-atos* pack-saddle: cf. SUMMER[2]]

sumptuary /ˈsʌmptjʊərɪ/ *adj.* **1** regulating expenditure. **2** (of a law or edict etc.) limiting private expenditure in the interests of the State. [L *sumptuarius* f. *sumptus* cost f. *sumere* sumpt- take]

sumptuous /ˈsʌmptjʊəs/ *adj.* rich, lavish, costly (*a sumptuous setting*). □□ **sumptuosity** /-ˈɒsɪtɪ/ *n.* **sumptuously** *adv.* **sumptuousness** *n.* [ME f. OF *somptueux* f. L *sumptuosus* (as SUMPTUARY)]

Sun. *abbr.* Sunday.

sun /sʌn/ *n. & v.* —*n.* **1 a** (also **Sun**) the star round which the Earth orbits and from which it receives light and warmth. (See below.) **b** any similar star in the universe with or without planets. **2** the light or warmth received from the sun (*pull down the blinds and keep out the sun*). **3** *poet.* a day or a year. **4** *poet.* a person or thing regarded as a source of glory, radiance, etc. —*v.* (**sunned**, **sunning**) **1** *refl.* bask in the sun. **2** *tr.* expose to the sun. **3** *intr.* sun oneself. □ **against the sun** anticlockwise. **beneath** (or **under**) **the sun** anywhere in the world. **in the sun** exposed to the sun's rays. **on which the sun never sets** (of an empire etc.) worldwide. **sun and planet** a system of gearing cog wheels. **sun-baked** dried or hardened or baked from the heat of the sun. **sun-bath** a period of exposing the body to the sun. **sun bear** a small black bear, *Helarctos malayanus*, of SE Asia, with a light-coloured mark on its chest. **sun-blind** *Brit.* a window awning. **sun-bonnet** a bonnet of cotton etc. covering the neck and shading the face, esp. for children. **sun-bow** a spectrum of colours like a rainbow produced by the sun shining on spray etc. **sun-dance** a dance of N. American Indians in honour of the sun. **sun-deck** the upper deck of a steamer. **sun-disc** a winged disc, emblematic of the sun-god. **sun-dog** = PARHELION. **sun-dress** a dress without sleeves and with a low neck. **sun-dried** dried by the sun, not by artificial heat. **sun-glasses** glasses tinted to protect the eyes from sunlight or glare. **sun-god** the sun worshipped as a deity. **sun-hat** a hat designed to protect the head from the sun. **sun-helmet** a helmet of cork etc. formerly worn by White people in the tropics. **sun in splendour** *Heraldry* the sun with rays and a human face. **one's sun is set** the time of one's prosperity is over. **Sun King** Louis XIV of France, so called from the magnificence of his reign. **sun-kissed** warmed or affected by the sun. **sun-lamp 1** a lamp giving ultraviolet rays for an artificial suntan, therapy, etc. **2** *Cinematog.* a large lamp with a parabolic reflector used in film-making. **sun lounge** a room with large windows, designed to receive sunlight. **sun parlor** *US* = *sun lounge*. **sun-rays 1** sunbeams. **2** ultraviolet rays used therapeutically. **sun-roof** a sliding roof on a car. **sun-stone** a cat's eye gem, esp. feldspar with embedded flecks of haematite etc. **sun-suit** a play-suit, esp. for children, suitable for sunbathing. **sun-up** esp. *US* sunrise. **sun visor** a fixed or movable shield at the top of a vehicle windscreen to shield the eyes from the sun. **take** (or **shoot**) **the sun** *Naut.* ascertain the altitude of the sun with a sextant in order to fix the latitude. **with the sun** clockwise. □□ **sunless** *adj.* **sunlessness** *n.* **sunlike** *adj.* **sunproof** *adj.* **sunward** *adj. & adv.* **sunwards** *adv.* [OE *sunne*, *sunna*]

The central body of the solar system, the Sun is a luminous body which provides the light and energy which sustains living creatures on Earth. It is a star of the type known to astronomers as a G2 subdwarf, a sphere of hydrogen and helium 1.4 million km in diameter which obtains its energy from nuclear fusion reactions deep within its interior. Temperatures at the centre must be high enough to sustain these reactions, say twenty million degrees or so; but the surface temperature is a little under 6000 °C. The visible surface is marked by occasional sunspots, local regions where temperatures are 2000 ° cooler than the rest of the surface, which appear to arise from local intense magnetic fields. Above this region, known as the photosphere, are the chromosphere and corona, regions of much higher temperature. The apparent path of the Sun across the sky (which is merely a reflection of the Earth's orbit about the Sun) determines the terrestrial seasons.

sunbathe /'sʌnbeɪð/ v.intr. bask in the sun, esp. to tan the body. □□ **sunbather** n.

sunbeam /'sʌnbiːm/ n. a ray of sunlight.

sunbed /'sʌnbed/ n. **1** a lightweight, usu. folding, chair with a seat long enough to support the legs, used for sunbathing. **2** a bed for lying on under a sun-lamp.

sunbelt /'sʌnbelt/ n. a strip of territory receiving a high amount of sunshine, esp. (**the Sunbelt**) the region in the southern US stretching from California to Florida.

sunbird /'sʌnbɜːd/ n. any small bright-plumaged Old World bird of the family Nectariniidae, resembling a humming-bird.

sunblock /'sʌnblɒk/ n. a cream or lotion for protecting the skin from the sun.

sunburn /'sʌnbɜːn/ n. & v. —n. tanning and inflammation of the skin caused by over-exposure to the sun. —v.intr. **1** suffer from sunburn. **2** (as **sunburnt** or **sunburned** adj.) suffering from sunburn; brown or tanned.

sunburst /'sʌnbɜːst/ n. **1** something resembling the sun and its rays, esp.: **a** an ornament, brooch, etc. **b** a firework. **2** the sun shining suddenly from behind clouds.

Sun City a resort centre in the Mankwe district of Bophuthatswana, South Africa.

sundae /'sʌndeɪ, -dɪ/ n. a dish of ice-cream with fruit, nuts, syrup, etc. [perh. f. SUNDAY, either because the dish orig. included left-over ice-cream sold cheaply on Monday, or because it was at first sold only on Sunday, having been devised (according to some accounts) to circumvent Sunday legislation. The spelling is sometimes said to have been altered from *Sunday* out of deference to religious people's feelings]

Sunda Islands /'sʌndə/ islands of the Malay Archipelago, Indonesia, divided into two groups, the **Greater Sunda Islands** which include Borneo, Sumatra, Java, and the islands of Sulawesi, and the **Lesser Sunda Islands** which lie to the east of Java and include Sumbawa, Flores, Sumba, and Timor.

Sunday /'sʌndeɪ, -dɪ/ n. & adv. —n. **1** the first day of the week, a Christian holiday and day of worship. (See below.) **2** a newspaper published on a Sunday. —adv. colloq. **1** on Sunday. **2** (**Sundays**) on Sundays; each Sunday. □ **Sunday best** joc. a person's best clothes, kept for Sunday use. **Sunday letter** = dominical letter. **Sunday painter** an amateur painter, esp. one with little training. **Sunday school** a school held on Sundays for children, now only for religious instruction. Although there were earlier examples of schools for poor children on Sundays, the movement owes its success to Robert Raikes (1735–1811), a native of Gloucester, who in 1780 started a school in his own parish which became widely imitated. [OE *sunnandæg*, transl. of L *dies solis*, Gk *hēmera hēliou* day of the sun]

The old pagan 'day of the sun' was given a Christian interpretation and referred to Christ, the 'sun of righteousness' (Mal. 4: 2), being called the 'day of the Lord'. Already in New Testament times Sunday began to replace (for Christians) the Jewish sabbath, chiefly in commemoration of the Resurrection. Its observance as a day of rest, consecrated especially to the service of God, began to be regulated by both ecclesiastical and civil legislation from the 4th c. In the 19th c. Sunday was still a day mainly devoted to duties of piety, but the increasing secularization of life in the 20th c. has considerably reduced its religious observance, though requirement to work on that day is regarded as unsocial.

sunder /'sʌndə(r)/ v.tr. & intr. archaic or literary □ **in sunder**

apart. [OE *sundrian*, f. *āsundrian* etc.: *in sunder* f. ME f. o(n)*sunder* ASUNDER]

Sunderbans /'sʌndəbənz/ a swamp region at the mouth of the Ganges Delta in Bangladesh and the Indian State of West Bengal.

Sunderland /'sʌndələnd/ an industrial city in NE England, at the mouth of the River Wear; pop. (1981) 195,900.

sundew /'sʌndjuː/ n. any small insect-consuming bog-plant of the family Droseraceae, esp. of the genus *Drosera* with hairs secreting drops of moisture.

sundial /'sʌndaɪəl/ n. an instrument showing the time by the shadow of a pointer cast by the sun on to a graduated dial. It is probably the most ancient time-measuring instrument. Sundials in which the edge of the gnomon is parallel to the Earth's axis (so that it points to the north celestial pole) can show solar time to an accuracy of a minute or two; for centuries they were used as a check on the accuracy of the clocks and watches which eventually superseded them, until telegraphic and radio time signals became available.

sundown /'sʌndaʊn/ n. sunset.

sundowner /'sʌnˌdaʊnə(r)/ n. **1** Austral. a tramp who arrives at a sheep station etc. in the evening for food and shelter. **2** Brit. colloq. an alcoholic drink taken at sunset.

sundry /'sʌndrɪ/ adj. & n. —adj. various; several (*sundry items*). —n. (pl. **-ies**) **1** (in pl.) items or oddments not mentioned individually. **2** Austral. Cricket = EXTRA n. 5. [OE *syndrig* separate, rel. to SUNDER]

sunfast /'sʌnfɑːst/ adj. US (of dye) not subject to fading by sunlight.

sunfish /'sʌnfɪʃ/ n. any of various almost spherical fish, esp. a large ocean fish, *Mola mola*.

sunflower /'sʌnˌflaʊə(r)/ n. any very tall plant of the genus *Helianthus*, esp. *H. annus* with very large showy golden-rayed flowers, grown also for its seeds which yield an edible oil.

Sung /sʊŋ/ the name of the dynasty which ruled in China 960–1279.

sung past part. of SING.

sunk past and past part. of SINK.

sunken /'sʌŋkən/ adj. **1** that has been sunk. **2** beneath the surface; submerged. **3** (of the eyes, cheeks, etc.) hollow, depressed. □ **sunken garden** a garden placed below the general level of its surroundings. [past part. of SINK]

sunlight /'sʌnlaɪt/ n. light from the sun.

sunlit /'sʌnlɪt/ adj. illuminated by sunlight.

sunn /sʌn/ n. (in full **sunn hemp**) an E. Indian hemplike fibre. [Urdu & Hindi *san* f. Skr. *śāṇā* hempen]

Sunna /'sʌnə/ n. a traditional portion of Muslim law based on Muhammad's words or acts but not written by him, accepted as authoritative by many Muslims but rejected by the Shiites. [Arab., = form, way, course, rule]

Sunni /'sʌnɪ/ n. & adj. —n. (pl. same or **Sunnis**) **1** one of the two main branches of Islam, regarding the Sunna as equal in authority to the Koran (cf. SHIAH). **2** an adherent of this branch of Islam. (See below.) —adj. of or relating to Sunni.

Sunnis comprise the main community in most Muslim countries other than Iran. The split occurred early in the history of Islam over the question of allegiance to the nascent Ummayyad dynasty (supported by the Sunnis) versus the family of Ali, son-in-law of the Prophet Muhammad and fourth caliph. After his assassination and that of his son Husayn at the Battle of Kerbala (in present-day Iraq) in 680, one group of Muslims broke away from the main body, declaring their allegiance to the martyred sons, and calling themselves the Shia (= party). What became known as the Sunni Muslims continued to follow the reigning caliph. From the basic split in attitudes to leadership of the community have followed other differences in community organization and legal practice, but doctrinally Sunni and Shiite Muslims adhere to the same body of tenets.

Sunnite /'sʌnaɪt/ n. & adj. —n. an adherent of the Sunni branch of Islam. —adj. of or relating to Sunni.

sunny /'sʌnɪ/ adj. (**sunnier, sunniest**) **1 a** bright with sunlight. **b** exposed to or warmed by the sun. **2** cheery and bright in temperament. □ **the sunny side 1** the side of a house, street, etc. that gets most sun. **2** the more cheerful aspect of circumstances etc. (*always looks on the sunny side*). □□ **sunnily** *adv.* **sunniness** *n.*

sunrise /ˈsʌnraɪz/ *n.* **1** the sun's rising at dawn. **2** the coloured sky associated with this. **3** the time at which sunrise occurs. □ **sunrise industry** any newly established industry, esp. in electronics and telecommunications, regarded as signalling prosperity.

sunset /ˈsʌnset/ *n.* **1** the sun's setting in the evening. **2** the coloured sky associated with this. **3** the time at which sunset occurs. **4** the declining period of life.

Sunset Boulevard a road which links the centre of Los Angeles with the Pacific Ocean 48 km (30 miles) to the west. The eastern section of the road between Fairfax Avenue and Beverly Hills is known as Sunset Strip.

sunshade /ˈsʌnʃeɪd/ *n.* **1** a parasol. **2** an awning.

sunshine /ˈsʌnʃaɪn/ *n.* **1 a** the light of the sun. **b** an area lit by the sun. **2** fine weather. **3** cheerfulness; joy (*brought sunshine into her life*). **4** *Brit. colloq.* a form of address. □ **sunshine roof** = *sun-roof.* □□ **sunshiny** *adj.*

sunspot /ˈsʌnspɒt/ *n.* one of the dark patches, changing in shape and size and lasting for varying periods, observed on the sun's surface.

sunstar /ˈsʌnstɑː(r)/ *n.* any starfish of the genus *Solaster*, with many rays.

sunstroke /ˈsʌnstrəʊk/ *n.* acute prostration or collapse from the excessive heat of the sun.

suntan /ˈsʌntæn/ *n. & v.* —*n.* the brownish colouring of skin caused by exposure to the sun. —*v.intr.* (**-tanned, -tanning**) colour the skin with a suntan.

suntrap /ˈsʌntræp/ *n.* a place sheltered from the wind and suitable for catching the sunshine.

Sun Yat-sen /suːn jætˈsen/ (also **Sun Yixian**) (1866–1925), Chinese statesman, generally considered to be the 'Father of the Revolution'. Sun Yat-sen spent the period 1895–1911 in exile after an unsuccessful attempt to overthrow the Manchus, but returned to play a crucial part in the successful revolution and to organize the Kuomintang (1911–12). In the chaotic period that followed he was briefly provisional president of the Chinese Republic and a decade later president of the Southern Chinese Republic before dying of cancer.

sup[1] /sʌp/ *v. & n.* —*v.tr.* (**supped, supping**) **1** take (soup, tea, etc.) by sips or spoonfuls. **2** esp. *N.Engl. colloq.* drink (alcohol). —*n.* a sip of liquid. [OE *sūpan*]

sup[2] /sʌp/ *v.intr.* (**supped, supping**) (usu. foll. by *off, on*) *archaic* take supper. [OF *super, soper*]

sup- /sʌp, səp/ *prefix* assim. form of SUB- before *p.*

super /ˈsuːpə(r), ˈsjuː-/ *adj. & n.* —*adj.* **1** (also **super-duper** /-ˈduːpə(r)/) *colloq.* (also as *int.*) exceptional; splendid. **2** *Commerce* superfine. **3** *Commerce* (of a measure) superficial, in square (not lineal or solid) measure (*120 super ft.; 120 ft. super*). —*n. colloq.* **1** *Theatr.* a supernumerary actor. **2** a superintendent. **3** superphosphate. **4** an extra, unwanted, or unimportant person; a supernumerary. **5** *Commerce* superfine cloth or manufacture. [abbr.]

super- /ˈsuːpə(r), ˈsjuː-/ *comb. form* forming nouns, adjectives, and verbs, meaning: **1** above, beyond, or over in place or time or conceptually (*superstructure; supernormal; superimpose*). **2** to a great or extreme degree (*superabundant; superhuman*). **3** extra good or large of its kind (*supertanker*). **4** of a higher kind, esp. in names of classificatory divisions (*superclass*). [from or after L *super-* f. *super* above, beyond]

superable /ˈsuːpərəb(ə)l, ˈsjuː-/ *adj.* able to be overcome. [L *superabilis* f. *superare* overcome]

superabound /ˌsuːpərəˈbaʊnd, ˌsjuː-/ *v.intr.* be very or too abundant. [LL *superabundare* (as SUPER-, ABOUND)]

superabundant /ˌsuːpərəˈbʌnd(ə)nt, ˌsjuː-/ *adj.* abounding beyond what is normal or right. □□ **superabundance** *n.* **superabundantly** *adv.* [ME f. LL *superabundare*: see SUPERABOUND]

superadd /ˌsuːpərˈæd, ˌsjuː-/ *v.tr.* add over and above. □□ **superaddition** /-əˈdɪʃ(ə)n/ *n.* [ME f. L *superaddere* (as SUPER-, ADD)]

superaltar /ˈsuːpərˌɔːltə(r), ˈsjuː-, -ˌɒltə(r)/ *n. Eccl.* a portable slab of stone consecrated for use on an unconsecrated altar etc. [ME f. med.L *superaltare* (as SUPER-, ALTAR)]

superannuate /ˌsuːpərˈænjʊˌeɪt, ˌsjuː-/ *v.tr.* **1** retire (a person) with a pension. **2** dismiss or discard as too old for use, work, etc. **3** (as **superannuated** *adj.*) too old for work or use; obsolete. □□ **superannuable** *adj.* [back-form. f. *superannuated* f. med.L *superannuatus* f. L SUPER- + *annus* year]

superannuation /ˌsuːpərˌænjʊˈeɪʃ(ə)n, ˌsjuː-/ *n.* **1** a pension paid to a retired person. **2** a regular payment made towards this by an employed person. **3** the process or an instance of superannuating.

superaqueous /ˌsuːpərˈeɪkwɪəs, ˌsjuː-/ *adj.* above water.

superb /suːˈpɜːb, sjuː-/ *adj.* **1** of the most impressive, splendid, grand, or majestic kind (*superb courage; a superb specimen*). **2** *colloq.* excellent; fine. □□ **superbly** *adv.* **superbness** *n.* [F *superbe* or L *superbus* proud]

Super Bowl the championship game of the National Football League in US professional football, played annually in January from 1967 onwards.

supercalender /ˌsuːpəˈkælɪndə(r), ˌsjuː-/ *v.tr.* give a highly glazed finish to (paper) by extra calendering.

supercargo /ˌsuːpəˈkɑːɡəʊ, ˈsjuː-/ *n.* (pl. **-oes**) an officer in a merchant ship managing sales etc. of cargo. [earlier *supracargo* f. Sp. *sobrecargo* f. *sobre* over + *cargo* CARGO]

supercelestial /ˌsuːpəsɪˈlestɪəl, ˌsjuː-/ *adj.* **1** above the heavens. **2** more than heavenly. [LL *supercaelestis* (as SUPER-, CELESTIAL)]

supercharge /ˈsuːpəˌtʃɑːdʒ, ˈsjuː-/ *v.tr.* **1** (usu. foll. by *with*) charge (the atmosphere etc.) with energy, emotion, etc. **2** use a supercharger on (an internal-combustion engine).

supercharger /ˈsuːpəˌtʃɑːdʒə(r), ˈsjuː-/ *n.* a device supplying air or fuel to an internal-combustion engine at above normal pressure to increase efficiency.

superciliary /ˌsuːpəˈsɪlɪərɪ, ˌsjuː-/ *adj. Anat.* of or concerning the eyebrow; over the eye. [L *supercilium* eyebrow (as SUPER-, *cilium* eyelid)]

supercilious /ˌsuːpəˈsɪlɪəs, ˌsjuː-/ *adj.* assuming an air of contemptuous indifference or superiority. □□ **superciliously** *adv.* **superciliousness** *n.* [L *superciliosus* (as SUPERCILIARY)]

superclass /ˈsuːpəˌklɑːs, ˈsjuː-/ *n.* a taxonomic category between class and phylum.

supercolumnar /ˌsuːpəkəˈlʌmnə(r), ˌsjuː-/ *adj. Archit.* having one order or set of columns above another. □□ **supercolumniation** /-nɪˈeɪʃ(ə)n/ *n.*

supercomputer /ˌsuːpəkəmˈpjuːtə(r), ˌsjuː-/ *n.* a powerful computer capable of dealing with complex problems. □□ **supercomputing** *n.*

superconductivity /ˌsuːpəˌkɒndʌkˈtɪvɪtɪ, ˌsjuː-/ *n. Physics* the property of zero electrical resistance in some substances at very low absolute temperatures. Discovered in 1911 by H. Kamerlingh Onnes and at first regarded merely as a scientific curiosity, superconductivity can now be explained in terms of quantum theory. Knowledge of the phenomenon has made possible the construction of large electromagnets which are able to operate without expending large quantities of electrical energy. □□ **superconducting** /-kənˈdʌktɪŋ/ *adj.* **superconductive** /-kənˈdʌktɪv/ *adj.*

superconductor /ˌsuːpəkənˈdʌktə(r), ˌsjuː-/ *n. Physics* a substance having superconductivity.

superconscious /ˌsuːpəˈkɒnʃəs, ˌsjuː-/ *adj.* transcending human consciousness. □□ **superconsciously** *adv.* **superconsciousness** *n.*

supercool /ˈsuːpəˌkuːl, -ˈkuːl, ˈsjuː-/ *v. & adj.* —*v. Chem.* **1** *tr.* cool (a liquid) below its freezing-point without solidification or crystallization. **2** *intr.* (of a liquid) be cooled in this way. —*adj. sl.* very cool, relaxed, fine, etc.

supercritical /ˌsuːpəˈkrɪtɪk(ə)l, ˌsjuː-/ *adj. Physics* of more than critical mass etc.

super-duper var. of SUPER *adj.* 1.

superego /ˌsuːpərˈiːgəʊ, -ˈegəʊ, ˌsjuː-/ n. (pl. **-os**) Psychol. the part of the mind that acts as a conscience and responds to social rules.

superelevation /ˌsuːpərˌelɪˈveɪʃ(ə)n, ˌsjuː-/ n. the amount by which the outer edge of a curve on a road or railway is above the inner edge.

supereminent /ˌsuːpərˈemɪnənt, ˌsjuː-/ adj. supremely eminent, exalted, or remarkable. □□ **supereminence** n. **supereminently** adv. [L supereminēre rise above (as SUPER-, EMINENT)]

supererogation /ˌsuːpərˌerəˈgeɪʃ(ə)n, ˌsjuː-/ n. the performance of more than duty requires. □ **works of supererogation** RC Ch. actions believed to form a reserve fund of merit that can be drawn on by prayer in favour of sinners. □□ **supererogatory** /-rɪˈrɒgətərɪ/ adj. [LL supererogatio f. supererogare pay in addition (as SUPER-, erogare pay out)]

superexcellent /ˌsuːpərˈeksələnt, ˌsjuː-/ adj. very or supremely excellent. □□ **superexcellence** n. **superexcellently** adv. [LL superexcellens (as SUPER-, EXCELLENT)]

superfamily /ˈsuːpəˌfæmɪlɪ, ˈsjuː-/ n. (pl. **-ies**) a taxonomic category between family and order.

superfatted /ˌsuːpəˈfætɪd, ˌsjuː-/ adj. (of soap) containing extra fat.

superfecundation /ˌsuːpəˌfiːkənˈdeɪʃ(ə)n, ˌsjuː-/ n. = SUPERFETATION 1.

superfetation /ˌsuːpəfiːˈteɪʃ(ə)n, ˌsjuː-/ n. 1 Med. & Zool. a second conception during pregnancy giving rise to embryos of different ages in the uterus. 2 Bot. the fertilization of the same ovule by different kinds of pollen. 3 the accretion of one thing on another. [F superfétation or f. mod.L superfetatio f. L superfetare (as SUPER-, fetus FOETUS)]

superficial /ˌsuːpəˈfɪʃ(ə)l, ˌsjuː-/ adj. 1 of or on the surface; lacking depth (a superficial knowledge; superficial wounds). 2 swift or cursory (a superficial examination). 3 apparent but not real (a superficial resemblance). 4 (esp. of a person) having no depth of character or knowledge; trivial; shallow. 5 Commerce (of a measure) square (cf. SUPER adj. 3). □□ **superficiality** /-ʃɪˈælɪtɪ/ n. (pl. **-ies**). **superficially** adv. **superficialness** n. [LL superficialis f. L (as SUPERFICIES)]

superficies /ˌsuːpəˈfɪʃɪˌiːz, ˌsjuː-/ n. (pl. same) Geom. a surface. [L (as SUPER-, facies face)]

superfine /ˈsuːpəˌfaɪn, ˈsjuː-/ adj. 1 Commerce of extra quality. 2 pretending great refinement. [med.L superfinus (as SUPER-, FINE[1])]

superfluity /ˌsuːpəˈfluːɪtɪ, ˌsjuː-/ n. (pl. **-ies**) 1 the state of being superfluous. 2 a superfluous amount or thing. [ME f. OF superfluité f. LL superfluitas -tatis f. L superfluus: see SUPERFLUOUS]

superfluous /suːˈpɜːfluəs, sjuː-/ adj. more than enough, redundant, needless. □□ **superfluously** adv. **superfluousness** n. [ME f. L superfluus (as SUPER-, fluere to flow)]

supergiant /ˈsuːpəˌdʒaɪənt, ˈsjuː-/ n. a star of very great luminosity and size.

superglue /ˈsuːpəˌgluː/ n. any of various adhesives with an exceptional bonding capability.

supergrass /ˈsuːpəˌgrɑːs, ˈsjuː-/ n. colloq. a police informer who implicates a large number of people.

superheat /ˌsuːpəˈhiːt, ˌsjuː-/ v.tr. Physics 1 heat (a liquid) above its boiling-point without vaporization. 2 heat (a vapour) above its boiling-point (superheated steam). □□ **superheater** n.

superhet /ˌsuːpəˈhet, ˌsjuː-/ n. colloq. = SUPER-HETERODYNE.

superheterodyne /ˌsuːpəˈhetərəʊˌdaɪn, ˌsjuː-/ adj. & n. —adj. denoting or characteristic of a system of radio reception in which a local variable oscillator is tuned to beat at a constant ultrasonic frequency with carrier-wave frequencies, making it unnecessary to vary the amplifier tuning and securing greater selectivity. —n. a superheterodyne receiver. [SUPERSONIC + HETERODYNE]

superhighway /ˈsuːpəˌhaɪweɪ, ˈsjuː-/ n. US a broad main road for fast traffic.

superhuman /ˌsuːpəˈhjuːmən, ˌsjuː-/ adj. 1 beyond normal human capability. 2 higher than man. □□ **superhumanly** adv. [LL superhumanus (as SUPER-, HUMAN)]

superhumeral /ˌsuːpəˈhjuːmər(ə)l, ˌsjuː-/ n. Eccl. a vestment worn over the shoulders, e.g. an amice, ephod, or pallium. [LL superhumerale (as SUPER-, HUMERAL)]

superimpose /ˌsuːpərɪmˈpəʊz, ˌsjuː-/ v.tr. (usu. foll. by on) lay (a thing) on something else. □□ **superimposition** /-pəˈzɪʃ(ə)n/ n.

superincumbent /ˌsuːpərɪnˈkʌmbənt, ˌsjuː-/ adj. lying on something else.

superinduce /ˌsuːpərɪnˈdjuːs, ˌsjuː-/ v.tr. introduce or induce in addition. [L superinducere cover over, bring from outside (as SUPER-, INDUCE)]

superintend /ˌsuːpərɪnˈtend, ˌsjuː-/ v.tr. & intr. be responsible for the management or arrangement of (an activity etc.); supervise and inspect. □□ **superintendence** n. **superintendency** n. [eccl.L superintendere (as SUPER-, INTEND), transl. Gk episkopō]

superintendent /ˌsuːpərɪnˈtend(ə)nt, ˌsjuː-/ n. & adj. —n. 1 a a person who superintends. b a director of an institution etc. 2 a Brit. a police officer above the rank of inspector. b US the head of a police department. 3 US the caretaker of a building. —adj. superintending. [eccl.L superintendent- part. stem of superintendere: see SUPERINTEND]

superior /suːˈpɪərɪə(r), sjuː-, sʊ-/ adj. & n. —adj. 1 in a higher position; of higher rank (a superior officer; a superior court). 2 a above the average in quality etc. (made of superior leather). b having or showing a high opinion of oneself; supercilious (had a superior air). 3 (often foll. by to) a better or greater in some respect (superior to its rivals in speed). b above yielding, making concessions, paying attention, etc. (is superior to bribery; superior to temptation). 4 further above or out; higher, esp.: a Astron. (of a planet) having an orbit further from the Sun than the Earth's. b Zool. (of an insect's wings) folding over others. c Printing (of figures or letters) placed above the line. d Bot. (of the calyx) above the ovary. e Bot. (of the ovary) above the calyx. —n. 1 a person superior to another in rank, character, etc. (is deferential to his superiors; is his superior in courage). 2 (fem. **superioress** /-rɪs/) Eccl. the head of a monastery or other religious institution (Mother Superior; Father Superior). 3 Printing a superior letter or figure. □ **superior numbers** esp. Mil. more men etc. or their strength (overcome by superior numbers). **superior persons** esp. iron. the better educated or élite; prigs. □□ **superiorly** adv. [ME f. OF superiour f. L superior -oris, compar. of superus that is above f. super above]

Superior, Lake one of the five Great Lakes of North America and the largest freshwater lake in the world.

superiority /suːˌpɪərɪˈɒrɪtɪ, sjuː-, sʊ-/ n. the state of being superior. □ **superiority complex** Psychol. an undue conviction of one's own superiority to others.

superjacent /ˌsuːpəˈdʒeɪs(ə)nt, ˌsjuː-/ adj. overlying; superincumbent. [L superjacēre (as SUPER-, jacēre lie)]

superlative /suːˈpɜːlətɪv, sjuː-/ adj. & n. —adj. 1 of the highest quality or degree (superlative wisdom). 2 Gram. (of an adjective or adverb) expressing the highest or a very high degree of a quality (e.g. bravest, most fiercely) (cf. POSITIVE, COMPARATIVE). —n. 1 Gram. a the superlative expression or form of an adjective or adverb. b a word in the superlative. 2 something embodying excellence; the highest form of a thing. □□ **superlatively** adv. **superlativeness** n. [ME f. OF superlatif -ive f. LL superlativus f. L superlatus (as SUPER-, latus past part. of ferre take)]

superlunary /ˌsuːpəˈluːnərɪ, ˌsjuː-, -ˈljuːnərɪ/ adj. 1 situated beyond the moon. 2 belonging to a higher world, celestial. [med.L superlunaris (as SUPER-, LUNAR)]

superman /ˈsuːpəˌmæn, ˈsjuː-/ n. (pl. **-men**) 1 esp. Philos. the ideal superior man of the future, held by Nietzsche to be able to be evolved from the normal human type. 2 colloq. a man of exceptional strength or ability. [SUPER- + MAN, formed by G. B. Shaw after Nietzsche's G Übermensch]

supermarket /ˈsuːpəˌmɑːkɪt, ˈsjuː-/ n. a large self-service store selling foods, household goods, etc.

supermundane /ˌsuːpəˈmʌndeɪn, ˌsjuː-/ adj. superior to earthly things.

supernal /suːˈpɜːn(ə)l, sjuː-/ adj. esp. poet. 1 heavenly; divine. 2 of or concerning the sky. 3 lofty. □□ **supernally** adv. [ME f. OF supernal or med.L supernalis f. L supernus f. super above]

supernatant /ˌsuːpəˈneɪt(ə)nt, ˌsjuː-/ adj. & n. esp. Chem. —adj. floating on the surface of a liquid. —n. a supernatant substance. [SUPER- + natant swimming (as NATATION)]

supernatural /ˌsuːpəˈnætʃər(ə)l, ˌsjuː-/ adj. & n. —adj. attributed to or thought to reveal some force above the laws of nature; magical; mystical. —n. (prec. by the) supernatural, occult, or magical forces, effects, etc. □□ **supernaturalism** n. **supernaturalist** n. **supernaturalize** v.tr. (also -ise). **supernaturally** adv. **supernaturalness** n.

supernormal /ˌsuːpəˈnɔːm(ə)l, ˌsjuː-/ adj. beyond what is normal or natural. □□ **supernormality** /-ˈmælɪtɪ/ n.

supernova /ˌsuːpəˈnəʊvə, ˌsjuː-/ n. (pl. -novae /-viː/ or -novas) Astron. a star that suddenly increases very greatly in brightness because of an explosion disrupting its structure and ejecting debris at speeds of up to a tenth that of light and temperatures of hundreds of thousands of degrees Within the resulting shell of material may be left a pulsar or a black hole. Though frequently observed in other galaxies, only three have been recorded in our own Galaxy: by Chinese astronomers in 1054, by Tycho Brahe in 1572, and by Kepler in 1604.

supernumerary /ˌsuːpəˈnjuːmərərɪ, ˌsjuː-/ adj. & n. —adj. 1 in excess of the normal number; extra. 2 (of a person) engaged for extra work. 3 (of an actor) appearing on stage but not speaking. —n. (pl. -ies) 1 an extra or unwanted person or thing. 2 a supernumerary actor. 3 a person engaged for extra work. [LL supernumerarius (soldier) added to a legion already complete, f. L super numerum beyond the number]

superorder /ˈsuːpərˌɔːdə(r), ˈsjuː-/ n. Biol. a taxonomic category between order and class. □□ **superordinal** /-ˈɔːdɪn(ə)l/ adj.

superordinate /ˌsuːpərˈɔːdɪnət, ˌsjuː-/ adj. (usu. foll. by to) of superior importance or rank. [SUPER-, after subordinate]

superphosphate /ˌsuːpəˈfɒsfeɪt, ˌsjuː-/ n. a fertilizer made by treating phosphate rock with sulphuric or phosphoric acid.

superphysical /ˌsuːpəˈfɪzɪk(ə)l, ˌsjuː-/ adj. 1 unexplainable by physical causes; supernatural. 2 beyond what is physical.

superpose /ˌsuːpəˈpəʊz, ˌsjuː-/ v.tr. (usu. foll. by on) esp. Geom. place (a thing or a geometric figure) on or above something else, esp. so as to coincide. □□ **superposition** /-pəˈzɪʃ(ə)n/ n. [F superposer (as SUPER-, POSE[1])]

superpower /ˈsuːpəˌpaʊə(r), ˈsjuː-/ n. a nation or State having a dominant position in world politics, one with the power to act decisively in pursuit of interests affecting the whole world, esp. the US and the USSR since the Second World War.

supersaturate /ˌsuːpəˈsætʃəˌreɪt, ˌsjuː-, -tjʊˌreɪt/ v.tr. add to (esp. a solution) beyond saturation point. □□ **supersaturation** /-ˈreɪʃ(ə)n/ n.

superscribe /ˈsuːpəˌskraɪb, ˈsjuː-, -ˈskraɪb/ v.tr. 1 write (an inscription) at the top of or on the outside of a document etc. 2 write an inscription over or on (a thing). □□ **superscription** /-ˈskrɪpʃ(ə)n/ n. [L superscribere (as SUPER-, scribere script- write)]

superscript /ˈsuːpəskrɪpt, ˈsjuː-/ adj. & n. —adj. written or printed above the line, esp. Math. (of a symbol) written above and to the right of another. —n. a superscript number or symbol. [L superscriptus past part. of superscribere: see SUPERSCRIBE]

supersede /ˌsuːpəˈsiːd, ˌsjuː-/ v.tr. 1 a adopt or appoint another person or thing in place of. b set aside; cease to employ. 2 (of a person or thing) take the place of. □□ **supersedence** n. **supersedure** /-dʒə(r)/ n. **supersession** /-ˈseʃ(ə)n/ n. [OF superseder f. L supersedēre be superior to (as SUPER-, sedēre sess- sit)]

supersonic /ˌsuːpəˈsɒnɪk, ˌsjuː-/ adj. designating or having a speed greater than that of sound. □□ **supersonically** adv.

supersonics /ˌsuːpəˈsɒnɪks, ˌsjuː-/ n.pl. (treated as sing.) = ULTRASONICS.

superstar /ˈsuːpəˌstɑː(r), ˈsjuː-/ n. an extremely famous or renowned actor, film star, musician, etc. □□ **superstardom** n.

superstition /ˌsuːpəˈstɪʃ(ə)n, ˌsjuː-/ n. 1 credulity regarding the supernatural. 2 an irrational fear of the unknown or mysterious. 3 misdirected reverence. 4 a practice, opinion, or religion based on these tendencies. 5 a widely held but unjustified idea of the effects or nature of a thing. □□ **superstitious** adj.

superstitiously adv. **superstitiousness** n. [ME f. OF superstition or L superstitio (as SUPER-, stare stat- stand)]

superstore /ˈsuːpəˌstɔː(r), ˈsjuː-/ n. a large supermarket selling a wide range of goods.

superstratum /ˈsuːpəˌstrɑːtəm, ˈsjuː-/ n. (pl. -strata /-tə/) an overlying stratum.

superstructure /ˈsuːpəˌstrʌktʃə(r), ˈsjuː-/ n. 1 the part of a building above its foundations. 2 a structure built on top of something else. 3 a concept or idea based on others. □□ **superstructural** adj.

supersubtle /ˌsuːpəˈsʌt(ə)l, ˌsjuː-/ adj. extremely or excessively subtle. □□ **supersubtlety** n.

supertanker /ˈsuːpəˌtæŋkə(r), ˈsjuː-/ n. a very large tanker ship.

supertax /ˈsuːpəˌtæks, ˈsjuː-/ n. a tax on incomes above a certain level, esp. a surtax.

superterrestrial /ˌsuːpətəˈrestrɪəl, ˌsjuː-/ adj. 1 in or belonging to a region above the earth. 2 celestial.

supertonic /ˌsuːpəˈtɒnɪk, ˌsjuː-/ n. Mus. the note above the tonic, the second note of the diatonic scale of any key.

supervene /ˌsuːpəˈviːn, ˌsjuː-/ v.intr. occur as an interruption in or a change from some state. □□ **supervenient** adj. **supervention** /-ˈvenʃ(ə)n/ n. [L supervenire supervent- (as SUPER-, venire come)]

supervise /ˈsuːpəˌvaɪz, ˈsjuː-/ v.tr. 1 superintend, oversee the execution of (a task etc.). 2 oversee the actions or work of (a person). □□ **supervision** /-ˈvɪʒ(ə)n/ n. **supervisor** n. **supervisory** adj. [med.L supervidēre supervis- (as SUPER-, vidēre see)]

superwoman /ˈsuːpəˌwʊmən, ˈsjuː-/ n. (pl. -women) colloq. a woman of exceptional strength or ability.

supinate /ˈsuːpɪˌneɪt, ˈsjuː-/ v.tr. put (a hand or foreleg etc.) into a supine position (cf. PRONATE). □□ **supination** /-ˈneɪʃ(ə)n/ n. [back-form. f. supination f. L supinatio f. supinare f. supinus: see SUPINE]

supinator /ˈsuːpɪˌneɪtə(r), ˈsjuː-/ n. Anat. a muscle in the forearm effecting supination.

supine /ˈsuːpaɪn, ˈsjuː-/ adj. & n. —adj. 1 lying face upwards (cf. PRONE). 2 having the front or ventral part upwards; (of the hand) with the palm upwards. 3 inert, indolent; morally or mentally inactive. —n. a Latin verbal noun used only in the accusative and ablative cases, esp. to denote purpose (e.g. mirabile dictu wonderful to relate). □□ **supinely** adv. **supineness** n. [L supinus, rel. to super: (n.) f. LL supinum neut. (reason unkn.)]

supper /ˈsʌpə(r)/ n. a light evening meal. □ **sing for one's supper** do something in return for a benefit. □□ **supperless** adj. [ME f. OF soper, super]

supplant /səˈplɑːnt/ v.tr. dispossess and take the place of, esp. by underhand means. □□ **supplanter** n. [ME f. OF supplanter or L supplantare trip up (as SUB-, planta sole)]

supple /ˈsʌp(ə)l/ adj. —adj. (**suppler**, **supplest**) 1 flexible, pliant; easily bent. 2 compliant; avoiding overt resistance; artfully or servilely submissive. —v. tr. & intr. make or become supple. □□ **suppleness** n. [ME f. OF souple ult. f. L supplex supplicis submissive]

supplejack /ˈsʌp(ə)lˌdʒæk/ n. any of various strong twining tropical shrubs, esp. Berchemia scandens. [SUPPLE + JACK[1]]

supplely var. of SUPPLY[2].

supplement n. & v. —n. /ˈsʌplɪmənt/ 1 a thing or part added to remedy deficiencies (dietary supplement). 2 a part added to a book etc. to provide further information. 3 a separate section, esp. a colour magazine, added to a newspaper or periodical. 4 Geom. the amount by which an angle is less than 180° (cf. COMPLEMENT). —v.tr. /ˈsʌplɪmənt, ˌsʌplɪˈment/ provide a supplement for. □□ **supplemental** /-ˈment(ə)l/ adj. **supplementally** /-ˈmentəlɪ/ adv. **supplementation** /-ˈteɪʃ(ə)n/ n. [ME f. L supplementum (as SUB-, plēre fill)]

supplementary /ˌsʌplɪˈmentərɪ/ adj. forming or serving as a supplement; additional. □ **supplementary benefit** (in the UK) a weekly allowance paid by the State to those not in full-time employment and with an income below a certain level (cf. family credit). □□ **supplementarily** adv.

suppletion /səˈpliːʃ(ə)n/ n. the act or an instance of supplementing, esp. *Linguistics* the occurrence of unrelated forms to supply gaps in conjugation (e.g. *went* as the past of *go*). □□ **suppletive** adj. [ME f. OF f. med.L *suppletio -onis* (as SUPPLY[1])]

suppliant /ˈsʌplɪənt/ adj. & n. —adj. 1 supplicating. 2 expressing supplication. —n. a supplicating person. □□ **suppliantly** adv. [ME f. F *supplier* beseech f. L (as SUPPLICATE)]

supplicate /ˈsʌplɪˌkeɪt/ v. 1 tr. petition humbly to (a person) or for (a thing). 2 intr. (foll. by *to, for*) make a petition. □□ **supplicant** adj. & n. **supplication** /-ˈkeɪʃ(ə)n/ n. **supplicatory** adj. [ME f. L *supplicare* (as SUB-, *plicare* bend)]

supply[1] /səˈplaɪ/ v. & n. —v.tr. (**-ies, -ied**) 1 provide or furnish (a thing needed). 2 (often foll. by *with*) provide (a person etc. with a thing needed). 3 meet or make up for (a deficiency or need etc.). 4 fill (a vacancy, place, etc.) as a substitute. —n. (pl. **-ies**) 1 the act or an instance of providing what is needed. 2 a stock, store, amount, etc., of something provided or obtainable (*a large supply of water; the gas-supply*). 3 (in pl.) **a** the collected provisions and equipment for an army, expedition, etc. **b** a grant of money by Parliament for the costs of government. **c** a money allowance to a person. 4 (often *attrib.*) a person, esp. a schoolteacher or clergyman, acting as a temporary substitute for another. 5 (*attrib.*) providing supplies or a supply (*supply officer*). □ **in short supply** available in limited quantity. **on supply** (of a schoolteacher etc.) acting as a supply. **supply and demand** *Econ.* quantities available and required as factors regulating the price of commodities. **supply-side** *Econ.* denoting a policy of low taxation and other incentives to produce goods and invest. □□ **supplier** n. [ME f. OF *so(u)pleer* etc. f. L *supplēre* (as SUB-, *plēre* fill)]

supply[2] /ˈsʌplɪ/ adv. (also **supplely** /ˈsʌpəlɪ/) in a supple manner.

support /səˈpɔːt/ v. & n. —v.tr. 1 carry all or part of the weight of. 2 keep from falling or sinking or failing. 3 provide with a home and the necessities of life (*has a family to support*). 4 enable to last out; give strength to; encourage. 5 bear out; tend to substantiate or corroborate (a statement, charge, theory, etc.). 6 give help or countenance to, back up; second, further. 7 speak in favour of (a resolution etc.). 8 be actively interested in (a particular team or sport). 9 take a part that is secondary to (a principal actor etc.). 10 assist (a lecturer etc.) by one's presence. 11 endure, tolerate (*can no longer support the noise*). 12 maintain or represent (a part or character) adequately. 13 subscribe to the funds of (an institution). —n. 1 the act or an instance of supporting; the process of being supported. 2 a person or thing that supports. □ **in support of** in order to support. **supporting film** (or **picture** etc.) a less important film in a cinema programme. **support price** a minimum price guaranteed to a farmer for agricultural produce and maintained by subsidy etc. □□ **supportable** adj. **supportability** /-təˈbɪlɪtɪ/ n. **supportably** adv. **supportingly** adv. **supportless** adj. [ME f. OF *supporter* f. L *supportare* (as SUB-, *portare* carry)]

supporter /səˈpɔːtə(r)/ n. 1 a person or thing that supports, esp. a person supporting a team or sport. 2 *Heraldry* the representation of an animal etc., usu. one of a pair, holding up or standing beside an escutcheon.

supportive /səˈpɔːtɪv/ adj. providing support or encouragement. □□ **supportively** adv. **supportiveness** n.

suppose /səˈpəʊz/ v.tr. (often foll. by *that* + clause) 1 assume, esp. in default of knowledge; be inclined to think (*I suppose they will return; what do you suppose he meant?*). 2 take as a possibility or hypothesis (*let us suppose you are right*). 3 (in *imper.*) as a formula of proposal (*suppose we go to the party*). 4 (of a theory or result etc.) require as a condition (*design in creation supposes a creator*). 5 (in *imper.* or *pres. part.* forming a question) in the circumstances that; if (*suppose he won't let you; supposing we stay*). 6 (as **supposed** adj.) generally accepted as being so; believed (*his supposed brother; generally supposed to be wealthy*). 7 (in *passive*; foll. by *to* + infin.) **a** be expected or required (*was supposed to write to you*). **b** (with neg.) not have to; not be allowed to (*you are not supposed to go in there*). □ **I suppose so** an expression of hesitant agreement. □□ **supposable** adj. [ME f. OF *supposer* (as SUB-, POSE[1])]

supposedly /səˈpəʊzɪdlɪ/ adv. as is generally supposed.

supposition /ˌsʌpəˈzɪʃ(ə)n/ n. 1 a fact or idea etc. supposed. 2 the act or an instance of supposing. □□ **suppositional** adj.

supposititious /ˌsʌpəˈzɪʃəs/ adj. hypothetical, assumed. □□ **suppositiously** adv. **suppositiousness** n. [partly f. SUPPOSITITIOUS, partly f. SUPPOSITION + -OUS]

supposititious /səˌpɒzɪˈtɪʃəs/ adj. spurious; substituted for the real. □□ **supposititiously** adv. **supposititiousness** n. [L *supposititius, -icius* f. *supponere supposit-* substitute (as SUB- *ponere* place)]

suppository /səˈpɒzɪtərɪ/ n. (pl. **-ies**) a medical preparation in the form of a cone, cylinder, etc., to be inserted into the rectum or vagina to melt. [ME f. med.L *suppositorium*, neut. of LL *suppositorius* placed underneath (as SUPPOSITITIOUS)]

suppress /səˈpres/ v.tr. 1 end the activity or existence of, esp. forcibly. 2 prevent (information, feelings, a reaction, etc.) from being seen, heard, or known (*tried to suppress the report; suppressed a yawn*). 3 **a** partly or wholly eliminate (electrical interference etc.). **b** equip (a device) to reduce such interference due to it. 4 *Psychol.* keep out of one's consciousness. □□ **suppressible** adj. **suppression** n. **suppressive** adj. **suppressor** n. [ME f. L *supprimere suppress-* (as SUB-, *premere* press)] **suppressant** /səˈpres(ə)nt/ n. a suppressing or restraining agent, esp. a drug that suppresses the appetite.

suppurate /ˈsʌpjʊˌreɪt/ v.intr. 1 form pus. 2 fester. □□ **suppuration** /-ˈreɪʃ(ə)n/ n. **suppurative** /-rətɪv/ adj. [L *suppurare* (as SUB-, *purare* as PUS)]

supra /ˈsuːprə, ˈsjuː-/ adv. above or earlier on (in a book etc.). [L, = above]

supra- /ˈsuːprə, ˈsjuː-/ prefix 1 above. 2 beyond, transcending (*supranational*). [from or after L *supra-* f. *supra* above, beyond, before in time]

supramaxillary /ˌsuːprəmækˈsɪlərɪ, ˌsjuː-/ adj. of or relating to the upper jaw.

supramundane /ˌsuːprəˈmʌndeɪn, ˌsjuː-/ adj. above or superior to the world.

supranational /ˌsuːprəˈnæʃən(ə)l, ˌsjuː-/ adj. transcending national limits. □□ **supranationalism** n. **supranationality** /-ˈnælɪtɪ/ n.

supraorbital /ˌsuːprəˈɔːbɪt(ə)l, ˌsjuː-/ adj. situated above the orbit of the eye.

suprarenal /ˌsuːprəˈriːn(ə)l, ˌsjuː-/ adj. situated above the kidneys.

supremacist /suːˈpreməsɪst, sjuː-/ n. & adj. —n. an advocate of the supremacy of a particular group, esp. determined by race or sex. —adj. relating to or advocating such supremacy. □□ **supremacism** n.

supremacy /suːˈpreməsɪ, sjuː-/ n. (pl. **-ies**) 1 the state of being supreme. 2 the highest authority. □ **Act of Supremacy** any Act of Parliament laying down the position of the sovereign as supreme head on earth of the Church of England (and excluding the authority of the pope) or supreme governor of England in spiritual and temporal matters, especially that of 1534.

supreme /suːˈpriːm, sjuː-/ adj. & n. —adj. 1 highest in authority or rank. 2 greatest; most important. 3 (of a penalty or sacrifice etc.) involving death. —n. 1 a rich cream sauce. 2 a dish served in this. □ **the Supreme Being** a name for God. **Supreme Court** the highest judicial court in a State etc. **supreme pontiff** see PONTIFF. **Supreme Soviet** see SOVIET. □□ **supremely** adv. **supremeness** n. [L *supremus*, superl. of *superus* that is above f. *super* above]

suprême /suːˈprem/ n. = SUPREME n. [F]

supremo /suːˈpriːməʊ, sjuː-/ n. (pl. **-os**) 1 a supreme leader or ruler. 2 a person in overall charge. [Sp., = SUPREME]

Supt. abbr. Superintendent.

sur-[1] /sɜː(r), sə(r)/ prefix = SUPER- (*surcharge; surrealism*). [OF]

sur-[2] /sɜː(r), sə(r)/ prefix assim. form of SUB- before r.

sura /ˈsʊərə/ n. (also **surah**) a chapter or section of the Koran. [Arab. *sūra*]

Surabaya /ˌsʊərəˈbaɪə/ a seaport and the principal naval base of Indonesia, capital of the province of East Java; pop. (1980) 2,027,900.

surah /ˈsjʊərə/ n. a soft twilled silk for scarves etc. [F pronunc. of Surat in India, where it was orig. made]

sural /ˈsjʊər(ə)l/ adj. of or relating to the calf of the leg (sural artery). [mod.L suralis f. L sura calf]

Surat /ˈsʊərət, sʊˈraːt/ a port in the State of Gujarat in west central India; pop. (1981) 913,000. Here the East India Company established its first trading post in 1612; Surat was a major city of India in the late 17th–18th c.

surcease /sɜːˈsiːs/ n. & v. literary —n. a cessation. —v.intr. & tr. cease. [ME f. OF sursis, -ise (cf. AF sursise omission), past part. of OF surseoir refrain, delay f. L (as SUPERSEDE), with assim. to CEASE]

surcharge n. & v. —n. /ˈsɜːtʃɑːdʒ/ 1 an additional charge or payment. 2 a charge made by assessors as a penalty for false returns of taxable property. 3 a mark printed on a postage stamp changing its value. 4 an additional or excessive load. 5 Brit. an amount in an official account not passed by the auditor and having to be refunded by the person responsible. 6 the showing of an omission in an account for which credit should have been given. —v.tr. /ˈsɜːtʃɑːdʒ, -ˈtʃɑːdʒ/ 1 exact a surcharge from. 2 exact (a sum) as a surcharge. 3 mark (a postage stamp) with a surcharge. 4 overload. 5 fill or saturate to excess. [ME f. OF surcharger (as SUR-¹, CHARGE)]

surcingle /ˈsɜːˌsɪŋɡ(ə)l/ n. a band round a horse's body usu. to keep a pack etc. in place. [ME f. OF surcengle (as SUR-¹, cengle girth f. L cingula f. cingere gird)]

surcoat /ˈsɜːkəʊt/ n. 1 hist. a loose robe worn over armour, esp. in the 13th–14th c. 2 a similar sleeveless garment worn as part of the insignia of an order of knighthood. 3 hist. an outer coat of rich material. [ME f. OF surcot (as SUR-¹, cot coat)]

surculose /ˈsɜːkjʊˌləʊs/ adj. Bot. producing suckers. [L surculosus f. surculus twig]

surd /sɜːd/ adj. & n. —adj. 1 Math. (of a number) irrational. 2 Phonet. (of a sound) uttered with the breath and not the voice (e.g. f, k, p, s, t). —n. 1 Math. a surd number, esp. the root of an integer. 2 Phonet. a surd sound. [L surdus deaf, mute: sense 1 by mistransl. into L of Gk alogos irrational, speechless, through Arab. jaḍr aṣamm deaf root]

sure /ʃʊə(r), ʃɔː(r)/ adj. & adv. —adj. 1 having or seeming to have adequate reason for a belief or assertion. 2 (often foll. by of, or that + clause) convinced. 3 (foll. by of) having a certain prospect or confident anticipation or satisfactory knowledge of. 4 reliable or unfailing (there is one sure way to find out). 5 (foll. by to + infin.) certain. 6 undoubtedly true or truthful. —adv. colloq. certainly. □ as sure as eggs is eggs see EGG¹. as sure as fate quite certain. be sure (in imper. or infin.; foll. by that + clause or to + infin.) take care to; not fail to (be sure to turn the lights out). for sure colloq. without doubt. make sure 1 make or become certain; ensure. 2 (foll. by of) establish the truth or ensure the existence or happening of. sure enough colloq. 1 in fact; certainly. 2 with near certainty (they will come sure enough). sure-fire colloq. certain to succeed. sure-footed never stumbling or making a mistake. sure-footedly in a sure-footed way. sure-footedness being sure-footed. sure thing int. esp. US colloq. certainly. to be sure 1 it is undeniable or admitted. 2 it must be admitted. □□ sureness n. [ME f. OF sur sure (earlier seür) f. L securus SECURE]

surely /ˈʃʊəlɪ/ adv. 1 with certainty (the time approaches slowly but surely). 2 as an appeal to likelihood or reason (surely that can't be right). 3 with safety; securely (the goat plants its feet surely).

surety /ˈʃʊərɪtɪ, ˈʃʊətɪ/ n. (pl. -ies) 1 a person who takes responsibility for another's performance of an undertaking, e.g. to appear in court, or payment of a debt. 2 archaic a certainty. □ of (or for) a surety archaic certainly. stand surety become a surety, go bail. □□ suretyship n. [ME f. OF surté, seürté f. L securitas -tatis SECURITY]

surf /sɜːf/ n. & v. —n. 1 the swell of the sea breaking on the shore or reefs. 2 the foam produced by this. —v.intr. go surf-riding. □ surf-casting fishing by casting a line into the sea from the shore. surf-riding the sport of being carried over the surf to the shore on a surfboard. Surfing or surf-riding originated in primitive societies living in coastal areas facing the open sea. It was a pastime for the peoples of the South Sea Islands before European mariners made their historic voyages,

and was observed by Captain Cook in Tahiti in 1777. Body surfing (without a board) was practised by the early Hawaiians. □□ **surfer** n. **surfy** adj. [app. f. obs. suff, perh. assim. to surge: orig. applied to the Indian coast]

surface /ˈsɜːfɪs/ n. & v. —n. 1 **a** the outside of a material body. **b** the area of this. 2 any of the limits terminating a solid. 3 the upper boundary of a liquid or of the ground etc. 4 the outward aspect of anything; what is apparent on a casual view or consideration (presents a large surface to view; all is quiet on the surface). 5 Geom. a set of points that has length and breadth but no thickness. 6 (attrib.) **a** of or on the surface (surface area). **b** superficial (surface politeness). —v. 1 tr. give the required surface to (a road, paper, etc.). 2 intr. & tr. rise or bring to the surface. 3 intr. become visible or known. 4 intr. colloq. become conscious; wake up. □ come to the surface become perceptible after being hidden. surface-active (of a substance, e.g. a detergent) able to affect the wetting properties of a liquid. surface mail mail carried over land and by sea, and not by air. surface noise extraneous noise in playing a gramophone record, caused by imperfections in the grooves. surface tension the tension of the surface-film of a liquid, tending to minimize its surface area. □□ surfaced adj. (usu. in comb.). surfacer n. [F (as SUR-¹, FACE)]

surfactant /sɜːˈfækt(ə)nt/ n. a substance which reduces surface tension. [surface-active]

surfboard /ˈsɜːfbɔːd/ n. a long narrow board used in surf-riding.

surfeit /ˈsɜːfɪt/ n. & v. —n. 1 an excess esp. in eating or drinking. 2 a feeling of satiety or disgust resulting from this. —v. (surfeited, surfeiting) 1 tr. overfeed. 2 intr. overeat. 3 intr. & tr. (foll. by with) be or cause to be wearied through excess. [ME f. OF sorfe(i)t, surfe(i)t (as SUPER-, L facere fact- do)]

surficial /sɜːˈfɪʃ(ə)l/ adj. Geol. of or relating to the earth's surface. □□ **surficially** adv. [SURFACE after superficial]

surge /sɜːdʒ/ n. & v. —n. 1 a sudden or impetuous onset (a surge of anger). 2 the swell of the waves at sea. 3 a heavy forward or upward motion. 4 a rapid increase in price, activity, etc. over a short period. 5 a sudden marked increase in voltage of an electric current. —v.intr. 1 (of waves, the sea, etc.) rise and fall or move heavily forward. 2 (of a crowd etc.) move suddenly and powerfully forwards in large numbers. 3 (of an electric current etc.) increase suddenly. 4 Naut. (of a rope, chain, or windlass) slip back with a jerk. □ surge chamber (or tank) a chamber designed to neutralize sudden changes of pressure in a flow of liquid. [OF sourdre sourge-, or sorgir f. Cat., f. L surgere rise]

surgeon /ˈsɜːdʒ(ə)n/ n. 1 a medical practitioner qualified to practise surgery. 2 a medical officer in a navy or army or military hospital. □ surgeon fish any tropical marine fish of the genus Acanthurus with movable lancet-shaped spines on each side of the tail. surgeon general (pl. surgeons general) US the head of a public health service or of an army etc. medical service. surgeon's knot a reef-knot with a double twist. [ME f. AF surgien f. OF serurgien (as SURGERY)]

surgery /ˈsɜːdʒərɪ/ n. (pl. -ies) 1 the branch of medicine concerned with treatment of injuries or disorders of the body by incision, manipulation or alteration of organs etc., with the hands or with instruments. (See below.) 2 Brit. **a** a place where a doctor, dentist, etc., treats patients. **b** the occasion of this (the doctor will see you after surgery). 3 Brit. **a** a place where an MP, lawyer, or other professional person gives advice. **b** the occasion of this. [ME f. OF surgerie f. L chirurgia f. Gk kheirourgia handiwork, surgery f. kheir hand + erg- work]

The beginnings of surgery can be traced back to prehistoric times, when sharpened flints were used for opening abscesses, scarifying the skin, and for the serious operation of trepanning the skull. In the Middle Ages the practice of surgery became separated from that of medicine, largely because at different periods the Church forbade the practice of surgery by its clerics, who included not only those in monasteries (which played a great part in caring for the sick) but most educated doctors. Consequently surgery was left to barber-surgeons and other lowly practitioners, and for centuries the status of the surgeon was markedly inferior to that of the physician. In 1745 the Company of Surgeons was formed, becoming the Royal College of Surgeons in 1800. Advances in surgery in the 19th c. were made possible by overcoming two great problems—pain (see ANAESTHETIC), and infection (see ANTISEPTIC); an operation was no longer a desperate procedure undertaken only as a last resort. In the 20th c. the technical efficiency of the surgeon has been supplemented by a number of discoveries and techniques, including X-rays, safer anaesthetics, prompt replacement of blood and fluid loss, and effective antibiotics, while the present high level of surgical skill is partly due to the high degree of specialization which is one of the most striking features of modern medicine. Recent advances include open-heart surgery, cryosurgery, microsurgery, and the use of tomography.

surgical /'sɜːdʒɪk(ə)l/ *adj.* **1** of or relating to or done by surgeons or surgery. **2** resulting from surgery (*surgical fever*). **3 a** used in surgery. **b** (of a special garment etc.) worn to correct a deformity etc. □ **surgical spirit** methylated spirit used in surgery for cleansing etc. □□ **surgically** *adv.* [earlier *chirurgical* f. *chirurgy* f. OF *sirurgie*: see SURGEON]

suricate /'sʊərɪˌkeɪt/ *n.* a South African burrowing mongoose, *Suricata suricatta*, with grey and black stripes. [F f. S.Afr. native name]

Suriname /ˌsʊərɪˈnæm/ a country on the NE coast of South America; pop. (est. 1988) 395,000; official language, Dutch; capital, Paramaribo. The climate is subtropical and the population is largely concentrated on the coast. Suriname has large timber resources, but the economy is chiefly dependent on bauxite, which makes up over three-quarters of its exports. Settled by the English in 1650, the country was ceded to the Dutch in 1667 but twice returned to British control before finally reverting to The Netherlands in 1815. Known until 1948 as Dutch Guiana, it attained a measure of autonomy in 1950 and 1954 followed by full independence in 1975. □ **Suriname toad** = PIPA. □□ **Surinamer** *n.* **Surinamese** /-ˈmiːz/ *adj.* & *n.*

surly /'sɜːlɪ/ *adj.* (**surlier**, **surliest**) bad-tempered and unfriendly; churlish. □□ **surlily** *adv.* **surliness** *n.* [alt. spelling of obs. *sirly* haughty f. SIR + -LY¹]

surmise /səˈmaɪz/ *n.* & *v.* —*n.* a conjecture or suspicion about the existence or truth of something. —*v.* **1** *tr.* (often foll. by *that* + clause) infer doubtfully; make a surmise about. **2** *tr.* suspect the existence of. **3** *intr.* make a guess. [ME f. AF & OF fem. past part. of *surmettre* accuse f. LL *supermittere supermiss-* (as SUPER-, *mittere* send)]

surmount /səˈmaʊnt/ *v.tr.* **1** overcome or get over (a difficulty or obstacle). **2** (usu. in *passive*) cap or crown (*peaks surmounted with snow*). □□ **surmountable** *adj.* [ME f. OF *surmonter* (as SUR-¹, MOUNT¹)]

surmullet /sɜːˈmʌlɪt/ *n.* the red mullet. [F *surmulet* f. OF *sor* red + *mulet* MULLET]

surname /'sɜːneɪm/ *n.* & *v.* —*n.* **1** a hereditary name common to all members of a family, as distinct from a Christian or first name. **2** *archaic* an additional descriptive or allusive name attached to a person, sometimes becoming hereditary. —*v.tr.* **1** give a surname to. **2** give (a person a surname). **3** (as **surnamed** *adj.*) having as a family name. [ME, alt. of *surnoun* f. AF (as SUR-¹, NOUN name)]

surpass /səˈpɑːs/ *v.tr.* **1** outdo, be greater or better than. **2** (as **surpassing** *adj.*) pre-eminent, matchless (*of surpassing intelligence*). □□ **surpassingly** *adv.* [F *surpasser* (as SUR-¹, PASS¹)]

surplice /'sɜːplɪs/ *n.* a loose white linen vestment reaching the knees, worn over a cassock by clergy and choristers at services. □□ **surpliced** *adj.* [ME f. AF *surplis*, OF *sourpelis*, f. med.L *superpellicium* (as SUPER-, *pellicia* PELISSE)]

surplus /'sɜːpləs/ *n.* & *adj.* —*n.* **1** an amount left over when requirements have been met. **2 a** an excess of revenue over expenditure in a given period, esp. a financial year (opp. DEFICIT). **b** the excess value of a company's assets over the face value of its stock. —*adj.* exceeding what is needed or used. □ **surplus value** *Econ.* the difference between the value of work done and wages paid. [ME f. AF *surplus*, OF *s(o)urplus* f. med.L *superplus* (as SUPER-, + *plus* more)]

surprise /səˈpraɪz/ *n.* & *v.* —*n.* **1** an unexpected or astonishing event or circumstance. **2** the emotion caused by this. **3** the act of catching a person etc. unawares, or the process of being

caught unawares. **4** (*attrib.*) unexpected; made or done etc. without warning (*a surprise visit*). —*v.tr.* **1** affect with surprise; turn out contrary to the expectations of (*your answer surprised me; I surprised her by arriving early*). **2** (usu. in *passive*; foll. by *at*) shock, scandalize (*I am surprised at you*). **3** capture or attack by surprise. **4** come upon (a person) unawares (*surprised him taking a biscuit*). **5** (foll. by *into*) startle (a person) by surprise into an action etc. (*surprised them into consenting*). □ **take by surprise** affect with surprise, esp. by an unexpected encounter or statement. □□ **surprisedly** /-zɪdlɪ/ *adv.* **surprising** *adj.* **surprisingly** *adv.* **surprisingness** *n.* [OF, fem. past part. of *surprendre* (as SUR-¹, *prendre* f. L *praehendere* seize)]

surra /'sʊərə, 'sʌrə/ *n.* a febrile disease transmitted by bites of flies and affecting horses and cattle in the tropics. [Marathi]

surreal /səˈrɪəl/ *adj.* **1** having the qualities of surrealism. **2** strange, bizarre. □□ **surreality** /-ˈælɪtɪ/ *n.* **surreally** *adv.* [backform. f. SURREALISM etc.]

surrealism /səˈrɪəlɪz(ə)m/ *n.* a 20th-c. movement in art and literature aiming at expressing the unconscious mind, e.g. by depicting the phenomena of dreams etc. and by the irrational juxtaposition of images. (See below.) □□ **surrealist** *n.* & *adj.* **surrealistic** /-ˈlɪstɪk/ *adj.* **surrealistically** /-ˈlɪstɪkəlɪ/ *adv.* [F *surréalisme* (as SUR-¹, REALISM)]

This influential European movement, which began in literature with André Breton's manifesto of 1924, belongs to the 1920s and 1930s, but its elements are found also in later decades. It grew out of symbolism and Dada, and its participants (influenced by the ideas of Freud) sought to push beyond the accepted conventions of reality by representing in poetry and art the irrational imagery of dreams and the unconscious mind. This the poets achieved by 'automatic' writing, setting down words unfettered by the conscious mind, while in the visual arts surrealism hovered between a fluid abstracting style analogous to this (as in the works of Masson, Breton, Arp, Miro, and Cocteau) and a more photographic style which relied on deliberately ambiguous combinations of recognizable forms, with Magritte and Dali creating a disorientating realist imagery often based on dreams, hallucination, and paranoia. The surrealists readily experimented with new media: Ernst developed Dadaist collage and invented frottage (a rubbing process), while Man Ray and others experimented with photography and photomontage. In 1928 the collaboration of Dali and Buñuel on *Un Chien andalou* initiated a phase of surrealist film-making.

surrebutter /ˌsʌrɪˈbʌtə(r)/ *n. Law* the plaintiff's reply to the defendant's rebutter. [SUR-¹ + REBUTTER, after SURREJOINDER]

surrejoinder /ˌsʌrɪˈdʒɔɪndə(r)/ *n. Law* the plaintiff's reply to the defendant's rejoinder. [SUR-¹ + REJOINDER]

surrender /səˈrendə(r)/ *v.* & *n.* —*v.* **1** *tr.* hand over; relinquish possession of, esp. on compulsion or demand; give into another's power or control. **2** *intr.* **a** accept an enemy's demand for submission. **b** give oneself up; cease from resistance; submit. **3** *intr.* & *refl.* (foll. by *to*) give oneself over to a habit, emotion, influence, etc. **4** *tr.* give up rights under (a life-insurance policy) in return for a smaller sum received immediately. **5** *tr.* give up (a lease) before its expiry. **6** *tr.* abandon (hope etc.). —*n.* the act or an instance of surrendering. □ **surrender to bail** duly appear in a lawcourt after release on bail. **surrender value** the amount payable to one who surrenders a life-insurance policy. [ME f. AF & OF *surrendre* (as SUR-¹, RENDER)]

surreptitious /ˌsʌrəpˈtɪʃəs/ *adj.* **1** covert; kept secret. **2** done by stealth; clandestine. □□ **surreptitiously** *adv.* **surreptitiousness** *n.* [ME f. L *surrepticius -itius* f. *surripere surrept-* (as SUR-¹, *rapere* seize)]

Surrey /'sʌrɪ/ a county of SE England; pop. (1981) 1,017,000; county town, Guildford.

surrey /'sʌrɪ/ *n.* (pl. **surreys**) *US* a light four-wheeled carriage with two seats facing forwards. [orig. of an adaptation of the *Surrey cart*, orig. made in *Surrey* in England]

surrogate /'sʌrəgət/ *n.* **1** a substitute, esp. for a person in a specific role or office. **2** *Brit.* a deputy, esp. of a bishop in granting marriage licences. **3** *US* a judge in charge of probate, inheritance, and guardianship. □ **surrogate mother 1** a person acting the role of mother. **2** a woman who bears a child on behalf of another woman, from her own egg fertilized by the other woman's partner. □□ **surrogacy** n. **surrogateship** n. [L *surrogatus* past part. of *surrogare* elect as a substitute (as SUR-¹, *rogare* ask)]

surround /səˈraʊnd/ v. & n. —v.tr. **1** come or be all round; encircle, enclose. **2** (in *passive*; foll. by *by, with*) have on all sides (*the house is surrounded by trees*). —n. **1** *Brit.* **a** a border or edging, esp. an area between the walls and carpet of a room. **b** a floor-covering for this. **2** an area or substance surrounding something. □□ **surrounding** adj. [ME = overflow, f. AF *sur(o)under*, OF *s(o)uronder* f. LL *superundare* (as SUPER-, *undare* flow f. *unda* wave)]

surroundings /səˈraʊndɪŋz/ n.pl. the things in the neighbourhood of, or the conditions affecting, a person or thing.

surtax /ˈsɜːtæks/ n. & v. —n. an additional tax, esp. levied on incomes above a certain level. —v.tr. impose a surtax on. [F *surtaxe* (as SUR-¹, TAX)]

Surtees /ˈsɜːtiːz/, Robert Smith (1805–64), English journalist and novelist, who built up a reputation as a sporting journalist with his comic sketches of Mr Jorrocks, the sporting Cockney grocer, collected in *Jorrocks's Jaunts and Jollities* (1838). His second great character, Mr Soapy Sponge, appears in *Mr Sponge's Sporting Tour* (1853), and the celebrated Mr Facey Romford in his last novel *Mr Facey Romford's Hounds* (1865). These works deal convincingly with the characteristic aspects of English fox-hunting society and the illustrations by Leech, Alken, and Phiz have contributed to their success.

surtitle /ˈsɜːˌtaɪt(ə)l/ n. (esp. in opera) each of a sequence of captions projected above the stage, translating the text being sung.

surtout /sɜːˈtuː, -ˈtuːt/ n. hist. a greatcoat or frock-coat. [F f. *sur* over + *tout* everything]

Surtsey /ˈsɜːtsɪ/ a small island to the south of Iceland, which rose from the sea during a volcanic eruption in 1963.

surveillance /sɜːˈveɪləns/ n. close observation, esp. of a suspected person. [F f. *surveiller* (as SUR-¹, *veiller* f. L *vigilare* keep watch)]

survey v. & n. —v.tr. /səˈveɪ/ **1** take or present a general view of. **2** examine the condition of (a building etc.). **3** determine the boundaries, extent, ownership, etc., of (a district etc.). —n. /ˈsɜːveɪ/ **1** a general view or consideration of something. **2 a** the act of surveying property. **b** the result or findings of this, esp. in a written report. **3** an inspection or investigation. **4** a map or plan made by surveying an area. **5** a department carrying out the surveying of land. [ME f. AF *survei(e)r*, OF *so(u)rveeir* (pres. stem *survey-*) f. med.L *supervidēre* (as SUPER-, *vidēre* see)]

surveyor /səˈveɪə(r)/ n. **1** a person who surveys land and buildings, esp. professionally. **2** *Brit.* an official inspector, esp. for measurement and valuation. **3** a person who carries out surveys. □□ **surveyorship** n. (esp. in sense 2). [ME f. AF & OF *surve(i)our* (as SURVEY)]

survival /səˈvaɪv(ə)l/ n. **1** the process or an instance of surviving. **2** a person, thing, or practice that has remained from a former time. □ **survival kit** emergency rations etc., esp. carried by servicemen. **survival of the fittest** the process or result of natural selection.

survive /səˈvaɪv/ v. **1** intr. continue to live or exist; be still alive or existent. **2** tr. live or exist longer than. **3** tr. remain alive after going through, or continue to exist in spite of (a danger, accident, etc.). [ME f. AF *survivre*, OF *sourvivre* f. L *supervivere* (as SUPER-, *vivere* live)]

survivor /səˈvaɪvə(r)/ n. **1** a person who survives or has survived. **2** *Law* a joint tenant who has the right to the whole estate on the other's death.

Surya /ˈsʊərɪə/ *Hinduism* one of several solar deities in the Vedic religion. He became the sun-god of later Hindu mythology. [Skr., = sun]

Sus. *abbr.* Susanna (Apocrypha).

sus var. of SUSS.

sus- /sʌs, səs/ *prefix* assim. form of SUB- before *c, p, t*.

Susa /ˈsuːsə/ an ancient city of SW Iran, the capital of Elam and later of Persia in Achaemenid times.

Susanna /suːˈzænə/ a book of the Apocrypha telling of the false accusation of adultery brought against Susanna, a woman of Babylon, by the two elders, her condemnation, and her final deliverance by the sagacity of Daniel.

susceptibility /səˌseptɪˈbɪlɪtɪ/ n. (pl. **-ies**) **1** the state of being susceptible. **2** (in pl.) a person's sensitive feelings. **3** *Physics* the ratio of magnetization to a magnetizing force.

susceptible /səˈseptɪb(ə)l/ adj. **1** impressionable, sensitive; easily moved by emotion. **2** (foll. by *to*) likely to be affected by; liable or vulnerable to (*susceptible to pain*). **b** (foll. by *of*) allowing; admitting of (*facts not susceptible of proof*). □□ **susceptibly** adv. [LL *susceptibilis* f. L *suscipere suscept-* (as SUB-, *capere* take)]

susceptive /səˈseptɪv/ adj. **1** concerned with the receiving of emotional impressions or ideas. **2** receptive. **3** = SUSCEPTIBLE. [LL *susceptivus* (as SUSCEPTIBLE)]

sushi /ˈsuːʃɪ/ n. a Japanese dish of balls of cold rice flavoured and garnished. [Jap.]

suslik /ˈsʌslɪk/ n. an E. European and Asian ground squirrel, *Citellus citellus*. [Russ.]

suspect v., n., & adj. —v.tr. /səˈspekt/ **1** have an impression of the existence or presence of (*suspects poisoning*). **2** (foll. by *to be*) believe tentatively, without clear ground. **3** (foll. by *that* + clause) be inclined to think. **4** (often foll. by *of*) be inclined to mentally accuse; doubt the innocence of (*suspect him of complicity*). **5** doubt the genuineness or truth of. —n. /ˈsʌspekt/ a suspected person. —adj. /ˈsʌspekt/ subject to or deserving suspicion or distrust; not sound or trustworthy. [ME f. L *suspicere suspect-* (as SUB-, *specere* look)]

suspend /səˈspend/ v.tr. **1** hang up. **2** keep inoperative or undecided for a time; defer. **3** debar temporarily from a function, office, privilege, etc. **4** (as **suspended** adj.) (of solid particles or a body in a fluid medium) sustained somewhere between top and bottom. □ **suspended animation** a temporary cessation of the vital functions without death. **suspended sentence** a judicial sentence left unenforced subject to good behaviour during a specified period. **suspend payment** (of a company) fail to meet its financial engagements; admit insolvency. □□ **suspensible** adj. [ME f. OF *suspendre* or L *suspendere suspens-* (as SUB-, *pendere* hang)]

suspender /səˈspendə(r)/ n. **1** an attachment to hold up a stocking or sock by its top. **2** (in pl.) *US* a pair of braces. □ **suspender belt** a woman's undergarment with suspenders.

suspense /səˈspens/ n. **1** a state of anxious uncertainty or expectation. **2** *Law* a suspension; the temporary cessation of a right etc. □ **keep in suspense** delay informing (a person) of urgent information. **suspense account** an account in which items are entered temporarily before allocation to the right account. □□ **suspenseful** adj. [ME f. AF & OF *suspens* f. past part. of L *suspendere* SUSPEND]

suspension /səˈspenʃ(ə)n/ n. **1** the act of suspending or the condition of being suspended. **2** the means by which a vehicle is supported on its axles. **3** a substance consisting of particles suspended in a medium. **4** *Mus.* the prolongation of a note of a chord to form a discord with the following chord. □ **suspension bridge** a bridge with a roadway suspended from cables supported by structures at each end. (See BRIDGE¹.) [F *suspension* or L *suspensio* (as SUSPEND)]

suspensive /səˈspensɪv/ adj. **1** having the power or tendency to suspend or postpone. **2** causing suspense. □□ **suspensively** adv. **suspensiveness** n. [F *suspensif -ive* or med.L *suspensivus* (as SUSPEND)]

suspensory /səˈspensərɪ/ adj. (of a ligament, muscle, bandage, etc.) holding an organ etc. suspended. [F *suspensoire* (as SUSPENSION)]

suspicion /səˈspɪʃ(ə)n/ n. **1** the feeling or thought of a person who suspects. **2** the act or an instance of suspecting; the state of being suspected. **3** (foll. by *of*) a slight trace of. □ **above suspicion** too obviously good etc. to be suspected. **under sus-**

picion suspected. [ME f. AF *suspeciun* (OF *sospeçon*) f. med.L *suspectio* *-onis* f. L *suspicere* (as SUSPECT): assim. to F *suspicion* & L *suspicio*]

suspicious /sə'spɪʃəs/ *adj.* **1** prone to or feeling suspicion. **2** indicating suspicion (*a suspicious glance*). **3** inviting or justifying suspicion (*a suspicious lack of surprise*). □□ **suspiciously** *adv.* **suspiciousness** *n.* [ME f. AF & OF f. L *suspiciosus* (as SUSPICION)]

suss /sʌs/ *v.* & *n.* (also **sus**) *Brit. sl.* —*v.tr.* (**sussed, sussing**) **1** suspect of a crime. **2** (usu. foll. by *out*) **a** investigate, inspect (*go and suss out the restaurants*). **b** work out; grasp, understand, realize (*he had the market sussed*). —*n.* **1** a suspect. **2** a suspicion; suspicious behaviour. □ **on suss** on suspicion (of having committed a crime). [abbr. of SUSPECT, SUSPICION]

Sussex /'sʌsɪks/ a former county of southern England, now divided into East Sussex and West Sussex. —*n.* **1** a speckled or red domestic fowl of an English breed. **2** this breed.

sustain /sə'steɪn/ *v.tr.* **1** support, bear the weight of, esp. for a long period. **2** give strength to; encourage, support. **3** (of food) give nourishment to. **4** endure, stand; bear up against. **5** undergo or suffer (defeat or injury etc.). **6** (of a court etc.) uphold or decide in favour of (an objection etc.). **7** substantiate or corroborate (a statement or charge). **8** maintain or keep (a sound, effort, etc.) going continuously. **9** continue to represent (a part, character, etc.) adequately. □ □**sustainable** *adj.* **sustainedly** /-nɪdlɪ/ *adv.* **sustainer** *n.* **sustainment** *n.* [ME f. AF *sustein-*, OF *so(u)stein-* stressed stem of *so(u)stenir* f. L *sustinēre* *sustent-* (as SUB-, *tenēre* hold)]

sustenance /'sʌstɪnəns/ *n.* **1 a** nourishment, food. **b** the process of nourishing. **2** a means of support; a livelihood. [ME f. AF *sustenaunce*, OF *so(u)stenance* (as SUSTAIN)]

sustentation /ˌsʌstən'teɪʃ(ə)n/ *n. formal* **1** the support of life. **2** maintenance. [ME f. OF *sustentation* or L *sustentatio* f. *sustentare* frequent. of *sustinēre* SUSTAIN]

susurration /ˌsju:sə'reɪʃ(ə)n, ˌsuː-/ *n.* (also **susurrus** /sjuː'sʌrəs, suː-/) *literary* a sound of whispering or rustling. [ME f. LL *susurratio* f. L *susurrare*]

Sutherland[1] /'sʌðələnd/, Graham (1903–80), English painter. During the Second World War he was an official war artist, producing poignant pictures of ruined and shattered buildings. Among his portraits are those of Somerset Maugham and the controversial portrait of Sir Winston Churchill (destroyed by Churchill's family). Religious works include the *Crucifixion* for St Matthew's, Northampton (1944) and the tapestry, a figure of Christ in Glory, for the rebuilt Coventry Cathedral (1954–7).

Sutherland[2] /'sʌðələnd/, Dame Joan (1926–), Australian operatic soprano, noted for her performances in dramatic coloratura roles. She scored an enormous success in 1959 in the title role of Donizetti's *Lucia di Lammermoor*.

Sutlej /'sʌtlɪdʒ/ a river that rises in SW Tibet and flows west through the Indian States of Himachal Pradesh and Punjab before entering Pakistan (Punjab province), where it joins the Chenab River to form the Panjnad. It is one of the 'five rivers' that gave Punjab its name.

sutler /'sʌtlə(r)/ *n. hist.* a person following an army and selling provisions etc. to the soldiers. [obs. Du. *soeteler* f. *soetelen* befoul, perform mean duties, f. Gmc]

Sutra /'suːtrə/ *n.* **1** an aphorism or set of aphorisms in Hindu literature. **2** a narrative part of Buddhist literature. **3** Jainist scripture. [Skr. *sūtra* thread, rule, f. *siv* SEW]

suttee /sʌ'tiː, 'sʌtɪ/ *n.* (also **sati**) (*pl.* **suttees** or **satis**) esp. *hist.* **1** the Hindu practice of a widow immolating herself on her husband's funeral pyre. **2** a widow who undergoes or has undergone this. [Hindi & Urdu f. Skr. *satī* faithful wife f. *sat* good]

Sutton Hoo /ˌsʌt(ə)n 'huː/ an estate in Suffolk, site of a group of barrows, one of which was found (1939) to cover the remains of a Saxon ship burial (or perhaps a cenotaph; no body was discovered) of the 7th c. AD. The timbers had decayed and only their impression was left in the soil, with the iron bolts still in place, and in the centre was a magnificent collection of grave goods, including exotic jewellery, an iron standard, decorated shield, bronze helmet, and Merovingian gold coins.

suture /'suːtʃə(r)/ *n.* & *v.* —*n.* **1** *Surgery* **a** the joining of the edges of a wound or incision by stitching. **b** the thread or wire

used for this. **2** the seamlike junction of two bones, esp. in the skull. **3** *Bot.* & *Zool.* a similar junction of parts. —*v.tr. Surgery* stitch up (a wound or incision) with a suture. □□ **sutural** *adj.* **sutured** *adj.* [F *suture* or L *sutura* f. *suere sut-* sew]

Suva /'suːvə/ the capital of Fiji, situated on the island of Viti Levu; pop. (1986) 71,600.

suzerain /'suːzərən/ *n.* **1** a feudal overlord. **2** a sovereign or State having some control over another State that is internally autonomous. □□ **suzerainty** *n.* [F, app. f. *sus* above f. L *su(r)sum* upward, after *souverain* SOVEREIGN]

s.v. *abbr.* **1** a side valve. **2** (in a reference) under the word or heading given. [sense 2 f. L *sub voce* (or *verbo*)]

Svalbard /'svaːlbaːd/ a group of islands, comprising Spitsbergen and other groups, in the Arctic Ocean about 640 km (400 miles) north of Norway, to which country they have belonged since 1925. There are important coal and mineral deposits.

svelte /svelt/ *adj.* slender, lissom, graceful. [F f. It. *svelto*]

Svengali /sveŋ'gaːlɪ/ the name of a character in George du Maurier's novel *Trilby* (1894). He is a musician who trains Trilby's voice and controls her stage singing through hypnotic power; his influence over her is such that when he dies her voice collapses and she loses her eminence.

Sverdlovsk /svead'lɒfsk/ a city of the Soviet Union, in the eastern foothills of the Ural Mountains; pop. (est. 1987) 1,331,000. It was founded by Peter the Great in 1721 and named Ekaterinburg after his wife Catherine (Russian *Ekaterina*). The Czar Nicholas II and his family were held prisoner here after the revolution of 1917 and killed in 1918. The city was renamed in 1924 after a Communist leader.

SW *abbr.* **1** south-west. **2** south-western.

swab /swɒb/ *n.* & *v.* (also **swob**) —*n.* **1** a mop or other absorbent device for cleaning or mopping up. **2 a** an absorbent pad used in surgery. **b** a specimen of a possibly morbid secretion taken with a swab for examination. **3** *sl.* a term of contempt for a person. —*v.tr.* (**swabbed, swabbing**) **1** clean with a swab. **2** (foll. by *up*) absorb (moisture) with a swab. [back-form. f. *swabber* f. early mod.Du. *zwabber* f. a Gmc base = 'splash, sway']

Swabia /'sweɪbɪə/ a former German duchy (German *Schwaben*). The region is now divided between Germany, Switzerland, and France. □□ **Swabian** *adj.* & *n.*

swaddle /'swɒd(ə)l/ *v.tr.* swathe (esp. an infant) in garments or bandages etc. □ **swaddling-clothes** narrow bandages formerly wrapped round a newborn child to restrain its movements and quieten it. [ME f. SWATHE + -LE[4]]

swag /swæg/ *n.* & *v.* —*n.* **1** *sl.* **a** the booty carried off by burglars etc. **b** illicit gains. **2 a** an ornamental festoon of flowers etc. **b** a carved etc. representation of this. **c** drapery of similar appearance. **3** *Austral.* & *NZ* a traveller's or miner's bundle of personal belongings. —*v.* (**swagged, swagging**) **1** *tr.* arrange (a curtain etc.) in swags. **2** *intr.* **a** hang heavily. **b** sway from side to side. **3** *tr.* cause to sway or sag. [16th c.: prob. f. Scand.]

swage /sweɪdʒ/ *n.* & *v.* —*n.* **1** a die or stamp for shaping wrought iron etc. by hammering or pressure. **2** a tool for bending metal etc. —*v.tr.* shape with a swage. □ **swage-block** a block with various perforations, grooves, etc. for shaping metal. [F *s(o)uage* decorative groove, of unkn. orig.]

swagger /'swægə(r)/ *v.*, *n.*, & *adj.* —*v.intr.* **1** walk arrogantly or self-importantly. **2** behave arrogantly; be domineering. —*n.* **1** a swaggering gait or manner. **2** swaggering behaviour. **3** a dashing or confident air or way of doing something. **4** smartness. —*adj.* **1** *colloq.* smart or fashionable. **2** (of a coat) cut with a loose flare from the shoulders. □ **swagger stick** a short cane carried by a military officer. □□ **swaggerer** *n.* **swaggeringly** *adv.* [app. f. SWAG *v.* + -ER[4]]

swagman /'swægmæn/ *n.* (*pl.* **-men**) *Austral.* & *NZ* a tramp carrying a swag (see SWAG *n.* 3).

Swahili /swə'hiːlɪ, swɑː'hiːlɪ/ *n.* (*pl.* same) **1** a member of a Bantu people of Zanzibar and adjacent coasts. **2** their language, a Bantu language of the Niger-Congo group with a vocabulary heavily influenced by Arabic. It is the most important language in East Africa, spoken also in the central and southern regions and expanding rapidly to the west and north, and while it is the first language of only about a million people it is used as a common language by about 20 million who speak different mother tongues. It is the official language of Kenya and Tanzania. [Arab. *sawāḥil* pl. of *sāḥil* coast]

swain /sweɪn/ n. **1** archaic a country youth. **2** poet. a young lover or suitor. [ME *swein* f. ON *sveinn* lad = OE *swān* swineherd, f. Gmc]

swallow[1] /ˈswɒləʊ/ v. & n. —v. **1** tr. cause or allow (food etc.) to pass down the throat. **2** intr. perform the muscular movement of the oesophagus required to do this. **3** tr. **a** accept meekly; put up with (an affront etc.). **b** accept credulously (an unlikely assertion etc.). **4** tr. repress; resist the expression of (a feeling etc.) (*swallow one's pride*). **5** tr. articulate (words etc.) indistinctly. **6** tr. (often foll. by *up*) engulf or absorb; exhaust; cause to disappear. —n. **1** the act of swallowing. **2** an amount swallowed in one action. □ **swallow-hole** Brit. = *sink-hole* (see SINK n. 6). □□ **swallowable** adj. **swallower** n. [OE *swelg* (n.), *swelgan* (v.) f. Gmc]

swallow[2] /ˈswɒləʊ/ n. any of various migratory swift-flying insect-eating birds of the family Hirundinidae, esp. *Hirundo rustica*, with a forked tail and long pointed wings. □ **one swallow does not make a summer** a warning against a hasty inference from one instance. **swallow-dive** a dive with the arms outspread until close to the water. **swallow-tail 1** a deeply forked tail. **2** anything resembling this shape. **3** any butterfly of the family Papilionidae with wings extended at the back to this shape. **swallow-tailed** having a swallow-tail. [OE *swealwe* f. Gmc]

swam past of SWIM.

swami /ˈswɑːmɪ/ n. (pl. **swamis**) a Hindu male religious teacher. [Hindi *swāmī* master, prince, f. Skr. *svāmin*]

Swammerdam /ˈswɑːməˌdæm/, Jan (1637–80), one of a number of Dutch investigators into what is now called biology. Qualified in medicine, he preferred to commit himself to research, and worked extensively on insects, describing their anatomy and life histories and classifying them into four groups. A pioneer in the use of lenses, he was the first to observe red blood cells; other work included an elegant demonstration of the fact that muscles do not change in volume during motion.

swamp /swɒmp/ n. & v. —n. a piece of waterlogged ground; a bog or marsh. —v. **1 a** tr. overwhelm, flood, or soak with water. **b** intr. become swamped. **2** tr. overwhelm or make invisible etc. with an excess or large amount of something. □□ **swampy** adj. (**swampier**, **swampiest**). [17th c., = dial. *swamp* sunk (14th c.), prob. of Gmc orig.]

Swan /swɒn/, Sir Joseph Wilson (1828–1914), English physicist and chemist, a pioneer of electric lighting. In 1860 he devised an electric light-bulb consisting of a carbon filament inside a glass bulb, and for nearly twenty years worked to perfect it. He formed a partnership in 1883 with the American inventor, Edison, to manufacture the bulbs. Swan also devised a dry photographic plate and (in 1878) bromide paper for the printing of negatives.

swan /swɒn/ n. & v. —n. **1** a large water-bird of the genus *Cygnus* etc., having a long flexible neck, webbed feet, and in most species snow-white plumage. **2** literary a poet. —v.intr. (**swanned**, **swanning**) (usu. foll. by *about*, *off*, etc.) colloq. move or go aimlessly or casually or with a superior air. □ **swan-dive** US = *swallow-dive* (see SWALLOW[2]). **swan-neck** a curved structure shaped like a swan's neck. **Swan of Avon** literary Shakespeare. **swan-upping** Brit. the annual taking up and marking of Thames swans. □□ **swanlike** adj. & adv. [OE f. Gmc]

swank /swæŋk/ n., v., & adj. colloq. —n. ostentation, swagger, bluff. —v.intr. behave with swank; show off. —adj. esp. US = SWANKY. [19th c.: orig. uncert.]

swankpot /ˈswæŋkpɒt/ n. Brit. colloq. a person behaving with swank.

swanky /ˈswæŋkɪ/ adj. (**swankier**, **swankiest**) **1** marked by swank; ostentatiously smart or showy. **2** (of a person) inclined to swank; boastful. □□ **swankily** adv. **swankiness** n.

swannery /ˈswɒnərɪ/ n. (pl. **-ies**) a place where swans are bred.

swansdown /ˈswɒnzdaʊn/ n. **1** the fine down of a swan, used in trimmings and esp. in powder-puffs. **2** a kind of thick cotton cloth with a soft nap on one side.

Swansea /ˈswɒnzɪ/ a city in South Wales, at the mouth of the River Tawe; pop. (1981) 167,800.

swansong /ˈswɒnsɒŋ/ n. **1** a person's last work or act before death or retirement etc. **2** a song like that fabled to be sung by a dying swan.

swap /swɒp/ v. & n. (also **swop**) —v.tr. & intr. (**swapped**, **swapping**) exchange or barter (one thing for another). —n. **1** an act of swapping. **2** a thing suitable for swapping. **3** a thing swapped. □□ **swapper** n. [ME, orig. = 'hit': prob. imit.]

SWAPO /ˈswɑːpəʊ/ abbr. South West Africa People's Organization, an organization formed in Namibia in 1964–6 from a combination of existing nationalist groups after the South African government began to try to extend formal authority in the region. Driven from the country, SWAPO began a guerrilla campaign, operating largely from neighbouring Angola.

Swaraj /swəˈrɑːdʒ/ n. hist. self-government or independence for India. □□ **Swarajist** n. [Skr., = self-ruling: cf. RAJ]

sward /swɔːd/ n. literary **1** an expanse of short grass. **2** turf. □□ **swarded** adj. [OE *sweard* skin]

sware /sweə(r)/ archaic past of SWEAR.

swarf /swɔːf/ n. **1** fine chips or filings of stone, metal, etc. **2** wax etc. removed in cutting a gramophone record. [ON *svarf* file-dust]

swarm[1] /swɔːm/ n. & v. —n. **1** a cluster of bees leaving the hive with the queen to establish a new colony. **2** a large number of insects or birds moving in a cluster. **3** a large group of people, esp. moving over or filling a large area. **4** (in pl.; foll. by *of*) great numbers. **5** a group of zoospores. —v.intr. **1** move in or form a swarm. **2** gather or move in large numbers. **3** (foll. by *with*) (of a place) be overrun, crowded, or infested (*was swarming with tourists*). [OE *swearm* f. Gmc]

swarm[2] /swɔːm/ v.intr. (foll. by *up*) & tr. climb (a rope or tree etc.), in a rush, by clasping or clinging with the hands and knees etc. [16th c.: orig. unkn.]

swart /swɔːt/ adj. archaic swarthy, dark-hued. [OE *sweart* f. Gmc]

swarthy /ˈswɔːðɪ/ adj. (**swarthier**, **swarthiest**) dark, dark-complexioned. □□ **swarthily** adv. **swarthiness** n. [var. of obs. *swarty* (as SWART)]

swash[1] /swɒʃ/ v. & n. —v. **1** intr. (of water etc.) wash about; make the sound of washing or rising and falling. **2** tr. archaic strike violently. **3** intr. archaic swagger. —n. the motion or sound of swashing water. [imit.]

swash[2] /swɒʃ/ adj. **1** inclined obliquely. **2** (of a letter) having a flourished stroke or strokes. □ **swash-plate** an inclined disc revolving on an axle and giving reciprocating motion to a part in contact with it. [17th c.: orig. unkn.]

swashbuckler /ˈswɒʃˌbʌklə(r)/ n. a swaggering bully or ruffian. □□ **swashbuckling** adj. & n. [SWASH[1] + BUCKLER]

swastika /ˈswɒstɪkə/ n. **1** an ancient symbol formed by an equal-armed cross with each arm continued at a right angle. **2** this with clockwise continuations as the symbol of Nazi Germany. [Skr. *svastika* f. *svasti* well-being f. *sú* good + *astí* being]

swat /swɒt/ v. & n. —v.tr. (**swatted**, **swatting**) **1** crush (a fly etc.) with a sharp blow. **2** hit hard and abruptly. —n. a swatting blow. [17th c. in the sense 'sit down': N.Engl. dial. & US var. of SQUAT]

swatch /swɒtʃ/ n. **1** a sample, esp. of cloth or fabric. **2** a collection of samples. [17th c.: orig. unkn.]

swath /swɔːθ/ n. (also **swathe** /sweɪð/) (pl. **swaths** /swɔːθs, swɔːðs/ or **swathes**) **1** a ridge of grass or corn etc. lying after being cut. **2** a space left clear after the passage of a mower etc. **3** a broad strip. □ **cut a wide swath** be effective in destruction. [OE *swæth*, *swathu*]

swathe /sweɪð/ v. & n. —v.tr. bind or enclose in bandages or garments etc. —n. a bandage or wrapping. [OE *swathian*]

swatter /ˈswɒtə(r)/ n. an implement for swatting flies.

sway /sweɪ/ v. & n. —v. **1** intr. lean or cause to lean unsteadily in different directions alternately. **2** intr. oscillate irregularly; waver. **3** tr. **a** control the motion or direction of. **b**

have influence or rule over. —*n.* **1** rule, influence, or government (*hold sway*). **2** a swaying motion or position. □ **sway-back** an abnormally hollowed back (esp. of a horse); lordosis. **sway-backed** (esp. of a horse) having a sway-back. [ME: cf. LG *swäjen* be blown to and fro, Du. *zwaaien* swing, wave]

Swazi /ˈswɑːzɪ/ *n.* **1 a** a member of a people of mixed stock inhabiting Swaziland and parts of eastern Transvaal in the Republic of South Africa. **2** their language, of the Niger-Congo group, an official language of Swaziland. [*Mswati*, name of a former king of the Swazi]

Swaziland /ˈswɑːzɪˌlænd/ a small landlocked country of southern Africa, bounded by Transvaal, Natal, and Mozambique; pop. (est. 1988) 735,300; official languages, Swazi and English; capital, Mbabane. The country takes its name from the Swazis who occupied it from the mid-18th c. It was a South African protectorate from 1894 and came under British rule in 1902 after the second Boer War. In 1968 it became a fully independent kingdom within the Commonwealth.

swear /sweə(r)/ *v.* & *n.* —*v.* (*past* **swore** /swɔː(r)/; *past part.* **sworn** /swɔːn/) **1** *tr.* **a** (often foll. by *to* + infin. or *that* + clause) state or promise solemnly or on oath. **b** take (an oath). **2** *tr. colloq.* say emphatically; insist (*swore he had not seen it*). **3** *tr.* cause to take an oath (*swore them to secrecy*). **4** *intr.* (often foll. by *at*) use profane or indecent language, esp. as an expletive or from anger. **5** *tr.* (often foll. by *against*) make a sworn affirmation of (an offence) (*swear treason against*). **6** *intr.* (foll. by *by*) **a** appeal to as a witness in taking an oath (*swear by Almighty God*). **b** *colloq.* have or express great confidence in (*swears by yoga*). **7** *intr.* (foll. by *to*; usu. in *neg.*) admit the certainty of (*could not swear to it*). **8** *intr.* (foll. by *at*) *colloq.* (of colours etc.) fail to harmonize with. —*n.* a spell of swearing. □ **swear blind** *colloq.* affirm emphatically. **swear in** induct into office etc. by administering an oath. **swear off** *colloq.* promise to abstain from (drink etc.). **swear-word** a profane or indecent word, esp. uttered as an expletive. □□ **swearer** *n.* [OE *swerian* f. Gmc, rel. to ANSWER]

sweat /swet/ *n.* & *v.* —*n.* **1** moisture exuded through the pores of the skin, esp. from heat or nervousness. **2** a state or period of sweating. **3** *colloq.* a state of anxiety (*was in a sweat about it*). **4** *colloq.* **a** drudgery, effort. **b** a laborious task or undertaking. **5** condensed moisture on a surface. —*v.* (*past* and *past part.* **sweated** or *US* **sweat**) **1** *intr.* exude sweat; perspire. **2** *intr.* be terrified, suffering, etc. **3** *intr.* (of a wall etc.) exhibit surface moisture. **4** *intr.* drudge, toil. **5** *tr.* heat (meat or vegetables) slowly in fat or water to extract the juices. **6** *tr.* emit (blood, gum, etc.) like sweat. **7** *tr.* make (a horse, athlete, etc.) sweat by exercise. **8** *tr.* **a** cause to drudge or toil. **b** (as **sweated** *adj.*) (of goods, workers, or labour) produced by or subjected to long hours under poor conditions. **9** *tr.* subject (hides or tobacco) to fermentation in manufacturing. □ **by the sweat of one's brow** by one's own hard work. **no sweat** *colloq.* there is no need to worry. **sweat-band** a band of absorbent material inside a hat or round a wrist etc. to soak up sweat. **sweat blood** *colloq.* **1** work strenuously. **2** be extremely anxious. **sweat gland** *Anat.* a spiral tubular gland below the skin secreting sweat. **sweating-sickness** an epidemic fever with sweating prevalent in England in the 15th–16th c. **sweat it out** *colloq.* endure a difficult experience to the end. [ME *swet(e)*, alt. (after *swete* v. f. OE *swǽtan* OHG *sweizzen* roast) of *swote* f. OE *swāt* f. Gmc]

sweater /ˈswetə(r)/ *n.* **1** a jersey or pullover of a kind worn before, during, or after exercise, or as an informal garment. **2** an employer who works employees hard in poor conditions for low pay.

sweatshirt /ˈswetʃɜːt/ *n.* a sleeved cotton sweater of a kind worn by athletes before and after exercise.

sweatshop /ˈswetʃɒp/ *n.* a workshop where sweated labour is used.

sweatsuit /ˈswetsuːt, -sjuːt/ *n.* a suit of a sweatshirt and loose trousers, as worn by athletes etc.

sweaty /ˈswetɪ/ *adj.* (**sweatier**, **sweatiest**) **1** sweating; covered with sweat. **2** causing sweat. □□ **sweatily** *adv.* **sweatiness** *n.*

Swede /swiːd/ *n.* **1 a** a native or national of Sweden. **b** a person of Swedish descent. **2** (**swede**) (in full **swede turnip**) a large

yellow-fleshed turnip, *Brassica napus*, orig. from Sweden. [MLG & MDu. *Swēde*, prob. f. ON *Svíthjóth* f. *Svíar* Swedes + *thjóth* people]

Sweden /ˈswiːd(ə)n/ a country occupying the eastern part of the Scandinavian peninsula; pop. (est. 1988) 8,393,000, official language, Swedish; capital, Stockholm. Its Germanic and Gothic inhabitants took part in the Viking raids. Originally united in the 12th c., Sweden formed part of the Union of Kalmar with Denmark and Norway from 1397 until its re-emergence as an independent State under Gustavus Vasa in 1523. The following two centuries saw the country's rise and fall as the prominent Baltic power, influence on the European mainland peaking during the reign of Gustavus Adolphus in the early 17th c. and collapsing following the defeat of Charles XII in the Great Northern War at the beginning of the 18th c. Between 1814 and 1905, Sweden was united with Norway. She maintained her neutrality in the two World Wars, while her economy prospered through increasing industrialization, and the political hegemony of the Social Democratic party led to the creation of an extensive system of social security.

Swedenborg /ˈswiːdənˌbɔːg/, Emanuel (1688–1772), Swedish scientist and mystical thinker. Endowed with unusual mental fertility and inventiveness and considerable mathematical ability, he anticipated many subsequent hypotheses and discoveries (nebular theory, magnetic theory, machine-gun, aeroplane), and is also claimed as the founder of crystallography. As time went on he became increasingly concerned to show by scientific means the fundamentally spiritual structure of the universe. In 1743–5 he became conscious of visions both in dreams and while awake, and felt called to make known his doctrines to mankind at large. He spent the rest of his life writing assiduously, with doctrines that were a blend of pantheism and theosophy, and maintaining his scientific interests to the end. Swedenborg himself wished his teaching to be propagated within existing Churches but his followers set up an independent body, the New Jerusalem Church. The movement is especially strong in Lancashire.

Swedish /ˈswiːdɪʃ/ *adj.* & *n.* —*adj.* of or relating to Sweden or its people or language. —*n.* the official language of Sweden, spoken by its 8 million inhabitants, by another 300,000 in Finland (where it is one of the two official languages), and by 600,000 in the US. It belongs to the Scandinavian language group.

Sweeney /ˈswiːnɪ/ *n.* (prec. by *the*) *Brit. sl.* the members of a flying squad. [rhyming sl. f. *Sweeney* Todd, a barber who murdered his customers]

sweep /swiːp/ *v.* & *n.* —*v.* (*past* and *past part.* **swept** /swept/) **1** *tr.* clean or clear (a room or area etc.) with or as with a broom. **2** *intr.* (often foll. by *up*) clean a room etc. in this way. **3** *tr.* (often foll. by *up*) collect or remove (dirt or litter etc.) by sweeping. **4** *tr.* (foll. by *aside*, *away*, etc.) **a** push with or as with a broom. **b** dismiss or reject abruptly (*their objections were swept aside*). **5** *tr.* (foll. by *along*, *down*, etc.) carry or drive along with force. **6** *tr.* (foll. by *off*, *away*, etc.) remove or clear forcefully. **7** *tr.* traverse swiftly or lightly (*the wind swept the hillside*). **8** *tr.* impart a sweeping motion to (*swept his hand across*). **9** *tr.* swiftly cover or affect (*a new fashion swept the country*). **10** *intr.* **a** glide swiftly; speed along with unchecked motion. **b** go majestically. **11** *intr.* (of geographical features etc.) have continuous extent. **12** *tr.* drag (a river-bottom etc.) to search for something. **13** *tr.* (of artillery etc.) include in the line of fire; cover the whole of. **14** *tr.* propel (a barge etc.) with sweeps. —*n.* **1** the act or motion or an instance of sweeping. **2** a curve in the road, a sweeping line of a hill, etc. **3** range or scope (*beyond the sweep of the human mind*). **4** = *chimney-sweep*. **5** a sortie by aircraft. **6** *colloq.* = SWEEPSTAKE. **7** a long oar worked from a barge etc. **8** the sail of a windmill. **9** a long pole mounted as a lever for raising buckets from a well. **10** *Electronics* the movement of a beam across the screen of a cathode-ray tube. □ **make a clean sweep of 1** completely abolish or expel. **2** win all the prizes etc. in (a competition etc.). **sweep away 1** abolish swiftly. **2** (usu. in *passive*) powerfully affect, esp. emotionally. **sweep the board 1** win all the money in a gambling-game. **2** win all possible prizes etc. **sweep-second**

hand a second-hand on a clock or watch, moving on the same dial as the other hands. **sweep under the carpet** see CARPET. **swept-back** (of an aircraft wing) fixed at an acute angle to the fuselage, inclining outwards towards the rear. **swept-up** (of hair) = UPSWEPT. **swept-wing** (of an aircraft) having swept-back wings. [ME *swepe* (earlier *swōpe*) f. OE *swāpan*]

sweepback /'swiːpbæk/ *n.* the angle at which an aircraft's wing is set back from a position at right angles to the body.

sweeper /'swiːpə(r)/ *n.* **1** a person who cleans by sweeping. **2** a device for sweeping carpets etc. **3** *Football* a defensive player positioned close to the goalkeeper.

sweeping /'swiːpɪŋ/ *adj.* & *n.* —*adj.* **1** wide in range or effect (*sweeping changes*). **2** taking no account of particular cases or exceptions (*a sweeping statement*). —*n.* (in *pl.*) dirt etc. collected by sweeping. □□ **sweepingly** *adv.* **sweepingness** *n.*

sweepstake /'swiːpsteɪk/ *n.* **1** a form of gambling on horse-races etc. in which all competitors' stakes are paid to the winners. **2** a race with betting of this kind. **3** a prize or prizes won in a sweepstake.

sweet /swiːt/ *adj.* & *n.* —*adj.* **1** having the pleasant taste characteristic of sugar. **2** smelling pleasant like roses or perfume etc.; fragrant. **3** (of sound etc.) melodious or harmonious. **4 a** not salt, sour, or bitter. **b** fresh, with flavour unimpaired by rottenness. **c** (of water) fresh and readily drinkable. **5** (of wine) having a sweet taste (opp. DRY). **6** highly gratifying or attractive. **7** amiable, pleasant (*has a sweet nature*). **8** *colloq.* (of a person or thing) pretty, charming, endearing. **9** (foll. by *on*) *colloq.* fond of; in love with. —*n.* **1** *Brit.* a small shaped piece of confectionery usu. made with sugar or sweet chocolate. **2** *Brit.* a sweet dish forming a course of a meal. **3** a sweet part of something; sweetness. **4** (in *pl.*) delights, gratification. **5** (esp. as a form of address) sweetheart etc. □ **she's sweet** *Austral. sl.* all is well. **sweet-and-sour** cooked in a sauce containing sugar and vinegar or lemon etc. **sweet basil** see BASIL. **sweet bay** = BAY². **sweet-brier** see BRIER¹. **sweet chestnut** see CHESTNUT. **sweet cicely** a white-flowered aromatic plant, *Myrrhis odorata*. **sweet corn** **1** a kind of maize with kernels having a high sugar content. **2** these kernels, eaten as a vegetable when young. **sweet flag** = *sweet rush*. **sweet-gale** see GALE². **sweet pea** any climbing plant of the genus *Lathyrus*, esp. *L. odoratus* with fragrant flowers in many colours. **sweet pepper** see PEPPER. **sweet potato 1** a tropical climbing plant, *Ipomoea batatas*, with sweet tuberous roots used for food. **2** the root of this. **sweet rocket** see ROCKET². **sweet rush** (or **sedge**) a kind of sedge with a thick creeping aromatic rootstock used in medicine and confectionery. **sweet sultan** a sweet-scented plant, *Centaurea moschata* or *C. suaveoleus*. **sweet talk** *colloq.* flattery, blandishment. **sweet-talk** *v.tr. colloq.* flatter in order to persuade. **sweet-tempered** amiable. **sweet tooth** a liking for sweet-tasting things. **sweet violet** a sweet-scented violet, *Viola odorata*. **sweet william** a plant, *Dianthus barbatus*, with clusters of vivid fragrant flowers. □□ **sweetish** *adj.* **sweetly** *adv.* [OE *swēte* f. Gmc]

sweetbread /'swiːtbred/ *n.* the pancreas or thymus of an animal, esp. as food.

sweeten /'swiːt(ə)n/ *v.tr.* & *intr.* **1** make or become sweet or sweeter. **2** make agreeable or less painful. □ **sweeten the pill** see PILL. □□ **sweetening** *n.*

sweetener /'swiːtənə(r)/ *n.* **1** a substance used to sweeten food or drink. **2** *colloq.* a bribe or inducement.

sweetheart /'swiːthɑːt/ *n.* **1** a lover or darling. **2** a term of endearment (esp. as a form of address). □ **sweetheart agreement** (or **deal**) *colloq.* an industrial agreement reached privately by employers and trade unions in their own interests.

sweetie /'swiːtɪ/ *n. colloq.* **1** *Brit.* a sweet. **2** (also **sweetie-pie**) a term of endearment (esp. as a form of address).

sweeting /'swiːtɪŋ/ *n.* **1** a sweet-flavoured variety of apple. **2** *archaic* darling.

sweetmeal /'swiːtmiːl/ *n.* **1** sweetened wholemeal. **2** a sweetmeal biscuit.

sweetmeat /'swiːtmiːt/ *n.* **1** a sweet (see SWEET *n.* 1). **2** a small fancy cake.

sweetness /'swiːtnɪs/ *n.* the quality of being sweet; fragrance,

melodiousness, etc. □ **sweetness and light** a display of (esp. uncharacteristic) mildness and reason.

sweetshop /'swiːtʃɒp/ *n. Brit.* a shop selling sweets as its main item.

sweetsop /'swiːtsɒp/ *n.* **1** a tropical American evergreen shrub, *Annona squamosa*. **2** the fruit of this, having a green rind and a sweet pulp.

swell /swel/ *v.*, *n.*, & *adj.* —*v.* (*past part.* **swollen** /'swəʊlən/ or **swelled**) **1** *intr.* & *tr.* grow or cause to grow bigger or louder or more intense; expand; increase in force or intensity. **2** *intr.* (often foll. by *up*) & *tr.* rise or raise up from the surrounding surface. **3** *intr.* (foll. by *out*) bulge. **4** *intr.* (of the heart as the seat of emotion) feel full of joy, pride, relief, etc. **5** *intr.* (foll. by *with*) be hardly able to restrain (pride etc.). —*n.* **1** an act or the state of swelling. **2** the heaving of the sea with waves that do not break, e.g. after a storm. **3 a** a crescendo. **b** a mechanism in an organ etc. for obtaining a crescendo or diminuendo. **4** *colloq.* a person of distinction or of dashing or fashionable appearance. **5** a protuberant part. —*adj.* **1** esp. *US colloq.* fine, splendid, excellent. **2** *colloq.* smart, fashionable. □ **swell-box** *Mus.* a box in which organ-pipes are enclosed, with a shutter for controlling the sound-level. **swelled** (or **swollen**) **head** *colloq.* conceit. **swell-organ** *Mus.* a section of an organ with pipes in a swell-box. □□ **swellish** *adj.* [OE *swellan* f. Gmc]

swelling /'swelɪŋ/ *n.* an abnormal protuberance on or in the body.

swelter /'sweltə(r)/ *v.* & *n.* —*v.intr.* (of the atmosphere, or a person etc. suffering from it) be uncomfortably hot. —*n.* a sweltering atmosphere or condition. □□ **swelteringly** *adv.* [base of (now dial.) *swelt* f. OE *sweltan* perish f. Gmc]

swept *past* and *past part.* of SWEEP.

swerve /swɜːv/ *v.* & *n.* —*v.intr.* & *tr.* change or cause to change direction, esp. abruptly. —*n.* **1** a swerving movement. **2** divergence from a course. □□ **swerveless** *adj.* **swerver** *n.* [ME, repr. OE *sweorfan* SCOUR¹]

SWG *abbr.* standard wire gauge.

Swift /swɪft/, Jonathan (1667–1745), Anglo-Irish poet and satirist, nicknamed 'the Dean'. He was born in Dublin, a cousin of Dryden, and divided his life between London and Ireland. His *Journal to Stella* (letters to Esther Johnson, 1710–13) give a vivid account of life in London, where he was close to Tory ministers. Swift's relations with Stella have remained obscure; whether he ultimately married her is uncertain. Another woman, Esther Vanhomrigh ('Vanessa'), entered his life in 1708, and their romance is related in the poem *Cadenus and Vanessa* (1713). While in England he wrote *A Tale of a Tub* (1697), a satire on 'corruptions in religion and learning'. He also wrote many political pamphlets, and involved himself in Irish affairs. In 1713 he was made Dean of St Patrick's in Dublin, where he wrote his greatest work *Gulliver's Travels* (1726), a powerful satire on man and human institutions, with a fantastic tale of travels in wonderland which appeals to all ages. Macaulay, Thackeray, and many other writers were alienated by his ferocity and coarseness, but the 20th c. has seen a revival of critical interest stressing his vigour and satirical inventiveness rather than his alleged misanthropy. Nearly all his works were published anonymously and for only one, *Gulliver's Travels*, did he receive any payment (£200).

swift /swɪft/ *adj.*, *adv.*, & *n.* —*adj.* **1** quick, rapid; soon coming or passing. **2** speedy, prompt (*a swift response; was swift to act*). —*adv.* (*archaic* except in *comb.*) swiftly (*swift-moving*). —*n.* **1** any swift-flying insect-eating bird of the family Apodidae, with long wings and a superficial resemblance to a swallow. **2** a revolving frame for winding yarn etc. from. □□ **swiftly** *adv.* **swiftness** *n.* [OE, rel. to *swīfan* move in a course]

swiftie /'swɪftɪ/ *n. Austral. sl.* **1** a deceptive trick. **2** a person who acts or thinks quickly.

swiftlet /'swɪftlɪt/ *n.* a small swift of the genus *Collocalia*.

swig /swɪg/ *v.* & *n.* —*v.tr.* & *intr.* (**swigged**, **swigging**) *colloq.* drink in large draughts. —*n.* a swallow of drink, esp. a large amount. □□ **swigger** *n.* [16th c., orig. as noun in obs. sense 'liquor': orig. unkn.]

swill /swɪl/ *v.* & *n.* —*v.* **1** *tr.* (often foll. by *out*) rinse or flush;

pour water over or through. **2** *tr.* & *intr.* drink greedily. —*n.* **1** an act of rinsing. **2** mainly liquid refuse as pig-food. **3** inferior liquor. □□ **swiller** *n.* [OE *swillan*, *swilian*, of unkn. orig.]

swim /swɪm/ *v.* & *n.* —*v.* (**swimming**; past **swam** /swæm/; past part. **swum** /swʌm/) **1** *intr.* propel the body through water by working the arms and legs, or (of a fish) the fins and tail. **2** *tr.* **a** traverse (a stretch of water or its distance) by swimming. **b** compete in (a race) by swimming. **c** use (a particular stroke) in swimming. **3** *intr.* float on or at the surface of a liquid (*bubbles swimming on the surface*). **4** *intr.* appear to undulate or reel or whirl. **5** *intr.* have a dizzy effect or sensation (*my head swam*). **6** *intr.* (foll. by *in*, *with*) be flooded. —*n.* **1** a spell or the act of swimming. **2** a deep pool frequented by fish in a river. □ **in the swim** involved in or acquainted with what is going on. **swim-bladder** a gas-filled sac in fishes used to maintain buoyancy. **swimming-bath** (or **-pool**) an artificial indoor or outdoor pool for swimming. **swimming-costume** *Brit.* a garment worn for swimming. □□ **swimmable** *adj.* **swimmer** *n.* [OE *swimman* f. Gmc]

swimmeret /ˈswɪməˌret/ *n.* a swimming-foot in crustaceans.

swimmingly /ˈswɪmɪŋlɪ/ *adv.* with easy and unobstructed progress.

swimsuit /ˈswɪmsuːt, -sjuːt/ *n.* a one-piece swimming-costume worn by women. □□ **swimsuited** *adj.*

swimwear /ˈswɪmweə(r)/ *n.* clothing worn for swimming.

Swinburne /ˈswɪnbɜːn/, Algernon Charles (1837–1909), English poet and critic, associated with Rossetti and the Pre-Raphaelite circle. He achieved celebrity with *Atalanta in Calydon* (1865), a drama in classical Greek form which revealed his great metrical skills. *Poems and Ballads* (1866) demonstrates his preoccupation with de Sade and masochism, and his outspoken repudiation of Christianity caused the volume to be censured; *A Song of Italy* (1867) and *Songs before Sunrise* (1871) expressed his support for Mazzini in the struggle for Italian independence and his hatred of authority. His health was seriously affected by heavy drinking and in 1879 he moved to Putney to be cared for by his friend the critic T. Watts-Dunton. As a critic Swinburne showed perception and originality, contributed to the revival of interest in Elizabethan drama, and influenced modern criticism with his studies of Blake, the Brontës, and others.

swindle /ˈswɪnd(ə)l/ *v.* & *n.* —*v.tr.* (often foll. by *out of*) **1** cheat (a person) of money, possessions, etc. (*was swindled out of all his savings*). **2** cheat a person of (money etc.) (*swindled all his savings out of him*). —*n.* **1** an act of swindling. **2** a person or thing represented as what it is not. **3** a fraudulent scheme. □□ **swindler** *n.* [back-form. f. *swindler* f. G *Schwindler* extravagant maker of schemes, swindler, f. *schwindeln* be dizzy]

swine /swaɪn/ *n.* (pl. same) **1** *formal* or *US* a pig. **2** *colloq.* (pl. **swine** or **swines**) **a** a term of contempt or disgust for a person. **b** a very unpleasant or difficult thing. □ **swine fever** an intestinal virus disease of pigs. □□ **swinish** *adj.* (esp. in sense 2). **swinishly** *adv.* **swinishness** *n.* [OE *swīn* f. Gmc]

swineherd /ˈswaɪnhɜːd/ *n.* a person who tends pigs.

swing /swɪŋ/ *v.* & *n.* —*v.* (past and past part. **swung** /swʌŋ/) **1** *intr.* & *tr.* move or cause to move with a to-and-fro or curving motion, as of an object attached at one end and hanging free at the other. **2** *intr.* & *tr.* **a** sway. **b** hang so as to be free to sway. **c** oscillate or cause to oscillate. **3** *intr.* & *tr.* revolve or cause to revolve. **4** *intr.* move by gripping something and leaping etc. (*swung from tree to tree*). **5** *intr.* go with a swinging gait (*swung out of the room*). **6** *intr.* (foll. by *round*) move round to the opposite direction. **7** *intr.* change from one opinion or mood to another. **8** *intr.* (foll. by *at*) attempt to hit or punch. **9 a** *intr.* (also **swing it**) play music with a swing rhythm. **b** *tr.* play (a tune) with swing. **10** *intr. colloq.* **a** be lively or up to date; enjoy oneself. **b** be promiscuous. **11** *intr. colloq.* (of a party etc.) be lively, successful, etc. **12** *tr.* have a decisive influence on (esp. voting etc.). **13** *tr. colloq.* deal with or achieve; manage. **14** *intr. colloq.* be executed by hanging. **15** *Cricket* **a** *intr.* (of the ball) deviate from a straight course in the air. **b** *tr.* cause (the ball) to do this. —*n.* **1** the act or an instance of swinging. **2** the motion of swinging. **3** the extent of swinging. **4** a swinging or smooth gait or rhythm or

action. **5 a** a seat slung by ropes or chains etc. for swinging on or in. **b** a spell of swinging on this. **6** an easy but vigorous continued action. **7 a** jazz or dance music with an easy flowing rhythm. Since the mid-1930s (esp. for a decade) the term has been applied to a variety of big dance-band music played in this style. **b** the rhythmic feeling or drive of this music. **8 a** discernible change in opinion, esp. the amount by which votes or points scored etc. change from one side to another. □ **swing-boat** a boat-shaped swing at fairs. **swing-bridge** a bridge that can be swung to one side to allow the passage of ships. **swing-door** a door able to open in either direction and close itself when released. **swing the lead** *Brit. colloq.* malinger; shirk one's duty. **swings and roundabouts** a situation affording no eventual gain or loss (from the phr. *lose on the swings what you make on the roundabouts*). **swing shift** *US* a work shift from afternoon to late evening. **swing-wing** an aircraft wing that can move from a right-angled to a swept-back position. **swung dash** a dash (~) with alternate curves. □□ **swinger** *n.* (esp. in sense 10 of *v.*). [OE *swingan* to beat f. Gmc]

swinge /swɪndʒ/ *v.tr.* (**swingeing**) *archaic* strike hard; beat. [alt. f. ME *swenge* f. OE *swengan* shake, shatter, f. Gmc]

swingeing /ˈswɪndʒɪŋ/ *adj.* esp. *Brit.* **1** (of a blow) forcible. **2** huge or far-reaching, esp. in severity (*swingeing economies*). □□ **swingeingly** *adv.*

swinging /ˈswɪŋɪŋ/ *adj.* **1** (of gait, melody, etc.) vigorously rhythmical. **2** *colloq.* **a** lively; up to date; excellent. **b** promiscuous. □□ **swingingly** *adv.*

swingle /ˈswɪŋɡ(ə)l/ *n.* & *v.* —*n.* **1** a wooden instrument for beating flax and removing the woody parts from it. **2** the swinging part of a flail. —*v.tr.* clean (flax) with a swingle. [ME f. MDu. *swinghel* (as SWING, -LE¹)]

swingletree /ˈswɪŋɡ(ə)lˌtriː/ *n.* a crossbar pivoted in the middle, to which the traces are attached in a cart, plough, etc.

swingy /ˈswɪŋɪ/ *adj.* (**swingier**, **swingiest**) **1** (of music) characterized by swing (see SWING *n.* 7). **2** (of a skirt or dress) designed to swing with body movement.

swipe /swaɪp/ *v.* & *n. colloq.* —*v.* **1** *tr.* & (often foll. by *at*) *intr.* hit hard and recklessly. **2** *tr.* steal. —*n.* a reckless hard hit or attempted hit. □□ **swiper** *n.* [perh. var. of SWEEP]

swipple /ˈswɪp(ə)l/ *n.* the swingle of a flail. [ME, prob. formed as SWEEP + -LE¹]

swirl /swɜːl/ *v.* & *n.* —*v.intr.* & *tr.* move or flow or carry along with a whirling motion. —*n.* **1** a swirling motion of or in water, air, etc. **2** the act of swirling. **3** a twist or curl, esp. as part of a pattern or design. □□ **swirly** *adj.* [ME (orig. as noun): orig. Sc., perh. of LG or Du. orig.]

swish /swɪʃ/ *v.*, *n.*, & *adj.* —*v.* **1** *tr.* swing (a scythe or stick etc.) audibly through the air, grass, etc. **2** *intr.* move with or make a swishing sound. **3** *tr.* (foll. by *off*) cut (a flower etc.) in this way. —*n.* a swishing action or sound. —*adj. colloq.* smart, fashionable. □□ **swishy** *adj.* [imit.]

Swiss /swɪs/ *adj.* & *n.* —*adj.* of or relating to Switzerland or its people. —*n.* (pl. same) **1** a native or national of Switzerland. **2** a person of Swiss descent. □ **Swiss chard** = CHARD. **Swiss cheese plant** a climbing house-plant, *Monstera deliciosa*, with aerial roots and holes in the leaves (as in some Swiss cheeses). **Swiss guards** Swiss mercenary troops employed formerly by sovereigns of France etc. and still at the Vatican. **Swiss roll** a cylindrical cake with a spiral cross-section, made from a flat piece of sponge cake spread with jam etc. and rolled up. [F *Suisse* f. MHG *Swīz*]

switch /swɪtʃ/ *n.* & *v.* —*n.* **1** a device for making and breaking the connection in an electric circuit. **2 a** a transfer, change-over, or deviation. **b** an exchange. **3** a slender flexible shoot cut from a tree. **4** a light tapering rod. **5** *US* a device at the junction of railway tracks for transferring a train from one track to another; = POINT *n.* 17. **6** a tress of false or detached hair tied at one end used in hairdressing. —*v.* **1** *tr.* (foll. by *on*, *off*) turn (an electrical device) on or off. **2** *intr.* change or transfer position, subject, etc. **3** *tr.* change or transfer. **4** *tr.* reverse the positions of; exchange (*switched chairs*). **5** *tr.* swing or snatch (a thing) suddenly (*switched it out of my hand*). **6** *tr.* beat or flick with a switch. □ **switch-blade**

a pocket knife with the blade released by a spring. **switched-on** *colloq.* **1** up to date; aware of what is going on. **2** excited; under the influence of drugs. **switch off** *colloq.* cease to pay attention. **switch over** change or exchange. **switch-over** *n.* a change or exchange. □□ **switcher** *n.* [earlier *swits, switz*, prob. f. LG]

switchback /ˈswɪtʃbæk/ *n.* **1** *Brit.* a railway at a fair etc., in which the train's ascents are effected by the momentum of its previous descents. **2** (often *attrib.*) a railway or road with alternate sharp ascents and descents.

switchboard /ˈswɪtʃbɔːd/ *n.* an apparatus for varying connections between electric circuits, esp. in telephony.

swither /ˈswɪðə(r)/ *v. & n. Sc.* —*v.intr.* hesitate; be uncertain. —*n.* doubt or uncertainty. [16th c.: orig. unkn.]

Swithin /ˈswɪðɪn/, St (d. 862), chaplain to Egbert king of Wessex, and bishop of Winchester from 852. The tradition that any rain on St Swithin's day (15 July) will remain for the next forty days may refer to the heavy rain said to have occurred when his relics were to be transferred to a shrine in the cathedral.

Switzerland /ˈswɪtsələnd/ a small country in central Europe, dominated by the Alps and Jura Mountains; pop. (est. 1988) 6,592,550; official languages, French, German, Italian, and Romansch; capital, Berne. The area (occupied by a Celtic people, the Helvetii) was under Roman rule from the 1st c. BC until the 5th c. AD, and from the 10th c. formed part of the Holy Roman Empire. Switzerland emerged as an independent country in the Middle Ages when the local cantons joined in league to defeat first their Hapsburg overlords (14th c.; see SCHWYZ) and then their Burgundian neighbours (15th c.). The Swiss Confederation maintained neutrality in international affairs through the 17th and 18th centuries, and after a period of French domination (1798–1815), the Confederation's neutrality was guaranteed by the other European powers. Neutral in both World Wars, Switzerland has emerged as the headquarters of such international organizations as the Red Cross. The population is divided linguistically into French-, German-, and Italian-speaking areas, while the economy is centred on precision engineering, dairy products, and tourism, also benefiting from the country's position as an international financial centre.

swivel /ˈswɪv(ə)l/ *n. & v.* —*n.* a coupling between two parts enabling one to revolve without turning the other. —*v.tr. & intr.* (**swivelled, swivelling**; *US* **swiveled, swiveling**) turn on or as on a swivel. □ **swivel chair** a chair with a seat able to be turned horizontally. [ME f. weak grade *swif-* of OE *swīfan* sweep + -LE¹: cf. SWIFT]

swizz /swɪz/ *n.* (also **swiz**) (*pl.* **swizzes**) *Brit. colloq.* **1** something unfair or disappointing. **2** a swindle. [abbr. of SWIZZLE²]

swizzle¹ /ˈswɪz(ə)l/ *n. & v. colloq.* —*n.* a mixed alcoholic drink esp. of rum or gin and bitters made frothy. —*v.tr.* stir with a swizzle-stick. □ **swizzle-stick** a stick used for frothing or flattening drinks. [19th c.: orig. unkn.]

swizzle² /ˈswɪz(ə)l/ *n. Brit. colloq.* = SWIZZ. [20th c.: prob. alt. of SWINDLE]

swob var. of SWAB.

swollen *past part.* of SWELL.

swoon /swuːn/ *v. & n. literary* —*v.intr.* faint; fall into a fainting-fit. —*n.* an occurrence of fainting. [ME *swoune* perh. back-form. f. *swogning* (n.) f. *iswogen* f. OE *geswogen* overcome]

swoop /swuːp/ *v. & n.* —*v.* **1** *intr.* (often foll. by *down*) descend rapidly like a bird of prey. **2** *intr.* (often foll. by *on*) make a sudden attack from a distance. **3** *tr.* (often foll. by *up*) *colloq.* snatch the whole of at one swoop. —*n.* a swooping or snatching movement or action. □ **at** (or **in**) **one fell swoop** see FELL⁴. [perh. dial. var. of obs. *swōpe* f. OE *swāpan*: see SWEEP]

swoosh /swʊʃ/ *n. & v.* —*n.* the noise of a sudden rush of liquid, air, etc. —*v.intr.* move with this noise. [imit.]

swop var. of SWAP.

sword /sɔːd/ *n.* **1** a weapon usu. of metal with a long blade and hilt with a handguard, used esp. for thrusting or striking, and often worn as part of ceremonial dress. (See below.) **2** (prec. by *the*) **a** war. **b** military power. □ **put to the sword** kill, esp. in war. **sword-bearer** an official carrying the sovereign's etc. sword on a formal occasion. **sword dance** a dance in which the performers brandish swords or step about swords laid on the ground. **sword grass** a grass, *Scirpus americanus*, with swordlike leaves. **sword knot** a ribbon or tassel attached to a sword-hilt orig. for securing it to the wrist. **sword lily** = GLADIOLUS. **sword of Damocles** see DAMOCLES. **the sword of justice** judicial authority. **Sword of State** a sword borne before the sovereign on State occasions. **sword-swallower** a person ostensibly or actually swallowing sword blades as entertainment. □□ **swordlike** *adj.* [OE *sw(e)ord* f. Gmc]

The sword evolved in the Bronze Age, when metal-smelting became known, and developed in various forms—as a rapier, for cut-and-thrust, and for slashing; with a straight blade, and with the curved blade which was believed to deal a deeper wound. It became obsolete as an infantry weapon after the development of explosives, but remained in use as a weapon of cavalry units until the early 20th c.

swordbill /ˈsɔːdbɪl/ *n.* a long-billed humming-bird, *Ensifera ensifera*.

swordfish /ˈsɔːdfɪʃ/ *n.* a large marine fish, *Xiphias gladius*, with an extended swordlike upper jaw.

swordplay /ˈsɔːdpleɪ/ *n.* **1** fencing. **2** repartee; cut-and-thrust argument.

swordsman /ˈsɔːdzmən/ *n.* (*pl.* **-men**) a person of (usu. specified) skill with a sword. □□ **swordsmanship** *n.*

swordstick /ˈsɔːdstɪk/ *n.* a hollow walking-stick containing a blade that can be used as a sword.

swordtail /ˈsɔːdteɪl/ *n.* **1** a tropical fish, *Xiphophorus helleri*, with a long tail. **2** = *horseshoe crab*.

swore *past* of SWEAR.

sworn /swɔːn/ **1** *past part.* of SWEAR. **2** *adj.* bound by or as by an oath (*sworn enemies*).

swot /swɒt/ *v. & n. Brit. colloq.* —*v.* (**swotted, swotting**) **1** *intr.* study assiduously. **2** *tr.* (often foll. by *up*) study (a subject) hard or hurriedly. —*n.* **1** a person who swots. **2 a** hard study. **b** a thing that requires this. [dial. var. of SWEAT]

swum *past part.* of SWIM.

swung *past* and *past part.* of SWING.

swy /swaɪ/ *n. Austral.* two-up. [G *zwei* two]

SY *abbr.* steam yacht.

sybarite /ˈsɪbəˌraɪt/ *n. & adj.* —*n.* a person who is self-indulgent or devoted to sensuous luxury. —*adj.* fond of luxury or sensuousness. □□ **sybaritic** /-ˈrɪtɪk/ *adj.* **sybaritical** /-ˈrɪtɪk/ *adj.* **sybaritically** /-ˈrɪtɪkəlɪ/ *adv.* **sybaritism** *n.* [orig. an inhabitant of Sybaris in S. Italy, noted for luxury, f. L *sybarita* f. Gk *subarītēs*]

sycamine /ˈsɪkəˌmaɪn, -mɪn/ *n. Bibl.* the black mulberry tree, *Morus nigra* (see Luke 17: 6; in modern versions translated as 'mulberry tree'). [L *sycaminus* f. Gk *sukaminos* mulberry-tree f. Heb. *šiḳmāh* sycamore, assim. to Gk *sukon* fig]

sycamore /ˈsɪkəˌmɔː(r)/ *n.* **1** (in full **sycamore maple**) **a** a large maple, *Acer pseudoplatanus*, with winged seeds, grown for its shade and timber. **b** its wood. **2** *US* the plane-tree or its wood. **3** *Bibl.* a fig-tree, *Ficus sycomorus*, growing in Egypt, Syria, etc. [var. of SYCOMORE]

syce /saɪs/ *n.* (also **sice**) *Anglo-Ind.* a groom. [Hind. f. Arab. *sā'is, sāyis*]

sycomore /ˈsɪkəˌmɔː(r)/ *n. Bot.* = SYCAMORE 3. [ME f. OF *sic(h)amor* f. L *sycomorus* f. Gk *sukomoros* f. *sukon* fig + *moron* mulberry]

syconium /saɪˈkəʊnɪəm/ *n.* (*pl.* **syconia**) *Bot.* a fleshy hollow receptacle developing into a multiple fruit as in the fig. [mod.L f. Gk *sukon* fig]

sycophant /ˈsɪkəˌfænt/ *n.* a servile flatterer; a toady. □□ **sycophancy** *n.* **sycophantic** /-ˈfæntɪk/ *adj.* **sycophantically** /-ˈfæntɪkəlɪ/ *adv.* [F *sycophante* or L *sycophanta* f. Gk *sukophantēs* informer f. *sukon* fig + *phainō* show: the reason for the name is uncert., and association with informing against the illegal exportation of figs from ancient Athens (recorded by Plutarch) cannot be substantiated]

sycosis /saɪˈkəʊsɪs/ *n.* a skin-disease of the bearded part of the face with inflammation of the hair-follicles. [mod.L f. Gk *sukōsis* f. *sukon* fig: orig. of a figlike ulcer]

Sydenham /ˈsɪdənəm/, Thomas (c.1624–89), 'the English Hippocrates', so called for his contemporary reputation as a physician and his scepticism of theoretical medicine. He emphasized the healing power of nature, made a study of epidemics, wrote a treatise on gout (from which he suffered), and explained the nature of chorea (St Vitus's dance).

Sydney /ˈsɪdnɪ/ the capital of New South Wales, the largest city and chief port of Australia; pop. (1986) 3,430,600.

syenite /ˈsaɪəˌnaɪt/ n. a grey crystalline rock of feldspar and hornblende with or without quartz. □□ **syenitic** /-ˈnɪtɪk/ adj. [F syénite f. L Syenites (lapis) (stone) of Syene in Egypt]

syl- /sɪl/ prefix assim. form of SYN- before l.

syllabary /ˈsɪləbərɪ/ n. (pl. -ies) a list of characters representing syllables and (in some languages or stages of writing) serving the purpose of an alphabet. [mod.L syllabarium (as SYLLABLE)]

syllabi pl. of SYLLABUS.

syllabic /sɪˈlæbɪk/ adj. 1 of, relating to, or based on syllables. 2 Prosody based on the number of syllables. 3 (of a symbol) representing a whole syllable. 4 articulated in syllables. □□ **syllabically** adv. **syllabicity** /-ˈbɪsɪtɪ/ n. [F syllabique or LL syllabicus f. Gk sullabikos (as SYLLABLE)]

syllabication /ˌsɪlæbɪˈkeɪʃ(ə)n/ n. (also **syllabification** /-fɪˈkeɪʃ(ə)n/) division into or articulation by syllables. □□ **syllabify** v.tr. (-ies, -ied). [med.L syllabicatio f. syllabicare f. L syllaba: see SYLLABLE]

syllabize /ˈsɪləˌbaɪz/ v.tr. (also -ise) divide into or articulate by syllables. [med.L syllabizare f. Gk sullabizō (as SYLLABLE)]

syllable /ˈsɪləb(ə)l/ n. & v. —n. 1 a unit of pronunciation uttered without interruption, forming the whole or a part of a word and usu. having one vowel sound often with a consonant or consonants before or after: there are two syllables in water and three in inferno. 2 a character or characters representing a syllable. 3 (usu. with neg.) the least amount of speech or writing (did not utter a syllable). —v.tr. pronounce by syllables; articulate distinctly. □ **in words of one syllable** expressed plainly or bluntly. □□ **syllabled** adj. (also in comb.). [ME f. AF sillable f. OF sillabe f. L syllaba f. Gk sullabē (as SYN-, lambanō take)]

syllabub /ˈsɪləˌbʌb/ n. (also **sillabub**) a dessert made of cream or milk flavoured, sweetened, and whipped to thicken it. [16th c.: orig. unkn.]

syllabus /ˈsɪləbəs/ n. (pl. **syllabuses** or **syllabi** /-ˌbaɪ/) 1 a the programme or outline of a course of study, teaching, etc. b a statement of the requirements for a particular examination. 2 RC Ch. a summary of points decided by papal decree regarding heretical doctrines or practices. [mod.L, orig. a misreading of L sittybas accus. pl. of sittyba f. Gk sittuba title-slip or label]

syllepsis /sɪˈlepsɪs/ n. (pl. **syllepses** /-siːz/) a figure of speech in which a word is applied to two others in different senses (e.g. caught the train and a bad cold) or to two others of which it grammatically suits one only (e.g. neither they nor it is working) (cf. ZEUGMA). □□ **sylleptic** adj. **sylleptically** adv. [LL f. Gk sullēpsis taking together f. sullambanō: see SYLLABLE]

syllogism /ˈsɪləˌdʒɪz(ə)m/ n. 1 a form of reasoning in which a conclusion is drawn from two given or assumed propositions (premises): a common or middle term is present in the two premises but not in the conclusion, which may be invalid (e.g. all trains are long; some buses are long; therefore some buses are trains: the common term is long). Aristotle listed the types of syllogism and showed of each whether it was valid. 2 deductive reasoning as distinct from induction. □□ **syllogistic** /-ˈdʒɪstɪk/ adj. **syllogistically** /-ˈdʒɪstɪkəlɪ/ adv. [ME f. OF silogisme or L syllogismus f. Gk sullogismos f. sullogizomai (as SYN-, logizomai to reason f. logos reason)]

syllogize /ˈsɪləˌdʒaɪz/ v. (also -ise) 1 intr. use syllogisms. 2 tr. put (facts or an argument) in the form of syllogism. [ME f. OF sillogiser or LL syllogizare f. Gk sullogizomai (as SYLLOGISM)]

sylph /sɪlf/ n. 1 an elemental spirit of the air. 2 a slender graceful woman or girl. 3 any humming-bird of the genus Aglaiocercus with a long forked tail. □□ **sylphlike** adj. [mod.L sylphes, G Sylphen (pl.), perh. based on L sylvestris of the woods + nympha nymph]

sylva /ˈsɪlvə/ n. (also **silva**) (pl. **sylvae** /-viː/ or **sylvas**) 1 the trees of a region, epoch, or environment. 2 a treatise on or a list of such trees. [L silva a wood]

sylvan /ˈsɪlv(ə)n/ adj. (also **silvan**) 1 a of the woods. b having woods; wooded. 2 rural. [F sylvain (obs. silvain) or L Silvanus woodland deity f. silva a wood]

sylviculture var. of SILVICULTURE.

sym- /sɪm/ prefix assim. form of SYN- before b, m, p.

symbiont /ˈsɪmbɪənt/ n. an organism living in symbiosis. [Gk sumbiōn -ountos part. of sumbioō live together (as SYMBIOSIS)]

symbiosis /ˌsɪmbaɪˈəʊsɪs, ˌsɪmbɪ-/ n. (pl. **symbioses** /-siːz/) 1 a an interaction between two different organisms living in close physical association, usu. to the advantage of both (cf. ANTIBIOSIS). b an instance of this. 2 a a mutually advantageous association or relationship between persons. b an instance of this. □□ **symbiotic** /-ˈɒtɪk/ adj. **symbiotically** /-ˈɒtɪkəlɪ/ adv. [mod.L f. Gk sumbiōsis a living together f. sumbioō live together, sumbios companion (as SYN-, bios life)]

symbol /ˈsɪmb(ə)l/ n. & v. —n. 1 a thing conventionally regarded as typifying, representing, or recalling something, esp. an idea or quality (white is a symbol of purity). 2 a mark or character taken as the conventional sign of some object, idea, function, or process, e.g. the letters standing for the chemical elements or the characters in musical notation. —v.tr. (**symbolled**, **symbolling**; US **symboled**, **symboling**) symbolize. □□ **symbology** /-ˈbɒlədʒɪ/ n. [ME f. L symbolum f. Gk sumbolon mark, token (as SYN-, ballō throw)]

symbolic /sɪmˈbɒlɪk/ adj. (also **symbolical** /-ˈbɒlɪk(ə)l/) 1 of or serving as a symbol. 2 involving the use of symbols or symbolism. □ **symbolic logic** the use of symbols to denote propositions etc. in order to assist reasoning. □□ **symbolically** adv. [F symbolique or LL symbolicus f. Gk sumbolikos]

symbolism /ˈsɪmbəˌlɪz(ə)m/ n. 1 a the use of symbols to represent ideas. b symbols collectively. 2 an artistic and poetic movement or style using symbols and indirect suggestion to express ideas, emotions, etc. (See below.) □□ **symbolist** n. **symbolistic** /-ˈlɪstɪk/ adj.

In a literary and art historical sense, symbolism is the idealist movement of the 1880s and 1890s in France. Primarily a literary concept, it was launched as an identifiable movement by the radical poet Jean Moréas in 1886. Symbolism was seen as the expression of an idea through form, the word or object represented being no more than a sign to open up the world of the imagination; symbolist poets include Mallarmé, Verlaine, and Rimbaud. In the visual arts, the term is widely applied to both French and non-French painters of the fin de siècle who reacted against the prevailing standards of classicism, positivism, and naturalism, preferring to paint enigmatic, mysterious, and dreamlike subjects. Redon, Moreau, Rops, and Ensor are the best known, but the movement was much wider; the critic Aurier in 1891–2 identified Gauguin and the Nabis as symbolist painters. Symbolism was important in the development of later theories of abstraction and surrealism.

symbolize /ˈsɪmbəˌlaɪz/ v.tr. (also -ise) 1 be a symbol of. 2 represent by means of symbols. □□ **symbolization** /-ˈzeɪʃ(ə)n/ n. [F symboliser f. symbole SYMBOL]

symbology /sɪmˈbɒlədʒɪ/ n. 1 the study of symbols. 2 a the use of symbols. b symbols collectively.

symmetry /ˈsɪmɪtrɪ/ n. (pl. -ies) 1 a correct proportion of the parts of a thing; balance, harmony. b beauty resulting from this. 2 a a structure that allows an object to be divided into parts of an equal shape and size and similar position to the point or line or plane of division. b the possession of such a structure. c approximation to such a structure. 3 the repetition of exactly similar parts facing each other or a centre. 4 Bot. the possession by a flower of sepals and petals and stamens and pistils in the same number or multiples of the same number. □□ **symmetric** /sɪˈmetrɪk/ adj. **symmetrical** /-ˈmetrɪk(ə)l/ adj. **symmetrically** /-ˈmetrɪkəlɪ/ adv. **symmetrize** v.tr. (also -ise). [obs. F symmétrie or L summetria f. Gk (as SYN-, metron measure)]

Symons /ˈsaɪmənz/, Julian Gustave (1912–), English author of crime fiction and of works on this subject. His writing career extends over more than fifty years. Among his best-known works are *The Immaterial Murder Case* (1945), *The Colour of Murder* (1957), *The Man Whose Dreams Came True* (1968), and *The Tell-Tale Heart* (1978).

sympathectomy /ˌsɪmpəˈθektəmɪ/ n. (pl. **-ies**) the surgical removal of a sympathetic ganglion etc.

sympathetic /ˌsɪmpəˈθetɪk/ adj. 1 of, showing, or expressing sympathy. 2 due to sympathy. 3 likeable or capable of evoking sympathy. 4 (of a person) friendly and cooperative. 5 (foll. by *to*) inclined to favour (a proposal etc.) (*was most sympathetic to the idea*). 6 (of a landscape etc.) that touches the feelings by association etc. 7 (of a pain etc.) caused by a pain or injury to someone else or in another part of the body. 8 (of a sound, resonance, or string) sounding by a vibration communicated from another vibrating object. 9 (of a nerve or ganglion) belonging to the sympathetic nervous system. □ **sympathetic magic** a type of magic that seeks to achieve an effect by performing an associated action or using an associated thing. **sympathetic nervous system** see NERVOUS SYSTEM. □□ **sympathetically** adv. [SYMPATHY, after *pathetic*]

sympathize /ˈsɪmpəˌθaɪz/ v.intr. (also **-ise**) (often foll. by *with*) 1 feel or express sympathy; share a feeling or opinion. 2 agree with a sentiment or opinion. □□ **sympathizer** n. [F *sympathiser* (as SYMPATHY)]

sympathy /ˈsɪmpəθɪ/ n. (pl. **-ies**) 1 a the state of being simultaneously affected with the same feeling as another. b the capacity for this. 2 (often foll. by *with*) a the act of sharing or tendency to share (with a person etc.) in an emotion or sensation or condition of another person or thing. b (in *sing.* or *pl.*) compassion or commiseration; condolences. 3 (often foll. by *for*) a favourable attitude; approval. 4 (in *sing.* or *pl.*; often foll. by *with*) agreement (with a person etc.) in opinion or desire. 5 (*attrib.*) in support of another cause (*sympathy strike*). □ **in sympathy** (often foll. by *with*) 1 having or showing or resulting from sympathy (with another). 2 by way of sympathetic action (*working to rule in sympathy*). [L *sympathia* f. Gk *sumpatheia* (as SYN-, *pathēs* f. *pathos* feeling)]

sympetalous /sɪmˈpetələs/ adj. Bot. having the petals united.

symphonic /sɪmˈfɒnɪk/ adj. (of music) relating to or having the form or character of a symphony. □ **symphonic poem** an extended orchestral piece, usu. in one movement, on a descriptive or rhapsodic theme. □□ **symphonically** adv.

symphonist /ˈsɪmfənɪst/ n. a composer of symphonies.

symphony /ˈsɪmfənɪ/ n. (pl. **-ies**) 1 an elaborate composition usu. for full orchestra, and in several movements with one or more in sonata form. (See below.) 2 an interlude for orchestra alone in a large-scale vocal work. 3 = *symphony orchestra*. □ **symphony orchestra** a large orchestra suitable for playing symphonies etc. [ME, = harmony of sound, f. OF *symphonie* f. L *symphonia* f. Gk *sumphōnia* (as SYN-, *-phōnos* f. *phōnē* sound)]

In the 16th c. the term denoted a piece of music for an instrumental ensemble, but since the 18th c. it has been applied to an orchestral work typically in four movements (in the early years, three) in a standard order and each conforming to a certain type. Towards the mid-19th c., after the formidable achievements of Beethoven in the genre, the symphony gave way in popularity to the symphonic poem and concert overture but continued to be an important test of a composer's mastery of form. From the time of Brahms onwards great symphonies have been and are still being written and performed, combining Beethoven's expansion of the terms of reference (adding voices to the orchestra, sharing motives between movements, writing with an extra-musical 'programme' in mind, etc.) with a flexible attitude towards the structure and number of movements.

symphyllous /sɪmˈfɪləs/ adj. Bot. having the leaves united. [SYN- + Gk *phullon* leaf]

symphysis /ˈsɪmfɪsɪs/ n. (pl. **symphyses** /-ˌsiːz/) 1 the process of growing together. 2 a a union between two bones esp. in the median plane of the body. b the place or line of this. □□ **symphyseal** /-ˈfɪzɪəl/ adj. **symphysial** /-ˈfɪzɪəl/ adj. [mod.L f. Gk *sumphusis* (as SYN-, *phusis* growth)]

sympodium /sɪmˈpəʊdɪəm/ n. (pl. **sympodia** /-dɪə/) Bot. the apparent main axis or stem of a vine etc., made up of successive

secondary axes. □□ **sympodial** adj. [mod.L (as SYN-, Gk *pous podos* foot)]

symposium /sɪmˈpəʊzɪəm/ n. (pl. **symposia** /-zɪə/) 1 a a conference or meeting to discuss a particular subject. b a collection of essays or papers for this purpose. 2 a philosophical or other friendly discussion. 3 a drinking-party, esp. of the ancient Greeks with conversation etc. after a banquet. [L f. Gk *sumposion* in sense 3 (as SYN-, *-potēs* drinker)]

symptom /ˈsɪmptəm/ n. 1 Med. a change in the physical or mental condition of a person, regarded as evidence of a disease (cf. SIGN 5). 2 a sign of the existence of something. [ME *synthoma* f. med.L *sinthoma*, & f. LL *symptoma* f. Gk *sumptōma -atos* chance, symptom, f. *sumpiptō* happen (as SYN-, *piptō* fall)]

symptomatic /ˌsɪmptəˈmætɪk/ adj. serving as a symptom. □□ **symptomatically** adv.

symptomatology /ˌsɪmptəməˈtɒlədʒɪ/ n. the branch of medicine concerned with the study and interpretation of symptoms.

syn- /sɪn/ prefix with, together, alike. [from or after Gk *sun-* f. *sun* with]

synaeresis /sɪˈnɪərɪsɪs/ n. (US **syneresis**) (pl. **synaereses** /-ˌsiːz/) the contraction of two vowels into a diphthong or single vowel. [LL f. Gk *sunairesis* (as SYN-, *hairesis* f. *haireō* take)]

synaesthesia /ˌsɪniːsˈθiːzɪə/ n. (US **synesthesia**) 1 Psychol. the production of a mental sense-impression relating to one sense by the stimulation of another sense. 2 a sensation produced in a part of the body by stimulation of another part. □□ **synaesthetic** /-ˈθetɪk/ adj. [mod.L f. SYN- after *anaesthesia*]

synagogue /ˈsɪnəˌɡɒɡ/ n. 1 the building where a Jewish assembly or congregation meets for religious observance and instruction. 2 the assembly itself. □□ **synagogal** /-ˈɡɒɡ(ə)l/ adj. **synagogical** /-ˈɡɒdʒɪk(ə)l/ adj. [ME f. OF *sinagoge* f. LL *synagoga* f. Gk *sunagōgē* meeting (as SYN-, *agō* bring)]

synallagmatic /ˌsɪnəlæɡˈmætɪk/ adj. (of a treaty or contract) imposing reciprocal obligations. [SYN- + Gk *allassō* exchange]

synapse /ˈsaɪnæps, ˈsɪn-/ n. Anat. a junction of two nerve-cells. [Gk *synapsis* (as SYN-, *hapsis* f. *haptō* join)]

synapsis /sɪˈnæpsɪs/ n. (pl. **synapses** /-ˌsiːz/) 1 Anat. = SYNAPSE. 2 Biol. the fusion of chromosome-pairs at the start of meiosis. □□ **synaptic** /-ˈnæptɪk/ adj. **synaptically** /-ˈnæptɪkəlɪ/ adv.

synarthrosis /ˌsɪnɑːˈθrəʊsɪs/ n. (pl. **synarthroses** /-ˌsiːz/) Anat. an immovably fixed bone-joint, e.g. the sutures of the skull. [SYN- + Gk *arthrōsis* jointing f. *arthron* joint]

sync /sɪŋk/ n. & v. (also **synch**) colloq. —n. synchronization. —v.tr. & intr. synchronize. □ **in** (or **out of**) **sync** (often foll. by *with*) according or agreeing well or badly). [abbr.]

syncarp /ˈsɪnkɑːp/ n. a compound fruit from a flower with several carpels, e.g. a blackberry. [SYN- + Gk *karpos* fruit]

syncarpous /sɪnˈkɑːpəs/ adj. (of a flower or fruit) having the carpels united (opp. APOCARPOUS). [SYN- + Gk *karpos* fruit]

synch var. of SYNC.

synchondrosis /ˌsɪŋkɒnˈdrəʊsɪs/ n. (pl. **synchondroses** /-ˌsiːz/) Anat. an almost immovable bone-joint bound by a layer of cartilage, as in the spinal vertebrae. [SYN- + Gk *khondros* cartilage]

synchro- /ˈsɪŋkrəʊ/ comb. form synchronized, synchronous.

synchrocyclotron /ˌsɪŋkrəʊˈsaɪklə₍tron/ n. a cyclotron able to achieve higher energies by decreasing the frequency of the accelerating electric field as the particles increase in energy and mass.

synchromesh /ˈsɪŋkrəʊˌmeʃ/ n. & adj. —n. a system of gear-changing, esp. in motor vehicles, in which the driving and driven gearwheels are made to revolve at the same speed during engagement by means of a set of friction clutches, thereby easing the change. —adj. relating to or using this system. [abbr. of *synchronized mesh*]

synchronic /sɪŋˈkrɒnɪk, sɪn-/ adj. describing a subject (esp. a language) as it exists at one point in time (opp. DIACHRONIC). □□ **synchronically** adv. [LL *synchronus*: see SYNCHRONOUS]

synchronism /ˈsɪŋkrəˌnɪz(ə)m/ n. 1 = SYNCHRONY. 2 the process of synchronizing sound and picture in cinematography, television, etc. □□ **synchronistic** /-ˈnɪstɪk/ adj.

synchronistically /-'nistikəli/ adv. [Gk sugkhronismos (as SYNCHRONOUS)]

synchronize /'siŋkrə,naiz/ v. (also **-ise**) **1** intr. (often foll. by with) occur at the same time; be simultaneous. **2** tr. cause to occur at the same time. **3** tr. carry out the synchronism of (a film). **4** tr. ascertain or set forth the correspondence in the date of (events). **5 a** tr. cause (clocks etc.) to show a standard or uniform time. **b** intr. (of clocks etc.) be synchronized. □ **synchronized swimming** a form of swimming in which participants make coordinated leg and arm movements in time to music. □□ **synchronization** /-'zeiʃ(ə)n/ n. **synchronizer** n.

synchronous /'siŋkrənəs/ adj. (often foll. by with) existing or occurring at the same time. □**synchronous motor** Electr. a motor having a speed exactly proportional to the current frequency. □□ **synchronously** adv. [LL synchronus f. Gk sugkhronos (as SYN-, khronos time)]

synchrony /'siŋkrəni/ n. **1** the state of being synchronic or synchronous. **2** the treatment of events etc. as being synchronous. [Gk sugkhronos: see SYNCHRONOUS]

synchrotron /'siŋkrə,trɒn/ n. Physics a cyclotron in which the magnetic field strength increases with the energy of the particles to keep their orbital radius constant.

syncline /'siŋklain/ n. a rock-bed forming a trough. □□ **synclinal** /-'klain(ə)l/ adj. [synclinal (as SYN-, Gk klinō lean)]

syncopate /'siŋkə,peit/ v.tr. **1** Mus. displace the beats or accents in (a passage) so that strong beats become weak and vice versa. **2** shorten (a word) by dropping interior sounds or letters, as symbology for symbolology, Gloster for Gloucester. □□ **syncopation** /-'peiʃ(ə)n/ n. **syncopator** n. [LL syncopare swoon (as SYNCOPE)]

syncope /'siŋkəpi/ n. **1** Gram. the omission of interior sounds or letters in a word (see SYNCOPATE 2). **2** Med. a temporary loss of consciousness caused by a fall in blood pressure. □□ **syncopal** adj. [ME f. LL syncopē f. Gk sugkopē (as SYN-, koptō strike, cut off)]

syncretism /'siŋkrə,tiz(ə)m/ n. **1** Philos. & Theol. the process or an instance of syncretizing (see SYNCRETIZE). **2** Philol. the merging of different inflectional varieties in the development of a language. □□ **syncretic** /-'kretik/ adj. **syncretist** n. **syncretistic** /-'tistik/ adj. [mod.L syncretismus f. Gk sugkrētismos f. sugkrētizō (of two parties) combine against a third f. krēs Cretan (orig. of ancient Cretan communities)]

syncretize /'siŋkrə,taiz/ v.tr. (also **-ise**) Philos. & Theol. attempt, esp. inconsistently, to unify or reconcile differing schools of thought.

syncytium /sin'sitiəm/ n. (pl. **syncytia** /-tiə/) Biol. a mass of cytoplasm with several nuclei, not divided into separate cells. □□ **syncytial** adj. [formed as SYN- + -CYTE + -IUM]

syndactyl /sin'dæktil/ adj. (of an animal) having digits united as in webbed feet etc. □□ **syndactylism** n. **syndactylous** adj.

syndesis /'sindisis/ n. (pl. **syndeses** /-si:z/) Biol. = SYNAPSIS 2. [mod.L f. Gk syndesis binding together f. sundeō bind together]

syndesmosis /,sindez'məʊsis/ n. the union and articulation of bones by means of ligaments. [mod.L f. Gk sundesmos binding, fastening + -OSIS]

syndetic /sin'detik/ adj. Gram. of or using conjunctions. [Gk sundetikos (as SYNDESIS)]

syndic /'sindik/ n. **1** a government official in various countries. **2** Brit. a business agent of certain universities and corporations, esp. (at Cambridge University) a member of a committee of the senate. □□ **syndical** adj. [F f. LL syndicus f. Gk sundikos (as SYN-, -dikos f. dikē justice)]

syndicalism /'sindikə,liz(ə)m/ n. hist. a movement for transferring the ownership and control of the means of production and distribution to workers' unions. □□ **syndicalist** n. [F syndicalisme f. syndical (as SYNDIC)]

syndicate n. & v. —n. /'sindikət/ **1** a combination of individuals or commercial firms to promote some common interest. **2** an association or agency supplying material simultaneously to a number of newspapers or periodicals. **3** a group of people who combine to buy or rent property, gamble, organize crime, etc. **4** a committee of syndics. —v.tr. /'sindi,keit/ **1** form into a syndicate. **2** publish (material) through a syndicate. □□

syndication /-'keiʃ(ə)n/ n. [F syndicat f. med.L syndicatus f. LL syndicus: see SYNDIC]

syndrome /'sindrəʊm/ n. **1** a group of concurrent symptoms of a disease. **2** a characteristic combination of opinions, emotions, behaviour, etc. □□ **syndromic** /-'drɒmik/ adj. [mod.L f. Gk sundromē (as SYN-, dromē f. dramein to run)]

syne /sain/ adv., conj., & prep. Sc. since. [contr. f. ME sithen SINCE]

synecdoche /si'nekdəki/ n. a figure of speech in which a part is made to represent the whole or vice versa (e.g. new faces at the meeting; England lost by six wickets). □□ **synecdochic** /-'dɒkik/ adj. [ME f. L f. Gk sunekdokhē (as SYN-, ekdokhē f. ekdekhomai take up)]

synecology /,sini'kɒlədʒi/ n. the ecological study of plant or animal communities. □□ **synecological** /-,i:kə'lɒdʒik(ə)l/ adj. **synecologist** n.

syneresis US var. of SYNAERESIS.

synergism /'sinə,dʒiz(ə)m/ n. (also **synergy** /'sinədʒi/) the combined effect of drugs, organs, etc., that exceeds the sum of their individual effects. □□ **synergetic** /-'dʒetik/ adj. **synergic** /-'nə:dʒik/ adj. **synergistic** /-'dʒistik/ adj. **synergistically** /-'dʒistikəli/ adv. [Gk sunergos working together (as SYN-, ergon work)]

synergist /'sinədʒist/ n. a medicine or a bodily organ (e.g. a muscle) that cooperates with another or others.

synesthesia US var. of SYNAESTHESIA.

syngamy /'siŋgəmi/ n. Biol. the fusion of gametes or nuclei in reproduction. □□ **syngamous** adj. [SYN- + Gk gamos marriage]

Synge /siŋ/, (Edmund) John Millington (1871–1909), Irish dramatist. In Paris he was encouraged by Yeats to observe Irish peasant life in the Aran Islands; this resulted in his description The Aran Islands (1907) and his best-known play, The Playboy of the Western World (1907), which caused outrage and riots at the Abbey Theatre, Dublin, for its frankness and the implication that Irish peasants would condone a brutal murder, but his skilful fusion of the language of ordinary people with his own dramatic rhetoric has made it a classic. His other plays include The Tinker's Wedding (1908) and Deirdre of the Sorrows (1910), in which a spare rhythmic prose achieves powerful and resonant effects, but many of his countrymen objected to the ironic wit and realism. Many of the poems in Poems and Translations (1909) foreshadow his imminent death from Hodgkin's disease.

syngenesis /sin'dʒenəsis/ n. sexual reproduction from combined male and female elements.

synod /'sinəd/ n. **1** a Church council attended by delegated clergy and sometimes laity (see also General Synod). **2** a Presbyterian ecclesiastical court above the presbyteries and subject to the General Assembly. **3** any meeting for debate. [ME f. LL synodus f. Gk sunodos meeting (as SYN-, hodos way)]

synodic /si'nɒdik/ adj. Astron. relating to or involving the conjunction of stars, planets, etc. □**synodic period** the time between the successive conjunctions of a planet with the sun. [LL synodicus f. Gk sunodikos (as SYNOD)]

synodical /si'nɒdik(ə)l/ adj. **1** (also **synodal** /'sinəd(ə)l/) of, relating to, or constituted as a synod. **2** = SYNODIC.

synoecious /si'ni:ʃəs/ adj. Bot. having male and female organs in the same flower or receptacle. [SYN- after dioecious etc.]

synonym /'sinənim/ n. **1** a word or phrase that means exactly or nearly the same as another in the same language (e.g. shut and close). **2** a word denoting the same thing as another but suitable to a different context (e.g. serpent for snake, Hellene for Greek) or containing a different emphasis (e.g. blindworm for slow-worm). **3** a word equivalent to another in some but not all senses (e.g. ship and vessel). □□ **synonymic** /-'nimik/ adj. **synonymity** /-'nimiti/ n. [ME f. L synonymum f. Gk sunōnumon neut. of sunōnumos (as SYN-, onoma name): cf. ANONYMOUS]

synonymous /si'nɒniməs/ adj. (often foll. by with) **1** having the same meaning; being a synonym (of). **2** (of a name, idea, etc.) suggestive of or associated with another (excessive drinking regarded as synonymous with violence). □□ **synonymously** adv. **synonymousness** n.

synonymy /si'nɒnimi/ n. (pl. **-ies**) **1** the state of being synonymous. **2** the collocation of synonyms for emphasis (e.g. in *any shape or form*). **3 a** a system or collection of synonyms. **b** a treatise on synonyms. [LL *synonymia* f. Gk *sunōnumia* (as SYNONYM)]

synopsis /sɪ'nɒpsɪs/ *n.* (*pl.* **synopses** /-siːz/) **1** a summary or outline. **2** a brief general survey. □□ **synopsize** *v.tr.* (also *-ise*). [LL f. Gk (as SYN-, *opsis* seeing)]

synoptic /sɪ'nɒptɪk/ *adj.* & *n.* —*adj.* **1** of, forming, or giving a synopsis. **2** taking or affording a comprehensive mental view. **3** of the Synoptic Gospels. **4** giving a general view of weather conditions. —*n.* **1** a Synoptic Gospel. **2** the writer of a Synoptic Gospel. □ **Synoptic Gospels** the Gospels of Matthew, Mark, and Luke, describing events from a similar point of view and having many similarities (whereas that of John differs greatly). □□ **synoptical** *adj.* **synoptically** *adv.* [Gk *sunoptikos* (as SYNOPSIS)]

synoptist /sɪ'nɒptɪst/ *n.* the writer of a Synoptic Gospel.

synostosis /ˌsɪnɒ'stəʊsɪs/ *n.* the joining of bones by ankylosis etc. [SYN- + Gk *osteon* bone + -OSIS]

synovia /saɪ'nəʊvɪə, sɪn-/ *n.* *Physiol.* a viscous fluid lubricating joints and tendon sheaths. □ **synovial membrane** a dense membrane of connective tissue secreting synovia. □□ **synovial** *adj.* [mod.L, formed prob. arbitrarily by Paracelsus]

synovitis /ˌsaɪnəʊ'vaɪtɪs, sɪn-/ *n.* inflammation of the synovial membrane.

syntactic /sɪn'tæktɪk/ *adj.* of or according to syntax. □□ **syntactical** *adj.* **syntactically** *adv.* [Gk *suntaktikos* (as SYNTAX)]

syntagma /sɪn'tægmə/ *n.* (*pl.* **syntagmas** or **syntagmata** /-mətə/) **1** a word or phrase forming a syntactic unit. **2** a systematic collection of statements. □□ **syntagmatic** /-'mætɪk/ *adj.* **syntagmic** *adj.* [LL f. Gk *suntagma* (as SYNTAX)]

syntax /'sɪntæks/ *n.* **1** the grammatical arrangement of words, showing their connection and relation. **2** a set of rules for or an analysis of this. [F *syntaxe* or LL *syntaxis* f. Gk *suntaxis* (as SYN-, *taxis* f. *tassō* arrange)]

synth /sɪnθ/ *n.* *colloq.* = SYNTHESIZER.

synthesis /'sɪnθɪsɪs/ *n.* (*pl.* **syntheses** /-ˌsiːz/) **1** the process or result of building up separate elements, esp. ideas, into a connected whole, esp. into a theory or system. **2** a combination or composition. **3** *Chem.* the artificial production of compounds from their constituents (as distinct from extraction from plants etc. **4** *Gram.* **a** the process of making compound and derivative words. **b** the tendency in a language to use inflected forms rather than groups of words, prepositions, etc. **5** the joining of divided parts in surgery. □□ **synthesist** *n.* [L f. Gk *sunthesis* (as SYN-, THESIS)]

synthesize /'sɪnθɪˌsaɪz/ *v.tr.* (also **synthetize** /-ˌtaɪz/, *-ise*) **1** make a synthesis of. **2** combine into a coherent whole.

synthesizer /'sɪnθɪˌsaɪzə(r)/ *n.* an electronic musical instrument, esp. operated by a keyboard, producing a wide variety of sounds by generating and combining signals of different frequencies. A musical instrument produces a fundamental pure tone and a series of other pure tones of lesser intensity (the *overtones*, each with its own intensity and frequency) which are characteristic of that instrument and which together give it its timbre. The synthesizer, by generating a combination of pure tones, can simulate this. Its development as a musical instrument dates from the late 1950s, in the US.

synthetic /sɪn'θetɪk/ *adj.* & *n.* —*adj.* **1** made by chemical synthesis, esp. to imitate a natural product (*synthetic rubber*). **2** (of emotions etc.) affected, insincere. **3** *Logic* (of a proposition) having truth or falsity determinable by recourse to experience (cf. ANALYTIC 3). **4** *Philol.* using combinations of simple words or elements in compounded or complex words (cf. ANALYTICAL). —*n.* *Chem.* a synthetic substance. □ **synthetic resin** *Chem.* see RESIN *n.* 2. □□ **synthetical** *adj.* **synthetically** *adv.* [F *synthétique* or mod.L *syntheticus* f. Gk *sunthetikos* f. *sunthetos* f. *suntithēmi* (as SYN-, *tithēmi* put)]

syphilis /'sɪfɪlɪs/ *n.* a contagious venereal disease progressing from infection of the genitals via the skin and mucous membrane to the bones, muscles, and brain. □□ **syphilitic** /-'lɪtɪk/ *adj.* **syphilize** /-ˌlaɪz/ *v.tr.* (also *-ise*). **syphiloid** /-ˌlɔɪd/ *adj.* [mod.L f. title (*Syphilis, sive Morbus Gallicus*) of a Latin poem (1530), f.

Syphilus, a character in it, the supposed first sufferer from the disease]

syphon var. of SIPHON.

Syracuse /'saɪrəˌkjuːz/ (Italian **Siracusa** /ˌsɪrə'kuːzə/) a port on the south-east coast of Sicily; pop. (1981) 117,600. Founded by the Corinthians *c.*734 BC, it was a flourishing centre of Greek culture especially in the 5th–4th c. BC under its rulers Dionysius the Elder and Dionysius the Younger.

Syria /'sɪrɪə/ a country in SW Asia with a coastline on the eastern Mediterranean Sea; pop. (est. 1988) 11,569,650; official language, Arabic; capital, Damascus. In ancient times the name was applied to a much wider area, which included also the present countries of Lebanon, Israel, Jordan, and adjacent parts of Iraq and Saudi Arabia. It was the site of various early civilizations, trading with Egypt and Crete; the Phoenicians were settled on the coastal plain. The country was greatly enriched by the transit trade from Babylonia, Arabia, and the Far East. Falling successively within the empires of Persia, Macedon, and Rome it became a centre of Islamic power and civilization from the 7th c. and a province of the Ottoman empire in 1516. After the Turkish defeat in the First World War, Syria was mandated to France and achieved independence with the ejection of Vichy troops by the Allies in 1941. The last three and a half decades of Syrian history have been dominated by continuing antagonism towards Israel, involvement in Middle Eastern wars and in the internal affairs of Lebanon, and domestic political instability. Although largely agricultural, Syria is becoming more industrialized, and has benefited in recent years from increasing oil exports. □□ **Syrian** *adj.* & *n.*

Syriac /'sɪrɪˌæk/ *n.* & *adj.* —*n.* the liturgical language of the Maronite and Syrian Catholic Churches, the Syrian Jacobite Church, and the Nestorian Church. It is descended from the Aramaic spoken near the city of Edessa (now Urfa) in SE Turkey from shortly before the Christian era, and was extensively used in the early Church owing to the active Christian communities in those parts. After Greek it was the most important language in the eastern Roman Empire until the rise of Islam in the 8th c. The Syriac alphabet developed from a late form of Aramaic used at Palmyra in Syria. —*adj.* in or relating to this language. [L *Syriacus* f. Gk *Suriakos* f. *Suria* Syria]

syringa /sɪ'rɪŋgə/ *n.* *Bot.* **1** = *mock orange*. **2** any plant of the genus *Syringa*, esp. the lilac. [mod.L, formed as SYRINX (with ref. to the use of its stems as pipe-stems)]

syringe /sɪ'rɪndʒ, 'sɪr-/ *n.* & *v.* —*n.* **1** *Med.* **a** a tube with a nozzle and piston or bulb for sucking in and ejecting liquid in a fine stream, used in surgery. **b** (in full **hypodermic syringe**) a similar device with a hollow needle for insertion under the skin. **2** any similar device used in gardening, cooking, etc. —*v.tr.* sluice or spray (the ear, a plant, etc.) with a syringe. [ME f. med.L *syringa* (as SYRINX)]

syrinx /'sɪrɪŋks/ *n.* (*pl.* **syrinxes** or **syringes** /sɪ'rɪndʒiːz/) **1** a set of pan-pipes. **2** *Archaeol.* a narrow gallery cut in rock in an ancient Egyptian tomb. **3** the lower larynx or song-organ of birds. □□ **syringeal** /sɪ'rɪndʒɪəl/ *adj.* [L *syrinx -ngis* f. Gk *surigx suriggos* pipe, channel]

Syro- /'saɪrəʊ/ *comb. form* Syrian; Syrian and (*Syro-Phoenician*). [Gk *Suro-* f. *Suros* a Syrian]

syrup /'sɪrəp/ *n.* (US **sirup**) **1 a** a sweet sauce made by dissolving sugar in boiling water, often used for preserving fruit etc. **b** a similar sauce of a specified flavour as a drink, medicine, etc. (*rose-hip syrup*). **2** condensed sugar-cane juice; part of this remaining uncrystallized at various stages of refining; molasses, treacle. **3** excessive sweetness of style or manner. □□ **syrupy** *adj.* [ME f. OF *sirop* or med.L *siropus* f. Arab. *šarāb* beverage: cf. SHERBET, SHRUB²]

syssarcosis /ˌsɪsɑː'kəʊsɪs/ *n.* (*pl.* **syssarcoses** /-siːz/) *Anat.* a connection between bones formed by intervening muscle. [mod.L f. Gk *sussarkōsis* (as SYN-, *sarx, sarkos* flesh)]

systaltic /sɪ'stæltɪk/ *adj.* (esp. of the heart) contracting and dilating rhythmically; pulsatory (cf. SYSTOLE, DIASTOLE). [LL *systalticus* f. Gk *sustaltikos* (as SYN-, *staltos* f. *stellō* put)]

system /'sɪstəm/ *n.* **1** a complex whole; a set of connected things or parts; an organized body of material or immaterial things. **2** a set of devices (e.g. pulleys) functioning together. **3** *Physiol.* **a** a set of organs in the body with a common structure or function (*the digestive system*). **b** the human or animal body as a whole. **4** **a** method; considered principles of procedure or classification. **b** classification. **5** orderliness. **6** **a** a body of theory or practice relating to or prescribing a particular form of government, religion, etc. **b** (prec. by *the*) the prevailing political or social order, esp. regarded as oppressive and intransigent. **7** a method of choosing one's procedure in gambling etc. **8** *Computing* a group of related hardware units or programs or both, esp. when dedicated to a single application. **9** one of seven general types of crystal structure. **10** a major group of geological strata (*the Devonian system*). **11** *Physics* a group of associated bodies moving under mutual gravitation etc. **12** *Mus.* the braced staves of a score. □ **get a thing out of one's system** *colloq.* be rid of a preoccupation or anxiety. **systems analysis** the analysis of a complex process or operation in order to improve its efficiency, esp. by applying a computer system. □□ **systemless** *adj.* [F *système* or LL *systema* f. Gk *sustēma -atos* (as SYN-, *histēmi* set up)]

systematic /ˌsɪstəˈmætɪk/ *adj.* **1** methodical; done or conceived according to a plan or system. **2** regular, deliberate (*a systematic liar*). □ **systematic theology** a form of theology in which the aim is to arrange religious truths in a self-consistent whole. □□ **systematically** *adv.* **systematism** /ˈsɪstəmə ˌtɪz(ə)m/ *n.*

systematist /ˈsɪstəmətɪst/ *n.* [F *systématique* f. LL *systematicus* f. late Gk *sustēmatikos* (as SYSTEM)]

systematics /ˌsɪstəˈmætɪks/ *n.pl.* (usu. treated as *sing.*) the study or a system of classification; taxonomy.

systematize /ˈsɪstəmə ˌtaɪz/ *v.tr.* (also **-ise**) **1** make systematic. **2** devise a system for. □□ **systematization** /-ˈzeɪʃ(ə)n/ *n.* **systematizer** *n.*

systemic /sɪˈstemɪk/ *adj.* **1** *Physiol.* **a** of or concerning the whole body, not confined to a particular part (*systemic infection*). **b** (of blood circulation) other than pulmonary. **2** *Hort.* (of an insecticide, fungicide, etc.) entering the plant via the roots or shoots and passing through the tissues. □□ **systemically** *adv.* [irreg. f. SYSTEM]

systemize /ˈsɪstəˌmaɪz/ *v.tr.* = SYSTEMATIZE. □□ **systemization** /-ˈzeɪʃ(ə)n/ *n.* **systemizer** *n.*

systole /ˈsɪstəlɪ/ *n. Physiol.* the contraction of the heart, when blood is pumped into the arteries (cf. DIASTOLE). □□ **systolic** /-ˈstɒlɪk/ *adj.* [LL f. Gk *sustolē* f. *sustellō* contract (as SYSTALTIC)]

syzygy /ˈsɪzɪdʒɪ/ *n.* (pl. **-ies**) **1** *Astron.* conjunction or opposition, esp. of the moon with the sun. **2** a pair of connected or correlated things. [LL *syzygia* f. Gk *suzugia* f. *suzugos* yoked, paired (as SYN-, *zugon* yoke)]

Szczecin /ˈʃtɛtsiːn/ (also **Stettin** /ʃteˈtiːn/) a port on the Oder River in NW Poland; pop. (1985) 391,000.

Szechwan see SICHUAN.

Szeged /ˈsɛgɛd/ a port on the River Tisza, in southern Hungary; pop. (1988) 188,000.

T

T¹ /tiː/ *n.* (also **t**) (*pl.* **Ts** or **T's**) **1** the twentieth letter of the alphabet. **2** a T-shaped thing (esp. *attrib.*: *T-joint*). □ **to a T** exactly; to a nicety.

T² *abbr.* **1** tera-. **2** tesla.

T³ *symb. Chem.* the isotope tritium.

t. *abbr.* **1** ton(s). **2** tonne(s).

't *pron. contr.* of IT¹ (*'tis*).

-t¹ /t/ *suffix* = -ED¹ (*crept; sent*).

-t² /t/ *suffix* = -EST² (*shalt*).

TA *abbr.* (in the UK) Territorial Army.

Ta *symb. Chem.* the element tantalum.

ta /tɑː/ *int. Brit. colloq.* thank you. [infantile form]

Taal /tɑːl/ *n.* (prec. *by the*) *hist.* an early form of Afrikaans. [Du., = language, rel. to TALE]

TAB *abbr.* **1** typhoid-paratyphoid A and B vaccine. **2** *Austral.* Totalizator Agency Board.

tab¹ /tæb/ *n. & v.* —*n.* **1 a** a small flap or strip of material attached for grasping, fastening, or hanging up, or for identification. **b** a similar object as part of a garment etc. **2** *US colloq.* a bill or price (*picked up the tab*). **3** *Brit. Mil.* a marking on the collar distinguishing a staff officer. **4 a** a stage-curtain. **b** a loop for suspending this. —*v.tr.* (**tabbed, tabbing**) provide with a tab or tabs. □ **keep tabs** (or **a tab**) **on** *colloq.* **1** keep account of. **2** have under observation or in check. [prob. f. dial.: cf. TAG¹]

tab² /tæb/ *n.* **1** = TABULATOR 2. **2** = TABULATOR 3. [abbr.]

tabard /ˈtæbəd/ *n.* **1** a short-sleeved or sleeveless jerkin emblazoned with the arms of the sovereign and forming the official dress of a herald or pursuivant. **2** *hist.* a short surcoat open at the sides and with short sleeves, worn by a knight over armour and emblazoned with armorial bearings. **3** a woman's or girl's sleeveless jerkin open at the sides. [ME f. OF *tabart*, of unkn. orig.]

tabaret /ˈtæbərɪt/ *n.* an upholstery fabric of alternate satin and plain stripes. [prob. f. TABBY]

Tabasco /təˈbæskəʊ/ a State of eastern Mexico; pop. (est. 1988) 1,299,500; capital, Villahermosa.

tabasco /təˈbæskəʊ/ *n.* **1** a pungent pepper made from the fruit of *Capsicum frutescens.* **2** (**Tabasco**) *propr.* a sauce made from this used to flavour food. [TABASCO]

tabbouleh /təˈbuːleɪ/ *n.* an Arabic vegetable salad made with cracked wheat. [Arab. *tabbūla*]

tabby /ˈtæbɪ/ *n.* (*pl.* **-ies**) **1** (in full **tabby cat**) **a** a grey or brownish cat mottled or streaked with dark stripes. **b** any domestic cat, esp. female. **2** a kind of watered silk. **3** a plain weave. [F *tabis* (in sense 2) f. Arab. *al-'attabiya* the quarter of Baghdad where tabby was manufactured: connection of other senses uncert.]

tabernacle /ˈtæbəˌnæk(ə)l/ *n.* **1** (in the Bible) **a** a fixed or movable habitation, usually of light construction. **b** a tent containing the Ark of the Covenant, used as a portable shrine by the Israelites during their wanderings in the wilderness. **2 a** a meeting-place for worship used by nonconformists (e.g. Baptists) or by Mormons. **b** *hist.* any of the temporary structures used during the rebuilding of churches after the Fire of London. **3 a** a canopied niche or recess in the wall of a church etc. **b** an ornamental receptacle for the pyx or consecrated elements of the Eucharist. **4** *Naut.* a socket or double post for a hinged mast that can be lowered to pass under low bridges. □ **feast of Tabernacles** = SUCCOTH. □□ **tabernacled** *adj.* [ME f. OF *tabernacle* or L *tabernaculum* tent, dimin. of *taberna* hut]

tabes /ˈteɪbiːz/ *n. Med.* **1** emaciation. **2** locomotor ataxy; a form of neurosyphilis. □□ **tabetic** /təˈbetɪk/ *adj.* [L, = wasting away]

tabla /ˈtæblə, ˈtɑː-/ *n. Ind. Mus.* a pair of small drums played with the hands. [Hind. f. Arab. *ṭabla* drum]

tablature /ˈtæblətʃə(r)/ *n. Mus.* a system of writing down music to be performed, where figures, letters, and similar signs are used instead of notes. Such systems emerged in the late 15th c. Systems for the lute and the organ used a tablature in which the symbols represented the position of the player's fingers, not the pitch. The diagrammatic notation used today in popular music for the guitar, ukelele, etc. is a type of tablature. [F f. It. *tavolatura* f. *tavolare* set to music]

table /ˈteɪb(ə)l/ *n. & v.* —*n.* **1 a** a piece of furniture with a flat top and one or more legs, providing a level surface for eating, writing, or working at, playing games on, etc. **2** a flat surface serving a specified purpose (*altar table; bird table*). **3 a** food provided in a household (*keeps a good table*). **b** a group seated at table for dinner etc. **4 a** a set of facts or figures systematically displayed, esp. in columns (*a table of contents*). **b** matter contained in this. **c** = *multiplication table.* **5** a flat surface for working on or for machinery to operate on. **6 a** a slab of wood or stone etc. for bearing an inscription. **b** matter inscribed on this. **7** = TABLELAND. **8** *Archit.* **a** a flat usu. rectangular vertical surface. **b** a horizontal moulding, esp. a cornice. **9 a** a flat surface of a gem. **b** a cut gem with two flat faces. **10** each half or quarter of a folding board for backgammon. **11** (prec. *by the*) *Bridge* the dummy hand. —*v.tr.* **1** bring forward for discussion or consideration at a meeting. **2** postpone consideration of (a matter). **3** *Naut.* strengthen (a sail) with a wide hem. □ **at table** taking a meal at a table. **lay on the table 1** submit for discussion. **2** postpone indefinitely. **on the table** offered for discussion. **table knife** a knife for use at meals, esp. in eating a main course. **table licence** a licence to serve alcoholic drinks only with meals. **table linen** tablecloths, napkins, etc. **table manners** decorum or correct behaviour while eating at table. **table-mat** a mat for protecting a tabletop from hot dishes, etc. **Table of the House** the central table in either of the Houses of Parliament. **table salt** salt that is powdered or easy to powder for use at meals. **table talk** miscellaneous informal talk at table. **table tennis** an indoor game based on lawn tennis, played with small bats and a ball bounced on a table divided by a net. No precise date of its origin or invention is known; equipment for it is mentioned in a sports goods catalogue of 1884. **table wine** ordinary wine for drinking with a meal. **turn the tables** (often foll. by *on*) reverse one's relations (with), esp. by turning an inferior into a superior position (orig. in backgammon). **under the table** *colloq.* drunken after a meal. □□ **tableful** *n.* (*pl.* **-fuls**). **tabling** *n.* [ME f. OF f. L *tabula* plank, tablet, list]

tableau /ˈtæbləʊ/ *n.* (*pl.* **tableaux** /-ləʊz/) **1** a picturesque presentation. **2** = TABLEAU VIVANT. **3** a dramatic or effective situation suddenly brought about. □ **tableau curtains** *Theatr.* a pair of curtains drawn open by a diagonal cord. [F, = picture, dimin. of *table*: see TABLE]

tableau vivant /ˌtæbləʊ ˈviːvã/ *n.* (*pl.* **tableaux vivants** *pronunc.* same) *Theatr.* a silent and motionless group of people arranged to represent a scene. [F, lit. 'living picture']

tablecloth /ˈteɪb(ə)lˌklɒθ/ *n.* a cloth spread over the top of a table, esp. for meals.

table d'hôte /ˌtɑːb(ə)l ˈdəʊt/ *n.* a meal consisting of a set menu at a fixed price, esp. in a hotel (cf. À LA CARTE). [F, = host's table]

tableland /ˈteɪb(ə)lˌlænd/ *n.* an extensive elevated region with a level surface; a plateau.

Table Mountain a flat-topped mountain overlooking Cape Town in South Africa, rising to a height of 1,087 m (3,563 ft.).

tablespoon /ˈteɪb(ə)lˌspuːn/ *n.* **1** a large spoon for serving food. **2** an amount held by this. □□ **tablespoonful** *n.* (*pl.* **-fuls**).

tablet /ˈtæblɪt/ *n.* **1** a small measured and compressed amount of a substance, esp. of a medicine or drug. **2** a small flat piece of soap etc. **3** a flat slab of stone or wood, esp. for display or an inscription. **4** *Archit.* = TABLE 8. **5** *US* a writing-pad. [ME f. OF *tablete* f. Rmc, dimin. of L *tabula* TABLE]

tabletop /'teɪb(ə)lˌtɒp/ *n.* **1** the top or surface of a table. **2** (*attrib.*) that can be placed or used on a tabletop.

tableware /'teɪb(ə)lˌweə(r)/ *n.* dishes, plates, implements, etc., for use at meals.

tablier /'tæblɪˌeɪ/ *n. hist.* an apron-like part of a woman's dress. [F]

tabloid /'tæblɔɪd/ *n.* **1** a newspaper, usu. popular in style with bold headlines and large photographs, having pages of half size. **2** anything in a compressed or concentrated form. [orig. the propr. name of a medicine sold in tablets]

taboo /tə'buː/ *n., adj., & v.* (also **tabu**) —*n.* (*pl.* **taboos** or **tabus**) **1** a system or the act of setting a person or thing apart as sacred or accursed. **2** a prohibition or restriction imposed by social custom. —*adj.* **1** avoided or prohibited, esp. by social custom (*taboo words*). **2** designated as sacred and prohibited. —*v.tr.* (**taboos, tabooed** or **tabus, tabued**) **1** put (a thing, practice, etc.) under taboo. **2** exclude or prohibit by authority or social influence. [Tongan *tabu*]

tabor /'teɪbə(r)/ *n. hist.* a small drum, esp. one used to accompany a pipe. [ME f. OF *tabour, tabur*: cf. TABLA, Pers. *tabīra* drum]

tabouret /'tæbərɪt/ *n.* (*US* **taboret**) a low seat usu. without arms or a back. [F, = stool, dimin. as TABOR]

tabu var. of TABOO.

tabular /'tæbjʊlə(r)/ *adj.* **1** of or arranged in tables or lists. **2** broad and flat like a table. **3** (of a crystal) having two broad flat faces. **4** formed in thin plates. □□ **tabularly** *adv.* [L *tabularis* (as TABLE)]

tabula rasa /ˌtæbjʊlə 'rɑːzə/ *n.* **1** an erased tablet. **2** the human mind (esp. at birth) viewed as having no innate ideas. [L, = scraped tablet]

tabulate /'tæbjʊˌleɪt/ *v.tr.* arrange (figures or facts) in tabular form. □□ **tabulation** /-'leɪʃ(ə)n/ *n.* [LL *tabulare tabulat-* f. *tabula* table]

tabulator /'tæbjʊˌleɪtə(r)/ *n.* **1** a person or thing that tabulates. **2** a device on a typewriter for advancing to a sequence of set positions in tabular work. **3** *Computing* a machine that produces lists or tables from a data storage medium such as punched cards.

tacamahac /'tækəməˌhæk/ *n.* **1** a resinous gum obtained from certain tropical trees esp. of the genus *Calophyllum*. **2 a** the balsam poplar. **b** the resin of this. [obs. Sp. *tacamahaca* f. Aztec *tecomahiyac*]

tac-au-tac /ˌtækəʊ'tæk/ *n. Fencing* a parry combined with a riposte. [F: imit.]

tacet /'tæsɪt, 'teɪ-/ *v.intr. Mus.* an instruction for a particular voice or instrument to be silent. [L, = is silent]

tachism /'tæʃɪz(ə)m/ *n.* (also **tachisme**) a form of action painting with dabs of colour arranged randomly to evoke a subconscious feeling. [F *tachisme* f. *tache* stain]

tachistoscope /tə'kɪstəˌskəʊp/ *n.* an instrument for very brief measured exposure of objects to the eye. □□ **tachistoscopic** /-'skɒpɪk/ *adj.* [Gk *takhistos* swiftest + -SCOPE]

tacho /'tækəʊ/ *n.* (*pl.* **-os**) *colloq.* = TACHOMETER. [abbr.]

tacho- /'tækəʊ/ *comb. form* speed. [Gk *takhos* speed]

tachograph /'tækəˌgrɑːf/ *n.* a device used esp. in heavy goods vehicles and coaches etc. for automatically recording speed and travel time.

tachometer /tə'kɒmɪtə(r)/ *n.* an instrument for measuring the rate of rotation of a shaft and hence the speed or velocity of a vehicle.

tachy- /'tækɪ/ *comb. form* swift. [Gk *takhus* swift]

tachycardia /ˌtækɪ'kɑːdɪə/ *n. Med.* an abnormally rapid heart rate. [TACHY- + Gk *kardia* heart]

tachygraphy /tə'kɪgrəfɪ/ *n.* **1** stenography, esp. that of the ancient Greeks and Romans. **2** the abbreviated medieval writing of Greek and Latin. □□ **tachygrapher** *n.* **tachygraphic** /-'græfɪk/ *adj.* **tachygraphical** /-'græfɪk(ə)l/ *adj.*

tachymeter /tə'kɪmɪtə(r)/ *n.* **1** *Surveying* an instrument used to locate points rapidly. **2** a speed-indicator.

tacit /'tæsɪt/ *adj.* understood or implied without being stated (*tacit consent*). □□ **tacitly** *adv.* [L *tacitus* silent f. *tacēre* be silent]

taciturn /'tæsɪˌtɜːn/ *adj.* reserved in speech; saying little; uncommunicative. □□ **taciturnity** /-'tɜːnɪtɪ/ *n.* **taciturnly** *adv.* [F *taciturne* or L *taciturnus* (as TACIT)]

Tacitus /'tæsɪtəs/, Cornelius (born c.56), Roman senator and historian, whose works are pervaded by a deep pessimism (partly the product of personal experience under Domitian) about the course of Roman history since the end of the Republic. His major works on imperial history, only partially preserved, the *Annals* (covering the period from 14 to 68) and the *Histories* (beginning in 69), are a piercingly ironic but scrupulously accurate record of the period, conveyed in a highly individual style, elevated, rapid, and intense.

tack[1] /tæk/ *n. & v.* —*n.* **1** a small sharp broad-headed nail. **2** *US* a drawing-pin. **3** a long stitch used in fastening fabrics etc. lightly or temporarily together. **4 a** the direction in which a ship moves as determined by the position of its sails and regarded in terms of the direction of the wind (*starboard tack*). **b** a temporary change of direction in sailing to take advantage of a side wind etc. **5** a course of action or policy (*try another tack*). **6** *Naut.* **a** a rope for securing the corner of some sails. **b** the corner to which this is fastened. **7** a sticky condition of varnish etc. **8** *Brit.* an extraneous clause appended to a bill in Parliament. —*v.* **1** *tr.* (often foll. by *down* etc.) fasten with tacks. **2** *tr.* stitch (pieces of cloth etc.) lightly together. **3** *tr.* (foll. by *to, on*) annex (a thing). **4** *intr.* (often foll. by *about*) **a** change a ship's course by turning its head to the wind (cf. WEAR[2]). **b** make a series of tacks. **5** *intr.* change one's conduct or policy etc. **6** *tr. Brit.* append (a clause) to a bill. □□ **tacker** *n.* [ME *tak* etc., of uncert. orig.: cf. Bibl. *tache* clasp, link f. OF *tache*]

tack[2] /tæk/ *n.* the saddle, bridle, etc., of a horse. [shortened f. TACKLE]

tackle /'tæk(ə)l/ *n. & v.* —*n.* **1** equipment for a task or sport (*fishing-tackle*). **2** a mechanism, esp. of ropes, pulley-blocks, hooks, etc., for lifting weights, managing sails, etc. (*block and tackle*). **3** a windlass with its ropes and hooks. **4** an act of tackling in football etc. **5** *Amer. Football* **a** the position next to the end of the forward line. **b** the player in this position. —*v.tr.* **1** try to deal with (a problem or difficulty). **2** grapple with or try to overcome (an opponent). **3** enter into discussion with. **4** obstruct, intercept, or seize and stop (a player running with the ball). **5** secure by means of tackle. □□ **tackle-block** a pulley over which a rope runs. **tackle-fall** a rope for applying force to the blocks of a tackle. □□ **tackler** *n.* **tackling** *n.* [ME, prob. f. MLG *takel* f. *taken* lay hold of]

tacky[1] /'tækɪ/ *adj.* (**tackier, tackiest**) (of glue or paint etc.) still slightly sticky after application. □□ **tackiness** *n.* [TACK[1] + -Y[1]]

tacky[2] /'tækɪ/ *adj.* (**tackier, tackiest**) esp. *US colloq.* **1** showing poor taste or style. **2** tatty or seedy. □□ **tackily** *adv.* **tackiness** *n.* [19th c.: orig. unkn.]

taco /'tɑːkəʊ/ *n.* (*pl.* **-os**) a Mexican dish of meat etc. in a folded or rolled tortilla. [Mex. Sp.]

tact /tækt/ *n.* **1** adroitness in dealing with others or with difficulties arising from personal feeling. **2** intuitive perception of the right thing to do or say. [F f. L *tactus* touch, sense of touch f. *tangere tact-* touch]

tactful /'tæktfʊl/ *adj.* having or showing tact. □□ **tactfully** *adv.* **tactfulness** *n.*

tactic /'tæktɪk/ *n.* **1** a tactical manoeuvre. **2** = TACTICS. [mod.L *tactica* f. Gk *taktikē* (*tekhnē* art): see TACTICS]

tactical /'tæktɪk(ə)l/ *adj.* **1** of, relating to, or constituting tactics (*a tactical retreat*). **2** (of bombing or weapons) done or for use in immediate support of military or naval operations (opp. STRATEGIC). **3** adroitly planning or planned. **4** (of voting) aimed at preventing the strongest candidate from winning by supporting the next strongest. □□ **tactically** *adv.* [Gk *taktikos* (as TACTICS)]

tactics /'tæktɪks/ *n.pl.* **1** (also treated as *sing.*) the art of disposing armed forces esp. in contact with an enemy (cf. STRATEGY). **2 a** the plans and means adopted in carrying out a scheme or achieving some end. **b** a skilful device or devices. □□ **tactician** /tækˈtɪʃ(ə)n/ n. [mod.L tactica f. Gk taktika neut.pl. f. taktos ordered f. tassō arrange]

tactile /ˈtæktaɪl/ adj. **1** of or connected with the sense of touch. **2** perceived by touch. **3** tangible. **4** Art (in painting) producing or concerning the effect of three-dimensional solidity. □□ **tactual** /ˈtæktjʊəl/ adj. (in senses 1, 2). **tactility** /-ˈtɪlɪtɪ/ n. [L tactilis f. tangere tact- touch]

tactless /ˈtæktlɪs/ adj. having or showing no tact. □□ **tactlessly** adv. **tactlessness** n.

tad /tæd/ n. US colloq. a small amount (often used adverbially: a tad too salty). [19th c.: orig. unkn.]

Tadjikistan /ˌtædʒɪkɪˈstɑːn/ the Tadjik SSR, a constituent republic of the USSR, in central Asia; pop. (est. 1987) 4,807,000; capital, Dushanbe.

tadpole /ˈtædpəʊl/ n. a larva of an amphibian, esp. a frog, toad, or newt in its aquatic stage and breathing through gills. [ME taddepolle (as TOAD, POLL¹ from the size of its head)]

taedium vitae /ˌtiːdɪəm ˈviːtaɪ, ˈvaɪtiː/ n. weariness of life (often as a pathological state, with a tendency to suicide). [L]

Taegu /ˈtaɪguː/ a city in SE Korea; pop. (1985) 2,030,650. Near the city is the Haeinsa temple, established in AD 802, which contains 80,000 wooden printing-blocks dating from the 13th c., engraved with compilations of Buddhist scriptures.

taenia /ˈtiːnɪə/ n. (US tenia) (pl. **taeniae** /-nɪˌiː/ or **taenias**) **1** Archit. a fillet between a Doric architrave and frieze. **2** Anat. any flat ribbon-like structure, esp. the muscles of the colon. **3** any large tapeworm of the genus Taenia, esp. T. saginata and T. soleum, parasitic on humans. **4** Gk Antiq. a fillet or headband. □□ **taenioid** adj. [L f. Gk tainia ribbon]

taffeta /ˈtæfɪtə/ n. a fine lustrous silk or silklike fabric. [ME f. OF taffetas or med.L taffata, ult. f. Pers. tāfta past part. of tāftan twist]

taffrail /ˈtæfreɪl/ n. Naut. a rail round a ship's stern. [earlier tafferel f. Du. taffereel panel, dimin. of tafel (as TABLE): assim. to RAIL¹]

Taffy /ˈtæfɪ/ n. (pl. **-ies**) colloq. often offens. a Welshman. [supposed Welsh pronunc. of Davy = David (Welsh Dafydd)]

taffy /ˈtæfɪ/ n. (pl. **-ies**) US **1** a confection like toffee. **2** insincere flattery. [19th c.: orig. unkn.]

tafia /ˈtæfɪə/ n. W.Ind. rum distilled from molasses etc. [18th c.: orig. uncert.]

Taft /tæft/, William Howard (1857–1930), 27th President of the US, 1909–13. His Presidency is remembered for its 'dollar diplomacy' in foreign affairs and for its tariff laws which were attacked as being too favourable to big business.

tag¹ /tæg/ n. & v. —n. **1** a label, esp. one for tying on an object to show its address, price, etc. **2** a metal or plastic point at the end of a lace etc. to assist insertion. **3** a loop at the back of a boot used in pulling it on. **4** US a licence plate of a motor vehicle. **5** a loose or ragged end of anything. **6** a ragged lock of wool on a sheep. **7** Theatr. a closing speech addressed to the audience. **8** a trite quotation or stock phrase. **9 a** the refrain of a song. **b** a musical phrase added to the end of a piece. **10** an animal's tail, or its tip. —v.tr. (**tagged**, **tagging**) **1** provide with a tag or tags. **2** (often foll. by on, on to) join or attach. **3** colloq. follow closely or trail behind. **4** Computing identify (an item of data) by its type for later retrieval. **5** label radioactively (see LABEL v. 3). **6 a** find rhymes for (verses). **b** string (rhymes) together. **7** shear away tags from (sheep). □ **tag along** (often foll. by with) go along or accompany passively. **tag end** esp. US the last remnant of something. [ME: orig. unkn.]

tag² /tæg/ n. & v. —n. **1** a children's game in which one chases the rest, and anyone who is caught then becomes the pursuer. **2** Baseball the act of tagging a runner. —v.tr. (**tagged**, **tagging**) **1** touch in a game of tag. **2** (often foll. by out) put (a runner) out by touching with the ball or with the hand holding the ball. [18th c.: orig. unkn.]

Tagalog /təˈgɑːlɒg/ n. & adj. —n. **1** a member of the principal people of the Philippine Islands. **2** the language of this people, which belongs to the Malayo-Polynesian language group although its vocabulary has been heavily influenced by Spanish with some adaptions from Chinese and Arabic. —adj. of or relating to this people or language. [Tagalog f. taga native + ilog river]

tagetes /təˈdʒiːtiːz/ n. any plant of the genus Tagetes, esp. any of various marigolds with bright orange or yellow flowers. [mod.L f. L Tages an Etruscan god]

tagliatelle /ˌtæljəˈtelɪ/ n. a form of pasta in narrow ribbons. [It.]

tagmemics /tægˈmiːmɪks/ n. the study and description of language in terms of tagmemes (the smallest meaningful units of grammatical form), based on the work of K. L. Pike (1912–), which stresses the functional and structural relations of grammatical units. [Gk tagma arrangement, after phoneme]

Tagore /təˈgɔː(r)/, Sir Rabindranath (1861–1941), Bengali poet and philosopher, who was awarded the Nobel Prize for literature in 1913 for his Gitanjali: Song-Offering (1912), poems modelled on medieval Indian devotional lyrics. He wrote philosophical plays such as Chitra (1913), novels (The Home and the World, 1919; Gora, 1929), and short fiction which often comments powerfully and courageously on Indian national and social concerns. He founded the Santiniketan communal school to encourage links between Eastern and Western educational and philosophical systems.

Tagus /ˈteɪgəs/ (Spanish **Tajo** /ˈtɑːxəʊ/, Portuguese **Tejo** /ˈteɪʒuː/) a river of Spain and Portugal, flowing into the Atlantic near Lisbon.

Tahiti /təˈhiːtɪ/ one of the Society Islands in the South Pacific, administered by France; pop. (1983) 115,800; capital, Papeete. The island is famous as the location of the Bounty mutiny in 1789. □□ **Tahitian** /-ʃ(ə)n/ adj. & n.

tahr /tɑː(r)/ n. any goatlike mammal of the genus Hemitragus, esp. H. jemlahicus of the Himalayas. [native name in Nepal]

tahsil /tɑːˈsiːl/ n. an administrative area in parts of India. [Urdu taḥsīl f. Arab., = collection]

t'ai chi chu'an /ˌtaɪ tʃiː ˈtʃwɑːn/ n. (also **t'ai chi** /taɪ ˈtʃiː/) a Chinese martial art and system of callisthenics consisting of sequences of very slow controlled movements. [Chin., = great ultimate boxing]

Ta'if /ˈtɑːɪf/ the unofficial seat of government of Saudi Arabia during the summer, situated in the Asir Mountains to the south-east of Mecca; pop. 204,850.

Taig /teɪg/ n. sl. offens. (in Northern Ireland) a Protestant name for a Catholic. [var. of Teague, Anglicized spelling of the Irish name Tadhg, a nickname for an Irishman]

taiga /ˈtaɪgə/ n. coniferous forest lying between tundra and steppe, esp. in Siberia. [Russ.]

tail¹ /teɪl/ n. & v. —n. **1** the hindmost part of an animal, esp. when prolonged beyond the rest of the body. **2 a** a thing like a tail in form or position, esp. something extending downwards or outwards at an extremity. **b** the rear end of anything, e.g. of a procession. **c** a long train or line of people, vehicles, etc. **3 a** the rear part of an aeroplane, with the tailplane and rudder, or of a rocket. **b** the rear part of a motor vehicle. **4** the luminous trail of particles following a comet. **5 a** the inferior or weaker part of anything, esp. in a sequence. **b** Cricket the end of the batting order, with the weakest batsmen. **6 a** the part of a shirt below the waist. **b** the hanging part of the back of a coat. **7** (in pl.) colloq. **a** a tailcoat. **b** evening dress including this. **8** (in pl.) the reverse of a coin as a choice when tossing. **9** colloq. a person following or shadowing another. **10** an extra strip attached to the lower end of a kite. **11** the stem of a note in music. **12** the part of a letter (e.g. y) below the line. **13 a** the exposed end of a slate or tile in a roof. **b** the unexposed end of a brick or stone in a wall. **14** the slender backward prolongation of a butterfly's wing. **15** a comparative calm at the end of a gale. **16** a calm stretch following rough water in a stream. —v. **1** tr. remove the stalks of (fruit). **2** tr. & (foll. by after) intr. colloq. shadow or follow closely. **3** tr. provide with a tail. **4** tr. dock the tail of (a lamb etc.). **5** tr. (often foll. by on to) join (one thing to another). □ **on a person's tail** closely following a person. **tail back** (of traffic) form a tailback. **tail covert** any of the feathers covering the base of a bird's tail feathers. **tail-end 1** the hindmost or lowest or last part. **2** (sense 5 of the *n.*). **tail-ender** a person at the tail-end of something, esp. in cricket and athletic races. **tail in** fasten (timber) by one end into a wall etc. **tail-light** (or **-lamp**) *US* a light at the rear of a train, motor vehicle, or bicycle. **tail off** (or **away**) **1** become fewer, smaller, or slighter. **2** fall behind or away in a scattered line. **tail-off** *n.* a decline or gradual reduction, esp. in demand. **tail-race** the part of a mill-race below the water-wheel. **tail-skid** a support for the tail of an aircraft when on the ground. **tail wind** a wind blowing in the direction of travel of a vehicle or aircraft etc. **with one's tail between one's legs** in a state of dejection or humiliation. **with one's tail up** in good spirits; cheerful. □□ **tailed** *adj.* (also in *comb.*). **tailless** *adj.* [OE *tægl, tægel* f. Gmc]

tail² /teɪl/ *n.* & *adj. Law* —*n.* limitation of ownership, esp. of an estate limited to a person and that person's heirs. —*adj.* so limited (*estate tail; fee tail*). □ **in tail** under such a limitation. [ME f. OF *taille* notch, cut, tax, f. *taillier* cut ult. f. L *talea* twig]

tailback /ˈteɪlbæk/ *n.* a long line of traffic extending back from an obstruction.

tailboard /ˈteɪlbɔːd/ *n.* a hinged or removable flap at the rear of a lorry etc.

tailcoat /ˈteɪlkəʊt/ *n.* a man's morning or evening coat with a long skirt divided at the back into tails and cut away in front, worn as part of formal dress.

tailgate /ˈteɪlɡeɪt/ *n.* & *v.* —*n.* **1** esp. *US* **a** = TAILBOARD. **b** the tail door of an estate car or hatchback. **2** the lower end of a canal lock. —*v. US colloq.* **1** *intr.* drive too closely behind another vehicle. **2** *tr.* follow (a vehicle) too closely. □□ **tailgater** *n.*

tailing /ˈteɪlɪŋ/ *n.* **1** (in *pl.*) the refuse or inferior part of grain or ore etc. **2** the part of a beam or projecting brick etc. embedded in a wall.

Tailleferre /taɪˈfeə(r)/, Germaine (1892–), French composer and pianist, a pupil of Ravel. Although a member of 'Les Six' (see SIX), unlike most of the group she emerged as a composer of graceful music in the French tradition. Her works include concertos for unusual combinations, including one for baritone, piano, and orchestra.

tailor /ˈteɪlə(r)/ *n.* & *v.* —*n.* a maker of clothes, esp. one who makes men's outer garments to measure. —*v.* **1** *tr.* make (clothes) as a tailor. **2** *tr.* make or adapt for a special purpose. **3** *intr.* work as or be a tailor. **4** *tr.* (esp. as **tailored** *adj.*) make clothes for (*he was immaculately tailored*). **5** *tr.* (as **tailored** *adj.*) = tailor-made. □ **tailor-bird** any small Asian etc. bird of the genus *Orthotomus* that stitches leaves together to form a nest. **tailor-made** *adj.* **1** (of clothing) made to order by a tailor. **2** made or suited for a particular purpose (*a job tailor-made for me*). —*n.* a tailor-made garment. **tailor's chair** a chair without legs for sitting cross-legged like a tailor at work. **tailor's twist** a fine strong silk thread used by tailors. □□ **tailoring** *n.* [ME & AF *taillour*, OF *tailleur* cutter, formed as TAIL²]

tailored /ˈteɪləd/ *adj.* (of clothing) well or closely fitted.

tailpiece /ˈteɪlpiːs/ *n.* **1** an appendage at the rear of anything. **2** the final part of a thing. **3** a decoration in a blank space at the end of a chapter etc. in a book. **4** a piece of wood to which the strings of some musical instruments are attached at their lower ends.

tailpipe /ˈteɪlpaɪp/ *n.* the rear section of the exhaust pipe of a motor vehicle.

tailplane /ˈteɪlpleɪn/ *n.* a horizontal aerofoil at the tail of an aircraft.

tailspin /ˈteɪlspɪn/ *n.* & *v.* —*n.* **1** a spin (see SPIN *n.* 2) by an aircraft with the tail spiralling. **2** a state of chaos or panic. —*v.intr.* (**-spinning**; *past* and *past part.* **-spun**) perform a tailspin.

tailstock /ˈteɪlstɒk/ *n.* the adjustable part of a lathe holding the fixed spindle.

Taimyr Peninsula /taɪˈmɪə/ a peninsula forming the northernmost point of mainland USSR and of Asia.

taint /teɪnt/ *n.* & *v.* —*n.* **1** a spot or trace of decay, infection, or some bad quality. **2** a corrupt condition or infection. —*v.* **1** *tr.* affect with a taint. **2** *tr.* (foll. by *with*) affect slightly. **3** *intr.*

become tainted. □□ **taintless** *adj.* [ME, partly f. OF *teint(e)* f. L *tinctus* f. *tingere* dye, partly f. ATTAINT]

taipan¹ /ˈtaɪpæn/ *n.* the head of a foreign business in China. [Chin.]

taipan² /ˈtaɪpæn/ *n.* a large venomous Australian snake, *Oxyuranus microlepidotus*. [Aboriginal]

Taipei /taɪˈpeɪ/ the capital of Taiwan; pop. (est. 1987) 2,640,000.

Taiwan /taɪˈwæn/ an island, mountainous and densely forested on its east side, off the SE coast of China; pop. (est. 1988) 20,004,400; official language, Chinese; capital, Taipei. Settled for centuries by the Chinese, the island was sighted by the Portuguese in 1590; they named it Formosa (= beautiful). It was ceded to Japan by China in 1895 but returned to China after the Second World War. General Chiang Kai-shek withdrew there in 1949 with 500,000 troops towards the end of the war with the Communist regime, and it became the headquarters of the Chinese Nationalists. Since the 1950s Taiwan has undergone steady economic growth, particularly in its export-oriented industries. In 1971 it lost its seat in the United Nations to the People's Republic of China, which regards Taiwan as one of its provinces. □□ **Taiwanese** /-ˈniːz/ *adj.* & *n.*

Taiyuan /ˌtaɪʊˈɑːn/ a city in northern China, capital of Shanxi province; pop. (est. 1986) 1,880,000.

Ta'iz /tæˈiz/ the administrative capital of Yemen from 1948 to 1962; pop. (1986) 178,000.

taj /tɑːdʒ/ *n.* a tall conical cap worn by a dervish. [Arab. *tāj*]

Taj Mahal /tɑːʒ məˈhɑːl/ a mausoleum at Agra in northern India, by the River Jumna. Completed *c*.1648, it was built by the Mogul emperor Shah Jahan in memory of his favourite wife who had borne him fourteen children. Set in formal gardens, the domed building in white marble is reflected in a pool flanked by cypresses. [perh. corrupt. of Pers. *Mumtaz Mahal*, title of wife of Shah Jahan, f. *mumtāz* chosen one, *mahal* abode]

Tajo see TAGUS.

takahe /ˈtɑːkəhiː/ *n.* = NOTORNIS. [Maori]

take /teɪk/ *v.* & *n.* —*v.* (*past* **took** /tʊk/; *past part.* **taken** /ˈteɪkən/) **1** *tr.* lay hold of; get into one's hands. **2** *tr.* acquire, get possession of, capture, earn, or win. **3** *tr.* get the use of by purchase or formal agreement (*take lodgings*). **4** *tr.* (in a recipe) avail oneself of; use. **5** *tr.* use as a means of transport (*took a taxi*). **6** *tr.* regularly buy or subscribe to (a particular newspaper or periodical etc.). **7** *tr.* obtain after fulfilling the required conditions (*take a degree*). **8** *tr.* occupy (*take a chair*). **9** *tr.* make use of (*take the next turning on the left*). **10** *tr.* consume as food or medicine (*take tea; took the pills*). **11** *intr.* **a** be successful or effective (*the inoculation did not take*). **b** (of a plant, seed, etc.) begin to grow. **12** *tr.* require or use up (*will only take a minute; these things take time*). **13** *tr.* cause to come or go with one; convey (*take the book home; the bus will take you all the way*). **14** *tr.* remove; dispossess a person of (*someone has taken my pen*). **15** *tr.* catch or be infected with (fire or fever etc.). **16** *tr.* **a** experience or be affected by (*take fright; take pleasure*). **b** give play to (*take comfort*). **c** exert (*take courage; take no notice*). **17** *tr.* find out and note (a name and address; a person's temperature etc.) by enquiry or measurement. **18** *tr.* grasp mentally; understand (*I take your point; I took you to mean yes*). **19** *tr.* treat or regard in a specified way (*took the news calmly; took it badly*). **20** *tr.* (foll. by *for*) regard as being (*do you take me for an idiot?*). **21** *tr.* **a** accept (*take the offer*). **b** submit to (*take a joke; take no nonsense; took a risk*). **22** *tr.* choose or assume (*took a different view; took a job; took the initiative*). **23** *tr.* derive (*takes its name from the inventor*). **24** *tr.* (foll. by *from*) subtract (*take 3 from 9*). **25** *tr.* execute, make, or undertake; perform or effect (*take notes; take an oath; take a decision; take a look*). **26** *tr.* occupy or engage oneself in; indulge in; enjoy (*take a rest; take exercise; take a holiday*). **27** *tr.* conduct (*took the school assembly*). **28** *tr.* deal with in a certain way (*took the corner too fast*). **29** *tr.* **a** teach or be taught (a subject). **b** be examined in (a subject). **30** *tr.* make (a photograph) with a camera; photograph (a person or thing). **31** *tr.* use as an instance (*let us take Napoleon*). **32** *tr. Gram.* have or require as part of the appropriate construction (*this verb takes an object*). **33** *tr.* have sexual intercourse with (a woman). **34** *tr.* (in *passive*; foll. by *by, with*) be attracted or charmed by. —*n.* **1** an amount taken or caught in one session or attempt etc. **2** a scene or sequence of film photographed continuously at one time. **3** esp. *US* takings, esp. money received at a theatre for seats. **4** *Printing* the amount of copy set up at one time. □ **be taken ill** become ill, esp. suddenly. **have what it takes** *colloq.* have the necessary qualities etc. for success. **take account of** see ACCOUNT. **take action** see ACTION. **take advantage of** see ADVANTAGE. **take advice** see ADVICE. **take after** resemble (esp. a parent or ancestor). **take against** begin to dislike, esp. impulsively. **take aim** see AIM. **take apart 1** dismantle. **2** *colloq.* beat or defeat. **take aside** see ASIDE. **take as read** accept without reading or discussing. **take away 1** remove or carry elsewhere. **2** subtract. **3** *Brit.* buy (food etc.) at a shop or restaurant for eating elsewhere. **take-away** *Brit. attrib.adj.* (of food) bought at a shop or restaurant for eating elsewhere. —*n.* **1** an establishment selling this. **2** the food itself (*let's get a take-away*). **take back 1** retract (a statement). **2** convey (a person or thing) to his or her or its original position. **3** carry (a person) in thought to a past time. **4** *Printing* transfer to the previous line. **take the biscuit** (or **bun** or **cake**) *colloq.* be the most remarkable. **take a bow** see BOW². **take care of** see CARE. **take a chance** etc. see CHANCE. **take down 1** write down (spoken words). **2** remove (a structure) by separating it into pieces. **3** humiliate. **take effect** see EFFECT. **take for granted** see GRANT. **take fright** see FRIGHT. **take from** diminish; weaken; detract from. **take heart** be encouraged. **take hold** see HOLD¹. **take-home pay** the pay received by an employee after the deduction of tax etc. **take ill** (*US* **sick**) *colloq.* be taken ill. **take in 1** receive as a lodger etc. **2** undertake (work) at home. **3** make (a garment etc.) smaller. **4** understand (*did you take that in?*). **5** cheat (*managed to take them all in*). **6** include or comprise. **7** *colloq.* visit (a place) on the way to another (*shall we take in Avebury?*). **8** furl (a sail). **9** *Brit.* regularly buy (a newspaper etc.). **take-in** *n.* a deception. **take in hand 1** undertake; start doing or dealing with. **2** undertake the control or reform of (a person). **take into account** see ACCOUNT. **take it 1** (often foll. by *that* + clause) assume (*I take it that you have finished*). **2** *colloq.* endure a difficulty or hardship in a specified way (*took it badly*). **take it easy** see EASY. **take it from me** (or **take my word for it**) I can assure you. **take it ill** resent it. **take it into one's head** see HEAD. **take it on one** (or **oneself**) (foll. by *to* + infin.) venture or presume. **take it or leave it** (esp. in *imper.*) an expression of indifference or impatience about another's decision after making an offer. **take it out of 1** exhaust the strength of. **2** have revenge on. **take it out on** relieve one's frustration by attacking or treating harshly. **take one's leave of** see LEAVE². **take a lot of** (or **some**) **doing** be hard to do. **take a person's name in vain** see VAIN. **take off 1 a** remove (clothing) from one's or another's body. **b** remove or lead away. **2** deduct (part of an amount). **3** depart, esp. hastily (*took off in a fast car*). **4** *colloq.* mimic humorously. **5** jump from the ground. **6** become airborne. **7** (of a scheme, enterprise, etc.) become successful or popular. **8** have (a period) away from work. **take-off 1** the act of becoming airborne. **2** an act of mimicking. **3** a place from which one jumps. **take oneself off** go away. **take on 1** undertake (work etc.). **2** engage (an employee). **3** be willing or ready to meet (an adversary in sport, argument, etc., esp. a stronger one). **4** acquire (a new meaning etc.). **5** *colloq.* show strong emotion. **take orders** see ORDER. **take out 1** remove from within a place; extract. **2** escort on an outing. **3** get (a licence or summons etc.) issued. **4** *US* = *take away* 3. **5** *Bridge* remove (a partner or a partner's call) from a suit by bidding a different one or one no trumps. **6** *sl.* murder or destroy. **take a person out of himself** or **herself** make a person forget his or her worries. **take over 1** succeed to the management or ownership of. **2** take control. **3** *Printing* transfer to the next line. **take-over** *n.* the assumption of control (esp. of a business); the buying-out of one company by another. **take part** see PART. **take place** see PLACE. **take a person's point** see POINT. **take shape** assume a distinct form; develop into something definite. **take sides** see SIDE. **take stock** see STOCK. **take the sun** see SUN. **take that!** an exclamation accompanying a blow etc. **take one's time** not hurry. **take to 1** begin or fall into the habit of (*took to smoking*). **2** have recourse to. **3** adapt oneself to. **4** form a liking for. **take to heart** see HEART. **take to one's heels** see HEEL¹. **take to pieces** see PIECE. **take the**

trouble see TROUBLE. **take up 1** become interested or engaged in (a pursuit). **2** adopt as a protégé. **3** occupy (time or space). **4** begin (residence etc.). **5** resume after an interruption. **6** interrupt or question (a speaker). **7** accept (an offer etc.). **8** shorten (a garment). **9** lift up. **10** absorb (*sponges take up water*). **11** take (a person) into a vehicle. **12** pursue (a matter etc.) further. **take a person up on** accept (a person's offer etc.). **take up with** begin to associate with. □□ **takable** *adj.* (also **takeable**). [OE *tacan* f. ON *taka*]

taker /ˈteɪkə(r)/ *n.* **1** a person who takes a bet. **2** a person who accepts an offer.

takin /ˈtɑːkɪn/ *n.* a large Tibetan horned ruminant, *Budorcas taxicolor*. [Mishmi]

taking /ˈteɪkɪŋ/ *adj.* & *n.* —*adj.* **1** attractive or captivating. **2** catching or infectious. —*n.* (in *pl.*) an amount of money taken in business. □□ **takingly** *adv.* **takingness** *n.*

Taklimakan Desert /ˌtæklɪməˈkɑːn/ a desert forming the greater part of the Tarim Basin of Xinjiang autonomous region, NW China.

Takoradi /ˌtɑːkəˈrɑːdɪ/ a major West African seaport on the Gulf of Guinea, in west Ghana, part of the joint urban area of Sekondi-Takoradi; pop. (1984) 93,400.

tala /ˈtɑːlə/ *n.* any of the traditional rhythmic patterns of Indian music. [Skr.]

talapoin /ˈtæləˌpɔɪn/ *n.* **1** a Buddhist monk or priest. **2** a small West African monkey, *Miopithecus talapoin*. [Port. *talapão* f. Talaing *tala pói* my lord]

talaria /təˈleərɪə/ *n.pl. Rom. Mythol.* winged sandals as an attribute of Mercury, Iris, and others. [L, neut. pl. of *talaris* f. *talus* ankle]

Talbot /ˈtɔːlbət, ˈtɒl-/, William Henry Fox (1800–77), English chemist, archaeologist, and pioneer of photography. Working independently of Daguerre, by 1841 he had developed a process for producing a negative from which multiple positive prints could be made.

talc /tælk/ *n.* & *v.* —*n.* **1** talcum powder. **2** any crystalline form of magnesium silicate that occurs in soft flat plates, usu. white or pale green in colour and used as a lubricator etc. —*v.tr.* (**talcked, talcking**) treat (a surface) with talc to lubricate or dry it. □□ **talcose** *adj.* **talcous** *adj.* **talcy** *adj.* (in sense 1). [F *talc* or med.L *talcum*, f. Arab. *ṭalḳ* f. Pers. *ṭalḳ*]

talcum /ˈtælkəm/ *n.* **1** = TALC. **2** (in full **talcum powder**) powdered talc for toilet and cosmetic use, usu. perfumed. [med.L: see TALC]

tale /teɪl/ *n.* **1** a narrative or story, esp. fictitious and imaginatively treated. **2** a report of an alleged fact, often malicious or in breach of confidence (*all sorts of tales will get about*). **3** *archaic* or *literary* a number or total (*the tale is complete*). □ **tale of a tub** an idle fiction. [OE *talu* f. Gmc: cf. TELL¹]

talebearer /ˈteɪlˌbeərə(r)/ *n.* a person who maliciously gossips or reveals secrets. □□ **talebearing** *n.* & *adj.*

talent /ˈtælənt/ *n.* **1** a special aptitude or faculty (*a talent for music; has real talent*). **2** high mental ability. **3 a** a person or persons of talent (*is a real talent; plenty of local talent*). **b** *colloq.* members of the opposite sex regarded in terms of sexual promise. **4** an ancient weight and unit of currency, esp. among the ancient Greeks. □ **talent-scout** (or **-spotter**) a person looking for talented performers, esp. in sport and entertainment. □□ **talented** *adj.* **talentless** *adj.* [OE *talente* & OF *talent* f. L *talentum* inclination of mind f. Gk *talanton* balance, weight, sum of money]

tales /ˈteɪliːz/ *n. Law* **1** a writ for summoning jurors to supply a deficiency. **2** a list of persons who may be summoned. [ME f. L *tales* (*de circumstantibus*) such (of the bystanders), the first words of the writ]

talesman /ˈteɪliːzmən, ˈteɪlz-/ *n.* (*pl.* **-men**) *Law* a person summoned by a *tales*.

taleteller /ˈteɪlˌtelə(r)/ *n.* **1** a person who tells stories. **2** a person who spreads malicious reports.

tali *pl.* of TALUS¹.

talion /ˈtælɪən/ *n.* = LEX TALIONIS. [ME f. OF f. L *talio -onis* f. *talis* such]

talipes /'tælɪˌpiːz/ n. Med. = club-foot. [mod.L f. L talus ankle + pes foot]

talipot /'tælɪˌpɒt/ n. a tall S. Indian palm, Corypha umbraculifera, with very large fan-shaped leaves that are used as sunshades etc. [Malayalam tālipat, Hindi tālpāt f. Skr. tālapattra f. tāla palm + pattra leaf]

talisman /'tælɪzmən/ n. (pl. **talismans**) 1 an object, esp. an inscribed ring or stone, supposed to be endowed with magic powers esp. of averting evil from or bringing good luck to its holder. 2 a charm or amulet; a thing supposed capable of working wonders. □□ **talismanic** /-'mænɪk/ adj. [F & Sp., = It. talismano, f. med.Gk telesmon, Gk telesma completion, religious rite f. teleō complete f. telos end]

talk /tɔːk/ v. & n. —v. 1 intr. (often foll. by to, with) converse or communicate ideas by spoken words. 2 intr. have the power of speech. 3 intr. (foll. by about) a have as the subject of discussion. b (in imper.) colloq. as an emphatic statement (talk about expense! It cost me £50). 4 tr. express or utter in words; discuss (you are talking nonsense; talked cricket all day). 5 tr. use (a language) in speech (is talking Spanish). 6 intr. (foll. by at) address pompously. 7 tr. (usu. foll. by into, out of) bring into a specified condition etc. by talking (talked himself hoarse; how did you talk them into it?; talked them out of the difficulty). 8 intr. reveal (esp. secret) information; betray secrets. 9 intr. gossip (people are beginning to talk). 10 intr. have influence (money talks). 11 intr. communicate by radio. —n. 1 conversation or talking. 2 a particular mode of speech (baby-talk). 3 an informal address or lecture. 4 a rumour or gossip (there is talk of a merger). b its theme (their success was the talk of the town). 5 (often in pl.) extended discussions or negotiations. □ **know what one is talking about** be expert or authoritative. **now you're talking** colloq. I like what you say, suggest, etc. **talk away** 1 consume (time) in talking. 2 carry on talking (talk away! I'm listening). **talk back** 1 reply defiantly. 2 respond on a two-way radio system. **talk big** colloq. talk boastfully. **talk down to** speak patronizingly or condescendingly to. **talk a person down 1** silence a person by greater loudness or persistence. 2 bring (a pilot or aircraft) to landing by radio instructions from the ground. **talk the hind leg off a donkey** talk incessantly. **talk nineteen to the dozen** see DOZEN. **talk of 1** discuss or mention. 2 (often foll. by verbal noun) express some intention of (talked of moving to London). **talk of the town** what is being talked about generally. **talk out** Brit. block the course of (a bill in Parliament) by prolonging discussion to the time of adjournment. **talk over** discuss at length. **talk a person over** (or **round**) gain agreement or compliance from a person by talking. **talk shop** talk, esp. tediously or inopportunely, about one's occupation, business, etc. **talk show** = chat show (see CHAT¹). **talk tall** boast. **talk through one's hat** (or **neck**) colloq. 1 exaggerate. 2 bluff. 3 talk wildly or nonsensically. **talk to** reprove or scold (a person). **talk to oneself** soliloquize. **talk turkey** see TURKEY. **talk up** discuss (a subject) in order to arouse interest in it. **you can't** (or **can**) **talk** colloq. a reproof that the person addressed is just as culpable etc. in the matter at issue. □□ **talker** n. [ME talken frequent. verb f. TALE or TELL¹]

talkathon /'tɔːkəˌθɒn/ n. colloq. a prolonged session of talking or discussion. [TALK + MARATHON]

talkative /'tɔːkətɪv/ adj. fond of or given to talking. □□ **talkatively** adv. **talkativeness** n.

talkback /'tɔːkbæk/ n. 1 (often attrib.) a system of two-way communication by loudspeaker. 2 Austral. & NZ = phone-in (see PHONE¹).

talkie /'tɔːkɪ/ n. esp. US colloq. a film with a soundtrack, as distinct from a silent film. [TALK + -IE, after movie]

talking /'tɔːkɪŋ/ adj. & n. —adj. 1 that talks. 2 having the power of speech (a talking parrot). 3 expressive (talking eyes). —n. in senses of TALK v. □ **talking book** a recorded reading of a book, esp. for the blind. **talking film** (or **picture**) a film with a soundtrack. **talking head** colloq. a presenter etc. on television, speaking to the camera and viewed in close-up. **talking of** while we are discussing (talking of food, what time is lunch?). **talking-point** a topic for discussion or argument.

talking-shop derog. an institution regarded as a place of argument rather than action. **talking-to** colloq. a reproof or reprimand (gave them a good talking-to).

tall /tɔːl/ adj. & adv. —adj. 1 of more than average height. 2 of a specified height (looks about six feet tall). 3 higher than the surrounding objects (a tall building). 4 colloq. extravagant or excessive (a tall story; tall talk). —adv. as if tall; proudly; in a tall or extravagant way (sit tall). □ **tall drink** a drink served in a tall glass. **tall hat** = top hat (see TOP¹). **tall order** an exorbitant or unreasonable demand. **tall ship** a sailing ship with a high mast. □□ **tallish** adj. **tallness** n. [ME, repr. OE getæl swift; prompt]

tallage /'tælɪdʒ/ n. hist. 1 a form of taxation on towns etc., abolished in the 14th c. 2 a tax on feudal dependants etc. [ME f. OF taillage f. tailler cut: see TAIL²]

tallboy /'tɔːlbɔɪ/ n. a tall chest of drawers sometimes in lower and upper sections or mounted on legs.

Talleyrand /'tælɪˌrænd/ Charles Maurice de Talleyrand-Périgord (1754–1838), French cleric, diplomat, and statesman, who contrived to hold high office during several regimes. He was foreign minister (1797) under the Directory, but involved himself in the coup that brought Napoleon to power and held the same position under the new leader (1799–1807), becoming his trusted adviser, then resigned office and engaged in secret negotiations to have him deposed. After the fall of Napoleon (1814) he became head of the new government and recalled Louis XVIII to the throne, but towards 1830, aware of the growing unpopularity of the government of Charles X, he entered into diplomatic relations with Louis Philippe (see entry), who rewarded him with the post of ambassador to Great Britain (1830–4).

Tallinn /'tælɪn/ a port on the Gulf of Finland, capital of Estonia; pop. (est. 1987) 478,000.

Tallis /'tælɪs/, Thomas (c.1505–85), English composer and organist, Gentleman of the Chapel Royal 1540–85, serving under Henry VIII, Edward VI, Mary, and Elizabeth I, and organist jointly with Byrd. In 1575 Elizabeth gave Tallis and Byrd a twenty-one-year monopoly in printing music. In that year they published Cantiones sacrae, a collection of 34 of their motets. Tallis is known mainly for his church music, especially the forty-part motet Spem in alium.

tallith /'tælɪθ/ n. a scarf worn by Jews esp. at prayer. [Rabbinical Heb. ṭallīt f. ṭillel to cover]

tallow /'tæləʊ/ n. & v. —n. the harder kinds of (esp. animal) fat melted down for use in making candles, soap, etc. —v.tr. grease with tallow. □ **tallow-tree** any of various trees, esp. Sapium sebiferum of China, yielding vegetable tallow. **vegetable tallow** a vegetable fat used as tallow. □□ **tallowish** adj. **tallowy** adj. [ME talg, talug, f. MLG talg, talch, of unkn. orig.]

tally /'tælɪ/ n. & v. —n. (pl. **-ies**) 1 the reckoning of a debt or score. 2 a total score or amount. 3 a a mark registering a fixed number of objects delivered or received. b such a number as a unit. 4 hist. a a piece of wood scored across with notches for the items of an account and then split into halves, each party keeping one. b an account kept in this way. 5 a ticket or label for identification. 6 a corresponding thing, counterpart, or duplicate. —v. (-ies, -ied) (often foll. by with) 1 intr. agree or correspond. 2 tr. record or reckon by tally. □ **tally clerk** an official who keeps a tally of goods, esp. those loaded or unloaded in docks. **tally sheet** a paper on which a tally is kept. **tally system** a system of sale on short credit or instalments with an account kept by tally. □□ **tallier** n. [ME f. AF tallie, AL tallia, talia f. L talea: cf. TAIL²]

tally-ho /ˌtælɪ'həʊ/ int., n., & v. —int. a huntsman's cry to the hounds on sighting a fox. —n. (pl. **-hos**) an utterance of this. —v. (-hoes, -hoed) 1 intr. utter a cry of 'tally-ho'. 2 tr. indicate (a fox) or urge (hounds) with this cry. [cf. F taiaut]

tallyman /'tælɪmən/ n. (pl. **-men**) 1 a person who keeps a tally. 2 a person who sells goods on credit, esp. from door to door.

Talmud /'tælmʊd, -məd/ n. the body of Jewish civil and ceremonial law and legend comprising the Mishnah and the Gemara, dating from the 5th c. BC but including earlier material.

□□ **Talmudic** /-ˈmʊdɪk/ adj. **Talmudical** /-ˈmʊdɪk(ə)l/ adj. **Talmudist** n. [late Heb. talmûḏ instruction f. Heb. lāmaḏ learn]

talon /ˈtælən/ n. **1** a claw, esp. of a bird of prey. **2** the cards left after the deal in a card-game. **3** the last part of a dividend-coupon sheet, entitling the holder to a new sheet on presentation. **4** the shoulder of a bolt against which the key presses in shooting it in a lock. **5** an ogee moulding. □□ **taloned** adj. (also in comb.). [ME f. OF, = heel, ult. f. L talus: see TALUS¹]

talus¹ /ˈteɪləs/ n. (pl. **tali** /-laɪ/) Anat. the ankle-bone supporting the tibia. Also called ASTRAGALUS. [L, = ankle, heel]

talus² /ˈteɪləs/ n. (pl. **taluses**) **1** the slope of a wall that tapers to the top or rests against a bank. **2** Geol. a sloping mass of fragments at the foot of a cliff. [F: orig. unkn.]

TAM abbr. television audience measurement, denoting a measure of the number of people watching a particular television programme as estimated by the company Television Audience Measurement Ltd.

tam /tæm/ n. a tam-o'-shanter. [abbr.]

tamable var. of TAMEABLE.

tamale /təˈmɑːlɪ/ n. a Mexican food of seasoned meat and maize flour steamed or baked in maize husks. [Mex. Sp. tamal, pl. tamales]

tamandua /təˈmændjuːə/ n. any small Central and S. American arboreal anteater of the genus Tamandua, with a prehensile tail used in climbing. [Port. f. Tupi tamanduá]

tamarack /ˈtæməˌræk/ n. **1** an American larch, Larix laricina. **2** the wood from this. [Amer. Ind.]

tamarillo /ˌtæməˈrɪləʊ/ n. (pl. **-os**) esp. Austral. & NZ = tree tomato. [arbitrary marketing name: cf. Sp. tomatillo dimin. of tomate TOMATO]

tamarin /ˈtæmərɪn/ n. any S. American usu. insect-eating monkey of the genus Saguinus, having hairy crests and moustaches. [F f. Carib]

tamarind /ˈtæmərɪnd/ n. **1** a tropical evergreen tree, Tamarindus indica. **2** the fruit of this, containing an acid pulp used as food and in making drinks. [med.L tamarindus f. Arab. tamr-hindī Indian date]

tamarisk /ˈtæmərɪsk/ n. any shrub of the genus Tamarix, usu. with long slender branches and small pink or white flowers, that thrives by the sea. [ME f. LL tamariscus, L tamarix]

Tamaulipas /ˌtæmaʊˈliːpæs/ a State of NE Mexico; pop. (est. 1988) 2,226,700; capital, Ciudad Victoria.

Tambo /ˈtæmbəʊ/, Oliver (1917–   ), Black South African politician, a prominent member of the African National Congress (see entry) and business partner of Nelson Mandela in a law firm. When the ANC was banned in South Africa in 1960 he left the Republic in order to organize activities elsewhere, and during Mandela's imprisonment he became acting president of the ANC (in Zambia) in 1967 and president in 1977.

tambour /ˈtæmbʊə(r)/ n. & v. —n. **1** a drum. **2 a** a circular frame for holding fabric taut while it is being embroidered. **b** material embroidered in this way. **3** Archit. each of a sequence of cylindrical stones forming the shaft of a column. **4** Archit. the circular part of various structures. **5** Archit. a lobby with a ceiling and folding doors in a church porch etc. to obviate draughts. **6** a sloping buttress or projection in a fives-court etc. —v.tr. (also absol.) decorate or embroider on a tambour. [F f. tabour TABOR]

tamboura /tæmˈbʊərə/ n. Mus. an Indian stringed instrument used as a drone. [Arab. ṭanbūra]

tambourin /ˈtæmbərɪn/ n. **1** a long narrow drum used in Provence. **2 a** a dance accompanied by a tambourin. **b** the music for this. [F, dimin. of TAMBOUR]

tambourine /ˌtæmbəˈriːn/ n. a percussion instrument consisting of a hoop with a parchment stretched over one side and jingling discs in slots round the hoop. □□ **tambourinist** n. [F, dimin. of TAMBOUR]

tame /teɪm/ adj. & v. —adj. **1** (of an animal) domesticated; not wild or shy. **2** insipid; lacking spirit or interest; dull (tame acquiescence). **3** (of a person) amenable and available. **4** US **a** (of land) cultivated. **b** (of a plant) produced by cultivation. —v.tr. **1** make tame; domesticate; break in. **2** subdue, curb, humble;

break the spirit of. □□ **tamely** adv. **tameness** n. **tamer** n. (also in comb.). [OE tam f. Gmc]

tameable /ˈteɪməb(ə)l/ adj. (also **tamable**) capable of being tamed. □□ **tameability** /-ˈbɪlɪtɪ/ n. **tameableness** n.

Tamerlane /ˈtæməˌleɪn/ (d. 1405) Timur Lenk or Lang (= 'lame Timur'), ruler of Turkestan who conquered large parts of Asia in the late 14th and early 15th c., ancestor of the Mogul dynasty in India.

Tamil /ˈtæmɪl/ n. & adj. —n. **1** a member of a Dravidian people inhabiting South India and Sri Lanka. **2** their language, of the Dravidian group, one of the major languages of southern India, spoken by about 88 million people together with about another 4 million in Sri Lanka and Malaysia. —adj. of this people or their language. □□ **Tamilian** /-ˈmɪlɪən/ adj. [native name Tamil, rel. to DRAVIDIAN]

Tamil Nadu /ˈtæmɪl næˈduː/ a State in SE India; pop. (1981) 48,297,450; capital, Madras.

Tammany /ˈtæmənɪ/ **1** a fraternal and benevolent society of New York City, founded in 1789, developed out of one of the earlier patriotic societies. **2** a political organization of the Democratic Party, identified with this society and notorious in the 19th c. for corruption, maintaining power by the use of bribes etc. It dominated the political life of New York City during the 19th and early 20th c. before being reduced in power by Franklin Roosevelt in 1932. □ **Tammany Hall 1** any of the successive buildings used as the headquarters of Tammany. **2** the members of Tammany. [name of Indian chief (late 17th c.) said to have welcomed William Penn and regarded (c.1770–90) as 'patron saint' of Pennsylvania and other northern colonies]

Tammerfors see TAMPERE.

Tammuz /ˈtæmʊz/ a Babylonian or Syrian deity, lover of Astarte, corresponding to the Greek Adonis. He became the personification of the seasonal decay and revival of crops.

tammy /ˈtæmɪ/ n. (pl. **-ies**) = TAM-O'-SHANTER.

tam-o'-shanter /ˌtæməˈʃæntə(r)/ n. a round woollen or cloth cap of Scottish origin fitting closely round the brows but large and full above. [the hero of Burns's Tam o' Shanter]

tamp /tæmp/ v.tr. **1** pack (a blast-hole) full of clay etc. to get the full force of an explosion. **2** ram down (road material etc.). □□ **tamper** n. **tamping** n. (in sense 1). [perh. back-form. f. F tampin (var. of TAMPION, taken as = tamping]

tamper /ˈtæmpə(r)/ v.intr. (foll. by with) **1** meddle with or make unauthorized changes in. **2** exert a secret or corrupt influence upon; bribe. □□ **tamperer** n. **tamper-proof** adj. [var. of TEMPER]

Tampere /ˈtæmpəˌreɪ/ (Swedish **Tammerfors** /ˈtɑːməˌfɔːs/) the second-largest city in Finland; pop. (1987) 170,533.

Tampico /tæmˈpiːkəʊ/ one of Mexico's principal seaports, on the Gulf of Mexico; pop. (1980) 268,000.

tampion /ˈtæmpɪən/ n. (also **tompion** /ˈtɒm-/) **1** a wooden stopper for the muzzle of a gun. **2** a plug e.g. for the top of an organ-pipe. [ME f. F tampon, nasalized var. of tapon, rel. to TAP¹]

tampon /ˈtæmpɒn/ n. & v. —n. a plug of soft material used to stop a wound or absorb secretions, esp. one inserted into the vagina. —v.tr. (**tamponed**, **tamponing**) plug with a tampon. [F: see TAMPION]

tamponade /ˌtæmpəˈneɪd/ n. compression of the heart by an accumulation of fluid in the pericardial sac.

tamponage /ˈtæmpənɪdʒ/ n. = TAMPONADE.

tam-tam /ˈtæmtæm/ n. a large metal gong. [Hindi: see TOM-TOM]

Tamworth Manifesto /ˈtæmwəθ/ an election speech by Sir Robert Peel in 1834 in his Tamworth constituency, in which he accepted the changes instituted by the Reform Act and expressed his belief in moderate political reform. The manifesto is often held to signal the emergence of the Conservative Party from the old loose grouping of Tory interests.

tan¹ /tæn/ n., adj., & v. —n. **1** a brown skin colour resulting from exposure to ultraviolet light. **2** a yellowish-brown colour. **3** bark, esp. of oak, bruised and used to tan hides. **4** (in full **spent tan**) tan from which the tannic acid has been extracted, used for covering roads etc. —*adj.* yellowish-brown. —*v.* (**tanned, tanning**) **1** *tr.* & *intr.* make or become brown by exposure to ultraviolet light. **2** *tr.* convert (raw hide) into leather by soaking in a liquid containing tannic acid or by the use of mineral salts etc. **3** *tr. sl.* beat, thrash. □□ **tannable** *adj.* **tanning** *n.* **tannish** *adj.* [OE *tannian,* prob. f. med.L *tanare, tannare,* perh. f. Celtic]

tan² /tæn/ *abbr.* tangent.

tanager /'tænədʒə(r)/ *n.* any small American bird of the subfamily Thraupinae, the male usu. having brightly-coloured plumage. [mod.L *tanagra* f. Tupi *tangara*]

Tanagra /'tænəgrə/ *n.* a terracotta figurine of a type dating chiefly from the 3rd c. BC, many of which were found at Tanagra in Boeotia, Greece. Carefully modelled and painted, their most usual subject consists of elegantly draped young women.

tanbark /'tænbɑːk/ *n.* the bark of oak and other trees, used to obtain tannin.

tandem /'tændəm/ *n.* & *adv.* —*n.* **1** a bicycle or tricycle with two or more seats one behind another. **2** a group of two persons or machines etc. with one behind or following the other. **3** a carriage driven tandem. —*adv.* with two or more horses harnessed one behind another (*drive tandem*). □ **in tandem** one behind another. [L, = at length (of time), used punningly]

tandoor /'tænduə(r)/ *n.* a clay oven. [Hind.]

tandoori /tæn'duəri/ *n.* food cooked over charcoal in a tandoor (often *attrib.: tandoori chicken*). [Hind.]

Tang /tæŋ/ the name of the dynasty which ruled in China from 618 to *c.*906, a period noted for territorial conquest and great wealth and regarded as the golden age of Chinese poetry and art. —*n.* (*attrib.*) designating art and artefacts of this period. [Chin. *táng*]

tang¹ /tæŋ/ *n.* **1** a strong taste or flavour or smell. **2** a characteristic quality. **3** the projection on the blade of a tool, esp. a knife, by which the blade is held firm in the handle. [ME f. ON *tange* point, tang of a knife]

tang² /tæŋ/ *v.* & *n.* —*v.tr.* & *intr.* ring, clang; sound loudly. —*n.* a tanging sound. [imit.]

Tanga /'tæŋgə/ the second-largest seaport in Tanzania; pop. 103,400.

tanga /'tæŋgə/ *n.* a skimpy bikini of small panels connected with strings. [Port.]

Tanganyika /ˌtæŋgə'niːkə/ see TANZANIA. □ **Lake Tanganyika** a large lake in central Africa between Tanzania and Zaïre.

tangelo /'tændʒəˌləʊ/ *n.* (*pl.* -**os**) a hybrid of the tangerine and grapefruit. [TANGERINE + POMELO]

tangent /'tændʒ(ə)nt/ *n.* & *adj.* —*n.* **1** a straight line, curve, or surface that meets another curve or curved surface at a point, but if extended does not intersect it at that point. **2** the ratio of the sides opposite and adjacent to an angle in a right-angled triangle. —*adj.* **1** (of a line or surface) that is a tangent. **2** touching. □ **at a tangent** diverging from a previous course of action or thought etc. (*go off at a tangent*). **tangent galvanometer** a galvanometer with a coil through which the current to be measured is passed, its strength being proportional to the tangent of the angle of deflection. □□ **tangency** *n.* [L *tangere tangent-* touch]

tangential /tæn'dʒenʃ(ə)l/ *adj.* **1** of or along a tangent. **2** divergent. **3** peripheral. □□ **tangentially** *adv.*

tangerine /ˌtændʒə'riːn/ *n.* **1** a small sweet orange-coloured citrus fruit with a thin skin; a mandarin. **2** a deep orange-yellow colour. [TANGIER]

tangible /'tændʒɪb(ə)l/ *adj.* **1** perceptible by touch. **2** definite; clearly intelligible; not elusive or visionary (*tangible proof*). □□ **tangibility** /-'bɪlɪtɪ/ *n.* **tangibleness** *n.* **tangibly** /-blɪ/ *adv.* [F *tangible* or LL *tangibilis* f. *tangere* touch]

Tangier /tæn'dʒɪə(r)/ a seaport of Morocco, situated nearly opposite Gibraltar and commanding the western entrance to the Mediterranean; pop. (1982) 266,300. It had its beginning in the Roman port and town of Tingis, but the present walled city was built in the Middle Ages by the Moors. It was taken by the Portuguese towards the end of the 15th c., and given to Britain as part of the dowry of Princess Catherine of Braganza when she married Charles II in 1662. Britain abandoned it twenty-two years later to the sultan of Morocco, who retained control of the port and the surrounding countryside until 1904. From then until 1956 (except for five years in the Second World War, when it was seized by Spain) the zone was under international control. In 1956 it passed to the newly independent monarchy of Morocco.

tangle¹ /'tæŋg(ə)l/ *v.* & *n.* —*v.* **1 a** *tr.* intertwine (threads or hairs etc.) in a confused mass; entangle. **b** *intr.* become tangled. **2** *intr.* (foll. by *with*) *colloq.* become involved (esp. in conflict or argument) with (*don't tangle with me*). **3** *tr.* complicate (*a tangled affair*). —*n.* **1** a confused mass of intertwined threads etc. **2** a confused or complicated state (*be in a tangle; a love tangle*). [ME var. of obs. *tagle,* of uncert. orig.]

tangle² /'tæŋg(ə)l/ *n.* any of various seaweeds, esp. of the genus *Laminaria* or *Fucus.* [prob. f. Norw. *taangel* f. ON *þöngull*]

tangly /'tæŋglɪ/ *adj.* (**tanglier, tangliest**) tangled.

tango¹ /'tæŋgəʊ/ *n.* & *v.* —*n.* (*pl.* -**os**) **1** a slow S. American ballroom dance. **2** the music for this. —*v.intr.* (-**oes, -oed**) dance the tango. [Amer. Sp.]

tango² /'tæŋgəʊ/ *n.* a tangerine colour. [abbr. after TANGO¹]

tangram /'tæŋgræm/ *n.* a Chinese puzzle square cut into seven pieces to be combined into various figures. [19th c.: orig. unkn.]

tangy /'tæŋɪ/ *adj.* (**tangier, tangiest**) having a strong usu. spicy tang. □□ **tanginess** *n.*

tanh /θæn, tænʃ, tæn'eɪtʃ/ *abbr.* hyperbolic tangent.

tanist /'tænɪst/ *n. hist.* the heir apparent to a Celtic chief, usu. his most vigorous adult relation, chosen by election. □□ **tanistry** *n.* [Ir. & Gael. *tánaiste* heir]

Tanjungkarang /ˌtændʒʊŋkə'ræŋ/ a city of Indonesia, capital of the province of Lampung at the southern tip of the island of Sumatra; pop. (1980) 284,275.

tank /tæŋk/ *n.* & *v.* —*n.* **1** a large receptacle or storage chamber usu. for liquid or gas. **2** a heavy armoured fighting vehicle carrying guns and moving on a tracked carriage. (See below.) **3** a container for the fuel supply in a motor vehicle. **4** the part of a locomotive tender containing water for the boiler. **5 a** *Ind.* & *Austral.* a reservoir. **b** *dial.* esp. *US* a pond. —*v.* (usu. foll. by *up*) esp. *Brit.* **1** *tr.* fill the tank of (a vehicle etc.) with fuel. **2** *intr.* & *colloq. tr.* (in *passive*) drink heavily; become drunk. □ **tank engine** a railway engine carrying fuel and water receptacles in its own frame, not in a tender. **tank-farming** the practice of growing plants in tanks of water without soil. **tank top** a sleeveless close-fitting upper garment with a scoop-neck. □□ **tankful** *n.* (*pl.* -**fuls**). **tankless** *adj.* [Gujarati *tānkh* etc., perh. f. Skr. *taḍāga* pond]

Early designs for a mechanical armoured vehicle include one by Leonardo da Vinci (1484), to be driven by an arrangement of crank handles and geared wheels, and protected by a covering of smooth armour. Later inventors tried to use steam power, but it was not until the invention of the internal-combustion engine and the development of track mechanism that a really successful vehicle was constructed. This tank was a British invention, developed secretly during the First World War with the intention of opening the way to a decisive victory by introducing it suddenly in large numbers. (The name 'tank' for these vehicles was adopted for purposes of secrecy during manufacture.) Many senior army officers, however, were hostile to the new weapon, so that fewer than a dozen tanks effectively took the field in their first battle on the Somme (Sept. 1916), and they were not used in mass until Nov. 1917 when they were immediately successful; their use in battle meant that in the Second World War there was no repetition of the static trench warfare of 1914–18. It was soon apparent that different types of tanks and other armoured vehicles should be designed for different roles in battle. Their importance has increased with the development of tactical nuclear weapons, since they are mobile, have a relatively high weapon-power to manpower, and offer some protection against blast and radioactivity.

tanka /'tæŋkə/ *n.* a Japanese poem in five lines and thirty-one syllables giving a complete picture of an event or mood. [Jap.]

tankage /ˈtæŋkɪdʒ/ n. 1 **a** storage in tanks. **b** a charge made for this. 2 the cubic content of a tank. 3 a kind of fertilizer obtained from refuse bones etc.

tankard /ˈtæŋkəd/ n. 1 a tall mug with a handle and sometimes a hinged lid, esp. of silver or pewter for beer. 2 the contents of or an amount held by a tankard (drank a tankard of ale). [ME: orig. unkn.: cf. MDu. tanckaert]

tanker /ˈtæŋkə(r)/ n. a ship, aircraft, or road vehicle for carrying liquids, esp. mineral oils, in bulk.

tanner[1] /ˈtænə(r)/ n. a person who tans hides.

tanner[2] /ˈtænə(r)/ n. Brit. hist. sl. a sixpence. [19th c.: orig. unkn.]

tannery /ˈtænərɪ/ n. (pl. -ies) a place where hides are tanned.

Tannhäuser /ˈtænhɔɪzə(r)/, (c.1200–c.1270), German poet whose work, which reveals humour with irony and an alert sense of parody, marks a historical decline in the minnesinger school. Because of his years in the Near East and the sensuality of his love poetry he became a legendary figure as the knight who visited Venus's grotto, repented, and sought absolution from the pope, and as such he is commemorated in Wagner's opera.

tannic /ˈtænɪk/ adj. of or produced from tan. □ **tannic acid** a complex natural organic compound of a yellowish colour used as a mordant and astringent. □□ **tannate** /-neɪt/ n. [F tannique (as TANNIN)]

tannin /ˈtænɪn/ n. any of a group of complex organic compounds found in certain tree-barks and oak-galls, used in leather production and ink manufacture. [F tanin (as TAN[1], -IN)]

tannish see TAN[1].

Tannoy /ˈtænɔɪ/ n. propr. a type of public-address system. [20th c.: orig. uncert.]

tanrec var. of TENREC.

tansy /ˈtænzɪ/ n. (pl. -ies) any plant of the genus Tanacetum, esp. T. vulgare with yellow button-like flowers and aromatic leaves, formerly used in medicines and cookery. [ME f. OF tanesie f. med.L athanasia immortality f. Gk]

tantalite /ˈtæntəˌlaɪt/ n. a rare dense black mineral, the principal source of the element tantalum. [G & Sw. tantalit (as TANTALUM)]

tantalize /ˈtæntəˌlaɪz/ v.tr. (also -ise) 1 torment or tease by the sight or promise of what is unobtainable. 2 raise and then dash the hopes of; torment with disappointment. □□ **tantalization** /-ˈzeɪʃ(ə)n/ n. **tantalizer** n. **tantalizingly** adv. [Gk Tantalos TANTALUS]

tantalum /ˈtæntələm/ n. Chem. a rare hard white metallic element, first discovered in 1802. It can occur uncombined in nature as well as in a number of ores, where it is usually associated with niobium. The metal, which is very hard and resistant to corrosion, was formerly used for the filaments of electric light bulbs, and it is currently used for manufacturing capacitors, parts of aircraft, and surgical and other equipment. ¶ Symb.: **Ta**; atomic number 73. □□ **tantalic** adj. [TANTALUS with ref. to its non-absorbent quality]

Tantalus /ˈtæntələs/ Gk Mythol. a Lydian king, son of Zeus and father of Pelops. He is represented as being punished eternally (for he was immortal): he is hungry and thirsty, but the water in which he stands recedes when he tries to drink it and the fruit above his head is blown aside from his hand. His crime is variously related: some say that he revealed the secrets of the gods, others that he gave their food to mortals, others that he killed his son Pelops and offered his flesh to the gods. His penalty became almost proverbial to the Greeks for 'tantalizing' in the modern sense.

tantalus /ˈtæntələs/ n. 1 a stand in which spirit-decanters may be locked up but visible. 2 a wood ibis, Mycteria americana. [TANTALUS]

tantamount /ˈtæntəˌmaʊnt/ predic.adj. (foll. by to) equivalent to (was tantamount to a denial). [f. obs. verb f. It. tanto montare amount to so much]

tantivy /tænˈtɪvɪ/ n. & adj. archaic —n. (pl. -ies) 1 a hunting cry. 2 a swift movement; a gallop or rush. —adj. swift. [17th c.: perh. an imit. of hoof-beats]

tant mieux /tɑ̃ ˈmjø:/ int. so much the better. [F]

tant pis /tɑ̃ ˈpi:/ int. so much the worse. [F]

tantra /ˈtæntrə/ n. any of a class of Hindu, Buddhist, or Jain sacred texts that deal with mystical and magical practices. □□ **tantric** adj. **tantrism** n. **tantrist** n. [Skr., = loom, groundwork, doctrine f. tan stretch]

tantrum /ˈtæntrəm/ n. an outburst of bad temper or petulance (threw a tantrum). [18th c.: orig. unkn.]

Tanzania /ˌtænzəˈniːə/ a country in East Africa with a coastline on the Indian Ocean, consisting of a mainland area (the former republic of Tanganyika) and the island of Zanzibar; pop. (1988) 24,295,200; official languages, Swahili and English; capital, Dodoma. A German colony from the late 19th c., Tanganyika became a British mandate after the First World War and a trust territory, administered by Britain, after the Second, before achieving independence as a member State of the Commonwealth in 1961. It was named Tanzania after its union with Zanzibar in 1964. Like most of its neighbours Tanzania is largely dependent on agriculture, exporting sisal, cloves, cotton, and coffee. □□ **Tanzanian** adj. & n.

Tao /tau, ˈtaːəʊ/ n. the metaphysical concept central to all systems of Chinese philosophy, the absolute principle underlying the universe, combining within itself the principles of yin and yang. To Confucius, it is the Way of the superior man; to Lao-tzu, it is the Way of nature. The latter interpretation developed into the philosophical religion of Taoism. [Chin. dao (right) way]

Taoiseach /ˈtiːʃəx/ n. the Prime Minister of the Irish Republic. [Ir., = chief, leader]

Taoism /ˈtauɪz(ə)m, ˈtaːəʊ-/ n. one of the two major Chinese religious and philosophical systems (the other is Confucianism), traditionally founded by Lao-tzu in about the 6th c. BC (its texts are slightly later). The central concept and goal is the Tao, an elusive term denoting here the force inherent in nature and, by extension, the code of behaviour that is in harmony with the natural order. Its most sacred scripture is the Tao-te-Ching (also called Lao-tzu), ascribed to its founder. □□ **Taoist** /-ɪst/ n. **Taoistic** /-ˈɪstɪk/ adj. [TAO]

Taormina /ˌtaːɔːˈmiːnə/ a town and resort on the east coast of Sicily; pop. (1981) 10,085.

tap[1] /tæp/ n. & v. —n. 1 a device by which a flow of liquid or gas from a pipe or vessel can be controlled. 2 an act of tapping a telephone etc. 3 Brit. a taproom. 4 an instrument for cutting the thread of a female screw. —v.tr. (tapped, tapping) 1 **a** provide (a cask) with a tap. **b** let out (a liquid) by means of, or as if by means of, a tap. 2 draw sap from (a tree) by cutting into it. 3 **a** obtain information or supplies or resources from. **b** establish communication or trade with. 4 connect a listening device to (a telephone or telegraph line etc.) to listen to a call or transmission. 5 cut a female screw-thread in. □ **on tap 1** ready to be drawn off by tap. 2 colloq. ready for immediate use; freely available. **tap root** a tapering root growing vertically downwards. **tap water** water from a piped supply. □□ **tapless** adj. **tappable** adj. [OE tæppian (v.), tæppa (n.) f. Gmc]

tap[2] /tæp/ v. & n. —v. (tapped, tapping) 1 intr. (foll. by at, on) strike a gentle but audible blow. 2 tr. strike lightly (tapped me on the shoulder). 3 tr. (foll. by against etc.) cause (a thing) to strike lightly (tapped a stick against the window). 4 intr. = TAP-DANCE v. (can you tap?). —n. 1 **a** a light blow; a rap. **b** the sound of this (heard a tap at the door). 2 **a** = TAP-DANCE n. (goes to tap classes). **b** a piece of metal attached to the toe and heel of a tap-dancer's shoe to make the tapping sound. 3 (in pl., usu. treated as sing.) US **a** a bugle call for lights to be put out in army quarters. **b** a similar signal at a military funeral. □□ **tapper** n. [ME tappe (imit.), perh. through F taper]

tapa /ˈtaːpə/ n. 1 the bark of a paper-mulberry tree. 2 cloth made from this, used in the Pacific islands. [Polynesian]

tap-dance /ˈtæpdaːns/ n. & v. —n. a form of display dance performed wearing shoes fitted with metal taps, with rhythmical tapping of the toes and heels. —v.intr. perform a tap-dance. □□ **tap-dancer** n. **tap-dancing** n.

tape /teɪp/ n. & v. —n. 1 a narrow strip of woven material for tying up, fastening, etc. 2 **a** a strip of material stretched across the finishing line of a race. **b** a similar strip for marking off an area or forming a notional barrier. **3** (in full **adhesive tape**) a strip of opaque or transparent paper or plastic etc., esp. coated with adhesive for fastening, sticking, masking, insulating, etc. **4 a** = *magnetic tape*. **b** a tape recording or tape cassette. **5** = *tape-measure*. —*v.tr.* **1 a** tie up or join etc. with tape. **b** apply tape to. **2** (foll. by *off*) seal or mark off an area or thing with tape. **3** record on magnetic tape. **4** measure with tape. □ **breast the tape** win a race. **have** (or **get**) **a person** or **thing taped** *Brit. colloq.* understand a person or thing fully. **on tape** recorded on magnetic tape. **tape deck** a platform with capstans for using magnetic tape. **tape machine** a machine for receiving and recording telegraph messages. **tape-measure** a strip of tape or thin flexible metal marked for measuring lengths. **tape-record** record (sounds) on magnetic tape. **tape recorder** apparatus for recording sounds on magnetic tape and afterwards reproducing them. **tape recording** a recording on magnetic tape. □□ **tapeable** *adj.* (esp. in sense 3 of *v.*). **tapeless** *adj.* **tapelike** *adj.* [OE *tæppa, tæppe*, of unkn. orig.]

taper /ˈteɪpə(r)/ *n. & v.* —*n.* **1** a wick coated with wax etc. for conveying a flame. **2** a slender candle. —*v.* (often foll. by *off*) **1** *intr. & tr.* diminish or reduce in thickness towards one end. **2** *tr. & intr.* make or become gradually less. [OE *tapur, -or, -er* wax candle, f. L PAPYRUS, whose pith was used for candle-wicks]

tapestry /ˈtæpɪstrɪ/ *n.* (*pl.* **-ies**) **1 a** a thick textile fabric in which coloured weft threads are woven to form pictures or designs. **b** embroidery imitating this, usu. in wools on canvas. **c** a piece of such embroidery. **2** events or circumstances etc. compared with a tapestry in being intricate, interwoven, etc. (*life's rich tapestry*). □□ **tapestried** *adj.* [ME, alt. f. *tapissery* f. OF *tapisserie* f. *tapissier* tapestry-worker or *tapisser* to carpet, f. *tapis*: see TAPIS]

tapetum /təˈpiːtəm/ *n.* a light-reflecting part of the choroid membrane in the eyes of certain mammals, e.g. cats. [LL f. L *tapete* carpet]

tapeworm /ˈteɪpwɜːm/ *n.* any flatworm of the class Cestoda, with a body like segmented tape, living as a parasite in the intestines.

tapioca /ˌtæpɪˈəʊkə/ *n.* a starchy substance in hard white grains obtained from cassava and used for puddings etc. [Tupi-Guarani *tipioca* f. *tipi* dregs + *og, ok* squeeze out]

tapir /ˈteɪpə(r), -pɪə(r)/ *n.* any nocturnal hoofed mammal of the genus *Tapirus*, native to Central and S. America and Malaysia, having a short flexible protruding snout used for feeding on vegetation. □□ **tapiroid** *adj. & n.* [Tupi *tapira*]

tapis /ˈtæpiː/ *n.* a covering or tapestry. □ **on the tapis** (of a subject) under consideration or discussion. [ME, a kind of cloth, f. OF *tapiz* f. LL *tapetium* f. Gk *tapētion* dimin. of *tapēs tapētos* tapestry]

tapotement /təˈpəʊtmənt/ *n.* *Med.* rapid and repeated striking of the body as massage treatment. [F f. *tapoter* tap]

tapper see TAP[2].

tappet /ˈtæpɪt/ *n.* a lever or projecting part used in machinery to give intermittent motion, often in conjunction with a cam. [app. f. TAP[2] + -ET[1]]

taproom /ˈtæpruːm, -rʊm/ *n.* a room in which alcoholic drinks are available on tap.

tapster /ˈtæpstə(r)/ *n.* a person who draws and serves alcoholic drinks at a bar. [OE *tæppestre* orig. fem. (as TAP[1], -STER)]

tapu /ˈtɑːpuː/ *n. & adj.* NZ = TABOO. [Maori]

tar[1] /tɑː(r)/ *n. & v.* —*n.* **1** a dark thick inflammable liquid distilled from wood or coal etc. and used as a preservative of wood and iron, in making roads, as an antiseptic, etc. **2** a similar substance formed in the combustion of tobacco etc. —*v.tr.* (**tarred, tarring**) cover with tar. □ **tar and feather** smear with tar and then cover with feathers as a punishment. **tar-brush** a brush for applying tar. **tarred with the same brush** having the same faults. [OE *te(o)ru* f. Gmc, rel. to TREE]

tar[2] /tɑː(r)/ *n. colloq.* a sailor. [abbr. of TARPAULIN]

Tara /ˈtɑːrə/ a hill in County Meath, Ireland, site in early times of the residence of the high kings of Ireland, still marked by ancient earthworks.

taradiddle /ˈtærəˌdɪd(ə)l/ *n.* (also **tarradiddle**) *colloq.* **1** a petty lie. **2** pretentious nonsense. [18th c.: cf. DIDDLE]

taramasalata /ˌtærəməsəˈlɑːtə/ *n.* (also **tarama** /ˈtærəmə/) a pinkish pâté made from the roe of mullet or other fish with olive oil, seasoning, etc. [mod.Gk *taramas* roe (f. Turk. *tarama*) + *salata* SALAD]

Taranaki /ˌtærəˈnækɪ/ an administrative region of North Island, New Zealand; pop. (1986) 107,600; chief town, New Plymouth. The region takes its name from the Maori name for Mount Egmont, which dominates it.

tarantass /ˌtærənˈtæs/ *n.* a springless four-wheeled Russian vehicle. [Russ. *tarantas*]

tarantella /ˌtærənˈtelə/ *n.* (also **tarantelle** /-ˈtel/) **1** a rapid whirling S. Italian dance. **2** the music for this. [It., f. *Taranto* in Italy (because the dance was once thought to be a cure for a tarantula bite): cf. TARANTISM]

tarantism /ˈtærənˌtɪz(ə)m/ *n.* *hist.* dancing mania, esp. that originating in S. Italy among those who had (actually or supposedly) been bitten by a tarantula. [mod.L *tarantismus*, It. *tarantismo* f. TARANTO]

Taranto /təˈræntəʊ/ a seaport and naval base in Apulia region, SE Italy; pop. (1981) 244,100. It is the site of the ancient city of Tarentum, founded by the Greeks in the 8th c. BC.

tarantula /təˈræntjʊlə/ *n.* **1** any large hairy tropical spider of the family Theraphosidae. **2** a large black S. European spider, *Lycosa tarentula*, whose bite was formerly held to cause tarantism. [med.L f. It. *tarantola* (as TARANTISM)]

Tarawa /ˈtærəwə, təˈrɑːwə/ the capital of Kiribati, on the Pacific atoll of Tarawa; pop. (1985) 21,200.

taraxacum /təˈræksəkəm/ *n.* **1** any composite plant of the genus *Taraxacum*, including the dandelion. **2** a tonic etc. prepared from the dried roots of this. [med.L f. Arab. *ṭarakšaḳūk* f. Pers. *talḳ* bitter + *chaḳūk* purslane]

tarboosh /tɑːˈbuːʃ/ *n.* a cap like a fez, sometimes worn as part of a turban. [Egypt. Arab. *ṭarbūš*, ult. f. Pers. *sar-būš* head-cover]

Tardenoisian /ˌtɑːdɪˈnɔɪzɪən/ *adj. & n.* —*adj.* of a late mesolithic industry of western and central Europe, named after the type-site at Tardenois in NE France. —*n.* this industry.

tardigrade /ˈtɑːdɪˌɡreɪd/ *n. & adj.* —*n.* any minute freshwater animal of the phylum Tardigrada, having a short plump body and four pairs of short legs. Also called *water bear*. —*adj.* of or relating to this phylum. [F *tardigrade* f. L *tardigradus* f. *tardus* slow + *gradi* walk]

tardy /ˈtɑːdɪ/ *adj.* (**tardier, tardiest**) **1** slow to act or come or happen. **2** delaying or delayed beyond the right or expected time. □□ **tardily** *adv.* **tardiness** *n.* [F *tardif, tardive* ult. f. L *tardus* slow]

tare[1] /teə(r)/ *n.* **1** vetch, esp. as corn-weed or fodder. **2** (in *pl.*) *Bibl.* an injurious corn-weed (Matt. 13: 24–30). [ME: orig. unkn.]

tare[2] /teə(r)/ *n.* **1** an allowance made for the weight of the packing or wrapping around goods. **2** the weight of a motor vehicle without its fuel or load. □ **tare and tret** the arithmetical rule for computing a tare. [ME f. F, = deficiency, tare, f. med.L *tara* f. Arab. *ṭarḥa* what is rejected f. *ṭaraḥa* reject]

targe /tɑːdʒ/ *n. archaic* = TARGET *n.* 5. [ME f. OF]

target /ˈtɑːɡɪt/ *n. & v.* —*n.* **1** a mark or point fired or aimed at, esp. a round or rectangular object marked with concentric circles. **2** a person or thing aimed at, or exposed to gunfire etc. (*they were an easy target*). **3** (also *attrib.*) an objective or result aimed at (*our export targets; target date*). **4** a person or thing against whom criticism, abuse, etc., is or may be directed. **5** *archaic* a shield or buckler, esp. a small round one. —*v.tr.* (**targeted, targeting**) **1** identify or single out (a person or thing) as an object of attention or attack. **2** aim or direct (*missiles targeted on major cities; should target our efforts where needed*). □□ **targetable** *adj.* [ME, dimin. of ME and OF *targe* shield]

Targum /ˈtɑːɡəm/ *n.* any of various ancient Aramaic paraphrases or interpretations of the Hebrew scriptures, made from at least the 1st c. AD when Hebrew was ceasing to be a spoken language. [Chaldee, = interpretation]

tariff /ˈtærɪf/ *n. & v.* —*n.* **1** a table of fixed charges (*a hotel tariff*).

2 a a duty on a particular class of imports or exports. **b** a list of duties or customs to be paid. **3** standard charges agreed between insurers etc. —*v.tr.* subject (goods) to a tariff. [F *tarif* f. It. *tariffa* f. Turk. *tarife* f. Arab. *ta'rīf(a)* f. *'arrafa* notify]

Tarim /tɑːˈriːm/ a river of NW China formed by the junction of the Yarkan and Hotan rivers in the west of Xinjiang autonomous region. The Tarim Basin, which lies between the Kunlun and Tien Shan mountains, includes the vast Taklimakan Desert and the Turfan Depression.

tarlatan /ˈtɑːlət(ə)n/ *n.* a thin stiff open-weave muslin. [F *tarlatane*, prob. of Ind. orig.]

Tarmac /ˈtɑːmæk/ *n. & v.* —*n. propr.* **1** = TARMACADAM. **2** a surface made of this, e.g. a runway. —*v.tr.* (**tarmac**) (**tarmacked, tarmacking**) apply tarmacadam to. [abbr.]

tarmacadam /ˌtɑːməˈkædəm/ *n.* a material of stone or slag bound with tar, used in paving roads etc. [TAR¹ + MACADAM]

Tarn /tɑːn/ a river of southern France which rises in the Cévennes and flows south-west through deep gorges before meeting the Garonne.

tarn /tɑːn/ *n.* a small mountain lake. [ME *terne, tarne* f. ON]

tarnish /ˈtɑːnɪʃ/ *v. & n.* —*v.* **1** *tr.* lessen or destroy the lustre of (metal etc.). **2** *tr.* impair (one's reputation etc.). **3** *intr.* (of metal etc.) lose lustre. —*n.* **1 a** a loss of lustre. **b** a film of colour formed on an exposed surface of a mineral or metal. **2** a blemish; a stain. □□ **tarnishable** *adj.* [F *ternir* f. *terne* dark]

taro /ˈtɑːrəʊ/ *n.* (*pl.* **-os**) a tropical aroid plant, *Colocasia esculenta*, with tuberous roots used as food. Also called EDDO. [Polynesian]

tarot /ˈtærəʊ/ *n.* **1** (in *sing.* or *pl.*) **a** any of several games played with a pack of cards having five suits, the last of which is a set of permanent trumps. **b** a similar pack used in fortune-telling. (See below and PLAYING-CARDS.) **2 a** any of the trump cards. **b** any of the cards from a fortune-telling pack. [F *tarot*, It. *tarocchi*, of unkn. orig.]

Tarot cards are thought to go back to the 12th c. in Europe, though the earliest surviving set is from 1390. Their origin and symbolism is obscure. Part of the tarot pack consisted of 56 cards arranged in 4 suits of 14 each, numbered similarly to a 52-card pack except that a Knight was included among the court cards. The suits were called Cups, Swords, Money, and Batons (Clubs). The rest of the pack was composed of a series of pictures representing various aspects of life and drawn from legend and folklore. The Devil was included, and there were emblematic pictures of Death, the Sun, the Moon, etc. There was also an extra unnumbered card called Le Fou (the fool), ancestor of the modern Joker. In the game played the emblem cards always had a special power over the others. In fortune-telling the cards are interpreted according to the meaning assigned to them. Renewed interest in the occult has led to a recent revival in the use of tarots.

tarp /tɑːp/ *n.* US & Austral. colloq. tarpaulin. [abbr.]

tarpan /ˈtɑːpæn/ *n.* an extinct N. European primitive wild horse. [Kirghiz Tartar]

tarpaulin /tɑːˈpɔːlɪn/ *n.* **1** heavy-duty waterproof cloth esp. of tarred canvas. **2** a sheet or covering of this. **3 a** a sailor's tarred or oilskin hat. **b** *archaic* a sailor. [prob. f. TAR¹ + PALL¹ + -ING¹]

Tarpeian rock /tɑːˈpiːən/ a cliff, probably at the SW corner of the Capitoline Hill, over which murderers and traitors were hurled in ancient Rome. [name of *Tarpeia*, legendary daughter of the commander of the citadel, which she betrayed to the Sabines; she is said to be buried at the foot of the hill]

tarpon /ˈtɑːpɒn/ *n.* **1** a large silvery fish, *Tarpon atlanticus*, common in the tropical Atlantic. **2** a similar fish, *Megalops cyprinoides*, of the Pacific Ocean. [Du. *tarpoen*, of unkn. orig.]

Tarquin /ˈtɑːkwɪn/ the name of two kings of ancient Rome, Tarquinius Priscus and Tarquinius Superbus ('the Proud'; traditionally 534–510 BC). After his expulsion from the city, and the founding of the republic, the latter engaged in a number of vain attacks on Rome.

tarradiddle var. of TARADIDDLE.

tarragon /ˈtærəgən/ *n.* a bushy herb, *Artemisia dracunculus*, with leaves used to flavour salads, stuffings, vinegar, etc. [= med.L

tarchon f. med. Gk *tarkhōn*, perh. through Arab. f. Gk *drakōn* dragon]

tarras var. of TRASS.

tarry¹ /ˈtɑːrɪ/ *adj.* (**tarrier, tarriest**) of or like or smeared with tar. □□ **tarriness** *n.*

tarry² /ˈtærɪ/ *v.intr.* (**-ies, -ied**) archaic or literary **1** defer coming or going. **2** linger, stay, wait. **3** be tardy. □□ **tarrier** *n.* [ME: orig. uncert.]

tarsal /ˈtɑːs(ə)l/ *adj. & n.* —*adj.* of or relating to the bones in the ankle. —*n.* a tarsal bone. [TARSUS + -AL]

tarsi *pl.* of TARSUS.

tarsi- /ˈtɑːsɪ/ *comb. form* (also **tarso-** /ˈtɑːsəʊ/) tarsus.

tarsia /ˈtɑːsɪə/ *n.* = INTARSIA. [It.]

tarsier /ˈtɑːsɪə(r)/ *n.* any small large-eyed arboreal nocturnal primate of the genus *Tarsius*, native to Borneo, the Philippines, etc., with a long tail and long hind legs used for leaping from tree to tree. [F (as TARSUS), from the structure of its foot]

Tarski /ˈtɑːskɪ/, Alfred (1902–83), Polish-born mathematician and logician, author of works on a wide variety of topics, especially the concept of truth and the relations between language and the world.

tarso- *comb. form* var. of TARSI-.

Tarsus /ˈtɑːsəs/ a city in SW Turkey, birthplace of St Paul; pop. (1980) 121,000.

tarsus /ˈtɑːsəs/ *n.* (*pl.* **tarsi** /-saɪ/) **1 a** the group of bones forming the ankle and upper foot. **b** the shank of a bird's leg. **c** the terminal segment of a limb in insects. **2** the fibrous connective tissue of the eyelid. [mod.L f. Gk *tarsos* flat of the foot, rim of the eyelid]

tart¹ /tɑːt/ *n.* **1** an open pastry case containing jam etc. **2** esp. Brit. a pie with a fruit or sweet filling. □□ **tartlet** *n.* [ME f. OF *tarte* = med.L *tarta*, of unkn. orig.]

tart² /tɑːt/ *n. & v.* —*n. sl.* **1** a prostitute; a promiscuous woman. **2** *sl. offens.* a girl or woman. —*v.* (foll. by *up*) esp. Brit. colloq. **1** *tr.* (usu. *refl.*) smarten (oneself or a thing) up, esp. flashily or gaudily. **2** *intr.* dress up gaudily. [prob. abbr. of SWEETHEART]

tart³ /tɑːt/ *adj.* **1** sharp or acid in taste. **2** (of a remark etc.) cutting, bitter. □□ **tartly** *adv.* **tartness** *n.* [OE *teart*, of unkn. orig.]

tartan¹ /ˈtɑːt(ə)n/ *n.* **1** a pattern of coloured stripes crossing at right angles, esp. the distinctive plaid worn by the Scottish Highlanders to denote their clan. **2** woollen cloth woven in this pattern (often *attrib.*: a tartan scarf). [perh. f. OF *tertaine, tiretaine*]

tartan² /ˈtɑːt(ə)n/ *n.* a lateen-sailed single-masted ship used in the Mediterranean. [F *tartane* f. It. Catalan, perh. f. Arab. *ṭarīda*]

Tartar /ˈtɑːtə(r)/ *n. & adj.* (also **Tatar** except in sense 3 of *n.*) —*n.* **1 a** a member of any of numerous mostly Muslim and Turkic tribes inhabiting various parts of European and Asiatic Russia, especially parts of Siberia, Crimea, N. Caucasus, and districts along the Volga. **b** a member of the mingled host of Central Asian peoples, including Mongols and Turks, who under the leadership of Genghis Khan overran and devastated much of Asia and eastern Europe in the early 13th c., and under Tamerlane (14th c.) established a large empire in central Europe with its capital at Samarkand. **c** a descendant of this people. **2** the Turkic language of these peoples. **3** (**tartar**) a violent-tempered or intractable person. —*adj.* **1** of or relating to the Tartars. **2** of or relating to Central Asia east of the Caspian Sea. □ **tartar sauce** a sauce of mayonnaise and chopped gherkins, capers, etc. □□ **Tartarian** /-ˈteəriən/ *adj.* [ME *tartre* f. OF *Tartare* or med.L *Tartarus*]

tartar /ˈtɑːtə(r)/ *n.* **1** a hard deposit of saliva, calcium phosphate, etc., that forms on the teeth. **2** a deposit of acid potassium tartrate that forms a hard crust on the inside of a cask during the fermentation of wine. □ **tartar emetic** potassium antimony tartrate used as a mordant and in medicine (formerly as an emetic). □□ **tartarize** *v.tr.* (also **-ise**). [ME f. med.L f. med.Gk *tartaron*]

tartare /tɑːˈtɑː(r)/ *adj.* (in full **sauce tartare**) = *tartar sauce* (see TARTAR). [F, = tartar]

tartaric /tɑːˈtærɪk/ *adj.* Chem. of or produced from tartar. □

tartaric acid a natural carboxylic acid found esp. in unripe grapes, used in baking powders and as a food additive. [F *tartarique* f. med.L *tartarum*: see TARTAR]

Tartarus /ˈtɑːtərəs/ *Gk Mythol.* **1** a god, sone of Aither (Sky) and Gaia (Earth). **2** a part of the Underworld where the wicked suffer punishment for their misdeeds, especially those such as Ixion and Tantalus who have committed some outrage against the gods. □□ **Tartarean** /-ˈteərɪən/ *adj.* [L f. Gk *Tartaros*]

Tartary /ˈtɑːtərɪ/ the Tartar regions of Asia and eastern Europe, especially the high plateau of Asia and its NW slopes.

tartrate /ˈtɑːtreɪt/ *n. Chem.* any salt or ester of tartaric acid. [F (as TARTAR, -ATE¹)]

tartrazine /ˈtɑːtrəˌziːn/ *n. Chem.* a brilliant yellow dye derived from tartaric acid and used to colour food, drugs, and cosmetics. [as TARTAR + AZO- + -INE⁴]

tarty /ˈtɑːtɪ/ *adj. colloq.* (**tartier, tartiest**) (esp. of a woman) vulgar, gaudy; promiscuous. □□ **tartily** *adv.* **tartiness** *n.* [TART² + -Y¹]

Tarzan /ˈtɑːz(ə)n/ a character in novels by the American author Edgar Rice Burroughs (1875–1950) and subsequent films and television series. He is a white man (Lord Greystoke by birth), orphaned in West Africa in his infancy and reared by apes in the jungle. —*n.* a man of great agility and powerful physique.

Tas. *abbr.* Tasmania.

Tashi Lama /ˈtæʃɪ ˌlɑːmə/ *n.* = PANCHEN LAMA.

Tashkent /tæʃˈkent/ the capital of the Soviet republic of Uzbekistan, in the western foothills of the Tien Shan Mountains; pop. (est. 1987) 2,124,000.

task /tɑːsk/ *n. & v.* —*n.* a piece of work to be done or undertaken. —*v.tr.* **1** make great demands on (a person's powers etc.). **2** assign a task to. □ **take to task** rebuke, scold. **task force** (or **group**) **1** *Mil.* an armed force organized for a special operation. **2** a unit specially organized for a task. [ME f. ONF *tasque* = OF *tasche* f. med.L *tasca*, perh. f. *taxa* f. L *taxare* TAX]

taskmaster /ˈtɑːskˌmɑːstə(r)/ *n.* (*fem.* **taskmistress** /-ˌmɪstrɪs/) a person who imposes a task or burden, esp. regularly or severely.

TASM *abbr.* tactical air-to-surface missile.

Tasman /ˈtæzmən/, Abel Janszoon (1603–59), Dutch explorer. Sent from the Dutch East Indies by their Governor, van Diemen, to explore Australian waters (1642–3), Tasman arrived at Tasmania (which he named Van Diemen's Land), New Zealand, and some of the Friendly Islands. On a second voyage in 1644 he also reached the Gulf of Carpentaria on the north coast of Australia.

Tasmania /tæzˈmeɪnɪə/ a State of the Commonwealth of Australia consisting of one large and several smaller islands southeast of the continent; pop. (1986) 448,200; capital, Hobart. Like mainland Australia, Tasmania was inhabited in prehistoric times (see ABORIGINES). The first European explorer to arrive there was Tasman (see entry), who called the island Van Diemen's Land, a name which it bore until 1855. Settled by a British party from New South Wales in 1803, it became a separate colony in 1825 and was federated with the other States of Australia in 1901. □□ **Tasmanian** *adj. & n.*

Tasmanian devil *n.* a bearlike nocturnal flesh-eating marsupial, *Sarcophilus harrisii*, now found only in Tasmania.

Tasman Sea the part of the South Pacific that lies between Australia and New Zealand.

Tass /tæs/ *n.* the official news agency of the Soviet Union. [the initials of Russ. *Telegrafnoe agentstvo Sovetskogo Soyuza* Telegraphic Agency of the Soviet Union]

tass /tæs/ *n. Sc.* **1** a cup or small goblet. **2** a small draught of brandy etc. [ME f. OF *tasse* cup f. Arab. *ṭāsa* basin f. Pers. *tast*]

tassel¹ /ˈtæs(ə)l/ *n. & v.* —*n.* **1** a tuft of loosely hanging threads or cords etc. attached for decoration to a cushion, scarf, cap, etc. **2** a tassel-like head of some plants, esp. a flower-head with prominent stamens at the top of a maize stalk. —*v.* (**tasselled, tasselling**; *US* **tasseled, tasseling**) **1** *tr.* provide with a tassel or tassels. **2** *intr. US* (of maize etc.) form tassels. [ME f. OF *tas(s)el* clasp, of unkn. orig.]

tassel² /ˈtæs(ə)l/ *n.* (also **torsel** /ˈtɔː-/) a small piece of stone, wood, etc., supporting the end of a beam or joist. [OF ult. f. L *taxillus* small die, and *tessella*: see TESSELLATE]

tassie /ˈtæsɪ/ *n. Sc.* a small cup.

taste /teɪst/ *n. & v.* —*n.* **1 a** the sensation characteristic of a soluble substance caused in the mouth and throat by contact with that substance (*disliked the taste of garlic*). **b** the faculty of perceiving this sensation (*was bitter to the taste*). **2** a small portion of food or drink taken as a sample. **3** a slight experience (*a taste of success*). **4** (often foll. by *for*) a liking or predilection (*has expensive tastes; is not to my taste*). **5** aesthetic discernment in art, literature, conduct, etc., esp. of a specified kind (*a person of taste; dresses in poor taste*). —*v.* **1** *tr.* sample or test the flavour of (food etc.) by taking it into the mouth. **2** (also *absol.*) perceive the flavour of (*could taste the lemon; cannot taste with a cold*). **3** *tr.* (esp. with *neg.*) eat or drink a small portion of (*had not tasted food for days*). **4** *tr.* have experience of (*had never tasted failure*). **5** *intr.* (often foll. by *of*) have a specified flavour (*tastes bitter; tastes of onions*). □ **a bad** (or **bitter** etc.) **taste** *colloq.* a strong feeling of regret or unease. **taste blood** see BLOOD. **taste bud** any of the cells or nerve-endings on the surface of the tongue by which things are tasted. **to taste** in the amount needed for a pleasing result (*add salt and pepper to taste*). □□ **tasteable** *adj.* [ME, = touch, taste, f. OF *tast*, *taster* touch, try, taste, ult. perh. f. L *tangere* touch + *gustare* taste]

tasteful /ˈteɪstfʊl/ *adj.* having, or done in, good taste. □□ **tastefully** *adv.* **tastefulness** *n.*

tasteless /ˈteɪstlɪs/ *adj.* **1** lacking flavour. **2** having, or done in, bad taste. □□ **tastelessly** *adv.* **tastelessness** *n.*

taster /ˈteɪstə(r)/ *n.* **1** a person employed to test food or drink by tasting it, esp. for quality or *hist.* to detect poisoning. **2** a small cup used by a wine-taster. **3** an instrument for extracting a small sample from within a cheese. **4** a sample of food etc. [ME f. AF *tastour*, OF *tasteur* f. *taster*: see TASTE]

tasting /ˈteɪstɪŋ/ *n.* a gathering at which food or drink (esp. wine) is tasted and evaluated.

tasty /ˈteɪstɪ/ *adj.* (**tastier, tastiest**) (of food) pleasing in flavour; appetizing. □□ **tastily** *adv.* **tastiness** *n.*

tat¹ /tæt/ *n. colloq.* **1 a** tatty or tasteless clothes; worthless goods. **b** rubbish, junk. **2** a shabby person. [back-form. f. TATTY]

tat² /tæt/ *v.* (**tatted, tatting**) **1** *intr.* do tatting. **2** *tr.* make by tatting. [19th c.: orig. unkn.]

tat³ see TIT².

ta-ta /tæˈtɑː/ *int. Brit. colloq.* goodbye (said esp. to or by a child). [19th c.: orig. unkn.]

Tatar var. of TARTAR.

Tate /teɪt/, Nahum (1652–1715), English playwright, whose plays were mainly adaptations from earlier writers. His version of *King Lear* omits the Fool, makes Edgar and Cordelia lovers, and ends happily. He wrote (with Dryden) the second part of *Absalom and Achitophel*, the libretto for Purcell's *Dido and Aeneas*, and in 1696, with Nicholas Brady, published the metrical version of the psalms that bears their names. He was appointed Poet Laureate in 1692.

Tate Gallery /teɪt/ a national gallery of British art at Millbank, London, which originated in the dissatisfaction felt at the inadequate representation of English schools in the National Gallery. The Tate Gallery, opened in 1897, was built at the expense of (Sir) Henry Tate (1819–99), sugar manufacturer, to house the collection presented by him (in 1890) and other works accumulated by various bequests (including that of Turner) to the nation. In the 20th c. modern foreign paintings and sculpture (both British and foreign) were added. On foundation the gallery was subordinate to the National Gallery, but it was made fully independent in 1955.

tater /ˈteɪtə(r)/ *n.* (also **tatie** /-tɪ/, **tato** /-təʊ/) *sl.* = POTATO. [abbr.]

Tati /ˈtɑːtɪ/ Jacques (1908–82), real name Tatischeff, French film director and actor. His first full-length film *Jour de Fête* (1947) was followed by *Monsieur Hulot's Holiday* (1951), which saw the creation of a gangling comic hero (played by himself) at odds with modern gadgetry. Financial problems and his passionate perfectionism account for the smallness of his output.

---

b *but*   d *dog*   f *few*   g *get*   h *he*   j *yes*   k *cat*   l *leg*   m *man*   n *no*   p *pen*   r *red*   s *sit*   t *top*   v *voice*

tatler *archaic* var. of TATTLER 1.

Tatra Mountains /ˈtɑːtrə/ (also **Tatras**) a range of the Carpathians in eastern Czechoslovakia and southern Poland, rising to over 2,460 m (8,000 ft.).

tatter /ˈtætə(r)/ n. (usu. in *pl.*) a rag; an irregularly torn piece of cloth or paper etc. □ **in tatters** *colloq.* (of a negotiation, argument, etc.) ruined, demolished. □□ **tattery** *adj.* [ME f. ON *tötrar* rags: cf. Icel. *töturr*]

tattered /ˈtætəd/ *adj.* in tatters.

tattersall /ˈtætəˌsɔːl/ n. (in full **tattersall check**) a fabric with a pattern of coloured lines forming squares like a tartan. [R. *Tattersall*, Engl. horseman d. 1795: from the traditional design of horse blankets]

Tattersalls /ˈtætəˌsɔːlz/ an English firm of horse auctioneers founded in 1776 by Richard Tattersall.

tatting /ˈtætɪŋ/ n. **1** a kind of knotted lace made by hand with a small shuttle and used for trimming etc. **2** the process of making this. [19th c.: orig. unkn.]

tattle /ˈtæt(ə)l/ v. & n. —v. **1** *intr.* prattle, chatter; gossip idly. **2** *tr.* utter (words) idly. —n. gossip; idle or trivial talk. □ **tattle-tale** *US* a tell-tale, esp. a child. [ME f. MFlem. *tatelen, tateren* (imit.)]

tattler /ˈtætlə(r)/ n. a prattler; a gossip.

tattoo¹ /təˈtuː/ n. **1** an evening drum or bugle signal recalling soldiers to their quarters. **2** an elaboration of this with music and marching, presented as an entertainment. **3** a rhythmic tapping or drumming. [17th-c. *tap-too* f. Du. *taptoe*, lit. 'close the tap' (of the cask)]

tattoo² /təˈtuː, tæ-/ v. & n. —v.tr. (**tattoos, tattooed**) **1** mark (the skin) with an indelible design by puncturing it and inserting pigment. **2** make (a design) in this way. —n. a design made by tattooing. □□ **tattooer** n. **tattooist** n. [Polynesian]

tatty /ˈtætɪ/ *adj.* (**tattier, tattiest**) *colloq.* **1** tattered; worn and shabby. **2** inferior. **3** tawdry. □□ **tattily** *adv.* **tattiness** n. [orig. Sc., = shaggy, app. rel. to OE *tættec* rag, TATTER]

Tatum /ˈteɪtəm/, Arthur ('Art') (1910–56), American jazz pianist of great technical accomplishment. He first became famous in the 1930s, and in 1943 founded his own influential trio.

tau /taʊ, tɔː/ n. the nineteenth letter of the Greek alphabet (*T*, *τ*). □ **tau cross** a T-shaped cross. **tau particle** *Physics* an unstable, heavy, and charged elementary particle of the lepton class. [ME f. Gk]

taught *past* and *past part.* of TEACH.

taunt /tɔːnt/ n. & v. —n. a thing said in order to anger or wound a person. —v.tr. **1** assail with taunts. **2** reproach (a person) contemptuously. □□ **taunter** n. **tauntingly** *adv.* [16th c., in phr. *taunt for taunt* f. F *tant pour tant* tit for tat, hence a smart rejoinder]

taupe /təʊp/ n. a grey with a tinge of another colour, usu. brown. [F, = MOLE¹]

Taupo /ˈtaʊpəʊ/ **1** the capital of Tongariro region, North Island, New Zealand; pop. (1986) 15,900. **2** the largest lake of New Zealand, in central North Island.

Tauranga /taʊˈræŋə/ a seaport on the Bay of Plenty, North Island, New Zealand; pop. (1988) 61,800.

taurine /ˈtɔːriːn, -raɪn/ *adj.* of or like a bull; bullish. [L *taurinus* f. *taurus* bull]

tauromachy /tɔːˈrɒməkɪ/ n. (*pl.* **-ies**) *archaic* **1** a bullfight. **2** bullfighting. [Gk *tauromakhia* f. *tauros* bull + *makhē* fight]

Taurus /ˈtɔːrəs/ **1** a constellation containing the star Aldebaran, the galactic clusters of the Hyades and Pleiades, and the Crab Nebula. **2** the second sign of the zodiac (the Bull), which the sun enters about 21 April. —n. a person born when the sun is in this sign. □□ **Taurean** *adj.* & n. [ME f. L, = bull]

Taurus Mountains /ˈtɔːrəs/ a range of mountains in SW Turkey, rising to over 3,700 m (12,000 ft.).

taut /tɔːt/ *adj.* **1** (of a rope, muscles, etc.) tight; not slack. **2** (of nerves) tense. **3** (of a ship etc.) in good order or condition. □□ **tauten** *v.tr.* & *intr.* **tautly** *adv.* **tautness** n. [ME *touht, togt*, perh. = TOUGH, infl. by *tog-* past part. stem of obs. *tee* (OE *tēon*) pull]

tauto- /ˈtɔːtəʊ/ *comb. form* the same. [Gk, f. *tauto, to auto* the same]

tautog /tɔːˈtɒg/ n. a fish, *Tautoga onitis*, found off the Atlantic coast of N. America, used as food. [Narraganset *tautauog* (pl.)]

tautology /tɔːˈtɒlədʒɪ/ n. (*pl.* **-ies**) **1** the saying of the same thing twice over in different words, esp. as a fault of style (e.g. *arrived one after the other in succession*). **2** a statement that is necessarily true. □□ **tautologic** /-təˈlɒdʒɪk/ *adj.* **tautological** /-təˈlɒdʒɪk(ə)l/ *adj.* **tautologically** /-təˈlɒdʒɪkəlɪ/ *adv.* **tautologist** n. **tautologize** /-ˌdʒaɪz/ *v.intr.* (also **-ise**). **tautologous** /-ləgəs/ *adj.* [LL *tautologia* f. Gk (as TAUTO-, -LOGY)]

tautomer /ˈtɔːtəˌmɑː(r)/ n. *Chem.* a substance that exists as two mutually convertible isomers in equilibrium. □□ **tautomeric** /-ˈmerɪk/ *adj.* **tautomerism** /-ˈtɒməˌrɪz(ə)m/ n. [TAUTO- + -MER]

tautophony /tɔːˈtɒfənɪ/ n. repetition of the same sound. [TAUTO- + Gk *phōnē* sound]

tavern /ˈtæv(ə)n/ n. *literary* an inn or public house. [ME f. OF *taverne* f. L *taberna* hut, tavern]

taverna /təˈvɜːnə/ n. a Greek eating house. [mod. Gk (as TAVERN)]

TAVR *abbr.* (in the UK) Territorial and Army Volunteer Reserve. ¶ The name in use 1967–79: now **TA**.

taw¹ /tɔː/ v.tr. make (hide) into leather without the use of tannin, esp. by soaking in a solution of alum and salt. □□ **tawer** n. [OE *tawian* f. Gmc]

taw² /tɔː/ n. **1** a large marble. **2** a game of marbles. **3** a line from which players throw marbles. [18th c.: orig. unkn.]

tawdry /ˈtɔːdrɪ/ *adj.* & n. —*adj.* (**tawdrier, tawdriest**) **1** showy but worthless. **2** over-ornamented, gaudy, vulgar. —n. cheap or gaudy finery. □□ **tawdrily** *adv.* **tawdriness** n. [earlier as noun: short for *tawdry lace*, orig. *St Audrey's lace* f. *Audrey* = *Etheldrida*, patron saint of Ely]

tawny /ˈtɔːnɪ/ *adj.* (**tawnier, tawniest**) of an orange- or yellow-brown colour. □ **tawny eagle** a brownish African or Asian eagle, *Aquila rapax*. **tawny owl** a reddish-brown European owl, *Strix aluco*. □□ **tawniness** n. [ME f. AF *tauné*, OF *tané* f. *tan* TAN¹]

taws /tɔːz/ n. (also **tawse**) *Sc. hist.* a thong with a slit end formerly used in schools for punishing children. [app. pl. of obs. *taw* tawed leather, f. TAW¹]

tax /tæks/ n. & v. —n. **1** a contribution to State revenue compulsorily levied on individuals, property, or businesses (often foll. by *on*: *a tax on luxury goods*). **2** (usu. foll. by *on, upon*) a strain or heavy demand; an oppressive or burdensome obligation. —v.tr. **1** impose a tax on (persons or goods etc.). **2** deduct tax from (income etc.). **3** make heavy demands on (a person's powers or resources etc.) (*you really tax my patience*). **4** (foll. by *with*) confront (a person) with a wrongdoing etc. **5** call to account. **6** *Law* examine and assess (costs etc.). □ **tax avoidance** the arrangement of financial affairs to minimize payment of tax. **tax-deductible** (of expenditure) that may be paid out of income before the deduction of income tax. **tax disc** *Brit.* a paper disc displayed on the windscreen of a motor vehicle, certifying payment of excise duty. **tax evasion** the illegal non-payment or underpayment of income tax. **tax-free** exempt from taxes. **tax haven** a country etc. where income tax is low. **tax return** a declaration of income for taxation purposes. **tax shelter** a means of organizing business affairs to minimize payment of tax. **tax year** see *financial year*. □□ **taxable** *adj.* **taxer** n. **taxless** *adj.* [ME f. OF *taxer* f. L *taxare* censure, charge, compute, perh. f. Gk *tassō* fix]

taxa *pl.* of TAXON.

taxation /tækˈseɪʃ(ə)n/ n. the imposition or payment of tax. [ME f. AF *taxacioun*, OF *taxation* f. L *taxatio -onis* f. *taxare*: see TAX]

taxi /ˈtæksɪ/ n. & v. —n. (*pl.* **taxis**) **1** (in full **taxi-cab**) a motor car licensed to ply for hire and usu. fitted with a taximeter. **2** a boat etc. similarly used. —v. (**taxis, taxied, taxiing** or **taxying**) **1 a** *intr.* (of an aircraft or pilot) move along the ground under the machine's own power before take-off or after landing. **b** *tr.* cause (an aircraft) to taxi. **2** *intr.* & *tr.* go or convey in a taxi. □ **taxi dancer** a dancing partner available for hire. **taxi-driver** a driver of a taxi. **taxi rank** (*US* **stand**) a place where taxis wait to be hired. [abbr. of *taximeter cab*]

taxidermy /ˈtæksɪˌdɜːmɪ/ n. the art of preparing, stuffing, and mounting the skins of animals with lifelike effect. □□

taxidermal /-ˈdɜːm(ə)l/ *adj.* **taxidermic** /-ˈdɜːmɪk/ *adj.* **taxidermist** *n.* [Gk *taxis* arrangement + *derma* skin]

taximeter /ˈtæksɪˌmiːtə(r)/ *n.* an automatic device fitted to a taxi, recording the distance travelled and the fare payable. [F *taximètre* f. *taxe* tariff, TAX + -METER]

taxis /ˈtæksɪs/ *n.* **1** *Surgery* the restoration of displaced bones or organs by manual pressure. **2** *Biol.* the movement of a cell or organism in response to an external stimulus. **3** *Gram.* order or arrangement of words. [Gk f. *tassō* arrange]

taxman /ˈtæksmæn/ *n. colloq.* (*pl.* **-men**) an inspector or collector of taxes.

taxon /ˈtæks(ə)n/ *n.* (*pl.* **taxa** /ˈtæksə/) any taxonomic group. [back-form. f. TAXONOMY]

taxonomy /tækˈsɒnəmɪ/ *n.* **1** the science of the classification of living and extinct organisms. **2** practice of this. □□ **taxonomic** /-səˈnɒmɪk/ *adj.* **taxonomical** /-səˈnɒmɪk(ə)l/ *adj.* **taxonomically** /-səˈnɒmɪkəlɪ/ *adv.* **taxonomist** *n.* [F *taxonomie* (as TAXIS, Gk *-nomia* distribution)]

taxpayer /ˈtæksˌpeɪə(r)/ *n.* a person who pays taxes.

Tay /teɪ/ a river of Scotland flowing into the North Sea. The first Tay Bridge, a railway bridge across the Firth of Tay, opened in 1877, was blown down in 1879 while a passenger train was crossing it.

tayberry /ˈteɪbərɪ/ *n.* (*pl.* **-ies**) a dark red soft fruit produced by crossing the blackberry and raspberry. [*Tay* in Scotland (where introduced in 1977)]

Taylor[1] /ˈteɪl(ə)r/, Elizabeth (1932–), British film actress, whose career began as a child star in *Lassie Come Home* (1943) and *National Velvet* (1944). Later she had particular success in *Cat on a Hot Tin Roof* (1958), *Butterfield 8* (1961), and *Who's Afraid of Virginia Woolf?* (1966). Her image as a beautiful passionate woman was exploited by studio promotion and helped by her own penchant for husbands and high living. She was twice married to Richard Burton, with whom she starred in *Cleopatra* (1962) and other films.

Taylor[2] /ˈteɪlə(r)/, Jeremy (1613–67), English Anglican churchman and writer, chaplain to Archbishop Laud and Charles I, and (after the Restoration) bishop of Down and Connor (1660) and vice-chancellor of Dublin University. He is famous for his devotional writings, especially *Holy Living* (1650) and *Holy Dying* (1651), and the *Unum Necessarium* (1655), a treatise on sin and repentance, written in beautiful prose combining lucidity with rhetorical vigour and powerful imagery, qualities which made him one of the most celebrated preachers of his day.

Taylor[3] /ˈteɪlə(r)/, Zachary (1784–1850), 12th President of the US, 1849–50. He was one of the most famous US soldiers of the mid-19th c., and his victories in the war with Mexico made him a national hero.

Tayside /ˈteɪsaɪd/ a local government region in eastern Scotland; pop. (1981) 393,750.

tazza /ˈtɑːtsə/ *n.* a saucer-shaped cup, esp. one mounted on a foot. [It.]

TB *abbr.* **1 a** tubercle bacillus. **b** tuberculosis. **2** torpedo boat.

Tb *symb. Chem.* the element terbium.

Tblisi /təbɪˈliːsɪ/ (formerly **Tiflis** /ˈtɪflɪs/ the capital of the Soviet republic of Georgia; pop. (est. 1987) 1,194,000.

T-bone /ˈtiːbəʊn/ *n.* a T-shaped bone, esp. in steak from the thin end of a loin.

tbsp. *abbr.* tablespoonful.

Tc *symb. Chem.* the element technetium.

TCD *abbr.* Trinity College, Dublin.

Tchaikovsky /tʃaɪˈkɒfskɪ/, Pyotr (1840–93), Russian composer, who had embarked on a career as a civil servant before beginning to study music seriously in St Petersburg and then at the Moscow Conservatory. His feeling for Russian nationalism is apparent in such works as his Second ('Little Russian' or 'Ukrainian') Symphony (1872) and the incidental music to *The Snow Maiden* (1873), but an equally important influence, that of classical music and in particular Mozart's, is revealed in the opera *The Queen of Spades* (1890). But before this had come the opera

for which he is best known today, *Eugene Onegin* (1879); composition of this work coincided with his marriage to a young admirer, a commitment which was to last no longer than a few days. He is popularly known for the ballets *Swan Lake* (1877), *The Sleeping Beauty* (1890), and *The Nutcracker* (1892), and for the *1812 Overture* (1880), but for the darker side of his nature one must look to the six symphonies (1866–93): of the Sixth ('Pathetic') he wrote, 'I have put my whole soul into this work'. It was once thought that Tchaikovsky died from cholera after drinking impure water, but there is now a theory that he took poison because of a potential scandal arising from an alleged homosexual relationship with a member of the royal family.

TCP *abbr. propr.* a disinfectant and germicide. [trichlorophenylmethyliodasalicyl]

TD *abbr.* **1** (in the UK) Territorial (Officer's) Decoration. **2** *Ir.* Teachta Dála, Member of the Dáil.

Te *symb. Chem.* the element tellurium.

te /tiː/ *n.* (also **ti**) **1** (in tonic sol-fa) the seventh note of a major scale. **2** the note B in the fixed-doh system. [earlier *si*: F f. It., perh. f. Sancte Iohannes: see GAMUT]

tea /tiː/ *n. & v.* —*n.* **1 a** (in full **tea plant**) an evergreen shrub or small tree, *Camellia sinensis*, of India, China, etc. **b** its dried leaves. (See below.) **2** a drink made by infusing tea-leaves in boiling water. **3** a similar drink made from the leaves of other plants or from another substance (*camomile tea*; *beef tea*). **4 a** a light afternoon meal consisting of tea, bread, cakes, etc. **b** *Brit.* a cooked evening meal. —*v.* (**teaed** or **tea'd** /tiːd/) **1** *intr.* take tea. **2** *tr.* give tea to (a person). □ **tea and sympathy** *colloq.* hospitable behaviour towards a troubled person. **tea bag** a small perforated bag of tea for infusion. **tea-ball** esp. *US* a ball of perforated metal to hold tea for infusion. **tea-bread** light or sweet bread for eating at tea. **tea break** *Brit.* a pause in work etc. to drink tea. **tea caddy** a container for tea. **tea ceremony** an elaborate Japanese ritual of serving and drinking tea, as an expression of Zen Buddhist philosophy. **tea chest** a light metal-lined wooden box in which tea is transported. **tea cloth** = *tea towel*. **tea cosy** a cover to keep a teapot warm. **tea dance** an afternoon tea with dancing. **tea garden** a garden in which afternoon tea is served to the public. **tea lady** a woman employed to make tea in offices etc. **tea-leaf 1** a dried leaf of tea, used to make a drink of tea. **2** (esp. in *pl.*) these after infusion or as dregs. **3** *rhyming sl.* a thief. **tea party** a party at teatime. **tea-planter** a proprietor or cultivator of a tea plantation. **tea rose** a hybrid shrub, *Rosa odorata*, with a scent resembling that of tea. **tea towel** a towel for drying washed crockery etc. **tea-tree** *Austral. & NZ* an aromatic evergreen flowering shrub, *Leptospermum scoparium*, the manuka. **tea trolley** (*US* **wagon**) a small wheeled trolley from which tea is served. [17th-c. *tay*, *tey*, prob. f. Du. *tee* f. Chin. (Amoy dial.) *te*, = Mandarin dial. *cha*]

The tea plant has been cultivated for thousands of years in China. When tea was first introduced into Europe in the 17th c. it was so scarce and costly that tea caddies were fitted with locks and keys. China continued to be the main tea-producing country until the 19th c., when it was discovered that tea grew also in Assam, a district of NE India. In 1870, when rust destroyed the coffee crop in Sri Lanka, tea was planted there, and later it was introduced into the East Indies, the Transcaucasian region of Russia, and Africa. It grows best in areas of moderate to high rainfall, equable temperatures, and high humidity.

teacake /ˈtiːkeɪk/ *n. Brit.* a light yeast-based usu. sweet bun eaten at tea, often toasted.

teach /tiːtʃ/ *v.tr.* (*past and past part.* **taught** /tɔːt/) **1 a** give systematic information to (a person) or about (a subject or skill). **b** (*absol.*) practise this professionally. **c** enable (a person) to do something by instruction and training (*taught me to swim*; *taught me how to dance*). **2** advocate as a moral etc. principle (*my parents taught me tolerance*). **3** (foll. by *to* + infin.) **a** induce (a person) by example or punishment to do or not to do a thing (*that will teach you to sit still*; *that will teach you not to laugh*). **b** *colloq.* make (a person) disinclined to do a thing (*I will teach you to interfere*). □ **teach-in 1** an informal lecture and discussion on a subject of public interest. **2** a series of these. **teach a person a lesson** see

LESSON. **teach school** *US* be a teacher in a school. [OE *tæcan* f. a Gmc root = 'show']

teachable /'tiːtʃəb(ə)l/ *adj.* **1** apt at learning. **2** (of a subject) that can be taught. □□ **teachability** /-'bɪlɪtɪ/ *n.* **teachableness** *n.*

teacher /'tiːtʃə(r)/ *n.* a person who teaches, esp. in a school. □□ **teacherly** *adj.*

teaching /'tiːtʃɪŋ/ *n.* **1** the profession of a teacher. **2** (often in *pl.*) what is taught; a doctrine. □ **teaching hospital** a hospital where medical students are taught. **teaching machine** any of various devices for giving instruction according to a programme measuring pupils' responses.

teacup /'tiːkʌp/ *n.* **1** a cup from which tea is drunk. **2** an amount held by this, about 150 ml. □□ **teacupful** *n.* (*pl.* **-fuls**).

teak /tiːk/ *n.* **1** a large deciduous tree, *Tectona grandis*, native to India and SE Asia. **2** its hard durable timber, much used in shipbuilding and furniture. [Port. *teca* f. Malayalam *tēkka*]

teal /tiːl/ *n.* (*pl.* same) **1** any of various small freshwater ducks of the genus *Anas*, esp. *A. crecca*. **2** a dark greenish-blue colour. [rel. to MDu. *tēling*, of unkn. orig.]

team /tiːm/ *n. & v.* —*n.* **1** a set of players forming one side in a game (*a cricket team*). **2** two or more persons working together. **3 a** a set of draught animals. **b** one animal or more in harness with a vehicle. —*v.* **1** *intr. & tr.* (usu. foll. by *up*) join in a team or in common action (*decided to team up with them*). **2** *tr.* harness (horses etc.) in a team. **3** *tr.* (foll. by *with*) match or coordinate (clothes). □ **team-mate** a fellow-member of a team or group. **team spirit** willingness to act as a member of a group rather than as an individual. **team-teaching** teaching by a team of teachers working together. [OE *tēam* offspring f. a Gmc root = 'pull', rel. to TOW¹]

teamster /'tiːmstə(r)/ *n.* **1** *US* a lorry-driver. **2** a driver of a team of animals.

teamwork /'tiːmwɜːk/ *n.* the combined action of a team, group, etc., esp. when effective and efficient.

teapot /'tiːpɒt/ *n.* a pot with a handle, spout, and lid, in which tea is brewed and from which it is poured.

teapoy /'tiːpɔɪ/ *n.* a small three- or four-legged table esp. for tea. [Hindi *tīn*, *tir-* three + Pers. *pāī* foot: sense and spelling infl. by TEA]

tear¹ /teə(r)/ *v. & n.* —*v.* (*past* **tore** /tɔː(r)/; *past part.* **torn** /tɔːn/) **1** *tr.* (often foll. by *up*) pull apart or to pieces with some force (*tear it in half*; *tore up the letter*). **2** *tr.* **a** make a hole or rent in by tearing (*have torn my coat*). **b** make (a hole or rent). **3** *tr.* (foll. by *away, off,* etc.) pull violently or with some force (*tore the book away from me*; *tore off the cover*; *tore a page out*; *tore down the notice*). **4** *tr.* violently disrupt or divide (*the country was torn by civil war*; *torn by conflicting emotions*). **5** *intr. colloq.* go or travel hurriedly or impetuously (*tore across the road*). **6** *intr.* undergo tearing (*the curtain tore down the middle*). **7** *intr.* (foll. by *at* etc.) pull violently or with some force. —*n.* **1** a hole or other damage caused by tearing. **2** a torn part of cloth etc. □ **be torn between** have difficulty in choosing between. **tear apart 1** search (a place) exhaustively. **2** criticize forcefully. **tear one's hair out** behave with extreme desperation or anger. **tear into 1** attack verbally; reprimand. **2** make a vigorous start on (an activity). **tear oneself away** leave despite a strong desire to stay. **tear sheet** a page that can be removed from a newspaper or magazine etc. for use separately. **tear to shreds** *colloq.* refute or criticize thoroughly. **that's torn it** *Brit. colloq.* that has spoiled things, caused a problem, etc. □□ **tearable** *adj.* **tearer** *n.* [OE *teran* f. Gmc]

tear² /tɪə(r)/ *n.* **1** a drop of clear salty liquid secreted by glands, that serves to moisten and wash the eye and is shed from it in grief or other strong emotions. **2** a tearlike thing; a drop. □ **in tears** crying; shedding tears. **tear-drop** a single tear. **tear-duct** a drain for carrying tears to the eye or from the eye to the nose. **tear-gas** gas that disables by causing severe irritation to the eyes. **tear-jerker** *colloq.* a story, film, etc., calculated to evoke sadness or sympathy. **without tears** presented so as to be learned or done easily. □□ **tearlike** *adj.* [OE *tēar*]

tearaway /'teərə‚weɪ/ *n. Brit.* **1** an impetuous or reckless young person. **2** a hooligan.

tearful /'tɪəfʊl/ *adj.* **1** crying or inclined to cry. **2** causing or

accompanied with tears; sad (*a tearful event*). □□ **tearfully** *adv.* **tearfulness** *n.*

tearing /'teərɪŋ/ *adj.* extreme, overwhelming, violent (*in a tearing hurry*).

tearless /'tɪəlɪs/ *adj.* not shedding tears. □□ **tearlessly** *adv.* **tearlessness** *n.*

tearoom /'tiːruːm, -rʊm/ *n.* a small restaurant or café where tea is served.

tease /tiːz/ *v. & n.* —*v.tr.* (also *absol.*) **1 a** make fun of (a person or animal) playfully or unkindly or annoyingly. **b** tempt or allure, esp. sexually, while refusing to satisfy the desire aroused. **2** pick (wool, hair, etc.) into separate fibres. **3** dress (cloth) esp. with teasels. —*n.* **1** *colloq.* a person fond of teasing. **2** an instance of teasing (*it was only a tease*). □ **tease out** separate by disentangling. □□ **teasingly** *adv.* [OE *tǣsan* f. WG]

teasel /'tiːz(ə)l/ *n. & v.* (also **teazel, teazle**) —*n.* **1** any plant of the genus *Dipsacus*, with large prickly heads that are dried and used to raise the nap on woven cloth. **2** a device used as a substitute for teasels. —*v.tr.* dress (cloth) with teasels. □□ **teaseler** *n.* [OE *tǣs(e)l*, = OHG *zeisala* (as TEASE)]

teaser /'tiːzə(r)/ *n.* **1** *colloq.* a hard question or task. **2** a teasing person. **3** esp. *US* a short introductory advertisement etc.

teaset /'tiːset/ *n.* a set of crockery for serving tea.

teashop /'tiːʃɒp/ *n.* esp. *Brit.* = TEAROOM.

teaspoon /'tiːspuːn/ *n.* **1** a small spoon for stirring tea. **2** an amount held by this. □□ **teaspoonful** *n.* (*pl.* **-fuls**).

teat /tiːt/ *n.* **1** a mammary nipple, esp. of an animal. **2** a thing resembling this, esp. a device of rubber etc. for sucking milk from a bottle. [ME f. OF *tete*, prob. of Gmc orig., replacing TIT³]

teatime /'tiːtaɪm/ *n.* the time in the afternoon when tea is served.

teazel (also **teazle**) var. of TEASEL.

tec /tek/ *n. colloq.* a detective. [abbr.]

tech /tek/ *n.* (also **tec**) *colloq.* a technical college. [abbr.]

technetium /tek'niːʃ(ə)m/ *n. Chem.* an artificially produced radioactive metallic element occurring in the fission products of uranium. Technetium was the first new element to be created artificially, in 1937. Chemically related to rhenium, it has been used in certain alloys to impart resistance to corrosion. ¶ Symb.: **Tc**; atomic number 43. [mod.L f. Gk *tekhnētos* artificial f. *tekhnē* art]

technic /'teknɪk/ *n.* **1** (usu. in *pl.*) **a** a technology. **b** technical terms, details, methods, etc. **2** technique. □□ **technicist** /-sɪst/ *n.* [L *technicus* f. Gk *tekhnikos* f. *tekhnē* art]

technical /'teknɪk(ə)l/ *adj.* **1** of or involving or concerned with the mechanical arts and applied sciences (*technical college*; *a technical education*). **2** of or relating to a particular subject or craft etc. or its techniques (*technical terms*; *technical merit*). **3** (of a book or discourse etc.) using technical language; requiring special knowledge to be understood. **4** due to mechanical failure (*a technical hitch*). **5** legally such; such in strict interpretation (*technical assault*; *lost on a technical point*). □ **technical hitch** a temporary breakdown or problem in machinery etc. **technical knockout** *Boxing* a termination of a fight by the referee on the grounds of a contestant's inability to continue, the opponent being declared the winner. □□ **technically** *adv.* **technicalness** *n.*

technicality /‚teknɪ'kælɪtɪ/ *n.* (*pl.* **-ies**) **1** the state of being technical. **2** a technical expression. **3** a technical point or detail (*was acquitted on a technicality*).

technician /tek'nɪʃ(ə)n/ *n.* **1** an expert in the practical application of a science. **2** a person skilled in the technique of an art or craft. **3** a person employed to look after technical equipment and do practical work in a laboratory etc.

Technicolor /'teknɪ‚kʌlə(r)/ *n.* (often *attrib.*) **1** *propr.* a process of colour cinematography using synchronized monochrome films, each of a different colour, to produce a colour print. **2** (usu. **technicolor**) *colloq.* **a** vivid colour. **b** artificial brilliance. □□ **technicolored** *adj.* [TECHNICAL + COLOR]

technique /tek'niːk/ *n.* **1** mechanical skill in an art. **2** a means of achieving one's purpose, esp. skilfully. **3** a manner of artistic execution in music, painting, etc. [F (as TECHNIC)]

technocracy /tekˈnɒkrəsɪ/ n. (pl. **-ies**) **1** the government or control of society or industry by technical experts. **2** an instance or application of this. [Gk *tekhnē* art + -CRACY]

technocrat /ˈteknəˌkræt/ n. an exponent or advocate of technocracy. □□ **technocratic** /-ˈkrætɪk/ adj. **technocratically** /-ˈkrætɪkəlɪ/ adv.

technological /ˌteknəˈlɒdʒɪk(ə)l/ adj. of or using technology. □□ **technologically** adv.

technology /tekˈnɒlədʒɪ/ n. (pl. **-ies**) **1** the study or use of the mechanical arts and applied sciences. **2** these subjects collectively. □□ **technologist** n. [Gk *tekhnologia* systematic treatment f. *tekhnē* art]

techy var. of TETCHY.

tectonic /tekˈtɒnɪk/ adj. **1** of or relating to building or construction. **2** Geol. relating to the deformation of the earth's crust or to the structural changes caused by this (see *plate tectonics*). □□ **tectonically** adv. [LL *tectonicus* f. Gk *tektonikos* f. *tektōn -onos* carpenter]

tectonics /tekˈtɒnɪks/ n.pl. (usu. treated as *sing*.) **1** Archit. the art and process of producing practical and aesthetically pleasing buildings. **2** Geol. the study of large-scale structural features (cf. *plate tectonics*).

tectorial /tekˈtɔːrɪəl/ adj. Anat. **1** forming a covering. **2** (in full **tectorial membrane**) the membrane covering the organ of Corti (see CORTI) in the inner ear. [L *tectorium* a cover (as TECTRIX)]

tectrix /ˈtektrɪks/ n. (pl. **tectrices** /-ˌsiːz, -ˈtraɪsiːz/) = COVERT n. [mod.L f. L *tegere tect-* cover]

Ted /ted/ n. (also **ted**) Brit. colloq. a Teddy boy. [abbr.]

ted /ted/ v.tr. (**tedded, tedding**) turn over and spread out (grass, hay, or straw) to dry or for a bedding etc. □□ **tedder** n. [ME f. ON *tethja* spread manure f. *tad* dung, *toddi* small piece]

teddy /ˈtedɪ/ n. (pl. **-ies**) **1** (also **Teddy**; in full **teddy bear**) a soft toy bear. President Theodore Roosevelt's bear-hunting expeditions occasioned a celebrated comic poem, accompanied by cartoons, in the *New York Times* of 7 Jan. 1906, concerning the adventures of two bears named 'Teddy B' and 'Teddy G'. These names were transferred to two bears (also known as the 'Roosevelt bears') presented to Bronx Zoo in the same year. Finally, the fame of these bears was turned to advantage by toy dealers, whose toy 'Roosevelt bears', imported from Germany, became an instant fashion in the US. **2** a woman's undergarment resembling camiknickers. [sense 1 from *Teddy*, pet-name of *Theodore* Roosevelt, d. 1919]

Teddy boy /ˈtedɪ/ n. Brit. colloq. **1** a youth, esp. of the 1950s, affecting an Edwardian style of dress and appearance. **2** a young rowdy male. [*Teddy*, pet-form of *Edward*]

Te Deum /tiː ˈdiːəm, teɪ ˈdeɪəm/ **1 a** an ancient Latin hymn of praise beginning *Te Deum laudamus* 'We praise thee, O God', sung at matins, or on special occasions as a thanksgiving. **b** the music for this. **2** an expression of thanksgiving or exultation. [L]

tedious /ˈtiːdɪəs/ adj. tiresomely long; wearisome. □□ **tediously** adv. **tediousness** n. [ME f. OF *tedieus* or LL *taediosus* (as TEDIUM)]

tedium /ˈtiːdɪəm/ n. the state of being tedious; boredom. [L *taedium* f. *taedēre* to weary]

tee¹ /tiː/ n. = T¹. [phonet. spelling]

tee² /tiː/ n. & v. —n. **1** Golf **a** a cleared space from which a golf ball is struck at the beginning of play for each hole. **b** a small support of wood or plastic from which a ball is struck at a tee. **2** a mark aimed at in bowls, quoits, curling, etc. —v.tr. (**tees, teed**) (often foll. by *up*) Golf place (a ball) on a tee ready to strike it. □ **tee off 1** Golf play a ball from a tee. **2** colloq. start, begin. [earlier (17th-c.) *teaz*, of unkn. orig.: in sense 2 perh. = TEE¹]

tee-hee /tiːˈhiː/ n. & v. (also **te-hee**) —n. **1** a titter. **2** a restrained or contemptuous laugh. —v.intr. (**tee-hees, tee-heed**) titter or laugh in this way. [imit.]

teem¹ /tiːm/ v.intr. **1** be abundant (*fish teem in these waters*). **2** (foll. by *with*) be full of or swarming with (*teeming with fish; teeming with ideas*). [OE *tēman* etc. give birth to f. Gmc, rel. to TEAM]

teem² /tiːm/ v.intr. (often foll. by *down*) (of water etc.) flow copiously; pour (*it was teeming with rain*). [ME *tēmen* f. ON *tœma* f. *tómr* (adj.) empty]

teen /tiːn/ adj. & n. —adj. = TEENAGE. —n. = TEENAGER. [abbr. of TEENAGE, TEENAGER]

-teen /tiːn/ suffix forming the names of numerals from 13 to 19. [OE inflected form of TEN]

teenage /ˈtiːneɪdʒ/ adj. relating to or characteristic of teenagers. □□ **teenaged** adj.

teenager /ˈtiːnˌeɪdʒə(r)/ n. a person from 13 to 19 years of age.

teens /tiːnz/ n.pl. the years of one's age from 13 to 19 (*in one's teens*).

teensy /ˈtiːnzɪ/ adj. (**teensier, teensiest**) colloq. = TEENY. □ **teensy-weensy** = *teeny-weeny*.

teeny /ˈtiːnɪ/ adj. (**teenier, teeniest**) colloq. tiny. □ **teeny-weeny** very tiny. [var. of TINY]

teeny-bopper /ˈtiːnɪˌbɒpə(r)/ n. colloq. a young teenager, usu. a girl, who keenly follows the latest fashions in clothes, pop music, etc.

teepee var. of TEPEE.

teeshirt var. of T-SHIRT.

teeter /ˈtiːtə(r)/ v.intr. **1** totter; stand or move unsteadily. **2** hesitate; be indecisive. □ **teeter on the brink** (or **edge**) be in imminent danger (of disaster etc.). [var. of dial. *titter*]

teeth pl. of TOOTH.

teethe /tiːð/ v.intr. grow or cut teeth, esp. milk teeth. □ **teething-ring** a small ring for an infant to bite on while teething. **teething troubles** initial difficulties in an enterprise etc., regarded as temporary. □□ **teething** n.

teetotal /tiːˈtəʊt(ə)l/ adj. advocating or characterized by total abstinence from alcoholic drink. □□ **teetotalism** n. [redupl. of TOTAL]

teetotaller /tiːˈtəʊtələ(r)/ n. (US **teetotaler**) a person advocating or practising abstinence from alcoholic drink.

teetotum /tiːˈtəʊtəm/ n. **1** a spinning-top with four sides lettered to determine whether the spinner has won or lost. **2** any top spun with the fingers. [T (the letter on one side) + L *totum* the whole (stakes), for which T stood]

teff /tef/ n. an African cereal, *Eragrostis tef*. [Amharic *ṭēf*]

TEFL /ˈtef(ə)l/ abbr. teaching of English as a foreign language.

Teflon /ˈteflɒn/ n. propr. polytetrafluoroethylene, esp. used as a non-stick coating for kitchen utensils. [*tetra-* + *fluor-* + *-on*]

teg /teg/ n. a sheep in its second year. [ME *tegge* (recorded in place-names), repr. OE (unrecorded) *tegga* ewe]

Tegucigalpa /teˌɡuːsɪˈɡælpə/ the capital of Honduras; pop. (1986) 604,600.

tegular /ˈteɡjʊlə(r)/ adj. **1** of or like tiles. **2** arranged like tiles. □□ **tegularly** adv. [L *tegula* tile f. *tegere* cover]

tegument /ˈteɡjʊmənt/ n. the natural covering of an animal's body or part of its body. □□ **tegumental** /-ˈment(ə)l/ adj. **tegumentary** /-ˈmentərɪ/ adj. [L *tegumentum* f. *tegere* cover]

te-hee var. of TEE-HEE.

Tehran /teəˈrɑːn/ the capital of Iran; pop. (1986) 6,042,600.

Teilhard de Chardin /taɪˈɑːd də ʃɑːˈdæ̃/, Pierre (1881–1955), French Jesuit philosopher and palaeontologist, best known for his evolutionary theory, blending science and theology, that man is evolving mentally and socially towards a perfect spiritual state.

Tejo see TAGUS.

Te Kanawa /te ˈkɑːnəwə/, Dame Kiri (1944–), New Zealand operatic soprano, who has sung in the world's leading opera houses, especially in works by Mozart, Strauss, and Verdi.

tektite /ˈtektaɪt/ n. Geol. a small roundish glassy body of unknown origin occurring in various parts of the earth. [G *Tektit* f. Gk *tēktos* molten f. *tēkō* melt]

Tel. abbr. **1** Telephone. **2 a** Telegraph. **b** Telegraphic.

telaesthesia /ˌtelɪsˈθiːzɪə/ n. (US **telesthesia**) Psychol. the supposed perception of distant occurrences or objects otherwise than by the recognized senses. □□ **telaesthetic** /-ˈθetɪk/ adj. [mod.L, formed as TELE- + Gk *aisthēsis* perception]

telamon /'telə‚məʊn/ n. (pl. **telamones** /-'məʊniːz/) Archit. a male figure used as a pillar to support an entablature. [L telamones f. Gk telamōnes pl. of Telamōn, name of a mythical hero]

Tel Aviv /tel ə'viːv/ a city on the Mediterranean coast of Israel, founded as a suburb of the port of Jaffa by Russian Jewish immigrants in 1909 and named Tel Aviv a year later; pop. (1987) 319,500 (with Jaffa).

tele- /'telɪ/ comb. form 1 at or to a distance (telekinesis). 2 forming names of instruments for operating over long distances (telescope). 3 television (telecast). 4 done by means of the telephone (telesales). [Gk tēle- f. tēle far off: sense 3 f. TELEVISION: sense 4 f. TELEPHONE]

tele-ad /'telɪ‚æd/ n. an advertisement placed in a newspaper etc. by telephone.

telecamera /'telɪ‚kæmrə, -mərə/ n. 1 a television camera. 2 a telephotographic camera.

telecast /'telɪ‚kɑːst/ n. & v. —n. a television broadcast. —v.tr. transmit by television. □□ **telecaster** n. [TELE- + BROADCAST]

telecine /'telɪ‚sɪnɪ/ n. 1 the broadcasting of cinema film on television. 2 equipment for doing this. [TELE- + CINE]

telecommunication /‚telɪkə‚mjuːnɪ'keɪʃ(ə)n/ n. 1 communication over a distance by cable, telegraph, telephone, or broadcasting. 2 (usu. in pl.) the branch of technology concerned with this. [F télé- communication (as TELE-, COMMUNICATION)]

teleconference /'telɪ‚kɒnfərəns/ n. a conference with participants in different locations linked by telecommunication devices. □□ **teleconferencing** n.

teledu /'telɪ‚duː/ n. a badger, Mydaus javanensis, of Java and Sumatra, that secretes a foul-smelling liquid when attacked. [Jav.]

telefacsimile /‚telɪfæk'sɪmɪlɪ/ n. facsimile transmission (see FACSIMILE n. 2).

telefax /'telɪ‚fæks/ n. = TELEFACSIMILE. [abbr.]

telefilm /'telɪfɪlm/ n. = TELECINE.

telegenic /‚telɪ'dʒenɪk/ adj. having an appearance or manner that looks pleasing on television. [TELEVISION + -genic in PHOTOGENIC]

telegony /tɪ'legənɪ/ n. Biol. the supposed influence of a previous sire on the offspring of a dam with other sires. □□ **telegonic** /‚telɪ'gɒnɪk/ adj. [TELE- + Gk -gonia begetting]

telegram /'telɪ‚græm/ n. a message sent by telegraph and then usu. delivered in written form. ¶ In UK official use since 1981 only for international messages. [TELE- + -GRAM, after TELEGRAPH]

telegraph /'telɪ‚grɑːf, -‚græf/ n. & v. —n. 1 a a system of or device for transmitting messages or signals to a distance esp. by making and breaking an electrical connection. (See below.) b (attrib.) used in this system (telegraph pole; telegraph wire). 2 (in full **telegraph board**) a board displaying scores or other information at a match, race meeting, etc. —v. 1 tr. send a message by telegraph to. 2 tr. send by telegraph. 3 tr. give an advance indication of. 4 intr. make signals (telegraphed to me to come up). □ **telegraph key** a device for making and breaking the electric circuit of a telegraph system. **telegraph plant** an E. Indian plant, Desmodium gyrans, whose leaves have a spontaneous jerking motion. □□ **telegrapher** /'telɪ‚grɑːfə(r), tɪ'legrəfə(r)/ n. [F télégraphe (as TELE-, -GRAPH)]

Electric telegraphy began just before the middle of the 19th c. The many inventors who helped to devise a working system were spurred on by the demands of the newly built railways for some means of conveying messages between signalmen to ensure the safety of trains. Samuel Morse, inventor of the Morse code, made use of the electromagnet and had made his first working model of a telegraph by 1835. The first practical telegraph in England was set up in 1837, linking Euston railway station in London with Camden station a mile away. A few years later, when the railway telegraph helped to bring about the arrest of a murderer, public interest in the invention was assured, and until c.1880, when telephones became more generally available, the telegraph was the standard means of rapid communication within a district. Telegraph wires and cables may be above or below ground or on the sea bed. Optical fibres

and radio waves are also used to carry the signals, and satellites relay them from one part of the globe to another.

telegraphese /‚telɪgrə'fiːz/ n. colloq. or joc. an abbreviated style usual in telegrams.

telegraphic /‚telɪ'græfɪk/ adj. 1 of or by telegraphs or telegrams. 2 economically worded. □ **telegraphic address** an abbreviated or other registered address for use in telegrams. □□ **telegraphically** adv.

telegraphist /tɪ'legrəfɪst/ n. a person skilled or employed in telegraphy.

telegraphy /tɪ'legrəfɪ/ n. the science or practice of using or constructing communication systems for the reproduction of information.

Telegu var. of TELUGU.

telekinesis /‚telɪkaɪ'niːsɪs, -kɪ'niːsɪs/ n. Psychol. movement of objects at a distance supposedly by paranormal means. □□ **telekinetic** /-'netɪk/ adj. [mod.L (as TELE-, Gk kinēsis motion f. kineō move)]

Telemachus /tɪ'leməkəs/ Gk legend the son of Ulysses and Penelope.

Telemann /'teɪlə‚mæn/, Georg Philipp (1681–1767), German composer and organist. His voluminous output included 600 overtures, 44 Passions, 12 complete services, and 40 operas. In his lifetime his reputation far exceeded that of his contemporary, J. S. Bach.

telemark /'telɪ‚mɑːk/ n. & v. Skiing —n. a swing turn with one ski advanced and the knee bent, used to change direction or stop short. —v.intr. perform this turn. [Telemark in Norway]

telemarketing /'telɪ‚mɑːkɪtɪŋ/ n. the marketing of goods etc. by means of usu. unsolicited telephone calls. □□ **telemarketer** n.

telemessage /'telɪ‚mesɪdʒ/ n. a message sent by telephone or telex and delivered in written form. ¶ In UK official use since 1981 for inland messages, replacing telegram.

telemeter /'telɪ‚miːtə(r), tɪ'lemɪtə(r)/ n. & v. —n. an apparatus for recording the readings of an instrument and transmitting them by radio. —v. 1 intr. record readings in this way. 2 tr. transmit (readings etc.) to a distant receiving set or station. □□ **telemetric** /-'metrɪk/ adj. **telemetry** /tɪ'lemətrɪ/ n.

teleology /‚telɪ'ɒlədʒɪ, ‚tiː-/ n. (pl. **-ies**) Philos. 1 the explanation of phenomena by the purpose they serve rather than by postulated causes. 2 Theol. the doctrine of design and purpose in the material world. □□ **teleologic** /-ə'lɒdʒɪk/ adj. **teleological** /-ə'lɒdʒɪk(ə)l/ adj. **teleologically** /-ə'lɒdʒɪkəlɪ/ adv. **teleologism** n. **teleologist** n. [mod.L teleologia f. Gk telos teleos end + -LOGY]

teleost /'telɪ‚ɒst/ n. any fish of the subclass Teleostei of bony fish, including eels, plaice, salmon, etc. [Gk teleo- complete + osteon bone]

telepath /'telɪ‚pæθ/ n. a telepathic person. [back-form. f. TELEPATHY]

telepathy /tɪ'lepəθɪ/ n. the supposed communication of thoughts or ideas otherwise than by the known senses. □□ **telepathic** /‚telɪ'pæθɪk/ adj. **telepathically** /‚telɪ'pæθɪkəlɪ/ adv. **telepathist** n. **telepathize** v.tr. & intr. (also **-ise**).

telephone /'telɪ‚fəʊn/ n. & v. —n. 1 an apparatus for transmitting sound (esp. speech) to a distance by wire or cord or radio, esp. by converting acoustic vibrations to electrical signals. (See below.) 2 a transmitting and receiving instrument used in this. 3 a system of communication using a network of telephones. —v. 1 tr. speak to (a person) by telephone. 2 tr. send (a message) by telephone. 3 intr. make a telephone call. □ **on the telephone 1** having a telephone. **2** by use of or using the telephone. **over the telephone** by use of or using the telephone. **telephone book** = telephone directory. **telephone booth** (or **kiosk**) a public booth or enclosure from which telephone calls can be made. **telephone box** Brit. = telephone booth. **telephone call** = CALL n. 4. **telephone directory** a book listing telephone subscribers and numbers in a particular area. **telephone exchange** = EXCHANGE n. 3. **telephone number** a number assigned to a particular telephone and used in making connections to it. **telephone operator** esp. US an operator in a telephone exchange. □□ **telephoner** *n.* **telephonic** /-ˈfɒnɪk/ *adj.* **telephonically** /-ˈfɒnɪkəlɪ/ *adv.*

The 'Electrical Speaking Telephone' was invented by Alexander Graham Bell and patented in the US in 1875–7. The German experimenter P. Reis had already (in 1861) devised an instrument transmitting sound of constant pitch but did not succeed in reproducing a voice. The three basic essentials of a telephone system are a telephone set to convert sound into electrical signals and back again, a transmission system to carry these signals over a distance, within acceptable limits of distortion and attenuation, and a switching system to connect any two telephone sets. Such connections are now usually made automatically as the caller, by dialling the receiver's number, sends out a series of pulses which actuate the switching system, and are monitored electronically. Methods of transmission of signals are the same as those used for telegraphy (see TELEGRAPH).

telephonist /tɪˈlefənɪst/ *n. Brit.* an operator in a telephone exchange or at a switchboard.

telephony /tɪˈlefənɪ/ *n.* the use or a system of telephones.

telephoto /ˌtelɪˈfəʊtəʊ/ *n.* (*pl.* **-os**) (in full **telephoto lens**) a lens used in telephotography.

telephotographic /ˌtelɪˌfəʊtəˈgræfɪk/ *adj.* of or for or using telephotography. □□ **telephotographically** *adv.*

telephotography /ˌtelɪfəˈtɒgrəfɪ/ *n.* the photographing of distant objects with a system of lenses giving a large image.

teleport /ˈtelɪˌpɔːt/ *v.tr. Psychol.* move by telekinesis. □□ **teleportation** /-ˈteɪʃ(ə)n/ *n.* [TELE- + PORT⁴ 3]

teleprinter /ˈtelɪˌprɪntə(r)/ *n.* a device for transmitting telegraph messages as they are keyed, and for printing messages received.

teleprompter /ˈtelɪˌprɒmptə(r)/ *n.* a device beside a television or cinema camera that slowly unrolls a speaker's script out of sight of the audience (cf. AUTOCUE).

telerecord /ˈtelɪrɪˌkɔːd/ *v.tr.* record for television broadcasting.

telerecording /ˈtelɪrɪˌkɔːdɪŋ/ *n.* a recorded television broadcast.

telesales /ˈtelɪˌseɪlz/ *n.pl.* selling by means of the telephone.

telescope /ˈtelɪˌskəʊp/ *n. & v.* —*n.* **1** an optical instrument using lenses or mirrors or both to make distant objects appear nearer and larger. (See below.) **2** = radio telescope. (See separate entry.) —*v.* **1** *tr.* press or drive (sections of a tube, colliding vehicles, etc.) together so that one slides into another like the sections of a folding telescope. **2** *intr.* close or be driven or be capable of closing in this way. **3** *tr.* compress so as to occupy less space or time. [It. *telescopio* or mod.L *telescopium* (as TELE-, -SCOPE)]

The optical telescope was probably invented independently many times before Galileo turned it on the heavens in 1609; the claim that it was invented in Holland by Hans Lippershey, a Dutch lens-maker (early 17th c.), is false. Its development not only advanced scientific knowledge but brought consequences for religious and philosophical thought (see COPERNICUS). Subsequent improvements of its design were made by Kepler, Galileo, Huygens, and Newton. Classically made from a collection of lenses mounted in a tube, or with a concave mirror and lens system, modern astronomical telescopes built on similar principles but from different materials are also used to observe radio waves and infrared radiation. Higher energy radiation may also be measured from telescopes carried beyond the atmosphere by artificial satellites. The largest optical telescope is in Crimea and has a mirror 6 metres in diameter.

telescopic /ˌtelɪˈskɒpɪk/ *adj.* **1 a** of, relating to, or made with a telescope (*telescopic observations*). **b** visible only through a telescope (*telescopic stars*). **2** (esp. of a lens) able to focus on and magnify distant objects. **3** consisting of sections that telescope. □ **telescopic sight** a telescope used for sighting on a rifle etc. □□ **telescopically** *adv.*

telesoftware /ˌtelɪˈsɒftweə(r)/ *n.* software transmitted or broadcast to receiving terminals.

telesthesia *US* var. of TELAESTHESIA.

Teletex /ˈtelɪˌteks/ *n. propr.* an electronic text transmission system.

teletext /ˈtelɪˌtekst/ *n.* a news and information service, in the form of text and graphics, from a computer source transmitted to televisions with appropriate receivers (cf. CEEFAX, ORACLE).

telethon /ˈtelɪˌθɒn/ *n. esp. US* an exceptionally long television programme, esp. to raise money for a charity. [TELE- + -*thon* in MARATHON]

Teletype /ˈtelɪˌtaɪp/ *n. & v.* —*n. propr.* a kind of teleprinter. —*v.* (**teletype**) **1** *intr.* operate a teleprinter. **2** *tr.* send by means of a teleprinter.

teletypewriter /ˌtelɪˈtaɪpˌraɪtə(r)/ *n. esp. US* = TELEPRINTER.

televiewer /ˈtelɪˌvjuːə(r)/ *v.tr.* a person who watches television. □□ **televiewing** *adj.*

televise /ˈtelɪˌvaɪz/ *v.tr.* transmit by television. □□ **televisable** *adj.* [back-form. f. TELEVISION]

television /ˈtelɪˌvɪʒ(ə)n, -ˈvɪʒ(ə)n/ *n.* **1** a system for reproducing on a screen visual images transmitted (usu. with sound) by radio signals. (See below and CATHODE-RAY TUBE.) **2** (in full **television set**) a device with a screen for receiving these signals. **3** television broadcasting generally.

When electric telegraphy came into use in the mid-19th c. inventors began to think of transmitting pictures by electric wire. The broad principle is that of cinematography, reproduction of a series of successive images which the human brain registers as a continuous picture because of the persistence of vision. Variations of light and shade are converted by a television camera into variations of electric current which can then be transmitted by radio or cable and picked up by a receiver to be changed back into variations of light and shade on the screen. For colour television light from the scene is split by the camera into its constituent colours and reconstituted from these by the television receiver. Television was first demonstrated by J. L. Baird in 1926.

televisual /ˌtelɪˈvɪʒʊəl, -ˈvɪzjʊəl/ *adj.* relating to or suitable for television. □□ **televisually** *adv.*

telex /ˈteleks/ *n. & v.* (also **Telex**) —*n.* an international system of telegraphy with printed messages transmitted and received by teleprinters using the public telecommunications network. A telex service opened in London in 1932. —*v.tr.* send or communicate with by telex. [TELEPRINTER + EXCHANGE]

Telford /ˈtelfəd/, Thomas (1757–1834), called by Southey the 'Colossus of Roads', the greatest road-builder, greatest bridge-builder, and greatest canal-builder, son of a Scottish shepherd. He was responsible for hundreds of miles of new roads in the Scottish Highlands and for the London-Holyhead road, the main route to Ireland, of which the most notable feature is the suspension bridge crossing the Menai Strait, opened in 1826. His canals include the Caledonian Canal across Scotland and the Gotha Canal across Sweden, and he was also responsible for a number of dock and harbour works. It is fitting that such a great civil engineer should have become the first president of the Institution of Civil Engineers, the first such engineering institution.

Tell /tel/, William. A legendary hero of the liberation of Switzerland from Austrian oppression, who was required to hit with an arrow an apple placed on the head of his son; this he successfully did. The events are placed in the 14th c. but there is no evidence for a historical person of this name. Similar legends of a marksman shooting at an object placed on the head of a man or child are of widespread occurrence.

tell¹ /tel/ *v.* (*past* and *past part.* **told** /təʊld/) **1** *tr.* relate or narrate in speech or writing; give an account of (*tell me a story*). **2** *tr.* make known; express in words; divulge (*tell me your name; tell me what you want*). **3** *tr.* reveal or signify to (a person) (*your face tells me everything*). **4** *tr.* utter (*don't tell lies*). **b** warn (*I told you so*). **5** *intr.* **a** (often foll. by *of, about*) divulge information or a description; reveal a secret (*I told of the plan; promise you won't tell*). **b** (foll. by *on*) *colloq.* inform against (a person). **6** *tr.* (foll. by *to* + *infin.*) give (a person) a direction or order (*tell them to wait; do as you are told*). **7** *tr.* assure (*it's true, I tell you*). **8** *tr.* explain in writing; instruct (*this book tells you how to cook*). **9** *tr.* decide, determine, distinguish (*cannot tell which button to press; how do you tell one from the other?*). **10** *intr.* **a** (often foll. by *on*) produce a noticeable effect (*every disappointment tells; the strain was beginning to tell on me*). **b** reveal the truth (*time will tell*). **c** have an influence (*the evidence tells against you*). **11** *tr.* (often *absol.*) count (votes) at a meeting, election, etc. □ **as far as one can tell** judging from the available information. **tell apart** distinguish between (usu. with *neg.* or *interrog.*: *could not tell them apart*). **tell me another** *colloq.* an expression of incredulity. **tell off 1** *colloq.* reprimand, scold. **2** count off or detach for duty. **tell a tale** (or **its own tale**) be significant or revealing. **tell tales** report a discreditable fact about another. **tell that to the marines** see MARINE. **tell the time** determine the time from the face of a clock or watch. **there is no telling** it is impossible to know (*there's no telling what may happen*). **you're telling me** *colloq.* I agree wholeheartedly. □□ **tellable** *adj.* [OE *tellan* f. Gmc, rel. to TALE]

tell[2] /tel/ *n. Archaeol.* an artificial mound in the Middle East etc. formed by the accumulated remains of ancient settlements. [Arab. *tall* hillock]

teller /'telə(r)/ *n.* **1** a person employed to receive and pay out money in a bank etc. **2** a person who counts (votes). **3** a person who tells esp. stories (*a teller of tales*). □□ **tellership** *n.*

telling /'telɪŋ/ *adj.* **1** having a marked effect; striking. **2** significant. □□ **tellingly** *adv.*

telling-off /ˌtelɪŋ'ɒf/ *n.* (*pl.* **tellings-off**) *colloq.* a reproof or reprimand.

tell-tale /'telteɪl/ *n.* **1** a person who reveals (esp. discreditable) information about another's private affairs or behaviour. **2** (*attrib.*) that reveals or betrays (*a tell-tale smile*). **3** a device for automatic monitoring or registering of a process etc. **4** a metal sheet extending across the front wall of a squash court, above which the ball must strike the wall.

tellurian /te'ljʊərɪən/ *adj.* & *n.* —*adj.* of or inhabiting the Earth. —*n.* an inhabitant of the Earth. [L *tellus -uris* earth]

telluric /te'ljʊərɪk/ *adj.* **1** of the Earth as a planet. **2** of the soil. **3** *Chem.* of tellurium, esp. in its higher valency. □□ **tellurate** /-rət/ *n.* [L *tellus -uris* earth: sense 3 f. TELLURIUM]

tellurium /te'ljʊərɪəm/ *n. Chem.* a rare brittle lustrous silver-white element, chemically related to sulphur and selenium. First discovered in 1782, tellurium occasionally occurs uncombined in nature but more often in ores with metals. The element has two allotropic forms: a silvery crystalline substance and an amorphous powder. It is used as a catalyst, as a colouring agent, and in some electrical devices and alloys. ¶ Symb.: **Te**; atomic number 52. □□ **telluride** /'teljʊəˌraɪd/ *n.* **tellurite** /'teljʊəˌraɪt/ *n.* **tellurous** *adj.* [L *tellus -uris* earth, prob. named in contrast to *uranium*]

telly /'telɪ/ *n.* (*pl.* **-ies**) esp. *Brit. colloq.* **1** television. **2** a television set. [abbr.]

telpher /'telfə(r)/ *n.* a system for transporting goods etc. by electrically driven trucks or cable-cars. □□ **telpherage** *n.* [TELE- + -PHORE]

telson /'tels(ə)n/ *n.* the last segment in the abdomen of Crustacea etc. [Gk, = limit]

Telstar /'telstɑ:(r)/ the first of the active communications satellites (i.e. both receiving and retransmitting signals, not merely reflecting signals from their surface). It was launched by the US in 1962 and used in the transmission of television broadcasting and telephone communication.

Telugu /'teləˌgu:/ *n.* (also **Telegu**) (*pl.* same or **Telegus**) **1** a member of a Dravidian people in SE India. **2** their language, the most widespread of the Dravidian languages in India, spoken by about 45 million people mainly in Andhra Pradesh. [Telugu]

temerarious /ˌteməˈreərɪəs/ *adj. literary* reckless, rash. [L *temerarius* f. *temere* rashly]

temerity /tɪˈmerɪtɪ/ *n.* **1** rashness. **2** audacity, impudence. [L *temeritas* f. *temere* rashly]

temp /temp/ *n.* & *v. colloq.* —*n.* a temporary employee, esp. a secretary. —*v.intr.* work as a temp. [abbr.]

temp.[1] /temp/ *abbr.* temperature.

temp.[2] /temp/ *abbr.* in the time of (*temp. Henry I*). [L *tempore* ablat. of *tempus* time]

temper /'tempə(r)/ *n.* & *v.* —*n.* **1** habitual or temporary disposition of mind esp. as regards composure (*a person of a placid temper*). **2** irritation or anger (*in a fit of temper*). **3** a tendency to have fits of anger (*have a temper*). **4** composure or calmness (*keep one's temper; lose one's temper*). **5** the condition of metal as regards hardness and elasticity. —*v.tr.* **1** bring (metal or clay) to a proper hardness or consistency. **2** (foll. by *with*) moderate or mitigate (*temper justice with mercy*). **3** tune or modulate (a piano etc.) so as to distance intervals correctly. □ **in a bad temper** angry, peevish. **in a good temper** in an amiable mood. **out of temper** angry, peevish. **show temper** be petulant. □□ **temperable** *adj.* **temperative** /-ətɪv/ *adj.* **tempered** *adj.* **temperedly** *adv.* **temperer** *n.* [OE *temprian* (v.) f. L *temperare* mingle: infl. by OF *temprer, tremper*]

tempera /'tempərə/ *n.* a method of painting using an emulsion e.g. of pigment with egg, esp. in fine art on canvas. It was used in Europe from the 12th or early 13th c. until the 15th c., when it began to give way to oil painting. [It.: cf. DISTEMPER[1]]

temperament /'temprəmənt/ *n.* **1** a person's distinct nature and character, esp. as determined by physical constitution and permanently affecting behaviour (*a nervous temperament; the artistic temperament*). **2** a creative or spirited personality (*was full of temperament*). **3 a** an adjustment of intervals in tuning a piano etc. so as to fit the scale for use in all keys. **b** (**equal temperament**) an adjustment in which the 12 semitones are at equal intervals. [ME f. L *temperamentum* (as TEMPER)]

temperamental /ˌtemprəˈment(ə)l/ *adj.* **1** of or having temperament. **2 a** (of a person) liable to erratic or moody behaviour. **b** (of a thing, e.g. a machine) working unpredictably; unreliable. □□ **temperamentally** *adv.*

temperance /'tempərəns/ *n.* **1** moderation or self-restraint esp. in eating and drinking. **2 a** total or partial abstinence from alcoholic drink. **b** (*attrib.*) advocating or concerned with abstinence. [ME f. AF *temperaunce* f. L *temperantia* (as TEMPER)]

temperate /'tempərət/ *adj.* **1** avoiding excess; self-restrained. **2** moderate. **3** (of a region or climate) characterized by mild temperatures. **4** abstemious. □ **temperate zone** the belt of the earth between the frigid and the torrid zones. □□ **temperately** *adv.* **temperateness** *n.* [ME f. L *temperatus* past part. of *temperare*: see TEMPER]

temperature /'temprɪtʃə(r)/ *n.* **1** the degree or intensity of heat of a body in relation to others, esp. as shown by a thermometer or perceived by touch etc. **2** *Med.* the degree of internal heat of the body. **3** *colloq.* a body temperature above the normal (*have a temperature*). **4** the degree of excitement in a discussion etc. □ **take a person's temperature** ascertain a person's body temperature, esp. as a diagnostic aid. **temperature-humidity index** a quantity giving the measure of discomfort due to the combined effects of the temperature and humidity of the air. [F *température* or L *temperatura* (as TEMPER)]

-tempered /'tempəd/ *comb. form* having a specified temper or disposition (*bad-tempered; hot-tempered*). □□ **-temperedly** *adv.* **-temperedness** *n.*

Tempest /'tempɪst/, Dame Marie (1864–1942), English actress, real name Mary Susan Etherington. Though trained as a singer she made her name in comedy, becoming noted for her playing of charming elegant middle-aged women.

tempest /'tempɪst/ *n.* **1** a violent windy storm. **2** violent agitation or tumult. [ME f. OF *tempest(e)* ult. f. L *tempestas* season, storm, f. *tempus* time]

tempestuous /tem'pestjʊəs/ *adj.* **1** stormy. **2** (of a person, emotion, etc.) turbulent, violent, passionate. □□ **tempestuously** *adv.* **tempestuousness** *n.* [LL *tempestuosus* (as TEMPEST)]

tempi *pl.* of TEMPO.

Templar /'templə(r)/ *n.* **1** a lawyer or law student with chambers in the Temple, London. **2** (in full **Knight Templar**) *hist.* a member of the Knights Templars (see entry). [ME f. AF *templer*, OF *templier*, med.L *templarius* (as TEMPLE[1])]

template /'templɪt, -pleɪt/ *n.* (also **templet**) **1 a** a pattern or gauge, usu. a piece of thin board or metal plate, used as a guide in cutting or drilling metal, stone, wood, etc. **b** a flat card or plastic pattern esp. for cutting cloth for patchwork etc. **2** a timber or plate used to distribute the weight in a wall or under a beam etc. **3** *Biochem.* the molecular pattern governing the assembly of a protein etc. [orig. *templet*: prob. f. TEMPLE³ + -ET¹, alt. after *plate*]

Temple /'temp(ə)l/, Shirley (1928–), American film actress, the most famous of all child stars, who from 1934 played leading parts in a succession of winsome stories, often adapted from children's classics. After her second marriage, as Shirley Temple Black she was active in politics for the Republican Party, represented the US at the United Nations, and served as ambassador in various countries.

temple¹ /'temp(ə)l/ *n.* **1** a building devoted to the worship, or regarded as the dwelling-place, of a god or gods or other objects of religious reverence. **2** *hist.* any of three successive religious buildings of the Jews in Jerusalem. **3** *US* a synagogue. **4** a place of Christian public worship, esp. a Protestant church in France. **5** a place in which God is regarded as residing, esp. a Christian's person or body. □ **temple block** a percussion instrument consisting of a hollow block of wood which is struck with a stick. [OE *temp(e)l*, reinforced in ME by OF *temple*, f. L *templum* open or consecrated space]

temple² /'temp(ə)l/ *n.* the flat part of either side of the head between the forehead and the ear. [ME f. OF ult. f. L *tempora* pl. of *tempus*]

temple³ /'temp(ə)l/ *n.* a device in a loom for keeping the cloth stretched. [ME f. OF, orig. the same word as TEMPLE²]

templet var. of TEMPLATE.

tempo /'tempəʊ/ *n.* (*pl.* **-os** or **tempi** /-piː/) **1** *Mus.* the speed at which music is or should be played, esp. as characteristic (*waltz tempo*). **2** the rate of motion or activity (*the tempo of the war is quickening*). [It. f. L *tempus* time]

temporal /'tempər(ə)l/ *adj.* **1** of worldly as opposed to spiritual affairs; of this life; secular. **2** of or relating to time. **3** *Gram.* relating to or denoting time or tense (*temporal conjunction*). **4** of the temples of the head (*temporal artery; temporal bone*). □ **temporal power** the power of an ecclesiastic, esp. the Pope, in temporal matters. □□ **temporally** *adv.* [ME f. OF *temporel* or f. L *temporalis* f. *tempus* -*oris* time]

temporality /ˌtempə'rælɪtɪ/ *n.* (*pl.* **-ies**) **1** temporariness. **2** (usu. in pl.) a secular possession, esp. the properties and revenues of a religious corporation or an ecclesiastic. [ME f. LL *temporalitas* (as TEMPORAL)]

temporary /'tempərərɪ/ *adj.* & *n.* —*adj.* lasting or meant to last only for a limited time (*temporary buildings; temporary relief*). —*n.* (*pl.* **-ies**) a person employed temporarily (cf. TEMP). □□ **temporarily** *adv.* **temporariness** *n.* [L *temporarius* f. *tempus* -*oris* time]

temporize /'tempəˌraɪz/ *v.intr.* (also **-ise**) **1** avoid committing oneself so as to gain time; employ delaying tactics. **2** comply temporarily with the requirements of the occasion, adopt a time-serving policy. □□ **temporization** /-'zeɪʃ(ə)n/ *n.* **temporizer** *n.* [F *temporiser* bide one's time f. med. L *temporizare* delay f. *tempus* -*oris* time]

tempt /tempt/ *v.tr.* **1** entice or incite (a person) to do a wrong or forbidden thing (*tempted him to steal it*). **2** allure, attract. **3** risk provoking (esp. an abstract force or power) (*would be tempting fate to try it*). **4** *archaic* make trial of; try the resolution of (*God did tempt Abraham*). □ **be tempted to** be strongly disposed to (*I am tempted to question this*). □□ **temptable** *adj.* **temptability** /-'bɪlɪtɪ/ *n.* [ME f. OF *tenter*, *tempter* test f. L *temptare* handle, test, try]

temptation /temp'teɪʃ(ə)n/ *n.* **1 a** the act or an instance of tempting; the state of being tempted; incitement esp. to wrong-doing. **b** (**the Temptation**) the tempting of Christ by the Devil (see Matt. 4). **2** an attractive thing or course of action. **3** *archaic* putting to the test. [ME f. OF *tentacion*, *temptacion* f. L *temptatio* -*onis* (as TEMPT)]

tempter /'temptə(r)/ *n.* (*fem.* **temptress** /-trɪs/) **1** a person who tempts. **2** (**the Tempter**) the Devil. [ME f. OF *tempteur* f. eccl.L *temptator* -*oris* (as TEMPT)]

tempting /'temptɪŋ/ *adj.* **1** attractive, inviting. **2** enticing to evil. □□ **temptingly** *adv.*

tempura /'tempʊərə/ *n.* a Japanese dish of fish, shellfish, or vegetables, fried in batter. [Jap.]

ten /ten/ *n.* & *adj.* —*n.* **1** one more than nine. **2** a symbol for this (10, x, X). **3** a size etc. denoted by ten. **4** the time of ten o'clock (*is it ten yet?*). **5** a card with ten pips. **6** a set of ten. —*adj.* **1** that amount to ten. **2** (as a round number) several (*ten times as easy*). □ **the Ten Commandments** see COMMANDMENT. **ten-gallon hat** a cowboy's large broad-brimmed hat. **ten-week stock** a variety of stock, *Matthiola incana*, said to bloom ten weeks after the sowing of the seed. [OE *tien*, *tēn* f. Gmc]

ten. *abbr.* tenuto.

tenable /'tenəb(ə)l/ *adj.* **1** that can be maintained or defended against attack or objection (*a tenable position; a tenable theory*). **2** (foll. by *for*, *by*) (of an office etc.) that can be held for (a specified period) or by (a specified class of person). □□ **tenability** /-'bɪlɪtɪ/ *n.* **tenableness** *n.* [F f. *tenir* hold f. L *tenēre*]

tenace /'tenəs/ *n.* **1** two cards, one ranking next above, and the other next below, a card held by an opponent. **2** the holding of such cards. [F f. Sp. *tenaza*, lit. 'pincers']

tenacious /tɪ'neɪʃəs/ *adj.* **1** (often foll. by *of*) keeping a firm hold of property, principles, life, etc.; not readily relinquishing. **2** (of memory) retentive. **3** holding fast. **4** strongly cohesive. **5** persistent, resolute. **6** adhesive, sticky. □□ **tenaciously** *adv.* **tenaciousness** *n.* **tenacity** /tɪ'næsɪtɪ/ *n.* [L *tenax* -*acis* f. *tenēre* hold]

tenaculum /tɪ'nækjʊləm/ *n.* (*pl.* **tenacula** /-lə/) a surgeon's sharp hook for picking up arteries etc. [L, = holding instrument, f. *tenēre* hold]

tenancy /'tenənsɪ/ *n.* (*pl.* **-ies**) **1** the status of a tenant; possession as a tenant. **2** the duration or period of this.

tenant /'tenənt/ *n.* & *v.* —*n.* **1** a person who rents land or property from a landlord. **2** (often foll. by *of*) the occupant of a place. **3** *Law* a person holding real property by private ownership. —*v.tr.* occupy as a tenant. □ **tenant farmer** a person who farms rented land. **tenant right** *Brit.* the right of a tenant to continue a tenancy at the termination of the lease. □□ **tenantable** *adj.* **tenantless** *adj.* [ME f. OF, pres. part. of *tenir* hold f. L *tenēre*]

tenantry /'tenəntrɪ/ *n.* the tenants of an estate etc.

tench /tentʃ/ *n.* (*pl.* same) a European freshwater fish, *Tinca tinca*, of the carp family. [ME f. OF *tenche* f. LL *tinca*]

tend¹ /tend/ *v.intr.* **1** (usu. foll. by *to*) be apt or inclined (*tends to lose his temper*). **2** serve, conduce. **3** be moving; be directed; hold a course (*tends in our direction; tends downwards; tends to the same conclusion*). [ME f. OF *tendre* stretch f. L *tendere* tens- or tent-]

tend² /tend/ *v.* **1** *tr.* take care of, look after (a person esp. an invalid, animals esp. sheep, a machine). **2** *intr.* (foll. by *on*, *upon*) wait on. **3** *intr.* (foll. by *to*) esp. *US* give attention to. □□ **tendance** *n.* *archaic.* [ME f. ATTEND]

tendency /'tendənsɪ/ *n.* (*pl.* **-ies**) **1** (often foll. by *to*, *towards*) a leaning or inclination, a way of tending. **2** a group within a larger political party or movement. [med.L *tendentia* (as TEND¹)]

tendentious /ten'denʃəs/ *adj.* *derog.* (of writing etc.) calculated to promote a particular cause or viewpoint; having an underlying purpose. □□ **tendentiously** *adv.* **tendentiousness** *n.* [as TENDENCY + -OUS]

tender¹ /'tendə(r)/ *adj.* (**tenderer**, **tenderest**) **1** easily cut or chewed, not tough (*tender steak*). **2** easily touched or wounded, susceptible to pain or grief (*a tender heart; a tender conscience*). **3** easily hurt, sensitive (*tender skin; a tender place*). **4** delicate, fragile (*a tender reputation*). **5** loving, affectionate, fond (*tender parents; wrote tender verses*). **6** requiring tact or careful handling, ticklish (*a tender subject*). **7** (of age) early, immature (*of tender years*). **8** (usu. foll. by *of*) solicitous, concerned (*tender of his honour*). □ **tender-eyed** **1** having gentle eyes. **2** weak-eyed. **tender-hearted** having a tender heart, easily moved by pity etc. **tender-heartedness** being tender-hearted. **tender mercies** *iron.* attention or treatment which is not in the best interests of its recipient. **tender spot** a subject on which a person is touchy. □□ **tenderly** *adv.* **tenderness** *n.* [ME f. OF *tendre* f. L *tener*]

tender² /'tendə(r)/ *v.* & *n.* —*v.* **1** *tr.* **a** offer, present (one's services, apologies, resignation, etc.). **b** offer (money etc.) as payment. **2** *intr.* (often foll. by *for*) make a tender for the supply of a thing or the execution of work. —*n.* an offer, esp. an offer in writing to execute work or supply goods at a fixed price. □ **plea of tender** *Law* a plea that the defendant has always been ready to satisfy the plaintiff's claim and now brings the sum into court. **put out to tender** seek tenders in respect of (work etc.). □□ **tenderer** *n.* [OF *tendre*: see TEND¹]

tender³ /ˈtendə(r)/ *n.* **1** a person who looks after people or things. **2** a vessel attending a larger one to supply stores, convey passengers or orders, etc. **3** a special truck closely coupled to a steam locomotive to carry fuel, water, etc. [ME f. TEND² or f. ATTENDER (as ATTEND)]

tenderfoot /ˈtendəˌfʊt/ *n.* a newcomer or novice, esp. in the bush or in the Scouts or Guides.

tenderize /ˈtendəˌraɪz/ *v.tr.* (also **-ise**) make tender, esp. make (meat) tender by beating etc. □□ **tenderizer** *n.*

tenderloin /ˈtendəˌlɔɪn/ *n.* **1 a** *Brit.* the middle part of a pork loin. **b** *US* the undercut of a sirloin. **2** *US sl.* a district of a city where vice and corruption are prominent.

tendon /ˈtend(ə)n/ *n.* **1** a cord or strand of strong tissue attaching a muscle to a bone etc. **2** (in a quadruped) = HAMSTRING. □□ **tendinitis** /ˌtendɪˈnaɪtɪs/ *n.* **tendinous** /-dɪnəs/ *adj.* [F *tendon* or med.L *tendo* *-dinis* f. Gk *tenōn* sinew f. *teinō* stretch]

tendril /ˈtendrɪl/ *n.* **1** each of the slender leafless shoots by which some climbing plants cling for support. **2** a slender curl of hair etc. [prob. f. obs. F *tendrillon* dimin. of obs. *tendron* young shoot ult. f. L *tener* TENDER¹]

Tenebrae /ˈtenəˌbreɪ/ *n.pl.* **1** *RC Ch. hist.* matins and lauds for the last three days of Holy Week, at which candles are successively extinguished. **2** this office set to music. [L, = darkness]

tenebrous /ˈtenɪbrəs/ *adj.* *literary* dark, gloomy. [ME f. OF *tenebrus* f. L *tenebrosus* (as TENEBRAE)]

tenement /ˈtenɪmənt/ *n.* **1** a room or a set of rooms forming a separate residence within a house or block of flats. **2** *US* & *Sc.* a house divided into and let in tenements. **3** a dwelling-place. **4 a** a piece of land held by an owner. **b** *Law* any kind of permanent property, e.g. lands or rents, held from a superior. □ **tenement-house** *US* & *Sc.* = sense 2. □□ **tenemental** /-ˈment(ə)l/ *adj.* **tenementary** /-ˈmentəri/ *adj.* [ME f. OF f. med.L *tenementum* f. *tenēre* hold]

Tenerife /ˌtenəˈriːf/ a volcanic island which is the largest of the Canary Islands, pop. (1986) 759,400; capital, Santa Cruz.

tenesmus /tɪˈnezməs/ *n.* *Med.* a continual inclination to evacuate the bowels or bladder accompanied by painful straining. [med.L f. Gk *teinesmos* straining f. *teinō* stretch]

tenet /ˈtenɪt, ˈtiːnet/ *n.* a doctrine, dogma, or principle held by a group or person. [L, = he etc. holds f. *tenēre* hold]

tenfold /ˈtenfəʊld/ *adj.* & *adv.* **1** ten times as much or as many. **2** consisting of ten parts.

tenia *US* var. of TAENIA.

Teniers /ˈtenɪəz/, David (1610–90), Flemish painter known as the Younger in distinction from his father, David the Elder (1582–1649). A wide-ranging and prolific artist, he worked in Antwerp and Brussels and is best known for his peasant scenes in the style of Brouwer, and scenes of everyday life. In 1651 he was appointed court painter to Archduke Leopold Wilhelm, and was much admired by Philip IV of Spain. The sensitivity and sureness of touch in his paintings was influential until well into the 19th c.

Tenn. *abbr.* Tennessee.

Tennant Creek /ˈtenənt/ a mining town between Alice Springs and Darwin in Northern Territory, Australia; pop. (1986) 3,300.

tenné /ˈtenɪ/ *n.* & (usu. placed after noun) *adj.* (also **tenny**) *Heraldry* orange-brown. [obs. F, var. of *tanné* TAWNY]

tenner /ˈtenə(r)/ *n.* *colloq.* a ten-pound or ten-dollar note. [TEN]

Tennessee /ˌtenɪˈsiː/ a State in the central south-eastern US; pop. (est. 1985) 4,591,100; capital, Nashville. Ceded by Britain to the US in 1783, it became the 16th State in 1796. □ **Tennessee Valley Authority** an independent federal government agency in the US. Created in 1933 as part of the New Deal proposals to

offset unemployment by a programme of public works, its aim was to provide for the development of the whole Tennessee River basin. It was authorized to construct or improve dams that would control flooding and generate cheap hydroelectric power, to check erosion, and to provide afforestation across seven States.

Tenniel /ˈtenɪəl/, Sir John (1820–1914), English draughtsman, known chiefly for his work as an illustrator for Lewis Carroll's *Alice* books. He also worked prolifically for *Punch* between 1851 and 1901 as a cartoonist.

tennis /ˈtenɪs/ *n.* **1** lawn tennis (see LAWN). **2** (also **real, royal,** or (*US*) **court tennis**) an indoor game for two or four persons in which a small solid ball is struck with rackets over a net, or rebounds from side walls, in a walled court. A net divides the court into equal but dissimilar halves: the service side, from which service is always delivered, and the hazard side, on which service is received. A similar game was played in monastery cloisters in the 11th c., and early references associate tennis with the clergy. From the Church it spread to the Crown, and became a royal and aristocratic game which spread from France to the rest of Europe. At first it was played with a bare (or gloved) hand, and development to the present sophisticated racket was gradual. Crude wooden boards were followed by the short-handled bat, at first of solid wood, later covered with parchment like a drum. The long-handled racket, strung with sheep's intestines, was not invented until *c.*1500. Until *c.*1700 the stringing was diagonal, and only in 1875 was it strengthened by threading the cross-strings through the main strings, which greatly increased the pace of the game. Its popularity declined partly because of the need for special courts, whose owners found it more profitable to hire them out as theatres: when Molière went on tour in the provinces he acted in tennis courts, and the French theatre still retains the shape of a tennis court. □ **tennis-ball** a ball used in playing tennis. **tennis-court** a court used in playing tennis. **tennis elbow** a sprain caused by or as by playing tennis. **tennis-racket** a racket used in playing tennis. **tennis shoe** a light canvas or leather soft-soled shoe suitable for tennis or general casual wear. [ME *tenetz, tenes*, etc., app. f. OF *tenez* 'take, receive', called by the server to an opponent, imper. of *tenir* take]

tenno /ˈtenəʊ/ *n.* (*pl.* **-os**) the Emperor of Japan viewed as a divinity. [Jap.]

tenny var. of TENNÉ.

Tennyson /ˈtenɪs(ə)n/, Alfred, 1st Baron Tennyson (1809–92), English poet, educated by his father, a Lincolnshire rector, and at Cambridge University, where he met A. H. Hallam whose death (1833) he mourned in his greatest work, *In Memoriam* (1850), which expresses his own anxieties about immortality, change, and evolution. His early volumes of poetry include 'Mariana', 'The Lotos-Eaters', 'The Lady of Shalott', and 'Morte d'Arthur' (1842), the germ of his later *Idylls of the King* (1859), a series of twelve poems of Arthurian legend. By the middle of the century he was firmly established as the voice of his age, Prince Albert and Queen Victoria being among his admirers, and was made Poet Laureate in 1850. Among his many later works are the narrative poem *Enoch Arden* (1864) and several dramas of which *Becket* (1884) appeared in the year he was made a peer. His reputation in the early 20th c. declined but he is now widely acknowledged for his masterly metrical skill and lyrical genius.

tenon /ˈtenən/ *n.* & *v.* —*n.* a projecting piece of wood made for insertion into a corresponding cavity (esp. a mortise) in another piece. —*v.tr.* **1** cut as a tenon. **2** join by means of a tenon. □ **tenon-saw** a small saw with a strong brass or steel back for fine work. □□ **tenoner** *n.* [ME f. F f. *tenir* hold f. L *tenēre*]

tenor /ˈtenə(r)/ *n.* **1 a** a singing-voice between baritone and alto or counter-tenor, the highest of the ordinary adult male range. (See below.) **b** a singer with this voice. **c** a part written for it. **2 a** an instrument, esp. a viola, recorder, or saxophone, of which the range is roughly that of a tenor voice. **b** (in full **tenor bell**) the largest bell of a peal or set. **3** (usu. foll. by *of*) the general purport or drift of a document or speech. **4** (usu. foll. by *of*) a settled or prevailing course or direction, esp. the course of a person's life or habits. **5** *Law* **a** the actual wording of a document. **b** an exact copy. **6** the subject to which a metaphor refers (opp. VEHICLE 4). □ **tenor clef** *Mus.* a clef placing middle C on the second highest line of the staff. [ME f. AF *tenur*, OF *tenour* f. L *tenor* -*oris* f. *tenēre* hold]

In music before the 16th c. *tenor* referred to a voice part (rather than a voice), so called because it formed the basis of a composition, 'holding' a melody (usually pre-existing) against which the other voices were composed. Later, the tenor became the highest male voice using normal voice production, with a range of about two octaves.

tenosynovitis /ˌtenəʊˌsaɪnəʊ'vaɪtɪs/ n. inflammation and swelling of a tendon, usu. in the wrist, often caused by repetitive movements such as typing. [Gk *tenōn* tendon + SYNOVITIS]

tenotomy /tə'nɒtəmɪ/ n. (pl. **-ies**) the surgical cutting of a tendon, esp. as a remedy for a club-foot. [F *ténotomie*, irreg. f. Gk *tenōn* -*ontos* tendon]

tenpin /'tenpɪn/ n. **1** a pin used in tenpin bowling. **2** (in pl.) US = tenpin bowling. □ **tenpin bowling** a game developed from ninepins in which ten pins are set up at the end of an alley and bowled down with hard rubber balls. (See BOWLING.)

tenrec /'tenrek/ n. (also **tanrec** /'tæn-/) any hedgehog-like tailless insect-eating mammal of the family Tenrecidae, esp. *Tenrec ecaudatus* native to Madagascar. [F *tanrec*, f. Malagasy *tàndraka*]

tense[1] /tens/ adj. & v. —adj. **1** stretched tight, strained (*tense cord*; *tense muscle*; *tense nerves*; *tense emotion*). **2** causing tenseness (*a tense moment*). **3** *Phonet.* pronounced with the vocal muscles tense. —v.tr. & intr. make or become tense. □ **tense up** become tense. □□ **tensely** adv. **tenseness** n. **tensity** n. [L *tensus* past part. of *tendere* stretch]

tense[2] /tens/ n. *Gram.* **1** a form taken by a verb to indicate the time (also the continuance or completeness) of the action etc. (*present tense*; *imperfect tense*). **2** a set of such forms for the various persons and numbers. □□ **tenseless** adj. [ME f. OF *tens* f. L *tempus* time]

tensile /'tensaɪl/ adj. **1** of or relating to tension. **2** capable of being drawn out or stretched. □□ **tensile strength** resistance to breaking under tension. □□ **tensility** /ten'sɪlɪtɪ/ n. [med.L *tensilis* (as TENSE[1])]

tensimeter /ten'sɪmɪtə(r)/ n. **1** an instrument for measuring vapour pressure. **2** a manometer. [TENSION + -METER]

tension /'tenʃ(ə)n/ n. & v. —n. **1** the act or an instance of stretching; the state of being stretched; tenseness. **2** mental strain or excitement. **3** a strained (political, social, etc.) state or relationship. **4** *Mech.* the stress by which a bar, cord, etc. is pulled when it is part of a system in equilibrium or motion. **5** electromagnetic force (*high tension*; *low tension*). —v.tr. subject to tension. □□ **tensional** adj. **tensionally** adv. **tensionless** adj. [F *tension* or L *tensio* (as TEND[1])]

tenson /'tens(ə)n/ n. (also **tenzon** /'tenz(ə)n/) **1** a contest in verse-making between troubadours. **2** a piece of verse composed for this. [F *tenson*, = Prov. *tenso* (as TENSION)]

tensor /'tensə(r)/ n. **1** *Anat.* a muscle that tightens or stretches a part. **2** *Math.* a generalized form of vector involving an arbitrary number of indices. □□ **tensorial** /-'sɔːrɪəl/ adj. [mod.L (as TEND[1])]

tent[1] /tent/ n. & v. —n. **1** a portable shelter or dwelling of canvas, cloth, etc., supported by a pole or poles and stretched by cords attached to pegs driven into the ground. **2** *Med.* a tentlike enclosure for control of the air supply to a patient. —v. **1** tr. cover with or as with a tent. **2** intr. **a** encamp in a tent. **b** dwell temporarily. □ **tent-bed** a bed with a tentlike canopy, or for a patient in a tent. **tent coat** (or **dress**) a coat (or dress) cut very full. **tent-fly** (pl. **-flies**) **1** a flap at the entrance to a tent. **2** a piece of canvas stretched over the ridge-pole of a tent leaving an open space but keeping off sun and rain. **tent-peg** any of the pegs to which the cords of a tent are attached. **tent-pegging** a sport in which a rider tries at full gallop to carry off on the point of a lance a tent-peg fixed in the ground. **tent-stitch 1** a series of parallel diagonal stitches. **2** such a stitch. [ME f. OF *tente* ult. f. L *tendere* stretch: *tent-stitch* may be f. another word]

tent[2] /tent/ n. a deep-red sweet wine chiefly from Spain, used esp. as sacramental wine. [Sp. *tinto* deep-coloured f. L *tinctus* past part.: see TINGE]

tent[3] /tent/ n. *Surgery* a piece (esp. a roll) of lint, linen, etc., inserted into a wound or natural opening to keep it open. [ME f. OF *tente* f. *tenter* probe (as TEMPT)]

tentacle /'tentək(ə)l/ n. **1** a long slender flexible appendage of an (esp. invertebrate) animal, used for feeling, grasping, or moving. **2** a thing used like a tentacle as a feeler etc. **3** *Bot.* a sensitive hair or filament. □□ **tentacled** adj. (also in comb.). **tentacular** /-'tækjʊlə(r)/ adj. **tentaculate** /-'tækjʊlət/ adj. [mod.L *tentaculum* f. L *tentare* = *temptare* (see TEMPT) + -*culum* -CULE]

tentative /'tentətɪv/ adj. & n. —adj. **1** done by way of trial, experimental. **2** hesitant, not definite (*tentative suggestion*; *tentative acceptance*). —n. an experimental proposal or theory. □□ **tentatively** adv. **tentativeness** n. [med.L *tentativus* (as TENTACLE)]

tenter[1] /'tentə(r)/ n. **1** a machine for stretching cloth to dry in shape. **2** = TENTERHOOK. [ME ult. f. med.L *tentorium* (as TEND[1])]

tenter[2] /'tentə(r)/ n. *Brit.* **1** a person in charge of something, esp. of machinery in a factory. **2** a workman's unskilled assistant. [*tent* (now Sc.) pay attention, perh. f. *tent* attention f. INTENT or obs. *attent* (as ATTEND)]

tenterhook /'tentəˌhʊk/ n. any of the hooks to which cloth is fastened on a tenter. □ **on tenterhooks** in a state of suspense or mental agitation due to uncertainty.

tenth /tenθ/ n. & adj. —n. **1** the position in a sequence corresponding to the number 10 in the sequence 1–10. **2** something occupying this position. **3** one of ten equal parts of a thing. **4** *Mus.* **a** an interval or chord spanning an octave and a third in the diatonic scale. **b** a note separated from another by this interval. —adj. that is the tenth. □ **tenth-rate** of extremely poor quality. □□ **tenthly** adv. [ME *tenthe*, alt. of OE *teogotha*]

tenuis /'tenjʊɪs/ n. (pl. **tenues** /-jʊˌiːz/) *Phonet.* a voiceless stop, e.g. k, p, t. [L, = thin, transl. Gk *psilos* smooth]

tenuity /tɪ'njuːɪtɪ/ n. **1** slenderness. **2** (of a fluid, esp. air) rarity, thinness. [L *tenuitas* (as TENUIS)]

tenuous /'tenjʊəs/ adj. **1** slight, of little substance (*tenuous connection*). **2** (of a distinction etc.) oversubtle. **3** thin, slender, small. **4** rarefied. □□ **tenuously** adv. **tenuousness** n. [L *tenuis*]

tenure /'tenjə(r)/ n. **1** a condition, or form of right or title, under which (esp. real) property is held. **2** (often foll. by *of*) **a** the holding or possession of an office or property. **b** the period of this (*during his tenure of office*). **3** guaranteed permanent employment, esp. as a teacher or lecturer after a probationary period. [ME f. OF f. *tenir* hold f. L *tenēre*]

tenured /'tenjəd/ adj. **1** (of an official position) carrying a guarantee of permanent employment. **2** (of a teacher, lecturer, etc.) having guaranteed tenure of office.

tenurial /ten'jʊərɪəl/ adj. of the tenure of land. □□ **tenurially** adv. [med.L *tenūra* TENURE]

tenuto /tə'nuːtəʊ/ adv., adj., & n. *Mus.* —adv. & adj. (of a note etc.) sustained, given its full time-value (cf. LEGATO, STACCATO). —n. (pl. **-os**) a note or chord played tenuto. [It., = held]

Tenzing Norgay /ˌtensɪŋ 'nɔːgeɪ/ (1914–86), Sherpa mountaineer who, with Sir Edmund Hillary, was the first to reach the summit of Mount Everest (1953).

tenzon var. of TENSON.

teocalli /ˌtiːə'kælɪ/ n. (pl. **teocallis**) a temple of the Aztecs or other Mexican peoples, usu. on a truncated pyramid. [Nahuatl f. *teotl* god + *calli* house]

Teotihuacán /teɪˌəʊtɪwə'kɑːn/ the largest city of pre-Columban America, about 40 km (25 miles) north-east of Mexico City. Built *c*.300 BC it reached its zenith *c*. AD 300–600, when it was the centre of an influential culture, but by 650 it had declined as a major power and was sacked by the invading Toltec *c*.750. Among its monuments are palatial buildings, plazas, and temples, including the Pyramidal of the Sun and of the Moon and the temple of Quetzalcóatl.

tepee /'tiːpiː/ n. (also **teepee**) a N. American Indian's conical tent, made of skins, cloth, or canvas on a frame of poles. [Sioux or Dakota Indian *tīpī*]

tephra /ˈtefrə/ n. fragmented rock etc. ejected by a volcanic eruption. [Gk, = ash]

tepid /ˈtepɪd/ adj. **1** slightly warm. **2** unenthusiastic. □□ **tepidity** /tɪˈpɪdɪtɪ/ n. **tepidly** adv. **tepidness** n. [L tepidus f. tepēre be lukewarm]

tequila /teˈkiːlə/ n. a Mexican liquor made from an agave. [Tequila in Mexico]

ter- /tɜː(r)/ comb. form three; threefold (tercentenary; tervalent). [L ter thrice]

tera- /ˈterə/ comb. form denoting a factor of 10^{12}. [Gk teras monster]

terai /təˈraɪ/ n. (in full **terai hat**) a wide-brimmed felt hat, often with a double crown, worn by travellers etc. in subtropical regions. [Terai, belt of marshy jungle between Himalayan foothills and plains, f. Hindi tarāī moist (land)]

terametre /ˈterəˌmiːtə(r)/ n. a unit of length equal to 10^{12} metres.

teraph /ˈterəf/ n. (pl. **teraphim**, also used as sing.) a small image as a domestic deity or oracle of the ancient Hebrews. [ME f. LL theraphin, Gk theraphin f. Heb. ʈʼrāpîm]

terato- /ˈterətəʊ/ comb. form monster. [Gk teras -atos monster]

teratogen /təˈrætədʒ(ə)n/ n. Med. an agent or factor causing malformation of an embryo. □□ **teratogenic** /ˌterətəˈdʒenɪk/ adj. **teratogeny** /ˌterəˈtɒdʒənɪ/ n.

teratology /ˌterəˈtɒlədʒɪ/ n. **1** Biol. the scientific study of animal or vegetable monstrosities. **2** mythology relating to fantastic creatures, monsters, etc. □□ **teratological** /-təˈlɒdʒɪk(ə)l/ adj. **teratologist** n.

teratoma /ˌterəˈtəʊmə/ n. Med. a tumour of heterogeneous tissues, esp. of the gonads.

terbium /ˈtɜːbɪəm/ n. Chem. a silvery metallic element of the lanthanide series, first discovered in 1843. It has few commercial uses. ¶ Symb.: **Tb**; atomic number 65. [mod.L f. Ytterby in Sweden]

terce /tɜːs/ n. Eccl. **1** the office of the canonical hour of prayer appointed for the third daytime hour (i.e. 9 a.m.). **2** this hour. [var. of TIERCE]

tercel /ˈtɜːs(ə)l/ n. (also **tiercel** /ˈtɪəs(ə)l/) Falconry the male of the hawk, esp. a peregrine or goshawk. [ME f. OF tercel, ult. a dimin. of L tertius third, perh. from a belief that the third egg of a clutch produced a male bird, or that the male was one-third smaller than the female]

tercentenary /ˌtɜːsenˈtiːnərɪ, -ˈtenərɪ, tɜːˈsentɪnərɪ/ n. & adj. —n. (pl. **-ies**) **1** a three-hundredth anniversary. **2** a celebration of this. —adj. of this anniversary.

tercentennial /ˌtɜːsenˈtenɪəl/ adj. & n. —adj. **1** occurring every three hundred years. **2** lasting three hundred years. —n. a tercentenary.

tercet /ˈtɜːsɪt/ n. (also **tiercet** /ˈtɪə-/) Prosody a set or group of three lines rhyming together or connected by rhyme with an adjacent triplet. [F f. It. terzetto dimin. of terzo third f. L tertius]

terebene /ˈterɪˌbiːn/ n. a mixture of terpenes prepared by treating oil of turpentine with sulphuric acid, used as an expectorant etc. [TEREBINTH + -ENE]

terebinth /ˈterɪbɪnθ/ n. a small Southern European tree, Pistacia terebinthus, yielding turpentine. [ME f. OF terebinte or L terebinthus f. Gk terebinthos]

terebinthine /ˌterɪˈbɪnθaɪn/ adj. **1** of the terebinth. **2** of turpentine. [L terebinthinus f. Gk terebinthinos (as TEREBINTH)]

teredo /təˈriːdəʊ/ n. (pl. **-os**) any bivalve mollusc of the genus Teredo, esp. T. navalis, that bores into wooden ships etc. Also called SHIPWORM. [L f. Gk terēdōn f. teirō rub hard, wear away, bore]

Terence /ˈterəns/ (Publius Terentius Afer, c.190–159 BC) Roman comic playwright, originally a slave from North Africa, the author of six comedies based on models from Greek comedy. His plays, all set in Athens, are marked by realism in character and language, consistency of plot, and an urbanity quite different from the extravagance of Plautus. He is an important ancestor of the modern 'comedy of manners'.

Terengganu see TRENGGANU.

Teresa /təˈriːzə/, Mother (1910–), Roman Catholic nun, born Agnes Gonxha Bojaxhiu of Albanian parents in Yugoslavia, who is known as 'the Saint of the Gutters' for bringing comfort and dignity to the destitute. She founded an order (Missionaries of Charity) which is noted for its work among the poor and the dying in Calcutta, India, and throughout the world. She was awarded the Nobel Peace Prize in 1979.

Teresa of Ávila /təˈriːzə, ˈævɪlə/, St (1515–82), Spanish Carmelite nun and mystic. Her importance is twofold. As the reformer of the Carmelite Order her work has survived in the great number of discalced monasteries which venerate her as their foundress; she was a woman of strong character, shrewdness, and great practical ability. As a spiritual writer her influence was epoch-making, giving a description of the entire life of prayer from meditation to the so-called 'mystic marriage' or union with God. Her combination of mystic experience with ceaseless activity as a reformer and organizer make her life the classical instance for those who contend that the highest contemplation is not incompatible with great practical achievements.

Teresa of Lisieux /tɪˈriːzə, liːzɪˈɜː/, St (1873–97), French Carmelite nun. After her death from tuberculosis her cult grew through the circulation of her autobiography, L'Histoire d'une âme, teaching that sanctity can be attained through continual renunciation in small matters, and not only through extreme self-mortification.

Tereshkova /ˌterɪʃˈkəʊvə/, Valentina (1937–), Soviet cosmonaut, who became the first woman to fly in space (June 1963).

terete /təˈriːt/ adj. Biol. smooth and rounded; cylindrical. [L teres -etis]

tergal /ˈtɜːg(ə)l/ adj. of or relating to the back; dorsal. [L tergum back]

tergiversate /ˈtɜːdʒɪˌvɜːseɪt/ v.intr. **1** be apostate; change one's party or principles. **2** equivocate; make conflicting or evasive statements. **3** turn one's back on something. □□ **tergiversation** /-ˈseɪʃ(ə)n/ n. **tergiversator** n. [L tergiversari turn one's back f. tergum back + vertere vers- turn]

-teria /ˈtɪərɪə/ suffix denoting self-service establishments (washeteria). [after CAFETERIA]

term /tɜːm/ n. & v. —n. **1** a word used to express a definite concept, esp. in a particular branch of study etc. (a technical term). **2** (in pl.) language used; mode of expression (answered in no uncertain terms). **3** (in pl.) a relation or footing (we are on familiar terms). **4** (in pl.) **a** conditions or stipulations (cannot accept your terms; do it on your own terms). **b** charge or price (his terms are £20 a lesson). **5 a** a limited period of some state or activity (for a term of five years). **b** a period over which operations are conducted or results contemplated (in the short term). **c** a period of some weeks, alternating with holiday or vacation, during which instruction is given in a school, college, or university, or Brit. during which a lawcourt holds sessions. **d** a period of imprisonment. **e** a period of tenure. **6** Logic a word or words that may be the subject or predicate of a proposition. **7** Math. **a** each of the two quantities in a ratio. **b** each quantity in a series. **c** a part of an expression joined to the rest by + or − (e.g. a, b, c in a + b − c). **8** the completion of a normal length of pregnancy. **9** an appointed day, esp. a Scottish quarter day. **10** (in full Brit. **term of years** or US **term for years**) Law an interest in land for a fixed period. **11** = TERMINUS 6. **12** archaic a boundary or limit, esp. of time. —v.tr. denominate, call; assign a term to (the music termed classical). □ **bring to terms** cause to accept conditions. **come to terms** yield, give way. **come to terms with 1** reconcile oneself to (a difficulty etc.). **2** conclude an agreement with. **in set terms** in definite terms. **in terms** explicitly. **in terms of** in the language peculiar to, using as a basis of expression or thought. **make terms** conclude an agreement. **on terms** on terms of friendship or equality. **term paper** US an essay or dissertation representative of the work done during a term. **terms of reference** Brit. points referred to an individual or body of persons for decision or report; the scope of an inquiry etc.; a definition of this. **terms of trade** Brit. the ratio between prices paid for imports and those received for exports. □□ **termless** adj. **termly** adj. & adv. [ME f. OF terme f. L TERMINUS]

termagant /ˈtɜːməgənt/ n. & adj. —n. 1 an overbearing or brawling woman; a virago or shrew. 2 (**Termagant**) hist. an imaginary deity of violent and turbulent character, often appearing in morality plays. —adj. violent, turbulent, shrewish. [ME Tervagant f. OF Tervagan f. It. Trivigante]

terminable /ˈtɜːmɪnəb(ə)l/ adj. 1 that may be terminated. 2 coming to an end after a certain time (terminable annuity). □□ **terminableness** n.

terminal /ˈtɜːmɪn(ə)l/ adj. & n. —adj. 1 a (of a disease) ending in death, fatal. b (of a patient) in the last stage of a fatal disease. c (of a morbid condition) forming the last stage of a fatal disease. d colloq. ruinous, disastrous, very great (terminal laziness). 2 of or forming a limit or terminus (terminal station). 3 a Zool. etc. ending a series (terminal joints). b Bot. borne at the end of a stem etc. 4 of or done etc. each term (terminal accounts; terminal examinations). —n. 1 a terminating thing; an extremity. 2 a terminus for trains or long-distance buses. 3 a departure and arrival building for air passengers. 4 a point of connection for closing an electric circuit. 5 an apparatus for transmission of messages between a user and a computer, communications system, etc. 6 (in full **terminal figure**) = TERMINUS 6. 7 an installation where oil is stored at the end of a pipeline or at a port. 8 a patient suffering from a terminal illness. □ **terminal velocity** a velocity of a falling body such that the resistance of the air etc. prevents further increase of speed under gravity. □□ **terminally** adv. [L terminalis (as TERMINUS)]

terminate /ˈtɜːmɪˌneɪt/ v. 1 tr. & intr. bring or come to an end. 2 intr. (foll. by in) (of a word) end in (a specified letter or syllable etc.). 3 tr. end (a pregnancy) before term by artificial means. 4 tr. bound, limit. [L terminare (as TERMINUS)]

termination /ˌtɜːmɪˈneɪʃ(ə)n/ n. 1 the act or an instance of terminating; the state of being terminated. 2 Med. an induced abortion. 3 an ending or result of a specified kind (a happy termination). 4 a word's final syllable or letters or letter esp. as an element in inflection or derivation. □ **put a termination to** (or **bring to a termination**) make an end of. □□ **terminational** adj. [ME f. OF termination or L terminatio (as TERMINATE)]

terminator /ˈtɜːmɪˌneɪtə(r)/ n. 1 a person or thing that terminates. 2 the dividing line between the light and dark part of a planetary body.

terminer see OYER AND TERMINER.

termini pl. of TERMINUS.

terminism /ˈtɜːmɪˌnɪz(ə)m/ n. 1 the doctrine that everyone has a limited time for repentance. 2 = NOMINALISM. □□ **terminist** n. [L]

terminological /ˌtɜːmɪnəˈlɒdʒɪk(ə)l/ adj. of terminology. □ **terminological inexactitude** joc. a lie. □□ **terminologically** adv.

terminology /ˌtɜːmɪˈnɒlədʒɪ/ n. (pl. -ies) 1 the system of terms used in a particular subject. 2 the science of the proper use of terms. □□ **terminologist** n. [G Terminologie f. med.L TERMINUS term]

terminus /ˈtɜːmɪnəs/ n. (pl. **termini** /-ˌnaɪ/ or **terminuses**) 1 a station at the end of a railway or bus route. 2 a point at the end of a pipeline etc. 3 a final point, a goal. 4 a starting-point. 5 Math. the end-point of a vector etc. 6 Archit. a figure of a human bust or an animal ending in a square pillar from which it appears to spring, orig. as a boundary-marker. □ **terminus ad quem** /æd ˈkwem/ the finishing-point of an argument, policy, period, etc. **terminus ante quem** /ˌæntɪ ˈkwem/ the finishing-point of a period. **terminus a quo** /ɑː ˈkwəʊ/ the starting-point of an argument, policy, period, etc. **terminus post quem** /pəʊst ˈkwem/ the starting-point of a period. [L, = end, limit, boundary]

termitary /ˈtɜːmɪtərɪ/ n. (pl. -ies) a nest of termites, usu. a large mound of earth.

termite /ˈtɜːmaɪt/ n. a small antlike social insect of the order Isoptera, chiefly tropical and destructive to timber. [LL termes -mitis, alt. of L tarmes after terere rub]

termor /ˈtɜːmə(r)/ n. Law a person who holds lands etc. for a term of years, or for life. [ME f. AF termer (as TERM)]

tern¹ /tɜːn/ n. any marine bird of the subfamily Sterninae, like

a gull but usu. smaller and with a long forked tail. [of Scand. orig.: cf. Da. terne, Sw. tärna f. ON therna]

tern² /tɜːn/ n. 1 a set of three, esp. three lottery numbers that when drawn together win a large prize. 2 such a prize. [F terne f. L terni three each]

ternary /ˈtɜːnərɪ/ adj. 1 composed of three parts. 2 Math. using three as a base (ternary scale). □ **ternary form** Mus. the form of a movement in which the first subject is repeated after an interposed second subject in a related key. [ME f. L ternarius f. terni three each]

ternate /ˈtɜːneɪt/ adj. 1 arranged in threes. 2 Bot. (of a leaf): a having three leaflets. b whorled in threes. □□ **ternately** adv. [mod.L ternatus (as TERNARY)]

terne /tɜːn/ n. (in full **terne-plate**) inferior tin-plate alloyed with much lead. [prob. f. F terne dull: cf. TARNISH]

terotechnology /ˌtɪərəʊtekˈnɒlədʒɪ, ˌtɪə-/ n. the branch of technology and engineering concerned with the installation and maintenance of equipment. [Gk tēreō take care of + TECHNOLOGY]

terpene /ˈtɜːpiːn/ n. Chem. any of a large group of unsaturated cyclic hydrocarbons found in the essential oils of plants, esp. conifers and oranges. [terpentin obs. var. of TURPENTINE]

Terpsichore /tɜːpˈsɪkərɪ/ Gk & Rom. Mythol. the Muse of lyric poetry and dance. [Gk, = delighting in dance]

Terpsichorean /ˌtɜːpsɪkəˈriːən/ adj. of or relating to dancing.

terra alba /ˌterə ˈælbə/ n. a white mineral, esp. pipeclay or pulverized gypsum. [L, = white earth]

terrace /ˈterəs, -rɪs/ n. & v. —n. 1 each of a series of flat areas formed on a slope and used for cultivation. 2 a level paved area next to a house. 3 a a row of houses on a raised level or along the top or face of a slope. b a row of houses built in one block of uniform style. 4 a flight of wide shallow steps as for spectators at a sports ground. 5 Geol. a raised beach, or a similar formation beside a river etc. —v.tr. form into or provide with a terrace or terraces. □ **terraced house** Brit. = terrace house. **terraced roof** a flat roof esp. of an Indian or Eastern house. **terrace house** Brit. any of a row of houses joined by party-walls. [OF ult. f. L terra earth]

terracotta /ˌterəˈkɒtə/ n. 1 a unglazed usu. brownish-red earthenware used chiefly as an ornamental building-material and in modelling. b a statuette of this. 2 its colour. [It. terra cotta baked earth]

terra firma /ˌterə ˈfɜːmə/ n. dry land, firm ground. [L, = firm land]

terrain /teˈreɪn, tə-/ n. a tract of land as regarded by the physical geographer or the military tactician. [F, ult. f. L terrenum neut. of terrenus TERRENE]

terra incognita /ˌterə ɪŋˈkɒgnɪtə, ˌɪnkɒgˈniːtə/ n. an unknown or unexplored region. [L, = unknown land]

terramara /ˌterəˈmɑːrə/ n. (pl. **terramare** /-reɪ/) = TERRAMARE. [It. dial.: see TERRAMARE]

terramare /ˌterəˈmɑːrɪ, -ˈmeə(r)/ n. 1 an ammoniacal earthy deposit found in mounds in prehistoric lake-dwellings or settlements esp. in Italy. 2 such a dwelling or settlement. [F f. It. dial. terra mara f. marna marl]

terrapin /ˈterəpɪn/ n. 1 any of various N. American edible freshwater turtles of the family Emydidae. 2 (**Terrapin**) propr. a type of prefabricated one-storey building. [Algonquian]

terrarium /teˈreərɪəm/ n. (pl. **terrariums** or **terraria** /-rɪə/) 1 a vivarium for small land animals. 2 a sealed transparent globe etc. containing growing plants. [mod.L f. L terra earth, after AQUARIUM]

terra sigillata /ˌterə ˌsɪdʒɪˈleɪtə/ n. 1 astringent clay from Lemnos or Samos. 2 Samian ware. [med.L, = sealed earth]

terrazzo /teˈrætsəʊ/ n. (pl. -os) a flooring-material of stone chips set in concrete and given a smooth surface. [It., = terrace]

terrene /teˈriːn/ adj. 1 of the earth; earthy, worldly. 2 of earth, earthy. 3 of dry land; terrestrial. [ME f. AF f. L terrenus f. terra earth]

terreplein /ˈteəpleɪn/ n. a level space where a battery of guns is mounted. [orig. a sloping bank behind a rampart f. F terre-plein

f. It. *terrapieno* f. *terrapienare* fill with earth f. *terra* earth + *pieno* f. L *plenus* full]

terrestrial /tə'restrɪəl, tɪ-/ *adj.* & *n.* —*adj.* **1** of or on or relating to the Earth; earthly. **2 a** of or on dry land. **b** *Zool.* living on or in the ground (opp. AQUATIC, ARBOREAL, AERIAL). **c** *Bot.* growing in the soil (opp. AQUATIC, EPIPHYTIC). **3** *Astron.* (of a planet) similar in size or composition to the Earth. **4** of this world, worldly (*terrestrial sins*; *terrestrial interests*). —*n.* an inhabitant of the Earth. □ **a terrestrial globe** a globe representing the Earth. **the terrestrial globe** the Earth. **terrestrial magnetism** the magnetic properties of the Earth as a whole. **terrestrial telescope** a telescope giving an erect image for observation of terrestrial objects. □□ **terrestrially** *adv.* [ME f. L *terrestris* f. *terra* earth]

terret /'terɪt/ *n.* (also **territ**) each of the loops or rings on a harness-pad for the driving-reins to pass through. [ME, var. of *toret* (now dial.) f. OF *to(u)ret* dimin. of TOUR]

terre-verte /teə'veət/ *n.* a soft green earth used as a pigment. [F, = green earth]

terrible /'terɪb(ə)l/ *adj.* **1** *colloq.* very great or bad (*a terrible bore*). **2** *colloq.* very incompetent (*terrible at tennis*). **3** causing terror; fit to cause terror; awful, dreadful, formidable. □□ **terribleness** *n.* [ME f. F f. L *terribilis* f. *terrēre* frighten]

terribly /'terɪblɪ/ *adv.* **1** *colloq.* very, extremely (*he was terribly nice about it*). **2** in a terrible manner.

terricolous /te'rɪkələs/ *adj.* living on or in the earth. [L *terricola* earth-dweller f. *terra* earth + *colere* inhabit]

terrier[1] /'terɪə(r)/ *n.* **1 a** a small dog of various breeds originally used for turning out foxes etc. from their earths. **b** any of these breeds. **2** an eager or tenacious person or animal. **3** (**Terrier**) *Brit. colloq.* a member of the Territorial Army etc. [ME f. OF (*chien*) *terrier* f. med.L *terrarius* f. L *terra* earth]

terrier[2] /'terɪə(r)/ *n. hist.* **1** a book recording the site, boundaries, etc., of the land of private persons or corporations. **2** a rent-roll. **3** a collection of acknowledgements of vassals or tenants of a lordship. [ME f. OF *terrier* (adj.) = med.L *terrarius liber* (as TERRIER[1])]

terrific /tə'rɪfɪk/ *adj.* **1** *colloq.* **a** of great size or intensity. **b** excellent (*did a terrific job*). **c** excessive (*making a terrific noise*). **2** causing terror. □□ **terrifically** *adv.* [L *terrificus* f. *terrēre* frighten]

terrify /'terɪˌfaɪ/ *v.tr.* (**-ies**, **-ied**) fill with terror; frighten severely (*terrified them into submission*; *is terrified of dogs*). □□ **terrifier** *n.* **terrifyingly** *adv.* [L *terrificare* (as TERRIFIC)]

terrigenous /te'rɪdʒɪnəs/ *adj.* produced by the earth or the land (*terrigenous deposits*). [L *terrigenus* earth-born]

terrine /tə'riːn/ *n.* **1** pâté or similar food. **2** an earthenware vessel, esp. one in which such food is cooked or sold. [orig. form of TUREEN]

territ var. of TERRET.

territorial /ˌterɪ'tɔːrɪəl/ *adj.* & *n.* —*adj.* **1** of territory (*territorial possessions*). **2** limited to a district (*the right was strictly territorial*). **3** (of a person or animal etc.) tending to defend an area of territory. **4** (usu. **Territorial**) of any of the Territories of the US or Canada. —*n.* (**Territorial**) (in the UK) a member of the Territorial Army. □ **Territorial Army** (in the UK) a volunteer force locally organized to provide a reserve of trained and disciplined manpower for use in an emergency (known as *Territorial and Army Volunteer Reserve* 1967–79). **territorial waters** the waters under the jurisdiction of a State, esp. the part of the sea within a stated distance of the shore (traditionally three miles from low-water mark). □□ **territoriality** /-'ælɪtɪ/ *n.* **territorialize** *v.tr.* (also **-ise**). **territorialization** /-laɪ'zeɪʃ(ə)n/ *n.* **territorially** *adv.* [LL *territorialis* (as TERRITORY)]

territory /'terɪtərɪ, -trɪ/ *n.* (*pl.* **-ies**) **1** the extent of the land under the jurisdiction of a ruler, State, city, etc. **2** (**Territory**) an organized division of a country, esp. one not yet admitted to the full rights of a State. **3** a sphere of action or thought; a province. **4** the area over which a commercial traveller or goods-distributor operates. **5** *Zool.* an area defended by an animal or animals against others of the same species. **6** an area defended by a team or player in a game. **7** a large tract of land. [ME f. L *territorium* f. *terra* land]

terror /'terə(r)/ *n.* **1** extreme fear. **2 a** a person or thing that causes terror. **b** (also **holy terror**) *colloq.* a formidable person; a troublesome person or thing (*the twins are little terrors*). **3** the use of organized intimidation; terrorism. □ **the Terror** or **Reign of Terror** the period of the French Revolution between mid-1793 and July 1794 when the ruling Jacobin faction, dominated by Robespierre, ruthlessly executed opponents and anyone else considered a threat to their regime. It ended with the fall and execution of Robespierre, but in its last six weeks more than 1,300 people were guillotined in Paris alone. **reign of terror** a period of remorseless repression or bloodshed. **terror-stricken** (or **-struck**) affected with terror. [ME f. OF *terrour* f. L *terror* -*oris* f. *terrēre* frighten]

terrorist /'terərɪst/ *n.* a person who uses or favours violent and intimidating methods of coercing a government or community. □□ **terrorism** *n.* **terroristic** /-'rɪstɪk/ *adj.* **terroristically** /-'rɪstɪkəlɪ/ *adv.* [F *terroriste* (as TERROR)]

terrorize /'terəˌraɪz/ *v.tr.* (also **-ise**) **1** fill with terror. **2** use terrorism against. □□ **terrorization** /-'zeɪʃ(ə)n/ *n.* **terrorizer** *n.*

Terry /'terɪ/, Dame Ellen Alice (1847–1928), English actress. She was already well known when in 1878 Henry Irving engaged her as his leading lady at the Lyceum, beginning a partnership which was to become one of the outstanding features of the London theatrical scene for the next 25 years. She played many Shakespearian roles, notably Ophelia, Beatrice, Desdemona, Juliet, Viola, Lady Macbeth, and Imogen, and (in 1906) Lady Cicely Waynflete in *Captain Brassbound's Conversion*, a part specially written for her by Shaw. She celebrated her stage jubilee in the same year, but thereafter acted very little.

terry /'terɪ/ *n.* & *adj.* —*n.* (*pl.* **-ies**) a pile fabric with the loops uncut, used esp. for towels. —*adj.* of this fabric. [18th c.: orig. unkn.]

terse /tɜːs/ *adj.* (**terser**, **tersest**) **1** (of language) brief, concise, to the point. **2** curt, abrupt. □□ **tersely** *adv.* **terseness** *n.* [L *tersus* past part. of *tergēre* wipe, polish]

tertian /'tɜːʃ(ə)n/ *adj.* (of a fever) recurring every third day by inclusive counting. [ME (*fever*) *tersiane* f. L (*febris*) *tertiana* (as TERTIARY)]

tertiary /'tɜːʃərɪ/ *adj.* & *n.* —*adj.* **1** third in order or rank etc. **2** (**Tertiary**) *Geol.* of or relating to the first period in the Cenozoic era, so called because it follows the Mesozoic, which was formerly also called *Secondary*. It lasted from about 65 to 2 million years ago, and comprises the Palaeocene, Eocene, Oligocene, Miocene, and Pliocene epochs. World temperatures were generally warm except towards the close of the period, and mammals evolved rapidly, becoming the dominant land vertebrates. —*n.* **1** *Geol.* this period or system. **2** a member of the third order of a monastic body. □ **tertiary education** education, esp. in a college or university, that follows secondary education. [L *tertiarius* f. *tertius* third]

tertium quid /ˌtɜːtɪəm 'kwɪd, ˌtɜːtjəm/ *n.* a third something, esp. intermediate between mind and matter or between opposite things. [L, app. transl. Gk *triton ti*]

Tertullian /tɜː'tʌlɪən/ (Quintus Septimius Floreas Tertullianus, *c.*160–*c.*240) Latin Church Father from Carthage. Converted to Christianity *c.*195, he was the author of many treatises in which he devoted his gifts of rhetoric and irony to the defence of Christianity and the castigation of pagan idolatry and Gnostic heresy. His enthusiasm for the martyrs, and his puritanism, were intensified when he joined the Montanists.

tervalent /'tɜːˌvələnt, -'veɪlənt/ *adj. Chem.* having a valency of three. [TER- + VALENT- part. stem (as VALENCE[1])]

Terylene /'terɪliːn/ *n. propr.* a synthetic polyester used as a textile fibre. [*terephthalic* acid (f. *terebic* f. TEREBINTH + PHTHALIC ACID) + ETHYLENE]

terza rima /ˌteətsə 'riːmə/ *n. Prosody* an arrangement of (esp. iambic pentameter) triplets rhyming *aba bcb cdc* etc. as in Dante's *Divina Commedia*. [It., = third rhyme]

terzetto /teət'setəʊ, -tsɛt-/ *n.* (*pl.* **-os** or **terzetti** /-tiː/) *Mus.* a vocal or instrumental trio. [It.: see TERCET]

TESL /'tes(ə)l/ *abbr.* teaching of English as a second language.

Tesla /'teslə/, Nikola (1856–1943), American electrical engineer and prolific inventor, born in Croatia of Serbian family. In 1884 he emigrated to the US, where he worked briefly on motors and direct-current generators with Edison before joining the Westinghouse company and concentrating on alternating-current devices, with which the future of the industry in fact lay. He developed the first alternating-current induction motor in 1888, and with this and his contributions to long-distance electrical power transmission revolutionized the industry. He studied high-frequency current, developing several forms of oscillators and the famous Tesla coil, an induction coil that was widely used in radio technology and subsequently in television and other electronic equipment, and developed a wireless guidance system for ships. Although his inventions paved the way for many of the technological developments of modern times he never reaped the material rewards that might have been his; a recluse in later life, he died in poverty.

tesla /'teslə/ n. the SI unit of magnetic flux density. [N. TESLA]

TESOL /'tesɒl/ abbr. teaching of English to speakers of other languages.

TESSA n. (also **Tessa**) Brit. tax exempt special savings account, a form of tax-free investment introduced in 1991. [abbr.]

tessellate /'tesə,leɪt/ v.tr. **1** make from tesserae. **2** Math. cover (a plane surface) by repeated use of a single shape. [L tessellare f. tessella dimin. of TESSERA]

tessellated /'tesə,leɪtɪd/ adj. **1** of or resembling mosaic. **2** Bot. & Zool. regularly chequered. [L tessellatus or It. tessellato (as TESSELLATE)]

tessellation /,tesə'leɪʃ(ə)n/ n. **1** the act or an instance of tessellating; the state of being tessellated. **2** an arrangement of polygons without gaps or overlapping, esp. in a repeated pattern.

tessera /'tesərə/ n. (pl. **tesserae** /-,riː/) **1** a small square block used in mosaic. **2** Gk & Rom. Antiq. a small square of bone etc. used as a token, ticket, etc. □□ **tesseral** adj. [L f. Gk, neut. of tesseres, tessares four]

tessitura /,tesɪ'tʊərə/ n. Mus. the range within which most tones of a voice-part fall. [It., = TEXTURE]

test[1] /test/ n. & v. —n. **1** a critical examination or trial of a person's or thing's qualities. **2** the means of so examining; a standard for comparison or trial; circumstances suitable for this (success is not a fair test). **3** a minor examination, esp. in school (spelling test). **4** colloq. a test match. **5** a ground of admission or rejection (is excluded by our test). **6** Chem. a reagent or a procedure employed to reveal the presence of another in a compound. **7** Brit. a movable hearth in a reverberating furnace with a cupel used in separating gold or silver from lead. —v.tr. **1** put to the test; make trial of (a person or thing or quality). **2** try severely; tax a person's powers of endurance etc. **3** Chem. examine by means of a reagent. **4** Brit. refine or assay (metal). □ **put to the test** cause to undergo a test. **Test Act** hist. **1** an act in force 1672–1828, requiring all persons before holding office in Britain to take oaths of supremacy and allegiance or an equivalent test. **2** an act of 1871 relaxing conditions for university degrees. **test bed** equipment for testing aircraft engines before acceptance for general use. **test card** a still television picture transmitted outside normal programme hours and designed for use in judging the quality and position of the image. **test case** Law a case setting a precedent for other cases involving the same question of law. **test drive** a drive taken to determine the qualities of a motor vehicle with a view to its regular use. **test-drive** v.tr. (past **-drove**; past part. **-driven**) drive (a vehicle) for this purpose. **test flight** a flight during which the performance of an aircraft is tested. **test-fly** v.tr. (**-flies**; past **-flew**; past part. **-flown**) fly (an aircraft) for this purpose. **test match** a cricket or Rugby match between teams of certain countries, usu. each of a series in a tour. **test meal** a meal of specified quantity and composition, eaten to assist tests of gastric secretion. **test out** put (a theory etc.) to a practical test. **test paper** **1** a minor examination paper. **2** Chem. a paper impregnated with a substance changing colour under known conditions. **test pilot** a pilot who test-flies aircraft. **test-tube** a thin glass tube closed at one end used for chemical tests etc. **test-tube baby** colloq. a baby conceived by in vitro fertilization.

□□ **testable** adj. **testability** /-ə'bɪlɪtɪ/ n. **testee** /tes'tiː/ n. [ME f. OF f. L testu(m) earthen pot, collateral form of testa TEST[2]]

test[2] /test/ n. the shell of some invertebrates, esp. foraminiferars and tunicates. [L testa tile, jug, shell, etc.: cf. TEST[1]]

testa /'testə/ n. (pl. **testae** /-tiː/) Bot. a seed-coat. [L (as TEST[2])]

testaceous /te'steɪʃəs/ adj. **1** Biol. having a hard continuous outer covering. **2** Bot. & Zool. of a brick-red colour. [L testaceus (as TEST[2])]

testament /'testəmənt/ n. **1** a will (esp. last will and testament). **2** (usu. foll. by to) evidence, proof (is testament to his loyalty). **3** Bibl. **a** a covenant or dispensation. **b** (**Testament**) a division of the Christian Bible (see Old Testament, New Testament). **c** (**Testament**) a copy of the New Testament. [ME f. L testamentum will (as TESTATE): in early Christian L testamentum rendering Gk diathēkē covenant]

testamentary /,testə'mentərɪ/ adj. of or by or in a will. [L testamentarius (as TESTAMENT)]

testate /'testeɪt/ adj. & n. —adj. having left a valid will at death. —n. a testate person. □□ **testacy** n. (pl. **-ies**). [L testatus past part. of testari testify, make a will, f. testis witness]

testator /te'steɪtə(r)/ n. (fem. **testatrix** /te'steɪtrɪks/) a person who has made a will, esp. one who dies testate. [ME f. AF testatour f. L testator (as TESTATE)]

tester[1] /'testə(r)/ n. **1** a person or thing that tests. **2** a sample of a cosmetic etc., allowing customers to try it before purchase.

tester[2] /'testə(r)/ n. a canopy, esp. over a four-poster bed. [ME f. med.L testerium, testrum, testura, ult. f. L testa tile]

testes pl. of TESTIS.

testicle /'testɪk(ə)l/ n. a male organ that produces spermatozoa etc., esp. one of a pair enclosed in the scrotum behind the penis of a man and most mammals. □□ **testicular** /-'stɪkjʊlə(r)/ adj. [ME f. L testiculus dimin. of testis witness (of virility)]

testiculate /te'stɪkjʊlət/ adj. **1** having or shaped like testicles. **2** Bot. (esp. of an orchid) having pairs of tubers so shaped. [LL testiculatus (as TESTICLE)]

testify /'testɪ,faɪ/ v. (**-ies**, **-ied**) **1** intr. (of a person or thing) bear witness (testified to the facts). **2** intr. Law give evidence. **3** tr. affirm or declare (testified his regret; testified that she had been present). **4** tr. (of a thing) be evidence of, evince. □□ **testifier** n. [ME f. L testificari f. testis witness]

testimonial /,testɪ'məʊnɪəl/ n. **1** a certificate of character, conduct, or qualifications. **2** a gift presented to a person (esp. in public) as a mark of esteem, in acknowledgement of services, etc. [ME f. OF testimoignal (adj.) f. tesmoin or LL testimonialis (as TESTIMONY)]

testimony /'testɪmənɪ/ n. (pl. **-ies**) **1** Law an oral or written statement under oath or affirmation. **2** declaration or statement of fact. **3** evidence, demonstration (called him in testimony; produce testimony). **4** Bibl. the Ten Commandments. **5** archaic a solemn protest or confession. [ME f. L testimonium f. testis witness]

testis /'testɪs/ n. (pl. **testes** /-tiːz/) Anat. & Zool. a testicle. [L, = witness: cf. TESTICLE]

testosterone /te'stɒstə,rəʊn/ n. a steroid androgen formed in the testicles. [TESTIS + STEROL + -ONE]

testudinal /te'stjuː,dɪn(ə)l/ adj. of or shaped like a tortoise. [as TESTUDO]

testudo /te'stjuː,dəʊ, te'stuː-/ n. (pl. **-os** or **testudines** /-dɪ,niːz/) Rom.Hist. **1** a screen formed by a body of troops in close array with overlapping shields. **2** a movable screen to protect besieging troops. [L testudo -dinis, lit. 'tortoise' (as TEST[2])]

testy /'testɪ/ adj. (**testier**, **testiest**) irritable, touchy. □□ **testily** adv. **testiness** n. [ME f. AF testif f. OF teste head (as TEST[2])]

tetanic /tɪ'tænɪk/ adj. of or such as occurs in tetanus. □□ **tetanically** adv. [L tetanicus f. Gk tetanikos (as TETANUS)]

tetanus /'tetənəs/ n. **1** a bacterial disease affecting the nervous system and marked by tonic spasm of the voluntary muscles. **2** Physiol. the prolonged contraction of a muscle caused by rapidly repeated stimuli. □□ **tetanize** v.tr. (also **-ise**). **tetanoid** adj. [ME f. L f. Gk tetanos muscular spasm f. teinō stretch]

tetany /'tetənɪ/ n. a disease with intermittent muscular spasms caused by malfunction of the parathyroid glands and a consequent deficiency of calcium. [F tétanie (as TETANUS)]

tetchy /ˈtetʃɪ/ adj. (also **techy**) (**-ier**, **-iest**) peevish, irritable. □□ **tetchily** adv. **tetchiness** n. [prob. f. tecche, tache blemish, fault f. OF teche, tache]

tête-à-tête /ˌteɪtɑːˈteɪt/ n., adv., & adj. —n. **1** a private conversation or interview usu. between two persons. **2** an S-shaped sofa for two people to sit face to face. —adv. together in private (dined tête-à-tête). —adj. **1** private, confidential. **2** concerning only two persons. [F, lit. 'head-to-head']

tête-bêche /teɪtˈbeʃ/ adj. (of a postage stamp) printed upside down or sideways relative to another. [F f. tête head + bêchevet double bed-head]

tether /ˈteðə(r)/ n. & v. —n. **1** a rope etc. by which an animal is tied to confine it to the spot. **2** the extent of one's knowledge, authority, etc.; scope, limit. —v.tr. tie (an animal) with a tether. □ **at the end of one's tether** having reached the limit of one's patience, resources, abilities, etc. [ME f. ON tjóthr f. Gmc]

Tétouan /teɪˈtwɑːn/ a city in northern Morocco, formerly the capital of Spanish Morocco; pop. (1982) 199,600.

tetra- /ˈtetrə/ comb. form (also **tetr-** before a vowel) **1** four (tetrapod). **2** Chem. (forming names of compounds) containing four atoms or groups of a specified kind (tetroxide). [Gk f. tettares four]

tetrachord /ˈtetrəkɔːd/ n. Mus. **1** a scale-pattern of four notes, the interval between the first and last being a perfect fourth. **2** a musical instrument with four strings.

tetracyclic /ˌtetrəˈsɪklɪk/ adj. **1** Bot. having four circles or whorls. **2** Chem. (of a compound) having a molecular structure of four fused hydrocarbon rings.

tetracycline /ˌtetrəˈsaɪkliːn/ n. an antibiotic with a molecule of four rings. [TETRACYCLIC + -INE⁴]

tetrad /ˈtetræd/ n. **1** a group of four. **2** the number four. [Gk tetras -ados (as TETRA-)]

tetradactyl /ˌtetrəˈdæktɪl/ n. Zool. an animal with four toes on each foot. □□ **tetradactylous** adj.

tetraethyl lead /ˌtetrəˈiːθaɪl/ n. a liquid added to petrol as an antiknock agent.

tetragon /ˈtetrəɡɒn/ n. a plane figure with four angles and four sides. [Gk tetragōnon quadrangle (as TETRA-, -GON)]

tetragonal /tɪˈtræɡən(ə)l/ adj. **1** of or like a tetragon. **2** Crystallog. (of a crystal) having three axes at right angles, two of them equal. □□ **tetragonally** adv.

tetragram /ˈtetrəɡræm/ n. a word of four letters.

Tetragrammaton /ˌtetrəˈɡræməˌtɒn/ n. the Hebrew name of God written in four letters, articulated as Yahweh etc. [Gk (as TETRA-, gramma, -atos letter)]

tetragynous /tɪˈtrædʒɪnəs/ adj. Bot. having four pistils.

tetrahedron /ˌtetrəˈhiːdrən, -ˈhedrən/ n. (pl. **tetrahedra** /-drə/ or **tetrahedrons**) a four-sided solid; a triangular pyramid. □□ **tetrahedral** adj. [late Gk tetraedron neut. of tetraedros four-sided (as TETRA-, -HEDRON)]

tetralogy /tɪˈtrælədʒɪ/ n. (pl. **-ies**) **1** a group of four related literary or operatic works. **2** Gk Antiq. a trilogy of tragedies with a satyric drama.

tetramerous /tɪˈtræmərəs/ adj. having four parts.

tetrameter /tɪˈtræmɪtə(r)/ n. Prosody a verse of four measures. [LL tetrametrus f. Gk tetrametros (as TETRA-, metron measure)]

tetrandrous /tɪˈtrændrəs/ adj. Bot. having four stamens.

tetraplegia /ˌtetrəˈpliːdʒɪə, -dʒə/ n. Med. = QUADRIPLEGIA. □□ **tetraplegic** adj. & n. [mod.L (as TETRA-, Gk plēgē blow, strike)]

tetraploid /ˈtetrəplɔɪd/ adj. & n. Biol. —adj. (of an organism or cell) having four times the haploid set of chromosomes. —n. a tetraploid organism or cell.

tetrapod /ˈtetrəpɒd/ n. **1** Zool. an animal with four feet. **2** a structure supported by four feet radiating from a centre. □□ **tetrapodous** /tɪˈtræpədəs/ adj. [mod.L tetrapodus f. Gk tetrapous (as TETRA-, pous podos foot)]

tetrapterous /tɪˈtræptərəs/ adj. Zool. having four wings. [mod.L tetrapterus f. Gk tetrapteros (as TETRA-, pteron wing)]

tetrarch /ˈtetrɑːk/ n. **1** Rom.Hist. **a** the governor of a fourth part of a country or province. **b** a subordinate ruler. **2** one of four joint rulers. □□ **tetrarchate** /-ˌkeɪt/ n. **tetrarchical** /-ˈrɑːkɪk(ə)l/ adj. **tetrarchy** n. (pl. **-ies**). [ME f. LL tetrarcha f. L tetrarches f. Gk tetrarkhēs (as TETRA-, arkhō rule)]

tetrastich /ˈtetrəstɪk/ n. Prosody a group of four lines of verse. [L tetrastichon f. Gk (as TETRA-, stikhon line)]

tetrastyle /ˈtetrəˌstaɪl/ n. & adj. —n. a building with four pillars esp. forming a portico in front or supporting a ceiling. —adj. (of a building) built in this way. [L tetrastylos f. Gk tetrastulos (as TETRA-, STYLE)]

tetrasyllable /ˈtetrəˌsɪləb(ə)l/ n. a word of four syllables. □□ **tetrasyllabic** /-ˈlæbɪk/ adj.

tetrathlon /teˈtræθlən/ n. a contest comprising four events, esp. riding, shooting, swimming, and running. [TETRA- + Gk athlon contest, after PENTATHLON]

tetratomic /ˌtetrəˈtɒmɪk/ adj. Chem. having four atoms (of a specified kind) in the molecule.

tetravalent /ˌtetrəˈveɪlənt/ adj. Chem. having a valency of four; quadrivalent.

tetrode /ˈtetrəʊd/ n. a thermionic valve having four electrodes. [TETRA- + Gk hodos way]

tetter /ˈtetə(r)/ n. archaic or dial. a pustular skin-eruption, e.g. eczema. [OE teter: cf. OHG zittaroh, G dial. Zitteroch, Skr. dadru]

Teut. abbr. Teutonic.

Teuto- /ˈtjuːtəʊ/ comb. form = TEUTON.

Teuton /ˈtjuːt(ə)n/ n. **1** a member of a Teutonic nation, esp. a German. **2** hist. a member of a N. European tribe mentioned in the 4th c. BC and combining with others to carry out raids on NE and southern France during the Roman period until heavily defeated in 102 BC. [L Teutones, Teutoni, f. an IE base meaning 'people' or 'country']

Teutonic /tjuːˈtɒnɪk/ adj. & n. —adj. **1** relating to or characteristic of the Germanic peoples or their languages. **2** German. —n. the early language usu. called Germanic. □□ **Teutonicism** /-ˌsɪz(ə)m/ n. [F teutonique f. L Teutonicus (as TEUTON)]

Teutonic Knights a military order of German Knights, originally enrolled c. 1191 as the Teutonic Knights of St Mary of Jerusalem, for service in the Holy Land. Their first seat was at Acre; after the fall of the Latin kingdom of Jerusalem they settled at Marienburg on the Vistula, and carried on a crusade against the neighbouring heathen nations of Prussia, Livonia, etc. Their conquests made them a great sovereign power, but from the 15th c. they rapidly declined and were abolished by Napoleon in 1809. The order was reestablished in Vienna as an honorary ecclesiastical institution in 1834 and maintains a titular existence.

Tex. abbr. Texas.

Texan /ˈteks(ə)n/ n. & adj. —n. a native of Texas in the US. —adj. of or relating to Texas.

Texas /ˈteksəs/ a State in the southern US, bordering on the Gulf of Mexico; pop. (est. 1985) 14,227,800; capital, Austin. The area was opened up by Spanish explorers (16th-17th c.) and formed part of Mexico until it became an independent republic in 1836 and the 28th State of the US in 1845.

text /tekst/ n. **1** the main body of a book as distinct from notes, appendices, pictures, etc. **2** the original words of an author or document, esp. as distinct from a paraphrase of or commentary on them. **3** a passage quoted from Scripture, esp. as the subject of a sermon. **4** a subject or theme. **5** (in pl.) books prescribed for study. **6** US a textbook. **7** (in full **text-hand**) a fine large kind of handwriting esp. for manuscripts. □ **text editor** Computing a system or program allowing the user to enter and edit text. **text processing** Computing the manipulation of text, esp. transforming it from one format to another. □□ **textless** adj. [ME f. ONF tixte, texte f. L textus tissue, literary style (in med.L = Gospel) f. L texere text- weave]

textbook /ˈtekstbʊk/ n. & adj. —n. a book for use in studying, esp. a standard account of a subject. —attrib.adj. **1** exemplary, accurate (cf. COPYBOOK). **2** instructively typical. □□ **textbookish** adj.

textile /ˈtekstaɪl/ n. & adj. —n. **1** any woven material. **2** any cloth. —adj. **1** of weaving or cloth (textile industry). **2** woven (*textile fabrics*). **3** suitable for weaving (*textile materials*). [L *textilis* (as TEXT)]

textual /'tekstjʊəl/ *adj.* of, in, or concerning a text (*textual errors*). □ **textual criticism** the process of attempting to ascertain the correct reading of a text. □□ **textually** *adv.* [ME f. med.L *textualis* (as TEXT)]

textualist /'tekstjʊəlɪst/ *n.* a person who adheres strictly to the letter of the text. □□ **textualism** *n.*

texture /'tekstʃə(r)/ *n.* & *v.* —*n.* **1** the feel or appearance of a surface or substance. **2** the arrangement of threads etc. in textile fabric. **3** the arrangement of small constituent parts. **4** *Art* the representation of the structure and detail of objects. **5** *Mus.* the quality of sound formed by combining parts. **6** the quality of a piece of writing, esp. with reference to imagery, alliteration, etc. **7** quality or style resulting from composition (*the texture of her life*). —*v.tr.* (usu. as **textured** *adj.*) provide with a texture. □□ **textural** *adj.* **texturally** *adv.* **textureless** *adj.* [ME f. L *textura* weaving (as TEXT)]

texturize /'tekstʃəraɪz/ *v.tr.* (also **-ise**) (usu. as **texturized** *adj.*) impart a particular texture to (fabrics or food).

TG *abbr.* transformational grammar.

TGV /,tiːdʒiː'viː/ *n.* a type of high-speed French passenger train. [F, abbr. of *train à grande vitesse*]

TGWU *abbr.* (in the UK) Transport and General Workers' Union.

Th *symb. Chem.* the element thorium.

Th. *abbr.* Thursday.

-th¹ /θ/ *suffix* (also **-eth** /ɪθ/) forming ordinal and fractional numbers from *four* onwards (*fourth*; *thirtieth*). [OE *-tha, -the, -otha, -othe*]

-th² /θ/ *suffix* forming nouns denoting an action or process: **1** from verbs (*birth*; *growth*). **2** from adjectives (*breadth*; *filth*; *length*). [OE *-thu, -tho, -th*]

-th³ var. of -ETH².

Thackeray /'θækərɪ/, William Makepeace (1811–63), English novelist, no cynic but a satirist, born in Calcutta and educated in England. After leaving Cambridge University (where he made friends with Tennyson and others) without a degree, he entered London literary society as a journalist and illustrator, publishing a variety of works in periodicals. The turning point of his career came with his masterpiece, *Vanity Fair* (1847–8; illustrated by the author), a vivid portrayal of early 19th-c. society, satirizing the pretentions of the upper-middle classes through its central character, the socially ambitious, unscrupulous, low-born Becky Sharp. He consolidated his success with *Pendennis* (1848–50), *The Newcomes* (1853–5), *Henry Esmond* (1852), a virtuoso historical novel set in the 18th c., and its sequel *The Virginians* (1857–9), and *The Rose and the Ring* (1855), one of his Christmas books. In 1860 he became the first editor of the *Cornhill Magazine* in which appeared many of his later novels.

Thai /taɪ/ *n.* & *adj.* —*n.* (*pl.* same or **Thais**) **1 a** a native or national of Thailand; a member of the largest ethnic group in Thailand. **b** a person of Thai descent. **2** the language of Thailand, a tonal language of the Sino-Tibetan language group, spoken by 35 million people. —*adj.* of or relating to Thailand or its people or language. [Thai, = free]

Thailand /'taɪlænd/ a country in SE Asia on the Gulf of Thailand, with Burma on its western border; pop. (est. 1988) 54,588,700; official language, Thai; capital, Bangkok. The country was known as Siam until 1939, when it changed its name to Thailand (lit. = 'land of the free'). Its early history is uncertain. For centuries Thais had filtered into the area and by the 13th c. had established a number of principalities in what is now Thailand and in adjacent regions. A powerful kingdom emerged in the 14th c. and engaged in a series of wars with its neighbour Burma before increasing exposure to European powers in the 19th c. resulted in the loss of territory in the east to France and in the south to Britain, though Thailand itself succeeded in retaining its independence. Politically unstable for much of the 20th c., Thailand was occupied by the Japanese in the Second World War, and supported the US in the Vietnam campaign; later it had border difficulties with Cambodia. The country is the world's largest exporter of rice, but mining and industry also play an important role in its economy. □ **Gulf of**

Thailand an inlet of the South China Sea between the Malay Peninsula and Thailand/Cambodia. □□ **Thailander** *n.*

thalamus /'θæləməs/ *n.* (*pl.* **thalami** /-ˌmaɪ/) **1** *Anat.* either of two masses of grey matter in the forebrain, serving as relay stations for sensory tracts. **2** *Bot.* the receptacle of a flower. **3** *Gk Antiq.* an inner room or women's apartment. □□ **thalamic** /θə'læmɪk, 'θæləmɪk/ *adj.* (in senses 1 and 2). [L f. Gk *thalamos*]

thalassic /θə'læsɪk/ *adj.* of the sea or seas, esp. small or inland seas. [F *thalassique* f. Gk *thalassa* sea]

thaler /'taːlə(r)/ *n. hist.* a German silver coin. [G T(h)*aler*: see DOLLAR]

Thales /'θeɪliːz/ (early 6th c. BC) Greek philosopher from Miletus in Ionia, universally accounted one of the Seven Sages. Aristotle held him to be the founder of physical science; he is also credited with the founding of geometry. Seeking a primary substance from which all things are derived, he identified this substance as water, and represented the earth as floating on an underlying ocean; his cosmology had Egyptian and Semitic affinities.

Thalia /θə'laɪə/ *Gk* & *Rom. Mythol.* the Muse of comedy. [Gk, = rich, plentiful]

thalidomide /θə'lɪdəˌmaɪd/ *n.* a drug formerly used as a sedative but found in 1961 to cause foetal malformation when taken by a mother early in pregnancy. □ **thalidomide baby** (or **child**) a baby or child born deformed from the effects of thalidomide. [ph*thalimidoglutarimide*]

thalli *pl.* of THALLUS.

thallium /'θælɪəm/ *n. Chem.* a rare soft white metallic element, occurring naturally in zinc blende and some iron ores, discovered spectroscopically by Sir William Crookes in 1861. Its compounds were formerly used as insecticides and rat poison and have some use in specialized optical and infrared equipment. ¶ Symb.: Tl; atomic number 81. □□ **thallic** *adj.* **thallous** *adj.* [formed as THALLUS, from the green line in its spectrum]

thallophyte /'θæləˌfaɪt/ *n. Bot.* a plant having a thallus, e.g. alga, fungus, or lichen. [mod.L *Thallophyta* (as THALLUS) + -PHYTE]

thallus /'θæləs/ *n.* (*pl.* **thalli** /-laɪ/) a plant-body without vascular tissue and not differentiated into root, stem, and leaves. □□ **thalloid** *adj.* [L f. Gk *thallos* green shoot f. *thallō* bloom]

thalweg /'taːlveg/ *n.* **1** *Geog.* a line where opposite slopes meet at the bottom of a valley, river, or lake. **2** *Law* a boundary between States along the centre of a river etc. [G f. *Thal* valley + *Weg* way]

Thames /temz/ a river of southern England, flowing eastwards 338 km (210 miles) from the Cotswolds in Gloucestershire through London to the North Sea. A flood barrier across the river to protect London from high tides was completed in 1982.

Thames Valley /temz/ **1** the region around the valley of the River Thames in southern England. **2** an administrative region on North Island, New Zealand; pop. (1986) 58,665; chief town, Thames.

than /ðən, ðæn/ *conj.* **1** introducing the second element in a comparison (*you are older than he is*; *you are older than he*). ¶ It is also possible to say *you are older than him*, with *than* treated as a preposition, esp. in less formal contexts. **2** introducing the second element in a statement of difference (*anyone other than me*). [OE *thanne* etc., orig. the same word as THEN]

thanage /'θeɪnɪdʒ/ *n. hist.* **1** the rank of thane. **2** the land granted to a thane. [ME f. AF *thanage* (as THANE)]

thanatology /,θænə'tɒlədʒɪ/ *n.* the scientific study of death and its associated phenomena and practices. [Gk *thanatos* death + -LOGY]

thane /θeɪn/ *n. hist.* **1** a man who held land from an English king or other superior by military service, ranking between ordinary freemen and hereditary nobles. **2** a man who held land from a Scottish king and ranked with an earl's son; the chief of a clan. □□ **thanedom** *n.* [OE *theg(e)n* servant, soldier f. Gmc]

thank /θæŋk/ *v.* & *n.* —*v.tr.* **1** express gratitude to (*thanked him for the present*). **2** hold responsible (*you can thank yourself for this*). —*n.* (in *pl.*) **1** gratitude (*expressed his heartfelt thanks*). **2** an expression of gratitude (*give thanks to Heaven*). **3** (as a formula) thank you (*thanks for your help*; *thanks very much*). □ **give thanks** say grace at a meal. **I will thank you** a polite formula, now usu. *iron.* implying reproach (*I will thank you to go away*). **no** (or **small**) **thanks to** despite. **thank goodness** (or **God** or **heavens** etc.) **1** *colloq.* an expression of relief or pleasure. **2** an expression of pious gratitude. **thank-offering** an offering made as an act of thanksgiving. **thanks to** as the (good or bad) result of (*thanks to my foresight; thanks to your obstinacy*). **thank you** a polite formula acknowledging a gift or service or an offer accepted or refused. **thank-you** *n. colloq.* an instance of expressing thanks. [OE *thancian, thanc* f. Gmc, rel. to THINK]

thankful /ˈθæŋkfʊl/ *adj.* **1** grateful, pleased. **2** (of words or acts) expressive of thanks. □□ **thankfulness** *n.* [OE *thancful* (as THANK, -FUL)]

thankfully /ˈθæŋkfʊlɪ/ *adv.* **1** in a thankful manner. **2** *disp.* let us be thankful; fortunately (*thankfully, nobody was hurt*). [OE *thancfullice* (as THANKFUL, -LY²)]

thankless /ˈθæŋklɪs/ *adj.* **1** not expressing or feeling gratitude. **2** (of a task etc.) giving no pleasure or profit. **3** not deserving thanks. □□ **thanklessly** *adv.* **thanklessness** *n.*

thanksgiving /ˈθæŋksˌgɪvɪŋ, -ˈgɪvɪŋ/ *n.* **1 a** the expression of gratitude, esp. to God. **b** a form of words for this. **2** (**Thanksgiving** or **Thanksgiving Day**) a national holiday for giving thanks to God, the fourth Thursday in November in the US, usu. the second Monday in October in Canada. A festival of this kind was first held by Plymouth Colony in 1621 in thankfulness for a successful harvest after a year of hardship. Turkey and pumpkin pie are traditionally eaten. □ **General Thanksgiving** a form of thanksgiving in the Book of Common Prayer or the Alternative Service Book.

thar var. of TAHR.

Thar Desert /tɑː(r)/ (also **Great Indian Desert**) a desert region to the east of the Indus River in the Rajasthan and Gujarat States of NW India and the Punjab and Sind regions of SE Pakistan.

that /ðæt/ *pron., adj., adv., & conj.* —*demons.pron.* (*pl.* **those** /ðəʊz/) **1** the person or thing indicated, named, or understood, esp. when observed by the speaker or when familiar to the person addressed (*I heard that; who is that in the garden?; I knew all that before; that is not fair*). **2** (contrasted with *this*) the further or less immediate or obvious etc. of two (*this bag is much heavier than that*). **3** the action, behaviour, or circumstances just observed or mentioned (*don't do that again*). **4** *Brit.* (on the telephone etc.) the person spoken to (*who is that?*). **5** *colloq.* referring to a strong feeling just mentioned ('*Are you glad?' 'I am that'*). **6** (esp. in relative constructions) the one, the person, etc., described or specified in some way (*those who have cars can take the luggage; those unfit for use; a table like that described above*). **7** /ðət/ (*pl.* **that**) used instead of *which* or *whom* to introduce a defining clause, esp. one essential to identification (*the book that you sent me; there is nothing here that matters*). ¶ As a relative *that* usually specifies, whereas *who* or *which* need not: compare *the book that you sent me is lost* with *the book, which I gave you, is lost.* —*demons.adj.* (*pl.* **those** /ðəʊz/) **1** designating the person or thing indicated, named, understood, etc. (cf. sense 1 of *pron.*) (*look at that dog; what was that noise?; things were easier in those days*). **2** contrasted with *this* (cf. sense 2 of *pron.*) (*this bag is heavier than that one*). **3** expressing strong feeling (*shall not easily forget that day*). —*adv.* **1** to such a degree; so (*have done that much; will go that far*). **2** *Brit. colloq.* very (*not that good*). **3** /ðət/ at which, on which, etc. (*at the speed that he was going he could not stop; the day that I first met her*). ¶ Often omitted in this sense: *the day I first met her.* —*conj.* /ðət/ except when stressed/ introducing a subordinate clause indicating: **1** a statement or hypothesis (*they say that he is better; there is no doubt that he meant it; the result was that the handle fell off*). **2** a purpose (*we live that we may eat*). **3** a result (*am so sleepy that I cannot keep my eyes open*). **4** a reason or clause (*it is rather that he lacks the time*). **5** a wish (*Oh, that summer were here!*). ¶ Often omitted in senses 1, 3: *they say he is better.* □ **all that** very (*not all that good*). **and all that** (or **and that** *colloq.*) and all or various things associated with or similar to what has been mentioned; and so forth. **like that 1** of that kind (*is fond of books like that*). **2** in that manner, as you are doing, as he has been doing, etc. (*wish they would not talk like that*). **3** *colloq.* without effort (*did the job like*

that). **4** of that character (*he would not accept any payment—he is like that*). **that is** (or **that is to say**) a formula introducing or following an explanation of a preceding word or words. **that's** *colloq.* you are (by virtue of present or future obedience etc.) (*that's a good boy*). **that's more like it** an acknowledgement of improvement. **that's right** an expression of approval or *colloq.* assent. **that's that** a formula concluding a narrative or discussion or indicating completion of a task. **that there** *sl.* = sense 1 of *adj.* **that will do** no more is needed or desirable. [OE *thæt*, nom. & acc. sing. neut. of demons. pron. & adj. *se, sẽo, thæt* f. Gmc; *those* f. OE *thãs* pl. of *thes* THIS]

thatch /θætʃ/ *n. & v.* —*n.* **1** a roof-covering of straw, reeds, palm-leaves, or similar material. **2** *colloq.* the hair of the head. —*v.tr.* (also *absol.*) cover (a roof or a building) with thatch. □□ **thatcher** *n.* [n. late collateral form of *thack* (now dial.) f. OE *thæc*, after v. f. OE *theccan* f. Gmc, assim. to *thack*]

Thatcher /ˈθætʃə(r)/, Margaret Hilda (1925–), British stateswoman, the first woman Prime Minister of the UK and the longest-serving British Prime Minister of the 20th c. Her period in office was marked by trade-union reform, greatly increased privatization, abolition of exchange controls, and heavy reduction of public spending, and she played an important role internationally. In 1982 military force was successfully used against an Argentine invasion of the Falkland Islands. Mrs Thatcher has been criticized for authoritarian management of government, and accused by her opponents of dividing society by not protecting the less able while allowing the able to prosper.

Thatcherism /ˈθætʃəˌrɪz(ə)m/ *n.* the political and economic policies advocated by Mrs Margaret Thatcher, especially as contrasted with those of earlier Conservative leaders. They include emphasis on individual responsibility and enterprise, in reaction to the collectivism and corporatism of previous decades. □□ **Thatcherite** *n.*

thaumatrope /ˈθɔːməˌtrəʊp/ *n. hist.* **1** a disc or card with two different pictures on its two sides, which combine into one by the persistence of visual impressions when the disc is rapidly rotated. **2** a zoetrope. [irreg. f. Gk *thauma* marvel + *-tropos* -turning]

thaumaturge /ˈθɔːməˌtɜːdʒ/ *n.* a worker of miracles; a wonder-worker. □□ **thaumaturgic** /-ˈtɜːdʒɪk/ *adj.* **thaumaturgical** /-ˈtɜːdʒɪk(ə)l/ *adj.* **thaumaturgist** *n.* **thaumaturgy** *n.* [med.L *thaumaturgus* f. Gk *thaumatourgos* (adj.) f. *thauma -matos* marvel + *-ergos* -working]

thaw /θɔː/ *v. & n.* —*v.* **1** *intr.* (often foll. by *out*) (of ice or snow or a frozen thing) pass into a liquid or unfrozen state. **2** *intr.* (usu. prec. by *it* as subject) (of the weather) become warm enough to melt ice etc. (*it began to thaw*). **3** *intr.* become warm enough to lose numbness etc. **4** *intr.* become less cold or stiff in manner; become genial. **5** *tr.* (often foll. by *out*) cause to thaw. **6** *tr.* make cordial or animated. —*n.* **1** the act or an instance of thawing. **2** the warmth of weather that thaws (*a thaw has set in*). **3** *Polit.* a relaxation of control or restriction. □□ **thawless** *adj.* [OE *thawian* f. WG; orig. unkn.]

the /before a vowel ðɪ, before a consonant ðə, when stressed ðiː/ *adj. & adv.* —*adj.* (called the definite article) **1** denoting one or more persons or things already mentioned, under discussion, implied, or familiar (*gave the man a wave; shall let the matter drop; hurt myself in the arm; went to the theatre*). **2** serving to describe as unique (*the Queen; the Thames*). **3 a** (foll. by defining adj.) which is, who are, etc. (*ignored the embarrassed Mr Smith; Edward the Seventh*). **b** (foll. by adj. used *absol.*) denoting a class described (*from the sublime to the ridiculous*). **4** best known or best entitled to the name (with the stressed: *no relation to the Kipling; this is the book on this subject*). **5** used to indicate a following defining clause or phrase (*the book that you borrowed; the best I can do for you; the bottom of a well*). **6 a** used to indicate that a singular noun represents a species, class, etc. (*the cat loves comfort; has the novel a future?; plays the harp well*). **b** used with a noun which figuratively represents an occupation, pursuit, etc. (*went on the stage; too fond of the bottle*). **c** (foll. by the name of a unit) a, per (*5p in the pound; £5 the square metre; allow 8 minutes to the mile*). **d** *colloq.* or archaic designating a disease, affliction, etc. (*the measles; the toothache; the blues*). **7** (foll. by a unit of time) the present, the current (*man of*

theandric

the moment; *questions of the day; book of the month*). **8** *Brit. colloq.* my, our (*the dog; the fridge*). **9** used before the surname of the chief of a Scottish or Irish clan (*the Macnab*). **10** *dial.* (esp. in Wales) used with a noun characterizing the occupation of the person whose name precedes (*Jones the Bread*). —*adv.* (preceding comparatives in expressions of proportional variation) in or by that (or such a) degree; on that account (*the more the merrier; the more he gets the more he wants*). □ **all the** in the full degree to be expected (*that makes it all the worse*). **so much the** (tautologically) so much, in that degree (*so much the worse for him*). [(adj.) OE, replacing *se, sēo, thæt* (= THAT), f. Gmc: (adv.) f. OE *thý, thē,* instrumental case]

theandric /θiːˈændrɪk/ *adj.* of the union, or by the joint agency, of the divine and human natures in Christ. [eccl.Gk *theandrikos* f. *theos* god + *anēr andros* man]

theanthropic /ˌθiːənˈθrɒpɪk/ *adj.* **1** both divine and human. **2** tending to embody deity in human form. [eccl.Gk *theanthrōpos* god-man f. *theos* god + *anthrōpos* human being]

thearchy /ˈθiːɑːkɪ/ *n.* (*pl.* **-ies**) **1** government by a god or gods. **2** a system or order of gods (*the Olympian thearchy*). [eccl.Gk *thearkhia* godhead f. *theos* god + *-arkhia* f. *arkhō* rule]

theatre /ˈθɪətə(r)/ *n.* (*US* **theater**) **1 a** a building or outdoor area for dramatic performances. **b** a cinema. **2 a** the writing and production of plays. **b** effective material for the stage (*makes good theatre*). **3** a room or hall for lectures etc. with seats in tiers. **4** *Brit.* an operating theatre. **5 a** a scene or field of action (*the theatre of war*). **b** (*attrib.*) designating weapons intermediate between tactical and strategic (*theatre nuclear missiles*). **6** a natural land-formation in a gradually rising part-circle like ancient Greek and Roman theatres. □ **theatre-goer** a frequenter of theatres. **theatre-going** frequenting theatres. **theatre-in-the-round** a form of play presentation in which the audience is seated all round the acting area. One of the earliest forms of theatre, it was probably used for open-air performances, street theatres, and such rustic sports as the May Day games and the mummers' play. It was revived in the 20th c.— beginning in the Soviet Union in the 1930s—by those who rebelled against the proscenium arch which they felt to be a barrier between actors and audience. **Theatre of the Absurd** the name given to the works of a group of dramatists, including Beckett, Ionesco, and Pinter, who share the belief that man's life is without meaning or purpose and that human beings cannot communicate. Such dramatists abandoned conventional dramatic form and coherent dialogue, the futility of existence being conveyed by illogical and meaningless speeches and ultimately by complete silence. The first and perhaps most characteristic play in this style was Beckett's *Waiting for Godot* (1952). **theatre sister** a nurse supervising the nursing team in an operating theatre. [ME f. OF *t(h)eatre* or f. L *theatrum* f. Gk *theatron* f. *theaomai* behold]

theatric /θɪˈætrɪk/ *adj. & n.* —*adj.* = THEATRICAL. —*n.* (in *pl.*) theatrical actions.

theatrical /θɪˈætrɪk(ə)l/ *adj. & n.* —*adj.* **1** of or for the theatre; of acting or actors. **2** (of a manner, speech, gesture, or person) calculated for effect; showy, artificial, affected. —*n.* (in *pl.*) **1** dramatic performances (*amateur theatricals*). **2** theatrical actions. □□ **theatricalism** *n.* **theatricality** /-ˈkælɪtɪ/ *n.* **theatricalize** *v.tr.* (also **-ise**). **theatricalization** /-laɪˈzeɪʃ(ə)n/ *n.* **theatrically** *adv.* [LL *theatricus* f. Gk *theatrikos* f. *theatron* THEATRE]

Thebes /θiːbz/ **1** the Greek name for a city of Upper Egypt, about 675 km (420 miles) south of modern Cairo, that was the capital of ancient Egypt under the 18th Dynasty (*c.*1550–1290 BC). Its monuments (on both banks of the Nile) were the richest in the land, with the town and major temples at Luxor and Karnak on the east bank, and the necropolis, with tombs of royalty and nobles, on the west bank. It was already a tourist attraction in the 2nd c. AD. **2** a city of Greece, in Boeotia, about 74 km (46 miles) NW of Athens, leader of the whole of Greece for a short period after the defeat of the Spartans at the battle of Leuctra in 371 BC. □□ **Theban** *adj. & n.*

theca /ˈθiːkə/ *n.* (*pl.* **thecae** /-siː/) **1** *Bot.* a part of a plant serving as a receptacle. **2** *Zool.* a case or sheath enclosing an organ or organism. □□ **thecate** *adj.* [L f. Gk *thēkē* case]

thé dansant /ˌteɪ dɑ̃ˈsɑ̃/ *n.* = *tea dance.* [F]

thee /ðiː/ *pron.* objective case of THOU¹. [OE]

theft /θeft/ *n.* **1** the act or an instance of stealing. **2** *Law* dishonest appropriation of another's property with intent to deprive him or her of it permanently. [OE *thīefth, thēofth,* later *thēoft,* f. Gmc (as THIEF)]

thegn /θeɪn/ *n. hist.* an English thane. [OE: see THANE]

theine /ˈθiːɪn, ˈθiːiːn/ *n.* = CAFFEINE. [mod.L *thea* tea + -INE⁴]

their /ðeə(r)/ *poss.pron.* (*attrib.*) **1** of or belonging to them or themselves (*their house; their own business*). **2** (**Their**) (in titles) that they are (*Their Majesties*). **3** *disp.* as a third person sing. indefinite meaning 'his or her' (*has anyone lost their purse?*). [ME f. ON *their(r)a* of them, genit. pl. of *sá* THE, THAT]

theirs /ðeəz/ *poss.pron.* the one or ones belonging to or associated with them (*it is theirs; theirs are over here*). □ **of theirs** of or belonging to them (*a friend of theirs*). [ME f. THEIR]

theism /ˈθiːɪz(ə)m/ *n.* belief in the existence of gods or a god, esp. a God supernaturally revealed to man (cf. DEISM) and sustaining a personal relation to his creatures. □□ **theist** *n.* **theistic** /-ˈɪstɪk/ **theistical** /-ˈɪstɪk(ə)l/ *adj.* **theistically** /-ˈɪstɪkəlɪ/ *adv.* [Gk *theos* god + -ISM]

them /ð(ə)m, or, when stressed, ðem/ *pron. & adj.* —*pron.* **1** objective case of THEY (*I saw them*). **2** *colloq.* they (*it's them again; is older than them*). **3** *archaic* themselves (*they fell and hurt them*). —*adj. sl.* or *dial.* those (*them bones*). [ME *theim* f. ON: see THEY]

thematic /θɪˈmætɪk/ *adj.* **1** of or relating to subjects or topics (*thematic philately; the arrangement of the anthology is thematic*). **2** *Mus.* of melodic subjects (*thematic treatment*). **3** *Gram.* **a** of or belonging to a theme (*thematic vowel; thematic form*). **b** (of a form of a verb) having a thematic vowel. □ **thematic catalogue** *Mus.* a catalogue giving the opening themes of works as well as their names and other details. □□ **thematically** *adv.* [Gk *thematikos* (as THEME)]

theme /θiːm/ *n.* **1** a subject or topic on which a person speaks, writes, or thinks. **2** *Mus.* a prominent or frequently recurring melody or group of notes in a composition. **3** *US* a school exercise, esp. an essay, on a given subject. **4** *Gram.* the stem of a noun or verb; the part to which inflections are added, esp. composed of the root and an added vowel. **5** *hist.* any of the 29 provinces in the Byzantine empire. □ **theme park** an amusement park organized round a unifying idea. **theme song** (or **tune**) **1** a recurrent melody in a musical play or film. **2** a signature tune. [ME *teme* ult. f. Gk *thema -matos* f. *tithēmi* set, place]

Themis /ˈθemɪs/ *Gk Mythol.* a goddess originally akin to or even identical with Gaia (Earth). Her name probably means 'steadfast'. In Hesiod she is a daughter of Earth and is Zeus's second consort, but, as her name is used also to mean 'firmly established custom or law, justice', she tends to become an abstraction, Justice or Righteousness.

Themistocles /θɪˈmɪstəˌkliːz/ (*c.*528–462 BC) Athenian democratic statesman who was instrumental in building up the Athenian fleet in the 480s BC, and as a general in 480 BC was responsible for the defeat of the Persian fleet at Salamis. In the following years he lost influence to his conservative opponents, and was ostracized; eventually he fled from Greece to the Persians in Asia Minor, where he died.

themselves /ðəmˈselvz/ *pron.* **1 a** *emphat. form* of THEY or THEM. **b** *refl. form* of THEM; (cf. HERSELF). **2** in their normal state of body or mind (*are quite themselves again*). □ **be themselves** act in their normal, unconstrained manner.

then /ðen/ *adv., adj., & n.* —*adv.* **1** at that time; at the time in question (*was then too busy; then comes the trouble; the then existing laws*). **2 a** next, afterwards; after that (*then he told me to come in*). **b** and also (*then, there are the children to consider*). **3 a** in that case; therefore; it follows that (*then you should have said so*). **b** if what you say is true (*but then why did you take it?*). **c** (implying grudging or impatient concession) if you must have it so (*all right then, have it your own way*). **d** used parenthetically to resume a narrative etc. (*the policeman, then, knocked on the door*). —*adj.* that or who was such at the time in question (*the then Duke*). —*n.* that time (*until*

æ cat ɑː arm e bed ɜː her ɪ sit iː see ɒ hot ɔː saw ʌ run ʊ put uː too ə ago aɪ my

then). □ **then and there** immediately and on the spot. [OE *thanne, thonne,* etc., f. Gmc, rel. to THAT, THE]

thenar /ˈθiːnə(r)/ *n. Anat.* the ball of muscle at the base of the thumb. [earlier = palm of the hand: mod.L f. Gk]

thence /ðens/ *adv.* (also **from thence**) *archaic* or *literary* **1** from that place or source. **2** for that reason. [ME *thannes, thennes* f. *thanne, thenne* f. OE *thanon(e)* etc. f. WG]

thenceforth /ðensˈfɔːθ/ *adv.* (also **from thenceforth**) *archaic* or *literary* from that time onward.

thenceforward /ðensˈfɔːwəd/ *adv. archaic* or *literary* thenceforth.

theo- /ˈθiːəʊ/ *comb. form* God or gods. [Gk f. *theos* god]

theobromine /θiəˈbrəʊmɪn, -miːn/ *n.* a bitter white alkaloid obtained from cacao seeds, related to caffeine. [*Theobroma* cacao genus: mod.L f. Gk *theos* god + *brōma* food, + -INE⁴]

theocentric /θiəˈsentrɪk/ *adj.* having God as its centre.

theocracy /θiˈɒkrəsɪ/ *n.* (*pl.* **-ies**) **1** a form of government by God or a god directly or through a priestly order etc. **2** (**the Theocracy**) the Jewish commonwealth from Moses to the monarchy. □□ **theocrat** /ˈθiːəˌkræt/ *n.* **theocratic** /θiəˈkrætɪk/ *adj.* **theocratically** /θiəˈkrætɪkəlɪ/ *adv.*

theocrasy /ˈθiːəˌkreɪsɪ, θiˈɒkrəsɪ/ *n.* **1** the mingling of deities into one personality. **2** the union of the soul with God through contemplation (among Neoplatonists etc.). [THEO- + Gk *krasis* mingling]

Theocritus /θiˈɒkrɪtəs/ (*c*.300–*c*.260 BC) Hellenistic poet originally from Syracuse, who subsequently wrote in Cos and Alexandria. His poems, known under the title *Idylls,* include hymns, short epic narratives, and dramatic mimes, but he is most famous for the bucolic idylls, hexameter poems in dramatic form presenting the song-contests and love-songs of imaginary shepherds; these poems were immensely influential as the model of Virgil's *Eclogues* and of all subsequent pastoral poetry.

theodicy /θiˈɒdɪsɪ/ *n.* (*pl.* **-ies**) **1** the vindication of divine providence in view of the existence of evil. **2** an instance of this. □□ **theodicean** /-ˈsiːən/ *adj.* [THEO- + Gk *dikē* justice]

theodolite /θiˈɒdəˌlaɪt/ *n.* a surveying-instrument for measuring horizontal and vertical angles with a rotating telescope. □□ **theodolitic** /-ˈlɪtɪk/ *adj.* [16th c. *theodelitus,* of unkn. orig.]

Theodora /ˌθiːəˈdɔːrə/ (*c*.500–48), Byzantine empress, wife of Justinian. Although she is reputed to have lived a very dissolute life in her earlier years, she was undoubtedly a woman of outstanding intellect and learning, and exercised a very considerable influence upon political affairs and the complicated theological questions of the time. Her portrait in mosaic can be seen in the church of San Vitale at Ravenna.

Theodoric /θiˈɒdərɪk/ 'the Great' (*c*.454–526), king of the Ostrogoths from 474, who invaded Italy in 488 and completed its conquest in 493, establishing a kingdom with its capital at Ravenna. At its greatest extent his empire included not only the Italian mainland, but Sicily, Dalmatia, and parts of Germany.

Theodosius I /ˌθiːəˈdəʊsɪəs/ 'the Great' (*c*.346–395), eastern Roman emperor 379–95. War with the Goths was ended by treaty in 382; subsequently he successfully defeated two usurpers, Magnus Maximus and Eugenius, to the western throne, on which he installed his son Honorius. A pious Christian and rigid upholder of Nicene orthodoxy, in 391 he banned all forms of pagan cult, probably under the influence of St Ambrose.

theogony /θiˈɒgənɪ/ *n.* (*pl.* **-ies**) **1** the genealogy of the gods. **2** an account of this. [THEO- + Gk *-gonia* begetting]

theologian /θiəˈləʊdʒɪən, -dʒ(ə)n/ *n.* a person trained in theology. [ME f. OF *theologien* (as THEOLOGY)]

theological /θiəˈlɒdʒɪk(ə)l/ *adj.* of theology. □ **theological virtues** faith, hope, and charity. □□ **theologically** *adv.* [med.L *theologicalis* f. L *theologicus* f. Gk *theologikos* (as THEOLOGY)]

theology /θiˈɒlədʒɪ/ *n.* (*pl.* **-ies**) **1 a** the study of theistic (esp. Christian) religion. **b** a system of theistic (esp. Christian) religion. **c** the rational analysis of a religious faith. **2** a system of theoretical principles, esp. an impractical or rigid ideology.

□□ **theologist** *n.* **theologize** *v.tr.* & *intr.* (also **-ise**). [ME f. OF *theologie* f. L *theologia* f. Gk (as THEO-, -LOGY)]

theomachy /θiˈɒməkɪ/ *n.* (*pl.* **-ies**) strife among or against the gods. [THEO- + Gk *makhē* fight]

theophany /θiˈɒfənɪ/ *n.* (*pl.* **-ies**) a visible manifestation of God or a god to man.

theophoric /θiəˈfɒrɪk/ *adj.* bearing the name of a god.

Theophrastus /ˌθiəˈfræstəs/ (*c*.370–288/5 BC) Greek philosopher and scientist, the pupil and successor of Aristotle, whose method and researches he continued, with a particular emphasis on empirical observation. His few surviving works include treatises on botany and other scientific subjects, and the *Characters,* a collection of sketches of psychological types, which in post-classical times was the most influential of his works.

theophylline /θiəˈfɪlɪn, -liːn/ *n.* an alkaloid similar to theobromine, found in tea-leaves. [irreg. f. mod.L *thea* tea + Gk *phullon* leaf + -INE⁴]

theorbo /θiˈɔːbəʊ/ *n.* (*pl.* **-os**) a two-necked musical instrument of the lute class much used in the seventeenth c. □□ **theorbist** *n.* [It. *tiorba,* of unkn. orig.]

theorem /ˈθiərəm/ *n.* esp. *Math.* **1** a general proposition not self-evident but proved by a chain of reasoning; a truth established by means of accepted truths (cf. PROBLEM). **2** a rule in algebra etc., esp. one expressed by symbols or formulae (*binomial theorem*). □□ **theorematic** /-ˈmætɪk/ *adj.* [F *théorème* or LL *theorema* f. Gk *theōrēma* speculation, proposition f. *theōreō* look at]

theoretic /θiəˈretɪk/ *adj.* & *n.* —*adj.* = THEORETICAL. —*n.* (in *sing.* or *pl.*) the theoretical part of a science etc. [LL *theoreticus* f. Gk *theōrētikos* (as THEORY)]

theoretical /θiəˈretɪk(ə)l/ *adj.* **1** concerned with knowledge but not with its practical application. **2** based on theory rather than experience or practice. □□ **theoretically** *adv.*

theoretician /ˌθiərɪˈtɪʃ(ə)n/ *n.* a person concerned with the theoretical aspects of a subject.

theorist /ˈθiərɪst/ *n.* a holder or inventor of a theory or theories.

theorize /ˈθiəraɪz/ *v.intr.* (also **-ise**) evolve or indulge in theories. □□ **theorizer** *n.*

theory /ˈθiərɪ/ *n.* (*pl.* **-ies**) **1** a supposition or system of ideas explaining something, esp. one based on general principles independent of the particular things to be explained (opp. HYPOTHESIS) (*atomic theory; theory of evolution*). **2** a speculative (esp. fanciful) view (*one of my pet theories*). **3** the sphere of abstract knowledge or speculative thought (*this is all very well in theory, but how will it work in practice?*). **4** the exposition of the principles of a science etc. (*the theory of music*). **5** *Math.* a collection of propositions to illustrate the principles of a subject (*probability theory; theory of equations*). [LL *theoria* f. Gk *theōria* f. *theōros* spectator f. *theōreō* look at]

theosophy /θiˈɒsəfɪ/ *n.* (*pl.* **-ies**) any of various philosophies professing to achieve a knowledge of God by spiritual ecstasy, direct intuition, or special individual relations, esp. a modern movement professing Hindu and Buddhist teachings and seeking universal brotherhood. It was founded as the Theosophical Society by the Russian adventuress H. P. Blavatsky and Col. H. S. Olcott, teaching the transmigration of souls, the brotherhood of man irrespective of race or creed, and complicated systems of psychology and cosmology, and denying a personal god. □□ **theosopher** *n.* **theosophic** /θiəˈsɒfɪk/ *adj.* **theosophical** /θiəˈsɒfɪk(ə)l/ *adj.* **theosophically** /θiəˈsɒfɪkəlɪ/ *adv.* **theosophist** *n.* [med.L *theosophia* f. late Gk *theosophia* f. *theosophos* wise concerning God (as THEO-, *sophos* wise)]

Thera see SANTORINI.

therapeutic /ˌθerəˈpjuːtɪk/ *adj.* **1** of, for, or contributing to the cure of disease. **2** contributing to general, esp. mental, well-being (*finds walking therapeutic*). □□ **therapeutical** *adj.* **therapeutically** *adv.* **therapeutist** *n.* [attrib. use of *therapeutic,* orig. form of THERAPEUTICS]

therapeutics /ˌθerəˈpjuːtɪks/ *n.pl.* (usu. treated as *sing.*) the branch of medicine concerned with the treatment of disease and the action of remedial agents. [F *thérapeutique* or LL *thera-*

peutica (pl.) f. Gk therapeutika neut. pl. of therapeutikos f. therapeuō wait on, cure]

therapy /ˈθerəpɪ/ n. (pl. **-ies**) **1** the treatment of physical or mental disorders, other than by surgery. **2** a particular type of such treatment. □□ **therapist** n. [mod.L therapia f. Gk therapeia healing]

Theravada /ˌθerəˈvɑːdə/ n. the only surviving ancient school of Buddhism (see HINAYANA). It is practised today in Sri Lanka, Burma, Thailand, Cambodia, and Laos. [Pali theravāda f. thera elder, old + vāda speech, doctrine]

there /ðeə(r)/ adv., n., & int. —adv. **1** in, at, or to that place or position (lived there for some years; goes there every day). **2** at that point (in speech, performance, writing, etc.) (there he stopped). **3** in that respect (I agree with you there). **4** used for emphasis in calling attention (you there!; there goes the bell). **5** used to indicate the fact or existence of something (there is a house on the corner). —n. that place (lives somewhere near there). —int. **1** expressing confirmation, triumph, dismay, etc. (there! what did I tell you?). **2** used to soothe a child etc. (there, there, never mind). □ **have been there before** sl. know all about it. **so there** colloq. that is my final decision (whether you like it or not). **there and then** immediately and on the spot. **there it is 1** that is the trouble. **2** nothing can be done about it. **there's** colloq. you are (by virtue of present or future obedience etc.) (there's a dear). **there you are** (or **go**) colloq. **1** this is what you wanted etc. **2** expressing confirmation, triumph, resignation, etc. [OE thǣr, thēr f. Gmc, rel. to THAT, THE]

thereabouts /ˈðeərəˌbaʊts, -ˈbaʊts/ adv. (also **thereabout**) **1** near that place (ought to be somewhere thereabouts). **2** near that number, quantity, etc. (two litres or thereabouts).

thereafter /ðeərˈɑːftə(r)/ adv. formal after that.

thereanent /ˌðeərəˈnent/ adv. Sc. about that matter.

thereat /ðeərˈæt/ adv. archaic **1** at that place. **2** on that account. **3** after that.

thereby /ðeəˈbaɪ, ˈðeə-/ adv. by that means, as a result of that. □ **thereby hangs a tale** much could be said about that.

therefor /ðeəˈfɔː(r)/ adv. archaic for that object or purpose.

therefore /ˈðeəfɔː(r)/ adv. for that reason; accordingly, consequently.

therefrom /ðeəˈfrɒm/ adv. archaic from that or it.

therein /ðeərˈɪn/ adv. formal **1** in that place etc. **2** in that respect.

thereinafter /ˌðeərɪnˈɑːftə(r)/ adv. formal later in the same document etc.

thereinbefore /ðeərɪnbɪˈfɔː(r)/ adv. formal earlier in the same document etc.

thereinto /ðeərˈɪntʊ/ adv. archaic into that place.

thereof /ðeərˈɒv/ adv. formal of that or it.

thereon /ðeərˈɒn/ adv. archaic on that or it (of motion or position).

thereout /ðeərˈaʊt/ adv. archaic out of that, from that source.

therethrough /ðeəˈθruː/ adv. archaic through that.

thereto /ðeəˈtuː/ adv. formal **1** to that or it. **2** in addition, to boot.

theretofore /ðeətʊˈfɔː(r)/ adv. formal before that time.

thereunto /ðeərˈʌntʊ/ adv. archaic to that or it.

thereupon /ˌðeərəˈpɒn/ adv. **1** in consequence of that. **2** soon or immediately after that. **3** archaic upon that (of motion or position).

therewith /ðeəˈwɪð/ adv. archaic **1** with that. **2** soon or immediately after that.

therewithal /ˌðeəwɪˈðɔːl/ adv. archaic in addition, besides.

theriac /ˈθɪərɪˌæk/ n. archaic an antidote to the bites of poisonous animals, esp. snakes. [L theriaca f. Gk thēriakē antidote, fem. of thēriakos f. thēr wild beast]

therianthropic /ˌθɪərɪænˈθrɒpɪk/ adj. of or worshipping beings represented in combined human and animal forms. [Gk thērion dimin. of thēr wild beast + anthrōpos human being]

theriomorphic /ˌθɪərɪəˈmɔːfɪk/ adj. (esp. of a deity) having an animal form. [as THERIANTHROPIC + Gk morphē form]

therm /θɜːm/ n. a unit of heat, esp. as the statutory unit of gas supplied in the UK equivalent to 100,000 British thermal units or 1.055×10^8 joules. [Gk thermē heat]

thermae /ˈθɜːmiː/ n.pl. Gk & Rom. Antiq. public baths. [L f. Gk thermai (pl.) (as THERM)]

thermal /ˈθɜːm(ə)l/ adj. & n. —adj. **1** of, for, or producing heat. **2** promoting the retention of heat (thermal underwear). —n. a rising current of heated air (used by gliders, balloons, and birds to gain height). □ **British thermal unit** the amount of heat needed to raise 1 lb. of water at maximum density through one degree Fahrenheit, equivalent to 1.055×10^3 joules. **thermal capacity** the number of heat units needed to raise the temperature of a body by one degree. **thermal neutron** a neutron in thermal equilibrium with its surroundings. **thermal reactor** a nuclear reactor using thermal neutrons. **thermal springs** springs of naturally hot water. **thermal unit** a unit for measuring heat. □□ **thermalize** v.tr. & intr. (also **-ise**). **thermalization** /-laɪˈzeɪʃ(ə)n/ n. **thermally** adv. [F (as THERM)]

thermic /ˈθɜːmɪk/ adj. of or relating to heat.

thermidor see LOBSTER.

thermion /ˈθɜːmɪˌɒn/ n. an ion or electron emitted by a substance at high temperature. [THERMO- + ION]

thermionic /ˌθɜːmɪˈɒnɪk/ adj. of or relating to electrons emitted from a substance at very high temperature. □ **thermionic emission** the emission of electrons from a heated source. **thermionic valve** (US **tube**) a device consisting of a sealed tube containing two or more electrodes, one of which is heated to produce a flow of electrons in one direction. The diode valve (which has two electrodes) functions as a rectifier and was so used by the English scientist, Sir John Ambrose Fleming, in 1904. The triode valve (with two electrodes and a grid) was invented in 1906 by an American engineer Lee de Forest and functioned as an amplifier—a weak signal received in the grid produced a stronger signal in the anode circuit. Before the development of semiconductor devices such as transistors (which have now largely replaced it) the thermionic tube was used in all electronic equipment such as radio, radar, and computers.

thermionics /ˌθɜːmɪˈɒnɪks/ n.pl. (treated as sing.) the branch of science and technology concerned with thermionic emission.

thermistor /θɜːˈmɪstə(r)/ n. Electr. a resistor whose resistance is greatly reduced by heating, used for measurement and control. [thermal resistor]

thermite /ˈθɜːmaɪt/ n. (also **thermit** /-mɪt/) a mixture of finely powdered aluminium and iron oxide that produces a very high temperature on combustion (used in welding and for incendiary bombs). [G Thermit (as THERMO-, -ITE¹)]

thermo- /ˈθɜːməʊ/ comb. form denoting heat. [Gk f. thermos hot, thermē heat]

thermochemistry /ˌθɜːməʊˈkemɪstrɪ/ n. the branch of chemistry dealing with the quantities of heat evolved or absorbed during chemical reactions. □□ **thermochemical** adj.

thermocouple /ˈθɜːməʊˌkʌp(ə)l/ n. a pair of different metals in contact at a point, generating a thermoelectric voltage that can serve as a measure of temperature at this point relative to their other parts.

thermodynamics /ˌθɜːməʊdaɪˈnæmɪks/ n.pl. (usu. treated as sing.) the science of the relations between heat and other (mechanical, electrical, etc.) forms of energy, and, by extension, of the relationships and interconvertibility of all forms of energy. (See below.) □□ **thermodynamic** adj. **thermodynamical** adj. **thermodynamically** adv. **thermodynamicist** /-sɪst/ n.

Thermodynamics deals with the place of energy in any material system: the forms it takes, its distribution, and the changes liable to take place in the system if the energy distribution is 'unbalanced'. The principles of thermodynamics can therefore be regarded as governing the direction of all physical changes taking place in the universe. Most material systems consist of large numbers of particles (atoms and molecules). Thermodynamics states that, with time, the energy in such a system will inevitably tend to become distributed in the most probable pattern, which consists of all the individual particles of the system engaging in random motion. We perceive such random motion as heat. Other types of change in a system, such as the intermingling of two different types of particles, also lead to greater randomness or disorder. It appears, in fact, that the universe is gradually 'running down' because this randomness or entropy (see ENTROPY) is continually increasing. The historical development of thermodynamics is complicated; it arose from consideration of the efficiency of steam engines in the early 19th c. (especially by Sadi Carnot), and its main laws were introduced in the 1850s without explicit reference to the random motion of individual particles. The first law states that heat is indeed a form of energy (not a special 'fluid' as had once been thought), and then reaffirms the law of conservation of energy. The second law deals with the tendency of entropy to increase, as described above. Although most, if not all, physical changes are nominally governed by the laws of thermodynamics, many everyday processes of change can be adequately described in terms of ordinary mechanics. Among areas in which the principles and methods of thermodynamics are of great practical importance are the study and design of engines, and the rules governing the direction of chemical and biochemical reactions.

thermoelectric /ˌθɜːməʊɪˈlektrɪk/ adj. producing electricity by a difference of temperatures. □□ **thermoelectrically** adv. **thermoelectricity** /-ˌɪlekˈtrɪsɪtɪ/ n.

thermogenesis /ˌθɜːməʊˈdʒenɪsɪs/ n. the production of heat, esp. in a human or animal body.

thermogram /ˈθɜːməˌɡræm/ n. a record made by a thermograph.

thermograph /ˈθɜːməˌɡrɑːf/ n. **1** an instrument that gives a continuous record of temperature. **2** an apparatus used to obtain an image produced by infrared radiation from a human or animal body. □□ **thermographic** /-ˈɡræfɪk/ adj.

thermography /θɜːˈmɒɡrəfɪ/ n. Med. the taking or use of infrared thermograms, esp. to detect tumours.

thermolabile /ˌθɜːməʊˈleɪbaɪl, -bɪl/ adj. (of a substance) unstable when heated.

thermoluminescence /ˌθɜːməʊˌluːmɪˈnes(ə)ns/ n. the property of becoming luminescent when pretreated and subjected to high temperatures, used as a means of dating ancient artefacts. □□ **thermoluminescent** adj.

thermolysis /θɜːˈmɒlɪsɪs/ n. decomposition by the action of heat. □□ **thermolytic** /-ˈlɪtɪk/ adj.

thermometer /θəˈmɒmɪtə(r)/ n. an instrument for measuring temperature by means of a substance whose expansion and contraction under different degrees of heat and cold are capable of accurate measurement. The earliest form was an air-thermometer invented and used by Galileo before 1597 for indicating the temperature of the atmosphere; alcohol thermometers were used c.1650. The device of a fixed zero (originally the freezing-point) was introduced by Hooke, 1665; the fixing of the zero as an arbitrary point below the freezing-point is attributed to Fahrenheit, who made mercurial thermometers c.1720; many other famous figures have contributed to the design of graduated scales. The most familiar type of thermometer consists of a slender hermetically sealed glass tube with a fine bore, having a bulb at the lower end filled with mercury, which rises as a conspicuous column in the tube (which is graduated) on expansion. □□ **thermometric** /ˌθɜːməˈmetrɪk/ adj. **thermometrical** /ˌθɜːməˈmetrɪk(ə)l/ adj. **thermometry** n. [F *thermomètre* or mod.L *thermometrum* (as THERMO-, -METER)]

thermonuclear /ˌθɜːməʊˈnjuːklɪə(r)/ adj. **1** relating to or using nuclear reactions that occur only at very high temperatures. **2** relating to or characterized by weapons using thermonuclear reactions.

thermophile /ˈθɜːməʊˌfaɪl/ n. & adj. (also **thermophil** /-fɪl/) —n. a bacterium etc. growing optimally at high temperatures. —adj. of or being a thermophile. □□ **thermophilic** /-ˈfɪlɪk/ adj.

thermopile /ˈθɜːməʊˌpaɪl/ n. a set of thermocouples esp. arranged for measuring small quantities of radiant heat.

thermoplastic /ˌθɜːməʊˈplæstɪk/ adj. & n. —adj. (of a substance) that becomes plastic on heating and hardens on cooling,

and is able to repeat these processes. —n. a thermoplastic substance.

Thermopylae /θəˈmɒpɪˌliː/ a pass in Greece, about 200 km (120 miles) NW of Athens, originally narrow but now much widened by the recession of the sea. It was the scene of the heroic defence (480 BC) against the Persian army of Xerxes by 6,000 Greeks including 300 Spartans under their commander Leonidas. The defenders were outflanked then, and by the Gauls in 279 BC, and by Cato in 191 BC.

Thermos /ˈθɜːmɒs/ n. (in full **Thermos flask**) propr. a vacuum flask. [Gk (as THERMO-)]

thermosetting /ˌθɜːməʊˈsetɪŋ/ adj. (of plastics) setting permanently when heated. □□ **thermoset** /ˈθɜː-/ adj.

thermosphere /ˈθɜːməˌsfɪə(r)/ n. the region of the atmosphere between the mesopause and the height at which it ceases to have the properties of a continuous medium, characterized throughout by an increase in temperature with height.

thermostable /ˌθɜːməʊˈsteɪb(ə)l/ adj. (of a substance) stable when heated.

thermostat /ˈθɜːməˌstæt/ n. a device that automatically regulates temperature, or that activates a device when the temperature reaches a certain point. □□ **thermostatic** /-ˈstætɪk/ adj. **thermostatically** /-ˈstætɪkəlɪ/ adv. [THERMO- + Gk *statos* standing]

thermotaxis /ˌθɜːməʊˈtæksɪs/ n. **1** the regulation of heat or temperature esp. in warm-blooded animals. **2** movement or stimulation in a living organism caused by heat. □□ **thermotactic** adj. **thermotaxic** adj.

thermotropism /θɜːˈmɒtrəˌpɪz(ə)m/ n. the growing or bending of a plant towards or away from a source of heat. □□ **thermotropic** /ˌθɜːməʊˈtrɒpɪk/ adj.

thesaurus /θɪˈsɔːrəs/ n. (pl. **thesauri** /-raɪ/ or **thesauruses**) **1 a** a collection of concepts or words arranged according to sense. **b** US a book of synonyms and antonyms. **2** a dictionary or encyclopedia. [L f. Gk *thēsauros* treasure]

these pl. of THIS.

Theseus /ˈθiːsjəs/ Gk legend the son of Poseidon (or of Aegeus, king of Athens) and national hero of Athens. He slew the Cretan Minotaur with the help of Ariadne and was successful in numerous other exploits.

thesis /ˈθiːsɪs/ n. (pl. **theses** /-siːz/) **1** a proposition to be maintained or proved. **2** a dissertation, esp. by a candidate for a degree. **3** /ˈθiːsɪs, ˈθesɪs/ an unstressed syllable or part of a metrical foot in Greek or Latin verse (opp. ARSIS). [ME f. LL f. Gk, = putting, placing, a proposition etc. f. *the-* root of *tithēmi* place]

Thespian /ˈθespɪən/ adj. & n. —adj. of or relating to tragedy or drama. —n. an actor or actress. [THESPIS]

Thespis /ˈθespɪs/ (6th c. BC) Greek dramatic poet, regarded as the father of Greek tragedy.

Thess. abbr. Thessalonians (New Testament).

Thessalonian /ˌθesəˈləʊnɪən/ adj. & n. —adj. of ancient Thessalonica (modern Salonica), a city in NE Greece. —n. a native of ancient Thessalonica. □ **(Epistle to the) Thessalonians** either of two books of the New Testament, the earliest letters of St Paul, written from Corinth to the new Church at Thessalonica.

Thessalonica, Thessaloniki see SALONICA.

Thessaly /ˈθesəlɪ/ a region of NE Greece; pop. (1981) 695,650. □□ **Thessalian** /θeˈseɪlɪən/ adj. & n.

theta /ˈθiːtə/ n. the eighth letter of the Greek alphabet (Θ, θ). [Gk]

Thetis /ˈθetɪs/ Gk Mythol. a sea-nymph, mother of Achilles.

theurgy /ˈθiːɜːdʒɪ/ n. **1 a** a supernatural or divine agency esp. in human affairs. **b** the art of securing this. **2** the magical science of the Neoplatonists. □□ **theurgic** /-ˈɜːdʒɪk/ adj. **theurgical** /-ˈɜːdʒɪk(ə)l/ adj. **theurgist** n. [LL *theurgia* f. Gk *theourgia* f. *theos* god + *-ergos* working]

thew /θjuː/ n. (often in pl.) literary **1** muscular strength. **2** mental or moral vigour. [OE *thēaw* usage, conduct, of unkn. orig.]

they /ðeɪ/ pron. (obj. **them**; poss. **their, theirs**) **1** the people, animals, or things previously named or in question (pl. of HE, SHE, IT[1]). **2** people in general (*they say we are wrong*). **3** those in authority (*they have raised the fees*). **4** disp. as a third person sing.

---

w we   z zoo   ʃ she   ʒ decision   θ thin   ð this   ŋ ring   x loch   tʃ chip   dʒ jar   (see over for vowels)

indefinite pronoun meaning 'he or she' (*anyone can come if they want to*). [ME *thei*, obj. *theim*, f. ON *their* nom. pl. masc., *theim* dat. pl. of *sá* THE that]

they'd /ðeɪd/ *contr.* **1** they had. **2** they would.

they'll /ðeɪl, ðel/ *contr.* **1** they will. **2** they shall.

they're /ðe(r), ˈðeɪə(r)/ *contr.* they are.

they've /ðeɪv/ *contr.* they have.

THI *abbr.* temperature-humidity index.

thiamine /ˈθaɪəmɪn, -ˌmiːn/ *n.* (also **thiamin**) a vitamin of the B complex, found in unrefined cereals, beans, and liver, a deficiency of which causes beriberi. Also called *vitamin B₁*, or ANEURIN. [THIO- + *amin* from VITAMIN]

thick /θɪk/ *adj., n.,* & *adv.* —*adj.* **1 a** of great or specified extent between opposite surfaces (*a thick wall; a wall two metres thick*). **b** of large diameter (*a thick rope*). **2 a** (of a line etc.) broad; not fine. **b** (of script or type, etc.) consisting of thick lines. **3 a** arranged closely; crowded together; dense. **b** numerous (*fell thick as peas*). **4** (usu. foll. by *with*) densely covered or filled (*air thick with snow*). **5 a** firm in consistency; containing much solid matter; viscous (*a thick paste; thick soup*). **b** made of thick material (*a thick coat*). **6** muddy, cloudy; impenetrable by sight (*thick darkness*). **7** *colloq.* (of a person) stupid, dull. **8** (of a voice) indistinct. **9** *colloq.* intimate or very friendly (esp. *thick as thieves*). —*n.* a thick part of anything. —*adv.* thickly (*snow was falling thick; blows rained down thick and fast*). □ **a bit thick** *Brit. colloq.* unreasonable or intolerable. **in the thick of 1** at the busiest part of. **2** heavily occupied with. **thick ear** *Brit. sl.* the external ear swollen as a result of a blow (esp. *give a person a thick ear*). **thick-skinned** not sensitive to reproach or criticism. **thick-skulled** (or **-witted**) stupid, dull; slow to learn. **through thick and thin** under all conditions; in spite of all difficulties. □□ **thickish** *adj.* **thickly** *adv.* [OE *thicce* (adj. & adv.) f. Gmc]

thicken /ˈθɪkən/ *v.* **1** *tr.* & *intr.* make or become thick or thicker. **2** *intr.* become more complicated (*the plot thickens*). □□ **thickener** *n.*

thickening /ˈθɪkənɪŋ/ *n.* **1** the process of becoming thick or thicker. **2** a substance used to thicken liquid. **3** a thickened part.

thicket /ˈθɪkɪt/ *n.* a tangle of shrubs or trees. [OE *thiccet* (as THICK, -ET¹)]

thickhead /ˈθɪkhed/ *n.* **1** *colloq.* a stupid person; a blockhead. **2** *Austral.* any bird of the genus *Pachycephala*; a whistler. □□ **thickheaded** /-ˈhedɪd/ *adj.* **thickheadedness** /-ˈhedɪdnɪs/ *n.*

thickness /ˈθɪknɪs/ *n.* **1** the state of being thick. **2** the extent to which a thing is thick. **3** a layer of material of a certain thickness (*three thicknesses of cardboard*). **4** a part that is thick or lies between opposite surfaces (*steps cut in the thickness of the wall*). [OE *thicnes* (as THICK, -NESS)]

thickset /θɪkˈset/ *adj.* & *n.* —*adj.* **1** heavily or solidly built. **2** set or growing close together. —*n.* a thicket.

thief /θiːf/ *n.* (*pl.* **thieves** /θiːvz/) a person who steals esp. secretly and without violence. [OE *thēof* f. Gmc]

thieve /θiːv/ *v.* **1** *intr.* be a thief. **2** *tr.* steal (a thing). [OE *thēofian* (as THIEF)]

thievery /ˈθiːvəri/ *n.* the act or practice of stealing.

thieves *pl.* of THIEF.

thievish /ˈθiːvɪʃ/ *adj.* given to stealing. □□ **thievishly** *adv.* **thievishness** *n.*

thigh /θaɪ/ *n.* **1** the part of the human leg between the hip and the knee. **2** a corresponding part in other animals. □ **thigh-bone** = FEMUR. □□ **-thighed** *adj.* (in *comb.*). [OE *thēh, thēoh, thīoh,* OHG *dioh,* ON *thjó* f. Gmc]

thill /θɪl/ *n.* a shaft of a cart or carriage, esp. one of a pair. [ME: orig. unkn.]

thill-horse /ˈθɪlhɔːs/ *n.* (also **thiller** /ˈθɪlə(r)/) a horse put between thills.

thimble /ˈθɪmb(ə)l/ *n.* **1** a metal or plastic cap, usu. with a closed end, worn to protect the finger and push the needle in sewing. **2** *Mech.* a short metal tube or ferrule etc. **3** *Naut.* a metal ring concave on the outside and fitting in a loop of spliced rope to prevent chafing. [OE *thȳmel* (as THUMB, -LE¹)]

thimbleful /ˈθɪmb(ə)lˌfʊl/ *n.* (*pl.* **-fuls**) a small quantity, esp. of liquid to drink.

thimblerig /ˈθɪmb(ə)lrɪg/ *n.* a game often involving sleight of hand, in which three inverted thimbles or cups are moved about, contestants having to spot which is the one with a pea or other object beneath. □□ **thimblerigger** *n.* [THIMBLE + RIG² in sense 'trick, dodge']

Thimphu /ˈtɪmpuː/ the capital of Bhutan; pop. (1987) 15,000.

thin /θɪn/ *adj., adv.,* & *v.* —*adj.* (**thinner, thinnest**) **1** having the opposite surfaces close together; of small thickness or diameter. **2 a** (of a line) narrow or fine. **b** (of a script or type etc.) consisting of thin lines. **3** made of thin material (*a thin dress*). **4** lean; not plump. **5 a** not dense or copious (*thin hair; a thin haze*). **b** not full or closely packed (*a thin audience*). **6** of slight consistency (*a thin paste*). **7** weak; lacking an important ingredient (*thin blood; a thin voice*). **8** (of an excuse, argument, disguise, etc.) flimsy or transparent. —*adv.* thinly (*cut the bread very thin*). —*v.* (**thinned, thinning**) **1** *tr.* & *intr.* make or become thin or thinner. **2** *tr.* & *intr.* (often foll. by *out*) reduce; make or become less dense or crowded or numerous. **3** *tr.* (often foll. by *out*) remove some of a crop of (seedlings, saplings, etc.) or some young fruit from (a vine or tree) to improve the growth of the rest. □ **have a thin time** *colloq.* have a wretched or uncomfortable time. **on thin ice** see ICE. **thin air** a state of invisibility or non-existence (*vanished into thin air*). **thin end of the wedge** see WEDGE¹. **thin on the ground** see GROUND¹. **thin on top** balding. **thin-skinned** sensitive to reproach or criticism; easily upset. □□ **thinly** *adv.* **thinness** *n.* **thinnish** *adj.* [OE *thynne* f. Gmc]

thine /ðaɪn/ *poss.pron. archaic* or *dial.* **1** (*predic.* or *absol.*) of or belonging to thee. **2** (*attrib.* before a vowel) = THY. [OE *thīn* f. Gmc]

thing /θɪŋ/ *n.* **1** a material or non-material entity, idea, action, etc., that is or may be thought about or perceived. **2** an inanimate material object (*take that thing away*). **3** an unspecified object or item (*have a few things to buy*). **4** an act, idea, or utterance (*a silly thing to do*). **5** an event (*an unfortunate thing to happen*). **6** a quality (*patience is a useful thing*). **7** (with ref. to a person) expressing pity, contempt, or affection (*poor thing!; a dear old thing*). **8** a specimen or type of something (*the latest thing in hats*). **9** *colloq.* one's special interest or concern (*not my thing at all*). **10** *colloq.* something remarkable (*now there's a thing!*). **11** (prec. by *the*) *colloq.* **a** what is conventionally proper or fashionable. **b** what is needed or required (*your suggestion was just the thing*). **c** what is to be considered (*the thing is, shall we go or not?*). **d** what is important (*the thing about them is their reliability*). **12** (in *pl.*) personal belongings or clothing (*where have I left my things?*). **13** (in *pl.*) equipment (*painting things*). **14** (in *pl.*) affairs in general (*not in the nature of things*). **15** (in *pl.*) circumstances or conditions (*things look good*). **16** (in *pl.* with a following adjective) all that is so describable (*all things Greek*). **17** (in *pl.*) *Law* property. □ **do one's own thing** *colloq.* pursue one's own interests or inclinations. **do things to** *colloq.* affect remarkably. **have a thing about** *colloq.* be obsessed or prejudiced about. **make a thing of** *colloq.* **1** regard as essential. **2** cause a fuss about. **one** (or **just one**) **of these things** *colloq.* something unavoidable or to be accepted. [OE f. Gmc]

thingummy /ˈθɪŋəmi/ *n.* (*pl.* **-ies**) (also **thingamy**, **thingumabob** /-məˌbɒb/, **thingumajig** /-məˌdʒɪg/) *colloq.* a person or thing whose name one has forgotten or does not know or does not wish to mention. [THING + meaningless suffix]

thingy /ˈθɪŋi/ *n.* (*pl.* **-ies**) = THINGUMMY.

think /θɪŋk/ *v.* & *n.* —*v.* (*past* and *past part.* **thought** /θɔːt/) **1** *tr.* (foll. by *that* + clause) be of the opinion (*we think that they will come*). **2** *tr.* (foll. by *that* + clause or *to* + infin.) judge or consider (*is thought to be a fraud*). **3** *intr.* exercise the mind with one's ideas etc. (*let me think for a moment*). **4** *tr.* (foll. by *of* or *about*) **a** consider; be or become mentally aware of (*think of you constantly*). **b** form or entertain the idea of; imagine to oneself (*couldn't think of such a thing*). **c** choose mentally; hit upon (*think of a number*). **5** *tr.* have a half-formed intention (*I think I'll stay*). **6** *tr.* form a conception of (*cannot think how you do it*). **7** *tr.* reduce to a specified condition by thinking (*cannot think away a toothache*). **8** *tr.* recognize the presence or existence of (*the child thought no harm*). **9** *tr.* (foll. by *to* + infin.) intend or expect (*thinks to deceive*

æ cat ɑː arm e bed ɜː her ɪ sit iː see ɒ hot ɔː saw ʌ run ʊ put uː too ə ago aɪ my

us). **10** *tr.* (foll. by *to* + infin.) remember (*did not think to lock the door*). —*n. colloq.* an act of thinking (*must have a think about that*). □ **think again** revise one's plans or opinions. **think aloud** utter one's thoughts as soon as they occur. **think back to** recall (a past event or time). **think better of** change one's mind about (an intention) after reconsideration. **think big** see BIG. **think fit** see FIT¹. **think for oneself** have an independent mind or attitude. **think little** (or **nothing**) **of** consider to be insignificant or unremarkable. **think much** (or **highly**) **of** have a high opinion of. **think on** (or **upon**) *archaic* think of or about. **think out 1** consider carefully. **2** produce (an idea etc.) by thinking. **think over** reflect upon in order to reach a decision. **think through** reflect fully upon (a problem etc.). **think twice** use careful consideration, avoid hasty action, etc. **think up** *colloq.* devise; produce by thought. □□ **thinkable** *adj.* [OE *thencan thōhte gethōht* f. Gmc]

thinker /ˈθɪŋkə(r)/ *n.* **1** a person who thinks, esp. in a specified way (*an original thinker*). **2** a person with a skilled or powerful mind.

thinking /ˈθɪŋkɪŋ/ *adj. & n.* —*adj.* using thought or rational judgement. —*n.* **1** opinion or judgement. **2** (in *pl.*) thoughts; courses of thought. □ **put on one's thinking cap** *colloq.* meditate on a problem.

think-tank /ˈθɪŋktæŋk/ *n.* a body of experts providing advice and ideas on specific national and commercial problems.

thinner /ˈθɪnə(r)/ *n.* a volatile liquid used to dilute paint etc.

thio- /ˈθaɪəʊ/ *comb. form* sulphur, esp. replacing oxygen in compounds (*thio-acid*). [Gk *theion* sulphur]

thiol /ˈθaɪɒl/ *n. Chem.* any organic compound containing an alcohol-like group but with sulphur in place of oxygen. [THIO- + -OL¹]

thiosulphate /ˌθaɪəʊˈsʌlfeɪt/ *n.* a sulphate in which one oxygen atom is replaced by sulphur.

thiourea /ˌθaɪəʊˈjʊərɪə/ *n.* a crystalline compound used in photography and the manufacture of synthetic resins.

Thira see SANTORINI.

third /θɜːd/ *n. & adj.* —*n.* **1** the position in a sequence corresponding to that of the number 3 in the sequence 1–3. **2** something occupying this position. **3** each of three equal parts of a thing. **4** = **third gear**. **5** *Mus.* **a** an interval or chord spanning three consecutive notes in the diatonic scale (e.g. C to E). **b** a note separated from another by this interval. **6 a** a place in the third class in an examination. **b** a person having this. —*adj.* that is the third. □ **third-best** *adj.* of third quality. —*n.* a thing in this category. **third class** the third-best group or category, esp. of hotel and train accommodation. **third-class** *adj.* **1** belonging to or travelling by the third class. **2** of lower quality; inferior. —*adv.* by the third class (*travels third-class*). **third degree** long and severe questioning esp. by police to obtain information or a confession. **third-degree** *Med.* denoting burns of the most severe kind, affecting lower layers of tissue. **third eye 1** *Hinduism & Buddhism* the 'eye of insight' in the forehead of an image of a deity, esp. the god Siva. **2** the faculty of intuitive insight. **third force** a political group or party acting as a check on conflict between two opposing parties. **third gear** the third (and often next to highest) in a sequence of gears. **third man** *Cricket* **1** a fielder positioned near the boundary behind the slips. **2** this position. **third part** each of three equal parts into which a thing is or might be divided. **third party 1** another party besides the two principals. **2** a bystander etc. **third-party** *adj.* (of insurance) covering damage or injury suffered by a person other than the insured. **third person 1** = **third party**. **2** *Gram.* see PERSON. **third-rate** inferior; very poor in quality. **third reading** a third presentation of a bill to a legislative assembly, in the UK to debate committee reports and in the US to consider it for the last time. **Third Reich** see REICH. **Third World** (usu. prec. by *the*) the developing countries of Asia, Africa, and Latin America (orig. countries considered as not politically aligned with Communist or Western nations). □□ **thirdly** *adv.* [OE *third(d)a, thridda* f. Gmc]

thirst /θɜːst/ *n. & v.* —*n.* **1** a physical need to drink liquid, or the feeling of discomfort caused by this. **2** a strong desire or

craving (*a thirst for power*). —*v.intr.* (often foll. by *for* or *after*) **1** feel thirst. **2** have a strong desire. [OE *thurst, thyrstan* f. WG]

thirsty /ˈθɜːstɪ/ *adj.* (**thirstier, thirstiest**) **1** feeling thirst. **2** (of land, a season, etc.) dry or parched. **3** (often foll. by *for* or *after*) eager. **4** *colloq.* causing thirst (*thirsty work*). □□ **thirstily** *adv.* **thirstiness** *n.* [OE *thurstig, thyrstig* (as THIRST, -Y¹)]

thirteen /θɜːˈtiːn, ˈθɜː-/ *n. & adj.* —*n.* **1** one more than twelve, or three more than ten. **2** a symbol for this (13, xiii, XIII). **3** a size etc. denoted by thirteen. —*adj.* that amount to thirteen. □□ **thirteenth** *adj. & n.* [OE *thrēotīene* (as THREE, -TEEN)]

thirty /ˈθɜːtɪ/ *n. & adj.* —*n.* (*pl.* **-ies**) **1** the product of three and ten. **2** a symbol for this (30, xxx, XXX). **3** (in *pl.*) the numbers from 30 to 39, esp. the years of a century or of a person's life. —*adj.* that amount to thirty. □ **thirty-first, -second**, etc. the ordinal numbers between thirtieth and fortieth. **thirty-one, -two**, etc. the cardinal numbers between thirty and forty. **thirty-second note** esp. *US Mus.* = DEMISEMIQUAVER. **thirty-two-mo** a book with 32 leaves to the printing-sheet. □□ **thirtieth** *adj. & n.* **thirtyfold** *adj. & adv.* [OE *thrītig* (as THREE, -TY²)]

Thirty-nine Articles the set of points of doctrine finally adopted by the Church of England (1571) as a statement of its dogmatic position. Many, perhaps intentionally, allow a wide variety of interpretation. Since 1865 clergy have been asked to give a general assent to them; previously a more particular subscription was demanded.

Thirty Years War a prolonged European war of the 17th c. Beginning as a struggle between the Catholic Holy Roman Emperor and some of his German Protestant States, the war gradually drew in most of the major European military powers and developed into a fight for continental hegemony with France, Sweden, Spain, and the Empire as the major protagonists. The result of three decades of intermittent hostilities was the emergence of Bourbon France as the pre-eminent European power and the devastation of much of Germany, where military activity had remained centred throughout.

this /ðɪs/ *pron., adj., & adv.* —*demons.pron.* (*pl.* **these** /ðiːz/) **1** the person or thing close at hand or indicated or already named or understood (*can you see this?; this is my cousin*). **2** (contrasted with *that*) the person or thing nearer to hand or more immediately in mind. **3** the action, behaviour, or circumstances under consideration (*this won't do at all; what do you think of this?*). **4** (on the telephone): **a** *Brit.* the person speaking. **b** *US* the person spoken to. —*demons.adj.* (*pl.* **these** /ðiːz/) **1** designating the person or thing close at hand etc. (cf. senses 1, 2 of *pron.*). **2** (of time): **a** the present or current (*am busy all this week*). **b** relating to today (*this morning*). **c** just past or to come (*have been asking for it these three weeks*). **3** *colloq.* (in narrative) designating a person or thing previously unspecified (*then up came this policeman*). —*adv.* to this degree or extent (*knew him when he was this high; did not reach this far*). □ **this and that** *colloq.* various unspecified examples of things (esp. trivial). **this here** *sl.* this particular (person or thing). **this much** the amount or extent about to be stated (*I know this much, that he was not there*). **this world** mortal life. [OE, neut. of *thes*]

Thisbe /ˈθɪsbɪ/ *Rom. legend* lover of Pyramus (see entry).

thistle /ˈθɪs(ə)l/ *n.* **1** any of various prickly composite herbaceous plants of the genus *Cirsium, Carlina*, or *Carduus* etc., usu. with globular heads of purple flowers. **2** a figure of this as the heraldic emblem of Scotland, and part of the insignia of the distinctively Scottish order of knighthood, the **Order of the Thistle**, instituted in 1687 by James II and revived in 1703 by Queen Anne. [OE *thistel* f. Gmc]

thistledown /ˈθɪs(ə)l,daʊn/ *n.* a light fluffy stuff attached to thistle-seeds and blown about in the wind.

thistly /ˈθɪslɪ/ *adj.* overgrown with thistles.

thither /ˈðɪðə(r)/ *adv. archaic* or *formal* to or towards that place. [OE *thider*, alt. (after HITHER) of *thæder*]

thixotropy /θɪkˈsɒtrəpɪ/ *n.* the property of becoming temporarily liquid when shaken or stirred etc., and returning to a gel on standing. □□ **thixotropic** /ˌθɪksəˈtrɒpɪk/ *adj.* [Gk *thixis* touching + *tropē* turning]

tho' var. of THOUGH.

thole[1] /θəʊl/ n. (in full **thole-pin**) **1** a pin in the gunwale of a boat as the fulcrum for an oar. **2** each of two such pins forming a rowlock. [OE *thol* fir-tree, peg]

thole[2] /θəʊl/ v.tr. *Sc.* or *archaic* **1** undergo or suffer (pain, grief, etc.). **2** permit or admit of. [OE *tholian* f. Gmc]

tholos /ˈθɒlɒs/ n. (pl. **tholoi** /-lɔɪ/) *Gk Antiq.* a dome-shaped tomb, esp. of the Mycenaean period. [Gk]

Thomas[1] /ˈtɒməs/, Dylan Marlais (1914–53), Welsh-born poet. He moved to London in 1934 and embarked on a career of journalism, broadcasting, and film-making. Thomas's romantic, affirmative, rhetorical style was new and influential and much imitated by his contemporaries. He won recognition with *Deaths and Entrances* (1946), which contains some of his best-known poems, and continued his success with *Collected Poems 1934–1952* (1952), *Portrait of the Artist as a Young Dog* (1955; prose and verse), and *Adventures in the Skin Trade* (1955; stories). Shortly before his death in New York, hastened by wild living and hard drinking, he read his most famous single work, *Under Milk Wood*, a radio drama in which the poetic alliterative prose is interspersed with songs and ballads.

Thomas[2] /ˈtɒməs/, (Philip) Edward (1878–1917), English poet, who produced much biographical and topographical prose before turning to poetry with the encouragement of the American poet Robert Frost. His work combines a loving and accurate observation of the English pastoral scene with colloquial speech-rhythms. He was killed at Arras on active service; most of his poems appeared posthumously.

Thomas[3] /ˈtɒməs/, St, an Apostle, who refused to believe that Christ had risen again unless he could see and touch his wounds (John 20; 24–9). Feast day, 21 Dec. □ **doubting Thomas** a sceptic.

Thomas à Kempis /ˈtɒməs ə ˈkempɪs/ (c.1380–1471) German ascetical writer. Born Thomas Hemerken at Kempen, near Cologne, he became an Augustinian canon in Holland. He is the probable author of the *Imitation of Christ*, an important manual of spiritual devotion.

Thomas Aquinas see AQUINAS.

Thomism /ˈtəʊmɪz(ə)m/ n. the doctrine of Thomas Aquinas or of his followers. □□ **Thomist** n. **Thomistic** /-ˈmɪstɪk/ adj. **Thomistical** /-ˈmɪstɪk(ə)l/ adj.

Thompson[1] /ˈtɒms(ə)n/, Daley (1958–   ), English athlete, winner of the decathlon in the Olympic Games of 1980 and 1984.

Thompson[2] /ˈtɒms(ə)n/, Francis (1859–1907), English poet, rescued from destitution by Alice and Wilfred Meynell who secured him literary recognition. His finest work, which conveys intense religious experience in imagery of great power, includes the poems 'The Hound of Heaven' and 'The Kingdom of God'. He published three volumes of verse (1893–7) and much literary criticism in periodicals. Opium addiction together with tuberculosis caused his early death.

Thomson[1] /ˈtɒms(ə)n/, James (1700–48), Scottish poet. He came to London in 1725, where he met Arbuthnot, Gay, and Pope, found patrons, and through the influence of Lord Lyttelton received a sinecure. *The Seasons* (1726–30), one of the most popular English poems, both in style and subject inaugurated a new era by its sentiment for nature; the text was adapted for Haydn's oratorio (1801). His other works include his patriotic poem *Liberty* (1735–6), the tragedies *Sophonisba* (1730) and *Tancred and Sigismunda* (1745), the masque *Alfred* (1740), containing 'Rule, Britannia', and *The Castle of Indolence* (1748), which contains a portrait of the poet which mocks his notorious love of idleness.

Thomson[2] /ˈtɒms(ə)n/, James (1834–82), Scottish poet, whose most famous poem is 'The City of Dreadful Night' (1874), a powerful evocation of a half-ruined city, through which flows the River of the Suicides, where the narrator encounters tormented shades wandering in a Dantesque version of a living hell, presided over by Melancolia.

Thomson[3] /ˈtɒms(ə)n/, Sir Joseph John (1856–1940), English physicist, discoverer of the electron. During his tenure as Cavendish professor of physics at Cambridge from 1884 until 1918 he consolidated the worldwide reputation of the Cavendish Laboratory; seven of his former pupils were to win Nobel Prizes. His own experiments of the bending of cathode rays in magnetic and electric fields began in 1897. He deduced from these deflexions that he was dealing with particles smaller than the atom, which he initially called 'corpuscles' but later 'electrons', adopting the word coined a few years previously by the physicist G. J. Stoney. His model of the atom, incorporating the negatively-charged electron for the first time, was abandoned in favour of Rutherford's more satisfactory model in 1911. Thomson received the 1906 Nobel Prize for physics for his researches into the electrical conductivity of gases and was knighted in 1908. His son Sir George Paget Thomson (1892–1975), also a physicist, shared the 1937 Nobel Prize with Clinton Davisson for his discovery of the effect of electron diffraction.

thong /θɒŋ/ n. & v. —n. **1** a narrow strip of hide or leather used as the lash of a whip, as a halter or rein, etc. **2** *Austral., NZ, & US* = FLIP-FLOP. —v.tr. **1** provide with a thong. **2** strike with a thong. [OE *thwang, thwong* f. Gmc]

Thor /θɔː(r)/ *Scand. Mythol.* the god of thunder, the weather, agriculture, and the home. He is represented as armed with a hammer. Thursday is named after him.

thorax /ˈθɔːræks/ n. (pl. **thoraces** /ˈθɔːrəˌsiːz/ or **thoraxes**) **1** *Anat. & Zool.* the part of the trunk between the neck and the abdomen. **2** *Gk Antiq.* a breastplate or cuirass. □□ **thoracal** /ˈθɔːrək(ə)l/ adj. **thoracic** /θɔːˈræsɪk/ adj. [L f. Gk *thōrax -akos*]

Thoreau /ˈθɔːrəʊ/, Henry David (1817–62), American writer, best known for his book *Walden, or Life in the Woods* (1854), an account of his two-year experiment in self-sufficiency (1845–7), when he built himself a wooden hut on the edge of Walden Pond near his native Concord in Massachusetts. He describes his domestic economy, neighbours, plants and wild life, and sense of the Indian past, and questions the materialism and the prevailing work ethnic of the age; he has been hailed as a pioneer ecologist. Equally influential in future years was his essay on civil disobedience (1849), in which he argues the right of the individual to refuse to pay taxes when conscience dictates; his technique of passive resistance was adopted by Gandhi.

thoria /ˈθɔːrɪə/ n. the oxide of thorium.

thorium /ˈθɔːrɪəm/ n. *Chem.* a radioactive metallic element, first discovered in 1828. Thorium became economically important after 1885 when its oxide, which can become brightly incandescent, began to be widely used in gas mantles. Thorium's radioactive properties were discovered in 1898. The major isotope found in nature has a very long half-life and is thought, along with uranium and radioactive potassium, to be responsible for most of the heat generated inside the earth. Nowadays thorium has a variety of industrial uses and is of increasing importance as a nuclear fuel. ¶ Symb.: **Th**; atomic number 90. [*Thor*, Scand. god of thunder]

thorn /θɔːn/ n. **1** a stiff sharp-pointed projection on a plant. **2** a thorn-bearing shrub or tree. **3** the name of an Old English and Icelandic runic letter, = th. □ **on thorns** continuously uneasy esp. in fear of being detected. **thorn-apple 1** a poisonous plant of the nightshade family, *Datura stramonium*. **2** the prickly fruit of this. **a thorn in one's flesh** (or **side**) a constant annoyance. □□ **thornless** adj. **thornproof** adj. [OE f. Gmc]

thornback /ˈθɔːnbæk/ n. a ray, *Raja clavata*, with spines on the back and tail.

thornbill /ˈθɔːnbɪl/ n. **1** any Australian warbler of the genus *Acanthiza*. **2** any of various South American humming-birds, esp. of the genus *Chalcostigma*.

Thorndike /ˈθɔːndaɪk/, Dame (Agnes) Sybil (1882–1976), English actress, who played a wide range of Shakespearean roles in England and in the US, and gave one of her finest performances in the title role of the first London production of G. B. Shaw's *St Joan* (1924).

thorntail /ˈθɔːnteɪl/ n. any S. American humming-bird of the genus *Popelairia*.

thorny /ˈθɔːnɪ/ adj. (**thornier, thorniest**) **1** having many thorns. **2** (of a subject) hard to handle without offence; problematic. □□ **thornily** adv. **thorniness** n.

b but   d dog   f few   g get   h he   j yes   k cat   l leg   m man   n no   p pen   r red   s sit   t top   v voice

thorough /ˈθʌrə/ *adj.* **1** complete and unqualified; not superficial (*needs a thorough change*). **2** acting or done with great care and completeness (*the report is most thorough*). **3** absolute (*a thorough nuisance*). □ **thorough bass** a bass part for a keyboard player with numerals and symbols below to indicate the harmony. **thorough-paced 1** (of a horse) trained to all paces. **2** complete or unqualified. □□ **thoroughly** *adv.* **thoroughness** *n.* [orig. as adv. and prep. in the senses of *through*, f. OE *thuruh* var. of *thurh* THROUGH]

thoroughbred /ˈθʌrəˌbred/ *adj. & n.* —*adj.* **1** of pure breed. **2** high-spirited. —*n.* **1** a thoroughbred animal, esp. a horse. **2** (**Thoroughbred**) **a** a breed of racehorses originating from English mares and Arab stallions. **b** a horse of this breed.

thoroughfare /ˈθʌrəˌfeə(r)/ *n.* a road or path open at both ends, esp. for traffic.

thoroughgoing /ˈθʌrəˌɡəʊɪŋ, -ˈɡəʊɪŋ/ *adj.* **1** uncompromising; not superficial. **2** (usu. *attrib.*) extreme; out and out.

thorp /θɔːp/ *n.* (also **thorpe**) *archaic* a village or hamlet. ¶ Now usually only in place-names. [OE *thorp, throp*, f. Gmc]

Thorvaldsen or **Thorwaldsen** /ˈtɔːvæls(ə)n/, Bertel (1768 or 1770–1844), Danish neoclassical sculptor, who worked for many years in Rome. He made his name with the statue *Jason* (1802–3), which was based on the *Doryphoros* of Polyclitus; other major works include the tomb of Pius VII at St Peter's in Rome (1824–31) and a monument to Lord Byron (1829). In Copenhagen a museum was built for him (1839–48), itself a remarkable piece of neo-antique architecture, the courtyard of which was to contain his tomb.

Thos. *abbr.* Thomas.

those *pl.* of THAT.

Thoth /θəʊθ, təʊt/ *Egyptian Mythol.* a moon-god, the god of wisdom and of scribes and writing, patron of the sciences. He was also regarded as a god of justice, protector of laws. Thoth was closely associated with Ra and was his messenger, which led the Greeks to identify him with Hermes. He is most often represented in human form with the head of an ibis surmounted by the moon's disc and crescent.

thou[1] /ðaʊ/ *pron.* (*obj.* **thee** /ðiː/; *poss.* **thy** or **thine**; *pl.* **ye** or **you**) second person singular pronoun, now replaced by *you* except in some formal, liturgical, dialect, and poetic uses. [OE *thu* f. Gmc]

thou[2] /θaʊ/ *n.* (*pl.* same or **thous**) *colloq.* **1** a thousand. **2** one thousandth. [abbr.]

though /ðəʊ/ *conj. & adv.* (also **tho'**) —*conj.* **1** despite the fact that (*though it was early we went to bed; though annoyed, I agreed*). **2** (introducing a possibility) even if (*ask him though he may refuse; would not attend though the Queen herself were there*). **3** and yet; nevertheless (*she read on, though not to the very end*). **4** in spite of being (*ready though unwilling*). —*adv. colloq.* however; all the same (*I wish you had told me, though*). [ME *thoh* etc. f. ON *thó* etc., corresp. to OE *thēah*, f. Gmc]

thought[1] /θɔːt/ *n.* **1** the process or power of thinking; the faculty of reason. **2** a way of thinking characteristic of or associated with a particular time, people, group, etc. (*medieval European thought*). **3** sober reflection or consideration (*gave it much thought*). **4** an idea or piece of reasoning produced by thinking (*many good thoughts came out of the discussion*). **5** (foll. by *of* + verbal noun or *to* + infin.) a partly formed intention or hope (*gave up all thoughts of winning; had no thought to go*). **6** (usu. in *pl.*) what one is thinking; one's opinion (*have you any thoughts on this?*). **7** the subject of one's thinking (*my one thought was to get away*). **8** (prec. by *a*) somewhat (*seems to me a thought arrogant*). □ **give thought to** consider; think about. **in thought** thinking, meditating. **take thought** consider matters. **thought-provoking** stimulating serious thought. **thought-reader** a person supposedly able to perceive another's thoughts. **thought-reading** the supposed perception of what another is thinking. **thought transference** telepathy. **thought-wave** an undulation of the supposed medium of thought transference. □□ **-thoughted** *adj.* (in *comb.*). [OE *thōht* (as THINK)]

thought[2] *past* and *past part.* of THINK.

thoughtful /ˈθɔːtfʊl/ *adj.* **1** engaged in or given to meditation. **2** (of a book, writer, remark, etc.) giving signs of serious thought.

3 (often foll. by *of*) (of a person or conduct) considerate; not haphazard or unfeeling. □□ **thoughtfully** *adv.* **thoughtfulness** *n.*

thoughtless /ˈθɔːtlɪs/ *adj.* **1** careless of consequences or of others' feelings. **2** due to lack of thought. □□ **thoughtlessly** *adv.* **thoughtlessness** *n.*

thousand /ˈθaʊz(ə)nd/ *n. & adj.* —*n.* (*pl.* **thousands** or (in sense 1) **thousand**) (in *sing.* prec. by *a* or *one*) **1** the product of a hundred and ten. **2** a symbol for this (1,000, m, M). **3** a set of a thousand things. **4** (in *sing.* or *pl.*) *colloq.* a large number. —*adj.* that amount to a thousand. □ **Thousand and One Nights** see ARABIAN NIGHTS. □□ **thousandfold** *adj. & adv.* **thousandth** *adj. & n.* [OE *thūsend* f. Gmc]

Thousand Islands 1 a group of about 1500 islands in a widening of the St Lawrence River, just below Kingston. Some of the islands belong to Canada and some to the US. **2** a group of about 100 small islands in the SW Java Sea, forming part of Indonesia.

Thrace /θreɪs/ **1** an ancient country lying west of Istanbul and the Black Sea and north of the Aegean, part of modern Turkey, Greece, and Bulgaria, inhabited by a primitive warlike Indo-European people. It became a Roman province in 46. **2** a region of modern Greece, in the north-east of the country; pop. (1981) 345,200. □□ **Thracian** /ˈθreɪʃ(ə)n/ *adj. & n.*

thrall /θrɔːl/ *n. literary* **1** (often foll. by *of, to*) a slave (of a person, or a power or influence). **2** bondage; a state of slavery or servitude (*in thrall*). □□ **thraldom** *n.* (also **thralldom**). [OE *thrǣl* f. ON *thrǣll*, perh. f. a Gmc root = run]

thrash /θræʃ/ *v. & n.* —*v.* **1** *tr.* beat severely, esp. with a stick or whip. **2** *tr.* defeat thoroughly in a contest. **3** *intr.* (of a paddle wheel, branch, etc.) act like a flail; deliver repeated blows. **4** *intr.* (foll. by *about, around*) move or fling the limbs about violently or in panic. **5** *intr.* (of a ship) keep striking the waves; make way against the wind or tide (*thrash to windward*). **6** *tr.* = THRESH 1. —*n.* **1** an act of thrashing. **2** *colloq.* a party, esp. a lavish one. □ **thrash out** discuss to a conclusion. □□ **thrashing** *n.* [OE *therscan*, later *threscan*, f. Gmc]

thrasher[1] /ˈθræʃə(r)/ *n.* **1** a person or thing that thrashes. **2** = THRESHER.

thrasher[2] /ˈθræʃə(r)/ *n.* any of various long-tailed N. American thrushlike birds of the family Mimidae. [perh. f. E dial. *thrusher* = THRUSH[1]]

thrawn /θrɔːn/ *adj. Sc.* **1** perverse or ill-tempered. **2** misshapen, crooked. [Sc. form of *thrown* in obs. senses]

thread /θred/ *n. & v.* —*n.* **1 a** a spun-out filament of cotton, silk, or glass etc.; yarn. **b** a length of this. **2** a thin cord of twisted yarns used esp. in sewing and weaving. **3** anything regarded as threadlike with reference to its continuity or connectedness (*the thread of life; lost the thread of his argument*). **4** the spiral ridge of a screw. **5** (in *pl.*) *sl.* clothes. **6** a thin seam or vein of ore. —*v.tr.* **1** pass a thread through the eye of (a needle). **2** put (beads) on a thread. **3** arrange (material in a strip form, e.g. film or magnetic tape) in the proper position on equipment. **4** make (one's way) carefully through a crowded place, over a difficult route, etc. **5** streak (hair etc.) as with threads. **6** form a screw-thread on. □ **hang by a thread** be in a precarious state, position, etc. **thread mark** a mark in the form of a thin line made in banknote paper with highly coloured silk fibres to prevent photographic counterfeiting. □□ **threader** *n.* **threadlike** *adj.* [OE *thrǣd* f. Gmc]

threadbare /ˈθredbeə(r)/ *adj.* **1** (of cloth) so worn that the nap is lost and the thread visible. **2** (of a person) wearing such clothes. **3 a** hackneyed. **b** feeble or insubstantial (*a threadbare excuse*).

threadfin /ˈθredfɪn/ *n.* any small tropical fish of the family Polynemidae, with long streamers from its pectoral fins.

Threadneedle Street a street in the City of London containing the premises of the Bank of England (the **Old Lady of Threadneedle Street**; see OLD). [earlier *three-needle*, possibly from a tavern with the arms of the Needlemakers]

threadworm /ˈθredwɜːm/ *n.* any of various esp. parasitic threadlike nematode worms, e.g. the pinworm.

w we z zoo ʃ she ʒ decision θ thin ð this ŋ ring x loch tʃ chip dʒ jar (*see over for vowels*)

thready /ˈθredɪ/ adj. (**threadier, threadiest**) **1** of or like a thread. **2** (of a person's pulse) scarcely perceptible.

threat /θret/ n. **1 a** a declaration of an intention to punish or hurt. **b** Law a menace of bodily hurt or injury, such as may restrain a person's freedom of action. **2** an indication of something undesirable coming (the threat of war). **3** a person or thing as a likely cause of harm etc. [OE thrēat affliction etc. f. Gmc]

threaten /ˈθret(ə)n/ v.tr. **1** make a threat or threats against. **2** be a sign or indication of (something undesirable). **3** (foll. by to + infin.) announce one's intention to do an undesirable or unexpected thing (threatened to resign). **4** (also absol.) give warning of the infliction of (harm etc.) (the clouds were threatening rain). □□ **threatener** n. **threateningly** adv. [OE thrēatnian (as THREAT)]

three /θriː/ n. & adj. —n. **1 a** one more than two, or seven less than ten. **b** a symbol for this (3, iii, III). **2** a size etc. denoted by three. **3** the time of three o'clock. **4** a set of three. **5** a card with three pips. —adj. that amount to three. □ **three-card trick** a game in which bets are made on which is the queen among three cards lying face downwards. **three cheers** see CHEER. **three-colour process** a process of reproducing natural colours by combining photographic images in the three primary colours. **three-cornered 1** triangular. **2** (of a contest etc.) between three parties as individuals. **three-decker 1** a warship with three gun-decks. **2** a novel in three volumes. **3** a sandwich with three slices of bread. **three-dimensional** having or appearing to have length, breadth, and depth. **three-handed 1** having or using three hands. **2** involving three players. **three-legged race** a running-race between pairs, one member of each pair having the left leg tied to the right leg of the other. **three-line whip** a written notice, underlined three times to denote urgency, to members of a political party to attend a parliamentary vote. **three parts** three quarters. **three-phase** see PHASE. **three-piece** consisting of three items (esp. of a suit of clothes or a suite of furniture). **three-ply** adj. of three strands, webs, or thicknesses. —n. **1** three-ply wool. **2** three-ply wood made by gluing together three layers with the grain in different directions. **three-point landing** Aeron. the landing of an aircraft on the two main wheels and the tail wheel or skid simultaneously. **three-point turn** a method of turning a vehicle round in a narrow space by moving forwards, backwards, and forwards again in a sequence of arcs. **three-quarter** n. (also **three-quarter back**) Rugby Football any of three or four players just behind the half-backs. —adj. **1** consisting of three-fourths of something. **2** (of a portrait) going down to the hips or showing three-fourths of the face (between full face and profile). **three-quarters** three parts out of four. **three-ring circus** esp. US **1** a circus with three rings for simultaneous performances. **2** an extravagant display. **the three Rs** reading, writing, and arithmetic, regarded as the fundamentals of learning. **three-way** involving three ways or participants. **three-wheeler** a vehicle with three wheels. [OE thrī f. Gmc]

threefold /ˈθriːfəʊld/ adj. & adv. **1** three times as much or as many. **2** consisting of three parts.

Three Mile Island an island near Harrisburg, Pennsylvania, site of a nuclear power station. In 1979 an accident caused damage to uranium in the reactor core; reactions against the nuclear industry as a whole were immediate and severe.

threepence /ˈθrepəns, ˈθrʊpəns/ n. Brit. the sum of three pence, esp. before decimalization.

threepenny /ˈθrepənɪ, ˈθrʊpənɪ/ adj. Brit. costing three pence, esp. before decimalization. □ **threepenny bit** hist. a former coin worth three old pence.

threescore /ˈθriːskɔː(r)/ n. archaic sixty.

threesome /ˈθriːsəm/ n. **1** a group of three persons. **2** a game etc. for three, esp. Golf one against two.

thremmatology /ˌθreməˈtɒlədʒɪ/ n. the science of breeding animals and plants. [Gk thremma -matos nursling + -LOGY]

threnody /ˈθrenədɪ/ n. (also **threnode** /ˈθrenəʊd/) (pl. **-ies** or **threnodes**) **1** a lamentation, esp. on a person's death. **2** a song of lamentation. □□ **threnodial** /-ˈnəʊdɪəl/ adj. **threnodic** /-ˈnɒdɪk/ adj. **threnodist** /ˈθrenədɪst/ n. [Gk thrēnōidia f. thrēnos wailing + ōidē ODE]

threonine /ˈθriːəˌniːn, -nɪn/ n. Biochem. an amino acid, considered essential for growth. [threose (name of a tetrose sugar) ult. f. Gk eruthros red + -INE⁴]

thresh /θreʃ/ v. **1** tr. beat out or separate grain from (corn etc.). **2** intr. = THRASH v. 4. **3** tr. (foll. by over) analyse (a problem etc.) in search of a solution. □ **threshing-floor** a hard level floor for threshing esp. with flails. **threshing-machine** a power-driven machine for separating the grain from the straw or husk. **thresh out** = thrash out. [var. of THRASH]

thresher /ˈθreʃə(r)/ n. **1** a person or machine that threshes. **2** a shark, Alopias vulpinus, with a long upper lobe to its tail, that it can lash about.

threshold /ˈθreʃəʊld, -həʊld/ n. **1** a strip of wood or stone forming the bottom of a doorway and crossed in entering a house or room etc. **2** a point of entry or beginning (on the threshold of a new century). **3** Physiol. & Psychol. a limit below which a stimulus causes no reaction (pain threshold). **4** Physics a limit below which no reaction occurs, esp. a minimum dose of radiation producing a specified effect. **5** (often attrib.) a step in a scale of wages or taxation, usu. operative in specified conditions. [OE therscold, threscold, etc., rel. to THRASH in the sense 'tread']

threw past of THROW.

thrice /θraɪs/ adv. archaic or literary **1** three times. **2** (esp. in comb.) highly (thrice-blessed). [ME thries f. thrie (adv.) f. OE thrīwa, thrīga (as THREE, -S³)]

thrift /θrɪft/ n. **1** frugality; economical management. **2** a plant of the genus Armeria, esp. the sea pink. □ **thrift shop** (or **store**) a shop selling second-hand items usu. for charity. [ME f. ON (as THRIVE)]

thriftless /ˈθrɪftlɪs/ adj. wasteful, improvident. □□ **thriftlessly** adv. **thriftlessness** n.

thrifty /ˈθrɪftɪ/ adj. (**thriftier, thriftiest**) **1** economical, frugal. **2** thriving, prosperous. □□ **thriftily** adv. **thriftiness** n.

thrill /θrɪl/ n. & v. —n. **1** a wave or nervous tremor of emotion or sensation (a thrill of joy; a thrill of recognition). **2** a throb or pulsation. **3** Med. a vibratory movement or resonance heard in auscultation. —v. **1** intr. & tr. feel or cause to feel a thrill (thrilled to the sound; a voice that thrilled millions). **2** intr. quiver or throb with or as with emotion. **3** intr. (foll. by through, over, along) (of an emotion etc.) pass with a thrill through etc. (fear thrilled through my veins). □□ **thrilling** adj. **thrillingly** adv. [thirl (now dial.) f. OE thyrlian pierce f. thȳrel hole f. thurh THROUGH]

thriller /ˈθrɪlə(r)/ n. an exciting or sensational story or play etc., esp. one involving crime or espionage.

thrips /θrɪps/ n. (pl. same) any insect of the order Thysanoptera, esp. a pest injurious to plants. [L f. Gk, = woodworm]

thrive /θraɪv/ v.intr. (past **throve** /θrəʊv/ or **thrived**; past part. **thriven** /ˈθrɪv(ə)n/ or **thrived**) **1** prosper or flourish. **2** grow rich. **3** (of a child, animal, or plant) grow vigorously. [ME f. ON thrífask refl. of thrífa grasp]

thro' var. of THROUGH.

throat /θrəʊt/ n. **1 a** the windpipe or gullet. **b** the front part of the neck containing this. **2** literary **a** a voice, esp. of a songbird. **b** a thing compared to a throat, esp. a narrow passage, entrance, or exit. **3** Naut. the forward upper corner of a fore-and-aft sail. □ **cut one's own throat** bring about one's own downfall. **ram** (or **thrust**) **down a person's throat** force (a thing) on a person's attention. □□ **-throated** adj. (in comb.). [OE throte, throtu f. Gmc]

throaty /ˈθrəʊtɪ/ adj. (**throatier, throatiest**) **1** (of a voice) deficient in clarity; hoarsely resonant. **2** guttural; uttered in the throat. **3** having a prominent or capacious throat. □□ **throatily** adv. **throatiness** n.

throb /θrɒb/ v. & n. —v.intr. (**throbbed, throbbing**) **1** palpitate or pulsate, esp. with more than the usual force or rapidity. **2** vibrate or quiver with a persistent rhythm or with emotion. —n. **1** a throbbing. **2** a palpitation or (esp. violent) pulsation. [ME, app. imit.]

throe /θrəʊ/ n. (usu. in pl.) **1** a violent pang, esp. of childbirth or death. **2** anguish. □ **in the throes of** struggling with the task of. [ME throwe perh. f. OE thrēa, thrawu calamity, alt. perh. by assoc. with woe]

thrombi *pl.* of THROMBUS.

thrombin /ˈθrɒmbɪn/ *n.* an enzyme promoting the clotting of blood. [as THROMBUS + -IN]

thrombocyte /ˈθrɒmbəˌsaɪt/ *n.* a blood platelet, a small plate of protoplasm concerned in the coagulation of blood. [as THROMBUS + -CYTE]

thrombose /θrɒmˈbəʊz/ *v.tr.* & *intr.* affect with or undergo thrombosis. [back-form. f. THROMBOSIS]

thrombosis /θrɒmˈbəʊsɪs/ *n.* (*pl.* **thromboses** /-siːz/) the coagulation of the blood in a blood-vessel or organ. □□ **thrombotic** /-ˈbɒtɪk/ *adj.* [mod.L f. Gk *thrombōsis* curdling (as THROMBUS)]

thrombus /ˈθrɒmbəs/ *n.* (*pl.* **thrombi** /-baɪ/) a blood-clot formed in the vascular system and impeding the blood flow. [mod.L f. Gk *thrombos* lump, blood-clot]

throne /θrəʊn/ *n.* & *v.* —*n.* **1** a chair of State for a sovereign or bishop etc. **2** sovereign power (*came to the throne*). **3** (in *pl.*) the third order of the ninefold celestial hierarchy. **4** *colloq.* a lavatory seat and bowl. —*v.tr.* place on a throne. □□ **throneless** *adj.* [ME f. OF *trone* f. L *thronus* f. Gk *thronos* high seat]

throng /θrɒŋ/ *n.* & *v.* —*n.* **1** a crowd of people. **2** (often foll. by *of*) a multitude, esp. in a small space. —*v.* **1** *intr.* come in great numbers (*crowds thronged to the stadium*). **2** *tr.* flock into or crowd round; fill with or as with a crowd (*crowds thronged the streets*). [ME *thrang*, *throng*, OE *gethrang*, f. verbal stem *thring- thrang-*]

throstle /ˈθrɒs(ə)l/ *n.* **1** a song thrush. **2** (in full **throstle-frame**) a machine for continuously spinning wool or cotton etc. [OE f. Gmc: rel. to THRUSH[1]]

throttle /ˈθrɒt(ə)l/ *n.* & *v.* —*n.* **1 a** (in full **throttle-valve**) a valve controlling the flow of fuel or steam etc. in an engine. **b** (in full **throttle-lever**) a lever or pedal operating this valve. **2** the throat, gullet, or windpipe. —*v.tr.* **1** choke or strangle. **2** prevent the utterance etc. of. **3** control (an engine or steam etc.) with a throttle. □ **throttle back** (or **down**) reduce the speed of (an engine or vehicle) by throttling. □□ **throttler** *n.* [ME *throtel* (v.), perh. f. THROAT + -LE[4] (n.) perh. a dimin. of THROAT]

through /θruː/ *prep.*, *adv.*, & *adj.* (also **thro'**, *US* **thru**) —*prep.* **1 a** from end to end or from side to side of. **b** going in one side or end and out the other of. **2** between or among (*swam through the waves*). **3** from beginning to end (*read through the letter*; *went through many difficulties*). **4** because of; by the agency, means, or fault of (*lost it through carelessness*). **5** *US* up to and including (*Monday through Friday*). —*adv.* **1** through a thing; from side to side, end to end, or beginning to end (*went through to the garden*; *would not let us through*). **2** having completed (esp. successfully) (*are through their exams*). **3** so as to be connected by telephone (*will put you through*). —*attrib.adj.* **1** (of a journey, route, etc.) done without a change of line or vehicle etc. or with one ticket. **2** (of traffic) going through a place to its destination. □ **be through** *colloq.* **1** (often foll. by *with*) have finished. **2** (often foll. by *with*) cease to have dealings. **3** have no further prospects (*is through as a politician*). **no through road** = *no thoroughfare*. **through and through** **1** thoroughly, completely. **2** through again and again. [OE *thurh* f. WG]

throughout /θruːˈaʊt/ *prep.* & *adv.* —*prep.* right through; from end to end of (*throughout the town*; *throughout the 18th century*). —*adv.* in every part or respect (*the timber was rotten throughout*).

throughput /ˈθruːpʊt/ *n.* the amount of material put through a process, esp. in manufacturing or computing.

throughway /ˈθruːweɪ/ *n.* (also **thruway**) *US* a thoroughfare, esp. a motorway.

throve *past* of THRIVE.

throw /θrəʊ/ *v.* & *n.* —*v.tr.* (*past* **threw** /θruː/; *past part.* **thrown** /θrəʊn/) **1** propel with some force through the air or in a particular direction. **2** force violently into a specified position or state (*the ship was thrown on the rocks*; *threw themselves down*). **3** compel suddenly to be in a specified condition (*was thrown out of work*). **4** turn or move (part of the body) quickly or suddenly (*threw an arm out*). **5** project or cast (light, a shadow, a spell, etc.). **6 a** bring to the ground in wrestling. **b** (of a horse) unseat (its rider). **7** *colloq.* disconcert (*the question threw me for a moment*). **8** (foll. by *on*, *off*, etc.) put (clothes etc.) hastily on or off etc. **9 a** cause (dice) to fall on a table. **b** obtain (a specified number) by

throwing dice. **10** cause to pass or extend suddenly to another state or position (*threw in the army*; *threw a bridge across the river*). **11** move (a switch or lever) so as to operate it. **12 a** form (ceramic ware) on a potter's wheel. **b** turn (wood etc.) on a lathe. **13** have (a fit or tantrum etc.). **14** give (a party). **15** *colloq.* lose (a contest or race etc.) intentionally. **16** *Cricket* bowl (a ball) with an illegitimate sudden straightening of the elbow. **17** (of a snake) cast (its skin). **18** (of an animal) give birth to (young). **19** twist (silk etc.) into thread or yarn. **20** (often foll. by *into*) put into another form or language etc. —*n.* **1** an act of throwing. **2** the distance a thing is or may be thrown (*a record throw with the hammer*). **3** the act of being thrown in wrestling. **4** *Geol.* & *Mining* **a** a fault in strata. **b** the amount of vertical displacement caused by this. **5** a machine or device giving rapid rotary motion. **6 a** the movement of a crank or cam etc. **b** the extent of this. **7** the distance moved by the pointer of an instrument etc. **8** (in full **throw rug**) *US* **a** a light cover for furniture. **b** a light rug. **9** (prec. by *a*) *sl.* each; per item (*sold at £10 a throw*). □ **throw about** (or **around**) **1** throw in various directions. **2** spend (one's money) ostentatiously. **throw away** **1** discard as useless or unwanted. **2** waste or fail to make use of (an opportunity etc.). **3** discard (a card). **4** *Theatr.* speak (lines) with deliberate underemphasis. **5** (in *passive*; often foll. by *on*) be wasted (*the advice was thrown away on him*). **throw-away** *adj.* **1** meant to be thrown away after (one) use. **2** (of lines etc.) deliberately underemphasized. —*n.* a thing to be thrown away after (one) use. **throw back** **1** revert to ancestral character. **2** (usu. in *passive*; foll. by *on*) compel to rely on (*was thrown back on his savings*). **throw-back** *n.* **1** reversion to ancestral character. **2** an instance of this. **throw cold water on** see COLD. **throw down** cause to fall. **throw down the gauntlet** (or **glove**) issue a challenge. **throw dust in a person's eyes** mislead a person by misrepresentation or distraction. **throw good money after bad** incur further loss in a hopeless attempt to recoup a previous loss. **throw one's hand in 1** abandon one's chances in a card game, esp. poker. **2** give up; withdraw from a contest. **throw in 1** interpose (a word or remark). **2** include at no extra cost. **3** throw (a football) from the edge of the pitch where it has gone out of play. **4** *Cricket* return (the ball) from the outfield. **5** *Cards* give (a player) the lead, to the player's disadvantage. **throw-in** *n.* the throwing in of a football during play. **throw in one's lot with** see LOT. **throw in the towel** admit defeat. **throw light on** see LIGHT[1]. **throw off 1** discard; contrive to get rid of. **2** write or utter in an offhand manner. **3** (of hounds or a hunt) begin hunting; make a start. **throw-off** the start in a hunt or race. **throw oneself at** seek blatantly as a spouse or sexual partner. **throw oneself into** engage vigorously in. **throw oneself on** (or **upon**) **1** rely completely on. **2** attack. **throw open** (often foll. by *to*) **1** cause to be suddenly or widely open. **2** make accessible. **throw out 1** put out forcibly or suddenly. **2** discard as unwanted. **3** expel (a troublemaker etc.). **4** build (a wing of a house, a pier, or a projecting or prominent thing). **5** put forward tentatively. **6** reject (a proposal or bill in Parliament). **7** confuse or distract (a person speaking, thinking, or acting) from the matter in hand. **8** *Cricket* & *Baseball* put out (an opponent) by throwing the ball to the wicket or base. **throw over** desert or abandon. **throw stones** cast aspersions. **throw together 1** assemble hastily. **2** bring into casual contact. **throw up 1** abandon. **2** resign from. **3** *colloq.* vomit. **4** erect hastily. **5** bring to notice. **6** lift (a sash-window) quickly. **throw up** (or **in**) **the sponge 1** (of a boxer or his attendant) throw the sponge used between rounds into the air as a token of defeat. **2** abandon a contest; admit defeat. **throw one's weight about** (or **around**) *colloq.* act with unpleasant self-assertiveness. □□ **throwable** *adj.* **thrower** *n.* (also in *comb.*). [OE *thrāwan* twist, turn f. WG]

throwster /ˈθrəʊstə(r)/ *n.* a person who throws silk.

thru *US* var. of THROUGH.

thrum[1] /θrʌm/ *v.* & *n.* —*v.* (**thrummed**, **thrumming**) **1** *tr.* play (a stringed instrument) monotonously or unskilfully. **2** *intr.* (often foll. by *on*) drum idly. —*n.* **1** such playing. **2** the resulting sound. [imit.]

thrum[2] /θrʌm/ *n.* & *v.* —*n.* **1** the unwoven end of a warp-thread, or the whole of such ends, left when the finished web is cut away. **2** any short loose thread. —*v.tr.* (**thrummed, thrumming**) make of or cover with thrums. □□ **thrummer** *n.* **thrummy** *adj.* [OE f. Gmc]

thrush[1] /θrʌʃ/ *n.* any small or medium-sized songbird of the family Turdidae, esp. a song thrush or mistle thrush (see MISTLE THRUSH, *song thrush*). [OE *thrysce* f. Gmc: cf. THROSTLE]

thrush[2] /θrʌʃ/ *n.* **1 a** a disease, esp. of children, marked by whitish fungous vesicles in the mouth and throat. **b** a similar disease of the vagina. **2** inflammation affecting the frog of a horse's foot. [17th c.: orig. unkn.]

thrust /θrʌst/ *v.* & *n.* —*v.* (*past* and *past part.* **thrust**) **1** *tr.* push with a sudden impulse or with force (*thrust the letter into my pocket*). **2** *tr.* (foll. by *on*) impose (a thing) forcibly; enforce acceptance of (a thing) (*had it thrust on me*). **3** *intr.* (foll. by *at, through*) pierce or stab; make a sudden lunge. **4** *tr.* make (one's way) forcibly. **5** *intr.* (foll. by *through, past,* etc.) force oneself (*thrust past me abruptly*). —*n.* **1** a sudden or forcible push or lunge. **2** the propulsive force developed by a jet or rocket engine. **3** a strong attempt to penetrate an enemy's line or territory. **4** a remark aimed at a person. **5** the stress between the parts of an arch etc. **6** (often foll. by *of*) the chief theme or gist of remarks etc. **7** an attack with the point of a weapon. **8** (in full **thrust fault**) *Geol.* a low-angle reverse fault, with older strata displaced horizontally over newer. □ **thrust-block** a casting or frame carrying or containing the bearings on which the collars of a propeller shaft press. **thrust oneself** (or **one's nose**) in obtrude, interfere. **thrust stage** a stage extending into the audience. [ME *thruste* etc. f. ON *thrýsta*]

thruster /ˈθrʌstə(r)/ *n.* **1** a person or thing that thrusts. **2** a small rocket engine used to provide extra or correcting thrust on a spacecraft.

thruway *US* var. of THROUGHWAY.

Thucydides /θjuːˈsɪdɪˌdiːz/ (*c.*455–*c.*400 BC) Greek historian from Athens, whose *History* records the events of the Peloponnesian War between Athens and Sparta, in which he himself took part. The work, written to be 'a possession for ever', presents a scientific analysis of the origins and course of the war, based on painstaking inquiry into what actually happened and aided by the application of historical imagination in the reconstruction of political speeches. He does not conceal his admiration for the achievements of Pericles. His idiosyncratic style has a poetic flavour, with an energy and conciseness that matches the power of his thought.

thud /θʌd/ *n.* & *v.* —*n.* a low dull sound as of a blow on a non-resonant surface. —*v.intr.* (**thudded, thudding**) make or fall with a thud. □□ **thuddingly** *adv.* [prob. f. OE *thyddan* thrust]

thug /θʌg/ *n.* **1** a vicious or brutal ruffian. **2** (**Thug**) *hist.* a member of an association of professional robbers and murderers in India, who strangled their victims. Their methods were described by travellers from *c.*1665, and their suppression was rigidly prosecuted from 1831. □□ **thuggery** *n.* **thuggish** *adj.* **thuggishly** *adv.* **thuggishness** *n.* [Hindi & Marathi *ṭhag* swindler]

thuggee /θʌˈgiː/ *n.* *hist.* murder practised by the Thugs. □□ **thuggism** *n.* [Hindi *ṭhagī* (as THUG)]

thuja /ˈθuːjə/ *n.* (also **thuya**) any evergreen coniferous tree of the genus *Thuja*, with small leaves closely pressed to the branches; arbor vitae. [mod.L f. Gk *thuia*, an Afr. tree]

Thule /ˈθjuːlɪ, ˈθuːlɪ/ **1** a name given by the ancient Greek explorer Pytheas (*c.*310 BC) to a country described by him as six days' sail north of Britain, and regarded by the ancients as the northernmost point of the world. It has been variously identified with Iceland, one of the Shetland Islands, and part of Scandinavia. **2** (usu. *attrib.*) a prehistoric Eskimo culture widely distributed from Alaska to Greenland *c.* AD 500–1400, named after a small Eskimo settlement on the NW coast of Greenland.

thulium /ˈθjuːlɪəm/ *n.* *Chem.* a soft metallic element of the lanthanide series, occurring naturally in apatite. ¶ Symb.: **Tm**; atomic number 69. [mod.L f. L *Thule* (see THULE 1)]

thumb /θʌm/ *n.* & *v.* —*n.* **1 a** a short thick terminal projection on the human hand, set lower and apart from the other four and opposable to them. **b** a digit of other animals corresponding to this. **2** part of a glove etc. for a thumb. —*v.* **1** *tr.* wear or soil (pages etc.) with a thumb (*a well-thumbed book*). **2** *intr.* turn over pages with or as with a thumb (*thumbed through the directory*). **3** *tr.* request or obtain (a lift in a passing vehicle) by signalling with a raised thumb. **4** *tr.* use the thumb in a gesture. □ **be all thumbs** be clumsy with one's hands. **thumb index** *n.* a set of lettered grooves cut down the side of a diary, dictionary, etc. for easy reference. —*v.tr.* provide (a book etc.) with these. **thumb one's nose** = *cock a snook* (see SNOOK[1]). **thumb-nut** a nut shaped for turning with the thumb and forefinger. **thumbs down** an indication of rejection or failure. **thumbs up** an indication of satisfaction or approval. **under a person's thumb** completely dominated by a person. □□ **thumbed** *adj.* (also in *comb.*). **thumbless** *adj.* [OE *thūma* f. a WG root = swell]

thumbnail /ˈθʌmneɪl/ *n.* **1** the nail of a thumb. **2** (*attrib.*) denoting conciseness (*a thumbnail sketch*).

thumbprint /ˈθʌmprɪnt/ *n.* an impression of a thumb esp. as used for identification.

thumbscrew /ˈθʌmskruː/ *n.* **1** an instrument of torture for crushing the thumbs. **2** a screw with a flattened head for turning with the thumb and forefinger.

thumbtack /ˈθʌmtæk/ *n.* esp. *US* a drawing-pin.

thump /θʌmp/ *v.* & *n.* —*v.* **1** *tr.* beat or strike heavily esp. with the fist (*threatened to thump me*). **2** *intr.* throb or pulsate strongly (*my heart was thumping*). **3** *intr.* (foll. by *at, on,* etc.) deliver blows, esp. to attract attention (*thumped on the door*). **4** *tr.* (often foll. by *out*) play (a tune on a piano etc.) with a heavy touch. **5** *intr.* tread heavily. —*n.* **1** a heavy blow. **2** the sound of this. □□ **thumper** *n.* [imit.]

thumping /ˈθʌmpɪŋ/ *adj.* *colloq.* big, prominent (*a thumping majority; a thumping lie*).

thunder /ˈθʌndə(r)/ *n.* & *v.* —*n.* **1** a loud rumbling or crashing noise heard after a lightning flash and due to the expansion of rapidly heated air. **2** a resounding loud deep noise (*thunders of applause*). **3** strong censure or denunciation. —*v.* **1** *intr.* (prec. by *it* as subject) thunder sounds (*it is thundering; if it thunders*). **2** *intr.* make or proceed with a noise suggestive of thunder (*the applause thundered in my ears; the traffic thundered past*). **3** *tr.* utter or communicate (approval, disapproval, etc.) loudly or impressively. **4** *intr.* (foll. by *against* etc.) **a** make violent threats etc. against. **b** criticize violently. □ **steal a person's thunder** spoil the effect of another's idea, action, etc. by expressing or doing it first. [from the remark of John Dennis, English dramatist (*c.*1710), when the stage thunder he had intended for his own play was used for another] **thunder-box** *colloq.* a primitive lavatory. □□ **thunderer** *n.* **thunderless** *adj.* **thundery** *adj.* [OE *thunor* f. Gmc]

Thunder Bay a city on an inlet of Lake Superior in SW Ontario; pop. (1986) 112,300. Now one of Canada's major ports, Thunder Bay was created in 1970 by the amalgamation of the twin cities of Fort William and Port Arthur and two adjoining townships.

thunderbolt /ˈθʌndəbəʊlt/ *n.* **1 a** a flash of lightning with a simultaneous crash of thunder. **b** a stone etc. imagined to be a destructive bolt. **2** a sudden or unexpected occurrence or item of news. **3** a supposed bolt or shaft as a destructive agent, esp. as an attribute of a god.

thunderclap /ˈθʌndəklæp/ *n.* **1** a crash of thunder. **2** something startling or unexpected.

thundercloud /ˈθʌndəklaʊd/ *n.* a cumulus cloud with a tall diffuse top, charged with electricity and producing thunder and lightning.

thunderhead /ˈθʌndəhed/ *n.* esp. *US* a rounded cumulus cloud projecting upwards and heralding thunder.

thundering /ˈθʌndərɪŋ/ *adj.* *colloq.* very big or great (*a thundering nuisance*). □□ **thunderingly** *adv.*

thunderous /ˈθʌndərəs/ *adj.* **1** like thunder. **2** very loud. □□ **thunderously** *adv.* **thunderousness** *n.*

thunderstorm /ˈθʌndəstɔːm/ *n.* a storm with thunder and lightning and usu. heavy rain or hail.

thunderstruck /ˈθʌndəstrʌk/ *adj.* amazed; overwhelmingly surprised or startled.

Thur. abbr. Thursday.

Thurber /ˈθɜːbə(r)/, James (Grove) (1894–1961), American humorist, writer, and cartoonist. In 1927 began his lifelong association with the *New Yorker* in which he published many of his essays, stories, and sketches, including 'The Secret Life of Walter Mitty' (1932). Among his many collections are *Men, Women and Dogs* (1943; drawings) and *The Thurber Carnival* (1945).

thurible /ˈθjʊərɪb(ə)l/ n. a censer. [ME f. OF *thurible* or L *t(h)uribulum* f. *thus thur-* incense (as THURIFER)]

thurifer /ˈθjʊərɪfə(r)/ n. an acolyte carrying a censer. [LL f. *thus thuris* incense f. Gk *thuos* sacrifice + *-fer* -bearing]

Thuringia /θjʊəˈrɪndʒɪə/ a densely forested 'Land' (State) of Germany, lying to the north of the Ore Mountains; pop. (est. 1990) 2,500,000; capital, Erfurt.

Thurs. abbr. Thursday.

Thursday /ˈθɜːzdeɪ, -dɪ/ n. & adv. —n. the fifth day of the week, following Wednesday. —adv. colloq. **1** on Thursday. **2** (**Thursdays**) on Thursdays; each Thursday. [OE *thunresdæg, thur(e)sdæg*, day of thunder, named after THOR, whose name was substituted for that of Jove or JUPITER, representing LL *Jovis dies* day of Jupiter]

thus /ðʌs/ adv. formal **1 a** in this way. **b** as indicated. **2 a** accordingly. **b** as a result or inference. **3** to this extent; so (*thus far; thus much*). [OE (= OS *thus*), of unkn. orig.]

thuya var. of THUJA.

thwack /θwæk/ v. & n. —v.tr. hit with a heavy blow; whack. —n. a heavy blow. [imit.]

thwaite /θweɪt/ n. Brit. dial. a piece of wild land made arable. ¶ Now usually only in place-names. [ON *thveit(i)* paddock, rel. to OE *thwītan* to cut]

thwart /θwɔːt/ v., n., prep., & adv. —v.tr. frustrate or foil (a person or purpose etc.). —n. a rower's seat placed across a boat. —prep. & adv. archaic across, athwart. [ME *thwert* (adv.) f. ON *thvert* neut. of *thverr* transverse = OE *thwe(o)rh* f. Gmc]

thy /ðaɪ/ poss.pron. (attrib.) (also **thine** /ðaɪn/ before a vowel) of or belonging to thee: now replaced by *your* except in some formal, liturgical, dialect, and poetic uses. [ME *thī*, reduced f. *thīn* THINE]

Thyestes /θaɪˈestiːz/ Gk legend brother of Atreus (see entry). □□ **Thyestean** /-ˈestɪən/ adj.

thyme /taɪm/ n. any herb or shrub of the genus *Thymus* with aromatic leaves, esp. *T. vulgare* grown for culinary use. □□ **thymy** adj. [ME f. OF *thym* f. *thymum* f. Gk *thumon* f. *thuō* burn a sacrifice]

thymi pl. of THYMUS.

thymine /ˈθaɪmiːn/ n. Biochem. a pyrimidine derivative found in all living tissue as a component base of DNA. [*thymic* (as THYMUS) + -INE⁴]

thymol /ˈθaɪmɒl/ n. Chem. a white crystalline phenol obtained from oil of thyme and used as an antiseptic. [as THYME + -OL¹]

thymus /ˈθaɪməs/ n. (pl. **thymi** /-maɪ/) (in full **thymus gland**) Anat. a lymphoid organ situated in the neck of vertebrates (in humans becoming much smaller at the approach of puberty) producing lymphocytes for the immune response. [mod.L f. Gk *thumos*]

thyristor /θaɪˈrɪstə(r)/ n. Electronics a semiconductor rectifier in which the current between two electrodes is controlled by a signal applied to a third electrode. [Gk *thura* gate + TRANSISTOR]

thyro- /ˈθaɪrəʊ/ comb. form (also **thyreo-** /-rɪəʊ/) thyroid.

thyroid /ˈθaɪrɔɪd/ n. & adj. —n. (in full **thyroid gland**) **1** a large ductless gland in the neck of vertebrates secreting a hormone which regulates growth and development through the rate of metabolism. **2** an extract prepared from the thyroid gland of animals and used in treating goitre and cretinism etc. —adj. Anat. & Zool. **1** connected with the thyroid cartilage (*thyroid artery*). **2** shield-shaped. □ **thyroid cartilage** a large cartilage of the larynx, the projection of which in man forms the Adam's apple. [obs.F *thyroïde* or mod.L *thyroïdes*, irreg. f. Gk *thureoeidēs* f. *thureos* oblong shield]

thyroxine /θaɪˈrɒksiːn/ n. the main hormone produced by the thyroid gland, involved in controlling the rate of metabolic processes. [THYROID + OX- + -INE⁴]

thyrsus /ˈθɜːsəs/ n. (pl. **thyrsi** /-saɪ/) **1** Gk & Rom. Antiq. a staff tipped with an ornament like a pine-cone, an attribute of Bacchus. **2** Bot. an inflorescence as in lilac, with the primary axis racemose and the secondary axis cymose. [L f. Gk *thursos*]

thyself /ðaɪˈself/ pron. archaic emphat. & refl. form of THOU¹, THEE.

Ti symb. Chem. the element titanium.

ti¹ /tiː/ n. any woody liliaceous plant of the genus *Cordyline*, esp. *C. terminalis* with edible roots. [Tahitian, Maori, etc.]

ti² var. of TE.

Tianjin /ˌtɪenˈdʒɪn/ (also **Tientsin** /-ˈtsɪn/ a port and the third-largest city of China, in Hubei province; pop. (est. 1986) 5,380,000.

tiara /tɪˈɑːrə/ n. **1** a jewelled ornamental band worn on the front of a woman's hair. **2** a three-crowned diadem worn by a pope. **3** hist. a turban worn by ancient Persian kings. □□ **tiaraed** adj. (also **tiara'd**). [L f. Gk, of unkn. orig.]

Tiber /ˈtaɪbə(r)/ a river of central Italy, upon which Rome stands, flowing 405 km (252 miles) westwards from the Tuscan Apennines to the sea at Ostia.

Tiberius /taɪˈbɪərɪəs/ (Tiberius Julius Caesar Augustus, 42 BC– AD 37) Roman emperor AD 14–37, the adopted successor of his stepfather Augustus. He pursued a brilliant military career under Augustus, whose policies he faithfully continued when he became emperor. His reign was marked by an increasing number of treason trials. In AD 26 he retired to Capri and never again visited Rome; business with the Senate was conducted by letter. Morose and suspicious, Tiberius was not a popular emperor.

Tibesti Mountains /tɪˈbestɪ/ a mountain range in north central Africa on the frontier between Chad and Libya. The highest peak is Emi Koussi which rises to a height of 3,415 m (2,134 ft.).

Tibet /tɪˈbet/ (Chinese **Xizang** /ʃiːˈzæŋ/) a mountainous country (the highest plateau in the world) on the northern frontier of India, an autonomous region of China since 1965; pop. (est. 1986) 2,030,000; capital, Lhasa. □ **Little Tibet** see BALTISTAN.

Tibetan /tɪˈbet(ə)n/ n. & adj. —n. **1 a** a native of Tibet. **b** a person of Tibetan descent. **2** the language of Tibet, spoken by about 2 million people there, a similar number in neighbouring provinces of China, and a million people in Nepal. It belongs to the Sino-Tibetan language group and is most closely related to Burmese. Its alphabet is based on that of Sanskrit and dates from the 7th c. —adj. of or relating to Tibet or its people or language.

tibia /ˈtɪbɪə/ n. (pl. **tibiae** /-bɪˌiː/) **1** Anat. the inner and usu. larger of two bones extending from the knee to the ankle. **2** the tibiotarsus of a bird. **3** the fourth segment of the leg in insects. □□ **tibial** adj. [L, = shin-bone]

tibiotarsus /ˌtɪbɪəʊˈtɑːsəs/ n. (pl. **tibiotarsi** /-saɪ/) the bone in a bird corresponding to the tibia fused at the lower end with some bones of the tarsus. [TIBIA + TARSUS]

Tibullus /tɪˈbʌləs/, Albius (c.50–19 BC), Roman poet. His smooth and simply-written verses exalt a nostalgic ideal of peaceful rural life over the harsh realities of war and foreign travel.

tic /tɪk/ n. a habitual spasmodic contraction of the muscles esp. of the face. □ **tic douloureux** /ˌduːləˈruː, -ˈrɜː/ trigeminal neuralgia. [F f. It. *ticchio: douloureux* F, = painful]

tice /taɪs/ n. **1** Cricket = YORKER. **2** Croquet a stroke tempting an opponent to aim at one's ball. [*tice* (now dial.), = ENTICE]

Tichborne claimant /ˈtɪtʃbɔːn/ Arthur Orton (1834–98), a butcher, who came from Australia to claim the rich Tichborne estate after the heir, eldest son of the 10th baronet, was lost at sea. After a long trial (1871) he lost his claim and was imprisoned for perjury.

tick¹ /tɪk/ n. & v. —n. **1** a slight recurring click esp. that of a watch or clock. **2** esp. Brit. colloq. a moment; an instant. **3** a mark (√) to denote correctness, check items in a list, etc. —v. **1** intr. **a** (of a clock etc.) make ticks. **b** (foll. by *away*) (of time etc.) pass. **2** intr. (of a mechanism) work, function (*take it apart to see how it ticks*). **3** tr. **a** mark (a written answer etc.) with a tick. **b** (often foll. by *off*) mark (an item in a list etc.) with a tick in checking.

□ **in two ticks** *Brit. colloq.* in a very short time. **tick off** *colloq.* reprimand. **tick over 1** (of an engine etc.) idle. **2** (of a person, project, etc.) be working or functioning at a basic or minimum level. **tick-tack** (or **tic-tac**) *Brit.* a kind of manual semaphore signalling used by racecourse bookmakers to exchange information. **tick-tack-toe** *US* noughts and crosses. **tick-tock** the ticking of a large clock etc. **what makes a person tick** *colloq.* a person's motivation. □□ **tickless** *adj.* [ME: cf. Du. *tik*, LG *tikk* touch, tick]

tick² /tɪk/ *n.* **1** any of various arachnids of the order Acarina, parasitic on the skin of dogs and cattle etc. **2** any of various insects of the family Hippoboscidae, parasitic on sheep and birds etc. **3** *colloq.* an unpleasant or despicable person. □ **tick-bird** = *ox-pecker*. **tick fever** a bacterial or rickettsial fever transmitted by the bite of a tick. [OE *ticca* (recorded as *ticia*); ME *teke*, *tyke*: cf. MDu., MLG *tēke*, OHG *zēcho*]

tick³ /tɪk/ *n. colloq.* credit (*buy goods on tick*). [app. an abbr. of TICKET in phr. *on the ticket*]

tick⁴ /tɪk/ *n.* **1** the cover of a mattress or pillow. **2** = TICKING. [ME *tikke*, *tēke* f. WG f. L *theca* f. Gk *thēkē* case]

ticker /ˈtɪkə(r)/ *n. colloq.* **1** the heart. **2** a watch. **3** *US* a tape machine. □ **ticker-tape 1** a paper strip from a tape machine. **2** this or similar material thrown from windows etc. to greet a celebrity.

ticket /ˈtɪkɪt/ *n. & v.* —*n.* **1** a written or printed piece of paper or card entitling the holder to enter a place, participate in an event, travel by public transport, use a public amenity, etc. **2** an official notification of a traffic offence etc. (*parking ticket*). **3** *Brit.* a certificate of discharge from the army. **4** a certificate of qualification as a ship's master, pilot, etc. **5** a label attached to a thing and giving its price or other details. **6** *esp. US* **a** a list of candidates put forward by one group esp. a political party. **b** the principles of a party. **7** (prec. by *the*) *colloq.* what is correct or needed. —*v.tr.* (**ticketed**, **ticketing**) attach a ticket to. □ **have tickets on oneself** *Austral. colloq.* be conceited. **ticket-day** *Brit. Stock Exch.* the day before settling day, when the names of actual purchasers are handed to stockbrokers. **ticket office** an office or kiosk where tickets are sold for transport, entertainment, etc. **ticket-of-leave man** *Brit. hist.* a prisoner or convict who had served part of his time and was granted certain concessions, esp. leave. □□ **ticketed** *adj.* **ticketless** *adj.* [obs.F *étiquet* f. OF *estiquet(te)* f. *estiquier*, *estechier* fix f. MDu. *steken*]

tickety-boo /ˌtɪkətɪˈbuː/ *adj. Brit. colloq.* all right; in order. [20th c.: orig. uncert.]

ticking /ˈtɪkɪŋ/ *n.* a stout usu. striped material used to cover mattresses etc. [TICK⁴ + -ING¹]

tickle /ˈtɪk(ə)l/ *v. & n.* —*v.* **1 a** *tr.* apply light touches or strokes to (a person or part of a person's body) so as to excite the nerves and usu. produce laughter and spasmodic movement. **b** *intr.* feel this sensation (*my foot tickles*). **2** *tr.* excite agreeably; amuse or divert (a person, a sense of humour, vanity, etc.) (*was highly tickled at the idea*; *this will tickle your fancy*). **3** *tr.* catch (a trout etc.) by rubbing it so that it moves backwards into the hand. —*n.* **1** an act of tickling. **2** a tickling sensation. □ **tickled pink** (or **to death**) *colloq.* extremely amused or pleased. □□ **tickler** *n.* **tickly** *adj.* [ME, prob. frequent. of TICK¹]

ticklish /ˈtɪklɪʃ/ *adj.* **1** sensitive to tickling. **2** (of a matter or person to be dealt with) difficult; requiring careful handling. □□ **ticklishly** *adv.* **ticklishness** *n.*

tic-tac var. of *tick-tack* (see TICK¹).

tidal /ˈtaɪd(ə)l/ *adj.* relating to, like, or affected by tides (*tidal basin*; *tidal river*). □ **tidal bore** a large wave or bore caused by constriction of the spring tide as it enters a long narrow shallow inlet. **tidal flow** the regulated movement of traffic in opposite directions on the same stretch of road at different times of the day. **tidal wave 1** *Geog.* an exceptionally large ocean wave, esp. one caused by an underwater earthquake or volcanic eruption. **2** a widespread manifestation of feeling etc. □□ **tidally** *adv.*

tidbit *US* var. of TITBIT.

tiddledy-wink *US* var. of TIDDLY-WINK.

tiddler /ˈtɪdlə(r)/ *n. Brit. colloq.* **1** a small fish, esp. a stickleback

or minnow. **2** an unusually small thing or person. [perh. rel. to TIDDLY² and *tittlebat*, a childish form of *stickleback*]

tiddly¹ /ˈtɪdlɪ/ *adj.* (**tiddlier**, **tiddliest**) *esp. Brit. colloq.* slightly drunk. [19th c., earlier = a drink: orig. unkn.]

tiddly² /ˈtɪdlɪ/ *adj.* (**tiddlier**, **tiddliest**) *Brit. colloq.* little.

tiddly-wink /ˈtɪdlɪwɪŋk/ *n.* (*US* **tiddledy-** /ˈtɪdəldɪ-/) **1** a counter flicked with another into a cup etc. **2** (in *pl.*) this game. [19th c.: perh. rel. to TIDDLY¹]

tide /taɪd/ *n. & v.* —*n.* **1 a** the periodic rise and fall of the sea due to the attraction of the moon and sun (see EBB *n.* 1, FLOOD *n.* 3). **b** the water as affected by this. **2** a time or season (usu. in *comb.*: *Whitsuntide*). **3** a marked trend of opinion, fortune, or events. —*v.intr.* drift with the tide, esp. work in or out of harbour with the help of the tide. □ **tide-mill** a mill with a water-wheel driven by the tide. **tide over** enable or help (a person) to deal with an awkward situation, difficult period, etc. (*the money will tide me over until Friday*). **tide-rip** (or **-rips**) rough water caused by opposing tides. **work double tides** work twice the normal time, or extra hard. □□ **tideless** *adj.* [OE *tīd* f. Gmc, rel. to TIME]

tideland /ˈtaɪdlænd/ *n. US* land that is submerged at high tide.

tidemark /ˈtaɪdmɑːk/ *n.* **1** a mark made by the tide at high water. **2** *esp. Brit.* **a** a mark left round a bath at the level of the water in it. **b** a line on a person's body marking the extent to which it has been washed.

tidetable /ˈtaɪdˌteɪb(ə)l/ *n.* a table indicating the times of high and low tides at a place.

tidewaiter /ˈtaɪdˌweɪtə(r)/ *n. hist.* a customs officer who boarded ships on their arrival to enforce the customs regulations.

tidewater /ˈtaɪdˌwɔːtə(r)/ *n.* **1** water brought by or affected by tides. **2** (*attrib.*) *US* affected by tides (*tidewater region*).

tidewave /ˈtaɪdweɪv/ *n.* an undulation of water passing round the earth and causing high and low tides.

tideway /ˈtaɪdweɪ/ *n.* **1** a channel in which a tide runs, esp. the tidal part of a river. **2** the ebb or flow in a tidal channel.

tidings /ˈtaɪdɪŋz/ *n.* (as *sing.* or *pl.*) *literary* news, information. [OE *tīdung*, prob. f. ON *títhindi* events f. *títhr* occurring]

tidy /ˈtaɪdɪ/ *adj.*, *n.*, & *v.* —*adj.* (**tidier**, **tidiest**) **1** neat, orderly; methodically arranged. **2** (of a person) methodically inclined. **3** *colloq.* considerable (*it cost a tidy sum*). —*n.* (*pl.* **-ies**) **1** a receptacle for holding small objects or waste scraps, esp. in a kitchen sink. **2** an act or spell of tidying. **3** *esp. US* a detachable ornamental cover for a chair-back etc. —*v.tr.* (**-ies**, **-ied**) (also *absol.*; often foll. by *up*) put in good order; make (oneself, a room, etc.) tidy. □□ **tidily** *adv.* **tidiness** *n.* [ME, = timely etc., f. TIDE + -Y¹]

tie /taɪ/ *v. & n.* —*v.* (**tying**) **1** *tr.* attach or fasten with string or cord etc. (*tie the dog to the gate*; *tie his hands together*; *tied on a label*). **2** *tr.* **a** form (a string, ribbon, shoelace, necktie, etc.) into a knot or bow. **b** form (a knot or bow) in this way. **3** *tr.* restrict or limit (a person) as to conditions, occupation, place, etc. (*is tied to his family*). **4** *intr.* (often foll. by *with*) achieve the same score or place as another competitor (*they tied at ten games each*; *tied with her for first place*). **5** *tr.* hold (rafters etc.) together by a crosspiece etc. **6** *tr. Mus.* **a** unite (written notes) by a tie. **b** perform (two notes) as one unbroken note. —*n.* **1** a cord or chain etc. used for fastening. **2** a strip of material worn round the collar and tied in a knot at the front with the ends hanging down. **3** a thing that unites or restricts persons; a bond or obligation (*family ties*; *ties of friendship*; *children are a real tie*). **4** a draw, dead heat, or equality of score among competitors. **5** *Brit.* a match between any pair from a group of competing players or teams. **6** (also **tie-beam** etc.) a rod or beam holding parts of a structure together. **7** *Mus.* a curved line above or below two notes of the same pitch indicating that they are to be played for the combined duration of their time values. **8** *US* a railway sleeper. **9** *US* a shoe tied with a lace. □ **fit to be tied** *colloq.* very angry. **tie-break** (or **-breaker**) a means of deciding a winner from competitors who have tied. **tie-dye** (or **tie and dye**) a method of producing dyed patterns by tying string etc. to protect parts of the fabric from the dye. **tie in** (foll. by *with*) bring into or have a close association or agreement. **tie-in** *n.* **1** a connection or association. **2** (often *attrib.*) *esp. US* a form of sale or advertising that offers or requires more than a single purchase. **3** the joint promotion of related commodities etc. (e.g. a book and a film). **tie-line** a transmission line connecting parts of a system, esp. a telephone line connecting two private branch exchanges. **tie-pin** (or **-clip**) an ornamental pin or clip for holding a tie in place. **tie up 1** bind or fasten securely with cord etc. **2** invest or reserve (capital etc.) so that it is not immediately available for use. **3** moor (a boat). **4** secure (an animal). **5** obstruct; prevent from acting freely. **6** secure or complete (an undertaking etc.). **7** (often foll. by *with*) = *tie in*. **8** (usu. in *passive*) fully occupy (a person). □□ **tieless** adj. [OE *tígan*, *tēgan* (v.), *tēah*, *tēg* (n.) f. Gmc]

tied /taɪd/ adj. Brit. **1** (of a house) occupied subject to the tenant's working for its owner. **2** (of a public house etc.) bound to supply the products of a particular brewery only.

Tien Shan /tɪen ˈʃæn/ a range of mountains lying to the north of the Tarim Basin in Xinjiang autonomous region, NW China. Extending into the Soviet republic of Khirgizia, it rises to a height of 7,439 m (24,406 ft.) at Pik Pobeda.

Tientsin see TIANJIN.

Tiepolo /ˈtjeɪpəˌləʊ/, Giovanni Battista or Giambattista (1696–1770), Italian painter and graphic artist, the last of the great Venetian fresco painters. His early work is indebted to Veronese in its sumptuous colour and lavish settings. By the 1740s he had developed an individual style of exotic imagery, translucent colour, and theatrical splendour almost operatic in effect (e.g. the *Antony and Cleopatra* frescoes, Palazzo Labia, Venice, 1746–7). His international fame led to a commission from the Prince-Bishop at Würzburg whose residence he decorated (1751–2) with the greatest fresco cycle of the entire 18th c., a perfect fusion of architecture, painting, and stucco work. In 1762, at the request of Charles III, he moved to Madrid where he spent the rest of his life. His religious paintings for the royal chapel at Aranjuez reveal a more tragic vision and new intensity of feeling. His sons Giandomenico (1727–1804) and Lorenzo (1736–76) worked with him on many commissions, the former working competently in his father's manner as well as producing genre scenes.

tier /tɪə(r)/ n. **1** a row or rank or unit of a structure, as one of several placed one above another (*tiers of seats*). **2** *Naut.* **a** a circle of coiled cable. **b** a place for a coiled cable. □□ **tiered** adj. (also in comb.). [earlier *tire* f. F f. *tirer* draw, elongate f. Rmc]

tierce /tɪəs/ n. **1** *Eccl.* = TERCE. **2** *Mus.* an interval of two octaves and a major third. **3** a sequence of three cards. **4** *Fencing* **a** the third of eight parrying positions. **b** the corresponding thrust. **5** archaic **a** a former wine-measure of one-third of a pipe. **b** a cask containing a certain quantity (varying with the goods) esp. of provisions. [ME f. OF *t(i)erce* f. L *tertia* fem. of *tertius* third]

tierced /tɪəst/ adj. *Heraldry* divided into three parts of different tinctures.

tiercel var. of TERCEL.

tiercet var. of TERCET.

Tierra del Fuego /tɪˌerə del ˈfweɪɡəʊ/ an archipelago separated from the southern tip of South America by the Strait of Magellan; its main island. It was discovered by Magellan in 1520 and is now divided between Chile and Argentina. [Sp., = land of fire]

tiff /tɪf/ n. **1** a slight or petty quarrel. **2** a fit of peevishness. [18th c.: orig. unkn.]

Tiffany /ˈtɪfənɪ/, Louis Comfort (1848–1933), American painter, decorator, and architect, one of the leading American masters of the art nouveau style. The immensely successful interior decorating firm he established in New York in 1881 is famous above all for its highly distinctive glass vases and lamps, although until 1900 it was better known for stained glass and mosaic work.

tiffany /ˈtɪfənɪ/ n. (pl. **-ies**) thin gauze muslin. [orig. dress worn on Twelfth Night, f. OF *tifanie* f. eccl.L *theophania* f. Gk *theophaneia* Epiphany]

tiffin /ˈtɪfɪn/ n. & v. Ind. —n. a light meal, esp. lunch. —v.intr. (**tiffined**, **tiffining**) take lunch etc. [app. f. *tiffing* sipping]

Tiflis see TBILISI.

tig /tɪɡ/ n. = TAG². [var. of TICK¹]

tiger /ˈtaɪɡə(r)/ n. **1** a large Asian flesh-eating feline, *Panthera tigris*, having a yellow-brown coat with black stripes. **2** a fierce, energetic, or formidable person. □ **tiger beetle** any flesh-eating beetle of the family Cicindelidae, with spotted or striped wing-covers. **tiger-cat 1** any moderate-sized feline resembling the tiger, e.g. the ocelot, serval, or margay. **2** *Austral.* any of various flesh-eating marsupials of the genus *Dasyurus*, including the Tasmanian devil. **tiger-eye** (or **tiger's-eye**) **1** a yellow-brown striped gem of brilliant lustre. **2** *US* a pottery-glaze of similar appearance. **tiger lily** a tall garden lily, *Lilium tigrinum*, with flowers of dull orange spotted with black or purple. **tiger moth** any moth of the family Arctiidae, esp. *Arctia caja*, having richly spotted and streaked wings suggesting a tiger's skin. **tiger-wood** a striped or streaked wood used for cabinet-making. □□ **tigerish** adj. **tigerishly** adv. [ME f. OF *tigre* f. L *tigris* f. Gk *tigris*]

Tigers n.pl. a Tamil military organization in Sri Lanka, seeking independence for the Tamil community.

tight /taɪt/ adj., n., & adv. —adj. **1** closely held, drawn, fastened, fitting, etc. (a tight hold; a tight skirt). **2** closely and firmly put together (a tight joint). **3** (of clothes etc.) too closely fitting (my shoes are rather tight). **4** impermeable, impervious, esp. (in comb.) to a specified thing (watertight). **5** tense; stretched so as to leave no slack (a tight bowstring). **6** colloq. drunk. **7** colloq. (of a person) mean, stingy. **8 a** (of money or materials) not easily obtainable. **b** (of a money market) in which money is tight. **9 a** (of precautions, a programme, etc.) stringent, demanding. **b** presenting difficulties (a tight situation). **10** produced by or requiring great exertion or pressure (a tight squeeze). **11** (of control etc.) strictly imposed. —adv. tightly (hold tight!). □ **tight corner** (or **place** or **spot**) a difficult situation. **tight-fisted** stingy. **tight-fitting** (of a garment) fitting (often too) close to the body. **tight-lipped** with or as with the lips compressed to restrain emotion or speech. □□ **tightly** adv. **tightness** n. [prob. alt. of *thight* f. ON *théttr* watertight, of close texture]

tighten /ˈtaɪt(ə)n/ v.tr. & intr. make or become tight or tighter. □ **tighten one's belt** see BELT.

tightrope /ˈtaɪtrəʊp/ n. a rope stretched tightly high above the ground, on which acrobats perform.

tights /taɪts/ n.pl. **1** a thin close-fitting wool or nylon etc. garment covering the legs and the lower part of the torso, worn by women in place of stockings. **2** a similar garment worn by a dancer, acrobat, etc.

Tiglath-Pileser /ˌtɪɡlæθpaɪˈliːzə(r)/ the name of three kings of Assyria:

Tiglath-Pileser I (reigned c.1115–1077 BC), dealt effectively with his enemies, consolidated Assyrian influence, and extended its territory over Armenia, Cappadocia, and modern Lebanon. Best known for his prowess in battle and in hunting, he also built or rebuilt a number of temples, reinforced the city walls of Nineveh, and was a patron of literature, collected in one of the oldest extant libraries.

Tiglath-Pileser III (reigned 745–727 BC), brought the Assyrian empire to the height of its power, and (under the name Pulu) assumed the position of governor of Babylonia, uniting the two crowns in the person of one ruler bearing different names.

tigon /ˈtaɪɡən/ n. the offspring of a tiger and a lioness (cf. LIGER). [portmanteau word f. TIGER + LION]

Tigray /ˈtiːɡreɪ/ (also **Tigre**) a province in the arid northern highlands of Ethiopia; capital, Mekele. Secessionist rebels have waged a guerrilla war against the government of Ethiopia since 1975.

tigress /ˈtaɪɡrɪs/ n. **1** a female tiger. **2** a fierce or passionate woman.

Tigris /ˈtaɪɡrɪs/ the more easterly of the two rivers of Mesopotamia, 1850 km (1,150 miles) long, rising in the mountains of eastern Turkey and flowing through Iraq to join the Euphrates, forming the Shatt al-Arab which flows into the Persian Gulf. The city of Baghdad lies upon it.

Tijuana /tɪˈwɑːnə/ a town in NW Mexico, situated just south of the US frontier; pop. (1980) 461,250.

Tikal /tiːˈkæl/ an ancient Maya city in the tropical Petén region of northern Guatemala, with great plazas, pyramids, and palaces. It flourished especially in AD 300–800, reaching its peak towards the end of that period.

tike var. of TYKE.

tiki /ˈtiːkɪ/ n. (pl. **tikis**) NZ a large wooden or small ornamental greenstone image representing a human figure. [Maori]

tilbury /ˈtɪlbərɪ/ n. (pl. **-ies**) hist. a light open two-wheeled carriage fashionable in the first half of the 19th c. [after the inventor's name]

tilde /ˈtɪldə/ n. a mark (˜), put over a letter, e.g. over a Spanish n when pronounced ny (as in señor) or a Portuguese a or o when nasalized (as in São Paulo). [Sp., ult. f. L titulus TITLE]

tile /taɪl/ n. & v. —n. 1 a thin slab of concrete or baked clay etc. used in series for covering a roof or pavement etc. 2 a similar slab of glazed pottery, cork, linoleum, etc., for covering a floor, wall, etc. 3 a thin flat piece used in a game (esp. mah-jong). —v.tr. cover with tiles. □ **on the tiles** colloq. having a spree. [OE tigule, -ele, f. L tegula]

tiler /ˈtaɪlə(r)/ n. 1 a person who makes or lays tiles. 2 the doorkeeper of a Freemasons' lodge.

tiling /ˈtaɪlɪŋ/ n. 1 the process of fixing tiles. 2 an area of tiles.

till¹ /tɪl/ prep. & conj. —prep. 1 up to or as late as (wait till six o'clock; did not return till night). 2 up to the time of (faithful till death; waited till the end). —conj. 1 up to the time when (wait till I return). 2 so long that (laughed till I cried). ¶ Until is more usual when beginning a sentence. [OE & ON til to, rel. to TILL³]

till² /tɪl/ n. a drawer for money in a shop or bank etc., esp. with a device recording the amount of each purchase. [ME: orig. unkn.]

till³ /tɪl/ v.tr. prepare and cultivate (land) for crops. □□ **tillable** adj. **tiller** n. [OE tilian strive for, cultivate, f. Gmc]

till⁴ /tɪl/ n. stiff clay containing boulders, sand, etc. deposited by melting glaciers and ice-sheets. [17th c. (Sc.): orig. unkn.]

tillage /ˈtɪlɪdʒ/ n. 1 the preparation of land for crop-bearing. 2 tilled land.

tiller¹ /ˈtɪlə(r)/ n. a horizontal bar fitted to the head of a boat's rudder to turn it in steering. [ME f. AF telier weaver's beam f. med.L telarium f. L tela web]

tiller² /ˈtɪlə(r)/ n. & v. —n. 1 a shoot of a plant springing from the bottom of the original stalk. 2 a sapling. 3 a sucker. —v.intr. put forth tillers. [app. repr. OE telgor extended f. telga bough]

Tillich /ˈtɪlɪk/, Paul Johannes (1886–1965), German-born American philosopher and Protestant theologian, whose distinctive form of Christian existentialism proposed a reconciliation of religion and secular society. His developed views are expounded in his Systematic Theology (1951–63).

tilt /tɪlt/ v. & n. —v. 1 intr. & tr. assume or cause to assume a sloping position; heel over. 2 intr. (foll. by at) strike, thrust, or run at, with a weapon, esp. in jousting. 3 intr. (foll. by with) engage in a contest. 4 tr. forge or work (steel etc.) with a tilt-hammer. —n. 1 the act or an instance of tilting. 2 a sloping position. 3 (of medieval knights etc.) the act of charging with a lance against an opponent or at a mark, done for exercise or as a sport. 4 an encounter between opponents; an attack esp. with argument or satire (have a tilt at). 5 = tilt-hammer. □ **full** (or **at full**) **tilt** 1 at full speed. 2 with full force. **tilt-hammer** a heavy pivoted hammer used in forging. **tilt-yard** hist. a place where tilts (see sense 3 of n.) took place. □□ **tilter** n. [ME tilte perh. f. an OE form rel. to tealt unsteady f. Gmc: weapon senses of unkn. orig.]

tilth /tɪlθ/ n. 1 tillage, cultivation. 2 the condition of tilled soil (in good tilth). [OE tilth(e) (as TILL³)]

Tim. abbr. Timothy (New Testament).

Timaru /ˈtɪməˌruː/ a seaport and resort on the east coast of South Island, New Zealand; pop. (1988) 28,400.

timbal /ˈtɪmb(ə)l/ n. archaic a kettledrum. [F timbale, earlier tamballe f. Sp. atabal f. Arab. aṭ-ṭabl the drum]

timbale /tãˈbɑːl/ n. a drum-shaped dish of minced meat or fish in a pastry shell. [F: see TIMBAL]

timber /ˈtɪmbə(r)/ n. 1 wood prepared for building, carpentry, etc. 2 a piece of wood or beam, esp. as the rib of a vessel. 3 large standing trees suitable for timber; woods or forest. 4 (esp. as int.) a warning cry that a tree is about to fall. □ **timber hitch** a knot used in attaching a rope to a log or spar. **timber wolf** a type of large N. American grey wolf. □□ **timbering** n. [OE, = building, f. Gmc]

timbered /ˈtɪmbəd/ adj. 1 (esp. of a building) made wholly or partly of timber. 2 (of country) wooded.

timberland /ˈtɪmbəˌlænd/ n. US land covered with forest yielding timber.

timberline /ˈtɪmbəˌlaɪn/ n. (on a mountain) the line or level above which no trees grow.

timbre /ˈtæmbə(r), ˈtæbrə/ n. the distinctive character of a musical sound or voice apart from its pitch and intensity. [F f. Rmc f. med.Gk timbanon f. Gk tumpanon drum]

timbrel /ˈtɪmbr(ə)l/ n. archaic a tambourine or similar instrument. [dimin. of ME timbre f. OF (as TIMBRE, -LE²)]

Timbuktu /ˌtɪmbʌkˈtuː/ 1 (also **Tombouctou**) a town of Mali in Africa; pop. (est.) 20,500. 2 (**Timbuctoo**) any distant or remote place.

time /taɪm/ n. & v. —n. 1 the indefinite continued progress of existence, events, etc., in past, present, and future regarded as a whole. 2 **a** the progress of this as affecting persons or things (stood the test of time). **b** (**Time**) (in full **Father Time**) the personification of time, esp. as an old man, bald but with a forelock, carrying a scythe and hourglass. 3 a more or less definite portion of time belonging to particular events or circumstances (the time of the Plague; prehistoric times; the scientists of the time). 4 an allotted, available, or measurable portion of time; the period of time at one's disposal (am wasting my time; had no time to visit; how much time do you need?). 5 a point of time esp. in hours and minutes (the time is 7.30; what time is it?). 6 (prec. by a) an indefinite period (waited for a time). 7 time or an amount of time as reckoned by a conventional standard (the time allowed is one hour; ran the mile in record time; eight o'clock New York time). 8 **a** an occasion (last time I saw you). **b** an event or occasion qualified in some way (had a good time). 9 a moment or definite portion of time destined or suitable for a purpose etc. (now is the time to act; shall we fix a time?). 10 (in pl.) expressing multiplication (is four times as old; five times six is thirty). 11 a lifetime (will last my time). 12 (in sing. or pl.) **a** the conditions of life or of a period (hard times; times have changed). **b** (prec. by the) the present age, or that being considered. 13 colloq. a prison sentence (is doing time). 14 an apprenticeship (served his time). 15 a period of gestation. 16 the date or expected date of childbirth (is near her time) or of death (my time is drawing near). 17 measured time spent in work (put them on short time). 18 **a** any of several rhythmic patterns of music (in waltz time). **b** the duration of a note as indicated by a crotchet, minim, etc. 19 Brit. the moment at which the opening hours of a public house end. —v.tr. 1 choose the time or occasion for (time your remarks carefully). 2 do at a chosen or correct time. 3 arrange the time of arrival of. 4 ascertain the time taken by (a process or activity, or a person doing it). 5 regulate the duration or interval of; set times for (trains are timed to arrive every hour). □ **against time** with utmost speed, so as to finish by a specified time (working against time). **ahead of time** earlier than expected. **ahead of one's time** having ideas too enlightened or advanced to be accepted by one's contemporaries. **all the time 1** during the whole of the time referred to (often despite some contrary expectation etc.) (we never noticed, but he was there all the time). 2 constantly (nags all the time). 3 at all times (leaves a light on all the time). **at one time 1** in or during a known but unspecified past period. 2 simultaneously (ran three businesses at one time). **at the same time 1** simultaneously; at a time that is the same for all. 2 nevertheless (at the same time, I do not want to offend you). **at a time** separately in the specified groups or numbers (came three at a time). **at times** occasionally, intermittently. **before time** (usu. prec. by not) before the due or expected time. **before one's time** prematurely (old before his time). **for the time being** for the present; until some cther arrangement is made. **half the time** colloq. as often as not. **have no time for 1** be unable or unwilling to spend time on. **2** dislike. **have the time 1** be able to spend the time needed. **2** know from a watch etc. what time it is. **have a time of it** undergo trouble or difficulty. **in no** (or **less than no**) **time 1** very soon. **2** very quickly. **in one's own good time** at a time and a rate decided by oneself. **in one's own time** outside working hours. **in time 1** not late, punctual (*was in time to catch the bus*). **2** eventually (*in time you may agree*). **3** in accordance with a given rhythm or tempo, esp. of music. **in one's time** at or during some previous period of one's life (*in his time he was a great hurdler*). **keep good** (or **bad**) **time 1** (of a clock etc.) record time accurately (or inaccurately). **2** be habitually punctual (or not punctual). **keep time** move or sing etc. in time. **know the time of day** be well informed. **lose no time** (often foll. by *in* + verbal noun) act immediately (*lost no time in cashing the cheque*). **not before time** not too soon; timely. **no time** *colloq.* a very short interval (*it was no time before they came*). **out of time** unseasonable; unseasonably. **pass the time of day** *colloq.* exchange a greeting or casual remarks. **time after time 1** repeatedly, on many occasions. **2** in many instances. **time and** (or **time and time**) **again** on many occasions. **time and a half** a rate of payment for work at one and a half times the normal rate. **time-and-motion** (usu. *attrib.*) concerned with measuring the efficiency of industrial and other operations. **time bomb** a bomb designed to explode at a pre-set time. **time capsule** a box etc. containing objects typical of the present time, buried for discovery in the future. **time clock 1** a clock with a device for recording workers' hours of work. **2** a switch mechanism activated at pre-set times by a built-in clock. **time-consuming** using much or too much time. **time exposure** the exposure of photographic film for longer than the maximum normal shutter setting. **time factor** the passage of time as a limitation on what can be achieved. **time-fuse** a fuse calculated to burn for or explode at a given time. **time-honoured** esteemed by tradition or through custom. **time immemorial** (or **out of mind**) a longer time than anyone can remember or trace. **time-lag** an interval of time between an event, a cause, etc. and its effect. **time-lapse** (of photography) using frames taken at long intervals to photograph a slow process, and shown continuously as if at normal speed. **time-limit** the limit of time within which a task must be done. **the time of day** the hour by the clock. **time off** time for rest or recreation etc. **the time of one's life** a period or occasion of exceptional enjoyment. **time out** esp. *US* **1** a brief intermission in a game etc. **2** = *time off.* **time-scale** the time allowed for or taken by a sequence of events in relation to a broader period of time. **time-served** having completed a period of apprenticeship or training. **time-server** a person who changes his or her views to suit the prevailing circumstances, fashion, etc. **time-share** a share in a property under a time-sharing scheme. **time-sharing 1** the operation of a computer system by several users for different operations at one time. **2** the use of a holiday home at agreed different times by several joint owners. **time sheet** a sheet of paper for recording hours of work etc. **time signal** an audible (esp. broadcast) signal or announcement of the exact time of day. **time signature** *Mus.* an indication of tempo following a clef, expressed as a fraction with the numerator giving the number of beats in each bar and the denominator giving the duration of each beat. **time switch** a switch acting automatically at a pre-set time. **time warp** an imaginary distortion of space in relation to time, whereby persons or objects of one age can be moved to another. **time was** there was a time (*time was when I could do that*). **time-work** work paid for by the time it takes. **time-worn** impaired by age. **time zone** a range of longitudes where a common standard time is used. [OE *tīma* f. Gmc]

timekeeper /'taɪmˌkiːpə(r)/ *n.* **1** a person who records time, esp. of workers or in a game. **2 a** a watch or clock as regards accuracy (*a good timekeeper*). **b** a person as regards punctuality. □□ **timekeeping** *n.*

timeless /'taɪmlɪs/ *adj.* not affected by the passage of time; eternal. □□ **timelessly** *adv.* **timelessness** *n.*

timely /'taɪmlɪ/ *adj.* (**timelier, timeliest**) opportune; coming at the right time. □□ **timeliness** *n.*

timepiece /'taɪmpiːs/ *n.* an instrument, such as a clock or watch, for measuring time.

timer /'taɪmə(r)/ *n.* **1** a person or device that measures or records time taken. **2** an automatic mechanism for activating a device etc. at a pre-set time.

timetable /'taɪmˌteɪb(ə)l/ *n. & v.* —*n.* a list of times at which events are scheduled to take place, esp. the arrival and departure of buses or trains etc., or a sequence of lessons in a school or college. —*v.tr.* include in or arrange to a timetable; schedule.

timid /'tɪmɪd/ *adj.* (**timider, timidest**) easily frightened; apprehensive, shy. □□ **timidity** /-'mɪdɪtɪ/ *n.* **timidly** *adv.* **timidness** *n.* [F *timide* or L *timidus* f. *timēre* fear]

timing /'taɪmɪŋ/ *n.* **1** the way an action or process is timed, esp. in relation to others. **2** the regulation of the opening and closing of valves in an internal-combustion engine.

Timişoara /ˌtɪmɪ'ʃwaːrə/ an industrial city in western Romania; pop. (1985) 319,000. Incidents in this city gave rise to the revolution that brought to an end the Ceauşescu regime in 1989.

timocracy /tɪ'mɒkrəsɪ/ *n.* (*pl.* **-ies**) **1** a form of government in which possession of property is required in order to hold office. **2** a form of government in which rulers are motivated by love of honour. □□ **timocratic** /-ə'krætɪk/ *adj.* [OF *timocracie* f. med.L *timocratia* f. Gk *timokratia* f. *timē* honour, worth + *kratia* -CRACY]

Timor /'tiːmɔː(r)/ the largest of the Lesser Sunda Islands in the southern Malay Archipelago. The island was formerly divided into Dutch West Timor and Portuguese East Timor. In 1950 West Timor was absorbed into the newly formed Republic of Indonesia and in 1976 East Timor was annexed by Indonesia following the outbreak of civil war in the previous year. □ **Timor Sea** the part of the Indian Ocean between Timor and NW Australia.

timorous /'tɪmərəs/ *adj.* **1** timid; easily alarmed. **2** frightened. □□ **timorously** *adv.* **timorousness** *n.* [ME f. OF *temoreus* f. med.L *timorosus* f. L *timor* f. *timēre* fear]

Timothy /'tɪməθɪ/, St (1st c. AD), a convert and colleague of St Paul. □ (**Epistle to**) **Timothy** either of two Pauline epistles of the New Testament addressed to him.

timothy /'tɪməθɪ/ *n.* (in full **timothy grass**) a fodder grass, *Phleum pratense*. [*Timothy* Hanson, who introduced it in Carolina *c.*1720]

timpani /'tɪmpənɪ/ *n.pl.* (also **tympani**) kettle-drums. □□ **timpanist** *n.* [It., pl. of *timpano* = TYMPANUM]

tin /tɪn/ *n. & v.* **1** *Chem.* a silvery-white malleable metallic element. (See below.) ¶ Symb.: **Sn**; atomic number 50. **2 a** a vessel or container made of tin or tinned iron. **b** *Brit.* an airtight sealed container made of tin plate or aluminium for preserving food. **3** = *tin plate.* **4** *Brit. sl.* money. —*v.tr.* (**tinned, tinning**) **1** seal (food) in an airtight tin for preservation. **2** cover or coat with tin. □ **put the tin lid on** see LID. **tin can** a tin container (see sense 2 of *n.*), esp. an empty one. **tin foil** foil made of tin, aluminium, or tin alloy, used for wrapping food for cooking or storing. **tin-glaze** a glaze made white and opaque by the addition of tin oxide. **tin god 1** an object of unjustified veneration. **2** a self-important person. **tin hat** *colloq.* a military steel helmet. **tin Lizzie** *colloq.* an old or decrepit car. **tin-opener** a tool for opening tins. **tin plate** sheet iron or sheet steel coated with tin. **tin-plate** *v.tr.* coat with tin. **tin soldier** a toy soldier made of metal. **tin-tack** an iron tack. **tin whistle** = *penny whistle.* [OE f. Gmc]

Tin can occur native but is more often found as ores, especially cassiterite. It has two major allotropic forms: white tin, the normal metallic form, and grey tin, a powdery form to which white tin tends to change at low temperatures. The metal takes a high polish and is resistant to corrosion. It is used in a number of important alloys (with lead, copper, or antimony to form solder, white-metal, pewter, bronze, etc.), or for plating iron and steel sheets to form tin plate for containers, kitchen utensils, toys, etc. Its use in making bronze dates from ancient times.

tinamou /'tɪnəˌmuː/ *n.* any South American bird of the family Tinamidae, resembling a grouse but related to the rhea. [F f. Galibi *tinamu*]

Tinbergen[1] /'tɪnbɜːgən/, Jan (1903–), Dutch economist, brother of the zoologist Nikolaas Tinbergen. In 1969 he shared with Ragnar Frisch the first Nobel Prize for economics, awarded for his pioneering work on econometrics.

Tinbergen[2] /'tɪnbɜːgən/, Nikolaas (1907–), Dutch zoologist, noted for his studies of animal behaviour, which helped to establish ethology as a distinct discipline, with relevance also to human psychology and sociology. He was awarded a Nobel Prize in 1973.

tinctorial /tɪŋk'tɔːrɪəl/ adj. **1** of or relating to colour or dyeing. **2** producing colour. [L tinctorius f. tinctor dyer: see TINGE]

tincture /'tɪŋktʃə(r), -tʃə(r)/ n. & v. —n. (often foll. by of) **1** a slight flavour or trace. **2** a tinge (of a colour). **3** a medicinal solution (of a drug) in alcohol (tincture of quinine). **4** Heraldry an inclusive term for the metals, colours, and furs used in coats of arms. **5** colloq. an alcoholic drink. —v.tr. **1** colour slightly; tinge, flavour. **2** (often foll. by with) affect slightly (with a quality). [ME f. L tinctura dyeing (as TINGE)]

tinder /'tɪndə(r)/ n. a dry substance such as wood that readily catches fire from a spark. □ **tinder-box** hist. a box containing tinder, flint, and steel, formerly used for kindling fires. □□ **tindery** adj. [OE tynder, tyndre f. Gmc]

tine /taɪn/ n. a prong or tooth or point of a fork, comb, antler, etc. □□ **tined** adj. (also in comb.). [OE tind]

tinea /'tɪnɪə/ n. Med. ringworm. [L, = moth, worm]

ting /tɪŋ/ n. & v. —n. a tinkling sound as of a bell. —v.intr. & tr. emit or cause to emit this sound. [imit.]

tinge /tɪndʒ/ v. & n. —v.tr. (also **tingeing**) (often foll. by with; often in passive) **1** colour slightly (is tinged with red). **2** affect slightly (regret tinged with satisfaction). —n. **1** a tendency towards or trace of some colour. **2** a slight admixture of a feeling or quality. [ME f. L tingere tinct- dye, stain]

tingle /'tɪŋg(ə)l/ v. & n. —v. **1** intr. **a** feel a slight prickling, stinging, or throbbing sensation. **b** cause this (the reply tingled in my ears). **2** tr. make (the ear etc.) tingle. —n. a tingling sensation. [ME, perh. var. of TINKLE]

tingly /'tɪŋglɪ/ adj. (**tinglier**, **tingliest**) causing or characterized by tingling.

tinhorn /'tɪnhɔːn/ n. & adj. US sl. —n. a pretentious but unimpressive person. —adj. cheap, pretentious.

tinker /'tɪŋkə(r)/ n. & v. —n. **1** an itinerant mender of kettles and pans etc. **2** Sc. & Ir. a gypsy. **3** colloq. a mischievous person or animal. **4** a spell of tinkering. **5** a rough-and-ready worker. —v. **1** intr. (foll. by at, with) work in an amateurish or desultory way, esp. to adjust or mend machinery etc. **2 a** intr. work as a tinker. **b** tr. repair (pots and pans). □□ **tinkerer** n. [ME: orig. unkn.]

tinkle /'tɪŋk(ə)l/ v. & n. —v. **1** intr. & tr. make or cause to make a succession of short light ringing sounds. **2** intr. colloq. urinate. —n. **1** a tinkling sound. **2** Brit. colloq. a telephone call (will give you a tinkle on Monday). **3** colloq. an act of urinating. [ME f. obs. tink to chink (imit.)]

tinner /'tɪnə(r)/ n. **1** a tin-miner. **2** a tinsmith.

tinnitus /tɪ'naɪtəs/ n. Med. a ringing in the ears. [L f. tinnire tinnit- ring, tinkle, of imit. orig.]

tinny /'tɪnɪ/ adj. & n. —adj. (**tinnier**, **tinniest**) **1** of or like tin. **2** (of a metal object) flimsy, insubstantial. **3 a** sounding like struck tin. **b** (of reproduced sound) thin and metallic, lacking low frequencies. **4** Austral. sl. lucky. —n. (also **tinnie**) (pl. **-ies**) Austral. sl. a can of beer. □□ **tinnily** adv. **tinniness** n.

Tin Pan Alley originally the name given to a district in New York (28th Street, between 5th Avenue and Broadway) where many songwriters, arrangers, and music publishers were based. The district gave its name to the American popular music industry between the late 1880s and the mid-20th c., particularly to such composers as Irving Berlin, Jerome Kern, George Gershwin, Cole Porter, and Richard Rodgers. The term was also applied to Denmark Street in London.

tinpot /'tɪnpɒt/ adj. Brit. cheap, inferior.

tinsel /'tɪns(ə)l/ n. & v. —n. **1** glittering metallic strips, threads, etc., used as decoration to give a sparkling effect. **2** a fabric adorned with tinsel. **3** superficial brilliance or splendour. **4** (attrib.) showy, gaudy, flashy. —v.tr. (**tinselled**, **tinselling**) adorn with or as with tinsel. □□ **tinselled** adj. **tinselly** adj. [OF estincele spark f. L scintilla]

tinsmith /'tɪnsmɪθ/ n. a worker in tin and tin plate.

tinsnips /'tɪnsnɪps/ n. a pair of clippers for cutting sheet metal.

tinstone /'tɪnstəʊn/ n. Geol. = CASSITERITE.

tint /tɪnt/ n. & v. —n. **1** a variety of a colour, esp. one made lighter by adding white. **2** a tendency towards or admixture of a different colour (red with a blue tint). **3** a faint colour spread over a surface, esp. as a background for printing on. **4** a set of parallel engraved lines to give uniform shading. —v.tr. apply a tint to; colour. □□ **tinter** n. [alt. of earlier tinct f. L tinctus dyeing (as TINGE), perh. infl. by It. tinto]

Tintagel /tɪn'tædʒ(ə)l/ a village on the coast of northern Cornwall, with ruins of a castle. It is the traditional birthplace of King Arthur.

tintinnabulation /ˌtɪntɪˌnæbjʊ'leɪʃ(ə)n/ n. a ringing or tinkling of bells. [as L tintinnabulum tinkling bell f. tintinnare redupl. form of tinnire ring]

Tintoretto /ˌtɪntə'retəʊ/, Jacopo Robusti (1518–94), Venetian painter, given his nickname because his father was a dyer (tintore). Little is known of his early life but he began his artistic career in about 1537 and some sources claim he did work, however briefly, in Titian's studio. He spent nearly all his life in Venice, personally unpopular and considered professionally unscrupulous. Although he received both religious and State commissions, he did not attract aristocratic patronage as much as he appealed to the monied middle classes. From 1550 the influence of Titian and Veronese can be seen and Tintoretto's works take on a mannerist religious intensity, where the mood dominates. His work can be distinguished by unusual viewpoints, bold colour, lively sometimes rushed brushwork, and the hint of the bizarre, highlighted by bold chiaroscuro effects.

tinware /'tɪnweə(r)/ n. articles made of tin or tin plate.

tiny /'taɪnɪ/ adj. (**tinier**, **tiniest**) very small or slight. □□ **tinily** adv. **tininess** n. [obs. tine, tyne (adj. & n.) small, a little: ME, of unkn. orig.]

-tion /ʃ(ə)n/ suffix forming nouns of action, condition, etc. (see -ION, -ATION, -ITION, -UTION). [from or after F -tion or L -tio -tionis]

tip[1] /tɪp/ n. & v. —n. **1** an extremity or end, esp. of a small or tapering thing (tips of the fingers). **2** a small piece or part attached to the end of a thing, e.g. a ferrule on a stick. **3** a leaf-bud of tea. —v.tr. (**tipped**, **tipping**) **1** provide with a tip. **2** tr. (foll. by in) attach (a loose sheet) to a page at the inside edge. □ **on the tip of one's tongue** about to be said, esp. after difficulty in recalling to mind. **the tip of the iceberg** a small evident part of something much larger or more significant. □□ **tipless** adj. **tippy** adj. (in sense 3). [ME f. ON typpi (n.), typpa (v.), typptr tipped f. Gmc (rel. to TOP[1]): prob. reinforced by MDu. & MLG tip]

tip[2] /tɪp/ v. & n. —v. (**tipped**, **tipping**) **1 a** intr. lean or slant. **b** tr. cause to do this. **2** tr. (foll. by into etc.) **a** overturn or cause to overbalance (was tipped into the pond). **b** discharge the contents of (a container etc.) in this way. —n. **1 a** a slight push or tilt. **b** a light stroke, esp. in baseball. **2** Brit. a place where material (esp. refuse) is tipped. □ **tip the balance** make the critical difference. **tip the scales** see SCALE[2]. **tip-up** able to be tipped, e.g. of a seat in a theatre to allow passage past. [17th c.: orig. uncert.]

tip[3] /tɪp/ v. & n. —v. (**tipped**, **tipping**) (often foll. by over, up) **1** tr. make a small present of money to, esp. for a service given (have you tipped the porter?). **2** tr. name as the likely winner of a race or contest etc. **3** tr. strike or touch lightly. **4** tr. sl. give, hand, pass (esp. in tip the wink below). —n. **1** a small money present, esp. for a service given. **2** a piece of private or special information, esp. regarding betting or investment. **3** a small or casual piece of advice. □ **tip off 1** give (a person) a hint or piece of special information or warning, esp. discreetly or confidentially. **2** Basketball start play by throwing the ball up between two opponents. **tip-off** a hint or warning etc. given discreetly or confidentially. **tip a person the wink** give a person private information. □□ **tipper** n. [ME: orig. uncert.]

tipcat /'tɪpkæt/ n. **1** a game with a short piece of wood tapering at the ends and struck with a stick. **2** this piece of wood.

tipper /'tɪpə(r)/ n. (often attrib.) a road haulage vehicle that tips at the back to discharge its load.

Tipperary /ˌtɪpə'reərɪ/ a county of central Ireland, in the province of Munster; divided into North and South Ridings; pop. (est. 1986) 137,000.

tippet /'tɪpɪt/ n. **1** a covering of fur etc. for the shoulders formerly worn by women. **2** a similar garment worn as part of some official costumes, esp. by the clergy. **3** hist. a long narrow strip of cloth as part of or an attachment to a hood etc. [ME, prob. f. TIP[1]]

Tippett /'tɪpɪt/, Sir Michael Kemp (1905–), English composer. In 1938–9 he composed the Concerto for Double String Orchestra, a work which bears many of his stylistic fingerprints—in particular the marked rhythmic drive. He was a conscientious objector in the Second World War, and his concerns with the different strands which make up human nature—light and dark, warm and shrinking, calm and violent—is expressed in much of his music, particularly the oratorio A Child of our Time (1939–41) and his four operas (1955–77), as well as in his writings. He has not shunned traditional instrumental forms, and other works include four symphonies (1944–77), four string quartets (1934–79), and three piano sonatas (1936–73).

tipple /'tɪp(ə)l/ v. & n. —v. **1** intr. drink intoxicating liquor habitually. **2** tr. drink (liquor) repeatedly in small amounts. —n. colloq. a drink, esp. a strong one. □□ **tippler** n. [ME, backform. f. tippler, of unkn. orig.]

tipstaff /'tɪpstɑːf/ n. **1** a sheriff's officer. **2** a metal-tipped staff carried as a symbol of office. [contr. of tipped staff, i.e. tipped with metal]

tipster /'tɪpstə(r)/ n. a person who gives tips, esp. about betting at horse-races.

tipsy /'tɪpsɪ/ adj. (**tipsier, tipsiest**) **1** slightly intoxicated. **2** caused by or showing intoxication (a tipsy leer). □ **tipsy-cake** Brit. a sponge cake soaked in wine or spirits and served with custard. □□ **tipsily** adv. **tipsiness** n. [prob. f. TIP[2] = inclined to lean, unsteady: for -sy cf. FLIMSY, TRICKSY]

tiptoe /'tɪptəʊ/ n., v., & adv. —n. the tips of the toes. —v.intr. (**tiptoes, tiptoed, tiptoeing**) walk on tiptoe, or very stealthily. —adv. (also **on tiptoe**) with the heels off the ground and the weight on the balls of the feet.

tiptop /'tɪptɒp/ adj., adv., & n. colloq. —adj. & adv. highest in excellence; very best. —n. the highest point of excellence.

TIR abbr. international road transport (esp. with ref. to EEC regulations). [F, = transport international routier]

tirade /taɪ'reɪd, tɪ-/ n. a long vehement denunciation or declamation. [F, = long speech, f. It. tirata volley f. tirare pull f. Rmc]

tirailleur /ˌtiːraː'jɜː(r), ˌtɪrə'lɜː(r)/ n. **1** a sharpshooter. **2** a skirmisher. [F f. tirailler shoot independently f. tirer shoot, draw, f. Rmc]

Tiranë /tɪ'rɑːnə/ the capital of Albania; pop. (1983) 206,000.

tire[1] /'taɪə(r)/ v. **1** tr. & intr. make or grow weary. **2** tr. exhaust the patience or interest of; bore. **3** tr. (in passive; foll. by of) have had enough of; be fed up with (was tired of arguing). [OE tēorian, of unkn. orig.]

tire[2] /'taɪə(r)/ n. **1** a band of metal placed round the rim of a wheel to strengthen it. **2** US var. of TYRE. [ME, perh. = archaic tire head-dress]

tired /'taɪəd/ adj. **1** weary, exhausted; ready for sleep. **2** (of an idea etc.) hackneyed. □□ **tiredly** adv. **tiredness** n.

Tiree /taɪ'riː/ an island in the Inner Hebrides west of Mull.

tireless /'taɪəlɪs/ adj. having inexhaustible energy. □□ **tirelessly** adv. **tirelessness** n.

Tiresias /taɪ'riːsɪəs/ Gk legend a blind Theban prophet, so wise that even his ghost had its wits and was not a mere phantom. Legends account variously for his wisdom and blindness.

tiresome /'taɪəsəm/ adj. **1** wearisome, tedious. **2** colloq. annoying (how tiresome of you!). □□ **tiresomely** adv. **tiresomeness** n.

Tir-nan-Og /ˌtɪənæ'nəʊg/ Irish Mythol. a land of perpetual youth, the Irish equivalent of Elysium. [Ir., = land of the young]

tiro /'taɪəˌrəʊ/ n. (also **tyro**) (pl. **-os**) a beginner or novice. [L tiro, med.L tyro, recruit]

Tirol see TYROL.

Tiruchirapalli /ˌtɪrətʃɪ'raːpəlɪ/ a city in Tamil Nadu State in southern India; pop. (1981) 608,000.

'tis /tɪz/ archaic it is. [contr.]

tisane /tɪ'zæn/ n. an infusion of dried herbs etc. [F: see PTISAN]

Tisiphone /tɪ'sɪfənɪ/ Gk Mythol. one of the Furies. [Gk, = the avenger of blood]

tissue /'tɪʃuː, 'tɪsjuː/ n. **1** any of the coherent collections of specialized cells of which animals or plants are made (muscular tissue; nervous tissue). **2** = tissue-paper. **3** a disposable piece of thin soft absorbent paper for wiping, drying, etc. **4** fine woven esp. gauzy fabric. **5** (foll. by of) a connected series (a tissue of lies). □ **tissue-paper** thin soft unsized paper for wrapping or protecting fragile or delicate articles. [ME f. OF tissu rich material, past part. of tistre f. L texere weave]

Tisza /'tiːsə/ the longest tributary of the Danube in eastern Europe. Rising in the Carpathian Mountains of Ukraine, it flows 962 km (600 miles) southwards through Romania and Hungary before meeting the Danube in Yugoslavia, south-west of Belgrade.

Tit. abbr. Titus (New Testament).

tit[1] /tɪt/ n. any of various small birds esp. of the family Paridae. [prob. f. Scand.]

tit[2] /tɪt/ n. □ **tit for tat** /tæt/ blow for blow; retaliation. [= earlier tip (TIP[2]) for tap]

tit[3] /tɪt/ n. **1** colloq. a nipple. **2** coarse sl. a woman's breast. ¶ Usually considered a taboo word in sense 2. [OE: cf. MLG titte]

tit[4] /tɪt/ n. coarse sl. a term of contempt for a person. [20th c.: perh. f. TIT[3]]

Titan /'taɪt(ə)n/ n. **1** Gk Mythol. any of the older gods who preceded the Olympians and were the children of Heaven and Earth. They are believed to be pre-Greek gods, but the evidence is slight. **2** (often **titan**) a person of very great strength, intellect, or importance. □□ **Titaness** n. fem. [ME f. L f. Gk]

Titanic /taɪ'tænɪk/ a British passenger liner, the largest ship in the world when she was built, that struck an iceberg in the North Atlantic on her maiden voyage in April 1912 and sank with the loss of 1,490 lives. The disaster led to new regulations requiring ships to carry sufficient lifeboats for all on board, a more southerly liner track across the Atlantic, and an ice patrol which continues to this day.

titanic[1] /taɪ'tænɪk/ adj. **1** of or like the Titans. **2** gigantic, colossal. □□ **titanically** adv. [Gk titanikos (as TITAN)]

titanic[2] /taɪ'tænɪk, tɪ-/ adj. Chem. of titanium, esp. in quadrivalent form. □□ **titanate** /'taɪtəˌneɪt, 'tɪ-/ n.

titanium /taɪ'teɪnɪəm, tɪ-/ n. Chem. a grey metallic element occurring naturally in many clays etc., widespread in the earth's crust. It is not found uncombined in nature. First discovered (as the oxide) in 1791, titanium did not become commercially significant until after the Second World War. Since then its lightness, strength, and resistance to corrosion have found use in alloys for parts of aircraft, space vehicles, etc. Of its various compounds, titanium dioxide is noteworthy: it is a very opaque white solid which is widely used in paints and other surface coatings. ¶ Symb.: Ti; atomic number 22. □ **titanium dioxide** (or **oxide**) a white oxide occurring naturally and used as a white pigment. [Gk (as TITAN) + -IUM, after uranium]

titbit /'tɪtbɪt/ n. (US **tidbit** /'tɪd-/) **1** a dainty morsel. **2** a piquant item of news etc. [perh. f. dial. tid tender + BIT[1]]

titch /tɪtʃ/ n. (also **tich**) colloq. a small person. [Tich, stage name of Harry Relph (d. 1928), Engl. music-hall comedian]

titchy /'tɪtʃɪ/ adj. (**titchier, titchiest**) colloq. very small.

titer US var. of TITRE.

titfer /'tɪtfə(r)/ n. Brit. sl. a hat. [abbr. of tit for tat, rhyming sl.]

tithe /taɪð/ n. & v. —n. **1** one tenth of the annual produce of land or labour, formerly taken as a tax for the support of the Church and clergy. **2** a tenth part. —v. **1** tr. subject to tithes. **2** intr. pay tithes. □ **tithe barn** a barn built to hold tithes paid in kind. □□ **tithable** adj. [OE teogotha tenth]

tithing /'taɪðɪŋ/ n. **1** the practice of taking or paying a tithe. **2** *hist.* **a** ten householders living near together and collectively responsible for each other's behaviour. **b** the area occupied by them. [OE *tīgething* (as TITHE, -ING¹)]

Tithonus /tɪ'θəʊnəs/ *Gk Mythol.* a Trojan prince with whom the goddess Aurora fell in love. She asked Zeus to make him immortal but omitted to ask for eternal youth, and he became very old and decrepit although he talked perpetually. Tithonus prayed her to remove him from this world and she changed him into a grasshopper, which chirps ceaselessly.

titi /'ti:ti:/ n. (pl. **titis**) any South American monkey of the genus *Callicebus*. [Tupi]

Titian /'tɪʃ(ə)n/ (Tiziano Vecellio, *c.*1488–1576), Italian painter, who dominated Venetian art during its greatest period. Trained in the studio of Giovanni Bellini, he was inspired by Giorgione, after whose early death (1510) it fell to Titian to complete a number of his unfinished paintings. On Bellini's death in 1516 Titian became official painter to the Republic. Among his most famous works are the enigmatic *Sacred and Profane Love* (*c.*1516), the *Assumption* (1516–18), and classical subjects such as *Bacchus and Ariadne* (1518–23). His fame spread throughout Europe; Charles V appointed him court painter and knighted him. Titian painted many noble portraits, conveying the sitters' personalities and not merely recording their features. His last great work was the *Pietà* (1573–6) intended for his own tomb. Titian's influence on later painters has been profound. His greatness as an artist, it appears, was not matched by his character; he was of a mercenary disposition.

His name is used to denote the colour of hair which he favoured in his pictures (e.g. *Ariadne*, *The Magdalene*, and *Flora*), described as 'a bright golden auburn' and more loosely used as a polite or appreciative word for 'red'.

Titicaca /ˌtɪtɪ'kɑːkə/, **Lake** a lake in the Andes, between Peru and Bolivia, at an altitude of 3,809 m (12,497 ft.), the highest large lake in the world.

titillate /'tɪtɪˌleɪt/ v.tr. **1** excite pleasantly. **2** tickle. □□ **titillatingly** adv. **titillation** /-'leɪʃ(ə)n/ n. [L *titillare titillat-*]

titivate /'tɪtɪˌveɪt/ v.tr. (also **tittivate**) *colloq.* **1** adorn, smarten. **2** (often *refl.*) put the finishing touches to. □□ **titivation** /-'veɪʃ(ə)n/ n. [earlier *tidivate*, perh. f. TIDY after *cultivate*]

titlark /'tɪtlɑːk/ n. a pipit, esp. the meadow pipit.

title /'taɪt(ə)l/ n. & v. —n. **1** the name of a book, work of art, piece of music, etc. **2** the heading of a chapter, poem, document, etc. **3 a** the contents of the title-page of a book. **b** a book regarded in terms of its title (*published 20 new titles*). **4** a caption or credit in a film, broadcast, etc. **5** a form of nomenclature indicating a person's status (e.g. *professor, queen*) or used as a form of address or reference (e.g. *Lord, Mr, Your Grace*). **6** a championship in sport. **7** *Law* **a** the right to ownership of property with or without possession. **b** the facts constituting this. **c** (foll. by *to*) a just or recognized claim. **8** *Eccl.* **a** a fixed sphere of work and source of income as a condition for ordination. **b** a parish church in Rome under a cardinal. —v.tr. give a title to. □ **title-deed** a legal instrument as evidence of a right, esp. to property. **title-page** a page at the beginning of a book giving the title and particulars of authorship etc. **title role** the part in a play etc. that gives it its name (e.g. Othello). [ME f. OF f. L *titulus* placard, title]

titled /'taɪt(ə)ld/ adj. having a title of nobility or rank.

titling¹ /'taɪtlɪŋ/ n. the impressing of a title in gold leaf etc. on the cover of a book.

titling² /'tɪtlɪŋ/ n. **1** a titlark. **2** a titmouse.

titmouse /'tɪtmaʊs/ n. (pl. **titmice** /-maɪs/) any of various small tits, esp. of the genus *Parus*. [ME *titmōse* f. TIT¹ + OE *māse* titmouse, assim. to MOUSE]

Tito /'tiːtəʊ/ (Josip Broz, 1892–1980), Yugoslavian statesman. An NCO in the Austro-Hungarian army, Tito was captured by the Russians in 1915 and after escaping participated in the Russian Revolution and Civil War on the Red side. He returned to Yugoslavia in 1920 and became an active Communist organizer. With the German invasion in 1941 he became a guerrilla leader, gradually establishing his Partisans as the most effective resistance movement, winning Allied support, and emerging as head of the new government at the end of the war. He defied Stalin over policy in the Balkans in 1948 and established Yugoslavia as a non-aligned Communist State, being elected President in 1953 and after successive re-elections being named President for life in 1974.

Titograd /'tiːtəʊˌɡræd/ the capital of the republic of Montenegro in western Yugoslavia; pop. (1981) 132,400. Formerly named Podgorica, it was renamed in honour of Marshal Tito in 1948.

titrate /'taɪtreɪt, 'tɪ-/ v.tr. *Chem.* ascertain the amount of a constituent in (a solution) by measuring the volume of a known concentration of reagent required to complete the reaction. □□ **titratable** adj. **titration** /-'treɪʃ(ə)n/ n.

titre /'taɪtə(r)/ n. (*US* **titer**) *Chem.* the strength of a solution or the quantity of a constituent as determined by titration. [F, = TITLE]

titter /'tɪtə(r)/ v. & n. —v.intr. laugh in a furtive or restrained way; giggle. —n. a furtive or restrained laugh. □□ **titterer** n. **titteringly** adv. [imit.]

tittivate var. of TITIVATE.

tittle /'tɪt(ə)l/ n. **1** a small written or printed stroke or dot. **2** a particle; a whit (esp. in *not one jot or tittle*). [ME f. L (as TITLE)]

tittlebat /'tɪt(ə)lˌbæt/ n. *Brit.* a stickleback. [fanciful var.]

tittle-tattle /'tɪt(ə)lˌtæt(ə)l/ n. & v. —n. petty gossip. —v.intr. gossip, chatter. [redupl. of TATTLE]

tittup /'tɪtəp/ v. & n. —v.intr. (**tittuped, tittuping** or **tittupped, tittupping**) go about friskily or jerkily; bob up and down; canter. —n. such a gait or movement. [perh. imit. of hoof-beats]

titty /'tɪtɪ/ n. (pl. **-ies**) *sl.* = TIT³ (esp. as a child's term).

titubation /ˌtɪtjʊ'beɪʃ(ə)n/ n. *Med.* unsteadiness esp. as caused by nervous disease. [L *titubatio* f. *titubare* totter]

titular /'tɪtjʊlə(r)/ adj. & n. —adj. **1** of or relating to a title (*the book's titular hero*). **2** existing, or being what is specified, in name or title only (*titular ruler; titular sovereignty*). —n. **1** the holder of an office etc. esp. a benefice, without the corresponding functions or obligations. **2** a titular saint. □ **titular bishop** a bishop, esp. in a non-Christian country, with a see named after a Christian see no longer in existence. **titular saint** the patron saint of a particular church. □□ **titularly** adv. [F *titulaire* or mod.L *titularis* f. *titulus* TITLE]

Titus¹ /'taɪtəs/ (Titus Flavius Vespasianus, 39–81) Roman emperor 79–81, elder son of Vespasian. In 70 he ended a revolt in Judaea and destroyed Jerusalem. A popular and generous emperor, he completed the Colosseum and provided relief for the destruction caused by the eruption of Vesuvius in 79.

Titus² /'taɪtəs/, St (1st c. AD), a convert and helper of St Paul. □ **(Epistle to) Titus** a Pauline epistle of the New Testament addressed to him.

tizzy /'tɪzɪ/ n. (pl. **-ies**) (also **tizz, tiz**) *colloq.* a state of nervous agitation (*in a tizzy*). [20th c.: orig. unkn.]

T-junction /'tiːˌdʒʌŋkʃ(ə)n/ n. a road junction at which one road joins another at right angles without crossing it.

TKO abbr. *Boxing* technical knockout.

Tl symb. *Chem.* the element thallium.

Tlaxcala /tlɑːsˈkɑːlə/ **1** a State of east central Mexico; pop. (est. 1988) 665,600. **2** its capital city; pop. (est.) 16,000.

TLC abbr. *colloq.* tender loving care.

TLS abbr. *Times Literary Supplement*.

TM abbr. Transcendental Meditation.

Tm symb. *Chem.* the element thulium.

tmesis /'tmiːsɪs/ n. (pl. **tmeses** /-siːz/) *Gram.* the separation of parts of a compound word by an intervening word or words (esp. in colloq. speech, e.g. *can't find it any-blooming-where*). [Gk *tmēsis* cutting f. *temnō* cut]

TN abbr. *US* Tennessee (in official postal use).

tn abbr. **1** *US* ton(s). **2** town.

---

b *but* d *dog* f *few* g *get* h *he* j *yes* k *cat* l *leg* m *man* n *no* p *pen* r *red* s *sit* t *top* v *voice*

TNT *abbr.* trinitrotoluene, a high explosive formed from toluene by substitution of three hydrogen atoms with nitro groups.

to /tə, *before a vowel* tʊ, *emphat.* tu:/ *prep. & adv.* —*prep.* **1** introducing a noun: **a** expressing what is reached, approached, or touched (*fell to the ground; went to Paris; put her face to the window; five minutes to six*). **b** expressing what is aimed at: often introducing the indirect object of a verb (*throw it to me; explained the problem to them*). **c** as far as; up to (*went on to the end; have to stay from Tuesday to Friday*). **d** to the extent of (*were all drunk to a man; was starved to death*). **e** expressing what is followed (*according to instructions; made to order*). **f** expressing what is considered or affected (*am used to that; that is nothing to me*). **g** expressing what is caused or produced (*turn to stone; tear to shreds*). **h** expressing what is compared (*nothing to what it once was; comparable to any other; equal to the occasion; won by three goals to two*). **i** expressing what is increased (*add it to mine*). **j** expressing what is involved or composed as specified (*there is nothing to it; more to him than meets the eye*). **k** expressing the substance of a debit entry in accounting (*to four chairs, sixty pounds*). **l** *archaic* for; by way of (*took her to wife*). **2** introducing the infinitive: **a** as a verbal noun (*to get there is the priority*). **b** expressing purpose, consequence, or cause (*we eat to live; left him to starve; am sorry to hear that*). **c** as a substitute for *to* + infinitive (*wanted to come but was unable to*). —*adv.* **1** in the normal or required position or condition (*come to; heave to*). **2** (of a door) in a nearly closed position. □ **to and fro 1** backwards and forwards. **2** repeatedly between the same points. [OE tō (adv. & prep.) f. WG]

toad /təʊd/ *n.* **1** any froglike amphibian of the family Bufonidae, esp. of the genus *Bufo*, breeding in water but living chiefly on land. **2** any of various similar amphibians including the Surinam toad. **3** a repulsive or detestable person. □ **toad-eater** *archaic* a toady. **toad-in-the-hole** *Brit.* sausages or other meat baked in batter. □□ **toadish** *adj.* [OE tādige, tādde, tāda, of unkn. orig.]

toadfish /ˈtəʊdfɪʃ/ *n.* any marine fish of the family Batrachoididae, with a large head and wide mouth, making grunting noises by vibrating the walls of its swim-bladder.

toadflax /ˈtəʊdflæks/ *n.* **1** any plant of the genus *Linaria* or *Chaenorrhinum*, with flaxlike leaves and spurred yellow or purple flowers. **2** a related plant, *Cymbalaria muralis*, with lilac flowers and ivy-shaped leaves.

toadstone /ˈtəʊdstəʊn/ *n.* a stone, sometimes precious, supposed to resemble or to have been formed in the body of a toad, formerly used as an amulet etc.

toadstool /ˈtəʊdstuːl/ *n.* the spore-bearing structure of various fungi, usu. poisonous, with a round top and slender stalk.

toady /ˈtəʊdɪ/ *n. & v.* —*n.* (*pl.* **-ies**) a sycophant; an obsequious hanger-on. —*v.tr. &* (foll. by *to*) *intr.* (**-ies, -ied**) behave servilely to; fawn upon. □□ **toadyish** *adj.* **toadyism** *n.* [contr. of *toad-eater*, orig. the attendant of a charlatan, employed to eat or pretend to eat toads (held to be poisonous) to enable his master to exhibit his skill in expelling poison]

toast /təʊst/ *n. & v.* —*n.* **1** bread in slices browned on both sides by radiant heat. **2 a** a person (orig. esp. a woman) or thing in whose honour a company is requested to drink. **b** a call to drink or an instance of drinking in this way. —*v.* **1** *tr.* cook or brown (bread, a teacake, cheese, etc.) by radiant heat. **2** *intr.* (of bread etc.) become brown in this way. **3** *tr.* warm (one's feet, oneself, etc.) at a fire etc. **4** *tr.* drink to the health or in honour of (a person or thing). □ **have a person on toast** *colloq.* be in a position to deal with a person as one wishes. **toasting-fork** a long-handled fork for making toast before a fire. **toast rack** a rack for holding slices of toast at table. [ME (orig. as verb) f. OF *toster* roast, ult. f. L *torrēre tost-* parch: sense 2 of the noun reflects the notion that a woman's name flavours the drink as spiced toast would]

toaster /ˈtəʊstə(r)/ *n.* an electrical device for making toast.

toastmaster /ˈtəʊst,mɑːstə(r)/ *n.* (*fem.* **toastmistress** /-,mɪstrɪs/) an official responsible for announcing toasts at a public occasion.

tobacco /təˈbækəʊ/ *n.* (*pl.* **-os**) **1** (in full **tobacco-plant**) any plant of the genus *Nicotiana*, of American origin, with narcotic leaves used for smoking, chewing, or snuff. **2** its leaves, esp. as prepared for smoking. Tobacco was introduced into England in the reign of Queen Elizabeth I. Although it can be grown in temperate climates its cultivation as a crop is carried out mainly in tropical and subtropical countries. □ **tobacco mosaic virus** a virus that causes mosaic disease in tobacco, much used in biochemical research. **tobacco-pipe** see PIPE *n.* 2. **tobacco-stopper** an instrument for pressing down the tobacco in a pipe. [Sp. *tabaco*, of Amer. Ind. orig.]

tobacconist /təˈbækənɪst/ *n.* a retail dealer in tobacco and cigarettes etc.

Tobit /ˈtəʊbɪt/ a book of the Apocrypha, a romance of the Jewish captivity telling the story of Tobit, a pious Jew.

toboggan /təˈbɒɡən/ *n. & v.* —*n.* a long light narrow sledge for sliding downhill esp. over compacted snow or ice. —*v.intr.* ride on a toboggan. As a winter recreation, tobogganing is recorded in 16th-c. documents. Its development as a racing sport dates from the mid-19th c. □□ **tobogganer** *n.* **tobogganing** *n.* **tobogganist** *n.* [Can. F *tabaganne* f. Algonquian]

Tobruk /təˈbrʊk/ (Arabic **Tubruq**) a port on the Mediterranean coast of NE Libya; pop. (1984) 94,000. Tobruk was the scene of fierce fighting during the North African campaign in the Second World War.

Toby /ˈtəʊbɪ/ the name of the trained dog introduced (in the first half of the 19th c.) into the Punch and Judy show, which wears a frill round its neck. [familiar form of the name *Tobias*]

toby jug /ˈtəʊbɪ/ *n.* a jug or mug for ale etc., usu. in the form of a stout old man wearing a three-cornered hat. [familiar form of the name *Tobias*]

Tocantins /,təʊkənˈtiːns/ a river of South America which rises in west central Brazil and flows 2,639 km (1,640 miles) north to join the Pará River.

toccata /təˈkɑːtə/ *n.* a musical composition for a keyboard instrument designed to exhibit the performer's touch and technique. [It., fem. past part. of *toccare* touch]

Toc H /tɒkˈeɪtʃ/ *n. Brit.* a society, orig. of ex-servicemen and -women, founded after the First World War for promoting Christian fellowship and social service. [*toc* (former telegraphy code for *T*) + *H*, for Talbot House, a soldier's club established in Belgium in 1915]

Tocharian /təˈkeərɪən/ *n. & adj.* —*n.* **1** an extinct Indo-European language of a central Asian people in the first millennium AD. **2** a member of the people speaking this language. —*adj.* of or in this language. [F *tocharien* f. L *Tochari* f. Gk *Tokharoi* a Scythian tribe]

tocopherol /,təʊkəʊˈfɪərɒl/ *n.* any of several closely related vitamins, found in wheat-germ oil, egg yolk, and leafy vegetables, and important in the stabilization of cell membranes etc. Also called *vitamin E*. [Gk *tokos* offspring + *pherō* bear + -OL¹]

tocsin /ˈtɒksɪn/ *n.* an alarm bell or signal. [F f. OF *touquesain, toquassen* f. Prov. *tocasenh* f. *tocar* TOUCH + *senh* signal-bell]

tod /tɒd/ *n. Brit. sl.* □ **on one's tod** alone; on one's own. [20th c.: perh. f. rhyming sl. *on one's Tod Sloan* (name of a jockey)]

today /təˈdeɪ/ *adv. & n.* —*adv.* **1** on or in the course of this present day (*shall we go today?*). **2** nowadays, in modern times. —*n.* **1** this present day (*today is my birthday*). **2** modern times. □ **today week** (or **fortnight** etc.) a week (or fortnight etc.) from today. [OE tō dæg on (this) day (as TO, DAY)]

Todd /tɒd/, Sweeney. A barber who murdered his customers, the central character of a play by George Dibdin Pitt (1799–1855), and of later plays.

toddle /ˈtɒd(ə)l/ *v. & n.* —*v.intr.* **1** walk with short unsteady steps like those of a small child. **2** *colloq.* **a** (often foll. by *round, to,* etc.) take a casual or leisurely walk. **b** (usu. foll. by *off*) depart. —*n.* **1** a toddling walk. **2** *colloq.* a stroll or short walk. [16th-c. *todle* (Sc. & N.Engl.), of unkn. orig.]

toddler /ˈtɒdlə(r)/ *n.* a child who is just beginning to walk. □□ **toddlerhood** *n.*

toddy /ˈtɒdɪ/ *n.* (*pl.* **-ies**) **1** a drink of spirits with hot water and sugar or spices. **2** the sap of some kinds of palm, fermented to produce arrack. [Hind. *tāṛī* f. *tār* palm f. Skr. *tāla* palmyra]

to-do /təˈduː/ *n.* a commotion or fuss. [*to do* as in *what's to do* (= to be done)]

tody /'təʊdɪ/ n. (pl. **-ies**) any small insect-eating West Indian bird of the genus *Todus*, related to the kingfisher. [F *todier* f. L *todus*, a small bird]

toe /təʊ/ n. & v. —n. **1** any of the five terminal projections of the foot. **2** the corresponding part of an animal. **3** the part of an item of footwear that covers the toes. **4** the lower end or tip of an implement etc. **5** *Archit.* a projection from the foot of a buttress etc. to give stability. —v. (**toes, toed, toeing**) **1** tr. touch (a starting-line etc.) with the toes before starting a race. **2** tr. **a** mend the toe of (a sock etc.). **b** provide with a toe. **3** intr. (foll. by *in, out*) **a** walk with the toes pointed in (or out). **b** (of a pair of wheels) converge (or diverge) slightly at the front. **4** tr. *Golf* strike (the ball) with a part of the club too near the toe. □ **on one's toes** alert, eager. **toe-clip** a clip on a bicycle-pedal to prevent the foot from slipping. **toe-hold 1** a small foothold. **2** a small beginning or advantage. **toe the line** conform to a general policy or principle, esp. unwillingly or under pressure. **turn up one's toes** *colloq.* die. □□ **toed** adj. (also in *comb.*). **toeless** adj. [OE *tā* f. Gmc]

toecap /'təʊkæp/ n. the (usu. strengthened) outer covering of the toe of a boot or shoe.

toenail /'təʊneɪl/ n. **1** the nail at the tip of each toe. **2** a nail driven obliquely through the end of a board etc.

toerag /'təʊræg/ n. *Brit. sl.* a term of contempt for a person. [earlier = tramp, vagrant, f. the rag wrapped round the foot in place of a sock]

toey /'təʊɪ/ adj. *Austral. sl.* restless, nervous, touchy.

toff /tɒf/ n. & v. *Brit. sl.* —n. a distinguished or well-dressed person; a dandy. —v.tr. (foll. by *up*) dress up smartly. [perh. a perversion of *tuft* = titled undergraduate (from the gold tassel formerly worn on the academic cap)]

toffee /'tɒfɪ/ n. (also **toffy**) (pl. **toffees** or **toffies**) **1** a kind of firm or hard sweet softening when sucked or chewed, made by boiling sugar, butter, etc. **2** *Brit.* a small piece of this. □ **for toffee** *sl.* (prec. by *can't* etc.) (denoting incompetence) at all (*they couldn't sing for toffee*). **toffee-apple** an apple with a thin coating of toffee. **toffee-nosed** esp. *Brit. sl.* snobbish, pretentious. [earlier TAFFY]

toft /tɒft/ n. *Brit.* **1** a homestead. **2** land once occupied by this. [OE f. ON *topt*]

tofu /'təʊfuː/ n. (esp. in China and Japan) a curd made from mashed soya beans. [Jap. *tōfu* f. Chin., = rotten beans]

tog[1] /tɒg/ n. & v. *colloq.* —n. (usu. in *pl.*) an item of clothing. —v.tr. & intr. (**togged, togging**) (foll. by *out, up*) dress, esp. elaborately. [app. abbr. of 16th-c. cant *togeman(s)*, *togman*, f. F *toge* or L *toga*: see TOGA]

tog[2] /tɒg/ n. a unit of thermal resistance used to express the insulating properties of clothes and quilts. [arbitrary, prob. f. TOG[1]]

toga /'təʊgə/ n. *hist.* an ancient Roman citizen's loose flowing outer garment. □□ **togaed** adj. (also **toga'd**). [L, rel. to *tegere* cover]

together /tə'geðə(r)/ adv. & adj. —adv. **1** in company or conjunction (*walking together; built it together; were at school together*). **2** simultaneously; at the same time (*both shouted together*). **3** one with another (*were talking together*). **4** into conjunction; so as to unite (*tied them together; put two and two together*). **5** into company or companionship (*came together in friendship*). **6** uninterruptedly (*could talk for hours together*). —adj. *colloq.* well organized or controlled. □ **together with** as well as; and also. [OE *tōgædere* f. TO + *gædre* together: cf. GATHER]

togetherness /tə'geðənɪs/ n. **1** the condition of being together. **2** a feeling of comfort from being together.

toggery /'tɒgərɪ/ n. *colloq.* clothes, togs.

toggle /'tɒg(ə)l/ n. & v. —n. **1** a device for fastening (esp. a garment), consisting of a crosspiece which can pass through a hole or loop in one position but not in another. **2** a pin or other crosspiece put through the eye of a rope, a link of a chain, etc., to keep it in place. **3** a pivoted barb on a harpoon. **4** *Computing* a switch action that is operated the same way but with opposite effect on successive occasions. —v.tr. provide or fasten with a toggle. □ **toggle joint** a device for exerting pressure along two

jointed rods by applying a transverse force at the joint. **toggle switch** an electric switch with a projecting lever to be moved usu. up and down. [18th-c. Naut.: orig. unkn.]

Togliatti /tɒl'jætɪ/ a city of the Soviet Union founded in 1738 but relocated in the mid-1950s in order to make way for the Kuibishev reservoir; pop. (est. 1987) 627,000. Formerly called Stavropol, it was renamed in 1964 after Palmiro Togliatti (1893–1964), Ukrainian-born politician who led the Italian Communist Party for nearly forty years.

Togo /'təʊgəʊ/ a country in West Africa between Ghana and Benin with a short coastline on the Gulf of Guinea; pop. (est. 1988) 3,336,400; official language, French; capital, Lomé. Annexed by Germany in 1884, the district called Togoland was divided between France and Britain after the First World War. The British western section joined Ghana on the latter's independence (1957). The remainder of the area became a United Nations mandate under French administration after the Second World War and achieved independence, as a republic with the name Togo, in 1960. The economy is mainly agricultural but phosphates (of which there are rich deposits) form the principal source of export earnings. □□ **Togolese** /-gə'liːz/ adj. & n..

Tohoku /təʊ'həʊkuː/ the largest of the five regions on Honshu Island, Japan; pop. (1986) 9,737,000; capital, Sendai.

toil /tɔɪl/ v. & n. —v.intr. **1** work laboriously or incessantly. **2** make slow painful progress (*toiled along the path*). —n. prolonged or intensive labour; drudgery. □ **toil-worn** worn or worn out by toil. □□ **toiler** n. [ME f. AF *toiler* (v.), *toil* (n.), dispute, OF *tooilier, tooil,* f. L *tudiculare* stir about f. *tudicula* machine for bruising olives, rel. to *tundere* beat]

toile /twɑːl/ n. **1** cloth esp. for garments. **2** a garment reproduced in muslin or other cheap material for fitting or for making copies. [F *toile* cloth f. L *tela* web]

toilet /'tɔɪlɪt/ n. **1** = LAVATORY. **2** the process of washing oneself, dressing, etc. (*make one's toilet*). **3** the cleansing of part of the body after an operation or at the time of childbirth. □ **toilet paper** (or **tissue**) paper for cleaning oneself after excreting. **toilet roll** a roll of toilet paper. **toilet set** a set of hairbrushes, combs, etc. **toilet soap** soap for washing oneself. **toilet table** a dressing-table usu. with a mirror. **toilet-train** cause (a young child) to undergo toilet-training. **toilet-training** the training of a young child to use the lavatory. **toilet water** a dilute form of perfume used after washing. [F *toilette* cloth, wrapper, dimin. f. *toile*: see TOILE]

toiletry /'tɔɪlɪtrɪ/ n. (pl. **-ies**) (usu. in *pl.*) any of various articles or cosmetics used in washing, dressing, etc.

toilette /twɑː'let/ n. = TOILET 2. [F: see TOILET]

toils /tɔɪlz/ n.pl. a net or snare. [pl. of *toil* f. OF *toile* cloth f. L *tela* web]

toilsome /'tɔɪlsəm/ adj. involving toil; laborious. □□ **toilsomely** adv. **toilsomeness** n.

toing and froing /ˌtuːɪŋ ənd 'frəʊɪŋ/ n. constant movement to and fro; bustle; dispersed activity. [TO adv. + FRO + -ING[1]]

Tokay /tə'keɪ/ n. **1** a sweet aromatic wine made near Tokaj in Hungary. **2** a similar wine produced elsewhere.

Tokelau /ˌtəʊkə'lɑːuː/ a group of islands between Kiribati and Western Samoa in the western Pacific Ocean, forming an overseas territory of New Zealand; pop. (1986) 1,690.

token /'təʊkən/ n. & adj. —n. **1 a** a thing serving as a symbol, reminder, or distinctive mark of something (*as a token of affection; in token of my esteem*). **2** a thing serving as evidence of authenticity or as a guarantee. **3** a voucher exchangeable for goods (often of a specified kind), given as a gift. **4** anything used to represent something else, esp. a metal disc etc. used instead of money in coin-operated machines etc. **5** (*attrib.*) **a** nominal or perfunctory (*token effort*). **b** conducted briefly to demonstrate strength of feeling (*token resistance; token strike*). **c** serving to acknowledge a principle only (*token payment*). **d** chosen by way of tokenism to represent a particular group (*the token woman on the committee*). □ **by this** (or **the same**) **token 1** similarly. **2** moreover. **token money** coins having a higher face value than their worth as metal. **token vote** a parliamentary vote of money, the stipulated amount of which is not meant to be binding. [OE *tāc(e)n* f. Gmc, rel. to TEACH]

tokenism /ˈtəʊkəˌnɪz(ə)m/ *n*. **1** esp. *Polit.* the principle or practice of granting minimum concessions, esp. to appease radical demands etc. (cf. TOKEN 5d). **2** making only a token effort.

Tokyo /ˈtəʊkjəʊ/ the capital of Japan; pop. (1987) 8,209,000. The city was formerly called Edo and was the centre of the military government under the shoguns; it was renamed Tokyo in 1868 when it became the imperial capital. [Jap., = eastern capital]

tolbooth var. of TOLLBOOTH.

Tolbukhin /tɒlˈbuːxɪn/ an agricultural centre in NE Bulgaria; pop. (1987) 111,000.

told *past* and *past part.* of TELL¹.

Toledo¹ /təˈleɪdəʊ/ a city of Spain, the Spanish capital 1087–1560, long famous for the manufacture of finely-tempered sword-blades.

Toledo² /təˈliːdəʊ/ an industrial city and Great Lakes shipping centre on Lake Erie in NW Ohio; pop. (1982) 350,550.

tolerable /ˈtɒlərəb(ə)l/ *adj*. **1** able to be endured. **2** fairly good; mediocre. □□ **tolerability** /-ˈbɪlɪtɪ/ *n*. **tolerableness** *n*. **tolerably** *adv*. [ME f. OF f. L *tolerabilis* (as TOLERATE)]

tolerance /ˈtɒlərəns/ *n*. **1** a willingness or ability to tolerate; forbearance. **2** the capacity to tolerate. **3** an allowable variation in any measurable property. **4** the ability to tolerate the effects of a drug etc. after continued use. [ME f. OF f. L *tolerantia* (as TOLERATE)]

tolerant /ˈtɒlərənt/ *adj*. **1** disposed or accustomed to tolerate others or their acts or opinions. **2** (foll. by *of*) enduring or patient. □□ **tolerantly** *adv*. [F *tolérant* f. L *tolerare* (as TOLERATE)]

tolerate /ˈtɒləˌreɪt/ *v.tr*. **1** allow the existence or occurrence of without authoritative interference. **2** leave unmolested. **3** endure or permit, esp. with forbearance. **4** sustain or endure (suffering etc.). **5** be capable of continued subjection to (a drug, radiation, etc.) without harm. **6** find or treat as endurable. □□ **tolerator** *n*. [L *tolerare tolerat-* endure]

toleration /ˌtɒləˈreɪʃ(ə)n/ *n*. the process or practice of tolerating, esp. the allowing of differences in religious opinion without discrimination. [F *tolération* f. L *toleratio* (as TOLERATE)]

Toleration Act an act of 1689 granting freedom of worship to dissenters (excluding Roman Catholics and Unitarians) on certain conditions. Its real purpose was to unite all Protestants under William III against the deposed Roman Catholic James II.

Tolkien /ˈtɒlkiːn/, John Ronald Reuel (1892–1973), Professor of Anglo-Saxon and later of English Language and Literature at Oxford, born in South Africa, author of *The Hobbit* (1937) and *The Lord of the Rings* (1954–5), two fantasies written for child and adult readers, set in an imaginary Middle Earth peopled by hobbits (shy human-like creatures of dwarfish stature) and other strange races. The books have attracted a huge following since the mid-1960s.

toll¹ /təʊl/ *n*. **1** a charge payable for permission to pass a barrier or use a bridge or road etc. **2** the cost or damage caused by a disaster, battle, etc., or incurred in an achievement (*death toll*). **3** *US* a charge for a long distance telephone call. □ **take its toll** be accompanied by loss or injury etc. **toll-bridge** a bridge at which a toll is charged. **toll-gate** a gate preventing passage until a toll is paid. **toll-house** a house at a toll-gate or -bridge, for the use of the keeper, usually hexagonal in shape so that the windows commanded a view in all directions. **toll-road** a road maintained by the tolls collected on it. [OE f. med.L *toloneum* f. LL *teloneum* f. Gk *telōnion* toll-house f. *telos* tax]

toll² /təʊl/ *v*. & *n*. —*v*. **1 a** *intr*. (of a bell) sound with a slow uniform succession of strokes. **b** *tr*. ring (a bell) in this way. **c** *tr*. (of a bell) announce or mark (a death etc.) in this way. **2** *tr*. strike (the hour). —*n*. **1** the act of tolling. **2** a stroke of a bell. [ME, special use of (now dial.) *toll* entice, pull, f. an OE root -*tyllan* (recorded in *fortyllan* seduce)]

tollbooth /ˈtəʊlbuːð, -buːθ/ *n*. (also **tolbooth**) **1** a booth at the roadside from which tolls are collected. **2** *Sc. archaic* a town hall. **3** *Sc. archaic* a town gaol.

Tollund /ˈtɒlənd/ a fen in central Jutland, Denmark, where the well-preserved corpse of an Iron Age man (*c*.500 BC–400 AD) was found in a peat bog in 1950. The body was naked save for a leather cap and belt, and round the neck was a plaited leather noose: Tollund Man had met his death by hanging, a victim of murder or ritual slaughter.

Tolpuddle martyrs /ˈtɒlpʌd(ə)l/ six farm labourers of the village of Tolpuddle, Dorset, who attempted to form a union to obtain an increase in wages and were sentenced in 1834 to seven years' transportation on a charge of administering unlawful oaths. Their harsh sentences caused widespread protests, and two years later they were pardoned and repatriated from Australia.

Tolstoy /ˈtɒlstɔɪ, -ˈstɔɪ/, Count Lev Nikolaevich (1828–1910), Russian writer. His first published work, *Childhood* (1852), began the perceptive trilogy of his early years (continued in *Boyhood*, 1854 and *Youth*, 1857). His unromantic view of war, expressed in *Sevastopol Sketches* (1855–6), was inspired by his experiences in the Crimea. The next decade was mainly devoted to the creation of his masterpiece *War and Peace* (1863–9), an epic novel of the Napoleonic invasion and the lives of three aristocratic families; *Anna Karenina* (1873–7) describes a married woman's passion for a young officer and her tragic fate. His constant concern with moral questions developed into a spiritual crisis which led to radical changes in his life and works, including *The Death of Ivan Ilich* (1886), *The Kreutzer Sonata* (1889), and *Resurrection* (1899). Tolstoy's moral stance regarding non-resistance to evil, renunciation of property, abolition of governments and churches, but a belief in God and man, led to his excommunication from the Russian Orthodox Church (1901) and the banning of many of his works, but brought him a moral authority and influence and his home, Yasnaya Polyana, became a place of pilgrimage.

Toltec /ˈtɒltek/ *n*. & *adj*. —*n*. (*pl*. same or **Toltecs**) a member of a Nahuatl-speaking people who dominated central Mexico *c*.900–1200. (See below.) —*adj*. of the Toltec. [Sp. f. Nahuatl]

The Toltec were a warrior aristocracy whose period of domination was violent and innovative. They founded or developed cities (their capital was Tula), but were unable to consolidate their hold on the conquered area, which developed into a number of States, mostly independent. In the 12th–13th c. famine and drought (perhaps caused by climatic changes) brought catastrophe, and the disunited area fell to invading barbarian tribes from the north.

tolu /təˈluː, ˈtəʊluː/ *n*. a fragrant brown balsam obtained from either of two South American trees, *Myroxylon balsamum* or *M. toluifera*, and used in perfumery and medicine. [Santiago de *Tolu* in Colombia]

toluene /ˈtɒljʊˌiːn/ *n*. a colourless aromatic liquid hydrocarbon derivative of benzene, orig. obtained from tolu, used in the manufacture of explosives etc. Also called *methyl benzene*. □□ **toluic** *adj*. **toluol** *n*. [TOLU + -ENE]

tom /tɒm/ *n*. a male of various animals, esp. (in full **tom-cat**) a male cat. [abbr. of the name *Thomas*]

tomahawk /ˈtɒməˌhɔːk/ *n*. & *v*. —*n*. **1** a N. American Indian war-axe with a stone or iron head. **2** *Austral*. a hatchet. —*v.tr*. strike, cut, or kill with a tomahawk. [Renape *tämähāk* f. *tämäham* he etc. cuts]

tomato /təˈmɑːtəʊ/ *n*. (*pl*. **-oes**) **1** a glossy red or yellow pulpy edible fruit. **2** a solanaceous plant, *Lycopersicon esculentum*, native to tropical America bearing this. Originally called the love-apple (a translation of the French *pomme d'amour*, German *Liebesapfel*) and hence considered to be an aphrodisiac, it arrived in Europe from South America at the end of the 16th c. and became widely cultivated in Italy for use with pasta. In Britain its reputation delayed its acceptability; the Puritans circulated a story that tomatoes were poisonous, and until the 19th c. they were grown as decorative plants, not for eating. □□ **tomatoey** *adj*. [17th-c. *tomate*, = F or Sp. & Port., f. Mex. *tomatl*]

tomb /tuːm/ *n*. **1** a large esp. underground vault for the burial of the dead. **2** an enclosure cut in the earth or in rock to receive a dead body. **3** a sepulchral monument. **4** (prec. by *the*) the state of death. [ME *t(o)umbe* f. AF *tumbe*, OF *tombe* f. LL *tumba* f. Gk *tumbos*]

tombac /ˈtɒmbæk/ n. an alloy of copper and zinc used esp. as material for cheap jewellery. [F f. Malay *tambāga* copper]

tombola /tɒmˈbəʊlə/ n. *Brit.* a kind of lottery with tickets usu. drawn from a turning drum-shaped container, esp. at a fête or fair. [F *tombola* or It. f. *tombolare* tumble]

tombolo /ˈtɒmbəˌləʊ/ n. (*pl.* **-os**) a spit joining an island to the mainland. [It., = sand-dune]

Tombouctou see TIMBUKTU.

tomboy /ˈtɒmbɔɪ/ n. a girl who behaves in a rough boyish way. □□ **tomboyish** adj. **tomboyishness** n.

tombstone /ˈtuːmstəʊn/ n. a stone standing or laid over a grave, usu. with an epitaph.

Tom Collins /tɒm ˈkɒlɪnz/ n. an iced cocktail of gin with soda, lemon or lime juice, and sugar. [20th c.: orig. unkn.]

Tom, Dick, and Harry /ˌtɒm dɪk ənd ˈhærɪ/ n. (usu. prec. by *any*, *every*) usu. *derog.* ordinary people taken at random.

tome /təʊm/ n. a large heavy book or volume. [F f. L *tomus* f. Gk *tomos* section, volume f. *temnō* cut]

-tome /təʊm/ comb. form forming nouns meaning: **1** an instrument for cutting (*microtome*). **2** a section or segment. [Gk *tomē* a cutting, *-tomos* -cutting, f. *temnō* cut]

tomentum /təˈmentəm/ n. (*pl.* **tomenta** /-tə/) **1** *Bot.* matted woolly down on stems and leaves. **2** *Anat.* the tufted inner surface of the pia mater in the brain. □□ **tomentose** /təˈmentəʊs, ˈtəʊ-/ adj. **tomentous** adj. [L, = cushion-stuffing]

tomfool /tɒmˈfuːl/ n. **1** a foolish person. **2** (*attrib.*) silly, foolish (*a tomfool idea*).

tomfoolery /tɒmˈfuːlərɪ/ n. (*pl.* **-ies**) **1** foolish behaviour; nonsense. **2** an instance of this.

Tommy /ˈtɒmɪ/ n. (*pl.* **-ies**) *colloq.* a British private soldier. [*Tommy* (*Thomas*) *Atkins*, a name used in specimens of completed official forms]

tommy-bar /ˈtɒmɪˌbɑː(r)/ n. a short bar for use with a box spanner.

tommy-gun /ˈtɒmɪˌɡʌn/ n. a type of sub-machine-gun. [J. T. *Thompson*, US Army officer d. 1940, its co-inventor]

tommy-rot /ˈtɒmɪˌrɒt/ n. *sl.* nonsense.

tomogram /ˈtɒməˌɡræm/ n. a record obtained by tomography.

tomography /təˈmɒɡrəfɪ/ n. a method of radiography in which an image of a selected plane in the body or other object is obtained by rotating the detector and the source of radiation in such a way that points outside the plane give a blurred image. The technique, devised in the early 1930s and later sophisticated, is as important in the history of medicine as the discovery of X-rays. [Gk *tomē* a cutting + -GRAPHY]

Tomor /ˈtɒmɔː(r)/, **Mount** a mountain in southern Albania rising to a height of 2,480 m (8,050 ft.).

tomorrow /təˈmɒrəʊ/ adv. & n. —adv. **1** on the day after today. **2** at some future time. —n. **1** the day after today. **2** the near future. □ **tomorrow morning** (or **afternoon** etc.) in the morning (or afternoon etc.) of tomorrow. **tomorrow week** a week from tomorrow. [TO + MORROW: cf. TODAY]

Tompion /ˈtɒmpɪən/, Thomas (c.1639–1713), the most famous of the early English clock- and watch-makers, making in 1675 one of the first balance-spring watches invented by Robert Hooke. For the Royal Observatory, Greenwich, he made two large pendulum clocks which needed winding only once a year, and he collaborated with Edward Barlow in patenting the horizontal-wheel cylinder escapement needed to produce flat watches. His achievement in raising the level of the industry was recognized by his burial in Westminster Abbey. Two of his nephews also became famous clockmakers.

tompion var. of TAMPION.

Tomsk /tɒmsk/ an industrial city of the Soviet Union on the River Tom in west central Siberia; pop. (est. 1987) 489,000.

Tom Thumb /tɒm ˈθʌm/ the title of an old nursery tale, of which there are several versions. He was said to be the son of a ploughman in the time of King Arthur, and was as tall as his father's thumb. —n. **1** a diminutive person. **2** a dwarf variety of various plants.

tomtit /ˈtɒmtɪt/ n. a tit, esp. a blue tit.

tom-tom /ˈtɒmtɒm/ n. **1** a primitive drum beaten with the hands. **2** a tall drum beaten with the hands and used in jazz bands etc. [Hindi *tamtam*, imit.]

-tomy /təmɪ/ comb. form forming nouns denoting cutting, esp. in surgery (*laparotomy*). [Gk *-tomia* cutting f. *temnō* cut]

ton[1] /tʌn/ n. **1** (in full **long ton**) a unit of weight equal to 2,240 lb. avoirdupois (1016.05 kg). **2** (in full **short ton**) a unit of weight equal to 2,000 lb. avoirdupois (907.19 kg). **3** (in full **metric ton**) = TONNE. **4 a** (in full **displacement ton**) a unit of measurement of a ship's weight or volume in terms of its displacement of water with the loadline just immersed, equal to 2,240 lb. or 35 cu. ft. (0.99 cubic metres). **b** (in full **freight ton**) a unit of weight or volume of cargo, equal to a metric ton (1,000 kg) or 40 cu. ft. **5 a** (in full **gross ton**) a unit of gross internal capacity, equal to 100 cu. ft. (2.83 cubic metres). **b** (in full **net** or **register ton**) an equivalent unit of net internal capacity. **6** a unit of refrigerating power able to freeze 2,000 lb. of ice at 0°C in 24 hours. **7** a measure of capacity for various materials, esp. 40 cu. ft. of timber. **8** (usu. in *pl.*) *colloq.* a large number or amount (*tons of money*). **9** esp. *Brit. sl.* **a** a speed of 100 m.p.h. **b** a sum of £100. **c** a score of 100. □ **ton-mile** one ton of goods carried one mile, as a unit of traffic. **ton-up** *Brit. sl.* n. a speed of 100 m.p.h. —attrib.adj. **1** (of a motor cyclist) achieving this, esp. habitually and recklessly (*ton-up kid*). **2** fond or capable of travelling at high speed. **weigh a ton** *colloq.* be very heavy. [orig. the same word as TUN: differentiated in the 17th c.]

ton[2] /tɔ̃/ n. **1** a prevailing mode or fashion. **2** fashionable society. [F]

tonal /ˈtəʊn(ə)l/ adj. **1** of or relating to tone or tonality. **2** (of a fugue etc.) having repetitions of the subject at different pitches in the same key. □□ **tonally** adv. [med.L *tonalis* (as TONE)]

tonality /təˈnælɪtɪ/ n. (*pl.* **-ies**) **1** *Mus.* **a** the relationship between the tones of a musical scale. **b** the observance of a single tonic key as the basis of a composition. **2** the tone or colour scheme of a picture.

tondo /ˈtɒndəʊ/ n. (*pl.* **tondi** /-dɪ/) a circular painting or relief. [It., = round (plate), f. *rotondo* f. L *rotundus* round]

tone /təʊn/ n. & v. —n. **1** a musical or vocal sound, esp. with reference to its pitch, quality, and strength. **2** (often in *pl.*) modulation of the voice expressing a particular feeling or mood (*a cheerful tone; suspicious tones*). **3** a manner of expression in writing. **4** *Mus.* **a** a musical sound, esp. of a definite pitch and character. **b** an interval of a major second, e.g. C–D. **5 a** the general effect of colour or of light and shade in a picture. **b** the tint or shade of a colour. **6 a** the prevailing character of the morals and sentiments etc. in a group. **b** an attitude or sentiment expressed esp. in a letter etc. **7** the proper firmness of bodily organs. **8** a state of good or specified health or quality. **9** *Phonet.* **a** an accent on one syllable of a word. **b** a way of pronouncing a word to distinguish it from others of a similar sound (*Mandarin Chinese has four tones*). —v. **1** tr. give the desired tone to. **2** tr. modify the tone of. **3** intr. (often foll. by *to*) attune. **4** intr. (foll. by *with*) be in harmony (esp. of colour) (*does not tone with the wallpaper*). **5** tr. *Photog.* give (a monochrome picture) an altered colour in finishing by means of a chemical solution. **6** intr. undergo a change in colour by toning. □ **tone-arm** the movable arm supporting the pick-up of a record-player. **tone control** a switch for varying the proportion of high and low frequencies in reproduced sound. **tone-deaf** unable to perceive differences of musical pitch accurately. **tone-deafness** the condition of being tone-deaf. **tone down 1** make or become softer in tone of sound or colour. **2** make (a statement etc.) less harsh or emphatic. **tone language** a language that uses variations in pitch to distinguish words which would otherwise sound identical. **tone poem** = *symphonic poem*. **tone-row** = SERIES 8. **tone up 1** make or become stronger in tone of sound or colour. **2** make (a statement etc.) more emphatic. **whole-tone scale** see WHOLE. □□ **toneless** adj. **tonelessly** adv. **toner** n. [ME f. OF *ton* or L *tonus* f. Gk *tonos* tension, tone f. *teinō* stretch]

toneburst /ˈtəʊnbɜːst/ n. an audio signal used in testing the transient response of audio components.

toneme /ˈtəʊniːm/ n. a phoneme distinguished from another only by its tone. □□ **tonemic** /-'ni:mɪk/ *adj.* [TONE after *phoneme*]

tong /tɒŋ/ *n.* a Chinese guild, association, or secret society. [Chin. *tang* meeting-place]

Tonga /'tɒŋə/ a country in the South Pacific consisting of over 150 small volcanic and coral islands, SE of Fiji; pop. (est. 1988) 99,600; official languages, Tongan and English; capital, Nuku'alofa. Discovered by the Dutch in the early 17th c., the islands were visited by Cook who named them the Friendly Islands. The people were converted to Christianity by Methodist missionaries in the early 19th c. and the kingdom became a British protectorate in 1900, gaining independence as a member State of the Commonwealth in 1970. The soil is generally fertile and the main exports are copra and bananas.

tonga /'tɒŋgə/ *n.* a light horse-drawn two-wheeled vehicle used in India. [Hindi *tāṅgā*]

Tongan /'tɒŋən/ *adj. & n.* —*adj.* of Tonga or its people or language. —*n.* **1** a native of Tonga. **2** the Polynesian language spoken in Tonga.

Tongariro /ˌtɒŋgəˈriəˌrəʊ/ an administrative region on North Island, New Zealand; pop. (1986) 40,800; chief town, Taupo. The region takes its name from Tongariro, a sacred mountain of the Maori which rises to a height of 2,007 m (6,516 ft.) at the centre of North Island.

tongs /tɒŋz/ *n.pl.* (also **pair of tongs** *sing.*) an instrument with two hinged or sprung arms for grasping and holding. [pl. of *tong* f. OE *tang(e)* f. Gmc]

tongue /tʌŋ/ *n. & v.* —*n.* **1** the fleshy muscular organ in the mouth used in tasting, licking, and swallowing, and (in man) for speech. **2** the tongue of an ox etc. as food. **3** the faculty of or a tendency in speech (*a sharp tongue*). **4** a particular language (*the German tongue*). **5** a thing like a tongue in shape or position, esp.: **a** a long low promontory. **b** a strip of leather etc., attached at one end only, under the laces in a shoe. **c** the clapper of a bell. **d** the pin of a buckle. **e** the projecting strip on a wooden etc. board fitting into the groove of another. **f** a vibrating slip in the reed of some musical instruments. **g** a jet of flame. —*v.* (**tongues, tongued, tonguing**) **1** *tr.* produce staccato etc. effects with (a flute etc.) by means of tonguing. **2** *intr.* use the tongue in this way. □ **find** (or **lose**) **one's tongue** be able (or unable) to express oneself after a shock etc. **the gift of tongues** the power of speaking in unknown languages, regarded as one of the gifts of the Holy Spirit (Acts 2). **keep a civil tongue in one's head** avoid rudeness. **tongue-and-groove** applied to boards in which a tongue along one edge fits into a groove along the edge of the next, each board having a tongue on one edge and a groove on the other. **tongue-in-cheek** *adj.* ironic; slyly humorous. —*adv.* insincerely or ironically. **tongue-lashing** a severe scolding or reprimand. **tongue-tie** a speech impediment due to a malformation of the tongue. **tongue-tied 1** too shy or embarrassed to speak. **2** having a tongue-tie. **tongue-twister** a sequence of words difficult to pronounce quickly and correctly. **with one's tongue hanging out** eagerly or expectantly. **with one's tongue in one's cheek** insincerely or ironically. □□ **tongued** *adj.* (also in *comb.*). **tongueless** *adj.* [OE *tunge* f. Gmc, rel. to L *lingua*]

tonguing /'tʌŋɪŋ/ *n. Mus.* the technique of playing a wind instrument using the tongue to articulate certain notes.

tonic /'tɒnɪk/ *n. & adj.* —*n.* **1** an invigorating medicine. **2** anything serving to invigorate. **3** = *tonic water*. **4** *Mus.* the first degree of a scale, forming the keynote of a piece (see KEYNOTE 3). —*adj.* **1** serving as a tonic; invigorating. **2** *Mus.* denoting the first degree of a scale. **3 a** producing tension, esp. of the muscles. **b** restoring normal tone to organs. □ **tonic accent** an accent marked by a change of pitch within a syllable. **tonic spasm** continuous muscular contraction (cf. CLONUS). **tonic water** a carbonated mineral water containing quinine. □□ **tonically** *adv.* [F *tonique* f. Gk *tonikos* (as TONE)]

tonic sol-fa /sɒl'fɑ:/ *n.* a system of musical notation used especially in teaching the notes in singing. It was developed by Sarah Ann Glover (1785–1867) as *Norwich Sol-fa*, and promulgated by John Curwen (1816–80) in the 1840s. In it the seven notes of the major scale in any key are sung to syllables written *doh, ray, me,*

fah, soh, lah, te (modifications of earlier forms; see GAMUT); doh always denotes the tonic or keynote, and the remaining syllables indicate the relation to it of the other notes of the scale. Time-values are shown by vertical lines, colons, etc. *The New Curwen Method*, a revised version aimed at training the ear and leading to reading from standard musical notation, was published in 1980.

tonicity /tə'nɪsɪtɪ/ *n.* **1** the state of being tonic. **2** a healthy elasticity of muscles etc.

tonight /tə'naɪt/ *adv. & n.* —*adv.* on the present or approaching evening or night. —*n.* the evening or night of the present day. [TO + NIGHT: cf. TODAY]

tonka bean /'tɒŋkə/ *n.* the black fragrant seed of a South American tree, *Dipteryx odorata*, used in perfumery etc. [*tonka*, its name in Guyana, + BEAN]

Tonkin /tɒn'kɪn/, **Gulf of** a north-western arm of the South China Sea between Vietnam and China.

Tonlé Sap /'tɒnleɪ 'sæp/ a lake in central Cambodia, linked to the Mekong River by the Tonlé Sap River. The area of the lake is tripled during the wet season (June–November). On the north-west shore stand the ruins of the ancient Khmer city of Angkor.

tonnage /'tʌnɪdʒ/ *n.* **1** a ship's internal cubic capacity or freight-carrying capacity measured in tons. **2** the total carrying capacity esp. of a country's mercantile marine. **3** a charge per ton on freight or cargo. [orig. in sense 'duty on a tun of wine': OF *tonnage* f. *tonne* TUN: later f. TON¹]

tonne /tʌn/ *n.* a metric ton equal to 1,000 kg. [F: see TUN]

tonneau /'tɒnəʊ/ *n.* the part of a motor car occupied by the back seats, esp. in an open car. □ **tonneau cover** a removable flexible cover for the passenger seats in an open car, boat, etc., when they are not in use. [F, lit. cask, tun]

tonometer /tə'nɒmɪtə(r)/ *n.* **1** a tuning-fork or other instrument for measuring the pitch of tones. **2** an instrument for measuring the pressure of fluid. [formed as TONE + -METER]

tonsil /'tɒns(ə)l, -sɪl/ *n.* either of two small masses of lymphoid tissue on each side of the root of the tongue. □□ **tonsillar** *adj.* [F *tonsilles* or L *tonsillae* (pl.)]

tonsillectomy /ˌtɒnsɪ'lektəmɪ/ *n.* (pl. **-ies**) the surgical removal of the tonsils.

tonsillitis /ˌtɒnsɪ'laɪtɪs/ *n.* inflammation of the tonsils.

tonsorial /tɒn'sɔːrɪəl/ *adj.* usu. *joc.* of or relating to a hairdresser or hairdressing. [L *tonsorius* f. *tonsor* barber f. *tondēre tons-* shave]

tonsure /'tɒnsjə(r), 'tɒnʃə(r)/ *n. & v.* —*n.* **1** the rite of shaving the crown of the head (in the RC Church until 1972) or the whole head (in the Orthodox Church), esp. of a person entering a priesthood or monastic order. **2** a bare patch made in this way. —*v.tr.* give a tonsure to. [ME f. OF *tonsure* or L *tonsura* (as TONSORIAL)]

tontine /tɒn'tiːn, 'tɒn-/ *n.* an annuity shared by subscribers to a loan, the shares increasing as subscribers die until the last survivor gets all, or until a specified date when the remaining survivors share the proceeds. [F, f. the name of Lorenzo *Tonti* of Naples, originator of tontines in France *c.*1653]

tony /'təʊnɪ/ *adj.* (**tonier, toniest**) *US colloq.* having 'tone'; stylish, fashionable.

too /tuː/ *adv.* **1** to a greater extent than is desirable, permissible, or possible for a specified or understood purpose (*too colourful for my taste; too large to fit*). **2** *colloq.* extremely (*you're too kind*). **3** in addition (*are they coming too?*). **4** moreover (*we must consider, too, the time of year*). □ **none too 1** rather less than (*feeling none too good*). **2** barely. **too bad** see BAD. **too much, too much for** see MUCH. **too right** see RIGHT. **too-too** *adj. & adv. colloq.* extreme, excessive(ly). [stressed form of TO, f. 16th-c. spelling *too*]

took past of TAKE.

tool /tuːl/ *n. & v.* —*n.* **1** any device or implement used to carry out mechanical functions whether manually or by a machine. **2** a thing used in an occupation or pursuit (*the tools of one's trade; literary tools*). **3** a person used as a mere instrument by another. **4** *coarse sl.* the penis. ¶ Usually considered a taboo use. **5 a** a distinct figure in the tooling of a book. **b** a small stamp or roller used to make this. —*v.tr.* **1** dress (stone) with a chisel. **2** impress a design on (a leather book-cover). **3** (foll. by *along, around,* etc.) *sl.* drive or ride, esp. in a casual or leisurely manner. **4** (often foll. by *up*) equip with tools. □ **tool-box** a box or container for keeping tools in. **tool-pusher** a worker directing the drilling on an oil rig. **tool up 1** *sl.* arm oneself. **2** equip oneself. □□ **tooler** *n.* [OE *tōl* f. Gmc]

tooling /'tu:lɪŋ/ *n.* **1** the process of dressing stone with a chisel. **2** the ornamentation of a book-cover with designs impressed by heated tools.

toolmaker /'tu:lˌmeɪkə(r)/ *n.* a person who makes precision tools, esp. tools used in a press. □□ **toolmaking** *n.*

toot[1] /tu:t/ *n. & v.* —*n.* **1** a short sharp sound as made by a horn, trumpet, or whistle. **2** *US sl.* cocaine or a snort (see SNORT *n.* 4) of cocaine. —*v.* **1** *tr.* sound (a horn etc.) with a short sharp sound. **2** *intr.* give out such a sound. □□ **tooter** *n.* [prob. f. MLG *tūten*, or imit.]

toot[2] /tu:t/ *n. Austral. sl.* a lavatory. [20th c.: orig. unkn.]

tooth /tu:θ/ *n. & v.* —*n.* (*pl.* **teeth** /ti:θ/) **1** each of a set of hard bony enamel-coated structures in the jaws of most vertebrates, used for biting and chewing. **2** a toothlike part or projection, e.g. the cog of a gearwheel, the point of a saw or comb, etc. **3** (often foll. by *for*) one's sense of taste; an appetite or liking. **4** (in *pl.*) force or effectiveness (*the penalties give the contract teeth*). —*v.* **1** *tr.* provide with teeth. **2** *intr.* (of cog-wheels) engage, interlock. □ **armed to the teeth** completely and elaborately armed or equipped. **fight tooth and nail** fight very fiercely. **get one's teeth into** devote oneself seriously to. **in the teeth of 1** in spite of (opposition or difficulty etc.). **2** contrary to (instructions etc.). **3** directly against (the wind etc.). **set a person's teeth on edge** see EDGE. **tooth-billed** (of a bird) having toothlike projections on the cutting edges of the bill. **tooth-comb** = *fine-tooth comb* (see FINE[1]). **tooth powder** powder for cleaning the teeth. **tooth shell** = *tusk shell*. □□ **toothed** *adj.* (also in *comb.*). **toothless** *adj.* **toothlike** *adj.* [OE *tōth* (*pl.* *tēth*) f. Gmc]

toothache /'tu:θeɪk/ *n.* a (usu. prolonged) pain in a tooth or teeth.

toothbrush /'tu:θbrʌʃ/ *n.* a brush for cleaning the teeth.

toothing /'tu:θɪŋ/ *n.* projecting bricks or stones left at the end of a wall to allow its continuation.

toothpaste /'tu:θpeɪst/ *n.* a paste for cleaning the teeth.

toothpick /'tu:θpɪk/ *n.* a small sharp instrument for removing small pieces of food lodged between the teeth.

toothsome /'tu:θsəm/ *adj.* (of food) delicious, appetizing. □□ **toothsomely** *adv.* **toothsomeness** *n.*

toothwort /'tu:θwɜ:t/ *n.* a parasitic plant, *Lathraea squamaria,* with toothlike root scales.

toothy /'tu:θɪ/ *adj.* (**toothier, toothiest**) having or showing large, numerous, or prominent teeth (*a toothy grin*). □□ **toothily** *adv.*

tootle /'tu:t(ə)l/ *v.intr.* **1** toot gently or repeatedly. **2** (usu. foll. by *along, around,* etc.) *colloq.* move casually or aimlessly. □□ **tootler** *n.*

tootsy /'tʊtsɪ/ *n.* (also **tootsie**) (*pl.* **-ies**) *sl.* usu. *joc.* a foot. [E joc. dimin.: cf. FOOTSIE]

Toowoomba /tu:'wu:mbə/ an agricultural centre to the west of Brisbane in the Darling Downs region of Queensland in NE Australia; pop. (est. 1987) 79,100.

top[1] /tɒp/ *n., adj., & v.* —*n.* **1** the highest point or part (*the top of the house*). **2 a** the highest rank or place (*at the top of the school*). **b** a person occupying this (*was top in maths*). **c** the upper end or head (*the top of the table*). **3** the upper surface of a thing, esp. of the ground, a table, etc. **4** the upper part of a thing, esp.: **a** a blouse, jumper, etc. for wearing with a skirt or trousers. **b** the upper part of a shoe or boot. **c** the stopper of a bottle. **d** the lid of a jar, saucepan, etc. **e** the creamy part of milk. **f** the folding roof of a car, pram, or carriage. **g** the upper edge or edges of a page or pages in a book (*gilt top*). **5** the utmost degree; height (*called at the top of his voice*). **6** (in *pl.*) *colloq.* a person or thing of the best quality (*he's tops at cricket*). **7** (esp. in *pl.*) the leaves etc.

of a plant grown esp. for its root (*turnip-tops*). **8** (usu. in *pl.*) a bundle of long wool fibres prepared for spinning. **9** *Naut.* a platform round the head of the lower mast, serving to extend the topmost rigging or carry guns. **10** (in *pl.*) esp. *Bridge* the two or three highest cards of a suit. **11** *Brit.* = *top gear* (*climbed the hill in top*). **12** = TOPSPIN. —*adj.* **1** highest in position (*the top shelf*). **2** highest in degree or importance (*at top speed; the top job*). —*v.tr.* (**topped, topping**) **1** provide with a top, cap, etc. (*cake topped with icing*). **2** remove the top of (a plant, fruit, etc.), esp. to improve growth, prepare for cooking, etc. **3** be higher or better than; surpass; be at the top of (*topped the list*). **4** *sl.* **a** execute esp. by hanging, kill. **b** (*refl.*) commit suicide. **5** reach the top of (a hill etc.). **6** *Golf* **a** hit (a ball) above the centre. **b** make (a stroke) in this way. □ **at the top** (or **at the top of the tree**) in the highest rank of a profession etc. **come to the top** win distinction. **from top to toe** from head to foot; completely. **off the top of one's head** see HEAD. **on top 1** in a superior position; above. **2** on the upper part of the head (*bald on top*). **on top of 1** fully in command of. **2** in close proximity to. **3** in addition to. **on top of the world** *colloq.* exuberant. **over the top 1** over the parapet of a trench (and into battle). **2** into a final or decisive state. **3** to excess, beyond reasonable limits (*that joke was over the top*). **top-boot** esp. *hist.* a boot with a high top esp. of a different material or colour. **top brass** esp. *Mil. colloq.* the highest-ranking officers, heads of industries, etc. **top copy** the uppermost typed copy (cf. *carbon copy*). **top dog** *colloq.* a victor or master. **top drawer 1** the uppermost drawer in a chest etc. **2** *colloq.* high social position or origin. **top-dress** apply manure or fertilizer on the top of (earth) instead of ploughing it in. **top-dressing 1** this process. **2** manure so applied. **3** a superficial show. **top-flight** in the highest rank of achievement. **top fruit** *Brit.* fruit grown on trees, not bushes. **top gear** *Brit.* the highest gear in a motor vehicle or bicycle. **top-hamper** an encumbrance on top, esp. the upper sails and rigging of a ship. **top hat** a man's tall silk hat. **top-hole** *Brit. colloq.* first-rate. **top-level** of the highest level of importance, prestige, etc. **top-notch** *colloq.* first-rate. **top-notcher** *colloq.* a first-rate person or thing. **top off** (or **up**) put an end or the finishing touch to (a thing). **top out** put the highest stone on (a building). **top one's part** esp. *Theatr.* act or discharge one's part to perfection. **top-sawyer 1** a sawyer in the upper position in a saw-pit. **2** a person who holds a superior position; a distinguished person. **top secret** of the highest secrecy. **top ten** (or **twenty** etc.) the first ten (or twenty etc.) gramophone records in the charts. **top up** esp. *Brit.* **1 a** complete (an amount or number). **b** fill up (a glass or other partly full container). **2** top up something for (a person) (*may I top you up with sherry?*). **top-up** *n.* an addition; something that serves to top up (esp. a partly full glass). □□ **topmost** *adj.* [OE *topp*]

top[2] /tɒp/ *n.* a wooden or metal toy, usu. conical, spherical, or pear-shaped, spinning on a point when set in motion by hand, string, etc. [OE, of uncert. orig.]

topaz /'təʊpæz/ *n.* **1** a transparent or translucent aluminium silicate mineral, usu. yellow, used as a gem. **2** any South American humming-bird of the genus *Topaza.* [ME f. OF *topace, topaze* f. L *topazus* f. Gk *topazos*]

topazolite /tə'pæzəˌlaɪt/ *n.* a yellow or green kind of garnet. [TOPAZ + -LITE]

topcoat /'tɒpkəʊt/ *n.* **1** an overcoat. **2** an outer coat of paint etc.

tope[1] /təʊp/ *v.intr. archaic* or *literary* drink alcohol to excess, esp. habitually. □□ **toper** *n.* [perh. f. obs. *top quaff*]

tope[2] /təʊp/ *n. Ind.* a grove, esp. of mangoes. [Telugu *tōpu,* Tamil *tōppu*]

tope[3] /təʊp/ *n.* = STUPA. [Punjab *tōp* f. Prakrit & Pali *thūpo* f. Skr. STUPA]

tope[4] /təʊp/ *n.* a small shark, *Galeorhinus galeus.* [perh. f. Corn.]

topee var. of TOPI.

Topeka /tə'pi:kə/ the capital of Kansas; pop. (1980) 115,266.

topgallant /tɒp'gælənt, tə'gælənt/ *n. Naut.* the mast, sail, yard, or rigging immediately above the topmast and topsail.

top-heavy /tɒp'hevɪ/ *adj.* **1** disproportionately heavy at the top so as to be in danger of toppling. **2 a** (of an organization, business, etc.) having a disproportionately large number of people in senior administrative positions. **b** overcapitalized. **3** *colloq.* (of a woman) having a disproportionately large bust. □□ **top-heavily** *adv.* **top-heaviness** *n.*

Tophet /ˈtəʊfɪt/ *Bibl.* hell. [name of a place in the Valley of Hinnom near Jerusalem used for idolatrous worship and later for burning refuse: f. Heb. *tōpeṯ*]

tophus /ˈtəʊfəs/ *n.* (*pl.* **tophi** /-faɪ/) **1** *Med.* a gouty deposit of crystalline uric acid and other substances at the surface of joints. **2** *Geol.* = TUFA. [L, name of loose porous stones]

topi /ˈtəʊpɪ/ *n.* (also **topee**) (*pl.* **topis** or **topees**) *Anglo-Ind.* a hat, esp. a sola topi. [Hindi *ṭopī*]

topiary /ˈtəʊpɪərɪ/ *adj. & n.* —*adj.* concerned with or formed by clipping shrubs, trees, etc. into ornamental shapes. —*n.* (*pl.* **-ies**) **1** topiary art. **2** an example of this. □□ **topiarian** /-pɪˈeərɪən/ *adj.* **topiarist** *n.* [F *topiaire* f. L *topiarius* landscape-gardener f. *topia opera* fancy gardening f. Gk *topia* pl. dimin. of *topos* place]

topic /ˈtɒpɪk/ *n.* **1** a theme for a book, discourse, essay, sermon, etc. **2** the subject of a conversation or argument. [L *topica* f. Gk (*ta*) *topika* topics, as title of a treatise by Aristotle f. *topos* a place, a commonplace]

topical /ˈtɒpɪk(ə)l/ *adj.* **1** dealing with the news, current affairs, etc. (*a topical song*). **2** dealing with a place; local. **3** *Med.* (of an ailment, medicine, etc.) affecting a part of the body. **4** of or concerning topics. □□ **topicality** /-ˈkælɪtɪ/ *n.* **topically** *adv.*

Topkapi Palace /tɒpˈkɑːpɪ/ the former Seraglio or residence in Istanbul of the sultans of the Ottoman empire, last occupied by Mahmut II (1808–39) and now a museum.

topknot /ˈtɒpnɒt/ *n.* a knot, tuft, crest, or bow of ribbon, worn or growing on the head.

topless /ˈtɒplɪs/ *adj.* **1** without or seeming to be without a top. **2 a** (of clothes) having no upper part. **b** (of a person) wearing such clothes; bare-breasted. **c** (of a place, esp. a beach) where women go topless. □□ **toplessness** *n.*

toplofty /tɒpˈlɒftɪ/ *adj.* *US colloq.* haughty.

topman /ˈtɒpmən/ *n.* (*pl.* **-men**) **1** a top-sawyer. **2** *Naut.* a man doing duty in a top.

topmast /ˈtɒpmɑːst/ *n.* *Naut.* the mast next above the lower mast.

topography /təˈpɒɡrəfɪ/ *n.* **1 a** a detailed description, representation on a map, etc., of the natural and artificial features of a town, district, etc. **b** such features. **2** *Anat.* the mapping of the surface of the body with reference to the parts beneath. □□ **topographer** *n.* **topographic** /-ˈɡræfɪk/ *adj.* **topographical** /-ˈɡræfɪk(ə)l/ *adj.* **topographically** /-ˈɡræfɪkəlɪ/ *adv.* [ME f. LL *topographia* f. Gk f. *topos* place]

topoi *pl.* of TOPOS.

topology /təˈpɒlədʒɪ/ *n.* *Math.* the study of geometrical properties and spatial relations unaffected by the continuous change of shape or size of figures. □□ **topological** /ˌtɒpəˈlɒdʒɪk(ə)l/ *adj.* **topologically** /ˌtɒpəˈlɒdʒɪkəlɪ/ *adv.* **topologist** *n.* [G *Topologie* f. Gk *topos* place]

toponym /ˈtɒpənɪm/ *n.* **1** a place-name. **2** a descriptive place-name, usu. derived from a topographical feature of the place. [TOPONYMY]

toponymy /təˈpɒnɪmɪ/ *n.* the study of the place-names of a region. □□ **toponymic** /-ˈnɪmɪk/ *adj.* [Gk *topos* place + *onoma* name]

topos /ˈtɒpɒs/ *n.* (*pl.* **topoi** /ˈtɒpɔɪ/) a stock theme in literature etc. [Gk, = commonplace]

topper /ˈtɒpə(r)/ *n.* **1** a thing that tops. **2** *colloq.* = top hat (see TOP[1]). **3** *colloq.* a good fellow; a good sort.

topping /ˈtɒpɪŋ/ *adj. & n.* —*adj.* **1** pre-eminent in position, rank, etc. **2** *Brit. archaic sl.* excellent. —*n.* anything that tops something else, esp. icing etc. on a cake.

topple /ˈtɒp(ə)l/ *v.intr. & tr.* (usu. foll. by *over, down*) **1** fall or cause to fall as if top-heavy. **2** totter or cause to totter and fall. [TOP[1] + -LE[4]]

topsail /ˈtɒpseɪl, -s(ə)l/ *n.* a square sail next above the lowest fore-and-aft sail on a gaff.

topside /ˈtɒpsaɪd/ *n.* **1** *Brit.* the outer side of a round of beef. **2** the side of a ship above the water-line.

topsoil /ˈtɒpsɔɪl/ *n.* the top layer of soil (opp. SUBSOIL).

topspin /ˈtɒpspɪn/ *n.* a fast forward spinning motion imparted to a ball in tennis etc. by hitting it forward and upward.

topsy-turvy /ˌtɒpsɪˈtɜːvɪ/ *adv., adj., & n.* —*adv.* **1** upside down. **2** in utter confusion. —*n.* utter confusion. □□ **topsy-turvily** *adv.* **topsy-turviness** *n.* [app. f. TOP[1] + obs. *terve* overturn]

toque /təʊk/ *n.* **1** a woman's small brimless hat. **2** *hist.* a small cap or bonnet for a man or woman. [F, app. = It. *tocca*, Sp. *toca*, of unkn. orig.]

toquilla /təˈkiːjə/ *n.* **1** a palmlike tree, *Carludovica palmata*, native to S. America. **2** a fibre produced from the leaves of this. [Sp., = small gauze head-dress, dimin. of *toca* toque]

tor /tɔː(r)/ *n.* a hill or rocky peak, esp. in Devon or Cornwall. [OE *torr*: cf. Gael. *tòrr* bulging hill]

Torah /ˈtɔːrə/ *n.* **1** (usu. prec. by *the*) **a** the Pentateuch. **b** a scroll containing this. **2** the will of God as revealed in Mosaic law. [Heb. *tōrāh* instruction]

torc var. of TORQUE 1.

torch /tɔːtʃ/ *n. & v.* —*n.* **1** (also **electric torch**) *Brit.* a portable battery-powered electric lamp. **2 a** a piece of wood, cloth, etc., soaked in tallow and lighted for illumination. **b** any similar lamp, e.g. an oil-lamp on a pole. **3** a source of heat, illumination, or enlightenment (*bore aloft the torch of freedom*). **4** esp. *US* a blowlamp. **5** *US sl.* an arsonist. —*v.tr.* esp. *US sl.* set alight with a torch. □ **carry a torch for** suffer from unrequited love for. **put to the torch** destroy by burning. **torch-fishing** catching fish by torchlight at night. **torch-race** *Gk Antiq.* a festival performance of runners handing lighted torches to others in relays. **torch singer** a woman who sings torch songs. **torch song** a popular song of unrequited love. **torch-thistle** any tall cactus of the genus *Cereus*, with funnel-shaped flowers which open at night. [ME f. OF *torche* f. L *torqua* f. *torquēre* twist]

torchère /tɔːˈʃeə(r)/ *n.* a tall stand with a small table for a candlestick etc. [F (as TORCH)]

torchlight /ˈtɔːtʃlaɪt/ *n.* the light of a torch or torches.

torchon /ˈtɔːʃ(ə)n, -ʃɔ̃/ *n.* (in full **torchon lace**) coarse bobbin lace with geometrical designs. [F, = duster, dishcloth f. *torcher* wipe]

tore[1] *past* of TEAR[1].

tore[2] /tɔː(r)/ *n.* = TORUS 1, 4. [F f. L *torus*: see TORUS]

toreador /ˈtɒrɪəˌdɔː(r)/ *n.* a bullfighter, esp. on horseback. □ **toreador pants** close-fitting calf-length women's trousers. [Sp. f. *torear* fight bulls f. *toro* bull f. L *taurus*]

torero /tɒˈreərəʊ/ *n.* (*pl.* **-os**) a bullfighter. [Sp. f. *toro*: see TOREADOR]

toreutic /təˈruːtɪk/ *adj. & n.* —*adj.* of or concerning the chasing, carving, and embossing of esp. metal. —*n.* (in *pl.*) the art or practice of this. [Gk *toreutikos* f. *toreuō* work in relief]

torgoch /ˈtɔːɡɒx/ *n.* a kind of red-bellied char found in some Welsh lakes. [Welsh f. *tor* belly + *coch* red]

tori *pl.* of TORUS.

toric /ˈtɒrɪk/ *adj.* *Geom.* having the form of a torus or part of a torus.

torii /ˈtɔːrɪɪ/ *n.* (*pl.* same) the gateway of a Shinto shrine, with two uprights and two crosspieces. [Jap.]

Torino see TURIN.

torment *n. & v.* —*n.* /ˈtɔːment/ **1** severe physical or mental suffering (*was in torment*). **2** a cause of this. **3** *archaic* **a** torture. **b** an instrument of torture. —*v.tr.* /tɔːˈment/ **1** subject to torment (*tormented with worry*). **2** tease or worry excessively (*enjoyed tormenting the teacher*). □□ **tormentedly** *adv.* **tormentingly** *adv.* **tormentor** /-ˈmentə(r)/ *n.* [ME f. OF *torment, tormenter* f. L *tormentum* missile-engine f. *torquēre* to twist]

tormentil /ˈtɔːməntɪl/ *n.* a low-growing plant, *Potentilla erecta*, with bright yellow flowers and a highly astringent rootstock used in medicine. [ME f. OF *tormentille* f. med.L *tormentilla*, of unkn. orig.]

torn *past part.* of TEAR[1].

tornado /tɔːˈneɪdəʊ/ *n.* (*pl.* **-oes**) **1** a violent storm of small extent with whirling winds, esp.: **a** in West Africa at the beginning and end of the rainy season. **b** in the US etc. over a narrow path often accompanied by a funnel-shaped cloud. **2** an outburst or volley of cheers, hisses, missiles, etc. □□ **tornadic** /-ˈnædɪk/ *adj.* [app. assim. of Sp. *tronada* thunderstorm (f. *tronar* to thunder) to Sp. *tornar* to turn]

Tornio /ˈtɔːnɪəʊ/ **1** (Swedish **Tornea**) a town in NW Finland at the head of the Gulf of Bothnia; pop. (1987) 22,538. **2** (Swedish **Torne**) a river that rises in NE Sweden and flows south along the Sweden–Finland frontier before emptying into the Gulf of Bothnia.

toroid /ˈtɔːrɔɪd/ *n.* a figure of toroidal shape.

toroidal /tɔːˈrɔɪd(ə)l/ *adj.* *Geom.* of or resembling a torus. □□ **toroidally** *adv.*

Toronto /təˈrɒntəʊ/ the capital of Ontario and largest city in Canada; pop. (1986) 612,300; metropolitan area pop. 3,427,200.

torose /ˈtɔːrəʊs/ *adj.* **1** *Bot.* (of plants, esp. their stalks) cylindrical with bulges at intervals. **2** *Zool.* knobby. [L *torosus* f. *torus*: see TORUS]

torpedo /tɔːˈpiːdəʊ/ *n. & v.* —*n.* (*pl.* **-oes**) **1 a** a cigar-shaped self-propelled underwater missile fired at a ship and exploding on impact. (See below.) **b** (in full **aerial torpedo**) a similar device dropped from an aircraft. **2** *Zool.* an electric ray. **3** *US* an explosive device or firework. —*v.tr.* (**-oes, -oed**) **1** destroy or attack with a torpedo. **2** make (a policy, institution, plan, etc.) ineffective or inoperative; destroy. □ **torpedo-boat** a small fast lightly armed warship for carrying or discharging torpedoes. **torpedo-net** (or **-netting**) netting of steel wire hung round a ship to intercept torpedoes. **torpedo-tube** a tube from which torpedoes are fired. □□ **torpedo-like** *adj.* [L, = numbness, electric ray f. *torpēre* be numb]

The term was originally applied to a case charged with gunpowder designed to explode under water after a given interval so as to destroy any vessel in its immediate vicinity. This submarine mine was either towed by a ship or moored and allowed to drift. The first self-propelled torpedo was designed in 1866 by Robert Whitehead, a British engineer, and the first successful use of the weapon in war was by the Japanese against the Russians in 1904. Torpedoes can be launched by ships or aircraft but have been used most successfully by submarines, and accounted for heavy shipping losses in the Second World War. Since then developments have included sophisticated acoustic devices that enable the torpedo to home in on its target.

torpefy /ˈtɔːpɪˌfaɪ/ *v.tr.* (**-ies, -ied**) make numb or torpid. [L *torpefacere* f. *torpēre* be numb]

torpid /ˈtɔːpɪd/ *adj.* **1** sluggish, inactive, dull, apathetic. **2** numb. **3** (of a hibernating animal) dormant. □□ **torpidity** /-ˈpɪdɪtɪ/ *n.* **torpidly** *adv.* **torpidness** *n.* [L *torpidus* (as TORPOR)]

torpor /ˈtɔːpə(r)/ *n.* torpidity. □□ **torporific** /-ˈrɪfɪk/ *adj.* [L f. *torpēre* be sluggish]

torquate /ˈtɔːkweɪt/ *adj.* *Zool.* (of an animal) with a ring of distinctive colour or texture of hair or plumage round the neck. [L *torquatus* (as TORQUE)]

torque /tɔːk/ *n.* **1** (also **torc**) *hist.* a necklace of twisted metal, esp. of the ancient Gauls and Britons. **2** *Mech.* the moment of a system of forces tending to cause rotation. □ **torque converter** a device to transmit the correct torque from the engine to the axle in a motor vehicle. [(sense 1 F f. L *torques*) f. L *torquēre* to twist]

Torquemada /ˌtɔːkɪˈmɑːdə/, Tomás de (c.1420–98), Spanish cleric, a Dominican monk who became Inquisitor-General of Spain and Grand Inquisitor, and transformed the Inquisition into an instrument of the State. He earned a reputation for ruthlessness and ferocious repression of religious heterodoxy and was the prime mover in the expulsion of the Jews from Spain from 1492 onwards.

torr /tɔː(r)/ *n.* (*pl.* same) a unit of pressure used in measuring partial vacuums, equal to 133.32 pascals. [E. TORRICELLI]

torrefy /ˈtɒrɪˌfaɪ/ *v.tr.* (**-ies, -ied**) **1** roast or dry (metallic ore, a drug, etc.). **2** parch or scorch with heat. □□ **torrefaction** /-ˈfækʃ(ə)n/ *n.* [F *torréfier* f. L *torrefacere* f. *torrēre* scorch]

torrent /ˈtɒrənt/ *n.* **1** a rushing stream of water, lava, etc. **2** (in pl.) a great downpour of rain (*came down in torrents*). **3** (usu. foll. by *of*) a violent or copious flow (*uttered a torrent of abuse*). □□ **torrential** /təˈrenʃ(ə)l/ *adj.* **torrentially** /təˈrenʃəlɪ/ *adv.* [F f. It. *torrente* f. L *torrens -entis* scorching, boiling, roaring f. *torrēre* scorch]

Torres Strait /ˈtɒrɪs/ a channel linking the Arafura Sea and Coral Sea and separating the north tip of Queensland, Australia, from the island of New Guinea.

Torricelli /ˌtɒrɪˈtʃelɪ/, Evangelista (1608–47), Italian mathematician and physicist, a disciple of Galileo whom he succeeded as mathematician to the court of Tuscany. A law or theorem that bears his name deals with the velocity of liquids flowing under the force of gravity from orifices. His most important invention was the mercury barometer in 1643, with which he demonstrated that the atmosphere exerts a pressure by showing that it could support a column of mercury in an inverted closed tube, and he was the first person to produce a sustained vacuum.

torrid /ˈtɒrɪd/ *adj.* **1 a** (of the weather) very hot and dry. **b** (of land etc.) parched by such weather. **2** (of language or actions) emotionally charged; passionate, intense. □ **torrid zone** the central belt of the earth between the Tropics of Cancer and Capricorn. □□ **torridity** /-ˈrɪdɪtɪ/ *n.* **torridly** *adv.* **torridness** *n.* [F *torride* or L *torridus* f. *torrēre* parch]

torse /tɔːs/ *n.* *Heraldry* a wreath. [obs. F *torse, torce* wreath ult. f. L *torta* fem. past part. (as TORT)]

torsel var. of TASSEL[2].

Tórshavn /ˈtɔːshaʊn/ the capital of the Faeroe Islands, situated on the island of Strømø; pop. (1986) 15,300.

torsion /ˈtɔːʃ(ə)n/ *n.* **1** twisting, esp. of one end of a body while the other is held fixed. **2** *Math.* the extent to which a curve departs from being planar. **3** *Bot.* the state of being twisted into a spiral. **4** *Med.* the twisting of the cut end of an artery after surgery etc. to impede bleeding. □ **torsion balance** an instrument for measuring very weak forces by their effect upon a system of fine twisted wire. **torsion bar** a bar forming part of a vehicle suspension, twisting in response to the motion of the wheels, and absorbing their vertical movement. **torsion pendulum** a pendulum working by rotation rather than by swinging. □□ **torsional** *adj.* **torsionally** *adv.* **torsionless** *adj.* [ME f. OF f. LL *torsio -onis* f. L *tortio* (as TORT)]

torsk /tɔːsk/ *n.* a fish of the cod family, *Brosmius brosme*, abundant in northern waters and often dried for food. [Norw. *to(r)sk* f. ON *tho(r)skr* prob. rel. to *thurr* dry]

torso /ˈtɔːsəʊ/ *n.* (*pl.* **-os**) **1** the trunk of the human body. **2** a statue of a human consisting of the trunk alone, without head or limbs. **3** an unfinished or mutilated work (esp. of art, literature, etc.). [It., = stalk, stump, torso, f. L *thyrsus*]

tort /tɔːt/ *n.* *Law* a breach of duty (other than under contract) leading to liability for damages. [ME f. OF f. med.L *tortum* wrong, neut. past part. of L *torquēre tort-* twist]

torte /ˈtɔːtə/ *n.* (*pl.* **torten** /ˈtɔːt(ə)n/ or **tortes**) an elaborate sweet cake or tart. [G]

tortfeasor /ˈtɔːtˌfiːzə(r)/ *n.* *Law* a person guilty of tort. [OF *tort-fesor, tort-faiseur,* etc. f. *tort* wrong, *-fesor, faiseur* doer]

torticollis /ˌtɔːtɪˈkɒlɪs/ *n.* *Med.* a rheumatic etc. disease of the muscles of the neck, causing twisting and stiffness. [mod.L f. L *tortus* crooked + *collum* neck]

tortilla /tɔːˈtiːjə, -ˈtiːljə/ *n.* a thin flat orig. Mexican maize cake eaten hot or cold with or without a filling. [Sp. dimin. of *torta* cake f. LL]

tortious /ˈtɔːʃəs/ *adj.* *Law* constituting a tort; wrongful. □□ **tortiously** *adv.* [AF *torcious* f. *torcion* extortion f. LL *tortio* torture: see TORSION]

tortoise /ˈtɔːtəs/ *n.* **1** any slow-moving land or freshwater reptile of the family Testudinidae, encased in a scaly or leathery domed shell, and having a retractile head and elephantine legs. **2** *Rom. Antiq.* = TESTUDO. □□ **tortoise-like** *adj. & adv.* [ME *tortuce*, OF *tortue,* f. med.L *tortuca*, of uncert. orig.]

tortoiseshell /ˈtɔːtəsˌʃel/ n. & adj. —n. 1 the yellowish-brown mottled or clouded outer shell of some turtles, used for decorative hair-combs, jewellery, etc. 2 **a** = tortoiseshell cat. **b** = tortoiseshell butterfly. —adj. having the colouring or appearance of tortoiseshell. □ **tortoiseshell butterfly** any of various butterflies, esp. of the genus *Aglais* or *Nymphalis*, with wings mottled like tortoiseshell. **tortoiseshell cat** a domestic cat with markings resembling tortoiseshell.

Tortola /tɔːˈtəʊlə/ the principal island of the British Virgin Islands in the West Indies; chief town, Road Town.

tortrix /ˈtɔːtrɪks/ n. any moth of the family Tortricidae, esp. *Tortrix viridana*, the larvae of which live inside rolled leaves. [mod.L, fem. of L *tortor* twister: see TORT]

tortuous /ˈtɔːtjʊəs/ adj. 1 full of twists and turns (*followed a tortuous route*). 2 devious, circuitous, crooked (*has a tortuous mind*). □□ **tortuosity** /-ˈɒsɪtɪ/ n. (pl. -ies). **tortuously** adv. **tortuousness** n. [ME f. OF f. L *tortuosus* f. *tortus* a twist (as TORT)]

torture /ˈtɔːtʃə(r)/ n. & v. —n. 1 the infliction of severe bodily pain esp. as a punishment or a means of persuasion. 2 severe physical or mental suffering (*the torture of defeat*). —v.tr. 1 subject to torture (*tortured by guilt*). 2 force out of a natural position or state; deform; pervert. □□ **torturable** adj. **torturer** n. **torturous** adj. **torturously** adv. [F f. LL *tortura* twisting (as TORT)]

torula /ˈtɒrʊlə/ n. (pl. **torulae** /-ˌliː/) 1 a yeast, *Candida utilis*, used medicinally as a food additive. 2 any yeast-like fungus of the genus *Torula*, growing on dead vegetation. [mod.L, dimin. of *torus*: see TORUS]

torus /ˈtɔːrəs/ n. (pl. **tori** /-raɪ/) 1 *Archit.* a large convex bun-shaped moulding esp. as the lowest part of the base of a column. 2 *Bot.* the receptacle of a flower. 3 *Anat.* a smooth ridge of bone or muscle. 4 *Geom.* a surface or solid formed by rotating a closed curve, esp. a circle, about a line in its plane but not intersecting it. [L, = swelling, bulge, cushion, etc.]

Torvill /ˈtɔːvɪl/, Jayne (1957–), English skater, who in partnership with Christopher Dean won many championships in ice-dancing in 1981–4.

Tory /ˈtɔːrɪ/ n. & adj. —n. (pl. -ies) 1 *colloq.* = CONSERVATIVE n. 2. 2 *hist.* a member of the party that opposed the exclusion of James II and later supported the established religious and political order and gave rise to the Conservative party (opp. WHIG). (See below.) 3 *US hist. derog.* a colonist loyal to the British during the War of American Independence. —adj. *colloq.* = CONSERVATIVE adj. 3. □□ **Toryism** n. [orig. = Irish outlaw, prob. f. Ir. f. *tóir* pursue. The term was used in the 17th c. of the dispossessed Irish, who became outlaws and subsisted by plundering and killing the English settlers and soldiers. It became used as an abusive nickname (1679–80) for those who opposed the exclusion of James, Duke of York (a Roman Catholic), from the succession to the Crown—reputedly because the Duke was seen to favour Irishmen.]

Historically the Tories were associated with the Church of England and with non-toleration of religious nonconformists and Catholics. They suffered as a result of their links with the Jacobites and were excluded from office in the first half of the 18th c. After 1760 they accepted George III and the established order in Church and State. Their fortunes rose as opponents of the French Revolution, but after the end of the Napoleonic Wars they became increasingly reactionary, a trend which led to their eventual defeat in 1830. In the following decades, particularly under the influence of Peel, the nature of the party changed, and it became known by the name Conservative.

Toscana see TUSCANY.

Toscanini /ˌtɒskəˈniːnɪ/, Arturo (1867–1957), Italian conductor and cellist. He conducted at La Scala, Milan, and at the Metropolitan Opera in New York. The NBC (National Broadcasting Company) formed a new orchestra in New York for him, which he conducted from 1937 to 1954, giving public concerts and many famous concert performances of operas. He always conducted from memory.

tosh /tɒʃ/ n. *colloq.* rubbish, nonsense. [19th c.: orig. unkn.]

toss /tɒs/ v. & n. —v. 1 *tr.* throw up (a ball etc.) esp. with the hand. 2 *tr.* & *intr.* roll about, throw, or be thrown, restlessly or from side to side (*the ship tossed on the ocean; was tossing and turning all night; tossed her head angrily*). 3 *tr.* (usu. foll. by *to, away, aside, out*, etc.) throw (a thing) lightly or carelessly (*tossed the letter away*). 4 *tr.* **a** throw (a coin) into the air to decide a choice etc. by the side on which it lands. **b** (also *absol.*; often foll. by *for*) settle a question or dispute with (a person) in this way (*tossed him for the armchair; tossed for it*). 5 *tr.* **a** (of a bull etc.) throw (a person etc.) up with the horns. **b** (of a horse etc.) throw (a rider) off its back. 6 *tr.* coat (food) with dressing etc. by shaking. 7 *tr.* bandy about in debate; discuss (*tossed the question back and forth*). —n. 1 the act or an instance of tossing (a coin, the head, etc.). 2 *Brit.* a fall, esp. from a horse. □ **toss one's head** throw it back esp. in anger, impatience, etc. **tossing the caber** the Scottish sport of throwing a tree-trunk. **toss oars** raise oars to an upright position in salute. **toss off** 1 drink off at a draught. 2 dispatch (work) rapidly or without effort (*tossed off an omelette*). 3 *Brit. coarse sl.* masturbate. ¶ Usually considered a taboo use in sense 3. **toss a pancake** throw it up so that it flips on to the other side in the frying-pan. **toss up** toss a coin to decide a choice etc. **toss-up** n. 1 a doubtful matter; a close thing (*it's a toss-up whether he wins*). 2 the tossing of a coin. [16th c.: orig. unkn.]

tosser /ˈtɒsə(r)/ n. 1 *Brit. coarse sl.* an unpleasant or contemptible person. 2 a person or thing that tosses.

tot[1] /tɒt/ n. 1 a small child (*a tiny tot*). 2 a dram of liquor. [18th c., of dial. orig.]

tot[2] /tɒt/ v. & n. —v. (**totted, totting**) 1 *tr.* (usu. foll. by *up*) add (figures etc.). 2 *intr.* (foll. by *up*) (of items) mount up. —n. *Brit. archaic* a set of figures to be added. □ **totting-up** 1 the adding of separate items. 2 *Brit.* the adding of convictions for driving offences to cause disqualification. **tot up to** amount to. [abbr. of TOTAL or of L *totum* the whole]

tot[3] /tɒt/ v. & n. *Brit. sl.* —v.intr. (**totted, totting**) collect saleable items from refuse as an occupation. —n. an article collected from refuse. [19th c.: orig. unkn.]

total /ˈtəʊt(ə)l/ adj., n., & v. —adj. 1 complete, comprising the whole (*the total number of people*). 2 absolute, unqualified (*in total ignorance; total abstinence*). —n. a total number or amount. —v. (**totalled, totalling**; *US* **totaled, totaling**) 1 *tr.* **a** amount in number to (*they totalled 131*). **b** find the total of (things, a set of figures, etc.). 2 *intr.* (foll. by *to, up to*) amount to, mount up to. 3 *tr. US sl.* wreck completely. □ **total abstinence** abstaining completely from alcohol. **total eclipse** an eclipse in which the whole disc (of the sun, moon, etc.) is obscured. **total internal reflection** reflection without refraction of a light-ray meeting the interface between two media at more than a certain critical angle to the normal. **total recall** the ability to remember every detail of one's experience clearly. **total war** a war in which all available weapons and resources are employed. □□ **totally** adv. [ME f. OF f. med.L *totalis* f. *totus* entire]

totalitarian /təʊˌtælɪˈteərɪən/ adj. & n. —adj. of or relating to a centralized dictatorial form of government requiring complete subservience to the State. —n. a person advocating such a system. □□ **totalitarianism** n.

totality /təʊˈtælɪtɪ/ n. 1 the complete amount or sum. 2 *Astron.* the time during which an eclipse is total.

totalizator /ˈtəʊtəlaɪˌzeɪtə(r)/ n. (also **totalisator**) 1 a device showing the number and amount of bets staked on a race, to facilitate the division of the total among those backing the winner. 2 a system of betting based on this.

totalize /ˈtəʊtəˌlaɪz/ v.tr. (also **-ise**) collect into a total; find the total of. □□ **totalization** /-ˈzeɪʃ(ə)n/ n.

totalizer /ˈtəʊtəˌlaɪzə(r)/ n. = TOTALIZATOR.

tote[1] /təʊt/ n. *sl.* 1 a totalizator. 2 a lottery. [abbr.]

tote[2] /təʊt/ v.tr. esp. *US colloq.* carry, convey, esp. a heavy load (*toting a gun*). □ **tote bag** a woman's large bag for shopping etc. **tote box** *US* a small container for goods. □□ **toter** n. (also in comb.). [17th-c. US, prob. of dial. orig.]

totem /ˈtəʊtəm/ n. 1 a natural object, esp. an animal, adopted by North American Indians as an emblem of a clan or an individual. 2 an image of this. □ **totem-pole** 1 a pole on which totems are carved or hung. 2 a hierarchy. □□ **totemic** /-ˈtemɪk/

adj. **totemism** *n.* **totemist** *n.* **totemistic** /-ˈmɪstɪk/ *adj.* [Algonquian]

tother /ˈtʌðə(r)/ *adj.* & *pron.* (also **t'other**) *dial.* or *joc.* the other. □ **tell tother from which** *joc.* tell one from the other. [ME *the tother*, for earlier *thet other* 'that other'; now understood as = *the other*]

totter /ˈtɒtə(r)/ *v.* & *n.* —*v.intr.* **1** stand or walk unsteadily or feebly (*tottered out of the pub*). **2 a** (of a building etc.) shake or rock as if about to collapse. **b** (of a system of government etc.) be about to fall. —*n.* an unsteady or shaky movement or gait. □□ **totterer** *n.* **tottery** *adj.* [ME f. MDu. *touteren* to swing].

toucan /ˈtuːkən/ *n.* any tropical American fruit-eating bird of the family Ramphastidae, with an immense beak and brightly coloured plumage. [Tupi *tucana*, Guarani *tucã*]

touch /tʌtʃ/ *v.* & *n.* —*v.* **1** *tr.* come into or be in physical contact with (another thing) at one or more points. **2** *tr.* (often foll. by *with*) bring the hand etc. into contact with (*touched her arm*). **3 a** *intr.* (of two things etc.) be in or come into contact with one another (*the balls were touching*). **b** *tr.* bring (two things) into mutual contact (*they touched hands*). **4** *tr.* rouse tender or painful feelings in (*was touched by his appeal*). **5** *tr.* strike lightly (*just touched the wall with the back bumper*). **6** *tr.* (usu. with *neg.*) **a** disturb or harm (*don't touch my things*). **b** have any dealings with (*won't touch bricklaying*). **c** consume; use up; make use of (*dare not touch alcohol; has not touched her breakfast; need not touch your savings*). **d** cope with; affect; manage (*soap won't touch this dirt*). **7** *tr.* **a** deal with (a subject) lightly or in passing (*touched the matter of their expenses*). **b** concern (*it touches you closely*). **8** *tr.* **a** reach or rise as far as, esp. momentarily (*the thermometer touched 90°*). **b** (usu. with *neg.*) approach in excellence etc. (*can't touch him for style*). **9** *tr.* affect slightly; modify (*pity touched with fear*). **10** *tr.* (as **touched** *adj.*) slightly mad. **11** *tr.* (often foll. by *in*) esp. *Art* mark lightly, put in (features etc.) with a brush, pencil, etc. **12** *tr.* **a** strike (the keys, strings, etc. of a musical instrument). **b** strike the keys or strings of (a piano etc.). **13** *tr.* (usu. foll. by *for*) *sl.* ask for and get money etc. from (a person) as a loan or gift (*touched him for £5*). **14** *tr.* injure slightly (*blossom touched by frost*). **15** *tr. Geom.* be tangent to (a curve). —*n.* **1** the act or an instance of touching, esp. with the body or hand (*felt a touch on my arm*). **2 a** the faculty of perception through physical contact, esp. with the fingers (*has no sense of touch in her right arm*). **b** the qualities of an object etc. as perceived in this way (*the soft touch of silk*). **3** a small amount; a slight trace (*a touch of salt; a touch of irony*). **4 a** a musician's manner of playing keys or strings. **b** the manner in which the keys or strings respond to touch. **c** an artist's or writer's style of workmanship, writing, etc. (*has a delicate touch*). **5** a distinguishing quality or trait (*a professional touch*). **6** (esp. in *pl.*) **a** a light stroke with a pen, pencil, etc. **b** a slight alteration or improvement (*speech needs a few touches*). **7** = TAG². **8** (prec. by *a*) slightly (*is a touch too arrogant*). **9** *sl.* **a** the act of asking for and getting money etc. from a person. **b** a person from whom money etc. is so obtained. **10** *Football* the part of the field outside the side limits. **11** *archaic* a test with or as if with a touchstone (*put it to the touch*). □ **at a touch** if touched, however lightly (*opened at a touch*). **easy touch** *sl.* a person who readily parts with money. **finishing touch** (or **touches**) the final details completing and enhancing a piece of work etc. **get** (or **put**) **in** (or **into**) **touch with** come or cause to come into communication with; contact. **in touch** (often foll. by *with*) **1** in communication (*we're still in touch after all these years*). **2** up to date, esp. regarding news etc. (*keeps in touch with events*). **3** aware, conscious, empathetic (*not in touch with her own feelings*). **keep in touch** (often foll. by *with*) **1** remain informed (*kept in touch with the latest developments*). **2** continue correspondence, a friendship, etc. **lose touch** (often foll. by *with*) **1** cease to be informed. **2** cease to correspond with or be in contact with another person. **lose one's touch** not show one's customary skill. **the Nelson touch** a masterly or sympathetic approach to a problem (from Horatio Nelson, Admiral at Trafalgar). **out of touch** (often foll. by *with*) **1** not in correspondence. **2** not up to date or modern. **3** lacking in awareness or sympathy (*out of touch with his son's beliefs*). **personal touch** a characteristic or individual approach to a situation. **soft touch** = *easy touch* (see TOUCH). **to the touch** when touched

(*was cold to the touch*). **touch-and-go** uncertain regarding a result; risky (*it was touch-and-go whether we'd catch the train*). **touch at** (of a ship) call at (a port etc.). **touch bottom 1** reach the bottom of water with one's feet. **2** be at the lowest or worst point. **3** be in possession of the full facts. **touch down 1** *Rugby Football* & *Amer. Football* touch the ground with the ball being one's own or the opponent's goal. **2** (of an aircraft) make contact with the ground in landing. **touch football** US football with touching in place of tackling. **touch-hole** a small hole in a gun for igniting the charge. **touch-in-goal** *Football* each of the four corners enclosed by continuations of the touch-lines and goal-lines. **touch-judge** *Rugby Football* a linesman. **touch-line** (in various sports) either of the lines marking the side boundaries of the pitch. **touch-mark** the maker's mark on pewter. **touch-me-not** any of various plants of the genus *Impatiens*, with ripe seed-capsules jerking open when touched. **touch-needle** a needle of gold or silver alloy of known composition used as a standard in testing other alloys on a touchstone. **touch off 1** represent exactly (in a portrait etc.). **2** explode by touching with a match etc. **3** initiate (a process) suddenly (*touched off a run on the pound*). **touch of nature 1** a natural trait. **2** *colloq.* an exhibition of human feeling with which others sympathize (from a misinterpretation of Shakesp. *Troilus and Cressida* III. iii. 169). **touch of the sun 1** a slight attack of sunstroke. **2** a little sunlight. **touch on** (or **upon**) **1** treat (a subject) briefly, refer to or mention casually. **2** verge on (*that touches on impudence*). **touch-paper** paper impregnated with nitre, for firing gunpowder, fireworks, etc. **touch the spot** *colloq.* find out or do exactly what was needed. **touch-type** type without looking at the keys. **touch-typing** this skill. **touch-typist** a person who touch-types. **touch up 1** give finishing touches to or retouch (a picture, writing, etc.). **2** *Brit. sl.* **a** caress so as to excite sexually. **b** sexually molest. **3** strike (a horse) lightly with a whip. **touch wood** touch something wooden with the hand to avert ill luck. **would not touch with a bargepole** see BARGEPOLE. □□ **touchable** *adj.* [ME f. OF *tochier, tuchier* (v.), *touche* (n.): prob. imit., imitating a knock]

touchdown /ˈtʌtʃdaʊn/ *n.* **1** the act or an instance of an aircraft making contact with the ground during landing. **2** *Rugby Football* & *Amer. Football* the act or an instance of touching down.

touché /tuːˈʃeɪ/ *int.* **1** the acknowledgement of a hit by a fencing-opponent. **2** the acknowledgement of a justified accusation, a witticism, or a point made in reply to one's own. [F, past part. of *toucher* TOUCH]

toucher /ˈtʌtʃə(r)/ *n.* **1** a person or thing that touches. **2** *Bowls* a wood that touches the jack.

touching /ˈtʌtʃɪŋ/ *adj.* & *prep.* —*adj.* moving; pathetic (*a touching incident; touching confidence*). —*prep. literary* concerning; about. □□ **touchingly** *adv.* **touchingness** *n.* [ME f. TOUCH: (prep.) f. OF *touchant* pres. part. (as TOUCH)]

touchstone /ˈtʌtʃstəʊn/ *n.* **1** a fine-grained dark schist or jasper used for testing alloys of gold etc. by marking it with them and observing the colour of the mark. **2** a standard or criterion.

touchwood /ˈtʌtʃwʊd/ *n.* readily inflammable wood, esp. when made soft by fungi, used as tinder.

touchy /ˈtʌtʃɪ/ *adj.* (**touchier, touchiest**) apt to take offence; over-sensitive. □□ **touchily** *adv.* **touchiness** *n.* [perh. alt. of TETCHY after TOUCH]

tough /tʌf/ *adj.* & *n.* —*adj.* **1** hard to break, cut, tear, or chew; durable; strong. **2** (of a person) able to endure hardship; hardy. **3** unyielding, stubborn, difficult (*it was a tough job; a tough customer*). **4** *colloq.* **a** acting sternly; hard (*get tough with*). **b** (of circumstances, luck, etc.) severe, unpleasant, hard, unjust. **5** *colloq.* criminal or violent (*tough guys*). —*n.* a tough person, esp. a ruffian or criminal. □ **tough guy** *colloq.* **1** a hard unyielding person. **2** a violent aggressive person. **tough it** (or **tough it out**) *colloq.* endure or withstand difficult conditions. **tough-minded** realistic, not sentimental. **tough-mindedness** being tough-minded. □□ **toughen** *v.tr.* & *intr.* **toughener** *n.* **toughish** *adj.* **toughly** *adv.* **toughness** *n.* [OE *tōh*]

toughie /ˈtʌfɪ/ *n. colloq.* a tough person or problem.

Toulon /tuːˈlɔ̃/ a port and naval base on the Mediterranean coast of southern France; pop. (1982) 182,000.

æ cat ɑː arm e bed ɜː her ɪ sit iː see ɒ hot ɔː saw ʌ run ʊ put uː too ə ago aɪ my

Toulouse /tuːˈluːz/ a city of SW France on the River Garonne, capital of the Midi-Pyrénées region; pop. (1982) 354,300. It was the capital of the Visigoths (419–507), and later the chief town of Aquitaine; its university was founded in 1229. Toulouse is now a centre of the aerospace industry.

Toulouse-Lautrec /tuːˈluːz ləʊˈtrek/ Henri de (1864–1901), French painter, draughtsman, and print-maker, the son of Count Alphonse de Toulouse-Lautrec Monfa. His highly original style, often bordering on caricature, adopts the technical apparatus of post-impressionism, and his delicate calligraphic line, strongly influenced by Japanese prints, readily reflects the spirit of art nouveau. Lautrec revelled in the Bohemian life, and his depictions of theatre, music-halls, cafés, and brothels sum up the earthier side of the life of Montmartre. Lautrec participated in the 1890s' revival of colour lithography, and his printed works, particularly the large posters, are today regarded as perfect examples of the spirit of the settled and comfortable Parisian life at that time.

toupee /ˈtuːpeɪ/ n. (also **toupet** /tuːˈpeɪ/) a wig or artificial hair-piece to cover a bald spot. [F *toupet* hair-tuft dimin. of OF *toup* tuft (as TOP¹)]

tour /tʊə(r)/ n. & v. —n. **1 a** a journey from place to place as a holiday. **b** an excursion, ramble, or walk (*made a tour of the garden*). **2 a** a spell of duty on military or diplomatic service. **b** the time to be spent at a particular post. **3** a series of performances, matches, etc., at different places on a route through a country etc. —v. **1** intr. (usu. foll. by *through*) make a tour (*toured through India*). **2** tr. make a tour of (a country etc.). □ **on tour** (esp. of a team, theatre company, etc.) touring. **touring-car** a car with room for passengers and much luggage. **tour operator** a travel agent specializing in package holidays. [ME f. OF *to(u)r* f. L *tornus* f. Gk *tornos* lathe]

touraco var. of TURACO.

tour de force /ˌtʊə də ˈfɔːs/ n. a feat of strength or skill. [F]

tourer /ˈtʊərə(r)/ n. a vehicle, esp. a car, for touring. [TOUR]

tourism /ˈtʊərɪz(ə)m/ n. the organization and operation of (esp. foreign) holidays, esp. as a commercial enterprise.

tourist /ˈtʊərɪst/ n. a person making a visit or tour as a holiday; a traveller, esp. abroad (often attrib.: *tourist accommodation*). □ **tourist class** the lowest class of passenger accommodation in a ship, aircraft, etc. **Tourist Trophy** motor-cycle races held annually on the Isle of Man from 1907. □□ **touristic** /-ˈrɪstɪk/ adj. **touristically** /-ˈrɪstɪkəlɪ/ adv.

touristy /ˈtʊərɪstɪ/ adj. usu. derog. appealing to or visited by many tourists.

tourmaline /ˈtʊəməlɪn, -ˌliːn/ n. a boron aluminium silicate mineral of various colours, possessing unusual electrical properties, and used in electrical and optical instruments and as a gemstone. [F f. Sinh. *toramalli* porcelain]

Tournai /tʊəˈneɪ/ (Flemish **Doornik** /ˈdɔːniːk/) a textile manufacturing town of Belgium, on the River Scheldt near the Belgian–French frontier; pop. (1988) 66,750.

tournament /ˈtʊənəmənt/ n. **1** any contest of skill between a number of competitors, esp. played in heats (*chess tournament; tennis tournament*). **2** a display of military exercises etc. (*Royal Tournament*). **3** hist. a pageant in which jousting with blunted weapons took place. **b** a meeting for jousting between single knights for a prize etc. [ME f. OF *torneiement* f. *torneier* TOURNEY]

tournedos /ˈtʊənəˌdəʊ/ n. (pl. same /-ˌdəʊz/) a small round thick cut from a fillet of beef. [F]

tourney /ˈtʊənɪ/ n. & v. —n. (pl. **-eys**) a tournament. —v.intr. (**-eys, -eyed**) take part in a tournament. [ME f. OF *tornei* (n.), *torneier* (v.), ult. f. L *tornus* a turn]

tourniquet /ˈtʊənɪˌkeɪ/ n. a device for stopping the flow of blood through an artery by twisting a bar etc. in a ligature or bandage. [F prob. f. OF *tournicle* coat of mail, TUNICLE, infl. by *tourner* TURN]

Tours /tʊə(r)/ an industrial city in west central France; pop. (1982) 136,500.

tousle /ˈtaʊz(ə)l/ v.tr. **1** make (esp. the hair) untidy; rumple. **2** handle roughly or rudely. [frequent. of (now dial.) *touse*, ME f. OE rel. to OHG *-zuson*]

tous-les-mois /ˌtuːleɪˈmwɑː/ n. **1** food starch obtained from tubers of a canna, *Canna indica*. **2** this plant. [F, lit. = every month, prob. corrupt. of W.Ind. *toloman*]

tout /taʊt/ v. & n. —v. **1** intr. (usu. foll. by *for*) solicit custom persistently; pester customers (*touting for business*). **2** tr. solicit the custom of (a person) or for (a thing). **3** tr. a Brit. spy out the movements and condition of racehorses in training. **b** US offer racing tips for a share of the resulting profit. —n. a person employed in touting. □□ **touter** n. [ME *tūte* look out = ME (now dial.) *toot* (OE *tōtian*) f. Gmc]

tout court /tuː ˈkʊə(r)/ adv. without addition; simply (*called James tout court*). [F, lit. very short]

tovarish /təˈvɑːrɪʃ/ n. (also **tovarich**) (in the USSR) comrade (esp. as a form of address). [Russ. *tovarishch*]

tow¹ /təʊ/ v. & n. —v.tr. **1** (of a motor vehicle, horse, or person controlling it) pull (a boat, another motor vehicle, a caravan, etc.) along by a rope, tow-bar, etc. **2** pull (a person or thing) along behind one. —n. the act or an instance of towing; the state of being towed. □ **have in** (or **on**) **tow 1** be towing. **2** be accompanied by and often in charge of (a person). **tow-bar** a bar for towing esp. a trailer or caravan. **tow-** (or **towing-**) **line** (or **rope**) a line etc. used in towing. **tow-** (or **towing-**) **net** a net used for dragging through water to collect specimens. **tow-** (or **towing-**) **path** a path beside a river or canal used for towing a boat by horse. □□ **towable** adj. **towage** /-ɪdʒ/ n. [OE *togian* f. Gmc, rel. to TUG]

tow² /təʊ/ n. **1** the coarse and broken part of flax or hemp prepared for spinning. **2** a loose bunch of rayon etc. strands. □ **tow-coloured** (of hair) very light. **tow-head** tow-coloured or unkempt hair. **tow-headed** having very light or unkempt hair. □□ **towy** /ˈtəʊɪ/ adj. [ME f. MLG *touw* f. OS *tou*, rel. to ON *tó* wool: cf. TOOL]

toward prep. & adj. —prep. /təˈwɔːd, tɔːd/ = TOWARDS. —adj. /ˈtəʊəd/ archaic **1** about to take place; in process. **2** docile, apt. **3** promising, auspicious. □□ **towardness** /ˈtəʊədnɪs/ n. (in sense of adj.).

towards /təˈwɔːdz, twɔːdz, tɔːdz/ prep. **1** in the direction of (*set out towards town*). **2** as regards; in relation to (*his attitude towards death*). **3** as a contribution to; for (*put this towards your expenses*). **4** near (*towards the end of our journey*). [OE *tōweard* (adj.) future (as TO, -WARD)]

towel /ˈtaʊəl/ n. & v. —n. **1 a** a piece of rough-surfaced absorbent cloth used for drying oneself or a thing after washing. **b** absorbent paper used for this. **c** a cloth used for drying plates, dishes, etc.; a tea towel. **2** Brit. = sanitary towel. —v. (**towelled, towelling**; US **toweled, toweling**) **1** tr. (often refl.) wipe or dry with a towel. **2** intr. wipe or dry oneself with a towel. **3** tr. sl. thrash. □ **towel-horse** (or **-rail**) a frame for hanging towels on. □□ **towelling** n. [ME f. OF *toail(l)e* f. Gmc]

tower /ˈtaʊə(r)/ n. & v. —n. **1 a** a tall esp. square or circular structure, often part of a church, castle, etc. **b** a fortress etc. comprising or including a tower. **c** a tall structure housing machinery, apparatus, operators, etc. (*cooling tower; control tower*). **2** a place of defence; a protection. —v.intr. **1** (usu. foll. by *above, high*) reach or be high or above; be superior. **2** (of a bird) soar or hover. **3** (as **towering** adj.) **a** high, lofty (*towering intellect*). **b** violent (*towering rage*). □ **the Tower** the Tower of London (see separate entry). **tower block** a tall building containing offices or flats. **tower of silence** a tall open-topped structure on which Parsees place their dead. **tower of strength** a person who gives strong and reliable support. □□ **towered** /ˈtaʊəd/ adj. **towery** adj. [OE *torr*, & ME *tūr*, AF & OF *tur* etc., f. L *turris* f. Gk]

Tower of London a fortress by the Thames just east of the City of London. The oldest part, the White Tower, was begun in 1078. It was later used as a State prison, and is now a repository of ancient armour and weapons and other objects of public interest, including the Crown jewels (which have been kept there since the time of Henry III).

town /taʊn/ n. **1 a** a large urban area with a name, defined boundaries, and local government, being larger than a village and usu. not created a city. **b** any densely populated area, esp. as opposed to the country or suburbs. **c** the people of a town (the whole town knows of it). **2 a** Brit. London or the chief city or town in one's neighbourhood (went up to town). **b** the central business or shopping area in a neighbourhood (just going into town). **3** the permanent residents of a university town as distinct from the members of the university (cf. GOWN). **4** US = TOWNSHIP 2. □ **go to town** colloq. act or work with energy or enthusiasm. **on the town** colloq. enjoying the entertainments, esp. the night-life, of a town; celebrating. **town clerk 1** US & hist. the officer of the corporation of a town in charge of records etc. **2** Brit. hist. the secretary and legal adviser of a town corporation until 1974. **town council** the elective governing body in a municipality. **town councillor** an elected member of this. **town crier** see CRIER. **town gas** manufactured gas for domestic and commercial use. **town hall** a building for the administration of local government, having public meeting rooms etc. **town house 1** a town residence, esp. of a person with a house in the country. **2** a terrace house, esp. of a stylish modern type. **3** a house in a planned group in a town. **4** Brit. a town hall. **town-major** hist. the chief executive officer in a garrison town or fortress. **town mayor** Brit. the chairman of a town council. **town meeting** US a meeting of the voters of a town for the transaction of public business. **town planning** the planning of the construction and growth of towns. □□ **townish** adj. **townless** adj. **townlet** n. **townward** adj. & adv. **townwards** adv. [OE tūn enclosure f. Gmc]

townee /taʊˈniː/ n. (also **townie** /ˈtaʊnɪ/) derog. a person living in a town, esp. as opposed to a countryman or (in a university town) a student etc.

townscape /ˈtaʊnskeɪp/ n. **1** the visual appearance of a town or towns. **2** a picture of a town.

townsfolk /ˈtaʊnzfəʊk/ n. the inhabitants of a particular town or towns.

township /ˈtaʊnʃɪp/ n. **1** S.Afr. **a** an urban area set aside for Black (usu. African) occupation. **b** a White urban area (esp. if new or about to be developed). **2** US & Can. **a** a division of a county with some corporate powers. **b** a district six miles square. **3** Brit. hist. **a** a community inhabiting a manor, parish, etc. **b** a manor or parish as a territorial division. **c** a small town or village forming part of a large parish. **4** Austral. & NZ a small town; a town-site. [OE tūnscipe (as TOWN, -SHIP)]

townsman /ˈtaʊnzmən/ n. (pl. **-men**; fem. **townswoman**, pl. **-women**) an inhabitant of a town; a fellow citizen.

townspeople /ˈtaʊnzˌpiːp(ə)l/ n.pl. the people of a town.

Townsville /ˈtaʊnzvɪl/ an industrial port and resort town of Queensland, on the NE coast of Australia; pop. (1986) 103,700.

towy see TOW².

toxaemia /tɒkˈsiːmɪə/ n. (US **toxemia**) **1** blood-poisoning. **2** a condition in pregnancy characterized by increased blood pressure. □□ **toxaemic** adj. [as TOXI- + -AEMIA]

toxi- /ˈtɒksɪ/ comb. form (also **toxico-** /ˈtɒksɪˌkəʊ/, **toxo-** /ˈtɒksəʊ/) poison; poisonous, toxic.

toxic /ˈtɒksɪk/ adj. **1** of or relating to poison (toxic symptoms). **2** poisonous (toxic gas). **3** caused by poison (toxic anaemia). □□ **toxically** adv. **toxicity** /-ˈsɪsɪtɪ/ n. [med.L toxicus poisoned f. L toxicum f. Gk toxikon (pharmakon) (poison for) arrows f. toxon bow, toxa arrows]

toxicology /ˌtɒksɪˈkɒlədʒɪ/ n. the scientific study of poisons. □□ **toxicological** /-kəˈlɒdʒɪk(ə)l/ adj. **toxicologist** n.

toxin /ˈtɒksɪn/ n. a poison produced by a living organism, esp. one formed in the body and stimulating the production of anti-bodies. [TOXIC + -IN]

toxocara /ˌtɒksəʊˈkɑːrə/ n. any nematode worm of the genus Toxocara, parasitic in the alimentary canal of dogs and cats. □□ **toxocariasis** /-kəˈraɪəsɪs/ n. [TOXO- (see TOXI-) + Gk kara head]

toxophilite /tɒkˈsɒfɪˌlaɪt/ n. & adj. —n. a student or lover of archery. —adj. of or concerning archery. □□ **toxophily** n. [Ascham's Toxophilus (1545) f. Gk toxon bow + -philos -PHILE]

toy /tɔɪ/ n. & v. —n. **1 a** a plaything, esp. for a child. **b** (often attrib.) a model or miniature replica of a thing, esp. as a plaything (toy gun). **2 a** a thing, esp. a gadget or instrument, regarded as providing amusement or pleasure. **b** a task or undertaking regarded in an unserious way. **3** (usu. attrib.) a diminutive breed

or variety of dog etc. —v.intr. (usu. foll. by with) **1** trifle, amuse oneself, esp. with a person's affections; flirt (toyed with the idea of going to Africa). **2 a** move a material object idly (toyed with her necklace). **b** nibble at food etc. unenthusiastically (toyed with a peach). □ **toy-box** a usu. wooden box for keeping toys in. **toy boy** colloq. a woman's much younger male lover. **toy soldier 1** a miniature figure of a soldier. **2** sl. a soldier in a peacetime army. [16th c.: earlier = dallying, fun, jest, whim, trifle: orig. unkn.]

Toynbee /ˈtɔɪnbɪ/, Arnold Joseph (1889–1975), English histor-ian, who held various university posts and became Director of Studies at the Royal Institute of International Affairs (1925–55). His greatest work is his twelve-volume Study of History (1934–61), in which he surveys the history of 21 civilizations, tracing a pattern of growth, maturity, and decay in them all and con-cluding that the present Western civilization is in the last of these stages. His suggestion that its fragmentation and waning could be saved by a new universal religion, with one spiritually oriented world society, was not well received.

Tpr. abbr. Trooper.

trabeation /ˌtreɪbɪˈeɪʃ(ə)n/ n. the use of beams instead of arches or vaulting in construction. □□ **trabeate** /ˈtreɪbɪət/ adj. [L trabs trabis beam]

trabecula /trəˈbekjʊlə/ n. (pl. **trabeculae** /-ˌliː/) **1** Anat. a sup-porting band or bar of connective or bony tissue, esp. dividing an organ into chambers. **2** Bot. a beamlike projection or process within a hollow structure. □□ **trabecular** adj. **trabeculate** /-lət/ adj. [L, dimin. of trabs beam]

Trabzon /ˈtræbz(ə)n/ (formerly **Trebizond** /ˈtrebɪˌzɒnd/) a city and port of Turkey, on the Black Sea; pop. (1985) 155,960. Tra-ditionally founded by Greek colonists in 756 BC, its ancient name was Trapezus. From 1204 to 1461 it was the capital of an empire established by Alexis Comnenus.

tracasserie /trəˈkæsərɪ/ n. **1** a state of annoyance. **2** a fuss; a petty quarrel. [F f. tracasser bustle]

trace¹ /treɪs/ v. & n. —v.tr. **1 a** observe, discover, or find vestiges or signs of by investigation. **b** (often foll. by along, through, to, etc.) follow or mark the track or position of (traced their footprints in the mud; traced the outlines of a wall). **c** (often foll. by back) follow to its origins (can trace my family to the 12th century; the report has been traced back to you). **2** (often foll. by over) copy (a drawing etc.) by drawing over its lines on a superimposed piece of translucent paper, or by using carbon paper. **3** (often foll. by out) mark out, delineate, sketch, or write esp. laboriously (traced out a plan of the district; traced out his vision of the future). **4** pursue one's way along (a path etc.). —n. **1 a** a sign or mark or other indication of something having existed; a vestige (no trace remains of the castle; has the traces of a vanished beauty). **b** a very small quantity. **c** an amount of rainfall etc. too small to be measured. **2** a track or footprint left by a person or animal. **3** a track left by the moving pen of an instrument etc. **4** a line on the screen of a cathode-ray tube showing the path of a moving spot. **5** a curve's projection on or intersection with a plane etc. **6** a change in the brain caused by learning processes. □ **trace element 1** a chemical element occurring in minute amounts. **2** a chemical element required only in minute amounts by living organisms for normal growth. **trace fossil** a fossil that represents a burrow, footprint, etc., of an organism. □□ **traceable** adj. **traceability** /-ˈbɪlɪtɪ/ n. **traceless** adj. [ME f. OF trace (n.), tracier (v.) f. L tractus drawing: see TRACT¹]

trace² /treɪs/ n. each of the two side-straps, chains, or ropes by which a horse draws a vehicle. □ **kick over the traces** become insubordinate or reckless. **trace-horse** a horse that draws in traces or by a single trace, esp. one hitched on to help uphill etc. [ME f. OF trais, pl. of TRAIT]

tracer /ˈtreɪsə(r)/ n. **1** a person or thing that traces. **2** Mil. a bullet etc. that is visible in flight because of flames etc. emitted, enabling the gunner to correct the aim. **3** an artificially pro-duced radioactive isotope capable of being followed through the body by the radiation it produces.

tracery /ˈtreɪsərɪ/ n. (pl. **-ies**) **1** ornamental stone openwork esp. in the upper part of a Gothic window. **2** a fine decorative pattern. **3** a natural object finely patterned. □□ **traceried** adj.

trachea /trəˈkiːə, ˈtreɪkɪə/ n. (pl. **tracheae** /-ˈkiːiː/) 1 the passage reinforced by rings of cartilage, through which air reaches the bronchial tubes from the larynx; the windpipe. 2 each of the air passages in the body of an insect etc. 3 any duct or vessel in a plant. □□ **tracheal** /ˈtreɪkɪəl/ adj. **tracheate** /ˈtreɪkɪˌeɪt/ adj. [ME f. med.L, = LL trachia f. Gk trakheia (artēria) rough (artery), f. trakhus rough]

tracheo- /ˈtreɪkɪəʊ/ comb. form.

tracheotomy /ˌtrækɪˈɒtəmɪ/ n. (also **tracheostomy** /-ˈɒstəmɪ/) (pl. **-ies**) an incision made in the trachea to relieve an obstruction to breathing. □ **tracheotomy tube** a breathing-tube inserted into this incision.

trachoma /trəˈkəʊmə/ n. a contagious disease of the eye with inflamed granulation on the inner surface of the lids. □□ **trachomatous** /-ˈkəʊmətəs, -ˈkɒmətəs/ adj. [mod.L f. Gk trakhōma f. trakhus rough]

trachyte /ˈtreɪkaɪt, ˈtræk-/ n. a light-coloured volcanic rock rough to the touch. □□ **trachytic** /trəˈkɪtɪk/ adj. [F f. Gk trakhutēs roughness (as TRACHOMA)]

tracing /ˈtreɪsɪŋ/ n. 1 a copy of a drawing etc. made by tracing. 2 = TRACE¹ n. 3. 3 the act or an instance of tracing. □ **tracing-paper** translucent paper used for making tracings.

track¹ /træk/ n. & v. —n. 1 **a** a mark or marks left by a person, animal, or thing in passing. **b** (in pl.) such marks esp. footprints. 2 a rough path, esp. one beaten by use. 3 a continuous railway line (laid three miles of track). 4 **a** a racecourse for horses, dogs, etc. **b** a prepared course for runners etc. 5 **a** a groove on a gramophone record. **b** a section of a gramophone record containing one song etc. (this side has six tracks). **c** a lengthwise strip of magnetic tape containing one sequence of signals. 6 **a** a line of travel, passage, or motion (followed the track of the hurricane; America followed in the same track). **b** the path travelled by a ship, aircraft, etc. (cf. COURSE n. 2c). 7 a continuous band round the wheels of a tank, tractor, etc. 8 the transverse distance between a vehicle's wheels. 9 = SOUNDTRACK. 10 a line of reasoning or thought (this track proved fruitless). —v. 1 tr. follow the track of (an animal, person, spacecraft, etc.). 2 tr. make out (a course, development, etc.); trace by vestiges. 3 intr. (often foll. by back, in, etc.) (of a film or television camera) move in relation to the subject being filmed. 4 intr. (of wheels) run so that the back ones are exactly in the track of the front ones. 5 intr. (of a gramophone stylus) follow a groove. 6 tr. US **a** make a track with (dirt etc.) from the feet. **b** leave such a track on (a floor etc.). □ **in one's tracks** colloq. where one stands, there and then (stopped him in his tracks). **keep** (or **lose**) **track of** follow (or fail to follow) the course or development of. **make tracks** colloq. go or run away. **make tracks for** colloq. go in pursuit of or towards. **off the track** away from the subject. **on a person's track** 1 in pursuit of him or her. 2 in possession of a clue to a person's conduct, plans, etc. **on the wrong side of** (or **across**) **the tracks** colloq. in an inferior or dubious part of town. **on the wrong** (or **right**) **track** following the wrong (or right) line of inquiry. **track down** reach or capture by tracking. **track events** running-races as opposed to jumping etc. (cf. field events). **tracking station** an establishment set up to track objects in the sky. **track-laying** (of a vehicle) having a caterpillar tread. **track record** a person's past performance or achievements. **track shoe** a spiked shoe worn by a runner. **track suit** a loose warm suit worn by an athlete etc. for exercising or jogging. **track system** US streaming in education. **track with** Austral. sl. associate with, court. □□ **trackage** US n. [ME f. OF trac, perh. f. LG or Du. tre(c)k draught etc.]

track² /træk/ v. 1 tr. tow (a boat) by rope etc. from a bank. 2 intr. travel by being towed. [app. f. Du. trekken to draw etc., assim. to TRACK¹]

tracker /ˈtrækə(r)/ n. 1 a person or thing that tracks. 2 a police dog tracking by scent. 3 a wooden connecting-rod in the mechanism of an organ. 4 = black tracker.

tracking /ˈtrækɪŋ/ n. Electr. the formation of a conducting path over the surface of an insulating material.

tracklayer /ˈtrækˌleɪə(r)/ n. 1 US = TRACKMAN. 2 a tractor or other vehicle equipped with continuous tracks (see TRACK¹ n. 7).

tracklement /ˈtrækəlmənt/ n. an item of food, esp. a jelly, served with meat. [20th c.: orig. unkn.]

trackless /ˈtræklɪs/ adj. 1 without a track or tracks; untrodden. 2 leaving no track or trace. 3 not running on a track. □ **trackless trolley** US a trolleybus.

trackman /ˈtrækmən/ n. (pl. **-men**) a platelayer.

trackway /ˈtrækweɪ/ n. a beaten path; an ancient roadway.

tract¹ /trækt/ n. 1 a region or area of indefinite, esp. large, extent (pathless desert tracts). 2 Anat. an area of an organ or system (respiratory tract). 3 Brit. archaic a period of time etc. [L tractus drawing f. trahere tract- draw, pull]

tract² /trækt/ n. a short treatise in pamphlet form esp. on a religious subject. [app. abbr. of L tractatus TRACTATE]

tract³ /trækt/ n. RC Ch. & Mus. an anthem replacing the alleluia in some masses. [med.L tractus (cantus) drawn-out (song), past part. of L trahere draw]

tractable /ˈtræktəb(ə)l/ adj. 1 (of a person) easily handled; manageable; docile. 2 (of material etc.) pliant, malleable. □□ **tractability** /-ˈbɪlɪtɪ/ n. **tractableness** n. **tractably** adv. [L tractabilis f. tractare handle, frequent. of trahere tract- draw]

Tractarianism /trækˈteərɪəˌnɪz(ə)m/ n. hist. = OXFORD MOVEMENT. □□ **Tractarian** adj. & n. [after Tracts for the Times, a series of 90 pamphlets published in Oxford 1833–41 and outlining the movement's principles]

tractate /ˈtrækteɪt/ n. a treatise. [L tractatus f. tractare: see TRACTABLE]

traction /ˈtrækʃ(ə)n/ n. 1 the act of drawing or pulling a thing over a surface, esp. a road or track (steam traction). 2 **a** a sustained pulling on a limb, muscle, etc., by means of pulleys, weights, etc. **b** contraction, e.g. of a muscle. 3 the grip of a tyre on a road, a wheel on a rail, etc. 4 US the public transport service. □ **traction-engine** a steam or diesel engine for drawing heavy loads on roads, fields, etc. **traction-wheel** the driving-wheel of a locomotive etc. □□ **tractional** adj. **tractive** /ˈtræktɪv/ adj. [F traction or med.L tractio f. L trahere tract- draw]

tractor /ˈtræktə(r)/ n. 1 a motor vehicle used for hauling esp. farm machinery, heavy loads, etc. 2 a traction-engine. [LL tractor (as TRACTION)]

Tracy /ˈtreɪsɪ/, Spencer (1900–67), American film actor, who won his first Oscar for his performance in Captain Courageous (1937) and his second in the following year for Boys Town. He is noted for his partnership with Katherine Hepburn in films that include Adam's Rib (1949) and his last film Guess Who's Coming to Dinner? (1967).

trad /træd/ n. & adj. esp. Brit. colloq. —n. traditional jazz. —adj. traditional. [abbr.]

trade /treɪd/ n. & v. —n. 1 **a** buying and selling. **b** buying and selling conducted between nations etc. **c** business conducted for profit (esp. as distinct from a profession) (a butcher by trade). **d** business of a specified nature or time (Christmas trade; tourist trade). 2 a skilled handicraft esp. requiring an apprenticeship (learnt a trade; his trade is plumbing). 3 (usu. prec. by the) **a** the people engaged in a specific trade (the trade will never agree to it; trade enquiries only). **b** Brit. colloq. licensed victuallers. **c** colloq. the submarine service. 4 US a transaction, esp. a swap. 5 (usu. in pl.) a trade wind. —v. 1 intr. (often foll. by in, with) engage in trade; buy and sell (trades in plastic novelties; we trade with Japan). 2 tr. **a** exchange in commerce; barter (goods). **b** exchange (insults, blows, etc.). 3 intr. (usu. foll. by with, for) have a transaction with a person for a thing. 4 intr. (usu. foll. by to) carry goods to a place. □ **be in trade** esp. derog. be in commerce, esp. keep a shop. **foreign trade** international trade. **Trade Board** Brit. hist. a statutory body for settling disputes etc. in certain industries. **trade book** a book published by a commercial publisher and intended for general readership. **trade cycle** Brit. recurring periods of boom and recession. **trade gap** the extent by which a country's imports exceed its exports. **trade in** (often foll. by for) exchange (esp. a used car etc.) in esp. part payment for another. **trade-in** n. a thing, esp. a car, exchanged in this way. **trade journal** a periodical containing news etc. concerning a particular trade. **trade-last** US a compliment from a third person which is reported to the person complimented in exchange for one to the reporter. **trade mark 1** a device, word, or words, secured by legal registration or established by use as representing a company, product, etc. **2** a distinctive characteristic etc. **trade name 1** a name by which a thing is called in a trade. **2** a name given to a product. **3** a name under which a business trades. **trade off** exchange, esp. as a compromise. **trade-off** *n.* such an exchange. **trade on** take advantage of (a person's credulity, one's reputation, etc.). **trade paper** = *trade journal.* **trade plates** number-plates used by a car-dealer etc. on unlicensed cars. **trade price** a wholesale price charged to the dealer before goods are retailed. **trade secret 1** a secret device or technique used esp. in a trade. **2** *joc.* any secret. **trade union** see separate entry. **trade wind** see separate entry. □□ **tradable** *adj.* **tradeable** *adj.* [ME f. MLG *trade* track f. OS *trada*, OHG *trata*: cf. TREAD]

trader /ˈtreɪdə(r)/ *n.* **1** a person engaged in trade. **2** a merchant ship.

tradescantia /ˌtrædɪˈskæntɪə/ *n.* any usu. trailing plant of the genus *Tradescantia*, with large blue, white, or pink flowers. [mod.L f. J. *Tradescant*, Engl. naturalist d. 1638]

tradesman /ˈtreɪdzmən/ *n.* (*pl.* **-men**; *fem.* **tradeswoman**, *pl.* **-women**) a person engaged in trading or a trade, esp. a shop-keeper or skilled craftsman.

tradespeople /ˈtreɪdzˌpiːp(ə)l/ *n.pl.* people engaged in trade, regarded collectively.

Trades Union Congress the official representative body of British trade unions, founded in 1868, which meets annually to discuss matters of common concern. It is made up of delegates of the affiliated unions.

trade union *n.* (also **trades union**) an organized association of workers in a trade, group of trades, or a profession, formed to protect and further their rights and interests. (See below.) □ **trade-** (or **trades-**) **unionism** this system or association. **trade-** (or **trades-**) **unionist** a member of a trade union.

A product of the Industrial Revolution, the trade unions expanded in size and importance in the 19th c., although often subject, particularly in the earlier years, to repressive legislation (see COMBINATION ACTS), assuming a more aggressive and socialist outlook towards the end of the century and playing a central role in the formation of the Labour Party. The trade-union movement achieved true national power in the early 20th c., with smaller unions tending to amalgamate into organizations with memberships in the hundreds of thousands covering the entire country.

trade wind *n.* a constant wind blowing towards the equator from the north-east or south-east. The name had in its origin nothing to do with 'trade' in the commercial sense of 'passage for the purpose of trading', though the importance of those winds to navigation led 18th-c. etymologists (and perhaps even navigators) so to understand the term. It was originally applied to any wind that 'blows trade', i.e. in a constant course or way (a 'track' or 'trodden path'), but as it became gradually known that the only winds of which this is approximately true were the Indian monsoons and the winds now called 'trade winds' on each side of the equator in the Atlantic and Pacific Oceans, the name became restricted to these and eventually to the latter.

trading /ˈtreɪdɪŋ/ *n.* the act of engaging in trade. □ **trading estate** esp. *Brit.* a specially-designed industrial and commercial area. **trading post** a store etc. established in a remote or unsettled region. **trading-stamp** a stamp given to customers by some stores which is exchangeable in large numbers for various articles.

tradition /trəˈdɪʃ(ə)n/ *n.* **1 a** a custom, opinion, or belief handed down to posterity esp. orally or by practice. **b** this process of handing down. **2** esp. *joc.* an established practice or custom (*it's a tradition to complain about the weather*). **3** artistic, literary, etc. principles based on experience and practice; any one of these (*stage tradition; traditions of the Dutch School*). **4** *Theol.* doctrine or a particular tradition etc. claimed to have divine authority without documentary evidence, esp.: **a** the oral teaching of Christ and the Apostles. **b** the laws held by the Pharisees to have been delivered by God to Moses. **c** the words and deeds of Muhammad not in the Koran. **5** *Law* the formal delivery of property etc. □□

traditionary *adj.* **traditionist** *n.* **traditionless** *adj.* [ME f. OF *tradicion* or L *traditio* f. *tradere* hand on, betray (as TRANS-, *dare* give)]

traditional /trəˈdɪʃən(ə)l/ *adj.* **1** of, based on, or obtained by tradition. **2** (of jazz) in the style of the early 20th c. □□ **traditionally** *adv.*

traditionalism /trəˈdɪʃənəˌlɪz(ə)m/ *n.* **1** respect, esp. excessive, for tradition, esp. in religion. **2** a philosophical system referring all religious knowledge to divine revelation and tradition. □□ **traditionalist** *n.* **traditionalistic** /-ˈlɪstɪk/ *adj.*

traditor /ˈtrædɪtə(r)/ *n.* (*pl.* **traditors** or **traditores** /-ˈtɔːriːz/) *hist.* an early Christian who surrendered copies of Scripture or Church property to his or her persecutors to save his or her life. [L: see TRAITOR]

traduce /trəˈdjuːs/ *v.tr.* speak ill of; misrepresent. □□ **traducement** *n.* **traducer** *n.* [L *traducere* disgrace (as TRANS-, *ducere duct-* lead)]

Trafalgar /trəˈfælgə(r)/ a cape on the south coast of Spain, near which a decisive battle of the Napoleonic Wars was fought on 21 Oct. 1805. The British fleet under Nelson (who was killed in the action) achieved a great victory over the combined fleets of France and Spain which were attempting to clear the way for Napoleon's projected invasion of Britain. Superior British seamanship and gunnery ensured the surrender of more than half the Franco-Spanish fleet after several hours of hard fighting, and after this battle Napoleon was never again able to mount a serious threat to British naval supremacy.

traffic /ˈtræfɪk/ *n. & v.* —*n.* **1** (often *attrib.*) **a** vehicles moving in a public highway, esp. of a specified kind, density, etc. (*heavy traffic on the M1; traffic warden*). **b** such movement in the air or at sea. **2** (usu. foll. by *in*) trade, esp. illegal (*the traffic in drugs*). **3 a** the transportation of goods, the coming and going of people or goods by road, rail, air, sea, etc. **b** the persons or goods so transported. **4** dealings or communication between people etc. (*had no traffic with them*). **5** the messages, signals, etc., transmitted through a communications system; the flow or volume of such business. —*v.* (**trafficked, trafficking**) **1** *intr.* (usu. foll. by *in*) deal in something, esp. illegally (*trafficked in narcotics; traffics in innuendo*). **2** *tr.* deal in; barter. □ **traffic circle** *US* a roundabout. **traffic cop** esp. *US colloq.* a traffic policeman. **traffic island** a paved or grassed area in a road to divert traffic and provide a refuge for pedestrians. **traffic jam** traffic at a standstill because of roadworks, an accident, etc. **traffic sign** a sign conveying information, a warning, etc., to vehicle-drivers. **traffic warden** *Brit.* a uniformed official employed to help control road traffic and esp. parking. □□ **trafficker** *n.* **trafficless** *adj.* [F *traff(f)ique*, Sp. *tráfico*, It. *traffico*, of unkn. orig.]

trafficator /ˈtræfɪˌkeɪtə(r)/ *n. Brit. hist.* a signal raised automatically to indicate a change of direction in a motor vehicle. [TRAFFIC + INDICATOR]

traffic-light *n.* (also **traffic-lights** *or* **-signal**) a signal controlling road traffic by means of coloured lights. A traffic signal, with an official in charge, was tried out in Westminster, London, in 1868; this seems to be the first instance of the use of a mechanical device for street-traffic control. It was a modification of the railway signalling system and consisted of a semaphore arm with red and green gas lamps for night use. The experiment was terminated by the explosion of the lamps. Electric traffic lights were introduced in Cleveland, Ohio, in 1914, and in New York in 1918; *c.*1925 an attempt was made to coordinate the actions of the police in Piccadilly in London by a series of railway colour-light signals. In 1926 a traffic signal was installed at a busy road junction in Wolverhampton, but was not retained in use because there was no legislation to enforce obedience to its indications. Early road signals were manually operated, and were followed by fixed-time signals; modern traffic-actuated systems of control sometimes involve the processing of information by means of a computer.

tragacanth /ˈtrægəˌkænθ/ *n.* a white or reddish gum from a plant, *Astragalus gummifer*, used in pharmacy, calico-printing, etc., as a vehicle for drugs, dye, etc. [F *tragacante* f. L *tragacantha* f. Gk *tragakantha*, name of a shrub, f. *tragos* goat + *akantha* thorn]

æ cat ɑː arm e bed ɜː her ɪ sit iː see ɒ hot ɔː saw ʌ run ʊ put uː too ə ago aɪ my

tragedian /trə'dʒiːdɪən/ n. 1 a writer of tragedies. 2 an actor in tragedy. [ME f. OF *tragediane* (as TRAGEDY)]

tragedienne /trə,dʒiːdɪ'en/ n. an actress in tragedy. [F fem. (as TRAGEDIAN)]

tragedy /'trædʒɪdɪ/ n. (pl. **-ies**) 1 a serious accident, crime, or natural catastrophe. 2 a sad event; a calamity (*the team's defeat is a tragedy*). 3 **a** a play in verse or prose dealing with tragic events and with an unhappy ending, esp. concerning the downfall of the protagonist. **b** tragic plays as a genre (cf. COMEDY). [ME f. OF *tragedie* f. L *tragoedia* f. Gk *tragōidia* app. goat-song f. *tragos* goat + *ōidē* song. Many theories have been offered to account for the name (e.g. that a goat was given as a prize for a play at the ancient Greek festival of Dionysus, at which tragedies were presented), but some dispute the connection with 'goat'.]

tragic /'trædʒɪk/ adj. 1 (also **tragical** /-k(ə)l/) sad; calamitous; greatly distressing (*a tragic tale*). 2 of, or in the style of, tragedy (*tragic drama; a tragic actor*). □ **tragic irony** a device, orig. in Greek tragedy, by which words carry a tragic, esp. prophetic, meaning to the audience (occas. also to the speaker), unknown to the character speaking. □□ **tragically** adv. [F *tragique* f. L *tragicus* f. Gk *tragikos* f. *tragos* goat: see TRAGEDY]

tragicomedy /,trædʒɪ'kɒmɪdɪ/ n. (pl. **-ies**) 1 **a** a play having a mixture of comedy and tragedy. **b** plays of this kind as a genre. 2 an event etc. having tragic and comic elements. □□ **tragicomic** adj. **tragicomically** adv. [F *tragicomédie* or It. *tragicomedia* f. LL *tragicomoedia* f. L *tragico-comoedia* (as TRAGIC, COMEDY)]

tragopan /'trægə,pæn/ n. any Asian pheasant of the genus *Tragopan*, with erect fleshy horns on its head. [L f. Gk f. *tragos* goat + *Pan* the god Pan]

Traherne /trə'hɜːn/, Thomas (1637–74), English writer of religious works in prose and verse. *Centuries*, his major achievement, is written in unconventional verse expressing rapturous joy; manuscripts of these and many of his poems were discovered on a London bookstall in 1896–7 and published as *Poetical Works* (1903) and *Centuries of Meditation* (1908). The boundless potential of man's mind and spirit is his recurrent theme, as is the need for man to regain the wonder and simplicity of childhood.

trahison des clercs /,traːiˌzɔ̃ deɪ 'kleər/ n. the betrayal of standards, scholarship, etc., by intellectuals. [F, title of a book by J. Benda (1927)]

trail /treɪl/ n. & v. —n. 1 **a** a track left by a thing, person, etc., moving over a surface (*left a trail of wreckage; a slug's slimy trail*). **b** a track or scent followed in hunting, seeking, etc. (*he's on the trail*). 2 a beaten path or track, esp. through a wild region. 3 a part dragging behind a thing or person; an appendage (*a trail of smoke; a condensation trail*). 4 the rear end of a gun-carriage stock. —v. 1 tr. & intr. draw or be drawn along behind, esp. on the ground. 2 intr. (often foll. by *behind*) walk wearily; lag; straggle. 3 tr. follow the trail of; pursue (*trailed him to his home*). 4 intr. be losing in a game or other contest (*trailing by three points*). 5 intr. (usu. foll. by *away, off*) peter out; tail off. 6 intr. **a** (of a plant etc.) grow or hang over a wall, along the ground etc. **b** (of a garment etc.) hang loosely. 7 tr. (often *refl.*) drag (oneself, one's limbs, etc.) along wearily etc. 8 tr. advertise (a film, a radio or television programme, etc.) in advance by showing extracts etc. 9 tr. apply (slip) through a nozzle or spout to decorate ceramic ware. □ **at the trail** Mil. with arms trailed. **trail arms** Mil. let a rifle etc. hang balanced in one hand and, Brit., parallel to the ground. **trail bike** a light motor cycle for use in rough terrain. **trail-blazer** 1 a person who marks a new track through wild country. 2 a pioneer; an innovator. **trail-blazing** n. the act or process of blazing a trail. —*attrib.adj.* that blazes a trail; pioneering. **trail one's coat** deliberately provoke a quarrel, fight, etc. **trailing edge** 1 the rear edge of an aircraft's wing etc. 2 *Electronics* the part of a pulse in which the amplitude diminishes (opp. *leading edge* (see LEADING¹)). **trailing wheel** a wheel not given direct motive power. **trail-net** a drag-net. [ME (earlier as verb) f. OF *traillier* to tow, or f. MLG *treilen* haul f. L *tragula* drag-net]

trailer /'treɪlə(r)/ n. 1 a person or thing that trails. 2 a series of brief extracts from a film etc., used to advertise it in advance. 3

a vehicle towed by another, esp.: **a** the rear section of an articulated lorry. **b** an open cart. **c** a platform for transporting a boat etc. **d** *US* a caravan. 4 a trailing plant.

train /treɪn/ v. & n. —v. 1 **a** tr. (often foll. by *to* + infin.) teach (a person, animal, oneself, etc.) a specified skill esp. by practice (*trained the dog to beg; was trained in midwifery*). **b** intr. undergo this process (*trained as a teacher*). 2 tr. & intr. bring or come into a state of physical efficiency by exercise, diet, etc.; undergo physical exercise, esp. for a specific purpose (*trained me for the high jump; the team trains every evening*). 3 tr. cause (a plant) to grow in a required shape (*trained the peach tree up the wall*). 4 (usu. as **trained** adj.) make (the mind, eye, etc.) sharp or discerning as a result of instruction, practice, etc. 5 tr. (often foll. by *on*) point or aim (a gun, camera, etc.) at an object etc. 6 *colloq.* **a** intr. go by train. **b** tr. (foll. by *it* as object) make a journey by train (*trained it to Aberdeen*). 7 tr. (usu. foll. by *away*) *archaic* entice, lure. —n. 1 a series of railway carriages or trucks drawn by an engine. 2 something dragged along behind or forming the back part of a dress, robe, etc. (*wore a dress with a long train; the train of the peacock*). 3 a succession or series of people, things, events, etc. (*a long train of camels; interrupted my train of thought; a train of ideas*). 4 a body of followers; a retinue (*a train of admirers*). 5 a succession of military vehicles etc., including artillery, supplies, etc. (*baggage train*). 6 a line of gunpowder etc. to fire an explosive charge. 7 a series of connected wheels or parts in machinery. □ **in train** properly arranged or directed. **in a person's train** following behind a person. **in the train of** as a sequel of. **train-bearer** a person employed to hold up the train of a robe etc. **train down** train with exercise or diet to lower one's weight. **train-ferry** (pl. **-ies**) a ship that conveys a railway train across water. **train-mile** one mile travelled by one train, as a unit of traffic. **train-spotter** a person who collects locomotive numbers as a hobby. **train-spotting** this hobby. □□ **trainable** adj. **trainability** /-'bɪlɪtɪ/ n. **trainee** /-'niː/ n. **trainless** adj. [ME f. OF *trainer*, *trahiner*, ult. f. L *trahere* draw]

trainband /'treɪnbænd/ n. *hist.* any of several divisions of London citizen soldiers, esp. in the Stuart period.

trainer /'treɪnə(r)/ n. 1 a person who trains. 2 a person who trains horses, athletes, footballers, etc., as a profession. 3 an aircraft or device simulating it used to train pilots. 4 Brit. a soft running shoe of leather, canvas, etc.

training /'treɪnɪŋ/ n. the act or process of teaching or learning a skill, discipline, etc. (*physical training*). □ **go into training** begin physical training. **in training** 1 undergoing physical training. 2 physically fit as a result of this. **out of training** 1 no longer training. 2 physically unfit. **training-college** a college or school for training esp. prospective teachers. **training-ship** a ship on which young people are taught seamanship etc.

trainman /'treɪnmæn/ n. (pl. **-men**) a railway employee working on trains.

train-oil /'treɪnɔɪl/ n. oil obtained from the blubber of a whale (esp. of a right whale). [obs. *train*, *trane* train-oil f. MLG *trān*, MDu. *traen*, app. = TEAR²]

trainsick /'treɪnsɪk/ adj. affected with nausea by the motion of a train. □□ **trainsickness** n.

traipse /treɪps/ v. & n. (also **trapes**) *colloq.* or *dial.* —v.intr. 1 tramp or trudge wearily. 2 (often foll. by *about*) go on errands. —n. 1 a tedious journey on foot. 2 *archaic* a slattern. [16th-c. *trapes* (v.), of unkn. orig.]

trait /treɪ, treɪt/ n. a distinguishing feature or characteristic esp. of a person. [F f. L *tractus* (as TRACT¹)]

traitor /'treɪtə(r)/ n. (fem. **traitress** /-trɪs/) (often foll. by *to*) a person who is treacherous or disloyal, esp. to his country. □□ **traitorous** adj. **traitorously** adv. [ME f. OF *traīt(o)ur* f. L *traditor -oris* f. *tradere*: see TRADITION]

Trajan /'treɪdʒ(ə)n/ (Marcus Ulpius Traianus, 53–117) Roman emperor 98–117, born in Spain, the adopted successor of Nerva. He was a popular and respected emperor, efficient in administration and energetic in public works. The Dacian wars of 101–6 ended in the annexation of Dacia as a province (the campaigns are illustrated on Trajan's Column in Rome); his final years were taken up with a war against the Parthians.

aʊ *how* eɪ *day* əʊ *no* eə *hair* ɪə *near* ɔɪ *boy* ʊə *poor* aɪə *fire* aʊə *sour* (*see over for consonants*)

trajectory /trə'dʒektəri, 'trædʒik-/ n. (pl. **-ies**) **1** the path described by a projectile flying or an object moving under the action of given forces. **2** Geom. a curve or surface cutting a system of curves or surfaces at a constant angle. [(orig. adj.) f. med.L trajectorius f. L traicere traject- (as TRANS-, jacere throw)]

tra-la /trɑː'lɑː/ int. an expression of joy or gaiety. [imit. of song]

tram[1] /træm/ n. **1** Brit. an electrically-powered passenger vehicle running on rails laid in a public road. (See below.) **2** a four-wheeled vehicle used in coal-mines. □ **tram-road** hist. a road with wooden, stone, or metal wheel-tracks. [MLG & MDu. trame balk, beam, barrow-shaft]

The tram (or tramcar, US streetcar), was invented in New York in 1830 by John Stephenson, an Irish coach-builder. Trams were originally horse-drawn (see RAILWAYS), and then steam power was used so that they were either self-propelled or hauled by cables using stationary engines. The great expansion in their use came with electric traction in the 1890s, with current collected either from overhead wires or sometimes from a conductor rail beneath the road surface. The rise of the motor bus and the electric trolleybus with their greater flexibility of the course caused a decline in the use of trams in both Britain and the US, but some transport planners forecast a return to the tram on grounds of economy and ability to use electric power rather than the oil fuel needed for buses.

tram[2] /træm/ n. (in full **tram silk**) double silk thread used for the weft of some velvets and silks. [F trame f. L trama weft]

tramcar /'træmkɑː(r)/ n. Brit. = TRAM[1] 1.

tramlines /'træmlaɪnz/ n.pl. **1** rails for a tramcar. **2** colloq. **a** either pair of two sets of long parallel lines at the sides of a lawn-tennis court. **b** similar lines at the side or back of a badminton court. **3** inflexible principles or courses of action etc.

trammel /'træm(ə)l/ n. & v. —n. **1** (usu. in pl.) an impediment to free movement; a hindrance (the trammels of domesticity). **2** a triple drag-net for fish, which are trapped in a pocket formed when they attempt to swim through. **3** an instrument for drawing ellipses etc. with a bar sliding in upright grooves. **4** a beam-compass. **5** US a hook in a fireplace for a kettle etc. —v.tr. (**trammelled, trammelling**; US **trammeled, trammeling**) confine or hamper with or as if with trammels. [in sense 'net' ME f. OF tramail f. med.L tramacula, tremaculum, perh. formed as TRI- + macula (MAIL[2]): later history uncert.]

tramontana /ˌtrɑːmɒn'tɑːnə/ n. a cold north wind in the Adriatic. [It.: see TRAMONTANE]

tramontane /trə'mɒnteɪn/ adj. & n. —adj. **1** situated or living on the other side of mountains, esp. the Alps as seen from Italy. **2** (from the Italian point of view) foreign; barbarous. —n. **1** a tramontane person. **2** = TRAMONTANA. [ME f. It. tramontano f. L transmontanus beyond the mountains (as TRANS-, mons montis mountain)]

tramp /træmp/ v. & n. —v. **1** intr. **a** walk heavily and firmly (tramping about upstairs). **b** go on foot, esp. a distance. **2** tr. **a** cross on foot, esp. wearily or reluctantly. **b** cover (a distance) in this way (tramped forty miles). **3** tr. (often foll. by down) tread on; trample; stamp on. **4** tr. Austral. colloq. dismiss from employment, sack. **5** intr. live as a tramp. —n. **1** an itinerant vagrant or beggar. **2** the sound of a person, or esp. people, walking, marching, etc., or of horses' hooves. **3** a journey on foot, esp. protracted. **4 a** an iron plate protecting the sole of a boot used for digging. **b** the part of a spade that it strikes. **5** esp. US sl. derog. a promiscuous woman. **6** = ocean tramp. □ **tramper** n. **trampish** adj. [ME trampe f. Gmc]

trample /'træmp(ə)l/ v. & n. —v.tr. **1** tread under foot. **2** press down or crush in this way. —n. the sound or act of trampling. □ **trample on 1** tread heavily on. **2** treat roughly or with contempt; disregard (a person's feelings etc.). □ **trampler** n. [ME f. TRAMP + -LE[4]]

trampoline /'træmpəˌliːn/ n. & v. —n. a strong fabric sheet connected by springs to a horizontal frame, used by gymnasts etc. for somersaults, as a springboard, etc. Trampolining as a sport was introduced into Britain from the US, though it was known in Europe as a circus act centuries before the earliest competitions, which were held in the US in the late 1940s.

—v.intr. use a trampoline. □□ **trampolinist** n. [It. trampolino f. trampoli stilts]

tramway /'træmweɪ/ n. **1** = tram-road (see TRAM[1]). **2 a** rails for a tramcar. **b** a tramcar system.

trance /trɑːns/ n. & v. —n. **1 a** a sleeplike or half-conscious state without response to stimuli. **b** a hypnotic or cataleptic state. **2** such a state as entered into by a medium. **3** a state of extreme exaltation or rapture; ecstasy. —v.tr. poet. = ENTRANCE[2]. □□ **trancelike** adj. [ME f. OF transe f. transir depart, fall into trance f. L transire: see TRANSIT]

tranche /trɑːnʃ/ n. a portion, esp. of income, or of a block of shares. [F, = slice (as TRENCH)]

tranny /'trænɪ/ n. (pl. **-ies**) esp. Brit. colloq. a transistor radio. [abbr.]

tranquil /'træŋkwɪl/ adj. calm, serene, unruffled. □□ **tranquillity** /-'kwɪlɪtɪ/ n. **tranquilly** adv. [F tranquille or L tranquillus]

tranquillize /'træŋkwɪˌlaɪz/ v.tr. (US **tranquilize, -ise**) make tranquil, esp. by a drug etc.

tranquillizer /'træŋkwɪˌlaɪzə(r)/ n. (US **tranquilizer, -iser**) a drug used to diminish anxiety.

trans- /trænz, trɑːns, -nz/ prefix **1** across, beyond (transcontinental; transgress). **2** on or to the other side of (transatlantic) (opp. CIS-). **3** through (transonic). **4** into another state or place (transform; transcribe). **5** surpassing, transcending (transfinite). **6** Chem. **a** (of an isomer) having the same atom or group on opposite sides of a given plane in the molecule (cf. CIS- 4). **b** having a higher atomic number than (transuranic). [from or after L trans across]

transact /træn'zækt, trɑː-, -'sækt/ v.tr. perform or carry through (business). □□ **transactor** n. [L transigere transact- (as TRANS-, agere do)]

transaction /træn'zækʃ(ə)n, trɑː-, -'sækʃ(ə)n/ n. **1 a** a piece of esp. commercial business done; a deal (a profitable transaction). **b** the management of business etc. **2** (in pl.) published reports of discussions, papers read, etc., at the meetings of a learned society. □□ **transactional** adj. **transactionally** adv. [ME f. LL transactio (as TRANSACT)]

transalpine /trænz'ælpaɪn, trɑː-, -s'ælpaɪn/ adj. beyond the Alps, esp. from the Italian point of view. [L transalpinus (as TRANS-, alpinus ALPINE)]

transatlantic /ˌtrænzət'læntɪk, ˌtrɑː-, -sət'læntɪk/ adj. **1** beyond the Atlantic, esp.: **a** Brit. American. **b** US European. **2** crossing the Atlantic (a transatlantic flight).

Transcaucasia /ˌtrænzkɔː'keɪzɪə/ that part of the Soviet Union lying to the south of the Caucasus Mountains. □□ **Transcaucasian** adj.

transceiver /træn'siːvə(r), trɑː-/ n. a combined radio transmitter and receiver.

transcend /træn'send, trɑː-/ v.tr. **1** be beyond the range or grasp of (human experience, reason, belief, etc.). **2** excel; surpass. [ME f. OF transcendre or L transcendere (as TRANS-, scandere climb)]

transcendent /træn'send(ə)nt, trɑː-/ adj. & n. —adj. **1** excelling, surpassing (transcendent merit). **2** transcending human experience. **3** Philos. **a** higher than or not included in any of Aristotle's ten categories in scholastic philosophy. **b** not realizable in experience in Kantian philosophy. **4** (esp. of the supreme being) existing apart from, not subject to the limitations of, the material universe (opp. IMMANENT). —n. Philos. a transcendent thing. □□ **transcendence** n. **transcendency** n. **transcendently** adv.

transcendental /ˌtrænsen'dent(ə)l, ˌtrɑː-/ adj. & n. —adj. **1** = TRANSCENDENT. **2 a** (in Kantian philosophy) presupposed in and necessary to experience; a priori. **b** (in Schelling's philosophy) explaining matter and objective things as products of the subjective mind. **c** (esp. in Emerson's philosophy) regarding the divine as the guiding principle in man. **3 a** visionary, abstract. **b** vague, obscure. **4** Math. (of a function) not capable of being produced by the algebraical operations of addition, multiplication, and involution, or the inverse operations.

—*n.* a transcendental term, conception, etc. □ **transcendental cognition** a priori knowledge. **Transcendental Meditation** a method of detaching oneself from problems, anxiety, etc., by silent meditation and repetition of a mantra. **transcendental object** a real (unknown and unknowable) object. **transcendental unity** unity brought about by cognition. □□ **transcendentally** *adv.* [med.L *transcendentalis* (as TRANSCENDENT)]

transcendentalism /ˌtrænsenˈdentəˌlɪz(ə)m, ˌtrɑːn-/ *n.* **1** transcendental philosophy. **2** exalted or visionary language. □□ **transcendentalist** *n.* **transcendentalize** *v.tr.* (also **-ise**).

transcode /trænzˈkəʊd, trɑːnz-/ *v.tr.* & *intr.* convert from one form of coded representation to another.

transcontinental /trænzˌkɒntɪˈnent(ə)l, trɑːnz-, træns-, trɑːns-/ *adj.* & *n.* —*adj.* (of a railway etc.) extending across a continent. —*n.* a transcontinental railway or train. □□ **transcontinentally** *adv.*

transcribe /trænˈskraɪb, trɑːn-/ *v.tr.* **1** make a copy of, esp. in writing. **2** transliterate. **3** write out (shorthand, notes, etc.) in ordinary characters or continuous prose. **4 a** record for subsequent reproduction. **b** broadcast in this form. **5** arrange (music) for a different instrument etc. □□ **transcriber** *n.* **transcription** /-ˈskrɪpʃ(ə)n/ *n.* **transcriptional** /-ˈskrɪpʃ(ə)n(ə)l/ *adj.* **transcriptive** /-ˈskrɪptɪv/ *adj.* [L *transcribere transcript-* (as TRANS-, *scribere* write)]

transcript /ˈtrænskrɪpt, ˈtrɑːn-/ *n.* **1 a** written or recorded copy. **2** any copy. [ME f. OF *transcrit* f. L *transcriptum* neut. past part.: see TRANSCRIBE]

Transdanubian Highlands /ˌtrænzdænˈjuːbɪən/ a hilly region to the west of the Danube in western Hungary.

transducer /trænsˈdjuːsə(r), trɑːns-, -zˈdjuːsə(r)/ *n.* any device for converting a non-electrical signal into an electrical one e.g. pressure into voltage. [L *transducere* lead across (as TRANS-, *ducere* lead)]

transect /trænˈsekt, trɑːn-, -ˈzekt/ *v.tr.* cut across or transversely. □□ **transection** *n.* [TRANS- + L *secare sect-* cut]

transept /ˈtrænsept, ˈtrɑːn-/ *n.* **1** either arm of the part of a cross-shaped church at right angles to the nave (*north transept*; *south transept*). **2** this part as a whole. □□ **transeptal** /-ˈsept(ə)l/ *adj.* [mod.L *transeptum* (as TRANS-, SEPTUM)]

transexual var. of TRANSSEXUAL.

transfer *v.* & *n.* —*v.* /trænsˈfɜː(r), trɑːns-/ (**transferred**, **transferring**) **1** *tr.* (often foll. by *to*) **a** convey, remove, or hand over (a thing etc.) (*transferred the bag from the car to the station*). **b** make over the possession of (property, a ticket, rights, etc.) to a person (*transferred his membership to his son*). **2** *tr.* & *intr.* change or move to another group, club, department, etc. **3** *intr.* change from one station, route, etc., to another on a journey. **4** *tr.* **a** convey (a drawing etc.) from one surface to another, esp. to a lithographic stone by means of transfer-paper. **b** remove (a picture) from one surface to another, esp. from wood or a wall to canvas. **5** *tr.* change (the sense of a word etc.) by extension or metaphor. —*n.* /ˈtrænsfɜː(r), ˈtrɑːns-/ **1** the act or an instance of transferring or being transferred. **2 a** a design etc. conveyed or to be conveyed from one surface to another. **b** a small usu. coloured picture or design on paper, which is transferable to another surface. **3** a football player etc. who is or is to be transferred. **4 a** the conveyance of property, a right, etc. **b** a document effecting this. **5** US a ticket allowing a journey to be continued on another route etc. □ **transfer-book** a register of transfers of property, shares, etc. **transfer company** US a company conveying passengers or luggage between stations. **transfer fee** a fee paid for the transfer of esp. a professional footballer. **transfer ink** ink used for making designs on a lithographic stone or transfer-paper. **transfer list** a list of footballers available for transfer. **transfer-paper** specially coated paper to receive the impression of transfer ink and transfer it to stone. **transfer RNA** RNA conveying an amino-acid molecule from the cytoplasm to a ribosome for use in protein synthesis etc. □□ **transferee** /-ˈriː/ *n.* **transferor** /-ˈfɜː(r)/ esp. Law *n.* **transferrer** /-ˈfɜːrə(r)/ *n.* [ME f. F *transférer* or L *transferre* (as TRANS-, *ferre lat-* bear)]

transferable /trænsˈfɜːrəb(ə)l, trɑːns-, ˈtr-/ *adj.* capable of being transferred. □ **transferable vote** a vote that can be transferred to another candidate if the first choice is eliminated. □□ **transferability** /-ˈbɪlɪtɪ/ *n.*

transference /ˈtrænsfərəns, ˈtrɑː-/ *n.* **1** the act or an instance of transferring; the state of being transferred. **2** *Psychol.* the redirection of childhood emotions to a new object, esp. to a psychoanalyst.

transferral /trænsˈfɜːr(ə)l, trɑːns-/ *n.* = TRANSFER *n.* 1.

transferrin /trænsˈfɜːrɪn, trɑː-/ *n.* a protein transporting iron in the blood of animals. [TRANS- + L *ferrum* iron]

transfiguration /trænsˌfɪgjʊˈreɪʃ(ə)n, trɑː-/ *n.* **1** a change of form or appearance. **2 a** Christ's appearance in radiant glory to three of his disciples (Matt. 17: 2, Mark 9: 2–3). **b** (**Transfiguration**) the festival of Christ's transfiguration, 6 Aug. [ME f. OF *transfiguration* or L *transfiguratio* (as TRANSFIGURE)]

transfigure /trænsˈfɪgə(r), trɑː-/ *v.tr.* change in form or appearance, esp. so as to elevate or idealize. [ME f. OF *transfigurer* or L *transfigurare* (as TRANS-, FIGURE)]

transfinite /trænsˈfaɪnaɪt, trɑː-/ *adj.* **1** beyond or surpassing the finite. **2** *Math.* (of a number) exceeding all finite numbers.

transfix /trænsˈfɪks, trɑː-/ *v.tr.* **1** pierce with a sharp implement or weapon. **2** root (a person) to the spot with horror or astonishment; paralyse the faculties of. □□ **transfixion** /-ˈfɪkʃ(ə)n/ *n.* [L *transfigere transfix-* (as TRANS-, FIX)]

transform /trænsˈfɔːm, trɑː-/ *v.* & *n.* —*v.* **1 a** *tr.* make a thorough or dramatic change in the form, outward appearance, character, etc., of. **b** *intr.* (often foll. by *into*, *to*) undergo such a change. **2** *tr.* *Electr.* change the voltage etc. of (a current). **3** *tr.* *Math.* change (a mathematical entity) by transformation. —*n.* /ˈtrænsfɔːm, ˈtrɑːns-/ *Math.* & *Linguistics* the product of a transformation. □□ **transformable** *adj.* **transformative** *adj.* [ME f. OF *transformer* or L *transformare* (as TRANS-, FORM)]

transformation /ˌtrænsfəˈmeɪʃ(ə)n, ˌtrɑː-/ *n.* **1** the act or an instance of transforming; the state of being transformed. **2** *Zool.* a change of form at metamorphosis, esp. of insects, amphibia, etc. **3** the induced or spontaneous change of one element into another. **4** *Math.* a change from one geometrical figure, expression, or function to another of the same value, magnitude, etc. **5** *Biol.* the modification of a eukaryotic cell from its normal state to a malignant state. **6** *Linguistics* a process, with reference to particular rules, by which one grammatical pattern of sentence structure can be converted into another, or the underlying meaning of a sentence can be converted into a statement of syntax. **7** *archaic* a woman's wig. **8** a sudden dramatic change of scene on stage. [ME f. OF *transformation* or LL *transformatio* (as TRANSFORM)]

transformational /ˌtrænsfəˈmeɪʃən(ə)l/ *adj.* relating to or involving transformation. □ **transformational grammar** see GRAMMAR. □□ **transformationally** *adv.*

transformer /trænsˈfɔːmə(r), trɑː-, -zˈfɔːmə(r)/ *n.* **1** an apparatus for reducing or increasing the voltage of an alternating current. **2** a person or thing that transforms.

transfuse /trænsˈfjuːz, trɑː-/ *v.tr.* **1** permeate (*purple dye transfused the water*; *was transfused with gratitude*). **2 a** transfer (blood) from one person or animal to another. **b** inject (liquid) into a blood-vessel to replace lost fluid. **3** cause (fluid etc.) to pass from one vessel etc. to another. □□ **transfusion** /-ˈfjuːʒ(ə)n/ *n.* [ME f. L *transfundere transfus-* (as TRANS-, *fundere* pour)]

transgenic /trænsˈdʒenɪk/ *adj.* *Biol.* (of an animal or plant) having genetic material introduced from another species.

transgress /trænzˈgres, trɑː-, -sˈgres/ *v.tr.* (also *absol.*) **1** go beyond the bounds or limits set by (a commandment, law, etc.); violate; infringe. **2** *Geol.* (of the sea) to spread over (the land). □□ **transgression** /-ˈgreʃ(ə)n/ *n.* **transgressive** *adj.* **transgressor** *n.* [F *transgresser* or L *transgredi transgress-* (as TRANS-, *gradi* go)]

tranship var. of TRANSSHIP.

transhumance /trænsˈhjuːməns, trɑː-/ *n.* the seasonal moving of livestock to a different region. [F f. *transhumer* f. L TRANS- + *humus* ground]

transient /ˈtrænzɪənt, ˈtrɑː-, -sɪənt/ *adj.* & *n.* —*adj.* **1** of short duration; momentary; passing; impermanent (*life is transient; of transient interest*). **2** *Mus.* serving only to connect; inessential (*a transient chord*). —*n.* **1** a temporary visitor, worker, etc. **2** *Electr.* a brief current etc. □□ **transience** *n.* **transiency** *n.* **transiently** *adv.* [L *transire* (as TRANS-, *ire* go)]

transilluminate /ˌtrænzɪˈluːmɪˌneɪt, ˌtrɑː-/ *v.tr.* pass a strong light through for inspection, esp. for medical diagnosis. □□ **transillumination** /-ˈneɪʃ(ə)n/ *n.*

transire /trænˈsaɪə(r)/ *n. Brit.* a customs permit for the passage of goods. [L *transire* go across (as TRANSIENT)]

transistor /trænˈzɪstə(r), trɑː-, -ˈsɪstə(r)/ *n.* **1** a semiconductor device, usually having three terminals and two junctions, in which the load current can be made to be proportional to a small input current, so that it is functionally equivalent to a valve but is much smaller and more robust, operates at lower voltages, and consumes less power and produces less heat. (See below.) **2** (in full **transistor radio**) a portable radio with transistors. [portmanteau word, f. TRANSFER + RESISTOR]

Transistors were developed at the Bell Telephone Laboratories in the US in 1947 after an intensive programme of research; the inventors were awarded the Nobel Prize for physics in 1956. They are used to amplify electronic signals, are the active elements of silicon integrated circuits, and have now largely replaced thermionic valves.

transistorize /trænˈzɪstəˌraɪz, trɑː-, -ˈsɪstəˌraɪz/ *v.tr.* (also **-ise**) design or equip with, or convert to, transistors rather than valves. □□ **transistorization** /-ˈzeɪʃ(ə)n/ *n.*

transit /ˈtrænzɪt, ˈtrɑː-, -sɪt/ *n. & v.* —*n.* **1** the act or process of going, conveying, or being conveyed, esp. over a distance (*transit by rail; made a transit of the lake*). **2** a passage or route (*the overland transit*). **3 a** the apparent passage of a celestial body across the meridian of a place. **b** such an apparent passage across the sun or a planet. **4** *US* the local conveyance of passengers on public routes. —*v.* (**transited, transiting**) **1** *tr.* make a transit across. **2** *intr.* make a transit. □ **in transit** while going or being conveyed. **transit camp** a camp for the temporary accommodation of soldiers, refugees, etc. **transit-circle** (or **-instrument**) an instrument for observing the transit of a celestial body across the meridian. **transit-compass** (or **-theodolite**) a surveyor's instrument for measuring a horizontal angle. **transit-duty** duty paid on goods passing through a country. **transit lounge** a lounge at an airport for passengers waiting between flights. **transit visa** a visa allowing only passage through a country. [ME f. L *transitus* f. *transire* (as TRANSIENT)]

transition /trænˈzɪʃ(ə)n, trɑː-, -ˈsɪʃ(ə)n/ *n.* **1** a passing or change from one place, state, condition, etc., to another (*an age of transition; a transition from plain to hills*). **2** *Mus.* a momentary modulation. **3** *Art* a change from one style to another, esp. *Archit.* from Norman to Early English. **4** *Physics* a change in an atomic nucleus or orbital electron with emission or absorption of radiation. □ **transition element** *Chem.* any of a set of elements in the periodic table characterized by partly filled *d* or *f* orbitals and the ability to form coloured complexes. **transition point** *Physics* the point at which different phases of the same substance can be in equilibrium. □□ **transitional** *adj.* **transitionally** *adv.* **transitionary** *adj.* [F *transition* or L *transitio* (as TRANSIT)]

transitive /ˈtrænsɪtɪv, ˈtrɑː-, -zɪtɪv/ *adj.* **1** *Gram.* (of a verb or sense of a verb) that takes a direct object (whether expressed or implied), e.g. *saw* in *saw the donkey, saw that she was ill* (opp. INTRANSITIVE). **2** *Logic* (of a relation) such as to be valid for any two members of a sequence if it is valid for every pair of successive members. □□ **transitively** *adv.* **transitiveness** *n.* **transitivity** /-ˈtɪvɪtɪ/ *n.* [LL *transitivus* (as TRANSIT)]

transitory /ˈtrænsɪtərɪ, ˈtrɑː-, -zɪtərɪ/ *adj.* not permanent, brief, transient. □ **transitory action** *Law* an action that can be brought in any country irrespective of where the transaction etc. started. □□ **transitorily** *adv.* **transitoriness** *n.* [ME f. AF *transitorie*, OF *transitoire* f. L *transitorius* (as TRANSIT)]

Transjordan /trænzˈdʒɔːd(ə)n/ the former name of an area of Palestine east of the Jordan, now the major part of the Hashemite Kingdom of Jordan.

Transkei /trænˈskaɪ/ an independent tribal homeland of the Xhosa people in South Africa; pop. (1985) 2,947,000.

translate /trænˈsleɪt, trɑː-, -ˈzleɪt/ *v.* **1** *tr.* (also *absol.*) **a** (often foll. by *into*) express the sense of (a word, sentence, speech, book, etc.) in another language. **b** do this as a profession etc. (*translates for the UN*). **2** *intr.* (of a literary work etc.) be translatable, bear translation (*does not translate well*). **3** *tr.* express (an idea, book, etc.) in another, esp. simpler, form. **4** *tr.* interpret the significance of; infer as (*translated his silence as dissent*). **5** *tr.* move or change, esp. from one person, place, or condition, to another (*was translated by joy*). **6** *intr.* (foll. by *into*) result in; be converted into; manifest itself as. **7** *tr. Eccl.* **a** remove (a bishop) to another see. **b** remove (a saint's relics etc.) to another place. **8** *tr. Bibl.* convey to heaven without death; transform. **9** *tr. Mech.* **a** cause (a body) to move so that all its parts travel in the same direction. **b** impart motion without rotation to. □□ **translatable** *adj.* **translatability** /-ˈbɪlɪtɪ/ *n.* [ME f. L *translatus*, past part. of *transferre*: see TRANSFER]

translation /trænsˈleɪʃ(ə)n, trɑː-, -zˈleɪʃ(ə)n/ *n.* **1** the act or an instance of translating. **2** a written or spoken expression of the meaning of a word, speech, book, etc. in another language. □□ **translational** *adj.* **translationally** *adv.*

translator /trænsˈleɪtə(r), trɑː-, -zˈleɪtə(r)/ *n.* **1** a person who translates from one language into another. **2** a television relay transmitter. **3** a program that translates from one (esp. programming) language into another.

transliterate /trænzˈlɪtəˌreɪt, trɑː-, -sˈlɪtəˌreɪt/ *v.tr.* represent (a word etc.) in the closest corresponding letters of a different alphabet or language. □□ **transliteration** /-ˈreɪʃ(ə)n/ *n.* **transliterator** *n.* [TRANS- + L *littera* letter]

translocate /ˌtrænzləʊˈkeɪt, ˌtrɑː-, -sləʊˈkeɪt/ *v.tr.* **1** move from one place to another. **2** (usu. in *passive*) *Bot.* move (substances in a plant) from one part to another. □□ **translocation** *n.*

translucent /trænzˈluːs(ə)nt, trɑː-, -ˈljuːs(ə)nt, -sˈl-/ *adj.* **1** allowing light to pass through diffusely; semi-transparent. **2** transparent. □□ **translucence** *n.* **translucency** *n.* **translucently** *adv.* [L *translucēre* (as TRANS-, *lucēre* shine)]

translunar /trænzˈluːnə(r), -ˈljuːnə(r), -sˈl-/ *adj.* **1** lying beyond the moon. **2** of or relating to space travel or a trajectory towards the moon.

transmarine /ˌtrænzməˈriːn, ˌtrɑː-, -sməˈriːn/ *adj.* situated or going beyond the sea. [L *transmarinus* f. *marinus* MARINE]

transmigrant /trænzˈmaɪgrənt, trɑː-, -sˈmaɪgrənt/ *adj. & n.* —*adj.* passing through, esp. a country on the way to another. —*n.* a migrant or alien passing through a country etc. [L *transmigrant-*, part. stem of *transmigrare* (as TRANSMIGRATE)]

transmigrate /ˌtrænzmaɪˈgreɪt, ˌtrɑː-, -smaɪˈgreɪt/ *v.intr.* **1** (of the soul) pass into a different body; undergo metempsychosis. **2** migrate. □□ **transmigration** /-ˈgreɪʃ(ə)n/ *n.* **transmigrator** *n.* **transmigratory** /-ˈmaɪgrətərɪ/ *adj.* [ME f. L *transmigrare* (as TRANS-, MIGRATE)]

transmission /trænzˈmɪʃ(ə)n, trɑː-, -sˈmɪʃ(ə)n/ *n.* **1** the act or an instance of transmitting; the state of being transmitted. **2** a broadcast radio or television programme. **3** the mechanism by which power is transmitted from an engine to the axle in a motor vehicle. □ **transmission line** a conductor or conductors carrying electricity over large distances with minimum losses. [L *transmissio* (as TRANS-, MISSION)]

transmit /trænzˈmɪt, trɑː-, -sˈmɪt/ *v.tr.* (**transmitted, transmitting**) **1 a** pass or hand on; transfer (*transmitted the message; how diseases are transmitted*). **b** communicate (ideas, emotions, etc.). **2 a** allow (heat, light, sound, electricity, etc.) to pass through; be a medium for. **b** be a medium for (ideas, emotions, etc.) (*his message transmits hope*). **3** broadcast (a radio or television programme). □□ **transmissible** /-ˈmɪsəb(ə)l/ *adj.* **transmissive** /-ˈmɪsɪv/ *adj.* **transmittable** *adj.* **transmittal** *n.* [ME f. L *transmittere* (as TRANS-, *mittere miss-* send)]

transmitter /trænzˈmɪtə(r), trɑː-, -zˈmɪtə(r)/ *n.* **1** a person or thing that transmits. **2** a set of equipment used to generate and transmit electromagnetic waves carrying messages, signals, etc., esp. those of radio or television. **3** = NEUROTRANSMITTER.

transmogrify /trænzˈmɒgrɪˌfaɪ, trɑː-, -sˈmɒgrɪˌfaɪ/ *v.tr.* (**-ies, -ied**) *joc.* transform, esp. in a magical or surprising manner. □□ **transmogrification** /-fɪˈkeɪʃ(ə)n/ *n.* [17th c.: orig. unkn.]

transmontane /trænz'mɒnteɪn, trɑː-, -s'mɒnteɪn, -'teɪn/ adj. = TRAMONTANE. [L transmontanus: see TRAMONTANE]

transmutation /ˌtrænzmjuː'teɪʃ(ə)n, ˌtrɑː-, -smjuː'teɪʃ(ə)n/ n. **1** the act or an instance of transmuting or changing into another form etc. **2** Alchemy hist. the supposed process of changing base metals into gold. **3** Physics the changing of one element into another by nuclear bombardment etc. **4** Geom. the changing of a figure or body into another of the same area or volume. **5** Biol. Lamarck's theory of the change of one species into another. □□ **transmutational** adj. **transmutationist** n. [ME f. OF transmutation or LL transmutatio (as TRANSMUTE)]

transmute /trænz'mjuːt, trɑː-, -s'mjuːt/ v.tr. **1** change the form, nature, or substance of. **2** Alchemy hist. subject (base metals) to transmutation. □□ **transmutable** adj. **transmutability** /-'bɪlɪtɪ/ n. **transmutative** /-tətɪv/ adj. **transmuter** n. [ME f. L transmutare (as TRANS-, mutare change)]

transnational /trænz'næʃ(ə)l, trɑː-, -s'næʃən(ə)l/ adj. extending beyond national boundaries.

transoceanic /trænz,əʊʃɪ'ænɪk, trɑː-, -s,əʊʃɪ'ænɪk/ adj. **1** situated beyond the ocean. **2** concerned with crossing the ocean (transoceanic flight).

transom /'trænsəm/ n. **1** a horizontal bar of wood or stone across a window or the top of a door (cf. MULLION). **2** each of several beams fixed across the stern-post of a ship. **3** a beam across a saw-pit to support a log. **4** a strengthening crossbar. **5** US = transom window. □ **transom window 1** a window divided by a transom. **2** a window placed above the transom of a door or larger window; a fanlight. □□ **transomed** adj. [ME traversayn, transyn, -ing, f. OF traversin f. traverse TRAVERSE]

transonic /træn'sɒnɪk, trɑː-/ adj. (also **trans-sonic**) relating to speeds close to that of sound. [TRANS- + SONIC, after supersonic etc.]

transpacific /ˌtrænzpə'sɪfɪk, ˌtrɑː-, -spə'sɪfɪk/ adj. **1** beyond the Pacific. **2** crossing the Pacific.

transparence /træns'pærəns, trɑː-, -'peərəns/ n. = TRANSPARENCY 1.

transparency /træns'pærənsɪ, trɑː-, -'peərənsɪ/ n. (pl. **-ies**) **1** the condition of being transparent. **2** Photog. a positive transparent photograph on glass or in a frame to be viewed using a slide projector etc. **3** a picture, inscription, etc., made visible by a light behind it. [med.L transparentia (as TRANSPARENT)]

transparent /træns'pærənt, trɑː-, -'peərənt/ adj. **1** allowing light to pass through so that bodies can be distinctly seen (cf. TRANSLUCENT). **2 a** (of a disguise, pretext, etc.) easily seen through. **b** (of a motive, quality, etc.) easily discerned; evident; obvious. **3** (of a person etc.) easily understood; frank; open. **4** Physics transmitting heat or other electromagnetic rays without distortion. □□ **transparently** adv. **transparentness** n. [ME f. OF f. med.L transparens f. L transparēre shine through (as TRANS-, parēre appear)]

transpierce /træns'pɪəs, trɑː-/ v.tr. pierce through.

transpire /træn'spaɪə(r), trɑː-/ v. **1** intr. (of a secret or something unknown) leak out; come to be known. **2** intr. disp. **a** (prec. by it as subject) turn out; prove to be the case (it transpired he knew nothing about it). **b** occur; happen. **3** tr. & intr. emit (vapour, sweat, etc.), or be emitted, through the skin or lungs; perspire. **4** intr. (of a plant or leaf) release water vapour. □□ **transpirable** adj. **transpiration** /-spɪ'reɪʃ(ə)n/ n. **transpiratory** /-rətərɪ/ adj. [F transpirer or med.L transpirare (as TRANS-, L spirare breathe)]

transplant v. & n. —v.tr. /træns'plɑːnt, trɑː-/ **1 a** plant in another place (transplanted the daffodils). **b** move to another place (whole nations were transplanted). **2** Surgery transfer (living tissue or an organ) and implant in another part of the body or in another body. —n. /'trænsplɑːnt, 'trɑː-/ **1** Surgery **a** the transplanting of an organ or tissue. **b** such an organ etc. **2** a thing, esp. a plant, transplanted. □□ **transplantable** /-'plɑːntəb(ə)l/ adj. **transplantation** /-'teɪʃ(ə)n/ n. **transplanter** /-'plɑːntə(r)/ n. [ME f. LL transplantare (as TRANS-, PLANT)]

transponder /træn'spɒndə(r), trɑː-/ n. a device for receiving a radio signal and automatically transmitting a different signal. [TRANSMIT + RESPOND]

transpontine /træns'pɒntaɪn, trɑː-, -z'pɒntaɪn/ adj. on the other side of a bridge, esp. on the south side of the Thames. [TRANS- + L pons pontis bridge]

transport v. & n. —v.tr. /træns'pɔːt, trɑː-/ **1** take or carry (a person, goods, troops, baggage, etc.) from one place to another. **2** hist. take (a criminal) to a penal colony; deport. **3** (as **transported** adj.) (usu. foll. by with) affected with strong emotion. —n. /'trænspɔːt, 'trɑː-/ **1 a** a system of conveying people, goods, etc., from place to place. **b** the means of this (our transport has arrived). **2** a ship, aircraft, etc. used to carry soldiers, stores, etc. **3** (esp. in pl.) vehement emotion (transports of joy). **4** hist. a transported convict. □ **transport café** Brit. a roadside café for (esp. commercial) drivers. [ME f. OF transporter or L transportare (as TRANS-, portare carry)]

transportable /træns'pɔːtəb(ə)l, trɑː-/ adj. **1** capable of being transported. **2** hist. (of an offender or an offence) punishable by transportation. □□ **transportability** /-'bɪlɪtɪ/ n.

transportation /ˌtrænspɔː'teɪʃ(ə)n, ˌtrɑː-/ n. **1** the act of conveying or the process of being conveyed. **2 a** a system of conveying. **b** esp. US the means of this. **3** hist. removal to a penal colony.

transporter /træns'pɔːtə(r), trɑː-/ n. **1** a person or device that transports. **2** a vehicle used to transport other vehicles or large pieces of machinery etc. by road. □ **transporter bridge** a bridge carrying vehicles etc. across water on a suspended moving platform.

transpose /træns'pəʊz, trɑː-, -z'pəʊz/ v.tr. **1 a** cause (two or more things) to change places. **b** change the position of (a thing) in a series. **2** change the order or position of (words or a word) in a sentence. **3** Mus. write or play in a different key. **4** Algebra transfer (a term) with a changed sign to the other side of an equation. □ **transposing instrument** Mus. an instrument producing notes different in pitch from the written notes. **transposing piano** etc. Mus. a piano etc. on which a transposition may be effected mechanically. □□ **transposable** adj. **transposal** n. **transposer** n. [ME, = transform f. OF transposer (as TRANS-, L ponere put)]

transposition /ˌtrænspə'zɪʃ(ə)n, ˌtrɑː-, -zpə'zɪʃ(ə)n/ n. the act or an instance of transposing; the state of being transposed. □□ **transpositional** adj. **transpositive** /-'pɒzɪtɪv/ adj. [F transposition or LL transpositio (as TRANS-, POSITION)]

transputer /træns'pjuːtə(r), trɑː-, -z'pjuːtə(r)/ n. a microprocessor with integral memory designed for parallel processing. [TRANSISTOR + COMPUTER]

transsexual /træns'seksjʊəl, trɑː-, -ʃʊəl/ adj. & n. (also **transexual**) —adj. having the physical characteristics of one sex and the supposed psychological characteristics of the other. —n. **1** a transsexual person. **2** a person whose sex has been changed by surgery. □□ **transsexualism** n.

transship /træn'ʃɪp, trɑː-, trænz-/ v.tr. (also **tranship**) intr. (**-shipped**, **-shipping**) transfer from one ship or form of transport to another. □□ **transshipment** n.

Trans-Siberian Railway a railway built in 1891–1904 from Moscow east around Lake Baikal to Vladivostok on the Sea of Japan, a distance of 9,311 km (5,786 miles). It opened up Siberia and advanced Russian interest in East Asia.

trans-sonic var. of TRANSONIC.

transubstantiation /ˌtrænsəb,stænʃɪ'eɪʃ(ə)n, ˌtrɑː-/ n. the Roman Catholic doctrine that in the Eucharist the whole substance of the bread and wine, after consecration, is converted into the body and blood of Christ, only the 'accidents' (i.e. appearances) of bread and wine remaining. The belief was defined in 1215, and the terminology is based on medieval philosophy with its acceptance of Aristotelian theories on the nature of substance. (See CONSUBSTANTIATION.) [med.L (as TRANS-, SUBSTANCE)]

transude /træn'sjuːd/ v.intr. (of a fluid) pass through the pores or interstices of a membrane etc. □□ **transudation** /-deɪʃ(ə)n/ n. **transudatory** /-dətərɪ/ adj. [F transsuder f. OF tressuer (as TRANS-, L sudare sweat)]

transuranic /ˌtrænsjʊə'rænɪk, ˌtrɑː-/ adj. Chem. (of an element) having a higher atomic number than uranium. There are at least 13 transuranic elements known, all of which are radioactive and were first obtained artificially in nuclear reactors or after nuclear explosions.

Transvaal /trænz'vɑːl/ a province of the Republic of South Africa, lying north of the Orange Free State and separated from it by the River Vaal; pop. (1986) 7,532,200; capital, Pretoria. Inhabited by Ndebele Africans, it was first settled by Whites c.1840. In the second half of the 19th c. the right of self-government was lost, regained, and (after defeat in the Second Boer War) lost again, and in 1900 the Transvaal was once more annexed by Britain. Self-government was granted in 1906, and it became a founding province of the Union of South Africa. (1910). [L *trans* across + *Vaal* name of river]

transversal /trænz'vɜːs(ə)l, trɑː-, -'vɜːs(ə)l/ *adj.* & *n.* —*adj.* (of a line) cutting a system of lines. —*n.* a transversal line. □□ **transversality** /-'sælɪtɪ/ *n.* **transversally** *adv.* [ME f. med.L *transversalis* (as TRANSVERSE)]

transverse /'trænzvɜːs, 'trɑː-, -'vɜːs, -ns-/ *adj.* situated, arranged, or acting in a crosswise direction. □ **transverse magnet** a magnet with poles at the sides and not the ends. **transverse wave** *Physics* a wave in which the medium vibrates at right angles to the direction of its propagation. □□ **transversely** *adv.* [L *transvertere transvers-* turn across (as TRANS-, *vertere* turn)]

transvestism /trænz'vestɪz(ə)m, trɑː-, -s'vestɪz(ə)n/ *n.* the practice of wearing the clothes of the opposite sex, esp. as a sexual stimulus. □□ **transvestist** *n.* [G *Transvestismus* f. TRANS- + L *vestire* clothe]

transvestite /trænz'vestaɪt, trɑː-, -s'vestaɪt/ *n.* a person given to transvestism.

Transylvania /ˌtrænsɪl'veɪnɪə/ a large tableland region of NW Romania separated from the rest of the country by the Carpathian Mountains and the Transylvanian Alps. Formerly part of Hungary, Transylvania was annexed by Romania in 1918. Its name means 'beyond the forest'. □□ **Transylvanian** *adj.*

trap[1] /træp/ *n.* & *v.* —*n.* **1 a** an enclosure or device, often baited, for catching animals, usu. by affording a way in but not a way out. **b** a device with bait for killing vermin, esp. = MOUSETRAP. **2** a trick betraying a person into speech or an act (*is this question a trap?*). **3** an arrangement to catch an unsuspecting person, e.g. a speeding motorist. **4** a device for hurling an object such as a clay pigeon into the air to be shot at. **5** a compartment from which a greyhound is released at the start of a race. **6** a shoe-shaped wooden device with a pivoted bar that sends a ball from its heel into the air on being struck at the other end with a bat. **7 a** a curve in a downpipe etc. that fills with liquid and forms a seal against the upward passage of gases. **b** a device for preventing the passage of steam etc. **8** *Golf* a bunker. **9** a device allowing pigeons to enter but not leave a loft. **10** a two-wheeled carriage (*a pony and trap*). **11** = TRAPDOOR. **12** *sl.* the mouth (esp. *shut one's trap*). **13** (esp. in *pl.*) *colloq.* a percussion instrument esp. in a jazz band. —*v.tr.* (**trapped, trapping**) **1** catch (an animal) in a trap. **2** catch or catch out (a person) by means of a trick, plan, etc. **3** stop and retain in or as in a trap. **4** provide (a place) with traps. □ **trap-ball** a game played with a trap (see sense 6 of *n.*). **trap-shooter** a person who practises trap-shooting. **trap-shooting** the sport of shooting at objects released from a trap. □□ **traplike** *adj.* [OE *treppe, træppe*, rel. to MDu. *trappe*, med.L *trappa*, of uncert. orig.]

trap[2] /træp/ *v.tr.* (**trapped, trapping**) (often foll. by *out*) **1** provide with trappings. **2** adorn. [obs. *trap* (n.): ME f. OF *drap*: see DRAPE]

trap[3] /træp/ *n.* (in full **trap-rock**) any dark-coloured igneous rock, fine-grained and columnar in structure, esp. basalt. [Sw. *trapp* f. *trappa* stair, f. the often stairlike appearance of its outcroppings]

trapdoor /'træpdɔː(r)/ *n.* a door or hatch in a floor, ceiling, or roof, usu. made flush with the surface. □ **trapdoor spider** any of various spiders, esp. of the family Ctenizidae, that make a hinged trapdoor at the top of their nest.

trapes var. of TRAIPSE.

trapeze /trə'piːz/ *n.* a crossbar or set of crossbars suspended by ropes as a swing for acrobatics etc. [F *trapèze* f. LL *trapezium*: see TRAPEZIUM]

trapezium /trə'piːzɪəm/ *n.* (*pl.* **trapezia** /-zɪə/ or **trapeziums**) **1** *Brit.* a quadrilateral with only one pair of sides parallel. **2** *US* = TRAPEZOID 1. [LL f. Gk *trapezion* f. *trapeza* table]

trapezoid /'træpɪzɔɪd/ *n.* **1** *Brit.* a quadrilateral with no two sides parallel. **2** *US* = TRAPEZIUM 1. □□ **trapezoidal** *adj.* [mod.L *trapezoides* f. Gk *trapezoeidēs* (as TRAPEZIUM)]

trapper /'træpə(r)/ *n.* a person who traps wild animals esp. to obtain furs.

trappings /'træpɪŋz/ *n.pl.* **1** ornamental accessories, esp. as an indication of status (*the trappings of office*). **2** the harness of a horse esp. when ornamental. [ME (as TRAP[2])]

Trappist /'træpɪst/ *n.* & *adj.* —*n.* a member of a branch of the Cistercian order founded in 1664 at La Trappe in Normandy and noted for an austere rule including a vow of silence. —*adj.* of or relating to this order. [F *trappiste* f. *La Trappe*]

traps /træps/ *n.pl.* *colloq.* personal belongings; baggage. [perh. contr. f. TRAPPINGS]

trash /træʃ/ *n.* & *v.* —*n.* **1** esp. *US* worthless or waste stuff; rubbish, refuse. **2** a worthless person or persons. **3** a thing of poor workmanship or material. **4** (in full **cane-trash**) *W.Ind.* the refuse of crushed sugar canes and dried stripped leaves and tops of sugar cane used as fuel. —*v.tr.* **1** esp. *US colloq.* wreck. **2** strip (sugar canes) of their outer leaves to speed up the ripening process. **3** esp. *US colloq.* expose the worthless nature of; disparage. □ **trash can** *US* a dustbin. **trash-ice** (on a sea, lake, etc.) broken ice mixed with water. [16th c.: orig. unkn.]

trashy /'træʃɪ/ *adj.* (**trashier, trashiest**) worthless; poorly made. □□ **trashily** *adv.* **trashiness** *n.*

Trás-os-Montes /ˌtrɑːzuːʒ'mɒnteʃ/ a mountainous region of NE Portugal beyond the Douro River. Its name means 'beyond the mountains'.

trass /træs/ *n.* (also **tarras** /tə'ræs/) a light-coloured tuff used as cement-material. [Du. *trass*, earlier *terras, tiras* f. Rmc: cf. TERRACE]

trattoria /ˌtrætə'riːə/ *n.* an Italian restaurant. [It.]

trauma /'trɔːmə, 'trau-/ *n.* (*pl.* **traumata** /-mətə/ or **traumas**) **1** any physical wound or injury. **2** physical shock following this, characterized by a drop in body temperature, mental confusion, etc. **3** *Psychol.* emotional shock following a stressful event, sometimes leading to long-term neurosis. □□ **traumatize** *v.tr.* (also **-ise**). **traumatization** /-taɪ'zeɪʃ(ə)n/ *n.* [Gk *trauma traumatos* wound]

traumatic /trɔː'mætɪk, trau-/ *adj.* **1** of or causing trauma. **2** *colloq.* (in general use) distressing; emotionally disturbing (*a traumatic experience*). **3** of or for wounds. □□ **traumatically** *adv.* [LL *traumaticus* f. Gk *traumatikos* (as TRAUMA)]

traumatism /'trɔːmətɪz(ə)m, 'trau-/ *n.* **1** the action of a trauma. **2** a condition produced by this.

travail /'træveɪl/ *n.* & *v.* *literary* —*n.* **1** painful or laborious effort. **2** the pangs of childbirth. —*v.intr.* undergo a painful effort, esp. in childbirth. [ME f. OF *travail, travaillier* ult. f. med.L *trepalium* instrument of torture f. L *tres* three + *palus* stake]

travel /'træv(ə)l/ *v.* & *n.* —*v.intr.* & *tr.* (**travelled, travelling**; *US* **traveled, traveling**) **1** *intr.* go from one place to another; make a journey esp. of some length or abroad. **2** *tr.* **a** journey along or through (a country). **b** cover (a distance) in travelling. **3** *intr. colloq.* withstand a long journey (*wines that do not travel*). **4** *intr.* go from place to place as a salesman. **5** *intr.* move or proceed in a specified manner or at a specified rate (*light travels faster than sound*). **6** *intr. colloq.* move quickly. **7** *intr.* pass esp. in a deliberate or systematic manner from point to point (*the photographer's eye travelled over the scene*). **8** *intr.* (of a machine or part) move or operate in a specified way. **9** *intr.* (of deer etc.) move onwards in feeding. —*n.* **1 a** the act of travelling, esp. in foreign countries. **b** (often in *pl.*) a spell of this (*have returned from their travels*). **2** the range, rate, or mode of motion of a part in machinery. □ **travel agency** (or **bureau**) an agency that makes the necessary arrangements for travellers. **travel agent** a person or firm acting as a travel agency. **travelling crane** a crane able to move on rails, esp. along an overhead support. **travelling-rug** a rug used for warmth on a journey. **travelling wave** *Physics* a wave in which the medium moves in the direction of propagation. **travel-sick** suffering from nausea caused by motion in travelling. **travel-sickness** the condition of being travel-sick. [ME, orig. = TRAVAIL]

travelled /ˈtræv(ə)ld/ *adj.* experienced in travelling (also in *comb.*: *much-travelled*).

traveller /ˈtrævələ(r)/ *n.* (*US* **traveler**) **1** a person who travels or is travelling. **2** a travelling salesman. **3** a Gypsy. **4** *Austral.* an itinerant workman; a swagman. **5** a moving mechanism, esp. a travelling crane. □ **traveller's cheque** (*US* **check**) a cheque for a fixed amount that may be cashed on signature, usu. internationally. **traveller's joy** a wild clematis, *Clematis vitalba.* **traveller's tale** an incredible and probably untrue story.

travelogue /ˈtrævəˌlɒg/ *n.* a film or illustrated lecture about travel. [TRAVEL after *monologue* etc.]

traverse /ˈtrævəs, trəˈvɜːs/ *v.* & *n.* —*v.* **1** *tr.* travel or lie across (*traversed the country; a pit traversed by a beam*). **2** *tr.* consider or discuss the whole extent of (a subject). **3** *tr.* turn (a large gun) horizontally. **4** *tr. Law* deny (an allegation) in pleading. **5** *tr.* thwart, frustrate, or oppose (a plan or opinion). **6** *intr.* (of the needle of a compass etc.) turn on or as on a pivot. **7** *intr.* (of a horse) walk obliquely. **8** *intr.* make a traverse in climbing. —*n.* **1** a sideways movement. **2** an act of traversing. **3** a thing, esp. part of a structure, that crosses another. **4** a gallery extending from side to side of a church or other building. **5 a** a single line of survey, usu. plotted from compass bearings and chained or paced distances between angular points. **b** a tract surveyed in this way. **6** *Naut.* a zigzag line taken by a ship because of contrary winds or currents. **7** a skier's similar movement on a slope. **8** the sideways movement of a part in a machine. **9 a** a sideways motion across a rock-face from one practicable line of ascent or descent to another. **b** a place where this is necessary. **10** *Mil.* a pair of right-angle bends in a trench to avoid enfilading fire. **11** *Law* a denial, esp. of an allegation of a matter of fact. **12** the act of turning a large gun horizontally to the required direction. □□ **traversable** *adj.* **traversal** *n.* **traverser** *n.* [OF *traverser* f. LL *traversare, transversare* (as TRANSVERSE)]

travertine /ˈtrævəˌtiːn/ *n.* a white or light-coloured calcareous rock deposited from springs. [It. *travertino, tivertino* f. L *tiburtinus* of Tibur (Tivoli) near Rome]

travesty /ˈtrævɪstɪ/ *n.* & *v.* —*n.* (*pl.* **-ies**) a grotesque misrepresentation or imitation (*a travesty of justice*). —*v.tr.* (**-ies, -ied**) make or be a travesty of. [(orig. adj.) f. F *travesti* past part. of *travestir* disguise, change the clothes of, f. It. *travestire* (as TRANS-, *vestire* clothe)]

travois /trəˈvɔɪ/ *n.* (*pl.* same /-ˈvɔɪz/) a N. American Indian vehicle of two joined poles pulled by a horse etc. for carrying a burden. [earlier *travail* f. F, perh. the same word as TRAVAIL]

trawl /trɔːl/ *v.* & *n.* —*v.* **1** *intr.* **a** fish with a trawl or seine. **b** seek a suitable candidate etc. by sifting through a large number. **2** *tr.* **a** catch by trawling. **b** seek a suitable candidate etc. from (a certain area or group etc.) (*trawled the schools for new trainees*). —*n.* **1** an act of trawling. **2** (in full **trawl-net**) a large widemouthed fishing-net dragged by a boat along the bottom. **3** (in full **trawl-line**) *US* a long sea-fishing line buoyed and supporting short lines with baited hooks. [prob. f. MDu. *traghelen* to drag (cf. *traghel* drag-net), perh. f. L *tragula*]

trawler /ˈtrɔːlə(r)/ *n.* **1** a boat used for trawling. **2** a person who trawls.

tray /treɪ/ *n.* **1** a flat shallow vessel usu. with a raised rim for carrying dishes etc. or containing small articles, papers, etc. **2** a shallow lidless box forming a compartment of a trunk. □□ **trayful** *n.* (*pl.* **-fuls**). [OE *trīg* f. Gmc, rel. to TREE]

treacherous /ˈtretʃərəs/ *adj.* **1** guilty of or involving treachery. **2** (of the weather, ice, the memory, etc.) not to be relied on; likely to fail or give way. □□ **treacherously** *adv.* **treacherousness** *n.* [ME f. OF *trecherous* f. *trecheor* a cheat f. *trechier, trichier*: see TRICK]

treachery /ˈtretʃərɪ/ *n.* (*pl.* **-ies**) **1** violation of faith or trust; betrayal. **2** an instance of this.

treacle /ˈtriːk(ə)l/ *n.* **1** esp. *Brit.* **a** a syrup produced in refining sugar. **b** molasses. **2** cloying sentimentality or flattery. □□ **treacly** *adj.* [ME *triacle* f. OF f. L *theriaca* f. Gk *thēriakē* antidote against venom, fem. of *thēriakos* (adj.) f. *thērion* wild beast]

tread /tred/ *v.* & *n.* —*v.* (**trod** /trɒd/; **trodden** /ˈtrɒd(ə)n/ or **trod**) **1** *intr.* (often foll. by *on*) **a** set down one's foot; walk or step (*do not tread on the grass; trod on a snail*). **b** (of the foot) be set down. **2** *tr.* walk on. **b** (often foll. by *down*) press or crush with the feet. **3** *tr.* perform (steps etc.) by walking (*trod a few paces*). **4** *tr.* make (a hole etc.) by treading. **5** *intr.* (foll. by *on*) suppress; subdue mercilessly. **6** *tr.* make a track with (dirt etc.) from the feet. **7** *tr.* (often foll. by *in, into*) press down into the ground with the feet (*trod dirt into the carpet*). **8** *tr.* (also *absol.*) (of a male bird) copulate with (a hen). —*n.* **1** a manner or sound of walking (*recognized the heavy tread*). **2** (in full **tread-board**) the top surface of a step or stair. **3** the thick moulded part of a vehicle tyre for gripping the road. **4 a** the part of a wheel that touches the ground or rail. **b** the part of a rail that the wheels touch. **5** the part of the sole of a shoe that rests on the ground. **6** (of a male bird) copulation. □ **tread the boards** (or **stage**) be an actor; appear on the stage. **tread on air** see AIR. **tread on a person's toes** offend a person or encroach on a person's privileges etc. **tread out 1** stamp out (a fire etc.). **2** press out (wine or grain) with the feet. **tread water** maintain an upright position in the water by moving the feet with a walking movement and the hands with a downward circular motion. □□ **treader** *n.* [OE *tredan* f. WG]

treadle /ˈtred(ə)l/ *n.* & *v.* —*n.* a lever worked by the foot and imparting motion to a machine. —*v.intr.* work a treadle. [OE *tredel* stair (as TREAD)]

treadmill /ˈtredmɪl/ *n.* **1** a wide mill-wheel turned by people treading on steps fixed along the length of its circumference, formerly worked by prisoners as a punishment. The treadmill, which enforced monotonous and hard work, was first introduced as a prison punishment in 1817. The machines it operated were used for pumping or grinding, or often as mere labour without any other purpose. **2** a similar device used for exercise. **3** tiring monotonous routine work.

treadwheel /ˈtredwiːl/ *n.* a treadmill or similar appliance.

treason /ˈtriːz(ə)n/ *n.* **1** (in full **high treason**: see note below) violation by a subject of allegiance to the sovereign or to the State, esp. by attempting to kill or overthrow the sovereign or to overthrow the government. **2** (in full **petty treason**) *hist.* murder of one's master or husband, regarded as a form of treason. ¶ The crime of *petty treason* was abolished in 1828; the term *high treason*, originally distinguished from *petty treason*, now has the same meaning as *treason.* □□ **treasonous** *adj.* [ME f. AF *treisoun* etc., OF *traïson*, f. L *traditio* handing over (as TRADITION)]

treasonable /ˈtriːzənəb(ə)l/ *adj.* involving or guilty of treason. □□ **treasonably** *adv.*

treasure /ˈtreʒə(r)/ *n.* & *v.* —*n.* **1 a** precious metals or gems. **b** a hoard of these. **c** accumulated wealth. **2 a** thing valued for its rarity, workmanship, associations, etc. (*art treasures*). **3** *colloq.* a much loved or highly valued person. —*v.tr.* **1** (often foll. by *up*) store up as valuable. **2** value (esp. a long-kept possession) highly. □ **treasure hunt 1** a search for treasure. **2** a game in which players seek a hidden object from a series of clues. **treasure trove** *Law* treasure of unknown ownership found hidden. [ME f. OF *tresor*, ult. f. Gk *thēsauros*: see THESAURUS]

treasurer /ˈtreʒərə(r)/ *n.* **1** a person appointed to administer the funds of a society or municipality etc. **2** an officer authorized to receive and disburse public revenues. □□ **treasurership** *n.* [ME f. AF *tresorer*, OF *tresorier* f. *tresor* (see TREASURE) after LL *thesaurarius*]

treasury /ˈtreʒərɪ/ *n.* (*pl.* **-ies**) **1** a place or building where treasure is stored. **2** the funds or revenue of a State, institution, or society. **3** (**Treasury**) **a** the department managing the public revenue of a country. (See below.) **b** the offices and officers of this. **c** the place where the public revenues are kept. □ **Treasury bench** (in the UK) the front bench in the House of Commons occupied by the Prime Minister, Chancellor of the Exchequer, etc. **treasury bill** a bill of exchange issued by the government to raise money for temporary needs. **treasury note** *US* & *hist.* a note issued by the Treasury for use as currency. [ME f. OF *tresorie* (as TREASURE)]

In Britain, the Treasury began to supersede the functions of the Exchequer from the time of Elizabeth I, under Lord Burghley, and in the 18th c. the First Lord gradually assumed the role of Prime Minister. The office of First Lord of the Treasury is now always held by the Prime Minister, but the functions of the office are carried out by the Chancellor of the Exchequer. (See EXCHEQUER.)

treat /triːt/ v. & n. —v. **1** tr. act or behave towards or deal with (a person or thing) in a certain way (*treated me kindly; treat it as a joke*). **2** tr. deal with or apply a process to; act upon to obtain a particular result (*treat it with acid*). **3** tr. apply medical care or attention to. **4** tr. present or deal with (a subject) in literature or art. **5** tr. (often foll. by *to*) provide with food or drink or entertainment at one's own expense (*treated us to dinner*). **6** intr. (often foll. by *with*) negotiate terms (with a person). **7** intr. (often foll. by *of*) give a spoken or written exposition. —n. **1** an event or circumstance (esp. when unexpected or unusual) that gives great pleasure. **2** a meal, entertainment, etc., provided by one person for the enjoyment of another or others. **3** (prec. by *a*) extremely good or well (*they looked a treat; has come on a treat*). □□ **treatable** adj. **treater** n. **treating** n. [ME f. AF *treter*, OF *traitier* f. L *tractare* handle, frequent. of *trahere tract-* draw, pull]

treatise /ˈtriːtɪs, -ɪz/ n. a written work dealing formally and systematically with a subject. [ME f. AF *tretis* f. OF *traitier* TREAT]

treatment /ˈtriːtmənt/ n. **1** a process or manner of behaving towards or dealing with a person or thing (*received rough treatment*). **2** the application of medical care or attention to a patient. **3** a manner of treating a subject in literature or art. **4** (prec. by *the*) colloq. the customary way of dealing with a person, situation, etc. (*got the full treatment*).

treaty /ˈtriːtɪ/ n. (pl. **-ies**) **1** a formally concluded and ratified agreement between States. **2** an agreement between individuals or parties, esp. for the purchase of property. □ **treaty port** hist. a port that a country was bound by treaty to keep open to foreign trade. [ME f. AF *treté* f. L *tractatus* TRACTATE]

Trebizond see TRABZON.

treble /ˈtreb(ə)l/ adj., n., & v. —adj. **1 a** threefold. **b** triple. **c** three times as much or many (*treble the amount*). **2** (of a voice) high-pitched. **3** Mus. = SOPRANO (esp. of an instrument or with ref. to a boy's voice). —n. **1** a treble quantity or thing. **2** Darts a hit on the narrow ring enclosed by the two middle circles of a dartboard, scoring treble. **3 a** Mus. = SOPRANO (esp. a boy's voice or part, or an instrument). **b** a high-pitched voice. **4** the high-frequency output of a radio, record-player, etc., corresponding to the treble in music. **5** a system of betting in which the winnings and stake from the first bet are transferred to a second and then (if successful) to a third. **6** Sport three victories or championships in the same game, sport, etc. —v. **1** tr. & intr. make or become three times as much or many; increase threefold; multiply by three. **2** tr. amount to three times as much as. □ **treble chance** a method of competing in a football pool in which the chances of winning depend on the number of draws and home and away wins predicted by the competitors. **treble clef** a clef placing G above middle C on the second lowest line of the staff. **treble rhyme** a rhyme including three syllables. □□ **trebly** adv. (in sense 1 of adj.). [ME f. OF f. L *triplus* TRIPLE]

Treblinka /treˈblɪŋkə/ a Nazi concentration camp in Poland in the Second World War, where the Jews of the Warsaw ghetto were put to death.

trebuchet /ˈtrebjuˌʃet/ n. (also **trebucket** /ˈtrebʌkɪt, ˈtriː-/) hist. **1** a military machine used in siege warfare for throwing stones etc. **2** a tilting balance for accurately weighing light articles. [ME f. OF f. *trebucher* overthrow, ult. f. Frank.]

trecento /treɪˈtʃentəʊ/ n. the style of Italian art and literature of the 14th c. □□ **trecentist** n. [It., = 300 used with reference to the years 1300–99]

tree /triː/ n. & v. **1 a** a perennial plant with a woody self-supporting main stem or trunk when mature and usu. unbranched for some distance above the ground (cf. SHRUB[1]). **b** any similar plant having a tall erect usu. single stem, e.g. palm tree. **2** a piece or frame of wood etc. for various purposes (*shoe-tree*). **3** archaic or poet. **a** a gibbet. **b** a cross, esp. the one used for Christ's crucifixion. **4** (in full **tree diagram**) Math. a diagram with a structure of branching connecting lines. **5** = *family tree*. —v.tr. **1** force to take refuge in a tree. **2** esp. US put into a difficult position. **3** stretch on a shoe-tree. □ **grow on trees** (usu. with *neg.*) be plentiful. **tree agate** agate with treelike markings. **tree calf** a calf binding for books stained with a treelike design. **tree-fern** a large fern, esp. of the family Cyatheaceae, with an upright trunklike stem. **tree frog** any arboreal tailless amphibian, esp. of the family Hylidae, climbing by means of adhesive discs on its digits. **tree hopper** any insect of the family Membracidae, living in trees. **tree house** a structure in a tree for children to play in. **tree line** = TIMBERLINE. **tree of heaven** an ornamental Asian tree, *Ailanthus altissima*, with evil-smelling flowers. **tree of knowledge** the branches of knowledge as a whole. **tree of life** = ARBOR VITAE. **tree ring** a ring in a cross section of a tree, from one year's growth. **tree shrew** any small insect-eating arboreal mammal of the family Tupaiidae having a pointed nose and bushy tail. **tree sparrow 1** Brit. a sparrow, *Passer montanus*, inhabiting woodland areas. **2** US a N. American finch, *Spizella arborea*, inhabiting grassland areas. **tree surgeon** a person who treats decayed trees in order to preserve them. **tree surgery** the art or practice of such treatment. **tree toad** = *tree frog*. **tree tomato** a South American shrub, *Cyphomandra betacea*, with egg-shaped red fruit. **tree-trunk** the trunk of a tree. **up a tree** esp. US cornered; nonplussed. □□ **treeless** adj. **treelessness** n. **tree-like** adj. [OE *trēow* f. Gmc]

treecreeper /ˈtriːˌkriːpə(r)/ n. any small creeping bird, esp. of the family Certhiidae, feeding on insects in the bark of trees.

treen /triːn/ n. (treated as *pl.*) small domestic wooden objects, esp. antiques. [*treen* (adj.) wooden f. OE *trēowen* (as TREE)]

treenail /ˈtriːneɪl/ n. (also **trenail**) a hard wooden pin for securing timbers etc.

treetop /ˈtriːtɒp/ n. the topmost part of a tree.

trefa /ˈtreɪfə/ adj. (also **tref** /treɪf/ and other variants) not kosher. [Heb. *ṭᵉrēpāh* the flesh of an animal torn f. *ṭārap* rend]

trefoil /ˈtrefɔɪl, ˈtriː-/ n. & adj. —n. **1** any leguminous plant of the genus *Trifolium*, with leaves of three leaflets and flowers of various colours, esp. clover. **2** any plant with similar leaves. **3** a three-lobed ornamentation, esp. in tracery windows. **4** a thing arranged in or with three lobes. —adj. of or concerning a three-lobed plant, window tracery, etc. □□ **trefoiled** adj. (also in *comb.*). [ME f. AF *trifoil* f. L *trifolium* (as TRI-, *folium* leaf)]

trek /trek/ v. & n. orig. S.Afr. —v.intr. (**trekked, trekking**) **1** travel or make one's way arduously (*trekking through the forest*). **2** esp. hist. migrate or journey with one's belongings by ox-wagon. **3** (of an ox) draw a vehicle or pull a load. —n. **1 a** a journey or walk made by trekking (*it was a trek to the nearest launderette*). **b** each stage of such a journey. **2** an organized migration of a body of persons. □□ **trekker** n. [S.Afr. Du. *trek* (n.), *trekken* (v.) draw, travel]

trellis /ˈtrelɪs/ n. & v. —n. (in full **trellis-work**) a lattice or grating of light wooden or metal bars used esp. as a support for fruit-trees or creepers and often fastened against a wall. —v.tr. (**trellised, trellising**) **1** provide with a trellis. **2** support (a vine etc.) with a trellis. [ME f. OF *trelis, trelice* ult. f. L *trilix* three-ply (as TRI-, *licium* warp-thread)]

trematode /ˈtreməˌtəʊd/ n. any parasitic flatworm of the class Trematoda, esp. a fluke, equipped with hooks or suckers, e.g. a liver fluke. [mod.L *Trematoda* f. Gk *trēmatōdēs* perforated f. *trēma* hole]

tremble /ˈtremb(ə)l/ v. & n. —v.intr. **1** shake involuntarily from fear, excitement, weakness, etc. **2** be in a state of extreme apprehension (*trembled at the very thought of it*). **3** move in a quivering manner (*leaves trembled in the breeze*). —n. **1** a trembling state or movement; a quiver (*couldn't speak without a tremble*). **2** (in *pl.*) a disease (esp. of cattle) marked by trembling. □ **all of a tremble** colloq. **1** trembling all over. **2** extremely agitated. **trembling poplar** an aspen. □□ **tremblingly** adv. [ME f. OF *trembler* f. med.L *tremulare* f. L *tremulus* TREMULOUS]

trembler /ˈtremblə(r)/ n. an automatic vibrator for making and breaking an electrical circuit.

trembly /ˈtremblɪ/ adj. (**tremblier**, **trembliest**) colloq. trembling; agitated.

tremendous /trɪˈmendəs/ adj. **1** awe-inspiring, fearful, overpowering. **2** colloq. remarkable, considerable, excellent (a tremendous explosion; gave a tremendous performance). □□ **tremendously** adv. **tremendousness** n. [L tremendus, gerundive of tremere tremble]

tremolo /ˈtremələʊ/ n. Mus. **1** a tremulous effect in playing stringed and keyboard instruments or singing, esp. by rapid reiteration of a note; in other instruments, by rapid alternation between two notes (cf. VIBRATO). **2** a device in an organ producing a tremulous effect. [It. (as TREMULOUS)]

tremor /ˈtremə(r)/ n. & v. —n. **1** a shaking or quivering. **2** a thrill (of fear or exultation etc.). **3** (in full **earth tremor**) a slight earthquake. —v.intr. undergo a tremor or tremors. [ME f. OF tremour & L tremor f. tremere tremble]

tremulous /ˈtremjʊləs/ adj. **1** trembling or quivering (in a tremulous voice). **2** (of a line etc.) drawn by a tremulous hand. **3** timid or vacillating. □□ **tremulously** adv. **tremulousness** n. [L tremulus f. tremere tremble]

trenail var. of TREENAIL.

trench /trentʃ/ n. & v. —n. **1** a long narrow usu. deep depression or ditch. **2** Mil. **a** this dug by troops to stand in and be sheltered from enemy fire. **b** (in pl.) a defensive system of these. **3** a long narrow deep depression in the ocean bed. —v. **1** tr. dig a trench or trenches in (the ground). **2** tr. turn over the earth of (a field, garden, etc.) by digging a succession of adjoining ditches. **3** intr. (foll. by on, upon) archaic **a** encroach. **b** verge or border closely. □ **trench coat 1** a soldier's lined or padded water-proof coat. **2** a loose belted raincoat. **trench fever** a highly infectious disease transmitted by lice, that infested soldiers in the trenches in the First World War. **trench mortar** a light simple mortar throwing a bomb from one's own into the enemy trenches. **trench warfare** hostilities carried on from more or less permanent trenches. [ME f. OF trenche (n.) trenchier (v.), ult. f. L truncare TRUNCATE]

trenchant /ˈtrentʃ(ə)nt/ adj. **1** (of a style or language etc.) incisive, terse, vigorous. **2** archaic or poet. sharp, keen. □□ **trenchancy** n. **trenchantly** adv. [ME f. OF, part. of trenchier: see TRENCH]

trencher /ˈtrentʃə(r)/ n. **1** hist. a wooden or earthenware platter for serving food. **2** (in full **trencher cap**) a stiff square academic cap; a mortarboard. [ME f. AF trenchour, OF trencheoir f. trenchier: see TRENCH]

trencherman /ˈtrentʃəmən/ n. (pl. **-men**) a person who eats well, or in a specified manner (a good trencherman).

trend /trend/ n. & v. —n. a general direction and tendency (esp. of events, fashion, or opinion etc.). —v.intr. **1** bend or turn away in a specified direction. **2** be chiefly directed; have a general and continued tendency. □ **trend-setter** a person who leads the way in fashion etc. **trend-setting** establishing trends or fashions. [ME 'revolve' etc. f. OE trendan f. Gmc: cf. TRUNDLE]

trendy /ˈtrendɪ/ adj. & n. colloq. —adj. (**trendier**, **trendiest**) often derog. fashionable; following fashionable trends. —n. (pl. **-ies**) a fashionable person. □□ **trendily** adv. **trendiness** n.

Trengganu /trenˈɡɑːnuː/ (also **Terengganu**) a State on the east coast of the Malaysian peninsula; pop. (1980) 540,600; capital, Kuala Terengganu.

Trent /trent/ the anglicized name of Trento, a city of northern Italy, scene of an ecumenical Church council, meeting from time to time between 1545 and 1563, which defined the doctrines of the Church in opposition to those of the Reformation, reformed discipline, and strengthened the authority of the papacy.

trente-et-quarante /ˌtrɑ̃teɪkæˈrɑ̃t/ n. = rouge-et-noir. [F, = thirty and forty]

Trentino-Alto Adige /trenˈtiːnəʊˌæltəʊˈædɪ ˌdʒeɪ/ a region of NE Italy, comprising the autonomous provinces of Bolzano and Trento; pop. (1981) 873,400.

Trenton /ˈtrent(ə)n/ the capital of New Jersey; pop. (1980) 92,124.

trepan /trɪˈpæn/ n. & v. —n. **1** a cylindrical saw formerly used by surgeons for removing part of the bone of the skull. **2** a borer for sinking shafts. —v.tr. (**trepanned**, **trepanning**) perforate (the skull) with a trepan. □□ **trepanation** /ˌtrepəˈneɪʃ(ə)n/ n. **trepanning** n. [ME f. med.L trepanum f. Gk trupanon f. trupaō bore f. trupē hole]

trepang /trɪˈpæŋ/ n. = BÊCHE-DE-MER 1. [Malay trīpang]

trephine /trɪˈfaɪn, -ˈfiːn/ n. & v. —n. an improved form of trepan with a guiding centre-pin. —v.tr. operate on with this. □□ **trephination** /ˌtrefɪˈneɪʃ(ə)n/ n. [orig. trafine, f. L tres fines three ends, app. formed after TREPAN]

trepidation /ˌtrepɪˈdeɪʃ(ə)n/ n. **1** a feeling of fear or alarm; perturbation of the mind. **2** tremulous agitation. **3** the trembling of limbs, e.g. in paralysis. [L trepidatio f. trepidare be agitated, tremble, f. trepidus alarmed]

trespass /ˈtrespəs/ v. & n. —v.intr. **1** (usu. foll. by on, upon) make an unlawful or unwarrantable intrusion (esp. on land or property). **2** (foll. by on) make unwarrantable claims (shall not trespass on your hospitality). **3** (foll. by against) literary or archaic offend. —n. **1** Law a voluntary wrongful act against the person or property of another, esp. unlawful entry to a person's land or property. **2** archaic a sin or offence. □ **trespass on a person's preserves** meddle in another person's affairs. □□ **trespasser** n. [ME f. OF trespasser pass over, trespass, trespas (n.), f. med.L transpassare (as TRANS-, PASS¹)]

tress /tres/ n. & v. —n. **1** a long lock of human (esp. female) hair. **2** (in pl.) a woman's or girl's head of hair. —v.tr. arrange (hair) in tresses. □□ **tressed** adj. (also in comb.). **tressy** adj. [ME f. OF tresse, perh. ult. f. Gk trikha threefold]

tressure /ˈtreʃə(r)/ n. Heraldry a narrow orle. [ME, orig. = hair-ribbon, f. OF tressour etc. (as TRESS)]

trestle /ˈtres(ə)l/ n. **1** a supporting structure for a table etc., consisting of two frames fixed at an angle or hinged or of a bar supported by two divergent pairs of legs. **2** (in full **trestle-table**) a table consisting of a board or boards laid on trestles or other supports. **3** (in full **trestle-work**) an open braced framework to support a bridge etc. **4** (in full **trestle-tree**) Naut. each of a pair of horizontal pieces on a lower mast supporting the top-mast etc. [ME f. OF trestel ult. f. L transtrum]

tret /tret/ n. hist. an allowance of extra weight formerly made to purchasers of some goods for waste in transportation. [ME f. AF & OF, var. of trait draught: see TRAIT]

trevally /trɪˈvælɪ/ n. (pl. **-ies**) any Australian fish of the genus Caranx, used as food. [prob. alt. f. cavally, a kind of fish, f. Sp. caballo horse f. L (as CAVALRY)]

Trevithick /ˈtrevɪθɪk/, Richard (1771–1833), known as the Cornish Giant, the most notable and original engineer to emerge from the Cornish mining industry, where steam engines were first widely used. His particular contribution was in the use of high-pressure steam to drive a piston which then could send out exhaust against atmospheric pressure, giving a compact and therefore portable engine; this led to the first railway locomotive in 1804, at a colliery in South Wales. He also applied it to a steam-dredger, a threshing machine, and a cultivator. In 1816 he sailed for Peru to apply steam power in the silver-mines, but this proved a disastrous enterprise and he returned penniless in 1827. Trevithick was a man of boundless energy, with schemes for refrigeration, tunnelling, wreck salvage, agricultural machinery, land reclamation, and gun-mountings.

trews /truːz/ n.pl. esp. Brit. trousers, esp. close-fitting tartan trousers worn by women. [Ir. trius, Gael. triubhas (sing.): cf. TROUSERS]

trey /treɪ/ n. (pl. **treys**) the three on dice or cards. [ME f. OF trei, treis three f. L tres]

TRH abbr. Their Royal Highnesses.

tri- /traɪ/ comb. form forming nouns and adjectives meaning: **1** three or three times. **2** Chem. (forming the names of compounds) containing three atoms or groups of a specified kind (triacetate). [L & Gk f. L tres, Gk treis three]

triable /ˈtraɪəb(ə)l/ adj. **1** liable to a judicial trial. **2** that may be tried or attempted. [ME f. AF (as TRY)]

triacetate /traɪˈæsɪˌteɪt/ n. a cellulose derivative containing three acetate groups, esp. as a base for man-made fibres.

triad /ˈtraɪæd/ n. **1** a group of three (esp. notes in a chord). **2** the number three. **3** a Chinese secret society, usu. criminal. (See TRIAD SOCIETY.) **4** a Welsh form of literary composition with an arrangement in groups of three. □□ **triadic** /-ˈædɪk/ adj. **triadically** /-ˈædɪkəlɪ/ adv. [F triade or LL trias triad- f. Gk trias -ados f. treis three]

triadelphous /ˌtraɪəˈdelfəs/ adj. Bot. having stamens united in three bundles. [TRI- + Gk adelphos brother]

Triad Society a secret Chinese society formed c.1730 with the alleged purpose of ousting the Manchu dynasty. The name was given to various related organizations sharing a similar ritual and acting as both fraternal and criminal organizations. In the mid-19th c. they grew in strength and thereafter played an erratic and violent role in China. Such societies, often of a criminal character, often flourish among overseas Chinese. [tr. Chin. San Ho Hui lit. 'three unite society', i.e. triple union society, thought to mean 'the union of Heaven, Earth, and Man']

triage /ˈtraɪɑːʒ/ n. **1** the act of sorting according to quality. **2** the assignment of degrees of urgency to decide the order of treatment of wounds, illnesses, etc. [F f. trier: cf. TRY]

trial /ˈtraɪəl/ n. **1** a judicial examination and determination of issues between parties by a judge with or without a jury (stood trial for murder). **2 a** a process or mode of testing qualities. **b** experimental treatment. **c** a test (will give you a trial). **3** a trying thing or experience or person, esp. hardship or trouble (the trials of old age). **4** a sports match to test the ability of players eligible for selection to a team. **5** a test of individual ability on a motor cycle over rough ground or on a road. **6** any of various contests involving performance by horses, dogs, or other animals. □ **on trial 1** being tried in a court of law. **2** being tested; to be chosen or retained only if suitable. **trial and error** repeated (usu. varied and unsystematic) attempts or experiments continued until successful. **trial balance** (of a ledger in double-entry book-keeping), a comparison of the totals on either side, the inequality of which reveals errors in posting. **trial jury** = petty jury. **trial run** a preliminary test of a vehicle, vessel, machine, etc. [AF trial, triel f. trier TRY]

trialist /ˈtraɪəlɪst/ n. **1** a person who takes part in a sports trial, motor-cycle trial, etc. **2** a person involved in a judicial trial.

triandrous /traɪˈændrəs/ adj. Bot. having three stamens.

triangle /ˈtraɪˌæŋg(ə)l/ n. **1** a plane figure with three sides and angles. **2** any three things not in a straight line, with imaginary lines joining them. **3** an implement of this shape. **4** a musical instrument consisting of a steel rod bent into a triangle and sounded by striking it with a small steel rod. **5** a situation, esp. an emotional relationship, involving three people. **6** a right-angled triangle of wood etc. as a drawing-implement. **7** Naut. a device of three spars for raising weights. **8** hist. a frame of three halberds joined at the top to which a soldier was bound for flogging. □ **triangle of forces** a triangle whose sides represent in magnitude and direction three forces in equilibrium. [ME f. OF triangle or L triangulum neut. of triangulus three-cornered (as TRI-, ANGLE¹)]

triangular /traɪˈæŋgjʊlə(r)/ adj. **1** triangle-shaped, three-cornered. **2** (of a contest or treaty etc.) between three persons or parties. **3** (of a pyramid) having a three-sided base. □□ **triangularity** /-ˈlærɪtɪ/ n. **triangularly** adv. [LL triangularis (as TRIANGLE)]

triangulate v. & adj. —v.tr. /traɪˈæŋgjʊˌleɪt/ **1** divide (an area) into triangles for surveying purposes. **2 a** measure and map (an area) by the use of triangles with a known base length and base angles. **b** determine (a height, distance, etc.) in this way. —adj. /traɪˈæŋgjʊlət/ Zool. marked with triangles. □□ **triangulately** /-lətlɪ/ adv. **triangulation** /-ˈleɪʃ(ə)n/ n. [L triangulatus triangular (as TRIANGLE)]

Trianon /ˈtriːɑˌnɔ̃/ either of two small palaces in the great park at Versailles. The larger (**Grand Trianon**) was built by Louis XIV in 1687; the smaller (**Petit Trianon**), built by Louis XV 1762–8, belonged first to Madame du Barry and afterwards to Marie Antoinette.

Triassic /traɪˈæsɪk/ adj. & n. Geol. —adj. of or relating to the earliest period of the Mesozoic era, following the Permian and

preceding the Jurassic, lasting from about 248 to 213 million years ago. Dinosaurs became numerous during this period, which also saw the appearance of the first mammals. —n. this period or system. [LL trias (as TRIAD), because the strata are divisible into three groups]

triathlon /traɪˈæθlɒn/ n. an athletic contest consisting of three different events. □□ **triathlete** n. [TRI- after DECATHLON]

triatomic /ˌtraɪəˈtɒmɪk/ adj. Chem. **1** having three atoms (of a specified kind) in the molecule. **2** having three replacement atoms or radicals.

triaxial /traɪˈæksɪəl/ adj. having three axes.

tribade /ˈtrɪbɑːd/ n. a woman who takes part in a simulation of sexual intercourse with another woman. □□ **tribadism** n. [F tribade or L tribas f. Gk f. tribō rub]

tribal /ˈtraɪb(ə)l/ adj. of, relating to, or characteristic of a tribe or tribes. □□ **tribally** adv.

tribalism /ˈtraɪbəˌlɪz(ə)m/ n. tribal organization. □□ **tribalist** n. **tribalistic** /-ˈlɪstɪk/ adj.

tribasic /traɪˈbeɪsɪk/ adj. Chem. (of an acid) having three replaceable hydrogen atoms.

tribe /traɪb/ n. **1** a group of (esp. primitive) families or communities, linked by social, economic, religious, or blood ties, and usu. having a common culture and dialect, and a recognized leader. **2** any similar natural or political division. **3** Rom.Hist. each of the political divisions of the Roman people. **4** each of the 12 divisions of the Israelites, each traditionally descended from one of the patriarchs. **5** usu. derog. a set or number of persons esp. of one profession etc. or family (the whole tribe of actors). **6** Biol. a group of organisms usu. ranking between genus and the subfamily. **7** (in pl.) large numbers. [ME, orig. in pl. form tribuz, tribus f. OF or L tribus (sing. & pl.)]

tribesman /ˈtraɪbzmən/ n. (pl. -men) a member of a tribe or of one's own tribe.

triblet /ˈtrɪblɪt/ n. a mandrel used in making tubes, rings, etc. [F triboulet, of unkn. orig.]

tribo- /ˈtrɪbəʊ-, ˈtraɪ-/ comb. form rubbing, friction. [Gk tribos rubbing]

triboelectricity /ˌtrɪbəʊˌɪlekˈtrɪsɪtɪ, ˌtraɪbəʊ-/ n. the generation of an electric charge by friction.

tribology /traɪˈbɒlədʒɪ/ n. the study of friction, wear, lubrication, and the design of bearings; the science of interacting surfaces in relative motion. □□ **tribologist** n.

triboluminescence /ˌtrɪbəʊˌluːmɪˈnes(ə)ns, ˌtraɪ-/ n. the emission of light from a substance when rubbed, scratched, etc. □□ **triboluminescent** adj.

tribometer /traɪˈbɒmɪtə(r)/ n. an instrument for measuring friction in sliding.

tribrach /ˈtraɪbræk, ˈtrɪ-/ n. Prosody a foot of three short or unstressed syllables. □□ **tribrachic** /-ˈbrækɪk/ adj. [L tribrachys f. Gk tribrakhus (as TRI-, brakhus short)]

tribulation /ˌtrɪbjʊˈleɪʃ(ə)n/ n. **1** great affliction or oppression. **2** a cause of this (was a real tribulation to me). [ME f. OF f. eccl.L tribulatio -onis f. L tribulare press, oppress, f. tribulum sledge for threshing, f. terere trit- rub]

tribunal /traɪˈbjuːn(ə)l, trɪ-/ n. **1** Brit. a board appointed to adjudicate in some matter, esp. one appointed by the government to investigate a matter of public concern. **2** a court of justice. **3** a seat or bench for a judge or judges. **4 a** a place of judgement. **b** judicial authority (the tribunal of public opinion). [F tribunal or L tribunus (as TRIBUNE²)]

tribune¹ /ˈtrɪbjuːn/ n. **1** a popular leader or demagogue. **2** (in full **tribune of the people**) an official in ancient Rome chosen by the people to protect their interests. **3** (in full **military tribune**) a Roman legionary officer. □□ **tribunate** /-nət/ n. **tribuneship** n. [ME f. L tribunus, prob. f. tribus tribe]

tribune² /ˈtrɪbjuːn/ n. **1 a** a bishop's throne in a basilica. **b** an apse containing this. **2** a dais or rostrum. **3** a raised area with seats. [F f. It. f. med.L tribuna TRIBUNAL]

Tribune Group a group within the British Labour Party consisting of supporters of the extreme left-wing views put forward in the weekly journal Tribune.

tributary /'trɪbjʊtərɪ/ n. & adj. —n. (pl. -ies) 1 a river or stream flowing into a larger river or lake. 2 hist. a person or State paying or subject to tribute. —adj. 1 (of a river etc.) that is a tributary. 2 hist. a paying tribute. b serving as tribute. □□ **tributarily** adv. **tributariness** n. [ME f. L *tributarius* (as TRIBUTE)]

tribute /'trɪbjuːt/ n. 1 a thing said or done or given as a mark of respect or affection etc. (*paid tribute to their achievements; floral tributes*). 2 hist. a a payment made periodically by one State or ruler to another, esp. as a sign of dependence. b an obligation to pay this (*was laid under tribute*). 3 (foll. by *to*) an indication of (some praiseworthy quality) (*their success is a tribute to their perseverance*). 4 a proportion of ore or its equivalent paid to a miner for his work, or to the owner of a mine. [ME f. L *tributum* neut. past part. of *tribuere tribut-* assign, orig. divide between tribes (*tribus*)]

tricar /'traɪkɑː(r)/ n. Brit. a three-wheeled motor car.

trice /traɪs/ n. □ **in a trice** in a moment; instantly. [ME *trice* (v.) pull, haul f. MDu. *trīsen*, MLG *trīssen*, rel. to MDu. *trīse* windlass, pulley]

tricentenary /ˌtraɪsenˈtiːnərɪ/ n. (pl. -ies) = TERCENTENARY.

triceps /'traɪseps/ adj. & n. —adj. (of a muscle) having three heads or points of attachment. —n. any triceps muscle, esp. the large muscle at the back of the upper arm. [L, = three-headed (as TRI-, *-ceps* f. *caput* head)]

triceratops /ˌtraɪˈserəˌtɒps/ n. a plant-eating dinosaur with three sharp horns on the forehead and a wavy-edged collar round the neck. [mod.L f. Gk *trikeratos* three-horned + *ōps* face]

trichiasis /trɪˈkaɪəsɪs/ n. Med. ingrowth or introversion of the eyelashes. [LL f. Gk *trikhiasis* f. *trikhiaō* be hairy]

trichina /trɪˈkaɪnə/ n. (pl. **trichinae** /-niː/) any hairlike parasitic nematode worm of the genus *Trichinella*, esp. *T. spiralis*, the adults of which live in the small intestine, and whose larvae become encysted in the muscle tissue of humans and flesh-eating animals. □□ **trichinous** adj. [mod.L f. Gk *trikhinos* of hair: see TRICHO-]

Trichinopoly see TIRUCHIRAPALLI.

trichinosis /ˌtrɪkɪˈnəʊsɪs/ n. a disease caused by trichinae, usu. ingested in meat, and characterized by digestive disturbance, fever, and muscular rigidity.

tricho- /'trɪkəʊ/ comb. form hair. [Gk *thrix trikhos* hair]

trichogenous /trɪˈkɒdʒənəs/ adj. causing or promoting the growth of hair.

trichology /trɪˈkɒlədʒɪ, traɪ-/ n. the study of the structure, functions, and diseases of the hair. □□ **trichologist** n.

trichome /'traɪkəʊm/ n. Bot. a hair, scale, prickle, or other outgrowth from the epidermis of a plant. [Gk *trikhōma* f. *trikhoō* cover with hair (as TRICHO-)]

trichomonad /ˌtrɪkəˈmɒnæd/ n. any flagellate protozoan of the genus *Trichomonas*, parasitic in humans, cattle, and fowls.

trichomoniasis /ˌtrɪkəməˈnaɪəsɪs/ n. any of various infections caused by trichomonads parasitic on the urinary tract, vagina, or digestive system.

trichopathy /trɪˈkɒpəθɪ/ n. the treatment of diseases of the hair. □□ **trichopathic** /ˌtrɪkəˈpæθɪk/ adj.

trichotomy /traɪˈkɒtəmɪ/ n. (pl. -ies) a division (esp. sharply defined) into three categories, esp. of human nature into body, soul, and spirit. □□ **trichotomic** /-kəˈtɒmɪk/ adj. [Gk *trikha* threefold f. *treis* three, after DICHOTOMY]

trichroic /traɪˈkrəʊɪk/ adj. (esp. of a crystal viewed in different directions) showing three colours. □□ **trichroism** /'traɪkrəʊˌɪz(ə)m/ n. [Gk *trikhroos* (as TRI-, *khrōs* colour)]

trichromatic /ˌtraɪkrəˈmætɪk/ adj. 1 having or using three colours. 2 (of vision) having the normal three colour-sensations, i.e. red, green, and purple. □□ **trichromatism** /-ˈkrəʊməˌtɪz(ə)m/ n.

trick /trɪk/ n. & v. —n. 1 an action or scheme undertaken to fool, outwit, or deceive. 2 an optical or other illusion (*a trick of the light*). 3 a special technique; a knack or special way of doing something. 4 a a feat of skill or dexterity. b an unusual action (e.g. begging) learned by an animal. 5 a mischievous, foolish, or discreditable act; a practical joke (*a mean trick to play*). 6 a peculiar

or characteristic habit or mannerism (*has a trick of repeating himself*). 7 a the cards played in a single round of a card-game, usu. one from each player. b such a round. c a point gained as a result of this. 8 (*attrib.*) done to deceive or mystify or to create an illusion (*trick photography; trick question*). 9 Naut. a sailor's turn at the helm, usu. two hours. —v.tr. 1 deceive by a trick; outwit. 2 (often foll. by *out of*, or *into* + verbal noun) cheat; treat deceitfully so as to deprive (*were tricked into agreeing; were tricked out of their savings*). 3 (of a thing) foil or baffle; take by surprise; disappoint the calculations of. □ **do the trick** colloq. accomplish one's purpose; achieve the required result. **how's tricks?** colloq. how are you? **not miss a trick** see MISS[1]. **trick cyclist** 1 a cyclist who performs tricks, esp. in a circus. 2 sl. a psychiatrist. **trick of the trade** a special usu. ingenious technique or method of achieving a result in an industry or profession etc. **trick or treat** US a children's custom of calling at houses at Hallowe'en with the threat of pranks if they are not given a small gift. **trick out** (or **up**) dress, decorate, or deck out esp. showily. **up to one's tricks** colloq. misbehaving. **up to a person's tricks** aware of what a person is likely to do by way of mischief. □□ **tricker** n. **trickish** adj. **trickless** adj. [ME f. OF dial. *trique*, OF *triche* f. *trichier* deceive, of unkn. orig.]

trickery /'trɪkərɪ/ n. (pl. -ies) 1 the practice or an instance of deception. 2 the use of tricks.

trickle /'trɪk(ə)l/ v. & n. —v. 1 intr. & tr. flow or cause to flow in drops or a small stream (*water trickled through the crack*). 2 tr. come or go slowly or gradually (*information trickles out*). —n. a trickling flow. □ **trickle charger** an electrical charger for batteries that works at a steady slow rate from the mains. [ME *trekel*, *trikle*, prob. imit.]

trickster /'trɪkstə(r)/ n. a deceiver or rogue.

tricksy /'trɪksɪ/ adj. (**tricksier**, **tricksiest**) full of tricks; playful. □□ **tricksily** adv. **tricksiness** n. [TRICK: for *-sy* cf. FLIMSY, TIPSY]

tricky /'trɪkɪ/ adj. (**trickier**, **trickiest**) 1 difficult or intricate; requiring care and adroitness (*a tricky job*). 2 crafty or deceitful. 3 resourceful or adroit. □□ **trickily** adv. **trickiness** n.

triclinic /traɪˈklɪnɪk/ adj. 1 (of a mineral) having three unequal oblique axes. 2 denoting the system classifying triclinic crystalline substances. [Gk TRI- + *klinō* incline]

triclinium /traɪˈklɪnɪəm, trɪ-/ n. (pl. **triclinia** /-nɪə/) Rom. Antiq. 1 a dining-table with couches along three sides. 2 a room containing this. [L f. Gk *triklinion* (as TRI-, *klīnē* couch)]

tricolour /'trɪkələ(r), 'traɪˌkʌlə(r)/ n. & adj. (*US* **tricolor**) —n. a flag of three colours, esp. the French national flag of blue, white, and red. —adj. (also **tricoloured**) having three colours. [F *tricolore* f. LL *tricolor* (as TRI-, COLOUR)]

tricorn /'traɪkɔːn/ adj. & n. (also **tricorne**) —adj. 1 having three horns. 2 (of a hat) having a brim turned up on three sides. —n. 1 an imaginary animal with three horns. 2 a tricorn hat. [F *tricorne* or L *tricornis* (as TRI-, *cornu* horn)]

tricot /'trɪkəʊ, 'triː-/ n. 1 a hand-knitted woollen fabric. b an imitation of this. 2 a ribbed woollen cloth. [F, = knitting f. *tricoter* knit, of unkn. orig.]

tricrotic /traɪˈkrɒtɪk/ adj. (of the pulse) having a triple beat. [TRI- after DICROTIC]

tricuspid /traɪˈkʌspɪd/ adj. & n. —n. 1 a tooth with three cusps or points. 2 a heart-valve formed of three triangular segments. —adj. (of a tooth) having three cusps or points.

tricycle /'traɪsɪk(ə)l/ n. & v. —n. 1 a vehicle having three wheels, two on an axle at the back and one at the front, driven by pedals in the same way as a bicycle. 2 a three-wheeled motor vehicle for a disabled driver. —v.intr. ride on a tricycle. □□ **tricyclist** n.

tridactyl /traɪˈdæktɪl/ adj. (also **tridactylous** /-ˈdæktɪləs/) having three fingers or toes.

trident /'traɪd(ə)nt/ n. 1 a three-pronged spear, esp. as an attribute of Poseidon (Neptune) or Britannia. 2 (**Trident**) a US type of submarine-launched ballistic missile. [L *tridens trident-* (as TRI-, *dens* tooth)]

tridentate /traɪˈdenteɪt/ adj. having three teeth or prongs. [TRI- + L *dentatus* toothed]

Tridentine /traɪˈdentaɪn, trɪ-/ *adj. & n.* —*adj.* of or relating to the Council of Trent (see TRENT), esp. as the basis of Roman Catholic doctrine. —*n.* a Roman Catholic adhering to this traditional doctrine. □ **Tridentine mass** the eucharistic liturgy used by the Roman Catholic Church from 1570 to 1964. [med.L *Tridentinus* f. *Tridentum* Trent]

triduum /ˈtrɪdjʊəm/ *n. RC Ch.* esp. *hist.* three days' prayer in preparation for a saint's day or other religious occasion. [L (as TRI-, *dies* day)]

tridymite /ˈtrɪdɪˌmaɪt/ *n.* a crystallized form of silica, occurring in cavities of volcanic rocks. [G *Tridymit* f. Gk *tridumos* threefold (as TRI-, *didumos* twin), from its occurrence in groups of three crystals]

tried *past* and *past part.* of TRY.

triennial /traɪˈenɪəl/ *adj. & n.* —*adj.* 1 lasting three years. 2 recurring every three years. —*n.* a visitation of an Anglican diocese by its bishop every three years. □□ **triennially** *adv.* [LL *triennis* (as TRI-, L *annus* year)]

triennium /traɪˈenɪəm/ *n.* (*pl.* **trienniums** or **triennia** /-nɪə/) a period of three years. [L (as TRIENNIAL)]

Trier /ˈtrɪə(r)/ a city at the centre of the wine-producing Moselle region of Rhineland-Palatinate in western Germany; pop. (1983) 94,700.

trier /ˈtraɪə(r)/ *n.* 1 a person who perseveres (*is a real trier*). 2 a tester, esp. of foodstuffs. 3 a person appointed to decide whether a challenge to a juror is well-founded.

Trieste /trɪˈest/ a city of NE Italy, the largest seaport on the Adriatic and capital of Friuli-Venezia Giulia region; pop. (1981) 252,350. Formerly held by Austria, Trieste was annexed by Italy after the First World War and retained in 1954 following a failed attempt to make the area a Free Territory.

trifacial nerve /traɪˈfeɪʃ(ə)l/ *n.* = TRIGEMINAL NERVE.

trifecta /traɪˈfektə/ *n. US, Austral.,* & *NZ* a form of betting in which the first three places in a race must be predicted in the correct order. [TRI- + PERFECTA]

trifid /ˈtraɪfɪd/ *adj.* esp. *Biol.* partly or wholly split into three divisions or lobes. [L *trifidus* (as TRI-, *findere fid-* split)]

trifle /ˈtraɪf(ə)l/ *n. & v.* —*n.* 1 a thing of slight value or importance. 2 a a small amount esp. of money (*was sold for a trifle*). b (prec. by *a*) somewhat (*seems a trifle annoyed*). 3 *Brit.* a confection of sponge cake with custard, jelly, fruit, cream, etc. —*v.* 1 *intr.* talk or act frivolously. 2 *intr.* (foll. by *with*) a treat or deal with frivolously or derisively; flirt heartlessly with. b refuse to take seriously. 3 *tr.* (foll. by *away*) waste (time, energies, money, etc.) frivolously. □□ **trifler** *n.* [ME f. OF *truf(f)le* by-form of *trufe* deceit, of unkn. orig.]

trifling /ˈtraɪflɪŋ/ *adj.* 1 unimportant, petty. 2 frivolous. □□ **triflingly** *adv.*

trifocal /traɪˈfəʊk(ə)l/ *adj. & n.* —*adj.* having three focuses, esp. of a lens with different focal lengths. —*n.* (in *pl.*) trifocal spectacles.

trifoliate /traɪˈfəʊlɪət/ *adj.* 1 (of a compound leaf) having three leaflets. 2 (of a plant) having such leaves.

triforium /traɪˈfɔːrɪəm/ *n.* (*pl.* **triforia** /-rɪə/) a gallery or arcade above the arches of the nave, choir, and transepts of a church. [AL, of unkn. orig.]

triform /ˈtraɪfɔːm/ *adj.* (also **triformed**) 1 formed of three parts. 2 having three forms or bodies.

trifurcate *v. & adj.* —*v.tr.* & *intr.* /ˈtraɪfəˌkeɪt/ divide into three branches. —*adj.* /-ˈfɜːkət/ divided into three branches.

trig[1] /trɪg/ *n. colloq.* trigonometry. [abbr.]

trig[2] /trɪg/ *adj. & v. archaic* or *dial.* —*adj.* trim or spruce. —*v.tr.* (**trigged**, **trigging**) make trim; smarten. [ME, = trusty, f. ON *tryggr*, rel. to TRUE]

trigamous /ˈtrɪgəməs/ *adj.* 1 a three times married. b having three wives or husbands at once. 2 *Bot.* having male, female, and hermaphrodite flowers in the same head. □□ **trigamist** *n.* **trigamy** *n.* [Gk *trigamos* (as TRI-, *gamos* marriage)]

trigeminal nerve /traɪˈdʒemɪn(ə)l/ *n. Anat.* the largest cranial nerve which divides into the ophthalmic, maxillary, and mandibular nerves. □ **trigeminal neuralgia** *Med.* neuralgia involving one or more of these branches, and often causing severe pain. [as TRIGEMINUS]

trigeminus /traɪˈdʒemɪnəs/ *n.* (*pl.* **trigemini** /-ˌnaɪ/) the trigeminal nerve. [L, = born as a triplet (as TRI-, *geminus* born at the same birth)]

trigger /ˈtrɪgə(r)/ *n. & v.* —*n.* 1 a movable device for releasing a spring or catch and so setting off a mechanism (esp. that of a gun). 2 an event, occurrence, etc., that sets off a chain reaction. —*v.tr.* 1 (often foll. by *off*) set (an action or process) in motion; initiate, precipitate. 2 fire (a gun) by the use of a trigger. □ **quick on the trigger** quick to respond. **trigger fish** any usu. tropical marine fish of the family Balistidae with a first dorsal fin-spine which can be depressed by pressing on the second. **trigger-happy** apt to shoot without or with slight provocation. □□ **triggered** *adj.* [17th-c. *tricker* f. Du. *trekker* f. *trekken* pull: cf. TREK]

triglyph /ˈtraɪglɪf/ *n. Archit.* each of a series of tablets with three vertical grooves, alternating with metopes in a Doric frieze. □□ **triglyphic** /-ˈglɪfɪk/ *adj.* **triglyphical** /-ˈglɪfɪk(ə)l/ *adj.* [L *triglyphus* f. Gk *trigluphos* (as TRI-, *gluphē* carving)]

trigon /ˈtraɪgɒn/ *n.* 1 a triangle. 2 an ancient triangular lyre or harp. 3 the cutting region of an upper molar tooth. [L *trigonum* f. Gk *trigōnon* neuter of *trigōnos* three-cornered (as TRI-, -GON)]

trigonal /ˈtrɪgən(ə)l/ *adj.* 1 triangular; of or relating to a triangle. 2 *Biol.* triangular in cross-section. 3 (of a crystal etc.) having an axis with threefold symmetry. □□ **trigonally** *adv.* [med.L *trigonalis* (as TRIGON)]

trigonometry /ˌtrɪgəˈnɒmɪtrɪ/ *n.* the branch of mathematics dealing with the relations of the sides and angles of triangles and with the relevant functions of any angles. □□ **trigonometric** /-nəˈmetrɪk/ *adj.* **trigonometrical** /-nəˈmetrɪk(ə)l/ *adj.* [mod.L *trigonometria* (as TRIGON, -METRY)]

trigraph /ˈtraɪgrɑːf/ *n.* (also **trigram** /-græm/) 1 a group of three letters representing one sound. 2 a figure of three lines.

trigynous /ˈtrɪdʒɪnəs/ *adj. Bot.* having three pistils.

trihedral /traɪˈhedr(ə)l, -ˈhiːdr(ə)l/ *adj.* having three surfaces.

trihedron /traɪˈhedrən, -ˈhiːdrən/ *n.* a figure of three intersecting planes.

trihydric /traɪˈhaɪdrɪk/ *adj. Chem.* containing three hydroxyl groups.

trike /traɪk/ *n. & v.intr. colloq.* tricycle. [abbr.]

trilabiate /traɪˈleɪbɪət/ *adj. Bot.* & *Zool.* three-lipped.

trilateral /traɪˈlætər(ə)l/ *adj. & n.* —*adj.* 1 of, on, or with three sides. 2 shared by or involving three parties, countries, etc. (*trilateral negotiations*). —*n.* a figure having three sides.

trilby /ˈtrɪlbɪ/ *n.* (*pl.* **-ies**) *Brit.* a soft felt hat with a narrow brim and indented crown. □□ **trilbied** *adj.* [name of the heroine in G. du Maurier's novel *Trilby* (1894), in the stage version of which such a hat was worn]

trilinear /traɪˈlɪnɪə(r)/ *adj.* of or having three lines.

trilingual /traɪˈlɪŋgw(ə)l/ *adj.* 1 able to speak three languages, esp. fluently. 2 spoken or written in three languages. □□ **trilingualism** *n.*

triliteral /traɪˈlɪtər(ə)l/ *adj.* 1 of three letters. 2 (of a Semitic language) having (most) roots with three consonants.

trilith /ˈtraɪlɪθ/ *n.* (also **trilithon** /-lɪθ(ə)n/) a monument consisting of three stones, esp. of two uprights and a lintel. □□ **trilithic** /-ˈlɪθɪk/ *adj.* [Gk *trilithon* (as TRI-, *lithos* stone)]

trill /trɪl/ *n. & v.* —*n.* 1 a quavering or vibratory sound, esp. a rapid alternation of sung or played notes. 2 a bird's warbling sound. 3 the pronunciation of *r* with a vibration of the tongue. —*v.* 1 *intr.* produce a trill. 2 *tr.* warble (a song) or pronounce (*r* etc.) with a trill. [It. *trillo* (n.), *trillare* (v.)]

trillion /ˈtrɪljən/ *n.* (*pl.* same or (in sense 3) **trillions**) 1 a million million (1,000,000,000,000 or 10^{12}). 2 (formerly, esp. *Brit.*) a million million million (1,000,000,000,000,000,000 or 10^{18}). 3 (in *pl.*) *colloq.* a very large number (*trillions of times*). ¶ Senses 1–2 correspond to the change in sense of *billion*. □□ **trillionth** *adj. & n.* [F *trillion* or It. *trilione* (as TRI-, MILLION), after *billion*]

æ *cat* ɑː *arm* e *bed* ɜː *her* ɪ *sit* iː *see* ɒ *hot* ɔː *saw* ʌ *run* ʊ *put* uː *too* ə *ago* aɪ *my*

trilobite /ˈtraɪləˌbaɪt/ n. any fossil marine arthropod of the class Trilobita of Palaeozoic times, characterized by a three-lobed body. [mod.L *Trilobites* (as TRI-, Gk *lobos* lobe)]

trilogy /ˈtrɪlədʒɪ/ n. (pl. **-ies**) **1** a group of three related literary or operatic works. **2** Gk Antiq. a set of three tragedies performed as a group. [Gk *trilogia* (as TRI-, -LOGY)]

trim /trɪm/ v., n., & adj. —v. (**trimmed, trimming**) **1** tr. **a** set in good order. **b** make neat or of the required size or form, esp. by cutting away irregular or unwanted parts. **2** tr. (foll. by *off*, *away*) remove by cutting off (such parts). **3** tr. **a** (often foll. by *up*) make (a person) neat in dress and appearance. **b** ornament or decorate (esp. clothing, a hat, etc. by adding ribbons, lace, etc.). **4** tr. adjust the balance of (a ship or aircraft) by the arrangement of its cargo etc. **5** tr. arrange (sails) to suit the wind. **6** intr. **a** associate oneself with currently prevailing views, esp. to advance oneself. **b** hold a middle course in politics or opinion. **7** tr. colloq. **a** rebuke sharply. **b** thrash. **c** get the better of in a bargain etc. —n. **1** the state or degree of readiness or fitness (*found everything in perfect trim*). **2** ornament or decorative material. **3** dress or equipment. **4** the act of trimming a person's hair. **5** the inclination of an aircraft to the horizontal. —adj. **1** neat or spruce. **2** in good order; well arranged or equipped. □ **in trim 1** looking smart, healthy, etc. **2** Naut. in good order. □□ **trimly** adv. **trimness** n. [perh. f. OE *trymman*, *trymian* make firm, arrange: but there is no connecting evidence between OE and 1500]

trimaran /ˈtraɪməˌræn/ n. a vessel like a catamaran, with three hulls side by side. [TRI- + CATAMARAN]

trimer /ˈtraɪmə(r)/ n. Chem. a polymer comprising three monomer units. □□ **trimeric** /-ˈmerɪk/ adj. [TRI- + -MER]

trimerous /ˈtraɪmərəs, ˈtrɪ-/ adj. having three parts.

trimester /traɪˈmestə(r)/ n. a period of three months, esp. of human gestation or US as a university term. □□ **trimestral** adj. **trimestrial** adj. [F *trimestre* f. L *trimestris* (as TRI-, -*mestris* f. *mensis* month)]

trimeter /ˈtrɪmɪtə(r)/ n. Prosody a verse of three measures. □□ **trimetric** /traɪˈmetrɪk/ adj. **trimetrical** /traɪˈmetrɪk(ə)l/ adj. [L *trimetrus* f. Gk *trimetros* (as TRI-, *metron* measure)]

trimmer /ˈtrɪmə(r)/ n. **1** a person who trims articles of dress. **2** a person who trims in politics etc.; a time-server. **3** an instrument for clipping etc. **4** Archit. a short piece of timber across an opening (e.g. for a hearth) to carry the ends of truncated joists. **5** a small capacitor etc. used to tune a radio set. **6** Austral. colloq. a striking or outstanding person or thing.

trimming /ˈtrɪmɪŋ/ n. **1** ornamentation or decoration, esp. for clothing. **2** (in pl.) colloq. the usual accompaniments, esp. of the main course of a meal. **3** (in pl.) pieces cut off in trimming.

trimorphism /traɪˈmɔːfɪz(ə)m/ n. Bot., Zool., & Crystallog. existence in three distinct forms. □□ **trimorphic** adj. **trimorphous** adj.

Trincomalee /ˌtrɪŋkəməˈliː/ the principal seaport of Sri Lanka; pop. (1981) 44,300. Described by Lord Nelson as the 'finest harbour in the world', Trincomalee was the chief British naval base in South-East Asia during the Second World War after the fall of Singapore.

trine /traɪn/ adj. & n. —adj. **1** threefold, triple; made up of three parts. **2** Astrol. denoting the aspect of two heavenly bodies 120° (one-third of the zodiac) apart. —n. Astrol. a trine aspect. □□ **trinal** adj. [ME f. OF *trin* *trine* f. L *trinus* threefold f. *tres* three]

Trinidad and Tobago /ˈtrɪnɪˌdæd, təˈbeɪɡəʊ/ a country in the West Indies consisting of the main island of Trinidad, off the NE coast of Venezuela, and the much smaller island of Tobago (further to the north-east); pop. (est. 1988) 1,279,900; official language, English; capital, Port of Spain. Discovered by Columbus in 1498, the islands became British during the Napoleonic Wars and were formally amalgamated as a Crown Colony in 1888. After a short period as a member of the West Indies Federation between 1958 and 1962, Trinidad and Tobago became an independent member State of the Commonwealth in 1962 and finally a republic in 1976. A substantial part of the national income is generated by the export of petroleum products while the capital Port of Spain is a major seaport. □□

Trinidadian /-ˈdeɪdɪən/ adj. & n. **Tobagan** adj. & n. **Tobagonian** /-ˈɡəʊnɪən/ adj. & n.

Trinitarian /ˌtrɪnɪˈteərɪən/ n. & adj. —n. a person who believes in the doctrine of the Trinity. —adj. of or relating to this belief. □□ **Trinitarianism** n.

trinitrotoluene /traɪˌnaɪtrəˈtɒljʊˌiːn/ n. (also **trinitrotoluol** /-ˈtɒljʊˌɒl/) = TNT.

trinity /ˈtrɪnɪtɪ/ n. (pl. **-ies**) **1** the state of being three. **2** a group of three. **3** (**the Trinity** or **Holy Trinity**) Theol. the three persons of the Christian Godhead (Father, Son, and Holy Spirit). □ **Trinity Brethren** the members of Trinity House (see separate entry). **Trinity Sunday** the next Sunday after Whit Sunday, celebrated in honour of the Holy Trinity. **Trinity term** Brit. the university and law term beginning after Easter. [ME f. OF *trinité* f. L *trinitas* -*tatis* triad (as TRINE)]

Trinity House a corporation founded in 1514, in the reign of Henry VIII, which has official responsibility for the licensing of ships' pilots in the UK and the erection and maintenance of lighthouses, buoys, etc., round the coasts of England and Wales. In Scotland this latter function is discharged by the Commissioners of Northern Lighthouses.

trinket /ˈtrɪŋkɪt/ n. a trifling ornament, jewel, etc., esp. one worn on the person. □□ **trinketry** n. [16th c.: orig. unkn.]

trinomial /traɪˈnəʊmɪəl/ adj. & n. —adj. consisting of three terms. —n. a scientific name or algebraic expression of three terms. [TRI- after BINOMIAL]

trio /ˈtriːəʊ/ n. (pl. **-os**) **1** a set or group of three. **2** Mus. **a** a composition for three performers. **b** a group of three performers. **c** the central, usu. contrastive, section of a minuet, scherzo, or march. **3** (in piquet) three aces, kings, queens, or jacks in one hand. [F & It. f. L *tres* three, after *duo*]

triode /ˈtraɪəʊd/ n. **1** a thermionic valve having three electrodes. (See DE FOREST.) **2** a semiconductor rectifier having three connections. [TRI- + ELECTRODE]

trioecious /traɪˈiːʃəs/ adj. Bot. having male, female, and hermaphrodite organs each on separate plants. [TRI- + Gk *oikos* house]

triolet /ˈtriːəlɪt, ˈtraɪəlɪt/ n. a poem of eight (usu. eight-syllabled) lines rhyming *abaaabab*, the first line recurring as the fourth and seventh and the second as the eighth. [F (as TRIO)]

trioxide /traɪˈɒksaɪd/ n. Chem. an oxide containing three oxygen atoms.

trip /trɪp/ v. & n. —v.intr. & tr. (**tripped, tripping**) **1** intr. **a** walk or dance with quick light steps. **b** (of a rhythm etc.) run lightly. **2 a** intr. & tr. (often foll. by *up*) stumble or cause to stumble, esp. by catching or entangling the feet. **b** intr. & tr. (foll. by *up*) make or cause to make a slip or blunder. **3** tr. detect (a person) in a blunder. **4** intr. make an excursion to a place. **5** tr. release (part of a machine) suddenly by knocking aside a catch etc. **6 a** release and raise (an anchor) from the bottom by means of a cable. **b** turn (a yard etc.) from a horizontal to a vertical position for lowering. **7** intr. colloq. have a hallucinatory experience caused by a drug. —n. **1** a journey or excursion, esp. for pleasure. **2 a** a stumble or blunder. **b** the act of tripping or the state of being tripped up. **3** a nimble step. **4** colloq. a hallucinatory experience caused by a drug. **5** a contrivance for a tripping mechanism etc. □ **trip-hammer** a large tilt-hammer operated by tripping. **trip-wire** a wire stretched close to the ground, operating an alarm etc. when disturbed. [ME f. OF *triper*, *tripper*, f. MDu. *trippen* skip, hop]

tripartite /traɪˈpɑːtaɪt/ adj. **1** consisting of three parts. **2** shared by or involving three parties. **3** Bot. (of a leaf) divided into three segments almost to the base. □□ **tripartitely** adv. **tripartition** /-ˈtɪʃ(ə)n/ n. [ME f. L *tripartitus* (as TRI-, *partitus* past part. of *partiri* divide)]

tripe /traɪp/ n. **1** the first or second stomach of a ruminant, esp. an ox, as food. **2** colloq. nonsense, rubbish (*don't talk such tripe*). [ME f. OF, of unkn. orig.]

triphibious /traɪˈfɪbɪəs/ adj. (of military operations) on land, on sea, and in the air. [irreg. f. TRI- after *amphibious*]

triphthong /ˈtrɪfθɒŋ/ n. **1** a union of three vowels (letters or sounds) pronounced in one syllable (as in *fire*). **2** three vowel characters representing the sound of a single vowel (as in b*eau*). □□ **triphthongal** /-'θɒŋg(ə)l/ *adj.* [F *triphtongue* (as TRI-, DIPHTHONG)]

Tripitaka /ˌtrɪpɪ'tɑːkə/ *n.* the sacred canon of Theravada Buddhism, written in the Pali language. [Skr., = the three baskets or collections]

triplane /'traɪpleɪn/ *n.* an early type of aeroplane having three sets of wings, one above the other.

triple /'trɪp(ə)l/ *adj., n.,* & *v.* —*adj.* **1** consisting of three usu. equal parts or things; threefold. **2** involving three parties. **3** three times as much or many (*triple the amount; triple thickness*). —*n.* **1** a threefold number or amount. **2** a set of three. **3** (in *pl.*) a peal of changes on seven bells. —*v.tr.* & *intr.* multiply or increase by three. □ **triple crown 1** *RC Ch.* the pope's tiara. **2** the act of winning all three of a group of important events in horse-racing, rugby football, etc. **triple jump** an athletic exercise or contest comprising a hop, a step, and a jump. **triple play** *Baseball* the act of putting out three runners in a row. **triple point** the temperature and pressure at which the solid, liquid, and vapour phases of a pure substance can coexist in equilibrium. **triple rhyme** a rhyme including three syllables. **triple time** *Mus.* that with three beats to the bar; waltz time. □□ **triply** *adv.* [OF *triple* or L *triplus* f. Gk *triplous*]

Triple Alliance an alliance of three States etc.: in 1668, between England, The Netherlands, and Sweden against France; in 1717, between Britain, France, and the Netherlands against Spain; in 1865, between Argentina, Brazil, and Uruguay against Paraguay; in 1882, between Germany, Austria–Hungary, and Italy against France and Russia.

Triple Entente an early 20th-c. alliance between Great Britain, France, and Russia. Originally a series of loose agreements, the Entente began to assume the nature of a more formal alliance as the prospect of war with the Central Powers became more likely. The original Entente Cordiale with France was signed in 1904, the agreement with Russia in 1907.

triplet /'trɪplɪt/ *n.* **1** each of three children or animals born at one birth. **2** a set of three things, esp. of equal notes played in the time of two or of verses rhyming together. [TRIPLE + -ET[1], after *doublet*]

triplex /'trɪpleks/ *adj.* & *n.* —*adj.* triple or threefold. —*n.* (**Triplex**) *Brit. propr.* toughened or laminated safety glass for car windows etc. [L *triplex -plicis* (as TRI-, *plic-* fold)]

triplicate *adj., n.,* & *v.* —*adj.* /'trɪplɪkət/ **1** existing in three examples or copies. **2** having three corresponding parts. **3** tripled. —*n.* /'trɪplɪkət/ each of a set of three copies or corresponding parts. —*v.tr.* /'trɪplɪˌkeɪt/ **1** make in three copies. **2** multiply by three. □ **in triplicate** consisting of three exact copies. □□ **triplication** /-'keɪʃ(ə)n/ *n.* [ME f. L *triplicatus* past part. of *triplicare* (as TRIPLEX)]

triplicity /trɪ'plɪsɪtɪ/ *n.* (*pl.* **-ies**) **1** the state of being triple. **2** a group of three things. **3** *Astrol.* a set of three zodiacal signs. [ME f. LL *triplicitas* f. L TRIPLEX]

triploid /'trɪplɔɪd/ *n.* & *adj. Biol.* —*n.* an organism or cell having three times the haploid set of chromosomes. —*adj.* of or being a triploid. [mod.L *triploides* f. Gk (as TRIPLE)]

triploidy /'trɪplɔɪdɪ/ *n.* the condition of being triploid.

tripmeter /'trɪpˌmiːtə(r)/ *n.* a vehicle instrument that can be set to record the distance of individual journeys.

tripod /'traɪpɒd/ *n.* **1** a three-legged stand for supporting a camera etc. **2** a stool, table, or utensil resting on three feet or legs. **3** *Gk Antiq.* a bronze altar at Delphi on which a priestess sat to utter oracles. □□ **tripodal** /'trɪpəd(ə)l/ *adj.* [L *tripus tripodis* f. Gk *tripous* (as TRI-, *pous podos* foot)]

Tripoli[1] /'trɪpəlɪ/ the capital and chief port of Libya; pop. (1984) 990,700.

Tripoli[2] /'trɪpəlɪ/ a seaport in NW Lebanon; pop. (1980) 175,000.

tripoli /'trɪpəlɪ/ *n.* = *rotten-stone*. [F f. TRIPOLI[1], TRIPOLI[2]]

Tripolitania /ˌtrɪpɒlɪ'teɪnɪə/ the region surrounding Tripoli in North Africa, now part of Libya. □□ **Tripolitanian** *adj.* & *n.* [L *Tripolis* three cities, i.e. the ancient cities of Oea (now Tripoli), Sabratha, and Leptis Magna]

tripos /'traɪpɒs/ *n. Brit.* (at Cambridge University) the honours examination for the BA degree. [as TRIPOD, with ref. to the stool on which graduates sat to deliver a satirical speech at the degree ceremony]

tripper /'trɪpə(r)/ *n.* **1** *Brit.* a person who goes on a pleasure trip or excursion. **2** *colloq.* a person experiencing hallucinatory effects of a drug.

triptych /'trɪptɪk/ *n.* **1 a** a picture or relief carving on three panels, usu. hinged vertically together and often used as an altarpiece. **b** a set of three associated pictures placed in this way. **2** a set of three writing-tablets hinged or tied together. **3** a set of three artistic works. [TRI-, after DIPTYCH]

triptyque /trɪp'tiːk/ *n.* a customs permit serving as a passport for a motor vehicle. [F, as TRIPTYCH (orig. having three sections)]

Tripura /'trɪpʊrə/ a State in NE India; pop. (1981) 2,060,200; capital, Agartala.

triquetra /traɪ'ketrə/ *n.* (*pl.* **triquetrae** /-triː/) a symmetrical ornament of three interlaced arcs. [L, fem. of *triquetrus* three-cornered]

trireme /'traɪriːm/ *n.* an ancient Greek warship, with three files of oarsmen on each side. [F *trirème* or L *triremis* (as TRI-, *remus* oar)]

trisaccharide /traɪ'sækəˌraɪd/ *n. Chem.* a sugar consisting of three linked monosaccharides.

Trisagion /trɪ'sægɪɒn/ *n.* a hymn, esp. in the Eastern Churches, with a triple invocation of God as holy. [ME f. Gk, neut. of *trisagios* f. *tris* thrice + *hagios* holy]

trisect /traɪ'sekt/ *v.tr.* cut or divide into three (usu. equal) parts. □□ **trisection** *n.* **trisector** *n.* [TRI- + L *secare sect-* cut]

trishaw /'traɪʃɔː/ *n.* a light three-wheeled pedalled vehicle used in the Far East. [TRI- + RICKSHAW]

triskelion /trɪ'skelɪən/ *n.* a symbolic figure of three legs or lines from a common centre. [Gk TRI- + *skelos* leg]

trismus /'trɪzməs/ *n. Med.* a variety of tetanus with tonic spasm of the jaw muscles causing the mouth to remain tightly closed. [mod.L f. Gk *trismos* = *trigmos* a scream, grinding]

Tristan da Cunha /ˌtrɪst(ə)n də 'kuːnjə/ the largest of a small group of volcanic islands in the South Atlantic, 2,112 km (1,320 miles) south-west of St Helena of which it is a dependency; pop. (1988) 313. In 1961 the entire population was evacuated when the island volcano erupted.

triste /triːst/ *adj.* sad, melancholy, dreary. [F f. L *tristis*]

Tristram /'trɪstrəm/ (in medieval legend) a knight who was the lover of Iseult (see ISEULT).

trisyllable /traɪ'sɪləb(ə)l, trɪ-/ *n.* a word or metrical foot of three syllables. □□ **trisyllabic** /-'læbɪk/ *adj.*

tritagonist /traɪ'tægənɪst, trɪ-/ *n.* the third actor in a Greek play (cf. DEUTERAGONIST). [Gk *tritagōnistēs* (as TRITO-, *agōnistēs* actor)]

trite /traɪt/ *adj.* (of a phrase, opinion, etc.) hackneyed, worn out by constant repetition. □□ **tritely** *adv.* **triteness** *n.* [L *tritus* past part. of *terere* rub]

tritiate /'trɪtɪˌeɪt/ *v.tr.* replace the ordinary hydrogen in (a substance) by tritium. □□ **tritiation** /-'eɪʃ(ə)n/ *n.*

tritium /'trɪtɪəm/ *n. Chem.* a radioactive isotope of hydrogen with a mass about three times that of ordinary hydrogen. ¶ Symb.: T. [mod.L f. Gk *tritos* third]

trito- /'traɪtəʊ, 'trɪtəʊ/ *comb. form* third. [Gk *tritos* third]

Triton /'traɪt(ə)n/ *Gk Mythol.* the son of Poseidon and Amphitrite. —*n.* **1** *Gk Mythol.* a member of a class of minor sea-gods, usually represented as a man with a fish's (sometimes a horse's) tail carrying a trident and shell-trumpet. (See MERMAID.) **2** (**triton**) any marine gastropod mollusc of the family Cymatiidae, with a long conical shell. **3** (**triton**) a newt. [L f. Gk *Tritōn*]

triton /'traɪt(ə)n/ *n.* a nucleus of a tritium atom, consisting of a proton and two neutrons.

tritone /'traɪtəʊn/ *n. Mus.* an interval of an augmented fourth, comprising three tones.

triturate /'trɪtjʊˌreɪt/ *v.tr.* **1** grind to a fine powder. **2** masticate thoroughly. □□ **triturable** *adj.* **trituration** /-'reɪʃ(ə)n/ *n.* **triturator** *n.* [L *triturare* thresh corn f. *tritura* rubbing (as TRITE)]

triumph /ˈtraɪəmf, -ʌmf/ n. & v. —n. **1 a** the state of being victorious or successful (returned home in triumph). **b** a great success or achievement. **2** a supreme example (a triumph of engineering). **3** joy at success; exultation (could see triumph in her face). **4** the processional entry of a victorious general into ancient Rome. —v.intr. **1** (often foll. by over) gain a victory; be successful; prevail. **2** ride in triumph. **3** (often foll. by over) exult. [ME f. OF triumphe (n.), triumpher (v.), f. L triump(h)us prob. f. Gk thriambos hymn to Bacchus]

triumphal /traɪˈʌmf(ə)l/ adj. of or used in or celebrating a triumph. [ME f. OF triumphal or L triumphalis (as TRIUMPH)]

triumphant /traɪˈʌmf(ə)nt/ adj. **1** victorious or successful. **2** exultant. □□ **triumphantly** adv. [ME f. OF triumphant or L triumphare (as TRIUMPH)]

triumvir /ˈtraɪəmvɪə(r), -ˈʌmvə(r)/ n. (pl. **triumvirs** or **triumviri** /-raɪ/) **1** each of three men holding a joint office. **2** a member of a triumvirate. □□ **triumviral** adj. [L, orig. in pl. triumviri, back-form. f. trium virorum genit. of tres viri three men]

triumvirate /traɪˈʌmvɪrət/ n. **1** a board or ruling group of three men, esp. in ancient Rome. The term is used specifically of the office to which Antony, Lepidus, and Octavian were appointed in 43 BC (the **Second Triumvirate**) and, improperly, of the unofficial coalition of Julius Caesar, Pompey, and Crassus in 60 BC (the **First Triumvirate**). **2** the office of triumvir.

triune /ˈtraɪjuːn/ adj. three in one, esp. with ref. to the Trinity. □□ **triunity** /-ˈjuːnɪtɪ/ n. (pl. **-ies**). [TRI- + L unus one]

trivalent /traɪˈveɪlənt/ adj. Chem. having a valency of three; tervalent. □□ **trivalency** n.

Trivandrum /trɪˈvændrəm/ the capital of the State of Kerala in SW India; pop. (1981) 520,000.

trivet /ˈtrɪvɪt/ n. **1** an iron tripod or bracket for a cooking pot or kettle to stand on. **2** an iron bracket designed to hook on to bars of a grate for a similar purpose. □ **as right as a trivet** colloq. in a perfectly good state, esp. healthy. **trivet table** a table with three feet. [ME trevet, app. f. L tripes (as TRI-, pes pedis foot)]

trivia /ˈtrɪvɪə/ n.pl. trifles or trivialities. [mod.L, pl. of TRIVIUM, infl. by TRIVIAL]

trivial /ˈtrɪvɪəl/ adj. **1** of small value or importance; trifling (raised trivial objections). **2** (of a person) concerned only with trivial things. **3** archaic commonplace or humdrum (the trivial round of daily life). **4** Biol. & Chem. of a name: **a** popular; not scientific. **b** specific, as opposed to generic. **5** Math. giving rise to no difficulty or interest. □□ **triviality** /-ˈælɪtɪ/ n. (pl. **-ies**). **trivially** adv. **trivialness** n. [L trivialis commonplace f. trivium: see TRIVIUM]

trivialize /ˈtrɪvɪəlaɪz/ v.tr. (also **-ise**) make trivial or apparently trivial; minimize. □□ **trivialization** /-ˈzeɪʃ(ə)n/ n.

trivium /ˈtrɪvɪəm/ n. hist. a medieval university course of grammar, rhetoric, and logic. [L, = place where three roads meet (as TRI-, via road)]

tri-weekly /traɪˈwiːklɪ/ adj. produced or occurring three times a week or every three weeks.

-trix /trɪks/ suffix (pl. **-trices** /trɪsɪz, ˈtraɪsiːz/ or **-trixes**) forming feminine agent nouns corresponding to masculine nouns in -tor, esp. in Law (executrix). [L -trix -tricis]

tRNA abbr. transfer RNA.

Troad /ˈtrəʊæd/ an ancient region of NW Asia Minor of which ancient Troy was the chief city.

trocar /ˈtrəʊkɑː(r)/ n. an instrument used for withdrawing fluid from a body cavity, esp. in oedema etc. [F trois-quarts, trocart f. trois three + carre side, face of an instrument, after its triangular form]

trochaic /trəˈkeɪɪk/ adj. & n. Prosody —adj. of or using trochees. —n. (usu. in pl.) trochaic verse. [L trochaicus f. Gk trokhaikos (as TROCHEE)]

trochal /ˈtrəʊk(ə)l/ adj. Zool. wheel-shaped. □ **trochal disc** Zool. the retractable disc on the head of a rotifer bearing a crown of cilia, used for drawing in food or for propulsion. [Gk trokhos wheel]

trochanter /trəˈkæntə(r)/ n. **1** Anat. any of several bony protuberances by which muscles are attached to the upper part of the thigh-bone. **2** Zool. the second segment of the leg in insects. [F f. Gk trokhantēr f. trekhō run]

troche /trəʊʃ/ n. a small usu. circular medicated tablet or lozenge. [obs. trochisk f. OF trochisque f. LL trochiscus f. Gk trokhiskos dimin. of trokhos wheel]

trochee /ˈtrəʊkiː, -kɪ/ n. Prosody a foot consisting of one long or stressed syllable followed by one short or unstressed syllable. [L trochaeus f. Gk trokhaios (pous) running (foot) f. trekhō run]

trochlea /ˈtrɒklɪə/ n. (pl. **trochleae** /-lɪiː/) Anat. a pulley-like structure or arrangement of parts, e.g. the groove at the lower end of the humerus. □□ **trochlear** adj. [L, = pulley f. Gk trokhilia]

trochoid /ˈtrəʊkɔɪd/ adj. & n. —adj. **1** Anat. rotating on its own axis. **2** Geom. (of a curve) traced by a point on a radius of a circle rotating along a straight line or another circle. —n. a trochoid joint or curve. □□ **trochoidal** /-ˈkɔɪd(ə)l/ adj. [Gk trokhoeidēs wheel-like f. trokhos wheel]

trod past and past part. of TREAD.

trodden past part. of TREAD.

trog /trɒg/ n. sl. a term of contempt for a person; a lout or hooligan. [abbr. of TROGLODYTE]

troglodyte /ˈtrɒglədaɪt/ n. **1** a cave-dweller, esp. of prehistoric times. **2** a hermit. **3** derog. a wilfully obscurantist or old-fashioned person. □□ **troglodytic** /-ˈdɪtɪk/ adj. **troglodytical** /-ˈdɪtɪk(ə)l/ adj. **troglodytism** n. [L troglodyta f. Gk trōglodutēs f. the name of an Ethiopian people, after trōglē hole]

trogon /ˈtrəʊgɒn/ n. any tropical bird of the family Trogonidae, with a long tail and brilliantly coloured plumage. [mod.L f. Gk trōgōn f. trōgō gnaw]

troika /ˈtrɔɪkə/ n. **1 a** a Russian vehicle with a team of three horses abreast. **b** this team. **2** a group of three people, esp. as an administrative council. [Russ. f. troe three]

troilism /ˈtrɔɪlɪz(ə)m/ n. sexual activity involving three participants. [perh. f. F trois three]

Troilus /ˈtrɔɪləs/ **1** Gk legend the son of Priam and Hecuba, killed by Achilles. **2** (in medieval legend) the forsaken lover of Cressida.

Trojan /ˈtrəʊdʒ(ə)n/ adj. & n. —adj. of or relating to ancient Troy. —n. **1** a native or inhabitant of Troy. **2** a person who works, fights, etc. courageously (works like a Trojan). □ **Trojan Horse 1** a hollow wooden horse said to have been used by the Greeks to enter Troy. **2** a person or device planted to bring about an enemy's downfall. **Trojan War** the ten-year siege of Troy by the Greeks in Greek legend (see TROY), which ended with the capture of the city after a band of Greek warriors had entered by a trick, concealed in a hollow wooden horse so large that the city walls had had to be breached for it to be drawn inside. [ME f. L Troianus f. Troia Troy]

troll¹ /trəʊl/ n. (in Scandinavian folklore) a fabulous being, esp. a giant or dwarf dwelling in a cave. [ON & Sw. troll, Da. trold]

troll² /trəʊl/ v. & n. —v. **1** intr. sing out in a carefree jovial manner. **2** tr. & intr. fish by drawing bait along in the water. **3** intr. esp. Brit. walk, stroll. —n. **1** the act of trolling for fish. **2 a** line or bait used in this. □□ **troller** n. [ME 'stroll, roll': cf. OF troller quest, MHG trollen stroll]

trolley /ˈtrɒlɪ/ n. (pl. **-eys**) **1** esp. Brit. a table, stand, or basket on wheels or castors for serving food, transporting luggage or shopping, gathering purchases in a supermarket, etc. **2** esp. Brit. a low truck running on rails. **3** (in full **trolley-wheel**) a wheel attached to a pole etc. used for collecting current from an overhead electric wire to drive a vehicle. **4 a** US = trolley-car. **b** Brit. = trolley bus. □ **trolley bus** Brit. an electric bus running on the road and using a trolley-wheel. **trolley-car** US an electric tram using a trolley-wheel. [of dial. orig., perh. f. TROLL²]

trollop /ˈtrɒləp/ n. **1** a disreputable girl or woman. **2** a prostitute. □□ **trollopish** adj. **trollopy** adj. [17th c.: perh. rel. to TRULL]

Trollope /ˈtrɒləp/, Anthony (1815–82), English novelist. His career in the General Post Office began in London in 1834 and took him to Ireland (1841–59) and other parts of the world; in this capacity he introduced the pillar-box for letters. He retired in 1867 and stood unsuccessfully for Parliament as a Liberal candidate in 1868. His literary career became established with his fourth novel *The Warden* (1855), the first of the six 'Barsetshire' novels which included *Barchester Towers* (1857) and ended with *The Last Chronicle of Barset* (1867); they are set in an imaginary English West Country and portray a solid rural society of curates and landed gentry, with characters who reappear in one or more of the series. This technique he developed in his six political 'Palliser' novels; in these, which begin with *Can You Forgive Her?* (1864) and include *The Eustace Diamonds* (1873), he expresses his own political views. Trollope was admired for his treatment of family and professional life, the variety and delicacy of his heroines, and his accurate pictures of social life. His remarkable output included 47 novels, travel books, biographies, and short stories.

trombone /trɒmˈbəʊn/ *n*. **1 a** a large brass wind instrument with a forward-pointing extendable slide, the oldest brass instrument to possess a full chromatic compass. The trombone was introduced towards the mid-15th c., when it was often called 'sackbut', and was a favourite member of both instrumental and sacred and secular vocal music, particularly in Italy. It never really lost its early popularity, and its association with church music developed in 18th-c. Germany and Austria, leading Mozart to bring it in for dramatic and solemn effect in *Don Giovanni* and in the 'Tuba mirum' of his Requiem Mass. **b** its player. **2** an organ stop with the quality of a trombone. □□ **trombonist** *n*. [F or It. f. It. *tromba* TRUMPET]

trommel /ˈtrɒm(ə)l/ *n*. Mining a revolving cylindrical sieve for cleaning ore. [G, = drum]

tromometer /trəˈmɒmɪtə(r)/ *n*. an instrument for measuring very slight earthquake shocks. [Gk *tromos* trembling + -METER]

trompe /trɒmp/ *n*. an apparatus for producing a blast in a furnace by using falling water to displace air. [F, = trumpet: see TRUMP[1]]

trompe-l'œil /trɔ̃pˈləːɪ/ *n*. a still-life painting etc. designed to give an illusion of reality. [F, lit. 'deceives the eye']

Tromsø /ˈtrɒmsɜː/ the principal city of Arctic Norway, situated on an island just west of the mainland; pop. (1988) 49,450.

-tron /trɒn/ *suffix* Physics forming nouns denoting: **1** an elementary particle (*positron*). **2** a particle accelerator. **3** a thermionic valve. [after ELECTRON]

Trondheim /ˈtrɒndhaɪm/ a fishing port and the second-largest city of Norway; pop. (1988) 135,500. Trondheim is situated on a peninsula in west central Norway. It was the capital city during the Viking period, founded by Olaf I Tryggvason and becoming a pilgrimage centre as the burial place of Olaf II Haraldsson (St Olaf) who died in battle nearby in 1030.

troop /truːp/ *n*. & *v*. —*n*. **1** an assembled company; an assemblage of people or animals. **2** (in *pl*.) soldiers or armed forces. **3** a cavalry unit commanded by a captain. **4** a unit of artillery and armoured formation. **5** a grouping of three or more Scout patrols. —*v*. **1** *intr*. (foll. by *in*, *out*, *off*, etc.) come together or move in large numbers. **2** *tr*. form (a regiment) into troops. □ **troop the colour** esp. Brit. transfer a flag ceremonially at a public mounting of garrison guards. **troop-ship** a ship used for transporting troops. [F *troupe*, back-form. f. *troupeau* dimin. of med.L *troppus* flock, prob. of Gmc orig.]

trooper /ˈtruːpə(r)/ *n*. **1** a private soldier in a cavalry or armoured unit. **2** *Austral*. & *US* a mounted or motor-borne policeman. **3** a cavalry horse. **4** esp. Brit. a troop-ship. □ **swear like a trooper** swear extensively or forcefully.

tropaeolum /trəˈpiːələm/ *n*. a trailing or climbing plant of the genus *Tropaeolum*, with trumpet-shaped yellow, orange, or red flowers. [mod.L f. L *tropaeum* trophy, with ref. to the likeness of the flower and leaf to a helmet and shield]

trope /trəʊp/ *n*. a figurative (e.g. metaphorical or ironical) use of a word. [L *tropus* f. Gk *tropos* turn, way, trope f. *trepō* turn]

trophic /ˈtrɒfɪk/ *adj*. of or concerned with nutrition (*trophic nerves*). [Gk *trophikos* f. *trophē* nourishment f. *trephō* nourish]

-trophic /ˈtrɒfɪk/ *comb*. *form* relating to nutrition.

tropho- /ˈtrɒfəʊ/ *comb*. *form* nourishment. [Gk *trophē*: see TROPHIC]

trophoblast /ˈtrɒfəʊˌblæst/ *n*. a layer of tissue on the outside of a mammalian blastula, providing nourishment to an embryo.

trophy /ˈtrəʊfɪ/ *n*. (*pl*. **-ies**) **1** a cup or other decorative object awarded as a prize or memento of victory or success in a contest etc. **2** a memento or souvenir, e.g. a deer's antlers, taken in hunting. **3** *Gk* & *Rom*. Antiq. the weapons etc. of a defeated army set up as a memorial of victory. **4** an ornamental group of symbolic or typical objects arranged for display. □□ **trophied** *adj*. (also in *comb*.). [F *trophée* f. L *trophaeum* f. Gk *tropaion* f. *tropē* rout f. *trepō* turn]

tropic /ˈtrɒpɪk/ *n*. & *adj*. —*n*. **1** the parallel of latitude 23° 27′ north (**tropic of Cancer**) or south (**tropic of Capricorn**) of the Equator. **2** each of two corresponding circles on the celestial sphere where the sun appears to turn after reaching its greatest declination. **3** (**the Tropics**) the region between the tropics of Cancer and Capricorn. —*adj*. **1** = TROPICAL 1. **2** of tropism. □ **tropic bird** any sea bird of the family Phaethontidae, with very long central tail-feathers. [ME f. L *tropicus* f. Gk *tropikos* f. *tropē* turning f. *trepō* turn]

-tropic /ˈtrɒpɪk/ *comb*. *form* **1** = -TROPHIC. **2** turning towards (*heliotropic*).

tropical /ˈtrɒpɪk(ə)l/ *adj*. **1** of, peculiar to, or suggesting the Tropics (*tropical fish*; *tropical diseases*). **2** very hot; passionate, luxuriant. **3** of or by way of a trope. □ **tropical year** see YEAR 1. □□ **tropically** *adv*.

tropism /ˈtrəʊpɪz(ə)m/ *n*. Biol. the turning of all or part of an organism in a particular direction in response to an external stimulus. [Gk *tropos* turning f. *trepō* turn]

tropology /trəˈpɒlədʒɪ/ *n*. **1** the figurative use of words. **2** figurative interpretation, esp. of the Scriptures. □□ **tropological** /ˌtrɒpəˈlɒdʒɪk(ə)l/ *adj*. [LL *tropologia* f. Gk *tropologia* (as TROPE)]

tropopause /ˈtrɒpəˌpɔːz, ˈtrəʊ-/ *n*. the interface between the troposphere and the stratosphere. [TROPOSPHERE + PAUSE]

troposphere /ˈtrɒpəˌsfɪə(r), ˈtrəʊ-/ *n*. a layer of atmospheric air extending from about 6–10 km upwards from the earth's surface, in which the temperature falls with increasing height (cf. STRATOSPHERE, IONOSPHERE). □□ **tropospheric** /-ˈsfɛrɪk/ *adj*. [Gk *tropos* turning + SPHERE]

troppo[1] /ˈtrɒpəʊ/ *adv*. Mus. too much (qualifying a tempo indication). □ **ma non troppo** but not too much so. [It.]

troppo[2] /ˈtrɒpəʊ/ *adj*. Austral. sl. mentally ill from exposure to a tropical climate.

Trossachs /ˈtrɒsəks/, **the** a picturesque wooded valley in Central region, Scotland, between Loch Achray and the lower end of Loch Katrine.

Trot /trɒt/ *n*. colloq. usu. derog. a Trotskyist. [abbr.]

trot /trɒt/ *v*. & *n*. —*v*. (**trotted**, **trotting**) **1** *intr*. (of a person) run at a moderate pace esp. with short strides. **2** *intr*. (of a horse) proceed at a steady pace faster than a walk lifting each diagonal pair of legs alternately. **3** *intr*. colloq. walk or go. **4** *tr*. cause (a horse or person) to trot. **5** *tr*. traverse (a distance) at a trot. —*n*. **1** the action or exercise of trotting (*proceed at a trot*; *went for a trot*). **2** (**the trots**) *sl*. an attack of diarrhoea. **3** a brisk steady movement or occupation. **4** (in *pl*.) Austral. colloq. **a** trotting-races. **b** a meeting for these. □ **on the trot** colloq. **1** continually busy (*kept them on the trot*). **2** in succession (*five weeks on the trot*). **trot out 1** cause (a horse) to trot to show his paces. **2** produce or introduce (as if) for inspection and approval, esp. tediously or repeatedly. [ME f. OF *troter* f. Rmc & med.L *trottare*, of Gmc orig.]

troth /trəʊθ/ *n*. archaic **1** faith, loyalty. **2** truth. □ **pledge** (or **plight**) **one's troth** pledge one's word esp. in marriage or betrothal. [ME *trowthe*, for OE *trēowth* TRUTH]

Trotsky /ˈtrɒtskɪ/, Leon, originally Lev Davidovich Bronstein (1879–1940), Russian revolutionary. An early member of the Bolshevik party, Trotsky became Lenin's principal lieutenant in the troubled years following the Russian Revolution, organizing the Red Armies which eventually defeated the opposing Whites in the Russian Civil War. After Lenin's death, he unsuccessfully contested the leadership with Stalin and was eventually banished in 1929. For some years he moved around the world, settling in Mexico in 1937, but was murdered there by a Stalinist assassin three years later.

Trotskyist /ˈtrɒtskɪˌɪst/ *n*. a supporter of Leon Trotsky, who believed in the theory of continuing revolution rather than the more pragmatic ideas of State Communism generally accepted in Russia in the post-Revolutionary era. With the defeat and disgrace of their leader in the power struggle following the death of Lenin, the Trotskyists were generally branded by the successful Stalinists as perverters of the Revolution. Trotskyism has generally included a fair mixture of anarchist–syndicalist ideology, but the term has come to be used indiscriminately to describe all forms of radical left-wing Communism. □□ **Trotskyism** n. **Trotskyite** n. derog.

trotter /ˈtrɒtə(r)/ n. **1** a horse bred or trained for trotting. **2** (usu. in pl.) **a** an animal's foot as food (pig's trotters). **b** joc. a human foot.

trotting /ˈtrɒtɪŋ/ n. a form of horse-racing (also called harness-racing) in which a horse pulls a two-wheeled vehicle (a sulky) and its driver. Trotting-races were held in Asia Minor as early as 1350 BC. In the Roman Empire chariot racing became one of the favourite sports, and it is probably from the Romans that trotting took its roots as a worldwide sport.

troubadour /ˈtruːbə,dɔː(r)/ n. **1** any of a number of French medieval lyric poets composing and singing in Provençal during the 12th and early 13th c. (and perhaps earlier), famous for the complexity of their verse forms and for the conception of chivalry and courtly love which prevails in their poems. They flourished in the courts of Spain, Italy, and France and through their influence on the northern French poets and on the German Minnesingers they had a major effect on all the subsequent development of European lyric poetry. As well as love poetry they also composed moralizing, satirical, and political poems (sirventes), and military poems. **2** a singer or poet. [F f. Prov. trobador f. trobar find, invent, compose in verse]

trouble /ˈtrʌb(ə)l/ n. & v. —n. **1** difficulty or distress; vexation, affliction (am having trouble with my car). **2 a** inconvenience; unpleasant exertion; bother (went to a lot of trouble). **b** a cause of this (the child was no trouble). **3** a cause of annoyance or concern (the trouble with you is that you can't say no). **4** a faulty condition or operation (kidney trouble; engine trouble). **5 a** fighting, disturbance (crowd trouble; don't want any trouble). **b** (in pl.) political or social unrest, public disturbances; **the Troubles** any of various rebellions, civil wars, and unrest in Ireland, especially in 1919–23 and (in Northern Ireland) from 1968. **6** disagreement, strife (is having trouble at home). —v. **1** tr. cause distress or anxiety to; disturb (were much troubled by their debts). **2** intr. be disturbed or worried (don't trouble about it). **3** tr. afflict; cause pain etc. to (am troubled with arthritis). **4** tr. & intr. (often refl.) subject or be subjected to inconvenience or unpleasant exertion (sorry to trouble you; don't trouble yourself; don't trouble to explain). □ **ask (or look) for trouble** colloq. invite trouble or difficulty by one's actions, behaviour, etc.; behave rashly or indiscreetly. **be no trouble** cause no inconvenience etc. **go to the trouble** (or **some trouble** etc.) exert oneself to do something. **in trouble 1** involved in a matter likely to bring censure or punishment. **2** colloq. pregnant while unmarried. **take trouble** (or **the trouble**) exert oneself to do something. **trouble and strife** rhyming sl. wife. **trouble spot** a place where difficulties regularly occur. □□ **troubler** n. [ME f. OF truble (n.), trubler, turbler (v.) ult. f. L turbidus TURBID]

troubled /ˈtrʌb(ə)ld/ adj. showing, experiencing, or reflecting trouble, anxiety, etc. (a troubled mind; a troubled childhood).

troublemaker /ˈtrʌb(ə)l,meɪkə(r)/ n. a person who habitually causes trouble. □□ **troublemaking** n.

troubleshooter /ˈtrʌb(ə)l,ʃuːtə(r)/ n. **1** a mediator in industrial or diplomatic etc. disputes. **2** a person who traces and corrects faults in machinery etc. □□ **troubleshooting** n.

troublesome /ˈtrʌb(ə)lsəm/ adj. **1** causing trouble. **2** vexing, annoying. □□ **troublesomely** adv. **troublesomeness** n.

troublous /ˈtrʌbləs/ adj. archaic or literary full of troubles; agitated, disturbed (troublous times). [ME f. OF troubleus (as TROUBLE)]

trough /trɒf/ n. **1** a long narrow open receptacle for water, animal feed, etc. **2** a channel for conveying a liquid. **3** an elongated region of low barometric pressure. **4** a hollow between two wave crests. **5** the time of lowest economic performance etc. **6** a region around the minimum on a curve of variation of a quantity. **7** a low point or depression. [OE trog f. Gmc]

trounce /traʊns/ v.tr. **1** defeat heavily. **2** beat, thrash. **3** punish severely. □□ **trouncer** n. **trouncing** n. [16th c., = afflict: orig. unkn.]

troupe /truːp/ n. a company of actors or acrobats etc. [F, = TROOP]

trouper /ˈtruːpə(r)/ n. **1** a member of a theatrical troupe. **2** a staunch colleague.

trousers /ˈtraʊzəz/ n.pl. **1** an outer garment reaching from the waist usu. to the ankles, divided into two parts to cover the legs. **2** (**trouser**) (attrib.) designating parts of this (trouser leg). □ **trouser-clip** = bicycle-clip. **trouser suit** a woman's suit of trousers and jacket. **wear the trousers** be the dominant partner in a marriage. □□ **trousered** adj. **trouserless** adj. [archaic trouse (sing.) f. Ir. & Gael. triubhas TREWS: pl. form after drawers]

trousseau /ˈtruːsəʊ/ n. (pl. **trousseaus** or **trousseaux** /-səʊz/) the clothes collected by a bride for her marriage. [F, lit. bundle, dimin. of trousse TRUSS]

trout /traʊt/ n. (pl. same or **trouts**) **1** any of various freshwater fish of the genus Salmo of the northern hemisphere, valued as food. **2** a similar fish of the family Salmonidae (see also salmon trout). **3** sl. derog. a woman, esp. an old or ill-tempered one (usu. old trout). □□ **troutlet** n. **troutling** n. **trouty** adj. [OE truht f. LL tructa]

trouvaille /ˈtruːvaɪl/ n. a lucky find; a windfall. [F f. trouver find]

trouvère /truːˈveə(r)/ n. a medieval epic poet in Northern France in the 11th–14th c. [OF trovere f. trover find: cf. TROUBADOUR]

trove /trəʊv/ n. = treasure trove. [AF trové f. trover find]

trover /ˈtrəʊvə(r)/ n. Law **1** finding and keeping personal property. **2** common-law action to recover the value of personal property wrongfully taken etc. [OF trover find]

trow /traʊ, trəʊ/ v.tr. archaic think, believe. [OE trūwian, trēowian, rel. to TRUCE]

trowel /ˈtraʊəl/ n. & v. —n. **1** a small hand-held tool with a flat pointed blade, used to apply and spread mortar etc. **2** a similar tool with a curved scoop for lifting plants or earth. —v.tr. (**trowelled, trowelling**; US **troweled, troweling**) **1** apply (plaster etc.). **2** dress (a wall etc.) with a trowel. [ME f. OF truele f. med.L truella f. L trulla scoop, dimin. of trua ladle etc.]

Troy /trɔɪ/ also called Ilium, in Homeric legend the city of King Priam that was besieged for ten years by the Greeks in their endeavour to recover Helen, wife of Menelaus, who had been abducted. It was believed to be a figment of Greek legend until a stronghold called by the Turks Hissarlik, in Asiatic Turkey near the Dardanelles, was identified as the site of Troy by the German archaeologist H. Schliemann, who in 1870 began excavations of the mound which proved to be composed of 46 strata, dating from the early Bronze Age to the Roman era. The stratum known as Troy VII, believed to be that of the Homeric city, was sacked c.1210 BC. Again destroyed c.1100 BC, the site was resettled by the Greeks c.700 BC and finally abandoned in the Roman period.

troy /trɔɪ/ n. (in full **troy weight**) a system of weights used for precious metals and gems, with a pound of 12 ounces or 5,760 grains. [ME, prob. f. Troyes in France]

trs. abbr. transpose (letters or words etc.).

truant /ˈtruːənt/ n., adj., & v. —n. **1** a child who stays away from school without leave or explanation. **2** a person missing from work etc. —adj. (of a person, conduct, thoughts, etc.) shirking, idle, wandering. —v.intr. (also **play truant**) stay away as a truant. □□ **truancy** n. [ME f. OF, prob. ult. f. Celt.: cf. Welsh truan, Gael. truaghan wretched]

truce /truːs/ n. **1** a temporary agreement to cease hostilities. **2** a suspension of private feuding or bickering. □□ **truceless** adj. [ME trew(e)s (pl.) f. OE trēow, rel. to TRUE]

Trucial States /ˈtruːʃ(ə)l/ the name applied to seven Arab sheikhdoms on the Persian Gulf, which since 1971 have been known as the United Arab Emirates (see entry). It refers to the maritime truce made with Britain in 1836 (and subsequently renewed and extended) by which local rulers undertook to abstain from maritime warfare.

truck[1] /trʌk/ n. & v. —n. **1** Brit. an open railway wagon for carrying freight. **2** esp. *US* a vehicle for carrying heavy goods; a lorry. **3** a vehicle for transporting troops, supplies, etc. **4** a railway bogie. **5** a wheeled stand for transporting goods. **6 a** *Naut.* a wooden disc at the top of a mast with holes for halyards. **b** a small solid wheel. —v. **1** *tr.* convey on or in a truck. **2** *intr.* *US* drive a truck. **3** *intr.* *US sl.* proceed; go, stroll. □□ **truckage** *n.* [perh. short for TRUCKLE in sense 'wheel, pulley']

truck² /trʌk/ *n.* & *v.* —*n.* **1** dealings; exchange, barter. **2** small wares. **3** *US* market-garden produce (*truck farm*). **4** *colloq.* odds and ends. **5** *hist.* the payment of workers in kind. —*v.tr.* & *intr.* *archaic* barter, exchange. □ **have no truck with** avoid dealing with. **Truck Acts** (in the UK) a series of Acts directed, from 1830 onwards, against the 'truck system', common in the 19th c., whereby workmen received their wages in the form of vouchers for goods redeemable only at a special shop (often run by the employer). The Acts required wages to be paid in cash. [ME f. OF *troquer* (unrecorded) = *trocare*, of unkn. orig.]

trucker /ˈtrʌkə(r)/ *n.* esp. *US* **1** a long-distance lorry-driver. **2** a firm dealing in long-distance carriage of goods.

truckie /ˈtrʌki/ *n.* *Austral. colloq.* a lorry-driver; a trucker.

trucking /ˈtrʌkɪŋ/ *n.* *US* conveyance of goods by lorry.

truckle /ˈtrʌk(ə)l/ *n.* & *v.* —*n.* **1** (in full **truckle-bed**) a low bed on wheels that can be stored under a larger bed. **2** *orig. dial.* a small barrel-shaped cheese. —*v.intr.* (foll. by *to*) submit obsequiously. □□ **truckler** *n.* [orig. = wheel, pulley, f. AF *trocle* f. L *trochlea* pulley]

truculent /ˈtrʌkjʊlənt/ *adj.* **1** aggressively defiant. **2** aggressive, pugnacious. **3** fierce, savage. □□ **truculence** *n.* **truculency** *n.* **truculently** *adv.* [L *truculentus* f. *trux trucis* fierce]

Trudeau /ˈtruːdəʊ/, Pierre Elliott (1919–), French-Canadian statesman, Prime Minister of Canada 1968–79 and 1980–4. His terms of office were marked by the rejection of separatism in Quebec and by the securing of Canada's final constitutional independence from the British Parliament (1982).

trudge /trʌdʒ/ *v.* & *n.* —*v.* **1** *intr.* go on foot esp. laboriously. **2** *tr.* traverse (a distance) in this way. —*n.* a trudging walk. □□ **trudger** *n.* [16th c.: orig. unkn.]

trudgen /ˈtrʌdʒ(ə)n/ *n.* a swimming stroke like the crawl with a scissors movement of the legs. [J. *Trudgen*, 19th-c. English swimmer]

true /truː/ *adj.*, *adv.*, & *v.* —*adj.* **1** in accordance with fact or reality (*a true story*). **2** genuine; rightly or strictly so called; not spurious or counterfeit (*a true friend; the true heir to the throne*). **3** (often foll. by *to*) loyal or faithful (*true to one's word*). **4** (foll. by *to*) accurately conforming (to a standard or expectation etc.) (*true to form*). **5** correctly positioned or balanced; upright, level. **6** exact, accurate (*a true aim; a true copy*). **7** (*absol.*) (also **it is true**) certainly, admittedly (*true, it would cost more*). **8** (of a note) exactly in tune. **9** *archaic* honest, upright (*twelve good men and true*). —*adv.* **1** truly (*tell me true*). **2** accurately (*aim true*). **3** without variation (*breed true*). —*v.tr.* (**trues, trued, truing** or **trueing**) bring (a tool, wheel, frame, etc.) into the exact position or form required. □ **come true** actually happen or be the case. **out of true** (or **the true**) not in the correct or exact position. **true bill** *US* & *hist.* a bill of indictment endorsed by a grand jury as being sustained by evidence. **true-blue** *adj.* extremely loyal or orthodox. —*n.* such a person, esp. a Conservative. **true-born** genuine (*a true-born Englishman*). **true-bred** of a genuine or good breed. **true-hearted** faithful, loyal. **true horizon** see HORIZON 1c. **true-love** a sweetheart. **true-love** (or **-lover's**) **knot** a kind of knot with interlacing bows on each side, symbolizing true love. **true north** etc. north etc. according to the earth's axis, not magnetic north. **true rib** a rib joined directly to the breastbone. **true to form** (or **type**) being or behaving etc. as expected. **true to life** accurately representing life. □□ **trueish** *adj.* **trueness** *n.* [OE *trēowe*, *trȳwe*, f. the Gmc noun repr. by TRUCE]

truffle /ˈtrʌf(ə)l/ *n.* **1** any strong-smelling underground fungus of the order Tuberales, used as a culinary delicacy and found esp. in France by trained dogs or pigs. **2** a usu. round sweet made of chocolate mixture covered with cocoa etc. [prob. f. Du. *truffel* f. obs. F *truffle* ult. f. L *tubera* pl. of TUBER]

trug /trʌg/ *n.* *Brit.* **1** a shallow oblong garden-basket usu. of wood

strips. **2** *archaic* a wooden milk-pan. [perh. a dial. var. of TROUGH]

truism /ˈtruːɪz(ə)m/ *n.* **1** an obviously true or hackneyed statement. **2** a proposition that states nothing beyond what is implied in any of its terms. □□ **truistic** /-ˈɪstɪk/ *adj.*

Trujillo Molina /truːˌxiːəʊ mɒˈliːnə/, Rafael Léonidas (1891–1961), dictator of the Dominican Republic 1930–61. As commander of the army he seized power in 1930, and his regime employed authoritarian measures to accomplish some material progress and used terrorist methods to repress opposition. He was assassinated in 1961.

trull /trʌl/ *n.* *archaic* a prostitute. [16th c.: cf. G *Trulle*, TROLLOP]

truly /ˈtruːlɪ/ *adv.* **1** sincerely, genuinely (*am truly grateful*). **2** really, indeed (*truly, I do not know*). **3** faithfully, loyally (*served them truly*). **4** accurately, truthfully (*is not truly depicted; has been truly stated*). **5** rightly, properly (*well and truly*). [OE *trēowlice* (as TRUE, -LY²)]

Truman /ˈtruːmən/, Harry S (1884–1972), 33rd President of the US, 1945–53. At home he largely continued Roosevelt's 'New Deal' policies but in foreign affairs he was faced with new problems. He authorized the use of the atomic bomb against Japan, abruptly ended Lend-Lease in 1945, and enunciated the so-called 'Truman Doctrine' in 1947 in response to a perceived threat of Soviet expansion in the Cold War period, promising US military and economic aid to countries whose stability was threatened by a Communist take-over.

trumeau /truːˈməʊ/ *n.* (*pl.* **trumeaux** /-ˈməʊz/) a section of wall or a pillar between two openings, e.g. a pillar dividing a large doorway. [F]

trump¹ /trʌmp/ *n.* & *v.* —*n.* **1** a playing-card of a suit ranking above the others. **2** an advantage esp. involving surprise. **3** *colloq.* **a** a helpful or admired person. **b** *Austral.* & *NZ* a person in authority. —*v.* **1 a** *tr.* defeat (a card or its player) with a trump. **b** *intr.* play a trump card when another suit has been led. **2** *tr. colloq.* gain a surprising advantage over (a person, proposal, etc.). □ **trump card 1** a card belonging to, or turned up to determine, a trump suit. **2** *colloq.* **a** a valuable resource. **b** a surprise move to gain an advantage. **trump up** fabricate or invent (an accusation, excuse, etc.) (*on a trumped-up charge*). **turn up trumps** *Brit. colloq.* **1** turn out better than expected. **2** be greatly successful or helpful. [corrupt. of TRIUMPH in the same (now obs.) sense]

trump² /trʌmp/ *n.* *archaic* a trumpet-blast. □ **the last trump** the trumpet-blast to wake the dead on Judgement Day. [ME f. OF *trompe* f. Frank.: prob. imit.]

trumpery /ˈtrʌmpərɪ/ *n.* & *adj.* —*n.* (*pl.* **-ies**) **1 a** worthless finery. **b** a worthless article. **2** rubbish. —*adj.* **1** showy but worthless (*trumpery jewels*). **2** delusive, shallow (*trumpery arguments*). [ME f. OF *tromperie* f. *tromper* deceive]

trumpet /ˈtrʌmpɪt/ *n.* & *v.* —*n.* **1 a** a tubular or conical brass instrument with a flared bell and a bright penetrating tone. (See below.) **b** its player. **c** an organ stop with a quality resembling a trumpet. **2 a** the tubular corona of a daffodil etc. **b** a trumpet-shaped thing (*ear-trumpet*). **3** a sound of or like a trumpet. —*v.* (**trumpeted, trumpeting**) **1** *intr.* **a** blow a trumpet. **b** (of an enraged elephant etc.) make a loud sound as of a trumpet. **2** *tr.* proclaim loudly (a person's or thing's merit). □ **trumpet-call** an urgent summons to action. **trumpet major** the chief trumpeter of a cavalry regiment. □□ **trumpetless** *adj.* [ME f. OF *trompette* dimin. (as TRUMP²)]

One of the ancient instruments (two are preserved from the tomb of Tutankhamun), in its early days it produced only 'natural' notes and was particularly associated with fanfares and flourishes, from pageantry to stirring military music. In the 18th c. crooks were added to allow a wider selection of notes, and in the early 19th c. the valved trumpet made possible a far greater and less typecast contribution to orchestral music.

trumpeter /ˈtrʌmpɪtə(r)/ *n.* **1** a person who plays or sounds a trumpet, esp. a cavalry soldier giving signals. **2** a bird making a trumpet-like sound, esp.: **a** a variety of domestic pigeon. **b** a large black S. American cranelike bird of the genus *Psophia*. □ **trumpeter swan** a large N. American wild swan, *Cygnus buccinator*.

truncal /'trʌŋk(ə)l/ adj. of or relating to the trunk of a body or a tree.

truncate v. & adj. —v.tr. /trʌŋ'keɪt, 'trʌŋ-/ **1** cut the top or the end from (a tree, a body, a piece of writing, etc.). **2** Crystallog. replace (an edge or an angle) by a plane. —adj. /'trʌŋkeɪt/ Bot. & Zool. (of a leaf or feather etc.) ending abruptly as if cut off at the base or tip. □□ **truncately** /'trʌŋkeɪtlɪ/ adv. **truncation** /-'keɪʃ(ə)n/ n. [L truncare truncat- maim]

truncheon /'trʌntʃ(ə)n/ n. **1** esp. Brit. a short club or cudgel, esp. carried by a policeman. **2** a staff or baton as a symbol of authority, esp. that of the Earl Marshal. [ME f. OF tronchon stump ult. f. L truncus trunk]

trundle /'trʌnd(ə)l/ v.tr. & intr. roll or move heavily or noisily esp. on or as on wheels. □ **trundle-bed** = TRUCKLE[1]. [var. of obs. or dial. trendle, trindle, f. OE trendel circle (as TREND)]

trunk /trʌŋk/ n. **1** the main stem of a tree as distinct from its branches and roots. **2** a person's or animal's body apart from the limbs and head. **3** the main part of any structure. **4** a large box with a hinged lid for transporting luggage, clothes, etc. **5** US the luggage compartment of a motor car. **6** an elephant's elongated prehensile nose. **7** (in pl.) men's close-fitting shorts worn for swimming, boxing, etc. **8** the main body of an artery, nerve, etc. **9** an enclosed shaft or conduit for cables, ventilation, etc. □ **trunk call** esp. Brit. a telephone call on a trunk line with charges made according to distance. **trunk line** a main line of a railway, telephone system, etc. **trunk road** esp. Brit. an important main road. □□ **trunkful** n. (pl. **-fuls**). **trunkless** adj. [ME f. OF tronc f. L truncus]

trunking /'trʌŋkɪŋ/ n. **1** a system of shafts or conduits for cables, ventilation, etc. **2** the use or arrangement of trunk lines.

trunnion /'trʌnjən/ n. **1** a supporting cylindrical projection on each side of a cannon or mortar. **2** a hollow gudgeon supporting a cylinder in a steam engine and giving passage to the steam. [F trognon core, tree-trunk, of unkn. orig.]

truss /trʌs/ n. & v. —n. **1** a framework, e.g. of rafters and struts, supporting a roof or bridge etc. **2** a surgical appliance worn to support a hernia. **3** Brit. a bundle of old hay (56 lb.) or new hay (60 lb.) or straw (36 lb.). **4** a compact terminal cluster of flowers or fruit. **5** a large corbel supporting a monument etc. **6** Naut. a heavy iron ring securing the lower yards to a mast. —v.tr. **1** tie up (a fowl) compactly for cooking. **2** (often foll. by up) tie (a person) up with the arms to the sides. **3** support (a roof or bridge etc.) with a truss or trusses. □□ **trusser** n. [ME f. OF trusser (v.), trusse (n.), of unkn. orig.]

trust /trʌst/ n. & v. —n. **1 a** a firm belief in the reliability or truth or strength etc. of a person or thing. **b** the state of being relied on. **2** a confident expectation. **3 a** a thing or person committed to one's care. **b** the resulting obligation or responsibility (am in a position of trust; have fulfilled my trust). **4** a person or thing confided in (is our sole trust). **5** reliance on the truth of a statement etc. without examination. **6** commercial credit (obtained goods on trust). **7** Law a confidence placed in a person by making that person the nominal owner of property to be used for another's benefit. **b** the right of the latter to benefit by such property. **c** the property so held. **d** the legal relation between the holder and the property so held. **8 a** a body of trustees. **b** an organization managed by trustees. **c** an organized association of several companies for the purpose of reducing or defeating competition etc., esp. one in which all or most of the stock is transferred to a central committee and shareholders lose their voting power although remaining entitled to profits. —v. **1** tr. place trust in; believe in; rely on the character or behaviour of. **2** tr. (foll. by with) allow (a person) to have or use (a thing) from confidence in its proper use (was reluctant to trust them with my books). **3** tr. (often foll. by that + clause) have faith or confidence or hope that a thing will take place (I trust you will not be late; I trust that she is recovering). **4** tr. (foll. by to) consign (a thing) to (a person) with trust. **5** tr. (foll. by for) allow credit to (a customer) for (goods). **6** intr. (foll. by in) place reliance in (we trust in you). **7** intr. (foll. by to) place (esp. undue) reliance on (shall have to trust to luck). □ **in trust** Law held on the basis of trust (see sense 7 of n.). **on trust 1** on credit. **2** on the basis of trust or confidence. **take on trust** accept (an assertion, claim, etc.)

without evidence or investigation. **trust company** a company formed to act as a trustee or to deal with trusts. **trust fund** a fund of money etc. held in trust. **trust territory** a territory under the trusteeship of the United Nations or of a State designated by them. □□ **trustable** adj. **truster** n. [ME troste, truste (n.) f. ON traust f. traustr strong: (v.) f. ON treysta, assim. to the noun]

trustee /trʌs'tiː/ n. **1** Law a person or member of a board given control or powers of administration of property in trust with a legal obligation to administer it solely for the purposes specified. **2** a State made responsible for the government of an area. □□ **trusteeship** n.

trustful /'trʌstfʊl/ adj. **1** full of trust or confidence. **2** not feeling or showing suspicion. □□ **trustfully** adv. **trustfulness** n.

trusting /'trʌstɪŋ/ adj. having trust (esp. characteristically); trustful. □□ **trustingly** adv. **trustingness** n.

trustworthy /'trʌst,wɜːðɪ/ adj. deserving of trust; reliable. □□ **trustworthily** adv. **trustworthiness** n.

trusty /'trʌstɪ/ adj. & n. —adj. (**trustier, trustiest**) **1** archaic or joc. trustworthy (a trusty steed). **2** archaic loyal (to a sovereign) (my trusty subjects). —n. (pl. **-ies**) a prisoner who is given special privileges for good behaviour. □□ **trustily** adv. **trustiness** n.

truth /truːθ/ n. (pl. **truths** /truːðz, truːθs/) **1** the quality or a state of being true or truthful (doubted the truth of the statement; there may be some truth in it). **2 a** what is true (tell us the whole truth; the truth is that I forgot). **b** what is accepted as true (one of the fundamental truths). □ **in truth** literary truly, really. **to tell the truth** (or **truth to tell**) to be frank. **truth drug** any of various drugs supposedly able to induce a person to tell the truth. **truth table** a list indicating the truth or falsity of various propositions in logic etc. □□ **truthless** adj. [OE trīewth, trēowth (as TRUE)]

truthful /'truːθfʊl/ adj. **1** habitually speaking the truth. **2** (of a story etc.) true. **3** (of a likeness etc.) corresponding to reality. □□ **truthfully** adv. **truthfulness** n.

try /traɪ/ v. & n. —v. (**-ies, -ied**) **1** intr. make an effort with a view to success (often foll. by to + infin.; colloq. foll. by and + infin.: tried to be on time; try and be early; I shall try hard). ¶ Use with and is uncommon in the past tense and in negative contexts (except in imper.). **2** tr. make an effort to achieve (tried my best; had better try something easier). **3** tr. **a** test (the quality of a thing) by use or experiment. **b** test the qualities of (a person or thing) (try it before you buy). **4** tr. make severe demands on (a person, quality, etc.) (my patience has been sorely tried). **5** tr. examine the effectiveness or usefulness of for a purpose (try cold water; try the off-licence; have you tried kicking it?). **6** tr. ascertain the state of fastening of (a door, window, etc.). **7** tr. **a** investigate and decide (a case or issue) judicially. **b** subject (a person) to trial (will be tried for murder). **8** tr. make an experiment in order to find out (let us try which takes longest). **9** intr. (foll. by for) **a** apply or compete for. **b** seek to reach or attain (am going to try for a gold medal). **10** tr. (often foll. by out) extract (oil) from fat by heating. **b** treat (fat) in this way. **11** tr. (often foll. by up) smooth (roughly-planed wood) with a plane to give an accurately flat surface. —n. (pl. **-ies**) **1** an effort to accomplish something; an attempt (give it a try). **2** Rugby Football the act of touching the ball down behind the opposing goal-line, scoring points and entitling the scoring side to a kick at goal. **3** Amer. Football an attempt to score an extra point in various ways after a touchdown. □ **try conclusions with** see CONCLUSION. **try a fall with** contend with. **try for size** try out or test for suitability. **try one's hand** see how skilful one is, esp. at the first attempt. **trying-plane** a plane used in trying (see sense 11 of v.). **try it on** colloq. **1** test another's patience. **2** attempt to outwit or deceive another person. **try on** put on (clothes etc.) to see if they fit or suit the wearer. **try-on** n. Brit. colloq. **1** an act of trying it on. **2** an attempt to fool or deceive. **try out 1** put to the test. **2** test thoroughly. **try-out** n. an experimental test of efficiency, popularity, etc. **try-sail** /'traɪs(ə)l/ a small strong fore-and-aft sail set on the mainmast or other mast of a sailing-vessel in heavy weather. **try-square** a carpenter's square, usu. with one wooden and one metal limb. [ME, = separate, distinguish, etc., f. OF trier sift, of unkn. orig.]

trying /ˈtraɪɪŋ/ adj. annoying, vexatious; hard to endure. □□ **tryingly** adv.

trypanosome /ˈtrɪpənəˌsəʊm/ n. Med. any protozoan parasite of the genus Trypanosoma having a long trailing flagellum and infesting the blood etc. [Gk trupanon borer + -SOME³]

trypanosomiasis /ˌtrɪpənəsəˈmaɪəsɪs/ n. any of several diseases caused by a trypanosome including sleeping sickness and Chagas' disease.

trypsin /ˈtrɪpsɪn/ n. a digestive enzyme acting on proteins and present in the pancreatic juice. □□ **tryptic** adj. [Gk tripsis friction f. tribō rub (because it was first obtained by rubbing down the pancreas with glycerine)]

trypsinogen /trɪpˈsɪnədʒən/ n. a substance in the pancreas from which trypsin is formed.

tryptophan /ˈtrɪptəˌfæn/ n. Biochem. an amino acid essential in the diet of vertebrates. [as TRYPSIN + -phan f. Gk phainō appear]

tryst /trɪst/ n. & v. archaic —n. 1 a time and place for a meeting, esp. of lovers. 2 such a meeting (keep a tryst; break one's tryst). —v.intr. (foll. by with) make a tryst. □□ **tryster** n. [ME, = obs. trist (= TRUST) f. OF triste an appointed station in hunting]

tsar /zɑː(r)/ n. (also **czar**) 1 hist. the title of the former emperor of Russia. 2 a person with great authority. □□ **tsardom** n. **tsarism** n. **tsarist** n. [Russ. tsar′, ult. f. L Caesar]

tsarevich /ˈzɑːrɪvɪtʃ/ n. (also **czarevich**) hist. the eldest son of an emperor of Russia. [Russ. tsarevich son of a tsar]

tsarina /zɑːˈriːnə/ n. (also **czarina**) hist. the title of the former empress of Russia. [It. & Sp. (c)zarina f. G Czarin, Zarin, fem. of Czar, Zar′]

Tsavo /ˈsɑːvəʊ/ an extensive national park in SE Kenya, established in 1948.

tsetse /ˈtsetsi, ˈtetsi/ n. any fly of the genus Glossina native to Africa, that feeds on human and animal blood with a needle-like proboscis and transmits trypanosomiasis. [Tswana]

TSH abbr. 1 thyroid-stimulating hormone. 2 Their Serene Highnesses.

T-shirt /ˈtiːʃɜːt/ n. (also **teeshirt**) a short-sleeved casual top, usu. of knitted cotton and having the form of a T when spread out.

Tsinghai see QINGHAI.

Tsitsikamma Forest /ˌsɪtsɪˈkɑːmə/ an area of dense natural forest on the south coast of Cape Province, South Africa.

tsp. abbr. (pl. **tsps.**) teaspoonful.

T-square /ˈtiːskweə(r)/ n. a T-shaped instrument for drawing or testing right angles.

tsunami /tsuːˈnɑːmɪ/ n. (pl. **tsunamis**) a long high sea wave caused by underwater earthquakes or other disturbances. [Jap. f. tsu harbour + nami wave]

Tswana /ˈtswɑːnə/ n. (also **Setswana** /seˈtswɑːnə/) 1 a southern African people living in Botswana and neighbouring areas. 2 a member of this people. 3 the Bantu language of this people. ¶ Setswana is now the preferred form for the language. [native name]

TT abbr. 1 Tourist Trophy. 2 tuberculin-tested. 3 a teetotal. b teetotaller.

TU abbr. Trade Union.

Tu. abbr. Tuesday.

Tuareg /ˈtwɑːreg/ n. & adj. —n. (pl. same or **Tuaregs**) 1 a member of a Berber group of nomadic pastoralists of North Africa, the legendary blue-veiled warriors of Timbuktu and the romance of Beau Geste. The main concentrations of Tuareg population are now in Algeria, Mali, Niger, and Western Libya, with smaller groups to be found in Nigeria, the Sudan, etc. 2 their Berber dialect, which is the only Berber language to have an indigenous written form (its alphabet is related to ancient Phoenician script). —adj. of or relating to this people or their language. [native name]

tuatara /ˌtuːəˈtɑːrə/ n. a large lizard-like reptile, Sphenodon punctatus, unique to certain small islands of New Zealand, having a crest of soft spines extending along its back, and a third eye on top of its head. [Maori f. tua on the back + tara spine]

tub /tʌb/ n. & v. —n. 1 an open flat-bottomed usu. round container for various purposes. 2 a tub-shaped (usu. plastic) carton. 3 the amount a tub will hold. 4 colloq. a bath. 5 a colloq. a clumsy slow boat. b a stout roomy boat for rowing practice. 6 (in mining) a container for conveying ore, coal, etc. —v. (**tubbed, tubbing**) 1 tr. & intr. plant, bathe, or wash in a tub. 2 tr. enclose in a tub. 3 tr. line (a mine-shaft) with a wooden or iron casing. □ **tub chair** a chair with solid arms continuous with a usu. semicircular back. **tub-thumper** colloq. a ranting preacher or orator. **tub-thumping** colloq. ranting oratory. □□ **tubbable** adj. **tubbish** adj. **tubful** n. (pl. **-fuls**). [ME, prob. of LG or Du. orig.: cf. MLG, MDu. tubbe]

tuba /ˈtjuːbə/ n. (pl. **tubas**) 1 a a low-pitched brass wind instrument. b its player. 2 an organ stop with the quality of a tuba. [It. f. L, = trumpet]

tubal /ˈtjuːb(ə)l/ adj. Anat. of or relating to a tube, esp. the bronchial or Fallopian tubes.

tubby /ˈtʌbɪ/ adj. (**tubbier, tubbiest**) 1 (of a person) short and fat; tub-shaped. 2 (of a violin) dull-sounding, lacking resonance. □□ **tubbiness** n.

tube /tjuːb/ n. & v. —n. 1 a long hollow rigid or flexible cylinder, esp. for holding or carrying air, liquids, etc. 2 a soft metal or plastic cylinder sealed at one end and having a screw cap at the other, for holding a semi-liquid substance ready for use (a tube of toothpaste). 3 Anat. & Zool. a hollow cylindrical organ in the body (bronchial tubes; Fallopian tubes). 4 (often prec. by the) colloq. the London underground railway system (went by tube). 5 a a cathode-ray tube esp. in a television set. b (prec. by the) esp. US colloq. television. 6 US a thermionic valve. 7 = inner tube. 8 the cylindrical body of a wind instrument. 9 Austral. sl. a can of beer. —v.tr. 1 equip with tubes. 2 enclose in a tube. □□ **tubeless** adj. (esp. in sense 7 of n.). **tubelike** adj. [F tube or L tubus]

tubectomy /tjuːˈbektəmɪ/ n. (pl. **-ies**) Surgery removal of a Fallopian tube.

tuber /ˈtjuːbə(r)/ n. 1 a the short thick rounded part of a stem or rhizome, usu. found underground and covered with modified buds, e.g. in a potato. b the similar root of a dahlia etc. 2 Anat. a lump or swelling. [L, = hump, swelling]

tubercle /ˈtjuːbək(ə)l/ n. 1 a small rounded protuberance esp. on a bone. 2 a small rounded swelling on the body or in an organ, esp. a nodular lesion characteristic of tuberculosis in the lungs etc. 3 a small tuber; a wartlike growth. □ **tubercle bacillus** a bacterium causing tuberculosis. □□ **tuberculate** /-ˈbɜːkjʊlət/ adj. **tuberculous** /-ˈbɜːkjʊləs/ adj. [L tuberculum, dimin. of tuber: see TUBER]

tubercular /tjʊˈbɜːkjʊlə(r)/ adj. & n. —adj. of or having tubercles or tuberculosis. —n. a person with tuberculosis. [f. L tuberculum (as TUBERCLE)]

tuberculation /tjʊˌbɜːkjʊˈleɪʃ(ə)n/ n. 1 the formation of tubercles. 2 a growth of tubercles. [f. L tuberculum (as TUBERCLE)]

tuberculin /tjʊˈbɜːkjʊlɪn/ n. a sterile liquid from cultures of tubercle bacillus, used in the diagnosis and treatment of tuberculosis. □ **tuberculin test** a hypodermic injection of tuberculin to detect a tubercular infection. **tuberculin-tested** (of milk) from cows giving a negative response to a tuberculin test. [f. L tuberculum (as TUBERCLE)]

tuberculosis /tjʊˌbɜːkjʊˈləʊsɪs/ n. an infectious disease caused by the bacillus Mycobacterium tuberculosis, characterized by tubercles, esp. in the lungs (see also pulmonary tuberculosis). The disease occurs throughout the world and has grave social importance because some three million people die from it each year and many more suffer long incapacitating illnesses. It was common in Europe in the 19th c.; Keats developed the illness shortly after nursing his sick brother, and Anne and Emily Brontë and their brother Branwell died of it. Today in the countries that enjoy good living conditions and medical services the situation is very different, but the disease is still widespread in the developing countries. The most common form, formerly popularly known as consumption, affects the lungs, which are invaded by bacteria (tubercle bacilli) first identified by the German bacteriologist Robert Koch in 1882. Tuberculosis was once called the 'white plague' and considered to be incurable, but now treatment, which has been transformed by the use of new drugs and by lung operations, can arrest the disease and restore the patient to normal health. In consequence the death rate from it has been dramatically reduced. This decline is due also to early diagnosis of the disease by X-rays, to the use of vaccines, and to improved standards of living and hygiene, for tuberculosis flourishes among the overcrowded and underfed. Its control by public health authorities is one of the finest examples of the success of a carefully planned and well-directed campaign against a disease.

Tuberculosis can affect parts of the body other than the lungs, in particular the bones and joints and the central nervous system. There is also a type known as bovine tuberculosis which attacks cattle, and infection can be passed on to human beings by the milk of infected cows. Elimination of tuberculosis from dairy herds, and pasteurization of milk, have greatly reduced such transmission of the disease.

tuberose[1] /ˈtjuːbəˌrəʊs/ adj. **1** covered with tubers; knobby. **2** of or resembling a tuber. **3** bearing tubers. □□ **tuberosity** /-ˈrɒsɪtɪ/ n. [L tuberosus f. TUBER]

tuberose[2] /ˈtjuːbəˌrəʊz/ n. a plant, Polianthes tuberosa, native to Mexico, having heavily scented white funnel-like flowers and strap-shaped leaves. [L tuberosa fem. (as TUBEROSE[1])]

tuberous /ˈtjuːbərəs/ adj. = TUBEROSE[1]. □ **tuberous root** a thick and fleshy root like a tuber but without buds. [F tubéreux or L tuberosus f. TUBER]

tubifex /ˈtjuːbɪˌfeks/ n. any red annelid worm of the genus Tubifex, found in mud at the bottom of rivers and lakes and used as food for aquarium fish. [mod.L f. L tubus tube + -fex f. facere make]

tubiform /ˈtjuːbɪˌfɔːm/ adj. tube-shaped.

tubing /ˈtjuːbɪŋ/ n. **1** a length of tube. **2** a quantity of tubes.

Tubruq see TOBRUK.

Tubuai Islands /tuːˈbwaɪ/ (also **Austral Islands**) a group of volcanic islands in the southern Pacific Ocean forming part of French Polynesia; pop. (1983) 6,300.

tubular /ˈtjuːbjʊlə(r)/ adj. **1** tube-shaped. **2** having or consisting of tubes. **3** (of furniture etc.) made of tubular pieces. □ **tubular bells** an orchestral instrument consisting of a row of vertically suspended brass tubes that are struck with a hammer.

tubule /ˈtjuːbjuːl/ n. a small tube in a plant or an animal body. [L tubulus, dimin. of tubus tube]

tubulous /ˈtjuːbjʊləs/ adj. = TUBULAR.

TUC abbr. (in the UK) Trades Union Congress.

tuck /tʌk/ v. & n. —v. **1** tr. (often foll. by in, up) **a** draw, fold, or turn the outer or end parts of (cloth or clothes etc.) close together so as to be held; thrust in the edge of (a thing) so as to confine it (tucked his shirt into his trousers; tucked the sheet under the mattress). **b** thrust in the edges of bedclothes around (a person) (came to tuck me in). **2** tr. draw together into a small space (tucked her legs under her; the bird tucked its head under its wing). **3** tr. stow (a thing) away in a specified place or way (tucked it in a corner; tucked it out of sight). **4** tr. **a** make a stitched fold in (material, a garment, etc.). **b** shorten, tighten, or ornament with stitched folds. **5** tr. hit (a ball) to the desired place. —n. **1** a flattened usu. stitched fold in material, a garment, etc., often one of several parallel folds for shortening, tightening, or ornament. **2** Brit. colloq. food, esp. cakes and sweets eaten by children (also attrib.: tuck box). **3** Naut. the part of a ship's hull where the planks meet under the stern. **4** (in full **tuck position**) (in diving, gymnastics, etc.) a position with the knees bent upwards into the chest and the hands clasped round the shins. □ **tuck in** colloq. eat food heartily. **tuck-in** n. Brit. colloq. a large meal. **tuck into** (or **away**) colloq. eat (food) heartily (tucked into their dinner; could really tuck it away). **tuck-net** (or **-seine**) a small net for taking caught fish from a larger net. **tuck shop** Brit. a small shop, esp. near or in a school, selling food to children. [ME tukke, tokke, f. MDu., MLG tucken, = OHG zucchen pull, rel. to TUG]

tucker /ˈtʌkə(r)/ n. & v. —n. **1** a person or thing that tucks. **2** hist. a piece of lace or linen etc. in or on a woman's bodice. **3** Austral. colloq. food. —v.tr. (esp. in passive; often foll. by out) US

colloq. tire, exhaust. □ **best bib and tucker** see BIB[1]. **tucker-bag** (or **-box**) Austral. colloq. a container for food.

tucket /ˈtʌkɪt/ n. archaic a flourish on a trumpet. [ONF toquer beat (a drum)]

tucking /ˈtʌkɪŋ/ n. a series of usu. stitched tucks in material or a garment.

Tucson /ˈtuːsɒn/ a resort city in SE Arizona; pop. (1982) 352,450.

-tude /tjuːd/ suffix forming abstract nouns (altitude; attitude; solitude). [from or after F -tude f. L -tudo -tudinis]

Tudor /ˈtjuːdə(r)/ n. the name of the English royal house descended from Owen Tudor who married Catherine, widowed queen of Henry V, which ruled England from 1485 (Henry VII) until the death of Elizabeth I (1603). —attrib. or adj. **1** of the architectural style (the latest development of Perpendicular) prevailing in England during the reigns of the Tudors. **2** of or resembling the domestic architecture of this period, with much half-timbering, brickwork frequently in patterns, elaborate chimneys, many gables, rich oriel windows, and much interior panelling and moulded plasterwork. □ **Tudor rose** a conventionalized five-lobed decorative figure of a rose, especially a combination of the red and white roses of York and Lancaster adopted as a badge by Henry VII.

Tues. abbr. (also **Tue.**) Tuesday.

Tuesday /ˈtjuːzdeɪ, -dɪ/ n. & adv. —n. the third day of the week, following Monday. —adv. **1** colloq. on Tuesday. **2** (**Tuesdays**) on Tuesdays; each Tuesday. [OE Tiwesdæg f. Tiw the Gmc god identified with Roman Mars]

tufa /ˈtjuːfə/ n. **1** a porous rock composed of calcium carbonate and formed round mineral springs. **2** = TUFF. □□ **tufaceous** /-ˈfeɪʃəs/ adj. [It., var. of tufo: see TUFF]

tuff /tʌf/ n. rock formed by the consolidation of volcanic ash. □□ **tuffaceous** /-ˈfeɪʃəs/ adj. [F tuf, tuffe f. It. tufo f. LL tofus, L TOPHUS]

tuffet /ˈtʌfɪt/ n. **1** = TUFT 1. **2** a low seat. [var. of TUFT]

tuft /tʌft/ n. & v. —n. **1** a bunch or collection of threads, grass, feathers, hair, etc., held or growing together at the base. **2** Anat. a bunch of small blood-vessels. —v. **1** tr. provide with a tuft or tufts. **2** tr. make depressions at regular intervals in (a mattress etc.) by passing a thread through. **3** intr. grow in tufts. □□ **tufty** adj. [ME, prob. f. OF tofe, toffe, of unkn. orig.: for -t cf. GRAFT[1]]

tufted /ˈtʌftɪd/ adj. **1** having or growing in a tuft or tufts. **2** (of a bird) having a tuft of feathers on the head.

Tu Fu /tuː ˈfuː/ (712–70), a major (according to some, the greatest) Chinese poet, noted for his bitter satiric poems attacking social injustice and corruption at court. Intense personal suffering during the turbulent 750s added a note of universal pathos to his verse and inspired some of his finest work.

tug /tʌg/ v. & n. —v. (**tugged**, **tugging**) **1** tr. & (foll. by at) intr. pull hard or violently; jerk (tugged it from my grasp; tugged at my sleeve). **2** tr. tow (a ship etc.) by means of a tugboat. —n. **1** a hard, violent, or jerky pull (gave a tug on the rope). **2** a sudden strong emotional feeling (felt a tug as I watched them go). **3** a small powerful boat for towing larger boats and ships. **4** an aircraft towing a glider. **5** (of a horse's harness) a loop from a saddle supporting a shaft or trace. □ **tug of love** colloq. a dispute over the custody of a child. **tug of war 1** a trial of strength between two sides pulling against each other on a rope. **2** a decisive or severe contest. □□ **tugger** n. [ME togge, tugge, intensive f. Gmc: see TOW[1]]

tugboat /ˈtʌgbəʊt/ n. = TUG n. 3.

tui /ˈtuːɪ/ n. NZ a large honey-eater, Prosthemadura novaeseelandiae, native to New Zealand and having a long protrusible bill and glossy bluish-black plumage with two white tufts at the throat. [Maori]

tuition /tjuːˈɪʃ(ə)n/ n. **1** teaching or instruction, esp. if paid for (driving tuition; music tuition). **2** a fee for this. □□ **tuitional** adj. [ME f. OF f. L tuitio -onis f. tueri tuit- watch, guard]

Tula[1] /ˈtuːlə/ an industrial city of the Soviet Union to the south of Moscow; pop. (est. 1987) 538,000.

Tula[2] /ˈtuːlə/ the ancient capital city of the Toltecs in Mexico, usually identified with a site near the town of Tula in Hidalgo State, central Mexico.

tularaemia /ˌtuːləˈriːmɪə/ n. (US **tularemia**) a severe infectious disease of animals transmissible to man, caused by the bacterium *Pasteurella tularense* and characterized by ulcers at the site of infection, fever, and loss of weight. □□ **tularaemic** adj. [mod.L f. *Tulare* County in California, where it was first observed]

tulip /ˈtjuːlɪp/ n. **1** any bulbous spring-flowering plant of the genus *Tulipa*, esp. one of the many cultivated forms with showy cup-shaped flowers of various colours and markings. **2** a flower of this plant. □ **tulip-root** a disease of oats etc. causing the base of the stem to swell. **tulip-tree** any of various trees esp. of the genus *Liriodendron*, producing tulip-like flowers. **tulip-wood** a fine-grained pale timber produced by the N. American tree *Liriodendron tulipifera*. [orig. *tulipa*(n) f. mod.L *tulipa* f. Turk. *tul(i)band* f. Pers. *dulband* TURBAN (from the shape of the expanded flower)]

Tull /tʌl/, Jethro (1674–1741), the progenitor of the agricultural revolution in England, which preceded the Industrial Revolution, whose major invention in 1701 was the seed-drill for sowing seeds in accurately spaced rows at a controlled rate. This made possible the control of weeds by horse-drawn hoe and so reduced the need for farm labourers, freeing them to work in factories. His methods were adopted abroad also, particularly in France and the US.

tulle /tjuːl/ n. a soft fine silk etc. net for veils and dresses. [*Tulle* in SW France, where it was first made]

Tulsa /ˈtʌlsə/ a port on the Arkansas River in NE Oklahoma; pop. (1982) 375,300.

tum /tʌm/ n. colloq. stomach. [abbr. of TUMMY]

tumble /ˈtʌmb(ə)l/ v. & n. —v. **1** intr. & tr. fall or cause to fall suddenly, clumsily, or headlong. **2** intr. fall rapidly in amount etc. (*prices tumbled*). **3** intr. (often foll. by *about*, *around*) roll or toss erratically or helplessly to and fro. **4** intr. move or rush in a headlong or blundering manner (*the children tumbled out of the car*). **5** intr. (often foll. by *to*) colloq. grasp the meaning or hidden implication of an idea, circumstance, etc. (*they quickly tumbled to our intentions*). **6** tr. overturn; fling or push roughly or carelessly. **7** intr. perform acrobatic feats, esp. somersaults. **8** tr. rumple or disarrange; pull about; disorder. **9** tr. dry (washing) in a tumble-drier. **10** tr. clean (castings, gemstones, etc.) in a tumbling-barrel. **11** intr. (of a pigeon) turn over backwards in flight. —n. **1** a sudden or headlong fall. **2** a somersault or other acrobatic feat. **3** an untidy or confused state. □ **tumble-drier** n. a machine for drying washing in a heated rotating drum. **tumble-dry** v.tr. & intr. (**-dries**, **-dried**) dry in a tumble-drier. **tumbling-barrel** (or **-box** etc.) a revolving device containing an abrasive substance, in which castings, gemstones, etc., are cleaned by friction. **tumbling-bay 1** the outfall of a river, reservoir, etc. **2** a pool into which this flows. [ME *tumbel* f. MLG *tummelen*, OHG *tumalōn* frequent. of *tūmōn*: cf. OE *tumbian* dance]

tumbledown /ˈtʌmb(ə)lˌdaʊn/ adj. falling or fallen into ruin; dilapidated.

tumbler /ˈtʌmblə(r)/ n. **1** a drinking-glass with no handle or foot (formerly with a rounded bottom so as not to stand upright). **2** an acrobat, esp. one performing somersaults. **3** (in full **tumbler-drier**) = *tumble-drier*. **4 a** a pivoted piece in a lock that holds the bolt until lifted by a key. **b** a notched pivoted plate in a gunlock. **5** a kind of pigeon that turns over backwards in flight. **6** an electrical switch worked by pushing a small sprung lever. **7** a toy figure that rocks when touched. **8** = *tumbling-barrel* (see TUMBLE). □□ **tumblerful** n. (pl. **-fuls**).

tumbleweed /ˈtʌmb(ə)lˌwiːd/ n. US & Austral. a plant, *Amaranthus albus*, that forms a globular bush that breaks off in late summer and is tumbled about by the wind.

tumbrel /ˈtʌmbr(ə)l/ n. (also **tumbril** /-rɪl/) hist. **1** an open cart in which condemned persons were conveyed to their execution, esp. to the guillotine during the French Revolution. **2** a two-wheeled covered cart for carrying tools, ammunition, etc. **3** a cart that tips to empty its load, esp. one carrying dung. [ME f. OF *tumberel*, *tomberel* f. *tomber* fall]

tumefy /ˈtjuːmɪˌfaɪ/ v. (**-ies**, **-ied**) **1** intr. swell, inflate; be inflated. **2** tr. cause to do this. □□ **tumefacient** /-ˈfeɪʃ(ə)nt/ adj.

tumefaction /-ˈfækʃ(ə)n/ n. [F *tuméfier* f. L *tumefacere* f. *tumēre* swell]

tumescent /tjʊˈmes(ə)nt/ adj. **1** becoming tumid; swelling. **2** swelling as a response to sexual stimulation. □□ **tumescence** n. **tumescently** adv. [L *tumescere* (as TUMEFY)]

tumid /ˈtjuːmɪd/ adj. **1** (of parts of the body etc.) swollen, inflated. **2** (of a style etc.) inflated, bombastic. □□ **tumidity** /-ˈmɪdɪtɪ/ n. **tumidly** adv. **tumidness** n. [L *tumidus* f. *tumēre* swell]

tummy /ˈtʌmɪ/ n. (pl. **-ies**) colloq. the stomach. □ **tummy-button** the navel. [childish pronunc. of STOMACH]

tumour /ˈtjuːmə(r)/ n. (US **tumor**) a swelling, esp. from an abnormal growth of tissue. □□ **tumorous** adj. [L *tumor* f. *tumēre* swell]

tumult /ˈtjuːmʌlt/ n. **1** an uproar or din, esp. of a disorderly crowd. **2** an angry demonstration by a mob; a riot; a public disturbance. **3** a conflict of emotions in the mind. [ME f. OF *tumulte* or L *tumultus*]

tumultuous /tjʊˈmʌltjʊəs/ adj. **1** noisily vehement; uproarious; making a tumult (*a tumultuous welcome*). **2** disorderly. **3** agitated. □□ **tumultuously** adv. **tumultuousness** n. [OF *tumultuous* or L *tumultuosus* (as TUMULT)]

tumulus /ˈtjuːmjʊləs/ n. (pl. **tumuli** /-ˌlaɪ/) an ancient burial mound or barrow. □□ **tumular** adj. [L f. *tumēre* swell]

tun /tʌn/ n. & v. —n. **1** a large beer or wine cask. **2** a brewer's fermenting-vat. **3** a measure of capacity, equal to 252 wine gallons. —v.tr. (**tunned**, **tunning**) store (wine etc.) in a tun. [OE *tunne* f. med.L *tunna*, prob. of Gaulish orig.]

tuna[1] /ˈtjuːnə/ n. (pl. same or **tunas**) **1** any marine fish of the family Scombridae native to tropical and warm waters, having a round body and pointed snout, and used for food. Also called TUNNY. **2** (in full **tuna-fish**) the flesh of the tuna or tunny, usu. tinned in oil or brine. [Amer. Sp., perh. f. Sp. *atún* tunny]

tuna[2] /ˈtjuːnə/ n. **1** a prickly pear, esp. *Opuntia tuna*. **2** the fruit of this. [Sp. f. Haitian]

Tunb Islands /ˈtuːnəb/ two small islands (Greater and Lesser Tunb) in the Persian Gulf, administered by the emirate of Ras al Khaimah until occupied by Iran in 1971.

tundish /ˈtʌndɪʃ/ n. **1** a wooden funnel esp. in brewing. **2** an intermediate reservoir in metal-founding.

tundra /ˈtʌndrə/ n. a vast level treeless Arctic region usu. with a marshy surface and underlying permafrost. [Lappish]

tune /tjuːn/ n. & v. —n. a melody with or without harmony. —v. **1** tr. put (a musical instrument) in tune. **2 a** tr. adjust (a radio receiver etc.) to the particular frequency of the required signals. **b** intr. (foll. by *in*) adjust a radio receiver to the required signal (*tuned in to Radio 2*). **3** tr. adjust (an engine etc.) to run smoothly and efficiently. **4** tr. (foll. by *to*) adjust or adapt to a required or different purpose, situation, etc. **5** intr. (foll. by *with*) be in harmony with. □ **in tune 1** having the correct pitch or intonation (*sings in tune*). **2** (usu. foll. by *with*) harmonizing with one's company, surroundings, etc. **out of tune 1** not having the correct pitch or intonation (*always plays out of tune*). **2** (usu. foll. by *with*) clashing with one's company etc. **to the tune of** colloq. to the considerable sum or amount of. **tune up 1** (of an orchestra) bring the instruments to the proper or uniform pitch. **2** begin to play or sing. **3** bring to the most efficient condition. □□ **tunable** adj. (also **tuneable**). [ME: unexpl. var. of TONE]

tuneful /ˈtjuːnfʊl/ adj. melodious, musical. □□ **tunefully** adv. **tunefulness** n.

tuneless /ˈtjuːnlɪs/ adj. **1** unmelodious, unmusical. **2** out of tune. □□ **tunelessly** adv. **tunelessness** n.

tuner /ˈtjuːnə(r)/ n. **1** a person who tunes musical instruments, esp. pianos. **2** a device for tuning a radio receiver.

tung /tʌŋ/ n. (in full **tung-tree**) a tree, *Aleurites fordii*, native to China, bearing poisonous fruits containing seeds that yield oil. □ **tung oil** this oil used in paints and varnishes. [Chin. *tong*]

tungsten /ˈtʌŋst(ə)n/ n. Chem. a steel-grey dense metallic element (also known as wolfram), first isolated in 1783. Tungsten is a strong hard metal with a very high melting-point. It has become of importance in the 20th c. as the chief material from which electric light bulb filaments are made. Tungsten is also used in special steels, and the compound tungsten carbide, which is extremely hard, is used to form the cutting edges of saws, the tips of drill-bits, etc. ¶ Symb.: W; atomic number 74. □□ **tungstate** /-steɪt/ n. **tungstic** adj. **tungstous** adj. [Sw. f. *tung* heavy + *sten* stone]

Tungus /ˈtʌŋʌs/ n. (pl. same) **1** a member of a Mongoloid people of eastern Siberia. **2** an Altaic language or group of languages, spoken in parts of Siberia, since 1931 set down in an alphabet based on the Russian alphabet. □□ **Tungusian** /tʌŋˈgjuːsɪən/ adj. & n. **Tungusic** /-ˈgjuːsɪk/ adj. & n. [native name]

tunic /ˈtjuːnɪk/ n. **1 a** a close-fitting short coat of police or military etc. uniform. **b** a loose, often sleeveless garment usu. reaching to about the knees, as worn in ancient Greece and Rome. **c** any of various loose, pleated dresses gathered at the waist with a belt or cord. **d** a tunicle. **2** Zool. the rubbery outer coat of an ascidian etc. **3** Bot. **a** any of the concentric layers of a bulb. **b** the tough covering of a part of this. **4** Anat. a membrane enclosing or lining an organ. [F *tunique* or L *tunica*]

tunica /ˈtjuːnɪkə/ n. (pl. **tunicae** /-ˌkiː/) Bot. & Anat. = TUNIC 3, 4. [L]

tunicate /ˈtjuːnɪkət, -ˌkeɪt/ n. & adj. —n. any marine animal of the subphylum Urochordata having a rubbery or hard outer coat, including sea squirts. —adj. **1** Zool. of or relating to this subphylum. **2 a** Zool. enclosed in a tunic. **b** Bot. having concentric layers. [L *tunicatus* past part. of *tunicare* clothe with a tunic (as TUNICA)]

tunicle /ˈtjuːnɪk(ə)l/ n. a short vestment worn by a bishop or subdeacon at the Eucharist etc. [ME f. OF *tunicle* or L *tunicula* dimin. of TUNICA]

tuning /ˈtjuːnɪŋ/ n. the process or a system of putting a musical instrument in tune. □ **tuning-fork** a two-pronged steel fork that gives a particular note when struck, used in tuning. **tuning-peg** (or **pin** etc.) a peg or pin etc. attached to the strings of a stringed instrument and turned to alter their tension in tuning.

Tunis /ˈtjuːnɪs/ the capital of Tunisia, situated near the Mediterranean coast; pop. (1984) 596,650.

Tunisia /tjuːˈnɪsɪə/ a country in North Africa, on the Mediterranean Sea; pop. (est. 1988) 7,738,000; official language, Arabic; capital, Tunis. Phoenician settlements on the coast developed into the Carthaginian commercial empire which came into conflict with Rome, and after defeat in the Punic Wars became a Roman province. The area was conquered by the Vandals in the 5th c. AD and subsequently by the Arabs (7th c.); in the 16th c. it became part of the Ottoman empire. Under loose Turkish rule, Tunisia became a centre of piratical activity in the 16th–19th c. before its establishment as a French protectorate in 1886. The rise of nationalist activity after the Second World War led to independence and the establishment of a republic in 1956–7. Considerable efforts have been made to improve the economy, which is based almost entirely on agriculture and mining (there are large deposits of phosphates in the better-watered coastal strip, but economic difficulties have led to severe social problems. Tourism is developing as an industry. □□ **Tunisian** adj. & n.

tunnel /ˈtʌn(ə)l/ n. & v. —n. **1** an artificial underground passage through a hill or under a road or river etc., esp. for a railway or road to pass through, or in a mine. **2** an underground passage dug by a burrowing animal. **3** a prolonged period of difficulty or suffering (esp. in metaphors, e.g. *the end of the tunnel*). **4** a tube containing a propeller shaft etc. —v. (**tunnelled, tunnelling**; US **tunneled, tunneling**) **1** intr. (foll. by *through*, *into*, etc.) make a tunnel through (a hill etc.). **2** tr. make (one's way) by tunnelling. **3** intr. Physics pass through a potential barrier. □ **tunnel diode** Electronics a two-terminal semiconductor diode using tunnelling electrons to perform high-speed switching operations. **tunnel-kiln** a kiln in which ceramic ware is carried on trucks along a continuously-heated passage. **tunnel-net** a fishing-net wide at the mouth and narrow at the other end. **tunnel vision 1** vision that is defective in not adequately including objects away from the centre of the field of view. **2** colloq. inability to grasp the wider implications of a situation. □□ **tunneller** n. [ME f. OF *tonel* dimin. of *tonne* TUN]

tunny /ˈtʌnɪ/ n. (pl. same or **-ies**) = TUNA[1]. [F *thon* f. Prov. *ton*, f. L *thunnus* f. Gk *thunnos*]

tup /tʌp/ n. & v. —n. **1** esp. Brit. a male sheep; a ram. **2** the striking-head of a pile-driver, etc. —v.tr. (**tupped, tupping**) esp. Brit. (of a ram) copulate with (a ewe). [ME *toje*, *tupe*, of unkn. orig.]

Tupamaro /ˌtuːpəˈmɑːrəʊ/ n. (pl. **-os**) a Marxist urban guerrilla in Uruguay. [*Tupac Amaru*, the names of two Inca leaders]

Tupelo /ˈtjuːpəˌləʊ/ a city in NE Mississippi, scene of a Civil War battle in July 1864, when Union forces defeated the Confederates, and birthplace of the singer Elvis Presley (1935–77); pop. (1980) 23,900.

tupelo /ˈtjuːpɪˌləʊ/ n. (pl. **-os**) **1** any of various Asian and N. American deciduous trees of the genus *Nyssa*, with colourful foliage and growing in swampy conditions. **2** the wood of this tree. [Creek f. *ito* tree + *opilwa* swamp]

Tupi /ˈtuːpiː/ n. & adj. —n. (pl. same or **Tupis**) **1** a member of an American Indian people native to the Amazon valley. **2** the language of this people. —adj. of or relating to this people or language. [native name]

tuppence /ˈtʌpəns/ n. Brit. = TWOPENCE. [phonet. spelling]

tuppenny /ˈtʌpənɪ/ adj. Brit. = TWOPENNY. [phonet. spelling]

Tupperware /ˈtʌpəˌweə(r)/ n. propr. a range of plastic containers for storing food. [*Tupper*, name of the US manufacturer, + WARE[1]]

tuque /tuːk/ n. a Canadian stocking cap. [Can. F form of TOQUE]

turaco /ˈtʊərəˌkəʊ/ n. (also **touraco**) (pl. **-os**) any African bird of the family Musophagidae, with crimson and green plumage and a prominent crest. [F f. native W.Afr. name]

Turanian /tjʊˈreɪnɪən/ n. & adj. —n. the group of Asian languages that are neither Semitic nor Indo-European, esp. the Ural-Altaic family. —adj. of or relating to this group. [Pers. *Tūrān* region beyond the Oxus]

turban /ˈtɜːbən/ n. **1** a man's headdress of cotton or silk wound round a cap or the head, worn esp. by Muslims and Sikhs. **2** a woman's headdress or hat resembling this. □□ **turbaned** adj. [16th c. (also *tulbant* etc.), ult. f. Turk. *tülbent* f. Pers. *dulband*: cf. TULIP]

turbary /ˈtɜːbərɪ/ n. (pl. **-ies**) Brit. **1** the right of digging turf on common ground or on another's ground. **2** a place where turf or peat is dug. [ME f. AF *turberie*, OF *tourberie* f. *tourbe* TURF]

turbellarian /ˌtɜːbɪˈleərɪən/ n. & adj. —n. any usu. free-living flatworm of the class Turbellaria, having a ciliated surface. —adj. of or relating to this class. [mod.L *Turbellaria* f. L *turbella* dimin. of *turba* crowd: see TURBID]

turbid /ˈtɜːbɪd/ adj. **1** (of a liquid or colour) muddy, thick; not clear. **2** (of a style etc.) confused, disordered. □□ **turbidity** /-ˈbɪdɪtɪ/ n. **turbidly** adv. **turbidness** n. [L *turbidus* f. *turba* a crowd, a disturbance]

turbinate /ˈtɜːbɪnət/ adj. **1** shaped like a spinning-top or inverted cone. **2** (of a shell) with whorls decreasing rapidly in size. **3** Anat. (esp. of some nasal bones) shaped like a scroll. □□ **turbinal** adj. **turbination** /-ˈneɪʃ(ə)n/ n. [L *turbinatus* (as TURBINE)]

turbine /ˈtɜːbaɪn/ n. a device for producing continuous mechanical power, in which a fluid (water, steam, air, or a gas) is accelerated to a high speed in a channel or nozzle and the resulting jet(s) directed at a rotating wheel with vanes or scoop-shaped buckets round its rim. A force is created on the wheel and hence a torque on its shaft, as in a water-wheel (used to work machinery), and in the 19th c. these were developed (chiefly in France and Germany) to drive machinery in factories. The steam turbine was invented 2,000 years ago by Hero of Alexandria, but the first practical one was devised by Sir Charles Parsons in 1884, and contributions to its development were made by the Swedish engineer de Laval and others. Steam-driven turbines have replaced the steam engine in electrical power stations. Gas turbines are a form of internal-combustion engine in which air is compressed, heated by means of fuel sprayed into a combustion chamber, then expanded in a turbine to produce enough power both to drive the compressor and to provide a surplus. They are much used for aircraft propulsion, having a high specific power output (i.e. high power for low weight). [F f. L *turbo-binis* spinning-top, whirlwind]

turbit /'tɜːbɪt/ *n.* a breed of domestic pigeon of stout build with a neck frill and short beak. [app. f. L *turbo* top, from its figure]

turbo /'tɜːbəʊ/ *n.* (*pl.* **-os**) = TURBOCHARGER.

turbo- /'tɜːbəʊ/ *comb. form* turbine.

turbocharger /'tɜːbəʊˌtʃɑːdʒə(r)/ *n.* a supercharger driven by a turbine powered by the engine's exhaust gases.

turbofan /'tɜːbəʊˌfæn/ *n. Aeron.* **1** a jet engine in which jet gases also operate a turbine-driven compressor for supplying compressed air to the combustion chamber. **2** an aircraft powered by this. The turbojet engine was experimentally devised in the decade before the Second World War by a young RAF officer, Frank Whittle, who at first found it difficult to interest British aircraft engine manufacturers in the design or to secure financial backing for his experiments. German designers, starting slightly later than Whittle, were more fortunate, since the German Air Ministry (unlike the British) appreciated the military potential of the engine, and they were able to develop an engine reliable enough to propel the first turbo-jet aeroplane in 1939.

turbojet /'tɜːbəʊˌdʒet/ *n. Aeron.* **1** a jet engine in which jet also operates a turbine-driven compressor for the air drawn into the engine. **2** an aircraft powered by this.

turboprop /'tɜːbəʊˌprɒp/ *n. Aeron.* **1** a jet engine in which a turbine is used as in a turbojet and also to drive a propeller. **2** an aircraft powered by this.

turboshaft /'tɜːbəʊˌʃɑːft/ *n.* a gas turbine that powers a shaft for driving heavy vehicles, generators, pumps, etc.

turbosupercharger /ˌtɜːbəʊˈsuːpəˌtʃɑːdʒə(r)/ *n.* = TURBOCHARGER.

turbot /'tɜːbət/ *n.* **1** a flatfish, *Scophthalmus maximus*, having large bony tubercles on the body and head and prized as food. **2** any of various similar fishes including halibut. [ME f. OF f. OSw. *törnbut* f. *törn* thorn + *but* BUTT³]

turbulence /'tɜːbjʊləns/ *n.* **1** an irregularly fluctuating flow of air or fluid. **2** *Meteorol.* stormy conditions as a result of atmospheric disturbance. **3** a disturbance, commotion, or tumult.

turbulent /'tɜːbjʊlənt/ *adj.* **1** disturbed; in commotion. **2** (of a flow of air etc.) varying irregularly; causing disturbance. **3** tumultuous. **4** insubordinate, riotous. □□ **turbulently** *adv.* [L *turbulentus* f. *turba* crowd]

Turco /'tɜːkəʊ/ *n.* (*pl.* **-os**) *hist.* an Algerian soldier in the French army. [Sp., Port., & It., = TURK]

Turco- /'tɜːkəʊ/ *comb. form* (also **Turko-**) Turkish; Turkish and. [med.L (as TURK)]

Turcoman var. of TURKOMAN.

turd /tɜːd/ *n. coarse sl.* **1** a lump of excrement. **2** a term of contempt for a person. ¶ Often considered a taboo word, esp. in sense 2. [OE *tord* f. Gmc]

turdoid /'tɜːdɔɪd/ *adj.* thrushlike. [L *turdus* THRUSH¹]

tureen /tjʊəˈriːn, tə-/ *n.* a deep covered dish for serving soup etc. [earlier *terrine*, *-ene* f. F *terrine* large circular earthenware dish, fem. of OF *terrin* earthen ult. f. L *terra* earth]

turf /tɜːf/ *n.* & *v.* —*n.* (*pl.* **turfs** or **turves**) **1 a** a layer of grass etc. with earth and matted roots as the surface of grassland. **b** a piece of this cut from the ground. **2** a slab of peat for fuel. **3** (prec. by *the*) **a** a horse-racing generally. **b** a general term for racecourses. —*v.tr.* **1** cover (ground) with turf. **2** (foll. by *out*) esp. *Brit. colloq.* expel or eject (a person or thing). □ **turf accountant** *Brit.* a bookmaker. [OE f. Gmc]

Turfan Depression /'tʊəfɑːn, -'fæn/ a deep depression in western China, in the Tarim basin, with an area of 50,000 sq. km (20,000 sq. miles) and a depth of 154 m (505 ft.), China's lowest point below sea level.

turfman /'tɜːfmən/ *n.* (*pl.* **-men**) esp. *US* a devotee of horse-racing.

turfy /'tɜːfɪ/ *adj.* (**turfier, turfiest**) like turf; grassy.

Turgenev /tɜːˈɡeɪnjef/, Ivan Sergievich (1818–83), Russian novelist and playwright, who studied at Moscow and St Petersburg Universities and in Berlin (1838–41), then served in the Russian

Civil Service which he abandoned for literature in 1845. His first major prose work *A Hunter's Notes* (1847–51) led to a period of confinement at his country estate for its evocative portrayal of Russian serfdom. Partly because of his love for the singer Pauline Garcia Viardot he spent most of his remaining life abroad (mainly in Baden-Baden and Paris) where he met Flaubert and other literary figures, and thus developed a closeness in both sensibility and literary practice to Western Europe. His series of novels in which individual lives are examined to illuminate the social, political, and philosophical issues of the day includes *Rudin* (1856), *On the Eve* (1860), *Fathers and Sons* (1862) in which in *Bazarov* he created a Nihilist hero, and *Virgin Soil* (1877). His short stories include 'Asya' (1858) and 'First Love' (1860); his greatest play was *A Month in the Country* (1850).

turgescent /tɜːˈdʒes(ə)nt/ *adj.* becoming turgid; swelling. □□ **turgescence** *n.*

turgid /'tɜːdʒɪd/ *adj.* **1** swollen, inflated, enlarged. **2** (of language) pompous, bombastic. □□ **turgidity** /-'dʒɪdɪtɪ/ *n.* **turgidly** *adv.* **turgidness** *n.* [L *turgidus* f. *turgēre* swell]

turgor /'tɜːɡə(r)/ *n. Bot.* the rigidity of cells due to the absorption of water. [LL (as TURGID)]

Turin /tjʊəˈrɪn/ (Italian **Torino** /tɒˈriːnəʊ/) a city in NW Italy, capital of Piedmont region; pop. (1981) 1,117,150. Turin was the capital of the kingdom of Sardinia from 1720 and a centre of the Risorgimento in the 19th c.; it was the first capital of a unified Italy (1861–4).

turion /'tʊərɪən/ *n. Bot.* **1** a young shoot or sucker arising from an underground bud. **2** a bud formed by certain aquatic plants. [F f. L *turio -onis* shoot]

Turk /tɜːk/ *n.* **1 a** a native or national of Turkey. **b** a person of Turkish descent. **2** a member of a Central Asian people from whom the Ottomans derived, speaking Turkic languages. **3** *offens.* a ferocious, wild, or unmanageable person. □ **Turk's cap** a martagon lily or other plant with turban-like flowers. **Turk's head** a turban-like ornamental knot. [ME, = F *Turc*, It. etc. *Turco*, med.L *Turcus*, Pers. & Arab. *Turk*, of unkn. orig.]

Turkana /tɜːˈkɑːnə/, Lake (formerly **Lake Rudolf** /'ruːdɒlf/) a salt lake in NW Kenya, with no surface outlet.

Turkey /'tɜːkɪ/ a country in SW Asia comprising the whole of the Anatolian peninsula, extending from the Aegean Sea to the western boundaries of the USSR and Iran, and with a small enclave in SE Europe; pop. (est. 1988) 54,167,850; official language, Turkish; capital, Ankara. (See ANATOLIA.) Modern Turkey is descended from the Ottoman empire, established in the late Middle Ages and largely maintained until its collapse at the end of the First World War. The nationalist leader Kemal Ataturk moulded a new westernized State, centred upon Anatolia, from the ruins of the empire, and Turkey successfully avoided involvement in the Second World War. The economy is predominantly agricultural, although the land is generally poor for such purposes, but some industrialization has taken place using its oil and mineral resources. The country suffers from a certain degree of political instability, resulting in the imposition of military rule.

turkey /'tɜːkɪ/ *n.* (*pl.* **-eys**) **1** a large American bird of the genus *Meleagris*, especially *M. gallopavo* which was found domesticated in the Aztec civilization in Mexico when that country was discovered in 1518. It was soon introduced into Europe and thence to Britain, where it ousted peacock and swan as a table fowl. It has dark plumage with a green or bronze sheen and is prized as food esp. on festive occasions including Christmas and, in the US, Thanksgiving. **2** the flesh of the turkey as food. **3** *US sl.* **a** a theatrical failure; a flop. **b** a stupid or inept person. □ **talk turkey** *US colloq.* talk frankly and straightforwardly; get down to business. **turkey buzzard** (or **vulture**) an American vulture, *Cathartes aura*. [16th c.: short for *turkeycock* or *turkeyhen*, orig. applied to the guinea-fowl which was imported through Turkey, and then erron. to the Amer. bird]

Turkey carpet /'tɜːkɪ/ *n.* = Turkish carpet.

turkeycock /'tɜːkɪˌkɒk/ *n.* **1** a male turkey. **2** a pompous or self-important person.

Turkey red /ˈtɜːkɪ/ n. **1** a scarlet pigment obtained from the madder or alizarim. **2** a cotton cloth dyed with this.

Turki /ˈtɜːkɪ/ adj. & n. —adj. of or relating to a group of about 20 Ural-Altaic languages (including Turkish) and the peoples speaking them. —n. the Turki group of languages, spoken in Turkey, Iran, and the southern part of the Soviet Union. □□ **Turkic** adj. [Pers. turkī (as TURK)]

Turkish /ˈtɜːkɪʃ/ adj. & n. —adj. of or relating to Turkey or to the Turks or their language. —n. the official language of Turkey, spoken by about 50 million people, the most important of the Turkic group. It was originally written in Arabic script but changed over to the Roman alphabet in 1928. □ **Turkish bath 1** a hot-air or steam bath followed by washing, massage, etc. **2** (in sing. or pl.) a building for this. **Turkish carpet** a wool carpet with a thick pile and traditional bold design. **Turkish coffee** a strong black coffee. **Turkish delight** a sweet of lumps of flavoured gelatine coated in powdered sugar. **Turkish towel** a towel made of cotton terry.

Turkistan /tɜːkɪˈstɑːn/ a region of central Asia east of the Caspian Sea, largely in the USSR.

Turkmenistan /tɜːkmenɪˈstɑːn/ the Turkoman SSR, a constituent republic of the USSR, lying between the Caspian Sea and Afghanistan; pop. (est. 1987) 3,361,000; capital, Ashkhabad.

Turko- var. of TURCO-.

Turkoman /ˈtɜːkəʊmən/ n. (also **Turcoman**) (pl. -**mans**) **1** a member of any of various Turkic peoples in Turkmenistan in SW Middle Asia. **2** the language of these peoples. □ **Turkoman carpet** a traditional rich-coloured carpet with a soft long nap. [Pers. Turkumān (as TURK, mānistan resemble)]

Turks and Caicos Islands /tɜːks, ˈkeɪkɒs/ a British dependency in the Caribbean, a group of over 30 islands (of which 8 are inhabited) about 80 km (50 miles) SE of the Bahamas; pop. (est. 1988) 9,300; capital, Cockburn Town (on the island of Grand Turk).

Turku /ˈtʊəkuː/ (Swedish **Åbo** /ˈɔːbuː/) an industrial port in SW Finland; pop. (1987) 160,456.

turmeric /ˈtɜːmərɪk/ n. **1** an E. Indian plant, Curcuma longa, of the ginger family, yielding aromatic rhizomes used as a spice and for yellow dye. **2** this powdered rhizome used as a spice esp. in curry-powder. [16th-c. forms tarmaret etc. perh. f. F terre mérite and mod.L terra merita, of unkn. orig.]

turmoil /ˈtɜːmɔɪl/ n. **1** violent confusion; agitation. **2** din and bustle. [16th c.: orig. unkn.]

turn /tɜːn/ v. & n. —v. **1** tr. & intr. move around a point or axis so that the point or axis remains in a central position; give a rotary motion to or receive a rotary motion (turned the wheel; the wheel turns; the key turns in the lock). **2** tr. & intr. change in position so that a different side, end, or part becomes outermost or uppermost etc.; invert or reverse or cause to be inverted or reversed (turned inside out; turned it upside down). **3 a** tr. give a new direction to (turn your face this way). **b** intr. take a new direction (turn left here; my thoughts have often turned to you). **4** tr. aim in a certain way (turned the hose on them). **5** intr. & tr. (foll. by into) change in nature, form, or condition to (turned into a dragon; then turned him into a frog; turned the book into a play). **6** intr. (foll. by to) **a** apply oneself to; set about (turned to doing the ironing). **b** have recourse to; begin to indulge in habitually (turned to drink; turned to me for help). **c** go on to consider next (let us now turn to your report). **7** intr. & tr. become or cause to become (turned hostile; has turned informer; your comment turned them angry). **8 a** tr. & intr. (foll. by against) make or become hostile to (has turned them against us). **b** intr. (foll. by on, upon) become hostile to; attack (suddenly turned on them). **9** intr. (of hair or leaves) change colour. **10** intr. (of milk) become sour. **11** intr. (of the stomach) be nauseated. **12** intr. (of the head) become giddy. **13** tr. cause (milk) to become sour, (the stomach) to be nauseated, or (the head) to become giddy. **14** tr. translate (turn it into French). **15** tr. move to the other side of; go round (turned the corner). **16** tr. pass the age or time of (he has turned 40; it has now turned 4 o'clock). **17** intr. (foll. by on) depend on; be determined by (it all turns on the weather tomorrow). **18** tr. send or put into a specified place or condition; cause to go (was turned loose; turned the water out into a basin). **19** tr. perform (a somersault etc.) with rotary motion. **20** tr. remake (a garment or, esp., a sheet) putting the worn outer side on the inside. **21** tr. make (a profit). **22** tr. divert (a bullet). **23** tr. blunt (the edge of a knife, slot of a screw-head, etc.). **24** tr. shape (an object) on a lathe. **25** tr. give an (esp. elegant) form to (turn a compliment). **26** intr. Golf begin the second half of a round. **27** tr. (esp. as **turned** adj.) Printing invert (type) to make it appear upside down (a turned comma). **28** tr. pass round (the flank etc. of an army) so as to attack it from the side or rear. **29** intr. (of the tide) change from flood to ebb or vice versa. —n. **1** the act or process or an instance of turning; rotary motion (a single turn of the handle). **2 a** a changed or a change of direction or tendency (took a sudden turn to the left). **b** a deflection or deflected part (full of twists and turns). **3** a point at which a turning or change occurs. **4** a turning of a road. **5** a change of the tide from ebb to flow or from flow to ebb. **6** a change in the course of events. **7** a tendency or disposition (is of a mechanical turn of mind). **8** an opportunity or obligation etc. that comes successively to each of several persons etc. (your turn will come; my turn to read). **9** a short walk or ride (shall take a turn in the garden). **10** a short performance on stage or in a circus etc. **11** service of a specified kind (did me a good turn). **12** purpose (served my turn). **13** colloq. a momentary nervous shock or ill feeling (gave me quite a turn). **14** Mus. an ornament consisting of the principal note with those above and below it. **15** one round in a coil of rope etc. **16** Printing a temporary substitute for a missing letter. **b** a letter turned wrong side up. **17 a** Brit. the difference between the buying and selling price of stocks etc. **b** a profit made from this. □ **at every turn** continually; at each new stage etc. **by turns** in rotation of individuals or groups; alternately. **in turn** in succession; one by one. **in one's turn** when one's turn or opportunity comes. **not know which way** (or **where**) **to turn** be completely at a loss, unsure how to act, etc. **not turn a hair** see HAIR. **on the turn 1** changing. **2** (of milk) becoming sour. **3** at the turning-point. **out of turn 1** at a time when it is not one's turn. **2** inappropriately; inadvisedly or tactlessly (did I speak out of turn?). **take turns** (or **take it in turns**) act or work alternately or in succession. **to a turn** (esp. cooked) to exactly the right degree etc. **turn about** move so as to face in a new direction. **turn-about** n. **1** an act of turning about. **2** an abrupt change of policy etc. **turn and turn about** alternately. **turn around** esp. US = turn round. **turn away 1** turn to face in another direction. **2** refuse to accept; reject. **3** send away. **turn back 1** begin or cause to retrace one's steps. **2** fold back. **turn one's back on** see BACK. **turn-bench** a watchmaker's portable lathe. **turn-buckle** a device for tightly connecting parts of a metal rod or wire. **turn-cap** a revolving chimney-top. **turn the corner 1** pass round it into another street. **2** pass the critical point in an illness, difficulty, etc. **turn a deaf ear** see DEAF. **turn down 1** reject (a proposal, application, etc.). **2** reduce the volume or strength of (sound, heat, etc.) by turning a knob etc. **3** fold down. **4** place downwards. **turn-down** (of a collar) turned down. **turn one's hand to** see HAND. **turn a person's head** see HEAD. **turn an honest penny** see HONEST. **turn in 1** hand in or return. **2** achieve or register (a performance, score, etc.). **3** colloq. go to bed in the evening. **4** fold inwards. **5** incline inwards (his toes turn in). **6** colloq. abandon (a plan etc.). **turn in one's grave** see GRAVE[1]. **turn off 1 a** stop the flow or operation of (water, electricity, etc.) by means of a tap, switch, etc. **b** operate (a tap, switch, etc.) to achieve this. **2 a** enter a side-road. **b** (of a side-road) lead off from another road. **3** colloq. repel; cause to lose interest (turned me right off with their complaining). **4** dismiss from employment. **turn-off** n. **1** a turning off a main road. **2** colloq. something that repels or causes a loss of interest. **turn of speed** the ability to go fast when necessary. **turn on 1 a** start the flow or operation of (water, electricity, etc.) by means of a tap, switch, etc. **b** operate (a tap, switch, etc.) to achieve this. **2** colloq. excite; stimulate the interest of, esp. sexually. **3** tr. & intr. colloq. intoxicate or become intoxicated with drugs. **turn-on** n. colloq. a person or thing that causes (esp. sexual) arousal. **turn on one's heel** see HEEL[1]. **turn out 1** expel. **2** extinguish (an electric light etc.). **3** dress or equip (well turned out). **4** produce (manufactured goods etc.). **5** empty or clean out (a room etc.). **6** empty (a pocket) to see the contents. **7** colloq. **a**

get out of bed. **b** go out of doors. **8** *colloq.* assemble; attend a meeting etc. **9** (often foll. by *to* + infin. or *that* + clause) prove to be the case; result (*turned out to be true; we shall see how things turn out*). **10** *Mil.* call (a guard) from the guardroom. **turn over 1** reverse or cause to reverse vertical position; bring the under or reverse side into view (*turn over the page*). **2** upset; fall or cause to fall over. **3 a** cause (an engine) to run. **b** (of an engine) start running. **4** consider thoroughly. **5** (foll. by *to*) transfer the care or conduct of (a person or thing) to (a person) (*shall turn it all over to my deputy; turned him over to the authorities*). **6** do business to the amount of (*turns over £5000 a week*). **turn over a new leaf** improve one's conduct or performance. **turn round 1** turn so as to face in a new direction. **2 a** *Commerce* unload and reload (a ship, vehicle, etc.). **b** receive, process, and send out again; cause to progress through a system. **3** adopt new opinions or policy. **turn-round** *n.* **1 a** the process of loading and unloading. **b** the process of receiving, processing, and sending out again; progress through a system. **2** the reversal of an opinion or tendency. **turn the scales** see SCALE². **turn the tables** see TABLE. **turn tail** turn one's back; run away. **turn the tide** reverse the trend of events. **turn to** set about one's work (*came home and immediately turned to*). **turn to account** see ACCOUNT. **turn turtle** see TURTLE. **turn up 1** increase the volume or strength of (sound, heat, etc.) by turning a knob etc. **2** place upwards. **3** discover or reveal. **4** be found, esp. by chance (*it turned up on a rubbish dump*). **5** happen or present itself; (of a person) put in an appearance (*a few people turned up late*). **6** *colloq.* cause to vomit (*the sight turned me up*). **7** shorten (a garment) by increasing the size of the hem. **turn-up** *n.* **1** *Brit.* the lower turned-up end of a trouser leg. **2** *colloq.* an unexpected (esp. welcome) happening; a surprise. [OE *tyrnan, turnian* f. L *tornare* f. *tornus* lathe f. Gk *tornos* lathe, circular movement: prob. reinforced in ME f. OF *turner, torner*]

turncoat /ˈtɜːnkəʊt/ *n.* a person who changes sides in a conflict, dispute, etc.

turncock /ˈtɜːnkɒk/ *n.* an official employed to turn on water for the mains supply etc.

Turner /ˈtɜːnə(r)/, Joseph Mallord William (1775–1851), English landscape painter, eccentric, recognized in his own day as a revolutionary genius. The son of a barber, he trained as a topographical draughtsman, but made his name with paintings of mountain scenery, seascapes, and classical compositions, influenced by Claude Lorraine. His most characteristic work is dominated by the power of light, expressed through the primary colours (especially yellow) and often arranged in a swirling vortex. Throughout his career he made careful studies from nature, but he is also seen as a forerunner of abstract art. In the 1830s and 1840s he adopted watercolour techniques for his 'colour-beginnings' in oil, which he worked up to finished paintings during varnishing days at the Royal Academy. Turner left the entire contents of his studio to the nation: some 300 paintings (now at the Tate Gallery and National Gallery) and 20,000 watercolours and drawings (British Museum).

turner /ˈtɜːnə(r)/ *n.* **1** a person or thing that turns. **2** a person who works with a lathe. [ME f. OF *tornere -eor* f. LL *tornator* (as TURN)]

turnery /ˈtɜːnərɪ/ *n.* **1** objects made on a lathe. **2** work with a lathe.

turning /ˈtɜːnɪŋ/ *n.* **1 a** a road that branches off another. **b** a place where this occurs. **2 a** use of the lathe. **b** (in *pl.*) chips or shavings from a lathe. □ **turning-circle** the smallest circle in which a vehicle can turn without reversing. **turning-point** point at which a decisive change occurs.

turnip /ˈtɜːnɪp/ *n.* **1** a cruciferous plant, *Brassica rapa*, with a large white globular root and sprouting leaves. **2** this root used as a vegetable. **3** a large thick old-fashioned watch. □ **turnip-top** the leaves of the turnip eaten as a vegetable. □□ **turnipy** *adj.* [earlier *turnep(e)* f. *neep* f. L *napus*: first element of uncert. orig.]

turnkey /ˈtɜːnkiː/ *n.* & *adj.* —*n.* (*pl.* -**eys**) *archaic* a gaoler. —*adj.* (of a contract etc.) providing for a supply of equipment in a state ready for operation.

turnout /ˈtɜːnaʊt/ *n.* **1** the number of people attending a meeting, voting at an election, etc. (*rain reduced the turnout*). **2**

the quantity of goods produced in a given time. **3** a set or display of equipment, clothes, etc.

turnover /ˈtɜːnəʊvə(r)/ *n.* **1** the act or an instance of turning over. **2** the amount of money taken in a business. **3** the number of people entering and leaving employment etc. **4** a small pie or tart made by folding a piece of pastry over a filling.

turnpike /ˈtɜːnpaɪk/ *n.* **1** *hist.* a defensive frame of spikes. **2** *hist.* **a** a toll-gate. **b** a road on which a toll was collected at a toll-gate. (See below.) **3** *US* a motorway on which a toll is charged.

In Britain private companies were authorized by separate Acts of Parliament to build and maintain roads between set points and to charge a small toll for usage at turnpike gates at each end of the road. The first Turnpike Act was passed in 1663, but most became law in the 18th c. in response to the increasing need for good roads. The turnpikes fell into decline during the 19th c. through competition from the railways and tolls were progressively abolished between the 1870s and 1890s. The road system remained in a state of neglect until the advent of the motor car in the early 20th c.

turnsick /ˈtɜːnsɪk/ *n.* = STURDY *n.*

turnside /ˈtɜːnsaɪd/ *n.* giddiness in dogs and cattle.

turnsole /ˈtɜːnsəʊl/ *n.* any of various plants supposed to turn with the sun. [OF *tournesole* f. Prov. *tournasol* f. L *tornare* TURN + *sol* sun]

turnspit /ˈtɜːnspɪt/ *n.* *hist.* a person or small dog used to turn a spit.

turnstile /ˈtɜːnstaɪl/ *n.* a gate for admission or exit, with revolving arms allowing people through singly.

turnstone /ˈtɜːnstəʊn/ *n.* any wading bird of the genus *Arenaria*, related to the plover, that looks under stones for small animals to eat.

turntable /ˈtɜːnˌteɪb(ə)l/ *n.* **1** a circular revolving plate supporting a gramophone record that is being played. **2** a circular revolving platform for turning a railway locomotive or other vehicle.

turpentine /ˈtɜːpənˌtaɪn/ *n.* & *v.* —*n.* an oleo-resin secreted by several trees esp. of the genus *Pinus, Pistacia, Syncarpia*, or *Copaifera*, and used in various commercial preparations. —*v.tr.* apply turpentine to. □ **Chian turpentine** the type of turpentine secreted by the terebinth. **oil of turpentine** a volatile pungent oil distilled from turpentine, used in mixing paints and varnishes, and in medicine. [ME f. OF *ter(e)bentine* f. L *ter(e)binthina* (*resina* resin) (as TEREBINTH)]

turpeth /ˈtɜːpɪθ/ *n.* (in full **turpeth root**) the root of an E. Indian plant, *Ipomoea turpethum*, used as a cathartic. [ME f. med.L *turbit(h)um* f. Arab. & Pers. *turbiḍ*]

Turpin /ˈtɜːpɪn/, Dick (1706–39), English highwayman, hanged at York for horse-stealing in 1739. Turpin was the most famous of the 18th-c. highwaymen, whose exploits, which were in reality criminal and often bloody, were made legendary by the popular literature of the day.

turpitude /ˈtɜːpɪˌtjuːd/ *n.* *formal* baseness, depravity, wickedness. [F *turpitude* or L *turpitudo* f. *turpis* disgraceful, base]

turps /tɜːps/ *n.* *colloq.* oil of turpentine. [abbr.]

turquoise /ˈtɜːkwɔɪz, -kwɑːz/ *n.* **1** a semiprecious stone, usu. opaque and greenish- or sky-blue, consisting of hydrated copper aluminium phosphate. **2** a greenish-blue colour. [ME *turkeis* etc. f. OF *turqueise* (later -*oise*) Turkish (stone)]

turret /ˈtʌrɪt/ *n.* **1** a small tower, usu. projecting from the wall of a building as a decorative addition. **2** a low flat usu. revolving armoured tower for a gun and gunners in a ship, aircraft, fort, or tank. **3** a rotating holder for tools in a lathe etc. □ **turret lathe** = capstan lathe. □□ **turreted** *adj.* [ME f. OF *to(u)rete* dimin. of *to(u)r* TOWER]

turtle /ˈtɜːt(ə)l/ *n.* **1** any of various marine or freshwater reptiles of the order Chelonia, encased in a shell of bony plates, and having flippers or webbed toes used in swimming. **2** the flesh of the turtle, esp. used for soup. **3** *Computing* a directional cursor in a computer graphics system which can be instructed to move around a screen. □ **turn turtle** capsize. **turtle-neck 1** a high close-fitting neck on a knitted garment. **2** *US* = polo-neck. [app. alt. of *tortue*: see TORTOISE]

turtle-dove /'tɜːt(ə)lˌdʌv/ n. any wild dove of the genus *Streptopelia*, esp. *S. turtur*, noted for its soft cooing and its affection for its mate and young. [archaic *turtle* (in the same sense) f. OE *turtla*, *turtle* f. L *turtur*, of imit. orig.]

turves pl. of TURF.

Tuscan /'tʌskən/ n. & adj. —n. 1 an inhabitant of Tuscany. 2 the classical Italian language of Tuscany. —adj. 1 of or relating to Tuscany or the Tuscans. 2 *Archit.* denoting the least ornamented of the classical orders. □ **Tuscan straw** fine yellow wheat-straw used for hats etc. [ME f. F f. L *Tuscanus* f. *Tuscus* Etruscan]

Tuscany /'tʌskəni/ (Italian **Toscana** /tɒs'kɑːnə/) a region of west central Italy; pop. (1981) 3,581,000; capital, Florence.

tush[1] /tʌʃ/ int. archaic expressing strong disapproval or scorn. [ME: imit.]

tush[2] /tʌʃ/ n. 1 a long pointed tooth, esp. a canine tooth of a horse. 2 an elephant's short tusk. [OE *tusc* TUSK]

tusk /tʌsk/ n. & v. —n. 1 a long pointed tooth, esp. protruding from a closed mouth, as in the elephant, walrus, etc. 2 a tusklike tooth or other object. —v.tr. gore, thrust at, or tear up with a tusk or tusks. □ **tusk shell** 1 any of various molluscs of the class Scaphopoda. 2 its long tubular tusk-shaped shell. □□ **tusked** adj. (also in comb.). **tusky** adj. [ME alt. of OE *tux* var. of *tusc*: cf. TUSH[2]]

tusker /'tʌskə(r)/ n. an elephant or wild boar with well-developed tusks.

tussah US var. of TUSSORE.

Tussaud /'tuːsəʊ/, Marie (née Grosholtz, 1760–1850), Swiss founder of 'Madame Tussaud's', a permanent exhibition in London of wax models of eminent or notorious people (originally victims of the French Revolution) from 1802 onwards.

tusser var. of TUSSORE.

tussive /'tʌsɪv/ adj. of or relating to a cough. [L *tussis* cough]

tussle /'tʌs(ə)l/ n. & v. —n. a struggle or scuffle. —v.intr. engage in a tussle. [orig. Sc. & N.Engl., perh. dimin. of *touse*: see TOUSLE]

tussock /'tʌsək/ n. 1 a clump of grass etc. 2 (in full **tussock moth**) any moth of the genus *Orgyia* etc., with tufted larvae. □ **tussock grass** grass growing in tussocks, esp. *Poa flabellata* from Patagonia etc. □□ **tussocky** adj. [16th c.: perh. alt. f. dial. *tusk* tuft]

tussore /'tʌsɔː(r), 'tʌsə(r)/ n. (also **tusser**, US **tussah** /'tʌsə(r)/) 1 an Indian or Chinese silkworm, *Antheraea mylitta*, yielding strong but coarse brown silk. 2 (in full **tussore-silk**) silk from this and some other silkworms. [Urdu f. Hindi *tasar* f. Skr. *tasara* shuttle]

tut var. of TUT-TUT.

Tutankhamun /ˌtuːtənkɑː'muːn/ (c.1370–1352 BC, reigned c.1361–1352 BC) an Egyptian pharaoh of the 18th Dynasty, who acceded to the throne while still a boy. He abandoned the worship of the sun-god, instituted by Akhenaten, and reinstated the worship of Amun, with Thebes once again the capital city. Although insignificant in the history of Egypt he has become world-famous because of the variety and richness of the contents of his tomb, discovered by the English archaeologist Howard Carter in 1922, which was found virtually intact, its entrance having remained covered by debris from the building of the tomb of Rameses VI nearby.

tutelage /'tjuːtɪlɪdʒ/ n. 1 guardianship. 2 the state or duration of being under this. 3 instruction, tuition. [L *tutela* f. *tuēri* *tuit-* or *tut-* watch]

tutelary /'tjuːtɪləri/ adj. (also **tutelar** /-tɪlə(r)/) 1 **a** serving as guardian. **b** relating to a guardian (*tutelary authority*). 2 giving protection (*tutelary saint*). [LL *tutelaris*, L *-arius* f. *tutela*: see TUTELAGE]

tutenag /'tjuːtɪˌnæg/ n. 1 zinc imported from China and the E. Indies. 2 a white alloy like German silver. [Marathi *tuttināg* perh. f. Skr. *tuttha* copper sulphate + *nāga* tin, lead]

Tuthmosis /tʌθ'məʊsɪs/ the name of three Egyptian pharaohs:
Tuthmosis III (1479–1425 BC, 18th Dynasty), initially co-ruler with his aunt Hatshepsut. He launched campaigns in Palestine and Syria and in Nubia, and built extensively.

tutor /'tjuːtə(r)/ n. & v. —n. 1 a private teacher, esp. in general charge of a person's education. 2 a university teacher supervising the studies or welfare of assigned undergraduates. 3 *Brit.* a book of instruction in a subject. —v. 1 tr. act as a tutor to. 2 intr. work as a tutor. 3 tr. restrain, discipline. 4 intr. US receive tuition. □□ **tutorage** n. tutorship n. [ME f. AF, OF *tutour* or L *tutor* f. *tuēri* *tut-* watch]

tutorial /tjuː'tɔːrɪəl/ adj. & n. —adj. of or relating to a tutor or tuition. —n. a period of individual tuition given by a tutor. □□ **tutorially** adv. [L *tutorius* (as TUTOR)]

tutsan /'tʌts(ə)n/ n. a species of St John's wort, *Hypericum androsaemum*, formerly used to heal wounds etc. [ME f. AF *tutsaine* all healthy]

tutti /'tʊti/ adv. & n. Mus. —adv. with all voices or instruments together. —n. (pl. **tuttis**) a passage to be performed in this way. [It., pl. of *tutto* all]

tutti-frutti /ˌtuːtɪ'fruːtɪ/ n. (pl. **-fruttis**) a confection, esp. ice-cream, of or flavoured with mixed fruits. [It., = all fruits]

tut-tut /tʌt'tʌt/ int., n., & v. (also **tut** /tʌt/) —int. expressing rebuke, impatience, or contempt. —n. such an exclamation. —v.intr. (**-tutted**, **-tutting**) exclaim this. [imit. of a click of the tongue against the teeth]

tutty /'tʌtɪ/ n. impure zinc oxide or carbonate used as a polishing powder. [ME f. OF *tutie* f. med.L *tutia* f. Arab. *tūtiyā*]

Tutu /'tuːtuː/, Desmond (Mpilo) (1931–), South African clergyman, who became Johannesburg's first Black Anglican bishop. In 1984 he was awarded the Nobel Peace Prize for his role in opposition to the apartheid system in South Africa.

tutu[1] /'tuːtuː/ n. a ballet dancer's short skirt of stiffened projecting frills. [F]

tutu[2] /'tuːtuː/ n. Bot. a shrub, *Coriaria arborea*, native to New Zealand, bearing poisonous purplish-black berries. [Maori]

Tuvalu /tuː'vɑːluː/ a small country in the SW Pacific, consisting of a group of nine islands, the former Ellice Islands; pop. (est. 1988) 8,500; official languages, English and Tuvaluan; capital, Funafuti. The islands formed part of the British colony of the Gilbert and Ellice Islands until they separated after a referendum (see KIRIBATI) and became independent within the Commonwealth in 1978. □□ **Tuvaluan** adj. & n.

tu-whit, tu-whoo /tʊˌwɪt tʊ'wuː/ n. a representation of the cry of an owl. [imit.]

tux /tʌks/ n. US colloq. = TUXEDO.

tuxedo /tʌk'siːdəʊ/ n. (pl. **-os** or **-oes**) US 1 a dinner-jacket. 2 a suit of clothes including this. [after a country club at *Tuxedo Park*, New York]

tuyère /twiː'jeə(r), tuː-/ n. (also **tuyere**, **twyer** /'twaɪə(r)/) a nozzle through which air is forced into a furnace etc. [F f. *tuyau* pipe]

TV abbr. television.

TVA abbr. Tennessee Valley Authority.

TVP abbr. propr. textured vegetable protein (in foods made from vegetable but given a meatlike texture).

twaddle /'twɒd(ə)l/ n. & v. —n. useless, senseless, or dull writing or talk. —v.intr. indulge in this. □□ **twaddler** n. [alt. of earlier *twattle*, alt. of TATTLE]

Twain /tweɪn/, Mark (pseudonym of Samuel Langhorne Clemens, 1835–1910), American writer, brought up in Missouri. After working as a printer's apprentice and a river pilot on the Mississippi (later related in his autobiographical *Life on the Mississippi*, 1883), he established himself as a leading humourist in *The Celebrated Jumping Frog of Calvaleras County, and Other Sketches* (1867), a reputation consolidated by *The Innocents Abroad* (1869). England provided the background for his democratic historical fantasy *The Prince and the Pauper* (1882). His most famous works, both deeply rooted in his own childhood, were *The Adventures of Tom Sawyer* (1876) and its sequel *The Adventures of Huckleberry Finn* (1885), which powerfully evoke Mississippi frontier life, combining picaresque adventure with satire and great technical innovative power.

twain /tweɪn/ adj. & n. archaic two (usu. in *twain*). [OE *twegen*, masc. form of *twā* TWO]

twang /twæŋ/ n. & v. —n. 1 a strong ringing sound made by the plucked string of a musical instrument or bow. 2 the nasal quality of a voice compared to this. —*v.* **1** *intr.* & *tr.* emit or cause to emit this sound. **2** *tr.* usu. *derog.* play (a tune or instrument) in this way. **3** *tr.* utter with a nasal twang. □□ **twangy** *adj.* [imit.]

'twas /twɒz, twəz/ *archaic* it was. [contr.]

twat /twɒt/ *n.* *coarse sl.* ¶ Usually considered a taboo word. **1** the female genitals. **2** *Brit.* a term of contempt for a person. [17th c.: orig. unkn.]

twayblade /ˈtweɪbleɪd/ *n.* any orchid of the genus *Listera* etc., with green or purple flowers and a single pair of leaves. [*tway* var. of TWAIN + BLADE]

tweak /twiːk/ *v.* & *n.* —*v.tr.* **1** pinch and twist sharply; pull with a sharp jerk; twitch. **2** make fine adjustments to (a mechanism). —*n.* an instance of tweaking. [prob. alt. of dial. *twick* & TWITCH¹]

twee /twiː/ *adj.* (**tweer** /ˈtwiːə(r)/) *Brit.* usu. *derog.* affectedly dainty or quaint. □□ **tweely** *adv.* **tweeness** *n.* [childish pronunc. of SWEET]

Tweed /twiːd/ a river flowing largely through the southern uplands of Scotland for a distance of 155 km (97 miles) before entering the North Sea at Berwick-upon-Tweed in NE England.

tweed /twiːd/ *n.* **1** a rough-surfaced woollen cloth, usu. of mixed flecked colours, orig. produced in Scotland. **2** (in *pl.*) clothes made of tweed. [orig. a misreading of *tweel*, Sc. form of TWILL, infl. by assoc. with the river TWEED]

Tweedledum and Tweedledee /ˌtwiːd(ə)lˈdʌm, ˌtwiːd(ə)lˈdiː/ *n.* two persons or things differing only or chiefly in name (originally applied to the composers Handel and Bononcini in a satire by John Byrom containing the lines 'Strange all this Difference should be Twixt Tweedle-dum and Tweedle-dee!').

tweedy /ˈtwiːdɪ/ *adj.* (**tweedier**, **tweediest**) **1** of or relating to tweed cloth. **2** characteristic of the country gentry, heartily informal. □□ **tweedily** *adv.* **tweediness** *n.*

'tween /twiːn/ *prep.* *archaic* = BETWEEN. □ **'tween-decks** *Naut.* the space between decks. [contr.]

tweet /twiːt/ *n.* & *v.* —*n.* the chirp of a small bird. —*v.intr.* make a chirping noise. [imit.]

tweeter /ˈtwiːtə(r)/ *n.* a loudspeaker designed to reproduce high frequencies.

tweezers /ˈtwiːzəz/ *n.pl.* a small pair of pincers for taking up small objects, plucking out hairs, etc. [extended form of *tweezes* (cf. *pincers* etc.) pl. of obs. *tweeze* case for small instruments, f. *etweese* = *étuis*, pl. of ÉTUI]

twelfth /twelfθ/ *n.* & *adj.* —*n.* **1** the position in a sequence corresponding to the number 12 in the sequence 1–12. **2** something occupying this position. **3** each of twelve equal parts of a thing. **4** *Mus.* **a** an interval or chord spanning an octave and a fifth in the diatonic scale. **b** a note separated from another by this interval. —*adj.* that is the twelfth. □ **Twelfth Day** 6 Jan., the twelfth day after Christmas, the festival of the Epiphany. **twelfth man** a reserve member of a cricket team. **Twelfth Night** the evening of 5 Jan., the eve of the Epiphany, formerly the last day of Christmas festivities and observed as a time of merrymaking. **twelfth part** = sense 3 of *n.* □□ **twelfthly** *adv.* [OE *twelfta* (as TWELVE)]

twelve /twelv/ *n.* & *adj.* —*n.* **1** one more than eleven; the product of two units and six units. **2** a symbol for this (12, xii, XII). **3** a size etc. denoted by twelve. **4** the time denoted by twelve o'clock (*is it twelve yet?*). **5** (**the Twelve**) the twelve apostles. **6** (**12**) *Brit.* (of films) classified as suitable for persons of 12 years and over. —*adj.* that amount to twelve. □ **twelve-note** (or **-tone**) *Mus.* using the twelve chromatic notes of the octave on an equal basis without dependence on a key system. This technique of musical composition was developed by the composer Schoenberg (see entry). **Twelve Tables** a set of laws drawn up in ancient Rome in 451 and 450 BC, embodying the most important rules of Roman law. **Twelve Tribes** those of ancient Israel (see TRIBE *n.* 4). [OE *twelf(e)* f. Gmc, prob. rel. to TWO]

twelvefold /ˈtwelvfəʊld/ *adj.* & *adv.* **1** twelve times as much or as many. **2** consisting of twelve parts.

twelvemo /ˈtwelvməʊ/ *n.* = DUODECIMO.

twelvemonth /ˈtwelvmʌnθ/ *n.* *archaic* a year; a period of twelve months.

twenty /ˈtwentɪ/ *n.* & *adj.* —*n.* (*pl.* **-ies**) **1** the product of two and ten. **2** a symbol for this (20, xx, XX). **3** (in *pl.*) the numbers from 20 to 29, esp. the years of a century or of a person's life. **4** *colloq.* a large indefinite number (*have told you twenty times*). —*adj.* that amount to twenty. □ **twenty-first**, **-second**, etc. the ordinal numbers between twentieth and thirtieth. **twenty-one**, **-two**, etc. the cardinal numbers between twenty and thirty. **twenty-twenty** (or 20/20) **1** denoting vision of normal acuity. **2** *colloq.* denoting clear perception or hindsight. □□ **twentieth** *adj.* & *n.* **twentyfold** *adj.* & *adv.* [OE *twentig* (perh. as TWO, -TY²)]

'twere /twɜː(r)/ *archaic* it were. [contr.]

twerp /twɜːp/ *n.* (also **twirp**) *sl.* a stupid or objectionable person. [20th c.: orig. unkn.]

Twi /twiː, tʃwiː/ *n.* & *adj.* —*n.* (*pl.* **Twi** or **Twis**) **1** the chief language spoken in Ghana, consisting of several mutually intelligible dialects. **2** the people speaking this language. —*adj.* of or relating to the Twi or their language.

twibill /ˈtwaɪbɪl/ *n.* a double-bladed battleaxe. [OE f. *twi-* double + BILL³]

twice /twaɪs/ *adv.* **1** two times (esp. of multiplication); on two occasions. **2** in double degree or quantity (*twice as good*). [ME *twiges* f. OE *twige* (as TWO, -S³)]

twiddle /ˈtwɪd(ə)l/ *v.* & *n.* —*v.* **1** *tr.* & (foll. by *with* etc.) *intr.* twirl, adjust, or play randomly or idly. **2** *intr.* move twirlingly. —*n.* **1** an act of twiddling. **2** a twirled mark or sign. □ **twiddle one's thumbs 1** make them rotate round each other. **2** have nothing to do. □□ **twiddler** *n.* **twiddly** *adj.* [app. imit., after *twirl*, *twist*, and *fiddle*, *piddle*]

twig¹ /twɪg/ *n.* **1** a small branch or shoot of a tree or shrub. **2** *Anat.* a small branch of an artery etc. □□ **twigged** *adj.* (also in *comb.*). **twiggy** *adj.* [OE *twigge* f. a Gmc root *twi-* (unrecorded) as in TWICE, TWO]

twig² /twɪg/ *v.tr.* (**twigged**, **twigging**) *colloq.* **1** (also *absol.*) understand; grasp the meaning or nature of. **2** perceive, observe. [18th c.: orig. unkn.]

twilight /ˈtwaɪlaɪt/ *n.* **1** the soft glowing light from the sky when the sun is below the horizon, esp. in the evening. **2** the period of this. **3** a faint light. **4** a state of imperfect knowledge or understanding. **5** a period of decline or destruction. □ **twilight of the gods** *Scand. Mythol.* the destruction of the gods and of the world in conflict with the powers of evil. **twilight sleep** *Med.* a state of partial narcosis, esp. to ease the pain of childbirth. **twilight zone 1** an urban area that is becoming dilapidated. **2** any physical or conceptual area which is undefined or intermediate. [ME f. OE *twi-* two (in uncert. sense) + LIGHT¹]

twilit /ˈtwaɪlɪt/ *adj.* (also **twilighted** /-ˌlaɪtɪd/) dimly illuminated by or as by twilight. [past part. of *twilight* (v.) f. TWILIGHT]

twill /twɪl/ *n.* & *v.* —*n.* a fabric so woven as to have a surface of diagonal parallel ridges. —*v.tr.* (esp. as **twilled** *adj.*) weave (fabric) in this way. □□ **twilled** *adj.* [N.Engl. var. of obs. *twilly*, OE *twili*, f. *twi-* double, after L *bilix* (as BI-, *licium* thread)]

'twill /twɪl/ *archaic* it will. [contr.]

twin /twɪn/ *n.*, *adj.*, & *v.* —*n.* **1** each of a closely related or associated pair, esp. of children or animals born at a birth. **2** the exact counterpart of a person or thing. **3** a compound crystal one part of which is in a reversed position with reference to the other. **4** (**the Twins**) the zodiacal sign or constellation Gemini. —*adj.* **1** forming, or being one of, such a pair (*twin brothers*). **2** *Bot.* growing in pairs. **3** consisting of two closely connected and similar parts. —*v.* (**twinned**, **twinning**) **1** *tr.* & *intr.* **a** join intimately together. **b** (foll. by *with*) pair. **2** *intr.* bear twins. **3** *intr.* grow as a twin crystal. **4** *intr.* & *tr.* *Brit.* link or cause (a town) to link with one in a different country, for the purposes of friendship and cultural exchange. □ **twin bed** each of a pair of single beds. **twin-engined** having two engines. **twin-screw** (of a ship) having two propellers on separate shafts with opposite twists. **twin set** esp. *Brit.* a woman's matching cardigan and jumper. **twin town** *Brit.* a town which is twinned with another. □□ **twinning** *n.* [OE *twinn* double, f. *twi-* two: cf. ON *tvinnr*]

twine /twaɪn/ *n.* & *v.* —*n.* **1** a strong thread or string of two or more strands of hemp or cotton etc. twisted together. **2** a coil or twist. **3** a tangle; an interlacing. —*v.* **1** *tr.* form (a string or thread etc.) by twisting strands together. **2** *tr.* form (a garland etc.) of interwoven material. **3** *tr.* (often foll. by *with*) garland (a brow etc.). **4** *intr.* (often foll. by *round*, *about*) coil or wind. **5** *intr.* & *refl.* (of a plant) grow in this way. □□ **twiner** *n.* [OE *twīn*, *twigin* linen, ult. f. the stem of *twi-* two]

twinge /twɪndʒ/ *n.* & *v.* —*n.* a sharp momentary local pain or pang (*a twinge of toothache*; *a twinge of conscience*). —*v.intr.* & *tr.* experience or cause to experience a twinge. [*twinge* (v.) pinch, wring f. OE *twengan* f. Gmc]

twinkle /ˈtwɪŋk(ə)l/ *v.* & *n.* —*v.* **1** *intr.* (of a star or light etc.) shine with rapidly intermittent gleams. **2** *intr.* (of the eyes) sparkle. **3** *intr.* (of the feet in dancing) move lightly and rapidly. **4** *tr.* emit (a light or signal) in quick gleams. **5** *tr.* blink or wink (one's eyes). —*n.* **1 a** a sparkle or gleam of the eyes. **b** a blink or wink. **2** a slight flash of light; a glimmer. **3** a short rapid movement. □ **in a twinkle** (or **a twinkling** or **the twinkling of an eye**) in an instant. □□ **twinkler** *n.* **twinkly** *adj.* [OE *twinclian*]

twirl /twɜːl/ *v.* & *n.* —*v.tr.* & *intr.* spin or swing or twist quickly and lightly round. —*n.* **1** a twirling motion. **2** a form made by twirling, esp. a flourish made with a pen. □□ **twirler** *n.* **twirly** *adj.* [16th c.: prob. alt. (after *whirl*) of obs. *tirl* TRILL]

twirp var. of TWERP.

twist /twɪst/ *v.* & *n.* —*v.* **1 a** *tr.* change the form of by rotating one end and not the other or the two ends in opposite directions. **b** *intr.* undergo such a change; take a twisted position (*twisted round in his seat*). **c** *tr.* wrench or pull out of shape with a twisting action (*twisted my ankle*). **2** *tr.* **a** wind (strands etc.) about each other. **b** form (a rope etc.) by winding the strands. **c** (foll. by *with*, *in with*) interweave. **d** form by interweaving or twining. **3 a** *tr.* give a spiral form to (a rod, column, cord, etc.) as by rotating the ends in opposite directions. **b** *intr.* take a spiral form. **4** *tr.* (foll. by *off*) break off or separate by twisting. **5** *tr.* distort or misrepresent the meaning of (words). **6 a** *intr.* take a curved course. **b** *tr.* make (one's way) in a winding manner. **7** *tr. Brit. colloq.* cheat (*twisted me out of £20*). **8** *tr.* cause (the ball, esp. in billiards) to rotate while following a curved path. **9** *tr.* (as **twisted** *adj.*) (of a person or mind) emotionally unbalanced. **10** *intr.* dance the twist. —*n.* **1** the act or an instance of twisting. **2 a** a twisted state. **b** the manner or degree in which a thing is twisted. **3** a thing formed by or as by twisting, esp. a thread or rope etc. made by winding strands together. **4** the point at which a thing twists or bends. **5** usu. *derog.* a peculiar tendency of mind or character etc. **6** an unexpected development of events, esp. in a story etc. **7** a fine strong silk thread used by tailors etc. **8** a roll of bread, tobacco, etc., in the form of a twist. **9** *Brit.* a paper packet with screwed-up ends. **10** a curled piece of lemon etc. peel to flavour a drink. **11** a spinning motion given to a ball in cricket etc. to make it take a special curve. **12 a** a twisting strain. **b** the amount of twisting of a rod etc., or the angle showing this. **c** forward motion combined with rotation about an axis. **13** *Brit.* a drink made of two ingredients mixed together. **14** *Brit. colloq.* a swindle. **15** (prec. by *the*) a dance with a twisting movement of the body, popular in the 1960s. □ **round the twist** *Brit. sl.* crazy. **twist a person's arm** *colloq.* apply coercion, esp. by moral pressure. **twist round one's finger** see FINGER. □□ **twistable** *adj.* **twisty** *adj.* (**twistier, twistiest**). [ME, rel. to TWIN, TWINE]

twister /ˈtwɪstə(r)/ *n.* **1** *Brit. colloq.* a swindler; a dishonest person. **2** a twisting ball in cricket or billiards. **3** *US* a tornado, waterspout, etc.

twit[1] /twɪt/ *n.* esp. *Brit. sl.* a silly or foolish person. [orig. dial.: perh. f. TWIT[2]]

twit[2] /twɪt/ *v.tr.* (**twitted, twitting**) reproach or taunt, usu. good-humouredly. [16th-c. *twite* f. *atwite* f. OE *ætwītan* reproach with f. *æt* at + *wītan* blame]

twitch /twɪtʃ/ *v.* & *n.* —*v.* **1** *intr.* (of the features, muscles, limbs, etc.) move or contract spasmodically. **2** *tr.* give a short sharp pull at. —*n.* **1** a sudden involuntary contraction or movement. **2** a sudden pull or jerk. **3** *colloq.* a state of nervousness. **4** a noose and stick for controlling a horse during a veterinary operation.

□□ **twitchy** *adj.* (**twitchier, twitchiest**) (in sense 3 of *n.*). [ME f. Gmc: cf. OE *twiccian*, dial. *twick*]

twitcher /ˈtwɪtʃə(r)/ *n.* **1** *colloq.* a bird-watcher who tries to get sightings of rare birds. **2** a person or thing that twitches.

twitch grass /twɪtʃ/ *n.* = COUCH[2]. [var. of QUITCH]

twite /twaɪt/ *n.* a moorland finch, *Carduelis flavirostris*, resembling the linnet. [imit. of its cry]

twitter /ˈtwɪtə(r)/ *v.* & *n.* —*v.* **1** *intr.* (of or like a bird) emit a succession of light tremulous sounds. **2** *tr.* utter or express in this way. —*n.* **1** the act or an instance of twittering. **2** a tremulously excited state. □□ **twitterer** *n.* **twittery** *adj.* [ME, imit.: cf. -ER[4]]

'twixt /twɪkst/ *prep. archaic* = BETWIXT. [contr.]

two /tuː/ *n.* & *adj.* —*n.* **1** one more than one; the sum of one unit and another unit. **2** a symbol for this (2, ii, II). **3** a size etc. denoted by two. **4** the time of two o'clock (*is it two yet?*). **5** a set of two. **6** a card with two pips. —*adj.* that amount to two. □ **in two** in or into two pieces. **in two shakes** (or **ticks**) see SHAKE, TICK[1]. **or two** denoting several (*a thing or two* = several things). **put two and two together** make (esp. an obvious) inference from what is known or evident. **that makes two of us** *colloq.* that is true of me also. **two-bit** *US colloq.* cheap, petty. **two-by-four** a length of timber with a rectangular cross-section 2 in. by 4 in. **two by two** (or **two and two**) in pairs. **two can play at that game** *colloq.* another person's behaviour can be copied to that person's disadvantage. **two-dimensional 1** having or appearing to have length and breadth but no depth. **2** lacking depth or substance; superficial. **two-edged** double-edged. **two-faced 1** having two faces. **2** insincere; deceitful. **two-handed 1** having, using, or requiring the use of two hands. **2** (of a card-game) for two players. **two a penny** see PENNY. **two-piece** *adj.* (of a suit etc.) consisting of two matching items. —*n.* a two-piece suit etc. **two-ply** *adj.* of two strands, webs, or thicknesses. —*n.* **1** two-ply wool. **2** two-ply wood made by gluing together two layers with the grain in different directions. **two-seater 1** a vehicle or aircraft with two seats. **2** a sofa etc. for two people. **two-sided 1** having two sides. **2** having two aspects; controversial. **two-step** a round dance with a sliding step in march or polka time. **two-stroke** esp. *Brit.* (of an internal-combustion engine) having its power cycle completed in one up-and-down movement (i.e. two strokes) of the piston, with the fuel/air mixture entering and exhaust gases leaving the cylinder through inlet and exhaust ports in its walls, opened and closed by movements of the piston, instead of through the more complicated valves used in a four-stroke engine. **two-time** *colloq.* **1** deceive or be unfaithful to (esp. a partner or lover). **2** swindle, double-cross. **two-timer** *colloq.* a person who is deceitful or unfaithful. **two-tone** having two colours or sounds. **two-up** *Austral.* & *NZ* a gambling game with bets placed on a showing of two heads or two tails. **two-way 1** involving two ways or participants. **2** (of a switch) permitting a current to be switched on or off from either of two points. **3** (of a radio) capable of transmitting and receiving signals. **4** (of a tap etc.) permitting fluid etc. to flow in either of two channels or directions. **5** (of traffic etc.) moving in two esp. opposite directions. **two-way mirror** a panel of glass that can be seen through from one side and is a mirror on the other. **two-wheeler** a vehicle with two wheels. [OE *twā* (fem. & neut.), *tū* (neut.), with Gmc cognates and rel. to Skr. *dwau*, *dwe*, Gk & L *duo*]

twofold /ˈtuːfəʊld/ *adj.* & *adv.* **1** twice as much or as many. **2** consisting of two parts.

twopence /ˈtʌpəns/ *n. Brit.* **1** the sum of two pence, esp. before decimalization. **2** *colloq.* (esp. with *neg.*) a thing of little value (*don't care twopence*).

twopenny /ˈtʌpnɪ/ *adj. Brit.* **1** costing two pence, esp. before decimalization. **2** *colloq.* cheap, worthless. □ **twopenny-halfpenny** /ˌtʌpnɪˈheɪpnɪ/ cheap, insignificant.

twosome /ˈtuːsəm/ *n.* **1** two persons together. **2** a game, dance, etc., for two persons.

'twould /twʊd/ *archaic* it would. [contr.]

twyer var. of TUYÈRE.

TX *abbr. US* Texas (in official postal use).

-ty[1] /tɪ/ *suffix* forming nouns denoting quality or condition (*cruelty*; *plenty*). [ME *-tie, -tee, -te* f. OF *-té, -tet* f. L *-tas -tatis*: cf. *-ITY*]

-ty[2] /tɪ/ *suffix* denoting tens (*twenty*; *thirty*; *ninety*). [OE *-tig*]

Tyburn /ˈtaɪbɜːn/ a place in London, near the site of Marble Arch, where public hangings were held *c.*1300–1783.

tychism /ˈtaɪkɪz(ə)m/ *n. Philos.* the theory that chance controls the universe. [Gk *tukhē* chance]

tycoon /taɪˈkuːn/ *n.* **1** a business magnate. **2** *hist.* a title applied by foreigners to the shogun of Japan 1854–68. [Jap. *taikun* great lord]

tying *pres. part.* of TIE.

tyke /taɪk/ *n.* (also **tike**) **1** esp. *Brit.* an unpleasant or coarse man. **2** a mongrel. **3** a small child. **4** *Brit. sl.* a Yorkshireman. **5** *Austral.* & *NZ sl. offens.* a Roman Catholic. [ME f. ON *tík* bitch: sense 5 assim. from TAIG]

Tyler[1] /ˈtaɪlə(r)/, John (1790–1862), 10th President of the US, 1841–5. His alliance with the Southern Democrats on the issue of States' rights aggravated the polarization of politics between the North and the South in the years preceding the American Civil War. At the end of his Presidency he secured the annexation of Texas.

Tyler[2] /ˈtaɪlə(r)/, Wat (d. 1381), the leader of the English Peasants' Revolt of 1381, who successfully led the rebels from Kent into London but was killed during a parley with the young king Richard II by the Lord Mayor of London and several other royal supporters.

tylopod /ˈtaɪləˌpɒd/ *n.* & *adj. Zool.* —*n.* any animal that bears its weight on the sole-pads of the feet rather than on the hoofs, esp. the camel. —*adj.* (of an animal) bearing its weight in this way. □□ **tylopodous** /-ˈlɒpədəs/ *adj.* [Gk *tulos* knob or *tulē* callus, cushion + *pous podos* foot]

tympan /ˈtɪmpən/ *n.* **1** *Printing* an appliance in a printing-press used to equalize pressure between the platen etc. and a printing-sheet. **2** *Archit.* = TYMPANUM. [F *tympan* or L *tympanum*: see TYMPANUM]

tympana *pl.* of TYMPANUM.

tympani *var.* of TIMPANI.

tympanic /tɪmˈpænɪk/ *adj.* **1** *Anat.* of, relating to, or having a tympanum. **2** resembling or acting like a drumhead. □ **tympanic bone** *Anat.* the bone supporting the tympanic membrane. **tympanic membrane** *Anat.* the membrane separating the outer ear and middle ear and transmitting vibrations resulting from sound waves to the inner ear.

tympanites /ˌtɪmpəˈnaɪtiːz/ *n.* a swelling of the abdomen caused by gas in the intestine etc. □□ **tympanitic** /-ˈnɪtɪk/ *adj.* [LL f. Gk *tumpanitēs* of a drum (as TYMPANUM)]

tympanum /ˈtɪmpənəm/ *n.* (*pl.* **tympanums** or **tympana** /-nə/) **1** *Anat.* **a** the middle ear. **b** the tympanic membrane. **2** *Zool.* the membrane covering the hearing organ on the leg of an insect. **3** *Archit.* **a** a vertical triangular space forming the centre of a pediment. **b** a similar space over a door between the lintel and the arch; a carving on this space. **4** a drum-wheel etc. for raising water from a stream. [L f. Gk *tumpanon* drum f. *tuptō* strike]

Tyndale /ˈtɪnd(ə)l/, William (*c.*1494–1536), English translator of the Bible and a leading figure of the Reformation in England. Faced with ecclesiastical opposition to his project for translating the Bible, Tyndale went abroad, never to return to his own country, and his translation of the New Testament was published in Germany. His vigorous translations from the Greek and Hebrew became widely popular in England and were the basis of both the Authorized and the Revised Version. In 1535 he was arrested on a charge of heresy, and later strangled and burnt at the stake.

Tyne and Wear /taɪn, wɪə(r)/ a metropolitan county of NE England; pop. (1981) 1,154,700; county town, Newcastle-upon-Tyne.

Tynwald /ˈtɪnwɒld/ *n.* the legislative assembly of the Isle of Man, which meets annually to proclaim newly enacted laws. It consists of the governor (representing the sovereign) and council acting as the upper house, and the House of Keys (an elective

assembly). [ON *thing-völlr* place of assembly f. *thing* assembly + *völlr* field]

type /taɪp/ *n.* & *v.* —*n.* **1 a** a class of things or persons having common characteristics. **b** a kind or sort (*would like a different type of car*). **2** a person, thing, or event serving as an illustration, symbol, or characteristic specimen of another, or of a class. **3** (in *comb.*) made of, resembling, or functioning as (*ceramic-type material*; *Cheddar-type cheese*). **4** *colloq.* a person, esp. of a specified character (*is rather a quiet type*; *is not really my type*). **5** an object, conception, or work of art serving as a model for subsequent artists. **6** *Printing* **a** a piece of metal etc. with a raised letter or character on its upper surface for use in printing. **b** a kind or size of such pieces (*printed in large type*). **c** a set or supply of these (*ran short of type*). **7** a device on either side of a medal or coin. **8** *Theol.* a foreshadowing in the Old Testament of a person or event of the Christian dispensation. **9** *Biol.* an organism having or chosen as having the essential characteristics of its group and giving its name to the next highest group. —*v.* **1** *tr.* be a type or example of. **2** *tr.* & *intr.* write with a typewriter. **3** *tr.* esp. *Biol.* & *Med.* assign to a type; classify. **4** *tr.* = TYPECAST. □ **in type** *Printing* composed and ready for printing. **type-founder** a designer and maker of metal types. **type-foundry** a foundry where type is made. **type-metal** *Printing* an alloy of lead etc., used for casting printing-types. **type site** *Archaeol.* a site where objects regarded as defining the characteristics of a period etc. are found. **type specimen** *Biol.* the specimen used for naming and describing a new species. □□ **typal** *adj.* [ME f. F *type* or L *typus* f. Gk *tupos* impression, figure, type, f. *tuptō* strike]

typecast /ˈtaɪpkɑːst/ *v.tr.* (*past* and *past part.* **-cast**) assign (an actor or actress) repeatedly to the same type of role, esp. one in character.

typeface /ˈtaɪpfeɪs/ *n. Printing* **1** a set of types or characters in a particular design. **2** the inked part of type, or the impression made by this.

typescript /ˈtaɪpskrɪpt/ *n.* a typewritten document.

typesetter /ˈtaɪpˌsetə(r)/ *n. Printing* **1** a person who composes type. **2** a composing-machine. □□ **typesetting** *n.*

typewrite /ˈtaɪpraɪt/ *v.tr.* & *intr.* (*past* **-wrote**; *past part.* **-written**) *formal* = TYPE *v.* 2.

typewriter /ˈtaɪpˌraɪtə(r)/ *n.* a machine for producing characters similar to those of print, with keys that are pressed to cause raised metal characters to strike the paper (inserted round a roller), usually through inked ribbon. As early as 1714 an Englishman, Henry Mill, was granted a patent for a machine to impress or transcribe letters singly, as in writing, but it is not certain whether he ever made one. For a long time inventors concentrated on writing-machines for the use of blind people, but the first practical typewriter was produced in 1873 when the firm of Remington and Sons manufactured that designed by two Americans, Sholes and Gliddon. It had 44 keys, so arranged that the letters which most commonly occur together were placed far apart in order to slow the typist down and prevent the bars which carried the letters from jamming as they struck to and from the roller carrying the paper—an arrangement which has survived in spite of technological advances which make it unnecessary. The history of the typewriter has consisted mainly of a series of improvements upon the original device; the electric typewriter dates from 1935. Typing was considered an acceptable occupation for women at a time when 'working' was thought to be unbecoming but being 'in business' was socially acceptable, and 'lady typewriters' (as they were then called) became a feature of office life.

typewritten /ˈtaɪpˌrɪt(ə)n/ *adj.* produced with a typewriter.

typhlitis /tɪfˈlaɪtɪs/ *n.* inflammation of the caecum. □□ **typhlitic** /-ˈlɪtɪk/ *adj.* [mod.L f. Gk *tuphlon* caecum or blind gut f. *tuphlos* blind + *-ITIS*]

typhoid /ˈtaɪfɔɪd/ *n.* & *adj.* —*n.* **1** (in full **typhoid fever**) an infectious bacterial fever with an eruption of red spots on the chest and abdomen and severe intestinal irritation. Prince Albert died of typhoid fever in 1861, and the disease was formerly a scourge of armies, spread by contaminated water and by infection; in the Boer War more lives were lost by this than

b *but* d *dog* f *few* g *get* h *he* j *yes* k *cat* l *leg* m *man* n *no* p *pen* r *red* s *sit* t *top* v *voice*

by enemy action. A vaccine has been developed which gives temporary immunity. **2** a similar disease of animals. —*adj.* like typhus. □ **typhoid condition** (or **state**) a state of depressed vitality occurring in many acute diseases. □□ **typhoidal** *adj.* [TYPHUS + -OID]

typhoon /taɪˈfuːn/ *n.* a violent hurricane in E. Asian seas. □□ **typhonic** /-ˈfɒnɪk/ *adj.* [partly f. Port. *tufão* f. Arab. *ṭūfān* perh. f. Gk *tuphōn* whirlwind; partly f. Chin. dial. *tai fung* big wind]

typhus /ˈtaɪfəs/ *n.* an infectious fever caused by rickettsiae, characterized by a purple rash, headaches, fever, and usu. delirium. Until 1849 it was confused with typhoid fever, a quite different disease. Formerly known as gaol fever, ship fever, putrid fever, and camp fever, it was always associated with conditions of squalor and overcrowding, spread by lice; prevalent in Europe in the 18th–19th c., it became rare when people became more fastidious. Other forms of the disease are spread by rat fleas, ticks, and mites. A vaccine is now available. □□ **typhous** *adj.* [mod.L f. Gk *tuphos* smoke, stupor f. *tuphō* to smoke]

typical /ˈtɪpɪk(ə)l/ *adj.* **1** serving as a characteristic example; representative. **2** characteristic of or serving to distinguish a type. **3** (often foll. by *of*) conforming to expected behaviour, attitudes, etc. (*is typical of them to forget*). **4** symbolic. □□ **typicality** /-ˈkælɪtɪ/ *n.* **typically** *adv.* [med.L *typicalis* f. L *typicus* f. Gk *tupikos* (as TYPE)]

typify /ˈtɪpɪˌfaɪ/ *v.tr.* (**-ies**, **-ied**) **1** be a representative example of; embody the characteristics of. **2** represent by a type or symbol; serve as a type, figure, or emblem of; symbolize. □□ **typification** /-fɪˈkeɪʃ(ə)n/ *n.* **typifier** *n.* [L *typus* TYPE + -FY]

typist /ˈtaɪpɪst/ *n.* a person who uses a typewriter, esp. professionally.

typo /ˈtaɪpəʊ/ *n.* (*pl.* **-os**) *colloq.* **1** a typographical error. **2** a typographer. [abbr.]

typographer /taɪˈpɒɡrəfə(r)/ *n.* a person skilled in typography.

typography /taɪˈpɒɡrəfɪ/ *n.* **1** printing as an art. **2** the style and appearance of printed matter. □□ **typographic** /-pəˈɡræfɪk/ *adj.* **typographical** /-pəˈɡræfɪk(ə)l/ *adj.* **typographically** /-pəˈɡræfɪkəlɪ/ *adv.* [F *typographie* or mod.L *typographia* (as TYPE, -GRAPHY)]

typology /taɪˈpɒlədʒɪ/ *n.* the study and interpretation of (esp. biblical) types. □□ **typological** /-əˈlɒdʒɪk(ə)l/ *adj.* **typologist** *n.* [Gk *tupos* TYPE + -LOGY]

Tyr /tɪə(r)/ *Scand. Mythol.* the god of battle.

tyrannical /tɪˈrænɪk(ə)l/ *adj.* **1** acting like a tyrant; imperious, arbitrary. **2** given to or characteristic of tyranny. □□ **tyrannically** *adv.* [OF *tyrannique* f. L *tyrannicus* f. Gk *turannikos* (as TYRANT)]

tyrannicide /tɪˈrænɪˌsaɪd/ *n.* **1** the act or an instance of killing a tyrant. **2** the killer of a tyrant. □□ **tyrannicidal** /-ˈsaɪd(ə)l/ *adj.* [F f. L *tyrannicida*, *-cidium* (as TYRANT, -CIDE)]

tyrannize /ˈtɪrəˌnaɪz/ *v.tr.* & (foll. by *over*) *intr.* (also **-ise**) behave like a tyrant towards; rule or treat despotically or cruelly. [F *tyranniser* (as TYRANT)]

tyrannosaurus /tɪˌrænəˈsɔːrəs/ *n.* (also **tyrannosaur**) any bipedal flesh-eating dinosaur of the genus *Tyrannosaurus*, esp. *T. rex* having powerful hind legs, small clawlike front legs, and a long well-developed tail. It was the largest known carnivorous animal. [Gk *turannos* TYRANT, after *dinosaur*]

tyranny /ˈtɪrənɪ/ *n.* (*pl.* **-ies**) **1** the cruel and arbitrary use of authority. **2** a tyrannical act; tyrannical behaviour. **3 a** rule by a tyrant. **b** a period of this. **c** a State ruled by a tyrant. □□ **tyrannous** *adj.* **tyrannously** *adv.* [ME f. OF *tyrannie* f. med.L *tyrannia* f. Gk *turannia* (as TYRANT)]

tyrant /ˈtaɪərənt/ *n.* **1** an oppressive or cruel ruler. **2** a person exercising power arbitrarily or cruelly. **3** *Gk Hist.* an absolute ruler who seized power without the legal right. [ME *tyran*, *-ant*, f. OF *tiran*, *tyrant* f. L *tyrannus* f. Gk *turannos*]

Tyre /taɪə(r)/ a city and seaport of the Phoenicians, south of Sidon, now in Lebanon; pop. (1980) 14,000.

tyre /ˈtaɪə(r)/ *n.* (*US* **tire**) a rubber covering, usu. inflated, placed round a wheel to form a soft contact with the road. (See below.) □ **tyre-gauge** a portable device for measuring the air-pressure in a tyre. [var. of TIRE²]
  Early wheels were of wood, with protection given (when iron-working technology was available) by a strip of iron attached round the felloe. In the mid-19th c. tyres for carriage wheels began to be made of solid rubber, which mitigated the damage to road-surfaces but still gave a hard 'ride'. It was a Belfast veterinary surgeon, John Dunlop (see entry), who in 1888 devised (for use on his son's tricycle) the first practical type of pneumatic tyre, consisting of an air-filled tube inside a canvas cover with rubber treads, and by the early 20th c. such tyres had superseded solid rubber tyres on motor vehicles. Modern tyre design has dispensed with the inner tube.

Tyrian /ˈtɪrɪən/ *adj.* & *n.* —*adj.* of or relating to ancient Tyre in Phoenicia. —*n.* a native or citizen of Tyre. □ **Tyrian purple** see PURPLE n. 2. [L *Tyrius* f. *Tyrus* Tyre]

tyro var. of TIRO.

Tyrol /ˈtɪr(ə)l, -ˈrɒl/ (German **Tirol**) an Alpine province of western Austria, the southern part of which was ceded to Italy after the First World War; pop. (1981) 586,100; capital, Innsbruck. □□ **Tyrolean** /-ˈliːən/ *adj.* **Tyrolese** /-ˈliːz/ *adj.* & *n.*

Tyrone /tɪˈrəʊn/ a county of Northern Ireland; pop. (1981) 143,900; county town, Omagh.

Tyrrhene /ˈtɪriːn/ *adj.* & *n.* (also **Tyrrhenian** /tɪˈriːnɪən/) *archaic* or *poet.* = ETRUSCAN. [L *Tyrrhenus*]

Tyrrhenian Sea /tɪˈriːnɪən/ a part of the Mediterranean Sea bounded by mainland Italy, Sicily, Sardinia, Corsica, and the Ligurian Sea.

tzatziki /tsætˈsiːkɪ/ *n.* a Greek side dish of yoghurt with cucumber. [mod. Gk]

tzigane /tsɪˈɡɑːn/ *n.* **1** a Hungarian gypsy. **2** (*attrib.*) characteristic of the tziganes or (esp.) their music. [F f. Magyar *c(z)igány*]

U

U¹ /juː/ n. (also **u**) (pl. **Us** or **U's**) **1** the twenty-first letter of the alphabet. **2** a U-shaped object or curve (esp. in comb.: *U-bolt*).

U² /juː/ adj. esp. Brit. colloq. **1** upper class. **2** supposedly characteristic of the upper class. [abbr.; coined by A. S. C. Ross (1954)]

U³ /uː/ adj. a Burmese title of respect before a man's name. [Burmese]

U⁴ abbr. (also **U.**) **1** Brit. universal (of films classified as suitable without restriction). **2** university.

U⁵ symb. Chem. the element uranium.

u prefix = MU 2 (μ).

UAE abbr. United Arab Emirates.

Ubaid /uːˈbaɪd/ adj. of a mesolithic culture in Mesopotamia that flourished during the 5th millennium BC, named after tell Al 'Ubaid near the ancient city of Ur.

ubiety /juːˈbaɪətɪ/ n. the fact or condition of being in a definite place; local relation. [med.L ubietas f. L ubi where]

-ubility /jʊˈbɪlɪtɪ/ suffix forming nouns from, or corresponding to, adjectives in -uble (solubility; volubility). [L -ubilitas: cf. -ITY]

ubiquitarian /juːˌbɪkwɪˈteərɪən/ adj. & n. Theol. —adj. relating to or believing in the doctrine of the omnipresence of Christ's body. —n. a believer in this. □□ **ubiquitarianism** n. [mod.L ubiquitarius (as UBIQUITOUS)]

ubiquitous /juːˈbɪkwɪtəs/ adj. **1** present everywhere or in several places simultaneously. **2** often encountered. □□ **ubiquitously** adv. **ubiquitousness** n. **ubiquity** n. [mod.L ubiquitas f. L ubique everywhere f. ubi where]

-uble /jʊb(ə)l/ suffix forming adjectives meaning 'that may or must be' (see -ABLE) (soluble; voluble). [F f. L -ubilis]

-ubly /jʊblɪ/ suffix forming adverbs corresponding to adjectives in -uble.

U-boat /ˈjuːbəʊt/ n. hist. a German submarine; esp. in the First and Second World War. [G U-boot = Unterseeboot under-sea boat]

UC abbr. University College.

u.c. abbr. upper case.

UCATT abbr. (in the UK) Union of Construction, Allied Trades, and Technicians.

UCCA /ˈʌkə/ abbr. (in the UK) Universities Central Council on Admissions.

Uccello /uːˈtʃeləʊ/, Paolo (properly Paolo di Dono, 1397–1495), Florentine painter, whose nickname (uccello means 'bird') is said to refer to his love of animals, especially birds. His surviving works include the series of three panels (c.1455) on the Battle of San Romano, in which his enthusiasm for perspective is clearly seen, and The Hunt in the Forest, with its atmosphere of fairy-tale romance and darting energy, which is one of the earliest known Italian paintings on canvas.

UCW abbr. (in the UK) Union of Communication Workers.

UDA abbr. Ulster Defence Association (a loyalist paramilitary organization) in Northern Ireland, formed in 1971.

udal /ˈjuːd(ə)l/ n. (also **odal** /ˈəʊd(ə)l/) the kind of freehold right based on uninterrupted possession prevailing in N. Europe before the feudal system and still in use in Orkney and Shetland. [ON óthal f. Gmc]

UDC abbr. hist. (in the UK) Urban District Council.

udder /ˈʌdə(r)/ n. the mammary gland of cattle, sheep, etc., hanging as a baglike organ with several teats. □□ **uddered** adj. (also in comb.). [OE ūder f. WG]

UDI abbr. unilateral declaration of independence.

udometer /juːˈdɒmɪtə(r)/ n. formal a rain-gauge. [F udomètre f. L udus damp]

UDR abbr. Ulster Defence Regiment.

UEFA /juːˈiːfə/ abbr. Union of European Football Associations.

Ufa /uːˈfɑː/ the capital of the autonomous Soviet republic of Bashkir, in the Ural Mountains; pop. (est. 1987) 1,092,000.

UFO /ˈjuːfəʊ/ n. (also **ufo**) (pl. **UFOs** or **ufos**) an unidentified flying object. The term is often applied to supposed vehicles ('flying saucers') piloted by beings from outer space, for which no convincing evidence has ever been produced. Most UFO sightings are eventually identified as weather balloons, aircraft, or high-flying birds. A small number are reported in the Press as encounters with intelligent denizens of other worlds, but these are of so sensational a nature as to provoke widespread scepticism about their veracity. [abbr.]

ufology /juːˈfɒlədʒɪ/ n. the study of UFOs. □□ **ufologist** n.

Uganda /juːˈgændə/ a landlocked country in East Africa, a member State of the Commonwealth, of which a large part is covered by lakes, notably Lake Victoria; pop. (est. 1988) 16,446,900; official language, English; capital, Kampala. First explored by Europeans in the mid-19th c., Uganda became a British protectorate in 1894 and achieved full independence in 1962. Since that time the country has been severely troubled by political instability (largely owing to tribal divisions), which continues today, despite the overthrow of the dictator Idi Amin in 1979. Nevertheless, the Ugandan economy is relatively well developed, particularly with regard to the production of agricultural commodities such as tea, coffee, tobacco, and cotton for export. □□ **Ugandan** adj. & n.

Ugarit /ˈuːgærɪt/ (modern Ras Shamra) an ancient North Syrian seaport occupied from neolithic times until its destruction by the Sea Peoples in about the 12th c. BC. Ugarit was an important commercial city during the Late Bronze Age, to which period belong a palace, temples, and private residences containing legal, religious, and administrative cuneiform texts in Sumerian, Akkadian, Hurrian, Hittite, and Ugaritic languages. The last of these was written in an early form of the alphabet which is related to Phoenician. □□ **Ugaritic** /-ˈrɪtɪk/ adj. & n.

ugh /əx, ʌg, ʌx/ int. **1** expressing disgust or horror. **2** the sound of a cough or grunt. [imit.]

Ugli /ˈʌglɪ/ n. (pl. **Uglis** or **Uglies**) propr. a mottled green and yellow citrus fruit, a hybrid of a grapefruit and tangerine developed in Jamaica c.1930. [UGLY]

uglify /ˈʌglɪfaɪ/ v.tr. (-ies, -ied) make ugly. □□ **uglification** /-fɪˈkeɪʃ(ə)n/ n.

ugly /ˈʌglɪ/ adj. (**uglier**, **ugliest**) **1** unpleasing or repulsive to see or hear (an ugly scar; spoke with an ugly snarl). **2** unpleasantly suggestive; discreditable (ugly rumours are about). **3** threatening, dangerous (the sky has an ugly look). **4** morally repulsive; vile (ugly vices). □ **ugly customer** an unpleasantly formidable person. **ugly duckling** a person who turns out to be beautiful or talented etc. against all expectations (with ref. to a cygnet in a brood of ducks in a tale by Andersen). □□ **uglily** adv. **ugliness** n. [ME f. ON ugglígr to be dreaded f. ugga to dread]

Ugrian /ˈuːgrɪən/ adj. & n. (also **Ugric** /ˈuːgrɪk/) —adj. of or relating to the eastern branch of Finnic peoples, esp. the Finns and Magyars, or their languages. —n. **1** a member of this people. **2** any of the languages of this people. [Russ. Ugry name of a race dwelling E. of the Urals]

UHF abbr. ultra-high frequency.

uh-huh /ˈʌhʌ/ int. colloq. expressing assent. [imit.]

uhlan /ˈuːlɑːn, ˈjuːlən/ n. hist. a cavalryman armed with a lance in some European armies, esp. the former German army. [F & G f. Pol. (h)ulan f. Turk. oglan youth, servant]

UHT abbr. ultra heat treated (esp. of milk, for long keeping).

Uist /ˈjuːɪst/ two small islands (**North Uist** and **South Uist**) of the Outer Hebrides.

Uitlander /ˈeɪtlɒndə(r)/ n. S.Afr. hist. any of the non-Boer immigrants into the Transvaal, who came after the discovery of gold (1886). To the Boers, these immigrants, with foreign capital and different life-styles, constituted a cultural and economic threat; the Transvaal government denied them citizenship, taxed them heavily, and excluded them from the government. [Afrik. f. Du. *uit* out + *land* land]

Ujjain /uːˈdʒeɪn/ a city of west central India in the State of Madhya Pradesh, a holy city of the Hindus; pop. (1981) 278,454.

Ujung Padang /uːˌdʒʊŋ pæˈdæŋ/ (formerly **Makassar** /məˈkæsə(r)/) the chief seaport of the Sulawesi Islands, Indonesia; pop. (1980) 709,000.

UK abbr. United Kingdom.

UKAEA abbr. United Kingdom Atomic Energy Authority.

ukase /juːˈkeɪz/ n. **1** an arbitrary command. **2** hist. an edict of the Tsarist Russian government. [Russ. *ukaz* ordinance, edict f. *ukazat'* show, decree]

ukiyo-e /ˌuːkiːˈjəʊjeɪ/ n. a school of Japanese art using subjects from everyday life and simple treatment. It was the dominant movement in Japanese art in the 17th–19th centuries, favoured by such celebrated artists as Hokusai and Utamaro. [Jap., = genre picture]

Ukraine /juːˈkreɪn/ formerly the name of a district (**the Ukraine**) north of the Black Sea, now the Ukrainian SSR, the third-largest constituent republic of the Soviet Union; pop. (est. 1987) 51,201,000; capital, Kiev. In July 1990 it passed a declaration of sovereignty and independence of Moscow. □□ **Ukrainian** adj. & n. [Russ. *ukraina* frontier region f. *u* at + *krai* edge]

ukulele /ˌjuːkəˈleɪlɪ/ n. a small four-stringed Hawaiian (orig. Portuguese) guitar. [Hawaiian, = jumping flea]

Ulan Bator /ˌʊlɑːn ˈbɑːtɔː(r)/ the capital of Mongolia; pop. (est. 1988) 500,000.

-ular /jʊlə(r)/ suffix forming adjectives, sometimes corresp. to nouns in *-ule* (*pustular*) but often without diminutive force (*angular*; *granular*). □□ **-ularity** /-ˈlærɪtɪ/ suffix forming nouns. [from or after L *-ularis* (as -ULE, -AR¹)]

ulcer /ˈʌlsə(r)/ n. **1** an open sore on an external or internal surface of the body, often forming pus. **2 a** a moral blemish. **b** a corroding or corrupting influence etc. □□ **ulcered** adj. **ulcerous** adj. [ME f. L *ulcus -eris*, rel. to Gk *helkos*]

ulcerate /ˈʌlsəˌreɪt/ v.tr. & intr. form into or affect with an ulcer. □□ **ulcerable** adj. **ulceration** /-ˈreɪʃ(ə)n/ n. **ulcerative** /-rətɪv/ adj. [ME f. L *ulcerare ulcerat-* (as ULCER)]

-ule /juːl/ suffix forming diminutive nouns (*capsule*; *globule*). [from or after L *-ulus, -ula, -ulum*]

Uleåborg see OULU.

ulema /ˈuːlɪmə/ n. **1** a body of Muslim doctors of sacred law and theology. **2** a member of this. [Arab. *'ulamā* pl. of *'ālim* learned f. *'alama* know]

-ulent /jʊlənt/ suffix forming adjectives meaning 'abounding in, full of' (*fraudulent*; *turbulent*). □□ **-ulence** suffix forming nouns. [L *-ulentus*]

Ulfilas /ˈʊlfɪˌlæs/ (311–81), a Christian of Cappadocian origin, who became bishop of the Arian Visigoths in 341. He translated the Bible from the Greek into Gothic, inventing (it is said) an alphabet for the purpose and omitting the Books of Kings as their warlike deeds might have a bad influence upon a nation so fond of war as the Goths. Fragments of this translation survive.

Ulhasnagar /ˌuːlhəsˈnɑːgə(r)/ a city in Maharashtra State in western India; pop. (1981) 648,000.

uliginose /juːˈlɪdʒɪˌnəʊs/ adj. (also **uliginous** /-nəs/) Bot. growing in wet or swampy places. [L *uliginosus* f. *uligo -ginis* moisture]

ullage /ˈʌlɪdʒ/ n. **1** the amount by which a cask etc. falls short of being full. **2** loss by evaporation or leakage. [ME f. AF *ulliage*, OF *ouillage* f. *ouiller* fill up, ult. f. L *oculus* eye, with ref. to the bung-hole]

Ulm /ʊlm/ an industrial city on the Danube in Baden-Württemberg in Germany; pop. (1987) 100,700. Napoleon defeated the Austrians at the battle of Ulm in 1805. The city is the birthplace of Albert Einstein.

ulna /ˈʌlnə/ n. (pl. **ulnae** /-niː/) **1** the thinner and longer bone in the forearm, on the side opposite to the thumb (cf. RADIUS 3). **2**

Zool. a corresponding bone in an animal's foreleg or a bird's wing. □□ **ulnar** adj. [L, rel. to Gk *ōlenē* and ELL]

ulotrichan /juːˈlɒtrɪkən/ adj. & n. —adj. (also **ulotrichous** /-kəs/) having tightly-curled hair, esp. denoting a human type. —n. a person having such hair. [mod.L *Ulotrichi* f. Gk *oulos* woolly, crisp + *thrix trikhos* hair]

-ulous /jʊləs/ suffix forming adjectives (*fabulous*; *populous*). [L *-ulosus, -ulus*]

Ulpian /ˈʌlpɪən/ (Domitius Ulpianus, d. 223) Roman jurist active under Caracalla. His numerous legal writings, chiefly syntheses of earlier learning, provided one of the chief sources for the *Digest* of Justinian.

Ulster /ˈʌlstə(r)/ **1** a former province of Ireland comprising the present Northern Ireland and the counties of Cavan, Donegal, and Monaghan (which are now in the Republic of Ireland). **2** (loosely) Northern Ireland (see entry). □ **Ulster Unionist, Ulster Democratic Unionist** a member of the political parties in Northern Ireland seeking to maintain the union of Northern Ireland with Britain. After the rest of Ireland gained its independence in 1920, Unionist politicians continued to dominate Northern Ireland and still provide much of its representation at Westminster.

ulster /ˈʌlstə(r)/ n. a man's long loose overcoat of rough cloth. [*Ulster* in Ireland, where it was orig. sold]

Ulsterman /ˈʌlstəmən/ n. (pl. **-men**; fem. **Ulsterwoman**; pl. **-women**) a native of Ulster.

ult. abbr. ultimo.

ulterior /ʌlˈtɪərɪə(r)/ adj. **1** existing in the background, or beyond what is evident or admitted; hidden, secret (esp. *ulterior motive*). **2** situated beyond. **3** more remote; not immediate; in the future. □□ **ulteriorly** adv. [L, = further, more distant]

ultima /ˈʌltɪmə/ n. the last syllable of a word. [L *ultima* (*syllaba*), fem. of *ultimus* last]

ultimata pl. of ULTIMATUM.

ultimate /ˈʌltɪmət/ adj. & n. —adj. **1** last, final. **2** beyond which no other exists or is possible (*the ultimate analysis*). **3** fundamental, primary, unanalysable (*ultimate truths*). **4** maximum (*ultimate tensile strength*). —n. **1** (prec. by *the*) the best achievable or imaginable. **2** a final or fundamental fact or principle. □□ **ultimately** adv. **ultimateness** n. [LL *ultimatus* past part. of *ultimare* come to an end]

ultima Thule /ˌʌltɪmə ˈθuːliː/ n. a far-away unknown region. [L, = furthest Thule, a remote northern region]

ultimatum /ˌʌltɪˈmeɪtəm/ n. (pl. **ultimatums** or **ultimata** /-tə/) a final demand or statement of terms by one party, the rejection of which by another could cause a breakdown in relations, war, or an end of cooperation etc. [L neut. past part.: see ULTIMATE]

ultimo /ˈʌltɪˌməʊ/ adj. Commerce of last month (*the 28th ultimo*). [L *ultimo mense* in the last month]

ultimogeniture /ˌʌltɪməʊˈdʒɛnɪtʃə(r)/ n. a system in which the youngest son has the right of inheritance (cf. PRIMOGENITURE 2). [L *ultimus* last, after PRIMOGENITURE]

ultra /ˈʌltrə/ adj. & n. —adj. favouring extreme views or measures, esp. in religion or politics. —n. an extremist. [orig. as abbr. of F *ultra-royaliste*: see ULTRA-]

ultra- /ˈʌltrə/ comb. form **1** beyond; on the other side of (opp. CIS-). **2** extreme(ly), excessive(ly) (*ultra-conservative*; *ultra-modern*). [L *ultra* beyond]

ultracentrifuge /ˌʌltrəˈsentrɪˌfjuːdʒ/ n. a high-speed centrifuge used to separate small particles and large molecules by their rate of sedimentation from sols.

ultra-high /ˌʌltrəˈhaɪ/ adj. (of a frequency) in the range 300 to 3000 megahertz.

ultraist /ˈʌltrəɪst/ n. the holder of extreme positions in politics, religion, etc. □□ **ultraism** n.

ultramarine /ˌʌltrəməˈriːn/ n. & adj. —n. **1 a** a brilliant blue pigment orig. obtained from lapis lazuli. **b** an imitation of this from powdered fired clay, sodium carbonate, sulphur, and resin. **2** the colour of this. —adj. **1** of this colour. **2** archaic situated beyond the sea. [obs. It. *oltramarino* & med.L *ultramarinus* beyond the sea (as ULTRA-, MARINE), because lapis lazuli was brought from beyond the sea]

ultramicroscope /ˌʌltrəˈmaɪkrəˌskəʊp/ n. an optical microscope used to reveal very small particles by means of light scattered by them.

ultramicroscopic /ˌʌltrəˌmaɪkrəˈskɒpɪk/ adj. **1** too small to be seen by an ordinary optical microscope. **2** of or relating to an ultramicroscope.

ultramontane /ˌʌltrəˈmɒnteɪn/ adj. & n. —adj. **1** situated on the other side of the Alps from the point of view of the speaker. **2** advocating supreme papal authority in matters of faith and discipline (cf. GALLICAN). The principle was firmly established by the declaration of papal infallibility (1870). —n. **1** a person living on the other side of the Alps. **2** a person advocating supreme papal authority. [med.L ultramontanus (as ULTRA-, L mons montis mountain)]

ultramundane /ˌʌltrəˈmʌndeɪn/ adj. lying beyond the world or the solar system. [L ultramundanus (as ULTRA-, mundanus f. mundus world)]

ultrasonic /ˌʌltrəˈsɒnɪk/ adj. of or involving sound waves with a frequency above the upper limit of human hearing. Methods of producing ultrasonic waves include certain applications of magnetism and application of a rapidly alternating voltage across a piezoelectric crystal. Uses of ultrasonic waves include sonar, detection of faults or cracks in metals, cleaning processes, and destruction of bacteria. Cutting-tools of relatively soft metals can be ultrasonically vibrated to cut shapes or holes in glassy or ceramic materials that cannot be machined by conventional techniques. □□ **ultrasonically** adv.

ultrasonics /ˌʌltrəˈsɒnɪks/ n.pl. (usu. treated as sing.) the science and application of ultrasonic waves.

ultrasound /ˈʌltrəˌsaʊnd/ n. **1** sound having an ultrasonic frequency. **2** ultrasonic waves. □ **ultrasound cardiography** = ECHOCARDIOGRAPHY.

ultrastructure /ˈʌltrəˌstrʌktʃə(r)/ n. Biol. fine structure not visible with an optical microscope.

ultraviolet /ˌʌltrəˈvaɪələt/ adj. Physics **1** having a wavelength (just) beyond the violet end of the visible spectrum. **2** of or using such radiation.

ultra vires /ˌʌltrə ˈvaɪəˌriːz, ˌʊltrə ˈviːreɪz/ adv. & predic.adj. beyond one's legal power or authority. [L]

ululate /ˈjuːlʊˌleɪt/ v.intr. howl, wail; make a hooting cry. □□ **ululant** adj. **ululation** /-ˈleɪʃ(ə)n/ n. [L ululare ululat- (imit.)]

Ulyanov /ʊlˈjɑːnɒf/, Vladimir Ilyich, see LENIN.

Ulyanovsk /ʊlˈjɑːnɒfsk/ a city of the Soviet Union, on the River Volga; pop. (est. 1987) 589,000. Formerly called Sibirsk, it was the birthplace of Lenin and was renamed in his honour in 1924.

Ulysses /ˈjuːlɪˌsiːz/ **1** the Roman name for Odysseus (see entry). **2** a space probe launched in 1990 to inspect the unseen parts of the sun.

um /ʌm, əm/ int. expressing hesitation or a pause in speech. [imit.]

-um var. of -IUM 1.

Umayyad /ʊˈmaɪjæd/ adj. & n. —adj. of a Muslim dynasty, which included the family of the prophet Muhammad, that ruled Islam from 660 (or 661) to 750 and later ruled Moorish Spain 756–1031. —n. a member of this dynasty.

umbel /ˈʌmb(ə)l/ n. Bot. a flower-cluster in which stalks nearly equal in length spring from a common centre and form a flat or curved surface, as in parsley. □□ **umbellar** adj. **umbellate** /-bəˌleɪt/ adj. **umbellule** /-ˈbeljuːl/ adj. [obs. F umbelle or L umbella sunshade, dimin. of UMBRA]

umbellifer /ʌmˈbelɪfə(r)/ n. any plant of the family Umbelliferae bearing umbels, including parsley and parsnip. □□ **umbelliferous** /-bəˈlɪfərəs/ adj. [obs. F umbellifère L (as UMBEL, -fer bearing)]

umber /ˈʌmbə(r)/ n. & adj. —n. **1** a natural pigment like ochre but darker and browner. **2** the colour of this. —adj. **1** of this colour. **2** dark, dusky. [F (terre d')ombre or It. (terra di) ombra = shadow (earth), f. L UMBRA or Umbra fem. of Umber Umbrian]

umbilical /ʌmˈbɪlɪk(ə)l, ˌʌmbɪˈlaɪk(ə)l/ adj. **1** of, situated near, or affecting the navel. **2** centrally placed. □ **umbilical cord 1** a flexible cordlike structure attaching a foetus to the placenta. **2** Astronaut. a supply cable linking a missile to its launcher, or an astronaut in space to a spacecraft. [obs. F umbilical or f. UMBILICUS]

umbilicate /ʌmˈbɪlɪkət/ adj. **1** shaped like a navel. **2** having an umbilicus.

umbilicus /ʌmˈbɪlɪkəs, ˌʌmbɪˈlaɪkəs/ n. (pl. **umbilici** /-ˌsaɪ/ or **umbilicuses**) **1** Anat. the navel. **2** Bot. & Zool. a navel-like formation. **3** Geom. a point in a surface through which all cross-sections have the same curvature. [L, rel. to Gk omphalos and to NAVEL]

umbles /ˈʌmb(ə)lz/ n.pl. the edible offal of deer etc. (cf. humble pie). [ME var. of NUMBLES]

umbo /ˈʌmbəʊ/ n. (pl. **-os** or **umbones** /-ˈbəʊniːz/) **1** the boss of a shield, esp. in the centre. **2** Bot. & Zool. a rounded knob or protuberance. □□ **umbonal** adj. **umbonate** /-nət/ adj. [L umbo -onis]

umbra /ˈʌmbrə/ n. (pl. **umbras** or **umbrae** /-briː/) Astron. **1** a total shadow usu. cast on the earth by the moon during a solar eclipse. **2** the dark central part of a sunspot (cf. PENUMBRA). □□ **umbral** adj. [L, = shade]

umbrage /ˈʌmbrɪdʒ/ n. **1** offence; a sense of slight or injury (esp. give or take umbrage at). **2** archaic **a** a shade. **b** what gives shade. [ME f. OF ult. f. L umbraticus f. umbra: see UMBRA]

umbrella /ʌmˈbrelə/ n. **1** a light portable device for protection against rain, strong sun, etc., consisting of a usu. circular canopy of cloth mounted by means of a collapsible metal frame on a central stick, used for protection against sunshine or (esp.) as a portable protection against rain, or as a symbol of rank and authority in some Oriental and African countries. **2** protection or patronage. **3** (often attrib.) a coordinating or unifying agency (umbrella organization). **4** a screen of fighter aircraft or a curtain of fire put up as a protection against enemy aircraft. **5** Zool. the gelatinous disc of a jellyfish etc., which it contracts and expands to move through the water. □ **umbrella bird** any S. American bird of the genus Cephalopterus, with a black radiating crest and long wattles. **umbrella pine 1** = stone pine. **2** a tall Japanese evergreen conifer, Sciadopitys verticillata, with leaves in umbrella-like whorls. **umbrella stand** a stand for holding closed upright umbrellas. **umbrella tree** a small magnolia, Magnolia tripetala, with leaves in a whorl like an umbrella. □□ **umbrellaed** /-ləd/ adj. **umbrella-like** adj. [It. ombrella, dimin. of ombra shade f. L umbra: see UMBRA]

Umbria /ˈʌmbrɪə/ **1** a district of ancient central Italy. **2** a corresponding region of modern Italy; pop. (1981) 807,550; capital, Perugia. □□ **Umbrian** adj. & n.

umbriferous /ʌmˈbrɪfərəs/ adj. formal providing shade. [L umbrifer f. umbra shade: see -FEROUS]

umiak /ˈuːmɪˌæk/ n. an Eskimo skin-and-wood open boat propelled by women with paddles. [Eskimo]

umlaut /ˈʊmlaʊt/ n. & v. —n. **1** a mark (¨) used over a vowel, esp. in Germanic languages, to indicate a vowel change. **2** such a vowel change, e.g. German Mann, Männer, English man, men, due to i, j, etc. (now usu. lost or altered) in the following syllable. —v.tr. modify (a form or a sound) by an umlaut. [G f. um about + Laut sound]

Umm al Qaiwain /ʊm æl kaɪˈwaɪn/, **1** the second-smallest of the seven States of the United Arab Emirates; pop. (1980) 12,300. **2** its capital city.

umpire /ˈʌmpaɪə(r)/ n. & v. —n. **1** a person chosen to enforce the rules and settle disputes in various sports. **2** a person chosen to arbitrate between disputants, or to see fair play. —v. **1** intr. (usu. foll. by for, in, etc.) act as umpire. **2** tr. act as umpire in (a game etc.). □□ **umpirage** /-rɪdʒ/ n. **umpireship** n. [ME, later form of noumpere f. OF nonper not equal (as NON-, PEER²): for loss of n- cf. ADDER]

umpteen /ʌmpˈtiːn/ adj. & pron. sl. —adj. indefinitely many; a lot of. —pron. indefinitely many. □□ **umpteenth** adj. **umpty** /ˈʌmptɪ/ adj. (joc. form. on -TEEN)

UN abbr. United Nations.

un-¹ /ʌn/ prefix **1** added to adjectives and participles and their derivative nouns and adverbs, meaning: **a** not: denoting the absence of a quality or state (*unusable; uncalled-for; uneducated; unfailing; unofficially; unhappiness*). **b** the reverse of, usu. with an implication of approval or disapproval, or with some other special connotation (*unselfish; unsociable; unscientific*). ¶ Words formed in this way often have neutral counterparts in *non-* (see NON- 6) and counterparts in *-in* (see IN-[1]), e.g. *unadvisable*. **2** (less often) added to nouns, meaning 'a lack of' (*unrest; untruth*). ¶ The number of words that can be formed with this prefix (and similarly with *un-[2]*) is potentially as large as the number of adjectives in use; consequently only a selection, being considered the most current or semantically noteworthy, can be given here. [OE f. Gmc, rel. to L *in-*]

un-[2] /ʌn/ *prefix* added to verbs and (less often) nouns, forming verbs denoting: **1** the reversal or cancellation of an action or state (*undress; unlock; unsettle*). **2** deprivation or separation (*unmask*). **3** release from (*unburden; uncage*). **4** causing to be no longer (*unman*). ¶ See the note at un-[1]. Both *un-[1]* and *un-[2]* can be understood in some forms in *-able, -ed* (especially), and *-ing*: for example, *undressed* can mean either 'not dressed' or 'no longer dressed'. [OE *un-, on-* f. Gmc]

un-[3] *prefix* Chem. denoting 'one', combined with other numerical roots *nil* (= 0), *un* (= 1), *bi* (= 2), etc., to form names of elements based on the atomic number. The roots are put together in order of the digits which make up the atomic number and are terminated by *-ium* (*unnilquadium* = 104, *ununbium* = 112, etc.). [L *unus* one]

'un /ən/ *pron. colloq.* one (*that's a good 'un*). [dial. var.]

UNA *abbr.* United Nations Association.

unabashed /ˌʌnəˈbæʃt/ *adj.* not abashed. □□ **unabashedly** /-ʃɪdlɪ/ *adv.*

unabated /ˌʌnəˈbeɪtɪd/ *adj.* not abated; undiminished. □□ **unabatedly** *adv.*

unable /ʌnˈeɪb(ə)l/ *adj.* (usu. foll. by *to* + infin.) not able; lacking ability.

unabridged /ˌʌnəˈbrɪdʒd/ *adj.* (of a text etc.) complete; not abridged.

unabsorbed /ˌʌnəbˈzɔːbd, -ˈsɔːbd/ *adj.* not absorbed.

unacademic /ˌʌnækəˈdemɪk/ *adj.* **1** not academic (esp. not scholarly or theoretical). **2** (of a person) not suited to academic study.

unaccented /ˌʌnækˈsentɪd/ *adj.* not accented; not emphasized.

unacceptable /ˌʌnəkˈsept(ə)l/ *adj.* not acceptable. □□ **unacceptableness** *n.* **unacceptably** *adv.*

unacclaimed /ˌʌnəˈkleɪmd/ *adj.* not acclaimed.

unaccommodating /ˌʌnəˈkɒməˌdeɪtɪŋ/ *adj.* not accommodating; disobliging.

unaccompanied /ˌʌnəˈkʌmpənɪd/ *adj.* **1** not accompanied. **2** *Mus.* without accompaniment.

unaccomplished /ˌʌnəˈkʌmplɪʃt, -ˈkɒmplɪʃt/ *adj.* **1** not accomplished; uncompleted. **2** lacking accomplishments.

unaccountable /ˌʌnəˈkaʊntəb(ə)l/ *adj.* **1** unable to be explained. **2** unpredictable or strange in behaviour. **3** not responsible. □□ **unaccountability** /-ˈbɪlɪtɪ/ *n.* **unaccountableness** *n.* **unaccountably** *adv.*

unaccounted /ˌʌnəˈkaʊntɪd/ *adj.* of which no account is given. □ **unaccounted for** unexplained; not included in an account.

unaccustomed /ˌʌnəˈkʌstəmd/ *adj.* **1** (usu. foll. by *to*) not accustomed. **2** not customary; unusual (*his unaccustomed silence*). □□ **unaccustomedly** *adv.*

unacknowledged /ˌʌnəkˈnɒlɪdʒd/ *adj.* not acknowledged.

unacquainted /ˌʌnəˈkweɪntɪd/ *adj.* (usu. foll. by *with*) not acquainted.

unadaptable /ˌʌnəˈdæptəb(ə)l/ *adj.* not adaptable.

unadapted /ˌʌnəˈdæptɪd/ *adj.* not adapted.

unaddressed /ˌʌnəˈdrest/ *adj.* (esp. of a letter etc.) without an address.

unadjacent /ˌʌnəˈdʒeɪs(ə)nt/ *adj.* not adjacent.

unadopted /ˌʌnəˈdɒptɪd/ *adj.* **1** not adopted. **2** *Brit.* (of a road) not taken over for maintenance by a local authority.

unadorned /ˌʌnəˈdɔːnd/ *adj.* not adorned; plain.

unadulterated /ˌʌnəˈdʌltəˌreɪtɪd/ *adj.* **1** not adulterated; pure; concentrated. **2** sheer, complete, utter (*unadulterated nonsense*).

unadventurous /ˌʌnədˈventʃərəs/ *adj.* not adventurous. □□ **unadventurously** *adv.*

unadvertised /ʌnˈædvəˌtaɪzd/ *adj.* not advertised.

unadvisable /ˌʌnədˈvaɪzəb(ə)l/ *adj.* **1** not open to advice. **2** (of a thing) inadvisable.

unadvised /ˌʌnədˈvaɪzd/ *adj.* **1** indiscreet; rash. **2** not having had advice. □□ **unadvisedly** /-zɪdlɪ/ *adv.* **unadvisedness** *n.*

unaffected /ˌʌnəˈfektɪd/ *adj.* **1** (usu. foll. by *by*) not affected. **2** free from affectation; genuine; sincere. □□ **unaffectedly** *adv.* **unaffectedness** *n.*

unaffiliated /ˌʌnəˈfɪlɪˌeɪtɪd/ *adj.* not affiliated.

unafraid /ˌʌnəˈfreɪd/ *adj.* not afraid.

unaided /ʌnˈeɪdɪd/ *adj.* not aided; without help.

unalienable /ʌnˈeɪlɪənəb(ə)l/ *adj. Law* = INALIENABLE.

unaligned /ˌʌnəˈlaɪnd/ *adj.* **1** = NON-ALIGNED. **2** not physically aligned.

unalike /ˌʌnəˈlaɪk/ *adj.* not alike; different.

unalive /ˌʌnəˈlaɪv/ *adj.* **1** lacking in vitality. **2** (foll. by *to*) not fully susceptible or awake to.

unalleviated /ˌʌnəˈliːvɪˌeɪtɪd/ *adj.* not alleviated; relentless.

unallied /ˌʌnəˈlaɪd/ *adj.* not allied; having no allies.

unallowable /ˌʌnəˈlaʊəb(ə)l/ *adj.* not allowable.

unalloyed /ˌʌnəˈlɔɪd, ʌnˈæl-/ *adj.* **1** not alloyed; pure. **2** complete; utter (*unalloyed joy*).

unalterable /ʌnˈɔːltərəb(ə)l, ʌnˈɒl-/ *adj.* not alterable. □□ **unalterableness** *n.* **unalterably** *adv.*

unaltered /ʌnˈɔːltəd, ʌnˈɒl-/ *adj.* not altered; remaining the same.

unamazed /ˌʌnəˈmeɪzd/ *adj.* not amazed.

unambiguous /ˌʌnæmˈbɪgjʊəs/ *adj.* not ambiguous; clear or definite in meaning. □□ **unambiguity** /-ˈgjuːɪtɪ/ *n.* **unambiguously** *adv.*

unambitious /ˌʌnæmˈbɪʃəs/ *adj.* not ambitious; without ambition. □□ **unambitiously** *adv.* **unambitiousness** *n.*

unambivalent /ˌʌnæmˈbɪvələnt/ *adj.* (of feelings etc.) not ambivalent; straightforward. □□ **unambivalently** *adv.*

un-American /ˌʌnəˈmerɪkən/ *adj.* **1** not in accordance with American characteristics etc. **2** contrary to the interests of the US; (in the US) treasonable. □□ **un-Americanism** *n.*

unamiable /ʌnˈeɪmɪəb(ə)l/ *adj.* not amiable.

unamplified /ʌnˈæmplɪˌfaɪd/ *adj.* not amplified.

unamused /ˌʌnəˈmjuːzd/ *adj.* not amused.

unanalysable /ʌnˈænəˌlaɪzəb(ə)l/ *adj.* not able to be analysed.

unanalysed /ʌnˈænəˌlaɪzd/ *adj.* not analysed.

unaneled /ˌʌnəˈniːld/ *adj. archaic* not having received extreme unction.

unanimous /juːˈnænɪməs/ *adj.* **1** all in agreement (*the committee was unanimous*). **2** (of an opinion, vote, etc.) held or given by general consent (*the unanimous choice*). □□ **unanimity** /-nəˈnɪmɪtɪ/ *n.* **unanimously** *adv.* **unanimousness** *n.* [LL *unanimis*, L *unanimus* f. *unus* one + *animus* mind]

unannounced /ˌʌnəˈnaʊnst/ *adj.* not announced; without warning (of arrival etc.).

unanswerable /ʌnˈɑːnsərəb(ə)l/ *adj.* **1** unable to be refuted (*has an unanswerable case*). **2** unable to be answered (*an unanswerable question*). □□ **unanswerableness** *n.* **unanswerably** *adv.*

unanswered /ʌnˈɑːnsəd/ *adj.* not answered.

unanticipated /ˌʌnænˈtɪsɪˌpeɪtɪd/ *adj.* not anticipated.

unapparent /ˌʌnəˈpærənt/ *adj.* not apparent.

unappealable /ˌʌnəˈpiːləb(ə)l/ *adj. esp. Law* not able to be appealed against.

unappealing /ˌʌnəˈpiːlɪŋ/ *adj.* not appealing; unattractive. □□ **unappealingly** *adv.*

unappeasable /ˌʌnəˈpiːzəb(ə)l/ *adj.* not appeasable.

unappeased /ˌʌnəˈpiːzd/ *adj.* not appeased.

unappetizing /ʌnˈæpɪˌtaɪzɪŋ/ *adj.* not appetizing. ☐☐ **unappetizingly** *adv.*

unapplied /ˌʌnəˈplaɪd/ *adj.* not applied.

unappreciated /ˌʌnəˈpriːʃɪˌeɪtɪd/ *adj.* not appreciated.

unappreciative /ˌʌnəˈpriːʃətɪv/ *adj.* not appreciative.

unapproachable /ˌʌnəˈprəʊtʃəb(ə)l/ *adj.* **1** not approachable; remote, inaccessible. **2** (of a person) unfriendly. ☐☐ **unapproachability** /-ˈbɪlɪti/ *n.* **unapproachableness** *n.* **unapproachably** *adv.*

unappropriated /ˌʌnəˈprəʊprɪˌeɪtɪd/ *adj.* **1** not allocated or assigned. **2** not taken into possession by anyone.

unapproved /ˌʌnəˈpruːvd/ *adj.* not approved or sanctioned.

unapt /ʌnˈæpt/ *adj.* **1** (usu. foll. by *for*) not suitable. **2** (usu. foll. by *to* + infin.) not apt. ☐☐ **unaptly** *adv.* **unaptness** *n.*

unarguable /ʌnˈɑːgjʊəb(ə)l/ *adj.* not arguable; certain.

unarm /ʌnˈɑːm/ *v.tr.* deprive or free of arms or armour.

unarmed /ʌnˈɑːmd/ *adj.* not armed; without weapons.

unarresting /ˌʌnəˈrestɪŋ/ *adj.* uninteresting, dull. ☐☐ **unarrestingly** *adv.*

unarticulated /ˌʌnɑːˈtɪkjʊˌleɪtɪd/ *adj.* not articulated or distinct.

unartistic /ˌʌnɑːˈtɪstɪk/ *adj.* not artistic, esp. not concerned with art. ☐☐ **unartistically** *adv.*

unascertainable /ˌʌnæsəˈteɪnəb(ə)l/ *adj.* not ascertainable.

unascertained /ˌʌnæsəˈteɪnd/ *adj.* not ascertained; unknown.

unashamed /ˌʌnəˈʃeɪmd/ *adj.* **1** feeling no guilt, shameless. **2** blatant; bold. ☐☐ **unashamedly** /-mɪdli/ *adv.* **unashamedness** /-mɪdnɪs/ *n.*

unasked /ʌnˈɑːskt/ *adj.* (often foll. by *for*) not asked, requested, or invited.

unassailable /ˌʌnəˈseɪləb(ə)l/ *adj.* unable to be attacked or questioned; impregnable. ☐☐ **unassailability** /-ˈbɪlɪti/ *n.* **unassailableness** *n.* **unassailably** *adv.*

unassertive /ˌʌnəˈsɜːtɪv/ *adj.* (of a person) not assertive or forthcoming; reticent. ☐☐ **unassertively** *adv.* **unassertiveness** *n.*

unassignable /ˌʌnəˈsaɪnəb(ə)l/ *adj.* not assignable.

unassigned /ˌʌnəˈsaɪnd/ *adj.* not assigned.

unassimilated /ˌʌnəˈsɪmɪˌleɪtɪd/ *adj.* not assimilated. ☐☐ **unassimilable** *adj.*

unassisted /ˌʌnəˈsɪstɪd/ *adj.* not assisted.

unassuaged /ˌʌnəˈsweɪdʒd/ *adj.* not assuaged. ☐☐ **unassuageable** *adj.*

unassuming /ˌʌnəˈsjuːmɪŋ/ *adj.* not pretentious or arrogant; modest. ☐☐ **unassumingly** *adv.* **unassumingness** *n.*

unatoned /ˌʌnəˈtəʊnd/ *adj.* not atoned for.

unattached /ˌʌnəˈtætʃt/ *adj.* **1** (often foll. by *to*) not attached, esp. to a particular body, organization, etc. **2** not engaged or married.

unattackable /ˌʌnəˈtækəb(ə)l/ *adj.* unable to be attacked or damaged.

unattainable /ˌʌnəˈteɪnəb(ə)l/ *adj.* not attainable. ☐☐ **unattainableness** *n.* **unattainably** *adv.*

unattempted /ˌʌnəˈtemptɪd/ *adj.* not attempted.

unattended /ˌʌnəˈtendɪd/ *adj.* **1** (usu. foll. by *to*) not attended. **2** (of a person, vehicle, etc.) not accompanied; alone; uncared for.

unattractive /ˌʌnəˈtræktɪv/ *adj.* not attractive. ☐☐ **unattractively** *adv.* **unattractiveness** *n.*

unattributable /ˌʌnəˈtrɪbjʊtəb(ə)l/ *adj.* (esp. of information) that cannot or may not be attributed to a source etc. ☐☐ **unattributably** *adv.*

unauthentic /ˌʌnɔːˈθentɪk/ *adj.* not authentic. ☐☐ **unauthentically** *adv.*

unauthenticated /ˌʌnɔːˈθentɪˌkeɪtɪd/ *adj.* not authenticated.

unauthorized /ʌnˈɔːθəˌraɪzd/ *adj.* (also **unauthorised**) not authorized.

unavailable /ˌʌnəˈveɪləb(ə)l/ *adj.* not available. ☐☐ **unavailability** /-ˈbɪlɪti/ *n.* **unavailableness** *n.*

unavailing /ˌʌnəˈveɪlɪŋ/ *adj.* not availing; achieving nothing; ineffectual. ☐☐ **unavailingly** *adv.*

unavoidable /ˌʌnəˈvɔɪdəb(ə)l/ *adj.* not avoidable; inevitable. ☐☐ **unavoidability** /-ˈbɪlɪti/ *n.* **unavoidableness** *n.* **unavoidably** *adv.*

unavowed /ˌʌnəˈvaʊd/ *adj.* not avowed.

unaware /ˌʌnəˈweə(r)/ *adj. & adv.* —*adj.* **1** (usu. foll. by *of*, or *that* + clause) not aware; ignorant (*unaware of her presence*). **2** (of a person) insensitive; unperceptive. —*adv.* = UNAWARES. ☐☐ **unawareness** *n.*

unawares /ˌʌnəˈweəz/ *adv.* **1** unexpectedly (*met them unawares*). **2** inadvertently (*dropped it unawares*). [earlier *unware(s)* f. OE *unwær(es)*: see WARE²]

unbacked /ʌnˈbækt/ *adj.* **1** not supported. **2** (of a horse etc.) having no backers. **3** (of a chair, picture, etc.) having no back or backing.

unbalance /ʌnˈbæləns/ *v. & n.* —*v.tr.* **1** upset the physical or mental balance of (*unbalanced by the blow; the shock unbalanced him*). **2** (as **unbalanced** *adj.*) **a** not balanced. **b** (of a mind or a person) unstable or deranged. —*n.* lack of balance; instability, esp. mental.

unban /ʌnˈbæn/ *v.tr.* (**unbanned**, **unbanning**) cease to ban; remove a ban from.

unbar /ʌnˈbɑː(r)/ *v.tr.* (**unbarred**, **unbarring**) **1** remove a bar or bars from (a gate etc.). **2** unlock, open.

unbearable /ʌnˈbeərəb(ə)l/ *adj.* not bearable. ☐☐ **unbearableness** *n.* **unbearably** *adv.*

unbeatable /ʌnˈbiːtəb(ə)l/ *adj.* not beatable; excelling.

unbeaten /ʌnˈbiːt(ə)n/ *adj.* **1** not beaten. **2** (of a record etc.) not surpassed. **3** *Cricket* (of a player) not out.

unbeautiful /ʌnˈbjuːtɪˌfʊl/ *adj.* not beautiful; ugly. ☐☐ **unbeautifully** *adv.*

unbecoming /ˌʌnbɪˈkʌmɪŋ/ *adj.* **1** (esp. of clothing) not flattering or suiting a person. **2** (usu. foll. by *to*, *for*) not fitting; indecorous or unsuitable. ☐☐ **unbecomingly** *adv.* **unbecomingness** *n.*

unbefitting /ˌʌnbɪˈfɪtɪŋ/ *adj.* not befitting; unsuitable. ☐☐ **unbefittingly** *adv.* **unbefittingness** *n.*

unbefriended /ˌʌnbɪˈfrendɪd/ *adj.* not befriended.

unbegotten /ˌʌnbɪˈgɒt(ə)n/ *adj.* not begotten.

unbeholden /ˌʌnbɪˈhəʊld(ə)n/ *predic.adj.* (usu. foll. by *to*) under no obligation.

unbeknown /ˌʌnbɪˈnəʊn/ *adj.* (also **unbeknownst** /-ˈnəʊnst/) (foll. by *to*) without the knowledge of (*was there all the time unbeknown to us*). [UN-¹ + *beknown* (archaic) = KNOWN]

unbelief /ˌʌnbɪˈliːf/ *n.* lack of belief, esp. in religious matters. ☐☐ **unbeliever** *n.* **unbelieving** *adj.* **unbelievingly** *adv.* **unbelievingness** *n.*

unbelievable /ˌʌnbɪˈliːvəb(ə)l/ *adj.* not believable; incredible. ☐☐ **unbelievability** /-ˈbɪlɪti/ *n.* **unbelievableness** *n.* **unbelievably** *adv.*

unbeloved /ˌʌnbɪˈlʌvd/ *adj.* not beloved.

unbelt /ʌnˈbelt/ *v.tr.* remove or undo the belt of (a garment etc.).

unbend /ʌnˈbend/ *v.* (*past and past part.* **unbent**) **1** *tr. & intr.* change from a bent position; straighten. **2** *intr.* relax from strain or severity; become affable (*likes to unbend with a glass of beer*). **3** *tr. Naut.* **a** unfasten (sails) from yards and stays. **b** cast (a cable) loose. **c** untie (a rope).

unbending /ʌnˈbendɪŋ/ *adj.* **1** not bending; inflexible. **2** firm; austere (*unbending rectitude*). **3** relaxing from strain, activity, or formality. ☐☐ **unbendingly** *adv.* **unbendingness** *n.*

unbiased /ʌnˈbaɪəst/ *adj.* (also **unbiassed**) not biased; impartial.

unbiblical /ʌnˈbɪblɪk(ə)l/ *adj.* **1** not in or authorized by the Bible. **2** contrary to the Bible.

unbiddable /ʌnˈbɪdəb(ə)l/ *adj. Brit.* disobedient; not docile.

unbidden /ʌnˈbɪd(ə)n/ *adj.* not commanded or invited (*arrived unbidden*).

unbind /ʌnˈbaɪnd/ *v.tr.* (*past and past part.* **unbound**) release from bonds or binding.

unbirthday /ʌnˈbɜːθdeɪ/ n. (often attrib.) joc. any day but one's birthday (an unbirthday party).

unbleached /ʌnˈbliːtʃt/ adj. not bleached.

unblemished /ʌnˈblemɪʃt/ adj. not blemished.

unblessed /ʌnˈblest/ adj. (also **unblest**) not blessed.

unblinking /ʌnˈblɪŋkɪŋ/ adj. 1 not blinking. 2 steadfast; not hesitating. 3 stolid; cool. □□ **unblinkingly** adv.

unblock /ʌnˈblɒk/ v.tr. 1 remove an obstruction from (esp. a pipe, drain, etc.). 2 (also absol.) Cards allow the later unobstructed play of (a suit) by playing a high card.

unblown /ʌnˈbləʊn/ adj. 1 not blown. 2 archaic (of a flower) not yet in bloom.

unblushing /ʌnˈblʌʃɪŋ/ adj. 1 not blushing. 2 unashamed; frank. □□ **unblushingly** adv.

unbolt /ʌnˈbəʊlt/ v.tr. release (a door etc.) by drawing back the bolt.

unbolted /ʌnˈbəʊltɪd/ adj. 1 not bolted. 2 (of flour etc.) not sifted.

unbonnet /ʌnˈbɒnɪt/ v. (**unbonneted, unbonneting**) 1 tr. remove the bonnet from. 2 intr. archaic remove one's hat or bonnet esp. in respect.

unbookish /ʌnˈbʊkɪʃ/ adj. 1 not academic; not often inclined to read. 2 free from bookishness.

unboot /ʌnˈbuːt/ v.intr. & tr. remove one's boots or the boots of (a person).

unborn /ʌnˈbɔːn/ adj. 1 not yet born (an unborn child). 2 never to be brought into being (unborn hopes).

unbosom /ʌnˈbʊz(ə)m/ v.tr. 1 disclose (thoughts, secrets, etc.). 2 (refl.) unburden (oneself) of one's thoughts, secrets, etc.

unbothered /ʌnˈbɒðəd/ adj. not bothered; unconcerned.

unbound[1] /ʌnˈbaʊnd/ adj. 1 not bound or tied up. 2 unconstrained. 3 a (of a book) not having a binding. b having paper covers. 4 (of a substance or particle) in a loose or free state.

unbound[2] past and past part. of UNBIND.

unbounded /ʌnˈbaʊndɪd/ adj. not bounded; infinite (unbounded optimism). □□ **unboundedly** adv. **unboundedness** n.

unbrace /ʌnˈbreɪs/ v.tr. 1 (also absol.) free from tension; relax (the nerves etc.). 2 remove a brace or braces from.

unbreachable /ʌnˈbriːtʃəb(ə)l/ adj. not able to be breached.

unbreakable /ʌnˈbreɪkəb(ə)l/ adj. not breakable.

unbreathable /ʌnˈbriːðəb(ə)l/ adj. not able to be breathed.

unbribable /ʌnˈbraɪbəb(ə)l/ adj. not bribable.

unbridgeable /ʌnˈbrɪdʒəb(ə)l/ adj. unable to be bridged.

unbridle /ʌnˈbraɪd(ə)l/ v.tr. 1 remove a bridle from (a horse). 2 remove constraints from (one's tongue, a person, etc.). 3 (as **unbridled** adj.) unconstrained (unbridled insolence).

unbroken /ʌnˈbrəʊkən/ adj. 1 not broken. 2 not tamed (an unbroken horse). 3 not interrupted (unbroken sleep). 4 not surpassed (an unbroken record). □□ **unbrokenly** adv. **unbrokenness** /-ənnɪs/ n.

unbruised /ʌnˈbruːzd/ adj. not bruised.

unbuckle /ʌnˈbʌk(ə)l/ v.tr. release the buckle of (a strap, shoe, etc.).

unbuild /ʌnˈbɪld/ v.tr. (past and past part. **unbuilt**) 1 demolish or destroy (a building, theory, system, etc.). 2 (as **unbuilt** adj.) not yet built or (of land etc.) not yet built on.

unburden /ʌnˈbɜːd(ə)n/ v.tr. 1 relieve of a burden. 2 (esp. refl.; often foll. by to) relieve (oneself, one's conscience, etc.) by confession etc. □□ **unburdened** adj.

unburied /ʌnˈberɪd/ adj. not buried.

unbury /ʌnˈberɪ/ v.tr. (-ies, -ied) 1 remove from the ground etc. after burial. 2 unearth (a secret etc.).

unbusinesslike /ʌnˈbɪznɪsˌlaɪk/ adj. not businesslike.

unbutton /ʌnˈbʌt(ə)n/ v.tr. 1 a unfasten (a coat etc.) by taking the buttons out of the buttonholes. b unbutton the clothes of (a person). 2 (absol.) colloq. relax from tension or formality, become communicative. 3 (as **unbuttoned** adj.) a not buttoned. b colloq. communicative; informal.

uncage /ʌnˈkeɪdʒ/ v.tr. 1 release from a cage. 2 release from constraint; liberate.

uncalled /ʌnˈkɔːld/ adj. not summoned or invited. □ **uncalled-for** (of an opinion, action, etc.) impertinent or unnecessary (an uncalled-for remark).

uncandid /ʌnˈkændɪd/ adj. not candid; disingenuous.

uncanny /ʌnˈkænɪ/ adj. (**uncannier, uncanniest**) seemingly supernatural; mysterious. □□ **uncannily** adv. **uncanniness** n. [(orig. Sc. & N.Engl.) f. UN-[1] + CANNY]

uncanonical /ˌʌnkəˈnɒnɪk(ə)l/ adj. not canonical. □□ **uncanonically** adv.

uncap /ʌnˈkæp/ v.tr. (**uncapped, uncapping**) 1 remove the cap from (a jar, bottle, etc.). 2 remove a cap from (the head or another person).

uncared-for /ʌnˈkeədfɔː(r)/ adj. disregarded; neglected.

uncase /ʌnˈkeɪs/ v.tr. remove from a cover or case.

uncashed /ʌnˈkæʃt/ adj. not cashed.

uncaught /ʌnˈkɔːt/ adj. not caught.

unceasing /ʌnˈsiːsɪŋ/ adj. not ceasing; continuous (unceasing effort). □□ **unceasingly** adv.

uncensored /ʌnˈsensəd/ adj. not censored.

uncensured /ʌnˈsensjəd/ adj. not censured.

unceremonious /ˌʌnserɪˈməʊnɪəs/ adj. 1 lacking ceremony or formality. 2 abrupt; discourteous. □□ **unceremoniously** adv. **unceremoniousness** n.

uncertain /ʌnˈsɜːt(ə)n/ adj. 1 not certainly knowing or known (uncertain what it means; the result is uncertain). 2 unreliable (his aim is uncertain). 3 changeable, erratic (uncertain weather). □ **in no uncertain terms** clearly and forcefully. □□ **uncertainly** adv.

uncertainty /ʌnˈsɜːtəntɪ/ n. (pl. **-ies**) 1 the fact or condition of being uncertain. 2 an uncertain matter or circumstance. □ **uncertainty principle** 1 (in full **Heisenberg uncertainty principle** after W. Heisenberg; see entry) Physics the principle that the momentum and position of a particle cannot both be precisely determined at the same time. (See QUANTUM.) 2 any of various similar restrictions on the accuracy of measurement.

uncertified /ʌnˈsɜːtɪˌfaɪd/ adj. 1 not attested as certain. 2 not guaranteed by a certificate of competence etc. 3 not certified as insane.

unchain /ʌnˈtʃeɪn/ v.tr. 1 remove the chains from. 2 release; liberate.

unchallengeable /ʌnˈtʃælɪndʒəb(ə)l/ adj. not challengeable; unassailable. □□ **unchallengeably** adv.

unchallenged /ʌnˈtʃælɪndʒd/ adj. not challenged.

unchangeable /ʌnˈtʃeɪndʒəb(ə)l/ adj. not changeable; immutable, invariable. □□ **unchangeability** /-ˈbɪlɪtɪ/ n. **unchangeableness** n. **unchangeably** adv.

unchanged /ʌnˈtʃeɪndʒd/ adj. not changed; unaltered.

unchanging /ʌnˈtʃeɪndʒɪŋ/ adj. not changing; remaining the same. □□ **unchangingly** adv. **unchangingness** n.

unchaperoned /ʌnˈʃæpəˌrəʊnd/ adj. without a chaperone.

uncharacteristic /ˌʌnkærɪktəˈrɪstɪk/ adj. not characteristic. □□ **uncharacteristically** adv.

uncharged /ʌnˈtʃɑːdʒd/ adj. not charged (esp. in senses 3, 7, 8 of CHARGE v.).

uncharitable /ʌnˈtʃærɪtəb(ə)l/ adj. censorious, severe in judgement. □□ **uncharitableness** n. **uncharitably** adv.

uncharted /ʌnˈtʃɑːtɪd/ adj. not charted, mapped, or surveyed.

unchartered /ʌnˈtʃɑːtəd/ adj. 1 not furnished with a charter; not formally privileged or constituted. 2 unauthorized; illegal.

unchaste /ʌnˈtʃeɪst/ adj. not chaste. □□ **unchastely** adv. **unchasteness** n. **unchastity** /-ˈtʃæstɪtɪ/ n.

unchecked /ʌnˈtʃekt/ adj. 1 not checked. 2 freely allowed; unrestrained (unchecked violence).

unchivalrous /ʌnˈʃɪvəlrəs/ adj. not chivalrous; rude. □□ **unchivalrously** adv.

unchosen /ʌnˈtʃəʊz(ə)n/ adj. not chosen.

unchristian /ʌnˈkrɪstjən/ adj. **1 a** contrary to Christian principles, esp. uncaring or selfish. **b** not Christian. **2** colloq. outrageous. ☐☐ **unchristianly** adv.

unchurch /ʌnˈtʃɜːtʃ/ v.tr. **1** excommunicate. **2** deprive (a building) of its status as a church.

uncial /ˈʌnsɪəl, -ʃ(ə)l/ adj. & n. —adj. **1** of or written in majuscule writing with rounded unjoined letters found in manuscripts of the 4th–8th c., from which modern capitals are derived. **2** of or relating to an inch or an ounce. —n. **1** an uncial letter. **2** an uncial style or MS. [L uncialis f. uncia inch: sense 1 in LL sense of unciales litterae, the orig. application of which is unclear]

unciform /ˈʌnsɪfɔːm/ adj. = UNCINATE.

uncinate /ˈʌnsɪnət/ adj. esp. Anat. hooked; crooked. [L uncinatus f. uncinus hook]

uncircumcised /ʌnˈsɜːkəmˌsaɪzd/ adj. **1** not circumcised. **2** spiritually impure; heathen. ☐☐ **uncircumcision** /-ˈsɪʒ(ə)n/ n.

uncivil /ʌnˈsɪvɪl/ adj. **1** ill-mannered; impolite. **2** not public-spirited. ☐☐ **uncivilly** adv.

uncivilized /ʌnˈsɪvɪˌlaɪzd/ adj. (also **uncivilised**) **1** not civilized. **2** rough; uncultured.

unclad /ʌnˈklæd/ adj. not clad; naked.

unclaimed /ʌnˈkleɪmd/ adj. not claimed.

unclasp /ʌnˈklɑːsp/ v.tr. **1** loosen the clasp or clasps of. **2** release the grip of (a hand etc.).

unclassifiable /ʌnˈklæsɪˌfaɪəb(ə)l/ adj. not classifiable.

unclassified /ʌnˈklæsɪˌfaɪd/ adj. **1** not classified. **2** (of State information) not secret.

uncle /ˈʌŋk(ə)l/ n. **1 a** the brother of one's father or mother. **b** an aunt's husband. **2** colloq. a name given by children to a male family friend. **3** sl. esp. hist. a pawnbroker. ☐ **Uncle Sam** see separate entry. **Uncle Tom** derog. a Black man considered to be servile, cringing, etc. (from the hero of H. B. Stowe's Uncle Tom's Cabin, 1852). [ME f. AF uncle, OF oncle f. LL auunculus f. L avunculus maternal uncle: see AVUNCULAR]

-uncle /ˈʌŋk(ə)l/ suffix forming nouns, usu. diminutives (carbuncle). [OF -uncle, -oncle or L -unculus, -la, a special form of -ulus -ULE]

unclean /ʌnˈkliːn/ adj. **1** not clean. **2** unchaste. **3** unfit to be eaten; ceremonially impure. **4** Bibl. (of a spirit) wicked. ☐☐ **uncleanly** adv. **uncleanly** /-ˈklenlɪ/ adj. **uncleanliness** /-ˈklenlɪnɪs/ n. **uncleanness** n. [OE unclǣne (as UN-¹, CLEAN)]

unclear /ʌnˈklɪə(r)/ adj. **1** not clear or easy to understand; obscure, uncertain. **2** (of a person) doubtful, uncertain (I'm unclear as to what you mean). ☐☐ **unclearly** adv. **unclearness** n.

unclench /ʌnˈklentʃ/ v. **1** tr. release (clenched hands, features, teeth, etc.). **2** intr. (of clenched hands etc.) become relaxed or open.

Uncle Sam colloq. a personification of the government or people of the United States of America. The suggestion that it arose as a facetious interpretation of the letters US is as old as the first recorded instance, and later statements connecting it with different government officials of the name of Samuel appear to be unfounded.

unclinch /ʌnˈklɪntʃ/ v.tr. & intr. release or become released from a clinch.

uncloak /ʌnˈkləʊk/ v.tr. **1** expose, reveal. **2** remove a cloak from.

unclog /ʌnˈklɒg/ v.tr. (**unclogged, unclogging**) unblock (a drain, pipe, etc.).

unclose /ʌnˈkləʊz/ v. **1** tr. & intr. open. **2** tr. reveal; disclose.

unclothe /ʌnˈkləʊð/ v.tr. **1** remove the clothes from. **2** strip of leaves or vegetation (trees unclothed by the wind). **3** expose, reveal. ☐☐ **unclothed** adj.

unclouded /ʌnˈklaʊdɪd/ adj. **1** not clouded; clear; bright. **2** untroubled (unclouded serenity).

uncluttered /ʌnˈklʌtəd/ adj. not cluttered; austere, simple.

unco /ˈʌŋkəʊ/ adj., adv., & n. Sc. —adj. strange, unusual; notable. —adv. remarkably; very. —n. (pl. -os) **1** a stranger. **2** (in pl.) news. ☐ **the unco guid** /gɪd/ esp. derog. the rigidly religious. [ME, var. of UNCOUTH]

uncoil /ʌnˈkɔɪl/ v.tr. & intr. unwind.

uncoloured /ʌnˈkʌləd/ adj. (US **uncolored**) **1** having no colour. **2** not influenced; impartial. **3** not exaggerated.

uncombed /ʌnˈkəʊmd/ adj. (of hair or a person) not combed.

uncome-at-able /ˌʌnkʌmˈætəb(ə)l/ adj. colloq. inaccessible; unattainable. [UN-¹ + come-at-able: see COME]

uncomely /ʌnˈkʌmlɪ/ adj. **1** improper; unseemly. **2** ugly.

uncomfortable /ʌnˈkʌmftəb(ə)l/ adj. **1** not comfortable. **2** uneasy; causing or feeling disquiet (an uncomfortable silence). ☐☐ **uncomfortableness** n. **uncomfortably** adv.

uncommercial /ˌʌnkəˈmɜːʃ(ə)l/ adj. **1** not commercial. **2** contrary to commercial principles.

uncommitted /ˌʌnkəˈmɪtɪd/ adj. **1** not committed. **2** unattached to any specific political cause or group.

uncommon /ʌnˈkɒmən/ adj. & adv. —adj. **1** not common; unusual; remarkable. **2** remarkably great etc. (an uncommon fear of spiders). —adv. archaic uncommonly (he was uncommon fat). ☐☐ **uncommonly** adv. **uncommonness** /-mənnɪs/ n.

uncommunicative /ˌʌnkəˈmjuːnɪkətɪv/ adj. not wanting to communicate; taciturn. ☐☐ **uncommunicatively** adv. **uncommunicativeness** n.

uncompanionable /ˌʌnkəmˈpænjənəb(ə)l/ adj. unsociable.

uncompensated /ʌnˈkɒmpenˌseɪtɪd/ adj. not compensated.

uncompetitive /ˌʌnkəmˈpetɪtɪv/ adj. not competitive.

uncomplaining /ˌʌnkəmˈpleɪnɪŋ/ adj. not complaining; resigned. ☐☐ **uncomplainingly** adv.

uncompleted /ˌʌnkəmˈpliːtɪd/ adj. not completed; incomplete.

uncomplicated /ʌnˈkɒmplɪˌkeɪtɪd/ adj. not complicated; simple; straightforward.

uncomplimentary /ˌʌnkɒmplɪˈmentərɪ/ adj. not complimentary; insulting.

uncompounded /ˌʌnkəmˈpaʊndɪd/ adj. not compounded; unmixed.

uncomprehending /ˌʌnkɒmprɪˈhendɪŋ/ adj. not comprehending. ☐☐ **uncomprehendingly** adv. **uncomprehension** /-ˈʃ(ə)n/ n.

uncompromising /ʌnˈkɒmprəˌmaɪzɪŋ/ adj. unwilling to compromise; stubborn; unyielding. ☐☐ **uncompromisingly** adv. **uncompromisingness** n.

unconcealed /ˌʌnkənˈsiːld/ adj. not concealed; obvious.

unconcern /ˌʌnkənˈsɜːn/ n. lack of concern; indifference; apathy. ☐☐ **unconcerned** adj. **unconcernedly** /-nɪdlɪ/ adv.

unconcluded /ˌʌnkənˈkluːdɪd/ adj. not concluded.

unconditional /ˌʌnkənˈdɪʃ(ə)n(ə)l/ adj. not subject to conditions; complete (unconditional surrender). ☐☐ **unconditionality** /-ˈnælɪtɪ/ n. **unconditionally** adv.

unconditioned /ˌʌnkənˈdɪʃ(ə)nd/ adj. **1** not subject to conditions or to an antecedent condition. **2** (of behaviour etc.) not determined by conditioning; natural. ☐ **unconditioned reflex** an instinctive response to a stimulus.

unconfined /ˌʌnkənˈfaɪnd/ adj. not confined; boundless.

unconfirmed /ˌʌnkənˈfɜːmd/ adj. not confirmed.

unconformable /ˌʌnkənˈfɔːməb(ə)l/ adj. **1** not conformable or conforming. **2** (of rock strata) not having the same direction of stratification. **3** hist. not conforming to the provisions of the Act of Uniformity. ☐☐ **unconformableness** n. **unconformably** adv.

unconformity /ˌʌnkənˈfɔːmɪtɪ/ n. an instance of a break in the chronological sequence of layers of rock.

uncongenial /ˌʌnkənˈdʒiːnɪəl/ adj. not congenial.

unconjecturable /ˌʌnkənˈdʒektʃərəb(ə)l/ adj. not conjecturable.

unconnected /ˌʌnkəˈnektɪd/ adj. **1** not physically joined. **2** not connected or associated. **3** (of speech etc.) disconnected; not joined in order or sequence (unconnected ideas). **4** not related by family ties. ☐☐ **unconnectedly** adv. **unconnectedness** n.

unconquerable /ʌnˈkɒŋkərəb(ə)l/ adj. not conquerable. ☐☐ **unconquerableness** n. **unconquerably** adv.

unconquered /ʌnˈkɒŋkəd/ adj. not conquered or defeated.

unconscionable /ʌnˈkɒnʃənəb(ə)l/ adj. **1 a** having no

conscience. **b** contrary to conscience. **2 a** unreasonably excessive (*an unconscionable length of time*). **b** not right or reasonable. □□ **unconscionableness** *n.* **unconscionably** *adv.* [UN-¹ + obs. *conscionable* f. *conscions* obs. var. of CONSCIENCE]

unconscious /ʌnˈkɒnʃəs/ *adj. & n.* —*adj.* not conscious (*unconscious of any change; fell unconscious on the floor; an unconscious prejudice*). —*n.* that part of the mind which is inaccessible to the conscious mind but which affects behaviour, emotions, etc. (cf. *collective unconscious*). □□ **unconsciously** *adv.* **unconsciousness** *n.*

unconsecrated /ʌnˈkɒnsɪˌkreɪtɪd/ *adj.* not consecrated.

unconsenting /ˌʌnkənˈsentɪŋ/ *adj.* not consenting.

unconsidered /ˌʌnkənˈsɪdəd/ *adj.* **1** not considered; disregarded. **2** (of a response etc.) immediate; not premeditated.

unconsolable /ˌʌnkənˈsəʊləb(ə)l/ *adj* unable to be consoled; inconsolable. □□ **unconsolably** *adv.*

unconstitutional /ˌʌnkɒnstɪˈtjuːʃ(ə)n(ə)l/ *adj.* not in accordance with the political constitution or with procedural rules. □□ **unconstitutionality** /-ˈnælɪtɪ/ *n.* **unconstitutionally** *adv.*

unconstrained /ˌʌnkənˈstreɪnd/ *adj.* not constrained or compelled. □□ **unconstrainedly** /-nɪdlɪ/ *adv.*

unconstraint /ˌʌnkənˈstreɪnt/ *n.* freedom from constraint.

unconstricted /ˌʌnkənˈstrɪktɪd/ *adj.* not constricted.

unconsumed /ˌʌnkənˈsjuːmd/ *adj.* not consumed.

unconsummated /ʌnˈkɒnsjʊˌmeɪtɪd/ *adj.* not consummated.

uncontainable /ˌʌnkənˈteɪnəb(ə)l/ *adj.* not containable.

uncontaminated /ˌʌnkənˈtæmɪˌneɪtɪd/ *adj.* not contaminated.

uncontested /ˌʌnkənˈtestɪd/ *adj.* not contested. □□ **uncontestedly** *adv.*

uncontradicted /ˌʌnkɒntrəˈdɪktɪd/ *adj.* not contradicted.

uncontrollable /ˌʌnkənˈtrəʊləb(ə)l/ *adj.* not controllable. □□ **uncontrollableness** *n.* **uncontrollably** *adv.*

uncontrolled /ˌʌnkənˈtrəʊld/ *adj.* not controlled; unrestrained, unchecked.

uncontroversial /ˌʌnkɒntrəˈvɜːʃ(ə)l/ *adj.* not controversial. □□ **uncontroversially** *adv.*

uncontroverted /ˌʌnkɒntrəˈvɜːtɪd, ʌnˈkɒn-/ *adj.* not controverted. □□ **uncontrovertible** *adj.*

unconventional /ˌʌnkənˈvenʃ(ə)n(ə)l/ *adj.* not bound by convention or custom; unusual; unorthodox. □□ **unconventionalism** *n.* **unconventionality** /-ˈnælɪtɪ/ *n.* **unconventionally** *adv.*

unconverted /ˌʌnkənˈvɜːtɪd/ *adj.* not converted.

unconvinced /ˌʌnkənˈvɪnst/ *adj.* not convinced.

unconvincing /ˌʌnkənˈvɪnsɪŋ/ *adj.* not convincing. □□ **unconvincingly** *adv.*

uncooked /ʌnˈkʊkt/ *adj.* not cooked; raw.

uncool /ʌnˈkuːl/ *adj. sl.* **1** unrelaxed; unpleasant. **2** (of jazz) not cool.

uncooperative /ˌʌnkəʊˈɒpərətɪv/ *adj.* not cooperative. □□ **uncooperatively** *adv.*

uncoordinated /ˌʌnkəʊˈɔːdɪˌneɪtɪd/ *adj.* **1** not coordinated. **2** (of a person's movements etc.) clumsy.

uncopiable /ʌnˈkɒpɪəb(ə)l/ *adj.* not able to be copied.

uncord /ʌnˈkɔːd/ *v.tr.* remove the cord from.

uncork /ʌnˈkɔːk/ *v.tr.* **1** draw the cork from (a bottle). **2** allow (feelings etc.) to be vented.

uncorroborated /ˌʌnkəˈrɒbəˌreɪtɪd/ *adj.* (esp. of evidence etc.) not corroborated.

uncorrupted /ˌʌnkəˈrʌptɪd/ *adj.* not corrupted.

uncountable /ʌnˈkaʊntəb(ə)l/ *adj.* **1** inestimable, immense (*uncountable wealth*). **2** *Gram.* (of a noun) that cannot form a plural or be used with the indefinite article (e.g. *happiness*). □□ **uncountability** /-ˈbɪlɪtɪ/ *n.* **uncountably** *adv.*

uncounted /ʌnˈkaʊntɪd/ *adj.* **1** not counted. **2** very many; innumerable.

uncouple /ʌnˈkʌp(ə)l/ *v.tr.* **1** release (wagons) from couplings. **2** release (dogs etc.) from couples. □□ **uncoupled** *adj.*

uncourtly /ʌnˈkɔːtlɪ/ *adj.* not courteous; ill-mannered.

uncouth /ʌnˈkuːθ/ *adj.* **1** (of a person, manners, appearance, etc.) lacking in ease and polish; uncultured, rough (*uncouth voices; behaviour was uncouth*). **2** *archaic* not known; desolate; wild; uncivilized (*an uncouth place*). □□ **uncouthly** *adv.* **uncouthness** *n.* [OE *uncūth* unknown (as UN-¹ + *cūth* past part. of *cunnan* know, CAN¹)]

uncovenanted /ʌnˈkʌvənəntɪd/ *adj.* **1** not bound by a covenant. **2** not promised by or based on a covenant, esp. God's covenant.

uncover /ʌnˈkʌvə(r)/ *v.* **1** *tr.* **a** remove a cover or covering from. **b** make known; disclose (*uncovered the truth at last*). **2** *intr. archaic* remove one's hat, cap, etc. **3** *tr.* (as **uncovered** *adj.*) **a** not covered by a roof, clothing, etc. **b** not wearing a hat.

uncreate /ˌʌnkriːˈeɪt/ *v.tr. literary* annihilate.

uncreated /ˌʌnkriːˈeɪtɪd/ *adj.* existing without having been created; not created. [UN-¹ + obs. *create* f. L *creatus* past part. of *creare*: see CREATE]

uncreative /ˌʌnkriːˈeɪtɪv/ *adj.* not creative.

uncritical /ʌnˈkrɪtɪk(ə)l/ *adj.* **1** not critical; complacently accepting. **2** not in accordance with the principles of criticism. □□ **uncritically** *adv.*

uncropped /ʌnˈkrɒpt/ *adj.* not cropped.

uncross /ʌnˈkrɒs/ *v.tr.* **1** remove (the limbs, knives, etc.) from a crossed position. **2** (as **uncrossed** *adj.*) **a** *Brit.* (of a cheque) not crossed. **b** not thwarted or challenged. **c** not wearing a cross.

uncrown /ʌnˈkraʊn/ *v.tr.* **1** deprive (a monarch etc.) of a crown. **2** deprive (a person) of a position. **3** (as **uncrowned** *adj.*) **a** not crowned. **b** having the status but not the name of (*the uncrowned king of boxing*).

uncrushable /ʌnˈkrʌʃəb(ə)l/ *adj.* not crushable.

uncrushed /ʌnˈkrʌʃt/ *adj.* not crushed.

UNCSTD *abbr.* United Nations Conference on Science and Technology for Development.

UNCTAD *abbr.* United Nations Conference on Trade and Development. Its headquarters are in Geneva.

unction /ˈʌŋkʃ(ə)n/ *n.* **1 a** the act of anointing with oil etc. as a religious rite. **b** the oil etc. so used. **2 a** soothing words or thought. **b** excessive or insincere flattery. **3 a** the act of anointing for medical purposes. **b** an ointment so used. **4 a** a fervent or sympathetic quality in words or tone caused by or causing deep emotion. **b** a pretence of this. [ME f. L *unctio* f. *ung(u)ere unct-* anoint]

unctuous /ˈʌŋktjʊəs/ *adj.* **1** (of behaviour, speech, etc.) unpleasantly flattering; oily. **2** (esp. of minerals) having a greasy or soapy feel; oily. □□ **unctuously** *adv.* **unctuousness** *n.* [ME f. med.L *unctuosus* f. L *unctus* anointing (as UNCTION)]

unculled /ʌnˈkʌld/ *adj.* not culled.

uncultivated /ʌnˈkʌltɪˌveɪtɪd/ *adj.* (esp. of land) not cultivated.

uncultured /ʌnˈkʌltʃəd/ *adj.* **1** not cultured, unrefined. **2** (of soil or plants) not cultivated.

uncurb /ʌnˈkɜːb/ *v.tr.* remove a curb or curbs from. □□ **uncurbed** *adj.*

uncured /ʌnˈkjʊəd/ *adj.* **1** not cured. **2** (of pork etc.) not salted or smoked.

uncurl /ʌnˈkɜːl/ *v.intr. & tr.* relax from a curled position, untwist.

uncurtailed /ˌʌnkəˈteɪld/ *adj.* not curtailed.

uncurtained /ʌnˈkɜːt(ə)nd/ *adj.* not curtained.

uncut /ʌnˈkʌt/ *adj.* **1** not cut. **2** (of a book) with the pages not cut open or with untrimmed margins. **3** (of a book, film, etc.) complete; uncensored. **4** (of a stone, esp. a diamond) not shaped by cutting. **5** (of fabric) having its pile-loops intact (*uncut moquette*).

undamaged /ʌnˈdæmɪdʒd/ *adj.* not damaged; intact.

undated /ʌnˈdeɪtɪd/ *adj.* not provided or marked with a date.

undaunted /ʌnˈdɔːntɪd/ *adj.* not daunted. □□ **undauntedly** *adv.* **undauntedness** *n.*

undecagon /ʌnˈdekəgən/ *n.* = HENDECAGON. [L *undecim* eleven, after *decagon*]

undeceive /ˌʌndɪˈsiːv/ *v.tr.* (often foll. by *of*) free (a person) from a misconception, deception, or error.

undecided /ˌʌndɪˈsaɪdɪd/ *adj.* **1** not settled or certain (*the question* is *undecided*). **2** hesitating; irresolute (*undecided about their relative merits*). □□ **undecidedly** *adv.*

undecipherable /ˌʌndɪˈsaɪfərəb(ə)l/ *adj.* not decipherable.

undeclared /ˌʌndɪˈkleəd/ *adj.* not declared.

undefeated /ˌʌndɪˈfiːtɪd/ *adj.* not defeated.

undefended /ˌʌndɪˈfendɪd/ *adj.* (esp. of a lawsuit) not defended.

undefiled /ˌʌndɪˈfaɪld/ *adj.* not defiled; pure.

undefined /ˌʌndɪˈfaɪnd/ *adj.* **1** not defined. **2** not clearly marked; vague, indefinite. □□ **undefinable** *adj.* **undefinably** *adv.*

undelivered /ˌʌndɪˈlɪvəd/ *adj.* **1** not delivered or handed over. **2** not set free or released. **3 a** (of a pregnant woman) not yet having given birth. **b** (of a child) not yet born.

undemanding /ˌʌndɪˈmɑːndɪŋ/ *adj.* not demanding; easily satisfied. □□ **undemandingness** *n.*

undemocratic /ˌʌndeməˈkrætɪk/ *adj.* not democratic. □□ **undemocratically** *adv.*

undemonstrated /ʌnˈdemənˌstreɪtɪd/ *adj.* not demonstrated.

undemonstrative /ˌʌndɪˈmɒnstrətɪv/ *adj.* not expressing feelings etc. outwardly; reserved. □□ **undemonstratively** *adv.* **undemonstrativeness** *n.*

undeniable /ˌʌndɪˈnaɪəb(ə)l/ *adj.* **1** unable to be denied or disputed; certain. **2** excellent (*was of undeniable character*). □□ **undeniableness** *n.* **undeniably** *adv.*

undenied /ˌʌndɪˈnaɪd/ *adj.* not denied.

undependable /ˌʌndɪˈpendəb(ə)l/ *adj.* not to be depended upon; unreliable.

under /ˈʌndə(r)/ *prep., adv., & adj.* —*prep.* **1 a** in or to a position lower than; below; beneath (*fell under the table; under the left eye*). **b** within, on the inside of (a surface etc.) (*wore a vest under his shirt*). **2 a** inferior to; less than (*a captain is under a major; is under 18*). **b** at or for a lower cost than (*was under £20*). **3 a** subject or liable to; controlled or bound by (*lives under oppression; under pain of death; born under Saturn; the country prospered under him*). **b** undergoing (*is under repair*). **c** classified or subsumed in (*that book goes under biology; goes under many names*). **4** at the foot of or sheltered by (*hid under the wall; under the cliff*). **5** planted with (a crop). **6** powered by (sail, steam, etc.). **7** following (another player in a card game). **8** *archaic* attested by (esp. *under one's hand and seal* = signature). —*adv.* **1** in or to a lower position or condition (*kept him under*). **2** *colloq.* in or into a state of unconsciousness (*put him under for the operation*). —*adj.* lower (*the under jaw*). □ **under age** see AGE. **under one's arm** see ARM¹. **under arms** see ARM². **under one's belt** see BELT. **under one's breath** see BREATH. **under canvas** see CANVAS. **under a cloud** see CLOUD. **under control** see CONTROL. **under the counter** see COUNTER¹. **under cover** see COVER *n.* 4. **under fire** see FIRE. **under foot** see FOOT. **under hatches** see HATCH¹. **under a person's nose** see NOSE. **under the rose** see ROSE¹. **under separate cover** in another envelope. **under the sun** anywhere in the world. **under water** in and covered by water. **under way** in motion; in progress. **under the weather** see WEATHER. □□ **undermost** *adj.* [OE f. Gmc]

under- /ˈʌndə(r)/ *prefix* in senses of UNDER: **1** below, beneath (*undercarriage; underground*). **2** lower in status; subordinate (*under-secretary*). **3** insufficiently, incompletely (*undercook; underdeveloped*). [OE (as UNDER)]

underachieve /ˌʌndərəˈtʃiːv/ *v.intr.* do less well than might be expected (esp. scholastically). □□ **underachievement** *n.* **underachiever** *n.*

underact /ˌʌndərˈækt/ *v.* **1 tr.** act (a part etc.) with insufficient force. **2** *intr.* act a part in this way.

underarm /ˈʌndərˌɑːm/ *adj. & adv.* **1** *Sport*, esp. *Cricket* with the arm below shoulder-level. **2** under the arm. **3** in the armpit.

underbelly /ˈʌndəˌbelɪ/ *n.* (pl. **-ies**) the under surface of an animal, vehicle, etc., esp. as an area vulnerable to attack.

underbid *v. & n.* —*v.tr.* /ˌʌndəˈbɪd/ (**-bidding**; *past* and *past part.* **-bid**) **1** make a lower bid than (a person). **2** (also *absol.*) *Bridge* etc. bid less on (one's hand) than its strength warrants. —*n.* /ˈʌndəˌbɪd/ **1** such a bid. **2** the act or an instance of underbidding.

underbidder /ˌʌndəˈbɪdə(r)/ *n.* **1** the person who makes the bid next below the highest. **2** *Bridge* etc. a player who underbids.

underbody /ˈʌndəˌbɒdɪ/ *n.* (pl. **-ies**) the under surface of the body of an animal, vehicle, etc.

underbred /ˌʌndəˈbred/ *adj.* **1** ill-bred, vulgar. **2** not of pure breeding.

underbrush /ˈʌndəˌbrʌʃ/ *n. US* undergrowth in a forest.

undercarriage /ˈʌndəˌkærɪdʒ/ *n.* **1** a wheeled structure beneath an aircraft, usu. retracted when not in use, to receive the impact on landing and support the aircraft on the ground etc. **2** the supporting frame of a vehicle.

undercart /ˈʌndəˌkɑːt/ *n. Brit. colloq.* the undercarriage of an aircraft.

undercharge /ˌʌndəˈtʃɑːdʒ/ *v.tr.* **1** charge too little for (a thing) or to (a person). **2** give less than the proper charge to (a gun, an electric battery, etc.).

underclass /ˈʌndəˌklɑːs/ *n.* a subordinate social class.

underclay /ˈʌndəˌkleɪ/ *n.* a clay bed under a coal seam.

undercliff /ˈʌndəklɪf/ *n.* a terrace or lower cliff formed by a landslip.

underclothes /ˈʌndəˌkləʊðz, -ˌkləʊz/ *n.pl.* clothes worn under others, esp. next to the skin.

underclothing /ˈʌndəˌkləʊðɪŋ/ *n.* underclothes collectively.

undercoat /ˈʌndəˌkəʊt/ *n.* **1 a** a preliminary layer of paint under the finishing coat. **b** the paint used for this. **2** an animal's under layer of hair or down. **3** a coat worn under another. □□ **undercoating** *n.*

undercover /ˌʌndəˈkʌvə(r), ˈʌn-/ *adj.* (usu. *attrib.*) **1** surreptitious. **2** engaged in spying, esp. by working with or among those to be observed (*undercover agent*).

undercroft /ˈʌndəˌkrɒft/ *n.* a crypt. [ME f. UNDER- + *croft* crypt f. MDu. *crofte* cave f. med.L *crupta* for L *crypta*: see CRYPT]

undercurrent /ˈʌndəˌkʌrənt/ *n.* **1** a current below the surface. **2** an underlying often contrary feeling, activity, or influence (*an undercurrent of protest*).

undercut *v. & n.* —*v.tr.* /ˌʌndəˈkʌt/ (**-cutting**; *past* and *past part.* **-cut**) **1** sell or work at a lower price or lower wages than. **2** *Golf* strike (a ball) so as to make it rise high. **3 a** cut away the part below or under (a thing). **b** cut away material to show (a carved design etc.) in relief. **4** render unstable or less firm, undermine. —*n.* /ˈʌndəˌkʌt/ **1** *Brit.* the underside of a sirloin. **2** *US* a notch cut in a tree-trunk to guide its fall when felled. **3** any space formed by the removal or absence of material from the lower part of something.

underdeveloped /ˌʌndədɪˈveləpt/ *adj.* **1** not fully developed; immature. **2** (of a country etc.) below its potential economic level. **3** *Photog.* not developed sufficiently to give a normal image. □□ **underdevelopment** *n.*

underdog /ˈʌndəˌdɒg/ *n.* **1** a dog, or usu. a person, losing a fight. **2** a person who is in a state of inferiority or subjection.

underdone /ˌʌndəˈdʌn, ˈʌn-/ *adj.* **1** not thoroughly done. **2** (of food) lightly or insufficiently cooked.

underdress /ˌʌndəˈdres/ *v.tr. & intr.* dress too plainly or too lightly.

underemphasis /ˌʌndərˈemfəsɪs/ *n.* (pl. **-emphases** /-ˌsiːz/) an insufficient degree of emphasis. □□ **underemphasize** *v.tr.* (also **-ise**).

underemployed /ˌʌndərɪmˈplɔɪd/ *adj.* not fully employed. □□ **underemployment** *n.*

underestimate *v. & n.* —*v.tr.* /ˌʌndərˈestɪˌmeɪt/ form too low an estimate of. —*n.* /ˌʌndərˈestɪmət/ an estimate that is too low. □□ **underestimation** /-ˈmeɪʃ(ə)n/ *n.*

underexpose /ˌʌndərɪkˈspəʊz/ *v.tr. Photog.* expose (film) for too short a time or with insufficient light. □□ **underexposure** *n.*

underfed /ˌʌndəˈfed/ *adj.* insufficiently fed.

underfelt /ˈʌndəˌfelt/ *n.* felt for laying under a carpet.

underfloor /ˈʌndəˌflɔː(r)/ *attrib.adj.* situated or operating beneath the floor (*underfloor heating*).

underflow /ˈʌndəˌfləʊ/ *n.* an undercurrent.

underfoot /ˌʌndəˈfʊt/ adv. **1** under one's feet. **2** on the ground. **3** in a state of subjection. **4** so as to obstruct or inconvenience.

undergarment /ˈʌndəˌgɑːmənt/ n. a piece of underclothing.

undergird /ˌʌndəˈgɜːd/ v.tr. **1** make secure underneath. **2** strengthen, support.

underglaze /ˈʌndəˌgleɪz/ adj. & n. —adj. **1** (of painting on porcelain etc.) done before the glaze is applied. **2** (of colours) used in such painting. —n. underglaze painting.

undergo /ˌʌndəˈgəʊ/ v.tr. (3rd sing. present **-goes**; past **-went**; past part. **-gone**) be subjected to; suffer; endure. [OE undergān (as UNDER-, GO[1])]

undergrad /ˌʌndəˈgræd/ n. colloq. = UNDERGRADUATE. [abbr.]

undergraduate /ˌʌndəˈgrædjʊət/ n. a student at a university who has not yet taken a first degree.

underground adv., adj., n., & v. —adv. /ˌʌndəˈgraʊnd/ **1** beneath the surface of the ground. **2** in or into secrecy or hiding. —adj. /ˈʌndəˌgraʊnd/ **1** situated underground. **2** secret, hidden, esp. working secretly to subvert a ruling power. **3** unconventional, experimental (underground press). —n. /ˈʌndəˌgraʊnd/ **1** an underground railway. **2** a secret group or activity, esp. aiming to subvert the established order. —v.tr. /ˈʌndəˌgraʊnd/ lay (cables) below ground level.

undergrowth /ˈʌndəˌgrəʊθ/ n. a dense growth of shrubs etc., esp. under large trees.

underhand adj. & adv. —adj. /ˈʌndəˌhænd/ **1** secret, clandestine, not above-board. **2** deceptive, crafty. **3** Sport, esp. Cricket underarm. —adv. /ˌʌndəˈhænd/ in an underhand manner. [OE (as UNDER-, HAND)]

underhanded /ˌʌndəˈhændɪd/ adj. & adv. = UNDERHAND.

underhung /ˈʌndəˌhʌŋ, -ˈhʌŋ/ adj. **1** (of the lower jaw) projecting beyond the upper jaw. **2** having an underhung jaw.

underlay[1] v. & n. —v.tr. /ˌʌndəˈleɪ/ (past and past part. **-laid**) lay something under (a thing) to support or raise it. —n. /ˈʌndəˌleɪ/ a thing laid under another, esp. material laid under a carpet or mattress as protection or support. [OE underlecgan (as UNDER-, LAY[1])]

underlay[2] past of UNDERLIE.

underlease /ˈʌndəˌliːs/ n. & v.tr. = SUBLEASE.

underlet /ˌʌndəˈlet/ v.tr. (**-letting**; past and past part. **-let**) **1** sublet. **2** let at less than the true value.

underlie /ˌʌndəˈlaɪ/ v.tr. (**-lying**; past **-lay**; past part. **-lain**) **1** (also absol.) lie or be situated under (a stratum etc.). **2** (also absol.) (esp. as **underlying** adj.) (of a principle, reason, etc.) be the basis of (a doctrine, law, conduct, etc.). **3** exist beneath the superficial aspect of. [OE underlicgan (as UNDER-, LIE[1])]

underline v. & n. —v.tr. /ˌʌndəˈlaɪn/ **1** draw a line under (a word etc.) to give emphasis or draw attention or indicate italic or other special type. **2** emphasize, stress. —n. /ˈʌndəˌlaɪn/ **1** a line drawn under a word etc. **2** a caption below an illustration.

underlinen /ˈʌndəˌlɪnɪn/ n. underclothes esp. of linen.

underling /ˈʌndəlɪŋ/ n. usu. derog. a subordinate.

underlying pres. part. of UNDERLIE.

undermanned /ˌʌndəˈmænd/ adj. having too few people as crew or staff.

undermentioned /ˌʌndəˈmenʃ(ə)nd, ˈʌn-/ adj. Brit. mentioned at a later place in a book etc.

undermine /ˌʌndəˈmaɪn/ v.tr. **1** injure (a person, reputation, influence, etc.) by secret or insidious means. **2** weaken, injure, or wear out (health etc.) imperceptibly or insidiously. **3** wear away the base or foundation of (rivers undermine their banks). **4** make a mine or excavation under. □□ **underminer** n.

underminingly adv. [ME f. UNDER- + MINE[2]]

underneath /ˌʌndəˈniːθ/ prep., adv., n., & adj. —prep. **1** at or to a lower place than, below. **2** on the inside of, within. —adv. **1** at or to a lower place. **2** inside. —n. the lower surface or part. —adj. lower. [OE underneothan (as UNDER + neothan: cf. BENEATH)]

undernourished /ˌʌndəˈnʌrɪʃt/ adj. insufficiently nourished. □□ **undernourishment** n.

underpaid past and past part. of UNDERPAY.

underpants /ˈʌndəˌpænts/ n.pl. an undergarment, esp. men's, covering the lower part of the body and part of the legs.

under-part /ˈʌndəˌpɑːt/ n. **1** a lower part, esp. of an animal. **2** a subordinate part in a play etc.

underpass /ˈʌndəˌpɑːs/ n. **1** a road etc. passing under another. **2** a crossing of this form.

underpay /ˌʌndəˈpeɪ/ v.tr. (past and past part. **-paid**) pay too little to (a person) or for (a thing). □□ **underpayment** n.

underpin /ˌʌndəˈpɪn/ v.tr. (**-pinned**, **-pinning**) **1** support from below with masonry etc. **2** support, strengthen.

underplant /ˌʌndəˈplɑːnt/ v.tr. (usu. foll. by with) plant or cultivate the ground about (a tall plant) with smaller ones.

underplay /ˌʌndəˈpleɪ/ v. **1** tr. play down the importance of. **2** intr. & tr. Theatr. **a** perform with deliberate restraint. **b** underact.

underplot /ˈʌndəˌplɒt/ n. a subordinate plot in a play etc.

underpopulated /ˌʌndəˈpɒpjʊˌleɪtɪd/ adj. having an insufficient or very small population.

underprice /ˌʌndəˈpraɪs/ v.tr. price lower than what is usual or appropriate.

underprivileged /ˌʌndəˈprɪvɪlɪdʒd/ adj. **1** less privileged than others. **2** not enjoying the normal standard of living or rights in a society.

underproduction /ˌʌndəprəˈdʌkʃ(ə)n/ n. production of less than is usual or required.

underproof /ˈʌndəˌpruːf/ adj. containing less alcohol than proof spirit does.

underprop /ˌʌndəˈprɒp/ v.tr. (**-propped**, **-propping**) **1** support with a prop. **2** support, sustain.

underquote /ˌʌndəˈkwəʊt/ v.tr. **1** quote a lower price than (a person). **2** quote a lower price than others for (goods etc.).

underrate /ˌʌndəˈreɪt/ v.tr. have too low an opinion of.

underscore v. & n. —v.tr. /ˌʌndəˈskɔː(r)/ = UNDERLINE v. —n. /ˈʌndəˌskɔː(r)/ = UNDERLINE n. 1.

undersea /ˈʌndəˌsiː/ adj. below the sea or the surface of the sea, submarine.

underseal /ˈʌndəˌsiːl/ v. & n. —v.tr. seal the under-part of (esp. a motor vehicle against rust etc.). —n. a protective coating for this.

under-secretary /ˌʌndəˈsekrətərɪ/ n. (pl. **-ies**) a subordinate official, esp. a junior minister or senior civil servant.

undersell /ˌʌndəˈsel/ v.tr. (past and past part. **-sold**) **1** sell at a lower price than (another seller). **2** sell at less than the true value.

underset v. & n. —v.tr. /ˌʌndəˈset/ (**-setting**; past and past part. **-set**) place something under (a thing). —n. /ˈʌndəˌset/ Naut. an undercurrent.

undersexed /ˌʌndəˈsekst/ adj. having unusually weak sexual desires.

under-sheriff /ˈʌndəˌʃerɪf/ n. a deputy sheriff.

undershirt /ˈʌndəˌʃɜːt/ n. esp. US an undergarment worn under a shirt; a vest.

undershoot v. & n. —v.tr. /ˌʌndəˈʃuːt/ (past and past part. **-shot**) **1** (of an aircraft) land short of (a runway etc.). **2** shoot short of or below. —n. /ˈʌndəˌʃuːt/ the act or an instance of undershooting.

undershorts /ˈʌndəˌʃɔːts/ n. US short underpants; trunks.

undershot /ˈʌndəˌʃɒt/ adj. **1** (of a water-wheel) turned by water flowing under it. **2** = UNDERHUNG.

undershrub /ˈʌndəˌʃrʌb/ n. = SUBSHRUB.

underside /ˈʌndəˌsaɪd/ n. the lower or under side or surface.

undersigned /ˈʌndəˌsaɪnd, -ˈsaɪnd/ adj. whose signature is appended (we, the undersigned, wish to state . . .).

undersized /ˈʌndəˌsaɪzd, -ˈsaɪzd/ adj. of less than the usual size.

underskirt /ˈʌndəˌskɜːt/ n. a skirt worn under another; a petticoat.

underslung /ˈʌndəˌslʌŋ/ adj. **1** supported from above. **2** (of a vehicle chassis) hanging lower than the axles.

undersold past and past part. of UNDERSELL.

undersow /ˈʌndəˌsəʊ/ v.tr. (past part. **-sown**) **1** sow (a later-growing crop) on land already seeded with another crop. **2**

(foll. by *with*) sow land already seeded with (a crop) with a later-growing crop.

underspend /ˌʌndəˈspend/ *v.* (*past* and *past part.* **-spent**) **1** *tr.* spend less than (a specified amount). **2** *intr. & refl.* spend too little.

understaffed /ˌʌndəˈstɑːft/ *adj.* having too few staff.

understand /ˌʌndəˈstænd/ *v.* (*past* and *past part.* **-stood** /-ˈstʊd/) **1** *tr.* perceive the meaning of (words, a person, a language, etc.) (*does not understand what you say; understood you perfectly; cannot understand French*). **2** *tr.* perceive the significance or explanation or cause of (*do not understand why he came; could not understand what the noise was about; do not understand the point of his remark*). **3** *tr.* be sympathetically aware of the character or nature of, know how to deal with (*quite understand your difficulty; cannot understand him at all; could never understand algebra*). **4** *tr.* **a** (often foll. by *that* + clause) infer esp. from information received, take as implied, take for granted (*I understand that it begins at noon; I understand him to be a distant relation; am I to understand that you refuse?*). **b** (*absol.*) believe or assume from knowledge or inference (*he is coming tomorrow, I understand*). **5** *tr.* supply (a word) mentally (*the verb may be either expressed or understood*). **6** *intr.* have understanding (in general or in particular). □ **understand each other 1** know each other's views or feelings. **2** be in agreement or collusion. □□ **understandable** *adj.* **understandably** *adv.* **understander** *n.* [OE *understandan* (as UNDER-, STAND)]

understanding /ˌʌndəˈstændɪŋ/ *n. & adj.* —*n.* **1 a** the ability to understand or think; intelligence. **b** the power of apprehension; the power of abstract thought. **2** an individual's perception or judgement of a situation etc. **3** an agreement; a thing agreed upon, esp. informally (*had an understanding with the rival company; consented only on this understanding*). **4** harmony in opinion or feeling (*disturbed the good understanding between them*). **5** sympathetic awareness or tolerance. —*adj.* **1** having understanding or insight or good judgement. **2** sympathetic to others' feelings. □□ **understandingly** *adv.* [OE (as UNDERSTAND)]

understate /ˌʌndəˈsteɪt/ *v.tr.* **1** express in greatly or unduly restrained terms. **2** represent as being less than it actually is. □□ **understatement** /ˌʌndəˈsteɪtmənt, ˈʌndə-/ *n.* **understater** *n.*

understeer /ˈʌndəstɪə(r)/ *n. & v.* —*n.* a tendency of a motor vehicle to turn less sharply than was intended. —*v.intr.* have such a tendency.

understood *past* and *past part.* of UNDERSTAND.

understorey /ˈʌndəˌstɔːrɪ/ *n.* (*pl.* **-eys**) **1** a layer of vegetation beneath the main canopy of a forest. **2** the plants forming this.

understudy /ˈʌndəˌstʌdɪ/ *n. & v.* esp. *Theatr.* —*n.* (*pl.* **-ies**) a person who studies another's role or duties in order to act at short notice in the absence of the other. —*v.tr.* (**-ies**, **-ied**) **1** study (a role etc.) as an understudy. **2** act as an understudy to (a person).

undersubscribed /ˌʌndəsəbˈskraɪbd/ *adj.* without sufficient subscribers, participants, etc.

undersurface /ˈʌndəˌsɜːfɪs/ *n.* the lower or under surface.

undertake /ˌʌndəˈteɪk/ *v.tr.* (*past* **-took**; *past part.* **-taken**) **1** bind oneself to perform, make oneself responsible for, engage in, enter upon (work, an enterprise, a responsibility). **2** (usu. foll. by *to* + infin.) accept an obligation, promise. **3** guarantee, affirm (*I will undertake that he has not heard a word*).

undertaker /ˈʌndəˌteɪkə(r)/ *n.* **1** a person whose business is to make arrangements for funerals. **2** (also -ˈteɪkə(r)) a person who undertakes to do something. **3** *hist.* an influential person in 17th-century England who undertook to procure particular legislation, esp. to obtain supplies from the House of Commons if the king would grant some concession.

undertaking /ˌʌndəˈteɪkɪŋ/ *n.* **1** work etc. undertaken, an enterprise (*a serious undertaking*). **2** a pledge or promise. **3** /ˈʌn-/ the management of funerals as a profession.

undertenant /ˈʌndəˌtenənt/ *n.* a subtenant. □□ **undertenancy** *n.* (*pl.* **-ies**).

underthings /ˈʌndəθɪŋz/ *n.pl. colloq.* underclothes.

undertint /ˈʌndətɪnt/ *n.* a subdued tint.

undertone /ˈʌndəˌtəʊn/ *n.* **1** a subdued tone of sound or colour. **2** an underlying quality. **3** an undercurrent of feeling.

undertook *past* of UNDERTAKE.

undertow /ˈʌndəˌtəʊ/ *n.* a current below the surface of the sea moving in the opposite direction to the surface current.

undertrick /ˈʌndətrɪk/ *n. Bridge* a trick by which the declarer falls short of his or her contract.

undervalue /ˌʌndəˈvæljuː/ *v.tr.* (**-values**, **-valued**, **-valuing**) **1** value insufficiently. **2** underestimate. □□ **undervaluation** /-juːˈeɪʃ(ə)n/ *n.*

undervest /ˈʌndəˌvest/ *n.* *Brit.* an undergarment worn on the upper part of the body; a vest.

underwater /ˌʌndəˈwɔːtə(r)/ *adj. & adv.* —*adj.* situated or done under water. —*adv.* under water.

underwear /ˈʌndəˌweə(r)/ *n.* underclothes.

underweight *adj. & n.* —*adj.* /ˌʌndəˈweɪt/ weighing less than is normal or desirable. —*n.* /ˈʌndəˌweɪt/ insufficient weight.

underwent *past* of UNDERGO.

underwhelm /ˌʌndəˈwelm/ *v.tr. joc.* fail to impress. [after OVERWHELM]

underwing /ˈʌndəwɪŋ/ *n.* a wing placed under or partly covered by another.

underwood /ˈʌndəˌwʊd/ *n.* undergrowth.

underwork /ˌʌndəˈwɜːk/ *v.* **1** *tr.* impose too little work on. **2** *intr.* do too little work.

underworld /ˈʌndəˌwɜːld/ *n.* **1** the part of society comprising those who live by organized crime and immorality. **2** the mythical abode of the dead under the earth. **3** the antipodes.

underwrite /ˌʌndəˈraɪt, ˈʌn-/ *v.* (*past* **-wrote**; *past part.* **-written**) **1 a** *tr.* sign, and accept liability under (an insurance policy, esp. on shipping etc.). **b** *tr.* accept (liability) in this way. **c** *intr.* practise (marine) insurance. **2** *tr.* undertake to finance or support. **3** *tr.* engage to buy all the stock in (a company etc.) not bought by the public. **4** *tr.* write below (*the underwritten names*). □□ **underwriter** /ˈʌn-/ *n.*

undescended /ˌʌndɪˈsendɪd/ *adj. Med.* (of a testicle) remaining in the abdomen instead of descending normally into the scrotum.

undeserved /ˌʌndɪˈzɜːvd/ *adj.* not deserved (as reward or punishment). □□ **undeservedly** /-vɪdlɪ/ *adv.*

undeserving /ˌʌndɪˈzɜːvɪŋ/ *adj.* not deserving. □□ **undeservingly** *adv.*

undesigned /ˌʌndɪˈzaɪnd/ *adj.* unintentional. □□ **undesignedly** /-nɪdlɪ/ *adv.*

undesirable /ˌʌndɪˈzaɪərəb(ə)l/ *adj. & n.* —*adj.* not desirable, objectionable, unpleasant. —*n.* an undesirable person. □□ **undesirability** /-ˈbɪlɪtɪ/ *n.* **undesirableness** *n.* **undesirably** *adv.*

undesired /ˌʌndɪˈzaɪəd/ *adj.* not desired.

undesirous /ˌʌndɪˈzaɪərəs/ *adj.* not desirous.

undetectable /ˌʌndɪˈtektəb(ə)l/ *adj.* not detectable. □□ **undetectability** /-ˈbɪlɪtɪ/ *n.* **undetectably** *adv.*

undetected /ˌʌndɪˈtektɪd/ *adj.* not detected.

undetermined /ˌʌndɪˈtɜːmɪnd/ *adj.* = UNDECIDED.

undeterred /ˌʌndɪˈtɜːd/ *adj.* not deterred.

undeveloped /ˌʌndɪˈveləpt/ *adj.* not developed.

undeviating /ʌnˈdiːvɪˌeɪtɪŋ/ *adj.* not deviating; steady, constant. □□ **undeviatingly** *adv.*

undiagnosed /ʌnˈdaɪəgˌnəʊzd, ˌʌndaɪəgˈnəʊzd/ *adj.* not diagnosed.

undid *past* of UNDO.

undies /ˈʌndɪz/ *n.pl. colloq.* (esp. women's) underclothes. [abbr.]

undifferentiated /ˌʌndɪfəˈrenʃɪˌeɪtɪd/ *adj.* not differentiated; amorphous.

undigested /ˌʌndɪˈdʒestɪd, ˌʌndaɪ-/ *adj.* **1** not digested. **2** (esp. of information, facts, etc.) not properly arranged or considered.

undignified /ʌnˈdɪgnɪˌfaɪd/ *adj.* lacking dignity.

undiluted /ˌʌndaɪˈljuːtɪd/ *adj.* not diluted.

undiminished /ˌʌndɪˈmɪnɪʃt/ adj. not diminished or lessened.

undine /ˈʌndiːn/ n. a female water-spirit. [mod.L undina (word invented by Paracelsus) f. L unda wave]

undiplomatic /ˌʌndɪpləˈmætɪk/ adj. tactless. □□ **undiplomatically** adv.

undischarged /ˌʌndɪsˈtʃɑːdʒd/ adj. (esp. of a bankrupt or a debt) not discharged.

undiscipline /ʌnˈdɪsɪplɪn/ n. lack of discipline.

undisciplined /ʌnˈdɪsɪplɪnd/ adj. lacking discipline; not disciplined.

undisclosed /ˌʌndɪsˈkləʊzd/ adj. not revealed or made known.

undiscoverable /ˌʌndɪˈskʌvərəb(ə)l/ adj. that cannot be discovered.

undiscovered /ˌʌndɪˈskʌvəd/ adj. not discovered.

undiscriminating /ˌʌndɪˈskrɪmɪˌneɪtɪŋ/ adj. not showing good judgement.

undisguised /ˌʌndɪsˈɡaɪzd/ adj. not disguised. □□ **undisguisedly** /-zɪdlɪ/ adv.

undismayed /ˌʌndɪsˈmeɪd/ adj. not dismayed.

undisputed /ˌʌndɪˈspjuːtɪd/ adj. not disputed or called in question.

undissolved /ˌʌndɪˈzɒlvd/ adj. not dissolved.

undistinguishable /ˌʌndɪˈstɪŋɡwɪʃəb(ə)l/ adj. (often foll. by from) indistinguishable.

undistinguished /ˌʌndɪˈstɪŋɡwɪʃt/ adj. not distinguished; mediocre.

undistributed /ˌʌndɪˈstrɪbjuːtɪd/ adj. not distributed. □ **undistributed middle** Logic a fallacy resulting from the failure of the middle term of a syllogism to refer to all the members of a class.

undisturbed /ˌʌndɪˈstɜːbd/ adj. not disturbed or interfered with.

undivided /ˌʌndɪˈvaɪdɪd/ adj. not divided or shared; whole, entire (gave him my undivided attention).

undo /ʌnˈduː/ v.tr. (3rd sing. present **-does**; past **-did**; past part. **-done**) **1 a** unfasten or untie (a coat, button, parcel, etc.). **b** unfasten the clothing of (a person). **2** annul, cancel (cannot undo the past). **3** ruin the prospects, reputation, or morals of. [OE undōn (as UN-², DO¹)]

undock /ʌnˈdɒk/ v.tr. **1** (also absol.) separate (a spacecraft) from another in space. **2** take a (ship) out of a dock.

undocumented /ʌnˈdɒkjʊˌmentɪd/ adj. **1** US not having the appropriate document. **2** not proved by or recorded in documents.

undoing /ʌnˈduːɪŋ/ n. **1** ruin or a cause of ruin. **2** the process of reversing what has been done. **3** the action of opening or unfastening.

undomesticated /ˌʌndəˈmestɪˌkeɪtɪd/ adj. not domesticated.

undone /ʌnˈdʌn/ adj. **1** not done; incomplete (left the job undone). **2** not fastened (left the buttons undone). **3** archaic ruined.

undoubtable /ʌnˈdaʊtəb(ə)l/ adj. that cannot be doubted; indubitable.

undoubted /ʌnˈdaʊtɪd/ adj. certain, not questioned, not regarded as doubtful. □□ **undoubtedly** adv.

UNDP abbr. United Nations Development Programme. Its headquarters are in New York.

undrained /ʌnˈdreɪnd/ adj. not drained.

undraped /ʌnˈdreɪpt/ adj. **1** not covered with drapery. **2** naked.

undreamed /ʌnˈdriːmd, ʌnˈdremt/ adj. (also **undreamt** /ʌnˈdremt/) (often foll. by of) not dreamed or thought of or imagined.

undress /ʌnˈdres/ v. & n. —v. **1** intr. take off one's clothes. **2** tr. take the clothes off (a person). —n. **1** ordinary dress as opposed to full dress or uniform. **2** casual or informal dress.

undressed /ʌnˈdrest/ adj. **1** not or no longer dressed; partly or wholly naked. **2** (of leather etc.) not treated. **3** (of food) not having a dressing.

undrinkable /ʌnˈdrɪŋkəb(ə)l/ adj. unfit for drinking.

UNDRO abbr. United Nations Disaster Relief Office. Its headquarters are in Geneva.

undue /ʌnˈdjuː/ adj. **1** excessive, disproportionate. **2** not suitable. **3** not owed. □ **undue influence** Law influence by which a person is induced to act otherwise than by his or her own free will, or without adequate attention to the consequences. □□ **unduly** adv.

undulant /ˈʌndjʊlənt/ adj. moving like waves; fluctuating. □ **undulant fever** brucellosis in humans. [L undulare (as UNDULATE)]

undulate v. & adj. —v. /ˈʌndjʊleɪt/ intr. & tr. have or cause to have a wavy motion or look. —adj. /ˈʌndjʊlət/ wavy, going alternately up and down or in and out (leaves with undulate margins). □□ **undulately** adv. [LL undulatus f. L unda wave]

undulation /ˌʌndjʊˈleɪʃ(ə)n/ n. **1** a wavy motion or form, a gentle rise and fall. **2** each wave of this. **3** a set of wavy lines.

undulatory /ˈʌndjʊlətərɪ/ adj. **1** undulating, wavy. **2** of or due to undulation.

undutiful /ʌnˈdjuːtɪˌfʊl/ adj. not dutiful. □□ **undutifully** adv. **undutifulness** n.

undyed /ʌnˈdaɪd/ adj. not dyed.

undying /ʌnˈdaɪɪŋ/ adj. **1** immortal. **2** never-ending (undying love). □□ **undyingly** adv.

unearned /ʌnˈɜːnd/ adj. not earned. □ **unearned income** income from interest payments etc. as opposed to salary, wages, or fees. **unearned increment** an increase in the value of property not due to the owner's labour or outlay.

unearth /ʌnˈɜːθ/ v.tr. **1 a** discover by searching or in the course of digging or rummaging. **b** dig out of the earth. **2** drive (a fox etc.) from its earth.

unearthly /ʌnˈɜːθlɪ/ adj. **1** supernatural, mysterious. **2** colloq. absurdly early or inconvenient (an unearthly hour). **3** not earthly. □□ **unearthliness** n.

unease /ʌnˈiːz/ n. lack of ease, discomfort, distress.

uneasy /ʌnˈiːzɪ/ adj. (**uneasier**, **uneasiest**) **1** disturbed or uncomfortable in mind or body (passed an uneasy night). **2** disturbing (had an uneasy suspicion). □□ **uneasily** adv. **uneasiness** n.

uneatable /ʌnˈiːtəb(ə)l/ adj. not able to be eaten, esp. because of its condition (cf. INEDIBLE).

uneaten /ʌnˈiːt(ə)n/ adj. not eaten; left undevoured.

uneconomic /ˌʌniːkəˈnɒmɪk, ˌʌnek-/ adj. not economic; incapable of being profitably operated etc. □□ **uneconomically** adv.

uneconomical /ˌʌniːkəˈnɒmɪk(ə)l, ˌʌnek-/ adj. not economical; wasteful.

unedifying /ʌnˈedɪˌfaɪɪŋ/ adj. not edifying, esp. uninstructive or degrading. □□ **unedifyingly** adv.

unedited /ʌnˈedɪtɪd/ adj. not edited.

uneducated /ʌnˈedjʊˌkeɪtɪd/ adj. not educated. □□ **uneducable** /-kəb(ə)l/ adj.

unelectable /ˌʌnɪˈlektəb(ə)l/ adj. (of a candidate, party, etc.) holding views likely to bring defeat at an election.

unembellished /ˌʌnɪmˈbelɪʃt/ adj. not embellished or decorated.

unemotional /ˌʌnɪˈməʊʃən(ə)l/ adj. not emotional; lacking emotion. □□ **unemotionally** adv.

unemphatic /ˌʌnɪmˈfætɪk/ adj. not emphatic. □□ **unemphatically** adv.

unemployable /ˌʌnɪmˈplɔɪəb(ə)l/ adj. & n. —adj. unfitted for paid employment. —n. an unemployable person. □□ **unemployability** /-ˈbɪlɪtɪ/ n.

unemployed /ˌʌnɪmˈplɔɪd/ adj. **1** not having paid employment; out of work. **2** not in use.

unemployment /ˌʌnɪmˈplɔɪmənt/ n. **1** the state of being unemployed. **2** the condition or extent of this in a country or region etc. (the North has higher unemployment). □ **unemployment benefit** a payment made by the State or (in the US) a trade union to an unemployed person.

unenclosed /ˌʌnɪnˈkləʊzd/ adj. not enclosed.

unencumbered /ˌʌnɪnˈkʌmbəd/ adj. **1** (of an estate) not having any liabilities (e.g. a mortgage) on it. **2** having no encumbrance; free.

unending /ʌnˈendɪŋ/ adj. having or apparently having no end. □□ **unendingly** adv. **unendingness** n.

unendowed /ˌʌnɪnˈdaʊd/ adj. not endowed.

unendurable /ˌʌnɪnˈdjʊərəb(ə)l/ adj. that cannot be endured. □□ **unendurably** adv.

unengaged /ˌʌnɪnˈɡeɪdʒd/ adj. not engaged; uncommitted.

un-English /ʌnˈɪŋɡlɪʃ/ adj. **1** not characteristic of the English. **2** not English.

unenjoyable /ˌʌnɪnˈdʒɔɪəb(ə)l/ adj. not enjoyable.

unenlightened /ˌʌnɪnˈlaɪt(ə)nd/ adj. not enlightened.

unenterprising /ʌnˈentəˌpraɪzɪŋ/ adj. not enterprising.

unenthusiastic /ˌʌnɪnˌθjuːziˈæstɪk, ˌʌnɪnˌθuː-/ adj. not enthusiastic. □□ **unenthusiastically** adv.

unenviable /ʌnˈenvɪəb(ə)l/ adj. not enviable. □□ **unenviably** adv.

unenvied /ʌnˈenvɪd/ adj. not envied.

UNEP abbr. United Nations Environment Programme. Its headquarters are in Nairobi.

unequal /ʌnˈiːkw(ə)l/ adj. **1** (often foll. by to) not equal. **2** of varying quality. **3** lacking equal advantage to both sides (an unequal bargain). □□ **unequally** adv.

unequalize /ʌnˈiːkwəˌlaɪz/ v.tr. (also **-ise**) make unequal.

unequalled /ʌnˈiːkw(ə)ld/ adj. superior to all others.

unequipped /ˌʌnɪˈkwɪpt/ adj. not equipped.

unequivocal /ˌʌnɪˈkwɪvək(ə)l/ adj. not ambiguous, plain, unmistakable. □□ **unequivocally** adv. **unequivocalness** n.

unerring /ʌnˈɜːrɪŋ/ adj. not erring, failing, or missing the mark; true, certain. □□ **unerringly** adv. **unerringness** n.

unescapable /ˌʌnɪˈskeɪpəb(ə)l/ adj. inescapable.

UNESCO /juːˈneskəʊ/ abbr. (also **Unesco**) United Nations Educational, Scientific, and Cultural Organization, an agency of the United Nations set up in 1945 to promote the exchange of information, ideas, and culture. Its headquarters are in Paris.

unescorted /ˌʌnɪˈskɔːtɪd/ adj. not escorted.

unessential /ˌʌnɪˈsenʃ(ə)l/ adj. & n. —adj. **1** not essential (cf. INESSENTIAL). **2** not of the first importance. —n. an unessential part or thing.

unestablished /ˌʌnɪˈstæblɪʃt/ adj. not established.

unethical /ʌnˈeθɪk(ə)l/ adj. not ethical, esp. unscrupulous in business or professional conduct. □□ **unethically** adv.

unevangelical /ˌʌniːvænˈdʒelɪk(ə)l/ adj. not evangelical.

uneven /ʌnˈiːv(ə)n/ adj. **1** not level or smooth. **2** not uniform or equable. **3** (of a contest) unequal. □□ **unevenly** adv. **unevenness** n. [OE unefen (as UN-1, EVEN1)]

uneventful /ˌʌnɪˈventfʊl/ adj. not eventful. □□ **uneventfully** adv. **uneventfulness** n.

unexamined /ˌʌnɪɡˈzæmɪnd/ adj. not examined.

unexampled /ˌʌnɪɡˈzɑːmp(ə)ld/ adj. having no precedent or parallel.

unexceptionable /ˌʌnɪkˈsepʃənəb(ə)l/ adj. with which no fault can be found; entirely satisfactory. □□ **unexceptionableness** n. **unexceptionably** adv.

unexceptional /ˌʌnɪkˈsepʃ(ə)n(ə)l/ adj. not out of the ordinary; usual, normal. □□ **unexceptionally** adv.

unexcitable /ˌʌnɪkˈsaɪtəb(ə)l/ adj. not easily excited. □□ **unexcitability** /-ˈbɪlɪtɪ/ n.

unexciting /ˌʌnɪkˈsaɪtɪŋ/ adj. not exciting; dull.

unexecuted /ʌnˈeksɪˌkjuːtɪd/ adj. not carried out or put into effect.

unexhausted /ˌʌnɪɡˈzɔːstɪd/ adj. **1** not used up, expended, or brought to an end. **2** not emptied.

unexpected /ˌʌnɪkˈspektɪd/ adj. not expected; surprising. □□ **unexpectedly** adv. **unexpectedness** n.

unexpired /ˌʌnɪkˈspaɪəd/ adj. that has not yet expired.

unexplainable /ˌʌnɪkˈspleɪnəb(ə)l/ adj. inexplicable. □□ **unexplainably** adv.

unexplained /ˌʌnɪkˈspleɪnd/ adj. not explained.

unexploited /ˌʌnɪkˈsplɔɪtɪd/ adj. (of resources etc.) not exploited.

unexplored /ˌʌnɪkˈsplɔːd/ adj. not explored.

unexposed /ˌʌnɪkˈspəʊzd/ adj. not exposed.

unexpressed /ˌʌnɪkˈsprest/ adj. not expressed or made known (unexpressed fears).

unexpurgated /ʌnˈekspəˌɡeɪtɪd/ adj. (esp. of a text etc.) not expurgated; complete.

unfaceable /ʌnˈfeɪsəb(ə)l/ adj. that cannot be faced or confronted.

unfading /ʌnˈfeɪdɪŋ/ adj. that never fades. □□ **unfadingly** adv.

unfailing /ʌnˈfeɪlɪŋ/ adj. **1** not failing. **2** not running short. **3** constant. **4** reliable. □□ **unfailingly** adv. **unfailingness** n.

unfair /ʌnˈfeə(r)/ adj. **1** not equitable or honest (obtained by unfair means). **2** not impartial or according to the rules (unfair play). □□ **unfairly** adv. **unfairness** n. [OE unfæger (as UN-1, FAIR1)]

unfaithful /ʌnˈfeɪθfʊl/ adj. **1** not faithful, esp. adulterous. **2** not loyal. **3** treacherous. □□ **unfaithfully** adv. **unfaithfulness** n.

unfaltering /ʌnˈfɔːltərɪŋ, ʌnˈfɒl-/ adj. not faltering; steady, resolute. □□ **unfalteringly** adv.

unfamiliar /ˌʌnfəˈmɪljə(r)/ adj. not familiar. □□ **unfamiliarity** /-lɪˈærɪtɪ/ n.

unfashionable /ʌnˈfæʃənəb(ə)l/ adj. not fashionable. □□ **unfashionableness** n. **unfashionably** adv.

unfashioned /ʌnˈfæʃ(ə)nd/ adj. not made into its proper shape.

unfasten /ʌnˈfɑːs(ə)n/ v. **1** tr. & intr. make or become loose. **2** tr. open the fastening(s) of. **3** tr. detach.

unfastened /ʌnˈfɑːs(ə)nd/ adj. **1** that has not been fastened. **2** that has been loosened, opened, or detached.

unfathered /ʌnˈfɑːðəd/ adj. **1** having no known or acknowledged father; illegitimate. **2** of unknown origin (unfathered rumours).

unfatherly /ʌnˈfɑːðəlɪ/ adj. not befitting a father. □□ **unfatherliness** n.

unfathomable /ʌnˈfæðəməb(ə)l/ adj. incapable of being fathomed. □□ **unfathomableness** n. **unfathomably** adv.

unfathomed /ʌnˈfæðəmd/ adj. **1** of unascertained depth. **2** not fully explored or known.

unfavourable /ʌnˈfeɪvərəb(ə)l/ adj. (US **unfavorable**) not favourable; adverse, hostile. □□ **unfavourableness** n. **unfavourably** adv.

unfavourite /ʌnˈfeɪvərɪt/ adj. (US **unfavorite**) colloq. least favourite; most disliked.

unfazed /ʌnˈfeɪzd/ adj. colloq. untroubled; not disconcerted.

unfeasible /ʌnˈfiːzɪb(ə)l/ adj. not feasible; impractical. □□ **unfeasibility** /-ˈbɪlɪtɪ/ n. **unfeasibly** adv.

unfed /ʌnˈfed/ adj. not fed.

unfeeling /ʌnˈfiːlɪŋ/ adj. **1** unsympathetic, harsh, not caring about others' feelings. **2** lacking sensation or sensitivity. □□ **unfeelingly** adv. **unfeelingness** n. [OE unfelende (as UN-1, FEELING)]

unfeigned /ʌnˈfeɪnd/ adj. genuine, sincere. □□ **unfeignedly** adv.

unfelt /ʌnˈfelt/ adj. not felt.

unfeminine /ʌnˈfemɪnɪn/ adj. not in accordance with, or appropriate to, female character. □□ **unfemininity** /-ˈnɪnɪtɪ/ n.

unfenced /ʌnˈfenst/ adj. **1** not provided with fences. **2** unprotected.

unfermented /ˌʌnfəˈmentɪd/ adj. not fermented.

unfertilized /ʌnˈfɜːtɪˌlaɪzd/ adj. (also **unfertilised**) not fertilized.

unfetter /ʌnˈfetə(r)/ v.tr. release from fetters.

unfettered /ʌnˈfetəd/ adj. unrestrained, unrestricted.

unfilial /ʌnˈfɪlɪəl/ adj. not befitting a son or daughter. □□ **unfilially** adv.

unfilled /ʌnˈfɪld/ adj. not filled.

unfiltered /ʌnˈfɪltəd/ adj. **1** not filtered. **2** (of a cigarette) not provided with a filter.

unfinished /ʌnˈfɪnɪʃt/ adj. not finished; incomplete.

æ cat ɑː arm e bed ɜː her ɪ sit iː see ɒ hot ɔː saw ʌ run ʊ put uː too ə ago aɪ my

unfit /ʌnˈfɪt/ *adj. & v.* —*adj.* (often foll. by *for*, or *to* + infin.) not fit. —*v.tr.* (**unfitted**, **unfitting**) (usu. foll. by *for*) make unsuitable. □□ **unfitly** *adv.* **unfitness** *n.*

unfitted /ʌnˈfɪtɪd/ *adj.* **1** not fit. **2** not fitted or suited. **3** not provided with fittings.

unfitting /ʌnˈfɪtɪŋ/ *adj.* not fitting or suitable, unbecoming. □□ **unfittingly** *adv.*

unfix /ʌnˈfɪks/ *v.tr.* **1** release or loosen from a fixed state. **2** detach.

unfixed /ʌnˈfɪkst/ *adj.* not fixed.

unflagging /ʌnˈflæɡɪŋ/ *adj.* tireless, persistent. □□ **unflaggingly** *adv.*

unflappable /ʌnˈflæpəb(ə)l/ *adj. colloq.* imperturbable; remaining calm in a crisis. □□ **unflappability** /-ˈbɪlɪti/ *n.* **unflappably** *adv.*

unflattering /ʌnˈflætərɪŋ/ *adj.* not flattering. □□ **unflatteringly** *adv.*

unflavoured /ʌnˈfleɪvəd/ *adj.* not flavoured.

unfledged /ʌnˈfledʒd/ *adj.* **1** (of a person) inexperienced. **2** (of a bird) not yet fledged.

unfleshed /ʌnˈfleʃt/ *adj.* **1** not covered with flesh. **2** stripped of flesh.

unflinching /ʌnˈflɪntʃɪŋ/ *adj.* not flinching. □□ **unflinchingly** *adv.*

unfocused /ʌnˈfəʊkəst/ *adj.* (also **unfocussed**) not focused.

unfold /ʌnˈfəʊld/ *v.* **1** *tr.* open the fold or folds of, spread out. **2** *tr.* reveal (thoughts etc.). **3** *intr.* become opened out. **4** *intr.* develop. □□ **unfoldment** *n. US.* [OE *unfealdan* (as UN-², FOLD¹)]

unforced /ʌnˈfɔːst/ *adj.* **1** not produced by effort; easy, natural. **2** not compelled or constrained. □□ **unforcedly** *adv.*

unfordable /ʌnˈfɔːdəb(ə)l/ *adj.* that cannot be forded.

unforeseeable /ˌʌnfɔːˈsiːəb(ə)l/ *adj.* not foreseeable.

unforeseen /ˌʌnfɔːˈsiːn/ *adj.* not foreseen.

unforetold /ˌʌnfɔːˈtəʊld/ *adj.* not foretold; unpredicted.

unforgettable /ˌʌnfəˈɡetəb(ə)l/ *adj.* that cannot be forgotten; memorable, wonderful (*an unforgettable experience*). □□ **unforgettably** *adv.*

unforgivable /ˌʌnfəˈɡɪvəb(ə)l/ *adj.* that cannot be forgiven. □□ **unforgivably** *adv.*

unforgiven /ˌʌnfəˈɡɪv(ə)n/ *adj.* not forgiven.

unforgiving /ˌʌnfəˈɡɪvɪŋ/ *adj.* not forgiving. □□ **unforgivingly** *adv.* **unforgivingness** *n.*

unforgotten /ˌʌnfəˈɡɒt(ə)n/ *adj.* not forgotten.

unformed /ʌnˈfɔːmd/ *adj.* **1** not formed. **2** shapeless. **3** not developed.

unformulated /ʌnˈfɔːmjʊleɪtɪd/ *adj.* not formulated.

unforthcoming /ˌʌnfɔːθˈkʌmɪŋ/ *adj.* not forthcoming.

unfortified /ʌnˈfɔːtɪfaɪd/ *adj.* not fortified.

unfortunate /ʌnˈfɔːtjʊnət, -tʃənət/ *adj. & n.* —*adj.* **1** having bad fortune; unlucky. **2** unhappy. **3** regrettable. **4** disastrous. —*n.* an unfortunate person.

unfortunately /ʌnˈfɔːtjʊnətlɪ, -tʃənətlɪ/ *adv.* **1** (qualifying a whole sentence) it is unfortunate that. **2** in an unfortunate manner.

unfounded /ʌnˈfaʊndɪd/ *adj.* having no foundation (*unfounded hopes*; *unfounded rumour*). □□ **unfoundedly** *adv.* **unfoundedness** *n.*

UNFPA *abbr.* United Nations Fund for Population Activities. Its headquarters are in New York.

unframed /ʌnˈfreɪmd/ *adj.* (esp. of a picture) not framed.

unfreeze /ʌnˈfriːz/ *v.* (*past* **unfroze**; *past part.* **unfrozen**) **1** *tr.* cause to thaw. **2** *intr.* thaw. **3** *tr.* remove restrictions from, make (assets, credits, etc.) realizable.

unfrequented /ˌʌnfrɪˈkwentɪd/ *adj.* not frequented.

unfriended /ʌnˈfrendɪd/ *adj. literary* without friends.

unfriendly /ʌnˈfrendlɪ/ *adj.* (**unfriendlier**, **unfriendliest**) not friendly. □□ **unfriendliness** *n.*

unfrock /ʌnˈfrɒk/ *v.tr.* = DEFROCK.

unfroze *past of* UNFREEZE.

unfrozen *past part.* of UNFREEZE.

unfruitful /ʌnˈfruːtfʊl/ *adj.* **1** not producing good results, unprofitable. **2** not producing fruit or crops. □□ **unfruitfully** *adv.* **unfruitfulness** *n.*

unfulfilled /ˌʌnfʊlˈfɪld/ *adj.* not fulfilled. □□ **unfulfillable** *adj.*

unfunded /ʌnˈfʌndɪd/ *adj.* (of a debt) not funded.

unfunny /ʌnˈfʌnɪ/ *adj.* (**unfunnier**, **unfunniest**) not amusing (though meant to be). □□ **unfunnily** *adv.* **unfunniness** *n.*

unfurl /ʌnˈfɜːl/ *v.* **1** *tr.* spread out (a sail, umbrella, etc.). **2** *intr.* become spread out.

unfurnished /ʌnˈfɜːnɪʃt/ *adj.* **1** (usu. foll. by *with*) not supplied. **2** without furniture.

ungainly /ʌnˈɡeɪnlɪ/ *adj.* (of a person, animal, or movement) awkward, clumsy. □□ **ungainliness** *n.* [UN-¹ + obs. *gainly* graceful ult. f. ON *gegn* straight]

ungallant /ʌnˈɡælənt/ *adj.* not gallant. □□ **ungallantly** *adv.*

ungenerous /ʌnˈdʒenərəs/ *adj.* not generous; mean. □□ **ungenerously** *adv.* **ungenerousness** *n.*

ungenial /ʌnˈdʒiːnɪəl/ *adj.* not genial.

ungentle /ʌnˈdʒent(ə)l/ *adj.* not gentle. □□ **ungentleness** *n.* **ungently** *adv.*

ungentlemanly /ʌnˈdʒentəlmənlɪ/ *adj.* not gentlemanly. □□ **ungentlemanliness** *n.*

unget-at-able /ˌʌnɡetˈætəb(ə)l/ *adj. colloq.* inaccessible.

ungifted /ʌnˈɡɪftɪd/ *adj.* not gifted or talented.

ungird /ʌnˈɡɜːd/ *v.tr.* **1** release the girdle, belt, or girth of. **2** release or take off by undoing a belt or girth.

unglazed /ʌnˈɡleɪzd/ *adj.* not glazed.

ungloved /ʌnˈɡlʌvd/ *adj.* not wearing a glove or gloves.

ungodly /ʌnˈɡɒdlɪ/ *adj.* **1** impious, wicked. **2** *colloq.* outrageous (*an ungodly hour to arrive*). □□ **ungodliness** *n.*

ungovernable /ʌnˈɡʌvənəb(ə)l/ *adj.* uncontrollable, violent. □□ **ungovernability** /-ˈbɪlɪtɪ/ *n.* **ungovernably** *adv.*

ungraceful /ʌnˈɡreɪsfʊl/ *adj.* not graceful. □□ **ungracefully** *adv.* **ungracefulness** *n.*

ungracious /ʌnˈɡreɪʃəs/ *adj.* **1** not kindly or courteous; unkind. **2** unattractive. □□ **ungraciously** *adv.* **ungraciousness** *n.*

ungrammatical /ˌʌnɡrəˈmætɪk(ə)l/ *adj.* contrary to the rules of grammar. □□ **ungrammaticality** /-ˈkælɪtɪ/ *n.* **ungrammatically** *adv.* **ungrammaticalness** *n.*

ungraspable /ʌnˈɡrɑːspəb(ə)l/ *adj.* that cannot be grasped or comprehended.

ungrateful /ʌnˈɡreɪtfʊl/ *adj.* **1** not feeling or showing gratitude. **2** not pleasant or acceptable. □□ **ungratefully** *adv.* **ungratefulness** *n.*

ungrounded /ʌnˈɡraʊndɪd/ *adj.* **1** having no basis or justification; unfounded. **2** *Electr.* not earthed. **3** (foll. by *in* a subject) not properly instructed. **4** (of an aircraft, ship, etc.) no longer grounded.

ungrudging /ʌnˈɡrʌdʒɪŋ/ *adj.* not grudging. □□ **ungrudgingly** *adv.*

ungual /ˈʌŋɡw(ə)l/ *adj.* of, like, or bearing a nail, hoof, or claw. [L UNGUIS]

unguard /ʌnˈɡɑːd/ *v.tr. Cards* discard a low card that was protecting (a high card) from capture.

unguarded /ʌnˈɡɑːdɪd/ *adj.* **1** incautious, thoughtless (*an unguarded remark*). **2** not guarded; without a guard. □□ **unguardedly** *adv.* **unguardedness** *n.*

unguent /ˈʌŋɡwənt/ *n.* a soft substance used as ointment or for lubrication. [L *unguentum* f. *unguere* anoint]

unguessable /ʌnˈɡesəb(ə)l/ *adj.* that cannot be guessed or imagined.

unguiculate /ʌŋˈɡwɪkjʊlət/ *adj.* **1** *Zool.* having one or more nails or claws. **2** *Bot.* (of petals) having an unguis. [mod.L *unguiculatus* f. *unguiculus* dimin. of UNGUIS]

unguided /ʌnˈɡaɪdɪd/ *adj.* not guided in a particular path or direction; left to take its own course.

unguis /ˈʌŋɡwɪs/ *n.* (*pl.* **ungues** /-wiːz/) **1** *Bot.* the narrow base of a petal. **2** *Zool.* a nail or claw. [L]

ungula /ˈʌŋgjʊlə/ n. (pl. **ungulae** /-ˌliː/) a hoof or claw. [L, dimin. of UNGUIS]

ungulate /ˈʌŋgjʊlət, -ˌleɪt/ adj. & n. —adj. hoofed. —n. a hoofed mammal. [LL ungulatus f. UNGULA]

unhallowed /ʌnˈhæləʊd/ adj. 1 not consecrated. 2 not sacred; unholy, wicked.

unhampered /ʌnˈhæmpəd/ adj. not hampered.

unhand /ʌnˈhænd/ v.tr. rhet. or joc. 1 take one's hands off (a person). 2 release from one's grasp.

unhandsome /ʌnˈhænsəm/ adj. not handsome.

unhandy /ʌnˈhændɪ/ adj. 1 not easy to handle or manage; awkward. 2 not skilful in using the hands. □□ **unhandily** adv. **unhandiness** n.

unhang /ʌnˈhæŋ/ v.tr. (past and past part. **unhung**) take down from a hanging position.

unhappy /ʌnˈhæpɪ/ adj. (**unhappier**, **unhappiest**) 1 not happy, miserable. 2 unsuccessful, unfortunate. 3 causing misfortune. 4 disastrous. 5 inauspicious. □□ **unhappily** adv. **unhappiness** n.

unharbour /ʌnˈhɑːbə(r)/ v.tr. Brit. dislodge (a deer) from a covert.

unharmed /ʌnˈhɑːmd/ adj. not harmed.

unharmful /ʌnˈhɑːmfʊl/ adj. not harmful.

unharmonious /ˌʌnhɑːˈməʊnɪəs/ adj. not harmonious.

unharness /ʌnˈhɑːnɪs/ v.tr. remove a harness from.

unhasp /ʌnˈhɑːsp/ v.tr. free from a hasp or catch; unfasten.

unhatched /ʌnˈhætʃt/ adj. (of an egg etc.) not hatched.

UNHCR abbr. United Nations High Commissioner for Refugees. Its headquarters are in Geneva.

unhealthful /ʌnˈhelθfʊl/ adj. harmful to health, unwholesome. □□ **unhealthfulness** n.

unhealthy /ʌnˈhelθɪ/ adj. (**unhealthier**, **unhealthiest**) 1 not in good health. 2 a (of a place etc.) harmful to health. b unwholesome. c sl. dangerous to life. □□ **unhealthily** adv. **unhealthiness** n.

unheard /ʌnˈhɜːd/ adj. 1 not heard. 2 (usu. **unheard-of**) unprecedented, unknown.

unheated /ʌnˈhiːtɪd/ adj. not heated.

unheeded /ʌnˈhiːdɪd/ adj. not heeded; disregarded.

unheedful /ʌnˈhiːdfʊl/ adj. heedless; taking no notice.

unheeding /ʌnˈhiːdɪŋ/ adj. not giving heed; heedless. □□ **unheedingly** adv.

unhelpful /ʌnˈhelpfʊl/ adj. not helpful. □□ **unhelpfully** adv. **unhelpfulness** n.

unheralded /ʌnˈherəldɪd/ adj. not heralded; unannounced.

unheroic /ˌʌnhɪˈrəʊɪk/ adj. not heroic. □□ **unheroically** adv.

unhesitating /ʌnˈhezɪˌteɪtɪŋ/ adj. without hesitation. □□ **unhesitatingly** adv. **unhesitatingness** n.

unhindered /ʌnˈhɪndəd/ adj. not hindered.

unhinge /ʌnˈhɪndʒ/ v.tr. 1 take (a door etc.) off its hinges. 2 (esp. as **unhinged** adj.) unsettle or disorder (a person's mind etc.), make (a person) crazy.

unhistoric /ˌʌnhɪˈstɒrɪk/ adj. not historic or historical.

unhistorical /ˌʌnhɪˈstɒrɪk(ə)l/ adj. not historical. □□ **unhistorically** adv.

unhitch /ʌnˈhɪtʃ/ v.tr. 1 release from a hitched state. 2 unhook, unfasten.

unholy /ʌnˈhəʊlɪ/ adj. (**unholier**, **unholiest**) 1 impious, profane, wicked. 2 colloq. dreadful, outrageous (made an unholy row about it). 3 not holy. □□ **unholiness** n. [OE unhālig (as UN-[1], HOLY)]

unhonoured /ʌnˈɒnəd/ adj. not honoured.

unhook /ʌnˈhʊk/ v.tr. 1 remove from a hook or hooks. 2 unfasten by releasing a hook or hooks.

unhoped /ʌnˈhəʊpt/ adj. (foll. by for) not hoped for or expected.

unhorse /ʌnˈhɔːs/ v.tr. 1 throw or drag from a horse. 2 (of a horse) throw (a rider). 3 dislodge, overthrow.

unhouse /ʌnˈhaʊz/ v.tr. deprive of shelter; turn out of a house.

unhuman /ʌnˈhjuːmən/ adj. 1 not human. 2 superhuman. 3 inhuman, brutal.

unhung[1] /ʌnˈhʌŋ/ adj. 1 not (yet) executed by hanging. 2 not hung up (for exhibition).

unhung[2] past and past part. of UNHANG.

unhurried /ʌnˈhʌrɪd/ adj. not hurried. □□ **unhurriedly** adv.

unhurt /ʌnˈhɜːt/ adj. not hurt.

unhusk /ʌnˈhʌsk/ v.tr. remove a husk or shell from.

unhygienic /ˌʌnhaɪˈdʒiːnɪk/ adj. not hygienic. □□ **unhygienically** adv.

unhyphenated /ʌnˈhaɪfəˌneɪtɪd/ adj. not hyphenated.

uni /ˈjuːnɪ/ n. (pl. **unis**) esp. Austral. & NZ colloq. a university. [abbr.]

uni- /ˈjuːnɪ/ comb. form one; having or consisting of one. [L f. unus one]

Uniat /ˈjuːnɪˌæt, -ɪət/ adj. & n. (also **Uniate** /-ˌeɪt/) —adj. of or relating to any of the Churches in eastern Europe and the Near East that acknowledge the pope's supremacy and are in communion with Rome but retain their respective languages, rites, and canon law in accordance with the terms of their union. —n. a member of such a community. [Russ. uniyat f. uniya f. L unio UNION]

uniaxial /ˌjuːnɪˈæksɪəl/ adj. having a single axis. □□ **uniaxially** adv.

unicameral /ˌjuːnɪˈkæmər(ə)l/ adj. with a single legislative chamber.

UNICEF /ˈjuːnɪˌsef/ abbr. United Nations Children's (orig. International Children's Emergency) Fund, established in 1946 to assist governments to meet the long-term needs of maternal and child welfare. Its headquarters are in New York.

unicellular /ˌjuːnɪˈseljʊlə(r)/ adj. (of an organism, organ, tissue, etc.) consisting of a single cell.

unicolour /ˈjuːnɪˌkʌlə(r)/ adj. (also **unicoloured**) of one colour.

unicorn /ˈjuːnɪˌkɔːn/ n. 1 a a mythical animal usually regarded as having the body of a horse with a single straight horn projecting from its forehead, first portrayed on Assyrian reliefs. Its horn was reputed to have medicinal or magical properties. The unicorn has been identified at various times with the rhinoceros, certain species of antelope, etc. b a heraldic representation of this, with a twisted horn, a deer's feet, a goat's beard, and a lion's tail, esp. as a supporter of the royal arms of Great Britain or Scotland. c used in old translations of the Old Testament for the Hebrew rĕˈem, a two-horned animal, probably a wild ox. 2 a a pair of horses and a third horse in front. b an equipage with these. 3 (in full **unicorn whale** or **sea-unicorn**) the narwhal. [ME f. OF unicorne f. L unicornis f. UNI- + cornu horn, transl. Gk monocerōs]

unicuspid /ˌjuːnɪˈkʌspɪd/ adj. & n. —adj. with one cusp. —n. a unicuspid tooth.

unicycle /ˈjuːnɪˌsaɪk(ə)l/ n. a single-wheeled cycle, esp. as used by acrobats. □□ **unicyclist** n.

unidea'd /ˌʌnaɪˈdɪəd/ adj. having no ideas.

unideal /ˌʌnaɪˈdɪəl/ adj. not ideal.

unidentifiable /ˌʌnaɪˈdentɪˌfaɪəb(ə)l/ adj. unable to be identified.

unidentified /ˌʌnaɪˈdentɪˌfaɪd/ adj. not identified.

unidimensional /ˌjuːnɪdaɪˈmenʃ(ə)n(ə)l/ adj. having (only) one dimension.

unidirectional /ˌjuːnɪdɪˈrekʃ(ə)n(ə)l, ˌjuːnɪdaɪ-/ adj. having only one direction of motion, operation, etc. □□ **unidirectionality** /-ˈnælɪtɪ/ n. **unidirectionally** adv.

UNIDO abbr. United Nations Industrial Development Organization, an organization operating under this name since 1966 and an agency of the United Nations from 1986, whose aim is to promote the industrialization of developing countries. Its headquarters are in Vienna.

unification /ˌjuːnɪfɪˈkeɪʃ(ə)n/ n. the act or an instance of unifying; the state of being unified. □□ **unificatory** adj.

Unification Church the Holy Spirit Association for the Unification of World Christianity, an evangelistic religious and political organization founded in 1954 in Korea by Sun Myung Moon. Its headquarters were moved to New York State in 1973,

b but d dog f few g get h he j yes k cat l leg m man n no p pen r red s sit t top v voice

and it became known as a cult religion in the US and elsewhere. Its basic scripture is Moon's book *The Divine Principle* (1952), in which he claimed Messianic status, believing that he was chosen by God to save mankind from Satanism and regarding Communists as Satan's representatives. The organization aroused controversy by its fund-raising techniques and by the methods by which young people were drawn into the movement. Its adherents are sometimes contemptuously called Moonies.

uniflow /ˈjuːnɪˌfləʊ/ *adj.* involving flow (esp. of steam or waste gases) in one direction only.

uniform /ˈjuːnɪfɔːm/ *adj., n., & v.* —*adj.* **1** not changing in form or character; the same, unvarying (*present a uniform appearance*; *all of uniform size and shape*). **2** conforming to the same standard, rules, or pattern. **3** constant in the course of time (*uniform acceleration*). **4** (of a tax, law, etc.) not varying with time or place. —*n.* uniform distinctive clothing worn by members of the same body, e.g. by soldiers, police, and schoolchildren. —*v.tr.* **1** clothe in uniform (*a uniformed officer*). **2** make uniform. □□ **uniformly** *adv.* [F *uniforme* or L *uniformis* (as UNI-, FORM)]

uniformitarian /ˌjuːnɪˌfɔːmɪˈteərɪən/ *adj. & n.* —*adj.* of the theory that geological processes are always due to continuously and uniformly operating forces. —*n.* a holder of this theory. □□ **uniformitarianism** *n.*

uniformity /ˌjuːnɪˈfɔːmɪti/ *n.* (pl. **-ies**) **1** being uniform; sameness, consistency. **2** an instance of this. □ **Act of Uniformity** legislation for securing uniformity in public worship and use of a particular Book of Common Prayer. The first such Acts, establishing the foundations of the English Protestant Church, were passed in the reign of Edward VI but repealed under his Catholic successor Mary I; a third was passed in the reign of Elizabeth I, and a final Act in 1662 after the Restoration. [ME f. OF *uniformité* or LL *uniformitas* (as UNIFORM)]

unify /ˈjuːnɪfaɪ/ *v.tr.* (also *absol.*) (**-ies**, **-ied**) reduce to unity or uniformity. □ **unified field theory** *Physics* a theory that seeks to explain all the field phenomena (e.g. gravitation and electromagnetism: see FIELD *n.* 9) formerly treated by separate theories. □□ **unifier** *n.* [F *unifier* or LL *unificare* (as UNI-, -FY)]

unilateral /ˌjuːnɪˈlætər(ə)l/ *adj.* **1** performed by or affecting only one person or party (*unilateral disarmament*; *unilateral declaration of independence*). **2** one-sided. **3** (of the parking of vehicles) restricted to one side of the street. **4** (of leaves) all on the same side of the stem. **5** (of a line of descent) through ancestors of one sex only. □ **Unilateral Declaration of Independence** the declaration of independence from the United Kingdom made by Rhodesia under Ian Smith in 1965. □□ **unilaterally** *adv.*

unilateralism /ˌjuːnɪˈlætərəˌlɪz(ə)m/ *n.* **1** unilateral disarmament. **2** *US* the pursuit of a foreign policy without allies. □□ **unilateralist** *n. & adj.*

unilingual /ˌjuːnɪˈlɪŋgw(ə)l/ *adj.* of or in only one language. □□ **unilingually** *adv.*

uniliteral /ˌjuːnɪˈlɪtər(ə)l/ *adj.* consisting of one letter.

unilluminated /ˌʌnɪˈluːmɪˌneɪtɪd, ˌʌnɪˈljuː-/ *adj.* not illuminated.

unillustrated /ʌnˈɪləˌstreɪtɪd/ *adj.* (esp. of a book) without illustrations.

unilocular /ˌjuːnɪˈlɒkjʊlə(r)/ *adj. Bot. & Zool.* single-chambered.

unimaginable /ˌʌnɪˈmædʒɪnəb(ə)l/ *adj.* impossible to imagine. □□ **unimaginably** *adv.*

unimaginative /ˌʌnɪˈmædʒɪnətɪv/ *adj.* lacking imagination; stolid, dull. □□ **unimaginatively** *adv.* **unimaginativeness** *n.*

unimpaired /ˌʌnɪmˈpeəd/ *adj.* not impaired.

unimpassioned /ˌʌnɪmˈpæʃ(ə)nd/ *adj.* not impassioned.

unimpeachable /ˌʌnɪmˈpiːtʃəb(ə)l/ *adj.* giving no opportunity for censure; beyond reproach or question. □□ **unimpeachably** *adv.*

unimpeded /ˌʌnɪmˈpiːdɪd/ *adj.* not impeded. □□ **unimpededly** *adv.*

unimportance /ˌʌnɪmˈpɔːt(ə)ns/ *n.* lack of importance.

unimportant /ˌʌnɪmˈpɔːt(ə)nt/ *adj.* not important.

unimposing /ˌʌnɪmˈpəʊzɪŋ/ *adj.* unimpressive. □□ **unimposingly** *adv.*

unimpressed /ˌʌnɪmˈprest/ *adj.* not impressed.

unimpressionable /ˌʌnɪmˈpreʃənəb(ə)l/ *adj.* not impressionable.

unimpressive /ˌʌnɪmˈpresɪv/ *adj.* not impressive. □□ **unimpressively** *adv.* **unimpressiveness** *n.*

unimproved /ˌʌnɪmˈpruːvd/ *adj.* **1** not made better. **2** not made use of. **3** (of land) not used for agriculture or building; not developed.

unincorporated /ˌʌnɪnˈkɔːpəˌreɪtɪd/ *adj.* **1** not incorporated or united. **2** not formed into a corporation.

uninfected /ˌʌnɪnˈfektɪd/ *adj.* not infected.

uninflamed /ˌʌnɪnˈfleɪmd/ *adj.* not inflamed.

uninflammable /ˌʌnɪnˈflæməb(ə)l/ *adj.* not inflammable.

uninflected /ˌʌnɪnˈflektɪd/ *adj.* **1** *Gram.* (of a language) not having inflections. **2** not changing or varying. **3** not bent or deflected.

uninfluenced /ʌnˈɪnflʊənst/ *adj.* (often foll. by *by*) not influenced.

uninfluential /ˌʌnɪnflʊˈenʃ(ə)l/ *adj.* having little or no influence.

uninformative /ˌʌnɪnˈfɔːmətɪv/ *adj.* not informative; giving little information.

uninformed /ˌʌnɪnˈfɔːmd/ *adj.* **1** not informed or instructed. **2** ignorant, uneducated.

uninhabitable /ˌʌnɪnˈhæbɪtəb(ə)l/ *adj.* that cannot be inhabited. □□ **uninhabitableness** *n.*

uninhabited /ˌʌnɪnˈhæbɪtɪd/ *adj.* not inhabited.

uninhibited /ˌʌnɪnˈhɪbɪtɪd/ *adj.* not inhibited. □□ **uninhibitedly** *adv.* **uninhibitedness** *n.*

uninitiated /ˌʌnɪˈnɪʃɪˌeɪtɪd/ *adj.* not initiated; not admitted or instructed.

uninjured /ʌnˈɪndʒəd/ *adj.* not injured.

uninspired /ˌʌnɪnˈspaɪəd/ *adj.* **1** not inspired. **2** (of oratory etc.) commonplace.

uninspiring /ˌʌnɪnˈspaɪərɪŋ/ *adj.* not inspiring. □□ **uninspiringly** *adv.*

uninstructed /ˌʌnɪnˈstrʌktɪd/ *adj.* not instructed or informed.

uninsurable /ˌʌnɪnˈʃʊərəb(ə)l/ *adj.* that cannot be insured.

uninsured /ˌʌnɪnˈʃʊəd/ *adj.* not insured.

unintelligent /ˌʌnɪnˈtelɪdʒ(ə)nt/ *adj.* not intelligent. □□ **unintelligently** *adv.*

unintelligible /ˌʌnɪnˈtelɪdʒɪb(ə)l/ *adj.* not intelligible. □□ **unintelligibility** /-ˈbɪlɪti/ *n.* **unintelligibleness** *n.* **unintelligibly** *adv.*

unintended /ˌʌnɪnˈtendɪd/ *adj.* not intended.

unintentional /ˌʌnɪnˈtenʃən(ə)l/ *adj.* not intentional. □□ **unintentionally** *adv.*

uninterested /ʌnˈɪntrəstɪd, -trɪstɪd/ *adj.* **1** not interested. **2** unconcerned, indifferent. □□ **uninterestedly** *adv.* **uninterestedness** *n.*

uninteresting /ʌnˈɪntrəstɪŋ, -trɪstɪŋ/ *adj.* not interesting. □□ **uninterestingly** *adv.* **uninterestingness** *n.*

uninterpretable /ˌʌnɪnˈtɜːprɪtəb(ə)l/ *adj.* that cannot be interpreted.

uninterruptable /ˌʌnɪntəˈrʌptəb(ə)l/ *adj.* that cannot be interrupted.

uninterrupted /ˌʌnɪntəˈrʌptɪd/ *adj.* not interrupted. □□ **uninterruptedly** *adv.* **uninterruptedness** *n.*

uninucleate /ˌjuːnɪˈnjuːklɪˌeɪt, -ɪət/ *adj. Biol.* having a single nucleus.

uninventive /ˌʌnɪnˈventɪv/ *adj.* not inventive. □□ **uninventively** *adv.* **uninventiveness** *n.*

uninvestigated /ˌʌnɪnˈvestɪˌgeɪtɪd/ *adj.* not investigated.

uninvited /ˌʌnɪnˈvaɪtɪd/ *adj.* not invited. □□ **uninvitedly** *adv.*

uninviting /ˌʌnɪnˈvaɪtɪŋ/ *adj.* not inviting, unattractive, repellent. □□ **uninvitingly** *adv.*

uninvoked /ˌʌnɪnˈvəʊkt/ *adj.* not invoked.

uninvolved /ˌʌnɪnˈvɒlvd/ *adj.* not involved.

union /ˈjuːnjən, -nɪən/ *n.* **1 a** the act or an instance of uniting;

the state of being united. **b** (**the Union**) *hist.* the uniting of the English and Scottish crowns in 1603, of the English and Scottish parliaments in 1707, or of Great Britain and Ireland in 1801. **2 a** a whole resulting from the combination of parts or members. **b** a political unit formed in this way, esp. the US, the UK, the USSR, or South Africa. **3** = *trade union.* **4** marriage, matrimony. **5** concord, agreement (*lived together in perfect union*). **6** (**Union**) **a** a general social club and debating society at some universities and colleges. **b** the buildings or accommodation of such a society. **7** *Math.* the totality of the members of two or more sets. **8** *Brit. hist.* **a** two or more parishes consolidated for the administration of the Poor Laws. **b** (in full **union workhouse**) a workhouse erected by this. **9** *Brit.* an association of independent (esp. Congregational or Baptist) Churches for purposes of cooperation. **10** a part of a flag with a device emblematic of union, normally occupying the upper corner next to the staff. **11** a joint or coupling for pipes etc. **12** a fabric of mixed materials, e.g. cotton with linen or silk. □ **union-bashing** *Brit. colloq.* active opposition to trade unions and their rights. **union catalogue** a catalogue of the combined holdings of several libraries. **union down** (of a flag) hoisted with the union below as a signal of distress. **Union Jack** see separate entry. **union shop** a shop, factory, trade, etc., in which employees must belong to a trade union or join one within an agreed time. **union suit** *US* a single undergarment for the body and legs; combinations. [ME f. OF *union* or eccl.L *unio* unity f. L *unus* one]

unionist /ˈjuːnjənɪst, ˈjuːnɪən-/ *n.* **1 a** a member of a trade union. **b** an advocate of trade unions. **2** (usu. **Unionist**) an advocate of union, esp.: **a** *US* a supporter or advocate of the Federal Union of the United States of America, especially one who during the Civil War (1861–5) was opposed to secession. **b** (in British politics) a member of a political party advocating or supporting maintenance of the parliamentary Union between Great Britain and Ireland (later, between Great Britain and Northern Ireland). This party was formed in 1886 by the coalition of the Conservatives with those Liberals (Liberal Unionists) who were opposed to Gladstone's policy of home rule for Ireland. While the chief tenet of this party was the maintenance of the Union, its general policy and principles gradually became identified with those of the Conservative Party, and in 1909 the coalition officially adopted the name of 'Conservative and Unionist Party'. □□ **unionism** *n.* **unionistic** /-ˈnɪstɪk/ *adj.*

unionize /ˈjuːnjəˌnaɪz, ˈjuːnɪən-/ *v.tr.* & *intr.* (also **-ise**) bring or come under trade-union organization or rules. □□ **unionization** /-ˈzeɪʃ(ə)n/ *n.*

un-ionized /ʌnˈaɪəˌnaɪzd/ *adj.* (also **-ised**) not ionized.

Union Jack 1 (also **Union flag**) the national flag or ensign of the United Kingdom (formerly of Great Britain), formed by combining the crosses of the three patron saints St George, St Andrew, and St Patrick, retaining the blue ground of the banner of St Andrew. This flag was introduced to symbolize the union of the crowns of England and Scotland (1603) and was formed by surmounting the cross saltire of St Andrew by the cross of St George; the cross saltire of St Patrick was added on the union of the parliaments of Great Britain and Ireland (1801). Originally and properly the term 'Union Jack' denoted a small British Union flag flown as the jack of a ship; in later and more extended use it denoted any size or adaptation of the Union flag (even when not used as a jack). **2** (**union jack**) *US* a jack consisting of the union from the national flag.

Union of Soviet Socialist Republics the world's largest country, with 15 constituent republics, occupying the northern half of Asia (part of it lies within the Arctic Circle) and part of eastern Europe; pop. (est. 1988) 286,434,800; official language, Russian; capital, Moscow. (For its history before 1917 see RUSSIA.) The overthrow of the Tsar in the Russian Revolution of 1917 led to the triumph of the Bolsheviks, the withdrawal of Russia from the First World War, and the establishment of a Communist State. Between the wars Soviet history was dominated by the attempted economic overhaul of the country, the imposition of Communist systems and values throughout the country, and Soviet involvement in attempted Communist revolutions elsewhere in the world. The German invasion of 1941 led to a long

and bloody campaign in the western USSR, leaving millions dead and resulting in the Soviet conquest of eastern Europe. In the postwar era, the USSR emerged as one of two antagonistic superpowers, rivalling the US, in the polarization of the Communist and non-Communist worlds. The Soviet economy has been characterized by strong central planning and continued attempts to open up the large Russian hinterlands. In the late 1980s Mikhail Gorbachev sought to reform the whole Communist system, with economic changes that would lead to the establishment of a market economy. Unrest in the republics of the USSR from 1989 onwards, with a rise in nationalist feeling, challenged the fabric of the Union.

Union Territory any of the six administrative territories within the Republic of India.

uniparous /juːˈnɪpərəs/ *adj.* **1** producing one offspring at a birth. **2** *Bot.* having one axis or branch.

uniped /ˈjuːnɪˌped/ *n.* & *adj.* —*n.* a person having only one foot or leg. —*adj.* one-footed, one-legged. [UNI- + *pes pedis* foot]

unipersonal /ˌjuːnɪˈpɜːsən(ə)l/ *adj.* (of the Deity) existing only as one person.

uniplanar /ˌjuːnɪˈpleɪnə(r)/ *adj.* lying in one plane.

unipod /ˈjuːnɪˌpɒd/ *n.* a one-legged support for a camera etc. [UNI-, after TRIPOD]

unipolar /ˌjuːnɪˈpəʊlə(r)/ *adj.* **1** (esp. of an electric or magnetic apparatus) showing only one kind of polarity. **2** *Biol.* (of a nerve cell etc.) having only one pole. □□ **unipolarity** /-ˈlærɪtɪ/ *n.*

unique /jʊˈniːk, juːˈniːk/ *adj.* & *n.* —*adj.* **1** of which there is only one; unequalled; having no like, equal, or parallel (*his position was unique; this vase is considered unique*). **2** *disp.* unusual, remarkable (*the most unique man I ever met*). —*n.* a unique thing or person. □□ **uniquely** *adv.* **uniqueness** *n.* [F f. L *unicus* f. *unus* one]

unironed /ʌnˈaɪənd/ *adj.* (esp. of clothing, linen, etc.) not ironed.

uniserial /ˌjuːnɪˈsɪərɪəl/ *adj. Bot.* & *Zool.* arranged in one row.

unisex /ˈjuːnɪˌseks/ *adj.* (of clothing, hairstyles, etc.) designed to be suitable for both sexes.

unisexual /ˌjuːnɪˈseksjʊəl, -kʃʊəl/ *adj.* **1 a** of one sex. **b** *Bot.* having stamens or pistils but not both. **2** unisex. □□ **unisexuality** /-ʊˈælɪtɪ/ *n.* **unisexually** *adv.*

unison /ˈjuːnɪs(ə)n/ *n.* & *adj.* —*n.* **1** *Mus.* **a** coincidence in pitch of sounds or notes. **b** this regarded as an interval. **2** *Mus.* a combination of voices or instruments at the same pitch or at pitches differing by one or more octaves (*sang in unison*). **3** agreement, concord (*acted in perfect unison*). —*adj. Mus.* coinciding in pitch. □ **unison string** a string tuned in unison with another string and meant to be sounded with it. □□ **unisonant** /jʊˈnɪsənənt/ *adj.* **unisonous** /jʊˈnɪsənəs/ *adj.* [OF *unison* or LL *unisonus* (as UNI-, *sonus* SOUND¹)]

unissued /ʌnˈɪʃuːd, ʌnˈɪsjuːd/ *adj.* not issued.

unit /ˈjuːnɪt/ *n.* **1 a** an individual thing, person, or group regarded as single and complete, esp. for purposes of calculation. **b** each of the (smallest) separate individuals or groups into which a complex whole may be analysed (*the family as the unit of society*). **2** a quantity chosen as a standard in terms of which other quantities may be expressed (*unit of heat; SI unit; mass per unit volume*). **3** *Brit.* the smallest share in a unit trust. **4** a device with a specified function forming part of a complex mechanism. **5** a piece of furniture for fitting with others like it or made of complementary parts. **6** a group with a special function in an organization. **7** a group of buildings, wards, etc., in a hospital. **8** the number 'one'. □ **unit cell** *Crystallog.* the smallest repeating group of atoms, ions, or molecules in a crystal. **unit cost** the cost of producing one item of manufacture. **unit-holder** *Brit.* a person with a holding in a unit trust. **unit price** the price charged for each unit of goods supplied. **unit trust** *Brit.* an investment company investing combined contributions from many persons in various securities and paying them dividends (calculated on the average return of the securities) in proportion to their holdings. [L *unus*, prob. after DIGIT]

UNITAR *abbr.* United Nations Institute for Training and Research. Its headquarters are in New York.

Unitarian /ˌjuːnɪˈteərɪən/ n. & adj. —n. **1** a person who believes that God is not a Trinity but one person. **2** a member of a religious body maintaining this and advocating freedom from formal dogma or doctrine. (See below.) —adj. of or relating to the Unitarians. □□ **Unitarianism** n. [mod.L unitarius f. L unitas UNITY]

Unitarians have no formal creed; originally their teaching was based on scriptural authority, but now reason and conscience have become their criteria for belief and practice. A similar doctrine was voiced in the early Church, but modern Unitarianism dates historically from the Reformation era; as an organized community it became established in the 16th–17th c. in Poland, Hungary, and England, emerging as a full denomination in England when T. Lindsey seceded from the Church of England in 1773.

unitary /ˈjuːnɪtərɪ/ adj. **1** of a unit or units. **2** marked by unity or uniformity. □□ **unitarily** adv. **unitarity** /-ˈtærɪtɪ/ n.

unite /joˈnaɪt, juː-/ v. **1** tr. & intr. join together; make or become one; combine. **2** tr. & intr. join together for a common purpose or action (united in their struggle against injustice). **3** tr. & intr. join in marriage. **4** tr. possess (qualities, features, etc.) in combination (united anger with mercy). **5** intr. & tr. form or cause to form a physical or chemical whole (oil will not unite with water). □ **United Brethren** Eccl. the Moravians. □□ **unitedly** adv. **unitive** /ˈjuːnɪtɪv/ adj. **unitively** /ˈjuːnɪtɪvlɪ/ adv. [ME f. L unire unit- f. unus one]

United Arab Emirates an independent State formed in 1971 by the union of seven independent sheikhdoms (formerly called the Trucial States and enjoying special treaty relations with Britain) along the south coast of the Persian Gulf westwards from the entrance to the Gulf of Oman. The member States are Abu Dhabi, Ajman, Dubai, Fujairah, Ras al Khaimah (which joined early in 1972), Sharjah, and Umm al Qaiwain; total pop. (est. 1988) 1,980,350.

United Kingdom the kingdom of Great Britain (see BRITAIN) and, since 1922, Northern Ireland. The term referred to Great Britain and the whole of Ireland from 1801 (when the two countries were united by Act of Parliament) until 1920, when Ireland was partitioned.

United Nations an international organization of countries set up in 1945, in succession to the League of Nations, to promote international peace, security, and cooperation, with its headquarters in New York. Its members, originally the countries that fought against the Axis in the Second World War, now number 159 and include most sovereign States of the world, the chief exceptions being Switzerland and North and South Korea. Administration is by the Secretariat, headed by the Secretary-General. The chief deliberative body is the General Assembly, in which each member State has one vote; recommendations are passed but the UN has no power to impose its will. The Security Council bears the primary responsibility for the maintenance of peace and security; other bodies carry out the functions of the UN with regard to international economic, social, judicial, cultural, educational, health, and other matters.

United Provinces hist. the seven Dutch provinces of Friesland, Gelderland, Groningen, Holland, Overijssel, Utrecht, and Zeeland which formed a union under the Treaty of Utrecht in 1579 following their successful rebellion against Spanish rule, leading to the formation of the Dutch Republic or The Netherlands. **2** an administrative division of British India formed by the union of Agra and Oudh. It has been the State of Uttar Pradesh since 1950 when India became a republic.

United Reformed Church the Church formed in 1972 by the union of the greater part of the Congregational Church in England and Wales with the Presbyterian Church in England.

United States (in full **United States of America**) a country occupying most of the southern half of North America and including also Alaska in the north and Hawaii in the Pacific Ocean, comprising 50 States and the Federal District of Columbia; pop. (est. 1988) 246,042,500; official language, English; capital, Washington DC. The east coast of North America was colonized by the British in the 17th c., while the south was penetrated by the Spanish from Mexico and the centre taken

possession of, but barely colonized, by the French. The modern US grew out of the successful rebellion of the east coast colonies against British rule in 1775–83. The Louisiana territory was purchased from France in 1803 and the south-west was taken from Mexico after the war of 1846–8. The second half of the 19th c. saw the gradual opening up of the western half of the country after the interruption caused by the Civil War between the northern States and those of the south. In the 20th c. the United States has been the world's principal economic power, participating on the Allied side in both World Wars and becoming one of the two antagonistic superpowers, dominating the non-Communist world in the era following the Second World War.

unity /ˈjuːnɪtɪ/ n. (pl. **-ies**) **1** oneness; being one, single, or individual; being formed of parts that constitute a whole; due interconnection and coherence of parts (disturbs the unity of the idea; the pictures lack unity; national unity). **2** harmony or concord between persons etc. (lived together in unity). **3** a thing forming a complex whole (a person regarded as a unity). **4** Math. the number 'one', the factor that leaves unchanged the quantity on which it operates. **5** Theatr. each of the three dramatic principles requiring limitation of the supposed time of a drama to that occupied in acting it or to a single day (**unity of time**), use of one scene throughout (**unity of place**), and concentration on the development of a single plot (**unity of action**). [ME f. OF unité f. L unitas -tatis f. unus one]

Univ. abbr. University.

univalent adj. & n. —adj. **1** /ˌjuːnɪˈveɪlənt/ Chem. having a valency of one. **2** /juːˈnɪvələnt/ Biol. (of a chromosome) remaining unpaired during meiosis. —n. /juːˈnɪvələnt/ Biol. a univalent chromosome. [UNI- + valent- pres. part. stem (as VALENCE¹)]

univalve /ˈjuːnɪvælv/ adj. & n. Zool. —adj. having one valve. —n. a univalve mollusc.

universal /ˌjuːnɪˈvɜːs(ə)l/ adj. & n. —adj. **1** of, belonging to, or done etc. by all persons or things in the world or in the class concerned; applicable to all cases (the feeling was universal; met with universal approval). **2** Logic (of a proposition) in which something is asserted of all of a class (opp. PARTICULAR). —n. **1** Logic a universal proposition. **2** Philos. **a** a term or concept of general application. **b** a nature or essence signified by a general term. □ **universal agent** an agent empowered to do all that can be delegated. **universal compass** a compass with legs that may be extended for large circles. **universal coupling** (or **joint**) a coupling or joint which can transmit rotary power by a shaft at any selected angle. **universal language** an artificial language intended for use by all nations. **universal proposition** Logic a proposition in which the predicate is affirmed or denied of all members of a class (opp. particular proposition). **universal suffrage** a suffrage extending to all adults with minor exceptions. **universal time** that used for astronomical reckoning at all places. □□ **universality** /-ˈsælɪtɪ/ n. **universalize** v.tr. (also **-ise**). **universalization** /-ˈzeɪʃ(ə)n/ n. **universally** adv. [ME f. OF universal or L universalis (as UNIVERSE)]

universalist /ˌjuːnɪˈvɜːsəlɪst/ n. Theol. **1** a person who holds that all mankind will eventually be saved. **2** a member of an organized body of Christians who hold this. □□ **universalism** n. **universalistic** /-ˈlɪstɪk/ adj.

Universal Postal Union a UN inter-governmental agency that regulates international postal affairs. Founded in 1874 as the General Postal Union, it came into effect in 1875; the name was changed to Universal Postal Union in 1878, and it became a UN agency in 1948. Its headquarters are in Berne.

universe /ˈjuːnɪvɜːs/ n. **1** (also **Universe**) all existing things including the Earth and its creatures and all the heavenly bodies; the cosmos. (See below.) **2** all mankind. **3** Statistics & Logic all the objects under consideration. □ **universe of discourse** Logic = sense 3. [F univers f. L universum neut. of universus combined into one, whole f. UNI- + versus past part. of vertere turn]

Ancient and medieval ideas confined all known things to the surface of Earth, apart from the relatively few heavenly bodies visible to the naked eye, which were supposed to orbit Earth on idealized crystal spheres. This geocentric world-picture was replaced by the system of Copernicus, which placed the sun at the centre of the system of worlds. In turn, the privileged position of the sun was displaced by the realization of Herschel that the Milky Way was a great host of stars, of which our sun was part. Only in the 20th c. was it conclusively shown that even this system of stars occupied no special position, and that there were millions of other star systems, or galaxies, many bigger than our own. The known Universe is believed to be at least ten thousand million light-years in diameter; its formation and evolution are the province of the science of cosmology (see also HUBBLE'S LAW).

university /ˌjuːnɪˈvɜːsɪtɪ/ n. (pl. **-ies**) **1** an educational institution designed for instruction, examination, or both, of students in many branches of advanced learning, conferring degrees in various faculties, and often embodying colleges and similar institutions. **2** the members of this collectively. **3** a team, crew, etc., representing a university. □ **at university** studying at a university. [ME f. OF université f. L universitas -tatis the whole (world), in LL college, guild (as UNIVERSE)]

univocal /juːˈnɪvək(ə)l, ˌjuːnɪˈvəʊk(ə)l/ adj. & n. —adj. (of a word etc.) having only one proper meaning. —n. a univocal word. □□ **univocality** /ˌjuːnɪvəʊˈkælɪtɪ/ n. **univocally** adv.

unjoin /ʌnˈdʒɔɪn/ v.tr. detach from being joined; separate.

unjoined /ʌnˈdʒɔɪnd/ adj. not joined.

unjoint /ʌnˈdʒɔɪnt/ v.tr. **1** separate the joints of. **2** disunite.

unjust /ʌnˈdʒʌst/ adj. not just, contrary to justice or fairness. □□ **unjustly** adv. **unjustness** n.

unjustifiable /ʌnˈdʒʌstɪˌfaɪəb(ə)l/ adj. not justifiable. □□ **unjustifiably** adv.

unjustified /ʌnˈdʒʌstɪˌfaɪd/ adj. not justified.

unkempt /ʌnˈkempt/ adj. **1** untidy, of neglected appearance. **2** uncombed, dishevelled. □□ **unkemptly** adv. **unkemptness** n. [UN-¹ + archaic kempt past part. of kemb comb f. OE cemban]

unkept /ʌnˈkept/ adj. **1** (of a promise, law, etc.) not observed; disregarded. **2** not tended; neglected.

unkillable /ʌnˈkɪləb(ə)l/ adj. that cannot be killed.

unkind /ʌnˈkaɪnd/ adj. **1** not kind. **2** harsh, cruel. **3** unpleasant. □□ **unkindly** adv. **unkindness** n.

unking /ʌnˈkɪŋ/ v.tr. **1** deprive of the position of king; dethrone. **2** deprive (a country) of a king.

unkink /ʌnˈkɪŋk/ v. **1** tr. remove the kinks from; straighten. **2** intr. lose kinks; become straight.

unknit /ʌnˈnɪt/ v.tr. (**unknitted**, **unknitting**) separate (things joined, knotted, or interlocked).

unknot /ʌnˈnɒt/ v.tr. (**unknotted**, **unknotting**) release the knot or knots of, untie.

unknowable /ʌnˈnəʊəb(ə)l/ adj. & n. —adj. that cannot be known. —n. **1** an unknowable thing. **2** (**the Unknowable**) the postulated absolute or ultimate reality.

unknowing /ʌnˈnəʊɪŋ/ adj. & n. —adj. (often foll. by of) not knowing; ignorant, unconscious. —n. ignorance (cloud of unknowing). □□ **unknowingly** adv. **unknowingness** n.

unknown /ʌnˈnəʊn/ adj. & n. —adj. (often foll. by to) not known, unfamiliar (his purpose was unknown to me). —n. **1** an unknown thing or person. **2** an unknown quantity (equation in two unknowns). □ **unknown country** see COUNTRY. **unknown quantity** a person or thing whose nature, significance, etc., cannot be determined. **Unknown Soldier** an unidentified representative member of a country's armed forces killed in war, given burial with special honours in a national memorial. **unknown to** without the knowledge of (did it unknown to me). **Unknown Warrior** = Unknown Soldier. □□ **unknownness** n.

unlabelled /ʌnˈleɪb(ə)ld/ adj. (US **unlabeled**) not labelled; without a label.

unlaboured /ʌnˈleɪbəd/ adj. (US **unlabored**) not laboured.

unlace /ʌnˈleɪs/ v.tr. **1** undo the lace or laces of. **2** unfasten or loosen in this way.

unlade /ʌnˈleɪd/ v.tr. **1** take the cargo out of (a ship). **2** discharge (a cargo etc.) from a ship.

unladen /ʌnˈleɪd(ə)n/ adj. not laden. □ **unladen weight** the weight of a vehicle etc. when not loaded with goods etc.

unladylike /ʌnˈleɪdɪˌlaɪk/ adj. not ladylike.

unlaid¹ /ʌnˈleɪd/ adj. not laid.

unlaid² past and past part. of UNLAY.

unlamented /ˌʌnləˈmentɪd/ adj. not lamented.

unlash /ʌnˈlæʃ/ v.tr. unfasten (a thing lashed down etc.).

unlatch /ʌnˈlætʃ/ v. **1** tr. release the latch of. **2** tr. & intr. open or be opened in this way.

unlawful /ʌnˈlɔːfʊl/ adj. not lawful; illegal, not permissible. □□ **unlawfully** adv. **unlawfulness** n.

unlay /ʌnˈleɪ/ v.tr. (past and past part. **unlaid**) Naut. untwist (a rope). [UN-² + LAY¹]

unleaded /ʌnˈledɪd/ adj. **1** (of petrol etc.) without added lead. **2** not covered, weighted, or framed with lead. **3** Printing not spaced with leads.

unlearn /ʌnˈlɜːn/ v.tr. (past and past part. **unlearned** or **unlearnt**) **1** discard from one's memory. **2** rid oneself of (a habit, false information, etc.).

unlearned¹ /ʌnˈlɜːnɪd/ adj. not well educated; untaught, ignorant. □□ **unlearnedly** adv.

unlearned² /ʌnˈlɜːnd/ adj. (also **unlearnt** /-ˈlɜːnt/) that has not been learnt.

unleash /ʌnˈliːʃ/ v.tr. **1** release from a leash or restraint. **2** set free to engage in pursuit or attack.

unleavened /ʌnˈlev(ə)nd/ adj. not leavened; made without yeast or other raising agent.

unless /ʌnˈles, ənˈles/ conj. if not; except when (shall go unless I hear from you; always walked unless I had a bicycle). [ON or IN + LESS, assim. to UN-¹]

unlettered /ʌnˈletəd/ adj. **1** illiterate. **2** not well educated.

unliberated /ʌnˈlɪbəˌreɪtɪd/ adj. not liberated.

unlicensed /ʌnˈlaɪs(ə)nst/ adj. not licensed, esp. without a licence to sell alcoholic drink.

unlighted /ʌnˈlaɪtɪd/ adj. **1** not provided with light. **2** not set burning.

unlike /ʌnˈlaɪk/ adj. & prep. —adj. **1** not like; different from (is unlike both his parents). **2** uncharacteristic of (such behaviour is unlike him). **3** dissimilar, different. —prep. differently from (acts quite unlike anyone else). □ **unlike signs** Math. plus and minus. □□ **unlikeness** n. [perh. f. ON ūlíkr, OE ungelic: see LIKE¹]

unlikeable /ʌnˈlaɪkəb(ə)l/ adj. (also **unlikable**) not easy to like; unpleasant.

unlikely /ʌnˈlaɪklɪ/ adj. (**unlikelier**, **unlikeliest**) **1** improbable (unlikely tale). **2** (foll. by to + infin.) not to be expected to do something (he's unlikely to be available). **3** unpromising (an unlikely candidate). □□ **unlikelihood** n. **unlikeliness** n.

unlimited /ʌnˈlɪmɪtɪd/ adj. without limit; unrestricted; very great in number or quantity (has unlimited possibilities; an unlimited expanse of sea). □□ **unlimitedly** adv. **unlimitedness** n.

unlined¹ /ʌnˈlaɪnd/ adj. **1** (of paper etc.) without lines. **2** (of a face etc.) without wrinkles.

unlined² /ʌnˈlaɪnd/ adj. (of a garment etc.) without lining.

unlink /ʌnˈlɪŋk/ v.tr. **1** undo the links of (a chain etc.). **2** detach or set free by undoing or unfastening a link or chain.

unliquidated /ʌnˈlɪkwɪˌdeɪtɪd/ adj. not liquidated.

unlisted /ʌnˈlɪstɪd/ adj. not included in a published list, esp. of Stock Exchange prices or of telephone numbers.

unlit /ʌnˈlɪt/ adj. not lit.

unlivable /ʌnˈlɪvəb(ə)l/ adj. that cannot be lived or lived in.

unlived-in /ʌnˈlɪvdɪn/ adj. **1** appearing to be uninhabited. **2** unused by the inhabitants.

unload /ʌnˈləʊd/ v.tr. **1** (also absol.) remove a load from (a vehicle etc.). **2** remove (a load) from a vehicle etc. **3** remove the charge from (a firearm etc.). **4** colloq. get rid of. **5** (often foll. by on) colloq. **a** divulge (information). **b** (also absol.) give vent to (feelings). □□ **unloader** n.

unlock /ʌnˈlɒk/ v.tr. **1 a** release the lock of (a door, box, etc.). **b** release or disclose by unlocking. **2** release thoughts, feelings, etc., from (one's mind etc.).

unlocked /ʌnˈlɒkt/ adj. not locked.

unlooked-for /ʌnˈlʊktfɔː(r)/ *adj.* unexpected, unforeseen.

unloose /ʌnˈluːs/ *v.tr.* (also **unloosen**) loose; set free.

unlovable /ʌnˈlʌvəb(ə)l/ *adj.* not lovable.

unloved /ʌnˈlʌvd/ *adj.* not loved.

unlovely /ʌnˈlʌvlɪ/ *adj.* not attractive; unpleasant, ugly. □□ **unloveliness** *n.*

unloving /ʌnˈlʌvɪŋ/ *adj.* not loving. □□ **unlovingly** *adv.* **unlovingness** *n.*

unlucky /ʌnˈlʌkɪ/ *adj.* (**unluckier, unluckiest**) 1 not fortunate or successful. 2 wretched. 3 bringing bad luck. 4 ill-judged. □□ **unluckily** *adv.* **unluckiness** *n.*

unmade /ʌnˈmeɪd/ *adj.* 1 not made. 2 destroyed, annulled.

unmake /ʌnˈmeɪk/ *v.tr.* (*past* and *past part.* **unmade**) undo the making of; destroy, depose, annul.

unmalleable /ʌnˈmælɪəb(ə)l/ *adj.* not malleable.

unman /ʌnˈmæn/ *v.tr.* (**unmanned, unmanning**) 1 deprive of supposed manly qualities (e.g. self-control, courage); cause to weep etc., discourage. 2 deprive (a ship etc.) of men.

unmanageable /ʌnˈmænɪdʒəb(ə)l/ *adj.* not (easily) managed, manipulated, or controlled. □□ **unmanageableness** *n.* **unmanageably** *adv.*

unmanly /ʌnˈmænlɪ/ *adj.* not manly. □□ **unmanliness** *n.*

unmanned /ʌnˈmænd/ *adj.* 1 not manned. 2 overcome by emotion etc.

unmannerly /ʌnˈmænəlɪ/ *adj.* 1 without good manners. 2 (of actions, speech, etc.) showing a lack of good manners. □□ **unmannerliness** *n.*

unmarked /ʌnˈmɑːkt/ *adj.* 1 not marked. 2 not noticed.

unmarketable /ʌnˈmɑːkɪtəb(ə)l/ *adj.* not marketable.

unmarried /ʌnˈmærɪd/ *adj.* not married; single.

unmask /ʌnˈmɑːsk/ *v.* 1 *tr.* **a** remove the mask from. **b** expose the true character of. 2 *intr.* remove one's mask. □□ **unmasker** *n.*

unmatchable /ʌnˈmætʃəb(ə)l/ *adj.* that cannot be matched. □□ **unmatchably** *adv.*

unmatched /ʌnˈmætʃt/ *adj.* not matched or equalled.

unmatured /ˌʌnməˈtjʊəd/ *adj.* not yet matured.

unmeaning /ʌnˈmiːnɪŋ/ *adj.* having no meaning or significance; meaningless. □□ **unmeaningly** *adv.* **unmeaningness** *n.*

unmeant /ʌnˈment/ *adj.* not meant or intended.

unmeasurable /ʌnˈmeʒərəb(ə)l/ *adj.* that cannot be measured. □□ **unmeasurably** *adv.*

unmeasured /ʌnˈmeʒəd/ *adj.* 1 not measured. 2 limitless.

unmelodious /ˌʌnmɪˈləʊdɪəs/ *adj.* not melodious; discordant. □□ **unmelodiously** *adv.*

unmelted /ʌnˈmeltɪd/ *adj.* not melted.

unmemorable /ʌnˈmemərəb(ə)l/ *adj.* not memorable. □□ **unmemorably** *adv.*

unmentionable /ʌnˈmenʃənəb(ə)l/ *adj.* & *n.* —*adj.* that cannot (properly) be mentioned. —*n.* 1 (in *pl.*) *joc.* **a** undergarments. **b** *archaic* trousers. 2 a person or thing not to be mentioned. □□ **unmentionability** /-ˈbɪlɪtɪ/ *n.* **unmentionableness** *n.* **unmentionably** *adv.*

unmentioned /ʌnˈmenʃ(ə)nd/ *adj.* not mentioned.

unmerchantable /ʌnˈmɜːtʃəntəb(ə)l/ *adj.* not merchantable.

unmerciful /ʌnˈmɜːsɪfʊl/ *adj.* merciless. □□ **unmercifully** *adv.* **unmercifulness** *n.*

unmerited /ʌnˈmerɪtɪd/ *adj.* not merited.

unmet /ʌnˈmet/ *adj.* (of a quota, demand, goal, etc.) not achieved or fulfilled.

unmetalled /ʌnˈmet(ə)ld/ *adj.* *Brit.* (of a road etc.) not made with road-metal.

unmethodical /ˌʌnmɪˈθɒdɪk(ə)l/ *adj.* not methodical. □□ **unmethodically** *adv.*

unmetrical /ʌnˈmetrɪk(ə)l/ *adj.* not metrical.

unmilitary /ʌnˈmɪlɪtərɪ/ *adj.* not military.

unmindful /ʌnˈmaɪndfʊl/ *adj.* (often foll. by *of*) not mindful. □□ **unmindfully** *adv.* **unmindfulness** *n.*

unmissable /ʌnˈmɪsəb(ə)l/ *adj.* that cannot or should not be missed.

unmistakable /ˌʌnmɪˈsteɪkəb(ə)l/ *adj.* that cannot be mistaken or doubted, clear. □□ **unmistakability** /-ˈbɪlɪtɪ/ *n.* **unmistakableness** *n.* **unmistakably** *adv.*

unmistaken /ˌʌnmɪˈsteɪkən/ *adj.* not mistaken; right, correct.

unmitigated /ʌnˈmɪtɪˌɡeɪtɪd/ *adj.* 1 not mitigated or modified. 2 absolute, unqualified (*an unmitigated disaster*). □□ **unmitigatedly** *adv.*

unmixed /ʌnˈmɪkst/ *adj.* not mixed. □ **unmixed blessing** a thing having advantages and no disadvantages.

unmodified /ʌnˈmɒdɪˌfaɪd/ *adj.* not modified.

unmodulated /ʌnˈmɒdjʊˌleɪtɪd/ *adj.* not modulated.

unmolested /ˌʌnməˈlestɪd/ *adj.* not molested.

unmoor /ʌnˈmʊə(r), ʌnˈmɔː(r)/ *v.tr.* 1 (also *absol.*) release the moorings of (a vessel). 2 weigh all but one anchor of (a vessel).

unmoral /ʌnˈmɒr(ə)l/ *adj.* not concerned with morality (cf. IMMORAL). □□ **unmorality** /ˌʌnmɒˈrælɪtɪ/ *n.* **unmorally** *adv.*

unmotherly /ʌnˈmʌðəlɪ/ *adj.* not motherly.

unmotivated /ʌnˈməʊtɪˌveɪtɪd/ *adj.* without motivation; without a motive.

unmounted /ʌnˈmaʊntɪd/ *adj.* not mounted.

unmourned /ʌnˈmɔːnd/ *adj.* not mourned.

unmoved /ʌnˈmuːvd/ *adj.* 1 not moved. 2 not changed in one's purpose. 3 not affected by emotion. □□ **unmovable** *adj.* (also **unmoveable**).

unmown /ʌnˈməʊn/ *adj.* not mown.

unmuffle /ʌnˈmʌf(ə)l/ *v.tr.* 1 remove a muffler from (a face, bell, etc.). 2 free of something that muffles or conceals.

unmurmuring /ʌnˈmɜːmərɪŋ/ *adj.* not complaining. □□ **unmurmuringly** *adv.*

unmusical /ʌnˈmjuːzɪk(ə)l/ *adj.* 1 not pleasing to the ear. 2 unskilled in or indifferent to music. □□ **unmusicality** /-ˈkælɪtɪ/ *n.* **unmusically** *adv.* **unmusicalness** *n.*

unmutilated /ʌnˈmjuːtɪˌleɪtɪd/ *adj.* not mutilated.

unmuzzle /ʌnˈmʌz(ə)l/ *v.tr.* 1 remove a muzzle from. 2 relieve of an obligation to remain silent.

unnail /ʌnˈneɪl/ *v.tr.* unfasten by the removal of nails.

unnameable /ʌnˈneɪməb(ə)l/ *adj.* that cannot be named, esp. too bad to be named.

unnamed /ʌnˈneɪmd/ *adj.* not named.

unnatural /ʌnˈnætʃər(ə)l/ *adj.* 1 contrary to nature or the usual course of nature; not normal. 2 **a** lacking natural feelings. **b** extremely cruel or wicked. 3 artificial. 4 affected. □□ **unnaturally** *adv.* **unnaturalness** *n.*

unnavigable /ʌnˈnævɪɡəb(ə)l/ *adj.* not navigable. □□ **unnavigability** /-ˈbɪlɪtɪ/ *n.*

unnecessary /ʌnˈnesəsərɪ/ *adj.* & *n.* —*adj.* 1 not necessary. 2 more than is necessary (*with unnecessary care*). —*n.* (*pl.* **-ies**) (usu. in *pl.*) an unnecessary thing. □□ **unnecessarily** *adv.* **unnecessariness** *n.*

unneeded /ʌnˈniːdɪd/ *adj.* not needed.

unneighbourly /ʌnˈneɪbəlɪ/ *adj.* not neighbourly. □□ **unneighbourliness** *n.*

unnerve /ʌnˈnɜːv/ *v.tr.* deprive of strength or resolution. □□ **unnervingly** *adv.*

unnoticeable /ʌnˈnəʊtɪsəb(ə)l/ *adj.* not easily seen or noticed. □□ **unnoticeably** *adv.*

unnoticed /ʌnˈnəʊtɪst/ *adj.* not noticed.

unnumbered /ʌnˈnʌmbəd/ *adj.* 1 not marked with a number. 2 not counted. 3 countless.

UNO /ˈjuːnəʊ/ *abbr.* United Nations Organization.

unobjectionable /ˌʌnəbˈdʒekʃənəb(ə)l/ *adj.* not objectionable; acceptable. □□ **unobjectionableness** *n.* **unobjectionably** *adv.*

unobliging /ˌʌnəˈblaɪdʒɪŋ/ *adj.* not obliging; unhelpful, uncooperative.

unobscured /ˌʌnəbˈskjʊəd/ *adj.* not obscured.

unobservable /ˌʌnəbˈzɜːvəb(ə)l/ *adj.* not observable; imperceptible.

unobservant /ˌʌnəbˈzɜːv(ə)nt/ adj. not observant. □□ **unobservantly** adv.

unobserved /ˌʌnəbˈzɜːvd/ adj. not observed. □□ **unobservedly** /-vɪdlɪ/ adv.

unobstructed /ˌʌnəbˈstrʌktɪd/ adj. not obstructed.

unobtainable /ˌʌnəbˈteɪnəb(ə)l/ adj. that cannot be obtained.

unobtrusive /ˌʌnəbˈtruːsɪv/ adj. not making oneself or itself noticed. □□ **unobtrusively** adv. **unobtrusiveness** n.

unoccupied /ʌnˈɒkjʊˌpaɪd/ adj. not occupied.

unoffending /ˌʌnəˈfendɪŋ/ adj. not offending; harmless, innocent. □□ **unoffended** adj.

unofficial /ˌʌnəˈfɪʃ(ə)l/ adj. 1 not officially authorized or confirmed. 2 not characteristic of officials. □ **unofficial strike** a strike not formally approved by the strikers' trade union. □□ **unofficially** adv.

unoiled /ʌnˈɔɪld/ adj. not oiled.

unopened /ʌnˈəʊpənd/ adj. not opened.

unopposed /ˌʌnəˈpəʊzd/ adj. not opposed.

unordained /ˌʌnɔːˈdeɪnd/ adj. not ordained.

unordinary /ʌnˈɔːdɪnərɪ/ adj. not ordinary.

unorganized /ʌnˈɔːgəˌnaɪzd/ adj. (also **-ised**) not organized (cf. DISORGANIZE).

unoriginal /ˌʌnəˈrɪdʒɪn(ə)l/ adj. lacking originality; derivative. □□ **unoriginality** /-ˈnælɪtɪ/ n. **unoriginally** adv.

unornamental /ˌʌnɔːnəˈment(ə)l/ adj. not ornamental; plain.

unornamented /ʌnˈɔːnəˌmentɪd/ adj. not ornamented.

unorthodox /ʌnˈɔːθəˌdɒks/ adj. not orthodox. □□ **unorthodoxly** adv. **unorthodoxy** n.

unostentatious /ˌʌnɒstenˈteɪʃəs/ adj. not ostentatious. □□ **unostentatiously** adv. **unostentatiousness** n.

unowned /ʌnˈəʊnd/ adj. 1 unacknowledged. 2 having no owner.

unpack /ʌnˈpæk/ v.tr. 1 (also absol.) open and remove the contents of (a package, luggage, etc.). 2 take (a thing) out from a package etc. □□ **unpacker** n.

unpaged /ʌnˈpeɪdʒd/ adj. with pages not numbered.

unpaid /ʌnˈpeɪd/ adj. (of a debt or a person) not paid.

unpainted /ʌnˈpeɪntɪd/ adj. not painted.

unpaired /ʌnˈpeəd/ adj. 1 not arranged in pairs. 2 not forming one of a pair.

unpalatable /ʌnˈpælətəb(ə)l/ adj. 1 not pleasant to taste. 2 (of an idea, suggestion, etc.) disagreeable, distasteful. □□ **unpalatability** /-ˈbɪlɪtɪ/ n. **unpalatableness** n.

unparalleled /ʌnˈpærəˌleld/ adj. having no parallel or equal.

unpardonable /ʌnˈpɑːdənəb(ə)l/ adj. that cannot be pardoned. □□ **unpardonableness** n. **unpardonably** adv.

unparliamentary /ˌʌnpɑːləˈmentərɪ/ adj. contrary to proper parliamentary usage. □ **unparliamentary language** oaths or abuse.

unpasteurized /ʌnˈpɑːstjəˌraɪzd, -tʃəˌraɪzd, ʌnˈpæs-/ adj. not pasteurized.

unpatented /ʌnˈpeɪtəntɪd, ʌnˈpæt-/ adj. not patented.

unpatriotic /ˌʌnpætrɪˈɒtɪk, ˌʌnpeɪt-/ adj. not patriotic. □□ **unpatriotically** adv.

unpaved /ʌnˈpeɪvd/ adj. not paved.

unpeeled /ʌnˈpiːld/ adj. not peeled.

unpeg /ʌnˈpeg/ v.tr. (**unpegged**, **unpegging**) 1 unfasten by the removal of pegs. 2 cease to maintain or stabilize (prices etc.).

unpeople v. & n. —v.tr. /ʌnˈpiːp(ə)l/ depopulate. —n.pl. /ˈʌnˌpiːp(ə)l/ unpersons.

unperceived /ˌʌnpəˈsiːvd/ adj. not perceived; unobserved.

unperceptive /ˌʌnpəˈseptɪv/ adj. not perceptive. □□ **unperceptively** adv. **unperceptiveness** n.

unperfected /ˌʌnpəˈfektɪd/ adj. not perfected.

unperforated /ʌnˈpɜːfəˌreɪtɪd/ adj. not perforated.

unperformed /ˌʌnpəˈfɔːmd/ adj. not performed.

unperfumed /ˌʌnpɜːˈfjuːmd/ adj. not perfumed.

unperson /ˈʌnˌpɜːs(ə)n/ n. a person whose name or existence is denied or ignored.

unpersuadable /ˌʌnpəˈsweɪdəb(ə)l/ adj. not able to be persuaded; obstinate.

unpersuaded /ˌʌnpəˈsweɪdɪd/ adj. not persuaded.

unpersuasive /ˌʌnpəˈsweɪsɪv/ adj. not persuasive. □□ **unpersuasively** adv.

unperturbed /ˌʌnpəˈtɜːbd/ adj. not perturbed. □□ **unperturbedly** /-bɪdlɪ/ adv.

unphilosophical /ˌʌnfɪləˈsɒfɪk(ə)l/ adj. (also **unphilosophic**) 1 not according to philosophical principles. 2 lacking philosophy. □□ **unphilosophically** adv.

unphysiological /ˌʌnfɪzɪəˈlɒdʒɪk(ə)l/ adj. (also **unphysiologic**) not in accordance with normal physiological functioning. □□ **unphysiologically** adv.

unpick /ʌnˈpɪk/ v.tr. undo the sewing of (stitches, a garment, etc.).

unpicked /ʌnˈpɪkt/ adj. 1 not selected. 2 (of a flower) not plucked.

unpicturesque /ˌʌnpɪktʃəˈresk/ adj. not picturesque.

unpin /ʌnˈpɪn/ v.tr. (**unpinned**, **unpinning**) 1 unfasten or detach by removing a pin or pins. 2 Chess release (a piece that has been pinned).

unpitied /ʌnˈpɪtɪd/ adj. not pitied.

unpitying /ʌnˈpɪtɪɪŋ/ adj. not pitying. □□ **unpityingly** adv.

unplaceable /ʌnˈpleɪsəb(ə)l/ adj. that cannot be placed or classified (his accent was unplaceable).

unplaced /ʌnˈpleɪst/ adj. not placed, esp. not placed as one of the first three finishing in a race etc.

unplanned /ʌnˈplænd/ adj. not planned.

unplanted /ʌnˈplɑːntɪd/ adj. not planted.

unplausible /ʌnˈplɔːzɪb(ə)l/ adj. not plausible.

unplayable /ʌnˈpleɪəb(ə)l/ adj. 1 Sport (of a ball) that cannot be struck or returned. 2 that cannot be played. □□ **unplayably** adv.

unpleasant /ʌnˈplez(ə)nt/ adj. not pleasant; displeasing; disagreeable. □□ **unpleasantly** adv. **unpleasantness** n.

unpleasing /ʌnˈpliːzɪŋ/ adj. not pleasing. □□ **unpleasingly** adv.

unploughed /ʌnˈplaʊd/ adj. not ploughed.

unplucked /ʌnˈplʌkt/ adj. not plucked.

unplug /ʌnˈplʌg/ v.tr. (**unplugged**, **unplugging**) 1 disconnect (an electrical device) by removing its plug from the socket. 2 unstop.

unplumbed /ʌnˈplʌmd/ adj. 1 not plumbed. 2 not fully explored or understood. □□ **unplumbable** adj.

unpoetic /ˌʌnpəʊˈetɪk/ adj. (also **unpoetical**) not poetic.

unpointed /ʌnˈpɔɪntɪd/ adj. 1 having no point or points. 2 a not punctuated. b (of written Hebrew etc.) without vowel points. 3 (of masonry or brickwork) not pointed.

unpolished /ʌnˈpɒlɪʃt/ adj. 1 not polished; rough. 2 without refinement; crude.

unpolitic /ʌnˈpɒlɪtɪk/ adj. impolitic, unwise.

unpolitical /ˌʌnpəˈlɪtɪk(ə)l/ adj. not concerned with politics. □□ **unpolitically** adv.

unpolled /ʌnˈpəʊld/ adj. 1 not having voted at an election. 2 not included in an opinion poll.

unpolluted /ˌʌnpəˈluːtɪd/ adj. not polluted.

unpopular /ʌnˈpɒpjʊlə(r)/ adj. not popular; not liked by the public or by people in general. □□ **unpopularity** /-ˈlærɪtɪ/ n. **unpopularly** adv.

unpopulated /ʌnˈpɒpjʊˌleɪtɪd/ adj. not populated.

unpossessed /ˌʌnpəˈzest/ adj. 1 (foll. by of) not in possession of. 2 not possessed.

unpractical /ʌnˈpræktɪk(ə)l/ adj. 1 not practical. 2 (of a person) not having practical skill. □□ **unpracticality** /-ˈkælɪtɪ/ n. **unpractically** adv.

unpractised /ʌnˈpræktɪst/ adj. (US **unpracticed**) 1 not experienced or skilled. 2 not put into practice.

unprecedented /ʌnˈpresɪˌdentɪd/ adj. 1 having no precedent; unparalleled. 2 novel. □□ **unprecedentedly** adv.

unpredictable /ˌʌnprɪˈdɪktəb(ə)l/ adj. that cannot be predicted.

□□ **unpredictability** /-'bɪlɪtɪ/ n. **unpredictableness** n. **unpredictably** adv.

unpredicted /ˌʌnprɪ'dɪktɪd/ adj. not predicted or foretold.

unprejudiced /ʌn'predʒʊdɪst/ adj. not prejudiced.

unpremeditated /ˌʌnprɪ'medɪˌteɪtɪd/ adj. not previously thought over, not deliberately planned, unintentional. □□ **unpremeditatedly** adv.

unprepared /ˌʌnprɪ'peəd/ adj. not prepared (in advance); not ready. □□ **unpreparedly** adv. **unpreparedness** n.

unprepossessing /ˌʌnpriːpə'zesɪŋ/ adj. not prepossessing; unattractive.

unprescribed /ˌʌnprɪ'skraɪbd/ adj. (esp. of drugs) not prescribed.

unpresentable /ˌʌnprɪ'zentəb(ə)l/ adj. not presentable.

unpressed /ʌn'prest/ adj. not pressed, esp. (of clothing) unironed.

unpresuming /ˌʌnprɪ'zjuːmɪŋ/ adj. not presuming; modest.

unpresumptuous /ˌʌnprɪ'zʌmptjʊəs/ adj. not presumptuous.

unpretending /ˌʌnprɪ'tendɪŋ/ adj. unpretentious. □□ **unpretendingly** adv. **unpretendingness** n.

unpretentious /ˌʌnprɪ'tenʃəs/ adj. not making a great display; simple, modest. □□ **unpretentiously** adv. **unpretentiousness** n.

unpriced /ʌn'praɪst/ adj. not having a price or prices fixed, marked, or stated.

unprimed /ʌn'praɪmd/ adj. not primed.

unprincipled /ʌn'prɪnsɪp(ə)ld/ adj. lacking or not based on good moral principles. □□ **unprincipledness** n.

unprintable /ʌn'prɪntəb(ə)l/ adj. that cannot be printed, esp. because too indecent or libellous or blasphemous. □□ **unprintably** adv.

unprinted /ʌn'prɪntɪd/ adj. not printed.

unprivileged /ʌn'prɪvɪlɪdʒd/ adj. not privileged.

unproblematic /ˌʌnprɒblə'mætɪk/ adj. causing no difficulty. □□ **unproblematically** adv.

unproclaimed /ˌʌnprəʊ'kleɪmd/ adj. not proclaimed.

unprocurable /ˌʌnprə'kjʊərəb(ə)l/ adj. that cannot be procured.

unproductive /ˌʌnprə'dʌktɪv/ adj. not productive. □□ **unproductively** adv. **unproductiveness** n.

unprofessional /ˌʌnprə'feʃən(ə)l/ adj. 1 contrary to professional standards of behaviour etc. 2 not belonging to a profession; amateur. □□ **unprofessionally** adv.

unprofitable /ʌn'prɒfɪtəb(ə)l/ adj. not profitable. □□ **unprofitableness** n. **unprofitably** adv.

unprogressive /ˌʌnprə'gresɪv/ adj. not progressive.

unpromising /ʌn'prɒmɪsɪŋ/ adj. not likely to turn out well. □□ **unpromisingly** adv.

unprompted /ʌn'prɒmptɪd/ adj. spontaneous.

unpronounceable /ˌʌnprə'naʊnsəb(ə)l/ adj. that cannot be pronounced. □□ **unpronounceably** adv.

unpropitious /ˌʌnprə'pɪʃəs/ adj. not propitious. □□ **unpropitiously** adv.

unprosperous /ʌn'prɒspərəs/ adj. not prosperous. □□ **unprosperously** adv.

unprotected /ˌʌnprə'tektɪd/ adj. not protected. □□ **unprotectedness** n.

unprotesting /ˌʌnprə'testɪŋ/ adj. not protesting. □□ **unprotestingly** adv.

unprovable /ʌn'pruːvəb(ə)l/ adj. that cannot be proved. □□ **unprovability** /-'bɪlɪtɪ/ n. **unprovableness** n.

unproved /ʌn'pruːvd/ adj. (also **unproven** /-v(ə)n/) not proved.

unprovided /ˌʌnprə'vaɪdɪd/ adj. (usu. foll. by with) not furnished, supplied, or equipped.

unprovoked /ˌʌnprə'vəʊkt/ adj. (of a person or act) without provocation.

unpublished /ʌn'pʌblɪʃt/ adj. not published. □□ **unpublishable** adj.

unpunctual /ʌn'pʌŋktjʊəl/ adj. not punctual. □□ **unpunctuality** /-tjʊ'ælɪtɪ/ n.

unpunctuated /ʌn'pʌŋktjʊˌeɪtɪd/ adj. not punctuated.

unpunishable /ʌn'pʌnɪʃəb(ə)l/ adj. that cannot be punished.

unpunished /ʌn'pʌnɪʃt/ adj. not punished.

unpurified /ʌn'pjʊərɪˌfaɪd/ adj. not purified.

unputdownable /ˌʌnpʊt'daʊnəb(ə)l/ adj. colloq. (of a book) so engrossing that one has to go on reading it.

unqualified /ʌn'kwɒlɪˌfaɪd/ adj. 1 not competent (unqualified to give an answer). 2 not legally or officially qualified (an unqualified practitioner). 3 not modified or restricted; complete (unqualified assent; unqualified success).

unquenchable /ʌn'kwentʃəb(ə)l/ adj. that cannot be quenched. □□ **unquenchably** adv.

unquenched /ʌn'kwentʃt/ adj. not quenched.

unquestionable /ʌn'kwestʃənəb(ə)l/ adj. that cannot be disputed or doubted. □□ **unquestionability** /-'bɪlɪtɪ/ n. **unquestionableness** n. **unquestionably** adv.

unquestioned /ʌn'kwestʃ(ə)nd/ adj. 1 not disputed or doubted; definite, certain. 2 not interrogated.

unquestioning /ʌn'kwestʃənɪŋ/ adj. 1 asking no questions. 2 done etc. without asking questions. □□ **unquestioningly** adv.

unquiet /ʌn'kwaɪət/ adj. 1 restless, agitated, stirring. 2 perturbed, anxious. □□ **unquietly** adv. **unquietness** n.

unquotable /ʌn'kwəʊtəb(ə)l/ adj. that cannot be quoted.

unquote /ʌn'kwəʊt/ v.tr. (as int.) (in dictation, reading aloud, etc.) indicate the presence of closing quotation marks (cf. QUOTE v. 5 b).

unquoted /ʌn'kwəʊtɪd/ adj. not quoted, esp. on the Stock Exchange.

unravel /ʌn'ræv(ə)l/ v. (**unravelled**, **unravelling**; US **unraveled**, **unraveling**) 1 tr. cause to be no longer ravelled, tangled, or intertwined. 2 tr. probe and solve (a mystery etc.). 3 tr. undo (a fabric, esp. a knitted one). 4 intr. become disentangled or unknitted.

unreachable /ʌn'riːtʃəb(ə)l/ adj. that cannot be reached. □□ **unreachableness** n. **unreachably** adv.

unread /ʌn'red/ adj. 1 (of a book etc.) not read. 2 (of a person) not well-read.

unreadable /ʌn'riːdəb(ə)l/ adj. 1 too dull or too difficult to be worth reading. 2 illegible. □□ **unreadability** /-'bɪlɪtɪ/ n. **unreadably** adv.

unready[1] /ʌn'redɪ/ adj. 1 not ready. 2 not prompt in action. □□ **unreadily** adv. **unreadiness** n.

unready[2] /ʌn'redɪ/ adj. archaic lacking good advice; rash (Ethelred the Unready). [UN-[1] + REDE, assim. to UNREADY[1]]

unreal /ʌn'rɪəl/ adj. 1 not real. 2 imaginary, illusory. 3 US & Austral. sl. incredible, amazing. □□ **unreality** /-'ælɪtɪ/ n. **unreally** adv.

unrealistic /ˌʌnrɪə'lɪstɪk/ adj. not realistic. □□ **unrealistically** adv.

unrealizable /ʌn'rɪəlaɪzəb(ə)l/ adj. that cannot be realized.

unrealized /ʌn'rɪəlaɪzd/ adj. not realized.

unreason /ʌn'riːz(ə)n/ n. lack of reasonable thought or action. [ME, = injustice, f. UN-[1] + REASON]

unreasonable /ʌn'riːzənəb(ə)l/ adj. 1 going beyond the limits of what is reasonable or equitable (unreasonable demands). 2 not guided by or listening to reason. □□ **unreasonableness** n. **unreasonably** adv.

unreasoned /ʌn'riːz(ə)nd/ adj. not reasoned.

unreasoning /ʌn'riːzənɪŋ/ adj. not reasoning. □□ **unreasoningly** adv.

unreceptive /ˌʌnrɪ'septɪv/ adj. not receptive.

unreciprocated /ˌʌnrɪ'sɪprəˌkeɪtɪd/ adj. not reciprocated.

unreckoned /ʌn'rekənd/ adj. not calculated or taken into account.

unreclaimed /ˌʌnrɪ'kleɪmd/ adj. not reclaimed.

unrecognizable /ʌn'rekəgˌnaɪzəb(ə)l/ adj. (also **-isable**) that cannot be recognized. □□ **unrecognizableness** n. **unrecognizably** adv.

unrecognized /ʌnˈrekəgˌnaɪzd/ adj. (also **-ised**) not recognized.

unrecompensed /ʌnˈrekəmˌpenst/ adj. not recompensed.

unreconciled /ʌnˈrekənˌsaɪld/ adj. not reconciled.

unreconstructed /ˌʌnriːkənˈstrʌktɪd/ adj. **1** not reconciled or converted to the current political orthodoxy. **2** not rebuilt.

unrecorded /ˌʌnrɪˈkɔːdɪd/ adj. not recorded. □□ **unrecordable** adj.

unrectified /ʌnˈrektɪˌfaɪd/ adj. not rectified.

unredeemable /ˌʌnrɪˈdiːməb(ə)l/ adj. that cannot be redeemed. □□ **unredeemably** adv.

unredeemed /ˌʌnrɪˈdiːmd/ adj. not redeemed.

unredressed /ˌʌnrɪˈdrest/ adj. not redressed.

unreel /ʌnˈriːl/ v.tr. & intr. unwind from a reel.

unreeve /ʌnˈriːv/ v.tr. (past **unrove**) withdraw (a rope etc.) from being reeved.

unrefined /ˌʌnrɪˈfaɪnd/ adj. not refined.

unreflecting /ˌʌnrɪˈflektɪŋ/ adj. not thoughtful. □□ **unreflectingly** adv. **unreflectingness** n.

unreformed /ˌʌnrɪˈfɔːmd/ adj. not reformed.

unregarded /ˌʌnrɪˈgɑːdɪd/ adj. not regarded.

unregenerate /ˌʌnrɪˈdʒenərət/ adj. not regenerate; obstinately wrong or bad. □□ **unregeneracy** n. **unregenerately** adv.

unregistered /ʌnˈredʒɪstəd/ adj. not registered.

unregulated /ʌnˈregjʊˌleɪtɪd/ adj. not regulated.

unrehearsed /ˌʌnrɪˈhɜːst/ adj. not rehearsed.

unrelated /ˌʌnrɪˈleɪtɪd/ adj. not related. □□ **unrelatedness** n.

unrelaxed /ˌʌnrɪˈlækst/ adj. not relaxed.

unrelenting /ˌʌnrɪˈlentɪŋ/ adj. **1** not relenting or yielding. **2** unmerciful. **3** not abating or relaxing. □□ **unrelentingly** adv. **unrelentingness** n.

unreliable /ˌʌnrɪˈlaɪəb(ə)l/ adj. not reliable; erratic. □□ **unreliability** /-ˈbɪlɪtɪ/ n. **unreliableness** n. **unreliably** adv.

unrelieved /ˌʌnrɪˈliːvd/ adj. **1** lacking the relief given by contrast or variation. **2** not aided or assisted. □□ **unrelievedly** adv.

unreligious /ˌʌnrɪˈlɪdʒəs/ adj. **1** not concerned with religion. **2** irreligious.

unremarkable /ˌʌnrɪˈmɑːkəb(ə)l/ adj. not remarkable; uninteresting. □□ **unremarkably** adv.

unremembered /ˌʌnrɪˈmembəd/ adj. not remembered; forgotten.

unremitting /ˌʌnrɪˈmɪtɪŋ/ adj. never relaxing or slackening, incessant. □□ **unremittingly** adv. **unremittingness** n.

unremorseful /ˌʌnrɪˈmɔːsfʊl/ adj. lacking remorse. □□ **unremorsefully** adv.

unremovable /ˌʌnrɪˈmuːvəb(ə)l/ adj. that cannot be removed.

unremunerative /ˌʌnrɪˈmjuːnərətɪv/ adj. bringing no, or not enough, profit or income. □□ **unremuneratively** adv. **unremunerativeness** n.

unrenewable /ˌʌnrɪˈnjuːəb(ə)l/ adj. that cannot be renewed. □□ **unrenewed** adj.

unrepealed /ˌʌnrɪˈpiːld/ adj. not repealed.

unrepeatable /ˌʌnrɪˈpiːtəb(ə)l/ adj. **1** that cannot be done, made, or said again. **2** too indecent to be said again. □□ **unrepeatability** /-ˈbɪlɪtɪ/ n.

unrepentant /ˌʌnrɪˈpent(ə)nt/ adj. not repentant, impenitent. □□ **unrepentantly** adv.

unreported /ˌʌnrɪˈpɔːtɪd/ adj. not reported.

unrepresentative /ˌʌnreprɪˈzentətɪv/ adj. not representative. □□ **unrepresentativeness** n.

unrepresented /ˌʌnreprɪˈzentɪd/ adj. not represented.

unreproved /ˌʌnrɪˈpruːvd/ adj. not reproved.

unrequested /ˌʌnrɪˈkwestɪd/ adj. not requested or asked for.

unrequited /ˌʌnrɪˈkwaɪtɪd/ adj. (of love etc.) not returned. □□ **unrequitedly** adv. **unrequitedness** n.

unreserve /ˌʌnrɪˈzɜːv/ n. lack of reserve; frankness.

unreserved /ˌʌnrɪˈzɜːvd/ adj. **1** not reserved (unreserved seats). **2**

without reservations; absolute (unreserved confidence). **3** free from reserve (an unreserved nature). □□ **unreservedly** /-vɪdlɪ/ adv. **unreservedness** n.

unresisted /ˌʌnrɪˈzɪstɪd/ adj. not resisted. □□ **unresistedly** adv.

unresisting /ˌʌnrɪˈzɪstɪŋ/ adj. not resisting. □□ **unresistingly** adv. **unresistingness** n.

unresolvable /ˌʌnrɪˈzɒlvəb(ə)l/ adj. (of a problem, conflict, etc.) that cannot be resolved.

unresolved /ˌʌnrɪˈzɒlvd/ adj. **1 a** uncertain how to act, irresolute. **b** uncertain in opinion, undecided. **2** (of questions etc.) undetermined, undecided, unsolved. **3** not broken up or dissolved. □□ **unresolvedly** /-vɪdlɪ/ adv. **unresolvedness** n.

unresponsive /ˌʌnrɪˈspɒnsɪv/ adj. not responsive. □□ **unresponsively** adv. **unresponsiveness** n.

unrest /ʌnˈrest/ n. **1** lack of rest. **2** restlessness, disturbance, agitation.

unrested /ʌnˈrestɪd/ adj. not refreshed by rest.

unrestful /ʌnˈrestfʊl/ adj. not restful. □□ **unrestfully** adv.

unresting /ʌnˈrestɪŋ/ adj. not resting. □□ **unrestingly** adv.

unrestored /ˌʌnrɪˈstɔːd/ adj. not restored.

unrestrained /ˌʌnrɪˈstreɪnd/ adj. not restrained. □□ **unrestrainedly** /-nɪdlɪ/ adv. **unrestrainedness** n.

unrestricted /ˌʌnrɪˈstrɪktɪd/ adj. not restricted. □□ **unrestrictedly** adv. **unrestrictedness** n.

unreturned /ˌʌnrɪˈtɜːnd/ adj. **1** not reciprocated or responded to. **2** not having returned or been returned.

unrevealed /ˌʌnrɪˈviːld/ adj. not revealed; secret.

unreversed /ˌʌnrɪˈvɜːst/ adj. (esp. of a decision etc.) not reversed.

unrevised /ˌʌnrɪˈvaɪzd/ adj. not revised; in an original form.

unrevoked /ˌʌnrɪˈvəʊkt/ adj. not revoked or annulled; still in force.

unrewarded /ˌʌnrɪˈwɔːdɪd/ adj. not rewarded.

unrewarding /ˌʌnrɪˈwɔːdɪŋ/ adj. not rewarding or satisfying.

unrhymed /ʌnˈraɪmd/ adj. not rhymed.

unrhythmical /ʌnˈrɪðmɪk(ə)l/ adj. not rhythmical. □□ **unrhythmically** adv.

unridable /ʌnˈraɪdəb(ə)l/ adj. that cannot be ridden.

unridden /ʌnˈrɪd(ə)n/ adj. not ridden.

unriddle /ʌnˈrɪd(ə)l/ v.tr. solve or explain (a mystery etc.). □□ **unriddler** n.

unrig /ʌnˈrɪg/ v.tr. (**unrigged**, **unrigging**) **1** remove the rigging from (a ship). **2** dial. undress.

unrighteous /ʌnˈraɪtʃəs/ adj. not righteous; unjust, wicked, dishonest. □□ **unrighteously** adv. **unrighteousness** n. [OE unrihtwīs (as UN-¹, RIGHTEOUS)]

unrip /ʌnˈrɪp/ v.tr. (**unripped**, **unripping**) open by ripping.

unripe /ʌnˈraɪp/ adj. not ripe. □□ **unripeness** n.

unrisen /ʌnˈrɪz(ə)n/ adj. that has not risen.

unrivalled /ʌnˈraɪv(ə)ld/ adj. (US **unrivaled**) having no equal; peerless.

unrivet /ʌnˈrɪvɪt/ v.tr. (**unriveted**, **unriveting**) **1** undo, unfasten, or detach by the removal of rivets. **2** loosen, relax, undo, detach.

unrobe /ʌnˈrəʊb/ v.tr. & intr. **1** disrobe. **2** undress.

unroll /ʌnˈrəʊl/ v.tr. & intr. **1** open out from a rolled-up state. **2** display or be displayed in this form.

unromantic /ˌʌnrəˈmæntɪk/ adj. not romantic. □□ **unromantically** adv.

unroof /ʌnˈruːf/ v.tr. remove the roof of.

unroofed /ʌnˈruːft/ adj. not provided with a roof.

unroot /ʌnˈruːt/ v.tr. **1** uproot. **2** eradicate.

unrope /ʌnˈrəʊp/ v. **1** tr. detach by undoing a rope. **2** intr. Mountaineering detach oneself from a rope.

unrounded /ʌnˈraʊndɪd/ adj. not rounded.

unrove past of UNREEVE.

unroyal /ʌnˈrɔɪəl/ adj. not royal.

unruffled /ʌnˈrʌf(ə)ld/ *adj.* **1** not agitated or disturbed; calm. **2** not physically ruffled.

unruled /ʌnˈruːld/ *adj.* **1** not ruled or governed. **2** not having ruled lines.

unruly /ʌnˈruːlɪ/ *adj.* (**unrulier, unruliest**) not easily controlled or disciplined, disorderly. □□ **unruliness** *n.* [ME f. UN-¹ + *ruly* f. RULE]

UNRWA /ˈʌnrɑː/ *abbr.* United Nations Relief and Works Agency for Palestine Refugees in the Near East. Its headquarters are in Vienna.

unsaddle /ʌnˈsæd(ə)l/ *v.tr.* **1** remove the saddle from (a horse etc.). **2** dislodge from a saddle.

unsafe /ʌnˈseɪf/ *adj.* not safe. □□ **unsafely** *adv.* **unsafeness** *n.*

unsaid¹ /ʌnˈsed/ *adj.* not said or uttered.

unsaid² *past* and *past part.* of UNSAY.

unsalaried /ʌnˈsælərɪd/ *adj.* not salaried.

unsaleable /ʌnˈseɪləb(ə)l/ *adj.* not saleable. □□ **unsaleability** /-ˈbɪlɪtɪ/ *n.*

unsalted /ʌnˈsɔːltɪd, ʌnˈsɒl-/ *adj.* not salted.

unsanctified /ʌnˈsæŋktɪˌfaɪd/ *adj.* not sanctified.

unsanctioned /ʌnˈsæŋkʃ(ə)nd/ *adj.* not sanctioned.

unsanitary /ʌnˈsænɪtərɪ/ *adj.* not sanitary.

unsatisfactory /ˌʌnsætɪsˈfæktərɪ/ *adj.* not satisfactory; poor, unacceptable. □□ **unsatisfactorily** *adv.* **unsatisfactoriness** *n.*

unsatisfied /ʌnˈsætɪsˌfaɪd/ *adj.* not satisfied. □□ **unsatisfiedness** *n.*

unsatisfying /ʌnˈsætɪsˌfaɪɪŋ/ *adj.* not satisfying. □□ **unsatisfyingly** *adv.*

unsaturated /ʌnˈsætʃəˌreɪtɪd, -tjʊˌreɪtɪd/ *adj.* **1** *Chem.* (of a compound, esp. a fat or oil) having double or triple bonds in its molecule and therefore capable of further reaction. **2** not saturated. □□ **unsaturation** /-ˈreɪʃ(ə)n/ *n.*

unsaved /ʌnˈseɪvd/ *adj.* not saved.

unsavoury /ʌnˈseɪvərɪ/ *adj.* (US **unsavory**) **1** disagreeable to the taste, smell, or feelings; disgusting. **2** disagreeable, unpleasant (*an unsavoury character*). **3** morally offensive. □□ **unsavourily** *adv.* **unsavouriness** *n.*

unsay /ʌnˈseɪ/ *v.tr.* (*past* and *past part.* **unsaid**) retract (a statement).

unsayable /ʌnˈseɪəb(ə)l/ *adj.* that cannot be said.

unscalable /ʌnˈskeɪləb(ə)l/ *adj.* that cannot be scaled.

unscarred /ʌnˈskɑːd/ *adj.* not scarred or damaged.

unscathed /ʌnˈskeɪðd/ *adj.* without suffering any injury.

unscented /ʌnˈsentɪd/ *adj.* not scented.

unscheduled /ʌnˈʃedjuːld/ *adj.* not scheduled.

unscholarly /ʌnˈskɒləlɪ/ *adj.* not scholarly. □□ **unscholarliness** *n.*

unschooled /ʌnˈskuːld/ *adj.* **1** uneducated, untaught. **2** not sent to school. **3** untrained, undisciplined. **4** not made artificial by education.

unscientific /ˌʌnsaɪənˈtɪfɪk/ *adj.* **1** not in accordance with scientific principles. **2** not familiar with science. □□ **unscientifically** *adv.*

unscramble /ʌnˈskræmb(ə)l/ *v.tr.* restore from a scrambled state, esp. interpret (a scrambled transmission etc.). □□ **unscrambler** *n.*

unscreened /ʌnˈskriːnd/ *adj.* **1 a** (esp. of coal) not passed through a screen or sieve. **b** not investigated or checked, esp. for security or medical problems. **2** not provided with a screen. **3** not shown on a screen.

unscrew /ʌnˈskruː/ *v.* **1** *tr.* & *intr.* unfasten or be unfastened by turning or removing a screw or screws or by twisting like a screw. **2** *tr.* loosen (a screw).

unscripted /ʌnˈskrɪptɪd/ *adj.* (of a speech etc.) delivered without a prepared script.

unscriptural /ʌnˈskrɪptʃər(ə)l, -tʃʊər(ə)l/ *adj.* against or not in accordance with Scripture. □□ **unscripturally** *adv.*

unscrupulous /ʌnˈskruːpjʊləs/ *adj.* having no scruples, unprincipled. □□ **unscrupulously** *adv.* **unscrupulousness** *n.*

unseal /ʌnˈsiːl/ *v.tr.* break the seal of; open (a letter, receptacle, etc.).

unsealed /ʌnˈsiːld/ *adj.* not sealed.

unsearchable /ʌnˈsɜːtʃəb(ə)l/ *adj.* inscrutable. □□ **unsearchableness** *n.* **unsearchably** *adv.*

unsearched /ʌnˈsɜːtʃt/ *adj.* not searched.

unseasonable /ʌnˈsiːzənəb(ə)l/ *adj.* **1** not appropriate to the season. **2** untimely, inopportune. □□ **unseasonableness** *n.* **unseasonably** *adv.*

unseasoned /ʌnˈsiːz(ə)nd/ *adj.* **1** not flavoured with salt, herbs, etc. **2** (esp. of timber) not matured. **3** not habituated.

unseat /ʌnˈsiːt/ *v.tr.* **1** remove from a seat, esp. in an election. **2** dislodge from a seat, esp. on horseback.

unseaworthy /ʌnˈsiːˌwɜːðɪ/ *adj.* not seaworthy.

unsecured /ˌʌnsɪˈkjʊəd/ *adj.* not secured.

unseeable /ʌnˈsiːəb(ə)l/ *adj.* that cannot be seen.

unseeded /ʌnˈsiːdɪd/ *adj. Sport* (of a player) not seeded.

unseeing /ʌnˈsiːɪŋ/ *adj.* **1** unobservant. **2** blind. □□ **unseeingly** *adv.*

unseemly /ʌnˈsiːmlɪ/ *adj.* (**unseemlier, unseemliest**) **1** indecent. **2** unbecoming. □□ **unseemliness** *n.*

unseen /ʌnˈsiːn/ *adj.* & *n.* —*adj.* **1** not seen. **2** invisible. **3** (of a translation) to be done without preparation. —*n. Brit.* an unseen translation.

unsegregated /ʌnˈsegrɪˌgeɪtɪd/ *adj.* not segregated.

unselect /ˌʌnsɪˈlekt/ *adj.* not select.

unselective /ˌʌnsɪˈlektɪv/ *adj.* not selective.

unselfconscious /ˌʌnselfˈkɒnʃəs/ *adj.* not self-conscious. □□ **unselfconsciously** *adv.* **unselfconsciousness** *n.*

unselfish /ʌnˈselfɪʃ/ *adj.* mindful of others' interests. □□ **unselfishly** *adv.* **unselfishness** *n.*

unsensational /ˌʌnsenˈseɪʃən(ə)l/ *adj.* not sensational. □□ **unsensationally** *adv.*

unsentimental /ˌʌnsentɪˈment(ə)l/ *adj.* not sentimental. □□ **unsentimentality** /-ˈtælɪtɪ/ *n.* **unsentimentally** *adv.*

unseparated /ʌnˈsepəˌreɪtɪd/ *adj.* not separated.

unserviceable /ʌnˈsɜːvɪsəb(ə)l/ *adj.* not serviceable; unfit for use. □□ **unserviceability** /-ˈbɪlɪtɪ/ *n.*

unset /ʌnˈset/ *adj.* not set.

unsettle /ʌnˈset(ə)l/ *v.* **1** *tr.* disturb the settled state or arrangement of; discompose. **2** *tr.* derange. **3** *intr.* become unsettled. □□ **unsettlement** *n.*

unsettled /ʌnˈset(ə)ld/ *adj.* **1** not (yet) settled. **2** liable or open to change or further discussion. **3** (of a bill etc.) unpaid. □□ **unsettledness** *n.*

unsewn /ʌnˈsəʊn/ *adj.* not sewn. □ **unsewn binding** = *perfect binding.*

unsex /ʌnˈseks/ *v.tr.* deprive (a person, esp. a woman) of the qualities of her or his sex.

unsexed /ʌnˈsekst/ *adj.* having no sexual characteristics.

unshackle /ʌnˈʃæk(ə)l/ *v.tr.* **1** release from shackles. **2** set free.

unshaded /ʌnˈʃeɪdɪd/ *adj.* not shaded.

unshakeable /ʌnˈʃeɪkəb(ə)l/ *adj.* that cannot be shaken; firm, obstinate. □□ **unshakeability** /-ˈbɪlɪtɪ/ **unshakeably** *adv.*

unshaken /ʌnˈʃeɪkən/ *adj.* not shaken. □□ **unshakenly** *adv.*

unshapely /ʌnˈʃeɪplɪ/ *adj.* not shapely. □□ **unshapeliness** *n.*

unshared /ʌnˈʃeəd/ *adj.* not shared.

unsharp /ʌnˈʃɑːp/ *adj. Photog.* not sharp. □□ **unsharpness** *n.*

unshaved /ʌnˈʃeɪvd/ *adj.* not shaved.

unshaven /ʌnˈʃeɪv(ə)n/ *adj.* not shaved.

unsheathe /ʌnˈʃiːð/ *v.tr.* remove (a knife etc.) from a sheath.

unshed /ʌnˈʃed/ *adj.* not shed.

unshell /ʌnˈʃel/ *v.tr.* (usu. as **unshelled** *adj.*) extract from its shell.

unsheltered /ʌnˈʃeltəd/ *adj.* not sheltered.

unshielded /ʌnˈʃiːldɪd/ *adj.* not shielded or protected.

unship /ʌnˈʃɪp/ *v.tr.* (**unshipped, unshipping**) **1** remove or discharge (a cargo or passenger) from a ship. **2** esp. *Naut.* remove (an object, esp. a mast or oar) from a fixed position.

unshockable /ʌnˈʃɒkəb(ə)l/ *adj.* that cannot be shocked. □□ **unshockability** /-ˈbɪlɪtɪ/ *n.* **unshockably** *adv.*

unshod /ʌnˈʃɒd/ *adj.* not wearing shoes.

unshorn /ʌnˈʃɔːn/ *adj.* not shorn.

unshrinkable /ʌnˈʃrɪŋkəb(ə)l/ *adj.* (of fabric etc.) not liable to shrink. □□ **unshrinkability** /-ˈbɪlɪtɪ/ *n.*

unshrinking /ʌnˈʃrɪŋkɪŋ/ *adj.* unhesitating, fearless. □□ **unshrinkingly** *adv.*

unsighted /ʌnˈsaɪtɪd/ *adj.* **1** not sighted or seen. **2** prevented from seeing, esp. by an obstruction.

unsightly /ʌnˈsaɪtlɪ/ *adj.* unpleasant to look at, ugly. □□ **unsightliness** *n.*

unsigned /ʌnˈsaɪnd/ *adj.* not signed.

unsinkable /ʌnˈsɪŋkəb(ə)l/ *adj.* unable to be sunk. □□ **unsinkability** /-ˈbɪlɪtɪ/ *n.*

unsized[1] /ʌnˈsaɪzd/ *adj.* **1** not made to a size. **2** not sorted by size.

unsized[2] /ʌnˈsaɪzd/ *adj.* not treated with size.

unskilful /ʌnˈskɪlfʊl/ *adj.* (US **unskillful**) not skilful. □□ **unskilfully** *adv.* **unskilfulness** *n.*

unskilled /ʌnˈskɪld/ *adj.* lacking or not needing special skill or training.

unskimmed /ʌnˈskɪmd/ *adj.* (of milk) not skimmed.

unslakeable /ʌnˈsleɪkəb(ə)l/ *adj.* (also **unslakable**) that cannot be slaked or quenched.

unsleeping /ʌnˈsliːpɪŋ/ *adj.* not or never sleeping. □□ **unsleepingly** *adv.*

unsliced /ʌnˈslaɪst/ *adj.* (esp. of a loaf of bread when it is bought) not having been cut into slices.

unsling /ʌnˈslɪŋ/ *v.tr.* (*past* and *past part.* **unslung**) free from being slung or suspended.

unsmiling /ʌnˈsmaɪlɪŋ/ *adj.* not smiling. □□ **unsmilingly** *adv.* **unsmilingness** *n.*

unsmoked /ʌnˈsməʊkt/ *adj.* **1** not cured by smoking (*unsmoked bacon*). **2** not consumed by smoking (*an unsmoked cigar*).

unsnarl /ʌnˈsnɑːl/ *v.tr.* disentangle. [UN-[2] + SNARL[2]]

unsociable /ʌnˈsəʊʃəb(ə)l/ *adj.* not sociable, disliking the company of others. □□ **unsociability** /-ˈbɪlɪtɪ/ *n.* **unsociableness** *n.* **unsociably** *adv.*

unsocial /ʌnˈsəʊʃ(ə)l/ *adj.* **1** not social; not suitable for, seeking, or conforming to society. **2** outside the normal working day (*unsocial hours*). **3** antisocial. □□ **unsocially** *adv.*

unsoiled /ʌnˈsɔɪld/ *adj.* not soiled or dirtied.

unsold /ʌnˈsəʊld/ *adj.* not sold.

unsolder /ʌnˈsəʊldə(r), ʌnˈsɒl-/ *v.tr.* undo the soldering of.

unsoldierly /ʌnˈsəʊldʒəlɪ/ *adj.* not soldierly.

unsolicited /ˌʌnsəˈlɪsɪtɪd/ *adj.* not asked for; given or done voluntarily. □□ **unsolicitedly** *adv.*

unsolvable /ʌnˈsɒlvəb(ə)l/ *adj.* that cannot be solved, insoluble. □□ **unsolvability** /-ˈbɪlɪtɪ/ *n.* **unsolvableness** *n.*

unsolved /ʌnˈsɒlvd/ *adj.* not solved.

unsophisticated /ˌʌnsəˈfɪstɪˌkeɪtɪd/ *adj.* **1** artless, simple, natural, ingenuous. **2** not adulterated or artificial. □□ **unsophisticatedly** *adv.* **unsophisticatedness** *n.* **unsophistication** /-ˈkeɪʃ(ə)n/ *n.*

unsorted /ʌnˈsɔːtɪd/ *adj.* not sorted.

unsought /ʌnˈsɔːt/ *adj.* **1** not searched out or sought for. **2** unasked; without being requested.

unsound /ʌnˈsaʊnd/ *adj.* **1** unhealthy, diseased. **2** rotten, weak. **3 a** ill-founded, fallacious. **b** unorthodox, heretical. **4** unreliable. **5** wicked. □ **of unsound mind** insane. □□ **unsoundly** *adv.* **unsoundness** *n.*

unsounded[1] /ʌnˈsaʊndɪd/ *adj.* **1** not uttered or pronounced. **2** not made to sound.

unsounded[2] /ʌnˈsaʊndɪd/ *adj.* unfathomed.

unsoured /ʌnˈsaʊəd/ *adj.* not soured.

unsown /ʌnˈsəʊn/ *adj.* not sown.

unsparing /ʌnˈspeərɪŋ/ *adj.* **1** lavish, profuse. **2** merciless. □□ **unsparingly** *adv.* **unsparingness** *n.*

unspeakable /ʌnˈspiːkəb(ə)l/ *adj.* **1** that cannot be expressed in words. **2** indescribably bad or objectionable. □□ **unspeakableness** *n.* **unspeakably** *adv.*

unspecialized /ʌnˈspeʃəˌlaɪzd/ *adj.* not specialized.

unspecified /ʌnˈspesɪˌfaɪd/ *adj.* not specified.

unspectacular /ˌʌnspekˈtækjʊlə(r)/ *adj.* not spectacular; dull. □□ **unspectacularly** *adv.*

unspent /ʌnˈspent/ *adj.* **1** not expended or used. **2** not exhausted or used up.

unspilled /ʌnˈspɪld/ *adj.* not spilt.

unspilt /ʌnˈspɪlt/ *adj.* not spilt.

unspiritual /ʌnˈspɪrɪtjʊəl/ *adj.* not spiritual; earthly, worldly. □□ **unspirituality** /-ʊˈælɪtɪ/ *n.* **unspiritually** *adv.* **unspiritualness** *n.*

unspoiled /ʌnˈspɔɪld/ *adj.* **1** unspoilt. **2** not plundered.

unspoilt /ʌnˈspɔɪlt/ *adj.* not spoilt.

unspoken /ʌnˈspəʊkən/ *adj.* **1** not expressed in speech. **2** not uttered as speech.

unsporting /ʌnˈspɔːtɪŋ/ *adj.* not sportsmanlike; not fair or generous. □□ **unsportingly** *adv.* **unsportingness** *n.*

unsportsmanlike /ʌnˈspɔːtsmənˌlaɪk/ *adj.* unsporting.

unspotted /ʌnˈspɒtɪd/ *adj.* **1 a** not marked with a spot or spots. **b** morally pure. **2** unnoticed.

unsprung /ʌnˈsprʌŋ/ *adj.* not provided with a spring or springs; not resilient.

unstable /ʌnˈsteɪb(ə)l/ *adj.* (**unstabler**, **unstablest**) **1** not stable. **2** changeable. **3** showing a tendency to sudden mental or emotional changes. □ **unstable equilibrium** a state in which a body when disturbed tends to move farther from equilibrium. □□ **unstableness** *n.* **unstably** *adv.*

unstained /ʌnˈsteɪnd/ *adj.* not stained.

unstamped /ʌnˈstæmpt/ *adj.* **1** not marked by stamping. **2** not having a stamp affixed.

unstarched /ʌnˈstɑːtʃt/ *adj.* not starched.

unstated /ʌnˈsteɪtɪd/ *adj.* not stated or declared.

unstatesmanlike /ʌnˈsteɪtsmənˌlaɪk/ *adj.* not statesmanlike.

unstatutable /ʌnˈstætjʊtəb(ə)l/ *adj.* contrary to a statute or statutes. □□ **unstatutably** *adv.*

unsteadfast /ʌnˈstedfɑːst/ *adj.* not steadfast.

unsteady /ʌnˈstedɪ/ *adj.* (**unsteadier**, **unsteadiest**) **1** not steady or firm. **2** changeable, fluctuating. **3** not uniform or regular. □□ **unsteadily** *adv.* **unsteadiness** *n.*

unstick *v. & n.* —*v.* /ʌnˈstɪk/ (*past* and *past part.* **unstuck**) **1** *tr.* separate (a thing stuck to another). **2** *Aeron. colloq.* **a** *intr.* take off. **b** *tr.* cause (an aircraft) to take off. —*n.* /ˈʌnstɪk/ *Aeron. colloq.* the moment of take-off. □ **come unstuck** *colloq.* come to grief, fail.

unstinted /ʌnˈstɪntɪd/ *adj.* not stinted. □□ **unstintedly** *adv.*

unstinting /ʌnˈstɪntɪŋ/ *adj.* ungrudging, lavish. □□ **unstintingly** *adv.*

unstirred /ʌnˈstɜːd/ *adj.* not stirred.

unstitch /ʌnˈstɪtʃ/ *v.tr.* undo the stitches of.

unstop /ʌnˈstɒp/ *v.tr.* (**unstopped**, **unstopping**) **1** free from obstruction. **2** remove the stopper from.

unstoppable /ʌnˈstɒpəb(ə)l/ *adj.* that cannot be stopped or prevented. □□ **unstoppability** /-ˈbɪlɪtɪ/ *n.* **unstoppably** *adv.*

unstopper /ʌnˈstɒpə(r)/ *v.tr.* remove the stopper from.

unstrained /ʌnˈstreɪnd/ *adj.* **1** not subjected to straining or stretching. **2** not injured by overuse or excessive demands. **3** not forced or produced by effort. **4** not passed through a strainer.

unstrap /ʌnˈstræp/ *v.tr.* (**unstrapped**, **unstrapping**) undo the strap or straps of.

unstreamed /ʌnˈstriːmd/ *adj. Brit.* (of schoolchildren) not arranged in streams.

unstressed /ʌnˈstrest/ *adj.* **1** (of a word, syllable, etc.) not pronounced with stress. **2** not subjected to stress.

unstring /ʌnˈstrɪŋ/ *v.tr.* (*past* and *past part.* **unstrung**) **1** remove or relax the string or strings of (a bow, harp, etc.). **2** remove from a string. **3** (esp. as **unstrung** adj.) unnerve.

unstructured /ʌnˈstrʌktʃəd/ adj. **1** not structured. **2** informal.

unstuck past and past part. of UNSTICK.

unstudied /ʌnˈstʌdɪd/ adj. easy, natural, spontaneous. □□ **unstudiedly** adv.

unstuffed /ʌnˈstʌft/ adj. not stuffed.

unstuffy /ʌnˈstʌfɪ/ adj. **1** informal, casual. **2** not stuffy.

unsubdued /ˌʌnsəbˈdjuːd/ adj. not subdued.

unsubjugated /ʌnˈsʌbdʒʊˌɡeɪtɪd/ adj. not subjugated.

unsubstantial /ˌʌnsəbˈstænʃ(ə)l/ adj. having little or no solidity, reality, or factual basis. □□ **unsubstantiality** /-ʃɪˈælɪtɪ/ n. **unsubstantially** adv.

unsubstantiated /ˌʌnsəbˈstænʃɪˌeɪtɪd/ adj. not substantiated.

unsuccess /ˌʌnsəkˈses/ n. **1** lack of success; failure. **2** an instance of this.

unsuccessful /ˌʌnsəkˈsesfʊl/ adj. not successful. **unsuccessfully** adv. **unsuccessfulness** n.

unsugared /ʌnˈʃʊɡəd/ adj. not sugared.

unsuggestive /ˌʌnsəˈdʒestɪv/ adj. not suggestive.

unsuitable /ʌnˈsuːtəb(ə)l, ʌnˈsjuː-/ adj. not suitable. □□ **unsuitability** /-ˈbɪlɪtɪ/ n. **unsuitableness** n. **unsuitably** adv.

unsuited /ʌnˈsuːtɪd, ʌnˈsjuː-/ adj. **1** (usu. foll. by for) not fit for a purpose. **2** (usu. foll. by to) not adapted.

unsullied /ʌnˈsʌlɪd/ adj. not sullied.

unsummoned /ʌnˈsʌmənd/ adj. not summoned.

unsung /ʌnˈsʌŋ/ adj. **1** not celebrated in song; unknown. **2** not sung.

unsupervised /ʌnˈsuːpəˌvaɪzd, ʌnˈsjuː-/ adj. not supervised.

unsupportable /ˌʌnsəˈpɔːtəb(ə)l/ adj. **1** that cannot be endured. **2** indefensible. □□ **unsupportably** adv.

unsupported /ˌʌnsəˈpɔːtɪd/ adj. not supported. □□ **unsupportedly** adv.

unsure /ʌnˈʃʊə(r), ʌnˈʃɔː(r)/ adj. not sure. □□ **unsurely** adv. **unsureness** n.

unsurpassable /ˌʌnsəˈpɑːsəb(ə)l/ adj. that cannot be surpassed. □□ **unsurpassably** adv.

unsurpassed /ˌʌnsəˈpɑːst/ adj. not surpassed.

unsurprising /ˌʌnsəˈpraɪzɪŋ/ adj. not surprising. □□ **unsurprisingly** adv.

unsusceptible /ˌʌnsəˈseptɪb(ə)l/ adj. not susceptible. □□ **unsusceptibility** /-ˈbɪlɪtɪ/ n.

unsuspected /ˌʌnsəˈspektɪd/ adj. not suspected. □□ **unsuspectedly** adv.

unsuspecting /ˌʌnsəˈspektɪŋ/ adj. not suspecting. □□ **unsuspectingly** adv. **unsuspectingness** n.

unsuspicious /ˌʌnsəˈspɪʃəs/ adj. not suspicious. □□ **unsuspiciously** adv. **unsuspiciousness** n.

unsustained /ˌʌnsəˈsteɪnd/ adj. not sustained.

unswathe /ʌnˈsweɪð/ v.tr. free from being swathed.

unswayed /ʌnˈsweɪd/ adj. uninfluenced, unaffected.

unsweetened /ʌnˈswiːt(ə)nd/ adj. not sweetened.

unswept /ʌnˈswept/ adj. not swept.

unswerving /ʌnˈswɜːvɪŋ/ adj. **1** steady, constant. **2** not turning aside. □□ **unswervingly** adv.

unsworn /ʌnˈswɔːn/ adj. **1** (of a person) not subjected to or bound by an oath. **2** not confirmed by an oath.

unsymmetrical /ˌʌnsɪˈmetrɪk(ə)l/ adj. not symmetrical. □□ **unsymmetrically** adv.

unsympathetic /ˌʌnsɪmpəˈθetɪk/ adj. not sympathetic. □□ **unsympathetically** adv.

unsystematic /ˌʌnsɪstəˈmætɪk/ adj. not systematic. □□ **unsystematically** adv.

untack /ʌnˈtæk/ v.tr. detach, esp. by removing tacks.

untainted /ʌnˈteɪntɪd/ adj. not tainted.

untalented /ʌnˈtæləntɪd/ adj. not talented.

untameable /ʌnˈteɪməb(ə)l/ adj. that cannot be tamed.

untamed /ʌnˈteɪmd/ adj. not tamed, wild.

untangle /ʌnˈtæŋɡ(ə)l/ v.tr. **1** free from a tangled state. **2** free from entanglement.

untanned /ʌnˈtænd/ adj. not tanned.

untapped /ʌnˈtæpt/ adj. not (yet) tapped or wired (untapped resources).

untarnished /ʌnˈtɑːnɪʃt/ adj. not tarnished.

untasted /ʌnˈteɪstɪd/ adj. not tasted.

untaught /ʌnˈtɔːt/ adj. **1** not instructed by teaching; ignorant. **2** not acquired by teaching; natural, spontaneous.

untaxed /ʌnˈtækst/ adj. not required to pay or not attracting taxes.

unteach /ʌnˈtiːtʃ/ v.tr. (past and past part. **untaught**) **1** cause (a person) to forget or discard previous knowledge. **2** remove from the mind (something known or taught) by different teaching.

unteachable /ʌnˈtiːtʃəb(ə)l/ adj. **1** incapable of being instructed. **2** that cannot be imparted by teaching.

untearable /ʌnˈteərəb(ə)l/ adj. that cannot be torn.

untechnical /ʌnˈteknɪk(ə)l/ adj. not technical. □□ **untechnically** adv.

untempered /ʌnˈtempəd/ adj. (of metal etc.) not brought to the proper hardness or consistency.

untenable /ʌnˈtenəb(ə)l/ adj. not tenable; that cannot be defended. □□ **untenability** /-ˈbɪlɪtɪ/ n. **untenableness** n. **untenably** adv.

untended /ʌnˈtendɪd/ adj. not tended; neglected.

untested /ʌnˈtestɪd/ adj. not tested or proved.

untether /ʌnˈteðə(r)/ v.tr. release (an animal) from a tether.

untethered /ʌnˈteðəd/ adj. not tethered.

unthanked /ʌnˈθæŋkt/ adj. not thanked.

unthankful /ʌnˈθæŋkfʊl/ adj. not thankful. □□ **unthankfully** adv. **unthankfulness** n.

unthinkable /ʌnˈθɪŋkəb(ə)l/ adj. **1** that cannot be imagined or grasped by the mind. **2** colloq. highly unlikely or undesirable. □□ **unthinkability** /-ˈbɪlɪtɪ/ n. **unthinkableness** n. **unthinkably** adv.

unthinking /ʌnˈθɪŋkɪŋ/ adj. **1** thoughtless. **2** unintentional, inadvertent. □□ **unthinkingly** adv. **unthinkingness** n.

unthought /ʌnˈθɔːt/ adj. (often foll. by of) not thought of.

unthoughtful /ʌnˈθɔːtfʊl/ adj. unthinking, unmindful; thoughtless. □□ **unthoughtfully** adv. **unthoughtfulness** n.

unthread /ʌnˈθred/ v.tr. **1** take the thread out of (a needle etc.). **2** find one's way out of (a maze).

unthrifty /ʌnˈθrɪftɪ/ adj. **1** wasteful, extravagant, prodigal. **2** not thriving or flourishing. □□ **unthriftily** adv. **unthriftiness** n.

unthrone /ʌnˈθrəʊn/ v.tr. dethrone.

untidy /ʌnˈtaɪdɪ/ adj. (**untidier**, **untidiest**) not neat or orderly. □□ **untidily** adv. **untidiness** n.

untie /ʌnˈtaɪ/ v.tr. (pres. part. **untying**) **1** undo (a knot etc.). **2** unfasten the cords etc. of (a package etc.). **3** release from bonds or attachment. [OE untīgan (as UN-², TIE)]

untied /ʌnˈtaɪd/ adj. not tied.

until /ənˈtɪl, ʌn-/ prep. & conj. = TILL¹. ¶ Used esp. when beginning a sentence and in formal style, e.g. until you told me, I had no idea; he resided there until his decease. [orig. northern ME untill f. ON und as far as + TILL¹]

untilled /ʌnˈtɪld/ adj. not tilled.

untimely /ʌnˈtaɪmlɪ/ adj. & adv. —adj. **1** inopportune. **2** (of death) premature. —adv. archaic **1** inopportunely. **2** prematurely. □□ **untimeliness** n.

untinged /ʌnˈtɪndʒd/ adj. not tinged.

untiring /ʌnˈtaɪərɪŋ/ adj. tireless. □□ **untiringly** adv.

untitled /ʌnˈtaɪt(ə)ld/ adj. having no title.

unto /ˈʌntʊ, ˈʌntə/ prep. archaic = TO prep. (in all uses except as the sign of the infinitive); (do unto others; faithful unto death; take unto oneself). [ME f. UNTIL, with TO replacing northern TILL¹]

untold /ʌnˈtəʊld/ adj. **1** not told. **2** not (able to be) counted or measured (untold misery). [OE untĕald (as UN-¹, TOLD)]

untouchable /ʌnˈtʌtʃəb(ə)l/ adj. & n. —adj. that may not or cannot be touched. —*n.* a member of a hereditary Hindu group held to defile members of higher castes on contact. ¶ Use of the term, and social restrictions accompanying it, were declared illegal under the constitution of India in 1949 and in Pakistan in 1953. □□ **untouchability** /-ˈbɪlɪtɪ/ *n.* **untouchableness** *n.*

untouched /ʌnˈtʌtʃt/ *adj.* **1** not touched. **2** not affected physically, not harmed, modified, used, or tasted. **3** not affected by emotion. **4** not discussed.

untoward /ˌʌntəˈwɔːd, ʌnˈtəʊəd/ *adj.* **1** inconvenient, unlucky. **2** awkward. **3** perverse, refractory. **4** unseemly. □□ **untowardly** *adv.* **untowardness** *n.*

untraceable /ʌnˈtreɪsəb(ə)l/ *adj.* that cannot be traced. □□ **untraceably** *adv.*

untraced /ʌnˈtreɪst/ *adj.* not traced.

untrained /ʌnˈtreɪnd/ *adj.* not trained.

untrammelled /ʌnˈtræm(ə)ld/ *adj.* not trammelled, unhampered.

untransferable /ˌʌntrænsˈfɜːrəb(ə)l, ˌʌntrɑːns-, ʌnˈt-/ *adj.* not transferable.

untranslatable /ˌʌntrænsˈleɪtəb(ə)l, ˌʌntrɑːns-, -zˈleɪtəb(ə)l/ *adj.* that cannot be translated satisfactorily. □□ **untranslatability** /-ˈbɪlɪtɪ/ *n.* **untranslatably** *adv.*

untransportable /ˌʌntrænsˈpɔːtəb(ə)l, ˌʌntrɑːn-/ *adj.* that cannot be transported.

untravelled /ʌnˈtræv(ə)ld/ *adj.* (*US* **untraveled**) **1** that has not travelled. **2** that has not been travelled over or through.

untreatable /ʌnˈtriːtəb(ə)l/ *adj.* (of a disease etc.) that cannot be treated.

untreated /ʌnˈtriːtɪd/ *adj.* not treated.

untried /ʌnˈtraɪd/ *adj.* **1** not tried or tested. **2** inexperienced. **3** not yet tried by a judge.

untrodden /ʌnˈtrɒd(ə)n/ *adj.* not trodden, stepped on, or traversed.

untroubled /ʌnˈtrʌb(ə)ld/ *adj.* not troubled; calm, tranquil.

untrue /ʌnˈtruː/ *adj.* **1** not true, contrary to what is the fact. **2** (often foll. by *to*) not faithful or loyal. **3** deviating from an accepted standard. □□ **untruly** *adv.* [OE *untrēowe* etc. (as UN-[1], TRUE)]

untruss /ʌnˈtrʌs/ *v.tr.* unfasten (a trussed fowl).

untrustworthy /ʌnˈtrʌstˌwɜːðɪ/ *adj.* not trustworthy. □□ **untrustworthiness** *n.*

untruth /ʌnˈtruːθ/ *n.* (pl. /-ˈtruːðz, -ˈtruːθs/) **1** the state of being untrue, falsehood. **2** a false statement (*told me an untruth*). [OE *untrēowth* etc. (as UN-[1], TRUTH)]

untruthful /ʌnˈtruːθfʊl/ *adj.* not truthful. □□ **untruthfully** *adv.* **untruthfulness** *n.*

untuck /ʌnˈtʌk/ *v.tr.* free (bedclothes etc.) from being tucked in or up.

untunable /ʌnˈtjuːnəb(ə)l/ *adj.* (of a piano etc.) that cannot be tuned.

untuned /ʌnˈtjuːnd/ *adj.* **1** not in tune, not made tuneful. **2** (of a radio receiver etc.) not tuned to any one frequency. **3** not in harmony or concord, disordered.

untuneful /ʌnˈtjuːnfʊl/ *adj.* not tuneful. □□ **untunefully** *adv.* **untunefulness** *n.*

unturned /ʌnˈtɜːnd/ *adj.* **1** not turned over, round, away, etc. **2** not shaped by turning.

untutored /ʌnˈtjuːtəd/ *adj.* uneducated, untaught.

untwine /ʌnˈtwaɪn/ *v.tr.* & *intr.* untwist, unwind.

untwist /ʌnˈtwɪst/ *v.tr.* & *intr.* open from a twisted or spiralled state.

untying *pres. part.* of UNTIE.

unusable /ʌnˈjuːzəb(ə)l/ *adj.* not usable.

unused *adj.* **1** /ʌnˈjuːzd/ **a** not in use. **b** never having been used. **2** /ʌnˈjuːst/ (foll. by *to*) not accustomed.

unusual /ʌnˈjuːʒʊəl/ *adj.* **1** not usual. **2** exceptional, remarkable. □□ **unusually** *adv.* **unusualness** *n.*

unutterable /ʌnˈʌtərəb(ə)l/ *adj.* inexpressible; beyond description (*unutterable torment; an unutterable fool*). □□ **unutterableness** *n.* **unutterably** *adv.*

unuttered /ʌnˈʌtəd/ *adj.* not uttered or expressed.

unvaccinated /ʌnˈvæksɪˌneɪtɪd/ *adj.* not vaccinated.

unvalued /ʌnˈvæljuːd/ *adj.* **1** not regarded as valuable. **2** not having been valued.

unvanquished /ʌnˈvæŋkwɪʃt/ *adj.* not vanquished.

unvaried /ʌnˈveərɪd/ *adj.* not varied.

unvarnished /ʌnˈvɑːnɪʃt/ *adj.* **1** not varnished. **2** (of a statement or person) plain and straightforward (*the unvarnished truth*).

unvarying /ʌnˈveərɪɪŋ/ *adj.* not varying. □□ **unvaryingly** *adv.* **unvaryingness** *n.*

unveil /ʌnˈveɪl/ *v.* **1** *tr.* remove a veil from. **2** *tr.* remove a covering from (a statue, plaque, etc.) as part of the ceremony of the first public display. **3** *tr.* disclose, reveal, make publicly known. **4** *intr.* remove one's veil.

unventilated /ʌnˈventɪˌleɪtɪd/ *adj.* **1** not provided with a means of ventilation. **2** not discussed.

unverifiable /ʌnˈverɪˌfaɪəb(ə)l/ *adj.* that cannot be verified.

unverified /ʌnˈverɪˌfaɪd/ *adj.* not verified.

unversed /ʌnˈvɜːst/ *adj.* (usu. foll. by *in*) not experienced or skilled.

unviable /ʌnˈvaɪəb(ə)l/ *adj.* not viable. □□ **unviability** /-ˈbɪlɪtɪ/ *n.*

unviolated /ʌnˈvaɪəˌleɪtɪd/ *adj.* not violated.

unvisited /ʌnˈvɪzɪtɪd/ *adj.* not visited.

unvitiated /ʌnˈvɪʃɪˌeɪtɪd/ *adj.* not vitiated.

unvoiced /ʌnˈvɔɪst/ *adj.* **1** not spoken. **2** *Phonet.* not voiced.

unwaged /ʌnˈweɪdʒd/ *adj.* not receiving a wage; out of work.

unwanted /ʌnˈwɒntɪd/ *adj.* not wanted.

unwarlike /ʌnˈwɔːlaɪk/ *adj.* not warlike.

unwarmed /ʌnˈwɔːmd/ *adj.* not warmed.

unwarned /ʌnˈwɔːnd/ *adj.* not warned or forewarned.

unwarrantable /ʌnˈwɒrəntəb(ə)l/ *adj.* indefensible, unjustifiable. □□ **unwarrantableness** *n.* **unwarrantably** *adv.*

unwarranted /ʌnˈwɒrəntɪd/ *adj.* **1** unauthorized. **2** unjustified.

unwary /ʌnˈweərɪ/ *adj.* **1** not cautious. **2** (often foll. by *of*) not aware of possible danger etc. □□ **unwarily** *adv.* **unwariness** *n.*

unwashed /ʌnˈwɒʃt/ *adj.* **1** not washed. **2** not usually washed or clean. □ **the great unwashed** *colloq.* the rabble.

unwatched /ʌnˈwɒtʃt/ *adj.* not watched.

unwatchful /ʌnˈwɒtʃfʊl/ *adj.* not watchful.

unwatered /ʌnˈwɔːtəd/ *adj.* not watered.

unwavering /ʌnˈweɪvərɪŋ/ *adj.* not wavering. □□ **unwaveringly** *adv.*

unweaned /ʌnˈwiːnd/ *adj.* not weaned.

unwearable /ʌnˈweərəb(ə)l/ *adj.* that cannot be worn.

unwearied /ʌnˈwɪərɪd/ *adj.* **1** not wearied or tired. **2** never becoming weary, indefatigable. **3** unremitting. □□ **unweariedly** *adv.* **unweariedness** *n.*

unweary /ʌnˈwɪərɪ/ *adj.* not weary.

unwearying /ʌnˈwɪərɪɪŋ/ *adj.* **1** persistent. **2** not causing or producing weariness. □□ **unwearyingly** *adv.*

unwed /ʌnˈwed/ *adj.* unmarried.

unwedded /ʌnˈwedɪd/ *adj.* unmarried. □□ **unweddedness** *n.*

unweeded /ʌnˈwiːdɪd/ *adj.* not cleared of weeds.

unweighed /ʌnˈweɪd/ *adj.* **1** not considered; hasty. **2** (of goods) not weighed.

unwelcome /ʌnˈwelkəm/ *adj.* not welcome or acceptable. □□ **unwelcomely** *adv.* **unwelcomeness** *n.*

unwell /ʌnˈwel/ *adj.* **1** not in good health; (somewhat) ill. **2** indisposed.

unwept /ʌnˈwept/ *adj.* **1** not wept for. **2** (of tears) not wept.

unwetted /ʌnˈwetɪd/ *adj.* not wetted.

unwhipped /ʌnˈwɪpt/ *adj.* **1** not punished by or as by whipping. **2** *Brit.* not subject to a party whip.

unwholesome /ʌnˈhəʊlsəm/ *adj.* **1** not promoting, or detrimental to, physical or moral health. **2** unhealthy, insalubrious. **3** unhealthy-looking. □□ **unwholesomely** *adv.* **unwholesomeness** *n.*

unwieldy /ʌnˈwiːldɪ/ adj. (**unwieldier, unwieldiest**) cumbersome, clumsy, or hard to manage, owing to size, shape, or weight. □□ **unwieldily** adv. **unwieldiness** n. [ME f. UN-¹ + wieldy active (now dial.) f. WIELD]

unwilling /ʌnˈwɪlɪŋ/ adj. not willing or inclined; reluctant. □□ **unwillingly** adv. **unwillingness** n. [OE unwillende (as UN-¹, WILLING)]

unwind /ʌnˈwaɪnd/ v. (past and past part. **unwound**) **1 a** tr. draw out (a thing that has been wound). **b** intr. become drawn out after having been wound. **2** intr. & tr. colloq. relax.

unwinking /ʌnˈwɪŋkɪŋ/ adj. **1** not winking. **2** watchful, vigilant. □□ **unwinkingly** adv.

unwinnable /ʌnˈwɪnəb(ə)l/ adj. that cannot be won.

unwisdom /ʌnˈwɪzdəm/ n. lack of wisdom, folly, imprudence. [OE unwīsdōm (as UN-¹, WISDOM)]

unwise /ʌnˈwaɪz/ adj. **1** foolish, imprudent. **2** injudicious. □□ **unwisely** adv. [OE unwīs (as UN-¹, WISE¹)]

unwished /ʌnˈwɪʃt/ adj. (usu. foll. by for) not wished for.

unwithered /ʌnˈwɪðəd/ adj. not withered; still vigorous or fresh.

unwitnessed /ʌnˈwɪtnɪst/ adj. not witnessed.

unwitting /ʌnˈwɪtɪŋ/ adj. **1** unaware of the state of the case (an unwitting offender). **2** unintentional. □□ **unwittingly** adv. **unwittingness** n. [OE unwitende (as UN-¹, WIT²)]

unwomanly /ʌnˈwʊmənlɪ/ adj. not womanly; not befitting a woman. □□ **unwomanliness** n.

unwonted /ʌnˈwəʊntɪd/ adj. not customary or usual. □□ **unwontedly** adv. **unwontedness** n.

unwooded /ʌnˈwʊdɪd/ adj. not wooded, treeless.

unworkable /ʌnˈwɜːkəb(ə)l/ adj. not workable; impracticable. □□ **unworkability** /-ˈbɪlɪtɪ/ n. **unworkableness** n. **unworkably** adv.

unworked /ʌnˈwɜːkt/ adj. **1** not wrought into shape. **2** not exploited or turned to account.

unworkmanlike /ʌnˈwɜːkmənˌlaɪk/ adj. badly done or made.

unworldly /ʌnˈwɜːldlɪ/ adj. **1** spiritually-minded. **2** spiritual. □□ **unworldliness** n.

unworn /ʌnˈwɔːn/ adj. not worn or impaired by wear.

unworried /ʌnˈwʌrɪd/ adj. not worried; calm.

unworthy /ʌnˈwɜːðɪ/ adj. (**unworthier, unworthiest**) **1** (often foll. by of) not worthy or befitting the character of a person etc. **2** discreditable, unseemly. **3** contemptible, base. □□ **unworthily** adv. **unworthiness** n.

unwound¹ /ʌnˈwaʊnd/ adj. not wound or wound up.

unwound² past and past part. of UNWIND.

unwounded /ʌnˈwuːndɪd/ adj. not wounded, unhurt.

unwoven /ʌnˈwəʊv(ə)n/ adj. not woven.

unwrap /ʌnˈræp/ v. (**unwrapped, unwrapping**) **1** tr. remove the wrapping from. **2** tr. open or unfold. **3** intr. become unwrapped.

unwrinkled /ʌnˈrɪŋk(ə)ld/ adj. free from wrinkles, smooth.

unwritable /ʌnˈraɪtəb(ə)l/ adj. that cannot be written.

unwritten /ʌnˈrɪt(ə)n/ adj. **1** not written. **2** (of a law etc.) resting originally on custom or judicial decision, not on statute.

unwrought /ʌnˈrɔːt/ adj. (of metals) not hammered into shape or worked into a finished condition.

unyielding /ʌnˈjiːldɪŋ/ adj. **1** not yielding to pressure etc. **2** firm, obstinate. □□ **unyieldingly** adv. **unyieldingness** n.

unyoke /ʌnˈjəʊk/ v. **1** tr. release from a yoke. **2** intr. cease work.

unzip /ʌnˈzɪp/ v.tr. (**unzipped, unzipping**) unfasten the zip of.

up /ʌp/ adv., prep., adj., n., & v. —adv. **1** at, in, or towards a higher place or position (jumped up in the air; what are they doing up there?). **2** to or in a place regarded as higher, esp.: **a** northwards (up in Scotland). **b** Brit. towards a major city or a university (went up to London). **3** colloq. ahead etc. as indicated (went up front). **4 a** to or in an erect position or condition (stood it up). **b** to or in a prepared or required position (wound up the watch). **c** in or into a condition of efficiency, activity, or progress (stirred up trouble; the house is up for sale; the hunt is up). **5** Brit. in a stronger or winning position

or condition (our team was three goals up; am £10 up on the transaction). **6** (of a computer) running and available for use. **7** to the place or time in question or where the speaker etc. is (a child came up to me; went straight up to the door; has been fine up till now). **8** at or to a higher price or value (our costs are up; shares are up). **9 a** completely or effectually (burn up; eat up; tear up; use up). **b** more loudly or clearly (speak up). **10** in a state of completion; denoting the end of availability, supply, etc. (time is up). **11** into a compact, accumulated, or secure state (pack up; save up; tie up). **12** out of bed (are you up yet?). **13** (of the sun etc.) having risen. **14** happening, esp. unusually or unexpectedly (something is up). **15** taught or informed (is well up in French). **16** (usu. foll. by before) appearing for trial etc. (was up before the magistrate). **17** (of a road etc.) being repaired. **18** (of a jockey) in the saddle. **19** towards the source of a river. **20** inland. **21** (of the points etc. in a game): **a** registered on the scoreboard. **b** forming the total score for the time being. **22** upstairs, esp. to bed (are you going up yet?). **23** (of a theatre-curtain) raised etc. to reveal the stage. **24** (as int.) get up. **25** (of a ship's helm) with rudder to leeward. **26** in rebellion. —prep. **1** upwards along, through, or into (climbed up the ladder). **2** from the bottom to the top of. **3** along (walked up the road). **4 a** at or in a higher part of (is situated up the street). **b** towards the source of (a river). —adj. **1** directed upwards (up stroke). **2** Brit. of travel towards a capital or centre (the up train; the up platform). **3** (of beer etc.) effervescent, frothy. —n. a spell of good fortune. —v. (**upped, upping**) **1** intr. colloq. start up; begin abruptly to say or do something (upped and hit him). **2** intr. (foll. by with) raise; pick up (upped with his stick). **3** tr. increase or raise, esp. abruptly (upped all their prices). □ **be all up with** be disastrous or hopeless for (a person). **on the up and up** colloq. **1** Brit. steadily improving. **2** esp. US honest(ly); on the level. **something is up** colloq. something unusual or undesirable is afoot or happening. **up against 1** close to. **2** in or into contact with. **3** colloq. confronted with (up against a problem). **up against it** colloq. in great difficulties. **up-anchor** Naut. weigh anchor. **up and about** (or **doing**) having risen from bed; active. **up-and-coming** colloq. (of a person) making good progress and likely to succeed. **up and down 1** to and fro (along). **2** in every direction. **3** colloq. in varying health or spirits. **up-and-over** (of a door) opened by being raised and pushed back into a horizontal position. **up draught** an upward draught, esp. in a chimney. **up for** available for or being considered for (office etc.). **up hill and down dale** up and down hills on an arduous journey. **up in arms** see ARM². **up-market** adj. & adv. towards or relating to the dearer or more affluent sector of the market. **up the pole** see POLE¹. **ups and downs 1** rises and falls. **2** alternate good and bad fortune. **up the spout** see SPOUT. **up stage** at or to the back of a theatre stage. **up sticks** see STICK¹. **up-stroke** a stroke made or written upwards. **up to 1** until (up to the present). **2** not more than (you can have up to five). **3** less than or equal to (sums up to £10). **4** incumbent on (it is up to you to say). **5** capable of or fit for (am not up to a long walk). **6** occupied or busy with (what have you been up to?). **up to date** see DATE¹. **up to the mark** see MARK¹. **up to the minute** see MINUTE¹. **up to snuff** see SNUFF². **up to one's tricks** see TRICK. **up to a person's tricks** see TRICK. **up with** int. expressing support for a stated person or thing. **what's up?** colloq. **1** what is going on? **2** what is the matter? [OE up(p), uppe, rel. to OHG ūf]

up- /ʌp/ prefix in senses of UP, added: **1** as an adverb to verbs and verbal derivations, = 'upwards' (upcurved; update). **2** as a preposition to nouns forming adverbs and adjectives (up-country; uphill). **3** as an adjective to nouns (upland; up-stroke). [OE up(p)-, = UP]

Upanishad /uːˈpænɪˌʃæd/ n. each of a series of esoteric Sanskrit treatises based on the Vedas, dating from 800 BC onwards. Held to teach 'the conclusion of the Veda' (Vedanta), the Upanishads mark the transition from ritual sacrifice to a mystical concern with the nature of reality. Polytheism is superseded by a pantheistic monism derived from the basic concepts of atman and Brahman. [Skr., = sitting near, i.e. at the feet of a master, f. upa near + ni-ṣad sit down]

upas /ˈjuːpəs/ n. **1** (in full **upas-tree**) **a** a Javanese tree, Antiaris toxicaria, yielding a milky sap used as arrow-poison. **b** Mythol. a

Javanese tree thought to be fatal to whatever came near it. **c** a pernicious influence, practice, etc. **2** the poisonous sap of upas and other trees. [Malay *ūpas* poison]

upbeat /ˈʌpbiːt/ *n. & v.* —*n.* an unaccented beat in music. —*adj. colloq.* optimistic or cheerful.

upbraid /ʌpˈbreɪd/ *v.tr.* (often foll. by *with, for*) chide or reproach (a person). □□ **upbraiding** *n.* [OE *upbrēdan* (as UP-, *brēdan* = *bregdan* BRAID in obs. sense 'brandish')]

upbringing /ˈʌpˌbrɪŋɪŋ/ *n.* the bringing up of a child; education. [obs. *upbring* to rear (as UP-, BRING)]

upcast *n. & v.* —*n.* /ˈʌpkɑːst/ **1** the act of casting up; an upward throw. **2** *Mining* a shaft through which air leaves a mine. **3** *Geol.* = UPTHROW. —*v.tr.* /ʌpˈkɑːst/ (*past* and *past part.* **upcast**) cast up.

upcoming /ʌpˈkʌmɪŋ/ *adj.* esp. *US* forthcoming; about to happen.

up-country /ʌpˈkʌntrɪ, ˈʌp-/ *adv. & adj.* inland; towards the interior of a country.

update *v. & n.* —*v.tr.* /ʌpˈdeɪt/ bring up to date. —*n.* /ˈʌpdeɪt/ **1** the act or an instance of updating. **2** an updated version; a set of updated information. □□ **updater** *n.*

Updike /ˈʌpdaɪk/, John Hoyer (1932–), American novelist and short-story writer. His novels include the series *Rabbit, Run* (1960), *Rabbit Redux* (1971), *Rabbit is Rich* (1981), and *Rabbit at Rest* (1990), a small-town domestic tragedy which traces the career of an ex-basketball-player from his marriage through the social upheavals of the 1960s to the compromise of middle age; *Couples* (1968), a portrait of sexual passion and realignment amongst a group of couples in Massachusetts; and *The Coup* (1979), an exotic first-person narration by the fictitious ex-dictator of an African State. His writing is marked by an ornate highly charged prose.

up-end /ʌpˈend/ *v.tr.* set or rise up on end.

upfield /ˈʌpfiːld/ *adv.* in or to a position nearer to the opponents' end of a football etc. field.

upfold /ˈʌpfəʊld/ *n. Geol.* an anticline.

upfront /ʌpˈfrʌnt, ˈʌp-/ *adv. & adj. colloq.* —*adv.* (usu. **up front**) **1** at the front; in front. **2** (of payments) in advance. —*adj.* **1** honest, open, frank. **2** (of payments) made in advance. **3** at the front or most prominent.

upgrade *v. & n.* —*v.tr.* /ʌpˈgreɪd/ **1** raise in rank etc. **2** improve (equipment, machinery, etc.) esp. by replacing components. —*n.* /ˈʌpgreɪd/ **1** the act or an instance of upgrading. **2** an upgraded piece of equipment etc. □ **on the upgrade 1** improving in health etc. **2** advancing, progressing. □□ **upgrader** *n.*

upgrowth /ˈʌpgrəʊθ/ *n.* the process or result of growing upwards.

upheaval /ʌpˈhiːv(ə)l/ *n.* **1** a violent or sudden change or disruption. **2** *Geol.* an upward displacement of part of the earth's crust. **3** the act or an instance of heaving up.

upheave /ʌpˈhiːv/ *v.* **1** *tr.* heave or lift up, esp. forcibly. **2** *intr.* rise up.

uphill *adv., adj., & n.* —*adv.* /ʌpˈhɪl/ in an ascending direction up a hill, slope, etc. —*adj.* /ˈʌphɪl/ **1** sloping up; ascending. **2** arduous, difficult (*an uphill task*). —*n.* /ˈʌphɪl/ an upward slope.

uphold /ʌpˈhəʊld/ *v.tr.* (*past* and *past part.* **upheld**) **1** confirm or maintain (a decision etc., esp. of another). **2** give support or countenance to (a person, practice, etc.). □□ **upholder** *n.*

upholster /ʌpˈhəʊlstə(r)/ *v.tr.* **1** provide (furniture) with upholstery. **2** furnish (a room etc.) with furniture, carpets, etc. □ **well-upholstered** *joc.* (of a person) fat. [back-form. f. UPHOLSTERER]

upholsterer /ʌpˈhəʊlstərə(r)/ *n.* a person who upholsters furniture, esp. professionally. [obs. *upholster* (n.) f. UPHOLD (in obs. sense 'keep in repair') + -STER]

upholstery /ʌpˈhəʊlstərɪ/ *n.* **1** textile covering, padding, springs, etc., for furniture. **2** an upholsterer's work.

upkeep /ˈʌpkiːp/ *n.* **1** maintenance in good condition. **2** the cost or means of this.

upland /ˈʌplənd/ *n. & adj.* —*n.* the higher or inland parts of a country. —*adj.* of or relating to these parts.

uplift *v. & n.* —*v.tr.* /ʌpˈlɪft/ **1** raise; lift up. **2** elevate or stimulate

morally or spiritually. —*n.* /ˈʌplɪft/ **1** the act or an instance of being raised. **2** *Geol.* the raising of part of the earth's surface. **3** *colloq.* a morally or spiritually elevating influence. **4** support for the bust etc. from a garment. □□ **uplifter** /-ˈlɪftə(r)/ *n.* **uplifting** /-ˈlɪftɪŋ/ *adj.* (esp. in sense 2 of *v.*).

upmost var. of UPPERMOST.

upon /əˈpɒn/ *prep.* = ON. ¶ *Upon* is sometimes more formal, and is preferred in *once upon a time* and *upon my word*, and in uses such as *row upon row of seats* and *Christmas is almost upon us.* [ME f. UP + ON *prep.*, after ON *upp á*]

upper[1] /ˈʌpə(r)/ *adj. & n.* —*adj.* **1** higher in place; situated above another part (*the upper atmosphere; the upper lip*). **2** higher in rank or dignity etc. (*the upper class*). **3** situated on higher ground (and usu. further inland; *Upper Egypt*). **4** (of a geological or archaeological period) later (called 'upper' because its rock formations or remains lie above those of the period called 'lower'). —*n.* the part of a boot or shoe above the sole. □ **on one's uppers** *colloq.* extremely short of money. **upper case** see CASE[2]. **upper class** the highest class of society, esp. the aristocracy. **upper-class** *adj.* of the upper class. **the upper crust** *colloq.* the aristocracy. **upper-cut** *n.* an upwards blow delivered with the arm bent. —*v.tr.* hit with an upper-cut. **the upper hand** dominance or control. **Upper House** the higher house (sometimes non-elected) in a legislature, esp. the House of Lords. **the upper regions 1** the sky. **2** heaven. **upper works** the part of a ship that is above the water when fully laden. [ME f. UP + -ER[2]]

upper[2] /ˈʌpə(r)/ *n. sl.* a stimulant drug, esp. an amphetamine. [UP *v.* + -ER[1]]

Upper Austria a province of northern Austria; pop. (1981) 1,270,400; capital, Linz.

uppermost /ˈʌpəˌməʊst/ *adj. & adv.* —*adj.* (also **upmost** /ˈʌpməʊst/) **1** highest in place or rank. **2** predominant. —*adv.* at or to the highest or most prominent position.

uppish /ˈʌpɪʃ/ *adj.* esp. *Brit. colloq.* self-assertive or arrogant. □□ **uppishly** *adv.* **uppishness** *n.*

uppity /ˈʌpɪtɪ/ *adj. colloq.* uppish, snobbish. [fanciful f. UP]

Uppsala /ʊpˈsɑːlə/ a city in eastern Sweden; pop. (1987) 160,000. Founded in 1477, its university is the oldest in northern Europe. The botanist Linnaeus is buried here.

upraise /ʌpˈreɪz/ *v.tr.* raise to a higher level.

upright /ˈʌpraɪt/ *adj. & n.* —*adj.* **1** erect, vertical (*an upright posture; stood upright*). **2** (of a piano) with vertical strings. **3** (of a person or behaviour) righteous; strictly honourable or honest. **4** (of a picture, book, etc.) greater in height than breadth. —*n.* **1** a post or rod fixed upright esp. as a structural support. **2** an upright piano. □□ **uprightly** *adv.* **uprightness** *n.* [OE *upriht* (as UP, RIGHT)]

uprise /ʌpˈraɪz/ *v.intr.* (**uprose, uprisen**) rise (to a standing position, etc.).

uprising /ˈʌpˌraɪzɪŋ/ *n.* a rebellion or revolt.

uproar /ˈʌprɔː(r)/ *n.* a tumult; a violent disturbance. [Du. *oproer* f. *op* up + *roer* confusion, assoc. with ROAR]

uproarious /ʌpˈrɔːrɪəs/ *adj.* **1** very noisy. **2** provoking loud laughter. □□ **uproariously** *adv.* **uproariousness** *n.*

uproot /ʌpˈruːt/ *v.tr.* **1** pull (a plant etc.) up from the ground. **2** displace (a person) from an accustomed location. **3** eradicate, destroy. □□ **uprooter** *n.*

uprose *past* of UPRISE.

uprush /ˈʌprʌʃ/ *n.* an upward rush, esp. *Psychol.* from the subconscious.

ups-a-daisy var. of UPSY-DAISY.

upset *v., n., & adj.* —*v.* /ʌpˈset/ (**upsetting**; *past* and *past part.* **upset**) **1** *tr. & intr.* overturn or be overturned. **2** *tr.* disturb the composure or digestion of (*was very upset by the news; ate something that upset me*). **3** *tr.* disrupt. **4** *tr.* shorten and thicken (metal, esp. a tire) by hammering or pressure. —*n.* /ˈʌpset/ **1** a condition of upsetting or being upset (*a stomach upset*). **2** a surprising result in a game etc. —*adj.* /ˈʌpset/ disturbed (*an upset stomach*). □ **upset price** the lowest acceptable selling price of a property

in an auction etc.; a reserve price. □□ **upsetter** /-ˈsetə(r)/ n.
upsettingly /-ˈsetɪŋlɪ/ adv.

upshot /ˈʌpʃɒt/ n. the final or eventual outcome or conclusion.

upside down /ˌʌpsaɪd ˈdaʊn/ adv. & adj. —adv. **1** with the
upper part where the lower part should be; in an inverted
position. **2** in or into total disorder (everything was turned upside
down). —adj. (also **upside-down** attrib.) that is positioned
upside down; inverted. □ **upside-down cake** a sponge cake
baked with fruit in a syrup at the bottom, and inverted for
serving. [ME, orig. up so down, perh. = 'up as if down']

upsides /ˈʌpˈsaɪdz/ adv. Brit. colloq. (foll. by with) equal with (a
person) by revenge, retaliation, etc. [upside = top part]

upsilon /ˈjuːpsɪˌlɒn, ˌʌpˈsaɪlɒn/ n. the twentieth letter of the
Greek alphabet (Y, υ). [Gk, = slender U f. psilos slender, with ref.
to its later coincidence in sound with Gk oi]

upstage /ˌʌpˈsteɪdʒ/ adj., adv., & v. —adj. & adv. **1** nearer the
back of a theatre stage. **2** snobbish(ly). —v.tr. **1** (of an actor)
move upstage to make (another actor) face away from the audience. **2** divert attention from (a person) to oneself; outshine.

upstairs adv., adj., & n. —adv. /ˌʌpˈsteəz/ to or on an upper floor.
—adj. /ˈʌpsteəz/ (also **upstair**) situated upstairs. —n. /ˈʌpˈsteəz/
an upper floor.

upstanding /ˌʌpˈstændɪŋ/ adj. **1** standing up. **2** strong and
healthy. **3** honest or straightforward.

upstart /ˈʌpstɑːt/ n. & adj. —n. a person who has risen suddenly
to prominence, esp. one who behaves arrogantly. —adj. **1** that
is an upstart. **2** of or characteristic of an upstart.

upstate /ˈʌpsteɪt/ n., adj., & adv. US —n. part of a State remote
from its large cities, esp. the northern part. —adj. of or relating
to this part. —adv. in or to this part. □□ **upstater** n.

upstream /ˈʌpstriːm/ adv. & adj. —adv. against the flow of a
stream etc. —adj. moving upstream.

upsurge /ˈʌpsɜːdʒ/ n. an upward surge; a rise (esp. in feelings
etc.).

upswept /ˈʌpswept/ adj. **1** (of the hair) combed to the top of the
head. **2** curved or sloped upwards.

upswing /ˈʌpswɪŋ/ n. an upward movement or trend.

upsy-daisy /ˈʌpsɪˌdeɪzɪ/ int. (also **ups-a-daisy**) expressing
encouragement to a child who is being lifted or has fallen.
[earlier up-a-daisy: cf. LACKADAISICAL]

uptake /ˈʌpteɪk/ n. **1** colloq. understanding; comprehension (esp.
quick or slow on the uptake). **2** the act or an instance of taking up.

upthrow /ˈʌpθrəʊ/ n. **1** the act or an instance of throwing
upwards. **2** Geol. an upward dislocation of strata.

upthrust /ˈʌpθrʌst/ n. **1** upward thrust, e.g. of a fluid on an
immersed body. **2** Geol. = UPHEAVAL.

uptight /ʌpˈtaɪt, ˈʌptaɪt/ adj. colloq. **1** nervously tense or angry.
2 US rigidly conventional.

uptown /ˈʌptaʊn/ adj., adv., & n. US —adj. of or in the residential
part of a town or city. —adv. in or into this part. —n. this part.
□□ **uptowner** n.

upturn n. & v. —n. /ˈʌptɜːn/ **1** an upward trend; an improvement. **2** an upheaval. —v.tr. /ʌpˈtɜːn/ turn up or upside down.

UPU abbr. Universal Postal Union.

upward /ˈʌpwəd/ adv. & adj. —adv. (also **upwards**) towards
what is higher, superior, larger in amount, more important, or
earlier. —adj. moving, extending, pointing, or leading upward.
□ **upwards of** more than (found upwards of forty specimens). [OE
upweard(es) (as UP, -WARD)]

upwardly /ˈʌpwədlɪ/ adv. in an upward direction. □ **upwardly
mobile** able or aspiring to advance socially or professionally.

upwarp /ˈʌpwɔːp/ n. Geol. a broad surface elevation; an anticline.

upwind /ˈʌpwɪnd/ adj. & adv. against the direction of the wind.

Ur /ɜː(r)/ an ancient Sumerian city in what is now southern Iraq,
formerly (until the river changed its course) on the Euphrates,
a city of the moon-god Nanna (Sin) and his spouse Ningal. There
is no evidence supporting the Biblical statement that it was
Abraham's place of origin, and the connection of Ur with the
people known as 'Chaldees' (Chaldeans) dates only from c.8th c.
BC, many centuries later than any plausible date for Abraham

as a historical figure. The site was excavated in 1922–34 by Sir
Leonard Woolley, who discovered there spectacularly rich royal
tombs of c.2600–2000 BC. The city was sacked by invaders c.2000
BC, and superseded by Babylon.

ur- /uː(r)/ comb. form primitive, original, earliest. [G]

uracil /ˈjʊərəsɪl/ n. Biochem. a pyrimidine derivative found in
living tissue as a component base of RNA. [UREA + ACETIC]

uraemia /jʊˈriːmɪə/ n. (US **uremia**) Med. a morbid condition
due to the presence in the blood of urinary matter normally
eliminated by the kidneys. □□ **uraemic** adj. [Gk ouron urine +
haima blood]

uraeus /jʊˈriːəs/ n. the sacred serpent as an emblem of power
represented on the head-dress of Egyptian divinities and sovereigns. [mod.L f. Gk ouraios, repr. the Egypt. word for 'cobra']

Ural-Altaic /ˌjʊər(ə)lælˈteɪɪk/ n. & adj. —n. Philol. a group of
languages, thought to be sufficiently close to be considered
together, comprising the Uralic and Altaic languages. —adj. **1**
of or relating to this group of languages. **2** of or relating to the
Ural and Altaic mountain ranges in the USSR and central Asia.

Uralic /jʊəˈrælɪk/ n. & adj. —n. Philol. a family of languages
comprising the Finno-Ugric group and Samoyed, spoken over a
wide area in Europe, Asia, and the Scandinavian contries.
—adj. of or relating to this family of languages. [URAL]

Ural Mountains /ˈjʊər(ə)l/ (also **Urals**) a mountain range in
the USSR. It extends 1,600 km (1,000 miles) south from within
the Arctic Circle to Kazakhstan, and forms a natural boundary
between Europe and Asia.

Urania /jʊəˈreɪnɪə/ Gk & Rom. Mythol. the Muse of astronomy.
[Gk, = heavenly]

uranium /jʊˈreɪnɪəm/ n. Chem. a radioactive grey dense metallic
element, used as a source of nuclear energy. Not found uncombined in nature, it was discovered in 1789 and first isolated in
1841, but did not become economically important until the 20th
c. Becquerel discovered radioactivity in uranium in 1896, and
its capacity to undergo fission, first revealed in 1938, pointed
the way to its use as a source of energy. The main natural
isotope of uranium, uranium 238, is not fissile, however, and
the fissile isotope, uranium 235, had to be separated from it by
a laborious process before it could be used. The atomic bomb
exploded over Hiroshima in 1945 contained uranium 235. This
isotope has since been used to produce power in nuclear reactors, as has the more common uranium 238, which can be
transmuted into the artificial fissile element plutonium.
Uranium compounds have been used as colouring agents for
ceramics, glass, etc. ¶ Symb.: U; atomic number 92. □□ **uranic**
/-ˈrænɪk/ adj. [mod.L, f. URANUS: cf. tellurium]

urano-¹ /ˈjʊərənəʊ/ comb. form the heavens. [Gk ouranos
heaven(s)]

urano-² /ˈjʊərənəʊ/ comb. form uranium.

uranography /ˌjʊərəˈnɒgrəfɪ/ n. the branch of astronomy concerned with describing and mapping the stars, planets, etc. □□
uranographer n. **uranographic** /-nəˈgræfɪk/ adj.

Uranus /ˈjʊərənəs, jʊˈreɪnəs/ **1** Gk Mythol. a personification of
the sky, the most ancient of the Greek gods and first ruler of
the universe. In a cosmological myth he was overthrown by his
son Cronus. **2** Astron. the seventh of the major planets, the first
planet to be discovered by the telescope, by Sir William Herschel
in 1781. [L f. Gk Ouranos heaven]

urban /ˈɜːbən/ adj. of, living in, or situated in a town or city (an
urban population) (opp. RURAL). □ **urban district** Brit. hist. a
group of urban communities governed by an elected council.
urban guerrilla a terrorist operating in an urban area. **urban
renewal** slum clearance and redevelopment in a city or town.
urban sprawl the uncontrolled expansion of urban areas. [L
urbanus f. urbs urbis city]

urbane /ɜːˈbeɪn/ adj. courteous; suave; elegant and refined in
manner. □□ **urbanely** adv. **urbaneness** n. [F urbain or L urbanus:
see URBAN]

urbanism /ˈɜːbənɪz(ə)m/ n. **1** urban character or way of life. **2**
a study of urban life. □□ **urbanist** n.

urbanite /ˈɜːbənaɪt/ n. a dweller in a city or town.

urbanity /ɜːˈbænɪtɪ/ n. **1** an urbane quality; refinement of manner. **2** urban life. [F *urbanité* or L *urbanitas* (as URBAN)]

urbanize /ˈɜːbənaɪz/ v.tr. (also **-ise**) **1** make urban. **2** destroy the rural quality of (a district). □□ **urbanization** /-ˈzeɪʃ(ə)n/ n. [F *urbaniser* (as URBAN)]

urceolate /ˈɜːsɪələt/ adj. Bot. having the shape of a pitcher, with a large body and small mouth. [L *urceolus* dimin. of *urceus* pitcher]

urchin /ˈɜːtʃɪn/ n. **1** a mischievous child, esp. young and raggedly dressed. **2** = *sea urchin*. **3** archaic **a** a hedgehog. **b** a goblin. [ME *hirchon*, *urcheon* f. ONF *herichon*, OF *heriçon* ult. f. L *(h)ericius* hedgehog]

Urdu /ˈʊɔduː, ˈɜː-/ n. an Indic language allied to Hindi, which it resembles in grammar and structure, but with a large admixture of Arabic and Persian words, having been built up from the language of the early Muslim invaders, and usually written in Persian script. It is the language of the Muslim population, spoken as a first language by over 5 million people in Pakistan (where it is an official language), as a second language by another 40 million there, and by about 30 million in India. [Hind. (*zabān i*) *urdū* (language of the) camp, f. Pers. *urdū* f. Turki *ordū*: see HORDE]

-ure /jə(r)/ suffix forming **1** nouns of action or process (*censure*; *closure*; *seizure*). **2** nouns of result (*creature*; *scripture*). **3** collective nouns (*legislature*; *nature*). **4** nouns of function (*judicature*; *ligature*). [from or after OF *-ure* f. L *-ura*]

urea /ˈjʊɔrɪə, -ˈriːə/ n. Biochem. a soluble colourless crystalline nitrogenous compound contained esp. in the urine of mammals. □□ **ureal** adj. [mod.L f. F *urée* f. Gk *ouron* urine]

uremia US var. of URAEMIA.

ureter /jʊɔˈriːtə(r)/ n. the duct by which urine passes from the kidney to the bladder or cloaca. □□ **ureteral** adj. **ureteric** /ˌjʊɔrɪˈterɪk/ adj. **ureteritis** /-ˈraɪtɪs/ n. [F *uretère* or mod.L *ureter* f. Gk *ourētēr* f. *oureō* urinate]

urethane /jʊˈriːθeɪn, ˈjʊɔrɪθeɪn/ n. Chem. a crystalline amide, ethyl carbamate, used in plastics and paints. [F *uréthane* (as UREA, ETHANE)]

urethra /jʊɔˈriːθrə/ n. (pl. **urethrae** /-riː/ or **urethras**) the duct by which urine is discharged from the bladder. □□ **urethral** adj. **urethritis** /-rɪˈθraɪtɪs/ n. [LL f. Gk *ourēthra* (as URETER)]

urge /ɜːdʒ/ v. & n. —v.tr. **1** (often foll. by *on*) drive forcibly; impel; hasten (*urged them on*; *urged the horses forward*). **2** (often foll. by *to* + infin. or *that* + clause) encourage or entreat earnestly or persistently (*urged them to go*; *urged them to action*; *urged that they should go*). **3** (often foll. by *on*, *upon*) advocate (an action or argument etc.) pressingly or emphatically (to a person). **4** adduce forcefully as a reason or justification (*urged the seriousness of the problem*). **5** ply (a person etc.) hard with argument or entreaty. —n. **1** an urging impulse or tendency. **2** a strong desire. □□ **urger** n. [L *urgēre* press, drive]

urgent /ˈɜːdʒ(ə)nt/ adj. **1** requiring immediate action or attention (*an urgent need for help*). **2** importunate; earnest and persistent in demand. □□ **urgency** n. **urgently** adv. [ME f. F (as URGE)]

URI abbr. upper respiratory infection.

-uria /ˈjʊɔrɪə/ comb. form forming nouns denoting that a substance is (esp. excessively) present in the urine. [mod.L f. Gk *-ouria* (as URINE)]

Uriah /jʊɔˈraɪə/ an officer in David's army, husband of Bathsheba, whom David caused to be killed in battle (2 Sam. 11).

uric /ˈjʊɔrɪk/ adj. of or relating to urine. □ **uric acid** a crystalline acid forming a constituent of urine. [F *urique* (as URINE)]

urinal /jʊɔˈraɪn(ə)l, ˈjʊɔrɪn(ə)l/ n. **1** a sanitary fitting, usu. against a wall, for men to urinate into. **2** a place or receptacle for urination. [ME f. OF f. LL *urinal* neut. of *urinalis* (as URINE)]

urinalysis /ˌjʊɔrɪˈnælɪsɪs/ n. (pl. **urinalyses** /-ˌsiːz/) the chemical analysis of urine esp. for diagnostic purposes.

urinary /ˈjʊɔrɪnərɪ/ adj. **1** of or relating to urine. **2** affecting or occurring in the urinary system (*urinary diseases*).

urinate /ˈjʊɔrɪneɪt/ v.intr. discharge urine. □□ **urination** /-ˈneɪʃ(ə)n/ n. [med.L *urinare* (as URINE)]

urine /ˈjʊɔrɪn/ n. a pale-yellow fluid secreted as waste from the

blood by the kidneys, stored in the bladder, and discharged through the urethra. □□ **urinous** adj. [ME f. OF f. L *urina*]

urn /ɜːn/ n. & v. —n. **1** a vase with a foot and usu. a rounded body, esp. for storing the ashes of the cremated dead or as a vessel or measure. **2** a large vessel with a tap, in which tea or coffee etc. is made or kept hot. **3** poet. anything in which a dead body or its remains are preserved, e.g. a grave. —v.tr. enclose in an urn. □□ **urnful** n. (pl. **-fuls**). [ME f. L *urna*, rel. to *urceus* pitcher]

urnfield /ˈɜːnfiːld/ n. a necropolis in which cremated remains are placed in pottery vessels (cinerary urns) and buried, especially one belonging to a group of Bronze Age cultures of central Europe and associated with peoples who were later identified as Celts.

uro-¹ /ˈjʊɔrəʊ/ comb. form urine. [Gk *ouron* urine]

uro-² /ˈjʊɔrəʊ/ comb. form tail. [Gk *oura* tail]

urochord /ˈjʊɔrəʊˌkɔːd/ n. the notochord of a tunicate.

urodele /ˈjʊɔrəʊˌdiːl/ n. any amphibian of the order Urodela, having a tail when in the adult form, including newts and salamanders. [URO-² + Gk *dēlos* evident]

urogenital /ˌjʊɔrəʊˈdʒenɪt(ə)l/ adj. of or relating to urinary and genital products or organs.

urology /jʊɔˈrɒlədʒɪ/ n. the scientific study of the urinary system. □□ **urologic** /-rəˈlɒdʒɪk/ adj. **urologist** n.

uropygium /ˌjʊɔrəʊˈpɪdʒɪəm/ n. the rump of a bird. [med.L f. Gk *ouropugion*]

uroscopy /jʊɔˈrɒskəpɪ/ n. Med. hist. the examination of urine, esp. in diagnosis.

Ursa Major /ˌɜːsə ˈmeɪdʒə(r)/ the most familiar of the constellations, variously named the Great Bear, Plough, Big Dipper, or Charles's Wain. According to legend Callisto, daughter of Lycaon, was transformed by Zeus into a bear to escape the wrath of Juno. Her son Arcas, not recognizing her, was about to slay the bear when both were transported into the heavens, Callisto as the Great Bear, Arcas as the Little Bear. [L, = greater (she-)bear]

Ursa Minor /ˌɜːsə ˈmaɪnə(r)/ the constellation of the Little Bear, containing the north celestial pole and Polaris. It is known also as the Little Dipper, and its two bright stars beta and gamma are known as Guardians of the Pole. [L, = lesser (she-)bear]

ursine /ˈɜːsaɪn/ adj. of or like a bear. [L *ursinus* f. *ursus* bear]

Ursula /ˈɜːsjʊlə/, St, legendary British saint and martyr, said to have been put to death with 11,000 virgins after being captured by Huns near Cologne while on a pilgrimage. The legend developed from the veneration of some nameless virgin martyrs at Cologne, dating from before the 4th–5th c.; in later forms of the story Ursula, whose name now came to be affixed to their leader, was a British princess.

Ursuline /ˈɜːsjʊlaɪn, -lɪn/ n. & adj. —n. a nun of an order founded by St Angela Merici at Brescia in 1537 for nursing the sick and teaching girls. It is the oldest teaching order of women in the Roman Catholic Church. —adj. of or relating to this order. [St *Ursula*, the founder's patron saint]

urticaria /ˌɜːtɪˈkeərɪə/ n. Med. nettle-rash. [mod.L f. L *urtica* nettle f. *urere* burn]

urticate /ˈɜːtɪˌkeɪt/ v.tr. sting like a nettle. □□ **urtication** /-ˈkeɪʃ(ə)n/ n. [med.L *urticare* f. L *urtica*: see URTICARIA]

Uruguay /ˈjʊɔrəˌgwaɪ/ a country in South America lying south of Brazil, with a coastline on the Atlantic Ocean; pop. (1985) 2,940,200; official language, Spanish; capital, Montevideo. Not permanently settled by Europeans until the 17th c., Uruguay became an area of long-standing Spanish–Portuguese rivalry. Liberated in 1825, it remained relatively backward and disunited through the 19th c., but in the 20th c., despite its small size (it is the smallest of the South American republics) it has emerged as one of the most prosperous and literate nations in the continent, boasting an extensive social welfare system and a balanced economy. □□ **Uruguayan** adj. & n.

Uruk /ˈʊrək/ (Biblical *Erech*, modern Arabic *Warka*) a leading city of Sumer and Babylonia, founded in the 5th millennium BC and associated with the legendary hero Gilgamesh and the god Dumuzi.

Urumqi /ʊˈrʊmtʃɪ/ (also **Urumchi**) the capital of Xinjiang autonomous region in NW China; pop. (est. 1986) 1,000,000.

urus /ˈjʊərəs/ n. = AUROCHS. [L f. Gmc]

US abbr. **1** United States (of America). **2** Under-Secretary. **3** unserviceable.

us /ʌs, əs/ pron. **1** objective case of WE (they saw us). **2** colloq. = WE (it's us again). **3** colloq. = ME¹ (give us a kiss). [OE ūs f. Gmc]

USA abbr. **1** United States of America. **2** US United States Army.

usable /ˈjuːzəb(ə)l/ adj. that can be used. □□ **usability** /-ˈbɪlɪtɪ/ n. **usableness** n.

USAF abbr. United States Air Force.

usage /ˈjuːsɪdʒ/ n. **1** a manner of using or treating; treatment (damaged by rough usage). **2** habitual or customary practice, esp. as creating a right, obligation, or standard. [ME f. OF f. us USE n.]

usance /ˈjuːz(ə)ns/ n. the time allowed by commercial usage for the payment of foreign bills of exchange. [ME f. OF (as USE)]

USDAW /ˈʌzdɔː/ abbr. (in the UK) Union of Shop, Distributive, and Allied Workers.

use v. & n. —v.tr. /juːz/ **1** cause to act or serve for a purpose; bring into service; avail oneself of (rarely uses the car; use your discretion). **2** treat (a person) in a specified manner (they used him shamefully). **3** exploit for one's own ends (they are just using you). **4** (in past /juːst/; foll. by to + infin.) did or had in the past (but no longer) as a customary practice or state (I used to be an archaeologist; it used not (or did not use) to rain so often). **5** (as **used** adj.) second-hand. **6** (as **used** /juːst/ predic. adj.) (foll. by to) familiar by habit; accustomed (not used to hard work). **7** apply (a name or title etc.) to oneself. —n. /juːs/ **1** the act of using or the state of being used; application to a purpose (put it to good use; is in daily use; worn and polished with use). **2** the right or power of using (lost the use of my right arm). **3 a** the ability to be used (a torch would be of use). **b** the purpose for which a thing can be used (it's no use talking). **4** custom or usage (long use has reconciled me to it). **5** the characteristic ritual and liturgy of a church or diocese etc. **6** Law hist. the benefit or profit of lands, esp. in the possession of another who holds them solely for the beneficiary. □ **could use** colloq. would be glad to have; would be improved by having. **have no use for 1** be unable to find a use for. **2** dislike or be impatient with. **make use of 1** employ, apply. **2** benefit from. **use and wont** established custom. **use a person's name** quote a person as an authority or reference etc. **use up 1** consume completely, use the whole of. **2** find a use for (something remaining). **3** exhaust or wear out e.g. with overwork. [ME f. OF us, user, ult. f. L uti us- use]

useful /ˈjuːsfʊl/ adj. **1 a** of use; serviceable. **b** producing or able to produce good results (gave me some useful hints). **2** colloq. highly creditable or efficient (a useful performance). □ **make oneself useful** perform useful services. **useful load** the load carried by an aircraft etc. in addition to its own weight. □□ **usefully** adv. **usefulness** n.

useless /ˈjuːslɪs/ adj. **1** serving no purpose; unavailing (the contents were made useless by damp; protest is useless). **2** colloq. feeble or ineffectual (am useless at swimming). □□ **uselessly** adv. **uselessness** n.

user /ˈjuːzə(r)/ n. **1** a person who uses (esp. a particular commodity or service, or a computer). **2** colloq. a drug addict. **3** Law the continued use or enjoyment of a right etc. □ **right of user** Law **1** a right to use. **2** a presumptive right arising from the user. **user-friendly** esp. Computing (of a machine or system) designed to be easy to use.

ushabti /ʊˈʃæbtɪ/ n. each of a set of wooden, stone, or faience figurines, in the form of mummies, placed in an ancient Egyptian tomb to serve the dead person by taking his place in any work that he might be called upon to do in the afterlife. They were often 365 in number, one for each day of the year, with a number of overseers. [Egyptian, = answerer]

usher /ˈʌʃə(r)/ n. & v. —n. **1** a person who shows people to their seats in a hall or theatre etc. **2** a doorkeeper at a court etc. **3** Brit. an officer walking before a person of rank. **4** archaic or joc.

an assistant teacher. —v.tr. **1** act as usher to. **2** (usu. foll. by in) announce or show in etc. (ushered us into the room; ushered in a new era). □□ **ushership** n. [ME f. AF usser, OF uissier, var. of huissier f. med.L ustiarius for L ostiarius f. ostium door]

usherette /ˌʌʃəˈret/ n. a female usher esp. in a cinema.

Ushuaia /uːˈswaɪə/ a port in Tierra del Fuego; pop. (1980) 11,000. Founded as a penal colony in 1884, it is the most southerly town in the world.

USM abbr. Stock Exch. Unlisted Securities Market.

USN abbr. United States Navy.

Uspallata Pass /ˌuspæˈjɑːtə/ the principal route across the Andes, linking Argentina with Chile. At its highest point stands a statue of 'Christ of the Andes'.

usquebaugh /ˈʌskwɪbɔː/ n. esp. Ir. & Sc. whisky. [Ir. & Sc. Gael. uisge beatha water of life: cf. WHISKY]

USS abbr. United States Ship.

USSR abbr. Union of Soviet Socialist Republics.

Ustinov /ˈjuːstɪˌnɒf/, Sir Peter Alexander (1921–), British actor, director, novelist, and dramatist, of Russian descent. He wrote and acted in plays including The Love of Four Colonels (1951) and Romanoff and Juliet (1956; he also directed the film version, 1961); his many films include Spartacus (1960), Topkapi (1964), and Death on the Nile (1978). Large, ebullient, a witty impersonator and raconteur, Ustinov's particular vein of satirical fantasy has been expressed more pungently in his stage plays than in his films.

usual /ˈjuːʒʊəl/ adj. **1** such as commonly occurs, or is observed or done; customary, habitual (the usual formalities; it is usual to tip them; forgot my keys as usual). **2** (prec. by the, my, etc.) colloq. a person's usual drink etc. □□ **usually** adv. **usualness** n. [ME f. OF usual, usuel or LL usualis (as USE)]

usucaption /ˌjuːzjuːˈkæpʃ(ə)n/ n. (also **usucapion** /ˌjuːzjuːˈkeɪpɪən/) (in Roman and Scots law) the acquisition of a title or right to property by uninterrupted and undisputed possession for a prescribed term. [OF usucap(t)ion or L usucap(t)io f. usucapere acquire by prescription f. usu by use + capere capt- take]

usufruct /ˈjuːzjuːˌfrʌkt/ n. & v. —n. (in Roman and Scots law) the right of enjoying the use and advantages of another's property short of the destruction or waste of its substance. —v.tr. hold in usufruct. □□ **usufructuary** /-ˈfrʌktjʊərɪ/ adj. & n. [med.L usufructus f. L usus (et) fructus f. usus USE + fructus FRUIT]

usurer /ˈjuːʒərə(r)/ n. a person who practises usury. [ME f. AF usurer, OF usureor f. usure f. L usura: see USURY]

usurious /juːˈʒʊərɪəs/ adj. of, involving, or practising usury. □□ **usuriously** adv.

usurp /juːˈzɜːp/ v. **1** tr. seize or assume (a throne or power etc.) wrongfully. **2** intr. (foll. by on, upon) encroach. □□ **usurpation** /ˌjuːzəˈpeɪʃ(ə)n/ n. **usurper** n. [ME f. OF usurper f. L usurpare seize for use]

usury /ˈjuːʒərɪ/ n. **1** the act or practice of lending money at interest, esp. Law at an exorbitant rate. **2** interest at this rate. □ **with usury** rhet. or poet. with increased force etc. [ME f. med.L usuria f. L usura (as USE)]

UT abbr. **1** universal time. **2** US Utah (in official postal use).

Utah /ˈjuːtɑː, US -tɔː/ a State in the western US; pop. (est. 1985) 1,461,000; capital, Salt Lake City. The area was ceded to the US by Mexico in 1848 and was settled by Mormons; statehood was refused until these abandoned their practise of polygamy—a dispute which led to a brief war (1857) of settlers against US troops. Utah became the 45th State of the US in 1896.

Utamaro /ˌuːtəˈmɑːrəʊ/, Kitagawa (1753–1806), Japanese print-maker, one of the greatest masters of ukiyo-e. His books of woodblock prints range from his Insects (1788) to his better-known The Poem of the Pillow (1788), and The Twelve Hours of the Green Houses (1795) with its sensual and elegant depictions of women. His expressive simple design was greatly admired by the modern movement in Europe in the second half of the 19th c.

UTC abbr. co-ordinated universal time (see GREENWICH).

ute /juːt/ n. Austral. & NZ sl. a utility truck. [abbr.]

utensil /juːˈtens(ə)l/ n. an implement or vessel, esp. for domestic

w we　z zoo　ʃ she　ʒ decision　θ thin　ð this　ŋ ring　x loch　tʃ chip　dʒ jar　(see over for vowels)

use (*cooking utensils*). [ME f. OF *utensile* f. med.L, neut. of L *utensilis* usable (as USE)]

uterine /ˈjuːtəˌraɪn, -rɪn/ *adj.* **1** of or relating to the uterus. **2** born of the same mother but not the same father (*sister uterine*). [ME f. LL *uterinus* (as UTERUS)]

uterus /ˈjuːtərəs/ *n.* (*pl.* **uteri** /-ˌraɪ/) the womb. □□ **uteritis** /-ˈraɪtɪs/ *n.* [L]

Uther Pendragon /ˌjuːθə penˈdrægən/ (in Arthurian legend) king of the Britons and father of Arthur.

utile /ˈjuːtaɪl/ *adj.* useful; having utility. [ME f. OF f. L *utilis* f. *uti* use]

utilitarian /ˌjuːtɪlɪˈteərɪən/ *adj.* & *n.* —*adj.* **1** designed to be useful for a purpose rather than attractive; severely practical. **2** of utilitarianism. —*n.* an adherent of utilitarianism.

utilitarianism /ˌjuːtɪlɪˈteərɪəˌnɪz(ə)m/ *n.* **1** the theory, famously advocated by Bentham and J. S. Mill, that the guiding principle of conduct should be to achieve the greatest happiness of the greatest number. **2** the theory that the usefulness (or otherwise) of an action is the criterion of whether it is right (or wrong).

utility /juːˈtɪlɪtɪ/ *n.* (*pl.* **-ies**) **1** the condition of being useful or profitable. **2** a useful thing. **3** = *public utility*. **4** (*attrib.*) **a** severely practical and standardized (*utility furniture*). **b** made or serving for utility. □ **utility room** a room equipped with appliances for washing, ironing, and other domestic work. **utility vehicle** (or **truck** etc.) a vehicle capable of serving various functions. [ME f. OF *utilité* f. L *utilitas -tatis* (as UTILE)]

utilize /ˈjuːtɪˌlaɪz/ *v.tr.* (also **-ise**) make practical use of; turn to account; use effectively. □□ **utilizable** *adj.* **utilization** /-ˈzeɪʃ(ə)n/ *n.* **utilizer** *n.* [F *utiliser* f. It. *utilizzare* (as UTILE)]

-ution /ˈjuːʃ(ə)n, ˈuːʃ(ə)n/ *suffix* forming nouns, = -ATION (*solution*). [F f. L *-utio*]

utmost /ˈʌtməʊst/ *adj.* & *n.* furthest, extreme, or greatest (*the utmost limits*; *showed the utmost reluctance*). —*n.* (prec. by *the*) the utmost point or degree etc. □ **do one's utmost** do all that one can. [OE *ūt(e)mest* (as OUT, -MOST)]

Utopia /juːˈtəʊpɪə/ *n.* an imagined perfect place or state of things. [name of an imaginary island, governed on a perfect political and social system, in a book of that title by Sir Thomas More (1516): mod.L f. Gk *ou* not + *topos* place]

Utopian /juːˈtəʊpɪən/ *adj.* & *n.* (also **utopian**) —*adj.* characteristic of Utopia; idealistic. —*n.* an idealistic reformer. □□ **Utopianism** *n.*

Utrecht /juːˈtrext/ a city and province of The Netherlands; pop. (1987) 230,373. □ **Peace of Utrecht** a series of treaties (1713) ending the War of the Spanish Succession. By their terms the disputed throne of Spain was given to the French aspirant Philip V, but the union of the French and Spanish thrones was forbidden, while the succession of the House of Hanover to the British throne was secured and the former Spanish territories in Italy were ceded to the Hapsburgs.

utricle /ˈjuːtrɪk(ə)l/ *n.* a small cell or sac in an animal or plant,

esp. one in the inner ear. □□ **utricular** /juːˈtrɪkjʊlə(r)/ *adj.* [F *utricule* or L *utriculus* dimin. of *uter* leather bag]

Uttar Pradesh /ˌʊtɑː prəˈdeʃ/ a State in Northern India, bordering on Tibet and Nepal; pop. (1981) 110,858,000; capital, Lucknow.

utter[1] /ˈʌtə(r)/ *attrib.adj.* complete, total, absolute (*utter misery*; *saw the utter absurdity of it*). □□ **utterly** *adv.* **utterness** *n.* [OE *ūtera*, *ūttra*, compar. adj. f. *ūt* OUT: cf. OUTER]

utter[2] /ˈʌtə(r)/ *v.tr.* **1** emit audibly (*uttered a startled cry*). **2** express in spoken or written words. **3** *Law* put (esp. forged money) into circulation. □□ **utterable** *adj.* **utterer** *n.* [ME f. MDu. *ūteren* make known, assim. to UTTER[1]]

utterance /ˈʌtərəns/ *n.* **1** the act or an instance of uttering. **2** a thing spoken. **3 a** the power of speaking. **b** a manner of speaking. **4** *Linguistics* an uninterrupted chain of spoken or written words not necessarily corresponding to a single or complete grammatical unit.

uttermost /ˈʌtəˌməʊst/ *adj.* furthest, extreme.

Uttley /ˈʌtlɪ/, Alison (1884–1976), English author of children's books, remembered especially for her 'Little Grey Rabbit' series (published from 1929 onwards) and for her 'Sam Pig' stories (1940 onwards).

U-turn /ˈjuːtɜːn/ *n.* **1** the turning of a vehicle in a U-shaped course so as to face in the opposite direction. **2** a reversal of policy.

UV *abbr.* ultraviolet.

uvea /ˈjuːvɪə/ *n.* the pigmented layer of the eye, lying beneath the outer layer. [med.L f. L *uva* grape]

uvula /ˈjuːvjʊlə/ *n.* (*pl.* **uvulae** /-ˌliː/) **1** a fleshy extension of the soft palate hanging above the throat. **2** a similar process in the bladder or cerebellum. [ME f. LL, dimin. of L *uva* grape]

uvular /ˈjuːvjʊlə(r)/ *adj.* & *n.* —*adj.* **1** of or relating to the uvula. **2** articulated with the back of the tongue and the uvula, as in *r* in French. —*n.* a uvular consonant.

uxorial /ʌkˈsɔːrɪəl/ *adj.* of or relating to a wife.

uxoricide /ʌkˈsɒrɪˌsaɪd/ *n.* **1** the killing of one's wife. **2** a person who does this. □□ **uxoricidal** /-ˈsaɪd(ə)l/ *adj.* [L *uxor* wife + -CIDE]

uxorious /ʌkˈsɔːrɪəs/ *adj.* **1** greatly or excessively fond of one's wife. **2** (of behaviour etc.) showing such fondness. □□ **uxoriously** *adv.* **uxoriousness** *n.* [L *uxoriosus* f. *uxor* wife]

Uzbek /ˈʌzbek, ˈʊz-/ *n.* (also **Uzbeg** /-beg/) **1** a member of a Turkic people living mainly in Uzbekistan. **2** the language of Uzbekistan, the most widely spoken non-Slavonic language in the USSR with some 9 million speakers, a Turkic language belonging to the Altaic language group. Originally it was written in the Arabic script but that was replaced by the Roman alphabet in 1927 and the Cyrillic in 1940. [Uzbek]

Uzbekistan /ˌʊzbekɪˈstɑːn, ˌʌ-/ the Uzbek Soviet Socialist Republic, a constituent republic of the USSR, lying south and south-east of the Aral Sea; pop. (est. 1987) 19,026,000; capital, Tashkent.

V

V¹ /viː/ *n.* (also **v**) (*pl.* **Vs** or **V's**) **1** the twenty-second letter of the alphabet. **2** a V-shaped thing. **3** (as a Roman numeral) five.

V² *abbr.* (also **V.**) volt(s).

V³ *abbr.* Vergeltungswaffe. □ **V-1, V-2** German missiles used in the Second World War. V1 was a flying bomb; V2 was a type of rocket bomb (see von BRAUN). [G, = reprisal weapon]

V⁴ *symb. Chem.* the element vanadium.

v. *abbr.* **1** verse. **2** verso. **3** versus. **4** very. **5** *vide.*

VA *abbr.* **1** *US* Veterans' Administration. **2** Vicar Apostolic. **3** Vice Admiral. **4** *US* Virginia (in official postal use). **5** (in the UK) Order of Victoria and Albert.

Va. *abbr.* Virginia.

Vaal /vɑːl/ a river of South Africa, the chief tributary of the Orange River. For much of its course it forms the border between Transvaal and Orange Free State.

Vaasa /ˈvɑːsə/ (Swedish **Vasa**) **1** a province of western Finland; pop. (1987) 444,405. **2** its capital, a port on the Gulf of Bothnia; pop. (1987) 53,780.

vac /væk/ *n. Brit. colloq.* vacation (esp. of universities). [abbr.]

vacancy /ˈveɪkənsɪ/ *n.* (*pl.* **-ies**) **1** the state of being vacant or empty. **2** an unoccupied post or job (*there are three vacancies for typists*). **3** an available room in a hotel etc. **4** emptiness of mind; idleness, listlessness.

vacant /ˈveɪkənt/ *adj.* **1** not filled or occupied; empty. **2** not mentally active; showing no interest (*had a vacant stare*). □ **vacant possession** *Brit.* ownership of a house etc. with any previous occupant having moved out. □□ **vacantly** *adv.* [ME f. OF *vacant* or L *vacare* (as VACATE)]

vacate /vəˈkeɪt, veɪ-/ *v.tr.* **1** leave vacant or cease to occupy (a house, room, etc.). **2** give up tenure of (a post etc.). **3** *Law* annul (a judgement or contract etc.). □□ **vacatable** *adj.* [L *vacare vacat-* be empty]

vacation /vəˈkeɪʃ(ə)n/ *n. & v.* —*n.* **1** a fixed period of cessation from work, esp. in universities and lawcourts. **2** *US* a holiday. **3** the act of vacating (a house or post etc.). —*v.intr.* *US* take a holiday. □ **vacation land** *US* an area providing attractions for holidaymakers. □□ **vacationer** *n.* **vacationist** *n.* [ME f. OF *vacation* or L *vacatio* (as VACATE)]

vaccinate /ˈvæksɪˌneɪt/ *v.tr.* inoculate with a vaccine to procure immunity from a disease; immunize. □□ **vaccination** /-ˈneɪʃ(ə)n/ *n.* **vaccinator** *n.*

vaccine /ˈvæksiːn/ *n. & adj.* —*n.* **1** an antigenic preparation used to stimulate the production of antibodies and procure immunity from one or several diseases. **2** *hist.* the cowpox virus used in vaccination against smallpox. —*adj.* of or relating to cowpox or vaccination. □□ **vaccinal** /-sɪn(ə)l/ *adj.* [L *vaccinus* f. *vacca* cow]

vaccinia /vækˈsɪnɪə/ *n. Med.* a virus used as a vaccine against smallpox. [mod.L (as VACCINE)]

vacillate /ˈvæsɪˌleɪt/ *v.intr.* **1** fluctuate in opinion or resolution. **2** move from side to side; oscillate, waver. □□ **vacillation** /-ˈleɪʃ(ə)n/ *n.* **vacillator** *n.* [L *vacillare vacillat-* sway]

vacua *pl.* of VACUUM.

vacuole /ˈvækjʊˌəʊl/ *n. Biol.* a tiny space within the cytoplasm of a cell containing air, fluid, food particles, etc. □□ **vacuolar** /ˈvækjʊələ(r)/ *adj.* **vacuolation** /-ˈleɪʃ(ə)n/ *n.* [F, dimin. of L *vacuus* empty]

vacuous /ˈvækjʊəs/ *adj.* **1** lacking expression (*a vacuous stare*). **2** unintelligent (*a vacuous remark*). **3** empty. □□ **vacuity** /vəˈkjuːɪtɪ/ *n.* **vacuously** *adv.* **vacuousness** *n.* [L *vacuus* empty (as VACATE)]

vacuum /ˈvækjʊəm/ *n. & v.* —*n.* (*pl.* **vacuums** or **vacua** /-jʊə/) **1** a space entirely devoid of matter. **2** a space or vessel from which the air has been completely or partly removed by a pump etc. **3 a** the absence of the normal or previous content of a place,

environment, etc. **b** the absence of former circumstances, activities, etc. **4** (*pl.* **vacuums**) *colloq.* a vacuum cleaner. **5** a decrease of pressure below the normal atmospheric value. —*v. colloq.* **1** *tr.* clean with a vacuum cleaner. **2** *intr.* use a vacuum cleaner. □ **vacuum brake** a brake in which pressure is caused by the exhaustion of air. **vacuum-clean** clean with a vacuum cleaner. **vacuum cleaner** see separate entry. **vacuum flask** *Brit.* a vessel with a double wall enclosing a vacuum so that the liquid in the inner receptacle retains its temperature. The modern flask was invented by Sir James Dewar, Scottish physicist, in the 1890s. **vacuum gauge** a gauge for testing the pressure after the production of a vacuum. **vacuum-packed** sealed after the partial removal of air. **vacuum pump** a pump for producing a vacuum. **vacuum tube** a tube with a near-vacuum for the free passage of electric current. [mod.L, neut. of L *vacuus* empty]

vacuum cleaner *n.* an electric appliance for taking up dust, dirt, etc. by suction. The first vacuum cleaner was invented and named by H. C. Booth (1871–1955), English engineer, in 1901. He founded a company providing a cleaning service using his machines, which were large and cumbersome and required a horse-drawn cart to convey the electric motor which powered them. Smaller domestic models were developed some years later.

VAD *abbr.* **1** Voluntary Aid Detachment. **2** a member of this.

vade-mecum /ˌvɑːdɪˈmeɪkəm, ˌveɪdɪˈmiːkəm/ *n.* a handbook etc. carried constantly for use. [F f. mod.L, = go with me]

Vaduz /væˈdʊts/ the capital of Liechtenstein; pop. (est. 1987) 4,900.

vagabond /ˈvægəˌbɒnd/ *n., adj., & v.* —*n.* **1** a wanderer or vagrant, esp. an idle one. **2** *colloq.* a scamp or rascal. —*adj.* having no fixed habitation; wandering. —*v.intr.* wander about as a vagabond. □□ **vagabondage** *n.* [ME f. OF *vagabond* or L *vagabundus* f. *vagari* wander]

vagal see VAGUS.

vagary /ˈveɪgərɪ/ *n.* (*pl.* **-ies**) a caprice; an eccentric idea or act (*the vagaries of Fortune*). □□ **vagarious** /vəˈgeərɪəs/ *adj.* [L *vagari* wander]

vagi *pl.* of VAGUS.

vagina /vəˈdʒaɪnə/ *n.* (*pl.* **vaginas** or **vaginae** /-niː/) **1** the canal between the uterus and vulva of a woman or other female mammal. **2** a sheath formed round a stem by the base of a leaf. □□ **vaginal** *adj.* **vaginitis** /ˌvædʒɪˈnaɪtɪs/ *n.* [L, = sheath, scabbard]

vaginismus /ˌvædʒɪˈnɪzməs/ *n.* a painful spasmodic contraction of the vagina, usu. in response to pressure. [mod.L (as VAGINA)]

vagrant /ˈveɪgrənt/ *n. & adj.* —*n.* **1** a person without a settled home or regular work. **2** a wanderer or vagabond. —*adj.* **1** wandering or roving (*a vagrant musician*). **2** being a vagrant. □□ **vagrancy** *n.* **vagrantly** *adv.* [ME f. AF *vag(a)raunt*, perh. alt. f. AF *wakerant* etc. by assoc. with L *vagari* wander]

vague /veɪg/ *adj.* **1** of uncertain or ill-defined meaning or character (*gave a vague answer; has some vague idea of emigrating*). **2** (of a person or mind) imprecise; inexact in thought, expression, or understanding. □□ **vaguely** *adv.* **vagueness** *n.* **vaguish** *adj.* [F *vague* or L *vagus* wandering, uncertain]

vagus /ˈveɪgəs/ *n.* (*pl.* **vagi** /-gaɪ/) *Anat.* either of the tenth pair of cranial nerves with branches to the heart, lungs, and viscera. □□ **vagal** *adj.* [L: see VAGUE]

vail /veɪl/ *v. archaic* **1** *tr.* lower or doff (one's plumes, pride, crown, etc.) esp. in token of submission. **2** *intr.* yield; give place; remove one's hat as a sign of respect etc. [ME f. obs. *avale* f. OF *avaler* to lower f. *a val* down, f. *val* VALE¹]

vain /veɪn/ *adj.* **1** excessively proud or conceited, esp. about one's own attributes. **2** empty, trivial, unsubstantial (*vain boasts; vain* triumphs). **3** useless; followed by no good result (*in the vain hope of dissuading them*). □ **in vain** without result or success (*it was in vain that we protested*). **take a person's name in vain** use it lightly or profanely. □□ **vainly** *adv.* **vainness** *n.* [ME f. OF f. L *vanus* empty, without substance]

vainglory /veɪnˈglɔːrɪ/ *n.* literary boastfulness; extreme vanity. □□ **vainglorious** *adj.* **vaingloriously** *adv.* **vaingloriousness** *n.* [ME, after OF *vaine gloire*, L *vana gloria*]

vair /veə(r)/ *n.* **1** archaic or hist. a squirrel-fur widely used for medieval linings and trimmings. **2** Heraldry fur represented by small shield-shaped or bell-shaped figures usu. alternately azure and argent. [ME f. OF f. L (as VARIOUS)]

Vaishnava /ˈvaɪʃnɑːˌvɑ/ *n.* Hinduism a devotee of Vishnu. [Skr. *vaiṣṇavá*]

Vaisya /ˈvaɪsjə/ *n.* **1** the third of the four great Hindu classes, comprising the merchants and agriculturalists. **2** a member of this class. [Skr. *vaiśya* peasant, labourer]

valance /ˈvæləns/ *n.* (also **valence**) a short curtain round the frame or canopy of a bedstead, above a window, or under a shelf. □□ **valanced** *adj.* [ME ult. f. OF *avaler* descend: see VAIL]

vale¹ /veɪl/ *n.* archaic or poet. (except in place-names) a valley (*Vale of the White Horse*). □ **vale of tears** literary the world as a scene of life, trouble, etc. [ME f. OF *val* f. L *vallis*, *valles*]

vale² /ˈvɑːleɪ/ *int.* & *n.* —*int.* farewell. —*n.* a farewell. [L, impr. of *valēre* be well or strong]

valediction /ˌvælɪˈdɪkʃ(ə)n/ *n.* **1** the act or an instance of bidding farewell. **2** the words used in this. [L *valedicere valedict-* (as VALE², *dicere* say), after *benediction*]

valedictorian /ˌvælɪdɪkˈtɔːrɪən/ *n.* US a person who gives a valedictory, esp. the highest-ranking member of a graduating class.

valedictory /ˌvælɪˈdɪktərɪ/ *adj.* & *n.* —*adj.* serving as a farewell. —*n.* (pl. **-ies**) a farewell address.

valence¹ /ˈveɪləns/ *n.* Chem. esp. US = VALENCY. □ **valence electron** an electron in the outermost shell of an atom involved in forming a chemical bond.

valence² var. of VALANCE.

Valencia /vəˈlensɪə/ **1** a city and port of eastern Spain, capital of the former Moorish kingdom of Valencia; pop. (1986) 738,575. **2** a region of eastern Spain, on the Mediterranean, a Moorish kingdom 1021–1238.

Valenciennes /væˌlɑːnsɪˈen/ *n.* a rich kind of lace. [*Valenciennes* in NE France, where it was made in the 17th and 18th c.]

valency /ˈveɪlənsɪ/ *n.* (pl. **-ies**) Brit. Chem. the combining power of an atom measured by the number of hydrogen atoms it can displace or combine with. [LL *valentia* power, competence f. *valēre* be well or strong]

Valentine /ˈvælənˌtaɪn/, St. The name of an early Italian saint (or possibly two saints), traditionally commemorated on 14 Feb.—a Roman priest martyred c.269, and a bishop of Terni martyred at Rome. St Valentine was regarded as the patron of lovers, a tradition which may be connected with the old belief that birds pair on 14 Feb., or with the pagan fertility festival of Lupercalia (mid-Feb.).

valentine /ˈvælənˌtaɪn/ *n.* **1** a card or gift sent, often anonymously, as a mark of love or affection on St Valentine's Day (14 Feb.). (See below.) **2** a sweetheart chosen on this day. [ME f. OF *Valentin* f. L *Valentinus*, name of two saints]

Valentines as we know them first appeared in the 18th c., and were cards with drawings and verses made by the sender. In the 19th c. shop-made valentines appeared and became increasingly elaborate, adorned with lace, real flowers, feathers, and moss; their dispatch was aided by the introduction of the penny post. Today the custom offers an opportunity for indulging in gentle or humorous sentimentality.

Valentino /ˌvælənˈtiːnəʊ/, Rudolph (1895–1926), real name Rodolfo Guglielmi di Valentino, Italian-born American film actor who in his short career held an unrivalled place in the imagination of female audiences. The dismissive description 'Latin lover' fails to convey his audacious yet fundamentally romantic sexuality in *The Sheikh* (1921) and subsequent films. At his

funeral there were scenes of mass hysteria and his death was said to be the cause of several suicides.

valerian /vəˈlɪərɪən/ *n.* **1** any of various flowering plants of the family Valerianaceae. **2** the root of any of these used as a medicinal sedative. □ **common valerian 1** a valerian, *Valeriana officinalis*, with pink or white flowers and a strong smell liked by cats: also called SETWALL. **2** the root of this used as a medicinal sedative. [ME f. OF *valeriane* f. med.L *valeriana* (*herba*), app. fem. of *Valerianus* of Valerius]

valeric acid /vəˈlerɪk, -ˈlɪərɪk/ *n.* Chem. = PENTANOIC ACID. [VALERIAN + -IC]

Valéry /ˌvæleˈriː/, Paul Ambroise (1871–1945), French poet, critic, and man of letters. His best-known poems are *La Jeune Parque* (*The Young Fate*, 1917), and *Le Cimetière marin* (1922; translated by C. Day Lewis as *The Graveyard by the Sea*, 1946). His notebooks (*Cahiers*, published posthumously) covering the years 1894 to 1945, show his preoccupation with the workings of the human mind, especially his own. Valéry wrote with great elegance on a number of subjects—literary, philosophical, and aesthetic—made lecture tours, and delivered speeches on national occasions. He had been elected to the Académie Française in 1925, and on his death he was given a State funeral.

valet /ˈvælɪt, -leɪ/ *n.* & *v.* —*n.* **1** a gentleman's personal attendant who looks after his clothes etc. **2** a hotel etc. employee with similar duties. —*v.* (**valeted**, **valeting**) **1** *intr.* work as a valet. **2** *tr.* act as a valet to. **3** *tr.* clean or clean out (a car). [F, = OF *valet*, *vaslet*, VARLET: rel. to VASSAL]

valeta var. of VELETA.

valetudinarian /ˌvælɪˌtjuːdɪˈneərɪən/ *n.* & *adj.* —*n.* a person of poor health or unduly anxious about health. —*adj.* **1** of or being a valetudinarian. **2** of poor health. **3** seeking to recover one's health. □□ **valetudinarianism** *n.* [L *valetudinarius* in ill health f. *valetudo -dinis* health f. *valēre* be well]

valetudinary /ˌvælɪˈtjuːdɪnərɪ/ *adj.* & *n.* (pl. **-ies**) = VALETUDINARIAN.

valgus /ˈvælgəs/ *n.* a deformity involving the outward displacement of the foot or hand from the midline. [L, = knock-kneed]

Valhalla /vælˈhælə/ **1** Scand. Mythol. the hall assigned to heroes who have died in battle, in which they feast with Odin. **2** a building used for honouring the illustrious. [mod.L f. ON *Valhöll* f. *valr* the slain + *höll* HALL]

valiant /ˈvæljənt/ *adj.* (of a person or conduct) brave, courageous. □□ **valiantly** *adv.* [ME f. AF *valiaunt*, OF *vaillant* ult. f. L *valēre* be strong]

valid /ˈvælɪd/ *adj.* **1** (of a reason, objection, etc.) sound or defensible; well-grounded. **2 a** executed with the proper formalities (*a valid contract*). **b** legally acceptable (*a valid passport*). **c** not having reached its expiry date. □□ **validity** /vəˈlɪdɪtɪ/ *n.* **validly** *adv.* [F *valide* or L *validus* strong (as VALIANT)]

validate /ˈvælɪˌdeɪt/ *v.tr.* make valid; ratify, confirm. □□ **validation** /-ˈdeɪʃ(ə)n/ *n.* [med.L *validare* f. L (as VALID)]

valine /ˈveɪliːn/ *n.* Biochem. an amino acid that is an essential nutrient for vertebrates and a general constituent of proteins. [VALERIC (ACID) + -INE⁴]

valise /vəˈliːz/ *n.* **1** a kitbag. **2** US a small portmanteau. [F f. It. *valigia* corresp. to med.L *valisia*, of unkn. orig.]

Valium /ˈvælɪəm/ *n.* propr. the drug diazepam used as a tranquillizer and relaxant. [20th c.: orig. uncert.]

Valkyrie /vælˈkɪərɪ, ˈvælkɪrɪ/ *n.* Scand. Mythol. each of Odin's twelve handmaidens hovering over battlefields and carrying slain warriors designated by the gods to Valhalla. [ON *Valkyrja*, lit. 'chooser of the slain' f. *valr* the slain + (unrecorded) *kur-*, *kuz-* rel. to CHOOSE]

Valladolid /ˌvælədəˈliːd/ the capital of Castilla-León region in northern Spain; pop. (1986) 341,200.

vallecula /vəˈlekjʊlə/ *n.* (pl. **valleculae** /-ˌliː/) Anat. & Bot. a groove or furrow. □□ **vallecular** *adj.* **valleculate** /-ˌleɪt/ *adj.* [LL, dimin. of L *vallis* valley]

Valle d'Aosta /ˌvæleɪ dɑːˈɒstə/ a region in the north-west corner of Italy; pop. (1981) 112,350; capital, Aosta.

Valletta /vəˈletə/ the capital and port of Malta; pop. (1987) 9,239.

valley /ˈvælɪ/ n. (pl. **-eys**) **1** a low area more or less enclosed by hills and usu. with a stream flowing through it. **2** any depression compared to this. **3** *Archit.* an internal angle formed by the intersecting planes of a roof. [ME f. AF *valey*, OF *valee* ult. f. L *vallis, valles*: cf. VALE¹]

Valley Forge the site on the Schuylkill River in Pennsylvania, about 32 km (20 miles) north-west of Philadelphia, where George Washington's Continental Army spent the bitterly cold winter of 1777–8, during the War of American Independence, in conditions of extreme hardship.

vallum /ˈvæləm/ n. *Rom. Antiq.* a rampart and stockade as a defence. [L, collect. f. *vallus* stake]

Valois¹ /ˈvælwɑː/ a medieval duchy of France; the name of the French royal family from the time of Philip VI (1328) to the death of Henry III (1589), when the throne passed to the Bourbons.

Valois² /ˈvælwɑː/, Ninette de (1898–   ), real name Edris Stannus, British dancer, choreographer, teacher, and ballet director, born in Ireland. In 1931 she opened the official ballet school of the Sadler's Wells Theatre, where her company, the Vic-Wells Ballet, appeared, later becoming the Sadler's Wells Ballet and then the Royal Ballet in 1956. As a choreographer her most successful years were the 1930s, when she created such works as *Job* (1931), *The Rake's Progress* (1935), *The Gods Go a-Begging* (1936), and *Checkmate* (1937).

Valona see VLORË.

valonia /vəˈləʊnɪə/ n. acorn-cups of an evergreen oak, *Quercus macrolepsis*, used in tanning, dyeing, and making ink. [It. *vallonia* ult. f. Gk *balanos* acorn]

valor US var. of VALOUR.

valorize /ˈvæləˌraɪz/ v.tr. (also **-ise**) raise or fix the price of (a commodity etc.) by artificial means, esp. by government action. □□ **valorization** /-ˈzeɪʃ(ə)n/ n. [back-form. f. *valorization* f. F *valorisation* (as VALOUR)]

valour /ˈvælə(r)/ n. (US **valor**) personal courage, esp. in battle. □□ **valorous** adj. [ME f. OF f. LL *valor -oris* f. *valēre* be strong]

Valparaiso /ˌvælpəˈraɪzəʊ/ the principal port of Chile and terminus of the trans-Andean railway; pop. 1987) 278,800.

valse /vɑːls, vɔːls/ n. a waltz. [F f. G (as WALTZ)]

valuable /ˈvæljʊəb(ə)l/ adj. & n. —adj. of great value, price, or worth (*a valuable property; valuable information*). —n. (usu. in pl.) a valuable thing, esp. a small article of personal property. □□ **valuably** adv.

valuation /ˌvæljʊˈeɪʃ(ə)n/ n. **1 a** an estimation (esp. by a professional valuer) of a thing's worth. **b** the worth estimated. **2** the price set on a thing. □□ **valuate** /ˈvæ-/ v.tr. esp. US.

valuator /ˈvæljʊˌeɪtə(r)/ n. a person who makes valuations; a valuer.

value /ˈvæljuː/ n. & v. —n. **1** the worth, desirability, or utility of a thing, or the qualities on which these depend (*the value of regular exercise*). **2** worth as estimated; valuation (*set a high value on my time*). **3** the amount of money or goods for which a thing can be exchanged in the open market; purchasing power. **4** the equivalent of a thing; what represents or is represented by or may be substituted for a thing (*paid them the value of their lost property*). **5** (in full **value for money**) something well worth the money spent. **6** the ability of a thing to serve a purpose or cause an effect (*news value; nuisance value*). **7** (in pl.) one's principles or standards; one's judgement of what is valuable or important in life. **8** *Mus.* the duration of the sound signified by a note. **9** *Math.* the amount denoted by an algebraic term or expression. **10** (foll. by *of*) **a** the meaning (of a word etc.). **b** the quality (of a spoken sound). **11** the relative rank or importance of a playing-card, chess-piece, etc., according to the rules of the game. **12** the relation of one part of a picture to others in respect of light and shade; the part being characterized by a particular tone. **13** *Physics & Chem.* the numerical measure of a quantity or a number denoting magnitude on some conventional scale (*the value of gravity at the equator*). —v.tr. (**values, valued, valuing**) **1** estimate the value of; appraise (esp. professionally) (*valued the property at £200,000*). **2** have a high or specified opinion of; attach importance to (*a valued friend*). □ **value added tax** a tax on the amount

by which the value of an article has been increased at each stage of its production, introduced into the UK in 1973 to conform with other EEC countries. **value judgement** a subjective estimate of quality etc. **value received** money or its equivalent given for a bill of exchange. [ME f. OF, fem. past part. of *valoir* be worth f. L *valēre*]

valueless /ˈvæljʊlɪs/ adj. having no value. □□ **valuelessness** n.

valuer /ˈvæljʊə(r)/ n. a person who estimates or assesses values, esp. professionally.

valuta /vəˈljuːtə/ n. **1** the value of one currency with respect to another. **2** a currency considered in this way. [It., = VALUE]

valve /vælv/ n. **1** a device for controlling the passage of fluid through a pipe etc., esp. an automatic device allowing movement in one direction only. **2** *Anat. & Zool.* a membranous part of an organ etc. allowing a flow of blood etc. in one direction only. **3** *Brit.* = *thermionic valve*. **4** a device to vary the effective length of the tube in a brass musical instrument. **5** each of the two shells of an oyster, mussel, etc. **6** *Bot.* each of the segments into which a capsule or dry fruit dehisces. **7** *archaic* a leaf of a folding door. □□ **valvate** /-veɪt/ adj. **valved** adj. (also in comb.). **valveless** adj. **valvule** n. [ME f. L *valva* leaf of a folding door]

valvular /ˈvælvjʊlə(r)/ adj. **1** having a valve or valves. **2** having the form or function of a valve. [mod.L *valvula*, dimin. of L *valva*]

valvulitis /ˌvælvjʊˈlaɪtɪs/ n. inflammation of the valves of the heart.

vambrace /ˈvæmbreɪs/ n. *hist.* defensive armour for the forearm. [ME f. AF *vaunt-bras*, OF *avant-bras* f. *avant* before (see AVAUNT) + *bras* arm]

vamoose /vəˈmuːs/ v.intr. US (esp. as *int.*) *sl.* depart hurriedly. [Sp. *vamos* let us go]

vamp¹ /væmp/ n. & v. —n. **1** the upper front part of a boot or shoe. **2** a patched-up article. **3** an improvised musical accompaniment. —v. **1** tr. (often foll. by *up*) repair or furbish. **2** tr. (foll. by *up*) make by patching or from odds and ends. **3 a** tr. & intr. improvise a musical accompaniment (to). **b** tr. improvise (a musical accompaniment). **4** tr. put a new vamp to (a boot or shoe). [ME f. OF *avantpié* f. *avant* before (see AVAUNT) + *pied* foot]

vamp² /væmp/ n. & v. *colloq.* —n. **1** an unscrupulous flirt. **2** a woman who uses sexual attraction to exploit men. —v. **1** tr. allure or exploit (a man). **2** intr. act as a vamp. [abbr. of VAMPIRE]

vampire /ˈvæmpaɪə(r)/ n. **1** a ghost or reanimated corpse supposed to leave its grave at night to suck the blood of persons sleeping. (See below.) **2** a person who preys ruthlessly on others. **3** (in full **vampire bat**) any tropical (esp. South American) bat of the family Desmodontidae, with incisors for (actually or supposedly) piercing flesh and feeding on blood. **4** *Theatr.* a small spring trapdoor used for sudden disappearances. □□ **vampiric** /-ˈpɪrɪk/ adj. [F *vampire* or G *Vampir* f. Magyar *vampir* perh. f. Turk. *uber* witch]

The vampire legend is widespread in Europe and Asia but is particularly associated with the folklore of eastern Europe, and its continual popularity in the 20th c. is largely due to the success of Bram Stoker's novel *Dracula* (1897). A number of superstitions have arisen: that vampires cast no shadow, are not reflected in mirrors, attack only at night, and can be warded off by garlic or by a crucifix; that the body of a vampire can be destroyed by being beheaded or burnt, or by a stake being driven through its heart.

vampirism /ˈvæmpaɪəˌrɪz(ə)m/ n. **1** belief in the existence of vampires. **2** the practices of a vampire.

vamplate /ˈvæmpleɪt/ n. *hist.* an iron plate on a lance protecting the hand when the lance was couched. [ME f. AF *vauntplate* (as VAMBRACE, PLATE)]

Van /væn/, Lake the largest lake in Turkey, situated in the mountains of eastern Anatolia.

van¹ /væn/ n. **1** a covered vehicle for conveying goods etc. **2** *Brit.* a railway carriage for luggage or for the use of the guard. **3** *Brit.* a gypsy caravan. [abbr. of CARAVAN]

van² /væn/ n. **1** a vanguard. **2** the forefront (*in the van of progress*). [abbr. of VANGUARD]

van³ /væn/ n. **1** the testing of ore quality by washing on a shovel or by machine. **2** *archaic* a winnowing fan. **3** *archaic* or *poet.* a wing. [ME, southern & western var. of FAN¹, perh. partly f. OF *van* or L *vannus*]

van⁴ /væn/ *n. Brit. Tennis colloq.* = ADVANTAGE. [abbr.]

vanadium /vəˈneɪdɪəm/ *n. Chem.* a hard grey metallic transition element, discovered in 1801 and first isolated in 1867. It is not found in the uncombined state in nature. The main use of the metal is in certain steels, where it improves strength and hardness. Its compounds are widely employed as catalysts and in the ceramic and glass industries. ¶ Symb.: **V**; atomic number 23. □□ **vanadate** /ˈvænəˌdeɪt/ *n.* **vanadic** /-ˈnædɪk/ *adj.* **vanadous** /ˈvænədəs/ *adj.* [mod.L f. ON *Vanadís* name of the Scand. goddess Freyja + -IUM]

Van Allen belt /væn ˈælən/ *n.* (also **Van Allen layer**) each of two regions of intense radiation partly surrounding the earth at heights of several thousand kilometres. [J. A. *Van Allen*, US physicist b. 1914]

Vanbrugh /ˈvænbrə/, Sir John (1664–1726), English architect, one of the chief exponents of the baroque in England. In early life he was a soldier and a playwright, author of two famous comedies *The Relapse* or *Virtue in Danger* and *The Provok'd Wife* (1697), but from 1699 became known chiefly as an architect. His masterpieces were Seaton Delaval Hall in Northumberland and (produced in collaboration with Hawksmoor) Castle Howard in Yorkshire and Blenheim Palace in Oxfordshire.

Van Buren /væn ˈbjʊərən/, Martin (1782–1862), 8th President of the US, 1837–41.

Vancouver¹ /vænˈkuːvə(r)/, George (1757–98), English explorer who commanded a naval expedition exploring the coasts of Australia, New Zealand, and Hawaii in 1791–2, and then went on to circumnavigate Vancouver Island, which is named after him, and chart the west coast of North America (1792–4).

Vancouver² /vænˈkuːvə(r)/ a city and seaport of British Columbia, Canada; pop. (1986) 431,150; metropolitan area pop. 1,380,700. □ **Vancouver Island** a large island off the Pacific coast of Canada, opposite Vancouver.

Vanda see VANTAA.

V. & A. *abbr.* Victoria & Albert Museum (in London).

vandal /ˈvænd(ə)l/ *n. & adj.* —*n.* **1** a person who wilfully or maliciously destroys or damages property. **2 (Vandal)** a member of a Germanic people that overran part of Roman Europe in the 4th–5th c., establishing kingdoms in Gaul and Spain, and finally (428–9) migrated to North Africa. They sacked Rome in 455 in a marauding expedition, but were eventually defeated by the Byzantine general Belisarius, after which their North African kingdom fell prey to Muslim invaders. —*adj.* of or relating to the Vandals. □□ **Vandalic** /-ˈdælɪk/ *adj.* (in sense 2 of *n.*). [L *Vandalus* f. Gmc]

vandalism /ˈvændəˌlɪz(ə)m/ *n.* wilful or malicious destruction or damage to works of art or other property. □□ **vandalistic** /-ˈlɪstɪk/ *adj.* **vandalistically** /-ˈlɪstɪkəlɪ/ *adv.*

vandalize /ˈvændəˌlaɪz/ *v.tr.* (also **-ise**) destroy or damage wilfully or maliciously.

van de Graaff generator /væn də ˈɡrɑːf/ *n. Electr.* a machine devised to generate electrostatic charge by means of a vertical endless belt collecting charge from a voltage source and transferring it to a large insulated metal dome, where a high voltage is produced. [R. J. *van de Graaff*, US physicist d. 1967]

Vanderbilt /ˈvændəˌbɪlt/, Cornelius (1794–1877), American shipping and railway magnate. From his vast fortune he made an endowment to found Vanderbilt University in Nashville, Tennessee (1873).

van der Waals forces /væn də ˈwɑːlz/ *n.pl. Chem.* short-range attractive forces between uncharged molecules arising from the interaction of dipole moments. [J. *van der Waals*, Dutch physicist d. 1923]

Van de Velde see VELDE.

Van Diemen's Land /væn ˈdiːmənz/ the former name of Tasmania (see entry). Its name commemorates Anthony van Diemen (1593–1645), Dutch governor of Java, who sent Tasman on his voyage.

Van Dyck /væn ˈdaɪk/, Sir Anthony (1599–1641), Flemish painter. From 1618–20 he worked in Rubens's workshop, rapidly becoming his most brilliant assistant. In 1621–8 he was in Italy where he studied Titian and the Venetians. The portraits he produced at Genoa marked the onset of his artistic maturity in their acute characterization, superlative brushwork, and shimmering colour. In 1628–32 he worked in Antwerp, at the height of his powers, and was then invited to England by Charles I, who knighted him. His subsequent portraits of the Caroline court determined the course of portraiture in England for over 200 years with their sensitivity and refinement of style, glittering surface, and elegant composition.

vandyke /vænˈdaɪk/ *n. & adj.* —*n.* **1** each of a series of large points forming a border to lace or cloth etc. **2** a cape or collar etc. with these. —*adj.* **(Vandyke)** in the style of dress, esp. with pointed borders, common in portraits by Van Dyck. □ **Vandyke beard** a neat pointed beard. **Vandyke brown** a deep rich brown. [Sir A. VAN DYCK, Anglicized *Vandyke*]

vane /veɪn/ *n.* **1** (in full **weather-vane**) a revolving pointer mounted on a church spire or other high place to show the direction of the wind (cf. WEATHERCOCK). **2** a blade of a screw propeller or a windmill etc. **3** the sight of surveying instruments, a quadrant, etc. **4** the flat part of a bird's feather formed by the barbs. □□ **vaned** *adj.* **vaneless** *adj.* [ME, southern & western var. of obs. *fane* f. OE *fana* banner f. Gmc]

Vänern /ˈvenən/ the largest lake in Sweden and the third-largest in Europe.

vanessa /vəˈnesə/ *n.* any butterfly of the genus *Vanessa*, including the red admiral and the painted lady. [mod.L]

Van Eyck /væn ˈaɪk/, Jan (died 1441), Flemish painter. Vasari attributes to him the invention of oil painting, and though it is known that oils were used as a medium in the Middle Ages long before his time there is no doubt that he made an innovative contribution to the technique of their use, bringing greater flexibility, richer and denser colour, and a wider range from light to dark. His most famous works, the Ghent altarpiece and the portrait *Arnolfini and his Wife* (1434), justify his contemporary fame with their superb control of oil paint, clarity of exposition, and representational skill. His brother Hubert (d. 1426) remains a shadowy figure but may have collaborated on the Ghent altarpiece.

vang /væŋ/ *n. Naut.* each of two guy-ropes running from the end of a gaff to the deck. [earlier *fang* = gripping-device: OE f. ON *fang* grasp f. Gmc]

Van Gogh /væn ɡɒf/, Vincent Willem (1853–90), Dutch postimpressionist painter, who lived as art dealer, lay preacher, and tramp before deciding to become an artist in 1881. After a period of study at Antwerp, where his humanitarian ideals were reflected in paintings of peasants such as *The Potato Eaters*, he moved to Paris in 1886, coming under the influence of the impressionists and of Japanese woodcuts. Rejecting the optical realism of the impressionists he began to use colours for their expressive or symbolic values, and abandoned the delicate manner of the pointillists for broad, vigorous, swirling brushstrokes. In 1888 he settled at Arles, where he produced many paintings but suffered poverty, depression, and hallucinations. There he was joined by Gauguin, but they quarrelled, precipitating a crisis in which Van Gogh cut off his own ear; he subsequently spent a year in an asylum near by, where he painted *Starry Night*. His prodigious activity continued—he painted 70 canvases in the last 70 days of his life—but his acute depression culminated in his suicide. His letters to his brother Theo, of which more than 750 are extant, provide abundant information about his aesthetic aims and mental disturbances.

vanguard /ˈvænɡɑːd/ *n.* **1** the foremost part of an army or fleet advancing or ready to advance. **2** the leaders of a movement or of opinion etc. [earlier *vandgard, (a)vantgard*, f. OF *avan(t)garde* f. *avant* before (see AVAUNT) + *garde* GUARD]

vanilla /vəˈnɪlə/ *n.* **1 a** any tropical climbing orchid of the genus *Vanilla*, esp. *V. planifolia*, with fragrant flowers. **b** (in full **vanilla-pod**) the fruit of these. **2** a substance obtained from the vanilla-pod or synthesized and used to flavour ice-cream, chocolate, etc. [Sp. *vanilla* pod, dimin. of *vaina* sheath, pod, f. L VAGINA]

vanillin /vəˈnɪlɪn/ *n.* the fragrant principle of vanilla.

vanish /ˈvænɪʃ/ *v.* **1** *intr.* **a** disappear suddenly. **b** disappear gradually; fade away. **2** *intr.* cease to exist. **3** *intr. Math.* become zero. **4** *tr.* cause to disappear. □ **vanishing cream** an ointment that leaves no visible trace when rubbed into the skin. **vanishing-point 1** the point at which receding parallel lines viewed in perspective appear to meet. **2** the state of complete disappearance of something. [ME f. OF *e(s)vaniss-* stem of *e(s)vanir* ult. f. L *evanescere* (as EX-1, *vanus* empty)]

Vanitory /ˈvænɪtərɪ/ *n.* (*pl.* **-ies**) *propr.* = vanity unit.

vanity /ˈvænɪtɪ/ *n.* (*pl.* **-ies**) **1** conceit and desire for admiration of one's personal attainments or attractions. **2 a** futility or unsubstantiality (*the vanity of human achievement*). **b** an unreal thing. **3** ostentatious display. **4** *US* a dressing-table. □ **vanity bag** (or **case**) a bag or case carried by a woman and containing a small mirror, make-up, etc. **Vanity Fair** the world (allegorized in Bunyan's *Pilgrim's Progress*) as a scene of vanity. **vanity unit** a unit consisting of a wash-basin set into a flat top with cupboards beneath. [ME f. OF *vanité* f. L *vanitas -tatis* (as VAIN)]

vanquish /ˈvæŋkwɪʃ/ *v.tr.* literary conquer or overcome. □□ **vanquishable** *adj.* **vanquisher** *n.* [ME *venkus, -quis*, etc., f. OF *vencus* past part. and *venquis* past tenses of *veintre* f. L *vincere*: assim. to -ISH²]

Vantaa /ˈvæntɑː/ (Swedish **Vanda**) a suburb of Helsinki, established as a separate city in 1972; pop. (1987) 149,063.

vantage /ˈvɑːntɪdʒ/ *n.* **1** (also **vantage point** or **ground**) a place affording a good view or prospect. **2** *Tennis* = ADVANTAGE. **3** *archaic* an advantage or gain. [ME f. AF f. OF *avantage* ADVANTAGE]

Vanuatu /ˌvænwɑːˈtuː/ a country consisting of a group of islands in the SW Pacific; pop. (est. 1980) 154,700; official languages, English and French; capital, Vila. Discovered by the Portuguese in the early 17th c., the islands were administered jointly by Britain and France as the condominium of the New Hebrides. They became an independent republic within the Commonwealth in 1980.

vapid /ˈvæpɪd/ *adj.* insipid; lacking interest; flat, dull (*vapid moralizing*). □□ **vapidity** /vəˈpɪdɪtɪ/ *n.* **vapidly** *adv.* **vapidness** *n.* [L *vapidus*]

vapor *US* var. of VAPOUR.

vaporific /ˌveɪpəˈrɪfɪk/ *adj.* concerned with or causing vapour or vaporization.

vaporimeter /ˌveɪpəˈrɪmɪtə(r)/ *n.* an instrument for measuring the amount of vapour.

vaporize /ˈveɪpəˌraɪz/ *v.tr. & intr.* (also **-ise**) convert or be converted into vapour. □□ **vaporizable** *adj.* (also **vaporable**). **vaporization** /-ˈzeɪʃ(ə)n/ *n.*

vaporizer /ˈveɪpəˌraɪzə(r)/ *n.* a device that vaporizes substances, esp. for medicinal inhalation.

vapour /ˈveɪpə(r)/ *n. & v.* (*US* **vapor**) —*n.* **1** moisture or another substance diffused or suspended in air, e.g. mist or smoke. **2** *Physics* a gaseous form of a normally liquid or solid substance (cf. GAS). **3** a medicinal agent for inhaling. **4** (in *pl.*) *archaic* a state of depression or melancholy thought to be caused by exhalations of vapour from the stomach. —*v.intr.* **1** rise as vapour. **2** make idle boasts or empty talk. □ **vapour density** the density of a gas or vapour relative to hydrogen etc. **vapour pressure** the pressure of a vapour in contact with its liquid or solid form. **vapour trail** a trail of condensed water from an aircraft or rocket at high altitude, seen as a white streak against the sky. □□ **vaporous** *adj.* **vaporously** *adv.* **vaporousness** *n.* **vapourer** *n.* **vapouring** *n.* **vapourish** *adj.* **vapoury** *adj.* [ME f. OF *vapour* or L *vapor* steam, heat]

var. *abbr.* **1** variant. **2** variety.

varactor /vəˈræktə(r)/ *n.* a semiconductor diode with a capacitance dependent on the applied voltage. [*varying* re*actor*]

Varah /ˈvɑːrə/, (Edward) Chad (1911–), English clergyman, founder of The Samaritans (see entry).

Varanasi /vəˈrɑːnəsɪ/ (formerly **Benares** /bɪˈnɑːrɪz/) a Hindu holy city on the Ganges in the State of Uttar Pradesh, India; pop.

(1981) 794,000. Said to contain 1,500 temples and shrines, it is a place of pilgrimage for devout Hindus, who undergo ritual purification in the river.

Varangian /vəˈrændʒɪən/ *n. & adj.* —*n.* a Norse rover, especially one of those who penetrated into Russia in the 9th–10th c. —*adj.* of the Varangians. [med. L *Varangus*, ult. f. ON, = confederate]

varec /ˈværek/ *n.* **1** seaweed. **2** = KELP. [F *varec(h)* f. ON: rel. to WRECK]

Varèse /ˈvɑːrez/, Edgard (1883–1965), French-born composer. He emigrated to the US in 1915, and it is the works performed in his adopted country that are known today, virtually all others being lost. His music employed traditional forces until the 1950s, when he began to experiment with tape-recordings and electronic instruments.

variable /ˈveərɪəb(ə)l/ *adj. & n.* —*adj.* **1 a** that can be varied or adapted (*a rod of variable length; the pressure is variable*). **b** (of a gear) designed to give varying speeds. **2** apt to vary; not constant; unsteady (*a variable mood; variable fortunes*). **3** *Math.* (of a quantity) indeterminate; able to assume different numerical values. **4** (of wind or currents) tending to change direction. **5** *Bot. & Zool.* (of a species) including individuals or groups that depart from the type. **6** *Biol.* (of an organism or part of it) tending to change in structure or function. —*n.* **1** a variable thing or quantity. **2** *Math.* a variable quantity. **3** *Naut.* **a** a shifting wind. **b** (in *pl.*) the region between the NE and SE trade winds. □ **variable star** any star whose brightness changes, either irregularly because of unpredictable changes in the physical state of the star, or regularly. Irregular variables include those which undergo a single outburst, such as novae or supernovae. Periodic variables show regular changes in light intensity either because of eclipses by binary companions or because of regular changes within the stellar interior, as in the case of Cepheid variables. The period of variability may range from a few hours to several years. □□ **variability** /-ˈbɪlɪtɪ/ *n.* **variableness** *n.* **variably** *adv.* [ME f. OF f. L *variabilis* (as VARY)]

variance /ˈveərɪəns/ *n.* **1** difference of opinion; dispute, disagreement; lack of harmony (*at variance among ourselves; a theory at variance with all known facts*). **2** *Law* a discrepancy between statements or documents. **3** *Statistics* a quantity equal to the square of the standard deviation. [ME f. OF f. L *variantia* difference (as VARY)]

variant /ˈveərɪənt/ *adj. & n.* —*adj.* **1** differing in form or details from the main one (*a variant spelling*). **2** having different forms (*forty variant types of pigeon*). **3** variable or changing. —*n.* a variant form, spelling, type, reading, etc. [ME f. OF (as VARY)]

variate /ˈveərɪət/ *n. Statistics* **1** a quantity having a numerical value for each member of a group. **2** a variable quantity, esp. one whose values occur according to a frequency distribution. [past part. of L *variare* (as VARY)]

variation /ˌveərɪˈeɪʃ(ə)n/ *n.* **1** the act or an instance of varying. **2** departure from a former or normal condition, action, or amount, or from a standard or type (*prices are subject to variation*). **3** the extent of this. **4** a thing that varies from a type. **5** *Mus.* a repetition (usu. one of several) of a theme in a changed or elaborated form. **6** *Astron.* a deviation of a heavenly body from its mean orbit or motion. **7** *Math.* a change in a function etc. due to small changes in the values of constants etc. **8** *Ballet* a solo dance. □□ **variational** *adj.* [ME f. OF *variation* or L *variatio* (as VARY)]

varicella /ˌværɪˈselə/ *n. Med.* = CHICKENPOX. [mod.L, irreg. dimin. of VARIOLA]

varices *pl.* of VARIX.

varicocele /ˈværɪkəˌsiːl/ *n.* a mass of varicose veins in the spermatic cord. [formed as VARIX + -CELE]

varicoloured /ˈveərɪˌkʌləd/ *adj.* (*US* **varicolored**) **1** variegated in colour. **2** of various or different colours. [L *varius* VARIOUS + COLOURED]

varicose /ˈværɪˌkəʊs/ *adj.* (esp. of the veins of the legs) affected by a condition causing them to become dilated and swollen. □□ **varicosity** /-ˈkɒsɪtɪ/ *n.* [L *varicosus* f. VARIX]

varied /ˈveərɪd/ *adj.* showing variety; diverse. □□ **variedly** *adv.*

variegate /ˈveərɪˌɡeɪt, -rɪəˌɡeɪt/ *v.tr.* **1** mark with irregular patches of different colours. **2** diversify in appearance, esp. in colour. **3** (as **variegated** adj.) Bot. (of plants) having leaves containing two or more colours. □□ **variegation** /-'geɪʃ(ə)n/ n. [L variegare variegat- f. varius various]

varietal /və'raɪət(ə)l/ adj. **1** esp. Bot. & Zool. of, forming, or designating a variety. **2** (of wine) made from a single designated variety of grape. □□ **varietally** adv.

varietist /və'raɪətɪst/ n. a person whose habits etc. differ from what is normal.

variety /və'raɪətɪ/ n. (pl. -ies) **1** diversity; absence of uniformity; many-sidedness; the condition of being various (not enough variety in our lives). **2** a quantity or collection of different things (for a variety of reasons). **3 a** a class of things different in some common qualities from the rest of a larger class to which they belong. **b** a specimen or member of such a class. **4** (foll. by of) a different form of a thing, quality, etc. **5** Biol. **a** a subspecies. **b** a cultivar. **c** an individual or group usually fertile within the species to which it belongs but differing from the species type in some qualities capable of perpetuation. **6** a mixed sequence of dances, songs, comedy acts, etc. (usu. attrib.: a variety show). □ **variety store** US a shop selling many kinds of small items. [F variété or L varietas (as VARIOUS)]

varifocal /ˌveərɪ'fəʊk(ə)l/ adj. & n. —adj. having a focal length that can be varied, esp. of a lens that allows an infinite number of focusing distances for near, intermediate, and far vision. —n. (in pl.) varifocal spectacles.

variform /'veərɪfɔːm/ adj. having various forms. [L varius + -FORM]

variola /və'raɪələ/ n. Med. smallpox. □□ **variolar** adj. **varioloid** /'veərɪəˌlɔɪd/ adj. **variolous** adj. [med.L, = pustule, pock (as VARIOUS)]

variole /'veərɪˌəʊl/ n. **1** a shallow pit like a smallpox mark. **2** a small spherical mass in variolite. [med.L variola: see VARIOLA]

variolite /'veərɪəˌlaɪt/ n. a rock with embedded small spherical masses causing on its surface an appearance like smallpox pustules. □□ **variolitic** /-'lɪtɪk/ adj. [as VARIOLE + -ITE[1]]

variometer /ˌveərɪ'ɒmɪtə(r)/ n. **1** a device for varying the inductance in an electric circuit. **2** a device for indicating an aircraft's rate of change of altitude. [as VARIOUS + -METER]

variorum /ˌveərɪ'ɔːrəm/ adj. & n. —adj. **1** (of an edition of a text) having notes by various editors or commentators. **2** (of an edition of an author's works) including variant readings. —n. a variorum edition. [L f. editio cum notis variorum edition with notes by various (commentators): genit. pl. of varius VARIOUS)]

various /'veərɪəs/ adj. **1** different, diverse (too various to form a group). **2** more than one, several (for various reasons). □□ **variously** adv. **variousness** n. [L varius changing, diverse]

varistor /və'rɪstə(r)/ n. a semiconductor diode with resistance dependent on the applied voltage. [varying resistor]

varix /'veərɪks/ n. (pl. **varices** /'værɪˌsiːz/) **1** Med. **a** a permanent abnormal dilation of a vein or artery. **b** a vein etc. dilated in this way. **2** each of the ridges about the whorls of a univalve shell. [ME f. L varix -icis]

varlet /'vɑːlɪt/ n. archaic or joc. **1** a menial or rascal. **2** hist. a knight's attendant. □□ **varletry** n. [ME f. OF, var. of vaslet: see VALET]

varmint /'vɑːmɪnt/ n. US or dial. a mischievous or discreditable person or animal, esp. a fox. [var. of varmin, VERMIN]

Varna /'vɑːnə/ a port and resort of Bulgaria, on the coast of the Black Sea; pop. (1987) 305,900.

varna /'vɑːnə/ n. any of the four great Hindu classes. In Vedic religion, the first three classes of Aryan society were Brahmin, Kshatriya, and Vaisya. The fourth class, Sudra, was probably recruited later from the indigenous people of India. Each class was considered equally necessary to the social order, the separate functions being complementary. In modern India, varna has largely given way to the more specific requirements of caste and sub-caste. [Skr., = colour, class]

varnish /'vɑːnɪʃ/ n. & v. —n. **1** a resinous solution used to give a hard shiny transparent coating to wood, metal, paintings, etc. **2** any other preparation for a similar purpose (nail varnish). **3** external appearance or display without an underlying reality. **4** artificial or natural glossiness. **5** a superficial polish of manner. —v.tr. **1** apply varnish to. **2** gloss over (a fact). □□ **varnisher** n. [ME f. OF vernis f. med.L veronix fragrant resin, sandarac or med.Gk bereníkē prob. f. Berenice in Cyrenaica]

Varro /'værəʊ/, Marcus Terentius (116–27 BC), Roman scholar and encyclopedist. Of his voluminous works, which covered almost every branch of ancient knowledge and were a mine of information for later pagan and Christian authors, there survive (apart from fragments) only a work on agriculture and part of a work on the Latin language. He was also the author of literary satires and dialogues.

varsity /'vɑːsɪtɪ/ n. (pl. -ies) **1** Brit. colloq. (esp. with ref. to sports) university. **2** US a university etc. first team in a sport. [abbr.]

Varuna /'vʌrʊnə/ Hinduism one of the oldest of the gods in the Rig-Veda. Originally the sovereign lord of the universe and guardian of cosmic law, he is known in later Hinduism as god of the waters.

varus /'veərəs/ n. a deformity involving the inward displacement of the foot or hand from the midline. [L, = bent, crooked]

varve /vɑːv/ n. a pair of layers of silt deposited in lakes where a glacier melts, one being of fine silt (deposited in winter, when there is little melting) and one of coarser silt (deposited in summer, when the ice melts more freely), used to determine the chronology of glacial sediments. □□ **varved** adj. [Sw. varv layer]

vary /'veərɪ/ v. (-ies, -ied) **1** tr. make different; modify, diversify (seldom varies the routine; the style is not sufficiently varied). **2** intr. **a** undergo change; become or be different (the temperature varies from 30° to 70°). **b** be of different kinds (his mood varies). **3** intr. (foll. by as) be in proportion to. □□ **varyingly** adv. [ME f. OF varier or L variare (as VARIOUS)]

vas /væs/ n. (pl. **vasa** /'veɪsə/) Anat. a vessel or duct. □ **vas deferens** /'defəˌrenz/ (pl. **vasa deferentia** /ˌdefə'renʃɪə/) Anat. the spermatic duct from the testicle to the urethra. □□ **vasal** /'veɪs(ə)l/ adj. [L, = vessel]

Vasari /və'sɑːrɪ/, Giorgio (1511–74), Italian painter, architect, and biographer whose pioneering Lives of the Most Excellent Painters, Sculptors and Architects (1550, enlarged 1568) remains influential today and the starting-point for the study of Renaissance art, tracing the rise of Renaissance naturalism and humanism from the experiments of Cimabue and Giotto to the sophisticated styles of the 16th c.; he celebrated the art of Leonardo, Raphael, and particularly Michelangelo, whom he knew and admired, as the pinnacle of achievement. His own considerable achievements as painter and architect have sometimes been overshadowed by his importance as 'the first art historian worthy of the title'. His painting style can be classified as mannerist, and his major works are the vast frescoes, depicting the history of Florence and the Medici, in the Palazzo Vecchio in Florence, and those in the Sala Regia in the Vatican. Vasari was the architect of the Uffizi Palace in Florence and designed the tomb of Michelangelo in Sta Croce.

Vasco da Gama see GAMA.

vascular /'væskjʊlə(r)/ adj. of, made up of, or containing vessels for conveying blood or sap etc. (vascular functions; vascular tissue). □ **vascular plant** a plant with conducting tissue. □□ **vascularity** /-'lærɪtɪ/ n. **vascularize** v.tr. (also -ise). **vascularly** adv. [mod.L vascularis f. L VASCULUM]

vasculum /'væskjʊləm/ n. (pl. **vascula** /-lə/) a botanist's (usu. metal) collecting-case with a lengthwise opening. [L, dimin. of VAS]

vase /vɑːz/ n. a vessel, usu. tall and circular, used as an ornament or container, esp. for flowers. □□ **vaseful** n. (pl. -fuls). [F f. L VAS]

vasectomy /və'sektəmɪ/ n. (pl. -ies) the surgical removal of part of each vas deferens esp. as a means of sterilization. □□ **vasectomize** v.tr. (also -ise).

Vaseline /'væsɪˌliːn/ n. & v. —n. propr. a type of petroleum jelly used as an ointment, lubricant, etc. —v.tr. (**vaseline**) treat with Vaseline. [irreg. f. G Wasser + Gk elaion oil]

vasiform /ˈveɪzɪˌfɔːm/ adj. **1** duct-shaped. **2** vase-shaped. [L vasif. VAS + -FORM]

vaso- /ˈveɪzəʊ/ comb. form a vessel, esp. a blood-vessel (vasoconstrictive). [L vas: see VAS]

vasoactive /ˌveɪzəʊˈæktɪv/ adj. = VASOMOTOR.

vasoconstrictive /ˌveɪzəʊkənˈstrɪktɪv/ adj. causing constriction of blood-vessels.

vasodilating /ˌveɪzəʊdaɪˈleɪtɪŋ/ adj. causing dilatation of blood-vessels. □□ **vasodilation** n.

vasomotor /ˈveɪzəʊˌməʊtə(r)/ adj. causing constriction or dilatation of blood-vessels.

vasopressin /ˌveɪzəʊˈpresɪn/ n. a pituitary hormone acting to reduce diuresis and increase blood pressure. Also called ANTIDIURETIC HORMONE.

vassal /ˈvæs(ə)l/ n. **1** hist. a holder of land by feudal tenure on conditions of homage and allegiance. **2** rhet. a humble dependant. □□ **vassalage** n. [ME f. OF f. med.L vassallus retainer, of Celt. orig.: the root vassus corresp. to OBret. uuas, Welsh gwas, Ir. foss: cf. VAVASOUR]

vast /vɑːst/ adj. & n. —adj. **1** immense, huge; very great (a vast expanse of water; a vast crowd). **2** colloq. great, considerable (makes a vast difference). —n. poet. or rhet. a vast space (the vast of heaven). □□ **vastly** adv. **vastness** n. [L vastus void, immense]

Västerås /ˈvɑːstərɔːs/ a port on Lake Mälaren in eastern Sweden; pop. (1987) 117,500.

VAT /ˌviːeɪˈtiː, væt/ abbr. (in the UK) value added tax.

vat /væt/ n. & v. —n. **1** a large tank or other vessel, esp. for holding liquids or something in liquid in the process of brewing, tanning, dyeing, etc. **2** a dyeing liquor in which a textile is soaked to take up a colourless soluble dye afterwards coloured by oxidation in air. —v.tr. (**vatted**, **vatting**) place or treat in a vat. □□ **vatful** n. (pl. **-fuls**). [ME, southern & western var. of fat, OE fæt f. Gmc]

vatic /ˈvætɪk/ adj. formal prophetic or inspired. [L vates prophet]

Vatican /ˈvætɪkən/ n. **1** the palace and official residence of the Pope in Rome. **2** papal government. □ **Vatican Council** an ecumenical council of the Roman Catholic Church, esp. that held in 1869–70, proclaiming the infallibility of the pope when speaking ex cathedra, or that held in 1962–5. □□ **Vaticanism** n. **Vaticanist** n. [F Vatican or L Vaticanus name of a hill in Rome]

Vatican City an independent papal State in Rome, the seat of government of the Roman Catholic Church; pop. (est. 1988) 750. The former papal States became incorporated into a unified Italy in 1870, and the temporal power of the pope was in suspense until the Lateran Treaty of 1929, signed between Pope Pius XI and Mussolini, which recognized the full and independent sovereignty of the Holy See in the City of the Vatican. It covers an area of 44 hectares (109 acres), and has its own police force, diplomatic service, postal service, coinage, and radio station.

vaticinate /vəˈtɪsɪˌneɪt/ v.tr. & intr. formal prophesy. □□ **vaticinal** adj. **vaticination** /-ˈneɪʃ(ə)n/ n. **vaticinator** n. [L vaticinari f. vates prophet]

VATman /ˈvætmæn/ n. (pl. **-men**) colloq. a customs and excise officer who administers VAT.

Vättern /ˈvet(ə)n/ the second-largest lake in Sweden.

vaudeville /ˈvɔːdəvɪl, ˈvəʊ-/ n. **1** esp. US variety entertainment popular from about 1880 to 1932, by which time films and radio had driven it into decline. **2** a stage play on a trivial theme with interspersed songs. **3** a satirical or topical song with a refrain. □□ **vaudevillian** /-ˈvɪlɪən/ adj. & n. [F, orig. of convivial song esp. any of those composed by O. Basselin, 15th-c. poet born at Vau de Vire in Normandy]

Vaudois[1] /ˈvəʊdwɑː/ n. & adj. —n. (pl. same) **1** a native of Vaud in W. Switzerland. **2** the French dialect spoken in Vaud. —adj. of or relating to Vaud or its dialect. [F]

Vaudois[2] /ˈvəʊdwɑː/ n. & adj. —n. (pl. same) a member of the Waldenses. —adj. of or relating to the Waldenses. [F, repr. med.L Valdensis (as WALDENSES)]

Vaughan /vɔːn/, Henry (1621–95), British poet, born in Wales, who probably studied law and is known to have practised medicine. One of the Metaphysical Poets, his volumes of religious poetry include Silex Scintillans (1650, 1655), in which he acknowledges his debt to George Herbert, and The Mount of Olives, or Solitary Devotions (1652). His poems have a distinctive limpid ethereal quality which has classed him as a mystic.

Vaughan Williams /vɔːn ˈwɪljəmz/, Ralph (1872–1958), English composer. His music is often thought of as quintessentially English, and this is only partly due to the influence of folk music: he had a keen interest in English folk-songs, which he collected and arranged. He composed in almost every genre, from operas and symphonies to choral works for amateurs and for professional choirs, concertos for neglected instruments such as harmonica and tuba, a suite for pipes, etc. The basis of his work is melody; its visionary quality, broad humanity, and appeal at several levels make it a remarkable expression of the national spirit in music, just as the man himself personified all that was best in the liberal 19th-c. tradition of which he was a scion.

vault /vɔːlt, vɒlt/ n. & v. —n. **1 a** an arched roof. **b** a continuous arch. **c** a set or series of arches whose joints radiate from a central point or line. **2** a vaultlike covering (the vault of heaven). **3** an underground chamber: **a** as a place of storage (bank vaults). **b** as a place of interment beneath a church or in a cemetery etc. (family vault). **4** an act of vaulting. **5** Anat. the arched roof of a cavity. —v. **1** intr. leap or spring, esp. while resting on one or both hands or with the help of a pole. **2** tr. spring over (a gate etc.) in this way. **3** tr. (esp. as **vaulted**) **a** make in the form of a vault. **b** provide with a vault or vaults. □□ **vaulter** n. [OF voute, vaute, ult. f. L volvere roll]

vaulting /ˈvɔːltɪŋ, ˈvɒltɪŋ/ n. **1** arched work in a vaulted roof or ceiling. **2** a gymnastic or athletic exercise in which participants vault over obstacles. □ **vaulting-horse** a wooden block to be vaulted over by gymnasts.

vaunt /vɔːnt/ v. & n. literary —v. **1** intr. boast, brag. **2** tr. boast of; extol boastfully. —n. a boast. □□ **vaunter** n. **vauntingly** adv. [ME f. AF vaunter, OF vanter f. LL vantare f. L vanus VAIN: partly obs. avaunt (v.) f. avanter f. a- intensive + vanter]

vavasory /ˈvævəsərɪ/ n. (pl. **-ies**) hist. the estate of a vavasour. [OF vavasorie or med.L vavasoria (as VAVASOUR)]

vavasour /ˈvævəˌsʊə(r)/ n. hist. a vassal owing allegiance to a great lord and having other vassals under him. [ME f. OF vavas(s)our f. med.L vavassor, perh. f. vassus vassorum VASSAL of vassals]

VC abbr. **1** Victoria Cross. **2** Vice-Chairman. **3** Vice-Chancellor. **4** Vice-Consul.

VCR abbr. video cassette recorder.

VD abbr. venereal disease.

VDU abbr. visual display unit.

VE abbr. Victory in Europe (in 1945). □ **VE day** 8 May, the day marking this.

've abbr. (chiefly after pronouns) = HAVE (I've; they've).

veal /viːl/ n. calf's flesh as food. □□ **vealy** adj. [ME f. AF ve(e)l, OF veiaus veel f. L vitellus dimin. of vitulus calf]

vector /ˈvektə(r)/ n. & v. —n. **1** Math. & Physics a quantity having direction as well as magnitude, esp. as determining the position of one point in space relative to another (radius vector). **2** a carrier of disease. **3** a course to be taken by an aircraft. —v.tr. direct (an aircraft in flight) to a desired point. □□ **vectorial** /-ˈtɔːrɪəl/ adj. **vectorize** v.tr. (also **-ise**) (in sense 1 of n.). **vectorization** /-təraɪˈzeɪʃ(ə)n/ n. [L, = carrier, f. vehere vect- convey]

Veda /ˈveɪdə, ˈviː-/ n. (in sing. or pl.) the most ancient and sacred literature of the Hindus, believed to have been revealed directly to the early seers. It contains ritual utterances of the early Aryans in India, composed in old Sanskrit and preserved by oral tradition, manuals for the priests of Vedic religion. The term applies first to the Rig-Veda; the 'triple Veda' includes the Sama-Veda and Yajur-Veda; the Atharva-Veda was added later. In its wider sense, the term also includes the Brahmanas and the mystical Aranyakas and Upanishads. [Skr. veda, lit. (sacred) knowledge]

Vedanta /vɪˈdæntə, veˈdɑː-/ n. **1** the Upanishads. **2** the Hindu philosophy based on these, esp. in its monistic form. □□ **Vedantic** adj. **Vedantist** n. [Skr. vedānta (as VEDA, anta end)]

w we z zoo ʃ she ʒ decision θ thin ð this ŋ ring x loch tʃ chip dʒ jar (see over for vowels)

Vedda /ˈvedə/ n. a Sri Lankan aboriginal. [Sinh. *veddā* hunter]

vedette /vɪˈdet/ n. a mounted sentry positioned beyond an army's outposts to observe the movements of the enemy. [F, = scout, f. It. *vedetta, veletta* f. Sp. *vela*(r) watch f. L *vigilare*]

Vedic /ˈveɪdɪk, ˈviː-/ adj. & n. —adj. of or relating to the Veda or Vedas. —n. the language of the Vedas, an older form of Sanskrit. □ **Vedic religion** the ancient religion of the Aryan tribes who entered NW India *c.*1500 BC; the religious beliefs and practices contained in the Veda. It was a religion of ritual sacrifice to many gods, especially Indra, Varuna, Soma, and Agni; animal, vegetable, and human sacrifice are described. Vedic society is divided into four distinct classes (varna) that are still in evidence in Hinduism today. The increasing complexity of Vedic ritual led to the dominance of the specialist priesthood, the composition of the Brahmanas, and the rigidity of orthodox Brahmanism (*c.*900 BC onwards). The transition to classical Hinduism began in about the 5th c. BC. [F *Védique* or G *Vedisch* (as VEDA)]

vee /viː/ n. 1 the letter V. 2 a thing shaped like a V. [name of the letter]

veer[1] /vɪə(r)/ v. & n. —v.intr. 1 change direction, esp. (of the wind) clockwise (cf. BACK v. 5). 2 change in course, opinion, conduct, emotions, etc. 3 *Naut.* = WEAR[2]. —n. a change of course or direction. [F *virer* f. Rmc, perh. alt. f. L *gyrare* GYRATE]

veer[2] /vɪə(r)/ v.tr. *Naut.* slacken or let out (a rope, cable, etc.). [ME f. MDu. *vieren*]

veg /vedʒ/ n. *colloq.* a vegetable or vegetables. [abbr.]

Vega /ˈviːɡə/ n. the brightest star in the constellation Lyra, discovered to have a system of tiny particles (gathered round the star) which may eventually coalesce into planets. [Sp. or med.L *Vega* f. Arab., = the falling vulture (i.e. the constellation Lyra)]

Vega Carpio /ˌveɪɡə ˈkɑːpɪəʊ/, Lope Felix de (1562–1635), Spanish poet and playwright, who sailed with the Armada in 1588, an experience which inspired one of his less-regarded works, an epic which violently attacked England and Drake. A celebrated wit, idolized by his contemporaries, he was immensely prolific in many genres. He is said to have written 1,500 plays, of which several hundred survive, and is regarded as the founder of Spanish drama.

vegan /ˈviːɡən/ n. & adj. —n. a person who does not eat or use animal products. —adj. using or containing no animal products. [contr. of VEGETARIAN]

vegetable /ˈvedʒtəb(ə)l, ˈvedʒtəb(ə)l/ n. & adj. —n. 1 *Bot.* any of various plants, esp. a herbaceous plant used wholly or partly for food, e.g. a cabbage, potato, turnip, or bean. 2 *colloq.* **a** a person who is incapable of normal intellectual activity, esp. through brain injury etc. **b** a person lacking in animation or living a monotonous life. —adj. 1 of, derived from, relating to, or comprising plants or plant life, esp. as distinct from animal life or mineral substances. 2 of or relating to vegetables as food. 3 **a** unresponsive to stimulus (*vegetable behaviour*). **b** uneventful, monotonous (*a vegetable existence*). □ **vegetable butter** a vegetable fat with the consistency of butter. **vegetable ivory** see IVORY. **vegetable marrow** see MARROW 1. **vegetable oyster** = SALSIFY. **vegetable parchment** see PARCHMENT 2. **vegetable spaghetti** 1 a variety of marrow with flesh resembling spaghetti. 2 its flesh. **vegetable sponge** = LOOFAH. **vegetable tallow** see TALLOW. **vegetable wax** an exudation of certain plants such as sumac. [ME f. OF *vegetable* or LL *vegetabilis* animating (as VEGETATE)]

vegetal /ˈvedʒɪt(ə)l/ adj. 1 of or having the nature of plants (*vegetal growth*). 2 vegetative. [med.L *vegetalis* f. L *vegetare* animate]

vegetarian /ˌvedʒɪˈteərɪən/ n. & adj. —n. a person who abstains from animal food, esp. that from slaughtered animals, though often not eggs and dairy products. —adj. excluding animal food, esp. meat (*a vegetarian diet*). □□ **vegetarianism** n. [irreg. f. VEGETABLE + -ARIAN]

vegetate /ˈvedʒɪˌteɪt/ v.intr. 1 live an uneventful or monotonous life. 2 grow as plants do; fulfil vegetal functions. [L *vegetare* animate f. *vegetus* f. *vegēre* be active]

vegetation /ˌvedʒɪˈteɪʃ(ə)n/ n. 1 plants collectively; plant life (*luxuriant vegetation*; *no sign of vegetation*). 2 the process of

vegetating. □□ **vegetational** adj. [med.L *vegetatio* growth (as VEGETATE)]

vegetative /ˈvedʒɪtətɪv/ adj. 1 concerned with growth and development as distinct from sexual reproduction. 2 of or relating to vegetation or plant life. □□ **vegetatively** adv. **vegetativeness** n. [ME f. OF *vegetatif* -*ive* or med.L *vegetativus* (as VEGETATE)]

vegie /ˈvedʒɪ/ n. (also **veggie**) *colloq.* a vegetarian. [abbr.]

vehement /ˈviːəmənt/ adj. showing or caused by strong feeling; forceful, ardent (*a vehement protest*; *vehement desire*). □□ **vehemence** n. **vehemently** adv. [ME f. F *véhément* or L *vehemens* -*entis*, perh. f. *vemens* (unrecorded) deprived of mind, assoc. with *vehere* carry]

vehicle /ˈviːɪk(ə)l, ˈviːək(ə)l/ n. 1 any conveyance for transporting people, goods, etc., esp. on land. 2 a medium for thought, feeling, or action (*the stage is the best vehicle for their talents*). 3 a liquid etc. as a medium for suspending pigments, drugs, etc. 4 the literal meaning of a word or words used metaphorically (opp. TENOR 6). □□ **vehicular** /vɪˈhɪkjʊlə(r)/ adj. [F *véhicule* or L *vehiculum* f. *vehere* carry]

veil /veɪl/ n. & v. —n. 1 a piece of usu. more or less transparent fabric attached to a woman's hat etc., esp. to conceal the face or protect against the sun, dust, etc. 2 a piece of linen etc. as part of a nun's head-dress, resting on the head and shoulders. 3 a curtain, esp. that separating the sanctuary in the Jewish Temple. 4 a disguise; a pretext; a thing that conceals (*under the veil of friendship*; *a veil of mist*). 5 *Photog.* slight fogging. 6 huskiness of the voice. 7 = VELUM. —v.tr. 1 cover with a veil. 2 (esp. as **veiled** adj.) partly conceal (*veiled threats*). □ **beyond the veil** in the unknown state of life after death. **draw a veil over** avoid discussing or calling attention to. **take the veil** become a nun. □□ **veilless** adj. [ME f. AF *veil*(e), OF *voil*(e) f. L *vela* pl. of VELUM]

veiling /ˈveɪlɪŋ/ n. light fabric used for veils etc.

vein /veɪn/ n. & v. —n. 1 **a** any of the tubes by which blood is conveyed to the heart (cf. ARTERY). **b** (in general use) any blood-vessel (*has royal blood in his veins*). 2 a nervure of an insect's wing. 3 a slender bundle of tissue forming a rib in the framework of a leaf. 4 a streak or stripe of a different colour in wood, marble, cheese, etc. 5 a fissure in rock filled with ore or other deposited material. 6 a source of a particular characteristic (*a rich vein of humour*). 7 a distinctive character or tendency; a cast of mind or disposition; a mood (*spoke in a sarcastic vein*). —v.tr. fill or cover with or as with veins. □□ **veinless** n. **veinlet** n. **veinlike** adj. **veiny** adj. (**veinier, veiniest**). [ME f. OF *veine* f. L *vena*]

veining /ˈveɪnɪŋ/ n. a pattern of streaks or veins.

veinstone /ˈveɪnstəʊn/ n. = GANGUE.

vela pl. of VELUM.

velamen /vɪˈleɪmən/ n. (pl. **velamina** /-mɪnə/) an enveloping membrane esp. of an aerial root of an orchid. [L f. *velare* cover]

velar /ˈviːlə(r)/ adj. 1 of a veil or velum. 2 *Phonet.* (of a sound) pronounced with the back of the tongue near the soft palate. [L *velaris* f. *velum*: see VELUM]

Velázquez[1] /vɪˈlæskwɪz/, Diego (*c.* 1465–1524), Spanish conquistador, who in 1511 began the conquest of Cuba, founding a number of settlements including Havana (La Habana, 1515), and initiated expeditions to conquer the Mexican mainland.

Velázquez[2] /vɪˈlæskwɪz/, Diego Rodríguez de Silva y (1599–1660), Spanish painter. His religious works are naturalistic portraits rather than idealized types, and at the same time he painted a series of everyday subjects from Spanish domestic life and still lifes before becoming court painter to Philip IV in 1623. There his portraits humanized the stiff and formal Spanish tradition of idealized figures and tended towards naturalness and simplicity, rendering the character of the sitter with startling perception. In *Las Meninas* (*The Maids of Honour*, *c.*1656) the Infanta and her attendants are shown watching a sitting for a portrait of the king and queen, with the royal couple reflected in a mirror in the background, and the painter himself at work; it so impressed Picasso (who saw it at the age of 15) that in 1957 he painted 44 variations upon its theme.

Velcro /ˈvelkrəʊ/ n. *propr.* a fastener for clothes etc. consisting of two strips of nylon fabric, one looped and one burred, which adhere when pressed together. ☐☐ **Velcroed** adj. [F velours croché hooked velvet]

veld /velt/ n. (also **veldt**) S.Afr. open country; grassland. [Afrik. f. Du., = FIELD]

Velde /velt/, **van de** Dutch family of painters. Willem I (1611–93) executed detailed portraits of ships and was for a time official artist to the Dutch fleet; his sons were Adriaen (1636–72) and Willem II (1633–1707). Adriaen, the more versatile and gifted of the brothers, painted landscapes, biblical and genre scenes, and portraits, producing hundreds of paintings and also etchings. Willem II was one of Holland's greatest marine painters, known for the sensitive details of weather and light on his paintings of ships at sea. He went to England in 1672 and from 1674 Charles II gave him a retaining fee of £100 yearly, royal patronage enjoyed by his father before him.

veldskoen /'feltskuːn, 'fels-/ n. a strong suede or leather shoe or boot. [Afrik., = field-shoe]

veleta /vəˈliːtə/ n. (also **valeta**) a ballroom dance in triple time. [Sp., = weather-vane]

velitation /ˌvelɪˈteɪʃ(ə)n/ n. archaic a slight skirmish or controversy. [L velitatio f. velitari skirmish f. veles velitis light-armed skirmisher]

velleity /veˈliːɪtɪ/ n. literary 1 a low degree of volition not conducive to action. 2 a slight wish or inclination. [med.L velleitas f. L velle to wish]

Velleius Paterculus /veˌleɪəs pəˈtɜːkjʊləs/ (c.19 BC– after AD 30) Roman historian who in early life served abroad with the future emperor Tiberius. His Roman History in two books, reaching from the early history of Greece and Rome to AD 30, is notable for its rhetorical manner and for its adulation of Tiberius.

vellum /'veləm/ n. 1 **a** fine parchment orig. from the skin of a calf. **b** a manuscript written on this. 2 smooth writing-paper imitating vellum. [ME f. OF velin (as VEAL)]

velocimeter /ˌveləˈsɪmɪtə(r)/ n. an instrument for measuring velocity.

velocipede /vɪˈlɒsɪpiːd/ n. 1 hist. an early form of bicycle propelled by pressure from the rider's feet on the ground. 2 US a child's tricycle. ☐☐ **velocipedist** n. [F vélocipède f. L velox -ocis swift + pes pedis foot]

velocity /vɪˈlɒsɪtɪ/ n. (pl. **-ies**) 1 the measure of the rate of movement of a usu. inanimate object in a given direction. 2 speed in a given direction. 3 (in general use) speed. ☐ **velocity of escape** = escape velocity. [F vélocité or L velocitas f. velox -ocis swift]

velodrome /'veləˌdrəʊm/ n. a special place or building with a track for cycle-racing. [F vélodrome f. vélo bicycle (as VELOCITY, -DROME)]

velour /vəˈlʊə(r)/ n. (also **velours**) 1 a plushlike woven fabric or felt. 2 archaic a hat of this felt. [F velours velvet f. OF velour, velous f. L villosus hairy f. villus: see VELVET]

velouté /vəˈluːteɪ/ n. a sauce made from a roux of butter and flour with white stock. [F, = velvety]

velum /'viːləm/ n. (pl. **vela** /-lə/) a membrane, membranous covering, or flap. [L, = sail, curtain, covering, veil]

velutinous /vɪˈluːtɪnəs/ adj. covered with soft fine hairs. [perh. f. It. vellutino f. velluto VELVET]

velvet /'velvɪt/ n. & adj. —n. 1 a closely woven fabric of silk, cotton, etc., with a thick short pile on one side. 2 the furry skin on a deer's growing antler. 3 anything smooth and soft like velvet. —adj. of, like, or soft as velvet. ☐ **on velvet** in an advantageous or prosperous position. **velvet glove** outward gentleness, esp. cloaking firmness or strength (cf. iron hand). **velvet revolution** a non-violent political revolution, esp. the smooth change from communism to a western-style democracy in Czechoslovakia at the end of 1989. ☐☐ **velveted** adj. **velvety** adj. [ME f. OF veluotte f. velu velvety f. med.L villutus f. L villus tuft, down]

velveteen /ˌvelvɪˈtiːn/ n. 1 a cotton fabric with a pile like velvet. 2 (in pl.) trousers etc. made of this.

Ven. abbr. Venerable (as the title of an archdeacon).

vena cava /ˌviːnə ˈkeɪvə/ n. (pl. **venae cavae** /-niː -viː/) each of usu. two veins carrying blood into the heart. [L, = hollow vein]

venal /'viːn(ə)l/ adj. 1 (of a person) able to be bribed or corrupted. 2 (of conduct etc.) characteristic of a venal person. ☐☐ **venality** /-ˈnælɪtɪ/ n. **venally** adv. [L venalis f. venum thing for sale]

venation /vɪˈneɪʃ(ə)n/ n. the arrangement of veins in a leaf or an insect's wing etc., or the system of venous blood vessels in an organism. ☐☐ **venational** adj. [L vena vein]

vend /vend/ v.tr. 1 offer (small wares) for sale. 2 Law sell. ☐ **vending-machine** a machine that dispenses small articles for sale when a coin or token is inserted. ☐☐ **vender** n. (usu. in comb.). **vendible** adj. [F vendre or L vendere sell (as VENAL, dare give)]

Venda /'vendə/ an independent tribal homeland of the Vhavenda people (1985) 455,000.

vendace /'vendeɪs/ n. a small delicate fish, Coregonus albula, found in some British lakes. [OF vendese, -oise f. Gaulish]

vendee /venˈdiː/ n. Law the buying party in a sale, esp. of property.

vendetta /venˈdetə/ n. 1 **a** a blood feud in which the family of a murdered person seeks vengeance on the murderer or the murderer's family. **b** this practice as prevalent in Corsica and Sicily. 2 a prolonged bitter quarrel. [It. f. L vindicta: see VINDICTIVE]

vendeuse /vɑ̃ˈdɜːz/ n. a saleswoman, esp. in a fashionable dress-shop. [F]

vendor /'vendə(r), -dɔ:(r)/ n. 1 Law the seller in a sale, esp. of property. 2 = vending-machine (see VEND). [AF vendour (as VEND)]

vendue /venˈdjuː/ n. US a public auction. [Du. vendu(e) f. F vendue sale f. vendre VEND]

veneer /vɪˈnɪə(r)/ n. & v. —n. 1 **a** a thin covering of fine wood or other surface material applied to a coarser wood. **b** a layer in plywood. 2 (often foll. by of) a deceptive outward appearance of a good quality etc. —v.tr. 1 apply a veneer to (wood, furniture, etc.). 2 disguise (an unattractive character etc.) with a more attractive manner etc. [earlier fineer f. G furni(e)ren f. OF fournir FURNISH]

veneering /vɪˈnɪərɪŋ/ n. material used as veneer.

venepuncture /'viːnɪˌpʌŋktʃə(r)/ n. (also **venipuncture**) Med. the puncture of a vein esp. with a hypodermic needle to withdraw blood or for an intravenous injection. [L vena vein + PUNCTURE]

venerable /'venərəb(ə)l/ adj. 1 entitled to veneration on account of character, age, associations, etc. (a venerable priest; venerable relics). 2 as the title of an archdeacon in the Church of England. 3 RC Ch. as the title of a deceased person who has attained a certain degree of sanctity but has not been fully beatified or canonized. ☐☐ **venerability** /-ˈbɪlɪtɪ/ n. **venerableness** n. **venerably** adv. [ME f. OF venerable or L venerabilis (as VENERATE)]

venerate /'venəˌreɪt/ v.tr. 1 regard with deep respect. 2 reverence on account of sanctity etc. ☐☐ **veneration** /-ˈreɪʃ(ə)n/ n. **venerator** n. [L venerari adore, revere]

venereal /vɪˈnɪərɪəl/ adj. 1 of or relating to sexual desire or intercourse. 2 relating to venereal disease. ☐ **venereal disease** any of various diseases contracted chiefly by sexual intercourse with a person already infected. ☐☐ **venereally** adv. [ME f. L venereus f. venus veneris sexual love]

venereology /vɪˌnɪərɪˈɒlədʒɪ/ n. the scientific study of venereal diseases. ☐☐ **venereological** /-əˈlɒdʒɪk(ə)l/ adj. **venereologist** n.

venery[1] /'venərɪ/ n. archaic sexual indulgence. [med.L veneria (as VENEREAL)]

venery[2] /'venərɪ/ n. archaic hunting. [ME f. OF venerie f. vener to hunt ult. f. L venari]

venesection /'viːnɪˌsekʃ(ə)n/ n. (also **venisection**) phlebotomy. [med.L venae sectio cutting of a vein (as VEIN, SECTION)]

Venetia /vɪˈniːʃə/ (Italian **Veneto** /'veneˌtəʊ/) a region of NE Italy; pop. (1981) 4,345,000; capital, Venice. The region takes its name from the pre-Roman inhabitants, the Veneti.

Venetian /vɪˈniːʃ(ə)n/ n. & adj. —n. 1 a native or citizen of Venice in NE Italy. 2 the Italian dialect of Venice. 3 (**venetian**)

= *venetian blind.* —*adj.* of Venice. □ **venetian blind** a window-blind of adjustable horizontal slats to control the light. **Venetian glass** delicate glassware made at Murano near Venice. **Venetian red** a reddish pigment of ferric oxides. **Venetian window** a window with three separate openings, the central one being arched and highest. □□ **venetianed** *adj.* (in sense 3 of *n.*). [ME f. OF *Venicien*, assim. to med.L *Venetianus* f. *Venetia* Venice]

Venezia see VENICE.

Venezuela /ˌveneˈzweɪlə/ a country on the north coast of South America, with a coastline on the Caribbean Sea; pop. (est. 1988) 18,770,000; official language, Spanish; capital, Caracas. Columbus discovered the mouth of the Orinoco River in 1498, and in the following year Vespucci explored the coast. It was the early Italian explorers who gave the country its name (= little Venice), when they saw native Indian houses built on stilts over water and were reminded of the city of Venice. Settled by the Spanish in the 16th c., Venezuela won its independence in 1821 after a ten-year struggle, but did not finally emerge as a separate nation until its secession from the Federation of Grand Colombia in 1830. Its history since then has been characterized by endemic political instability, civil war, and dictatorship, and by the generation of considerable wealth from its well-established oil industry. □□ **Venezuelan** *adj.* & *n.*

vengeance /ˈvendʒ(ə)ns/ *n.* punishment inflicted or retribution exacted for wrong to oneself or to a person etc. whose cause one supports. □ **with a vengeance** in a higher degree than was expected or desired; in the fullest sense (*punctuality with a vengeance*). [ME f. OF f. *venger* avenge f. L (as VINDICATE)]

vengeful /ˈvendʒfʊl/ *adj.* vindictive; seeking vengeance. □□ **vengefully** *adv.* **vengefulness** *n.* [obs. *venge* avenge (as VENGEANCE)]

venial /ˈviːnɪəl/ *adj.* (of a sin or fault) pardonable, excusable; not mortal. □□ **veniality** /-ˈælɪtɪ/ *n.* **venially** *adv.* **venialness** *n.* [ME f. OF f. LL *venialis* f. *venia* forgiveness]

Venice /ˈvenɪs/ (Italian **Venezia** /veˈnetsɪə/) a city of NE Italy, on a lagoon of the Adriatic Sea, built on numerous islands that are separated by canals and linked by bridges; pop. (1981) 346,150. It was a powerful republic in the Middle Ages, and from the 13th to the 16th c. a leading sea-power, controlling trade to the Levant and ruling parts of the eastern Mediterranean. Its commercial importance declined after the Cape route to India was discovered at the end of the 16th c., but it remained an important centre of art and music. After the Napoleonic Wars Venice was placed under Austrian rule; it was incorporated into a unified Italy in 1866.

venipuncture var. of VENEPUNCTURE.

venisection var. of VENESECTION.

venison /ˈvenɪs(ə)n, -z(ə)n/ *n.* a deer's flesh as food. [ME f. OF *veneso(u)n* f. L *venatio -onis* hunting f. *venari* to hunt]

Venite /vɪˈnaɪtɪ/ *n.* 1 a canticle consisting of Psalm 95. 2 a musical setting of this. [ME f. L, = 'come ye', its first word]

Venn diagram /ven/ *n.* a diagram of usu. circular areas representing mathematical sets, the areas intersecting where they have elements in common. [J. *Venn*, Engl. logician d. 1923]

venom /ˈvenəm/ *n.* 1 a poisonous fluid secreted by snakes, scorpions, etc., usu. transmitted by a bite or sting. 2 malignity; virulence of feeling, language, or conduct. □□ **venomed** *adj.* [ME f. OF *venim*, var. of *venin* ult. f. L *venenum* poison]

venomous /ˈvenəməs/ *adj.* 1 a containing, secreting, or injecting venom. b (of a snake etc.) inflicting poisonous wounds by this means. 2 (of a person etc.) virulent, spiteful, malignant. □□ **venomously** *adv.* **venomousness** *n.* [ME f. OF *venimeux* f. *venim*: see VENOM]

venose /ˈviːnəʊz/ *adj.* having many or very marked veins. [L *venosus* f. *vena* vein]

venous /ˈviːnəs/ *adj.* of, full of, or contained in veins. □□ **venosity** /vɪˈnɒsɪtɪ/ *n.* **venously** *adv.* [L *venosus* VENOSE or L *vena* vein + -OUS]

vent[1] /vent/ *n.* & *v.* —*n.* 1 (also **vent-hole**) a hole or opening allowing motion of air etc. out of or into a confined space. 2 an outlet; free passage or play (*gave vent to their indignation*). 3 the anus esp. of a lower animal, serving for both excretion and reproduction. 4 the venting of an otter, beaver, etc. 5 an aperture or outlet through which volcanic products are discharged at the earth's surface. 6 a touch-hole of a gun. 7 a finger-hole in a musical instrument. 8 a flue of a chimney. —*v.* 1 *tr.* a make a vent in (a cask etc.). b provide (a machine) with a vent. 2 *tr.* give vent or free expression to (*vented my anger on the cat*). 3 *intr.* (of an otter or beaver) come to the surface for breath. □ **vent one's spleen on** scold or ill-treat without cause. □□ **ventless** *adj.* [partly F *vent* f. L *ventus* wind, partly F *évent* f. *éventer* expose to air f. OF *esventer* ult. f. L *ventus* wind]

vent[2] /vent/ *n.* a slit in a garment, esp. in the lower edge of the back of a coat. [ME, var. of *fent* f. OF *fente* slit ult. f. L *findere* cleave]

ventiduct /ˈventɪdʌkt/ *n.* *Archit.* an air-passage, esp. for ventilation. [L *ventus* wind + *ductus* DUCT]

ventifact /ˈventɪfækt/ *n.* a stone shaped by wind-blown sand. [L *ventus* wind + *factum* neut. past part. of *facere* make]

ventil /ˈventɪl/ *n.* *Mus.* 1 a valve in a wind instrument. 2 a shutter for regulating the air-flow in an organ. [G f. It. *ventile* f. med.L *ventile* sluice f. L *ventus* wind]

ventilate /ˈventɪleɪt/ *v.tr.* 1 cause air to circulate freely in (a room etc.). 2 submit (a question, grievance, etc.) to public consideration and discussion. 3 *Med.* a oxygenate (the blood). b admit or force air into (the lungs). □□ **ventilation** /-ˈleɪʃ(ə)n/ *n.* **ventilative** /-ˈleɪtɪv/ *adj.* [L *ventilare ventilat-* blow, winnow, f. *ventus* wind]

ventilator /ˈventɪleɪtə(r)/ *n.* 1 an appliance or aperture for ventilating a room etc. 2 *Med.* = RESPIRATOR 2.

ventral /ˈventr(ə)l/ *adj.* 1 *Anat.* & *Zool.* of or on the abdomen (cf. DORSAL). 2 *Bot.* of the front or lower surface. □ **ventral fin** either of the ventrally placed fins on a fish. □□ **ventrally** *adv.* [obs. *venter* abdomen f. L *venter ventr-*]

ventre à terre /ˌvɑːntr ɑː ˈteə(r)/ *adv.* at full speed. [F, lit. with belly to the ground]

ventricle /ˈventrɪk(ə)l/ *n.* *Anat.* 1 a cavity in the body. 2 a hollow part of an organ, esp. in the brain or heart. □□ **ventricular** /-ˈtrɪkjʊlə(r)/ *adj.* [ME f. L *ventriculus* dimin. of *venter* belly]

ventricose /ˈventrɪkəʊz/ *adj.* 1 having a protruding belly. 2 *Bot.* distended, inflated. [irreg. f. VENTRICLE + -OSE[1]]

ventriloquism /venˈtrɪləkwɪz(ə)m/ *n.* the skill of speaking or uttering sounds so that they seem to come from the speaker's dummy or a source other than the speaker. □□ **ventriloquial** /ˌventrɪˈləʊkwɪəl/ *adj.* **ventriloquist** *n.* **ventriloquize** *v.intr.* (also **-ise**). [ult. f. L *ventriloquus* ventriloquist f. *venter* belly + *loqui* speak]

ventriloquy /venˈtrɪləkwɪ/ *n.* = VENTRILOQUISM.

venture /ˈventʃə(r)/ *n.* & *v.* —*n.* 1 a an undertaking of a risk. b a risky undertaking. 2 a commercial speculation. —*v.* 1 *intr.* dare; not be afraid (*did not venture to stop them*). 2 *intr.* (usu. foll. by *out* etc.) dare to go (out), esp. outdoors. 3 *tr.* dare to put forward (an opinion, suggestion, etc.). 4 a *tr.* expose to risk; stake (a bet etc.). b *intr.* take risks. 5 *intr.* (foll. by *on, upon*) dare to engage in etc. (*ventured on a longer journey*). □ **at a venture** at random; without previous consideration. **venture capital** = risk capital. **Venture Scout** *Brit.* a member of the Scout Association (see entry) aged between 16 and 20. [*aventure* for ADVENTURE]

venturer /ˈventʃərə(r)/ *n.* *hist.* a person who undertakes or shares in a trading venture.

venturesome /ˈventʃəsəm/ *adj.* 1 disposed to take risks. 2 risky. □□ **venturesomely** *adv.* **venturesomeness** *n.*

venturi /venˈtjʊərɪ/ *n.* (*pl.* **venturis**) a device consisting of a short section of tube which is narrower than the parts at each end, so that gas or liquid under pressure flows through it faster, used to produce an effect of suction or in measuring the rate of flow. [G. B. *Venturi*, It. physicist d. 1822]

venue /ˈvenjuː/ *n.* 1 a an appointed meeting-place esp. for a sports event, meeting, concert, etc. b a rendezvous. 2 *Law hist.* the county or other place within which a jury must be gathered and a cause tried (orig. the neighbourhood of the crime etc.). [F, = a coming, fem. past part. of *venir* come f. L *venire*]

w we z zoo ʃ she ʒ decision θ thin ð this ŋ ring x loch tʃ chip dʒ jar (*see over for vowels*)

venule /ˈvenjuːl/ *n. Anat.* a small vein adjoining the capillaries. [L *venula* dimin. of *vena* vein]

Venus /ˈviːnəs/ **1** *Rom. Mythol.* an Italian goddess, not originally Roman. In classical Rome she was identified with Aphrodite, though she seems to have been formerly a spirit of kitchen gardens and their fertility. Famous statues of her include the Venus of Milo (see separate entry). **2** *Astron.* the second planet of the solar system, almost equal in size to Earth and orbiting 108 million km from the sun, known to the Greeks as 'Hesperus' and 'Phosphorus'—the morning and evening star—in recognition of its appearances in the twilight sky, where it outshines all celestial objects other than the sun and moon. The early telescopic observations of Galileo revealed its phases clearly, demonstrating that it did orbit the sun. Because of the total cloud cover no surface detail can be seen through even the largest telescope. The clouds, rich in sulphuric acid, are supported in a dense atmosphere of carbon dioxide which traps the light and heat of the sun to produce surface temperatures of 460 °C. The topography of the planet is largely flat, but with two raised 'continental' plateaux. The surface has been revealed by space probes to be a rocky plain, sweltering under a dull orange sky. —*n.* (*pl.* **Venuses**) *poet.* **1** a beautiful woman. **2** sexual love; amorous influences or desires. □ **Venus** (or **Venus's**) **fly-trap** a flesh-consuming plant, *Dionaea muscipula*, with leaves that close on insects etc. **Venus's comb** = *shepherd's needle* (see SHEPHERD). **Venus's looking-glass** any of various plants of the genus *Legousia* with small blue flowers. □□ **Venusian** /vɪˈnjuːzɪən/ *adj.* & *n.*

Venus of Milo /ˈmaɪləʊ, ˈmiː-/ a classical sculpture of Aphrodite dated to *c.*100 BC. It was discovered on the Greek island of Melos in 1820 and is now in the Louvre, having formed part of the war loot acquired by Napoleon on his campaigns. The most famous antique sculpture, it is essentially an eclectic piece, the head being in 5th-c. style while the spiral movement of the body betrays a Hellenistic concern for dynamic sculptural effect.

veracious /vəˈreɪʃəs/ *adj. formal* **1** speaking or disposed to speak the truth. **2** (of a statement etc.) true or meant to be true. □□ **veraciously** *adv.* **veraciousness** *n.* [L *verax veracis* f. *verus* true]

veracity /vəˈræsɪtɪ/ *n.* **1** truthfulness, honesty. **2** accuracy (of a statement etc.). [F *véracité* or med.L *veracitas* (as VERACIOUS)]

Veracruz /ˌveərəˈkruːz/ **1** a State of eastern Mexico; pop. (est. 1988) 6,659,000; capital, Jalapa Enriquez. **2** a city and port of Mexico, on the Gulf of Mexico; pop. (1980) 305,456. It was originally founded by Hernán Cortés in 1519 as La Villa Rica de la Veracruz (= Rich Town of the True Cross).

veranda /vəˈrændə/ *n.* (also **verandah**) **1** a portico or external gallery, usu. with a roof, along the side of a house. **2** *Austral.* & *NZ* a roof over a pavement in front of a shop. [Hindi *varandā* f. Port. *varanda*]

veratrine /ˈverəˌtriːn, -ɪn/ *n.* a poisonous compound obtained from sabadilla etc., and used esp. as a local irritant in the treatment of neuralgia and rheumatism. [F *vératrine* f. L *veratrum* hellebore]

verb /vɜːb/ *n. Gram.* a word used to indicate an action, state, or occurrence, and forming the main part of the predicate of a sentence (e.g. *hear*, *become*, *happen*). [ME f. OF *verbe* or L *verbum* word, verb]

verbal /ˈvɜːb(ə)l/ *adj., n.,* & *v.* —*adj.* **1** of or concerned with words (*made a verbal distinction*). **2** oral, not written (*gave a verbal statement*). **3** *Gram.* of or in the nature of a verb (*verbal inflections*). **4** literal (*a verbal translation*). **5** talkative, articulate. —*n.* **1** *Gram.* **a** a verbal noun. **b** a word or words functioning as a verb. **2** *sl.* a verbal statement, esp. one made to the police. **3** *sl.* an insult; abuse (*gave them the verbal*). —*v.tr.* (**verballed**, **verballing**) *Brit. sl.* attribute a damaging statement to (a suspect). □ **verbal noun** *Gram.* a noun formed as an inflection of a verb and partly sharing its constructions (e.g. *smoking* in *smoking is forbidden*: see -ING[1]). □□ **verbally** *adv.* [ME f. F *verbal* or LL *verbalis* (as VERB)]

verbalism /ˈvɜːbəˌlɪz(ə)m/ *n.* **1** minute attention to words: verbal criticism. **2** merely verbal expression. □□ **verbalist** *n.* **verbalistic** /-ˈlɪstɪk/ *adj.*

verbalize /ˈvɜːbəˌlaɪz/ *v.* (also **-ise**) **1** *tr.* express in words. **2** *intr.* be verbose. **3** *tr.* make (a noun etc.) into a verb. □□ **verbalizable** *adj.* **verbalization** /-ˈzeɪʃ(ə)n/ *n.* **verbalizer** *n.*

verbatim /vɜːˈbeɪtɪm/ *adv.* & *adj.* in exactly the same words; word for word (*copied it verbatim; a verbatim report*). [ME f. med.L (adv.), f. L *verbum* word: cf. LITERATIM]

verbena /vɜːˈbiːnə/ *n.* any plant of the genus *Verbena*, bearing clusters of fragrant flowers. [L, = sacred bough of olive etc., in med.L vervain]

verbiage /ˈvɜːbɪɪdʒ/ *n.* needless accumulation of words; verbosity. [F f. obs. *verbeier* chatter f. *verbe* word: see VERB]

verbose /vɜːˈbəʊs/ *adj.* using or expressed in more words than are needed. □□ **verbosely** *adv.* **verboseness** *n.* **verbosity** /-ˈbɒsɪtɪ/ *n.* [L *verbosus* f. *verbum* word]

verboten /fɜːˈbəʊt(ə)n/ *adj.* forbidden, esp. by an authority. [G]

verb. sap. /vɜːb ˈsæp/ *int.* expressing the absence of the need for a further explicit statement. [abbr. of L *verbum sapienti sat est* a word is enough for the wise person]

verdant /ˈvɜːd(ə)nt/ *adj.* **1** (of grass etc.) green, fresh-coloured. **2** (of a field etc.) covered with green grass etc. **3** (of a person) unsophisticated, raw, green. □□ **verdancy** *n.* **verdantly** *adv.* [perh. f. OF *verdeant* part. of *verdoier* be green ult. f. L *viridis* green]

verd-antique /ˌvɜːdænˈtiːk/ *n.* **1** ornamental usu. green serpentine. **2** a green incrustation on ancient bronze. **3** green porphyry. [obs. F, = antique green]

verderer /ˈvɜːdərə(r)/ *n. Brit.* a judicial officer of royal forests. [AF (earlier *verder*), OF *verdier* ult. f. L *viridis* green]

Verdi /ˈveədiː/, Giuseppe (1813–1901), Italian composer. His first major operatic success was *Nabucco* (*Nabucodonosor*, 1842); he followed it with a period of sustained activity which he described as his 'years in the galleys', which resulted in a series of operas. The 1850s saw the completion of two further masterpieces, *Rigoletto* (1851), based on Hugo's *Le Roi s'amuse*, and *La Traviata* (1853), a failure on its first production but since then known as one of the most popular of operas. He was involved in the movement for Italian unity, his name being identified with the cause as an acrostic (VIVA VERDI, 'Viva Vittorio Emanuele, Re d'Italia'), and in 1868 accepted a commission to compose an opera in honour of the opening of the Suez Canal: *Aida* was in the event first performed at La Scala in 1871. Two operas based on Shakespeare followed, *Otello* (1884–7) and the glorious comedy *Falstaff* (1889–93), the contradiction to any accusation that Verdi's talents were limited to tragedy and high drama. Indeed, Verdi's strength lies in his strong feeling for characterization as much as in his original and nearly always effective orchestration, and more than in his gift for memorable tunes, so often the butt of unsympathetic criticism. His Requiem Mass (1873–4) is a powerful work which offsets the dramatic force of the Day of Judgement against a moving expression of human faith.

verdict /ˈvɜːdɪkt/ *n.* **1** a decision on an issue of fact in a civil or criminal cause or an inquest. **2** a decision; a judgement. [ME f. AF *verdit*, OF *voirdit* f. *voir, veir* true f. L *verus* + *dit* f. L DICTUM saying]

verdigris /ˈvɜːdɪgrɪs, -ˌgriːs/ *n.* **1 a** a green crystallized substance formed on copper by the action of acetic acid. **b** this used as a medicine or pigment. **2** green rust on copper or brass. [ME f. OF *verte-gres, vert de Grece* green of Greece]

Verdon-Roe /ˌvɜːd(ə)n ˈrəʊ/, Sir Edwin Alliott Verdon (1877–1958), English engineer and aircraft designer. He built the first British seaplane to rise from the water and (in 1912) the first cabin aircraft, and invented anti-dazzle car headlights. With his brother H. V. Roe he founded the Avro Company (1910–28) and built a number of planes of which the Avro 504 was the most successful; in 1928 he formed the Saunders-Roe Company to design and manufacture flying boats.

Verdun /vɜːˈdʌn/ a fortified town on the River Meuse in NE France, scene of a long and severe battle in the First World War (1916), where the French suffered heavy losses.

verdure /ˈvɜːdjə(r)/ *n.* **1** green vegetation. **2** the greenness of this. **3** *poet.* freshness. □□ **verdured** *adj.* **verdurous** *adj.* [ME f. OF f. *verd* green f. L *viridis*]

Vereeniging /fəˈriːnɪkɪŋ/ a city in Transvaal, South Africa; pop.

(1985) 540,100. □ **Treaty of Vereeniging** the treaty which terminated the Boer War in 1902.

verge[1] /vɜːdʒ/ *n.* **1** an edge or border. **2** an extreme limit beyond which something happens (*on the verge of tears*). **3** *Brit.* a grass edging of a road, flower-bed, etc. **4** *Archit.* an edge of tiles projecting over a gable. **5** a wand or rod carried before a bishop, dean, etc., as an emblem of office. [ME f. OF f. L *virga* rod]

verge[2] /vɜːdʒ/ *v.intr.* **1** incline downwards or in a specified direction (*the now verging sun; verge to a close*). **2** (foll. by *on*) border on; approach closely (*verging on the ridiculous*). [L *vergere* bend, incline]

verger /ˈvɜːdʒə(r)/ *n.* (also **virger**) **1** an official in a church who acts as caretaker and attendant. **2** an officer who bears the staff before a bishop etc. □□ **vergership** *n.* [ME f. AF (as VERGE[1])]

verglas /ˈvɛəglɑː/ *n.* a thin coating of ice or frozen rain. [F]

veridical /vɪˈrɪdɪk(ə)l/ *adj.* **1** *formal* truthful. **2** *Psychol.* (of visions etc.) coinciding with reality. □□ **veridicality** /-ˈkælɪtɪ/ *n.* **veridically** *adv.* [L *veridicus* f. *verus* true + *dicere* say]

veriest /ˈvɛrɪɪst/ *adj.* (*superl.* of VERY). *archaic* real, extreme (*the veriest fool knows that*).

verification /ˌvɛrɪfɪˈkeɪʃ(ə)n/ *n.* **1** the process or an instance of establishing the truth or validity of something. **2** *Philos.* the establishment of the validity of a proposition empirically. **3** the process of verifying procedures laid down in weapons agreements.

verify /ˈvɛrɪfaɪ/ *v.tr.* (**-ies, -ied**) **1** establish the truth or correctness of by examination or demonstration (*must verify the statement; verified my figures*). **2** (of an event etc.) bear out or fulfil (a prediction or promise). **3** *Law* append an affidavit to (pleadings); support (a statement) by testimony or proofs. □□ **verifiable** *adj.* **verifiably** *adv.* **verifier** *n.* [ME f. OF *verifier* f. med.L *verificare* f. *verus* true]

verily /ˈvɛrɪlɪ/ *adv.* *archaic* really, truly. [ME f. VERY + -LY[2], after OF & AF]

verisimilitude /ˌvɛrɪsɪˈmɪlɪtjuːd/ *n.* **1** the appearance or semblance of being true or real. **2** a statement etc. that seems true. □□ **verisimilar** /-ˈsɪmɪlə(r)/ *adj.* [L *verisimilitudo* f. *verisimilis* probable f. *veri* genit. of *verus* true + *similis* like]

verism /ˈvɪərɪz(ə)m/ *n.* realism in literature or art. □□ **verist** *n.* **veristic** /-ˈrɪstɪk/ *adj.* [L *verus* or It. *vero* true + -ISM]

verismo /veˈrɪzməʊ/ *n.* (esp. of opera) realism. [It. (as VERISM)]

veritable /ˈvɛrɪtəb(ə)l/ *adj.* real; rightly so called (*a veritable feast*). □□ **veritably** *adv.* [OF (as VERITY)]

verity /ˈvɛrɪtɪ/ *n.* (*pl.* **-ies**) **1** a true statement, esp. one of fundamental import. **2** truth. **3** a really existent thing. [ME f. OF *verité, verté* f. L *veritas -tatis* f. *verus* true]

verjuice /ˈvɜːdʒuːs/ *n.* **1** an acid liquor obtained from crab-apples, sour grapes, etc., and formerly used in cooking and medicine. **2** bitter feelings, thoughts, etc. [ME f. OF *vertjus* f. VERT green + *jus* JUICE]

verkrampte /feəˈkræmptə/ *adj.* & *n.* *S.Afr.* —*adj.* politically or socially conservative or reactionary, esp. as regards apartheid. —*n.* a person holding such views. [Afrik., lit. narrow, cramped]

verligte /feəˈlɪxtə/ *adj.* & *n.* *S.Afr.* —*adj.* progressive or enlightened, esp. as regards apartheid. —*n.* a person holding such views. [Afrik., = enlightened]

Vermeer /vɜːˈmɪə(r)/, Jan (Johannes) (1632–75), Dutch painter whose short life was spent in Delft. Little is known of him other than that he took over the family silk business in 1655 in order to support his ever-growing family of children. It appears that he made no money from his art in his lifetime and as few as 36 paintings are known to be by his hand. Most of these are simple genre pictures, often with a single figure (his wife as the model) or views of streets and towns; his work is distinguished by its clear design and simple form, and its harmonious balance of predominant yellows, blues, and greys. No other artist has enjoyed so dramatic a change from obscurity to fame. Virtually unknown, until the later 19th c. Vermeer was as neglected after his death as he had apparently been in his lifetime.

vermeil /ˈvɜːmeɪl, -mɪl/ *n.* **1** silver gilt. **2** an orange-red garnet. **3** *poet.* vermilion. [ME f. OF: see VERMILION]

vermi- /ˈvɜːmɪ/ *comb. form* worm. [L *vermis* worm]

vermian /ˈvɜːmɪən/ *adj.* of worms; wormlike. [L *vermis* worm]

vermicelli /ˌvɜːmɪˈsɛlɪ, -ˈtʃɛlɪ/ *n.* **1** pasta made in long slender threads. **2** shreds of chocolate used as cake decoration etc. [It., pl. of *vermicello* dimin. of *verme* f. L *vermis* worm]

vermicide /ˈvɜːmɪˌsaɪd/ *n.* a substance that kills worms.

vermicular /vəˈmɪkjʊlə(r)/ *adj.* **1** like a worm in form or movement; vermiform. **2** *Med.* of or caused by intestinal worms. **3** marked with close wavy lines. [med.L *vermicularis* f. L *vermiculus* dimin. of *vermis* worm]

vermiculate /vəˈmɪkjʊlət/ *adj.* **1** = VERMICULAR. **2** wormeaten. [L *vermiculatus* past part. of *vermiculari* be full of worms (as VERMICULAR)]

vermiculation /vəˌmɪkjʊˈleɪʃ(ə)n/ *n.* **1** the state or process of being eaten or infested by or converted into worms. **2** a vermicular marking. **3** a wormeaten state. [L *vermiculatio* (as VERMICULATE)]

vermiculite /vəˈmɪkjʊˌlaɪt/ *n.* a hydrous silicate mineral usu. resulting from alteration of mica, and expandable into sponge by heating, used as an insulation material. [as VERMICULATE + -ITE[1]]

vermiform /ˈvɜːmɪˌfɔːm/ *adj.* worm-shaped. □ **vermiform appendix** see APPENDIX 1.

vermifuge /ˈvɜːmɪˌfjuːdʒ/ *adj.* & *n.* —*adj.* that expels intestinal worms. —*n.* a drug that does this.

vermilion /vəˈmɪljən/ *n.* & *adj.* —*n.* **1** cinnabar. **2 a** a brilliant red pigment made by grinding this or artificially. **b** the colour of this. —*adj.* of this colour. [ME f. OF *vermeillon* f. *vermeil* f. L *vermiculus* dimin. of *vermis* worm]

vermin /ˈvɜːmɪn/ *n.* (usu. treated as *pl.*) **1** mammals and birds injurious to game, crops, etc., e.g. foxes, rodents, and noxious insects. **2** parasitic worms or insects. **3** vile persons. □□ **verminous** *adj.* [ME f. OF *vermin, -ine* ult. f. L *vermis* worm]

verminate /ˈvɜːmɪˌneɪt/ *v.intr.* **1** breed vermin. **2** become infested with parasites. □□ **vermination** /-ˈneɪʃ(ə)n/ *n.* [L *verminare verminat-* f. *vermis* worm]

vermivorous /vɜːˈmɪvərəs/ *adj.* feeding on worms.

Vermont /vɜːˈmɒnt/ a State in the north-eastern US, bordering on Canada; pop. (est. 1985) 511,450; capital, Montpelier. Explored and settled by the French (17th–18th c.) it became an independent republic in 1777 and the 14th State of the US in 1791.

vermouth /ˈvɜːməθ, vəˈmuːθ/ *n.* a wine flavoured with aromatic herbs. [F *vermout* f. G *Wermut* WORMWOOD]

vernacular /vəˈnækjʊlə(r)/ *n.* & *adj.* —*n.* **1** the language or dialect of a particular country (*Latin gave place to the vernacular*). **2** the language of a particular clan or group. **3** homely speech. —*adj.* **1** (of language) of one's native country; not of foreign origin or of learned formation. **2** (of architecture) concerned with ordinary houses and monumental buildings. □□ **vernacularism** *n.* **vernacularity** /-ˈlærɪtɪ/ *n.* **vernacularize** *v.tr.* (also **-ise**). **vernacularly** *adv.* [L *vernaculus* domestic, native f. *verna* home-born slave]

vernal /ˈvɜːn(ə)l/ *adj.* of, in, or appropriate to spring (*vernal equinox; vernal breezes*). □ **vernal grass** a sweet-scented European grass, *Anthoxanthum odoratum*, grown for hay. □□ **vernally** *adv.* [L *vernalis* f. *vernus* f. *ver* spring]

vernalization /ˌvɜːnəlaɪˈzeɪʃ(ə)n/ *n.* (also **-isation**) the cooling of seed before planting, in order to accelerate flowering. □□ **vernalize** /ˈvɜːnəˌlaɪz/ *v.tr.* (also **-ise**). [(transl. of Russ. *yarovizatsiya*) f. VERNAL]

vernation /vɜːˈneɪʃ(ə)n/ *n.* *Bot.* the arrangement of leaves in a leaf-bud (cf. AESTIVATION). [mod.L *vernatio* f. L *vernare* bloom (as VERNAL)]

Verne /veən/, Jules (1828–1905), French novelist who achieved great and enduring popularity by the combination of adventure and popular science in his tales, which included *De la terre à la lune* (1865), a story of an earth-to-moon journey, launched by a cannon. His work anticipates the principle adopted by later writers of science fiction: a hypothesis, and an examination of its consequences, made interesting by a story woven around it.

vernicle /'vɜ:nɪk(ə)l/ n. = VERONICA 2. [ME f. OF (earlier ver(o)nique), f. med.L VERONICA]

vernier /'vɜ:nɪə(r)/ n. a small movable graduated scale for obtaining fractional parts of subdivisions on a fixed main scale of a barometer, sextant, etc. □ vernier engine an auxiliary engine for slight changes in the motion of a space rocket etc. [P. Vernier, Fr. mathematician d. 1637]

Verona /vəˈrəʊnə/ a city at the south end of Lake Garda in NE Italy; pop. (1981) 265,900.

veronal /'verən(ə)l/ n. propr. a sedative drug, a derivative of barbituric acid. [G, f. Verona in Italy]

Veronese /ˌverəˈneɪzɪ/ (Paolo Caliari, c.1528–88), Italian painter, born at Verona, whose use of cool silvery colours and soft yellows persisted in all his work. By about 1553 he had established himself in Venice and was already popular. Apart from his frescos, his masterpieces were great feast-scenes of pageantry and splendour (e.g. The Marriage Feast at Cana, 1562). With the help of a large workshop, including three of his sons and his brother, his output was enormous. Unfortunately the treatment of religious themes was not always felt to be sufficiently respectful, and in 1573 Veronese was summoned before the Inquisition on a charge of irreverence in his painting of the Feast in the House of Levi.

Veronica /vəˈrɒnɪkə/, St, a woman of Jerusalem said to have offered her headcloth to Christ on the way to Calvary, to wipe the blood and sweat from his face. The cloth is said to have retained the image of his features.

veronica /vəˈrɒnɪkə/ n. 1 any plant of the genus Veronica or Hebe, esp. speedwell. 2 a a cloth supposedly impressed with an image of Christ's face. b any similar picture of Christ's face. (See VERONICA.) 3 Bullfighting the movement of a matador's cape away from a charging bull. [med.L f. the name Veronica: in sense 2 from the association with St Veronica]

verruca /vəˈruːkə/ n. (pl. verrucae /-siː/ or verrucas) a wart or similar growth. □□ verrucose /ˈverʊˌkəʊz/ adj. verrucous /'verʊkəs/ adj. [L]

Versailles /veəˈsaɪ/ a town SW of Paris, noted for its royal palace, of which the central portion was built by Louis XIII and the wings and other edifices by Louis XIV. The grandeur of its design in the French classical style, and the elaborate gardens full of fountains and statuary, embody the whole spirit of the French monarchy and the courtly culture for which it stood. Its active life terminated and its raison d'être was gone when in October 1789 the Paris revolutionaries forced Louis XVI to leave for the city. □ Treaty of Versailles 1 a treaty which terminated the War of American Independence in 1783. 2 a treaty signed in 1919 which, along with a series of associated agreements, brought a formal end to the First World War, redivided the territory of the defeated Central Powers, and restricted Germany's armed forces. The Treaty in fact represented an unhappy compromise between conciliation and punishment, leaving Germany smarting under what she considered a vindictive settlement while not sufficiently restricting her ability eventually to rearm and seek forcible redress.

versant /'vɜ:s(ə)nt/ n. 1 the extent of land sloping in one direction. 2 the general slope of land. [F f. verser f. L versare frequent. of vertere vers- turn]

versatile /'vɜ:səˌtaɪl/ adj. 1 turning easily or readily from one subject or occupation to another; capable of dealing with many subjects (a versatile mind). 2 (of a device etc.) having many uses. 3 Bot. & Zool. moving freely about or up and down on a support (versatile antenna). 4 archaic changeable, inconstant. □□ versatilely adv. versatility /-ˈtɪlɪtɪ/ n. [F versatile or L versatilis (as VERSANT)]

verse /vɜ:s/ n. & v. —n. 1 a metrical composition in general (wrote pages of verse). b a particular type of this (English verse). 2 a a metrical line in accordance with the rules of prosody. b a group of a definite number of such lines. c a stanza of a poem or song with or without refrain. 3 each of the short numbered divisions of a chapter in the Bible or other scripture. 4 a a versicle. b a passage (of an anthem etc.) for solo voice. —v.tr. 1 express in verse. 2 (usu. refl.; foll. by in) instruct; make

knowledgeable. □□ verselet n. [OE fers f. L versus a turn of the plough, a furrow, a line of writing f. vertere vers- turn: in ME reinforced by OF vers f. L versus]

versed[1] /vɜ:st/ adj. (foll. by in) experienced or skilled in; knowledgeable about. [F versé or L versatus past part. of versari be engaged in (as VERSANT)]

versed[2] /vɜ:st/ adj. Math. reversed. □ versed sine unity minus cosine. [mod.L (sinus) versus turned (sine), formed as VERSE]

verset /'vɜ:sɪt/ n. Mus. a short prelude or interlude for organ. [F: dimin. of vers VERSE]

versicle /'vɜ:sɪk(ə)l/ n. each of the short sentences in a liturgy said or sung by a priest etc. and alternating with responses. □□ versicular /-ˈsɪkjʊlə(r)/ adj. [ME f. OF versicule or L versiculus dimin. of versus: see VERSE]

versicoloured /'vɜ:sɪˌkʌləd/ adj. 1 changing from one colour to another in different lights. 2 variegated. [L versicolor f. versus past part. of vertere turn + color colour]

versify /'vɜ:sɪˌfaɪ/ v. (-ies, -ied) 1 tr. turn into or express in verse. 2 intr. compose verses. □□ versification /-fɪˈkeɪʃ(ə)n/ n. versifier n. [ME f. OF versifier f. L versificare (as VERSE)]

versin /'vɜ:saɪn/ n. (also versine) Math. = versed sine (see VERSED[2]).

version /'vɜ:ʃ(ə)n/ n. 1 an account of a matter from a particular person's point of view (told them my version of the incident). 2 a book or work etc. in a particular edition or translation (Authorized Version). 3 a form or variant of a thing as performed, adapted, etc. 4 a piece of translation, esp. as a school exercise. 5 Med. the manual turning of a foetus in the womb to improve presentation. □□ versional adj. [F version or med.L versio f. L vertere vers- turn]

vers libre /veə ˈliːbrə/ n. irregular or unrhymed verse in which the traditional rules of prosody are disregarded. [F, = free verse]

verso /'vɜ:səʊ/ n. (pl. -os) 1 a the left-hand page of an open book. b the back of a printed leaf of paper or manuscript (opp. RECTO). 2 the reverse of a coin. [L verso (folio) on the turned (leaf)]

verst /vɜ:st/ n. a Russian measure of length, about 1.1 km (0.66 mile). [Russ. versta]

versus /'vɜ:səs/ prep. against (esp. in legal and sports use). ¶ Abbr.: v., vs. [L, = towards, in med.L against]

vert /vɜ:t/ n. & (usu. placed after noun) adj. Heraldry green. [ME f. OF f. L viridis green]

vertebra /'vɜ:tɪbrə/ n. (pl. vertebrae /-briː/) 1 each segment of the backbone. 2 (in pl.) the backbone. □□ vertebral adj. [L f. vertere turn]

vertebrate /'vɜ:tɪbrət, -ˌbreɪt/ n. & adj. —n. any animal of the subphylum Vertebrata, having a spinal column, including mammals, birds, reptiles, amphibians, and fishes. —adj. of or relating to the vertebrates. [L vertebratus jointed (as VERTEBRA)]

vertebration /ˌvɜ:tɪˈbreɪʃ(ə)n/ n. division into vertebrae or similar segments.

vertex /'vɜ:teks/ n. (pl. vertices /-tɪˌsiːz/ or vertexes) 1 the highest point; the top or apex. 2 Geom. a each angular point of a polygon, polyhedron, etc. b a meeting-point of two lines that form an angle. c the point at which an axis meets a curve or surface. 3 Anat. the crown of the head. [L vertex -ticis whirlpool, crown of a head, vertex, f. vertere turn]

vertical /'vɜ:tɪk(ə)l/ adj. & n. —adj. 1 at right angles to a horizontal plane, perpendicular. 2 in a direction from top to bottom of a picture etc. 3 of or at the vertex or highest point. 4 at, or passing through, the zenith. 5 Anat. of or relating to the crown of the head. 6 involving all the levels in an organizational hierarchy or stages in the production of a class of goods (vertical integration). —n. a vertical line or plane. □ out of the vertical not vertical. vertical angles Math. each pair of opposite angles made by two intersecting lines. vertical fin Zool. a dorsal, anal, or caudal fin. vertical plane a plane at right angles to the horizontal. vertical take-off the take-off of an aircraft directly upwards. □□ verticality /-ˈkælɪtɪ/ n. verticalize v.tr. (also -ise). vertically adv. [F vertical or LL verticalis (as VERTEX)]

verticil /'vɜ:tɪsɪl/ n. Bot. & Zool. a whorl; a set of parts arranged in a circle round an axis. □□ verticillate /-ˈtɪsɪlət/ adj. [L verticillus whorl of a spindle, dimin. of VERTEX]

vertiginous /vəˈtɪdʒɪnəs/ adj. of or causing vertigo. □□ **vertiginously** adv. [L vertiginosus (as VERTIGO)]

vertigo /ˈvɜːtɪˌɡəʊ/ n. a condition with a sensation of whirling and a tendency to lose balance; dizziness, giddiness. [L vertigo -ginis whirling f. vertere turn]

vertu var. of VIRTU.

vervain /ˈvɜːveɪn/ n. Bot. any of various herbaceous plants of the genus Verbena, esp. V. officinalis with small blue, white, or purple flowers. [ME f. OF verveine f. L VERBENA]

verve /vɜːv/ n. enthusiasm, vigour, spirit, esp. in artistic or literary work. [F, earlier = a form of expression, f. L verba words]

vervet /ˈvɜːvɪt/ n. a small grey African monkey, Cercopithecus aethiops. [F]

Verviers /ˈveəvɪˌeɪ/ a manufacturing town of Belgium, in the province of Liège; pop. (1988) 53,355.

very /ˈverɪ/ adv. & adj. —adv. **1** in a high degree (did it very easily; had a very bad cough; am very much better). **2** in the fullest sense (foll. by own or superl. adj.: at the very latest; do your very best; my very own room). —adj. **1** real, true, actual; truly such (usu. prec. by the, this, his, etc. emphasizing identity, significance, or extreme degree: the very thing we need; those were his very words). **2** archaic real, genuine (very God). □ **not very 1** in a low degree. **2** far from being. **very good** (or **well**) a formula of consent or approval. **very high frequency** (of radio frequency) in the range 30–300 megahertz. **Very Reverend** the title of a dean. **the very same** see SAME. [ME f. OF verai ult. f. L verus true]

Very light /ˈverɪ, ˈvɪərɪ/ n. a flare projected from a pistol for signalling or temporarily illuminating the surroundings. [E. W. Very, Amer. inventor d. 1910]

Very pistol /ˈverɪ, ˈvɪərɪ/ n. a gun for firing a Very light.

Vesalius /vɪˈseɪlɪəs/, Andreas (1514–64), Flemish anatomist who challenged traditional theories of anatomy which he held to be seriously flawed in being based upon the bodies of apes. This was a guess, but one borne out by later studies. His major work De humani corporis fabrica (1543), containing accurate descriptions of human anatomy, owed its great historical impact, however, more to the woodcuts of his dissections (drawn and engraved by someone else) than to Vesalius' text. He became physician to the emperor Charles V but died at the age of 49 as the result of a shipwreck.

vesica /ˈvesɪkə/ n. **1** Anat. & Zool. a bladder, esp. the urinary bladder. **2** (in full **vesica piscis** or **piscium**) Art a pointed oval used as an aureole in medieval sculpture and painting. □□ **vesical** adj. [L]

vesicate /ˈvesɪˌkeɪt/ v.tr. raise blisters on. □□ **vesicant** adj. & n. **vesication** /-ˈkeɪʃ(ə)n/ n. **vesicatory** /-ˈkeɪtərɪ/ adj. & n. [LL vesicare vesicat- (as VESICA)]

vesicle /ˈvesɪk(ə)l/ n. **1** Anat., Zool., & Bot. a small bladder, bubble, or hollow structure. **2** Geol. a small cavity in volcanic rock produced by gas bubbles. **3** Med. a blister. □□ **vesicular** /vɪˈsɪkjʊlə(r)/ adj. **vesiculate** /vɪˈsɪkjʊlət/ adj. **vesiculation** /vɪˌsɪkjʊˈleɪʃ(ə)n/ n. [F vésicule or L vesicula dimin. of VESICA]

Vespasian /vesˈpeɪʒ(ə)n/ (Titus Flavius Vespasianus, AD 9–79) the first Flavian Roman emperor 69–79. A distinguished general (he played a leading part in Claudius' invasion of Britain), he was acclaimed emperor by the legions in Egypt during the civil wars that followed the death of Nero, and gained control of Italy after the defeat of Vitellius. He restored financial and military order after the chaos of civil war and was able to restore the Capitol, build his Forum and Temple of Peace, and start work on the Colosseum.

vesper /ˈvespə(r)/ n. **1** Venus as the evening star. **2** poet. evening. **3** (in pl.) **a** the sixth of the canonical hours of prayer. **b** evensong. [L vesper evening (star): sense 3 partly f. OF vespres f. eccl.L vesperas f. L vespera evening]

vespertine /ˈvespəˌtaɪn, -tɪn/ adj. **1** Bot. (of a flower) opening in the evening. **2** Zool. active in the evening. **3** Astron. setting near the time of sunset. **4** of or occurring in the evening. [L vespertinus f. vesper evening]

vespiary /ˈvespɪərɪ/ n. (pl. **-ies**) a nest of wasps. [irreg. f. L vespa wasp, after apiary]

vespine /ˈvespaɪn/ adj. of or relating to wasps. [L vespa wasp]

Vespucci /veˈspuːtʃɪ/, Amerigo (1451–1512), Florentine merchant and explorer. While in the service of the king of Portugal, Vespucci made several voyages to the New World and claimed, on dubious authority, to have been the first to sight the mainland of South America (1497). The name America is said to have been derived from his own first name, but there are other suggestions of its origin.

vessel /ˈves(ə)l/ n. **1** a hollow receptacle esp. for liquid, e.g. a cask, cup, pot, bottle, or dish. **2** a ship or boat, esp. a large one. **3 a** Anat. a duct or canal etc. holding or conveying blood or other fluid, esp. = blood-vessel. **b** Bot. a woody duct carrying or containing sap etc. **4** Bibl. or joc. a person regarded as the recipient or exponent of a quality (a weak vessel). [ME f. AF vessel(e), OF vaissel(le) f. LL vascellum dimin. of vas vessel]

vest /vest/ n. & v. —n. **1** an undergarment worn on the upper part of the body. **2** US & Austral. a waistcoat. **3** a usu. V-shaped piece of material to fill the opening at the neck of a woman's dress. —v. **1** tr. (esp. in passive; foll. by with) bestow or confer (powers, authority, etc.) on (a person). **2** tr. (foll. by in) confer (property or power) on (a person) with an immediate fixed right of immediate or future possession. **3** intr. (foll. by in) (of property, a right, etc.) come into the possession of (a person). **4 a** tr. poet. clothe. **b** intr. Eccl. put on vestments. □ **vested interest 1** Law an interest (usu. in land or money held in trust) recognized as belonging to a person. **2** a personal interest in a state of affairs, usu. with an expectation of gain. [(n.) F veste f. It. veste f. L vestis garment: (v.) ME, orig. past part. f. OF vestu f. vestir f. L vestire vestit- clothe]

Vesta /ˈvestə/ **1** Rom. Mythol. the goddess of the hearth and household. Her S̟tate worship was not in a temple but in a round building (doubtless an imitation in stone of the ancient round hut), which contained no image but a fire which was kept constantly burning and was tended by the Vestal Virgins. **2** Astron. one of the minor planets, with orbit between Mars and Jupiter, discovered in 1807. [L f. Gk hestia hearth]

vesta /ˈvestə/ n. hist. a short wooden or wax match. [VESTA 1]

Vestal /ˈvest(ə)l/ adj. & n. —adj. **1** of the Roman goddess Vesta. **2** (**vestal**) chaste, pure. —n. **1** a Vestal Virgin, a virgin consecrated to Vesta and vowed to chastity. In historical times there were normally six, serving for 30 years. Vestals wore the old sacral dress otherwise reserved for brides. Their duty was to tend the undying fire burning in the shrine of Vesta in the Forum of ancient Rome, and to remain virgin: an unchaste Vestal was punished by being entombed alive. **2** a chaste woman, esp. a nun. [ME f. L vestalis (adj. & n.) (as VESTA)]

vestee /veˈstiː/ n. = VEST n. 3.

Vesterålen /ˈvestəˌrɒlən/ an island group of NW Norway, to the north of the Lofoten Islands.

vestiary /ˈvestɪərɪ/ n. & adj. —n. (pl. **-ies**) **1** a vestry. **2** a robing-room; a cloakroom. —adj. of or relating to clothes or dress. [ME f. OF vestiarie, vestiaire: see VESTRY]

vestibule /ˈvestɪˌbjuːl/ n. **1 a** an antechamber, hall, or lobby next to the outer door of a building. **b** a porch of a church etc. **2** US an enclosed entrance to a railway-carriage. **3** Anat. **a** a chamber or channel communicating with others. **b** part of the mouth outside the teeth. **c** the central cavity of the labyrinth of the inner ear. □□ **vestibular** /-ˈstɪbjʊlə(r)/ adj. [F vestibule or L vestibulum entrance-court]

vestige /ˈvestɪdʒ/ n. **1** a trace or piece of evidence; a sign (vestiges of an earlier civilization; found no vestige of their presence). **2** a slight amount; a particle (without a vestige of clothing; showed not a vestige of decency). **3** Biol. a part or organ of an organism that is reduced or functionless but was well developed in its ancestors. [F f. L vestigium footprint]

vestigial /veˈstɪdʒɪəl, -dʒ(ə)l/ adj. **1** being a vestige or trace. **2** Biol. (of an organ) atrophied or functionless from the process of evolution (a vestigial wing). □□ **vestigially** adv.

vestiture /ˈvestɪtʃə(r)/ n. **1** Zool. hair, scales, etc., covering a surface. **2** archaic **a** clothing. **b** investiture. [ME f. med.L vestitura f. L vestire: see VEST]

vestment /ˈvestmənt/ n. **1** any of the official robes of clergy, choristers, etc., worn during divine service, esp. a chasuble. **2** a garment, esp. an official or state robe. [ME f. OF *vestiment, vestement* f. L *vestimentum* (as VEST)]

vestry /ˈvestrɪ/ n. (pl. **-ies**) **1** a room or building attached to a church for keeping vestments in. **2** hist. **a** a meeting of parishioners usu. in a vestry for parochial business. **b** a body of parishioners meeting in this way. □□ **vestral** adj. [ME f. OF *vestiaire, vestiarie,* f. L *vestiarium* (as VEST)]

vestryman /ˈvestrɪmən/ n. (pl. **-men**) a member of a vestry.

vesture /ˈvestʃə(r)/ n. & v. —n. *poet.* **1** garments, dress. **2** a covering. —v.tr. clothe. [ME f. OF f. med.L *vestitura* (as VEST)]

Vesuvius /vɪˈsuːvɪəs/ an active volcano near Naples in Italy, 1,277 m (4,190 ft.) high. It erupted violently in AD 79, burying the towns of Pompeii and Herculaneum.

vet[1] /vet/ n. & v. —n. *colloq.* a veterinary surgeon. —v.tr. (**vetted, vetting**) **1** make a careful and critical examination of (a scheme, work, candidate, etc.). **2** examine or treat (an animal). [abbr.]

vet[2] /vet/ n. *US colloq.* a veteran. [abbr.]

vetch /vetʃ/ n. any plant of the genus *Vicia,* esp. *V. sativa,* largely used for silage or fodder. □□ **vetchy** adj. [ME f. AF & ONF *veche* f. L *vicia*]

vetchling /ˈvetʃlɪŋ/ n. any of various plants of the genus *Lathyrus,* related to vetch.

veteran /ˈvetərən/ n. **1** a person who has grown old in or had long experience of esp. military service or an occupation (a *war veteran; a veteran of the theatre; a veteran marksman*). **2** *US* an ex-serviceman or servicewoman. **3** (attrib.) of or for veterans. □ **veteran car** *Brit.* a car made before 1916, or (strictly) before 1905. [F *vétéran* or L *veteranus* (adj. & n.) f. *vetus -eris* old]

veterinarian /ˌvetərɪˈneərɪən/ n. *US* a veterinary surgeon. [L *veterinarius* (as VETERINARY)]

veterinary /ˈvetərɪnərɪ/ adj. & n. —adj. of or for diseases and injuries of farm and domestic animals, or their treatment. —n. (pl. **-ies**) a veterinary surgeon. □ **veterinary surgeon** *Brit.* a person qualified to treat diseased or injured animals. [L *veterinarius* f. *veterinae* cattle]

vetiver /ˈvetɪvə(r)/ n. = CUSCUS[1]. [F *vétiver* f. Tamil *veṭṭiveru* f. *vēr* root]

veto /ˈviːtəʊ/ n. & v. —n. (pl. **-oes**) **1 a** a constitutional right to reject a legislative enactment. **b** the right of a permanent member of the UN Security Council to reject a resolution. **c** such a rejection. **d** an official message conveying this. **2** a prohibition (*put one's veto on a proposal*). —v.tr. (**-oes, -oed**) **1** exercise a veto against (a measure etc.). **2** forbid authoritatively. □□ **vetoer** n. [L, = I forbid, with ref. to its use by Roman tribunes of the people in opposing measures of the Senate]

vex /veks/ v.tr. **1** anger by a slight or a petty annoyance; irritate. **2** *archaic* grieve, afflict. □□ **vexer** n. **vexing** adj. **vexingly** adv. [ME f. OF *vexer* f. L *vexare* shake, disturb]

vexation /vekˈseɪʃ(ə)n/ n. **1** the act or an instance of vexing; the state of being vexed. **2** an annoying or distressing thing. [ME f. OF *vexation* or L *vexatio -onis* (as VEX)]

vexatious /vekˈseɪʃəs/ adj. **1** such as to cause vexation. **2** *Law* not having sufficient grounds for action and seeking only to annoy the defendant. □□ **vexatiously** adv. **vexatiousness** n.

vexed /vekst/ adj. **1** irritated, angered. **2** (of a problem, issue, etc.) difficult and much discussed; problematic. □□ **vexedly** /ˈveksɪdlɪ/ adv.

vexillology /ˌveksɪˈlɒlədʒɪ/ n. the study of flags. □□ **vexillological** /-ləˈlɒdʒɪk(ə)l/ adj. **vexillologist** n. [L *vexillum* flag + -LOGY]

vexillum /vekˈsɪləm/ n. (pl. **vexilla** /-lə/) **1** *Rom. Antiq.* **a** a military standard, esp. of a maniple. **b** a body of troops under this. **2** *Bot.* the large upper petal of a papilionaceous flower. **3** *Zool.* the vane of a feather. **4** *Eccl.* **a** a flag attached to a bishop's staff. **b** a processional banner or cross. [L f. *vehere vect-* carry]

VG abbr. **1** very good. **2** Vicar-General.

VHF abbr. very high frequency.

VI abbr. Virgin Islands.

via /ˈvaɪə/ prep. by way of; through (*London to Rome via Paris; send it via your secretary*). [L, ablat. of *via* way, road]

viable /ˈvaɪəb(ə)l/ adj. **1** (of a plan etc.) feasible; practicable esp. from an economic standpoint. **2 a** (of a plant, animal, etc.) capable of living or existing in a certain climate etc. **b** (of a foetus or newborn child) capable of maintaining life. **3** (of a seed or spore) able to germinate. □□ **viability** /-ˈbɪlɪtɪ/ n. **viably** adv. [F f. *vie* life f. L *vita*]

viaduct /ˈvaɪədʌkt/ n. **1** a long bridgelike structure, esp. a series of arches, carrying a road or railway across a valley or dip in the ground. **2** such a road or railway. [L *via* way, after AQUEDUCT]

vial /ˈvaɪəl/ n. a small (usu. cylindrical glass) vessel esp. for holding liquid medicines. □□ **vialful** n. (pl. **-fuls**). [ME, var. of *fiole* etc.: see PHIAL]

via media /ˌvaɪə ˈmiːdɪə, ˌviːə ˈmeɪdɪə/ n. *literary* a middle way or compromise between extremes. [L]

viand /ˈvaɪənd/ n. *formal* **1** an article of food. **2** (in pl.) provisions, victuals. [ME f. OF *viande* food, ult. f. L *vivenda,* neut. pl. gerundive of *vivere* to live]

viaticum /vaɪˈætɪkəm/ n. (pl. **viatica** /-kə/) **1** the Eucharist as given to a person near or in danger of death. **2** provisions or an official allowance of money for a journey. [L, neut. of *viaticus* f. *via* road]

vibes /vaɪbz/ n.pl. *colloq.* **1** vibrations, esp. in the sense of feelings or atmosphere communicated (*the house had bad vibes*). **2** = VIBRAPHONE. [abbr.]

vibraculum /vaɪˈbrækjʊləm/ n. (pl. **vibracula** /-lə/) *Zool.* a whiplike structure of bryozoans used to bring food within reach by lashing movements. □□ **vibracular** adj. [mod.L (as VIBRATE)]

vibrant /ˈvaɪbrənt/ adj. **1** vibrating. **2** (often foll. by with) (of a person or thing) thrilling, quivering (*vibrant with emotion*). **3** (of sound) resonant. □□ **vibrancy** n. **vibrantly** adv. [L *vibrare:* see VIBRATE]

vibraphone /ˈvaɪbrəfəʊn/ n. a percussion instrument of tuned metal bars with motor-driven resonators and metal tubes giving a vibrato effect. □□ **vibraphonist** n. [VIBRATO + -PHONE]

vibrate /vaɪˈbreɪt/ v. **1** intr. & tr. move or cause to move continuously and rapidly to and fro; oscillate. **2** intr. *Physics* move unceasingly to and fro, esp. rapidly. **3** intr. (of a sound) throb; continue to be heard. **4** intr. (foll. by with) quiver, thrill (*vibrating with passion*). **5** intr. (of a pendulum) swing to and fro. □□ **vibrative** /-rətɪv/ adj. [L *vibrare vibrat-* shake, swing]

vibratile /ˈvaɪbrətaɪl/ adj. **1** capable of vibrating. **2** *Biol.* (of cilia etc.) used in vibratory motion. [VIBRATORY, after *pulsatile* etc.]

vibration /vaɪˈbreɪʃ(ə)n/ n. **1** the act or an instance of vibrating; oscillation. **2** *Physics* (esp. rapid) motion to and fro esp. of the parts of a fluid or an elastic solid whose equilibrium has been disturbed or of an electromagnetic wave. **3** (in pl.) **a** a mental (esp. occult) influence. **b** a characteristic atmosphere or feeling in a place, regarded as communicable to people present in it. □□ **vibrational** adj. [L *vibratio* (as VIBRATE)]

vibrato /vɪˈbrɑːtəʊ/ n. *Mus.* a rapid slight variation in pitch in singing or playing a stringed or wind instrument, producing a tremulous effect (cf. TREMOLO). [It., past part. of *vibrare* VIBRATE]

vibrator /vaɪˈbreɪtə(r)/ n. **1** a device that vibrates or causes vibration, esp. an electric or other instrument used in massage or for sexual stimulation. **2** *Mus.* a reed in a reed-organ.

vibratory /ˈvaɪbrətərɪ, -ˈbreɪtərɪ/ adj. causing vibration.

vibrissae /vaɪˈbrɪsiː/ n.pl. **1** stiff coarse hairs near the mouth of most mammals (e.g. a cat's whiskers) and in the human nostrils. **2** bristle-like feathers near the mouth of insect-eating birds. [L (as VIBRATE)]

viburnum /vaɪˈbɜːnəm, vɪ-/ n. *Bot.* any shrub of the genus *Viburnum,* usu. with white flowers, e.g. the guelder rose and wayfaring-tree. [L, = wayfaring-tree]

Vic. abbr. Victoria.

vicar /ˈvɪkə(r)/ n. **1 a** (in the Church of England) an incumbent of a parish where tithes formerly passed to a chapter or religious house or layman (cf. RECTOR). **b** (in an Episcopal Church) a member of the clergy deputizing for another. **2** *RC Ch.* a representative or deputy of a bishop. **3** (in full **lay vicar** or **vicar choral**) a cleric or choir member appointed to sing certain parts of a cathedral service. □ **vicar apostolic** *RC Ch.* a Roman

Catholic missionary or titular bishop. **vicar-general** (*pl.*
vicars-general) **1** an Anglican official assisting or representing
a bishop esp. in administrative matters. **2** *RC Ch.* a bishop's
assistant in matters of jurisdiction etc. **Vicar of Christ** the
Pope. □□ **vicariate** /-ˈkeərɪət/ *n.* **vicarship** *n.* [ME f. AF *viker(e)*,
OF *vicaire* f. L *vicarius* substitute f. *vicis*: see VICE³]

vicarage /ˈvɪkərɪdʒ/ *n.* the residence or benefice of a vicar.

vicarial /vɪˈkeərɪəl/ *adj.* of or serving as a vicar.

vicarious /vɪˈkeərɪəs/ *adj.* **1** experienced in the imagination
through another person (*vicarious pleasure*). **2** acting or done
for another (*vicarious suffering*). **3** deputed, delegated (*vicarious
authority*). □□ **vicariously** *adv.* **vicariousness** *n.* [L *vicarius*: see
VICAR]

vice¹ /vaɪs/ *n.* **1 a** evil or grossly immoral conduct. **b** a particular
form of this, esp. involving prostitution, drugs, etc. **2 a** depravity, evil. **b** an evil habit; a particular form of depravity (*has the
vice of gluttony*). **3** a defect of character or behaviour (*drunkenness
was not among his vices*). **4** a fault or bad habit in a horse etc. □
vice ring a group of criminals involved in organizing illegal
prostitution. **vice squad** a police department enforcing laws
against prostitution, drug abuse, etc. □□ **viceless** *adj.* [ME f. OF
f. L *vitium*]

vice² /vaɪs/ *n. & v.* —*n.* (*US* **vise**) an instrument, esp. attached
to a workbench, with two movable jaws between which an
object may be clamped so as to leave the hands free to work on
it. —*v.tr.* secure in a vice. □□ **vicelike** *adj.* [ME, = winding
stair, screw, f. OF *vis* f. L *vitis* vine]

vice³ /ˈvaɪsɪ/ *prep.* in the place of; in succession to. [L, ablat. of
vix (recorded in oblique forms in *vic-*) change]

vice⁴ /vaɪs/ *n. colloq.* = VICE-PRESIDENT, VICE ADMIRAL, etc. [abbr.]

vice- /vaɪs/ *comb. form* forming nouns meaning: **1** acting as a
substitute or deputy for (*vice-president*). **2** next in rank to (*vice
admiral*). [as VICE³]

vice admiral /vaɪsˈædmər(ə)l/ *n.* a naval officer ranking below
admiral and above rear admiral. □□ **vice-admiralty** *n.* (*pl.* **-ies**)

vice-chamberlain /vaɪsˈtʃeɪmbəlɪn/ *n.* a deputy chamberlain,
esp. the deputy of the Lord Chamberlain.

vice-chancellor /vaɪsˈtʃɑːnsələ(r)/ *n.* a deputy chancellor (esp.
of a British university, discharging most of the administrative
duties).

vicegerent /vaɪsˈdʒerənt/ *adj. & n.* —*adj.* exercising delegated
power. —*n.* a vicegerent person; a deputy. □□ **vicegerency** *n.*
(*pl.* **-ies**) [med.L *vicegerens* (as VICE³, L *gerere* carry on)]

vicennial /vaɪˈsenɪəl/ *adj.* lasting for or occurring every twenty
years. [LL *vicennium* period of 20 years f. *vicies* 20 times f. *viginti*
20 + *annus* year]

Vicente /vɪˈsentɪ/, Gil (c.1465–1536), Portuguese poet and playwright. His plays (some in Portuguese, some in Spanish) include
dramas on religious themes and comedies which satirize the
nobility and clergy. He has been identified with a goldsmith of
the same name, and has sometimes been called the Portuguese
Shakespeare.

vice-president /vaɪsˈprezɪd(ə)nt/ *n.* an official ranking below
and deputizing for a president. □□ **vice-presidency** *n.* (*pl.* **-ies**).
vice-presidential /-ˈdenʃ(ə)l/ *adj.*

viceregal /vaɪsˈriːg(ə)l/ *adj.* of or relating to a viceroy. □□
viceregally *adv.*

vicereine /ˈvaɪsreɪn/ *n.* **1** the wife of a viceroy. **2** a woman
viceroy. [F (as VICE-, *reine* queen)]

viceroy /ˈvaɪsrɔɪ/ *n.* a ruler exercising authority on behalf of a
sovereign in a colony, province, etc. □□ **viceroyal** /-ˈrɔɪəl/ *adj.*
viceroyalty /-ˈrɔɪəltɪ/ *n.* **viceroyship** *n.* [F (as VICE-, *roy* king)]

vicesimal /vaɪˈsezɪm(ə)l/ *adj.* = VIGESIMAL. [L *vicesimus*
twentieth]

vice versa /ˌvaɪsɪ ˈvɜːsə/ *adv.* with the order of the terms or
conditions changed; the other way round (*could go from left to
right or vice versa*). [L, = the position being reversed (as VICE³,
versa ablat. fem. past part. of *vertere* turn)]

Vichy /ˈviːʃiː/ a town in central France noted for its mineral
waters; pop. (1982) 35,000. It was the headquarters of the French

government under Petain administering Southern France following the Franco-German armistice in 1940.

vichyssoise /ˌviːʃiːˈswɑːz/ *n.* a creamy soup of leeks and
potatoes, usu. served chilled. [F *vichyssois -oise* of Vichy (in
France)]

vicinage /ˈvɪsɪnɪdʒ/ *n.* **1** a neighbourhood; a surrounding
district. **2** relation in terms of nearness etc. to neighbours. [ME
f. OF *vis(e)nage* ult. f. L *vicinus* neighbour]

vicinal /ˈvɪsɪn(ə)l, -ˈsaɪn(ə)l/ *adj.* **1** neighbouring, adjacent. **2** of a
neighbourhood; local. [F *vicinal* or L *vicinalis* f. *vicinus* neighbour]

vicinity /vɪˈsɪnɪtɪ/ *n.* (*pl.* **-ies**) **1** a surrounding district. **2** (foll.
by *to*) nearness or closeness of place or relationship. □ **in the
vicinity** (often foll. by *of*) near (to). [L *vicinitas* (as VICINAL)]

vicious /ˈvɪʃəs/ *adj.* **1** bad-tempered, spiteful (*a vicious dog; vicious
remarks*). **2** violent, severe (*a vicious attack*). **3** of the nature of or
addicted to vice. **4** (of language or reasoning etc.) faulty or
unsound. □ **vicious circle** see CIRCLE *n.* 11. **vicious spiral**
continual harmful interaction of causes and effects, esp. as
causing repeated rises in both prices and wages. □□ **viciously**
adv. **viciousness** *n.* [ME f. OF *vicious* or L *vitiosus* f. *vitium* VICE¹]

vicissitude /vɪˈsɪsɪtjuːd, vaɪ-/ *n.* **1** a change of circumstances,
esp. variation of fortune. **2** *archaic* or *poet.* regular change;
alternation. □□ **vicissitudinous** /-ˈtjuːdɪnəs/ *adj.* [F *vicissitude* or
L *vicissitudo -dinis* f. *vicissim* by turns (as VICE³)]

Vicksburg /ˈvɪksbɜːg/ a city on the Mississippi; pop. (1980)
25,434. It was successfully besieged by Federal forces under
General Grant in 1863. It was the last Confederate-held outpost
on this river and its loss effectively split the secessionist States
in half, bringing the end of the American Civil War much nearer.

victim /ˈvɪktɪm/ *n.* **1** a person injured or killed as a result of an
event or circumstance (*a road victim; the victims of war*). **2** a person
or thing injured or destroyed in pursuit of an object or in
gratification of a passion etc. (*the victim of their ruthless ambition*).
3 a prey; a dupe (*fell victim to a confidence trick*). **4** a living creature
sacrificed to a deity or in a religious rite. [L *victima*]

victimize /ˈvɪktɪˌmaɪz/ *v.tr.* (also **-ise**) **1** single out (a person)
for punishment or unfair treatment, esp. dismissal from
employment. **2** make (a person etc.) a victim. □□ **victimization**
/-ˈzeɪʃ(ə)n/ *n.* **victimizer** *n.*

victor /ˈvɪktə(r)/ *n.* a winner in battle or in a contest. [ME f. AF
victo(u)r or L *victor* f. *vincere* *vict-* conquer]

Victor Emmanuel /ˌvɪktər ɪˈmænjuəl/ the name of three
kings of Sardinia, two of whom became kings of Italy:
  Victor Emmanuel II (1820–78), first king of a unified Italy
(1861–78).
  Victor Emmanuel III (1869–1947), king of Italy 1900–46,
forced to abdicate after the defeat and death of Mussolini, whose
policies he had supported.

Victoria¹ /vɪkˈtɔːrɪə/ (1819–1901), queen of the United Kingdom
1837–1901, the longest reign in British history. Brought up in
stifling seclusion, she succeeded to the throne on the death of
her uncle, William IV, and at once showed qualities of determination and obstinacy coupled with a pleasure-loving disposition. After her marriage to her cousin Prince Albert in 1840
Victoria became more serious, more conscious of her responsibilities, and more businesslike; she took an active interest in
the policies of her ministers in both home and foreign affairs,
ably advised by the Prince, who persuaded her that the Crown
should not be aligned with any political party—a principle that
has endured. The idea of duty, rather solemnly performed, came
to the forefront of her life; the age of Victorian respectability
had begun. She was hostile to Palmerston and never liked or
understood Gladstone; Melbourne was her trusted adviser, and
Disraeli (who in 1876 gained for her the title of Empress
of India) was similarly esteemed. Albert's death in 1861 was a
shock from which Victoria never recovered; her ensuing retirement from public life was unpopular, but from Disraeli's time
onwards she gradually emerged and the old lady in her widow's
weeds became a national figure, grandmother (through her nine
children) to half the royal houses of Europe, and her Diamond
Jubilee in 1897 was made an occasion for a demonstration of
public loyalty and imperial splendour. During Queen Victoria's

æ cat ɑː arm e bed ɜː her ɪ sit iː see ɒ hot ɔː saw ʌ run ʊ put uː too ə ago aɪ my

reign Britain reached the summit of her power and prosperity, and the Crown became the link between parts of an Imperial Commonwealth. Her death was rightly felt to be the end of an era.

Victoria[2] /vɪkˈtɔːrɪə/ a State of south-east Australia; pop. (1986) 4,183,500; capital, Melbourne. Originally known as the Port Philip district of New South Wales, it became a separate colony in 1851 and was federated with the other States of Australia in 1901.

Victoria[3] /vɪkˈtɔːrɪə/ a seaport on the island of Mahé and capital of the Seychelles Islands; pop. (est. 1985) 23,000.

Victoria[4] /vɪkˈtɔːrɪə/, Tomás Luis de (1548–1611), the leading Spanish composer of his generation. While working in Rome he may have studied with Palestrina, and his music, all of it sacred, resembles that of the Roman composer in its smoothly flowing counterpoint, undisturbed by subjective emotion, although where called for by the text an impassioned depiction of anguish and drama is one of the notable features of his style.

Victoria[5] /vɪkˈtɔːrɪə/, **Lake** (also **Victoria Nyanza** /nɪˈænzə/) the largest lake in Africa and the chief reservoir of the Nile, discovered by Speke in 1858. Sections of it lie within the boundaries of Uganda, Tanzania, and Kenya.

victoria /vɪkˈtɔːrɪə/ n. 1 a low light four-wheeled carriage with a collapsible top, seats for two passengers, and a raised driver's seat. 2 a gigantic S. American water lily, *Victoria amazonica*. 3 a a species of crowned pigeon. b a variety of domestic pigeon. 4 (also **victoria plum**) *Brit.* a large red luscious variety of plum. [VICTORIA[1]]

Victoria and Albert Museum a national museum of fine and applied art in South Kensington, London, created out of the surplus funds of the Great Exhibition of 1851 from which a nucleus of objects was purchased. This 'Museum of Ornamental Art', linked with an art library, was moved to its present site in 1857. In 1899 it was renamed after Queen Victoria and her consort, and the foundation-stone of the present building was laid by her. Its principal collections are of pictures (including the Raphael cartoons belonging to the Crown), textiles, ceramics, and furniture.

Victoria Cross a decoration awarded to members of the Commonwealth armed services for a conspicuous act of bravery, founded by Queen Victoria in 1856 and struck from the metal of guns captured at Sebastopol during the Crimean War. The most prized of all decorations, it consists of a bronze cross, with the royal crown surmounted by a lion in the centre, and with the words 'For Valour' beneath.

Victoria Falls a spectacular waterfall 109 m (355 ft.) high on the River Zambezi at the border of Zimbabwe and Zambia, discovered by David Livingstone in 1855.

Victoria Island an island in the Canadian Arctic, the third-largest island of Canada.

Victorian /vɪkˈtɔːrɪən/ adj. & n. —adj. of or characteristic of the time of Queen Victoria. Among the characteristics of the age in allusion to which the term is sometimes used are its improved standards of decency and morality; a self-satisfaction engendered by the great increase of wealth, the prosperity of the nation as a whole, and the immense industrial and scientific development; conscious rectitude and deficient sense of humour; an unquestioning acceptance of authority and orthodoxy. —n. a person, esp. a writer, of this time. □ **Royal Victorian Order** an order founded by Queen Victoria in 1896 and awarded for personal service to the sovereign. □□ **Victorianism** n.

Victoriana /vɪkˌtɔːrɪˈɑːnə/ n.pl. 1 articles, esp. collectors' items, of the Victorian period. 2 attitudes characteristic of this period.

Victoria Peak a mountain on Hong Kong Island rising to a height of 554 m (1,818 ft.)

Victoria sandwich n. (also **Victoria sponge**) a sponge cake consisting of two layers of sponge with a jam filling.

victorious /vɪkˈtɔːrɪəs/ adj. 1 having won a victory; conquering, triumphant. 2 marked by victory (*victorious day*). □□ **victoriously** adv. **victoriousness** n. [ME f. AF *victorious*, OF *victorieux*, f. L *victoriosus* (as VICTORY)]

victor ludorum /ˌvɪktə luːˈdɔːrəm/ n. the overall champion in a sports competition. [L, = victor of the games]

Victory the flagship of Lord Nelson at the battle of Trafalgar, now restored and on display in dry dock at Portsmouth.

victory /ˈvɪktərɪ/ n. (pl. **-ies**) 1 the process of defeating an enemy in battle or war or an opponent in a contest. 2 an instance of this; a triumph. [ME f. AF *victorie*, OF *victoire*, f. L *victoria* (as VICTOR)]

victual /ˈvɪt(ə)l/ n. & v. —n. (usu. in pl.) food, provisions, esp. as prepared for use. —v. (**victualled**, **victualling**; US **victualed**, **victualing**) 1 tr. supply with victuals. 2 intr. obtain stores. 3 intr. eat victuals. □□ **victualless** adj. [ME f. OF *vitaille* f. LL *victualia*, neut. pl. of L *victualis* f. *victus* food, rel. to *vivere* live]

victualler /ˈvɪtlə(r)/ n. (US **victualer**) 1 a a person etc. who supplies victuals. b (in full **licensed victualler**) *Brit.* a publican etc. licensed to sell alcoholic liquor. 2 a ship carrying stores for other ships. [ME f. OF *vitaill(i)er*, *vitaillour* (as VICTUAL)]

vicuña /vɪˈkjuːnə/ n. 1 a S. American mammal, *Vicugna vicugna*, related to the llama, with fine silky wool. 2 a cloth made from its wool. b an imitation of this. [Sp. f. Quechua]

Vidal /viːˈdæl/, Gore (Eugene Luther Vidal, 1925–), American novelist, playwright (for stage, cinema, and television), and essayist, noted for his witty satirical observations and for his outspoken political comments. His novels include *Williwaw* (1946), based on his wartime experiences, *The City and the Pillar* (1948), a sympathetic portrait of a homosexual, the comedy *Myra Breckenridge* (1968), and *Creation* (1981), set in the world of Darius, Xerxes, and Confucius. Among his plays are *Visit to a Small Planet* (1956) and *Suddenly Last Summer* (1958). *The Second American Revolution* (1982) is a collection of essays.

vide /ˈvɪdeɪ, ˈviː-, ˈvaɪdɪ/ v.tr. (as an instruction in a reference to a passage in a book etc.) see, consult. [L, imper. of *vidēre* see]

videlicet /vɪˈdeliˌset/ adv. = VIZ. [ME f. L f. *vidēre* see + *licet* it is permissible]

video /ˈvɪdɪəʊ/ adj., n., & v. —adj. 1 relating to the recording, reproducing, or broadcasting of visual images on magnetic tape. 2 relating to the broadcasting of television pictures. —n. (pl. **-os**) 1 the process of recording, reproducing, or broadcasting visual images on magnetic tape. 2 the visual element of television broadcasts. 3 colloq. = video recorder. 4 a film etc. recorded on a videotape. —v.tr. (**-oes**, **-oed**) make a video recording of. □ **video cassette** a cassette of videotape. **video frequency** a frequency in the range used for video signals in television. **video game** a game played by electronically manipulating images produced by a computer program on a television screen. **video nasty** colloq. an explicitly horrific or pornographic video film. **video** (or **video cassette**) **recorder** an apparatus for recording and playing videotapes. **video signal** a signal containing information for producing a television image. [L *vidēre* see, after AUDIO]

videodisc /ˈvɪdɪəʊˌdɪsk/ n. a metal-coated disc on which visual material is recorded for reproduction on a television screen.

videophone /ˈvɪdɪəʊˌfəʊn/ n. a telephone device transmitting a visual image as well as sound.

videotape /ˈvɪdɪəʊˌteɪp/ n. & v. —n. magnetic tape for recording television pictures and sound. —v.tr. make a recording of (broadcast material etc.) with this. □ **videotape recorder** = *video recorder*.

videotex /ˈvɪdɪəʊˌteks/ n. (also **videotext** /-ˌtekst/) any electronic information system, esp. teletext or viewdata.

vidimus /ˈvaɪdɪməs/ n. an inspection or certified copy of accounts etc. [L, = we have seen f. *vidēre* see]

vie /vaɪ/ v.intr. (**vying**) (often foll. by *with*) compete; strive for superiority (*vied with each other for recognition*). [prob. f. ME (as ENVY)]

vielle /vɪˈel/ n. a hurdy-gurdy. [F f. OF *viel(l)e*: see VIOL]

Vienna /vɪˈenə/ (German **Wien** /viːn/) the capital of Austria, situated on the River Danube; pop. (1981) 1,531,346. It was an important military centre (*Vindobona*) under the Romans, and from 1278 to 1918 the seat of the Hapsburgs. It has long been a centre of the arts and especially music, Mozart and Beethoven being among the great composers associated with it. □ **Vienna Circle** a group of empiricist philosophers, scientists, and mathematicians, active in Vienna from the 1920s to 1938, who were concerned chiefly with methods of verification of statements (see LOGICAL POSITIVISM), the formalization of language, and the unifying of scientific systems. **Vienna schnitzel** see SCHNITZEL. □□ **Viennese** /ˌvɪəˈniːz/ adj. & n.

Vientiane /vɪˌentɪˈɑːn/ the capital and chief port of Laos, on the Mekong River; pop. (1985) 377,400.

Vietcong /vjetˈkɒŋ/ n. (pl. same) a member of the Communist guerrilla force(s) active in Vietnam 1954–76. [Vietnamese, lit. = Vietnamese Communist]

Vietminh /vjetˈmɪn/ n. (pl. same) **1 a** a nationalist independence movement (1941–50) in French Indo-China. **b** the movement succeeding this. **2** a member of one of these movements. [Vietnamese Viet-Nam Dôc-Lâp Dong-Minh Vietnamese Independence League]

Vietnam /vjetˈnæm/ a country in SE Asia, with its eastern coastline on the South China Sea; pop. (est. 1988) 65,185,300; official language, Vietnamese; capital, Hanoi. Traditionally dominated by China, Vietnam came under increasing French influence in the second half of the 19th c. The country was occupied by the Japanese during the Second World War, and postwar hostilities between the French and the Communist Vietminh ended with French defeat and the partition of Vietnam along the 17th parallel in 1954. A prolonged war between North and South Vietnam, fought largely as a guerrilla campaign in the south, ended with the withdrawal of direct American military assistance to South Vietnam and its conquest by Communist forces in 1976, after which a reunited socialist republic was proclaimed. Since then Vietnam has been involved in border disputes with China and military intervention in Cambodia, while its predominantly agricultural economy, now largely collectivized, has been slowly recovering from wartime destruction and dislocation. [Vietnamese Viet tribal name, nam south]

Vietnamese /ˌvjetnəˈmiːz/ adj. & n. —adj. of or relating to Vietnam or its people or language. —n. (pl. same) **1** a native or inhabitant of Vietnam. **2** the language of Vietnam, spoken by about 60 million people. Its origin is uncertain but it may be distantly related to Chinese, from which it derives about half its vocabulary.

vieux jeu /vjɜː ˈʒɜː/ adj. old-fashioned, hackneyed. [F, lit. old game]

view /vjuː/ n. & v. —n. **1** range of vision; extent of visibility (came into view; in full view of the crowd). **2 a** what is seen from a particular point; a scene or prospect (a fine view of the downs; a room with a view). **b** a picture etc. representing this. **3** an inspection by the eye or mind; a visual or mental survey. **4** an opportunity for visual inspection; a viewing (a private view of the exhibition). **5 a** an opinion (holds strong views on morality). **b** a mental attitude (took a favourable view of the matter). **c** a manner of considering a thing (took a long-term view of it). —v. **1** tr. look at; survey visually; inspect (we are going to view the house). **2** tr. examine; survey mentally (different ways of viewing a subject). **3** tr. form a mental impression or opinion of; consider (does not view the matter in the same light). **4** intr. watch television. **5** tr. see (a fox) break cover. □ **have in view 1** have as one's object. **2** bear (a circumstance) in mind in forming a judgement etc. **in view of** having regard to; considering. **on view** being shown (for observation or inspection); being exhibited. **view halloo** Hunting a shout on seeing a fox break cover. **with a view to 1** with the hope or intention of. **2** with the aim of attaining (with a view to marriage). □□ **viewable** adj. [ME f. AF v(i)ewe, OF věue fem. past part. f. věoir see f. L vidēre]

viewdata /ˈvjuːˌdeɪtə/ n. a news and information service from a computer source to which a television screen is connected by telephone link.

viewer /ˈvjuːə(r)/ n. **1** a person who views. **2** a person watching television. **3** a device for looking at film transparencies etc.

viewfinder /ˈvjuːˌfaɪndə(r)/ n. a device on a camera showing the area covered by the lens in taking a photograph.

viewing /ˈvjuːɪŋ/ n. **1** an opportunity or occasion to view; an exhibition. **2** the act or practice of watching television.

viewless /ˈvjuːlɪs/ adj. **1** not having or affording a view. **2** lacking opinions.

viewpoint /ˈvjuːpɔɪnt/ n. a point of view, a standpoint.

vigesimal /vɪˈdʒesɪm(ə)l, vaɪ-/ adj. **1** of twentieths or twenty. **2** reckoning or reckoned by twenties. □□ **vigesimally** adv. [L vigesimus f. viginti twenty]

vigil /ˈvɪdʒɪl/ n. **1 a** keeping awake during the time usually given to sleep, esp. to keep watch or pray (keep vigil). **b** a period of this. **2** Eccl. the eve of a festival or holy day. **3** (in pl.) nocturnal devotions. [ME f. OF vigile f. L vigilia f. vigil awake]

vigilance /ˈvɪdʒɪləns/ n. watchfulness, caution, circumspection. □ **vigilance committee** US a self-appointed body for the maintenance of order etc. [F vigilance or L vigilantia f. vigilare keep awake (as VIGIL)]

vigilant /ˈvɪdʒɪlənt/ adj. watchful against danger, difficulty, etc. □□ **vigilantly** adv. [L vigilans -antis (as VIGILANCE)]

vigilante /ˌvɪdʒɪˈlænti/ n. a member of a vigilance committee or similar body. [Sp., = vigilant]

vigneron /ˈviːnjərɒ̃/ n. a vine-grower. [F f. vigne VINE]

vignette /viːˈnjet/ n. & v. —n. **1** a short descriptive essay or character sketch. **2** an illustration or decorative design, esp. on the title-page of a book, not enclosed in a definite border. **3** a photograph or portrait showing only the head and shoulders with the background gradually shaded off. —v.tr. **1** make a portrait of (a person) in vignette style. **2** shade off (a photograph or portrait). □□ **vignettist** n. [F, dimin. of vigne VINE]

Vignola /vɪnˈjəʊlə/, Giacomo Barozzi da (1507–73), Italian architect, author of a treatise on the five orders of architecture. His most important churches are in Rome. The design of Il Gesù, the mother-church of the Jesuits, was enormously influential; based on Alberti's church of S. Andrea, Mantua, it has a Latin cross plan, with the nave broadened and the dome area increased, in accordance with Counter-Reformation ideas and the new importance attached to preaching.

Vigny /ˈviːnjɪ/, Alfred de (1797–1863), French poet, novelist, and dramatist. His ten-year undistinguished career as an army officer ended in 1827. His poems (collected in Les Destinées, 1864) reveal his philosophy of stoical resignation to the world, a place of suffering, as the only valid response to the inflexibility of Divine Justice. Other works include his historical novel Cinq-Mars (1826) and the play Chatterton (1835), his masterpiece.

Vigo /ˈviːgəʊ/ the principal seaport on the Atlantic coast of Galicia in NW Spain; pop. (1986) 264,000.

vigor US var. of VIGOUR.

vigoro /ˈvɪgəˌrəʊ/ n. Austral. a team ball game combining elements of cricket and baseball. [app. f. VIGOROUS]

vigorous /ˈvɪgərəs/ adj. **1** strong and active; robust. **2** (of a plant) growing strongly. **3** forceful; acting or done with physical or mental vigour; energetic. **4** full of vigour; showing or requiring physical strength or activity. □□ **vigorously** adv. **vigorousness** n. [ME f. OF f. med.L vigorosus f. L vigor (as VIGOUR)]

vigour /ˈvɪgə(r)/ n. (US **vigor**) **1** active physical strength or energy. **2** a flourishing physical condition. **3** healthy growth; vitality; vital force. **4 a** mental strength or activity shown in thought or speech or in literary style. **b** forcefulness; trenchancy, animation. □□ **vigourless** adj. [ME f. OF vigour f. L vigor -oris f. vigēre be lively]

vihara /vɪˈhɑːrə/ n. a Buddhist temple or monastery. [Skr.]

Viking /ˈvaɪkɪŋ/ n. & adj. —n. a member of the Scandinavian traders and pirates who ravaged much of northern Europe, and spread eastwards to Russia and Byzantium, between the 8th and 11th centuries. While their early expeditions were generally little more than raids in search of plunder, in later years they tended to end in conquest and colonization. Much of eastern England was occupied by the Vikings and eventually Cnut, king of Denmark, succeeded to the English throne. —adj. of or relating to the Vikings or their time. [ON víkingr, perh. f. OE wícing f. wíc camp]

Vila /ˈviːlə/ also **Port Vila**) the capital of Vanuatu, on the southwest coast of the island of Efate.

vile /vaɪl/ adj. **1** disgusting. **2** morally base; depraved, shameful. **3** colloq. abominably bad (vile weather). **4** archaic worthless. □□ **vilely** adv. **vileness** n. [ME f. OF vil vile f. L vilis cheap, base]

vilify /'vɪlɪˌfaɪ/ v.tr. (-ies, -ied) defame; speak evil of. □□ **vilification** /-fɪ'keɪʃ(ə)n/ n. **vilifier** n. [ME in sense 'lower in value', f. LL vilificare (as VILE)]

vill /vɪl/ n. hist. a feudal township. [AF f. OF vile, ville farm f. L (as VILLA)]

Villa /'viːjə/, Francisco ('Pancho') (1877–1923), Mexican revolutionary. Pancho Villa was one of the strongest revolutionary leaders during the chaotic period of Mexican history at the beginning of the 20th c., playing a prominent role in the Madero revolution of 1910 and the uprising against Carranzo in 1914–15. Driven out of the country, he invaded the US but was forced back into Mexico by the American army in 1916. He was eventually assassinated.

villa /'vɪlə/ n. **1** Rom. Antiq. a large country house with an estate. **2** a country residence. **3** Brit. a detached or semi-detached house in a residential district. **4** a rented holiday home, esp. abroad. [It. & L]

village /'vɪlɪdʒ/ n. **1 a** a group of houses and associated buildings, larger than a hamlet and smaller than a town, esp. in a rural area. **b** the inhabitants of a village regarded as a community. **2** Brit. a self-contained district or community within a town or city, regarded as having features characteristic of village life. **3** US a small municipality with limited corporate powers. **4** Austral. a select suburban shopping centre. □□ **villager** n. **villagey** adj. [ME f. OF f. L villa]

villain /'vɪlən/ n. **1** a person guilty or capable of great wickedness. **2** colloq. usu. joc. a rascal or rogue. **3** (also **villain of the piece**) (in a play etc.) a character whose evil actions or motives are important in the plot. **4** Brit. colloq. a professional criminal. **5** archaic a rustic; a boor. [ME f. OF vilein, vilain ult. f. L villa: see VILLA]

villainous /'vɪlənəs/ adj. **1** characteristic of a villain; wicked. **2** colloq. abominably bad; vile (villainous weather). □□ **villainously** adv. **villainousness** n.

villainy /'vɪləni/ n. (pl. -ies) **1** villainous behaviour. **2** a wicked act. [OF vilenie (as VILLAIN)]

villanelle /ˌvɪlə'nel/ n. a usu. pastoral or lyrical poem of 19 lines, with only two rhymes throughout, and some lines repeated. [F f. It. villanella fem. of villanello rural, dimin. of villano (as VILLAIN)]

-ville /vɪl/ comb. form colloq. forming the names of fictitious places with ref. to a particular quality etc. (dragsville; squaresville). [F ville town, as in many US town-names]

villein /'vɪlɪn/ n. hist. a feudal tenant entirely subject to a lord or attached to a manor. [ME, var. of VILLAIN]

villeinage /'vɪlɪnɪdʒ/ n. hist. the tenure or status of a villein.

villus /'vɪləs/ n. (pl. villi /-laɪ/) **1** Anat. each of the short finger-like processes on some membranes, esp. on the mucous membrane of the small intestine. **2** Bot. (in pl.) long soft hairs covering fruit, flowers, etc. □□ **villiform** adj. **villose** adj. **villosity** /-'lɒsɪtɪ/ n. **villous** adj. [L, = shaggy hair]

Vilnius /'vɪlnɪəs/ the capital of the Soviet republic of Lithuania; pop. (est. 1987) 566,000.

vim /vɪm/ n. colloq. vigour. [perh. f. L, accus. of vis energy]

vimineous /vɪ'mɪnɪəs/ adj. Bot. of or producing twigs or shoots. [L vimineus f. vimen viminis osier]

vina /'viːnə/ n. an Indian four-stringed musical instrument with a fretted finger-board and a half-gourd at each end. In its most common (northern Indian) form it comprises a wide bamboo tube about a yard long to which are attached towards each end half-gourds acting as resonators; the strings, of steel and brass, are plucked with wire finger-picks and the sound, while delicate in tone, is characteristically bright, with a slightly 'buzzing' quality. [Skr. & Hindi viṇā]

vinaceous /vaɪ'neɪʃəs/ adj. wine-red. [L vinaceus f. vinum wine]

vinaigrette /ˌvɪnɪ'gret/ n. **1** (in full **vinaigrette sauce**) a salad dressing of oil, wine vinegar, and seasoning. **2** a small ornamental bottle for holding smelling-salts. [F, dimin. of vinaigre VINEGAR]

Vincent de Paul /ˌvɪns(ə)nt də 'pɔːl/, St (c.1580–1660), French priest who devoted his life to work among the poor, the sick, and the oppressed, and inspired similar devotion in others. In 1625 he established the Congregation of the Mission (or Lazarists), secular priests living under vows, for missions to rural areas, and in 1633 was co-founder of the Sisters of Charity, the first congregation of 'unenclosed' women devoted entirely to the care of the poor and the sick. He was strongly opposed to Jansenism.

vincible /'vɪnsɪb(ə)l/ adj. literary that can be overcome or conquered. □□ **vincibility** /-'bɪlɪtɪ/ n. [L vincibilis f. vincere overcome]

vinculum /'vɪŋkjʊləm/ n. (pl. **vincula** /-lə/) **1** Algebra a horizontal line drawn over a group of terms to show they have a common relation to what follows or precedes (e.g. $\overline{a + b} \times c = ac + bc$, but $a + b \times c = a + bc$). **2** Anat. a ligament; a fraenum. [L, = bond, f. vincire bind]

vindicate /'vɪndɪˌkeɪt/ v.tr. **1** clear of blame or suspicion. **2** establish the existence, merits, or justice of (one's courage, conduct, assertion, etc.). **3** justify (a person, oneself, etc.) by evidence or argument. □□ **vindicable** /-kəb(ə)l/ adj. **vindication** /-'keɪʃ(ə)n/ n. **vindicative** /-kətɪv/ adj. **vindicator** n. [L vindicare claim, avenge f. vindex -dicis claimant, avenger]

vindicatory /'vɪndɪˌkeɪtərɪ/ adj. **1** tending to vindicate. **2** (of laws) punitive.

vindictive /vɪn'dɪktɪv/ adj. **1** tending to seek revenge. **2** spiteful. □ **vindictive damages** Law damages exceeding simple compensation and awarded to punish the defendant. □□ **vindictively** adv. **vindictiveness** n. [L vindicta vengeance (as VINDICATE)]

vine /vaɪn/ n. **1** any climbing or trailing woody-stemmed plant, esp. of the genus Vitis, bearing grapes. **2** a slender trailing or climbing stem. □ **vine-dresser** a person who prunes, trains, and cultivates vines. □□ **viny** adj. [ME f. OF vi(g)ne f. L vinea vineyard f. vinum wine]

vinegar /'vɪnɪgə(r)/ n. **1** a sour liquid obtained from wine, cider, etc., by fermentation and used as a condiment or for pickling. **2** sour behaviour or character. □ **Vinegar Bible** the edition of 1717 with parable of the vinegar (for vineyard) in the heading above Luke 20. □□ **vinegarish** adj. **vinegary** adj. [ME f. OF vyn egre ult. f. L vinum wine + acer, acre sour]

vinery /'vaɪnərɪ/ n. (pl. -ies) **1** a greenhouse for grapevines. **2** a vineyard.

vineyard /'vɪnjɑːd, -jəd/ n. **1** a plantation of grapevines, esp. for wine-making. **2** Bibl. a sphere of action or labour (see Matt. 20: 1). [ME f. VINE + YARD²]

vingt-et-un /ˌvæ̃teɪ'ɜː/ n. = PONTOON¹. [F, = twenty-one]

vini- /'vɪnɪ/ comb. form wine. [L vinum]

viniculture /'vɪnɪˌkʌltʃə(r)/ n. the cultivation of grapevines. □□ **vinicultural** /-'kʌltʃər(ə)l/ adj. **viniculturist** /-'kʌltʃərɪst/ n.

vinification /ˌvɪnɪfɪ'keɪʃ(ə)n/ n. the conversion of grape-juice etc. into wine.

vining /'vaɪnɪŋ/ n. the separation of leguminous crops from their vines and pods.

Vinland /'vɪnlənd/ a region of North America, probably near Cape Cod, discovered and briefly settled in the 11th c. by Norsemen under Leif Ericsson. It was so named from the report that grapevines were found growing there.

vino /'viːnəʊ/ n. sl. wine, esp. of an inferior kind. [Sp. & It., = wine]

vin ordinaire /ˌvæ̃ ɔːdɪ'neə(r)/ n. cheap (usu. red) wine as drunk in France mixed with water. [F, = ordinary wine]

vinous /'vaɪnəs/ adj. **1** of, like, or associated with wine. **2** addicted to wine. □□ **vinosity** /-'nɒsɪtɪ/ n. [L vinum wine]

vin rosé /ˌvæ̃ rəʊ'zeɪ/ n. = ROSÉ. [F]

vint¹ /vɪnt/ v.tr. make (wine). [back-form. f. VINTAGE]

vint² /vɪnt/ n. a Russian card-game like auction bridge. [Russ., = screw]

vintage /'vɪntɪdʒ/ n. & adj. —n. **1 a** a season's produce of grapes. **b** the wine made from this. **2 a** the gathering of grapes for wine-making. **b** the season of this. **3** a wine of high quality from a single identified year and district. **4 a** the year etc. when a thing was made etc. **b** a thing made etc. in a particular year etc. **5** *poet.* or *rhet.* wine. —*adj.* **1** of high quality, esp. from the past or characteristic of the best period of a person's work. **2** of a past season. □ **vintage car** *Brit.* a car made between 1917 and 1930. **vintage festival** a carnival to celebrate the beginning of the vintage. [alt. (after VINTNER) of ME *vendage, vindage* f. OF *vendange* f. L *vindemia* f. *vinum* wine + *demere* remove]

vintager /ˈvɪntɪdʒə(r)/ *n.* a grape-gatherer.

vintner /ˈvɪntnə(r)/ *n.* a wine-merchant. [ME f. AL *vintenarius, vinetarius* f. AF *vineter,* OF *vinetier* f. med.L *vinetarius* f. L *vinetum* vineyard f. *vinum* wine]

viny see VINE.

vinyl /ˈvaɪnɪl/ *n.* any plastic made by polymerizing a compound containing the vinyl group, esp. polyvinyl chloride. □ **vinyl group** the organic radical or group CH_2CH. [L *vinum* wine + -YL]

viol /ˈvaɪəl/ *n.* a stringed musical instrument of the Renaissance and baroque periods, with six strings and (unlike the instruments of the violin family) gut frets tied round the neck. The music for viol consort from 16th- and 17th-c. England by such composers as William Byrd, Orlando Gibbons, and Henry Purcell represents the heyday of the instrument, but already in other countries the violin was assuming greater popularity, and the viol fell into disuse until its revival in the early 20th c. [ME *viel* etc. f. OF *viel(l)e,* alt. of *viole* f. Prov. *viola, viula,* prob. ult. f. L *vitulari* be joyful: cf. FIDDLE]

viola[1] /vɪˈəʊlə/ *n.* **1 a** an instrument of the violin family, larger than the violin and of lower pitch, and therefore sometimes known as the 'alto' or 'tenor violin'. **b** a viola-player. **2** a viol. □ **viola da braccio** /də ˈbrɑːtʃəʊ/ a viol corresponding to the modern viola. **viola da gamba** /də ˈɡæmbə/ a viol held between the player's legs, esp. one corresponding to the modern cello. **viola d'amore** /dæˈmɔːreɪ/ a sweet-toned tenor viol. [It. & Sp., prob. f. Prov.: see VIOL]

viola[2] /ˈvaɪələ/ *n.* **1** any plant of the genus *Viola,* including the pansy and violet. **2** a cultivated hybrid of this genus. [L, = violet]

violaceous /ˌvaɪəˈleɪʃəs/ *adj.* **1** of a violet colour. **2** *Bot.* of the violet family Violaceae. [L *violaceus* (as VIOLA[2])]

violate /ˈvaɪəleɪt/ *v.tr.* **1** disregard; fail to comply with (an oath, treaty, law, etc.). **2** treat (a sanctuary etc.) profanely or with disrespect. **3** break in upon, disturb (a person's privacy etc.). **4** assault sexually; rape. □□ **violable** *adj.* **violation** /-ˈleɪʃ(ə)n/ *n.* **violator** *n.* [ME f. L *violare* treat violently]

violence /ˈvaɪələns/ *n.* **1** the quality of being violent. **2** violent conduct or treatment, outrage, injury. **3** *Law* **a** the unlawful exercise of physical force. **b** intimidation by the exhibition of this. □ **do violence to** act contrary to; outrage. [ME f. OF f. L *violentia* (as VIOLENT)]

violent /ˈvaɪələnt/ *adj.* **1** involving or using great physical force (*a violent person; a violent storm; came into violent collision*). **2 a** intense, vehement, passionate, furious (*a violent contrast; violent dislike*). **b** vivid (*violent colours*). **3** (of death) resulting from external force or from poison (cf. NATURAL *adj.* 2). **4** involving an unlawful exercise of force (*laid violent hands on him*). □□ **violently** *adv.* [ME f. OF f. L *violentus*]

violet /ˈvaɪələt/ *n.* & *adj.* —*n.* **1 a** any plant of the genus *Viola,* esp. the sweet violet, with usu. purple, blue, or white flowers. **b** any of various plants resembling the sweet violet. **2** the bluish-purple colour seen at the end of the spectrum opposite red. **3 a** a pigment of this colour. **b** clothes or material of this colour. —*adj.* of this colour. [ME f. OF *violet(te)* dimin. of *viole* f. L VIOLA[2]]

violin /ˌvaɪəˈlɪn/ *n.* **1** a musical instrument with four strings of treble pitch played with a bow. (See below.) **2** a violin-player. □□ **violinist** *n.* [It. *violino* dimin. of VIOLA[1]]

The violin family comprises the double-bass, cello, viola, and the violin itself. All the instruments are bowed and have four strings, smooth unfretted necks (unlike the viol), and *f*-shaped sound-holes. The violin is the treble of the family, with a compass of over three-and-a-half octaves and a magnificent range of expression and technique. Many of the instruments of the

great Italian makers such as the Amatis (including Andrea, early 16th c.), Antonio Stradivari (d. 1737), and the Guarneri family (including Giuseppe 'del Gesù', d. 1744), are still in use today and are taken as models for new instruments. The violin is perfectly suited to the baroque style of melody and more or less subordinate accompaniment, and soon replaced the viol, first in Italy and then in France and elsewhere. Its solo repertory is immense and it is an indispensable member of the orchestra.

violist /ˈvaɪəlɪst/ *n.* a viol- or viola-player.

violoncello /ˌvaɪələnˈtʃeləʊ, ˌviː.ə-/ *n.* (*pl.* **-os**) *formal* = CELLO. □□ **violoncellist** *n.* [It., dimin. of VIOLONE]

violone /vɪəˈləʊnɪ/ *n.* a double-bass viol. [It., augment. of VIOLA[1]]

VIP *abbr.* very important person.

viper /ˈvaɪpə(r)/ *n.* **1** any venomous snake of the family Viperidae, esp. the common viper (see ADDER). **2** a malignant or treacherous person. □ **viper in one's bosom** a person who betrays those who have helped him or her. **viper's bugloss** a stiff bristly blue-flowered plant, *Echium vulgare.* **viper's grass** scorzonera. □□ **viperine** /-ˌraɪn/ *adj.* **viperish** *adj.* **viper-like** *adj.* **viperous** *adj.* [F *vipère* or L *vipera* f. *vivus* alive + *parere* bring forth]

virago /vɪˈrɑːɡəʊ, -ˈreɪɡəʊ/ *n.* (*pl.* **-os**) **1** a fierce or abusive woman. **2** *archaic* a woman of masculine strength or spirit. [OE f. L, = female warrior, f. *vir* man]

viral /ˈvaɪər(ə)l/ *adj.* of or caused by a virus. □□ **virally** *adv.*

Virchow /ˈvɜːkəʊ/, Rudolf Karl (1821–1902), German physician and pathologist, who laid the basis of cellular pathology. He was a great believer in the use of the microscope and saw the cell as the basis of life, and he stated that diseases were equivalent to particular types of cellular abnormality. In 1858 he published *Die Cellularpathologie* where he set out different types of abnormal cell, thus giving a scientific basis to pathology. Of a liberal if somewhat dogmatic character, Virchow joined in the 1848 uprising in Berlin. His interest in society and politics showed itself in his work on improving the sanitary conditions in Berlin and more generally in his view that social conditions played a crucial role in causing disease. Despite his wish to marry science to medicine, Virchow believed that environmental factors such as poor living conditions could cause disease just as much as specific agents such as germs. As professor of pathological anatomy in Berlin from 1856 Virchow helped to make the city a European centre of medicine.

virelay /ˈvɪrɪˌleɪ/ *n.* a short (esp. old French) lyric poem with two rhymes to a stanza variously arranged. [ME f. OF *virelai*]

virement /ˈvaɪəmənt, ˈvɪəmɑ̃/ *n.* the transfer of items from one financial account to another. [F f. *virer* turn: see VEER[1]]

vireo /ˈvɪrɪəʊ/ *n.* (*pl.* **-os**) any small American songbird of the family Vireonidae. [L, perh. = greenfinch]

virescence /vɪˈres(ə)ns/ *n.* **1** greenness. **2** *Bot.* abnormal greenness in petals etc. normally of some bright colour. □□ **virescent** *adj.* [L *virescere,* incept. of *virēre* be green]

virgate[1] /ˈvɜːɡət/ *adj.* *Bot.* & *Zool.* slim, straight, and erect. [L *virgatus* f. *virga* rod]

virgate[2] /ˈvɜːɡət/ *n.* *Brit. hist.* a varying measure of land, esp. 30 acres. [med.L *virgata* (rendering OE *gierd-land* yard-land) f. L *virga* rod]

virger var. of VERGER.

Virgil /ˈvɜːdʒɪl/ (Publius Vergilius Maro, 70–19 BC) Roman poet. Born near Mantua and educated in Cremona, Milan, and Rome, he studied Epicureanism in Naples. The loss of his paternal estate in the confiscations of 41 BC, following the civil war, is reflected in the imaginary scenes of his first major work, the *Eclogues,* ten pastoral poems in which the traditional themes of Greek bucolic poetry are blended with contemporary political and literary themes. His next work, the *Georgics,* is a didactic poem on farming, which also treats the wider themes of the relationship between man and nature and outlines an ideal of national revival after civil war. His last and most famous work was the *Aeneid,* an epic poem in twelve books (see AENEID). He died at Brindisi while returning from a journey to Greece. His works quickly established themselves as the greatest classics of Latin poetry and exerted an immense influence on later classical and post-classical literature.

virgin /ˈvɜːdʒɪn/ n. & adj. —n. **1** a person (esp. a woman) who has never had sexual intercourse. **2 a (the Virgin)** Christ's mother the Blessed Virgin Mary. **b** a picture or statue of the Virgin. **3 (the Virgin)** the zodiacal sign or constellation Virgo. **4** *colloq.* a naïve, innocent, or inexperienced person (*a political virgin*). **5** a member of any order of women under a vow to remain virgins. **6** a female insect producing eggs without impregnation. —adj. **1** that is a virgin. **2** of or befitting a virgin (*virgin modesty*). **3** not yet used, penetrated, or tried (*virgin soil*). **4** undefiled, spotless. **5** (of clay) not fired. **6** (of metal) made from ore by smelting. **7** (of wool) not yet, or only once, spun or woven. **8** (of an insect) producing eggs without impregnation. □ **virgin birth 1** the doctrine that Christ had no human father but was conceived by the Virgin Mary by the power of the Holy Spirit. **2** parthenogenesis. **virgin comb** a honeycomb that has been used only once for honey and never for brood. **virgin forest** a forest in its untouched natural state. **virgin honey** honey taken from a virgin comb, or drained from the comb without heat or pressure. **virgin queen** an unfertilized queen bee. **the Virgin Queen** Queen Elizabeth I of England. **virgin's bower** a clematis, *Clematis viticella*. □□ **virginhood** n. [ME f. AF & OF *virgine* f. L *virgo -ginis*]

virginal /ˈvɜːdʒɪn(ə)l/ adj. & n. —adj. that is or befits or belongs to a virgin. —n. (usu. in *pl.*) (in full **pair of virginals**) an early form of spinet in a box, used in the sixteenth and seventeenth centuries. □□ **virginalist** n. **virginally** adv. [ME f. OF *virginal* or L *virginalis* (as VIRGIN): name of the instrument perh. from its use by young women]

Virginia /vəˈdʒɪnɪə/ a State on the Atlantic coast of the US; pop. (est. 1985) 5,346,800; capital, Richmond. The site of the first permanent settlement in North America (1607), Virginia was named in honour of Elizabeth I, the 'Virgin Queen'. It was one of the original 13 States of the US. —n. **1** tobacco from Virginia. **2** a cigarette made of this. □ **Virginia creeper** a N. American vine, *Parthenocissus quinquefolia*, cultivated for ornament. **Virginia reel** *US* a country dance. **Virginia** (or **Virginian**) **stock** a cruciferous plant, *Malcolmia maritima*, with white or pink flowers. □□ **Virginian** n. & adj.

Virgin Islands a group of Caribbean islands at the eastern extremity of the Greater Antilles, discovered by Columbus in 1493 and now divided between British and US administration. Those which are a British dependency number about 42 (the largest is Tortola); pop. (est. 1988) 12,100; capital, Road Town. The remainder constitute an overseas territory of the US; pop. (est. 1988) 112,600; capital, Charlotte Amalie. These were purchased from Denmark in 1917 for strategic reasons. The small population is concentrated on the three major islands of St Thomas, St John, and St Croix. All the islands are increasingly dependent on tourism.

virginity /vəˈdʒɪnɪtɪ/ n. the state of being a virgin. [OF *virginité* f. L *virginitas* (as VIRGIN)]

Virgo /ˈvɜːɡəʊ/ **1** a constellation, traditionally regarded as contained in the figure of a woman. **2** the sixth sign of the zodiac (the Virgin), which the sun enters about 23 Aug., containing the bright star Spica and a rich cluster of galaxies. —n. (*pl.* **-os**) a person born when the sun is in this sign. □□ **Virgoan** n. & adj. [OE f. L, = virgin]

virgule /ˈvɜːɡjuːl/ n. **1** a slanting line used to mark division of words or lines. **2** = SOLIDUS 1. [F, = comma, f. L *virgula* dimin. of *virga* rod]

viridescent /ˌvɪrɪˈdes(ə)nt/ adj. greenish, tending to become green. □□ **viridescence** n. [LL *viridescere* f. L *viridis*: see VIRIDIAN]

viridian /vɪˈrɪdɪən/ n. & adj. —n. **1** a bluish-green chromium oxide pigment. **2** the colour of this. —adj. bluish-green. [L *viridis* green f. *virēre* be green]

viridity /vɪˈrɪdɪtɪ/ n. *literary* greenness, verdancy. [ME f. OF *viridité* or L *viriditas* f. *viridis*: see VIRIDIAN]

virile /ˈvɪraɪl/ adj. **1** of or characteristic of a man; having masculine (esp. sexual) vigour or strength. **2** of or having procreative power. **3** of a man as distinct from a woman or child. □□ **virility** /vɪˈrɪlɪtɪ/ n. [ME f. F *viril* or L *virilis* f. *vir* man]

virilism /ˈvɪrɪˌlɪz(ə)m/ n. *Med.* the development of secondary male characteristics in a female or precociously in a male.

viroid /ˈvaɪrɔɪd/ n. an infectious entity affecting plants, similar to a virus but smaller and consisting only of nucleic acid without a protein coat.

virology /vaɪˈrɒlədʒɪ/ n. the scientific study of viruses. □□ **virological** /-rəˈlɒdʒɪk(ə)l/ adj. **virologically** /-rəˈlɒdʒɪkəlɪ/ adv. **virologist** n.

virtu /vɜːˈtuː/ n. (also **vertu**) **1** a knowledge of or expertise in the fine arts. **2** virtuosity. □ **article** (or **object**) **of virtu** an article interesting because of its workmanship, antiquity, rarity, etc. [It. *virtù* VIRTUE, virtu]

virtual /ˈvɜːtjʊəl/ adj. **1** that is such for practical purposes though not in name or according to strict definition (*is the virtual manager of the business; take this as a virtual promise*). **2** *Optics* relating to the points at which rays would meet if produced backwards (*virtual focus; virtual image*). **3** *Mech.* relating to an infinitesimal displacement of a point in a system. **4** *Computing* not physically existing as such but made by software to appear to do so (*virtual memory*). □□ **virtuality** /-jʊˈælɪtɪ/ n. **virtually** adv. [ME f. med.L *virtualis* f. L *virtus* after LL *virtuosus*]

virtue /ˈvɜːtjuː, -tʃuː/ n. **1** moral excellence; uprightness, goodness. **2** a particular form of this (*patience is a virtue*). **3** chastity, esp. of a woman. **4** a good quality (*has the virtue of being adjustable*). **5** efficacy; inherent power (*no virtue in such drugs*). **6** an angelic being of the seventh order of the celestial hierarchy (see ORDER n. 19). □ **by** (or **in**) **virtue of** on the strength or ground of (*got the job by virtue of his experience*). **make a virtue of necessity** derive some credit or benefit from an unwelcome obligation. □□ **virtueless** adj. [ME f. OF *vertu* f. L *virtus -tutis* f. *vir* man]

virtuoso /ˌvɜːtjʊˈəʊsəʊ, -zəʊ/ n. (*pl.* **virtuosi** /-iː/ or **-os**) **1 a** a person highly skilled in the technique of a fine art, esp. music. **b** (*attrib.*) displaying the skills of a virtuoso. **2** a person with a special knowledge of or taste for works of art or virtu. □□ **virtuosic** /-ˈɒsɪk/ adj. **virtuosity** /-ˈɒsɪtɪ/ n. **virtuosoship** n. [It., = learned, skilful, f. LL (as VIRTUOUS)]

virtuous /ˈvɜːtjʊəs, -tʃʊəs/ adj. **1** possessing or showing moral rectitude. **2** chaste. □ **virtuous circle** a beneficial recurring cycle of cause and effect (cf. *vicious circle* (see CIRCLE n. 11)). □□ **virtuously** adv. **virtuousness** n. [ME f. OF *vertuous* f. LL *virtuosus* f. *virtus* VIRTUE]

virulent /ˈvɪrʊlənt, ˈvɪrjʊ-/ adj. **1** strongly poisonous. **2** (of a disease) violent or malignant. **3** bitterly hostile (*virulent animosity; virulent abuse*). □□ **virulence** n. **virulently** adv. [ME, orig. of a poisoned wound, f. L *virulentus* (as VIRUS)]

virus /ˈvaɪərəs/ n. **1** any of a group of minute infective and disease-producing agents consisting essentially of a length of DNA (or RNA) enveloped in a protein coat. Different viruses may infect animals, plants, and bacteria; in man, viruses cause, for example, the common cold, influenza, measles, rabies, and smallpox. Viruses can reproduce only within a host cell, utilizing the cell's own biochemical 'machinery' to assemble replica viruses which are then released into the organism. Outside the cell they are inert and show no metabolism of their own, so that it is arguable whether they are really 'alive' or not. The electron microscope reveals them to be mainly cylindrical or polyhedral in form, but systematic classification is difficult, and their origin (in evolutionary terms) remains obscure. **2** *Computing* = *computer virus*. **3** *archaic* a poison, a source of disease. **4** a harmful or corrupting influence. [L, = slimy liquid, poison]

Vis. abbr. Viscount.

visa /ˈviːzə/ n. & v. —n. an endorsement on a passport etc. showing that it has been found correct, esp. as allowing the holder to enter or leave a country. —v.tr. (**visas, visaed** /-zəd/ or **visa'd, visaing**) mark with a visa. [F f. L *visa* neut. pl. past part. of *vidēre* see]

visage /ˈvɪzɪdʒ/ n. *literary* a face, a countenance. □□ **visaged** adj. (also in *comb.*). [ME f. OF f. L *visus* sight (as VISA)]

Visakhapatnam /vɪˌʃækəˈpʌtnəm/ a seaport on the coast of Andhra Pradesh in SE India; pop. (1981) 594,000.

vis-à-vis /ˌviːzɑːˈviː/ prep., adv., & n. —prep. **1** in relation to. **2** opposite to. —adv. facing one another. —n. (*pl.* same) **1** a person or thing facing another, esp. in some dances. **2** a person occupying a corresponding position in another group. **3** *US* a social partner. [F, = face to face, f. *vis* face f. L (as VISAGE)]

Visc. *abbr.* Viscount.

viscacha /vɪsˈkætʃə/ *n.* (also **vizcacha** /vɪzˈk-/) any S. American burrowing rodent of the genus *Lagidium*, having valuable fur. [Sp. f. Quechua (h)uiscacha]

viscera /ˈvɪsərə/ *n.pl.* the interior organs in the great cavities of the body (e.g. brain, heart, liver), esp. in the abdomen (e.g. the intestines). [L, pl. of *viscus*: see VISCUS]

visceral /ˈvɪsər(ə)l/ *adj.* **1** of the viscera. **2** relating to inward feelings rather than conscious reasoning. □ **visceral nerve** a sympathetic nerve (see SYMPATHETIC *adj.* 9). □□ **viscerally** *adv.*

viscid /ˈvɪsɪd/ *adj.* **1** glutinous, sticky. **2** semifluid. □□ **viscidity** /vɪˈsɪdɪtɪ/ *n.* [LL *viscidus* f. L *viscum* birdlime]

viscometer /vɪsˈkɒmɪtə(r)/ *n.* an instrument for measuring the viscosity of liquids. □□ **viscometric** /ˌvɪskəˈmetrɪk/ *adj.* **viscometrically** /ˌvɪskəˈmetrɪkəlɪ/ *adv.* **viscometry** *n.* [var. of *viscosimeter* (as VISCOSITY)]

Visconti /vɪsˈkɒntɪ/, Luchino (1906–76), Italian film director, of aristocratic family background and professed Marxist sympathies. He worked for a time with Renoir, absorbing his naturalistic technique, and his first film *Ossessione* (*Obsession*, 1942) was hailed as a masterpiece of realism. Visconti worked also in the theatre, an innovative director of plays and later of operas. His best work in the cinema is characterized by a distinctive visual richness and formality which developed as his theatrical experience tended more towards the grandiose.

viscose /ˈvɪskəʊz, -kəʊs/ *n.* **1** a form of cellulose in a highly viscous state suitable for drawing into yarn. **2** rayon made from this. [LL *viscosus* (as VISCOUS)]

viscosity /vɪˈskɒsɪtɪ/ *n.* (*pl.* **-ies**) **1** the quality or degree of being viscous. **2** *Physics* **a** (of a fluid) internal friction, the resistance to flow. **b** a quantity expressing this. □ **dynamic viscosity** a quantity measuring the force needed to overcome internal friction. **kinematic viscosity** a quantity measuring the dynamic viscosity per unit density. □□ **viscosimeter** /-kəˈsɪmɪtə(r)/ *n.* [ME f. OF *viscose* or med.L *viscositas* (as VISCOUS)]

viscount /ˈvaɪkaʊnt/ *n.* a British nobleman ranking between an earl and a baron. This use of the title dates from 1440, during the reign of Henry VI. □□ **viscountcy** *n.* (*pl.* **-ies**). **viscountship** *n.* **viscounty** *n.* (*pl.* **-ies**). [ME f. AF *viscounte*, OF *vi(s)conte* f. med.L *vicecomes -mitis* (as VICE-, COUNT[2])]

viscountess /ˈvaɪkaʊntɪs/ *n.* **1** a viscount's wife or widow. **2** a woman holding the rank of viscount in her own right.

viscous /ˈvɪskəs/ *adj.* **1** glutinous, sticky. **2** semifluid. **3** *Physics* having a high viscosity; not flowing freely. □□ **viscously** *adv.* **viscousness** *n.* [ME f. AF *viscous* or LL *viscosus* (as VISCID)]

viscus /ˈvɪskəs/ *n.* (*pl.* **viscera** /ˈvɪsərə/) (usu. in *pl.*) any of the soft internal organs of the body. [L]

vise *US* var. of VICE[2].

Vishnu /ˈvɪʃnuː/ one of the major gods of modern Hinduism. Originally a minor Vedic god, he became the preserver in the Hindu triad with Siva and Brahma. To his devotees, he is the supreme being from whom the whole universe emanates. His consort is Lakshmi; his mount, the eagle Garuda. According to the avatar doctrine, Vishnu has descended to earth nine times to save the world: as a fish, a tortoise, a boar, half-man half-lion, a dwarf, the legendary Parasurama, Rama (the perfect hero of the Ramayana), the god Krishna, and the historical Buddha. The tenth incarnation, Kalkin, depicted as a man on a white horse carrying a flaming sword, will herald the end of the world. □□ **Vishnuism** *n.* **Vishnuite** *n.* & *adj.* [Skr. *Vishṇu* pervader f. *viṣ* pervade]

visibility /ˌvɪzɪˈbɪlɪtɪ/ *n.* **1** the state of being visible. **2** the range or possibility of vision as determined by the conditions of light and atmosphere (*visibility was down to 50 yards*). [F *visibilité* or LL *visibilitas* f. L *visibilis*: see VISIBLE]

visible /ˈvɪzɪb(ə)l/ *adj.* **1 a** that can be seen by the eye. **b** (of light) within the range of wavelengths to which the eye is sensitive. **2** that can be perceived or ascertained; apparent, open (*has no*

visible means of support; *spoke with visible impatience*). **3** (of exports etc.) consisting of actual goods (cf. *invisible exports*). □ **the Church visible** the whole body of professed Christian believers. **visible horizon** see HORIZON 1b. □□ **visibleness** *n.* **visibly** *adv.* [ME f. OF *visible* or L *visibilis* f. *vidēre vis-* see]

Visigoth /ˈvɪzɪˌɡɒθ/ *n.* a West Goth, a member of the branch of the Goths who invaded the Roman Empire between the 3rd and 5th c. and eventually established in Spain a kingdom that was overthrown by the Moors in 711–12. [LL *Visigothus*]

vision /ˈvɪʒ(ə)n/ *n.* & *v.* —*n.* **1** the act or faculty of seeing, sight (*has impaired his vision*). **2 a** a thing or person seen in a dream or trance. **b** a supernatural or prophetic apparition. **3** a thing or idea perceived vividly in the imagination (*the romantic visions of youth; had visions of warm sandy beaches*). **4** imaginative insight. **5** statesmanlike foresight; sagacity in planning. **6** a person etc. of unusual beauty. **7** what is seen on a television screen; television images collectively. —*v.tr.* see or present in or as in a vision. □ **field of vision** all that comes into view when the eyes are turned in some direction. **vision-mixer** a person whose job is to switch from one image to another in television broadcasting or recording. □□ **visional** *adj.* **visionless** *adj.* [ME f. OF f. L *visio -onis* (as VISIBLE)]

visionary /ˈvɪʒənərɪ/ *adj.* & *n.* —*adj.* **1** given to seeing visions or to indulging in fanciful theories. **2** existing only in a vision or in the imagination. **3** not practicable. —*n.* (*pl.* **-ies**) a visionary person. □□ **visionariness** *n.*

visit /ˈvɪzɪt/ *v.* & *n.* —*v.* (**visited**, **visiting**) **1 a** *tr.* (also *absol.*) go or come to see (a person, place, etc.) as an act of friendship or ceremony, on business or for a purpose, or from interest. **b** *tr.* go or come to see for the purpose of official inspection, supervision, consultation, or correction. **2** *tr.* reside temporarily with (a person) or at (a place). **3** *intr.* be a visitor. **4** *tr.* (of a disease, calamity, etc.) come upon, attack. **5** *tr. Bibl.* **a** (foll. by *with*) punish (a person). **b** (often foll. by *upon*) inflict punishment for (a sin). **6** *intr. US* **a** (foll. by *with*) go to see (a person) esp. socially. **b** (usu. foll. by *with*) converse, chat. **7** *tr. archaic* (often foll. by *with*) comfort, bless (with salvation etc.). —*n.* **1 a** an act of visiting, a call on a person or at a place (*was on a visit to some friends; paid him a long visit*). **b** temporary residence with a person or at a place. **2** (foll. by *to*) an occasion of going to a doctor, dentist, etc. **3** a formal or official call for the purpose of inspection etc. **4** *US* a chat. □ **right of visit** = *right of visitation* (see VISITATION). □□ **visitable** *adj.* [ME f. OF *visiter* or L *visitare* go to see, frequent. of *visare* view f. *vidēre vis-* see: (n.) perh. f. F *visite*]

visitant /ˈvɪzɪt(ə)nt/ *n.* & *adj.* —*n.* **1** a visitor, esp. a supposedly supernatural one. **2** = VISITOR 2. —*adj. archaic* or *poet.* visiting. [F *visitant* or L *visitare* (as VISIT)]

visitation /ˌvɪzɪˈteɪʃ(ə)n/ *n.* **1** an official visit of inspection, esp. a bishop's examination of a church in his diocese. **2** trouble or difficulty regarded as a divine punishment. **3** (**Visitation**) **a** the visit of the Virgin Mary to Elizabeth related in Luke 1: 39–56. **b** the festival commemorating this on 2 July. **4** *colloq.* an unduly protracted visit or social call. **5** the boarding of a vessel belonging to another State to learn its character and purpose. □ **right of visitation** the right to conduct a visitation of a vessel, not including the right of search. [ME f. OF *visitation* or LL *visitatio* (as VISIT)]

visitatorial /ˌvɪzɪtəˈtɔːrɪəl/ *adj.* of an official visitor or visitation. [ult. f. L *visitare* (see VISIT)]

visiting /ˈvɪzɪtɪŋ/ *n.* & *adj.* —*n.* paying a visit or visits. —*attrib.adj.* (of an academic) spending some time at another institution (*a visiting professor*). □ **visiting-card** a card with a person's name etc., sent or left in lieu of a formal visit. **visiting fireman** (*pl.* **-men**) *US sl.* a visitor given especially cordial treatment.

visitor /ˈvɪzɪtə(r)/ *n.* **1** a person who visits a person or place. **2** a migratory bird present in a locality for part of the year (*winter visitor*). **3** *Brit.* (in a college etc.) an official with the right or duty of occasionally inspecting and reporting. □ **visitors' book** a book in which visitors to a hotel, church, embassy, etc., write their names and addresses and sometimes remarks. [ME f. AF *visitour*, OF *visiteur* (as VISIT)]

visitorial /ˌvɪzɪˈtɔːrɪəl/ *adj.* of an official visitor or visitation.

visor /ˈvaɪzə(r)/ n. (also **vizor**) **1 a** a movable part of a helmet covering the face. **b** hist. a mask. **c** the projecting front part of a cap. **2** a shield (fixed or movable) to protect the eyes from unwanted light, esp. one at the top of a vehicle windscreen. □□ **visored** adj. **visorless** adj. [ME f. AF viser, OF visiere f. vis face f. L visus: see VISAGE]

vista /ˈvɪstə/ n. **1** a long narrow view as between rows of trees. **2** a mental view of a long succession of remembered or anticipated events (opened up new vistas to his ambition). □□ **vistaed** adj. [It., = view, f. visto seen, past part. of vedere see f. L vidēre]

Vistula /ˈvɪstjʊlə/ a river of Poland flowing from the Carpathians to the Baltic at Gdansk.

visual /ˈvɪzjʊəl, ˈvɪʒj-/ adj. & n. —adj. of, concerned with, or used in seeing. —n. (usu. in pl.) a visual image or display, a picture. □ **visual aid** a film, model, etc., as an aid to learning. **visual angle** the angle formed at the eye by rays from the extremities of an object viewed. **visual display unit** Computing a device displaying data as characters on a screen and usu. incorporating a keyboard. **visual field** field of vision. **visual purple** a light-sensitive pigment in the retina, rhodopsin. **visual ray** Optics a line extended from an object to the eye. □□ **visuality** /-ˈʊælɪtɪ/ n. **visually** adv. [ME f. LL visualis f. L visus sight f. vidēre see]

visualize /ˈvɪzjʊəˌlaɪz, ˈvɪʒj-/ v.tr. (also **-ise**) **1** make visible esp. to one's mind (a thing not visible to the eye). **2** make visible to the eye. □□ **visualizable** adj. **visualization** /-ˈzeɪʃ(ə)n/ n.

vital /ˈvaɪt(ə)l/ adj. & n. —adj. **1** of, concerned with, or essential to organic life (vital functions). **2** essential to the existence of a thing or to the matter in hand (a vital question; secrecy is vital). **3** full of life or activity. **4** affecting life. **5** fatal to life or to success etc. (a vital error). **6** disp. important. —n. (in pl.) the body's vital organs, e.g. the heart and brain. □ **vital capacity** the volume of air that can be expelled from the lungs after taking the deepest possible breath. **vital force 1** (in Bergson's philosophy) life-force. **2** any mysterious vital principle. **vital power** the power to sustain life. **vital statistics 1** the number of births, marriages, deaths, etc. **2** colloq. the measurements of a woman's bust, waist, and hips. □□ **vitally** adv. [ME f. OF f. L vitalis f. vita life]

vitalism /ˈvaɪtəˌlɪz(ə)m/ n. Biol. the doctrine that life originates in a vital principle distinct from chemical and other physical forces. □□ **vitalist** n. **vitalistic** /-ˈlɪstɪk/ adj. [F vitalisme or f. VITAL]

vitality /vaɪˈtælɪtɪ/ n. **1** liveliness, animation. **2** the ability to sustain life, vital power. **3** (of an institution, language, etc.) the ability to endure and to perform its functions. [L vitalitas (as VITAL)]

vitalize /ˈvaɪtəˌlaɪz/ v.tr. (also **-ise**) **1** endow with life. **2** infuse with vigour. □□ **vitalization** /-ˈzeɪʃ(ə)n/ n.

vitally /ˈvaɪtəlɪ/ adv. essentially, indispensably.

vitamin /ˈvɪtəmɪn, ˈvaɪt-/ n. any of a number of unrelated organic compounds, essential for normal growth and nutrition, which are required in small quantities in the diet because they cannot be synthesized by the body. A lack of any specific vitamin leads to a characteristic deficiency disease. Substances that are vitamins for one animal need not be so for another — vitamin C, for example, is required in the diet of only a few animals other than man. **vitamin A** (retinol) contributes to the pigments of the eye. Deficiency causes night-blindness and other symptoms. It can be obtained from various animal products, especially liver, and from vegetables such as carrots. **vitamin B** is a general term for any of a group of vitamins, formerly thought to be one substance, that are essential for the working of various different enzymes. They are found in a wide variety of animal and plant foods. **vitamin C** (ascorbic acid) serves to aid cells to adhere to one another and to maintain connective tissue. Deficiency results in scurvy. It is found mainly in fresh fruits and vegetables. **vitamin D** (calciferol) is involved in the absorption and deposition in the bone of calcium and phosphorus. It is obtained especially from fish oils and liver, but can be synthesized in the skin in the presence of sunlight. Deficiency results in rickets. **vitamin E** protects some types of molecule in the body from oxidation. It is found in a wide variety of foods. **vitamin K,** also widely distributed in foods, is needed to synthesize a substance essential for blood clotting. [orig. vitamine f. L vita life + AMINE, because orig. thought to contain an amino acid]

vitaminize /ˈvɪtəmɪˌnaɪz/ v.tr. (also **-ise**) add vitamins to.

vitellary /vɪˈtelərɪ, vaɪ-/ adj. of or relating to the vitellus.

vitelli pl. of VITELLUS.

vitellin /vɪˈtelɪn, vaɪ-/ n. Chem. the chief protein constituent of the yolk of egg. [VITELLUS + -IN]

vitelline /vɪˈtelaɪn, vaɪ-, -lɪn/ adj. of the vitellus. □ **vitelline membrane** the yolk-sac. [med.L vitellinus (as VITELLUS)]

Vitellius /vɪˈtelɪəs/, Aulus (15–69), Roman emperor in 69. Acclaimed emperor by the legions in Germany during the civil wars that followed the death of Nero, he entered Rome after the defeat of Otho but was in turn defeated and killed by the supporters of Vespasian. His gluttony was notorious.

vitellus /vɪˈteləs, vaɪ-/ n. (pl. **vitelli** /-laɪ/) **1** the yolk of an egg. **2** the contents of the ovum. [L, = yolk]

vitiate /ˈvɪʃɪˌeɪt/ v.tr. **1** impair the quality or efficiency of; corrupt, debase, contaminate. **2** make invalid or ineffectual. □□ **vitiation** /-ˈeɪʃ(ə)n/ n. **vitiator** n. [L vitiare f. vitium VICE¹]

viticulture /ˈvɪtɪˌkʌltʃə(r)/ n. the cultivation of grapevines; the science or study of this. □□ **viticultural** /-ˈkʌltʃərəl/ adj. **viticulturist** /-ˈkʌltʃərɪst/ n. [L vitis vine + CULTURE]

Viti Levu /ˌviːtiː ˈleɪvuː/ the largest of the islands of Fiji; chief settlement, Suva (capital of Fiji).

Vitoria /vɪˈtɔːrɪə/ a town in NE Spain, capital of the Basque provinces; pop. (1986) 207,500. Here in 1813 the British army under Wellington defeated a French force under Napoleon's brother, Joseph Bonaparte, and thus freed Spain from French domination. The French were forced back over the Pyrenees, leaving the way clear for Wellington's invasion of France early in 1814.

Vitosha /ˈviːtɒʃə/ a ski resort, the largest in Bulgaria, situated in the mountains to the east of Sofia.

vitreous /ˈvɪtrɪəs/ adj. **1** of, or of the nature of, glass. **2** like glass in hardness, brittleness, transparency, structure, etc. (vitreous enamel). □ **vitreous humour** (or **body**) see HUMOUR □□ **vitreousness** n. [L vitreus f. vitrum glass]

vitrescent /vɪˈtres(ə)nt/ adj. tending to become glass. □□ **vitrescence** n.

vitriform /ˈvɪtrɪˌfɔːm/ adj. having the form or appearance of glass.

vitrify /ˈvɪtrɪˌfaɪ/ v.tr. & intr. (**-ies**, **-ied**) convert or be converted into glass or a glasslike substance esp. by heat. □□ **vitrifaction** /-ˈfækʃ(ə)n/ n. **vitrifiable** adj. **vitrification** /-fɪˈkeɪʃ(ə)n/ n. [F vitrifier or med.L vitrificare (as VITREOUS)]

vitriol /ˈvɪtrɪəl/ n. **1** sulphuric acid or a sulphate, orig. one of glassy appearance. **2** caustic or hostile speech, criticism, or feeling. □ **copper vitriol** copper sulphate. **oil of vitriol** concentrated sulphuric acid. [ME f. OF vitriol or med.L vitriolum f. L vitrum glass]

vitriolic /ˌvɪtrɪˈɒlɪk/ adj. (of speech or criticism) caustic or hostile.

Vitruvius /vɪˈtruːvɪəs/ (Vitruvius Pol(l)io or Mamurra, late 1st c. BC) Roman architect and military engineer, who wrote a comprehensive treatise on architecture, based on Greek sources and on his own experience. He dealt with all aspects of building, including the health aspects of planning, and with acoustics, water supply, sundials, water-clocks, and many other mechanical contrivances as well as the more obvious aspects of architectural design, decoration, and building. His influence was profound, both immediately and in the Renaissance.

vitta /ˈvɪtə/ n. (pl. **vittae** /ˈvɪtiː/) **1** Bot. an oil-tube in the fruit of some plants. **2** Zool. a stripe of colour. □□ **vittate** adj. [L, = band, chaplet]

vituperate /vɪˈtjuːpəˌreɪt, vaɪ-/ v.tr. & intr. revile, abuse. □□ **vituperation** /-ˈreɪʃ(ə)n/ n. **vituperative** /-rətɪv/ adj. **vituperator** n. [L vituperare f. vitium VICE¹]

Vitus /ˈvaɪtəs/, St (c.300), a martyr of the persecution in the reign of Diocletian. He was invoked against epilepsy and certain nervous diseases, including 'St Vitus's dance' (= chorea), and against rabies. Feast day, 15 June.

viva[1] /ˈvaɪvə/ n. & v. Brit. colloq. —n. = VIVA VOCE n. —v.tr. (**vivas, vivaed** /-vəd/ or **viva'd, vivaing**) = VIVA VOCE v. [abbr.]

viva[2] /ˈviːvə/ int. & n. —int. long live. —n. a cry of this as a salute etc. [It., 3rd sing. pres. subj. of vivere live f. L]

vivace /vɪˈvɑːtʃɪ/ adv. Mus. in a lively brisk manner. [It. f. L (as VIVACIOUS)]

vivacious /vɪˈveɪʃəs/ adj. lively, sprightly, animated. □□ **vivaciously** adv. **vivaciousness** n. **vivacity** /vɪˈvæsɪtɪ/ n. [L vivax -acis f. vivere live]

Vivaldi /vɪˈvældɪ/, Antonio (1678–1741), Italian composer and violinist, known in his lifetime as 'Il prete rosso' (the red priest; he entered the Church in 1703) because of his red hair. Throughout his life he served an orphanage for girls in Venice as violin teacher and composer, but he also travelled a good deal in Italy and abroad where his reputation was higher than at home; he died in Vienna, being buried in a pauper's grave. Bach studied his music and copied and arranged several of the concertos, which number around 500. His feeling for texture and melody is evident not only in his most popular works, L'Estro armonico (Harmonic inspiration, 1711), a set of concertos for violins, and The Four Seasons (1725), but also in the surviving operas and in the solo motets that he wrote for the orphanage. Vivaldi's prolific output has led to his being accused of over-facility and repetitiveness, but the 20th c. has seen his work re-estimated, especially since the revival of interest in authentic methods of performing baroque music.

vivarium /vaɪˈveərɪəm, vɪ-/ n. (pl. **vivaria** /-rɪə/) a place artificially prepared for keeping animals in (nearly) their natural state. [L, = warren, fishpond, f. vivus living f. vivere live]

vivat /ˈvaɪvæt, ˈviːvæt/ int. & n. = VIVA[2]. [L, 3rd sing. pres. subj. of vivere live]

viva voce /ˌvaɪvə ˈvəʊtʃɪ, ˈvəʊsɪ/ adj., adv., n., & v. —adj. oral. —adv. orally. —n. an oral examination for an academic qualification. —v.tr. (**viva-voce**) (**-voces, -voceed, -voceing**) examine orally. [med.L, = with the living voice]

Vivekananda /ˌviːvəkəˈnʌndə/ Narendranath Datta (1863–1902), Indian spiritual leader and reformer, who spread the teachings of the Hindu mystic Ramakrishna and in 1897 founded the Ramakrishna Mission near Calcutta, devoted to charitable work among the poor in India. He became the major exponent in Western countries, where he travelled extensively, of Vedanta philosophy.

viverrid /vɪˈvɛrɪd, vaɪ-/ n. & adj. —n. any mammal of the family Viverridae, including civets, mongooses, and genets. —adj. of or relating to this family. [L viverra ferret + -ID[3]]

vivers /ˈvaɪvəz/ n.pl. Sc. food, victuals. [F vivres f. vivre live f. L vivere]

vivid /ˈvɪvɪd/ adj. 1 (of light or colour) strong, intense, glaring (a vivid flash of lightning; of a vivid green). 2 (of a mental faculty, impression, or description) clear, lively, graphic (has a vivid imagination; have a vivid recollection of the scene). 3 (of a person) lively, vigorous. □□ **vividly** adv. **vividness** n. [L vividus f. vivere live]

vivify /ˈvɪvɪˌfaɪ/ v.tr. (**-ies, -ied**) enliven, animate, make lively or living. □□ **vivification** /-fɪˈkeɪʃ(ə)n/ n. [F vivifier f. LL vivificare f. L vivus living f. vivere live]

viviparous /vɪˈvɪpərəs, vaɪ-/ adj. 1 Zool. bringing forth young alive, not hatching them by means of eggs (cf. OVIPAROUS). 2 Bot. producing bulbs or seeds that germinate while still attached to the parent plant. □□ **viviparity** /ˌvɪvɪˈpærɪtɪ/ n. **viviparously** adv. **viviparousness** n. [L viviparus f. vivus: see VIVIFY]

vivisect /ˈvɪvɪˌsekt/ v.tr. perform vivisection on. [back-form. f. VIVISECTION]

vivisection /ˌvɪvɪˈsekʃ(ə)n/ n. 1 dissection or other painful treatment of living animals for purposes of scientific research. 2 unduly detailed or ruthless criticism. □□ **vivisectional** adj. **vivisectionist** n. **vivisector** /ˈvɪvɪˌsektə(r)/ n. [L vivus living (see VIVIFY), after DISSECTION (as DISSECT)]

vixen /ˈvɪks(ə)n/ n. 1 a female fox. 2 a spiteful or quarrelsome

woman. □□ **vixenish** adj. **vixenly** adj. [ME fixen f. OE, fem. of FOX]

viz. /vɪz, or by substitution ˈneɪmlɪ/ adv. (usu. introducing a gloss or explanation) namely; that is to say; in other words (came to a firm conclusion, viz. that we were right). [abbr. of VIDELICET, z being med.L symbol for abbr. of -et]

vizard /ˈvɪzəd/ n. archaic a mask or disguise. [VISOR + -ARD]

vizcacha var. of VISCACHA.

vizier /vɪˈzɪə(r), ˈvɪzɪə(r)/ n. hist. a high official in some Muslim countries, esp. in Turkey under Ottoman rule. □□ **vizierate** /-rət/ n. **vizierial** /vɪˈzɪərɪəl/ adj. **viziership** n. [ult. f. Arab. wazīr caliph's chief counsellor]

vizor var. of VISOR.

Vlach /vlæk/ n. & adj. —n. a member of a people inhabiting Romania and parts of the Soviet Union. —adj. of or relating to this people. [Bulg. f. OSlav. Vlachŭ Romanian etc. f. Gmc, = foreigner]

Vladimir /ˈvlædɪˌmɪə(r)/, St (956–1015), the apostle of the Russians and Ruthenians. In 978 he took Kiev from the rule of his elder brother and conquered large areas of White Russia. After marrying a sister of the Greek emperor Basil II he became an ardent promoter of Christianity, which he imposed by force.

Vladivostok /ˌvlædɪˈvɒstɒk/ the principal seaport of the Soviet Union, on the Pacific east coast; pop. (est. 1987) 615,000.

Vlaminck /vlæˈmæŋk/, Maurice de (1876–1958), French painter, graphic artist, and writer. Largely self-taught, he became a leading exponent of fauvism (see FAUVE), mainly in landscapes, and was later influenced by Cézanne. He wrote novels and memoirs and was a pioneer collector of African art.

vlei /fleɪ/ n. S.Afr. a hollow in which water collects during the rainy season. [Du. dial. f. Du. vallei valley]

Vlorë /ˈvlɔːrə/ (also **Vlona** /ˈvlɒnʌ/, Italian **Valona**) a port of SW Albania, on the Adriatic coast; pop. (1983) 61,000.

V-neck /ˈviːnek, ˈviː-/ n. (often attrib.) 1 a neck of a pullover etc. with straight sides meeting at an angle in the front to form a V. 2 a garment with this.

VO abbr. (in the UK) Royal Victorian Order.

vocable /ˈvəʊkəb(ə)l/ n. a word, esp. with reference to form rather than meaning. [F vocable or L vocabulum f. vocare call]

vocabulary /vəˈkæbjʊlərɪ/ n. (pl. **-ies**) 1 the (principal) words used in a language or a particular book or branch of science etc. or by a particular author (scientific vocabulary; the vocabulary of Shakespeare). 2 a list of these, arranged alphabetically with definitions or translations. 3 the range of words known to an individual (his vocabulary is limited). 4 a set of artistic or stylistic forms or techniques, esp. a range of set movements in ballet etc. [med.L vocabularius, -um (as VOCABLE)]

vocal /ˈvəʊk(ə)l/ adj. & n. —adj. 1 of or concerned with or uttered by the voice (a vocal communication). 2 expressing one's feelings freely in speech (was very vocal about his rights). 3 Phonet. voiced. 4 poet. (of trees, water, etc.) endowed with a voice or a similar faculty. 5 (of music) written for or produced by the voice with or without accompaniment (cf. INSTRUMENTAL). —n. 1 (in sing. or pl.) the sung part of a musical composition. 2 a musical performance with singing. □ **vocal cords** folds of the lining membrane of the larynx near the opening of the glottis, with edges vibrating in the air-stream to produce the voice. **vocal score** a musical score showing the voice parts in full. □□ **vocality** /vəˈkælɪtɪ/ n. **vocally** adv. [ME f. L vocalis (as VOICE)]

vocalic /vəˈkælɪk/ adj. of or consisting of a vowel or vowels.

vocalism /ˈvəʊkəˌlɪz(ə)m/ n. 1 the use of the voice in speaking or singing. 2 a vowel sound or system.

vocalist /ˈvəʊkəlɪst/ n. a singer, esp. of jazz or popular songs.

vocalize /ˈvəʊkəˌlaɪz/ v. (also **-ise**) 1 tr. a form (a sound) or utter (a word) with the voice. b make sonant (f is vocalized into v). 2 intr. utter a vocal sound. 3 tr. write (Hebrew etc.) with vowel points. 4 intr. Mus. sing with several notes to one vowel. □□ **vocalization** /-ˈzeɪʃ(ə)n/ n. **vocalizer** n.

vocation /vəˈkeɪʃ(ə)n/ n. 1 a strong feeling of fitness for a particular career or occupation (in religious contexts regarded as a divine call). 2 a a person's employment, esp. regarded as requiring dedication. **b** a trade or profession. [ME f. OF *vocation* or L *vocatio* f. *vocare* call]

vocational /vəˈkeɪʃən(ə)l/ *adj.* **1** of or relating to an occupation or employment. **2** (of education or training) directed at a particular occupation and its skills. □□ **vocationalism** *n.* **vocationalize** *v.tr.* (also **-ise**). **vocationally** *adv.*

vocative /ˈvɒkətɪv/ *n. & adj. Gram.* —*n.* the case of nouns, pronouns, and adjectives used in addressing or invoking a person or thing. —*adj.* of or in this case. [ME f. OF *vocatif -ive* or L *vocativus* f. *vocare* call]

vociferate /vəˈsɪfəˌreɪt/ *v.* **1** *tr.* utter (words etc.) noisily. **2** *intr.* shout, bawl. □□ **vociferance** *n.* **vociferant** *adj. & n.* **vociferation** /-ˈreɪʃ(ə)n/ *n.* **vociferator** *n.* [L *vociferari* f. *vox* voice + *ferre* bear]

vociferous /vəˈsɪfərəs/ *adj.* **1** (of a person, speech, etc.) noisy, clamorous. **2** insistently and forcibly expressing one's views. □□ **vociferously** *adv.* **vociferousness** *n.*

vocoder /vəʊˈkəʊdə(r)/ *n.* a synthesizer that produces sounds from an analysis of speech input. [VOICE + CODE]

vodka /ˈvɒdkə/ *n.* an alcoholic spirit made esp. in Russia by distillation of rye etc. [Russ., dimin. of *voda* water]

voe /vəʊ/ *n.* a small bay or creek in Orkney or Shetland. [Norw. *vaag*, ON *vágr*]

vogue /vəʊg/ *n.* **1** (prec. by *the*) the prevailing fashion. **2** popular use or currency (*has had a great vogue*). □ **in vogue** in fashion, generally current. **vogue-word** a word currently fashionable. □□ **voguish** *adj.* [F f. It. *voga* rowing, fashion f. *vogare* row, go well]

voice /vɔɪs/ *n. & v.* —*n.* **1 a** sound formed in the larynx etc. and uttered by the mouth, esp. human utterance in speaking, shouting, singing, etc. (*heard a voice; spoke in a low voice*). **b** the ability to produce this (*has lost her voice*). **2 a** the use of the voice; utterance, esp. in spoken or written words (esp. *give voice*). **b** an opinion so expressed. **c** the right to express an opinion (*I have no voice in the matter*). **d** an agency by which an opinion is expressed. **3** *Gram.* a form or set of forms of a verb showing the relation of the subject to the action (*active voice; passive voice*). **4** *Mus.* **a** a vocal part in a composition. **b** a constituent part in a fugue. **5** *Phonet.* sound uttered with resonance of the vocal cords, not with mere breath. **6** (usu. in *pl.*) the supposed utterance of an invisible guiding or directing spirit. —*v.tr.* **1** give utterance to; express (*the letter voices our opinion*). **2** (esp. as **voiced** *adj.*) *Phonet.* utter with vibration of the vocal cords (e.g. *b, d, g, v, z*). **3** *Mus.* regulate the tone-quality of (organ-pipes). □ **in voice** (or **good voice**) in proper vocal condition for singing or speaking. **voice-box** the larynx. **the voice of God** the expression of God's will, wrath, etc. **voice-over** narration in a film etc. not accompanied by a picture of the speaker. **voice-print** a visual record of speech, analysed with respect to frequency, duration, and amplitude. **voice vote** *US* a vote taken by noting the relative strength of calls of *aye* and *no*. **with one voice** unanimously. □□ **-voiced** *adj.* **voicer** *n.* (in sense 3 of v.). [ME f. AF *voiz*, OF *vois* f. L *vox vocis*]

voiceful /ˈvɔɪsfʊl/ *adj. poet.* or *rhet.* **1** vocal. **2** sonorous.

voiceless /ˈvɔɪslɪs/ *adj.* **1** dumb, mute, speechless. **2** *Phonet.* uttered without vibration of the vocal cords (e.g. *f, k, p, s, t*). □□ **voicelessly** *adv.* **voicelessness** *n.*

void /vɔɪd/ *adj., n., & v.* —*adj.* **1 a** empty, vacant. **b** (foll. by *of*) lacking; free from (*a style void of affectation*). **2** esp. *Law* (of a contract, deed, promise, etc.) invalid, not binding (*null and void*). **3** useless, ineffectual. **4** (often foll. by *in*) *Cards* (of a hand) having no cards in a given suit. **5** (of an office) vacant (esp. *fall void*). —*n.* **1** an empty space, a vacuum (*vanished into the void; cannot fill the void made by death*). **2** an unfilled space in a wall or building. **3** (often foll. by *in*) *Cards* the absence of cards in a particular suit. —*v.tr.* **1** render invalid. **2** (also *absol.*) excrete. □□ **voidable** *adj.* **voidness** *n.* [ME f. OF dial. *voide*, OF *vuide, vuit*, rel. to L *vacare* VACATE: v. partly f. AVOID, partly f. OF *voider*]

voidance /ˈvɔɪd(ə)ns/ *n.* **1** *Eccl.* a vacancy in a benefice. **2** the act or an instance of voiding; the state of being voided. [ME f. OF (as VOID)]

voided /ˈvɔɪdɪd/ *adj. Heraldry* (of a bearing) having the central area cut away so as to show the field.

voile /vɔɪl, vwɑːl/ *n.* a thin semi-transparent dress-material of cotton, wool, or silk. [F, = VEIL]

Vojvodina /ˌvɔɪvəˈdiːnə/ an autonomous province of the republic of Serbia, Yugoslavia; pop. (1981) 2,034,700; capital, Novi Sad.

vol. *abbr.* volume.

volant /ˈvəʊlənt/ *adj.* **1** *Zool.* flying, able to fly. **2** *Heraldry* represented as flying. **3** *literary* nimble, rapid. [F f. *voler* f. L *volare* fly]

volar /ˈvəʊlə(r)/ *adj. Anat.* of the palm or sole. [L *vola* hollow of hand or foot]

volatile /ˈvɒləˌtaɪl/ *adj. & n.* —*adj.* **1** evaporating rapidly (*volatile salts*). **2** changeable, fickle. **3** lively, light-hearted. **4** apt to break out into violence. **5** transient. —*n.* a volatile substance. □ **volatile oil** see OIL. □□ **volatileness** *n.* **volatility** /-ˈtɪlɪtɪ/ *n.* [OF *volatil* or L *volatilis* f. *volare* *volat-* fly]

volatilize /vəˈlætɪˌlaɪz/ *v.* (also **-ise**) **1** *tr.* cause to evaporate. **2** *intr.* evaporate. □□ **volatilizable** *adj.* **volatilization** /-ˈzeɪʃ(ə)n/ *n.*

vol-au-vent /ˈvɒləʊˌvɑ̃/ *n.* a (usu. small) round case of puff pastry filled with meat, fish, etc., and sauce. [F, lit. 'flight in the wind']

volcanic /vɒlˈkænɪk/ *adj.* (also **vulcanic** /vʌl-/) of, like, or produced by a volcano. □ **volcanic bomb** a mass of ejected lava usu. rounded and sometimes hollow. **volcanic glass** obsidian. □□ **volcanically** *adv.* **volcanicity** /ˌvɒlkəˈnɪsɪtɪ/ *n.* [F *volcanique* f. *volcan* VOLCANO]

volcano /vɒlˈkeɪnəʊ/ *n.* (*pl.* **-oes**) **1** a mountain or hill having an opening or openings in the earth's crust through which lava, cinders, steam, gases, etc., are or have been expelled continuously or at intervals. **2 a** a state of things likely to cause a violent outburst. **b** a violent esp. suppressed feeling. [It. f. L *Volcanus* Vulcan, Roman god of fire]

volcanology var. of VULCANOLOGY.

vole[1] /vəʊl/ *n.* any small ratlike or mouselike plant-eating rodent of the family Cricetidae. [orig. *vole-mouse* f. Norw. f. *voll* field + *mus* mouse]

vole[2] /vəʊl/ *n. archaic* the winning of all tricks at cards. [F f. *voler* fly f. L *volare*]

volet /ˈvɒleɪ/ *n.* a panel or wing of a triptych. [F f. *voler* fly f. L *volare*]

Volga /ˈvɒlgə/ the longest river in Europe (3,688 km, 2,292 miles) rising in the north-west of the USSR and flowing to the Caspian Sea. It has been dammed at several points to provide a water supply and hydroelectric power.

Volgograd /ˈvɒlgəˌgræd/ an industrial city of the USSR at the junction of the Don and Volga rivers; pop. (est. 1987) 988,000. The city was called Tsaritsyn until 1925, and Stalingrad from then until 1961. During the Second World War it was the scene of a long and bitterly fought battle in 1942–3, in which the German advance into the Soviet Union was halted.

volitant /ˈvɒlɪt(ə)nt/ *adj. Zool.* volant. [L *volitare* frequent. of *volare* fly]

volition /vəˈlɪʃ(ə)n/ *n.* **1** the exercise of the will. **2** the power of willing. □ **of** (or **by**) **one's own volition** voluntarily. □□ **volitional** *adj.* **volitionally** *adv.* **volitive** /ˈvɒlɪtɪv/ *adj.* [F *volition* or med.L *volitio* f. *volo* I wish]

Völkerwanderung /ˈfɜːlkəˌvɑːndəˌrʊŋ/ *n.* a migration of peoples, esp. that of Germanic and Slavic peoples into Europe from the second to the eleventh centuries. [G]

volley /ˈvɒlɪ/ *n. & v.* —*n.* (*pl.* **-eys**) **1 a** the simultaneous discharge of a number of weapons. **b** the bullets etc. discharged in a volley. **2** (usu. foll. by *of*) a noisy emission of oaths etc. in quick succession. **3** *Tennis* the return of a ball in play before it touches the ground. **4** *Football* the kicking of a ball in play before it touches the ground. **5** *Cricket* **a** a ball pitched right up to the batsman or the stumps without bouncing. **b** the pitching of the ball in this way. —*v.* (**-eys**, **-eyed**) **1** *tr.* (also *absol.*) *Tennis & Football* return or send (a ball) by a volley. **2** *tr. & absol.* discharge (bullets, abuse, etc.) in a volley. **3** *intr.* (of bullets etc.) fly in a volley. **4** *intr.* (of guns etc.) sound together. **5** *intr.* make a sound like a volley of artillery. □□ **volleyer** n. [F *volée* ult. f. L *volare* fly]

volleyball /'vɒlɪˌbɔːl/ n. a game for two teams of six volleying a large ball by hand over a net. It was developed in the US from 1895, when W. G. Morgan, a physical fitness instructor at the YMCA at Holyoke, Massachusetts, formulated the game for middle-aged men who found basketball too vigorous.

Volos /'vɒlɒs/ a port on an inlet of the Aegean Sea in Thessaly in eastern Greece; pop. (1981) 107,400.

volplane /'vɒlpleɪn/ n. & v. *Aeron.* —n. a glide. —v.intr. glide. [F *vol plané* f. *vol* flight + *plané* past part. of *planer* hover, rel. to PLANE¹]

vols. abbr. volumes.

volt¹ /vəʊlt/ n. the SI unit of electromotive force, the difference of potential that would carry one ampere of current against one ohm resistance. ¶ Abbr.: **V**. [A. VOLTA²]

volt² /vɒlt, vəʊlt/ v. & n. —v.intr. *Fencing* make a volte. —n. var. of VOLTE. [F *volter* (as VOLTE)]

Volta¹ /'vɒltə/ a river formed in central Ghana by the junction of the headwaters, the Black and White Volta, which rise in Burkina. At Akosombo in SE Ghana the river has been dammed, creating Lake Volta which is one of the world's largest man-made lakes, completed in 1965. The lake serves for navigation, fishing, and irrigation; hydroelectric power generated at the dam meets Ghana's needs and provides a surplus.

Volta² /'vɒltə/, Alessandro Giuseppe Antonio Anastasio, Count (1745–1824), Italian physicist, the discoverer of a number of important electrical instruments, including the electrophorus (for generating static electricity), the condensing electroscope, and, most significant of all, the voltaic pile or electrochemical battery, the first device to produce a continuous electric current, which he announced in 1800. The impetus for this invention was Galvani's contention in 1791 that he had discovered a new kind of electricity, 'animal electricity', produced in animal tissue, which Volta ascribed to normal electricity produced by the contact of two dissimilar metals. He was made a Count when he demonstrated his battery to Napoleon in 1801. The volt is named in his honour.

voltage /'vəʊltɪdʒ/ n. electromotive force or potential difference expressed in volts.

voltaic /vɒl'teɪɪk/ adj. *archaic* of electricity from a primary battery; galvanic (*voltaic battery*).

Voltaire /'vɒlteə(r)/ (pseudonym of François-Marie Arouet, 1694–1778) French writer, author of plays, poetry, and histories, not so much a philosopher as a publicizer of the philosophical ideas of others. During a period in the Bastille (as author of a pungent political satire) he completed his tragedy *Oedipe* (1719) and his epic poem *La Henriade* (1723, 1728); both reveal his nascent political revolt. He spent a period in exile in England (1726–9) and was introduced there to the scientific theories of Newton and the empiricist philosophy of Locke. He also became acquainted with the political institutions of England, and extolled them as against the royal autocracy and nobles' privileges of France. Much of the rest of his life was spent outside France, or in a house from which he could make a quick escape across the border. He rejected all claims to revelation and came to be openly and fiercely hostile to Christianity and the Roman Catholic Church. His relentless attacks on the civil and ecclesiastical establishments, with every resource of wit and satire, were the source of both his immense prestige and his persecution.

voltameter /vɒl'tæmɪtə(r)/ n. an instrument for measuring an electric charge.

volte /vɒlt, vəʊlt/ n. (also **volt**) **1** *Fencing* a quick movement to escape a thrust. **2** a sideways circular movement of a horse. [F f. It. *volta* turn, fem. past part. of *volgere* turn f. L *volvere* roll]

volte-face /vɒlt'faːs/ n. **1** a complete reversal of position in argument or opinion. **2** the act or an instance of turning round. [F f. It. *voltafaccia*, ult. f. L *volvere* roll + *facies* appearance, face]

voltmeter /'vəʊltˌmiːtə(r)/ n. an instrument for measuring electric potential in volts.

voluble /'vɒljʊb(ə)l/ adj. **1** speaking or spoken vehemently, incessantly, or fluently (*voluble spokesman*; *voluble excuses*). **2** *Bot.*

twisting round a support, twining. □□ **volubility** /-'bɪlɪtɪ/ n. **volubleness** n. **volubly** adv. [F *voluble* or L *volubilis* f. *volvere* roll]

volume /'vɒljuːm/ n. **1 a** a set of sheets of paper, usu. printed, bound together and forming part or the whole of a work or comprising several works (*issued in three volumes; a library of 12,000 volumes*). **b** *hist.* a scroll of papyrus etc., an ancient form of book. **2 a** solid content, bulk. **b** the space occupied by a gas or liquid. **c** (foll. by *of*) an amount or quantity (*large volume of business*). **3 a** quantity or power of sound. **b** fullness of tone. **4** (foll. by *of*) **a** a moving mass of water etc. **b** (usu. in *pl.*) a wreath or coil or rounded mass of smoke etc. □□ **volumed** adj. (also in *comb.*). [ME f. OF *volum(e)* f. L *volumen -minis* roll f. *volvere* to roll]

volumetric /ˌvɒljʊ'metrɪk/ adj. of or relating to measurement by volume. □□ **volumetrically** adv. [VOLUME + METRIC]

voluminous /və'ljuːmɪnəs, və'luː-/ adj. **1** large in volume; bulky. **2** (of drapery etc.) loose and ample. **3** consisting of many volumes. **4** (of a writer) producing many books. □□ **voluminosity** /-'nɒsɪtɪ/ n. **voluminously** adv. **voluminousness** n. [LL *voluminosus* (as VOLUME)]

voluntarism /'vɒləntəˌrɪz(ə)m/ n. **1** the principle of relying on voluntary action rather than compulsion. **2** *Philos.* the doctrine that the will is a fundamental or dominant factor in the individual or the universe. **3** *hist.* the doctrine that the Church or schools should be independent of the State and supported by voluntary contributions. □□ **voluntarist** n. [irreg. f. VOLUNTARY]

voluntary /'vɒləntərɪ/ adj. & n. —adj. **1** done, acting, or able to act of one's own free will; not constrained or compulsory; intentional (*a voluntary gift*). **2** unpaid (*voluntary work*). **3** (of an institution) supported by voluntary contributions. **4** *Brit.* (of a school) built by a voluntary institution but maintained by a local education authority. **5** brought about, produced, etc., by voluntary action. **6** (of a movement, muscle, or limb) controlled by the will. **7** (of a confession by a criminal) not prompted by a promise or threat. **8** *Law* (of a conveyance or disposition) made without return in money or other consideration. —n. (pl. **-ies**) **1 a** an organ solo played before, during, or after a church service. **b** the music for this. **c** *archaic* an extempore performance esp. as a prelude to other music. **2** (in competitions) a special performance left to the performer's choice. **3** *hist.* a person who holds that the Church or schools should be independent of the State and supported by voluntary contributions. □ **Voluntary Aid Detachment** (in the UK) a group of organized voluntary first-aid and nursing workers. **Voluntary Service Overseas** a British organization promoting voluntary work in underdeveloped countries. □□ **voluntarily** adv. **voluntariness** n. [ME f. OF *voluntaire* or L *voluntarius* f. *voluntas* will]

voluntaryism /'vɒləntərɪˌɪz(ə)m/ n. *hist.* = VOLUNTARISM 1, 3. □□ **voluntaryist** n.

volunteer /ˌvɒlən'tɪə(r)/ n. & v. —n. **1** a person who voluntarily undertakes a task or enters military or other service, esp. *Mil. hist.* a member of any of the corps of voluntary soldiers formerly organized in the UK and provided with instructors, arms, etc., by the State. **2** (usu. *attrib.*) a self-sown plant. —v. **1** tr. (often foll. by *to* + infin.) undertake or offer (one's services, a remark or explanation, etc.) voluntarily. **2** intr. (often foll. by *for*) make a voluntary offer of one's services; be a volunteer. [F *volontaire* (as VOLUNTARY), assim. to -EER]

voluptuary /və'lʌptjʊərɪ/ n. & adj. —n. (pl. **-ies**) a person given up to luxury and sensual pleasure. —adj. concerned with luxury and sensual pleasure. [L *volupt(u)arius* (as VOLUPTUOUS)]

voluptuous /və'lʌptjʊəs/ adj. of, tending to, occupied with, or derived from, sensuous or sensual pleasure. □□ **voluptuously** adv. **voluptuousness** n. [ME f. OF *voluptueux* or L *voluptuosus* f. *voluptas* pleasure]

volute /və'ljuːt/ n. & adj. —n. **1** *Archit.* a spiral scroll characteristic of Ionic capitals and also used in Corinthian and composite capitals. **2 a** any marine gastropod mollusc of the genus *Voluta*. **b** the spiral shell of this. —adj. esp. *Bot.* rolled up. □□ **voluted** adj. [F *volute* or L *voluta* fem. past part. of *volvere* roll]

volution /və'luːʃ(ə)n, və'ljuː-/ n. **1** a rolling motion. **2** a spiral turn. **3** a whorl of a spiral shell. **4** *Anat.* a convolution. [as VOLUTE, after REVOLUTION etc.]

vomer /ˈvəʊmə(r)/ n. Anat. the small thin bone separating the nostrils in man and most vertebrates. [L, = ploughshare]

vomit /ˈvɒmɪt/ v. & n. —v.tr. (**vomited, vomiting**) **1** (also absol.) eject (matter) from the stomach through the mouth. **2** (of a volcano, chimney, etc.) eject violently, belch forth. —n. **1** matter vomited from the stomach. **2** archaic an emetic. □□ **vomiter** n. [ME ult. f. L vomere vomit- or frequent. L vomitare]

vomitorium /ˌvɒmɪˈtɔːrɪəm/ n. (pl. **vomitoria** /-rɪə/) Rom. Antiq. a vomitory. [L; see VOMITORY]

vomitory /ˈvɒmɪtərɪ/ adj. & n. —adj. emetic. —n. (pl. **-ies**) Rom. Antiq. each of a series of passages for entrance and exit in an amphitheatre or theatre. [L vomitorius (adj.), -um (n.) (as VOMIT)]

V-1 /viːˈwʌn/ n. see V³.

Vonnegut /ˈvɒnɪɡət/, Kurt (1922–), American novelist and writer of short stories, whose works mingle realism, science fiction, fantasy, and satire. They include Cat's Cradle (1963) and Slaughterhouse-five (1969); the latter is based on the fire-bombing of Dresden in 1945, which Vonnegut himself experienced as a prisoner of war.

von Neumann see NEUMANN.

voodoo /ˈvuːduː/ n. & v. —n. **1** use of or belief in religious witchcraft as practised among Blacks esp. in Haiti and elsewhere in the Caribbean area. (See below.) **2** a person skilled in this. **3** a voodoo spell. —v.tr. (**voodoos, voodooed**) affect by voodoo; bewitch. □□ **voodooism** n. **voodooist** n. [Ewe vodu]

In voodoo some debased elements of Roman Catholic ritual, dating from the French colonial period before 1804, are blended with African religious and magical elements derived from the former slave population. Trances induced by spirit possession are central to its ritual. Professed belief in a supreme God is combined with service to the loa, who are local (or African) gods, deified ancestors, or Catholic saints. The cult is strongly opposed by both the Catholic and the Protestant Church.

voracious /vəˈreɪʃəs/ adj. **1** greedy in eating, ravenous. **2** very eager in some activity (a voracious reader). □□ **voraciously** adv. **voraciousness** n. **voracity** /vəˈræsɪtɪ/ n. [L vorax f. vorare devour]

Vorarlberg /ˈfɔːrɑːlˌbeək/ an Alpine province of western Austria; pop. (1981) 305,600; capital, Bregenz.

Voronezh /vəˈrɒnjeʒ/ a city of the Soviet Union on the River Voronezh, north-east of Kharkov; pop. (est. 1987) 872,000.

Voroshilovgrad /ˌvɒrəˈʃiːlɒfɡræd/ an industrial city of the Ukrainian SSR, in the Donets Basin; pop. (est. 1987) 509,000. Known as Lugansk until 1935 and 1958–70, it was renamed in honour of the Soviet military and political leader Marshal Voroshilov (1881–1969).

-vorous /vərəs/ comb. form forming adjectives meaning 'feeding on' (carnivorous). □□ **-vora** /vərə/ comb. form forming names of groups. **-vore** /vɔː(r)/ comb. form forming names of individuals. [L -vorus f. vorare devour]

vortex /ˈvɔːteks/ n. (pl. **vortexes** or **vortices** /-tɪˌsiːz/) **1** a mass of whirling fluid, esp. a whirlpool or whirlwind. **2** any whirling motion or mass. **3** a system, occupation, pursuit, etc., viewed as swallowing up or engrossing those who approach it (the vortex of society). **4** Physics a portion of fluid whose particles have rotatory motion. □ **vortex-ring** a vortex whose axis is a closed curve, e.g. a smoke-ring. □□ **vortical** adj. **vortically** adv. **vorticity** /vɔːˈtɪsɪtɪ/ n. **vorticose** adj. **vorticular** /vɔːˈtɪkjʊlə(r)/ adj. [L vortex -icis eddy, var. of VERTEX]

vorticella /ˌvɔːtɪˈselə/ n. any sedentary protozoan of the family Vorticellidae, consisting of a tubular stalk with a bell-shaped ciliated opening. [mod.L, dimin. of VORTEX]

vorticism /ˈvɔːtɪsɪz(ə)m/ n. **1** an aggressive literary and artistic movement that flourished from 1912 to 1915. It attacked the sentimentality of 19th-c. art and celebrated violence, energy, and the machine. The vorticists, dominated by Wyndham Lewis, included Ezra Pound (who suggested the idea of a vortex from which ideas were constantly rushing), the sculptor Gaudier-Brzeska, and the painter Edward Wadsworth; they were associated with the philosopher T. E. Hulme, the novelist Ford Madox Ford, and the sculptor Jacob Epstein. In the visual arts their style was expressed in bold abstract compositions and was indebted to cubism and futurism. A vorticist exhibition was

held in 1915 at which there was manifested a tendency towards simplification into angular machine-like objects, but owing to wartime conditions the movement did not persist. **2** Metaphysics the theory regarding the universe, with Descartes, as a plenum in which motion propagates itself in circles. □□ **vorticist** n.

Vosges /vəʊʒ/ a mountain system of eastern France.

votary /ˈvəʊtərɪ/ n. (pl. **-ies**; fem. **votaress**) (usu. foll. by of) **1** a person vowed to the service of God or a god or cult. **2** a devoted follower, adherent, or advocate of a person, system, occupation, etc. □□ **votarist** n. [L vot-: see VOTE]

vote /vəʊt/ n. & v. —n. **1** a formal expression of choice or opinion by means of a ballot, show of hands, etc., concerning a choice of candidate, approval of a motion or resolution, etc. (let us take a vote on it; gave my vote to the independent candidate). **2** (usu. prec. by the) the right to vote, esp. in a State election. **3 a** an opinion expressed by a majority of votes. **b** Brit. money granted by a majority of votes. **4** the collective votes that are or may be given by or for a particular group (will lose the Welsh vote; the Conservative vote increased). **5** a ticket etc. used for recording a vote. —v. **1** intr. (often foll. by for, against, or to + infin.) give a vote. **2** tr. **a** (often foll. by that + clause) enact or resolve by a majority of votes. **b** grant (a sum of money) by a majority of votes. **c** cause to be in a specified position by a majority of votes (was voted off the committee). **3** tr. colloq. pronounce or declare by general consent (was voted a failure). **4** tr. (often foll. by that + clause) colloq. announce one's proposal (I vote that we all go home). □ **put to a** (or **the**) **vote** submit to a decision by voting. **vote down** defeat (a proposal etc.) in a vote. **vote in** elect by votes. **vote of censure** = vote of no confidence. **vote of confidence** (or **no confidence**) a vote showing that the majority support (or do not support) the policy of the governing body etc. **vote with one's feet** colloq. indicate an opinion by one's presence or absence. **voting- machine** (esp. in the US) a machine for the automatic registering of votes. **voting-paper** a paper used in voting by ballot. **voting stock** stock entitling the holder to a vote. □□ **votable** adj. **voteless** adj. [ME f. past part. stem vot- of L vovēre vow]

voter /ˈvəʊtə(r)/ n. **1** a person with the right to vote at an election. **2** a person voting.

votive /ˈvəʊtɪv/ adj. offered or consecrated in fulfilment of a vow (votive offering; votive picture). □ **votive mass** Eccl. a mass celebrated for a special purpose or occasion. [L votivus (as VOTE)]

vouch /vaʊtʃ/ v. **1** intr. (foll. by for) answer for, be surety for (will vouch for the truth of this; can vouch for him; could not vouch for his honesty). **2** tr. archaic cite as an authority. **3** tr. archaic confirm or uphold (a statement) by evidence or assertion. [ME f. OF vo(u)cher summon etc., ult. f. L vocare call]

voucher /ˈvaʊtʃə(r)/ n. **1** a document which can be exchanged for goods or services as a token of payment made or promised by the holder or another. **2** a document establishing the payment of money or the truth of accounts. **3** a person who vouches for a person, statement, etc. [AF voucher (as VOUCH) or f. VOUCH]

vouchsafe /vaʊtʃˈseɪf/ v.tr. formal **1** condescend to give or grant (vouchsafed me no answer). **2** (foll. by to + infin.) condescend. [ME f. VOUCH in sense 'warrant' + SAFE]

voussoir /ˈvuːswɑː(r)/ n. each of the wedge-shaped or tapered stones forming an arch. [OF vossoir etc. f. pop.L volsorium ult. f. L volvere roll]

vow /vaʊ/ n. & v. —n. **1** Relig. a solemn promise esp. in the form of an oath to God or another deity or to a saint. **2** (in pl.) the promises by which a monk or nun is bound to poverty, chastity, and obedience. **3** a promise of fidelity (lovers' vows; marriage vows). **4** (usu. as **baptismal vows**) the promises given at baptism by the baptized person or by sponsors. —v. **1** promise solemnly (vowed obedience). **2** dedicate to a deity. **3** (also absol.) archaic declare solemnly. □ **under a vow** having made a vow. [ME f. AF v(o)u, OF vo(u), f. L (as VOTE): (v.) f. OF vouer, in sense 2 partly f. AVOW]

vowel /ˈvaʊəl/ n. **1** a speech-sound made with vibration of the vocal cords but without audible friction, more open than a consonant and capable of forming a syllable. **2** a letter or letters representing this, as a, e, i, o, u, aw, ah. □ **vowel gradation** =

ABLAUT. **vowel mutation** = UMLAUT 2. **vowel-point** each of a set of marks indicating vowels in Hebrew etc. □□ **vowelled** *adj.* (also in *comb.*). **vowelless** *adj.* **vowelly** *adj.* [ME f. OF *vouel*, *voiel* f. L *vocalis* (*littera*) VOCAL (letter)]

vowelize /ˈvaʊəˌlaɪz/ *v.tr.* (also **-ise**) insert the vowels in (shorthand, Hebrew, etc.).

vox angelica /ˌvɒks ænˈdʒelɪkə/ *n.* an organ-stop with a soft tremulous tone. [LL, = angelic voice]

vox humana /ˌvɒks hjuːˈmɑːnə/ *n.* an organ-stop with a tone supposed to resemble a human voice. [L, = human voice]

vox pop /vɒks ˈpɒp/ *n. Broadcasting colloq.* popular opinion as represented by informal comments from members of the public; statements or interviews of this kind. [abbr. of VOX POPULI]

vox populi /ˌvɒks ˈpɒpjʊˌliː, -ˌlaɪ/ *n.* public opinion, the general verdict, popular belief or rumour. [L, = the people's voice]

voyage /ˈvɔɪɪdʒ/ *n.* & *v.* —*n.* **1** a journey, esp. a long one by water, air, or in space. **2** an account of this. —*v.* **1** *intr.* make a voyage. **2** *tr.* traverse, esp. by water or air. □□ **voyageable** *adj.* **voyager** *n.* [ME f. AF & OF *veiage*, *voiage* f. L *viaticum*]

Voyager each of two US space probes launched in 1977 to Jupiter, Saturn, Uranus, and Neptune. One reached Saturn in Nov. 1980, the other reached Neptune in August 1989.

voyageur /ˌvwɑːjɑːˈʒɜː(r)/ *n.* a Canadian boatman, esp. *hist.* one employed in transporting goods and passengers between trading posts. [F, = voyager (as VOYAGE)]

voyeur /vwɑːˈjɜː(r)/ *n.* a person who obtains sexual gratification from observing others' sexual actions or organs. □□ **voyeurism** *n.* **voyeuristic** /-ˈrɪstɪk/ *adj.* **voyeuristically** /-ˈrɪstɪkəlɪ/ *adj.* [F f. *voir* see]

VP *abbr.* Vice-President.

VR *abbr.* **1** Queen Victoria. **2** variant reading. [sense 1 f. L *Victoria Regina*]

VS *abbr.* Veterinary Surgeon.

vs. *abbr.* versus.

V-sign /ˈviːsaɪn/ *n.* **1** *Brit.* a sign of the letter V made with the first two fingers pointing up and the back of the hand facing outwards, as a gesture of abuse, contempt, etc. **2** a similar sign made with the palm of the hand facing outwards, as a symbol of victory.

VSO *abbr.* Voluntary Service Overseas.

VSOP *abbr.* Very Special Old Pale (brandy).

VT *abbr. US* Vermont (in official postal use).

Vt. *abbr.* Vermont.

VTO *abbr.* vertical take-off.

VTOL /ˈviːtɒl/ *abbr.* vertical take-off and landing.

V-2 /viːˈtuː/ *n.* see V³

vug /vʌg/ *n.* a rock-cavity lined with crystals. □□ **vuggy** *adj.* **vugular** *adj.* [Corn. *vooga*]

Vuillard /vwiːˈjɑːr/, Jean Edouard (1868–1940), French painter and lithographer, a member of the Nabis, whose subject-matter was often drawn from the tranquil everyday life of middle-class homes, with scenes from Montmartre, especially the tiny square, Vintimille.

Vulcan /ˈvʌlkən/ *Rom. Mythol.* the god of fire. (See HEPHAESTUS.)

vulcanic var. of VOLCANIC.

Vulcanist /ˈvʌlkənɪst/ *n.* a holder of the plutonic theory in geology (see PLUTONIST).

vulcanite /ˈvʌlkəˌnaɪt/ *n.* a hard black vulcanized rubber, ebonite. [as VULCANIZE]

vulcanize /ˈvʌlkəˌnaɪz/ *v.tr.* (also **-ise**) treat (rubber or rubberlike material) with sulphur etc. esp. at a high temperature to increase its strength. □□ **vulcanizable** *adj.* **vulcanization** /-ˌzeɪʃ(ə)n/ *n.* **vulcanizer** *n.* [VULCAN]

vulcanology /ˌvʌlkəˈnɒlədʒɪ/ *n.* (also **volcanology** /ˌvɒl-/) the scientific study of volcanoes. □□ **vulcanological** /-nəˈlɒdʒɪk(ə)l/ *adj.* **vulcanologist** *n.*

vulgar /ˈvʌlgə(r)/ *adj.* **1 a** of or characteristic of the common people, plebeian. **b** coarse in manners; low (*vulgar expressions; vulgar tastes*). **2** in common use; generally prevalent (*vulgar errors*). □ **vulgar fraction** a fraction expressed by numerator and denominator, not decimally. **vulgar Latin** see LATIN. **the vulgar tongue** the national or vernacular language, esp. formerly as opposed to Latin. □□ **vulgarly** *adv.* [ME f. L *vulgaris* f. *vulgus* common people]

vulgarian /vʌlˈgeərɪən/ *n.* a vulgar (esp. rich) person.

vulgarism /ˈvʌlgəˌrɪz(ə)m/ *n.* **1** a word or expression in coarse or uneducated use. **2** an instance of coarse or uneducated behaviour.

vulgarity /vʌlˈgærɪtɪ/ *n.* (*pl.* **-ies**) **1** the quality of being vulgar. **2** an instance of this.

vulgarize /ˈvʌlgəˌraɪz/ *v.tr.* (also **-ise**) **1** make (a person, manners, etc.) vulgar, infect with vulgarity. **2** spoil (a scene, sentiment, etc.) by making it too common, frequented, or well known. **3** popularize. □□ **vulgarization** /-ˈzeɪʃ(ə)n/ *n.*

Vulgate /ˈvʌlgeɪt, -gət/ *n.* **1** the Latin version of the Bible prepared mainly by Jerome in the late 4th c., translated directly from the Hebrew text of the Old Testament. It is used by the Roman Catholic Church in the recension of 1592, the Council of Trent having decreed in 1546 that the Vulgate was to be the sole Latin authority for the Bible. **2** (**vulgate**) the traditionally accepted text of any author. **3** (**vulgate**) common or colloquial speech. [L *vulgata* (*editio* edition), fem. past part. of *vulgare* make public f. *vulgus*: see VULGAR]

vulnerable /ˈvʌlnərəb(ə)l/ *adj.* **1** that may be wounded or harmed. **2** (foll. by *to*) exposed to damage by a weapon, criticism, etc. **3** *Bridge* having won one game towards rubber and therefore liable to higher penalties. □□ **vulnerability** /-ˈbɪlɪtɪ/ *n.* **vulnerableness** *n.* **vulnerably** *adv.* [LL *vulnerabilis* f. L *vulnerare* to wound f. *vulnus -eris* wound]

vulnerary /ˈvʌlnərərɪ/ *adj.* & *n.* —*adj.* useful or used for the healing of wounds. —*n.* (*pl.* **-ies**) a vulnerary drug, plant, etc. [L *vulnerarius* f. *vulnus*: see VULNERABLE]

vulpine /ˈvʌlpaɪn/ *adj.* **1** of or like a fox. **2** crafty, cunning. [L *vulpinus* f. *vulpes* fox]

vulture /ˈvʌltʃə(r)/ *n.* **1** any of various large birds of prey of the family Cathartidae or Accipitridae, with the head and neck more or less bare of feathers, feeding chiefly on carrion and reputed to gather with others in anticipation of a death. **2** a rapacious person. □□ **vulturine** /-ˌraɪn/ *adj.* **vulturish** *adj.* **vulturous** *adj.* [ME f. AF *vultur*, OF *voltour* etc., f. L *vulturius*]

vulva /ˈvʌlvə/ *n.* (*pl.* **vulvas**) *Anat.* the external female genitals, esp. the external opening of the vagina. □□ **vulvar** *adj.* **vulvitis** /-ˈvaɪtɪs/ *n.* [L, = womb]

vv. *abbr.* **1** verses. **2** volumes.

vying *pres. part.* of VIE.

W

W[1] /ˈdʌb(ə)ljuː/ n. (also **w**) (pl. **Ws** or **W's**) the twenty-third letter of the alphabet.

W[2] abbr. (also **W.**) **1** watt(s). **2** West; Western. **3** women's (size). **4** Welsh.

W[3] symb. Chem. the element tungsten.

w. abbr. **1** wicket(s). **2** wide(s). **3** with. **4** wife.

WA abbr. **1** Western Australia. **2** US Washington (State) (in official postal use).

Waac /wæk/ n. hist. a member of the Women's Army Auxiliary Corps (Brit. 1917–19 or US 1942–8). [initials WAAC]

Waaf /wæf/ n. Brit. hist. a member of the Women's Auxiliary Air Force (1939–48). [initials WAAF]

WAC abbr. (in the US) Women's Army Corps.

wack[1] /wæk/ n. esp. US sl. a crazy person. [prob. back-form. f. WACKY]

wack[2] /wæk/ n. dial. a familiar term of address. [perh. f. wacker Liverpudlian]

wacke /ˈwækə/ n. hist. a greyish-green or brownish rock resulting from the decomposition of basaltic rock. [G f. MHG wacke large stone, OHG wacko pebble]

wacko /ˈwækəʊ/ adj. & n. US sl. —adj. crazy. —n. (pl. **-os** or **-oes**) a crazy person. [WACKY + -o]

wacky /ˈwækɪ/ adj. & n. (also **whacky**) sl. —adj. (**-ier, -iest**) crazy. —n. (pl. **-ies**) a crazy person. □□ **wackily** adv. **wackiness** n. [orig. dial., = left-handed, f. WHACK]

wad /wɒd/ n. & v. —n. **1** a lump or bundle of soft material used esp. to keep things apart or in place or to stuff up an opening. **2** a disc of felt etc. keeping powder or shot in place in a gun. **3** a number of banknotes or documents placed together. **4** Brit. sl. a bun, sandwich, etc. **5** (in sing. or pl.) a large quantity esp. of money. —v.tr. (**wadded, wadding**) **1** stop up (an aperture or a gun-barrel) with a wad. **2** keep (powder etc.) in place with a wad. **3** line or stuff (a garment or coverlet) with wadding. **4** protect (a person, walls, etc.) with wadding. **5** press (cotton etc.) into a wad or wadding. [perh. rel. to Du. watten, F ouate padding, cotton wool]

wadding /ˈwɒdɪŋ/ n. **1** soft pliable material of cotton or wool etc. used to line or stuff garments, quilts, etc., or to pack fragile articles. **2** any material from which gun-wads are made.

waddle /ˈwɒd(ə)l/ v. & n. —v.intr. walk with short steps and a swaying motion, like a stout short-legged person or a bird with short legs set far apart (e.g. a duck or goose). —n. a waddling gait. □□ **waddler** n. [perh. frequent. of WADE]

waddy /ˈwɒdɪ/ n. (pl. **-ies**) **1** an Australian Aboriginal's war-club. **2** Austral. & NZ any club or stick. [Aboriginal, perh. f. WOOD]

Wade /weɪd/, George (1673–1748), British field-marshal and road-builder, responsible for the construction of a network of modern roads and bridges in the 1720s and 1730s in the Highlands of Scotland in order to enable the government to control the Jacobite clans, who had hitherto enjoyed a certain freedom from interference owing to the inaccessibility of their homeland.

wade /weɪd/ v. & n. —v. **1** intr. walk through water or some impeding medium e.g. snow, mud, or sand. **2** intr. make one's way with difficulty or by force. **3** intr. (foll. by through) read (a book etc.) in spite of its dullness etc. **4** intr. (foll. by into) colloq. attack (a person or task) vigorously. **5** tr. ford (a stream etc.) on foot. —n. a spell of wading. □ **wade in** colloq. make a vigorous attack or intervention. **wading bird** any long-legged water-bird that wades. □□ **wadable** adj. (also **wadeable**). [OE wadan f. Gmc, = go (through)]

wader /ˈweɪdə(r)/ n. **1 a** a person who wades. **b** a wading bird, esp. any of various birds of the order Charadriiformes. **2** (in pl.) high waterproof boots, or a waterproof garment for the legs and body, worn in fishing etc.

wadi /ˈwɒdɪ, ˈwɑːdɪ/ n. (also **wady**) (pl. **wadis** or **wadies**) a rocky watercourse in N. Africa etc., dry except in the rainy season. [Arab. wādī]

Wadi Halfa /ˌwɒdɪ ˈhælfə/ a town on the Nile in the extreme north of Sudan. The railway from Khartoum to Wadi Halfa was built to support Lord Kitchener's campaign to retake Sudan from the Mahdi (1896–8).

WAF abbr. (in the US) Women in the Air Force.

w.a.f. abbr. with all faults.

wafer /ˈweɪfə(r)/ n. & v. —n. **1** a very thin light crisp sweet biscuit, esp. of a kind eaten with ice-cream. **2** a thin disc of unleavened bread used in the Eucharist. **3** a disc of red paper stuck on a legal document instead of a seal. **4** Electronics a very thin slice of a semiconductor crystal used as the substrate for solid-state circuitry. **5** hist. a small disc of dried paste formerly used for fastening letters, holding papers together, etc. —v.tr. fasten or seal with a wafer. □ **wafer-thin** very thin. □□ **wafery** adj. [ME f. AF wafre, ONF waufre, OF gaufre (cf. GOFFER) f. MLG wāfel waffle: cf. WAFFLE[2]]

waffle[1] /ˈwɒf(ə)l/ n. & v. esp. Brit. colloq. —n. verbose but aimless or ignorant talk or writing. —v.intr. indulge in waffle. □□ **waffler** n. **waffly** adj. [orig. dial., frequent. of waff = yelp, yap (imit.)]

waffle[2] /ˈwɒf(ə)l/ n. esp. US a small crisp batter cake. □ **waffle-iron** a utensil, usu. of two shallow metal pans hinged together, for baking waffles. [Du. wafel, waefel f. MLG wāfel: cf. WAFER]

waft /wɒft, wɑːft/ v. & n. —v.tr. & intr. convey or travel easily as through air or over water; sweep smoothly and lightly along. —n. **1** (usu. foll. by of) a whiff or scent. **2** a transient sensation of peace, joy, etc. **3** (also **weft** /weft/) Naut. a distress signal, e.g. an ensign rolled or knotted or a garment flown in the rigging. [orig. 'convoy (ship etc.)', back-form. f. obs. waughter, wafter armed convoy-ship, f. Du. or LG wachter f. wachten to guard]

wag[1] /wæg/ v. & n. —v. (**wagged, wagging**) **1** tr. & intr. shake or wave rapidly or energetically to and fro. **2** intr. archaic (of the world, times, etc.) go along with varied fortune or characteristics. —n. a single wagging motion (with a wag of his tail). □ **the tail wags the dog** the less or least important member of a society, section of a party, or part of a structure has control. **tongues** (or **beards** or **chins** or **jaws**) **wag** there is talk. [ME waggen f. root of OE wagian sway]

wag[2] /wæg/ n. **1** a facetious person, a joker. **2** Brit. sl. a truant (play the wag). [prob. f. obs. waghalter one likely to be hanged (as WAG[1], HALTER)]

wage /weɪdʒ/ n. & v. —n. **1** (in sing. or pl.) a fixed regular payment, usu. daily or weekly, made by an employer to an employee, esp. to a manual or unskilled worker (cf. SALARY). **2** (in sing. or pl.) requital (the wages of sin is death). **3** (in pl.) Econ. the part of total production that rewards labour rather than remunerating capital. —v.tr. carry on (a war, conflict, or contest). □ **living wage** a wage that affords the means of normal subsistence. **wage-claim** = pay-claim (see PAY[1]). **wage-earner** a person who works for wages. **wages council** a board of workers' and employers' representatives determining wages where there is no collective bargaining. **wage slave** a person dependent on income from labour in conditions like slavery. [ME f. AF & ONF wage, OF g(u)age, f. Gmc, rel. to GAGE[1], WED]

wager /ˈweɪdʒə(r)/ n. & v.tr. & intr. = BET. □ **wager of battle** hist. an ancient form of trial by personal combat between the parties or their champions. **wager of law** hist. a form of trial in which the defendant was required to produce witnesses who

---

aʊ how eɪ day əʊ no eə hair ɪə near ɔɪ boy ʊə poor aɪə fire aʊə sour (see over for consonants)

would swear to his or her innocence. [ME f. AF *wageure* f. *wager* (as WAGE)]

Wagga Wagga /ˌwɒgə ˈwɒgə/ an agricultural centre in New South Wales, Australia; pop. (est. 1987), 50,930.

waggery /ˈwægərɪ/ n. (pl. **-ies**) **1** waggish behaviour, joking. **2** a waggish action or remark, a joke.

waggish /ˈwægɪʃ/ adj. playful, facetious. □□ **waggishly** adv. **waggishness** n.

waggle /ˈwæg(ə)l/ v. & n. colloq. —v. **1** intr. & tr. wag. **2** intr. Golf swing the club-head to and fro over the ball before playing a shot. —n. a waggling motion. [WAG¹ + -LE⁴]

waggly /ˈwæglɪ/ adj. unsteady.

Wagner /ˈvɑːgnə(r)/, Richard (1813–83), German composer and conductor. His life has attracted notoriety—because of his marriage to Liszt's daughter Cosima after an affair which involved deceiving her husband, his association with the deranged Ludwig II of Bavaria, his anti-Semitism, and the way in which his music and the festival opera-house he built at Bayreuth became a focal point for all that Hitler intended for the new Germany. In *The Flying Dutchman* (1841), inspired by a sea journey to London in which the ship was driven into a Norwegian fjord, *Tannhäuser* (1845), and *Lohengrin* (1848) can be seen the basic concerns of Wagner's approach to opera: myth and legend, often as recounted by early German writers; redemption through love, both Christian and secular; and above all unification of music and drama. The sheer mastery of *The Ring*, the sustaining of such an imposing achievement at a white heat of inspiration for something like twenty hours of music, is among the most amazing triumphs of the human spirit.

wagon /ˈwægən/ n. (also Brit. **waggon**) **1** a four-wheeled vehicle for heavy loads, often with a removable tilt or cover. **2** Brit. a railway vehicle for goods, esp. an open truck. **3** a trolley for conveying tea etc. **4** (in full **water-wagon**) a vehicle for carrying water. **5** US a light horse-drawn vehicle. **6** colloq. a motor car, esp. an estate car. □ **on the wagon** (or **water-wagon**) sl. teetotal. **wagon-roof** (or **-vault**) = *barrel vault*. [earlier *wagon*, *wag(h)en*, f. Du. *wag(h)en*, rel. to OE *wægn* WAIN]

wagoner /ˈwægənə(r)/ n. (also Brit. **waggoner**) the driver of a wagon. [Du. *wagenaar* (as WAGON)]

wagonette /ˌwægəˈnet/ n. (also Brit. **waggonette**) a four-wheeled horse-drawn pleasure vehicle, usu. open, with facing side-seats.

wagon-lit /ˌvægɔ̃ˈliː/ n. (pl. **wagons-lits** pronunc. same) a sleeping-car on a Continental railway. [F]

wagtail /ˈwægteɪl/ n. any small bird of the genus *Motacilla* with a long tail in frequent motion.

Wahabi /wəˈhɑːbɪ/ n. (also **Wahhabi**) (pl. **-is**) a member of a sect of Muslim puritans following strictly the original words of the Koran, named after Muhammad ibn Abd al-Wahab (1703–92), a native of Najd in central Arabia. Dissatisfied with the practices of his contemporaries in the capitals of Islamic learning, Abd al-Wahab called for a return to the earliest doctrines and practices of Islam as embodied in the Koran and Sunna, and for the abolition of accretions and corruptions which had pervaded the medieval Muslim community through the activities and preachings of mystical groups (see SUFI) and also through the blind subservience of the ulama—scholars and legislators of the community—to the dictates of earlier scholars. Forming an alliance with Muhammad ibn Saud, prince of a small adjacent kingdom, he showed his awareness of the inseparability of spiritual and temporal in Islam. The two leaders forged a State which came to encompass most of the Arabian peninsula, but their expansion and especially their attacks on sites holy to followers of Islam brought a response in the form of a successful military campaign undertaken by Muhammad Ali, Viceroy of Egypt, acting for the Ottoman government, which was nominal sovereign over the Arabian peninsula. The reconquest of Ottoman territory and dissolution of the Wahabi State was completed in 1919. The term 'Wahabi', however, was appropriated by various movements seeking reform and purification of the faith in the 19th c., and became almost a generic name for such movements.

wahine /wɑːˈhiːnɪ/ n. NZ a woman or wife. [Maori]

Wahran see ORAN.

wah-wah /ˈwɑːwɑː/ n. (also **wa-wa**) Mus. an effect achieved on brass instruments by alternately applying and removing a mute and on an electric guitar by controlling the output from the amplifier with a pedal. [imit.]

waif /weɪf/ n. **1** a homeless and helpless person, esp. an abandoned child. **2** an ownerless object or animal, a thing cast up by or drifting in the sea or brought by an unknown agency. □ **waifs and strays 1** homeless or neglected children. **2** odds and ends. □□ **waifish** adj. [ME f. AF *waif*, *weif*, ONF *gaif*, prob. of Scand. orig.]

Waikato /waɪˈkɑːtəʊ/ **1** the longest river of New Zealand, flowing north and north-west for 434 km (270 miles) from Lake Taupo at the centre of North Island to the Tasman Sea. **2** an administrative region of North Island, New Zealand; pop. (1986) 228,300; chief town, Hamilton.

Waikiki /waɪˈkiːkiː/ a beach resort forming a SE suburb of Honolulu.

wail /weɪl/ n. & v. —n. **1** a prolonged plaintive inarticulate loud high-pitched cry of pain, grief, etc. **2** a sound like or suggestive of this. —v. **1** intr. utter a wail. **2** intr. lament or complain persistently or bitterly. **3** intr. (of the wind etc.) make a sound like a person wailing. **4** tr. poet. or rhet. bewail; wail over. □□ **wailer** n. **wailful** adj. poet. **wailingly** adv. [ME f. ON, rel. to WOE]

Wailing Wall a high wall in Jerusalem, known in Jewish tradition as the 'Western Wall'. Originally part of the Temple structure erected by Herod the Great, since the 7th c. it has formed the western wall of the sanctuary enclosing the Dome of the Rock and other buildings, the third most holy place to Muslims after Mecca and Medina. Jews have been accustomed, probably since the Middle Ages, to lament at this wall the destruction of the Temple and the Holy City in AD 70 and to pray for its restoration.

wain /weɪn/ n. archaic a wagon. □ **the Wain** (also **Charles's Wain**) the constellation Ursa Major. In its name, Charles = Charlemagne; it was originally called the Wain of Arcturus (a neighbouring star); Arcturus was confused with Arturus, King Arthur, who is associated with Charlemagne in legend. [OE *wæg(e)n*, *wæn*, f. Gmc, rel. to WAY, WEIGH¹]

wainscot /ˈweɪnskət/ n. & v. —n. **1** boarding or wooden panelling on the lower part of a room-wall. **2** Brit. hist. imported oak of fine quality. —v.tr. (**wainscoted**, **wainscoting**) line with wainscot. [ME f. MLG *wagenschot*, app. f. *wagen* WAGON + *schot* of uncert. meaning]

wainscoting /ˈweɪnskətɪŋ/ n. **1** a wainscot. **2** material for this.

wainwright /ˈweɪnraɪt/ n. a wagon-builder.

Wairarapa /ˌwaɪrəˈrɑːpə/ an administrative region of North island, New Zealand; pop. (1986) 39,600; chief town, Masterton.

waist /weɪst/ n. **1 a** the part of the human body below the ribs and above the hips, usu. of smaller circumference than these; the narrower middle part of the normal human figure. **b** the circumference of this. **2** a similar narrow part in the middle of a violin, hourglass, wasp, etc. **3 a** the part of a garment encircling or covering the waist. **b** the narrow middle part of a woman's dress etc. **c** US a blouse or bodice. **4** the middle part of a ship, between the forecastle and the quarterdeck. □ **waist-cloth** a loincloth. **waist-deep** (or **-high**) up to the waist (*waist-deep in water*). □□ **waisted** adj. (also in comb.). **waistless** adj. [ME *wast*, perh. f. OE f. the root of WAX²]

waistband /ˈweɪstbænd/ n. a strip of cloth forming the waist of a garment.

waistcoat /ˈweɪskəʊt, ˈweɪstkəʊt, ˈweskət/ n. Brit. a close-fitting waist-length garment, without sleeves or collar but usu. buttoned, worn usu. by men over a shirt and under a jacket.

waistline /ˈweɪstlaɪn/ n. the outline or the size of a person's body at the waist.

wait /weɪt/ v. & n. —v. **1** intr. **a** defer action or departure for a specified time or until some expected event occurs (*wait a minute*; *wait till I come*; *wait for a fine day*). **b** be expectant or on the watch (*waited to see what would happen*). **c** (foll. by *for*) refrain from going so fast that (a person) is left behind (*wait for me!*). **2** *tr.* await (an opportunity, one's turn, etc.). **3** *tr.* defer (a meal etc.) until a person's arrival. **4** *intr.* (usu. as **waiting** *n.*) park a vehicle for a short time at the side of a road etc. (*no waiting*). **5** *intr.* **a** (in full **wait at** or *US* **on table**) act as a waiter or as a servant with similar functions. **b** act as an attendant. **6** *intr.* (foll. by *on, upon*) **a** await the convenience of. **b** serve as an attendant to. **c** pay a respectful visit to. —*n.* **1** a period of waiting (*had a long wait for the train*). **2** (usu. foll. by *for*) watching for an enemy; ambush (*lie in wait; lay wait*). **3** (in *pl.*) *Brit.* **a** *archaic* street singers of Christmas carols. **b** *hist.* official bands of musicians maintained by a city or town. □ **cannot wait 1** is impatient. **2** needs to be dealt with immediately. **can wait** need not be dealt with immediately. **wait-a-bit** a plant with hooked thorns etc. that catch the clothing. **wait and see** await the progress of events. **wait for it!** *colloq.* **1** do not begin before the proper moment. **2** used to create an interval of suspense before saying something unexpected or amusing. **wait on** *Austral., NZ, & N.Engl.* be patient, wait. **wait up** (often foll. by *for*) not go to bed until a person arrives or an event happens. **you wait!** used to imply a threat, warning, or promise. [ME f. ONF *waitier* f. Gmc, rel. to WAKE¹]

Waitangi /waɪˈtæŋgɪ/ a settlement in New Zealand at which in 1840 was negotiated the **Treaty of Waitangi**, forming the basis of British annexation of New Zealand, by which the Maori chiefs of North Island accepted British sovereignty in exchange for protection. Subsequent encroachment on the lands set aside for them led eventually to the Maori Wars of 1860–72 in which Maori independence was finally destroyed. □ **Waitangi Day** 6 Feb., celebrated in New Zealand since 1960 as a public holiday.

waiter /ˈweɪtə(r)/ *n.* **1** a man who serves at table in a hotel or restaurant etc. **2** a person who waits for a time, event, or opportunity. **3** a tray or salver.

waiting /ˈweɪtɪŋ/ *n.* **1** in senses of WAIT v. **2 a** official attendance at court. **b** one's period of this. □ **waiting game** abstention from early action in a contest etc. so as to act more effectively later. **waiting-list** a list of people waiting for a thing not immediately available. **waiting-room** a room provided for people to wait in, esp. by a doctor, dentist, etc., or at a railway or bus station.

waitress /ˈweɪtrɪs/ *n.* a woman who serves at table in a hotel or restaurant etc.

waive /weɪv/ *v.tr.* refrain from insisting on or using (a right, claim, opportunity, legitimate plea, etc.). [ME f. AF *weyver*, OF *gaiver* allow to become a WAIF, abandon]

waiver /ˈweɪvə(r)/ *n. Law* the act or an instance of waiving. [as WAIVE]

wake¹ /weɪk/ *v. & n.* —*v.* (*past* **woke** /wəʊk/ or **waked**; *past part.* **woken** /ˈwəʊkən/ or **waked**) **1** *intr. & tr.* (often foll. by *up*) cease or cause to cease to sleep. **2** *intr. & tr.* (often foll. by *up*) become or cause to become alert, attentive, or active (*needs something to wake him up*). **3** *intr.* (*archaic* except as **waking** *adj. & n.*) be awake (*in her waking hours; waking or sleeping*). **4** *tr.* disturb (silence or a place) with noise; make re-echo. **5** *tr.* evoke (an echo). **6** *intr. & tr.* rise or raise from the dead. —*n.* **1** a watch beside a corpse before burial; lamentation and (less often) merrymaking in connection with this. **2** (usu. in *pl.*) an annual holiday in (industrial) northern England. **3** *hist.* **a** a vigil commemorating the dedication of a church. **b** a fair or merrymaking on this occasion. □ **be a wake-up** (often foll. by *to*) *Austral. sl.* be alert or aware. **wake-robin 1** *Brit.* an arum, esp. the cuckoo-pint. **2** *US* any plant of the genus *Trillium*. □□ **waker** *n.* [OE *wacan* (recorded only in past *woc*), *wacian* (weak form), rel. to WATCH: sense 'vigil' perh. f. ON]

wake² /weɪk/ *n.* **1** the track left on the water's surface by a moving ship. **2** turbulent air left behind a moving aircraft etc. □ **in the wake of** behind, following, as a result of, in imitation of. [prob. f. MLG f. ON *vök* hole or opening in ice]

wakeful /ˈweɪkfʊl/ *adj.* **1** unable to sleep. **2** (of a night etc.) passed with little or no sleep. **3** vigilant. □□ **wakefully** *adv.* **wakefulness** *n.*

waken /ˈweɪkən/ *v.tr. & intr.* make or become awake. [ON *vakna* f. Gmc, rel. to WAKE¹]

Wakhan Salient /wəˈkɑːn/ *n.pl.* a narrow corridor of land forming a 300 km-long 'panhandle' at the north-east corner of Afghanistan. Demarcated by the Anglo-Russian Pamir Commission in 1895–6, the Salient once formed a buffer between Russian and British spheres of influence in Asia.

Walachia see WALLACHIA.

Waldenses /wɒlˈdensiːz/ *n.pl.* a puritan religious sect founded in southern France *c.*1173 by Peter Waldo (L *Valdus*), a merchant of Lyons, and despite much former persecution by the Roman Catholic Church still surviving, notably in Piedmont. □□ **Waldensian** *adj. & n.* [med.L f. Peter *Waldo* of Lyons, founder]

Waldheim /ˈvældhaɪm/, Kurt (1918–), Austrian diplomat and politician, Secretary-General of the United Nations 1972–81. In 1986 he was elected President of Austria; during the campaign allegations were made (which he denied) that he had been personally involved in or had direct knowledge of Nazi atrocities during the Second World War.

wale /weɪl/ *n. & v.* —*n.* **1** = WEAL¹. **2** a ridge on a woven fabric, e.g. corduroy. **3** *Naut.* a broad thick timber along a ship's side. **4** a specially woven strong band round a woven basket. —*v.tr.* provide or mark with wales. □ **wale-knot** a knot made at the end of a rope by intertwining strands to prevent unravelling or act as a stopper. [OE *walu* stripe, ridge]

Wales /weɪlz/ the western part of Great Britain; pop. (1981) 2,791,851; capital Cardiff. The earliest inhabitants appear to have been overrun by Celtic peoples in the Bronze and Iron Age. The Romans fortified the north and south of Wales and established a system of forts and outposts linked by roads that traversed the country. After the Roman withdrawal in the 5th c., the Celtic inhabitants of Wales successfully maintained their independence against the Anglo-Saxons who settled in England, and in the 8th c. Offa king of Mercia built an earthwork (see OFFA'S DYKE) marking the frontier established by his struggles against them. Largely isolated from historical developments in the rest of England until the Middle Ages, Wales was conquered by Edward I in the late 13th c. but continued a sporadic resistance to English rule until finally incorporated into the larger country by Henry VIII in 1536. Despite its absorption into the British State, Wales has retained a distinct cultural identity, but has suffered increasingly from the closure or stagnation of its coal and steel industries.

Walesa /væˈwensə/, Lech (1943–), Polish trade-unionist, leader of Solidarity (see entry). After the collapse of Communism he was elected President of his country in Dec. 1990.

walk /wɔːk/ *v. & n.* —*v.* **1** *intr.* **a** (of a person or other biped) progress by lifting and setting down each foot in turn, never having both feet off the ground at once. **b** progress with similar movements (*walked on his hands*). **c** go with the gait usual except when speed is desired. **d** (of a quadruped) go with the slowest gait, always having at least two feet on the ground at once. **2** *intr.* **a** travel or go on foot. **b** take exercise in this way (*walks for two hours each day*). **3** *tr.* perambulate, traverse on foot at walking speed; tread the floor or surface of. **4** *tr.* **a** cause to walk with one. **b** accompany in walking. **c** ride or lead (a horse, dog, etc.) at walking pace. **d** take charge of (a puppy) at walk (see sense 4 of *n.*). **5** *intr.* (of a ghost) appear. **6** *intr. Cricket* leave the wicket on being out. **7** *Baseball* **a** *intr.* reach first base on balls. **b** *tr.* allow to do this. **8** *intr. archaic* live in a specified manner, conduct oneself (*walk humbly; walk with God*). **9** *intr. US sl.* be released from suspicion or from a charge. —*n.* **1 a** an act of walking, the ordinary human gait (*go at a walk*). **b** the slowest gait of an animal. **c** a person's manner of walking (*know him by his walk*). **2 a** taking a (usu. specified) time to walk a distance (*is only ten minutes' walk from here; it's quite a walk to the bus-stop*). **b** an excursion on foot, a stroll or constitutional (*go for a walk*). **c** a journey on foot completed to earn money promised for a charity etc. **3 a** a place, track, or route intended or suitable for walking; a promenade, colonnade, or footpath. **b** a person's favourite place or route for walking. **c** the round of a postman, hawker, etc. **4** a farm etc. where a hound-puppy is sent to accustom it to various surroundings. **5** the place where a gamecock is kept. **6** a part of a forest under one keeper. □ **in a walk** without effort (*won in a walk*). **walk about** stroll. **walk all over** *colloq.* **1** defeat easily. **2** take advantage of. **walk away from 1** easily outdistance. **2** refuse to become involved with; fail to deal with. **3** survive (an accident etc.) without serious injury. **walk away with** *colloq.* = *walk off with*. **walk the boards** be an actor. **walk the hospitals** = *walk the wards*. **walk in** (often foll. by *on*) enter or arrive, esp. unexpectedly or easily. **walk into 1** *colloq.* encounter through unwariness (*walked into the trap*). **2** *sl. archaic* attack forcefully. **3** *sl. archaic* eat heartily. **walk it 1** make a journey on foot, not ride. **2** *colloq.* achieve something (esp. a victory) easily. **walk Matilda** see MATILDA. **walk off 1** depart (esp. abruptly). **2** get rid of the effects of (a meal, ailment, etc.) by walking (*walked off his anger*). **walk a person off his** or **her feet** (or **legs**) exhaust a person with walking. **walk off with** *colloq.* **1** steal. **2** win easily. **walk of life** an occupation, profession, or calling. **walk-on 1** (in full **walk-on part**) = *walking-on part*. **2** the player of this. **walk on air** see AIR. **walk out 1** depart suddenly or angrily. **2** (usu. foll. by *with*) *Brit. archaic* go for walks in courtship. **walk-out** *n.* a sudden angry departure, esp. as a protest or strike. **walk out on** desert, abandon. **walk over 1** *colloq.* = *walk all over.* **2** (often *absol.*) traverse (a racecourse) without needing to hurry, because one has no opponents or only inferior ones. **walk-over** *n.* an easy victory or achievement. **walk the plank** see PLANK. **walk the streets 1** be a prostitute. **2** traverse the streets esp. in search of work etc. **walk tall** *colloq.* feel justifiable pride. **walk up!** a showman's invitation to a circus etc. **walk-up** *US adj.* (of a building) allowing access to the upper floors only by stairs. —*n.* a walk-up building. **walk up to** approach (a person) for a talk etc. **walk the wards** be a medical student. □□ **walkable** *adj.* [OE *wealcan* roll, toss, wander, f. Gmc]

walkabout /ˈwɔːkəˌbaʊt/ *n.* **1** an informal stroll among a crowd by a visiting dignitary. **2** a period of wandering in the bush by an Australian Aboriginal.

walkathon /ˈwɔːkəˌθɒn/ *n.* an organized fund-raising walk. [WALK, after MARATHON]

walker /ˈwɔːkə(r)/ *n.* **1** a person or animal that walks. **2 a** a wheeled or footed framework in which a baby can learn to walk. **b** = *walking frame.*

Walker Cup /ˈwɔːkə(r)/ a golf tournament played between teams of men amateurs of the US and Great Britain and Ireland, held every second year in May, alternately in the US and Great Britain, from 1922; the trophy for this, donated by George H. Walker, a former president of the US Golf Association, who organized the competition.

walkie-talkie /ˌwɔːkɪˈtɔːkɪ/ *n.* a two-way radio carried on the person, esp. by policemen etc.

walking /ˈwɔːkɪŋ/ *n. & adj.* in senses of WALK *v.* □ **walking delegate** a trade-union official who visits members and their employers for discussions. **walking dictionary** (or **encyclopedia**) *colloq.* a person having a wide general knowledge. **walking fern** any American evergreen fern of the genus *Camptosorus,* with fronds that root at the ends. **walking frame** a usu. tubular metal frame with rubberized ferrules, used by disabled or old people to help them walk. **walking gentleman** (or **lady**) *Theatr.* a non-speaking extra; a supernumerary. **walking leaf** = *walking fern.* **walking-on part** a non-speaking dramatic role. **walking papers** *colloq.* dismissal (*gave him his walking papers*). **walking-tour** a holiday journey on foot, esp. of several days. **walking wounded 1** (of soldiers etc.) able to walk despite injuries; not bedridden. **2** *colloq.* a person or people having esp. mental or emotional difficulties.

walking-stick *n.* **1** a stick held or used as a support when walking. The walking-stick with a pommel held in the hand seems to have been introduced during the 15th c., but it was not until the 17th c. that the cane, or walking-stick, became an essential part of the dress of a fine gentleman. In the early 19th c. such sticks were notably fashionable, having entirely replaced swords which were no longer carried, and remained popular up to the beginning of the First World War, but now the traditional 'stick and gloves' of the man about town have almost completely vanished. **2** *US* = stick insect (see STICK[1]).

Walkman /ˈwɔːkmən/ *n.* (*pl.* **-mans**) *propr.* a type of personal stereo equipment.

walkway /ˈwɔːkweɪ/ *n.* a passage or path for walking along, esp.: **1** a raised passageway connecting different sections of a building. **2** a wide path in a garden etc.

wall /wɔːl/ *n. & v.* —*n.* **1 a** a continuous and usu. vertical structure of usu. brick or stone, having little width in proportion to its length and height and esp. enclosing, protecting, or dividing a space or supporting a roof. **b** the surface of a wall, esp. inside a room (*hung the picture on the wall*). **2** anything like a wall in appearance or effect, esp.: **a** the steep side of a mountain. **b** a protection or obstacle (*a wall of steel bayonets; a wall of indifference*). **c** *Anat.* the outermost layer or enclosing membrane etc. of an organ, structure, etc. **d** the outermost part of a hollow structure (*stomach wall*). **e** *Mining* rock enclosing a lode or seam. —*v.tr.* **1** (esp. as **walled** *adj.*) surround or protect with a wall (*walled garden*). **2 a** (usu. foll. by *up, off*) block or seal (a space etc.) with a wall. **b** (foll. by *up*) enclose (a person) within a sealed space (*walled them up in the dungeon*). □ **go to the wall** be defeated or pushed aside. **off the wall** *US sl.* unorthodox, unconventional. **up the wall** *colloq.* crazy or furious (*went up the wall when he heard*). **wall bar** one of a set of parallel bars, attached to the wall of a gymnasium, on which exercises are performed. **wall-barley** wild barley as a weed. **wall-board** a type of wall-covering made from wood pulp etc. **wall cress** = ARABIS. **wall-fern** an evergreen polypody, *Polypodium vulgare,* with very large leaves. **wall-fruit** fruit grown on trees trained against a wall for protection and warmth. **wall game** *Brit.* a form of football played at Eton beside a wall. (See ETON.) **wall-knot** = *wale-knot.* **wall-painting** a mural or fresco. **wall pepper** a succulent stonecrop, *Sedum acre,* with a pungent taste. **wall-plate** timber laid in or on a wall to distribute the pressure of a girder etc. **wall rocket** see ROCKET[2]. **wall rue** a small fern, *Adiantum ruta-muraria,* with leaves like rue, growing on walls and rocks. **walls have ears** it is unsafe to speak openly, as there may be eavesdroppers. **wall-to-wall 1** (of a carpet) fitted to cover a whole room etc. **2** *colloq.* profuse, ubiquitous (*wall-to-wall pop music*). □□ **walling** *n.* **wall-less** *adj.* [OE f. L *vallum* rampart f. *vallus* stake]

wallaby /ˈwɒləbɪ/ *n.* (*pl.* **-ies**) **1** any of various marsupials of the family Macropodidae, smaller than kangaroos, and having large hind feet and long tails. **2** (**Wallabies**) an Australian international Rugby Union team, so called from the animal found extensively in Australia. □ **on the wallaby** (or **wallaby track**) *Austral.* vagrant; unemployed. [Aboriginal *wolabā*]

Wallace[1] /ˈwɒlɪs/, Alfred Russel (1823–1913), British naturalist who independently formulated a theory of the origin of species that was identical with that of Charles Darwin, to whom he communicated his conclusions. He travelled extensively in South America and the East Indies, collecting specimens and studying the geographical distribution of animals. In 1858 a summary of the joint views of Wallace and Darwin concerning natural selection was read to the Linnaean Society in London, and credit for the theory has attached somewhat unfairly to Darwin. □ **Wallace's line** a hypothetical line, proposed by Wallace, extending from the Indian Ocean northward between Borneo and the Celebes into the Philippine Sea, dividing the regions where Australasian fauna are found from those of Asian fauna. The former are (in evolutionary terms) more primitive than the latter, and the line indicates the stage at which the continents became separated.

Wallace[2] /ˈwɒlɪs/, (Richard Horatio) Edgar (1875–1932), English novelist, playwright, and journalist. After working as a newspaper correspondent in South Africa he became the first editor of the *Rand Daily Mail* in Johannesburg before returning to England and embarking on the novels that were to make him famous. His *Sanders* stories, set in West Africa, are among the best of his writings, but it is for his thrillers that he is chiefly remembered. In 28 years of authorship more than 170 of his books were published; his style was simple and racy, his plots varied, the speed of his output was a byword, and meanwhile he sometimes had two or three plays running simultaneously in London. Notable among his works are *The Four Just Men* (1905) and its sequels, *The Ringer* (novel 1925; play 1926), *The Crimson Circle* (1922), and *The Mind of Mr. J. G. Reeder* (1925). He died in

Hollywood, California, where he had been writing motion picture stories, the first of which, *King Kong*, was produced shortly after his death.

Wallace[3] /ˈwɒlɪs/, Sir William (c.1270–1305), a national hero of Scotland, a leader of Scottish resistance to Edward I. Following his victory over an English army at Stirling in 1297 he briefly became official Guardian of the Realm, but his defeat at Falkirk a year later reduced him to little more than a guerrilla leader. He was eventually captured and executed by the English.

Wallace Collection /ˈwɒlɪs/ a museum in Manchester Square, London, containing a fine representation of French 18th-c. paintings and furniture, English 18th-c. portraits, and medieval armour. The collection was built up by the Seymour-Conway family, Earls and later Marquesses of Hertford, and was given to the nation in 1897.

Wallachia /wɒˈleɪkɪə/ (also **Walachia**) a former principality of SE Europe, between the Danube and the Transylvanian Alps, united in 1859 with Moldavia to form Romania. □□ **Wallachian** *adj. & n.* [as VLACH]

wallah /ˈwɒlə/ *n.* orig. *Anglo-Ind.*, now *sl.* **1** a person concerned with or in charge of a usu. specified thing, business, etc. (*asked the ticket wallah*). **2** a person doing a routine administrative job; a bureaucrat. [Hindi -*wālā* suffix = -ER[1]]

wallaroo /ˌwɒləˈruː/ *n.* a large brownish-black kangaroo, *Macropus robustus*. [Aboriginal *wolarū*]

Waller /ˈwɒlə(r)/, Fats (Thomas Wright Waller, 1904–43), American jazz pianist and songwriter, whose compositions include 'Ain't Misbehavin'' (1928) and 'Honeysuckle Rose' (1929).

wallet /ˈwɒlɪt/ *n.* **1** a small flat esp. leather case for holding banknotes etc. **2** *archaic* a bag for carrying food etc. on a journey, esp. as used by a pilgrim or beggar. [ME *walet*, prob. f. AF *walet* (unrecorded), perh. f. Gmc]

wall-eye /ˈwɔːlaɪ/ *n.* **1 a** an eye with a streaked or opaque white iris. **b** an eye squinting outwards. **2** an American perch, *Stizostedion vitreum*, with large prominent eyes. □□ **wall-eyed** *adj.* [back-form. f. *wall-eyed*: ME f. ON *vagleygr* f. *vagl* (unrecorded: cf. Icel. *vagl* film over the eye) + *auga* EYE]

wallflower /ˈwɔːlˌflaʊə(r)/ *n.* **1 a** a fragrant spring garden-plant, *Cheiranthus cheiri*, with esp. brown, yellow, or dark-red clustered flowers. **b** any of various flowering plants of the genus *Cheiranthus* or *Erysimum*, growing wild on old walls. **2** *colloq.* a neglected or socially awkward person, esp. a woman sitting out at a dance for lack of partners.

Wallis /ˈwɒlɪs/, Sir Barnes Neville (1887–1979), English inventor who patented over 140 designs. He designed the R100 airship, used geodetic construction on his famous Wellington bomber of the Second World War, invented radio telescopes and rangefinders for use over water, worked on guided missiles and swing-wing aircraft, and later designed supersonic aircraft. His bomb designs included the famous bouncing bomb used to destroy the Ruhr dams in Germany in 1943.

Wallis and Fatuna Islands /ˈwɒlɪs, fəˈtjuːnə/ an overseas territory of France comprising two groups of islands to the west of Samoa in the central Pacific; pop. (1982) 15,400; capital, Mata-Utu.

Walloon /wɒˈluːn/ *n. & adj.* —*n.* **1** a member of a people, of Gaulish origin and speaking a French dialect, living in southern Belgium (where they form the chief part of the population) and neighbouring parts of France. (See also FLEMING[1].) **2** the French dialect spoken by this people. —*adj.* of or concerning the Walloons or their language. [F *Wallon* f. med.L *Wallo -onis* f. Gmc: cf. WELSH]

wallop /ˈwɒləp/ *v. & n. sl.* —*v.tr.* (**walloped, walloping**) **1 a** thrash; beat. **b** hit hard. **2** (as **walloping** *adj.*) big; strapping; thumping (*a walloping profit*). —*n.* **1** a heavy blow; a thump. **2** *Brit.* beer or any alcoholic drink. □□ **walloping** *n.* [earlier senses 'gallop', 'boil', f. ONF (*walop* n. f.) *waloper*, OF *galoper*: cf. GALLOP]

walloper /ˈwɒləpə(r)/ *n.* **1** a person or thing that wallops. **2** *Austral. sl.* a policeman.

wallow /ˈwɒləʊ/ *v. & n.* —*v.intr.* **1** (esp. of an animal) roll about in mud, sand, water, etc. **2** (usu. foll. by *in*) indulge in unrestrained sensuality, pleasure, misery, etc. (*wallows in nostalgia*). —*n.* **1** the act or an instance of wallowing. **2 a** a place used by buffalo etc. for wallowing. **b** the depression in the ground caused by this. □□ **wallower** *n.* [OE *walwian* roll f. Gmc]

wallpaper /ˈwɔːlˌpeɪpə(r)/ *n. & v.* —*n.* **1** paper sold in rolls for pasting on to interior walls as decoration. **2** an unobtrusive background, esp. (usu. *derog.*) with ref. to sound, music, etc. —*v.tr.* (often *absol.*) decorate with wallpaper.

Wall Street a street at the south end of Manhattan, New York, where the New York Stock Exchange and other leading American financial institutions are located, whence the allusive use of its name to refer to the American money-market or financial interests. (See STOCK EXCHANGE.)

wally /ˈwɒlɪ/ *n.* (*pl.* **-ies**) *Brit. sl.* a foolish or inept person. [orig. uncert., perh. shortened form of *Walter*]

walnut /ˈwɔːlnʌt/ *n.* **1** any tree of the genus *Juglans*, having aromatic leaves and drooping catkins. **2** the nut of this tree containing an edible kernel in two half shells shaped like boats. **3** the timber of the walnut-tree used in cabinet-making. [OE *walh-hnutu* f. Gmc NUT]

Walpole[1] /ˈwɔːlpəʊl/, Horace, 4th Earl of Orford (1717–97), English writer and connoisseur, an MP 1741–67. In 1747, supported by various sinecures, he settled in Twickenham at Strawberry Hill which he made into his 'little Gothic castle'. There he collected curios, established his own printing press, and printed Gray's Pindaric Odes and his own *Anecdotes of Painting in England* (1762). His novel *The Castle of Otranto* (1764) set a fashion for 'Gothic' tales of mystery and horror. His literary reputation rests largely on his letters which are remarkable for their charm and wit and for their autobiographical, political, and social interest.

Walpole[2] /ˈwɔːlpəʊl/, Sir Hugh (1884–1941), British novelist, born in New Zealand, educated in England. His short experience as a schoolmaster is reflected in *Mr. Perrin and Mr. Traill* (1911) which set a vogue for novels and plays about schoolmasters. Among his many novels are *The Dark Forest* (1916), based on his wartime service with the Russian Red Cross, and *The Herries Chronicle* (1930–3), a historical sequence set in Cumberland (where he lived from 1924).

Walpole[3] /ˈwɔːlpəʊl/, Sir Robert, 1st Earl of Orford (1676–1745), British statesman. A career Whig politician, whose colourful life included a spell in the Tower of London on a charge of venality in office, Walpole is generally recognized as the first modern British Prime Minister. He held office between 1715–17 and 1721–42, presiding over a period of considerable peace and prosperity, although eventually failing to prevent war with Spain in 1739.

Walpurgis Night /vælˈpʊəgɪs/ the eve of 1 May, on which, according to German legend, a witches' Sabbath took place on the Brocken, a peak of the Harz mountains. It is named after St Walburga, an English nun who in the 8th c. helped to convert the Germans to Christianity; one of her feast days coincided with an ancient pagan feast with rites protecting from witchcraft.

walrus /ˈwɔːlrəs, ˈwɒl-/ *n.* a large amphibious long-tusked arctic mammal, *Odobenus rosmarus*, related to the seal and sea lion. □ **walrus moustache** a long thick drooping moustache. [prob. f. Du. *walrus, -ros*, perh. by metath. after *walvisch* 'whale-fish' f. word repr. by OE *horschwæl* 'horse-whale']

Walsall /ˈwɔːlsɔːl/ an industrial town in West Midlands, England; pop. (1981) 265,900.

Walton[1] /ˈwɔːlt(ə)n/, Izaak (1593–1683), English writer, chiefly known for *The Compleat Angler* (1653, largely rewritten in the second edition, 1655), a discourse on fishing which combines practical information with folklore, pastoral interludes of songs and ballads, and glimpses of an idyllic rural life. His biographies of Donne (1640), Wotton (1651), Hooker (1665), and George Herbert (1670) are gentle and admiring in tone.

Walton[2] /ˈwɔːlt(ə)n/, Sir William Turner (1902–83), English composer. He was a chorister and later an undergraduate at Christ Church, Oxford, but left without taking a degree and was unofficially adopted by the Sitwell family. *Façade* (1921–3), his music for a recitation of poems by Edith Sitwell, won him a reputation as a musical wit and iconoclast. There followed the bustling overture *Portsmouth Point* (1925), the deeply serious Viola Concerto (1928–9), then the flamboyantly-scored cantata *Belshazzar's Feast* (1930–1) to words arranged by Osbert Sitwell from the Bible, and the First Symphony (1932–5). Two Coronation Marches (1937 and 1953), skilful scores for the films of three Shakespeare plays, the opera *Troilus and Cressida* (1950–4), and further orchestral, chamber, and choral works have confirmed Walton's importance in the history of 20th-c. English music.

waltz /wɔːls, wɔːlts, wɒ–/ *n. & v.* —*n.* **1** a dance in triple time performed by couples who rotate and progress round the floor. **2** the usu. flowing and melodious music for this. In its early years in the late 18th c. the waltz was seen as conducive to lasciviousness and immorality because of the physical closeness of the couples. The most famous examples today are those by 19th-c. Viennese composers, particularly Joseph Lanner and Johann Strauss I and II, father and son. —*v.* **1** *intr.* dance a waltz. **2** *intr.* (often foll. by *in, out, round,* etc.) *colloq.* move lightly, casually, with deceptive ease, etc. (*waltzed in and took first prize*). **3** *tr.* move (a person) in or as if in a waltz, with ease (*was waltzed off to Paris*). □ **waltz Matilda** see MATILDA. □□ **waltzer** *n.* [G *Walzer* f. *walzen* revolve]

Waltzing Matilda an Australian song with words by A. B. Paterson (1895). A 'Matilda' is a bushman's bundle of belongings; to 'waltz Matilda' is to travel with this. The tune has been identified as that of a march arranged from an old Scottish ballad 'Thou Bonnie Wood of Craigielea' which in turn was an adaptation of 'The Bold Fusilier', a song that was popular with soldiers going to Marlborough's wars (early 18th c.).

Walvis Bay /ˈwɒlvɪs/ an enclave of South Africa on the Atlantic coast of Namibia; pop. 25,000. Administered by South West Africa during most of the period of South African control of that territory, it was eventually restored to the Cape Province of South Africa in 1977.

wampum /ˈwɒmpəm/ *n.* beads made from shells and strung together for use as money, decoration, or as aids to memory by N. American Indians. [Algonquin *wampumpeag* f. *wap* white + *umpe* string + *-ag* pl. suffix]

wan /wɒn/ *adj.* **1** (of a person's complexion or appearance) pale; exhausted; worn. **2** (of a star etc. or its light) partly obscured; faint. **3** *archaic* (of night, water, etc.) dark, black. □□ **wanly** *adv.* **wanness** *n.* [OE *wann* dark, black, of unkn. orig.]

wand /wɒnd/ *n.* **1 a** a supposedly magic stick used in casting spells by a fairy, magician, etc. **b** a stick used by a conjurer for effect. **2** a slender rod carried or used as a marker in the ground. **3** a staff symbolizing some officials' authority. **4** *colloq.* a conductor's baton. **5** a hand-held electronic device which can be passed over a bar-code to read the data this represents. [ME prob. f. Gmc: cf. WEND, WIND²]

wander /ˈwɒndə(r)/ *v. & n.* —*v.* **1** *intr.* (often foll. by *in, off,* etc.) go about from place to place aimlessly. **2** *intr.* **a** (of a person, river, road, etc.) wind about; diverge; meander. **b** (of esp. a person) get lost; leave home; stray from a path etc. **3** *intr.* talk or think incoherently; be inattentive or delirious. **4** *tr.* cover while wandering (*wanders the world*). —*n.* the act or an instance of wandering (*went for a wander round the garden*). □ **wandering Jew 1 a** a person of medieval legend condemned to wander the earth until the Day of Judgement, as a punishment for having insulted Christ on the way to the Crucifixion. **b** a person who never settles down. **2 a** a climbing plant, *Tradescantia albiflora*, with stemless variegated leaves. **b** a trailing plant, *Zebrina pendula*, with pink flowers. **wandering sailor** the moneywort. **wander-plug** a plug that can be fitted into any of various sockets in an electrical device. □□ **wanderer** *n.* **wandering** *n.* (esp. in *pl.*). [OE *wandrian* (as WEND)]

wanderlust /ˈwɒndəˌlʌst, ˈvændəˌlʊst/ *n.* an eagerness for travelling or wandering. [G]

wanderoo /ˌwɒndəˈruː/ *n.* a langur, *Semnopithecus vetulus*, of Sri Lanka. [Sinh. *wanderu* monkey]

wane /weɪn/ *v. & n.* —*v.intr.* **1** (of the moon) decrease in apparent size after the full moon (cf. WAX²). **2** decrease in power, vigour, importance, brilliance, size, etc.; decline. —*n.* **1** the process of waning. **2** a defect of a plank etc. that lacks square corners. □ **on the wane** waning; declining. □□ **waney** *adj.* (in sense 2 of *n.*). [OE *wanian* lessen f. Gmc]

Wanganui /ˌwɒŋɡəˈnuːɪ/ a seaport on the west coast of North Island, New Zealand; pop. (1988) 41,000.

wangle /ˈwæŋɡ(ə)l/ *v. & n. colloq.* —*v.tr.* **1** (often *refl.*) to obtain (a favour etc.) by scheming etc. (*wangled himself a free trip*). **2** alter or fake (a report etc.) to appear more favourable. —*n.* the act or an instance of wangling. □□ **wangler** *n.* [19th-c. printers' sl.: orig. unkn.]

wank /wæŋk/ *v. & n. coarse sl.* ¶ Usually considered a taboo word. —*v.intr. & tr.* masturbate. —*n.* an act of masturbating. [20th c.: orig. unkn.]

Wankel /ˈwæŋk(ə)l, ˈvæŋ-/, Felix (1902–88), German engineer, inventor of a rotary-piston internal-combustion engine which bears his name. Its main advantage over the conventional reciprocating-piston design is its freedom from vibration, which enables it to be used at a higher rotational speed and so to be more compact and lighter for a given capacity, but its many problems include sealing at the tips of the rotor lobes, higher fuel consumption, and increased pollutants in the exhaust.

wanker /ˈwæŋkə(r)/ *n. coarse sl.* ¶ Usually considered a taboo word. **1** a contemptible or ineffectual person. **2** a person who masturbates.

Wankie see HWANGE.

want /wɒnt/ *v. & n.* —*v.* **1** *tr.* **a** (often foll. by *to* + infin.) desire; wish for possession of; need (*wants a toy train*; *wants it done immediately*; *wanted to leave*; *wanted him to leave*). **b** need or desire (a person, esp. sexually). **c** esp. *Brit.* require to be attended to in esp. a specified way (*the garden wants weeding*). **d** (foll. by *to* + infin.) *colloq.* ought; should; need (*you want to pull yourself together*; *you don't want to overdo it*). **2** *intr.* (usu. foll. by *for*) lack; be deficient (*wants for nothing*). **3** *tr.* be without or fall short by (esp. a specified amount or thing) (*the drawer wants a handle*). **4** *intr.* (foll. by *in, out*) esp. US *colloq.* desire to be in, out, etc. (*wants in on the deal*). **5** *tr.* (as **wanted** *adj.*) (of a suspected criminal etc.) sought by the police. —*n.* **1** (often foll. by *of*) **a** a lack, absence, or deficiency (*could not go for want of time*; *shows great want of judgement*). **b** poverty; need (*living in great want*; *in want of necessities*). **2 a** a desire for a thing etc. (*meets a long-felt want*). **b** a thing so desired (*can supply your wants*). □ **do not want to** am unwilling to. **want ad** US a classified newspaper advertisement for something sought. □□ **wanter** *n.* [ME f. ON *vant* neut. of *vanr* lacking = OE *wana*, formed as WANE]

wanting /ˈwɒntɪŋ/ *adj.* **1** lacking (in quality or quantity); deficient, not equal to requirements (*wanting in judgement*; *the standard is sadly wanting*). **2** absent, not supplied or provided. □ **be found wanting** fail to meet requirements.

wanton /ˈwɒnt(ə)n/ *adj., n., & v.* —*adj.* **1** licentious; lewd; sexually promiscuous. **2** capricious; random; arbitrary; motiveless (*wanton destruction*; *wanton wind*). **3** luxuriant; unrestrained (*wanton profusion*). **4** *archaic* playful; sportive (*a wanton child*). —*n.* *literary* an immoral or licentious person, esp. a woman. —*v.intr. literary* **1** gambol; sport; move capriciously. **2** (foll. by *with*) behave licentiously. □□ **wantonly** *adv.* **wantonness** *n.* [ME *wantowen* (wan- UN-¹ + *towen* f. OE *togen* past part. of *tēon* discipline, rel. to TEAM)]

wapentake /ˈwɒpənˌteɪk, ˈwæp-/ *n. Brit. hist.* (in areas of England with a large Danish population) a division of a shire; a hundred. [OE *wǣpen(ge)tæc* f. ON *vápnatak* f. *vápn* weapon + *tak* taking f. *taka* TAKE: perh. with ref. to voting in assembly by show of weapons]

wapiti /ˈwɒpɪtɪ/ *n.* (*pl.* **wapitis**) a N. American deer, *Cervus canadensis*. [Cree *wapitik* white deer]

War. *abbr.* Warwickshire.

war /wɔː(r)/ *n. & v.* —*n.* **1 a** armed hostilities between esp. nations; conflict (*war broke out*; *war zone*). **b** a specific conflict or the period of time during which such conflict exists (*was before the war*). **c** the suspension of international law etc. during such a conflict. **2** (as **the War**) a war in progress or recently ended;

the most recent major war. **3 a** a hostility or contention between people, groups, etc. (*war of words*). **b** (often foll. by *on*) a sustained campaign against crime, disease, poverty, etc. —*v.intr.* (**warred, warring**) **1** (as **warring** *adj.*) **a** a rival; fighting (*warring factions*). **b** conflicting (*warring principles*). **2** make war. □ **art of war** strategy and tactics. **at war** (often foll. by *with*) engaged in a war. **go to war** declare or begin a war. **go to the wars** *archaic* serve as a soldier. **have been in the wars** *colloq.* appear injured, bruised, unkempt, etc. **war baby** a child, esp. illegitimate, born in wartime. **war bride** a woman who marries a serviceman met during a war. **war chest** funds for a war or any other campaign. **war-cloud** a threatening international situation. **war correspondent** a correspondent reporting from a scene of war. **war crime** a crime violating the international laws of war. **war criminal** a person committing or sentenced for such crimes. **war cry 1** a phrase or name shouted to rally one's troops. **2** a party slogan etc. **war damage** damage to property etc. caused by bombing, shelling, etc. **war dance** a dance performed by primitive peoples etc. before a battle or to celebrate victory. **war department** the State office in charge of the army etc. **war-game 1** a military exercise testing or improving tactical knowledge etc. **2** a battle etc. conducted with toy soldiers. **war-gaming** the playing of war-games. **war grave** the grave of a serviceman who died on active service, esp. one in a special cemetery etc. **war loan** stock issued by the British Government to raise funds in wartime. **war memorial** a monument etc. commemorating those killed in a war. **War of American Independence** see AMERICAN INDEPENDENCE. **war of attrition** a war in which each side seeks to wear out the other over a long period. **war of the elements** *poet.* storms or natural catastrophes. **War Office** *hist.* the British State department in charge of the army. **war of nerves** an attempt to wear down an opponent by psychological means. **war-plane** a military aircraft. **war poet** a poet writing on war themes, esp. of the two world wars. **Wars of the Roses** see separate entry. **war-weary** (esp. of a population) exhausted and dispirited by war. **war widow** a woman whose husband has been killed in war. **war-worn** = *war-weary*. **war zone** an area in which a war takes place. [ME *werre* f. AF, ONF var. of OF *guerre*: cf. WORSE]

waratah /ˈwɒrətə/ *n.* an Australian crimson-flowered shrub, *Telopea speciosissima.* [Aboriginal]

Warbeck /ˈwɔːbek/, Perkin (1474–99), the second of two pretenders to the English Crown in the reign of Henry VII, both claiming to be Richard Duke of York. Warbeck presented a far more formidable threat to Henry than had Lambert Simnel before him, chiefly because various foreign powers were willing to recognize him for their own diplomatic ends. After a series of abortive plots and uprisings he was finally captured. At first he was treated leniently, but he continued to intrigue in captivity and was executed.

warble[1] /ˈwɔːb(ə)l/ *v.* & *n.* —*v.* **1** *intr.* & *tr.* sing in a gentle trilling manner. **2** *tr.* **a** speak or utter in a warbling manner. **b** express in a song or verse (*warbled his love*). —*n.* a warbled song or utterance. [ME f. ONF *werble(r)* f. Frank. *hwirbilōn* whirl, trill]

warble[2] /ˈwɔːb(ə)l/ *n.* **1** a hard lump on a horse's back caused by the galling of a saddle. **2 a** the larva of a warble fly beneath the skin of cattle etc. **b** a tumour produced by this. □ **warble fly** any of various flies of the genus *Hypoderma*, infesting the skin of cattle and horses. [16th c.: orig. uncert.]

warbler /ˈwɔːblə(r)/ *n.* **1** a person, bird, etc. that warbles. **2** any small insect-eating bird of the family Sylviidae or, in N. America, Parulidae, including the blackcap, whitethroat, and chiff-chaff, not always remarkable for their song.

Warburg[1] /ˈwɔːbɜːg/, Aby Moritz (1866–1929), German historian of art, who founded at Hamburg the library that was transferred to England in 1933 and now bears his name as an Institute of the University of London.

Warburg[2] /ˈwɔːbɜːg/, Otto Heinrich (1883–1970), German biochemist, who was awarded a Nobel Prize in 1931 for his work on cellular respiration. He was offered a second Nobel Prize in 1944, but because of his Jewish birth the Hitler regime prevented its acceptance, though his international eminence saved him from imprisonment.

Ward /wɔːd/, Mrs Humphry (née Mary Augusta Arnold, 1851–1920), English novelist, granddaughter of Thomas Arnold and niece of Matthew Arnold from whom she inherited a sense of high moral purpose. A leading figure in the intellectual life of her day, an active philanthropist and supporter of higher education for women, she wrote several novels dealing with social and religious themes, including *Robert Elsmere* (1888), a vivid evocation, in part, of the varieties of religious faith and doubt which succeeded the ferment of the Oxford Movement.

ward /wɔːd/ *n.* & *v.* —*n.* **1** a separate room or division of a hospital, prison, etc. (*men's surgical ward*). **2 a** *Brit.* an administrative division of a constituency, usu. electing a councillor or councillors etc. **b** esp. *US* a similar administrative division. **3 a** a minor under the care of a guardian appointed by the parents or a court. **b** (in full **ward of court**) a minor or mentally deficient person placed under the protection of a court. **4** (in *pl.*) the corresponding notches and projections in a key and a lock. **5** *archaic* **a** the act of guarding or defending a place etc. **b** the bailey of a castle. **c** a guardian's control; confinement; custody. —*v.tr. archaic* guard; protect. □ **ward-heeler** *US* a party worker in elections etc. **ward off 1** parry (a blow). **2** avert (danger, poverty, etc.). [OE *weard, weardian* f. Gmc: cf. GUARD]

-ward /wəd/ *suffix* (also **-wards**) added to nouns of place or destination and to adverbs of direction and forming: **1** adverbs (usu. **-wards**) meaning 'towards the place etc.' (*moving backwards; set off homewards*). **2** adjectives (usu. **-ward**) meaning 'turned or tending towards' (*a downward look; an onward rush*). **3** (less commonly) nouns meaning 'the region towards or about' (*look to the eastward*). [from or after OE *-weard* f. a Gmc root meaning 'turn']

warden /ˈwɔːd(ə)n/ *n.* **1** (usu. in *comb.*) a supervising official (*churchwarden; traffic warden*). **2 a** *Brit.* a president or governor of a college, school, hospital, youth hostel, etc. **b** esp. *US* a prison governor. □□ **wardenship** *n.* [ME f. AF & ONF *wardein* var. of OF *g(u)arden* GUARDIAN]

warder /ˈwɔːdə(r)/ *n.* **1** *Brit.* (*fem.* **wardress**) a prison officer. **2** a guard. [ME f. AF *wardere, -our* f. ONF *warder*, OF *garder* to GUARD]

wardrobe /ˈwɔːdrəʊb/ *n.* **1** a large movable or built-in cupboard with rails, shelves, hooks, etc., for storing clothes. **2** a person's entire stock of clothes. **3** the costume department or costumes of a theatre, a film company, etc. **4** a department of a royal household in charge of clothing. □ **wardrobe mistress** (or **master**) a person in charge of a theatrical or film wardrobe. **wardrobe trunk** a trunk fitted with rails, shelves, etc. for use as a travelling wardrobe. [ME f. ONF *warderobe*, OF *garderobe* (as GUARD, ROBE)]

wardroom /ˈwɔːdruːm, -rʊm/ *n.* a room in a warship for the use of commissioned officers.

-wards var. of -WARD.

wardship /ˈwɔːdʃɪp/ *n.* **1** a guardian's care or tutelage (*under his wardship*). **2** the condition of being a ward.

ware[1] /weə(r)/ *n.* **1** (esp. in *comb.*) things of the same kind, esp. ceramics, made usu. for sale (*chinaware; hardware*). **2** (usu. in *pl.*) **a** articles for sale (*displayed his wares*). **b** a person's skills, talents, etc. **3** ceramics etc. of a specified material, factory, or kind (*Wedgwood ware; Delft ware*). [OE *waru* f. Gmc, perh. orig. = 'object of care', rel. to WARE[3]]

ware[2] /weə(r)/ *v.tr.* (also **'ware**) (esp. in hunting) look out for; avoid (usu. in *imper.*: *ware hounds!*). [OE *warian* f. Gmc (as WARE[3]), & f. ONF *warer*]

ware[3] /weə(r)/ *predic.adj. poet.* aware. [OE *wær* f. Gmc: cf. WARD]

warehouse /ˈweəhaʊs/ *n.* & *v.* —*n.* **1** a building in which esp. retail goods are stored; a repository. **2** esp. *Brit.* a wholesale or large retail store. —*v.tr.* /also -haʊz/ store (esp. furniture or bonded goods) temporarily in a repository. □ **warehouse party 1** an organized public party with dancing, held in a warehouse or similar building. **2** an acid house party (see ACID HOUSE). □□ **warehouseman** *n.* (*pl.* **-men**).

warfare /ˈwɔːfeə(r)/ *n.* a state of war; campaigning, engaging in war (*chemical warfare*).

warfarin /ˈwɔːfərɪn/ *n.* a water-soluble anticoagulant used esp.

as a rat poison. [Wisconsin Alumni Research Foundation + -*arin*, after COUMARIN]

warhead /ˈwɔːhed/ *n.* the explosive head of a missile, torpedo, or similar weapon.

Warhol /ˈwɔːhɒl/ Andy (1930–87), American painter, graphic artist, and film maker whose work played a definitive role in New York pop art of the 1960s. Warhol's background in commercial art and advertising illustration was central to the pop movement's concern with the imagery of the mass media; his famous statement 'I like boring things' was expressed in the standardized, consciously banal, nature of his work. In the early 1960s he achieved notoriety for a series of silk-screen prints and acrylic paintings whose subjects included familiar objects (such as Campbell's soup tins), car accidents, and Marilyn Monroe, treated with industrial precision and complete artistic detachment. These interests were readily extended to film, and Warhol played an important part in the new American underground cinema. His first films were silent and (deliberately) technically unsophisticated, treating repetitive and often voyeuristic themes. Later films such as *Flesh* (1968) and *Trash* (1970) were technically smoother, more conventional in structure, and intended for wide commercial release.

warhorse /ˈwɔːhɔːs/ *n.* **1** *hist.* a knight's or trooper's powerful horse. **2** *colloq.* a veteran soldier, politician, etc.; a reliable hack.

warlike /ˈwɔːlaɪk/ *adj.* **1** threatening war; hostile. **2** martial; soldierly. **3** of or for war; military (*warlike preparations*).

warlock /ˈwɔːlɒk/ *n. archaic* a sorcerer or wizard. [OE *wǣr-loga* traitor f. *wǣr* covenant: *loga* rel. to LIE²]

warlord /ˈwɔːlɔːd/ *n.* a military commander or commander-in-chief.

warm /wɔːm/ *adj., v.,* & *n.* —*adj.* **1** of or at a fairly or comfortably high temperature. **2** (of clothes etc.) affording warmth (*needs warm gloves*). **3 a** (of a person, action, feelings, etc.) sympathetic; cordial; friendly; loving (*a warm welcome; has a warm heart*). **b** enthusiastic; hearty (*was warm in her praise*). **4** animated, heated, excited; indignant (*the dispute grew warm*). **5** *colloq. iron.* dangerous, difficult, or hostile (*met a warm reception*). **6** *colloq.* **a** (of a participant in esp. a children's game of seeking) close to the object etc. sought. **b** near to guessing or finding out a secret. **7** (of a colour, light, etc.) reddish, pink, or yellowish, etc., suggestive of warmth. **8** *Hunting* (of a scent) fresh and strong. **9 a** (of a person's temperament) amorous; sexually demanding. **b** erotic; arousing. —*v.* **1** *tr.* **a** make warm (*fire warms the room*). **b** excite; make cheerful (*warms the heart*). **2** *intr.* **a** (often foll. by *up*) warm oneself at a fire etc. (*warmed himself up*). **b** (often foll. by *to*) become animated, enthusiastic, or sympathetic (*warmed to his subject*). —*n.* **1** the act of warming; the state of being warmed (*gave it a warm; had a nice warm by the fire*). **2** the warmth of the atmosphere etc. **3** *Brit. archaic* a warm garment, esp. an army greatcoat. □ **warmed-up** (*US* **-over**) **1** (of food etc.) reheated or stale. **2** stale; second-hand. **warm front** an advancing mass of warm air. **warming-pan** *hist.* a usu. brass container for live coals with a flat body and a long handle, used for warming a bed. **warm up 1** (of an athlete, performer, etc.) prepare for a contest, performance, etc. by practising. **2** (of a room etc.) become warmer. **3** (of a person) become enthusiastic etc. **4** (of a radio, engine, etc.) reach a temperature for efficient working. **5** reheat (food). **warm-up** *n.* a period of preparatory exercise for a contest or performance. **warm work 1** work etc. that makes one warm through exertion. **2** dangerous conflict etc. □□ **warmer** *n.* (also in *comb.*). **warmish** *adj.* **warmly** *adv.* **warmness** *n.* **warmth** *n.* [OE *wearm* f. Gmc]

warm-blooded /wɔːmˈblʌdɪd/ *adj.* **1** (of an organism) having warm blood; mammalian (see HOMOEOTHERM). **2** ardent, passionate. □□ **warm-bloodedness** *n.*

warm-hearted /wɔːmˈhɑːtɪd/ *adj.* having a warm heart; kind, friendly. □□ **warm-heartedly** *adv.* **warm-heartedness** *n.*

warmonger /ˈwɔːˌmʌŋɡə(r)/ *n.* a person who seeks to bring about or promote war. □□ **warmongering** *n.* & *adj.*

warn /wɔːn/ *v.tr.* **1** (also *absol.*) **a** (often foll. by *of*, or *that* + clause, or *to* + infin.) inform of danger, unknown circumstances, etc. (*warned them of the danger; warned her that she was being watched;*

warned him to expect a visit). **b** (often foll. by *against*) inform (a person etc.) about a specific danger, hostile person, etc. (*warned her against trusting him*). **2** (usu. with *neg.*) admonish; tell forcefully (*has been warned not to go*). **3** give (a person) cautionary notice regarding conduct etc. (*shall not warn you again*). □ **warn off 1** tell (a person) to keep away (from). **2** prohibit from attending races, esp. at a specified course. □□ **warner** *n.* [OE *war(e)nian, wearnian* ult. f. Gmc: cf. WARE³]

warning /ˈwɔːnɪŋ/ *n.* **1** in senses of WARN *v.* **2** anything that serves to warn; a hint or indication of difficulty, danger, etc. **3** *archaic* = NOTICE *n.* 3b. □ **warning coloration** *Biol.* conspicuous colouring that warns a predator etc. against attacking. □□ **warningly** *adv.* [OE *war(e)nung* etc. (as WARN, -ING¹)]

warp /wɔːp/ *v.* & *n.* —*v.* **1** *tr.* & *intr.* **a** make or become bent or twisted out of shape, esp. by the action of heat, damp, etc. **b** make or become perverted, bitter, or strange (*a warped sense of humour*). **2 a** *tr.* haul (a ship) by a rope attached to a fixed point. **b** *intr.* progress in this way. **3** *tr.* fertilize by flooding with warp. **4** *tr.* (foll. by *up*) choke (a channel) with an alluvial deposit etc. **5** *tr.* arrange (threads) as a warp. —*n.* **1 a** a state of being warped, esp. of shrunken or expanded timber. **b** perversion, bitterness, etc. of the mind or character. **2** the threads stretched lengthwise in a loom to be crossed by the weft. **3** a rope used in towing or warping, or attached to a trawl-net. **4** sediment etc. left esp. on poor land by standing water. □□ **warpage** *n.* (esp. in sense 1a of *v.*). **warper** *n.* (in sense 5 of *v.*). [OE *weorpan* throw, *wearp* f. Gmc]

warpaint /ˈwɔːpeɪnt/ *n.* **1** paint used to adorn the body before battle, esp. by N. American Indians. **2** *colloq.* elaborate make-up.

warpath /ˈwɔːpɑːθ/ *n.* **1** a warlike expedition of N. American Indians. **2** *colloq.* any hostile course or attitude (*is on the warpath again*).

warragal var. of WARRIGAL.

warrant /ˈwɒrənt/ *n.* & *v.* —*n.* **1 a** anything that authorizes a person or an action (*have no warrant for this*). **b** a person so authorizing (*I will be your warrant*). **2 a** a written authorization, money voucher, travel document, etc. (*a dividend warrant*). **b** a written authorization allowing police to search premises, arrest a suspect, etc. **3** a document authorizing counsel to represent the principal in a lawsuit (*warrant of attorney*). **4** a certificate of service rank held by a warrant-officer. —*v.tr.* **1** serve as a warrant for; justify (*nothing can warrant his behaviour*). **2** guarantee or attest to esp. the genuineness of an article, the worth of a person, etc. □ **I** (or **I'll**) **warrant** I am certain; no doubt (*he'll be sorry, I'll warrant*). **warrant-officer** an officer ranking between commissioned officers and NCOs. □□ **warranter** *n.* **warrantor** *n.* [ME f. ONF *warant*, var. of OF *guarant*, -*and* f. Frank. *werend* (unrecorded) f. *giweren* be surety for]

warrantable /ˈwɒrəntəb(ə)l/ *adj.* **1** able to be warranted. **2** (of a stag) old enough to be hunted (5 or 6 years). □□ **warrantableness** *n.* **warrantably** *adv.*

warrantee /ˌwɒrənˈtiː/ *n.* a person to whom a warranty is given.

warranty /ˈwɒrəntɪ/ *n.* (*pl.* **-ies**) **1** an undertaking as to the ownership or quality of a thing sold, hired, etc., often accepting responsibility for defects or liability for repairs needed over a specified period. **2** (usu. foll. by *for* + verbal noun) an authority or justification. **3** an undertaking by an insured person of the truth of a statement or fulfilment of a condition. [ME f. AF *warantie*, var. of *garantie* (as WARRANT)]

warren /ˈwɒrən/ *n.* **1 a** a network of interconnecting rabbit burrows. **b** a piece of ground occupied by this. **2** a densely populated or labyrinthine building or district. **3** *hist.* a piece of ground on which game is preserved. [ME f. AF & ONF *warenne*, OF *garenne* game-park f. Gmc]

warrigal /ˈwɒrɪɡ(ə)l/ *n.* & *adj.* (also **warragal**) *Austral.* —*n.* **1 a** dingo dog. **2** an untamed horse. **3** a wild Aboriginal. —*adj.* wild, untamed. [Aboriginal]

warring /ˈwɔːrɪŋ/ *adj.* rival, antagonistic.

warrior /ˈwɒrɪə(r)/ *n.* **1** a person experienced or distinguished in fighting. **2** a fighting man, esp. of primitive peoples. **3** (*attrib.*) martial (*a warrior nation*). [ME f. ONF *werreior* etc., OF *guerreior* etc. f. *werreier, guerreier* make WAR]

Warsaw /ˈwɔːsɔː/ (Polish **Warszawa** /vɑːˈʃævə/) the capital of Poland, on the River Vistula; pop. (1985) 1,649,000. The city was systematically razed to the ground by German occupying forces during the Second World War. □ **Warsaw Pact** a treaty of mutual defence and military aid signed at Warsaw on 14 May 1955 by Communist States of Europe, under Soviet leadership, in response to the creation of NATO. In June 1990, following the changes in eastern Europe during the previous year, and the collapse of the Communist system, the members of the Pact decided to change its nature from a military alliance to a mainly political body that would be a force for peaceful change; it was finally dissolved in Feb. 1991.

warship /ˈwɔːʃɪp/ n. an armoured ship used in war.

Wars of the Roses a general name (popularized by Sir Walter Scott in the 19th c.) for the civil wars of the dynastic struggle between the followers of the house of York (with the white rose as its emblem) and the house of Lancaster (with the red rose) in 15th-c. England during the reigns of Henry VI, Edward IV, and Richard III. The struggle was ended (except for the rebellion of Lambert Simnel) by the accession in 1485 of the Lancastrian Henry Tudor (Henry VII) who united the two houses by marrying Elizabeth, daughter of Edward IV. (For the reputed adoption of the emblems of the roses see Shakespeare *I Henry VI* II iv. 27ff.)

wart /wɔːt/ n. 1 a small hardish roundish growth on the skin caused by a virus-induced abnormal growth of papillae and thickening of the epidermis. 2 a protuberance on the skin of an animal, surface of a plant, etc. 3 *colloq.* an objectionable person. □ **wart-hog** an African wild pig of the genus *Phacochoerus*, with a large head and warty lumps on its face, and large curved tusks. **warts and all** *colloq.* with no attempt to conceal blemishes or inadequacies. □□ **warty** adj. [OE *wearte* f. Gmc]

wartime /ˈwɔːtaɪm/ n. the period during which a war is waged.

Warwick /ˈwɒrɪk/, Richard Neville, Earl of (1428–71), English statesman, known as 'the Kingmaker'. During the Wars of the Roses he fought first on the Yorkist side, and was instrumental in placing Edward IV on the throne in 1461, then (having lost influence at court) he changed sides and briefly restored Henry VI in 1470. Warwick was killed in the following year when the Lancastrians were defeated at Barnet.

Warwickshire /ˈwɒrɪkˌʃɪə(r)/ a midland county of England; pop. (1981) 477,300; county town, Warwick.

wary /ˈweərɪ/ adj. (**warier**, **wariest**) 1 on one's guard; given to caution; circumspect. 2 (foll. by *of*) cautious, suspicious (*am wary of using lifts*). 3 showing or done with caution or suspicion (*a wary expression*). □□ **warily** adv. **wariness** n. [WARE² + -Y¹]

was 1st & 3rd sing. past of BE.

Wash /wɒʃ/, **the** an inlet of the North Sea on the east coast of England between Norfolk and Lincolnshire.

Wash. abbr. Washington.

wash /wɒʃ/ v. & n. —v. 1 tr. cleanse (oneself or a part of oneself, clothes, etc.) with liquid, esp. water. 2 tr. (foll. by *out, off, away*, etc.) remove a stain or dirt in this way. 3 intr. wash oneself or esp. one's hands and face. 4 intr. wash clothes etc. 5 intr. (of fabric or dye) bear washing without damage. 6 intr. (foll. by *off, out*) (of a stain etc.) be removed by washing. 7 tr. *poet.* moisten, water (*tear-washed eyes; a rose washed with dew*). 8 tr. (of a river, sea, etc.) touch (a country, coast, etc.) with its waters. 9 tr. (of moving liquid) carry along in a specified direction (*a wave washed him overboard; was washed up on the shore*). 10 tr. **a** scoop out (*the water had washed a channel*). **b** erode, denude (*sea-washed cliffs*). 11 intr. (foll. by *over, along*, etc.) sweep, move, or splash. 12 tr. sift (ore) by the action of water. 13 tr. **a** brush a thin coat of watery paint or ink over (paper in water-colour painting etc., or a wall). **b** (foll. by *with*) coat (inferior metal) with gold etc. —n. 1 **a** the act or an instance of washing; the process of being washed (*give them a good wash; only needed one wash*). **b** (prec. by *the*) treatment at a laundry etc. (*sent them to the wash*). 2 **a** quantity of clothes for washing or just washed. 3 the visible or audible motion of agitated water or air, esp. due to the passage of a ship etc. or aircraft. 4 **a** soil swept off by water; alluvium. **b** a sandbank exposed only at low tide. 5 kitchen slops and scraps given to pigs. 6 **a** thin, weak, or inferior liquid food. **b** liquid food for

animals. 7 a liquid to spread over a surface to cleanse, heal, or colour. 8 a thin coating of water-colour, wall-colouring, or metal. 9 malt etc. fermenting before distillation. 10 a lotion or cosmetic. □ **come out in the wash** *colloq.* be clarified, or (of contingent difficulties) be resolved or removed, in the course of time. **wash-and-wear** adj. (of a fabric or garment) easily and quickly laundered. **wash-basin** a basin for washing one's hands, face, etc. **wash one's dirty linen in public** see LINEN. **wash down** 1 wash completely (esp. a large surface or object). 2 (usu. foll. by *with*) accompany or follow (food) with a drink. **washed out** 1 faded by washing. 2 pale. 3 *colloq.* limp, enfeebled. **washed up** esp. *US sl.* defeated, having failed. **wash one's hands** *euphem.* go to the lavatory. **wash one's hands of** renounce responsibility for. **wash-hand stand** = WASHSTAND. **wash-house** a building where clothes are washed. **wash-leather** chamois or similar leather for washing windows etc. **wash out** 1 clean the inside of (a thing) by washing. 2 clean (a garment etc.) by brief washing. 3 **a** rain off (an event etc.). **b** *colloq.* cancel. 4 (of a flood, downpour, etc.) make a breach in (a road etc.). **wash-out** n. 1 *colloq.* a fiasco; a complete failure. 2 a breach in a road, railway track, etc., caused by flooding (see also WASHOUT). **wash up** 1 tr. (also *absol.*) esp. *Brit.* wash (crockery and cutlery) after use. 2 *US* wash one's face and hands. **won't wash** esp. *Brit. colloq.* (of an argument etc.) will not be believed or accepted. [OE *wæscan* etc. f. Gmc, rel. to WATER]

washable /ˈwɒʃəb(ə)l/ adj. that can be washed, esp. without damage. □□ **washability** /-ˈbɪlɪtɪ/ n.

washboard /ˈwɒʃbɔːd/ n. 1 a board of ribbed wood or a sheet of corrugated zinc on which clothes are scrubbed in washing. 2 this used as a percussion instrument, played with the fingers.

washday /ˈwɒʃdeɪ/ n. a day on which clothes etc. are washed.

washer /ˈwɒʃə(r)/ n. 1 **a** a person or thing that washes. **b** a washing-machine. 2 a flat ring of rubber, metal, leather, etc., inserted at a joint to tighten it and prevent leakage. 3 a similar ring placed under the head of a screw, bolt, etc., or under a nut, to disperse its pressure. 4 *Austral.* a cloth for washing the face. □ **washer-up** (pl. **washers-up**) a person who washes up dishes etc.

washerwoman /ˈwɒʃəˌwʊmən/ n. (pl. **-women**) a woman whose occupation is washing clothes; a laundress.

washeteria /ˌwɒʃəˈtɪərɪə/ n. = LAUNDERETTE.

washing /ˈwɒʃɪŋ/ n. a quantity of clothes for washing or just washed. □ **washing-machine** a machine for washing clothes and linen etc. **washing-powder** powder of soap or detergent for washing clothes. **washing-soda** sodium carbonate, used dissolved in water for washing and cleaning. **washing-up** *Brit.* 1 the process of washing dishes etc. after use. 2 used dishes etc. for washing.

Washington¹ /ˈwɒʃɪŋt(ə)n/ the capital and administrative centre of the US, coterminous with the District of Columbia, founded in the presidency of George Washington and named after him.

Washington² /ˈwɒʃɪŋt(ə)n/ the most northerly of the Pacific States of the US; pop. (est. 1985) 4,132,350; capital, Olympia. Occupied jointly by Britain and the US in the first half of the 19th c, it became the 42nd State of the US in 1889.

Washington³ /ˈwɒʃɪŋt(ə)n/, George (1732–99), 1st President of the US 1789–97. A soldier with a distinguished record in the French and Indian War, Washington was chosen as commander of the Continental Army in 1775 and served in that capacity throughout the War of Independence, contributing greatly to the eventual American victory through his military ability and strength of character. After a brief retirement he returned to public life and was unanimously elected first President after the adoption of the Constitution. He served two terms, following a policy of neutrality in international affairs, before declining a third term and retiring once again to private life. Rightly known as the father of his country, Washington probably did more than any other man to secure the independence of the United States.

washland /ˈwɒʃlænd/ n. land periodically flooded by a stream.

washout /ˈwɒʃaʊt/ n. Geol. a narrow river-channel that cuts into pre-existing sediments (see also wash-out).

washroom /ˈwɒʃruːm, -rʊm/ n. US a room with washing and toilet facilities.

washstand /ˈwɒʃstænd/ n. a piece of furniture to hold a basin, jug, soap, etc.

washtub /ˈwɒʃtʌb/ n. a tub or vessel for washing clothes etc.

washy /ˈwɒʃɪ/ adj. (**washier**, **washiest**) **1** (of liquid food) too watery or weak; insipid. **2** (of colour) faded-looking, thin, faint. **3** (of a style, sentiment, etc.) lacking vigour or intensity. □□ **washily** adv. **washiness** n.

wasn't /ˈwɒz(ə)nt/ contr. was not.

Wasp /wɒsp/ n. (also **WASP**) US usu. derog. a middle-class American White Protestant descended from early European settlers. □□ **Waspy** adj. (also **WASPy**). [White Anglo-Saxon Protestant]

wasp /wɒsp/ n. **1** a stinging often flesh-eating insect of the order Hymenoptera, esp. the common social wasp Vespa vulgaris, with black and yellow stripes and a very thin waist. **2** (in comb.) any of various insects resembling a wasp in some way (wasp-beetle). □ **wasp-waist** a very slender waist. **wasp-waisted** having a very slender waist. □□ **wasplike** adj. [OE wæfs, wæps, wæsp, f. WG: perh. rel. to WEAVE¹ (from the weblike form of its nest)]

waspish /ˈwɒspɪʃ/ adj. irritable, petulant; sharp in retort. □□ **waspishly** adv. **waspishness** n.

wassail /ˈwɒseɪl, ˈwɒs(ə)l/ n. & v. archaic — n. **1** a festive occasion; a drinking-bout. **2** a kind of liquor drunk on such an occasion. — v.intr. make merry; celebrate with drinking etc. □ **wassail-bowl** (or **-cup**) a bowl or cup from which healths were drunk, esp. on Christmas Eve and Twelfth Night. □□ **wassailer** n. [ME wæs hæil etc. f. ON ves heill, corresp. to OE wes hāl 'be in health', a form of salutation: cf. HALE¹]

Wassermann /ˈvɑːsəˌmɑːn/, August Paul von (1866–1925), German bacteriologist, remembered chiefly for his introduction of a diagnostic test for syphilis owing to his discovery of a distinctive reaction in the blood serum when that disease is present.

wast /wɒst, wəst/ archaic or dial. 2nd sing. past of BE.

wastage /ˈweɪstɪdʒ/ n. **1** an amount wasted. **2** loss by use, wear, or leakage. **3** Commerce loss of employees other than by redundancy.

waste /weɪst/ v., adj., & n. — v. **1** tr. use to no purpose or for inadequate result or extravagantly (waste time). **2** tr. fail to use (esp. an opportunity). **3** tr. (often foll. by on) give (advice etc.), utter (words etc.), without effect. **4** tr. & intr. wear gradually away; make or become weak; wither. **5** tr. ravage, devastate. **6** tr. treat as wasted or valueless. **7** intr. be expended without useful effect. — adj. **1** superfluous; no longer serving a purpose. **2** (of a district etc.) not inhabited or cultivated; desolate (waste ground). **3** presenting no features of interest. — n. **1** the act or an instance of wasting; extravagant or ineffectual use of an asset, of time, etc. **2** waste material or food; refuse; useless remains or by-products. **3** a waste region; a desert etc. **4** the state of being used up; diminution by wear and tear. **5** Law damage to an estate caused by an act or by neglect, esp. by a life-tenant. **6** = waste pipe. □ (**at** or **run**) **to waste** be wasted. **lay waste** ravage, devastate. **waste-basket** esp. US = waste-paper basket. **waste one's breath** see BREATH. **waste not, want not** extravagance leads to poverty. **waste paper** spoiled or valueless paper. **waste-paper basket** esp. Brit. a receptacle for waste paper. **waste pipe** a pipe to carry off waste material, e.g. from a sink. **waste products** useless by-products of manufacture or of an organism or organisms. **waste words** see WORD. □□ **wastable** adj. **wasteless** adj. [ME f. ONF wast(e), var. of OF g(u)ast(e), f. L vastus]

wasteful /ˈweɪstfʊl/ adj. **1** extravagant. **2** causing or showing waste. □□ **wastefully** adv. **wastefulness** n.

wasteland /ˈweɪstlænd/ n. **1** an unproductive or useless area of land. **2** a place or time considered spiritually or intellectually barren.

waster /ˈweɪstə(r)/ n. **1** a wasteful person. **2** colloq. a wastrel.

wastrel /ˈweɪstr(ə)l/ n. **1** a wasteful or good-for-nothing person. **2** a waif; a neglected child.

watch /wɒtʃ/ v. & n. — v. **1** tr. keep the eyes fixed on; look at attentively. **2** tr. **a** keep under observation; follow observantly. **b** monitor or consider carefully; pay attention to (have to watch my weight; watched their progress with interest). **3** intr. (often foll. by for) be in an alert state; be vigilant; take heed (watch for the holes in the road; watch for an opportunity). **4** intr. (foll. by over) look after; take care of. **5** intr. archaic remain awake for devotions etc. — n. **1** a small portable timepiece for carrying on one's person. **2** a state of alert or constant observation or attention. **3** Naut. **a** a four-hour spell of duty. **b** (in full **starboard** or **port watch**) each of the halves, divided according to the position of the bunks, into which a ship's crew is divided to take alternate watches. **4** hist. a watchman or group of watchmen, esp. patrolling the streets at night. **5** a former division of the night. **6** a period of wakefulness at night. **7** hist. irregular Highland troops in the 18th c. □ **on the watch** waiting for an expected or feared occurrence. **set the watch** Naut. station sentinels etc. **watch-case** the outer metal case enclosing the works of a watch. **watch-chain** a metal chain for securing a pocket-watch. **Watch Committee** hist. (in the UK) the committee of a county borough council dealing with policing etc. **watch-glass 1** a glass disc covering the dial of a watch. **2** a similar disc used in a laboratory etc. to hold material for use in experiments. **watching brief** see BRIEF. **watch it** (or **oneself**) colloq. be careful. **watch-night 1** the last night of the year. **2** a religious service held on this night. **watch out 1** (often foll. by for) be on one's guard. **2** as a warning of immediate danger. **watch-spring** the mainspring of a watch. **watch one's step** proceed cautiously. **watch-strap** esp. Brit. a strap for fastening a watch on the wrist. **watch-tower** a tower from which observation can be kept. □□ **watchable** adj. **watcher** n. (also in comb.). [OE wæcce (n.), rel. to WAKE¹]

watchband /ˈwɒtʃbænd/ n. US = watch-strap.

watchdog /ˈwɒtʃdɒg/ n. & v. — n. **1** a dog kept to guard property etc. **2** a person or body monitoring others' rights, behaviour, etc. — v.tr. (**-dogged**, **-dogging**) maintain surveillance over.

watchful /ˈwɒtʃfʊl/ adj. **1** accustomed to watching. **2** on the watch. **3** showing vigilance. **4** archaic wakeful. □□ **watchfully** adv. **watchfulness** n.

watchmaker /ˈwɒtʃˌmeɪkə(r)/ n. a person who makes and repairs watches and clocks. □□ **watchmaking** n.

watchman /ˈwɒtʃmən/ n. (pl. **-men**) **1** a man employed to look after an empty building etc. at night. **2** archaic or hist. a member of a night-watch.

watchword /ˈwɒtʃwɜːd/ n. **1** a phrase summarizing a guiding principle; a slogan. **2** hist. a military password.

water /ˈwɔːtə(r)/ n. & v. — n. **1** a colourless transparent odourless tasteless liquid compound of oxygen and hydrogen, convertible into steam by heat and ice by cold. ¶ Chem. formula: H_2O. **2** a liquid consisting chiefly of this and found in seas, lakes, and rivers, in rain, and in secretions of organisms. **3** an expanse of water; a sea, lake, river, etc. **4** (in pl.) part of a sea or river (in Icelandic waters). **5** (often as **the waters**) mineral water at a spa etc. **6** the state of a tide (high water). **7** a solution of a specified substance in water (lavender-water). **8** the quality of the transparency and brilliance of a gem, esp. a diamond. **9** Finance an amount of nominal capital added by watering (see sense 10 of v.). **10** (attrib.) **a** found in or near water. **b** of, for, or worked by water. **c** involving, using, or yielding water. — v. **1** tr. sprinkle or soak with water. **2** tr. supply (a plant) with water. **3** tr. give water to (an animal) to drink. **4** intr. (of the mouth or eyes) secrete water as saliva or tears. **5** tr. (as **watered** adj.) (of silk etc.) having irregular wavy glossy markings. **6** tr. adulterate (milk, beer, etc.) with water. **7** tr. (of a river etc.) supply (a place) with water. **8** intr. (of an animal) go to a pool etc. to drink. **9** intr. (of a ship, engine, etc., or the person in charge of it) take in a supply of water. **10** tr. Finance increase (a company's debt, or nominal capital) by the issue of new shares without a corresponding addition to assets. □ **by water** using a ship etc. for travel or transport. **cast one's bread upon the waters** see BREAD. **like water** lavishly, profusely. **like water off a duck's back** see DUCK¹. **make one's mouth water** cause one's saliva to flow, stimulate one's appetite or anticipation. **of the first**

water 1 (of a diamond) of the greatest brilliance and transparency. **2** of the finest quality or extreme degree. **on the water** on a ship etc. **on the water-wagon** see WAGON. **water-bag** a bag of leather, canvas, etc., for holding water. **water bailiff 1** an official enforcing fishing laws. **2** *hist.* a custom-house officer at a port. **water bear** = TARDIGRADE *n.* **water-bed** a mattress of rubber or plastic etc. filled with water. **water-biscuit** a thin crisp unsweetened biscuit made from flour and water. **water blister** a blister containing a colourless fluid, not blood or pus. **water-boatman** any aquatic bug of the family Notonectidae or Corixidae, swimming with oarlike hind legs. **water-borne 1** (of goods etc.) conveyed by or travelling on water. **2** (of a disease) communicated or propagated by contaminated water. **water-buck** any of various African antelopes of the genus *Kobus*, frequenting river-banks. **water-buffalo** the common domestic Indian buffalo, *Bubalus arnee.* **water bus** a boat carrying passengers on a regular run on a river, lake, etc. **water-butt** a barrel used to catch rainwater. **water-cannon** a device giving a powerful jet of water to disperse a crowd etc. **the Water-carrier** (or **-bearer**) the zodiacal sign or constellation Aquarius. **water chestnut 1** an aquatic plant, *Trapa natans*, bearing an edible seed. **2 a** (in full **Chinese water chestnut**) a sedge, *Eleocharis tuberosa*, with rushlike leaves arising from a corm. **b** this corm used as food. **water-clock** see separate entry. **water-closet 1** see separate entry. **2** a room containing this. **water-colour** (*US* **-color**) **1** artists' paint made of pigment to be diluted with water and not oil. **2** a picture painted with this. **3** the art of painting with water-colours. **water-colourist** (*US* **-colorist**) a painter in water-colours. **water-cooled** cooled by the circulation of water. **water-cooler** a tank of cooled drinking-water. **water cure** = HYDROPATHY. **water-diviner** *Brit.* a person who dowses (see DOWSE¹) for water. **water down 1** dilute with water. **2** make less vivid, forceful, or horrifying. **water gauge 1** a glass tube etc. indicating the height of water in a reservoir, boiler, etc. **2** pressure expressed in terms of a head of water. **water-glass 1** a solution of sodium or potassium silicate used for preserving eggs, as a vehicle for fresco-painting, and for hardening artificial stone. **2** a tube with a glass bottom enabling objects under water to be observed. **water-hammer** a knocking noise in a water-pipe when a tap is suddenly turned off. **water-heater** a device for heating (esp. domestic) water. **water hemlock** a poisonous plant, *Cicuta maculata*, found in marshes etc.: also called COWBANE. **water-hole** a shallow depression in which water collects (esp. in the bed of a river otherwise dry). **water hyacinth** a tropical river-weed, *Eichhornia crassipes.* **water-ice** a confection of flavoured and frozen water and sugar etc.; a sorbet. **water jump** a place where a horse in a steeplechase etc. must jump over water. **water-level 1 a** the surface of the water in a reservoir etc. **b** the height of this. **2 a** level below which the ground is saturated with water. **3** a level using water to determine the horizontal. **water lily** any aquatic plant of the family Nymphaeaceae, with broad flat floating leaves and large usu. cup-shaped floating flowers. **water-line 1** the line along which the surface of water touches a ship's side (marked on a ship for use in loading). **2** a linear watermark. **water main** the main pipe in a water-supply system. **water-meadow** a meadow periodically flooded by a stream. **water melon** a large smooth green melon, *Citrullus lanatus*, with red pulp and watery juice. **water meter** a device for measuring and recording the amount of water supplied to a house etc. **water-mill** a mill worked by a water-wheel. **water-nymph** a nymph regarded as inhabiting or presiding over water. **water of crystallization** water forming an essential part of the structure of some crystals. **water of life** *rhet.* spiritual enlightenment. **water ouzel** = DIPPER 1. **water-pepper** an aquatic herb, *Polygonum hydropiper*: also called SMARTWEED. **water-pipe 1** a pipe for conveying water. **2** a hookah. **water-pistol** a toy pistol shooting a jet of water. **water plantain** any ditch-plant of the genus *Alisma*, with plantain-like leaves. **water polo** a game played by swimmers, with a ball like a football. The game originated in Britain as far back as 1870 or earlier, though the early rules were primitive and varied from area to area. It was played at the Olympic Games in 1900. **water-power 1** mechanical force derived from the weight or motion of water. **2** a fall in the level of a river, as a source of this force. **water purslane** a creeping plant, *Lythrum portula*, growing in damp places. **water rail** a wading bird, *Rallus aquaticus*, frequenting marshes etc. **water-rat** = *water-vole*. **water-rate** a charge made for the use of the public water-supply. **water-repellent** not easily penetrated by water. **water-scorpion** any aquatic bug of the family Nepidae, living submerged and breathing through a bristle-like tubular tail. **water-softener** an apparatus or substance for softening hard water. **water-soluble** soluble in water. **water-splash** part of a road submerged by a stream or pool. **water starwort** any plant of the genus *Callitriche*, growing in water. **water-supply** the provision and storage of water, or the amount of water stored, for the use of a town, house, etc. **water-table** = *water-level* 2. **water torture** a form of torture in which the victim is exposed to the incessant dripping of water on the head, or the sound of dripping. **water-tower** a tower with an elevated tank to give pressure for distributing water. **water under the bridge** past events accepted as past and irrevocable. **water-vole** an aquatic vole, esp. *Arvicola amphibius*. **water-weed** any of various aquatic plants. **water-wheel** a wheel driven by water to work machinery, or to raise water. **water-wings** inflated floats fixed on the arms of a person learning to swim. □□ **waterer** *n.* **waterless** *adj.* [OE *wæter* f. Gmc, rel. to WET]

waterbrash /ˈwɔːtəˌbræʃ/ *n.* pyrosis. [WATER + BRASH³]

water-clock *n.* a device for measuring time by the flow of water. In ancient Egypt (*c.*1400 BC) such devices consisted of round vessels from which water flowed through a hole in the base, with a time-scale marked on the inside of the vessel; the sloping sides helped to regulate the pressure of the outflow. Similar vessels were used in ancient Greece. The Romans used a cylinder into which water dripped, with a float for taking readings against a scale. By the 1st c. BC they had developed one with a shaft, attached to the float, with teeth that engaged a cogwheel to which was fixed a pointer moving over a dial. Similar clocks were used in Europe until the 16th c.

water-closet *n.* **1** a lavatory with a means for flushing the pan by water. **2** a room containing this. Some ancient civilizations had elaborate systems of drainage and lavatories which in construction surpass anything of later periods up to the 19th c. The Elizabethan poet Sir John Harington designed the first English water-closet and installed it in his home near Bath; water pumped into a cistern descended through a pipe to flush the pan, the flow being regulated by a hand-operated tap and then released from the pan by means of a valve. Although Queen Elizabeth I is said to have had a model installed at her Richmond Palace, most of Sir John's contemporaries regarded the innovation as a joke and it was never patented. The first patent for a water-closet was taken out in 1755 by Alexander Cumming, a watchmaker, and in 1778 Joseph Bramah patented one with an improved valve. By mid-Victorian times most middle-class homes had indoor water-closets, but until near the end of the 19th c. these drained into cesspools, which were later connected by pipes to town sewers, and the inadequate water supply was insufficient to keep the complicated workings clean. Improvements on the basic design included ceramic pans to replace the earlier metal ones, an S-bend in the outlet pipe (in which trapped water prevented drain odours from rising), improved flushing systems, and the use of non-corroding plastic to replace metal parts.

watercourse /ˈwɔːtəˌkɔːs/ *n.* **1** a brook, stream, or artificial water-channel. **2** the bed along which this flows.

watercress /ˈwɔːtəˌkres/ *n.* a hardy perennial cress, *Nasturtium officinale*, growing in running water, with pungent leaves used in salad.

waterfall /ˈwɔːtəˌfɔːl/ *n.* a stream or river flowing over a precipice or down a steep hillside.

Waterford /ˈwɑːtəˌfəd/ **1** a county of southern Ireland, in the province of Connaught; pop. (est. 1986) 51,600. **2** its capital city, a port, noted for its clear colourless flint glass; pop. (1981) 39,636.

waterfowl /ˈwɔːtəˌfaʊl/ n. (usu. collect. as pl.) birds frequenting water, esp. swimming game-birds.

waterfront /ˈwɔːtəˌfrʌnt/ n. the part of a town adjoining a river, lake, harbour, etc.

Watergate /ˈwɔːtəˌgeɪt/ a building in Washington, DC, housing the offices of the Democratic Party, the scene of a bungled bugging attempt by Republicans during the US election campaign of 1972. The attempted cover-up and subsequent inquiry caused a massive political scandal, gravely weakened the prestige of the government, and finally led to the resignation of President Richard Nixon in August 1974.

watergate /ˈwɔːtəˌgeɪt/ n. **1** a floodgate. **2** a gate giving access to a river etc.

watering /ˈwɔːtərɪŋ/ n. the act or an instance of supplying water or (of an animal) obtaining water. □ **watering-can** a portable container with a long spout usu. ending in a perforated sprinkler, for watering plants. **watering-hole 1** a pool of water from which animals regularly drink; = *water-hole*. **2** sl. a bar. **watering-place 1** = *watering-hole*. **2** a spa or seaside resort. **3** a place where water is obtained. [OE *wæterung* (as WATER, -ING¹)]

waterlogged /ˈwɔːtəˌlɒgd/ adj. **1** saturated with water. **2** (of a boat etc.) hardly able to float from being saturated or filled with water. **3** (of ground) made useless by being saturated with water. [*waterlog* (v.), f. WATER + LOG¹, prob. orig. = 'reduce (a ship) to the condition of a log']

Waterloo /ˌwɔːtəˈluː/ a village in Belgium, south of Brussels (pop., 1981, 49,428), where on 18 June 1815 Napoleon's army was defeated by the British (under the Duke of Wellington) and Prussians. Attempting to exploit the temporary separation of the British and Prussian armies after the battles of Ligny and Quatre Bras, Napoleon attacked the outnumbered British force. Wellington was able to hold off the French until the arrival of the Prussians on his left flank forced them to retreat. Under the pressure of the Allied pursuit Napoleon's army disintegrated completely, effectively ending his bid to return to power. —n. a decisive defeat or contest (*meet one's Waterloo*).

waterman /ˈwɔːtəmən/ n. (pl. **-men**) **1** a boatman plying for hire. **2** an oarsman as regards skill in keeping the boat balanced.

watermark /ˈwɔːtəˌmɑːk/ n. & v. —n. a faint design made in some paper during manufacture, visible when held against the light, identifying the maker etc. —v.tr. mark with this.

waterproof /ˈwɔːtəˌpruːf/ adj., n., & v. —adj. impervious to water. —n. a waterproof garment or material. —v.tr. make waterproof.

watershed /ˈwɔːtəˌʃed/ n. **1** a line of separation between waters flowing to different rivers, basins, or seas. **2** a turning-point in affairs. [WATER + *shed* ridge of high ground (rel. to SHED²), after G *Wasserscheide*]

waterside /ˈwɔːtəˌsaɪd/ n. the margin of a sea, lake, or river.

water-ski /ˈwɔːtəˌskiː/ n. & v. —n. (pl. **-skis**) each of a pair of skis for skimming the surface of the water when towed by a motor boat. —v.intr. (**-skis**, **-ski'd** or **-skied** /-skiːd/; **-skiing**) travel on water-skis. □□ **water-skier** n.

waterspout /ˈwɔːtəˌspaʊt/ n. a gyrating column of water and spray formed by a whirlwind between sea and cloud.

watertight /ˈwɔːtəˌtaɪt/ adj. **1** (of a joint, container, vessel, etc.) closely fastened or fitted or made so as to prevent the passage of water. **2** (of an argument etc.) unassailable.

waterway /ˈwɔːtəˌweɪ/ n. **1** a navigable channel. **2** a route for travel by water. **3** a thick plank at the outer edge of a deck along which a channel is hollowed for water to run off by.

waterworks /ˈwɔːtəˌwɜːks/ n. **1** an establishment for managing a water-supply. **2** colloq. the shedding of tears. **3** Brit. colloq. the urinary system.

watery /ˈwɔːtərɪ/ adj. **1** containing too much water. **2** too thin in consistency. **3** of or consisting of water. **4** (of the eyes) suffused or running with water. **5** (of conversation, style, etc.) vapid, uninteresting. **6** (of colour) pale. **7** (of the sun, moon, or sky) rainy-looking. □ **watery grave** the bottom of the sea as a place where a person lies drowned. □□ **wateriness** n. [OE *wæterig* (as WATER, -Y¹)]

Watling Street /ˈwɒtlɪŋ/ a Roman road running NW across England from Richborough in Kent through London and St Albans to Wroxeter in Shropshire.

Watson¹ /ˈwɒts(ə)n/, Dr. A doctor who is the companion and assistant of Sherlock Holmes in stories by Sir Arthur Conan Doyle. A stolid upright citizen of sterling qualities, he is a foil to his friend's brilliance, being slightly (but only slightly) more stupid than the average reader.

Watson² /ˈwɒts(ə)n/, James Dewey (1928–), American biologist who together with F. H. C. Crick proposed a model for the structure of the DNA molecule, for which he was awarded a Nobel Prize in 1962.

Watson³ /ˈwɒts(ə)n/, John Broadus (1878–1958), American psychologist and founder of the school of behaviourism. He viewed behaviour as determined by an interplay between genetic endowment and environmental influences, and held that the role of the psychologist was to discern through observation and experimentation just which behaviour was innate and which was acquired. Seeking an objective study of psychology, he set the stage for the empirical study of animal and human behaviour which was to dominate the field of psychology, particularly in the US, throughout the 20th c.

Watt /wɒt/, James (1736–1819), Scottish engineer, not the inventor but the great improver of the steam engine. While repairing a Newcomen engine in 1764 he realized that it could be made more efficient by condensing the spent steam in a separate chamber, allowing the cylinder to remain hot. Progress in its development was slow until eventually he found a good business partner in Matthew Boulton, whose hearty enthusiasm balanced Watt's own tendency towards despondency and pessimism, and the improved engines became used for a variety of purposes. Watt continued inventing until the end of his life. He introduced rotatory engines and the centrifugal governor to control them, devised a chemical method of copying documents, and introduced the term 'horsepower' (see entry). The metric unit of power is named in his honour.

watt /wɒt/ n. the SI unit of power, equivalent to one joule per second, corresponding to the rate of energy in an electric circuit where the potential difference is one volt and the current one ampere. ¶ Symb.: **W**. □ **watt-hour** the energy used when one watt is applied for one hour. [J. WATT]

wattage /ˈwɒtɪdʒ/ n. an amount of electrical power expressed in watts.

Watteau /ˈwɒtəʊ/, Jean Antoine (1684–1721), French painter, of Flemish descent, an initiator of the rococo style in painting, who achieved fame with his new genre of elegant richly-coloured *fêtes galantes* (scenes of gallantry) and pastorals. Watteau deliberately created an imaginary rather theatrical world; his novel imagery, based largely on themes of the game of love and the pursuit of pleasure, was the antithesis of the serious religious and classical subject-matter approved by the French Academy. His finest and most characteristic work is *L'Embarquement pour l'Île de Cythère* (1717).

wattle¹ /ˈwɒt(ə)l/ n. & v. —n. **1 a** interlaced rods and split rods as a material for making fences, walls, etc. **b** (in *sing.* or *pl.*) rods and twigs for this use. **2** an Australian acacia with long pliant branches, with bark used in tanning and golden flowers used as the national emblem. **3** dial. a wicker hurdle. —v.tr. **1** make of wattle. **2** enclose or fill up with wattles. □ **wattle and daub** a network of rods and twigs plastered with mud or clay as a building material. [OE *watul*, of unkn. orig.]

wattle² /ˈwɒt(ə)l/ n. **1** a loose fleshy appendage on the head or throat of a turkey or other birds. **2** = BARB n. 3. □□ **wattled** adj. [16th c.: orig. unkn.]

wattmeter /ˈwɒtˌmiːtə(r)/ n. a meter for measuring the amount of electricity in watts.

Watts¹ /wɒts/, George Frederick (1817–1904), English painter and sculptor, from the 1880s a dominant figure in the Victorian art world, one of the first holders of the Order of Merit (1902). Like many of his contemporaries he saw his art as a vehicle for moral purpose. His allegorical pictures (e.g. *Hope*), once immensely popular, have lasted less well than the great series of portraits of Gladstone, Tennyson, J. S. Mill, etc. His first wife was the actress Ellen Terry, whom he married in 1864.

Watts[2] /wɒts/, Isaac (1674–1748), English hymn-writer and poet, who published four volumes of verse including *Divine Songs for the Use of Children* (1715) and is remembered for his well-known hymns such as 'O God, our help in ages past', and his songs for children ('How doth the little busy bee'), some of which foreshadow Blake. He also wrote theological works and Pindaric odes and made daring experiments with metre.

Waugh /wɔː/, Evelyn Arthur St John (1903–66), English novelist. Educated at Oxford, he then worked as a schoolmaster, a background which provided material for his first and immensely successful novel *Decline and Fall* (1928); he became a Roman Catholic in 1930. His novels *Vile Bodies* (1930), *Black Mischief* (1932), *A Handful of Dust* (1934), and *Scoop* (1938) were works of high comedy and social satire which capture the brittle, cynical, determined frivolity of the postwar generation; *Brideshead Revisited* (1945), a complex story of an ancient Roman Catholic family, struck a more serious note. Waugh's career continued to prosper with *The Loved One* (1948) and *The Ordeal of Gilbert Pinfold* (1957), a self-caricature which ends in salvation. His wartime experiences in Crete and Yugoslavia appear in his trilogy *Men at Arms* (1952), *Officers and Gentlemen* (1955), *Unconditional Surrender* (1961). Waugh also wrote travel books, biographies, and an autobiography (1964).

waul /wɔːl/ v.intr. (also **wawl**) give a loud plaintive cry like a cat. [imit.]

wave /weɪv/ v. & n. —v. **1 a** intr. (often foll. by *to*) move a hand etc. to and fro in greeting or as a signal (*waved to me across the street*). **b** tr. move (a hand etc.) in this way. **2 a** intr. show a sinuous or sweeping motion as of a flag, tree, or a cornfield in the wind; flutter, undulate. **b** tr. impart a waving motion to. **3** tr. brandish (a sword etc.) as an encouragement to followers etc. **4** tr. tell or direct (a person) by waving (*waved them away*; *waved them to follow*). **5** tr. express (a greeting etc.) by waving (*waved goodbye to them*). **6** tr. give an undulating form to (hair, drawn lines, etc.); make wavy. **7** intr. (of hair etc.) have such a form; be wavy. —n. **1** a ridge of water between two depressions. **2** a long body of water curling into an arched form and breaking on the shore. **3** a thing compared to this, e.g. a body of persons in one of successive advancing groups. **4** a gesture of waving. **5 a** the process of waving the hair. **b** an undulating form produced in the hair by waving. **6 a** a temporary occurrence or increase of a condition, emotion, or influence (*a wave of enthusiasm*). **b** a specified period of widespread weather (*heat wave*). **7** *Physics* **a** the disturbance of the particles of a fluid medium to form ridges and troughs for the propagation or direction of motion, heat, light, sound, etc., without the advance of the particles. (See below.) **b** a single curve in the course of this motion (see also *standing wave*, *travelling wave* (see TRAVEL)). **8** *Electr.* a similar variation of an electromagnetic field in the propagation of radiation through a medium or vacuum. **9** (in *pl.*; prec. by *the*) *poet.* the sea; water. □ **make waves** *colloq.* cause trouble. **wave aside** dismiss as intrusive or irrelevant. **wave down** wave to (a vehicle or its driver) as a signal to stop. **wave equation** a differential equation expressing the properties of motion in waves. **wave-form** *Physics* a curve showing the shape of a wave at a given time. **wave-front** *Physics* a surface containing points affected in the same way by a wave at a given time. **wave function** a function satisfying a wave equation and describing the properties of a wave. **wave mechanics** a particular mathematical formulation of quantum mechanics introduced by E. Schrödinger in which particles such as electrons are regarded as having some of the properties of waves. **wave number** *Physics* the number of waves in a unit distance. **wave theory** *hist.* the theory that light is propagated through the ether by a wave-motion imparted to the ether by the molecular vibrations of the radiant body. □□ **waveless** adj. **wavelike** adj. & adv. [OE *wafian* (v.) f. Gmc: (n.) also alt. of ME *wawe*, *wage*]

Waves can be longitudinal, transverse, or torsional. In longitudinal waves (e.g. sound waves) the to-and-fro vibration is parallel to the direction of propagation; in transverse waves (e.g. water waves or light waves) the vibration is at right angles to the direction of propagation; in torsional waves a 'twist' is propagated. Waves display their characteristic properties of reflection, refraction, diffraction, and interference, under appropriate conditions. When two waves travelling in opposite directions meet, a 'standing wave' can result, which vibrates up and down but is not propagated. Wave phenomena are of great importance throughout physics. In the 20th c. quantum theory has introduced the seemingly paradoxical idea of 'wave-particle duality', in which photons of light and subatomic particles such as electrons are considered to have a dual nature, sharing characteristics of both waves and particles.

waveband /ˈweɪvbænd/ n. a range of (esp. radio) wavelengths between certain limits.

waveguide /ˈweɪvgaɪd/ n. *Electr.* a metal tube etc. confining and conveying microwaves.

wavelength /ˈweɪvleŋθ, -leŋkθ/ n. **1** the distance between successive crests of a wave, esp. points in a sound wave or electromagnetic wave. ¶ Symb.: λ **2** this as a distinctive feature of radio waves from a transmitter. **3** *colloq.* a particular mode or range of thinking and communicating (*we don't seem to be on the same wavelength*).

wavelet /ˈweɪvlɪt/ n. a small wave on water.

waver /ˈweɪvə(r)/ v.intr. **1** be or become unsteady; falter; begin to give way. **2** be irresolute or undecided between different courses or opinions; be shaken in resolution or belief. **3** (of a light) flicker. □□ **waverer** n. **waveringly** adv. [ME f. ON *vafra* flicker f. Gmc, rel. to WAVE]

wavy /ˈweɪvɪ/ adj. (**wavier**, **waviest**) (of a line or surface) having waves or alternate contrary curves (*wavy hair*). □□ **wavily** adv. **waviness** n.

wa-wa var. of WAH-WAH.

wawl var. of WAUL.

wax[1] /wæks/ n. & v. —n. **1** a sticky plastic yellowish substance secreted by bees as the material of honeycomb cells; beeswax. **2** a white translucent material obtained from this by bleaching and purifying and used for candles, in modelling, as a basis of polishes, and for other purposes. **3** any similar substance, e.g. earwax. **4** *colloq.* **a** a gramophone record. **b** material for the manufacture of this. **5** (*attrib.*) made of wax. —v.tr. **1** cover or treat with wax. **2** *colloq.* record for the gramophone. □ **be wax in a person's hands** be entirely subservient to a person. **lost wax** = CIRE PERDUE. **wax-light** a taper or candle of wax. **wax-myrtle** a tree, *Myrtus cerifera*, yielding wax and oil used for candles. **wax-painting** = ENCAUSTIC. **wax palm 1** a South American palm, *Ceroxylon alpinum*, with its stem coated in a mixture of resin and wax. **2** a carnauba. **wax paper** paper waterproofed with a layer of wax. **wax-pod** a yellow-podded bean. **wax-tree** an Asian tree, *Rhus succedanea*, having white berries which yield wax. □□ **waxer** n. [OE *wæx*, *weax* f. Gmc]

wax[2] /wæks/ v.intr. **1** (of the moon between new and full) have a progressively larger part of its visible surface illuminated, increasing in apparent size. **2** become larger or stronger. **3** pass into a specified state or mood (*wax lyrical*). □ **wax and wane** undergo alternate increases and decreases. [OE *weaxan* f. Gmc]

wax[3] /wæks/ n. *sl.* a fit of anger. [19th c.: orig. uncert.: perh. f. WAX[2] *wroth* etc.]

waxberry /ˈwæksbərɪ/ n. (*pl.* **-ies**) **1** a wax-myrtle. **2** the fruit of this.

waxbill /ˈwæksbɪl/ n. any of various birds esp. of the family Estrildidae, with usu. red bills resembling the colour of sealing wax.

waxcloth /ˈwæksklɒθ/ n. oilcloth.

waxen /ˈwæks(ə)n/ adj. **1** having a smooth pale translucent surface as of wax. **2** able to receive impressions like wax; plastic. **3** *archaic* made of wax.

waxwing /ˈwækswɪŋ/ n. any bird of the genus *Bombycilla*, with small tips like red sealing-wax to some wing-feathers.

waxwork /ˈwækswɜːk/ n. **1 a** an object, esp. a lifelike dummy, modelled in wax. **b** the making of waxworks. **2** (in *pl.*) an exhibition of wax dummies.

waxy[1] /ˈwæksɪ/ *adj.* (**waxier, waxiest**) resembling wax in consistency or in its surface. □□ **waxily** *adv.* **waxiness** *n.* [WAX[1] + -Y[1]]

waxy[2] /ˈwæksɪ/ *adj.* (**waxier, waxiest**) *Brit. sl.* angry, quick-tempered. [WAX[3] + -Y[1]]

way /weɪ/ *n. & adv.* —*n.* **1** a road, track, path, etc., for passing along. **2** a course or route for reaching a place, esp. the best one (*asked the way to London*). **3** a place of passage into a building, through a door, etc. (*could not find the way out*). **4 a** a method or plan for attaining an object (*that is not the way to do it*). **b** the ability to obtain one's object (*has a way with him*). **5 a** a person's desired or chosen course of action. **b** a custom or manner of behaving; a personal peculiarity (*has a way of forgetting things; things had a way of going badly*). **6** a specific manner of life or procedure (*soon got into the way of it*). **7** the normal course of events (*that is always the way*). **8** a travelling distance; a length traversed or to be traversed (*is a long way away*). **9 a** an unimpeded opportunity of advance. **b** a space free of obstacles. **10** a region or ground over which advance is desired or natural. **11** advance in some direction; impetus, progress (*pushed my way through*). **12** movement of a ship etc. (*gather way; lose way*). **13** the state of being engaged in movement from place to place; time spent in this (*met them on the way home; with songs to cheer the way*). **14** a specified direction (*step this way; which way are you going?*). **15** (in *pl.*) parts into which a thing is divided (*split it three ways*). **16** *colloq.* the scope or range of something (*want a few things in the stationery way*). **17** a person's line of occupation or business. **18** a specified condition or state (*things are in a bad way*). **19** a respect (*is useful in some ways*). **20 a** (in *pl.*) a structure of timber etc. down which a new ship is launched. **b** parallel rails etc. as a track for the movement of a machine. —*adv. colloq.* to a considerable extent; far (*you're way off the mark*). □ **across** (or **over**) **the way** opposite. **any way** = ANYWAY. **be on one's way** set off; depart. **by the way 1** incidentally; as a more or less irrelevant comment. **2** during a journey. **by way of 1** through; by means of. **2** as a substitute for or as a form of (*did it by way of apology*). **3** with the intention of (*asked by way of discovering the truth*). **come one's way** become available to one; become one's lot. **find a way** discover a means of obtaining one's object. **get** (or **have**) **one's way** (or **have it one's own way** etc.) get what one wants; ensure one's wishes are met. **give way 1 a** make concessions. **b** fail to resist; yield. **2** (often foll. by *to*) concede precedence (to). **3** (of a structure etc.) be dislodged or broken under a load; collapse. **4** (foll. by *to*) be superseded by. **5** (foll. by *to*) be overcome by (an emotion etc.). **6** (of rowers) row hard. **go out of one's way** (often foll. by *to* + infin.) make a special effort; act gratuitously or without compulsion (*went out of their way to help*). **go one's own way** act independently, esp. against contrary advice. **go one's way 1** leave, depart. **2** (of events, circumstances, etc.) be favourable to one. **go a person's way** accompany a person (*are you going my way?*). **have it both ways** see BOTH. **in its way** if regarded from a particular standpoint appropriate to it. **in no way** not at all; by no means. **in a way** in a certain respect but not altogether or completely. **in the** (or **one's**) **way** forming an obstacle or hindrance. **lead the way 1** act as guide or leader. **2** show how to do something. **look the other way 1** ignore what one should notice. **2** disregard an acquaintance etc. whom one sees. **one way and another** taking various considerations into account. **one way or another** by some means. **on the** (or **one's**) **way 1** in the course of a journey etc. **2** having progressed (*is well on the way to completion*). **3** *colloq.* (of a child) conceived but not yet born. **on the way out** *colloq.* going down in status, estimation, or favour; going out of fashion. **the other way about** (or **round**) in an inverted or reversed position or direction. **out of the way 1** no longer an obstacle or hindrance. **2** disposed of; settled. **3** (of a person) imprisoned or killed. **4** (with *neg.*) common or unremarkable (*nothing out of the way*). **5** (of a place) remote, inaccessible. **out of one's way** not on one's intended route. **put a person in the way of** give a person the opportunity of. **way back** *colloq.* long ago. **way-leave** a right of way rented to another. **the way of the Cross** a series of paintings or representations of the events in Christ's passion, esp. in a church. **way of life** the principles or habits governing all

one's actions etc. **way of thinking** one's customary opinion of matters. **way of the world** conduct no worse than is customary. **way-out** *colloq.* **1** unusual, eccentric. **2** avant-garde, progressive. **3** excellent, exciting. **ways and means 1** methods of achieving something. **2** methods of raising government revenue. **way station** *US* **1** a minor station on a railway. **2** a point marking progress in a certain course of action etc. **way-worn** tired with travel. [OE *weg* f. Gmc: (adv.) f. AWAY]

-way /weɪ/ *suffix* = -WAYS.

waybill /ˈweɪbɪl/ *n.* a list of passengers or parcels on a vehicle.

waybread /ˈweɪbrɛd/ *n. Brit. archaic* a broad-leaved plantain (see PLANTAIN[1]). [OE *wegbrǣde* (as WAY, BROAD)]

wayfarer /ˈweɪˌfɛərə(r)/ *n.* a traveller, esp. on foot.

wayfaring /ˈweɪˌfɛərɪŋ/ *n.* travelling, esp. on foot. □ **wayfaring-tree** a white-flowered European and Asian shrub, *Viburnum lantana*, common along roadsides, with berries turning from green through red to black.

Wayland the Smith /ˈweɪlənd/ *Scand. Mythol.* a smith with supernatural powers, in English legend supposed to have his forge in a dolmen on the downs in SW Oxfordshire.

waylay /weɪˈleɪ/ *v.tr.* (*past* and *past part.* **waylaid**) **1** lie in wait for. **2** stop to rob or interview. □□ **waylayer** *n.*

waymark /ˈweɪmɑːk/ *n.* a natural or artificial object as a guide to travellers, esp. walkers.

Wayne /weɪn/, John (real name Marion Michael Morrison, 1907–79), American film actor, remembered as the archetypal hero of westerns—tough, self-sufficient, brutal but not vicious. His classic westerns include *Stagecoach* (1939), *Red River* (1948), and *Rio Bravo* (1959).

-ways /weɪz/ *suffix* forming adjectives and adverbs of direction or manner (*sideways*) (cf. -WISE). [WAY + -'s]

wayside /ˈweɪsaɪd/ *n.* **1** the side or margin of a road. **2** the land at the side of a road. □ **fall by the wayside** fail to continue in an endeavour or undertaking (after Luke 8: 5).

wayward /ˈweɪwəd/ *adj.* **1** childishly self-willed or perverse; capricious. **2** unaccountable or freakish. □□ **waywardly** *adv.* **waywardness** *n.* [ME f. obs. *awayward* turned away f. AWAY + -WARD: cf. FROWARD]

wayzgoose /ˈweɪzguːs/ *n.* (*pl.* **-gooses**) an annual summer dinner or outing held by a printing-house for its employees. [17th c. (earlier *waygoose*): orig. unkn.]

Wb *abbr.* weber(s).

WC *abbr.* **1** water-closet. **2** West Central.

WCC *abbr.* World Council of Churches.

W/Cdr. *abbr.* Wing Commander.

WD *abbr.* **1** War Department. **2** Works Department.

we /wiː, wɪ/ *pron.* (*obj.* **us**; *poss.* **our, ours**) **1** (*pl.* of I[2]) used by and with reference to more than one person speaking or writing, or one such person and one or more associated persons. **2** used for or by a royal person in a proclamation etc. and by a writer or editor in a formal context. **3** people in general (cf. ONE *pron.* 2). **4** *colloq.* = I[2] (*give us a chance*). **5** *colloq.* (often implying condescension) you (*how are we feeling today?*). [OE f. Gmc]

WEA *abbr.* (in the UK) Workers' Educational Association.

weak /wiːk/ *adj.* **1** deficient in strength, power, or number; fragile; easily broken or bent or defeated. **2** deficient in vigour; sickly, feeble (*weak health; a weak imagination*). **3 a** deficient in resolution; easily led (*a weak character*). **b** (of an action or features) indicating a lack of resolution (*a weak surrender; a weak chin*). **4** unconvincing or logically deficient (*weak evidence; a weak argument*). **5** (of a mixed liquid or solution) watery, thin, dilute (*weak tea*). **6** (of a style etc.) not vigorous or well-knit; diffuse, slipshod. **7** (of a crew) short-handed. **8** (of a syllable etc.) unstressed. **9** *Gram.* in Germanic languages: **a** (of a verb) forming inflections by the addition of a suffix to the stem. **b** (of a noun or adjective) belonging to a declension in which the stem originally ended in -*n* (opp. STRONG *adj.* 22). □ **weak ending** an unstressed syllable in a normally stressed place at the end of a verse-line. **the weaker sex** *derog.* women. **weak grade** *Gram.* an unstressed ablaut-form. **weak interaction** *Physics* the weakest form of interaction between elementary particles. **weak-kneed** *colloq.*

lacking resolution. **weak-minded 1** mentally deficient. **2** lacking in resolution. **weak-mindedness** the state of being weak-minded. **weak moment** a time when one is unusually compliant or temptable. **weak point** (or **spot**) **1** a place where defences are assailable. **2** a flaw in an argument or character or in resistance to temptation. □□ **weakish** adj. [ME f. ON veikr f. Gmc]

weaken /ˈwiːkən/ v.tr. & intr. make or become weak or weaker. □□ **weakener** n.

weakfish /ˈwiːkfɪʃ/ n. (pl. same or **-fishes**) US a marine fish of the genus Cynoscion, used as food. [obs. Du. weekvisch f. week soft (formed as WEAK) + visch FISH¹]

weakling /ˈwiːklɪŋ/ n. a feeble person or animal.

weakly /ˈwiːklɪ/ adv. & adj. —adv. ın a weak manner. —adj. (**weaklier, weakliest**) sickly, not robust. □□ **weakliness** n.

weakness /ˈwiːknɪs/ n. **1** the state or condition of being weak. **2** a weak point; a defect. **3** the inability to resist a particular temptation. **4** (foll. by for) a self-indulgent liking (have a weakness for chocolate).

weal¹ /wiːl/ n. & v. —n. a ridge raised on the flesh by a stroke of a rod or whip. —v.tr. mark with a weal. [var. of WALE, infl. by obs. wheal suppurate]

weal² /wiːl/ n. literary welfare, prosperity; good fortune. [OE wela f. WG (as WELL¹)]

Weald /wiːld/ n. (also **weald**) (prec. by the) Brit. a formerly wooded district including parts of Kent, Surrey, and East Sussex. □ **weald-clay** beds of clay, sandstone, limestone, and ironstone, forming the top of Wealden strata, with abundant fossil remains. [OE, = wald WOLD]

Wealden /ˈwiːld(ə)n/ adj. & n. Brit. —adj. **1** of the Weald. **2** resembling the Weald geologically. —n. a series of Lower Cretaceous freshwater deposits above Jurassic strata and below chalk, best exemplified in the Weald.

wealth /welθ/ n. **1** riches; abundant possessions; opulence. **2** the state of being rich. **3** (foll. by of) an abundance or profusion (a wealth of new material). **4** archaic welfare or prosperity. □ **wealth tax** a tax on personal capital. [ME welthe, f. WELL¹ or WEAL² + -TH², after health]

wealthy /ˈwelθɪ/ adj. (**wealthier, wealthiest**) having an abundance esp. of money. □□ **wealthily** adv. **wealthiness** n.

wean¹ /wiːn/ v.tr. **1** accustom (an infant or other young mammal) to food other than (esp. its mother's) milk. **2** (often foll. by from, away from) disengage (from a habit etc.) by enforced discontinuance. [OE wenian accustom f. Gmc: cf. WONT]

wean² /wiːn/ n. Sc. a young child. [contr. of wee little one]

weaner /ˈwiːnə(r)/ n. a young animal recently weaned.

weanling /ˈwiːnlɪŋ/ n. a newly-weaned child etc.

weapon /ˈwepən/ n. **1** a thing designed or used or usable for inflicting bodily harm (e.g. a gun or cosh). **2** a means employed for trying to gain the advantage in a conflict (irony is a double-edged weapon). □□ **weaponed** adj. (also in comb.). **weaponless** adj. [OE wæp(e)n f. Gmc]

weaponry /ˈwepənrɪ/ n. weapons collectively.

wear¹ /weə(r)/ v. & n. —v. (past **wore** /wɔː(r)/; past part. **worn** /wɔːn/) **1** tr. have on one's person as clothing or an ornament etc. (is wearing shorts; wears earrings). **2** tr. be dressed habitually in (wears green). **3** tr. exhibit or present (a facial expression or appearance) (wore a frown; the day wore a different aspect). **4** tr. Brit. colloq. (usu. with neg.) tolerate, accept (they won't wear that excuse). **5** (often foll. by away) **a** tr. injure the surface of, or partly obliterate or alter, by rubbing, stress, or use. **b** intr. undergo such injury or change. **6** tr. & intr. (foll. by off, away) rub or be rubbed off. **7** tr. make (a hole etc.) by constant rubbing or dripping etc. **8** tr. & intr. (often foll. by out) exhaust, tire or be tired. **9** tr. (foll. by down) overcome by persistence. **10** intr. **a** remain for a specified time in working order or a presentable state; last long. **b** (foll. by well, badly, etc.) endure continued use or life. **11 a** intr. (of time) pass, esp. tediously. **b** tr. pass (time) gradually away. **12** tr. (of a ship) fly (a flag). —n. **1** the act of wearing or the state of being worn (suitable for informal wear). **2**

things worn; fashionable or suitable clothing (sportswear; footwear). **3** (in full **wear and tear**) damage sustained from continuous use. **4** the capacity for resisting wear and tear (still a great deal of wear left in it). □ **in wear** being regularly worn. **wear one's heart on one's sleeve** see HEART. **wear off** lose effectiveness or intensity. **wear out 1** use or be used until no longer usable. **2** tire or be tired out. **wear thin** (of patience, excuses, etc.) begin to fail. **wear the trousers** see TROUSERS. **wear** (or **wear one's years**) **well** colloq. remain young-looking. □□ **wearable** adj. **wearability** /-ˈbɪlɪtɪ/ n. **wearer** n. **wearingly** adv. [OE werian f. Gmc]

wear² /weə(r)/ v. (past and past part. **wore** /wɔː(r)/) **1** tr. bring (a ship) about by turning its head away from the wind. **2** intr. (of a ship) come about in this way (cf. TACK¹ v. 4). [17th c.: orig. unkn.]

wearisome /ˈwɪərɪsəm/ adj. tedious; tiring by monotony or length. □□ **wearisomely** adv. **wearisomeness** n.

weary /ˈwɪərɪ/ adj. & v. —adj. (**wearier, weariest**) **1** unequal to or disinclined for further exertion or endurance; tired. **2** (foll. by of) dismayed at the continuing of; impatient of. **3** tiring or tedious. —v. (**-ies, -ied**) **1** tr. & intr. make or grow weary. **2** intr. esp. Sc. long. □□ **weariless** adj. **wearily** adv. **weariness** n. **wearyingly** adv. [OE wērig, wǣrig f. WG]

weasel /ˈwiːz(ə)l/ n. & v. —n. **1** a small reddish-brown flesh-eating mammal, Mustela nivalis, with a slender body, related to the stoat and ferret. **2** a stoat. **3** colloq. a deceitful or treacherous person. —v.intr. (**weaselled, weaselling**; US **weaseled, weaseling**) **1** esp. US equivocate or quibble. **2** (foll. by on, out) default on an obligation. □ **weasel-faced** having thin sharp features. **weasel word** (usu. in pl.) a word that is intentionally ambiguous or misleading (said to allude to the weasel's alleged habit of sucking out the contents of an egg and leaving only the shell). □□ **weaselly** adj. [OE wesle, wesule f. WG]

weather /ˈweðə(r)/ n. & v. —n. **1** the state of the atmosphere at a place and time as regards heat, cloudiness, dryness, sunshine, wind, and rain etc. **2** (attrib.) Naut. windward (on the weather side). —v. **1** tr. expose to or affect by atmospheric changes, esp. deliberately to dry, season, etc. (weathered timber). **2 a** tr. (usu. in passive) discolour or partly disintegrate (rock or stones) by exposure to air. **b** intr. be discoloured or worn in this way. **3** tr. make (boards or tiles) overlap downwards to keep out rain etc. **4** tr. **a** come safely through (a storm). **b** survive (a difficult period etc.). **5** tr. (of a ship or its crew) get to the windward of (a cape etc.). □ **keep a** (or **one's**) **weather eye open** be watchful. **make good** (or **bad**) **weather of it** Naut. (of a ship) behave well (or badly) in a storm. **make heavy weather of** colloq. exaggerate the difficulty or burden presented by (a problem, course of action, etc.). **under the weather** colloq. indisposed or out of sorts. **weather-beaten** affected by exposure to the weather. **weather-bound** unable to proceed owing to bad weather. **weather-chart** (or **-map**) a diagram showing the state of the weather over a large area. **weather forecast** an analysis of the state of the weather with an assessment of likely developments over a certain time. **weather-glass** a barometer. **weather side** the side from which the wind is blowing (opp. lee side). **weather station** an observation post for recording meteorological data. **weather-strip** a piece of material used to make a door or window proof against rain or wind. **weather-tiles** tiles arranged to overlap like weatherboards. **weather-vane** see VANE. **weather-worn** damaged by storms etc. [OE weder f. Gmc]

weatherboard /ˈweðəˌbɔːd/ n. & v. —n. **1** a sloping board attached to the bottom of an outside door to keep out the rain etc. **2** each of a series of horizontal boards with edges overlapping to keep out rain etc. —v.tr. fit or supply with weatherboards. □□ **weatherboarding** n. (in sense 2 of n.).

weathercock /ˈweðəˌkɒk/ n. **1** a weather-vane (see VANE) in the form of a cock. **2** an inconstant person.

weathering /ˈweðərɪŋ/ n. **1** the action of the weather on materials etc. exposed to it. **2** exposure to adverse weather conditions (see WEATHER v. 1).

weatherly /ˈweðəlɪ/ adj. Naut. **1** (of a ship) making little leeway. **2** capable of keeping close to the wind. □□ **weatherliness** n.

w we   z zoo   ʃ she   ʒ decision   θ thin   ð this   ŋ ring   x loch   tʃ chip   dʒ jar   (see over for vowels)

weatherman /ˈweðəˌmæn/ n. (pl. **-men**) a meteorologist, esp. one who broadcasts a weather forecast.

weatherproof /ˈweðəˌpruːf/ adj. & v. —adj. resistant to the effects of bad weather, esp. rain. —v.tr. make weatherproof. □□ **weatherproofed** adj.

weave[1] /wiːv/ v. & n. —v. (past **wove** /wəʊv/; past part. **woven** /ˈwəʊv(ə)n/ or **wove**) 1 tr. **a** form (fabric) by interlacing long threads in two directions. **b** form (thread) into fabric in this way. 2 intr. **a** make fabric in this way. **b** work at a loom. 3 tr. make (a basket or wreath etc.) by interlacing rods or flowers etc. 4 tr. **a** (foll. by into) make (facts etc.) into a story or connected whole. **b** make (a story) in this way. —n. a style of weaving. [OE wefan f. Gmc]

weave[2] /wiːv/ v.intr. 1 move repeatedly from side to side; take an intricate course to avoid obstructions. 2 colloq. manoeuvre an aircraft in this way; take evasive action. □ **get weaving** sl. begin action; hurry. [prob. f. ME weve, var. of waive f. ON veifa WAVE]

weaver /ˈwiːvə(r)/ n. 1 a person whose occupation is weaving. 2 (in full **weaver-bird**) any tropical bird of the family Ploceidae, building elaborately woven nests. □ **weaver's knot** a sheet bend (see SHEET[2]) used in weaving.

web /web/ n. & v. —n. 1 **a** a woven fabric. **b** an amount woven in one piece. 2 a complete structure or connected series (a web of lies). 3 a cobweb, gossamer, or a similar product of a spinning creature. 4 **a** a membrane between the toes of a swimming animal or bird. **b** the vane of a bird's feather. 5 **a** a large roll of paper used in a continuous printing process. **b** an endless wire mesh on rollers, on which this is made. 6 a thin flat part connecting thicker or more solid parts in machinery etc. —v. (**webbed**, **webbing**) 1 tr. weave a web on. 2 intr. weave a web. □ **web-footed** having the toes connected by webs. **web offset** offset printing on a web of paper. **web-wheel** a wheel having a plate or web instead of spokes, or with rim, spokes, and centre in one piece as in watch-wheels. **web-worm** US a gregarious caterpillar spinning a large web in which to sleep or to feed on enclosed foliage. □□ **webbed** adj. [OE web, webb f. Gmc]

Webb[1] /web/, (Gladys) Mary (1881–1927), English novelist. Her tales of rustic life, romantic, passionate, morbid, and frequently naïve, are written in a fervid prose easily ridiculed by Stella Gibbons in Cold Comfort Farm (1932), but retain a certain emotional power. They include Gone to Earth (1917) and Precious Bane (1924). Public praise of the latter by the Prime Minister Stanley Baldwin, after her death, brought her posthumous fame.

Webb[2] /web/, Sidney James (1859–1947), English socialist, who with his wife Beatrice (1858–1943), in a life of public service and private happiness, exerted considerable influence on political theory and social reform. They were prominent members of the Fabian Society, and launched the idea which culminated in the founding of the London School of Economics (1895), to which they gave unwearying service. Together they produced several important books on socio-political theory and history, most notably The History of Trade Unionism (1894) and Industrial Democracy (1897). Sidney's involvement with the Labour Party led to his decision to stand for Parliament; he became an MP in 1922 and was made a peer (Baron Passfield) in 1929.

webbing /ˈwebɪŋ/ n. strong narrow closely-woven fabric used for supporting upholstery, for belts, etc.

Weber[1] /ˈveɪbə(r)/, Carl Maria von (1786–1826), German composer, especially of operas, orchestral works, and piano music. His first major operatic success was Der Freischütz (The Freeshooter, 1817–21). The importance of this work for German opera was considerable: it became immensely popular at a time when Italian opera dominated, and it formed the focal point of Weber's influence on Wagner with its anticipation of Wagner's leitmotiv technique. His subsequent works were less successful as self-contained forms but contain some fine music; they include Euryanthe (1822–3) and Oberon (1825–6), composed for London, where he died of tuberculosis. In 1844 his coffin was shipped back to Germany and buried in Dresden after a funeral oration by Wagner.

Weber[2] /ˈveɪbə(r)/, Max (1864–1920), German economist, successively professor at Berlin, Freiburg, Heidelberg, and Munich, most famous for his work on the relationship between economy and society, which established him as one of the founders of modern sociology. His influential The Protestant Ethic and the Spirit of Capitalism (1904–5) put forward the theory that there was a direct relationship between the Calvinist work ethic and the rise of Western capitalism.

weber /ˈveɪbə(r)/ n. the SI unit of magnetic flux, causing the electromotive force of one volt in a circuit of one turn when generated or removed in one second. ¶ Abbr.: **Wb**. [W. E. Weber, Ger. physicist d. 1891]

Webern /ˈveɪbən/, Anton (1883–1945), Austrian composer, an important pupil of Schoenberg. His music is marked by its brevity and clarity of expression—from the atonality of his three sets of songs to verses by Stefan George (1907–17) and increasingly concise orchestral works, to the strict serialism of the Symphony (1928), the String Quartet (1937–8), and the Orchestral Variations (1940). Webern survived the Second World War in Vienna, despite having his music proscribed by the Nazis, but was shot, accidentally, by an American soldier during the postwar occupation of Austria.

Webster[1] /ˈwebstə(r)/, John (c.1578–c.1632), English dramatist, son of a London coachmaker. Little is known of his life. He wrote several plays in collaboration with other dramatists but his great reputation rests on his own two major tragedies The White Devil (1609–12) and The Duchess of Malfi (1623), both of which are marked by a rich poetic texture and an intense tragic power. In the 19th c. critics complained about Webster's excessive use of horror, but in recent years there has been a revival of interest in his plays as drama and in Webster as a satirist and moralist.

Webster[2] /ˈwebstə(r)/, Noah (1758–1843), American lexicographer and philologist, remembered for his scholarly American Dictionary of the English Language (2 vols., 1828; there were many subsequent revisions) in which he challenged the parochialism of British dictionaries and, with a strong national pride and spirit, recorded Americanisms and American usages.

Wed. abbr. Wednesday.

wed /wed/ v.tr. & intr. (**wedding**; past and past part. **wedded** or **wed**) 1 usu. formal or literary **a** tr. & intr. marry. **b** tr. join in marriage. 2 tr. unite (wed efficiency to economy). 3 tr. (as **wedded** adj.) of or in marriage (wedded bliss). 4 tr. (as **wedded** adj.) (foll. by to) obstinately attached or devoted (to a pursuit etc.). [OE weddian to pledge f. Gmc]

we'd /wiːd, wɪd/ contr. 1 we had. 2 we should; we would.

Weddell Sea /ˈwed(ə)l/ an arm of the Atlantic Ocean lying to the east of the Antarctic Peninsula. It is named after its discoverer, the British explorer James Weddell (1787–1834).

wedding /ˈwedɪŋ/ n. a marriage ceremony (considered by itself or with the associated celebrations). □ **wedding breakfast** a meal etc. usually served between a wedding and the departure for the honeymoon. **wedding cake** a rich iced cake served at a wedding reception. **wedding day** the day or anniversary of a wedding. **wedding march** a march played at the entrance of the bride or the exit of the couple at a wedding. **wedding night** the night after a wedding (esp. with ref. to its consummation). **wedding ring** a ring worn by a married person. [OE weddung (as WED, -ING[1])]

wedge[1] /wedʒ/ n. & v. —n. 1 a piece of wood or metal etc. tapering to a sharp edge, that is driven between two objects or parts of an object to secure or separate them. 2 anything resembling a wedge (a wedge of cheese; troops formed a wedge). 3 a golf club with a wedge-shaped head. 4 **a** a wedge-shaped heel. **b** a shoe with this. —v.tr. 1 tighten, secure, or fasten by means of a wedge (wedged the door open). 2 force open or apart with a wedge. 3 (foll. by in, into) pack or thrust (a thing or oneself) tightly in or into. □ **thin end of the wedge** colloq. an action or procedure of little importance in itself, but likely to lead to more serious developments. **wedge-shaped 1** shaped like a solid wedge. 2 V-shaped. □□ **wedgelike** adj. **wedgewise** adv. [OE wecg f. Gmc]

wedge[2] /wedʒ/ v.tr. Pottery prepare (clay) for use by cutting, kneading, and throwing down. [17th c.: orig. uncert.]

æ cat ɑː arm e bed ɜː her ɪ sit iː see ɒ hot ɔː saw ʌ run ʊ put uː too ə ago aɪ my

wedgie /ˈwedʒɪ/ n. colloq. a shoe with an extended wedge-shaped heel.

Wedgwood[1] /ˈwedʒwʊd/, Josiah (1730–95), English potter, whose artistic and entrepreneurial skills helped to establish a Staffordshire factory of international repute. He produced china which could be afforded by all classes, and his productions document the rise of neoclassical taste in England; his designs were often based on antique relief sculptures. The factory is perhaps best known for powder-blue pieces with white embossed cameos or patterns. Among the artists employed to produce designs were George Stubbs and John Flaxman.

Wedgwood[2] /ˈwedʒwʊd/ n. propr. **1** ceramic ware made by J. Wedgwood, and his successors, esp. a kind of fine stoneware usu. with a white cameo design. **2** the characteristic blue colour of this stoneware.

wedlock /ˈwedlɒk/ n. the married state. □ **born in** (or **out of**) **wedlock** born of married (or unmarried) parents. [OE wedlāc marriage vow f. wed pledge (rel. to WED) + -lāc suffix denoting action]

Wednesday /ˈwenzdeɪ, -dɪ/ n. & adv. —n. the fourth day of the week, following Tuesday. —adv. colloq. **1** on Wednesday. **2** (**Wednesdays**) on Wednesdays; each Wednesday. [ME wednesdei, OE wōdnesdæg day of (the god) Odin or Woden, the chief Norse god, whose name was substituted for that of Mercury; the Late Latin name was Mercurii dies day of Mercury]

Weds. abbr. Wednesday.

wee[1] /wiː/ adj. (**weer** /ˈwiːə(r)/; **weest** /ˈwiːɪst/) **1** esp. Sc. little; very small. **2** colloq. tiny; extremely small (a wee bit). [orig. Sc. noun, f. north.ME wei (small) quantity f. Anglian wēg: cf. WEY]

wee[2] /wiː/ n. esp. Brit. sl. = WEE-WEE.

weed /wiːd/ n. & v. —n. **1 a** a wild plant growing where it is not wanted. **2** a thin weak-looking person or horse. **3** (prec. by the) sl. **a** marijuana. **b** tobacco. —v. **1** tr. clear (an area) of weeds. **b** remove unwanted parts from. **2** tr. (foll. by out) **a** sort out (inferior or unwanted parts etc.) for removal. **b** rid (a quantity or company) of inferior or unwanted members etc. **3** intr. cut off or uproot weeds. □ **weed-grown** overgrown with weeds. **weed-killer a substance used to destroy weeds.** □□ **weeder** n. **weedless** adj. [OE wēod, of unkn. orig.]

weeds /wiːdʒ/ n.pl. (in full **widow's weeds**) archaic deep mourning worn by a widow. [OE wǣd(e) garment f. Gmc]

weedy /ˈwiːdɪ/ adj. (**weedier**, **weediest**) **1** having many weeds. **2** (esp. of a person) weak, feeble; of poor stature. □□ **weediness** n.

week /wiːk/ n. **1** a period of seven days reckoned usu. from and to midnight on Saturday–Sunday. (See below.) **2** a period of seven days reckoned from any point (would like to stay for a week). **3** the six days between Sundays. **4 a** the five days Monday to Friday. **b** a normal amount of work done in this period (a 35-hour week). **5** (in pl.) a long time; several weeks (have not seen you for weeks; did it weeks ago). **6** (prec. by a specified day) a week after (that day) (Tuesday week; tomorrow week). [OE wice f. Gmc, prob. orig. = sequence]

Days were grouped in sevens by the ancient Babylonians, who named them after the five planets known in ancient astronomy and the Sun and the Moon; each day bore the name of the planet supposed to govern its first hour. The system was later adopted by the Romans, though in ancient Italy it was customary to have market days at intervals of eight days, marked on calendars by a continuous series of letters A–H, the first day being market day. The planetary names were introduced into Roman usage shortly before the Christian era; their English names are the Teutonic equivalents of these (see the entries for individual days). The concept of a day of rest specially dedicated to God was taken over from Judaism by the first Christians, and soon transferred to the first day of the week in honour of the Resurrection, which took place on that day.

weekday /ˈwiːkdeɪ/ n. a day other than Sunday or other than at a weekend (often attrib.: a weekday afternoon).

weekend /wiːkˈend, ˈwiːk-/ n. & v. —n. **1** Sunday and Saturday or part of Saturday. **2** this period extended slightly esp. for a holiday or visit etc. (going away for the weekend; a weekend cottage). —v.intr. spend a weekend (decided to weekend in the country).

weekender /wiːkˈendə(r)/ n. **1** a person who spends weekends away from home. **2** Austral. colloq. a holiday cottage.

weeklong /ˈwiːklɒŋ/ adj. lasting for a week.

weekly /ˈwiːklɪ/ adj., adv., & n. —adj. done, produced, or occurring once a week. —adv. once a week; from week to week. —n. (pl. **-ies**) a weekly newspaper or periodical.

ween /wiːn/ v.tr. archaic be of the opinion; think, suppose. [OE wēnan f. Gmc]

weeny /ˈwiːnɪ/ adj. (**weenier**, **weeniest**) colloq. tiny. □ **weeny-bopper** a girl like a teeny-bopper but younger. [WEE[1] after tiny, teeny]

weep /wiːp/ v. & n. —v. (past and past part. **wept** /wept/) **1** intr. shed tears. **2 a** tr. & (foll. by for) intr. shed tears for; bewail, lament over. **b** tr. utter or express with tears ('Don't go,' he wept; wept her thanks). **3 a** intr. be covered with or send forth drops. **b** intr. & tr. come or send forth in drops; exude liquid (weeping sore). **4** intr. (as **weeping** adj.) (of a tree) having drooping branches (weeping willow). —n. a fit or spell of weeping. □ **Weeping Cross** hist. a wayside cross for penitents to pray at. **weep out** utter with tears. □□ **weepingly** adv. [OE wēpan f. Gmc (prob. imit.)]

weeper /ˈwiːpə(r)/ n. **1** a person who weeps, esp. hist. a hired mourner at a funeral. **2** a small image of a mourner on a monument. **3** (in pl.) hist. **a** a man's crape hatband for funerals. **b** a widow's black crape veil or white cuffs.

weepie /ˈwiːpɪ/ n. (also **weepy**) (pl. **-ies**) colloq. a sentimental or emotional film, play, etc.

weepy /ˈwiːpɪ/ adj. (**weepier**, **weepiest**) colloq. inclined to weep; tearful. □□ **weepily** adv. **weepiness** n.

weever /ˈwiːvə(r)/ n. any marine fish of the genus Trachinus, with sharp venomous dorsal spines. [perh. f. OF wivre, guivre, serpent, dragon, f. L vipera VIPER]

weevil /ˈwiːvɪl/ n. **1** any destructive beetle of the family Curculionidae, with its head extended into a beak or rostrum and feeding esp. on grain. **2** any insect damaging stored grain. □□ **weevily** adj. [ME f. MLG wevel f. Gmc]

wee-wee /ˈwiːwiː/ n. & v. esp. Brit. sl. —n. **1** the act or an instance of urinating. **2** urine. —v.intr. (**-wees**, **-weed**) urinate. [20th c.: orig. unkn.]

w.e.f. abbr. with effect from.

weft[1] /weft/ n. **1 a** the threads woven across a warp to make fabric. **b** yarn for these. **c** a thing woven. **2** filling-strips in basket-weaving. [OE weft(a) f. Gmc: rel. to WEAVE[1]]

weft[2] var. of WAFT n. 3.

Wegener /ˈveɪɡənə(r)/, Alfred Lothar (1880–1930), German meteorologist and geologist, who from 1910 onwards propounded a detailed theory of continental drift (see CONTINENTAL). The theory was not accepted by most geologists during his lifetime, partly because he could not provide a convincing motive force to account for continental movements, but it is now accepted as correct in principle. As well as his geological studies Wegener wrote a standard textbook of meteorology. He died on the Greenland ice-cap in 1930 during an expedition.

Wehrmacht /ˈveərmɑːxt/ n. hist. the German armed forces, esp. the army, from 1921 to 1945. [G, = defensive force]

Wei /weɪ/ the name of several dynasties which ruled in China, especially that of 386–535.

weigh[1] /weɪ/ v. **1** tr. find the weight of. **2** tr. balance in the hands to guess or as if to guess the weight of. **3** tr. (often foll. by out) **a** take a definite weight of; take a specified weight from a larger quantity. **b** distribute in exact amounts by weight. **4** tr. **a** estimate the relative value, importance, or desirability of; consider with a view to choice, rejection, or preference (weighed the consequences; weighed the merits of the candidates). **b** (foll. by with, against) compare (one consideration with another). **5** tr. be equal to (a specified weight) (weighs three kilos; weighs very little). **6** intr. **a** have (esp. a specified) importance; exert an influence. **b** (foll. by with) be regarded as important by (the point that weighs with me). **7** intr. (often foll. by on) be heavy or burdensome (to); be depressing (to). □ **weigh anchor** see ANCHOR. **weigh down 1** bring or keep down by exerting weight. **2** be oppressive or burdensome to (*weighed down with worries*). **weigh in** (of a boxer before a contest, or a jockey after a race) be weighed. **weigh-in** *n.* the weighing of a boxer before a fight. **weighing-machine** a machine for weighing persons or large weights. **weigh into** *colloq.* attack (physically or verbally). **weigh in with** *colloq.* advance (an argument etc.) assertively or boldly. **weigh out** (of a jockey) be weighed before a race. **weigh up** *colloq.* form an estimate of; consider carefully. **weigh one's words** carefully choose the way one expresses something. □□ **weighable** *adj.* **weigher** *n.* [OE *wegan* f. Gmc, rel. to WAY]

weigh[2] /weɪ/ *n.* □ **under weigh** *disp.* = *under way.* [18th c.: from an erron. assoc. with *weigh anchor*]

weighbridge /'weɪbrɪdʒ/ *n.* a weighing-machine for vehicles, usu. having a plate set into the road for vehicles to drive on to.

weight /weɪt/ *n. & v.* —*n.* **1** *Physics* **a** the force experienced by a body as a result of the earth's gravitation (cf. MASS[1] *n.* 8). **b** any similar force with which a body tends to a centre of attraction. **2** the heaviness of a body regarded as a property of it; its relative mass or the quantity of matter contained by it giving rise to a downward force (*is twice your weight; kept in position by its weight*). **3 a** the quantitative expression of a body's weight (*has a weight of three pounds*). **b** a scale of such weights (*troy weight*). **4** a body of a known weight for use in weighing. **5** a heavy body esp. used in a mechanism etc. (*a clock worked by weights*). **6** a load or burden (*a weight off my mind*). **7 a** influence, importance (*carried weight with the public*). **b** preponderance (*the weight of evidence was against them*). **8** a heavy object thrown as an athletic exercise; = SHOT[1] 7. **9** the surface density of cloth etc. as a measure of its suitability. —*v.tr.* **1 a** attach a weight to. **b** hold down with a weight or weights. **2** (foll. by *with*) impede or burden. **3** *Statistics* multiply the components of (an average) by factors to take account of their importance. **4** assign a handicap weight to (a horse). **5** treat (a fabric) with a mineral etc. to make it seem stouter. □ **put on weight 1** increase one's weight. **2** get fat. **throw one's weight about** (or **around**) *colloq.* be unpleasantly self-assertive. **weight training** a system of physical training using weights in the form of barbells or dumb-bells. **worth one's weight in gold** (of a person) exceedingly useful or helpful. [OE *(ge)wiht* f. Gmc: cf. WEIGH[1]]

weighting /'weɪtɪŋ/ *n.* an extra allowance paid in special cases, esp. to allow for a higher cost of living (*London weighting*).

weightless /'weɪtlɪs/ *adj.* (of a body, esp. in an orbiting space-craft etc.) not apparently acted on by gravity. □□ **weightlessly** *adv.* **weightlessness** *n.*

weightlifting /'weɪtˌlɪftɪŋ/ *n.* the athletic sport of lifting heavy objects. The ancient Greeks lifted heavy stones as a pastime, and the custom persisted in many parts of Europe through the Middle Ages. Modern weightlifting with barbells and dumb-bells became popular towards the end of the 19th c. and was fostered by strong-man acts in circuses and music-halls. □□ **weightlifter** *n.*

weighty /'weɪtɪ/ *adj.* (**weightier, weightiest**) **1** weighing much; heavy. **2** momentous, important. **3** (of utterances etc.) deserving consideration; careful and serious. **4** influential, authoritative. □□ **weightily** *adv.* **weightiness** *n.*

Weil /vaɪl/, Simone (1909–43), French essayist and philosopher, who devoted herself to resisting the oppression inherent in organized institutions and to achieving identification with the sufferings of its victims. She worked on the shop floor of the Renault factory, took part in the Spanish Civil War (1936), and joined the French Resistance movement. Her religious thinking is in the mystic tradition, but she remained outside the Church and uncommitted to any religious or political institution.

Weill /vaɪl/, Kurt (1900–50), German composer. He studied in Berlin, where he remained until 1933, employing the art of the cabaret in his collaborations with the dramatist Bertolt Brecht to produce satirical works such as *The Rise and Fall of the City of Mahagonny* (1930), *The Threepenny Opera* (1928), and *The Seven Deadly Sins* (1933). He married the Austrian-born singer Lotte Lenya, the supreme exponent of his songs, most memorably

'Pirate Jenny' and 'Surabaya Johnny'. Weill continued to compose after settling in the US but produced nothing to equal the works of his Berlin years, which brilliantly evoke the harsh decadence of the period leading up to Hitler's rise to power.

Weimar /'vaɪmɑː(r)/ a town in central Germany (pop., 1981, 63,725), famous as the residence of Goethe and Schiller and as the seat of the National Assembly of Germany 1919–33. □ **Weimar Republic** the German republic of this period, so called because its constitution was drawn up at Weimar.

Weimaraner /ˌvaɪmɑˈrɑːnə(r), ˌvaɪ-/ *n.* a usu. grey dog of a variety of pointer used as a gun dog. [G, f. WEIMAR, where it was developed]

weir /wɪə(r)/ *n.* **1** a dam built across a river to raise the level of water upstream or regulate its flow. **2** an enclosure of stakes etc. set in a stream as a trap for fish. [OE *wer* f. *werian* dam up]

weird /wɪəd/ *adj. & n.* —*adj.* **1** uncanny, supernatural. **2** *colloq.* strange, queer, incomprehensible. **3** *archaic* connected with fate. —*n.* esp. *Sc. archaic* fate, destiny. □ **the weird sisters 1** the Fates. **2** witches. □□ **weirdly** *adv.* **weirdness** *n.* [(earlier as noun) f. OE *wyrd* destiny f. Gmc]

weirdie /'wɪədɪ/ *n.* (also **weirdy**) (*pl.* -**ies**) *colloq.* = WEIRDO.

weirdo /'wɪədəʊ/ *n.* (*pl.* -**os**) *colloq.* an odd or eccentric person.

Weismann /'vaɪsman/, August Friedrich Leopold (1834–1914), German biologist, one of the founders of modern genetics. He expounded a theory of heredity which assumed the continuity of 'germ-plasm', a substance which he postulated bore the factors that determine the transmission of characters from parent to offspring, carried by the gametes and itself unchanged from generation to generation. The theory rules out transmission of acquired characteristics.

Weizmann /'vaɪtsman, 'waɪ-/ Chaim Azriel (1874–1952), Zionist leader and scientist. Born in Poland, he became a British subject in 1910. While Palestine was under British administration (1920–48) the World Zionist Organization, under his leadership, played a major part in developing the Jewish community there by facilitating immigration and by land purchase in the 1930s. Weizmann played a crucial role in persuading the US government to recognize the new State of Israel (1948) and became its first President (1948–52).

weka /'wekə/ *n.* any flightless New Zealand rail of the genus *Gallirallus.* [Maori: imit. of its cry]

Welch /welʃ/ var. of WELSH (now only in *Royal Welch Fusiliers*).

welch var. of WELSH.

welcome /'welkəm/ *n., int., v., & adj.* —*n.* the act or an instance of greeting or receiving (a person, idea, etc.) gladly; kind or glad reception (*gave them a warm welcome*). —*int.* expressing such a greeting (*welcome!; welcome home!*). —*v.tr.* receive with a welcome (*welcomed them home; would welcome the opportunity*). —*adj.* **1** that one receives with pleasure (*a welcome guest; welcome news*). **2** (foll. by *to*, or *to* + infin.) **a** cordially allowed or invited; released of obligation (*you are welcome to use my car*). **b** *iron.* gladly given (an unwelcome task, thing, etc.) (*here's my work and you are welcome to it*). □ **make welcome** receive hospitably. **outstay one's welcome** stay too long as a visitor etc. **you are welcome** there is no need for thanks. □□ **welcomely** *adv.* **welcomeness** *n.* **welcomer** *n.* **welcomingly** *adv.* [orig. OE *wilcuma* one whose coming is pleasing f. *wil-* desire, pleasure + *cuma* comer, with later change to *wel-* WELL[1] after OF *bien venu* or ON *velkominn*]

weld[1] /weld/ *v. & n.* —*v.tr.* **1 a** hammer or press (pieces of iron or other metal usu. heated but not melted) into one piece. **b** join by fusion with an electric arc etc. **c** form by welding into some article. **2** fashion (arguments, members of a group, etc.) into an effectual or homogeneous whole. —*n.* a welded joint. □□ **weldable** *adj.* **weldability** /-'bɪlɪtɪ/ *n.* **welder** *n.* [alt. of WELL[2] *v.* in obs. sense 'melt or weld (heated metal)', prob. infl. by past part.]

weld[2] /weld/ *n.* **1** a plant, *Reseda luteola*, yielding a yellow dye. **2** *hist.* this dye. [ME f. OE *w(e)alde* (unrecorded): cf. MDu. *woude*, MLG *walde*]

welfare /'welfeə(r)/ *n.* **1** well-being, happiness; health and prosperity (of a person or a community etc.). **2** (**Welfare**) **a** the maintenance of persons in such a condition esp. by statutory procedure or social effort. **b** financial support given for this purpose. □ **welfare state 1** a system whereby the State undertakes to protect the health and well-being of its citizens, esp. those in financial or social need, by means of grants, pensions, etc. **2** a country practising this system. **welfare work** organized effort for the welfare of the poor, disabled, etc. [ME f. WELL¹ + FARE]

welfarism /ˈwelfeəˌrɪz(ə)m/ *n.* principles characteristic of a welfare state. □□ **welfarist** *n.*

welkin /ˈwelkɪn/ *n. poet.* sky; the upper air. [OE *wolcen* cloud, sky]

well¹ /wel/ *adv., adj., & int.* —*adv.* (**better, best**) **1** in a satisfactory way (*you have worked well*). **2** in the right way (*well said; you did well to tell me*). **3** with some talent or distinction (*plays the piano well*). **4** in a kind way (*treated me well*). **5** thoroughly, carefully (*polish it well*). **6** with heartiness or approval; favourably (*speak well of; the book was well reviewed*). **7** probably, reasonably, advisably (*you may well be right; you may well ask; we might well take the risk*). **8** to a considerable extent (*is well over forty*). **9** successfully, fortunately (*it turned out well*). **10** luckily, opportunely (*well met!*). **11** with a fortunate outcome; without disaster (*were well rid of them*). **12** profitably (*did well for themselves*). **13** comfortably, abundantly, liberally (*we live well here; the job pays well*). —*adj.* (**better, best**) **1** (*usu. predic.*) in good health (*are you well?; was not a well person*). **2** (*predic.*) **a** in a satisfactory state or position (*all is well*). **b** advisable (*it would be well to enquire*). —*int.* expressing surprise, resignation, insistence, etc., or resumption or continuation of talk, used esp. after a pause in speaking (*well I never!; well, I suppose so; well, who was it?*). □ **as well 1** in addition; to an equal extent. **2** (also **just as well**) with equal reason; with no loss of advantage or need for regret (*may as well give up; it would be just as well to stop now*). **as well as** in addition to. **leave** (or **let**) **well alone** avoid needless change or disturbance. **well-acquainted** (*usu. foll. by with*) familiar. **well-adjusted 1** in a good state of adjustment. **2** *Psychol.* mentally and emotionally stable. **well-advised** (*usu. foll. by to* + *infin.*) (of a person) prudent (*would be well-advised to wait*). **well-affected** (often foll. by *to, towards*) favourably disposed. **well and good** expressing dispassionate acceptance of a decision etc. **well and truly** decisively, completely. **well-appointed** having all the necessary equipment. **well aware** certainly aware (*well aware of the danger*). **well away 1** having made considerable progress. **2** *colloq.* fast asleep or drunk. **well-balanced 1** sane, sensible. **2** equally matched. **well-behaved** see BEHAVE. **well-being** a state of being well, healthy, contented, etc. **well-beloved** *adj.* dearly loved. —*n.* (*pl. same*) a dearly loved person. **well-born** of noble family. **well-bred** having or showing good breeding or manners. **well-built 1** of good construction. **2** (of a person) big and strong and well-proportioned. **well-chosen** (of words etc.) carefully selected for effect. **well-conditioned** in good physical or moral condition. **well-conducted** (of a meeting etc.) properly organized and controlled. **well-connected** see CONNECTED. **well-covered** *colloq.* plump, corpulent. **well-defined** clearly indicated or determined. **well-deserved** rightfully merited or earned. **well-disposed** (often foll. by *towards*) having a good disposition or friendly feeling (for). **well done 1** (of meat etc.) thoroughly cooked. **2** (of a task etc.) performed well (also as *int.*). **well-dressed** fashionably smart. **well-earned** fully deserved. **well-endowed 1** well provided with talent etc. **2** *colloq.* sexually potent or attractive. **well-favoured** good-looking. **well-fed** having or having had plenty to eat. **well-found** = *well-appointed*. **well-founded** (of suspicions etc.) based on good evidence; having a foundation in fact or reason. **well-groomed** (of a person) with carefully tended hair, clothes, etc. **well-grounded 1** = *well-founded*. **2** having a good training in or knowledge of the groundwork of a subject. **well-heeled** *colloq.* wealthy. **well-hung** *colloq.* (of a man) having large genitals. **well-informed** having much knowledge or information about a subject. **well-intentioned** having or showing good intentions. **well-judged** opportunely, skilfully, or discreetly done. **well-kept** kept in good order or condition. **well-knit** (esp. of a person) compact; not loose-jointed or sprawling. **well-known 1** known to many. **2** known thoroughly. **well-made 1** strongly or skilfully manufactured. **2** (of a person or animal) having a

good build. **well-mannered** having good manners. **well-marked** distinct; easy to detect. **well-matched** see MATCH¹. **well-meaning** (or **-meant**) well-intentioned (but ineffective or unwise). **well off 1** having plenty of money. **2** in a fortunate situation or circumstances. **well-oiled** *colloq.* **1** drunk. **2** (of a compliment etc.) easily expressed through habitual use. **well-ordered** arranged in an orderly manner. **well-paid 1** (of a job) that pays well. **2** (of a person) amply rewarded for a job. **well-pleased** highly gratified or satisfied. **well-preserved** see PRESERVE. **well-read** knowledgeable through much reading. **well-received** welcomed; favourably received. **well-rounded 1** complete and symmetrical. **2** (of a phrase etc.) complete and well expressed. **3** (of a person) having or showing a fully developed personality, ability, etc. **well-spent** (esp. of money or time) used profitably. **well-spoken** articulate or refined in speech. **well-thought-of** having a good reputation; esteemed, respected. **well-thought-out** carefully devised. **well-thumbed** bearing marks of frequent handling. **well-timed** opportune, timely. **well-to-do** prosperous. **well-tried** often tested with good results. **well-trodden** much frequented. **well-turned 1** (of a compliment, phrase, or verse) elegantly expressed. **2** (of a leg, ankle, etc.) elegantly shaped or displayed. **well-upholstered** see UPHOLSTER. **well-wisher** a person who wishes one well. **well-woman** a woman who has undergone satisfactory gynaecological tests (often *attrib.: well-woman clinic*). **well-worn 1** much worn by use. **2** (of a phrase etc.) trite, hackneyed. **well worth** certainly worth (*well worth a visit; well worth visiting*). ¶ A hyphen is normally used in combinations of *well-* when used attributively, but not when used predicatively, e.g. *a well-made coat* but *the coat is well made*. □□ **wellness** *n.* [OE *wel, well* prob. f. the same stem as WILL¹]

well² /wel/ *n. & v.* —*n.* **1** a shaft sunk into the ground to obtain water, oil, etc. **2** an enclosed space like a well-shaft, e.g. in the middle of a building for stairs or a lift, or for light or ventilation. **3** (foll. by *of*) a source, esp. a copious one (*a well of information*). **4 a** a mineral spring. **b** (in *pl.*) a spa. **5** = *ink-well*. **6** *archaic* a water-spring or fountain. **7** *Brit.* a railed space for solicitors etc. in a lawcourt. **8** a depression for gravy etc. in a dish or tray, or for a mat in the floor. **9** *Physics* a region of minimum potential etc. —*v.intr.* (foll. by *out, up*) spring as from a fountain; flow copiously. □ **well-head** (or **-spring**) a source. [OE *wella* (= OHG *wella* wave, ON *vella* boiling heat), *wellan* boil, melt f. Gmc]

we'll /wiːl, wɪl/ *contr.* we shall; we will.

Welles /welz/, (George) Orson (1915–85), American film director and actor, a man of wayward talents whose career was both brilliant and erratic. The classic *Citizen Kane* (1941) was one of the peaks of his achievement.

wellies /ˈwelɪz/ *n.pl. Brit. colloq.* wellingtons. [abbr.]

Wellington¹ /ˈwelɪŋt(ə)n/ the capital of New Zealand, situated at the south end of North Island; pop. (1988) 325,200.

Wellington² /ˈwelɪŋt(ə)n/ Arthur Wellesley, 1st Duke of (1769–1852), British soldier and statesman, known as the 'Iron Duke'. The son of an Irish peer, Wellesley first achieved prominence as a result of his victory over the Marathas in India in 1803. As commander of British forces in the Spanish Peninsula (1809–14) he won a series of victories against French forces and finally drove them across the Pyrenees into southern France, then in 1815 he decisively defeated Napoleon at the Battle of Waterloo, bringing the Napoleonic Wars to an end. A convinced conservative, Wellington served in a variety of political posts between 1819 and 1846, including that of Prime Minister (1828–30 and briefly in 1834), often accepting change against his personal inclinations. He served as Commander-in-Chief of the army from 1842 until his death, being widely considered in his later years the senior statesman on the British scene.

wellington /ˈwelɪŋt(ə)n/ *n.* (in full **wellington boot**) *Brit.* a waterproof rubber or plastic boot usu. reaching the knee. [after the 1st Duke of WELLINGTON²]

wellnigh /ˈwelnaɪ/ *adv. archaic* or *rhet.* almost (*wellnigh impossible*).

Wells /welz/, Herbert George (1866–1946), English novelist, the

w *we* z *zoo* ʃ *she* ʒ *decision* θ *thin* ð *this* ŋ *ring* x *loch* tʃ *chip* dʒ *jar* (*see over for vowels*)

son of a tradesman and professional cricketer. He was apprenticed to a draper, and studied science under the influence of T. H. Huxley. In 1903 he joined the Fabian Society but his provocative independence caused a rift with Shaw and the Webbs. His vast and varied literary output included early examples of science fiction, such as *The Time Machine* (1895), *The Invisible Man* (1897), and *The War of the Worlds* (1898), which combine political satire, warnings about the dangers of scientific advancement, and a hope for the future. He also wrote novels evoking, in comic realistic style, the lower-middle-class world of his youth: *Kipps* (1905) and *The History of Mr Polly* (1910). Among his other writings are the highly successful *Tono-Bungay* (1909), which he described as 'a social panorama in the vein of Balzac', and many works of scientific and political speculation (including *The Shape of Things to Come*, 1933) which confirmed his position as a great popularizer and one of the most influential voices of his age.

Wells, Fargo & Co. /welz ˈfɑːgəʊ/ US express company founded in 1852 by an American businessman, Henry Wells (1805–78), William Fargo (1818–81), and others. It carried mail to and from the newly developed West, originally by sea from New York to San Francisco (travelling overland at the Isthmus of Panama), founded a San Francisco bank, and later ran a stagecoach service (having bought the Pony Express and Southern Overland Mail empire) until the development of a transcontinental railway service. In 1918 it merged with other companies to form the American Railway Express Company.

Welsh /welʃ/ *adj. & n.* —*adj.* of or relating to Wales or its people or language. —*n.* **1** the Celtic language of Wales. (See below.) **2** (prec. by *the*; treated as *pl.*) the people of Wales. □ **Welsh corgi** see CORGI. **Welsh dresser** a type of dresser with open shelves above a cupboard. **Welsh harp** a harp with three rows of strings. **Welsh onion** a species of onion, *Allium fistulosum*, forming clusters of bulbs. **Welsh rabbit** (or **rarebit** by folk etymology) a dish of melted cheese etc. on toast. [OE *Welisc, Wælisc*, etc., f. Gmc f. L *Volcae*, the name of a Celtic people]

Welsh belongs to the Brythonic group of the Celtic languages. It is spoken by about 500,000 people in Wales and has a substantial literature dating from the medieval period. When Wales was united with England in 1536 it seemed likely that Welsh would disappear as a living language, but the publication of a Bible in Welsh in 1588 played an important part in preserving it. Although under great pressure from English, Welsh is widely used and taught in Wales. It is written almost phonetically, each letter (except *y*) having one standard sound only.

welsh /welʃ/ *v.intr.* (also **welch** /weltʃ/) **1** (of a loser of a bet, esp. a bookmaker) decamp without paying. **2** evade an obligation. **3** (foll. by *on*) **a** fail to carry out a promise to (a person). **b** fail to honour (an obligation). □□ **welsher** *n.* [19th c.: orig. unkn.]

Welshman /ˈwelʃmən/ *n.* (*pl.* **-men**) a man who is Welsh by birth or descent.

Welshwoman /ˈwelʃwʊmən/ *n.* (*pl.* **-women**) a woman who is Welsh by birth or descent.

welt /welt/ *n. & v.* —*n.* **1** a leather rim sewn round the edge of a shoe-upper for the sole to be attached to. **2** = WEAL[1]. **3** a ribbed or reinforced border of a garment; a trimming. **4** a heavy blow. —*v.tr.* **1** provide with a welt. **2** rain welts on; thrash. [ME *welte, walt*, of unkn. orig.]

Weltanschauung /ˌveltanˈʃaʊʊŋ/ *n.* a particular philosophy or view of life; a conception of the world. [G f. *Welt* world + *Anschauung* perception]

welter[1] /ˈweltə(r)/ *v. & n.* —*v.intr.* **1** roll, wallow; be washed about. **2** (foll. by *in*) lie prostrate or be soaked or steeped in blood etc. —*n.* **1** a state of general confusion. **2** (foll. by *of*) a disorderly mixture or contrast of beliefs, policies, etc. [ME f. MDu., MLG *welteren*]

welter[2] /ˈweltə(r)/ *n.* **1** a heavy rider or boxer. **2** *colloq.* a heavy blow. **3** *colloq.* a big person or thing. [19th c.: orig. unkn.]

welterweight /ˈweltəˌweɪt/ *n.* **1** a weight in certain sports intermediate between lightweight and middleweight, in the amateur boxing scale 63.5–67 kg but differing for professionals, wrestlers, and weightlifters. **2** a sportsman of this weight. □ **junior welterweight 1** a weight in professional boxing of 61.2–

63.5 kg. **2** a professional boxer of this weight. **light welterweight 1** a weight in amateur boxing of 60–63.5 kg. **2** an amateur boxer of this weight.

Weltschmerz /ˈveltʃmeəts/ *n.* a feeling of pessimism; an apathetic or vaguely yearning outlook on life. [G f. *Welt* world + *Schmerz* pain]

wen[1] /wen/ *n.* **1** a benign tumour on the skin esp. of the scalp. **2** an outstandingly large or congested city. □ **the great wen** London. [OE *wen, wenn*, of unkn. orig.: cf. Du. *wen*, MLG *wene*, LG *wehne* tumour, wart]

wen[2] /wen/ *n.* (also **wyn** /wɪn/) a runic letter in Old and Middle English, later replaced by *w*. [OE, var. of *wyn* joy (see WINSOME), used because it begins with this letter: cf. THORN 3]

Wenceslas[1] /ˈwensɪsləs/ (also **Wenceslaus**), St (907–29), prince of Bohemia and patron saint of Czechoslovakia. He worked for the religious and cultural improvement of his people but was murdered by his brother and became venerated as a martyr. The story told in J. M. Neale's carol 'Good King Wenceslas' appears imaginary. Feast day, 28 Sept.

Wenceslas[2] /ˈwensɪsləs/ (also **Wenceslaus**) (1361–1419), king of Bohemia (as Wenceslaus IV) 1378–1419. He became king of Germany and Holy Roman Emperor at the same time as he succeeded to the throne of Bohemia, but was deposed by the German electors in 1400 and afterwards imprisoned in Vienna. He regained the Bohemian throne in 1404 and held it until his death.

wench /wentʃ/ *n. & v.* —*n.* **1** *joc.* a girl or young woman. **2** *archaic* a prostitute. —*v.intr. archaic* (of a man) consort with prostitutes. □□ **wencher** *n.* [ME *wenche, wenchel* f. OE *wencel* child: cf. OE *wancol* weak, tottering]

Wend /wend/ *n.* a member of a Slavic people of N. Germany, now inhabiting E. Saxony. □□ **Wendic** *adj.* **Wendish** *adj.* [G *Wende* f. OHG *Winida*, of unkn. orig.]

wend /wend/ *v.tr. & intr. literary or archaic* go. □ **wend one's way** make one's way. [OE *wendan* turn f. Gmc, rel. to WIND[2]]

Wendy house /ˈwendɪ/ *n.* a children's small houselike tent or structure for playing in. [after the house built around *Wendy* in Barrie's *Peter Pan*]

Wensleydale /ˈwenzlɪˌdeɪl/ *n.* **1** a variety of white or blue cheese. **2 a** a sheep of a breed with long wool. **b** this breed. [*Wensleydale* in Yorkshire]

went *past of* GO[1].

wentletrap /ˈwent(ə)lˌtræp/ *n.* any marine snail of the genus *Clathrus*, with a spiral shell of many whorls. [Du. *wenteltrap* winding stair, spiral shell]

wept *past of* WEEP.

were *2nd sing. past, pl. past, and past subj. of* BE.

we're /wɪə(r)/ *contr.* we are.

weren't /wɜːnt/ *contr.* were not.

werewolf /ˈwɪəwʊlf, ˈweə-/ *n.* (also **werwolf** /ˈwɜː-/) (*pl.* **-wolves**) a mythical being who at times changes from a person to a wolf. [OE *werewulf*: first element perh. f. OE *wer* man = L *vir*]

Werner[1] /ˈvɜːnə(r)/, Abraham Gottlob (1749–1817), German geologist, the chief exponent of the Neptunian theory (see NEPTUNIAN) which included the belief that rocks such as granites (now known to be of igneous origin) were formed as precipitates from a primeval ocean. Although this theory was invalid, the controversy that it stimulated prompted a rapid increase in geological research, and Werner's was probably the first attempt to establish a universal stratigraphic sequence.

Werner[2] /ˈvɜːnə(r)/, Alfred (1866–1919), French-born Swiss chemist, founder of coordination chemistry. He demonstrated that stereochemistry was not just the property of carbon compounds, but was general to the whole of organic and inorganic chemistry. In 1893 he announced the theory of 'coordinating compounds' which had come to him in a flash of inspiration and in which he proposed two types of valency bonds. This theory, which gave fresh insight into the structure of chemical compounds, is fundamental not only to modern inorganic chemistry but also to the analytical, organic, physical, and bio-chemical fields, and the related ones of mineralogy and crystallography. In 1913 he became the first Swiss to be awarded the Nobel Prize for chemistry.

wert archaic 2nd sing. past of BE.

Weser /ˈveɪzə(r)/ a river of NW Germany. Formed at the junction of the Werra and Fulda rivers in Lower Saxony, it flows 292 km (182 miles) northwards to meet the North Sea near Bremerhaven.

Wesker /ˈweskə(r)/, Arnold (1932–), English playwright. His plays are avowedly socialist in outlook; a frequent theme is the working class's need for a cultural identity, as in *Roots* (1959).

Wesley /ˈwezlɪ/, John (1703–91), founder of Methodism. An Anglican priest, he was the leader of an earnest, devout, and scholarly group in Oxford who became known by various names including 'Methodists', and included his brother Charles (1707–88), who later became the composer of many well-known hymns. In 1738 the brothers experienced a spiritual conversion on a visit to the Moravian Church in Saxony, and determined to devote their lives to evangelistic work. Finding the churches closed to him through Anglican opposition, John Wesley began preaching out of doors; his success led him to organize a body of lay pastors to follow up his evangelism, and societies for their many working-class converts. Thenceforward he travelled the British Isles on horseback, averaging 8,000 miles a year; despite some hostility from the clergy he was mostly received with enthusiasm. Wesley himself wished his movement to remain within the Church of England, but an increasingly independent system grew up.

Wesleyan /ˈwezlɪən/ adj. & n. —adj. of or relating to a Protestant denomination founded by John Wesley (d. 1791) (cf. METHODIST). —n. a member of this denomination. □□ **Wesleyanism** n.

Wessex /ˈwesɪks/ the kingdom of the West Saxons, established in Hampshire in the early 6th c. and gradually extended by conquest to include much of southern England. Under Alfred the Great and his successors it formed the nucleus for the Anglo-Saxon kingdom of England. The name was revived by Thomas Hardy to designate the south-western counties of England (especially Dorset) in which his novels are set, and is used in the titles of certain present-day regional authorities.

West[1] /west/, Benjamin (1738–1820), American painter who settled in England in 1763, becoming historical painter to George III and second President of the Royal Academy in 1792. West made his reputation with large historical canvases in the neo-classical style. Later paintings, such as *Saul and the Witch of Endor* (1777) and *Death on a Pale Horse* (1802), are early examples of the Romantic taste for melodrama and fantasy.

West[2] /west/, Mae (1892–1980), American stage and film actress, who perfected a unique image combining sexuality, suggestiveness, and humorous gusto. She wrote plays as vehicles for her standard role—a woman of easy morals, with a ready wit and a toughness that no man could either resist or counter—and had spectacular success on Broadway with *Sex* (1926) and with *Diamond Lil* (1928) which was adapted as a film *She Done Him Wrong* (1933). In an era when a slender boyish shape was the fashion for women, she emphasized her curvaceous hourglass figure. Her legend endured; airmen's inflatable life-jackets were christened 'Mae Wests'. She wrote an entertaining autobiography *Goodness had nothing to do with it* (1960).

West[3] /west/, Dame Rebecca (real name Cicily Isabel Fairfield, 1892–1983), English novelist, journalist, and feminist, much influenced by the Pankhursts and the Women's Suffrage Movement. She chose the name 'Rebecca West' (one of Ibsen's heroines) when writing for *The Freewoman*, a fiercely feminist journal. In her younger days she became known for her beauty and for her shrewd, witty, and combative pieces. Her outspoken review of H. G. Wells's novel *Marriage* (1912) led to their secret love affair and the birth of a son. Among her many novels are *The Return of the Soldier* (1918), describing the return home of a shell-shocked soldier, *The Judge* (1922), and *The Birds Fall Down* (1966). Her non-fiction works include *Black Lamb and Grey Falcon* (1941), a two-volume study on Yugoslavia, and *The Meaning of Treason* (1949; updated in 1965 to include more recent spy scandals), and reports of the Nuremberg war-crimes trials after the Second World War. She continued to write with exceptional vigour almost until her death at the age of 90.

west /west/ n., adj., & adv. —n. **1 a** the point of the horizon where the sun sets at the equinoxes (cardinal point 90° to the left of north). **b** the compass point corresponding to this. **c** the direction in which this lies. **2** (usu. **the West**) **a** European in contrast to Oriental civilization. **b** the non-Communist States of Europe and N. America. **c** the western part of the late Roman Empire. **d** the western part of a country, town, etc. **3** *Bridge* a player occupying the position designated 'west'. —adj. **1** towards, at, near, or facing west. **2** coming from the west (*west wind*). —adv. **1** towards, at, or near the west. **2** (foll. by *of*) further west than. □ **go west** sl. be killed or destroyed etc. **West Country** the south-western counties of England. **West End** the entertainment and shopping area of London to the west of the City. **west-north-** (or **south-**) **west** the direction or compass-point midway between west and north-west (or south-west). **West Side** US the western part of Manhattan. [OE f. Gmc]

West Bank a region west of the River Jordan and north-west of the Dead Sea which became part of Jordan in 1948 and was occupied by Israel in the war of 1967 (see SIX DAY WAR); pop. (est. 1988) 866,000.

West Bengal a State in eastern India, formed in 1947 from the Hindu area of former Bengal; pop. (1981) 54,485,560; capital, Calcutta.

westbound /ˈwestbaʊnd/ adj. travelling or leading westwards.

westering /ˈwestərɪŋ/ adj. (of the sun) nearing the west. [*wester* (v.) ME f. WEST]

westerly /ˈwestəlɪ/ adj., adv., & n. —adj. & adv. **1** in a western position or direction. **2** (of a wind) blowing from the west. —n. (pl. **-ies**) a wind blowing from the west. [*wester* (adj.) f. OE *westra* f. WEST]

western /ˈwest(ə)n/ adj. & n. —adj. **1** of or in the west; inhabiting the west. **2** lying or directed towards the west. **3** (**Western**) of or relating to the West (see WEST n. 2). —n. a film or novel about life in western North America during the wars with the Indians, or involving cowboys etc. (See below.) □ **Western Church** the Churches of western Christendom as distinct from the Eastern or Orthodox Church. **Western Empire** see ROMAN EMPIRE. **Western hemisphere** the half of the earth containing the Americas. **Western roll** a technique of turning the body over the bar in the high jump. □□ **westernmost** adj. [OE *westerne* (as WEST, -ERN)]

Westerns are the oldest and most enduring genre in cinema, their historical setting being traditionally the 1850s to 1890s. In 1908–14 D. W. Griffith made a number of one-reel westerns, and by the 1920s the western was an internationally accepted convention. In the late 1930s and early 1940s it reached maturity, led by *Stagecoach* (1939) directed by John Ford, the greatest director of the genre, and starring John Wayne, its most popular star. From the early 1950s its accepted modes provided a 20th-c. mythology within which a wide variety of ideas could be developed, and its conventions have influenced action films of other cultures.

Western Australia a State comprising the western part of Australia; pop. 1,477,700; capital, Perth. It was first settled by the British in 1826 and 1829, and was federated with the other States of Australia in 1901.

westerner /ˈwestənə(r)/ n. a native or inhabitant of the west.

Western Isles 1 the Hebrides. **2** an islands area of Scotland consisting of the Outer Hebrides; pop. (1981) 31,000.

Western Sahara a former Spanish colony (Spanish Sahara) on the Atlantic coast of NW Africa, annexed by Morocco and Mauritania in 1976 after it had ceased to become a Spanish province; pop. (est. 1988) 181,400; capital, La'youn (El Aaiún). When Mauritania withdrew from the territory in 1979, Morocco extended its control over the entire region. A liberation movement (*Frente Polisario*), which launched a guerrilla war against the Spanish in 1973, has continued its struggle against Morocco in an attempt to establish an independent Saharawi Arab Democratic Republic.

Western Samoa /səˈməʊə/ a country consisting of a group of nine islands in the SW Pacific; pop. (est. 1988) 178,000; official languages, Samoan and English; capital, Apia. Discovered by the Dutch in the early 18th c., the islands were administered by Germany from 1900. After the First World War they were mandated to New Zealand, and became an independent republic within the Commonwealth in 1962. Robert Louis Stevenson settled there in 1890 and died at Apia in 1894.

Western Somalia see OGADEN.

westernize /ˈwestənaɪz/ v.tr. (also **Westernize, -ise**) influence with or convert to the ideas and customs etc. of the West. □□ **westernization** /-ˈzeɪʃ(ə)n/ n. **westernizer** n.

West Glamorgan /gləˈmɔːg(ə)n/ a county of South Wales; pop. (1981) 372,000; county town, Swansea.

West Indies a chain of islands extending from the coast of Florida in North America to that of Venezuela in South America, enclosing the Caribbean Sea. Discovered by Columbus in 1492 and named in the belief that he had discovered the Asian coast, the islands were opened up by the Spanish in the 16th c. and thereafter were the theatre of rivalry between the European colonial powers. Cultivation of sugar was introduced and the population was transformed by the mass importation of West African slaves to work the agricultural plantations; their descendants form the largest group in the population. □□ **West Indian** adj. & n.

westing /ˈwestɪŋ/ n. Naut. the distance travelled or the angle of longitude measured westward from either a defined north–south grid line or a meridian.

Westinghouse /ˈwestɪŋˌhaʊs/, George (1846–1914), American engineer whose achievements covered several different fields: vacuum-operated brakes for railway vehicles which enabled the driver to apply brakes throughout the train and which would act automatically in case of failure in any part of the system; electrically controlled signals for railways; this led him into the generation and transmission of electric power and (through Nikola Tesla) he championed the use of alternating current rather than the direct current used by Thomas Edison. Westinghouse built up a huge enterprise to manufacture his products, both in the US and abroad. He also pioneered the use of natural gas and pneumatic power (compressed air), and installed water turbines at Niagara Falls; altogether he had over 400 patents to his name.

Westman Islands /ˈwestmən/ a group of 15 volcanic islands to the south of Iceland; pop. (1987) 4,700.

Westmeath /westˈmiːð/ a county of Ireland, in the province of Leinster; pop. (est. 1986) 63,300; capital, Mullingar.

West Midlands a metropolitan county of central England; pop. (1981) 2,673,100; county town, Birmingham.

Westminster /ˈwestmɪnstə(r)/ an inner London borough containing the Houses of Parliament (*Palace of Westminster*; see below) and many government offices etc., whence its allusive use to mean British parliamentary life or politics. □ **Palace of Westminster** a palace, supposed to date from Edward the Confessor, on the site now occupied by the Houses of Parliament. It was destroyed by fire in 1512 and ceased to be a royal residence, but a great part of it remained. The Houses of Lords and Commons for a long time sat in its buildings, until these were destroyed by fire in 1834. **Statute of Westminster** the statute of 1931 recognizing the equality of status of the Dominions as autonomous communities within the British Empire, and giving their legislatures independence from British control.

Westminster Abbey the collegiate church of St Peter in Westminster, London, originally the abbey church of a Benedictine monastery. The present building, begun by Henry III in 1245 and altered and added to by successive rulers, replaced an earlier church built by Edward the Confessor. Nearly all the kings and queens of England have been crowned in Westminster Abbey; it is also the burial-place of many of England's monarchs (up to George II) and of the nation's leading statesmen, poets

(in the section called Poets' Corner), and other celebrities, and of the Unknown Warrior.

Westphalia /westˈfeɪlɪə/ a former province of NW Germany which from 1815 formed part of Prussia, now part of the German 'Land' (State) of North Rhine–Westphalia; capital, Dusseldorf. □ **Peace of Westphalia** the peace (1648) which ended the Thirty Years War. □□ **Westphalian** adj. & n.

West Point (in full **West Point Academy**) the US Military Academy, founded in 1802, located on the site of a former strategic fort on the west bank of the Hudson River in New York State.

West Sussex /ˈsʌsɪks/ a county of SE England; pop. (1981) 666,400; county town, Chichester.

West Virginia /vəˈdʒɪnɪə/ a State of the US, to the west of Virginia; pop. (est. 1985) 1,950,200; capital, Charleston. It separated from Virginia during the American Civil War (1861), and became the 35th State of the US in 1863.

westward /ˈwestwəd/ adj., adv., & n. —adj. & adv. (also **westwards**) towards the west. —n. a westward direction or region.

West Yorkshire a metropolitan county of northern England; pop. (1981) 2,066,400; county town, Wakefield.

wet /wet/ adj., v., & n. —adj. (**wetter, wettest**) **1** soaked, covered, or dampened with water or other liquid (*a wet sponge; a wet surface; got my feet wet*). **2** (of the weather etc.) rainy (*a wet day*). **3** (of paint, ink, etc.) not yet dried. **4** used with water (*wet shampoo*). **5** Brit. colloq. feeble, inept. **6** Brit. Polit. colloq. Conservative with liberal tendencies, esp. as regarded by right-wing Conservatives. **7** sl. (of a country, of legislation, etc.) allowing the free sale of alcoholic drink. **8** (of a baby or young child) incontinent (*is still wet at night*). —v.tr. (**wetting**; past and past part. **wet** or **wetted**) **1** make wet. **2 a** urinate in or on (*wet the bed*). **b** refl. urinate involuntarily. —n. **1** moisture; liquid that wets something. **2** rainy weather; a time of rain. **3** Brit. colloq. a feeble or inept person. **4** Brit. Polit. colloq. a Conservative with liberal tendencies (see sense 6 of adj.). **5** colloq. a drink. □ **wet the baby's head** colloq. celebrate its birth with a (usu. alcoholic) drink. **wet behind the ears** immature, inexperienced. **wet blanket** see BLANKET. **wet dock** a dock in which a ship can float. **wet dream** an erotic dream with involuntary ejaculation of semen. **wet fly** an artificial fly used under water by an angler. **wet look** a shiny surface given to clothing materials. **wet-nurse** n. a woman employed to suckle another's child. —v.tr. **1** act as a wet-nurse to. **2** colloq. treat as if helpless. **wet pack** the therapeutic wrapping of the body in wet cloths etc. **wet suit** a close-fitting rubber garment worn by skin-divers etc. to keep warm. **wet through** (or **to the skin**) with one's clothes soaked. **wetting agent** a substance that helps water etc. to spread or penetrate. **wet one's whistle** colloq. drink. □□ **wetly** adv. **wetness** n. **wettable** adj. **wetting** n. **wettish** adj. [OE wǣt (adj. & n.), wǣtan (v.), rel. to WATER: in ME replaced by past part. of the verb]

wetback /ˈwetbæk/ n. US colloq. an illegal immigrant from Mexico to the US. [WET + BACK: from the practice of swimming the Rio Grande to reach the US]

wether /ˈweðə(r)/ n. a castrated ram. [OE f. Gmc]

wetlands /ˈwetləndz/ n.pl. swamps and other damp areas of land.

we've /wiːv/ contr. we have.

Wexford /ˈweksfəd/ **1** a county of Ireland, in the province of Leinster; pop. (est. 1986) 102,450. **2** its capital city, a seaport; pop. (1981) 15,364.

wey /weɪ/ n. a former unit of weight or volume varying with different kinds of goods, e.g. 3 cwt. of cheese. [OE wǣg(e) balance, weight f. Gmc, rel. to WEIGH[1]]

Weyden /ˈvaɪd(ə)n/, Rogier van der (c.1400–64), the leading Flemish painter of the 15th c. In 1435 he was appointed official painter to the city of Brussels, where he settled. An enigmatic figure, he produced no signed or dated works, but his paintings became widely known in Europe during his lifetime. Major works include the *Deposition*, showing the influence of Jan van Eyck, and the *Entombment*, which may show Italian influences from his visit to Italy in 1450. His influence on other artists was great, and Netherlands portraiture of the 15th c. looked to his lead.

w.f. *abbr. Printing* wrong fount.

WFC *abbr.* World Food Council, a United Nations organization with headquarters in Rome.

WFP *abbr.* World Food Programme, a United Nations operation (jointly administered by the UN and the FAO) with headquarters in Rome.

WFTU *abbr.* World Federation of Trade Unions.

Wg. Cdr. *abbr.* Wing Commander.

whack /wæk/ *v. & n. colloq.* —*v.tr.* **1** strike or beat forcefully with a sharp blow. **2** (as **whacked** *adj.*) esp. *Brit.* tired out; exhausted. —*n.* **1** a sharp or resounding blow. **2** *sl.* a share. □ **have a whack at** *sl.* attempt. **out of whack** *US sl.* out of order; malfunctioning. □□ **whacker** *n.* **whacking** *n.* [imit., or alt. of THWACK]

whacking /'wækɪŋ/ *adj. & adv. colloq.* —*adj.* very large. —*adv.* very (*a whacking great skyscraper*).

whacko /'wækəʊ/ *int. sl.* expressing delight or enjoyment.

whacky var. of WACKY.

whale[1] /weɪl/ *n.* (*pl.* same or **whales**) any of the larger marine mammals of the order Cetacea, having a streamlined body and horizontal tail, and breathing through a blowhole on the head. (See below.) □ **a whale of a** *colloq.* an exceedingly good or fine etc. **whale-oil** oil from the blubber of whales. **whale shark** a large tropical whalelike shark, *Rhincodon typus*, feeding close to the surface. [OE *hwæl*]

There are about 83 living species of whales. Unlike seals, whales spend no time on land, and they have a very fishlike appearance with a tapering body, fins, and no trace of hind limbs. There are two main groups: the toothed whales, comprising the majority of species, are carnivorous and include dolphins, porpoises, and the sperm whale; the baleen whales, of which the largest species, the blue whale, is the biggest animal that has ever lived, feed by sieving plankton through fibrous plates in their mouths. Although air-breathing, some whales can dive to great depths and stay under water for an hour or more. They navigate by using a form of sonar, and also communicate by sound, sometimes over very long distances. Most whales are intelligent and sociable creatures. In recent decades whaling has threatened some species with extinction.

whale[2] /weɪl/ *v.tr. esp. US colloq.* beat, thrash. [var. of WALE]

whaleback /'weɪlbæk/ *n.* anything shaped like a whale's back.

whaleboat /'weɪlbəʊt/ *n.* a double-bowed boat of a kind used in whaling.

whalebone /'weɪlbəʊn/ *n.* an elastic horny substance growing in thin parallel plates in the upper jaw of some whales, used as stiffening etc. □ **whalebone whale** a baleen whale.

whaler /'weɪlə(r)/ *n.* **1** a whaling ship or a seaman engaged in whaling. **2** an Australian shark of the genus *Carcharhinus*. **3** *Austral. sl.* a tramp.

whaling /'weɪlɪŋ/ *n.* the practice or industry of hunting and killing whales, esp. for their oil or whalebone. □ **whaling-master** the captain of a whaler.

wham /wæm/ *int., n., & v. colloq.* —*int.* expressing the sound of a forcible impact. —*n.* such a sound. —*v.* (**whammed**, **whamming**) **1** *intr.* make such a sound or impact. **2** *tr.* strike forcibly. [imit.]

whammy /'wæmɪ/ *n.* (*pl.* **-ies**) *US colloq.* an evil or unlucky influence. [20th c.: orig. unkn.]

whang /wæŋ/ *v. & n. colloq.* —*v.* **1** *tr.* strike heavily and loudly; whack. **2** *intr.* (of a drum etc.) sound under or as under a blow. —*n.* a whanging sound or blow. [imit.]

Whangarei /ˌwæŋɡə'reɪ/ a port on North Island, New Zealand; pop. (1988) 43,800.

whangee /wæŋ'ɡiː/ *n.* **1** a Chinese or Japanese bamboo of the genus *Phyllostachys*. **2** a cane made from this. [Chin. *huang* old bamboo-sprouts]

whare /'wɒrɪ/ *n.* a Maori hut or house. [Maori]

wharf /wɔːf/ *n. & v.* —*n.* (*pl.* **wharves** /wɔːvz/ or **wharfs**) a level quayside area to which a ship may be moved to load and unload.

—*v.tr.* **1** moor (a ship) at a wharf. **2** store (goods) on a wharf. [OE *hwearf*]

wharfage /'wɔːfɪdʒ/ *n.* **1** accommodation at a wharf. **2** a fee for this.

wharfie /'wɔːfɪ/ *n. Austral. & NZ colloq.* a waterside worker; a wharf-labourer.

wharfinger /'wɔːfɪndʒə(r)/ *n.* an owner or keeper of a wharf. [prob. ult. f. WHARFAGE]

Wharton /'wɔːt(ə)n/, Edith (née Newbold Jones, 1862–1937), American novelist who settled in France in 1907 and devoted considerable energy to a cosmopolitan social life, which included a close friendship with Henry James, and to a literary career. She established her reputation as a leading novelist with *The House of Mirth* (1905) and continued with other novels, short stories, poems, and an autobiography (*A Backward Glance*, 1934). Her chief preoccupation is with the conflict between social and individual fulfilment (which frequently leads to tragedy), and her observant satiric portrayal of social nuance, both in Europe and America, shows a keen interest in the 'tribal behaviour' of various groups.

wharves *pl.* of WHARF.

what /wɒt/ *adj., pron., & adv.* —*interrog.adj.* **1** asking for a choice from an indefinite number or for a statement of amount, number, or kind (*what books have you read?*; *what news have you?*). **2** *colloq.* = WHICH *interrog.adj.* (*what book have you chosen?*). —*adj.* (usu. in exclam.) how great or remarkable (*what luck!*). —*rel.adj.* the or any . . . that (*will give you what help I can*). —*pron.* (corresp. to the functions of the *adj.*) **1** what thing or things? (*what is your name?*; *I don't know what you mean*). **2** (asking for a remark to be repeated) = what did you say? **3** asking for confirmation or agreement of something not completely understood (*you did what?*; *what, you really mean it?*). **4** how much (*what you must have suffered!*). **5** (as *rel.pron.*) that or those which; a or the or any thing which (*what followed was worse; tell me what you think*). —*adv.* to what extent (*what does it matter?*). □ **what about** what is the news or position or your opinion of (*what about me?*; *what about a game of tennis?*). **what-d'you-call-it** (or **what's-its-name**) a substitute for a name not recalled. **what ever** what at all or in any way (*what ever do you mean?*) (see also WHATEVER). **what for** *colloq.* **1** for what reason? **2** a severe reprimand (*e.g. give a person what for*). **what have you** *colloq.* (prec. by *or*) anything else similar. **what if?** **1** what would result etc. if. **2** what would it matter if. **what is more** and as an additional point; moreover. **what next?** *colloq.* what more absurd, shocking, or surprising thing is possible? **what not** (prec. by *and*) other similar things. **what of?** what is the news concerning? **what of it?** why should that be considered significant? **what's-his** (or **-its**) **-name** = *what-d'you-call-it.* **what's what** *colloq.* what is useful or important etc. **what with** *colloq.* because of (usu. several things). [OE *hwæt* f. Gmc]

whate'er /wɒt'eər/ *poet.* var. of WHATEVER.

whatever /wɒt'evə(r)/ *adj. & pron.* **1** = WHAT (in relative uses) with the emphasis on indefiniteness (*lend me whatever you can*; *whatever money you have*). **2** though anything (*we are safe whatever happens*). **3** (with *neg.* or *interrog.*) at all; of any kind (*there is no doubt whatever*). **4** *colloq.* = what ever. □ **or whatever** *colloq.* or anything similar.

whatnot /'wɒtnɒt/ *n.* **1** an indefinite or trivial thing. **2** a stand with shelves for small objects.

whatso /'wɒtsəʊ/ *adj. & pron. archaic* = WHATEVER 1, 2. [ME, = WHAT + SO, f. OE *swā hwæt swā*]

whatsoe'er /ˌwɒtsəʊ'eə(r)/ *poet.* var. of WHATSOEVER.

whatsoever /ˌwɒtsəʊ'evə(r)/ *adj. & pron.* = WHATEVER 1, 2, 3.

whaup /wɔːp/ *n. esp. Sc.* a curlew. [imit. of its cry]

wheal var. of WEAL[1].

wheat /wiːt/ *n.* **1** any cereal plant of the genus *Triticum*, bearing dense four-sided seed-spikes. **2** its grain, used in making flour etc. □ **separate the wheat from the chaff** see CHAFF. **wheat-belt** a region where wheat is the chief agricultural product. **wheat germ** the embryo of the wheat grain, extracted as a source of vitamins. **wheat-grass** = *couch grass* (see COUCH[2]). [OE *hwǣte* f. Gmc, rel. to WHITE]

w we   z zoo   ʃ she   ʒ decision   θ thin   ð this   ŋ ring   x loch   tʃ chip   dʒ jar   (*see over for vowels*)

wheatear /ˈwiːtɪə(r)/ n. any small migratory bird of the genus *Oenanthe*, esp. with a white belly and rump. [app. f. *wheatears* (as WHITE, ARSE)]

wheaten /ˈwiːt(ə)n/ adj. made of wheat.

wheatmeal /ˈwiːtmiːl/ n. flour made from wheat with some of the bran and germ removed.

Wheatstone /ˈwiːtst(ə)n/, Sir Charles (1802–75), English physicist and inventor in acoustics, optics, electricity, and telegraphy, a member of a family of musical instrument-makers and dealers. He invented the kaleidoscope, stereoscope, and the concertina, but is probably best known for his electrical inventions, including an electric clock. In the 1830s he collaborated with Sir William Fothergill Cooke to develop the electric telegraph, and in 1843 he devised the Wheatstone bridge; based on an idea of the mathematician Samuel Christie) and the rheostat for measuring electrical resistance. □ **Wheatstone bridge** an apparatus for measuring electrical resistance by equalizing the potential at two points of a circuit.

whee /wiː/ int. expressing delight or excitement. [imit.]

wheedle /ˈwiːd(ə)l/ v.tr. **1** coax by flattery or endearments. **2** (foll. by *out*) **a** get (a thing) out of a person by wheedling. **b** cheat (a person) out of a thing by wheedling. □□ **wheedler** n. **wheedling** adj. **wheedlingly** adv. [perh. f. G *wedeln* fawn, cringe f. *Wedel* tail]

wheel /wiːl/ n. & v. —n. **1** a circular frame or disc arranged to revolve on an axle and used to facilitate the motion of a vehicle or for various mechanical purposes. (See below.) **2** a wheel-like thing (*Catherine wheel*; *potter's wheel*; *steering wheel*). **3** motion as of a wheel, esp. the movement of a line of people with one end as a pivot. **4** a machine etc. of which a wheel is an essential part. **5** (in pl.) sl. a car. **6** US sl. = big wheel 2. **7** a set of short lines concluding a stanza. —v. **1** intr. & tr. **a** turn on an axis or pivot. **b** swing round in line with one end as a pivot. **2 a** intr. (often foll. by *about*, *round*) change direction or face another way. **b** tr. cause to do this. **3** tr. push or pull (a wheeled thing esp. a barrow, bicycle, or pram, or its load or occupant). **4** intr. go in circles or curves (*seagulls wheeling overhead*). □ **at the wheel 1** driving a vehicle. **2** directing a ship. **3** in control of affairs. **on wheels** (or **oiled wheels**) smoothly. **wheel and deal** engage in political or commercial scheming. **wheel-back** adj. (of a chair) with a back shaped like or containing the design of a wheel. **wheel-lock 1** an old kind of gunlock having a steel wheel to rub against flint etc. **2** a gun with this. **wheel of Fortune** luck. **wheel-spin** rotation of a vehicle's wheels without traction. **wheels within wheels 1** intricate machinery. **2** colloq. indirect or secret agencies. □□ **wheeled** adj. (also in comb.). **wheelless** adj. [OE *hwēol*, *hwēogol* f. Gmc]

The wheel is regarded as one of the most important of mankind's inventions, first recorded in Mesopotamia about 3500 BC, made of solid wood; it was unknown in the pre-Columbian civilizations of Central America other than Mexico. Spoked wheels appeared soon after 2000 BC and were gradually improved and refined; iron tyres were used to protect and strengthen the rim, and the dished wheel of slightly conical form greatly increased strength and stiffness. A wheel using wire spokes in tension only was evolved for the bicycle: by arranging alternate spokes to lead to opposite flanges of the hub and be tangential to the hub in the forward and backward directions the result was a strong lightweight wheel able to transmit a torque from hub to rim. The final evolution of the wheel was in the use of pneumatic tyres, making it easier for vehicles to traverse uneven surfaces.

wheelbarrow /ˈwiːlˌbærəʊ/ n. a small cart with one wheel and two shafts for carrying garden loads etc.

wheelbase /ˈwiːlbeɪs/ n. the distance between the front and rear axles of a vehicle.

wheelchair /ˈwiːltʃeə(r)/ n. a chair on wheels for an invalid or disabled person.

wheeler /ˈwiːlə(r)/ n. **1** (in comb.) a vehicle having a specified number of wheels. **2** a wheelwright. **3** a horse harnessed next to the wheels and behind another. □ **wheeler-dealer** a person who wheels and deals.

wheel-house n. **1** a steersman's shelter. **2** a stone-built circular house with inner partition walls radiating like the spokes of a wheel, found in western and northern Scotland and dating chiefly from c.100 BC–c.100 AD.

wheelie /ˈwiːlɪ/ n. sl. the stunt of riding a bicycle or motor cycle for a short distance with the front wheel off the ground.

wheelman n. esp. US **1** a driver of a wheeled vehicle. **2** a helmsman.

wheelsman /ˈwiːlzmən/ n. (pl. **-men**) US a steersman.

wheelwright /ˈwiːlraɪt/ n. a person who makes or repairs esp. wooden wheels.

wheeze /wiːz/ v. & n. —v. **1** intr. breathe with an audible chesty whistling sound. **2** tr. (often foll. by *out*) utter in this way. —n. **1** a sound of wheezing. **2** colloq. **a** Brit. a clever scheme. **b** an actor's interpolated joke etc. **c** a catch-phrase. □□ **wheezer** n. **wheezingly** adv. **wheezy** adj. (**wheezier**, **wheeziest**). **wheezily** adv. **wheeziness** n. [prob. f. ON *hvæsa* to hiss]

whelk[1] /welk/ n. any predatory marine gastropod mollusc of the family Buccinidae, esp. the edible kind of the genus *Buccinum*, having a spiral shell. [OE *wioloc*, *weoloc*, of unkn. orig.: perh. infl. by WHELK[2]]

whelk[2] /welk/ n. a pimple. [OE *hwylca* f. *hwelian* suppurate]

whelm /welm/ v.tr. poet. **1** engulf, submerge. **2** crush with weight, overwhelm. [OE *hwelman* (unrecorded) = *hwylfan* overturn]

whelp /welp/ n. & v. —n. **1** a young dog; a puppy. **2** archaic a cub. **3** an ill-mannered child or youth. **4** (esp. in pl.) a projection on the barrel of a capstan or windlass. —v.tr. (also absol.) **1** bring forth (a whelp or whelps). **2** derog. (of a human mother) give birth to. **3** originate (an evil scheme etc.). [OE *hwelp*]

when /wen/ adv., conj., pron., & n. —interrog.adv. **1** at what time? **2** on what occasion? **3** how soon? **4** how long ago? —rel.adv. (prec. by *time* etc.) at or on which (*there are times when I could cry*). —conj. **1** at the or any time that; as soon as (*come when you like*; *come when ready*; *when I was your age*). **2** although; considering that (*why stand up when you could sit down?*). **3** after which; and then; but just then (*was nearly asleep when the bell rang*). —pron. what time? (*till when can you stay?*; *since when it has been better*). —n. time, occasion, date (*fixed the where and when*). [OE *hwanne*, *hwenne*]

whence /wens/ adv. & conj. formal —adv. from what place? (*whence did they come?*). —conj. **1** to the place from which (*return whence you came*). **2** (often prec. by *place* etc.) from which (*the source whence these errors arise*). **3** and thence (*whence it follows that*). ¶ Use of *from whence* (as in *the place from whence they came*), though common, is generally considered incorrect. [ME *whannes*, *whennes* f. *whanne*, *whenne* f. OE *hwanon(e)* whence, formed as WHEN + -s[3]: cf. THENCE]

whencesoever /ˌwensəʊˈevə(r)/ adv. & conj. formal from whatever place or source.

whene'er /wenˈeə(r)/ poet. var. of WHENEVER.

whenever /wenˈevə(r)/ conj. & adv. **1** at whatever time; on whatever occasion. **2** every time that. □ **or whenever** colloq. or at any similar time.

whensoe'er /ˌwensəʊˈeə(r)/ poet. var. of WHENSOEVER.

whensoever /ˌwensəʊˈevə(r)/ conj. & adv. formal = WHENEVER.

where /weə(r)/ adv., conj., pron., & n. —interrog.adv. **1** in or to what place or position? (*where is the milk?*; *where are you going?*). **2** in what direction or respect? (*where does the argument lead?*; *where does it concern us?*). **3** in what book etc.?; from whom? (*where did you read that?*; *where did you hear that?*). **4** in what situation or condition? (*where does that leave us?*). —rel.adv. (prec. by *place* etc.) in or to which (*places where they meet*). —conj. **1** in or to the or any place, direction, or respect in which (*go where you like*; *that is where you are wrong*; *delete where applicable*). **2** and there (*reached Crewe, where the car broke down*). —pron. what place? (*where do you come from?*; *where are you going to?*). —n. place; scene of something (see WHEN n.). [OE *hwǣr*, *hwār*]

whereabouts adv. & n. —adv. /ˌweərəˈbaʊts/ where or approximately where? (*whereabouts are they?*; *show me whereabouts to look*). —n. /ˈweərəˌbaʊts/ (as sing. or pl.) a person's or thing's location roughly defined.

whereafter /weər'ɑːftə(r)/ *conj. formal* after which.

whereas /weər'æz/ *conj.* **1** in contrast or comparison with the fact that. **2** (esp. in legal preambles) taking into consideration the fact that.

whereat /weər'æt/ *conj. archaic* **1** at which place or point. **2** for which reason.

whereby /weə'baɪ/ *conj.* by what or which means.

where'er /weər'eə(r)/ *poet. var. of* WHEREVER.

wherefore /'weəfɔː(r), -'fɔː(r)/ *adv. & n.* —*adv. archaic* **1** for what reason? **2** for which reason. —*n.* a reason (*the whys and wherefores*).

wherefrom /weə'frɒm/ *conj. archaic* from which, from where.

wherein /weər'ɪn/ *conj. & adv. formal* —*conj.* in what or which place or respect. —*adv.* in what place or respect?

whereof /weər'ɒv/ *conj. & adv. formal* —*conj.* of what or which (*the means whereof*). —*adv.* of what?

whereon /weər'ɒn/ *conj. & adv. archaic* —*conj.* on what or which. —*adv.* on what?

wheresoe'er /ˌweəsəʊ'eə(r)/ *poet. var. of* WHERESOEVER.

wheresoever /ˌweəsəʊ'evə(r)/ *conj. & adv. formal or literary* = WHEREVER.

whereto /weə'tuː/ *conj. & adv. formal* —*conj.* to what or which. —*adv.* to what?

whereupon /ˌweərə'pɒn, 'weər-/ *conj.* immediately after which.

wherever /weər'evə(r)/ *adv. & conj.* —*adv.* in or to whatever place. —*conj.* in every place that. □ **or wherever** *colloq.* or in any similar place.

wherewithal /'weəwɪˌðɔːl/ *n. colloq.* money etc. needed for a purpose (*has not the wherewithal to do it*).

wherry /'werɪ/ *n.* (*pl.* **-ies**) **1** a light rowing-boat usu. for carrying passengers. **2** a large light barge. [ME: orig. unkn.]

wherryman /'werɪmən/ *n.* (*pl.* **-men**) a man employed on a wherry.

whet /wet/ *v. & n.* —*v.tr.* (**whetted, whetting**) **1** sharpen (a scythe or other tool) by grinding. **2** stimulate (the appetite or a desire, interest, etc.). —*n.* **1** the act or an instance of whetting. **2** a small quantity stimulating one's appetite for more. □□ **whetter** *n.* (also in *comb.*). [OE *hwettan* f. Gmc]

whether /'weðə(r)/ *conj.* introducing the first or both of alternative possibilities (*I doubt whether it matters; I do not know whether they have arrived or not*). □ **whether or no** see NO². [OE *hwæther, hwether* f. Gmc]

whetstone /'wetstəʊn/ *n.* **1** a tapered stone used with water to sharpen curved tools, e.g. sickles, hooks (cf. OILSTONE). **2** a thing that sharpens the senses etc.

whew /hwjuː/ *int.* expressing surprise, consternation, or relief. [imit.: cf. PHEW]

whey /weɪ/ *n.* the watery liquid left when milk forms curds. □ **whey-faced** pale esp. with fear. [OE *hwæg, hweg* f. LG]

which /wɪtʃ/ *adj. & pron.* —*interrog.adj.* asking for choice from a definite set of alternatives (*which John do you mean?; say which book you prefer; which way shall we go?*). —*rel.adj.* being the one just referred to; and this or these (*ten years, during which time they admitted nothing; a word of advice, which action is within your power, will set things straight*). —*interrog.pron.* **1** which person or persons (*which of you is responsible?*). **2** which thing or things (*say which you prefer*). —*rel.pron.* (*poss.* **of which, whose** /huːz/) **1** which thing or things, usu. introducing a clause not essential for identification (cf. THAT *pron.* 7) (*the house, which is empty, has been damaged*). **2** used in place of *that* after *in* or *that* (*there is the house in which I was born; that which you have just seen*). □ **which is which** a phrase used when two or more persons or things are difficult to distinguish from each other. [OE *hwilc* f. Gmc]

whichever /wɪtʃ'evə(r)/ *adj. & pron.* **1** any which (*take whichever you like; whichever one you like*). **2** no matter which (*whichever one wins, they both get a prize*).

whichsoever /ˌwɪtʃsəʊ'evə(r)/ *adj. & pron. archaic* = WHICHEVER.

whidah var. of WHYDAH.

whiff /wɪf/ *n. & v.* —*n.* **1** a puff or breath of air, smoke, etc. (*went outside for a whiff of fresh air*). **2** a smell (*caught the whiff of a cigar*).

3 (foll. by *of*) a trace or suggestion of scandal etc. **4** a small cigar. **5** a minor discharge (of grapeshot etc.). **6** a light narrow outrigged sculling-boat. —*v.* **1** *tr. & intr.* blow or puff lightly. **2** *intr. Brit.* smell (esp. unpleasant). **3** *tr.* get a slight smell of. [imit.]

whiffle /'wɪf(ə)l/ *v. & n.* —*v.* **1** *intr. & tr.* (of the wind) blow lightly, shift about. **2** *intr.* be variable or evasive. **3** *intr.* (of a flame, leaves, etc.) flicker, flutter. **4** *intr.* make the sound of a light wind in breathing etc. —*n.* a slight movement of air. □□ **whiffler** *n.* [WHIFF + -LE⁴]

whiffletree /'wɪf(ə)lˌtriː/ *n. US* = SWINGLETREE. [var. of WHIPPLETREE]

whiffy /'wɪfɪ/ *adj. colloq.* (**whiffier, whiffiest**) having an unpleasant smell.

Whig /wɪg/ *n. hist.* **1** a 17th-c. Scottish Presbyterian. **2** a member of a former British political group (See below.) **3** (*US*) a supporter of the War of American Independence. **4** (*US*) a member of a political party of 1834–56, succeeded by the Republicans. □□ **Whiggery** *n.* **Whiggish** *adj.* **Whiggism** *n.* [prob. a shortening of Sc. *whiggamer, -more*, nickname of 17th-c. Sc. rebels, f. *whig* to drive + MARE¹]

The British political interest group (not really a party in the modern sense of the word) was composed of a loose alliance of the country aristocracy and various trading interests, functioning largely through patronage. Opponents of Jacobitism and advocates of the supremacy of Parliament and the Hanoverian succession, the Whigs dominated the English political scene in the late 17th and first half of the 18th c. In the early 19th c. they experienced a revival as the advocates of parliamentary reform, passing the Reform Bill of 1832, and in the middle of the century gradually metamorphosed into the Liberal party.

while /waɪl/ *n., conj., v., & adv.* —*n.* **1** a space of time, time spent in some action (*a long while ago; waited a while; all this while*). **2** (*prec. by the*) **a** during some other process. **b** *poet.* during the time that. **3** (*prec. by a*) for some time (*have not seen you a while*). —*conj.* **1** during the time that; for as long as; at the same time as (*while I was away, the house was burgled; fell asleep while reading*). **2** in spite of the fact that; although, whereas (*while I want to believe it, I cannot*). **3** *N.Engl.* until (*wait while Monday*). —*v.tr.* (foll. by *away*) pass (time etc.) in a leisurely or interesting manner. —*rel.adv.* (*prec. by time* etc.) during which (*the summer while I was abroad*). □ **all the while** during the whole time (that). **for a long while** for a long time past. **for a while** for some time. **a good** (or **great**) **while** a considerable time. **in a while** (or **little while**) soon, shortly. **worth while** (or **one's while**) worth the time or effort spent. [OE *hwīl* f. Gmc: (conj.) abbr. of OE *thā hwīle the*, ME *the while that*]

whiles /waɪlz/ *conj. archaic* = WHILE. [orig. in the adverbs *somewhiles, otherwhiles*]

whilom /'waɪləm/ *adv. & adj. archaic* —*adv.* formerly, once. —*adj.* former, erstwhile (*my whilom friend*). [OE *hwīlum* dative pl. of *hwīl* WHILE]

whilst /waɪlst/ *adv. & conj. esp. Brit.* while. [ME f. WHILES: cf. AGAINST]

whim /wɪm/ *n.* **1 a** a sudden fancy; a caprice. **b** capriciousness. **2** *archaic* a kind of windlass for raising ore or water from a mine. [17th c.: orig. unkn.]

whimbrel /'wɪmbrɪl/ *n.* a small curlew, esp. *Numenius phaeopus*. [WHIMPER (imit.): cf. *dotterel*]

whimper /'wɪmpə(r)/ *v. & n.* —*v.* **1** *intr.* make feeble, querulous, or frightened sounds; cry and whine softly. **2** *tr.* utter whimperingly. —*n.* **1** a whimpering sound. **2** a feeble note or tone (*the conference ended on a whimper*). □□ **whimperer** *n.* **whimperingly** *adv.* [imit., f. dial. *whimp*]

whimsical /'wɪmzɪk(ə)l/ *adj.* **1** capricious. **2** fantastic. **3** odd or quaint; fanciful, humorous. □□ **whimsicality** /-'kælɪtɪ/ *n.* **whimsically** *adv.* **whimsicalness** *n.*

whimsy /'wɪmzɪ/ *n.* (also **whimsey**) (*pl.* **-ies** or **-eys**) **1** a whim; a capricious notion or fancy. **2** capricious or quaint humour. [rel. to WHIM-WHAM: cf. *flimsy*]

whim-wham /'wɪmwæm/ *n. archaic* **1** a toy or plaything. **2** = WHIM 1. [redupl.: orig. uncert.]

au how eɪ day əʊ no eə hair ɪə near ɔɪ boy ʊə poor aɪə fire aʊə sour (*see over for consonants*)

whin[1] /wɪn/ n. (in sing. or pl.) furze, gorse. [prob. Scand.: cf. Norw. hvine, Sw. hven]

whin[2] /wɪn/ n. **1** hard dark esp. basaltic rock or stone. **2** a piece of this. [ME: orig. unkn.]

whinchat /ˈwɪntʃæt/ n. a small brownish songbird, Saxicola rubetra. [WHIN[1] + CHAT[2]]

whine /waɪn/ n. & v. —n. **1** a complaining long-drawn wail as of a dog. **2** a similar shrill prolonged sound. **3 a** a querulous tone. **b** an instance of feeble or undignified complaining. —v. **1** intr. emit or utter a whine. **2** intr. complain in a querulous tone or in a feeble or undignified way. **3** tr. utter in a whining tone. □□ **whiner** n. **whiningly** adv. **whiny** adj. (**whinier**, **whiniest**). [OE hwīnan]

whinge /wɪndʒ/ v. & n. colloq. —v.intr. whine; grumble peevishly. —n. a whining complaint; a peevish grumbling. □□ **whinger** n. **whingingly** adv. **whingy** adj. [OE hwinsian f. Gmc]

whinny /ˈwɪnɪ/ n. & v. —n. (pl. **-ies**) a gentle or joyful neigh. —v.intr. (**-ies**, **-ied**) give a whinny. [imit.: cf. WHINE]

whinstone /ˈwɪnstəʊn/ n. = WHIN[2].

whip /wɪp/ n. & v. —n. **1** a lash attached to a stick for urging on animals or punishing etc. **2 a** a member of a political party in Parliament appointed to control its parliamentary discipline and tactics, esp. ensuring attendance and voting in debates. **b** Brit. the whips' written notice requesting or requiring attendance for voting at a division etc., variously underlined according to the degree of urgency (three-line whip). **c** (prec. by the) party discipline and instructions (asked for the Labour whip). **3** a dessert made with whipped cream etc. **4** the action of beating cream, eggs, etc., into a froth. **5** = WHIPPER-IN. **6** a rope-and-pulley hoisting apparatus. —v. (**whipped**, **whipping**) **1** tr. beat or urge on with a whip. **2** tr. beat (cream or eggs etc.) into a froth. **3** tr. & intr. take or move suddenly, unexpectedly, or rapidly (whipped away the tablecloth; whipped out a knife; whip off your coat; whipped behind the door). **4** tr. Brit. sl. steal (who's whipped my pen?). **5** tr. sl. **a** excel. **b** defeat. **6** tr. bind with spirally wound twine. **7** tr. sew with overcast stitches. □ **whip-bird** any Australian bird of the genus Psophodes with a cry like the crack of a whip. **whip-crane** a light derrick with tackle for hoisting. **whip-graft** Hort. a graft with the tongue of the scion in a slot in the stock and vice versa. **whip hand 1** a hand that holds the whip (in riding etc.). **2** (usu. prec. by the) the advantage or control in any situation. **whip in** bring (hounds) together. **whip on** urge into action. **whip-round** esp. Brit. colloq. an informal collection of money from a group of people. **whip scorpion** any arachnid of the order Uropygi, with a long slender tail-like appendage, which secretes an irritating vapour. **whip snake** any of various long slender snakes of the family Colubridae. **whip-stitch** a stitch made by whipping. **whip up 1** excite or stir up (feeling etc.). **2** summon (attendance). □□ **whipless** adj. **whiplike** adj. **whipper** n. [ME (h)wippen (v.), prob. f. MLG & MDu. wippen swing, leap, dance]

whipcord /ˈwɪpkɔːd/ n. **1** a tightly twisted cord such as is used for making whiplashes. **2** a close-woven worsted fabric.

whiplash /ˈwɪplæʃ/ n. **1** the flexible end of a whip. **2** a blow with a whip. □ **whiplash injury** an injury to the neck caused by a jerk of the head, esp. as in a motor accident.

whipper-in /ˌwɪpəˈrɪn/ n. a huntsman's assistant who manages the hounds.

whippersnapper /ˈwɪpəˌsnæpə(r)/ n. **1** a small child. **2** an insignificant but presumptuous or intrusive (esp. young) person. [perh. for whipsnapper, implying noise and unimportance]

whippet /ˈwɪpɪt/ n. a cross-bred dog of the greyhound type used for racing. [prob. f. obs. whippet move briskly, f. whip it]

whipping /ˈwɪpɪŋ/ n. **1** a beating, esp. with a whip. **2** cord wound round in binding. □ **whipping-boy 1** a scapegoat. **2** hist. a boy educated with a young prince and punished instead of him. **whipping-cream** cream suitable for whipping. **whipping-post** hist. a post used for public whippings. **whipping-top** a top kept spinning by blows of a lash.

whippletree /ˈwɪp(ə)lˌtriː/ n. = SWINGLETREE. [app. f. WHIP + TREE]

whippoorwill /ˈwɪpʊəˌwɪl/ n. an American nightjar, Caprimulgus vociferus. [imit. of its cry]

whippy /ˈwɪpɪ/ adj. (**whippier**, **whippiest**) flexible, springy. □□ **whippiness** n.

whipsaw /ˈwɪpsɔː/ n. & v. —n. a saw with a narrow blade held at each end by a frame. —v. (past part. **-sawn** or **-sawed**) **1** tr. cut with a whipsaw. **2** US sl. **a** tr. cheat by joint action on two others. **b** intr. be cheated in this way.

whipstock /ˈwɪpstɒk/ n. the handle of a whip.

whir var. of WHIRR.

whirl /wɜːl/ v. & n. —v. **1** tr. & intr. swing round and round; revolve rapidly. **2** tr. & intr. (foll. by away) convey or go rapidly in a vehicle etc. **3** tr. & intr. send or travel swiftly in an orbit or a curve. **4** intr. **a** (of the brain, senses, etc.) seem to spin round. **b** (of thoughts etc.) be confused; follow each other in bewildering succession. —n. **1** a whirling movement (vanished in a whirl of dust). **2** a state of intense activity (the social whirl). **3** a state of confusion (my mind is in a whirl). **4** colloq. an attempt (give it a whirl). □ **whirling dervish** see DERVISH. □□ **whirler** n. **whirlingly** adv. [ME: (v.) f. ON hvirfla: (n.) f. MLG & MDu. wervel spindle & ON hvirfill circle f. Gmc]

whirligig /ˈwɜːlɪgɪg/ n. **1** a spinning or whirling toy. **2** a merry-go-round. **3** a revolving motion. **4** anything regarded as hectic or constantly changing (the whirligig of time). **5** any freshwater beetle of the family Gyrinidae that circles about on the surface. [ME f. WHIRL + obs. gig whipping-top]

whirlpool /ˈwɜːlpuːl/ n. a powerful circular eddy in the sea etc. often causing suction to its centre.

whirlwind /ˈwɜːlwɪnd/ n. **1** a mass or column of air whirling rapidly round and round in a cylindrical or funnel shape over land or water. **2** a confused tumultuous process. **3** (attrib.) very rapid (a whirlwind romance). □ **reap the whirlwind** suffer worse results of a bad action.

whirlybird /ˈwɜːlɪˌbɜːd/ n. colloq. a helicopter.

whirr /wɜː(r)/ n. & v. (also **whir**) —n. a continuous rapid buzzing or softly clicking sound as of a bird's wings or of cog-wheels in constant motion. —v.intr. (**whirred**, **whirring**) make this sound. [ME, prob. Scand.: cf. Da. hvirre, Norw. kvirra, perh. rel. to WHIRL]

whisht /hwɪʃt/ v. (also **whist** /hwɪst/) esp. Sc. & Ir. dial. **1** intr. (esp. as int.) be quiet; hush. **2** tr. quieten. [imit.]

whisk /wɪsk/ v. & n. —v. **1** tr. (foll. by away, off) **a** brush with a sweeping movement. **b** take with a sudden motion (whisked the plate away). **2** tr. whip (cream, eggs, etc.). **3** tr. & intr. convey or go (esp. out of sight) lightly or quickly (whisked me off to the doctor; the mouse whisked into its hole). **4** tr. wave or lightly brandish. —n. **1** a whisking action or motion. **2** a utensil for whisking eggs or cream etc. **3** a bunch of grass, twigs, bristles, etc., for removing dust or flies. [ME wisk, prob. Scand.: cf. ON visk wisp]

whisker /ˈwɪskə(r)/ n. **1** (usu. in pl.) the hair growing on a man's face, esp. on the cheek. **2** each of the bristles on the face of a cat etc. **3** colloq. a small distance (within a whisker of; won by a whisker). **4** a strong hairlike crystal of metal etc. □ **have** (or **have grown**) **whiskers** colloq. (esp. of a story etc.) be very old. □□ **whiskered** adj. **whiskery** adj. [WHISK + -ER[1]]

whisky /ˈwɪskɪ/ n. (Ir., US **whiskey**) (pl. **-ies** or **-eys**) **1** a spirit distilled esp. from malted barley, other grains, or potatoes, etc. **2** a drink of this. [abbr. of obs. whiskybae, var. of USQUEBAUGH]

whisper /ˈwɪspə(r)/ v. & n. —v. **1 a** intr. speak very softly without vibration of the vocal cords. **b** intr. & tr. talk or say in a barely audible tone or in a secret or confidential way. **2** intr. speak privately or conspiratorially. **3** intr. (of leaves, wind, or water) rustle or murmur. —n. **1** whispering speech (talking in whispers). **2** a whispering sound. **3** a thing whispered. **4** a rumour or piece of gossip. □ **it is whispered** there is a rumour. **whispering-gallery** a gallery esp. under a dome with acoustic properties such that a whisper may be heard round its entire circumference. □□ **whisperer** n. **whispering** n. [OE hwisprian f. Gmc]

whist[1] /wɪst/ n. a card-game of mingled skill and chance, using a pack of 52 cards, usually played between two pairs of players. It was in vogue in the 18th c.; Swift alluded to it as a favourite pastime for clergymen. □ **whist drive** a social occasion with the playing of progressive whist. [earlier *whisk*, perh. f. WHISK (with ref. to whisking away the tricks): perh. assoc. with WHIST²]

whist² var. of WHISHT.

whistle /ˈwɪs(ə)l/ n. & v. —n. **1** a clear shrill sound made by forcing breath through a small hole between nearly closed lips. **2** a similar sound made by a bird, the wind, a missile, etc. **3** an instrument used to produce such a sound. —v. **1** intr. emit a whistle. **2 a** intr. give a signal or express surprise or derision by whistling. **b** tr. (often foll. by *up*) summon or give a signal to (a dog etc.) by whistling. **3** tr. (also absol.) produce (a tune) by whistling. **4** intr. (foll. by *for*) vainly seek or desire. □ **as clean** (or **clear** or **dry**) **as a whistle** very clean or clear or dry. **blow the whistle on** colloq. bring (an activity) to an end; inform on (those responsible). **whistle down the wind** **1** let go, abandon. **2** turn (a hawk) loose. **whistle in the dark** pretend to be unafraid. **whistle-stop** **1** US a small unimportant town on a railway. **2** a politician's brief pause for an electioneering speech on tour. **3** (attrib.) with brief pauses (a whistle-stop tour). **whistling kettle** a kettle fitted with a whistle sounded by steam when the kettle is boiling. [OE (h)wistlian (v.), (h)wistle (n.) of imit. orig.: cf. ON hvísla whisper, MSw. hvísla whistle]

Whistler /ˈwɪslə(r)/, James Abbott McNeill (1834–1903), American-born, French-educated, and (mainly) English-domiciled painter and etcher. In Paris he became a devotee of the cult of the Japanese print and of Oriental art and decoration in general, and met Courbet, whose realism inspired much of his early work. Settling in London in 1859 he was immediately successful, specializing in portraits (e.g. *The Artist's Mother*, 1872) and landscapes, often mainly in one or two colours and showing a harmonious relationship between colour and tone. In 1877 Ruskin denounced his *Nocturne in Black and Gold*, accusing him of 'flinging a pot of paint in the public's face', and the costs of the subsequent libel action (which he won) left him bankrupt. After a year devoted mostly to making etchings and pastels in Venice he returned to London. A dandy, a wit, and an inveterate conversationalist, he there conducted a series of campaigns against the public and critics in the form of pamphlets, annotated exhibition catalogues, and letters to newspapers.

whistler /ˈwɪslə(r)/ n. **1** any bird of the genus *Pachycephala*, with a whistling cry. **2** a kind of marmot.

Whit /wɪt/ adj. connected with, belonging to, or following Whit Sunday (Whit Monday; Whit weekend). □ **Whit Sunday** the seventh Sunday after Easter, commemorating the descent of the Holy Spirit upon the Apostles at Pentecost (Acts 2). [OE Hwita Sunnandæg, lit. white Sunday, prob. f. the white robes of the newly-baptized at Pentecost; in the Western Church the festival became a date for baptisms]

whit /wɪt/ n. a particle; a least possible amount (not a whit better). □ **every whit** the whole; wholly. **no** (or **never a** or **not a**) **whit** not at all. [earlier w(h)yt app. alt. f. WIGHT in phr. no wight etc.]

Whitby /ˈwɪtbɪ/, **Synod of** a conference held in 664 chiefly to settle the method of calculating the date of Easter. The Northumbrian Christians had followed the Irish custom while those of the South had adopted the Roman system. King Oswy of Northumbria decided in favour of Rome and England effectively severed her connection with the Irish Church.

White /waɪt/, Patrick Victor Martindale (1912–), Australian novelist, born in England. After service in the RAF during the Second World War he returned to Australia, which was the setting of his first published novel *Happy Valley* (1939) and many others. White won an international reputation with two epics, *The Tree of Man* (1955) and *Voss* (1957); the latter, set in the heroic Australian past, relates the doomed attempt of visionary German hero Johann Voss to lead an expedition across the continent. He has also published plays, short stories, and a self-portrait *Flaws in the Glass* (1981). He was awarded the Nobel Prize for literature in 1973.

white /waɪt/ adj., n., & v. —adj. **1** resembling a surface reflecting sunlight without absorbing any of the visible rays; of the colour of milk or fresh snow. **2** approaching such a colour; pale esp. in the face (turned as white as a sheet). **3** less dark than other things of the same kind. **4** (**White**) **a** of the human group having

light-coloured skin. **b** of or relating to White people. **5** albino (white mouse). **6 a** (of hair) having lost its colour esp. in old age. **b** (of a person) white-haired. **7** colloq. innocent, untainted. **8** (in comb.) (of esp. animals) having some white on the body (white-throated). **9 a** (of a plant) having white flowers or pale-coloured fruit etc. (white hyacinth; white cauliflower). **b** (of a tree) having light-coloured bark etc. (white ash; white poplar). **10** (of wine) made from white grapes or dark grapes with the skins removed. **11** (of coffee) with milk or cream added. **12** transparent, colourless (white glass). **13** hist. counter-revolutionary or reactionary (white guard; white army). —n. **1** a white colour or pigment. **2 a** white clothes or material (dressed in white). **b** (in pl.) white garments as worn in cricket, tennis, etc. **3 a** (in a game or sport) a white piece, ball, etc. **b** the player using such pieces. **4** the white part or albumen round the yolk of an egg. **5** the visible part of the eyeball round the iris. **6** (**White**) a member of a light-skinned race. **7** a white butterfly. **8** a blank space in printing. —v.tr. archaic make white. □ **bleed white** drain (a person, country, etc.) of wealth etc. **white admiral** a butterfly, *Limenitis camilla*, with a white band across its wings. **white ant** a termite. **white cell** (or **corpuscle**) a leucocyte. **white Christmas** Christmas with snow on the ground. **white coal** water as a source of power. **white-collar** (of a worker) engaged in clerical or administrative rather than manual work. **white currant** a cultivar of redcurrant with pale edible berries. **whited sepulchre** see SEPULCHRE. **white dwarf** a star of high density, formed when a low-mass star has exhausted all its central nuclear fuel, losing its outer layers as a planetary nebula. Although as massive as many stars, the radius of a typical white dwarf is no greater than that of Earth, implying densities so great that a matchbox full of white dwarf material must weigh several tons. **white elephant** a useless and troublesome possession or thing. [from the story that the kings of Siam were accustomed to present an elephant of a rare white albino kind (venerated in some Asian countries) to courtiers who had rendered themselves obnoxious, in order to ruin the recipient by the cost of its maintenance] **white ensign** see ENSIGN. **white feather** a symbol of cowardice (a white feather in the tail of a game-bird being a mark of bad breeding). **white fish** fish with pale flesh, e.g. plaice, cod, etc. **white flag** a symbol of surrender or a period of truce. **White Friar** a Carmelite (so called from the white cloak worn). **white frost** see FROST. **white goods** **1** domestic linen. **2** large domestic electrical equipment. **white heat** **1** the temperature at which metal emits white light. **2** a state of intense passion or activity. **white hope** a person expected to achieve much for a group, organization, etc. **white horses** white-crested waves at sea. **white-hot** at white heat. **white lead** a mixture of lead carbonate and hydrated lead oxide used as pigment. **white lie** a harmless or trivial untruth. **white light** colourless light, e.g. ordinary daylight. **white lime** lime mixed with water as a coating for walls; whitewash. **white magic** magic used only for beneficent purposes. **white matter** the part of the brain and spinal cord consisting mainly of nerve fibres (see also grey matter). **white meat** poultry, veal, rabbit, and pork. **white metal** a white or silvery alloy. **white monk** a Cistercian. **white night** a sleepless night. **white noise** noise containing many frequencies with equal intensities. **white-out** a dense blizzard esp. in polar regions. **white ox-eye** = ox-eye daisy. **White Paper** (in the UK) a Government report giving information or proposals on an issue. **white pepper** see PEPPER. **white poplar** = ABELE. **white rose** the emblem of Yorkshire or the House of York. **White Russian** = BELORUSSIAN. **white sale** a sale of household linen. **white sauce** a sauce of flour, melted butter, and milk or cream. **White slave** a woman tricked or forced into prostitution, usu. abroad. **White slavery** traffic in White slaves. **white sock** = STOCKING 3. **white spirit** light petroleum as a solvent. **white sugar** purified sugar. **white tie** a man's white bow-tie as part of full evening dress. **white vitriol** Chem. zinc sulphate. **white water** a shallow or foamy stretch of water. **white wedding** a wedding at which the bride wears a formal white wedding dress. **white whale** a northern cetacean, *Delphinapterus leucas*, white when adult: also called BELUGA. □□ **whitely** adv. **whiteness** n. **whitish** adj. [OE hwīt f. Gmc]

whitebait /ˈwaɪtbeɪt/ n. (pl. same) **1** (usu. pl.) the small silvery-white young of herrings and sprats esp. as food. **2** NZ a young inanga.

whitebeam /ˈwaɪtbiːm/ n. a rosaceous tree, Sorbus aria, having red berries and leaves with a white downy under-side.

whiteface /ˈwaɪtfeɪs/ n. the white make-up of an actor etc.

whitefish /ˈwaɪtfɪʃ/ n. (pl. same or **-fishes**) any freshwater fish of the genus Coregonus etc., of the trout family, and used esp. for food.

whitefly /ˈwaɪtflaɪ/ n. (pl. **-flies**) any small insect of the family Aleyrodidae, having wings covered with white powder and feeding on the sap of shrubs, crops, etc.

Whitehall /ˈwaɪthɔːl/ a street in Westminster, London, in which many important government offices are located, whence the allusive use of its name to refer to the British government or its offices or policy. The name is taken from the former royal palace of White Hall, originally a residence of Cardinal Wolsey confiscated by Henry VIII.

Whitehead /ˈwaɪthed/, Alfred North (1861–1947), English philosopher and mathematician. He is remembered chiefly for Principia Mathematica (1910–13), on which he collaborated with his pupil Bertrand Russell, but he was concerned to explain more generally the connections between mathematics, theoretical science, and ordinary experience. The work on geometry which arose from Principia led to an interest in the philosophy of science, and he proposed an alternative to Einstein's theories of relativity. In his later years he developed a general and systematic metaphysical view, which has had little direct influence, in part because of its obscurity.

whitehead /ˈwaɪthed/ n. colloq. a white or white-topped skin-pustule.

Whitehorse /ˈwaɪthɔːs/ the capital of Yukon Territory in NW Canada; pop. (1986) 20,000. Situated on the Alaska Highway, Whitehorse is the centre of a copper-mining and fur-trapping region.

White House the official residence of the US President in Washington, DC. It was built in 1792–9 of greyish-white limestone from designs of the Irish-born architect James Hoban (1762–1831) on a site chosen by George Washington; President John Adams took up residence there in 1800. The building was restored in 1814 after being burnt by British troops, the smoke-stained walls being painted white. Although known informally as the White House from the early 19th c., it was not formally so designated until the time of Theodore Roosevelt (1902).

whiten /ˈwaɪt(ə)n/ v.tr. & intr. make or become white. □□ **whitener** n. **whitening** n.

White Sea an inlet of the Barents Sea on the NW coast of the Soviet Union. The chief port upon it is Archangel.

whitesmith /ˈwaɪtsmɪθ/ n. **1** a worker in tin. **2** a polisher or finisher of metal goods.

whitethorn /ˈwaɪtθɔːn/ n. the hawthorn.

whitethroat /ˈwaɪtθrəʊt/ n. a warbler, Sylvia communis, with a white patch on the throat.

whitewash /ˈwaɪtwɒʃ/ n. & v. —n. **1** a solution of quicklime or of whiting and size for whitening walls etc. **2** a means employed to conceal mistakes or faults in order to clear a person or institution of imputations. —v.tr. **1** cover with whitewash. **2** attempt by concealment to clear the reputation of. **3** (in passive) (of an insolvent) get a fresh start by passage through a bankruptcy court. **4** US defeat (an opponent) without allowing any opposing score. □□ **whitewasher** n.

whitewood /ˈwaɪtwʊd/ n. a light-coloured wood esp. prepared for staining etc.

Whitey /ˈwaɪtɪ/ n. (pl. **-eys**) sl. offens. **1** a White person. **2** White people collectively.

whither /ˈwɪðə(r)/ adv. & conj. archaic —adv. **1** to what place, position, or state? **2** (prec. by place etc.) to which (the house whither we were walking). —conj. **1** to the or any place to which (go whither you will). **2** and thither (we saw a house, whither we walked). [OE hwider f. Gmc: cf. WHICH, HITHER, THITHER]

whithersoever /ˌwɪðəsəʊˈevə(r)/ adj. & conj. archaic to any place to which.

whiting[1] /ˈwaɪtɪŋ/ n. a small white-fleshed fish, Merlangus merlangus, used as food. [ME f. MDu. wijting, app. formed as WHITE + -ING[3]]

whiting[2] /ˈwaɪtɪŋ/ n. ground chalk used in whitewashing, plate-cleaning, etc.

whitleather /ˈwɪtˌleðə(r)/ n. tawed leather. [ME f. WHITE + LEATHER]

whitlow /ˈwɪtləʊ/ n. an inflammation near a fingernail or toenail. [ME whitflaw, -flow, app. = WHITE + FLAW[1] in the sense 'crack', but perh. of LG orig.: cf. Du. fijt, LG fīt whitlow]

Whitman /ˈwɪtmən/, Walt (1819–92) American poet, with little formal education, who worked as a printer, wandering school-teacher, journalist, and politician. His experience of the frontier resulted in the first edition of Leaves of Grass (1855) which aimed at liberating the American mind from the 'anti-democratic authorities of Asiatic and European past'. His prose Memoranda during the War (1875) is a moving account of his experience as a hospital visitor during the Civil War, as are the poems collected in Drum-Taps (1865). Whitman's free vigorous verse, conveying subjects at once national, mystically sexual, and personal, proved a liberating force to many of his literary successors.

Whitney /ˈwɪtnɪ/, Eli (1765–1825), American inventor. He is chiefly remembered for his mechanical cotton-gin, which was immediately successful but brought him little money because his design was so simple to copy. More important (and more lucrative) was his concept of interchangeable parts. Having obtained a US government contract to supply muskets he manufactured these in standardized parts for reassembly—a pioneer invention, since for the first time worn parts could be replaced by spares and the weapons repaired instead of being wholly replaced.

Whitsun /ˈwɪts(ə)n/ n. & adj. —n. = WHITSUNTIDE. —adj. = WHIT. [ME, f. Whitsun Day = Whit Sunday]

Whitsuntide /ˈwɪts(ə)nˌtaɪd/ n. the weekend or week including Whit Sunday.

Whittier /ˈwɪtɪə(r)/, John Greenleaf (1807–92), American poet, who began life as a farmer's boy. Among his best-known works are 'The Barefoot Boy' (1856), a celebration of rural boyhood which manifests his admiration for Robert Burns, and Snow-Bound (1866), a recollection of winter evenings with his family in the old homestead.

Whittington /ˈwɪtɪŋt(ə)n/, Sir Richard (d. 1423), medieval Mayor of London. Whittington was a London mercer who rose to become Lord Mayor of London in 1397–8, 1406–7, and 1419–20, and left substantial sums to the city for the rebuilding of Newgate Prison and the establishment of a city library. His early career later became the subject of a very popular folk tale.

Whittle /ˈwɪt(ə)l/, Sir Frank (1907–), English engineer, inventor of the turbojet engine.

whittle /ˈwɪt(ə)l/ v. **1** tr. & (foll. by at) intr. pare (wood etc.) with repeated slicing with a knife. **2** tr. (often foll. by away, down) reduce by repeated subtractions. [var. of ME thwitel long knife f. OE thwītan to cut off]

Whitworth /ˈwɪtwəθ/, Sir Joseph (1803–87), English engineer whose name is remembered chiefly for his introduction in 1841 of standard screw-threads.

whity /ˈwaɪtɪ/ adj. whitish; rather white (usu. in comb.: whity-brown) (cf. WHITEY).

whiz /wɪz/ n. & v. (also **whizz**) colloq. —n. **1** the sound made by the friction of a body moving through the air at great speed. **2** (also **wiz**) colloq. a person who is remarkable or skilful in some respect (is a whiz at chess). —v.intr. (**whizzed**, **whizzing**) move with or make a whiz. □ **whiz-bang** colloq. **1** a high-velocity shell from a small-calibre gun, whose passage is heard before the gun's report. **2** a jumping kind of firework. **whiz-kid** colloq. a brilliant or highly successful young person. [imit.: in sense 2 infl. by WIZARD]

WHO abbr. World Health Organization.

who /huː/ pron. (obj. **whom** /huːm/ or colloq. **who**; poss. **whose** /huːz/) **1 a** what or which person or persons? (who called?; you know who it was; whom or who did you see?). ¶ In the last example whom is correct but who is common in less formal contexts. **b**

what sort of person or persons? (*who am I to object?*). **2** (a person) that (*anyone who wishes can come; the woman whom you met; the man who you saw*). ¶ In the last two examples *whom* is correct but *who* is common in less formal contexts. **3** and or but he, she, they, etc. (*gave it to Tom, who sold it to Jim*). **4** *archaic* the or any person or persons that (*whom the gods love die young*). □ **as who should say** like a person who said; as though one said. **who-does-what** (of a dispute etc.) about which group of workers should do a particular job. **who goes there?** see GO[1]. **who's who** 1 who or what each person is (*know who's who*). **2** a list or directory with facts about notable persons. [OE *hwā* f. Gmc: *whom* f. OE dat. *hwām, hwæm: whose* f. genit. *hwæs*]

whoa /wəʊ/ *int.* used as a command to stop or slow a horse etc. [var. of HO]

who'd /huːd/ *contr.* **1** who had. **2** who would.

whodunit /huːˈdʌnɪt/ *n.* (also **whodunnit**) *colloq.* a story or play about the detection of a crime etc., esp. murder. [= *who done* (illiterate for *did*) *it?*]

whoe'er /huːˈeə(r)/ *poet.* var. of WHOEVER.

whoever /huːˈevə(r)/ *pron.* (*obj.* **whomever** /huːm-/ or *colloq.* **whoever**; *poss.* **whosever** /huːz-/) **1** the or any person or persons who (*whoever comes is welcome*). **2** though anyone (*whoever else objects, I do not; whosever it is, I want it*). **3** *colloq.* (as an intensive) who ever; who at all (*whoever heard of such a thing?*).

whole /həʊl/ *adj. & n.* —*adj.* **1** in an uninjured, unbroken, intact, or undiminished state (*swallowed it whole; there is not a plate left whole*). **2** not less than; all there is of; entire, complete (*waited a whole year; tell the whole truth; the whole school knows*). **3** (of blood or milk etc.) with no part removed. —*n.* **1** a thing complete in itself. **2** all there is of a thing (*spent the whole of the summer by the sea*). **3** (foll. by *of*) all members, inhabitants, etc., of (*the whole of London knows it*). □ **as a whole** as a unity; not as separate parts. **go the whole hog** see HOG. **on the whole** taking everything relevant into account; in general (*it was, on the whole, a good report; they behaved well on the whole*). **whole cloth** cloth of full size as manufactured. **whole holiday** a whole day taken as a holiday (cf. *half holiday*). **whole-life insurance** life insurance for which premiums are payable throughout the remaining life of the person insured. **whole lot** see LOT. **whole note** esp. *US Mus.* = SEMIBREVE. **whole number** a number without fractions; an integer. **whole-tone scale** *Mus.* a scale consisting entirely of tones, with no semitones. □□ **wholeness** *n.* [OE *hāl* f. Gmc]

wholefood /ˈhəʊlfuːd/ *n.* food which has not been unnecessarily processed or refined.

wholegrain /ˈhəʊlɡreɪn/ *adj.* made with or containing whole grains (*wholegrain bread*).

wholehearted /həʊlˈhɑːtɪd/ *adj.* **1** (of a person) completely devoted or committed. **2** (of an action etc.) done with all possible effort, attention, or sincerity; thorough. □□ **wholeheartedly** *adv.* **wholeheartedness** *n.*

wholemeal /ˈhəʊlmiːl/ *n.* (usu. *attrib.*) *Brit.* meal of wheat or other cereals with none of the bran or germ removed.

wholesale /ˈhəʊlseɪl/ *n., adj., adv., & v.* —*n.* the selling of things in large quantities to be retailed by others (cf. RETAIL). —*adj. & adv.* **1** by wholesale; at a wholesale price (*can get it for you wholesale*). **2** on a large scale (*wholesale destruction*). —*v.tr.* sell wholesale. □□ **wholesaler** *n.* [ME: orig. *by whole sale*]

wholesome /ˈhəʊlsəm/ *adj.* **1** promoting or indicating physical, mental, or moral health (*wholesome pursuits; a wholesome appearance*). **2** prudent (*wholesome respect*). □□ **wholesomely** *adv.* **wholesomeness** *n.* [ME, prob. f. OE (unrecorded) *hālsum* (as WHOLE, -SOME[1])]

wholewheat /ˈhəʊlwiːt/ *n.* (usu. *attrib.*) wheat with none of the bran or germ removed; wholemeal.

wholism var. of HOLISM.

wholly /ˈhəʊllɪ/ *adv.* **1** entirely; without limitation or diminution (*I am wholly at a loss*). **2** purely, exclusively (*a wholly bad example*). [ME, f. OE (unrecorded) *hāllīce* (as WHOLE, -LY[2])]

whom *objective case* of WHO.

whomever *objective case* of WHOEVER.

whomso *archaic objective case* of WHOSO.

whomsoever *objective case* of WHOSOEVER.

whoop /huːp, wuːp/ *n. & v.* (also **hoop**) —*n.* **1** a loud cry of or as of excitement etc. **2** a long rasping indrawn breath in whooping cough. —*v.intr.* utter a whoop. □ **whooping cough** an infectious bacterial disease, esp. of children, with a series of short violent coughs followed by a whoop. **whooping swan** a swan, *Cygnus cygnus*, with a characteristic whooping sound in flight. **whoop it up** *colloq.* **1** engage in revelry. **2** *US* make a stir. [ME: imit.]

whoopee *int. & n. colloq.* —*int.* /wʊˈpiː/ expressing exuberant joy. —*n.* /ˈwʊpɪ/ exuberant enjoyment or revelry. □ **make whoopee** *colloq.* rejoice noisily or hilariously. **whoopee cushion** a rubber cushion that when sat on makes a sound like the breaking of wind.

whooper /ˈhuːpə(r)/ *n.* a whooping swan.

whoops /wʊps/ *int. colloq.* expressing surprise or apology, esp. on making an obvious mistake. [var. of OOPS]

whoosh /wʊʃ/ *v., n., & int.* (also **woosh**) —*v.intr. & tr.* move or cause to move with a rushing sound. —*n.* a sudden movement accompanied by a rushing sound. —*int.* an exclamation imitating this. [imit.]

whop /wɒp/ *v.tr.* (**whopped**, **whopping**) *sl.* **1** thrash. **2** defeat, overcome. [ME: var. of dial. *wap*, of unkn. orig.]

whopper /ˈwɒpə(r)/ *n. sl.* **1** something big of its kind. **2** a great lie.

whopping /ˈwɒpɪŋ/ *adj. sl.* very big (*a whopping lie; a whopping fish*).

whore /hɔː(r)/ *n. & v.* —*n.* **1** a prostitute. **2** *derog.* a promiscuous woman. —*v.intr.* **1** (of a man) seek or chase after whores. **2** *archaic* (foll. by *after*) commit idolatry or iniquity. □ **whore-house** a brothel. □□ **whoredom** *n.* **whorer** *n.* [OE *hōre* f. Gmc]

whoremaster /ˈhɔːˌmɑːstə(r)/ *n. archaic* = WHOREMONGER.

whoremonger /ˈhɔːˌmʌŋɡə(r)/ *n. archaic* a person who has dealings with whores.

whoreson /ˈhɔːs(ə)n/ *n. archaic* **1** a disliked person. **2** (*attrib.*) (of a person or thing) vile.

whorish /ˈhɔːrɪʃ/ *adj.* of or like a whore. □□ **whorishly** *adv.* **whorishness** *n.*

whorl /wɔːl, wɜːl/ *n.* **1** a ring of leaves or other organs round a stem of a plant. **2** one turn of a spiral, esp. on a shell. **3** a complete circle in a fingerprint. **4** *archaic* a small wheel on a spindle steadying its motion. □□ **whorled** *adj.* [ME *wharwyl, whorwil*, app. var. of WHIRL: infl. by *wharve* (n.) = whorl of a spindle]

whortleberry /ˈwɜːt(ə)lˌberɪ/ *n.* (*pl.* **-ies**) a bilberry. [16th c.: dial. form of *hurtleberry*, ME, of unkn. orig.]

whose /huːz/ *pron. & adj.* —*pron.* of or belonging to which person (*whose is this book?*). —*adj.* of whom or which (*whose book is this?; the man, whose name was Tim; the house whose roof was damaged*).

whoseso *archaic poss.* of WHOSO.

whosesoever *poss.* of WHOSOEVER.

whosever /huːzˈevə(r)/ *poss.* of WHOEVER.

whoso /ˈhuːsəʊ/ *pron.* (*obj.* **whomso** /huːm-/; *poss.* **whoseso** /huːz-/) *archaic* = WHOEVER. [ME, = WHO + SO[1], f. OE *swā hwā swā*]

whosoever /ˌhuːsəʊˈevə(r)/ *pron.* (*obj.* **whomsoever** /ˌhuːm-/; *poss.* **whosesoever** /ˌhuːz-/) *archaic* = WHOEVER.

why /waɪ/ *adv., int., & n.* —*adv.* **1 a** for what reason or purpose (*why do you do it?; I can't know why you came*). **b** on what grounds (*why do you say that?*). **2** (prec. by *reason* etc.) for which (*the reasons why I did it*). —*int.* expressing: **1** surprised discovery or recognition (*why, it's you!*). **2** impatience (*why, of course I do!*). **3** reflection (*why, yes, I think so*). **4** objection (*why, what is wrong with it?*). —*n.* (*pl.* **whys**) a reason or explanation (esp. *whys and wherefores*). □ **why so?** on what grounds?; for what reason or purpose? [OE *hwī, hwȳ* instr. of *hwæt* WHAT f. Gmc]

Whyalla /waɪˈælə/ a steel-manufacturing town on the Spencer Gulf in South Australia; pop. (est. 1987) 27,700.

whydah /ˈwɪdə/ *n.* (also **whidah**) any small African weaver-bird of the genus *Vidua*, the male having mainly black plumage and tail-feathers of great length. [orig. *widow-bird*, altered f. assoc. with *Whidah* (now Ouidah) in Benin]

Whymper /'wɪmpə(r)/, Edward (1840–1911), English pioneer mountaineer. In 1860 he was commissioned to make drawings of the Alps to illustrate a record of the adventures of members of the Alpine Club, and in the following year returned to climb mountains as well as draw them, making his first reconnaissance of the Matterhorn which was then considered impregnable. After a series of first ascents in the Dauphiné and Mont Blanc regions, he attained his life's ambition by climbing the Matterhorn in 1865, at the age of 25, only to see it turn to tragedy when on the way down four of his fellow climbers hurtled to their death. Whymper never recovered from the experience, which for a time aroused public opposition to mountain-climbing.

WI *abbr.* **1** West Indies. **2** *Brit.* Women's Institute. **3** *US* Wisconsin (in official postal use).

wich- var. of WYCH-.

wick[1] /wɪk/ *n.* **1** a strip or thread of fibrous or spongy material feeding a flame with fuel in a candle, lamp, etc. **2** *Surgery* a gauze strip inserted in a wound to drain it. □ **dip one's wick** *coarse sl.* (of a man) have sexual intercourse. **get on a person's wick** *Brit. colloq.* annoy a person. [OE *wēoce, -wēoc* (cf. MDu. *wiecke*, MLG *wēke*), of unkn. orig.]

wick[2] /wɪk/ *n. dial. exc.* in compounds e.g. *bailiwick*, and in place-names e.g. *Hampton Wick, Warwick* **1** a town, hamlet, or district. **2** a dairy farm. [OE *wīc*, prob. f. Gmc f. L *vicus* street, village]

wicked /'wɪkɪd/ *adj.* (**wickeder, wickedest**) **1** sinful, iniquitous, given to or involving immorality. **2** spiteful, ill-tempered; intending or intended to give pain. **3** playfully malicious. **4** *colloq.* foul; very bad; formidable (*wicked weather; a wicked cough*). **5** *sl.* excellent, remarkable. □ **Wicked Bible** an edition of 1631, with the misprinted commandment 'thou shalt commit adultery'. □□ **wickedly** *adv.* **wickedness** *n.* [ME f. obs. *wick* (perh. adj. use of OE *wicca* wizard) + -ED[1] as in *wretched*]

wicker /'wɪkə(r)/ *n.* plaited twigs or osiers etc. as material for chairs, baskets, mats, etc. [ME, f. E.Scand.: cf. Sw. *viker* willow, rel. to *vika* bend]

wickerwork /'wɪkəˌwɜːk/ *n.* **1** wicker. **2** things made of wicker.

wicket /'wɪkɪt/ *n.* **1** *Cricket* **a** a set of stumps (orig. two, now three) with the bails in position defended by a batsman. **b** the ground between two wickets. **c** the state of this (*a slow wicket*). **d** an instance of a batsman being got out (*bowler has taken four wickets*). **e** a pair of batsmen batting at the same time (*a third-wicket partnership*). **2** (in full **wicket-door** or **-gate**) a small door or gate esp. beside or in a larger one or closing the lower part only of a doorway. **3** *US* an aperture in a door or wall usu. closed with a sliding panel. **4** *US* a croquet hoop. □ **at the wicket** *Cricket* **1** batting. **2** by the wicket-keeper (*caught at the wicket*). **keep wicket** *Cricket* be a wicket-keeper. **on a good** (or **sticky**) **wicket** *colloq.* in a favourable (or unfavourable) position. **wicket-keeper** *Cricket* the fieldsman stationed close behind a batsman's wicket. [ME f. AF & ONF *wiket*, OF *guichet*, of uncert. orig.]

wickiup /'wɪkɪˌʌp/ *n.* an American Indian hut of a frame covered with grass etc. [Fox *wikiyap*]

Wicklow /'wɪkləʊ/ **1** a county of eastern Ireland, in the province of Leinster; pop. (est. 1986) 94,500. **2** its capital city, on the Irish Sea; pop. (1981) 5,341.

widdershins var. of WITHERSHINS.

wide /waɪd/ *adj., adv., & n.* —*adj.* **1 a** measuring much or more than other things of the same kind across or from side to side. **b** considerable; more than is needed (*a wide margin*). **2** (following a measurement) in width (*a metre wide*). **3** extending far; embracing much; of great extent (*has a wide range; has wide experience; reached a wide public*). **4** not tight or close or restricted; loose. **5 a** free, liberal; unprejudiced (*takes wide views*). **b** not specialized; general. **6** open to the full extent (*staring with wide eyes*). **7 a** (foll. by *of*) not within a reasonable distance of. **b** at a considerable distance from a point or mark. **8** *Brit. sl.* shrewd; skilled in sharp practice (*wide boy*). **9** (in comb.) extending over the whole of

(*nationwide*). —*adv.* **1** widely. **2** to the full extent (*wide awake*). **3** far from the target etc. (*is shooting wide*). —*n.* **1** *Cricket* a ball judged to pass the wicket beyond the batsman's reach and so scoring a run. **2** (prec. by *the*) the wide world. □ **give a wide berth to** see BERTH. **wide-angle** (of a lens) having a short focal length and hence a field covering a wide angle. **wide awake 1** fully awake. **2** *colloq.* wary, knowing. **wide ball** *Cricket* (sense 1 of *n.*). **wide-eyed** surprised or naïve. **wide of the mark** see MARK[1]. **wide open** (often foll. by *to*) exposed or vulnerable (to attack etc.). **wide-ranging** covering an extensive range. **the wide world** all the world great as it is. □□ **wideness** *n.* **widish** *adj.* [OE *wīd* (adj.), *wīde* (adv.) f. Gmc]

wideawake /'waɪdəˌweɪk/ *n.* a soft felt hat with a low crown and wide brim.

widely /'waɪdlɪ/ *adv.* **1** to a wide extent; far apart. **2** extensively (*widely read; widely distributed*). **3** by many people (*it is widely thought that*). **4** considerably; to a large degree (*holds a widely different view*).

widen /'waɪd(ə)n/ *v.tr. & intr.* make or become wider. □□ **widener** *n.*

widespread /'waɪdspred, -'spred/ *adj.* widely distributed or disseminated.

widgeon /'wɪdʒ(ə)n/ *n.* (also **wigeon**) a species of dabbling duck, esp. *Anas penelope* or *Anas americana*. [16th c.: orig. uncert.]

widget /'wɪdʒɪt/ *n. colloq.* any gadget or device. [perh. alt. of GADGET]

widow /'wɪdəʊ/ *n. & v.* —*n.* **1** a woman who has lost her husband by death and has not married again. **2** a woman whose husband is often away on a specified activity (*golf widow*). **3** extra cards dealt separately and taken by the highest bidder. **4** *Printing* the short last line of a paragraph at the top of a page or column. —*v.tr.* **1** make into a widow or widower. **2** (as **widowed** *adj.*) bereft by the death of a spouse (*my widowed mother*). **3** (foll. by *of*) deprive of. □ **widow-bird** a whydah. **widow's cruse** an apparently small supply that proves or seems inexhaustible (see 1 Kgs. 17: 10–16). **widow's mite** a small money contribution (see Mark 12: 42). **widow's peak** a V-shaped growth of hair towards the centre of the forehead. **widow's weeds** see WEEDS. [OE *widewe*, rel. to OHG *wituwa*, Skr. *vidhávā*, L *viduus* bereft, widowed, Gk *ēítheos* unmarried man]

widower /'wɪdəʊə(r)/ *n.* a man who has lost his wife by death and has not married again.

widowhood /'wɪdəʊˌhʊd/ *n.* the state or period of being a widow.

width /wɪtθ, wɪdθ/ *n.* **1** measurement or distance from side to side. **2** a large extent. **3** breadth or liberality of thought, views, etc. **4** a strip of material of full width as woven. □□ **widthways** *adv.* **widthwise** *adv.* [17th c. (as WIDE, -TH[2]) replacing *wideness*]

wield /wiːld/ *v.tr.* **1** hold and use (a weapon or tool). **2** exert or command (power or authority etc.). □□ **wielder** *n.* [OE *wealdan*, *wieldan* f. Gmc]

wieldy /'wiːldɪ/ *adj.* (**wieldier, wieldiest**) easily wielded, controlled, or handled.

Wien see VIENNA.

Wiener schnitzel /'viːnə ˌʃnɪts(ə)l/ *n.* a veal escalope breaded, fried, and garnished. [G, = Viennese slice]

Wiesbaden /'viːsbɑːd(ə)n/ the capital of the State of Hesse in western Germany; pop. (1987) 266,500.

Wiesenthal /'viːsənˌtɑːl/, Simon (1908–), Austrian organizer of a search for Nazis who had committed war crimes or crimes against humanity and had escaped prosecution. His agency tracked down some 1,000 such offenders, its most spectacular success being the tracing of Adolf Eichmann (see entry).

wife /waɪf/ *n.* (*pl.* **wives** /waɪvz/) **1** a married woman esp. in relation to her husband. **2** *archaic* a woman, esp. an old or uneducated one. **3** (in comb.) a woman engaged in a specified activity (*fishwife; housewife; midwife*). □ **have** (or **take**) **to wife** *archaic* marry (a woman). **wife-swapping** *colloq.* exchanging wives for sexual relations. □□ **wifehood** *n.* **wifeless** *adj.* **wifelike** *adj.* **wifely** *adj.* **wifeliness** *n.* **wifish** *adj.* [OE *wīf* woman: ult. orig. unkn.]

wig[1] /wɪg/ n. an artificial head of hair esp. to conceal baldness or as a disguise, or worn by a judge or barrister or as period dress. □□ **wigged** adj. (also in comb.). **wigless** adj. [abbr. of PERIWIG: cf. WINKLE]

wig[2] /wɪg/ v.tr. (**wigged, wigging**) colloq. rebuke sharply; rate. [app. f. WIG[1] in sl. or colloq. sense 'rebuke' (19th c.)]

wigeon var. of WIDGEON.

wigging /ˈwɪgɪŋ/ n. colloq. a reprimand.

wiggle /ˈwɪg(ə)l/ v. & n. colloq. —v.intr. & tr. move or cause to move quickly from side to side etc. —n. an act of wiggling. □□ **wiggler** n. [ME f. MLG & MDu. wiggelen: cf. WAG[1], WAGGLE]

wiggly /ˈwɪglɪ/ adj. (**wigglier, wiggliest**) colloq. **1** showing wiggles. **2** having small irregular undulations.

wight /waɪt/ n. archaic a person (wretched wight). [OE wiht = thing, creature, of unkn. orig.]

Wightman Cup /ˈwaɪtmən/ an annual lawn tennis contest between women players of the US and Britain, inaugurated in 1923; the trophy for this, a silver vase donated by the US player Mrs H. H. Wightman. The competition was suspended in 1990 because the standard of British lawn tennis was felt to be insufficiently competitive.

wigwag /ˈwɪgwæg/ v.intr. (**wigwagged, wigwagging**) colloq. **1** move lightly to and fro. **2** wave flags in this way in signalling. [redupl. f. WAG[1]]

wigwam /ˈwɪgwæm/ n. **1** a N. American Indian's hut or tent of skins, mats, or bark on poles. **2** a similar structure for children etc. [Ojibwa wigwaum, Algonquin wikiwam their house]

Wilberforce /ˈwɪlbəˌfɔːs/, William (1759–1833), English philanthropist. A prominent Evangelical who sought, as an MP, to give practical expression to his Christian beliefs, he is best known for his work for the abolition of the slave trade, achieved in 1807.

wilco /ˈwɪlkəʊ/ int. colloq. expressing compliance or agreement, esp. acceptance of instructions received by radio. [abbr. of will comply]

Wilcox /ˈwɪlkɒks/, Ella Wheeler (1850–1919), American poet whose many volumes of romantic, sentimental, and mildly erotic verse were enjoyed by a vast readership. She also wrote short stories, novels, and two volumes of autobiography.

wild /waɪld/ adj., adv., & n. —adj. **1** (of an animal or plant) in its original natural state; not domesticated or cultivated (esp. of species or varieties allied to others that are not wild). **2** not civilized; barbarous. **3** (of scenery etc.) having a conspicuously desolate appearance. **4** unrestrained, disorderly, uncontrolled (a wild youth; wild hair). **5** tempestuous, violent (a wild night). **6 a** intensely eager; excited, frantic (wild with excitement; wild delight). **b** (of looks, appearance, etc.) indicating distraction. **c** (foll. by about) colloq. enthusiastically devoted to (a person or subject). **7** colloq. infuriated, angry (makes me wild). **8** haphazard, ill-aimed, rash (a wild guess; a wild shot; a wild venture). **9** (of a horse, game-bird, etc.) shy; easily startled. **10** colloq. exciting, delightful. **11** (of a card) having any rank chosen by the player holding it (the joker is wild). —adv. in a wild manner (shooting wild). —n. **1** a wild tract. **2** a desert. □ **in the wild** in an uncultivated etc. state. **in** (or **out in**) **the wilds** colloq. far from normal habitation. **run wild** grow or stray unchecked or undisciplined. **sow one's wild oats** see OAT. **wild and woolly** uncouth; lacking refinement. **wild boar** see BOAR. **wild card 1** see sense 11 of adj. **2** Computing a character that will match any character or sequence of characters in a file name etc. **3** Sport an extra player or team chosen to enter a competition at the selectors' discretion. **wild cat** any of various smallish cats, esp. the European Felis sylvestris (cf. WILDCAT). **wild-goose chase** a foolish or hopeless and unproductive quest. **wild horse 1** a horse not domesticated or broken in. **2** (in pl.) colloq. even the most powerful influence etc. (wild horses would not drag the secret from me). **wild hyacinth 1** = BLUEBELL 1. **wild man of the woods** colloq. an orang-utan. **wild rice** any tall grass of the genus Zizania, yielding edible grains. **wild silk 1** silk from wild silkworms. **2** an imitation of this from short silk fibres. **Wild West** the western regions of the US at the time when they were lawless frontier

districts. □□ **wildish** adj. **wildly** adv. **wildness** n. [OE wilde f. Gmc]

wildcat /ˈwaɪldkæt/ n. & adj. —n. **1** a hot-tempered or violent person. **2** US a bobcat (cf. wild cat). **3** an exploratory oil well. —adj. (attrib.) **1** esp. US reckless; financially unsound. **2** (of a strike) sudden and unofficial.

Wilde /waɪld/, Oscar Fingal O'Flahertie Wills (1854–1900), British dramatist and poet, born in Dublin. His flamboyant aestheticism attracted attention, much of it hostile; he proclaimed himself a disciple of Pater and the cult of 'Art for Art's sake'. Early publications include the fairy stories The Happy Prince and other tales (1888) and his only novel, The Picture of Dorian Gray (1890), a Gothic melodrama which aroused scandalized protest. His epigrammatic brilliance and shrewd social observation brought theatrical success with Lady Windermere's Fan (1892), A Woman of No Importance (1893), An Ideal Husband (1895), and his masterpiece The Importance of Being Earnest (1895). Lord Alfred Douglas's father, the Marquess of Queensberry, disapproved of his son's friendship with Wilde and publicly insulted the playwright; this started a chain of events which led to Wilde's imprisonment (1895–7) for homosexual offences. In prison he was declared bankrupt, and his letter of bitter reproach to Lord Alfred was published in part as De Profundis (1905), providing an apologia for his own conduct; his prison experiences provided material for The Ballad of Reading Gaol (1898) written in France after his release.

wildebeest /ˈwɪldəˌbiːst, ˈvɪl-/ n. = GNU. [Afrik. (as WILD, BEAST)]

wilder /ˈwɪldə(r)/ v.tr. archaic **1** lead astray. **2** bewilder. [perh. based on WILDERNESS]

wilderness /ˈwɪldənɪs/ n. **1** a desert; an uncultivated and uninhabited region. **2** part of a garden left with an uncultivated appearance. **3** (foll. by of) a confused assemblage of things. □ **in the wilderness** out of political office. **voice in the wilderness** an unheeded advocate of reform (see Matt. 3: 3 etc.). [OE wildēornes f. wild dēor wild deer]

wildfire /ˈwaɪldˌfaɪə(r)/ n. hist. **1** a combustible liquid, esp. Greek fire, formerly used in warfare. **2** = WILL-O'-THE-WISP. □ **spread like wildfire** spread with great speed.

wildfowl /ˈwaɪldfaʊl/ n. (pl. same) a game-bird, esp. an aquatic one.

wilding /ˈwaɪldɪŋ/ n. (also **wildling** /-lɪŋ/) **1** a plant sown by natural agency, esp. a wild crab-apple. **2** the fruit of such a plant. [WILD + -ING[3]]

wildlife /ˈwaɪldlaɪf/ n. wild animals collectively.

wildwood /ˈwaɪldwʊd/ n. poet. uncultivated or unfrequented woodland.

wile /waɪl/ n. & v. —n. (usu. in pl.) a stratagem; a trick or cunning procedure. —v.tr. (foll. by away, into, etc.) lure or entice. [ME wīl, perh. f. Scand. (ON vél craft)]

wilful /ˈwɪlfʊl/ adj. (US **willful**) **1** (of an action or state) intentional, deliberate (wilful murder; wilful neglect; wilful disobedience). **2** (of a person) obstinate, headstrong. □□ **wilfully** adv. **wilfulness** n. [ME f. WILL[2] + -FUL]

wilga /ˈwɪlgə/ n. Austral. a small tree of the genus Geijera, with white flowers. [Aboriginal]

wiliness see WILY.

Wilkes Land /wɪlks/ an area of Antarctica, bordering the Indian Ocean, claimed by Australia. It is named after the American naval officer Charles Wilkes (1798–1877), who first sighted it.

Wilkie /ˈwɪlkɪ/, Sir David (1785–1841), Scottish painter, who attained wide popularity with pictures of village life in a style influenced by 17th-c. Dutch and Flemish genre painters. After travel abroad in 1825–8 his style was revolutionized by Spanish painting, and he began to work on historical subjects on a larger scale and in a broader technique. His success did much to establish the popularity of anecdotal or 'subject' painting, esteemed in an age which looked first to the 'story' of a painting and the moral lesson it contained.

will[1] /wɪl/ v.aux. & tr. (3rd sing. present **will**; past **would** /wʊd/) (foll. by infin. without to, or absol.; present and past only in use)

1 (in the 2nd and 3rd persons, and often in the 1st: see SHALL) expressing the future tense in statements, commands, or questions (*you will regret this; they will leave at once; will you go to the party?*). **2** (in the 1st person) expressing a wish or intention (*I will return soon*). ¶ For the other persons in senses 1, 2, see SHALL. **3** expressing desire, consent, or inclination (*will you have a sandwich?; come when you will; the door will not open*). **4** expressing ability or capacity (*the jar will hold a kilo*). **5** expressing habitual or inevitable tendency (*accidents will happen; will sit there for hours*). **6** expressing probability or expectation (*that will be my wife*). □ **will do** *colloq.* expressing willingness to carry out a request. [OE *wyllan*, (unrecorded) *willan* f. Gmc: rel. to L *volo*]

will² /wɪl/ *n. & v.* —*n.* **1** the faculty by which a person decides or is regarded as deciding on and initiating action (*the mind consists of the understanding and the will*). **2** (also **will-power**) control exercised by deliberate purpose over impulse; self-control (*has a strong will; overcame his shyness by will-power*). **3 a** deliberate or fixed desire or intention (*a will to live*). **4** energy of intention; the power of effecting one's intentions or dominating others. **5** directions (usu. written) in legal form for the disposition of one's property after death (*make one's will*). **6** disposition towards others (*good will*). **7** *archaic* what one desires or ordains (*thy will be done*). —*v.tr.* **1** have as the object of one's will; intend unconditionally (*what God wills; willed that we should succeed*). **2** (*absol.*) exercise will-power. **3** instigate or impel or compel by the exercise of will-power (*you can will yourself into contentment*). **4** bequeath by the terms of a will (*shall will my money to charity*). □ **at will 1** whenever one pleases. **2** *Law* able to be evicted without notice (*tenant at will*). **have one's will** obtain what one wants. **what is your will?** what do you wish done? **where there's a will there's a way** determination will overcome any obstacle. **a will of one's own** obstinacy; wilfulness of character. **with the best will in the world** however good one's intentions. **with a will** energetically or resolutely. □□ **willed** *adj.* (also in *comb.*). **willer** *n.* **will-less** *adj.* [OE *willa* f. Gmc]

Willard /ˈwɪlɑːd/, Emma Hart (1787–1870), American pioneer of women's education, who opened a seminary in Vermont (1814) to teach subjects not then available to women, and later one in New York State (1821) offering a college education which became a model for similar establishments in the US and Europe.

Willemstadt /ˈvɪləmˌstɑːt/ the capital of the Netherlands Antilles, situated on the SW coast of the island of Curaçao; pop. (est. 1986) 50,000.

willet /ˈwɪlɪt/ *n.* (pl. same) a large N. American wader, *Catoptrophorus semipalmatus*. [pill-will- willet, imit. of its cry]

willful *US* var. of WILFUL.

William¹ /ˈwɪlɪəm/ the name of two kings of England, one of Great Britain, and one of the United Kingdom:

William I 'the Conqueror' (*c.*1027–87), reigned 1066–87, the first Norman king of England, illegitimate son of Robert ('the Devil') Duke of Normandy. William claimed the English throne on the death of Edward the Confessor (who had no children), stating that Edward had promised it to him and that Harold Earl of Wessex (Harold II) had agreed to be his 'liege man'. He landed in England and defeated and killed Harold at the battle of Hastings (1066), and was crowned king on Christmas Day. He successfully repressed a series of uprisings in the following years, and imposed his rule on England, introducing Norman institutions and customs (including feudalism and administrative and legal practices); the effect on English culture was considerable.

William II (*c.*1060–1100), son of William I, reigned 1087–1100, known as Rufus because of his ruddy complexion. The chroniclers have transmitted a hostile picture of an irreligious and homosexual king, but in fact he seems to have been blunt but shrewd though unpopular for his temper and high-handedness. He was a good soldier, campaigning in the north of England, where he secured the frontier against the Scots along a line from the Solway Firth to the Tweed, and in Normandy, which he finally acquired peacefully by purchase. His death while out hunting may well have been at the hands of an assassin rather than by accident.

William III (1650–1702), grandson of Charles I, reigned 1689–1702, known as William of Orange. Son of the Prince of Orange and Mary, daughter of Charles I, William was Stadholder (chief magistrate) of The Netherlands from 1672 and married Mary, daughter of the future James II, in 1677. In 1688 he landed in England at the behest of disaffected politicians, deposed James II, and, having accepted the Declaration of Rights, was crowned along with his wife early in the following year. In 1689–90 he successfully defeated James's supporters in Scotland and Ireland, and thereafter devoted most of his energies towards opposing the territorial ambitions of Louis XIV of France.

William IV (1765–1837), son of George III, reigned 1830–7, known as 'the sailor king'. William IV succeeded his unpopular brother George IV in 1830. In political terms, William IV's reign was significant for his reluctant agreement to create 50 new peers to overcome the House of Lords' opposition to the First Reform Bill, and for his attempt in 1834 to choose a Prime Minister to his own taste (Peel) without regard to the composition of Parliament.

William² /ˈwɪlɪəm/ (1143–1214), king of Scotland (as William I) 1165–1214, known as 'the Lion', grandson of David I. He attempted to reassert Scottish independence but was captured by Henry II of England and forced to become his 'liege man'.

William³ /ˈwɪlɪəm/ (German *Wilhelm*) the name of two German emperors and kings of Prussia:

William I (1797–1888), king of Prussia 1861–88, first German emperor 1871–88.

William II (1859–1941), 'the Kaiser', emperor of Germany 1888–1918. A weak and unsteady leader, he was unable to exercise a strong or consistent influence over German policies and tended to be dominated by politicians and soldiers. Vilified by Allied propaganda as the plotter of the First World War, William was in reality more the pawn of others and fell increasingly under the dominance of the army as the war progressed. With Germany on the verge of collapse in November 1918, he went into exile in Holland and abdicated his throne, leaving the way clear for the formation of the Weimar Republic.

William of Occam /ˈwɪlɪəm, ˈɒkəm/ (*c.*1285–1349) English Franciscan friar who spent the first part of his career (until 1324) studying and teaching philosophy in Oxford and the last part (1333–47) in Munich writing anti-papal pamphlets. He is remembered for a maxim which has acquired the name of *Occam's razor*—'it is vain to do with more what can be done with fewer', i.e. the fewest possible assumptions should be made in explaining a thing. Occam distinguished sharply between faith and reason, advocated a radical separation of the Church from the world, denied the pope all temporal authority, and conceded large powers to the laity and their representatives. Occam was the last of the great scholastic philosophers. His ideas influenced Luther, and paved the way for the Reformation.

Williams¹ /ˈwɪlɪəmz/, Tennessee (real name Thomas Lanier Williams, 1911–83), American dramatist, born in Mississippi, brought up there and in St Louis. He achieved success with the semi-autobiographical *The Glass Menagerie* (1944), a poignant and painful family drama set in St Louis; the young heroine's cherished glass animals stand for the bright vulnerable creatures found in all his plays, subjected to increasingly harsh pressures. His next success was *A Streetcar Named Desire* (1947), a study of sexual frustration, violence, and aberration, set in New Orleans. He continued to write prolifically, largely in a Gothic and macabre vein, with deep insight into human passion and its perversions. Other works include *Cat on a Hot Tin Roof* (1955), *Suddenly Last Summer* (1958), *The Night of the Iguana* (1962), the novella *The Roman Spring of Mrs Stone* (1950), collections of poems, and his *Memoirs* (1975).

Williams² /ˈwɪlɪəmz/, William Carlos (1883–1963), American poet, novelist, and writer of short stories. For many years he was a paediatrician, and his profession as a doctor deeply affected his literary life, giving him, in his own words, an entry into 'the secret gardens of the self'. His most ambitious poem, *Paterson* (1948–56) is a long free-verse evocation of an industrial city; the title of his last collection, *Pictures from Brueghel* (1963) suggests the plain poverty-stricken subjects of some of his verse and prose. His skill at depicting the ordinary with freshness and compassion is seen in his short stories, collected as *The Farmers' Daughters* (1961). Other prose works include *In the American Grain* (1925), essays exploring the nature of American literature and the influence of Puritanism in American culture.

Williamsburg /ˈwɪlɪəmzˌbɜːg/ a city in SE Virginia, between the James and York rivers; pop. (1980) 9,900. First settled in 1633, it became the capital of Virginia from 1699 to 1799, being renamed in honour of King William III. A large section of the early colonial area has been restored to its 18th-c. appearance.

willie var. of WILLY.

willies /ˈwɪlɪz/ *n.pl. colloq.* nervous discomfort (esp. *give* or *get the willies*). [19th c.: orig. unkn.]

willing /ˈwɪlɪŋ/ *adj. & n.* —*adj.* **1** ready to consent or undertake (*a willing ally*; *am willing to do it*). **2** given or done etc. by a willing person (*willing hands*; *willing help*). —*n.* cheerful intention (*show willing*). □□ **willingly** *adv.* **willingness** *n.*

will-o'-the-wisp /ˌwɪlədəˈwɪsp/ *n.* **1** a phosphorescent light seen on marshy ground, perhaps resulting from the combustion of gases. **2** an elusive person. **3** a delusive hope or plan. [orig. *Will with the wisp*: *wisp* = handful of (lighted) hay etc.]

willow /ˈwɪləʊ/ *n.* **1** a tree or shrub of the genus *Salix*, growing usu. near water in temperate climates, with small flowers borne on catkins, and pliant branches yielding osiers and timber for cricket-bats, baskets, etc. **2** a cricket-bat. □ **willow grouse** a common European grouse, *Lagopus lagopus*, with brown breeding plumage and white winter plumage. **willow-herb** any plant of the genus *Epilobium* etc., esp. one with leaves like a willow and pale purple flowers. **willow-warbler** (or **-wren**) a small woodland bird, *Phylloscopus trochilus*, with a tuneful song. [OE *welig*]

willow-pattern *n.* a conventional 'Chinese' design of blue on white china etc., in which a willow-tree is a prominent feature. Origination of the pattern is attributed to Thomas Turner of Caughley *c.*1780 and also to Thomas Minton. The pattern was widely copied in the 19th c. As it became standardized *c.*1830 it shows a pagoda, two birds in the sky, a fence in the foreground, a boat, a three-arched bridge across which walk three Chinese figures, and a willow-tree overhanging the bridge.

willowy /ˈwɪləʊɪ/ *adj.* **1** having or bordered by willows. **2** lithe and slender.

Wills /wɪlz/, William John (1834–61), English explorer of Australia. (See BURKE[3].)

willy /ˈwɪlɪ/ *n.* (also **willie**) (*pl.* **-ies**) *Brit. sl.* the penis.

willy-nilly /ˌwɪlɪˈnɪlɪ/ *adv. & adj.* —*adv.* whether one likes it or not. —*adj.* existing or occurring willy-nilly. [later spelling of *will I, nill I* I am willing, I am unwilling]

willy-willy /ˈwɪlɪˌwɪlɪ/ *n.* (*pl.* **-ies**) *Austral.* a cyclone or dust-storm. [Aboriginal]

Wilson[1] /ˈwɪls(ə)n/, Sir Angus (Frank Johnstone) (1913–), English novelist and short-story writer. Born in Durban, South Africa, and educated in England, he became Deputy Superintendent of the Reading Room of the British Museum. His works include the novels *Hemlock and After* (1952), *Anglo-Saxon Attitudes* (1956), *The Middle Age of Mrs. Eliot* (1958), *No Laughing Matter* (1967), *Setting the World on Fire* (1980), and several volumes of short stories. These display a brilliant satiric wit, acute social observation, and a love of the macabre and the farcical. He has also written on Zola (1950), Dickens (1970), and Kipling (1977).

Wilson[2] /ˈwɪls(ə)n/, Edmund (1895–1972), American author and critic. His writings include verse, short stories, experimental plays, and the novel *I Thought of Daisy* (1929, 1967), but he is remembered chiefly for his works of literary and social criticism, which include *Axel's Castle* (1931), a study of symbolist literature, *To the Finland Station* (1940), tracing socialist and revolutionary theory, and *Studies in the Literature of the American Civil War* (1962). His third wife was the novelist Mary McCarthy, and he was a friend from college days of Scott Fitzgerald.

Wilson[3] /ˈwɪls(ə)n/, (James) Harold, Baron Wilson (1916–), British Labour statesman, Prime Minister 1964–70 and 1974–6. During these periods the country was plagued by economic problems: first, balance-of-payments deficits and sterling crises,

then (in 1974-6) inflation. Social reforms in the 1960s included the introduction of comprehensive schools, changes in laws on sexual relations and on divorce and abortion, the end of the death penalty, and the reduction of the age of adulthood to 18. Overseas, the government failed to solve the problem of Rhodesian UDI in 1965. In 1975, after a referendum, the last Wilson administration reluctantly confirmed British membership of the European Economic Community, a matter on which the country was deeply divided.

Wilson[4] /ˈwɪls(ə)n/, Thomas Woodrow (1856–1924), 28th President of the US 1913–21. Already possessed of a reputation as the pre-eminent American academic expert on law and political economy, as President he carried out a series of successful administrative and fiscal reforms. He was re-elected in 1916 on a platform of keeping America out of the First World War, but, following the German reintroduction of unrestricted submarine warfare, entered the war on the Allied side in April 1917. Wilson's 14 Points and plan for the formation of the League of Nations were crucial in the international negotiations surrounding the end of the war, but political opposition at home blocked full American participation in the peace settlement and Wilson's health collapsed before he could overcome Senatorial opposition to his policies.

wilt[1] /wɪlt/ *v. & n.* —*v.* **1** *intr.* (of a plant, leaf, or flower) wither, droop. **2** *intr.* (of a person) lose one's energy, flag, tire, droop. **3** *tr.* cause to wilt. —*n.* a plant-disease causing wilting. [orig. dial.: perh. alt. f. *wilk*, *welk*, of LG or Du. orig.]

wilt[2] /wɪlt/ *archaic 2nd person sing.* of WILL[1].

Wilton /ˈwɪlt(ə)n/ *n.* a kind of woven carpet with a thick pile. [Wilton in SW England]

Wilts. /wɪlts/ *abbr.* Wiltshire.

Wiltshire /ˈwɪltʃɪə)r/ a county of SW England; pop. (1981) 524,900; county town, Trowbridge.

wily /ˈwaɪlɪ/ *adj.* (**wilier, wiliest**) full of wiles; crafty, cunning. □□ **wilily** *adv.* **wiliness** *n.*

Wimbledon /ˈwɪmb(ə)ld(ə)n/ a suburb of London, the most famous of all lawn tennis centres, containing the headquarters of the All England Lawn Tennis and Croquet Club, scene of 'The Lawn Tennis Championships on Grass', the oldest tournament of this kind, since 1877.

wimp /wɪmp/ *n. colloq.* a feeble or ineffectual person. □□ **wimpish** *adj.* **wimpishly** *adv.* **wimpishness** *n.* **wimpy** *adj.* [20th c.: orig. uncert.]

wimple /ˈwɪmp(ə)l/ *n. & v.* —*n.* a linen or silk head-dress covering the neck and the sides of the face, formerly worn by women and still worn by some nuns. —*v.tr. & intr.* arrange or fall in folds. [OE *wimpel*]

Wimpy /ˈwɪmpɪ/ *n.* (*pl.* **-ies**) *propr.* a hamburger served in a plain bun.

Wimsey /ˈwɪmzɪ/, Lord Peter (Death Bredon), an aristocratic amateur detective in the novels of D. L. Sayers.

Wimshurst machine /ˈwɪmzhɜːst/ *n.* a device for generating an electric charge by turning glass discs in opposite directions. [J. Wimshurst, Engl. engineer d. 1903]

win /wɪn/ *v. & n.* —*v.* (**winning**; *past* and *past part.* **won** /wʌn/) **1** *tr.* acquire or secure as a result of a fight, contest, bet, litigation, or some other effort (*won some money*; *won my admiration*). **2** *tr.* be victorious in (a fight, game, race, etc.). **3** *intr.* **a** be the victor; win a race or contest etc. (*who won?*; *persevere, and you will win*). **b** (foll. by *through*, *free*, etc.) make one's way or become by successful effort. **4** *tr.* reach by effort (*win the summit*; *win the shore*). **5** *tr.* obtain (ore) from a mine. **6** *tr.* dry (hay etc.) by exposure to the air. —*n.* victory in a game or bet etc. □ **win the day** be victorious in battle, argument, etc. **win over** persuade, gain the support of. **win one's spurs 1** *colloq.* gain distinction or fame. **2** *hist.* gain a knighthood. **win through** (or **out**) overcome obstacles. **you can't win** *colloq.* there is no way to succeed. **you can't win them all** *colloq.* a resigned expression of consolation on failure. □□ **winnable** *adj.* [OE *winnan* toil, endure: cf. OHG *winnan*, ON *vinna*]

wince[1] /wɪns/ *n. & v.* —*n.* a start or involuntary shrinking movement showing pain or distress. —*v.intr.* give a wince. □□

wincer *n.* **wincingly** *adv.* [ME f. OF *guenchir* turn aside: cf. WINCH, WINK]

wince² /wɪns/ *n.* a roller for moving textile fabric through a dyeing-vat. [var. of WINCH]

wincey /ˈwɪnsɪ/ *n.* (*pl.* **winceys**) a strong lightweight fabric of wool and cotton or linen. [orig. Sc.: app. f. *woolsey* in LINSEY-WOOLSEY]

winceyette /ˌwɪnsɪˈet/ *n.* *Brit.* a lightweight napped flannelette used esp. for nightclothes.

winch /wɪntʃ/ *n.* & *v.* —*n.* **1** the crank of a wheel or axle. **2** a windlass. **3** the reel of a fishing-rod. **4** = WINCE². —*v.tr.* lift with a winch. □□ **wincher** *n.* [OE *wince* f. Gmc: cf. WINCE¹]

Winchester /ˈwɪntʃɪstə(r)/ *n.* **1** *propr.* a breech-loading repeating rifle. **2** (in full **Winchester disk**) *Computing* a hermetically sealed data-storage device with high capacity (so called because its original numerical designation corresponded to that of the rifle's calibre). [O. F. *Winchester* d. 1880, US manufacturer of the rifle]

wind¹ /wɪnd/ *n.* & *v.* —*n.* **1 a** air in more or less rapid natural motion, esp. from an area of high pressure to one of low pressure. **b** a current of wind blowing from a specified direction or otherwise defined (*north wind*; *contrary wind*). **2 a** breath as needed in physical exertion or in speech. **b** the power of breathing without difficulty while running or making a similar continuous effort (*let me recover my wind*). **c** a spot below the centre of the chest where a blow temporarily paralyses breathing. **3** mere empty words; meaningless rhetoric. **4** gas generated in the bowels etc. by indigestion; flatulence. **5 a** an artifically produced current of air, esp. for sounding an organ or other wind instrument. **b** air stored for use or used as a current. **c** the wind instruments of an orchestra collectively (*poor balance between wind and strings*). **6** a scent carried by the wind, indicating the presence or proximity of an animal etc. —*v.tr.* **1** exhaust the wind of by exertion or a blow. **2** renew the wind of by rest (*stopped to wind the horses*). **3** make breathe quickly and deeply by exercise. **4** make (a baby) bring up wind after feeding. **5** detect the presence of by a scent. **6** /waɪnd/ (*past* and *past part.* **winded** or **wound** /waʊnd/) *poet.* sound (a bugle or call) by blowing. □ **before the wind** helped by the wind's force. **between wind and water** at a vulnerable point. **close to** (or **near**) **the wind 1** sailing as nearly against the wind as is consistent with using its force. **2** *colloq.* verging on indecency or dishonesty. **get wind of 1** smell out. **2** begin to suspect; hear a rumour of. **get** (or **have**) **the wind up** *colloq.* be alarmed or frightened. **how** (or **which way**) **the wind blows** (or **lies**) **1** what is the state of opinion. **2** what developments are likely. **in the wind** happening or about to happen. **in the wind's eye** directly against the wind. **like the wind** swiftly. **off the wind** *Naut.* with the wind on the quarter. **on a wind** *Naut.* against a wind on either bow. **on the wind** (of a sound or scent) carried by the wind. **put the wind up** *colloq.* alarm or frighten. **take wind** be rumoured; become known. **take the wind out of a person's sails** frustrate a person by anticipating an action or remark etc. **to the winds** (or **four winds**) **1** in all directions. **2** into a state of abandonment or neglect. **wind and weather** exposure to the effects of the elements. **wind band** a group of wind instruments as a band or section of an orchestra. **wind-break** a row of trees or a fence or wall etc. serving to break the force of the wind. **wind-chill** the cooling effect of wind blowing on a surface. **wind-cone** = *wind-sock*. **wind-force** the force of the wind esp. as measured on the Beaufort etc. scale. **wind-gap** a dried-up former river valley through ridges or hills. **wind-gauge 1** an anemometer. **2** an apparatus attached to the sights of a gun enabling allowance to be made for the wind in shooting. **3** a device showing the amount of wind in an organ. **wind instrument** a musical instrument in which sound is produced by a current of air, esp. the breath. **wind-jammer** a merchant sailing-ship. **wind machine** a device for producing a blast of air or the sound of wind. **wind** (or **winds**) **of change** a force or influence for reform. **wind-rose** a diagram of the relative frequency of wind directions at a place. **wind-row** a line of raked hay, corn-sheaves, peats, etc., for drying by the wind. **wind-sail** a canvas funnel conveying air to the lower parts of a ship. **wind shear** a

variation in wind velocity at right angles to the wind's direction. **wind-sleeve** = *wind-sock*. **wind-sock** a canvas cylinder or cone on a mast to show the direction of the wind at an airfield etc. **wind-tunnel** a tunnel-like device to produce an air-stream past models of aircraft etc. for the study of wind effects on them. □□ **windless** *adj.* [OE f. Gmc]

wind² /waɪnd/ *v.* & *n.* —*v.* (*past* and *past part.* **wound** /waʊnd/) **1** *intr.* go in a circular, spiral, curved, or crooked course (*a winding staircase*; *the path winds up the hill*). **2** *tr.* make (one's way) by such a course (*wind your way up to bed*; *wound their way into our affections*). **3** *tr.* wrap closely; surround with or as with a coil (*wound the blanket round me*; *wound my arms round the child*; *wound the child in my arms*). **4 a** *tr.* coil; provide with a coiled thread etc. (*wind the ribbon on to the card*; *wound cotton on a reel*; *winding wool into a ball*). **b** *intr.* coil; (of wool etc.) coil into a ball (*the creeper winds round the pole*; *the wool wound into a ball*). **5** *tr.* wind up (a clock etc.). **6** *tr.* hoist or draw with a windlass etc. (*wound the cable-car up the mountain*). —*n.* **1** a bend or turn in a course. **2** a single turn when winding. □ **wind down 1** lower by winding. **2** (of a mechanism) unwind. **3** (of a person) relax. **4** draw gradually to a close. **wind-down** *n. colloq.* a gradual lessening of excitement or reduction of activity. **wind off** unwind (string, wool, etc.). **wind round one's finger** see FINGER. **wind up 1** coil the whole of (a piece of string etc.). **2** tighten the coiling or coiled spring of (esp. a clock etc.). **3 a** *colloq.* increase the tension or intensity of (*wound myself up to fever pitch*). **b** irritate or provoke (a person) to the point of anger. **4** bring to a conclusion; end (*wound up his speech*). **5** *Commerce* **a** arrange the affairs of and dissolve (a company). **b** (of a company) cease business and go into liquidation. **6** *colloq.* arrive finally; end in a specified state or circumstance (*you'll wind up in prison*; *wound up owing £100*). **wind-up** *n.* **1** a conclusion; a finish. **2** a state of anxiety; the provocation of this. **wound up** *adj.* (of a person) excited or tense or angry. [OE *windan* f. Gmc, rel. to WANDER, WEND]

windage /ˈwɪndɪdʒ/ *n.* **1** the friction of air against the moving part of a machine. **2 a** the effect of the wind in deflecting a missile. **b** an allowance for this. **3** the difference between the diameter of a gun's bore and its projectile, allowing the escape of gas.

windbag /ˈwɪndbæg/ *n. colloq.* a person who talks a lot but says little of any value.

windbound /ˈwɪndbaʊnd/ *adj.* unable to sail because of contrary winds.

windbreaker /ˈwɪndˌbreɪkə(r)/ *n. US* = WINDCHEATER.

windburn /ˈwɪndbɜːn/ *n.* inflammation of the skin caused by exposure to the wind.

windcheater /ˈwɪndˌtʃiːtə(r)/ *n.* a kind of wind-resistant outer jacket with close-fitting neck, cuffs, and lower edge.

winder /ˈwaɪndə(r)/ *n.* a winding mechanism esp. of a clock or watch.

Windermere /ˈwɪndəˌmɪə(r)/ the largest lake in England, in Cumbria.

windfall /ˈwɪndfɔːl/ *n.* **1** an apple or other fruit blown to the ground by the wind. **2** a piece of unexpected good fortune, esp. a legacy.

windflower /ˈwɪndˌflaʊə(r)/ *n.* an anemone.

Windhoek /ˈvɪnthuːk/ the capital of Namibia; pop. (est. 1988) 114,500.

windhover /ˈwɪndˌhɒvə(r)/ *n. Brit.* a kestrel.

winding /ˈwaɪndɪŋ/ *n.* **1** in senses of WIND² *v.* **2** curved or sinuous motion or movement. **3 a** a thing that is wound round or coiled. **b** *Electr.* coils of wire as a conductor round an armature etc. □ **winding-engine** a machine for hoisting. **winding-sheet** a sheet in which a corpse is wrapped for burial.

windlass /ˈwɪndləs/ *n.* & *v.* —*n.* a machine with a horizontal axle for hauling or hoisting. —*v.tr.* hoist or haul with a windlass. [alt. (perh. by assoc. with dial. *windle* to wind) of obs. *windas* f. OF *guindas* f. ON *vindáss* f. *vinda* WIND² + *áss* pole]

windlestraw /ˈwɪnd(ə)lstrɔː/ *n. archaic* an old dry stalk of grass. [OE *windelstrēaw* grass for plaiting f. *windel* basket (as WIND², -LE¹) + *strēaw* STRAW]

windmill /'wɪndmɪl/ n. **1** a mill worked by the action of the wind on its sails. (See below.) **2** esp. *Brit.* a toy consisting of a stick with curved vanes attached that revolve in a wind. □ **throw one's cap** (or **bonnet**) **over the windmill** act recklessly or unconventionally. **tilt at** (or **fight**) **windmills** attack an imaginary enemy or grievance (with ref. to Don Quixote, who attacked windmills, thinking that they were giants).

The windmill uses the power of the wind to drive a corn mill or for purposes such as pumping water or generating electricity. Originating in Persia in the 7th c., it spread to Europe in the 12th c. and was gradually improved, especially in England during the 18th c. where the millwrights evolved remarkably effective self-acting control mechanisms. The wind-pump was first developed in Holland for drainage purposes, while the deep-well pump for raising water for stock-watering originated in the US and was further developed in Australia. Most windmills use a rotor with a near-horizontal axis; the sails were originally of canvas, a type still used in Crete. English windmills adopted wooden sails, with pivoted slats for control, while US wind-pumps use a large number of sheet-metal sails; they are controlled by a tail vane which points the rotor into the wind but turns it edge-on to dangerously strong winds. Some windmills have a vertical axis, such as the Savonius rotor, which uses blades of S shape. The Darrieus windmill has flexible blades of aerofoil section which form catenaries; its high rotational speed makes it suitable for electricity generation. Since the energy crisis of the 1970s and an increase in concern over environmental issues there has been a revival of interest in the windmill.

window /'wɪndəʊ/ n. **1 a** an opening in a wall, roof, or vehicle etc., usu. with glass in fixed, sliding, or hinged frames, to admit light or air etc. and allow the occupants to see out. **b** the glass filling this opening (*have broken the window*). **2** a space for display behind the front window of a shop. **3** an aperture in a wall etc. through which customers are served in a bank, ticket office, etc. **4** an opportunity to observe or learn. **5** an opening or transparent part in an envelope to show an address. **6** a part of a VDU display selected to show a particular category or part of the data. **7 a** an interval during which atmospheric and astronomical circumstances are suitable for the launch of a spacecraft. **b** any interval or opportunity for action. **8** strips of metal foil dispersed in the air to obstruct radar detection. **9** a range of electromagnetic wavelengths for which a medium is transparent. □ **out of the window** *colloq.* no longer taken into account. **window-box** a box placed on an outside window-sill for growing flowers. **window-cleaner** a person who is employed to clean windows. **window-dressing 1** the art of arranging a display in a shop-window etc. **2** an adroit presentation of facts etc. to give a deceptively favourable impression. **window-ledge** = *window-sill*. **window-pane** a pane of glass in a window. **window-seat 1** a seat below a window, esp. in a bay or alcove. **2** a seat next to a window in an aircraft, train, etc. **window-shop** (**-shopped**, **-shopping**) look at goods displayed in shop-windows, usu. without buying anything. **window-shopper** a person who window-shops. **window-sill** a sill below a window. **window tax** *Brit. hist.* a tax on windows or similar openings (abolished in 1851). □□ **windowed** adj. (also in *comb.*). **windowless** adj. [ME f. ON *vindauga* (as WIND¹, EYE)]

windowing /'wɪndəʊɪŋ/ n. *Computing* the selection of part of a stored image for display or enlargement.

windpipe /'wɪndpaɪp/ n. the air-passage from the throat to the lungs; the trachea.

Windscale /'wɪndskeɪl/ the name of an industrial site in Cumbria from 1947 to 1981 (known before and after these dates as Sellafield; see entry) that became synonymous with the development of nuclear power in Britain, having produced plutonium for weapons and later for the atomic energy programme. In October 1957 a serious fire developed in a reactor there, causing an escape of radioactivity; it was the world's worst nuclear accident until that at Chernobyl (see entry) in 1986.

windscreen /'wɪndskriːn/ n. *Brit.* a screen of glass at the front of a motor vehicle. □ **windscreen wiper** a device consisting of a rubber blade on an arm, moving in an arc, for keeping a windscreen clear of rain etc.

windshield /'wɪndʃiːld/ n. *US* = WINDSCREEN.

Windsor /'wɪnzə(r)/ the name assumed by the British royal house in 1917. □ **Duke of Windsor** the title conferred on Edward VIII on his abdication in 1936. **Windsor Castle** a royal residence in Berkshire, founded by William the Conqueror and extended by his successors, particularly Edward III.

Windsor chair /'wɪnzə(r)/ n. a wooden dining chair with a semicircular back supported by upright rods.

windsurfing /'wɪnd,sɜːfɪŋ/ n. the sport of riding on water on a sailboard. □□ **windsurf** v.intr. **windsurfer** n.

windswept /'wɪndswept/ adj. exposed to or swept back by the wind.

windward /'wɪndwəd/ adj., adv., & n. —adj. & adv. on the side from which the wind is blowing (opp. LEEWARD). —n. the windward region, side, or direction (*to windward; on the windward of*). □ **get to windward of 1** place oneself there to avoid the smell of. **2** gain an advantage over.

Windward Islands a group of islands in the eastern Caribbean Sea which constitute the southern part of the Lesser Antilles. The largest are Dominica, Martinique, St Lucia, and Barbados. Their name refers to the fact that they are nearest to the direction of the prevailing winds, which are easterly.

windy /'wɪndɪ/ adj. (**windier, windiest**) **1** stormy with wind (*a windy night*). **2** exposed to the wind; windswept (*a windy plain*). **3** generating or characterized by flatulence. **4** *colloq.* wordy, verbose, empty (*a windy speech*). **5** *colloq.* nervous, frightened. □□ **windily** adv. **windiness** n. [OE *windig* (as WIND¹, -Y¹)]

wine /waɪn/ n. & v. —n. **1** fermented grape-juice as an alcoholic drink. **2** a fermented drink resembling this made from other fruits etc. as specified (*elderberry wine; ginger wine*). **3** the dark-red colour of red wine. —v. **1** intr. drink wine. **2** tr. entertain to wine. □ **wine and dine** entertain to or have a meal with wine. **wine bar** a bar or small restaurant where wine is the main drink available. **wine bottle** a glass bottle for wine, the standard size holding 75 cl or 26⅔ fl. oz. **wine box** a square carton of wine with a dispensing tap. **wine cellar 1** a cellar for storing wine. **2** the contents of this. **wine-grower** a cultivator of grapes for wine. **wine list** a list of wines available in a restaurant etc. **wine-tasting 1** judging the quality of wine by tasting it. **2** an occasion for this. **wine vinegar** vinegar made from wine as distinct from malt. **wine waiter** a waiter responsible for serving wine. □□ **wineless** adj. [OE *wīn* f. Gmc f. L *vinum*]

wineberry /'waɪnbərɪ/ n. (pl. **-ies**) **1 a** a deciduous bristly shrub, *Rubus phoenicolasius*, from China and Japan, producing scarlet berries used in cookery. **b** this berry. **2** = MAKO².

winebibber /'waɪn,bɪbə(r)/ n. a tippler or drunkard. □□ **winebibbing** n. & adj. [WINE + *bib* to tipple]

wineglass /'waɪnɡlɑːs/ n. **1** a glass for wine, usu. with a stem and foot. **2** the contents of this, a wineglassful.

wineglassful /'waɪnɡlɑːs,fʊl/ n. (pl. **-fuls**) **1** the capacity of a wineglass, esp. of the size used for sherry, as a measure of liquid, about four tablespoons. **2** the contents of a wineglass.

winepress /'waɪnpres/ n. a press in which grapes are squeezed in making wine.

winery /'waɪnərɪ/ n. (pl. **-ies**) esp. *US* an establishment where wine is made.

wineskin /'waɪnskɪn/ n. a whole skin of a goat etc. sown up and used to hold wine.

wing /wɪŋ/ n. & v. —n. **1** each of the limbs or organs by which a bird, bat, or insect is able to fly. **2** a rigid horizontal winglike structure forming a supporting part of an aircraft. **3** part of a building etc. which projects or is extended in a certain direction (*lived in the north wing*). **4 a** a forward player at either end of a line in football, hockey, etc. **b** the side part of a playing-area. **5** (in *pl.*) the sides of a theatre stage out of view of the audience. **6** a section of a political party in terms of the extremity of its views. **7** a flank of a battle array (*the cavalry were massed on the left wing*). **8** *Brit.* the part of a motor vehicle covering a wheel. **9 a** an air-force unit of several squadrons or groups. **b** (in *pl.*) a pilot's badge in the RAF etc. (*get one's wings*). **10** *Anat.* & *Bot.* a lateral part or projection of an organ or structure. —*v.* **1** *intr.* & *tr.* travel or traverse on wings or in an aircraft (*winging through the air; am winging my way home*). **2** *tr.* wound in a wing or an arm. **3** *tr.* equip with wings. **4** *tr.* enable to fly; send in flight (*fear winged my steps; winged an arrow towards them*). □ **give** (or **lend**) **wings** to speed up (a person or a thing). **on the wing** flying or in flight. **on a wing and a prayer** with only the slightest chance of success. **spread** (or **stretch**) **one's wings** develop one's powers fully. **take under one's wing** treat as a protégé. **take wing** fly away; soar. **waiting in the wings** holding oneself in readiness. **wing-beat** one complete set of motions with a wing in flying. **wing-case** the horny cover of an insect's wing. **wing-chair** a chair with side-pieces projecting forwards at the top of a high back. **wing-collar** a man's high stiff collar with turned-down corners. **wing commander** an RAF officer next below group captain. **winged words** highly apposite or significant words. **wing-game** game-birds. **wing-nut** a nut with projections for the fingers to turn it on a screw. **wing-span** (or **-spread**) measurement right across the wings of a bird or aircraft. **wing-stroke** = *wing-beat*. **wing-tip** the outer end of an aircraft's or a bird's wing. □□ **winged** *adj.* (also in *comb.*). **wingless** *adj.* **winglet** *n.* **winglike** *adj.* [ME pl. *wenge, -en, -es* f. ON *vængir*, pl. of *vængr*]

wingding /ˈwɪŋdɪŋ/ *n. sl.* **1** *esp. US* a wild party. **2** *US* a drug addict's real or feigned seizure. [20th c.: orig. unkn.]

Winged Victory a winged statue of Nike, the Greek goddess of victory, especially the Nike of Samothrace (*c.*200 BC) preserved in the Louvre.

winger /ˈwɪŋə(r)/ *n.* **1** a player on a wing in football, hockey, etc. **2** (in *comb.*) a member of a specified political wing (*left-winger*).

wink /wɪŋk/ *v.* & *n.* —*v.* **1 a** *tr.* close and open (one eye or both eyes) quickly. **b** *intr.* close and open an eye. **2** *intr.* (often foll. by *at*) wink one eye as a signal of friendship or greeting or to convey a message to a person. **3** *intr.* (of a light etc.) twinkle; shine or flash intermittently. —*n.* **1** the act or an instance of winking, esp. as a signal etc. **2** *colloq.* a brief moment of sleep (*didn't sleep a wink*). □ **as easy as winking** *colloq.* very easy. **in a wink** very quickly. **wink at 1** purposely avoid seeing; pretend not to notice. **2** connive at (a wrongdoing etc.). [OE *wincian* f. Gmc: cf. WINCE[1], WINCH]

winker /ˈwɪŋkə(r)/ *n.* **1** a flashing indicator light on a motor vehicle. **2** (usu. in *pl.*) a horse's blinker.

winkle /ˈwɪŋk(ə)l/ *n.* & *v.* —*n.* any edible marine gastropod mollusc of the genus *Littorina*; a periwinkle. —*v.tr.* (foll. by *out*) *esp. Brit.* extract or eject (*winkled the information out of them*). □ **winkle-picker** *sl.* a shoe with a long pointed toe. □□ **winkler** *n.* [abbr. of PERIWINKLE[2]: cf. WIG[1]]

winner /ˈwɪnə(r)/ *n.* **1** a person, racehorse, etc. that wins. **2** *colloq.* a successful or highly promising idea, enterprise, etc. (*the new scheme seemed a winner*).

winning /ˈwɪnɪŋ/ *adj.* & *n.* —*adj.* **1** having or bringing victory or an advantage (*the winning entry; a winning stroke*). **2** attractive, persuasive (*a winning smile; winning ways*). —*n.* (in *pl.*) money won esp. in betting etc. □ **winning-post** a post marking the end of a race. □□ **winningly** *adv.* **winningness** *n.*

Winnipeg /ˈwɪnɪˌpeg/ the capital of Manitoba, and the largest city of the prairie provinces of central Canada; pop. (1986) 594,550; metropolitan area pop. 623,300.

Winnipeg /ˈwɪnɪˌpeg/, **Lake** a large lake in Manitoba, Canada, north of the city of Winnipeg.

winnow /ˈwɪnəʊ/ *v.tr.* **1** blow (grain) free of chaff etc. by an air-current. **2** (foll. by *out, away, from,* etc.) get rid of (chaff etc.) from grain. **3 a** sift, separate; clear of refuse or inferior specimens. **b** sift or examine (evidence for falsehood etc.). **c** clear, sort, or weed out (rubbish etc.). **4** *poet.* **a** fan (the air with wings). **b** flap (wings). **c** stir (the hair etc.). □□ **winnower** *n.* (in senses 1, 2). [OE *windwian* (as WIND[1])]

wino /ˈwaɪnəʊ/ *n.* (*pl.* **-os**) *sl.* a habitual excessive drinker of cheap wine; an alcoholic.

winsome /ˈwɪnsəm/ *adj.* (of a person, looks, or manner) winning,

attractive, engaging. □□ **winsomely** *adv.* **winsomeness** *n.* [OE *wynsum* f. *wyn* JOY + -SOME[1]]

winter /ˈwɪntə(r)/ *n.* & *v.* —*n.* **1** the coldest season of the year, in the N. hemisphere from December to February and in the S. hemisphere from June to August. **2** *Astron.* the period from the winter solstice to the vernal equinox. **3** a bleak or lifeless period or region etc. (*nuclear winter*). **4** *poet.* a year (esp. of a person's age) (*a man of fifty winters*). **5** (*attrib.*) **a** characteristic of or suitable for winter (*winter light; winter clothes*). **b** (of fruit) ripening late or keeping until or during winter. **c** (of wheat or other crops) sown in autumn for harvesting the following year. —*v.* **1** *intr.* (usu. foll. by *at, in*) pass the winter (*likes to winter in the Canaries*). **2** *tr.* keep or feed (plants, cattle) during winter. □ **winter aconite** see ACONITE 2. **winter cress** any bitter-tasting cress of the genus *Barbarea*, esp. *B. vulgaris*. **winter garden** a garden or conservatory of plants flourishing in winter. **winter jasmine** a jasmine, *Jasminum nudiflorum*, with yellow flowers. **winter quarters** a place where soldiers spend the winter. **winter sleep** hibernation. **winter solstice** see SOLSTICE. **winter sports** sports performed on snow or ice esp. in winter (e.g. skiing and ice-skating). **winter-tide** *poet.* = WINTERTIME. □□ **winterer** *n.* **winterless** *adj.* **winterly** *adj.* [OE f. Gmc, prob. rel. to WET]

wintergreen /ˈwɪntəˌgriːn/ *n.* any of several plants esp. of the genus *Pyrola* or *Gaultheria* remaining green through the winter.

Winterhalter /ˈvɪntəˌhæltə(r)/, Franz Xavier (1806–73), German artist and international court-painter, whose sitters included Napoleon III, the emperor Francis Joseph, and Queen Victoria and her family. His work still has a clear-cut, waxen, decorative charm but is remembered as a reflection of the high society that he portrayed rather than as creative art.

winterize /ˈwɪntəˌraɪz/ *v.tr.* (also **-ise**) *esp. US* adapt for operation or use in cold weather. □□ **winterization** /-ˈzeɪʃ(ə)n/ *n.*

Winter Palace the former Russian imperial residence in Leningrad (St Petersburg), stormed in the Revolution of 1917, later used as a museum and art gallery.

wintertime /ˈwɪntəˌtaɪm/ *n.* the season of winter.

wintry /ˈwɪntrɪ/ *adj.* (also **wintery**) (/-tərɪ/; **wintrier, wintriest**) **1** characteristic of winter (*wintry weather; a wintry sun; a wintry landscape*). **2** (of a smile, greeting, etc.) lacking warmth or enthusiasm. □□ **wintrily** *adv.* **wintriness** *n.* [OE *wintrig*, or f. WINTER]

winy /ˈwaɪnɪ/ *adj.* (**winier, winiest**) resembling wine in taste or appearance. □□ **wininess** *n.*

wipe /waɪp/ *v.* & *n.* —*v.tr.* **1** clean or dry the surface of by rubbing with the hands or a cloth etc. **2** rub (a cloth) over a surface. **3** spread (a liquid etc.) over a surface by rubbing. **4** (often foll. by *away, off,* etc.) **a** clear or remove by wiping (*wiped the mess off the table; wipe away your tears*). **b** remove or eliminate completely (*the village was wiped off the map*). **5 a** erase (data, a recording, etc., from a magnetic medium). **b** erase data from (the medium). **6** *Austral.* & *NZ sl.* reject or dismiss (a person or idea). —*n.* **1** an act of wiping (*give the floor a wipe*). **2** a piece of disposable absorbent cloth, usu. treated with a cleansing agent, for wiping something clean (*antiseptic wipes*). □ **wipe down** clean (esp. a vertical surface) by wiping. **wipe a person's eye** *colloq.* get the better of a person. **wipe the floor with** *colloq.* inflict a humiliating defeat on. **wipe off** annul (a debt etc.). **wipe out 1 a** destroy, annihilate (*the whole population was wiped out*). **b** obliterate (*wiped it out of my memory*). **2** *sl.* murder. **3** clean the inside of. **4** avenge (an insult etc.). **wipe-out** *n.* **1** the obliteration of one radio signal by another. **2** an instance of destruction or annihilation. **3** *sl.* a fall from a surfboard. **wipe the slate clean** see SLATE. **wipe up 1** *Brit.* dry (dishes etc.). **2** take up (a liquid etc.) by wiping. □□ **wipeable** *adj.* [OE *wīpian*: cf. OHG *wīfan* wind round, Goth. *weipan* crown: rel. to WHIP]

wiper /ˈwaɪpə(r)/ *n.* **1** = *windscreen wiper*. **2** *Electr.* a moving contact. **3** a cam or tappet.

WIPO *abbr.* World Intellectual Property Organization.

wire /ˈwaɪə(r)/ *n.* & *v.* —*n.* **1 a** metal drawn out into the form of a thread or thin flexible rod. **b** a piece of this. **c** (*attrib.*) made of wire. **2** a length or quantity of wire used for fencing or to carry an electric current etc. **3** *esp. US colloq.* a telegram or cablegram. —*v.tr.* **1** provide, fasten, strengthen, etc., with wire. **2** (often foll. by *up*) *Electr.* install electrical circuits in (a building, piece of equipment, etc.). **3** esp. *US colloq.* telegraph (*wired me that they were coming*). **4** snare (an animal etc.) with wire. **5** (usu. in *passive*) *Croquet* obstruct (a ball, shot, or player) by a hoop. □ **by wire** by telegraph. **get one's wires crossed** become confused and misunderstood. **wire brush 1** a brush with tough wire bristles for cleaning hard surfaces, esp. metal. **2** a brush with wire strands brushed against cymbals to produce a soft metallic sound. **wire cloth** cloth woven from wire. **wire-cutter** a tool for cutting wire. **wire gauge 1** a gauge for measuring the diameter of wire etc. **2** a standard series of sizes in which wire etc. is made. **wire gauze** a stiff gauze woven from wire. **wire grass** any of various grasses with tough wiry stems. **wire-haired** (esp. of a dog) having stiff or wiry hair. **wire mattress** a mattress supported by wires stretched in a frame. **wire netting** netting of wire twisted into meshes. **wire rope** rope made by twisting wires together as strands. **wire-tapper** a person who indulges in wire-tapping. **wire-tapping** the practice of tapping (see TAP[1] *v.* 4) a telephone or telegraph line to eavesdrop. **wire-walker** an acrobat performing feats on a wire rope. **wire wheel** a vehicle-wheel with spokes of wire. **wire wool** a mass of fine wire for cleaning. □□ **wirer** *n.* [OE *wīr*]

wiredraw /ˈwaɪədrɔː/ *v.tr.* (*past* **-drew** /-ˌdruː/; *past part.* **-drawn** /-ˌdrɔːn/) **1** draw (metal) out into wire. **2** elongate; protract unduly. **3** (esp. as **wiredrawn** *adj.*) refine or apply or press (an argument etc.) with idle or excessive subtlety.

wireless /ˈwaɪəlɪs/ *n. & adj.* —*n.* **1** esp. *Brit.* **a** (in full **wireless set**) a radio receiving set. **b** the transmission and reception of radio signals. ¶ Now old-fashioned, esp. with ref. to broadcasting, and superseded by *radio* (see entry). The name *wireless* refers to the fact that whereas early telegraphic communication used wires for transmission, the system pioneered by Marconi (see entry) used electromagnetic waves, with no conducting wire between the transmitting and receiving stations. **2** = *wireless telegraphy.* —*adj.* lacking or not requiring wires. □ **wireless telegraphy** = RADIO-TELEGRAPHY.

wireman /ˈwaɪəmən/ *n.* (*pl.* **-men**) **1** esp. *US* an installer or repairer of electric wires. **2** a journalist working for a telegraphic news agency.

wirepuller /ˈwaɪəˌpʊlə(r)/ *n.* esp. *US* a politician etc. who exerts a hidden influence. □□ **wirepulling** *n.*

wireworm /ˈwaɪəˌwɜːm/ *n.* the larva of the click beetle causing damage to crop plants.

wiring /ˈwaɪərɪŋ/ *n.* **1** a system of wires providing electrical circuits. **2** the installation of this (*came to do the wiring*).

wiry /ˈwaɪərɪ/ *adj.* (**wirier, wiriest**) **1** tough and flexible as wire. **2** (of a person) thin and sinewy; untiring. **3** made of wire. □□ **wirily** *adv.* **wiriness** *n.*

Wis. *abbr.* Wisconsin.

wis /wɪs/ *v.intr. archaic* know well. [orig. *I wis* = obs. *iwis* 'certainly' f. OE *gewis*, erron. taken as 'I know' and as pres. tense of *wist* (WIT[2])]

Wisconsin /wɪsˈkɒnsɪn/ a State in the northern US, bordering on Lakes Superior and Michigan; pop. (est. 1985) 4,705,600; capital, Madison. Ceded to Britain by the French in 1763 and acquired by the US in 1783, it became the 30th State of the US in 1848.

Wisd. *abbr.* Wisdom of Solomon (Apocrypha).

Wisden /ˈwɪzd(ə)n/, John (1826–84), English cricketer. His name has been perpetuated in *Wisden Cricketers' Almanack*, an annual publication which first appeared in 1864.

wisdom /ˈwɪzdəm/ *n.* **1** the state of being wise. **2** experience and knowledge together with the power of applying them critically or practically. **3** sagacity, prudence; common sense. **4** wise sayings, thoughts, etc., regarded collectively. □ **in his** or **her** etc. **wisdom** usu. *iron.* thinking it would be best (*the committee in its wisdom decided to abandon the project*). **Wisdom of Solomon** see SOLOMON. **wisdom tooth** each of four hindmost molars not usu. cut before 20 years of age. [OE *wīsdōm* (as WISE[1], -DOM)]

wise[1] /waɪz/ *adj. & v.* —*adj.* **1 a** having experience and knowledge and judiciously applying them. **b** (of an action, behaviour, etc.) determined by or showing or in harmony with such experience and knowledge. **2** sagacious, prudent, sensible, discreet. **3** having knowledge. **4** suggestive of wisdom (*with a wise nod of the head*). **5** *US colloq.* **a** alert, crafty. **b** (often foll. by *to*) having (usu. confidential) information (about). —*v.tr. & intr.* (foll. by *up*) esp. *US colloq.* put or get wise. □ **be** (or **get**) **wise to** *colloq.* become aware of. **no** (or **none the** or **not much**) **wiser** knowing no more than before. **put a person wise** (often foll. by *to*) *colloq.* inform a person (about). **wise after the event** able to understand and assess an event or circumstance after its implications have become obvious. **wise guy** *colloq.* a know-all. **wise man** a wizard, esp. one of the Magi. **wise saw** a proverbial saying. **without anyone's being the wiser** undetected. □□ **wisely** *adv.* [OE *wīs* f. Gmc: see WIT[2]]

wise[2] /waɪz/ *n. archaic* way, manner, or degree (*in solemn wise; on this wise*). □ **in no wise** not at all. [OE *wīse* f. Gmc f. WIT[2]]

-wise /waɪz/ *suffix* forming adjectives and adverbs of manner (*crosswise; clockwise; lengthwise*) or respect (*moneywise*) (cf. -WAYS). ¶ More fanciful phrase-based combinations, such as *employment-wise* (= as regards employment), are *colloq.*, and restricted to informal contexts. [as WISE[2]]

wiseacre /ˈwaɪzˌeɪkə(r)/ *n.* a person who affects a wise manner. [MDu. *wijssegger* soothsayer, prob. f. OHG *wīssago, wīzago,* assim. to WISE[1], ACRE]

wisecrack /ˈwaɪzkræk/ *n. & v. colloq.* —*n.* a smart pithy remark. —*v.intr.* make a wisecrack. □□ **wisecracker** *n.*

wisent /ˈwiːz(ə)nt/ *n.* the European bison, *Bison bonasus.* [G: cf. BISON]

wish /wɪʃ/ *v. & n.* —*v.* **1** *intr.* (often foll. by *for*) have or express a desire or aspiration for (*wish for happiness*). **2** *tr.* (often foll. by *that* + clause, usu. with *that* omitted) have as a desire or aspiration (*I wish I could sing; I wished that I was dead*). **3** *tr.* want or demand, usu. so as to bring about what is wanted (*I wish to go; I wish you to do it; I wish it done*). **4** *tr.* express one's hopes for (*we wish you well; wish them no harm; wished us a pleasant journey*). **5** *tr.* (foll. by *on, upon*) *colloq.* foist on a person. —*n.* **1 a** a desire, request, or aspiration. **b** an expression of this. **2** a thing desired (*got my wish*). □ **best** (or **good**) **wishes** hopes felt or expressed for another's happiness. **wish-fulfilment** a tendency for subconscious desire to be satisfied in fantasy. **wishing-well** a well into which coins are dropped and a wish is made. **the wish is father to the thought** we believe a thing because we wish it true. □□ **wisher** *n.* (in sense 4 of *v.*); (also in *comb.*). [OE *wȳscan,* OHG *wunsken* f. Gmc, ult. rel. to WEEN, WONT]

wishbone /ˈwɪʃbəʊn/ *n.* **1** a forked bone between the neck and breast of a cooked bird: when broken between two people the longer portion entitles the holder to make a wish. **2** an object of similar shape.

wishful /ˈwɪʃfʊl/ *adj.* **1** (often foll. by *to* + infin.) desiring, wishing. **2** having or expressing a wish. □ **wishful thinking** belief founded on wishes rather than facts. □□ **wishfully** *adv.* **wishfulness** *n.*

wish-wash /ˈwɪʃwɒʃ/ *n.* **1** a weak or watery drink. **2** insipid talk or writing. [redupl. of WASH]

wishy-washy /ˈwɪʃɪˌwɒʃɪ/ *adj.* **1** feeble, insipid, or indecisive in quality or character. **2** (of tea, soup, etc.) weak, watery, sloppy. [redupl. of WASHY]

wisp /wɪsp/ *n.* **1** a small bundle or twist of straw etc. **2** a small separate quantity of smoke, hair, etc. **3** a small thin person etc. **4** a flock (of snipe). □□ **wispy** *adj.* (**wispier, wispiest**). **wispily** *adv.* **wispiness** *n.* [ME: orig. uncert.: cf. WFris. *wisp,* and WHISK]

wist *past* and *past part.* of WIT[2].

wisteria /wɪsˈtɪərɪə/ *n.* (also **wistaria** /-ˈsteərɪə/) any climbing plant of the genus *Wisteria,* with hanging racemes of blue, purple, or white flowers. [C. *Wistar* (or *Wister*), Amer. anatomist d. 1818]

wistful /ˈwɪstfʊl/ *adj.* (of a person, looks, etc.) yearningly or mournfully expectant or wishful. □□ **wistfully** *adv.* **wistfulness** *n.* [app. assim. of obs. *wistly* (adv.) intently (cf. WHISHT) to *wishful,* with corresp. change of sense]

wit[1] /wɪt/ *n.* **1** (in *sing.* or *pl.*) intelligence; quick understanding (*has quick wits; a nimble wit*). **2 a** the unexpected, quick, and humorous combining or contrasting of ideas or expressions (*conversation sparkling with wit*). **b** the power of giving intellectual pleasure by this. **3** a person possessing such a power, esp. a cleverly humorous person. □ **at one's wit's** (or **wits'**) **end** utterly at a loss or in despair. **have** (or **keep**) **one's wits about one** be alert or vigilant or of lively intelligence. **live by one's wits** live by ingenious or crafty expedients, without a settled occupation. **out of one's wits** mad, distracted. **set one's wits to** argue with. □□ **witted** adj. (in sense 1); (also in comb.). [OE *wit(t)*, *gewit(t)* f. Gmc]

wit² /wɪt/ v.tr. & intr. (1st & 3rd sing. present **wot** /wɒt/; past and past part. **wist**) (often foll. by *of*) archaic know. □ **to wit** that is to say; namely. [OE *witan* f. Gmc]

witan /ˈwɪt(ə)n/ n. see WITENAGEMOT. [OE]

witch /wɪtʃ/ n. & v. —n. **1** a sorceress, esp. a woman supposed to have dealings with the devil or evil spirits. **2** an ugly old woman; a hag. **3** a fascinating girl or woman. **4** a flat-fish, *Pleuronectes cynoglossus*, resembling the lemon sole. —v.tr. archaic **1** bewitch. **2** fascinate, charm, lure. □ **witch ball**, a coloured glass ball of the kind formerly hung up to keep witches away. **witch-doctor** a tribal magician of primitive people. **witches' sabbath** see SABBATH 3. **witch-hunt 1** hist. a search for and persecution of supposed witches. **2** a campaign directed against a particular group of those holding unpopular or unorthodox views, esp. communists. **the witching hour** midnight, when witches are supposedly active (after Shakesp. *Hamlet* III. ii. 377 *the witching time of night*). □□ **witching** adj. **witchlike** adj. [OE *wicca* (masc.), *wicce* (fem.), rel. to *wiccian* (v.) practise magic arts]

witch- var. of WYCH-.

witchcraft /ˈwɪtʃkrɑːft/ n. the use of magic; sorcery. Witchcraft, which has a long history around the world, rests on belief in a person's ability to injure others by occult means. Most witch-trials in early modern Europe arose from harm which a villager claimed had been inflicted on him by a neighbour (usually female). What was distinctive in this period was the concern of the Church and intellectuals, both Catholics and Protestants defining the witch as a heretic who obtained her power through a pact with the Devil. The papal bull of 1484 led to fierce persecution for about a century and a half. In England roughly a thousand people were hanged for witchcraft, mostly under Elizabeth and James I; the last execution was in 1685. On the Continent, and in Scotland, the use of torture produced far more victims and bizarre confessions of sabbaths and night-flying. The Church's concern with devil-worship probably grew out of a misinterpretation of late medieval heresies and popular practices and superstitions. Inflation and population increases produced social pressures which encouraged allegations, and in Protestant countries the Church's traditional remedies, such as holy water, were no longer available. Educated opinion came to reject witchcraft in the course of the 17th c., though popular rural belief survived much longer.

witchery /ˈwɪtʃərɪ/ n. **1** witchcraft. **2** power exercised by beauty or eloquence or the like.

witchetty /ˈwɪtʃətɪ/ n. (pl. **-ies**) Austral. a large white larva of a beetle or moth, eaten as food by Aborigines. [Aboriginal]

witch-hazel /ˈwɪtʃˌheɪz(ə)l/ n. (also **wych-hazel**) **1** any American shrub of the genus *Hamamelis*, with bark yielding an astringent lotion. **2** this lotion, esp. from the leaves of *H. virginiana*.

witenagemot /ˌwɪtənəɡəˈmoʊt/ n. hist. (also **witan**) the council that advised the Anglo-Saxon kings, consisting of nobles and churchmen chosen by the king himself. [OE f. *witena* genit. pl. of *wita* wise man (as WIT²) + *gemōt* meeting: cf. MOOT]

with /wɪð/ prep. expressing: **1** an instrument or means used (*cut with a knife*; *can walk with assistance*). **2** association or company (*lives with his mother*; *works with Shell*; *lamb with mint sauce*). **3** cause or origin (*shiver with fear*; *in bed with measles*). **4** possession, attribution (*the man with dark hair*; *a vase with handles*). **5** circumstances; accompanying conditions (*sleep with the window open*; *a holiday with all expenses paid*). **6** manner adopted or displayed (*behaved with dignity*; *spoke with vehemence*; *handle with care*; *won with ease*). **7** agreement or harmony (*sympathize with*; *I believe with you that it can be done*). **8** disagreement, antagonism, competition (*incompatible with*; *stop arguing with me*). **9** responsibility

or care for (*the decision rests with you*; *leave the child with me*). **10** material (*made with gold*). **11** addition or supply; possession of as a material, attribute, circumstance, etc. (*fill it with water*; *threaten with dismissal*; *decorate with holly*). **12** reference or regard (*be patient with them*; *how are things with you?*; *what do you want with me?*; *there's nothing wrong with expressing one's opinion*). **13** relation or causative association (*changes with the weather*; *keeps pace with the cost of living*). **14** an accepted circumstance or consideration (*with all your faults, we like you*). □ **away** (or **in** or **out** etc.) **with** (as int.) take, send, or put (a person or thing) away, in, out, etc. **be with a person 1** agree with and support a person. **2** colloq. follow a person's meaning (*are you with me?*). **one with** part of the same whole as. **with child** (or **young**) literary pregnant. **with it** colloq. **1** up to date; conversant with modern ideas etc. **2** alert and comprehending. **with-it** adj. colloq. (of clothes etc.) fashionable. **with that** thereupon. [OE, prob. shortened f. a Gmc prep. corresp. to OE *wither*, OHG *widar* against]

withal /wɪˈðɔːl/ adv. & prep. archaic —adv. moreover; as well; at the same time. —prep. (placed after its expressed or omitted object) with (*what shall he fill his belly withal?*). [ME f. WITH + ALL]

withdraw /wɪðˈdrɔː/ v. (past **withdrew** /-ˈdruː/; past part. **withdrawn** /-ˈdrɔːn/) **1** tr. pull or take aside or back (*withdrew my hand*). **2** tr. discontinue, cancel, retract (*withdrew my support*; *the promise was later withdrawn*). **3** tr. remove; take away (*withdrew the child from school*; *withdrew their troops*). **4** tr. take (money) out of an account. **5** intr. retire or go away; move away or back. **6** intr. (as **withdrawn** adj.) abnormally shy and unsociable; mentally detached. □ **withdrawing-room** archaic = DRAWING-ROOM 1. □□ **withdrawer** n. [ME f. with- away (as WITH) + DRAW]

withdrawal /wɪðˈdrɔːəl/ n. **1** the act or an instance of withdrawing or being withdrawn. **2** a process of ceasing to take addictive drugs, often with an unpleasant physical reaction (*withdrawal symptoms*). **3** = *coitus interruptus*.

withe /wɪθ, wɪð, waɪð/ (also **withy** /ˈwɪðɪ/) (pl. **withes** or **-ies**) n. a tough flexible shoot esp. of willow or osier used for tying a bundle of wood etc. [OE *withthe*, *withig* f. Gmc, rel. to WIRE]

wither /ˈwɪðə(r)/ v. **1** tr. & intr. (often foll. by *up*) make or become dry and shrivelled (*withered flowers*). **2** tr. & intr. (often foll. by *away*) deprive of or lose vigour, vitality, freshness, or importance. **3** intr. decay, decline. **4** tr. **a** blight with scorn etc. **b** (as **withering** adj.) scornful (*a withering look*). □□ **witheringly** adv. [ME, app. var. of WEATHER differentiated for certain senses]

withers /ˈwɪðəz/ n.pl. the ridge between a horse's shoulder-blades. [shortening of (16th-c.) *widersome* (or -*sone*) f. *wider-*, *wither-against* (cf. WITH), as the part that resists the strain of the collar: second element obscure]

withershins /ˈwɪðəʃɪnz/ adv. (also **widdershins** /ˈwɪd-/) esp. Sc. **1** in a direction contrary to the sun's course (considered as unlucky). **2** anticlockwise. [MLG *weddersins* f. MHG *widdersinnes* f. *wider* against + *sin* direction]

withhold /wɪðˈhoʊld/ v.tr. (past and past part. **-held** /-ˈheld/) **1** (often foll. by *from*) hold back; restrain. **2** refuse to give, grant, or allow (*withhold one's consent*; *withhold the truth*). □□ **withholder** n. [ME f. with- away (as WITH) + HOLD¹]

within /wɪˈðɪn/ adv. & prep. —adv. archaic or literary **1** inside; to, at, or on the inside; internally. **2** indoors (*is anyone within?*). **3** in spirit (*make me pure within*). **4** inside the city walls (*Bishopsgate within*). —prep. **1** inside; enclosed or contained by. **2 a** not beyond or exceeding (*within one's means*). **b** not transgressing (*within the law*; *within reason*). **3** not further off than (*within three miles of a station*; *within shouting distance*; *within ten days*). □ **within doors** in or into a house. **within one's grasp** see GRASP. **within reach** (or **sight**) **of** near enough to be reached or seen. [OE *withinnan* on the inside (as WITH, *innan* (adv. & prep.) within, formed as IN)]

without /wɪˈðaʊt/ prep. & adv. —prep. **1** not having, feeling, or showing (*came without any money*; *without hesitation*; *without any emotion*). **2** with freedom from (*without fear*; *without embarrassment*). **3** in the absence of (*cannot live without you*; *the train left without us*). **4** with neglect or avoidance of (*do not leave without telling me*). ¶ Use as a *conj.*, as in *do not leave without you tell me*, is non-standard. **5** *archaic* outside (*without the city wall*). —*adv.* *archaic* or *literary* **1** outside (*seen from without*). **2** out of doors (*remained shivering without*). **3** in outward appearance (*rough without but kind within*). **4** outside the city walls (*Bishopsgate without*). □ **without end** infinite, eternal. [OE *withūtan* (as WITH, *ūtan* from outside, formed as OUT)]

withstand /wɪð'stænd/ v. (*past* and *past part.* **-stood** /-'stʊd/) **1** *tr.* oppose, resist, hold out against (a person, force, etc.). **2** *intr.* make opposition; offer resistance. □□ **withstander** n. [OE *withstandan* f. *with-* against (as WITH) + STAND]

withy /'wɪðɪ/ n. (*pl.* **-ies**) **1** a willow of any species. **2** var. of WITHE.

witless /'wɪtlɪs/ adj. **1** lacking wits; foolish, stupid. **2** crazy. □□ **witlessly** adv. **witlessness** n. [OE *witlēas* (as WIT[1], -LESS)]

witling /'wɪtlɪŋ/ n. *archaic* usu. *derog.* a person who fancies himself or herself as a wit.

witness /'wɪtnɪs/ n. & v. —n. **1** a person present at some event and able to give information about it (cf. EYEWITNESS). **2 a** a person giving sworn testimony. **b** a person attesting another's signature to a document. **3** (foll. by *to*, *of*) a person or thing whose existence, condition, etc., attests or proves something (*is a living witness to their generosity*). **4** testimony, evidence, confirmation. —v. **1** *tr.* be a witness of (an event etc.) (*did you witness the accident?*). **2** *tr.* be witness to the authenticity of (a document or signature). **3** *tr.* serve as evidence or an indication of. **4** *intr.* (foll. by *against*, *for*, *to*) give or serve as evidence. □ **bear witness to** (or **of**) **1** attest the truth of. **2** state one's belief in. **call to witness** appeal to for confirmation etc. **witness-box** (US **-stand**) an enclosure in a lawcourt from which witnesses give evidence. [OE *witnes* (as WIT[1], -NESS)]

Wittenberg /'vɪtən,bɜːg/ a town in Germany, on the River Elbe; pop. (1981) 54,094. It is famous as the residence of Luther and starting-point of the Reformation, with an ancient university (merged with that of Halle in 1817) at which Luther taught.

witter /'wɪtə(r)/ v.intr. (often foll. by *on*) *colloq.* speak tediously on trivial matters. [20th c.: prob. imit.]

Wittgenstein /'vɪtgən,ʃtaɪn/, Ludwig Josef Johann (1889–1951), Austrian-born philosopher who came to England in 1911, studied at Cambridge under Bertrand Russell in 1912–13, and abandoned philosophy until the late 1920s, returning to Cambridge in 1929. From early training in engineering and a philosophical interest in mathematics he passed to the study of language and its relationship to the things of the world. In his earlier work, the *Tractatus Logico-philosophicus* (1921), he held that language 'pictures' things by established conventions. In his later works the topic is again language, which he now saw as a response to, not merely a reproduction of, what is real; traditional philosophical problems were seen as caused by mistaken analogies and simplistic generalizations, chiefly in attempts to understand the workings of language. The positive view which emerges is that correctness in any use of language is determined solely by the role of that use in human activities and practices. None of the work of this later period was published in his lifetime; the breadth of his influence was largely due to the powerful effect of his personality on friends, pupils, and colleagues at philosophical meetings.

witticism /'wɪtɪ,sɪz(ə)m/ n. a witty remark. [coined by Dryden (1677) f. WITTY, after *criticism*]

witting /'wɪtɪŋ/ adj. **1** aware. **2** intentional. □□ **wittingly** adv. [ME f. WIT[2] + -ING[2]]

witty /'wɪtɪ/ adj. (**wittier**, **wittiest**) **1** showing verbal wit. **2** characterized by wit or humour. □□ **wittily** adv. **wittiness** n. [OE *witig*, *wittig* (as WIT[1], -Y[1])]

Witwatersrand /wɪt'wɔːtəz,rænd/ a series of parallel ridges forming a watershed between the Vaal and Olifant rivers in the province of Transvaal, South Africa. The Witwatersrand or Rand area is South Africa's chief centre of gold mining. Its Afrikaans name means 'ridge of white waters'.

wivern var. of WYVERN.

wives *pl.* of WIFE.

wiz var. of WHIZ n. 2.

wizard /'wɪzəd/ n. & adj. —n. **1** a sorcerer; a magician. **2** a person of remarkable powers, a genius. **3** a conjuror. —adj. *sl.* esp. *Brit.* wonderful, excellent. □□ **wizardly** adj. **wizardry** n. [ME f. WISE[1] + -ARD]

wizened /'wɪz(ə)nd/ adj. (also **wizen**) (of a person or face etc.) shrivelled-looking. [past part. of *wizen* shrivel f. OE *wisnian* f. Gmc]

wk. *abbr.* **1** week. **2** work. **3** weak.

wks. *abbr.* weeks.

Wm. *abbr.* William.

WMO *abbr.* World Meteorological Organization.

WNW *abbr.* west-north-west.

WO *abbr.* Warrant Officer.

wo /wəʊ/ int. = WHOA. [var. of *who* (int.), HO]

w.o. *abbr.* walk-over.

woad /wəʊd/ n. *hist.* **1** a cruciferous plant, *Isatis tinctoria*, yielding a blue dye now superseded by indigo. **2** the dye obtained from this. [OE *wād* f. Gmc]

wobbegong /'wɒbɪ,gɒŋ/ n. an Australian brown shark, *Orectolobus maculatus*, with buff patterned markings. [Aboriginal]

wobble /'wɒb(ə)l/ v. & n. —v. **1 a** *intr.* sway or vibrate unsteadily from side to side. **b** *tr.* cause to do this. **2** *intr.* stand or go unsteadily; stagger. **3** *intr.* waver, vacillate; act inconsistently. **4** *intr.* (of the voice or sound) quaver, pulsate. —n. **1** a wobbling movement. **2** an instance of vacillation or pulsation. □ **wobble-board** *Austral.* a piece of fibreboard used as a musical instrument with a low booming sound. □□ **wobbler** n. [earlier *wabble*, corresp. to LG *wabbeln*, ON *vafla* waver f. Gmc: cf. WAVE, WAVER, -LE[4]]

wobbly /'wɒblɪ/ adj. (**wobblier**, **wobbliest**) **1** wobbling or tending to wobble. **2** wavy, undulating (*a wobbly line*). **3** unsteady; weak after illness (*feeling wobbly*). **4** wavering, vacillating, insecure (*the economy was wobbly*). □ **throw a wobbly** *sl.* have a fit of nerves. □□ **wobbliness** n.

Wodehouse /'wʊdhaʊs/, Sir Pelham Grenville (1881–1975), English humorous writer, an American citizen from 1955. In a writing career that spanned more than 70 years his prolific output included over 120 volumes, and he became Broadway's leading writer of musical comedy lyrics. His best-known characters include Jeeves, Bertie Wooster, and the vague absent-minded Lord Emsworth, owner of the prize sow the Empress of Blandings. Wodehouse's stories, told with exuberant vitality, most of them set in an upper-class world of his own invention, exist in a realm that is as oblivious of the external world as the author was when writing them. They are musical comedies without music, their plots ingenious and finely wrought, their construction faultless, cadence and nuance displaying fineness of ear and taste, the work of a consummate stylist, while the reader is treated to gleanings from a remarkable variety of poets, philosophers, and classical writers. Wodehouse has been the subject of overstated praise, and of stupid attacks during the Second World War when he was unjustly accused of being a traitor and producing propaganda for the Axis powers.

wodge /wɒdʒ/ n. *Brit. colloq.* a chunk or lump. [alt. of WEDGE[1]]

woe /wəʊ/ n. *archaic* or *literary* **1** affliction; bitter grief; distress. **2** (in *pl.*) calamities, troubles. **3** *joc.* problems (*told me a tale of woe*). □ **woe betide** there will be unfortunate consequences for (*woe betide you if you are late*). **woe is me** an exclamation of distress. [OE *wā*, *wǣ* f. Gmc, a natural exclam. of lament]

woebegone /'wəʊbɪ,gɒn/ adj. dismal-looking. [WOE + *begone* = surrounded f. OE *began* (as BE-, GO[1])]

woeful /'wəʊfʊl/ adj. **1** sorrowful; afflicted with distress (*a woeful expression*). **2** causing sorrow or affliction. **3** very bad; wretched (*woeful ignorance*). □□ **woefully** adv. **woefulness** n.

wog[1] /wɒg/ n. *sl. offens.* a foreigner, esp. a non-White one. [20th c.: orig. unkn.]

wog[2] /wɒg/ n. *Austral. sl.* an illness or infection. [20th c.: orig. unkn.]

woggle /'wɒg(ə)l/ n. a leather etc. ring through which the ends of a Scout's neckerchief are passed at the neck. [20th c.: orig. unkn.]

wok /wɒk/ n. a bowl-shaped frying-pan used in esp. Chinese cookery. [Cantonese]

woke past of WAKE¹.

woken past part. of WAKE¹.

wold /wəʊld/ n. a piece of high open uncultivated land or moor. [OE wald f. Gmc, perh. rel. to WILD: cf. WEALD]

Wolf /vɒlf/, Hugo (1860–1903), Austrian composer. Although his opera Der Corregidor (1895) is occasionally given, Wolf is known as a lieder composer. In under 20 years he produced some 300 songs, making full use of the resources of chromaticism but maintaining an essentially small scale. In his early songs he took the verse of German writers, especially Goethe, very often setting the same texts as his great predecessor Schubert but bringing to them an entirely different approach, introspective and complex, capable of expressing the celestial eroticism of Gannymede as well as the anguished cry of the mad harpist in the three Harfenspieler. In 1889–96 he turned to translations of Spanish and Italian verse for the three volumes of his Spanish Songbook and the two volumes of his Italian Songbook, but his composing career was cut short by mental illness resulting from a syphilitic infection, and his last years were spent in an asylum.

wolf /wʊlf/ n. & v. —n. (pl. **wolves** /wʊlvz/) **1** a wild flesh-eating tawny-grey mammal related to the dog, esp. Canis lupus, preying on sheep etc. and hunting in packs. **2** sl. a man given to seducing women. **3** a rapacious or greedy person. **4** Mus. **a** a jarring sound from some notes in a bowed instrument. **b** an out-of-tune effect when playing certain chords on old organs (before the present 'equal temperament' was in use). —v.tr. (often foll. by down) devour (food) greedily. □ **cry wolf** raise repeated false alarms (so that a genuine one is disregarded). **have** (or **hold**) **a wolf by the ears** be in a precarious position. **keep the wolf from the door** avert hunger or starvation. **lone wolf** a person who prefers to act alone. **throw to the wolves** sacrifice without compunction. **Wolf Cub** the former name for a Cub Scout. (See SCOUT ASSOCIATION.) **wolf-cub** a young wolf. **wolf-fish** any large voracious blenny of the genus Anarrhichas. **wolf in sheep's clothing** a hostile person who pretends friendship. **wolf-pack** an attacking group of submarines or aircraft. **wolf's-milk** spurge. **wolf-spider** any ground-dwelling spider of the family Lycosidae, hunting instead of trapping its prey. **wolf-whistle** n. a sexually admiring whistle by a man to a woman. —v.intr. make a wolf-whistle. □□ **wolfish** adj. **wolfishly** adv. **wolflike** adj. & adv. [OE wulf f. Gmc]

Wolfe /wʊlf/, James (1727–59), British general, captor of Quebec. As one of the leaders of the expedition sent to capture French Canada, he played a vital part in the siege of Louisburg before being charged with the attack on the enemy capital, Quebec City. He was mortally wounded while leading his troops to victory on the Plains of Abraham, the battle which effectively sealed the fate of France's Canadian empire.

wolfhound /'wʊlfhaʊnd/ n. a borzoi or other dog of a kind used orig. to hunt wolves.

wolfram /'wʊlfrəm/ n. **1** tungsten. **2** tungsten ore; a native tungstate of iron and manganese. [G: perh. f. Wolf WOLF + Rahm cream, or MHG rām dirt, soot]

wolframite /'wʊlfrə,maɪt/ n. = WOLFRAM 2.

wolfsbane /'wʊlfsbeɪn/ n. an aconite, esp. Aconitum lycoctonum.

wolfskin /'wʊlfskɪn/ n. **1** the skin of a wolf. **2** a mat, cloak, etc., made from this.

Wolfson /'wʊlfs(ə)n/, Sir Isaac (1897–), British businessman (founder of Great Universal Stores Ltd.) and philanthropist. He endowed the Wolfson Foundation (1955) for the advancement of health, education, and youth activities in Britain and the Commonwealth. A college is named after him both at Oxford University (1966) and at Cambridge, where University College was renamed in 1973, in recognition of grants received from the Wolfson Foundation; both are for graduate students.

Wollaston /'wʊləst(ə)n/, William Hyde (1766–1828), English chemist and physicist, pioneer of powder metallurgy, developed when attempting to produce malleable platinum, in the course of which he discovered palladium (1802) and rhodium (1804). The income he derived from his platinum process allowed him

to devote himself entirely to scientific research. He demonstrated in 1801 that frictional electricity (electrostatics) and current electricity were the same, was the first to observe the dark (Fraunhofer) lines in the solar spectrum, and invented a chemical slide-rule and several optical instruments, including the reflecting goniometer (for measuring the angles of crystals), a double-image prism, and an aberration-free lens. He supported Dalton's atomic theory and the wave theory of light. The mineral wollastonite is named after him.

Wolsey /'wʊlzɪ/, Thomas (c.1474–1530), English cardinal, archbishop of York (1514–30), Lord Chancellor (1515–29), a statesman rather than a churchman. Favoured by Henry VIII, he wielded an almost royal power and dominated foreign and domestic policy until he occurred royal displeasure through his failure to secure the papal dispensation necessary for the king's divorce from Catherine of Aragon, which led to his arrest on a charge of treason; he died on his way to trial in London. Wolsey had devoted his life to the aggrandizement of king and country, fostering the development of royal absolutism in politics as well as in ecclesiastical matters. His main interest was in foreign politics, in which he frequently changed sides, skilfully holding the balance of power between the Holy Roman Empire and France in a boldly conceived (but disastrously expensive) attempt to make England the arbiter of Europe, a dream that remained unrealized in his age.

Wolverhampton /ˌwʊlvə'hæmpt(ə)n/ an industrial city in the West Midlands; pop. (1981) 254,550.

wolverine /'wʊlvə,riːn/ n. (also **wolverene**) an animal (Gulo gulo), also known as the glutton, that is the largest of the weasel family, living in the cold pine forests of the northern continents, especially North America. The coarse shiny hairs of its brown fur are remarkable in that they do not collect and hold moisture; for this reason the fur is prized for trimming the openings of Eskimo clothing. [16th-c. wolvering, somehow derived f. wolv-, stem of WOLF]

wolves pl. of WOLF.

woman /'wʊmən/ n. (pl. **women** /'wɪmɪn/) **1** an adult human female. **2** the female sex; any or an average woman (how does woman differ from man?). **3** a wife or female sexual partner. **4** (prec. by the) emotions or characteristics traditionally associated with women (brought out the woman in him). **5** a man with characteristics traditionally associated with women. **6** (attrib.) female (woman driver; women friends). **7** (as second element in comb.) a woman of a specified nationality, profession, skill, etc. (Englishwoman; horsewoman). **8** colloq. a female domestic help. **9** archaic or hist. a queen's etc. female attendant ranking below lady (woman of the bedchamber). □ **woman of the streets** a prostitute. **women's lib** colloq. = women's liberation. **women's libber** colloq. a supporter of women's liberation. **women's liberation** the liberation of women from inequalities and subservient status in relation to men, and from attitudes causing these. **Women's Liberation** (or **Movement**) a movement campaigning for women's liberation. **women's rights** rights that promote a position of legal and social equality of women with men. □□ **womanless** adj. **womanlike** adj. [OE wīfmon, -man (as WIFE, MAN), a formation peculiar to English, the ancient word being WIFE]

womanhood /'wʊmən,hʊd/ n. **1** female maturity. **2** womanly instinct. **3** womankind.

womanish /'wʊmənɪʃ/ adj. usu. derog. **1** (of a man) effeminate, unmanly. **2** suitable to or characteristic of a woman. □□ **womanishly** adv. **womanishness** n.

womanize /'wʊmə,naɪz/ v. (also **-ise**) **1** intr. chase after women; philander. **2** tr. make womanish. □□ **womanizer** n.

womankind /'wʊmən,kaɪnd/ n. (also **womenkind** /'wɪmɪn-/) women in general.

womanly /'wʊmənlɪ/ adj. (of a woman) having or showing qualities traditionally associated with women; not masculine or girlish. □□ **womanliness** n.

womb /wuːm/ n. **1** the organ of conception and gestation in a woman and other female mammals; the uterus. **2** a place of origination and development. □□ **womblike** adj. [OE wamb, womb]

wombat /ˈwɒmbæt/ n. any burrowing plant-eating Australian marsupial of the family Vombatidae, resembling a small bear, with short legs. [Aboriginal]

women pl. of WOMAN.

womenfolk /ˈwɪmɪnˌfəʊk/ n. 1 women in general. 2 the women in a family.

womenkind var. of WOMANKIND.

Women's Institute an organization of women to enable those in rural areas to meet regularly and engage in crafts, cultural activities, social work, etc. Now worldwide, it was first set up in Ontario, Canada, in 1895, and in Britain in 1915.

won past and past part. of WIN.

Wonder /ˈwʌndə(r)/, Stevie (real name Stephen Judkins, 1950–), American singer and songwriter, noted for his innovations and versatility. His albums include Music of My Mind (1972) and Songs in the Key of Life (1976).

wonder /ˈwʌndə(r)/ n. & v. —n. 1 an emotion excited by what is unexpected, unfamiliar, or inexplicable, e.g. surprise mingled with admiration or curiosity etc. 2 a strange or remarkable person or thing, specimen, event, etc. 3 (attrib.) having marvellous or amazing properties etc. (a wonder drug). 4 a surprising thing (it is a wonder you were not hurt). —v. 1 intr. (often foll. by at, or to + infin.) be filled with wonder or great surprise. 2 tr. (foll. by that + clause) be surprised to find. 3 tr. desire or be curious to know (I wonder what the time is). 4 tr. expressing a tentative enquiry (I wonder whether you would mind?). □ **I shouldn't wonder** colloq. I think it likely. **I wonder** I very much doubt it. **no** (or **small**) **wonder** (often foll. by that + clause) one cannot be surprised; one might have guessed; it is natural. **the seven wonders of the world** seven buildings and monuments regarded in antiquity as specially remarkable. **wonder-struck** (or **-stricken**) reduced to silence by wonder. **wonders will never cease** an exclamation of extreme (usu. agreeable) surprise. **wonder-worker** a person who performs wonders. **work** (or **do**) **wonders** 1 do miracles. 2 succeed remarkably. □□ **wonderer** n. [OE wundor, wundrian, of unkn. orig.]

wonderful /ˈwʌndəˌfʊl/ adj. 1 very remarkable or admirable. 2 arousing wonder. □□ **wonderfully** adv. **wonderfulness** n. [OE wunderfull (as WONDER, -FUL)]

wondering /ˈwʌndərɪŋ/ adj. filled with wonder; marvelling (their wondering gaze). □□ **wonderingly** adv.

wonderland /ˈwʌndəˌlænd/ n. 1 a fairyland. 2 a land of surprises or marvels.

wonderment /ˈwʌndəmənt/ n. surprise, awe.

wondrous /ˈwʌndrəs/ adj. & adv. poet. —adj. wonderful. —adv. wonderfully (wondrous kind). □□ **wondrously** adv. **wondrousness** n. [alt. of obs. wonders (adj. & adv.), = genit. of WONDER (cf. -s³) after marvellous]

wonky /ˈwɒŋkɪ/ adj. (**wonkier**, **wonkiest**) Brit. sl. 1 crooked. 2 loose, unsteady. 3 unreliable. □□ **wonkily** adv. **wonkiness** n. [fanciful formation]

wont /wəʊnt/ adj., n., & v. —predic.adj. archaic or literary (foll. by to + infin.) accustomed (as we were wont to say). —n. formal or joc. what is customary, one's habit (as is my wont). —v.tr. & intr. (3rd sing. present **wonts** or **wont**; past **wont** or **wonted**) archaic make or become accustomed. [OE gewunod past part. of gewunian f. wunian dwell]

won't /wəʊnt/ contr. will not.

wonted /ˈwəʊntɪd/ attrib.adj. habitual, accustomed, usual.

woo /wuː/ v.tr. (**woos**, **wooed**) 1 court; seek the hand or love of (a woman). 2 try to win (fame, fortune, etc.). 3 seek the favour or support of. 4 coax or importune. □□ **wooable** adj. **wooer** n. [OE wōgian (intr.), āwōgian (tr.), of unkn. orig.]

Wood /wʊd/, Sir Henry (1869–1944), English conductor. He had many posts as a conductor before becoming, in 1894, music adviser to Felix Mottl's Wagner concerts at the new Queen's Hall, the setting a year later for the first of the Promenade Concerts re-established by Robert Newman and with Wood as conductor. He retained the conductorship until the year he died,

building the concerts from rudimentary beginnings to form a central feature of English musical life. He was a tireless champion of contemporary music, conducting the first performance of Schoenberg's Five Orchestral Pieces in 1912 and introducing the music of Janáček to England. He made many orchestral transcriptions and arranged the Fantasia on British Sea Songs which for many years was performed, with the participation of the audience, on the last night of every Prom season.

wood /wʊd/ n. 1 a a hard fibrous material that forms the main substance of the trunk or branches of a tree or shrub. b this cut for timber or for fuel, or for use in crafts, manufacture, etc. 2 (in sing. or pl.) growing trees densely occupying a tract of land. 3 (prec. by the) wooden storage, esp. a cask, for wine etc. (poured straight from the wood). 4 a wooden-headed golf club. 5 = BOWL² n. 1. □ **not see the wood for the trees** fail to grasp the main issue from over-attention to details. **out of the wood** (or **woods**) out of danger or difficulty. **wood alcohol** methanol. **wood anemone** a wild spring-flowering anemone, Anemone nemorosa. **wood-engraver** a maker of wood-engravings. **wood-engraving** 1 a relief cut on a block of wood sawn across the grain. 2 a print made from this. 3 the technique of making such reliefs and prints. **wood-fibre** fibre obtained from wood esp. as material for paper. **wood hyacinth** = BLUEBELL 1. **wood nymph** a dryad or hamadryad. **wood pulp** wood-fibre reduced chemically or mechanically to pulp as raw material for paper. **wood-screw** a metal male screw with a slotted head and sharp point. **wood sorrel** a small plant, Oxalis acetosella, with trifoliate leaves and white flowers streaked with purple. **wood spirit** crude methanol obtained from wood. **wood warbler** 1 a European woodland bird, Phylloscopus sibilatrix, with a trilling song. 2 any American warbler of the family Parulidae. **wood wool** fine pine etc. shavings used as a surgical dressing or for packing. □□ **woodless** adj. [OE wudu, wi(o)du f. Gmc]

woodbind /ˈwʊdbaɪnd/ n. = WOODBINE.

woodbine /ˈwʊdbaɪn/ n. 1 wild honeysuckle. 2 US Virginia creeper.

woodblock /ˈwʊdblɒk/ n. a block from which woodcuts are made.

woodchuck /ˈwʊdtʃʌk/ n. a reddish-brown and grey N. American marmot, Marmota monax. [Amer. Ind. name: cf. Cree wuchak, otchock]

woodcock /ˈwʊdkɒk/ n. (pl. same) any game-bird of the genus Scolopax, inhabiting woodland.

woodcraft /ˈwʊdkrɑːft/ n. esp. US 1 skill in woodwork. 2 knowledge of woodland esp. in camping, scouting, etc.

woodcut /ˈwʊdkʌt/ n. 1 a relief cut on a block of wood sawn along the grain. 2 a print made from this, esp. as an illustration in a book. 3 the technique of making such reliefs and prints.

woodcutter /ˈwʊdˌkʌtə(r)/ n. 1 a person who cuts wood. 2 a maker of woodcuts.

wooded /ˈwʊdɪd/ adj. having woods or many trees.

wooden /ˈwʊd(ə)n/ adj. 1 made of wood. 2 like wood. 3 a stiff, clumsy, or stilted; without animation or flexibility (wooden movements; a wooden performance). b expressionless (a wooden stare). □ **wooden-head** colloq. a stupid person. **wooden-headed** colloq. stupid. **wooden-headedness** colloq. stupidity. **wooden horse** = Trojan Horse. **wooden spoon** a booby prize (orig. a spoon given to the candidate coming last in the Cambridge mathematical tripos). □□ **woodenly** adv. **woodenness** n.

woodgrouse /ˈwʊdɡraʊs/ n. = CAPERCAILLIE.

woodland /ˈwʊdlənd/ n. wooded country, woods (often attrib.: woodland scenery). □□ **woodlander** n.

woodlark /ˈwʊdlɑːk/ n. a lark, Lullula arborea.

woodlouse /ˈwʊdlaʊs/ n. (pl. -lice /-laɪs/) any small terrestrial isopod crustacean of the genus Oniscus etc. feeding on rotten wood etc. and often able to roll into a ball.

woodman /ˈwʊdmən/ n. (pl. -men) 1 a forester. 2 a woodcutter.

woodmouse /ˈwʊdmaʊs/ n. (pl. -mice /-maɪs/) a fieldmouse.

woodnote /ˈwʊdnəʊt/ n. (often in pl.) a natural or spontaneous note of a bird etc.

woodpecker /ˈwʊdˌpekə(r)/ n. any bird of the family Picidae that climbs and taps tree-trunks in search of insects.

woodpie /ˈwʊdpaɪ/ n. a greater spotted woodpecker.

woodpigeon /ˈwʊdˌpɪdʒ(ə)n/ n. a dove, *Columba palumbus*, having white patches like a ring round its neck. Also called *ring-dove* (see RING[1]).

woodpile /ˈwʊdpaɪl/ n. a pile of wood, esp. for fuel.

woodruff /ˈwʊdrʌf/ n. a white-flowered plant of the genus *Galium*, esp. *G. odoratum* grown for the fragrance of its whorled leaves when dried or crushed.

woodrush /ˈwʊdrʌʃ/ n. any grassy herbaceous plant of the genus *Luzula*.

woodshed /ˈwʊdʃed/ n. a shed where wood for fuel is stored. □ **something nasty in the woodshed** *colloq.* a shocking or distasteful thing kept secret.

woodsman /ˈwʊdzmən/ n. (*pl.* **-men**) 1 a person who lives in or is familiar with woodland. 2 a person skilled in woodcraft.

Woodstock /ˈwʊdstɒk/ a town in the south-east of New York State, noted as an artists' colony. In August 1969 a rock festival held at the Woodstock Music and Art Fair near Bethel, NY, drew massive crowds and came to symbolize the youth culture of the period.

woodsy /ˈwʊdzɪ/ adj. US like or characteristic of woods. [irreg. f. WOOD + -Y[1]]

woodwasp /ˈwʊdwɒsp/ n. any sawfly of the family Siricidae, esp. *Urocerus gigas*, that hangs its nest in trees and inserts its eggs into the wood of conifers where the larvae bore damaging tunnels.

woodwind /ˈwʊdwɪnd/ n. (often *attrib.*) 1 (*collect.*) the wind instruments of the orchestra that were (mostly) orig. made of wood, e.g. the flute and clarinet. 2 (usu. in *pl.*) an individual instrument of this kind or its player (*the woodwinds are out of tune*).

woodwork /ˈwʊdwɜːk/ n. 1 the making of things in wood. 2 things made of wood, esp. the wooden parts of a building. □ **crawl** (or **come**) **out of the woodwork** *colloq.* (of something unwelcome) appear; become known. □□ **woodworker** n. **woodworking** n.

woodworm /ˈwʊdwɜːm/ n. 1 the wood-boring larva of the furniture beetle. 2 the damaged condition of wood affected by this.

woody /ˈwʊdɪ/ adj. (**woodier**, **woodiest**) 1 (of a region) wooded; abounding in woods. 2 like or of wood (*woody tissue*). □ **woody nightshade** see NIGHTSHADE. □□ **woodiness** n.

woodyard /ˈwʊdjɑːd/ n. a yard where wood is used or stored.

woof[1] /wʊf/ n. & v. —n. the gruff bark of a dog. —v.intr. give a woof. [imit.]

woof[2] /wuːf/ n. = WEFT[1]. [OE *ōwef*, alt. of *ōwebb* (after *wefan* WEAVE[1]), formed as A-[2], WEB: infl. by *warp*]

woofer /ˈwuːfə(r)/ n. a loudspeaker designed to reproduce low frequencies (cf. TWEETER). [WOOF[1] + -ER[1]]

wool /wʊl/ n. 1 fine soft wavy hair from the fleece of sheep, goats, etc. 2 **a** yarn produced from this hair. **b** cloth or clothing made from it. 3 any of various wool-like substances (*steel wool*). 4 soft short under-fur or down. 5 *colloq.* a person's hair, esp. when short and curly. □ **pull the wool over a person's eyes** deceive a person. **wool-fat** lanolin. **wool-fell** *Brit.* the skin of a sheep etc. with the fleece still on. **wool-gathering** absent-mindedness; dreamy inattention. **wool-grower** a breeder of sheep for wool. **wool-oil** suint. **wool-pack 1** a fleecy cumulus cloud. **2** *hist.* a bale of wool. **wool-skin** = *wool-fell*. **wool-sorters' disease** anthrax. **wool-stapler** a person who grades wool. □□ **wool-like** adj. [OE *wull* f. Gmc]

Woolf /wʊlf/, (Adeline) Virginia (1882–1941), English novelist, whose London house became the centre of the Bloomsbury Group. She began her literary career as a critic for the *Times Literary Supplement* and in 1912 married Leonard Woolf with whom she founded the Hogarth Press (1917), which published some of her finest works. Her third novel, *Jacob's Room* (1922), was recognized as a new development in the art of fiction and in her succeeding novels she firmly established her stream-of-consciousness technique and poetic impressionism, becoming a principal exponent of modernism; these include *Mrs.*

Dalloway (1925), *To the Lighthouse* (1927), *The Waves* (1931), and *The Years* (1937), interspersed with slighter works and her feminist classic *A Room of One's Own* (1929). She had meanwhile suffered recurring attacks of acute mental disturbance and shortly after completing her final and most experimental novel, *Between the Acts* (1941), drowned herself in the River Ouse. She is now acclaimed as one of the great innovative novelists of the 20th c. and many of her techniques have been absorbed into mainstream fiction. Her published letters and diaries are a dazzling evocation of the literary world of her time.

woollen /ˈwʊlən/ adj. & n. (*US* **woolen**) —adj. made wholly or partly of wool, esp. from short fibres. —n. 1 a fabric produced from wool. 2 (in *pl.*) woollen garments. [OE *wullen* (as WOOL, -EN[2])]

Woolley /ˈwʊlɪ/, Sir Charles Leonard (1880–1960), English archaeologist, noted for his excavations at Ur.

woolly /ˈwʊlɪ/ adj. & n. —adj. (**woollier**, **woolliest**) 1 bearing or naturally covered with wool or wool-like hair. 2 resembling or suggesting wool (*woolly clouds*). 3 (of a sound) indistinct. 4 (of thought) vague or confused. 5 *Bot.* downy. 6 lacking in definition, luminosity, or incisiveness. —n. (*pl.* **-ies**) *colloq.* a woollen garment, esp. a knitted pullover. □ **woolly-bear** a large hairy caterpillar, esp. of the tiger moth. □□ **woolliness** n.

Woolsack /ˈwʊlsæk/ n. 1 (in the UK) the usual seat, without back or arms, of the Lord Chancellor in the House of Lords, made of a large square bag of wool and covered with cloth. It is said to have been adopted in Edward III's reign as a reminder to the Lords of the importance to England of the wool trade. 2 the position of Lord Chancellor.

woolshed /ˈwʊlʃed/ n. *Austral.* & NZ a large shed for shearing and baling wool.

Woolworth /ˈwʊlwəθ/, Frank Winfield (1852–1919), American business man who from 1879 onwards opened a chain of shops, in the US and other countries, selling low-priced goods.

Woomera /ˈwuːmərə/ a location in central South Australia used as a nuclear testing site from 1952 to 1957.

woomera /ˈwuːmərə/ n. *Austral.* 1 an Aboriginal stick for throwing a dart or spear more forcibly. 2 a club used as a missile. [Aboriginal]

woop woop /ˈwuːpwuːp/ n. *Austral.* & NZ *sl.* 1 a jocular name for a remote outback town or district. 2 (**Woop Woop**) an imaginary remote place. [mock Aboriginal]

woosh var. of WHOOSH.

woozy /ˈwuːzɪ/ adj. (**woozier**, **wooziest**) *colloq.* 1 dizzy or unsteady. 2 dazed or slightly drunk. 3 vague. □□ **woozily** adv. **wooziness** n. [19th c.: orig. unkn.]

wop /wɒp/ n. *sl. offens.* an Italian or other S. European. [20th c.: orig. uncert.: perh. f. It. *guappo* bold, showy, f. Sp. *guapo* dandy]

Worcester /ˈwʊstə(r)/ a city in the county of Hereford and Worcester, on the River Severn, scene of a battle (1651) in which Cromwell defeated a Scottish army under Charles II; pop. (1981) 74,790. □ **Worcester china** (also **Royal Worcester**) porcelain made at Worcester in a factory founded in 1751. **Worcester sauce** a pungent sauce containing soy, vinegar, and condiments, first made at Worcester.

Worcs. *abbr.* Worcestershire.

word /wɜːd/ n. & v. —n. 1 a sound or combination of sounds forming a meaningful element of speech, usu. shown with a space on either side of it when written or printed, used as part (or occas. as the whole) of a sentence. 2 speech, esp. as distinct from action (*bold in word only*). 3 one's promise or assurance (*gave us their word*). 4 (in *sing.* or *pl.*) a thing said, a remark or conversation. 5 (in *pl.*) the text of a song or an actor's part. 6 (in *pl.*) angry talk (*they had words*). 7 news, intelligence; a message. 8 a command, password, or motto (*gave the word to begin*). 9 a basic unit of the expression of data in a computer. —v.tr. put into words; select words to express (*how shall we word that?*). □ **at a word** as soon as requested. **be as good as** (or **better than**) **one's word** fulfil (or exceed) what one has promised. **break one's word** fail to do what one has promised. **have no words for** be unable to express. **have a word** (often foll. by *with*) speak briefly (to). **in other words** expressing the same thing differently. **in so many words** explicitly or bluntly. **in a** (or **one**) **word** briefly. **keep one's word** do what one has promised. **my** (or **upon my**) **word** an exclamation of surprise or consternation. **not the word for it** not an adequate or appropriate description. **of few words** taciturn. **of one's word** reliable in keeping promises (*a woman of her word*). **on** (or **upon**) **my word** a form of asseveration. **put into words** express in speech or writing. **take a person at his** or **her word** interpret a person's words literally or exactly. **take a person's word for it** believe a person's statement without investigation etc. **too ... for words** too ... to be adequately described (*was too funny for words*). **waste words** talk in vain. **the Word** (or **Word of God**) **1** the Bible or a part of it. **2** the title of the Second Person of the Trinity, = Logos. **word-blind** incapable of identifying written or printed words owing to a brain defect. **word-blindness** this condition. **word-deaf** incapable of identifying spoken words owing to a brain defect. **word-deafness** this condition. **word for word** in exactly the same or (of translation) corresponding words. **word-game** a game involving the making or selection etc. of words. **word of honour** an assurance given upon one's honour. **word of mouth** speech (only). **word order** the sequence of words in a sentence, esp. affecting meaning etc. **word-painting** a vivid description in writing. **word-perfect** knowing one's part etc. by heart. **word-picture** a piece of word-painting. **word processor** a purpose-built computer system for electronically storing text entered from a keyboard, incorporating corrections, and providing a printout. **words fail me** an expression of disbelief, dismay, etc. **word-square** a set of words of equal length written one under another to read the same down as across (e.g. *too old ode*). **a word to the wise** = VERB. SAP. □□ **wordage** *n.* **wordless** *adj.* **wordlessly** *adv.* **wordlessness** *n.* [OE f. Gmc]

wordbook /ˈwɜːdbʊk/ *n.* a book with lists of words; a vocabulary or dictionary.

wording /ˈwɜːdɪŋ/ *n.* **1** a form of words used. **2** the way in which something is expressed.

wordplay /ˈwɜːdpleɪ/ *n.* use of words to witty effect, esp. by punning.

wordsmith /ˈwɜːdsmɪθ/ *n.* a skilled user or maker of words.

Wordsworth /ˈwɜːdzwəθ/, William (1770–1850), English poet, an enthusiastic worshipper of nature and simplicity and, with Coleridge, the creator of the English Romantic movement. He was born in the Lake District and describes the profound effect of his country childhood and sense of the living landscape in his posthumously published poetic autobiography *The Prelude* (1850). He spent some time in France, where he became an enthusiastic republican until disillusioned by the Terror, and had a love affair with Annette Vallon, who bore him a daughter, and then in Somerset, where, with Coleridge, he composed the *Lyrical Ballads*, 1798, which attacked conventional poetry of the 18th c. Then he settled with his sister Dorothy in Grasmere in 1799; with his wife (Mary Hutchinson, whom he married in 1802) they lived a life of 'plain living and high thinking', and he composed the poems that made him (after initial hostility) revered as the greatest poet of his time. These include his 'Immortality' ode (1807), many fine sonnets, and pastoral poems such as 'Michael' (1800). Radical in his youth, he became conservative with age, and in 1843 was made Poet Laureate.

wordy /ˈwɜːdɪ/ *adj.* (**wordier**, **wordiest**) **1** using or expressed in many or too many words; verbose. **2** consisting of words. □□ **wordily** *adv.* **wordiness** *n.* [OE *wordig* (as WORD, -Y¹)]

wore¹ *past* of WEAR¹.

wore² *past* and *past part.* of WEAR².

work /wɜːk/ *n.* & *v.* —*n.* **1** the application of mental or physical effort to a purpose; the use of energy. **2 a** a task to be undertaken. **b** the materials for this. **c** (*prec. by the*; foll. by *of*) a task occupying (no more than) a specified time (*the work of a moment*). **3** a thing done or made by work; the result of an action; an achievement; a thing made. **4** a person's employment or occupation etc., esp. as a means of earning income (*looked for work*; *is out of work*). **5 a** a literary or musical composition. **b** (in *pl.*) all such by an author or composer etc. **6** actions or experiences of a specified kind (*good work!*; *this is thirsty work*). **7 a** (in *comb.*)

things or parts made of a specified material or with specified tools etc. (*ironwork*; *needlework*). **b** *archaic* needlework. **8** (in *pl.*) the operative part of a clock or machine. **9** *Physics* the exertion of force overcoming resistance or producing molecular change (*convert heat into work*). **10** (in *pl.*) *colloq.* all that is available; everything needed. **11** (in *pl.*) operations of building or repair (*road works*). **12** (in *pl.*; often treated as *sing.*) a place where manufacture is carried on. **13** (usu. in *pl.*) *Theol.* a meritorious act. **14** (usu. in *pl.* or in *comb.*) a defensive structure (*earthworks*). **15** (in *comb.*) **a** ornamentation of a specified kind (*poker-work*). **b** articles having this. —*v.* (*past* and *past part.* **worked** or (esp. as *adj.*) **wrought**) **1** *intr.* (often foll. by *at*, *on*) do work; be engaged in bodily or mental activity. **2** *intr.* **a** be employed in certain work (*works in industry*; *works as a secretary*). **b** (foll. by *with*) be the workmate of (a person). **3** *intr.* (often foll. by *for*) make efforts; conduct a campaign (*works for peace*). **4** *intr.* (foll. by *in*) be a craftsman (in a material). **5** *intr.* operate or function, esp. effectively (*how does this machine work?*; *your idea will not work*). **6** *intr.* (of a part of a machine) run, revolve; go through regular motions. **7** *tr.* carry on, manage, or control (*cannot work the machine*). **8** *tr.* **a** put or keep in operation or at work; cause to toil (*this mine is no longer worked*; *works the staff very hard*). **b** cultivate (land). **9** *tr.* bring about; produce as a result (*worked miracles*). **10** *tr.* knead, hammer; bring to a desired shape or consistency. **11** *tr.* do, or make by, needlework etc. **12** *tr.* & *intr.* (cause to) progress or penetrate, or make (one's way), gradually or with difficulty in a specified way (*worked our way through the crowd*; *worked the peg into the hole*). **13** *intr.* (foll. by *loose* etc.) gradually become (loose etc.) by constant movement. **14** *tr.* artificially excite (*worked themselves into a rage*). **15** *tr.* solve (a sum) by mathematics. **16** *tr.* **a** purchase with one's labour instead of money (*work one's passage*). **b** obtain by labour the money for (one's way through university etc.). **17** *intr.* (foll. by *on*, *upon*) have influence. **18** *intr.* be in motion or agitated; cause agitation, ferment (*his features worked violently*; *the yeast began to work*). **19** *intr.* *Naut.* sail against the wind. □ **at work** in action or engaged in work. **give a person the works 1** *colloq.* give or tell a person everything. **2** *colloq.* treat a person harshly. **3** *sl.* kill a person. **have one's work cut out** be faced with a hard task. **set to work** begin or cause to begin operations. **work away** (or **on**) continue to work. **work-basket** (or **-bag** etc.) a basket or bag etc. containing sewing materials. **work camp** a camp at which community work is done esp. by young volunteers. **work one's fingers to the bone** see BONE. **work in** find a place for. **work it** *colloq.* bring it about; achieve a desired result. **work of art** a fine picture, poem, or building etc. **work off** get rid of by work or activity. **work out 1** solve (a sum) or find out (an amount) by calculation. **2** (foll. by *at*) be calculated (*the total works out at 230*). **3** give a definite result (*this sum will not work out*). **4** have a specified result (*the plan worked out well*). **5** provide for the details of (*has worked out a scheme*). **6** accomplish or attain with difficulty (*work out one's salvation*). **7** exhaust with work (*the mine is worked out*). **8** engage in physical exercise or training. **work over 1** examine thoroughly. **2** *colloq.* treat with violence. **works council** esp. *Brit.* a group of employees representing those employed in a works etc. in discussions with their employers. **work-shy** disinclined to work. **works of supererogation** see SUPEREROGATION. **work study** a system of assessing methods of working so as to achieve the maximum output and efficiency. **work table** a table for working at, esp. with a sewing-machine. **work to rule** (esp. as a form of industrial action) follow official working rules exactly in order to reduce output and efficiency. **work-to-rule** the act or an instance of working to rule. **work up 1** bring gradually to an efficient state. **2** (foll. by *to*) advance gradually to a climax. **3** elaborate or excite by degrees. **4** mingle (ingredients) into a whole. **5** learn (a subject) by study. **work one's will** (foll. by *on*, *upon*) *archaic* accomplish one's purpose on (a person or thing). **work wonders** see WONDER. □□ **workless** *adj.* [OE *weorc* etc. f. Gmc]

workable /ˈwɜːkəb(ə)l/ *adj.* **1** that can be worked or will work. **2** that is worth working; practicable, feasible (*a workable quarry*; *a workable scheme*). □□ **workability** (/-ˈbɪlɪtɪ/) *n.* **workableness** *n.* **workably** *adv.*

workaday /ˈwɜːkəˌdeɪ/ adj. **1** ordinary, everyday, practical. **2** fit for, used, or seen on workdays.

workaholic /ˌwɜːkəˈhɒlɪk/ n. colloq. a person addicted to working.

workbench /ˈwɜːkbentʃ/ n. a bench for doing mechanical or practical work, esp. carpentry.

workbox /ˈwɜːkbɒks/ n. a box for holding tools, materials for sewing, etc.

workday /ˈwɜːkdeɪ/ n. esp. US a day on which work is usually done.

worker /ˈwɜːkə(r)/ n. **1** a person who works, esp. a manual or industrial employee. **2** a neuter or undeveloped female of various social insects, esp. a bee or ant, that does the basic work of its colony. □ **worker priest** a French Roman Catholic or an Anglican priest who engages part-time in secular work.

workforce /ˈwɜːkfɔːs/ n. **1** the workers engaged or available in an industry etc. **2** the number of such workers.

workhorse /ˈwɜːkhɔːs/ n. a horse, person, or machine that performs hard work.

workhouse /ˈwɜːkhaʊs/ n. **1** Brit. hist. a public institution where people of a parish unable to support themselves were housed and (if able-bodied) made to work. Under the new Poor Law of 1834, able-bodied paupers could obtain public relief only by staying at workhouses, where conditions were made as uncomfortable as possible with a view to discouraging idlers; families were split up. Conditions gradually improved in the face of public protest, but workhouses were always dreaded as places of humiliation until their disappearance c.1930. **2** US a house of correction for petty offenders.

working /ˈwɜːkɪŋ/ adj. & n. —adj. **1** engaged in work, esp. in manual or industrial labour. **2** functioning or able to function. —n. **1** the activity of work. **2** the act or manner of functioning of a thing. **3 a** a mine or quarry. **b** the part of this in which work is being or has been done (a disused working). □ **working capital** the capital actually used in a business. **working class** the class of people who are employed for wages, esp. in manual or industrial work. **working-class** adj. of the working class. **working day** esp. Brit. **1** a workday. **2** the part of the day devoted to work. **working drawing** a drawing to scale, serving as a guide for construction or manufacture. **working hours** hours normally devoted to work. **working hypothesis** a hypothesis used as a basis for action. **working knowledge** knowledge adequate to work with. **working lunch** etc. a meal at which business is conducted. **working order** the condition in which a machine works (satisfactorily or as specified). **working-out** **1** the calculation of results. **2** the elaboration of details. **working party** a group of people appointed to study a particular problem or advise on some question.

workload /ˈwɜːkləʊd/ n. the amount of work to be done by an individual etc.

workman /ˈwɜːkmən/ n. (pl. **-men**) **1** a man employed to do manual labour. **2** a person considered with regard to skill in a job (a good workman).

workmanlike /ˈwɜːkmənˌlaɪk/ adj. characteristic of a good workman; showing practised skill.

workmanship /ˈwɜːkmənʃɪp/ n. **1** the degree of skill in doing a task or of finish in the product made. **2** a thing made or created by a specified person etc.

workmate /ˈwɜːkmeɪt/ n. a person engaged in the same work as another.

workout /ˈwɜːkaʊt/ n. a session of physical exercise or training.

workpeople /ˈwɜːkˌpiːp(ə)l/ n.pl. people in paid employment.

workpiece /ˈwɜːkpiːs/ n. a thing worked on with a tool or machine.

workplace /ˈwɜːkpleɪs/ n. a place at which a person works; an office, factory, etc.

workroom /ˈwɜːkruːm, -rʊm/ n. a room for working in, esp. one equipped for a certain kind of work.

worksheet /ˈwɜːkʃiːt/ n. **1** a paper for recording work done or in progress. **2** a paper listing questions or activities for students etc. to work through.

workshop /ˈwɜːkʃɒp/ n. **1** a room or building in which goods are manufactured. **2 a** a meeting for concerted discussion or activity (a dance workshop). **b** the members of such a meeting.

workstation /ˈwɜːkˌsteɪʃ(ə)n/ n. **1** the location of a stage in a manufacturing process. **2** a computer terminal or the desk etc. where this is located.

worktop /ˈwɜːktɒp/ n. a flat surface for working on, esp. in a kitchen.

workwoman /ˈwɜːkˌwʊmən/ n. (pl. **-women**) a female worker or operative.

world /wɜːld/ n. **1 a** the earth, or a planetary body like it. **b** its countries and their inhabitants. **c** all people; the earth as known or in some particular respect. **2 a** the universe or all that exists; everything. **b** everything that exists outside oneself (dead to the world). **3 a** the time, state, or scene of human existence. **b** (prec. by the, this) mortal life. **4** secular interests and affairs. **5** human affairs; their course and conditions; active life (how goes the world with you?). **6** average, respectable, or fashionable people or their customs or opinions. **7** all that concerns or all who belong to a specified class, time, domain, or sphere of activity (the medieval world; the world of sport). **8** (foll. by of) a vast amount (that makes a world of difference). **9** (attrib.) affecting many nations, of all nations (world politics; a world champion). □ **all the world and his wife 1** any large mixed gathering of people. **2** all with pretensions to fashion. **bring into the world** give birth to or attend at the birth of. **carry the world before one** have rapid and complete success. **come into the world** be born. **for all the world** (foll. by like, as if) precisely (looked for all the world as if they were real). **get the best of both worlds** benefit from two incompatible sets of ideas, circumstances, etc. **in the world** of all; at all (used as an intensifier in questions) (what in the world is it?). **man** (or **woman**) **of the world** a person experienced and practical in human affairs. **the next** (or **other**) **world** a supposed life after death. **out of this world** colloq. extremely good etc. (the food was out of this world). **see the world** travel widely; gain wide experience. **think the world of** have a very high regard for. **world-beater** a person or thing surpassing all others. **world-class** of a quality or standard regarded as high throughout the world. **world-famous** known throughout the world. **the world, the flesh, and the devil** the various kinds of temptation. **world language 1** an artificial language for international use. **2** a language spoken in many countries. **world-line** Physics a curve in space-time joining the positions of a particle throughout its existence. **the** (or **all the**) **world over** throughout the world. **world power** a nation having power and influence in world affairs. **the world's end** the farthest attainable point of travel. **world-shaking** of supreme importance. **the world to come** supposed life after death. **world-view** = WELTANSCHAUUNG. **world war** see separate entry. **world-weariness** being world-weary. **world-weary** weary of the world and life on it. **world without end** for ever. [OE w(e)orold, world f. a Gmc root meaning 'age': rel. to OLD]

World Bank the popular name of the International Bank for Reconstruction and Development, an agency set up by the United Nations in 1945 to promote the economic development of member nations by facilitating the investment of capital for productive purposes, encouraging private foreign investment, and if necessary lending money from its own funds. Its headquarters are in Washington, DC.

World Council of Churches an association established in 1948 to promote unity among the many different Christian Churches. Its 307 member Churches have adherents in over 100 countries, and virtually all Christian traditions are included except Roman Catholicism. Its headquarters are in Geneva.

World Cup any of various international sports competitions, or the trophies awarded for these; (in Association football) a competition instituted in 1930 and held every fourth year between teams who are winners from regional competitions.

World Federation of Trade Unions an association of trade unions, founded in 1945. Its headquarters are in Czechoslovakia. In 1949 a number of members withdrew and founded the International Confederation of Free Trade Unions (see entry).

World Health Organization an agency of the United

Nations, established in 1948. Its aim is the attainment by all peoples of the world of the highest possible level of health, and to this end its activities include cooperation with member governments in their efforts to promote health and control communicable diseases, and the advancement of biomedical research through some 500 collaborating research centres throughout the world. Its headquarters are in Geneva.

World Intellectual Property Organization an organization, established in 1967 and an agency of the United Nations from 1974, for cooperation between governments in matters concerning patents, trade marks, copyright, etc., and the transfer of technology between countries. Its headquarters are in Geneva.

worldling /ˈwɜːldlɪŋ/ n. a worldly person.

worldly /ˈwɜːldlɪ/ adj. (**worldlier, worldliest**) **1** temporal or earthly (*worldly goods*). **2** engrossed in temporal affairs, esp. the pursuit of wealth and pleasure. □ **worldly-minded** intent on worldly things. **worldly wisdom** prudence as regards one's own interests. **worldly-wise** having worldly wisdom. □□ **worldliness** n. [OE *woruldlic* (as WORLD, -LY¹)]

World Meteorological Organization an agency of the United Nations, established in 1950. Its aim is to facilitate worldwide cooperation in meteorological observations, research, and services. Its headquarters are in Geneva.

World Series a series of baseball championship matches played after the end of the season between the champions of the two major US professional baseball leagues, the American League and the National League. It was first played in 1903.

World's View a height in the Matopo Hills in Zimbabwe, south-east of Bulawayo. It is the burial place of Cecil Rhodes.

world war n. a war involving many important nations. The name is commonly given to the wars of 1914–18 and 1939–45, although only the second of these was truly global.

First World War (1914–18), a war between the Central Powers (Germany and Austria-Hungary, joined later by Turkey and Bulgaria) and the Allies (Britain, France, Russia, and minor European nations, joined later by Italy and the US). Most of the fighting took place in Europe, being characterized by a long and bloody stalemate in the west and the eventual collapse of Russia in the east. The war was ended by a series of armistices in late 1918, the most important being that with Germany on 11 November, and peace terms were finally settled at Versailles in 1919. One of the most important consequences of the war was the collapse of the German, Austro-Hungarian, and Russian empires.

Second World War (1939–45), a war between the Axis Powers (Germany, Italy, and Japan) and the Allies, including the three major powers Britain, Russia, and the US. It began with the German attack on Poland in September 1939, within a year of which the Germans had overrun most of Europe, including France, the Low Countries, Scandinavia (excluding neutral Sweden and allied Finland), and Poland. Fighting spread to the Mediterranean where Italy had joined Germany and finally to the USSR, which Germany attacked in June 1941. The war became world-wide following the Japanese attack on the US naval base at Pearl Harbor in December 1941. From 1942 onwards the Allies gradually began to turn the tide against the Axis, but although Italy surrendered in 1943, Germany did not give up until invaded (surrendering in May 1945) and Japan resisted until the first atomic bombs were dropped on the country in August 1945.

worldwide /ˈwɜːldwaɪd, -ˈwaɪd/ adj. & adv. —adj. affecting, occurring in, or known in all parts of the world. —adv. throughout the world.

World Wide Fund for Nature an international organization established (as the World Wildlife Fund) in 1961 to raise funds for projects including the conservation of species of animals or of special areas. Its headquarters are in Gland, Switzerland.

worm /wɜːm/ n. & v. —n. **1** any of various types of creeping or burrowing invertebrate animals with long slender bodies and no limbs, esp. segmented in rings or parasitic in the intestines or tissues. **2** the long slender larva of an insect, esp. in fruit or wood. **3** (in pl.) intestinal or other internal parasites. **4** a blindworm or slow-worm. **5** a maggot supposed to eat dead bodies in the grave. **6** an insignificant or contemptible person. **7 a** the spiral part of a screw. **b** a short screw working in a worm-gear. **8** the spiral pipe of a still in which the vapour is cooled and condensed. **9** the ligament under a dog's tongue. —v. **1** intr. & tr. (often refl.) move with a crawling motion (*wormed through the bushes; wormed our way through the bushes*). **2** intr. & refl. (foll. by *into*) insinuate oneself into a person's favour, confidence, etc. **3** tr. (foll. by *out*) obtain (a secret etc.) by cunning persistence (*managed to worm the truth out of them*). **4** tr. cut the worm of (a dog's tongue). **5** tr. rid (a plant or dog etc.) of worms. **6** tr. Naut. make (a rope etc.) smooth by winding thread between the strands. □ **food for worms** a dead person. **worm-cast** a convoluted mass of earth left on the surface by a burrowing earthworm. **worm-fishing** fishing with worms for bait. **worm-gear** an arrangement of a toothed wheel worked by a revolving spiral. **worm-hole** a hole left by the passage of a worm. **worm-seed 1** seed used to expel intestinal worms. **2** a plant e.g. santonica bearing this seed. **worm's-eye view** a view as seen from below or from a humble position. **worm-wheel** the wheel of a worm-gear. **a (or even a) worm will turn** the meekest will resist or retaliate if pushed too far. □□ **wormer** n. **wormlike** adj. [OE *wyrm* f. Gmc]

wormeaten /ˈwɜːmˌiːt(ə)n/ adj. **1 a** eaten into by worms. **b** rotten, decayed. **2** old and dilapidated.

Worms /wɜːmz, vɔːmz/ an industrial town on the Rhine in western Germany; pop. (1983) 73,000. □ **Diet of Worms** a meeting of Charles V's imperial Diet at Worms in 1521 at which Martin Luther was summoned to appear. Luther committed himself to the cause of Protestant reform, and on the last day of the Diet his teaching was formally condemned in the Edict of Worms.

wormwood /ˈwɜːmwʊd/ n. **1** any woody shrub of the genus *Artemisia*, with a bitter aromatic taste, used in the preparation of vermouth and absinthe and in medicine. **2** bitter mortification or a source of this. [ME, alt. f. obs. *wormod* f. OE *wormōd, wermōd*, after *worm, wood*: cf. VERMOUTH]

wormy /ˈwɜːmɪ/ adj. (**wormier, wormiest**) **1** full of worms. **2** wormeaten. □□ **worminess** n.

worn /wɔːn/ past part. of WEAR¹. —adj. **1** damaged by use or wear. **2** looking tired and exhausted. **3** (in full **well-worn**) (of a joke etc.) stale; often heard.

worriment /ˈwʌrɪmənt/ n. esp. US **1** the act of worrying or state of being worried. **2** a cause of worry.

worrisome /ˈwʌrɪsəm/ adj. causing or apt to cause worry or distress. □□ **worrisomely** adv.

worrit /ˈwʌrɪt/ n. colloq. = WORRY. [orig. alt. in general use of WORRY]

worry /ˈwʌrɪ/ v. & n. —v. (**-ies, -ied**) **1** intr. give way to anxiety or unease; allow one's mind to dwell on difficulty or troubles. **2** tr. harass, importune; be a trouble or anxiety to. **3** tr. **a** (of a dog etc.) shake or pull about with the teeth. **b** attack repeatedly. **4** (as **worried** adj.) **a** uneasy, troubled in the mind. **b** suggesting worry (*a worried look*). —n. (pl. **-ies**) **1** a thing that causes anxiety or disturbs a person's tranquillity. **2** a disturbed state of mind; anxiety; a worried state. **3** a dog's worrying of its quarry. □ **not to worry** colloq. there is no need to worry. **worry along** (or **through**) manage to advance by persistence in spite of obstacles. **worry beads** a string of beads manipulated with the fingers to occupy or calm oneself. **worry-guts** (or **-wart**) colloq. a person who habitually worries unduly. **worry oneself** (usu. in neg.) take needless trouble. **worry out** obtain (the solution to a problem etc.) by dogged effort. □□ **worriedly** adv. **worrier** n. **worryingly** adv. [OE *wyrgan* strangle f. WG]

worse /wɜːs/ adj., adv., & n. —adj. **1** more bad. **2** (predic.) in or into worse health or a worse condition (*is getting worse; is none the worse for it*). —adv. more badly or more ill. —n. **1** a worse thing or things (*you might do worse than*). **2** (prec. by the) a worse condition (*a change for the worse*). □ **none the worse** (often foll. by *for*) not adversely affected (by). **or worse** or as an even worse alternative. **the worse for drink** fairly drunk. **the worse for wear 1** damaged by use. **2** injured. **worse luck** see LUCK. **worse off** in a worse (esp. financial) position. [OE *wyrsa, wiersa* f. Gmc]

worsen /ˈwɜːs(ə)n/ *v.tr. & intr.* make or become worse.

worship /ˈwɜːʃɪp/ *n. & v.* —*n.* **1 a** homage or reverence paid to a deity, esp. in a formal service. **b** the acts, rites, or ceremonies of worship. **2** adoration or devotion comparable to religious homage shown towards a person or principle (*the worship of wealth; regarded them with worship in their eyes*). **3** *archaic* worthiness, merit; recognition given or due to these; honour and respect. —*v.* (**worshipped, worshipping**; *US* **worshiped, worshiping**) **1** *tr.* adore as divine; honour with religious rites. **2** *tr.* idolize or regard with adoration (*worships the ground she walks on*). **3** *intr.* attend public worship. **4** *intr.* be full of adoration. □ **Your** (or **His** or **Her**) **Worship** esp. *Brit.* a title of respect used to or of a mayor, certain magistrates, etc. □□ **worshipper** *n.* (*US* **worshiper**). [OE *weorthscipe* (as WORTH, -SHIP)]

worshipful /ˈwɜːʃɪpfʊl/ *adj.* **1** (usu. **Worshipful**) *Brit.* a title given to justices of the peace and to certain old companies or their officers etc. **2** *archaic* entitled to honour or respect. **3** *archaic* imbued with a spirit of veneration. □□ **worshipfully** *adv.* **worshipfulness** *n.*

worst /wɜːst/ *adj., adv., n., & v.* —*adj.* most bad. —*adv.* most badly. —*n.* the worst part, event, circumstance, or possibility (*the worst of the storm is over; prepare for the worst*). —*v.tr.* get the better of; defeat, outdo. □ **at its** etc. **worst** in the worst state. **at worst** (or **the worst**) in the worst possible case. **do your worst** an expression of defiance. **get** (or **have**) **the worst of it** be defeated. **if the worst comes to the worst** if the worst happens. [OE *wierresta, wyrresta* (adj.), *wyrst, wyrrest* (adv.), f. Gmc]

worsted /ˈwʊstɪd/ *n.* **1** a fine smooth yarn spun from combed long-staple wool. **2** fabric made from this. [*Worste(a)d* in S. England]

wort /wɜːt/ *n.* **1** *archaic* (except in names) a plant or herb (*liverwort; St John's wort*). **2** the infusion of malt which after fermentation becomes beer. [OE *wyrt*: rel. to ROOT¹]

Worth /wɜːθ/, Charles Frederick (1825–95), French couturier, born in England, founder of Parisian *haute couture*. He gained the patronage of the empress Eugénie, wife of Napoleon III, and is noted for designing crinolined gowns in the mid-19th c., making copious use of rich fabrics, and for introducing the bustle.

worth /wɜːθ/ *adj. & n.* —*predic.adj.* (governing a noun like a preposition) **1** of a value equivalent to (*is worth £50; is worth very little*). **2** such as to justify or repay; deserving; bringing compensation for (*worth doing; not worth the trouble*). **3** possessing or having property amounting to (*is worth a million pounds*). —*n.* **1** what a person or thing is worth; the (usu. specified) merit of (*of great worth; persons of worth*). **2** the equivalent of money in a commodity (*ten pounds' worth of petrol*). □ **for all one is worth** *colloq.* with one's utmost efforts; without reserve. **for what it is worth** without a guarantee of its truth or value. **worth it** *colloq.* worth the time or effort spent. **worth one's salt** see SALT. **worth while** (or **one's while**) see WHILE. [OE w(e)*orth*]

worthless /ˈwɜːθlɪs/ *adj.* without value or merit. □□ **worthlessly** *adv.* **worthlessness** *n.*

worthwhile /ˈwɜːθwaɪl, -ˈwaɪl/ *adj.* that is worth the time or effort spent; of value or importance. □□ **worthwhileness** *n.*

worthy /ˈwɜːðɪ/ *adj. & n.* —*adj.* (**worthier, worthiest**) **1** estimable; having some moral worth; deserving respect (*lived a worthy life*). **2** (of a person) entitled to (esp. condescending) recognition (*a worthy old couple*). **3 a** (foll. by *of* or *to* + infin.) deserving (*worthy of a mention; worthy to be remembered*). **b** (foll. by *of*) adequate or suitable to the dignity etc. of (*in words worthy of the occasion*). —*n.* (*pl.* **-ies**) **1** a worthy person. **2** a person of some distinction. **3** *joc.* a person. □□ **worthily** *adv.* **worthiness** *n.* [ME *wurthi* etc. f. WORTH]

-worthy /ˈwɜːðɪ/ *comb. form* forming adjectives meaning: **1** deserving of (*blameworthy; noteworthy*). **2** suitable or fit for (*newsworthy; roadworthy*).

wot see WIT².

wotcher /ˈwɒtʃə(r)/ *int. Brit. sl.* a form of casual greeting. [corrupt. of *what cheer*]

would /wʊd, wəd/ *v.aux.* (3rd *sing.* **would**) past of WILL¹, used esp.: **1** (in the 2nd and 3rd persons, and often in the 1st: see SHOULD). **a** in reported speech (*he said he would be home by evening*). **b** to express the conditional mood (*they would have been killed if they had gone*). **2** to express habitual action (*would wait for her every evening*). **3** to express a question or polite request (*would they like it?; would you come in, please?*). **4** to express probability (*I guess she would be over fifty by now*). **5** (foll. by *that* + clause) *literary* to express a wish (*would that you were here*). **6** to express consent (*they would not help*). □ **would-be** often *derog.* desiring or aspiring to be (*a would-be politician*). [OE *wolde*, past of *wyllan*: see WILL¹]

wouldn't /ˈwʊd(ə)nt/ *contr.* would not. □ **I wouldn't know** *colloq.* (as is to be expected) I do not know.

wouldst /wʊdst/ *archaic* 2nd *sing.* past of WOULD.

Woulfe bottle /wʊlf/ *n. Chem.* a jar with more than one neck, used for passing a gas through a liquid etc. [P. *Woulfe*, Engl. chemist d. 1803]

wound¹ /wuːnd/ *n. & v.* —*n.* **1** an injury done to living tissue by a cut or blow etc., esp. beyond the cutting or piercing of the skin. **2** an injury to a person's reputation or a pain inflicted on a person's feelings. **3** *poet.* the pangs of love. —*v.tr.* inflict a wound on (*wounded soldiers; wounded feelings*). □□ **woundingly** *adv.* **woundless** *adj.* [OE *wund* (n.), *wundian* (v.)]

wound² /waʊnd/ past and past part. of WIND² (cf. WIND¹ *v.* 6).

Wounded Knee the site in North Dakota of the last major battle (1890) between the US army and the Sioux Indians, in which over 150 Sioux were massacred. The event was recalled in 1973 when members of the American Indian Movement occupied the site; after a skirmish in which two Indians were killed they agreed to evacuate the area in exchange for negotiations on Indian grievances.

woundwort /ˈwuːndwɜːt/ *n.* any of various plants esp. of the genus *Stachys*, formerly supposed to have healing properties.

wove¹ past of WEAVE¹.

wove² /wəʊv/ *adj.* (of paper) made on a wire-gauze mesh and so having a uniform unlined surface. [var. of *woven*, past part. of WEAVE¹]

woven past part. of WEAVE¹.

wow¹ /waʊ/ *int., n., & v.* —*int.* expressing astonishment or admiration. —*n. sl.* a sensational success. —*v.tr. sl.* impress or excite greatly. [orig. Sc.: imit.]

wow² /waʊ/ *n.* a slow pitch-fluctuation in sound-reproduction, perceptible in long notes. [imit.]

wowser /ˈwaʊzə(r)/ *n. Austral. sl.* **1** a puritanical fanatic. **2** a spoilsport. **3** a teetotaller. [20th c.: orig. uncert.]

WP *abbr.* word processor or processing.

w.p. *abbr.* weather permitting.

w.p.b. *abbr.* waste-paper basket.

WPC *abbr.* (in the UK) woman police constable.

w.p.m. *abbr.* words per minute.

WRAC *abbr.* (in the UK) Women's Royal Army Corps.

wrack /ræk/ *n.* **1** seaweed cast up or growing on the shore. **2** destruction. **3** a wreck or wreckage. **4** = RACK². **5** = RACK⁵. [ME f. MDu. *wrak* or MLG *wra(c)k*, a parallel formation to OE *wræc*, rel. to *wrecan* WREAK: cf. WRECK, RACK⁵]

WRAF *abbr.* (in the UK) Women's Royal Air Force.

wraggle-taggle var. of RAGGLE-TAGGLE.

wraith /reɪθ/ *n.* **1** a ghost or apparition. **2** the spectral appearance of a living person supposed to portend that person's death. □□ **wraithlike** *adj.* [16th-c. Sc.: orig. unkn.]

Wrangel Island /ˈræŋg(ə)l/ an island of the eastern Soviet Union, in the Arctic Ocean, named after the Russian admiral and explorer Baron Ferdinand Wrangel (1794–1870).

wrangle /ˈræŋg(ə)l/ *n. & v.* —*n.* a noisy argument, altercation, or dispute. —*v.* **1** *intr.* engage in a wrangle. **2** *tr. US* herd (cattle). [ME, prob. f. LG or Du.: cf. LG *wrangelen*, frequent. of *wrangen* to struggle, rel. to WRING]

wrangler /ˈræŋglə(r)/ *n.* **1** a person who wrangles. **2** *US* a cowboy. **3** (at Cambridge University) a person placed in the first class of the mathematical tripos.

wrap /ræp/ *v. & n.* —*v.tr.* (**wrapped**, **wrapping**) **1** (often foll. by *up*) envelop in folded or soft encircling material (*wrap it up in paper; wrap up a parcel*). **2** (foll. by *round*, *about*) arrange or draw (a pliant covering) round (a person) (*wrapped the scarf closer around me*). **3** (foll. by *round*) *sl.* crash (a vehicle) into a stationary object. —*n.* **1** a shawl or scarf or other such addition to clothing; a wrapper. **2** esp. *US* material used for wrapping. □ **take the wraps off** disclose. **under wraps** in secrecy. **wrap-over** *adj.* (*attrib.*) (of a garment) having no seam at one side but wrapped around the body and fastened. —*n.* such a garment. **wrapped up in** engrossed or absorbed in. **wrap up 1** finish off, bring to completion (*wrapped up the deal in two days*). **2** put on warm clothes (*mind you wrap up well*). **3** (in *imper.*) *sl.* be quiet. [ME: orig. unkn.]

wraparound /ˈræpəˌraʊnd/ *adj. & n.* (also **wraparound** /ˈræpraʊnd/) —*adj.* **1** (esp. of clothing) designed to wrap round. **2** curving or extending round at the edges. —*n.* anything that wraps round.

wrappage /ˈræpɪdʒ/ *n.* a wrapping or wrappings.

wrapper /ˈræpə(r)/ *n.* **1** a cover for a sweet, chocolate, etc. **2** a cover enclosing a newspaper or similar packet for posting. **3** a paper cover of a book, usu. detachable. **4** a loose enveloping robe or gown. **5** a tobacco-leaf of superior quality enclosing a cigar.

wrapping /ˈræpɪŋ/ *n.* (esp. in *pl.*) material used to wrap; wraps, wrappers. □ **wrapping paper** strong or decorative paper for wrapping parcels.

wrapround var. of WRAPAROUND.

wrasse /ræs/ *n.* any bright-coloured marine fish of the family Labridae with thick lips and strong teeth. [Corn. *wrach*, var. of *gwrach*, = Welsh *gwrach*, lit. 'old woman']

wrath /rɒθ, rɔːθ/ *n. literary* extreme anger. [OE *wrǣththu* f. *wrāth* WROTH]

wrathful /ˈrɒθfʊl/ *adj. literary* extremely angry. □□ **wrathfully** *adv.* **wrathfulness** *n.*

wrathy /ˈrɔːθɪ/ *adj. US* = WRATHFUL.

wreak /riːk/ *v.tr.* **1** (usu. foll. by *upon*) give play or satisfaction to; put in operation (vengeance or one's anger etc.). **2** cause (damage etc.) (*the hurricane wreaked havoc on the crops*). **3** *archaic* avenge (a wrong or wronged person). □□ **wreaker** *n.* [OE *wrecan* drive, avenge, etc., f. Gmc: cf. WRACK, WRECK, WRETCH]

wreath /riːθ/ *n.* (*pl.* **wreaths** /riːðz, riːθs/) **1** flowers or leaves fastened in a ring esp. as an ornament for a person's head or a building or for laying on a grave etc. as a mark of honour or respect. **2 a** a similar ring of soft twisted material such as silk. **b** *Heraldry* a representation of this below a crest. **3** a carved representation of a wreath. **4** (foll. by *of*) a curl or ring of smoke or cloud. **5** a light drifting mass of snow etc. [OE *writha* f. weak grade of *wrīthan* WRITHE]

wreathe /riːð/ *v.* **1** *tr.* encircle as, with, or like a wreath. **2** *tr.* (foll. by *round*) put (one's arms etc.) round (a person etc.). **3** *intr.* (of smoke etc.) move in the shape of wreaths. **4** *tr.* form (flowers, silk, etc.) into a wreath. **5** *tr.* make (a garland). [partly back-form. f. archaic *wrethen* past part. of WRITHE; partly f. WREATH]

wreck /rek/ *n. & v.* —*n.* **1** the destruction or disablement esp. of a ship. **2** a ship that has suffered a wreck (*the shores are strewn with wrecks*). **3** a greatly damaged or disabled building, thing, or person (*had become a physical and mental wreck*). **4** (foll. by *of*) a wretched remnant or disorganized set of remains. **5** *Law* goods etc. cast up by the sea. —*v.* **1** *tr.* cause the wreck of (a ship etc.). **2** *tr.* completely ruin (hopes, chances, etc.). **3** *intr.* suffer a wreck. **4** *tr.* (as **wrecked** *adj.*) involved in a shipwreck (*wrecked sailors*). **5** *intr.* *US* deal with wrecked vehicles etc. □ **wreck-master** an officer appointed to take charge of goods etc. cast up from a wrecked ship. [ME f. AF *wrec* etc. (cf. VAREC) f. a Gmc root meaning 'to drive': cf. WREAK]

wreckage /ˈrekɪdʒ/ *n.* **1** wrecked material. **2** the remnants of a wreck. **3** the action or process of wrecking.

wrecker /ˈrekə(r)/ *n.* **1** a person or thing that wrecks or destroys. **2** esp. *hist.* a person on the shore who tries to bring about a shipwreck in order to plunder or profit by the wreckage. **3** esp. *US* a person employed in demolition, or in recovering a wrecked ship or its contents. **4** *US* a person who breaks up damaged vehicles for spares and scrap. **5** *US* a vehicle or train used in recovering a damaged one.

Wren[1] /ren/ *n.* (in the UK) a member of the Women's Royal Naval Service. [orig. in pl., f. abbr. WRNS]

Wren[2] /ren/, Sir Christopher (1632–1723), English architect and scientist, founder-member and later President of the Royal Society (1680). His early scientific training may well be responsible for the lucid and elegant architectural style Wren developed with St Paul's Cathedral (1675–1710) and the City churches (1670–86), whose spatial relations were clearly and logically expressed at a time when baroque exuberance tended towards a surcharged emotionalism. His unrealized town-plan for the rebuilding of London after the Great Fire (1666) would have made it one of the great European show-pieces of baroque architecture.

Wren[3] /ren/, Percival Christopher (1885–1941), English novelist, who had a varied and much-travelled life, working at one time as a member of the French Foreign Legion. He achieved popular success with the first of his Foreign Legion novels, *Beau Geste* (1924), a romantic adventure story.

wren /ren/ *n.* any small usu. brown short-winged songbird of the family Troglodytidae, esp. *Troglodytes troglodytes* of Europe, having an erect tail. [OE *wrenna*, rel. to OHG *wrendo*, *wrendilo*, Icel. *rindill*]

wrench /rentʃ/ *n. & v.* —*n.* **1** a violent twist or oblique pull or act of tearing off. **2** an adjustable tool like a spanner for gripping and turning nuts etc. **3** an instance of painful uprooting or parting (*leaving home was a great wrench*). **4** *Physics* a combination of a couple with the force along its axis. —*v.* **1** *tr.* twist or pull violently round or sideways. **2** (often foll. by *off*, *away*, etc.) pull off with a wrench. **3** distort (facts) to suit a theory etc. [(earlier as verb:) OE *wrencan* twist]

wrest /rest/ *v. & n.* —*v.tr.* **1** force or wrench away from a person's grasp. **2** (foll. by *from*) obtain by effort or with difficulty. **3** distort into accordance with one's interests or views (*wrest the law to suit themselves*). —*n. archaic* a key for tuning a harp or piano etc. □ **wrest-block** (or **-plank**) the part of a piano or harpsichord holding the wrest-pins. **wrest-pin** each of the pins to which the strings of a piano or harpsichord are attached. [OE *wræstan* f. Gmc, rel. to WRIST]

wrestle /ˈres(ə)l/ *n. & v.* —*n.* **1** a contest in which two opponents grapple and try to throw each other to the ground esp. as an athletic sport under a code of rules. (See below.) **2** a hard struggle. —*v.* **1** *intr.* (often foll. by *with*) take part in a wrestle. **2** *tr.* fight (a person) in a wrestle (*wrestled his opponent to the ground*). **3** *intr.* **a** (foll. by *with*, *against*) struggle, contend. **b** (foll. by *with*) do one's utmost to deal with (a task, difficulty, etc.). **4** *tr.* move with efforts as if wrestling. □□ **wrestler** *n.* **wrestling** *n.* [OE (unrecorded) *wrǣstlian*: cf. MLG *wrostelen*, OE *wraxlian*]

Wrestling is one of the oldest and most basic of all sports. Many of the holds and throws used now in international championship events are the same as those of ancient Egypt, China, and Greece. It was introduced to the Olympic Games in 704 BC.

wretch /retʃ/ *n.* **1** an unfortunate or pitiable person. **2** (often as a playful term of depreciation) a reprehensible or contemptible person. [OE *wrecca* f. Gmc]

wretched /ˈretʃɪd/ *adj.* (**wretcheder**, **wretchedest**) **1** unhappy or miserable. **2** of bad quality or no merit; contemptible. **3** unsatisfactory or displeasing. □ **feel wretched 1** be unwell. **2** be much embarrassed. □□ **wretchedly** *adv.* **wretchedness** *n.* [ME, irreg. f. WRETCH + -ED[1]: cf. WICKED]

wrick *Brit.* var. of RICK[2].

wriggle /ˈrɪg(ə)l/ *v. & n.* —*v.* **1** *intr.* (of a worm etc.) twist or turn its body with short writhing movements. **2** (of a person or animal) make wriggling motions. **3** *tr. & intr.* (foll. by *along* etc.) move or go in this way (*wriggled into the corner; wriggled his hand into the hole*). **4** *tr.* make (one's) way by wriggling. **5** *intr.* practise evasion. —*n.* an act of wriggling. □ **wriggle out of**

colloq. avoid on a contrived pretext. □□ **wriggler** *n.* **wriggly** *adj.* [ME f. MLG *wriggelen* frequent. of *wriggen*]

Wright[1] /raɪt/, Frank Lloyd (1869–1959), American architect, the leading exponent of 'organic' architecture, advocating a close relationship between building and landscape and the nature of the materials used. His 'prairie-style' houses revolutionized American domestic architecture in the first decade of the 20th c. with their long low horizontal lines and visual merging of an unbroken interior with the surrounding landscape. Pupils gathered round him and during his long and prolific career, which extended over a period of 74 years, he influenced whole generations of architects. His lecture *The Art and Craft of the Machine* (1901) carried his belief, that art must dominate the machine in an industrial society, to a wide audience.

Wright[2] /raɪt/, Orville (1871–1948) and Wilbur (1867–1912), American brothers who were the first to make brief powered sustained and controlled flights in an aeroplane (Kitty Hawk, North Carolina, 17 Dec. 1903). They were also the first to make and fly a fully practical powered aeroplane (1905) and passenger-carrying aeroplane (1908). With the profits from their bicycle-manufacturing business at Dayton, Ohio, they experimented first with gliders, developed their aerofoils in their own wind tunnel, invented wing-warping, and designed and built their own petrol engine for their *Flyer*. Both brothers became skilled pilots and in 1908 demonstrated in France that their aircraft was capable of long flights and manoeuvrability.

wright /raɪt/ *n.* a maker or builder (usu. in *comb.*: *playwright*; *shipwright*). [OE *wryhta*, *wyrhta* f. WG: cf. WORK]

wring /rɪŋ/ *v. & n.* —*v.tr.* (*past* and *past part.* **wrung** /rʌŋ/) **1 a** squeeze tightly. **b** (often foll. by *out*) squeeze and twist esp. to remove liquid. **2** twist forcibly; break by twisting. **3** distress or torture. **4** extract by squeezing. **5** (foll. by *out, from*) obtain by pressure or importunity; extort. —*n.* an act of wringing; a squeeze. □ **wring a person's hand** clasp it forcibly or press it with emotion. **wring one's hands** clasp them as a gesture of great distress. **wring the neck of** kill (a chicken etc.) by twisting its neck. [OE *wringan*, rel. to WRONG]

wringer /ˈrɪŋə(r)/ *n.* a device for wringing water from washed clothes etc.

wringing /ˈrɪŋɪŋ/ *adj.* (in full **wringing wet**) so wet that water can be wrung out.

wrinkle /ˈrɪŋk(ə)l/ *n. & v.* —*n.* **1** a slight crease or depression in the skin such as is produced by age. **2** a similar mark in another flexible surface. **3** *colloq.* a useful tip or clever expedient. —*v.* **1** *tr.* make wrinkles in. **2** *intr.* form wrinkles; become marked with wrinkles. [orig. repr. OE *gewrinclod* sinuous]

wrinkly /ˈrɪŋklɪ/ *adj. & n.* —*adj.* (**wrinklier, wrinkliest**) having many wrinkles. —*n.* (also **wrinklie**) (*pl.* **-ies**) *sl. offens.* an old or middle-aged person.

wrist /rɪst/ *n.* **1** the part connecting the hand with the forearm. **2** the corresponding part in an animal. **3** the part of a garment covering the wrist. **4 a** (in full **wrist-work**) the act or practice of working the hand without moving the arm. **b** the effect got in fencing, ball games, sleight of hand, etc., by this. **5** (in full **wrist-pin**) *Mech.* a stud projecting from a crank etc. as an attachment for a connecting-rod. □ **wrist-drop** the inability to extend the hand through paralysis of the forearm muscles. **wrist-watch** a small watch worn on a strap round the wrist. [OE f. Gmc, prob. f. a root rel. to WRITHE]

wristband /ˈrɪstbænd/ *n.* a band forming or concealing the end of a shirt-sleeve; a cuff.

wristlet /ˈrɪstlɪt/ *n.* a band or ring worn on the wrist to strengthen or guard it or as an ornament, bracelet, handcuff, etc.

wristy /ˈrɪstɪ/ *adj.* (esp. of a shot in cricket, tennis, etc.) involving or characterized by movement of the wrist.

writ[1] /rɪt/ *n.* **1** a form of written command in the name of a sovereign, court, State, etc., to act or abstain from acting in some way. **2** a Crown document summoning a peer to Parliament or ordering the election of a member or members of Parliament. □ **serve a writ on** deliver a writ to (a person). **one's writ runs** one has authority (as specified). [OE (as WRITE)]

writ[2] /rɪt/ *archaic past part.* of WRITE. □ **writ large** in magnified or emphasized form.

write /raɪt/ *v.* (*past* **wrote** /rəʊt/; *past part.* **written** /ˈrɪt(ə)n/) **1** *intr.* mark paper or some other surface by means of a pen, pencil, etc., with symbols, letters, or words. **2** *tr.* form or mark (such symbols etc.). **3** *tr.* form or mark the symbols that represent or constitute (a word or sentence, or a document etc.). **4** *tr.* fill or complete (a sheet, cheque, etc.) with writing. **5** *tr.* put (data) into a computer store. **6** *tr.* (esp. in *passive*) indicate (a quality or condition) by one's or its appearance (*guilt was written on his face*). **7** *tr.* compose (a text, article, novel, etc.) for written or printed reproduction or publication; put into literary etc. form and set down in writing. **8** *intr.* be engaged in composing a text, article, etc. (*writes for the local newspaper*). **9** *intr.* (foll. by *to*) write and send a letter (to a recipient). **10** *tr. US* or *colloq.* write and send a letter to (a person) (*wrote him last week*). **11** *tr.* convey (news, information, etc.) by letter (*wrote that they would arrive next Friday*). **12** *tr.* state in written or printed form (*it is written that*). **13** *tr.* cause to be recorded. **14** *tr.* underwrite (an insurance policy). **15** *tr.* (foll. by *into, out of*) include or exclude (a character or episode) in a story by suitable changes of the text. **16** *tr. archaic* describe in writing. □ **nothing to write home about** *colloq.* of little interest or value. **write down 1** record or take note of in writing. **2** write as if for those considered inferior. **3** disparage in writing. **4** reduce the nominal value of (stock, goods, etc.). **write in 1** send a suggestion, query, etc., in writing to an organization, esp. a broadcasting station. **2** *US* add (an extra name) on a list of candidates when voting. **write-in** *n. US* an instance of writing in (see *write in* 2). **write off 1** write and send a letter. **2** cancel the record of (a bad debt etc.); acknowledge the loss of or failure to recover (an asset). **3** damage (a vehicle etc.) so badly that it cannot be repaired. **4** compose with facility. **write-off** *n.* a thing written off, esp. a vehicle too badly damaged to be repaired. **write out 1** write in full or in finished form. **2** exhaust (oneself) by writing (*have written myself out*). **write up 1** write a full account of. **2** praise in writing. **3** make entries to bring (a diary etc.) up to date. **write-up** *n. colloq.* a written or published account, a review. □□ **writable** *adj.* [OE *wrītan* scratch, score, write, f. Gmc: orig. used of symbols inscribed with sharp tools on stone or wood]

writer /ˈraɪtə(r)/ *n.* **1** a person who writes or has written something. **2** a person who writes books; an author. **3** a clerk, esp. in the Navy or in government offices. **4** a scribe. □ **writer's cramp** a muscular spasm due to excessive writing. **Writer to the Signet** a Scottish solicitor conducting cases in the Court of Session. [OE *wrītere* (as WRITE)]

writhe /raɪð/ *v. & n.* —*v.* **1** *intr.* twist or roll oneself about in or as if in acute pain. **2** *intr.* suffer severe mental discomfort or embarrassment (*writhed with shame*; *writhed at the thought of it*). **3** *tr.* twist (one's body etc.) about. —*n.* an act of writhing. [OE *wrīthan*, rel. to WREATHE]

writing /ˈraɪtɪŋ/ *n.* **1** a group or sequence of letters or symbols. (See below.) **2** = HANDWRITING. **3** (usu. in *pl.*) a piece of literary work done; a book, article, etc. **4** (**Writings**) the Hagiographa. □ **in writing** in written form. **writing-desk** a desk for writing at, esp. with compartments for papers etc. **the writing on the wall** an ominously significant event or sign that something is doomed (with allusion to the Biblical story of the writing that appeared on the wall at Belshazzar's feast (Dan. 5: 5, 25–8), foretelling his doom). **writing-pad** a pad (see PAD[1] *n.* 2) of paper for writing on. **writing-paper** paper for writing (esp. letters) on.

Primitive drawings, as records of ideas, were the forerunners of writing which began in Mesopotamia with pictographic signs and developed into a formalized system of linear and then cuneiform signs representing first words or ideas, then syllables, and finally sounds. The cuneiform system was adopted from the Sumerians by the Akkadians and passed on to Syria, the Elamites, and the Hurrians in the 3rd millennium BC, the Assyrians, Hittites, Canaanites, and Egyptians in the 2nd millennium BC, and the Achaemenid Persians in the 1st millennium BC when it was gradually superseded by the alphabetic system of writing (see ALPHABET).

written *past part.* of WRITE.

WRNS *abbr.* (in the UK) Women's Royal Naval Service.

Wrocław /ˈvrɒtswɑːf/ (German **Breslau** /ˈbreslaʊ/) a port and industrial city on the Oder River in western Poland; pop. (1985) 636,000.

wrong /rɒŋ/ *adj., adv., n., & v.* —*adj.* **1** mistaken; not true; in error (*gave a wrong answer; we were wrong to think that*). **2** unsuitable; less or least desirable (*the wrong road; a wrong decision*). **3** contrary to law or morality (*it is wrong to steal*). **4** amiss; out of order, in or into a bad or abnormal condition (*something wrong with my heart; my watch has gone wrong*). —*adv.* (usually placed last) in a wrong manner or direction; with an incorrect result (*guessed wrong; told them wrong*). —*n.* **1** what is morally wrong; a wrong action. **2** injustice; unjust action or treatment (*suffer wrong*). —*v.tr.* **1** treat unjustly; do wrong to. **2** mistakenly attribute bad motives to; discredit. □ **do wrong** commit sin; transgress, offend. **do wrong to** malign or mistreat (a person). **get in wrong with** incur the dislike or disapproval of (a person). **get on the wrong side of** fall into disfavour with. **get wrong 1** misunderstand (a person, statement, etc.). **2** obtain an incorrect answer to. **get** (or **get hold of**) **the wrong end of the stick** misunderstand completely. **go down the wrong way** (of food) enter the windpipe instead of the gullet. **go wrong 1** take the wrong path. **2** stop functioning properly. **3** depart from virtuous or suitable behaviour. **in the wrong** responsible for a quarrel, mistake, or offence. **on the wrong side of 1** out of favour with (a person). **2** somewhat more than (a stated age). **wrong-foot** *colloq.* **1** (in tennis, football, etc.) play so as to catch (an opponent) off balance. **2** disconcert; catch unprepared. **wrong-headed** perverse and obstinate. **wrong-headedly** in a wrong-headed manner. **wrong-headedness** the state of being wrong-headed. **wrong side** the worse or undesired or unusable side of something, esp. fabric. **wrong side out** inside out. **wrong way round** in the opposite or reverse of the normal or desirable orientation or sequence etc. □□ **wronger** *n.* **wrongly** *adv.* **wrongness** *n.* [OE *wrang* f. ON *rangr* awry, unjust, rel. to WRING]

wrongdoer /ˈrɒŋˌduːə(r)/ *n.* a person who behaves immorally or illegally. □□ **wrongdoing** *n.*

wrongful /ˈrɒŋfʊl/ *adj.* **1** characterized by unfairness or injustice. **2** contrary to law. **3** (of a person) not entitled to the position etc. occupied. □□ **wrongfully** *adv.* **wrongfulness** *n.*

wrong'un /ˈrɒŋən/ *n. colloq.* a person of bad character. [contr. of *wrong one*]

wrote *past* of WRITE.

wroth /rəʊθ, rɒθ/ *predic.adj. archaic* angry. [OE *wrāth* f. Gmc]

wrought /rɔːt/ *archaic past* and *past part.* of WORK. —*adj.* (of metals) beaten out or shaped by hammering. □ **wrought iron** see IRON.

wrung *past* and *past part.* of WRING.

WRVS *abbr.* (in the UK) Women's Royal Voluntary Service.

wry /raɪ/ *adj.* (**wryer, wryest** or **wrier, wriest**) **1** distorted or turned to one side. **2** (of a face or smile etc.) contorted in disgust, disappointment, or mockery. **3** (of humour) dry and mocking. □□ **wryly** *adv.* **wryness** *n.* [*wry* (v.) f. OE *wrīgian* tend, incline, in ME deviate, swerve, contort]

wryneck /ˈraɪnek/ *n.* **1** = TORTICOLLIS. **2** any bird of the genus *Jynx* of the woodpecker family, able to turn its head over its shoulder.

WSW *abbr.* west-south-west.

wt. *abbr.* weight.

Wu /wuː/ *n.* a dialect of Chinese spoken in the Kiangsu and Chekiang Provinces. [Chin.]

Wuhan /wuːˈhæn/ a port on the Yangtze River in eastern China; pop. (est. 1986) 3,400,000.

Wulfila /ˈwʊlfɪlə/ var. of ULFILAS.

wunderkind /ˈvʊndəkɪnt/ *n. colloq.* a person who achieves great success while relatively young. [G f. *Wunder* wonder + *Kind* child]

Wundt /vʊnt/, Wilhelm (1832–1920), German philosopher, physiologist, and founder of psychology as an independent and scientific discipline in Leipzig, where he established a laboratory devoted to its study. He felt that the major task of the psychologist was to analyse human consciousness, which could be broken down into simpler fundamental units. He required subjects to report their sensory impressions under controlled conditions, and although this method of inquiry (*introspection*) was later rejected by experimental psychologists, Wundt's legacy includes the rigorous methodology upon which he insisted.

Wuppertal /ˈvʊpəˌtɑːl/ an industrial city of western Germany, in North Rhine-Westphalia; pop. (1987) 374,200.

Wurlitzer /ˈwɜːlɪtsə(r)/ *n. propr.* any of various musical instruments made by the Rudolf Wurlitzer Company, esp. a type of large electric organ, or a player-piano.

wurst /vʊəst, vɜːst/ *n.* German or Austrian sausage. [G]

WV *abbr.* US West Virginia (in official postal use).

W.Va. *abbr.* West Virginia.

WW *abbr.* US World War (I, II).

WX *abbr.* women's extra-large size.

WY *abbr.* US Wyoming (in official postal use).

Wyatt /ˈwaɪət/, Sir Thomas (1503–42), English poet, who held various diplomatic posts in the service of Henry VIII. His visit to Italy in 1527 probably stimulated him to translate and imitate the poems of Petrarch. His son, also named Sir Thomas Wyatt, was executed (1554) after leading an unsuccessful rebellion against the proposed marriage of Mary I to the future Philip II of Spain.

wych- /wɪtʃ/ *comb. form* (also **wich-, witch-**) in names of trees with pliant branches. [OE *wic(e)* app. f. a Gmc root meaning 'bend': rel. to WEAK]

wych-alder /ˈwɪtʃˌɔːldə(r)/ *n.* an American plant, *Fothergilla gardenii*, with alder-like leaves.

wych-elm /ˈwɪtʃelm/ *n.* a species of elm, *Ulmus glabra*.

Wycherley /ˈwɪtʃəlɪ/, William (1641–1715), English dramatist, whose Restoration comedies are highly regarded for their acute social criticism, particularly of sexual morality and the marriage conventions. They include *The Gentleman Dancing-Master* (1673), *The Country Wife* (1675), and *The Plain-Dealer* (1677).

wych-hazel /ˈwɪtʃˌheɪz(ə)l/ *n.* **1** var. of WITCH-HAZEL. **2** = WYCH-ELM.

Wyclif /ˈwɪklɪf/, John (*c.*1330–84), English reformer, a philosopher and theologian. A lecturer at Oxford (1361–82) and prolific writer, he criticized the wealth and power of the visible Church (which he constrasted with the eternal ideal Church), upheld the Bible as the sole guide for doctrine, and questioned the scriptural basis of the papacy. He instituted the first translation into English of the whole Bible, himself translating the Gospels and probably other parts. After his attacks on the doctrine of transubstantiation (1381) and on the Peasants' Revolt, widely but erroneously attributed to his teaching, he was compelled to retire from Oxford. His teaching cut at the roots of medieval theocracy and at current faith and dogma, and he has been called the 'Morning Star of the Reformation'.

Wykehamist /ˈwɪkəmɪst/ *adj. & n.* —*adj.* of or concerning Winchester College. —*n.* a past or present member of Winchester College. [mod.L *Wykehamista* f. William of *Wykeham*, bishop of Winchester and founder of the college (d. 1404)]

wyn var. of WEN².

wynd /waɪnd/ *n. Sc.* a narrow street or alley. [ME, app. f. the stem of WIND²]

Wyo. *abbr.* Wyoming.

Wyoming /waɪˈəʊmɪŋ/ a State in the western central US; pop. (est. 1985) 469,550; capital, Cheyenne. Acquired as part of the Louisiana Purchase in 1803, it became the 44th State of the US in 1890.

WYSIWYG /ˈwɪzɪwɪg/ *adj.* (also **wysiwyg**) *Computing* denoting the representation of text onscreen in a form exactly corresponding to its appearance on a printout. [acronym of *what you see is what you get*]

wyvern /ˈwaɪv(ə)n/ *n.* (also **wivern**) *Heraldry* a winged two-legged dragon with a barbed tail. [ME *wyver* f. OF *wivre, guivre* f. L *vipera*: for -*n* cf. BITTERN]

X

X¹ /eks/ *n.* (also **x**) (*pl.* **Xs** or **X's**) **1** the twenty-fourth letter of the alphabet. **2** (as a Roman numeral) ten. **3** (usu. **x**) *Algebra* the first unknown quantity. **4** *Geom.* the first coordinate. **5** an unknown or unspecified number or person etc. **6** a cross-shaped symbol esp. used to indicate position (*X marks the spot*) or incorrectness or to symbolize a kiss or a vote, or as the signature of a person who cannot write.

X² *symb.* (of films) classified as suitable for adults only. ¶ Formerly used in the UK to indicate that persons under 18 would not be admitted; it was replaced in 1983 by *18*, but is still used in the US.

-x /z/ *suffix* forming the plural of many nouns in *-u* taken from French (*beaux*; *tableaux*). [F]

xanthate /'zænθeɪt/ *n.* any salt or ester of xanthic acid.

Xanthian Marbles /'zænθɪən/ sculptures found in 1838 at Xanthus in ancient Lycia, which are now in the British Museum. The figures are Assyrian in character and it is believed they were executed before 500 BC; the subjects include processions, athletic activity, sieges, and tomb scenes.

xanthic /'zænθɪk/ *adj.* yellowish. □ **xanthic acid** any colourless unstable acid containing the $-OCS_2H$ group. [Gk *xanthos* yellow]

Xanthippe /zæn'θɪpɪ/ (also **Xantippe** /-'tɪpɪ/) (5th c. BC) wife of the philosopher Socrates. Her bad-tempered behaviour towards her husband has made her proverbial as a shrew.

xanthoma /zæn'θəʊmə/ *n.* (*pl.* **xanthomas** or **xanthomata** /-tə/) *Med.* **1** a skin disease characterized by irregular yellow patches. **2** such a patch. [as XANTHIC + -OMA]

xanthophyll /'zænθəfɪl/ *n.* any of various oxygen-containing carotenoids associated with chlorophyll, some of which cause the yellow colour of leaves in the autumn. [as XANTHIC + Gk *phullon* leaf]

Xavier /'zævɪə(r), 'zeɪ-/, St Francis (1506–52), Spanish missionary, known as the 'Apostle of the Indies' and 'of Japan'. While studying in Paris he met St Ignatius Loyola and became with him one of the original seven Jesuits, pledged to follow Christ and evangelize the heathen. He set out on a remarkable series of missionary journeys: to southern India, Malacca, the Molucca Islands, Sri Lanka, and Japan, and is said to have made more than 700,000 converts. He died, worn out from his labours, while on his way to China.

X-chromosome /'eks,krəʊmə,səʊm/ *n.* a sex chromosome of which the number in female cells is twice that in male cells. [X as an arbitrary label + CHROMOSOME]

x.d. *abbr.* ex dividend.

Xe *symb. Chem.* the element xenon.

xebec /'zi:bek/ *n.* (also **zebec, zebeck**) a small three-masted Mediterranean vessel with lateen and usu. some square sails. [alt. (after Sp. *xabeque*) of F *chebec* f. It. *sciabecco* f. Arab. *šabāk*]

Xenakis /ze'nɑːkɪs/, Iannis (1922–), French composer, born in Romania of Greek parents. He moved to Paris in 1947 and established the School of Mathematical and Automated Music there in 1965. He had had an early training as an engineer and architect, and his music employs the mathematical laws of probability, computer-aided calculations, and electronic instruments. In the works which make up *Polytope* he combined electronic sound with laser beams and other visual effects.

xeno- /'zenəʊ/ *comb. form* **1 a** foreign. **b** a foreigner. **2** other. [Gk *xenos* strange, foreign, stranger]

xenogamy /ze'nɒgəmɪ/ *n. Bot.* cross-fertilization. □□ **xenogamous** *adj.*

xenolith /'zenəlɪθ/ *n. Geol.* an inclusion within an igneous rock mass, usu. derived from the immediately surrounding rock.

xenon /'zenɒn/ *n. Chem.* a heavy colourless odourless inert gaseous element occurring in traces in the atmosphere discovered in 1898 by Sir William Ramsay and M. W. Travers. It is obtained by the distillation of liquefied air and is used in certain specialized electric lamps. A radioactive isotope produced in nuclear reactors is important in the control of the chain reaction. ¶ Symb.: **Xe**; atomic number 54. [Gk, neut. of *xenos* strange]

Xenophanes /ze'nɒfə,niːz/ (*c.*570–490 BC) Greek philosopher and poet, the first writer to consider the impact of natural theology on conduct. In ruthless criticism of Homer and Hesiod he denied that the gods resemble men in conduct, shape, or understanding, and argued that there is a single eternal self-sufficient Consciousness which sways the universe (with which it is identical) through thought.

xenophobe /'zenə,fəʊb/ *n.* a person given to xenophobia.

xenophobia /,zenə'fəʊbɪə/ *n.* a deep dislike of foreigners. □□ **xenophobic** *adj.*

Xenophon /'zenəfən/ (*c.*428/7–*c.*354 BC) Greek writer from Athens who spent many years in the service of Sparta. His writings reflect the viewpoint of a conventional and practical-minded gentleman who supported aristocratic ideals and virtues. His historical works include the *Anabasis*, an eyewitness account of the expedition of the Persian prince Cyrus II against Artaxerxes (401–399 BC) in which he led the Greek mercenaries in their retreat to the Black Sea after they had been left in a dangerous situation between the Tigris and Euphrates; the *Apology*, *Memorabilia*, and *Symposium* recall the life and teachings of his friend Socrates; the *Cyropaedia* is a historical romance on the education of Cyrus II, seen as the ideal prince. He also wrote treatises on politics, war, hunting, and horsemanship.

xeranthemum /zɪə'rænθɪməm/ *n.* a composite plant of the genus *Xeranthemum*, with dry everlasting composite flowers. [mod.L f. Gk *xēros* dry + *anthemon* flower]

xeric /'zɪərɪk/ *adj. Ecol.* having or characterized by dry conditions. [as XERO- + -IC]

xero- /'zɪərəʊ, 'zerəʊ/ *comb. form* dry. [Gk *xēros* dry]

xeroderma /,zɪərə'dɜːmə/ *n.* any of various diseases characterized by extreme dryness of the skin, esp. ichthyosis. [mod.L (as XERO-, Gk *derma* skin)]

xerograph /'zɪərə,grɑːf, 'ze-/ *n.* a copy produced by xerography.

xerography /zɪə'rɒgrəfɪ, ze-/ *n.* a dry copying process in which black or coloured powder adheres to parts of a surface remaining electrically charged after exposure of the surface to light from an image of the document to be copied. □□ **xerographic** /-rə'græfɪk/ *adj.* **xerographically** /-rə'græfɪkəlɪ/ *adv.*

xerophilous /zɪə'rɒfɪləs, ze-/ *adj.* (of a plant) adapted to extremely dry conditions.

xerophyte /'zɪərə,faɪt, 'ze-/ *n.* (also **xerophile** /-,faɪl/) a plant able to grow in very dry conditions, e.g. in a desert.

Xerox /'zɪərɒks, 'ze-/ *n. & v.* —*n. propr.* **1** a machine for copying by xerography. **2** a copy made using this machine. —*v.tr.* (**xerox**) reproduce by this process. [invented f. XEROGRAPHY]

Xerxes I /'zɜːksiːz/ the son of Darius, king of Persia 486–465 BC, who inherited the task of punishing the Greeks for their support of the cities of Ionia that had revolted against Persian rule. After victories in 480 BC by sea at Artemisium and by land at Thermopylae his fleet was defeated at Salamis, and his land forces were defeated at Plataea in the following year.

Xhosa /'kəʊsə, 'kɔː-/ *n. & adj.* —*n.* **1** (*pl.* same or **Xhosas**) a member of a Bantu people of Cape Province, South Africa. **2** the Bantu language of this people, similar to Zulu. —*adj.* of or relating to this people or language. [native name]

xi /saɪ, gzaɪ, zaɪ/ *n.* the fourteenth letter of the Greek alphabet (Ξ, ξ). [Gk]

Xian /ʃiː'æn/ an industrial city of northern China, capital of Shaanxi province; pop. (est. 1986) 2,330,000. It was the capital of China, bearing various names, under several ruling dynasties. The Qin emperor Shi Huangdi (*c.* 259–210 BC) is buried here in an elaborate tomb complex, guarded by 10,000 life-size pottery soldiers and horses, the 'terracotta army', discovered in 1974.

Ximenes /hiːˈmeɪneɪθ, *pop.* ˈzɪmɪˌniːz/ = Jiménez de CISNEROS.

Xingú /ʃɪŋˈguː/ a South American river which rises in the Mato Grosso of west Brazil and flows northwards for a distance of 1,979 km (1,230 miles) to join the Amazon.

Xinjiang /ˌʃɪntʃɪˈæŋ/ (also **Sinkiang**) an autonomous region of NW China; pop. (est. 1986) 13,840,000; capital, Urumqi.

-xion /kʃ(ə)n/ *suffix* forming nouns (see -ION) from Latin participial stems in -x- (*fluxion*).

Xiphias /ˈzɪfɪˌæs/ a southern constellation, also called Dorado. [Gk *xiphos* sword]

xiphisternum /ˌzɪfɪˈstɜːnəm/ *n. Anat.* = *xiphoid process.* [as XIPHOID + STERNUM]

xiphoid /ˈzɪfɔɪd/ *adj. Biol.* sword-shaped. □ **xiphoid process** the cartilaginous process at the lower end of the sternum. [Gk *xiphoeidēs* f. *xiphos* sword]

Xizang see TIBET.

Xmas /ˈkrɪsməs, ˈeksməs/ *n. colloq.* = CHRISTMAS. [abbr., with X for the initial chi of Gk *Khristos* Christ]

xoanon /ˈzəʊəˌnɒn/ *n.* (*pl.* **xoana** /-nə/) *Gk Antiq.* a primitive usu. wooden image of a deity supposed to have fallen from heaven. [Gk f. *xeō* carve]

X-ray /ˈeksreɪ/ *n. & v.* (also **x-ray**) —*n.* **1** (in *pl.*) electromagnetic radiation of short wavelength, able to pass through opaque bodies. (See below.) **2** an image made by the effect of X-rays on a photographic plate, esp. showing the position of bones etc. by their greater absorption of the rays. —*v.tr.* photograph, examine, or treat with X-rays. □ **X-ray astronomy** see separate entry. **X-ray crystallography** the study of crystals and their structure by means of the diffraction of X-rays by the regularly spaced atoms of a crystalline material. **X-ray tube** a device for generating X-rays by accelerating electrons to high energies and causing them to strike a metal target from which the X-rays are emitted. [transl. of G *x-Strahlen* f. *Strahl* ray, so called because when discovered in 1895 the nature of the rays was unknown]

X-rays were discovered in 1895 by Wilhelm Röntgen, who noticed the fluorescence of certain crystals in the vicinity of an operating cathode-ray tube. He attributed this to a new kind of radiation from the tube which he called X-rays. He discovered that the rays travel in straight lines, that they are not electrical, that they affect photographic plates, and that they have a considerable power of penetrating matter. Röntgen produced the first X-ray photograph or radiograph of the human hand. By 1912 it was recognized that X-rays are electromagnetic radiation of a very high frequency with wavelengths more than a thousand times smaller than those of visible light. The shorter the wavelength of the X-ray, the greater its penetrating power.

X-rays are produced when very high-velocity electrons are stopped suddenly by a target, as in an X-ray tube; the rapid deceleration of the electrons at the target produces a pulse of X-radiation. X-rays now have a great variety of applications in science, medicine, and industry. The best known of these include radiology, the spectroscopic analysis of the structure of solid crystalline materials, and the study of the structure of organic molecules. High doses of X-radiation can be damaging to living tissue and, in particular, can be used to treat cancerous tissue.

X-ray astronomy *n.* the observation of celestial objects with instruments capable of detecting and measuring high-energy electromagnetic radiation. Because the atmosphere absorbs practically all cosmic X-rays, it is necessary to place X-ray telescopes and spectrometers in Earth orbit aboard artificial satellites. Objects known to emit X-rays include the sun, certain cataclysmic variable stars, and clusters of galaxies which have been found to be permeated by a rarefied, but extremely hot, intergalactic gas. Temperatures characteristic of X-ray-emitting regions of stars and galaxies are in the millions of degrees. The detection of X-rays from certain close binary stars offers the best hope of detecting black holes.

xylem /ˈzaɪlem/ *n. Bot.* woody tissue (cf. PHLOEM). [Gk *xulon* wood]

xylene /ˈzaɪliːn/ *n. Chem.* one of three isomeric hydrocarbons formed from benzene by the substitution of two methyl groups, obtained from wood etc. [formed as XYLEM + -ENE]

xylo- /ˈzaɪləʊ/ *comb. form* wood. [Gk *xulon* wood]

xylocarp /ˈzaɪləˌkɑːp/ *n.* a hard woody fruit. □□ **xylocarpous** /-ˈkɑːpəs/ *adj.*

xylograph /ˈzaɪləˌɡrɑːf/ *n.* a woodcut or wood-engraving (esp. an early one).

xylography /zaɪˈlɒɡrəfɪ/ *n.* **1** the (esp. early or primitive) practice of making woodcuts or wood-engravings. **2** the use of wood blocks in printing.

Xylonite /ˈzaɪləˌnaɪt/ *n. propr.* a kind of celluloid. [irreg. f. *xyloidin* (as XYLO-) + -ITE[1]]

xylophagous /zaɪˈlɒfəɡəs/ *adj.* (of an insect or mollusc) eating, or boring into, wood.

xylophone /ˈzaɪləˌfəʊn/ *n.* a musical instrument of graduated wooden bars with tubular resonators suspended vertically beneath them, struck with small wooden etc. hammers. Its first appearance was in Africa and in Java, where it was known before the 9th c. In central Europe a different type was a popular instrument from the 15th c., known as the straw-fiddle because the bars lay on straw. It was first used in orchestral music by Saint-Saëns in *Danse macabre* (1874), its sound being particularly apt for the representation of rattling skeletons. □□ **xylophonic** /-ˈfɒnɪk/ *adj.* **xylophonist** *n.* [Gk *xulon* wood + -PHONE]

xystus /ˈzɪstəs/ *n.* (*pl.* **xysti** /-taɪ/) **1** a covered portico used by athletes in ancient Greece for exercise. **2** *Rom. Antiq.* a garden walk or terrace. [L f. Gk *xustos* smooth f. *xuō* scrape]

Y

Y¹ /waɪ/ n. (also **y**) (pl. **Ys** or **Y's**) **1** the twenty-fifth letter of the alphabet. **2** (usu. **y**) *Algebra* the second unknown quantity. **3** *Geom.* the second coordinate. **4 a** a Y-shaped thing, esp. an arrangement of lines, piping, roads, etc. **b** a forked clamp or support.

Y² *abbr.* (also **Y.**) **1** yen. **2** Yeomanry. **3** *US* = YMCA, YWCA.

Y³ *symb. Chem.* the element yttrium.

y. *abbr.* year(s).

y- /ɪ/ *prefix archaic* forming past participles, collective nouns, etc. (*yclept*). [OE *ge-* f. Gmc]

-y¹ /ɪ/ *suffix* forming adjectives: **1** from nouns and adjectives, meaning: **a** full of; having the quality of (*messy; icy; horsy*). **b** addicted to (*boozy*). **2** from verbs, meaning 'inclined to', 'apt to' (*runny; sticky*). [from or after OE *-ig* f. Gmc]

-y² /ɪ/ *suffix* (also **-ey, -ie**) forming diminutive nouns, pet names, etc. (*granny; Sally; nightie; Mickey*). [ME (orig. Sc.)]

-y³ /ɪ/ *suffix* forming nouns denoting: **1** state, condition, or quality (*courtesy; orthodoxy; modesty*). **2** an action or its result (*colloquy; remedy; subsidy*). [from or after F *-ie* f. L *-ia, -ium*, Gk *-eia, -ia*: cf. -ACY, -ERY, -GRAPHY, and others]

yabby /ˈjæbɪ/ n. (also **yabbie**) (pl. **-ies**) *Austral.* **1** a small freshwater crayfish, esp. of the genus *Cherax*. **2** a marine prawn, *Callianassa australiensis*, often used as bait. [Aboriginal]

yacht /jɒt/ n. & v. —n. **1** a light sailing-vessel, esp. equipped for racing. **2** a larger usu. power-driven vessel equipped for cruising. **3** a light vessel for travel on sand or ice. —v.intr. race or cruise in a yacht. □ **yacht-club** a club esp. for yacht-racing [early mod.Du. *jaghte* = *jaghtschip* fast pirate-ship f. *jag(h)t* chase f. *jagen* to hunt + *schip* SHIP]

yachting /ˈjɒtɪŋ/ n. racing or cruising in a yacht. Modern yachting was pioneered in Holland in the 17th c. when travel along the miles of sheltered Dutch waterways was difficult without boats. An early convert to the pastime was Charles II of England, who spent nearly ten years in exile in the Low Countries until the Restoration in 1660. His brother James (later James II) was almost as keen, and Pepys records that the royal brothers delighted in working the ship themselves 'like common seamen'. In the early 18th c. yachting (because of its inevitable discomforts) was regarded as an eccentric occupation, but in 1775 a revival of royal patronage and 'water parties' on the Thames gave rise to the organized yachting of today.

yachtsman /ˈjɒtsmən/ n. (pl. **-men**; *fem.* **yachtswoman**, pl. **-women**) a person who sails yachts.

yack /jæk/ n. & v. (also **yackety-yack** /ˌjækətɪˈjæk/) *sl. derog.* —n. trivial or unduly persistent conversation. —v.intr. engage in this. [imit.]

yacka (also **yacker**) var. of YAKKA.

yaffle /ˈjæf(ə)l/ n. *dial.* a green woodpecker, *Picus viridus*. [imit. of its laughing cry]

yager var. of JAEGER.

yah /jɑː/ *int.* expressing derision or defiance. [imit.]

yahoo /jəˈhuː, jɑː-/ n. a coarse bestial person. [name of an imaginary race of brutish creatures in Swift's *Gulliver's Travels* (1726)]

Yahweh /ˈjɑːweɪ/ n. (also **Yahveh** /-veɪ/) the Hebrew name of God in the Old Testament. [Heb. *YHVH* with added vowels: see JEHOVAH]

Yahwist /ˈjɑːwɪst/ n. (also **Yahvist** /-vɪst/) the postulated author or authors of parts of the Hexateuch in which God is regularly named *Yahweh*. (Cf. ELOHIST.)

Yajur-Veda /ˌjʌdʒʊlˈveɪdə, -ˈviːdə/ n. one of the four Vedas, a collection of sacrificial formulae in Old Sanscrit, used in the Vedic religion by the priest in charge of sacrificial ritual. [Skr., f. *yajus* ritual worship + *vēda* VEDA]

yak /jæk/ n. a long-haired humped Tibetan ox, *Bos grunniens*. [Tibetan *gyag*]

yakka /ˈjækə/ n. (also **yacka, yacker**) *Austral. sl.* work. [Aboriginal]

Yale lock /jeɪl/ n. *propr.* a type of lock for doors etc. with a cylindrical barrel turned by a flat key with a serrated edge. [L. *Yale*, Amer. inventor d. 1868]

Yale University /jeɪl/ an American university, now non-sectarian, originally a 'collegiate school' founded in 1701 at Killingworth and Saybrook, Connecticut, by a group of Congregational ministers. In 1716 it moved to its present site at New Haven and soon afterwards was renamed Yale College after Elihu Yale, a notable benefactor. In 1887 it became Yale University.

Yalta /ˈjæltə/ a port on the Black Sea in the USSR, site of a conference in February 1945 between the Allied leaders Churchill, Roosevelt, and Stalin, who met to plan the final stages of the Second World War and to agree the subsequent territorial division of Europe. In spite of the friendship displayed at the time the scene was set for East/West polarization; the Iron Curtain and the Cold War were to follow.

Yalu River /ˈjɑːluː/ a river rising in the mountains of Jilin province in NE China. Flowing about 800 km (500 miles) southwest to the Gulf of Korea, it forms part of the frontier between China and North Korea. The advance of UN troops towards the Yalu River precipitated the Chinese invasion of North Korea in November 1950.

yam /jæm/ n. **1 a** any tropical or subtropical climbing plant of the genus *Dioscorea*. **b** the edible starchy tuber of this. **2** *US* a sweet potato. [Port. *inhame* or Sp. *iñame*, of unkn. orig.]

Yama /ˈjæmə/ (in Hindu mythology) the first man to die. He became the guardian, judge, and ruler of the dead, and is represented as carrying a noose and riding a buffalo. [Skr. *yama* restraint (*yam* restrain)]

Yamato /jæˈmɑːtəʊ/ n. the style or school in Japan which culminated in the 12th and 13th c. and dealt with Japanese subjects in a distinctively Japanese (rather than Chinese) way. [Jap., = Japanese]

yammer /ˈjæmə(r)/ n. & v. *colloq. or dial.* —n. **1** a lament, wail, or grumble. **2** voluble talk. —v.intr. **1** utter a yammer. **2** talk volubly. □□ **yammerer** n. [OE *geōmrian* f. *geōmor* sorrowful]

Yamoussoukro /ˌjæmuːˈsuːkrəʊ/ the capital-designate of the Ivory Coast; pop. (1984) 120,000.

Yamuna /ˈjæmʊnə/ a river of India that rises in the Himalayas and flows south and south-east to meet the Ganges at Allahabad.

yandy /ˈjændɪ/ v. & n. *Austral.* —v.tr. (**-ies, -ied**) separate (grass seed) from refuse by special shaking. —n. (pl. **-ies**) a shallow dish used for this. [Aboriginal]

yang /jæŋ/ n. (in Chinese philosophy) the active principle of the universe, characterized as heaven, male, light, and penetrating (complemented by YIN). [Chin.]

Yangshao /yæŋˈʃaʊ/ *adj.* of an ancient civilization of northern China during the 3rd millennium BC, characterized by painted pottery with naturalistic designs of fish and human faces, and abstract patterns of triangles, spirals, arcs, and dots.

Yangtze Kiang /ˈjæntsɪ ˈkjæŋ/ the principal river of China, which rises in Tibet and flows 6,380 km (3,964 miles) through central China to the East China Sea. [Chin. *kiang* river]

Yank /jæŋk/ n. *colloq.* often *derog.* an inhabitant of the US; an American. [abbr.]

yank /jæŋk/ v. & n. *colloq.* —v.tr. pull with a jerk. —n. a sudden hard pull. [19th c.: orig. unkn.]

Yankee /ˈjæŋkɪ/ n. *colloq.* **1** often *derog.* = YANK. **2** *US* an inhabitant of New England or one of the northern States. **3** *hist.* a

---

æ *cat* ɑː *arm* e *bed* ɜː *her* ɪ *sit* iː *see* ɒ *hot* ɔː *saw* ʌ *run* ʊ *put* uː *too* ə *ago* aɪ *my*

Federal soldier in the Civil War. **4** a type of bet on four or more horses to win (or be placed) in different races. **5** (*attrib.*) of or as of the Yankees. □ **Yankee Doodle 1** a burlesque song to a jolly tune, first used by British troops, in the War of American Independence, to deride the American colonial revolutionaries. It was subsequently adopted by the Americans and turned to their own advantage, and is now regarded as a national air. **2** = YANKEE. [18th c.: orig. uncert.: perh. f. Du. *Janke* dimin. of *Jan* John attested (17th c.) as a nickname]

Yaoundé /jæ'ʊndeɪ/ the capital of Cameroon; pop. (est. 1984) 552,000.

yap /jæp/ v. & n. —*v.intr.* (**yapped**, **yapping**) **1** bark shrilly or fussily. **2** *colloq.* talk noisily, foolishly, or complainingly. —*n.* a sound of yapping. □□ **yapper** n. [imit.]

yapok /'jæpɒk/ n. = POSSUM. [*Oyapok, Oiapoque*, N. Brazilian river]

yapp /jæp/ n. *Brit.* a form of bookbinding with a limp leather cover projecting to fold over the edges of the leaves. [name of a London bookseller c.1860, for whom it was first made]

yarborough /'jɑːbərə/ n. a whist or bridge hand with no card above a 9. [Earl of *Yarborough* (d. 1897), said to have betted against its occurrence]

yard[1] /jɑːd/ n. **1** a unit of linear measure equal to 3 feet (0.9144 metre). (See below.) **2** this length of material (*a yard and a half of cloth*). **3** a square or cubic yard esp. (in building) of sand etc. **4** a cylindrical spar tapering to each end slung across a mast for a sail to hang from. **5** (in *pl.*; foll. by *of*) *colloq.* a great length (*yards of spare wallpaper*). □ **by the yard** at great length. **yard-arm** the outer extremity of a ship's yard. **yard of ale** *Brit.* **1** a deep slender beer glass, about a yard long and holding two to three pints. **2** the contents of this. [OE *gerd* f. WG]

The earlier standard was the ell (= 45 inches), and this was succeeded in 1353 by the *verge* of which 'yard' is the English equivalent; the yard was defined as the distance between two marks on a certain metallic bar, kept in the Tower of London, when this is at a temperature of 60 °F.

yard[2] /jɑːd/ n. & v. —*n.* **1** a piece of enclosed ground esp. attached to a building or used for a particular purpose. **2** *US* the garden of a house. —*v.tr.* put (cattle) into a stockyard. □ **the Yard** *Brit. colloq.* = SCOTLAND YARD. **yard-man 1** a person working in a railway-yard or timber-yard. **2** *US* a gardener or a person who does various outdoor jobs. **yard-master** the manager of a railway-yard. [OE *geard* enclosure, region, f. Gmc: cf. GARDEN]

yardage /'jɑːdɪdʒ/ n. **1** a number of yards of material etc. **2 a** the use of a stockyard etc. **b** payment for this.

yardbird /'jɑːdbɜːd/ n. *US sl.* **1** a new military recruit. **2** a convict.

Yardie /'jɑːdɪ/ n. a member of any of various West Indian gangs, originating in Jamaica, engaging in organized crime, esp. illegal drug-trafficking. [Jamaican Engl. *yard* home, Jamaica]

yardstick /'jɑːdstɪk/ n. **1** a standard used for comparison. **2** a measuring rod a yard long, usu. divided into inches etc.

yarmulke /'jɑːməlkə/ n. (also **yarmulka**) a skullcap worn by Jewish men. [Yiddish]

yarn /jɑːn/ n. & v. —*n.* **1** any spun thread, esp. for knitting, weaving, rope-making, etc. **2** *colloq.* a long or rambling story or discourse. —*v.intr. colloq.* tell yarns. [OE *gearn*]

yarran /'jærən/ n. any of several Australian acacias, esp. *Acacia homalophylla*, a small tree with scented wood used for fencing, fuel, etc. [Aboriginal]

yarrow /'jærəʊ/ n. any perennial herb of the genus *Achillea*, esp. milfoil. [OE *gearwe*, of unkn. orig.]

yashmak /'jæʃmæk/ n. a veil concealing the face except the eyes, worn by some Muslim women in public. [Arab. *yašmaḳ*, Turk. *yaşmak*]

yataghan /'jætəˌgæn/ n. a sword without a guard and often with a double-curved blade, used in Muslim countries. [Turk. *yātāġan*]

yaw /jɔː/ v. & n. —*v.intr.* (of a ship or aircraft etc.) fail to hold a straight course; fall off; go unsteadily (esp. turning from side to side). —*n.* the yawing of a ship etc. from its course. [16th c.: orig. unkn.]

yawl /jɔːl/ n. **1** a two-masted fore-and-aft sailing-boat with the mizen-mast stepped far aft. **2** a small kind of fishing-boat. **3** *hist.* a ship's jolly boat with four or six oars. [MLG *jolle* or Du. *jol*, of unkn. orig.: cf. JOLLY[2]]

yawn /jɔːn/ v. & n. —*v.* **1** *intr.* (as a reflex) open the mouth wide and inhale esp. when sleepy or bored. **2** *intr.* (of a chasm etc.) gape, be wide open. **3** *tr.* utter or say with a yawn. —*n.* **1** an act of yawning. **2** *colloq.* a boring or tedious idea, activity, etc. □□ **yawner** n. **yawningly** adv. [OE *ginian*, *geonian*]

yawp /jɔːp/ n. & v. —*n.* **1** a harsh or hoarse cry. **2** foolish talk. —*v.intr.* utter these. □□ **yawper** n. [ME (imit.)]

yaws /jɔːz/ *n.pl.* (usu. treated as *sing.*) a contagious tropical skin-disease with large red swellings. [17th c.: orig. unkn.]

Yayoi /jɑ'jɔɪ/ *adj.* & n. —*adj.* of a neolithic industry of Japan, dating from the 3rd c. BC, named after a street in Tokyo where its characteristic chiefly wheel-made pottery was first discovered. It is marked by the introduction of rice cultivation to Japan, and the appearance of large burial mounds has suggested the emergence of an increasingly powerful ruling class. —*n.* this industry. [Jap.]

Yb *symb. Chem.* the element ytterbium.

Y-chromosome /'waɪˌkrəʊməˌsəʊm/ n. a sex chromosome occurring only in male cells. [Y as an arbitrary label + CHROMOSOME]

yclept /ɪ'klept/ *adj.* *archaic* or *joc.* called (by the name of). [OE *gecleopod* past part. of *cleopian* call f. Gmc]

y.d. *abbr.* yard (measure).

yds. *abbr.* yards (measure).

ye[1] /jiː/ *pron. archaic* pl. of THOU[1]. □ **ye gods!** *joc.* an exclamation of astonishment. [OE *ge* f. Gmc]

ye[2] /jiː/ *adj. pseudo-archaic* = THE (*ye olde tea-shoppe*). [var. spelling f. the *y*-shaped letter THORN (representing *th*) in the 14th c.]

yea /jeɪ/ *adv.* & n. *archaic* —*adv.* **1** yes. **2** indeed, nay (*ready, yea eager*). —*n.* the word 'yea'. □ **yea and nay** shilly-shally. **yeas and nays** affirmative and negative votes. [OE *gea*, f. Gmc]

yeah /jeə/ *adv. colloq.* yes. □ **oh yeah?** expressing incredulity. [casual pronunc. of YES]

yean /jiːn/ *v.tr.* & *intr. archaic* bring forth (a lamb or kid). [perh. f. OE *geēanian* (unrecorded, as Y-, *ēanian* to lamb)]

yeanling /'jiːnlɪŋ/ n. *archaic* a young lamb or kid.

year /jɪə(r), jɜː(r)/ n. **1** (also **astronomical year**, **equinoctial year**, **natural year**, **solar year**, **tropical year**) the time occupied by the earth in one revolution round the sun, 365 days, 5 hours, 48 minutes, and 46 seconds in length (cf. *sidereal year*). **2** (also **calendar year**, **civil year**) the period of 365 days (**common year**) or 366 days (see *leap year*) from 1 Jan. to 31 Dec., used for reckoning time in ordinary affairs. **3 a** a period of the same length as this starting at any point (*four years ago*). **b** such a period in terms of a particular activity etc. occupying its duration (*school year; tax year*). **4** (in *pl.*) age or time of life (*young for his years*). **5** (usu. in *pl.*) *colloq.* a very long time (*it took years to get served*). **6** a group of students entering college etc. in the same academic year. □ **in the year of Our Lord** (foll. by the year) in a specified year AD. **of the year** chosen as outstanding in a particular year (*sportsman of the year*). **a year and a day** the period specified in some legal matters to ensure the completion of a full year. **the year dot** see DOT[1]. **year in, year out** continually over a period of years. **year-long** lasting a year or the whole year. **year of grace** the year AD. **year-round** existing etc. throughout the year. [OE *gē(a)r* f. Gmc]

yearbook /'jɪəbʊk, 'jɜː-/ n. an annual publication dealing with events or aspects of the (usu. preceding) year.

yearling /'jɪəlɪŋ, 'jɜː-/ n. & *adj.* —*n.* **1** an animal between one and two years old. **2** a racehorse in the calendar year after the year of foaling. —*adj.* **1** a year old; having existed or been such for a year (*a yearling heifer*). **2** intended to terminate after one year (*yearling bonds*).

yearly /'jɪəlɪ, 'jɜː-/ *adj.* & *adv.* —*adj.* **1** done, produced, or occurring once a year. **2** of or lasting a year. —*adv.* once a year; from year to year. [OE *gēarlic, -lice* (as YEAR)]

yearn /jɜːn/ *v.intr.* **1** (usu. foll. by *for, after*, or *to* + infin.) have a strong emotional longing. **2** (usu. foll. by *to*, *towards*) be filled with compassion or tenderness. □□ **yearner** *n.* **yearning** *n.* & *adj.* **yearningly** *adv.* [OE *giernan* f. a Gmc root meaning 'eager']

yeast /jiːst/ *n.* **1** a greyish-yellow fungous substance obtained esp. from fermenting malt liquors and used as a fermenting agent, to raise bread, etc. **2** any of various unicellular fungi in which vegetative reproduction takes place by budding or fission. □□ **yeastless** *adj.* **yeastlike** *adj.* [OE *gist*, *giest* (unrecorded): cf. MDu. *ghist*, MHG *jist*, ON *jöstr*]

yeasty /ˈjiːstɪ/ *adj.* (**yeastier**, **yeastiest**) **1** frothy or tasting like yeast. **2** in a ferment. **3** working like yeast. **4** (of talk etc.) light and superficial. □□ **yeastily** *adv.* **yeastiness** *n.*

Yeats /jeɪts/, William Butler (1865–1939), Irish poet and dramatist, son of J. B. Yeats and brother of Jack Yeats (both celebrated painters). Yeats developed a fascination for mystic religion and the supernatural while studying at the School of Art in Dublin. With Lady Gregory and others he established the Irish National Theatre (later based at the Abbey Theatre) and his play *The Countess Cathleen* (1892) began the Irish revival in the theatre. Irish lore and legend predominate in *The Celtic Twilight* (1893; stories) which became a generic phrase for the Irish literary revival of which Yeats is the acknowledged leader. Irish traditional and national themes and his unrequited love for revolutionary patriot Maude Gonne inspired *The Wanderings of Oisin and other Poems* (1889) and other volumes. In his later works he moved further from his early elaborate Pre-Raphaelite style towards a new spare colloquial lyricism. In 1917 he married Georgie Hyde-Lees, whose power of automatic writing stimulated his occultism; her 'communicators' ultimately provided him with the system of symbolism (described in *A Vision*, 1925) which underlies many of the poems in *The Tower* (1928) and *The Winding Stair* (1929). Yeats served as senator of the Irish Free State (1922–8) and was awarded the Nobel Prize for literature in 1923.

yegg /jeg/ *n.* US *sl.* a travelling burglar or safe-breaker. [20th c.: perh. a surname]

yell /jel/ *n.* & *v.* —*n.* **1** a loud sharp cry of pain, anger, fright, encouragement, delight, etc. **2** a shout. **3** US an organized cry, used esp. to support a sports team. **4** *sl.* an amusing person or thing. —*v.intr.* & *tr.* make or utter with a yell. [OE *g(i)ellan* f. Gmc]

yellow /ˈjeləʊ/ *adj.*, *n.*, & *v.* —*adj.* **1** of the colour between green and orange in the spectrum, of buttercups, lemons, egg-yolks, or gold. **2** of the colour of faded leaves, ripe wheat, etc. **3** having a yellow skin or complexion. **4** *colloq.* cowardly. **5** (of looks, feelings, etc.) jealous, envious, or suspicious. **6** (of newspapers etc.) unscrupulously sensational. —*n.* **1** a yellow colour or pigment. **2** yellow clothes or material (*dressed in yellow*). **3 a** a yellow ball, piece, etc., in a game or sport. **b** the player using such pieces. **4** (usu. in *comb.*) a yellow moth or butterfly. **5** (in *pl.*) jaundice of horses etc. **6** US a peach-disease with yellowed leaves. —*v.tr.* & *intr.* make or become yellow. □ **yellow arsenic** = ORPIMENT. **yellow-belly 1** *colloq.* a coward. **2** any of various fish with yellow underparts. **yellow card** *Football* a card shown by the referee to a player being cautioned. **yellow fever** see separate entry. **yellow flag 1** a flag displayed by a ship in quarantine. **2** an iridaceous plant, *Iris pseudacorus*, with slender sword-shaped leaves and yellow flowers. **yellow jack 1** = *yellow fever.* **2** = *yellow flag.* **yellow line** (in the UK) a line painted along the side of the road in yellow either singly or in pairs to denote parking restrictions. **yellow metal** brass of 60 parts copper and 40 parts zinc. **Yellow Pages** *propr.* a section of a telephone directory on yellow paper and listing business subscribers according to the goods or services they offer. **the yellow peril** the political or military threat regarded as emanating from Asian peoples, esp. the Chinese. **yellow rattle** a yellow-flowered plant of the genus *Rhinanthus*. **yellow rocket** see ROCKET². **yellow spot** the point of acutest vision in the retina. **yellow streak** *colloq.* a trait of cowardice. □□ **yellowish** *adj.* **yellowly** *adv.* **yellowness** *n.* **yellowy** *adj.* [OE *geolu*, *geolo* f. WG, rel. to GOLD]

yellowback /ˈjeləʊˌbæk/ *n.* a cheap novel etc. in a yellow cover.

yellow fever *n.* a tropical disease with fever and jaundice,

the notorious 'yellow jack' of the old sea-stories, carried from infected persons by the bite of a female mosquito of the genus *Aëdes aegyptii.* Primarily a disease of monkeys, it became established in humans many centuries ago and was probably carried from Africa to the West Indies when African slaves were first taken there. Yellow fever is often fatal; its prevention and control (as by inoculation) are all-important.

yellowhammer /ˈjeləʊˌhæmə(r)/ *n.* a bunting, *Emberiza citrinella*, of which the male has a yellow head, neck, and breast. [16th c.: orig. of *hammer* uncert.]

Yellowknife /ˌjeləʊˈnaɪf/ the capital of the Northwest Territories of Canada, on the north shore of the Great Slave Lake; pop. (1986) 11,000. Founded in 1935 as a gold-mining town, Yellowknife was named after an Indian tribe.

Yellow River (Chinese **Huang Ho** /hwæŋ ˈhəʊ/) the second-largest river in China. Rising in the mountains of west central China, it flows in a great circle for a distance of about 4,830 km (3,000 miles) before entering the Bo Hai Gulf.

Yellowstone /ˈjeləʊˌstəʊn/ an area of Wyoming and Montana in the US, reserved as a National Park since 1872. It is famous for its scenery, geysers, and wildlife. The Yellowstone River, which rises in the park, is a tributary of the Missouri.

yelp /jelp/ *n.* & *v.* —*n.* a sharp shrill cry of or as of a dog in pain or excitement. —*v.intr.* utter a yelp. □□ **yelper** *n.* [OE *gielp(an)* boast (imit.): cf. YAWP]

Yeltsin /ˈjeltsɪn/, Boris (1931–), Soviet politician. At first a close supporter of Mikhail Gorbachev's programme of reform, he soon became his leading radical opponent, impatient with party bureaucracy and the slowness of change. In 1990 Yeltsin was elected to the important post of President of the Russian Republic; shortly afterwards, in a dramatic move, he and his supporters resigned from the Communist Party, creating a powerful opposition movement.

Yemen /ˈjemən/ a country in the south and south-west of the Arabian peninsula, formerly divided into the People's Democratic Republic of Yemen (South Yemen; pop. (est. 1988) 2,425,600; official language, Arabic; capital, Aden) and the Yemen Arab Republic (North Yemen; pop. (est. 1988) 6,732,400; official language, Arabic; capital, Sana'a). An Islamic country since the mid-7th c., Yemen was part of the Ottoman empire from the 16th c. In the 19th c. it came under increasing British influence as a result of the strategic importance of Aden at the mouth of the Red Sea. Civil war between royalist and republican forces in the era following the Second World War ended with the British withdrawal and South Yemen's declaration of independence in 1967. North and South Yemen reunited to form the Yemeni Republic in 1990. □□ **Yemeni** *adj.* & *n.*

yen¹ /jen/ *n.* (*pl.* same) the chief monetary unit of Japan. [Jap. f. Chin. *yuan* round, dollar]

yen² /jen/ *n.* & *v.* *colloq.* —*n.* a longing or yearning. —*v.intr.* (**yenned**, **yenning**) feel a longing. [Chin. dial.]

Yenisei /ˌjenɪˈseɪ/ a river of the Soviet Union which rises in the mountains of southern Siberia near the frontier with Mongolia and flows 4,106 km (2,566 miles) northwards to the Kara Sea.

yeoman /ˈjəʊmən/ *n.* (*pl.* **-men**) **1** esp. *hist.* a man holding and cultivating a small landed estate. **2** *hist.* a person qualified by possessing free land of an annual value of 40 shillings to serve on juries, vote for the knight of the shire, etc. **3** *Brit.* a member of the yeomanry force. **4** *hist.* a servant in a royal or noble household. **5** (in full **yeoman of signals**) a petty officer in the Navy, concerned with visual signalling. **6** US a petty officer performing clerical duties on board ship. □ **Yeoman of the Guard** a member of the British sovereign's bodyguard, first established by Henry VII. Their functions are now entirely ceremonial, and along with the warders of the Tower of London (who, like them, wear Tudor dress as uniform) they are commonly known as beefeaters. **yeoman** (or **yeoman's**) **service** efficient or useful help in need. **Yeoman Usher** *Brit.* the deputy of Black Rod. □□ **yeomanly** *adj.* [ME *yoman*, *yeman*, etc., prob. f. YOUNG + MAN]

yeomanry /ˈjəʊmənrɪ/ *n.* (*pl.* **-ies**) **1** a body of yeomen. **2** *Brit.*

hist. a volunteer cavalry force raised from the yeoman class (1794–1908).

yep /jep/ *adv. & n.* (also **yup** /jʌp/) *US colloq.* = YES. [corrupt.]

-yer /jə(r)/ *suffix* var. of -IER esp. after *w* (*bowyer*; *lawyer*).

yerba maté /'jɜːbə ˌmæteɪ/ *n.* = MATÉ. [Sp., = herb maté]

Yerevan /ˌjerɪ'væn/ the capital of the Soviet republic of Armenia; pop. (est. 1987) 1,168,000.

yes /jes/ *adv. & n.* —*adv.* **1** equivalent to an affirmative sentence: the answer to your question is affirmative, it is as you say or as I have said, the statement etc. made is correct, the request or command will be complied with, the negative statement etc. made is not correct. **2** (in answer to a summons or address) an acknowledgement of one's presence. —*n.* an utterance of the word *yes*. □ **say yes** grant a request or confirm a statement. **yes?** **1** indeed? is that so? **2** what do you want? **yes and** a form for introducing a stronger phrase (*he came home drunk—yes, and was sick*). **yes and no** that is partly true and partly untrue. **yes-man** (*pl.* **-men**) *colloq.* a weakly acquiescent person. [OE *gēse, gīse*, prob. f. *gīa sīe* may it be (*gīa* is unrecorded)]

yester- /'jestə(r)/ *comb. form poet. or archaic* of yesterday; that is the last past (*yester-eve*). [OE *geostran*]

yesterday /'jestədeɪ/ *adv. & n.* —*adv.* **1** on the day before today. **2** in the recent past. —*n.* **1** the day before today. **2** the recent past. □ **yesterday morning** (or **afternoon** etc.) in the morning (or afternoon etc.) of yesterday. [OE *giestran dæg* (as YESTER-, DAY)]

yesteryear /'jestəjɪə(r)/ *n. literary* **1** last year. **2** the recent past.

yet /jet/ *adv. & conj.* —*adv.* **1** as late as, or until, now or then (*there is yet time; your best work yet*). **2** (with *neg.* or *interrog.*) so soon as, or by, now or then (*it is not time yet; have you finished yet?*). **3** again; in addition (*more and yet more*). **4** in the remaining time available; before all is over (*I will do it yet*). **5** (foll. by *compar.*) even (*a yet more difficult task*). **6** nevertheless; and in spite of that; but for all that (*it is strange, and yet it is true*). —*conj.* but at the same time; but nevertheless (*I won, yet what good has it done?*). □ **nor yet** and also not (*won't listen to me nor yet to you*). [OE *gīet(a)*, = OFris. *iēta*, of unkn. orig.]

yeti /'jetɪ/ *n.* = *Abominable Snowman*. [Tibetan]

yew /juː/ *n.* **1** any dark-leaved evergreen coniferous tree of the genus *Taxus*, having seeds enclosed in a fleshy red aril, and often planted in churchyards. **2** its wood, used formerly as a material for bows and still in cabinet-making. [OE *īw, ēow* f. Gmc]

Y-fronts /'waɪfrʌnts/ *n. propr.* men's or boys' briefs with a Y-shaped seam at the front.

Yggdrasil /'ɪgdrəsɪl/ *n. Scand. Mythol.* an ash-tree whose roots and branches join heaven, earth, and hell. The Norns sit beneath it. [ON *yg(g)drasill* f. *Yggr* Odin + *drasill* horse]

YHA *abbr.* (in the UK) Youth Hostels Association.

Yid /jɪd/ *n. sl. offens.* a Jew. [back-form. f. YIDDISH]

Yiddish /'jɪdɪʃ/ *n. & adj.* —*n.* a vernacular used by Jews in or from central and eastern Europe. Until 1939 it was widely spoken, but since the Second World War the number of speakers has declined in the face of the rise of Hebrew as a spoken language. It originated in the 9th c. among Jewish emigrants who settled in cities along the Rhine in Germany and adopted the German dialect of the area. Their German was heavily influenced by Hebrew which remained their literary language. In the 14th c. it was carried eastwards where it was again influenced by the Slavonic languages. From this amalgam arose Yiddish. When it was written down, the Hebrew characters were used with the difference that vowels were written with separate signs. —*adj.* of or relating to this language. [G *jüdisch* Jewish]

Yiddisher /'jɪdɪʃ(ə)r/ *n. & adj.* —*n.* a person speaking Yiddish. —*adj.* Yiddish-speaking.

yield /jiːld/ *v. & n.* —*v.* **1** *tr.* (also *absol.*) produce or return as a fruit, profit, or result (*the land yields crops; the land yields poorly; the investment yields 15%*). **2** *tr.* give up; surrender, concede; comply with a demand for (*yielded the fortress; yielded themselves prisoners*). **3** *intr.* (often foll. by *to*) **a** surrender; make submission. **b** give consent or change one's course of action in deference to; respond as required to (*yielded to persuasion*). **4** *intr.* (foll. by *to*) be inferior or confess inferiority to (*I yield to none in understanding*

the problem). **5** *intr.* (foll. by *to*) give right of way to other traffic. **6** *intr.* *US* allow another the right to speak in a debate etc. —*n.* an amount yielded or produced; an output or return. □ **yield point** *Physics* the stress beyond which a material becomes plastic. □□ **yielder** *n.* [OE *g(i)eldan* pay f. Gmc]

yielding /'jiːldɪŋ/ *adj.* **1** compliant, submissive. **2** (of a substance) able to bend; not stiff or rigid. □□ **yieldingly** *adv.* **yieldingness** *n.*

yin /jɪn/ *n.* (in Chinese philosophy) the passive principle of the universe, characterized as earth, female, dark, and absorbing (complemented by YANG). [Chin.]

yip /jɪp/ *v. & n. US* —*v.intr.* (**yipped, yipping**) = YELP *v.* —*n.* = YELP *n.* [imit.]

yippee /'jɪpiː, -'piː/ *int.* expressing delight or excitement. [natural excl.]

-yl /ɪl/ *suffix Chem.* forming nouns denoting a radical (*ethyl; hydroxyl; phenyl*).

ylang-ylang /'iːlæŋ,iːlæŋ/ *n.* (also **ilang-ilang**) **1** a Malayan tree, *Cananga odorata*, from the fragrant yellow flowers of which a perfume is distilled. **2** the perfume itself. [Tagalog *álang-ilang*]

YMCA 1 Young Men's Christian Association, a welfare movement that aims to develop high standards of Christian character. It was begun in London in 1844, originally for the 'improvement of the spiritual condition of young men in the drapery and other trades', and now has branches all over the world. The World Alliance of YMCAs was established in 1855; its headquarters are in Geneva. **2** a hostel run by this Association. [abbr.]

Ymir /'iːmə(r)/ *Scand. Mythol.* the primeval giant from whose body the gods created the world.

-yne /aɪn/ *suffix Chem.* forming names of unsaturated compounds containing a triple bond (*ethyne* = acetylene).

yob /jɒb/ *n. Brit. sl.* a lout or hooligan. □□ **yobbish** *adj.* **yobbishly** *adv.* **yobbishness** *n.* [back sl. for BOY]

yobbo /'jɒbəʊ/ *n.* (*pl.* **-os**) *Brit. sl.* = YOB.

yod /jɒd/ *n.* **1** the tenth and smallest letter of the Hebrew alphabet. **2** its semivowel sound /j/. [Heb. *yōd* f. *yad* hand]

yodel /'jəʊd(ə)l/ *v. & n.* —*v.tr. & intr.* (**yodelled, yodelling**; *US* **yodeled, yodeling**) sing with melodious inarticulate sounds and frequent changes between falsetto and the normal voice in the manner of the Swiss mountain-dwellers. —*n.* a yodelling cry. □□ **yodeller** *n.* [G *jodeln*]

yoga /'jəʊgə/ *n.* **1** a Hindu system of philosophic meditation and asceticism designed to effect reunion with the universal spirit. **2** = HATHA YOGA. □□ **yogic** /'jəʊgɪk/ *adj.* [Hind. f. Skr., = union]

yogh /jɒg/ *n.* a Middle English letter used for certain values of *g* and *y*. [ME]

yoghurt /'jɒgət/ *n.* (also **yogurt**) a semi-solid sourish food prepared from milk fermented by added bacteria. [Turk. *yoğurt*]

yogi /'jəʊgɪ/ *n.* a person proficient in yoga. □□ **yogism** *n.* [Hind. f. YOGA]

Yogyakarta see JOGJAKARTA.

yo-heave-ho /'jəʊhiːv,həʊ/ *int. & n.* = *heave-ho*.

yo-ho /jəʊ'həʊ/ *int.* (also **yo-ho-ho** /ˌjəʊhəʊ'həʊ/) **1** used to attract attention. **2** = YO-HEAVE-HO. [cf. YO-HEAVE-HO & HO]

yoicks /jɔɪks/ *int.* (also **hoicks** /hɔɪks/) a cry used by fox-hunters to urge on the hounds. [orig. unkn.: cf. *hyke* call to hounds, HEY[1]]

yoke /jəʊk/ *n. & v.* —*n.* **1** a wooden crosspiece fastened over the necks of two oxen etc. and attached to the plough or wagon to be drawn. **2** (*pl.* same or **yokes**) a pair (of oxen etc.). **3** an object like a yoke in form or function, e.g. a wooden shoulder-piece for carrying a pair of pails, the top section of a dress or skirt etc. from which the rest hangs. **4** sway, dominion, or servitude, esp. when oppressive. **5** a bond or union, esp. that of marriage. **6** *Rom.Hist.* an uplifted yoke, or an arch of three spears symbolizing it, under which a defeated army was made to march. **7** *archaic* the amount of land that one yoke of oxen could plough in a day. **8** a crossbar on which a bell swings. **9** the crossbar of a rudder to whose ends ropes are fastened. **10** a bar of soft iron between the poles of an electromagnet. —*v.* **1** *tr.* put a yoke on.

2 *tr.* couple or unite (a pair). **3** *tr.* (foll. by *to*) link (one thing) to (another). **4** *intr.* match or work together. [OE *geoc* f. Gmc]

yokel /ˈjəʊk(ə)l/ *n.* a rustic; a country bumpkin. [perh. f. dial. *yokel* green woodpecker]

Yokohama /ˌjəʊkəʊˈhɑːmə/ a seaport on Honshu Island, Japan; pop. (1987) 3,072,000. Originally a small fishing village, Yokohama is now the second-largest city in Japan.

yolk[1] /jəʊk/ *n.* **1** the yellow internal part of an egg that nourishes the young before it hatches. **2** *Biol.* the corresponding part of any animal ovum. □ **yolk-bag** (or **-sac**) a membrane enclosing the yolk of an egg. □□ **yolked** *adj.* (also in *comb.*). **yolkless** *adj.* **yolky** *adj.* [OE *geol(o)ca* f. *geolu* YELLOW]

yolk[2] /jəʊk/ *n.* = SUINT. [OE *eowoca* (unrecorded)]

Yom Kippur /jɒm ˈkɪpə(r)/ *n.* = *Day of Atonement* (see ATONEMENT). □ **Yom Kippur War** the Israeli name for the Arab–Israeli conflict in 1973, called by the Arabs the October War. Egyptian and Syrian forces attacked Israel on the festival of Yom Kippur (6 October), and the war lasted for nearly three weeks. Syrian forces were repulsed, Egypt took back part of the east bank of the Suez Canal, and Israel established a bridgehead on its west bank. [Heb.]

yomp /jɒmp/ *v.intr. Brit. sl.* march with heavy equipment over difficult terrain. [20th c.: orig. unkn.]

yon /jɒn/ *adj., adv.,* & *pron. literary* & *dial.* —*adj.* & *adv.* yonder. —*pron.* yonder person or thing. [OE *geon*]

yonder /ˈjɒndə(r)/ *adv.* & *adj.* —*adv.* over there; at some distance in that direction; in the place indicated by pointing etc. —*adj.* situated yonder. [ME: cf. OS *gendra*, Goth. *jaindrē*]

yoni /ˈjəʊnɪ/ *n.* a symbol of the female genitals venerated by Hindus etc. [Skr., = source, womb, female genitals]

yonks /jɒŋks/ *n.pl. sl.* a long time (*haven't seen them for yonks*). [20th c.: orig. unkn.]

yoo-hoo /ˈjuːhuː/ *int.* used to attract a person's attention. [natural excl.]

yore /jɔː(r)/ *n. literary* □ **of yore** formerly; in or of old days. [OE *geāra, gēare*, etc., adv. forms of uncert. orig.]

York /jɔːk/ **1** a city in North Yorkshire, seat of the archbishop, Primate of England; pop. (1981) 99,900. **2** the name of the English royal house descended from Edmund of Langley (1341–1402), 5th son of Edward III and (from 1385) 1st Duke of York, which ruled England from 1461 (Edward IV) until the death of Richard III (1485). It was united with the House of Lancaster when Henry VII married the eldest daughter of Edward IV (1486).

york /jɔːk/ *v.tr. Cricket* bowl with a yorker. [back-form. f. YORKER]

yorker /ˈjɔːkə(r)/ *n. Cricket* a ball bowled so that it pitches immediately under the bat. [prob. f. *York*, as having been introduced by Yorkshire players]

Yorkist /ˈjɔːkɪst/ *adj.* & *n.* —*adj.* of the family descended from the 1st Duke of York (see YORK) or of the White Rose party supporting it in the Wars of the Roses (cf. LANCASTRIAN). —*n.* a member or adherent of the Yorkist family.

Yorks. *abbr.* Yorkshire.

Yorkshire fog /ˈjɔːkʃə/ *n.* a fodder-grass, *Holcus lanatus*.

Yorkshireman /ˈjɔːkʃəmən/ *n.* (*pl.* **-men**; *fem.* **Yorkshirewoman**, *pl.* **-women**) a native of Yorkshire in N. England.

Yorkshire pudding /ˈjɔːkʃə/ *n.* a baked batter pudding usu. eaten with roast beef.

Yorkshire terrier /ˈjɔːkʃə/ *n.* a small long-haired blue-grey and tan kind of terrier.

Yoruba /ˈjɒrʊbə/ *n.* (*pl.* same or **Yorubas**) **1** a member of a Black people on the coast of West Africa, especially in Nigeria where they are numerically the largest ethnic group. **2** their language, which is one of the major languages of Nigeria and is spoken by 10 million people in the south-west of the country. It is a tonal language of the Niger-Congo language group. [native name]

Yosemite /jəʊˈsemɪˌtɪ/ a National Park in eastern California in the US, named after the Yosemite River which flows through it.

you /juː/ *pron.* (*obj.* **you**; *poss.* **your, yours**) **1** used with reference to the person or persons addressed or one such person and

one or more associated persons. **2** (as *int.* with a noun) in an exclamatory statement (*you fools!*). **3** (in general statements) one, a person, anyone, or everyone (*it's bad at first, but you get used to it*). □ **you-all** *US colloq.* you (usu. more than one person). **you and yours** you together with your family, property, etc. **you-know-what** (or **-who**) something or someone unspecified but understood. [OE *ēow* accus. & dative of *gē* YE[1] f. WG: supplanting *ye* because of the more frequent use of the obj. case, and *thou* and *thee* as the more courteous form]

you'd /juːd, jʊd/ *contr.* **1** you had. **2** you would.

you'll /juːl, jʊl, jɔːl/ *contr.* you will; you shall.

Young /jʌŋ/, Brigham (1801–77), Mormon leader (see MORMON).

young /jʌŋ/ *adj.* & *n.* —*adj.* (**younger** /ˈjʌŋgə(r)/; **youngest** /ˈjʌŋgɪst/) **1** not far advanced in life, development, or existence; not yet old. **2** immature or inexperienced. **3** felt in or characteristic of youth (*young love; young ambition*). **4** representing young people (*Young Conservatives; Young England*). **5** distinguishing a son from his father (*young Jones*). **6** (**younger**) **a** distinguishing one person from another of the same name (*the younger Pitt*). **b** *Sc.* the heir of a landed commoner. —*n.* (*collect.*) offspring, esp. of animals before or soon after birth. □ **with young** (of an animal) pregnant. **young blood** see BLOOD. **younger hand** *Cards* the second player of two. **young fustic** see FUSTIC. **young hopeful** see HOPEFUL. **young idea** the child's mind. **young lady** *colloq.* a girlfriend or sweetheart. **young man** a boyfriend or sweetheart. **young person** *Law* (in the UK) a person generally between 14 and 17 years of age. **Young Pretender** see PRETENDER. **young thing** *archaic* or *colloq.* an indulgent term for a young person. **Young Turk 1** a member of a group of reformers in the Ottoman empire in the late 19th c. and early 20th c. who carried out the revolution of 1908 and deposed the sultan Abdul Hamid II. **2** a young person eager for radical change to the established order. **young turk** *offens.* a violent child or youth. **young 'un** *colloq.* a youngster. **young woman** *colloq.* a girlfriend or sweetheart. □□ **youngish** *adj.* **youngling** *n.* [OE *g(e)ong* f. Gmc]

youngster /ˈjʌŋstə(r)/ *n.* a child or young person.

younker /ˈjʌŋkə(r)/ *n. archaic* = YOUNGSTER. [MDu. *jonckher* f. *jonc* YOUNG + *hēre* lord: cf. JUNKER]

your /jɔː(r), jʊə(r)/ *poss.pron.* (*attrib.*) **1** of or belonging to you or yourself or yourselves (*your house; your own business*). **2** *colloq.* usu. *derog.* much talked of; well known (*none so fallible as your self-styled expert*). [OE *ēower* genit. of *gē* YE[1]]

you're /jʊə(r), jə(r), jɔː(r)/ *contr.* you are.

yours /jɔːz, jʊəz/ *poss.pron.* **1** the one or ones belonging to or associated with you (*it is yours; yours are over there*). **2** your letter (*yours of the 10th*). **3** introducing a formula ending a letter (*yours ever; yours truly*). □ **of yours** of or belonging to you (*a friend of yours*).

yourself /jɔːˈself, jʊə-/ *pron.* (*pl.* **yourselves** /-ˈselvz/) **1 a** *emphat.* form of YOU. **b** *refl.* form of YOU. **2** in your normal state of body or mind (*are quite yourself again*). □ **be yourself** act in your normal, unconstrained manner. **how's yourself?** *sl.* how are you? (esp. after answering a similar enquiry).

youth /juːθ/ *n.* (*pl.* **youths** /juːðz/) **1** the state of being young; the period between childhood and adult age. **2** the vigour or enthusiasm, inexperience, or other characteristic of this period. **3** an early stage of development etc. **4** a young person (esp. male). **5** (*pl.*) young people collectively (*the youth of the country*). □ **youth club** (or **centre**) a place or organization provided for young people's leisure activities. **youth hostel** a place where (esp. young) holiday-makers can put up cheaply for the night. **youth hosteller** a user of a youth hostel. [OE *geoguth* f. Gmc, rel. to YOUNG]

youthful /ˈjuːθfʊl/ *adj.* **1** young, esp. in appearance or manner. **2** having the characteristics of youth (*youthful impatience*). **3** having the freshness or vigour of youth (*a youthful complexion*). □□ **youthfully** *adv.* **youthfulness** *n.*

you've /juːv, jʊv/ *contr.* you have.

yowl /jaʊl/ *n.* & *v.* —*n.* a loud wailing cry of or as of a cat or dog in pain or distress. —*v.intr.* utter a yowl. [imit.]

yo-yo /ˈjəʊjəʊ/ *n.* & *v.* —*n.* (*pl.* **yo-yos**) **1** a toy consisting of a pair of discs with a deep groove between them in which string is attached and wound, and which can be spun alternately downward and upward by its weight and momentum as the string unwinds and rewinds. **2** a thing that repeatedly falls and rises again. —*v.intr.* (**yo-yoes, yo-yoed**) **1** play with a yo-yo. **2** move up and down; fluctuate. [20th c.: orig. unkn.]

Ypres /ˈiːprə, *joc.* ˈwaɪpəz/ a town in Belgium, scene of some of the bitterest fighting on the Western Front during the First World War.

yr. *abbr.* **1** year(s). **2** younger. **3** your.

yrs. *abbr.* **1** years. **2** yours.

ytterbium /ɪˈtɜːbɪəm/ *n. Chem.* a silvery metallic element of the lanthanide series occurring naturally as various isotopes. It has few commercial uses. ¶ Symb.: **Yb**; atomic number 70. [mod.L f. *Ytterby* in Sweden]

yttrium /ˈɪtrɪəm/ *n. Chem.* a greyish metallic element resembling the lanthanides, included among the rare-earth metals. Yttrium compounds have a variety of uses, the most important being to make red phosphors for colour-television tubes. The metal itself is used in certain alloys and superconductors. ¶ Symb.: **Y**; atomic number 39. [formed as YTTERBIUM]

yuan /juːˈɑːn/ *n.* (*pl.* same) the chief monetary unit of China. [Chin.: see YEN[1]]

Yucatán /ˌjuːkəˈtɑːn/ a State of SE Mexico, at the northern tip of the Yucatán peninsula which is bounded by the Gulf of Mexico and the Caribbean Sea; pop. (est. 1988) 1,302,600; capital, Mérida.

yucca /ˈjʌkə/ *n.* any American white-flowered liliaceous plant of the genus *Yucca*, with swordlike leaves. [Carib]

yuck /jʌk/ *int.* & *n.* (also **yuk**) *sl.* —*int.* an expression of strong distaste or disgust. —*n.* something messy or repellent. [imit.]

yucky /ˈjʌkɪ/ *adj.* (also **yukky**) (**-ier, -iest**) *sl.* **1** messy, repellent. **2** sickly, sentimental.

Yugoslavia /ˌjuːɡəʊˈslɑːvɪə/ a country in SE Europe with a coastline on the Adriatic Sea and with frontiers that border seven nations; pop. (est. 1988) 23,580,150; no official language since all are constitutionally equal, but Serbo-Croat serves as the lingua franca; capital, Belgrade. The country was formed, as a kingdom, as a result of the peace settlement at the end of the First World War from Serbia, Montenegro, and the former Slavic provinces of the Austro-Hungarian empire, and assumed the name of Yugoslavia in 1929. Invaded by the Axis powers during the Second World War, Yugoslavia emerged from a long guerrilla war as a Communist State but refused to accept Soviet domination. Composed of a mixture of racial and religious groups, the country has maintained well-developed links with the West and has benefited from major industrialization and the promotion of tourism, but nationalist movements within the country have put a strain on the political unity of the republic. In 1990 its Congress voted to end single-party rule. □□ **Yugoslav** /ˈjuː-/ *adj.* & *n.*, **Yugoslavian** *adj.* & *n.* [Austrian G *Jugoslav* f. Serb. *jugo-* f. *jug* south + SLAV]

yuk var. of YUCK.

yukky var. of YUCKY.

Yukon /ˈjuːkɒn/ a river of North America 3,020 km (1,870 miles) long, rising in Canada on the border between Yukon Territory and British Columbia and flowing through Alaska into the Bering Sea.

Yukon Territory a territory of NW Canada, where gold was discovered in the Klondike River in 1896; pop. (1986) 23,500. It was constituted a separate political unit in 1898, with its capital at Dawson.

yule /juːl/ *n.* (in full **yule-tide**) *archaic* the Christmas festival. □ **yule-log 1** a large log burnt in the hearth on Christmas Eve. **2** a log-shaped chocolate cake eaten at Christmas. [OE *gēol(a)*: cf. ON *jól*]

yummy /ˈjʌmɪ/ *adj.* (**yummier, yummiest**) *colloq.* tasty, delicious. [YUM-YUM + -Y[1]]

yum-yum /jʌmˈjʌm/ *int.* expressing pleasure from eating or the prospect of eating. [natural excl.]

Yunnan /juːˈnæn/ a province of southern China; pop. (est. 1986) 34,560,000; capital, Kunming.

yup var. of YEP.

yuppy /ˈjʌpɪ/ *n.* (*pl.* **-ies**) *colloq.*, usu. *derog.* a young middle-class professional person working in a city. [young urban professional]

YWCA 1 Young Women's Christian Association, a welfare movement that began in Britain in 1855, originally 'to advance the physical, social, intellectual, moral, and spiritual interests of young women', and now has branches in many countries. The world organization, with headquarters in Geneva, was established in 1894. **2** a hostel run by this Association. [abbr.]

Z

Z /zed/ *n.* (also **z**) (*pl.* **Zs** or **Z's**) **1** the twenty-sixth letter of the alphabet. **2** (usu. **z**) *Algebra* the third unknown quantity. **3** *Geom.* the third coordinate. **4** *Chem.* atomic number.

zabaglione /ˌzɑːbɑːˈljəʊneɪ/ *n.* an Italian sweet of whipped and heated egg yolks, sugar, and (esp. Marsala) wine. [It.]

Zacatecas /ˌzækəˈteɪkəs/ **1** a State of north central Mexico; pop. (est. 1988) 1,252,500. **2** its capital city; pop. (1980) 80,088.

zaffre /ˈzæfə(r)/ *n.* (*US* **zaffer**) an impure cobalt oxide used as a blue pigment. [It. *zaffera* or F *safre*]

zag /zæg/ *n.* a sharp change of direction in a zigzag course. [ZIGZAG]

Zagreb /ˈzɑːɡreb/ the capital of the republic of Croatia in NW Yugoslavia; pop. (1981) 1,174,500. Zagreb was the birthplace of President Tito.

Zagros Mountains /ˈzæɡrɒs/ a range of mountains in western Iran. most of Iran's oilfields lie along the western foothills of the central Zagros Mountains.

Zaïre¹ /zɑːˈɪə(r)/ a major river of central Africa flowing into the Atlantic. It lies largely within the republic of Zaïre and is 4,630 km (2,880 miles) long.

Zaïre² /zɑːˈɪə(r)/ a country in central Africa with a short coastline on the Atlantic Ocean; pop. (est. 1988) 33,293,900; official language, French; capital, Kinshasa. Only gradually opened up by European exploration, the area became a Belgian colony in the late 19th and early 20th c., known as the Congo Free State (1885–1908) then as the Belgian Congo (1908–60). Independence (as a republic) in 1960 was followed by civil war and UN intervention and an even reasonably stable State was some time in emerging; the name Zaïre was adopted in 1971. The economy is largely based on mineral exports, particularly of copper, of which Zaïre is one of the world's major producers. □□ **Zaïrean** /-rɪən/ *adj. & n.*

Zákinthos /ˈzækɪnˌθɒs/ **1** the most southerly of the Greek islands in the Ionian Sea; pop. (1981) 30,000. **2** its capital city; pop. (1981) 9,764.

Zakopane /ˌzækəʊˈpænə/ a winter sports resort in the Tatra Mountains of southern Poland; pop. (1983) 29,700.

Zambezi /zæmˈbiːzɪ/ an African river 2,655 km (1,650 miles) long, flowing through Angola, Zambia, and Mozambique to the Indian Ocean. It forms the border between Zambia and Zimbabwe.

Zambia /ˈzæmbɪə/ a landlocked country in central Africa, a member State of the Commonwealth; pop. (est. 1988) 7,546,200; official language, English; capital, Lusaka. Explored by Livingstone in the mid-19th c., the area was administered by the British South Africa Company from 1889 until taken over as a protectorate by the British government in 1924, having been named Northern Rhodesia in 1911. After some disturbances full independence was gained in 1964, as a republic under President Kenneth Kaunda, subsequent economic reconstruction being assisted by Chinese financial aid and the redevelopment of the copper-mining industry. Zambia is the third-largest copper-producing country in the world after the US and USSR. □□ **Zambian** *adj. & n.*

Zamboanga /ˌsæmbəʊˈæŋɡə/ a port on the west coast of the island of Mindanao in the southern Philippines; pop. (1980) 343,700.

ZANU /ˈzɑːnuː/ *abbr.* Zimbabwe African National Union.

zany /ˈzeɪnɪ/ *adj. & n.* —*adj.* (**zanier**, **zaniest**) comically idiotic; crazily ridiculous. —*n.* **1** a buffoon or jester. **2** *hist.* an attendant clown awkwardly mimicking a chief clown in shows; a merry andrew. □□ **zanily** *adv.* **zaniness** *n.* [F *zani* or It. *zan(n)i*, Venetian form of *Gianni*, *Giovanni* John]

Zanzibar /ˌzænzɪˈbɑː(r)/ an island off the coast of East Africa that was (together with the islands of Pemba and Latham) a sultanate from 1856 and a British protectorate from 1890 until it gained independence as a member State of the Commonwealth in 1963; pop. (est. 1985) 571,000. In the following year the Sultan's government was overthrown and the country became a republic, uniting with Tanganyika (see TANZANIA).

zap /zæp/ *v., n., & int. sl.* —*v.* (**zapped, zapping**) **1** *tr.* **a** kill or destroy; deal a sudden blow to. **b** hit forcibly (*zapped the ball over the net*). **2** *intr. & tr.* move quickly and vigorously. **3** *tr.* overwhelm emotionally. **4** *tr. Computing* erase or change (an item in a program). **5** *intr.* (foll. by *through*) fast-wind a videotape to skip a section. —*n.* **1** energy, vigour. **2** a strong emotional effect. —*int.* expressing the sound or impact of a bullet, ray gun, etc., or any sudden event. [imit.]

Zapata /səˈpɑːtə/, Emiliano (*c.*1877–1919), Mexican revolutionary. Unlike most of the other Mexican leaders of the period Zapata was not associated with any particular faction, earning his fame as a champion of agrarianism. Like most of his contemporaries, however, he met a violent end, being assassinated in 1919.

zapateado /ˌzɑːpətɪˈɑːdəʊ/ *n.* (*pl.* -**os**) **1** a flamenco dance with rhythmic stamping of the feet. **2** this technique or action. [Sp. f. *zapato* shoe]

Zaporozhye /ˌzæpəˈrɒʒjɪ/ an industrial city of Ukraine, on the Dnieper River, site of a dam providing hydroelectric power; pop. (est. 1987) 875,000.

Zapotec /ˈzæpətek/ *n.* (*pl.* same or **Zapotecs**) a member or the language of an Indian people centred at Oaxaca in SW Mexico. [Sp. f. Nahuatl]

zappy /ˈzæpɪ/ *adj.* (**zappier, zappiest**) *colloq.* **1** lively, energetic. **2** striking.

ZAPU /ˈzɑːpuː/ *abbr.* Zimbabwe African People's Union.

zarape var. of SERAPE.

Zaragoza see SARAGOSSA.

Zarathustra /ˌzærəˈθʊstrə/ the Old Iranian name for Zoroaster. □□ **Zarathustrian** *adj. & n.*

zariba /zəˈriːbə/ *n.* (also **zareba**) **1** a hedged or palisaded enclosure for the protection of a camp or village in the Sudan etc. **2** a restricting or confining influence. [Arab. *zarība* cattle-pen]

zarzuela /θɑːˈθweɪlə/ *n.* a Spanish traditional form of musical comedy. [Sp.: app. f. a place-name]

Zatopek /ˈzɑːtɒˌpek/, Emil (1922–), Czechoslovakian long-distance runner, who broke records at various distances and in the 1952 Olympic Games at Helsinki won gold medals in the 5,000 metres, 10,000 metres, and marathon races.

zax var. of SAX².

zeal /ziːl/ *n.* **1** earnestness or fervour in advancing a cause or rendering service. **2** hearty and persistent endeavour. [ME *zele* f. eccl.L *zelus* f. Gk *zēlos*]

Zealand /ˈziːlənd/ (Danish **Sjælland** /ˈʃelənd/) the principal island of Denmark, situated between the Jutland peninsula and the south tip of Sweden. Its chief city is Copenhagen, capital of Denmark.

zealot /ˈzelət/ *n.* **1** an uncompromising or extreme partisan; a fanatic. **2** (**Zealot**) *hist.* a member of an ancient Jewish sect aiming at a world Jewish theocracy and resisting the Romans until AD 70. □□ **zealotry** *n.* [eccl.L *zelotes* f. Gk *zēlōtēs* (as ZEAL)]

zealous /ˈzeləs/ *adj.* full of zeal; enthusiastic. □□ **zealously** *adv.* **zealousness** *n.*

zebec (also **zebeck**) var. of XEBEC.

zebra /ˈzebrə, ˈziː-/ *n.* **1** any of various African quadrupeds, esp. *Equus burchelli*, related to the ass and horse, with black and white stripes. **2** (*attrib.*) with alternate dark and pale stripes. □ **zebra crossing** *Brit.* a striped street-crossing where pedestrians have precedence over vehicles. □□ **zebrine** /-braɪn/ *adj.* [It. or Port. f. Congolese]

zebu /ˈziːbuː/ *n.* a humped ox, *Bos indicus*, of India, E. Asia, and Africa. [F *zébu*, of unkn. orig.]

Zebulun /ˈzebjuːlən/ **1** a Hebrew patriarch, son of Jacob and Leah (Gen. 30: 20). **2** the tribe of Israel traditionally descended from him.

Zech. *abbr.* Zechariah (Old Testament).

Zechariah /ˌzekəˈraɪə/ **1** a Hebrew minor prophet of the 6th c. BC. **2** a book of the Old Testament containing his prophecies, urging the restoration of the Temple, and some later material.

zed /zed/ *n. Brit.* the letter Z. [F *zède* f. LL *zeta* f. Gk ZETA]

Zedekiah /ˌzedɪˈkaɪə/ the last king of Judah, who rebelled against Nebuchadnezzar and was carried off to Babylon into captivity (Kings 24–5, 2 Chron. 36).

zedoary /ˈzedəʊərɪ/ *n.* an aromatic ginger-like substance made from the rootstock of E. Indian plants of the genus *Curcuma* and used in medicine, perfumery, and dyeing. [ME f. med.L *zedoarium* f. Pers. *zidwār*]

zee /ziː/ *n. US* the letter Z. [17th c.: var. of ZED]

Zeebrugge /ziːˈbrʊgə/ a seaport on the coast of Belgium, linked by canal to Bruges and by ferry to Hull and Dover in England.

Zeeland /ˈziːlənd/ an agricultural province of south-east Netherlands, at the estuary of the Maas, Scheldt, and Rhine rivers; pop. (1988) 355,500; capital, Middelburg.

Zeeman /ˈziːmən/, Pieter (1865–1943), Dutch physicist, who in 1886 discovered the phenomenon now named after him—the Zeeman effect, the splitting of the spectral lines of a substance by a magnetic field. It has been used to detect and measure the magnetic fields of stars, and in studying atomic particles and nuclei. For this discovery Zeeman shared the 1902 Nobel Prize for physics with Lorentz, his former teacher, who had predicted the existence of such an effect.

zein /ˈziːɪn/ *n. Biochem.* the principal protein of maize. [*Zea* the generic name of maize + -IN]

Zeitgeist /ˈtsaɪtgaɪst/ *n.* **1** the spirit of the times. **2** the trend of thought and feeling in a period. [G f. *Zeit* time + *Geist* spirit]

Zen /zen/ *n.* a sect of Japanese Buddhism that teaches the attainment of enlightenment through meditation and intuition rather than through study of the scriptures. □□ **Zenist** *n.* (also **Zennist**). [Jap., = meditation]

zenana /zɪˈnɑːnə/ *n.* the part of a house for the seclusion of women of high-caste families in India and Iran. [Hind. *zenāna* f. Pers. *zanāna* f. *zan* woman]

Zend /zend/ *n.* an interpretation of the Avesta, each Zend being part of the Zend-Avesta. □ **Zend-Avesta** the Zoroastrian sacred writings of the Avesta or text and Zend or commentary. [Pers. *zand* interpretation]

Zener cards /ˈziːnə/ *n.* a set of 25 cards each with one of five different symbols, used in ESP research. [K. E. *Zener*, Amer. psychologist b. 1903]

zenith /ˈzenɪθ, ˈziː-/ *n.* **1** the part of the celestial sphere directly above an observer (opp. NADIR). **2** the highest point in one's fortunes; a time of great prosperity etc. □ **zenith distance** an arc intercepted between a celestial body and its zenith; the complement of a body's altitude. [ME f. OF *cenit* or med.L *cenit* ult. f. Arab. *samt (ar-ra's)* path (over the head)]

zenithal /ˈzenɪθ(ə)l/ *adj.* of or relating to a zenith. □ **zenithal projection** a projection of part of a globe on to a plane tangential to the centre of the part, showing the correct directions of all points from the centre.

Zeno /ˈziːnəʊ/ (5th c. BC) Greek philosopher from Elea in southern Italy, pupil of Parmenides whose theories he supported by demonstrating the paradoxical conclusions that follow from the premisses of its opponents—the paradox of Achilles and the tortoise, for example, by which it is shown that once Achilles has given the tortoise a start he can never overtake it, since by the time he arrives where it was it has already moved on.

Zenobia /zeˈnəʊbɪə/ (3rd c.) queen of Palmyra, who succeeded her murdered husband as ruler and then conquered Egypt and much of Asia Minor. When she proclaimed her son emperor, the Roman emperor Aurelian marched against her and eventually defeated and captured her. She was later given a pension and a villa in Italy.

zeolite /ˈziːəlaɪt/ *n.* each of a number of minerals consisting mainly of hydrous silicates of calcium, sodium, and aluminium, able to act as cation exchangers. □□ **zeolitic** /-ˈlɪtɪk/ *adj.* [Sw. & G *zeolit* f. Gk *zeō* boil + -LITE (from their characteristic swelling and fusing under the blowpipe)]

Zeph. *abbr.* Zephaniah (Old Testament).

Zephaniah /ˌzefəˈnaɪə/ **1** a Hebrew minor prophet of the 7th c. BC. **2** a book of the Old Testament containing his prophecies.

zephyr /ˈzefə(r)/ *n.* **1** *literary* a mild gentle wind or breeze. **2** a fine cotton fabric. **3** an athlete's thin gauzy jersey. [F *zéphyr* or L *zephyrus* f. Gk *zephuros* (god of the) west wind]

Zeppelin /ˈzepəlɪn/, Ferdinand Adolf August Heinrich, Count von (1838–1917), German airship pioneer who both designed and built airships as well as forming the world's first commercial passenger service. In the First World War his airships, known as Zeppelins, were used to bomb England. Later designs by the company he formed included the *Graf Zeppelin* and the *Hindenburg* (see AIRSHIP), and in the 1920s and 1930s achieved success with transatlantic commercial flights.

Zermatt /ˈzɜːmæt/ an Alpine ski resort and mountaineering centre near the Matterhorn in southern Switzerland.

zero /ˈzɪərəʊ/ *n. & v.* —*n.* (*pl.* -os) **1 a** the figure 0; nought. **b** no quantity or number; nil. **2** a point on the scale of an instrument from which a positive or negative quantity is reckoned. **3** (*attrib.*) having a value of zero; no, not any (*zero population growth*). **4** (in full **zero-hour**) **a** the hour at which a planned, esp. military, operation is timed to begin. **b** a crucial moment. **5** the lowest point; a nullity or nonentity. —*v.tr.* (-oes, -oed) **1** adjust (an instrument etc.) to zero point. **2** set the sights of (a gun) for firing. □ **zero in on 1** take aim at. **2** focus one's attention on. **zero option** a disarmament proposal for the total removal of certain types of weapons on both sides. **zero-rated** on which no value added tax is charged. **zero-sum** (of a game, political situation, etc.) in which whatever is gained by one side is lost by the other so that the net change is always zero. [F *zéro* or It. *zero* f. OSp. f. Arab. *ṣifr* CIPHER]

zeroth /ˈzɪərəʊθ/ *adj.* immediately preceding what is regarded as 'first' in a series.

zest /zest/ *n.* **1** piquancy; a stimulating flavour or quality. **2 a** keen enjoyment or interest. **b** (often foll. by *for*) relish. **c** gusto (*entered into it with zest*). **3** a scraping of orange or lemon peel as flavouring. □□ **zestful** *adj.* **zestfully** *adv.* **zestfulness** *n.* **zesty** *adj.* (**zestier, zestiest**). [F *zeste* orange or lemon peel, of unkn. orig.]

zeta /ˈziːtə/ *n.* the sixth letter of the Greek alphabet (Z, ζ). [Gk *zēta*]

zetetic /ziːˈtetɪk/ *adj.* proceeding by inquiry. [Gk *zētētikos* f. *zēteō* seek]

zeugma /ˈzjuːgmə/ *n.* a figure of speech using a verb or adjective with two nouns, to one of which it is strictly applicable while the word appropriate to the other is not used (e.g. *with weeping eyes* and [*sc. grieving*] *hearts*) (cf. SYLLEPSIS). □□ **zeugmatic** /-ˈmætɪk/ *adj.* [L f. Gk *zeugma -atos* f. *zeugnumi* to yoke, *zugon* yoke]

Zeus /zjuːs/ *Gk Mythol.* the supreme god, whose epithet is 'father' and whose name means 'sky'. He was the god of weather and atmospheric phenomena (rain, thunder, etc.), protector and ruler of the family, son of Cronus whom he dethroned after being brought up in Crete (see CRONUS). The Romans identified him with Jupiter. [Gk f. Skr., = sky]

Zeuxis /ˈzjuːksɪs/ (latter 5th c. BC) Greek painter, born at Heraclea in southern Italy. Our only knowledge of his works (none of which survive) comes through the records of ancient writers, who make reference to monochrome techniques and his use of shading to create an illusion of depth. There are many anecdotes of his verisimilitude; his paintings of grapes are said to have deceived the birds.

---

w we   z zoo   ʃ she   ʒ decision   θ thin   ð this   ŋ ring   x loch   tʃ chip   dʒ jar   (*see over for vowels*)

Zhejiang /ˌdʒɜːdʒɪˈæŋ/ (also **Chekiang** /ˌtʃekɪˈæŋ/) a province of eastern China; pop. (est. 1986) 40,700,000; capital, Hangzhou.

Zhengzhou /dʒeŋˈdʒəʊ/ (also **Chengchow** /tʃeŋˈtʃaʊ/) the capital of Henan province in NE central China; pop. (est. 1986) 1,590,000.

zho var. of DZHO.

Zhou Enlai see CHOU EN-LAI.

Zhukov /ˈʒuːkɒf/, Georgi Konstantinovich (1896–1974), Soviet military leader, responsible for much of the planning of the Soviet Union's campaigns in the Second World War. He defeated the Germans at Stalingrad (1943), lifted the siege of Leningrad (1944), led the final assault on Germany (1945), captured Berlin, and became commander of the Soviet zone in occupied Germany.

zibet /ˈzɪbɪt/ n. (US **zibeth**) **1** an Asian or Indian civet, *Viverra zibetha*. **2** its scent. [med.L *zibethum*: see CIVET]

zidovudine /ˌzaɪdəʊˈvjuːdiːn/ n. = AZT. [chem. name *azidothymidine*]

Ziegfeld /ˈziːɡfeld/, Florenz (1867–1932), American theatre manager, creator of a series of revues entitled the *Ziegfeld Follies* which began in 1907 and continued annually until his death, being seen intermittently thereafter until 1957. He based his show on that of the *Folies-Bergère*, with the emphasis on scenic splendour, comic sketches, vaudeville specialities, and attractive young women.

ziff /zɪf/ n. Austral. sl. a beard. [20th c.: orig. unkn.]

ziggurat /ˈzɪɡəˌræt/ n. a pyramidal stepped tower in ancient Mesopotamia, built in several stages which diminish in size towards the summit on which there may have been a shrine. Possibly derived from earlier platform temples, the ziggurat is first attested in the late 3rd millennium BC; the one at Babylon may be the 'Tower of Babel' of early Hebrew legend (Gen. 11: 1–9). [Assyr. *ziqquratu* pinnacle]

zigzag /ˈzɪɡzæɡ/ n., adj., adv., & v. —n. **1** a line or course having abrupt alternate right and left turns. **2** (often in pl.) each of these turns. —adj. having the form of a zigzag; alternating right and left. —adv. with a zigzag course. —v.intr. (**zigzagged**, **zigzagging**) move in a zigzag course. □□ **zigzaggedly** adv. [F f. G *zickzack*]

zilch /zɪltʃ/ n. esp. US sl. nothing. [20th c.: orig. uncert.]

zillah /ˈzɪlə/ n. an administrative district in India, containing several parganas. [Hind. *ḍilah* division]

zillion /ˈzɪljən/ n. colloq. an indefinite large number. □□ **zillionth** adj. & n. [Z (perh. = unknown quantity) + MILLION]

Zimbabwe /zɪmˈbɑːbwɪ/ a landlocked country in SE Africa, south of the River Zambezi, bordered by Zambia, Botswana, the Transvaal, and Mozambique; pop. (est. 1988) 9,728,500; official language, English; capital Harare. Known as Southern Rhodesia and then as Rhodesia, the country was a self-governing British colony from 1923. The ruling White minority sought independence from Britain when Northern Rhodesia became independent (as Zambia) in 1964, but Britain refused to grant this unless Black majority rule was to be guaranteed within a definite period. Led by its prime minister, Ian Smith, Rhodesia issued a unilateral declaration of independence (UDI) in 1965, which was countered by the imposition of economic sanctions by Britain and the UN. These, and even more the growing activity of nationalist guerrillas, forced Smith eventually to concede the principle of Black majority rule, and after an unsuccessful attempt to introduce this under the moderate Bishop Muzorewa, whose regime failed to come to terms with the guerrilla movement, national elections were held under British supervision in 1980. These resulted in the election of Robert Mugabe as Prime Minister and were followed by the formal granting of independence to the country as a republic and member State of the Commonwealth, taking its name from Great Zimbabwe. □ **Great Zimbabwe** a complex of imposing stone ruins in a fertile valley c.270 km (175 miles) south of Harare, discovered in 1868 and at first optimistically believed to be the city of Ophir, mentioned in the Bible as a place from which Solomon brought gold in great quantity, and of King Solomon's Mines, a belief which led to a great staking of mining

claims. The buildings consist of an acropolis, a stone enclosure, and scattered remains between these, covering an area of 24 hectares (60 acres). The city probably grew up as a focus of trade routes, and in the 14th–15th c. was the centre of a powerful and wealthy empire, where a Black civilization flourished centuries before the arrival of Europeans. What eventually happened to this place and the skills that built it remains unexplained. □□ **Zimbabwean** adj. & n. [Bantu, = stone house]

zinc /zɪŋk/ n. Chem. a white metallic element occurring naturally as zinc blende. (See below.) ¶ Symb.: **Zn**; atomic number 30. □ **flowers of zinc** = zinc oxide. **zinc blende** see BLENDE. **zinc chloride** a white crystalline deliquescent solid used as a preservative and flux. **zinc oxide** a powder used as a white pigment and in medicinal ointments. **zinc sulphate** a white water-soluble compound used as a mordant. □□ **zinced** adj. [G *Zink*, of unkn. orig.]

In ancient times the metal was known only in brass, an alloy of copper and zinc. It is now used as a component in a number of alloys, as well as for coating (galvanizing) iron and steel to protect against corrosion; its compounds have numerous industrial uses. Trace amounts of zinc are essential to the human body and to many other living organisms.

zinco /ˈzɪŋkəʊ/ n. & v. —n. (pl. **-os**) = ZINCOGRAPH. —v.tr. & intr. (**-oes**, **-oed**) = ZINCOGRAPH. [abbr.]

zincograph /ˈzɪŋkəˌɡrɑːf/ n. & v. —n. **1** a zinc plate with a design etched in relief on it for printing from. **2** a print taken from this. —v. **1** tr. & intr. etch on zinc. **2** tr. reproduce (a design) in this way. □□ **zincography** /-ˈkɒɡrəfɪ/ n.

zincotype /ˈzɪŋkəˌtaɪp/ n. = ZINCOGRAPH.

zing /zɪŋ/ n. & v. colloq. —n. vigour, energy. —v.intr. move swiftly or with a shrill sound. □□ **zingy** adj. (**zingier**, **zingiest**). [imit.]

Zingaro /ˈzɪŋɡəˌrəʊ/ n. (pl. **Zingari** /-ˌriː/) a gypsy. [It.]

zinger /ˈzɪŋə(r)/ n. US sl. an outstanding person or thing.

Zinjanthropus /zɪnˈdʒænθrəpəs/ n. a species of Australopithecus (A. boisei). [Arab. *Zinj* E. Africa + Gk *anthropos* man]

zinked see ZINC.

zinnia /ˈzɪnɪə/ n. a composite plant of the genus *Zinnia*, with showy rayed flowers of deep red and other colours. [J. G. *Zinn*, Ger. physician and botanist d. 1759]

Zion /ˈzaɪən/ n. (also **Sion** /ˈsaɪən/) **1** one of the two hills and also the citadel of ancient Jerusalem, taken by David from the Jebusites (2 Sam. 5: 6–7). The name came to signify Jerusalem itself (Is. 1: 27) and, allegorically, the heavenly city or kingdom of heaven (Heb. 12: 22). **2** the Jewish religion or people. **3** the Christian Church. **4** a non-conformist chapel. [OE f. eccl.L *Sion* f. Heb. *ṣîyôn*]

Zionism /ˈzaɪəˌnɪz(ə)m/ n. a political movement founded in 1897 under the leadership of Theodore Herzl that sought and has achieved the reestablishment of a Jewish nation in Palestine, reflecting the continuing nationalist attachment of the Jews and their religion to that country. (See also WEIZMANN.) □□ **Zionist** n.

zip /zɪp/ n. & v. —n. **1** a light fast sound, as of a bullet passing through air. **2** energy, vigour. **3** esp. Brit. **a** a zip-fastener (see entry). **b** (attrib.) having a zip-fastener (zip bag). —v. (**zipped**, **zipping**) **1** tr. & intr. (often foll. by up) fasten with a zip-fastener. **2** intr. move with zip or at high speed. [imit.]

Zip code /zɪp/ n. US a system of postal codes consisting of five-digit numbers. [zone improvement plan]

zip-fastener n. a fastening device of two flexible strips with interlocking projections closed or opened by a sliding clip pulled along them. Slide fasteners using hooks and eyes were exhibited at Chicago in 1893; a similar device using spring clips followed in 1912 in the US and in Europe, and in 1917 the US Navy used such fasteners on windproof flying-suits for its airmen. The zipper (patented under this name) was used in 1923 on boots made of rubber and fabric, and in the late 1920s these fasteners began to appear on other clothing.

zipper /ˈzɪpə(r)/ n. & v. esp. US —n. a zip-fastener (see entry). —v.tr. (often foll. by up) fasten with a zipper. □□ **zippered** adj.

æ cat ɑː arm e bed ɜː her ɪ sit iː see ɒ hot ɔː saw ʌ run ʊ put uː too ə ago aɪ my

zippy /ˈzɪpɪ/ adj. (**zippier**, **zippiest**) colloq. **1** bright, fresh, lively. **2** fast, speedy. □□ **zippily** adv. **zippiness** n.

zircon /ˈzɜːkɒn/ n. a zirconium silicate of which some translucent varieties are cut into gems (see HYACINTH 4, JARGON²). [G Zirkon: cf. JARGON²]

zirconium /zɜˈkəʊnɪəm/ n. Chem. a grey metallic element chemically related to titanium. First discovered (as the oxide) in 1789, zirconium and its compounds now have a variety of industrial uses. The metal's resistance to heat and corrosion and its transparency to neutrons have led to its becoming an important structural material within nuclear reactors. ¶ Symb.: **Zr**; atomic number 40. [mod.L f. ZIRCON + -IUM]

zit /zɪt/ n. esp. US sl. a pimple. [20th c.: orig. unkn.]

zither /ˈzɪðə(r)/ n. **1** a plucked stringed folk instrument of Austria and Bavaria, in its present most common form comprising a shallow wooden sound-box over which are stretched five melody strings and two sets of accompaniment strings tuned to form chords. The zither features in Anton Karas's theme music to the film The Third Man (1949). **2** any of various instruments in which the strings are stretched between the two ends of a flat body, such as a board or a stick. Members of the family include the psaltery, dulcimer, and vina. □□ **zitherist** n. [G (as CITTERN)]

zizz /zɪz/ n. & v. colloq. —n. **1** a whizzing or buzzing sound. **2** a short sleep. —v.intr. **1** make a whizzing sound. **2** doze or sleep. [imit.]

zloty /ˈzlɒtɪ/ n. (pl. same or **zlotys**) the chief monetary unit of Poland. [Pol., lit. 'golden']

Zn symb. Chem. the element zinc.

zodiac /ˈzəʊdɪˌæk/ n. **1 a** a belt of the heavens close to the sun's apparent annual path through the celestial sphere, as viewed from Earth, limited by lines about 8° from the ecliptic on each side, including all apparent positions of the sun, moon, and planets as known to ancient astronomers, and divided into twelve equal parts (**signs of the zodiac**), each formerly containing the similarly named constellation but now by precession of the equinoxes coinciding with the constellation that bears the name of the preceding sign: Aries, Taurus, Gemini, Cancer, Leo, Virgo, Libra, Scorpio, Sagittarius, Capricorn(us), Aquarius, Pisces. (See below.) **b** a diagram of these signs. **2** a complete cycle, circuit, or compass. [ME f. OF zodiaque f. L zodiacus f. Gk zōidiakos f. zōidion sculptured animal-figure, dimin. of zōion animal]

The zodiac, comprising stars immensely distant, appeared from Earth to be immutable. All the seven moving stars or planets known before modern times—the Sun, Moon, Mercury, Venus, Mars, Jupiter, and Saturn—moved within the zodiacal band, constantly changing their positions in relation to the Earth and each other, and these movements formed the basis of astrological science. Each sign governed a different part of the body, and a planet's influence changed as it moved from one to another. Many physicians thought it vital to choose the appropriate astrological moment in letting blood, giving medicines, or attempting surgery. The constellations are no longer located in the zodiacal signs named after them, a consequence of the fact that the Earth is not a perfect sphere and the polar axis changes slightly each year (see PRECESSION).

zodiacal /zəˈdaɪək(ə)l/ adj. of or in the zodiac. □ **zodiacal light** a diffuse band of light seen in the night sky on either side of the ecliptic and thought to be due to reflection of sunlight from minute particles of ice and dust within the plane of the solar system. It is best observed in the darkness of tropical skies. [F (as ZODIAC)]

zoetrope /ˈzəʊɪˌtrəʊp/ n. hist. an optical toy in the form of a cylinder with a series of pictures on the inner surface which give an impression of continuous motion when viewed through slits with the cylinder rotating. [irreg. f. Gk zōē life + -tropos turning]

Zoffany /ˈzɒfənɪ/, Johann (1734/5–1810), German-born painter who had settled in England by 1758. His introduction to Garrick led to his painting scenes from the contemporary theatre (e.g. The Clandestine Marriage), which brought him immediate success.

Zoffany received several royal commissions, the most important being The Tribune of the Uffizi for Queen Charlotte in 1770; in Vienna he painted portraits of the Austrian imperial family. In 1783–9 he made an extended sojourn in India. His paintings are for the most part of indifferent artistic merit.

zoic /ˈzəʊɪk/ adj. **1** of or relating to animals. **2** Geol. (of rock etc.) containing fossils; with traces of animal or plant life. [prob. back-form. f. AZOIC]

zollverein /ˈtsɒlfəˌraɪn/ n. hist. a customs union, esp. of German States in the 19th c. [G]

zombie /ˈzɒmbɪ/ n. **1** colloq. a dull or apathetic person. **2** a corpse said to be revived by witchcraft. [W.Afr. zumbi fetish]

zonation /zəʊˈneɪʃ(ə)n/ n. distribution in zones, esp. (Ecol.) of plants into zones characterized by the dominant species.

zonda /ˈzɒndə/ n. a hot dusty wind in Argentina. [Amer. Sp.]

zone /zəʊn/ n. & v. —n. **1** an area having particular features, properties, purpose, or use (danger zone; erogenous zone; smokeless zone). **2** any well-defined region of more or less beltlike form. **3 a** an area between two exact or approximate concentric circles. **b** a part of the surface of a sphere enclosed between two parallel planes, or of a cone or cylinder etc., between such planes cutting it perpendicularly to the axis. **4** (in full **time zone**) a range of longitudes where a common standard time is used. **5** Geol. etc. a range between specified limits of depth, height, etc., esp. a section of strata distinguished by characteristic fossils. **6** Geog. any of five divisions of the earth bounded by circles parallel to the equator (see FRIGID, TEMPERATE, TORRID). **7** an encircling band or stripe distinguishable in colour, texture, or character from the rest of the object encircled. **8** archaic a belt or girdle worn round the body. —v.tr. **1** encircle as or with a zone. **2** arrange or distribute by zones. **3** assign as or to a particular area. □□ **zonal** adj. **zoning** n. (in sense 3 of v.). [F zone or L zona girdle f. Gk zōnē]

zonk /zɒŋk/ v. & n. sl. —v. **1** tr. hit or strike. **2** (foll. **zonk** /zɒŋk/ v. & n. sl. —v. **1** tr. hit or strike. **2** (foll. by out) **a** tr. overcome with sleep; intoxicate. **b** intr. fall heavily asleep. —n. (often as int.) the sound of a blow or heavy impact. [imit.]

zoo /zuː/ n. a zoological garden. [abbr.]

zoo- /ˈzəʊə/ comb. form of animals or animal life. [Gk zōio- f. zōion animal]

zoogeography /ˌzəʊədʒɪˈɒgrəfɪ/ n. the branch of zoology dealing with the geographical distribution of animals. □□ **zoogeographic** /-ˌdʒiːəˈgræfɪk/ adj. **zoogeographical** /-ˌdʒiːəˈgræfɪk(ə)l/ adj. **zoogeographically** /-ˌdʒiːəˈgræfɪkəlɪ/ adv.

zoography /zəʊˈɒgrəfɪ/ n. descriptive zoology.

zooid /ˈzəʊɔɪd/ n. **1** a more or less independent invertebrate organism arising by budding or fission. **2** a distinct member of an invertebrate colony. □□ **zooidal** /-ˈɔɪd(ə)l/ adj. [formed as ZOO- + -OID]

zoolatry /zəʊˈɒlətrɪ/ n. the worship of animals.

zoological /ˌzəʊəˈlɒdʒɪk(ə)l, disp. ˌzuːə-/ adj. of or relating to zoology. □ **zoological garden** (or **gardens**) a public garden or park with a collection of animals for exhibition and study. □□ **zoologically** adv.

zoology /zəʊˈɒlədʒɪ, disp. ˌzuː-/ n. the scientific study of animals, esp. with reference to their structure, physiology, classification, and distribution. □□ **zoologist** n. [mod.L zoologia (as ZOO-, -LOGY)]

zoom /zuːm/ v. & n. —v. **1** intr. move quickly, esp. with a buzzing sound. **2 a** intr. cause an aeroplane to mount at high speed and a steep angle. **b** tr. cause (an aeroplane) to do this. **3 a** intr. (of a camera) close up rapidly from a long shot to a close-up. **b** tr. cause (a lens or camera) to do this. —n. **1** an aeroplane's steep climb. **2** a zooming camera shot. □ **zoom lens** a lens allowing a camera to zoom by varying the focal length. [imit.]

zoomancy /ˈzəʊəˌmænsɪ/ n. divination from the appearances or behaviour of animals.

zoomorphic /ˌzəʊəˈmɔːfɪk/ adj. **1** dealing with or represented in animal forms. **2** having gods of animal form. □□ **zoomorphism** n.

zoonosis /ˌzəʊəˈnəʊsɪs/ n. any of various diseases which can be transmitted to humans from animals. [ZOO- + Gk *nosos* disease]

zoophyte /ˈzəʊəˌfaɪt/ n. a plantlike animal, esp. a coral, sea anemone, or sponge. □□ **zoophytic** /-ˈfɪtɪk/ adj. [Gk *zōophuton* (as ZOO-, -PHYTE)]

zooplankton /ˌzəʊəˈplæŋkt(ə)n/ n. plankton consisting of animals.

zoospore /ˈzəʊəˌspɔː(r)/ n. a spore of fungi, algae, etc. capable of motion. □□ **zoosporic** /-ˈspɒrɪk/ adj.

zootomy /zəʊˈɒtəmɪ/ n. the dissection or anatomy of animals.

zoot suit /zuːt/ n. colloq. a man's suit with a long loose jacket and high-waisted tapering trousers. [rhyming on SUIT]

zori /ˈzɔrɪ/ n. (pl. **zoris**) a Japanese straw or rubber etc. sandal. [Jap.]

zoril /ˈzɒrɪl/ n. (also **zorille**) a flesh-eating African mammal, *Ictonyx striatus*, of the skunk and the weasel family. [F *zorille* f. Sp. *zorrilla* dimin. of *zorro* fox]

Zoroaster /ˌzɒrəʊˈæstə(r)/ (? c.628–551 BC, or perhaps considerably earlier) the Greek name for the Persian prophet Zarathustra, founder of Zoroastrianism.

Zoroastrianism /ˌzɒrəʊˈæstrɪəˌnɪz(ə)m/ n. a monotheistic religion of ancient Iran founded by Zoroaster (or Zarathustra) in the 6th c. BC. According to Zoroastrian mythology the supreme god, Ahura Mazda, created twin spirits, one of which chose truth and light, the other untruth and darkness. Later formulations pit Ahura Mazda (now called Ormazd) against his own evil twin (Ahriman). Zoroastrianism survives today in isolated areas of Iran and in India, where followers are known as Parsees. □□ **Zoroastrian** adj. & n.

Zouave /zuːˈɑːv, zwɑːv/ n. a member of a French light-infantry corps originally formed of Algerians and retaining their oriental uniform. [F f. *Zouaoua*, name of a tribe]

zounds /zaʊndz/ int. archaic expressing surprise or indignation. [(*God*)'s *wounds* (i.e. those of Christ on the Cross)]

ZPG abbr. zero population growth.

Zr symb. Chem. the element zirconium.

zucchetto /tsʊˈketəʊ/ n. (pl. **-os**) a Roman Catholic ecclesiastic's skullcap, black for a priest, purple for a bishop, red for a cardinal, and white for a pope. [It. *zucchetta* dimin. of *zucca* gourd, head]

zucchini /zuːˈkiːnɪ/ n. (pl. same or **zucchinis**) esp. US & Austral. a courgette. [It., pl. of *zucchino* dimin. of *zucca* gourd]

zugzwang /ˈtsʊktsvɑːŋ/ n. Chess an obligation to move in one's turn even when this must be disadvantageous. [G f. *Zug* move + *Zwang* compulsion]

Zuider Zee /ˌzaɪdə ˈziː/ a large shallow inlet of the North Sea in The Netherlands, large parts of which have been reclaimed for agricultural use in a programme started in 1924. [Du., = southern sea]

Zulu /ˈzuːluː/ n. & adj. —n. **1** a member of a South African Bantu people inhabiting the north-eastern part of Natal. **2** their language, one of the major Bantu languages of southern Africa, spoken by about 5 million people in the Zulu homeland in Natal. —adj. of or relating to the Zulus or their language. [native name]

Zululand see KWAZULU.

Zurbarán /ˌθʊərbəˈrɑːn/, Francisco (1598–1664), Spanish painter who became official painter to the town of Seville in 1628 and remained there until 1658, when he moved to Madrid. The influence of Caravaggio is evident in his works, which include narrative series of scenes from the lives of the saints, with simple colour and form in a profoundly realistic style.

Philip IV employed him in 1634 on a series *The Labours of Hercules* and a historical scene *The Defence of Cadiz*. In Spain Zurbarán was eclipsed during his lifetime by Murillo, but Courbet, Manet, and Picasso are among those who have paid tribute to him.

Zurich /ˈzjʊərɪk/ the largest city in Switzerland, situated on Lake Zurich; pop. (1987) 346,500.

Zwickau /ˈtsvɪkaʊ/ a mining and industrial city in SE Germany; pop. (1986) 120,600. It was the birthplace of the composer Robert Schumann.

zwieback /ˈzwiːbæk, ˈtsviːbɑːk/ n. a kind of biscuit rusk or sweet cake toasted in slices. [G, = twice baked]

Zwingli /ˈzvɪŋglɪ/, Ulrich (1484–1531), Swiss Protestant reformer, minister of Zurich from 1518, where he sought to carry through his political and religious ideals and met with strong local support. From 1522 he published articles advocating the liberation of believers from the control of the papacy and bishops, and upholding the Gospel as the sole basis of truth. His attacks on purgatory, invocation of saints, monasticism, and other orthodox doctrines seem to have owed little directly to Luther, of whose influence he always betrayed some jealousy, and he differed irreconcilably from Luther in his doctrine of the Eucharist, upholding a purely symbolic interpretation. The movement spread over Switzerland but met fierce resistance in some parts, and Zwingli was killed in the resulting civil war, when as chaplain of the Zurich forces he carried the banner.

zwitterion /ˈzwɪtəˌraɪən, ˈtsvɪ-/ n. a molecule or ion having separate positively and negatively charged groups. [G f. *Zwitter* a hybrid]

zygo- /ˈzaɪgəʊ/ comb. form joining, pairing. [Gk *zugo-* f. *zugon* yoke]

zygodactyl /ˌzaɪgəʊˈdæktɪl/ adj. & n. —adj. (of a bird) having two toes pointing forward and two backward. —n. such a bird. □□ **zygodactylous** adj.

zygoma /zaɪˈgəʊmə, zɪ-/ n. (pl. **zygomata** /-tə/) the bony arch of the cheek formed by connection of the zygomatic and temporal bones. [Gk *zugōma -atos* f. *zugon* yoke]

zygomatic /ˌzaɪgəˈmætɪk, ˌzɪ-/ adj. of or relating to the zygoma. □ **zygomatic arch** = ZYGOMA. **zygomatic bone** the bone that forms the prominent part of the cheek.

zygomorphic /ˌzaɪgəˈmɔːfɪk/ adj. (also **zygomorphous** /-ˈfəs/) (of a flower) divisible into similar halves only by one plane of symmetry.

zygospore /ˈzaɪgəˌspɔː(r)/ n. a thick-walled spore formed by certain fungi.

zygote /ˈzaɪgəʊt/ n. Biol. a cell formed by the union of two gametes. □□ **zygotic** /-ˈgɒtɪk/ adj. **zygotically** /-ˈgɒtɪkəlɪ/ adv. [Gk *zugōtos* yoked f. *zugoō* to yoke]

zymase /ˈzaɪmeɪs/ n. the enzyme fraction in yeast which catalyses the alcoholic fermentation of glucose. [F f. Gk *zumē* leaven]

zymology /zaɪˈmɒlədʒɪ/ n. Chem. the scientific study of fermentation. □□ **zymological** /-məˈlɒdʒɪk(ə)l/ adj. **zymologist** n. [as ZYMASE + -LOGY]

zymosis /zaɪˈməʊsɪs, zɪ-/ n. archaic fermentation. [mod.L f. Gk *zumōsis* (as ZYMASE)]

zymotic /zaɪˈmɒtɪk, zɪ-/ adj. archaic of or relating to fermentation. □ **zymotic disease** archaic an epidemic, endemic, contagious, infectious, or sporadic disease regarded as caused by the multiplication of germs introduced from outside. [Gk *zumōtikos* (as ZYMOSIS)]

zymurgy /ˈzaɪmɜːdʒɪ/ n. the branch of applied chemistry dealing with the use of fermentation in brewing etc. [Gk *zumē* leaven, after *metallurgy*]

CHRONOLOGY OF WORLD EVENTS

Chronology of World Events

Palaeolithic Man

All dates BP (before present)

c.5,500,000–3,000,000	Early *hominids* (Australopithecines) evolve in African woodland; bipedal; herbivorous; found in East and Southern Africa.

Lower Palaeolithic

c.2,100,000	*Homo habilis* evolving in Africa, shaping and using stones as tools. Omnivore, killing small game; also a scavenger.
c.1,800,000	*Homo erectus* evolving in Africa descended from *Homo habilis*.
c.1,500,000	*Homo erectus* (formerly Pithecanthropus) disperses from Africa; uses fabricated stone tools; omnivore, killing small animals, scavenging remains of large ones; camps by lakes and in river valleys.
c.1,500,000	Acheulian hand-axes and cleavers in East and Southern Africa.
c.1,000,000	*Homo erectus* in East and SE Asia.
c.700,000	Evidence in Europe.
c.500,000	Fire?
c.250,000	*Homo erectus presapiens* emerging; evidence through Europe; possible hut-dwellings.

Middle Palaeolithic

c.120,000	*Homo sapiens* (anatomically modern humans) evolving in East and Southern Africa. Hand-axes and cleavers disappear; emphasis on tools made from stone flakes, probably hafted.
c.80,000	*Homo (sapiens) neanderthalensis* as cave-dweller in Europe; flint scrapers for preparing furs; burial of dead; absorbed(?) into populations of *Homo sapiens* by c.30,000.
c.50,000	*Homo sapiens sapiens* (modern humans) spreading from Africa through Asia, China, Australia, America (?c.25,000). Variety of tools (knives, axes, scrapers, harpoons, needles, awls, etc.) and materials (wood, bone, antler, stone, reed, leather, flint, fur, etc.).

Upper Palaeolithic

c.35,000	Early round houses in South Russia.
c.30,000	First cave-painting and carving SW France (Lascaux). Female figurines across Europe and Russia.
c.27,000	First painting on stone tablets in Southern Africa (Namibia).
c.20,000	Finger-drawings on clay walls, e.g. Koonalda Cave, Australia. Paintings on rock surfaces in Australia.
c.15,000	Tools made on elongate blades of stone in Europe, Western Asia, East and Southern Africa. High level of art. Personal adornment (beads, pendants).
c.12,000	Siberia first peopled as ice age ends. Earliest potters in Japan. Microlithic tools widely made throughout the world. Bows, spears, knives in use.
c.10,000	Climatic change stimulates new economies and techniques. Beginning of farming in several parts of the world.

Near East, Mediterranean, and Europe	Rest of the World

All dates BC

	Near East, Mediterranean, and Europe	Rest of the World
9000	Sedentary societies emerging: *Natufian culture* in Syria and Palestine; collection of *wild cereals*, first domestication of *dog*.	*Jomon culture* on coastal sites of Japan for fishing and collecting.
8300	*Post-glacial warming* and spread of forests begins.	
8000	*Pre-pottery neolithic* societies in Syria and Palestine, with cultivated cereals and mud-brick villages (Jericho). Rapid *ice-retreat* in northern Europe and spread of light forest: *mesolithic* societies, e.g. *Maglemose culture* in birch and pine forest, hunting elk and wild cattle; first evidence of dugout *canoes*.	*Cattle-keeping groups*, making pottery, spread into the Sahara, then wetter than today.
7000	Domestication of *goat*, *sheep*, *pig* at various places in Near East, followed by *cattle*: animals used mainly for meat, not milk or wool. *Linen textiles*. First use of *copper* for small ornaments, made by hammering and heating pure copper. *Obsidian* imported to mainland Greece from island of Melos.	Cultivation of *root crops* in New Guinea and South America.
6000	First pottery in Near East; use of *smelting* (lead). Major site of Çatal Hüyük in central Turkey. Domestication of *cattle*. *Farming* spreads to SE Europe; first *neolithic cultures* there. Oak forests spread to northern Europe; *deer* and *pig* hunted.	Tropical *millet* first cultivated in the southern Sahara; temperate millet in China. *Wheat* and *barley* introduced to Pakistan.

Near East, Mediterranean, and Europe

Cattle first used for traction in Near East (*plough*, *sledge*). First evidence of *irrigation*, in Iraq.

5000   *Copper-smelting* in Turkey and Iran (*Chalcolithic*). *Woollen textiles*; use of animals for milk; domestication of *horse* and *donkey*.

Tree crops (olive, fig, vine) cultivated in the Levant.

Growth of population in lowland Mesopotamia; *date-palm* cultivated.

Farming spreads into central Europe.

Use of *skin boats* in Baltic; permanent coastal fishing and collecting sites (*Ertebølle culture*); adoption of simple pottery.

4000   *Copper-casting* and alloying in Near East; development of simple copper metallurgy in SE Europe. *Gold-working* in Near East and Europe.

First *urban civilization* develops in Sumer, with extensive *irrigation*. Trading colonies established in Syria; temple-building, craft workshops with extensive importation of raw materials such as metals and precious stones. First *wheeled vehicles* and *sailing-boats* on Euphrates and Nile; use of *writing* (cuneiform script); spread of *advanced farming* (plough, tree crops, wool) and *technology* (wheel, alloy metallurgy) to SE Europe.

Farming spreads to western and northern Europe; construction of monumental *tombs* in *megalithic* technique in Portugal, Brittany, British Isles, Scandinavia.

Use of *horse* leads to expansion of first *pastoralist communities* on steppes north of Black Sea: burial mounds covering pit-graves. *Plough* and *cart* widely adopted in Europe.

3200   Unification of *Upper and Lower Egypt*; trading expeditions by donkey up into the Levant, where urban societies now exist. *Troy* an important trading centre in north Aegean; *Cycladic culture* in the Greek islands. Copper-working in Iberia (Los Millares).

3000   Egyptian *hieroglyphic script* develops; *pyramid* building begins. Royal tombs in Mesopotamia (e.g. Ur) demonstrate high level of craftsmanship in secular city-states.

Spread of burial mounds and *corded-ware culture* in northern Europe replaces megalithic tradition, though ceremonial monuments (Avebury, first phase of Stonehenge) continue in British Isles. Stone-built temples in Malta.

2500   Extensive Egyptian maritime trade with *Byblos* (Lebanon); *Ebla* a major centre in Syria, in contact with both Byblos and Mesopotamia.

Exploration of eastern Mediterranean maritime routes along southern coast of Turkey to *Crete*, using boats with sails.

Beaker cultures bring innovations (copper-working, horses, drinking cups, woollen textiles) to Atlantic seaboard.

2300   Empire of *Agade* (Akkad) unites Mesopotamian city-states. Trade with *Indus valley civilization* in Pakistan. *Akkadian* becomes diplomatic language of the Near East.

2200   Collapse of Old Kingdom in Egypt, and of Empire of Agade. *Ur* revives as political centre in southern Mesopotamia.

2000   *Middle Kingdom* established in Egypt; revival of Levantine cities (Ugarit); beginnings of *Middle Minoan* (palatial) period in Crete.

Revival of northern Mesopotamian centres (Assur and Mari); Assyrian *merchant colonies* established in Anatolia. *Hittite Old Kingdom* develops; Babylonian empire expands.

1700   Egypt dominated by Asiatic rulers ('Hyksos').

Cretan palaces reconstructed after earthquake; expanded trade-links with mainland Greece: growth of *Mycenaean civilization*.

Hittite empire expands; Assyria dominated by *Mitanni*.

Tin-bronze now standard in Europe.

Appearance of *chariot*.

1500   *Kassite dynasty* in Babylon; *New Kingdom* in Egypt following expulsion of the Hyksos; expansion of Egyptian empire in the Levant. Rulers buried in Valley of the Kings. During brief Armarna period, *c.*1350, Akhenaton introduces *monotheism* and founds new capital. Increasing conflict with Hittites.

Canaanite cities flourish in the Levant, evolving the use of the *alphabet*.

1200   General recession and political collapse in many parts of eastern Mediterranean: end of Mycenaean and Hittite palace centres, decline of Egyptian power; appearance of '*Sea Peoples*', probably as foreign mercenaries.

Rest of the World

Beginning of *maize* cultivation in Mexico; *rice* cultivation in China.

Rice cultivation in India.

Llama domesticated in highland Peru, as pack animal; cotton cultivated in lowland Peru.

Pottery comes into use in South America.

Jade traded in China.

Introduction of *dog* to Australia.

Copper and *bronze* metallurgy in China and SE Asia; *silk* production.

Permanent *villages* with temple mounds and ceremonial centres in Peru. First *towns* in China (*Longshan culture*) with trade and specialized production.

Spread of pottery-making and *maize* cultivation in Middle and South America.

Emergence of *Shang civilization* in China.

Metal-working (copper, gold) in Peru.

Expansion of *Lapita culture* into western Polynesia.

Olmec civilization, with temple mounds and massive stone sculptures, in Mexico.

Near East, Mediterranean, and Europe

Spread of *iron* metallurgy.

Expansion of nomadic Aramaean tribes in Levant.

Temporary expansion of Assyria, and capture of *Babylon*.

Expansion of agriculture and bronze-working in temperate Europe, associated with expansion of *Urnfield cultures*. Links between Cyprus and Sardinia, where *Nuraghic culture* develops.

Rest of the World

	Near East, Mediterranean, and Europe	Rest of the World	Culture/Technology
1000	Development of *spice route* to Arabia; growth of coastal trade in Levant under *Phoenicians*; colonization of Cyprus and exploration of central and western Mediterranean.	*Zhou* (Chou) *dynasty* in China. *Adena culture* with rich burials under large mounds in Ohio and Mississippi valleys. *Chavín civilization* in Andes. Early cities in Ganges valley.	Hebrew and Greek *alphabets* developing from Phoenician.
	David king of Israel (*c*.1005–970); makes Jerusalem his capital.		
	Solomon king of Israel (*c*.970–930); extends kingdom to Egypt and Euphrates.		
	Temple of Jerusalem built.		Worship of *Dionysus* enters Greece from Thrace.
930	Israel divides into *Kingdom of Israel* in the north (*c*.930–721) and *Kingdom of Judah* in the south.		Early Hebrew texts (Psalms, Ecclesiastes).
	Phoenician contacts with *Crete* and Euboia.		
c.920	*Nubians* conquer *Egypt*; *Shabaka* rules from Thebes.		Early version of great Hindu epic the *Mahabharata*.
	Celts move west into Austria and Germany.	Farming villages on *Amazon* floodplain.	*Geometric style* pottery in Greece.
858	*Assyrian empire* reaches Mediterranean.		
814	Legendary date at which Phoenicians found *Carthage*.		
750	*Greek colonies* in southern Italy (*Cumae*) and Sicily.		*The Iliad* and *Odyssey* emerge from oral tradition.
	Greek city-state culture through Aegean; *Lydia* pioneers *coinage*. Colonies spread through Mediterranean; Sicily *Magna Graecia*.		
	Nomadic *Scythians* from southern Russia invade Asia Minor.		
753	Legendary date for *foundation of Rome*.		776 *First Olympiad*.
721	Assyrians under *Sargon II* (721–705) conquer Israel; under *Sennacherib* (704–681) empire expands and *conquers Egypt*. *Nineveh* the Assyrian capital.		*Taoism* founded in China, traditionally by Lao-tzu.
700	*Hallstatt* culture (Celtic iron-age warriors) in Austria moves west and down Rhône to Spain.		*Iron technology* enters India.
	Carthage expands through western Mediterranean, occupying *Sardinia* and *Ibiza*.	*Zhou* dynasty in China establishes *legal system*.	
	First Celtic *hill-forts*.	*Magadha kingdom* on Ganges in India.	*Zarathustra* in Iran. *Dionysiac* festivals in Greece leading to drama.
640	Assyrians under Ashurbanipal conquer *Elamites*.	660 traditional date for *Jimmu*, first Japanese emperor.	*Library* established in Nineveh under Ashurbanipal (*c*.668–627).
612	Assyria defeated by *Medes* and Babylonians; sack of *Nineveh*. Babylon under *Chaldean* dynasty.	New Nubian kingdom of *Cush* established at Meroë on Upper Nile.	

	Near East, Mediterranean, and Europe	Rest of the World	Culture/Technology
600			*Doric order* appears in Greek architecture.
			Trireme (warship) evolves.
594	Ionian Greeks found *Massilia* (Marseilles).		*Hanging Gardens of Babylon* built.
	Solon reforms *Athenian law*.		Jeremiah writing.
586	Chaldean *Nebuchadnezzar* conquers Jerusalem. Jews to Babylon in *Captivity*.	King Vishtaspa of Persia converted to *Zoroastrianism*.	*Thales* of Miletus developing *physical science* and *geometry*.
	Greeks colonize Spain; import *Cornish tin*.		
561	*Pisistratus* ('benevolent tyrant') controls Athens 561–527.	550 *Cyrus II* defeats Medes; establishes Persian empire from Susa; captures Babylon (539).	Greek lyric poetry (*Sappho*).
546	Persian empire extends to Aegean. *Ionian Greek cities* captured.		*Pythagoras* teaching in southern Italy.
538	*Jews return* and rebuild Temple.		*Ionic order* appears in Greek architecture.
509	*Roman republic* proclaimed; Etruscan rule ends.	Persian empire reaches *India*.	*Siddhartha Gautama* (the Buddha) teaching.
508	*Cleisthenes* establishes *democratic constitution* in Athens.	Chinese bronze coinage in form of miniature tools (knives and spades).	*Athenian pottery* at its zenith.
			Iron-working in China.
500	*Etruscans* at the height of their power.		Emergence of *Greek drama; theatres* built.
499	Revolt of *Ionian Greek* cities against the Persians.	First inscriptions from *Monte Albán*, Mexico.	Greek *philosophical thought* emerging (*Heraclitus* at Ephesus).
490	Persian emperor *Darius* invades Greece; his army defeated at *Marathon*.		*Confucius* (*d.* 479) teaching in China.
480	*Xerxes*, his son, crosses Hellespont by bridge of boats; invades Greece with army and navy. Allied with Thebes, he wins land battle at *Thermopylae*, devastates Attica, but is defeated by Greeks in sea battle at *Salamis*. Xerxes retreats.		*Aesop: Fables*.
472	Athens controls Aegean through *Delian League*.		*Aeschylus: The Persians*.
450	*Rome* extending power in *Latium* and against Etruscans. *Twelve Tables* (set of laws) drawn up.	*Persian empire* in decline.	
443	*Pericles* dominates Athenian democracy until 429. Athens rebuilt. *Parthenon* built, designed by Phidias.	Hanno the Carthaginian sails to *Senegal*.	*Sophocles: Antigone*.
			Herodotus: History.
	Celtic La Tène culture flourishes in Switzerland.	*Coinage* reaches India. Extensive trade links between Mediterranean and Asia.	*Phidias* leading Greek sculptor.
			Solar calendar in China.
431	*Peloponnesian War* begins; Athens against Sparta and her allies (431–404), with brief interlude (421–415) after *Peace of Nikias*.		*Democritus: theory of atom*.
			Euripides: The Trojans.
415	*Alcibiades* leads Athenian expedition to Sicily. Disastrous siege of *Syracuse*; many Athenians put to death.	*Nok culture* in West Africa (northern Nigeria), lasting until AD *c.*200. Iron metallurgy; clay figurines.	*Aristophanes: Comedies*.
405	Spartan victory at *Aegospotami*; Athens sues for peace (404).		*Thucydides: History of Peloponnesian War*.
390	Celts cross Brenner and *sack Rome*.	In China *Zhou* dynasty in decline.	399 *Socrates* condemned to death in Athens.
			387 *Plato* founds *Academy* in Athens.
			Hippocrates developing medicine on *Cos*.
371	*Thebes* led by *Epaminondas* defeats Sparta at *Leuctra* and briefly dominates Greece.		

Near East, Mediterranean, and Europe	Rest of the World	Culture/Technology
Rome dominates *Latium*, building roads and aqueducts.		
338 *Macedonia* defeats Thebes at battle of *Chaeronea*; controls all Greece under *Philip II* (359–336).		*Iron metallurgy* in Central Africa.
334 *Alexander* crosses Hellespont, defeats Darius III at *Granicus*, liberates Ionian cities; captures *Tyre* and *Egypt*; marches east.	*Alexander* master of Persian empire; invades *India*.	335 *Aristotle* founds *Lyceum* in Athens.
323 *Death of Alexander* in Babylon. His adoption of Persian life-style had been resented in Macedon. Empire disintegrates. His general *Antigonus* master of Macedonia.	*c.321 Chandragupta Maurya* (d. 296) establishes empire in India, overthrowing *Magadha kingdoms* and advancing west into lands occupied by Alexander; *Pataliputra* capital.	*Epicurean* and atomistic theory fashionable. *Hellenistic art* spreads throughout Asia. Menander: *Comedies*.
311 *Seleucid* power established in Babylon.		*Zhuangzi (Chuang-tzu)* in China writing on *Taoism*.
304 *Ptolemy* founds dynasty in Egypt.		
300 Hellenistic kingdom of Attalids established at *Pergamum*.	Early Classic *Maya* culture developing in Guatemala.	292–280 *Colossus* of Rhodes. 284 *Library* founded (100,000 volumes) at Alexandria. *Euclid* teaching there.
280 *Pyrrhus* of Epirus campaigns in Italy; defeats Romans in several battles but is unable to exploit victory and suffers heavy losses. He returns to Greece. *Rome* continues to advance into southern Italy.		*Catapult* and *quinquereme* warship invented at Syracuse. *Elephants* first used in battle.
264 *First Punic War* begins, Rome against Carthage. Rome expands navy and wins control of Sicily (but not Syracuse), Sardinia, and Corsica.	269 *Asoka* (*c.269–c.232*), Mauryan emperor of India. Enthusiastic convert to Buddhism.	*Zoroastrianism* spreading in Persia. Greek and Oriental cultures fusing in Hellenistic period. *Theocritus* writes *Idylls* idealizing bucolic life on island of Cos.
241 *Carthage admits defeat.*	256 *Zhou dynasty* ends in China.	
237 *Hamilcar* of Carthage conquers SE Iberia, based on Gades.	Extensive trade between China and Hellenistic world.	*Latin literature* beginning to emerge.
218 *Second Punic War* begins. *Hannibal* crosses Alps from Spain and wins battle at *Lake Trasimene*; defeats Romans at *Cannae*, but fails to take city.	221 *Qin Shi Huangdi* (*Ch'in Huang-ti*) establishes dynasty in China. Conquers Zhou provinces and unites country politically.	214 *Archimedes'* inventions resist Romans in siege of *Syracuse*. Archimedes put to death 212.
214 Romans fight *First Macedonian War* (214–205).	*c.210 Great Wall of China* constructed.	
202 *Scipio* defeats Carthage at *Zama* and Second Punic War ends (201).	206 *Han dynasty* established in China.	Horse collar and harness in China.
198 *Second Macedonian War* (198–196). Rome wins battle of *Cynoscephalae* (197) against Philip V.		
192 *Seleucid* Antiochus III occupies Athens and Greece.	*c.184 Mauryan empire* ends in India.	*Plautus* (d. 184) and *Terence* (d. 159) writing *comedies* in Rome.
172 *Third Macedonian War* (172–168/7). Rome wins battle of *Pydna* against Perseus (168). Macedonia subjugated.		
168 Revolt of Maccabees in Palestine against Seleucids; *Judas Maccabaeus* establishes Jewish dynasty in Jerusalem.	*Parthian empire* (*c.250–AD c.230*) at its height, from Caspian Sea and Euphrates to the Indus.	
149 *Third Punic War* begins.		
146 *Carthage destroyed.* Rome dominates western Mediterranean.		*Buddhism* spreading throughout SE Asia.
143 *Macedonia* becomes Roman province.		

Near East, Mediterranean, and Europe	Rest of the World	Culture/Technology
133 Rome master of *Iberia*, occupies *Balearic Islands* (123). The *brothers Gracchi* attempt social and legal reforms in Rome 133–121.	127–101 *Han armies* from China conquer Central Asia. Drift west of *Asiatic* tribes.	Polybius: *Histories* (40 volumes of Roman history, 220–146).
112 Outbreak of war between Rome and *Jugurtha*, king of Numidia.	Roman envoys to Han China.	*Parchment* invented in Pergamum to replace papyrus.
107 *Gaius Marius* first elected *Consul at Rome* (he was to be consul seven times before he died in 86 BC).	*Teotihuacán* and *Monte Albán* developing in Mexico.	
105 *Jugurtha* captured by Marius' quaestor *Sulla*.		
c.100 Celtic *Belgae* first settle in SE Britain.		Water-mill first described in Greek writings; came from China.

Mediterranean and Europe	Rest of the World	Culture/Technology
91 *Italian Confederacy* of tribes on Adriatic and Apennines rebel against Rome; civil war.		
90 *Lex Julia* extends Roman citizenship to the Latin and some Italian cities.		
88 *Mithridates VI*, king of Pontus, invades Greece; defeated by *Sulla* at *Chaeronea* (85).		*Buddhism* spreading in China.
73 *Spartacus* leads revolt of 40,000 slaves; suppressed by *Crassus* and *Pompey* (71); 6,000 *crucified* along Appian Way.		
66 *Mithridates* finally defeated by Pompey.	*Classic civilization of Peru* emerging (pyramids, palaces, etc.).	*Cicero* (106–43) pleading and writing in Rome.
63 *Catiline's conspiracy* at Rome.	Romans under *Pompey* conquer Syria and Palestine; end of *Seleucid empire*.	
60 *First Triumvirate* in Rome: Crassus, Pompey, and Caesar co-ordinate their political activities.		
58 Caesar campaigns against *Gauls*.		
55, 54 Caesar invades *Britain*.	*Teotihuacán civilization* of Mexico flourishes until 8th century. City of some 200,000 with complex of streets and apartment blocks. *Pyramid of the Sun* 700 ft. long and 200 ft. high.	
53 *Crassus* killed in battle against *Parthians*.		
52 *Vercingetorix* leader of Transalpine Gauls; defeated by *Caesar* (51).		
49 Caesar crosses *Rubicon* and begins civil war.		
48 Caesar defeats *Pompey* in battle of *Pharsalus*. Pompey murdered at Rome. Caesar campaigns in Egypt, Africa, and Spain (48–45).		*Library of Alexandria* burned, but re-established.
45 Caesar *dictator of Rome*.		46 Caesar introduces *Julian calendar*.
44 Caesar assassinated.		
43 *Second Triumvirate* (Octavian, Antony, Lepidus).		42 Virgil begins to write *Bucolics*.
31 Battle of *Actium*. Antony and Cleopatra commit suicide (30).		
27 Octavian accepts title of *Augustus*.		*Pantheon* built in Rome. 19 Virgil dies, leaving *Aeneid* unfinished. 17 *Herod* rebuilds Temple at Jerusalem.

Mediterranean and Europe	Rest of the World	Culture/Technology
6? Jesus of Nazareth born.	*c.9 Western Han* dynasty ends in China.	Strabo: *Geography.*
AD 9 Germans under *Arminius* annihilate 3 Roman legions. Rome withdraws to Rhine.		Vitruvius: *treatise on architecture.*
14 Death of *Augustus.* Julio-Claudian emperors follow. Empress *Livia* plots. *Tiberius* emperor (14–37).	*c.25 Eastern Han* dynasty established in China.	Ovid: *Metamorphoses.* *c.30 Crucifixion of Jesus,* followed by foundation of *Christianity.*
37 *Caligula* emperor; assassinated AD 41.		
41 *Claudius* emperor (AD 41–54).		
43 *Britain occupied* under Claudius.		
54 *Nero* emperor (AD 54–68).		*c.51 St Paul* writes first letters.
61 *Boudicca's revolt* in Britain crushed by Suetonius.	Kingdom of Axum (Ethiopia) flourishes from port of Adulis.	Cult of *Mithras* in Roman army.
64 Great fire of Rome: *Christians* blamed and *martyred* in Rome (64–7), including *St Paul* and *St Peter.*	66 *Revolt of Jews* in Palestine.	*Hero* invents various machines in Alexandria.
69 *Vespasian* emperor (69–79); first of *Flavian* emperors; restores imperial economy.	*Dead Sea Scrolls* hidden at Qumran near the Dead Sea.	*c.65* First *Gospel* (St Mark).
79 Eruption of *Vesuvius. Pompeii* and *Herculaneum* buried.	70 *Destruction* of *Temple* at *Jerusalem* under Titus, son of Vespasian. Jewish *Diaspora.*	*c.75 Colosseum* in Rome begun. *Paper, magnetic compass,* and *fireworks* invented in China. 90 Plutarch: *Lives.*
98 *Trajan* emperor (98–117); extends empire, defeating Dacians, Armenians, and Parthians. Empire at its fullest extent.	*Christianity* spreading.	Reform of *Buddhism* in India. *Iron-working* in Zambia.
100 *Pax Romana* throughout Europe, North Africa, and Middle East.		Juvenal (d. 130): *Satires.* Synod of Jamnia (in Palestine) fixes canon of *Old Testament* for Judaism.
117 *Hadrian* emperor (117–38).		*c.117* Tacitus: *Annals.*
122 *Hadrian's Wall* built in Britain against the Picts.		*c.125* Gaius Suetonius: *Lives of Caesars.*
132 *Bar-Cochba* leads revolt of Jews against the Romans.	Teotihuacán civilization in Mexico flourishing.	
138 *Antoninus Pius* emperor (138–61). Founds Antonine dynasty; streamlines imperial government.		Cult of *Mithras* continues to spread.
c.140 *Antonine Wall* built in Britain; abandoned *c.*163.		
161 *Marcus Aurelius* emperor (161–80); a Stoic philosopher, he campaigns on eastern and northern frontiers of empire.	*Parthian empire* weakening.	Astronomy developing in school of Alexandria. *c.180 Marcus Aurelius: Meditations.*
180 *Commodus* emperor (180–92); murdered for his wild extravagance and cruelty.	184 'Yellow Turban' revolt in China as Han dynasty declines.	Galen from Pergamum (d. 199) practising medicine in Rome.
193 *Septimius Severus* emperor (193–211); resumes *persecution of Christians;* long campaign in Britain against Picts; dies in York.		*c.197* Tertullian: *Apology* (defends Christianity against Greek philosophic thought).
211 *Caracalla* emperor (211–17); his reign one of cruelty and extortion; murdered on campaign in Parthia.	220 Han dynasty ends in China. 220–63 Period of the *'Three Kingdoms'* in China.	
212 *Edict of Caracalla* extends *Roman citizenship* to all freemen of empire.		Manes (*c.*215–75) from Persia develops *Manichaeism.* Egyptian *Coptic Church* to Ethiopia.
218 *Elagabalus* emperor (218–22); wild and decadent; seeks to impose worship of		Neoplatonism in Alexandria.

Mediterranean and Europe

Syrian sun-god Elah-Gabal. Murdered in Rome.

222   *Alexander Severus* emperor (222–35); under strong influence of Empress Mamaea; rule remembered as just; re-established authority of Rome.

235   Political tensions in Rome as empire begins to decline.

249   *Decius* emperor (249–51); intense persecution of Christians; Danube and the Balkans overrun by Goths.

253   *Valerian* (253–60) and *Gallienus* emperors (253–68). *Franks* invade empire and Sassanids take Syria. Gallienus defeats Alamanni (258).

270   Emperor *Aurelian* (270–5) abandons Dacia to Goths but *regains Rhine and Danube*.

284   *Diocletian* emperor (284–305); re-establishes frontiers and reorganizes government.

286   *Aurelius Carausius* seeks to separate Britain from empire.

293   Diocletian establishes *Tetrarchy*; he rules with *Galerius* in east, *Maximian* and *Constantius* in west.

296   *Constantius* re-establishes control of *Britain*.

303   Diocletian *persecutes Christians*.

306   *Constantius* campaigns in Scotland. He dies. *Constantine* proclaimed in York.

312   Constantine victorious at *Mulvian Bridge* against rival Maxentius.

313   *Edict of Milan* allows liberty of cult of Christianity.

315   *Constantine (303–37) sole emperor.*

324   Byzantium becomes capital of Empire as New Rome; named *Constantinopolis* (330).

353   *Constantius II* sole emperor (353–60); re-establishes control over empire and defeats Alamanni at *Battle of Strasbourg* (357).

      Saxons invading coasts of Britain.

360   *Julian (the Apostate)* emperor (360–3).

368   Order restored in Britain by *Count Theodosius*.

374   *St Ambrose* elected bishop of Milan (d. 397); influences emperor and dominates western Church.

378   *Visigoths* defeat Roman army at Adrianople.

Rest of the World

224 *Ardashir* of Persia defeats Parthians, whose empire collapses. The Persian *Sassanid empire* established.

232 Sassanid Ardashir II defeated by Emperor Alexander Severus.

c.250 Syrian kingdom of Palmyra rises in power under *Odaenathus* (d. 267).

259 Sassanid *Shapur* I captures Valerian.

Bantu tribes move into Southern Africa.

273 Kingdom of *Palmyra conquered* by Roman emperor Aurelian.

Classic *Maya civilization* emerging (Tikal, Uaxactún, Palenque); first Maya stele from Tikal 292.

Classic *Maya Old Empire* civilization (peaceful, civilian, highly literate; high levels of art; brick temples; priests very powerful with complex *religious ceremonies* and music).

317 Foundation of *Eastern Jin* (*Chin*) dynasty in China (317–420).

320 Foundation of *Gupta empire* (to c.550) by *Chandra Gupta I* in India (golden age of religion, philosophy, literature, and architecture).

Culture/Technology

Indian art (sculpture and painting) flourish. Chinese literature developing.

Gnostic Manichaeism spreads from Persia.

Roman *architecture* covers Europe and Mediterranean.

Christian theology emerging in Asia Minor and Egypt.

Monastic ideal (hermits) becoming popular (cf. *St Anthony*).

c.285 *Pappus Alexandrinus* last great mathematician of Alexandria.

Arius of Alexandria (c.250–c.336) founds *Arianism*, denying divinity of Christ.

325 *Council of Nicaea* denounces Arianism and agrees *Creed*.

Chinese mathematics reducing fractions and solving linear equations.

c.330–71 *St Martin* bishop of *Tours*.

Chinese *bucolic literature* flourishing.

Julian (the Apostate) restores paganism briefly.

Mediterranean and Europe	*Rest of the World*	*Culture/Technology*
379	*Flavius Theodosius (the Great)* emperor (379–95). Pious Christian; defeats usurpers and makes treaty with *Visigoths* (382).	*Huns* from Asia concentrate on River Volga; moving west.	
391	All *pagan cults banned* in empire by Theodosius.		Greek and Latin Fathers continue to define Christian theology; *Athanasian Creed* agreed.
395	Empire divided on death of Theodosius: *Honorius* (395–423) rules from Milan, *Arcadius* (395–408) from Constantinople.		
396–8	Roman victories in Britain against Picts, Scots, and Saxons.		*c.*400 Text of Palestinian *Talmud* finalized.
404	Western capital moves from Milan to *Ravenna*.		*c.*405 *St Jerome* (d. 420) completes *Vulgate* (Latin Bible).
407	*Constantius III* proclaimed in Britain.		
410	*Visigoths*, led by Alaric, *sack Rome*. *Romans evacuate Britain. Franks* occupy northern Gaul and *Celts* move into Breton peninsula.	420 *End of Eastern Jin dynasty* in China.	
476	*Romulus Augustulus*, last western emperor (475–6), is *deposed.* *Saxon* settlement in Sussex.		*Shinto* (worship of sun-goddess, reverence of ancestors and nature-spirits) in Japan.
481	*Clovis I*, king of Salian Franks (481–511), defeats Alamanni (496) and Visigoths (507).	Ecuadorean pottery dated *c.*500 found in *Galapagos Islands*. Evidence of *Pacific trade?*	*Buddhism* dominant in China.
488	Theodoric and *Ostrogoths* invade Italy.		
496	*Clovis baptized*; establishes *Merovingian* Frankish kingdom. *Wessex* occupied by Saxons.		
*c.*500	*British victory* over Saxons at Badon Hill. Visigoths established in Spain; Vandals in Africa (429–534).		

Britain and Europe	*Rest of the World*	*Culture/Technology*
552	*Ostrogoths* finally defeated by *General Narses*.	*c.*550 End of *Gupta empire* in India following attacks by *Huns*.	*c.*550 *St David* founds monastery.
560	*Aethelbert* king of Kent.		*Buddhism* in Japan along with *Shintoism*.
563	*St Columba* founds Iona.		
568	*Lombards* invade northern Italy. Anglo-Saxon kingdoms in Britain emerging. *Venice* established as retreat from Lombards.	*c.*570 Birth of *Muhammad*.	*Byzantine architecture* spreads throughout eastern empire and southern Italy.
577	*West Saxons* take Bath and Gloucester.	Chinese *Sui dynasty* 581–618; this short-lived dynasty reunites country and *rebuilds Great Wall*.	
590	Election of *Gregory the Great* as pope (590–604).	592 Prince *Shotoku Taishi* in Japan establishes mandarin-style bureaucracy.	*Gregorian chant* and Roman ritual, imposed by Gregory the Great.
		607 Unification of *Tibet*, which becomes *centre of Buddhism*.	
		618 *Tang dynasty* established in China (618–907); strong centralizing power restores order.	
627	Death of *Raedwald* of East Anglia. Possible burial at *Sutton Hoo*.	622 *Hegira* of Muhammad and friends: *Mecca to Medina*.	Christian missionaries to Germany and England (*St Augustine*, 597).

Britain and Europe	Rest of the World	Culture/Technology
Saxon kingdoms in Britain (*Mercia, Wessex,* and *Northumbria*) struggle for power.	632 *Death* of Muhammad. In Mexico Maya civilization at height; temples and palaces in stone (complex astronomical and mathematical knowledge).	c.625 Isidore of Seville: *Etymologies.* *Parchment* displacing papyrus.
629 *Dagobert,* king of Franks (629–39), reunites all Franks.		c.632 *Abu Bakr* collects the 114 chapters of the *Koran.*
635 *Cynegils* of Wessex baptized.	634 *Rapid spread of Islam* in Arabia, Syria, Iran, N. Africa under *Caliph Umar* (634–44). 636 Collapse of *Sassanid* empire.	c.641 The great *Library of Alexandria* destroyed by Arabs. 644 *Windmill* recorded in Persia.
664 *Synod of Whitby;* Roman practice imposed. 669 *Archbishop Theodore* in Britain.	660 Damascus capital of *Ummayad empire of Islam.*	
678 Constantinople successfully *resists Arabs.*		680 Divisions within Islam produce *Sunnites* and *Shiites.*
679 *Battle of Trent:* Mercia becomes major British power.	*Teotihuacán civilization* of Mexico declining, possibly owing to destruction of rain forests.	
685 *Battle of Nechtansmere:* Picts defeat Northumbrians. Wessex expanding; Kent, Surrey, Sussex taken.	*Monte Albán,* Zapotec civilization, flourishing; influenced by Teotihuacán.	
687 *Pepin II* reunites Merovingian kingdom.	*Afghanistan* conquered by Arabs who cross Khyber Pass and conquer the *Punjab.*	*Grand mosques* of Jerusalem (692) and Damascus (706–15) built.
711 Muslim Arabs enter *Spain,* conquer Seville (712).	*Hsuan Tsung* (Tang emperor, 712–56) suffers drastic incursions by Arabs and revolts.	
718 Bulgars pressing south towards Constantinople.		
732 *Battle of Tours;* decisive victory of *Charles Martel,* 'Mayor of Palace' of Merovingians, over Muslims.	8th c. *Kingdom of Ghana* established; to last till 1240.	*Block printing* in China for Buddhist texts. 731 Bede: *Ecclesiastical History.*
751 *Pepin III* (the Short), son of Charles Martel, ousts last Merovingian, *Childeric III,* and founds *Carolingian* dynasty. *Exarchate* of Ravenna lost by Byzantines to *Lombards.* Pope turns to Franks for protection.	Establishment of *Abbasid Caliphate* in Baghdad, 750–1258.	Golden age of Chinese poetry (*Li Po,* 701–61) and art (*Wu Tao-tzu,* d. 792).
754 *Pepin the Short* crowned in *St Denis* by Pope Stephen II; recognizes Papal States.		*Cordoba* centre of Muslim culture in Spain.
756 Abd al-Rahman founds *Caliphate of Cordoba.*		Irish *Book of Kells.*
757 *Offa* king of Mercia (757–96).		
768 *Charlemagne* king of Franks (768–814); campaigns against Avars and Saxons in east.		*Offa's Dyke* built. *Dravidian temples* in India.
774 Charlemagne annexes Lombardy, but checked in Spain (death of *Roland* at *Roncesvalles* 778).	Caliph *Haroun al-Raschid* (786–809) establishes close links with Constantinople and with Charlemagne. Patronage of learning and the arts (*1001 Nights*).	In Spain *cotton* grown.
794 *Viking raids* on England and Ireland; Jarrow and Iona (795) sacked.	Kyoto capital of Japan, dominated by *Fujiwara* family.	
800 *Charlemagne crowned* in Rome by *Pope Leo III.*		*Alcuin* at court of Charlemagne. 'Carolingian Renaissance'. 805 *Aachen cathedral* inspired by Byzantine models.

Britain and Europe	Rest of the World	Culture/Technology
812 *Treaty of Aix-la-Chapelle* (Aachen). Charlemagne recognized emperor of the West by eastern emperor Michael I.		*Beowulf*, Anglo-Saxon poem.
813 Byzantine army defeated by Bulgars at *Adrianople*. Constantinople besieged by Bulgars and Arab army.		
825 *Wessex* annexes *Essex*.		
827 Byzantine loss of *Sicily* and *Crete* to Arab Saracens.		833 *Observatory* in Baghdad; Arabs develop astronomy, mathematics (*algebra* from India), optics, medicine.
		Romanesque architecture developing in West.
843 *Treaty of Verdun*; Carolingian empire divided: *East Franks*, *West Franks*, and *Lotharingia*.	849 *Burma* unified by *Burmans* from Pagan.	843 Restoration of cult of *images* in Byzantine Church. *Icon art* to influence West through Venice.
Vikings trading to Volga and Baghdad.		845 *Buddhism outlawed* in China.
		*c.*850 *Windmills* in Europe.
862 *Novgorod* founded as trading centre; Viking and Byzantine merchants.	857 *Fujiwara family* in Japan extend power.	*c.*850 China develops *gunpowder*.
St Cyril's mission to Moravia; Bulgars accept Christianity.		
866 Danish *Great Army* lands on east coast of Britain; Northumbria conquered; *Danelaw* established.	*Tiahuanaco* in Andes flourishing city.	
867 *Basil I* founds Macedonian dynasty of Byzantine empire (867–1057).		
869 *St Edmund murdered* by Danes.		
871 *Alfred the Great* king of Wessex (871–99).		
878 Alfred wins battle of *Edington*; Guthrum baptized.		
*c.*880 *Kingdom of Kiev* established in Russia.		
885 *Paris besieged* by Vikings.		
896 *Magyars* settle in *Hungary*.	889 Classic Old Maya civilization in Mexico *ending*.	
	*c.*900 Teotihuacán civilization ends; rise of *Toltecs* in North Mexico based on Tula.	
910 Danelaw conquered by *Edward* and *Ethelred*.	907 Tang dynasty in China ends; *China fragments*.	Monastery of *Cluny* established. *Benedictine Order* spreads through Europe.
	908 Shiite dynasty from Morocco, the *Fatimites*, conquer North Africa.	
911 Treaty of *St-Clair-sur-Epte* establishes *Rollo the Norseman* in NW France; Duchy of *Normandy*.		
919 Vikings establish *Kingdom of York* under *Ragnald*.		
926 *Athelstan* king of England (926–39).	Arabs trading along *East African* coast.	*Stone* replacing *wood* as building material in western Europe.
936 *Otto I* king of East Franks and Saxons (936–73).	935 *Koryo kingdom* in Korea (935–1392), capital Kaesong; Buddhism flourishes.	Expansion of European agriculture.
937 Athelstan defeats Vikings and Scots at *Brunanburh*.		
939 *Edmund* king of England (939–46).		
945 Norsemen in *Constantinople* and *Kiev*.	947 *Liao dynasty* from *Manchuria* (947–1125) extends control over North China.	943 *Dunstan* (*c.*909–88) abbot of Glastonbury. Under his leadership *monasticism* re-established in England.
954 Viking kingdom of York *ends*.		

	Britain and Europe	Rest of the World	Culture/Technology
955	Decisive battle of *Lechfeld*. *Otto I* defeats *Magyars*.		
959	*Edgar* king of England (959–75).		
960	*Dunstan archbishop* of Canterbury.	960 *Sung dynasty* in China till 1279; gradually reunites country; high levels of art and literature.	
962	Otto I crowned *Holy Roman Emperor* in Rome by Pope John XII. Seeks to establish power in Italy.		
971	*Bulgaria and Phoenicia* conquered by Byzantine armies.	969 *Fatimites* conquer W. Arabia, Syria, and Egypt; *Cairo* capital (973).	c.970 Synod of Winchester approves Ethelwold's *Regularis Concordia*.
973	Dunstan *crowns* and *consecrates* Edgar.		
975	*Edward the Martyr* king (975–8); murdered by half-brother Ethelred.		
978	*Ethelred (the Unready)* king of England (978–1016).		
987	*Hugo Capet* king of France (987–96).	986 Viking settlements in Greenland. *New Maya Empire* emerging under Toltec influence.	988 Baptism of *Vladimir*, prince of Kiev (956–1015).
991	English treaty with Normans.	990 Ghana conquers Berber *kingdom of Audaghos* and gains gold and salt monopoly.	990 *School of Chartres* founded: early centre of western learning.
996	*Otto III* crowned in Rome (996–1002); establishes *capital in Rome* (999); with Pope Sylvester II aims to create universal Christian empire. *Balearic Islands* conquered by *Caliphate of Cordoba*.		*Avicenna* (980–1037) has lasting influence on West: philosophy, *Ash-Shifa* (Neoplatonic), and medicine *Qanun*; via Cordoba.
1001	Christian *kingdom of Hungary* established.		c.1000 Arabic description of magnifying properties of *glass lens*.
1003	*Swein Forkbeard*, king of Denmark, attacks England.	c.1000 *Chola Tamil dynasty* in S. India peaks under *Rajaraja I* (985–1016); stretches from Ganges to Malay archipelago.	
1013	*Swein invades England* and takes London.		
1014	Death of Swein. His son *Cnut* elected king by Danes in England.		
1016	Death of Ethelred; his son *Edmund Ironside* killed in battle. *Cnut* accepted as king of England (1017–35). Byzantine empire at height of power and influence under *Basil II* (976–1025).	*Mahmud of Ghazni* (971–1030) extends *Ghaznavid* empire into Persia and Punjab from Afghanistan.	
1035	*Harold* king of England (1035–40).		
1040	*Harthacnut* king of England and Denmark (1040–2).		
1042	*Edward the Confessor* king of England (1042–66).		c.1045 Printing by *movable type* in China.
1050	Bohemia, Poland, and Hungary become *fiefs* of Holy Roman Empire.	*Toltecs* flourish in Mexico; conspicuous Maya influence.	c.1050 *Salerno medical school* emerging; Arabic expertise. Cult of *Quetzalcóatl* in Toltec Mexico.
1054	*Schism* within Christian Church. Orthodox Eastern churches split from Catholic Rome.		
1066	*Normans* conquer England. *William I* king (1066–87).	1064 *Seljuk Turks* menace Byzantine empire.	1063 *St Mark's*, Venice, rebuilt. 1063 *Pisa Cathedral*.
1069	*'Harrowing of the North'* by William I.	1068 *Almoravid* Berber dynasty in N. Africa; fanatical Muslims; build *Marrakesh*.	

Britain and Europe	Rest of the World	Culture/Technology
1071 Normans established in southern *Italy*.	*Battle of Manzikert*; Seljuk Turks rout Byzantine army and threaten Asia Minor.	
1073 Hildebrand elected *Pope Gregory VII* (1073–85). '*Investiture Controversy*' with Emperor Henry IV (1056–1106).		
1077 Henry IV at *Canossa* accepts papal supremacy to invest bishops of Church.		*Bayeux Tapestry*.
1081 Normans invade *Balkans*; Venice aids Constantinople against Normans; *Venetian trade* expands.	1080 Under *Malik Shah* Turks control Asia Minor and interrupt Christian pilgrim routes to Jerusalem.	*c.*1080 *Chanson de Roland*.
1084 Foundation of Grande Chartreuse (*Carthusian Order* of monks).		
1086 *Domesday survey* in England.		
1087 *William II* king of England (1087–1100).		*Omar Khayyám* (*c.*1050–1123): algebra; astronomy; poetry (*Rubaiyat*).
		1090 Water-powered mechanical *clock* in China.
1095 *Pope Urban II* preaches *Crusade* at *Clermont* to rescue Holy Places from Turks.		1094 St Anselm: *Cur Deus Homo?*
1098 *Cistercian Order* of monks founded. Fairs of Champagne; *urban society* developing in Flanders, Germany, and Italy.	1099 Jerusalem captured by *Crusaders*.	*Feudal system* well established throughout Europe.
1100 *Henry I* king of England (1100–35).	*Christian States* in Palestine.	
1106 *Henry V* German emperor (1106–25).		
1108 *Louis the Fat* king of France (1108–37); *Capet power* expanding.		1115 St Bernard (1090–1153) abbot of *Clairvaux*; stresses *spiritualism* of monasticism.
1120 *White Ship* disaster; Henry I's son *William* drowned.	1116 *Jin* (*Chin*) dynasty in Manchuria. 1118 *Knights Templar* founded in Jerusalem.	'*Twelfth-Century Renaissance*'; rediscovery of *Aristotle*.
1122 *Concordat of Worms*; Henry V confirms end of Investiture Controversy.	1121 *Ibn Tumart*, claiming to be Mahdi, preaches puritanical Islam and founds *Almohades* dynasty in N. Africa.	
	1126 Song (Sung) capital *Kaifeng* in China sacked by Jin horsemen; retreat south to *Xingsai*.	
1135 Civil war in England: *Stephen* against *Matilda*.		Abelard (1079–1142) teaching in Paris.
1137 Catalonia linked by marriage with *Aragon*.		1136 Geoffrey of Monmouth: *History of the Kings of Britain* (Arthur).
1138 Henry of Bavaria of *Guelph* family disputes crown of Germany with *Conrad III* of Ghibellines; beginning of long medieval struggle: *Guelph* (for pope) against *Ghibelline* (for emperor).	*Anasazi* Indians in Colorado build *Mesa Verde*.	1140 Bernard obtains *condemnation* of Abelard. *Gothic architecture*; St Denis west front.
1147 The *Almohades* rule in southern Spain.	1147–8 *Second Crusade*; achieves little.	*c.*1150 Toledo school of translators transmits Arab learning to West.
1152 *Henry of Anjou* marries *Eleanor of Aquitaine*.	*c.*1150 *Khmer* temple *Angkor Wat* built in Cambodia.	*c.*1150 *Paris* University.
1154 *Henry II* king of England (1154–89).		
1155 *Frederick I* ('*Barbarossa*') crowned Holy Roman Emperor by Pope Hadrian IV (1155–90); seeks to extend power in Italy.	*Toltec* capital *Tula* overrun by *Chichimecs* from N. Mexico. Toltec power *declines*.	1158 University of *Bologna* granted charter by Frederick I.

Britain and Europe	Rest of the World	Culture/Technology
1165 *William ('the Lion') king of Scotland (1165–1214).*		
1166 *Assize of Clarendon establishes jury system in England.*	**1168** *Aztecs moving into Mexico; destroy Toltec Empire.*	**1167** *Catharist Manichaean heresy spreading.*
	1169 *Saladin (1137–93) founds dynasty of Ayyubids and conquers Egypt. Drives Christians from Acre and Jerusalem.*	**1167** *Oxford* University.
1170 Murder of *Thomas Becket.*		*c.*1170 *Tristan et Iseult.*
		Troubadour songs in France.
		Early *polyphonic music.*
1173 Henry II's sons rebel.		**1171** *Averroës* teaching in Cordoba.
1177 *Peace of Venice;* Frederick Barbarossa accepts that cardinals elect pope.		
1179 Third *Lateran Council* condemns *Catharism,* authorizes crusade against Albigensians.		
1180 *Philip II ('Augustus') king of France (1180–1223); greatly expands kingdom.*	**1181** *Khmer Empire* at height, under *Jayavarman VII.*	*Longbow* in Wales.
1182 *Massacre of Latin merchants in Constantinople.*	**1185** Japanese shogunate of *Minamoto Yoritomo* at Kamakura.	
1189 *Richard I king of England (1189–99).*	*Third Crusade;* Acre retaken (1191). Saladin grants pilgrims *access to Holy Places.*	**1193** *Zen Buddhism* in Japan.
1198 *Innocent III pope (1198–1216): papacy has maximum authority during these years.*		**1194** Chartres Cathedral rebuilding begun in Gothic style. Chartres windows.
1199 *John king of England (1199–1216).*	**1200** *Incas* developing civilization based on *Cuzco.*	
	Post-Classical civilization in Peru (*Chimu,* 1200–1465); large urban centres; elaborate irrigation.	
1204 *Fourth Crusade; Constantinople sacked.*	**1206** *Genghis Khan (1162–1227) proclaims Mongol empire.*	**1202** *Arabic mathematics* in Pisa (Fibonacci).
Philip Augustus victory in Normandy.	**1206** Muslim *Mameluke sultanate* in Delhi established.	*Louvre* built (fortress of Philip Augustus).
1212 *Children's Crusade;* thousands enslaved.		**1209** *Cambridge* University.
Battle of *Las Navas de Tolosa in Spain: Moors ejected from Castile.*		Franciscan (1209) and Dominican (1216) Orders.
1214 *Battle of Bouvines:* Philip Augustus against John and German emperor Otto IV. Philip gains *Normandy, Maine, Anjou,* and *Poitou* for France.		
1215 John accepts *Magna Carta* from barons.	Beijing (Peking) sacked and Jin empire destroyed by *Mongols.*	Islam spreading into SE Asia and Africa.
1216 *Henry III of England aged 9 (1216–72); William Marshall regent until 1227.*		
1220 *Frederick II emperor (1220–50); inherits S. Italy and Sicily, which he makes power-base.*		
1223 *Louis VIII of France (1223–6) conquers* Languedoc in *Albigensian Crusade* against Cathars (1224–6).		1224 Frederick II founds *Naples University:* Jews, Christians, and Arabs.
Mongols invade Russia.		Frederick's court at *Palermo* and *Lucca* centre of Byzantine and Arab culture.
1226 *Louis IX of France (1226–70).*	**1229** *Frederick II* negotiates access for pilgrims to *Jerusalem, Bethlehem,* and *Nazareth.*	
1236 *Cordoba* falls to Castile.	*c.*1235 *Sundjata* conquers Ghana and establishes *Mali empire* in West Africa.	*c.*1236 *Roman de la Rose.*
1241 Formation of Hanseatic League.	Mongol *'Golden Horde'* khanate.	

	Britain and Europe	*Rest of the World*	*Culture/Technology*
1250	*Italian cities* gain power on collapse of *Frederick II's* empire.	*Ayyubid dynasty* falls to Mongols and Christians are driven from Jerusalem. *Mongol Mamelukes* establish dynasty in Egypt.	1248 *Alhambra* begun. 1248 *Cologne* Cathedral begun.
1258	*Provisions of Oxford* limit royal power in England. Catalans under *James I of Aragon* (1213–76) *expel Moors* from Balearics.	Mongols take *Baghdad*.	Thomas Aquinas (1225–74): *Summa theologiae*. *Tin plate* for armour (Bohemia) and *screw-jack* (1271 in sketchbook of Villard de Honnecourt).
1261	Byzantines regain Constantinople.	1259 *Kublai Khan* elected Great Khan. Establishes capital in Beijing and founds *Yuan dynasty*.	Artists move from Apulia to Italian cities: *Nicola Pisano*, *Pulpit* c.1260; renaissance of classical style.
1264	*Battle of Lewes*; Simon de Montfort effective ruler of England until *Evesham* in 1265.		
1270	*Louis IX (St Louis)* dies on Crusade outside *Tunis*. *Philip III* succeeds (1270–85).	*Marco Polo* travelling 1271–95.	*Gothic architecture* throughout Europe.
1272	*Edward I* of England (1272–1307) begins conquest of *Wales*.		
1282	*Sicilian Vespers*; revolt against Angevins (ruled since 1266). Sicily goes to *Aragon*. Surrender of Harlech castle: Welsh revolt collapses.		*Duccio* (d. 1319) in Siena.
1284	*Statute of Rhuddlan*; English rule of Wales confirmed.		*Giotto* (c.1267–1337) establishes modern painting in Florence.
1285	*Philip IV* of France (1285–1314).	*Inca empire* expanding in Peru.	
1290	*Jews* expelled from England. *Scottish throne* vacant.		
1297	*William Wallace* defeats English army at *Stirling Bridge*.	New *empire of Maya* flourishing in Yucatán (Chichén Itzá); stone architecture; pottery; gold artefacts; elaborate temples.	*Roger Bacon*: *Opus maius* (1266); imprisoned for heresy.
1305	Edward I *executes* Wallace. *Clement V* pope (1305–14); papacy moves to *Avignon* (1309).		1303 *Spectacles* invented.
1306	*Jews* expelled from France.		*Duns Scotus* (c.1260–1308) and *nominalists* oppose Aquinas' theology.
1307	*Knights Templar suppressed* in France. *Edward II* king of England (1307–27). *Italian cities* flourish as German empire abandons control.	*Empire of Benin* emerging in southern Nigeria.	Dante: *Divina Commedia* begun c.1307.
1314	*Robert Bruce* defeats English at *Bannockburn*.		
1327	Edward II imprisoned and *murdered*. *Edward III* of England (1327–77); his mother *Isabella* and her lover *Mortimer* rule till 1330.	c.1325 *Tenochtitlán* founded by Aztecs; cult of *Quetzalcóatl* from Toltecs. *Ibn Batuta* (c.1304–68) travelling.	*Spinning-wheel* from India in Europe.
1328	*Scottish independence* recognized. Capet line of kings ends. *Philip VI* first *Valois* king of France (1328–50).	c.1330 Disease (plague) and famine weaken *Yuan dynasty*.	1329 *Meister Eckhart* (d. 1327) condemned posthumously.
1338	*Edward III* claims French throne and Hundred Years War begins.	1336 *Vijayanagar* city founded S. India; seat of Hindu empire till 1565. 1336 In Japan *Ashikaga* shogunate founded.	1335 *Mechanical clocks* at Milan and Wells.
1340	*Battle of Sluys*; English gain control of Channel.		*Paper-mill* at Fabriano. *Bruges* centre of *wool trade*; Flemish art emerging.

Britain and Europe	Rest of the World	Culture/Technology
1346 Battle of Crécy; English victory; cannon used; Calais occupied.		Petrarch: Canzoniere; crowned poet laureate 1341.
		c.1344 Order of Garter in England.
1348 Black Death arrives in England; one-third of population dies.	1348 Black Death reaches Europe from China.	Boccaccio: Decameron.
1351 English Statute of Labourers seeks to uphold feudalism.	Aztec Empire thriving; gold; copper; obsidian; calendar and hieroglyphic writing; mathematics based on 20 with zero; Tenochtitlán city of 300,000; pyramids with elaborate rituals with human sacrifice.	
1353 Ottoman Turks enter Europe.		
1356 Edward Black Prince wins Poitiers; French king John II captured.		
1358 Revolt of Étienne Marcel in Paris.		
1360 Treaty of Brétigny; England keeps western France, in peace with French.		1363 Guy de Chauliac advances medicine from Black Death studies.
		1364 Machaut: Mass of Nôtre Dame.
		William Langland: Piers Plowman.
1369 Hundred Years War resumed; French under Du Guesclin.	Mongol Tamerlane (Timur the Lame) conquers Turkestan, Delhi, Persia, Golden Horde, Syria, and Egypt (1363–1405).	Jean Froissart: Chronicles.
		Siena artists flourish.
	Ming dynasty in China founded by Zhu Yuanzhang (Chu Yuan-chang) (1368–1644); great period for pottery and bronze.	
1371 Robert II king of Scotland (1371–90); first Stuart.		
1377 Richard II king of England (1377–99). Papacy returns to Rome from Avignon.		
1378 Great Schism in Church; two popes.		Flamboyant architecture in Europe: Beauvais Cathedral.
1380 Charles VI king of France (1380–1422).		
1381 Peasants' Revolt in England; Wat Tyler defeated; poll tax withdrawn.		1382 Lollards (John Wyclif) condemned.
1386 Poland and Lithuania unite.	1392 Yi dynasty in Korea (1392–1910) under Ming influence.	1387 Chaucer: Canterbury Tales.
1396 Truce in Hundred Years War.		Ghiberti in Florence (1378–1455): Baptistery doors.
Battle of Nicopolis; Crusaders in Hungary defeated by Turks.		c.1389 Sluter in Dijon: Well of Moses.
1397 Union of Kalmar: crowns of Denmark, Norway, and Sweden unite (1397–1523).		
1399 Richard II deposed and murdered; Bolingbroke Henry IV 1399–1413.		
1402 Owen Glendower defeats English at Pilleth.	Timur defeats Ottomans at Ankara.	
	Foundation of Malacca by Srivijaya; becomes entrepôt.	
1403 Prince Henry ('Hal') defeats Percy ('Hotspur') and Glendower rebellions (1408).	Zheng He's (Cheng Ho's) voyages; reaches Persian Gulf and E. Africa from China (1405–33).	Metal screws in Europe.
1413 Henry V king of England (1413–22).	Portuguese voyages begin under Henry the Navigator (1394–1460).	St Andrews University.
		Duc de Berry: Très riches Heures.
1415 Henry wins Agincourt; occupies Normandy.		Hussites seek revenge for martyr Huss.
Council of Constance condemns John Huss to stake; ends Schism.		Painting in oil begins.

Britain and Europe	Rest of the World	Culture/Technology

Britain and Europe

1422 Henry VI king of England (infant); Council of Regency claims France. Charles VII king of France (1422–61).

1429 Joan of Arc relieves Orleans.

1431 Joan burnt at stake in Rouen.

1434 Cosimo de' Medici rules in Florence; patron of learning. Burgundy emerging under strong dukes.

1450 Jack Cade's peasant rebellion suppressed.

1452 Frederick III (1452–93) first Hapsburg Holy Roman Emperor.

1453 Constantinople falls to Ottoman Turks. Hundred Years War ends. Henry VI 'insane'; Richard duke of York protector; English 'Wars of Roses' begin.

1460 Richard of York killed at Wakefield.

1461 Edward of York seizes throne; Edward IV (1461–83). Louis XI king of France (1461–83).

1462 Ivan III of Russia rejects control of Horde.

1469 Ferdinand and Isabella marry; unite Aragon and Castile (1479).

1471 Lancastrians defeated at Tewkesbury; Henry VI killed; Edward IV accepted (1471–83).

1477 Death of Charles the Bold of Burgundy.

1480 Ivan III overthrows Mongol Golden Horde.

1483 Edward V; Richard III king of England (1483–5).

1485 Henry Tudor wins Bosworth; Henry VII (1485–1509).

1492 Reconquest of Spain complete.

1494 Treaty of Tordesillas divides New World between Spain and Portugal. Charles VIII invades Italy.

1498 Louis XII king of France (1498–1515).

1502 Death of Arthur Tudor in England. Margaret Tudor marries James IV of Scotland.

1503 Julius II pope (1503–13).

1509 Henry VIII king of England (1509–47).

1513 Scots defeated at Flodden; death of James IV.

Rest of the World

1431 Thais of Siam take Angkor. Phnom Penh new Khmer city.

1438 Inca ascendancy in Peru; high level of astronomical and surgical knowledge; cotton and potato grown.

1441 Maya city of Mayapán conquered by Uxmal.

1453 Hindu Majapahit empire in Java declining; Islam advancing.

1476 Incas conquer Chimú.

1492 Columbus reaches West Indies.

1493 Askia Muhammad emperor of Songhay on Niger, West Africa.

1497 John Cabot reaches mainland North America from Bristol.

1499 Vasco da Gama rounds Cape and reaches Calicut; beginning of Portuguese empire.

1502 Safavid dynasty in Iran: Ismael I (1501–24).

1511 Portuguese conquer Malacca.

Culture/Technology

Masaccio (d. 1428) frescoes.

1420 Dome of Florence Cathedral begun by Brunelleschi.

Donatello: David.

Van Eyck: Arnolfini portrait.

Thomas à Kempis (d. 1471): Imitation of Christ.

Nicholas of Cusa (d. 1464): astronomy; theology; revives Neo-Platonism.

1452–66 Piero della Francesca: Legend of Cross (Arezzo).

1456 Alberti: façade of Santa Maria Novella; Florence centre of artistic activity.

c.1456 Gutenberg Bible. c.40,000 editions printed 1450–1500.

1456–60 Uccello: Battle of S. Romano. Lace in France and Flanders.

1474 Caxton printing at Westminster.

1478 Topkapi Palace in Constantinople.

c.1478 Botticelli: Primavera.

Leonardo (1452–1519): anatomy; mechanics; painting, etc.

Nanak (1469–1539) founds the Sikh religion.

1501 Michelangelo carves David.

c.1504–5 Leonardo paints Mona Lisa.

1505–7 Dürer in Italy.

1506 Bramante designs St Peter's, Rome.

1508–12 Michelangelo: Sistine ceiling.

1509 Watch invented in Nuremberg.

Britain and Europe	Rest of the World	Culture/Technology
1515 *Francis I* king of France (1515–47).		1516 Grünewald: *Isenheim Altar*.
		1516 King's College Chapel, Cambridge completed.
1517 Start of *Protestant Reformation*, Germany.	Ottoman Turks conquer *Egypt*.	*Erasmus'* last visit to England.
1519 *Charles V* (Hapsburg) elected Holy Roman Emperor.	*Cortés* conquers *Aztecs*.	
	Magellan crosses Pacific.	
1521 *Diet of Worms* condemns Luther's teaching.	*Suleiman the Magnificent* sultan of Turkey (1520–66).	1522 Ignatius Loyola: *Spiritual Exercises* (pr. 1548).
1524 *Peasants' War* in Germany.		
1525 France loses control of N. Italy; *Battle of Pavia*.	*c.*1525 *Babur* from Kabul invades India and founds *Mughal dynasty*.	
Reformation moves to Switzerland.		
1526 Battle of *Mohács*. Ottoman Turks occupy Hungary.		
1527 Charles V's troops *sack Rome*.		*Paracelsus* in Basle (new concept of disease).
1529 Ottomans *besiege Vienna*.	Franciscan mission to Mexico.	Early Italian *madrigal*.
Fall of English chancellor *Wolsey*.	European *spice trade* with Asia; *sugar/slaves* with America.	
1533 Henry VIII marries *Anne Boleyn*.	1531–3 *Pizarro* conquers *Inca empire*. *Atahualpa* killed.	
1534 English *Act of Supremacy*; break with papacy.	*Iran* conquered by Ottoman Turks.	*Luther's Bible*.
Anabaptists revolt in Munster, Germany.		Rabelais: *Gargantua*.
		Jesuits founded.
1535 *John Calvin* in Geneva.		
1536 *Dissolution* of English and Welsh *monasteries*.		Calvin: *Institutes*.
1540 Henry VIII tries to impose political and religious settlement on *Ireland*.	1542 *Francis Xavier* in India, Sri Lanka, Japan (1549).	1543 Copernicus: *De revolutionibus*.
		1543 Vesalius: *De humani corporis fabrica*.
1545 *Council of Trent* begins (1545–63).		Calvin: *Letter on Usury*.
1547 *Edward VI* king of England (1547–53).	Portuguese settling coast of *Brazil*.	
Ivan the Terrible crowned tsar (1547–84).		
1553 *Mary Tudor* queen of England (1553–8); persecutes Protestants.		1550 Vasari: *Lives of the Most Excellent Painters* etc.
1555 *Peace of Augsburg*: pacification of Germany; Calvinists persecuted.		
1556 Charles V retires; *Philip II* king of Spain (1556–98).	*Akbar* emperor of India (1556–1605). Expands empire and unites its peoples.	
1558 France recaptures *Calais* from English.	1557 Portuguese found *Macao*.	
Elizabeth I queen (1558–1603).		
1559 *John Knox* active in Scotland.		*Tobacco* enters Europe.
1562 Start of French *Wars of Religion*.		
1563 *Religious settlement* in England; *39 Articles*.		
1567 *Dutch Revolt* begins.		1568–71 Palladio builds *Villa Rotonda* in Vicenza.
Mary Queen of Scots flees to England.		
1570 Pope excommunicates Elizabeth I.		1569 Mercator invents *map projection*.
		1569 Death of *Brueghel*.
1571 *Battle of Lepanto*; Turkish domination of Mediterranean ends.		
1572 *Massacre of St Bartholomew* (French Huguenots).	1573 *Oda Nobunaga*, Japanese warrior, imposes political order on *Japan*.	Camoens: *Os Lusíadas*.

Britain and Europe	Rest of the World	Culture/Technology
1577 Drake's *voyage round the world* begins.	**1576** Last Hindu kingdoms fall to Akbar, who welcomes Jesuits. Spanish expanding *New Spain* and *New Granada* in America.	**1576** Titian: *Pietà*. *El Greco* to Toledo. Tycho Brahe: *De nova stella*.
1579 *Union of Utrecht* unites Protestant Dutch. *Irish* rebels massacred; English *plant settlers*.		**1580–95** Montaigne: *Essais*.
1580 Spain occupies *Portugal*.		
1581 English *Levant Co.* founded.	**1582** Warrior Hideyoshi *unites Japan* and campaigns in Korea (1592, 1598).	
1585 *War of Three Henries* in France. England and Spain *at war*.	**1584** *Walter Raleigh* founds colony of *Virginia*.	
1587 Mary Queen of Scots *executed*.		
1588 *Spanish Armada* defeated. *Duke of Guise* murdered in France.		
1589 *Henry of Navarre* claims throne and besieges Paris.	**1591** *Morocco* conquers Islamic kingdom of *Songhay* on River Niger.	Early *ballet* in France. *c.*1590 Marlowe: *Faustus*. 1590, 1596 Spenser: *Faerie Queene*.
1593 *Henry IV* (1589–1610) accepts *Catholicism* in France.		**1592** *Monteverdi* to Mantua. Early *microscope*; *thermometer*; *water-closet*.
1594 Bad harvests in England (1594–7).		Death of *Palestrina* and *Lasso*.
1598 *Edict of Nantes* ends Wars of Religion in France. *Boris Godunov* Russian tsar (1598–1605).		**1596** Shakespeare: *Romeo and Juliet*.
1599 *Irish revolt* suppressed by Essex and Montjoy (1601).		*Globe Theatre* built.
1600 Rebellion of *Essex* against Elizabeth.	English *East India Co.* formed.	*Giordano Bruno* burnt for theory of universe. 1600–8 *Rubens* in Italy.
1603 *James VI* of Scotland and *James I* of England (1603–25).	*Tokugawa* shogunate established in Japan.	**1602** Shakespeare: *Hamlet*.
1604 Anglo/Spanish *Peace Treaty*.		
1605 *Gunpowder Plot* in English Parliament.	**1607** *Virginia* settled by British.	1605–6 Ben Jonson: *Volpone*. 1605, 1615 Cervantes: *Don Quixote*. **1607** First *opera* in Mantua: Monteverdi, *Orfeo*.
1609 *Dutch Republic* recognized.	**1608** *Quebec* settled by *Champlain* for France.	Shakespeare: *Sonnets*. Galileo: *telescope*. Kepler: *Laws of Planetary Motion*.
1610 *Ulster* planted with English and Scottish settlers. *Louis XIII* king of France (1610–43).		*Caravaggio* dies (1571–1610). 1611 *Authorized Version* of the *Bible*. Shakespeare: *Tempest*.
1613 Russian 'Time of Troubles' ends; *Romanov dynasty* established. *Elizabeth Stuart* marries Elector Palatine.		**1614** John Napier work on *logarithms*.
1618 *Thirty Years War* begins in Europe.	**1616** Japan ejects *Christian missionaries*. *Tobacco* plantations in *Virginia* expanding.	1616–21 *Inigo Jones* designs Banqueting House. **1618** French *salon* established under Marquise de Rambouillet.
1620 Emperor Ferdinand II wins battle of *White Mountain* in Bohemia.	*Pilgrim Fathers* arrive at Cape Cod on *Mayflower*.	F. Bacon: *Novum organum*.
1621 *Philip IV* king of Spain (1621–65).		
1624 *Richelieu* in power in France. Britain and Spain *renew war* (1624–30).		

Britain and Europe	Rest of the World	Culture/Technology
1625 *Charles I* king of England (1625–49).		
1626 *Count Wallenstein* leads Imperial armies in war.	Dutch purchase *Manhattan* (*New Amsterdam*).	
1627 Britain and France at war 1627–9. Richelieu defeats *Huguenots*.		
1629 Charles I governs *without Parliament*.	1630–42 Large-scale British emigration to *Massachusetts*.	1628 W. Harvey: *De motu cordis*.
1630 *Gustavus Adolphus* of Sweden joins Thirty Years War and is killed at *Lützen* (1632).		1632 *Van Dyck* to England.
1633 William Laud elected Archbishop of Canterbury; opposes Puritans in Britain.		Galileo before *Inquisition*; recants.
1634 *Wallenstein* assassinated.		
1635 *France* joins Thirty Years War.		
1637 Charles I faces *crisis in Scotland* over new liturgy.		Corneille: *Le Cid*. Descartes: *Co-ordinate geometry* and *Discours de la méthode*. Waterproof *umbrellas* used at court of Louis XIII of France.
1639 France occupies *Alsace*.	Japan *closed* to all Europeans.	
1640 *Long Parliament* begins. *Portugal* regains *independence* from Spain.		
1642 First *English Civil War* begins. Death of *Richelieu*.	1642–3 *Tasman* explores *Antipodes*.	Rembrandt: *Night Watch*. Pascal's *calculating machine*.
1643 *Louis XIV* king of France (1643–1715). *Mazarin* in power.		Torricelli invents *barometer*.
1644 Charles I defeated at *Marston Moor*.	*Qing* (*Ch'ing*) *dynasty* established in China.	
1645 *New Model Army* formed. Charles defeated at Naseby. War ends (1646).		
1647 *Leveller* influence in Army.		
1648 *Second Civil War*. King accepts defeat; tried and *executed* (1649). *Peace of Westphalia* ends Thirty Years War.	Atlantic *slave trade* expanding.	*c*.1648 *Taj Mahal* completed.
1649 *Cromwell* massacre at *Drogheda*, Ireland.		
1652 *First Anglo-Dutch War*. Cromwell conquers *Scots*.	1652 Dutch found *Cape Colony*.	1650 Air-pump (Germany). *c*.1650 Poussin: *Shepherds of Arcadia*. 1651 T. Hobbes: *Leviathan*.
1653 Oliver Cromwell '*Protector*' (1653–8).		
1654 *Queen Christina* of Sweden abdicates.		1656 Bernini completes piazza of *St Peter's*, Rome.
1658 *Peace of Roskilde* and *Treaty of Pyrenees* (1659) end period of war in Europe.	*Aurangzeb* Mughal emperor (1658–1707); expansion followed by decline after his death.	1656 Huygens invents *pendulum clock*. *c*.1656 Velázquez: *Las Meninas*.
1660 *Charles II* restored as king (1660–85).		*Vermeer* at work.
1661 Louis XIV begins *personal reign*. Colbert minister (1665–83).		1662 *Royal Society* in London. 1662 R. Boyle: *Boyle's law*.
1664 *Second Anglo-Dutch War* (1664–7).	Colbert founds *French East India Co.*	Molière: *Tartuffe*. Frans Hals: *The Regents*.
1665 *Great Plague* of London.		

Britain and Europe	Rest of the World	Culture/Technology
1666 Fire of London.	1667 Hindu Maratha kingdom founded by Sivaji in western India; challenges Mughals.	Academy of Science in France. 1666–7 Newton invents differential calculus. Spirit-level invented. 1667 Milton: Paradise Lost.
1670 French troops occupy Lorraine.	Rise of Ashanti in W. Africa.	1668 Versailles; palace rebuilt by Le Vau, Le Brun, and Le Nôtre. 1670–1720 Wren rebuilds London churches and St Paul's.
1672 Third Anglo-Dutch War (1672–4).	1675 In India Sikhism becomes military theocracy to resist Mughal power.	1671 Mme de Sévigné: correspondence.
1678 Franche-Comté to France.		1676 Van Leeuwenhoek finds microbes with the aid of microscope. 1677 Racine: Phèdre. 1678 Mme de Lafayette: Princesse de Clèves. 1678–84 Bunyan: Pilgrim's Progress.
1682 Peter the Great tsar of Russia (1682–1725).	1681 Pennsylvania founded. Carolinas flourish.	1681 Pressure-cooker invented.
1683 Turks under Kara Mustafa besiege Vienna.		
1685 Edict of Nantes revoked.		
1687 Hapsburgs recover Hungary.		Newton: Principia Mathematica.
1688 English 'Glorious Revolution'; William (1689–1702) and Mary (1689–94) reign.		
1689 War with France (War of League of Augsburg).	Treaty of Nerchinsk between China and Russia, fixing frontiers.	Purcell: Dido and Aeneas.
1690 Battle of the Boyne; Irish and French defeated. French fleet sunk.	1692 Witch trials in Salem.	Locke: Essay concerning Human Understanding.
1697 Treaty of Ryswick ends War of League of Augsburg.		1693 François Couperin to Versailles as court organist. 1698 T. Savery: steam engine.
1700 Charles II (Hapsburg) of Spain dies childless. Philip V (Bourbon) king of Spain (1700–46). Great Northern War (1700–21). Russians defeated by Sweden.		Congreve: Way of the World. Stradivarius: violins.
1701 War of Spanish Succession (1701–13): Britain, Netherlands, Austria, German princes, Savoy, and Portugal against France, Bavaria, and Castile.		
1702 Queen Anne (1702–14).		
1704 Marlborough wins battle of Blenheim. British take Gibraltar.		Newton: Optics (explains colour). 1705 Halley predicts return of his comet.
1706 Battle of Ramillies: Marlborough routs French.		
1707 Act of Union between England and Scotland.		
1708 Battle of Oudenarde: Marlborough's third victory.		J. S. Bach at Weimar.
1709 Battle of Poltava in Northern War ends Swedish hegemony in the Baltic. Last of Marlborough's victories at Malplaquet.	1710 British capture French Acadia (Nova Scotia).	First pianoforte in Italy. 1710 Jansenism persecuted in France.
1711 Queen Anne persuaded to dismiss Marlborough. Ministry led by Bolingbroke who seeks to end war.		Newcomen piston-operated steam engine in England. 1712 Handel to London.

	Britain and Europe	Rest of the World	Culture/Technology
1713	*Treaty of Utrecht*. Philip V confirmed in Spain. Southern Netherlands, Milan, Naples, and Sardinia to Austria. Britain gains *Assiento* to supply *slaves* to Spanish colonies. *Frederick William I* king of Prussia (1713–40).	*Newfoundland*, *St Kitts*, and *Hudson Bay* to Britain.	Bull *Unigenitus* against Jansenists.
1714	*George*, Elector of Hanover, great-grandson of James I, King George I of England and Scotland (1714–27).		*Fahrenheit* devises mercury thermometer.
1715	*Louis XV* king of France (1715–74); Philippe d'Orléans regent. *Jacobite rebellion* suppressed in Scotland and England.	1717 *Shenandoah Valley* settled. Indians evicted.	1716 F. Couperin: *Treatise on harpsichord playing*. 1717 Watteau: *Embarquement pour Cythère*.
1720	*South Sea Bubble*; major financial collapse in London.	Chinese invade *Tibet*.	1719 Defoe: *Robinson Crusoe*.
1721	*R. Walpole* first effective *Prime Minister*, as king often in Hanover (1721–42). Policy of peace and commercial expansion.	French and English *East India Cos.* rivals in India.	
1726	*Cardinal Fleury* chief minister in France (1726–43).		1724 *Bourse* opens in Paris. 1726 Swift: *Gulliver's Travels*. 1726 *Voltaire* liberated from Bastille; goes to England.
1727	Peaceful succession of *George II* (1727–60).	1728 Danish explorer *Bering* discovers Straits. 1729 *North and South Carolina* become Crown Colonies.	1728 Gay and Pepusch: *Beggar's Opera*. 1728 Pope: *Dunciad*. 1729 Bach: *St Matthew Passion*.
1733	*War of Polish Succession* (1733–8). Russia imposes *Augustus III*, elector of Saxony, on Poland.	1732 *James Oglethorpe* founds *Georgia* for 'poor debtors'.	1732 *Trevi Fountain* in Rome. 1733 J. Kay invents *flying shuttle* for weaving (England). 1734 *Fire extinguisher* invented by German physician M. Fuches. 1734 Voltaire: *Lettres philosophiques*. 1735 C. Linnaeus: *Systema naturae*. 1735 Rameau: *Les Indes galantes*.
1739	*War of Jenkins' Ear* between England and Spain.	1738 Sea Captain *R. Jenkins* advocates war in Caribbean against Spain. 1738 In W. Africa Yoruba kingdom of *Oyo* conquers Dahomey.	1738 *Wesley brothers* 'converted'.
1740	*Frederick II* king of Prussia (1740–86); claims *Silesia*, causing *War of Austrian Succession*: Austria, Britain, and Hanover against France, Spain, and Prussia. *Empress Maria Theresa*, queen of Hungary and Bohemia, wife of Francis I (1740–80).	1741 *Bering* discovers *Alaska*. 1741 *Dupleix* commandant-general for French in India.	Richardson: *Pamela*. 1742 *Celsius* devises centigrade scale. 1742 Handel: *Messiah*.
1743	King George II defeats French at *Dettingen*.		
1745	*Jacobite Rebellion* under 'Bonnie Prince Charlie'; ruthlessly suppressed (1746). French king's mistress the Marquise *de Pompadour* influences tastes (rococo) and policies. *Treaty of Dresden* confirms Frederick II in Silesia.	1744–8 *King George's War* in America along St Lawrence.	*Bow Street Runners* in London.
1746	*Battle of Culloden* in Scotland: defeat of Jacobites.	*Madras* taken but returned to Britain after war.	
1747	British win naval battle of *Belle-Isle*.	*Afghanistan* united.	*Sans-souci* palace in Prussia.

Britain and Europe	Rest of the World	Culture/Technology
1748 Treaty of Aix-la-Chapelle ends war in Europe.		Pompeii excavated. Montesquieu: Esprit des lois. 1749 Fielding: Tom Jones.
1750 Pombal, reformist minister, in power in Portugal (1750–82). Spirit of Enlightenment (Voltaire, Diderot, Montesquieu) influencing all of Europe.	East India Companies (English, French, Dutch) trading extensively in Asia: tea becomes fashionable drink in Europe.	Death of J. S. Bach. Symphonic form emerging in music.
1751 Death of Frederick, prince of Wales.		Diderot publishes vol. 1 of Encyclopédie.
1752 Britain adopts Gregorian calendar, leading to rioting.		Franklin devises lightning conductor (used kite to show electrical nature of lightning).
1753 Louis XV exiles Parlement de Paris. Kaunitz Austrian chancellor (1753–92).		Place de la Concorde in Paris. Jewish naturalization in Britain.
1754 Duke of Newcastle leads British ministry.		Buffon: Histoire naturelle (36 vols., 1749–88; revolutionizes thinking on animal kingdom).
1755 Lisbon earthquake.	Braddock expedition in North America against French and Indians; fails to take Fort Duquesne.	S. Johnson: Dictionary. Neoclassical art fashionable.
1756 Outbreak of Seven Years War: Britain, Hanover, Prussia, and Denmark against France, Austria, Russia, and Sweden. R. Pitt (the Elder, later Earl of Chatham) joins ministry.	Rivalry developing in India: French against British.	
1757 Frederick II wins at Rossbach and Leuthen.	Robert Clive commands East India Co. army. Battle of Plassey: Clive defeats Nawab of Bengal and controls the State.	Sextant designed by J. Campbell (England). French physiocrats exalt Nature and the Land. Stimulate agricultural reform in Britain and France.
1758 Choiseul first minister in France. Frederick II defeats Russia at Zorndorf.		Helvétius: De l'Esprit (book burnt for atheism).
1759 'Annus mirabilis': French defeated by Ferdinand of Brunswick at Minden and by Admiral Hawke at Quiberon Bay.	Wolfe captures city of Quebec and British then take Montreal and all colony of Quebec.	1759–67 L. Sterne: Tristram Shandy.
1760 George III, grandson of George II, king (1760–1820).		
1761 Chatham resigns; Bute British PM (1762–3).	Eyre Coote takes Pondicherry from French in India; later returned.	Haydn to court of Esterházy in Hungary.
1762 Accession of Catherine the Great in Russia, deposing her husband Peter III; empress 1762–96; influenced by Diderot and Voltaire and belief in 'Enlightened Despotism'. Russian landowners relieved of military service.	African slave trade begins to attract criticism.	J.-J. Rousseau: Émile and Contrat social. Gluck: Orphée et Euridice.
1763 Peace of Paris ends Seven Years War: France cedes Canada, the Mississippi, and control of India to Britain. J. Wilkes arrested for libel while an MP; expelled from Commons 1764.	American colonists move west into Ohio basin. Fort Duquesne becomes Pittsburgh.	Compulsory education in Prussia.
1764 Jesuits expelled from France.		Voltaire: Dictionnaire philosophique.
1765 Rockingham British PM. American Stamp Act to finance defence of colonies. Joseph II Hapsburg emperor, supported by mother Maria Theresa.	Clive recalled to govern Bengal; accused of corruption (1772).	1765–70 J.-J. Rousseau: Confessions.
1766 Stamp Act repealed. Chatham briefly PM. Lorraine integrated into France.	1766–9 Bougainville's voyage round world, exploring many Pacific islands.	H. Cavendish isolates hydrogen.

Britain and Europe	Rest of the World	Culture/Technology
1767 Catherine publishes *Instructions*, westernizing Russian law.	Increasing *opposition* in British American colonies to control from London through royal governors. W. African kingdom of *Benin* declining in power.	A. Young: *Farmer's Letters.*
1768 *Corsica* purchased by French.	*1768–71 Cook's* voyage in *Endeavour*; charts *New Zealand* and eastern *Australia.*	Robert and William *Adam architects*: Adelphi Terrace. Wright of Derby: *Experiment with an Air-Pump.*
1769 Russia advancing against Turks and Tartars. *Moldavia, Wallachia,* and *Crimea* occupied in war (1769–74). Birth of *Napoleon.*		Improved *steam engine* using condenser patented by J. *Watt.*
1770 *Lord North* ministry in Britain (1770–82). *Crime* increasing in London; Bow Street Runners developing (formed c.1745).	Policies of *North* government cause growing *resentment* in Virginia and Massachusetts. 'Boston Massacre' (5 die).	Edmund Burke: *Thoughts on the Present Discontents.* *Spinning-jenny* patented by J. *Hargreaves*; multiple spindles powered by water.
1771 Johann Struensee reforms in Denmark. Influence of *physiocrats* results in new attitudes to *agriculture* and *animal husbandry* (Arthur Young).		Gainsborough: *Blue Boy.* French *salons* dictate taste to Europe and America.
1772 First *partition of Poland* between Russia, Prussia, and Austria.		Horace Walpole (d. 1797) rebuilds *Strawberry Hill* in Neo-Gothic.
1773 *Russian uprising* to support bogus emperor, the Cossack *Pugachev*. Suppressed by Catherine with great cruelty.	'Boston tea-party' against taxation without representation.	*Iron bridge* at Coalbrookdale. Arthur Young: *Observations on the Present State of the Waste Lands of Great Britain.*
1774 Financial and administrative *chaos* at the end of Louis XV's reign. *Louis XVI* king (1774–93). British Parliament passes *Coercive Acts* against Boston and Massachusetts. Treaty of *Kutchuk Kainarji* recognizes Russian control of *Black Sea.*	*Warren Hastings* governor-general in India; consolidates Clive's conquests.	Goethe: *Sorrows of Young Werther.* J. *Priestley* discovers *oxygen* ('dephlogisticated air').
1776 *Turgot* French minister; tries to reform but condemned; *Necker* succeeds (1777–81). French support American colonies (*La Fayette*).	1775 Second *Continental Congress*, Philadelphia. American revolution; battle of *Bunker Hill.* *Declaration of Independence* signed 4 July by 11 rebel colonies.	1775 Beaumarchais: *Barber of Seville.* *Jenner* discovers principle of vaccination. 1776–88 Gibbon: *Decline and Fall of the Roman Empire.* 1776 Adam Smith: *Wealth of Nations.*
1777 Rapid growth of British *textile industry.*	British take *New York* and *Philadelphia* but are defeated at *Saratoga. Valley Forge*: Washington's winter camp: 11,000 die.	Sheridan: *School for Scandal.* *Lavoisier* theory of respiration. *Sturm und Drang* literary movement.
1778 *Bath* dominates polite British society. France joins *America* in war. *Evangelical churches* reviving in Britain (Methodism), Germany (Pietism), and America (Great Awakening).	1778 Washington revives hope as *France joins war.*	Mozart: *Paris Symphony.* *La Scala* in Milan.
1779 *Spain* joins American war. *Riots* against machines in England.		
1780 *Gordon Riots* in London (mob incitement against proposed easing of anti-Catholic laws); *Wilkes* helps to suppress.		*Bath Pump Room* rebuilt.
1781 *Joseph II* of Austria seeks to modernize the empire as 'Enlightened Despot'.	British take *Charleston* but *Cornwallis* surrenders at *Yorktown*. French admiral *de Grasse* had supremacy at sea (17 Oct. 1781).	Kant: *Critique of Pure Reason.* Planet *Uranus* discovered by *Herschel.*

	Britain and Europe	Rest of the World	Culture/Technology
1782	*Political crisis* in Britain. Fall of Lord North. Lord Rockingham briefly PM.		Laclos: *Les Liaisons dangereuses*. Goethe PM Weimar. *Watt* patents double-acting rotary steam engine.
1783	Fox-North Coalition. *Pitt the Younger* PM (1783–1801). *Treaty of Versailles*: Britain accepts independence of 13 Colonies but retains *West Indies* and *North American* Canadian colonies.	Defeated British *loyalists* leave victorious colonies and move to *New Brunswick* and Prince Edward Island.	*Hot-air balloon* (France).
1784	Russia annexes *Crimea* and founds *Sebastopol* (Potemkin). *East India Act* (East India Co.). *Methodists* split from Church of England.		*Cavendish* synthesizes water H + O.
1785	Pitt's attempt at *parliamentary reform* defeated. Catherine II grants *Charter* to nobility who exploit serfdom in Russia. *Eden commercial treaty* with France.	Warren Hastings returns to Britain to face 7-year trial for *corruption* in India.	David: *Le Serment des Horaces* (neoclassical). *Power loom* patented by *Cartwright* (England). 1786 Mozart: *Marriage of Figaro*.
1787			Schiller: *Don Carlos*. Charles formulates *Law*.
1788	George III's first *insanity*. France *bankrupt*; *Necker* restored.	First British convicts to *Botany Bay* under Philip. Settle in Sydney Bay and create *New South Wales*. *US Constitution* agreed. *George Washington* elected first US President.	Improved horse-drawn *threshing-machine* patented by Meikle.
1789	French Revolution: *Estates General* summoned (5 May); *Bastille* stormed (14 July); *National Assembly* called; French aristocrats flee to England and Germany. Torture ends in France as liberalization of government attempted. French *corvée* ended.	Washington inaugurated Jan. 1789. President until 1797. *Alexander Hamilton* to US Treasury.	Blake: *Songs of Innocence*. *Lavoisier* establishes *modern chemistry*.
1790	France: *Church* lands nationalized; 83 *French Departments*.	US Supreme Court meets in New York.	Burke: *Reflections on the French Revolution*. *Ambulances* in France.
1791	*Counter-revolutionaries* organize military invasion of France from Germany. Louis XVI and Marie Antoinette *under restraint* in Paris. Attempted escape foiled; arrested at *Varennes*. Revolutionary army trained.	Sydney NSW growing with *convict labour*. US *Congress* meets in Philadelphia; selects site of District of Columbia. Slave revolt in *Haiti* under *Toussaint L'Ouverture*.	Mozart dies in poverty. 1791–2 Thomas Paine: *Rights of Man*. *Louvre* becomes a museum.
1792	*Russian empire* extends beyond Black Sea. *French Republic* proclaimed (Sept.); beginning of *Terror*; victory at *Valmy* against Austria.		Mary Wollstonecraft: *Vindication of the Rights of Women*.
1793	*Louis XVI executed* (Jan.). Britain declares *war*; establishes *Board of Agriculture*. *Second partition* of Poland. *Committee of Public Safety* under *Robespierre*. Revolt of *Vendée*; crushed.	George Washington's second term as US President.	
1794	Robespierre *executed* (July).	*Toussaint* defeats Spanish and English force. 'Scottish Martyrs' transported to NSW.	Eli Whitney invents *cotton-gin* in US.

	Britain and Europe	Rest of the World	Culture/Technology
1795	Third partition of Poland. Rural depression and high inflation in Britain; Speenhamland system: poor relief. France under Directory.	'Whisky Rebellion' in US.	Hydraulic press in England.
1796	French campaign in Italy; Bonaparte victor.	John Adams elected US President (1797–1801).	Jenner succeeds with smallpox vaccine.
1797	Talleyrand French foreign minister. Treaty of Campo Formio with Austria; Cisalpine Republic formed; left bank of Rhine annexed. British navy mutinies at Nore.		Cherubini opera: Medea.
1798	Napoleon to Egypt. Helvetian Republic formed. Irish rebellion suppressed.	French invade Egypt.	Hansard: Parliamentary Reports. Malthus: Essay on Population. Lithography invented by Senefelder. Wordsworth: Lyrical Ballads. Coal-gas lighting patented in England.
1799	Napoleon returns to Paris and seizes power as First Consul. European coalition against France. Income tax in Britain and trade unions suppressed.	Nelson destroys French fleet at Aboukir Bay. French siege of Acre defeated by Sidney Smith. Napoleon returns to Paris.	Gas-fire patented (France).
1800	Napoleon defeats Austrians at Marengo. France dominates Italy except for Sicily and Sardinia.	Thomas Jefferson elected US President (1801–9).	Volta makes first battery. Fichte: The Destiny of Man.
1801	Irish Act of Union. First census in Britain. General Enclosure Act in Britain. Concordat between Napoleon and Pope. Alexander I tsar (1801–25).		Chateaubriand: Atala. Gauss: theory of number.
1802	Peace of Amiens. Napoleon annexes Piedmont.		Charlotte Dundas first steamship.
1803	Britain declares war and forms new coalition. Rebellion in Ireland suppressed.	Wellesley defeats Indians in Maratha War. Jefferson purchases Louisiana from Napoleon.	Beethoven: Eroica Symphony. Dalton: atomic theory.
1804	William Pitt again PM. Pope crowns Napoleon emperor. Execution of Duc d'Enghien shocks Europe.	Haiti independent; Toussaint imprisoned and dies in France. 1804–6 Lewis and Clark Expedition across US. Uthman dan Fodio leads jihad against Hausa in W. Africa (1804–8).	Code Civil in France. Trevithick: first steam rail locomotive in S. Wales.
1805	Nelson wins Battle of Trafalgar. Austrians defeated at Austerlitz and make peace.	Mehemet Ali Pasha of Egypt.	
1806	Death of William Pitt. Holy Roman Empire ends. Prussians defeated at Jena. Napoleon institutes Continental System. Confederation of Rhine formed.		Beaufort scale of wind velocity. Ingres: Napoleon on his Throne.
1807	British Orders in Council. Napoleon and Alexander I agree at Tilsit to divide Europe, east and west.	Colombia independence movement from Spain begins in Venezuela under Miranda and Bolivár.	Hegel: Philosophy of History. Fulton paddle-steamer.
1808	Spanish rising against French occupation; Peninsular War begins.	James Madison elected US President (1809–17). Rum Rebellion in NSW.	Gay-Lussac: law of gas expansion. 1808–32 Goethe: Faust.
1809	Renewed war with Austria, defeated at Wagram. British retreat from Corunna. France occupies Papal States.	Macquarie governor NSW. Ecuador independent.	Street lighting on Pall Mall, London.

	Britain and Europe	Rest of the World	Culture/Technology
1810	Wellington in command in Peninsular War.	Britain seizes Cape Colony. Fulani empire in Sokoto.	1810–14 Goya: Disasters of War.
1811	George III insane; prince regent installed (1811–20). British Orders in Council produce economic depression; Luddite riots against machines.	Mehemet Ali overthrows Mamelukes in Egypt. Rules with French advisers till 1849. Ashanti king Osei Bonsu crushes revolts and consolidates kingdom. Battle of Tippecanoe: US settlers defeat Indians. Paraguay independent.	Krupp factory at Essen. Avogadro: Law of atomicity of gases (Italy).
1812	Napoleon marches on Russia. Grand Army retreats from Moscow. British PM Spencer Perceval assassinated. Liverpool PM (1812–27).	War of 1812: US against Britain (1812–14).	Grimm: Fairy Tales. 1812–13 Byron: Childe Harold.
1813	Battle of Leipzig: allies defeat Napoleon. English East India Co. loses monopoly.		Davy: Elements of Agricultural Chemistry. Jane Austen: Pride and Prejudice.
1814	Napoleon abdicates to Elba. Louis XVIII (1814–24) and Ferdinand VII (1808, 1814–33) restored to France and Spain. Jesuits re-established. Congress of Vienna convened.	Treaty of Ghent ends war.	Machine press invented by Koenig prints The Times.
1815	Napoleon returns; 100 days; raises army; defeated at Waterloo; to St Helena. 38 German States form Confederation. Alexander I forms Holy Alliance.	Andrew Jackson wins Battle of New Orleans. US westward expansion begins.	Brighton Pavilion. Davy: miner's lamp.
1816		Congress of Tucumán proclaims United Provinces of South America; against Spain.	Rossini: Barber of Seville. Stethoscope invented (France).
1817	British Habeas corpus suspended; income tax ended. 'Blanketeers' (cotton operatives) march in slump; leaders imprisoned.	James Monroe US President (1817–25).	Ricardo: Principles of Political Economy. John Keats: Poems. 1817–21 Weber: Der Freischütz.
1818		Shaka (d. 1828) forms Zulu kingdom.	Mary Shelley: Frankenstein.
1819	Second Factory Act in Britain. Peterloo 'massacre' (11 killed). Six Acts to suppress unrest.	Raffles founds Singapore. US purchases Florida. Bolívar forms Gran Colombia.	Schubert: Trout Quintet. Géricault: Le Radeau de la Méduse. Macadamized roads stimulate coach travel.
1820	Abortive risings in Portugal, Sicily, Germany, and Spain (Ferdinand suppresses Liberals). Cato Street Conspiracy against Government. George IV king (1820–30).	Missouri Compromise (no slavery in northern part of Louisiana Purchase); settlers beyond the Mississippi.	Percy B. Shelley: Prometheus Unbound. Scott: Ivanhoe. Constable: The Hay Wain. 1820–2 Saint-Simon: Système industriel.
1821	Famine in Ireland. Queen Caroline excluded from coronation. Greek War of Independence starts.	Mexico independent.	Quincy: Confessions of an Opium-Eater.
1822	Castlereagh dies; Canning foreign secretary. Rapid industrialization of NW England and Lowland Scotland (textiles).	Liberia founded for US freed slaves.	Champollion deciphers Egyptian hieroglyphics (Rosetta Stone).
1823	Robert Peel initiates reform of prisons. Daniel O'Connell forms Catholic Association in Ireland.	Monroe Doctrine extends US protection to Spanish-American republics. First Anglo-Burmese War.	C. Macintosh rubberizes cotton (Scotland).
1824	British Combination Acts repealed to allow trade unions. Charles X in France (1824–30); repressive.	Peru independent.	Beethoven: Ninth Symphony. National Gallery founded.

	Britain and Europe	Rest of the World	Culture/Technology
1825	*Nicholas I* tsar of Russia (1825–55). *Decembrist* (rebel army officers) revolt suppressed.	Japan confirms laws of *European exclusion*. *Java War* (1825–30): Dutch establish firm control.	*Stockton and Darlington* railway.
1826	*Mehemet Ali* reconquers Peloponnese in Greek War.	*Brazil* independent. Britain establishes *Straits Settlement*: Penang, Malacca, and Singapore. Seku Ahmadu (Ahmad Lobbo) conquers *Timbuktu*.	J. F. Cooper: *Last of the Mohicans*.
1827	Britain and France send navies and destroy Turkish fleet at *Navarino*. *Canning* British PM; dies and succeeded by *Wellington* (1828–30).	France intervenes in *Algeria*.	*Beethoven* dies in Vienna.
1828	*O'Connell* (Catholic) elected to Parliament.		*BrahmoSamaj* (Hindu sect) formed in India.
1829	Full *Catholic emancipation* granted in Britain. *Metropolitan Police* formed. *Treaty of Adrianople* ends Russo-Turkish war; *Serbia* autonomous.	*Andrew Jackson* US President (1829–37). *Western Australia* founded.	*Braille* invented (France). *Sewing-machine* (France). Stephenson: *Rocket*. Abolition of *suttee* in India.
1830	First *cholera epidemics* in Europe. Charles X deposed; *Louis Philippe* king (1830–48). *William IV* king of England (1830–7). Lord Grey PM. *Swing Riots* in Britain; rural workers ruthlessly suppressed. *Polish rebellion* suppressed. *Belgium* independent.	Mehemet Ali encourages revival of *Arabic culture*. France takes *Algeria*. *Colombia* and *Venezuela* independent.	Stendhal: *Le Rouge et le noir*. Berlioz: *Symphonie fantastique*. *Joseph Smith* founds *Mormons*. Corot: *Chartres Cathedral*.
1831	Major *cholera* epidemic in Britain. *Mazzini* founds *Young Italy Movement*. *Greece* gains independence.		Delacroix: *La Liberté guidant le peuple*. *Darwin* begins voyage on *Beagle*. Bellini: *Norma*.
1832	First *Reform Act* in Britain. *Industrialization* in Belgium and NW France; railways.	*Black Hawk* war in US. His defeat leads to *Trail of Tears*; forcible settlement of Indians in Oklahoma.	*Morse* invents *code*.
1833	*British Factory Act*: child labour regulated.	Abolition of *slavery* in British Empire.	*Oxford Movement* to restore Anglicanism.
1834	British *Poor Law* reformed; *workhouses* created. Creation of German *Zollverein*. *Civil War* in Spain: Carlists against Liberals. Peel's *Tamworth Manifesto*.	Dorset *'Tolpuddle martyrs'* transported to Australia.	
1835	British *Municipal Reform Act*. *Railway boom* (1835–7); Irish labour.	1835–7 *Great Trek* by Afrikaners in Africa.	Donizetti: *Lucia di Lammermoor*. De Tocqueville: *Democracy in America*.
1836		*South Australia* becomes British Province. *Texas* independent from Mexico.	*Neo-Gothic* architecture triumphant. 1836–9 Chopin: *Twenty-four Preludes*.
1837	*Queen Victoria* (1837–1901).	*New Zealand* Association formed in London. Rebellions in *Canada*. *Alafin Atiba* rules *Oyo empire*, Nigeria (c.1837–59).	*Electric telegraph*.
1838	*People's Charter* drawn up in London for universal suffrage.	*Myall Creek* Massacre NSW. *Battle of Blood River* South Africa.	*Daguerreotype* photograph.
1839	*Anti-Corn Law League* founded in Manchester. *Chartist Movement* in Britain (riots).	First *Opium War* in China (1839–42). *Mehemet Ali* defeats Ottoman Turks. *Tanzimat* Reform in Ottoman Empire.	*Fox Talbot* invents negative-positive photo. Faraday: theory of *electromagnetism*. E. A. Poe: *Tales of the Grotesque and Arabesque*.

	Britain and Europe	*Rest of the World*	*Culture/Technology*
1840	Napoleon's ashes return to Paris.	Canadian Provinces *Act of Union*. *Treaty of Waitangi*, NZ: Maori and settlers. *Mzilikazi* leads *Ndebele* people into Transvaal and *Mashonaland*. *Matabeleland* founded by Ndebele.	First *bicycle* in Scotland. *Penny post* in Britain. Proudhon: *On Property*. Schumann: *Lieder cycles*.
1841	*Robert Peel* British PM (1841–6).	*Said ibn Sayyid* makes *Zanzibar* his capital. Britain takes *Hong Kong*.	
1842	*Income tax* reintroduced in Britain. British *Mines Act*: no women or children below 10 years.	Reforms in *Japan*. *US/Canadian border* agreed. *Treaty ports* in China (Treaty of Nanjing). France occupies *Tahiti*. 1842–3 France occupies *Guinea* and *Gabon*.	Verdi's *Nabucco* encourages Italian nationalism. Gogol: *Dead Souls*. Balzac begins *Comédie humaine*. Tennyson: *Morte d'Arthur*.
1843	Rural riots in Wales (*Rebecca*). *Free Church* of Scotland formed in protest against established Presbyterian Church.	Britain conquers *Sind*.	Joule: *theory of thermodynamics*. I. K. Brunel: *SS Great Britain*: first iron/screw ship.
1844	*Bank Charter Act* regularizes British banking. *Rochdale Co-operative Society* formed. *Royal Commission* on Public Health.		Dumas: *Count of Monte Cristo*. Turner: *Rain, Steam, Speed*. Kierkegaard: *Concept of Dread*.
1845	*Potato famine* in Ireland; 1 m. die; 8 m. emigrate. *Second Railway boom* in Britain (1845–7).	US annexes *Texas*. *Sikh Wars* (1845–8/9).	Engels: *Condition of the Working Class in England*. Disraeli: *Sybil*. 1845–9 Daumier: *Les Gens de justice*. *Galvanized corrugated iron* patented (England).
1846	Corn Laws repealed; *Peel resigns*; Lord *John Russell* PM (1846–52).	Second *Xhosa War*, Southern Africa. *Mexican-US War* (1846–8).	
1847	*Il Risorgimento* in Italy. *Factory Act* in Britain: 10-hour day.		Charlotte Brontë: *Jane Eyre*. Emily Brontë: *Wuthering Heights*.
1848	Charter *rejected*. British *Public Health Act*. Revolutions in Europe and Ireland. *Second French Republic*. Cholera in Europe.	*Gold* discovered in *California*. *Irish emigrants* to US. Abolition of *slavery* in French West Indies. Britain annexes *Punjab* and subdues *Sikhs*.	Liszt at Weimar. *Communist Manifesto*.
1849	Short-lived Roman Republic (Pope in exile). Revolutions *suppressed*; Garibaldi defeated in Italy and *Pope restored*; Austria defeats Hungarian nationalists. *Leopold II* restored in Tuscany; repressive regime.	California *gold-rush*.	*Safety-pin* patented.
1850		*Taiping Rebellion* in China; leader Hong Xiuquan (Hung Siu-tsuen); egalitarian beliefs; weakens Qing (Ch'ing) dynasty.	Millet: *Le Semeur*. Courbet: *L'Enterrement à Ornans* (salon scandal). Nathaniel Hawthorne: *Scarlet Letter*. Kelvin: *law of conservation of energy*.
1851	Fall of French Second Republic; coup by *Louis Napoleon*; plebiscite approves.	*Gold* in Australia; settlers moving into *Victoria*.	Paxton: Crystal Palace. *Great Exhibition* in Crystal Palace.
1852	*Aberdeen* British PM (1852–5). *Napoleon III* founds French *Second Empire*. *Cavour* premier of *Piedmont*.	Second *Anglo-Burmese War*. 1852–6 *Livingstone* crosses Africa. *Transvaal* independent.	W. H. Hunt: *Light of the World*.

	Britain and Europe	Rest of the World	Culture/Technology
1853	Gladstone's first budget. Fighting in Crimea; Russia against Turkey.	First railways and telegraph in India. Gadsden purchase by Mexico (US). Russia completes conquest of Kazakhstan.	Hypodermic syringe (France). Verdi: La Traviata.
1854	Crimean War develops; France and Britain join Turkey; Siege of Sebastopol; Nightingale to hospital at Scutari. British Civil Service reformed.	US forces Japan to end isolation (Treaty of Kanagawa). Eureka Rebellion in Victoria. Tukulor empire in Africa (al-Hajj Umar 1795–1864). US Republican Party founded. France annexes Senegal.	Catholic dogma of Immaculate Conception.
1855	Palmerston British PM (1855–8).	Railways in South America: Chile (1851), Brazil (1854), Argentina (1857).	Telegraph news stories of Crimean War. Walt Whitman: Leaves of Grass. Courbet: L'Atelier. 1855–6 Mendel discovers laws of heredity.
1856	Peace of Paris ends war; Danube open; Black Sea closed to warships.	Britain annexes Oudh. 1856–60 Second Chinese Opium War; Anglo-French force sacks Summer Palace and Peking; China open to European trade; Japanese trade agreement.	Synthetic colours invented.
1857	Mazzini hugely popular in London; Italian nationalism growing.	1857–8 Indian Mutiny; atrocities on both sides.	Baudelaire: Fleurs du mal. Flaubert: Madame Bovary. Trollope: Barchester Towers.
1858	Lionel Rothschild first Jewish MP. Government of India transferred from East India Co. to Crown.	Burton and Speke discover Lake Tanganyika. Fenians founded in US.	Lourdes miracles reported.
1859	Battles of Solferino and Magenta; French support Italians against Austria.	John Brown at Harper's Ferry.	J. S. Mill: On Liberty. Darwin: Origin of Species. Oil pumped in Pennsylvania.
1860	Garibaldi's 1000; Nice and Genoa to France.	1860–70 Taranaki Wars in New Zealand; Maori against settlers. Lincoln elected US President (1861–5); S. Carolina secedes from Union.	H. Bessemer mass production of steel. Huxley defends theory of evolution.
1861	Victor Emmanuel king of Italy (1861–78). Death of Prince Albert. Russia abolishes serfdom.	Bombardment of Fort Sumter leads to Civil War in US (1861–5). First Battle of Bull Run.	George Eliot: Silas Marner. Siemens developing open-hearth steel production.
1862	Bismarck minister-president of Prussia.	France annexes Cochin-China.	H. Spencer: First Principles (sociology). Victor Hugo: Les Misérables.
1863		Battle of Gettysburg; Union victory. Emancipation of US slaves. French protectorate of Cambodia.	Manet: Déjeuner sur l'herbe (salon scandal). Maxwell: theory of electromagnetism.
1864	Russia suppresses Polish revolt. First Socialist International in London (Karl Marx organizes). H. Dunant founds Red Cross.	French install Maximilian emperor of Mexico (shot 1867). Sherman march through Georgia.	Dickens: Our Mutual Friend. Jules Verne: Voyage to Centre of the Earth.
1865	Earl Russell British PM (1865–6).	1865–70 Paraguayan War: Brazil, Argentina, and Uruguay against Paraguay; ends in disaster for the latter. Lee surrenders at Appomattox. Lincoln assassinated; Andrew Johnson US President (1865–9).	Wagner: Tristan und Isolde. Lewis Carroll: Alice's Adventures in Wonderland. Pasteur publishes theory of germs causing disease.
1866	Lord Derby British PM (1866–8); Second Reform Bill.	1866–73 Livingstone third journey in Africa.	Dostoevsky: Crime and Punishment. Swinburne: Poems and Ballads.

Britain and Europe	Rest of the World	Culture/Technology
Prussia defeats Austria at *Sadova* (Seven Weeks War).	US *Reconstruction* Laws. US *Fourteenth Amendment* to Constitution.	
1867 Prussia forms *North German Confederation*; Austria forms *Austro-Hungarian* empire. *Fenian* rising. *Second British Reform Act.*	US purchases *Alaska* from Russia. *British North America Act* (Canada Dominion). *Meiji Restoration* in Japan; end of shogunates.	Karl Marx: *Das Kapital*. Ibsen: *Peer Gynt*. *Japanese art* arrives in West (Paris World Fair).
1868 *Gladstone* British PM (1868–74). British *TUC* formed.		W. Collins: *The Moonstone*. *Helium* discovered. First *refrigeration* ship. *Traffic signal* installed at Westminster, London.
1869 *Irish Church* disestablished.	Wyoming grants *women suffrage*.	*Suez Canal* opens. *Transcontinental Rail* (US). *Liquefaction of gases* (Andrews).
1870 Gladstone's *Irish Land Act*. British *elementary education*. Franco-Prussian War: Napoleon III defeated at *Sedan*; dethroned and exiled. *Papal Rome* annexed by Italy.	*Standard Oil* Company in US.	Doctrine of *papal infallibility*.
1871 French *Third Republic* suppresses *Paris Commune* and loses *Alsace-Lorraine* to *Second German empire*. British *trade unions* gain legality. *Bismarck* opposes Catholic church in '*Kulturkampf*' and establishes secular school system.	*Stanley* finds *Livingstone* at Ujiji. *Vancouver* and *British Columbia* join Canada. *Ku-Klux-Klan* suppressed in US.	
1872 *Scottish Education Act. Secret ballot* in Britain. British *Coal Mine Act.*		*Cézanne* settles in Provence. *Air brakes* patented (Westinghouse). Dewar: *vacuum flask*.
1873 *Marshall Mac-Mahon* President of France (1873–9).	Feudalism suppressed in Japan; modernization begins. *1873–1903 Aceh War*: Dutch suppress revolt in *Sumatra*.	Monet: *Impression: Sunrise*. Cézanne: *La Maison du pendu à Auvers*. *1873–7* Tolstoy: *Anna Karenina*. Remington *typewriter*.
1874 *Disraeli* forms British government (1874–80). *French Factory* act bans children under 12.	British Colony of *Gold Coast*. US Reconstruction *collapsing*; southern States impose *racist legislation*.	First *Impressionist Exhibition*: Monet, Sisley, Renoir, Pissarro, Degas, Cézanne.
1875 Britain buys control of *Suez Canal*. *Public Health Act; Artisans Dwelling Act.*	*New Zealand* Parliament formed. *Savorgnan de Brazza* to Congo.	*Bell* patents *telephone*. Bizet: *Carmen*.
1876 Turkish *massacre* of Bulgarians; European outcry.	Victoria *Empress of India*. Battle of *Little Bighorn* (Custer's death). *Indian nationalism* growing.	*Plimsoll line* for ships. Brahms: *First Symphony*.
1877 *Russo-Turkish War*; Russians threaten Constantinople; ended by *Treaty of San Stefano* (March 1878).	Last *Xhosa War* in South Africa. Britain annexes *Transvaal*. *Satsuma Rebellion* in Japan suppressed.	*Gramophone* (Edison). Tchaikovsky: *Swan Lake*. *c.1877 Microphones* developed by Berliner, Edison, and Hughes.
1878 *Congress of Berlin* settles Balkan crisis. *Salvation Army* created in Britain. *Serbian* independence.	Britain gains *Cyprus*. *1878–80* Britain fights *Second Afghan War*.	Gilbert and Sullivan: *HMS Pinafore*.
1879 *Dual Alliance*: Germany and Austria-Hungary. *Michael Davitt* forms *Irish Land League*; Parnell first President.	*Zulu War* in Africa. *1879–83 War of Pacific*: Peru and Bolivia against Chile (backed by Britain) for saltpetre; Bolivia land-locked.	First *tramways* (Berlin).

Britain and Europe	Rest of the World	Culture/Technology
1880 Gladstone's *Midlothian campaign* wins election.	1880–1 First *Boer War*: Britain releases *Transvaal* and *Orange Free State*.	Swan perfects *carbon-filament lamp*. Development of *seismograph*. Rodin: *La Porte de l'Enfer*.
1881 Irish *Land and Coercion Acts*. Assassination of *Alexander II*. *Jewish pogroms* in eastern Europe. *Alexander III* (1881–94).	1881–98 *Mahdi Holy War* in Sudan.	Nietzsche: *Aurora*. International *Electricity Exhibition* Paris.
1882 *Triple Alliance*: Germany, Austria, Italy. *Phoenix Park murders*, Dublin. Jules Ferry *'Loi scolaire'* secularizes French schools.	British occupy *Egypt*. French protectorate of *Tonkin*.	First *generating station* (New York). Manet: *Folies-Bergère*.
1883 *Plekhanov* founds Russian Marxist Party. Prussian *Social Security laws* (1883–7).	*Jewish* immigration to Palestine (Rothschild Colonies). Germany acquires *SW Africa*.	
1884 *Dreikaiserbund* renewed. *Third British Reform Act*. *Berlin Conference* on West African colonies.	1884–5 *Sino-French* war.	*Rayon* artificial fibres (France).
1885 *Lord Salisbury* British PM (1885–6). *Redistribution Act*.	Mahdi takes Khartoum; death of *Gordon* (Jan.). *Canadian Pacific* complete. All *Burma* occupied by British. *Gold* in Transvaal. *Belgian Congo* under *Leopold II*.	1885–98 Degas: *Femmes à leur toilette*. *Motor cycle* (Daimler). *Motor car* (Benz). *Pasteur* anti-*rabies* vaccine. Zola: *Germinal*.
1886 *Gladstone* British PM but resigns over Irish Home Rule. *Joseph Chamberlain* forms *Liberal Unionists*. Salisbury PM (1886–92). *Anti-Semitism* increasing throughout Europe.	*Slavery* ends in *Cuba*. *Tunisia* under French protectorate. *Royal Niger Co.* Charter. First Indian National *Congress* meets.	Rimbaud: *Les Illuminations*.
1887 Victoria *Golden Jubilee*. Industrial unrest in UK; *Trafalgar Square riots*. French General Boulanger fails to gain office.	British *East Africa Co.* Charter.	Conan Doyle: *Sherlock Holmes* stories. *Radio waves* (Hertz).
1888 British *match-girls* strike. *County Councils* formed. *William II* emperor of Germany (1888–1918).	French *Indo-China* established. *Slavery* ends in *Brazil*.	*Pneumatic tyre* (Dunlop). *Van Gogh* to Arles.
1889 *British South Africa Co.* chartered. *London Dock strike*. Second Socialist *International*.	Japanese *Meiji Constitution*. Italy takes *Somalia* and *Ethiopia*. *Oklahoma* Indian territory opened for settlers.	*Eiffel Tower*, Paris. *Linotype* printing machine (Germany). 1889–93 Verdi: *Falstaff*.
1890 Support for Boulanger wanes. *Parnell* resigns (*divorce* scandal). *Bismarck* dismissed.	Australian *Maritime strike*. Battle of *Wounded Knee*.	Death of *Van Gogh*. Mascagni: *Cavalleria rusticana*.
1891 *Social Democrats* in Germany adopt Kautsky's *Erfurt programme*. *Trans-Siberian Railway* begun.	*Shearers' Strike* in Australia. Australian demands for trade protection and unification. *Young Turk* movement founded.	*Gauguin* to Tahiti. Toulouse-Lautrec: *Le Bal du Moulin-Rouge*.
1892 *Sergei Witte* Russian finance minister (1892–1903); modernizes finance. *Alexander III* forms alliance with France. Gladstone's *Fourth Ministry*. First *Labour MP*. French *Factory Act*: 11-hour day for women and children aged 13–16.		Maeterlinck: *Pelléas et Mélisande*.

	Britain and Europe	Rest of the World	Culture/Technology
1893	Second Irish Home Rule Bill rejected by Lords. Independent Labour Party formed.	South Africa Co. of Rhodes wages Matabele War. France annexes Laos and Ivory Coast. Women's suffrage in New Zealand.	Tchaikovsky: Sixth Symphony. Dvořák: New World Symphony.
1894	French President Carnot assassinated. Nicholas II tsar (1894–1917). Lord Rosebery PM (1894–5). Death duties in Britain.	1894–5 Sino-Japanese War; China overwhelmingly defeated. Pullman strike in US.	Kipling: Jungle Book. Escalator lifts (US).
1895	Lord Salisbury PM (1895–1902); strongly imperialist government.	Cuban rebellion begins. Japan takes Taiwan (Formosa). In Transvaal Kruger seeks to exclude uitlanders; Jameson Raid (1896).	Lumière Brothers: cinema. X-rays discovered (Röntgen). Wilde: Importance of Being Earnest. Gillette safety-razor.
1896	Zionism founded by Herzl. First Olympic Games in Athens. Kaiser William supports Kruger.	Italian defeat at Adowa. French occupy Madagascar.	T. Hardy: Jude the Obscure. Radioactivity of uranium.
1897	Victoria Diamond Jubilee. Dreyfus Affair in France.	British destroy Benin City.	J. J. Thomson: the electron. Bergson: Matter and Memory. Compression ignition engine (Diesel). Monotype printing (US). Aspirin marketed.
1898	German naval expansion rapid under Tirpitz.	Spanish-American War: Spain loses Cuba, Puerto Rico, and Philippines. British conquer Sudan (Omdurman and Fashoda Incident). Hundred Days Reform in China defeated by Empress. Curzon viceroy in India. Sudan under Anglo-Egyptian protectorate.	Zola: J'accuse. Curies: radium.
1899	Second Boer War (1899–1902); strong Liberal objections. Dreyfus pardoned.	British disasters in South Africa; relief of Mafeking. Boxer Rising in China.	
1900	British 'Khaki' Election. Labour Representation Committee formed. Boer War concentration camps arouse European criticism.	First Pan-African Conference.	First Zeppelin. Planck: quantum theory. Freud: Interpretation of Dreams. Conrad: Lord Jim. Puccini: Tosca. First agricultural tractor.
1901	Death of Victoria, an end of era. Edward VII (1901–10).	Commonwealth of Australia formed. British protectorates in Nigeria. US President McKinley assassinated. Theodore Roosevelt President (1901–9).	Hearing-aid patented (US). Strindberg: Dance of Death. 1901–4 Picasso: Blue Period.
1902	Balfour British PM (1902–5). Education Act creates secondary schools. German investment in Ottoman empire.	Peace of Vereeniging ends Boer War. Anglo-Japanese Alliance.	Gide: L'Immoraliste.
1903	Bolshevik/Menshevik split. Pogroms in Russia. Suffragette movement begins (WSPU).	Mass European emigration to US. Panama Zone to US. Britain takes Sokoto; ends Fulani empire.	Electrocardiograph. Wright Brothers' flight. Henry James: The Ambassadors.
1904	Franco-British Entente Cordiale.	1904–5 Russo-Japanese War; Russian fleet sunk.	Chekhov: Cherry Orchard. Photoelectric cell.
1905	Germany opposes French expansion in Morocco; international crisis to be resolved by conference at Algeciras (1906). First Russian Revolution. Liberal government in Britain; Campbell-Bannerman PM (1905–8).	Japanese protectorate of Korea.	R. Strauss: Salome. Einstein: Special theory of relativity. Debussy: La Mer. Early brain surgery (Cushing in US).

	Britain and Europe	Rest of the World	Culture/Technology
1906	*Liberals* win election. *Russian Duma.* UK *Trade Disputes Act.* *Clemenceau* French PM (1906–9). French strikes suppressed.	Revolution in *Iran*; parliament granted. *Muslim League* founded India.	Matisse: *Bonheur de vivre.* Vitamins discovered (Hopkins). 1906–7 Gorky: *The Mother.*
1907	*Anglo-Russian Entente.* *Labour Party* formed.	*New Zealand* Dominion.	G. B. Shaw: *Major Barbara.* Electric *washing-machine.* *Diaghilev* Ballet.
1908	*Bulgaria* independent. *Bosnia-Herzegovina* occupied by Austrians. Asquith British PM (1908–16).		Borstal system in UK. 1908–9 Mahler: *Das Lied von der Erde.*
1909	Lloyd George 'People's Budget' rejected by Lords. *Old Age Pensions* begin. *Dreadnought* programme.	*Congo Free State* under Belgian parliament. *Young Turk* revolution in Turkey. US supports revolution in *Nicaragua.* *Oil-drilling* in Iran by British.	*Model T car* (Ford).
1910	British *constitutional crisis* over Lords. *George V* king (1910–36).	*Union of South Africa.* Japan annexes *Korea.*	E. M. Forster: *Howards End.* 1910–13 Russell: *Principia mathematica* (with Whitehead). Kandinsky: *Concerning the Spiritual in Art.* Brancusi: *La Muse endormie.* *Post-Impressionist* Exhibition, London.
1911	British *constitutional crisis* resolved; *Parliament Act* restricts Lords. *National Insurance* provides sickness benefits. Industrial unrest in UK.	Amundsen reaches *South Pole.* Chinese revolution; *Sun Yixian* (Sun Yatsen) establishes *republic* (1912).	Rutherford: *nuclear model of atom.* 1911–13 Stravinsky: *Sacre du printemps.*
1912	*Balkan Wars* 1912–13: Greece, Serbia, Bulgaria, and Montenegro against Ottoman Turks.	*Italy* conquers *Libya.* ANC formed in South Africa. *Titanic* sinks. French protectorate in *Morocco.* W. *Wilson* elected US President (1913–21).	Jung: *Psychology of Unconscious.* Schoenberg: *Pierrot lunaire.* A. Fournier: *Le Grand Meaulnes.* First *parachute* descent from aircraft. *Stainless steel.*
1913	*Ulster Volunteers* formed. Treaties of *London* and *Bucharest:* Turkey loses European lands except Constantinople. *Crisis* in Ireland. British *suffragettes.*		*Geiger-counter* invented. D. H. Lawrence: *Sons and Lovers.* Apollinaire: *Les Peintres cubistes.* 1913–27 Proust: *A la recherche du temps perdu.*
1914	Assassination at *Sarajevo* 28 June. Outbreak of *First World War.* BEF at *Mons;* first battle of *Ypres* and *Marne.* *Trench warfare.* Battle of *Tannenburg;* Hindenburg takes 100,000 Russians prisoner.	*Panama Canal* opens. *Egypt* British *protectorate.*	1914–21 Berg: *Wozzeck.*
1915	*Dardanelles/Gallipoli* (March 1915–Jan. 1916). Asquith forms *coalition.* *Zeppelin* raids.	Japan imposes *21 Demands* on China.	Einstein: *General theory of relativity.*
1916	Battles of *Verdun, Somme,* and *Jutland.* Irish *Easter Rising,* Dublin. Lloyd George PM (1916–22).	*Mesopotamia* campaign. British disaster of *Kut-el-Amara.* 1916–18 *Arab revolt* against Ottoman Turks.	*Dada* movement.
1917	*Russian Revolutions* ('Feb.' and 'Oct.'). *Nicholas II* abdicates. *Passchendaele.* British *convoy system.*	*US enters First World War.* British take *Baghdad.* *Balfour Declaration* on Palestine.	Pound: *Cantos.* Kafka: *Metamorphosis.* Lenin: *The State and Revolution.* New Orleans jazz: first recording. De Chirico: *Le Grand Métaphysique.*

Britain and Europe	Rest of the World	Culture/Technology
1918 Second battle of *Marne*; *tanks* help final allied advance. *Armistice* (Nov.). Women's *suffrage* UK.	British take *Palestine* and *Syria*; battle of *Megiddo*. Ottomans make peace.	G. M. Hopkins: *Poems* (posthumous). Spengler: *Decline of the West*.
1919 *Spartacist* revolt *Germany*. *Sinn Fein* in Ireland. *Poland, Hungary, Czechoslovakia, Estonia, Lithuania, Latvia* become republics. *Third International*, Moscow. *Versailles Peace Settlement*.	Arab rebellion in *Egypt* against British. *Amritsar Massacre* in India. *Prohibition* in US.	Elgar: *Cello Concerto*. *Alcock* and *Brown* fly Atlantic. Keynes: *Economic Consequences of the Peace*.
1920 IRA formed. *League of Nations*. *Weimar Republic* threatened by *Kapp Putsch*.	*Gandhi* dominates Indian Congress. *W. Wilson's* health fails; Senate *rejects* Versailles. *Marcus Garvey* in New York.	
1921 *Irish Civil War* (1921–4).	*1921–2 Washington Conference* on disarmament. *1921–6 Spanish war* against Berbers of Rif. *Chinese Communist Party* founded. *King Faisal* in Iraq.	C. Chaplin: *The Kid*. Pirandello: *Six Characters in Search of an Author*.
1922 USSR formed. Italian *fascists* march on Rome. *Mussolini* forms government. *Bonar Law* British PM (1922–3).	*King Fuad* installed in Egypt.	J. Joyce: *Ulysses*. T. S. Eliot: *Waste Land*. Max Weber: *Society and Economy*.
1923 German *hyper-inflation*. French occupy *Ruhr*. *Munich putsch* fails. *Baldwin* British PM.	*Ottoman empire ends*; Palestine, Transjordan, and Iraq to Britain; Syria to France.	S. Spencer: *The Resurrection*. Le Corbusier: *Vers une architecture*. First *talkie*.
1924 First *Labour government*; *MacDonald* PM. Death of *Lenin*. *Dawes Plan*. *Baldwin* PM (1924–9).	*Northern Rhodesia* British protectorate. US economy booming. *Achimota College* in Gold Coast.	
1925 *Stresemann* German foreign minister. *Locarno Pact*.	*Reza Khan* shah in Iran. *Chiang Kai-shek* launches campaign to unify China.	Hitler: *Mein Kampf*. Discovery of *ionosphere*. F. Scott Fitzgerald: *Great Gatsby*. *Surrealist* Exhibition in Paris. B. Keaton: *films*. Eisenstein: *Battleship Potemkin*.
1926 Germany joins League of Nations. British *General Strike* fails after nine days. *Gramsci* imprisoned in Italy.	France establishes Republic of *Lebanon*. *Emperor Hirohito* in Japan (1926–89).	First *television*.
1927 *Stalin* comes to power; *Trotsky* expelled from Party. *Red Army* develops in USSR. British *Trade Disputes Act* restricts trade unions. *Lindbergh* flies Atlantic.	Execution of *Sacco* and *Vanzetti* in US causes international outrage.	BBC founded.
1928 Soviet *collectivization*. *Nazis* and *Communists* compete in Germany. Women over 21 *enfranchised* in UK. *Stresemann* dies.	*Kellogg–Briand Pact* for peace.	Yeats: *Tower*. Ravel: *Bolero*. *Penicillin* discovered. W. Disney: *Mickey Mouse*. 1928–9 W. Walton: *Viola Concerto*.
1929 *Trotsky* exiled. *Lateran Treaty* in Italy. *Yugoslavia kingdom* under kings of Serbia.	*Wall Street Crash*. *Young Plan* for Germany.	

Britain and Europe	Rest of the World	Culture/Technology
Second *Labour government* under MacDonald. *Great Depression* begins.		
1930 London *Round-Table Conferences* on India 1930–2.	*Gandhi* leads *Salt March* in India. *Revolution* in Brazil; *Vargas* president.	E. Waugh: *Vile Bodies.* W. H. Auden: *Poems.* N. Coward: *Private Lives.* *Turbo-jet engine* patented by *Whittle.* Planet *Pluto* discovered. 1930–1 Walton: *Belshazzar's Feast.* 1930–1 Empire State Building in New York.
1931 *Global depression* worsens. *Alfonso XIII* flees; *Spanish Republic* formed. British *National government* under MacDonald (1931–5).	*Jiangxi Soviet* in China. *New Zealand* independent. *Japan* occupies *Manchuria.*	
1932 British *Union of Fascists* formed.	*Gandhi* campaigns for Indian *Untouchables.* *14 m. unemployed* in US. *Ottawa Conference.* Kingdoms of *Saudi Arabia* and *Iraq* independent.	*Cockcroft and Walton* split atom. James Chadwick: *neutron.* First *autobahn,* Cologne-Bonn, opened.
1933 *Nazi Party* wins *German elections. Hitler* appointed *chancellor; racist laws* (anti-Semitic) in Germany.	F. D. Roosevelt US President (1933–45); *New Deal. Batista* president of *Cuba.*	Malraux: *La Condition humaine.* Lorca: *Blood Wedding.*
1934 *Night of the Long Knives* in Germany; Hitler purges all rivals, including *Ernst Röhm; Third Reich* formed. Stalin *purges* begin.	1934–5 China *Long March. Purified National Party* in South Africa with ideology of *apartheid.*	H. Miller: *Tropic of Cancer.* A. Christie: *Murder on the Orient Express.*
1935 Nuremberg Laws: German *Jews* lose citizenship. *Stresa Agreement. Baldwin* British PM.	*Philippines* self-government. Italy invades *Ethiopia. Prempeh II Asantehene* in *Gold Coast.*	
1936 *Edward VIII* abdicates; *George VI* (1936–52). L. Blum *'Popular Front'* government in France. *Anti-Comintern Pact* (Japan and Germany). *Spanish Civil War* (1936–9). *Rhineland* reoccupied.	*Japan* signs *anti-Comintern Pact. Japan* invades *China;* war 1937–45.	Mao Zedong (Tse-tung): *Strategic Problems of Revolutionary War.* Dali: *Soft Construction with Boiled Beans: Premonition of Civil War.* A. J. Ayer: *Language, Truth, and Logic.* Prokofiev: *Peter and the Wolf.*
1937 *Chamberlain* British PM (1937–40).	*Arab/Jewish* conflict in Palestine. Chinese Civil War *truce;* massacre of *Nanjing.*	Picasso: *Guernica.* Orwell: *Road to Wigan Pier.* *Photocopier* patented US.
1938 Austrian *Anschluss* with Germany. *Munich Crisis.* Czechoslovakia cedes *Sudetenland. IRA* bombings in England.	*Pan-Africanism* gaining strength in East and West Africa.	*Fluorescent* lighting US. *Nylon* patented US. G. Greene: *Brighton Rock.* Marx Brothers: films (1929–46). *Nuclear fission* discovered. Pauling: *Nature of Chemical Bond.*
1939 *Nazi/Soviet Pact. Poland* invaded. *Franco* caudillo of Spain. Britain and France *declare war* on Germany.		
1940 Occupation by Germans of *France, Belgium,* the *Netherlands, Norway, Denmark.* British retreat from *Dunkirk. Vichy* government in France. *Churchill* PM (1940–5). German *bombing* of Britain (day, 1940; and night).		

Britain and Europe	Rest of the World	Culture/Technology
1941 Balkans occupied. German invasion of Soviet Union; scorched earth policy; siege of Leningrad.	Italians expelled from Somalia and Ethiopia and Eritrea. Lend-Lease by US. Atlantic Charter (Churchill and Roosevelt). Pearl Harbor: loss of Philippines and Pacific islands. US enters war. Malaya, Singapore, and Burma to Japan.	O. Wells: Citizen Kane. Messiaen to Paris Conservatoire.
1942 Dieppe raid disaster. Beveridge Report. Battle of Stalingrad; Germany surrenders (1943).	Midway Island (June) and El Alamein (Nov.) key battles. Brazil enters war.	Nuclear reactor built (Fermi). Camus: L'Étranger.
1943 Allied bombing of Germany. Battle of Kursk (4000 tanks). Allies invade Italy; Mussolini deposed and Fascist Party ends.		Cousteau and Gagnan: aqualung. Sartre: Being and Nothingness. Kidney machines. T. S. Eliot: Four Quartets.
1944 Normandy invasion; Paris liberated; NW Europe campaign. Arnhem disaster. British Education Act. Civil War in Greece (1944–9).	MacArthur begins reconquest. 1944–5 Burma recaptured. Battle of Leyte Gulf (Oct.). Burma Road to China reopened.	Holmes: Principles of Physical Geography. 1944–6 Eisenstein: Ivan the Terrible.
1945 Yalta Agreement. War ends Europe (May). United Nations formed. Labour wins British election; Attlee PM (1945–51). Potsdam Conference.	Death of Roosevelt; Truman US President (1945–53). Pan-African Conference (Manchester). Atomic bombs on Hiroshima and Nagasaki. War ends (Sept.). Wars of independence in Indo-China and Indonesia. Civil War in China (1945–9).	Olivier: Henry V. B. Britten: Peter Grimes. J. Pollock: abstract expressionist painting, New York.
1946 Cold War begins. In Britain National Health Service and National Insurance. Italian Republic formed.	Perón President in Argentina. Jordan independent.	
1947 Fuel, power, transport nationalized. Marshall Plan for Europe, rejected by Soviets. Puppet Communist States in eastern Europe.	India independent.	Transistor US. Genet: The Maids. Tennessee Williams: Streetcar named Desire.
1948 Berlin airlift.	Ceylon in Commonwealth. 1948–60 Malayan emergency. Apartheid legislation in South Africa. Gandhi assassination.	Brecht: Caucasian Chalk Circle.
1949 Comecon and NATO formed. Republic of Ireland formed. Communist regime in Hungary.	Truman's Point Four aid program. People's Republic in China.	Orwell: 1984. Manchester MkI computer. Simone de Beauvoir: The Second Sex.
1950 Schuman Plan: France and Germany to pool coal and steel industries. Labour Party wins election in Britain; retains power.	1950–3 Korean War. China conquers Tibet.	Stereophonic sound (2-track tape; phonograph record, 1958). Ionesco: The Bald Prima Donna. Rashomon; West discovers Japanese film. First successful kidney transplant. F. Hoyle: Nature of Universe.
1951 Conservatives win election; Churchill PM (1951–5).	Colombo Plan. Anzus pact in Pacific. Cyprus bid for independence.	Stravinsky: Rake's Progress. Matisse: Vence windows.
1952 Britain tests atomic bomb. European Coal and Steel Community formed; Britain refuses to join. Elizabeth II queen (1952–).		Hemingway: Old Man and the Sea. Beckett: Waiting for Godot.

	Britain and Europe	Rest of the World	Culture/Technology
1953	Death of *Stalin*. Conservative government in UK *denationalize* iron (1952), steel, and road transport.	*Egyptian Republic* formed. 1953–7 *Mau Mau* emergency Kenya. *McCarthy* era in US. *Eisenhower* US President (1953–61). *Central African Federation* formed (1953–63). *Korean War* ends.	Crick and Watson: double helix structure of *DNA*. Dylan Thomas: *Under Milk Wood*.
1954	Britain rejects French *European Defence Plan*, which collapses.	*Dien Bien Phu* falls. *Geneva* Conference on Vietnam. *Algerian revolt* begins. British troops withdraw from Egypt. *Nasser* in power.	*Fortran* in US.
1955	West Germany joins *NATO*. *Warsaw Pact* formed. *Messina Conference*. A. *Eden* British PM (1955–7).	*Bandung Conference* of Third World nations.	*Hovercraft* patented. Marcuse: *Eros and Civilization*. *Teilhard de Chardin* dies (1881–1955).
1956	*Twentieth Congress* of Soviet Communist Party; *Khrushchev* denounces Stalin. Britain and France *collude* with Israel on *Suez*. *Polish* and *Hungarian* revolts.	*Hundred Flowers* in China. *Castro* and *Guevara* land in *Cuba*. *Suez War*. *Morocco* independent. French colonies autonomous. *Civil War* in Vietnam begins.	Osborne: *Look back in Anger*. 1956–9 *Guggenheim Museum* New York. First commercial nuclear power stations (Britain 1956, US 1957).
1957	*Macmillan* British PM (1957–63). *Treaty of Rome; EEC* formed. Soviet *Sputnik* flight.	*Ghana* independent.	Robbe-Grillet: *Jealousy*. J. Kerouac: *On the Road*. 1957–60 L. Durrell: *Alexandria Quartet*.
1958	*Fifth French Republic. De Gaulle* president. Pope *John XXIII* elected. *Life peerages* in Britain.	*Great Leap Forward* in China. British *West Indies Federation* (1958–62). *French Community* (1958–61).	*Silicon chip* invented by Texas Instruments. Lévi-Strauss: *Structural Anthropology*. Achebe: *Things fall Apart*. *Fast breeder reactor* at Dounreay.
1959	*Conservatives* win British election. *EFTA* formed. *North Sea* natural gas discovered.	*Cuban revolution*. *Cyprus* joins Commonwealth.	G. Grass: *The Drum*. Ionesco: *The Rhinoceros*.
1960	*U2 spy plane* wrecks US/USSR summit. Soviet *technicians* withdrawn from China.	End of *Malayan emergency*. *Sharpeville Massacre* South Africa. *Belgian Congo* independent. *Vietnam War* (1960–75). *OPEC* formed. *Nigeria* independent.	*Lasers* built (US). Oral *contraceptives* marketed. Battery *razor*. *North Sea gas* flow.
1961	*Berlin Wall* erected.	*Bay of Pigs*. *South Africa* Republic.	Britten: *War Requiem*. Manned *space flight*.
1962	*Vatican II* (1962–5). *Cuban missile crisis* raises war threat. *Commonwealth Immigrants Act*.	*Cuban missile crisis*. Britain grants independence to *Jamaica, Trinidad and Tobago,* and *Uganda*.	*The Beatles*. *Satellite* television. A. Warhol: *Marilyn*.
1963	*French veto* Britain's EEC bid. *Test-ban Treaty* in Moscow. *Douglas-Home* PM (1963–4).	*Kenya* independent. J. F. *Kennedy* assassinated (President 1961–3). *OAU* formed. *Eritrea War* begins.	Hitchcock: *The Birds*. British *National Theatre* at Old Vic.
1964	Labour win British election; *H. Wilson* PM (1964–70). *Khrushchev* ousted by *Brezhnev* (1964–82). First *Race Relations Act* in Britain.	*Civil War* in the *Sudan*. US *Civil Rights Act* under President *Johnson* (1963–9). *PLO* formed.	*Word processor*.

	Britain and Europe	Rest of the World	Culture/Technology
1965	De Gaulle re-elected President. Wilson fails to solve Rhodesia crisis.	UDI in Rhodesia. Indo-Pakistan War. Military takeover in Indonesia.	Hoyle and Fowler: Nucleosynthesis in Massive Stars and Supernovae. H. Pinter: The Homecoming. J. Orton: Loot.
1966	Labour gains bigger majority.	Cultural Revolution in China (1966–8).	Chagall decorates Metropolitan Opera, New York.
1967	Economic problems result in devaluation of pound. EEC becomes EC. De Gaulle vetoes Britain's second bid to enter. Abortion legalized in Britain.	Biafra War (1967–70). Indira Gandhi Indian PM (1966–77, 1980–4). Six-Day War Israel.	Antonioni: Blow-Up. First heart transplant (Barnard).
1968	Warsaw Pact invade Czechoslovakia. Salazar resigns. Student protests throughout Europe.	Tet offensive in Vietnam. Martin Luther King shot.	Bell and Hewish discover first pulsar.
1969	Irish troubles begin. British army to Ulster. De Gaulle resigns. Pompidou president. Brandt German chancellor.	Nixon US President (1969–74). Sino-Soviet frontier war. Gadaffi in power in Libya. Nimeiri in power in the Sudan.	Open university in UK. First man on moon. Knox-Johnson: Non-stop circumnavigation of earth. Concorde flight. Woodstock pop festival.
1970	Conservatives win British election; Heath PM (1970–4). German policy of Ostpolitik. N. Ireland riots; IRA Provisionals recruit.	Allende president in Chile. Biafra War ends.	Saul Bellow: Mr. Sammler's Planet.
1971	N. Ireland internment policy. British Industrial Relations Act.		Visconti: Death in Venice. Decimal currency UK. Fellini: Roma.
1972	British miners strike. Uganda Asian refugees to UK. Direct rule of N. Ireland.	Bangladesh formed after Indo-Pakistan War. US/USSR detente. Amin seizes power in Uganda. SALT I signed. US recognizes Communist China. Allende killed in Chile.	1972–3 Berio: Concerto for Two Pianos. 1973–6 M. Tippett: The Ice Break.
1973	Denmark, Ireland, and UK enter European Community. Helsinki Conference. Widespread industrial unrest UK.	US withdraws from Vietnam War. OPEC raises oil prices. Yom Kippur War: Israel against Arab States.	US Skylab missions. Schumacher: Small is Beautiful. CT body-scanners. Microwave cooking becoming popular.
1974	Three-day week. Wilson PM (1974–6). IRA bombing of mainland Britain. Portugal restores democracy. N. Ireland Assembly fails.	Watergate scandal; Nixon resigns. Cyprus invaded by Turkey. Haile Selassie deposed in Ethiopia.	
1975	Franco dies; Juan Carlos restored to Spain. British Referendum confirms EC. Sex Discrimination Act. IMF assists Britain.	Angola and Mozambique independent. End of Vietnamese War. Khmer Rouge in Cambodia. Civil War in Lebanon.	Apollo and Soyuz dock in space.
1976	Callaghan British PM (1976–9).	Death of Mao Zedong; Gang of Four. Soweto massacre.	
1977	Democratic elections in Spain. Charter 77 launched. Terrorist activities in Germany and Italy.	Deng Xiaoping gains power in China.	Pompidou Centre, Paris.
1978	Pope John Paul II elected.	Camp David Accord (President Carter, Israel, and Egypt). Boat people leave Vietnam. Civil wars in Chad and Nicaragua.	I. Murdoch: The Sea, the Sea. First test-tube baby born.

	Britain and Europe	Rest of the World	Culture/Technology
1979	European Parliament direct elections. 'Winter of discontent' strikes in UK. Devolution referenda in Wales and Scotland fail. Conservatives win election; Thatcher British PM (1979–90).	Civil war in El Salvador. Shah of Iran deposed by Khomeini. Iran hostage crisis. USSR invades Afghanistan. Pol Pot deposed in Cambodia.	Islamic fundamentalism spreading. Coppola: Apocalypse Now.
1980	Solidarity in Poland; Catholic Church actively anti-Communist.	Zimbabwe independent. Iran–Iraq War (1980–8). US funds Contras in Nicaragua.	W. Golding: Rites of Passage. Anglican Church alternative service book.
1981	British Labour Party split; SDP formed. Riots in London and Liverpool. British Nationality Act. Privatization of public corporations. High unemployment. Mitterrand French President.	R. Reagan US President (1981–9). Sadat shot in Egypt.	Space shuttle Columbia. Pierre Boulez: Répons. Microprocessor in a variety of domestic appliances and gadgets.
1982	British victory over Argentina in Falklands War.	PLO takes refuge in Tunis. Israel invades Lebanon. Famine in Ethiopia.	Cordless telephone. Laser discs (CDs).
1983	Thatcher re-elected PM. Cruise missiles installed in UK and Germany; peace movements active.	US troops invade Grenada. Civilian government restored in Argentina.	R. Attenborough: Gandhi.
1984	Miners' strike UK (1984–5). IRA bomb attack on Cabinet at Brighton.	Hong Kong Agreement UK and China. Assassination of Indira Gandhi.	Thames Barrier completed. Office practices revolutionized by Fax, word processors, and PCs. Genetic fingerprinting in forensic science.
1985	Gorbachev general secretary of Soviet Communist Party; begins policy of liberalization. Anglo-Irish Agreement.	Eritrean Liberation Front continues war against Ethiopia. Anti-apartheid movement developing in South Africa. Military coup in the Sudan. Threat to tankers through Iran–Iraq War. Syria seeks to pacify Lebanon.	Electronic culture replacing literary.
1986	Spain and Portugal join EC. Jacques Chirac French PM; 'co-habitation' with President. British unemployment peaks at 3.5 m. Single European Act.	US bombs Libya.	Chernobyl disaster. Wole Soyinka gains Nobel Prize. Musée d'Orsay in Paris. Tarkovsky: The Sacrifice.
1987	Stock-market crisis (Oct.). Third Thatcher government.	China suppresses Tibet protests. US/USSR INF Treaty for intermediate missiles. Palestinian intifada.	
1988	SDP and Liberals merge to form Liberal Democrats. Mitterrand re-elected.	Iran–Iraq war ends. Polisario struggle against Morocco. PLO recognizes Israel.	Salman Rushdie: Satanic Verses. Hawking: Brief History of Time.
1989	Berlin Wall broken. Communist leaders deposed: Hungary, Poland, East Germany, Czechoslovakia, Bulgaria, Romania.	Khomeini dies. G. Bush US President (1989–). Tiananmen Square massacre (June). Namibia independent.	France celebrates the Revolution. Communist ideology collapsing throughout eastern Europe.
1990	East and West Germany reunited. Thatcher deposed; Major becomes PM.	Iraq invades and annexes Kuwait. ANC talks with De Klerk. Cold War formally ended.	800 m. watch World Cup.
1991		US-led coalition in Gulf War (Jan.–Feb.). Iraq surrenders after setting fire to Kuwaiti oil-wells.	

CHRONOLOGY OF SCIENTIFIC
DEVELOPMENTS

Chronology of Scientific Developments

Medical science

*c.*460 BC Hippocrates brings medicine from the realm of magic and the supernatural into that of natural phenomena (Greece)

*c.*160 Galen shows that arteries contain blood, not air, and founds *experimental physiology* (Greece & Italy)

*c.*1530 Paracelsus introduces *chemical treatment of disease* (Austria)

1625 *circulation of the blood* described by W. Harvey (Britain)

1676 presence of *microbes* first detected by A. van Leeuwenhoek (Holland)

1796 first effective *vaccine* (against smallpox) developed by E. Jenner (Britain)

1816 *monaural stethoscope* designed by R. Laënnec (France)

1825 *blood transfusion* successfully performed by J. Blundell (UK)

1842 *ether* first used as an anaesthetic by C. Long (US)

1860 *pasteurization* technique developed by L. Pasteur (France)

1863–4 *clinical thermometer* introduced by W. Aitken (UK)

1865 *germ theory of disease* published by L. Pasteur (France)

1867 first *antiseptic operation* performed by J. Lister (UK)

1885 *cholera bacillus* identified by R. Koch (Germany)

1891 concept of *chemotherapy* developed by P. Ehrlich (Germany)

1895 *X-rays* discovered by W. Röntgen (Germany)

1897 first synthetic *aspirin* produced by F. Hoffmann (Germany)

1898 medical properties of radiation discovered by P. and M. Curie (France)

1901 existence of *blood groups* discovered by K. Landsteiner (Austria)

1921 *insulin* isolated by F. Banting and C. Best (Canada)

1922 *tuberculosis vaccine* developed by L. Calmette and C. Guérin (France)

1928 *penicillin* discovered by A. Fleming (UK)

1929 *iron lung* designed by P. Drinker and C. McKhann (US)

1932 first *sulphonamide* developed by G. Domagk (Germany)

1938–40 *penicillin* isolated by H. Florey (Australia) and E. Chain (Germany)

1943 first *kidney machine* designed by W. Kolff (Holland)

1944 *DNA* determined as the genetic material of life by O. Avery (US)

1950 first successful *kidney transplant* performed by R. Lawler (US)

1953 *double helix structure of DNA* discovered by F. Crick (UK) and J. Watson (US)

1955 *ultrasound* successfully used in body scanning by I. Donald (UK)

1958 first *internal cardiac pacemaker* implanted by A. Senning (Sweden)

1960 *contraceptive pill* first available (US)

1967 first *heart transplant* performed by C. Barnard (S. Africa)

1971 *CAT* (computerized axial tomographic) scanner developed by G. Hounsfield (UK)

1978 first *test-tube baby* born (UK)

1980 World Health Organisation declares the *world free of smallpox* from 1 January 1980

1983 *HIV* or human immunodeficiency virus identified as responsible for causing Aids (US & France)

1984 *genetic fingerprinting* developed by A. Jeffreys (UK)

Telecommunications revolution

1794 *semaphore telegraph* designed by C. Chappe (France)

1837 *electric telegraph* patented by W. Cooke and C. Wheatstone (UK)

1838 *Morse code* introduced by S. Morse (US)

1839 first *commercial telegraph line* installed in London (UK)

1848 Associated Press *news wire service* begins in New York (US)

1851 first *underwater cable* laid under the English Channel

1851 Reuters *news wire service* begins in London (UK)

1858 first *transatlantic cable* laid between Ireland and Newfoundland

1858 *automatic telegraph system* patented by C. Wheatstone (UK)

1872 *duplex telegraphy* patented by J. Stearns (US)

1875 *telephone* patented by A. Bell (UK/US)

1877 *phonograph* (sound-recording machine) developed by T. Edison (US)

1878 first *telephone exchange* opened in Connecticut (US)

1887 existence of *radio waves* demonstrated by H. Hertz (Germany)

1889 first *automatic telephone exchange* introduced by A. Strowger (US)

1891 *discs for recording sound* pioneered by E. Berliner (Germany)

1895 G. Marconi (Italy) demonstrates *radio transmission* using Hertz's equipment

1897 *cathode-ray tube* invented by F. Braun (Germany)

1898 machine for *magnetic recording of sound* patented by V. Poulsen (Denmark)

1901 G. Marconi (Italy) sends first *radio signals* across the Atlantic

1906 *triode valve* invented by L. de Forest (US)

1920 regular *public radio broadcasting* established in Britain and US

1926 *television* first demonstrated by J. Baird (UK)

1927 first *transatlantic telephone links* opened between London and New York

1928 *magnetic tape* introduced by F. Pfleumer (Germany)

1936 *black and white television* service introduced by the BBC (UK)

1953 *colour television* successfully transmitted in US

1954 first *transistor radio* developed by Regency Company (US)

1956 first *transatlantic telephone cable* was laid underwater between Scotland and Newfoundland

1956 *video tape recorder* introduced by A. Poniatoff (US)

1960 Echo and Courier satellites (US) launched to relay first *satellite telephone calls* between US and Europe

1966 *fibre-optic cables* for telephone links pioneered by K. Kao and G. Hockham (UK)

1968 *pulse code modulation system* installed in London (UK)

1970 *videodisc* introduced by Decca (UK) and AEG (Germany)

1975 first *domestic videotape system* (Betamax) introduced by Sony (Japan)

1980s *teletext* system developed and introduced into Europe

1982 *compact disc* produced by Philips (Holland) and Sony (Japan)

1989 computers that run on *light pulses* rather than electricity developed by British Telecom (UK)

Computer technology

1642 machine for *adding and subtracting* designed by B. Pascal (France)

1674 machine for *multiplying and dividing* designed by G. Leibniz (Germany)

1834 *analytical engine* designed by C. Babbage (UK)

1849 *representation of logical events by symbols* enumerated by G. Boole (UK)

1855 *calculating engine* constructed by G. Schentz (Sweden) and exhibited at the Paris Exhibition

1889 *punched-card machine* patented by H. Hollerith (US) and used to tabulate the results of the US census

1924 Tabulating Machine Company of the US becomes International Business Machines (IBM)

1928 *magnetic tape* introduced by F. Pfleumer (Germany)

1943 code-breaking machine *Colossus* conceived by A. Turing (UK)

1945 *Electronic Numerical Integrator and Calculator* (ENIAC) designed by P. Eckert and J. Maunchly (US)

1947 *transistor* invented by J. Bardeen, W. Brattain, and W. Shockley at Bell Laboratories (US)

1948 first *computer, Manchester Mark I,* installed at Manchester University (UK)

1949–50 *printed electronic circuits* developed

1954 first *high-level programming language* (FORTRAN) published by J. Backus of IBM (US)

1958 first *integrated circuit* (or *silicon chip*) produced (US)

1962 Sinclair Radionics founded by C. Sinclair (UK)

1964 first *word processor* introduced by IBM (US)

1965 first *minicomputer* produced (US)

1968 Amstrad (UK) founded by A. M. Sugar to produce *microcomputers*

1969 *microprocessor* invented by E. Hoff of Intel (US)

1972 first *pocket calculator* introduced (UK)

1975 first *portable computer* produced by Altair (US)

1978 *magnetic discs* first introduced by Oyz (US)

1979 first *videotex* information system, Prestel, launched by British Telecom (UK)

1980s term *fifth generation* coined to describe computers designed for parallel processing (Japan)

1981 *desktop microcomputer* (IBM-PC) introduced by IBM (US)

1983 Esprit (European Strategic Programme for Research and Information Technology) established by the EEC to coordinate the European Information Technology industry

1984 *mouse* (movable desktop pointing device) introduced by Apple Macintosh (UK)

1984 *Data Protection Act* passed in UK, requiring disclosure of personal computer-held information to anyone requesting it

1985 *transputer* manufactured by Inmos (UK)

1985 *optical fibres* first used to link mainframe computers (US)

1986 class of *superconductors* discovered by G. Bednorz and A. Mueller at IBM laboratories (Zurich), with potential for superconducting computers in the future

1988 improved optical discs for general computing manufactured by ICL (UK) and Tender Electronic Systems (US)

1989 RISC (Reduced Instruction Set Computer) chip developed by INTEL (US), performing at ten times the speed of previous chips

Space exploration

1903 theory of *rocket propulsion* published by K. Tsiolkovsky (USSR)

1923 theory of *interplanetary flight* published by H. Oberth (Germany)

1926 first *liquid-fuel rocket* launched by R. Goddard (US)

1942 first *long-distance rocket* designed by W. von Braun (Germany)

1944 V-2 rocket, forerunner of *space rockets,* first used (Germany)

1949 first *multi-stage rocket* launched in US

1957 a *satellite, Sputnik 1* (USSR), first put into earth orbit

1957 satellite *Sputnik 2* (USSR) carries the *first space traveller,* the dog Laika

1958 US follows USSR and first puts a satellite, *Explorer 1* (US), into orbit

1959 space probe *Luna 2* (USSR) reaches the Moon

1961 Y. Gagarin becomes the *first man in space* in *Vostok 1* (USSR)

1963 V. Tereshkova becomes the *first woman in space* in *Vostok 6* (USSR)

1964 space probe *Ranger 7* (US) takes close pictures of the Moon

1965 France becomes third nation to launch a satellite

1965 A. Leonov makes the first *walk in space* from *Voskhod 2* (USSR)

1966 first *moon landing,* by space probe *Luna 9* (USSR)

1966 N. Armstrong and D. Scott in *Gemini 8* (US) make the *first docking in space* with *Gemini Agena* target vehicle

1968 F. Borman, J. Lovell, and W. Anders orbit the Moon in *Apollo 8* (US)

1969 N. Armstrong and E. Aldrin make the *first manned lunar landing* in the lunar module *Eagle,* with M. Collins in the command module *Apollo 11* (US). Armstrong and Aldrin walk on the Moon.

1970 Japan and China become the fourth and fifth satellite-launching nations

1971 Britain becomes the sixth satellite-launching nation

1971 *Soyuz 10* and *Salyut 1* (USSR) dock in orbit to form the first space station

1973 *Skylab* (US) launched for a series of zero-gravity experiments

1975 *Soyuz 19* (USSR) and *Apollo 18* (US) dock in orbit for the Apollo-Soyuz Test Project

1976 *Viking 1* (US) lands on Mars and sends back information on conditions and signs of life. No conclusive evidence of life on the planet

1977 Space Shuttle *Enterprise* (US) makes the *first shuttle test flight*

1977 *Voyager 2* (US) leaves on a mission to fly by Jupiter (1979), Saturn (1981), Uranus (1986), and Neptune (1989)

1981 Space Shuttle *Columbia* (US) makes the first shuttle mission

1983 European Spacelab launched into orbit by the Space Shuttle *Columbia* (US)

1986 European space probe *Giotto* investigates Halley's Comet

1986 Space Shuttle *Challenger* (US) explodes killing seven astronauts and halting the shuttle programme

1990 European Space Telescope Hubble launched in order to obtain clearer stellar images

APPENDICES

Appendix 1 Countries of the World

Country	Capital	Area	Currency unit
Afghanistan	Kabul	652,090 sq. km (251,773 sq. miles)	afghani = 100 puls
Albania	Tiranë	28,748 sq. km (11,000 sq. miles)	lek = 100 qindarka
Algeria	Algiers	2,381,741 sq. km (919,595 sq. miles)	dinar = 100 centimes
Andorra	Andorra la Vella	464 sq. km (179 sq. miles)	franc = 100 centimes / peseta = 100 céntimos
Angola	Luanda	1,246,700 sq. km (481,353 sq. miles)	kwanza = 100 lweis
Antigua and Barbuda	St John's	442 sq. km (171 sq. miles)	dollar = 100 cents
Argentina	Buenos Aires	2,758,829 sq. km (1,065,189 sq. miles)	austral
Australia	Canberra	7,682,300 sq. km (2,966,200 sq. miles)	dollar = 100 cents
Austria	Vienna	83,853 sq. km (32,376 sq. miles)	schilling = 100 groschen
Bahamas	Nassau	13,864 sq. km (5,353 sq. miles)	dollar = 100 cents
Bahrain	Manama	669 sq. km (258 sq. miles)	dinar = 1,000 fils
Bangladesh	Dhaka	143,998 sq. km (55,598 sq. miles)	taka = 100 poisha
Barbados	Bridgetown	430 sq. km (166 sq. miles)	dollar = 100 cents
Belgium	Brussels	30,521 sq. km (11,784 sq. miles)	franc = 100 centimes
Belize	Belmopan	22,965 sq. km (8,867 sq. miles)	dollar = 100 cents
Benin	Porto Novo	112,600 sq. km (43,475 sq. miles)	franc
Bhutan	Thimphu	46,100 sq. km (17,800 sq. miles)	ngultrum (or Indian rupee)
Bolivia	La Paz (legal capital, Sucre)	1,098,581 sq. km (424,165 sq. miles)	boliviano = 100 cents
Botswana	Gaborone	581,700 sq. km (224,600 sq. miles)	pula = 100 thebe
Brazil	Brasilia	8,512,000 sq. km (3,286,500 sq. miles)	cruzado = 1,000 cruzeiros
Brunei	Bandar Seri Begawan	5,765 sq. km (2,226 sq. miles)	dollar = 100 sen
Bulgaria	Sofia	110,912 sq. km (42,823 sq. miles)	lev = 100 stotinki
Burkina	Ouagadougou	274,122 sq. km (105,839 sq. miles)	franc
Burma (from 1989 called Myanmar)	Yangon (formerly Rangoon)	678,000 sq. km (261,789 sq. miles)	kyat = 100 pyas
Burundi	Bujumbura	27,834 sq. km (10,747 sq. miles)	franc
Cambodia	Phnom Penh	181,035 sq. km (69,898 sq. miles)	riel = 100 sen
Cameroon	Yaoundé	475,499 sq. km (183,591 sq. miles)	franc
Canada	Ottawa	9,976,147 sq. km (3,851,809 sq. miles)	dollar = 100 cents
Cape Verde Islands	Praia	4,033 sq. km (1,557 sq. miles)	escudo = 100 centavos
Central African Republic	Bangui	622,996 sq. km (240,540 sq. miles)	franc
Chad	N'Djamena	1,270,994 sq. km (490,733 sq. miles)	franc
Chile	Santiago	756,943 sq. km (292,257 sq. miles)	peso = 100 centavos
China	Peking	9,560,948 sq. km (3,691,500 sq. miles)	yuan = 10 jiao or 100 fen
Colombia	Bogotá	1,138,907 sq. km (439,734 sq. miles)	peso = 100 centavos
Comoros	Moroni	2,274 sq. km (878 sq. miles)	franc
Congo	Brazzaville	348,999 sq. km (134,749 sq. miles)	franc
Costa Rica	San José	50,899 sq. km (19,652 sq. miles)	colón = 100 céntimos
Cuba	Havana	114,524 sq. km (44,218 sq. miles)	peso = 100 centavos
Cyprus	Nicosia	9,251 sq. km (3,572 sq. miles)	pound = 100 cents
Czechoslovakia	Prague	127,870 sq. km (49,371 sq. miles)	koruna = 100 haléru
Denmark	Copenhagen	43,030 sq. km (16,614 sq. miles)	krone = 100 öre
Djibouti	Djibouti	21,699 sq. km (8,378 sq. miles)	franc
Dominica	Roseau	751 sq. km (290 sq. miles)	dollar = 100 cents
Dominican Republic	Santo Domingo	48,441 sq. km (18,703 sq. miles)	peso = 100 centavos
Ecuador	Quito	455,502 sq. km (175,870 sq. miles)	sucre = 100 centavos
Egypt	Cairo	1,000,250 sq. km (386,198 sq. miles)	pound = 100 piastres or 1,000 millièmes
El Salvador	San Salvador	20,865 sq. km (8,056 sq. miles)	colón = 100 centavos
Equatorial Guinea	Malabo	45,392 sq. km (17,526 sq. miles)	franc
Ethiopia	Addis Ababa	1,221,895 sq. km (471,776 sq. miles)	birr = 100 cents
Fiji	Suva	18,272 sq. km (7,055 sq. miles)	dollar = 100 cents
Finland	Helsinki	360,317 sq. km (139,119 sq. miles)	markka = 100 penniä
France	Paris	549,619 sq. km (212,209 sq. miles)	franc = 100 centimes

Country	Capital	Area	Currency unit
Gabon	Libreville	265,000 sq. km (102,317 sq. miles)	franc
Gambia, the	Banjul	10,368 sq. km (4,003 sq. miles)	dalasi = 100 bututs
Germany, Federal Republic of	Berlin (seat of government, Bonn)	356,388 sq. km (137,602 sq. miles)	Deutschmark = 100 pfennig
Ghana	Accra	238,538 sq. km (92,100 sq. miles)	cedi = 100 pesewa
Greece	Athens	131,955 sq. km (50,948 sq. miles)	drachma = 100 lepta
Grenada	St George's	345 sq. km (133 sq. miles)	dollar = 100 cents
Guatemala	Guatemala	108,888 sq. km (42,042 sq. miles)	quetzal = 100 centavos
Guinea	Conakry	245,855 sq. km (94,925 sq. miles)	franc
Guinea-Bissau	Bissau	36,125 sq. km (13,948 sq. miles)	peso = 100 centavos
Guyana	Georgetown	214,969 sq. km (83,000 sq. miles)	dollar = 100 cents
Haiti	Port-au-Prince	27,749 sq. km (10,714 sq. miles)	gourde = 100 centimes
Honduras	Tegucigalpa	112,087 sq. km (43,277 sq. miles)	lempira = 100 centavos
Hungary	Budapest	93,030 sq. km (35,919 sq. miles)	forint = 100 fillér
Iceland	Reykjavík	102,828 sq. km (39,702 sq. miles)	króna = 100 aurer
India	New Delhi	3,166,829 sq. km (1,261,816 sq. miles)	rupee = 100 paise
Indonesia	Jakarta	1,919,263 sq. km (741,031 sq. miles)	rupiah = 100 sen
Iran	Teheran	1,648,184 sq. km (636,367 sq. miles)	rial = 100 dinars
Iraq	Baghdad	433,999 sq. km (167,568 sq. miles)	dinar = 1,000 fils
Irish Republic	Dublin	70,282 sq. km (27,136 sq. miles)	pound (punt) = 100 pence
Israel	Jerusalem	20,770 sq. km (8,017 sq. miles)	new shekel
Italy	Rome	301,190 sq. km (116,290 sq. miles)	lira
Ivory Coast	Abidjan	319,820 sq. km (123,483 sq. miles)	franc
Jamaica	Kingston	11,425 sq. km (4,411 sq. miles)	dollar = 100 cents
Japan	Tokyo	369,698 sq. km (142,741 sq. miles)	yen
Jordan	Amman	97,739 sq. km (37,737 sq. miles)	dinar = 1,000 fils
Kenya	Nairobi	582,644 sq. km (224,960 sq. miles)	shilling = 100 cents
Kiribati	Tarawa	655 sq. km (253 sq. miles)	dollar = 100 cents
Korea, North	Pyongyang	121,248 sq. km (46,814 sq. miles)	won = 100 chon
Korea, South	Seoul	99,590 sq. km (38,452 sq. miles)	won = 100 jeon
Kuwait	Kuwait	20,150 sq. km (7,780 sq. miles)	dinar = 1,000 fils
Laos	Vientiane	236,798 sq. km (91,428 sq. miles)	kip = 100 ats
Lebanon	Beirut	10,399 sq. km (4,015 sq. miles)	pound = 100 piastres
Lesotho	Maseru	30,344 sq. km (11,716 sq. miles)	maloti = 100 lisente
Liberia	Monrovia	111,370 sq. km (43,000 sq. miles)	dollar = 100 cents
Libya	Tripoli	1,759,530 sq. km (679,358 sq. miles)	dinar = 1,000 dirhams
Liechtenstein	Vaduz	161 sq. km (62 sq. miles)	franc = 100 centimes
Luxembourg	Luxembourg	2,587 sq. km (999 sq. miles)	franc = 100 centimes
Madagascar	Antananarivo	587,042 sq. km (226,658 sq. miles)	franc malgache
Malawi	Lilongwe	94,485 sq. km (36,481 sq. miles)	kwacha = 100 tambala
Malaysia	Kuala Lumpur	330,669 sq. km (127,672 sq. miles)	dollar (ringgit) = 100 cents
Maldives	Malé	298 sq. km (115 sq. miles)	rufiyaa = 100 laris
Mali	Bamako	1,204,022 sq. km (464,875 sq. miles)	franc
Malta	Valletta	316 sq. km (122 sq. miles)	lira = 100 cents
Mauritania	Nouakchott	1,118,604 sq. km (431,895 sq. miles)	ouguiya = 5 khoums
Mauritius	Port Louis	1,865 sq. km (720 sq. miles)	rupee = 100 cents
Mexico	Mexico City	1,972,355 sq. km (761,530 sq. miles)	peso = 100 centavos
Monaco	Monaco	1.6 sq. km (0.6 sq. mile)	franc = 100 centimes
Mongolia	Ulan Bator	1,565,001 sq. km (604,250 sq. miles)	tugrik = 100 mongo
Morocco	Rabat (summer capital, Tangier)	622,012 sq. km (240,160 sq. miles)	dirham = 100 centimes
Mozambique	Maputo	784,961 sq. km (303,075 sq. miles)	metical = 100 centavos
Myanmar (see Burma)			
Namibia	Windhoek	824,293 sq. km (318,261 sq. miles)	rand = 100 cents
Nauru	Yaren	21 sq. km (8 sq. miles)	dollar = 100 cents
Nepal	Kathmandu	141,414 sq. km (54,600 sq. miles)	rupee = 100 paisa
Netherlands	Amsterdam (seat of government, The Hague)	36,174 sq. km (13,967 sq. miles)	guilder = 100 cents
New Zealand	Wellington	268,675 sq. km (103,736 sq. miles)	dollar = 100 cents
Nicaragua	Managua	148,005 sq. km (57,145 sq. miles)	córdoba = 100 centavos
Niger	Niamey	1,188,994 sq. km (459,073 sq. miles)	franc
Nigeria	Lagos	923,769 sq. km (356,669 sq. miles)	naira = 100 kobo
Norway	Oslo	324,218 sq. km (125,181 sq. miles)	krone = 100 öre

Country	Capital	Area	Currency unit
Oman	Muscat	212,379 sq. km (82,000 sq. miles)	rial = 1,000 baiza
Pakistan	Islamabad	803,941 sq. km (310,403 sq. miles)	rupee = 100 paisa
Panama	Panama	75,648 sq. km (29,208 sq. miles)	balboa = 100 centésimos
Papua New Guinea	Port Moresby	461,692 sq. km (178,260 sq. miles)	kina = 100 toea
Paraguay	Asunción	406,750 sq. km (157,047 sq. miles)	guarani = 100 céntimos
Peru	Lima	1,285,215 sq. km (496,224 sq. miles)	inti = 100 centimos
Philippines	Manila	299,765 sq. km (115,740 sq. miles)	peso = 100 centavos
Poland	Warsaw	311,700 sq. km (120,348 sq. miles)	zloty = 100 groszy
Portugal	Lisbon	91,970 sq. km (35,510 sq. miles)	escudo = 100 centavos
Qatar	Doha	10,360 sq. km (4,000 sq. miles)	riyal = 100 dirhams
Romania	Bucharest	237,500 sq. km (91,699 sq. miles)	leu = 100 bani
Rwanda	Kigali	26,338 sq. km (10,169 sq. miles)	franc
St Kitts and Nevis	Basseterre	311 sq. km (120 sq. miles)	dollar = 100 cents
St Lucia	Castries	616 sq. km (238 sq. miles)	dollar = 100 cents
St Vincent	Kingstown	389 sq. km (150 sq. miles)	dollar = 100 cents
San Marino	San Marino	60 sq. km (23 sq. miles)	lira
São Tomé and Principe	São Tomé	964 sq. km (372 sq. miles)	dobra = 100 centavos
Saudi Arabia	Riyadh	2,263,579 sq. km (873,972 sq. miles)	riyal = 20 qursh or 100 halalas
Senegal	Dakar	197,160 sq. km (76,124 sq. miles)	franc
Seychelles	Victoria	443 sq. km (171 sq. miles)	rupee = 100 cents
Sierra Leone	Freetown	72,326 sq. km (27,925 sq. miles)	leone = 100 cents
Singapore	Singapore	580 sq. km (224 sq. miles)	dollar = 100 cents
Solomon Islands	Honiara	29,785 sq. km (11,500 sq. miles)	dollar = 100 cents
Somalia	Mogadishu	637,539 sq. km (246,155 sq. miles)	shilling = 100 cents
South Africa	Pretoria (administrative); seat of legislature, Cape Town; judicial capital, Bloemfontein	1,221,038 sq. km (471,445 sq. miles)	rand = 100 cents
Spain	Madrid	504,745 sq. km (194,883 sq. miles)	peseta = 100 céntimos
Sri Lanka	Colombo	65,610 sq. km (25,332 sq. miles)	rupee = 100 cents
Sudan	Khartoum	2,505,792 sq. km (967,491 sq. miles)	pound = 100 piastres or 1,000 millièmes
Suriname	Paramaribo	163,820 sq. km (63,251 sq. miles)	guilder = 100 cents
Swaziland	Mbabane	17,366 sq. km (6,705 sq. miles)	lilangeni = 100 cents
Sweden	Stockholm	449,791 sq. km (173,665 sq. miles)	krona = 100 öre
Switzerland	Berne	41,287 sq. km (15,941 sq. miles)	franc = 100 centimes
Syria	Damascus	185,179 sq. km (71,498 sq. miles)	pound = 100 piastres
Tanzania	Dodoma	939,762 sq. km (362,844 sq. miles)	shilling = 100 cents
Thailand	Bangkok	513,517 sq. km (198,270 sq. miles)	baht = 100 stangs
Togo	Lomé	56,591 sq. km (21,850 sq. miles)	franc
Tonga	Nuku'alofa	699 sq. km (270 sq. miles)	pa'anga = 100 seniti
Trinidad and Tobago	Port of Spain	5,128 sq. km (1,980 sq. miles)	dollar = 100 cents
Tunisia	Tunis	164,148 sq. km (63,378 sq. miles)	dinar = 1,000 millimes
Turkey	Ankara	780,576 sq. km (301,382 sq. miles)	lira = 100 kurus
Tuvalu	Funafuti	24.6 sq. km (9.5 sq. miles)	dollar = 100 cents
Uganda	Kampala	236,036 sq. km (91,134 sq. miles)	shilling = 100 cents
Union of Soviet Socialist Republics	Moscow	22,272,000 sq. km (8,599,341 sq. miles)	rouble = 100 copecks
United Arab Emirates	Abu Dhabi	86,449 sq. km (33,378 sq. miles)	dirham = 100 fils
United Kingdom: England	London London	244,019 sq. km (94,216 sq. miles) 130,362 sq. km (50,333 sq. miles)	pound = 100 pence
Northern Ireland	Belfast	14,147 sq. km (5,462 sq. miles)	
Scotland	Edinburgh	78,749 sq. km (30,405 sq. miles)	
Wales	Cardiff	20,761 sq. km (8,016 sq. miles)	
United States of America	Washington	9,363,132 sq. km (3,615,123 sq. miles)	dollar = 100 cents
Uruguay	Montevideo	186,925 sq. km (72,172 sq. miles)	peso = 100 centésimos
Vanuatu	Vila	15,469 sq. km (6,050 sq. miles)	vatu
Vatican City	—	0.44 sq. km (0.17 sq. mile)	lira
Venezuela	Caracas	912,047 sq. km (352,143 sq. miles)	bolivar
Vietnam	Hanoi	334,331 sq. km (129,086 sq. miles)	dong = 10 hào or 100 xu

Country	Capital	Area	Currency unit
Western Samoa	Apia	2,841 sq. km (1,097 sq. miles)	tala = 100 sene
Yemen	Sana'a	485,273 sq. km (187,365 sq. miles)	riyal = 100 fils
Yugoslavia	Belgrade	255,803 sq. km (98,766 sq. miles)	dinar = 100 paras
Zaïre	Kinshasa	2,344,104 sq. km (905,063 sq. miles)	zaire = 100 makuta or 10,000 senghi
Zambia	Lusaka	752,620 sq. km (290,586 sq. miles)	kwacha = 100 ngwee
Zimbabwe	Harare	390,308 sq. km (150,699 sq. miles)	dollar = 100 cents

Dependencies

Dependency	Capital	Area	Currency
American Samoa (US)	Fagatogo	197 sq. km (76 sq. miles)	US dollar
Anguilla (Britain)	The Valley	91 sq. km (35 sq. miles)	East Caribbean dollar
Aruba (Netherlands)	Oranjestad	193 sq. km (75 sq. miles)	Aruban florin
Bermuda (Britain)	Hamilton	50 sq. km (21 sq. miles)	Bermuda dollar
Cayman Islands (Britain)	George Town	260 sq. km (100 sq. miles)	Cayman dollar
Christmas Island (Australia)		135 sq. km (52 sq. miles)	Australian dollar
Cocos Islands (Australia)	West Island	14 sq. km (5.4 sq. miles)	Australian dollar
Cook Islands (New Zealand)	Avarua	240 sq. km (93 sq. miles)	New Zealand dollar
Falkland Islands (Britain)	Stanley	12,170 sq. km (4,700 sq. miles)	Falkland Island pound
Faroe Islands (Denmark)	Tórshavn	1,400 sq. km (540 sq. miles)	Danish kroner
French Guiana (France)	Cayenne	83,533 sq. km (32,252 sq. miles)	French franc
French Polynesia (France)	Papeete	3,521 sq. km (1,359 sq. miles)	Colonial Franc Pacifique
Gibraltar (Britain)	Gibraltar	6.5 sq. km (2.5 sq. miles)	Gibraltar pound
Greenland (Denmark)	Godthab	2,175,600 sq. km (840,000 sq. miles)	Danish kroner
Guadeloupe (France)	Basse-Terre	1,705 sq. km (658 sq. miles)	French franc
Guam (US)	Agana	541 sq. km (209 sq. miles)	US dollar
Hong Kong (Britain)		1,072 sq. km (414 miles)	Hong Kong dollar
Macao (Portugal)		17 sq. km (6 sq. miles)	pataca
Marshall Islands (US)	Majuro	181 sq. km (70 sq. miles)	US dollar
Martinique (France)	Fort-de-France	1,079 sq. km (417 sq. miles)	French franc
Mayotte (France)	Dzaoudzi	373 sq. km (144 sq. miles)	French franc
Micronesia Federated States of (US)	Kolonia	702 sq. km (271 sq. miles)	US dollar
Montserrat (Britain)	Plymouth	100 sq. km (40 sq. miles)	East Caribbean dollar
Netherlands Antilles (The Netherlands)	Willemstad	839 sq. km (324 sq. miles)	Netherlands Antillean guilder
New Caledonia (France)	Nouméa	18,576 sq. km (7,175 sq. miles)	Colonial Franc Pacifique
Niue (New Zealand)		263 sq. km (102 sq. miles)	New Zealand dollar
Norfolk Island (Australia)	Kingston	34 sq. km (13 sq. miles)	Australian dollar
North Mariana Islands (US)	Saipan	477 sq. km (184 sq. miles)	US dollar
Palau (US)	Koror	497 sq. km (192 sq. miles)	US dollar
Pitcairn Island (Britain)	Adamstown	4.5 sq. km (1.75 sq. miles)	New Zealand dollar
Puerto Rico (US)	San Juan	8,955 sq. km (3,459 sq. miles)	US dollar
Réunion (France)	Saint-Denis	2,512 sq. km (968 sq. miles)	French franc

Dependency	Capital	Area	Currency
St Helena and dependencies of Ascension and Tristan da Cunha (Britain)	Jamestown	310 sq. km (119 sq. miles)	St Helena pound
St Pierre and Miquelon (France)	St Pierre	242 sq. km (93 sq. miles)	French franc
Svalbard (Norway)	Longyearbyen	62,000 sq. km (24,000 sq. miles)	Norwegian krone
Taiwan (Republic of China)	Taipei	35,981 sq. km (13,892 sq. miles)	New Taiwan dollar
Turks and Caicos Islands (Britain)	Grand Turk	430 sq. km (192 sq. miles)	US dollar
Virgin Islands American (US)	Charlotte Amalie	352 sq. km (136 sq. miles)	US dollar
Virgin Islands British (Britain)	Road Town	150 sq. km (59 sq. miles)	US dollar
Wallis and Futuna (France)	Mata-Utu	274 sq. km (106 sq. miles)	French franc
Western Sahara (Morocco)	La'youn	266,000 sq. km (102,742 sq. miles)	Moroccan dirham

Appendix 2 **The Commonwealth**

The Commonwealth is a free association of the 49 sovereign independent
States listed below, together with their associated States and dependencies

Antigua and Barbuda	Nauru
Australia	New Zealand
Bahamas	Nigeria
Bangladesh	Pakistan
Barbados	Papua New Guinea
Belize	St Christopher and Nevis
Botswana	St Lucia
Brunei	St Vincent and the Grenadines
Canada	Seychelles
Cyprus	Sierra Leone
Dominica	Singapore
Gambia, the	Solomon Islands
Ghana	Sri Lanka
Grenada	Swaziland
Guyana	Tanzania
India	Tonga
Jamaica	Trinidad and Tobago
Kenya	Tuvalu
Kiribati	Uganda
Lesotho	United Kingdom
Malawi	Vanuatu
Malaysia	Western Samoa
Maldives	Zambia
Malta	Zimbabwe
Mauritius	

Canada Provinces and Territories

(with official abbreviations)

Province	*Capital*
Alberta (Alta.)	Edmonton
British Columbia (BC)	Victoria
Manitoba (Man.)	Winnipeg
New Brunswick (NB)	Fredericton
Newfoundland and Labrador (Nfld.)	St John's
Nova Scotia (NS)	Halifax
Ontario (Ont.)	Toronto
Prince Edward Island (PEI)	Charlottetown
Quebec (Que.)	Quebec
Saskatchewan (Sask.)	Regina
Northwest Territories (NWT)	Yellowknife (seat of government)
Yukon Territory (YT)	Whitehorse ,,

Federal capital: Ottawa

The Commonwealth of Australia
States and Territories

State	*Capital*
New South Wales	Sydney
Queensland	Brisbane
South Australia	Adelaide
Tasmania	Hobart
Victoria	Melbourne
Western Australia	Perth
Australian Capital Territory	Canberra (federal capital)
Northern Territory	Darwin

India States and Union Territories

State	*Capital*
Andhra Pradesh	Hyderabad
Arunachal Pradesh	Itanagar
Assam	Dispur (temporary)
Bihar	Patna
Goa	Panaji
Gujarat	Gandhinagar
Haryana	Chandigarh
Himachal Pradesh	Shimla
Jammu and Kashmir	Srinagar (summer), Jammu (winter)
Karnataka	Bangalore
Kerala	Trivandrum
Madhya Pradesh	Bhopal
Maharashtra	Bombay
Manipur	Imphal
Meghalaya	Shillong
Mizoram	Aizawl
Nagaland	Kohima
Orissa	Bhubaneshwar
Punjab	Chandigarh
Rajasthan	Jaipur
Sikkim	Gangtok
Tamil Nadu	Madras
Tripura	Agartala
Uttar Pradesh	Lucknow
West Bengal	Calcutta

Union Territories	
Andaman and Nicobar Islands	Port Blair
Chandigarh	Chandigarh
Dadra and Nagar Haveli	Silvassa
Daman and Diu	Daman
Delhi	Delhi
Lakshadweep	Kavaratti
Pondicherry	Pondicherry

Appendix 3 States of the United States of America

(with official and postal abbreviations)

State	Capital	Popular name
Alabama (Ala., AL)	Montgomery	Yellowhammer State, Heart of Dixie, Cotton State
Alaska (Alas., AK)	Juneau	Great Land
Arizona (Ariz., AZ)	Phoenix	Grand Canyon State
Arkansas (Ark., AR)	Little Rock	Land of Opportunity
California (Calif., CA)	Sacramento	Golden State
Colorado (Col., CO)	Denver	Centennial State
Connecticut (Conn., CT)	Hartford	Constitution State, Nutmeg State
Delaware (Del., DE)	Dover	First State, Diamond State
Florida (Fla., FL)	Tallahassee	Sunshine State
Georgia (Ga., GA)	Atlanta	Empire State of the South, Peach State
Hawaii (HI)	Honolulu	The Aloha State
Idaho (ID)	Boise	Gem State
Illinois (Ill., IL)	Springfield	Prairie State
Indiana (Ind., IN)	Indianapolis	Hoosier State
Iowa (Ia., IA)	Des Moines	Hawkeye State
Kansas (Kan., KS)	Topeka	Sunflower State
Kentucky (Ky., KY)	Frankfort	Bluegrass State
Louisiana (La., LA)	Baton Rouge	Pelican State
Maine (Me., ME)	Augusta	Pine Tree State
Maryland (Md., MD)	Annapolis	Old Line State, Free State
Massachusetts (Mass., MA)	Boston	Bay State, Old Colony
Michigan (Mich., MI)	Lansing	Great Lake State, Wolverine State
Minnesota (Minn., MN)	St Paul	North Star State, Gopher State
Mississippi (Miss., MS)	Jackson	Magnolia State
Missouri (Mo., MO)	Jefferson City	Show Me State
Montana (Mont., MT)	Helena	Treasure State
Nebraska (Nebr., NB)	Lincoln	Cornhusker State
Nevada (Nev., NV)	Carson City	Sagebrush State, Battleborn State, Silver State
New Hampshire (NH)	Concord	Granite State
New Jersey (NJ)	Trenton	Garden State
New Mexico (N. Mex., NM)	Santa Fe	Land of Enchantment
New York (NY)	Albany	Empire State
North Carolina (NC)	Raleigh	Tar Heel State, Old North State
North Dakota (N. Dak., ND)	Bismarck	Peace Garden State
Ohio (OH)	Columbus	Buckeye State
Oklahoma (Okla., OK)	Oklahoma City	Sooner State
Oregon (Oreg., OR)	Salem	Beaver State
Pennsylvania (Pa., PA)	Harrisburg	Keystone State
Rhode Island (RI)	Providence	Little Rhody, Ocean State
South Carolina (SC)	Columbia	Palmetto State
South Dakota (S. Dak., SD)	Pierre	Coyote State, Sunshine State
Tennessee (Tenn., TN)	Nashville	Volunteer State
Texas (Tex., TX)	Austin	Lone Star State
Utah (UT)	Salt Lake City	Beehive State
Vermont (Vt., VT)	Montpelier	Green Mountain State
Virginia (Va., VA)	Richmond	Old Dominion
Washington (Wash., WA)	Olympia	Evergreen State
West Virginia (W. Va., WV)	Charleston	Mountain State
Wisconsin (Wis., WI)	Madison	Badger State
Wyoming (Wyo., WY)	Cheyenne	Equality State

Appendix 4 Soviet Union: Constituent Republics

Republic	Capital
Armenia	Yerevan
Azerbaijan	Baku
Belorussia	Minsk
Estonia	Tallinn
Georgia	Tbilisi (formerly Tiflis)
Kazakhstan	Alma-Ata
Kirghizia	Frunze
Latvia	Riga
Lithuania	Vilnius (formerly Vilna)
Moldavia	Kishinev (formerly Chişinău)
* Russia	Moscow
Tadjikistan	Dushanbe
Turkmenistan	Ashkhabad
Ukraine	Kiev
Uzbekistan	Tashkent

Capital: Moscow

* The Russian Soviet Federative Socialist Republic (RSFSR), the largest of the republics, consists of 16 autonomous republics, 5 autonomous provinces and 10 autonomous areas.

Appendix 5 The British Isles

1 Belfast
2 Newtownabbey
3 Carrickfergus
4 Castlereagh
5 North Down
6 Ards
7 Down
8 Newry & Mourne
9 Banbridge
10 Lisburn
11 Craigavon
12 Armagh
13 Dungannon
14 Fermanagh
15 Omagh
16 Cookstown
17 Magherafelt
18 Strabane
19 Derry
20 Limavady
21 Coleraine
22 Ballymoney
23 Moyle
24 Ballymena
25 Larne
26 Antrim

Appendix 6 **The British Constitution**

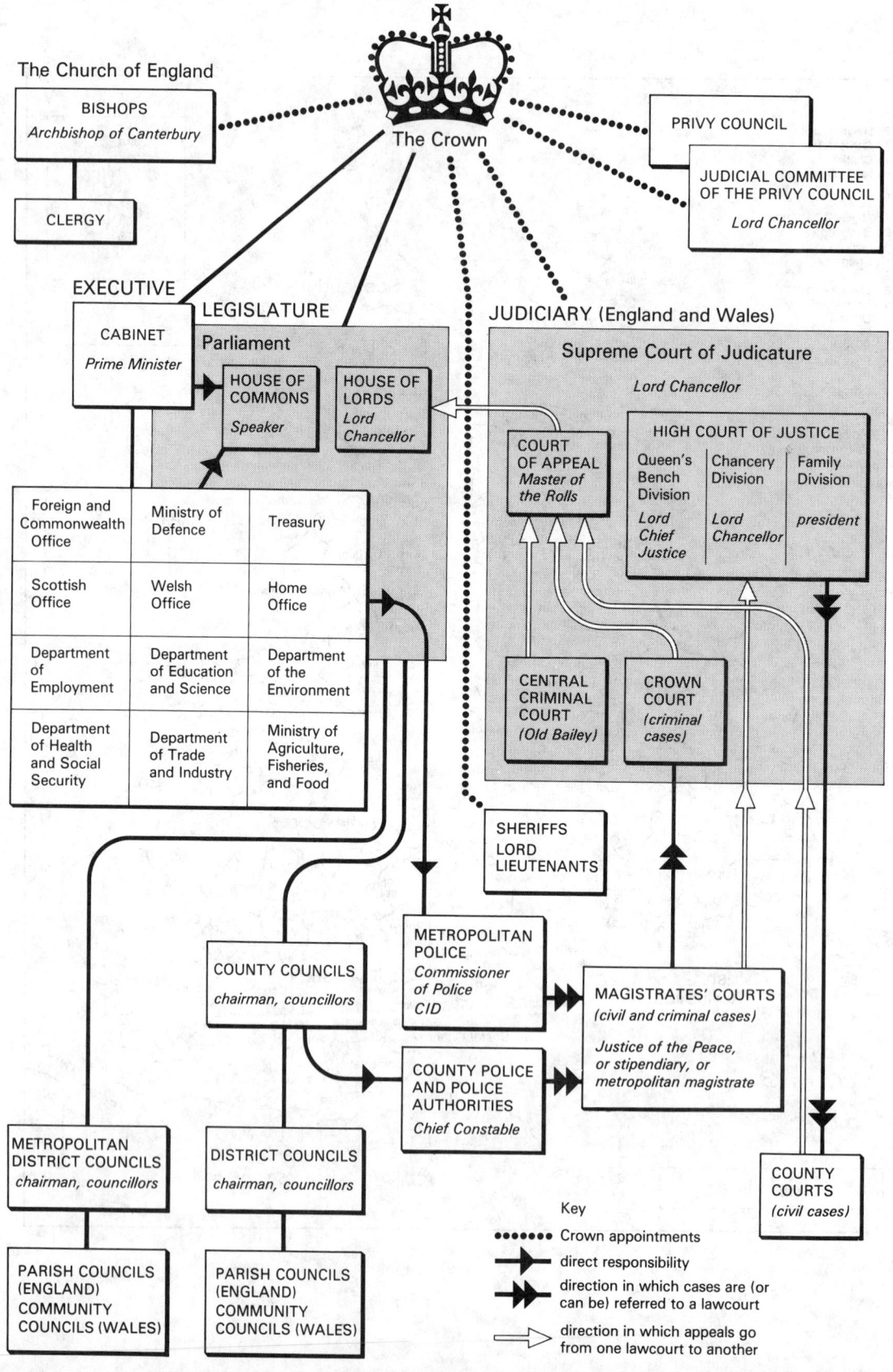

The Church of England

BISHOPS
Archbishop of Canterbury

CLERGY

The Crown

PRIVY COUNCIL

JUDICIAL COMMITTEE OF THE PRIVY COUNCIL
Lord Chancellor

EXECUTIVE

CABINET
Prime Minister

LEGISLATURE

Parliament

HOUSE OF COMMONS
Speaker

HOUSE OF LORDS
Lord Chancellor

Foreign and Commonwealth Office	Ministry of Defence	Treasury
Scottish Office	Welsh Office	Home Office
Department of Employment	Department of Education and Science	Department of the Environment
Department of Health and Social Security	Department of Trade and Industry	Ministry of Agriculture, Fisheries, and Food

JUDICIARY (England and Wales)

Supreme Court of Judicature
Lord Chancellor

COURT OF APPEAL
Master of the Rolls

HIGH COURT OF JUSTICE

Queen's Bench Division	Chancery Division	Family Division
Lord Chief Justice	*Lord Chancellor*	*president*

CENTRAL CRIMINAL COURT
(Old Bailey)

CROWN COURT
(criminal cases)

SHERIFFS LORD LIEUTENANTS

COUNTY COUNCILS
chairman, councillors

METROPOLITAN POLICE
Commissioner of Police
CID

COUNTY POLICE AND POLICE AUTHORITIES
Chief Constable

MAGISTRATES' COURTS
(civil and criminal cases)

Justice of the Peace, or stipendiary, or metropolitan magistrate

METROPOLITAN DISTRICT COUNCILS
chairman, councillors

DISTRICT COUNCILS
chairman, councillors

COUNTY COURTS
(civil cases)

PARISH COUNCILS (ENGLAND) COMMUNITY COUNCILS (WALES)

PARISH COUNCILS (ENGLAND) COMMUNITY COUNCILS (WALES)

Key

●●●●●● Crown appointments

➤ direct responsibility

➤➤ direction in which cases are (or can be) referred to a lawcourt

⇨ direction in which appeals go from one lawcourt to another

Appendix 7 The US Constitution

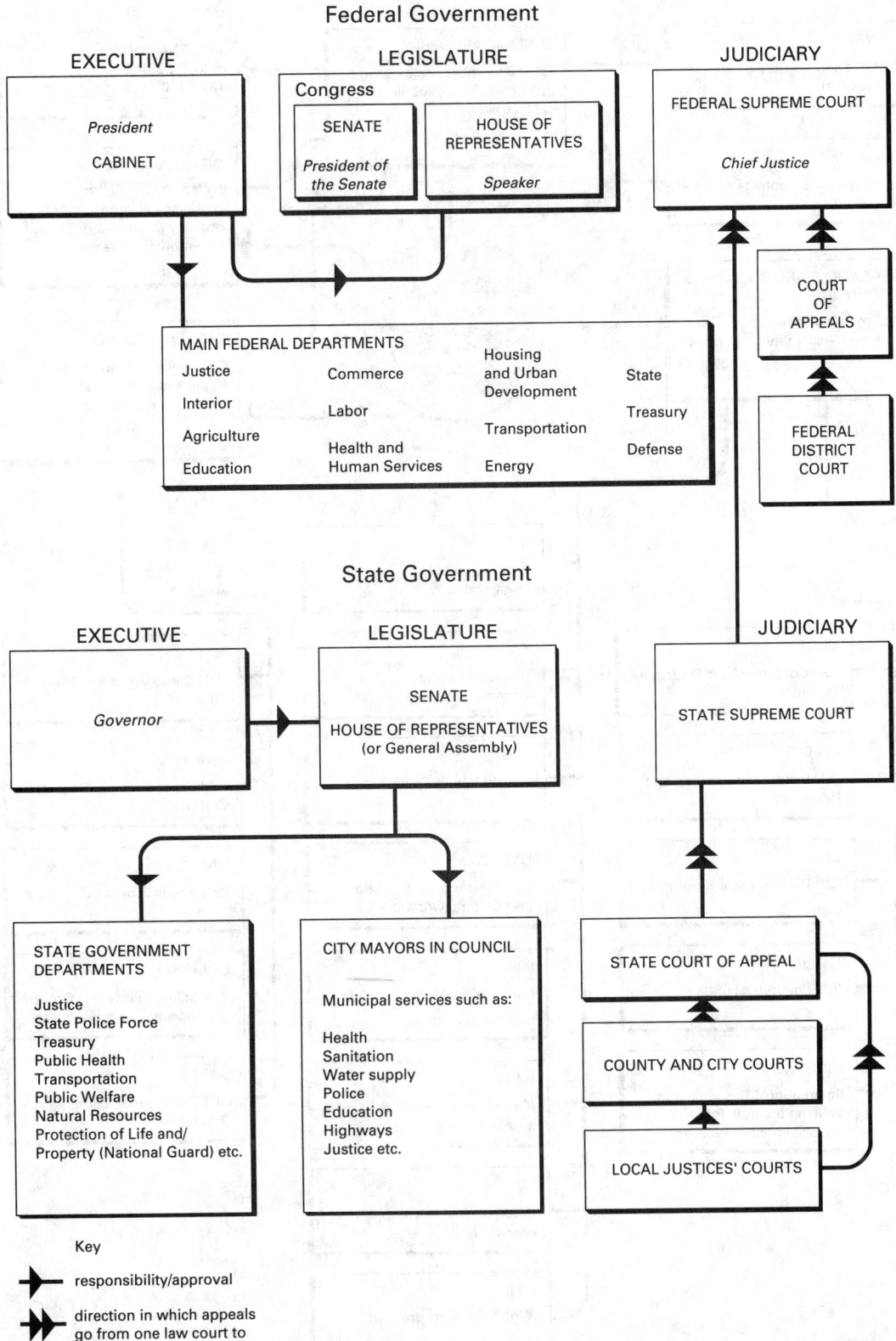

Federal Government

EXECUTIVE

President

CABINET

LEGISLATURE

Congress

SENATE

President of
the Senate

HOUSE OF
REPRESENTATIVES

Speaker

JUDICIARY

FEDERAL SUPREME COURT

Chief Justice

COURT
OF
APPEALS

FEDERAL
DISTRICT
COURT

MAIN FEDERAL DEPARTMENTS

Justice

Interior

Agriculture

Education

Commerce

Labor

Health and
Human Services

Housing
and Urban
Development

Transportation

Energy

State

Treasury

Defense

State Government

EXECUTIVE

Governor

LEGISLATURE

SENATE

HOUSE OF REPRESENTATIVES
(or General Assembly)

JUDICIARY

STATE SUPREME COURT

STATE GOVERNMENT
DEPARTMENTS

Justice
State Police Force
Treasury
Public Health
Transportation
Public Welfare
Natural Resources
Protection of Life and/
Property (National Guard) etc.

CITY MAYORS IN COUNCIL

Municipal services such as:

Health
Sanitation
Water supply
Police
Education
Highways
Justice etc.

STATE COURT OF APPEAL

COUNTY AND CITY COURTS

LOCAL JUSTICES' COURTS

Key

responsibility/approval

direction in which appeals
go from one law court to
another

Appendix 8 **The United Nations**

Structure of organization

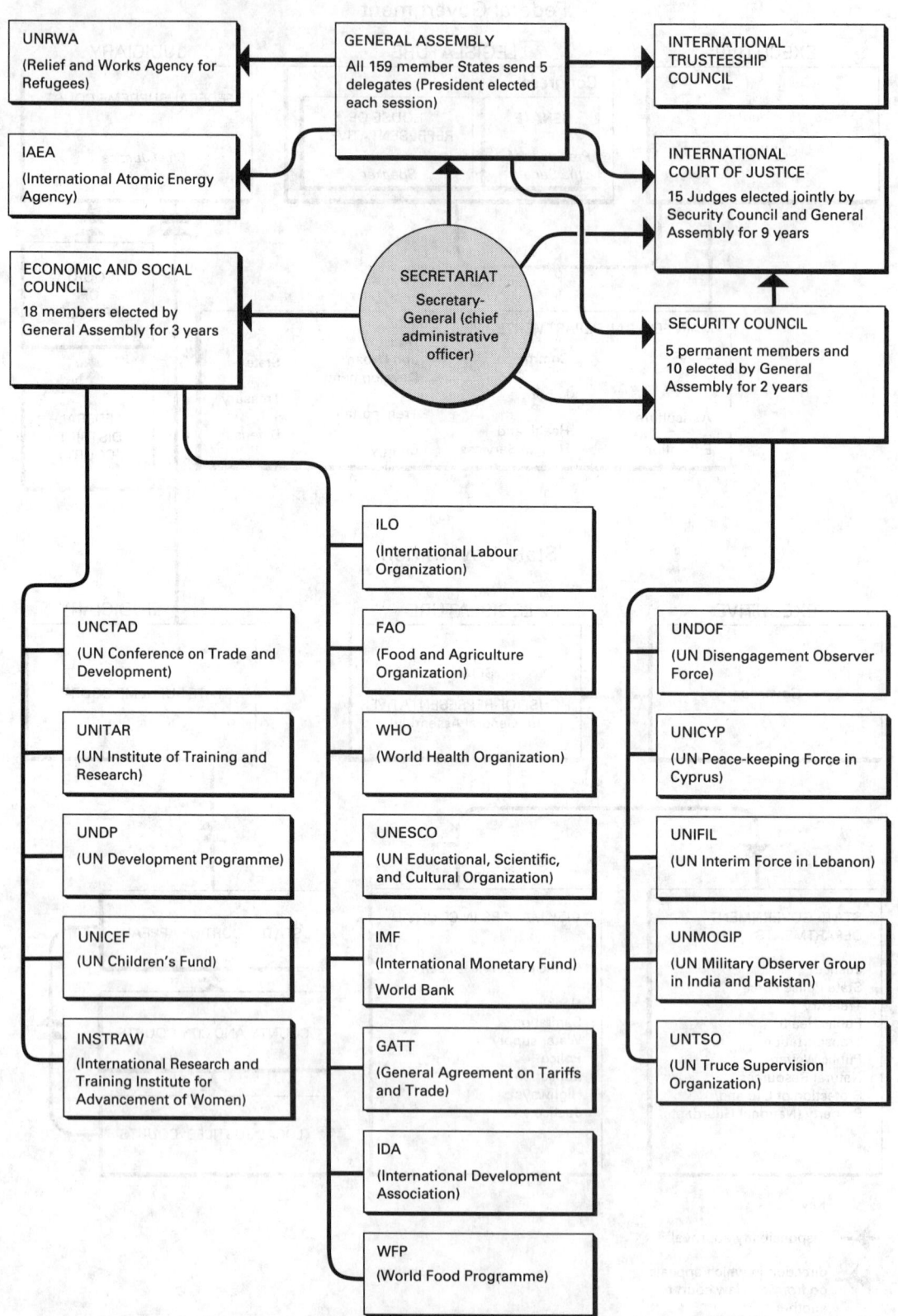

UNRWA
(Relief and Works Agency for Refugees)

IAEA
(International Atomic Energy Agency)

GENERAL ASSEMBLY
All 159 member States send 5 delegates (President elected each session)

INTERNATIONAL TRUSTEESHIP COUNCIL

INTERNATIONAL COURT OF JUSTICE
15 Judges elected jointly by Security Council and General Assembly for 9 years

ECONOMIC AND SOCIAL COUNCIL
18 members elected by General Assembly for 3 years

SECRETARIAT
Secretary-General (chief administrative officer)

SECURITY COUNCIL
5 permanent members and 10 elected by General Assembly for 2 years

UNCTAD
(UN Conference on Trade and Development)

UNITAR
(UN Institute of Training and Research)

UNDP
(UN Development Programme)

UNICEF
(UN Children's Fund)

INSTRAW
(International Research and Training Institute for Advancement of Women)

ILO
(International Labour Organization)

FAO
(Food and Agriculture Organization)

WHO
(World Health Organization)

UNESCO
(UN Educational, Scientific, and Cultural Organization)

IMF
(International Monetary Fund)
World Bank

GATT
(General Agreement on Tariffs and Trade)

IDA
(International Development Association)

WFP
(World Food Programme)

UNDOF
(UN Disengagement Observer Force)

UNICYP
(UN Peace-keeping Force in Cyprus)

UNIFIL
(UN Interim Force in Lebanon)

UNMOGIP
(UN Military Observer Group in India and Pakistan)

UNTSO
(UN Truce Supervision Organization)

Appendix 9 The European Community

Procedure for legislation

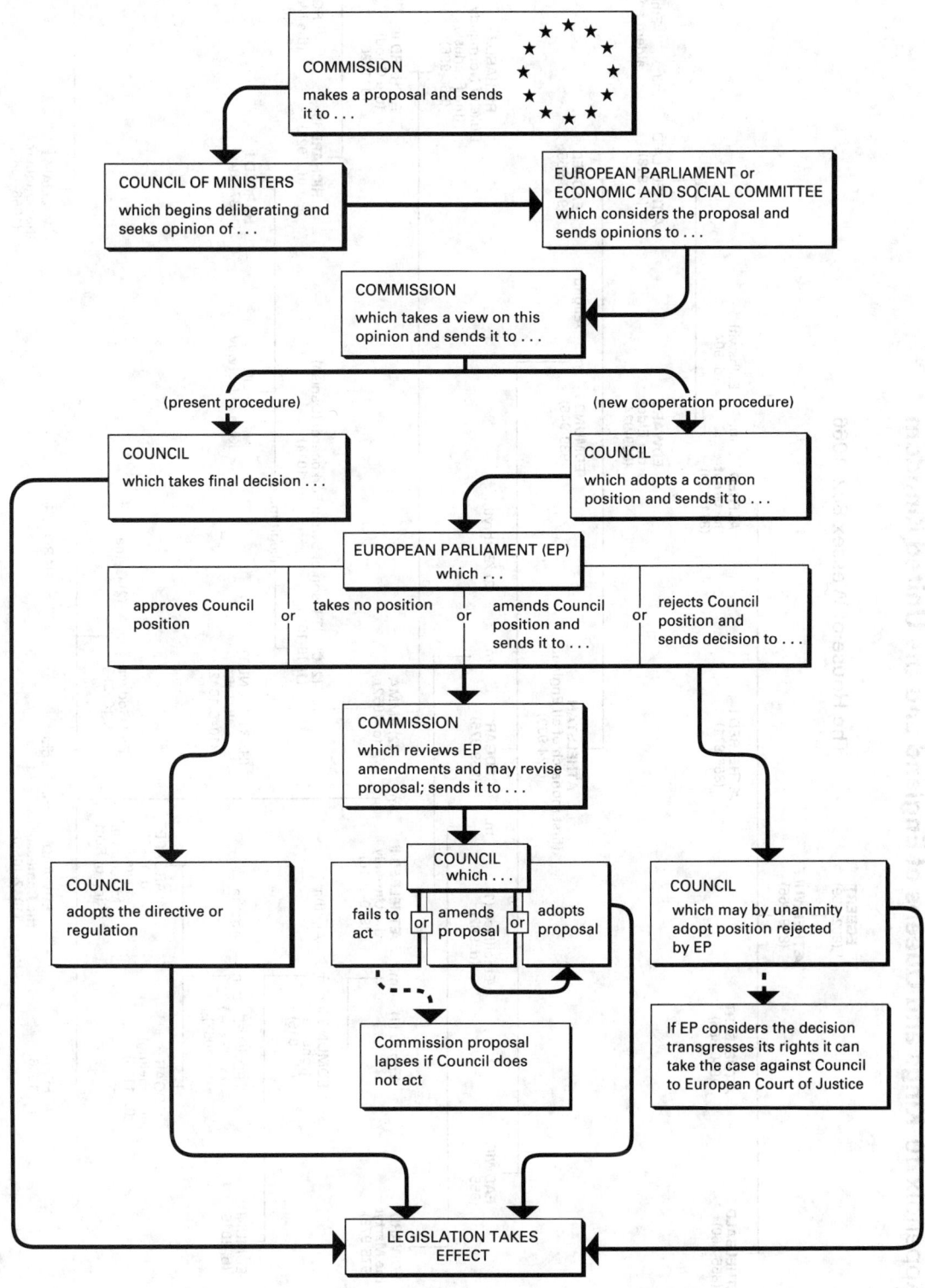

Appendix 10 Kings and Queens of England and the United Kingdom

The House of Wessex 802–1066

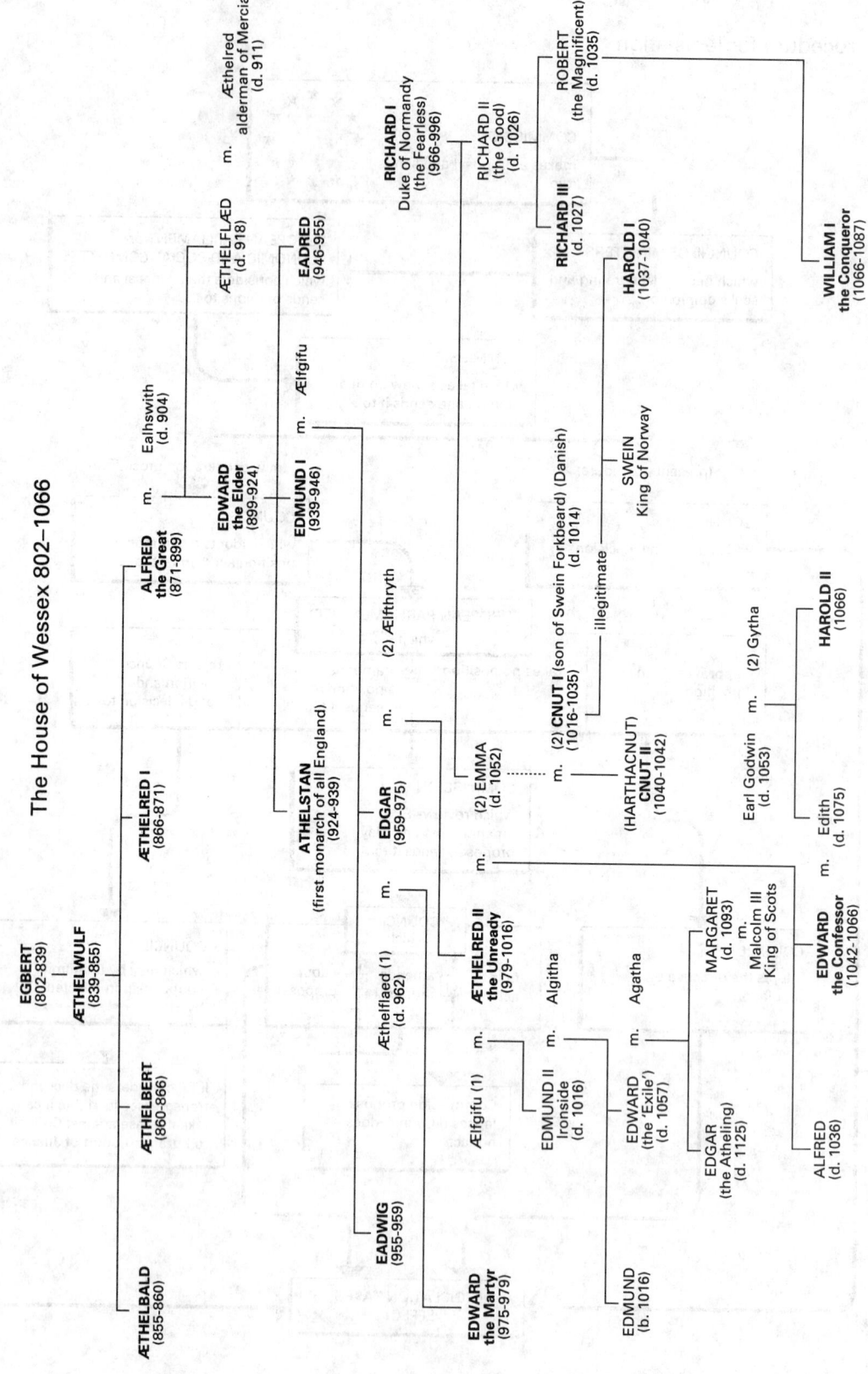

Norman and Plantagenet 1066–1327

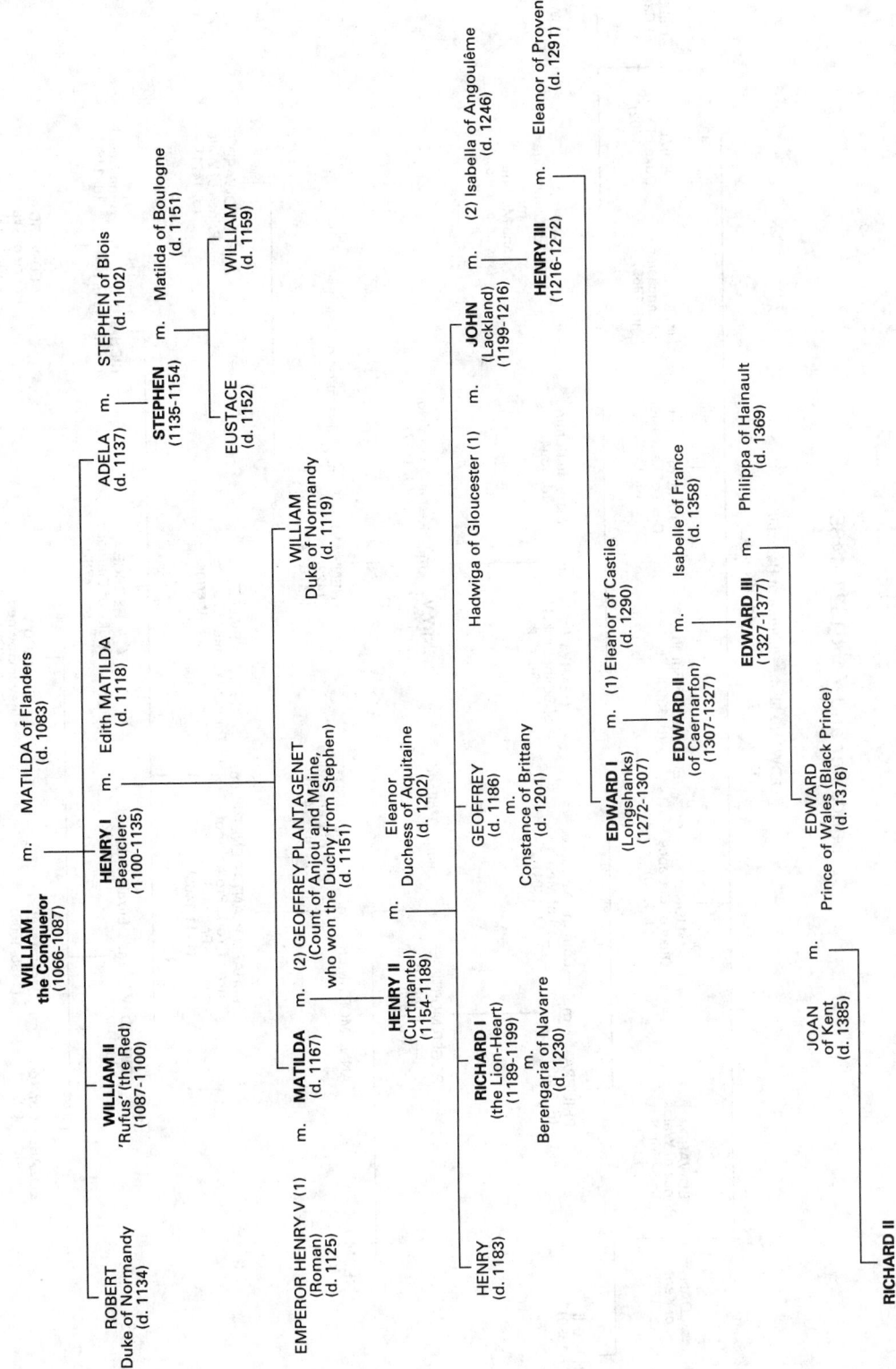

Lancaster and York 1327–1485

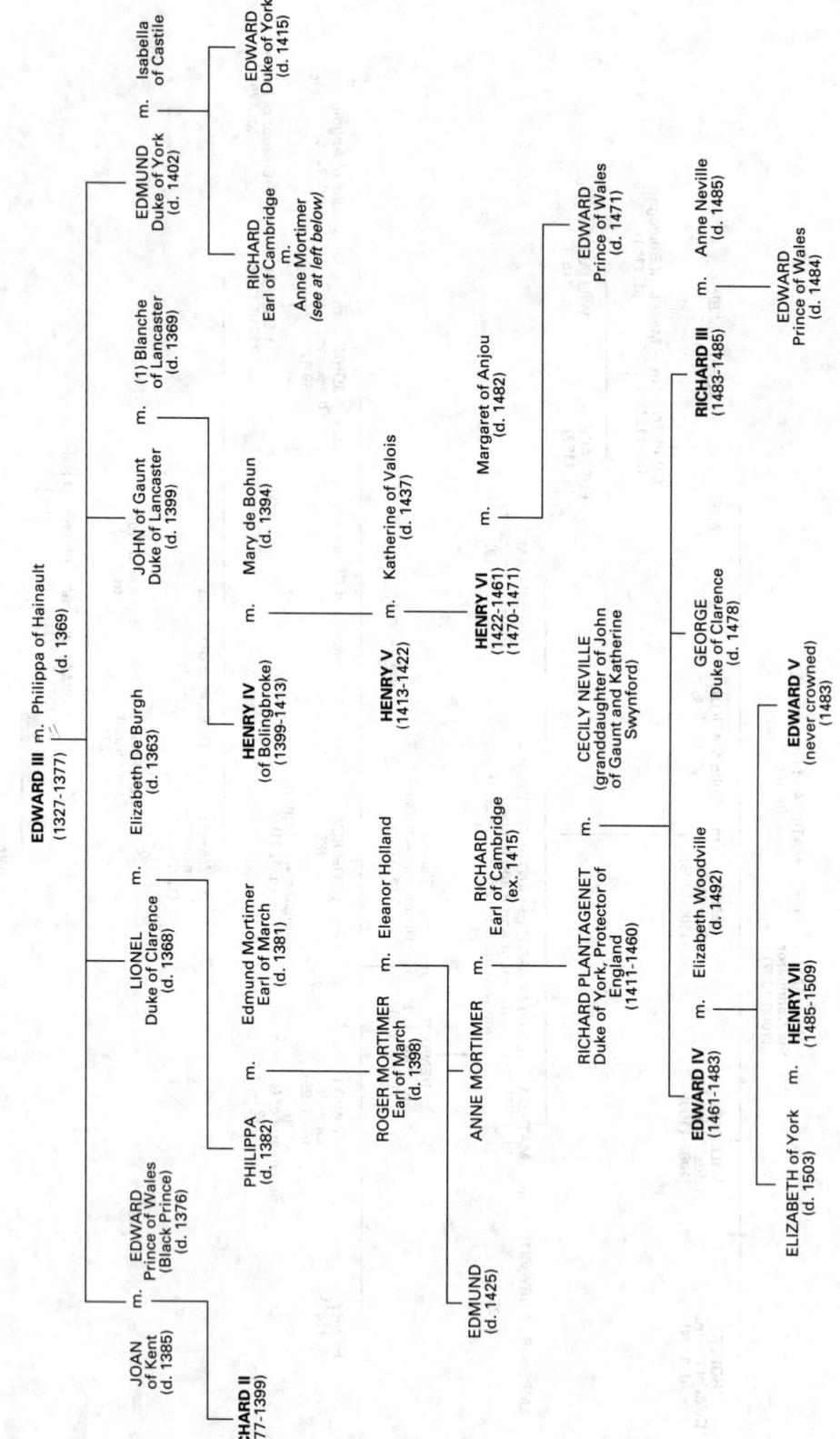

The Tudors 1485–1603

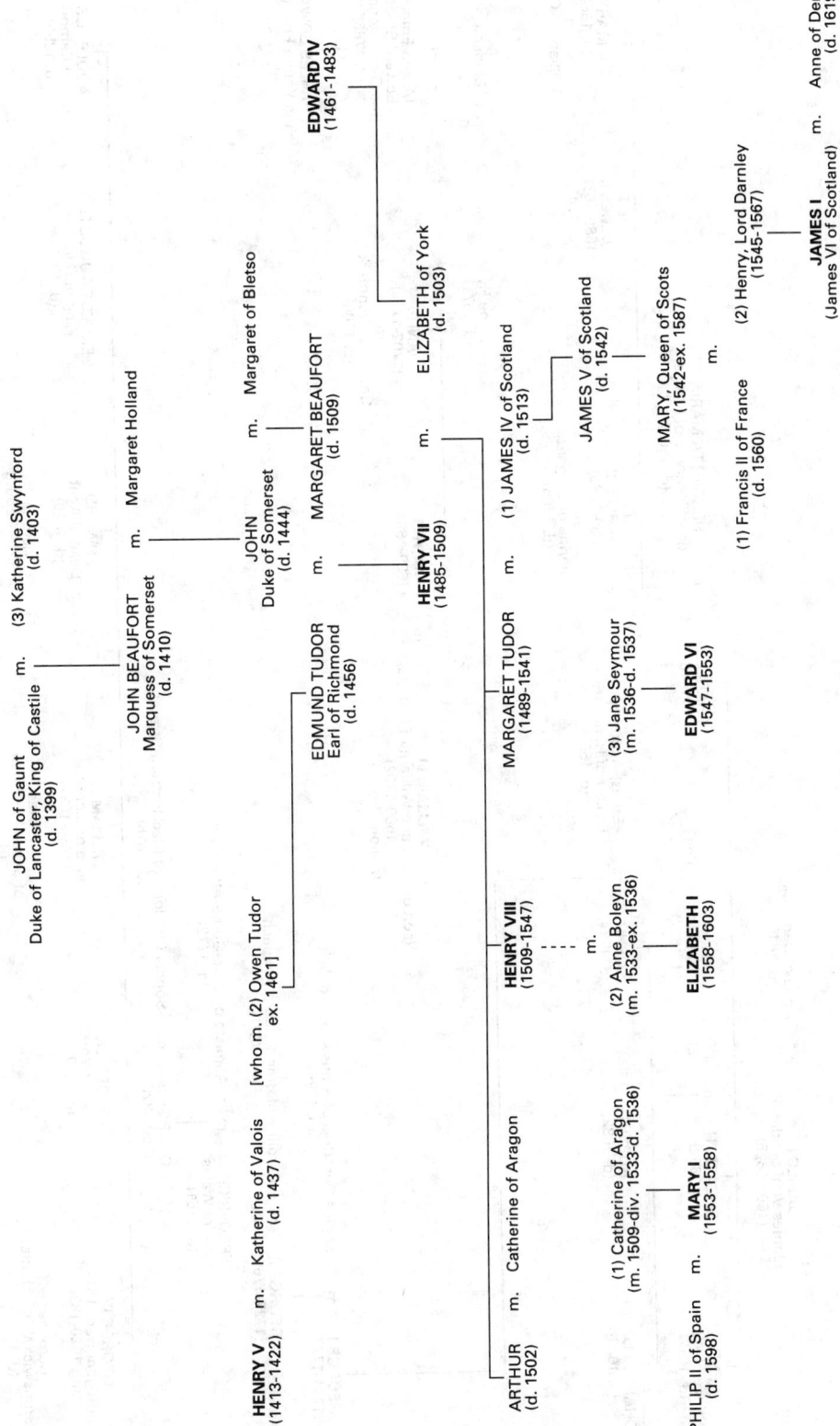

Stuarts and Hanoverians 1603–1837

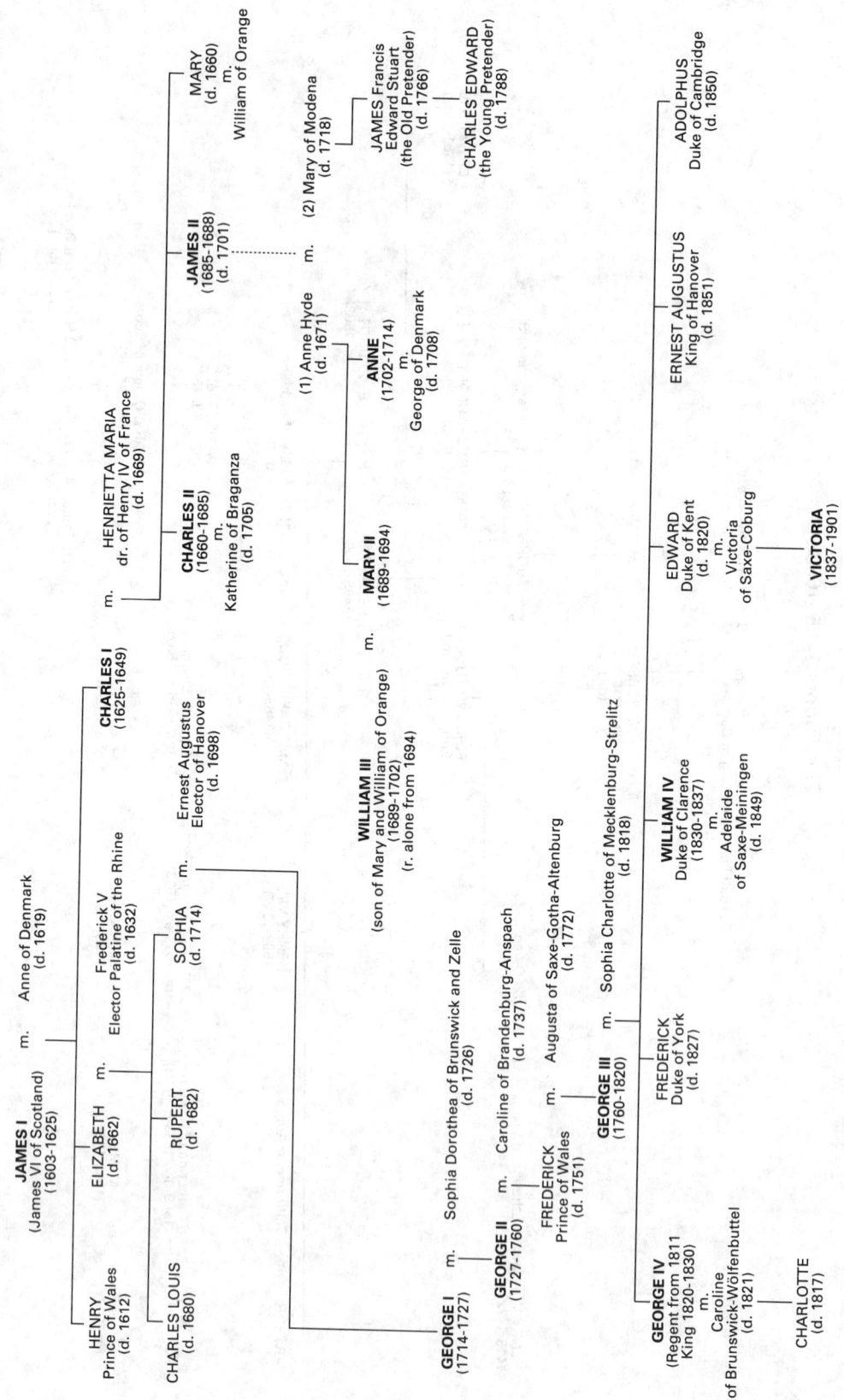

Descendants of Queen Victoria

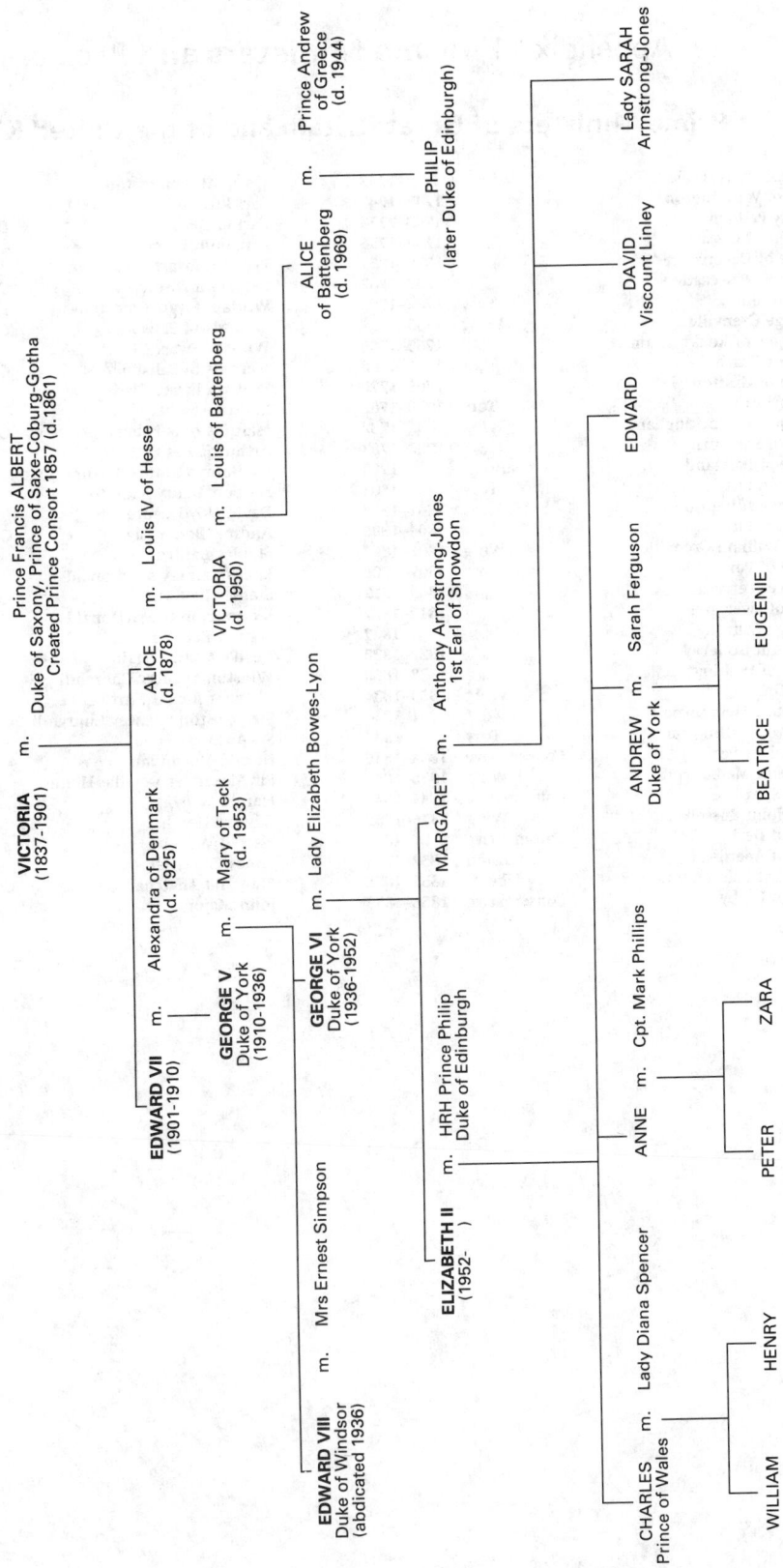

Appendix 11 Prime Ministers and Presidents

Prime Ministers of Great Britain and of the United Kingdom

Sir Robert Walpole	Whig	[1721]–1742
Earl of Wilmington	,,	1742–1743
Henry Pelham	,,	1743–1754
Duke of Newcastle	,,	1754–1756
Duke of Devonshire	,,	1756–1757
Duke of Newcastle	,,	1757–1762
Earl of Bute	Tory	1762–1763
George Grenville	Whig	1763–1765
Marquis of Rockingham	,,	1765–1766
Earl of Chatham	,,	1766–1768
Duke of Grafton	,,	1768–1770
Lord North	Tory	1770–1782
Marquis of Rockingham	Whig	1782
Earl of Shelburne	,,	1782–1783
Duke of Portland	coalition	1783
William Pitt	Tory	1783–1801
Henry Addington	,,	1801–1804
William Pitt	,,	1804–1806
Lord William Grenville	Whig	1806–1807
Duke of Portland	Tory	1807–1809
Spencer Perceval	,,	1809–1812
Earl of Liverpool	,,	1812–1827
George Canning	,,	1827
Viscount Goderich	,,	1827–1828
Duke of Wellington	,,	1828–1830
Earl Grey	Whig	1830–1834
Viscount Melbourne	,,	1834
Duke of Wellington	Tory	1834
Sir Robert Peel	Conservative	1834–1835
Viscount Melbourne	Whig	1835–1841
Sir Robert Peel	Conservative	1841–1846
Lord John Russell	Whig	1846–1852
Earl of Derby	Conservative	1852
Earl of Aberdeen	coalition	1852–1855
Viscount Palmerston	Liberal	1855–1858
Earl of Derby	Conservative	1858–1859
Viscount Palmerston	Liberal	1859–1865
Earl Russell	,,	1865–1866
Earl of Derby	Conservative	1866–1868
Benjamin Disraeli	,,	1868
William Ewart Gladstone	Liberal	1868–1874
Benjamin Disraeli	Conservative	1874–1880
William Ewart Gladstone	Liberal	1880–1885
Marquis of Salisbury	Conservative	1885–1886
William Ewart Gladstone	Liberal	1886
Marquis of Salisbury	Conservative	1886–1892
William Ewart Gladstone	Liberal	1892–1894
Earl of Rosebery	,,	1894–1895
Marquis of Salisbury	Conservative	1895–1902
Arthur James Balfour	,,	1902–1905
Sir Henry Campbell-Bannerman	Liberal	1905–1908
Herbert Henry Asquith	,,	1908–1916
David Lloyd George	coalition	1916–1922
Andrew Bonar Law	Conservative	1922–1923
Stanley Baldwin	,,	1923–1924
James Ramsay MacDonald	Labour	1924
Stanley Baldwin	Conservative	1924–1929
James Ramsay MacDonald	coalition	1929–1935
Stanley Baldwin	,,	1935–1937
Neville Chamberlain	,,	1937–1940
Winston Spencer Churchill	,,	1940–1945
Clement Richard Attlee	Labour	1945–1951
Sir Winston Spencer Churchill	Conservative	1951–1955
Sir Anthony Eden	,,	1955–1957
Harold Macmillan	,,	1957–1963
Sir Alexander Douglas-Home	,,	1963–1964
Harold Wilson	Labour	1964–1970
Edward Heath	Conservative	1970–1974
Harold Wilson	Labour	1974–1976
James Callaghan	,,	1976–1979
Margaret Thatcher	Conservative	1979–1990
John Major	,,	1990–

Prime Ministers of Canada

John A. Macdonald	1867–1873		W. L. Mackenzie King	1926–1930
Alexander Mackenzie	1873–1878		Richard B. Bennett	1930–1935
John A. Macdonald	1878–1891		W. L. Mackenzie King	1935–1948
John J. C. Abbott	1891–1892		Louis Stephen St Laurent	1948–1957
John S. D. Thompson	1892–1894		John George Diefenbaker	1957–1963
Mackenzie Bowell	1894–1896		Lester B. Pearson	1963–1968
Charles Tupper	1896		Pierre Elliott Trudeau	1968–1979
Wilfrid Laurier	1896–1911		Joseph Clark	1979–1980
Robert L. Borden	1911–1920		Pierre Elliott Trudeau	1980–1984
Arthur Meighen	1920–1921		John Turner	1984
W. L. Mackenzie King	1921–1926		Brian Mulroney	1984–
Arthur Meighen	1926			

Prime Ministers of Australia

Edmund Barton	1901–1903		Joseph A. Lyons	1932–1939
Alfred Deakin	1903–1904		Robert Gordon Menzies	1939–1941
John C. Watson	1904		Arthur William Fadden	1941
George Houstoun Reid	1904–1905		John Curtin	1941–1945
Alfred Deakin	1905–1908		Joseph Benedict Chifley	1945–1949
Andrew Fisher	1908–1909		Robert Gordon Menzies	1949–1966
Alfred Deakin	1909–1910		Harold Edward Holt	1966–1967
Andrew Fisher	1910–1913		John Grey Gorton	1968–1971
Joseph Cook	1913–1914		William McMahon	1971–1972
Andrew Fisher	1914–1915		Gough Whitlam	1972–1975
William M. Hughes	1915–1923		J. Malcolm Fraser	1975–1983
Stanley M. Bruce	1923–1929		Robert J. L. Hawke	1983–
James H. Scullin	1929–1931			

Prime Ministers of New Zealand

Henry Sewell	1856		Harry Albert Atkinson	1887–1891
William Fox	1856		John Ballance	1891–1893
Edward William Stafford	1856–1861		Richard John Seddon	1893–1906
William Fox	1861–1862		William Hall-Jones	1906
Alfred Domett	1862–1863		Joseph George Ward	1906–1912
Frederick Whitaker	1863–1864		Thomas Mackenzie	1912
Frederick Aloysius Weld	1864–1865		William Ferguson Massey	1912–1925
Edward William Stafford	1865–1869		Francis Henry Dillon Bell	1925
William Fox	1869–1872		Joseph Gordon Coates	1925–1928
Edward William Stafford	1872		Joseph George Ward	1928–1930
George Marsden Waterhouse	1872–1873		George William Forbes	1930–1935
William Fox	1873		Michael J. Savage	1935–1940
Julius Vogel	1873–1875		Peter Fraser	1940–1949
Daniel Pollen	1875–1876		Sidney G. Holland	1949–1957
Julius Vogel	1876		Keith J. Holyoake	1957 (Aug.–Nov.)
Harry Albert Atkinson	1876–1877		Walter Nash	1957–1960
George Grey	1877–1879		Keith J. Holyoake	1960–1972
John Hall	1879–1882		John R. Marshall	1972
Frederick Whitaker	1882–1883		Norman Kirk	1972–1974
Harry Albert Atkinson	1883–1884		Wallace Rowling	1974–1975
Robert Stout	1884		Robert D. Muldoon	1975–1984
Harry Albert Atkinson	1884		Hon. David Lange	1984–1989
Robert Stout	1884–1887		Geoffrey Palmer	1989–

Presidents of the United States of America

1. George Washington	Federalist	1789–1797
2. John Adams	„	1797–1801
3. Thomas Jefferson	Democratic-Republican	1801–1809
4. James Madison	„	1809–1817
5. James Monroe	„	1817–1825
6. John Quincy Adams	Independent	1825–1829
7. Andrew Jackson	Democrat	1829–1837
8. Martin Van Buren	„	1837–1841
9. William H. Harrison	Whig	1841
10. John Tyler	Whig, then Democrat	1841–1845
11. James K. Polk	Democrat	1845–1849
12. Zachary Taylor	Whig	1849–1850
13. Millard Fillmore	„	1850–1853
14. Franklin Pierce	Democrat	1853–1857
15. James Buchanan	„	1857–1861
16. Abraham Lincoln	Republican	1861–1865
17. Andrew Johnson	Democrat	1865–1869
18. Ulysses S. Grant	Republican	1869–1877
19. Rutherford B. Hayes	„	1877–1881
20. James A. Garfield	„	1881

21. Chester A. Arthur	Republican	1881–1885
22. Grover Cleveland	Democrat	1885–1889
23. Benjamin Harrison	Republican	1889–1893
24. Grover Cleveland	Democrat	1893–1897
25. William McKinley	Republican	1897–1901
26. Theodore Roosevelt	„	1901–1909
27. William H. Taft	„	1909–1913
28. Woodrow Wilson	Democrat	1913–1921
29. Warren G. Harding	Republican	1921–1923
30. Calvin Coolidge	„	1923–1929
31. Herbert Hoover	„	1929–1933
32. Franklin D. Roosevelt	Democrat	1933–1945
33. Harry S Truman	„	1945–1953
34. Dwight D. Eisenhower	Republican	1953–1961
35. John F. Kennedy	Democrat	1961–1963
36. Lyndon B. Johnson	„	1963–1969
37. Richard M. Nixon	Republican	1969–1974
38. Gerald R. Ford	„	1974–1977
39. James Earl Carter	Democrat	1977–1981
40. Ronald W. Reagan	Republican	1981–1989
41. George H. W. Bush	„	1989–

Appendix 12 Weather

The atmosphere

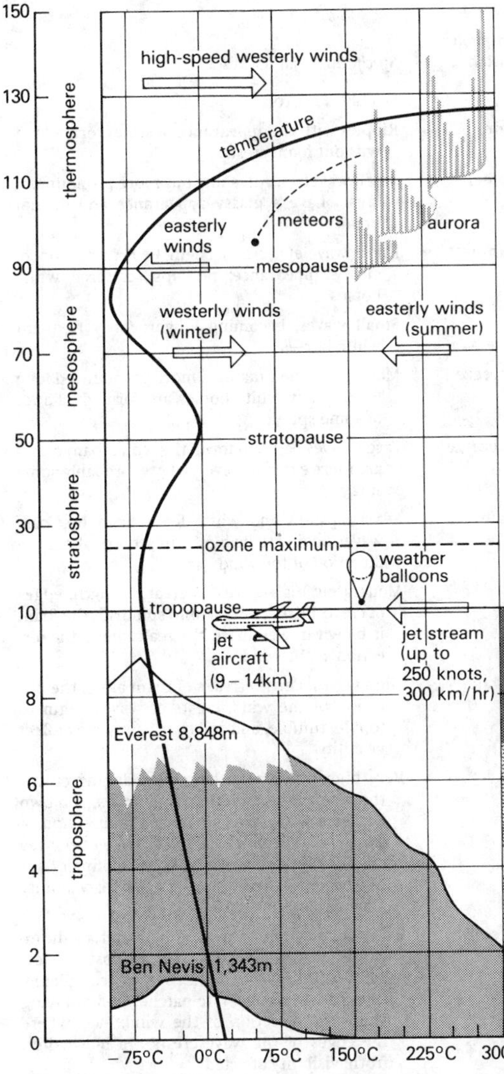

km

150 — thermosphere

high-speed westerly winds

130

temperature

110

easterly winds — meteors — aurora

90 — mesopause

mesosphere

westerly winds (winter) — easterly winds (summer)

70

50 — stratopause

30 — stratosphere

ozone maximum — weather balloons

10 — tropopause — jet aircraft (9 – 14km) — jet stream (up to 250 knots, 300 km/hr)

8

Everest 8,848m

6 — troposphere

4

2 — Ben Nevis 1,343m

0

−75°C 0°C 75°C 150°C 225°C 300°C

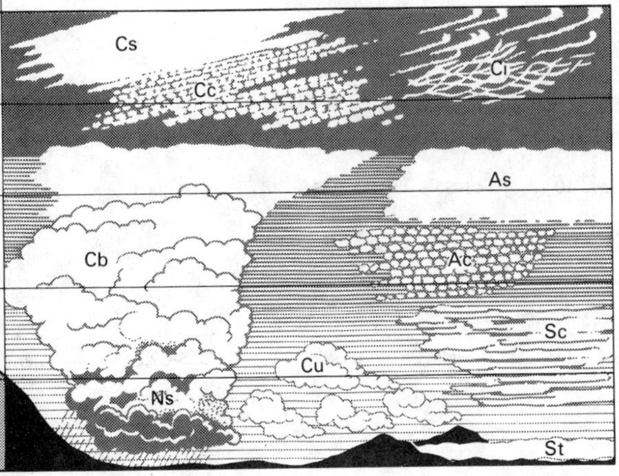

temperature in the atmosphere in a temperate zone, varying with altitude (°C)

Winds and pressure systems

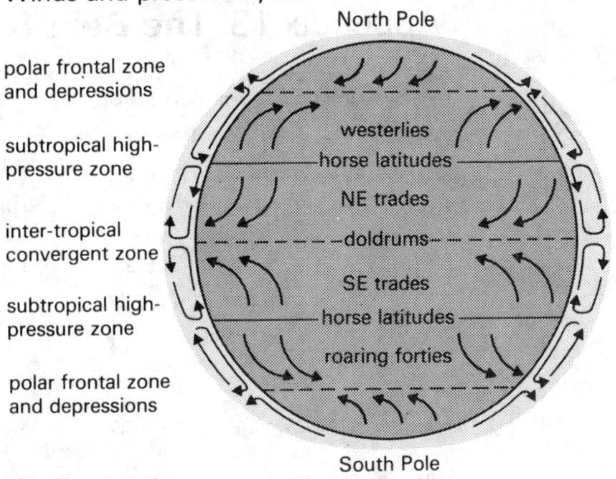

North Pole

polar frontal zone and depressions

subtropical high-pressure zone

inter-tropical convergent zone

subtropical high-pressure zone

polar frontal zone and depressions

South Pole

westerlies
horse latitudes
NE trades
doldrums
SE trades
horse latitudes
roaring forties

Clouds

high level (5 – 13km)
Cs cirrostratus
Cc cirrocumulus
Ci cirrus

middle level (2 – 7km)
Cb cumulonimbus
Ac altocumulus
As altostratus

low level (0 – 3km)
St stratus
Ns nimbo-stratus

Cu cumulus
Sc stratocumulus

Cs Cc Ci As Ac Cb Sc Cu Ns St

Thunderstorms

When the upper part of the cloud becomes positively charged and the lower part negatively charged to a sufficient extent, a giant spark of lightning occurs and the air expands rapidly, producing a thunderclap. Rain is typically (but not essentially) present.

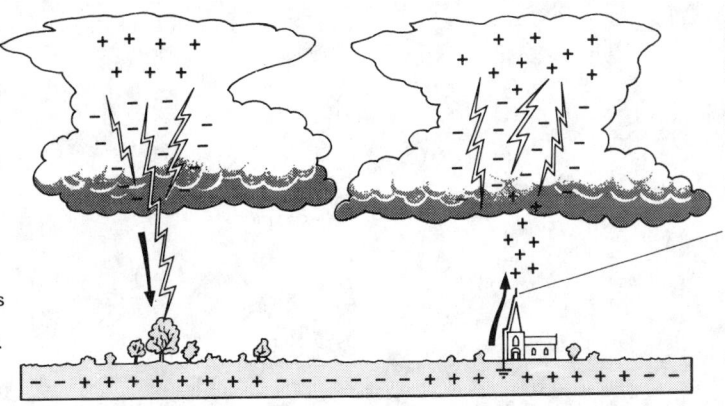

lightning

speed approx. 140,000km/sec

current up to 100,000 amps

heat release up to 30,000°C

a lightning-conductor lowers the charge difference by concentrating a positive 'electric wind' towards the base of the cloud

Appendix 13 The Beaufort Scale of Wind Force

Beaufort Number	Equivalent speed at 10 m above ground			Description of wind	Specifications for use at sea
	Knots	Miles per hour	Metres per second		
0	<1	<1	0.0–0.2	Calm	Sea like a mirror
1	1–3	1–3	0.3–1.5	Light air	Ripples with the appearance of scales formed but without foam crests
2	4–6	4–7	1.6–3.3	Light breeze	Small wavelets, still short but more pronounced; crests have a glassy appearance and do not break
3	7–10	8–12	3.4–5.4	Gentle breeze	Large wavelets; crests begin to break; foam of glassy appearance; perhaps scattered white horses
4	11–16	13–18	5.5–7.9	Moderate breeze	Small waves, becoming longer; fairly frequent white horses
5	17–21	19–24	8.0–10.7	Fresh breeze	Moderate waves, taking a more pronounced long form; many white horses are formed; chance of some spray
6	22–27	25–31	10.8–13.8	Strong breeze	Large waves begin to form; the white foam crests are more extensive everywhere; probably some spray
7	28–33	32–38	13.9–17.1	Near gale	Sea heaps up and white foam from breaking waves begins to be blown in streaks along the direction of the wind
8	34–40	39–46	17.2–20.7	Gale	Moderately high waves of greater length; edges of crests begin to break into spindrift; the foam is blown in well-marked streaks along the direction of the wind
9	41–47	47–54	20.8–24.4	Strong gale	High waves; dense streaks of foam along the direction of the wind; crests of waves begin to topple, tumble, and roll over; spray may affect visibility
10	48–55	55–63	24.5–28.4	Storm	Very high waves with long overhanging crests; the resulting foam, in great patches, is blown in dense white streaks along the direction of the wind; on the whole, the surface of the sea takes a white appearance; the tumbling of the sea becomes heavy and shock-like; visibility affected
11	56–63	64–72	28.5–32.6	Violent storm	Exceptionally high waves (small and medium-sized ships might be for a time lost to view behind the waves); the sea is completely covered with long white patches of foam lying along the direction of the wind; everywhere the edges of the wave crests are blown into froth; visibility affected
12	⩾64	⩾73	⩾32.7	Hurricane	The air is filled with foam and spray; sea completely white with driving spray; visibility very seriously affected

Appendix 14 Shapes and Forms in Mathematics

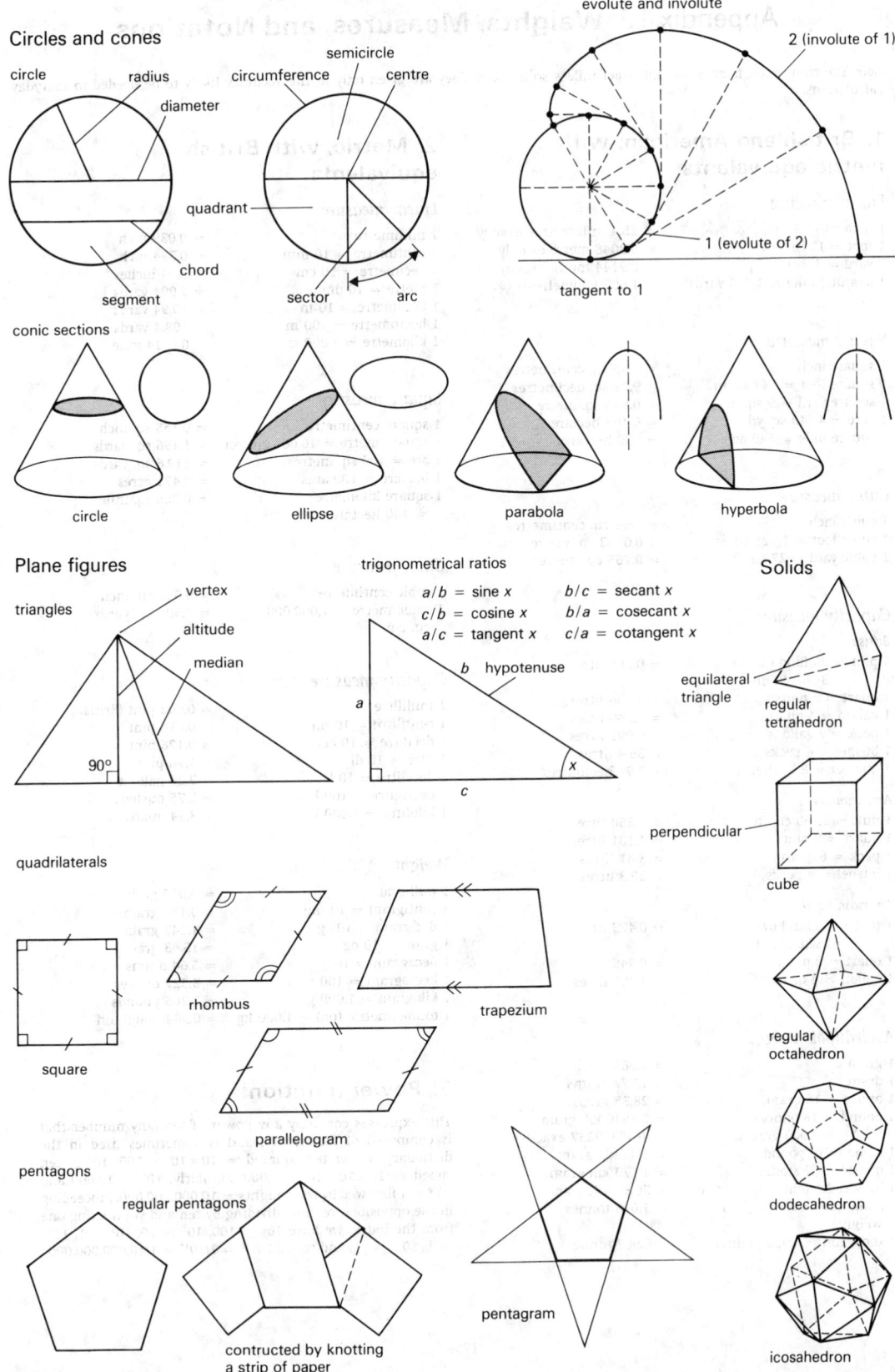

Circles and cones

evolute and involute

2 (involute of 1)
1 (evolute of 2)
tangent to 1

circle
radius
diameter
semicircle
circumference
centre
quadrant
chord
segment
sector
arc

conic sections

circle
ellipse
parabola
hyperbola

Plane figures

trigonometrical ratios

a/b = sine x b/c = secant x
c/b = cosine x b/a = cosecant x
a/c = tangent x c/a = cotangent x

triangles

vertex
altitude
median
$90°$

b hypotenuse
a
c
x

Solids

equilateral triangle
regular tetrahedron

perpendicular
cube

quadrilaterals

square
rhombus
trapezium
parallelogram

regular octahedron

pentagons

regular pentagons
contructed by knotting a strip of paper

pentagram

dodecahedron

icosahedron

Appendix 15 Weights, Measures, and Notations

Note. The conversion factors are not exact unless so marked. They are given only to the accuracy likely to be needed in everyday calculations.

1. British and American, with metric equivalents

Linear measure

1 inch	= 25.4 millimetres exactly
1 foot = 12 inches	= 0.3048 metre exactly
1 yard = 3 feet	= 0.9144 metre exactly
1 (statute) mile = 1,760 yards	= 1.609 kilometres

Square measure

1 square inch	= 6.45 sq. centimetres
1 square foot = 144 sq. in.	= 9.29 sq. decimetres
1 square yard = 9 sq. ft.	= 0.836 sq. metre
1 acre = 4,840 sq. yd.	= 0.405 hectare
1 square mile = 640 acres	= 259 hectares

Cubic measure

1 cubic inch	= 16.4 cu. centimetres
1 cubic foot = 1,728 cu. in.	= 0.0283 cu. metre
1 cubic yard = 27 cu. ft.	= 0.765 cu. metre

Capacity measure

British

1 pint = 20 fluid oz.	= 0.568 litre
= 34.68 cu. in.	
1 quart = 2 pints	= 1.136 litres
1 gallon = 4 quarts	= 4.546 litres
1 peck = 2 gallons	= 9.092 litres
1 bushel = 4 pecks	= 36.4 litres
1 quarter = 8 bushels	= 2.91 hectolitres

American dry

1 pint = 33.60 cu. in.	= 0.550 litre
1 quart = 2 pints	= 1.101 litres
1 peck = 8 quarts	= 8.81 litres
1 bushel = 4 pecks	= 35.3 litres

American liquid

1 pint = 16 fluid oz.	= 0.473 litre
= 28.88 cu. in.	
1 quart = 2 pints	= 0.946 litre
1 gallon = 4 quarts	= 3.785 litres

Avoirdupois weight

1 grain	= 0.065 gram
1 dram	= 1.772 grams
1 ounce = 16 drams	= 28.35 grams
1 pound = 16 ounces	= 0.4536 kilogram
= 7,000 grains	(0.45359237 exactly)
1 stone = 14 pounds	= 6.35 kilograms
1 quarter = 2 stones	= 12.70 kilograms
1 hundredweight = 4 quarters	= 50.80 kilograms
1 (long) ton = 20 hundred-weight	= 1.016 tonnes
1 short ton = 2,000 pounds	= 0.907 tonne

2. Metric, with British equivalents

Linear measure

1 millimetre	= 0.039 inch
1 centimetre = 10 mm	= 0.394 inch
1 decimetre = 10 cm	= 3.94 inches
1 metre = 10 dm	= 1.094 yards
1 decametre = 10 m	= 10.94 yards
1 hectometre = 100 m	= 109.4 yards
1 kilometre = 1,000 m	= 0.6214 mile

Square measure

1 square centimetre	= 0.155 sq. inch
1 square metre = 10,000 sq. cm	= 1.196 sq. yards
1 are = 100 sq. metres	= 119.6 sq. yards
1 hectare = 100 ares	= 2.471 acres
1 square kilometre = 100 hectares	= 0.386 sq. mile

Cubic measure

1 cubic centimetre	= 0.061 cu. inch
1 cubic metre = 1,000,000 cu. cm	= 1.308 cu. yards

Capacity measure

1 millilitre	= 0.002 pint (British)
1 centilitre = 10 ml	= 0.018 pint
1 decilitre = 10 cl	= 0.176 pint
1 litre = 10 dl	= 1.76 pints
1 decalitre = 10 l	= 2.20 gallons
1 hectolitre = 100 l	= 2.75 bushels
1 kilolitre = 1,000 l	= 3.44 quarters

Weight

1 milligram	= 0.015 grain
1 centigram = 10 mg	= 0.154 grain
1 decigram = 10 cg	= 1.543 grain
1 gram = 10 dg	= 15.43 grain
1 decagram = 10 g	= 5.64 drams
1 hectogram = 100 g	= 3.527 ounces
1 kilogram = 1,000 g	= 2.205 pounds
1 tonne (metric ton) = 1,000 kg	= 0.984 (long) ton

3. Power notation

This expresses concisely any power of ten (any number that is composed of factors 10), and is sometimes used in the dictionary. 10^2 or ten squared = 10×10 = 100; 10^3 or ten cubed = $10 \times 10 \times 10$ = 1,000. Similarly, 10^4 = 10,000 and 10^{10} = 1 followed by ten noughts = 10,000,000,000. Proceeding in the opposite direction, dividing by ten and subtracting one from the index, we have 10^2 = 100, 10^1 = 10, 10^0 = 1, 10^{-1} = $\frac{1}{10}$, 10^{-2} = $\frac{1}{100}$, and so on; 10^{-10} = $1/10^{10}$ = $1/10,000,000,000$.

4. Temperature

Fahrenheit: Water boils (under standard conditions) at 212° and freezes at 32°.
Celsius or Centigrade: Water boils at 100° and freezes at 0°.
Kelvin: Water boils at 373.15 K and freezes at 273.15 K.

Celsius	Fahrenheit
−17. 8°	0°
−10°	14°
0°	32°
10°	50°
20°	68°
30°	86°
40°	104°
50°	122°
60°	140°
70°	158°
80°	176°
90°	194°
100°	212°

To convert Celsius into Fahrenheit: multiply by 9, divide by 5, and add 32.
To convert Fahrenheit into Celsius: subtract 32, multiply by 5, and divide by 9.

5. Metric prefixes

	Abbreviation or Symbol	Factor
deca-	da	10
hecto-	h	10^2
kilo-	k	10^3
mega-	M	10^6
giga-	G	10^9
tera-	T	10^{12}
peta-	P	10^{15}
exa-	E	10^{18}
deci-	d	10^{-1}
centi-	c	10^{-2}
milli-	m	10^{-3}
micro-	μ	10^{-6}
nano-	n	10^{-9}
pico-	p	10^{-12}
femto-	f	10^{-15}
atto-	a	10^{-18}

Pronunciations and derivations of these are given at their alphabetical places in the dictionary. They may be applied to any units of the metric system: hectogram (abbr. hg) = 100 grams; kilowatt (abbr. kW) = 1,000 watts; megahertz (MHz) = 1 million hertz; centimetre (cm) = $\frac{1}{100}$ metre; microvolt (μV) = one millionth of a volt; picofarad (pF) = 10^{-12} farad, and are sometimes applied to other units (megabit, microinch).

6. Chemical notation

The symbol for a molecule (such as H_2O, CH_4, H_2SO_4) shows the symbols for the elements contained in it (C = carbon, H = hydrogen, etc.), followed by a subscript numeral denoting the number of atoms of each element in the molecule where this number is more than one. For example, the water molecule (H_2O) contains two atoms of hydrogen and one of oxygen.

7. SI units

Base units

Physical quantity	Name	Abbreviation or Symbol
length	metre	m
mass	kilogram	kg
time	second	s
electric current	ampere	A
temperature	kelvin	K
amount of substance	mole	mol
luminous intensity	candela	cd

Supplementary units

Physical quantity	Name	Abbreviation or Symbol
plane angle	radian	rad
solid angle	steradian	sr

Derived units with special names

Physical quantity	Name	Abbreviation or Symbol
frequency	hertz	Hz
energy	joule	J
force	newton	N
power	watt	W
pressure	pascal	Pa
electric charge	coulomb	C
electromotive force	volt	V
electric resistance	ohm	Ω
electric conductance	siemens	S
electric capacitance	farad	F
magnetic flux	weber	Wb
inductance	henry	H
magnetic flux density	tesla	T
luminous flux	lumen	lm
illumination	lux	lx

8. Binary system

Only two units (0 and 1) are used, and the position of each unit indicates a power of two.

One to ten written in binary form:

	eights (2^3)	fours (2^2)	twos (2^1)	one
1				1
2			1	0
3			1	1
4		1	0	0
5		1	0	1
6		1	1	0
7		1	1	1
8	1	0	0	0
9	1	0	0	1
10	1	0	1	0

i.e. ten is written as 1010 ($2^3 + 0 + 2^1 + 0$); one hundred is written as 1100100 ($2^6 + 2^5 + 0 + 0 + 2^2 + 0 + 0$)

Appendix 16 · Chemical Elements

Periodic Table of the Elements

IA	IIA	IIIB	IVB	VB	VIB	VIIB		VIII		IB	IIB	IIIA	IVA	VA	VIA	VIIA	O
1 H																	2 He
3 Li	4 Be											5 B	6 C	7 N	8 O	9 F	10 Ne
11 Na	12 Mg				Transitional metals							13 Al	14 Si	15 P	16 S	17 Cl	18 Ar
19 K	20 Ca	21 Sc	22 Ti	23 V	24 Cr	25 Mn	26 Fe	27 Co	28 Ni	29 Cu	30 Zn	31 Ga	32 Ge	33 As	34 Se	35 Br	36 Kr
37 Rb	38 Sr	39 Y	40 Zr	41 Nb	42 Mo	43 Tc	44 Ru	45 Rh	46 Pd	47 Ag	48 Cd	49 In	50 Sn	51 Sb	52 Te	53 I	54 Xe
55 Cs	56 Ba	*57 La	72 Hf	73 Ta	74 W	75 Re	76 Os	77 Ir	78 Pt	79 Au	80 Hg	81 Tl	82 Pb	83 Bi	84 Po	85 At	86 Rn
87 Fr	88 Ra	†89 Ac	104 Unq	105 Unp	106 Unh	107 Uns											

* Lanthanides	57 La	58 Ce	59 Pr	60 Nd	61 Pm	62 Sm	63 Eu	64 Gd	65 Tb	66 Dy	67 Ho	68 Er	69 Tm	70 Yb	71 Lu
† Actinides	89 Ac	90 Th	91 Pa	92 U	93 Np	94 Pu	95 Am	96 Cm	97 Bk	98 Cf	99 Es	100 Fm	101 Md	102 No	103 Lr

Element	Symbol	Element	Symbol	Element	Symbol	Element	Symbol
actinium	Ac	europium	Eu	mercury	Hg	samarium	Sm
aluminium	Al	fermium	Fm	molybdenum	Mo	scandium	Sc
americium	Am	fluorine	F	neodymium	Nd	selenium	Se
antimony	Sb	francium	Fr	neon	Ne	silicon	Si
argon	Ar	gadolinium	Gd	neptunium	Np	silver	Ag
arsenic	As	gallium	Ga	nickel	Ni	sodium	Na
astatine	At	germanium	Ge	niobium	Nb	strontium	Sr
barium	Ba	gold	Au	nitrogen	N	sulphur	S
berkelium	Bk	hafnium	Hf	nobelium	No	tantalum	Ta
beryllium	Be	hahnium[1]	Ha	osmium	Os	technetium	Tc
bismuth	Bi	helium	He	oxygen	O	tellurium	Te
boron	B	holmium	Ho	palladium	Pd	terbium	Tb
bromine	Br	hydrogen	H	phosphorus	P	thallium	Tl
cadmium	Cd	indium	In	platinum	Pt	thorium	Th
caesium	Cs	iodine	I	plutonium	Pu	thulium	Tm
calcium	Ca	iridium	Ir	polonium	Po	tin	Sn
californium	Cf	iron	Fe	potassium	K	titanium	Ti
carbon	C	krypton	Kr	praseodymium	Pr	tungsten	W
cerium	Ce	kurchatovium[1]	Ku	promethium	Pm	uranium	U
chlorine	Cl	lanthanum	La	protactinium	Pa	vanadium	V
chromium	Cr	lawrencium	Lr	radium	Ra	xenon	Xe
cobalt	Co	lead	Pb	radon	Rn	ytterbium	Yb
copper	Cu	lithium	Li	rhenium	Re	yttrium	Y
curium	Cm	lutetium	Lu	rhodium	Rh	zinc	Zn
dysprosium	Dy	magnesium	Mg	rubidium	Rb	zirconium	Zr
einsteinium	Es	manganese	Mn	ruthenium	Ru		
erbium	Er	mendelevium	Md	rutherfordium[1]	Rf		

[1] Names formed systematically and without attribution are preferred by IUPAC for numbers from 104 onward, and are used exclusively for numbers from 106 onward. Names based on the atomic number are formed on the numerical roots *nil* (= 0), *un* (= 1), *bi* (= 2), etc. (e.g. *unnilquadium* = 104, *ununbium* = 112, etc.)

Appendix 17 **Electronics**
Some symbols and components

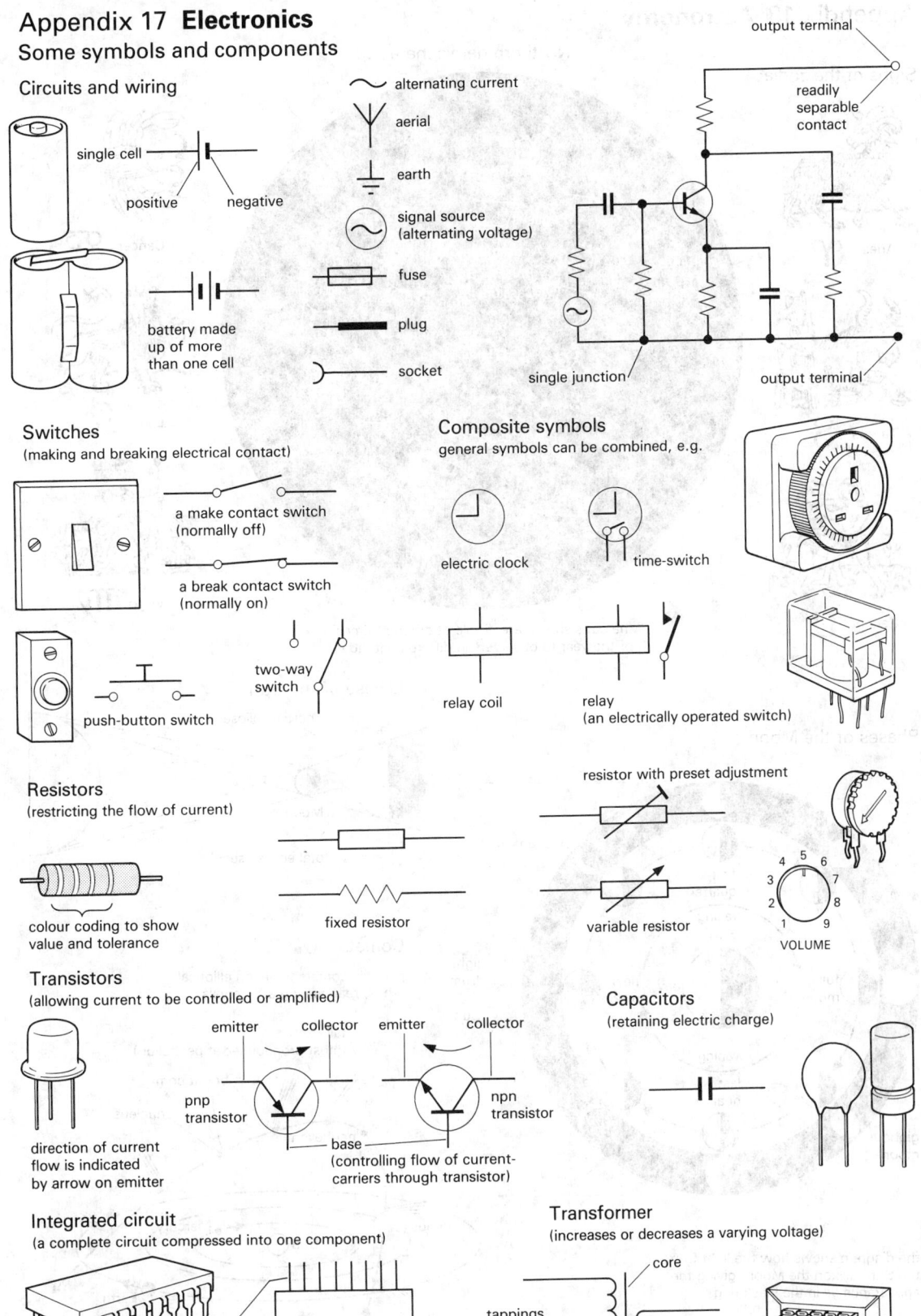

Circuits and wiring

single cell

positive   negative

battery made
up of more
than one cell

alternating current

aerial

earth

signal source
(alternating voltage)

fuse

plug

socket

output terminal

readily
separable
contact

single junction

output terminal

Switches
(making and breaking electrical contact)

a make contact switch
(normally off)

a break contact switch
(normally on)

two-way
switch

push-button switch

Composite symbols
general symbols can be combined, e.g.

electric clock

time-switch

relay coil

relay
(an electrically operated switch)

Resistors
(restricting the flow of current)

colour coding to show
value and tolerance

fixed resistor

resistor with preset adjustment

variable resistor

VOLUME

Transistors
(allowing current to be controlled or amplified)

emitter   collector   emitter   collector

pnp
transistor

npn
transistor

direction of current
flow is indicated
by arrow on emitter

base
(controlling flow of current-
carriers through transistor)

Capacitors
(retaining electric charge)

Integrated circuit
(a complete circuit compressed into one component)

inputs

outputs

Transformer
(increases or decreases a varying voltage)

core

tappings

winding

Appendix 18 **Astronomy**

Signs of the zodiac

Aries ♈

Taurus ♉

Gemini ♊

Northern hemisphere

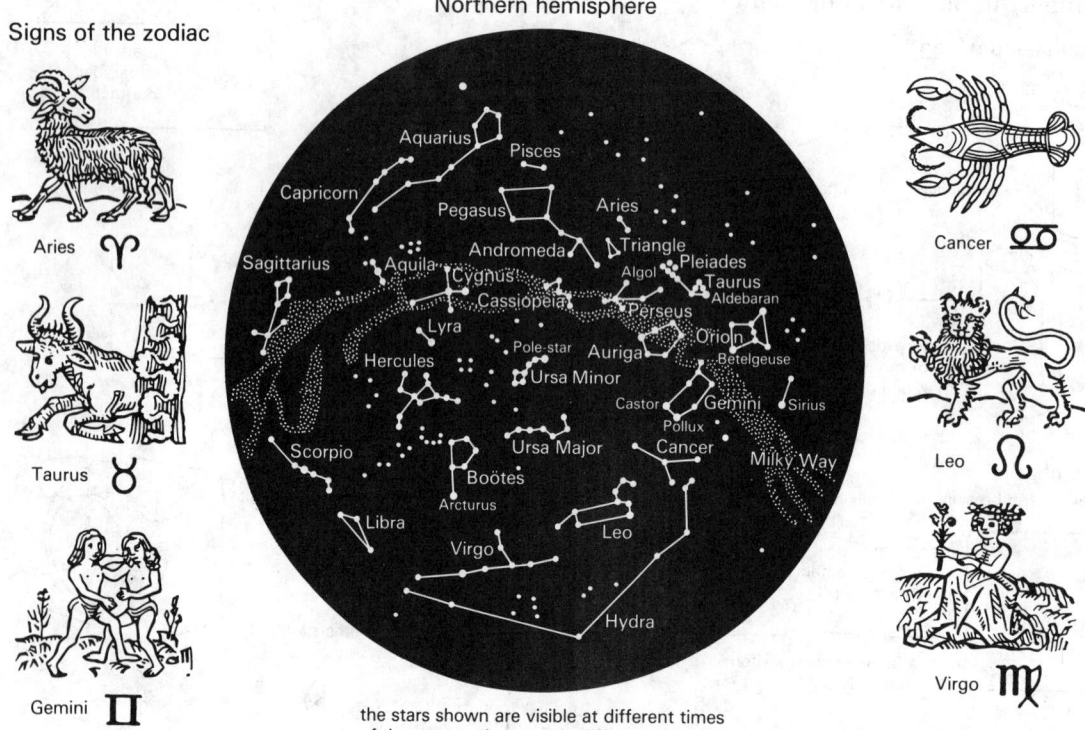

Aquarius
Pisces
Capricorn
Pegasus
Aries
Sagittarius
Aquila
Andromeda
Triangle
Pleiades
Algol
Taurus
Cygnus
Aldebaran
Cassiopeia
Perseus
Lyra
Orion
Pole-star
Auriga
Betelgeuse
Hercules
Ursa Minor
Castor
Gemini
Pollux
Sirius
Scorpio
Ursa Major
Cancer
Milky Way
Boötes
Arcturus
Libra
Leo
Virgo
Hydra

the stars shown are visible at different times
of the year to observers in different latitudes

Cancer ♋

Leo ♌

Virgo ♍

Eclipse of the Sun

Earth
partial eclipse seen
Moon
Sun
total eclipse seen

Phases of the Moon

crescent moon

first
quarter
waxing
Earth
full
moon
night
day
new
moon
light
from
the
Sun
waning
last
quarter

gibbous
moon

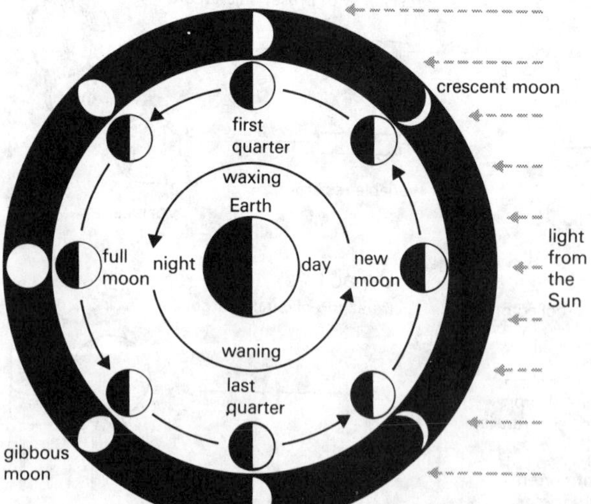

the diagram shows how the light from
the Sun falls on the Moon, giving the
appearance as in the black ring

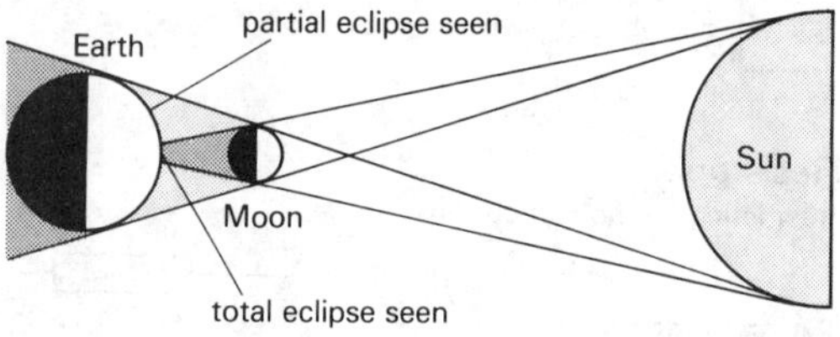

Comets

periodic comets travel on elliptical
orbits, reappearing at intervals

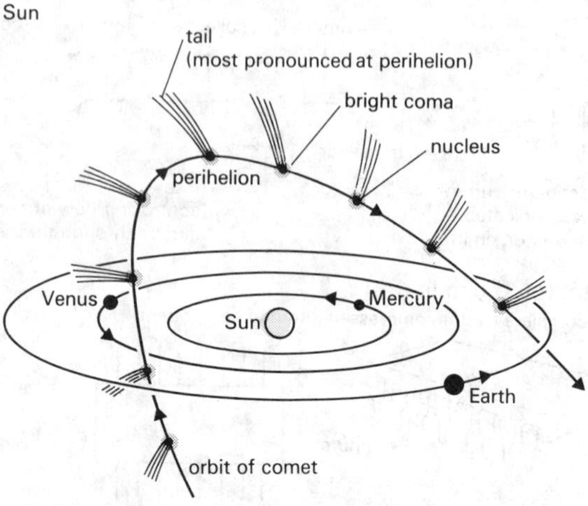

tail
(most pronounced at perihelion)
bright coma
nucleus
perihelion
Venus
Mercury
Sun
Earth

orbit of comet

Southern hemisphere

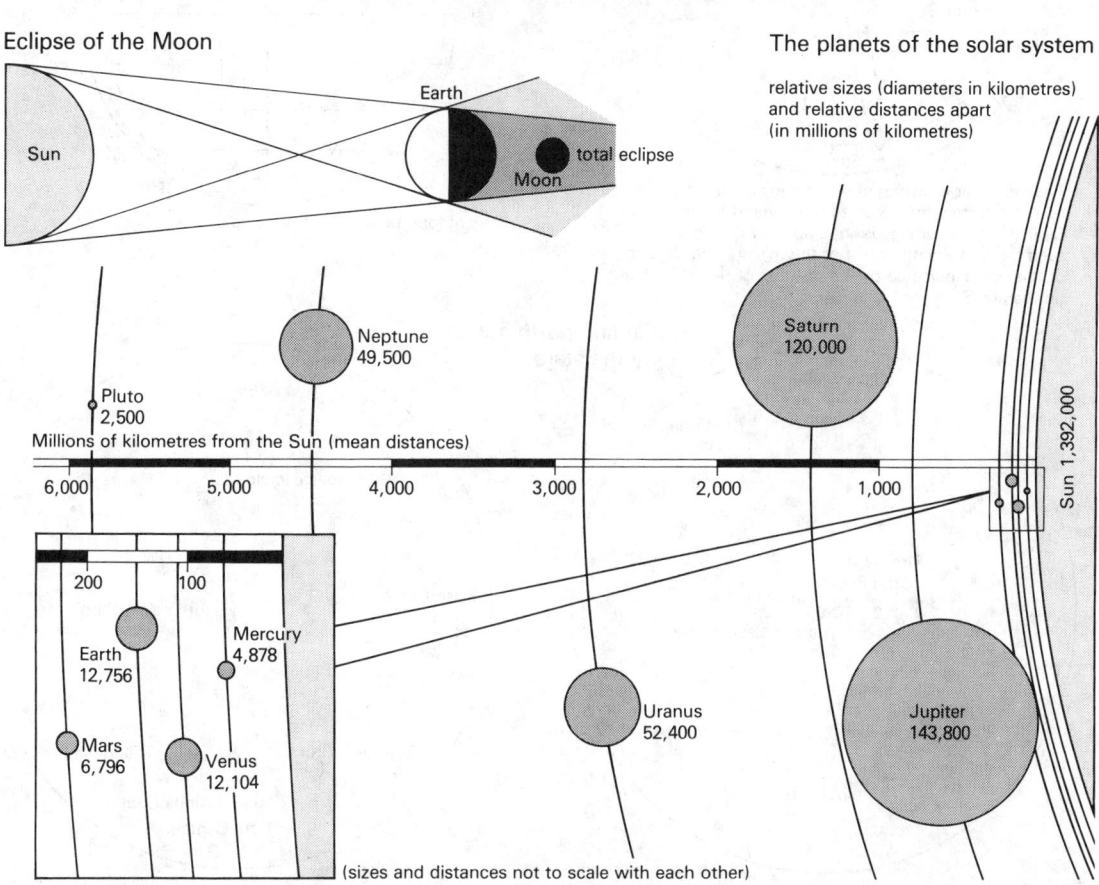

Libra ♎

Scorpio ♏

Sagittarius ♐

Capricorn ♑

Aquarius ♒

Pisces ♓

Southern hemisphere constellations shown:
Pegasus, Triangle, Aries, Pisces, Aquarius, Cygnus, Taurus, Pleiades, Phoenix, Capricorn, Aquila, Eridanus, Lyra, Auriga, Aldebaran, Orion, Betelgeuse, Sagittarius, Sirius, Southern Triangle, Gemini, Southern Cross, Scorpio, Hercules, Castor, Pollux, Milky Way, Centaurus, Libra, Hydra, Cancer, Virgo, Arcturus, Boötes, Leo

the shapes of some constellations appear different
in the two maps because of the different standpoints used

Eclipse of the Moon

Sun

Earth

total eclipse

Moon

The planets of the solar system

relative sizes (diameters in kilometres)
and relative distances apart
(in millions of kilometres)

Neptune
49,500

Saturn
120,000

Sun 1,392,000

Pluto
2,500

Millions of kilometres from the Sun (mean distances)

6,000   5,000   4,000   3,000   2,000   1,000

200   100

Mercury
4,878

Earth
12,756

Mars
6,796

Venus
12,104

Uranus
52,400

Jupiter
143,800

(sizes and distances not to scale with each other)

Celestial sphere

meridian and
azimuth circle
for point A

north celestial pole

zenith for
point A

winter
solstice

summer
solstice

Earth

ecliptic

equinox

celestial equator

nadir for
point A

south celestial pole

Points of the compass

N by W · N · N by E
NNW · NNE
NW by N · NE by N
NW · 0° · NE
NW by W · NE by E
WNW · ENE
315° · 45°
W by N · E by N
W · 270° · 90° · E
W by S · E by S
WSW · ESE
225° · 135°
SW by W · SE by E
SW · 180° · SE
SW by S · SE by S
SSW · SSE
S by W · S · S by E

modern compass roses are
usually marked in degrees only

Latitude and longitude

any point on the Earth's surface
can be defined by two references
(e.g. 51° 48′ N, 2° 27′ W)

lines of
latitude

North Pole

tropic of
Cancer
(23 ½° N)

west

75°N
60°N
45°N — meridian
30°N
15°N

75° 45° 30° 15° 0° 15° 30° 45° 75°
60° 60°

0° east

equator
15°S

30°S

tropic of
Capricorn
(23 ½° S)

45°S
60°S
75°S

lines of longitude

South Pole

Sextant

used to find
latitude at sea

star or sun

mirror A

half-silvered
mirror B

telescope

horizon

arc

60°

30°

0°

index bar

The index bar is swung until the chosen star is
reflected from mirror A on to the silvered half of mirror
B. The reflected image is lined up with the horizon
seen through the other half of the mirror. The altitude
of the star is indicated by the position of the index bar
on the arc.

Finding north and south by the stars

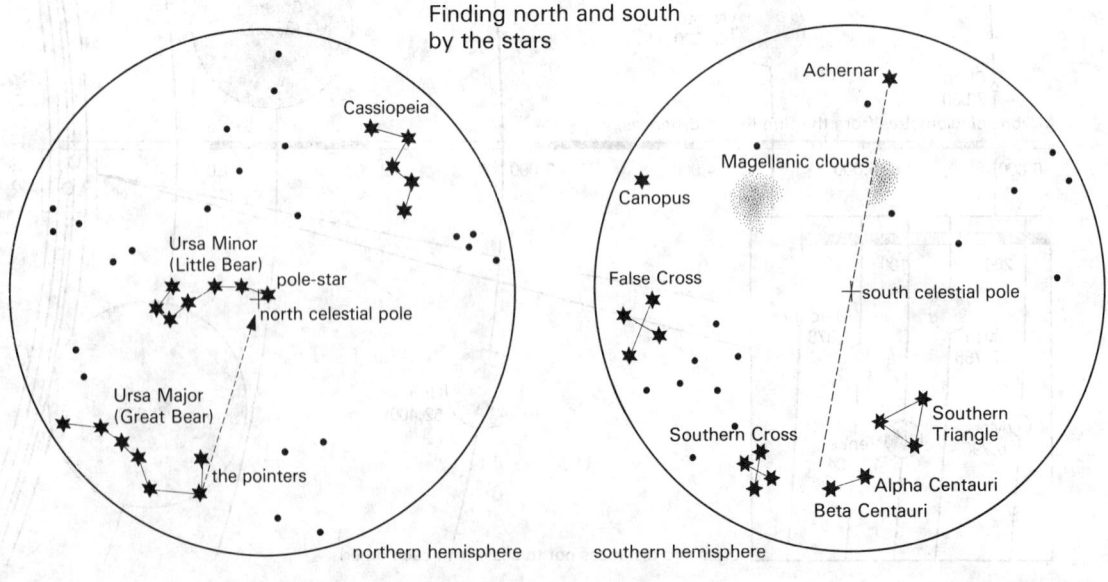

Cassiopeia

Ursa Minor
(Little Bear)

pole-star

north celestial pole

Ursa Major
(Great Bear)

the pointers

northern hemisphere

Achernar

Magellanic clouds

Canopus

False Cross

south celestial pole

Southern Cross

Southern
Triangle

Alpha Centauri
Beta Centauri

southern hemisphere

Appendix 20 Geology

Fossil history

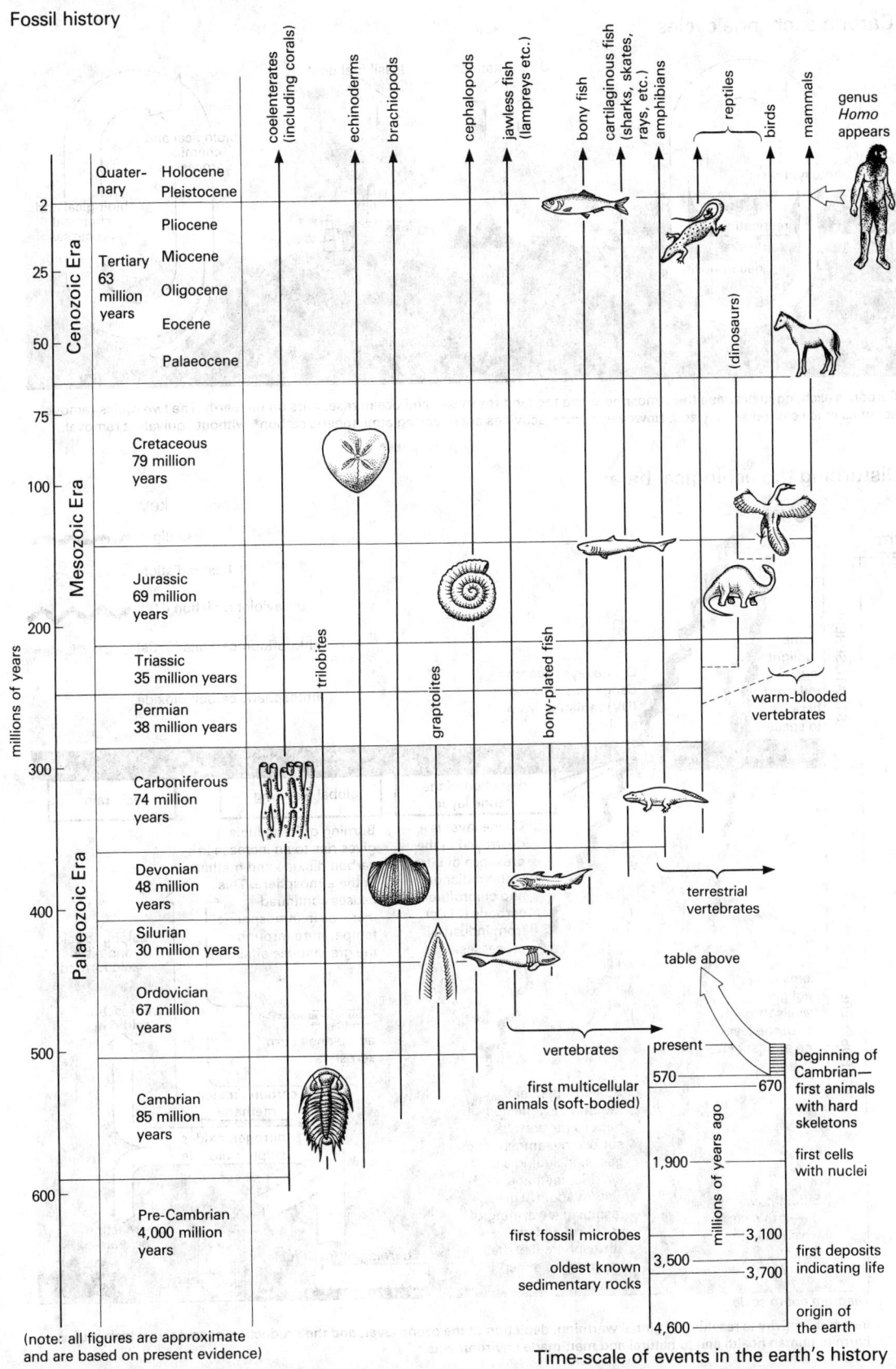

Time-scale of events in the earth's history

(note: all figures are approximate and are based on present evidence)

Appendix 21 **Ecology**

Carbon exchange cycles

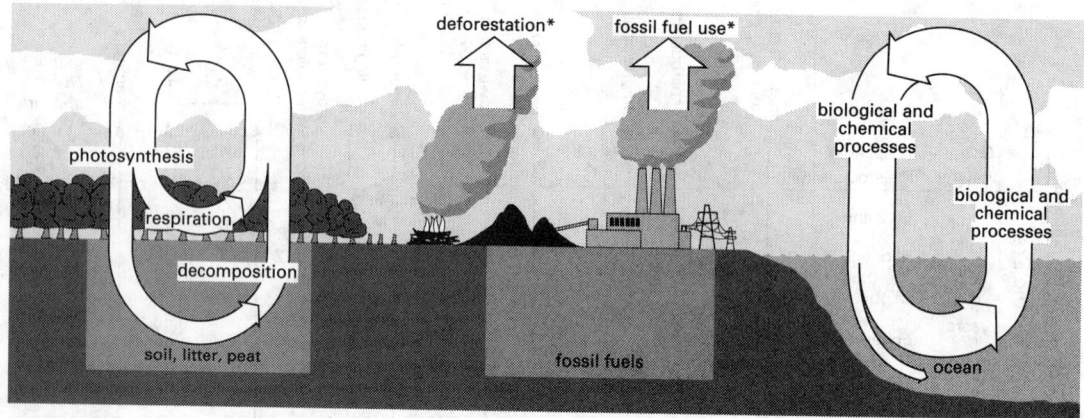

deforestation* fossil fuel use*

biological and chemical processes

photosynthesis

respiration

decomposition

biological and chemical processes

soil, litter, peat

fossil fuels

ocean

Carbon is exchanged between the atmosphere and the land reservoirs and ocean reservoirs on the earth. The two cycles remove about as much carbon as they add. However, human activities are releasing atmospheric carbon* without equivalent removal.

Disturbing the ecological balance

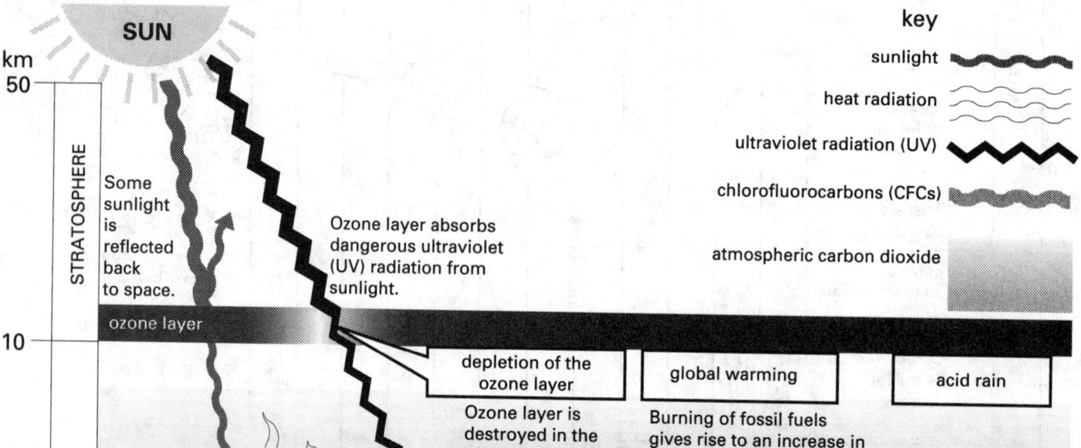

SUN

km
50

key

sunlight

heat radiation

ultraviolet radiation (UV)

chlorofluorocarbons (CFCs)

atmospheric carbon dioxide

STRATOSPHERE

Some sunlight is reflected back to space.

Ozone layer absorbs dangerous ultraviolet (UV) radiation from sunlight.

ozone layer

10

depletion of the ozone layer

global warming

acid rain

Ozone layer is destroyed in the presence of ultra-violet radiation, and chlorofluoro-carbons (CFCs) from industrial processes.

Burning of fossil fuels gives rise to an increase in carbon dioxide and methane in the atmosphere. This causes continued increase in atmospheric temperature through the greenhouse effect.

sulphuric acid and nitric acid formed

TROPOSPHERE

Remaining sunlight travels through the ozone layer and atmosphere.

aeroplanes burn kerosene

wet reaction acid rain

carbon dioxide methane

nitrogen oxides sulphur dioxide

Some of the heat radiation is reflected back to the earth's surface by atmospheric gases, including carbon dioxide, methane, and water vapour. This results in a warming of the earth and its atmosphere (i.e. the greenhouse effect).

Sunlight warms the earth's surface, which radiates heat.

burning of fossil fuels

dry reaction acid air

Diagram not to scale

Industrial activity is resulting in global warming, depletion of the ozone layer, and the production of acid rain which causes harm to human health and to natural and man-made environments.

Appendix 22 Terms for Groups of Animals etc.

Terms marked † belong to 15th-c. lists of 'proper terms', notably that in the *Book of St Albans* attributed to Dame Juliana Barnes (1486). Many of these are fanciful or humorous terms which probably never had any real currency, but have been taken up by Joseph Strutt in *Sports and Pastimes of England* (1801) and by other antiquarian writers.

a †shrewdness of apes
a herd or †pace of asses
a †cete of badgers
a †sloth or †sleuth of bears
a hive of bees; a swarm, drift, or bike of bees
a flock, flight, (*dial.*) parcel, pod (= small flock), †fleet, or †dissimulation of (small) birds; a volary of birds in an aviary
a sounder of wild boar
a †blush of boys
a herd or gang of buffalo
a †clowder or †glaring of cats; a †dowt (= ?do-out) or †destruction of wild cats
a herd, drove, (*dial.*) drift, or (*US & Austral.*) mob of cattle
a brood, (*dial.*) cletch or clutch, or †peep of chickens
a †chattering or †clattering of choughs
a †drunkship of cobblers
a †rag or †rake of colts
a †hastiness of cooks
a †covert of coots
a herd of cranes
a litter of cubs
a herd of curlew
a †cowardice of curs
a herd or mob of deer
a pack or kennel of dogs
a trip of dotterel
a flight, †dole, or †piteousness of doves
a raft, bunch, or †paddling of ducks on water; a team of wild ducks in flight
a fling of dunlins
a herd of elephants
a herd or (*US*) gang of elk
a †business of ferrets
a charm or †chirm of finches
a shoal of fish; a run of fish in motion
a cloud of flies
a †stalk of foresters
a †skulk of foxes
a gaggle or (in the air) a skein, team, or wedge of geese
a herd of giraffes
a flock, herd, or (*dial.*) trip of goats
a pack or covey of grouse
a †husk or †down of hares
a cast of hawks let fly
an †observance of hermits
a †siege of herons
a stud or †haras of (breeding) horses; (*dial.*) a team of horses
a kennel, pack, cry, or †mute of hounds
a flight or swarm of insects
a mob or troop of kangaroos
a kindle of kittens
a bevy of ladies
a †desert of lapwing

an †exaltation or bevy of larks
a †leap of leopards
a pride of lions
a †tiding of magpies
a †sord or †sute (= suit) of mallard
a †richesse of martens
a †faith of merchants
a †labour of moles
a troop of monkeys
a †barren of mules
a †watch of nightingales
a †superfluity of nuns
a covey of partridges
a †muster of peacocks
a †malapertness (= impertinence) of pedlars
a rookery of penguins
a head or (*dial.*) nye of pheasants
a kit of pigeons flying together
a herd of pigs
a stand, wing, or †congregation of plovers
a rush or flight of pochards
a herd, pod, or school of porpoises
a †pity of prisoners
a covey of ptarmigan
a litter of pups
a bevy or drift of quail
a string of racehorses
an †unkindness of ravens
a bevy of roes
a parliament or †building of rooks
a hill of ruffs
a herd or rookery of seals; a pod (= small herd) of seals
a flock, herd, (*dial.*) drift or trip, or (*Austral.*) mob of sheep
a †dopping of sheldrake
a wisp or †walk of snipe
a †host of sparrows
a †murmuration of starlings
a flight of swallows
a game or herd of swans; a wedge of swans in the air
a herd of swine; a †sounder of tame swine, a †drift of wild swine
a †glozing (= fawning) of taverners
a †spring of teal
a bunch or knob of waterfowl
a school, herd, or gam of whales; a pod (= small school) of whales; a grind of bottle-nosed whales
a company or trip of widgeon
a bunch, trip, or plump of wildfowl; a knob (less than 30) of wildfowl
a pack or †rout of wolves
a gaggle of women (*derisive*)
a †fall of woodcock
a herd of wrens

Appendix 23 The Animal Kingdom

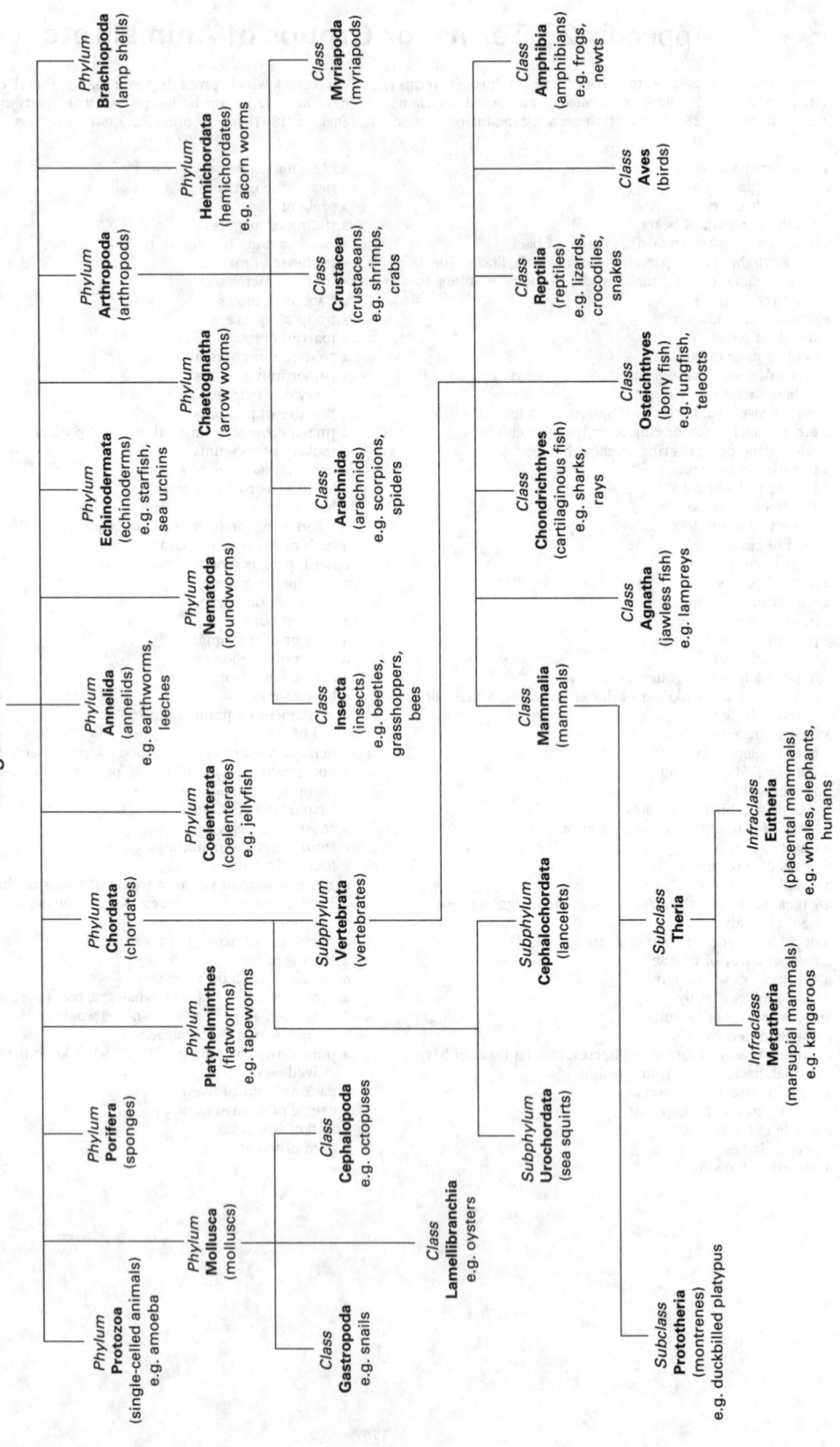

Appendix 24 The Plant Kingdom

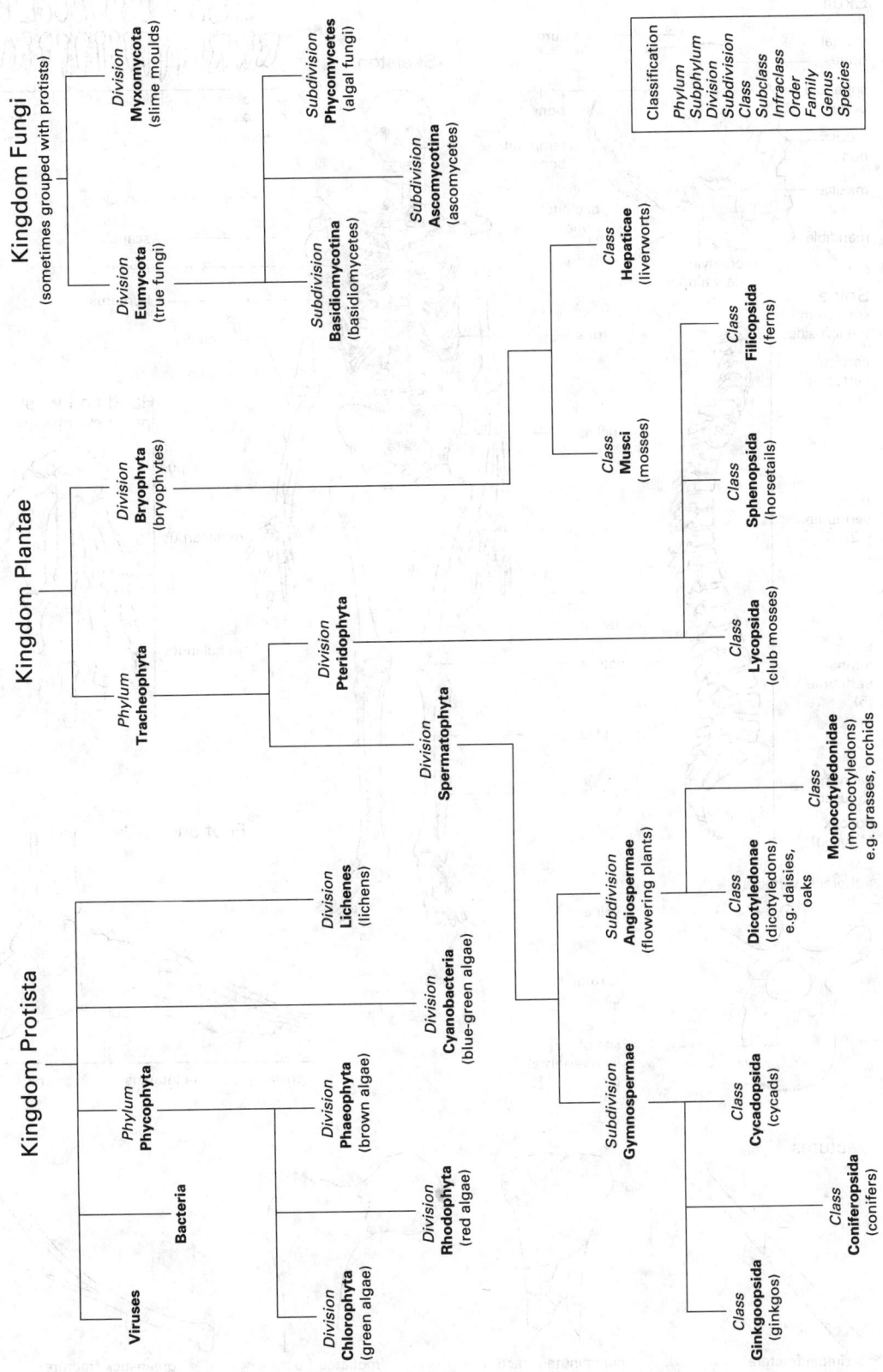

Appendix 25 The Body

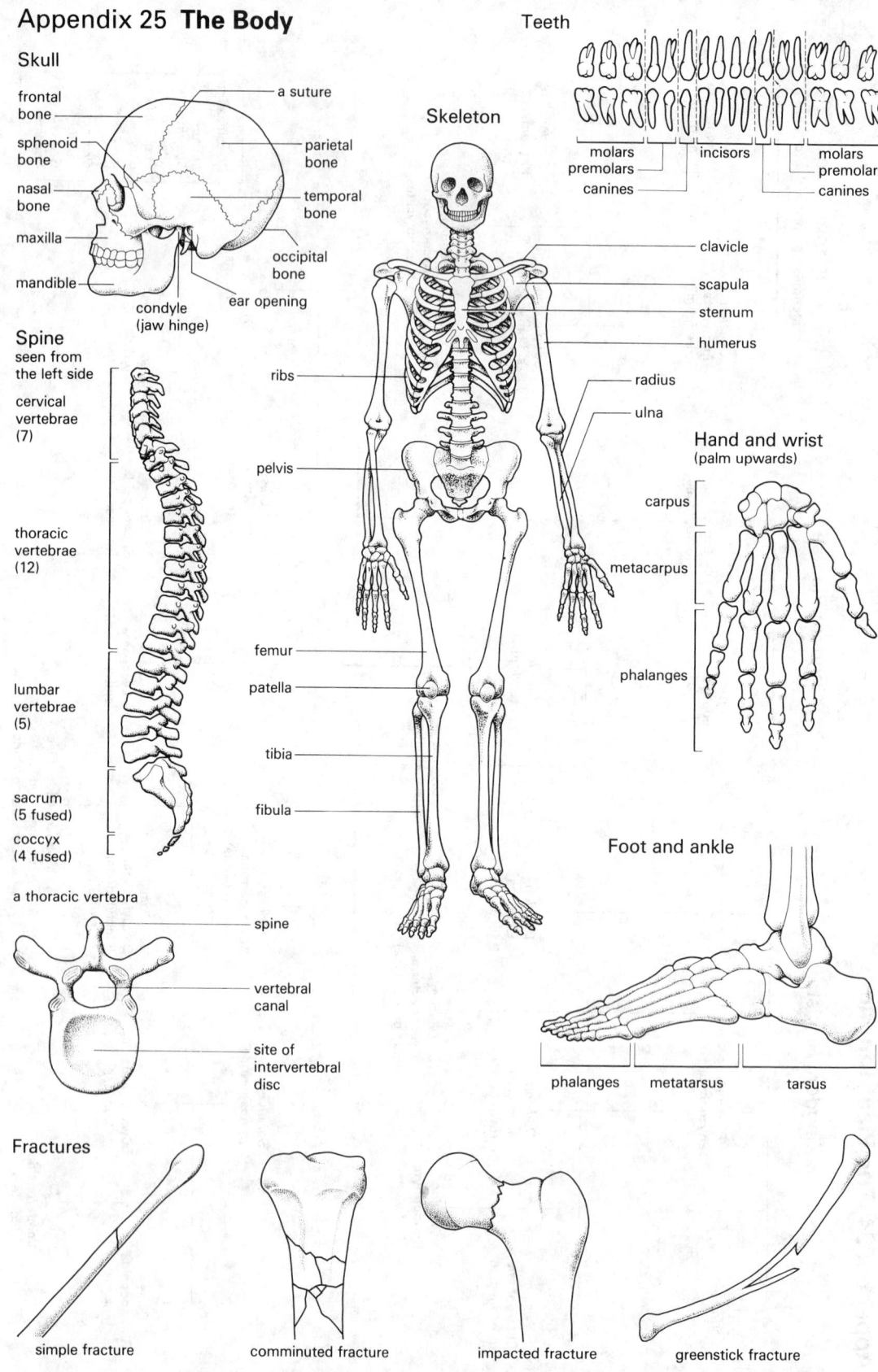

Skull

frontal bone
sphenoid bone
nasal bone
maxilla
mandible
a suture
parietal bone
temporal bone
occipital bone
ear opening
condyle (jaw hinge)

Spine
seen from the left side

cervical vertebrae (7)

thoracic vertebrae (12)

lumbar vertebrae (5)

sacrum (5 fused)

coccyx (4 fused)

a thoracic vertebra

spine
vertebral canal
site of intervertebral disc

Teeth

molars
premolars
canines
incisors
molars
premolars
canines

Skeleton

clavicle
scapula
sternum
humerus
ribs
radius
ulna
pelvis
femur
patella
tibia
fibula

Hand and wrist
(palm upwards)

carpus
metacarpus
phalanges

Foot and ankle

phalanges
metatarsus
tarsus

Fractures

simple fracture
comminuted fracture
impacted fracture
greenstick fracture

Ball and socket joint

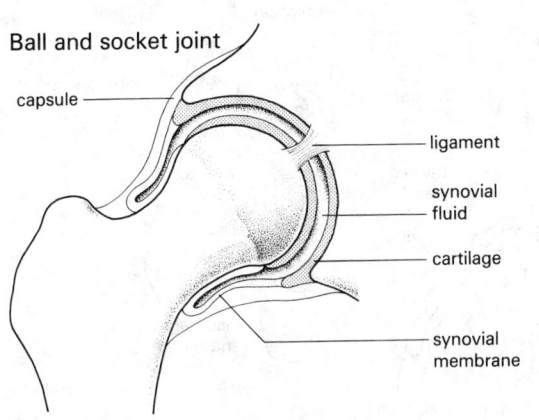

capsule

ligament

synovial fluid

cartilage

synovial membrane

Lower abdomen

male

spine   ureter

vas deferens

bladder

prostate gland

penis

scrotum enclosing testicles

rectum   urethra

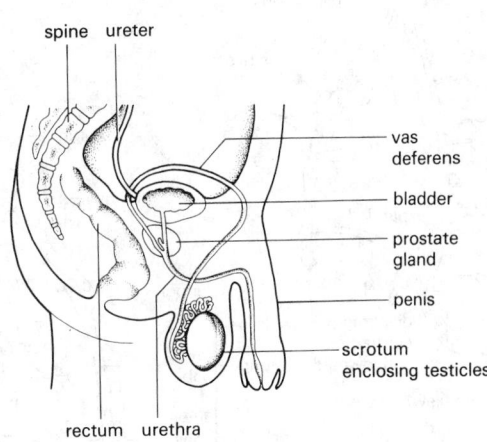

Parts of a muscle

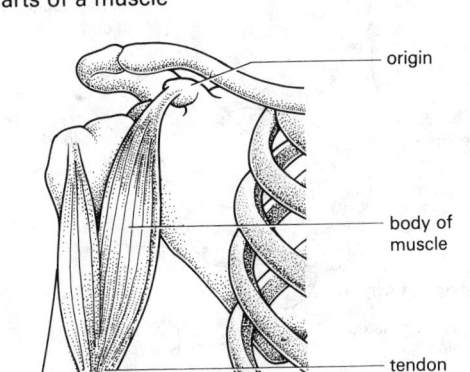

origin

body of muscle

tendon

insertion

spine   ovary

female

Fallopian tube

uterus

bladder

urethra

labium

rectum   cervix vagina

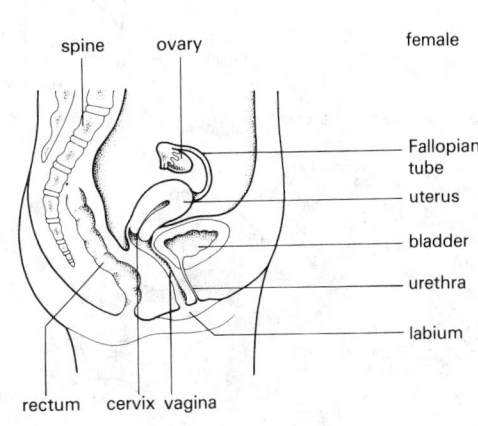

The alimentary canal

salivary gland

salivary glands

trachea

oesophagus

diaphragm

liver

gall bladder

bile duct

duodenum

ileum

caecum

appendix

anus

stomach

pancreas

jejunum

colon

rectum

Nose, mouth, and throat

sinuses

hard palate

soft palate

tongue

tonsil

pharynx

epiglottis

larynx

oesophagus

vocal cords

trachea

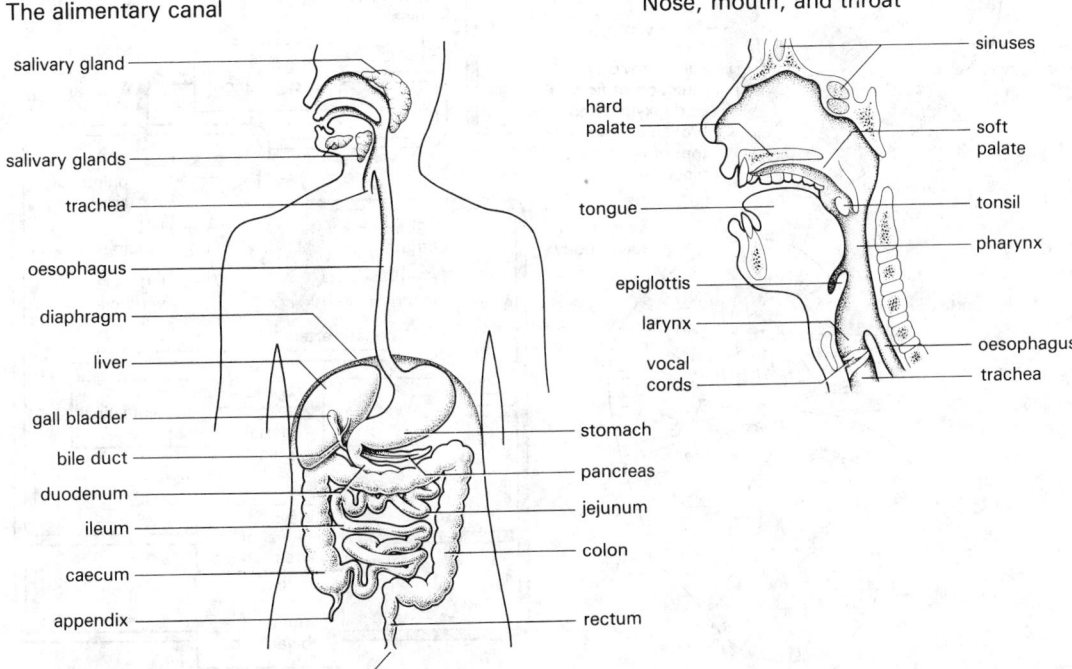

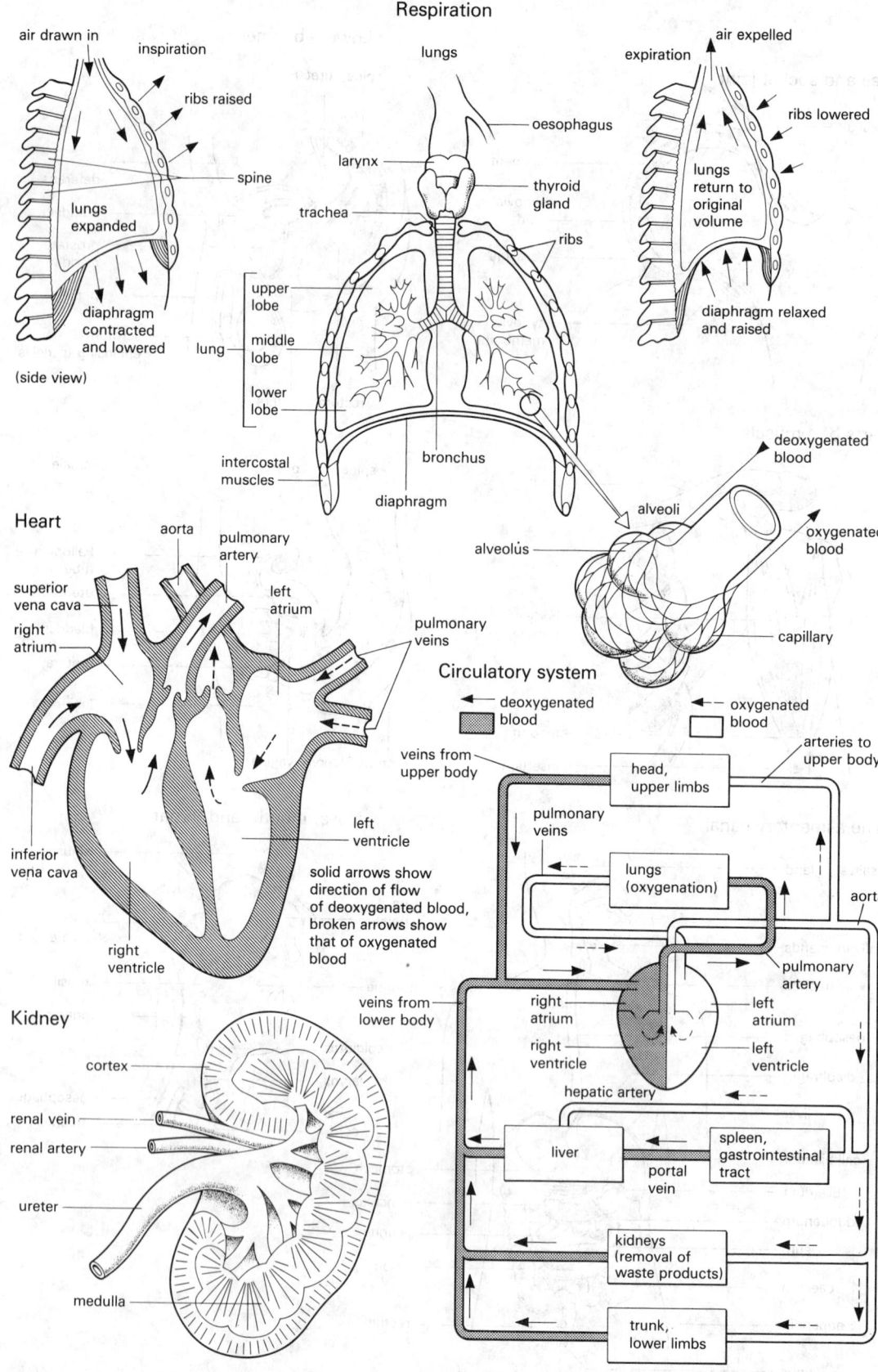

Respiration

air drawn in

inspiration

ribs raised

spine

lungs expanded

diaphragm contracted and lowered

(side view)

lungs

oesophagus

larynx

thyroid gland

trachea

ribs

upper lobe

middle lobe

lower lobe

lung

intercostal muscles

bronchus

diaphragm

air expelled

expiration

ribs lowered

lungs return to original volume

diaphragm relaxed and raised

deoxygenated blood

oxygenated blood

alveoli

alveolus

capillary

Heart

aorta

pulmonary artery

superior vena cava

right atrium

left atrium

pulmonary veins

inferior vena cava

left ventricle

solid arrows show direction of flow of deoxygenated blood, broken arrows show that of oxygenated blood

right ventricle

Kidney

cortex

renal vein

renal artery

ureter

medulla

Circulatory system

deoxygenated blood

oxygenated blood

veins from upper body

head, upper limbs

arteries to upper body

pulmonary veins

lungs (oxygenation)

aorta

pulmonary artery

veins from lower body

right atrium

left atrium

right ventricle

left ventricle

hepatic artery

liver

spleen, gastrointestinal tract

portal vein

kidneys (removal of waste products)

trunk, lower limbs

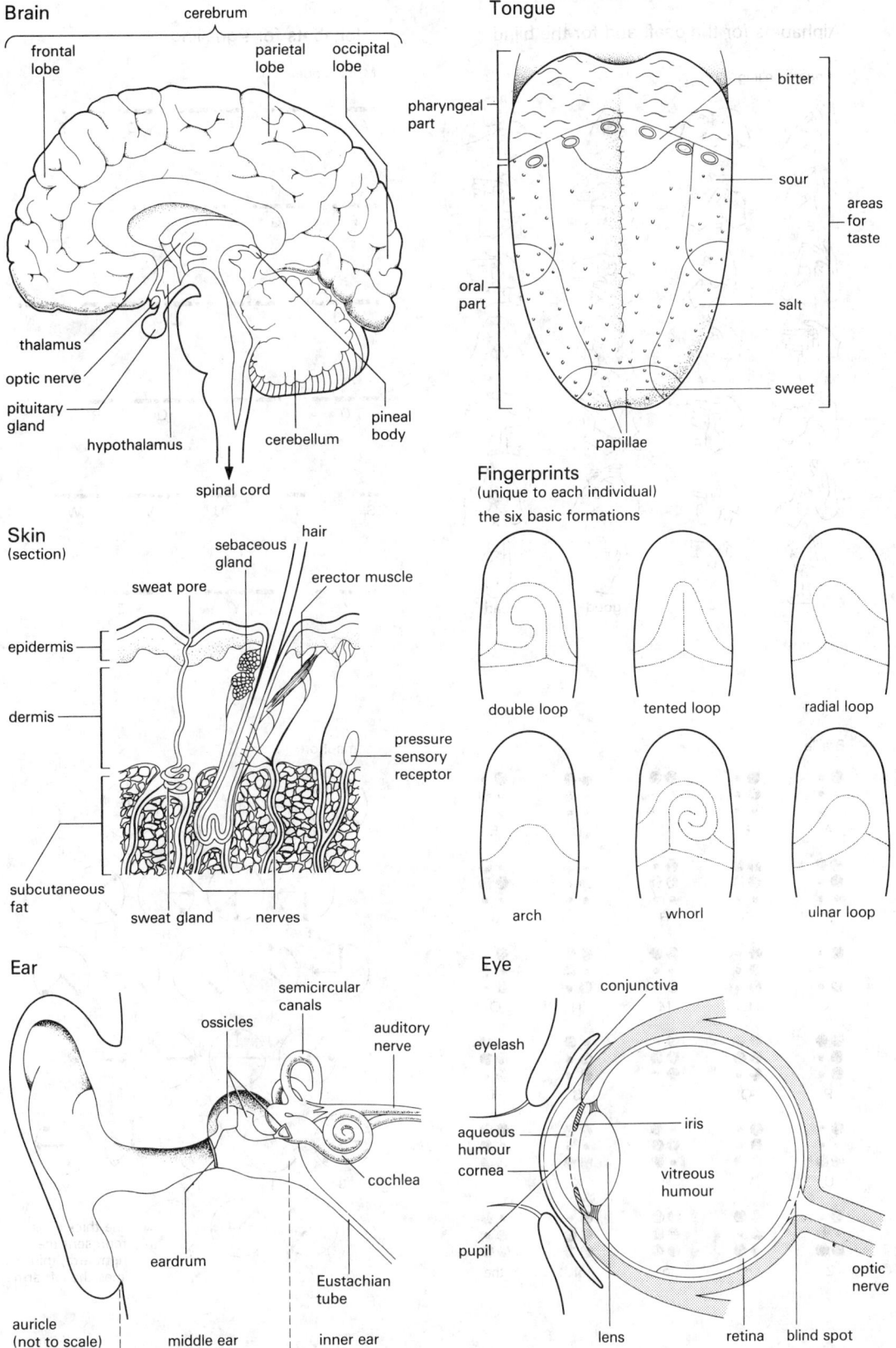

Brain

cerebrum

frontal lobe · parietal lobe · occipital lobe

thalamus · optic nerve · pituitary gland · hypothalamus · cerebellum · pineal body

spinal cord

Tongue

pharyngeal part

oral part

bitter · sour · salt · sweet

areas for taste

papillae

Skin
(section)

sweat pore · sebaceous gland · hair · erector muscle

epidermis

dermis

pressure sensory receptor

subcutaneous fat

sweat gland · nerves

Fingerprints
(unique to each individual)
the six basic formations

double loop · tented loop · radial loop

arch · whorl · ulnar loop

Ear

semicircular canals

ossicles

auditory nerve

cochlea

eardrum

Eustachian tube

auricle
(not to scale) · middle ear · inner ear

Eye

conjunctiva

eyelash

aqueous humour · cornea

iris

vitreous humour

pupil

lens · retina · blind spot

optic nerve

Appendix 26 **Alphabets**

Alphabets for the deaf, and for the blind

finger spelling

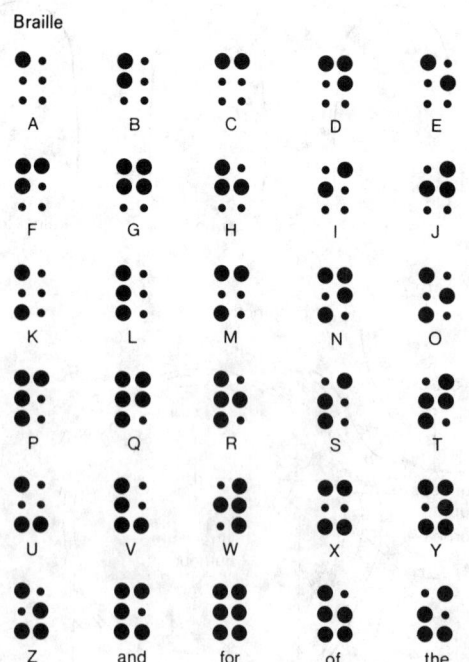

Alphabets for signalling

Morse code

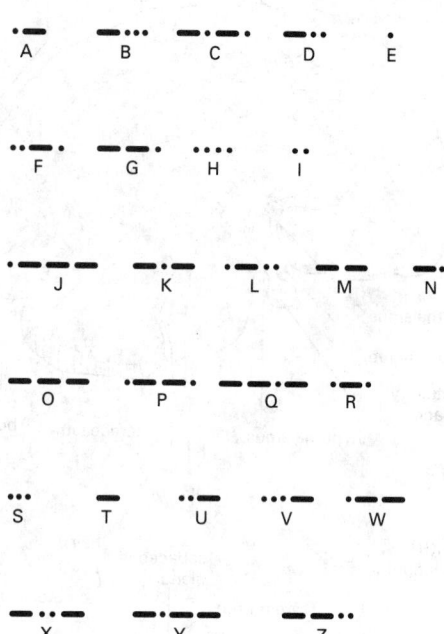

Braille

semaphore

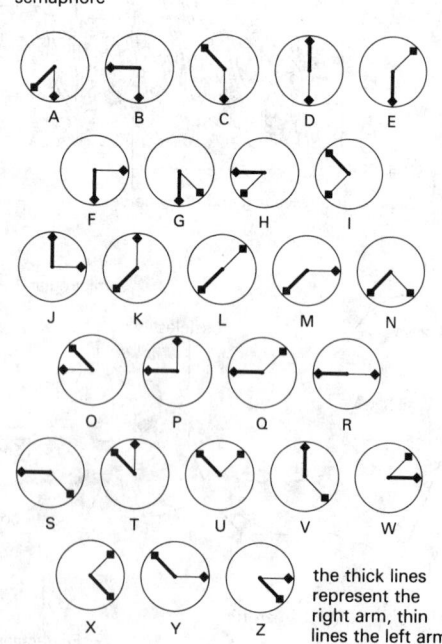

the thick lines represent the right arm, thin lines the left arm

Arabic

Forms				Name	Translit.
ا	ا			'alif	'
ب	ب	ـبـ	بـ	bā'	b
ت	ت	ـتـ	تـ	tā'	t
ث	ث	ـثـ	ثـ	thā'	th
ج	ج	ـجـ	جـ	jīm	j
ح	ح	ـحـ	حـ	ḥā'	ḥ
خ	خ	ـخـ	خـ	khā'	kh
د	ـد			dāl	d
ذ	ـذ			dhāl	dh
ر	ـر			rā'	r
ز	ـز			zay	z
س	س	ـسـ	سـ	sīn	s
ش	ش	ـشـ	شـ	shīn	sh
ص	ص	ـصـ	صـ	ṣād	ṣ
ض	ض	ـضـ	ضـ	ḍād	ḍ
ط	ط	ـطـ	طـ	ṭā'	ṭ
ظ	ظ	ـظـ	ظـ	ẓā'	ẓ
ع	ع	ـعـ	عـ	'ayn	'
غ	غ	ـغـ	غـ	ghayn	gh
ف	ف	ـفـ	فـ	fā'	f
ق	ق	ـقـ	قـ	qāf	q
ك	ك	ـكـ	كـ	kāf	k
ل	ل	ـلـ	لـ	lām	l
م	م	ـمـ	مـ	mīm	m
ن	ن	ـنـ	نـ	nūn	n
ه	ه	ـهـ	هـ	hā'	h
و	ـو			wāw	w
ى	ى	ـيـ	يـ	yā'	y

Hebrew

Letter	Name	Translit.
א	aleph	'
ב	beth	b, bh
ג	gimel	g, gh
ד	daleth	d, dh
ה	he	h
ו	waw	w
ז	zayin	z
ח	ḥeth	ḥ
ט	ṭeth	ṭ
י	yodh	y
כ ך	kaph	k, kh
ל	lamedh	l
מ ם	mem	m
נ ן	nun	n
ס	samekh	s
ע	'ayin	'
פ ף	pe	p, ph
צ ץ	ṣadhe	ṣ
ק	qoph	q
ר	resh	r
שׂ	śin	ś
שׁ	shin	sh
ת	taw	t, th

Greek

Letter	Name	Translit.
A α	alpha	a
B β	beta	b
Γ γ	gamma	g
Δ δ	delta	d
E ϵ	epsilon	e
Z ζ	zeta	z
H η	eta	ē
Θ θ	theta	th
I ι	iota	i
K κ	kappa	k
Λ λ	lambda	l
M μ	mu	m
N ν	nu	n
Ξ ξ	xi	x
O o	omicron	o
Π π	pi	p
P ρ	rho	r, rh
Σ σ ς	sigma	s
T τ	tau	t
Υ υ	upsilon	u
Φ φ	phi	ph
X χ	chi	kh
Ψ ψ	psi	ps
Ω ω	omega	ō

Russian

А а	a
Б б	b
В в	v
Г г	g
Д д	d
Е е	e
Ё ё	ë
Ж ж	zh
З з	z
И и	i
Й й	ĭ
К к	k
Л л	l
М м	m
Н н	n
О о	o
П п	p
Р р	r
С с	s
Т т	t
У у	u
Ф ф	f
Х х	kh
Ц ц	ts
Ч ч	ch
Ш ш	sh
Щ щ	shch
Ъ ъ	ˮ ('hard sign')
Ы ы	y
Ь ь	' ('soft sign')
Э э	é
Ю ю	yu
Я я	ya

Appendix 27 Indo-European Languages

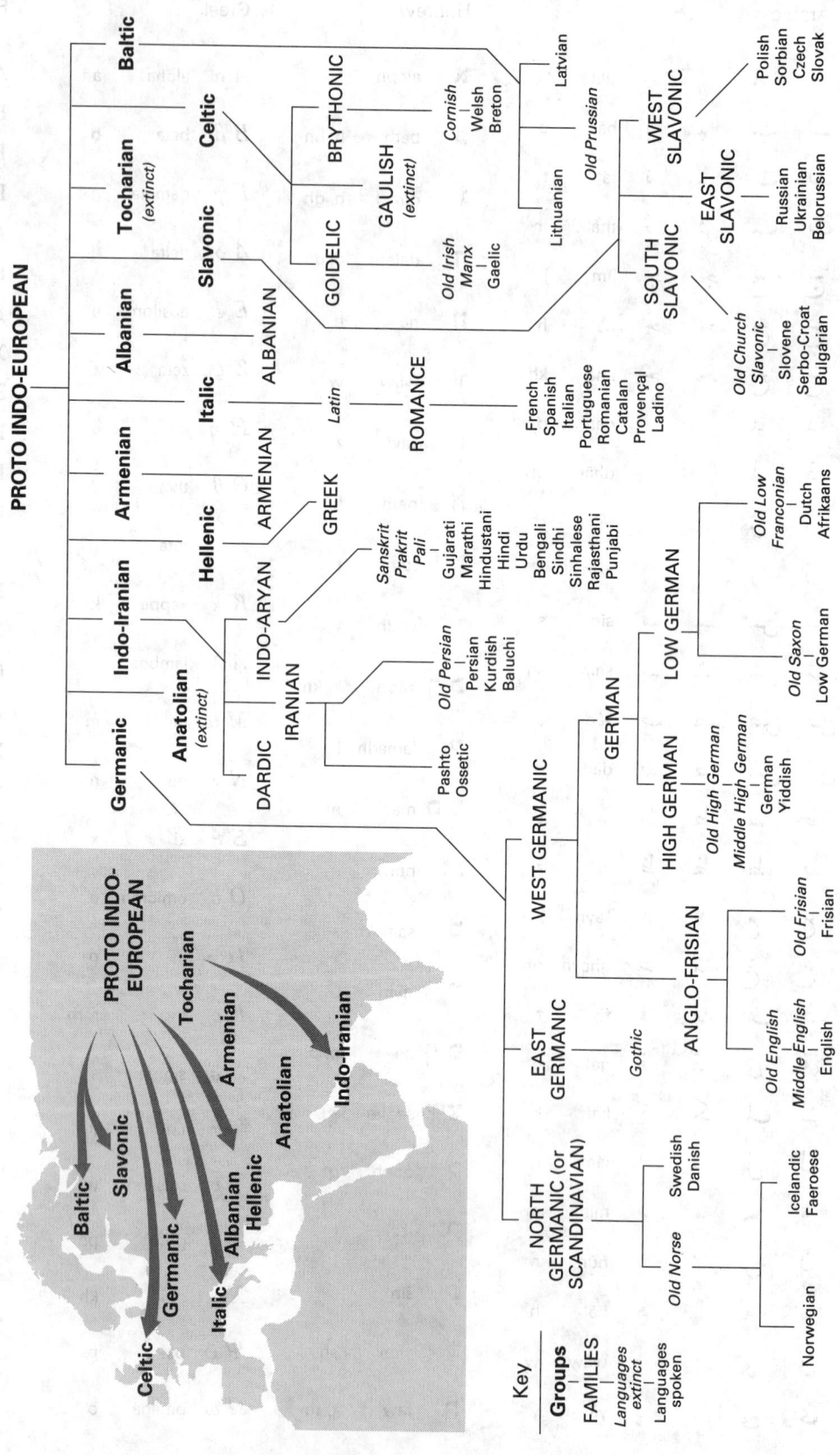

Appendix 28 **Hallmarks**

All marks shown relate to silver except where otherwise indicated

A hallmark

maker's mark   standard mark   Assay Office mark   date letter

Maker's mark (from 1363)
originally symbols, now initials

 symbol

 symbol and initials

 initials

Assay Office mark (from 1300)
now only London, Birmingham, Sheffield, and Edinburgh

London

Edinburgh

gold and silver (leopard's head uncrowned from 1821; mark includes platinum from 1975)

Britannia silver (prior to 1975)

gold and silver (also platinum from 1975)

Birmingham

Sheffield

gold (also platinum from 1975)

silver

silver (prior to 1975)

gold (also silver and platinum from 1975)

Some earlier Assay Office marks (with dates of closure)

Norwich (1702)	York (1856)	Exeter (1883)	Newcastle (1884)	Chester (1962)	Glasgow (1964)

Standard mark (from 1544)
Marks guaranteeing pure metal content of the percentage shown

sterling silver 92.5%

 marked in England

 marked in Scotland (from 1975)

 marked in Scotland (prior to 1975)

Britannia standard silver (1697–1720, also occasional use since) 95.8%

gold (crown followed by millesimal figure of the standard)

  i.e. 18 carat 75%

 22 carat 91.6%

 14 carat 58.5%

 9 carat 37.5%

(prior to 1975 marks incorporated the carat figure, and Scottish 18 and 22 carat gold bore a thistle mark instead of the crown)

Date letter (from 1478)
one letter per year before changing to next style of letter and/or shield

cycles vary between Assay Offices

London date letters (A–U used, excluding J) showing style of first letter and years of cycle

🅐	1498–1518[1]	🅐	1598–1618	🅐	1697[3]–1716	A	1796–1816	🅐	1896–1916
🅐	1518–1538	🅐	1618–1638	🅐	1716–1736	🅐	1816–1836	🅐	1916–1936
🅐	1538–1558	🅐	1638–1658	🅐	1736–1756	🅐	1836–1856	A	1936–1956
🅐	1558–1578	🅐	1658–1678	🅐	1756–1776	🅐	1856–1876	🅐	1956–1974[2]
A	1578–1598	🅐	1678–1697[2]	🅐	1776–1796	🅐	1876–1896	🅐	1975[4]–

Notes
1. Letter changed on 19 May until 1697
2. No U used in these cycles
3. A from 27 March–28 May 1697; year letters then changed on 29 May until 1975
4. Year letter changed with each calendar year; from 1975 all UK Offices use the same date letters and shield shape

Appendix 29 Musical Notation and the Orchestra

Values of notes and rests

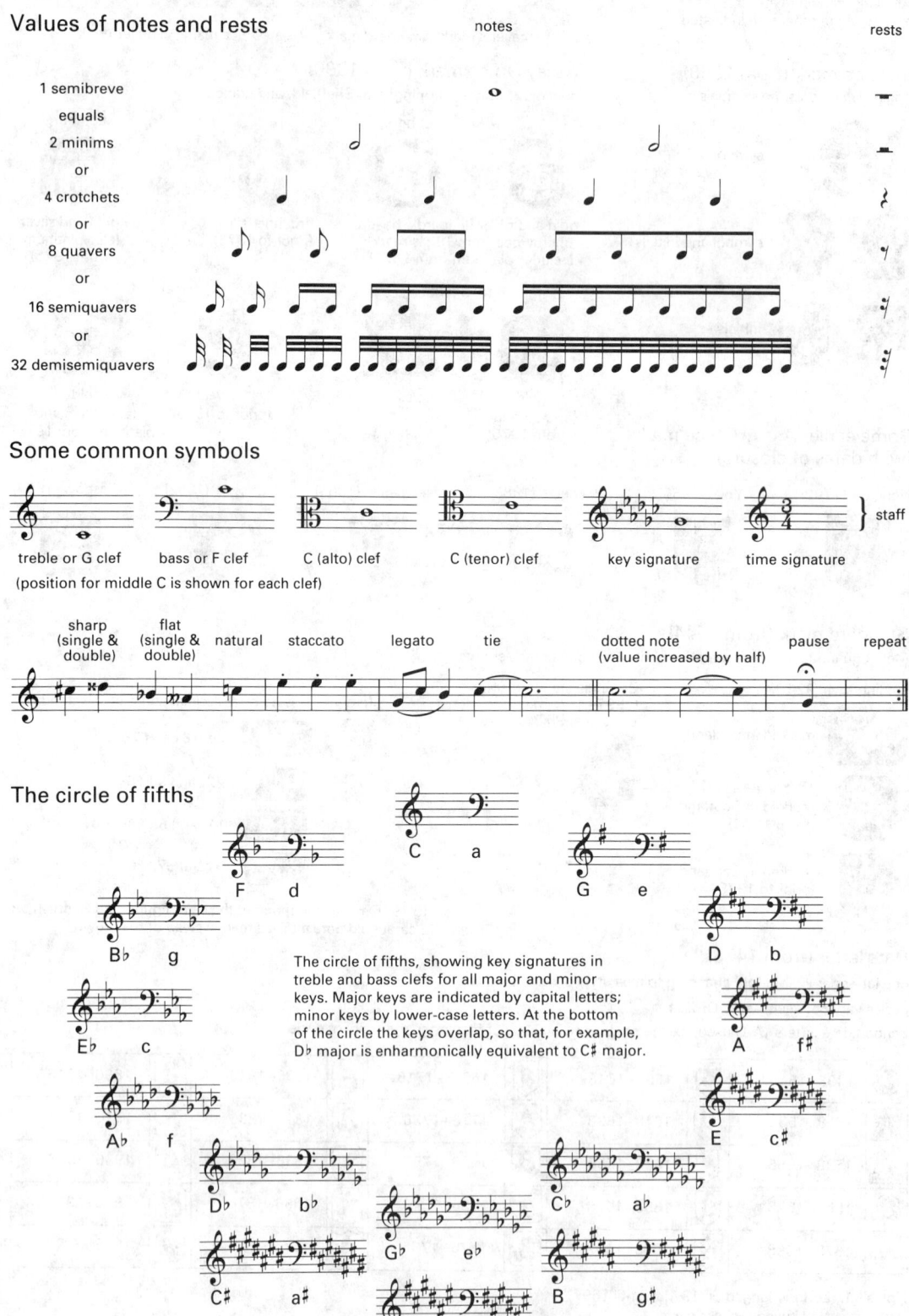

Some common symbols

The circle of fifths

The circle of fifths, showing key signatures in treble and bass clefs for all major and minor keys. Major keys are indicated by capital letters; minor keys by lower-case letters. At the bottom of the circle the keys overlap, so that, for example, D♭ major is enharmonically equivalent to C♯ major.

Orchestral layout

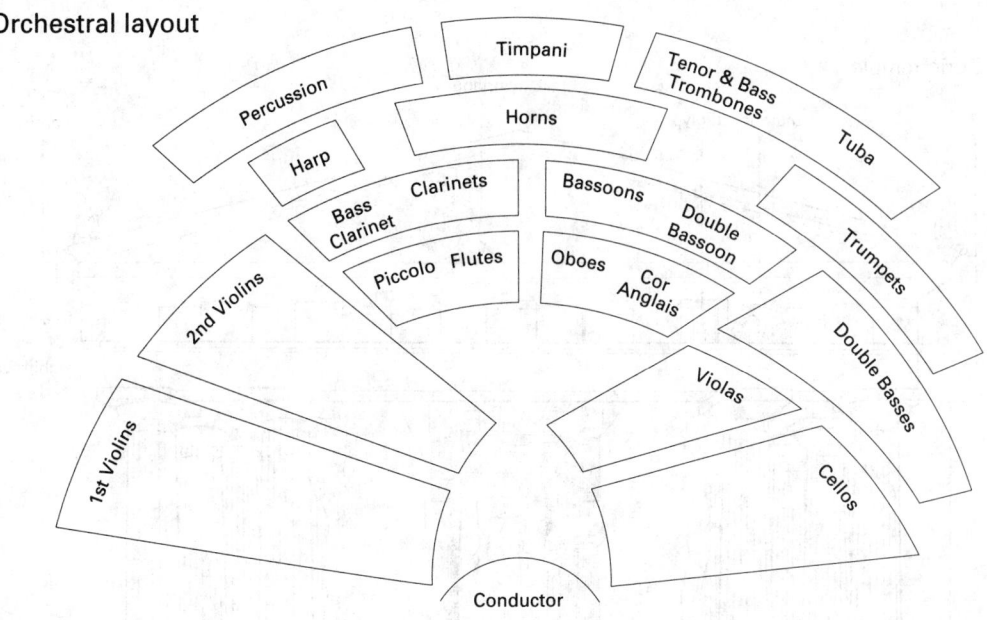

Dynamics

<	*crescendo*	get louder
>	*diminuendo*	get quieter
ppp		very, very quiet
pp	*pianissimo*	very quiet
p	*piano*	quiet
mp	*mezzopiano*	quite quiet
mf	*mezzoforte*	quite loud
f	*forte*	loud
ff	*fortissimo*	very loud
fff		very, very loud
sf	*sforzando*	suddenly very loud

Tempo indicators

adagio	slow
largo	slow and dignified
andante	flowing, at a walking pace
allegro	quick and bright
allegretto	not as quick as allegro
vivace	fast and lively
presto	very quick
accelerando	getting faster
ritenuto (rit.)	holding back
rallentando (rall.)	getting slower
rubato	flexible tempo

Interpretive indicators

cantabile	singing style	*legato*	smooth
dolce	soft and sweet	*staccato*	detached
espressivo	expressively		

Appendix 30 **Architecture**

Classical

A Greek Doric temple

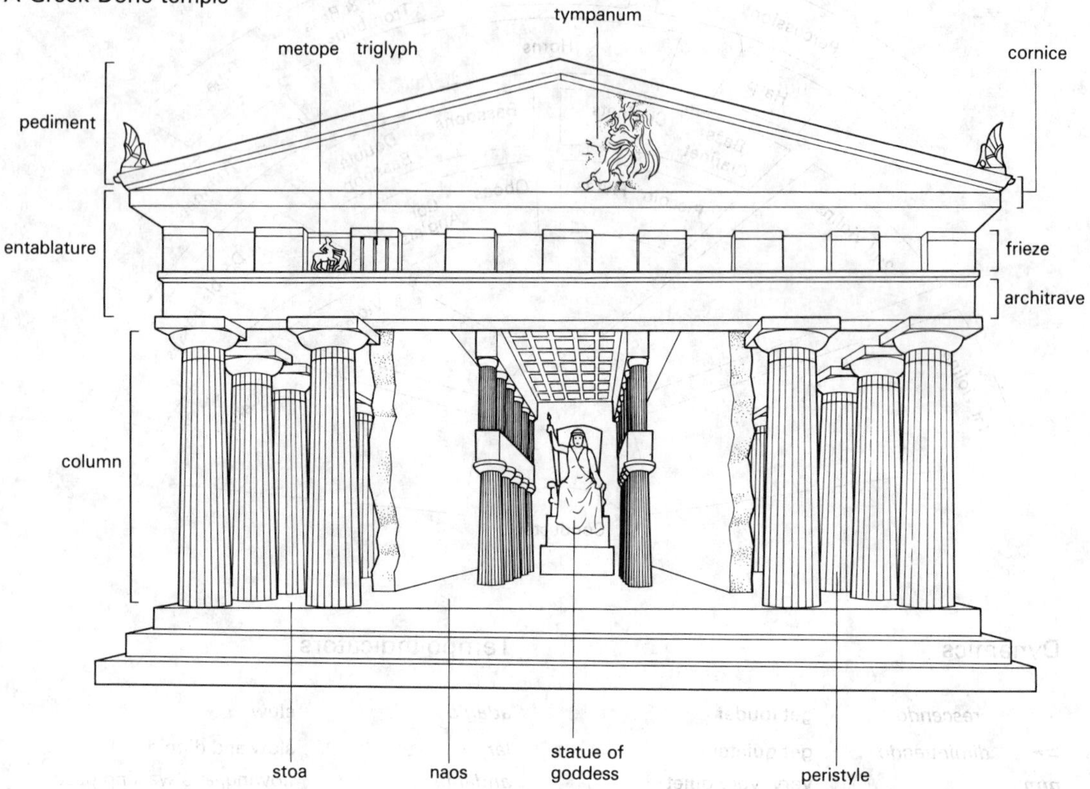

pediment

metope triglyph

tympanum

cornice

entablature

frieze

architrave

column

stoa

naos

statue of
goddess

peristyle

Orders of architecture: Greek origin

abacus

volute

acanthus

shaft

base

Doric

Ionic

Corinthian

Structure

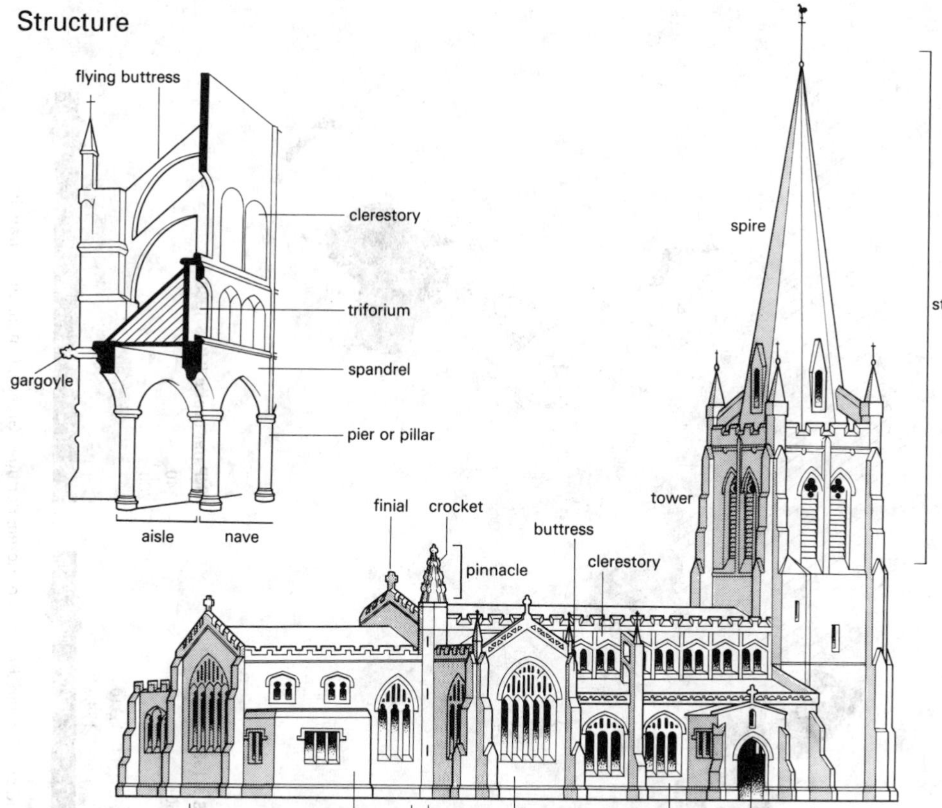

flying buttress

clerestory

triforium

spandrel

gargoyle

pier or pillar

aisle

nave

spire

steeple

tower

finial

crocket

buttress

pinnacle

clerestory

chancel

vestry

transept

nave

aisle

porch

Periods

(note: some churches include architectural details which are earlier or later than the main periods which they illustrate)

Windows

quatrefoil

cusp

embrasure
or splay

Norman, 12th c.

lancet, early 13th c.
(interior)

geometric bar tracery,
late 13th c.

Decorated curvilinear
tracery with ogee arch,
14th c.

Perpendicular
tracery, 15th c.

Vaults

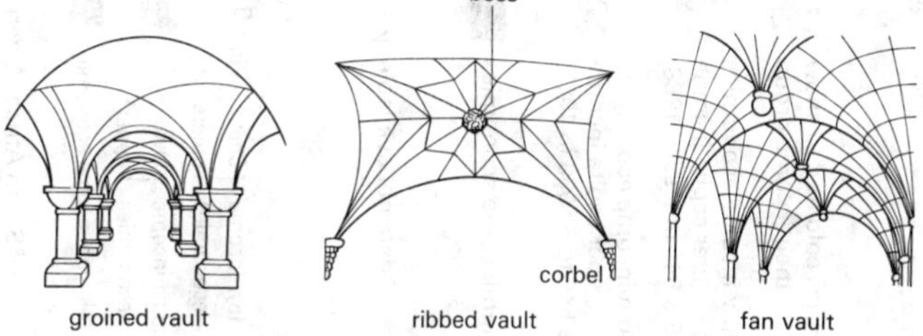

boss

corbel

groined vault

ribbed vault

fan vault

Hammer-beam roof

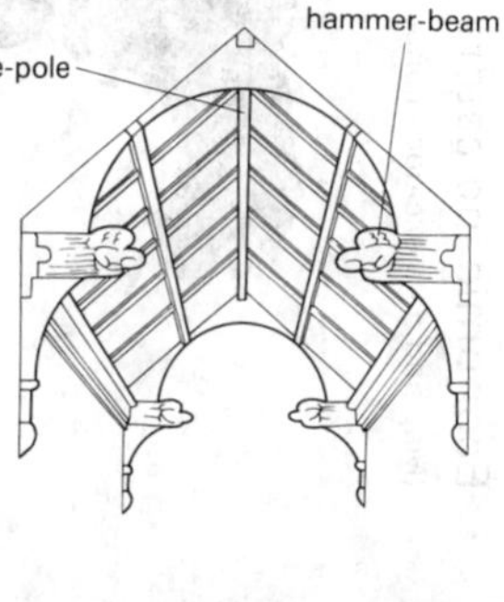

hammer-beam

ridge-pole

Appendix 31 Social Trends

Economic indicators

(Map and data exclude economies of less than one million population)

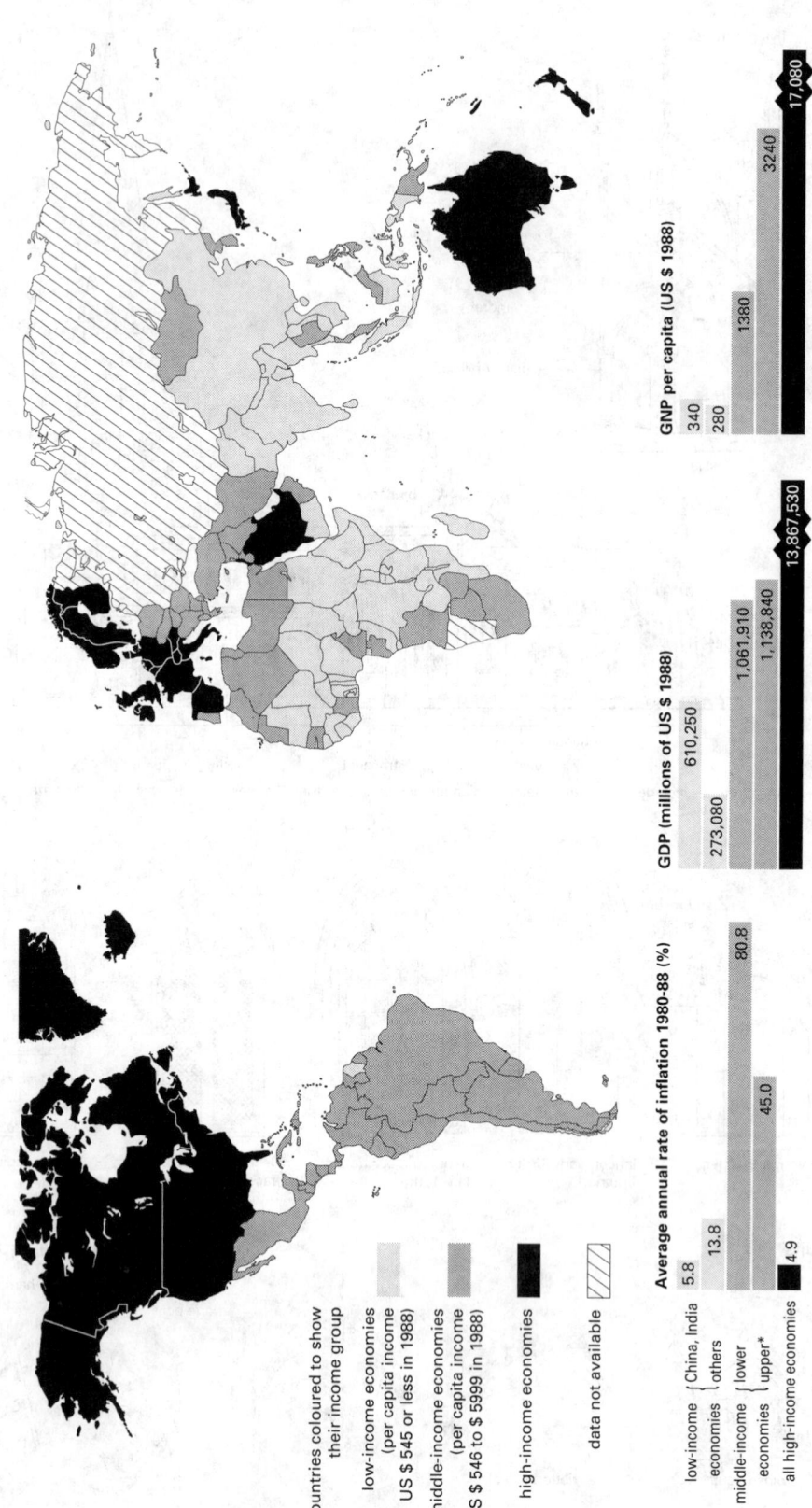

Countries coloured to show their income group

low-income economies (per capita income US $ 545 or less in 1988)

middle-income economies (per capita income US $ 546 to 5999 in 1988)

high-income economies

data not available

Average annual rate of inflation 1980-88 (%)

low-income economies {China, India} 5.8
{others} 13.8

middle-income economies {lower} 80.8
{upper*} 45.0

all high-income economies 4.9

GDP (millions of US $ 1988)

610,250
273,080
1,061,910
1,138,840
13,867,530

GNP per capita (US $ 1988)

340
280
1380
3240
17,080

*South Africa, Algeria, Hungary, Uruguay, Argentina, Yugoslavia, Gabon, Venezuela, Trinidad and Tobago, Republic of Korea, Portugal, Greece, Oman, Libya, Iran, Iraq

Health indicators

Population per physician 1984

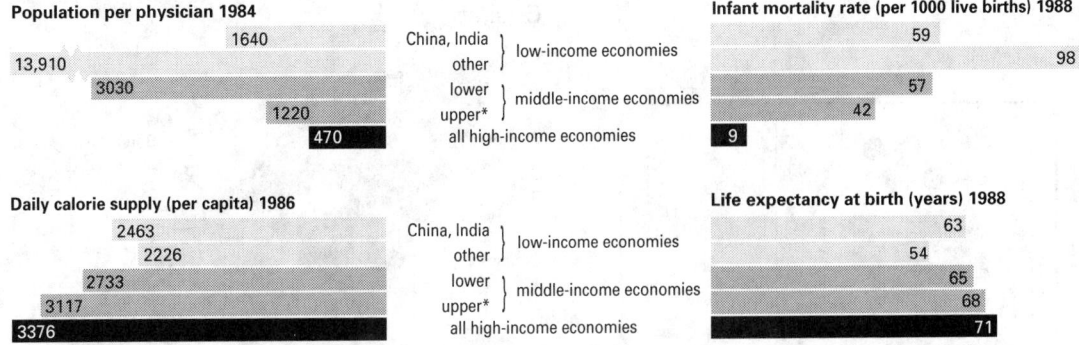

1640	China, India	} low-income economies
13,910	other	
3030	lower	} middle-income economies
1220	upper*	
470	all high-income economies	

Infant mortality rate (per 1000 live births) 1988

59	China, India	} low-income economies
98	other	
57	lower	} middle-income economies
42	upper*	
9	all high-income economies	

Daily calorie supply (per capita) 1986

2463	China, India	} low-income economies
2226	other	
2733	lower	} middle-income economies
3117	upper*	
3376	all high-income economies	

Life expectancy at birth (years) 1988

63	China, India	} low-income economies
54	other	
65	lower	} middle-income economies
68	upper*	
71	all high-income economies	

*South Africa, Algeria, Hungary, Uruguay, Argentina, Yugoslavia, Gabon, Venezuela, Trinidad and Tobago, Republic of Korea, Portugal, Greece, Oman, Libya, Iran, Iraq.

Population

Regional population in millions

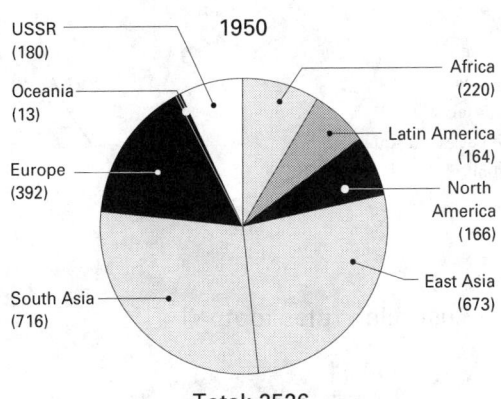

1950

USSR (180)
Oceania (13)
Europe (392)
South Asia (716)
Africa (220)
Latin America (164)
North America (166)
East Asia (673)

Total: 2526

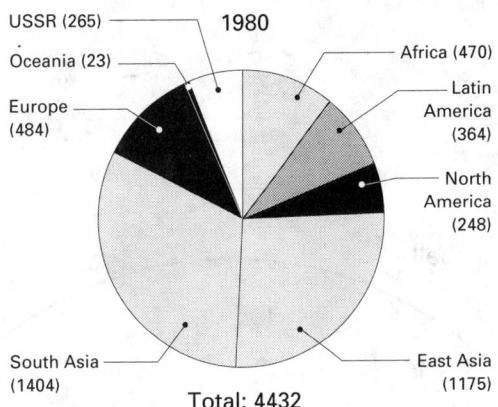

1980

USSR (265)
Oceania (23)
Europe (484)
South Asia (1404)
Africa (470)
Latin America (364)
North America (248)
East Asia (1175)

Total: 4432

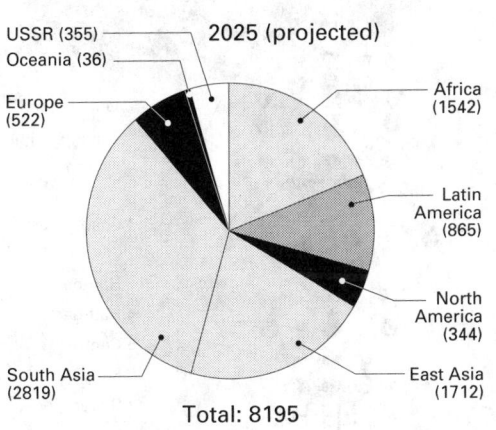

2025 (projected)

USSR (355)
Oceania (36)
Europe (522)
South Asia (2819)
Africa (1542)
Latin America (865)
North America (344)
East Asia (1712)

Total: 8195

World population growth

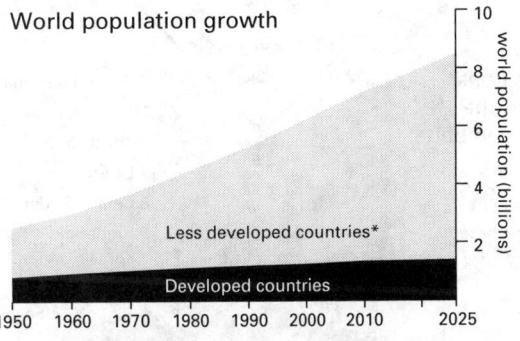

Less developed countries*

Developed countries

1950 1960 1970 1980 1990 2000 2010 2025

world population (billions): 10 8 6 4 2

*All regions of Africa, all regions of Latin America, all regions of Asia excluding Japan, Melanesia, Micronesia, and Polynesia.

Appendix 32 Sports and Games

Ice hockey

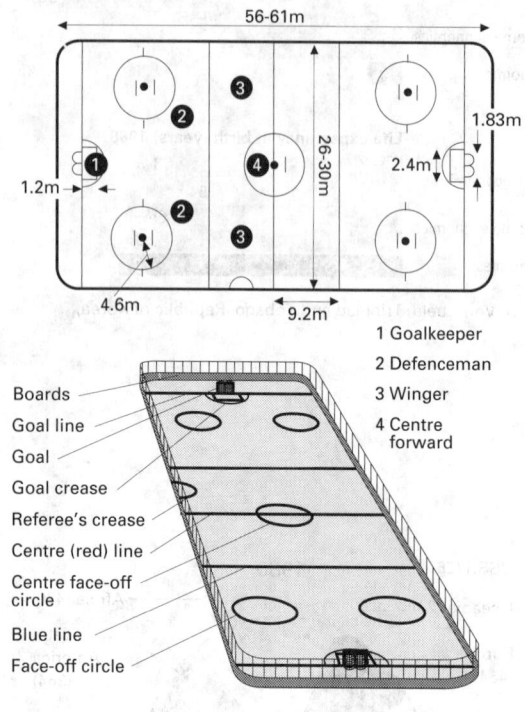

56-61m
1.83m
26-30m
2.4m
1.2m
4.6m
9.2m

1 Goalkeeper
2 Defenceman
3 Winger
4 Centre forward

Boards
Goal line
Goal
Goal crease
Referee's crease
Centre (red) line
Centre face-off circle
Blue line
Face-off circle

Cricket

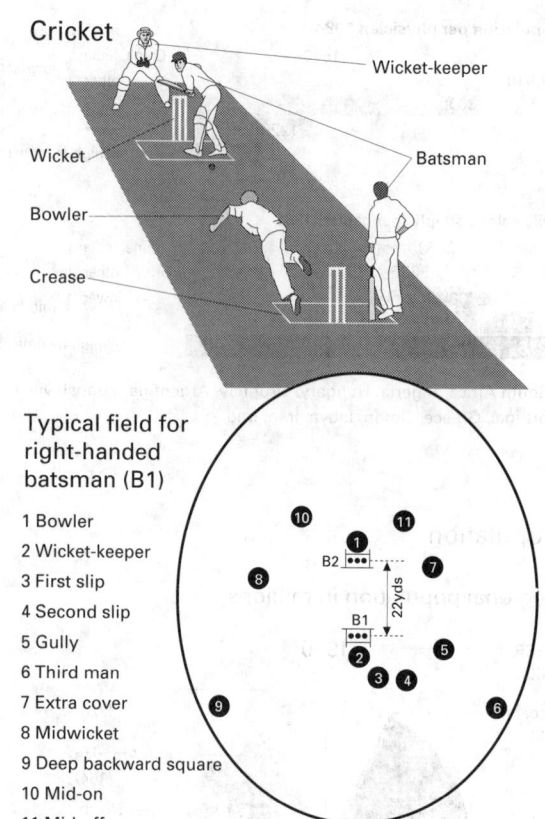

Wicket-keeper
Batsman
Wicket
Bowler
Crease

Typical field for right-handed batsman (B1)

1 Bowler
2 Wicket-keeper
3 First slip
4 Second slip
5 Gully
6 Third man
7 Extra cover
8 Midwicket
9 Deep backward square
10 Mid-on
11 Mid-off

22yds
B2
B1

Baseball

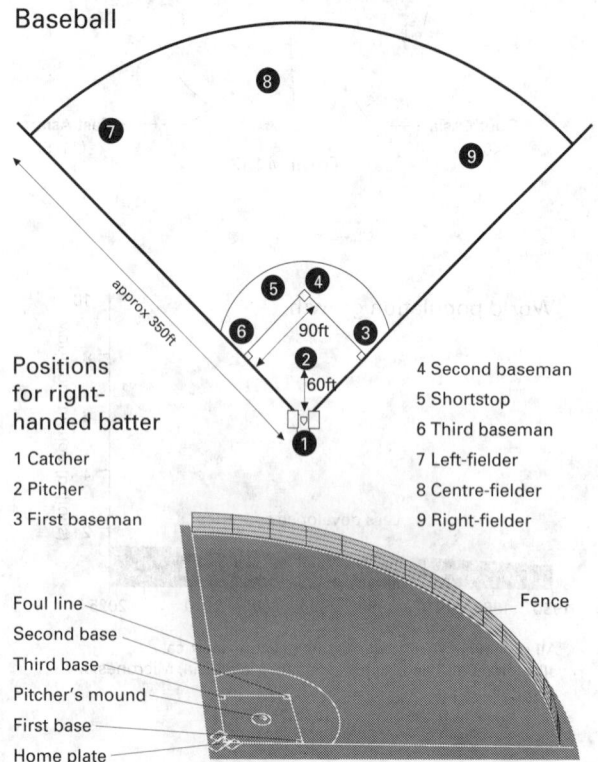

approx 350ft
90ft
60ft

Positions for right-handed batter

1 Catcher
2 Pitcher
3 First baseman
4 Second baseman
5 Shortstop
6 Third baseman
7 Left-fielder
8 Centre-fielder
9 Right-fielder

Foul line
Second base
Third base
Pitcher's mound
First base
Home plate
Fence

Australian rules football

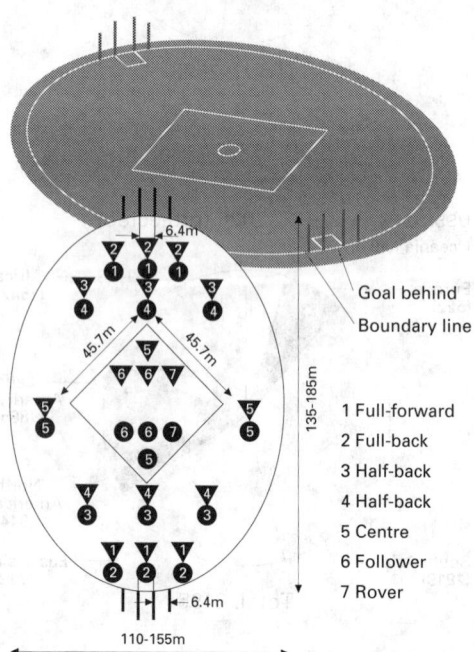

6.4m
45.7m
45.7m
135-185m
110-155m
6.4m

Goal behind
Boundary line

1 Full-forward
2 Full-back
3 Half-back
4 Half-back
5 Centre
6 Follower
7 Rover

Association Football

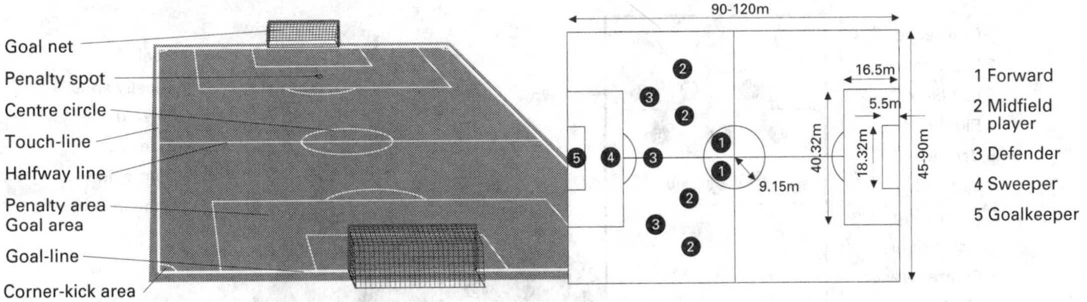

- Goal net
- Penalty spot
- Centre circle
- Touch-line
- Halfway line
- Penalty area
- Goal area
- Goal-line
- Corner-kick area

90-120m
16.5m
5.5m
40.32m
45-90m
18.32m
9.15m

1 Forward
2 Midfield player
3 Defender
4 Sweeper
5 Goalkeeper

Rugby Union

- Dead-ball line
- Touch-in-goal line
- In goal
- Goal-line
- Touch-line
- Halfway line

Rugby League

6-11m
100m
10m
22m
5.5m
68m

NB In Rugby League there are no flankers

100m
69m
15m
22m
5m
5.6m
22m
10m

1 Hooker
2 Prop
3 Lock
4 Number 8
5 Flanker
6 Scrum-half
7 Fly-half
8 Inside centre
9 Outside centre
10 Wing
11 Full back

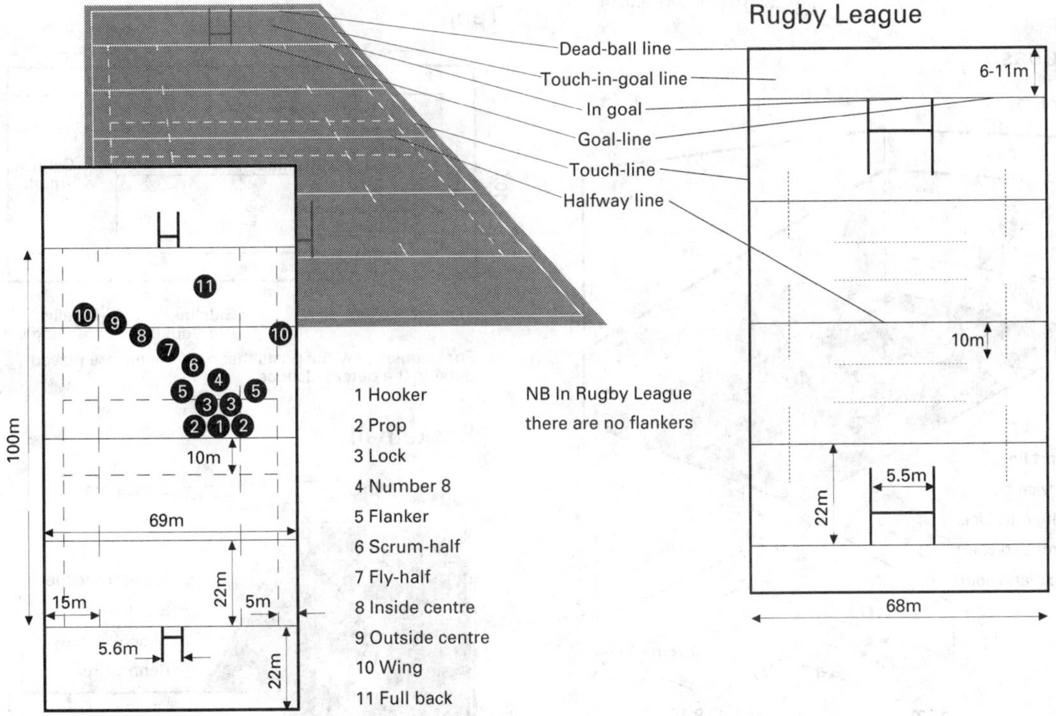

American Football

Offense ●

1 Center
2 Guard
3 Tackle
4 Tight end
5 Wide receiver
6 Quarterback
7 Running back

Defense ▲

3 Linebacker
1 Nose tackle
4 Safety
2 Defensive end
5 Cornerback

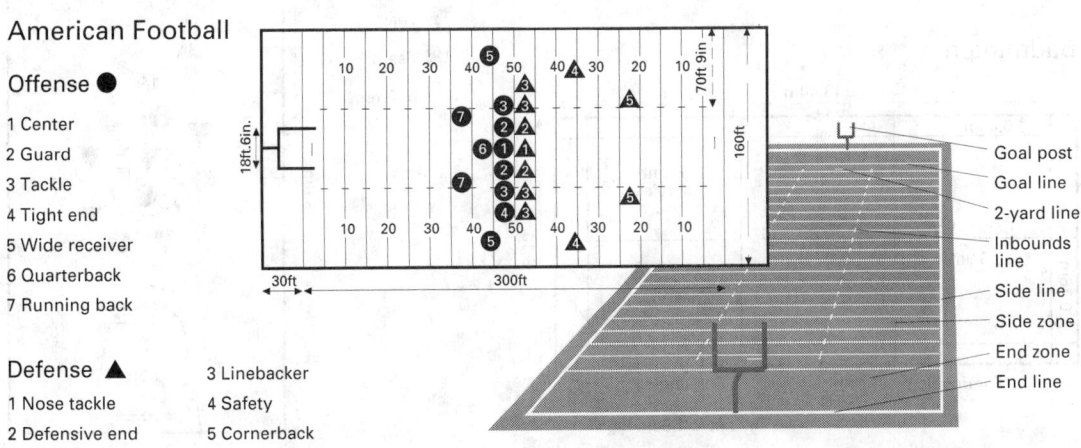

10 20 30 40 50 40 30 20 10 9in.
70ft 9in.
18ft.6in.
160ft
30ft
300ft

- Goal post
- Goal line
- 2-yard line
- Inbounds line
- Side line
- Side zone
- End zone
- End line

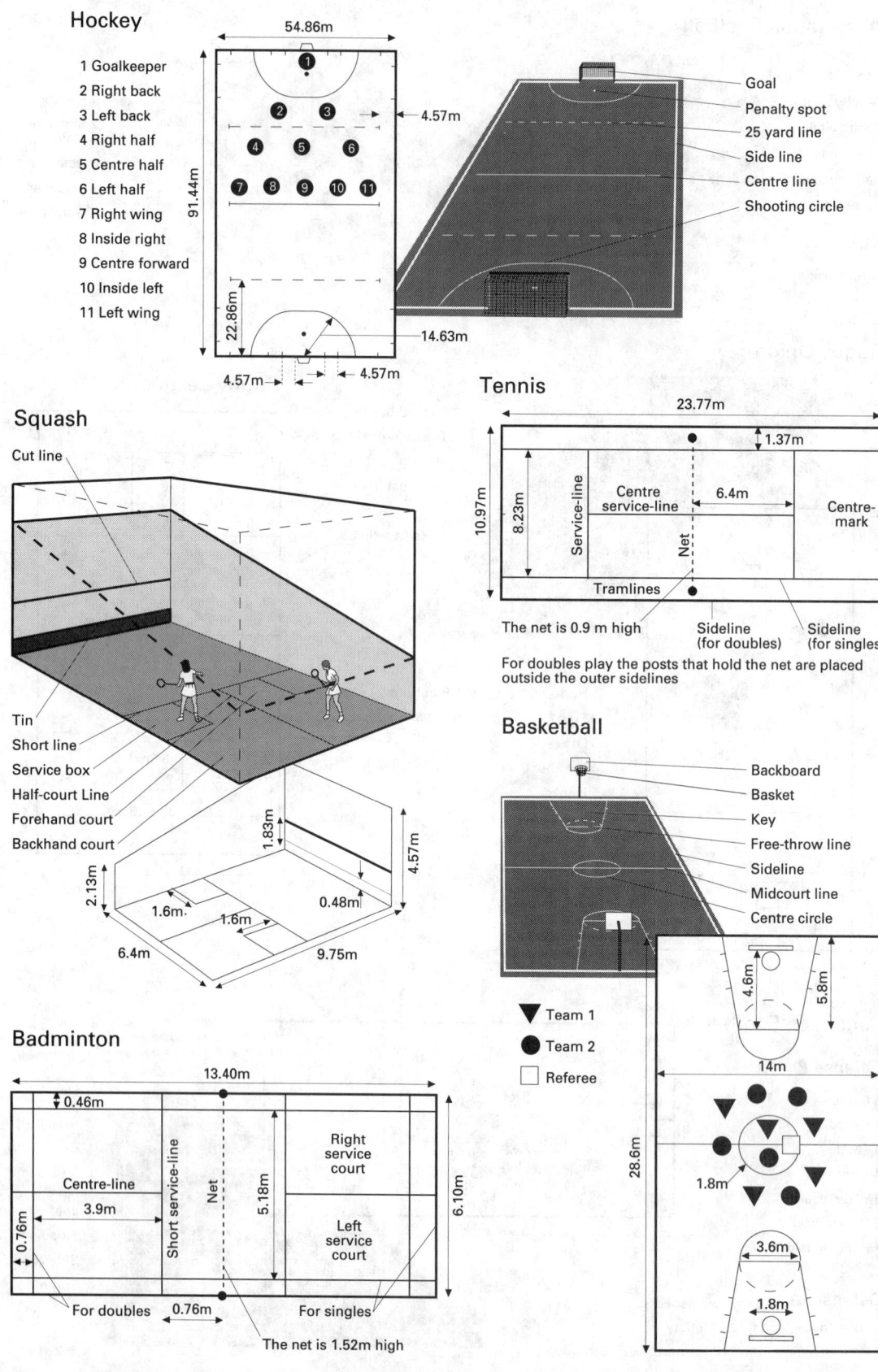

Hockey

1 Goalkeeper
2 Right back
3 Left back
4 Right half
5 Centre half
6 Left half
7 Right wing
8 Inside right
9 Centre forward
10 Inside left
11 Left wing

54.86m
91.44m
4.57m
22.86m
14.63m
4.57m
4.57m

Goal
Penalty spot
25 yard line
Side line
Centre line
Shooting circle

Squash

Cut line

Tin
Short line
Service box
Half-court Line
Forehand court
Backhand court

1.83m
2.13m
4.57m
1.6m.
1.6m
0.48m
6.4m
9.75m

Tennis

23.77m
1.37m
10.97m
8.23m
Service-line
Centre service-line
6.4m
Net
Centre-mark
Tramlines

The net is 0.9 m high

Sideline (for doubles)
Sideline (for singles)

For doubles play the posts that hold the net are placed outside the outer sidelines

Basketball

Backboard
Basket
Key
Free-throw line
Sideline
Midcourt line
Centre circle

▼ Team 1
● Team 2
□ Referee

4.6m
5.8m
14m
28.6m
1.8m
3.6m
1.8m

Badminton

13.40m
0.46m
Centre-line
3.9m
Short service-line
Net
Right service court
Left service court
5.18m
6.10m
0.76m
For doubles
0.76m
For singles

The net is 1.52m high

MAPS

British Isles

Boundaries

international

internal

Communications

motorway

other major road

railway

✈ major airport

Cities and towns

⬦ major built-up areas

■ over 1 million inhabitants

● more than 100,000 inhabitants

• smaller towns

Land height

metres
1000
500
200
100
sea level
land below sea level

▲ spot height in metres

Scale 1:5 500 000

0   50   100 km

Transverse Mercator Projection

© Oxford University Press

2 Europe

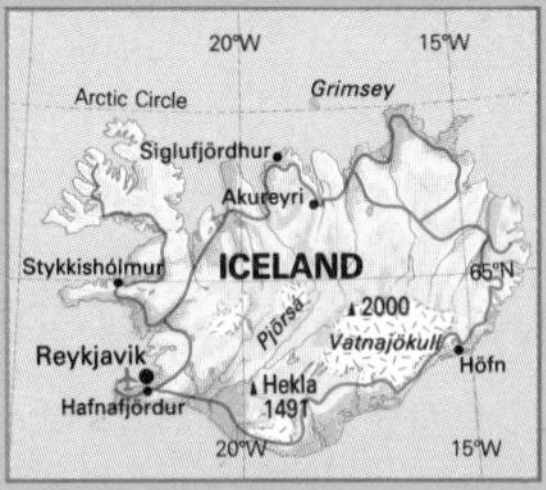

Boundaries

international

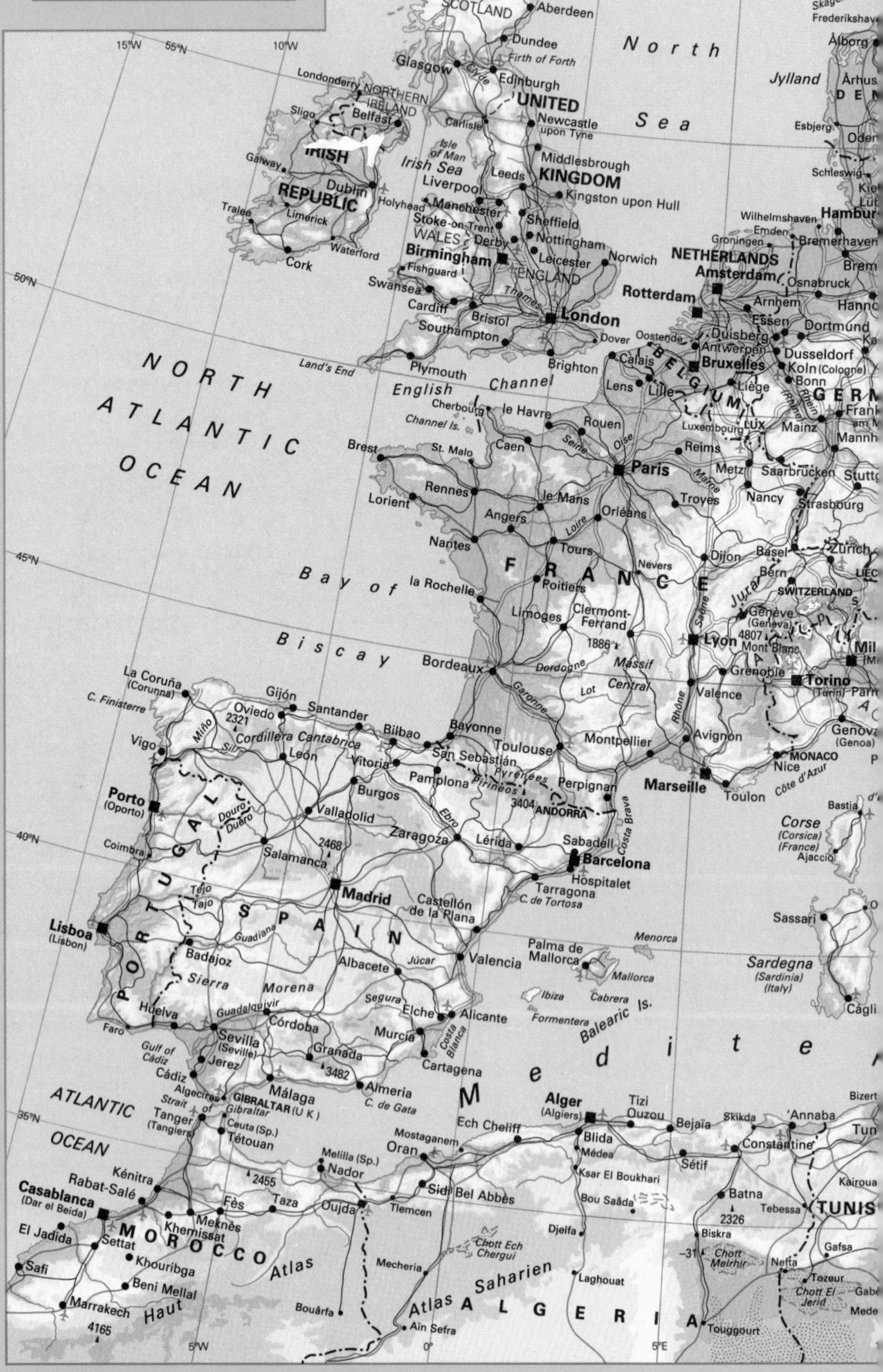

disputed
~~~~~~~~~~

internal
- - - - - -

Communications

motorway

other major road

railway

canal

✈ major airport

Cities and towns

■ over 1 million inhabitants

● more than 100 000 inhabitants

• smaller towns

Physical features

seasonal river/lake

marsh

salt pan

ice cap

sand dunes

Land height

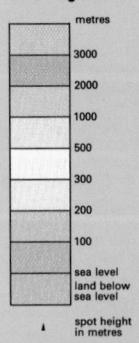

metres

3000
2000
1000
500
300
200
100
sea level
land below sea level

▲ spot height in metres

Scale 1:15 000 000

0   125   250 km

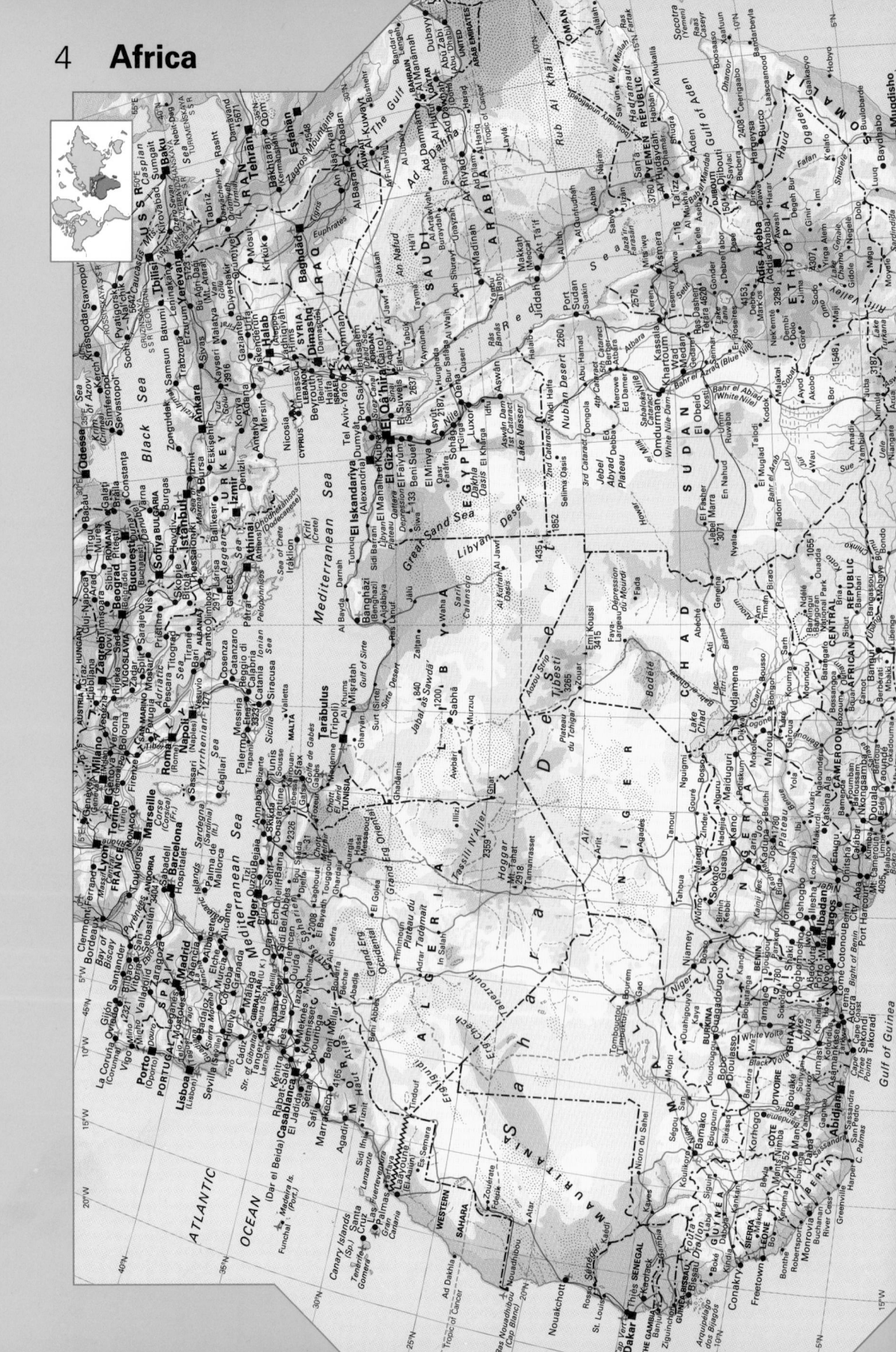

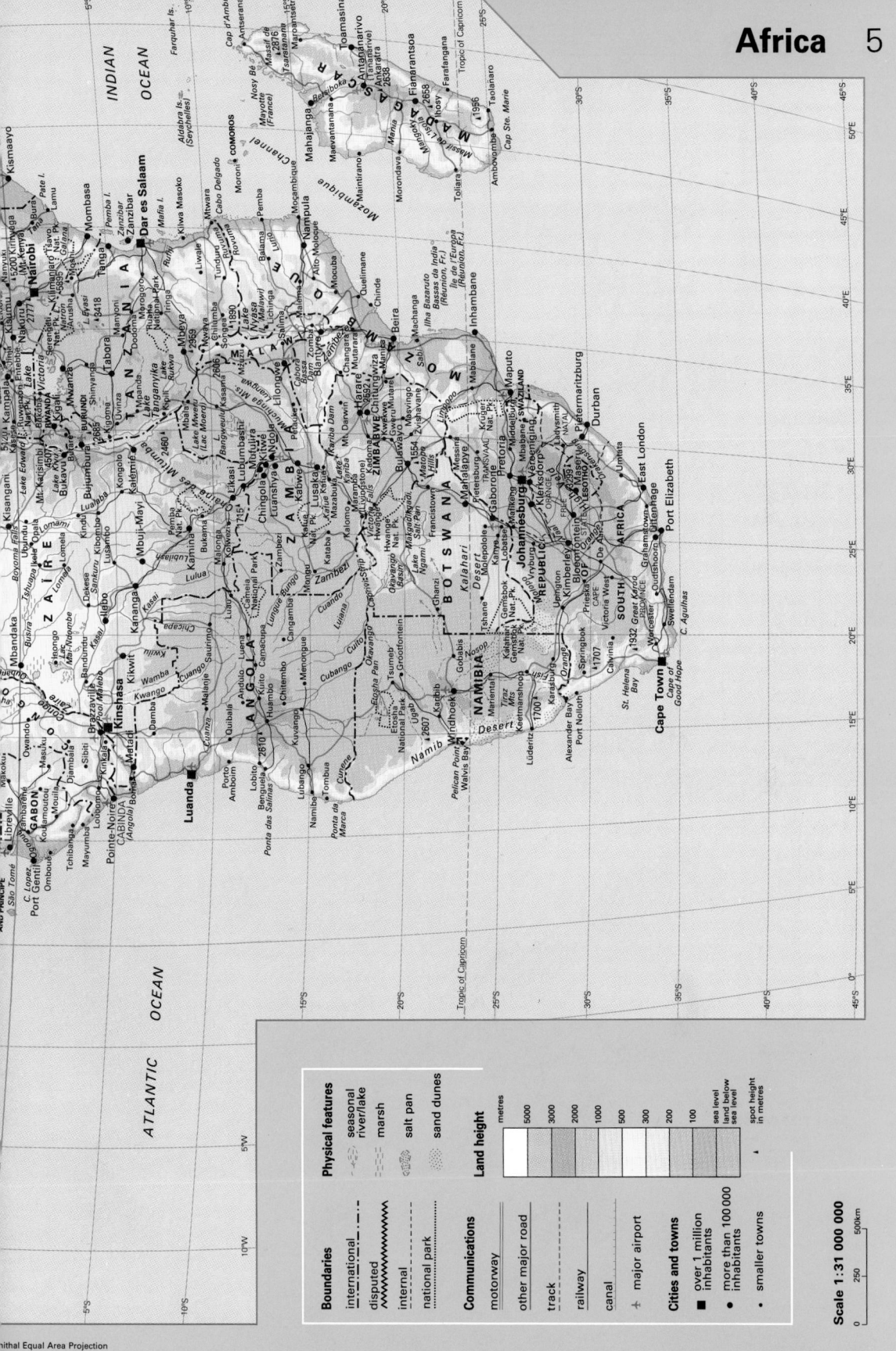

Boundaries
international
disputed
internal
national park

Communications
motorway
other major road
track
railway
canal
✈ major airport

Cities and towns
■ over 1 million inhabitants
● more than 100 000 inhabitants
• smaller towns

Physical features
seasonal river/lake
marsh
salt pan
sand dunes

Land height

metres	
5000	
3000	
2000	
1000	
500	
300	
200	
100	
sea level	
land below sea level	
▲ spot height in metres	

Scale 1:31 000 000

0   250   500km

Zenithal Equal Area Projection
Oxford University Press

Boundaries

international

disputed

internal

Communications

motorway

other major road

railway

canal

✈ major airport

Cities and towns

■ over 1 million inhabitants

● more than 100 000 inhabitants

· smaller towns

Physical features

seasonal river/lake

marsh

salt pan

ice cap

sand dunes

Land height

metres
5000
3000
2000
1000
500
300
200
100
sea level
land below sea level

▲ spot height in metres

Scale 1:30 000 000

0　250　500 km

Conical Orthomorphic Projection

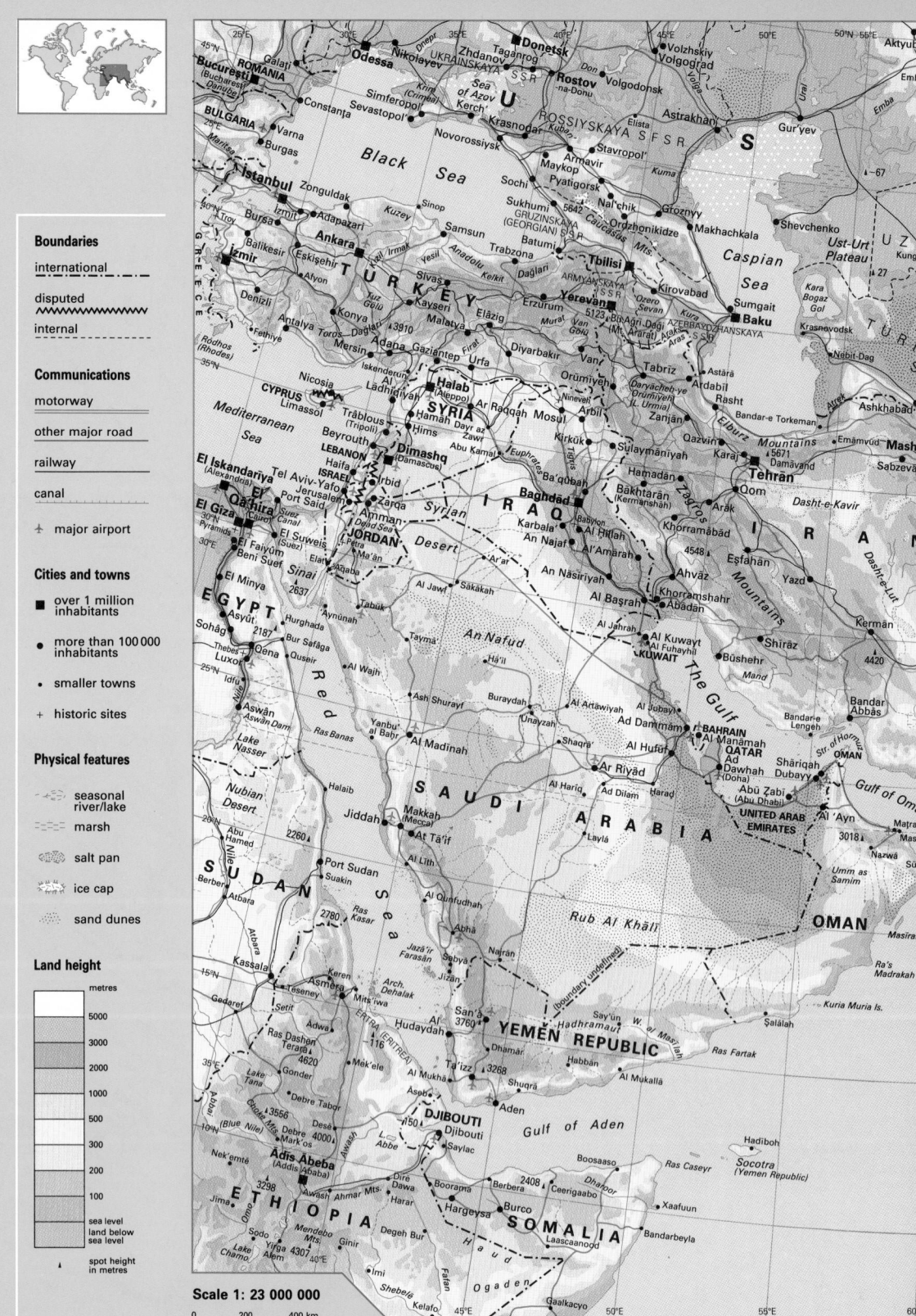

Scale 1: 23 000 000

Conical Orthomorphic Projection

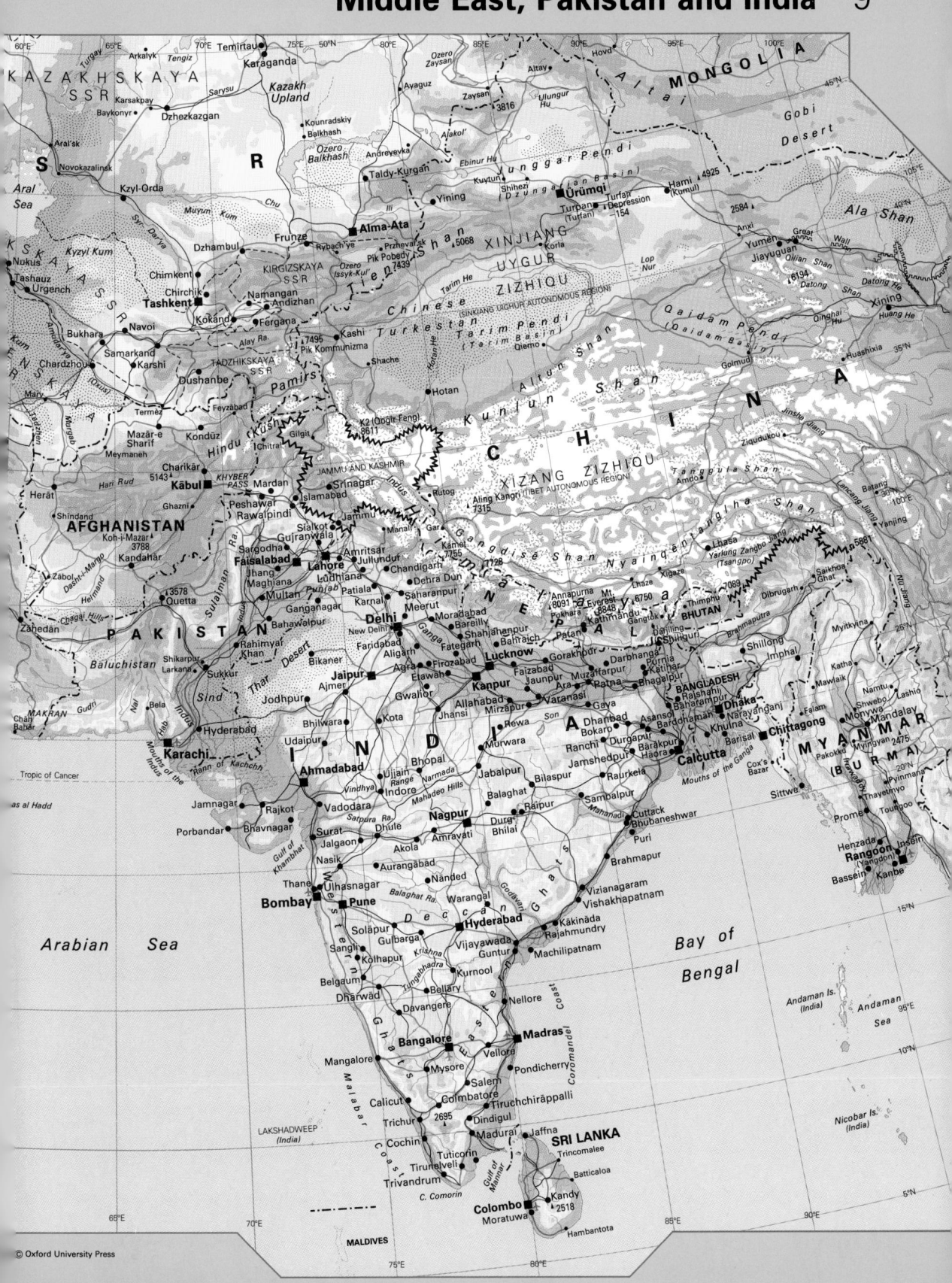

Middle East Pakistan

Physical features

Boundaries
- international
- disputed

seasonal
river/lake
marsh
salt pan
ice cap
sand dunes

Land height

metres	
5000	
3000	
2000	
1000	
500	
300	
200	
100	
sea level	land below sea level

spot height in metres

Communications

motorway
other major road
railway
canal

Cities and towns

■ over 1 million inhabitants
● more than 100 000 inhabitants
• smaller towns
✈ major airport

Scale 1:23 000 000

0   200   400 km

Conical Orthomorphic Projection   © Oxford University Press

Zenithal Equidistant Projection

Boundaries

international

internal

Communications

major road

railway

✈ major airport

Cities and towns

■ over 1 million inhabitants

● more than 100 000 inhabitants

• smaller towns

Physical features

seasonal river/lake

marsh

sand dunes

coral reef

Land height

metres
3000
2000
1000
500
300
200
100
sea level
land below sea level

▲ spot height in metres

Scale 1:26 500 000

0   250   500 km

Zenithal Equidistant Projection

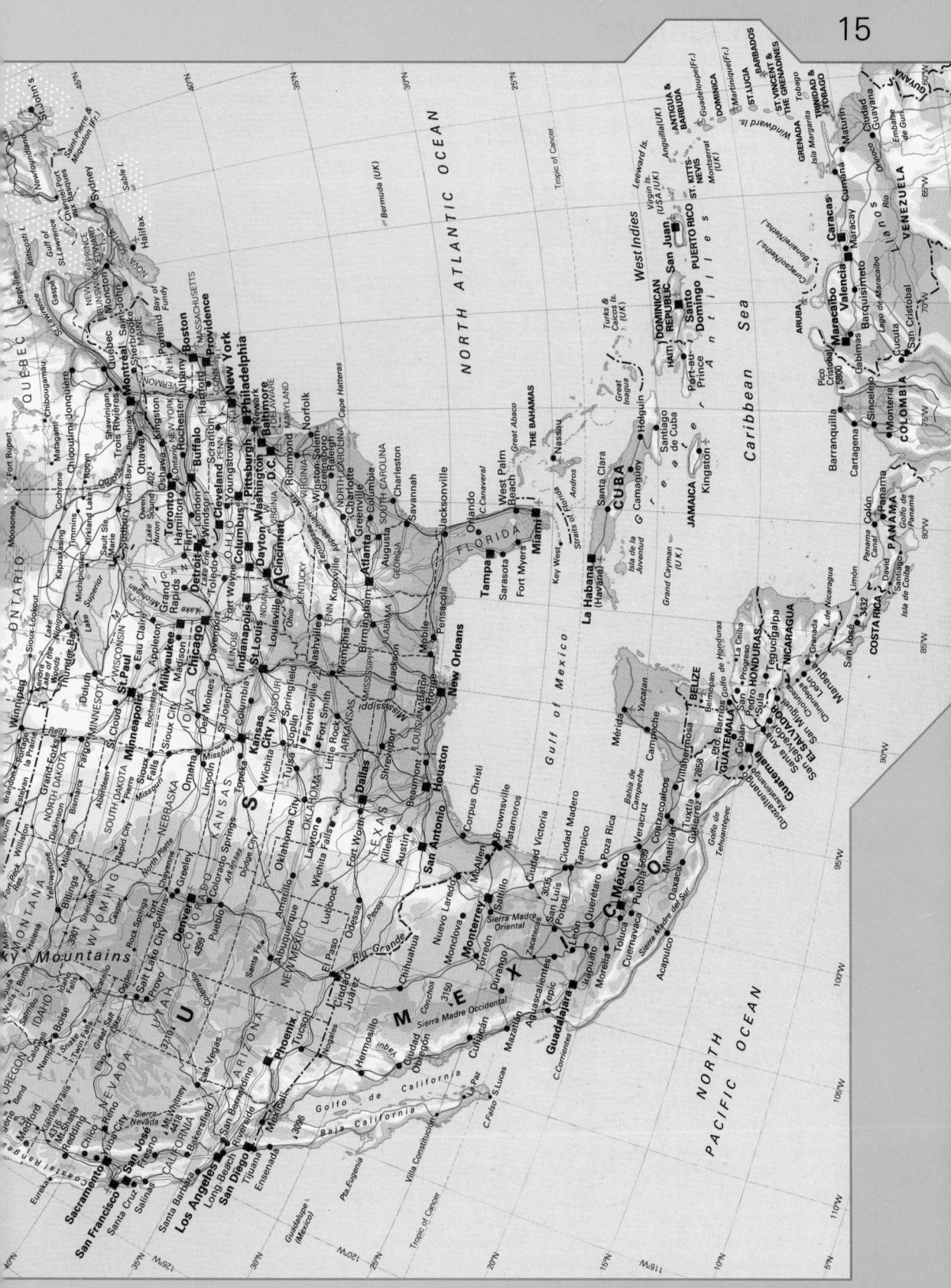

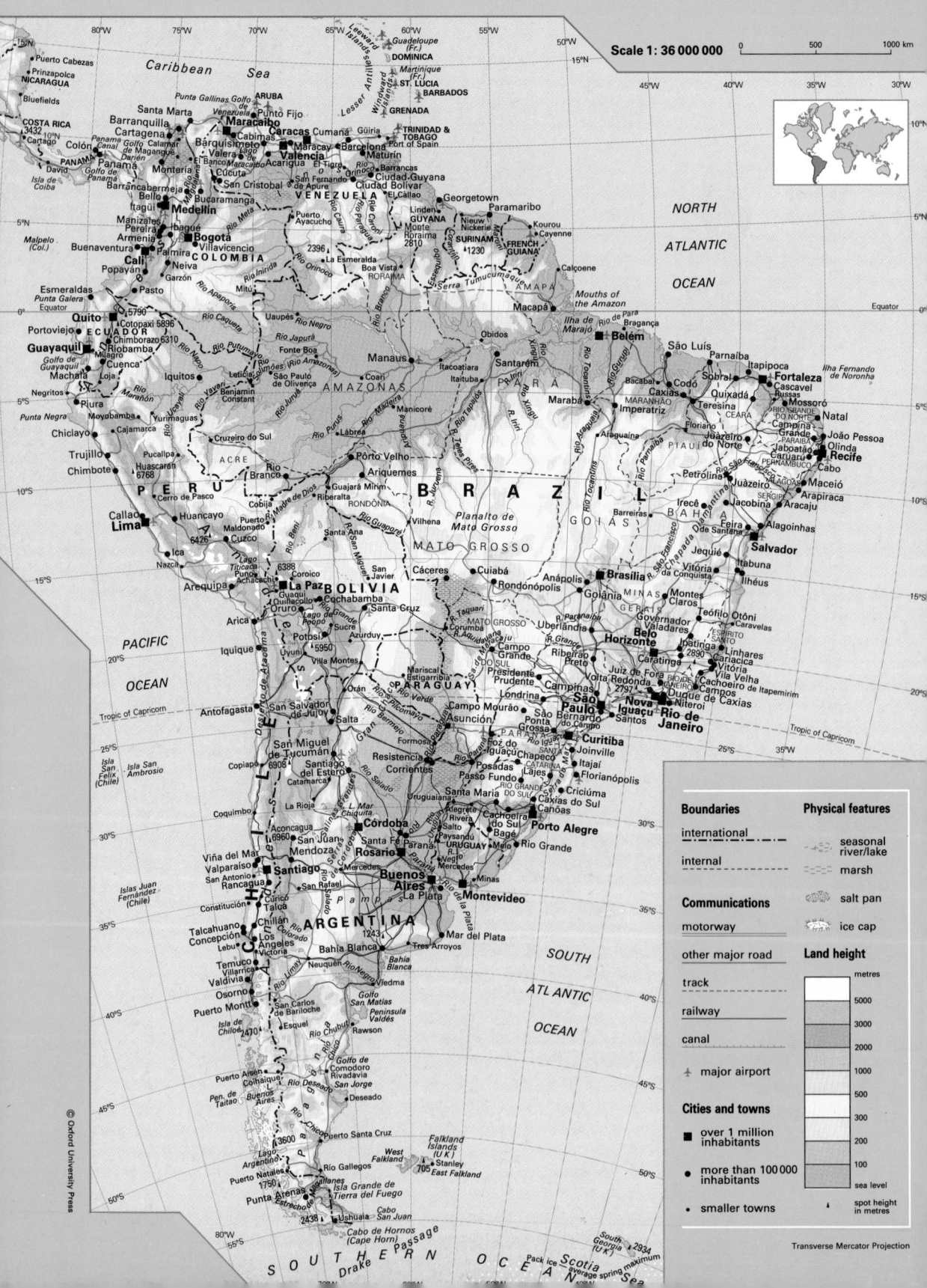

Scale 1 : 36 000 000

Boundaries

international

internal

Communications

motorway

other major road

track

railway

canal

✈ major airport

Cities and towns

■ over 1 million inhabitants

● more than 100 000 inhabitants

● smaller towns

Physical features

seasonal river/lake

marsh

salt pan

ice cap

Land height

metres
5000
3000
2000
1000
500
300
200
100
sea level

▲ spot height in metres

© Oxford University Press

Transverse Mercator Projection